THE GREEN BOOK OF SONGS BY SUBJECT

For 25 years, *The Green Book* has earned the praise of reviewers and industry professionals...

"Recommended…The only drawback is that it's hard to put down."
— **American Library Association** *Booklist/Reference Books Bulletin*

"First as a radio programmer, and now as an editor/journalist, I've always considered *The Green Book* to be among my most valuable reference books."
— **Ron Rodrigues, Editor-in-Chief,**
Radio & Records

"*The Green Book* is an invaluable resource—for programming, for research and for just plain entertainment. In fact, you'll probably need to buy two!"
— **Mark Hagen, Executive Producer,**
BBC Music Entertainment

"*The Green Book* is dangerous. Aside from its absolutely inestimable value in tracking down all manner of music information, this tome appeals to people— like Jeff Green and me—who have a lifelong tendency towards records trivia. And you know how twisted such people can be!"
— **Adam White, VP/Communications,** *Universal Music International*

"Revolutionary! One of the most fascinating reference books ever published. Stunning research and plain old fun!"
— **Robert K. Oermann, music scholar, author, journalist**

"*The Green Book* is the most exhaustive compendium imaginable of music organized by theme, mood, or topic. It's a must for scholars and the ideal tool for show biz insiders who need to match music to their specific cinematic or literary needs."
— **Ken Barnes, Music Editor,** *USA Today*

"Indispensable! *The Green Book* is the only reference book that classifies by theme, and you don't know how useful that is. It's a godsend."
— **Phil Sweetland, Country Music Correspondent,**
The New York Times **and BBC Radio 4**

"Curses! This book is too good, too powerful! Try as I may, I was unable to stump it. I accept defeat for now, but one day, victory may be mine…but probably not! Along with the chips and remote, this book should never be out of reach for the true music fan."
— **Lou Rufino, Engineer for** *Imus In The Morning*
nationally syndicated radio program

5TH EDITION • EXPANDED & UPDATED

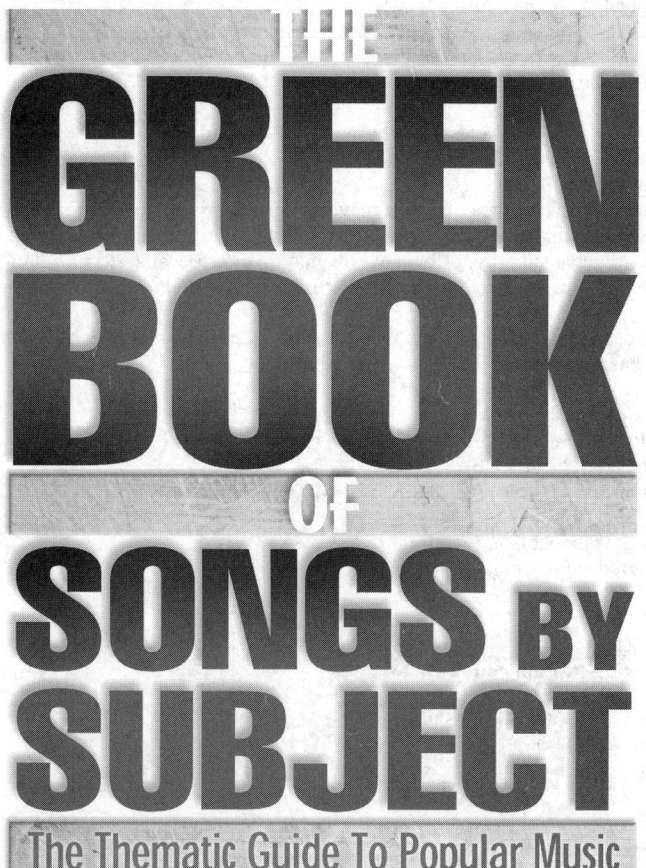

THE GREEN BOOK OF SONGS BY SUBJECT

The Thematic Guide To Popular Music

JEFF GREEN

Professional Desk References, Inc.
5543 Edmondson Pike, #183
Nashville, TN 37211   USA
www.greenbookofsongs.com

The Green Book Of Songs By Subject: The Thematic Guide To Popular Music
Fifth Edition – Expanded & Updated
By Jeff Green

® greenbookofsongs.com

Professional Desk References, Inc.
5543 Edmondson Pike, #183
Nashville, Tennessee 37211-5808 USA
Phone: (615) 832-1942; Toll Free (888) 335-SONG (7664)
Fax: (615) 331-1410
Email: info@greenbookofsongs.com
Website: www.greenbookofsongs.com

Publisher's Cataloging-in-Publication
Green, Jeff.
   The Green book of songs by subject : the thematic
 guide to popular music / by Jeff Green. — 5th ed.,
 expanded & updated.
   p. cm.
   Includes index.
   LCCN 2001099825
   ISBN 0-939735-10-5 (hard)
   ISBN 0-939735-20-2 (paper)

   1. Popular music—Literary themes, motives—
Discography. 2. Songs—Literary themes, motives—
Discography.   I. Title.

ML156.4.P6G73 2002   016.78242164'0266
                                       QBI02-701119

Composition by autobookcomp.

Printed In The United States Of America
First Printing: July, 2002
9 8 7 6 5 4 3 2 1

This book is dedicated to the songwriters who
create this music, the artists who perform it,
and the publishers and record companies
that make it available for us to enjoy.

CONTENTS

ACKNOWLEDGMENTS

Since the original published edition in 1982, the population of music colleagues in the entertainment and media industries who have contributed songs and ideas for the book has grown by leaps and bounds. It's impossible to list everyone, but to the many of you who have offered your musical knowledge and creativity I extend my sincere thanks.

Personal thanks go to my parents, Helene and Sheldon; my family members Mary Jo, Jeanne and Jim, and Jay and Dale; and my children Claire, Jarrett and Lara.

Special thanks to Dan Auerbach, Machgiel Bakker, Ken Barnes, Linda & Al Barten, David Bean, Terry Berne, Joey Boone, Bobbi Boyce, Ryan Burger, Jackie Byrom, Johnathan Chase, the Country Music Association, Norman Davis, Katie Dean, Daniel T. Dey, Rodolfo A. Di Iulio, Steve Dudugjian, Mark Edwards, Erica Farber, Chris Felder, Ron Fell, Cassie Fennell, Film House, Ben Fong-Torres, George Foster, the late Bill Gavin, Holly George-Warren, Pinky Gonzales, Jeff Heiman, Lon Helton, Ben & Amy Henderson, Karen Holt, Robin Mitchell Joyce, John Leader, Sam Marmorstein, Andy McQuade, Steven Miller, Mark Petrie, Mitchell Pindus, Jennifer Queen, Ron Rodrigues, Tom Roland, Theo Roos, Bobby Rosenbloum, Ken Rose, David Ross, Bruce Shindler, Dave Sholin, Bonnie Simmons, Yvonne Smith, Tom Sparks, Phyllis Stark, Dr. Roger Taylor, David Waldman, Howard Watkins, Isa Watkins, Adam White, Bob Wilson, Norm Winer and Brad Woodward.

In memory of Mickey and Milton Virshup.

Very special recognition and thanks to Rachel Petrie for her tireless dedication to this edition's development.

With great appreciation to Robert K. Oermann and Mark Schlicher.

Personal Dedication

This Fifth Edition is dedicated with love and gratitude to my wife Lauren, without whom this work would not have been possible. Her countless contributions are reflected in every page.

INTRODUCTION

Now celebrating its 25th anniversary with this revised, expanded and updated Fifth Edition, *The Green Book Of Songs By Subject* continues in its effort to provide a significant thematic guide to popular music. You'll find thousands of additional songs, artists and recordings, as well as hundreds of new categories and related themes, all cross-referenced in a new and more useful index.

Many people have asked how *The Green Book* began. On August 16, 1977, I was settling in for my weekly three-hour student DJ airshift at San Francisco State University radio station KSFS when the news of Elvis Presley's death came over the wire. There was only a little of Elvis's music in the station's record library; students usually brought in their own records for their shows. After playing a greatest hits collection, I started looking for whatever music I could think of that people might relate to him: songs about everything from Memphis to Las Vegas, from donuts to Cadillacs. It was hardly the most reverential tribute to Elvis, but it was fun to produce and generated several interesting listener calls.

Later that day, a fellow DJ asked me if I knew of songs fitting a particular theme for his show. I set to work to help him; before long I found myself filling recipe card boxes and then pages of a three-ring notebook with songs about all kinds of subjects. Within a few months, the one folder became two, and after some encouragement from a college label rep, I produced what eventually led to the book you now hold in your hands.

The 1982 first edition was in loose-leaf form and offered about 4,000 mostly rock and pop songs divided into about 100 subjects. Each of the subsequent editions has emphasized expanding the subjects, genres, eras and range of artistry. Interest has grown steadily: *The Green Book* is now used worldwide by ad agencies, television/radio programmers, film music supervisors, musicians, corporate marketers, libraries, universities, teachers, music therapists, mobile DJs, journalists, audio producers, songwriters and many other related professionals.

To keep *The Green Book* a realistic size, the general focus is on popular songs, artists and recordings. Having said that, you also will find thousands of relatively obscure titles and numerous lesser-known artists. The songs and discographies center chiefly on available recordings so that *The Green Book* may serve as a working reference book for industry professionals. But because there are countless important and/or useful songs and recordings that are no longer in print, many are included here. Copies of these records often can be found via specialty dealers, collectors and music libraries.

As for how *The Green Book* is maintained, I am fortunate to have many music industry friends and colleagues who regularly contribute songs and suggestions, in addition to the invaluable help of some key associates who've collaborated to bring this edition to publication. Beyond that, it just comes down to spadework: reading lyrics, researching artist books, interviews and articles, following the charts and reviews and, most important, listening to the music itself.

There's no question that the topics being discussed in music and the vernacular used in songwriting and storytelling have changed profoundly over the decades. Today's songwriters are increasingly addressing, in both plain and colorful terms, a number of important sociological issues. Therefore, included among the many new categories created for this edition are themes such as single-, step- and absentee parents, domestic abuse, AIDS, gender stereotypes and low self-esteem.

Meanwhile, this Fifth Edition also attempts for the first time to classify thousands of love songs, which are presented in 25 romance-related categories ranging from "falling in love" to "forbidden love" to "get lost!" As you can imagine, *The Green Book* cannot cover all of the great love-related songs; that would require several volumes alone (and a few lifetimes to do it!). This same situation applies to the new "Desire", "Feelings", "Lonely", "Pain & Healing" and "Sadness" categories; the number of songs about feeling down, wanting/needing and missing people or places is really limitless. The purpose of including these very broad themes now is to furnish a cross-section of artists and repertoire for your production and reference needs.

Therefore, you will undoubtedly find songs you know that are not included in this edition, and, as always, I welcome your suggestions and recommendations. The ever-widening community of contributors has played a major role in the development of *The Green Book* from the very beginning, and I look forward to hearing from you at any time. Feel free to email me at info@greenbookofsongs.com.

Of course, the more years I spend compiling *The Green Book*, the more I discover additional great music and artists that should be in it—both old and new. Like finding "Alps on Alps", this quest can never reach its destination, but if *The Green Book* helps you find music you need, then I consider the journey well worth making.

– Jeff Green

AUTHOR'S NOTES

What Is *The Green Book*?

The Green Book Of Songs By Subject: The Thematic Guide To Popular Music represents 25 years of music research undertaken to identify and classify music by theme. This Fifth Edition covers a century of recorded music from the early 1900s through early 2002, and offers over 35,000 songs classified into more than 86,000 listings across nearly 1,800 subjects and related themes. More than 9,100 artists are included on over 24,000 individual albums, compilations and soundtracks—CDs and vinyl—as well as some cassettes, 45s and even certain 78 RPM recordings on over 1,500 labels.

With the invaluable support of leading music industry authorities, these works were culled from the recordings themselves, sheet music, trade charts, individual collections, reference books and music specialists.

The Green Book covers all genres and generations of music, including popular standards, contemporary hits, oldies, rock, country, R&B, jazz of all styles and eras, folk, rap, hip hop, alternative, Broadway, blues, reggae, Americana, Cajun, TV theme songs, marching songs, college fight songs, instrumentals, children's songs, national anthems, advertising jingles, novelty records—you name it, it's in here!

How To Use *The Green Book*

The Green Book is divided into two sections:

The main body of the book, **Songs Categorized By Subject**, is organized alphabetically by subject category. At the top of each page, you'll find guide words to make browsing easier. At the beginning of each subject grouping is a boldface listing of the **MAIN CATEGORY** in capital letters, followed by **Subcategories**, if any, in boldface upper/lower case. Subcategories are concepts that are closely associated with the main category heading; songs relating to the subcategories are grouped with the songs relating to the main category.

Below the category/subcategory heading you often will find a *"See Also"* designation in italics offering cross-referencing to other related main categories. By turning to those categories, you will find not only additional related songs, but also *"See Also"* referrals that can further expand your search.

Each discography consists of a boldface **Song Title** and one or more artists, each accompanied by one or more recording discographies and affiliated record labels.

The second section is the **Subject Index**, a tool for browsing the subject categories and subcategories. Each main category is listed with its related subcategories, along with the page where its list of songs appears in the body of *The Green Book*. Each subcategory is also listed separately with a reference ("See") to the corresponding main category with its page number. Some subcategories include "See Also" references to additional categories which may be relevant to the subcategory concept.

For the first time, there also are thousands of additional search terms identified with one or more categories to help you find the songs you're looking for, especially when the category may not be easily discerned. In some cases, terms are included even when the book contains no songs specifically about that subject; however, the categories to which these terms are linked will contain songs about related concepts.

How The Subject Categories And Song Classifications Work

With nearly 1,800 subject themes and related subcategories, *The Green Book* attempts to cover a wide range of concepts, including living things, physical objects, romantic relationships, family matters, political and social issues, spiritual beliefs, entertainment, science, sports, places and much more.

Here are some of the organizational characteristics of *The Green Book* that may help you find what you're looking for faster:

- Where there are groups of three or more related categories that belong together, the Fifth Edition uses keywords to organize the list. For example, "Anatomy: Arms" heads a list of 15 categories covering the various parts of the body.

  Similarly, groupings of Ages, Animals, Cars, Cities, Colors, Communication, Countries, Days Of The Week, Directions, Drugs, Family, Food & Beverages, Love, Men's Names, Months & Dates, Musical Instruments, Numbers, Parents, Politics, Seasons, Sports, States and Women's Names are listed together.

Within these groups, there may be a "general" category including songs about the concept itself or about multiple examples of the concept. For example, "Love: General" lists songs about the nature of love, or the experience of being in love, as opposed to a particular phase of a relationship; "Animals: General" includes songs that mention a variety of animals, or are about the animal kingdom.

- With certain subjects, the opposite concept is often brought into the lyrics. That's why you'll see some categories such as "Fear & Courage" and "Pain & Healing" combined. In other cases, two concepts may be so closely connected that it would be impractical to separate song listings (e.g., "Danger & Disaster").

- There are some distinct similarities and strong connections between certain categories, yet each will have distinguishing characteristics.

  For example, "Pretend" and "Desire" both express concepts related to wishes. *The Green Book* has grouped in the "Pretend" category songs about fantasizing and wishing for things to be a certain way or for particular circumstances to occur. Among its related categories are "Dreams", "Hiding" and "Secrets". "Desire", on the other hand, covers states of wanting, needing, begging, asking, longing and craving, plus requests ("please"), favors and so on. It is related to many of the "Love" categories.

  Similarly, "Sounds" and "Nonsense Words" cover related themes. Songs in the "Sounds" list feature the concept of sound, as well as noises of objects (e.g., **Beep Beep**). The "Nonsense Words" category covers popular doo-wop titles, colloquialisms and, well, nonsense words!

  In such cases, subcategories that help expand a category's concept and "See Also" references to related categories should help users find the subjects that interest them.

- Many college fight songs are included, and you'll find them under "School" and "Sports: Football". Where they are state schools, you'll also find them under "States".

- Songs in the "Celebrities: Specific" category often have several names mentioned in them. This is also true in the "Cities: General" category, where many of the songs mention multiple cities. Cities were separated into their own group if 10 or more are listed.

- The "States" categories are only one place to look for compositions that refer to states. Also check "American West", "Cities", "Directions", "Mining", "Mountains", "Ocean", "Places" and "Rivers" for locations within specific states.

- Because Christmas songs are so seasonal, they are generally listed only in the "Christmas" category. Occasionally, though, you'll find these songs in additional categories, such as "Bells", "Seasons: Winter" and "Snow", when these other themes are strongly emphasized.

- Occasionally you will find songs that are essentially the same composition but are titled differently. An example is **Ain't Nobody's Business** and **'Tain't Nobody's Bus'ness If I Do**. Where this occurs, the songs will be listed separately under their individual titles as they appear on the recording.

- Similarly, an artist may go by different names (e.g., John Cougar/John Cougar Mellencamp/John Mellencamp, Count Basie/Count Basie & His Orchestra). Where entries such as these occur, the name appearing will be the one identified on the recording listed.

- TV theme songs are listed as **Theme From…**, along with the original song title if different. For example, the theme song for the TV show "Friends" is listed as **Theme From "Friends" (I'll Be There For You)**. Theme songs are found in both the "Television" category and the categories associated with the TV show's subject matter. Thus, **Theme from "Perry Mason"** also will appear under "Law & Order" and "Men's Names: P".

- Although many soundtrack albums are included, *The Green Book* does not attempt to classify most movie themes, owing to the tremendous number of them and the often diverse subject matter films can cover.

- As everyone knows, many thousands of songs have been written about having the blues. To keep *The Green Book* within a manageable size, the new "Sadness" category includes a very limited number of them, as does "Colors: Blue". As with other popular themes mentioned before ("Desire", "Lonely", "Love", "Pain & Healing", etc.), *The Green Book* offers a selection of songs as a reference tool and in no way attempts to be comprehensive (as much as I'd like it to be!). Though it will never be possible to include every song on every subject, your suggestions for additions are always welcome.

- Likewise, users are encouraged to submit category recommendations for future *Green Book* research. This edition features nearly 1,000 new categories and subcategories not found in the previous edition, and forthcoming *Green Book* editions will continue to establish new ones. As you'll see, some of the theme listings are much more developed than others. Many subjects are extremely common, whereas others are rarely written about. Every effort is taken to track down popular and/or relevant songs for all categories.

How Songs And Recordings Were Selected

The Green Book listings emphasize singles and album tracks released from U.S.-based record companies. Selections are made on the basis of popularity, production value, artist recognition, unique character and balance within each category.

Since this book has been created especially for those who work with audio production and programming, the vast majority of songs included are vocal selections. Instrumental recordings appearing in this book have been selected based on their popularity, familiar association with a particular category or to add depth to a subject of limited coverage.

The Green Book documents as many original versions of songs as possible, although some are no longer in print. I've also worked to recognize recordings performed by the songwriters themselves, even if their renditions are not the most widely known versions of the songs they've written.

Regarding popular standards and "oldies" which have been widely recorded by dozens of artists, I've tried to accommodate a cross-section of the many releases available.

How The Lyrics Have Been Interpreted

Because music is such a subjective experience, varying degrees of personal interpretation must be used to classify songs. Songwriters frequently employ metaphorical references, and it would be folly for me to claim to have determined the actual lyric intent of each song's composer. There is much room for opinion on thousands of songs, whether dealing with abstract existential themes or specific, yet variable, terms such as "Baby", "Candy", "Mama", "Daddy" and "Rock". Since every lyric is a potential metaphor, with the true meaning often known only by the songwriters themselves, I've tried to highlight each song's major themes as I believe the composers intended them.

It should also be kept in mind that the lyrics of some songs bear little, if any, actual relationship to the title. Determining the usefulness of a song under a particular heading will require a certain amount of individual interpretation by the reader.

Some songs are regarded as, frankly, too complex to fully classify in this book. To wit, Emmylou Harris's "The Pearl" covers profound themes of God and mankind that resist efforts to recognize it adequately. There are numerous other examples, and I thank you for accepting the inevitable limitations within which this book operates.

Thus, because the interpretations of certain songs may be inaccurate, and the status of labels and album releases is always in flux, there are bound to be errors and irregularities. I regret any misinterpretations or mistakes and appreciate learning of any distortion or inaccuracy that can be corrected in future *Green Book* materials.

Availability Of Songs And Format Configurations

The availability of any particular recording is constantly changing. In any given month, many titles and entire catalogs of certain artists are being licensed to other labels and distributors. Albums are also commonly repackaged, renamed, discontinued and perhaps later reissued by the original record companies or different labels.

The goal of *The Green Book* is to include songs on albums that are currently available as individual CDs, and secondarily as multiple CD sets. Occasionally you will find albums listed that, as best as can be determined, exist at retail only as cassettes. However, as mentioned before, there are many recordings in *The Green Book* that are out of print, owing to lack of demand or a label going out of business. Again, these records can often be tracked down through specialist dealers, collectors and music libraries.

Wherever possible, *The Green Book* attempts to include the original albums unless the songs are believed to exist currently only on different discographies. Titles thought to have gone out of print within recent years will carry their most recently known record company imprint or the original label. Some 45s and 78s are included with their original labels when I have not been able to locate albums containing those titles.

LEGEND

-C   Compilation album with several artists contributing songs

ST/   Soundtrack album

\#   Number, edition or volume in a set or series. Also precedes serial numbers for 45s and 78s.

45   45 RPM recording

78   78 RPM recording

Note: For duets appearing on a particular artist's album, that artist's name is typically listed first.

ADVICE, Lecturing, Recommendations, Suggestions

See Also: **DRUGS (various), MOTIVATION, SCHOOL, TEACHING
VALUES, THINKING & KNOWING, WARNINGS**

59th Street Bridge Song (Feelin' Groovy)
Harper's Bizarre; *Baby Boomer Classics-More Mellow
Sixties-C* . . . . (JCI Assoc. Labels)
Better Days-C . . . . (Rhino)
Simon & Garfunkel; *Collected Works* . . . . (Columbia)
Parsley Sage Rosemary & Thyme . . . . (Columbia)
Simon & Garfunkel's Greatest Hits . . . . (Columbia)
The Concert In Central Park . . . . (Warner Bros.)
Ac-Cent-Tchu-Ate The Positive
Andrews Sisters; *Andrews Sisters Greatest Hits* . . . . (Curb)
Bing Crosby; *Bing Crosby's Greatest Hits* . . . . (MCA)
Original Soundtrack; *ST/Bugsy* . . . . (Epic)
Ace In The Hole
George Strait; *Beyond The Blue Neon* . . . . (MCA)
Advice For The Young At Heart
Tears For Fears; *Seeds Of Love* . . . . (Fontana)
Alfie
Barbra Streisand; *What About Today* . . . . (Columbia)
Dionne Warwick; *Dionne Warwick Greatest Hits* . . . . . . (Everest)
Dionne Warwick-Anthology 1962-1971 . . . . (Rhino)
All For You
Janet; *All For You* . . . . (Virgin)
Now That's What I Call Music!-#7-C . . . . (Virgin)
All Mixed Up
311; *311* . . . . (Capricorn)
All Those Yesterdays
Pearl Jam; *Yield* . . . . (Epic)
All You Need Is Love
Beatles; *Beatles 1* . . . . (Capitol)
Compact Disc Singles Collection . . . . (Capitol)
Magical Mystery Tour . . . . (Capitol)
The Beatles/1967-1970 . . . . (Capitol)
Yellow Submarine . . . . (Capitol)
Analyse
Cranberries; *Wake Up And Smell The Coffee* . . . . (MCA)
Apple Tree
Erykah Badu; *Baduizm* . . . . (Kedar Entert./Universal)
April Love
Pat Boone; *Best Of Pat Boone* . . . . (MCA)
Pat Boone's Greatest Hits . . . . (Curb)
April Showers
Al Jolson; *Best Of Al Jolson* . . . . (MCA)
The Al Jolson Story-#2 . . . . (MCA)
Judy Garland; *Hits Of Judy Garland* . . . . (Capitol)
Judy . . . . (Capitol)
Are You Ready?
Creed; *Human Clay* . . . . (Wind-up)
Ask The Lonely
Vonda Shepard; *ST/Songs From ''Ally McBeal'' Featuring Vonda
Shepard* . . . . (550/Epic)
At My Front Door
Nilsson; *Son Of Schmilsson* . . . . (RCA)
Back 2 Good
Matchbox Twenty; *Yourself Or Someone Like You* . . . . (Lava)
Back In My Arms Again
Diana Ross & The Supremes; *Diana Ross & The Supremes'
Greatest Hits* . . . . (Motown)
Diana Ross & The Supremes-25th Anniversary . . . . (Motown)
Diana Ross & The Supremes-Anthology (1962-1969) . . . . (Motown)
Every Great #1 Hit . . . . (Motown)
Motown Story-First 25 Years-C . . . . (Motown)
Bad Advice
Chicago; *Chicago 16* . . . . (Full Moon/Warner Bros.)
Bad Moon Rising
Creedence Clearwater Revival; *1969* . . . . (Fantasy)
Creedence Clearwater Revival-Chronicle . . . . (Fantasy)
Creedence Clearwater Revival-Gold . . . . (Fantasy)
Green River . . . . (Fantasy)
Live In Europe . . . . (Fantasy)
Bag Lady
Erykah Badu; *Mama's Gun* . . . . (Motown)
Bawitdaba
Kid Rock; *Devil Without A Cause* . . . . . . (Top Dog/Lava/Atlantic)
Totally Hits-#1-C . . . . (Arista)
Be Glad
Del Reeves; *45-#50531* . . . . (United Artists)
Be Good To Yourself
Journey; *Journey's Greatest Hits* . . . . (Columbia)
Raised On Radio . . . . (Columbia)
Be Good To Yourself
Frankie Miller; *Full House* . . . . (Chrysalis)
Be Happy
Mary J. Blige; *My Life* . . . . (Uptown/MCA)

Be My Life's Companion
Mills Brothers; *Best Of The Mills Brothers* . . . . (MCA)
The Mills Brothers-Best Of The Decca Years . . . . (Decca)
Rosemary Clooney; *Rosemary Clooney-16 Most Requested Songs* . . . . (Legacy)
Be Somebody
Melissa Manchester; *Help Is On The Way* . . . . (Arista)
Be Thankful For What You Got
William DeVaughn; *Didn't It Blow Your Mind: Soul Hits Of The
'70s-#12-C* . . . . (Rhino)
Oldies But Goodies-#11-C . . . . (Original Sound)
Be True
Bruce Springsteen; *Tracks* . . . . (Columbia)
Be True
Rance Allen; *Up Above My Head* . . . . (Stax)
Be Your Own Best Friend
Ray Stevens; *Be Your Own Best Friend* . . . . (Warner Bros.)
Feeling's Not Right Again . . . . (Warner Bros.)
Be Your Own Girl
Wallflowers; *The Wallflowers* . . . . (Virgin)
Be Yourself
Patti LaBelle; *Be Yourself* . . . . (MCA)
Be Yourself
Cameo; *Alligator Woman* . . . . (Chocolate City)
Beat It
Michael Jackson; *Thriller* . . . . (Epic)
Beautiful
Carole King; *Tapestry* . . . . (Epic)
Beautiful Day
U2; *All That You Can't Leave Behind* . . . . (Interscope)
Now That's What I Call Music!-#6-C . . . . (Virgin)
Beauty Is Only Skin Deep
Temptations; *Good Feeling Music Of The Big Chill
Generation-#1-C* . . . . (Motown)
Motown Story-First 25 Years-C . . . . (Motown)
Motown's Mustang-A Motown Video-C . . . . (Motown)
Temptations-Anthology-The Best Of The Temptations . . . (Motown)
Been There
Clint Black with Steve Wariner; *D'lectrified* . . . . (RCA)
Bible Tells Me So
Don Cornell; *Rock 'N Roll Reunion: Class Of '55-C* . . . . . (Madacy)
Big Girls Don't Cry
4 Seasons; *4 Seasons' Greatest Hits-#1* . . . . (Rhino)
4 Seasons-Anthology . . . . (Rhino)
Billboard Top Rock 'N' Roll Hits-1962-C . . . . (Rhino)
More Dirty Dancing-C . . . . (RCA)
Big Money
Garth Brooks; *Scarecrow* . . . . (Capitol)
Book Of Love
Monotones; *Bedrock-Late '50s/'60s Rock 'N' Roll* . . . . . (Allegiance)
Best Of Chess Rock 'N' Roll-#1-C . . . . (Chess)
Original Golden Rock Oldies-#1-C . . . . (Specialty)
ST/American Graffiti . . . . (MCA)
Super Oldies Of The '50s-#2-C . . . . (Audio Fidelity)
Boy Named Sue
Johnny Cash; *Columbia Country Classics-#3-Americana-C* . . . . . (Columbia)
Johnny Cash's Biggest Hits . . . . (Columbia)
Johnny Cash's Greatest Hits-#2 . . . . (Columbia)
The Man In Black-His Greatest Hits . . . . (Legacy)
Breathe In The Air
Pink Floyd; *Dark Side Of The Moon* . . . . (Capitol)
Pink Floyd-Gift Set . . . . (Capitol)
Brush Up Your Shakespeare
Dick Hyman; *Cole Porter- All Through The Night* . . . . . (Musicmasters)
Keenan Wynn & James Whitmore; *ST/Kiss Me Kate* . . . . . (MCA)
Original Cast; *Kiss Me Kate* . . . . (Sony Music Classical)
Buy Me A Rose
Kenny Rogers; *She Rides Wild Horses* . . . . (Dreamcatcher)
Calling You
Hank Williams; *I Saw The Light* . . . . (Polydor)
Cancer
Filter; *Title Of Record* . . . . (Reprise)
Can't Buy Me Love
Beatles; *Beatles 1* . . . . (Capitol)
Hey Jude . . . . (Capitol)
Reel Music . . . . (Capitol)
ST/A Hard Day's Night . . . . (Capitol)
The Beatles At The Hollywood Bowl . . . . (Capitol)
The Beatles/1962-1966 . . . . (Capitol)
Can't Help But Wonder Where I'm Bound
Wyatt Rice; *Picture In A Tear* . . . . (Rounder)
Careful With That Mic...
Clutch; *Pure Rock Fury* . . . . (Atlantic)
Carry On
Crosby, Stills, Nash & Young; *Deja Vu* . . . . (Atlantic)
Catch A Falling Star
Perry Como; *Como's Golden Records* . . . . (RCA)
Nipper's Greatest Hits Of The '50s-#1-C . . . . (RCA)
Perry Como-Pure Gold . . . . (RCA)

Perry Como's All-Time Greatest Hits-#1 . . . . (RCA)
This Is Perry Como . . . . (RCA)

Change
Sheryl Crow; *Sheryl Crow* . . . . (A&M)

Change Your Mind
Sister Hazel; *Fortress* . . . . (Universal)

Chante's Got A Man
Chante Moore; *Now That's What I Call Music!-#3-C* . . . . . . (Virgin)
This Moment Is Mine . . . . (Silas)

Cigarettes & Alcohol
Oasis; *Definitely Maybe* . . . . (Epic)
Rod Stewart; *When We Were The New Boys* . . . . (Warner Bros.)

Coconut
Nilsson; *Nilsson Schmilsson* . . . . (RCA)
Nilsson's Greatest Hits . . . . (RCA)
Songwriter . . . . (RCA)

Come From The Heart
Don Williams; *Traces* . . . . (Capitol)
Kathy Mattea; *Willow In The Wind* . . . . (Mercury)

Come On Over
Shania Twain; *Come On Over* . . . . (Mercury)

Come Original
311; *Soundsystem* . . . . (Capricorn)

Come With Me
Shai; *Blackface* . . . . (Gasoline Alley)

Count Your Blessings (Instead Of Sheep)
Bing Crosby; *45-#29251* . . . . (Decca)
Eddie Fisher; *Best Of Eddie Fisher* . . . . (MCA)
Rosemary Clooney; *Essence Of Rosemary Clooney* . . . . (Legacy)

Cross Over The Bridge
Patti Page; *Patti Page-Golden Hits* . . . . (Mercury)
Patti Page's Greatest Hits . . . . (Columbia)

Cry
Crystal Gayle; *Best Of Crystal Gayle* . . . . (Warner Bros.)
Janie Fricke; *Celebration* . . . . (Columbia)
I'll Need To Hold Someone When I Cry . . . . (Columbia)
Johnnie Ray; *Best Of Johnnie Ray* . . . . (Exact)
Johnnie Ray-16 Most Requested Songs . . . . (Legacy)
Radio Classics Of The '50s-C . . . . (Columbia)
Lynn Anderson; *Lynn Anderson's Greatest Hits* . . . . (Columbia)
Ray Charles; *Ray Charles' Greatest Hits-#2* . . . . (Rhino)
Ray Charles-Anthology . . . . (Rhino)

Cry
Roxette; *Look Sharp!* . . . . (EMI)

Cry Ophelia
Adam Cohen; *Songs From Dawson's Creek* . . . . (Sony Music Soundtrax)

Crying In The Chapel
Elvis Presley; *Elvis-A Legendary Performer, Volume 3* . . . . (RCA)
How Great Thou Art . . . . (RCA)
The Top Ten Hits . . . . (RCA)
Worldwide 50 Gold Award Hits, Vol. 1, Parts 1 & 2 . . . . (RCA)
June Valli; *Nipper's Greatest Hits Of The '50s-#2-C* . . . . (RCA)
Little Richard; *Shut Up-Collection Of Rare Tracks-1951-1964* . . . . . . (Rhino)
Orioles; *Super Oldies Of The '50s-#1-C* . . . . (Audio Fidelity)
Rex Allen; *Only Country-1950-1954-C* . . . . (JCI Assoc. Labels)
Sonny Til & The Orioles; *Echoes Of A Rock Era-Early Years-C* . . . . . (Roulette)
Sonny Til & The Orioles' Greatest Hits . . . . (Collectables)
ST/American Graffiti . . . . (MCA)

Danny's Song
Anne Murray; *Anne Murray-Country* . . . . (Capitol)
Anne Murray's Greatest Hits . . . . (Capitol)
Danny's Song . . . . (Capitol)
Loggins & Messina; *Loggins & Messina-On Stage* . . . . (Columbia)
Sittin' In . . . . (Columbia)
The Best Of Friends . . . . (Columbia)

Desperado
Clint Black; *Common Thread-Songs Of The Eagles-C* . . . . (Giant)
Eagles; *Desperado* . . . . (Asylum)
Eagles Live . . . . (Asylum)
Eagles/Their Greatest Hits 1971-1975 . . . . (Asylum)
Hell Freezes Over . . . . (Geffen)
Linda Ronstadt; *Don't Cry Now* . . . . (Asylum)
Linda Ronstadt's Greatest Hits . . . . (Asylum)

Desperately Wanting
Better Than Ezra; *Friction, Baby* . . . . (Swell/Elektra)

Dig In
Lenny Kravitz; *Lenny* . . . . (Virgin)

Do Right Woman, Do Right Man
Aretha Franklin; *Aretha Franklin-30 Greatest Hits* . . . . (Rhino)
ST/Dead Presidents . . . . (Capitol)
Commitments; *ST/The Commitments* . . . . (MCA)

Do Something
Macy Gray; *On How Life Is* . . . . (Epic)
ST/Music Of The Heart . . . . (Epic/Sony Music Soundtrax)

Do What You Gotta Do
Garth Brooks; *Sevens* . . . . (Capitol)

Don't Be Stupid (You Know I Love You)
Shania Twain; *Come On Over* . . . . (Mercury)

Don't Get Above Your Raising
Lester Flatt, Earl Scruggs & The Foggy Mountain Boys; *Bluegrass Super Hits-C* . . . . (Columbia)

Don't Go Home With Your Hard On
Leonard Cohen; *Death Of A Ladies' Man* . . . . (Columbia)

Don't Laugh At Me
Mark Wills; *Wish You Were Here* . . . . (Mercury)

Don't Let It Bother You
Fats Waller; *Have A Little Dream On Me* . . . . (Eclipse)

Don't Look Back
Boston; *Boston's Greatest Hits* . . . . (Epic)
Don't Look Back . . . . (Epic)

Don't Look Back In Anger
Oasis; *What's The Story Morning Glory?* . . . . (Epic)

Don't Pick It Up
Offspring; *Ixnay On The Hombre* . . . . (Columbia)

Don't Rush (Take Love Slowly)
K-Ci & JoJo; *Love Always* . . . . (MCA)

Don't Stay Home
311; *311* . . . . (Capricorn)

Don't Take No For An Answer
Tom Robinson Band; *Power In The Darkness* . . . . (Harvest)

Don't Take Your Guns To Town
Johnny Cash; *Billboard Top Country Hits-1959-C* . . . . (Rhino)
Columbia Country Classics-#3-Americana-C . . . . (Columbia)
Johnny Cash-16 Biggest Hits-#2 . . . . (Legacy)
Johnny Cash's Greatest Hits . . . . (Columbia)
The Man In Black-His Greatest Hits . . . . (Legacy)

Don't Use Your Penis (For A Brain)
Romanovsky & Phillips; *Trouble In Paradise* . . . . (Fresh Fruit)

Don't Waste Your Heart
Dixie Chicks; *Fly* . . . . (Monument)

Don't Worry 'bout Me
Frank Sinatra; *Capitol Collectors Series-Frank Sinatra* . . . . . . (Capitol)

Doo Wop (That Thing)
Lauryn Hill; *The Miseducation Of Lauryn Hill* . . . . (Ruffhouse/Columbia)

Dream
Pied Pipers; *G.I. Jukebox-Songs From World War II-C* . . . . (Hip-O)

Dream On
Depeche Mode; *Exciter* . . . . (Mute/Reprise)

Dream On
Aerosmith; *Aerosmith* . . . . (Columbia)
Aerosmith-Classics Live . . . . (Columbia)
Aerosmith's Greatest Hits . . . . (Columbia)
Live! Bootleg . . . . (Columbia)

Drunk Is Better Than Dead
Push Stars; *ST/Malcolm In The Middle* . . . . (Restless)

Early To Bed
Morphine; *Like Swimming* . . . . (DreamWorks/Rykodisc)

Enemy
Days Of The New; *Days Of The New 2* . . . . (Outpost/Interscope)

Enjoy Yourself
Kylie Minogue; *Enjoy Yourself* . . . . (Geffen)

Everybody Be Yoself
Keb' Mo'; *Big Wide Grin* . . . . (Sony Wonder)

Everybody Hurts
R.E.M.; *Automatic For The People* . . . . (Warner Bros.)
Diana, Princess Of Wales-Tribute-C . . . . (Columbia)

Everybody Knows
Trisha Yearwood; *Everybody Knows* . . . . (MCA)

Everybody Needs Somebody To Love
Blues Brothers; *Best Of The Blues Brothers* . . . . (Atlantic)

Everybody's Free (To Wear Sunscreen)
Baz Luhrmann; *Now That's What I Call Music!-#2-C* . . . . . . (Virgin)
Something For Everybody . . . . (Capitol)

Everything Is Everything
Lauryn Hill; *The Miseducation Of Lauryn Hill* . . . . (Ruffhouse/Columbia)

Everything Must Change
Barbra Streisand; *Higher Ground* . . . . (Columbia)

Faith In Me
Crosby, Stills, Nash & Young; *Looking Forward* . . . . (Reprise)

Fire In The Hole
Van Halen; *Van Halen 3* . . . . (Warner Bros.)

Folsom Prison Blues
Brooks & Dunn with Johnny Cash; *Red Hot + Country-C* . . . . . . (Mercury)
Johnny Cash; *Billboard Top Country Hits-1968-C* . . . . (Rhino)
Classic Cash-Hall Of Fame Series . . . . (Mercury)
Hot Tracks-Train Super Hits-C . . . . (Epic)
Jailhouse Rock (Hits From The Big House)-C . . . . (Sony Music Special Prod.)
Johnny Cash At Folsom Prison & San Quentin . . . . (Columbia)
Johnny Cash-Original Golden Hits-#1 . . . . (Sun)
Johnny Cash's Greatest Hits-#2 . . . . (Columbia)
Superbilly . . . . (Sun)
The Man In Black-His Greatest Hits . . . . (Legacy)

For Crying Out Loud
Anita Cochran; *Anita* . . . . (Warner Bros.)

Forgive Them Father
Lauryn Hill featuring Shelly Thunder; *The Miseducation Of Lauryn Hill* . . . . (Ruffhouse/Columbia)
Friendly Advice
Tom Cochrane; *Mad Mad World* . . . . (Capitol)
Frozen
Madonna; *GHV2* . . . .(Warner Bros.)
Ray Of Light. . . . .(Maverick)
Gambler, The
Kenny Rogers; *Kenny Rogers' Greatest Hits* . . . . (EMI)
Kenny Rogers-Twenty Greatest Hits . . . .(EMI)
The Gambler . . . . (EMI)
Genie In A Bottle
Christina Aguilera; *Christina Aguilera*. . . . . (RCA)
Totally Hits-#2-C . . . . (Elektra)
Get Back
Beatles; *Beatles 1* . . . . (Capitol)
Beatles-20 Greatest Hits . . . . (Capitol)
Beatles-Box Set . . . . (Capitol)
Let It Be . . . . (Capitol)
Past Masters-Volume Two . . . . (Parlophone)
Reel Music . . . . (Capitol)
Rock 'N' Roll Music . . . . (Capitol)
The Beatles/1967-1970 . . . . (Capitol)
Get Born Again
Alice In Chains; *Nothing Safe* . . . . (Columbia)
Get Down On Your Knees And Pray
Marty Stuart; *Bluegrass Super Hits-C* . . . . (Columbia)
Get Happy
Benny Goodman; *Benny Goodman's Greatest Hits* . . . . (RCA Victor)
Ella Fitzgerald; *Harold Arlen Songbook-#2* . . . . (Verve)
Judy Garland; *Best Of Judy Garland In Hollywood* . . . . (Turner Classic Movies)
Nat Shilkret & The Victor Orchestra; *78-#22444* . . . . (Victor)
Get Rhythm
Johnny Cash; *Johnny Cash-Sun Years* . . . . (Rhino)
Ry Cooder; *Get Rhythm* . . . .(Warner Bros.)
Give The Girl A Kiss
Bruce Springsteen; *Tracks* . . . . (Columbia)
Go Let It Out
Oasis; *Standing On The Shoulders Of Giants* . . . .(Epic)
Go On
George Strait; *George Strait*. . . . .(MCA)
Good Advice
R.E.M.; *Fables Of The Reconstruction* . . . .(I.R.S.)
Good Advice
Texas; *White On Blonde* . . . . (Mercury)
Good Lovin' (Makes It Right)
Tammy Wynette; *Tammy Wynette-16 Biggest Hits* . . . . . . (Legacy)
Tammy Wynette-Anniversary-20 Years Of Hits . . . .(Epic)
Tears Of Fire-25th Anniversary Collection . . . .(Epic)
Got To Give It Up (Pt. 1)
Marvin Gaye; *Billboard Top Dance Hits-1977-C*. . . . . (Rhino)
Great Songs & Performances That Inspired The Motown 25th Anniversary Television Special-C . . . . (Motown)
Marvin Gaye Live At The London Palladium . . . . (Motown)
Gotta Serve Somebody
Bob Dylan; *Biograph* . . . . (Columbia)
Slow Train Coming . . . . (Columbia)
The Sopranos-Music From The HBO Original Series . . . . (Sony Music Soundtrax)
Bob Dylan & The Grateful Dead; *Dylan & The Dead*. . . . . (Columbia)
Grown Men Don't Cry
Tim McGraw; *Set This Circus Down* . . . . (Curb)
Guys & Dolls
Original Cast; *ST/Guys & Dolls* . . . .(MCA)
Hakuna Matata
Jimmy Cliff; *Disney's Greatest Pop Hits-C* . . . .(Disney)
Nathan Lane/Ernie Sabella/Jason Weaver/Joseph Williams; *ST/The Lion King* . . . . (Walt Disney)
Original Cast; *The Lion King* . . . .(Disney)
Rembrandts; *Disney's Music From The Park-C* . . . . (Disney)
Happiness Street
Georgia Gibbs; *Best Of Georgia Gibbs-The Mercury Years* . . . .(Chronicles)
Happy Talk
Original Cast; *South Pacific* . . . .(CBS Masterworks)
Hard Way, The
Mary Chapin Carpenter; *Come On Come On* . . . . (Columbia)
He Wasn't Man Enough
Toni Braxton; *The Heat* . . . . (LaFace)
Totally Hits-#3-C. . . . . (Atlantic)
Heart-Shaped Box
Nirvana; *In Utero* . . . . (David Geffen Co.)
Heaven And Hot Rods
Stone Temple Pilots; *No. 4* . . . . (Atlantic)
Hello, Young Lovers
Frank Sinatra; *Frank Sinatra Sings Rodgers & Hammerstein* . . . . . . (Columbia)
Mel Torme; *Jazz 'Round Midnight-Mel Torme* . . . . (Verve)
Original Broadway Cast; *The King And I* . . . .(RCA Victor)

Original Cast; *ST/The King And I* . . . . (Angel)
Hepcat's Advice, A
Elmore Nixon; *Best Of Duke-Peacock Blues-C*. . . . . (MCA Special Prod.)
Hey Jude
Beatles; *Beatles 1* . . . . (Capitol)
Beatles-20 Greatest Hits . . . . (Capitol)
Past Masters-Volume Two . . . . (Parlophone)
The Beatles/1967-1970. . . . . (Capitol)
Paul McCartney; *Knebworth-The Album-C* . . . . (Polydor)
Wilson Pickett; *Wilson Pickett's Greatest Hits* . . . . (Atlantic)
Hey There
Original Cast; *ST/Pajama Game* . . . . (Collectables)
Rosemary Clooney; *Essence Of Rosemary Clooney* . . . . (Legacy)
Hey Young World II
Macy Gray featuring Slick Rick; *The Id* . . . . (Epic)
Hold On (Change Is Comin')
Sounds Of Blackness; *Time For Healing* . . . . (Perspective/A&M)
Hold On To Your Dream
Stevie Wonder; *Song Review-A Greatest Hits Collection* . . . . (Motown)
ST/The Adventures Of Pinocchio . . . .(London)
Hold What You've Got
Joe Tex; *Atlantic Ultimate '60s Soul Smashes!-C* . . . . (Rhino)
Very Best Of Joe Tex. . . . . (Rhino)
House Of The Rising Sun
Animals; *Animals Greatest Hits* . . . . (Allegiance)
Best Of The Animals . . . .(Abkco)
Greatest Hits Live!-Rip It To Shreds. . . . . (I.R.S.)
Hank Williams, Jr.; *Hank Williams, Jr. "Live"* . . . . (WB/Curb)
Ronnie Milsap; *Ronnie Milsap-16 Greatest Hits-#2* . . . .(Trip)
How To Handle A Woman
Original Cast; *Camelot* . . . . (Columbia)
Richard Harris; *ST/Camelot* . . . . (Warner Bros.)
How To Succeed
New Broadway Cast; *How To Succeed In Business Without Really Trying* . . . . (RCA Victor)
Original Cast; *How To Succeed In Business Without Really Trying* . . . . . (RCA)
How Will I Know
Whitney Houston; *Soul Train 25th Anniv. Hall Of Fame-Box* . . . . (MCA)
Whitney Houston . . . . (Arista)
Whitney Houston's Greatest Hits . . . . (Arista)
Human Nature
Madonna; *Bedtime Stories* . . . .(Maverick/Sire)
GHV2 . . . . (Warner Bros.)
I Don't Want To Wait
Paula Cole; *Live On Letterman-From The Late Show* . . . . (Reprise)
Songs From Dawson's Creek . . . . (Sony Music Soundtrax)
This Fire . . . . (Imago)
I Hope You Dance
Lee Ann Womack; *I Hope You Dance*. . . . . (MCA)
I Know There's An Answer
Beach Boys; *Pet Sounds* . . . . (Capitol)
The Pet Sounds Sessions: A 30th Anniversary Collection . . . . (Capitol)
I Know What I Know
Paul Simon; *Graceland*. . . . . (Warner Bros.)
I Whistle A Happy Tune
Barbara Cook; *My Little Broadway*. . . . . (Sony Wonder)
Frank Sinatra; *Frank Sinatra Sings Rodgers & Hammerstein*. . . . . . . (Columbia)
Micky Dolenz; *Broadway Micky*. . . . .(Kid Rhino/Rhino 4 Kids)
Original Broadway Cast; *The King And I* . . . . (RCA Victor)
Original Cast; *The King And I* . . . . (MCA)
I Will Remember You
Sarah McLachlan; *Mirrorball* . . . . (Arista)
ST/Brothers McMullen. . . . . (Arista)
Surfacing . . . . (Arista)
Totally Hits-#2-C . . . . (Elektra)
If I Were You
Terri Clark; *Terri Clark*. . . . . (Mercury)
If You Ain't Lovin' (You Ain't Livin')
Faron Young; *Heroes Of Country Music-#3-Legends Of Nashville-C* . . . (Rhino)
Live Fast, Love Hard: Original Capitol Recordings-1952-1962-C . . . . (Country Music Foundation)
George Strait; *If You Ain't Lovin' You Ain't Livin'* . . . . (MCA)
Ten Strait Hits . . . . (MCA)
If You Love Me
Brownstone; *From The Bottom Up* . . . . (MJJ/Epic)
MTV Party To Go-#8-C . . . . (Tommy Boy)
If You Love Me, Baby
Beatles; *In The Beginning-The Early Tapes* . . . .(Polydor)
If You Wanna Be Happy
Jimmy Soul; *Best Of Jimmy Soul*. . . . . (Rhino)
Dick Bartley's One-Hit Wonders Of The '60s-#1-C . . . . (Rhino)
Son Of Frat Rock!-C . . . . (Rhino)
ST/Mermaids . . . . (Geffen)
ST/My Best Friend's Wedding . . . . (Work/Epic)
If You Wanna Touch Her, Ask!
Shania Twain; *Come On Over*. . . . . (Mercury)
I'll Be Around
Rappin' 4-Tay; *Don't Fight The Feelin'* . . . . (Rag Top/EMI)

I'm Flying
Original Cast/Mary Martin; *Peter Pan-The 1954 Broadway Production* . . . . (RCA Victor)
Imagination
Tamia; *Tamia* . . . . (Qwest)
Inner Light
Beatles; *Past Masters-Volume Two* . . . . (Parlophone)
Rarities . . . . (Capitol)
Insensitive
Jann Arden; *Living Under June* . . . . (A&M)
Women For Women-#2-C . . . . (Mercury)
Ironic
Alanis Morissette; *Jagged Little Pill* . . . . (Maverick)
It's All Coming Back
Keb' Mo'; *The Door* . . . . (550/Epic/Okeh)
It's How You Say It
Al Jarreau; *Tomorrow Today* . . . . (GRP/VMG)
It's Not Where You Start (It's Where You Finish)
Barbara Cook; *Dorothy Fields-Close As Pages In A Book* . . . . (DRG)
Original Broadway Cast; *See Saw* . . . . (DRG)
I've Been Down That Road Before
Hank Williams; *Alone And Forsaken* . . . . (Mercury)
Beyond The Sunset . . . . (Polydor)
Jump
Van Halen; *1984* . . . . (Warner Bros.)
Best Of Van Halen-#1 . . . . (Warner Bros.)
LIVE: Right here, right now . . . . (Warner Bros.)
Jumpin, Jumpin
Destiny's Child; *Now That's What I Call Music!-#5-C* . . . . (Virgin)
The Writing's On The Wall . . . . (Columbia)
Just Another Day
John Mellencamp; *Mr. Happy Go Lucky* . . . . (Mercury)
Just Be A Man About It
Toni Braxton; *The Heat* . . . . (LaFace)
Just Push Play
Aerosmith; *Just Push Play* . . . . (Columbia)
Just The Two Of Us
Will Smith; *Big Willie Style* . . . . (Columbia)
Keep A Lid On Things
Crash Test Dummies; *Give Yourself A Hand* . . . . (Arista)
Keep It Gay
Original Cast; *Me & Juliet* . . . . (RCA Victor)
Keep On Smilin'
Wet Willie; *Super Hits Of The '70s-Have A Nice Day-#13-C* . . . . . . (Rhino)
Wet Willie's Greatest Hits . . . . (Polydor)
Keep On Smilin'
Alfie; *45-#1827* . . . . (Motown)
Keep On The Sunny Side
Randy Scruggs with Earl Scruggs & Doc Watson; *Red Hot + Country-C* . . . . (Mercury)
Whites; *ST/O Brother, Where Art Thou?* . . . . (Mercury)
Keep Smiling At Trouble
Al Jolson; *Rainbow 'Round My Shoulder* . . . . (MCA Special Prod.)
Tony Bennett; *Forty Years-The Artistry Of Tony Bennett* . . . . (Columbia)
Keep Tryin'
Groove Theory; *Groove Theory* . . . . (Epic)
Keep Young And Beautiful
Annie Lennox; *Diva* . . . . (Arista)
Kicks
Paul Revere And The Raiders; *Legend Of Paul Revere And The Raiders* . . . . (Columbia)
Midnight Ride . . . . (Columbia)
Paul Revere And The Raiders' Greatest Hits . . . . . . (Columbia)
Kiss An Angel Good Mornin'
Charley Pride; *Charley Pride-24 Greatest Hits* . . . . . . (Tee Vee)
Pride! My 6 Latest And 6 Greatest . . . . (ISD/Intersound)
The Ultimate Charley Pride . . . . (Bransounds)
Kiss The Rain
Billie Myers; *A Taste Of '98-C* . . . . (Universal)
Growing Pains . . . . (Universal)
Last Cup Of Sorrow
Faith No More; *Album Of The Year* . . . . (Reprise)
Last Night On Earth
U2; *Pop* . . . . (Island)
Laugh Laugh
Beau Brummels; *Best Of The Beau Brummels* . . . . (Rhino)
Heart & Soul Of Rock 'N' Roll-#1-C . . . . (Rhino)
Introducing The Beau Brummels . . . . (Rhino)
Nuggets-#7-Early San Francisco-C . . . . (Rhino)
Leading With Your Heart
Barbra Streisand; *Higher Ground* . . . . (Columbia)
Learn To Be Still
Eagles; *Hell Freezes Over* . . . . (Geffen)
Leave Virginia Alone
Rod Stewart; *A Spanner In The Works* . . . . (Warner Bros.)
Lessons To Be Learned
Barbra Streisand; *Higher Ground* . . . . (Columbia)

Let A Smile Be Your Umbrella
Sammy Kaye & His Orchestra; *Best Of Sammy Kaye & His Orchestra* . . . (MCA)
Let 'Er Rip
Dixie Chicks; *Wide Open Spaces* . . . . (Monument)
Let Her Cry
Hootie & The Blowfish; *1996 Grammy Nominees-C* . . . . (Columbia)
Cracked Rear View . . . . (Atlantic)
Let It All Out (Let It All Hang Out)
Hombres; *Dick Bartley's One-Hit Wonders Of The '60s-#2-C* . . . . . (Rhino)
Let It Out (Let It All Hang Out) . . . . (Verve/Forecast)
Summer Of Love-#2-Turn On-Mind Expansion & Signs Of The Times-C . . . . (Rhino)
Let It Be
Aretha Franklin; *Aretha Franklin's Greatest Hits* . . . . . (Atlantic)
Beatles; *Beatles 1* . . . . (Capitol)
Beatles-20 Greatest Hits . . . . (Capitol)
Past Masters-Volume Two . . . . (Parlophone)
Reel Music . . . . (Capitol)
The Beatles/1967-1970 . . . . (Capitol)
Paul McCartney; *The Concert For New York City-C* . . . . (Columbia)
Tripping The Live Fantastic-Highlights! . . . . (Capitol)
Rockestra; *Kampuchea-C* . . . . (Atlantic)
Let That Pony Run
Pam Tillis; *Homeward Looking Angel* . . . . (Arista)
Let Your Love Flow
Bellamy Brothers; *Bellamy Brothers' Greatest Hits* . . . . . . (MCA)
Best Of The Bellamy Brothers . . . . (Curb)
Let Your Soul Be Your Pilot
Sting; *Mercury Falling* . . . . (A&M)
Let's Live For Today
Grass Roots; *At The Hop* . . . . (MCA)
Grass Roots-All-Time Greatest Hits . . . . (MCA)
Let's Live For Today . . . . (MCA Special Prod.)
Summer Of Love-#1-C . . . . (Rhino)
Vintage Music-#10-C . . . . (MCA)
Let's Think About Living
Bob Luman; *Bob Luman-Classic Country* . . . . (Simitar)
Life And How To Live It
R.E.M.; *Fables Of The Reconstruction* . . . . (I.R.S.)
Life Gets Away
Clint Black; *Clint Black-The Greatest Hits* . . . . (RCA)
One Emotion . . . . (RCA)
Life Is Just A Bowl Of Cherries
Ethel Merman; *The Ethel Merman Collection* . . . . . (Razor & Tie)
Jaye P. Morgan; *The Jaye P. Morgan Story* . . . . (Simitar)
Original Cast; *Fosse* . . . . (RCA Victor)
Rudy Vallee & His Connecticut Yankees; *As Time Goes By* . . . . (Varese Sarabande)
Life's A Dance
John Michael Montgomery; *Life's A Dance* . . . . (Atlantic)
Light In Your Eyes
LeAnn Rimes; *Blue* . . . . (MCG/Curb)
Listen
Collective Soul; *Disciplined Breakdown* . . . . (Atlantic)
Listen People
Herman's Hermits; *Herman's Hermits-Their Greatest Hits* . . . . . (Abkco)
Little Bit Of Soul
Music Explosion; *Best Of Ohio Express & Other Bubblegum Smashes-#1-C* . . . . (Rhino)
Cruisin'-1967-C . . . . (Increase)
Million-Dollar Memories #1-C . . . . (RCA)
Little Things
Tanya Tucker; *Complicated* . . . . (Capitol)
Little White Cloud That Cried
Johnnie Ray; *Best Of Johnnie Ray* . . . . (Columbia)
Best Of Johnnie Ray . . . . (Exact)
Johnnie Ray's Greatest Hits . . . . (Sony Music Special Prod.)
Lonely Women Make Good Lovers
Bob Luman; *Bob Luman-Classic Country* . . . . (Simitar)
Steve Wariner; *Best Of Steve Wariner* . . . . (RCA)
Midnight Fire . . . . (RCA)
Steve Wariner's Greatest Hits . . . . (RCA)
Steve Wariner-Super Hits . . . . (RCA)
Look For The Silver Lining
Alberta Hunter; *Look For The Silver Lining* . . . . (Columbia)
Chet Baker; *Let's Get Lost-Best Of Chet Baker Sings* . . . . . (Blue Note)
Dave Brubeck Quartet; *Stardust* . . . . (Fantasy)
Judy Garland; *Best Of Judy Garland In Hollywood* . . . . (Turner Classic Movies)
Marion Harris; *78-#3367* . . . . (Columbia)
Lose That Long Face
Judy Garland; *A Star Is Born* . . . . (Columbia)
Lost Ones
Lauryn Hill; *The Miseducation Of Lauryn Hill* . . . . . . (Ruffhouse/Columbia)
Love Don't Cost A Thing
Jennifer Lopez; *J. Lo* . . . . (Epic)
Now That's What I Call Music!-#6-C . . . . (Virgin)
Love Is A Good Thing
Sheryl Crow; *Sheryl Crow* . . . . (A&M)

Love Is All You Need For The Future
Nona Gaye; *Love For The Future* . . . . . (Third Stone)
Love Of Your Own, A
Average White Band; *Pickin' Up The Pieces-Best Of The Average White Band (1974-1980)* . . . . . (Rhino)
Smooth Grooves-A Sensual Collection-#1-C . . . . . (Rhino)
Soul Searching . . . . . (Rhino)
Love Potion Number 9
Clovers; *ST/American Graffiti* . . . . . (MCA)
Super Oldies Of The '50s-#7-C . . . . . (Audio Fidelity)
Herb Alpert & The Tijuana Brass; *Herb Alpert & The Tijuana Brass' Greatest Hits* . . . . . (A&M)
Herb Alpert & The Tijuana Brass-Classics-#1 . . . . . (A&M)
Searchers; *History Of British Rock-#3-C* . . . . . (Rhino)
Searchers' Greatest Hits . . . . . (Rhino)
Love The One You're With
Crosby, Stills & Nash; *Replay* . . . . . (Atlantic)
Crosby, Stills, Nash & Young; *4 Way Street* . . . . . (Atlantic)
Luther Vandross; *Songs* . . . . . (Epic)
Stephen Stills; *Hit Singles-1958-1977-C* . . . . . (Atlantic)
Stephen Stills . . . . . (Atlantic)
Still . . . . . (Atlantic)
Love Will Find A Way
Christina Aguilera; *Christina Aguilera* . . . . . (RCA)
Love Will Find Its Way To You
Reba McEntire; *Last One To Know* . . . . . (MCA)
Reba McEntire's Greatest Hits Volume Two . . . . . (MCA)
Mama Said
Shirelles; *Original Rock 'N' Roll Hits Of The '60s-C* . . . . . (Roulette)
Shirelles' Greatest Hits . . . . . (Everest)
Shirelles-Anthology 1959-1964 . . . . . (Rhino)
Shirelles-Classics . . . . . (Bac-Trac)
Super Oldies Of The '60s-#3-C . . . . . (Audio Fidelity)
Mama Told Me Not To Come
Randy Newman; *12 Songs* . . . . . (Reprise)
Randy Newman/Live . . . . . (Warner Archives)
Three Dog Night; *Best Of Three Dog Night* . . . . . (MCA)
Billboard Top Rock 'N' Roll Hits-1970-C . . . . . (Rhino)
Wilson Pickett; *Wilson Pickett's Greatest Hits* . . . . . (Atlantic)
Mammas Don't Let Your Babies Grow Up To Be Cowboys
Gibson/Miller Band; *Cowboy Super Hits-C* . . . . . (Columbia)
ST/The Cowboy Way . . . . . (Epic)
Waylon Jennings & Willie Nelson; *Waylon & Willie* . . . . . (RCA)
Waylon Jennings & Willie Nelson's Greatest Hits . . . . . (RCA)
Willie Nelson; *Greatest Hits (& Some That Will Be)* . . . . . (Columbia)
ST/The Electric Horseman . . . . . (Columbia)
Willie & Family Live . . . . . (Columbia)
Marry The Man Today
Original Cast; *ST/Guys & Dolls* . . . . . (MCA)
Mmm Bop
Hanson; *1998 Grammy Nominees-C* . . . . . (MCA)
Middle Of Nowhere . . . . . (Mercury)
Now That's What I Call Music!-#1-C . . . . . (Virgin)
Three Car Garage: The Independent Recordings . . . . . (Mercury)
My Best Was Never Good Enough
Bruce Springsteen; *The Ghost Of Tom Joad* . . . . . (Columbia)
Next Voice You Hear
Jackson Browne; *The Next Voice You Hear-Best Of Jackson Browne* . . (Elektra)
No Strings Attached
'N Sync; *No Strings Attached* . . . . . (Jive)
No Tears Left
Crosby, Stills, Nash & Young; *Looking Forward* . . . . . (Reprise)
Nobody's Got The Gun
Mark Knopfler; *Golden Heart* . . . . . (Warner Bros.)
Not For You
Pearl Jam; *Vitalogy* . . . . . (Epic)
Nowhere Man
Beatles; *"Yesterday"...And Today* . . . . . (Capitol)
Beatles-Box Set . . . . . (Capitol)
Compact Disc Singles Collection . . . . . (Capitol)
The Beatles/1962-1966 . . . . . (Capitol)
Now's The Time To Fall In Love
Eddie Cantor; *The Eddie Cantor Radio Show-1942-1943* . . . . . (Original Cast)
Gene Gardos & His Orchestra; *Brother Can You Spare A Dime? Great American Songs Of The Depression-C* . . . . . (Pro-Arte)
Off The Wall
Jacksons; *Jacksons Live* . . . . . (Epic)
Michael Jackson; *Off The Wall* . . . . . (Epic)
Old Man And Me
Hootie & The Blowfish; *Fairweather Johnson* . . . . . (Atlantic)
On The Sunny Side Of The Street
Diana Krall; *Stepping Out* . . . . . (Justin Time)
Frank Sinatra; *Come Swing With Me!* . . . . . (Capitol)
One More For The Road . . . . . (Capitol)
Sentimental Journey . . . . . (Capitol)
The Capitol Years . . . . . (Capitol)
Judy Garland; *Best Of Judy Garland* . . . . . (MCA)
Louis Armstrong; *Best Of Louis Armstrong* . . . . . (MCA)
Chicago Concert 1956 . . . . . (Columbia)
Jazz Club-Vocal . . . . . (Verve)
Music Autobiography . . . . . (MCA)
Ted Lewis & His Orchestra; *Charming Gents Of Stage & Screen-C* . . . . (Legacy)
Those Wonderful Years: Puttin' On The Ritz-C . . . . . (JCI Assoc. Labels)
One Hit Wonder
Everclear; *So Much For The Afterglow* . . . . . (Capitol)
One Step At A Time
Brenda Lee; *Brenda Lee-Anthology-#1 & #2* . . . . . (MCA)
Only The Strong Survive
Elvis Presley; *From Elvis In Memphis* . . . . . (RCA)
Memphis Record . . . . . (RCA)
Jerry Butler; *Best Of Jerry Butler* . . . . . (Mercury)
Best Of Jerry Butler . . . . . (Rhino)
Only Trust Your Heart
Diana Krall; *Only Trust Your Heart* . . . . . (GRP)
Open Up Your Eyes
Tonic; *Lemon Parade* . . . . . (Polydor)
Optimistic
Radiohead; *Kid A* . . . . . (Capitol)
Other Man's Grass Is Always Greener
Petula Clark; *Petula Clark's Greatest Hits* . . . . . (Crescendo)
Over Your Shoulder
Seven Mary Three; *Orange Ave.* . . . . . (Atlantic)
Pass You By
Boyz II Men; *Nathan Michael Shawn Wanya* . . . . . (Universal)
Passin' Thru
Earl Scruggs & Don Henley & Johnny Cash; *Earl Scruggs And Friends-C* . . . . . (MCA)
Randy Scruggs; *Crown Of Jewels* . . . . . (Reprise)
Randy Scruggs & Joan Osborne; *ST/Happy Texas* . . . . . (Arista)
Pick Yourself Up
Diana King; *When I Look In Your Eyes* . . . . . (GRP)
Frank Sinatra; *Sinatra and Swingin' Brass* . . . . . (Reprise)
Fred Astaire; *Starring Fred Astaire* . . . . . (Columbia)
That's Dancing . . . . . (EMI)
Please Don't Talk About Me When I'm Gone
Ann-Margret; *Let Me Entertain You* . . . . . (RCA)
Arlo Guthrie & Pete Seeger; *Precious Friend* . . . . . (Warner Bros.)
Billie Holiday; *Compact Jazz-Billie Holiday* . . . . . (Verve)
Music For Torching: Billie Holiday Story-#5 . . . . . (Verve)
The Ultimate Billie Holiday . . . . . (Verve)
Ella Fitzgerald & Count Basie; *Perfect Match* . . . . . (Pablo)
Frank Sinatra; *Swing Along With Me* . . . . . (Reprise)
Gene Austin; *The Voice Of The Southland* . . . . . (Living Era)
Harry Connick, Jr.; *20* . . . . . (Columbia)
Leon Redbone; *Champagne Charlie* . . . . . (Warner Bros.)
Ray Price; *Portrait Of A Singer* . . . . . (Step One)
Pop Ya Collar
Usher; *All About U* . . . . . (LaFace)
Popular
Nada Surf; *High/Low* . . . . . (Elektra)
Practice What You Preach
Santana; *Borboletta* . . . . . (Columbia)
Practice What You Preach
Barry White; *The Icon Is Love* . . . . . (A&M)
Practice What You Preach
American Girls; *American Girls* . . . . . (I.R.S.)
Practice What You Preach
Proven Innocent; *And Then There Were 2* . . . . . (First Priority)
Practice What You Preach
Alex Taylor; *Dancing With The Devil* . . . . . (Ichiban Int'l)
Practice What You Preach
Testament; *Practice What You Preach* . . . . . (Megaforce)
Pretend
Nat "King" Cole; *Capitol Collectors Series-Nat "King" Cole* . . . . . (Capitol)
The Nat "King" Cole Story . . . . . (Capitol)
Unforgettable . . . . . (Capitol)
Pure Morning
Placebo; *Without You I'm Nothing* . . . . . (Virgin)
Put Your Dreams Away (For Another Day)
Frank Sinatra; *Best Of The Columbia Years-1943-1952* . . . . . (Columbia)
Frank Sinatra-16 Most Requested Songs . . . . . (Columbia)
Sinatra: A Man And His Music . . . . . (Reprise)
The Capitol Years . . . . . (Capitol)
Mickey Gilley; *Put Your Dreams Away* . . . . . (Epic)
Ten Years Of Hits . . . . . (Epic)
Puttin' On The Ritz
Ella Fitzgerald; *Silver Collection-Songbooks* . . . . . (Verve)
Fred Astaire; *Irving Berlin Always-C* . . . . . (Verve)
Irving Berlin Songbook . . . . . (Verve)
Harry Richman; *Hollywood Sings-C* . . . . . (Living Era)
Those Wonderful Years: Puttin' On The Ritz-C . . . . . (JCI Assoc. Labels)
Judy Garland; *One & Only* . . . . . (Capitol)
Mandy Patinkin; *Mandy Patinkin* . . . . . (Columbia)
Taco; *After Eight* . . . . . (RCA)
Nipper's Greatest Hits Of The '80s-C . . . . . (RCA)
Que Sera, Sera
Doris Day; *Doris Day-16 Most Requested Songs-Encore!* . . . . . (Columbia)
Doris Day's Greatest Hits . . . . . (Columbia)

Radio Classics Of The '50s-C.................................(Columbia)
Sly & The Family Stone; *Fresh* ....(Legacy)
Sly & The Family Stone-Anthology ....(Epic)

Reach Out Of The Darkness
Friend And Lover; *Chicken Soup For The Soul: I'll Be There For You-Songs*
Of Friendship, Brotherhood And Sisterhood-C ....(Rhino)
Flower Power-Psychedelic Rock Classics-C ....(K-Tel)

Recover Your Soul
Elton John; *The Big Picture*..................................(Rocket)

Refugee
Tom Petty And The Heartbreakers; *Damn The Torpedoes* ....(MCA)
Pack Up The Plantation-Live! ....(MCA)

Remember (Christmas)
Nilsson; *Son Of Schmilsson*.................................(RCA)

Remember Me This Way
Jordan Hill; *Jordan Hill*..................................(Atlantic)
ST/Casper ....(MCA)

River, The
Garth Brooks; *Ropin' The Wind* ....(Liberty)
The Limited Series ....(Capitol)

Road You Leave Behind
David Lee Murphy; *Gettin' Out The Good Stuff* ....(MCA)

Roll With It
Steve Winwood; *Rock The First-#2-C*........(Sandstone Music)
Roll With It ....(Virgin)
ST/Nuns On The Run ....(Mercury)

Rosa Parks
Outkast; *Aquemini*.......................................(LaFace/Arista)

Rose Garden
k.d. lang; *Swingin' Country Favorites-C* ....(Warner Bros.)
k.d. lang and The Reclines; *Angel With A Lariat* ....(Sire)
Lynn Anderson; *All Time Legends Of Country Music-C* ....(Legacy)
Country Music Classics-#4-1970-1975-C ....(K-Tel)
Lynn Anderson's Greatest Hits ....(Columbia)
Rose Garden ....(Columbia)
Super Hits Of The '70s-Have A Nice Day-#4-C ....(Rhino)
Very Special Love Song-C ....(Fifty One West)

Safe Sex
Erick Sermon; *No Pressure* ....(Def Jam/IDJMG)

Safety In Numbers
Joan Osborne; *Righteous Love*.........................(Interscope)

San Francisco (Be Sure To Wear Some Flowers In Your Hair)
Scott McKenzie; *Nuggets-#10-Folk Rock-C* ....(Rhino)
Rock Artifacts-From The Vaults-#3-C ....(Columbia)
ST/Forrest Gump ....(Epic/Sony Music Soundtrax)
Summer Of Love-#1-C ....(Rhino)

Seven Angels
Bruce Springsteen; *Tracks*.............................(Columbia)

She Ain't The Girl For You
Kinleys; *Kinleys II* ....(Epic)

She Ain't Your Ordinary Girl
Alabama; *Alabama-Super Hits-#2* ....(RCA)
In Pictures ....(RCA)

She Loves You
Beatles; *Beatles 1*......................................(Capitol)
Beatles-20 Greatest Hits ....(Capitol)
Beatles-Box Set ....(Capitol)
Past Masters-Volume One ....(Parlophone)
The Beatles At The Hollywood Bowl ....(Capitol)
The Beatles' Second Album ....(Capitol)
The Beatles/1962-1966 ....(Capitol)

Sheep Go To Heaven
Cake; *Prolonging The Magic*..............................(Capricorn)

Shining Star
Earth, Wind & Fire; *Best Of Earth, Wind & Fire-#1* ....(Legacy)
Eternal Dance ....(Columbia)
Gratitude ....(Legacy)
That's The Way Of The World ....(Legacy)

Shoes You're Wearing
Clint Black; *Nothin' But The Taillights* ....(RCA)

Shop Around
Captain & Tennille; *Captain & Tennille's Greatest Hits*........(A&M)
Miracles; *Greatest Hits From The Beginning* ....(Motown)
Hi-We're The Miracles ....(Motown)
Smokey Robinson & The Miracles; *16 #1 Hits From The Early*
'60s-C ....(Motown)
Every Great Motown Song-First 25 Years-C ....(Motown)
Smokey Robinson & The Miracles' Anthology ....(Motown)

Shower The People
James Taylor; *In The Pocket* ....(Warner Bros.)
James Taylor's Greatest Hits ....(Warner Bros.)

Shut Up And Drive
Chely Wright; *Woman In The Moon* ....(Polydor Country)

Simple Creed
Live; *V*...(Radioactive/MCA)

Sing A Song
Earth, Wind & Fire; *Best Of Earth, Wind & Fire-#1* ....(Legacy)
Eternal Dance ....(Columbia)
Gratitude ....(Legacy)

Sing Something Simple
June Christy; *The Misty Miss Christy*......................(Capitol)

Sit Down, You're Rockin' The Boat
Don Henley; *ST/Leap Of Faith*.............................(MCA)
Original Cast; *Guys & Dolls*..............................(MCA)

Skinny
Filter; *Title Of Record*...................................(Reprise)

Sky Fits Heaven
Madonna; *Ray Of Light*..................................(Maverick)

Slow Ride
Foghat; *Best Of Foghat* ....(Rhino)
Best Of King Biscuit Live-#1-C ....(Sandstone Music)
Foghat-Live ....(Rhino)
Fool For The City ....(Rhino)

Smile
Dexter Gordon; *Best Of Dexter Gordon*....................(Blue Note)
Lyle Lovett; *ST/Hope Floats* ....(Capitol)
Nat "King" Cole; *The Nat "King" Cole Story* ....(Capitol)
Natalie Cole; *Unforgettable With Love* ....(Elektra)
Tony Bennett; *The Movie Song Album* ....(Columbia)
Tony Bennett's All-Time Greatest Hits ....(Columbia)

So You Want To Be A Rock 'N' Roll Star
Byrds; *Original Singles-#1-1965-1967* ....(Columbia)
Rock Classics Of The '60s-C ....(Columbia)
The Byrds ....(Columbia)
The Byrds (Untitled) ....(Legacy)
The Byrds' Greatest Hits ....(Columbia)
Patti Smith Group; *Wave* ....(Arista)
Tom Petty And The Heartbreakers; *Pack Up The Plantation-Live!* ......(MCA)
The Ultimate Rock Album-C ....(Foundation)

Some Days You Gotta Dance
Dixie Chicks; *Fly* ....(Monument)

Some Enchanted Evening
Jay & The Americans; *Come A Little Bit Closer-Best Of Jay & The*
Americans ....(Gold Rush)
Jay & The Americans' All-Time Greatest Hits ....(Rhino)
Original Cast; *South Pacific* ....(CBS Masterworks)
Perry Como; *Perry Como's All-Time Greatest Hits-#1* ....(RCA)
Rosanno Brazzi; *ST/South Pacific* ....(RCA)
Willie Nelson; *What A Wonderful World* ....(Columbia)

Sound Advice
Elvis Presley; *Elvis For Everyone!* ....(RCA)

Stand By Your Man
Elton John; *Tammy Wynette...Remembered-C* ....(Asylum)
Lyle Lovett and his Large Band; *Lyle Lovett and his*
Large Band ....(Curb/MCA)
Tammy Wynette; *Columbia Country Classics-#4-Nashville*
Sound-C ....(Columbia)
ST/Sleepless In Seattle ....(Epic/Sony Music Soundtrax)
Tammy Wynette's Biggest Hits ....(Epic)
Tears Of Fire-25th Anniversary Collection ....(Epic)

Stand On It
Mel McDaniel; *Hot Rod-Hot Rod Cowboys-C* ....(Right Stuff)

Stand On It
Bruce Springsteen; *Tracks* ....(Columbia)

Step By Step
Eddie Rabbitt; *Best Of Eddie Rabbitt/Greatest Hits-II* ....(Warner Bros.)
Number 1's ....(Warner Bros.)

Step Out Of Your Mind
American Breed; *Bend Me, Shape Me-Best Of The American*
Breed ....(Varese Vintage)

Straighten Up And Fly Right
Andrews Sisters; *Best Of The Andrews Sisters-#2* ....(MCA)
Diana Krall; *Stepping Out* ....(Justin Time)
Linda Ronstadt; *For Sentimental Reasons* ....(Asylum)
Nat "King" Cole; *Best Of Nat "King" Cole-Vol. 2* ....(Capitol)

Stuck In A Moment You Can't Get Out Of
U2; *All That You Can't Leave Behind* ....(Interscope)

Stupid Girl
Garbage; *Garbage*....................................(Almo Sounds)

Sweet Dreams (Are Made Of This)
Eurythmics; *Eurythmics' Greatest Hits* ....(Arista)
Sweet Dreams (Are Made Of This) ....(RCA)
Marilyn Manson; *Smells Like Children* ....(Interscope)

Sweet Rosalyn
Sheryl Crow; *Sheryl Crow* ....(A&M)

Sweet Talkin' Guy
Chiffons; *Best Of The Chiffons*...........................(Laurie)
Chiffons-Golden Classics ....(Collectables)
Collectables Presents The History Of Rock-#1-C ....(Collectables)
Everything You Always Wanted ....(Laurie)

Sweetest Days
Vanessa Williams; *The Sweetest Days* ....(Uptown/MCA)

Take Care Of Home
Dave Hollister; *Chicago '85 The Movie* ....(Def Squad/DreamWorks)

Take 'Em As They Come
Bruce Springsteen; *Tracks* ....(Columbia)

Take Good Care Of Her
Adam Wade; *45-#546* ....(Coed)

Sonny James; *Billboard Top Country Hits-1966-C* . . . . (Rhino)
Take Good Care Of My Baby
Bobby Vee; *Best Of Bobby Vee* . . . . (EMI)
Billboard Top Rock 'N' Roll Hits-1961-C . . . . (Rhino)
'Til My Dreamin' Comes True-C . . . . (Capitol)
Bobby Vinton; *Bobby Vinton-16 Most Requested Songs* . . . . (Legacy)
Dion; *Runaround Sue (Right Stuff)* . . . . (Right Stuff)
Take It Easy
Eagles; *Eagles* . . . . (Asylum)
Eagles Live . . . . (Asylum)
Eagles/Their Greatest Hits 1971-1975 . . . . (Asylum)
Hell Freezes Over . . . . (Geffen)
Jackson Browne; *For Everyman* . . . . (Asylum)
Travis Tritt; *Common Thread-Songs Of The Eagles-C* . . . . (Giant)
Take It Easy
Duke Ellington; *Brunswick Era-#1-1926-1929* . . . . (MCA)
Take It Easy
Crystal Gayle; *Crystal Gayle Greatest Hits* . . . . (Columbia)
These Days . . . . (Columbia)
Take Time To Know Her
Percy Sledge; *Best Of Percy Sledge* . . . . (Atlantic)
It Tears Me Up-Best Of Percy Sledge . . . . (Rhino)
Take Your Time (Do It Right) Part 1
Max-A-Million; *Club Hitz Of The '90s-#2-C* . . . . (Beast)
Take Your Time . . . . (S.O.S./Zoo)
S.O.S. Band; *Best Of The S.O.S. Band* . . . . (Tabu)
Billboard Top Hits-1980-C . . . . (Rhino)
Club Epic-#1-C . . . . (Legacy)
S.O.S. Band . . . . (Rhino)
Takes A Little Time
Amy Grant; *Behind The Eyes* . . . . (A&M)
Teach Your Children
Crosby, Stills & Nash; *CSN* . . . . (Atlantic)
Crosby, Stills, Nash & Young; *4 Way Street* . . . . (Atlantic)
Deja Vu . . . . (Atlantic)
So Far . . . . (Atlantic)
ST/The Wonder Years-Music From The Show & Era . . . . (Atlantic)
Suzy Bogguss/Alison Krauss/Kathy Mattea/Crosby, Stills & Nash; *Red Hot + Country-C* . . . . (Mercury)
Tell Her
Lonestar; *Lonely Grill* . . . . (BNA)
Tell Him
Exciters; *Best Of The Girl Groups-#2-C* . . . . (Rhino)
ST/Big Chill . . . . (Motown)
ST/My Best Friend's Wedding . . . . (Work/Epic)
Tell Him . . . . (Collectables)
Patti Drew; *Tell Him-Golden Classics* . . . . (Collectables)
Vonda Shepard; *ST/Songs From "Ally McBeal" Featuring Vonda Shepard* . . . . (550/Epic)
Tender Moment, A
Lee Roy Parnell; *Hits And Highways Ahead* . . . . (Arista)
Love Without Mercy . . . . (Arista)
Pure Country-Best Of The '90s-C . . . . (Priority)
Thank U
Alanis Morissette; *Supposed Former Infatuation Junkie* . . . . (Maverick)
That's Amore
Dean Martin; *Best Of Dean Martin* . . . . (CEMA Special Prod.)
Dean Martin's All Time Greatest Hits . . . . (Curb)
Dean Martin's Greatest Hits . . . . (EMI)
The Capitol Years-Dean Martin . . . . (Capitol)
That's Not Love
Keb' Mo'; *Just Like You* . . . . (Okeh)
That's The Way
Jo Dee Messina; *Burn* . . . . (Curb)
That's The Way It Is
Celine Dion; *All The Way...A Decade Of Song* . . . . (550 Music)
Collector's Series-Celine Dion-#1 . . . . (550 Music)
That's The Way Love Is
Marvin Gaye; *M.P.G.* . . . . (Motown)
Marvin Gaye-Anthology . . . . (Motown)
Marvin Gaye-Super Hits . . . . (Motown)
That's The Way Of The World
Earth, Wind & Fire; *Best Of Earth, Wind & Fire-#1* . . . . (Legacy)
Eternal Dance . . . . (Columbia)
Love Shouldn't Hurt-C . . . . (Qwest)
Pop Classics Of The '70s-C . . . . (Columbia)
That's The Way Of The World . . . . (Legacy)
Then What
Clay Walker; *Clay Walker's Greatest Hits* . . . . (Giant)
There's Your Trouble
Dixie Chicks; *Wide Open Spaces* . . . . (Monument)
They Like It Slow
H-Town; *Ladies Edition* . . . . (Relativity)
Thinking About Your Troubles
Nilsson; *The Point* . . . . (RCA)
This Door Swings Both Ways
Herman's Hermits; *Herman's Hermits-Their Greatest Hits* . . . . (Abkco)
This Lonely Place
Goldfinger; *Hang-Ups* . . . . (Mojo Music/Universal)
Through Your Hands
Don Henley; *ST/Michael* . . . . (Revolution)
Time Waits For No One
Hilltoppers; *P.S. I Love You (The Best Of The Hilltoppers)* . . . . . (Varese Vintage)
To Be Loved
Curtis Stigers; *Songs From Dawson's Creek* . . . . (Sony Music Soundtrax)
Tomorrow Never Knows
Beatles; *Beatles-Box Set* . . . . (Capitol)
Revolver . . . . (Capitol)
Phil Collins; *Face Value* . . . . (Atlantic)
Transfusion
Nervous Norvus; *Dr. Demento Presents The Greatest Novelty Records-#2-1950s-C* . . . . (Rhino)
Dr. Demento: 20th Anniversary Collection-C . . . . (Rhino)
Vintage Music-#3-C . . . . (MCA)
Wacky Weirdos-C . . . . (K-Tel)
Treat Her Like A Lady
Cornelius Brothers & Sister Rose; *Billboard Top Rock 'N' Roll Hits-1971-C* . . . . (Rhino)
Didn't It Blow Your Mind: Soul Hits Of The '70s-#5-C . . . . (Rhino)
Johnny Lee; *Best Of Johnny Lee* . . . . (Curb)
Treat Her Like A Lady
Celine Dion; *Let's Talk About Love-C* . . . . (550 Music)
Treat Her Like A Lady
Joe; *My Name Is Joe* . . . . (Jive)
Treat Her Like A Lady
Jimmy Buffett; *Boats Beaches Bars & Ballads* . . . . (Margaritaville)
Volcano . . . . (MCA)
Treat Her Like A Lady
Temptations; *Temptations-Anthology-The Best Of The Temptations* . . (Motown)
Truly For You . . . . (Motown)
Treat Her Right
Commitments; *ST/The Commitments* . . . . (MCA)
George Thorogood & The Destroyers; *Born To Be Bad* . . . . (Gold Rush)
Roy Head And The Traits; *Billboard Top Rock 'N' Roll Hits-1965-C* . . . (Rhino)
Treat Her Right
Sawyer Brown; *This Thing Called Wantin' & Havin' It All* . . . . (Curb)
Treat You Like A Queen
Rahsaan Patterson; *Love In Stereo* . . . . (MCA)
Troubles
Alicia Keys; *Songs In A Minor* . . . . (J)
Try Again
Aaliyah; *Now That's What I Call Music!-#4-C* . . . . (Virgin)
ST/Romeo Must Die . . . . (BlackGround Enterp./Atlantic)
Undo
Bjork; *Vespertine* . . . . (Elektra)
Voice Of The Heart
Diana Ross; *Take Me Higher* . . . . (Motown)
Waterfalls
TLC; *1996 Grammy Nominees-C* . . . . (Columbia)
CrazySexyCool . . . . (LaFace)
Weather
Amel Larrieux; *Infinite Possibilities* . . . . (Epic)
What Do The Simple Folk Do?
Julie Andrews; *Best Of Julie Andrews* . . . . (Rhino)
Julie Andrews & Richard Burton; *Camelot* . . . . (Columbia)
Original Soundtrack; *Camelot* . . . . (Warner Bros.)
What Do You Say
Reba McEntire; *So Good Together* . . . . (MCA)
What I Got
Sublime; *Now That's What I Call Music!-#2-C* . . . . (Virgin)
Sublime . . . . (Gasoline Alley)
What It's Like
Everlast; *Whitey Ford Sings The Blues* . . . . (Tommy Boy)
When The Lights Go Out
Bruce Springsteen; *Tracks* . . . . (Columbia)
When You Wish Upon A Star
Barbara Cook; *Disney Album* . . . . (Disney)
Billy Joel; *Simply Mad About The Mouse-C* . . . . (Columbia)
Cliff Edwards; *ST/Pinocchio* . . . . (Disney)
Dion; *The Wanderer* . . . . (Laurie)
Glenn Miller & Ray Eberle; *Chattanooga Choo Choo-#1 Hits* . . . . . . (Bluebird)
Linda Ronstadt; *For Sentimental Reasons* . . . . (Asylum)
Little Anthony And The Imperials; *We Are The Imperials* . . . . (Roulette)
Rosemary Clooney; *Rosemary Clooney-16 Most Requested Songs* . . . . (Legacy)
Stevie Wonder; *With A Song In My Heart* . . . . (Motown)
Wynton Marsalis; *Hot House Flowers* . . . . (Columbia)
Where Corn Don't Grow
Travis Tritt; *The Restless Kind* . . . . (Warner Bros.)
While You See A Chance
Steve Winwood; *Arc Of A Diver* . . . . (Island)
Steve Winwood-Chronicles . . . . (Island)
White Lines (Don't Do It)
Grandmaster Flash & Melle Mel; *Hip Hop Greats-Classic Raps-C* . . . . . (Rhino)

Why Don't You Get A Job?
Offspring; *Americana* . . . . (Columbia)
Wild World
Cat Stevens; *Cat Stevens Greatest Hits* . . . . (A&M)
  Tea For The Tillerman . . . . (A&M)
Jimmy Cliff; *In Concert-Best Of Jimmy Cliff* . . . . (Reprise)
  Reggae Spectacular-C . . . . (A&M)
Maxi Priest; *Best Of Me* . . . . (Charisma)
  Maxi . . . .(Virgin)
Wishin' & Hopin'
Ani DiFranco; *ST/My Best Friend's Wedding* . . . . (Work/Epic)
Dusty Springfield; *Dusty Springfield-Golden Hits* . . . . (Mercury)
  History Of British Rock-#6-C . . . . (Rhino)
With My Eyes Wide Open I'm Dreaming
Mandy Barnett; *I've Got A Right To Cry* . . . .(Sire)
Patti Page; *Patti Page-Golden Hits* . . . . (Mercury)
  Patti Page's Greatest Hits . . . . (Columbia)
Woman To Woman
Tammy Wynette; *Tammy Wynette-Anniversary-20 Years Of Hits* . . . . . . (Epic)
  Tammy Wynette's Greatest Hits-#3 . . . . (Epic)
  Tears Of Fire-25th Anniversary Collection . . . . (Epic)
Wynonna; *Tammy Wynette...Remembered-C* . . . . (Asylum)
Woman's Worth, A
Alicia Keys; *Songs In A Minor* . . . . (J)
Word, The
Beatles; *Beatles-Box Set* . . . . (Capitol)
  Rubber Soul . . . . (Capitol)
Words Of Love
Mamas & The Papas; *Best Of The Mamas & The Papas* . . . . (MCA)
  Farewell To The First Golden Era . . . . (MCA)
  Mamas & The Papas-16 Of Their Greatest Hits . . . . (MCA)
  Mama's Big Ones-Her Greatest Hits . . . . (MCA)
Working Man's Ph.D.
Aaron Tippin; *Call Of The Wild.* . . . .(RCA)
You Can Love Yourself
Keb' Mo'; *Just Like You* . . . . (Okeh)
You Can't Hurry Love
Diana Ross; *Diana Ross-The Ultimate Collection.* . . . . (Motown)
Diana Ross & The Supremes; *16 #1 Hits From The Early '60s-C* . . . . (Motown)
Phil Collins; *Hello, I Must Be Going* . . . . (Atlantic)
You Can't Run Away From It
Four Aces; *Four Aces-More Greatest Hits* . . . .(Varese Vintage)
You Don't Have To Cry
Crosby, Stills & Nash; *Crosby, Stills & Nash* . . . . (Atlantic)
You Don't Need The Wine To Have A Wonderful Time
Eddie Cantor; *Music From The New York Stage (1890-1920)-#4-1917-*
  1920-C . . . . (Pearl)
You Get What You Give
New Radicals; *Maybe You've Been Brainwashed Too* . . . . (MCA)
  Now That's What I Call Music!-#2-C . . . .(Virgin)
You Gotta Be
Des'ree; *Diana, Princess Of Wales-Tribute-C* . . . . (Columbia)
  I Ain't Movin' . . . . (550 Music)
You Gotta Have A Gimmick
Original Cast; *ST/Gypsy* . . . . (Columbia)
You Learn
Alanis Morissette; *Jagged Little Pill* . . . . (Maverick)
You Need To Be With Me
Susan Tedeschi; *Just Won't Burn* . . . . (Tone Cool)
You Should Be Mine (Don't Waste Your Time)
Brian McKnight; *Anytime* . . . . (Motown)
You'll Never Walk Alone
Andy Williams; *Unchained Melody-Greatest Songs* . . . .(Curb)
Jim Nabors; *Jim Nabors-16 Most Requested Songs* . . . . (Legacy)
Judy Garland; *Best Of The Capitol Masters-One & Only Box* . . . . (Capitol)
Mormon Tabernacle Choir; *Climb Ev'ry Mountain* . . . . (Columbia)
Original Broadway Cast; *Carousel* . . . . (Angel)
Original Cast; *Carousel* . . . . (MCA)
Pink Floyd; *Meddle* . . . . (Capitol)
Young Jews Be Proud
2 Live Jews; *As Kosher As They Wanna Be* . . . . (Kosher)
Young-At-Heart
Bing Crosby with Guy Lombardo & His Royal Canadians; *The Radio Years:*
  20 Songs. . . . . (Crescendo)
Frank Sinatra; *At The Movies.* . . . . (Capitol)
  Capitol Collectors Series-Frank Sinatra . . . . (Capitol)
  Classic Sinatra . . . . (Capitol)
  Sinatra's Sinatra . . . . (Reprise)
Ray Price; *Portrait Of A Singer* . . . . (Step One)
Rosemary Clooney; *Essence Of Rosemary Clooney* . . . . (Legacy)
You're Not In Kansas Anymore
Jo Dee Messina; *Jo Dee Messina.* . . . .(Curb)
You've Got To Hide Your Love Away
Beatles; *Beatles-Box Set* . . . . (Capitol)
  Beatles-Love Songs . . . . (Capitol)
  Reel Music . . . . (Capitol)
  ST/Help! . . . . (Capitol)

The Beatles/1962-1966 . . . . (Capitol)

AFRICA, Apartheid
See Also: **CITIES: A-Z, COUNTRIES: A-Z, FREEDOM, JUNGLES, PREJUDICE, PROTEST**

2nd Movement: African Lady
Randy Weston; *Uhuru Africa/Highlife.* . . . . (Roulette)
A.F.R.I.C.A.
Stetsasonic/Rev. Jesse Jackson/Olatunji; *A.F.R.I.C.A.-12''* . . . . (Tommy Boy)
Africa
Toto; *Past To Present 1977-1990.* . . . . (Columbia)
  Toto IV. . . . . (Columbia)
Africa
John Coltrane; *Best Of John Coltrane-His Greatest Years.* . . . . . (MCA)
Africa
Tony Wilson; *Catch One* . . . . (Bearsville)
Africa
Meters; *Rejuvenation* . . . . (Reprise)
Africa
Aldo Nova; *Subject...Aldo Nova* . . . .(Portrait)
Africa
Daryl Hall & John Oates; *Voices* . . . . (RCA)
Africa
Doug E. Fresh & The Get Fresh Crew; *World's Greatest Entertainer* . . .(Reality)
Africa Is For Me
Pablo Moses; *Pave The Way* . . . . (Mango)
Africa Talks To You-''The Asphalt Jungle''
Sly & The Family Stone; *There's A Riot Goin' On* . . . . (Epic)
Africa Unite
Bob Marley & The Wailers; *Survival.* . . . . (Island)
African
Peter Tosh; *Captured Live* . . . . (EMI)
  Equal Rights . . . . (Columbia)
African Dance
Soul II Soul; *Keep On Movin'* . . . . (Virgin)
African Dream
Stewart Copeland; *Rhythmatist* . . . . (A&M)
African Flame
Herb Alpert; *Wild Romance* . . . . (A&M)
African Friend
Jimmy Buffett; *Son Of A Son Of A Sailor* . . . . (MCA)
African Night Flight
David Bowie; *Lodger* . . . . (Rykodisc)
African Queen
Ali Thompson; *Take A Little Rhythm* . . . . (A&M)
African Ripples
Fats Waller; *Joint Is Jumpin'* . . . . (Bluebird)
  Piano Solos-1929-1941. . . . . (RCA)
  Turn On The Heat-Fats Waller Piano Solos . . . . (Bluebird)
African Shadow Man
Johnny Clegg & Savuka; *Shadow Man* . . . . (Capitol)
African Summer
Herb Alpert & Hugh Masekela; *Herb Alpert & Hugh Masekela* . . . . (A&M)
African Sunrise
John Denver; *Dreamland Express* . . . . (RCA)
African Sunset
Tommy Page; *Tommy Page* . . . . (Sire)
African Trilogy
Neil Diamond; *Tap Root Manuscript* . . . . (MCA)
African Waltz
Cannonball Adderley; *Original Jazz Classics-#1* . . . . (Riverside)
Cannonball Adderley & His Orchestra; *African Waltz* . . . (Original Jazz Classics)
African Woman
Third World; *Journey To Addis* . . . . (Island)
Africano
Earth, Wind & Fire; *Gratitude* . . . . (Legacy)
  That's The Way Of The World . . . . (Legacy)
Afrika
Jonathan Butler; *Introducing Jonathan Butler* . . . . (Jive)
Afro Blue
Cal Tjader; *Cal Tjader-Concert By The Sea.* . . . . (Fantasy)
  Cal Tjader's Greatest Hits . . . . (Fantasy)
  Monterey Concerts . . . . (Prestige)
John Coltrane; *Afro Blue Impressions* . . . . (Pablo)
  Best Of John Coltrane . . . . (Pablo)
  Best Of John Coltrane-His Greatest Years . . . . (MCA)
Mongo Santamaria; *Afro-Roots* . . . . (Prestige)
  Mongo Santamaria's Greatest Hits . . . . (Fantasy)
Apartheid
C. Chris & Rich E. Rich/Rudy Pardee; *Apartheid-12''* . . . . (MCA)
Apartheid
Peter Tosh; *Equal Rights* . . . . (Columbia)

Apartheid
  K-9 Posse; *On A Different Tip* ....(Arista)
Biko
  Peter Gabriel; *Peter Gabriel* ....(Geffen)
    Peter Gabriel/Plays Live ....(Geffen)
    Shaking The Tree-Sixteen Golden Greats ....(Geffen)
Black Africa
  Devonsquare; *Walking On Ice* ....(Atlantic)
Brass Band In African Chimes
  Simple Minds; *45-#2703* ....(A&M)
Carey
  Joni Mitchell; *Blue* ....(Reprise)
  Joni Mitchell with Tom Scott & The L.A. Express; *Miles Of Aisles* .... (Asylum)
Congo
  Genesis; *Calling All Stations* ....(Atlantic)
Cowboys In Africa
  Bush Tetras; *Better Late Than Never* ....(Roir)
December African Rain
  Juluka; *Best Of Juluka* ....(Rhythm Safari)
    Stand Your Ground ....(Warner Bros.)
Dial Africa
  John Coltrane & Wilbur Harden; *Africa-Savoy Sessions* .... (Savoy)
    Dial Africa ....(Savoy)
Echoes Of The African Forest
  Saka Acquaye Ensemble; *Voices Of Africa* ....(Nonesuch)
Exodus
  Bob Marley & The Wailers; *Babylon By Bus* ....(Tuff Gong)
    Exodus ....(Tuff Gong)
    Legend: The Best Of Bob Marley & The Wailers ....(Island)
Free Nelson Mandela
  Special AKA; *In The Studio* ....(Chrysalis)
Gold In Africa
  Tiger; *Where Was Butler?-Calypso Documentary* ....(Folklyric)
Gone A South Africa
  Yellowman & Charlie Chaplin; *Negril Chill-Live In Concert* ....(Roir)
Heart Is In Africa
  Rozalla; *Everybody's Free* ....(Epic)
Home Is Africa
  Horace Parlan; *Afro Blue: The Roots & Rhythms Of Jazz-C* .... (Blue Note)
I Never Was To Africa
  Ferron; *Shadows On A Dime* ....(Lucy)
Kilimanjaro
  Juluka; *Stand Your Ground* ....(Warner Bros.)
Madda Africa
  Sister Breeze; *Riddym Ravings* ....(Roir)
Man From South Africa
  Max Roach; *Percussion Bitter Sweet* ....(GRP)
Mbali Africa
  Sadao Watanabe; *Orange Express* ....(Columbia)
Meeting In Afrika
  Jimmy Cliff; *Give Thanx* ....(Warner Bros.)
Mother Africa
  Santana; *Welcome* ....(Columbia)
Motor-bike In Afrika
  Peter Hammill; *The Future Now* ....(Blue Plate)
New Africa
  Youssou N'Dour; *Eyes Open* .... (40 Acres & A Mule Musicworks)
New African Blues
  Cassandra Wilson; *She Who Weeps* ....(Jazz Music Today)
New African Whistler
  Roger Whittaker; *Live In Concert* .... (RCA)
Out Of Africa
  Deborah Franciose; *Almost Home* ....(North Star)
Out Of Africa Medley
  Danny Wright; *Black & White II* ....(Moulin D'Or)
Pata Pata
  Miriam Makeba; *Planet Africa: World Of African Music-C* ....(Priority)
    Welela ....(Verve)
Peace For South Africa
  Oscar Peterson Trio; *Live At The Blue Note* ....(Telarc)
Peace In Liberia
  Alpha Blondy; *Masada* ....(World Pacific)
Pieces Of Africa
  Boom Shaka; *Creation* .... (Moving Target)
Ponta De Lanca Africano (Umbabarauma)
  Jorge Ben; *To Scratch That Itch-Roots, Rock & Rhythm* ....(Luaka Bop)
Rhymin' Wit The African Symphony
  Legit Zimbabwe; *Basic Beats Sampler-C* ....(Hollywood Basic)
Ritmo Africano
  Cal Tjader; *Cal Tjader's Greatest Hits-#2* ....(Fantasy)
    Ritmos Calientes ....(Fantasy)
Rock The Casbah
  Clash; *Combat Rock* ....(Epic)
    On Broadway ....(Epic)
    Seems Like Yesterday-#4-Early '80s-C ....(K-Tel)

The Story Of The Clash, Volume 1 ....(Epic)
Sail Away
  Linda Ronstadt; *Don't Cry Now* ....(Asylum)
  Randy Newman; *Guilty: 30 Years Of Randy Newman* ....(Rhino)
    Sail Away ....(Reprise)
Scatterlings Of Africa
  Johnny Clegg & Savuka; *ST/Rain Man* ....(Capitol)
    Third World Child ....(Capitol)
Serengeti
  Cal Tjader; *Onda Va Bien* ....(Concord Picante Jazz)
  Chi; *Sun Lake* ....(Sonic Atmospheres)
  Cusco; *Cusco 2000* .... (Higher Octave)
  Eric Marienthal; *Round Trip* ....(GRP)
  Peter Seiler; *Dream Code* ....(Innovative Comm.)
    Flying Frames ....(Innovative Comm.)
    Sensitive Touch ....(Innovative Comm.)
Serengeti (The Adventure)
  H.M.A. Salsa/Jazz Orchestra; *California Salsa* .... (Sea Breeze)
Serengeti Long Walk
  Stewart Copeland; *Rhythmatist* ....(A&M)
Serengeti Trail
  Starr Parodi; *Change* ....(Gift Horse)
Serengeti Walk
  Dave Grusin; *Dave Grusin-Collection* ....(GRP)
    Out Of The Shadows ....(GRP)
  Dave Grusin & N.Y./L.A. Dream Band; *Dave Grusin & N.Y./L.A. Dream Band* ....(GRP)
Serengetti
  Grateful Dead; *Shakedown Street* .... (Arista)
Serenghetti
  Barefoot; *Barefoot* ....(Global Pacific)
Skokiaan
  Four Lads; *16 Most Requested Songs Of The '50s-#2-C* .... (Legacy)
Sorry Africa
  Tony Bird; *Sorry Africa* ....(Philo)
South Africa
  Sons Of Selassie; *Changes* .... (Rhythm Safari)
South Africa
  Cadillac Tramps; *Cadillac Tramps* ....(Dr. Dream Music Group)
South Africa
  Zawinul Syndicate; *Lost Tribes* .... (Columbia)
South Africa
  Gillan; *Magic* .... (Metal Blade)
South Africa National Anthem (Diestem Van Suid Afrika)
  Orlando Philharmonic Orchestra; *The National Anthems* ....(Madacy)
  Swarovski Musik Wattens; *National Anthems Of The World* ....(Koch International)
South African Blues
  Windy Rhythm Kings; *Chicago Jazz-#2 (1925-1929)-C* ....(Biograph)
South African Enlistment
  Abyssinians; *Arise* ....(Front Line)
Star Of Africa
  Gerry Mulligan & Chet Baker; *Gerry Mulligan & Chet Baker* .....(Crescendo)
Stole & Sold From Africa
  John McCutcheon; *Live At Wolf Trap* ....(Rounder)
Storms In Africa
  Enya; *Watermark* ....(Reprise)
Struggle (Free South Africa)
  Rochester/Easley Band; *One Minute Of Love* ....(Gramavision)
Sun City
  Artists United Against Apartheid; *Sun City-C* .... (Manhattan)
Taking Islands In Africa
  Japan; *Gentlemen Take Polaroids* ....(Blue Plate)
Teacher (African Teacher)
  Burning Spear; *Living Dub-#2* ....(Heartbeat)
Thank You For Talking To Me, Africa
  Miki Howard; *Femme Fatale* ....(Giant)
  Sly & The Family Stone; *Sly & The Family Stone-Anthology* ....(Epic)
    There's A Riot Goin' On ....(Epic)
Theme From "Out Of Africa"
  John Barry; *ST/Out Of Africa* ....(MCA)
Thoroughly African Man
  Red Clay Ramblers; *Chuckin' The Frizz* ....(Flying Fish)
Uncle Isak Goes To Africa
  Tom Wasinger; *Rock Music* ....(Invincible)
Under African Skies
  Paul Simon; *Graceland* .... (Warner Bros.)
War A Africa
  Jimmy Cliff; *Breakout* ....(JRS)
We Are The World
  USA For Africa; *We Are The World-C* ....(Columbia)
West Africa
  Willie Jackson; *West Africa* ....(Muse)
Whole World African
  Ska Danks; *H.E.A.L. Civilization Vs. Technology* ....(Elektra)
World Is Africa
  Black Uhuru; *Sinsemilla* ....(Mango)

AFTERNOON

See Also: **DAYS: GENERAL, MORNING, NIGHT, TIME: SPECIFIC**

Afternoon
Jonathan Richman & The Modern Lovers; *Beserkley Years-Best Of* . . . . . (Rhino)
Rock 'N' Roll With Jonathan Richman & The Modern Lovers . . . . (Rhino)
Afternoon Delight
Starland Vocal Band; *Starland Vocal Band* . . . . (Windsong)
Afternoon In Paris
Sonny Stitt; *Genesis* . . . . (Prestige)
Stitt/Bud Powell/J.J. Johnson . . . . (Prestige)
Afternoon In Paris
Anita O'Day; *Night Has A Thousand Eyes* . . . . (Emily)
Afternoon Of A Faun
Vikki Carr; *Live At The Greek Theatre* . . . . (Columbia)
Afternoon Sunshine
Edwin Starr; *Edwin Starr*. . . . . (20th Century Fox)
Afternoon Tea
Kinks; *Something Else*. . . . . (Reprise)
Afternoons In Utopia
Alphaville; *Afternoons In Utopia* . . . . (Atlantic)
April Afternoon
Joan Amalbert Latin Jazz Quintet; *Hot Sauce* . . . . (Prestige)
Arthur In The Afternoon
Liza Minnelli/Original Cast; *The Act*. . . . .(DRG)
August Afternoon
Mulgrew Miller; *The Countdown* . . . .(Landmark)
Every Sunday Afternoon
Bobby Short; *Bobby Short Celebrates Rodgers & Hart*. . . . . (Atlantic)
Groovin'
Aretha Franklin; *Lady Soul* . . . . (Atlantic)
Booker T. & The M.G.s; *Best Of Booker T. & The M.G.s* . . . . . . (Atlantic)
Soul Shots-#3-Soul Twist-C . . . . (Rhino)
Rascals; *Groovin'* . . . . (Warner Special Prod.)
Hit Singles-1958-1977-C . . . . (Atlantic)
Rascals' Greatest Hits . . . . (Atlantic)
ST/Platoon . . . . (Atlantic)
Interstate Love Song
Stone Temple Pilots; *Purple* . . . . (Atlantic)
It's Been A Great Afternoon
Merle Haggard; *For The Record: Merle Haggard-43 Legendary Hits* . . . .(BNA)
I'm Always On A Mountain When I Fall . . . . (MCA)
Merle Haggard's Greatest Hits . . . . (MCA)
More Of The Best . . . . (Rhino)
Lazy Afternoon
Barbra Streisand; *Lazy Afternoon* . . . . (Columbia)
Marlene Dietrich; *At The Cafe De Paris* . . . . (Columbia)
Patti Austin; *Real Me* . . . . (Qwest)
Tony Bennett; *Forty Years-The Artistry Of Tony Bennett* . . . . (Columbia)
Tony Bennett At Carnegie Hall. . . . . (Sony Music Special Prod.)
Lazy Day
Moody Blues; *On The Threshold Of A Dream*. . . . . (Polydor)
Long Afternoons
Jerry Jeff Walker; *A Man Must Carry On* . . . . (MCA)
Gypsy Songman . . . . (Rykodisc)
Louisiana Sunday Afternoon
Diane Schuur; *Diane Schuur-Collection* . . . .(GRP)
Talkin' 'Bout You . . . .(GRP)
Love In The Hot Afternoon
Gene Watson; *Best Of Gene Watson* . . . . (Capitol)
Gene Watson's Greatest Hits . . . . (Curb)
Great Records Of The Decade-'70s Hits-Country-C . . . . (Curb)
November Afternoon
Dizzy Gillespie; *Composer's Concepts*. . . . .(Emarcy)
James Moody; *Moving Forward* . . . .(Novus)
Paul Christopher; *Lavender* . . . .(Arylis)
Oh, How I Hate To Get Up In The Afternoon
Harry ''Sweets'' Edison; *Swing Trumpet Kings-C* . . . . (Verve)
Ohio Afternoon
Original New York Cast; *Oil City Symphony* . . . .(DRG)
On A Sunday Afternoon
Lighter Shade Of Brown & Huggy Boy; *Brown & Proud* . . . . (Pump)
On Rainy Afternoons
Barbra Streisand; *Wet* . . . . (Columbia)
On Saturday Afternoons In 1963
Rickie Lee Jones; *Rickie Lee Jones* . . . . (Warner Bros.)
On Sunday Afternoon
Harptones; *Echoes Of A Rock Era-The Harptones* . . . . (Roulette)
Quiet Afternoon
Stanley Clarke; *Live 1976-1977* . . . . (Epic)
School Days . . . . (Epic)
Quiet Afternoon
Paul Rebhan; *Colors* . . . . (Carmel)
Rainy Afternoon
Lee Konitz; *In Rio* . . . .(M-A Music Int'l)
Saturday Afternoon
Jefferson Airplane; *After Bathing At Baxters*. . . . .(RCA)

Flight Log (1966-1976) . . . .(Grunt)
Woodstock Two . . . . (Atlantic)
Saturday Afternoon
Thelonius Monk; *Next Saturday Afternoon* . . . .(Relativity)
Saturday Afternoon
Cassell Webb; *Thief Of Sadness*. . . . . (Venture)
Seattle Afternoon
Reilly & Maloney; *Reilly & Maloney-At Last* . . . . (Freckle)
Summer Afternoon
Vogues; *Vogues' Greatest Hits* . . . . (Rhino)
Sunday Afternoon
Candy Dulfer; *Sax-A-Go-Go* . . . . (RCA)
Sunday Afternoon In The Park
Van Halen; *Fair Warning*. . . . . (Warner Bros.)
Sunny Afternoon
Kinks; *Compleat Collection-20th Anniversary* . . . . (Compleat)
Kink Kronikles. . . . . (Reprise)
Kinks' Greatest Hits . . . . (Rhino)
Kinks-Live . . . . (Reprise)
Thursday Afternoon
Brian Eno; *Thursday Afternoon* . . . .(Editions E.G.)
Tuesday Afternoon
Moody Blues; *Caught Live Plus Five*. . . . . (Polydor)
Days Of Future Passed . . . . (Polydor)
ST/1969 . . . . (Polydor)
This Is The Moody Blues . . . . (Polydor)

AGES: 16

See Also: **AGES: 17, AGES: SPECIFIC, AGING, BIRTHDAY, CHILDREN, LOVE: CRUSHES, NUMBERS: 11-99, TEENAGERS, YOUNG**

16 Candles
Crests; *Alan Freed's Memory Lane-C* . . . . (MCA)
Billboard Top Rock 'N' Roll Hits-1959-C . . . . (Rhino)
Crests Greatest Hits . . . .(Collectables)
Cruisin'-1959-C . . . . (Increase)
Oldies But Goodies-#14-C . . . . (Original Sound)
Rock & Roll U.S.A.-21 Rock & Roll Favorites-#2-C . . . . (Laurie)
ST/American Graffiti . . . . (MCA)
Brown Sugar
Rolling Stones; *Classic Rock 1966-1988-C* . . . . (Atlantic)
Hot Rocks 1964-1971 . . . . (Abkco)
Made In The Shade . . . . (Rolling Stones)
Sticky Fingers . . . . (Virgin)
Christine 16
Kiss; *Alive II*. . . . . (Casablanca)
Love Gun. . . . . (Casablanca)
Good Times Bad Times
Led Zeppelin; *Led Zeppelin* . . . . (Atlantic)
Happy Birthday, Sweet Sixteen
Neil Sedaka; *Neil Sedaka Sings His Greatest Hits* . . . . (RCA)
Neil Sedaka Sings The Hits . . . . (RCA)
Neil Sedaka's All-Time Greatest Hits . . . . (RCA)
He Would Be Sixteen
Michelle Wright; *Now & Then*. . . . .(Arista)
Only Sixteen
Dr. Hook; *Bankrupt* . . . . (Capitol)
Dr. Hook-Greatest Hits & More . . . . (Capitol)
Great Records Of The Decade-'70s Hits-#2-C . . . .(Curb)
Little Bit More . . . . (Capitol)
Sam Cooke; *Best Of Sam Cooke* . . . . (RCA)
The Man And His Music . . . . (RCA)
This Is Sam Cooke . . . . (RCA)
Sixteen Going On Seventeen
Original Cast; *The Sound Of Music* . . . . (Sony Broadway)
Spirit Of A Boy, Wisdom Of A Man
Randy Travis; *Big Country Hits '99-C* . . . .(K-Tel)
You And You Alone . . . . (DreamWorks/SKG)
Sweet Little Sixteen
Beatles; *45-#1502* . . . .(Collectables)
Chuck Berry; *Best Of The Best Of Chuck Berry* . . . . .(International Mktg. Group)
Chuck Berry-Golden Hits . . . .(Mercury)
Chuck Berry-Greatest Hits Live . . . . (Quicksilver)
Cruisin'-1965-C . . . . (Increase)
Oldies But Goodies-#12-C . . . . (Original Sound)
Jerry Lee Lewis; *Jerry Lee Lewis-Original Golden Hits-#3* . . . . (Sun)
Jerry Lee Lewis & Friends; *Jerry Lee Lewis & Friends-Duets* . . . . (Sun)
John Lennon; *Lennon* . . . . (Capitol)
Rock 'N' Roll . . . . (Capitol)
Sweet Sixteen
B.B. King; *Back In The Alley* . . . . (MCA)
Best Of B.B. King. . . . . (MCA)
Electric B.B. King-His Best . . . . (MCA)
Live In Cook County Jail . . . . (MCA)

Sweet Sixteen
Destiny's Child; *The Writing's On The Wall* . . . . (Columbia)
Sweet Sixteen
Judy Garland; *Best Of Judy Garland* . . . . (MCA)
Sweet Sixteen
Big Joe Turner; *Big Joe Turner's Greatest Hits* . . . . (Atlantic)
Sweet Sixteen
Chuck Berry; *Chuck Berry's Greatest Hits* . . . . (Everest)
Teen Angel
Dion And The Belmonts; *Everything You Always Wanted* . . . . (Laurie)
Rock & Roll U.S.A.-21 Rock & Roll Favorites-#2-C . . . . (Laurie)
Mark Dinning; *Golden Years-1959-C* . . . . (Dominion Entert.)
Oldies But Goodies-#7-C . . . . (Original Sound)
ST/American Graffiti . . . . (MCA)
Teenage Tragedies-C . . . . (Rhino)
War Is Hell (On The Homefront Too)
T.G. Sheppard; *Perfect Stranger* . . . .(Warner Bros.)
T.G. Sheppard's All-Time Greatest Hits . . . .(Warner Bros.)
T.G. Sheppard's Greatest Hits . . . . (Warner Bros./Curb)
You're Sixteen
Johnny Burnette; *ST/American Graffiti* . . . .(MCA)
Ringo Starr; *Blast From Your Past* . . . .(Gold Rush)
Ringo . . . . (Capitol)

AGES: 17

*See Also: **AGES: 16, AGES: SPECIFIC, AGING, BIRTHDAY, CHILDREN, LOVE: CRUSHES, NUMBERS: 11-99, TEENAGERS, YOUNG***

17 Again
Eurythmics; *Peace* . . . . (Arista)
51st Anniversary
Jimi Hendrix Experience; *Are You Experienced?* . . . . (Reprise)
Adios
Jimmy Webb; *Suspending Disbelief* . . . . (Elektra)
Linda Ronstadt; *Cry Like A Rainstorm-Howl Like The Wind* . . . . (Elektra)
At Seventeen
Janis Ian; *Between The Lines* . . . . (Columbia)
Super Hits Of The '70s-Have A Nice Day-#15-C . . . . (Rhino)
Born In Chicago
George Thorogood & The Destroyers; *Boogie People* . . . .(EMI)
Paul Butterfield Blues Band; *Golden Butter* . . . . (Elektra)
Paul Butterfield Blues Band . . . . (Elektra)
Dancing Queen
Abba; *Abba Live* . . . . (Atlantic)
Abba's Greatest Hits-#2 . . . . (Atlantic)
Arrival . . . . (Polydor)
Gold-Greatest Hits . . . . (Polydor)
The Singles-First 10 Years . . . . (Atlantic)
Edge Of Seventeen
Stevie Nicks; *Bella Donna* . . . . (Modern)
Free To Go
Folk Implosion; *One Part Lullaby* . . . . (Interscope)
I Love Rock 'N Roll
Britney Spears; *Britney* . . . . (Jive)
Joan Jett & The Blackhearts; *I Love Rock 'n' Roll* . . . .(Blackheart)
ST/Wayne's World 2 . . . . (Reprise)
I Saw Her Standing There
Beatles; *Introducing...The Beatles* . . . .(Vee-Jay)
Meet The Beatles! . . . . (Capitol)
Please Please Me . . . . (Parlophone)
Rock 'N' Roll Music . . . . (Capitol)
The Beatles-Anthology-#1 . . . . (Capitol)
Paul McCartney; *Tripping The Live Fantastic-Highlights!* . . . . (Capitol)
I Saw Him Standing There
Tiffany; *Tiffany* . . . . (MCA)
Tiffany's Greatest Hits . . . . (Hip-O)
It Was A Very Good Year
Frank Sinatra; *Frank Sinatra-The Very Good Years* . . . . (Reprise)
September Of My Years . . . . (Reprise)
The Reprise Collection . . . . (Reprise)
The Sopranos-Music From The HBO Original
Series . . . . (Sony Music Soundtrax)
Frank Sinatra with Count Basie & The Orchestra; *Sinatra At The*
Sands . . . . (Reprise)
One Of These Days
Tim McGraw; *Everywhere* . . . . (Curb)
Rock Show, The
Blink-182; *Now That's What I Call Music!-#8-C* . . . . (Virgin)
Take Off Your Pants And Jacket . . . .(MCA)
Seventeen
Bobby Brown; *Dance!...Ya Know It!* . . . .(MCA)
King Of Stage . . . . (MCA)
Seventeen
Chambers Brothers; *Best Of The Chambers Brothers* . . . . (Fantasy)

Seventeen
Foreigner; *Head Games* . . . .(Atlantic)
Seventeen
Sex Pistols; *Never Mind The Bollocks, Here's The Sex Pistols* . . . (Warner Bros.)
Seventeen
Rusty Draper; *Rusty Draper's Greatest Hits* . . . . (Monument)
Seventeen
Winger; *Winger* . . . .(Atlantic)
Seventeen
Chris LeDoux; *Radio & Rodeo Hits* . . . . (Liberty)
Seventeen Goin' On 21
Brian Elliot; *Brian Elliot* . . . . (Warner Bros.)
Sexy + 17
Stray Cats; *Best Of Stray Cats-Rock This Town* . . . . (EMI)
Rant 'N' Rave With The Stray Cats . . . . (EMI)
She Is Always Seventeen
Harry Chapin; *Greatest Stories-Live* . . . . (Elektra)
Harry Chapin-Anthology . . . . (Elektra)
She Was Only Seventeen (He Was One Year More)
Marty Robbins; *American Originals-Marty Robbins* . . . . (Columbia)
Marty Robbins' Greatest Hits . . . . (Columbia)
Sixteen Going On Seventeen
Original Cast; *The Sound Of Music* . . . . (Sony Broadway)
Something Like That
Tim McGraw; *A Place In The Sun* . . . .(Curb)
Tim McGraw's Greatest Hits . . . . (Curb)
Strawberry Wine
Deana Carter; *Did I Shave My Legs For This?* . . . . (Capitol)
Walkaway Joe
Trisha Yearwood; *Hearts In Armor* . . . . (MCA)
Songbook-A Collection Of Hits . . . . (MCA)
Way Down The Line
Offspring; *Ixnay On The Hombre* . . . . (Columbia)
We Were In Love
Toby Keith; *Dream Walkin'* . . . . (Mercury)
Toby Keith's Greatest Hits, Volume One . . . . (Mercury)
Where Corn Don't Grow
Travis Tritt; *The Restless Kind* . . . . (Warner Bros.)

AGES: SPECIFIC

*See Also: **AGES: 16, AGES: 17, AGING, BIRTHDAY, CHILDREN, OLD, TEENAGERS, YOUNG***

18 Til I Die
Bryan Adams; *18 Til I Die* . . . . (A&M)
26 Cents (18)
Wilkinsons; *Nothing But Love* . . . .(Giant)
Almost Eighteen
Roy Orbison; *Get Hot Or Go Home-Vintage*
Rockabilly-C . . . . (Country Music Foundation)
Legendary Roy Orbison . . . . (Sony Music Special Prod.)
Baby Talk (He's 5, She's 3)
Jan & Dean; *Best Of Jan & Dean* . . . . (EMI)
Collectables Presents The History Of Rock-#9-C . . . . (Collectables)
One Summer Night-Live . . . . (Rhino)
Ballad Of Davy Crockett (3)
Bill Hayes; *Songs Of The West-#4-Movie & Television Themes-C* . . . . . . (Rhino)
Fess Parker; *16 Most Requested Songs Of The '50s-#1-C* . . . . (Legacy)
Columbia Country Classics-#3-Americana-C . . . . (Columbia)
Hollywood Magic-1950s-C . . . . (Columbia)
Kentucky HeadHunters; *Electric Barnyard* . . . . (Mercury)
Mac Wiseman; *45-#1240* . . . . (Dot)
Original Soundtrack; *Television's Greatest Hits-#4-Black & White*
Classics-C . . . . (TVT)
Tennessee Ernie Ford; *Capitol Collectors Series-Tennessee*
Ernie Ford . . . . (Capitol)
Be My Life's Companion
Mills Brothers; *Best Of The Mills Brothers* . . . . (MCA)
The Mills Brothers-Best Of The Decca Years . . . . (Decca)
Rosemary Clooney; *Rosemary Clooney-16 Most Requested Songs* . . . . (Legacy)
Bed Of Rose's (18, 35)
Statler Brothers; *Bed Of Rose's* . . . . (Mercury)
Best Day (7, 15)
George Strait; *Latest Greatest Straitest Hits* . . . . (MCA)
Body Bumpin' (18)
Mytown; *Mytown* . . . . (Cherry/Universal)
Born In Chicago (21)
George Thorogood & The Destroyers; *Boogie People* . . . . (EMI)
Paul Butterfield Blues Band; *Golden Butter* . . . . (Elektra)
Paul Butterfield Blues Band . . . . (Elektra)
Brenda's Got A Baby (12)
Tupac; *2Pacalypse Now* . . . . (Priority)
Cousin Dupree (3)
Steely Dan; *Two Against Nature* . . . .(Giant)
D-I-V-O-R-C-E (4)
Rosanne Cash; *Tammy Wynette...Remembered-C* . . . .(Asylum)

Tammy Wynette; *Super Hits Of The '60s-C* . . . . (Epic)
 Tammy Wynette-Anniversary-20 Years Of Hits . . . . (Epic)
 Tammy Wynette's Biggest Hits . . . . (Epic)
 Tammy Wynette's Greatest Hits . . . . (Epic)
Fly (25)
 Sugar Ray; *Floored* . . . . (Atlantic)
Footlights (41)
 Merle Haggard; *For The Record: Merle Haggard-43 Legendary Hits* . . . .(BNA)
Forty Again (also 10)
 John Berry; *Faces* . . . . (Capitol)
Graduation (Friends Forever) (25)
 Vitamin C; *Totally Hits-#3-C* . . . . (Atlantic)
 Vitamin C . . . . (Elektra)
He Was My Brother (23)
 Simon & Garfunkel; *Wednesday Morning 3 A.M.* . . . . (Columbia)
He Would Be Sixteen
 Michelle Wright; *Now & Then* . . . . (Arista)
Hey Nineteen
 Steely Dan; *Gaucho* . . . . (MCA)
 Steely Dan-Gold . . . . (MCA)
I Never Thought I'd Live To Be A Hundred
 Moody Blues; *To Our Children's Children's Children* . . . . (Polydor)
I Never Thought I'd Live To Be A Million
 Moody Blues; *To Our Children's Children's Children* . . . . (Polydor)
I Think About You (8)
 Collin Raye; *Best Of Collin Raye-Direct Hits* . . . . (Epic)
 I Think About You . . . . (Epic)
I'm A Man (5, 21)
 Bo Diddley; *Bo Diddley-His Best* . . . . (Chess)
 Super Blues . . . . (Chess)
 *The Sopranos-Music From The HBO Original
  Series* . . . . (Sony Music Soundtrax)
 Yardbirds; *Five Live Yardbirds* . . . . (Rhino)
 History Of British Rock-#3-C . . . . (Rhino)
 Yardbirds' Greatest Hits-#1 (1964-1966) . . . . (Rhino)
It Was A Very Good Year (21, 35)
 Frank Sinatra; *Frank Sinatra-The Very Good Years* . . . .(Reprise)
 September Of My Years . . . . (Reprise)
 The Reprise Collection . . . . (Reprise)
 *The Sopranos-Music From The HBO Original
  Series* . . . . (Sony Music Soundtrax)
 Frank Sinatra with Count Basie & The Orchestra; *Sinatra At The
  Sands* . . . . (Reprise)
Life's A Dance (14)
 John Michael Montgomery; *Life's A Dance* . . . . (Atlantic)
Love, Me (15)
 Collin Raye; *All I Can Be* . . . . (Epic)
 Greatest Country Hits Of The '90s-1992-C . . . . (Columbia)
Mama Tried (21)
 Grateful Dead; *Grateful Dead (Skull & Roses)* . . . . (Warner Bros.)
 John Anderson & Marty Stuart; *Mama's Hungry Eyes-Merle Haggard
  Tribute-C* . . . . (Arista)
 Merle Haggard; *Jailhouse Rock (Hits From The Big
  House)-C* . . . . (Sony Music Special Prod.)
 Merle Haggard & The Strangers; *Best Of Merle Haggard & The
  Strangers* . . . . (Capitol)
 For The Record: Merle Haggard-43 Legendary Hits . . . .(BNA)
 Okie From Muskogee . . . . (Capitol)
 Songs I'll Always Sing . . . . (Capitol)
 Very Best Of Merle Haggard . . . . (Capitol)
Memphis (6)
 Chuck Berry; *Chuck Berry* . . . . (Audio Fidelity)
 Chuck Berry-Golden Hits . . . . (Mercury)
 Chuck Berry's Greatest Hits . . . . (Everest)
 St. Louis To Liverpool . . . . (Chess)
 ST/Hail! Hail! Rock 'N' Roll . . . . (MCA)
 The Chess Box-Chuck Berry . . . . (Chess)
 Toronto Rock 'N' Roll Revival-#2-C . . . . (Accord)
 John Cale; *IRS Greatest Hits-#2 & #3-C* . . . . (I.R.S.)
 Johnny Rivers; *Best Of Johnny Rivers* . . . . (EMI)
 Johnny Rivers-Anthology 1964-1977 . . . . (Rhino)
 Lonnie Mack; *Teen Beat-Instrumental Rock-1957-1965-C* . . . . . (Capitol)
My Baby (11)
 Lil' Romeo; *My Baby* . . . . (Soulja/Priority)
My Next Thirty Years
 Tim McGraw; *A Place In The Sun* . . . . (Curb)
 Tim McGraw's Greatest Hits . . . . (Curb)
Nineteen
 Old 97's; *Fight Songs* . . . . (Elektra)
Old Friends (70)
 Barry Manilow; *Showstoppers* . . . . (Arista)
 Liza Minnelli; *Liza Minnelli-At Carnegie Hall* . . . .(Telarc)
 Original Cast; *Merrily We Roll Along* . . . . (RCA)
 Stephen Sondheim & Angela Lansbury & Co.; *Collector's Sondheim-C* . (RCA)
Only 12 Years Old
 Tony Adolescent & The Flower Leperds; *Dirges In
  The Dark* . . . . (Triple X Entert.)
Pardon Me (23)
 Incubus; *Make Yourself* . . . . (Immortal/Epic)

Pretty Little Miss (12)
 Patty Loveless; *Mountain Soul* . . . . (Epic)
Seventeen Come Sunday
 John Wright & Catherine Perrier; *Traditional Music Of
  Ireland* . . . . (Green Linnet)
Seventeen Goin' On 21
 Brian Elliot; *Brian Elliot* . . . . (Warner Bros.)
She Was Only Seventeen (He Was One Year More)
 Marty Robbins; *American Originals-Marty Robbins* . . . .(Columbia)
 Marty Robbins' Greatest Hits . . . . (Columbia)
She's A Little Past Forty
 Ronnie McDowell; *Best Of Ronnie McDowell* . . . .(Curb)
She's Nineteen Years Old
 Muddy Waters; *Best Of Blues-#1-C* . . . . (MCA Special Prod.)
 The Chess Box-Muddy Waters . . . . (Chess)
Someday Soon (21)
 Chris LeDoux; *Rodeo Songs Old & New* . . . .(Liberty)
 Ian & Sylvia; *Ian & Sylvia's Greatest Hits* . . . .(Vanguard)
 Northern Journey . . . . (Vanguard)
 Judy Collins; *Colors Of The Day-The Best Of Judy Collins* . . . .(Elektra)
 Who Knows Where The Time Goes . . . . (Elektra)
 Moe Bandy; *Moe Bandy's Greatest Hits* . . . . (Columbia)
 Rodeo Romeo . . . . (Columbia)
 Suzy Bogguss; *Aces* . . . . (Liberty)
Someone Else's Dream (27)
 Faith Hill; *It Matters To Me* . . . . (Warner Bros.)
Sweet Little Rock & Roller (9)
 Chuck Berry; *Chuck Berry Is On Top* . . . . (Chess)
 The Chess Box-Chuck Berry . . . . (Chess)
 Richard Thompson; *Guitar/Vocal* . . . . (Hannibal)
 Rod Stewart; *Absolutely Live* . . . . (Warner Bros.)
 Best Of Rod Stewart . . . . (Mercury)
 Storyteller/The Complete Anthology: 1964-1990 . . . . (Warner Bros.)
Theme From "James At 15"
 Original Soundtrack; *Television's Greatest Hits-#6-Remote Control-C* . . .(TVT)
Twelve Year Old Boy
 Elmore James; *Collectables Blues Collection-#1-C* . . . .(Collectables)
 Golden Classics-Elmore James . . . .(Collectables)
 The Sky Is Crying-History Of Elmore James . . . .(Rhino)
Two Little Girls (19)
 Ani DiFranco; *Little Plastic Castle* . . . . (Righteous Babe)
What's My Age Again? (23)
 Blink-182; *Enema Of The State* . . . . (MCA)
 Now That's What I Call Music!-#3-C . . . . (Virgin)
When I Was One & Twenty
 Cleo Laine; *Cleo Laine At Carnegie Hall-10th Anniversary
  Concert* . . . . (RCA Victor)
When I'm Sixty-Four
 Beatles; *Beatles-Box Set* . . . . (Capitol)
 Sgt. Pepper's Lonely Hearts Club Band . . . . (Capitol)
When You Are Sixty-Five
 Statler Brothers; *Entertainers...On And Off The Record* . . . .(Mercury)
Wild One (3)
 Faith Hill; *Take Me As I Am* . . . . (Warner Bros.)
Wrong Way (12)
 Sublime; *Sublime* . . . . (Gasoline Alley)
You Get What You Give (14)
 New Radicals; *Maybe You've Been Brainwashed Too* . . . .(MCA)
 Now That's What I Call Music!-#2-C . . . . (Virgin)
Young-At-Heart (105)
 Bing Crosby with Guy Lombardo & His Royal Canadians; *The Radio Years:
  20 Songs* . . . . (Crescendo)
 Frank Sinatra; *At The Movies* . . . . (Capitol)
 Capitol Collectors Series-Frank Sinatra . . . . (Capitol)
 Classic Sinatra . . . . (Capitol)
 Sinatra's Sinatra . . . . (Reprise)
 Ray Price; *Portrait Of A Singer* . . . . (Step One)
 Rosemary Clooney; *Essence Of Rosemary Clooney* . . . .(Legacy)

AGING, Growing Older, Growing Up, Innocence, Loss Of Innocence

See Also: AGES (various), BIRTHDAY, CHILDREN, CHILDREN LEAVING HOME, LIFE, OLD, PEOPLE, SCHOOL, TEENAGERS, THINKING & KNOWING, YOUNG

Adia
 Sarah McLachlan; *Mirrorball* . . . . (Arista)
 Surfacing . . . . (Arista)
Against The Wind
 Bob Seger & The Silver Bullet Band; *Against The Wind* . . . .(Capitol)
 Nine Tonight . . . . (Capitol)
 ST/Forrest Gump . . . . (Epic/Sony Music Soundtrax)
All By Myself
 Celine Dion; *Falling Into You* . . . . (550 Music)
 Eric Carmen; *Best Of Eric Carmen* . . . .(Arista)

Billboard Top Rock 'N' Roll Hits-1976-C . . . . (Rhino)

All Grown Up
Elvis Costello; *Mighty Like A Rose* . . . .(Warner Bros.)

All I Want
Offspring; *Ixnay On The Hombre* . . . . (Columbia)

All Star
Smash Mouth; *Astro Lounge* . . . . (Interscope)
Now That's What I Call Music!-#3-C . . . . (Virgin)

Almost Grown
Chuck Berry; *Berry Is On Top* . . . . (Chess)
Cruisin'-1959-C . . . .(Increase)
Roll Over Beethoven . . . .(Allegiance)
ST/American Graffiti . . . . (MCA)
The Chess Box-Chuck Berry . . . . (Chess)

An Innocent Man
Billy Joel; *An Innocent Man* . . . . (Columbia)

Angels
Earl Scruggs & Melissa Etheridge; *Earl Scruggs And Friends-C* . . . .(MCA)

Angels Of The Silences
Counting Crows; *Recovering The Satellites* . . . . (David Geffen Co.)

Another Way
Tevin Campbell; *Tevin Campbell* . . . . (Qwest)

Are U Still Down?
Jon B.; *Cool Relax* . . . . (Yab Yum/550)

At Seventeen
Janis Ian; *Between The Lines* . . . . (Columbia)
Super Hits Of The '70s-Have A Nice Day-#15-C . . . . (Rhino)

Awkward Age, The
Irene Franklin; *Music From The New York Stage (1890-1920)-#4-1917-*
1920-C . . . . (Pearl)

Be My Life's Companion
Mills Brothers; *Best Of The Mills Brothers* . . . .(MCA)
The Mills Brothers-Best Of The Decca Years . . . . (Decca)
Rosemary Clooney; *Rosemary Clooney-16 Most Requested Songs* . . . . (Legacy)

Believe Me If All Those Endearing Young Charms
Bronn Journey; *Celtic Journey* . . . . (Phileo)
Mitch Miller; *Favorite Irish Sing-Alongs* . . . . (Legacy)
Roger Whittaker; *Danny Boy & Other Irish Favorites* . . . .(RCA Victor)

Best Day
George Strait; *Latest Greatest Straitest Hits* . . . .(MCA)

Big Time
Neil Young & Crazy Horse; *Broken Arrow* . . . . (Reprise)
Year Of The Horse . . . . (Reprise)

Bittersweet Me
R.E.M.; *New Adventures In Hi-Fi* . . . .(Warner Bros.)

Blood Brothers
Bruce Springsteen; *Bruce Springsteen's Greatest Hits* . . . . (Columbia)

Bookends
Simon & Garfunkel; *Bookends* . . . . (Columbia)
Collected Works . . . . (Columbia)
Simon & Garfunkel's Greatest Hits . . . . (Columbia)

Broadway
Goo Goo Dolls; *Dizzy Up The Girl* . . . .(Warner Sunset/Reprise)

Carlene
Phil Vassar; *Phil Vassar* . . . . (Arista)

Caroline, No
Beach Boys; *Pet Sounds* . . . . (Capitol)
The Pet Sounds Sessions: A 30th Anniversary Collection . . . . (Capitol)

Carrie-Anne
Hollies; *Best Of The Hollies* . . . .(EMI)
Evolution . . . .(Epic)
Hollies-Epic Anthology From The Original Master Tapes . . . .(Epic)
The Hollies' Greatest Hits . . . .(Epic)

Cat's In The Cradle
Harry Chapin; *Greatest Stories-Live* . . . . (Elektra)
Harry Chapin-Anthology . . . . (Elektra)
Verities & Balderdash . . . . (Elektra)

Chattahoochee
Alan Jackson; *A Lot About Livin' (And A Little 'Bout Love)* . . . . (Arista)

Child Is Gone
Fiona Apple; *Tidal* . . . . (Clean Slate/Work)

Child's Song
Tom Rush; *Best Of Tom Rush: No Regrets* . . . . (Legacy)
Tom Rush . . . . (Columbia)

Circle Game, The
Buffy Sainte-Marie; *Best Of Buffy Sainte-Marie* . . . . (Vanguard)
Fire & Fleet & Candlelight . . . . (Vanguard)
Ian & Sylvia; *Ian & Sylvia's Greatest Hits* . . . . (Vanguard)
Joni Mitchell; *Ladies Of The Canyon* . . . . (Reprise)
Joni Mitchell with Tom Scott & The L.A. Express; *Miles Of Aisles* . . . . (Asylum)
Tom Rush; *Classic Rush* . . . . (Elektra)
The Circle Game . . . . (Elektra)

Close My Eyes
Mariah Carey; *Butterfly* . . . . (Columbia)

Come Back When You Grow Up
Bobby Vee; *Best Of Bobby Vee* . . . .(EMI)
Bobby Vee-Legendary Masters . . . .(EMI)
Good Vibrations (Sounds Of Top 40 Radio: 1964-1967)-C . . . . (Capitol)

Cousin Dupree
Steely Dan; *Two Against Nature* . . . .(Giant)

Cowboys To Girls
Intruders; *Intruders-Super Hits* . . . . (Philadelphia Int'l)
Soul Shots-C . . . . (Rhino)

Dammit (Growing Up)
Blink-182; *Dude Ranch* . . . . (Cargo)

Dancing In The Dark
Bruce Springsteen; *Born In The U.S.A.* . . . . (Columbia)
Bruce Springsteen's Greatest Hits . . . . (Columbia)

Desperados Waiting For A Train
Guy Clark; *Old No. 1* . . . . (Sugar Hill)
Jerry Jeff Walker; *Best Of Jerry Jeff Walker* . . . . (MCA)
Great Gonzos . . . . (MCA)
Viva Terlingua . . . . (MCA)
Waylon Jennings, Willie Nelson, Johnny Cash, Kris Kristofferson;
Highwayman . . . . (Columbia)
Hot Tracks-Train Super Hits-C . . . . (Epic)

Difference, The
Wallflowers; *Bringing Down The Horse* . . . .(Interscope)

Dream On
Aerosmith; *Aerosmith* . . . . (Columbia)
Aerosmith-Classics Live . . . . (Columbia)
Aerosmith's Greatest Hits . . . . (Columbia)
Live! Bootleg . . . . (Columbia)

End Of The Innocence
Don Henley; *The End Of The Innocence* . . . . (Geffen)

Everybody's Free (To Wear Sunscreen)
Baz Luhrmann; *Now That's What I Call Music!-#2-C* . . . . (Virgin)
Something For Everybody . . . . (Capitol)

Footlights
Merle Haggard; *For The Record: Merle Haggard-43 Legendary Hits* . . . .(BNA)

Free To Go
Folk Implosion; *One Part Lullaby* . . . .(Interscope)

Freshmen, The
Verve Pipe; *Villains* . . . . (RCA)

Girl Next Door
Musiq Soulchild; *Aijuswanaseing* . . . . (Def Soul/IDJMG)

Girl, You'll Be A Woman Soon
Neil Diamond; *Double Gold-Neil Diamond* . . . . (Bang)
Hot August Night . . . . (MCA)
Neil Diamond-Classics (Early Years) . . . . (Columbia)
Neil Diamond's Greatest Hits . . . . (Bang)

Give Me Wings
Michael Johnson; *Best Of Michael Johnson* . . . . (RCA)
Hits Of '86-C . . . . (RCA)
Wings . . . . (RCA)

Glory Days
Bruce Springsteen; *Born In The U.S.A.* . . . . (Columbia)
Bruce Springsteen's Greatest Hits . . . . (Columbia)

Goin' Back
Byrds; *20 Essential Tracks From The Box Set* . . . . (Columbia)
The Byrds . . . . (Columbia)
Dusty Springfield; *Dusty Springfield-Golden Greats* . . . . (Philips)
Neil Young; *Comes A Time* . . . . (Reprise)
Nils Lofgren; *Best Of Nils Lofgren* . . . . (A&M)
Night After Night . . . . (A&M)
Nils Lofgren . . . . (Rykodisc)

Goodbye Lament
Iommi; *Iommi* . . . . (Divine/Priority)

Graduate
Third Eye Blind; *Third Eye Blind* . . . . (Elektra)

Graduation (Friends Forever)
Vitamin C; *Totally Hits-#3-C* . . . .(Atlantic)
Vitamin C . . . . (Elektra)

Grow Old With Me
John Lennon; *The John Lennon Anthology* . . . . (Capitol)
Wonsaponatime . . . . (Capitol)
Mary Chapin Carpenter; *Party Doll And Other Favorites* . . . . (Columbia)

Growin' Up
Bruce Springsteen; *Greetings From Asbury Park, N.J.* . . . . (Columbia)
Live 1975-1985 . . . . (Legacy)
Tracks . . . . (Legacy)
Bruce Springsteen & The E Street Band; *Bruce Springsteen & The E Street*
Band Live/1975-85 . . . . (Legacy)

Growing Boy Needs His Lunch
Dead Kennedys; *Frankenchrist* . . . .(Alternative Tentacles)

Growing Up The Hard Way
Foreigner; *Agent Provocateur* . . . .(Atlantic)

Growing Up With Shiva
Information Society; *Information Society* . . . . (Tommy Boy)

Grown Up Wrong
Rolling Stones; *12 X 5* . . . .(Abkco)

Happy Birthday, Sweet Sixteen
Neil Sedaka; *Neil Sedaka Sings His Greatest Hits* . . . . (RCA)
Neil Sedaka Sings The Hits . . . . (RCA)
Neil Sedaka's All-Time Greatest Hits . . . . (RCA)

Hazy Shade Of Winter
Bangles; *Bangles' Greatest Hits* . . . . (Columbia)

ST/Less Than Zero .... (Def Jam)
Simon & Garfunkel; *Bookends* .... (Columbia)
 Collected Works .... (Columbia)

Heart Of Innocence
Jessica Simpson; *Sweet Kisses* .... (Columbia)

Help!
Beatles; *Beatles 1* .... (Capitol)
 Beatles-20 Greatest Hits .... (Capitol)
 Rarities .... (Capitol)
 Reel Music .... (Capitol)
 ST/Help! .... (Capitol)
 The Beatles At The Hollywood Bowl .... (Capitol)
 The Beatles/1962-1966 .... (Capitol)

Holding Back The Years
Simply Red; *Picture Book* .... (Elektra)
 Simply Red's Greatest Hits .... (East West)

How You've Grown
10,000 Maniacs; *Our Time In Eden* .... (Elektra)

I Choose
Offspring; *Ixnay On The Hombre* .... (Columbia)

I Don't Wanna Grow Up
Descendants; *I Don't Wanna Grow Up* .... (SST)

I Don't Wanna Grow Up
Tom Waits; *Bone Machine* .... (Island)

I Think About You
Collin Raye; *Best Of Collin Raye-Direct Hits* ... (Epic)
 I Think About You .... (Epic)

I Wanna Be Loved
Andrews Sisters; *Best Of The Andrews Sisters* ... (MCA)

I Wanna Grow Up To Be A Politician
Byrds; *20 Essential Tracks From The Box Set* ... (Columbia)
 Best Of The Byrds-Greatest Hits-#2 .... (Columbia)
 Byrdmaniax .... (Columbia)
 The Byrds .... (Columbia)

I Was Made To Love Her
Stevie Wonder; *16 #1 Hits From The Late '60s-C* .. (Motown)
 Stevie Wonder's Greatest Hits .... (Motown)

I Won't Grow Up
Original Cast/Mary Martin; *Peter Pan-The 1954 Broadway
 Production* .... (RCA Victor)

I'd Like That
XTC; *Homespun* .... (Idea/TVT)

I'll Be Here Awhile
311; *From Chaos* .... (Volcano Entertainment)

I'll Never Grow Up, Now
Twisted Sister; *Big Hits & Nasty Cuts* .... (Atlantic)

I'm Not A Girl, Not Yet A Woman
Britney Spears; *Britney* .... (Jive)

In Pictures
Alabama; *Alabama-Super Hits* .... (RCA)
 In Pictures .... (RCA)

Innocent
Fuel; *Something Like Human* .... (Epic)

Inside Of Me
Little Steven & The Disciples Of Soul; *The Sopranos-Music From The HBO
 Original Series* .... (Sony Music Soundtrax)

It Was A Very Good Year
Frank Sinatra; *Frank Sinatra-The Very Good Years* .. (Reprise)
 September Of My Years .... (Reprise)
 The Reprise Collection .... (Reprise)
 *The Sopranos-Music From The HBO Original
 Series* .... (Sony Music Soundtrax)
Frank Sinatra with Count Basie & The Orchestra; *Sinatra At The
 Sands* .... (Reprise)

It Wasn't God Who Made Honky Tonk Angels
Kitty Wells; *Grand Ole Opry-75 Years-#1-C* .... (MCA)
 Kitty Wells' Greatest Hits .... (Step One)
 The Kitty Wells Story .... (MCA)

It's Been Awhile
Staind; *Break The Cycle* .... (Flip/Elektra)

Jaded
Aerosmith; *Just Push Play* .... (Columbia)
 Now That's What I Call Music!-#7-C .... (Virgin)

James
Huffamoose; *We've Been Had Again* .... (Interscope)

Keep On Growing
Derek And The Dominos; *Layla* .... (Polydor)
Sheryl Crow; *ST/Boys On The Side* .... (Arista)

Kids Aren't Alright
Offspring; *Americana* .... (Columbia)

Kid's Grown Up
Leo Sayer; *Just A Boy* .... (Out Of Print)

Kisses Sweeter Than Wine
Jimmie Rodgers; *Best Of Jimmie Rodgers* ...... (Rhino)
 Cruisin'-1958-C .... (Increase)
Weavers; *Best Of The Weavers* .... (MCA)
 Reunion-At Carnegie Hall-1963 .... (Vanguard)
 Weavers At Carnegie Hall .... (Vanguard)

 Weavers' Greatest Hits .... (Vanguard)

Lack Of Water
Why Store; *The Why Store* .... (MCA)

Landslide
Fleetwood Mac; *25 Years-The Chain* ...... (Warner Bros.)
 Fleetwood Mac .... (Reprise)
 Fleetwood Mac Live .... (Warner Bros.)
 The Dance .... (Reprise)
Smashing Pumpkins; *Pisces Iscariot* .... (Virgin)

Learn To Fly
Foo Fighters; *There Is Nothing Left To Lose* .... (Roswell/RCA)

Let It Grow
Eric Clapton; *461 Ocean Boulevard* .... (Polydor)
 Eric Clapton-Crossroads-C .... (Polydor)

Let's Get Married
Jagged Edge; *J.E. Heartbreak* .... (So So Def/Columbia)

Life Gets Away
Clint Black; *Clint Black-The Greatest Hits* .... (RCA)
 One Emotion .... (RCA)

Little Sister
Elvis Presley; *Elvis' Golden Records, Volume 3* ... (RCA)
 Elvis In Concert .... (RCA)
 I Was The One .... (RCA)
 The Top Ten Hits .... (RCA)
 Worldwide 50 Gold Award Hits, Vol. 1, Parts 1 & 2 ... (RCA)

Maggie May
Rod Stewart; *Absolutely Live* .... (Warner Bros.)
 Best Of Rod Stewart .... (Mercury)
 Billboard Top Rock 'N' Roll Hits-1971-C .... (Rhino)
 Every Picture Tells A Story .... (Mercury)
 Rod Stewart's Greatest Hits .... (Warner Bros.)
 Sing It Again, Rod .... (Mercury)
 Storyteller/The Complete Anthology: 1964-1990 ... (Warner Bros.)

Mama
Spice Girls; *Diana, Princess Of Wales-Tribute-C* ... (Columbia)
 Spice .... (Virgin)

Mammas Don't Let Your Babies Grow Up To Be Cowboys
Gibson/Miller Band; *Cowboy Super Hits-C* ..... (Columbia)
 ST/The Cowboy Way .... (Epic)
Waylon Jennings & Willie Nelson; *Waylon & Willie* ... (RCA)
 Waylon Jennings & Willie Nelson's Greatest Hits ... (RCA)
Willie Nelson; *Greatest Hits (& Some That Will Be)* ... (Columbia)
 ST/The Electric Horseman .... (Columbia)
 Willie & Family Live .... (Columbia)

Man Of Me
Gary Allan; *Alright Guy* .... (MCA)

Me And Julio Down By The Schoolyard
Paul Simon; *Greatest Hits, Etc.* .... (Columbia)
 Negotiations And Love Songs, 1971-1986 .... (Warner Bros.)
 Paul Simon .... (Columbia)
 Paul Simon In Concert/Live Rhymin' .... (Columbia)
Simon & Garfunkel; *The Concert In Central Park* ... (Warner Bros.)

Memory Remains
Metallica; *Reload* .... (Elektra)

My Back Pages
Bob Dylan; *Another Side Of Bob Dylan* .... (Columbia)
 Bob Dylan's Greatest Hits-#2 .... (Columbia)
Byrds; *20 Essential Tracks From The Box Set* ... (Columbia)
 Byrds Play Dylan .... (Columbia)
 The Byrds' Greatest Hits .... (Columbia)
 Younger Than Yesterday .... (Columbia)

My Cup Runneth Over
Ed Ames; *My Cup Runneth Over* .... (RCA)
 Nipper's Greatest Hits Of The '60s-#2-C ..... (RCA)
George Jones; *Homecoming In Heaven* ...... (Razor & Tie)
Jim Nabors; *Jim Nabors-16 Most Requested Songs* ... (Legacy)
Original Broadway Cast; *I Do! I Do!* .... (RCA Victor)

My Hometown
Bruce Springsteen; *Born In The U.S.A.* .... (Columbia)
 Bruce Springsteen's Greatest Hits .... (Columbia)

My Next Thirty Years
Tim McGraw; *A Place In The Sun* .... (Curb)
 Tim McGraw's Greatest Hits .... (Curb)

My Way
Elvis Presley; *Aloha from Hawaii via Satellite* ... (RCA)
 Canadian Tribute .... (RCA)
 Elvis In Concert .... (RCA)
Frank Sinatra; *Frank Sinatra's Greatest Hits-#2* ... (Reprise)
 My Way .... (Reprise)
 Sinatra Reprise-The Very Good Years .... (Reprise)
 Sinatra-The Main Event Live .... (Reprise)
 The Reprise Collection .... (Reprise)
Paul Anka; *Very Best Of Paul Anka* .... (Ranwood)

Naked
Spice Girls; *Spice* .... (Virgin)

Neighborhood
Vonda Shepard; *ST/Songs From "Ally McBeal" Featuring Vonda
 Shepard* .... (550/Epic)

Never Never Land
Original Cast/Mary Martin; *Peter Pan-The 1954 Broadway Production* . . . .(RCA Victor)
Nineteen
Old 97's; *Fight Songs* . . . . (Elektra)
No Tears Left
Crosby, Stills, Nash & Young; *Looking Forward* . . . . (Reprise)
Nothing Really Matters
Madonna; *Ray Of Light* . . . .(Maverick)
Old
Paul Simon; *You're The One* . . . .(Warner Bros.)
Old Gray Mare, The
Original Soundtrack; *School Days-Kids Classics* . . . . (Benson)
Once In A Lifetime
Talking Heads; *Remain In Light* . . . . (Sire)
ST/Stop Making Sense . . . . (Sire)
One Step At A Time
Brenda Lee; *Brenda Lee-Anthology-#1 & #2* . . . . (MCA)
Oney
Johnny Cash; *Johnny Cash-16 Biggest Hits-#2* . . . . (Legacy)
Only Sixteen
Dr. Hook; *Bankrupt* . . . . (Capitol)
Dr. Hook-Greatest Hits & More . . . . (Capitol)
Great Records Of The Decade-'70s Hits-#2-C . . . . (Curb)
Little Bit More . . . . (Capitol)
Sam Cooke; *Best Of Sam Cooke* . . . . (RCA)
The Man And His Music . . . . (RCA)
This Is Sam Cooke . . . . (RCA)
Ooh La La
Rod Stewart; *When We Were The New Boys* . . . .(Warner Bros.)
Oops!...I Did It Again
Britney Spears; *Oops!...I Did It Again* . . . . (Jive)
Que Sera, Sera
Doris Day; *Doris Day-16 Most Requested Songs-Encore!* . . . . (Columbia)
Doris Day's Greatest Hits . . . . (Columbia)
Radio Classics Of The '50s-C . . . . (Columbia)
Sly & The Family Stone; *Fresh* . . . . (Legacy)
Sly & The Family Stone-Anthology . . . .(Epic)
Question Everything
8Stops7; *In Moderation* . . . . (Reprise)
Raised In The Alley Blues
Freddy Brown; *Barrelhouse Mamas: Born In The Alley, Raised In The Slums-C* . . . . (Yazoo)
Raised On Robbery
Joni Mitchell; *Court & Spark* . . . . (Asylum)
Razorblades
Chris Stills; *100 Year Thing* . . . . (Atlantic)
Rebecca Lynn
Bryan White; *Bryan White* . . . . (Asylum)
Reminiscing
Little River Band; *'70's Super Groups-C* . . . . (Rhino)
Reminiscing: The Twentieth Anniversary Collection . . . . (Rhino)
Restless Nights
Bruce Springsteen; *Tracks* . . . . (Columbia)
Rocking Chairs; *One Step Up/Two Steps Back-The Songs Of Bruce Springsteen-C* . . . . (Right Stuff)
Return To Innocence
Enigma; *The Cross Of Changes* . . . . (Virgin)
Ricky Wants A Man Of Her Own
Bruce Springsteen; *Tracks* . . . . (Columbia)
Rollin' Stoned
Great White; *Can't Get There From Here* . . . . (Portrait)
Roots Of My Raising
Merle Haggard & The Strangers; *Capitol Collectors Series-Merle Haggard & The Strangers* . . . . (Capitol)
For The Record: Merle Haggard-43 Legendary Hits . . . . (BNA)
Merle Haggard's Greatest Hits-#2 . . . . (Curb)
Sadder-But-Wiser Girl For Me
Original Cast; *The Music Man* . . . .(Gold Rush)
Robert Preston; *ST/The Music Man* . . . .(Warner Bros.)
San Antonio Rose To You
Rick Trevino; *Texas Super Hits-C* . . . . (Columbia)
Seen Enough
Crosby, Stills, Nash & Young; *Looking Forward* . . . . (Reprise)
September Song
Boston Pops Orchestra/Arthur Fiedler; *Greatest Hits Of The '30s* . . . . . . (RCA)
Mister Music U.S.A. . . . . (Deutsche Grammophon)
Music For Every Mood-Yesterday . . . . (RCA)
Eddy Duchin & Stanley Worth; *Best Of The Big Bands-C* . . . . . . (Columbia)
Eydie Gorme; *Best Of Eydie Gorme* . . . . (Curb)
Flamingos & Moonglows; *On The Dusty Road Of Hits* . . . . (Vee-Jay)
Frank Sinatra; *A Lovely Way To Spend An Evening* . . . . (ASV)
Point Of No Return . . . . (Capitol)
September Of My Years . . . . (Reprise)
Kate Wolf; *Safe At Anchor* . . . . (Kaleidoscope)
Lindsey Buckingham; *Law And Order* . . . . (Asylum)
Lou Reed; *Lost In The Stars-Music Of Kurt Weill-C* . . . . (A&M)
Roger Williams; *Roger Williams' Greatest Hits* . . . . (MCA)

Roy Clark; *Best Of Roy Clark* . . . . (MCA)
Sarah Vaughan & Clifford Brown; *Sarah Vaughan & Clifford Brown* . . . .(Emarcy)
Stan Kenton; *Comprehensive Stan Kenton* . . . . (Capitol)
Retrospective-Capitol Years . . . . (Blue Note)
Tony Bennett; *Forty Years-The Artistry Of Tony Bennett* . . . . . . (Columbia)
Willie Nelson; *Stardust* . . . . (Legacy)
Serve The Servants
Nirvana; *In Utero* . . . .(David Geffen Co.)
She Said
Collective Soul; *Dosage* . . . .(Atlantic)
ST/Scream 2 . . . .(Dimension/Capitol)
She's Leaving Home
Al Jarreau; *All Fly Home* . . . . (Warner Bros.)
Beatles; *Beatles-Box Set* . . . . (Capitol)
Beatles-Love Songs . . . . (Capitol)
Sgt. Pepper's Lonely Hearts Club Band . . . . (Capitol)
Shop Around
Captain & Tennille; *Captain & Tennille's Greatest Hits* . . . . (A&M)
Miracles; *Greatest Hits From The Beginning* . . . . (Motown)
Hi-We're The Miracles . . . . (Motown)
Smokey Robinson & The Miracles; *16 #1 Hits From The Early '60s-C* . . . . (Motown)
Every Great Motown Song-First 25 Years-C . . . . (Motown)
Smokey Robinson & The Miracles' Anthology . . . . (Motown)
Shy Of The Moon
Wallflowers; *The Wallflowers* . . . . (Virgin)
Simple Joys Of Maidenhood
Julie Andrews; *Camelot* . . . . (Columbia)
Various Artists; *ST/Camelot* . . . . (Warner Bros.)
Simple Lessons
Candlebox; *Lucy* . . . . (Maverick)
Sixteen Going On Seventeen
Original Cast; *The Sound Of Music* . . . . (Sony Broadway)
Social Disease
Elton John; *Goodbye Yellow Brick Road* . . . .(Polydor)
Soft
Second Coming; *Second Coming* . . . . (Capitol)
Softest Place On Earth
Xscape; *Traces Of My Lipstick* . . . . (So So Def/Columbia)
Solitude
Edwin McCain; *Honor Among Thieves* . . . . (Lava)
Edwin McCain & Darius Rucker; *VH-1 Crossroads-C* . . . .(Atlantic)
Son Of A Preacher Man
Dusty Springfield; *Dusty Springfield* . . . . (Rhino)
Dusty Springfield-Anthology . . . . (Mercury)
Spirit Of A Boy, Wisdom Of A Man
Randy Travis; *Big Country Hits '99-C* . . . . (K-Tel)
You And You Alone . . . .(DreamWorks/SKG)
Strawberry Wine
Deana Carter; *Did I Shave My Legs For This?* . . . . (Capitol)
Sweet Sixteen
Destiny's Child; *The Writing's On The Wall* . . . . (Columbia)
Sweet Summer
Diamond Rio; *One More Day* . . . . (Arista)
Sweet Surrender
Sarah McLachlan; *Mirrorball* . . . . (Arista)
Surfacing . . . . (Arista)
Swinging On A Star
Bing Crosby; *All-Time Best* . . . . (Curb)
Best Of Bing Crosby . . . . (MCA)
Dion And The Belmonts; *Dion And The Belmonts-Their Best* . . . . . . (Laurie)
Frank Sinatra; *Frank Sinatra Sings The Songs Of Van Heusen & Cahn* . . . . (Reprise)
That's Not Me
Beach Boys; *Pet Sounds* . . . . (Capitol)
The Pet Sounds Sessions: A 30th Anniversary Collection . . . (Capitol)
Theme From "A Different World"
Original Soundtrack; *Television's Greatest Hits-#7-Cable Ready-C* . . . . . (TVT)
Theme From "Beverly Hills 90210"
John Davis; *Beverly Hills 90210: Songs From The Peach Pit* . . . . (Rhino)
ST/Beverly Hills, 90210-College Years . . . . (Giant)
Television's Greatest Hits-#7-Cable Ready-C . . . . (TVT)
Theme From "Facts Of Life"
Original Soundtrack; *Television's Greatest Hits-#3-1970s & 1980s-C* . . . (TVT)
Theme From "Golden Girls"
Original Soundtrack; *Television's Greatest Hits-#6-Remote Control-C* . . . (TVT)
Theme From "Growing Pains"
Original Soundtrack; *Television's Greatest Hits-#6-Remote Control-C* . . . (TVT)
Theme From "James At 15"
Original Soundtrack; *Television's Greatest Hits-#6-Remote Control-C* . . . (TVT)
Theme From "My So-Called Life"
Original Soundtrack; *Television's Greatest Hits-#7-Cable Ready-C* . . . . (TVT)
Theme From "Thirtysomething"
Original Soundtrack; *Television's Greatest Hits-#7-Cable Ready-C* . . . . (TVT)
This Ole House
Rosemary Clooney; *Rosemary Clooney-16 Most Requested Songs* . . . . (Legacy)
Statler Brothers; *The World Of The Statler Brothers* . . . . (Columbia)

Stuart Hamblen; *Stuart Hamblen-A Man & His Music* . . . . (Lamb & Lion)
Throwing Stones
Paula Cole; *This Fire* . . . .(Imago)
Thunder Road
Bruce Springsteen; *Born To Run* . . . . (Columbia)
Bruce Springsteen's Greatest Hits . . . . (Columbia)
Bruce Springsteen & The E Street Band; *Bruce Springsteen & The E Street Band Live/1975-85* . . . .(Legacy)
Tiger
Paula Cole; *This Fire* . . . .(Imago)
Time
Pink Floyd; *Dark Side Of The Moon* . . . . (Capitol)
Delicate Sound Of Thunder . . . . (Columbia)
Pink Floyd-Gift Set . . . . (Capitol)
Too Old To Cut The Mustard
Carlisles; *45-#6348* . . . . (Mercury)
Ernest Tubb; *Ernest Tubb-Retrospective-#2* . . . . (MCA Special Prod.)
Trials
Jackopierce; *Finest Hour* . . . . (A&M)
Two Little Girls
Ani DiFranco; *Little Plastic Castle* . . . . (Righteous Babe)
Valleri
Monkees; *Birds Bees & The Monkees* . . . . (Rhino)
Missing Links . . . . (Rhino)
More Greatest Hits Of The Monkees . . . . (Arista)
Nuggets-Classic Collection From The Psychedelic '60s-C . . . . . (Rhino)
Vintage Eyes
Second Coming; *Second Coming* . . . . (Capitol)
Watching Scotty Grow
Bobby Goldsboro; *Bobby Goldsboro's All-Time Greatest Hits*. . . . . (Curb)
Honey-Best Of Bobby Goldsboro . . . . (EMI)
Mac Davis; *Mac Davis' Greatest Hits* . . . . (Columbia)
What I Didn't Know
Athenaeum; *Radiance* . . . . (Atlantic)
What's My Age Again?
Blink-182; *Enema Of The State* . . . . (MCA)
Now That's What I Call Music!-#3-C . . . . (Virgin)
When I Grow Too Old To Dream
Benny Goodman & His Orchestra; *Best Of Benny Goodman & His Orchestra* . . . .(Curb)
Linda Ronstadt; *Living In The USA* . . . . (Asylum)
Louis Armstrong; *Essential Louis Armstrong* . . . . (Vanguard)
When I Grow Up
Garbage; *Version 2.0* . . . . (Almo Sounds)
When I Grow Up (To Be A Man)
Beach Boys; *Absolute Best-#1* . . . . (Capitol)
Beach Boys-Gift Set . . . . (Capitol)
Dance Dance Dance . . . . (Capitol)
Made In The U.S.A. . . . . (Capitol)
Spirit Of America . . . . (Capitol)
When I Was Young
Animals; *Best Of The Animals* . . . . (Abkco)
Greatest Hits Live!-Rip It To Shreds . . . . (I.R.S.)
History Of British Rock-#8-C . . . . (Rhino)
When I'm Sixty-Four
Beatles; *Beatles-Box Set* . . . . (Capitol)
Sgt. Pepper's Lonely Hearts Club Band . . . . (Capitol)
When They're Old Enough To Know Better
Eddie Cantor; *Music From The New York Stage (1890-1920)-#4-1917-1920-C* . . . .(Pearl)
Where Corn Don't Grow
Travis Tritt; *The Restless Kind* . . . . (Warner Bros.)
Whiffenpoof Song
Bing Crosby & Fred Waring & His Glee Club; *Bing Crosby's Greatest Hits* . . . . (MCA)
Count Basie & Mills Brothers; *Count Basie & Mills Brothers-16 Great Performances* . . . . (MCA)
Louis Armstrong; *Best Of Louis Armstrong* . . . . (MCA)
Mitch Miller; *34 All-Time Great Sing-Along Selections-C* . . . . (Columbia)
Statler Brothers; *The World Of The Statler Brothers* . . . . (Columbia)
Wild One
Faith Hill; *Take Me As I Am* . . . . (Warner Bros.)
Woman In Me
Jessica Simpson featuring Destiny's Child; *Sweet Kisses* . . . . (Columbia)
Wouldn't It Be Nice
Beach Boys; *Absolutely Best-#2* . . . . (Capitol)
Made In The U.S.A. . . . . (Capitol)
Pet Sounds . . . . (Capitol)
Still Cruisin' . . . . (Capitol)
XXX's And OOO's
Trisha Yearwood; *Thinkin' About You* . . . . (MCA)
You Can Make History (Young Again)
Elton John; *Elton John-Love Songs* . . . . (MCA)
Younger Girl
Critters; *Sixties Rule! Chapter Two-C* . . . . (One Way)
Lovin' Spoonful; *Lovin' Spoonful-Anthology* . . . . (Rhino)
You're A Big Girl Now
Bob Dylan; *Blood On The Tracks* . . . . (Columbia)

AIDS

See Also: **PAIN & HEALING, SEX, SEX: RESISTING TEMPTATION**

A.I.D.S.
Luc Van Acker; *Industrial Machine Musick-C* . . . .(Cleopatra)
A.I.D.S.
Gregory Isaacs; *Dreaming* . . . . (Heartbeat)
A.I.D.S.
Method Of Destruction; *Loved By Thousands-Greatest Hits-#1* . . . . (Megaforce)
A.I.D.S. Infested Blood Of Christ
Hell On Earth; *Biomechanical Ejaculations Of The Damned* . . . . (Neptune)
A.I.D.S. Is A Four Letter Word
TVTV$; *Brainwashington* . . . . (Flipside)
A.I.D.S. Is Killing Me
Big Lucky Carter; *Lucky 13* . . . .(Blueside)
AIDS
Yellowman; *Message To The World* . . . . (Real Authentic Sound)
RAS Portraits . . . . (Real Authentic Sound)
Real Authentic Sampler-#2-C . . . . (Real Authentic Sound)
Yellowman Rides Again . . . . (Real Authentic Sound)
AIDS
Reverend Benjamin Cone, Jr.; *The House Is Open.* . . . .(Malaco)
AIDS & Armageddon
Fishbone & The Familyhood Nextperience; *Psychotic Friends Nutwerk* . . . .(Hollywood)
AIDS/Desolation
Ras Sam Brown; *Teacher.* . . . . (Real Authentic Sound)
Child Should Live Forever (Theme For The Eddie Cantor Fund For Children With AIDS)
Original Off-Broadway Cast; *A Hard Time To Be Single.* . . . . (Original Cast)
Cure For AIDS
Dan Bern; *Fifty Eggs* . . . . (Work)
Halloween Parade
Lou Reed; *New York.* . . . . (Sire)
Hell On High Heels
Motley Crue; *New Tattoo* . . . . (Motley/Beyond)
Hush Hush Hush
Paula Cole; *This Fire* . . . . (Imago)
Last Song
Elton John; *The One.* . . . . (MCA)
Living With AIDS
Romanovsky & Phillips; *Brave Boys-Best & More Of Romanovsky & Phillips* . . . .(Fresh Fruit)
Emotional Rollercoaster . . . .(Fresh Fruit)
Safe Sex
Erick Sermon; *No Pressure* . . . . (Def Jam/IDJMG)
She Thinks His Name Was John
Reba McEntire; *Read My Mind* . . . . (MCA)
Reba McEntire's Greatest Hits-#3: I'm A Survivor. . . . . (MCA)
Streets Of Philadelphia
Bruce Springsteen; *Bruce Springsteen's Greatest Hits* . . . . (Columbia)
Diana, Princess Of Wales-Tribute-C . . . .(Columbia)
ST/Philadelphia . . . . (Epic/Sony Music Soundtrax)

AIR, Breathing

See Also: **NATURE, SKY, WIND**

Air
Incredible String Band; *Relics Of The Incredible String Band* . . . .(Elektra)
Weetam . . . .(Elektra)
Air
Talking Heads; *Fear Of Music* . . . . (Sire)
Name Of This Band Is Talking Heads . . . . (Sire)
Air
Original Broadway Cast; *Hair* . . . . (RCA)
Air Dance
Black Sabbath; *Never Say Die* . . . . (Warner Bros.)
Air That I Breathe
Hollies; *Best Of The Hollies-#2* . . . . (EMI)
Hollies . . . . (Epic)
Hollies-Epic Anthology From The Original Master Tapes . . . . (Epic)
Barely Breathing
Duncan Sheik; *Duncan Sheik.* . . . . (Atlantic)
Breath Away From Heaven
George Harrison; *Cloud Nine* . . . . (Dark Horse)
Breath Of Life
Brian Setzer; *Knife Feels Like Justice* . . . . (EMI)
Breath Of Life
Erasure; *Chorus* . . . . (Sire)
Breath Taking Guy
Diana Ross & The Supremes; *Diana Ross & The Supremes-Anthology (1962-1969)* . . . .(Motown)

Marvelettes; *Marvelettes-Anthology* . . . . (Motown)
Supremes; *Where Did Our Love Go* . . . . (Motown)
Breathe
Ministry; *Just Say Da-#4 Of Just Say Yes-C* . . . . (Sire)
   The Mind Is A Terrible Thing To Taste . . . . (Sire)
Breathe
Faith Hill; *Breathe* . . . . (Warner Bros.)
Breathe
Collective Soul; *Hints, Allegations And Things Left Unsaid* . . . . (Atlantic)
Breathe
Nickelback; *State* . . . . (Roadrunner)
Breathe Again
Toni Braxton; *Toni Braxton* . . . . (LaFace)
Breathe In The Air
Pink Floyd; *Dark Side Of The Moon* . . . . (Capitol)
   Pink Floyd-Gift Set . . . . (Capitol)
Breathing
Kate Bush; *Never For Ever* . . . . (EMI)
   Whole Story . . . . (EMI)
Breathing
Fat; *Automat Hi-Life* . . . . (Cuneiform)
Breathing
Sextants; *Lucky You* . . . . (Imago)
Breathless
Jerry Lee Lewis; *18 Original Sun Greatest Hits* . . . . (Rhino)
   Jerry Lee Lewis-Original Golden Hits-#1 . . . . (Sun)
   Jerry Lee Lewis-Original Golden Hits-#1 . . . . (Sun)
   Oldies But Goodies-#6-C . . . . (Original Sound)
   The Golden Hits Of Jerry Lee Lewis . . . . (Smash)
Breathless
Corrs; *In Blue* . . . . (143/Lava/Atlantic)
   Totally Hits-#3-C . . . . (Atlantic)
Breathless
Quiet Riot; *Metal Health* . . . . (Pasha)
Breathless
Todd Rundgren; *Something/Anything?* . . . . (Rhino)
Breathless
Mtume; *Theater Of The Mind* . . . . (Epic)
Castles In The Air
Don McLean; *Best Of Don McLean* . . . . (EMI)
   Greatest Hits-Then & Now . . . . (EMI)
   Tapestry . . . . (Liberty)
Computers That Breathe
Tanner; *Ill-Gotten Gains* . . . . (Caroline)
Country Air
Beach Boys; *Smiley Smile/Wild Honey* . . . . (Capitol)
Death In The Autumn Air
Michael McDermott; *620 W. Surf* . . . . (Giant)
Dizzy Atmosphere
Dizzy Gillespie; *Dizzy's Diamonds-Best Of The Verve Years* . . . . (Verve)
Oscar Peterson & Dizzy Gillespie; *Oscar Peterson & Dizzy Gillespie* . . . . (Pablo)
Dog Breath
Frank Zappa; *Uncle Meat* . . . . (Barking Pumpkin)
Mothers Of Invention; *Just Another Band From L.A.* . . . . (Bizarre/Straight)
Every Breath I Take
Gene Pitney; *Gene Pitney-Anthology 1961-1968* . . . . (Rhino)
   Gene Pitney's Greatest Hits . . . . (Evergreen Music)
   Phil Spector-The Early Years-1958-1961-C . . . . (Rhino)
   Remember When-C . . . . (Garland)
   Super Oldies Of The '60s-#5-C . . . . (Audio Fidelity)
Every Breath You Take
Police; *Every Breath You Take-The Classics* . . . . (A&M)
   Synchronicity . . . . (A&M)
Tammy Wynette & Sting; *Without Walls-C* . . . . (Epic)
Exhale (Shoop Shoop)
Whitney Houston; *ST/Waiting To Exhale* . . . . (Arista)
   Whitney Houston's Greatest Hits . . . . (Arista)
Fresh Air
Quicksilver Messenger Service; *Quicksilver Messenger Service-*
   Anthology . . . . (Capitol)
Sons Of Mercury . . . . (Rhino)
Geek Stink Breath
Green Day; *Insomniac* . . . . (Reprise)
Hands In The Air
Bob Seger; *It's A Mystery* . . . . (Capitol)
I Can't Breathe Anymore
David Gilmour; *David Gilmour* . . . . (Columbia)
I Get Out Of Breath
Turtles; *Turtle Wax-Best Of The Turtles-#2* . . . . (Rhino)
I Need You
LeAnn Rimes; *ST/Jesus-The Epic Mini-Series* . . . . (Sparrow/Curb/Capitol)
Idiot Wind
Bob Dylan; *Blood On The Tracks* . . . . (Columbia)
   Hard Rain . . . . (Columbia)
   The Bootleg Series-Volumes 1-3 [Rare & Unreleased] . . . . (Columbia)
I'll Be There For You
Bon Jovi; *New Jersey* . . . . (Jambco)

In The Air Tonight
Phil Collins; *Classic Rock 1966-1988-C* . . . . (Atlantic)
   Face Value . . . . (Atlantic)
   Miami Vice-C . . . . (MCA)
   Prince's Trust 10th Anniversary Party-C . . . . (A&M)
   Serious Hits...Live! . . . . (Atlantic)
   The Secret Policeman's Other Ball/The Music . . . . (Rhino)
Letting Go
Sozzi; *Songs From Dawson's Creek* . . . . (Sony Music Soundtrax)
Life In The Air Age
Be Bop Deluxe; *Live! In The Air Age* . . . . (Harvest)
   Sunburst Finish . . . . (Capitol)
Like Humans Do
David Byrne; *Look Into The Eyeball* . . . . (Luaka Bop)
No Way Out
Stone Temple Pilots; *No. 4* . . . . (Atlantic)
On The Air
Peter Gabriel; *Peter Gabriel* . . . . (Atlantic)
   Peter Gabriel/Plays Live . . . . (Geffen)
   Revisited . . . . (Atlantic)
Out Of Thin Air
Howard Jones; *Cross That Line* . . . . (Elektra)
Possession
Sarah McLachlan; *Fumbling Towards Ecstasy* . . . . (Arista)
Reason For Breathing
Babyface; *Collection Of His Greatest Hits* . . . . (Arista/Epic)
Rollin'
Limp Bizkit; *Chocolate Starfish & The Hotdog Flavored*
   Water . . . . (Flip/Interscope)
Room To Breathe
Daryl Hall & John Oates; *Bigger Than Both Of Us* . . . . (RCA)
Room To Breathe
Downtown Science; *Downtown Science* . . . . (Def Jam)
Scum Of The Earth
Rob Zombie; *ST/Mission: Impossible 2* . . . . (Hollywood)
She Takes My Breath Away
Eddie Money; *Right Here* . . . . (Columbia)
She's A Rainbow
Rolling Stones; *Get Yer Ya-Ya's Out!* . . . . (Abkco)
   More Hot Rocks (big hits & fazed cookies) . . . . (Abkco)
   Singles Collection-The London Years . . . . (Abkco)
   Their Satanic Majesties Request . . . . (Abkco)
   Through The Past, Darkly (Big Hits Vol. 2) . . . . (Abkco)
Smog
Miracles; *City Of Angels* . . . . (Tamla)
Something About The Way You Look Tonight
Elton John; *The Big Picture* . . . . (Rocket)
Something In The Air
Thunderclap Newman; *History Of British Rock-#9-C* . . . . (Rhino)
   Hollywood Dream . . . . (MCA)
   ST/The Strawberry Statement . . . . (MCA)
Take My Breath Away
Berlin; *Best Of Berlin 1979-1988* . . . . (Geffen)
   Count Three & Pray . . . . (Geffen)
   ST/Top Gun . . . . (Columbia)

AIRPLANES, Airports, Flying In Planes, Helicopters, Pilots
See Also: *BIRDS, FLYING, TRAVELING*

Aeroplane
Red Hot Chili Peppers; *One Hot Minute* . . . . (Warner Bros.)
Air Algiers
Country Joe McDonald; *Hold On It's Coming* . . . . (Vanguard)
Air Crash Museum
Dead Milkmen; *Eat Your Paisley* . . . . (Restless)
Air Disaster
Albert Hammond; *45-#6030* . . . . (Mums)
Airplane
Beach Boys; *Love You* . . . . (Caribou)
Airplane
Ian Gomm; *Gomm With The Wind* . . . . (Stiff)
Airport
Wet Willie; *Drippin' Wet/Live!* . . . . (Capricorn)
   Wet Willie's Greatest Hits . . . . (Polydor)
Airport
Motors; *Approved By* . . . . (Blue Plate)
Airport
Smith Sisters; *Bluebird* . . . . (Flying Fish)
Airport Giveth
Rick Derringer; *All American Boy* . . . . (Blue Sky)
Amelia Earhart
BTO; *Rock 'N' Roll Nights* . . . . (Mercury)
Another Runway
Little River Band; *Diamantina Cocktail* . . . . (Capitol)

Army Air Corps
Fred Waring's Pennsylvanians; *Very Best Of Fred Waring & The*
Pennsylvanians ....(Reader's Digest Music)
Glenn Miller; *Best Of The Lost Recordings And The Secret*
Broadcasts.. (RCA Victor)
V-Disc Recordings-Glenn Miller ....(Collector's Choice)

Back In The U.S.A.
Chuck Berry; *Chuck Berry-Golden Hits* ....(Mercury)
Chuck Berry's Greatest Hits ....(Everest)
Roll Over Beethoven ....(Allegiance)
The Chess Box-Chuck Berry ....(Chess)
Linda Ronstadt; *Linda Ronstadt's Greatest Hits, Volume Two* ....(Asylum)
Living In The USA..(Asylum)

Back In The U.S.S.R.
Beatles; *Beatles-Box Set* ....(Capitol)
Rock 'N' Roll Music ....(Capitol)
The Beatles (White Album) ....(Capitol)
The Beatles/1967-1970...................................(Capitol)
Billy Joel; *KOHUEPT* ....(Columbia)

Bang The Drum Slowly
Emmylou Harris; *Red Dirt Girl* ....(Nonesuch)

Bennie And The Jets
Elton John; *Billboard Top Rock 'N' Roll Hits-1974-C* ...... (Rhino)
Classic Rock-#1-C ....(MCA)
Elton John's Greatest Hits ....(Polydor)
Goodbye Yellow Brick Road ....(Polydor)
Here And There..(Rocket)

Bermuda Triangle
Fleetwood Mac; *Heroes Are Hard To Find* ....(Reprise)

Bermuda Triangle Blues (Flight 45)
Blondie; *Plastic Letters* ....(Chrysalis)

Biggest Airport In The World
Moe Bandy; *Best Of Moe Bandy-Vol. 1* ....(Columbia)

Blues From An Airplane
Jefferson Airplane; *2400 Fulton Street-An Anthology*.......(RCA)
The Worst Of Jefferson Airplane..........................(RCA)

Bomber Medley
James Gang; *Best Of The James Gang*.......................(MCA)
James Gang Rides Again ....(MCA)

Brown Eyed Handsome Man (TWA)
Buddy Holly; *Buddy Holly-20 Golden Greats*................(MCA)
For The First Time Anywhere ....(MCA)
Rock & Roll Collection ....(MCA)
Chuck Berry; *Best Of The Best Of Chuck Berry*..... (International Mktg. Group)
Roll Over Beethoven ....(Allegiance)
The Chess Box-Chuck Berry ....(Chess)
Waylon Jennings; *Essential Waylon Jennings*...............(RCA)
Waylon Jennings-Super Hits...............................(RCA)

Budapest By Blimp
Thomas Dolby; *Aliens Ate My Buick* .... (EMI)

Can't Cry Anymore
Sheryl Crow; *MTV Party To Go-#8-C*........................(Tommy Boy)
Tuesday Night Music Club ....(A&M)

Comin' In On A Wing & A Prayer
Anita Ellis; *Songs That Won The War-C* ......(Columbia River Entert. Group)
Anne Shelton; *V-E Day 50th Anniversary-The Musical*
Memories-C .... (Living Era)
Four Vagabonds; *The Victory Collection: The Smithsonian Remembers When*
America Went To War-C ....(RCA)
Ry Cooder; *Boomer's Story* ....(Reprise)

Coming Into Los Angeles
Arlo Guthrie; *Best Of Arlo Guthrie* .... (Warner Bros.)
Running Down The Road ....(Reprise)
ST/Woodstock ....(Atlantic)

Danger Zone
Kenny Loggins; *ST/Top Gun* ....(Columbia)

Deportee (Plane Wreck At Los Gatos)
Arlo Guthrie & Pete Seeger; *Together In Concert*..........(Reprise)
Byrds; *The Byrds* ....(Columbia)
Cisco Houston; *Greatest Songs Of Woody Guthrie-C* ....(Vanguard)
Gene Clark & Carla Olson; *So Rebellious A Lover* ....(Rhino)
Judy Collins; *Tribute To Woody Guthrie-C*................ (Warner Bros.)
Waylon Jennings, Willie Nelson, Johnny Cash, Kris Kristofferson;
Highwayman ....(Columbia)

Do America
Mark Knopfler; *Sailing To Philadelphia* .... (Warner Bros.)

Don't Pull Your Love
Hamilton, Joe Frank & Reynolds; *'70s Biggest Hits-C* .... (MCA Special Prod.)
Hamilton, Joe Frank & Reynolds' Greatest Hits ....(MCA Special Prod.)
Rock Around The Oldies-#4-C ....(MCA Special Prod.)

Faith In Me
Crosby, Stills, Nash & Young; *Looking Forward* ....(Reprise)

Flight (505)
Rolling Stones; *Aftermath* ....(Abkco)

Flight 309 To Tennessee
Shelly West; *West By West* ....(Viva)

Flight 602
Chicago; *Chicago At Carnegie Hall* ....(Chicago)
Chicago III ....(Chicago)

Flyer
Saga; *Heads Or Tales*....................................(Portrait)

Flying Down To Rio
Bobby Short; *Ertegun's New York, N.Y. Cabaret Music-#5-C* .... (Atlantic)

Ghost Of Flight 401
Bob Welch; *Three Hearts* ....(Capitol)

I'm Mandy Fly Me
10 CC; *10 CC's Greatest Hits-1972-1978* .... (Polydor)
How Dare You! ....(Mercury)
Live & Let Live ....(Mercury)

I've Committed Murder
Macy Gray; *On How Life Is* .... (Epic)

Jet
Paul McCartney; *All The Best!* ....(Capitol)
Paul McCartney & Wings; *Band On The Run* ....(Capitol)
Wings; *Wings Greatest* ....(Capitol)
Wings Over America ....(Capitol)

Jet Airliner
Steve Miller Band; *Book Of Dreams* ....(Capitol)
Steve Miller Band-Gift Set ....(Capitol)
Steve Miller Band-Live ....(Capitol)
Steve Miller Band's Greatest Hits-1974-78 ....(Capitol)

Jet City Woman
Queensryche; *Empire*.................................... (EMI)

Jet Fighter
Three O'Clock; *Sixteen Tambourines* .... (Frontier)

Jet Lag
Nazareth; *Rampant*.......................................(A&M)

Jet Pilot
Bob Dylan; *Biograph*.....................................(Columbia)

Jet Silver & The Dolls Of Venus
Be Bop Deluxe; *Axe Victim* ....(Capitol)
Best Of Be Bop Deluxe-Raiding The Divine Archive ....(Capitol)

Jet Song
Original Cast; *ST/West Side Story* ....(Sony Broadway)

Jets At Dawn
Be Bop Deluxe; *Axe Victim* ....(Capitol)

L.A. International Airport
Susan Raye; *Best Of Susan Raye* ....(Capitol)

Leaving On A Jet Plane
Chantal Kreviazuk; *ST/Armageddon-The Album*..............(Columbia)
John Denver; *John Denver's Greatest Hits* .... (RCA)
Rhymes & Reasons .... (RCA)
Kendalls; *Super Country Hits Of The '70s-C* ....(Gusto)
Peter, Paul & Mary; *10 Years Together/The Best Of Peter, Paul*
and Mary ....(Warner Bros.)
Album 1700 ....(Warner Bros.)

Letter, The
Box Tops; *Billboard Top Rock 'N' Roll Hits-1967-C* ......(Rhino)
Box Tops' Greatest Hits ....(Rhino)
Cruisin'-1967-C ....(Increase)
Oldies But Goodies-#12-C .... (Original Sound)
Rockin' '60s-C .... (Priority)
Joe Cocker; *Joe Cocker Live* ....(Capitol)
Joe Cocker-Classics-#4.................................(A&M)
Joe Cocker's Greatest Hits ....(A&M)
Mad Dogs & Englishmen ....(A&M)
Vernon Green & The Medallions; *Oldies But Goodies-#1-C*... (Original Sound)
Vernon Green & The Medallions-Golden Classics ....(Collectables)

Meant To Be
Sammy Kershaw; *Politics Religion & Her*..................(Mercury)

Motels & Planes
Bill Morrissey; *Standing Eight*.......................... (Philo)

Next Plane To London
Rose Garden; *Only Love-1965-1969-C* .... (JCI Assoc. Labels)

Night Flight
Buddy Guy; *Buddy Guy-Complete Chess Studio Recordings* ....(Chess)

Night Flight
Led Zeppelin; *Physical Graffiti* ....(Swan Song)

No Plane On Sunday
Jimmy Buffett; *Floridays* .... (MCA)

Northwest 222
Harry Chapin; *Remember When The Music* ....(Dunhill Compact Classics)

On The Good Ship Lollipop
4 Seasons; *Rarities-#1* ....(Rhino)
Firehouse Five Plus Two; *Goes To Sea* ....(Good Time Jazz)

Out On The Airstrip
Urge Overkill; *Americruiser/Jesus Urge Superstar* ....(Touch & Go)

Outbound Plane
Nanci Griffith; *Little Love Affairs* .... (MCA)
Suzy Bogguss; *Aces* ....(Liberty)

Paper Airplanes
Seals & Crofts; *Year Of Sunday* ....(Warner Bros.)

Pilot
Heart; *Bebe Le Strange*..................................(Epic)

Pinkville Helicopter
Thom Parrott; *Best Of Broadside 1962-1968: Anthems Of The American Underground From The Pages Of Broadside Magazine-C* . . . . (Smithsonian Folkways)
Private Plane
Husker Du; *Flip Your Wig* . . . . (SST)
Promised Land
Band; *Moondog Matinee* . . . . (Capitol)
Chuck Berry; *Rock 'N' Roll Rarities-20 Magic Tracks*. . . . . (Chess)
The Chess Box-Chuck Berry . . . . (Chess)
Elvis Presley; *Promised Land* . . . . (RCA)
ST/This Is Elvis . . . . (RCA)
Freddy Weller; *Country Music Classics-#11-Early '70s-C* . . . . (K-Tel)
Freddy Weller's Greatest Hits . . . . (Columbia)
Gary Morris; *Full Moon Empty Heart* . . . . (Liberty)
Grateful Dead; *Steal Your Face* . . . . (Grateful Dead)
James Taylor; *Walking Man* . . . .(Warner Bros.)
Kingfish; *Kingfish/Alive In Eighty Five-Double Dose* . . . . (Relix)
Red Baron
David Benoit; *Here's To You Charlie Brown: 50th Great* . . . . (GRP/VMG)
Silver Wings
Merle Haggard; *More Of The Best* . . . . (Rhino)
The Seashores Of Old Mexico . . . .(Epic)
Merle Haggard & Jewel; *For The Record: Merle Haggard-43 Legendary Hits* . . . . (BNA)
Merle Haggard & The Strangers; *Okie From Muskogee*. . . . . (Capitol)
Songs I'll Always Sing . . . . (Capitol)
Pam Tillis; *Mama's Hungry Eyes-Merle Haggard Tribute-C* . . . . (Arista)
Sky Pilot
Eric Burdon & The Animals; *Eric Burdon & The Animals' Greatest Hits* . . . . (MGM)
History Of British Rock-#9-C . . . . (Rhino)
Songs Of Protest-C . . . . (Rhino)
Skywriter
Jackson 5; *Jackson 5-Anthology* . . . . (Motown)
Snoopy Vs. The Red Baron
Royal Guardsmen; *Best Of The Royal Guardsmen-#1* . . . . (Rhino)
Collectables Presents The History Of Rock-#9-C . . . . (Collectables)
Cruisin'-1967-C . . . .(Increase)
Million-Dollar Memories #1-C . . . . (RCA)
Super Oldies Of The '60s-#6-C . . . .(Audio Fidelity)
Sydney From A 727
Paul Kelly & The Messengers; *Comedy* . . . . (Dr. Dream Music Group)
Take A Picture
Filter; *Title Of Record*. . . . . (Reprise)
Totally Hits-#2-C. . . . . (Elektra)
Take Me To The Pilot
Elton John; *11-17-70* . . . . (Polydor)
Elton John . . . . (Polydor)
Here And There . . . .(Rocket)
Live In Australia With The Melbourne Symphony Orchestra. . . . . (MCA)
Talking Airplane Disaster
Phil Ochs; *Original New Folks* . . . . (Vanguard)
Thank You, Republic Airlines
Tom Paxton; *One Million Lawyers & Other Disasters* . . . . (Flying Fish)
Theme From "Airwolf"
Original Soundtrack; *Television's Greatest Hits-#6-Remote Control-C* . . (TVT)
Theme From "Dastardly & Muttley In Their Flying Machine"
Original Soundtrack; *Hanna-Barbera Pic-A-Nic Basket Of Cartoon Classics*. . . . . (Kid Rhino/Rhino 4 Kids)
Television's Greatest Hits-#3-1970s & 1980s-C . . . . (TVT)
Theme From "Twelve O'Clock High"
Original Soundtrack; *Television's Greatest Hits-#2-C* . . . . (TVT)
Theme From "Wings"
Original Soundtrack; *Television's Greatest Hits-#7-Cable Ready-C* . . . . . (TVT)
This Flight Tonight
Nazareth; *Hot Tracks* . . . . (A&M)
Nazareth-Classics-#16 . . . . (A&M)
This Flight Tonight
Joni Mitchell; *Blue* . . . . (Reprise)
Trains & Boats & Planes
Billy J. Kramer With The Dakotas; *Billy J. Kramer With The Dakotas-The Definitive Collection* . . . .(EMI)
History Of British Rock-#4-C . . . . (Rhino)
Dionne Warwick; *Dionne Warwick* . . . . (Everest)
Dionne Warwick Greatest Hits . . . . (Everest)
Dionne Warwick-Anthology 1962-1971 . . . . (Rhino)
Hot! Live & Otherwise . . . . (Arista)
Transatlantic Westbound Jet
Hollies; *Hollies* . . . .(Epic)
Twenty Flight Rock
Commander Cody & His Lost Planet Airmen; *Lost In The Ozone* . . . .(MCA)
Too Much Fun-Best Of Commander Cody & His Lost Planet Airmen . . .(MCA)
Eddie Cochran; *Eddie Cochran-Legendary Masters* . . . .(EMI)
Eddie Cochran's Greatest Hits . . . . (Curb)
On The Air . . . .(EMI)
Montrose; *Montrose* . . . .(Warner Bros.)
Paul McCartney; *CHOBA B CCCP-The Russian Album* . . . . (Capitol)
Rolling Stones; *"Still Life" (American Concert 1981)* . . . . (Virgin)

U.S. Air Force
Mormon Tabernacle Choir; *Stars And Stripes Together* . . . . (Columbia)
Who's Driving Your Plane?
Rolling Stones; *Singles Collection-The London Years* . . . .(Abkco)
Wing And A Prayer
Laurel MacDonald; *Chroma* . . . .(Wicklow)
Wingspan . . . .(Wicklow)
Wish You Were Here
Mark Wills; *Wish You Were Here* . . . . (Mercury)
You Belong To Me
Dean Martin; *Dean Martin's All Time Greatest Hits* . . . .(Curb)
Duprees; *13 Of The Best Doo Wop Love Songs-#2-C* . . . .(Original Sound)
Baby Boomer's Best-Mellow '60s-C . . . . (Priority)
Best Of The Duprees . . . . (Rhino)
Jo Stafford; *Billboard Pop Memories-1950-1954-C* . . . . (Rhino)
Jo Stafford's Greatest Hits . . . . (Curb)
Johnny Mathis; *In The Still Of The Night* . . . . (Columbia)
Patsy Cline; *Patsy Cline Sings Songs Of Love* . . . . (MCA Special Prod.)
Sentimentally Yours . . . . (MCA)
Vonda Shepard; *ST/Songs From "Ally McBeal" Featuring Vonda Shepard* . . . .(550/Epic)

ALCOHOL, Beer, Cocktails, Drinking, Getting Drunk, Hangover, Liquor, Whiskey, Wine

See Also: **ALCOHOL: RECOVERING ALCOHOLIC, BARS, CRAZY, FOOD & BEVERAGES: GENERAL, PARTY, ROAD ACCIDENTS**

3 Martini Lunch
Graham Parker; *Best Of Graham Parker 1988-1991*. . . . .(RCA)
51 Beers
Claude King; *Hi-Tone Poppa* . . . . (Collectables)
Abundance
Original Broadway Cast; *The Most Happy Fella*. . . . . . . (Sony Music Classical)
Add A Ring (Ballantine Premium Beer)
Original Soundtrack; *TeeVee Toons-The Commercials-#1-C* . . . . (TVT)
Alcohol
Kinks; *Everybody's In Show-Biz*. (Rhino)
Muswell Hillbillies . . . . (VelVel)
The Kinks' Greatest-Celluloid Heroes . . . . (RCA)
All You Ever Do Is Bring Me Down
Mavericks; *Best Of The Mavericks-Super Colossal Smash Hits Of The '90s* . . . . (Mercury)
Country Superstar Hits-C . . . . (Hip-O)
Honky Tonk Boogie-C . . . . (Hip-O)
Music For All Occasions . . . . (MCA)
Alligator Wine
Screamin' Jay Hawkins; *Voodoo Jive: Best Of Screamin' Jay Hawkins* . . . . (Rhino)
American Pie
Don McLean; *American Pie* . . . . (EMI)
Best Of Don McLean . . . . (EMI)
Greatest Hits Then & Now . . . . (EMI)
ST/Born On The Fourth Of July . . . . (MCA)
Madonna; *ST/The Next Big Thing* . . . . (Maverick)
And Her Tears Flowed Like Wine
Stan Kenton; *Lighter Side* . . . .(Creative World)
Stan Kenton's Greatest Hits . . . . (Capitol)
Stan Kenton & Anita O'Day; *Comprehensive Kenton* . . . . (Capitol)
Another Pack Of Cigarettes…
Marty Robbins; *The Performer* . . . . (Columbia)
Applejack
Dolly Parton; *Collector's Series-Dolly Parton* . . . . (RCA)
Dolly Parton's Greatest Hits . . . . (RCA)
Joe Morris; *Atlantic Rhythm & Blues 1947-1974-#1 (1947-1952)-C* . .(Atlantic)
Attack Of The Killer Beers
Murphy's Law; *Back With A Bong!*. . . . . (Profile)
Bad Whiskey
Lightnin' Hopkins; *Low Down Dirty Blues*. . . . . (Mainstream)
Ballad Of Ira Hayes, The
Johnny Cash; *The Man In Black-His Greatest Hits* . . . . (Legacy)
Peter La Farge; *Best Of Broadside 1962-1968: Anthems Of The American Underground From The Pages Of Broadside Magazine-C*. . . . .(Smithsonian Folkways)
Bar Exam
Derailers; *Here Come The Derailers*. . . . . (Lucky Dog)
Bartender's Blues
George Jones; *10 Years Of Hits* . . . . (Epic)
George Jones-16 Biggest Hits . . . . (Legacy)
George Jones-Super Hits . . . . (Epic)
The Bradley Barn Sessions . . . . (MCA)
Beer And Bones
John Michael Montgomery; *John Michael Montgomery's Greatest Hits* . . . .(Atlantic)
Life's A Dance . . . .(Atlantic)
Beer Barrel Polka
Andrews Sisters; *Andrews Sisters-16 Great Performances*. . . . . (MCA)

Best Of The Andrews Sisters . . . . (MCA)
Frankie Yankovic & His Yanks; *Frankie Yankovic & His Yanks'*
   Greatest Hits . . . . (Columbia)
Will Glahe; *This Is Will Glahe-Decade Of The '30s* . . . .(RCA)

Beer Drinkers & Hell Raisers
ZZ Top; *Best Of ZZ Top* . . . . (Warner Bros.)
   Six Pack . . . . (Warner Bros.)
   Tres Hombres . . . . (Warner Bros.)

Beer Drinkin' Song
Lacy J. Dalton; *Hot Country Rock-#2-C* . . . . (Epic)
   Lacy J. Dalton. . . . . (Columbia)

Beer Drinkin' Woman
Memphis Slim; *At The Gate Of Horn* . . . . (Vee-Jay)
   Raining The Blues . . . .(Fantasy)

Beer Run
Garth Brooks with George Jones; *Scarecrow* . . . . (Capitol)

Beer Run (B Double E Double Are You In?)
George Jones & Garth Brooks; *The Rock: Stone Cold Country 2001* . . . . .(BNA)

Big Ole Brew
Mel McDaniel; *Mel McDaniel's Greatest Hits* . . . . (Capitol)
   Take Me To The Country. . . . . (Capitol)

Blame The Whiskey
Paul David Wells; *Sounds Good To Me* . . . . (Capitol)

Blind Love & Whiskey
Little Mike & The Tornadoes; *Heart Attack* . . . . (Blind Pig)

Bling Bling
B.G.; *Chopper City In The Ghetto* . . . . (Cash Money/Universal)

Bloodshot Eyes
Wynonie Harris; *Bloodshot Eyes: The Best Of Wynonie Harris* . . . . (Rhino)
   Good Rockin' Blues . . . . (Gusto)

Bloody Mary
Original Cast; *South Pacific.* . . . . (CBS Masterworks)
Soundtrack; *South Pacific.* . . . . (RCA)

Bloody Mary
Whitesnake; *Snakebite* . . . . (Geffen)

Bloody Mary Morning
Willie Nelson; *Best Of Willie.* . . . .(RCA)
   Phases & Stages . . . . (Atlantic)
   ST/Honeysuckle Rose . . . . (Columbia)
   Willie & Family Live. . . . . (Columbia)

Blue Champagne
Manhattan Transfer; *The Manhattan Transfer* . . . . (Rhino)

Boat Drinks
Jimmy Buffett; *Songs You Know By Heart-Jimmy Buffett's Greatest*
   Hit(s) . . . . (MCA)
   Volcano. . . . . (MCA)

Bottle Of Red Wine
Derek And The Dominos; *Live At The Fillmore* . . . . (Polydor)
Eric Clapton; *Eric Clapton.* . . . . (Polydor)

Bottle Of Wine
Jimmy Gilmer And The Fireballs; *Frat Rock!-#4-C* . . . . (Rhino)
   Son Of Frat Rock!-C . . . . (Rhino)
   Super Hits-#1-C . . . . (Gusto)

Boyz-N-The-Hood
Dynamite Hack; *Superfast.* . . . . (Farm Club/Universal)

Brand New Whiskey
Gary Stewart; *Brand New* . . . . (Hightone)
   Gary's Greatest . . . . (Hightone)

Bubbles In My Beer
Bob Wills; *Sounds Of Texas* . . . . (Capitol)
Bob Wills & His Texas Playboys; *Bob Wills & His Texas Playboys-24*
   Great Hits . . . . (Polydor)
Bob Wills & His Texas Playboys-Anthology 1935-1973. . . . . (Rhino)
Willie Nelson; *Shotgun Willie* . . . . (Atlantic)

Bubbles In The Wine
Lawrence Welk; *Best Of Lawrence Welk-20 Great Hits* . . . . (Ranwood)
   Lawrence Welk-16 Most Requested Songs . . . . (Columbia)
Original Soundtrack; *Television's Greatest Hits-#4-Black & White*
   Classics-C . . . . (TVT)

California Wine
Bobby Goldsboro; *10th Anniversary Album-#2* . . . .(United Artists)

Carey
Joni Mitchell; *Blue.* . . . . (Reprise)
Joni Mitchell with Tom Scott & The L.A. Express; *Miles Of Aisles* . . . (Asylum)

Carolina Moonshiner
Porter Wagoner; *20 Great Country Hits-C* . . . . (RCA)
   Collector's Porter Wagoner. . . . . (RCA)

Case Of You
Joni Mitchell; *Blue.* . . . . (Reprise)
Joni Mitchell with Tom Scott & The L.A. Express; *Miles Of Aisles* . . . (Asylum)

Champagne & Rock & Roll
Climax Blues Band; *Shine On* . . . . (Sire)

Champagne And Wine
Otis Redding; *The Otis Redding Story.* . . . . (Atlantic)

Champagne Jam
Atlanta Rhythm Section; *Are You Ready!* . . . . (Polydor)
   Champagne Jam. . . . . (Polydor)

Champagne Supernova
Oasis; *What's The Story Morning Glory?* . . . . (Epic)

Cheap Seats, The
Alabama; *Cheap Seats* . . . . (RCA)

Cheap Tequila
Johnny Winter; *Still Alive & Well* . . . .(Columbia)
Rick Derringer; *All American Boy* . . . . (Blue Sky)

Cheers 2 U
Playa; *Cheers 2 U.* . . . . (Def Soul/Def Jam/RAL/Mercury)

Chug-A-Lug
Roger Miller; *Billboard Top Country Hits-1964-C* . . . .(Rhino)
   Frat Rock!-#3-Grandson Of Frat Rock!-C . . . . (Rhino)

Cigarettes & Alcohol
Oasis; *Definitely Maybe* . . . . (Epic)
Rod Stewart; *When We Were The New Boys* . . . . (Warner Bros.)

Cocktails For Two
Duke Ellington & His Orchestra; *No. 1 Hits Greatest Hits-C* . . . . . (RCA Victor)
Spike Jones; *Dinner Music...For People Who Aren't Very Hungry!* . . . .(Rhino)
   Dr. Demento Presents The Greatest Novelty Records-#1-1940s &
   Before-C . . . . (Rhino)
   Dr. Demento: 20th Anniversary Collection-C . . . . (Rhino)
   Nipper's Greatest Hits Of The '40s-#1-C . . . . (RCA)
Spike Jones & His City Slickers; *Best Of Spike Jones & His City*
   Slickers. . . . . (RCA)

Cold Hard Facts Of Life, The
Porter Wagoner; *Essential Porter Wagoner* . . . . (RCA)
   Porter Wagoner's Greatest Hits . . . . (Pair)

Completely Unique Experience, A (Colt 45 Malt Liquor)
Original Soundtrack; *TeeVee Toons-The Commercials-#1-C* . . . .(TVT)

Coors In Colorado
Ray Price; *Master Of The Art* . . . .(Warner Bros.)

Country State Of Mind
Hank Williams, Jr.; *Hank Williams, Jr.'s Greatest Hits III* . . . .(Curb)
   Montana Cafe . . . . (WB/Curb)

Cowboy Love
John Michael Montgomery; *John Michael Montgomery* . . . . (Atlantic)
   John Michael Montgomery's Greatest Hits. . . . . (Atlantic)

D.U.I.
Drink Small; *Round Two* . . . .(Ichiban Int'l)

Daddy's Drinking Up Our Christmas
Commander Cody; *Hillbilly Holiday-C* . . . .(Rhino)

Dance Tonight
Lucy Pearl; *Lucy Pearl.* . . . . (Overbrook/Pookie/Beyond)

Days Of Wine And Roses
Andy Williams; *Andy Williams' Greatest Hits* . . . .(Columbia)
   Andy Williams-16 Most Requested Songs . . . .(Legacy)
   Close Enough For Love. . . . .(Atco)
   Days Of Wine And Roses/Moon River & Other Great Movie
   Themes . . . .(Columbia)
Dream Syndicate; *Days Of Wine & Roses* . . . . (Slash)
   Live At Raji's. . . . . (Restless)
Frank Sinatra; *Days Of Wine And Roses, Moon River, And Other Academy*
   Award Winners. . . . . (Reprise)
Henry Mancini; *Best Of Henry Mancini.* . . . .(RCA)
   Henry Mancini-Pure Gold . . . . (RCA)
   Peter Gunn . . . . (RCA)

Delia's Gone
Johnny Cash; *American Recordings.* . . . .(American)

Don't Buy Me No Beer
Rockin' Louie; *It Will Stand.* . . . . (Ripete)

Don't Come Home A'Drinkin' (With Lovin' On Your Mind)
Loretta Lynn; *Loretta Lynn-Greatest Hits Live* . . . .(K-Tel)
   Loretta Lynn's Greatest Hits . . . . (MCA)
   MCA Records 30 Years Of Hits-1958-1988-C. . . . . (MCA)

Don't Drink & Drive
James Cannings; *Music For All Seasons* . . . . (J.C.)

Don't Drink That Wine
N.W.A.; *Efil4zaggin.* . . . . (Ruthless/Priority)

Don't Drink Whiskey
Johnny Winter; *Birds Can't Row Boats* . . . . (Relix)

Don't Drive Drunk
Stevie Wonder; *ST/Woman In Red* . . . . (Motown)

Don't Sell Daddy Any More Whiskey
Joe Val & The New England Bluegrass Boys; *Not A Word*
   From Home . . . . (Rounder)

Don't You Feel My Leg
Maria Muldaur; *Maria Muldaur.* . . . . (Reprise)

Drink A Round To Ireland
Judy Collins; *Times Of Our Lives.* . . . .(Elektra)

Drink To Me Only With Thine Eyes
Paul Robeson; *Essential Paul Robeson* . . . .(Vanguard)
Roger Whittaker; *Folk Songs Of Our Time* . . . . (RCA)

Drink, Swear, Steal & Lie
Michael Peterson; *Michael Peterson* . . . . (Reprise)

Drinkin' & Drivin'
Johnny Paycheck; *Encore-Johnny Paycheck* . . . . (Epic)
   Everybody's Got A Family. . . . . (Epic)
   Johnny Paycheck's Biggest Hits . . . . (Epic)

Drinkin' And Dreamin'
Waylon Jennings; *Best Of Waylon Jennings* . . . . (RCA)

Essential Waylon Jennings .... (RCA)
Turn The Page .... (RCA)

Drinkin' Beer
Jimmy Witherspoon; *Best Of Jimmy Witherspoon* ...... (Prestige)
Evenin' Blues .... (Prestige)

Drinkin' In My Sunday Dress
Maria McKee; *Maria McKee* .... (Geffen)

Drinkin' My Baby (Off My Mind)
Eddie Rabbitt; *Best Of Eddie Rabbitt/Greatest Hits-II* .... (Warner Bros.)
Great Divorce Songs For Him-C .... (Warner Bros.)
Number 1's .... (Warner Bros.)
Rocky Mountain Music .... (Elektra)

Drinkin' My Baby Goodbye
Charlie Daniels Band; *Me & The Boys* .... (Epic)

Drinkin' My Way Back Home
Gene Watson; *Gene Watson's Greatest Hits* .... (MCA)
Little By Little .... (MCA)
Texas Saturday Night .... (MCA)

Drinkin' Wine (Spo Dee O De)
"Stick" McGhee and His Buddies; *Atlantic Rhythm & Blues 1947-1974-#1*
(1947-1952)-C .... (Atlantic)
Soul Years-C .... (Atlantic)
Jerry Lee Lewis; *18 Original Sun Greatest Hits* .... (Rhino)
Best Of Town & Country-#3-C .... (Gusto)
I'm On Fire .... (Mercury)
Milestones .... (Rhino)

Drinking Again
Aretha Franklin; *Aretha Franklin Sings The Blues* .... (Columbia)
Bette Midler; *Bette Midler* .... (Atlantic)
Live At Last .... (Atlantic)

Drinking And Driving
Black Flag; *In My Head* .... (SST)

Drinking Champagne
George Strait; *Livin' It Up* .... (MCA)
Ten Strait Hits .... (MCA)

Drinking On The Job
Rainmakers; *Rainmakers* .... (Mercury)

Drinking Straight Whiskey
Johnny Young; *Chicago Blues* .... (Arhoolie)

Drunk Again
Champion Jack Dupree; *Collectables Blues Collection-#1-C* .... (Collectables)

Drunk In My Past
X; *More Fun In The New World* .... (Elektra)

Drunk Is Better Than Dead
Push Stars; *ST/Malcolm In The Middle* .... (Restless)

Drunk On The Moon
Tom Waits; *The Heart Of Saturday Night* .... (Asylum)

Drunken Blue Rooster
Todd Rundgren; *Todd* .... (Rhino)

Drunken Butterfly
Sonic Youth; *Dirty* .... (David Geffen Co.)

Drunken Driver
Ricky Skaggs and Kentucky Thunder; *Bluegrass Rules!* .... (Rounder)

Drunken Hearted Boy
Allman Brothers Band; *Dreams* .... (Polydor)

Drunken Hearted Man
Robert Johnson; *Robert Johnson-Complete Recordings* ...... (Columbia)

Dust On The Bottle
David Lee Murphy; *Out With A Bang* .... (MCA)

Elderberry Wine
Elton John; *Don't Shoot Me I'm Only The Piano Player* ...... (Polydor)

Empty Bottle Blues
Jerry Ricks; *Deep In The Well* .... (Rooster Blues)

Escape (Pina Colada Song)
Rupert Holmes; *Billboard Top Hits-1979-C* .... (Rhino)
Partners In Crime .... (MCA)

Everything I Love
Alan Jackson; *Everything I Love* .... (Arista)

Feelin' Single, Seein' Double
Emmylou Harris; *Elite Hotel* .... (Reprise)

Fifteen Beers
Johnny Paycheck; *Johnny Paycheck's Biggest Hits* .... (Epic)

Fool
Sanford Clark; *Billboard Top Rock 'N' Roll Hits-1956-C* ..... (Rhino)
Original Classic Oldies Of The '50s & '60s-#17-C .... (MCA)

From The Vine Came The Grape
Gaylords; *X-tra Cheese-Originals By The Originals-C* ...... (Compose)

Gimme A Pigfoot (And A Bottle Of Beer)
Billie Holiday; *Complete Decca Recordings* .... (Decca Jazz)
From The Original Decca Masters .... (MCA)

Gin And Juice
Snoop Doggy Dogg; *Doggystyle* .... (Death Row)

God Loves A Drunk
Richard Thompson; *Rumor & Sigh* .... (Capitol)

God Was Drunk When He Made Me
Jim White; *No Such Place* .... (Luaka Bop)

God's Own Drunk
Jimmy Buffett; *Living & Dying In 3/4 Time* .... (MCA)

You Had To Be There .... (MCA)

Good Friends & A Bottle Of Wine
Ted Nugent; *Weekend Warriors* .... (Epic)

Headache Tomorrow (Or A Heartache Tonight)
Mickey Gilley; *Mickey Gilley's Biggest Hits* .... (Epic)
Ten Years Of Hits .... (Epic)
That's All That Matters To Me .... (Epic)

Here I Am
Patty Loveless; *Patty Loveless-Classics* .... (Epic)
When Fallen Angels Fly .... (Epic)

Here's To Good Friends (Lowenbrau Beer)
Original Soundtrack; *TeeVee Toons-The Commercials-#1-C* ...... (TVT)

Here's To The Night
Eve 6; *Horrorscope* .... (RCA)
Totally Hits 2001-C .... (Arista)

Hey Bartender
Blues Brothers; *Briefcase Full Of Blues* .... (Atlantic)
Johnny Lee; *Hey Bartender* .... (Warner Bros.)
Honky Tonk Country-C .... (Warner Bros.)
Johnny Lee's Greatest Hits .... (Full Moon/Asylum)
Koko Taylor; *Blues Delux* .... (Alligator)
Earthshaker .... (Alligator)

Hey Get Your Cold Beer (Ballantine Premium Beer)
Original Soundtrack; *TeeVee Toons-The Commercials-#1-C* ...... (TVT)

Hey Nineteen
Steely Dan; *Gaucho* .... (MCA)
Steely Dan-Gold .... (MCA)

High And Dry
Marty Brown; *High And Dry* .... (MCA)

Honky Tonk Attitude
Joe Diffie; *Honky Tonk Attitude* .... (Epic)

Honky Tonk Truth
Brooks & Dunn; *Brooks & Dunn-The Greatest Hits Collection* .... (Arista)

How You Remind Me
Nickelback; *Silver Side Up* .... (Roadrunner)

However Much I Booze
Who; *By Numbers* .... (MCA)

I Ain't Drunk, I'm Just Drinking
Albert Collins; *Genuine Houserockin' Music II-C* ...... (Alligator)

I Don't Even Know Your Name
Alan Jackson; *Alan Jackson-The Greatest Hits Collection* .... (Arista)
Who I Am .... (Arista)

I Get A Kick Out Of You
Ethel Merman with Johnny Green & His Orchestra; *The Ethel Merman*
Collection .... (Razor & Tie)
This Is Art Deco-C .... (Columbia)
Frank Sinatra; *My One & Only Love* .... (Capitol)
Round #1 .... (Capitol)
Sinatra and Swingin' Brass .... (Reprise)
Sinatra-The Main Event Live .... (Reprise)
The Capitol Years .... (Capitol)
The Reprise Collection .... (Reprise)
Original Cast; *Anything Goes* .... (Epic)
Paul Whiteman & His Orchestra; *78-#24769* .... (Victor)

I Gotta Get Drunk
Willie Nelson; *Essential Willie Nelson* .... (RCA)
Honky Tonkin' .... (RCA)
Redneck Mothers-C .... (RCA)
Willie & Family Live .... (Columbia)
Willie Nelson-Live .... (RCA)

I Like Beer
Tom T. Hall; *Tom T. Hall In Concert* .... (RCA)
Tom T. Hall's Greatest Hits-#2 .... (Mercury)

I Spent My Last Ten Dollars (On Birth Control And Beer)
Two Nice Girls; *Lesbian Favorites-Women Like Us-C* ...... (Rhino)

I Think I'll Just Stay Here And Drink
Merle Haggard; *For The Record: Merle Haggard-43 Legendary Hits* .... (BNA)

If Drinkin' Don't Kill Me (Her Memory Will)
George Jones; *10 Years Of Hits* .... (Epic)
I Am What I Am .... (Epic)

If I Was A Drinkin' Man
Neal McCoy; *Neal McCoy's Greatest Hits* .... (Atlantic)
Neal McCoy-Super Hits .... (Atlantic)
You Gotta Love That! .... (Atlantic)

If I Were A Drinker
Travis Tritt; *Country Club* .... (Warner Bros.)

If The River Was Whiskey
Mississippi Fred McDowell; *Great Bluesmen At Newport-C* .... (Vanguard)

If You've Got The Money I've Got The Time
Lefty Frizzell; *American Originals-Lefty Frizzell* ...... (Columbia)
Columbia Country Classics-#2-Honky Tonk Heroes-C .... (Columbia)
Lefty Frizzell's Greatest Hits .... (Columbia)
Willie Nelson; *Greatest Hits (& Some That Will Be)* ..... (Columbia)
Sound In Your Mind .... (Columbia)
Willie & Family Live .... (Columbia)

If You've Got The Time (Miller High Life Beer)
Original Soundtrack; *TeeVee Toons-The Commercials-#1-C* ...... (TVT)

I'll Drink To That
Jimmy Smith; *Off The Top* .... (Elektra)

I'll Give You Something To Drink About
George Jones; *I Lived To Tell It All* . . . . (MCA)
I'm Gonna Hire A Wino To Decorate Our Home
David Frizzell; *Family's Fine But This One's All Mine* . . . . (Warner Bros.)
I'm Not Gonna Let It Bother Me Tonight
Atlanta Rhythm Section; *Are You Ready!* . . . . (Polydor)
Champagne Jam . . . . (Polydor)
In Praise Of Drugs & Alcohol
San Francisco Mime Troupe; *Steel Town* . . . .(Flying Fish)
Intoxicated Rat
New Lost City Ramblers; *American Moonshine & Prohibition Songs* . . . .(Smithsonian Folkways)
It Ain't In The Wine
Kate Wolf & Wildwood Flower; *Back Roads* . . . . (Rhino)
It Was A Very Good Year
Frank Sinatra; *Frank Sinatra-The Very Good Years* . . . .(Reprise)
September Of My Years . . . .(Reprise)
The Reprise Collection . . . .(Reprise)
The Sopranos-Music From The HBO Original Series . . . .(Sony Music Soundtrax)
Frank Sinatra with Count Basie & The Orchestra; *Sinatra At The Sands* . . . .(Reprise)
It's My Time
Martina McBride; *Emotion* . . . .(RCA)
Jack Daniel And Mr. Jim Beam
Philip Claypool; *Perfect World* . . . . (Curb)
Jack Daniel's If You Please
David Allan Coe; *David Allan Coe-Super Hits* . . . .(Columbia)
For The Record-The First 10 Years . . . .(Columbia)
Jack Daniel's Kind Of Day
Johnny Winter; *Lone Star Kind Of Day* . . . . (Relix)
Jack Daniel's Old No. 7
Jerry Lee Lewis; *Killer Country* . . . .(Mercury)
Jack Daniels, You Lied To Me Again
Ray Stevens; *20 Comedy Hits Special Collection* . . . . (Curb)
John Barleycorn
Traffic; *John Barleycorn Must Die* . . . . (Island)
Jose Cuervo
Shelly West; *West By West* . . . . (Viva)
Kansas City
Beatles; *Beatles VI*. . . . .(Capitol)
Beatles-Box Set . . . .(Capitol)
Rock 'N' Roll Music . . . .(Capitol)
Super Oldies Of The '60s-#10-C . . . . (Audio Fidelity)
Bill Haley & His Comets; *Bill Haley & His Comets' Greatest Hits* . . . . .(Everest)
Fats Domino; *Fats Domino's Greatest Hits*. . . . .(Everest)
Wilbert Harrison; *American Graffiti-#3-C* . . . . (MCA)
Billboard Top Rock 'N' Roll Hits-1959-C . . . .(Rhino)
Cruisin'-1959-C . . . .(Increase)
Echoes Of A Rock Era-Middle Years-C . . . .(Roulette)
Super Oldies Of The '50s-#2-C . . . . (Audio Fidelity)
Kentucky Moonshine
Pure Prairie League; *Takin' The Stage*. . . . .(RCA)
Two Lane Highway . . . .(RCA)
Kentucky Moonshiner
Dave Van Ronk; *Inside Dave Van Ronk* . . . .(Fantasy)
George Tucker; *George Tucker* . . . .(Rounder)
Killin' Time
Clint Black; *Killin' Time* . . . .(RCA)
RCA Award Winners-C. . . . .(RCA)
Kisses Sweeter Than Wine
Jimmie Rodgers; *Best Of Jimmie Rodgers*. . . . . (Rhino)
Cruisin'-1958-C . . . .(Increase)
Weavers; *Best Of The Weavers* . . . . (MCA)
Reunion-At Carnegie Hall-1963. . . . .(Vanguard)
Weavers At Carnegie Hall . . . .(Vanguard)
Weavers' Greatest Hits . . . .(Vanguard)
Last Night Of The World
Bruce Cockburn; *Breakfast In New Orleans, Dinner In Timbuktu* . . . . (Rykodisc)
Let Me Touch You For Awhile
Alison Krauss & Union Station; *New Favorite* . . . .(Rounder)
Let's Go Get Stoned
Joe Cocker; *Mad Dogs & Englishmen*. . . . .(A&M)
Ray Charles; *Ray Charles' Greatest Hits* . . . . (Rhino)
Ray Charles-Anthology . . . .(Rhino)
Ray Charles-His Greatest Hits-#1 . . . . (Dunhill Compact Classics)
Letter, The (That Johnny Walker Read)
Asleep At The Wheel; *Very Best Of Asleep At The Wheel Since 1970* . . . .(Relentless/Madacy)
Letting Go
Sozzi; *Songs From Dawson's Creek* . . . .(Sony Music Soundtrax)
Little Girl, The
John Michael Montgomery; *Brand New Me* . . . .(Atlantic)
Totally Hits-#3-C . . . .(Atlantic)
Little Miss Honky Tonk
Brooks & Dunn; *Waitin' On Sundown*. . . . .(Arista)
Little Old Wine Drinker Me
Dean Martin; *Dean Martin's Greatest Hits-#2* . . . .(Reprise)

Welcome To My World . . . .(Reprise)
Mel Tillis; *Best Of Mel Tillis* . . . .(MCA)
Lone Star Beer & Bob Wills Music
Red Steagall; *Lone Star Beer & Bob Wills Music* . . . .(MCA)
Texas Country . . . .(MCA)
Lone Star State Of Mind
Don Williams; *Currents* . . . .(RCA)
Nanci Griffith; *Country Classics-#8-1986-1987-C* . . . .(Universal)
Lone Star State Of Mind . . . .(MCA)
Pat Alger/Nanci Griffith/Trisha Yearwood; *True Love & Other Short Stories-C* . . . . (Sugar Hill)
Longneck Bottle
Garth Brooks; *Sevens* . . . .(Capitol)
Lost In The Ozone
Commander Cody; *We've Got A Live One Here!* . . . . (Warner Bros.)
Love Hangover
Diana Ross; *20 Greatest Songs In Motown History-C* . . . .(Motown)
20/20-C . . . .(Motown)
Diana Ross-All The Great Hits . . . .(Motown)
Diana Ross-Anthology . . . .(Motown)
Diana Ross-The Ultimate Collection . . . .(Motown)
Love Or Something Like It
Kenny Rogers; *Kenny Rogers-Twenty Greatest Hits* . . . . (EMI)
Loving Cup
Rolling Stones; *Exile On Main Street*. . . . . (Virgin)
Man Overboard
Blink-182; *The Mark, Tom & Travis Show-The Enema Strikes Back*. . . . .(MCA)
Margaritaville
Jimmy Buffett; *Changes In Latitudes, Changes In Attitudes* . . . .(MCA)
Songs You Know By Heart-Jimmy Buffett's Greatest Hit(s) . . . .(MCA)
You Had To Be There . . . .(MCA)
Mas Tequila
Sammy Hagar; *Red Voodoo* . . . .(MCA)
Misery And Gin
Merle Haggard; *Back To The Barrooms*. . . . .(MCA)
Merle Haggard's Greatest Hits . . . .(MCA)
Rainbow Stew-Live At Anaheim Stadium . . . .(MCA)
Molly
Sponge; *Rotting Pinata* . . . .(Work)
Moonlight Cocktail
Glenn Miller; *Best Of Glenn Miller-#2* . . . .(RCA)
Memorial-1944-1969 . . . .(Bluebird)
Nipper's Greatest Hits Of The '40s-#1-C . . . .(RCA)
Glenn Miller & His Orchestra; *Complete Glenn Miller & His Orchestra-#8* . . . .(Bluebird)
Rivieras; *45-#1134*. . . . .(Collectables)
Moonlight Cocktails . . . .(Collectables)
Moonshine Lullaby
Ethel Merman/Bruce Yarnell/Original Cast; *Annie Get Your Gun* . . . . (RCA Victor)
Ethel Merman/Ray Middleton/Original Cast; *Annie Get Your Gun* . . . . . . (MCA)
Original Broadway Cast; *Annie Get Your Gun*. . . . .(Angel)
More Wine Waiter Please
Poor; *Who Cares* . . . . (550 Music)
Mountain Dew
Charlie Daniels Band; *Volunteer Jam-C* . . . .(Capricorn)
Clancy Brothers; *Clancy Brothers Greatest Hits* . . . .(Vanguard)
Doc Watson; *Old Timey Concert* . . . .(Vanguard)
Eric Weissberg; *ST/Deliverance* . . . . (Warner Bros.)
Stanley Brothers; *Stanley Series-Vol. 1-#2* . . . . (Copper Creek)
Stanley Series-Vol. 2-#2 . . . . (Copper Creek)
Munich Beer Garden
Michigan Dutchmen; *German Polka Favorites* . . . .(Jay Jay)
My Beer Is Rheingold, The Dry Beer
Original Soundtrack; *TeeVee Toons-The Commercials-#1-C* . . . .(TVT)
My Own Worst Enemy
Lit; *A Place In The Sun*. . . . .(RCA)
My Whiskey Head Buddies
Elvin Bishop; *Don't Let The Bossman Get You Down* . . . . (Alligator)
My Wife
Who; *ST/The Kids Are Alright* . . . . (MCA)
Two's Missing . . . .(MCA)
Who Greatest Hits . . . .(MCA)
Who's next . . . .(MCA)
My Wife, She Got Drunk
Li'l Wally; *All American Polkas* . . . .(Jay Jay)
Nancy Whiskey
Ian & Sylvia; *Ian & Sylvia* . . . .(Vanguard)
Ian & Sylvia's Greatest Hits . . . .(Vanguard)
Irish Rovers; *Irish Rovers' Greatest Hits* . . . .(MCA)
Nashville Beer Garden
Andy Badale & The Beer Garden Band; *Nashville Beer Garden* . . . . .(Ranwood)
Neon Moon
Brooks & Dunn; *Brand New Man* . . . .(Arista)
Night They Invented Champagne
Betty Wand/Louis Jordan/Others; *ST/Gigi*. . . . .(Sony Music Special Prod.)
Original Cast; *Gigi* . . . . (RCA Victor)
No More Booze (On Tuesdays)
Freewheelers; *Freewheelers* . . . .(David Geffen Co.)

No Way Jose
Ray Kennedy; *Guitar Man* . . . . (Atlantic)
Old Dogs, Children & Watermelon Wine
Tom T. Hall; *Essential Tom T. Hall-20th Anniversary Collection* . . . . (Mercury)
Tom T. Hall's Greatest Hits-#2 . . . . (Mercury)
On Tap, In The Can, Or In The Bottle
Hank Thompson; *The Country Music Hall Of Fame-Hank Thompson* . . . . (MCA)
One Bourbon One Scotch One Beer
George Thorogood & The Destroyers; *George Thorogood & The Destroyers* . . . . (Rounder)
George Thorogood & The Destroyers-Live . . . . (EMI)
John Lee Hooker; *Best Of Chess Blues-C* . . . . (Chess)
John Lee Hooker-The Ultimate Collection-1948-1990 . . . . (Rhino)
Real Folk Blues-C . . . . (Chess)
One Mint Julep
Clovers; *Down In The Alley* . . . . (Rhino)
Love Potion No. 9 . . . . (EMI)
Ray Charles; *Ray Charles-His Greatest Hits-#1* . . . . (Dunhill Compact Classics)
Outlaws & Lone Star Beer
C.W. McCall; *C.W. McCall & Company* . . . . (Polydor)
Paddy Kelly's Brew
Tommy Makem; *Evening With Tommy Makem* . . . . (Shanachie)
Paper Cup
5th Dimension; *Up-Up And Away-The Definitive Collection* . . . . (Arista)
Party Ain't A Party
Queen Pen with Lost Boyz & Crew; *My Melody* . . . . (Lil' Man/Interscope)
The Source Presents Hip Hop Hits-#2-C . . . . (PolyGram TV)
Pass The 40 Ounce
Jena Si Qua; *Conquest Of A Nation* . . . . (Conquest)
Pass The Booze
Ernest Tubb; *Ernest Tubb-Retrospective-#2* . . . . (MCA Special Prod.)
Pink Cocktail For A Blue Lady
Glenn Miller & His Orchestra; *Complete Glenn Miller & His Orchestra* . . . . (Bluebird)
Complete Glenn Miller & His Orchestra-#9 . . . . (Bluebird)
Pink Elephants
Eddie Lang Blue Five & Joe Venuti; *Jazz In The Thirties-C* . . . . (Disques Swing)
Poison Whiskey
Lynyrd Skynyrd; *Pronounced Leh-nerd Skin-nerd* . . . . (MCA)
Poor Me
Joe Diffie; *Joe Diffie's Greatest Hits* . . . . (Epic)
Poor People Of Paris
Les Baxter & His Orchestra; *Memories Are Made Of This-C* . . . . (Capitol)
Pop A Top
Alan Jackson; *Under The Influence* . . . . (Arista)
Jim Ed Brown; *Essential Jim Ed Brown* . . . . (RCA)
Popcorn, Pretzels & Beer Waltz
Michigan Dutchmen; *Beer & Dutchmen Polkas* . . . . (Jay Jay)
Pour Me
Trick Pony; *Trick Pony* . . . . (H2E/Warner Bros.)
Pour Me Another Tequila
Eddie Rabbitt; *Eddie Rabbitt's All-Time Greatest Hits* . . . . (Warner Bros.)
Pour, O Pour The Pirate Sherry
Original Broadway Cast; *Pirates Of Penzance* . . . . (Elektra)
Power Of Positive Drinkin'
Mickey Gilley; *Mickey Gilley's Biggest Hits* . . . . (Epic)
Ten Years Of Hits . . . . (Epic)
Pretending To Be Drunk
Sparks; *Pulling Rabbits Out Of A Hat* . . . . (Atlantic)
Prohibition Blues
Nora Bayes; *Music From The New York Stage (1890-1920)-#4-1917-1920-C* . . . . (Pearl)
Prop Me Up Beside The Jukebox (If I Die)
Joe Diffie; *Honky Tonk Attitude* . . . . (Epic)
Punch Drunk
Sade; *Promise* . . . . (Portrait)
Rather Be Sloppy Drunk
Big Joe Williams; *Dark Muddy Bottom Blues-C* . . . . (Specialty)
Red Red Wine
Neil Diamond; *Double Gold-Neil Diamond* . . . . (Bang)
Hot August Night . . . . (MCA)
Neil Diamond-Classics (Early Years) . . . . (Columbia)
Neil Diamond's Greatest Hits . . . . (Bang)
Replacements; *Pleased To Meet Me* . . . . (Sire)
UB40; *Labour Of Love* . . . . (A&M)
Red Wine & Blue Memories
Joe Stampley; *Joe Stampley's Biggest Hits* . . . . (Epic)
Rednecks, White Socks And Blue Ribbon Beer
Johnny Russell; *Beer Redneck Mothers* . . . . (RCA)
Country Legends-C . . . . (Madacy)
Country's Greatest Drinking Songs-C . . . . (All-Star Music)
Rednecks, White Socks & Blue Ribbon Beer . . . . (RCA)
Rum & Coca-Cola
Andrews Sisters; *Andrews Sisters-16 Great Performances* . . . . (MCA)
Best Of The Andrews Sisters . . . . (MCA)
Boogie Woogie Bugle Girls . . . . (MCA)
Capitol Collectors Series-The Andrews Sisters . . . . (Capitol)
Professor Longhair; *Last Mardi Gras* . . . . (Atlantic)
Mardi Gras In Baton Rouge . . . . (Rhino)
Salt Of The Earth
Mick Jagger & Keith Richards; *The Concert For New York City-C* . . (Columbia)
Rolling Stones; *Beggars Banquet* . . . . (Abkco)
Sambuca Nights
Special EFX; *Special EFX* . . . . (GRP)
Same Old Wine
Loggins & Messina; *Sittin' In* . . . . (Columbia)
San Antonio Champagne
Troy Cory; *Real Country* . . . . (Video Record Albums)
Sangria
Tania Maria; *Come With Me* . . . . (Concord Picante Jazz)
The Real Tania Maria-Wild! . . . . (Concord Picante Jazz)
Sangria Wine
Jerry Jeff Walker; *Best Of Jerry Jeff Walker* . . . . (MCA)
Great Gonzos . . . . (MCA)
Viva Terlingua . . . . (MCA)
Saturday Night's Alright For Fighting
Elton John; *Elton John's Greatest Hits* . . . . (Polydor)
Goodbye Yellow Brick Road . . . . (Polydor)
Knebworth-The Album-C . . . . (Polydor)
Rock Classics-C . . . . (K-Tel)
Who; *Two Rooms-Celebrating The Songs Of Elton John & Bernie Taupin-C* . . . . (Polydor)
Save Tonight
Eagle-Eye Cherry; *Desireless* . . . . (Work)
Say It Ain't So
Weezer; *Weezer* . . . . (David Geffen Co.)
Schaefer Is The One Beer To Have
Original Soundtrack; *TeeVee Toons-The Commercials-#1-C* . . . . (TVT)
Scotch And Soda
Kingston Trio; *100 Proof Hits* . . . . (K-Tel)
25 Years Non-Stop . . . . (Xeres)
Best Of The Kingston Trio . . . . (Capitol)
Capitol Collectors Series-The Kingston Trio . . . . (Capitol)
Tom Dooley . . . . (Capitol)
Manhattan Transfer; *Coming Out* . . . . (Atlantic)
Secret Of Life
Faith Hill; *Faith* . . . . (Warner Bros.)
Gretchen Peters; *The Secret Of Life* . . . . (Purple Crayon Prod.)
Send Me No Wine
Moody Blues; *On The Threshold Of A Dream* . . . . (Polydor)
Set 'Em Up Joe
Vern Gosdin; *Chiseled In Stone* . . . . (Columbia)
Greatest Country Hits Of The '80s-1988-C . . . . (Columbia)
Set Up Two Glasses, Joe
Ernest Tubb/Ferlin Husky/Simon Crum; *Ernest Tubb Collection-C* . . (Step One)
She Said
Collective Soul; *Dosage* . . . . (Atlantic)
ST/Scream 2 . . . . (Dimension/Capitol)
Show Me The Way To Go Home
Artie Shaw; *Best Of Artie Shaw* . . . . (MCA)
Randy Erwin; *Back Home* . . . . (Really Outstanding Music)
Sin Wagon
Dixie Chicks; *Fly* . . . . (Monument)
Sister Moonshine
Supertramp; *Crisis? What Crisis?* . . . . (A&M)
Six Pack To Go, A
Hank Thompson and His Brazos Valley Boys; *Best Of The Best Of Hank Thompson* . . . . (Gusto)
Capitol Collectors Series-Hank Thompson . . . . (Capitol)
Country Comes To Carnegie Hall-C . . . . (MCA)
Hank Thompson . . . . (Dot)
Hank Thompson's Greatest Hits-#2 . . . . (Step One)
Six-Pack Summer
Phil Vassar; *Phil Vassar* . . . . (Arista)
Sloppy Drunk Blues
Lucille Bogan; *Barrelhouse Mamas: Born In The Alley, Raised In The Slums-C* . . . . (Yazoo)
Snortin' Whiskey
Pat Travers Band; *Boom Boom...The Best Of* . . . . (Polydor)
Crash & Burn . . . . (Polydor)
Sober
Tool; *Undertow* . . . . (Zoo/Volcano)
Social Disease
Elton John; *Goodbye Yellow Brick Road* . . . . (Polydor)
Soft Lips And Hard Liquor
Charlie Walker; *45-#0870* . . . . (RCA)
Somebody Buy This Cowgirl A Beer
Tanya Tucker; *Tanya Tucker Live* . . . . (MCA Special Prod.)
Sometimes It Hurts
Stabbing Westward; *Darkest Days* . . . . (Columbia)
Stein Song (University Of Maine)
Rudy Vallee & His Connecticut Yankees; *Billboard Pop Memories-The 1930s-C* . . . . (Rhino)
Heigh-Ho Everybody: This Is Rudy Vallee . . . . (Living Era)
Those Wonderful Years: Puttin' On The Ritz-C . . . . (JCI Assoc. Labels)
University Of Michigan Band; *Greatest College Football Marches* . . (Vanguard)

Stone Cold Sober
Rod Stewart; *Atlantic Crossing* . . . . . (Warner Bros.)
Storyteller/The Complete Anthology: 1964-1990 . . . . . (Warner Bros.)
Stoned At The Jukebox
Hank Williams, Jr.; *Best Of Hank Williams, Jr.* . . . . . (Curb)
Best Of Hank Williams, Jr.-#1-Roots & Branches . . . . . (Mercury)
Bocephus Box-Collection-1979-1992 . . . . . (Capricorn)
Lone Wolf . . . . . (WB/Curb)
Straight Tequila Night
John Anderson; *Seminole Wind* . . . . . (BNA)
Today's Hot Country-C . . . . . (K-Tel)
Straight, No Chaser
Miles Davis; *Milestones* . . . . . (Columbia)
Oscar Peterson; *Live At The North Sea Jazz Festival* . . . . . (Pablo)
Quincy Jones & His Orchestra; *Quintessence* . . . . . (MCA/Impulse)
Thelonius Monk; *Best Of Thelonius Monk* . . . . . (Blue Note)
ST/Thelonius Monk-Straight No Chaser . . . . . (Columbia)
Thelonius Monk-Composer . . . . . (Columbia)
Strawberry Wine
Band; *Stage Fright* . . . . . (Capitol)
Strawberry Wine
Deana Carter; *Did I Shave My Legs For This?* . . . . . (Capitol)
Suckin' A Big Bottle Of Gin
Joe Ely; *Joe Ely* . . . . . (MCA)
Sunday Morning Coming Down
Johnny Cash; *Classic Cash-Hall Of Fame Series* . . . . . (Mercury)
Johnny Cash's Greatest Hits-#2 . . . . . (Columbia)
The Man In Black-His Greatest Hits . . . . . (Legacy)
Kris Kristofferson; *Me & Bobby McGee* . . . . . (Columbia)
Songs Of Kris Kristofferson . . . . . (Columbia)
Vikki Carr; *Best Of Vikki Carr* . . . . . (EMI)
Willie Nelson; *Willie* . . . . . (RCA)
Willie Nelson Sings Kristofferson . . . . . (Columbia)
Swedish Schnapps
Charlie Parker; *Swedish Schnapps* . . . . . (Verve)
Verve Years-1950-1951 . . . . . (Verve)
Sweet Cherry Wine
Tommy James And The Shondells; *Tommy James And The Shondells-Anthology* . . . . . (Rhino)
Very Best Of Tommy James And The Shondells . . . . . (Pair)
Take Your Whiskey Home
Van Halen; *Women & Children First* . . . . . (Warner Bros.)
Tanqueray
Vern Gosdin; *Alone* . . . . . (Columbia)
Vern Gosdin's Greatest Hits . . . . . (Columbia)
Vern Gosdin-Super Hits . . . . . (Columbia)
Taste Of Honey
Barbra Streisand; *The Barbra Streisand Album* . . . . . (Columbia)
Beatles; *Beatles-Box Set* . . . . . (Capitol)
Please Please Me . . . . . (Parlophone)
The Early Beatles . . . . . (Capitol)
Herb Alpert; *Midnight Sun* . . . . . (A&M)
Herb Alpert & The Tijuana Brass; *Herb Alpert & The Tijuana Brass' Greatest Hits* . . . . . (A&M)
Herb Alpert & The Tijuana Brass-Classics-#1 . . . . . (A&M)
Tony Bennett; *Forty Years-The Artistry Of Tony Bennett* . . . . . (Columbia)
Tears Will Be The Chaser For Your Wine
Wanda Jackson; *Rockin' In The Country-Best Of Wanda Jackson* . . . . . (Rhino)
Wanda Jackson's Greatest Hits . . . . . (Gusto)
Ten Feet Tall And Bulletproof
Travis Tritt; *Ten Feet Tall And Bulletproof* . . . . . (Warner Bros.)
Tennessee Bottle
Kenny Rogers; *The Gambler* . . . . . (EMI)
Tennessee Toddy
Marty Robbins; *Essential Marty Robbins-1951-1982* . . . . . (Columbia)
Tennessee Whiskey
David Allan Coe; *David Allan Coe-17 Greatest Hits* . . . . . (Columbia)
David Allan Coe's Biggest Hits . . . . . (Legacy)
For The Record-The First 10 Years . . . . . (Columbia)
Tennessee Whiskey . . . . . (Columbia)
George Jones; *By Request* . . . . . (Epic)
First Time Live! . . . . . (Epic)
George Jones-Super Hits . . . . . (Epic)
Greatest Country Hits Of The '80s-1983-C . . . . . (Columbia)
Shine On . . . . . (Epic)
Merle Haggard; *19 Hot Country Requests-#2-C* . . . . . (Epic)
Tennessee Whiskey & Texas Women
Rayburn Anthony; *Audiograph Alive-C* . . . . . (Audiograph)
Dance Floor Crystal Ball . . . . . (Audiograph)
Tequila
Champs; *Billboard Top Rock 'N' Roll Hits-1958-C* . . . . . (Rhino)
Cruisin'-1958-C . . . . . (Increase)
Frat Rock!-#3-Grandson Of Frat Rock!-C . . . . . (Rhino)
Oldies But Goodies-#7-C . . . . . (Original Sound)
Super Oldies Of The '50s-#7-C . . . . . (Audio Fidelity)
Larry Carlton; *Friends* . . . . . (MCA)
Larry Carlton-Collection . . . . . (GRP)
Tequila
Pretenders; *Last Of The Independents* . . . . . (Sire)
Tequila Sheila
Bobby Bare; *Bobby Bare's Biggest Hits* . . . . . (Columbia)
Encore-Bobby Bare . . . . . (Columbia)
Mac Davis; *It's Hard To Be Humble* . . . . . (Casablanca)
Tequila Sunrise
Alan Jackson; *Common Thread-Songs Of The Eagles-C* . . . . . (Giant)
Eagles; *Desperado* . . . . . (Asylum)
Eagles/Their Greatest Hits 1971-1975 . . . . . (Asylum)
Hell Freezes Over . . . . . (Geffen)
Tequila Talkin'
Lonestar; *Lonestar* . . . . . (BNA)
There Stands The Glass
Carl Smith; *Best Of Carl Smith* . . . . . (Curb)
Webb Pierce; *Webb Pierce-Golden Hits* . . . . . (Plantation)
There's A Tear In My Beer
Hank Williams, Jr. & Hank Williams, Sr.; *Complete Hank Williams* . . . (Mercury)
Hank Williams, Jr.'s Greatest Hits III . . . . . (Curb)
They're All Out Of Liquor, Let's Find Another Party
Waitresses; *Best Of The Waitresses* . . . . . (Polydor)
This Bottle (In My Hand)
David Allan Coe & George Jones; *David Allan Coe-17 Greatest Hits* . . . . . (Columbia)
For The Record-The First 10 Years . . . . . (Columbia)
This Drinkin' Will Kill Me
Dwight Yoakam; *Hillbilly Deluxe* . . . . . (Reprise)
Three Drunk Newts
Barnes & Barnes; *Dr. Demento's Dementia Royale-C* . . . . . (Rhino)
Three Drunken Maidens
Maddy Prior & Tim Hart; *Summer Solstice* . . . . . (Shanachie)
Titties And Beer
Kiss; *Alive II* . . . . . (Casablanca)
Double Platinum . . . . . (Mercury)
Rock & Roll Over . . . . . (Casablanca)
Titties N' Beer
Frank Zappa; *Baby Snakes* . . . . . (Barking Pumpkin)
In New York . . . . . (Barking Pumpkin)
Tonight The Bottle Let Me Down
Brooks & Dunn; *Mama's Hungry Eyes-Merle Haggard Tribute-C* . . . . . (Arista)
Elvis Costello & The Attractions; *Almost Blue* . . . . . (Columbia)
Gram Parsons & The Flying Burrito Brothers; *Sleepless Nights* . . . . . (A&M)
Merle Haggard; *Swinging Doors* . . . . . (Out Of Print)
Tonight The Heartache's On Me
Dixie Chicks; *Wide Open Spaces* . . . . . (Monument)
Too Much Blood In My Alcohol System
Cold Shot; *Salt City Blues-C* . . . . . (Blue Wave)
Tubthumping
Chumbawamba; *Tubthumper* . . . . . (Universal)
Tumble In The Rough
Stone Temple Pilots; *Tiny Music...Songs From The Vatican Gift Shop* . . . . . (Atlantic)
Two Beers Away
Moe Bandy & Joe Stampley; *Moe Bandy & Joe Stampley's Greatest Hits* . . . . . (Columbia)
Two More Bottles Of Wine
Delbert McClinton; *Honky Tonkin'-I Done Me Some* . . . . . (Alligator)
Emmylou Harris; *Honky Tonk Country-C* . . . . . (Warner Bros.)
Profile/Best Of Emmylou Harris . . . . . (Warner Bros.)
Quarter Moon In A Ten Cent Town . . . . . (Warner Bros.)
Martina McBride; *Wild Angels* . . . . . (RCA)
Two Pina Coladas
Garth Brooks; *Sevens* . . . . . (Capitol)
Vintage Wine
Moody Blues; *Sur La Mer* . . . . . (Polydor)
Vodka
John Coltrane; *Prestige Recordings* . . . . . (Prestige)
John Coltrane & Paul Quinichette; *Cattin' With* . . . . . (Prestige)
Vodka Frenzy
Aversion; *Fit To Be Tied* . . . . . (Restless)
Warm Beer & Cold Women
Tom Waits; *Nighthawks At The Diner* . . . . . (Asylum)
Was It Just The Wine
Vern Gosdin; *10 Years Of Greatest Hits Newly Recorded* . . . . . (Columbia)
Water Into Wine
Bruce Cockburn; *In The Falling Dark* . . . . . (True North)
Water With The Wine
Joan Armatrading; *Joan Armatrading* . . . . . (A&M)
Watermelon Crawl
Tracy Byrd; *No Ordinary Man* . . . . . (MCA)
Way Down The Line
Offspring; *Ixnay On The Hombre* . . . . . (Columbia)
We Thuggin'
Fat Joe; *Jealous Ones Still Envy (J.O.S.E.)* . . . . . (Terror Squad/Atlantic)
Welcome To The Fold
Filter; *Title Of Record* . . . . . (Reprise)
Whalecatchers/Drunken Landlady
John Faulkner; *Kind Providence* . . . . . (Green Linnet)
What Part Of No
Lorrie Morgan; *Lorrie Morgan's Greatest Hits* . . . . . (BNA)

Watch Me . . . . (BNA)

What's Made Milwaukee Famous (Has Made A Loser Out Of Me)
Jerry Lee Lewis; *Heartbreak* . . . . (Tomato)
Milestones . . . . (Rhino)
Rod Stewart; *Best Of Rod Stewart* . . . . (Mercury)
Storyteller/The Complete Anthology: 1964-1990 . . . .(Warner Bros.)

When The Moon Shines On The Moonshine
Bert Williams; *Music From The New York Stage (1890-1920)-#4-1917-1920-C* . . . . (Pearl)

When You Say Bud (Budweiser Beer)
Original Soundtrack; *TeeVee Toons-The Commercials-#1-C*. . . . . (TVT)

When You're Out Of Schlitz (Schlitz Beer)
Original Soundtrack; *TeeVee Toons-The Commercials-#1-C*. . . . . (TVT)

Wherever You Go
Clint Black; *Clint Black-The Greatest Hits*. . . . . (RCA)
One Emotion . . . . (RCA)

Whiplash Liquor
Ugly Kid Joe; *As Ugly As They Wanna Be* . . . . (Stardog)

Whiskey
Charlie Daniels Band; *Volunteer Jam-C*. . . . . (Capricorn)
Whiskey . . . . (Epic)
Loggins & Messina; *Loggins And Messina*. . . . . (Columbia)

Whiskey Ain't Workin'
Travis Tritt & Marty Stuart; *It's All About To Change* . . . .(Warner Bros.)

Whiskey And Wimmen
John Lee Hooker; *Best Of John Lee Hooker* . . . .(Vee-Jay)
Best Of John Lee Hooker . . . . (Crescendo)
Infinite Boogie . . . . (Rhino)
Real Blues Brothers-C . . . .(Dunhill Compact Classics)
World's Greatest Blues Singer. . . . . (Vee-Jay)

Whiskey Bent & Hell Bound
Hank Williams, Jr.; *Hank Williams, Jr.'s Greatest Hits* . . . .(WB/Curb)
Whiskey Bent & Hell Bound. (WB/Curb)

Whiskey In The Jar
Metallica; *Garage Inc.* . . . . (Elektra)

Whiskey On A Sunday (Puppet Song)
Irish Rovers; *Irish Rovers' Greatest Hits* . . . .(MCA)

Whiskey River
Willie Nelson; *Greatest Hits (& Some That Will Be)* . . . . (Columbia)
Shotgun Willie . . . .(Atlantic)
ST/Honeysuckle Rose. . . . . (Columbia)
Willie & Family Live . . . . (Columbia)

Whiskey Rock A Roller
Lynyrd Skynyrd; *Gold & Platinum*. . . . . (MCA)
Nuthin' Fancy . . . . (MCA)
One More From The Road. . . . . (MCA)

Whiskey Train
Procol Harum; *Best Of Procol Harum* . . . . (A&M)
Home . . . . (A&M)
Procol Harum-Classics-#17 . . . . (A&M)
Procol Harum's Greatest Hits. . . . . (A&M)

Whiskey Under The Bridge
Brooks & Dunn; *Brooks & Dunn-The Greatest Hits Collection* . . . . (Arista)
Waitin' On Sundown . . . . (Arista)

Whiskey, If You Were A Woman
Highway 101; *Highway 101* . . . .(Warner Bros.)
Highway 101's Greatest Hits . . . .(Warner Bros.)

White Lightning
Big Bopper; *Hellooo Baby! Best Of The Big Bopper-1954-1959* . . . . . . (Rhino)
George Jones; *Best Of George Jones-1955-1967* . . . . (Rhino)
Billboard Top Country Hits-1959-C . . . . (Rhino)
George Jones' All-Time Greatest Hits. . . . .(Epic)
The Bradley Barn Sessions . . . . (MCA)
Hank Williams, Jr.; *Whiskey Bent & Hell Bound* . . . . (WB/Curb)

White Lightning & Wine
Heart; *Dreamboat Annie* . . . . (Capitol)

Why Am I Drinkin'
Merle Haggard; *Going Where The Lonely Go* . . . .(Epic)
Merle Haggard-Super Hits . . . .(Epic)

Why Don't We Get Drunk
Jimmy Buffett; *Boats Beaches Bars & Ballads* . . . .(Margaritaville)
Songs You Know By Heart-Jimmy Buffett's Greatest Hit(s) . . . . (MCA)
White Sport Coat & A Pink Crustacean . . . . (MCA)
You Had To Be There. . . . . (MCA)

Wine Me Up
Faron Young; *Faron Young-Golden Hits* . . . . (Mercury)
Faron Young-The Hits . . . . (Mercury)

Workin' Man Blues
Diamond Rio/Lee Roy Parnell/Steve Wariner; *Mama's Hungry Eyes-Merle Haggard Tribute-C* . . . . (Arista)
Gary Morris; *These Days* . . . . (Capitol)
Merle Haggard & The Strangers; *Best Of Country Blues* . . . . . . (Curb)
Capitol Collectors Series-Merle Haggard & The Strangers . . . . . . (Capitol)
For The Record: Merle Haggard-43 Legendary Hits . . . . . (BNA)
Okie From Muskogee . . . . (Capitol)
Songs I'll Always Sing . . . . (Capitol)
Ricky Van Shelton; *Wild-Eyed Dream* . . . . (Columbia)

WPLJ (White Port Lemon Juice)
Four Deuces; *Legends Of Doo-Wop-#3-C* . . . .(Juke Box Treasures)

Mothers Of Invention; *Burnt Weeny Sandwich* . . . . (Bizarre/Straight)

Yesterday's Wine
Merle Haggard & George Jones; *By Request*. . . . .(Epic)
Greatest Country Hits Of The '80s-1982-C . . . . (Columbia)
Taste Of Yesterday's Wine . . . .(Epic)
Walking The Line . . . .(Epic)
Willie Nelson; *Best Of Willie* . . . . (RCA)
Collector's Series-Willie Nelson . . . . (RCA)
The Outlaws . . . . (RCA)

Yo Ho Ho And A Bottle Of Rum
Original Cast; *Rugrats Sing-Along* . . . .(Interscope)

You Ain't Much Fun
Toby Keith; *Boomtown* . . . .(Polydor Country)

You Don't Need The Wine To Have A Wonderful Time
Eddie Cantor; *Music From The New York Stage (1890-1920)-#4-1917-1920-C* . . . . (Pearl)

Your Good Girl's Gonna Go Bad
Billie Jo Spears; *Best Of Billie Jo Spears* . . . . (CEMA Special Prod.)
Best Of Billie Jo Spears . . . .(Razor & Tie)
K.T. Oslin; *Tammy Wynette...Remembered-C* . . . .(Asylum)
Tammy Wynette; *Tammy Wynette-Anniversary-20 Years Of Hits* . . . . . . (Epic)
Tammy Wynette's Greatest Hits . . . .(Epic)
Your Good Girl's Gonna Go Bad . . . . (Legacy)

You're Still On My Mind
Byrds; *Sweetheart Of The Rodeo*. . . . . (Columbia)

ALCOHOL: RECOVERING ALCOHOLIC,
Alcoholism, Sober

See Also: **ALCOHOL, BACK ON MY FEET, BARS, DRUGS (various)**

Hitchin' A Ride
Green Day; *Nimrod* . . . .(Reprise)

If I Was A Drinkin' Man
Neal McCoy; *Neal McCoy's Greatest Hits* . . . .(Atlantic)
Neal McCoy-Super Hits . . . .(Atlantic)
You Gotta Love That! . . . .(Atlantic)

It's My Time
Martina McBride; *Emotion* . . . . (RCA)

Little Rock
Collin Raye; *Extremes* . . . . (Epic)

Thank God For Believers
Mark Chesnutt; *Thank God For Believers*. . . . . (Decca)

That's Why I'm Here
Kenny Chesney; *I Will Stand*. (BNA)

Wine Into Water
T. Graham Brown; *Wine Into Water* . . . .(ISD/Intersound)

AMERICAN WEST, Frontier, Pioneers

See Also: **ANIMALS: COWS (cattle), ANIMALS: HORSES, COUNTRY, COWBOYS, DIRECTIONS: WEST, FARMS, NATIVE AMERICANS, RODEO**

(Ghost) Riders In The Sky
Gene Autry; *50th Anniversary*. . . . . (Republic/Universal)
Cowboy Hall Of Fame . . . . (Republic/Universal)
Johnny Cash; *The Man In Black-His Greatest Hits* . . . . . (Legacy)
Outlaws; *Ghost Riders* . . . . (Arista)
Roy Clark; *Roy Clark In Concert* . . . . (MCA)
Roy Clark's Greatest Hits. . . . . (MCA)
Superpicker . . . . (MCA)
Vaughn Monroe; *Best Of Vaughn Monroe* . . . . (RCA)
This Is Vaughn Monroe/Decade Of The '40s . . . . (RCA)

Away Out On The Mountain
Jimmie Rodgers; *Best Of Jimmie Rodgers-Legendary Master Series* . . . . . (RCA)
Essential Jimmie Rodgers . . . . (RCA)
First Sessions-1927-1928-#1 . . . . (Rounder)
My Rough & Rowdy Ways . . . . (RCA)
This Is Jimmie Rodgers. . . . . (RCA)
Skip Gorman; *A Cowboy's Wild Song To His Herd*. . . . . . (Rounder)
Tim & Mollie O'Brien; *Away Out On The Mountain* . . . .(Sugar Hill)

Back In The Saddle Again
Gene Autry; *50th Anniversary* . . . . (Republic/Universal)
Columbia Country Classics-#1-Golden Age-C . . . . . . (Columbia)
Cowboy Hall Of Fame . . . . (Republic/Universal)
Cowboy Super Hits-C . . . . (Columbia)
Great American Singing Cowboys-C . . . . (Republic/Universal)
South Of The Border . . . . (Republic/Universal)

Billy The Kid
Charlie Daniels Band; *High Lonesome* . . . . (Epic)

Billy The Kid
Marty Robbins; *Gunfighter Ballads & Trail Songs* . . . . (Legacy)

Billy The Kid
Ry Cooder; *Into The Purple Valley* . . . . (Reprise)
Blanket On The Ground
Billie Jo Spears; *'70s Hits: Country-#1-C* . . . . (Curb)
Best Of Billie Jo Spears. . . . . (Razor & Tie)
Country Hits Of The '70s-C . . . . (CEMA Special Prod.)
Bonanza
Billy Strange; *Great Western Themes* . . . . (Crescendo)
Buttons And Bows
Dinah Shore; *16 Most Requested Songs Of The '40s-#1-C* . . . . (Legacy)
Golden Hits Of The '40s-C . . . . (Columbia Special Prod.)
Gene Autry; *Ridin' West-#2-C* . . . . (Crescendo)
Songs Of The West-#3-Gene Autry & Roy Rogers-C . . . . (Rhino)
Cattle Call
Eddy Arnold; *Best Of Eddy Arnold* . . . . (RCA)
Cattle Call . . . . (RCA)
Eddy Arnold-Pure Gold . . . . (RCA)
Nipper's Greatest Hits Of The '50s-#1-C . . . . (RCA)
Riders In The Sky; *Riders Radio Theater* . . . . (MCA)
Chant Of The Wanderer
Sons Of The Pioneers; *Sunset On The Range.* . . . . (Pair)
Colonel Buffalo Bill
Ethel Merman/Bruce Yarnell/Original Cast; *Annie Get*
Your Gun . . . . (RCA Victor)
Cowboy Love Song
Skip Gorman; *A Cowboy's Wild Song To His Herd.* . . . . (Rounder)
Cowboy's Wild Song To His Herd
Skip Gorman; *A Cowboy's Wild Song To His Herd.* . . . . (Rounder)
Don't Fence Me In
Andrews Sisters; *Andrews Sisters' All-Time Greatest Hits* . . . . (Decca)
Bing Crosby; *Best Of Bing Crosby* . . . . (MCA)
David Byrne; *Red Hot + Blue-Tribute To Cole Porter-C* . . . . (Chrysalis)
Ella Fitzgerald; *Cole Porter Songbook* . . . . (Verve)
Lari White/Shelby Lynne/Trisha Yearwood; *Don't Fence Me In* . . . . . . (RCA)
Willie Nelson & Leon Russell; *Cowboy Super Hits-C.* . . . . (Columbia)
Get Along Little Dogies
Riders In The Sky; *Saddle Pals* . . . . (Rounder)
Tex Ritter; *Tex Ritter: Country Music Hall Of Fame* . . . . . . (MCA Special Prod.)
Glendale Train
New Riders Of The Purple Sage; *Best Of New Riders Of The*
Purple Sage . . . . (Columbia)
New Riders Of The Purple Sage . . . . (Columbia)
Grand Coulee Dam
Bob Dylan; *Tribute To Woody Guthrie-C* . . . . (Warner Bros.)
Happy Trails
Michael Martin Murphey; *Cowboy Songs* . . . . (Warner Western)
Original Soundtrack; *Television's Greatest Hits-#1-C* . . . . (TVT)
Quicksilver Messenger Service; *Sons Of Mercury* . . . . (Rhino)
Randy Travis & Roy Rogers; *Heroes And Friends* . . . . (Warner Bros.)
Riders In The Sky; *Cowboy Way* . . . . (MCA)
Roy Rogers/Dale Evans/Dusty Rogers; *Roy Rogers Tribute-C* . . . . (RCA)
Van Halen; *Diver Down* . . . . (Warner Bros.)
I Wanna Be A Cowboy's Sweetheart
Patsy Montana & The Prairie Ramblers; *All Time Legends Of Country*
Music-C . . . . (Legacy)
Respect: A History Of Women In Music-C . . . . (Rhino)
I'm An Indian Too
Ethel Merman/Bruce Yarnell/Original Cast; *Annie Get*
Your Gun . . . . (RCA Victor)
Ethel Merman/Ray Middleton/Original Cast; *Annie Get Your Gun.* . . . . . (MCA)
Original Broadway Cast; *Annie Get Your Gun* . . . . (Angel)
Original Cast/Doris Day; *Annie Get Your Gun* . . . . (Columbia)
Last Cowboy Song
Ed Bruce; *16 Top Country Hits-#2-C* . . . . (MCA)
Ed Bruce's Greatest Hits . . . . (MCA)
Waylon Jennings, Willie Nelson, Johnny Cash, Kris Kristofferson; *Cowboy*
Super Hits-C . . . . (Columbia)
Highwayman. . . . . (Columbia)
Legend Of A Cowgirl
Imani Coppola; *Chupacabra* . . . . (Columbia)
Marlboro Song, The (Theme From "Magnificent 7")
Original Soundtrack; *TeeVee Toons-The Commercials-#1-C* . . . . (TVT)
O Bury Me Not On The Lone Prairie
Michael Martin Murphey; *Cowboy Songs* . . . . (Warner Western)
Sons Of The Pioneers; *Sunset On The Range.* . . . . (Pair)
Oklahoma Hills
Arlo Guthrie; *Tribute To Woody Guthrie-C.* . . . . (Warner Bros.)
Hank Thompson; *Hank Thompson's All-Time Greatest Hits* . . . . (Curb)
Jack Guthrie and his Oklahomans; *Birth Of A Dream-Capitol's Early*
Hits-C . . . . (Capitol)
Great Records Of The Decade-'40s-Country-C . . . . (Curb)
Kay Starr; *Kay Starr-Country* . . . . (Crescendo)
Prairie Wedding
Mark Knopfler; *Sailing To Philadelphia* . . . . (Warner Bros.)
Pretty Little Dogies
Skip Gorman; *A Cowboy's Wild Song To His Herd.* . . . . (Rounder)
Prisoner For Life
Skip Gorman; *A Cowboy's Wild Song To His Herd.* . . . . (Rounder)

Rebel-Johnny Yuma
Johnny Cash; *The Man In Black-His Greatest Hits* . . . . (Legacy)
Stampede
Chris LeDoux; *Chris LeDoux-20 Greatest Hits* . . . . (Capitol)
Theme From "Bat Masterson"
Original Soundtrack; *Television's Greatest Hits-#2-C* . . . . (TVT)
Theme From "Bonanza"
Al Caiola & His Orchestra; *Songs Of The West-#4-Movie & Television*
Themes-C . . . . (Rhino)
Cincinnati Pops Orchestra/Erich Kunzel; *Round-Up* . . . . (Telarc)
Original Soundtrack; *Television's Greatest Hits-#1-C* . . . . (TVT)
TV Classic Themes: 25th Anniversary Edition-C . . . . (Breakable)
Theme From "Branded"
Original Soundtrack; *Television's Greatest Hits-#1-C* . . . . (TVT)
Theme From "Bronco"
Original Soundtrack; *Television's Greatest Hits-#4-Black & White*
Classics-C . . . . (TVT)
Theme From "Cheyenne"
Original Soundtrack; *Television's Greatest Hits-#4-Black & White*
Classics-C . . . . (TVT)
Theme From "Colt .45"
Original Soundtrack; *Television's Greatest Hits-#4-Black & White*
Classics-C . . . . (TVT)
Theme From "Daniel Boone"
Original Soundtrack; *Television's Greatest Hits-#1-C* . . . . (TVT)
Theme From "F-Troop"
Original Soundtrack; *Television's Greatest Hits-#1-C* . . . . (TVT)
Theme From "Gunsmoke" (The Old Trail)
Billy Strange; *Great Western Themes* . . . . (Crescendo)
Original Soundtrack; *CBS: The First 50 Years.* . . . . (TVT)
Television's Greatest Hits-#4-Black & White Classics-C . . . . (TVT)
Theme From "Have Gun Will Travel" (Ballad Of Paladin)
Duane Eddy; *Duane Eddy-Pure Gold* . . . . (RCA)
Johnny Western; *Columbia Country Classics-#3-Americana-C* . . . (Columbia)
Television's Greatest Hits-#7-Cable Ready-C . . . . (TVT)
Theme From "Hopalong Cassidy"
Original Soundtrack; *Television's Greatest Hits-#4-Black & White*
Classics-C . . . . (TVT)
Theme From "Maverick"
Original Soundtrack; *Television's Greatest Hits-#2-C* . . . . (TVT)
Theme From "Rawhide"
Blues Brothers; *Original Soundtrack.* . . . . (Atlantic)
Frankie Laine; *CBS: The First 50 Years.* . . . . (TVT)
Cowboy Super Hits-C . . . . (Columbia)
Television's Greatest Hits-#2-C . . . . (TVT)
Riders In The Sky; *Cowboy Songs* . . . . (Rounder)
Theme From "The High Chapparal"
Original Soundtrack; *Television's Greatest Hits-#5-In Living Color-C.* . . . (TVT)
Theme From "The Lawman"
Original Soundtrack; *Television's Greatest Hits-#4-Black & White*
Classics-C . . . . (TVT)
Theme From "The Legend Of Jesse James"
Original Soundtrack; *Television's Greatest Hits-#4-Black & White*
Classics-C . . . . (TVT)
Theme From "The Life And Legend Of Wyatt Earp"
Original Soundtrack; *Television's Greatest Hits-#4-Black & White*
Classics-C . . . . (TVT)
Theme From "The Lone Ranger" (William Tell Overture)
Boston Pops Orchestra; *TV Classics-C* . . . . (RCA)
Boston Pops Orchestra/Arthur Fiedler; *Fiedler-Greatest Hits.* . . . . (RCA)
Original Soundtrack; *Television's Greatest Hits-#7-Cable Ready-C.* . . . . . (TVT)
Spike Jones & His City Slickers; *Best Of Spike Jones & His City*
Slickers. . . . . (RCA)
Theme From "The Rifleman"
Cincinnati Pops Orchestra/Erich Kunzel; *Round-Up* . . . . (Telarc)
Original Soundtrack; *Television's Greatest Hits-#1-C* . . . . (TVT)
Theme From "The Virginian"
101 Strings Orchestra; *Western Themes-#1* . . . . (Alshire)
Original Soundtrack; *Television's Greatest Hits-#2-C* . . . . (TVT)
Theme From "Wagon Train"
Original Soundtrack; *Television's Greatest Hits-#2-C* . . . . (TVT)
Theme From "Wild Wild West"
Original Soundtrack; *CBS: The First 50 Years.* . . . . (TVT)
Television's Greatest Hits-#1-C . . . . (TVT)
This Hard Land
Bruce Springsteen; *Bruce Springsteen's Greatest Hits* . . . . (Columbia)
Tracks . . . . (Columbia)
Tumbling Tumbleweeds
Billy Vaughn; *Billy Vaughn's Greatest Hits* . . . . (Curb)
Gene Autry; *Essential Gene Autry* . . . . (Columbia)
Meat Puppets; *Meat Puppets* . . . . (SST)
Michael Martin Murphey; *Cowboy Songs* . . . . (Warner Western)
Roy Rogers/K.T. Oslin/Restless Heart; *Roy Rogers Tribute-C* . . . . . . (RCA)
Sons Of The Pioneers; *The Country Music Hall Of Fame-Sons Of The*
Pioneers . . . . (MCA)
Utah Carol
Harry K. McClintock; *Cowboy Songs On*
Folkways-C . . . . (Smithsonian Folkways)
Marty Robbins; *Gunfighter Ballads & Trail Songs* . . . . (Legacy)

Way Out West In Texas
Don Edwards; *My Hero, Gene Autry: A Tribute* . . . . (Shanachie)
Western Movies (My Baby Loves)
Olympics; *All-Time Greatest Hits Of Rock 'N' Roll-C* . . . . (Curb)
American Graffiti-#3-C . . . . (MCA)
Best Of The Olympics . . . . (Vee-Jay)
Jumpin' Jive '50s-C . . . . (Priority)
When I Camped Under The Stars
Roy Rogers; *Songs Of The West-#3-Gene Autry & Roy Rogers-C* . . . . . . (Rhino)
When The Coyotes Come Near
Sons Of The Pioneers; *Horses, Cattle And Coyotes* . . . . (Shanachie)
Wild Wild West
Will Smith; *Willenium* . . . . (Columbia)

ANATOMY: ARMS

See Also: ANATOMY (various), HELP, HOLDING ON, HUG

(I Just) Died In Your Arms
Cutting Crew; *Broadcast* . . . . (Virgin)
Chicken Soup For The Woman's Soul-C . . . . (Rhino)
MTV-VH1 Powerplayers-C . . . .(EMI)
Angel
Sarah McLachlan; *Mirrorball* . . . . (Arista)
ST/City Of Angels . . . .(Warner Sunset/Reprise)
Surfacing . . . . (Arista)
Totally Hits-#1-C . . . . (Arista)
Angel In Your Arms
Barbara Mandrell; *Country Classics-#5-1985-1986-C* . . . . (Universal)
Get To The Heart . . . .(MCA)
Reba McEntire; *Reba McEntire* . . . . (Mercury)
Arms Of A Fool
Mel Tillis; *Brand New Mister Me* . . . . (Polydor)
Mel Tillis & The Statesiders; *Best Of Mel Tillis & The Statesiders* . . . . . (MGM)
Arms Of The One Who Loves You
Xscape; *Traces Of My Lipstick* . . . .(So So Def/Columbia)
Back In Baby's Arms
Patsy Cline; *Patsy Cline's 12 Greatest Hits* . . . .(MCA)
The Patsy Cline Story . . . .(MCA)
Back In My Arms Again
Diana Ross & The Supremes; *Diana Ross & The Supremes'*
Greatest Hits . . . . (Motown)
Diana Ross & The Supremes-25th Anniversary . . . . (Motown)
Diana Ross & The Supremes-Anthology (1962-1969) . . . . (Motown)
Every Great #1 Hit . . . . (Motown)
Motown Story-First 25 Years-C . . . . (Motown)
Back In Your Arms
Bruce Springsteen; *Tracks* . . . . (Columbia)
Back In Your Arms Again
Lorrie Morgan; *Lorrie Morgan's Greatest Hits* . . . . (BNA)
Circle Of Your Arms
Louis Armstrong; *Louis Armstrong* . . . . (Everest)
Crazy Arms
Chuck Berry; *The Chess Box-Chuck Berry* . . . . (Chess)
Jerry Lee Lewis; *18 Original Sun Greatest Hits* . . . . (Rhino)
Jerry Lee Lewis . . . . (Rhino)
The Golden Hits of Jerry Lee Lewis . . . . (Smash)
Linda Ronstadt; *Linda Ronstadt-Retrospective* . . . . (Capitol)
Patsy Cline; *Last Sessions* . . . .(MCA)
Portrait Of Patsy Cline . . . .(MCA)
Ray Price; *Columbia Country Classics-#2-Honky Tonk Heroes-C* . . (Columbia)
Ray Price's Greatest Hits . . . . (Columbia)
Ray Price's Greatest Hits-#1-3 . . . . (Step One)
Willie Nelson; *San Antonio Rose* . . . . (Columbia)
Death At One's Elbow
Smiths; *Strangeways Here We Come* . . . . (Sire)
Don't Let Go
Regina Belle; *Believe In Me* . . . .(MCA)
Embraceable You
Billie Holiday; *Body And Soul* . . . . (Verve)
Frank Sinatra; *The Capitol Years* . . . . (Capitol)
MGM Studio Orchestra; *ST/American In Paris* . . . . .(Sony Music Special Prod.)
Oleta Adams; *Glory Of Gershwin Featuring Larry Adler-C* . . . . (Mercury)
Sarah Vaughan; *Complete Sarah Vaughan On Mercury-#1-Great Jazz Years-*
1954-1956 . . . . (Mercury)
Empty Arms
Stevie Ray Vaughan and Double Trouble; *The Sky Is Crying* . . . . (Epic)
Fifty Miles Of Elbow Room
Iris DeMent; *Infamous Angel* . . . .(Warner Bros.)
Norman & Nancy Blake; *Blind Dog* . . . . (Rounder)
Red Clay Ramblers; *Twisted Laurel* . . . . (Flying Fish)
Full Moon And Empty Arms
Frank Sinatra; *A Lovely Way To Spend An Evening* . . . . (ASV)
Sarah Vaughan; *Slightly Classical* . . . . (Roulette)
Heaven In Your Arms
R.J.'s Latest Arrival; *Hold On* . . . . (Manhattan)
Hokey Pokey
Original Soundtrack; *Children's Favorites* . . . . (Kid Rhino/Rhino 4 Kids)

School Days-Kids Classics . . . . (Benson)
Ray Anthony; *Capitol Collectors Series-Ray Anthony* . . . . (Capitol)
Hold You Tight
Tara Kemp; *Tara Kemp* . . . .(Giant)
Holdin' Heaven
Tracy Byrd; *Tracy Byrd* . . . . (MCA)
I Got Lost In His Arms
Original Broadway Cast; *Annie Get Your Gun* . . . . (Angel)
I Need You
LeAnn Rimes; *ST/Jesus-The Epic Mini-Series* . . . . (Sparrow/Curb/Capitol)
If Ever You're In My Arms Again
Peabo Bryson; *Straight From The Heart* . . . . (Elektra)
I'll Hold You In My Heart (Till I Can Hold You In My Arms)
Eddy Arnold; *Best Of Eddy Arnold* . . . . (RCA)
Eddy Arnold-The Hits . . . . (Mercury)
Memories Are Made Of This . . . . (Mercury)
In The Arms Of Cocaine
Hank Williams, Jr.; *Strong Stuff* . . . . (Warner Bros.)
In These Arms
Bon Jovi; *Keep The Faith* . . . . (Mercury)
Into Your Arms
Lemonheads; *Come On Feel The Lemonheads* . . . .(Atlantic)
Lay Down Your Arms
Chordettes; *Best Of The Chordettes* . . . . (Rhino)
Loving Arms
Dixie Chicks; *Wide Open Spaces* . . . . (Monument)
My Arms Stay Open All Night
Tanya Tucker; *Tanya Tucker's Greatest Hits* . . . . (Liberty)
My Baby's Arms
John Steel; *Music From The New York Stage (1890-1920)#4-1917-*
1920-C . . . . (Pearl)
My Shoes Keep Walking Back To You
Ray Price; *All Time Legends Of Country Music-C* . . . . (Legacy)
Essential Ray Price-1951-1962 . . . . (Columbia)
Ray Price's Greatest Hits . . . . (Columbia)
Not Here In My Arms
Lisa Brokop; *Every Little Girl's Dream* . . . . (Patriot)
Open Arms
Journey; *Escape* . . . . (Columbia)
Journey's Greatest Hits . . . . (Columbia)
Seems Like Yesterday-#4-Early '80s-C . . . . (K-Tel)
ST/Heavy Metal . . . .(Asylum)
Other Arms
Robert Plant; *Principle Of Moments* . . . . (Es Paranza)
Put Your Arms Around Me, Honey
Fats Domino; *They Call Me The Fat Man* . . . . (EMI)
Judy Garland; *Best Of Judy Garland-From MGM Classic Films* . . . . (MCA)
Sammy Kaye & His Orchestra; *Best Of Sammy Kaye & His Orchestra* . . (MCA)
Rollin' In My Sweet Baby's Arms
Bill Monroe; *Bean Blossom* . . . .(MCA)
Del McCoury Band; *Appalachian Stomp: Bluegrass Classics-C* . . . . . . (Rhino)
Dillard & Clark; *Fantastic Expedition/Through The*
Morning . . . .(Mobile Fidelity Sound Lab)
Flatt & Scruggs; *Flatt & Scruggs At Carnegie Hall!* . . . . . . (Koch International)
Flatt & Scruggs-20 Greatest Hits . . . . (Deluxe)
Flying Burrito Brothers; *Close Encounters To The West Coast* . . . . (Relix)
Leon Russell; *Hank Wilson's Back, Vol. 1* . . . . (Right Stuff)
New Lost City Ramblers; *Greatest Folksingers Of The '60s-C* . . . . . . (Vanguard)
Ramblin' Jack Elliott; *Hard Travelin'* . . . . (Fantasy)
Ricky Skaggs and Kentucky Thunder; *History Of The Future* . . (Skaggs Family)
Tony Trischka; *Heartlands* . . . . (Rounder)
Willie Nelson; *Willie & Family Live* . . . . (Columbia)
Run Baby Run (Back Into My Arms)
Newbeats; *Collectables Presents The History Of Rock-#10-C* . . . . (Collectables)
Newbeats-Golden Classics Edition . . . . (Collectables)
Tremeloes; *Best Of The Tremeloes* . . . . (Rhino)
Run To My Lovin' Arms
Jay & The Americans; *Jay & The Americans'*
Greatest Hits . . . . (CEMA Special Prod.)
Safe In The Arms Of Love
Martina McBride; *ST/Switchback* . . . . (RCA)
Wild Angels . . . . (RCA)
Safe In The Arms Of Love
Martika; *Martika's Kitchen* . . . . (Columbia)
Turn The Tide . . . . (RCA)
Softly And Tenderly (I'll Hold You In My Arms)
Lewis Pruitt; *45-#31095* . . . . (Decca)
Take Me In Your Arms
Doobie Brothers; *Best Of The Doobies* . . . .(Warner Bros.)
Stampede . . . .(Warner Bros.)
Isley Brothers; *Motown Superstar Series-#6-Isley Brothers* . . . . (Motown)
The Isley Brothers Story-#1-Rockin' Soul-1959-1968 . . . . (Rhino)
Kim Weston; *25 Hard-To-Find Motown Classics-#3-C* . . . . (Motown)
Every Great Motown Song-First 25 Years-C . . . . (Motown)
Greatest By Holland/Dozier/Holland-C . . . . (Motown)
Motown Dance Party-#1-C . . . . (Motown)
Take Me In Your Arms & Hold Me
Eddy Arnold; *World Of Hits* . . . . (MGM)
Jim Reeves; *Don't Let Me Cross Over* . . . . (RCA)

I Love You Because . . . .(RCA)
Les Paul; *Legend & The Legacy-#1-4* . . . . (Capitol)

Take Me In Your Arms & Love Me
Gladys Knight & The Pips; *Everybody Needs Love/If I Were Your
Woman* . . . . (Motown)
Gladys Knight & The Pips-Anthology . . . . (Motown)

That's How You Know (When You're In Love)
Lari White; *Best Of Lari White* . . . . (RCA)
Wishes . . . . (RCA)

There Goes My Heart
Mavericks; *Best Of The Mavericks-Super Colossal Smash Hits Of
The '90s* . . . . (Mercury)
What A Crying Shame . . . . (MCA)

These Arms
All-4-One; *And The Music Speaks* . . . . (Blitzz)

These Arms Of Mine
Otis Redding; *Best Of Otis Redding* . . . . (Atco)
Good To Me . . . . (Stax)
ST/More Dirty Dancing . . . . (RCA)
The Otis Redding Story . . . . (Atlantic)
Very Best Of Otis Redding . . . . (Rhino)

Tree Hugger
Rugburns; *Taking The World By Donkey* . . . . (Priority)

Trying To Throw Your Arms Around The World
U2; *Achtung Baby* . . . . (Island)

Waltz Across Texas
Ernest Tubb; *Ernest Tubb's Greatest Hits* . . . . (MCA)
The Country Music Hall Of Fame-Ernest Tubb . . . . (MCA)
Ernest Tubb & Willie Nelson; *Ernest Tubb Collection-C* . . . .(Step One)

With Arms Wide Open
Creed; *Human Clay* . . . .(Wind-up)
Now That's What I Call Music!-#6-C . . . .(Virgin)

ANATOMY: BACK

See Also: ANATOMY (various)

Baby Scratch My Back
Slim Harpo; *Best Of Slim Harpo* . . . . (Rhino)
Sound Of The Swamp-Best Of Excello-#1-C . . . . (Rhino)

Better Watch Your Back
Daryl Hall & John Oates; *War Babies* . . . . (Atlantic)

Fishin' In The Dark
Nitty Gritty Dirt Band; *Billboard Top Country Hits-1987-C* . . . .(Rhino)
Hold On . . . . (Warner Bros.)
More Great Dirt-Best Of Nitty Gritty Dirt Band . . . . (Warner Bros.)

Get Off My Back Woman
B.B. King; *Live & Well* . . . . (MCA)

Monkey On My Back
Inspiral Carpets; *Life* . . . . (Elektra)

Monkey On My Back
Ten Years After; *A Space In Time* . . . . (Columbia)

Monkey On My Back
Aerosmith; *Pump* . . . . (Geffen)

Monkey On Your Back
Aldo Nova; *Portrait Of Aldo Nova* . . . . (Epic)
Subject...Aldo Nova . . . . (Portrait)

Never Let You Go
Third Eye Blind; *Blue* . . . . (Elektra)
Totally Hits-#2-C . . . . (Elektra)

Police On My Back
Clash; *On Broadway* . . . . (Epic)
Sandinista . . . . (Epic)

Ribbons Down My Back
Carol Channing/Original Cast; *Hello Dolly!* . . . .(RCA)

Scratch My Back
Otis Redding; *Soul Album* . . . . (Atco)

Scratch My Back
Fabulous Thunderbirds; *Fabulous Thunderbirds* . . . . (Chrysalis)

Scratch My Back
Smoove; *Smoove With A Ruffness* . . . .(East West)

Scratch My Back
Roxx Gang; *Things You've Never Done Before* . . . .(Virgin)

ANATOMY: BODY, Belly, Hips, Naked

See Also: ANATOMY (various)

36-22-36
Bobby Bland; *Best Of Bobby Bland-#2* . . . . (MCA)
Bobby Bland . . . . (MCA)
Here's The Man . . . . (MCA)

All Of Me
Billie Holiday; *Billie Holiday-Love Songs* . . . . (Legacy)
Count Basie; *Compact Jazz-The Standards* . . . . (Verve)
Diana Ross; *ST/Lady Sings The Blues* . . . . (Motown)

Dinah Washington; *Compact Jazz-Dinah Washington* . . . .(Verve)
Duke Ellington; *Jazz Party* . . . . (Legacy)
Esquivel; *Music From A Sparkling Planet* . . . .(Bar/None)
Frank Sinatra; *Sinatra Sings His Greatest Hits* . . . .(Legacy)
Helen O'Connell; *Great Girl Singers Sing 22 Original
Recordings-C* . . . . (Hindsight)
Louis Armstrong; *Louis Armstrong's Greatest Hits* . . . . (Legacy)
Martha Tilton; *Sweet And Lovely: Capitol's Great Ladies Of Song-C* . . .(Capitol)
Paul Whiteman & Mildred Bailey; *Those Wonderful Years: Happy Days Are
Here Again-C* . . . .(JCI Assoc. Labels)
Sarah Vaughan; *Essential Sarah Vaughan-The Great Songs* . . . .(Verve)
Willie Nelson; *Stardust* . . . . (Legacy)

Belly Button Window
Jimi Hendrix; *Cry Of Love* . . . . (Reprise)

Belly Up To The Bar, Boys
Debbie Reynolds; *ST/The Unsinkable Molly Brown* . . . . (MCA)
Original Cast; *The Unsinkable Molly Brown* . . . . (EMI-Angel)

Blistered
Johnny Cash; *Johnny Cash-16 Biggest Hits-#2* . . . .(Legacy)

Bodies
Sex Pistols; *Never Mind The Bollocks, Here's The Sex Pistols* . . .(Warner Bros.)

Bodies
Drowning Pool; *Sinner* . . . . (Wind-up)

Body And Soul
Benny Goodman & His Orchestra; *Benny Goodman's
Greatest Hits* . . . . (RCA Victor)
Benny Goodman Trio; *Ken Burns Jazz Collection-The Benny
Goodman Trio* . . . . (Legacy)
Billie Holiday; *Billie Holiday-16 Most Requested Songs* . . . .(Legacy)
Body And Soul . . . .(Verve)
The Billie Holiday Story-#2 . . . .(Columbia)
This Is Jazz #32: Billie Holiday Sings Standards . . . . (Columbia)
Verve Jazz Masters 47-Billie Holiday Sings Standards . . . .(Verve)
Carly Simon; *Torch* . . . . (Warner Bros.)
Coleman Hawkins; *Coleman Hawkins' Greatest Hits* . . . .(RCA Victor)
Verve Jazz Masters 34 . . . . (Verve)
Diana Krall; *Stepping Out* . . . . (Justin Time)
Eddie Jefferson; *Body And Soul* . . . . (Original Jazz Classics)
Letter From Home . . . . (Original Jazz Classics)
Main Man . . . . (Inner City)
The Jazz Singer . . . .(Evidence Music)
Louis Armstrong; *Essential Louis Armstrong* . . . .(Verve)
Louis Armstrong-Love Songs . . . . (Legacy)
Musical Autobiography-#2 . . . . (MCA)
Satchmo At Symphony Hall . . . .(Decca Jazz)
Verve Jazz Masters 1 . . . . (Verve)
Manhattan Transfer; *Best Of The Manhattan Transfer* . . . .(Atlantic)
Extensions . . . . (Rhino)
Manhattan Transfer-Anthology-Down In Birdland . . . . (Rhino)
Paul Whiteman & His Orchestra; *78-#2297* . . . . (Columbia)
Sarah Vaughan; *How Long Has This Been Going On?* . . . . (Pablo)
One Night Stand-The Town Hall Concert-1947 . . . . (Blue Note)
Sarah Vaughan . . . . (Everest)

Body And Soul
Anita Baker; *Rhythm Of Love* . . . . (Atlantic)

Body Bumpin'
Mytown; *Mytown* . . . .(Cherry/Universal)

Body Electric
Rush; *Grace Under Pressure* . . . .(Mercury)

Body Heavenly
Full Force; *Get Busy 1 Time* . . . .(Columbia)

Body Language
Pete Townshend; *Scoop* . . . .(Atco)

Body Language
Queen; *Hot Space* . . . .(Hollywood)

Body Language
INXS; *INXS* . . . .(Atco)

Body Slam!
Bootsy's Rubber Band; *Funk Nation-Free Your Mind And Your @'s Will
Follow-C* . . . . (Cold Front)

Body Talk
Ratt; *Dancing Undercover* . . . . (Atlantic)
Ratt & Roll 8191 . . . . (Atlantic)
ST/The Golden Child . . . . (Capitol)

Body Talk
Deele; *Body Talk* . . . . (Solar)
Street Beat . . . . (Solar)

Body Talk
Wallets; *Body Talk* . . . . (Twin-Tone)

Body Talk
Kix; *Cool Kids* . . . . (Atlantic)

Bullet-Ridden Bodies
Accused; *Grinning Like An Undertaker* . . . . (Nastymix)

Bury My Body
Animals; *Best Of The Animals* . . . . (Abkco)

Chest Pains
Greg "Fingers" Taylor; *Chest Pains* . . . . (MCA)

Da Dip
Freak Nasty; *Controversee...That's Life...And That's The Way It Is* . . . . (Power)

Dead Bodies Everywhere
Korn; *Follow The Leader* . . . .(Immortal/Epic)
Heartbeat/Free Your Body
Seduction; *Nothing Matters Without Love* . . . . (Vendettat)
Heavenly Bodies
Earl Thomas Conley; *Somewhere Between Right And Wrong* . . . . (RCA)
Heavenly Body
Chi-Lites; *Ear Candy-#2-C* . . . . (20th Century Fox)
Heavenly Body . . . . (20th Century Fox)
Hip Shake
Rolling Stones; *Exile On Main Street* . . . . (Virgin)
Hip Sway
Chris Standing; *Hip Sway* . . . . (Instinct)
Hippy Hippy Shake
Chan Romero; *Del-Fi Record Hop-C* . . . . (Del Fi)
Georgia Satellites; *Let It Rock-The Best Of The Georgia Satellites* . . . . (Elektra)
ST/Cocktail . . . . (Elektra)
Swinging Blue Jeans; *Hippy Hippy Shake-The Definition Collection*. . . . .(EMI)
I Love Your Guts
Elvis Hitler; *Disgraceland* . . . . (Restless)
I'll Go On Loving You
Alan Jackson; *High Mileage* . . . . (Arista)
In The Raw
Whispers; *Love Is Where You Find It* . . . . (Solar)
It's Your Body
Johnny Gill; *Let's Get The Mood Right* . . . . (Motown)
Let's Just Get Naked
Joan Osborne; *Relish* . . . . (Blue Gorilla/Mercury)
Linger
Jonatha Brooke; *Steady Pull* . . . . (Bad Dog)
Memphis Hip Shake
Cult; *Electric* . . . . (Sire)
My Body
LSG; *Levert-Sweat-Gill* . . . . (East West)
Naked
Goo Goo Dolls; *A Boy Named Goo* . . . .(Metal Blade)
Naked
Spice Girls; *Spice* . . . . (Virgin)
Naked & Nude
Lou & Peter Berryman; *Cupid's Trash Truck* . . . . (Cornbelt)
One Hit (To The Body)
Rolling Stones; *Dirty Work* . . . . (Virgin)
Shake Your Body (Down To The Ground)
Jacksons; *Destiny* . . . .(Epic)
Jacksons Live . . . .(Epic)
ST/Skatetown USA . . . . (Columbia)
Shake Your Groove Thing
Peaches & Herb; *2 Hot* . . . . (Polydor)
Billboard Top Dance Hits-1978-C . . . . (Rhino)
Mega Hits Dance Classics-#2-C . . . . (Priority)
Night At Studio 54-C . . . . (Casablanca)
Polydor Dance Classics-C . . . . (Polydor)
The Disco Years-#1-Turn The Beat Around-1974-1978-C . . . . . . (Rhino)
Shake Your Hips
Love Sculpture; *Blues Helping* . . . . (EMI)
Rolling Stones; *Exile On Main Street* . . . . (Virgin)
Slim Harpo; *Best Of Slim Harpo* . . . . (Rhino)
Shape Your Stomach's In (Alka-Seltzer)
Original Soundtrack; *TeeVee Toons-The Commercials-#1-C* . . . . (TVT)
Stiff Upper Lip (hip)
AC/DC; *Stiff Upper Lip* . . . . (East West)
This Body Is A Prison
Spencer Bohren; *Live In New Orleans* . . . . (Great Southern)
Touch Me (I Want Your Body)
Samantha Fox; *Samantha Fox's Greatest Hits* . . . . (Jive)
Touch Me (I Want Your Body) . . . . (Jive)
Waist Deep In The Big Muddy
Pete Seeger; *Best Of Broadside 1962-1968: Anthems Of The American
Underground From The Pages Of Broadside
Magazine-C* . . . . (Smithsonian Folkways)
What's It Gonna Be
Busta Rhymes Featuring Janet Jackson; *E.L.E.* . . . . (Elektra)
What's The Ugliest Part Of Your Body
Mothers Of Invention; *We're Only In It For The Money*. . . . .(Rykodisc)
Wiggle It
2 In A Room; *Cutting's Dance Express 3-C* . . . . (Cutting)
Woman (Sensuous Woman)
Don Gibson; *Don Gibson-18 Greatest Hits* . . . . (Curb)
Mark Chesnutt; *Almost Goodbye* . . . .(MCA)
Wrap My Body Tight
Johnny Gill; *Johnny Gill* . . . . (Motown)
X-Ray Hip
Bona Fide; *Royal Function* . . . . (N-Coded)
Your Body Is An Outlaw
Mel Tillis; *Your Body Is An Outlaw* . . . . (Elektra)
Your Body's Callin'
R. Kelly; *12 Play* . . . . (Jive)

Your Body's Here With Me
O'Jays; *My Favorite Person* . . . . (Philadelphia Int'l)

ANATOMY: FACE

See Also: ANATOMY (various), COSMETICS, EYES, SMILE

Angel Of The Morning
Juice Newton; *All-Time Country Classics-#2-C* . . . . (Capitol)
Juice . . . . (Capitol)
Juice Newton-Greatest Hits & More . . . . (Capitol)
Juice Newton's Greatest Hits . . . . (Gold Rush)
Merrilee Rush; *Dick Bartley's One-Hit Wonders Of The '60s-#2-C* . . . . (Rhino)
Mellow '60s-C . . . . (Priority)
Angels With Dirty Faces
Tommy Dorsey; *Complete Tommy Dorsey-#8* . . . . (RCA)
Angels With Dirty Faces
Los Lobos; *Kiko* . . . .(Slash)
Baby Face
Little Richard; *Compact Command Performances-Little Richard* . . . . (Motown)
Little Richard-His Greatest Hits . . . . (Vee-Jay)
Little Richard's Greatest Hits . . . . (Everest)
Tutti Frutti . . . . (Accord)
Baby Face
Bobby Darin; *Splish Splash-Best Of Bobby Darin-#1* . . . .(Atlantic)
Baby Face
Al Jolson; *The Al Jolson Story-#3* . . . . (MCA)
World's Greatest . . . . (MCA)
Kinks; *Everybody's In Show-Biz* . . . . (Rhino)
Blonde Hair, Brown Nose
Dweezil Zappa; *Havin' A Bad Day* . . . . (Rykodisc)
Breakout
Foo Fighters; *There Is Nothing Left To Lose* . . . .(Roswell/RCA)
Cheek To Cheek
Ella Fitzgerald; *Silver Collection-Songbooks* . . . . Verve)
Frank Sinatra; *Come Dance With Me!* . . . . (Capitol)
Fred Astaire; *Cheek To Cheek* . . . . (Pro-Arte)
Irving Berlin Songbook . . . . (Verve)
Mundell Lowe; *Mundell Lowe Quartet* . . . . (Riverside)
Pete Fountain; *Cheek To Cheek*. . . . . (Ranwood)
Tommy Dorsey; *Irving Berlin 100th Anniversary Collection-C* . . . . (MCA)
Tony Bennett; *Bennett/Berlin* . . . . (Columbia)
De Bat (Fly In Me Face)
Carly Simon; *Boys In The Trees* . . . . (Elektra)
Der Fuehrer's Face
Spike Jones & His City Slickers; *Best Of Spike Jones & His City
Slickers* . . . .(RCA)
Eyes Without A Face
Billy Idol; *Rebel Yell* . . . . (Chrysalis)
Flesheaters; *ST/Return Of The Living Dead* . . . .(Enigma)
Face Dances, Part 2
Pete Townshend; *All The Best Cowboys Have Chinese Eyes* . . . . (Atco)
Face In The Crowd
Michael Martin Murphey & Holly Dunn; *Americana* . . . . . (Warner Bros.)
Favorite Country Duets-C . . . . (Warner Bros.)
Milestones-Greatest Hits . . . . (Warner Bros.)
Face In The Crowd
Tom Petty; *Full Moon Fever* . . . . (MCA)
Face In The Crowd
Kinks; *Soap Opera* . . . . (Rhino)
Face In The Crowd
Lisa Lisa & Cult Jam; *Spanish Fly* . . . . (Columbia)
Face Of Love
Rosie O'Donnell & Jewel; *Another Rosie Christmas-C* . . . . (Columbia)
Face On The Cutting Room Floor
Nitty Gritty Dirt Band; *Live Two Five* . . . . (Capitol)
More Great Dirt-Best Of Nitty Gritty Dirt Band . . . . (Warner Bros.)
Face The Face
Pete Townshend; *White City* . . . . (Atco)
Who; *Join Together* . . . . (MCA)
Face To Face
Garth Brooks; *The Chase* . . . . (Liberty)
First Time Ever I Saw Your Face
Celine Dion; *All The Way...A Decade Of Song* . . . .(550 Music)
Roberta Flack; *Atlantic Rhythm & Blues 1947-1974-#6 (1966-
1969)-C* . . . .(Atlantic)
Best Of Roberta Flack . . . .(Atlantic)
First Take . . . .(Atlantic)
For Your Love
Stevie Wonder; *Conversation Peace* . . . . (Motown)
Natural Wonder . . . . (Motown)
Song Review-A Greatest Hits Collection . . . . (Motown)
Freckle Song
Larry Vincent; *Dr. Demento Presents The Greatest Novelty Records-#1-1940s
& Before-C* . . . . (Rhino)
Freshmen, The
Verve Pipe; *Villains* . . . . (RCA)

Funny Face
Donna Fargo; *Super Hits Of The '70s-Have A Nice Day-#11-C* . . . . (Rhino)
Funny Face
Original Cast; *My One And Only* . . . . (Atlantic)
Get The Funk Out Ma Face
Brothers Johnson; *Blast* . . . . (A&M)
Brothers Johnson-Classics-#11 . . . . (A&M)
Look Out For No. 1 . . . . (A&M)
Good Morning Beautiful
Steve Holy; *Blue Moon* . . . . (Curb)
Good To See You
Neil Young; *Silver & Gold* . . . . (Reprise)
Hide Your Face
Spade Cooley; *Columbia Historic Edition-Spade Cooley* . . . . (Columbia)
How Bizarre
OMC; *How Bizarre* . . . . (Huh!/Mercury)
I Belong To You (Every Time I See Your Face)
Rome; *Rome* . . . . (RCA)
I Can't See Your Face In My Mind
Doors; *Doors-Classics* . . . . (Elektra)
Strange Days . . . . (Elektra)
I Don't Know You Anymore
Savage Garden; *Affirmation.* . . . . (Columbia)
I Just Want To See His Face
Rolling Stones; *Exile On Main Street* . . . . (Virgin)
I See Your Face Before Me
Frank Sinatra; *In The Wee Small Hours* . . . . (Capitol)
Miles Davis; *Green Haze* . . . . (Prestige)
Miles Davis-Chronicle-Complete Prestige Recordings . . . . (Prestige)
I'm A Believer
Monkees; *Billboard Top Rock 'N' Roll Hits-1966-C* . . . . (Rhino)
Monkees' Greatest Hits . . . . (Rhino)
More Of The Monkees . . . . (Rhino)
Oldies But Goodies-#3-C . . . . (Original Sound)
Neil Diamond; *Live In America* . . . . (Columbia)
Neil Diamond's Greatest Hits-1966-1992 . . . . (Columbia)
September Morn . . . . (Columbia)
Smash Mouth; *Now That's What I Call Music!-#8-C* . . . . (Virgin)
ST/Shrek . . . . (Interscope)
I've Grown Accustomed To Her Face
Rex Harrison/Original Cast; *My Fair Lady* . . . . (Columbia)
Tony Bennett; *Big Band Bash* . . . . (Intermedia)
Chicago . . . . (Dunhill Compact Classics)
I've Just Seen A Face
Beatles; *Rubber Soul* . . . . (Capitol)
Paul McCartney; *Unplugged (The Official Bootleg)* . . . . (Capitol)
Wings; *Wings Over America* . . . . (Capitol)
I've Seen That Face Before
Grace Jones; *Island Life* . . . . (Island)
Nightclubbing . . . . (Island)
Jawbone
Band; *Stage Fright* . . . . (Capitol)
The Band-Gift Set . . . . (Capitol)
Jawbreaker
Judas Priest; *Defenders Of The Faith.* . . . . (Columbia)
Lines On My Face
Peter Frampton; *Comes Alive* . . . . (A&M)
Frampton's Camel . . . . (A&M)
Peter Frampton-Classics-#12 . . . . (A&M)
Lose That Long Face
Judy Garland; *A Star Is Born* . . . . (Columbia)
May The Bird Of Paradise Fly Up Your Nose
"Little" Jimmy Dickens; *Columbia Country Classics-#3-*
Americana-C . . . . (Columbia)
Super Hits Of The '60s-C . . . . (Epic)
Harlow Wilcox and the Oakies; *Cripple Cricket* . . . . (Plantation)
Moon-Faced, Starry-Eyed
Benny Goodman; *Jazz Collector Edition* . . . . (Laserlight)
Must You Throw Dirt In My Face
Elvis Costello; *Kojak Variety* . . . . (Warner Bros.)
Louvin Brothers; *45-#4822* . . . . (Capitol)
My Brave Face
Paul McCartney; *Flowers In The Dirt* . . . . (Capitol)
Tripping The Live Fantastic-Highlights! . . . . (Capitol)
Nancy (With The Laughing Face)
Frank Sinatra; *Sinatra Reprise-The Very Good Years* . . . . (Reprise)
Sinatra's Sinatra . . . . (Reprise)
John Coltrane; *The Gentle Side Of John Coltrane* . . . . (GRP)
Tony Bennett; *Perfectly Frank* . . . . (Columbia)
Needles And Pins
Jackie DeShannon; *Very Best Of Jackie DeShannon* . . . . (EMI)
Searchers; *History Of British Rock-#1-C* . . . . (Rhino)
Searchers' Greatest Hits. . . . . (Rhino)
Tom Petty And The Heartbreakers; *Pack Up The Plantation-Live!* . . . . . (MCA)
New Faces
Rolling Stones; *Voodoo Lounge* . . . . (Virgin)
One Angry Dwarf And 200 Solemn Faces
Ben Folds Five; *Whatever And Ever Amen* . . . . (Caroline/550)

Painted On My Heart
Cult; *ST/Gone In 60 Seconds* . . . .(Island)
People Are Strange
Doors; *Best Of The Doors* . . . .(Elektra)
Pizza Face
Barnes & Barnes; *Zabagabee-Best Of Barnes & Barnes* . . . .(Rhino)
Powder Your Face With Sunshine (Smile!)
Guy Lombardo & His Royal Canadians; *Best Of Guy Lombardo* . . . .(Curb)
Sammy Kaye & His Orchestra; *Sammy Kaye & His Orchestra Play 22*
Original Big Band Recordings . . . .(Hindsight)
Pretty
Korn; *Follow The Leader* . . . .(Immortal/Epic)
Put On A Happy Face
Dick Van Dyke; *Broadway Magic-The 1960s-C* . . . .(Columbia)
ST/Bye Bye Birdie . . . . (RCA)
Dick Van Dyke/Original Cast; *Bye Bye Birdie.* . . . .(Columbia)
Stevie Wonder; *With A Song In My Heart* . . . .(Motown)
Tony Bennett; *Forty Years-The Artistry Of Tony Bennett* . . . .(Columbia)
Tony Bennett's All-Time Greatest Hits . . . .(Columbia)
Razor Face
Elton John; *Madman Across The Water* . . . . (Polydor)
Shaddap You Face
Joe Dolce; *45-#51053* . . . .(MCA)
Smiling Faces Sometimes
Undisputed Truth; *Didn't It Blow Your Mind: Soul Hits Of The*
'70s-#5-C . . . .(Rhino)
Hard-To-Find Motown Classics-#2-C . . . .(Motown)
Stripper (Take It Off), The (Noxema Shave Cream)
Original Soundtrack; *TeeVee Toons-The Commercials-#1-C* . . . .(TVT)
Take A Look At My Face
Michael Bolton; *The Hunger* . . . .(Columbia)
Tell Me To My Face
Dan Fogelberg & Tim Weisberg; *Twin Sons Of Different*
Mothers . . . . (Full Moon)
There's Nothing Like The Face (Hershey's Chocolate Bars)
Original Soundtrack; *TeeVee Toons-The Commercials-#1-C* . . . .(TVT)
Tonight I Shall Sleep With A Smile On My Face
Duke Ellington; *Black, Brown & Beige: 1944-1946 Band*
Recordings . . . .(Bluebird)
Sarah Vaughan; *Duke Ellington Songbook Two* . . . .(Pablo)
Tracks Of My Tears, The
Bryan Ferry; *These Foolish Things* . . . . (Reprise)
Gladys Knight & The Pips; *Gladys Knight & The Pips-Anthology* . . . .(Motown)
Johnny Rivers; *Best Of Johnny Rivers* . . . .(EMI)
Linda Ronstadt; *Linda Ronstadt's Greatest Hits* . . . .(Asylum)
Prisoner In Disguise . . . .(Asylum)
Smokey Robinson & The Miracles; *Billboard Top R&B Hits-1965-*
1969-C . . . .(Rhino)
Smokey Robinson & The Miracles' Anthology . . . .(Motown)
Smokey Robinson & The Miracles' Greatest Hits-#2 . . . .(Motown)
ST/Big Chill. . . . .(Motown)
ST/Sound Of "Murphy Brown" . . . .(MCA)
Tripe Face Boogie
Little Feat; *Feats Don't Fail Me Now* . . . .(Warner Bros.)
Sailin' Shoes . . . .(Warner Bros.)
Waiting For Columbus . . . .(Warner Bros.)
Tulip Or Turnip (Tell Me Dream Face)
Duke Ellington & Teresa Brewer; *It Don't Mean A Thing If It Ain't Got That*
Swing . . . .(Columbia)
Two Faces
Bruce Springsteen; *Tunnel Of Love* . . . .(Columbia)
Two Faces Have I
Lou Christie; *Back To The '60s-#4-C* . . . .(Dominion Entert.)
Enlightnin'ment-Best Of Lou Christie . . . .(Rhino)
Two Teardrops
Steve Wariner; *Two Teardrops* . . . .(Capitol)
U Remind Me
Usher; *8701* . . . .(LaFace)
Totally Hits 2001-C . . . .(Arista)
Whiter Shade Of Pale
Annie Lennox; *Medusa* . . . .(Arista)
Procol Harum; *Best Of Procol Harum* . . . .(A&M)
Billboard Top Pop Hits-1967-C . . . .(Rhino)
History Of British Rock-#8-C . . . .(Rhino)
ST/Big Chill. . . . .(Motown)
Without Expression
John Mellencamp; *Best That I Could Do-1978-1988.* . . . .(Mercury)
Woman In Me
Jessica Simpson featuring Destiny's Child; *Sweet Kisses* . . . .(Columbia)
Written All Over Your Face
Rude Boys; *Rude Awakening* . . . . (Atlantic)
Your Smiling Face
James Taylor; *J.T.* . . . .(Columbia)
ST/FM . . . .(MCA)
You're So Sweet, Horseflies Keep Hangin' Round Your Face
Neil Diamond; *Brother Love's Traveling Salvation Show* . . . .(MCA)

ANATOMY: FEET

See Also: **ANATOMY (various), BACK ON MY FEET, SHOES, TRAVELING**

42nd Street
Diana Krall; *Stepping Out* . . . . (Justin Time)
Hal Kemp; *Best Of The Big Bands-C* . . . . (Columbia)
Mel Torme; *Cocktail Mix-#3-Swingin' Singles-C* . . . . (Rhino)
Original Broadway Cast; *42nd Street* . . . . (RCA Victor)

Amazing Bigfoot Diet
Mojo Nixon & Skid Roper; *Frenzy/Get Out Of My Way* . . . .(I.R.S.)

Back On My Feet Again
Babys; *Babys-Anthology* . . . . (Chrysalis)
Union Jacks . . . . (Chrysalis)

Back On My Feet Again
Furry Lewis; *Back On My Feet Again* . . . . (Prestige)
Shake 'Em On Down . . . . (Fantasy)

Back On My Feet Again
Randy Newman; *Good Old Boys* . . . . (Reprise)

Barefoot & Pregnant
Joan Armatrading; *To The Limit* . . . . (A&M)

Barefoot In Baltimore
Strawberry Alarm Clock; *Best Of The Strawberry Alarm Clock-#1* . . . (Bac-Trac)

Barefoot In Beverly Hills
Grace Jones; *Inside Story* . . . . (Manhattan)

Barefootin'
Robert Parker; *18 Soul Hits From The 60's-C* . . . . (JCI Assoc. Labels)
Billboard Top R&B Hits-1966-C . . . . (Rhino)
Golden Classics-Robert Palmer . . . . (Collectables)
Super Oldies Of The '60s-#4-C . . . .(Audio Fidelity)

Barefootin'
Barefoot Jerry; *Barefootin'* . . . . (Monument)

Barefootin'
Pete Townshend; *Pete Townshend's Deep End Live!* . . . . (Atco)

Barefootin'
Alabama; *Southern Star* . . . . (RCA)

Country Boy (You Got Your Feet In L.A.)
Glen Campbell; *Best Of Glen Campbell* . . . . (Capitol)
Glen Campbell-Classics Collection . . . . (Capitol)
Glen Campbell's Greatest Hits . . . . (Capitol)

Dancin' Feet
Montrose; *Montrose* . . . .(Warner Bros.)

Feet Up (Pat Him On The Po-Po)
Guy Mitchell; *Definitive Guy Mitchell* . . . . (Collector's Choice)

Footloose
Kenny Loggins; *ST/Footloose* . . . . (Columbia)

Footprints In The Snow
Bill Monroe; *Best Of Bill Monroe & His Blue Grass Boys* . . . .(MCA)
Clarence White; *Treasures Untold-C* . . . . (Vanguard)
Kentucky Colonels featuring Clarence White; *Kentucky Colonels featuring
Clarence White* . . . . (Rounder)

Footprints In The Snow
Emerson, Lake & Palmer; *Black Moon* . . . . (Rhino)

Footprints In The Snow
Isley Brothers; *Complete UA Sessions* . . . .(EMI)

Ground Beneath Her Feet, The
U2; *ST/The Million Dollar Hotel* . . . . (Interscope)

Has Anybody Seen Amy
John & Audrey Wiggins; *John & Audrey* . . . . (Mercury)

Head Over Feet
Alanis Morissette; *Jagged Little Pill* . . . .(Maverick)

Head Over Heels
Go-Go's; *Go-Go's Greatest* . . . .(I.R.S.)
Talk Show . . . .(I.R.S.)

Head Over Heels
Allure; *The Greatest Dance Album In The World-C* . . . .(Epic)
Allure featuring NAS; *Allure* . . . .(Track Masters/Crave)

Head Over Heels
Accept; *Balls To The Wall* . . . . (Portrait)

Head Over Heels
Tears For Fears; *Songs From The Big Chair* . . . . (Mercury)

Head Over Heels
Tony Terry; *Tony Terry* . . . . (Epic)

Head To Toe
Lisa Lisa & Cult Jam; *Spanish Fly* . . . . (Columbia)

Henry's Got Flat Feet (Can't Dance No More)
Hank Ballard And The Midnighters; *Sexy Ways: The Best Of Hank Ballard &
The Midnighters* . . . . (Rhino)

Hokey Pokey
Original Soundtrack; *Children's Favorites* . . . . . (Kid Rhino/Rhino 4 Kids)
School Days-Kids Classics . . . . (Benson)
Ray Anthony; *Capitol Collectors Series-Ray Anthony* . . . . (Capitol)

I Got Stripes
Johnny Cash; *Johnny Cash-16 Biggest Hits-#2* . . . . (Legacy)

If You're Happy & You Know It
Original Soundtrack; *Children's Favorites* . . . . (Kid Rhino/Rhino 4 Kids)

Knock Me Off My Feet
Stevie Wonder; *Songs In The Key Of Life* . . . . (Motown)

Living In The Footsteps Of Another Man
Chi-Lites; *Chi-Lites Greatest Hits* . . . . (Brunswick)
Half A Love . . . . (Brunswick)

My Head Hurts, My Feet Stink And I Don't Love Jesus
Jimmy Buffett; *Havana Daydreamin'* . . . . (MCA)

On Your Toes
Bobby Short; *Bobby Short Celebrates Rodgers & Hart* . . . .(Atlantic)

One Foot, Other Foot
Original Cast; *Allegro* . . . . (Out Of Print)

Ooh! My Feet!
Original Broadway Cast; *Most Happy Fella* . . . . (Sony Music Classical)

Popsicle Toes
Diana Krall; *When I Look In Your Eyes* . . . . (GRP)
Manhattan Transfer; *Coming Out* . . . .(Atlantic)
Michael Franks; *Art Of Tea* . . . .(Reprise)

Put Your Little Foot Right Out
Myron Floren; *22 Great Accordion Classics* . . . . (Ranwood)
Russ Morgan; *Best Of Russ Morgan* . . . . (MCA)

Shackles (Praise You)
Mary Mary; *Thankful* . . . . (C2/Columbia)

Shoe Goes On The Other Foot Tonight
George Jones; *20 Golden Pieces Of George Jones* . . . . (Bulldog)

Shoe Was On The Other Foot
Patti LaBelle; *Flame* . . . . (MCA)

Stand Up On Your Own Feet
Third World; *Arise In Harmony* . . . . (Island)

Sugarfoot Rag
Asleep At The Wheel; *Very Best Of Asleep At The Wheel
Since 1970* . . . .(Relentless/Madacy)
Bill Keith; *Something Auld, Something Newgrass, Something Borrowed,
Something Bluegrass* . . . . (Rounder)
Porter Wagoner; *Grand Ole Opry-75 Years-#2-C* . . . . (MCA)

Tickle Toe
Count Basie; *I Like Jazz-Essence Of Count Basie* . . . . (Columbia)
Count Basie & His Orchestra; *Best Of Count Basie & His Orchestra-The
Roulette Years* . . . . (Roulette)

Tip-Toe Through The Tulips With Me
Tiny Tim; *Dr. Demento Presents The Greatest Novelty Records-#3-
1960s-C* . . . . (Rhino)
Silly Songs-C . . . . (K-Tel)

Two Left Feet
Richard Thompson; *Hand Of Darkness* . . . .(Hannibal)
Watching The Dark-History Of Richard Thompson . . . . (Rykodisc)

When I'm Back On My Feet Again
Michael Bolton; *Soul Provider* . . . . (Columbia)

Where The Blacktop Ends
keith urban; *keith urban* . . . . (Capitol)

Your Feet's Too Big
Beatles; *45-#1503* . . . . (Collectables)
Fats Waller; *20 Golden Pieces Of Fats Waller* . . . .(Bulldog)
Ain't Misbehavin' . . . . (RCA)
Fats Waller-Legendary Performer . . . . (RCA)
Joint Is Jumpin' . . . . (Bluebird)
Original Cast; *Ain't Misbehavin'* . . . . (RCA)

ANATOMY: HAIR, Blonde, Brunette, Redhead

See Also: **ANATOMY (various)**

Almost Cut My Hair
Crosby, Stills, Nash & Young; *Deja Vu* . . . .(Atlantic)

Bald Head
Professor Longhair; *Crawfish Fiesta* . . . .(Alligator)
Last Mardi Gras . . . .(Atlantic)

Bald-Headed Woman
Lightnin' Hopkins; *Lightnin' Sam Hopkins* . . . . (Arhoolie)

Band Played On, The
Guy Lombardo & His Royal Canadians; *Guy Lombardo-All Time
Favorites* . . . . (MCA Special Prod.)

Barbie Girl
Aqua; *Aquarium* . . . . (MCA)
Now That's What I Call Music!-#1-C . . . .(Virgin)

Black Is The Color Of My True Love's Hair
Joan Baez; *Best Of Joan Baez* . . . . (A&M)
Joan Baez In Concert . . . . (Vanguard)
The Joan Baez Ballad Book . . . . (Vanguard)

Blonde Ambition
Billy Burnette; *Soldier Of Love* . . . . (Curb)

Blonde Hair, Brown Nose
Dweezil Zappa; *Havin' A Bad Day* . . . . (Rykodisc)

Blonde In The Bleachers
Joni Mitchell; *For The Roses* . . . . (Asylum)

Blondes (Have More Fun)
Rod Stewart; *Blondes Have More Fun* . . . . (Warner Bros.)

Blondes In Black Cars
Autograph; *That's The Stuff*. . . . .(RCA)
Blue Rock Montana/Red Headed Stranger
Willie Nelson; *Red Headed Stranger* . . . .(Columbia)
Brownsville Blues
Hammie Nixon; *Tappin' That Thing* . . . .(High Water)
Camarillo Brillo
Mothers; *Apostrophe/Overnite Sensation* . . . .(Rykodisc)
Curly Headed Baby
Pete Seeger; *Tribute To Woody Guthrie-C* . . . . (Warner Bros.)
Don't Mess With My Ducktail
Hank C. Burnette; *Don't Mess With My Ducktail* . . . .(Sun)
Fuzzy Wuzzy
Original Soundtrack; *Toddler Favorites* . . . . (Kid Rhino/Rhino 4 Kids)
Get A Haircut
George Thorogood & The Destroyers; *Haircut* . . . .(EMI)
Girl I Love
Led Zeppelin; *BBC Sessions* . . . .(Atlantic)
Give Me Back My Wig
Luther Allison; *Live In Chicago* . . . .(Alligator)
Mike Henderson & The Bluebloods; *First Blood* . . . .(Dead Reckoning)
Stevie Ray Vaughan; *Couldn't Stand The Weather* . . . .(Epic)
Gray Haired Young Man
Don Potter; *Over The Rainbow* . . . .(Mirror)
Hair
Cowsills; *Billboard Top Rock 'N' Roll Hits-1969-C* . . . .(Rhino)
Original Broadway Cast; *Hair*. . . . .(RCA)
Haircut Song
Ray Stevens; *I Have Returned* . . . .(MCA)
Ray Stevens' Greatest Hits-#2 . . . .(MCA)
Today's Country Classics-#2-C . . . .(MCA)
I Dream Of Jeanie With Light Brown Hair
Al Jolson; *The Al Jolson Story-#5* . . . .(MCA)
Joan Baez; *Diamonds & Rust* . . . . (A&M)
Mormon Tabernacle Choir; *Beautiful Dreamer* . . . .(Columbia)
Mormon Tabernacle Choir's Greatest Hits-#3. . . . .(Columbia)
Old Beloved Songs . . . .(Columbia)
I'm Gonna Wash That Man Right Outta My Hair
Mitzi Gaynor; *ST/South Pacific*. . . . .(RCA)
Original Cast; *South Pacific*. . . . .(CBS Masterworks)
Weather Girls; *Success* . . . .(Columbia)
Just Put A Ribbon In Your Hair
Riders In The Sky; *Christmas The Country Way* . . . .(Rounder)
Kinky Afro
Happy Mondays; *Pills 'N' Thrills & Bellyaches* . . . .(Elektra)
Lend Me Your Comb
Beatles; *The Beatles-Anthology-#1* . . . .(Capitol)
Carl Perkins; *Carl Perkins-Original Sun Greatest Hits* . . . .(Rhino)
Little Dab'll Do Ya (Brylcreem)
Original Soundtrack; *TeeVee Toons-The Commercials-#1-C* . . . . . .(TVT)
Long Hair Queer
Vandals; *Slippery When Ill* . . . .(Restless)
Long Haired Country Boy
Charlie Daniels Band; *A Decade Of Hits* . . . .(Epic)
Fire On The Mountain . . . .(Epic)
Me & The Boys . . . .(Epic)
South's Greatest Hits-#2-C . . . .(Capricorn)
Trucker's Jukebox-#2-C . . . .(Legacy)
Volunteer Jam 3 & 4 . . . .(Epic)
Long Haired Guys From England
Too Much Joy; *Cereal Killers* . . . . (Giant)
Longhaired Redneck
David Allan Coe; *David Allan Coe-17 Greatest Hits* . . . .(Columbia)
For The Record-The First 10 Years . . . .(Columbia)
Longhaired Redneck . . . .(Columbia)
Meet Virginia
Train; *Now That's What I Call Music!-#4-C* . . . .(Virgin)
Train . . . .(Aware/C2/Columbia)
Motorcycle Cowboy
Merle Haggard; *Merle Haggard-Live At Billy Bob's*. . . . . (Razor & Tie)
Party Doll
Buddy Knox; *Best Of Buddy Knox*. . . . .(Rhino)
Billboard Top Rock 'N' Roll Hits-1957-C . . . .(Rhino)
ST/American Graffiti . . . .(MCA)
Pencil Thin Mustache
Jimmy Buffett; *Boats Beaches Bars & Ballads* . . . . (Margaritaville)
Living & Dying In 3/4 Time . . . .(MCA)
Songs You Know By Heart-Jimmy Buffett's Greatest Hit(s) . . . . .(MCA)
You Had To Be There . . . .(MCA)
Permanent Waves
Kinks; *Misfits* . . . .(Arista)
Prairie Wedding
Mark Knopfler; *Sailing To Philadelphia* . . . . (Warner Bros.)
Pretty Ballerina
Left Banke; *History Of The Left Banke* . . . .(Rhino)
Nuggets-#11-Pop-Rock-4-C . . . .(Rhino)
Red Headed Irishman
J.P. Fraley & Annadeene; *Wild Rose Of The Mountain* . . . .(Rounder)

Red Headed Stranger
Willie Nelson; *Red Headed Stranger* . . . .(Columbia)
What A Wonderful World . . . .(Columbia)
San Francisco (Be Sure To Wear Some Flowers In Your Hair)
Scott McKenzie; *Nuggets-#10-Folk Rock-C* . . . .(Rhino)
Rock Artifacts-From The Vaults-#3-C . . . .(Columbia)
ST/Forrest Gump. . . . . (Epic/Sony Music Soundtrax)
Summer Of Love-#1-C . . . .(Rhino)
Scarlet Ribbons (For Her Hair)
Harry Belafonte; *Harry Belafonte-Legendary Performer* . . . .(RCA)
Harry Belafonte's All Time Greatest Hits-#1 . . . .(RCA)
This Is Harry Belafonte . . . .(RCA)
Jim Ed Brown & Maxine Brown; *Essential Jim Ed Brown* . . . .(RCA)
Kingston Trio; *At Large/Here We Go Again!*. . . . .(Capitol)
Capitol Collectors Series-The Kingston Trio . . . .(Capitol)
Lennon Sisters; *Best Of The Lennon Sisters* . . . .(Ranwood)
Les Paul; *Legend & The Legacy-#1-4* . . . .(Capitol)
NRBQ; *Diggin' Uncle Q* . . . .(Rounder)
Patti Page; *Patti Page-16 Most Requested Songs* . . . .(Legacy)
Roger Whittaker; *Roger Whittaker-Classics Collection-#2* . . . .(Liberty)
She Ain't Got No Hair
Professor Longhair; *Mardi Gras In Baton Rouge* . . . .(Rhino)
She's A Rainbow
Rolling Stones; *Get Yer Ya-Ya's Out!* . . . .(Abkco)
More Hot Rocks (big hits & fazed cookies) . . . .(Abkco)
Singles Collection-The London Years . . . .(Abkco)
Their Satanic Majesties Request . . . .(Abkco)
Through The Past, Darkly (Big Hits Vol. 2) . . . .(Abkco)
Signs
Five Man Electrical Band; *Songs Of Protest-C* . . . .(Rhino)
Silver Haired Daddy Of Mine
Frankie Yankovic & His Yanks; *I Wish I Was 18 Again* . . . .(Smash)
Sister Golden Hair
America; *America Live* . . . . (Warner Bros.)
Billboard Top Rock 'N' Roll Hits-1975-C . . . .(Rhino)
History-Greatest Hits . . . . (Warner Bros.)
Stacked Actors
Foo Fighters; *There Is Nothing Left To Lose* . . . .(Roswell/RCA)
Suicide Blonde
INXS; *Live Baby Live*. . . . .(Atlantic)
X . . . .(Atlantic)
That Silver Haired Daddy Of Mine
Doc Watson; *My Dear Old Southern Home* . . . . (Sugar Hill)
Gene Autry; *The Country Music Hall Of Fame-Gene Autry-15 Of His All-Time Greatest Hits* . . . .(Columbia)
Touch Of Grey
Grateful Dead; *Heart Of Rock-C* . . . .(Columbia)
In The Dark . . . .(Arista)
Uneasy Rider
Charlie Daniels Band; *A Decade Of Hits* . . . .(Epic)
Homesick Heroes . . . .(Epic)
Super Hits Of The '70s-Have A Nice Day-#11-C . . . .(Rhino)
Uneasy Rider . . . .(Epic)
Where The Blue Of The Night Meets The Gold Of The Day
Bing Crosby; *All-Time Best Of*. . . . .(Curb)
Best Of Bing Crosby . . . .(MCA)
Where The Blue Of The Night Meets The Gold Of The Day . . . . . .(Biograph)
Wind Blows Her Hair
Seeds; *Nuggets-#9-Acid Rock-C* . . . .(Rhino)
XXX's And OOO's
Trisha Yearwood; *Thinkin' About You*. . . . .(MCA)

ANATOMY: HANDS, Fingers
See Also: **ANATOMY (various)**, *TOUCH*

All Around The World Or The Myth Of Fingerprints
Paul Simon; *Graceland* . . . . (Warner Bros.)
Bird In The Hand
Velvelettes; *25 Hard-To-Find Motown Classics-#3-C* . . . .(Motown)
Burden In My Hand
Soundgarden; *Down On The Upside* . . . .(A&M)
Burning Fingers
Shawn Phillips; *Collaboration*. . . . .(A&M)
California Nights
Lesley Gore; *Summer & Sun-C* . . . .(Rhino)
Circle Of Hands
Uriah Heep; *Demons And Wizards*. . . . .(Mercury)
Uriah Heep-Live . . . .(Mercury)
Clap Hands, Here Comes Charlie
Barbra Streisand; *ST/Funny Lady*. . . . .(Arista)
Charlie Barnet; *Big Band-1967* . . . . (Mobile Fidelity Sound Lab)
Clap Hands, Here Comes Charlie . . . . (Bluebird)
Complete Charlie Barnet-#6 . . . .(RCA)
Cold Hands From New York
Gordon Lightfoot; *United Artists Collection* . . . .(EMI)

Country's In The Best Of Hands
Original Cast; *Li'l Abner* .... (Columbia)
Crack Pipe (Burnin' My Hand)
Coolies; *Doug (A Rock Opera & Comic Book)* .... (DB)
Daddy's Hands
Holly Dunn; *Country Love Songs-C* ....(Warner Bros.)
  Holly Dunn .... (MTM)
Devil's Right Hand
Steve Earle; *Essential Steve Earle* ....(MCA)
Steve Earle & The Dukes; *Early Tracks* ....(Epic)
  Shut Up And Die Like An Aviator ....(MCA)
Waylon Jennings; *Will The Wolf Survive* ....(MCA)
Empty-Handed Heart
Warren Zevon; *Bad Luck Streak In Dancing School.* .... (Asylum)
Everything You Touch
Smokey Robinson; *Love Smokey* .... (Motown)
Fingerprint File
Rolling Stones; *It's Only Rock 'N Roll* ....(Rolling Stones)
  Love You Live. .... (Virgin)
Fingerprints
Larry Carlton; *Fingerprints* ....(Warner Bros.)
Fingertips-Pt 2
Little Stevie Wonder; *Motown Classic Hits-#2-C* .... (Motown)
Stevie Wonder; *Stevie Wonder's Greatest Hits* .... (Motown)
Fire Of The Newly Alive
Rosanne Cash; *The Wheel.* .... (Columbia)
Generous Palmstroke
Bjork; *Vespertine* .... (Elektra)
Getaway
Earth, Wind & Fire; *Best Of Earth, Wind & Fire-#1.* .... (Legacy)
  Spirit .... (Columbia)
Goldfinger
Shirley Bassey; *13 Original James Bond Themes-C.* ....(EMI)
  Best Of Shirley Bassey ....(EMI)
  Great Performances. .... (Liberty)
  Shirley Bassey-Live At Carnegie Hall .... (United Artists)
  Shirley Bassey's Greatest Hits. ....(EMI)
  ST/Goldfinger. .... (United Artists)
Grandma's Hands
Al Jarreau; *Improvisations* .... (Blue Moon)
Barbra Streisand; *Butterfly* .... (Columbia)
Bill Withers; *Bill Withers' Greatest Hits* .... (Columbia)
  Bill Withers Live At Carnegie Hall .... (Columbia)
Keb' Mo'; *Big Wide Grin* .... (Sony Wonder)
Hand In Hand
Elmore James; *Collectables Blues Collection-#3-C* ..... (Collectables)
  Golden Classics-Elmore James .... (Collectables)
Hand In Hand
Three O'Clock; *Arrive Without Traveling* ....(I.R.S.)
Hand In Hand
Phil Collins; *Face Value.* .... (Atlantic)
Hand In Hand
BoDeans; *Home* .... (Slash)
Hand In Hand
Dire Straits; *Making Movies* ....(Warner Bros.)
Hand In Hand
Elvis Costello; *This Year's Model.* ....(Rykodisc)
Hand In My Pocket
Alanis Morissette; *Jagged Little Pill.* ....(Maverick)
Hand Of Fate
Rolling Stones; *Black And Blue* ....(Rolling Stones)
Hand Song, The
Nickel Creek; *Nickel Creek* .... (Sugar Hill)
Hand That Feeds
Aerosmith; *Draw The Line* .... (Columbia)
Hand That Rocks The Cradle
Glen Campbell; *Country Classics-#10-1987-C* .... (Universal)
  Still Within The Sound Of My Voice ....(MCA)
Hand That Rocks The Cradle
Smiths; *Smiths* .... (Sire)
Hand To Hold On To
John Cougar; *American Fool* .... (Riva)
Handful Of Dust
Patty Loveless; *When Fallen Angels Fly.* ....(Epic)
Hands
Jewel; *Spirit* .... (Atlantic)
Hands Across The Table
Art Tatum; *Tatum Group Masterpieces-#4-Part 2* ....(Pablo)
Hands In The Air
Bob Seger; *It's A Mystery* .... (Capitol)
Hands To Heaven
Breathe; *All That Jazz* .... (A&M)
Healing Hands
Elton John; *Sleeping With The Past* ....(MCA)
Healing Hands Of Time
Willie Nelson; *Healing Hands Of Time* .... (Liberty)
Hemorrhage (In My Hands)
Fuel; *Now That's What I Call Music!-#6-C* .... (Virgin)

Something Like Human .... (Epic)
He's Got The Whole World In His Hands
Laurie London; *Rock 'N Roll's Greatest Hits Of All Time-#10-
  '50s-C* ....(Platinum Disc)
Mormon Tabernacle Choir; *Mormon Tabernacle Choir's Greatest
  Hits-#2.* .... (Columbia)
Odetta; *Essential Odetta* .... (Vanguard)
Hip Shake
Rolling Stones; *Exile On Main Street* ....(Virgin)
Hold An Old Friend's Hand
Rita Coolidge; *Fall Into Spring* .... (A&M)
Tiffany; *Hold An Old Friend's Hand* ....(MCA)
Hold My Hand
Hootie & The Blowfish; *Cracked Rear View.* ....(Atlantic)
Hold My Hand
Don Cornell; *Hold My Hand* ....(MCA Special Prod.)
Holdin' A Good Hand
Lee Greenwood; *Holdin' A Good Hand* .... (Capitol)
Home In My Hand
Foghat; *Best Of Foghat* .... (Rhino)
  Energized .... (Rhino)
  Foghat-Live .... (Rhino)
Home In My Hand
Dave Edmunds; *Repeat When Necessary* .... (Swan Song)
Human Hands
Elvis Costello & The Attractions; *Imperial Bedroom* .... (Columbia)
I Got Id
Pearl Jam; *Merkinball* .... (Epic)
I Made A Fist
Original Broadway Cast; *The Most Happy Fella.* .... (Sony Music Classical)
I Want To Hold Your Hand
Beatles; *Beatles 1* .... (Capitol)
  Beatles-20 Greatest Hits .... (Capitol)
  Meet The Beatles! .... (Capitol)
  Past Masters-Volume One .... (Parlophone)
  The Beatles/1962-1966. .... (Capitol)
Lakeside; *Galactic Grooves/Best Of Lakeside* .... (Right Stuff)
  Your Wish Is My Command .... (Solar)
If You're Happy & You Know It
Original Soundtrack; *Children's Favorites* ....(Kid Rhino/Rhino 4 Kids)
Keep Your Hands Off My Baby
Trashmen; *Bird Call! The Twin City Stomp Of The
  Trashmen.* ....(Sundazed Music)
Kitty
Presidents Of The United States Of America; *The Presidents Of The United
  States Of America* ....(Columbia)
Lay Your Hands On Me
Thompson Twins; *Greatest Mixes-Best Of The Thompson Twins* .... (Arista)
  Greenpeace/Rainbow Warriors-C .... (Geffen)
  Here's To Future Days .... (Arista)
  ST/Perfect. .... (Arista)
Lay Your Hands On Me
Bon Jovi; *New Jersey* .... (Jambco)
Lay Your Hands On Me
Peter Gabriel; *Security* .... (Geffen)
Lend A Helpin' Hand
Lynyrd Skynyrd; *Skynyrd's First & Last* .... (MCA)
Linger
Cranberries; *Everybody Else Is Doing It, So Why Can't We?* .... (Island)
Linger
Jonatha Brooke; *Steady Pull* .... (Bad Dog)
Lipstick On A Fingertip
Victor Mecyssne; *Personal Mercury.* .... (Sweetfish)
Longneck Bottle
Garth Brooks; *Sevens* .... (Capitol)
Look Heart No Hands
Randy Travis; *Randy Travis' Greatest Hits-#2.* .... (Warner Bros.)
Lord Take My Hand
Maddox Brothers & Rose; *On The Air-#1 & 2* ....(Arhoolie)
Love Is In Control (Finger On The Trigger)
Donna Summer; *Donna Summer.* .... (Geffen)
Lovely Hula Hands
101 Strings Orchestra; *Sound Of Magnificence* .... (Alshire)
Magic Fingers (25 Cents)
Birdsongs Of The Mesozoic; *Faultline* .... (Cuneiform)
Man With The Golden Thumb
Jerry Reed; *Man With The Golden Thumb.* .... (RCA)
My Fate Is In Your Hands
Fats Waller; *Piano Solos-1929-1941.* ....(RCA)
  Rare Piano Roll Solos-#3. ....(Biograph)
  Turn On The Heat-Fats Waller Piano Solos. .... (Bluebird)
Nothin' But The Taillights
Clint Black; *Nothin' But The Taillights.* ....(RCA)
On The Other Hand
Randy Travis; *Randy Travis' Greatest Hits-#1* .... (Warner Bros.)
  Storms Of Life .... (Warner Bros.)
Our Hands
Bjork; *Vespertine* .... (Elektra)

Praying Hands
Devo; *Live-The Mongoloid Years* (Rykodisc)
Q: Are We Not Men? A: We Are Devo! (Warner Bros.)
Precious Lord, Take My Hand
Linda Hopkins; *How Blue Can You Get* (Quicksilver)
Preservation Hall Jazz Band; *Best Of The Preservation Hall Jazz Band* (Columbia)
Put That Ring On My Finger
Andrews Sisters; *50th Anniversary Collection-#2* (MCA)
Woody Herman; *Best Of The Big Bands-C* (Columbia)
Put Your Hand In The Hand
Anne Murray; *Anne Murray-Country* (Capitol)
Danny's Song (Capitol)
Snowbird (Capitol)
Elvis Presley; *Canadian Tribute* (RCA)
Elvis Now (RCA)
Ocean; *Super Hits Of The '70s-Have A Nice Day-#4-C* (Rhino)
Put Your Hands On The Screen
Martin Briley; *One Night With A Stranger* (Mercury)
Put Your Hands Together
O'Jays; *Live In London* (Philadelphia Int'l)
Ship Ahoy (Philadelphia Int'l)
Put Your Hands Where My Eyes Could See
Busta Rhymes; *When Disaster Strikes* (Elektra)
Raise Your Hand
Bruce Springsteen & The E Street Band; *Bruce Springsteen & The E Street Band Live/1975-85* (Legacy)
Eddie Floyd; *Knock On Wood* (Atlantic)
Stax/Volt Revue-#2-Live In Paris-C (Atlantic)
J. Geils Band; *Blow Your Face Out* (Rhino)
Raise Your Hands
Bon Jovi; *Slippery When Wet* (Jambco)
Reach Out And Touch
Diana Ross; *Diana Ross-All The Great Hits* (Motown)
Diana Ross-Anthology (Motown)
Live At Caesar's Palace (Motown)
Most Played Songs On America's Jukeboxes (Motown)
Motown Story-First 25 Years-C (Motown)
Ready, Willing And Able
Lari White; *Best Of Lari White* (RCA)
Don't Fence Me In (RCA)
Riding My Thumb To Mexico
Johnny Rodriguez; *40 Years Of Country Music-#3-1970-1979-C* (Mercury)
All I Ever Meant To Do (Mercury)
Desperado (Mercury)
Johnny Rodriguez's Greatest Hits (Mercury)
Right Hand Man
Eddy Raven; *Best Of Eddy Raven* (RCA)
Right Hand Man (RCA)
Right Hand Of God
Move; *Yeah Whatever* (Atlantic)
Right In The Palm Of Your Hand
Crystal Gayle; *Crystal* (EMI)
Favorites-Crystal Gayle (Liberty)
Mel McDaniel; *Countryfied* (Capitol)
Right Left Hand
George Jones; *Greatest Country Hits Of The '80s-1987-C* (Columbia)
More Hot Country Requests-#2-C (Epic)
Wine-Colored Glasses (Epic)
Ring On Her Finger, Time On Her Hands
Lee Greenwood; *Best Of Lee Greenwood-God Bless America* (Curb)
Inside Out/You've Got A Good Love Comin' (MCA)
Lee Greenwood's Greatest Hits (MCA)
Lee Greenwood-Super Hits (Epic)
Reba McEntire; *Starting Over* (MCA)
Rollin'
Limp Bizkit; *Chocolate Starfish & The Hotdog Flavored Water* (Flip/Interscope)
Sable On Blond
Stevie Nicks; *Wild Heart* (Modern)
Shackles (Praise You)
Mary Mary; *Thankful* (C2/Columbia)
Shake A Hand
LaVern Baker; *Soul On Fire* (Atlantic)
Little Richard; *Fabulous Little Richard* (Specialty)
Georgia Peach (Specialty)
Shake And Fingerpop
Junior Walker & The All Stars; *Junior Walker & The All Stars' Greatest Hits* (Motown)
Junior Walker & The All Stars-All The Great Hits (Motown)
Junior Walker & The All Stars-Anthology (Motown)
Shotgun (Motown)
Shake My Mother's Hand
Bill Monroe & His Blue Grass Boys; *Mule Skinner Blues* (RCA)
She Put Her Hand Where My Money Was
John Lee; *Down At The Depot* (Rounder)
Skin
Madonna; *Ray Of Light* (Maverick)
Slow Hand
Conway Twitty; *Conway Twitty's Greatest Hits* (Curb)
Latest Greatest Hits-#1 (Warner Bros.)
Number One's: The Warner Bros. Years (Warner Bros.)
Pointer Sisters; *Black & White* (Planet)
Pointer Sisters' Greatest Hits (RCA)
Sweet & Soulful (RCA)
Snap Your Fingers
Barbara Lewis; *Hello Stranger-The Best Of Barbara Lewis* (Rhino)
Dick Curless; *The Drag 'Em Off The Interstate, Sock It To 'Em Hits Of Dick Curless* (Razor & Tie)
Don Gibson; *Best Of Don Gibson-#1* (Curb)
Joe Henderson; *Discoveries Presents-Stereo Oldies-C* (Varese Vintage)
Ronnie Milsap; *Essential Ronnie Milsap* (RCA)
Heart & Soul (RCA)
Ronnie Milsap's Greatest Hits-#3 (RCA)
Snap Your Fingers
Teena Marie; *Ivory* (Epic)
Soul Finger
Bar-Kays; *Atlantic Rhythm & Blues 1947-1974-#6 (1966-1969)-C* (Atlantic)
Soul Finger (Rhino)
Soul Shots-#3-Soul Twist-C (Rhino)
Top Of The Stax-Twenty Greatest Hits-#2-C (Stax)
Stinkfist
Tool; *Aenima* (Freeworld/Capitol)
Sun In My Hand
Scorpions; *Best Of The Scorpions-#2* (RCA)
In Trance (RCA)
Take My Hand
Los Lobos; *The Neighborhood* (Slash)
Takin' Love Into My Own Hands
Sylvester; *12 By 12-Collection* (Megatone)
Taking My Life In Your Hands
Elvis Costello & The Brodsky Quartet; *Juliet Letters* (Warner Bros.)
Taking You Home
Don Henley; *Inside Job* (Warner Bros.)
Tear In Your Hand
Tori Amos; *Little Earthquakes* (Atlantic)
Tender Moment, A
Lee Roy Parnell; *Hits And Highways Ahead* (Arista)
Love Without Mercy (Arista)
Pure Country-Best Of The '90s-C (Priority)
This Bottle (In My Hand)
David Allan Coe & George Jones; *David Allan Coe-17 Greatest Hits* (Columbia)
For The Record-The First 10 Years (Columbia)
Through Your Hands
Don Henley; *ST/Michael* (Revolution)
Time On My Hands
Billie Holiday; *Billie Holiday* (Columbia)
Quintessential-#8-1939-1940 (Legacy)
The Billie Holiday Story-#2 (Columbia)
Duke Ellington; *Lullaby Of Birdland* (Intermedia)
Glenn Miller; *Best Of The Big Bands-C* (Columbia)
Time On My Hands
Sweet Honey In The Rock; *Good News* (Flying Fish)
Tips Of My Fingers
Bill Anderson; *Bill Anderson's Greatest Hits* (MCA)
The Bill Anderson Story (MCA)
Eddy Arnold; *Best Of Eddy Arnold-#2* (Dunhill Compact Classics)
Roy Clark; *Best Of Roy Clark* (MCA)
Roy Clark's Greatest Hits (MCA)
Yesterday When I Was Young (MCA)
Steve Wariner; *I Am Ready* (Arista)
Too Many Hands
Eagles; *One Of These Nights* (Asylum)
Too Much Time On My Hands
Styx; *Caught In The Act* (A&M)
Paradise Theater (A&M)
Styx-Classics-#15 (A&M)
Touch A Hand, Make A Friend
Oak Ridge Boys; *Country's Greatest Hits-#4-C* (MCA Special Prod.)
Oak Ridge Boys' Greatest Hits 3 (MCA)
Step On Out (MCA)
Staple Singers; *15 Original Big Hits-#4-C* (Stax)
Staple Singers-Chronicle (Stax)
Top Of The Stax-Twenty Greatest Hits-#2-C (Stax)
Touch Me (All Night Long)
Cathy Dennis; *Move To This* (Polydor)
Touch The Hand
Bryan Adams; *Waking Up The Neighbours* (A&M)
Under My Thumb
Rolling Stones; *''Still Life'' (American Concert 1981)* (Virgin)
12 X 5 (Abkco)
Aftermath (Abkco)
got Live if you want it! (Abkco)
Hot Rocks 1964-1971 (Abkco)
Who; *Odds & Sods* (MCA)
Who's Missing (MCA)

Walk Hand In Hand
Andy Williams; *I Like Your Kind Of Love-The Best Of The Cadence Years* . . . . (Varese Vintage)
Whatever Happens
Michael Jackson; *Invincible* . . . .(Epic)
When I Need You
Celine Dion; *Let's Talk About Love-C* . . . . (550 Music)
Leo Sayer; *'70s Greatest Rock Hits-#5-Kickin' Back-C* . . . . (Priority)
Show Must Go On-Anthology . . . . (Rhino)
When You Put Your Hands On Me
Christina Aguilera; *Christina Aguilera* . . . . (RCA)
White Knuckles
Elvis Costello & The Attractions; *Trust* . . . .(Rykodisc)
Wiggley Fingers
Patty Griffin; *Flaming Red* . . . . (A&M)
Will Jesus Wash The Bloodstains From Your Hands
Bill Frisell; *Nashville* . . . . (Nonesuch)
Exene Cervenka; *Running Sacred* . . . . (Rhino)
Willie & The Hand Jive
Eric Clapton; *461 Ocean Boulevard* . . . . (Polydor)
Time Pieces-#1-The Best Of Eric Clapton . . . . (Polydor)
George Thorogood & The Destroyers; *Maverick* . . . .(EMI)
Johnny Otis; *All-Time Greatest Hits Of Rock 'N' Roll-C* . . . . (Curb)
Capitol Years-Johnny Otis . . . . (Capitol)
Let The Good Times Roll-C . . . . (Capitol)
World Is Changing Hands
Dave Davies; *Dave Davies* . . . . (RCA)
Wrapped Around
Brad Paisley; *Brad Paisley-Part II* . . . . (Arista)
Wrapped Around Your Finger
Police; *Every Breath You Take-The Classics* . . . . (A&M)
Message In A Box-Complete Recordings . . . . (A&M)
Police-Live . . . . (A&M)
Synchronicity . . . . (A&M)
You Don't Know Me
Ray Charles; *Ray Charles-Complete Country & Western Recordings 1959-1986* . . . . (Rhino)
You're Gonna Get Your Fingers Burned
Alan Parsons Project; *Eye In The Sky* . . . . (Arista)
Very Best Live . . . . (RCA Victor)

ANATOMY: HEAD

See Also: ANATOMY (various), HATS

(Lay Your Head On My) Pillow
Tony Toni Tone; *Sons Of Soul* . . . . (Wing)
Anotherloverholenyohead
Prince and the Revolution; *Parade-Music From "Under The Cherry Moon"* . . . . (Paisley Park)
Bald Head
Professor Longhair; *Crawfish Fiesta* . . . . (Alligator)
Last Mardi Gras . . . . (Atlantic)
Banging My Head Against The Moon
John David Souther; *Black Rose* . . . . (Asylum)
Bird On My Head
David Seville; *45-#063* . . . . (United Artists)
Brain Damage
Pink Floyd; *Dark Side Of The Moon* . . . . (Capitol)
Pink Floyd-Gift Set . . . . (Capitol)
Works . . . . (Capitol)
Bullet In The Head
Rage Against The Machine; *Rage Against The Machine* . . (Epic Portrait Assoc.)
Caldonia (What Makes Your Big Head So Hard?)
Louis Jordan; *No Moe! Louis Jordan's Greatest Hits* . . . . (Verve)
Original Cast; *Five Guys Named Moe* . . . . (Columbia)
Woody Herman & His Orchestra; *Verve Jazz Masters 54* . . . . (Verve)
Can't Get It Out Of My Head
Electric Light Orchestra; *Eldorado* . . . . (Jet)
Electric Light Orchestra's Greatest Hits . . . . (Jet)
Exposition . . . . (Epic)
Ole ELO . . . . (Jet)
Crazy Baldhead
Bob Marley & The Wailers; *Rastaman Vibration* . . . . (Tuff Gong)
Rebel Music . . . . (Tuff Gong)
Songs Of Freedom . . . . (Tuff Gong)
Cuttin' Heads
John Mellencamp; *Cuttin' Heads* . . . . (Columbia)
Don't Talk (Put Your Head On My Shoulder)
Beach Boys; *Pet Sounds* . . . . (Capitol)
The Pet Sounds Sessions: A 30th Anniversary Collection . . . . (Capitol)
Linda Ronstadt; *Winter Light* . . . . (Elektra)
Dope Head Blues
Victoria Spivey; *News & The Blues-Telling It Like It Is-C* . . . . (Columbia)
Girl Inside My Head
Blues Traveler; *Bridge* . . . . (A&M)

Goin' Out Of My Head
Lettermen; *Best Of The Lettermen-#2* . . . . (Capitol)
The Lettermen's All-Time Greatest Hits . . . . (Capitol)
Little Anthony And The Imperials; *Best Of Little Anthony And The Imperials* . . . . (Rhino)
EMI Legends Of Rock & Roll-24 Greatest Hits-C . . . . (EMI)
Hard Headed Woman
Elvis Presley; *Billboard Top Rock 'N' Roll Hits-1958-C* . . . . (Rhino)
Number One Hits . . . . (RCA)
ST/King Creole . . . . (RCA)
The Top Ten Hits . . . . (RCA)
Worldwide 50 Gold Award Hits, Vol. 1, Parts 1 & 2 . . . . (RCA)
Hard Headed Woman
Cat Stevens; *Cat Stevens Greatest Hits* . . . . (A&M)
Tea For The Tillerman . . . . (A&M)
Head First
Babys; *Babys-Anthology* . . . . (Chrysalis)
Head First . . . . (Chrysalis)
Head Games
Foreigner; *Head Games* . . . .(Atlantic)
Records . . . .(Atlantic)
Head On
Jesus & Mary Chain; *Automatic* . . . . (Warner Bros.)
Head Over Feet
Alanis Morissette; *Jagged Little Pill* . . . . (Maverick)
Head Over Heels
Go-Go's; *Go-Go's Greatest* . . . . (I.R.S.)
Talk Show . . . . (I.R.S.)
Head Over Heels
Allure; *The Greatest Dance Album In The World-C* . . . . (Epic)
Allure featuring NAS; *Allure* . . . . (Track Masters/Crave)
Head Over Heels
Accept; *Balls To The Wall* . . . . (Portrait)
Head Over Heels
Tears For Fears; *Songs From The Big Chair* . . . . (Mercury)
Head Over Heels
Tony Terry; *Tony Terry* . . . . (Epic)
Head To Toe
Lisa Lisa & Cult Jam; *Spanish Fly* . . . . (Columbia)
Headkeeper
Dave Mason; *Classic Rock-#2-C* . . . . (MCA)
Headkeeper . . . . (MCA)
It's Like You Never Left . . . . (Columbia)
Very Best Of Dave Mason . . . . (MCA)
Headlong
Queen; *Classic Queen* . . . . (Hollywood)
Innuendo . . . . (Hollywood)
Queen-Collection . . . . (Hollywood)
Hemphead
P.O.L.; *Parade Of Losers* . . . .(Giant)
High Head Blues
Black Crowes; *Amorica* . . . . (American)
Hip Shake
Rolling Stones; *Exile On Main Street* . . . .(Virgin)
Hold Your Head Up
Argent; *Argent-Anthology-Collection Of Greatest Hits* . . . . (Epic)
Encore-Argent . . . . (Epic)
Rock Artifacts-From The Vaults-#1-C . . . . (Columbia)
ST/Queen's Logic . . . . (Epic)
Hole In My Head
Dixie Chicks; *Fly* . . . . (Monument)
Hopeless
Dionne Farris; *ST/Love Jones* . . . . (Columbia)
I Know What I Know
Paul Simon; *Graceland* . . . . (Warner Bros.)
I Wish You Could Have Turned My Head
Oak Ridge Boys; *Bobbie Sue* . . . . (MCA)
It's All In Your Head
Diamond Rio; *Diamond Rio IV* . . . . (Arista)
Diamond Rio's Greatest Hits . . . . (Arista)
Keep Their Heads Ringin'
Dr. Dre; *Hip Hop's Most Wanted-C* . . . . (Priority)
ST/Friday . . . . (Priority)
Keep Your Head To The Sky
Earth, Wind & Fire; *Best Of Earth, Wind & Fire-#2* . . . . (Columbia)
Elements Of Love: The Ballads . . . . (Legacy)
Head To The Sky . . . . (Columbia)
Knock It On The Head
Wood; *Songs From Stamford Hill* . . . . (Columbia)
Machinehead
Bush; *Sixteen Stone* . . . .(Trauma)
Man With The Lightbulb Head
Robyn Hitchcock & The Egyptians; *Fegmania* . . . .(Slash)
Maxwell's Silver Hammer
Beatles; *Abbey Road* . . . . (Parlophone)
My Head Hurts, My Feet Stink And I Don't Love Jesus
Jimmy Buffett; *Havana Daydreamin'* . . . . (MCA)

My Head's In Mississippi
ZZ Top; *Recycler*. . . . . (Warner Bros.)
ZZ Top's Greatest Hits . . . . (Warner Bros.)
Mystical Potato Head Groove Thing
Joe Satriani; *Flying In A Blue Dream*. . . . .(Relativity)
Over My Head
Fleetwood Mac; *25 Years-The Chain* . . . . (Warner Bros.)
Fleetwood Mac. . . . .(Reprise)
Fleetwood Mac Live . . . . (Warner Bros.)
Fleetwood Mac's Greatest Hits . . . . (Warner Bros.)
Potato Head Blues
Louis Armstrong; *Louis Armstrong-Best Of The Decca Years-#2-The*
Composer-C. . . . . (MCA)
You Rascal You. . . . .(Pro-Arte)
Pumpkin Head
Dharma Bums; *Bliss* . . . . (Frontier)
Put Your Head On My Shoulder
Lettermen; *Capitol Collectors Series-The Lettermen* . . . . (Capitol)
The Lettermen's All-Time Greatest Hits . . . . (Capitol)
Paul Anka; *Oldies But Goodies-#1-C* . . . .(Original Sound)
Paul Anka-30th Anniversary Anthology . . . .(Rhino)
Paul Anka's 21 Golden Hits . . . . (RCA)
Remember Diana . . . . (RCA)
Radio Head
Talking Heads; *True Stories* . . . . (Sire)
Raindrops Keep Fallin' On My Head
B.J. Thomas; *'70s Greatest Rock Hits-#9-#1 Hits-C* . . . .(Priority)
B.J. Thomas' Greatest Hits . . . . (Rhino)
B.J. Thomas-16 Greatest Hits . . . . (Trip)
Best Of B.J. Thomas . . . . (Dominion Entert.)
ST/Butch Cassidy & The Sundance Kid . . . . (A&M)
ST/Forrest Gump . . . . (Epic/Sony Music Soundtrax)
Screaming Skull
Fleshtones; *Living Legends* . . . . (I.R.S.)
Shake Your Heads
Accept; *Accept*. . . . . (Portrait)
Restless & Wild. . . . . (Portrait)
Suedehead
Morrissey; *Bona Drag* . . . .(Sire)
Viva Hate . . . .(Sire)
Turn My Head
Live; *Secret Samadhi* . . . . (Radioactive/MCA)
Two Headed Cow
Ennui; *Olive* . . . . (Slamdek)
Two Headed Dog (Red Temple Prayer)
Roky Erickson; *You're Gonna Miss Me-Best Of Roky Erickson* . . . . . . (Restless)
Two Headed Man
Lonnie Brooks; *Genuine Houserockin' Music-#3-C* . . . .(Alligator)
Two Headed Sex Change
Cramps; *Look Mom No Head!* . . . . (Restless)
Up Above My Head/Blind Bartimus
Marty Stuart with Jerry & Tammy Sullivan; *Red Hot + Country-C* . . . (Mercury)
Voices In My Head
Naked Eyes; *Best Of Naked Eyes*. . . . . (EMI)
Voices Inside My Head
Police; *Zenyatta Mondatta*. . . . . (A&M)
You Go To My Head
Billie Holiday; *At Storyville*. (Black Lion)
First Verve Sessions . . . . (Verve)
Bing Crosby; *The Radio Years: 20 Songs* . . . . (Crescendo)
Frank Sinatra; *Nice 'N' Easy* . . . . (Capitol)
Round #1 . . . . (Capitol)
Voice: The Columbia Years-1943-1952 . . . .(Columbia)
Linda Ronstadt; *For Sentimental Reasons* . . . . (Asylum)
You Wouldn't Believe
311; *From Chaos*. (Volcano Entertainment)

ANATOMY: LEGS, Knees

See Also: **ANATOMY (various)**

Ana's Song (Open Fire)
Silverchair; *Neon Ballroom*. . . . . (Epic)
By Your Side
Sade; *Lovers Rock* . . . . (Epic)
Cuyahoga
R.E.M.; *Life's Rich Pageant* . . . . (EMI-Capitol Entert. Properties)
Death On Two Legs
Queen; *A Night At The Opera* . . . .(Hollywood)
Live Killers . . . .(Hollywood)
Don't You Feel My Leg
Maria Muldaur; *Maria Muldaur* . . . .(Reprise)
Down On My Knees
Bread; *Baby I'm-A Want You*. . . . . (Elektra)
Best Of Bread . . . . (Elektra)
Bread-Anthology . . . . (Elektra)

Down On My Knees
Beth Nielsen Chapman; *Beth Nielsen Chapman* . . . . (Reprise)
Trisha Yearwood; *Hearts In Armor* . . . .(MCA)
Falling In Love (Is Hard On The Knees)
Aerosmith; *A Little South Of Sanity* . . . .(Geffen)
Nine Lives . . . .(Columbia)
Get A Leg Up
John Mellencamp; *Whenever We Wanted* . . . .(Mercury)
Hangman's Knee
Jeff Beck Group; *Beck-Ola* . . . . (Epic)
Hot Legs
Rod Stewart; *Absolutely Live* . . . .(Warner Bros.)
Footloose & Fancy Free . . . . (Warner Bros.)
Rod Stewart's Greatest Hits . . . . (Warner Bros.)
Storyteller/The Complete Anthology: 1964-1990 . . . . (Warner Bros.)
Just Another Thigh
Roxy Music; *Siren* . . . .(Atco)
Knee Deep In The Blues
Guy Mitchell; *Guy Mitchell-16 Most Requested Songs* . . . .(Legacy)
Marty Robbins; *Columbia Country Classics-#2-Honky Tonk*
Heroes-C . . . .(Columbia)
Lifetime Of Song-1951-1982 . . . .(Columbia)
Marty Robbins' Greatest Hits . . . . (Columbia)
Layla
Derek And The Dominos; *Classic Rock 1966-1988-C* . . . . (Atlantic)
Eric Clapton-Crossroads-C . . . . (Polydor)
Layla . . . . (Polydor)
ST/Goodfellas . . . . (Atlantic)
Eric Clapton; *Eric Clapton-Unplugged* . . . . (Reprise)
Legs
ZZ Top; *Eliminator* . . . . (Warner Bros.)
Long Legged Guitar Pickin' Man
Johnny Cash & June Carter; *Johnny Cash's Greatest Hits-#2* . . . .(Columbia)
Long Legged Hannah (From Butte, Montana)
Jesse Hunter; *A Man Like Me* . . . . (BNA)
Lord Of The Thighs
Aerosmith; *Aerosmith-Classics Live* . . . .(Columbia)
Gems . . . .(Columbia)
Get Your Wings . . . .(Columbia)
Live! Bootleg . . . .(Columbia)
Pandora's Box . . . .(Columbia)
On Bended Knee
Boyz II Men; *Boyz II Men II*. . . . .(Motown)
Skinny Legs And All
Joe Tex; *I Believe I'm Gonna Make It!-Best Of Joe Tex*. . . . .(Rhino)
Joe Tex's Greatest Hits . . . .(Curb)
Soul Years-C . . . . (Atlantic)
Televisions On My Leg
Squirrels; *What Gives?*. . . . . (Pop Llama Prod.)
Thigh Ride
Tawatha; *Welcome To My Dream* . . . .(Epic)
Thong Song
Sisqo; *Unleash The Dragon* . . . . (Dragon/Def Soul/IDJMG)

ANATOMY: LIPS

See Also: **ANATOMY (various), COSMETICS, KISSING**

Cautious Lip
Blondie; *Plastic Letters* . . . .(Chrysalis)
Cowboy Lips
Bobs; *The Bobs* . . . .(Rhino)
Fat Lip
Sum 41; *All Killer No Filler* . . . . (Island/IDJMG)
Now That's What I Call Music!-#8-C . . . . (Virgin)
Hip Shake
Rolling Stones; *Exile On Main Street*. . . . . (Virgin)
Hot Lips
Django Reinhardt; *Djangologie USA-#3 & 4* . . . . (DRG)
Harry James; *Mr. Trumpet* . . . .(Hindsight)
Stephane Grappelli; *Shades Of Django* . . . .(Verve)
I Wanna Hear It From Your Lips
Eric Carmen; *Eric Carmen*. . . . . (Geffen)
Louise Mandrell; *Dreamin'* . . . . (RCA)
If He Moves His Lips
Shemekia Copeland; *Wicked* . . . . (Alligator)
In The Mood
Andrews Sisters; *Andrews Sisters-16 Great Performances* . . . . (MCA)
Boogie Woogie Bugle Girls . . . . (MCA)
Chesterfield Broadcasts-#1 . . . . (RCA Victor)
Bette Midler; *Bette Midler* . . . . (Atlantic)
Live At Last . . . . (Atlantic)
Glenn Miller; *Best Of Glenn Miller* . . . . (RCA)
Glenn Miller-A Legendary Performer-#1 & 2 . . . .(Bluebird)
The Glenn Miller Story . . . . (RCA)
Glenn Miller & His Orchestra; *Glenn Miller & His Orchestra-*
Pure Gold . . . .(Bluebird)

The Unforgettable Glenn Miller & His Orchestra . . . . (RCA)
Kiss Of Fire
Georgia Gibbs; *Best Of Georgia Gibbs-The Mercury Years* . . . . (Chronicles)
Tony Martin; *Best Of Tony Martin On RCA* . . . . (Collector's Choice)
Kiss This
Aaron Tippin; *People Like Us* . . . . (Lyric Street)
Lip Service
Elvis Costello; *This Year's Model* . . . . (Rykodisc)
Lip Service
Michael Franks; *Camera Never Lies* . . . . (Warner Bros.)
Lip Service
John Astley; *Everyone Loves The Pilot Except The Crew* . . . . (Atlantic)
Lip Service
Jimmy Buffett; *Somewhere Over China* . . . . (MCA)
Lipgloss
Pulp; *His 'N' Hers* . . . . (Island)
Lips Like Sugar
Echo & The Bunnymen; *Echo & The Bunnymen* . . . . (Sire)
Just Say Yes...Sire's Winter CD Sampler-C . . . . (Sire)
Lipstick
Suzi Quatro; *The Wild One-Classic Quatro* . . . . (Razor & Tie)
Lipstick
Buzzcocks; *Operators Manual (Buzzcocks Best)* . . . . (I.R.S.)
Singles Going Steady . . . . (I.R.S.)
Lipstick And Leather
Y & T; *Best Of Y & T 81-85* . . . . (A&M)
Lipstick Don't Lie
Mark Collie; *Tennessee Plates* . . . . (Giant)
Lipstick Lies
Pat Benatar; *Live From Earth* . . . . (Chrysalis)
Lipstick On A Fingertip
Victor Mecyssne; *Personal Mercury* . . . . (Sweetfish)
Lipstick On My Dick
Luke; *Luke's Greatest Hits* . . . . (Lil' Joe)
Lipstick On The Radio
Neal McCoy; *Life Of The Party* . . . . (Atlantic)
Lipstick On Your Collar
Connie Francis; *Very Best Of Connie Francis* . . . . (Polydor)
Lipstick Promises
George Ducas; *George Ducas* . . . . (Capitol)
I Love Country-Hits Of The '90s-#4-C . . . . (Priority)
Lipstick Sunset
John Hiatt; *Bring The Family* . . . . (A&M)
Hiatt Comes Alive At Budokan . . . . (A&M)
John Hiatt's Greatest Hits The A&M Years '87-'94 . . . . (A&M)
Lipstick Traces (On A Cigarette)
Amazing Rhythm Aces; *Amazing Rhythm Aces* . . . . (MCA)
Benny Spellman; *Fortune Teller-Golden Classics* . . . . (Collectables)
History Of New Orleans R&B-#3-1962-1970-C . . . . (Rhino)
It Will Stand-Minit Records-1960-1963-C . . . . (EMI)
Delbert McClinton; *Live From Austin* . . . . (Alligator)
Plain From The Heart-Classics-#2 . . . . (Curb)
O'Jays; *Beg, Scream & Shout! The Big Ol' Box Of '60s Soul-C* . . . . . . (Rhino)
Soul Shots-#10-More Sweet Soul-C . . . . (Rhino)
Ringo Starr; *Bad Boy* . . . . (Epic)
Lipstick Vogue
Elvis Costello; *2 1/2 Years* . . . . (Rykodisc)
This Year's Model . . . . (Rykodisc)
Lipstick, Powder & Paint
Big Joe Turner; *Rhythm & Blues Years* . . . . (Rhino)
Delbert McClinton; *The Ultimate Collection-Delbert McClinton* . . . . . . (Hip-O)
Lollipop Lips
Connie Francis; *Connie Francis-Souvenirs* . . . . (Polydor)
Lyin' Comes So Easy To Your Lips
David Allan Coe; *D.A.C.* . . . . (Columbia)
My Lips Remember Your Kisses
Nat "King" Cole; *1941-1943* . . . . (Classics)
My Shoes Keep Walking Back To You
Ray Price; *All Time Legends Of Country Music-C* . . . . (Legacy)
Essential Ray Price-1951-1962 . . . . (Columbia)
Ray Price's Greatest Hits . . . . (Columbia)
Our Lips Are Sealed
Go-Go's; *Beauty & The Beat* . . . . (I.R.S.)
Go-Go's Greatest . . . . (I.R.S.)
Read My Lips
Mary Chapin Carpenter; *Hitchhiker Exampler-C* . . . . (Columbia)
Hot Country Rock-#2-C . . . . (Epic)
State Of The Heart . . . . (Columbia)
Read My Lips
Jimmy Somerville; *Jimmy Somerville-Singles Collection-1984-1990* . . (London)
Read My Lips
Duran Duran; *Liberty* . . . . (Capitol)
Read My Lips
Melba Moore; *Read My Lips* . . . . (Capitol)
Read My Lips
Betsy Rose; *Sacred Ground* . . . . (Kaleidoscope)
Read My Lips
Michael Franks; *Skin Dive* . . . . (Warner Bros.)

Read My Lips
Loverboy; *Wildside* . . . . (Columbia)
Soft Lips
Hank Thompson and His Brazos Valley Boys; *45-#40211* . . . . (Capitol)
Soft Lips And Hard Liquor
Charlie Walker; *45-#0870* . . . . (RCA)
Stiff Upper Lip
AC/DC; *Stiff Upper Lip* . . . . (East West)
Talk Back Trembling Lips
Ernest Ashworth; *Best Of Ernest Ashworth* . . . . (Curb)
Johnny Tillotson; *Cruisin'-1964-C* . . . . (Increase)
These Lips Don't Know How To Say Goodbye
Doug Stone; *Doug Stone* . . . . (Epic)
Greatest Country Hits Of The '90s-1991-C . . . . (Columbia)
Forester Sisters; *Sincerely* . . . . (Warner Bros.)
Touch Of Your Lips
Ben Webster; *Compact Jazz-Ben Webster-The Verve Years* . . . . (Verve)
Nat "King" Cole; *Nat "King" Cole (Box Set)* . . . . (Capitol)
Tony Bennett & Bill Evans; *Tony Bennett & Bill Evans* . . . . (Fantasy)
Wolverton Mountain
Claude King; *American Originals-Claude King* . . . . (Columbia)
Best Of Claude King . . . . (Gusto)
Billboard Top Country Hits-1962-C . . . . (Rhino)
Super Hits Of The '60s-C . . . . (Epic)
Workin' On A Groovy Thing
Patti Drew; *Soul Shots-#2-The "In" Crowd-Sweet Soul-C* . . . . (Rhino)
Tell Him-Golden Classics . . . . (Collectables)

ANATOMY: MISCELLANEOUS, Multiple Body
Parts, Neck
See Also: ANATOMY (various), EYES, HEART, SEX, SMILE

Achy Breaky Heart
Billy Ray Cyrus; *Some Gave All* . . . . (Mercury)
Ain't Got No (I Got Life)
Original Cast; *ST/Hair* . . . . (RCA)
Bad Liver & A Broken Heart
Tom Waits; *Small Change* . . . . (Asylum)
Brass In Pocket (I'm Special)
Pretenders; *Pretenders* . . . . (Sire)
Pretenders-The Singles . . . . (Sire)
Break Ya Neck
Busta Rhymes; *Genesis* . . . . (J)
If Your Heart Ain't Busy Tonight
Tanya Tucker; *What Do I Do With Me* . . . . (Capitol)
Jealous Bone
Patty Loveless; *Patty Loveless' Greatest Hits* . . . . (MCA)
Up Against My Heart . . . . (MCA)
Made To Love Ya
Gerald Levert; *Gerald's World* . . . . (East West)
No Matter What Shape (Your Stomach's In)
T-Bones; *Billboard Top Pop Hits-1966-C* . . . . (Rhino)
Otherside
Red Hot Chili Peppers; *Californication* . . . . (Warner Bros.)
Pencil Neck Geek
Fred Blassie; *Dr. Demento Presents The Greatest Novelty Records-#4-
1970s-C* . . . . (Rhino)
Dr. Demento: 20th Anniversary Collection-C . . . . (Rhino)
Dr. Demento's Dementia Royale-C . . . . (Rhino)
Physical
Olivia Newton-John; *Back To Basics-Essential Collection 1971-1992* . (Geffen)
Olivia Newton-John's Greatest Hits-#2 . . . . (MCA)
Physical . . . . (MCA)
Suck On The Jugular
Rolling Stones; *Voodoo Lounge* . . . . (Virgin)
Up The Neck
Pretenders; *Pretenders* . . . . (Sire)
Wear My Ring Around Your Neck
Elvis Presley; *50,000,000 Elvis Fans Can't Be Wrong-Elvis' Gold Records-
Volume 2* . . . . (RCA)
Hits Like Never Before-Essential-#3 . . . . (RCA)
The Top Ten Hits . . . . (RCA)
Worldwide 50 Gold Award Hits, Vol. 1, Parts 1 & 2 . . . . (RCA)
Ricky Van Shelton; *Ricky Van Shelton's Greatest Hits Plus* . . . . (Columbia)
Yummy Yummy Yummy
Ohio Express; *Billboard Top Rock 'N' Roll Hits-1968-C* . . . . (Rhino)
Bubblegum Classics-#1-C . . . . (Varese Vintage)

ANATOMY: MOUTH, Teeth, Tongue
See Also: ANATOMY (various), COSMETICS, SMILE

All I Want For Christmas (Is My Two Front Teeth)
David Seville & The Chipmunks; *Christmas With The Chipmunks-#2* . . . . (EMI)

Nat "King" Cole; *Let It Snow!-Cuddly Christmas Classics* . . . . (Capitol)
Spike Jones; *Dr. Demento Presents The Greatest Novelty Records-#6-Christmas-C* . . . . (Rhino)
   Spike Jones-Christmas . . . . (Rhino)
Big Mouth Blues
Gram Parsons; *G.P./Grievous Angel* . . . . (Reprise)
   Gram Parsons/Fallen Angels Live-1973 . . . . (Sierra)
Cloud On My Tongue
Tori Amos; *Under The Pink* . . . . (Atlantic)
Coming Down (Drug Tongue)
Cult; *The Cult* . . . . (Sire)
Fire In The Hole
Van Halen; *Van Halen 3* . . . . (Warner Bros.)
I Tan't Wait Till Quithmuth Day
Mel Blanc; *Christmas Comedy Classics-C* . . . . (Priority)
Idiot Wind
Bob Dylan; *Blood On The Tracks* . . . . (Columbia)
   Hard Rain . . . . (Columbia)
   The Bootleg Series-Volumes 1-3 [Rare & Unreleased] . . . . (Columbia)
I've Been Down That Road Before
Hank Williams; *Alone And Forsaken* . . . . (Mercury)
   Beyond The Sunset . . . . (Polydor)
Kicked In The Teeth
AC/DC; *Powerage* . . . . (Atlantic)
Linger
Jonatha Brooke; *Steady Pull* . . . . (Bad Dog)
Mouth
Merril Bainbridge; *The Garden* . . . . (Universal)
Mouth
Bush; *Deconstructed* . . . . (Trauma)
   Razorblade Suitcase . . . . (Trauma)
   ST/An American Werewolf In Paris . . . . (Hollywood)
Only Tongue Can Tell
Trash Can Sinatras; *Cake* . . . . (London)
Pulling Teeth
Green Day; *Dookie* . . . . (Reprise)
Pulling Teeth (Anesthesia)
Metallica; *Kill 'Em All* . . . . (Elektra)
Sun In My Mouth
Bjork; *Vespertine* . . . . (Elektra)
Taste Of India
Aerosmith; *Nine Lives* . . . . (Columbia)
Thank You For Loving Me
Bon Jovi; *Crush* . . . . (Island/IDJMG)
Tip Of My Tongue
Grass Roots; *Grass Roots-Anthology (1966-1975)* . . . . (Rhino)
John Hiatt; *Bring The Family* . . . . (A&M)
Tubes; *Best Of The Tubes* . . . . (Gold Rush)
Tip Of My Tongue
Tommy Quickly; *History Of British Rock-#1-C* . . . . (Rhino)
Your Gold Teeth
Steely Dan; *Countdown To Ecstasy* . . . . (MCA)
Your Gold Teeth II
Steely Dan; *Katy Lied* . . . . (MCA)

ANATOMY: REAR

See Also: **ANATOMY (various), DANCE, FIGHT, INSULTS, SEX**

American Bad Ass
Kid Rock; *History Of Rock* . . . . (Top Dog/Lava/Atlantic)
Asswhippin'
Fishbone; *Reality Of My Surroundings* . . . . (Columbia)
Baby Got Back
Sir Mix-A-Lot; *Mack Daddy* . . . . (Def American)
Back That Azz Up
Juvenile; *Back That Azz Up (single)* . . . . (Cash Money/Universal)
Backfield In Motion
Mel & Tim; *Collectables Presents The History Of Rock-#4-C* . . . . (Collectables)
   Oldies But Goodies-#2-C . . . . (Original Sound)
   Soul Shots-#2-The "In" Crowd-Sweet Soul-C . . . . (Rhino)
   Super Oldies Of The '60s-#10-C . . . . (Audio Fidelity)
Big Butt
Bobby Jimmy & The Critters; *West Coast Rap-First Dynasty-#3-C* . . . . . (Rhino)
Big Fat Funky Booty
Spin Doctors; *Up For Grabs...Live* . . . . (Epic Portrait Assoc.)
Boogie In Your Butt
Eddie Murphy; *Eddie Murphy* . . . . (Columbia)
Bootylicious
Destiny's Child; *Now That's What I Call Music!-#8-C* . . . . (Virgin)
   Survivor . . . . (Columbia)
Butt Fuck
Human Sexual Response; *Fig. 15* . . . . (Eat)
Butt Naked
Charm; *Atrophy* . . . . (Atlantic)
Dr. Jeckyll & Mr. Hyde; *Champagne Of Rap* . . . . (Profile)

Da Dip
Freak Nasty; *Controversee...That's Life...And That's The Way It Is* . . . . (Power)
Dance Your Ass Off
Bohannon; *Dance Your Ass Off* . . . . (Dakar)
Don't Kick Her In The Butt
Bobby Taylor & Carolyn Majors; *ST/Far Out Man* . . . . (Chameleon)
Fat Bottomed Girls
Queen; *Jazz* . . . . (Hollywood)
   Queen's Greatest Hits I & II . . . . (Hollywood)
Feet Up (Pat Him On The Po-Po)
Guy Mitchell; *Definitive Guy Mitchell* . . . . (Collector's Choice)
Get Off Your Ass And Jam
Parliament; *Parliament Live/P. Funk Earth Tour* . . . . (Casablanca)
Kick A Little
Little Texas; *Kick A Little* . . . . (Warner Bros.)
Kiss This
Aaron Tippin; *People Like Us* . . . . (Lyric Street)
Lyin' Ass Bitch
Fishbone; *Fishbone* . . . . (Columbia)
Meet De Boys On The Battlefront
Wild Tchoupitoulas; *Treacherous: A History Of The Neville Brothers* . . . (Rhino)
   Wild Tchoupitoulas . . . . (Island)
My Ass Is On Fire
Mr. Bungle; *Mr. Bungle* . . . . (Warner Bros.)
Nookie
Limp Bizkit; *Now That's What I Call Music!-#3-C* . . . . (Virgin)
   Significant Other . . . . (Flip/Interscope)
Pull Over
Trina; *Da Baddest B***h* . . . . (Slip 'N Slide)
Rhythm (Devoted To Art Of Moving Butts)
Tribe Called Quest; *People's Instinctive Travels And The Paths Of Rhythm* . . . . (Jive)
Rump Shaker
Wreckx-N-Effect; *Hard Or Smooth* . . . . (MCA)
Shake A Tail Feather
Five Du-Tones; *Toga Rock-#2-C* . . . . (Dunhill Compact Classics)
James & Bobby Purify; *Frat Rock!-#3-Grandson Of Frat Rock!-C* . . . . . (Rhino)
Shake Ya Ass
Mystikal; *Let's Get Ready* . . . . (Jive)
Shake Your Ass!
Blowfly; *Twisted World Of Blowfly* . . . . (Oops)
Shake Your Booty
KC And The Sunshine Band; *Best Of KC And The Sunshine Band* . . . . . (Rhino)
   KC And The Sunshine Band's Greatest Hits . . . . (TK)
   Mega Hits Dance Classics-#4-C . . . . (Priority)
   Part 3 . . . . (TK)
Shake Your Money Maker
Elmore James; *King Of The Slide Guitar* . . . . (Capricorn)
Fleetwood Mac; *Vintage Years* . . . . (Sire)
George Thorogood & The Destroyers; *Born To Be Bad* . . . . . (Gold Rush)
Paul Butterfield Blues Band; *Golden Butter* . . . . (Elektra)
   Paul Butterfield Blues Band . . . . (Elektra)
Shake Your Tailfeather
Blues Brothers & Ray Charles; *ST/The Blues Brothers* . . . . . (Atlantic)
Thong Song
Sisqo; *Unleash The Dragon* . . . . (Dragon/Def Soul/IDJMG)
Tush
ZZ Top; *Best Of ZZ Top* . . . . (Warner Bros.)
   Fandango . . . . (Warner Bros.)
   Six Pack . . . . (Warner Bros.)
   ST/An Officer And A Gentleman . . . . (Island)
   ZZ Top's Greatest Hits . . . . (Warner Bros.)

ANATOMY: SEXUAL

See Also: **ANATOMY (various), DESIRE, SEX, SEX: RESISTING TEMPTATION**

Baby Baby Please (Just A Little More Head)
2 Live Crew; *Sports Weekend (As Nasty As They Wanna Be Part II)* . . . . . (Luke)
Big Balls
AC/DC; *Dirty Deeds Done Dirt Cheap* . . . . (Atlantic)
Big Chested Girls
Prince Charles & The City Beat Band; *Stone Killers!* . . . . (Roir)
Boobs A Lot
Fugs; *Fugs 4 Rounders Score* . . . . (ESP Disk)
   Fugs' Greatest Hits . . . . (PVC)
   The Fugs First Album . . . . (ESP Disk)
Boobs A Lot
Holy Modal Rounders; *Dr. Demento's Delights-C* . . . . (Warner Bros.)
Bop Gun
Ice Cube & George Clinton; *Featuring...Ice Cube* . . . . (Priority)
Bounce Your Boobies
Rusty Warren; *Dr. Demento Presents The Greatest Novelty Records-#3-1960s-C* . . . . (Rhino)
Dance: Ten; Looks: Three
Original Cast; *A Chorus Line* . . . . (Columbia)

Davy's Dinghy
Ruth Wallis; *Dr. Demento Presents The Greatest Novelty Records-#2-*
1950s-C .... (Rhino)
Dr. Demento's Dementia Royale-C .... (Rhino)
Dick In The Dirt
Sammy Hagar; *VOA* .... (Geffen)
Don't Go Home With Your Hard On
Leonard Cohen; *Death Of A Ladies' Man*.............. (Columbia)
Don't Touch Me There
Tubes; *T.R.A.S.H. (Tubes Rarities And Smash Hits)*.............. (A&M)
What Do You Want From Live .... (A&M)
Young And Rich .... (A&M)
Don't Use Your Penis (For A Brain)
Romanovsky & Phillips; *Trouble In Paradise* .... (Fresh Fruit)
Fish & Tits
Barefoot Jerry; *Barefoot Jerry's Grocery*.................... (Monument)
Hold Me
Brian McKnight; *Anytime*................................. (Motown)
How Many Licks
Lil' Kim featuring Sisqo; *Notorious K.I.M.* ...... (Queen Bee/Undeas/Atlantic)
I Touch Myself
Divinyls; *Divinyls*...................................... (Virgin)
I.L.B.T.s (I Like Big Tits)
Joe Walsh; *Look What I Did! The Joe Walsh Anthology*.............. (MCA)
You Bought It-You Name It .... (Warner Bros.)
Lemon Song
Led Zeppelin; *Led Zeppelin II*........................ (Atlantic)
Lemon Squeezing Daddy
Sultans; *Risque Rhythms: Nasty '50s R&B-C* .... (Rhino)
Lipstick On My Dick
Luke; *Luke's Greatest Hits*............................. (Lil' Joe)
Longview
Green Day; *Dookie* .... (Reprise)
Love Gun
Kiss; *Alive II* .... (Casablanca)
Double Platinum .... (Mercury)
Love Gun .... (Casablanca)
Smashes, Thrashes & Hits .... (Mercury)
More Than Seven Dwarfs In Penis-Land
Ron Geesin; *ST/The Body*............................. (Restless)
Muscle Of Love
Alice Cooper; *Alice Cooper's Greatest Hits*..........(Warner Bros.)
Muscle Of Love ....(Warner Bros.)
My Ding-A-Ling
Chuck Berry; *Best Of The Best Of Chuck Berry* .... (International Mktg. Group)
Billboard Top Rock 'N' Roll Hits-1972-C .... (Rhino)
Roll Over Beethoven ....(Allegiance)
The Chess Box-Chuck Berry .... (Chess)
Toronto Rock 'N' Roll Revival-#2-C .... (Accord)
My Toot Toot
Fats Domino; *Fats Domino's Greatest Hits* ....(MCA)
Fats Domino & Doug Kershaw; *Alligator Stomp-#2-C* .... (Rhino)
Rockin' Sidney; *19 Hot Country Requests-#3-C* .... (Epic)
Alligator Stomp-#1-C .... (Rhino)
Nutted By Reality
Nick Lowe; *Pure Pop For Now People* .... (Columbia)
One More Chance
Notorious B.I.G.; *Ready To Die* .... (Bad Boy/Arista)
Pass The Pussy
A.T.E.E.M.; *A.T.E.E.M.* .... (Select)
Penis Dimension
Frank Zappa; *Disconnected Synapses*.................. (Rhino)
Penis Envy
Uncle Bonsai; *Lonely Grain Of Corn* .... (Freckle)
Penis Song (Not The Noel Coward Song)
Monty Python; *Monty Python Sings* .... (Virgin)
Phallic Marauder
Squadron; *Fatal Strike* ....(Warfare)
Pop My Dick Song
Sloppy Seconds; *First Seven Inches...& Then Some!* ....(Taang!)
Pop That Pussy
2 Live Crew; *Sports Weekend (As Nasty As They Wanna Be Part II)* ..... (Luke)
Push It
Garbage; *Version 2.0* .... (Almo Sounds)
Red Neck Friend
Jackson Browne; *For Everyman* .... (Asylum)
Rocket In My Pocket
Little Feat; *Hoy-Hoy!* ....(Warner Bros.)
Time Loves A Hero ....(Warner Bros.)
Waiting For Columbus.............................(Warner Bros.)
Silicone Sally
Slammin' Gladys; *Slammin' Gladys*................... (Priority)
Sugar Walls
Sheena Easton; *Dance Mix* ....(EMI)
Private Heaven ....(EMI)
Sweat Of My Balls
CB4 & Daddy-O-Hi-C; *ST/CB4* ....(MCA)

Testicle Of God (& It Was Good)
Gaye Bykers On Acid; *Stewed To The Gills* .... (Caroline)
Texas Tattoo
Gibson/Miller Band; *Steppin' Country-C* .... (Columbia)
Where There's Smoke .... (Epic)
Thinking With The Wrong Head
Little Charlie & The Nightcats; *Captured Live* .... (Alligator)
Thrill My Gorilla
Alice Cooper; *Constrictor*............................ (MCA)
Tit Photographer Blues
Fabulous Poodles; *Mirror Stars* .... (Epic)
Tits
Sparks; *Indiscreet* .... (Out Of Print)
Titties And Beer
Kiss; *Alive II* .... (Casablanca)
Double Platinum .... (Mercury)
Rock & Roll Over .... (Casablanca)
Titties N' Beer
Frank Zappa; *Baby Snakes* .... (Barking Pumpkin)
In New York .... (Barking Pumpkin)
Titty City
Nasty Niggas; *Banned From The Planet* .... (Critique)
Too Close
Next; *Rated Next* .... (Divine Mill/Arista)
U Can't Touch This
Hammer; *Please Hammer Don't Hurt 'Em*.................... (Capitol)
Vasectomy
Limeliters; *Singing For The Fun* ....(Crescendo)
Wang Dang Sweet Poontang
Ted Nugent; *Cat Scratch Fever*........................ (Epic)
Double Live Gonzo .... (Epic)
Who's Sucking On Grandpa's Balls Since Grandma Ain't Home
Tonight?
Frogs; *My Daughter The Broad*........................ (Matador)

ANATOMY: SHOULDER

See Also: ANATOMY (various), HELP

Angel On My Shoulder
Natalie Cole; *Natalie Cole's Greatest Hits-#1* .... (Elektra)
Cold On The Shoulder
Gordon Lightfoot; *Cold On The Shoulder*...............(Reprise)
Gord's Gold ....(Reprise)
Cry On My Shoulder
Bonnie Raitt; *Nick Of Time* .... (Capitol)
Cry On Your Own Shoulder
General Public; *Hand To Mouth* .... (I.R.S.)
Crying On Your Shoulder Again
Doug Stone; *Doug Stone* .... (Epic)
Don't Talk (Put Your Head On My Shoulder)
Beach Boys; *Pet Sounds* .... (Capitol)
The Pet Sounds Sessions: A 30th Anniversary Collection .. (Capitol)
Linda Ronstadt; *Winter Light* .... (Elektra)
Hey Jude
Beatles; *Beatles 1* .... (Capitol)
Beatles-20 Greatest Hits .... (Capitol)
Past Masters-Volume Two ....(Parlophone)
The Beatles/1967-1970.............................. (Capitol)
Paul McCartney; *Knebworth-The Album-C* ....(Polydor)
Wilson Pickett; *Wilson Pickett's Greatest Hits* ....(Atlantic)
I Got Stripes
Johnny Cash; *Johnny Cash-16 Biggest Hits-#2*.................. (Legacy)
I'm Walking Behind You
Eddie Fisher; *Very Best Of Eddie Fisher*................ (MCA)
Frank Sinatra; *Capitol Collectors Series-Frank Sinatra* .... (Capitol)
Concepts... (Capitol)
Point Of No Return .... (Capitol)
Lean On Me
Kirk Franklin; *The Nu Nation Project*...........(Gospo Centric/Interscope)
Make The World Go Away
Eddy Arnold; *Best Of Eddy Arnold* .... (RCA)
Billboard Top Country Hits-1965-C .... (Rhino)
Eddy Arnold-Pure Gold .... (RCA)
Nipper's Greatest Hits Of The '60s-#1-C .... (RCA)
World Of Hits .... (MGM)
Ray Price; *Ray Price-16 Biggest Hits* .... (Legacy)
Ray Price-20 Hits .... (Tee Vee)
Moon Is Still Over Her Shoulder
Michael Johnson; *Best Of Michael Johnson* .... (RCA)
Country Love Songs-C ....(Warner Bros.)
That's That .... (RCA)
Wings .... (RCA)
Over My Shoulder
Patty Loveless; *When Fallen Angels Fly* .... (Epic)
Over My Shoulder
Mike & The Mechanics; *Beggar On A Beach Of Gold* ....(Atlantic)

Over Your Shoulder
Seven Mary Three; *Orange Ave.* . . . . (Atlantic)
Put Your Head On My Shoulder
Lettermen; *Capitol Collectors Series-The Lettermen* . . . . . . (Capitol)
The Lettermen's All-Time Greatest Hits . . . . (Capitol)
Paul Anka; *Oldies But Goodies-#1-C* . . . . (Original Sound)
Paul Anka-30th Anniversary Anthology . . . . (Rhino)
Paul Anka's 21 Golden Hits . . . . (RCA)
Remember Diana . . . . (RCA)
Rabbit On My Shoulder
Peter Alsop/Dan Crow/Bruce Phillips/Happy Traum; *Silly Songs & Modern*
Lullabies . . . . (Briar)
Ready, Willing And Able
Lari White; *Best Of Lari White* . . . . (RCA)
Don't Fence Me In . . . . (RCA)
Sunshine On My Shoulders
John Denver; *John Denver's Greatest Hits* . . . . (RCA)
Take Me Home, Country Roads & Other Hits . . . . (RCA)
There's A New Moon Over My Shoulder
Gene Autry; *Columbia Historic Edition-Gene Autry* . . . . (Columbia)
Jimmie Davis; *Best Of Jimmie Davis* . . . . (MCA)
Jimmie Davis-Golden Hits . . . . (Plantation)
The Country Music Hall Of Fame-Jimmie Davis . . . . (MCA)
Tex Ritter; *Tex Ritter's Greatest Hits* . . . . (Curb)
There's A Rainbow 'Round My Shoulder
Al Jolson; *Jolson Sang 'Em* . . . . (Biograph)
Mammy . . . . (Pro-Arte)
When You Ask About Love
Crickets; *45-#9-55153* . . . . (Brunswick)
Whose Shoulder Will You Cry On
Kitty Wells; *Kitty Wells' Greatest Hits* . . . . (Step One)

ANATOMY: SKIN

See Also: **ANATOMY (various), TATTOO**

American Skin (41 Shots)
Bruce Springsteen & The E Street Band; *Live In New York City* . . . . . (Columbia)
Beauty Is Only Skin Deep
Temptations; *Good Feeling Music Of The Big Chill*
Generation-#1-C . . . . (Motown)
Motown Story-First 25 Years-C . . . . (Motown)
Motown's Mustang-A Motown Video-C . . . . (Motown)
Temptations-Anthology-The Best Of The Temptations . . . . (Motown)
Bittersweet Me
R.E.M.; *New Adventures In Hi-Fi* . . . . (Warner Bros.)
Blistered
Johnny Cash; *Johnny Cash-16 Biggest Hits-#2* . . . . (Legacy)
Brown Skin
India.Arie; *Acoustic Soul* . . . . (Motown)
Celebrity Skin
Hole; *Celebrity Skin* . . . . (David Geffen Co.)
Everybody's Free (To Wear Sunscreen)
Baz Luhrmann; *Now That's What I Call Music!-#2-C* . . . . (Virgin)
Something For Everybody . . . . (Capitol)
Flesh And Blood
Roxy Music; *Flesh + Blood* . . . . (Atco)
Flesh And Blood
Johnny Cash; *Johnny Cash's Biggest Hits* . . . . (Columbia)
The Man In Black-His Greatest Hits . . . . (Legacy)
Flesh For Fantasy
Billy Idol; *Rebel Yell* . . . . (Chrysalis)
Vital Idol . . . . (Chrysalis)
In The Flesh
Pink Floyd; *The Wall* . . . . (Columbia)
Roger Waters; *The Wall-Live In Berlin* . . . . (Mercury)
In The Flesh
Blondie; *Best Of Blondie* . . . . (Chrysalis)
Blondie . . . . (Chrysalis)
I've Got You Under My Skin
4 Seasons; *25th Anniversary Collection* . . . . (Rhino)
Diana Krall; *When I Look In Your Eyes* . . . . (GRP)
Frank Sinatra; *At The Sands* . . . . (Reprise)
Round #1 . . . . (Capitol)
Sinatra: A Man And His Music . . . . (Reprise)
Sinatra's Sinatra . . . . (Reprise)
The Reprise Collection . . . . (Reprise)
Frank Sinatra & Bono; *Frank Sinatra-Duets-C* . . . . . . (Capitol)
Frank Sinatra & Nelson Riddle Orchestra; *songs for Swingin'*
Lovers! . . . . (Capitol)
Jump Right In
Urge; *Master Of Styles.* . . . . (Immortal/Epic)
Livin' La Vida Loca
Ricky Martin; *Ricky Martin.* . . . . (Columbia)
Lose This Skin
Clash; *Sandinista.* . . . . (Epic)

Mr. Skin
Spirit; *12 Dreams Of Dr. Sardonicus* . . . . (Epic)
Best Of Spirit . . . . (Epic)
Spirit Of '84. . . . . (Mercury)
Time Circle . . . . (Epic)
Scar Tissue
Red Hot Chili Peppers; *Californication* . . . . (Warner Bros.)
Skin
Madonna; *Ray Of Light* . . . . (Maverick)
Skin & Bone
Kinks; *Celluloid Heroes* . . . . (RCA)
Everybody's In Show-Biz . . . . (Rhino)
Muswell Hillbillies . . . . (VelVel)
The Kinks' Greatest-Celluloid Heroes . . . . (RCA)
Skin & Bones
Hazies; *Vinnie Smokin' In The Big Room.* . . . . (EMI)
Skin I'm In
Cameo; *Machismo* . . . . (Atlanta Artists)
Sly & The Family Stone; *Fresh* . . . . (Legacy)
Streak, The
Ray Stevens; *Ray Stevens' Greatest Hits* . . . . (RCA)
Ray Stevens' Greatest Hits . . . . (MCA)
Ray Stevens-All-Time Greatest Comic Hits . . . . (Curb)
Super Hits Of The '70s-Have A Nice Day-#12-C . . . . (Rhino)
Tattoos & Scars
Montgomery Gentry; *Tattoos & Scars* . . . . (Columbia)
Under My Skin
Dandelion; *I Think I'm Gonna Be Sick* . . . . (Ruffhouse/Columbia)

ANGELS

See Also: **COMPLIMENTS, DEVILS, GOD, HEAVEN, HELL,**
HELP, SPIRITS

(Only Angels Wanna Wear My) Red Shoes
Elvis Costello; *Girls Girls Girls* . . . . (Columbia)
My Aim Is True . . . . (Columbia)
Elvis Costello & The Attractions; *Best Of Elvis Costello & The*
Attractions . . . . (Columbia)
(They Long To Be) Close To You
Carpenters; *Carpenters-Classics-#2* . . . . (A&M)
Carpenters-Love Songs . . . . (A&M)
Carpenters-The Singles 1969-1973. . . . . (A&M)
From The Top . . . . (A&M)
(You're The) Devil In Disguise
Elvis Presley; *Elvis' Gold Records, Volume 4* . . . . (RCA)
The Top Ten Hits . . . . (RCA)
And The Angels Sing
Ella Fitzgerald; *Lady Time* . . . . (Pablo)
Angel
Atlanta Rhythm Section; *3rd Annual Pipe Dream* . . . . . . (Polydor)
Are You Ready! . . . . (Polydor)
Angel
Sarah McLachlan; *Mirrorball* . . . . (Arista)
ST/City Of Angels . . . . (Warner Sunset/Reprise)
Surfacing . . . . (Arista)
Totally Hits-#1-C . . . . (Arista)
Angel
Shaggy; *Hotshot.* . . . . (MCA)
Angel
Fleetwood Mac; *25 Years-The Chain* . . . . (Warner Bros.)
Heroes Are Hard To Find . . . . (Reprise)
Tusk . . . . (Warner Bros.)
Angel
Aretha Franklin; *Aretha Franklin-30 Greatest Hits* . . . . (Rhino)
Angel
Buffy Sainte-Marie; *Best Of Buffy Sainte-Marie-#2* . . . . . . (Vanguard)
Illuminations . . . . (Vanguard)
Angel
Jimi Hendrix; *Cry Of Love* . . . . (Reprise)
Experience Hendrix: The Best Of Jimi Hendrix . . . . (MCA)
First Rays Of The New Rising Sun. . . . . (MCA)
Rod Stewart; *Best Of Rod Stewart* . . . . (Mercury)
Angel
Pure Prairie League; *Bustin' Out* . . . . (RCA)
Angel
Angela Winbush; *Billboard Top R&B Hits-1987-C.* . . . . . . (Rhino)
Sharp. . . . . (Mercury)
Angel
Poco; *Ride The Country* . . . . (Epic)
Angel
Aerosmith; *Permanent Vacation* . . . . (Geffen)
Angel
Iguanas; *Nuevo Boogaloo* . . . . (Margaritaville)
Angel
Bonnie Raitt; *Nine Lives.* . . . . (Warner Bros.)

Angel
New Kids On The Block; *New Kids On The Block* . . . . (Columbia)
Angel
Madonna; *Like A Virgin* . . . . (Sire)
Angel
Jon Secada; *Jon Secada* . . . . (SBK)
Angel
Bruce Springsteen; *Greetings From Asbury Park, N.J.* . . . . (Columbia)
Angel
Dirt Band; *Dirt Band* . . . . (United Artists)
Angel
Elvis Presley; *Elvis Sings For Children And Grownups Too!* . . . . (RCA)
Angel
Annie Lennox; *Diana, Princess Of Wales-Tribute-C* . . . . (Columbia)
Angel
Lionel Richie; *Renaissance* . . . . (Island/IDJMG)
Angel Angelina
George Strait; *Beyond The Blue Neon* . . . .(MCA)
Angel Baby
John Lennon; *Lennon* . . . . (Capitol)
Menlove Ave. . . . . (Capitol)
Rosie And The Originals; *Cruisin'-1960-C* . . . . (Increase)
Rock Gems-Classics From Small Label Era-C . . . . (Motown)
Super Oldies Of The '60s-#1-C . . . .(Audio Fidelity)
WCBS FM 101 History Of Rock-'60s-#1-C . . . . (Collectables)
Angel Band
Emmylou Harris; *Angel Band* . . . .(Warner Bros.)
Stanley Brothers; *ST/O Brother, Where Art Thou?* . . . . (Mercury)
Stanley Brothers & The Clinch Mountain Boys; *Best Of Bluegrass-#1-*
Standards-C . . . . (Mercury)
Angel Child
Lightnin' Hopkins; *How Many More Years I Got* . . . . (Fantasy)
Lightnin' Hopkins' Greatest Hits . . . . (Prestige)
Angel Come Home
Beach Boys; *L.A.-The Light Album* . . . . (Caribou)
Angel Eyes
Frank Sinatra; *At The Sands* . . . . (Reprise)
Frank Sinatra sings for Only The Lonely . . . . (Capitol)
Round #1 . . . . (Capitol)
Sinatra-The Main Event Live . . . . (Reprise)
Angel Eyes
Jeff Healey Band; *See The Light* . . . . (Arista)
Angel Eyes
Jim Brickman; *By Heart* . . . .(Windham Hill)
Angel Eyes
Abba; *Abba's Greatest Hits-#2.* . . . .(Atlantic)
Voulez-Vous. . . . . (Atlantic)
Angel Eyes
Roxy Music; *Manifesto.* . . . . (Atco)
Roxy Music-Atlantic Years 1973-1980 . . . . (Atco)
Angel Eyes
Ella Fitzgerald; *Best Of Ella Fitzgerald-#2.* . . . .(MCA)
Angel Flying Too Close To The Ground
Willie Nelson; *Greatest Hits (& Some That Will Be)* . . . . (Columbia)
ST/Honeysuckle Rose. . . . . (Columbia)
Angel Food Cake
Siegel-Schwall Band; *Best Of The Siegel-Schwall Band* . . . . (Vanguard)
Angel From Atlanta
Reddog; *Reddog* . . . . (Survival)
Angel From Montgomery
Bonnie Raitt; *Streetlights* . . . .(Warner Bros.)
Bonnie Raitt & John Prine; *Bonnie Raitt-Collection* . . . .(Warner Bros.)
John Prine; *John Prine* . . . . (Atlantic)
John Prine-Souvenirs. . . . . (Oh Boy)
Angel In Blue
J. Geils Band; *Freeze-Frame* . . . .(EMI)
Angel In Disguise
Earl Thomas Conley; *Don't Make It Easy For Me* . . . . (RCA)
Earl Thomas Conley's Greatest Hits . . . . (RCA)
Angel In My Eyes
John Michael Montgomery; *John Michael Montgomery's*
Greatest Hits . . . .(Atlantic)
Angel In The Sky
Rose Royce; *Rose Royce III/Strikes Again!* . . . . (Whitfield)
Angel In Your Arms
Barbara Mandrell; *Country Classics-#5-1985-1986-C.* . . . . (Universal)
Get To The Heart. . . . .(MCA)
Reba McEntire; *Reba McEntire* . . . . (Mercury)
Angel Lady
Boz Scaggs; *Slow Dancer* . . . . (Columbia)
Angel Loose In Houston
Larry Gatlin & The Gatlin Brothers Band; *Cookin' Up A Storm.* . . . . . . (Capitol)
Angel Number Nine
Pure Prairie League; *Bustin' Out* . . . . (RCA)
Angel Of Harlem
U2; *Rattle And Hum* . . . . (Island)
Angel Of Mercy
Albert King; *Albert King-Chronicle* . . . .(Stax)

Best Of Wattstax-C . . . . (Stax)
I'll Play The Blues For You . . . . (Stax)
Masterworks. . . . .(Atlantic)
New Orleans Heat . . . .(Tomato)
Angel Of Mercy
Dire Straits; *Communique* . . . . (Warner Bros.)
Angel Of Mine
Monica; *The Boy Is Mine.* . . . . (Arista)
Totally Hits-#1-C . . . . (Arista)
Angel Of The City
Robert Tepper; *No Easy Way Out* . . . .(Scotti Bros.)
ST/Cobra . . . .(Scotti Bros.)
Angel Of The Morning
Juice Newton; *All-Time Country Classics-#2-C* . . . . (Capitol)
Juice. . . . . (Capitol)
Juice Newton-Greatest Hits & More . . . . (Capitol)
Juice Newton's Greatest Hits . . . . (Gold Rush)
Merrilee Rush; *Dick Bartley's One-Hit Wonders Of The '60s-#2-C* . . . . . (Rhino)
Mellow '60s-C . . . .(Priority)
Angel Of The Night
Angela Bofill; *Angel Of The Night* . . . . (GRP)
Best Of Angela Bofill . . . . (Arista)
Angel On My Bike
Wallflowers; *Bringing Down The Horse* . . . .(Interscope)
Angel On My Shoulder
Natalie Cole; *Natalie Cole's Greatest Hits-#1* . . . . (Elektra)
Angel Spread Your Wings
Judy Collins; *Judith.* . . . . (Elektra)
Angel Without A Prayer
Deana Carter; *Love Shouldn't Hurt-C* . . . . (Qwest)
Angel Woman
Andrew Gold; *What's Wrong With This Picture?* . . . .(Asylum)
Angel You
Boz Scaggs; *Middle Man.* . . . . (Columbia)
Angels
Amy Grant; *Amy Grant-Collection* . . . . (A&M)
Straight Ahead . . . . (A&M)
Angels
Robbie Williams; *The Egg Has Landed* . . . . (Capitol)
Angels
BoDeans; *Love & Hope & Sex & Dreams* . . . .(Slash)
Angels
Heart; *Private Audition* . . . . (Epic)
Angels
Earl Scruggs & Melissa Etheridge; *Earl Scruggs And Friends-C* . . . . . . (MCA)
Angels And Sailors
Doors; *An American Prayer-Jim Morrison* . . . . (Elektra)
Angels Don't Cry
Psychedelic Furs; *Midnight To Midnight* . . . .(Columbia)
Angels Don't Fall In Love
Bangles; *Different Light* . . . . (Columbia)
Angels Don't Lie
Jim Reeves; *Best Of Jim Reeves-#4.* . . . . (RCA)
Angel's Eye
Aerosmith; *ST/Charlie's Angels* . . . . (Columbia)
Angels Get Lonesome Sometimes
Hank Williams, Jr.; *Hank Williams, Jr.-Early Years.* . . . . (WB/Curb)
One Night Stands . . . . (Warner Bros.)
Angels Have Fallen
Kansas; *Monolith* . . . . (Kirshner)
Angels In The Sky
Crew-Cuts; *Best Of The Crew-Cuts-The Mercury Years* . . . . (Mercury)
Angels In Waiting
Tammy Cochran; *Tammy Cochran* . . . . (Epic)
Angels Listened In
Crests; *Crests Greatest Hits* . . . .(Collectables)
Super Oldies Of The '50s-#3-C . . . .(Audio Fidelity)
WCBS FM 101 History Of Rock-'50s-#2-C . . . . (Collectables)
Angels Love Bad Men
Barbara Mandrell; *Sure Feels Good* . . . . (EMI)
Barbara Mandrell & Waylon Jennings; *Country Duets Two By*
Two-C . . . . (Capitol)
Angels Never Call
'Til Tuesday; *Welcome Home* . . . . (Epic)
Angels Of Atlanta
Marvin "Hannibal" Peterson; *Angels Of Atlanta* . . . . (Enja)
Angels Of Mercy
Glenn Miller & His Orchestra; *Complete Glenn Miller & His*
Orchestra. . . . .(Bluebird)
Angels Of The Silences
Counting Crows; *Recovering The Satellites* . . . . (David Geffen Co.)
Angels Rejoiced Last Night
Gram Parsons & The Flying Burrito Brothers; *Sleepless Nights* . . . . (A&M)
Angel's Son
Strait Up featuring Lajon of Sevendust; *Strait Up-C* . . . .(Immortal/Virgin)
Angel's Sunday
Jim Ed Brown; *Best Of Jim Ed Brown* . . . . (RCA)

Angels With Dirty Faces
Tommy Dorsey; *Complete Tommy Dorsey-#8* . . . . (RCA)
Angels With Dirty Faces
Los Lobos; *Kiko* . . . . (Slash)
Angels Would Fall
Melissa Etheridge; *Breakdown* . . . . (Island)
Back Door Angels
Jethro Tull; *War Child* . . . . (Chrysalis)
Black Balloon
Goo Goo Dolls; *Dizzy Up The Girl* . . . . (Warner Sunset/Reprise)
Blue Angel
Roy Orbison; *For The Lonely: 18 Greatest Hits* . . . . (Rhino)
In Dreams-Greatest Hits . . . . (Orbison)
Roy Orbison Greatest Hits . . . . (Monument)
Roy Orbison's All-Time Greatest Hits-#1 & 2 . . . . (Monument)
Very Best Of Roy Orbison . . . . (Monument)
Centerfold
J. Geils Band; *Flashback-Best Of The J. Geils Band* . . . . (EMI)
Freeze-Frame . . . . (EMI)
Showtime . . . . (EMI)
City Of Angels
10,000 Maniacs; *In My Tribe* . . . . (Elektra)
City Of Angels
Jay Ferguson; *Real Life Ain't This Way* . . . . (Asylum)
City Of Angels
Miracles; *City Of Angels* . . . . (Tamla)
City Of The Angels
Wang Chung; *ST/To Live And Die In L.A.* . . . . (Geffen)
City Of The Angels
Journey; *Evolution* . . . . (Columbia)
Come On Little Angel
Belmonts; *Lost Treasures* . . . . (Relic)
Devil In Her Heart
Beatles; *The Beatles' Second Album* . . . . (Capitol)
With The Beatles . . . . (Parlophone)
Donays; *Beatles Originals* . . . . (Rhino)
Devil Or Angel
Bobby Vee; *Best Of Bobby Vee* . . . . (EMI)
Bobby Vee-Golden Greats . . . . (Liberty)
Bobby Vee-Legendary Masters . . . . (EMI)
Clovers; *Atlantic Rhythm & Blues 1947-1974-#3 (1955-1958)-C* . . . . . (Atlantic)
Oldies But Goodies-#2-C . . . . (Original Sound)
Very Best Of The Clovers . . . . (Rhino)
Eagle Over Angel
Brother Phelps; *Let Go* . . . . (Asylum)
Earth Angel
Elvis Presley; *A Golden Celebration* . . . . (RCA)
New Edition; *ST/Under The Blue Moon* . . . . (MCA)
Penguins; *Billboard Top Rock 'N' Roll Hits-1955-C* . . . . (Rhino)
Golden Classics-Penguins . . . . (Collectables)
Oldies But Goodies-#1-C . . . . (Original Sound)
ST/American Graffiti . . . . (MCA)
Every Morning
Sugar Ray; *14:59* . . . . (Lava)
Fall From Grace
Amanda Marshall; *Amanda Marshall* . . . . (Epic)
Fallen Angel
Roger Daltrey; *Under A Raging Moon* . . . . (Atlantic)
Fallen Angel
Blue Oyster Cult; *Cultosaurus Erectus* . . . . (Columbia)
Fallen Angel
Fallen Angel; *Go For The Ride* . . . . (MCA)
Fallen Angel
Poison; *Open Up And Say...Ahh!* . . . . (Capitol)
Fallen Angel
Debbie Gibson; *Out Of The Blue* . . . . (Atlantic)
Fallen Angel
Robbie Robertson; *Robbie Robertson* . . . . (Geffen)
Fallen Angels
Kris Kristofferson; *Gift Of Song* . . . . (Polydor)
Shake Hands With The Devil . . . . (Columbia)
Fallen Angels
Aerosmith; *Nine Lives* . . . . (Columbia)
Fallen Angels
Dio; *Sacred Heart* . . . . (Warner Bros.)
Fly (The Angel Song)
Wilkinsons; *Nothing But Love* . . . . (Giant)
Fools Rush In (Where Angels Fear To Tread)
Brook Benton; *Super Oldies Of The '60s-#10-C* . . . . (Audio Fidelity)
Tommy Dorsey & Frank Sinatra; *Sessions-#1-February 1, 1940-July
17, 1940* . . . . (RCA)
Friday's Angels
Generation X; *Valley Of The Dolls* . . . . (Chrysalis)
Goodbye Angel
Fleetwood Mac; *25 Years-The Chain* . . . . (Warner Bros.)
Got A Date With An Angel
Hal Kemp; *Best Of The Big Bands-C* . . . . (Columbia)
Sammy Kaye & His Orchestra; *Best Of Sammy Kaye & His Orchestra* . . (MCA)

Guardian Angel
Judds; *Judds' Greatest Hits-#2* . . . . (MCA)
River Of Time . . . . (RCA)
Guardian Angel
Vels; *House Of Miracles* . . . . (Mercury)
Guardian Angel
Graham Parker; *Struck By Lightning* . . . . (RCA)
Guardian Angel
Lee Roy Parnell; *Tell The Truth* . . . . (Vanguard)
Guardian Angels
Pearls Before Swine; *Balaklava* . . . . (ESP Disk)
Best Of Pearls Before Swine . . . . (Adelphi)
Heaven Must Be Missing An Angel
Tavares; *Best Of Tavares* . . . . (Capitol)
Sky High . . . . (Capitol)
Help Me Angel
Steve Winwood; *Talking Back To The Night* . . . . (Island)
How Could An Angel Break My Heart
Kenny G with Toni Braxton; *Kenny G's Greatest Hits* . . . . (Arista)
Toni Braxton with Kenny G; *Diana, Princess Of Wales-Tribute-C* . . (Columbia)
Secrets . . . . (LaFace)
How Do You Speak To An Angel?
Etta James; *These Foolish Things-The Classic Balladry Of Etta James* . . . (MCA)
How Do You Talk To An Angel
Heights; *ST/Heights* . . . . (Capitol)
Hushabye
Mystics; *Doo-Wop Uptempo-#2-C* . . . . (Rhino)
Million-Dollar Memories #1-C . . . . (RCA)
Mystics-16 Golden Classics . . . . (Collectables)
I Can See An Angel
Patsy Cline; *20 Golden Pieces Of Patsy Cline* . . . . (Bulldog)
Hungry For Love-Her First Recordings-#2 . . . . (Rhino)
Today Tomorrow & Forever . . . . (MCA)
I Married An Angel
George Siravo; *Heritage Of Broadway-Rodgers & Hart* . . . . (Bainbridge)
I'm No Angel
Gregg Allman Band; *I'm No Angel* . . . . (Epic)
I'm Your Angel
Celine Dion & R. Kelly; *All The Way...A Decade Of Song* . . . . (550 Music)
These Are Special Times . . . . (550 Music)
R. Kelly & Celine Dion; *R.* . . . . (Jive)
Infamous Angel
Iris DeMent; *Infamous Angel* . . . . (Warner Bros.)
Iris
Goo Goo Dolls; *Dizzy Up The Girl* . . . . (Warner Sunset/Reprise)
ST/City Of Angels . . . . (Warner Sunset/Reprise)
It Wasn't God Who Made Honky Tonk Angels
Kitty Wells; *Grand Ole Opry-75 Years-#1-C* . . . . (MCA)
Kitty Wells' Greatest Hits . . . . (Step One)
The Kitty Wells Story . . . . (MCA)
Johnny Angel
Shelley Fabares; *Billboard Top Rock 'N' Roll Hits-1962-C* . . . . (Rhino)
ST/Mermaids . . . . (Geffen)
Kiss An Angel Good Mornin'
Charley Pride; *Charley Pride-24 Greatest Hits* . . . . (Tee Vee)
Pride! My 6 Latest And 6 Greatest . . . . (ISD/Intersound)
The Ultimate Charley Pride . . . . (Bransounds)
Let Me Be Your Angel
Stacy Lattisaw; *Very Best Of Stacy Lattisaw* . . . . (Rhino)
Lightning Crashes
Live; *Throwing Copper* . . . . (Radioactive/MCA)
Look Back In Anger
David Bowie; *Golden Years* . . . . (Rykodisc)
Lodger . . . . (Rykodisc)
Sound + Vision . . . . (Rykodisc)
ST/Chrisiane F. . . . . (RCA)
The Singles-1969-1993 . . . . (Rykodisc)
Love Is On The Way
Celine Dion; *Let's Talk About Love-C* . . . . (550 Music)
Dave Koz; *Dance* . . . . (Capitol)
Love Of My Life
Jim Brickman featuring Michael W. Smith; *Destiny* . . . . (Windham Hill)
Love Travels
Kathy Mattea; *Love Travels* . . . . (Mercury)
Malibu
Hole; *Celebrity Skin* . . . . (David Geffen Co.)
Maybe Angels
Sheryl Crow; *Sheryl Crow* . . . . (A&M)
Midnight Angel
Barbara Mandrell; *Best Of Barbara Mandrell* . . . . (MCA)
Midnight Angel . . . . (MCA)
Midnight Angel
Highway 101; *Paint The Town* . . . . (Warner Bros.)
My Angel
Stephen Stills; *Stills* . . . . (Columbia)
My Angel
Utopia; *Oops! Wrong Planet* . . . . (Rhino)

My Angel Baby
Toby Beau; *Toby Beau* . . . . (RCA)
My Baby Needs A Shepherd
Emmylou Harris; *Red Dirt Girl* . . . . (Nonesuch)
My Blue Angel
Aaron Tippin; *Read Between The Lines* . . . . (RCA)
My Special Angel
Bobby Helms; *American Graffiti-#3-C* . . . . (MCA)
Blue Ribbon Country-#3-C . . . . (Accord)
Oldies But Goodies-#14-C . . . . (Original Sound)
Pop A Billy . . . . (MCA)
Vintage Music-#2-C . . . . (MCA)
Vogues; *Vogues' Greatest Hits* . . . . (Rhino)
Vogues' Greatest Hits/Finest Performances . . . . (Sun)
Next Door To An Angel
Neil Sedaka; *Neil Sedaka Sings His Greatest Hits* . . . . (RCA)
Neil Sedaka's All-Time Greatest Hits . . . . (RCA)
On The Side Of Angels
LeAnn Rimes; *You Light Up My Life-Inspirational Songs* . . . . (Curb)
One Angel
Stir; *Stir* . . . . (Aware/C2/Columbia)
Overnight Angels
Ian Hunter & Mott The Hoople; *Shades Of Ian Hunter* . . . . (Chrysalis)
Play Me The Waltz Of The Angels
Derailers featuring Buck Owens; *Full Western Dress* . . . . (Sire)
Please
Bing Crosby; *Bing Crosby-16 Most Requested Songs* . . . . (Legacy)
Poison Angel
Winger; *Winger* . . . . (Atlantic)
Precious Angel
Bob Dylan; *Slow Train Coming* . . . . (Columbia)
Pretty Little Angel
Stevie Wonder; *Uptight (Everything's Alright)* . . . . (Motown)
Pretty Little Angel
Crests; *Crests Greatest Hits* . . . . (Collectables)
Pretty Little Angel Eyes
Curtis Lee; *Million-Dollar Memories-#2-C* . . . . (RCA)
Oldies But Goodies-#2-C . . . . (Original Sound)
Phil Spector-Back To Mono 1958-1969-C . . . . (Abkco)
Phil Spector-The Early Years-1958-1961-C . . . . (Rhino)
Rock & Roll U.S.A.-21 Rock & Roll Favorites-#2-C . . . . . (Laurie)
Psycho Man
Black Sabbath; *Reunion* . . . . (Epic)
Return Of The Grievous Angel
Gram Parsons; *GP/Grievous Angel* . . . . (Reprise)
Road Angel
Doobie Brothers; *What Were Once Vices Are Now Habits* . . . . (Warner Bros.)
Rock An' Roll Angels
Whitesnake; *Saints & Sinners* . . . . (Geffen)
Rock 'N' Roll Angel
Kentucky HeadHunters; *Pickin' On Nashville* . . . . (Mercury)
Send Down An Angel
Allison Moorer; *The Hardest Part* . . . . (MCA)
Send Me An Angel
Scorpions; *Crazy World* . . . . (Mercury)
Send Me An Angel '89
Real Life; *Send Me An Angel '89* . . . . (Curb)
Sending Me Angels
Kathy Mattea; *Love Travels* . . . . (Mercury)
Sent By Angels
Arc Angels; *Arc Angels* . . . . (David Geffen Co.)
Seven Angels
Bruce Springsteen; *Tracks* . . . . (Columbia)
Seven Spanish Angels
Willie Nelson & Ray Charles; *19 Hot Country Requests-#3-C* . . . . (Epic)
Friendship-C . . . . (Columbia)
Greatest Country Hits Of The '80s-1985-C . . . . . . (Columbia)
Half Nelson-C . . . . (Columbia)
Shangri La
Four Coins; *'50s Vocal Groups-C* . . . . (K-Tel)
Lettermen; *Capitol Collectors Series-The Lettermen* . . . . . . (Capitol)
The Lettermen's All-Time Greatest Hits . . . . (Capitol)
She Talks To Angels
Black Crowes; *Shake Your Money Maker* . . . . (Def American)
Sleeping In Paris
Rosanne Cash; *The Wheel* . . . . (Columbia)
Sleeps With Angels
Neil Young & Crazy Horse; *Sleeps With Angels* . . . . (Reprise)
Sleepwalker
Wallflowers; *Breach* . . . . (Interscope)
Somebody's Out There Watching
Kinleys; *Kinleys II* . . . . (Epic)
Stranger In Paradise
Arthur Lyman; *Pearly Shells* . . . . (Crescendo)
Bing Crosby; *The Radio Years: 20 Songs* . . . . (Crescendo)
Original Cast; *Kismet* . . . . (Columbia)
Tony Bennett; *Tony Bennett-16 Most Requested Songs* . . . . . (Legacy)
Tony Bennett's All-Time Greatest Hits . . . . (Columbia)

Sweet Black Angel
Rolling Stones; *Exile On Main Street* . . . . (Virgin)
Sweet Little Angel
B.B. King; *B.B. King-16 Original Big Hits* . . . . (Fantasy)
Back In The Alley . . . . (MCA)
Live & Well . . . . (MCA)
Live At The Regal . . . . (MCA)
Buddy Guy; *Best Of The Chicago Blues-C* . . . . (Vanguard)
Man & The Blues . . . . (Vanguard)
Etta James; *Late Show* . . . . (Fantasy)
Rocks The House . . . . (Chess)
Swing Low, Sweet Chariot
Eric Clapton; *Time Pieces-#1-The Best Of Eric Clapton* . . . . (Polydor)
Glenn Miller & His Orchestra; *Moonlight Serenade* . . . . (Ranwood)
Hi-Lo's; *Suddenly It's The Hi-Lo's* . . . . (Columbia)
Jerry Garcia Acoustic Band; *Almost Acoustic* . . . . (Grateful Dead)
Joan Baez; *From Every Stage* . . . . (A&M)
Peggy Lee; *Best Of Peggy Lee* . . . . (MCA)
Talking To My Angel
Melissa Etheridge; *Yes I Am* . . . . (Island)
Teen Angel
Dion And The Belmonts; *Everything You Always Wanted* . . . . (Laurie)
Rock & Roll U.S.A.-21 Rock & Roll Favorites-#2-C . . . . . . (Laurie)
Mark Dinning; *Golden Years-1959-C* . . . . (Dominion Entert.)
Oldies But Goodies-#7-C . . . . (Original Sound)
ST/American Graffiti . . . . (MCA)
Teenage Tragedies-C . . . . (Rhino)
Ten Thousand Angels
Mindy McCready; *Ten Thousand Angels* . . . . (BNA)
Ten Thousand Angels Cried
LeAnn Rimes; *You Light Up My Life-Inspirational Songs* . . . . (Curb)
Thank You For Sending Me An Angel
Talking Heads; *More Songs About Buildings & Food* . . . . (Sire)
That's How You Know (When You're In Love)
Lari White; *Best Of Lari White* . . . . (RCA)
Wishes . . . . (RCA)
Theme From "Charlie's Angels"
Original Soundtrack; *Television's Greatest Hits-#3-1970s & 1980s-C* . . . (TVT)
TV Classic Themes: 25th Anniversary Edition-C . . . . . . (Breakable)
Theme From "Highway To Heaven"
Original Soundtrack; *Television's Greatest Hits-#6-Remote Control-C* . . . (TVT)
There Must Be An Angel (Playing With My Heart)
Eurythmics; *Be Yourself Tonight* . . . . (RCA)
Eurythmics' Greatest Hits . . . . (Arista)
Live-1983-1989 . . . . (Arista)
There You Are
Martina McBride; *Emotion* . . . . (RCA)
They Don't Know
Jon B.; *Cool Relax* . . . . (Yab Yum/550)
Through Your Hands
Don Henley; *ST/Michael* . . . . (Revolution)
To See My Angel Cry
Conway Twitty; *Conway Twitty-Number Ones-#1* . . . . (Liberty)
Conway Twitty's Greatest Hits-#1 . . . . (MCA)
To See My Angel In Virginia
Livewire; *Wired* . . . . (Rounder)
Together Again
Janet Jackson; *Now That's What I Call Music!-#1-C* . . . . (Virgin)
Velvet Rope . . . . (Virgin)
Tonight The Heartache's On Me
Dixie Chicks; *Wide Open Spaces* . . . . (Monument)
True Love
Elton John & Kiki Dee; *Duets-C* . . . . (MCA)
Four Aces; *Best Of The Four Aces* . . . . (MCA)
Johnny Mathis & Henry Mancini; *Hollywood Musicals* . . . . . . (Columbia)
Patsy Cline; *Always* . . . . (MCA)
The Patsy Cline Story . . . . (MCA)
Roger Whittaker; *Best Loved Ballads-#2* . . . . (Liberty)
Visions Of Angels
Genesis; *Trespass* . . . . (MCA)
When I Think About Angels
Jamie O'Neal; *Shiver* . . . . (Mercury)
When The Fallen Angels Fly
Patty Loveless; *When Fallen Angels Fly* . . . . (Epic)
When We Dance
Sting; *All This Time* . . . . (Starwave)
Fields Of Gold-The Best Of Sting 1984-1994 . . . . (A&M)
Wild Angel
John Cougar; *Nothin' Matters And What If It Did* . . . . (Riva)
Wild Angels
Martina McBride; *Angels Among Us-C* . . . . (RCA)
Wild Angels . . . . (RCA)
Wild One
Faith Hill; *Take Me As I Am* . . . . (Warner Bros.)
Wild Side Of Life
Freddy Fender; *Before The Next Teardrop Falls* . . . . (Universal)
Best Of Freddy Fender . . . . (MCA)
Hank Thompson; *Best Of The Best Of Hank Thompson* . . . . . . (Gusto)

Capitol Collectors Series-Hank Thompson . . . . (Capitol)
Hank Thompson's All-Time Greatest Hits . . . .(Curb)
Traditions In Country Music-C. . . . . (Capitol)
Rod Stewart; *Night On The Town* . . . . (Warner Bros.)

You Angel You
Bob Dylan; *Biograph.* . . . . (Columbia)
Bob Dylan And The Band; *Planet Waves* . . . . (Columbia)
New Riders Of The Purple Sage; *Best Of New Riders Of The*
Purple Sage . . . . (Columbia)

ANGER

**See Also: DIVORCE, FEELINGS, FIGHT, HATE, INSULTS, LOVE
(various), WAR**

(I Can't Get No) Satisfaction
Devo; *Best Of Devo-Greatest Hits.* . . . . (Warner Bros.)
Q: Are We Not Men? A: We Are Devo! . . . . (Warner Bros.)
Otis Redding; *Best Of Otis Redding.* . . . . (Atlantic)
History Of Otis Redding . . . . (Atco)
Otis Redding . . . . (Atlantic)
The Otis Redding Story . . . . (Atlantic)
Rolling Stones; *Big Hits (High Tide & Green Grass)* . . . . (Abkco)
Flashpoint. . . . .(Virgin)
got Live if you want it!. . . . . (Abkco)
Hot Rocks 1964-1971 . . . . (Abkco)
Out Of Our Heads . . . . (Abkco)
Singles Collection-The London Years. . . . . (Abkco)

All Around The World
Oasis; *Be Here Now.* . . . . (Epic)

Angry
Eddy Arnold; *All Time Favorites.* . . . .(RCA)

Angry
Public Image Ltd.; *Happy?* . . . .(Virgin)

Angry
Paul McCartney; *Press To Play.* . . . . (Capitol)

Angry
Pat Benatar; *Innamorata* . . . .(CMC Int'l)

Angry Again
Megadeth; *Hidden Treasures* . . . . (Capitol)

Angry All The Time
Bruce Robison with Kelly Willis; *Wrapped* . . . .(Lucky Dog)
Tim McGraw with Faith Hill; *Set This Circus Down.* . . . . (Curb)

Angry Blues
James Taylor; *Gorilla* . . . . (Warner Bros.)

Angry Chair
Alice In Chains; *Dirt* . . . . (Columbia)

Angry Eyes
Loggins & Messina; *Best Of Friends.* . . . . (Columbia)
Loggins & Messina-On Stage . . . . (Columbia)
Loggins And Messina . . . . (Columbia)

Angry Johnny
Poe; *Hello* . . . . (Modern)

Angry Words
Willy Porter ; *Dog Eared Dream* . . . . (Private Music)

Angry Young Man
Steve Earle & The Dukes; *Exit 0* . . . . (MCA)

Angry Young Man
Corey Hart; *Fields Of Fire.* . . . . (EMI)

Angry Young Man
Billy Joel; *KOHUEPT* . . . . (Columbia)
Turnstiles . . . . (Columbia)

Angry Young Men
Christopher Cross; *Rendez Vous* . . . . (BMG)

Blame
Collective Soul; *Disciplined Breakdown* . . . . (Atlantic)

Bleed American
Jimmy Eat World; *Bleed American* . . . . (DreamWorks/SKG)

Blistering
Machine Head; *The More Things Change...* . . . . (Roadrunner)

Break Stuff
Limp Bizkit; *Significant Other* . . . .(Flip/Interscope)

Bug A Boo
Destiny's Child; *The Writing's On The Wall* . . . . (Columbia)

Bullet With Butterfly Wings
Smashing Pumpkins; *Mellon Collie And The Infinite Sadness* . . . .(Virgin)

Cold Contagious
Bush; *Razorblade Suitcase* . . . . (Trauma)

Country Boy's Tool Box
Aaron Tippin; *Tool Box.* . . . . (RCA)

Dammit (Growing Up)
Blink-182; *Dude Ranch* . . . . (Cargo)

Dangerous
Busta Rhymes; *When Disaster Strikes.* . . . . (Elektra)

Desperately Wanting
Better Than Ezra; *Friction, Baby.* . . . . (Swell/Elektra)

Don't Be Down On Me Baby
Journey; *Trial By Fire* . . . . (Columbia)

Don't Look Back In Anger
Oasis; *What's The Story Morning Glory?* . . . . (Epic)

Don't Stay Home
311; *311* . . . .(Capricorn)

Don't Take It Personal (Just One Of Dem Days)
Monica; *Miss Thang.* . . . . (Rowdy/Arista)

Don't You Get So Mad
Jeffrey Osborne; *Stay With Me Tonight* . . . .(A&M)

Down With The Sickness
Disturbed; *The Sickness* . . . . (Giant)

Fade
Staind; *Break The Cycle* . . . . (Flip/Elektra)

Fooling Yourself
Styx; *Caught In The Act* . . . .(A&M)
Grand Illusion . . . .(A&M)
Styx-Classics-#15 . . . .(A&M)

Forgot About Dre
Dr. Dre featuring Eminem; *Dr. Dre 2001.* . . . . (Aftermath/Interscope)

Gas Chamber (Angry Samoans)
Foo Fighters; *Foo Fighters.* . . . . (Roswell/RCA)

Groundzero (In Our Hearts You Remain)
Cash & Computa; *Groundzero (In Our Hearts You Remain)-CD*
Single . . . . (Select)

Home Is Where The Hatred Is
Esther Phillips; *Best Of Esther Phillips* . . . . (CBS Associated)
From A Whisper To A Scream . . . . (CBS Associated)
Gil Scott-Heron; *Gil Scott-Heron.* . . . .(Bluebird)
It's Your World . . . . (Arista)
Pieces Of A Man . . . . (Flying Dutchman)

Husbands And Wives
Brooks & Dunn; *Big Country Hits '99-C* . . . .(K-Tel)
If You See Her . . . .(Arista)
Neil Diamond; *Neil Diamond-Love Songs* . . . . (MCA)
Rainbow . . . . (MCA)
Stones . . . . (MCA)
Roger Miller; *Best Of Roger Miller* . . . . (Mercury)
Best Of Roger Miller-His Greatest Songs . . . .(Curb)
Roger Miller-Super Hits . . . . (Epic)
Roger Miller-The Hits . . . . (Mercury)

I Can't Stay Mad At You
Skeeter Davis; *Nipper's Greatest Hits Of The '60s-#2-C.* . . . . (RCA)

I Can't Tell You Why
Brownstone; *From The Bottom Up* . . . . (MJJ/Epic)
Eagles; *Eagles Greatest Hits, Volume 2* . . . . (Asylum)
Eagles Live . . . . (Asylum)
The Long Run . . . . (Asylum)
Vince Gill; *Common Thread-Songs Of The Eagles-C* . . . . (Giant)

I Do
Lisa Loeb; *Firecracker* . . . . (Geffen)

I Don't Care Anymore
Phil Collins; *Hello, I Must Be Going* . . . . (Atlantic)

I Made A Fist
Original Broadway Cast; *The Most Happy Fella* . . . . . . (Sony Music Classical)

If I Had A Rocket Launcher (Central America)
Bruce Cockburn; *Stealing Fire.* . . . . (Columbia)
Waiting For A Miracle-Singles 1970-1987 . . . . (Gold Castle)

I'm Not Angry
Elvis Costello; *My Aim Is True.* . . . . (Columbia)

Inner City Blues (Make Me Wanna Holler)
Marvin Gaye; *What's Going On.* . . . . (Motown)

Jeremy
Pearl Jam; *Ten* . . . . (Epic Portrait Assoc.)

Johnny Get Angry
Joanie Sommers; *Best Of The Girl Groups-#2-C* . . . . (Rhino)

Johnny Get Angry
Shelley Fabares; *Things We Did Last Summer* . . . . (Collectables)

Jumper
Third Eye Blind; *Third Eye Blind.* . . . . (Elektra)
Totally Hits-#1-C . . . .(Arista)

Kiss Off
Violent Femmes; *Violent Femmes* . . . . (Slash)

Last Day Of Our Acquaintance
Sinead O'Connor; *I Do Not Want What I Haven't Got.* . . . . (Ensign)

Leave It Behind
Offspring; *Ixnay On The Hombre.* . . . . (Columbia)

Like Strangers
Everly Brothers; *All They Had To Do Was Dream* . . . . (Rhino)
Everly Brothers' Greatest Hits . . . . (Delta)
Everly Brothers-Cadence Classics-Their 20 Greatest Hits . . . .(Rhino)

Look Back In Anger
David Bowie; *Golden Years.* . . . . (Rykodisc)
Lodger. . . . . (Rykodisc)
Sound + Vision . . . . (Rykodisc)
ST/Chrisiane F. . . . . (RCA)
The Singles-1969-1993 . . . . (Rykodisc)

Lose My Cool
SWF & Redman; *Release Some Tension* . . . . (RCA)

Make Em Say Uhh #2
Master P; *MP Da Last Don* . . . . (No Limit/Priority)
Monkey Wrench
Foo Fighters; *The Colour And The Shape* . . . . (Roswell/RCA)
Nothin' But The Taillights
Clint Black; *Nothin' But The Taillights* . . . . (RCA)
One
Metallica; *...And Justice For All* . . . . (Elektra)
One Angry Dwarf And 200 Solemn Faces
Ben Folds Five; *Whatever And Ever Amen* . . . . (Caroline/550)
One Week
Barenaked Ladies; *Stunt* . . . . (Reprise)
Totally Hits-#1-C . . . . (Arista)
Paper Sun
Def Leppard; *Euphoria* . . . . (Mercury)
Pardon Me
Incubus; *Make Yourself* . . . . (Immortal/Epic)
Pet Names
Smash Mouth; *Fush Yu Mang* . . . . (Interscope)
Push It
Garbage; *Version 2.0* . . . . (Almo Sounds)
Real Slim Shady
Eminem; *The Marshall Mathers LP* . . . . (Aftermath/Interscope)
Roulette
Bruce Springsteen; *Tracks* . . . . (Columbia)
Simple Creed
Live; *V* . . . . (Radioactive/MCA)
So Sad To Say
Mighty Mighty Bosstones; *Pay Attention* . . . . (Big Rig/DJMG)
Song For The Dumped
Ben Folds Five; *Naked Baby Photos* . . . . (Caroline)
ST/Mr. Wrong . . . . (Hollywood)
Whatever And Ever Amen . . . . (Caroline/550)
Stan
Eminem; *The Marshall Mathers LP* . . . . (Aftermath/Interscope)
Stay Together For The Kids
Blink-182; *Take Off Your Pants And Jacket* . . . . (MCA)
Stutter
Joe featuring Mystikal; *My Name Is Joe* . . . . (Jive)
Now That's What I Call Music!-#8-C . . . . (Virgin)
Sunny Came Home
Shawn Colvin; *1998 Grammy Nominees-C* . . . . (MCA)
A Few Small Repairs . . . . (Columbia)
Sweet Emotion
Aerosmith; *ST/Armageddon-The Album* . . . . (Columbia)
Tears Of Rage
Band; *Best Of The Band* . . . . (Capitol)
Music From Big Pink . . . . (Capitol)
To Kingdom Come-The Definitive Collection . . . . (Capitol)
Bob Dylan And The Band; *Basement Tapes* . . . . (Columbia)
The World Is Full Of Angry Young Men
XTC; *Rag & Bone Buffet* . . . . (Geffen)
This Ain't No Rag, It's A Flag
Charlie Daniels Band; *This Ain't No Rag, It's A Flag-CD Single* . . . . . (Blue Hat)
To The Moon And Back
Savage Garden; *Savage Garden* . . . . (Columbia)
Unconditional
Clay Davidson; *Unconditional* . . . . (Virgin)
Under A Raging Moon
Roger Daltrey; *Under A Raging Moon* . . . . (Atlantic)
Untouchable Face
Ani DiFranco; *Dilate* . . . . (Righteous Babe)
Living In Clip . . . . (Righteous Babe)
Way I Am
Eminem; *The Marshall Mathers LP* . . . . (Aftermath/Interscope)
We Can Work It Out
Beatles; *''Yesterday''...And Today* . . . . (Capitol)
Beatles 1 . . . . (Capitol)
Beatles-20 Greatest Hits . . . . (Capitol)
Beatles-Box Set . . . . (Capitol)
Past Masters-Volume Two . . . . (Parlophone)
The Beatles/1962-1966 . . . . (Capitol)
Paul McCartney; *Unplugged (The Official Bootleg)* . . . . (Capitol)
Stevie Wonder; *Beatles Songs By Greatest Stars* . . . . . (Motown)
Signed Sealed & Delivered . . . . (Motown)
Stevie Wonder's Greatest Hits-#2 . . . . (Motown)
Top 10 With A Bullet-Motown Solo Stars-C . . . . (Motown)
What Angry Blue?
Seven Mary Three; *RockCrown* . . . . (Mammoth)
When A Woman's Fed Up
R. Kelly; *Now That's What I Call Music!-#2-C* . . . . (Virgin)
R. . . . . (Jive)
When Doves Cry
Ginuwine; *The Bachelor* . . . . (550 Music)
Prince and the Revolution; *ST/Purple Rain* . . . . (Warner Bros.)
You Oughta Know
Alanis Morissette; *1996 Grammy Nominees-C* . . . . (Columbia)
Jagged Little Pill . . . . (Maverick)

ANIMALS: A

*See Also: **ANIMALS: A-Z, ANIMALS: GENERAL***

Apeman
Kinks; *Kink Kronikles* . . . . (Reprise)
Lola Versus Powerman And The Moneygoround, Part One . . . . (Reprise)
The Road . . . . (MCA)
Apeman Hop
Ramones; *Animal Boy* . . . . (Sire)
Escape From The Planet Of The Apes
They Might Be Giants; *Severe Tire Damage* . . . . (Restless)
Gator Tails And Monkey Ribs
Spats; *45-#10585* . . . . (ABC)
Harry The Hairy Ape
Ray Stevens; *Best Of Ray Stevens* . . . . (Mercury)
Home On The Range
Bing Crosby; *Crooner-Columbia Years-1928-1934* . . . . . . (Columbia)
Boston Pops Orchestra/Arthur Fiedler; *Yankee Doodle Dandy* . . . . . (RCA)
Gene Autry; *50th Anniversary* . . . . (Republic/Universal)
The Country Music Hall Of Fame-Gene Autry-15 Of His All-Time
Greatest Hits . . . . (Columbia)
Neil Young; *ST/Where The Buffalo Roam* . . . . (Backstreet)
Run Like An Antelope
Phish; *Lawn Boy* . . . . (Elektra)
See You Later, Alligator
Bill Haley & His Comets; *Bill Haley & His Comets* . . . . . (Everest)
Bill Haley & His Comets' Greatest Hits . . . . (MCA)
Bill Haley & His Comets-Golden Hits . . . . (MCA)
Billboard Top Rock 'N' Roll Hits-1956-C . . . . (Rhino)
Mr. Rock 'N' Roll . . . . (Accord)
Rock & Roll Is Here To Stay-C . . . . (Gusto)
Rockin' Rollin' . . . . (Accord)

ANIMALS: B

*See Also: **ANIMALS: A-Z, ANIMALS: BEARS, ANIMALS: BIRDS,
ANIMALS: GENERAL***

Bad Brahma Bull
Chris LeDoux; *Old Cowboy Classics* . . . . (Capitol)
Sing Me A Song Mr. Rodeo Man . . . . (Capitol)
Tex Ritter; *An American Legend* . . . . (Capitol)
Best Of Tex Ritter . . . . (Capitol)
Bat Out Of Hell
Meat Loaf; *Bat Out Of Hell* . . . . (Epic)
Batdance
Prince; *ST/Batman* . . . . (Warner Bros.)
Boy From Tupelo (buffalo)
Emmylou Harris; *Red Dirt Girl* . . . . (Nonesuch)
Buffalo Gun
Michael Murphey; *Swans Against The Sun* . . . . (Epic)
Buffalo River Home
John Hiatt; *Perfectly Good Guitar* . . . . (A&M)
Buffalo Skinners
Woody Guthrie; *Cowboy Songs On Folkways-C* . . . . . (Smithsonian Folkways)
Worried Man Blues-Golden Classics-#1 . . . . (Collectables)
Buffalo Stance
Neneh Cherry; *Raw Like Sushi* . . . . (Virgin)
ST/Slaves Of New York . . . . (Virgin)
Bulls On Parade
Rage Against The Machine; *Evil Empire* . . . . (Epic)
De Bat (Fly In Me Face)
Carly Simon; *Boys In The Trees* . . . . (Elektra)
Eager Beaver
Original Broadway Cast; *No Strings* . . . . (Angel)
Stan Kenton; *In Stereo* . . . . (Creative World)
Kenton In Hi-Fi . . . . (Blue Note)
Solo-Without His Orchestra . . . . (Creative World)
Great White Buffalo
Ted Nugent; *Double Live Gonzo* . . . . (Epic)
Home On The Range
Bing Crosby; *Crooner-Columbia Years-1928-1934* . . . . . . (Columbia)
Boston Pops Orchestra/Arthur Fiedler; *Yankee Doodle Dandy* . . . . . (RCA)
Gene Autry; *50th Anniversary* . . . . (Republic/Universal)
The Country Music Hall Of Fame-Gene Autry-15 Of His All-Time
Greatest Hits . . . . (Columbia)
Neil Young; *ST/Where The Buffalo Roam* . . . . (Backstreet)
Lonely Bull (El Solo Torro)
Herb Alpert & The Tijuana Brass; *Four Sider* . . . . (A&M)
Herb Alpert & The Tijuana Brass' Greatest Hits . . . . (A&M)
Herb Alpert & The Tijuana Brass-Classics-#1 . . . . . (A&M)
The Lonely Bull . . . . (A&M)
Now That The Buffalo's Gone
Buffy Sainte-Marie; *American Child* . . . . (Vanguard)
Best Of Buffy Sainte-Marie . . . . (Vanguard)

Greatest Folksingers Of The '60s-C ....(Vanguard)
I'm Gonna Be A Country Child ....(Vanguard)
On Wisconsin/If You Want To Be A Badger
University Of Wisconsin Marching Band; *Fifth Quarter* ...... (Fidelity Sound)
Release The Bats
Birthday Party; *Best & Rarest* ....(Missing Link)
Birthday Party-Collection ....(Missing Link)
Sadder & Wiser Beaver
Original Broadway Cast; *Beyond The Fringe* ....(Capitol)
Theme From "Batman"
Original Soundtrack; *Television's Greatest Hits-#1-C* ....(TVT)
Wynona's Big Brown Beaver
Primus; *Tales From The Punchbowl* ....(Interscope)
You Can't Roller Skate In A Buffalo Herd
Roger Miller; *Best Of Roger Miller-#2-King Of The Road* ....(Mercury)
Roger Miller-Golden Hits ....(Smash)

ANIMALS: BEARS

See Also: **ANIMALS: A-Z, ANIMALS: GENERAL**

(Let Me Be Your) Teddy Bear
Elvis Presley; *Elvis' Golden Records* ....(RCA)
Elvis In Concert ....(RCA)
Number One Hits ....(RCA)
ST/Loving You ....(RCA)
The Top Ten Hits ....(RCA)
Ballad Of Davy Crockett
Bill Hayes; *Songs Of The West-#4-Movie & Television Themes-C* .....(Rhino)
Fess Parker; *16 Most Requested Songs Of The '50s-#1-C* ....(Legacy)
Columbia Country Classics-#3-Americana-C ....(Columbia)
Hollywood Magic-1950s-C ....(Columbia)
Kentucky HeadHunters; *Electric Barnyard.* ....(Mercury)
Mac Wiseman; *45-#1240.* ....(Dot)
Original Soundtrack; *Television's Greatest Hits-#4-Black & White
Classics-C* ....(TVT)
Tennessee Ernie Ford; *Capitol Collectors Series-Tennessee
Ernie Ford* ....(Capitol)
Bear Went Over The Mountain, The
Original Soundtrack; *Children's Favorites* .... (Kid Rhino/Rhino 4 Kids)
Bears
Quicksilver Messenger Service; *Quicksilver Messenger Service-
Anthology.* ....(Capitol)
Sons Of Mercury ....(Rhino)
Bears
Lyle Lovett; *Step Inside This House* ....(Curb)
Black Bear Road
C.W. McCall; *C.W. McCall's Greatest Hits* ....(Polydor)
Fuzzy Wuzzy
Original Soundtrack; *Toddler Favorites* .... (Kid Rhino/Rhino 4 Kids)
House At Pooh Corner
Loggins & Messina; *Loggins & Messina-On Stage* ....(Columbia)
Sittin' In ....(Columbia)
The Best Of Friends ....(Columbia)
Nitty Gritty Dirt Band; *Best Of The Nitty Gritty Dirt Band* ....(Liberty)
Best Of The Nitty Gritty Dirt Band ....(Curb)
Dirt, Silver & Gold ....(One Way)
Uncle Charlie And His Dog Teddy ....(Liberty)
Preacher & The Bear
Andy Griffith; *American Originals-Andy Griffith* ....(Capitol)
Big Bopper; *Hellooo Baby! Best Of The Big Bopper-1954-1959* ....(Rhino)
Rufus Thomas & Carla Thomas; *Rufus Thomas & Carla Thomas-
Chronicle* ....(Stax)
Simon Smith & His Amazing Dancing Bear
Randy Newman; *Sail Away* ....(Reprise)
Sweet As Bear Meat
Johnny Hodges Orchestra; *Used To Be Duke* ....(Verve)
Teddy Bear Song
Barbara Fairchild; *Back To The '70s-Country-C* ....(Dominion Entert.)
Country Superstars-C ....(Dominion Entert.)
Teddy Bears
Barbra Streisand; *ST/Prince Of Tides* ....(Columbia)
Teddy Bears' Picnic
Anne Murray; *There's A Hippo In My Tub* ....(Capitol)
Frank DeVol; *Small Fry-Capitol Sings Kids Songs For Grownups-C* ..(Capitol)
Theme From "Gentle Ben"
Original Soundtrack; *Television's Greatest Hits-#5-In Living Color-C* ...(TVT)
Theme From "Yogi Bear"
Original Soundtrack; *Hanna-Barbera Classics-#1-Original Recordings Of
The World's Most Famous Cartoon Themes &
Scores* .... (Kid Rhino/Rhino 4 Kids)
*Hanna-Barbera Pic-A-Nic Basket Of Cartoon
Classics* .... (Kid Rhino/Rhino 4 Kids)
Television's Greatest Hits-#1-C ....(TVT)

ANIMALS: BIRDS, Fowl

See Also: **ANIMALS: A-Z, ANIMALS: GENERAL, FLYING,
FREEDOM, SKY**

After The Blackbird Sings
Wallflowers; *The Wallflowers* ....(Virgin)
Ain't Nobody Here But Us Chickens
Asleep At The Wheel; *Very Best Of Asleep At The Wheel
Since 1970* ....(Relentless/Madacy)
Louis Jordan; *Best Of Louis Jordan* ....(MCA)
Albatross
Judy Collins; *Colors Of The Day-The Best Of Judy Collins* ....(Elektra)
Wildflowers ....(Elektra)
Albatross
Fleetwood Mac; *25 Years-The Chain* ....(Warner Bros.)
Vintage Years ....(Sire)
Albatross
Public Image Ltd.; *Second Edition* ....(Island)
And Your Bird Can Sing
Beatles; *"Yesterday"...And Today* ....(Capitol)
Revolver ....(Capitol)
April Showers
Al Jolson; *Best Of Al Jolson* ....(MCA)
The Al Jolson Story-#2 ....(MCA)
Judy Garland; *Hits Of Judy Garland* ....(Capitol)
Judy ....(Capitol)
Baby, I Love Your Way/Free Bird Medley
Will To Power; *Billboard Top Hits-1988-C* ....(Rhino)
Will To Power ....(Epic)
Bad To Me
Billy J. Kramer With The Dakotas; *History Of British Rock-#1-C* ....(Rhino)
Rock Is Dead But It Won't Lie Down-C ....(Gold Rush)
Baltimore Oriole
George Harrison; *Somewhere In England* .... (Dark Horse)
Baltimore Oriole
Carmen McRae; *Greatest Of Carmen McRae* ....(MCA)
Bangkok Cockfight
Martin Denny; *Exotica-Best Of Martin Denny.* ....(Rhino)
Be Like The Bluebird
Cole Porter; *Cole Porter-A Centennial Celebration-C* .... (RCA)
Before I Go
John Hiatt; *Crossing Muddy Waters* ....(Vanguard)
Bird
Jerry Reed & Friends; *Bird.* .... (RCA)
Jerry Reed & Friends' Greatest Hits ....(RCA)
Bird
Time; *Ice Cream Castle* .... (Warner Bros.)
Bird
George Jones; *Too WIld Too Long* ....(Epic)
Bird Bathroom
Surf Punks; *My Beach* ....(Epic)
Bird Brain Baby
Mercy Dee Walton; *Back Luck 'N' Trouble* .... (Arhoolie)
Bird Dog
Everly Brothers; *Best Of The Everly Brothers* ....(Rhino)
Billboard Top Rock 'N' Roll Hits-1958-C ....(Rhino)
Everly Brothers-Cadence Classics-Their 20 Greatest Hits ....(Rhino)
Fabulous Style Of The Everly Brothers ....(Rhino)
Very Best Of The Everly Brothers .... (Warner Bros.)
Bird In A Gilded Cage
Joan Morris & William Bolcom; *After The Ball* ....(Nonesuch)
Bird In The Hand
Velvelettes; *25 Hard-To-Find Motown Classics-#3-C* ....(Motown)
Bird Of Beauty
Stevie Wonder; *Fulfillingness' First Finale* ....(Motown)
Bird Of Brazil
Joyce; *Music Inside* .... (Verve/Forecast)
Bird Of Japan
Joyce; *Music Inside* .... (Verve/Forecast)
Bird Of Prey
Uriah Heep; *Best Of Uriah Heep* ....(Mercury)
Bird On A Wire
Johnny Cash; *American Recordings.* ....(American)
Bird On My Head
David Seville; *45-#063* .... (United Artists)
Bird On The Wire
Jennifer Warnes; *Famous Blue Raincoat* .... (Private Music)
Joe Cocker; *Joe Cocker!.* ....(A&M)
Mad Dogs & Englishmen ....(A&M)
Judy Collins; *So Early In The Spring, The First 15 Years* ....(Elektra)
Who Knows Where The Time Goes ....(Elektra)
Leonard Cohen; *Best Of Leonard Cohen* ....(Columbia)
Bird That Whistles
Joni Mitchell; *Chalk Mark In A Rain Storm* ....(Geffen)
Birdbrain
Tom Buffalo; *Birdbrain.* .... (Beggar's Banquet)

Bird-Brain Rag
Max Morath; *The World Of Scott Joplin-#2* . . . . (Vanguard)
Birdhouse In Your Soul
They Might Be Giants; *Flood* . . . . (Elektra)
Birdland
Manhattan Transfer; *Atlantic Jazz Vocal Classics-C* . . . . (Rhino)
   Best Of The Manhattan Transfer . . . .(Atlantic)
   Billboard Top Contemporary Jazz Vocals-C . . . . (Rhino)
   Extensions . . . . (Rhino)
Quincy Jones; *Back On The Block* . . . . (Qwest)
Weather Report; *8:30* . . . . (Legacy)
   Heavy Weather . . . . (Legacy)
Birdland
Chubby Checker; *Chubby Checker's Greatest Hits* . . . . (Everest)
   Chubby Checker's Greatest Hits . . . . (Abkco)
Birdmad Girl
Cure; *Top* . . . . (Sire)
Birdman Of Alkatrash
Strawberry Alarm Clock; *Strawberry Alarm Clock-Anthology* . . . . . .(One Way)
Birds
Bette Midler; *Live At Last* . . . . (Atlantic)
Linda Ronstadt; *Linda Ronstadt* . . . . (Capitol)
Neil Young; *After The Gold Rush* . . . . (Reprise)
Birds And The Bees
Jewel Akens; *American Graffiti-#3-C* . . . . (MCA)
   Collectables Presents The History Of Rock-#4-C . . . . . . (Collectables)
   Cruisin'-1965-C . . . .(Increase)
   Oldies But Goodies-#9-C . . . . (Original Sound)
   Super Hits-#3-C . . . . (Gusto)
Birds In My Tree
Strawberry Alarm Clock; *Best Of The Strawberry Alarm Clock-#1* . . . (Bac-Trac)
Birds Of A Feather
Paul Revere And The Raiders; *Legend Of Paul Revere And The
   Raiders* . . . . (Columbia)
Birds Of A Feather
Phish; *The Story Of The Ghost* . . . . (Elektra)
Birds Of A Feather
Tim Curry; *Best Of Tim Curry* . . . . (A&M)
Birds Of Paradise
Ed Bruce; *Tell 'Em I've Gone Crazy* . . . . (MCA)
Birds Of Paradise
Pretenders; *Pretenders II* . . . . (Sire)
Birds Of Winter
Zamfir; *Return To Romance* . . . .(Philips)
Bird's The Word
Rivingtons; *Groove 'N' Grind-'50s & '60s Dance Hits-C* . . . . (Rhino)
   Let's Dance . . . . (Gusto)
   Super Oldies Of The '60s-#10-C . . . .(Audio Fidelity)
Black Crow
Joni Mitchell; *Hejira* . . . . (Asylum)
   Shadows & Light . . . . (Asylum)
Black Crow Blues
Bob Dylan; *Another Side Of Bob Dylan* . . . . (Columbia)
Blackbird
Beatles; *Beatles-Box Set* . . . . (Capitol)
   The Beatles (White Album) . . . . (Capitol)
Crosby, Stills & Nash; *CSN* . . . . (Atlantic)
Paul McCartney; *Unplugged (The Official Bootleg)* . . . . (Capitol)
Wings; *Wings Over America* . . . . (Capitol)
Blue Jay Way
Beatles; *Beatles-Box Set* . . . . (Capitol)
   Magical Mystery Tour . . . . (Capitol)
Bluebird
Buffalo Springfield; *Buffalo Springfield Again* . . . . (Atco)
   Buffalo Springfield-Retrospective . . . . (Atco)
   Classic Rock 1966-1988-C . . . . (Atlantic)
Bluebird
Paul McCartney & Wings; *Band On The Run* . . . . (Capitol)
Wings; *Wings Over America* . . . . (Capitol)
Bluebird
Robin Trower; *In City Dreams* . . . .(Chrysalis)
Bluebird
Electric Light Orchestra; *Secret Messages* . . . . (Jet)
Bluebird
Helen Reddy; *Live In London* . . . . (Capitol)
   No Way To Treat A Lady . . . . (Capitol)
Bluebird
Leon Russell; *Best Of Leon Russell* . . . . (MCA)
   Will O' The Wisp . . . . (MCA)
Bluebird Is Dead
Electric Light Orchestra; *Afterglow* . . . . (Epic)
   On The Third Day . . . . (Jet)
Bluebird Of Happiness
Lee Andrews And The Hearts; *Gotham Recording Sessions* . . . . . (Collectables)
   Lee Andrews And The Hearts' Biggest Hits . . . . (Collectables)
Bluebirds Over the Mountain
Beach Boys; *Absolute Best-#2* . . . . (Capitol)
   Beach Boys '69 (The Beach Boys Live In London) . . . . (Capitol)

Friends-20/20 . . . . (Capitol)
   Sunshine Dream . . . . (Capitol)
Ritchie Valens; *Best Of Ritchie Valens* . . . . (Rhino)
   History Of Ritchie Valens . . . . (Rhino)
   Ritchie Valens . . . . (Rhino)
Broken Wing
Martina McBride; *Evolution* . . . . (RCA)
Bubblegoose
Wyclef Jean; *Chef Aid-The South Park Album* . . . . (Columbia)
Wyclef Jean featuring Melky Sedeck; *Presents The Carnival F/Refugee
   Allstars* . . . . (Ruffhouse/Columbia)
Bye Bye Blackbird
Dean Martin; *Swingin' Down Yonder* . . . . (Capitol)
Joe Cocker; *With A Little Help From My Friends* . . . . (A&M)
Liza Minnelli; *ST/Liza With A "Z"* . . . . (Columbia)
Miles Davis; *Ballads* . . . . (Columbia)
   Miles Davis Quintet/Jazz Sampler #2 . . . . (Columbia)
Miles Davis Quintet; *Round About Midnight* . . . . (Columbia)
Cage The Songbird
Elton John; *Blue Moves* . . . . (MCA)
   Elton John . . . .(Polydor)
Caged Bird
Alicia Keys; *Songs In A Minor* . . . . (J)
California Saga (Beaks Of Eagles)
Beach Boys; *Holland* . . . .(Brother)
   Ten Years Of Harmony . . . .(Caribou)
Canary In A Coal Mine
Police; *Zenyatta Mondatta* . . . . (A&M)
Chicken Soup
Angel; *Helluva Band* . . . . (Mercury)
Chicken Stew Part I
Geoff Muldaur & Amos Garrett; *Geoff Muldaur & Amos
   Garrett* . . . . (Flying Fish)
Cluckin' Hen, Going Back To Kentucky
J.P. Fraley & Annadeene; *Wild Rose Of The Mountain* . . . . (Rounder)
Constipated Duck
Jeff Beck; *Blow By Blow* . . . . (Epic)
Cry Of The Wild Goose
Frankie Laine; *Frankie Laine-Golden Hits* . . . . (Mercury)
Didjerama
Jamiroquai; *Traveling Without Moving* . . . . (Work/Epic)
Disco Duck
Rick Dees And His Cast Of Idiots; *Original Disco Duck* . . . . (RSO)
Diving Duck Blues
Kingsnakes; *19 Lucky Strikes* . . . . (Blue Wave)
   Salt City Blues-C . . . . (Blue Wave)
Sleepy John Estes; *Legend Of Sleepy John Estes* . . . . (Delmark)
Taj Mahal; *Taj Mahal* . . . . (Columbia)
Dixie Chicken
Little Feat; *Dixie Chicken* . . . . (Warner Bros.)
   Waiting For Columbus . . . . (Warner Bros.)
Do The Bird
Dee Dee Sharp; *Let's Dance* . . . . (Gusto)
   Rock-O-Rama-#2-C . . . .(Abkco)
Do The Funky Chicken
Rufus Thomas; *15 Original Big Hits-#3-C* . . . . (Stax)
   Let's Dance . . . . (Gusto)
   Rufus Thomas-Chronicle . . . . (Stax)
Do The Funky Penguin
Rufus Thomas; *15 Original Big Hits-#3-C* . . . . (Stax)
   Rufus Thomas . . . . (Gusto)
   Rufus Thomas-Chronicle . . . . (Stax)
Don't Take Your Love From Me
Etta James; *These Foolish Things-The Classic Balladry Of Etta James* . . (MCA)
King Sisters; *Spotlight On The King Sisters* . . . . (Capitol)
Three Suns; *Very Best Of The Three Suns* . . . . (Taragon)
Drunken Blue Rooster
Todd Rundgren; *Todd* . . . . (Rhino)
Duck, The
Jackie Lee; *Only Dance 1965-1969-C* . . . .(JCI Assoc. Labels)
   Sock Hop-C . . . . (Dunhill Compact Classics)
   Super Oldies Of The '60s-#6-C . . . . (Audio Fidelity)
Olympics; *Best Of The Olympics* . . . . (Vee-Jay)
Eagle
Abba; *Abba's Greatest Hits-#2* . . . .(Atlantic)
   I Love Abba . . . .(Atlantic)
   The Album . . . .(Atlantic)
Eagle
Paul Winter; *Common Ground* . . . . (A&M)
Eagle
Waylon Jennings; *Eagle* . . . . (Epic)
   Greatest Country Hits Of The '90s-1991-C . . . . (Columbia)
Eagle & The Hawk
John Denver; *Aerie* . . . . (RCA)
   Evening With John Denver . . . . (RCA)
   John Denver's Greatest Hits . . . . (RCA)
Eagle Never Hunts The Fly
Music Machine; *Best Of Music Machine* . . . . (Rhino)
   Nuggets-#2-Punk-C . . . . (Rhino)

Eagle Over Angel
Brother Phelps; *Let Go* .... (Asylum)
Eagle Will Rise Again
Alan Parsons Project; *Pyramid* .... (Arista)
Eagles Fly
Sammy Hagar; *Sammy Hagar* .... (Geffen)
Flamingo (D.E.)
Duke Ellington; *Best Of Duke Ellington* .... (Capitol)
  Blanton-Webster Band .... (Bluebird)
  Do Nothin' Til You Hear From Me .... (Intermedia)
Flamingo Express
Royaltones; *45-#3011* .... (Goldisc)
Flamingos Fly
Sammy Hagar; *Nine On A Ten Scale* .... (Capitol)
Van Morrison; *Period Of Transition* .... (Warner Bros.)
Fly Like An Eagle
Seal; *ST/Space Jam* .... (Warner Sunset)
Steve Miller; *Fly Like An Eagle* .... (Capitol)
  ST/FM .... (MCA)
  Steve Miller Band-Gift Set .... (Capitol)
  Steve Miller Band-Live .... (Capitol)
  Steve Miller Band's Greatest Hits-1974-78 .... (Capitol)
Fly, Robin, Fly
Silver Convention; *Best Of Silver Convention-Get Up And Boogie*. . . (Hot Prod.)
Flying Turkey Trot
REO Speedwagon; *A Decade Of Rock And Roll 1970 To 1980* .... (Epic)
  R.E.O. .... (Epic)
  REO Speedwagon Live/You Get What You Play For ...... (Epic)
Fox, The (goose, ducks)
Nickel Creek; *Nickel Creek* .... (Sugar Hill)
Free As A Bird
Beatles; *The Beatles-Anthology-#1* .... (Capitol)
Free Bird
Lynyrd Skynyrd; *Gold & Platinum* .... (MCA)
  One More From The Road .... (MCA)
  Pronounced Leh-nerd Skin-nerd. .... (MCA)
  Southern By The Grace Of God-Tribute '87 .... (MCA)
Wynonna; *Skynyrd Frynds-C* .... (MCA)
Give Me Wings
Michael Johnson; *Best Of Michael Johnson* .... (RCA)
  Hits Of '86-C .... (RCA)
  Wings .... (RCA)
Golden Goose
Peter Frampton; *Somethin's Happening* .... (A&M)
Todd Rundgren; *Healing* .... (Rhino)
Golden Lark
Styx; *Man Of Miracles* .... (Wooden Nickel)
Gonna Find Me A Bluebird
Frank Ifield; *Best Of Frank Ifield* .... (Curb)
Marvin Rainwater; *Greatest Hits-1957-C* .... (Deluxe)
  Only Country-1955-1959-C .... (JCI Assoc. Labels)
Royal Wade Kimes; *ST/Traveller* .... (Asylum)
Grantchester Meadows
Pink Floyd; *Ummagumma* .... (Capitol)
Gray Eagle
Taylor's Kentucky Boys; *Traditional Country Classics 1927-1929* . . (Historical)
Great Speckled Bird
Roy Acuff; *Best Of Roy Acuff* .... (Liberty)
  Bluegrass Super Hits-C .... (Columbia)
  Roy Acuff's Greatest Hits .... (Columbia)
Green Finch & Linnet Bird
Original Cast/Angela Lansbury/Len Cariou; *Sweeney Todd* .... (RCA)
Grey Goose/Sixpenny Money
Joe Burke; *Traditional Music Of Ireland* .... (Green Linnet)
Hard Luck Stories
Neil Young; *Landing On Water* .... (Geffen)
Hey Little Bird
Buffy Sainte-Marie; *Best Of Buffy Sainte-Marie-#2* .... (Vanguard)
  Fire & Fleet & Candlelight. .... (Vanguard)
Hey, Mr. Bluebird
Ernest Tubb & Wilburn Brothers; *More Great Country Duets-C* .... (MCA Special Prod.)
High Flying Bird
Elton John; *Don't Shoot Me I'm Only The Piano Player* .... (Polydor)
His Eye Is On The Sparrow
Carmen McRae; *Greatest Of Carmen McRae* .... (MCA)
Marvin Gaye; *Musical Testament 1964-1984* .... (Motown)
Preservation Hall Jazz Band; *Best Of The Preservation Hall Jazz Band* .... (Columbia)
Soundtrack; *Streetcar Named Desire* .... (Allegiance)
Hole In My Head (goose)
Dixie Chicks; *Fly* .... (Monument)
Hummingbird
Seals & Crofts; *Seals & Crofts' Greatest Hits* ..... (Warner Bros.)
  Summer Breeze .... (Warner Bros.)
Hummingbird
B.B. King; *Best Of B.B. King* .... (MCA)
Hummingbird
Leon Russell; *Best Of Leon Russell* .... (MCA)

Hummingbird
Ricky Skaggs; *Kentucky Thunder* .... (Epic)
Hummingbird
Leon Russell; *Leon Russell* .... (MCA)
Hummingbird
Jimmy Page; *Outrider* .... (Geffen)
Hummingbird
Bob Seger; *Smokin' O.P.'s* .... (Capitol)
Hummingbird
Restless Heart; *Wheels* .... (RCA)
Hunting The Wren
Steeleye Span; *Live At Last* .... (Chrysalis)
I Tawt I Taw A Puddy Tat
Mel Blanc; *From The Vaults-#7-The Movies...-C* .... (Capitol)
I'm Like A Bird
Nelly Furtado; *Whoa Nelly!* .... (DreamWorks/SKG)
I'm So Lonesome I Could Cry
B.J. Thomas; *B.J. Thomas' Greatest Hits* .... (Rhino)
Cowboy Junkies; *Trinity Session* .... (RCA)
Hank Williams; *24 Of Hank Williams' Greatest Hits* ...... (Polydor)
  Hank Williams-40 Greatest Hits .... (Polydor)
  I'm So Lonesome I Could Cry-1949 .... (Polydor)
Hank Williams, Jr.; *Very Best Of Hank Williams, Jr.* ...... (Polydor)
Jim Rooney; *One Day At A Time* .... (Rounder)
Johnny Cash; *Hank Williams Songbook-C* .... (Columbia)
Keb' Mo'; *Timeless: Hank Williams Tribute-C* .... (Lost Highway/IDJMG)
Is A Bluebird Blue
Conway Twitty; *Rockin' Conway-MGM Years* .... (Mercury)
It Must Be Love
Alan Jackson; *Under The Influence* .... (Arista)
It Wouldn't Hurt To Have Wings
Mark Chesnutt; *Wings* .... (Decca)
Kentucky Bluebird
Keith Whitley; *Kentucky Bluebird* .... (RCA)
Kentucky Song Bird
Roger Whittaker; *Mirrors Of My Mind* .... (RCA)
Lady Bird
Nancy Sinatra & Lee Hazlewood; *Fairy Tales & Fantasies-Best Of* ..... (Rhino)
Last Lonely Eagle
New Riders Of The Purple Sage; *Best Of New Riders Of The Purple Sage* .... (Columbia)
  New Riders Of The Purple Sage .... (Columbia)
Listen To The Mocking Bird
Lester Flatt; *Lester Raymond Flatt.* .... (Flying Fish)
Little Bird
Jerry Jeff Walker; *Mr. Bojangles* .... (Bainbridge)
  Viva Terlingua. .... (MCA)
Little Bird
Sherrie Austin; *Love In The Real World* .... (Arista)
Little Bird
Beach Boys; *Friends-20/20* .... (Capitol)
Little Bird, Little Bird
Original London Cast; *Man Of La Mancha* .... (MCA)
Little Birdie
Stanley Brothers; *Stanley Brothers* .... (Melodian)
  Stanley Series-Vol. 2-#1 .... (Copper Creek)
Little Birdie
Joe Williams; *Happy Anniversary Charlie Brown!-C* .... (GRP)
Little Brown Bird
Elvin Bishop; *Live! Raisin' Hell* .... (Capricorn)
Little Red Hen
Johnny Otis; *Original Johnny Otis Show* .... (Savoy)
Little Red Rooster
B.B. King/Muddy Waters/Big Mama Thornton; *Live At Newport* ... (Intermedia)
Big Mama Thornton; *Jail* .... (Vanguard)
Rolling Stones; *Love You Live* .... (Virgin)
  The Rolling Stones, Now! .... (Abkco)
Sam Cooke; *Having A Party* .... (RCA)
  This Is Sam Cooke .... (RCA)
Little Turtle Dove
Bobby Day; *Best Of Bobby Day* .... (Rhino)
Little Wing
Derek And The Dominos; *Layla* .... (Polydor)
Jimi Hendrix; *Axis: Bold As Love* .... (Reprise)
  Concerts .... (Reprise)
  Essential Jimi Hendrix .... (Reprise)
  Lifelines/Jimi Hendrix Story .... (Reprise)
Sting; *...Nothing Like The Sun* .... (A&M)
Lullaby Of Birdland
Ella Fitzgerald; *Best Of Ella Fitzgerald-#2* .... (MCA)
  Ella Fitzgerald With Billie Holiday. .... (MCA)
Four Freshmen; *Greatest Hits-Four Freshman* .... (Curb)
Mel Torme; *Songs Of New York.* .... (Rhino)
Sarah Vaughan; *Sarah Vaughan-Golden Hits* .... (Mercury)
Tito Puente & His Latin Ensemble; *Mambo Diablo* .... (Concord Jazz)
May The Bird Of Paradise Fly Up Your Nose
"Little" Jimmy Dickens; *Columbia Country Classics-#3-Americana-C* .... (Columbia)
  Super Hits Of The '60s-C .... (Epic)

Harlow Wilcox and the Oakies; *Cripple Cricket* . . . . (Plantation)

Message To Michael
Dionne Warwick; *Dionne Warwick* . . . . (Everest)
   Dionne Warwick Greatest Hits . . . . (Everest)
   Dionne Warwick-Anthology 1962-1971 . . . . (Rhino)
   Hot! Live & Otherwise . . . . (Arista)
   Original Rock 'N' Roll Hits Of The '60s-C . . . . (Roulette)

Mexican Blackbird
ZZ Top; *Fandango* . . . . (Warner Bros.)
   Six Pack . . . . (Warner Bros.)

Mighty Quinn (Quinn The Eskimo)
Bob Dylan; *Biograph* . . . . (Columbia)
   Bob Dylan's Greatest Hits-#2 . . . . (Columbia)
   Self Portrait . . . . (Columbia)
Ian & Sylvia; *Ian & Sylvia's Greatest Hits* . . . . (Vanguard)
Manfred Mann; *Chapter Two-The Best Of The Fontana Years* . . . . . . (Fontana)

Miracle Of Love
Eileen Rodgers; *Hard To Find 45s On CD-#3-The Mid '50s-C* . . . . (Eric)

Mocking Bird Hill
Patti Page; *Patti Page-16 Most Requested Songs* . . . . (Legacy)
   Patti Page-Golden Hits . . . . (Mercury)
   Patti Page's Greatest Hits . . . . (Columbia)
Russ Morgan; *Best Of Russ Morgan* . . . . (MCA)

Mockingbird
Carly Simon & James Taylor; *Best Of Carly Simon & James Taylor* . . . (Elektra)
   Hotcakes . . . . (Elektra)
Inez Foxx with Charlie Foxx; *Billboard Top R&B Hits-1963-C* . . . . (Rhino)
   Oldies But Goodies-#8-C . . . . (Original Sound)
   Super Oldies Of The '60s-#4-C . . . . (Audio Fidelity)
Peter, Paul & Mary; *Peter, Paul & Mommy* . . . . (Warner Bros.)

Mockingbird Girl
Magnificent Bastards; *ST/Tank Girl* . . . . (Elektra)

Morse Moose & The Grey Goose
Wings; *London Town* . . . . (Capitol)

Mother Goose
Jethro Tull; *Aqualung* . . . . (Chrysalis)

My Canary Is Yellow
Chesterfield Kings; *Stop* . . . . (Mirror)

My Song Bird
Emmylou Harris; *Quarter Moon In A Ten Cent Town* . . . . . (Warner Bros.)
McCarters; *The Gift* . . . . (Warner Bros.)

Night Bird Flying
Jimi Hendrix; *Cry Of Love* . . . . (Reprise)
   Lifelines/Jimi Hendrix Story . . . . (Reprise)

Night Owl
Carly Simon; *Best Of Carly Simon* . . . . (Elektra)
   No Secrets . . . . (Elektra)

Night Owls
Little River Band; *Little River Band's Greatest Hits* . . . . (Capitol)
   Time Exposure . . . . (Capitol)

Nightingale Sang In Berkeley Square
Harry Connick, Jr.; *We Are In Love* . . . . (Columbia)
Manhattan Transfer; *Best Of The Manhattan Transfer* . . . . (Atlantic)
   Mecca For Moderns . . . . (Atlantic)
Tony Bennett; *Perfectly Frank* . . . . (Columbia)

North Star Grassman And The Ravens
Sandy Denny; *Gold Dust: Live At The Royalty-The Final Concert*. . . . . (Island)
   North Star Grassman And The Ravens. . . . . (Hannibal)

Norwegian Wood (This Bird Has Flown)
Beatles; *Beatles-Box Set* . . . . (Capitol)
   Beatles-Love Songs . . . . (Capitol)
   Rubber Soul . . . . (Capitol)
   The Beatles/1962-1966 . . . . (Capitol)

Oklahoma Rooster
Backwoods Banjo; *Jes' Fine* . . . . (Rounder)

On The Wings Of A Nightingale
Everly Brothers; *EB84* . . . . (Mercury)

One Big Love
Emmylou Harris; *Red Dirt Girl* . . . . (Nonesuch)
Patty Griffin; *Flaming Red* . . . . (A&M)

Ostrich
Steppenwolf; *Born To Be Wild-History Of Steppenwolf* . . . . (MCA)
   Steppenwolf . . . . (MCA)

Ostrich Walk
Bob Crosby & His Orchestra; *Bob Crosby-With June Christy & Polly Bergen*. . . . . (Hindsight)
Bob Scobey's Frisco Band; *Direct From San Francisco* . . . . . (Good Time Jazz)

Over The Rainbow
Barbra Streisand; *Just For The Record* . . . . (Columbia)
Dave Brubeck; *Greatest Hits From The Fantasy Years* . . . . (Fantasy)
Ella Fitzgerald; *Silver Collection-Songbooks* . . . . (Verve)
Judy Garland; *Best Of The Capitol Masters-One & Only Box* . . . . (Capitol)
   Judy Garland-At Carnegie Hall . . . . (Capitol)
   Judy Garland's Greatest Hits . . . . (Curb)
   Miss Show Business . . . . (Capitol)
   One & Only . . . . (Capitol)
   ST/The Wizard Of Oz. . . . . (Sony Music Special Prod.)

Painted Bird
Siouxsie And The Banshees; *Kiss In The Dream House*. . . . . (Geffen)

Nocturne. . . . . (Geffen)

Parakeet
R.E.M.; *Up* . . . . (Warner Bros.)

Phoenix
Cult; *Love* . . . . (Sire)

Phoenix
Wishbone Ash; *Live Dates* . . . . (MCA)

Phoenix
Dan Fogelberg; *Phoenix* . . . . (Full Moon)

Pigeon Song
America; *America* . . . . (Warner Bros.)

Pink Flamingos
Rickie Lee Jones; *Traffic From Paradise* . . . . (Geffen)

Please Mr. Sun
Johnnie Ray; *Back To The Early '50s* . . . . (Dominion Entert.)
   Johnnie Ray-16 Most Requested Songs . . . . (Legacy)
Vogues; *Vogues' Greatest Hits* . . . . (Rhino)

Poisoning Pigeons In The Park
Tom Lehrer; *Dr. Demento Presents The Greatest Novelty Records-C* . . . (Rhino)
   Dr. Demento: 20th Anniversary Collection-C . . . . (Rhino)
   Evening Wasted With Tom Lehrer . . . . (Reprise)

Pretty Flamingo
Manfred Mann; *Best Of Manfred Mann* . . . . (EMI Special Markets)
   History Of British Rock-#4-C . . . . (Rhino)
Rod Stewart; *Night On The Town* . . . . (Warner Bros.)

Ragtime Nightingale
Max Morath; *Max Morath Plays The Best Of Scott Joplin And Other Rags*. . . . . (Vanguard)

Ragtime Oriole
Max Morath; *The World Of Scott Joplin* . . . . (Vanguard)

Raven
Alan Parsons Project; *Tales Of Mystery & Imagination* . . . . (Mercury)

Raven
Genesis; *Lamb Lies Down On Broadway* . . . . (Atco)

Raven In The Snow
Bill Miller; *Raven In The Snow* . . . . (Reprise)

Red Bird Tennessee Waltz
Clark Kessinger & Gene Meade; *Clark Kessinger & Gene Meade* . . . . (Rounder)

Red Rooster
Howlin' Wolf; *The Chess Box-Howlin' Wolf* . . . . (Chess)
Paula Lockheart; *It Ain't The End Of The World* . . . . (Flying Fish)

Remember
Jimi Hendrix Experience; *Are You Experienced?* . . . . (Reprise)

Road Runner
Pretty Things; *History Of British Rock-#5-C* . . . . (Rhino)

Road Runner (I'm A)
Fleetwood Mac; *Penguin* . . . . (Reprise)
Humble Pie; *Eat It* . . . . (A&M)
   Smokin'. . . . . (A&M)
Junior Walker & The All Stars; *Junior Walker & The All Stars' Greatest Hits* . . . . (Motown)
   Junior Walker & The All Stars-Anthology . . . . (Motown)
   Motown Superstar Series-#5-Junior Walker & The All Stars . . . . . (Motown)
   Shotgun . . . . (Motown)

Roadrunner
Greg Kihn Band; *With The Naked Eye* . . . . (Beserkley)
Joan Jett; *The Hit List* . . . . (Epic)
Joan Jett & The Blackhearts; *Good Music* . . . . (Epic Portrait Assoc.)
Jonathan Richman & The Modern Lovers; *Beserkley Years-Best Of* . . . (Rhino)
Modern Lovers; *Modern Lovers* . . . . (Rhino)

Rockin' Goose
Johnny And The Hurricanes; *45-#1289*. . . . . (Collectables)

Rockin' Robin
Bobby Day; *Cruisin'-1958-C* . . . . (Increase)
   Oldies But Goodies-#5-C . . . . (Original Sound)
   Rockin' Robin . . . . (Collectables)
   Super Oldies Of The '50s-#2-C . . . . (Audio Fidelity)
Michael Jackson; *Best Of Michael Jackson*. . . . . (Motown)
   Got To Be There . . . . (Motown)
   Michael Jackson-Anthology . . . . (Motown)
   Original Soul Of Michael Jackson . . . . (Motown)

Rooster
Alice In Chains; *Dirt*. . . . . (Columbia)

Rooster Blues
Lightnin' Slim; *Sound Of The Swamp-Best Of Excello-#1-C* . . . . (Rhino)
Peter Wolf; *ST/Fried Green Tomatoes* . . . . (MCA)
Wade Walton; *I Have To Paint My Face: Mississippi Blues-1960* . . . (Arhoolie)

Rooster Song
Fats Domino; *They Call Me The Fat Man* . . . . (EMI)

Rudy The Magic Crow
Swamp Zombies; *Chicken Vulture Crow* . . . . (Dr. Dream Music Group)

Sacred Bird
Original London Cast; *Miss Saigon* . . . . (Geffen)

Shake A Tail Feather
Five Du-Tones; *Toga Rock-#2-C* . . . . (Dunhill Compact Classics)
James & Bobby Purify; *Frat Rock!-#3-Grandson Of Frat Rock!-C* . . . . . (Rhino)

Shoot That Turkey
Holy Modal Rounders; *Alleged In Their Own Time* . . . . (Rounder)

Silver Bird
Mark Lindsay; *Super Hits Of The '70s-Have A Nice Day-#4-C* . . . . (Rhino)
Silver Eagle
Merle Haggard & George Jones; *Taste Of Yesterday's Wine* . . . . (Epic)
Reba McEntire; *Just A Little Love* . . . . (MCA)
Silver Swan Rag
Scott Joplin; *Elite Syncopations* . . . . (Biograph)
Ragtime-#3-Early 1900s . . . . (Biograph)
Sing A Song Of Sixpence
Original Soundtrack; *Children's Favorites* . . . . (Kid Rhino/Rhino 4 Kids)
Sister Seagull
Be Bop Deluxe; *Best Of And The Rest Of Be Bop Deluxe* . . . . . (Capitol)
Best Of Be Bop Deluxe-Raiding The Divine Archive . . . . (Capitol)
Futurama . . . . (Harvest)
Live! In The Air Age . . . .(Harvest)
Skunk, The Goose & The Fly
Tower Of Power; *East Bay Grease* . . . . (Rhino)
Skybird
Neil Diamond; *Love At The Greek* . . . .(Columbia)
ST/Jonathan Livingston Seagull . . . .(Columbia)
Skylark
Anita O'Day; *1940s-The Singers-C* . . . .(Columbia)
Bette Midler; *Bette Midler* . . . . (Atlantic)
Erroll Garner Trio; *Greatest Garner* . . . . (Atlantic)
Glenn Miller; *Best Of Glenn Miller-#3* . . . .(RCA)
Hoagy Carmichael; *Hoagy Sings Carmichael* . . . .(EMI)
Too Marvelous For Words-Capitol Sings Jonny Mercer-C . . . (Capitol)
Linda Ronstadt; *Lush Life* . . . . (Asylum)
Tony Bennett; *Forty Years-The Artistry Of Tony Bennett* . . . .(Columbia)
Skyline Pigeon
Elton John; *Empty Sky* . . . . (Polydor)
Here And There . . . . (Rocket)
Snowbird
Anne Murray; *15 Of The Best* . . . . (Liberty)
Anne Murray-Country . . . .(Capitol)
Anne Murray's Greatest Hits . . . .(Capitol)
Snowbird . . . .(Capitol)
Elvis Presley; *Canadian Tribute* . . . .(RCA)
Elvis Country ("I'm 10,000 Years Old") . . . .(RCA)
Loretta Lynn; *Coal Miner's Daughter* . . . .(MCA)
Songbird
Barbra Streisand; *Barbra Streisand's Greatest Hits, Volume 2* . . . . . .(Columbia)
Lazy Afternoon . . . .(Columbia)
Songbird
Duncan Sheik; *Legacy-A Tribute To Fleetwood Mac's Rumours-C* . . . . .(Lava)
Fleetwood Mac; *25 Years-The Chain* . . . .(Warner Bros.)
Rumours . . . .(Warner Bros.)
Songbird
Kenny G; *Duotones* . . . . (Arista)
Kenny G-Live . . . . (Arista)
Songbird
Jesse Colin Young; *Songbird* . . . . (Warner Bros.)
Sparrow
Simon & Garfunkel; *Wednesday Morning 3 A.M.* . . . .(Columbia)
Sparrow In The Treetop
Guy Mitchell; *Guy Mitchell-16 Most Requested Songs* . . . .(Legacy)
Spread My Wings
Troop; *Attitude* . . . . (Atlantic)
Stereo Chickens
Jerry Jeff Walker; *A Man Must Carry On* . . . . (MCA)
Stone The Crows
Original Cast; *Joseph & The Amazing Technicolor Dreamcoat* . . . . . . (MCA)
Joseph & The Amazing Technicolor Dreamcoat . . . . (Polydor)
Suite: Judy Blue Eyes
Crosby, Stills & Nash; *Crosby, Stills & Nash* . . . . (Atlantic)
CSN . . . . (Atlantic)
ST/Woodstock . . . .(Atlantic)
Crosby, Stills, Nash & Young; *So Far* . . . .(Atlantic)
Surfin' Bird
Pee-Wee Herman; *ST/Back To The Beach* . . . .(Columbia)
Ramones; *All The Stuff & More-#2* . . . . (Sire)
Rocket To Russia . . . . (Sire)
Trashmen; *Collectables Presents The History Of Rock-#1-C* . . . . .(Collectables)
History Of Surf Music-#2-C . . . .(Rhino)
Monster Summer Hits-Wild Surf-C . . . .(Capitol)
ST/Full Metal Jacket . . . .(Warner Bros.)
Super Oldies Of The '60s-#11-C . . . . (Audio Fidelity)
Sweet Bird
Joni Mitchell; *Hissing Of Summer Lawns* . . . . (Asylum)
Tastes Just Like Chicken
Scatterbrain; *Scamboogery* . . . . (Elektra)
Tennessee Bird Walk
Blanchard & Morgan; *Super Hits-#2-C* . . . . (Gusto)
Tennessee Guitars; *20 Great Hits-C* . . . . (Plantation)
Golden Guitar Hits . . . . (SSS International)
Theme From "Duckman"
Original Soundtrack; *Television's Greatest Hits-#7-Cable Ready-C* . . . . .(TVT)
Theme From "Road Runner"
Original Soundtrack; *Television's Greatest Hits-#2-C* . . . .(TVT)

Theme From "Tennessee Tuxedo"
Original Soundtrack; *Television's Greatest Hits-#4-Black & White Classics-C* . . . .(TVT)
Theme From "The Sandpiper" (Shadow Of Your Smile)
Astrud Gilberto; *ST/Sandpiper* . . . . (Verve)
The Envelope Please-Academy Award Winning Songs-#3 (1958-1969)-C . . . .(Rhino)
Barbra Streisand; *My Name Is Barbra, Two* . . . .(Columbia)
Boston Pops Orchestra/Arthur Fiedler; *Greatest Hits Of The '60s-#2* . . . . (RCA)
Motion Picture Classics-#1 . . . . (RCA Victor)
Music For Every Mood-Yesterday . . . .(RCA)
Carmen McRae; *Carmen McRae-Alive* . . . . (Mainstream)
I Want You . . . . (Mainstream)
Frank Sinatra; *At The Sands* . . . . (Reprise)
The Reprise Collection . . . . (Reprise)
Henry Mancini; *Days Of Wine And Roses* . . . .(RCA)
James Morrison; *Snappy Doo* . . . . (Atlantic)
Jose Carreras; *Hollywood Golden Classics* . . . .(Atlantic)
Marvin Gaye; *Romantically Yours* . . . .(Columbia)
Tony Bennett; *Academy Award Winners: 16 Most Requested* . . . . . . (LeGrand)
The Movie Song Album . . . .(Columbia)
Tony Bennett-16 Most Requested Songs . . . .(Legacy)
Tony Bennett's All-Time Greatest Hits . . . .(Columbia)
Theme From "The Woody Woodpecker Show"
Original Soundtrack; *Television's Greatest Hits-#1-C* . . . .(TVT)
Theme From "Yakky Doodle"
Original Soundtrack; *Hanna-Barbera Classics-#1-Original Recordings Of The World's Most Famous Cartoon Themes & Scores* . . . . (Kid Rhino/Rhino 4 Kids)
Hanna-Barbera Pic-A-Nic Basket Of Cartoon Classics . . . . (Kid Rhino/Rhino 4 Kids)
There Ain't Nobody Here But Us Chickens
Original London Cast; *Five Guys Named Moe* . . . .(Relativity)
There'll Be Bluebirds Over The White Cliffs Of Dover
Kay Kyser & His Orchestra; *Best Of The Big Bands-C* . . . .(Columbia)
Thirty Dirty Birds
Red Hot Chili Peppers; *Freaky Styley* . . . .(EMI)
Thirty-Three (swans)
Smashing Pumpkins; *Mellon Collie And The Infinite Sadness* . . . . . (Virgin)
Three Little Birds
Bob Marley & The Wailers; *Exodus* . . . . (Tuff Gong)
Legend: The Best Of Bob Marley & The Wailers. . . . .(Island)
Songs Of Freedom . . . . (Tuff Gong)
Three Ravens
Peter, Paul & Mary; *Peter, Paul and Mary In Concert* . . . . (Warner Bros.)
Till There Was You
Beatles; *Beatles-Box Set.* . . . .(Capitol)
Meet The Beatles! . . . .(Capitol)
With The Beatles . . . . (Parlophone)
Original Cast; *ST/The Music Man* . . . . (Warner Bros.)
Tiny Sparrow
Peter, Paul & Mary; *Moving.* . . . . (Warner Bros.)
Tired Wings
Four Horsemen; *Nobody Said It Was Easy.* . . . . (Def American)
Toucan's Dance
Sergio Mendes; *Arara* . . . .(A&M)
Turkey In The Straw
Stanley Brothers; *Stanley Series-Vol. 1-#3* . . . . (Copper Creek)
Vassar Clements; *Grass Routes* . . . .(Rounder)
Turkey Lurky Time
Original Cast; *Promises Promises* . . . . (United Artists)
Turtle Dovin'
Coasters; *50 Coastin' Classics-C* . . . .(Rhino)
Coasters-Their Greatest Recordings-Early Years. . . . .(Atco)
Young Blood . . . . (Atlantic)
Two Sparrows In A Hurricane
Tanya Tucker; *Can't Run From Yourself* . . . .(Liberty)
Tanya Tucker's Greatest Hits-1990-1992 . . . . (Capitol)
Ugly Duckling
Danny Kaye; *Hans Christian Andersen* . . . . (MCA)
Up Where We Belong
Joe Cocker; *Joe Cocker Live* . . . .(Capitol)
Joe Cocker & Jennifer Warnes; *ST/An Officer And A Gentleman.* . . . . . .(Island)
The Island Story-1962-1987-25th Anniversary-C . . . .(Island)
Voice Of The Eagle
Robbie Basho; *Voice Of The Eagle* . . . .(Vanguard)
When Doves Cry
Ginuwine; *The Bachelor* . . . . (550 Music)
Prince and the Revolution; *ST/Purple Rain* . . . .(Warner Bros.)
When My Sugar Walks Down The Street
Ella Fitzgerald; *Ella Fitzgerald-The Early Years-#2 (1939-1941).* . . . . . .(GRP)
Nat "King" Cole; *The Billy May Sessions.* . . . .(Capitol)
Peggy Lee; *Capitol Sings Jimmy McHugh: I Feel A Song Comin' On-C* . . . .(Capitol)
When The Eagle Flies
Traffic; *When The Eagle Flies* . . . . (Asylum)
When The Red, Red Robin
Al Jolson; *Best Of Al Jolson* . . . . (MCA)
The Al Jolson Story-#3 . . . . (MCA)

Louis Armstrong; *I Like Jazz-Essence Of Louis Armstrong* . . . . (Columbia)
Mitch Miller; *Mitch Miller-16 Most Requested Songs* . . . . (Columbia)

When The Swallows Come Back To Capistrano
Glenn Miller; *In The Mood* . . . . (Pro-Arte)
Ink Spots; *Best Of The Ink Spots* . . . . (MCA)
Ink Spots' Greatest Hits-Original Recordings-1939-1946 . . . . (MCA)

Where Stars And Stripes And The Eagle Fly
Aaron Tippin; *CD Single-#164059* . . . . (Lyric Street)

Whisper To A Scream (Birds Fly)
Icicle Works; *Icicle Works* . . . . (Arista)

White Cliffs Of Dover
Kay Kyser & His Orchestra; *16 Most Requested Songs Of The
'40s-#1-C* . . . . (Legacy)
Lee Andrews And The Hearts; *Lee Andrews And The Hearts'
Biggest Hits* . . . . (Collectables)
Mystics; *Mystics-16 Golden Classics* . . . . (Collectables)
Righteous Brothers; *Righteous Brothers' Greatest Hits* . . . . (Verve)
Righteous Brothers-Anthology 1962-1974 . . . . (Verve)
Rosemary Clooney; *For The Duration* . . . .(Concord Jazz)

White Dove
Lynyrd Skynyrd; *First & Last* . . . . (MCA)

Wild Goose Grasses In Tarrytown
Weavers; *Weavers' Greatest Hits* . . . . (Vanguard)
Weavers-Classics . . . . (Vanguard)

Wild Turkey
Lacy J. Dalton; *Hot Country Rock-#1-C* . . . .(Epic)

Wings Of A Dove
Bob Marley & The Wailers; *Birth Of A Legend 1963-
1966* . . . . (Epic Portrait Assoc.)
Ferlin Husky; *Billboard Top Country Hits-1960-C* . . . . (Rhino)
Country Music Classics-#2-1960-1965-C . . . . (K-Tel)
Ferlin Husky's Greatest Hits . . . . (Curb)

Wolverton Mountain
Claude King; *American Originals-Claude King* . . . . (Columbia)
Best Of Claude King . . . . (Gusto)
Billboard Top Country Hits-1962-C . . . . (Rhino)
Super Hits Of The '60s-C . . . . (Epic)

Woody Woodpecker Song
Kay Kyser & His Orchestra; *Best Of The Big Bands-C* . . . . (Columbia)
Sentimental Favorites . . . . (Columbia)
Mel Blanc & The Sportsmen; *Small Fry-Capitol Sings Kids Songs For
Grownups-C* . . . . (Capitol)

Yellow Bird
Brothers Four; *Brothers Four-Greatest Hits* . . . . (Columbia)
Lawrence Welk; *Best Of Lawrence Welk-20 Great Hits* . . . .(Ranwood)
Mills Brothers; *Cab Driver* . . . .(Ranwood)
Mills Brothers-16 Great Performances . . . .(MCA)
Mills Brothers-22 Great Hits . . . . (Ranwood)
Roger Whittaker; *Roger Whittaker Greatest Hits* . . . . (RCA)

Yellow Raven
Scorpions; *Best Of The Ballads Hot & Slow-C* . . . . (RCA)
Virgin Killer . . . . (RCA)

ANIMALS: C

See Also: **ANIMALS: A-Z, ANIMALS: CATS, ANIMALS: COWS, ANIMALS: GENERAL**

Aba Daba Honeymoon
Debbie Reynolds; *Debbie Reynolds' Greatest Hits* . . . . (Curb)

Alvin For President
Alvin & The Chipmunks; *Greatest Hits: Still Squeaky After All These
Years* . . . . (Capitol)

Behind My Camel
Police; *Zenyatta Mondatta* . . . . (A&M)

Camel
Sonny Rollins; *Don't Stop The Carnival* . . . . (Milestone)

Chipmunk Song
Chipmunks; *Christmas With The Chipmunks-#1* . . . .(EMI)
David Seville & The Chipmunks; *Billboard's Greatest Christmas
Hits-C* . . . . (Rhino)
Dr. Demento's Greatest Christmas CD-C . . . . (Rhino)

Coyote
Joni Mitchell; *Hejira* . . . . (Asylum)
Shadows & Light . . . . (Asylum)
Joni Mitchell & The Band; *The Last Waltz* . . . .(Warner Bros.)

Coyote
Country Joe McDonald; *Into The Fray* . . . . (Rag Baby)
Rock & Roll Music From The Planet Earth . . . . (Fantasy)

Coyote, El
Kris Kristofferson; *Repossessed* . . . . (Mercury)

It Must Be A Camel
Frank Zappa; *Hot Rats* . . . .(Rykodisc)

Midnight At The Oasis (Camel)
Maria Muldaur; *Maria Muldaur* . . . . (Reprise)
Super Hits Of The '70s-Have A Nice Day-#13-C . . . . (Rhino)

Old Coyote Town
Don Williams; *Traces* . . . . (Capitol)

One Little Coyote
Riders In The Sky; *Harmony Ranch* . . . . (Columbia)

Piney Woods/Coyote Howl
Skip Gorman; *A Cowboy's Wild Song To His Herd.* . . . . (Rounder)

See You Later, Alligator (Crocodile)
Bill Haley & His Comets; *Bill Haley & His Comets* . . . . (Everest)
Bill Haley & His Comets' Greatest Hits . . . . (MCA)
Bill Haley & His Comets-Golden Hits . . . . (MCA)
Billboard Top Rock 'N' Roll Hits-1956-C . . . . (Rhino)
Mr. Rock 'N' Roll . . . . (Accord)
Rock & Roll Is Here To Stay-C . . . . (Gusto)
Rockin' & Rollin' . . . . (Accord)

Theme From "B.J. And The Bear" (chimpanzee)
Original Soundtrack; *Television's Greatest Hits-#6-Remote Control-C* . . . (TVT)

Theme From "The Alvin Show"
Original Soundtrack; *Television's Greatest Hits-#3-1970s & 1980s-C* . . . (TVT)

True Men Don't Kill Coyotes
Red Hot Chili Peppers; *Abbey Road E.P.* . . . . (EMI)
Red Hot Chili Peppers . . . . (EMI)
What Hits!? . . . . (EMI)

When The Coyotes Come Near
Sons Of The Pioneers; *Horses, Cattle And Coyotes* . . . .(Shanachie)

ANIMALS: CATS

See Also: **ANIMALS: A-Z, ANIMALS: GENERAL, ANIMALS: LIONS, ANIMALS: TIGERS**

Alaska Cats
Garrison Keillor & Frederica von Stade; *Songs Of The Cat* . . . .(RCA)

Alley Cat
Bent Fabric; *Those Wonderful Instrumentals-#3-C* . . . . (K-Tel)
Big Tiny Little; *Piano Memories* . . . .(Crescendo)

Alley Katz
Daryl Hall & John Oates; *Along The Red Ledge* . . . . (RCA)

Big Electric Cat
Adrian Belew; *Desire Of The Rhino King* . . . . (Island)

Black Cat
Janet Jackson; *Janet Jackson's Rhythm Nation 1814* . . . . (A&M)

Black Cat
Chris Daniels & The Kings; *In Your Face* . . . . (Flying Fish)

Black Cat Blues
John Lee Hooker; *...Alone.* . . . .(Specialty)
Memphis Minnie; *Hoodoo Lady-1933-1937.* . . . . (Columbia)

Black Cat Bone
Albert Collins & Johnny Copeland; *Alligator Records 20th Anniversary
Collection-C* . . . . (Alligator)
Johnny Winter; *Progressive Blues Experiment* . . . . (One Way)
Lightnin' Hopkins; *Dark Muddy Bottom Blues-C* . . . .(Specialty)
Mojo Hand-Anthology . . . . (Rhino)
Lonesome Sundown; *Been Gone Too Long.* . . . . (Hightone)
Roy Rogers; *Blues On The Range* . . . . (Blind Pig)

Black Cat Moan
Beck, Bogert & Appice; *Beck, Bogert & Appice* . . . . (Epic)
Beckology-C . . . . (Epic)

Black Cat Shuffle
Al DiMeola; *Electric Rendezvous* . . . . (Columbia)

Cat Fever
Little Feat; *Sailin' Shoes* . . . . (Warner Bros.)

Cat Melody
Pete Townshend & Ronnie Lane; *Rough Mix* . . . .(Atlantic)

Cat People (Putting Out Fire)
David Bowie; *Let's Dance* . . . . (EMI)
ST/Cat People . . . . (MCA)
The Singles-1969-1993. . . . . (Rykodisc)

Cat Scratch Fever
Ted Nugent; *Cat Scratch Fever* . . . . (Epic)
Double Live Gonzo. . . . . (Epic)

Cats In The Cradle
Ugly Kid Joe; *America's Least Wanted.* . . . . (Stardog)

Cat's In The Cradle
Harry Chapin; *Greatest Stories-Live* . . . . (Elektra)
Harry Chapin-Anthology . . . . (Elektra)
Verities & Balderdash . . . . (Elektra)

Cat's In The Cupboard
Pete Townshend; *Empty Glass* . . . . (Atco)

Cat's Squirrel
Cream; *Fresh Cream* . . . .(Polydor)
Jethro Tull; *This Was.* . . . . (Chrysalis)

Cats Under The Stars
Jerry Garcia; *Cats Under The Stars* . . . . (Arista)

Catwalk
Art Of Noise; *Below The Waste.* . . . . (China)
Saga; *Heads Or Tales* . . . . (Portrait)

China Cat Sunflower
Grateful Dead; *Aoxomoxoa* . . . . (Warner Bros.)
  Europe '72 . . . . (Warner Bros.)
  Without A Net . . . . (Arista)
Cleopatra's Cat
Spin Doctors; *Turn It Upside Down* . . . . (Epic)
Cool Cat
Queen; *Hot Space* . . . . (Hollywood)
Cool For Cats
Squeeze; *Cool For Cats* . . . . (A&M)
  Singles-45's and under . . . . (A&M)
  Squeeze-Classics-#25 . . . . (A&M)
Curiosity Killed The Cat
Curiosity Killed The Cat; *Keep Your Distance* . . . . (Mercury)
Dead Cat
Shelleyan Orphan; *Humroot* . . . . (Columbia)
Dead Cat Alley
Dirty White Boy; *Bad Reputation* . . . . (Polydor)
Dead Cat On The Line
Lucky Peterson; *Lucky Strikes!* . . . .(Alligator)
Eyes Like A Cat
Little Charlie & The Nightcats; *All The Way Crazy* . . . .(Alligator)
  Captured Live . . . . (Alligator)
Hell Cat
Scorpions; *Best Of The Scorpions* . . . .(RCA)
  Virgin Killer . . . . (RCA)
Honky Cat
Elton John; *Elton John's Greatest Hits* . . . . (Polydor)
  Here And There . . . . (Rocket)
  Honky Chateau . . . . (Rocket)
House-Cat
Danielle Dax; *Dark Adapted Eye* . . . . (Sire)
I Tawt I Taw A Puddy Tat
Mel Blanc; *From The Vaults-#7-The Movies...-C* . . . . (Capitol)
Intoxicated Rat
New Lost City Ramblers; *American Moonshine & Prohibition
  Songs* . . . . (Smithsonian Folkways)
Killed A Cat
Kenny Rankin; *Silver Morning* . . . . (Little David)
Kitten On The Keys
Claude Bolling; *Original Ragtime* . . . . (Columbia)
Dick Hyman; *Flip Side Of Red Seal* . . . .(RCA)
  Kitten On The Keys . . . .(RCA)
Liberace; *Liberace-16 Most Requested Songs* . . . . (Columbia)
Kitty
Presidents Of The United States Of America; *The Presidents Of The United
  States Of America* . . . . (Columbia)
Kitty Cat Song
Lee Dorsey; *Ride Your Pony* . . . . (Sundazed Music)
Leave My Kitten Alone
Beatles; *The Beatles-Anthology-#1* . . . . (Capitol)
Elvis Costello; *Kojak Variety* . . . . (Warner Bros.)
Little Willie John; *Best Of Little Willie John-Fever* . . . . (Rhino)
Life #9
Martina McBride; *The Way That I Am* . . . .(RCA)
Litterbox
Meat Puppets; *Meat Puppets* . . . . (SST)
Meow Meow Meow Meow (Meow Mix Cat Food)
Original Soundtrack; *TeeVee Toons-The Commercials-#1-C* . . . . (TVT)
Misty
Erroll Garner; *Other Voices* . . . . (Columbia)
Johnny Mathis; *First 25 Years-Silver Anniversary Album* . . . . (Columbia)
  Heavenly . . . . (Columbia)
  Johnny Mathis' All-Time Greatest Hits . . . . (Columbia)
  Johnny Mathis-Live . . . . (Columbia)
Sarah Vaughan; *Sarah Vaughan-Golden Hits* . . . . (Mercury)
Mr. Mistofelees
Original Broadway Cast; *Cats* . . . . (Geffen)
Original London Cast; *Cats* . . . . (Geffen)
My Cat Fell In The Well (Well Well Well)
Manhattan Transfer; *Bop doo-wopp* . . . . (Atlantic)
My Night To Howl
Lorrie Morgan; *War Paint* . . . .(BNA)
Nine Lives
Aerosmith; *Nine Lives* . . . . (Columbia)
Old Deuteronomy
Original Broadway Cast; *Cats* . . . . (Geffen)
Original London Cast; *Cats* . . . . (Geffen)
Old Gumbie Cat
Original Broadway Cast; *Cats* . . . . (Geffen)
Open Up The Doghouse (Two Cats Are Comin' In)
Nat "King" Cole; *Nat "King" Cole (Box Set)* . . . . (Capitol)
Parakeet
R.E.M.; *Up* . . . . (Warner Bros.)
Pattin' That Cat
Teddy Bunn; *Rare Blues Of The Twenties-1927-1930-C* . . . . (Historical)
Picasso And Me
Gretchen Peters; *Gretchen Peters* . . . .(Purple Crayon Prod.)

Pink Pussycat
Devo; *Duty Now For The Future* . . . . (Warner Bros.)
  Rest Of Devo-Greatest Misses . . . .(Warner Bros.)
Pink-Eyed Pussycat
Bill Haley & His Comets; *Rock Around The Country* . . . . (Crescendo)
  Rockin' Rollin' . . . . (Accord)
Pussy Cat Blues
Big Bill Broonzy; *Do That Guitar Rag* . . . . (Yazoo)
Pussy Cat Song (Nyow!)
Gordon MacRae & Jo Stafford; *Capitol Sings Kids Songs For Grown-
  ups-C* . . . . (Capitol)
Pussycat Meow
Deee-Lite; *Infinity Within* . . . . (Elektra)
Pussycat Moan
Katie Webster; *Alligator Records 20th Anniversary Collection-C* . . . . (Alligator)
Put Your Cat Clothes On
Carl Perkins; *Carl Perkins-Original Sun Greatest Hits* . . . .(Rhino)
  Legends Of Rock Guitar-'50s-#1-C . . . .(Rhino)
Rambo The Cat
Dave Valentin; *Two Amigos* . . . .(GRP)
Savannah Russel/Jete The Dancing Cat
Jeanne Newhall; *Novice* . . . . (Marzipan Music)
Stray Cat Blues
Rolling Stones; *Beggars Banquet* . . . . (Abkco)
  Get Yer Ya-Ya's Out! . . . . (Abkco)
Stray Cat Strut
Stray Cats; *Best Of Stray Cats-Rock This Town* . . . . (EMI)
  Built For Speed . . . . (EMI)
  Rock The First-#4-C . . . . (Sandstone Music)
Sweetest Kittens (Have The Sharpest Claws)
Meatmen; *Rock 'N' Roll Juggernaut* . . . . (Caroline)
Thanks To The Cat House
Johnny Paycheck; *Armed & Crazy* . . . . (Epic)
That Cat Is High
Manhattan Transfer; *Manhattan Transfer-Anthology-Down In
  Birdland* . . . .(Rhino)
  The Manhattan Transfer . . . .(Rhino)
Theme From "Courageous Cat & Minute Mouse"
Original Soundtrack; *Television's Greatest Hits-#2-C* . . . . (TVT)
Theme From "Felix The Cat"
Original Soundtrack; *Television's Greatest Hits-#1-C* . . . . (TVT)
Theme From "Josie & The Pussycats"
Original Soundtrack; *Hanna-Barbera Pic-A-Nic Basket Of Cartoon
  Classics* . . . . (Kid Rhino/Rhino 4 Kids)
  Television's Greatest Hits-#3-1970s & 1980s-C . . . . (TVT)
Theme From "Ren And Stimpy"
Original Soundtrack; *Television's Greatest Hits-#7-Cable Ready-C* . . . . . (TVT)
Theme From "Snagglepuss"
Original Soundtrack; *Hanna-Barbera Classics-#1-Original Recordings Of
  The World's Most Famous Cartoon Themes &
  Scores* . . . . (Kid Rhino/Rhino 4 Kids)
  *Hanna-Barbera Pic-A-Nic Basket Of Cartoon
  Classics* . . . . (Kid Rhino/Rhino 4 Kids)
  *Toon Tunes: 50 Classic Cartoon
  Songs-C* . . . . (Kid Rhino/Rhino 4 Kids)
Theme From "Tom & Jerry"
Henry Mancini; *ST/Tom & Jerry-The Movie* . . . . (MCA)
Theme From "Top Cat"
Original Soundtrack; *Hanna-Barbera Pic-A-Nic Basket Of Cartoon
  Classics* . . . . (Kid Rhino/Rhino 4 Kids)
  Television's Greatest Hits-#1-C . . . . (TVT)
There Are No Cats In America
Nehemiah Persoff/John Guarnieri/Warren Hays; *ST/An American Tail* . . (MCA)
This Black Cat Has 9 Lives
Louis Armstrong; *What A Wonderful World* . . . . (Bluebird)
Tom Cat Blues
Jelly Roll Morton; *Greatest Ragtime Of The Century-C* . . . . (Biograph)
Two Old Cats Like Us
Hank Williams, Jr. & Ray Charles; *Hank Williams, Jr.'s Greatest
  Hits-#2* . . . . (WB/Curb)
Ray Charles & Hank Williams, Jr.; *Friendship-C* . . . . (Columbia)
  Seven Spanish Angels & Other Hits . . . . (Columbia)
Walking My Cat Named Dog
Norma Tanega; *Peanut Butter Jam-C* . . . . (Sony Wonder)
Wash 'n Dry (There's A Cat In The Dryer)
Loudmouths; *Loudmouths* . . . .(New Red Archives)
What's New Pussycat
Tom Jones; *Tom Jones-London Collector-Greatest Hits* . . . . (London)
Wholly Cats
Charlie Christian; *Genius Of The Electric Guitar* . . . . (Columbia)
Wild As A Wildcat
Charlie Walker; *Charlie Walker-Golden Hits* . . . . (Plantation)
Wild Cat
UB40; *Present Arms* . . . . (Virgin)
Year Of The Cat
Al Stewart; *'70s Greatest Rock Hits-#5-Kickin' Back-C* . . . . (Priority)
  Best Of Al Stewart . . . . (Arista)
  Year Of The Cat . . . . (Arista)

Yellow Cat
John Denver; *Rhymes & Reasons* . . . . (RCA)
You Know Me Better Than That
George Strait; *Strait Out Of The Box* . . . . (MCA)
The Chill Of An Early Fall . . . .(MCA)

Frankie Laine; *CBS: The First 50 Years* . . . . (TVT)
Cowboy Super Hits-C . . . . (Columbia)
Television's Greatest Hits-#2-C . . . . (TVT)
Riders In The Sky; *Cowboy Songs* . . . . (Rounder)
There Ain't A Cow In Texas
Merle Travis; *Red, White & Bluegrass-C* . . . . (C.M.H. Prod.)
Vassar Clements & Buddy Emmons; *Saturday Night Shuffle-Merle Travis Celebration* . . . .(Shanachie)
Two Headed Cow
Ennui; *Olive* . . . . (Slamdek)
Utah Carol
Harry K. McClintock; *Cowboy Songs On Folkways-C* . . . .(Smithsonian Folkways)
Marty Robbins; *Gunfighter Ballads & Trail Songs* . . . . (Legacy)
Utah Carroll
Skip Gorman; *A Cowboy's Wild Song To His Herd* . . . . (Rounder)
Wild Cow Moan
Big Joe Turner & Sonny Boy Williamson; *Story Of The Blues-C* . . . . (Columbia)

ANIMALS: COWS, Cattle

*See Also: **AMERICAN WEST, ANIMALS: A-Z, ANIMALS: B (bulls), ANIMALS: GENERAL***

Callin' All Cows
Elvin Bishop; *Juke Joint Jump* . . . . (Capricorn)
Live! Raisin' Hell . . . . (Capricorn)
Cattle Call
Eddy Arnold; *Best Of Eddy Arnold* . . . . (RCA)
Cattle Call . . . . (RCA)
Eddy Arnold-Pure Gold . . . . (RCA)
Nipper's Greatest Hits Of The '50s-#1-C . . . . (RCA)
Riders In The Sky; *Riders Radio Theater* . . . . (MCA)
Cow Cow Boogie
Ella Fitzgerald; *Best Of Ella Fitzgerald-#2* . . . .(MCA)
Freddie Slack & Ella Mae Morse; *Jukebox Saturday Night-Great Vocal Hits-C* . . . . (Capitol)
Judds; *Heartland* . . . .(MCA)
Cowboy Night Herd Song
Roy Rogers & Sons Of The Pioneers; *Cowboy Super Hits-C* . . . . (Columbia)
Cowboy's Wild Song To His Herd
Skip Gorman; *A Cowboy's Wild Song To His Herd* . . . . (Rounder)
Cowtown
George Strait; *George Strait-Number 7* . . . .(MCA)
Webb Pierce; *Webb Pierce-Golden Hits-#2* . . . . (Plantation)
Cowtown
Carly Simon; *Another Passenger* . . . . (Elektra)
Farmer & The Cowman
Original Broadway Cast; *Oklahoma!* . . . . (RCA)
Get Along Little Dogies
Riders In The Sky; *Saddle Pals* . . . . (Rounder)
Tex Ritter; *Tex Ritter: Country Music Hall Of Fame* . . . . . .(MCA Special Prod.)
Holy Cow
54.40; *54.40* . . . . (Reprise)
Band; *Moondog Matinee* . . . . (Capitol)
Lee Dorsey; *Golden Classics-Lee Dorsey* . . . . (Collectables)
New Orleans Jazz & Heritage Festival-1976-C . . . . (Rhino)
Milk Cow Blues
Aerosmith; *Draw The Line* . . . . (Columbia)
Pandora's Box . . . . (Columbia)
Bob Wills & His Texas Playboys; *Best Of Bob Wills & His Texas Playboys* . . . .(MCA)
Tiffany Transcriptions-#3 . . . . (Rhino)
Eddie Cochran; *Eddie Cochran-Legendary Masters* . . . .(EMI)
Rick Nelson; *Rick Nelson-Souvenirs* . . . .(EMI)
Ricky Nelson; *Ricky Nelson-Legendary Masters* . . . .(EMI)
Tim McGraw & Asleep At The Wheel; *Ride With Bob-C* . . . (DreamWorks/SKG)
Milk Cow Blues Boogie
Elvis Presley; *A Date With Elvis* . . . . (RCA)
The Sun Sessions . . . . (RCA)
Rick Nelson; *Live In '85* . . . . (Rhino)
Party Till The Cows Come Home
Elvin Bishop Group; *Bill Graham Presents The Last Days Of The Fillmore-C* . . . . (Epic Portrait Assoc.)
Poor Cow
Donovan; *Troubadour-Definitive Collection* . . . .(Epic)
Poor Cow
Tanita Tikaram; *Ancient Heart* . . . . (Reprise)
Poor Cow
Elton John; *Reg Strikes Back* . . . .(MCA)
Pretty Girl Milking A Cow
Judy Garland; *Best Of Judy Garland* . . . .(MCA)
One & Only . . . . (Capitol)
Pretty Little Dogies
Skip Gorman; *A Cowboy's Wild Song To His Herd* . . . . (Rounder)
Quaker's Cow
Doc Watson; *On Stage (Featuring Merle Watson)* . . . . (Vanguard)
Saddle The Cow
Dr. John; *Brightest Smile In Town* . . . .(Clean Cuts)
Sat On A Cow Polka
Li'l Wally; *Old Country Polish Polkas* . . . .(Jay Jay)
Some Cow Fonque (More Tea, Vicar?)
Buckshot LeFonque; *ST/Men In Black* . . . . (Columbia)
Song Of A Cowboy
Skip Gorman; *A Cowboy's Wild Song To His Herd* . . . . (Rounder)
'Tain't A Cow In Texas
Margaret Whitmire; *Barrelhouse Mamas: Born In The Alley, Raised In The Slums-C* . . . . (Yazoo)
Theme From "Rawhide"
Blues Brothers; *Original Soundtrack* . . . .(Atlantic)

ANIMALS: D

*See Also: **ANIMALS: A-Z, ANIMALS: DOGS, ANIMALS: DOLPHINS, ANIMALS: GENERAL***

Be Kind To Your Web-Footed Friends
Mitch Miller; *Sing Along With Mitch* . . . . (Columbia)
Donkey Serenade
Allan Jones; *Allan Jones Sings Favorites* . . . . (Glendale)
Nipper's Greatest Hits Of The '30s-#1-C . . . . (RCA)
ST/Radio Days . . . .(Novus)
Artie Shaw; *Gloomy Sunday* . . . .(Pickwick)
This Is Artie Shaw . . . . (Bluebird)
Home On The Range
Bing Crosby; *Crooner-Columbia Years-1928-1934* . . . . (Columbia)
Boston Pops Orchestra/Arthur Fiedler; *Yankee Doodle Dandy* . . . . . .(RCA)
Gene Autry; *50th Anniversary* . . . . (Republic/Universal)
The Country Music Hall Of Fame-Gene Autry-15 Of His All-Time Greatest Hits . . . . (Columbia)
Neil Young; *ST/Where The Buffalo Roam* . . . .(Backstreet)
I Want A New Duck
"Weird Al" Yankovic; *Dare To Be Stupid* . . . .(Scotti Bros.)
Man & The Donkey
Chuck Berry; *Missing Berries-Rarities-#3* . . . . (Chess)
Monkey Wash Donkey Rinse
Warren Zevon; *Mutineer* . . . . (Giant)
One Way Donkey Ride
Sandy Denny; *Best Of Sandy Denny* . . . .(Hannibal)
Who Knows Where The Time Goes . . . .(Hannibal)
Ride Your Donkey
Joe Strummer; *Earthquake Weather* . . . . (Epic)
Run Like A Deer
Beers Family Sings; *Seasons Of Peace* . . . .(Biograph)

ANIMALS: DOGS

*See Also: **ANIMALS: A-Z, ANIMALS: GENERAL***

Amsterdam Dog Shit Blues
Mojo Nixon & Skid Roper; *Enigma Variations-#2-C* . . . . (Enigma Capitol)
Arkansas Dog
Pinkard & Bowden; *Writers In Disguise* . . . . (Warner Bros.)
Atomic Dog
George Clinton; *Best Of George Clinton* . . . . (Capitol)
Computer Games . . . . (Capitol)
Baby Do The Philly Dog
Olympics; *Official Record Album Of The Olympics* . . . . (Rhino)
Baby Ice Dog
Blue Oyster Cult; *Tyranny & Mutation* . . . . (Columbia)
Back In The Doghouse Again
Ray Stevens; *#1 With A Bullet* . . . . (Curb)
Ballad Of Mad Dogs & Englishmen
Ivan "Boogaloo Joe" Jones; *Black Whip* . . . .(Prestige)
Leon Russell; *Leon Russell & The Shelter People* . . . . (MCA)
Bark At The Moon
Ozzy Osbourne; *Bark At The Moon* . . . . (CBS Associated)
The Ozzman Cometh . . . . (Epic)
B-I-N-G-O
Original Soundtrack; *Mother Goose Songs* . . . .(Madacy)
Bird Dog
Everly Brothers; *Best Of The Everly Brothers* . . . . (Rhino)
Billboard Top Rock 'N' Roll Hits-1958-C . . . . (Rhino)
Everly Brothers-Cadence Classics-Their 20 Greatest Hits . . . . (Rhino)
Fabulous Style Of The Everly Brothers . . . . (Rhino)
Very Best Of The Everly Brothers . . . . (Warner Bros.)

Black Dog
Led Zeppelin; *Led Zeppelin IV* .... (Atlantic)
Led Zeppelin-Box Set .... (Atlantic)
Bow Wow (That's My Name)
Lil Bow Wow; *Beware Of Dog* .... (So So Def/Columbia)
Bride Of Rain Dog
Tom Waits; *Rain Dogs* .... (Island)
By-Tor & The Snow Dog Suite
Rush; *All The World's A Stage* .... (Mercury)
Archives .... (Mercury)
Fly By Night .... (Mercury)
Casual Affair
Tonic; *Lemon Parade* .... (Polydor)
Damned Old Dog
k.d. lang; *Tame Yourself-C* .... (Rhino)
Roches; *Roches* .... (Warner Bros.)
Dawgs (Are A Man's Best Friend)
Original Cast; *Dawgs* .... (Glendale)
Dead Puppies
Ogden Edsl; *Dr. Demento Presents The Greatest Novelty Records-#4-*
1970s-C .... (Rhino)
Dr. Demento Presents The Greatest Novelty Records-C .... (Rhino)
Diamond Dogs
David Bowie; *Changesbowie* .... (Rykodisc)
David Live .... (Rykodisc)
Diamond Dogs .... (Rykodisc)
The Singles-1969-1993 .... (Rykodisc)
Dirty Dawg
NKOTB; *Face The Music* .... (Columbia)
Dirty Old Egg-Sucking Dog
Johnny Cash; *Essential Johnny Cash* .... (Columbia)
Johnny Cash At Folsom Prison & San Quentin .... (Columbia)
Discount Dogs
Joe Perry Project; *Let The Music Do The Talking* .... (Columbia)
Dog
Rufus Thomas; *Walking The Dog* .... (Atlantic)
Dog & Butterfly
Heart; *Dog & Butterfly* .... (Portrait)
Heart's Greatest Hits/Live .... (Epic)
Dog Blue
Mimi & Richard Farina; *Best Of Mimi & Richard Farina* .... (Vanguard)
Dog Breath
Frank Zappa; *Uncle Meat* .... (Barking Pumpkin)
Mothers Of Invention; *Just Another Band From L.A.* .... (Bizarre/Straight)
Dog Days
Atlanta Rhythm Section; *Dog Days* .... (Polydor)
Dog Eat Dog
Adam Ant; *Antics In The Forbidden Zone* .... (Epic)
Kings Of The Wild Frontier .... (Epic)
Dog Eat Dog
Ted Nugent; *Free-For-All* .... (Epic)
Dog Eat Dog
AC/DC; *Let There Be Rock* .... (Atco)
Dog Eat Dog
"Weird Al" Yankovic; *Polka Party* .... (Scotti Bros.)
Doggie In The Window
Patti Page; *Patti Page-16 Most Requested Songs* .... (Legacy)
Patti Page-Golden Hits .... (Mercury)
Patti Page's Greatest Hits .... (Columbia)
Doggin' Around
Jackie Wilson; *Great Soul Hits* .... (Brunswick)
My Golden Favorites .... (Brunswick)
Reet Petite-Best Of Jackie Wilson .... (Columbia)
The Jackie Wilson Story .... (Epic)
Doggin' The Dog
Big Joe Turner; *Big Joe* .... (MCA)
Jazz Heritage-Blues & All That Jazz .... (MCA)
Jazz Heritage-Early Big Joe .... (MCA)
Doggone Right
Smokey Robinson & The Miracles; *Compact Command Performances-*
Smokey Robinson & The Miracles .... (Motown)
Smokey Robinson & The Miracles' Anthology .... (Motown)
Doggy Dogg World
Snoop Doggy Dogg; *Doggystyle* .... (Death Row)
Dogman
King's X; *Dogman* .... (Atlantic)
Dogs
Pink Floyd; *Animals* .... (Columbia)
Dogs
Motorhead; *Mega Metal-C* .... (K-Tel)
No Sleep At All .... (Roadracer)
Dogs
Stan Ridgway; *Mosquitos* .... (Geffen)
Dogs
Who; *Who's Missing* .... (MCA)
Dogs & Ferretts
Steeleye Span; *Commoner's Crown* .... (Chrysalis)

Dogs Among At Bushes
Chieftans; *8* .... (Columbia)
Dogs In The Yard
King Musker Band; *45-#800034* .... (Polydor)
Paul McCrane; *ST/Fame* .... (RSO)
Dog's Life
Gentle Giant; *Octopus* .... (Columbia)
Dogs Part 2
Who; *Who's Missing* .... (MCA)
Dogtown
Harry Chapin; *Heads & Tales* .... (Elektra)
Don't Let The Same Dog Bite You Twice
Robin Lee; *Heart On A Chain* .... (Atlantic)
Every Dog Has His Day
Charlie Gonzales; *Charlie Gonzales* .... (Collectables)
Every Dog Has Its Day
Eddie Bo; *Check Mr. Popeye* .... (Rounder)
Gonna Buy Me A Dog
Monkees; *Monkee Flips* .... (Rhino)
Monkees .... (Arista)
Got No More Home Than A Dog
Ian & Sylvia; *Ian & Sylvia* .... (Vanguard)
Ian & Sylvia's Greatest Hits .... (Vanguard)
Hair Of The Dog
Guns N' Roses; *The Spaghetti Incident?* .... (Geffen)
Nazareth; *Hair Of The Dog* .... (A&M)
Heavy Metal Memories-C .... (Rhino)
Hot Tracks .... (A&M)
Nazareth-Classics-#16 .... (A&M)
'Snaz .... (A&M)
Hangdog Hotel Room
Gordon Lightfoot; *Gord's Gold-#2* .... (Warner Bros.)
Hard Day's Night, A
Beatles; *Beatles 1* .... (Capitol)
Beatles-20 Greatest Hits .... (Capitol)
ST/A Hard Day's Night .... (Capitol)
The Beatles At The Hollywood Bowl .... (Capitol)
The Beatles/1962-1966 .... (Capitol)
He Treats Me Like A Dog
St. Louis Bessie; *Barrelhouse Mamas: Born In The Alley, Raised In The*
Slums-C .... (Yazoo)
Heaven And Hot Rods
Stone Temple Pilots; *No. 4* .... (Atlantic)
Hey Bulldog
Beatles; *Rock 'N' Roll Music* .... (Capitol)
Yellow Submarine .... (Capitol)
Hound Dog
Elvis Presley; *Aloha from Hawaii via Satellite* .... (RCA)
Elvis Aron Presley .... (RCA)
Elvis As Recorded At Madison Square Garden .... (RCA)
Elvis' Golden Records .... (RCA)
Elvis In Concert .... (RCA)
Elvis Recorded Live On Stage In Memphis .... (RCA)
Elvis-A Legendary Performer, Volume 3 .... (RCA)
From Memphis To Vegas/From Vegas To Memphis .... (RCA)
Number One Hits .... (RCA)
ST/Forrest Gump .... (Epic/Sony Music Soundtrax)
House The Dog Built
Jibri Wise One; *House The Dog Built (Single)* .... (Ear Candy)
I Buyed Me A Little Dog
Dave Van Ronk; *Van Ronk* .... (Fantasy)
I Love That Dog
Connie Kaldor; *Small Cafe* .... (Philo)
I Wanna Be A Drug-Sniffing Dog
Lard; *Pure Chewing Satisfaction* .... (Alternative Tentacles)
The Virus That Would Not Die!-C .... (Alternative Tentacles)
I Wanna Be Your Dog
Joan Jett & The Blackhearts; *Up Your Alley* .... (Epic Portrait Assoc.)
I Wanna Be Your Dog
Stooges; *Stooges* .... (Elektra)
I Wanna Be Your Puppy, Baby
John Lee Hooker; *Jazz Heritage-Lonesome Mood-C* .... (MCA)
I Want A Dog
Pet Shop Boys; *Introspective* .... (EMI)
If Dogs Run Free
Bob Dylan; *New Morning* .... (Columbia)
I'm Walking The Dog
Webb Pierce; *Best Of Webb Pierce* .... (MCA)
Webb Pierce-Golden Hits .... (Plantation)
Jealous Dogs
Pretenders; *Pretenders II* .... (Sire)
John Peel
Hermes Nye; *Anglo-American Songs* .... (Smithsonian Folkways)
King Of The Dogs
Spread Eagle; *Open To The Public* .... (MCA)
Leave My Kitten Alone
Beatles; *The Beatles-Anthology-#1* .... (Capitol)
Elvis Costello; *Kojak Variety* .... (Warner Bros.)

Little Willie John; *Best Of Little Willie John-Fever* . . . . (Rhino)
Let Me Play With Your Poodle
  Lightnin' Hopkins; *Lightnin' Hopkins-Complete Aladdin Recordings* . . . .(EMI)
Little Brown Dog
  Judy Collins; *Golden Apples Of The Sun* . . . . (Elektra)
Low Down Dog
  Big Joe Turner; *Boss Of The Blues* . . . .(Atlantic)
    Have No Fear Big Joe Is Here . . . . (Savoy)
Mad Dogs & Englishmen
  Noel Coward; *Live From Las Vegas & New York* . . . . (Columbia)
Man Bites Dog
  Plan 9; *Enigma Variations-#2-C* . . . . (Enigma Capitol)
Me & You & A Dog Named Boo
  Lobo; *Best Of Lobo* . . . . (Big Tree)
    Super Hits Of The '70s-Have A Nice Day-#5-C . . . . (Rhino)
Me And My Arrow
  Nilsson; *Nilsson's Greatest Hits* . . . . (RCA)
    The Point . . . . (RCA)
Move It On Over
  Hank Williams; *Complete Hank Williams* . . . . (Mercury)
My Dead Dog Rover
  Hank, Stu, Dave & Hank; *Dr. Demento Presents The Greatest Novelty
    Records-#4-1970s-C* . . . . (Rhino)
My Dog's Better Than Your Dog (Ken-L Ration Dog & Puppy Food)
  Original Soundtrack; *TeeVee Toons-The Commercials-#1-C* . . . . (TVT)
My Life As A Dog
  Active Ingredient; *Extrastrength* . . . . (Bainbridge)
Nasty Dogs & Funky Kings
  ZZ Top; *Fandango* . . . .(Warner Bros.)
    Six Pack . . . .(Warner Bros.)
No Dogs Allowed
  McSkat Kat And The Stray Mob; *Adventures Of McSkat Kat And The
    Stray Mob* . . . . (Captive)
  Original Cast; *Dawgs* . . . . (Glendale)
North To Alaska
  Dwight Yoakam; *Under The Covers* . . . . (Reprise)
  Johnny Horton; *American Originals-Johnny Horton* . . . . (Columbia)
    Billboard Top Country Hits-1961-C . . . . (Rhino)
    Johnny Horton's Greatest Hits . . . . (Columbia)
    Super Hits Of The '60s-C . . . .(Epic)
Not Much Of A Dog
  Michael Feinstein; *Pure Imagination* . . . . (Elektra)
Ol' Red
  Blake Shelton; *Blake Shelton* . . . .(Giant)
Old Dogs, Children & Watermelon Wine
  Tom T. Hall; *Essential Tom T. Hall-20th Anniversary Collection* . . . . (Mercury)
    Tom T. Hall's Greatest Hits-#2 . . . . (Mercury)
Open Up The Doghouse (Two Cats Are Comin' In)
  Nat "King" Cole; *Nat "King" Cole (Box Set)* . . . . (Capitol)
Peace Dog
  Cult; *Electric* . . . . (Sire)
Philly Dog
  Mar-Keys; *Back To Back: Mar-Keys & Booker T. & The M.G.s* . . . . . .(Atlantic)
    Great Memphis Sound . . . .(Atlantic)
    Stax/Volt Revue-#1-Live In London-C . . . .(Atlantic)
    Super Hits-#1-C . . . .(Atlantic)
Pilate
  Pearl Jam; *Yield* . . . .(Epic)
Play With Your Poodle
  B.B. King; *King Of The Blues* . . . .(MCA)
Please Throw This Poor Dog A Bone
  Junior Wells; *Blues Hit Big Town* . . . . (Delmark)
Police Dog Blues
  Blind Blake; *Georgia Blues-1927-1930* . . . . (Yazoo)
  Hot Tuna; *Splashdown* . . . . (Relix)
  Jorma Kaukonen & Tom Hobson; *Quah* . . . . (Relix)
  Ry Cooder; *Ry Cooder* . . . . (Reprise)
Poor White Hound Dog
  Merry Clayton; *ST/Performance* . . . .(Warner Bros.)
Promised Land
  Bruce Springsteen; *Darkness On The Edge Of Town* . . . . (Columbia)
  Bruce Springsteen & The E Street Band; *Bruce Springsteen & The E Street
    Band Live/1975-85* . . . . (Legacy)
Puppet Dog
  Thin White Rope; *Ruby Sea* . . . . (Frontier)
Puppy Love
  Donny Osmond; *Donny Osmond's Greatest Hits* . . . . (Curb)
  Ike & Tina Turner; *Ike & Tina Turner-Golden Classics* . . . . (Collectables)
  Little Jimmy Rivers & The Tops; *Memories Of Times Square Record
    Shop-#10-C* . . . . (Collectables)
  Paul Anka; *Paul Anka-30th Anniversary Anthology* . . . . (Rhino)
  Paul Anka's 21 Golden Hits* . . . . (RCA)
Puppy Song
  Nilsson; *Harry* . . . .(Dunhill Compact Classics)
  ST/You've Got Mail* . . . . (Atlantic)
Quarterdrawing Of The Dog
  Siouxsie And The Banshees; *Tinderbox* . . . .(Geffen)
Rain Dogs
  Tom Waits; *Big Time* . . . . (Island)

Rain Dogs . . . . (Island)
Rattling Dog
  Irish Rovers; *First Of The Irish Rovers* . . . . (MCA)
Return Of The Red Baron
  Royal Guardsmen; *Royal Guardsmen-Anthology* . . . . (One Way)
Rockin' Rollin' Rover
  Bill Haley & His Comets; *Bill Haley & His Comets-Golden Hits* . . . . (MCA)
Rockin' The Dog
  Hellecasters; *Town South Of Bakersfield-#3* . . . . (Restless)
Salty Dog Blues
  Flatt & Scruggs; *Earl Scruggs: His Family & Friends/Nashville
    Airplane* . . . . (Collectables)
    Flatt & Scruggs-20 Greatest Hits . . . . (Deluxe)
    Greatest Folksingers Of The '60s-C . . . . (Vanguard)
Salty Dog, A
  Procol Harum; *A Salty Dog* . . . . (A&M)
    Best Of Procol Harum . . . . (A&M)
    Procol Harum Live In Concert with the Edmonton Symphony . . . . (A&M)
    Procol Harum-Classics-#17 . . . . (A&M)
Shadow & Me
  Leon Russell; *Americana* . . . . (Paradise)
Shaggy Dog
  Lightnin' Hopkins; *Nothin' But The Blues-Golden Classics-#4* . . . (Collectables)
Sick As A Dog
  Aerosmith; *Live! Bootleg* . . . . (Columbia)
    Rocks . . . . (Columbia)
Snoopy Vs. The Red Baron
  Royal Guardsmen; *Best Of The Royal Guardsmen-#1* . . . . (Rhino)
    Collectables Presents The History Of Rock-#9-C . . . . (Collectables)
    Cruisin'-1967-C . . . . (Increase)
    Million-Dollar Memories-#1-C . . . . (RCA)
    Super Oldies Of The '60s-#6-C . . . . (Audio Fidelity)
Snoopy's Christmas
  Royal Guardsmen; *Snoopy & His Friends* . . . .(Laurie)
Song Dog
  Michael Murphey; *Lonewolf* . . . . (Epic)
Space Dog
  Tori Amos; *Under The Pink* . . . .(Atlantic)
Stop Doggin' Me
  Johnnie Taylor; *Chronicle: The 20 Greatest Hits* . . . . (Stax)
    Little Bluebird . . . . (Stax)
Stop Kicking My Dog Around
  Rufus Thomas; *Can't Get Away From This Dog* . . . . (Stax)
Tennessee Hound Dog
  Osborne Brothers; *Best Of The Osborne Brothers* . . . . (MCA)
Thanks To The Cat House
  Johnny Paycheck; *Armed & Crazy* . . . . (Epic)
That Dog Won't Hunt
  Waylon Jennings; *Will The Wolf Survive* . . . . (MCA)
That Hound Dog In The Window
  Homer & Jethro; *Duets-Collector's* . . . . (RCA)
Theme From "Dastardly & Muttley In Their Flying Machine"
  Original Soundtrack; *Hanna-Barbera Pic-A-Nic Basket Of Cartoon
    Classics* . . . .(Kid Rhino/Rhino 4 Kids)
    Television's Greatest Revue-#3-1970s & 1980s-C . . . . (TVT)
Theme From "Huckleberry Hound"
  Original Soundtrack; *Hanna-Barbera Classics-#1-Original Recordings Of
    The World's Most Famous Cartoon Themes &
    Scores* . . . .(Kid Rhino/Rhino 4 Kids)
    *Hanna-Barbera Pic-A-Nic Basket Of Cartoon
    Classics* . . . .(Kid Rhino/Rhino 4 Kids)
    Television's Greatest Hits-#2-C . . . . (TVT)
Theme From "Lassie"
  Original Soundtrack; *Television's Greatest Hits-#4-Black & White
    Classics-C* . . . . (TVT)
Theme From "Ren And Stimpy"
  Original Soundtrack; *Television's Greatest Hits-#7-Cable Ready-C* . . . . . (TVT)
Theme From "Rin Tin Tin"
  Original Soundtrack; *Television's Greatest Hits-#1-C* . . . . (TVT)
Theme From "Ruff And Reddy"
  Original Soundtrack; *Hanna-Barbera Classics-#1-Original Recordings Of
    The World's Most Famous Cartoon Themes &
    Scores* . . . .(Kid Rhino/Rhino 4 Kids)
    *Hanna-Barbera Pic-A-Nic Basket Of Cartoon
    Classics* . . . .(Kid Rhino/Rhino 4 Kids)
Theme From "Scooby Doo, Where Are You?"
  Original Soundtrack; *Hanna-Barbera Classics-#1-Original Recordings Of
    The World's Most Famous Cartoon Themes &
    Scores* . . . .(Kid Rhino/Rhino 4 Kids)
    *Hanna-Barbera Pic-A-Nic Basket Of Cartoon
    Classics* . . . .(Kid Rhino/Rhino 4 Kids)
    Television's Greatest Hits-#3-1970s & 1980s-C . . . . (TVT)
Theme From "Underdog"
  Original Soundtrack; *Television's Greatest Hits-#2-C* . . . . (TVT)
This Old Man
  Dana; *Dana's Best Sing & Play-Along Tunes!* . . . . (Real Music For Kidz)
  Original Soundtrack; *Children's Favorites* . . . .(Kid Rhino/Rhino 4 Kids)
Trashy Dog
  Steve Cropper/Albert King/Pops Staples; *Jammed Together* . . . . (Stax)

Two Headed Dog (Red Temple Prayer)
Roky Erickson; *You're Gonna Miss Me-Best Of Roky Erickson* . . . . . . (Restless)
Wag The Dog
Mark Knopfler; *ST/Wag The Dog* . . . . (Mercury)
Walk The Dog
Laurie Anderson; *United States Live* . . . . (Warner Bros.)
Walkin' The Dog
Aerosmith; *Aerosmith* . . . . (Columbia)
Pandora's Box . . . . (Columbia)
Luther Allison; *Atlantic Blues-Chicago-C* . . . . (Atlantic)
Rolling Stones; *England's Newest Hit Makers/The Rolling Stones* . . . . . (Abkco)
Rufus Thomas; *Can't Get Away From This Dog* . . . . (Stax)
Rufus Thomas . . . . (Gusto)
Super Hits-#2-C . . . . (Gusto)
Walkin' The Dog . . . . (Atlantic)
Walking My Cat Named Dog
Norma Tanega; *Peanut Butter Jam-C* . . . . (Sony Wonder)
Watch Dog
Etta James; *Tell Mama* . . . . (Chess)
Muddy Waters Blues Band; *Mud In Your Ear* . . . . (Muse)
Watchdogs Of The Night
UB40; *Live In Moscow* . . . . (A&M)
Rat In The Kitchen . . . . (A&M)
What I Got
Sublime; *Now That's What I Call Music!-#2-C* . . . . (Virgin)
Sublime . . . . (Gasoline Alley)
Where Did That Little Dog Go
Original Cast; *Snoopy* . . . . (DRG)
Where Has My Little Dog Gone
Horace Heidt & His Musical Knights; *The Uncollected Horace Heidt & His
Musical Knights-1939* . . . . (Hindsight)
White Minority
Black Flag; *First Four Years* . . . . (SST)
ST/Decline Of Western Civilization . . . . (Slash)
Who Let The Dogs Out
Baha Men; *Who Let The Dogs Out* . . . . (S-Curve)
Wild Dog Moon
Drivin' N' Cryin'; *Mystery Road* . . . . (Island)
Wild Dogs
Hank Williams, Jr.; *Bocephus Box-Collection-1979-1992* . . . . (Capricorn)
Wild Dogs
Tommy Bolin; *The Ultimate Tommy Bolin* . . . . (Geffen)
Wild West Show/Dog Act
Original Broadway Cast; *Will Rogers Follies* . . . . (Columbia)
Yellow Dog Blues
Bessie Smith; *Bessie Smith-The Complete Recordings-#2* . . . . . . (Legacy)
Eddie Condon; *Best Of Eddie Condon* . . . . (MCA)
You're In The Doghouse Now
Brenda Lee; *ST/Dick Tracy* . . . . (Sire)

ANIMALS: DOLPHINS, Porpoises

See Also: ANIMALS: A-Z, ANIMALS: GENERAL, ANIMALS: WHALES

D.O.L.F.I.N.
Emiko Kai; *Alternatives* . . . . (Columbia)
Digital Dolphins
Dolphins; *Malayan Breeze* . . . . (Digital Music Prod.)
Dolphin
Kenny Rankin; *Mindusters* . . . . (Out Of Print)
Stan Getz; *Dolphin* . . . . (Concord Jazz)
Dolphin Dance
Herbie Hancock; *Best Of Herbie Hancock-The Blue Note Years* . . . . (Blue Note)
Maiden Voyage . . . . (Blue Note)
Dolphin Dreams
Lee Ritenour; *Captain Fingers* . . . . (Epic)
Lee Ritenour-Collection . . . . (GRP)
On The Line . . . . (GRP)
Dolphin Field
Meat Puppets; *7-Inch Wonders Of The World-C* . . . . (SST)
Dolphin Morning
Paul Winter Consort; *Sun Singer* . . . . (Living Music)
Dolphin Story
Claudia Schmidt; *Midwestern Heart* . . . . (Flying Fish)
Dolphins
Mike Marshall & Darol Anger; *Chiaroscuro* . . . . (Windham Hill)
Windham Hill-First Ten Years-C . . . . (Windham Hill)
Dolphins
Tim Buckley; *Best Of Tim Buckley* . . . . (Rhino)
Sefronia . . . . (Bizarre/Straight)
Dolphins
Billy Bragg; *Don't Try This At Home* . . . . (Elektra)
Dolphins
Linda Ronstadt; *Hand Sown Home Grown* . . . . (Capitol)
Dolphins
Shelleyan Orphan; *Humroot* . . . . (Columbia)

Dolphins
The The; *Shades Of Blue* . . . . (Epic)
Dolphins & Whales (Come Home To The Sea)
Mannheim Steamroller; *Saving The Wildlife* . . . . (American Gramaphone)
Dolphin's Cry
Live; *The Distance To Here* . . . . (Radioactive/MCA)
Dolphin's Lullaby
Lani Hall; *Sweet Bird* . . . . (A&M)
Dolphin's Lullaby
Firefall; *Firefall* . . . . (Rhino)
Dolphin's Smile
Byrds; *Notorious Byrd Brothers* . . . . (Columbia)
The Byrds . . . . (Columbia)
Dolphin's Thoughts
Jay B. Jay; *Dream Machine* . . . . (Innovative Comm.)
Over Seas . . . . (Innovative Comm.)
Luminous Dolphin
Royal Trux; *End Of Music (As We Know It)* . . . . (Roir)
On Green Dolphin Street
Anita O'Day; *Anita O'Day* . . . . (Glendale)
Carmen McRae; *At The Great American Music Hall* . . . . (Blue Note)
Miles Davis; *Basic Miles* . . . . (Columbia)
Red Garland; *Saying Something* . . . . (Prestige)
Porpoise Mouth
Country Joe & The Fish; *Collected-1965-1970* . . . . (Vanguard)
Electric Music For The Mind & Body . . . . (Vanguard)
Life & Times Of Country Joe & The Fish . . . . (Vanguard)
Porpoise Song
Monkees; *Head* . . . . (Rhino)
Listen To The Band . . . . (Rhino)
Monkee Business . . . . (Rhino)
Nuggets-#9-Acid Rock-C . . . . (Rhino)
Promise, The (The Dolphin Song)
Olivia Newton-John; *Physical* . . . . (MCA)
Theme From "Flipper"
Original Soundtrack; *Television's Greatest Hits-#1-C* . . . . (TVT)
Various Tracks
Dr. John C. Lilly; *Sounds & Ultra-Sounds Of The Blue-
Nose* . . . . (Smithsonian Folkways)

ANIMALS: ELEPHANTS

See Also: ANIMALS: A-Z, ANIMALS: GENERAL

Ant & The Elephant
Chick Corea Elektric Band II; *Paint The World* . . . . (GRP)
Baby Elephant Walk
Henry Mancini; *Henry Mancini-Pure Gold* . . . . (RCA)
Peter Gunn . . . . (RCA)
Dat Dere
Rickie Lee Jones; *Pop Pop* . . . . (Geffen)
Tony Bennett; *The Playground* . . . . (Sony Wonder)
Elephant
Tanita Tikaram; *Eleven Kinds Of Loneliness* . . . . (Reprise)
Elephant Day Parade
Beat Farmers; *The Pursuit Of Happiness* . . . . (Curb)
Elephant Gun
David Lee Roth; *Eat 'Em & Smile* . . . . (Warner Bros.)
Elephant Ride
Squeeze; *Sweets From A Stranger* . . . . (A&M)
Elephant Song
Reilly & Maloney; *Profiles* . . . . (Freckle)
Elephant Stone
Stone Roses; *The Stone Roses* . . . . (Silvertone)
Turns Into Stone . . . . (Silvertone)
Elephant Talk
King Crimson; *Abbreviated* . . . . (Editions E.G.)
Compact . . . . (Editions E.G.)
Discipline . . . . (Editions E.G.)
Elephant Trainer
Liz Story; *Part Of Fortune* . . . . (Novus)
Elephants & Flowers
Prince; *ST/Graffiti Bridge* . . . . (Paisley Park)
Elephant's Graveyard
Boomtown Rats; *Boomtown Rats' Greatest Hits* . . . . (Columbia)
Mondo Bongo . . . . (Columbia)
Elephants In Love
Jean-Luc Ponty; *Fables* . . . . (Atlantic)
Great Beyond, The
R.E.M.; *Man On The Moon* . . . . (Warner Bros.)
Totally Hits-#2-C . . . . (Elektra)
L'Elephant
Tom Tom Club; *Tom Tom Club* . . . . (Sire)
One Bad Elephant
Brian Slawson; *Distant Drums* . . . . (Columbia)
Pink Elephants
Eddie Lang Blue Five & Joe Venuti; *Jazz In The Thirties-C* . . . (Disques Swing)

Pink Elephants On Parade
Barbara Cook; *Disney Album* . . . .(Disney)
Psychic Elephant
Shankar; *Vision* . . . . (ECM)
Seeing The Elephant
Debby McClatchy & The Red Clay Ramblers; *Debby McClatchy & The Red Clay Ramblers* . . . . (Green Linnet)
When I See An Elephant Fly
Barbara Cook; *Disney Album* . . . .(Disney)
Cliff Edwards/Jim Carmichael/The Hall Johnson Choir; *Disney Collection-#2-C* . . . .(Disney)

ANIMALS: FISH, Fishing, Sharks

See Also: **ANIMALS: A-Z, ANIMALS: DOLPHINS, ANIMALS: GENERAL, ANIMALS: WHALES, FOOD: FOOD & BEVERAGES, OCEAN, RIVERS, SAILING, SHIPS, WATER**

Any Little Fish
Bobby Short; *Bobby Noel & Cole* . . . .(Atlantic)
Bad Shark
Rick Dees And His Cast Of Idiots; *Original Disco Duck* . . . . (RSO)
Barracuda
Heart; *Heart's Greatest Hits/Live* . . . .(Epic)
Little Queen . . . . (Portrait)
Basket Of Oysters
Oscar Brand; *Bawdy Songs & Backroom Ballads* . . . .(Audio Fidelity)
Big Fish, Little Fish
Original Broadway Cast; *Purlie* . . . . (RCA)
Blue Oyster Cult
Blue Oyster Cult; *Imag[os]* . . . . (Columbia)
Bob Away My Blues
Clint Black; *D'lectrified* . . . . (RCA)
Catfish
Bob Dylan; *The Bootleg Series-Volumes 1-3 [Rare & Unreleased]* . . (Columbia)
Catfish
Danny O'Keefe; *Breezy Stories* . . . . (Atlantic)
Catfish
Joe Cocker; *Stingray* . . . . (A&M)
Catfish
John Lee Hooker; *Golden Classics-John Lee Hooker* . . . . (Collectables)
Catfish Blues
Ian & Sylvia; *Best Of Ian & Sylvia* . . . . (Vanguard)
Ian & Sylvia's Greatest Hits . . . . (Vanguard)
Jimi Hendrix Experience; *Radio One* . . . .(Rykodisc)
Catfish Fry
Red Meat; *Alameda County Line* . . . .(Ranchero)
Catfish John
Johnny Russell; *Johnny Russell's Greatest Hits* . . . . (Dominion Entert.)
Catfish Sam'ich
Charles Williams; *Charles Williams* . . . .(Mainstream)
Come On Down To My Boat
Every Mother's Son; *Battle Of The Bands-#3-C* . . . . (K-Tel)
Country State Of Mind
Hank Williams, Jr.; *Hank Williams, Jr.'s Greatest Hits III.* . . . . . . (Curb)
Montana Cafe . . . . (WB/Curb)
Crab Man's Call
Original Cast; *Porgy & Bess* . . . .(MCA)
Crawfish
Elvis Presley; *Hits Like Never Before-Essential-#3* . . . . (RCA)
ST/King Creole . . . . (RCA)
Do You Want My Job
Little Village; *Little Village* . . . . (Reprise)
Fins
Jimmy Buffett; *Songs You Know By Heart-Jimmy Buffett's Greatest Hit(s)* . . . .(MCA)
Volcano . . . .(MCA)
Fish
Yes; *Fragile* . . . .(Atlantic)
Yessongs . . . . (Atlantic)
Fish & Chips
Eddie & The Hot Rods; *Fish & Chips* . . . .(EMI)
Fish & Tits
Barefoot Jerry; *Barefoot Jerry's Grocery* . . . . (Monument)
Fish & Whistle
John Prine; *Bruised Orange* . . . . (Oh Boy)
Fish Ain't Bitin'
David Lee Murphy; *Out With A Bang* . . . .(MCA)
Lamont Dozier; *Deep Soul-#2-C* . . . . (Priority)
Fish Aren't Bitin' Today
David Allan Coe; *Compass Point* . . . . (Columbia)
Fish Heads
Barnes & Barnes; *20th Anniversary Collection* . . . . (Rhino)
Dr. Demento Presents The Greatest Novelty Records-#4-1970s-C . . . . (Rhino)
Fish In The Sea
Karen Alexander; *Isn't It Always Love* . . . . (Asylum)

Fish Song
Nitty Gritty Dirt Band; *All The Good Times* . . . . (United Artists)
Dirt, Silver & Gold . . . . (One Way)
Fisher's Hornpipe
Doc Watson; *Fresh Fish-C* . . . . (Flying Fish)
Fishes And Scorpions
Stephen Stills; *Stephen Stills 2* . . . .(Atlantic)
Fishin'
Elvin Bishop; *Let It Flow* . . . . (Capricorn)
Fishin' Blues
Jim Kweskin and His Jug Band; *Best Of Jim Kweskin* . . . . (Vanguard)
Jim Kweskin and His Jug Band. . . . . (Vanguard)
Lovin' Spoonful; *Lovin' Spoonful-Anthology* . . . . (Rhino)
Taj Mahal; *Best Of Taj Mahal* . . . . (Columbia)
Real Thing . . . . (Columbia)
Fishin' In The Dark
Nitty Gritty Dirt Band; *Billboard Top Country Hits-1987-C* . . . . (Rhino)
Hold On . . . . (Warner Bros.)
More Great Dirt-Best Of Nitty Gritty Dirt Band. . . . . (Warner Bros.)
Galveston Bay
Bruce Springsteen; *The Ghost Of Tom Joad* . . . . (Columbia)
Going Fishing
Jimmy Reed; *History Of Jimmy Reed* . . . .(Trip)
Wailin' Blues . . . .(Tradition)
Greenland Fisheries
Pete Seeger; *20 Golden Pieces Of Pete Seeger* . . . .(Bulldog)
Pete Seeger . . . . (Everest)
Pete Seeger Sings Folk Music Of The World . . . . (Tradition)
Hold Tight, Hold Tight (Sea Food)
Andrews Sisters; *Andrews Sisters-16 Great Performances* . . . . (MCA)
Best Of The Andrews Sisters. . . . . (MCA)
Boogie Woogie Bugle Girls . . . . (MCA)
I'm Gonna Go Fishing
Mel Torme; *Duke Ellington & Count Basie Songbook* . . . . (Verve)
Ray Charles; *My Kind Of Jazz-Part 3* . . . . (Crossover)
Joy To The World
Three Dog Night; *Best Of Three Dog Night* . . . . (MCA)
Good Feeling Music Of The Big Chill Generation-#2-C . . . . (Motown)
Good Feeling Music Of The Big Chill Generation-#3-C . . . . (Motown)
Joy To The World-Greatest Hits . . . . (MCA)
ST/Big Chill . . . . (Motown)
ST/Forrest Gump . . . .(Epic/Sony Music Soundtrax)
Just Like A Fish
Esther Phillips; *Atlantic Blues-Vocalists-C* . . . .(Atlantic)
Set Me Free . . . .(Atlantic)
Little Plastic Castle
Ani DiFranco; *Little Plastic Castle* . . . . (Righteous Babe)
Mack The Knife
Bobby Darin; *Bobby Darin-At The Copa* . . . . (Bainbridge)
Hit Singles-1958-1977-C . . . . (Atlantic)
The Bobby Darin Story. . . . . (Atlantic)
Frank Sinatra; *The Reprise Collection.* . . . . (Reprise)
Louis Armstrong; *Best Of Louis Armstrong* . . . . (Vanguard)
Mistress Of The Salmon Salt
Blue Oyster Cult; *Tyranny & Mutation* . . . . (Columbia)
Mud Shark, The
Mothers Of Invention; *Fillmore East-June 1971.* . . . . (Reprise)
My Barracuda
Jimmy Buffett; *Hot Water* . . . . (MCA)
No Anchovies Please
J. Geils Band; *Love Stinks* . . . . (EMI)
Octopus's Garden
Beatles; *Abbey Road* . . . . (Parlophone)
Beatles-Box Set. . . . . (Capitol)
The Beatles/1967-1970. . . . . (Capitol)
Promise Of A Fisherman
Paul Winter; *Common Ground* . . . . (A&M)
Sergio Mendes; *Sergio Mendes-Classics-#18* . . . . (A&M)
Pulling Mussels (From The Shell)
Squeeze; *Argybargy* . . . . (A&M)
Singles-45's and under. . . . . (A&M)
Rainbow Trout
Gordon Lightfoot; *Cold On The Shoulder* . . . . (Reprise)
Reach, The
Dan Fogelberg; *Innocent Age* . . . .(Full Moon)
Red Sharks
Crimson Glory; *Transcendance* . . . . (MCA)
Rock Lobster
B-52's; *B-52's* . . . . (Warner Bros.)
Saginaw, Michigan
Lefty Frizzell; *American Originals-Lefty Frizzell* . . . . (Columbia)
Billboard Top Country Hits-1964-C . . . . (Rhino)
Columbia Country Classics-#3-Americana-C . . . . (Columbia)
Lefty Frizzell's Greatest Hits . . . . (Columbia)
Same Ol' Fishing Hole
Blues Boy Willie; *Be-Who* . . . . (Ichiban Int'l)
Saturday Night Fish Fry
Louis Jordan; *Best Of Louis Jordan* . . . . (MCA)

No Moe! Louis Jordan's Greatest Hits . . . . (Verve)
Pearl Bailey; *Pearl Bailey-16 Most Requested Songs* . . . . . . (Legacy)
Saturday Night Fish Fry Drag
Joe Robichaux & The New Orleans Boys; *Joe Robichaux & The New
Orleans Boys-1933* . . . . (Folklyric)
Shark Attack
Split Enz; *True Colours* . . . . (A&M)
Shark Attack
Wailing Souls; *All Over The World* . . . . (Chaos)
Shark Walk
Shriekback; *Go Bang!* . . . . (Island)
Shooting Shark
Blue Oyster Cult; *Revolutionary By Night* . . . . (Columbia)
Son Of A Fisherman
Tom Jones; *Memories Don't Leave Like People Do* . . . . (Parrot)
Song Of The Shrimp
Elvis Presley; *ST/Girls! Girls! Girls!* . . . .(RCA)
Sushi Girl
Tubes; *Best Of The Tubes* . . . . (Gold Rush)
Completion Backward Principle. . . . . (Capitol)
Swish Fish
Showmen; *It Will Stand-15 More Golden Classics-C* . . . . (Collectables)
Talkin' Fishin'
Ramblin' Jack Elliott; *Greatest Songs Of Woody Guthrie-C* . . . . . . (Vanguard)
Talking Fishing Blues
Jack Elliot; *Greatest Songs Of Woody Guthrie-C* . . . . (Vanguard)
Tennessee Fish Fry
Helen O'Connell; *The Uncollected Helen O'Connell With Irv Orton's
Orchestra.* . . . . (Hindsight)
Theme From "Jaws"
John Williams; *ST/Jaws.* . . . . (MCA)
Three Little Fishes
Andrews Sisters; *Boogie Woogie Bugle Girls* . . . . (MCA)
Kay Kyser & His Orchestra; *Dr. Demento Presents The Greatest Novelty
Records-#1-1940s & Before-C* . . . . (Rhino)
Sentimental Favorites. . . . . (Columbia)
Throw Back The Little Ones
Steely Dan; *Katy Lied* . . . . (MCA)
Too Many Fish In The Sea
Marvelettes; *Marvelettes' Greatest Hits* . . . . (Motown)
Marvelettes-Anthology . . . . (Motown)
Mitch Ryder And The Detroit Wheels; *Mitch Ryder And The Detroit Wheels'
Greatest Hits* . . . . (Virgo)
Rascals; *Rascals-Anthology 1965-1972* . . . . (Rhino)
Tremeloes; *Best Of The Tremeloes* . . . . (Rhino)
Trout
Neneh Cherry & Michael Stipe; *Homebrew* . . . . (Virgin)
Unidentified Flying Tuna Trot
REO Speedwagon; *You Can Tune A Piano But You Can't Tuna Fish* . . . . . (Epic)
White Fishes
John Renbourn; *Sir Jon Alot Of Merrie Englanders* . . . . (Reprise)
Wynkin', Blinkin' & Nod
Doobie Brothers; *In Harmony-Sesame Street-C* . . . . (Columbia)
Irish Rovers; *Irish Rovers' Greatest Hits.* . . . . (MCA)
Simon Sisters; *Troubadours Of The Folk Era-#2-C* . . . . (Rhino)

ANIMALS: FOXES

*See Also: **ANIMALS: A-Z, ANIMALS: GENERAL***

Fox On The Run
George Jones; *First Time Live!* . . . . (Epic)
Sweet; *Desolation Boulevard* . . . . (Capitol)
Fox, The
Nickel Creek; *Nickel Creek* . . . . (Sugar Hill)
Foxey Lady
Jimi Hendrix; *Essential Jimi Hendrix, Volume 2.* . . . . (Reprise)
ST/Jimi Plays Monterey . . . . (Reprise)
ST/Wayne's World . . . . (Reprise)
Jimi Hendrix Experience; *Are You Experienced?* . . . . (Reprise)
Smash Hits . . . . (Reprise)
Mary's Danish; *Circa* . . . . (Morgan Creek)
Johnny The Fox Meets Jimmy The Weed
Thin Lizzy; *Live And Dangerous.* . . . . (Warner Bros.)
Run With The Fox
Yes; *Yesyears* . . . . (Atco)
Twentieth Century Fox
Doors; *Doors.* . . . . (Elektra)

ANIMALS: G

*See Also: **ANIMALS: A-Z, ANIMALS: GENERAL***

Bubblegoose
Wyclef Jean; *Chef Aid-The South Park Album* . . . . (Columbia)

Wyclef Jean featuring Melky Sedeck; *Presents The Carnival F/Refugee
Allstars* . . . . (Ruffhouse/Columbia)
Gorilla
James Taylor; *Gorilla* . . . . (Warner Bros.)
Gorilla, You're A Desperado
Warren Zevon; *Bad Luck Streak In Dancing School* . . . . (Asylum)
Green Gorilla
Spirit; *Time Circle* . . . .(Epic)
Ground Hog
Buffy Sainte-Marie; *Best Of Buffy Sainte-Marie* . . . .(Vanguard)
Many A Mile . . . .(Vanguard)
Dillards; *Bluegrass Breakdown* . . . .(Vanguard)
Doc Watson; *Essential Doc Watson.* . . . . (Vanguard)
New Lost City Ramblers; *20 Years Of Concert Performances.* . . . (Flying Fish)
Ground Hog Blues
John Lee Hooker; *Blues-#5-C* . . . .(Chess)
House Of The Blues . . . . (Chess)
Lonely Goatherd
Julie Andrews; *ST/The Sound Of Music* . . . . (RCA)
Original Cast/Mary Martin; *The Sound Of Music.* . . . . (Sony Broadway)
Papa's Billy Goat
Sarah Ogan Gunning; *Silver Dagger* . . . .(Rounder)
Rootin' Ground Hog
K.C. Douglas; *K.C.'s Blues* . . . . (Bluesville)
Shaved Gorilla
Flaming Lips; *Telepathic Surgery* . . . . (Restless)
Sheep Go To Heaven (Goats)
Cake; *Prolonging The Magic* . . . .(Capricorn)
Ten Tall Giraffes
Liquid Pink; *Liquid Pink* . . . .(Atomic)
Theme From "Magilla Gorilla"
Original Soundtrack; *Hanna-Barbera Classics-#1-Original Recordings Of
The World's Most Famous Cartoon Themes &
Scores* . . . . (Kid Rhino/Rhino 4 Kids)
*Hanna-Barbera Pic-A-Nic Basket Of Cartoon
Classics* . . . . (Kid Rhino/Rhino 4 Kids)
Television's Greatest Hits-#1-C . . . .(TVT)
Thrill My Gorilla
Alice Cooper; *Constrictor* . . . . (MCA)

ANIMALS: GENERAL, Multiple Animals, Zoos

*See Also: **ANIMALS: A-Z, ANIMALS: BEARS, BIRDS, CATS,
COWS, DOGS, DOLPHINS, ELEPHANTS, FISH, FOXES, HORSES,
INSECTS, KANGAROOS, LIONS, MICE, MONKEYS, MULES,
PIGS, RABBITS, RATS, REPTILES, SHEEP, TIGERS, WHALES,
WOLVES, FARMS***

Animal
Toto; *Past To Present 1977-1990.* . . . .(Columbia)
Animal
Bar-Kays; *Animal.* . . . .(Mercury)
Animal
Def Leppard; *Hysteria* . . . .(Mercury)
Animal
Pearl Jam; *Vs.* . . . . (Epic Portrait Assoc.)
Animal Boy
Ramones; *Animal Boy* . . . . (Sire)
Ramones Mania. . . . . (Sire)
Animal Crackers
Melanie; *Best Of Melanie.* . . . . (Buddah)
Animal Crackers
Anne Murray; *There's A Hippo In My Tub.* . . . .(Capitol)
Animal Fair
Original Soundtrack; *School Days-Kids Classics* . . . .(Benson)
Animal Farm
Kinks; *Are The Village Green Preservation Society* . . . . (Reprise)
Animal House
Stephen Bishop; *ST/Animal House.* . . . . (MCA)
Animal Instinct
Elvis Presley; *ST/Harum Scarum* . . . . (RCA)
Animal Instinct
Commodores; *Nightshift* . . . .(Motown)
Animal Magic
Belouis Some; *Animal Magic.* . . . . (Capitol)
Animal Magic
Blow Monkeys; *Animal Magic.* . . . . (RCA)
Animal Magic
Peter Gabriel; *Peter Gabriel.* . . . .(Atlantic)
Animal Song
Savage Garden; *Affirmation* . . . .(Columbia)
Animal Speaks
Golden Palominos; *Visions Of Excess* . . . .(Celluloid)

Animal Trainer & The Toad
Mountain; *Best Of Mountain* . . . . (Columbia)
Animal Zoo
Spirit; *12 Dreams Of Dr. Sardonicus* . . . .(Epic)
Best Of Spirit . . . .(Epic)
Animals
Talking Heads; *Fear Of Music* . . . . (Sire)
Animals In Jungles
China Crisis; *Working With Fire & Steel* . . . .(Warner Bros.)
At The Zoo
Simon & Garfunkel; *Bookends* . . . . (Columbia)
Collected Works . . . . (Columbia)
Bad Touch, The
Bloodhound Gang; *Hooray For Boobies* . . . . (Republic/Geffen)
Beast Of Burden
Bette Midler; *No Frills* . . . . (Atlantic)
Rolling Stones; *Rewind (1971-1984)* . . . .(Rolling Stones)
Some Girls . . . . (Virgin)
Sucking In The Seventies . . . .(Rolling Stones)
Carcass
Siouxsie And The Banshees; *The Scream* . . . .(Geffen)
Circle Of Life
Elton John; *Elton John-Love Songs* . . . .(MCA)
ST/The Lion King . . . . (Walt Disney)
Original Cast; *The Lion King* . . . .(Disney)
Continuing Story Of Bungalow Bill, The
Beatles; *The Beatles (White Album)* . . . . (Capitol)
Do The Evolution
Pearl Jam; *Yield* . . . .(Epic)
Don't Kill The Animals
Lene Lovich; *Animal Liberation-C* . . . . (Wax Trax)
Lene Lovich & Nina Hagen; *Tame Yourself-C* . . . . (Rhino)
Friendly Beasts
Garth Brooks; *Beyond The Season* . . . . (Liberty)
Peter, Paul & Mary & The New York Choral Society; *Holiday*
Celebration . . . .(Warner Bros.)
Riders In The Sky; *Christmas The Country Way* . . . . (Rounder)
Going To The Zoo
Peter, Paul & Mary; *Peter, Paul & Mommy* . . . .(Warner Bros.)
I Know An Old Lady Who Swallowed A Fly
Original Soundtrack; *More Silly Songs* . . . .(Disney)
Peter, Paul & Mary; *Peter, Paul & Mommy, Too* . . . . (Warner Bros.)
I'd Like To Be A Monkey In The Zoo
Frances White; *Music From The New York Stage (1890-1920)-#4-1917-*
1920-C . . . . (Pearl)
Let's Fall In Love
Diana Krall; *When I Look In Your Eyes* . . . . (GRP)
Frank Sinatra; *The Reprise Collection* . . . . (Reprise)
Louis Armstrong & Oscar Peterson; *Verve Elite Edition Collector's*
Disc-C . . . . (Verve)
Tony Bennett; *Tony Bennett Sings A String Of Harold*
Arlen . . . . (Columbia Special Prod.)
Old MacDonald Had A Farm
Original Soundtrack; *Toddler Favorites* . . . . (Kid Rhino/Rhino 4 Kids)
Pet Sematary
Ramones; *Brain Drain* . . . . (Sire)
Loco Live . . . . (Sire)
Red Football
Sinead O'Connor; *Universal Mother* . . . .(Ensign)
Several Species Of Small Furry Animals
Pink Floyd; *Ummagumma* . . . . (Capitol)
Works . . . . (Capitol)
Shakin' The Cage
Zoo; *Shakin' The Cage* . . . . (Capricorn)
Sweet Betsy From Pike
Cisco Houston; *Cowboy Ballads* . . . . (Smithsonian Folkways)
Mormon Tabernacle Choir; *This Land Is Your Land* . . . . (Columbia)
Talk To The Animals
Sammy Davis, Jr.; *Sammy Davis, Jr.'s Greatest Songs* . . . . (Curb)
Tie Me Kangaroo Down, Sport
Rolf Harris; *45-#213* . . . . (Eric)
Tie Me Kangaroo Down, Sport & Sun Arise . . . .(Epic)
Turkey In The Straw
Stanley Brothers; *Stanley Series-Vol. 1-#3* . . . . (Copper Creek)
Vassar Clements; *Grass Routes* . . . . (Rounder)
Tusk
Fleetwood Mac; *25 Years-The Chain* . . . .(Warner Bros.)
Tusk . . . .(Warner Bros.)
Unicorn
Irish Rovers; *Irish Rovers' Greatest Hits* . . . . (MCA)
Unicorn . . . . (MCA)
Vintage Music-#19-C . . . . (MCA)
Wildlife
Yellowjackets; *Four Corners* . . . . (MCA)
Live Wires . . . . (GRP)
Zooropa
U2; *Zooropa* . . . . (Island)

ANIMALS: H
See Also: **ANIMALS: A-Z, ANIMALS: GENERAL,**
ANIMALS: HORSES

Attack Of The Radioactive Hamsters
"Weird Al" Yankovic; *ST/UHF & Other Stuff* . . . .(Scotti Bros.)
Don't Be A Hog
Doctor Nerve; *Armed Observation* . . . . (Cuneiform)
I Am A Hog For Ya
Casey Jones; *Solid Blue* . . . .(Rooster Blues)
I Want A Hippopotamus For Christmas
Gayla Peevey; *Dr. Demento Presents The Greatest Novelty Records-#6-*
Christmas-C . . . . (Rhino)
Dr. Demento's Greatest Christmas CD-C . . . . (Rhino)
Three Stooges; *Christmas Time With The Three Stooges* . . . . (Rhino)
Screaming Night Hog
Steppenwolf; *Steppenwolf-16 Greatest Hits* . . . . (MCA)
Wart Hog
Ramones; *Ramones Mania* . . . .(Sire)
Too Tough To Die . . . .(Sire)
Who's Gonna Feed Them Hogs
Tom T. Hall; *Essential Tom T. Hall-20th Anniversary Collection* . . . . (Mercury)
Tom T. Hall's Greatest Hits-#2 . . . . (Mercury)

ANIMALS: HORSES, Ponies, Riding
See Also: **AMERICAN WEST, ANIMALS: A-Z, ANIMALS:**
GENERAL, COWBOYS, REBELS, RODEO, SPORTS: GENERAL

(Ghost) Riders In The Sky
Gene Autry; *50th Anniversary* . . . . (Republic/Universal)
Cowboy Hall Of Fame . . . . (Republic/Universal)
Johnny Cash; *The Man In Black-His Greatest Hits* . . . . (Legacy)
Outlaws; *Ghost Riders* . . . . (Arista)
Roy Clark; *Roy Clark In Concert* . . . . (MCA)
Roy Clark's Greatest Hits . . . . (MCA)
Superpicker . . . . (MCA)
Vaughn Monroe; *Best Of Vaughn Monroe* . . . . (RCA)
This Is Vaughn Monroe/Decade Of The '40s . . . . (RCA)
10,000 Horses
Candlebox; *Happy Pills* . . . . (Maverick)
All In Green Went My Love Riding
Joan Baez; *Love Song Album* . . . . (Vanguard)
All The King's Horses
Triumph; *Surveillance* . . . . (MCA)
All The King's Horses
Nazareth; *Expect No Mercy* . . . . (A&M)
All The King's Horses
Lynn Anderson; *Lynn Anderson's Greatest Hits-#2* . . . . (Columbia)
All The King's Horses
Firm; *Mean Business* . . . .(Atlantic)
All The King's Horses
Aretha Franklin; *Young, Gifted And Black* . . . .(Atlantic & Atco Remasters)
Appaloosa
Gino Vannelli; *Best Of Gino Vannelli* . . . . (A&M)
Brother To Brother . . . . (A&M)
Gino Vannelli-Classics-#7 . . . . (A&M)
Back In The Saddle
Aerosmith; *Aerosmith-Classics Live 2* . . . . (Columbia)
Aerosmith's Greatest Hits . . . . (Columbia)
Live! Bootleg . . . . (Columbia)
Pandora's Box . . . . (Columbia)
Rocks . . . . (Columbia)
Back In The Saddle Again
Gene Autry; *50th Anniversary* . . . . (Republic/Universal)
Columbia Country Classics-#1-Golden Age-C . . . . (Columbia)
Cowboy Hall Of Fame . . . . (Republic/Universal)
Cowboy Super Hits-C . . . . (Columbia)
Great American Singing Cowboys-C . . . . (Republic/Universal)
South Of The Border . . . . (Republic/Universal)
Bring On The Dancing Horses
Echo & The Bunnymen; *Songs To Learn & Sing-The Hits* . . . .(Sire)
ST/Pretty In Pink . . . . (A&M)
Caballo Diablo
Charlie Daniels Band; *Fire On The Mountain* . . . . (Epic)
Changing Horses
Dan Fogelberg; *Dan Fogelberg-Souvenirs* . . . .(Full Moon)
Chariots Of Fire
Vangelis; *ST/Chariots Of Fire* . . . .(Polydor)
Themes . . . .(Polydor)
Chestnut Mare
Byrds; *Best Of The Byrds-Greatest Hits-#2* . . . . (Columbia)
Rock Classics Of The '70s-C . . . . (Columbia)
The Byrds . . . . (Columbia)

The Byrds (Untitled) . . . . (Legacy)
Cowboy Love
John Michael Montgomery; *John Michael Montgomery* . . . . (Atlantic)
John Michael Montgomery's Greatest Hits . . . . (Atlantic)
Cowboy Rides Away
George Strait; *Country Classics-#1-C* . . . . (Universal)
Does Fort Worth Ever Cross Your Mind. . . . . (MCA)
George Strait's Greatest Hits-#2 . . . . (MCA)
Dark Horse
George Harrison; *Best Of George Harrison* . . . . (Capitol)
Dark Horse . . . . (Capitol)
Distance, The
Cake; *Fashion Nugget* . . . . (Capricorn)
Don't Change Horses
Tower Of Power; *Back To Oakland* . . . . (Warner Bros.)
Don't Need No Horse
Little Walter; *Chess Blues Box-C* . . . . (Chess)
Down At The Old Corral
Randy Travis; *Wind In The Wire* . . . . (Warner Bros.)
Elvira
Murry Kellum; *Country Comedy-20 Country Comedy Hits* . . . . (Plantation)
Oak Ridge Boys; *Fancy Free* . . . . (MCA)
MCA Records 30 Years Of Hits-1958-1988-C . . . . (MCA)
Oak Ridge Boys' Greatest Hits 2 . . . . (MCA)
Freedom Rider
Traffic; *John Barleycorn Must Die* . . . . (Island)
On The Road. . . . . (Island)
Goin' To Dallas To See My Pony Run
Lightnin' Hopkins; *Blues In My Bottle* . . . . (Bluesville)
Drinkin' In The Blues-Golden Classics-#1 . . . . (Collectables)
Lightnin' Hopkins . . . . (Everest)
Great White Horse
Guy & Ralna; *22 Golden Country Classics* . . . . (Ranwood)
Guy & Ralna-Country. . . . . (Ranwood)
Hi Ho Silver
Fleetwood Mac; *Kiln House* . . . . (Reprise)
High Horse
Nitty Gritty Dirt Band; *Plain Dirt Fashion* . . . . (Warner Bros.)
Twenty Years Of Dirt-Best Of The Nitty Gritty Dirt Band. . . . . . (Warner Bros.)
High Horse
Evelyn "Champagne" King; *Best Of Evelyn "Champagne" King-Love
Come Down* . . . . (RCA)
Horse & Carriage
Cam'ron featuring Mase; *Confessions Of Fire* . . . . (Untertainment/Epic)
Horse Latitudes
Doors; *Strange Days* . . . . (Elektra)
Horse With No Name
America; *America* . . . . (Warner Bros.)
America Live. . . . . (Warner Bros.)
Billboard Top Rock 'N' Roll Hits-1972-C . . . . (Rhino)
History-Greatest Hits . . . . (Warner Bros.)
Hundred And Sixty Acres
Marty Robbins; *Gunfighter Ballads & Trail Songs* . . . . (Legacy)
I Know You Rider
Big Brother & The Holding Company; *Big Brother & The Holding
Company Live* . . . . (Rhino)
Grateful Dead; *Europe '72* . . . . (Warner Bros.)
Hot Tuna; *Hot Tuna.* . . . . (RCA)
I Ride An Old Paint/Whoopee Ti-Yi-Yo/Git Along Little Doggies
Michael Martin Murphey; *Cowboy Songs* . . . . (Warner Western)
I Tipped My Hat And Slowly Rode Away
Gene Autry; *Sing Cowboy Sing: The Gene Autry Collection.* . . . . . (Rhino)
If I Had A Boat
Lyle Lovett; *Pontiac* . . . . (MCA)
Invisible City
Wallflowers; *Bringing Down The Horse* . . . . (Interscope)
I've Got The Horse Right Here
Original Cast; *Guys & Dolls* . . . . (MCA)
Legend Of A Cowgirl
Imani Coppola; *Chupacapra* . . . . (Columbia)
Let That Pony Run
Pam Tillis; *Homeward Looking Angel.* . . . . (Arista)
Little Joe The Wrangler's Sister Nell
Skip Gorman; *A Cowboy's Wild Song To His Herd* . . . . (Rounder)
Littlest Cowboy Rides Again
Chris LeDoux; *Songbook Of The American West* . . . . (Liberty)
Sounds Of The Western Country. . . . . (Liberty)
Midnight Rider
Allman Brothers Band; *Beginnings* . . . . (Polydor)
Best Of The Allman Brothers Band. . . . . (Polydor)
Decade Of Hits-1969-1979. . . . . (Polydor)
Idlewild South. . . . . (Polydor)
*The Road Goes On Forever, A Collection Of Their Greatest
Recordings.* . . . . (Polydor)
Duane Allman; *Duane Allman-An Anthology-Vol. II* . . . . (Capricorn)
Gregg Allman; *Laid Back* . . . . (Polydor)
South's Greatest Hits-C . . . . (Capricorn)
Willie Nelson; *ST/The Electric Horseman* . . . . (Columbia)

Montana
Frank Zappa; *You Can't Do That On Stage Anymore-#3* . . . . (Rykodisc)
Mothers Of Invention; *Apostrophe/Overnite Sensation* . . . . (Rykodisc)
Mustang Sally
Rascals; *Rascals' Greatest Hits* . . . . (Atlantic)
Wilson Pickett; *A Man & A Half-Best Of Wilson Pickett* . . . . (Rhino)
Atlantic Rhythm & Blues 1947-1974-#6 (1966-1969)-C . . . . (Atlantic)
Best Of Wilson Pickett. . . . . (Atlantic)
Wilson Pickett's Greatest Hits. . . . . (Atlantic)
Wilson Pickett-Super Hits. . . . . (Atlantic)
Young Rascals; *The Young Rascals* . . . . (Warner Special Prod.)
New Pony
Bob Dylan; *Street Legal* . . . . (Columbia)
Night Rider
Elvis Presley; *Collector's Gold* . . . . (RCA)
Live In Nashville . . . . (RCA)
ST/Pot Luck . . . . (RCA)
Night Rider
Electric Light Orchestra; *Face The Music* . . . . (Jet)
Night Rider's Lament
Chris LeDoux; *Chris LeDoux & The Saddle Boogie Band.* . . . . (Liberty)
Old Cowboy Classics . . . . (Capitol)
Paint Me Back Home In Wyoming. . . . . (Liberty)
Garth Brooks; *The Chase* . . . . (Liberty)
Jerry Jeff Walker; *Ridin' High.* . . . . (MCA)
Nanci Griffith; *Other Voices Other Rooms* . . . . (Elektra)
Suzy Bogguss; *Somewhere Between* . . . . (Capitol)
Old Gray Mare, The
Original Soundtrack; *School Days-Kids Classics* . . . . (Benson)
Old Paint
Chris LeDoux; *Old Cowboy Classics.* . . . . (Capitol)
Western Tunesmith . . . . (Liberty)
Linda Ronstadt; *Simple Dreams.* . . . . (Asylum)
Old Rockin' Horse
Slim Dusty; *Australia Is His Name* . . . . (Philo)
On A Carousel
Hollies; *Best Of The Hollies* . . . . (EMI)
History Of British Rock-#6-C . . . . (Rhino)
The Hollies' Greatest Hits. . . . . (Epic)
One Horse Town
Bobby Bland; *Introspective Of The Early Years* . . . . (MCA)
Touch Of The Blues. . . . . (MCA)
One Horse Town
Elton John; *Blue Moves* . . . . (MCA)
One Horse Town
David Frishberg; *Live At Vine Street* . . . . (Original Jazz Classics)
One Horse Town
Rembrandts; *Untitled.* . . . . (Atco)
One-Trick Pony
Paul Simon; *ST/One-Trick Pony* . . . . (Warner Bros.)
Pegasus
Mahavishnu Orchestra; *Visions Of The Emerald Beyond* . . . . . . (Columbia)
Pegasus
Allman Brothers Band; *Enlightened Rogues* . . . . (Polydor)
Philadelphia Fillies
Del Reeves; *Super Country Hits Of The '70s-C* . . . . (Gusto)
Pony
Ginuwine; *Ginuwine...The Bachelor* . . . . (550 Music)
Pony Boy
Allman Brothers Band; *Brothers & Sisters* . . . . (Polydor)
Pony Boy
Bruce Springsteen; *Human Touch* . . . . (Columbia)
Pony Express
Ted Nugent & The Amboy Dukes; *Call Of The Wild* . . . . . . (Bizarre/Straight)
Pony Man
Gordon Lightfoot; *Gord's Gold-#2* . . . . (Warner Bros.)
If You Could Read My Mind . . . . (Reprise)
Sit Down Young Stranger . . . . (Reprise)
Pony Ride
Olivia Newton-John; *Come On Over* . . . . (MCA)
Pony Time
Chubby Checker; *Chubby Checker's Greatest Hits* . . . . (Abkco)
Good Time Rock 'N' Roll-C . . . . (MCA)
Let's Dance. . . . . (Gusto)
Racehorse
Count Basie & His Kansas City 3; *For The Second Time* . . . . (Pablo)
Ride A Wild Horse
Kenny Nolan; *Night Miracles* . . . . (Casablanca)
Ride 'Em Cowboy
Roy Rogers & Sons Of The Pioneers; *Roy Rogers & Sons Of The
Pioneers* . . . . (Varese Sarabande)
Ride 'Em Cowboy
Paul Davis; *Ride 'Em Cowboy* . . . . (Bang)
Ride Like The Wind
Christopher Cross; *Christopher Cross* . . . . (Warner Bros.)
Ride On Cowboy
Alvin Lee/Ten Years Later; *Ride On* . . . . (RSO)

Ride On Pony
Free; *Free-Live* . . . . (A&M)
Highway . . . . (A&M)
Ride Your Pony
Lee Dorsey; *'60s Soul Party-C* . . . . (Era)
Golden Classics-Lee Dorsey . . . . (Collectables)
History Of New Orleans R&B-#3-1962-1970-C . . . . (Rhino)
Ride, Ride, Ride
Foghat; *Best Of Foghat* . . . . (Rhino)
Foghat . . . . (Rhino)
Ride, Ride, Ride
Tex Ritter; *The Country Music Hall Of Fame-Tex Ritter* . . . . (MCA)
Ride, The
David Allan Coe; *19 Hot Country Requests-C* . . . .(Epic)
Castles In The Sand . . . . (Columbia)
David Allan Coe-17 Greatest Hits . . . . (Columbia)
For The Record-The First 10 Years . . . . (Columbia)
Trucker's Jukebox-#2-C . . . . (Legacy)
Rider In The Rain
Randy Newman; *Little Criminals* . . . .(Warner Bros.)
Riders On The Storm
Doors; *Best Of The Doors* . . . . (Elektra)
Doors' Greatest Hits . . . . (Elektra)
L.A. Woman . . . . (Elektra)
ST/The Doors . . . . (Elektra)
Weird Scenes Inside The Gold Mine . . . . (Elektra)
Ridge Running Roan
Skip Gorman; *A Cowboy's Wild Song To His Herd* . . . . (Rounder)
Ridin' Down The Canyon
Gene Autry; *Columbia Historic Edition-Gene Autry* . . . . (Columbia)
Western Classics . . . . (Columbia)
Riders In The Sky; *Cowboy Way* . . . .(MCA)
Willie Nelson & Leon Russell; *One For The Road* . . . . (Columbia)
Riding High In Texas
Peter Rowan; *Medicine Trail* . . . . (Flying Fish)
Rockin' Horse
Bad English; *Bad English* . . . .(Epic)
Run For The Roses
Dan Fogelberg; *Dan Fogelberg/Greatest Hits* . . . .(Full Moon)
Innocent Age . . . . (Full Moon)
Live-Greetings From The West . . . . (Full Moon)
Saddle In The Rain
John Prine; *Common Sense* . . . . (Atlantic)
Prime Prine-The Best Of John Prine . . . . (Atlantic)
Saddle Tramp
Marty Robbins; *Gunfighter Ballads & Trail Songs* . . . . (Legacy)
Marty Robbins-More Greatest Hits . . . . (Columbia)
Saddle Up The Grey
New Lost City Ramblers; *20 Years Of Concert Performances* . . . . . (Flying Fish)
Saddle Up The Palomino
Neil Young, Crazy Horse & The Bullets; *American Stars 'N Bars* . . . . . (Reprise)
She'll Be Coming 'Round The Mountain
Four Freshmen & Stan Kenton & Orchestra; *Live At Butler
University* . . . . (Creative World)
Mormon Tabernacle Choir; *This Land Is Your Land* . . . . (Columbia)
Original Soundtrack; *Children's Favorites* . . . . (Kid Rhino/Rhino 4 Kids)
School Days-Kids Classics . . . . (Benson)
Shetland Pony Blues
Son House; *Delta Blues-Library Of Congress Sessions* . . . . (Biograph)
Silver Stallion
Waylon Jennings, Willie Nelson, Johnny Cash, Kris Kristofferson; *Greatest
Country Hits Of The '90s-1990-C* . . . . (Columbia)
Highwayman 2 . . . . (Columbia)
Strawberry Roan
Marty Robbins; *Gunfighter Ballads & Trail Songs* . . . . (Legacy)
Sunday Rider
David Gates; *First* . . . . (Elektra)
Goodbye Girl . . . . (Elektra)
Surrey With The Fringe On Top
Ellis Marsalis; *Heart Of Gold* . . . . (Columbia)
Original Broadway Cast; *Oklahoma!* . . . . (RCA)
Original Cast; *Oklahoma!* . . . .(MCA)
Swimming Horses
Siouxsie And The Banshees; *Hyaena* . . . . (Geffen)
Twice Upon A Time-The Singles . . . . (Geffen)
Theme From "Bronco"
Original Soundtrack; *Television's Greatest Hits-#4-Black & White
Classics-C* . . . . (TVT)
Theme From "Mr. Ed"
Original Soundtrack; *Television's Greatest Hits-#1-C* . . . . (TVT)
Theme From "The Lone Ranger" (William Tell Overture)
Boston Pops Orchestra; *TV Classics-C* . . . . (RCA)
Boston Pops Orchestra/Arthur Fiedler; *Fiedler-Greatest Hits* . . . . (RCA)
Original Soundtrack; *Television's Greatest Hits-#7-Cable Ready-C* . . . . . (TVT)
Spike Jones & His City Slickers; *Best Of Spike Jones & His City
Slickers* . . . . (RCA)
Tony The Pony
Morrissey; *Kill Uncle* . . . . (Sire)

Trick Rider
McBride & The Ride; *Sacred Ground* . . . . (MCA)
Two White Horses
John Lee Hooker; *That's Where It's At* . . . . (Stax)
White Horse
Laid Back; *Castles In The Sand* . . . .(Sire)
For The Record . . . . (Sire)
Greatest Hits Of The Street-C . . . . (Priority)
Keep Smiling . . . . (Sire)
White Horses
Outlaws; *Ghost Riders* . . . . (Arista)
Who's Gonna Ride Your Wild Horses
U2; *Achtung Baby* . . . . (Island)
Wild Horses
Rolling Stones; *Hot Rocks 1964-1971* . . . .(Abkco)
Made In The Shade . . . . (Rolling Stones)
Singles Collection-The London Years . . . .(Abkco)
Sticky Fingers . . . . (Virgin)
Wild Horses
Garth Brooks; *No Fences* . . . . (Capitol)
Wild Horses
Gino Vannelli; *Big Dreams Never Sleep* . . . . (Epic Portrait Assoc.)
Wild Horses
Sundays; *Blind* . . . . (David Geffen Co.)
Wild Horses
Flying Burrito Brothers; *Farther Along-Best Of The Flying Burrito
Brothers* . . . . (A&M)
Wild Horses
Suzy Bogguss; *Moment Of Truth* . . . . (Capitol)
Wild Horses
Prefab Sprout; *Jordan-The Comeback* . . . . (Epic)
Life Of Surprises-Best Of Prefab Sprout . . . . (Epic)
Wildfire
Michael Martin Murphey; *'70s Greatest Rock Hits-#3-High Times-C* . . (Priority)
Best Of Michael Martin Murphey . . . . (Liberty)
Blue Sky-Night Thunder . . . . (Epic)
Super Hits Of The '70s-Have A Nice Day-#14-C . . . . (Rhino)
Yankee Doodle
Boston Pops Orchestra/Arthur Fiedler; *Fiedler's Favorite Marches* . . . . . (RCA)
Music For All Occasions . . . . (RCA)

ANIMALS: INSECTS, Bugs, Butterflies, Spiders
*See Also: **ANIMALS: A-Z, ANIMALS: GENERAL***

Ain't No Bugs On Me
New Lost City Ramblers; *20 Years Of Concert Performances* . . . . . (Flying Fish)
An Ant Alone
Bob Telson & Little Village; *An Ant Alone-Songs From The
Warrior Ant* . . . . (Gramavision)
Ant & The Elephant
Chick Corea Elektric Band II; *Paint The World* . . . . (GRP)
Ant Farm
Young Fresh Fellows; *Men Who Loved Music* . . . .(Frontier)
Ant Farm
Night Soil Man; *Garden Of Delights* . . . . (Vinyl Comm.)
Ant Man Bee
Captain Beefheart & His Magic Band; *Trout Mask Replica* . . . . (Reprise)
Ant Rap
Adam Ant; *Antics In The Forbidden Zone* . . . . (Epic)
Prince Charming . . . . (Epic)
Ants
House Of Freaks; *Cakewalk* . . . .(Giant)
Ants Can Count
Bruce Fowler; *Ants Can Count* . . . . (Terra Nova)
Ants Go Marching, The
Original Soundtrack; *Mother Goose Songs* . . . .(Madacy)
Ants In My Pants
Bo Carter; *Rare Blues Of The Twenties-1927-1930-C* . . . . (Historical)
Ants In The Kitchen
Masters Of Reality; *Sunrise On The Sufferbus* . . . . (Chrysalis)
Ants Invasion
Adam Ant; *Kings Of The Wild Frontier* . . . . (Epic)
Ants Marching
Dave Matthews Band; *Under The Table And Dreaming* . . . . (RCA)
Attack Of The Giant Ants
Blondie; *Blondie* . . . . (Chrysalis)
Austrian Anthill
Brian Ritchie; *The Blend* . . . .(SST)
Be My Little Bumble Bee
Jonathan & Darlene Edwards; *Jonathan & Darlene Edwards'
Greatest Hits* . . . . (Corinthian)
Betcha The Love Bug Bitcha
Dr. Buzzard's Original "Savannah" Band; *Dr. Buzzard's Original
"Savannah" Band* . . . . (RCA)
Birds And The Bees
Jewel Akens; *American Graffiti-#3-C* . . . . (MCA)

Collectables Presents The History Of Rock-#4-C . . . . (Collectables)
Cruisin'-1965-C . . . . (Increase)
Oldies But Goodies-#9-C . . . . (Original Sound)
Super Hits-#3-C . . . . (Gusto)
Black Butterfly
Deniece Williams; *Let's Hear It For The Boy* . . . . (Columbia)
Black Butterfly
Duke Ellington; *Best Of Duke Ellington* . . . . (Pablo)
Black Widow
Alice Cooper; *The Alice Cooper Show* . . . . (Warner Bros.)
Welcome To My Nightmare . . . . (Atlantic)
Black Widow
Lita Ford; *Dangerous Curves* . . . . (RCA)
Black Widow
Jefferson Starship; *Winds Of Change* . . . . (Grunt)
Blue Tail Fly
Burl Ives; *Best Of Burl Ives* . . . . (MCA)
Pete Seeger; *20 Golden Pieces Of Pete Seeger* . . . . (Bulldog)
Boll Weevil Song
Brook Benton; *Brook Benton-Anthology* . . . . (Rhino)
It's Just A Matter Of Time-His Greatest Hits . . . . (Mercury)
Pick Of Brook Benton . . . . (Fifty One West)
Leadbelly; *Good Mornin' Blues-1936-1940* . . . . (Biograph)
Boris The Spider
Who; *Happy Jack* . . . . (MCA)
Meaty Beaty Big & Bouncy . . . . (MCA)
Who's Last . . . . (MCA)
Bug, The
Dire Straits; *On Every Street* . . . . (Warner Bros.)
Mary Chapin Carpenter; *Come On Come On* . . . . (Columbia)
Bullet With Butterfly Wings
Smashing Pumpkins; *Mellon Collie And The Infinite Sadness* . . . (Virgin)
Bumble Bee
Mance Lipscomb; *Texas Songwriter-#2* . . . . (Arhoolie)
You Got To Reap What You Sow . . . . (Arhoolie)
Bumble Bee
LaVern Baker; *Live In Hollywood '91* . . . . (Rhino)
Searchers; *Searchers' Greatest Hits* . . . . (Rhino)
Bumble Bee
Meryn Cadell; *Angel Food For Thought* . . . . (Sire)
Bumble Bee
Big Mama Thornton; *Ball N' Chain* . . . . (Arhoolie)
Bumble Bee Blues
Kansas Joe & Memphis Minnie; *Blues Masters-#12-Memphis Blues-C* . . (Rhino)
Memphis Minnie; *Country Blues Classics-#3* . . . . (Blues Classics)
Bumble Bee Blues
Brian Slawson & Stevie Ray Vaughan; *Distant Drums* . . . . (Columbia)
Bumble Bee Stomp
Benny Goodman; *On The Air-1937-1938* . . . . (Columbia)
Bumble Boogie
Freddy Martin; *Big Band In Hi Fi-#1-Let's Dance* . . . . (Capitol)
Bumble Boogie
Jo Ann Castle; *Legends Of Accordion-C* . . . . (Rhino)
Bumblebee
Eric Andersen; *Best Of Eric Andersen* . . . . (Vanguard)
Today Is The Highway . . . . (Vanguard)
Bumblebees
Christine Lavin; *Good Thing He Can't Read My Mind* . . . . (Philo)
Butterflies
Michael Jackson; *Invincible* . . . . (Epic)
Butterflies/Everytime I See A Butterfly
Les McCann; *Hustle To Survive* . . . . (Atlantic)
Butterfly
Charlie Gracie; *Rock-O-Rama-#1-C* . . . . (Abkco)
Butterfly
Crazy Town; *Gift Of Game* . . . . (Columbia)
Butterfly
Book Of Love; *Candy Carol* . . . . (Sire)
Butterfly
Terry Callier; *Fire On Ice* . . . . (Elektra)
Butterfly
Lenny Kravitz; *Mama Said* . . . . (Virgin)
Butterfly
Gladys Knight & The Pips; *One & Only* . . . . (Buddah)
Butterfly (I'll Set You Free)
Perry Como; *Perry Como Today* . . . . (RCA)
Butterfly For Bucky
Bobby Goldsboro; *Butterfly For Bucky* . . . . (United Artists)
Butterfly Kisses
Bob Carlisle; *Butterfly Kisses (Shades Of Grace)* . . . . (DMG/Jive)
Butterflyz
Alicia Keys; *Songs In A Minor* . . . . (J)
Catch Another Butterfly
John Denver; *Rhymes & Reasons* . . . . (RCA)
Caught In Your Web (Swear To Your Heart)
Russell Hitchcock; *ST/Arachnophobia* . . . . (Hollywood)
Centipede
Rebbie Jackson; *Centipede* . . . . (Columbia)

Change (In The House Of Flies)
Deftones; *White Pony* . . . . (Maverick)
Charlotte's Web
Statler Brothers; *10th Anniversary* . . . . (Mercury)
Cockroach
Albert King; *Years Gone By* . . . . (Stax)
Cockroach
Sweet; *Give Us A Wink* . . . . (Capitol)
Cockroach That Ate Cincinnati
Possum; *Dr. Demento's Delights-C* . . . . (Warner Bros.)
Rose & The Arrangement; *Dr. Demento Presents The Greatest Novelty
Records-#4-1970s-C* . . . . (Rhino)
Cricket Song
Donna Fargo; *Fargo Country* . . . . (Warner Bros.)
Daisys Up Your Butterfly
Cramps; *Stay Sick!* . . . . (Enigma Capitol)
Dancing Bumble Bee
Neil Diamond; *You Don't Bring Me Flowers* . . . . (Columbia)
Day Of The Locusts
Bob Dylan; *New Morning* . . . . (Columbia)
Diving To Be Deeper
Sinead Lohan; *No Mermaid* . . . . (Grapevine)
Dog & Butterfly
Heart; *Dog & Butterfly* . . . . (Portrait)
Heart's Greatest Hits/Live . . . . (Epic)
Drunken Butterfly
Sonic Youth; *Dirty* . . . . (David Geffen Co.)
Eagle Never Hunts The Fly
Music Machine; *Best Of Music Machine* . . . . (Rhino)
Nuggets-#2-Punk-C . . . . (Rhino)
Elusive Butterfly (Of Love)
Bob Lind; *Good Vibrations (Sounds Of Top 40 Radio: 1964-1967)-C* . . (Capitol)
Eye Of The Dragonfly
Friedemann; *Indian Summer* . . . . (Narada)
Fart Of The Bumblebee
Original Soundtrack; *Pull My Finger!-C* . . . . (Orchard)
Fireflies
Fleetwood Mac; *Fleetwood Mac Live* . . . . (Warner Bros.)
Fireflies
Gato Barbieri; *Caliente* . . . . (A&M)
Firefly
Tony Bennett; *Forty Years-The Artistry Of Tony Bennett* . . . . (Columbia)
Tony Bennett At Carnegie Hall . . . . (Sony Music Special Prod.)
Tony Bennett's All-Time Greatest Hits . . . . (Columbia)
Firefly
Temptations; *A Song For You* . . . . (Motown)
Firefly
Levitation; *Coterie* . . . . (Capitol)
Firefly
Emily Remler; *Firefly* . . . . (Concord Jazz)
Firefly Serenade
Lawrence Welk; *22 Great Songs For Dancing* . . . . (Ranwood)
Fishes And Scorpions
Stephen Stills; *Stephen Stills 2* . . . . (Atlantic)
Flies Of Texas Are Upon You
Ray Stevens; *Crackin' Up* . . . . (MCA)
Flight Of The Fly
Dan Hicks & His Hot Licks; *Striking It Rich!* . . . . (MCA)
Glow Worm
Mills Brothers; *Best Of The Mills Brothers* . . . . (MCA)
Cab Driver . . . . (Ranwood)
Mills Brothers' Greatest Hits . . . . (MCA)
Mills Brothers-16 Great Performances . . . . (MCA)
Greedy Fly
Bush; *Razorblade Suitcase* . . . . (Trauma)
High Hopes
Doris Day; *The Envelope Please-Academy Award Winning Songs (1934-
1993)-C* . . . . (Rhino)
Frank Sinatra; *Best Of The Capitol Years* . . . . (Capitol)
ST/Sinatra-CBS Mini-Series . . . . (Reprise)
Honey For The Bees
Patti Austin; *Gettin' Away With Murder* . . . . (Qwest)
Honey For The Bees
Alison Moyet; *Alf* . . . . (Columbia)
Honey To The Bee
Billie; *Honey To The B* . . . . (Virgin)
I Got Stung
Elvis Presley; *50,000,000 Elvis Fans Can't Be Wrong-Elvis' Gold Records-
Volume 2* . . . . (RCA)
The Top Ten Hits . . . . (RCA)
Worldwide 50 Gold Award Hits, Vol. 1, Parts 1 & 2 . . . . (RCA)
I Know An Old Lady Who Swallowed A Fly
Original Soundtrack; *More Silly Songs* . . . . (Disney)
Peter, Paul & Mary; *Peter, Paul & Mommy, Too* . . . . (Warner Bros.)
I'm A King Bee
Muddy Waters; *King Bee* . . . . (Blue Sky)
Rolling Stones; *England's Newest Hit Makers/The Rolling Stones* . . . . (Abkco)
Slim Harpo; *Best Of Slim Harpo* . . . . (Rhino)

Blues Classics-C . . . . (K-Tel)
I'm Nature's Mosquito
Jonathan Richman & The Modern Lovers; *Back In Your Life*. . . . . (Rhino)
Inchworm
Danny Kaye; *Billboard Presents Family Lullaby*
Classics-C. . . . . (Kid Rhino/Rhino 4 Kids)
Victoria Jackson; *Child's Celebration Of Song-#2-C*. . (Music For Little People)
Insects
Oingo Boingo; *Nothing To Fear* . . . . (A&M)
Skeletons In The Closet: The Best Of Oingo Boingo . . . . (A&M)
Insects
Altered Images; *Happy Birthday* . . . . (Portrait)
Internet Worm
Paul K.; *Achilles Heel* . . . . (Thirsty Ear)
Itsy Bitsy Spider, The
Original Soundtrack; *Mother Goose Songs*. . . . . (Madacy)
June Bug
Leo Kottke; *Best Of Leo Kottke* . . . . (Capitol)
Did You Hear Me . . . . (Capitol)
Mudlark . . . . (Capitol)
My Feet Are Smiling . . . . (Capitol)
June Bug
Lester Young; *Lester Young-Complete Savoy Recordings* . . . . (Savoy)
Master Takes . . . . (Savoy)
Killing The Fly
Union Underground; *...An Education In Rebellion* . . . . (Portrait)
King Cockroach
Chick Corea Elektric Band; *Chick Corea Elektric Band*. . . . . (GRP)
Kiss Me
Sixpence None The Richer; *Sixpence None The Richer* . . . . .(Squint/Columbia)
Songs From Dawson's Creek. . . . . (Sony Music Soundtrax)
Lady Bug
Anne Murray; *Together* . . . . (Capitol)
Lady Bug
Bumblebee Unlimited; *Sting Like A Bee*. . . . . (RCA)
Leech
Eve 6; *Eve 6* . . . . (RCA)
Let's Fall In Love
Diana Krall; *When I Look In Your Eyes* . . . . (GRP)
Frank Sinatra; *The Reprise Collection* . . . . (Reprise)
Louis Armstrong & Oscar Peterson; *Verve Elite Edition Collector's*
Disc-C. . . . . (Verve)
Tony Bennett; *Tony Bennett Sings A String Of Harold*
Arlen . . . . (Columbia Special Prod.)
Love Bug Leave My Heart Alone
Martha & The Vandellas; *Compact Command Performances-Martha Reeves*
& The Vandellas . . . . (Motown)
Martha Reeves & The Vandellas-Anthology . . . . (Motown)
Love Is Like A Butterfly
Dolly Parton; *Best Of Dolly Parton* . . . . (RCA)
Collector's Series-Dolly Parton . . . . (RCA)
Lovebug
George Jones; *Pick Of George Jones* . . . . (Fifty One West)
George Strait; *Easy Come Easy Go*. . . . . (MCA)
Miracle Of Love
Eileen Rodgers; *Hard To Find 45s On CD-#3-The Mid '50s-C* . . . . (Eric)
Moth & The Flame
Sky Saxon Blues Band; *Full Spoon Of Seedy Blues* . . . . (Crescendo)
Moth & The Flame, Parts 1-5
Keith Jarrett; *Invocations* . . . . (ECM)
Moth, The
Hearing Voices; *Hearing Voices* . . . . (Chase Music Group)
Moths
Jethro Tull; *20 Years Of Jethro Tull* . . . . (Chrysalis)
Heavy Horses. . . . . (Chrysalis)
My Cricket
Leon Russell; *Carney* . . . . (Right Stuff)
No Matter What They Say
Lil' Kim; *Notorious K.I.M.*. . . . . (Queen Bee/Undeas/Atlantic)
Ode To A Butterfly
Nickel Creek; *Nickel Creek* . . . . (Sugar Hill)
Pestilence
Icepick Trotsky; *Ultraviolet Catastrophe*. . . . . (SST)
Poor Butterfly
Sarah Vaughan; *Compact Jazz-Sarah Vaughan* . . . . (Verve)
Live In Japan . . . . (Mainstream)
Sarah Vaughan-Golden Hits . . . . (Mercury)
Sonny Rollins; *Best Of Sonny Rollins-The Blue Note Years* . . . . (Blue Note)
Sonny Rollins-Vol. 2 . . . . (Blue Note)
Queen Bee
Taj Mahal; *Evolution* . . . . (Warner Bros.)
Queen Bee
Barbra Streisand; *ST/A Star Is Born* . . . . (Columbia)
Queen Bee
John Lee Hooker; *Greatest Hits Of John Lee Hooker*. . . . . (Kent)
Queen Bee
Koko Taylor; *Queen Of The Blues* . . . . (Alligator)

Queen Bee
Grand Funk Railroad; *ST/Heavy Metal* . . . . (Asylum)
Rats & Roaches In My Kitchen
Silas Hogan; *Louisiana Blues* . . . . (Arhoolie)
Return Of The Spiders
Alice Cooper; *Easy Action* . . . . (Bizarre/Straight)
Roach Motel
Dead Youth; *Intense Brutality*. . . . . (Grind Core Int'l)
Roaches
Bobby Jimmy & The Critters; *Greatest Hits Of The Street-C* . . . . . . (Priority)
Rap Beginnings-#1-C . . . . (K-Tel)
Rapmasters 7-Best Of The Laughs-C . . . . (Priority)
You A Fool-Best Of Bobby Jimmy & The Critters. . . . . (K-Tel)
Roger's Bumble Bee (Latter Day)
Roger Williams; *Best Of Roger Williams* . . . . (MCA)
Roger Williams-Golden Hits . . . . (MCA)
Salt On A Slug
Black Flag; *Family Man* . . . . (SST)
Salting Of The Slug
Riders In The Sky; *Cowboy Way*. . . . . (MCA)
Several Species Of Small Furry Animals
Pink Floyd; *Ummagumma* . . . . (Capitol)
Works . . . . (Capitol)
Skunk, The Goose & The Fly
Tower Of Power; *East Bay Grease* . . . . (Rhino)
Sleepin' Bee
Al Jarreau; *1965* . . . . (Bainbridge)
Barbra Streisand; *Highlights From ''Just For The Record''* . . . . . . (Columbia)
Just For The Record . . . . (Columbia)
The Barbra Streisand Album . . . . (Columbia)
Bill Evans; *Compact Jazz-Bill Evans* . . . . (Verve)
Carmen McRae; *Setting Standards* . . . . (Pair)
Harold Arlen & Barbra Streisand; *Harold Sings Arlen (With*
Friend). (Sony Music Special Prod.)
Kiri Te Kanawa & Andre Previn; *Kiri Side Tracks-Jazz Album* . . . . . (Philips)
Mel Torme; *Swings Shubert Alley*. . . . . (Verve)
Original Cast; *House Of Flowers* . . . . (Sony Music Special Prod.)
Tony Bennett; *Consummate Collection-Classics Songs* . . . . (Columbia)
Forty Years-The Artistry Of Tony Bennett . . . . (Columbia)
Spanish Entomologist
Leo Kottke; *Best Of Leo Kottke* . . . . (Capitol)
Greenhouse . . . . (Capitol)
Very Best Of Leo Kottke . . . . (Capitol)
Spanish Flea
Herb Alpert & The Tijuana Brass; *Going Places* . . . . (A&M)
Herb Alpert & The Tijuana Brass' Greatest Hits . . . . (A&M)
Herb Alpert & The Tijuana Brass-Classics-#1 . . . . (A&M)
Spanish Fly
Van Halen; *Van Halen II* . . . . (Warner Bros.)
Spider
Kansas; *Point Of Know Return* . . . . (Kirshner)
Spider & The Fly
Rolling Stones; *Out Of Our Heads* . . . . (Abkco)
Singles Collection-The London Years . . . . (Abkco)
Spider Blues
John Koerner; *Spider Blues* . . . . (Elektra)
Spider In My Stew
Buster Benton; *Spider In My Stew*. . . . . (Ronn)
Spider Web
Joan Osborne; *Relish*. . . . . (Blue Gorilla/Mercury)
Spiders & Snakes
Jim Stafford; *Jim Stafford* . . . . (Polydor)
Super Hits Of The '70s-Have A Nice Day-#12-C . . . . (Rhino)
Loretta Lynn & Conway Twitty; *Very Best Of Loretta Lynn & Conway*
Twitty. . . . . (MCA)
Spiderwebs
No Doubt; *1997 Grammy Nominees-C* . . . . (Chronicles)
Tragic Kingdom . . . . (Trauma)
Staring At The Sun
U2; *Pop* . . . . (Island)
Sting Me
Black Crowes; *Southern Harmony & Musical Companion*. . . . . (Def American)
Sugar Bee
Boozoo Chavis & The Majic Sounds; *Stomp Down Zydeco-C* . . . . . (Rounder)
Jo-el Sonnier; *Jo-el Sonnier-Complete Mercury Sessions*. . . . . . . (Mercury)
Rockin' Dopsie & The Cajun Twisters; *Big Bad Zydeco*. . . . . . . (Crescendo)
Swattin' The Fly
Dawn Upshaw; *Dawn Upshaw Sings Vernon Duke* . . . . (Nonesuch)
Sweet Honey Sucking Bees
Miranda Sex Garden; *Madra*. . . . . (Mute/Reprise)
Tangled In The Web
Lynch Mob; *Lynch Mob* . . . . (Elektra)
Theme From ''Spiderman''
Original Soundtrack; *Television's Greatest Hits-#2-C* . . . . (TVT)
Theme From ''The Atom Ant Show''
Original Soundtrack; *Hanna-Barbera Pic-A-Nic Basket Of Cartoon*
Classics. . . . . (Kid Rhino/Rhino 4 Kids)
Television's Greatest Hits-#5-In Living Color-C . . . . (TVT)

Theme From "The Green Hornet"
Original Soundtrack; *Television's Greatest Hits-#2-C* . . . . (TVT)
There Ain't No Bugs On Me
Jerry Garcia & David Grisman; *Not For Kids Only* . . . . (Acoustic Disc)
There Is A Mountain
Donovan; *Donovan's Greatest Hits* . . . . (Epic)
Troubadour-Definitive Collection . . . . (Epic)
Toilet Licking Maggot
Hell On Earth; *Biomechanical Ejaculations Of The Damned* . . . . (Neptune)
Trouble
Coldplay; *Parachutes* . . . . (Nettwerk/Capitol)
Two Little Bees
Hollywood Flames; *Hollywood Flames* . . . . (Specialty)
Two Thousand Pound Bee
Ventures; *Radical Guitars* . . . . (Iloki)
ST/Wired . . . . (Varese Sarabande)
Venus Flytrap & The Bug
Stevie Wonder; *Journey Through The Secret Life Of Plants* . . . . . . (Motown)
Waiting For The Worms
Pink Floyd; *The Wall* . . . . (Columbia)
Roger Waters; *The Wall-Live In Berlin* . . . . (Mercury)
You're So Sweet, Horseflies Keep Hangin' Round Your Face
Neil Diamond; *Brother Love's Traveling Salvation Show* . . . . (MCA)

ANIMALS: KANGAROOS

See Also: **ANIMALS: A-Z, ANIMALS: GENERAL, COUNTRIES: AUSTRALIA**

I'll Bet You A Kangaroo
Olivia Newton-John; *Don't Stop Believin'* . . . . (MCA)
Kangaroo
Klaxons; *How Do You Do?* . . . . (Crescendo)
Les Paul; *Legend & The Legacy-#1-4* . . . . (Capitol)
Kangaroo Hop
Dee Clark; *Rain Drops* . . . . (Vee-Jay)
Theme From "Skippy, The Bush Kangaroo"
Original Soundtrack; *Television's Greatest Hits-#5-In Living Color-C* . . . (TVT)
Tie Me Kangaroo Down, Sport
Rolf Harris; *45-#213* . . . . (Eric)
Tie Me Kangaroo Down, Sport & Sun Arise . . . . (Epic)

ANIMALS: L

See Also: **ANIMALS: A-Z, ANIMALS: GENERAL, ANIMALS: LIONS**

Last Snow Leopard
Spencer Brewer; *Emerald* . . . . (Narada)
Leopard Skin Pillbox Hat
Bob Dylan; *Blonde On Blonde* . . . . (Columbia)
Leopards In Love
Zummos; *Modern Marriage* . . . . (A&M)
Ride My Llama
Neil Young & Crazy Horse; *Rust Never Sleeps* . . . . (Reprise)

ANIMALS: LIONS

See Also: **ANIMALS: A-Z, ANIMALS: GENERAL**

Can't Tame The Lion
Journey; *Trial By Fire* . . . . (Columbia)
I Am A Lion
Neil Diamond; *Tap Root Manuscript* . . . . (MCA)
Jungle, The
Kiss; *Carnival Of Souls: The Final Sessions* . . . . (Mercury)
Lion
Burning Spear; *Burning Spear-Live* . . . . (Island)
Man In The Hills . . . . (Island)
Toto; *Isolation* . . . . (Columbia)
Lion In The Winter
Hoyt Axton; *Road Songs* . . . . (A&M)
Southbound . . . . (A&M)
Lion's Den
Bruce Springsteen; *Tracks* . . . . (Columbia)
Listen To The Lion
Van Morrison; *It's Too Late To Stop Now* . . . . (Warner Bros.)
St. Dominic's Preview . . . . (Warner Bros.)
Mama Lion
David Crosby & Graham Nash; *Wind On The Water* . . . . (MCA)
Strong Like A Lion
Roots Radics; *Forward Ever-Backwards Never* . . . . (Heartbeat)

Theme From "Lippy The Lion & Hardy Har Har"
Original Soundtrack; *Hanna-Barbera Classics-#1-Original Recordings Of The World's Most Famous Cartoon Themes & Scores* . . . . (Kid Rhino/Rhino 4 Kids)
Hanna-Barbera Pic-A-Nic Basket Of Cartoon Classics . . . . (Kid Rhino/Rhino 4 Kids)
Wimoweh (Mbube)-The Lion Sleeps Tonight
Chet Atkins; *RCA Years* . . . . (RCA)
Kingston Trio; *Kingston Trio/From The Hungry i* . . . . (Capitol)
Nylons; *Seamless* . . . . (Open Air)
Pete Seeger; *Pete Seeger's Greatest Hits* . . . . (Columbia)
Tokens; *Billboard Top Rock 'N' Roll Hits-1961-C* . . . . (Rhino)
Nipper's Greatest Hits Of The '60s-#1-C . . . . (RCA)
Weavers; *Weavers' Greatest Hits* . . . . (Vanguard)

ANIMALS: M

See Also: **ANIMALS: A-Z, ANIMALS: GENERAL, ANIMALS: MICE, MONKEYS, MULES**

Morse Moose & The Grey Goose
Wings; *London Town* . . . . (Capitol)
Muskrat Love
America; *America Live* . . . . (Warner Bros.)
Hat Trick . . . . (Warner Bros.)
History-Greatest Hits . . . . (Warner Bros.)
Captain & Tennille; *Captain & Tennille's Greatest Hits* . . . . (A&M)
Muskrat Ramble
Dukes Of Dixieland; *Digital Dixieland* . . . . (Pro Jazz)
Kid Ory's Creole Jazz Band; *Kid Ory's Creole Jazz Band-1954* . . . . (Good Time Jazz)
Louis Armstrong; *Essential Louis Armstrong* . . . . (Vanguard)
Louis Armstrong's Greatest Hits . . . . (Curb)
McGuire Sisters; *McGuire Sisters' Greatest Hits* . . . . (MCA)
Pete Fountain; *High Society* . . . . (Bluebird)
Sly Mongoose
Charlie Parker; *Bebop & Bird-#2* . . . . (Rhino)
Monty Alexander Ivory & Steel; *Jamboree* . . . . (Concord Picante Jazz)
Strollin' (With My Moose)
Edgar Meyer; *Sampler '88-#2-C* . . . . (MCA)
Theme From "The Rocky & Bullwinkle Show" (moose)
Original Soundtrack; *Television's Greatest Hits-#2-C* . . . . (TVT)
Two Moose In A Caboose
Stan Kenton & His Orchestra; *The Uncollected Stan Kenton & His Orchestra-#5-1945-1947* . . . . (Hindsight)

ANIMALS: MICE

See Also: **ANIMALS: A-Z, ANIMALS: GENERAL**

And The Mouse Police Never Sleeps
Jethro Tull; *Heavy Horses* . . . . (Chrysalis)
Mickey Mouse
Sparks; *Angst In My Pants* . . . . (Atlantic)
Mickey Mouse Alma Mater
Mouseketeers; *Disney Collection-#1-C* . . . . (Disney)
Mickey Mouse March
Aaron Neville & Dr. John; *Stay Awake-Music Of Vintage Disney Films-C* . . . . (A&M)
Mouseketeers; *Disney Collection-#1-C* . . . . (Disney)
One Brown Mouse
Jethro Tull; *Bursting Out* . . . . (Chrysalis)
Heavy Horses . . . . (Chrysalis)
Pepino The Italian Mouse
Lou Monte; *Pepino The Italian Mouse & Other Songs* . . . . (Reprise)
Pretty Mouse
Fluid; *Glue* . . . . (Sub Pop)
Sugar Mice
Marillion; *Clutching At Straws* . . . . (Capitol)
Thieving Magpie . . . . (Capitol)
Theme From "Courageous Cat & Minute Mouse"
Original Soundtrack; *Television's Greatest Hits-#2-C* . . . . (TVT)
Theme From "Mighty Mouse"
Original Soundtrack; *Television's Greatest Hits-#2-C* . . . . (TVT)
Theme From "Pixie And Dixie"
Original Soundtrack; *Hanna-Barbera Classics-#1-Original Recordings Of The World's Most Famous Cartoon Themes & Scores* . . . . (Kid Rhino/Rhino 4 Kids)
Hanna-Barbera Pic-A-Nic Basket Of Cartoon Classics . . . . (Kid Rhino/Rhino 4 Kids)
Theme From "Tom & Jerry"
Henry Mancini; *ST/Tom & Jerry-The Movie* . . . . (MCA)
Three Blind Mice
Van Alexander; *Small Fry-Capitol Sings Kids Songs For Grownups-C* . . . . (Capitol)

ANIMALS: MONKEYS

See Also: *ANIMALS: A-Z, ANIMALS: GENERAL*

Constipated Monkey
Kain; *The Blue Guerilla* . . . . (Collectables)
Everybody's Got Something To Hide Except Me And My Monkey
Beatles; *The Beatles (White Album)* . . . . (Capitol)
Gator Tails And Monkey Ribs
Spats; *45-#10585* . . . . (ABC)
Hard Monkeys
Ten Years After; *A Space In Time* . . . . (Columbia)
I'd Like To Be A Monkey In The Zoo
Frances White; *Music From The New York Stage (1890-1920)-#4-1917-
1920-C* . . . . (Pearl)
King Kong's Monkey
Gary U.S. Bonds; *45-#1031* . . . . (LeGrand)
Mickey's Monkey
Miracles; *Greatest Hits From The Beginning* . . . . (Motown)
Smokey Robinson & The Miracles; *Compact Command Performances-
Smokey Robinson & The Miracles* . . . . (Motown)
*Great Songs & Performances That Inspired The Motown 25th Anniversary
Television Special-C* . . . . (Motown)
Motown Story-First 25 Years-C . . . . (Motown)
Smokey Robinson & The Miracles' Anthology . . . . (Motown)
Minnesota Man Claims Monkey Bowled Perfect Game
Jad Fair; *Strange But True* . . . . (Matador)
Monkey
Fabulous Thunderbirds; *T-Bird Rhythm* . . . . (Chrysalis)
George Michael; *Faith* . . . . (Columbia)
Monkey & The Engineer
Grateful Dead; *Reckoning* . . . . (Arista)
Jesse Fuller; *Lone Cat* . . . . (Good Time Jazz)
Monkey In Winter
Colourfield; *Deception* . . . . (Chrysalis)
Monkey In Your Soul
Steely Dan; *Pretzel Logic* . . . . (MCA)
Monkey Island
J. Geils Band; *Best Of The J. Geils Band* . . . . (Atlantic)
Monkey Island . . . . (Atlantic)
Monkey Man
Toots & The Maytals; *Toots & The Maytals-Live* . . . . (Mango)
Monkey Man
Rolling Stones; *Let It Bleed* . . . . (Abkco)
Monkey On My Back
Inspiral Carpets; *Life* . . . . (Elektra)
Monkey On My Back
Ten Years After; *A Space In Time* . . . . (Columbia)
Monkey On My Back
Aerosmith; *Pump* . . . . (Geffen)
Monkey On Your Back
Aldo Nova; *Portrait Of Aldo Nova* . . . . (Epic)
Subject...Aldo Nova . . . . (Portrait)
Monkey See, Monkey Do
Dickies; *Second Coming* . . . . (Enigma)
Melissa Manchester; *Help Is On The Way* . . . . (Arista)
Michael Franks; *Art Of Tea* . . . . (Reprise)
Ringo Starr; *Bad Boy* . . . . (Epic)
Monkey Shine
Head East; *Act Yourself Up* . . . . (A&M)
Head East-Live . . . . (A&M)
Monkey Time
Major Lance; *Back To The '60s-#3-C* . . . . (Dominion Entert.)
Groove 'N' Grind-'50s & '60s Dance Hits-C . . . . (Rhino)
Soul Shots-#2-The ''In'' Crowd-Sweet Soul-C . . . . (Rhino)
Tubes; *Best Of The Tubes* . . . . (Gold Rush)
Monkey Wash Donkey Rinse
Warren Zevon; *Mutineer* . . . . (Giant)
One Monkey Don't Stop No Show
Big Maybelle; *Okeh R&B Story-1949-1957* . . . . (Epic)
Honey Cone; *Honey Cone's Greatest Hits* . . . . (HDH)
Joe Tex; *I Believe I'm Gonna Make It!-Best Of Joe Tex* . . . . . . (Rhino)
Joe Tex's Greatest Hits . . . . (Curb)
Part Man, Part Monkey
Bruce Springsteen; *Tracks* . . . . (Columbia)
Sell My Monkey
B.B. King; *Blues 'N' Jazz/Electric B.B. King* . . . . (MCA)
Blues 'N' Jazz/Electric B.B. King . . . . (MCA)
Shock The Monkey
Peter Gabriel; *Greenpeace-C* . . . . (A&M)
Peter Gabriel/Plays Live . . . . (Geffen)
Security . . . . (Geffen)
Shaking The Tree-Sixteen Golden Greats . . . . (Geffen)
Space Monkey
Patti Smith Group; *Easter* . . . . (Arista)
Steel Monkey
Jethro Tull; *Crest Of A Knave* . . . . (Chrysalis)

Surf Monkey
Freddie King; *Just Pickin'* . . . . (Modern Blues)
Theme From ''The Monkees''
Monkees; *Monkees' Greatest Hits* . . . . (Rhino)
Original Soundtrack; *Television's Greatest Hits-#2-C* . . . . (TVT)
Too Much Monkey Business
Chuck Berry; *Classic Oldies From The '50s & '60s-#16-C* . . . . . . (MCA)
Roll Over Beethoven . . . . (Allegiance)
ST/Hail! Hail! Rock 'N' Roll . . . . (MCA)
Toronto Rock 'N' Roll Revival-#2-C . . . . (Accord)
Elvis Presley; *Guitar Man* . . . . (RCA)
Million-Dollar Quartet . . . . (RCA)
ST/This Is Elvis . . . . (RCA)
Yardbirds; *Five Live Yardbirds* . . . . (Rhino)
For Your Love . . . . (Accord)
Yardbirds' Greatest Hits-#1 (1964-1966) . . . . (Rhino)
Tweeter & The Monkey Man
Traveling Wilburys; *The Traveling Wilburys* . . . . (Wilbury/Warner Bros.)

ANIMALS: MULES

See Also: *ANIMALS: A-Z, ANIMALS: GENERAL*

Chinese Mule Train
Spike Jones; *Best Of Spike Jones-#2* . . . . (RCA)
Erie Canal
Burl Ives; *Best Of Burl Ives* . . . . (MCA)
Weavers; *Greatest Folksingers Of The '60s-C* . . . . (Vanguard)
Weavers' Greatest Hits . . . . (Vanguard)
Weavers-Classics . . . . (Vanguard)
Lickin'
Black Crowes; *Lions* . . . . (V2)
Mule Skinner Blues (Blue Yodel #8)
Bill Monroe; *Bean Blossom* . . . . (MCA)
Dolly Parton; *Best Of Dolly Parton* . . . . (RCA)
RCA Years-1967-1986 . . . . (RCA)
Fendermen; *Billboard Top Pop Hits-1960-C* . . . . (Rhino)
Hank Williams, Jr.; *Living Proof-MGM Recordings 1963-1975* . . . . (Mercury)
Mule Train
Gene Autry; *The Country Music Hall Of Fame-Gene Autry-15 Of His All-
Time Greatest Hits* . . . . (Columbia)
Tennessee Ernie Ford; *Best Of Tennessee Ernie Ford-16 Tons Of
Boogie* . . . . (Rhino)
Capitol Collectors Series-Tennessee Ernie Ford . . . . (Capitol)
Great Records Of The Decade-'40s-Country-C . . . . (Curb)
Rockin' The Mule
Barrence Whitfield & The Savages; *Ow Ow Ow Ow* . . . . (Rounder)
She Caught The Katy & Left Me A Mule To Ride
Blues Brothers; *Best Of The Blues Brothers* . . . . (Atlantic)
ST/The Blues Brothers . . . . (Atlantic)
Taj Mahal; *Best Of Taj Mahal* . . . . (Columbia)
Natch'l Blues . . . . (Columbia)
She Got A Mule Kick
Harry Crafton; *Harry Crafton* . . . . (Collectables)
She Left Me A Mule To Ride
Big Joe Williams; *Shake Your Boogie* . . . . (Arhoolie)
Swinging On A Star
Bing Crosby; *All-Time Best* . . . . (Curb)
Best Of Bing Crosby . . . . (MCA)
Dion And The Belmonts; *Dion And The Belmonts-Their Best* . . . . (Laurie)
Frank Sinatra; *Frank Sinatra Sings The Songs Of Van Heusen
& Cahn* . . . . (Reprise)

ANIMALS: P

See Also: *ANIMALS: A-Z, ANIMALS: GENERAL, ANIMALS:
HORSES (ponies), ANIMALS: PIGS*

Oh Mr. Possum
Jimmy Preston; *Jimmy Preston* . . . . (Collectables)
Panther In Michigan
Michael Smith; *Michael Smith* . . . . (Flying Fish)
Porcupine
Mary's Danish; *American Standard* . . . . (Morgan Creek)
Youth Gone Mad; *West/East* . . . . (Moving Target)
Porcupine Pie
Neil Diamond; *Hot August Night* . . . . (MCA)
Moods . . . . (MCA)
Possum Hunt
Lightnin' Hopkins; *Lost Texas Tapes-#4* . . . . (Collectables)
Possum Kingdom
Toadies; *ESPN Presents X Games-#1-C* . . . . (Tommy Boy)
Rubberneck . . . . (Interscope)
Possum Up A Gum Stump
Dick Fegy; *Flatpicking Guitar Festival-C* . . . . (Shanachie)

Run Possum Run!
Southern Rail; *Roadwork*....................................(Turquoise)
Theme From "The Pink Panther"
Henry Mancini; *Henry Mancini-Legendary Performer*...............(RCA)
Henry Mancini-Pure Gold......................................(RCA)
Peter Gunn...(RCA)
ST/Revenge Of The Pink Panther...............................(EMI)
Television's Greatest Hits-#2-C..............................(TVT)
Thing Called Love (Porcupine)
Bonnie Raitt; *Nick Of Time*..............................(Capitol)

ANIMALS: PIGS

See Also: *ANIMALS: A-Z, ANIMALS: GENERAL, FARMS*

Gimme A Pigfoot (And A Bottle Of Beer)
Billie Holiday; *Complete Decca Recordings*.................(Decca Jazz)
From The Original Decca Masters...........................(MCA)
I Am A Pig
Two; *The Best Of Rockline*................................(Nothing)
Voyeurs..(Nothing)
I'm A Pig
Angry Samoans; *Gimme Samoa-31 Garbage-Pit Hits*...............(PVC)
Paul Wants A Pig
John Jarvis; *Whatever Works*.............................(MCA)
Pig Feet
Fat Boys; *Coming Back Hard Again*..........................(Mercury)
Piggies
Beatles; *Beatles-Box Set*.................................(Capitol)
The Beatles (White Album)...............................(Capitol)
George Harrison; *Live In Japan*..........................(Dark Horse)
Piggy In the Mirror
Cure; *Top*..(Sire)
Piggy Pig Pig
Procol Harum; *Home*......................................(A&M)
Pigmeat
Leadbelly; *King Of The Twelve-String Guitar*..............(Columbia)
Pigmeat Is What I Crave
Bo Carter; *Legends Of The Blues-#1-C*....................(Columbia)
Pigs
Pink Floyd; *Animals*.....................................(Columbia)
Pigs (Three Different Ones)
Pink Floyd; *Animals*.....................................(Columbia)
Shine On...(Columbia)
Pigs In Zen
Jane's Addiction; *Jane's Addiction*..................(Triple X Entert.)
Nothing's Shocking..................................(Warner Bros.)
Pigs On The Wing
Pink Floyd; *Animals*.....................................(Columbia)
Shine On...(Columbia)
Pig's Song
Jim Croce; *Faces I've Been*..............................(Lifesong)
Pigs, Sheep & Wolves
Paul Simon; *You're The One*..........................(Warner Bros.)
Sad Pig Dance
Chris Proctor; *Delicate Dance*...........................(Flying Fish)
Swinging On A Star
Bing Crosby; *All-Time Best*...............................(Curb)
Best Of Bing Crosby......................................(MCA)
Dion And The Belmonts; *Dion And The Belmonts-Their Best*.......(Laurie)
Frank Sinatra; *Frank Sinatra Sings The Songs Of Van Heusen
& Cahn*...(Reprise)
This Little Pig
Living Colour; *Stain*....................................(Epic)
Three Little Pigs
Lloyd Price; *Lloyd Price's Greatest Hits*.................(MCA)
War Pigs
Black Sabbath; *Live Evil*............................(Warner Bros.)
Paranoid..(Warner Bros.)
We Sold Our Soul For Rock 'N' Roll..................(Warner Bros.)
Faith No More; *Real Thing*...............................(Slash)
Ozzy Osbourne; *Just Say Ozzy*.....................(Epic Portrait Assoc.)
Speak Of The Devil......................................(Jet)
The Ozzman Cometh.......................................(Epic)

ANIMALS: R

See Also: *ANIMALS: A-Z, ANIMALS: GENERAL, ANIMALS: RABBITS, RATS, REPTILES*

Breathe In The Air
Pink Floyd; *Dark Side Of The Moon*.......................(Capitol)
Pink Floyd-Gift Set.....................................(Capitol)
Lone Rhinoceros
Adrian Belew; *Desire Of The Rhino King*..................(Island)

Lone Rhino..(Island)
Raccoon Straits
Cal Tjader; *San Francisco Moods*.........................(Fantasy)
Rhinocerous
Smashing Pumpkins; *Gish*.................................(Virgin)
Ride The Rhino
Rhino Bucket; *Rhino Bucket*..............................(Reprise)
Rocky Raccoon
Beatles; *Beatles-Box Set*................................(Capitol)
The Beatles (White Album)...............................(Capitol)
Run Rudolph Run
Bryan Adams; *Very Special Christmas-C*...................(A&M)
Chuck Berry; *Billboard's Greatest R&B Christmas Hits-C*........(Rhino)
Rhythm & Blues Christmas-#1-C.......................(Collectables)
The Chess Box-Chuck Berry...............................(Chess)
Yuletide Soiree-C.......................................(Rhino)
Jimmy Buffett; *Christmas Island*.........................(MCA)
Southern Pacific; *Warner Bros. Christmas Tradition-C*........(Warner Bros.)
Sexy Rhino
Adrian Belew; *Desire Of The Rhino King*..................(Island)
Street Rats
Ted Nugent; *Free-For-All*................................(Epic)
Out Of Control..(Epic)

ANIMALS: RABBITS, Bunnies

See Also: *ANIMALS: A-Z, ANIMALS: GENERAL*

Cotton Tail
Duke Ellington; *Reminiscing In Tempo*....................(Columbia)
Duke Ellington & Ella Fitzgerald; *Compact Jazz-Best Of The Big
Bands-C*..(Verve)
Lambert, Hendricks & Ross; *Twisted-Best Of Lambert, Hendricks
& Ross*...(Rhino)
Wes Montgomery; *Artistry Of Wes Montgomery*..............(Riverside)
Pet Rabbit
Johnny Shines; *Traditional Delta Blues*..................(Biograph)
Rabbit Chase
New Lost City Ramblers; *New Lost City Ramblers-Early Years-1958-
1962*..(Smithsonian Folkways)
Rabbit In A Log
Stanley Brothers; *Long Journey Home*.....................(Rebel)
Rabbit In The Moon
Aztec Two-Step; *See It Was Like This...Acoustic Retrospective*...(Flying Fish)
Peter Erskine; *Transition*...............................(Denon)
Rabbit In The Pea Patch
Red Clay Ramblers; *Merchant's Lunch*.....................(Flying Fish)
Rabbit On My Shoulder
Peter Alsop/Dan Crow/Bruce Phillips/Happy Traum; *Silly Songs & Modern
Lullabies*..(Briar)
Run Little Rabbit
John & Jamie Hartford; *Hartford & Hartford*..............(Flying Fish)
Summer Bunnies
R. Kelly; *12 Play*.......................................(Jive)
Theme From "Bugs Bunny Overture"
Original Soundtrack; *Television's Greatest Hits-#1-C*.....(TVT)
White Rabbit
Damned; *Best Of The Damned*..............................(Roadracer)
Machine Gun Etiquette...................................(Roadracer)
George Benson; *George Benson-Collection*.................(Warner Bros.)
White Rabbit..(CBS Associated)
Jefferson Airplane; *2400 Fulton Street-An Anthology*.....(RCA)
Flight Log (1966-1976)..................................(Grunt)
Loves You...(RCA)
ST/Platoon..(Atlantic)
Surrealistic Pillow.....................................(RCA)
The Worst Of Jefferson Airplane.........................(RCA)

ANIMALS: RATS

See Also: *ANIMALS: A-Z, ANIMALS: GENERAL*

Ben
Michael Jackson; *Best Of Michael Jackson*................(Motown)
Jackson 5-16 Greatest Hits..............................(Motown)
Jackson 5-Anthology.....................................(Motown)
Jacksons Live...(Epic)
Michael Jackson-Anthology...............................(Motown)
Motown Superstar Series-#7-Michael Jackson..............(Motown)
Confident Rat
Ignorance; *Confident Rat*................................(Metal Blade)
Hotel Rats & Photostats
Jimmy Page; *ST/Death Wish 2*.............................(Swan Song)
Intoxicated Rat
New Lost City Ramblers; *American Moonshine & Prohibition
Songs*..(Smithsonian Folkways)

King Of Rats
Neighborhoods; *Neighborhoods* . . . . (Third Stone)
Pressed Rat & Warthog
Cream; *Wheels Of Fire* . . . . (Polydor)
Rat Bait
Swimming Pool Q's; *Deep End* . . . . (DB)
Rat In The Kitchen
UB40; *Live In Moscow* . . . . (A&M)
Rat In The Kitchen . . . . (A&M)
Rat Race
Bob Marley & The Wailers; *Babylon By Bus* . . . . (Tuff Gong)
Rastaman Vibration . . . . (Tuff Gong)
Rebel Music . . . . (Tuff Gong)
Rat Salad
Black Sabbath; *Paranoid* . . . . (Warner Bros.)
Rat Trap
Boomtown Rats; *Boomtown Rats' Greatest Hits* . . . . (Columbia)
Tonic For The Troops . . . . (Columbia)
Rats
Kinks; *Lola Versus Powerman And The Moneygoround, Part One* . . . . (Reprise)
Pearl Jam; *Vs.* . . . . (Epic Portrait Assoc.)
Syd Barrett; *Barrett* . . . . (Capitol)
Opel . . . . (Capitol)
Rats & Roaches In My Kitchen
Silas Hogan; *Louisiana Blues* . . . . (Arhoolie)
Rat's Eyes
Black Flag; *Slip It In* . . . . (SST)
Rats In My Kitchen
Sleepy John Estes; *Legend Of Sleepy John Estes* . . . . (Delmark)
Rats In The Cellar
Aerosmith; *Gems* . . . . (Columbia)
Pandora's Box . . . . (Columbia)
Rocks . . . . (Columbia)
Rats Motel
Lord Tracy; *Deaf Gods Of Babylon* . . . . (Uni)
Road Rats
Alice Cooper; *Lace And Whiskey* . . . . (Warner Bros.)

ANIMALS: REPTILES, Alligators, Crocodiles, Dinosaurs, Frogs, Snakes

See Also: *ANIMALS: A-Z, ANIMALS: GENERAL*

Alligator
Charlie Daniels Band; *Homesick Heroes* . . . . (Epic)
Alligator
Grateful Dead; *Anthem Of The Sun* . . . . (Warner Bros.)
Alligator Boogaloo
Clarence ''Gatemouth'' Brown; *Alright Again* . . . . (Rounder)
Alligator Crawl
Louis Armstrong; *Hot Fives & Hot Sevens-#2* . . . . (Columbia)
Alligator Man
Jimmy C. Newman; *Jimmy C. Newman's Greatest Hits* . . . . (Plantation)
Progressive CC . . . . (Plantation)
Souvenirs Of Music City U.S.A.-C . . . . (Plantation)
Alligator Wine
Screamin' Jay Hawkins; *Voodoo Jive: Best Of Screamin' Jay
Hawkins* . . . . (Rhino)
Alligator Woman
R.G. & Bayou Zydeco; *Fire On The Bayou* . . . . (Takoma)
Alligator Woman
Cameo; *Alligator Woman* . . . . (Chocolate City)
Animal Trainer & The Toad
Mountain; *Best Of Mountain* . . . . (Columbia)
Baby Snakes
Frank Zappa; *Baby Snakes* . . . . (Barking Pumpkin)
Sheik Yerbouti . . . . (Zappa)
Black Snake
John Lee Hooker; *Country Blues Of John Lee Hooker* . . . . (Riverside)
Ramblin' Jack Elliott; *Essential Ramblin' Jack Elliott* . . . . (Vanguard)
Black Snake Blues
Clifton Chenier; *Sixty Minutes With The King Of Zydeco* . . . . (Arhoolie)
Black Snake Dream Blues
Blind Lemon Jefferson; *Master Of The Blues-#2-1926-1929* . . . . . . (Biograph)
Black Snake Moan
Blind Lemon Jefferson; *Great Blues Guitarists-String Dazzlers-C* . . (Columbia)
Leadbelly; *Leadbelly* . . . . (Columbia)
Breakfast For Dinosaurs
Fowler Brothers; *Breakfast For Dinosaurs* . . . . (Fossil)
Bull Frog Blues
Jenny Pope; *Pot Hound Blues-1923-1930* . . . . (Historical)
Bull Frog Bounce
Leo Parker & Sax Gill; *Back To Back Baritones* . . . . (Collectables)
Bull Frog Patrol
Duncan Sisters; *Music From The New York Stage (1890-1920)-#4-1917-
1920-C* . . . . (Pearl)

Celebration Of The Lizard
Doors; *Absolutely Live* . . . . (Elektra)
Chameleon
Creedence Clearwater Revival; *1970* . . . . (Fantasy)
Pendulum . . . . (Fantasy)
Chameleon
Grover Washington, Jr.; *Love Affair-Music Of Ivan Lins-C* . . . . (Telarc)
Chameleon
Herbie Hancock; *Best Of Herbie Hancock* . . . . (Legacy)
Headhunters . . . . (Columbia)
Chameleon
Elton John; *Blue Moves* . . . . (MCA)
Chameleon
Labelle; *Chameleon* . . . . (Epic)
Chameleon Day
Talk Talk; *Colour Of Spring* . . . . (EMI)
Cold Hearted
Paula Abdul; *Forever Your Girl* . . . . (Virgin)
Get Up & Dance-Dance Mixes . . . . (Virgin)
Crawling King Snake
Doors; *L.A. Woman* . . . . (Elektra)
John Lee Hooker; *Best Of John Lee Hooker* . . . . (Crescendo)
World's Greatest Blues Singer . . . . (Vee-Jay)
Muddy Waters; *They Call Me Muddy Waters* . . . . (Chess)
Crocodile Rock
Elton John; *Billboard Top Rock 'N' Roll Hits-1973-C* . . . . (Rhino)
Don't Shoot Me I'm Only The Piano Player . . . . (Polydor)
Elton John's Greatest Hits . . . . (Polydor)
Here And There . . . . (Rocket)
Crocodiles
Echo & The Bunnymen; *Crocodiles* . . . . (Sire)
Dinosaur
Eyes Of The World; *Relix Bay Rock Sampler-#3-C* . . . . (Relix)
Dinosaur
Gabriel Bondage; *Angel Dust* . . . . (Deutsche Harmonia Mundi)
Dinosaur
Geezinslaws; *Geezinslaws* . . . . (Step One)
Dinosaur
Hank Williams, Jr.; *Habits Old & New* . . . . (Warner Bros.)
Dinosaur
Raw Youth; *Hot Diggity* . . . . (Giant)
Dinosaur
David Byrne; *The Catherine Wheel-Complete Broadway Score* . . . . (Sire)
Dinosaur
Thin White Rope; *The Ruby Sea* . . . . (Frontier)
Dinosaur Jesus
Barbie Bones; *Brake For Nobody* . . . . (Restless)
Dinosaur Tracks
Different World; *ST/Roadside Prophets* . . . . (Vanguard)
Dinosaurs
King Missile; *The Way To Salvation* . . . . (Atlantic)
Doin' The Frog
Duke Ellington & His Orchestra; *Brunswick Era-#1-1926-1929* . . . . . (MCA)
Dream Of The Blue Turtles
Sting; *Dream Of The Blue Turtles* . . . . (A&M)
Fattening Frogs For Snakes
Sonny Boy Williamson; *The Blues-#3-C* . . . . (Chess)
Frog Legs
Clifton Chenier; *Bon Ton Roulet & More* . . . . (Arhoolie)
Frog Song
May Irwin; *Music From The New York Stage (1890-1920)-#1-1890-
1908-C* . . . . (Pearl)
Froggie Went A Courtin'
Doc Watson; *Essential Doc Watson* . . . . (Vanguard)
Home Again . . . . (Vanguard)
Froggy Style
Nuttin' Nyce; *Down 4 Whateva* . . . . (Pocketown/Jive)
Frogs With Dirty Little Lips
Frank Zappa; *Them Or Us* . . . . (Rykodisc)
Gator Tails And Monkey Ribs
Spats; *45-#10585* . . . . (ABC)
I'm A Little Dinosaur
Jonathan Richman & The Modern Lovers; *Beserkley Years-Best Of* . . . (Rhino)
I'm In Love With A Big Blue Frog
Peter, Paul & Mary; *Album 1700* . . . . (Warner Bros.)
Karma Chameleon
Culture Club; *Colour By Numbers* . . . . (Virgin)
King Cobra
King Cobra; *Powerhouse Music* . . . . (AJK Music)
King Cobra
Herbie Hancock; *Best Of Herbie Hancock-The Blue Note Years* . . . (Blue Note)
King Cobra
Tom Scott & The L.A. Express; *Tom Scott & The L.A. Express* . . . . (Epic)
Kiss That Frog
Peter Gabriel; *Us* . . . . (Geffen)
Leap Frog
Les Brown & His Orchestra; *Best Of The Swing Bands-C* . . . . . . (Hindsight)
Big Band Sampler-C . . . . (Columbia)

Les Brown & His Orchestra's Greatest Hits . . . . (Curb)

Lizard Lady
Residents; *Duck Stab/Buster & Glenn/Goosebump* . . . . (East Side Digital)

Lizard Song
Max Demian Band; *Take It To The Max* . . . . (Out Of Print)

Pass The Snakes
Hot Tuna; *Live At Sweetwater* . . . . (Relix)

Peace Frog
Doors; *Doors-Classics* . . . . (Elektra)
Morrison Hotel/Hard Rock Cafe . . . . (Elektra)
Weird Scenes Inside The Gold Mine . . . . (Elektra)

Rattle My Snake
Amboy Dukes; *Survival Of The Fittest* . . . . (Polydor)

Rattlesnake
Live; *Secret Samadhi* . . . . (Radioactive/MCA)

Rattlesnake Mountain
Patrick Sky; *Patrick Sky* . . . . (Vanguard)

Rattlesnake Rock 'N' Roller
Blackfoot; *Marauder* . . . . (Atco)

Rattlesnake Shake
Fleetwood Mac; *25 Years-The Chain* . . . . (Warner Bros.)
Then Play On . . . . (Reprise)
Mick Fleetwood; *The Visitor* . . . . (RCA)

Rattlesnake Shake
Motley Crue; *Dr. Feelgood* . . . . (Elektra)

Rattlesnake Shake
Aerosmith; *Pandora's Box* . . . . (Columbia)

Rattlesnake Shake
Skid Row; *Skid Row* . . . . (Atlantic)

Rattlesnake Shake
Omar & The Howlers; *ST/Speed Zone* . . . . (Grudge)

Rattlesnakes
Lloyd Cole & The Commotions; *1984-1989* . . . . (Capitol)
Rattlesnakes . . . . (Geffen)

Reptile
Eric Clapton; *Reptile* . . . . (Duck/Reprise)

See You Later, Alligator
Bill Haley & His Comets; *Bill Haley & His Comets* . . . . (Everest)
Bill Haley & His Comets' Greatest Hits . . . . (MCA)
Bill Haley & His Comets-Golden Hits . . . . (MCA)
Billboard Top Rock 'N' Roll Hits-1956-C . . . . (Rhino)
Mr. Rock 'N' Roll . . . . (Accord)
Rock & Roll Is Here To Stay-C . . . . (Gusto)
Rockin' & Rollin' . . . . (Accord)

Senorita With A Necklace Of Tears (frogs)
Paul Simon; *You're The One* . . . . (Warner Bros.)

Snake
Luther Johnson & Muddy Waters; *Chicken Shack* . . . . (Muse)
Muddy Waters Blues Band; *Mud In Your Ear* . . . . (Muse)

Snake
Joe Satriani; *Not Of This Earth* . . . . (Relativity)

Snake Charmer
Blackmore's Rainbow; *Ritchie Blackmore's R-A-I-N-B-O-W* . . . . (Polydor)

Snake Charmer
John Hiatt; *ST/White Nights* . . . . (Atlantic)

Snake Charmer
Ted Nugent; *State Of Shock* . . . . (Epic)

Snake Drive
Eric Clapton; *Guitar Boogie* . . . . (RCA)

Snake Eyes
Alan Parsons Project; *Turn Of A Friendly Card* . . . . (Arista)

Snake Man
Doobie Brothers; *Toulouse Street* . . . . (Warner Bros.)

Snakebite
Jeff Lorber; *Kickin' It* . . . . (Samson)

Snakes Alive
Dreadful Snakes; *Dreadful Snakes* . . . . (Rounder)

Snakes And Ladders
Men At Work; *Two Hearts* . . . . (Columbia)

Snakes And Ladders
Joni Mitchell; *Chalk Mark In A Rain Storm* . . . . (Geffen)

Snakes Crawl At Night
Charley Pride; *Best Of Charley Pride* . . . . (RCA)

Snakes On Everything
Little Feat; *Little Feat* . . . . (Warner Bros.)

Spiders & Snakes
Jim Stafford; *Jim Stafford* . . . . (Polydor)
Super Hits Of The '70s-Have A Nice Day-#12-C . . . . (Rhino)
Loretta Lynn & Conway Twitty; *Very Best Of Loretta Lynn & Conway Twitty* . . . . (MCA)

Terrapin Station
Grateful Dead; *Terrapin Station* . . . . (Arista)

That Black Snake Moan
Blind Lemon Jefferson; *Blind Lemon Jefferson* . . . . (Milestone)

Theme From "Barney And Friends"
Original Soundtrack; *Television's Greatest Hits-#7-Cable Ready-C* . . . . . (TVT)

Theme From "Jurassic Park"
John Williams; *ST/Jurassic Park* . . . . (MCA)

Theme From "Touche Turtle"
Original Soundtrack; *Hanna-Barbera Classics-#1-Original Recordings Of The World's Most Famous Cartoon Themes & Scores* . . . . (Kid Rhino/Rhino 4 Kids)
Hanna-Barbera Pic-A-Nic Basket Of Cartoon Classics . . . . (Kid Rhino/Rhino 4 Kids)

Theme From "Wally Gator"
Original Soundtrack; *Hanna-Barbera Classics-#1-Original Recordings Of The World's Most Famous Cartoon Themes & Scores* . . . . (Kid Rhino/Rhino 4 Kids)
Hanna-Barbera Pic-A-Nic Basket Of Cartoon Classics . . . . (Kid Rhino/Rhino 4 Kids)

Toad In The Hole
Ian Anderson; *Walk Into Light* . . . . (Chrysalis)

Tree Frog
Count Basie; *Best Of Count Basie & His Orchestra* . . . . (Pablo)
Count Basie & His Orchestra; *I Told You So* . . . . (Pablo)

Tubesnake Boogie
ZZ Top; *El Loco* . . . . (Warner Bros.)
Six Pack . . . . (Warner Bros.)
ZZ Top's Greatest Hits . . . . (Warner Bros.)

Turtle Blues
Big Brother & The Holding Company; *Cheap Thrills* . . . . (Columbia)

T-U-R-T-L-E Power!
Partners In Kryme; *ST/Teenage Mutant Ninja Turtles* . . . . (SBK)

Turtle Rock
Bela Fleck & The Flecktones; *Flight Of The Cosmic Hippo* . . . . (Warner Bros.)

Turtle Shoes
Bobby McFerrin; *Spontaneous Inventions* . . . . (Blue Note)
Bobby McFerrin & Herbie Hancock; *ST/Twins* . . . . (WTG)

Union Of The Snake
Duran Duran; *Arena* . . . . (Capitol)
Decade . . . . (Capitol)
Seven And The Ragged Tiger . . . . (Capitol)

Venom Soup
Ted Nugent; *Weekend Warriors* . . . . (Epic)

Viper's Drag
Fats Waller; *Joint Is Jumpin'* . . . . (Bluebird)
Original Cast; *Ain't Misbehavin'* . . . . (RCA)

Voodoo
Godsmack; *Godsmack* . . . . (Republic/Universal)

Walk The Dinosaur
George Clinton & Goombas; *ST/Super Mario Brothers* . . . . (Capitol)

Walk The Dinosaur
Was (Not Was); *What Up Dog?* . . . . (Chrysalis)

Wrong Number
Cure; *Galore-The Singles-1987-1997* . . . . (Fiction/Elektra)

Yertle The Turtle
Red Hot Chili Peppers; *Freaky Styley* . . . . (EMI)

ANIMALS: S

See Also: **ANIMALS: A-Z, ANIMALS: GENERAL, ANIMALS: SHEEP**

Cat's Squirrel
Cream; *Fresh Cream* . . . . (Polydor)
Jethro Tull; *This Was* . . . . (Chrysalis)

Dead Skunk
Loudon Wainwright III; *Dr. Demento Presents The Greatest Novelty Records-#4-1970s-C* . . . . (Rhino)
Super Hits Of The '70s-Have A Nice Day-#10-C . . . . (Rhino)

Grey Seal
Elton John; *Goodbye Yellow Brick Road* . . . . (Polydor)

It's In The Book (Parts 1 & 2)
Johnny Standley; *Dr. Demento Gooses Mother-C* . . . . (Kid Rhino/Rhino 4 Kids)

Mississippi Squirrel Revival
Ray Stevens; *Country Classics-#1-C* . . . . (Universal)
He Thinks He's Ray Stevens . . . . (MCA)
Ray Stevens' Greatest Hits . . . . (MCA)

On Squirrel Hill
Ian Matthews; *Legacy-Collection Of New Folk Music-C* . . . . . . (Windham Hill)
Walking A Changing Line . . . . (Windham Hill)

Pissin' On A Skunk (No Need)
Saffire-Uppity Blues Women; *Hot Flash* . . . . (Alligator)

Playful Squirrels
Carlos Barbosa-Lima; *Music Of The Americas* . . . . (Concord Picante Jazz)

Sable On Blond
Stevie Nicks; *Wild Heart* . . . . (Modern)

Skunk (Sonically Speaking)
MC5; *High Times* . . . . (Rhino)

Skunk Creek
Poco; *Forgotten Trail-1969-1974* . . . . (Epic)

Skunk Funk
Brecker Brothers; *Collection-#1 & #2* . . . . (Novus)
Skunk, The Goose & The Fly
Tower of Power; *East Bay Grease* . . . . (Rhino)
Theme From "Secret Squirrel"
Original Soundtrack; *Hanna-Barbera Pic-A-Nic Basket Of Cartoon
Classics* . . . . (Kid Rhino/Rhino 4 Kids)
Television's Greatest Hits-#5-In Living Color-C . . . . (TVT)
Theme From "The Rocky & Bullwinkle Show" (flying squirrel)
Original Soundtrack; *Television's Greatest Hits-#2-C* . . . . (TVT)

ANIMALS: SHEEP

*See Also: **ANIMALS: A-Z, ANIMALS: GENERAL, ANIMALS: L
(lambs), FARMS***

10,432 Sheep
Doris Day Quartet & The Frank Comstock Orchestra; *Day At The
Movies* . . . . (Columbia)
And Dream Of Sheep
Kate Bush; *Hounds Of Love* . . . .(EMI)
Baa Baa Black Sheep
Original Soundtrack; *Toddler Favorites* . . . . (Kid Rhino/Rhino 4 Kids)
Black Sheep
John Anderson; *All The People Are Talkin'* . . . .(Warner Bros.)
John Anderson's Greatest Hits . . . .(Warner Bros.)
Black Sheep
Sam The Sham and The Pharaohs; *Pharaohization! (Best Of)* . . . . (Rhino)
Black Sheep Of The Family
Blackmore's Rainbow; *Ritchie Blackmore's R-A-I-N-B-O-W* . . . . (Polydor)
Count Your Blessings
Ashford & Simpson; *Best Of Ashford & Simpson* . . (EMI Special Markets)
Count Your Blessings (Instead Of Sheep)
Bing Crosby; *45-#29251* . . . . (Decca)
Eddie Fisher; *Best Of Eddie Fisher* . . . . (MCA)
Rosemary Clooney; *Essence Of Rosemary Clooney* . . . . (Legacy)
Dixie Chicken
Little Feat; *Dixie Chicken* . . . .(Warner Bros.)
Waiting For Columbus . . . .(Warner Bros.)
I'm On The Lamb, But I Ain't No Sheep
Blue Oyster Cult; *Blue Oyster Cult* . . . . (Columbia)
Lamb Lies Down On Broadway
Genesis; *Lamb Lies Down On Broadway* . . . . (Atco)
Seconds Out . . . .(Atlantic)
Little Lamb
Original Cast; *Gypsy* . . . . (Columbia)
Mary Had A Little Lamb
Garth Brooks; *The Magic Of Christmas: Songs From Call Me Claus* . . (Capitol)
Original Soundtrack; *Sesame Street: Kids' Favorite Songs-#2* . . (Sony Wonder)
Stevie Ray Vaughan and Double Trouble; *Live Alive* . . . .(Epic)
Texas Flood . . . .(Epic)
Wings; *Wild Life* . . . . (Capitol)
Pigs, Sheep & Wolves
Paul Simon; *You're The One* . . . .(Warner Bros.)
Searching For Lambs
June Tabor; *Aqaba* . . . . (Shanachie)
Peter Bellamy; *Peter Bellamy* . . . .(Green Linnet)
Sheep
Housemartins; *London O Hull 4* . . . . (Elektra)
Pink Floyd; *Animals* . . . . (Columbia)
Collection Of Great Dance Songs . . . . (Columbia)
Sheep Go To Heaven
Cake; *Prolonging The Magic* . . . . (Capricorn)
Someone To Watch Over Me
Ella Fitzgerald; *Ella Fitzgerald Sings The George & Ira Gershwin
Songbook* . . . . (Verve)
Elton John; *Glory Of Gershwin Featuring Larry Adler-C* . . . . (Mercury)
Frank Sinatra; *Nice 'N' Easy* . . . . (Capitol)
The Capitol Years . . . . (Capitol)
Jack Jones; *Gershwin Album* . . . . (Columbia)
Original Broadway Cast; *Crazy For You* . . . . (Angel)
Oscar Peterson; *My Favorite Instrument* . . . . (Verve)
Sarah Vaughan; *Sarah Vaughan Sings George Gershwin Songbook,
Vol. 2* . . . . (Emarcy)
Willie Nelson; *Stardust* . . . . (Legacy)
Try Counting Sheep
Black Sheep; *A Wolf In Sheep's Clothing* . . . . (Mercury)
Whiffenpoof Song
Bing Crosby & Fred Waring & His Glee Club; *Bing Crosby's
Greatest Hits* . . . .(MCA)
Count Basie & Mills Brothers; *Count Basie & Mills Brothers-16 Great
Performances* . . . . (MCA)
Louis Armstrong; *Best Of Louis Armstrong* . . . . (MCA)
Mitch Miller; *34 All-Time Great Sing-Along Selections-C* . . . . (Columbia)

Statler Brothers; *The World Of The Statler Brothers* . . . . (Columbia)

ANIMALS: TIGERS

*See Also: **ANIMALS: A-Z, ANIMALS: GENERAL***

Eye Of The Tiger
Survivor; *Eye Of The Tiger* . . . .(Scotti Bros.)
Frankenstein & Other Rock Monsters-C . . . . (CBS Associated)
Rocky Story-C . . . .(Scotti Bros.)
ST/Rocky III . . . . (EMI)
Hunting Tigers Out In India
Bonzo Dog Band; *Best Of The Bonzo Dog Band* . . . . (Rhino)
Tadpoles . . . . (Liberty)
I've Got A Tiger By The Tail
Buck Owens; *Billboard Top Country Hits-1965-C* . . . . (Rhino)
Buck Owens & The Buckaroos; *Buck Owens & The Buckaroos-Live At
Carnegie Hall* . . . . (Country Music Foundation)
Harlan Howard; *All-Time Favorite Country Songwriter* . . . . (Koch International)
Rick Springfield; *Living In Oz* . . . .(RCA)
Paper Tiger
Sue Thompson; *Collectables Presents The History Of
Rock-#4-C* . . . .(Collectables)
Golden Classics-Sue Thompson . . . .(Collectables)
Sue Thompson's Greatest Hits . . . . (Curb)
Paper Tiger
Painted Willie; *Relics Of The Incredible String Band* . . . . (Elektra)
Return Of The Tasmanian Tiger
John Fahey; *Live In Tasmania* . . . . (Takoma)
Ride The Tiger
Jefferson Starship; *Dragon Fly* . . . .(RCA)
Flight Log (1966-1976) . . . . (Grunt)
Jefferson Starship-Gold . . . .(RCA)
Taming The Tiger
Joni Mitchell; *Taming The Tiger* . . . . (Reprise)
Tiger
Fabian; *'50s Dance Party-C* . . . . (Dominion Entert.)
Best Of Fabian . . . . (MCA)
Fabian's Greatest Hits . . . . (Everest)
Partytime '50s-C . . . . (Priority)
Super Oldies Of The '50s-#7-C . . . . (Audio Fidelity)
Tiger
Paula Cole; *This Fire* . . . . (Imago)
Tiger In A Dress
Dan Reed Network; *Slam* . . . . (Mercury)
Tiger In The Rain
Michael Franks; *Tiger In The Rain* . . . . (Warner Bros.)
Tiger In Your Tank
Muddy Waters; *At Newport* . . . . (Chess)
Tiger Rag
Django Reinhardt; *Jazz Legacy* . . . .(Inner City)
Legendary Django Reinhardt . . . .(Crescendo)
Django Reinhardt & Stephane Grappelli; *Django Reinhardt & Stephane
Grappelli* . . . .(Crescendo)
Les Paul & Mary Ford; *Selections From "Legend & The Legacy"* . . . . (Capitol)
Louis Armstrong; *Essential Louis Armstrong* . . . . (Vanguard)
Mostly Blues . . . . (Olympic)
Stardust . . . . (Portrait)
Louis Armstrong & Friends; *20 Golden Pieces Of Louis Armstrong &
Friends* . . . .(Bulldog)
Louis Armstrong & His Orchestra; *Louis Armstrong & The Big
Bands* . . . . (Disques Swing)
Mills Brothers; *Mills Brothers-22 Great Hits* . . . . (Ranwood)
Preservation Hall Jazz Band; *Best Of The Preservation Hall
Jazz Band* . . . . (Columbia)
New Orleans-#1 . . . . (Columbia)
Tiger Rose
Robert Hunter; *Tiger Rose* . . . . (Rykodisc)
Tiger Woman
Claude King; *American Originals-Claude King* . . . . (Columbia)
Claude King's Best . . . . (Gusto)
Tiger, Tiger
Barbara Tiger/Original Cast; *Apple Tree* . . . . (Sony Music Special Prod.)

ANIMALS: U

*See Also: **ANIMALS: A-Z, ANIMALS: GENERAL***

Unicorn
Irish Rovers; *Irish Rovers' Greatest Hits* . . . . (MCA)
Unicorn . . . . (MCA)
Vintage Music-#19-C . . . . (MCA)

ANIMALS: W

See Also: **ANIMALS: A-Z, ANIMALS: GENERAL, ANIMALS: WHALES, ANIMALS: WOLVES**

Crazed Weasel
Ricky Peterson; *Night Watch* . . . . (Warner Bros.)
I Am The Walrus
Beatles; *Magical Mystery Tour* . . . . (Capitol)
  Rarities . . . . (Capitol)
  Reel Music . . . . (Capitol)
  The Beatles/1967-1970 . . . . (Capitol)
Pop Goes The Weasel
Bing Crosby; *Where The Blue Of The Night Meets The Gold Of The Day* . . . . (Biograph)
Boston Pops Orchestra/Arthur Fiedler; *Forever Fiedler* . . . . . (RCA)
Merry Macs; *Small Fry-Capitol Sings Kids Songs For Grownups-C* . . . (Capitol)
Pop Goes The Weasel
3rd Bass; *Derelicts Of Dialect* . . . . (Def Jam)
Pressed Rat & Warthog
Cream; *Wheels Of Fire* . . . . (Polydor)
Rock-N-Roll Weasel
Dead Serios; *Ralph Rules* . . . . (Long Song)

ANIMALS: WHALES

See Also: **ANIMALS: A-Z, ANIMALS: DOLPHINS, ANIMALS: FISH, ANIMALS: GENERAL, NATURE, OCEAN**

Arctic Whale Hunt
Mancini Pops Orchestra; *In Surround-Mostly Monsters Murders* . . . . (RCA)
Baby Beluga
Billy Gilman; *Country Goes Raffi-C* . . . . (Rounder)
Day Old Whale
Uncle Bonsai; *Lonely Grain Of Corn* . . . . (Freckle)
Dolphins & Whales (Come Home To The Sea)
Mannheim Steamroller; *Saving The Wildlife* . . . . (American Gramaphone)
Don't Kill The Whale
Yes; *Tormato* . . . . (Atlantic)
  Yesshows . . . . (Atlantic)
Drifting Like Whales In The Darkness
Sven Vath; *Accident In Paradise* . . . . (Warner Bros.)
Euphonius Whale
Dan Hicks & His Hot Licks; *Last Train To Hicksville* . . . . (MCA)
Farewell To Tarwathie
Judy Collins; *Colors Of The Day-The Best Of Judy Collins* . . . . (Elektra)
  So Early In The Spring, The First 15 Years . . . . (Elektra)
  Whales & Nightingales . . . . (Elektra)
Greenland Whale Fisheries
Judy Collins & Theodore Bikel; *Greatest Folksingers Of The '60s-C* . . . . (Vanguard)
Heroes
Wallflowers; *ST/Godzilla-The Album* . . . . (Epic/Sony Music Soundtrax)
Last Great American Whale
Lou Reed; *Greenpeace/Rainbow Warriors-C* . . . . (Geffen)
  New York . . . . (Sire)
Little Blue Whale
Country Joe McDonald; *Goodbye Blues* . . . . (Fantasy)
Moby Book
Stephen Goodman; *Jessie's Jig* . . . . (Asylum)
Moby Dick
Led Zeppelin; *Led Zeppelin II* . . . . (Atlantic)
  ST/The Song Remains The Same . . . . (Swan Song)
Ode To Big Blue
Gordon Lightfoot; *Don Quixote* . . . . (Warner Archives)
Odin
John Stewart; *Dream Babies Go To Hollywood* . . . . (RSO)
Prince Of Whales
Joachim Kuhn; *Dynamics* . . . . (Creative Music Prod.)
Prince Of Whales
Amy & Leslie; *Amy & Leslie* . . . . (Alcazar)
Rubber Blubber Whale
John McCutcheon; *Water From Another Time* . . . . (Rounder)
Save The Whale
Nik Kershaw; *The Riddle* . . . . (MCA)
Save The Whales
Country Joe McDonald; *Bread & Roses Festival Of Acoustic Music-#1-C* . . . . (Fantasy)
  Country Joe McDonald-Classics . . . . (Fantasy)
  Into The Fray . . . . (Rag Baby)
  Paradise With An Ocean View . . . . (Fantasy)
Save The Whales
Danny O'Keefe; *Global Blues* . . . . (Warner Bros.)
Theme From "The Great Whales"
Cincinnati Pops Orchestra/Erich Kunzel; *Sailing* . . . . (Telarc)

To The Last Whale Medley
Crosby, Stills & Nash; *CSN* . . . . (Atlantic)
  Replay . . . . (Atlantic)
David Crosby & Graham Nash; *Best Of David Crosby & Graham Nash* . . . . (MCA)
  Wind On The Water . . . . (MCA)
Various Tracks
Ewan MacColl/A.L. Lloyd/Peggy Seeger; *Other Songs Of The Whaling Era* . . . . (Smithsonian Folkways)
Various Tracks
Recorded Sounds; *Songs Of The Humpback Whale* . . . . (Capitol)
Various Tracks
Dr. Coates; *Sounds Of The Sea* . . . . (Smithsonian Folkways)
Various Tracks
Paul Clayton; *Whaling And Sailing Songs* . . . . (Tradition)
Various Tracks
Paul Clayton; *Whaling Songs And Ballads* . . . . (Stinson)
Whale
Electric Light Orchestra; *Out Of The Blue* . . . . (Jet)
Whale
Wall Matthews; *Gathering The World* . . . . (Clean Cuts)
Whale Meat Again
Jim Capaldi; *45-#9254* . . . . (Island)
Whale Of A Tale
Original London Cast; *Moby Dick* . . . . (RCA)
Whale Savers
Melbourne Symphony Orchestra; *Film & TV Themes Of Bruce Rowland* . . . . (Bay Cities)
Whale Song
Chris Michell; *Dolphin Love* . . . . (World Disc Music)
Whale Watch
Peter Kater; *Moments Dreams & Visions* . . . . (Silver Wave)
Whale, The-Part 1 & 2
John Tavener; *The Whale* . . . . (Capitol)
Whalecatchers/Drunken Landlady
John Faulkner; *Kind Providence* . . . . (Green Linnet)
Whaleheart
Marnie Jones; *Grace* . . . . (Thriving Productions)
Whaler
Montrose; *Montrose* . . . . (Warner Bros.)
Whaler Out Of New Bedford
Musical Film Score; *Whaler Out Of New Bedford* . . . . . (Smithsonian Folkways)
Whaler's Dues
Jethro Tull; *Rock Island* . . . . (Chrysalis)
Whales & Snow
Deep Jimi & The Zep Creams; *Funky Dinosaur* . . . . (East West)
Whale's Revenge
Original London Cast; *Moby Dick* . . . . (RCA)
Whales Tails
Cocteau Twins; *Victorialand* . . . . (Capitol)
Whales Weep Not (Overture)
Paul Winter Consort; *Whales Alive* . . . . (Living Music)
Paul Winter Consort & Paul Halley; *Living Music Collection II* . . . . (Living Music)
Whalesong
Michael Gettel; *San Juan Suite* . . . . (Sounding)
Whaling Stories
Procol Harum; *Home* . . . . (A&M)
  Procol Harum Live In Concert with the Edmonton Symphony . . . . (A&M)
  Procol Harum-Classics-#17 . . . . (A&M)

ANIMALS: WOLVES

See Also: **ANIMALS: A-Z, ANIMALS: GENERAL**

Brother Wolf, Sister Moon
Cult; *Love* . . . . (Sire)
Cry Wolf
Laura Branigan; *Touch* . . . . (Atlantic)
Stevie Nicks; *Other Side Of The Mirror* . . . . (Modern)
Cry Wolf
Victoria Shaw; *In Full View* . . . . (Reprise)
Dire Wolf
Grateful Dead; *Reckoning* . . . . (Arista)
  Workingman's Dead . . . . (Warner Bros.)
Hungry Like The Wolf
Duran Duran; *Arena* . . . . (Capitol)
  Decade . . . . (Capitol)
  Duran Duran (The Wedding Album) . . . . (Capitol)
  Rio . . . . (Capitol)
Li'l Red Riding Hood
Sam The Sham and The Pharaohs; *Best Of Sam The Sham and The Pharaohs* . . . . (Polydor)
  Cruisin'-1966-C . . . . (Increase)
  Pharaohization! (Best Of) . . . . (Rhino)

Lonesome Roving Wolves
Rosalie Sorrels; *Lonesome Roving Wolves-Songs & Ballads Of The West* . . . .(Green Linnet)
Peter And The Wolf
Dave Van Ronk; *Peter And The Wolf* . . . . (Alacazam)
Original Soundtrack; *Beethoven Wrote It...But It Swings* . . . . (Sony Music Classical)
Pigs, Sheep & Wolves
Paul Simon; *You're The One* . . . .(Warner Bros.)
Run Of The Wolf
Cris Williamson; *Wolf Moon* . . . . (Olivia)
Run With The Wolf
Blackmore's Rainbow; *Rainbow Rising* . . . . (Polydor)
Strolling Wolf
Creatures; *Boomerang* . . . .(Geffen)
Theme From "Dances With Wolves"
John Barry; *Moviola* . . . .(Epic)
Theme From "Hokey Wolf"
Original Soundtrack; *Hanna-Barbera Classics-#1-Original Recordings Of The World's Most Famous Cartoon Themes & Scores* . . . . (Kid Rhino/Rhino 4 Kids)
Hanna-Barbera Pic-A-Nic Basket Of Cartoon Classics . . . . (Kid Rhino/Rhino 4 Kids)
Werewolves Of London
Warren Zevon; *Excitable Boy* . . . . (Asylum)
Quiet Normal Life-Best Of Warren Zevon . . . . (Asylum)
ST/Color Of Money . . . . (MCA)
Stand In The Fire . . . . (Asylum)
Who's Afraid Of The Big Bad Wolf
Barbra Streisand; *Just For The Record* . . . . (Columbia)
The Barbra Streisand Album . . . . (Columbia)
L.L. Cool J; *Simply Mad About The Mouse-C* . . . . (Columbia)
Mormon Tabernacle Choir & Columbia Symphony Orchestra; *When You Wish Upon A Star-A Tribute To Walt Disney* . . . . . . (CBS Masterworks)
Will The Wolf Survive
Los Lobos; *How Will The Wolf Survive* . . . . (Slash)
Waylon Jennings; *Country Classics-#6-1985-1986-C* . . . . . . (Universal)
New Classic Waylon . . . . (MCA)
Will The Wolf Survive . . . . (MCA)
Witch Wolf
Styx; *Best Of Styx* . . . . (RCA)
Wolves
Garth Brooks; *No Fences* . . . . (Capitol)
You Cried Wolf
Todd Rundgren; *Hermit Of Mink Hollow* . . . . (Rhino)
Todd Rundgren-Anthology 1968-1985 . . . . (Rhino)

ANNIVERSARY
See Also: *MARRIAGE*

51st Anniversary
Jimi Hendrix Experience; *Are You Experienced?* . . . . (Reprise)
Anniversary
Robert Plant; *Manic Nirvana* . . . .(Es Paranza)
Anniversary
Tony Toni Tone; *MTV Party To Go-#5-C* . . . . (Tommy Boy)
Sons Of Soul . . . .(Wing)
Tony Toni Tone-Hits . . . . (Mercury)
Anniversary
Graham Parker; *Passion Is No Ordinary Word-Graham Parker Anthology-1976-1991* . . . . (Rhino)
Anniversary
Gerald Albright; *Smooth* . . . . (Atlantic)
Anniversary
Jonathan Butler; *Source, The* . . . . (N-Coded)
Anniversary Song
Cowboy Junkies; *Pale Sun, Crescent Moon* . . . . (RCA)
Anniversary Song
Al Jolson; *Al Jolson-Best Of The Decca Years* . . . . (MCA)
Cocktail Hour . . . . (Columbia River Entert. Group)
Dinah Shore; *Buttons & Bows* . . . . (ASV)
Dinah Shore-16 Most Requested Songs-Encore! . . . . (Legacy)
Django Reinhardt; *Verve Jazz Masters 38* . . . . (Verve)
Eva Cassidy; *Time After Time* . . . . (Blix Street)
Guy Lombardo & His Royal Canadians; *Enjoy Yourself, The Hits Of Guy Lombardo* . . . . (MCA)
Anniversary Waltz
Bing Crosby; *There Is Still Love-Anniversary Songs-C* . . . . (Scotti Bros.)
Eddy Howard; *Best Of Eddy Howard-The Mercury Years* . . . . . . (Mercury)
Check Yes Or No
George Strait; *Strait Out Of The Box* . . . . (MCA)
Happy Anniversary
Little River Band; *Diamantina Cocktail* . . . . (Capitol)
Little River Band's Greatest Hits . . . . (Capitol)
Happy Anniversary
Four Lads; *Moments To Remember-Very Best Of The Four Lads* . . . . . (Taragon)

Happy Anniversary
Slim Whitman; *Best Of Slim Whitman-Legendary Master Series* . . . . (EMI)
I Wish I Could Have Been There
John Anderson; *Solid Ground* . . . . (BNA)
Once-A-Year Day!
Original Cast; *ST/Pajama Game* . . . . (Collectables)
Our Anniversary
Fiestas; *Very Best Of The Fiestas* . . . . (Collectables)
Shep And The Limelites; *Very Best Of Shep & The Limelites-Daddy's Home* . . . . (Collectables)
Unhappy Anniversary
Vitamin C; *Vitamin C* . . . . (Elektra)
You
Jesse Powell; *'Bout It* . . . . (Silas)

ART & PHOTOGRAPHY, Cameras, Painting

(You Don't Have To) Paint Me A Picture
Gary Lewis And The Playboys; *Best Of Gary Lewis And The Playboys* . . . (EMI)
Gary Lewis And The Playboys' Greatest Hits . . . . (Rhino)
8 X 10
Bill Anderson; *The Bill Anderson Story* . . . . (MCA)
Absolutely (Story Of A Girl)
Nine Days; *Maddening Crowd* . . . .(550 Music)
Now That's What I Call Music!-#5-C . . . .(Virgin)
Art Decade
David Bowie; *Low* . . . . (Rykodisc)
Art For Art's Sake
10 CC; *10 CC's Greatest Hits-1972-1978* . . . .(Polydor)
How Dare You! . . . . (Mercury)
Live & Let Live . . . . (Mercury)
Art Lover
Kinks; *Give The People What They Want* . . . . (Arista)
The Road . . . . (MCA)
Artist
Jeannie C. Riley; *Things Go Better With Love* . . . .(Plantation)
Artist
Cat Stevens; *Back To Earth* . . . . (A&M)
Artistry In Rhythm
Stan Kenton; *Comprehensive Stan Kenton* . . . . (Capitol)
Live In Europe . . . . (Mercury)
Stan Kenton's Greatest Hits . . . . (Capitol)
Summer Of '51 . . . .(Garland)
Stan Kenton & His Orchestra; *Road Show* . . . . (Capitol)
Artists Only
Talking Heads; *More Songs About Buildings & Food* . . . .(Sire)
Name Of This Band Is Talking Heads . . . .(Sire)
Back On The Chain Gang
Pretenders; *Learning To Crawl* . . . .(Sire)
Pretenders-The Singles . . . .(Sire)
ST/King Of Comedy . . . . (Warner Bros.)
Bookends
Simon & Garfunkel; *Bookends* . . . . (Columbia)
Collected Works . . . . (Columbia)
Simon & Garfunkel's Greatest Hits . . . . (Columbia)
Boy In The Bubble
Paul Simon; *Graceland* . . . . (Warner Bros.)
Californication
Red Hot Chili Peppers; *Californication* . . . . (Warner Bros.)
Camera
Crosby, Stills & Nash; *After The Storm* . . . .(Atlantic)
R.E.M.; *Reckoning* . . . . (I.R.S.)
Camera Eye
Rush; *Moving Pictures* . . . . (Mercury)
Camera Never Lies
Elton John; *Reg Strikes Back* . . . . (MCA)
Camera Never Lies
Michael Franks; *Camera Never Lies* . . . . (Warner Bros.)
Camera One
Josh Joplin Group; *Useful Music* . . . .(Artemis)
Carlene
Phil Vassar; *Phil Vassar* . . . . (Arista)
Cathedrals
Jump, Little Children; *Magazine* . . . .(Breaking/Atlantic)
Centerfold
J. Geils Band; *Flashback-Best Of The J. Geils Band* . . . . (EMI)
Freeze-Frame . . . . (EMI)
Showtime . . . . (EMI)
Children And Art
Original Cast; *Sunday In The Park With George* . . . . (RCA Victor)
Easter Parade
Andy Russell; *Puttin' On The Ritz-Capitol Sings Berlin-C* . . . . (Capitol)
Bing Crosby; *All Time Best Of Bing Crosby* . . . .(Curb)
Judy Garland & Fred Astaire; *ST/Easter Parade* . . . . (Rhino)
Sarah Vaughan; *Complete Sarah Vaughan On Mercury-#2* . . . . (Mercury)

Every Picture Tells A Story
Rod Stewart; *Best Of Rod Stewart* . . . . (Mercury)
Every Picture Tells A Story . . . . (Mercury)
Storyteller/The Complete Anthology: 1964-1990 . . . . (Warner Bros.)
Eyes Of A Painter
Kate Wolf; *Close To You* . . . . (Kaleidoscope)
Evening In Austin . . . . (Kaleidoscope)
Gold In California-Retrospective-1975-1985 . . . . (Kaleidoscope)
Faded Pictures
Case Featuring Joe; *Personal Conversation* . . . . (Def Jam/IDJMG)
Family Snapshot
Peter Gabriel; *Peter Gabriel* . . . . (Geffen)
Peter Gabriel/Plays Live . . . . (Geffen)
Shaking The Tree-Sixteen Golden Greats . . . . (Geffen)
Few More Memories
Dolly Parton; *The Grass Is Blue* . . . . (Sugar Hill)
Freeze-Frame
J. Geils Band; *Flashback-Best Of The J. Geils Band* . . . . (EMI)
Freeze-Frame . . . . (EMI)
Girls On Film
Duran Duran; *Decade* . . . . (Capitol)
Duran Duran (The Wedding Album) . . . . (Capitol)
Great Work Of Art
T.G. Sheppard; *Livin' On The Edge* . . . . (Columbia)
T.G. Sheppard's Biggest Hits . . . . (Columbia)
Having My Picture Taken
Boomtown Rats; *Fine Art Of Surfacing* . . . . (Columbia)
Hotel Rats & Photostats
Jimmy Page; *ST/Death Wish 2* . . . . (Swan Song)
I Don't Know You Anymore
Savage Garden; *Affirmation* . . . . (Columbia)
I Wish I Was A Painter
Greg Brown; *One More Goodnight Kiss* . . . . (Red House)
If
Bread; *Best Of Bread* . . . . (Elektra)
Bread-Anthology . . . . (Elektra)
Bread-Retrospective . . . . (Rhino)
Manna . . . . (Rhino)
Illustrated Man
Johnny Winter; *Best Blues Album In The World...Ever!-C* . . . . (Virgin)
I'm Getting Tired So I Can Sleep
Dinah Shore; *The Eddie Cantor Radio Show-1942-1943* . . . . . . (Original Cast)
Image Of A Girl
Safaris; *Brown Eyed Soul...East L.A.-#3-C* . . . . (Rhino)
Imitation Of Life
R.E.M.; *Reveal* . . . . (Warner Bros.)
In Pictures
Alabama; *Alabama-Super Hits* . . . . (RCA)
In Pictures . . . . (RCA)
It's Hot Up Here
Mandy Patinkin/Bernadette Peters/Original Cast; *Sunday In The Park With George* . . . . (RCA Victor)
I've Got A Secret Miniature Camera
Peter Murphy; *ST/Pump Up The Volume* . . . . (MCA)
Kodachrome
Paul Simon; *Greatest Hits, Etc.* . . . . (Columbia)
Negotiations And Love Songs, 1971-1986 . . . . (Warner Bros.)
There Goes Rhymin' Simon . . . . (Columbia)
Simon & Garfunkel; *The Concert In Central Park* . . . . (Warner Bros.)
Let The Picture Paint Itself
Rodney Crowell; *Let The Picture Paint Itself* . . . . (MCA)
Like A Rembrandt
Badlees; *Diamonds In The Coal* . . . . (Rite-Off)
Love Spreads
Stone Roses; *Second Coming* . . . . (Geffen)
Masterpiece
Temptations; *Masterpiece* . . . . (Motown)
Temptations-Anthology-The Best Of The Temptations . . . . (Motown)
Masterpiece
Atlantic Starr; *Love Crazy* . . . . (Reprise)
Masterpiece
Grover Washington, Jr.; *Grover Washington, Jr.-At His Best* . . . . . (Motown)
Soul Box-#1 . . . . (Motown)
Meet The Swinger (Polaroid Swinger)
Original Soundtrack; *TeeVee Toons-The Commercials-#1-C* . . . . . . (TVT)
Mental Picture
Jon Secada; *Heart, Soul & A Voice* . . . . (SBK)
ST/The Specialist . . . . (Epic/Sony Music Soundtrax)
Miss Emily's Picture
John Conlee; *Country Gold-C* . . . . (Priority)
John Conlee With Love . . . . (MCA)
John Conlee's Greatest Hits . . . . (MCA)
Mona Lisa
Carl Mann; *Original Memphis Rock & Roll* . . . . (Sun)
Sun Story-C . . . . (Rhino)
Elvis Presley; *Elvis-A Legendary Performer, Volume 4* . . . . (RCA)
Jim Reeves; *Jim Reeves-Pure Gold* . . . . (RCA)
Nat "King" Cole; *Best Of Nat "King" Cole-Vol. 1* . . . . (Capitol)

Capitol Collectors Series-Nat "King" Cole . . . . (Capitol)
The Nat "King" Cole Story . . . . (Capitol)
Unforgettable . . . . (Capitol)
Neville Brothers; *Fiyo On The Bayou* . . . . (A&M)
Mona Lisa On Cruise Control
Dennis Robbins; *Born Ready* . . . . (Giant)
Mona Lisas And Mad Hatters
Elton John; *Honky Chateau* . . . . (Rocket)
Reg Strikes Back . . . . (MCA)
The Concert For New York City-C . . . . (Columbia)
Mona Lisa's Lost Her Smile
David Allan Coe; *19 Hot Country Requests-#2-C* . . . . (Epic)
David Allan Coe-17 Greatest Hits . . . . (Columbia)
For The Record-The First 10 Years . . . . (Columbia)
Greatest Country Hits Of The '80s-1984-C . . . . (Columbia)
Just Divorced . . . . (Columbia)
Museum
Herman's Hermits; *Herman's Hermits-Their Greatest Hits* . . . . (Abkco)
Museum
Greg Kihn; *Next Of Kihn* . . . . (Beserkley)
Museum
Wall Of Voodoo; *Seven Days In Sammystown* . . . . (I.R.S.)
Neighborhood
Vonda Shepard; *ST/Songs From "Ally McBeal" Featuring Vonda Shepard* . . . . (550/Epic)
Night Of Van Gogh
Boz Scaggs; *Other Roads* . . . . (Columbia)
Old Master Painter
Peggy Lee; *Capitol Collectors Series-Peggy Lee-#1-Early Years* . . . . (Capitol)
Old Photographs
Carlene Carter; *Two Sides To Every Woman* . . . . (Warner Bros.)
Old Photographs
Charley Pride; *Amazing Love* . . . . (RCA)
Old Photographs
Sawyer Brown; *Somewhere In The Night* . . . . (Liberty)
Only One You
T.G. Sheppard; *Best Of T.G. Sheppard* . . . . (Curb)
T.G. Sheppard's All-Time Greatest Hits . . . . (Warner Bros.)
Paint A Picture Of Yourself
Harry Chapin; *Dance Band On The Titanic* . . . . (Elektra)
Paint A Vulgar Picture
Smiths; *Strangeways Here We Come* . . . . (Sire)
Paint Another Picture
Darlene Love; *Paint Another Picture* . . . . (Columbia)
Paint Box
Pink Floyd; *Relics* . . . . (Capitol)
Paint By Numbers
Al Stewart; *24 Carrots* . . . . (Arista)
Paint It, Black
Eric Burdon; *Eric Burdon Sings The Animals' Greatest Hits* . . . . (Rhino)
Rolling Stones; *Aftermath* . . . . (Abkco)
Flashpoint . . . . (Virgin)
Hot Rocks 1964-1971 . . . . (Abkco)
Singles Collection-The London Years . . . . (Abkco)
Through The Past, Darkly (Big Hits Vol. 2) . . . . (Abkco)
Paint Me Back Home In Wyoming
Chris LeDoux; *Paint Me Back Home In Wyoming* . . . . (Liberty)
Sounds Of The Western Country . . . . (Liberty)
Paint Your Pretty Picture
Carmen McRae; *At The Great American Music Hall* . . . . (Blue Note)
Painted Bird
Siouxsie And The Banshees; *Kiss In The Dream House* . . . . (Geffen)
Nocturne . . . . (Geffen)
Painted On My Heart
Cult; *ST/Gone In 60 Seconds* . . . . (Island)
Painted Perfect
One Way Ride; *Strait Up!* . . . . (Refuge/MCA)
Painted Picture
Commodores; *Commodores-All The Great Hits* . . . . (Motown)
Painted Rhythm
Stan Kenton; *Comprehensive Stan Kenton* . . . . (Capitol)
Kenton In Hi-Fi . . . . (Blue Note)
Stan Kenton's Greatest Hits . . . . (Capitol)
Painted, Tainted Rose
Al Martino; *Best Of Al Martino* . . . . (Capitol)
Capitol Collectors Series-Al Martino . . . . (Capitol)
Painting Box
Incredible String Band; *5000 Spirits* . . . . (Elektra)
Relics Of The Incredible String Band . . . . (Elektra)
People Take Pictures Of Each Other
Kinks; *Are The Village Green Preservation Society* . . . . (Reprise)
Photograph
Ringo Starr; *Blast From Your Past* . . . . (Gold Rush)
Ringo . . . . (Capitol)
Photograph
Verve Pipe; *Villains* . . . . (RCA)
Photograph
Def Leppard; *Pyromania* . . . . (Mercury)

Photograph
Ella Fitzgerald; *Ella Abraca Jobim*. . . . .(Pablo)
Photograph Of You
Depeche Mode; *Broken Frame*. . . . . (Sire)
Photographic
Depeche Mode; *Speak & Spell*. . . . . (Sire)
Photographs & Memories
Jim Croce; *Photographs & Memories/His Greatest Hits* . . . .(Atlantic)
Time In A Bottle/Jim Croce's Greatest Love Songs . . . .(Atlantic)
You Don't Mess Around With Jim . . . .(Lifesong)
Picasso And Me
Gretchen Peters; *Gretchen Peters*. . . . . (Purple Crayon Prod.)
Picasso's Last Words
Paul McCartney & Wings; *Band On The Run*. . . . . (Capitol)
Wings; *Wings Over America* . . . . (Capitol)
Picture
Ricky Van Shelton; *Loving Proof*. . . . . (Columbia)
Picture Book
Kinks; *Are The Village Green Preservation Society*. . . . . (Reprise)
Picture Book
Simply Red; *Picture Book* . . . . (Elektra)
Picture From Life's Other Side
George Jones; *Hallelujah Weekend* . . . .(Epic)
Goebel Reeves; *Texas Drifter*. . . . .(Glendale)
Hank Williams; *Beyond The Sunset* . . . .(Polydor)
Hey Good Lookin' (December 1950-July 1951) . . . .(Polydor)
Picture In My Wallet
Darrell & The Oxfords; *Memories Of Times Square Record*
Shop-#11-C . . . . (Collectables)
Picture Of England
Sun & The Moon; *Sun & The Moon* . . . .(Geffen)
Picture Of Love
Continentals; *Doo-Wop Era-Harlem, New York-40 Hits-C* . . . . . .(Collectables)
Picture Of Me (Without You)
George Jones; *Best Of George Jones* . . . .(Epic)
Columbia Country Classics-#4-Nashville Sound-C . . . .(Columbia)
George Jones-Anniversary-Ten Years Of Hits . . . .(Epic)
George Jones-Super Hits. . . . .(Epic)
Lorrie Morgan; *Lorrie Morgan's Greatest Hits* . . . . (BNA)
Something In Red. . . . . (RCA)
Picture Of Our Love
Mickey Gilley; *Gilley* . . . .(Epic)
Picture On The Wall
Carter Family; *'Mid The Green Fields Of Virginia* . . . . (RCA)
Three Generations . . . . (Columbia)
Picture Postcards From L.A.
Joshua Kadison; *Painted Desert Serenade* . . . . (SBK)
Picture Puzzle
Kate Wolf; *Evening In Austin* . . . . (Kaleidoscope)
Give Yourself To Love . . . . (Kaleidoscope)
Lines On The Paper . . . . (Kaleidoscope)
Picture Show
John Prine; *The Missing Years* . . . . (Oh Boy)
Picture This
Jim Brickman; *Picture This* . . . . (Windham Hill)
Pictured Life
Scorpions; *Best Of The Scorpions*. . . . . (RCA)
Tokyo Tapes . . . . (RCA)
Virgin Killer . . . . (RCA)
Pictures
Statler Brothers; *Best Of The Statler Brothers* . . . . (Mercury)
Pictures Don't Lie
Billy Ray Cyrus; *Red Hot + Country-C* . . . . (Mercury)
Pictures Of Bernadette
Talk Talk; *45-#8326* . . . . (EMI)
Pictures Of Home
Deep Purple; *Machine Head*. . . . .(Warner Bros.)
Pictures Of Lily
Pete Townshend; *Another Scoop* . . . . (Atco)
Who; *Magic Bus-The Who On Tour* . . . . (MCA)
Meaty Beaty Big & Bouncy . . . .(MCA)
Pictures Of Matchstick Men
Camper Van Beethoven; *Edge Of Rock-C* . . . . (Era)
Key Lime Pie . . . . (Virgin)
Status Quo; *History Of British Rock-#8-C* . . . . (Rhino)
Sixties Rule! Chapter 1-C . . . . (One Way)
Pictures Of You
Cure; *Disintegration*. . . . . (Elektra)
Mixed Up . . . . (Elektra)
Show . . . . (Elektra)
Polaroids
Shawn Colvin; *Best Of The Columbia Records Radio Hour-#1-C* . . . (Columbia)
Fat City . . . . (Columbia)
Portrait
Kansas; *Point Of Know Return* . . . . (Kirshner)
Two For The Show . . . . (Kirshner)
Portrait
Damned; *Anything* . . . .(MCA)

Portrait
Enya; *Enya* . . . .(Atlantic)
Portrait In Atlanta
House Of Love; *Audience With The Mind* . . . .(Fontana)
Portrait Of Jennie
Nat "King" Cole; *Unforgettable* . . . . (Capitol)
Red Garland & Ray Barretto; *Manteca* . . . . (Prestige)
Portrait Of My Love
Dee Clark; *Best Of Dee Clark* . . . . (Vee-Jay)
Lettermen; *Best Of The Lettermen*. . . . . (Capitol)
Portraits Of Summer
Jim Bajor; *Gentle Images* . . . . (JBX)
Pretty Little Picture
Original Cast; *A Funny Thing Happened On The Way To The Forum*. . . . (Angel)
Stephen Sondheim; *Collector's Sondheim-C* . . . . (RCA)
Privacy
Michael Jackson; *Invincible* . . . . (Epic)
Robot Portrait
Quincy Jones & His Orchestra; *Quintessence* . . . . (MCA/Impulse)
Rudiger
Mark Knopfler; *Golden Heart* . . . . (Warner Bros.)
Self Portrait
Blackmore's Rainbow; *Ritchie Blackmore's R-A-I-N-B-O-W* . . . .(Polydor)
Send A Picture Of Mother
Johnny Cash; *Johnny Cash At Folsom Prison & San Quentin*. . . . . . . (Columbia)
She Drew A Broken Heart
Patty Loveless; *The Trouble With The Truth* . . . . (Epic)
She's Got You
Patsy Cline; *12 Greatest Hits* . . . . (MCA)
Billboard Top Country Hits-1962-C. . . . . (Rhino)
The Patsy Cline Story . . . . (MCA)
Snap Shot
Slave; *Show Time* . . . .(Cotillion)
Snapshot
Art Of Noise; *(Who's Afraid Of)* . . . . (Island)
Sylvia; *Snapshot* . . . . (RCA)
Sylvia's Greatest Hits . . . . (RCA)
Statue Of A Fool
Jack Greene; *Country Hits-C* . . . . (Exact)
Jack Greene Sings His Best . . . . (Step One)
Jack Greene's Greatest Hits. . . . . (International Mktg. Group)
MCA Records 30 Years Of Hits-1958-1988-C . . . . (MCA)
Ricky Van Shelton; *Ricky Van Shelton's Greatest Hits Plus*. . . . . . . (Columbia)
RVS III . . . . (Columbia)
Sunday In The Park With George
Original Cast; *Sunday In The Park With George* . . . . (RCA Victor)
Take A Picture
Filter; *Title Of Record* . . . .(Reprise)
Totally Hits-#2-C . . . . (Elektra)
Tapestry
Carole King; *Tapestry* . . . . (Epic)
Tear Me Out Of The Picture
George Jones; *High-Tech Redneck* . . . . (MCA)
Texas Tattoo
Gibson/Miller Band; *Steppin' Country-C* . . . . (Columbia)
Where There's Smoke . . . . (Epic)
That's Just About Right
BlackHawk; *BlackHawk* . . . . (Arista)
The Hits-Love & Gravity . . . . (Arista)
Theme From "Candid Camera"
Original Soundtrack; *Television's Greatest Hits-#4-Black & White*
Classics-C . . . . (TVT)
Theme From "Night Gallery"
Original Soundtrack-Sonny Curtis; *Television's Greatest Hits-#5-In Living*
Color-C . . . . (TVT)
Tit Photographer Blues
Fabulous Poodles; *Mirror Stars* . . . . (Epic)
Van Gogh's Left Ear
Kenny Garrett; *Black Hope* . . . . (Warner Bros.)
Vincent
Don McLean; *American Pie* . . . . (EMI)
Best Of Don McLean . . . . (EMI)
Greatest Hits Then & Now . . . . (EMI)
Visions Of Gaudi
Phil Woods; *Here's To My Lady* . . . . (Chesky)
When I Paint My Masterpiece
Band; *Bob Dylan 30th Anniversary Concert* . . . . (Columbia)
To Kingdom Come-The Definitive Collection . . . . (Capitol)
Bob Dylan; *Bob Dylan's Greatest Hits-#2* . . . . (Columbia)
Where Do I Fit In
Clay Walker; *Clay Walker*. . . . .(Giant)
Who Needs Pictures
Brad Paisley; *Who Needs Pictures* . . . . (Arista)
Wishing (If I Had A Photograph Of You)
A Flock Of Seagulls; *Best Of A Flock Of Seagulls* . . . . (Jive)
Listen . . . . (Jive)
XXX's And OOO's
Trisha Yearwood; *Thinkin' About You* . . . . (MCA)

You And The Mona Lisa
Shawn Colvin; *A Few Small Repairs* . . . . (Columbia)

ASTROLOGY, Horoscope, Tarot
See Also: **CIRCLES, FUTURE, LIFE, MAGIC, SPIRITS, STARS**

(You're A Fish And I'm A) Water Sign
Parliament; *Motor-Booty Affair* . . . .(Casablanca)
Ace Of Swords
Alan Parsons Project; *Turn Of A Friendly Card* . . . . (Arista)
Ace Of Wands
Steve Hackett; *Steve Hackett* . . . . (Chrysalis)
Voyage Of The Acolyte . . . . (Chrysalis)
Aquarian Cycle
Lonnie Liston Smith; *Song For The Children* . . . . (Columbia)
Aquarius
Original Broadway Cast; *Hair* . . . . (RCA)
Aquarius/Let The Sunshine In Medley
5th Dimension; *Billboard Top Rock 'N' Roll Hits-1969-C* . . . . (Rhino)
Greatest Hits On Earth . . . . (Arista)
ST/1969 . . . . (Polydor)
ST/Forrest Gump . . . . (Epic/Sony Music Soundtrax)
Aries
Supertramp; *Indelibly Stamped* . . . . (A&M)
Born Under A Bad Sign
Albert King; *Atlantic Blues-Guitar-C* . . . . (Atlantic)
Best Blues Album In The World...Ever!-C . . . . (Virgin)
Masterworks . . . . (Atlantic)
Stax Blues Masters-Blue Monday-C . . . . (Stax)
Booker T. & The M.G.s; *Best Of Booker T. & The M.G.s* . . . . . . (Atlantic)
Cream; *Strange Brew-Very Best Of Cream* . . . . (Polydor)
Wheels Of Fire . . . . (Polydor)
Jimi Hendrix; *Blues* . . . . (MCA)
Koko Taylor & Buddy Guy; *Force Of Nature* . . . .(Alligator)
Paul Butterfield Blues Band; *Paul Butterfield Blues Band-Live* . . . . (Elektra)
Rita Coolidge; *Rita Coolidge* . . . . (A&M)
Rita Coolidge's Greatest Hits . . . . (A&M)
Simpsons; *Simpsons Sing The Blues* . . . . (Geffen)
Born Under The Wrong Sign
Nazareth; *Close Enough For Rock 'N' Roll* . . . . (A&M)
Born With The Moon In Virgo
Michael Franks; *Previously Unavailable* . . . .(DRG)
Capricorn
Motorhead; *No Sleep 'Til Hammersmith* . . . . (Castle Music America)
Overkill . . . . (Castle Music America)
Capricorn
Barclay James Harvest; *Eyes Of The Universe* . . . . (Polydor)
Capricorn
Richard Elliot; *Initial Approach* . . . .(Blue Note)
Capricorn
Wayne Shorter; *Super Nova* . . . . (Blue Note)
Capricorn Kings
Lee Wright; *45-#7628* . . . .(Prairie Dog)
Capricorn Rising
Richard Evans; *Richard Evans* . . . . (A&M)
Capricorn Sister
Mother Love Bone; *Mother Love Bone* . . . .(Stardog)
Five Planets In Leo
Brew Moore Quintet; *Brew Moore Quintet* . . . .(Fantasy)
Gemini
Cannonball Adderley; *Cannonball Adderley In Europe-*
Collection-#7 . . . .(Landmark)
Cannonball Adderley Sextet-In New York . . . . (Riverside)
Coast To Coast . . . . (Milestone)
Gemini
Alan Parsons Project; *Eye In The Sky* . . . . (Arista)
Gemini
Miracles; *Miracles' Greatest Hits* . . . . (Motown)
Gemini Childe
Mamas & The Papas; *The Papas & The Mamas* . . . . (MCA)
Gemini Dream
Moody Blues; *Long Distance Voyager* . . . . (Polydor)
Voices In The Sky-The Best Of The Moody Blues . . . .(Threshold)
Gemini Girl
David Allan Coe; *Son Of The South* . . . . (Columbia)
I Feel Lucky
Mary Chapin Carpenter; *Come On Come On* . . . . (Columbia)
I, Capricorn
Shirley Bassey; *Shirley Bassey's Greatest Hits* . . . .(EMI)
I'm A Scorpio
Russ Ballard; *At The Third Stroke* . . . .(Epic)
Jesus Was a Capricorn
Kris Kristofferson; *Jesus Was a Capricorn* . . . . (Columbia)
Journey To Capricorn
Stan Kenton; *Journey Into Capricorn* . . . .(Creative World)

Leo Rising
Ronnie Montrose; *Open Fire* . . . . (Warner Bros.)
Magic Moon
Peter Frampton; *Something's Happening* . . . .(A&M)
Maybe I'm A Leo
Deep Purple; *Machine Head* . . . . (Warner Bros.)
My Aquarian
Juan Martin; *Through The Moving Window* . . . . (Novus)
Pisces
Lief Strand; *Zodiac* . . . .(Innovative Comm.)
Pisces
Matthew McCauley; *ST/Laserium Zodiac* . . . . (Polydor)
Pisces
Bobby Lyle; *The Genie* . . . .(Capitol)
Pisces Apple Lady
Leon Russell; *Leon Russell* . . . . (MCA)
Sagittarius
Burkard Schmidl; *Zodiac Symphony* . . . .(Innovative Comm.)
Scorpio
Grandmaster Flash & The Furious Five; *Street Jams-Hip-Hop From The*
Top-#2-C . . . .(Rhino)
Scorpio
Leif Strand; *Zodiac* . . . .(Innovative Comm.)
Scorpio Crew
Yellowman; *Don't Burn It Down* . . . . (Shanachie)
Scorpio Rising
10,000 Maniacs; *Wishing Chair* . . . .(Elektra)
Scorpio Rising
Army Of Lovers; *Army Of Lovers* . . . . (Giant)
Son Of Sagittarius
Eddie Kendricks; *Motown Superstar Series-#19-Eddie Kendricks* . . . .(Motown)
Southern Cross
Ozark Mountain Daredevils; *Car Over The Lake Album* . . . .(A&M)
Swinging Scorpio
Buddy Tate & Humphrey Lyttelton; *Swinging Scorpio* . . . .(Black Lion)
Tarot Woman
Blackmore's Rainbow; *Rainbow Rising* . . . . (Polydor)
Taurus
Spirit; *Spirit* . . . .(Epic)
Time Circle . . . .(Epic)
Taurus
Leif Strand; *Zodiac* . . . .(Innovative Comm.)
Turn Of A Friendly Card
Alan Parsons Project; *Best Of Alan Parsons Project-#2* . . . .(Arista)
Turn Of A Friendly Card . . . .(Arista)
Virgo
Wayne Shorter; *Best Of Wayne Shorter-TheBlue Note Years* . . . . . . (Blue Note)
Night Dreamer . . . . (Blue Note)
Virgo
Jose Feliciano; *And The Feeling's Good* . . . . (RCA)
Virgo
Matthew McCauley; *ST/Laserium Zodiac* . . . . (Polydor)
Virgo Clowns
Van Morrison; *His Band And The Street Choir* . . . . (Warner Bros.)
Water Sign
Gary Wright; *Light Of Smiles* . . . . (Warner Bros.)
Zodiac
Fatback Band; *Man With The Band* . . . . (Spring)
Zodiac
Down To The Bone; *The Urban Grooves-Album II* . . . . (Internal Bass)
Zodiacs
Roberta Kelly; *Zodiac Lady* . . . . (Casablanca)

BABY, Being Born, Pregnant
See Also: **AGING, BIRTHDAY, CHILDREN, FAMILY (various),**
FAMILY PLANNING, LIFE, PARENTS (various), PEOPLE, YOUNG

(You're) Having My Baby
Paul Anka; *'70s Party Killers-C* . . . .(Rhino)
Five Decades Of Hits . . . .(Curb)
Paul Anka-His Best . . . . (EMI)
Paul Anka-Live . . . .(Columbia)
Times Of Your Life . . . . (United Artists)
1-2-3
Len Barry; *24 Of The Grooviest Hits Of All Time! The '60s Ultimate*
Collection-#1-C . . . . (Sundazed Music)
Adventure Baby
Adventure Babies; *Laugh* . . . . (London)
All Through The Night
Judy Collins; *Baby's Bedtime* . . . .(Lightyear)
And The Baby Never Cries
Harry Chapin; *Sniper & Other Love Songs* . . . .(Elektra)
And The Cradle Will Rock
Van Halen; *Women & Children First* . . . . (Warner Bros.)

And When I Die
Blood, Sweat & Tears; *Blood, Sweat & Tears* . . . . (Columbia)
Blood, Sweat & Tears Greatest Hits . . . . (Columbia)
Blood, Sweat & Tears In Concert . . . . (Columbia)
Laura Nyro; *First Songs* . . . . (Columbia)
Live At The Bottom Line . . . . (Cypress)

Annie Had A Baby
Hank Ballard And The Midnighters; *Cruisin'-1955-C* . . . .(Increase)

Babies Makin' Babies
Sly & The Family Stone; *Fresh* . . . . (Legacy)
Sly & The Family Stone-Anthology . . . .(Epic)

Baby Beluga
Billy Gilman; *Country Goes Raffi-C* . . . . (Rounder)

Baby Blue
Gene Vincent and His Blue Caps; *Capitol Collectors Series-Gene Vincent
and His Blue Caps* . . . . (Gold Rush)

Baby Blue
George Strait; *If You Ain't Lovin' You Ain't Livin'* . . . .(MCA)

Baby Blue
Beach Boys; *L.A.-The Light Album* . . . . (Caribou)

Baby Blue
Paul Butterfield Blues Band; *North South* . . . . (Rhino)

Baby Blue
Echoes; *Super Oldies Of The '60s-#5-C* . . . .(Audio Fidelity)

Baby Boom Baby
James Taylor; *Never Die Young* . . . . (Columbia)

Baby Doll
Tony Toni Tone; *Who?* . . . .(Wing)

Baby Doll
Bessie Smith; *Bessie Smith-The Complete Recordings-#3* . . . . (Legacy)

Baby Doll
Ella Fitzgerald; *Best Of Ella Fitzgerald* . . . .(MCA)

Baby Doll
Raindogs; *Border Drive-In Theatre* . . . . (Atco)

Baby Doll
Marvin & Johnny; *Flipped Out.* . . . .(Specialty)

Baby Doll
Rita Remington; *Girls Girls Girls* . . . . (Plantation)

Baby Doll
Carlo; *La Bamba & Other Original Hits-C.* . . . . (Laurie)

Baby Doll
Memphis Slim; *Raining The Blues* . . . . (Fantasy)

Baby Doll
Farmers; *Rock Angel.* . . . . (Flying Fish)

Baby Doll
Devo; *Total Devo* . . . .(Enigma Capitol)

Baby Doll Polka
Frankie Yankovic & His Yanks; *America's Favorites* . . . .(Smash)
One More Time . . . .(Crescendo)

Baby Driver
Simon & Garfunkel; *Bridge Over Troubled Water* . . . . (Columbia)
Collected Works. . . . . (Columbia)

Baby Elephant Walk
Henry Mancini; *Henry Mancini-Pure Gold* . . . . (RCA)
Peter Gunn. . . . . (RCA)

Baby Face
Little Richard; *Compact Command Performances-Little Richard* . . . . (Motown)
Little Richard His Greatest Hits . . . . (Vee-Jay)
Little Richard's Greatest Hits . . . . (Everest)
Tutti Frutti . . . . (Accord)

Baby Face
Bobby Darin; *Splish Splash-Best Of Bobby Darin-#1* . . . .(Atlantic)

Baby Face
Al Jolson; *The Al Jolson Story-#3.* . . . .(MCA)
World's Greatest . . . .(MCA)
Kinks; *Everybody's In Show-Biz* . . . . (Rhino)

Baby Fat
Wet Willie; *Wet Willie's Greatest Hits* . . . . (Polydor)

Baby Mine
Barbara Cook; *Disney Album* . . . .(Disney)
Bette Midler; *ST/Beaches* . . . .(Atlantic)
Bonnie Raitt & Was (Not Was); *Stay Awake-Music Of Vintage Disney
Films-C* . . . . (A&M)

Baby Needs New Shoes
Restless Heart; *Matters Of The Heart* . . . . (RCA)

Baby Ruth
John Prine; *Storm Windows* . . . . (Asylum)

Baby Sitter
Betty Wright; *Golden Classics-Betty Wright* . . . . (Collectables)

Baby Talk
Jan & Dean; *Best Of Jan & Dean* . . . .(EMI)
Collectables Presents The History Of Rock-#9-C . . . . (Collectables)
One Summer Night-Live. . . . . (Rhino)

Baby Talk
Billy Idol; *Don't Stop* . . . .(Chrysalis)

Baby's House
Steve Miller Band; *Steve Miller Band-Anthology.* . . . . (Capitol)
Your Saving Grace. . . . . (Capitol)

Baby's Smile Woman's Kiss
Johnny Duncan; *Best Of Johnny Duncan* . . . . (Columbia)

Babysitter
Harry Chapin; *Portrait Gallery.* . . . . (Elektra)

Back On Earth
Ozzy Osbourne; *The Ozzman Cometh.* . . . . (Epic)

Barefoot & Pregnant
Joan Armatrading; *To The Limit* . . . . (A&M)

Biggest Hurt, The
Barbara Fairchild; *The Biggest Hurt* . . . . (Audiograph)

Billie Jean
Michael Jackson; *Thriller* . . . . (Epic)

Billion Dollar Babies
Alice Cooper; *Alice Cooper's Greatest Hits* . . . . (Warner Bros.)
Billion Dollar Babies . . . . (Warner Bros.)
The Alice Cooper Show . . . . (Warner Bros.)

Blessed Be
Alison Krauss; *Country Goes Raffi-C* . . . . (Rounder)

Born A Fool
Freddie Hart; *Best Of Freddie Hart* . . . . (MCA)

Born A Woman
Sandy Posey; *Best Of Sandy Posey-With Skeeter Davis* . . . . (Gusto)
Best Of Town & Country-#3-C. . . . . (Gusto)
Cruisin'-1966-C. . . . . (Increase)
Sandy Posey/Skeeter Davis/Wanda Jackson . . . . (Gusto)
Super Hits-#5-C . . . . (Gusto)

Born Again
Christians; *Christians* . . . . (Island)

Born Again Human
B.B. King; *There Must Be A Better World Somewhere* . . . . (MCA)

Born And Raised In Compton
DJ Quik; *Quik Is The Name* . . . .(Profile)

Born Country
Alabama; *Alabama's Greatest Hits-#2* . . . . (RCA)

Born Cross-Eyed
Grateful Dead; *Anthem Of The Sun* . . . . (Warner Bros.)
*What A Long Strange Trip It's Been: The Best Of The
Grateful Dead* . . . . (Warner Bros.)

Born Enchanter
Fleetwood Mac; *Heroes Are Hard To Find* . . . .(Reprise)

Born Fighter
Nick Lowe; *Basher: Best Of* . . . . (Columbia)
Labour Of Lust . . . . (Columbia)

Born For Adventure
Styx; *Equinox* . . . . (A&M)

Born Free
Andy Williams; *Andy Williams' Greatest Hits* . . . . (Columbia)
Andy Williams-16 Most Requested Songs. . . . . (Legacy)
John Barry; *Film Music Of John Barry* . . . . (Columbia)
Matt Monro; *ST/Born Free* . . . . (MGM)
Roger Williams; *Best Of Roger Williams* . . . . (MCA)
Roger Williams-Golden Hits . . . . (MCA)

Born In A Prison
John Lennon/Plastic Ono Band; *Sometime In New York City* . . . . (Capitol)

Born In America
Riot; *Born In America* . . . . (Quality)

Born In Chicago
George Thorogood & The Destroyers; *Boogie People* . . . . (EMI)
Paul Butterfield Blues Band; *Golden Butter* . . . . (Elektra)
Paul Butterfield Blues Band . . . . (Elektra)

Born In Chicago
Pixies; *Rubaiyat-Elektra's 40th Anniversary-C* . . . . (Elektra)

Born In East L.A.
Cheech & Chong; *Get Out Of My Room* . . . . (MCA)

Born In Georgia
Tinsley Ellis; *Fanning The Flames* . . . .(Alligator)

Born In Louisiana
Clarence "Gatemouth" Brown; *Alligator Records 20th Anniversary
Collection-C* . . . .(Alligator)
Standing My Ground . . . .(Alligator)

Born In Louisiana
Troy Turner; *Handful Of Aces* . . . . (Ichiban Int'l)

Born In Mississippi
Chris LeDoux; *Wild & Wooly* . . . . (Liberty)

Born In Moscow
Vasily Shumov; *My District* . . . .(Gold Castle)

Born In The Dark
Doug Stone; *Faith In Me Faith In You* . . . . (Columbia)
Steppin' Country-#2-C. . . . . (Columbia)

Born In The Fifties
Police; *Outlandos D'Amour* . . . . (A&M)

Born In The U.S.A.
Bruce Springsteen; *Born In The U.S.A.* . . . . (Columbia)
Bruce Springsteen's Greatest Hits . . . . (Columbia)
Tracks. . . . . (Columbia)
Bruce Springsteen & The E Street Band; *Bruce Springsteen & The E Street
Band Live/1975-85* . . . . (Legacy)

Born In The Water
Tragically Hip; *Road Apples* . . . . (MCA)
Born Late '58
Mott The Hoople; *Mott The Hoople's Greatest Hits* . . . . (Columbia)
The Ballad Of Mott: A Retrospective . . . . (Columbia)
Born Loose
Rod Stewart; *Footloose & Fancy Free* . . . . (Warner Bros.)
Born On A Friday
Cleo Laine; *Born On A Friday* . . . . (RCA)
Return To Carnegie . . . . (RCA)
Linda Hopkins; *How Blue Can You Get* . . . . (Quicksilver)
Born On A Monday
Michael Quatro; *Bottom Line* . . . . (Spector)
Born On The Bayou
Creedence Clearwater Revival; *Bayou Country* . . . . (Fantasy)
Chooglin' . . . . (Fantasy)
Creedence Clearwater Revival-Gold . . . . (Fantasy)
Creedence Gold . . . . (Fantasy)
Live In Europe . . . . (Fantasy)
The Concert . . . . (Fantasy)
Born Ready
Jesse Hunter; *A Man Like Me.* . . . . (BNA)
Born To Be Alive
Patrick Hernandez; *Let's Dance-DJ's Collection* . . . . (Columbia)
Born To Be Bad
George Thorogood & The Destroyers; *Born To Be Bad* . . . . (Gold Rush)
ST/Bull Durham . . . . (Capitol)
Born To Be Bad
Runaways; *Best Of The Runaways* . . . . (Mercury)
Born To Be Blue
George Shearing & Mel Torme; *Evening With George Shearing & Mel
Torme.* . . . . (Concord Jazz)
Judds; *Judds' Greatest Hits-#2* . . . . (MCA)
Love Can Build A Bridge . . . . (MCA)
Mel Torme; *Mel Torme-Compact Jazz* . . . . (Verve)
Steve Miller; *Born 2 B Blue* . . . . (Gold Rush)
Born To Be My Baby
Bon Jovi; *New Jersey.* . . . . (Jambco)
Born To Be Together
Ronettes; *Best Of The Ronettes* . . . . (Abkco)
Born To Be Wild
Steppenwolf; *Billboard Top Rock 'N' Roll Hits-1968-C* . . . . (Rhino)
Live Steppenwolf. . . . . (MCA)
Steppenwolf . . . . (MCA)
Steppenwolf-16 Greatest Hits . . . . (MCA)
Vintage Music-#9 & 10-C . . . . (MCA)
Born To Be With You
Chordettes; *Best Of The Chordettes.* . . . . (Rhino)
Chordettes Greatest Hits . . . . (Everest)
Lil' Bit Of Gold 3" CD Series-C . . . . (Rhino)
Born To Boogie
Hank Williams, Jr.; *Born To Boogie* . . . . (WB/Curb)
Hank Williams, Jr.'s Greatest Hits III . . . . (Curb)
Born To Boogie
T. Rex; *T. Rextasy: Best Of T. Rex 1970-1973.* . . . . (Warner Bros.)
Born To Cry
Dion And The Belmonts; *Dion And The Belmonts-20 Golden
Classics* . . . . (Collectables)
Dion-24 Original Classics . . . . (Arista)
Everything You've Always Wanted . . . . (Laurie)
More Great Hits . . . . (Laurie)
Born To Fly
Sara Evans; *Born To Fly* . . . . (RCA)
Born To Hand-Jive
Original Broadway Cast; *Grease* . . . . (Polydor)
Sha Na Na; *ST/Grease* . . . . (Polydor)
Born To Kill
Damned; *Damned Damned Damned* . . . . (Frontier)
Final Damnation . . . . (Restless)
Born To Kill
Gillan; *Double Trouble* . . . . (Metal Blade)
Born To Lose
Johnny Cash; *Johnny Cash* . . . . (Everest)
Original Johnny Cash. . . . . (Sun)
Rough Cut King Of Country Music . . . . (Sun)
The Man-The World-His Music . . . . (Sun)
Ray Charles; *Ray Charles-His Greatest Hits-#1* . . . . (Dunhill Compact Classics)
Born To Love Me
Roy Orbison; *Legendary Roy Orbison* . . . . (Sony Music Special Prod.)
Our Love Song . . . . (Monument)
Regeneration . . . . (Monument)
Born To Love You
Fabulous Thunderbirds; *Walk That Walk Talk That Talk.* . . (Epic Portrait Assoc.)
Born To Love You
Michael Nesmith; *Best Of (1970-1973)* . . . . (Rhino)
Born To Love You
Karen Brooks; *Hearts On Fire* . . . . (Warner Bros.)
Born To Love You
Mark Collie; *Mark Collie* . . . . (MCA)

Born To Love You
Temptations; *Temptin'.* . . . . (Motown)
Born To Move
Creedence Clearwater Revival; *1970.* . . . . (Fantasy)
Creedence Clearwater Revival-Chronicle-#2 . . . . (Fantasy)
Pendulum . . . . (Fantasy)
Born To Rock
Quiet Riot; *Condition Critical* . . . . (Epic Portrait Assoc.)
Born To Roll
Masta Ace Incorporated; *Sittin' On Chrome* . . . . (Delicious Vinyl)
Born To Run
Bruce Springsteen; *Born To Run* . . . . (Columbia)
Chimes Of Freedom . . . . (Columbia)
Bruce Springsteen & The E Street Band; *Bruce Springsteen & The E Street
Band Live/1975-85* . . . . (Legacy)
Melissa Etheridge; *The Concert For New York City-C* . . . . . . (Columbia)
Born To Run
Emmylou Harris; *Cimarron* . . . . (Warner Bros.)
Profile II-The Best Of Emmylou Harris . . . . (Warner Bros.)
Born To The Breed
Judy Collins; *Judith* . . . . (Elektra)
So Early In The Spring, The First 15 Years . . . . (Elektra)
Born To Wander
Rare Earth; *20 Hard-To-Find Motown Classics-#2-C* . . . . (Motown)
Ecology . . . . (Motown)
Hard-To-Find Motown Classics-#2-C . . . . (Motown)
Motown Superstar Series-#16-Rare Earth . . . . (Motown)
Born Too Late
Poni-Tails; *Original Classic Oldies Of The '50s-#4-C* . . . . (MCA)
Born Under A Bad Sign
Albert King; *Atlantic Blues-Guitar-C* . . . . (Atlantic)
Best Blues Album In The World...Ever!-C . . . . (Virgin)
Masterworks . . . . (Atlantic)
Stax Blues Masters-Blue Monday-C . . . . (Stax)
Booker T. & The M.G.s; *Best Of Booker T. & The M.G.s* . . . . . (Atlantic)
Cream; *Strange Brew-Very Best Of Cream* . . . . (Polydor)
Wheels Of Fire . . . . (Polydor)
Jimi Hendrix; *Blues* . . . . (MCA)
Koko Taylor & Buddy Guy; *Force Of Nature* . . . . (Alligator)
Paul Butterfield Blues Band; *Paul Butterfield Blues Band-Live* . . . (Elektra)
Rita Coolidge; *Rita Coolidge* . . . . (A&M)
Rita Coolidge's Greatest Hits . . . . (A&M)
Simpsons; *Simpsons Sing The Blues* . . . . (Geffen)
Born Under Punches
Talking Heads; *Remain In Light.* . . . . (Sire)
Born Under The Wrong Sign
Nazareth; *Close Enough For Rock 'N' Roll* . . . . (A&M)
Born With A Broken Heart
Kenny Wayne Shepherd; *Ledbetter Heights* . . . . (Giant)
Born With The Blues
Johnny Rodriguez; *Johnny Rodriguez's Biggest Hits* . . . . (Epic)
Born With The Moon In Virgo
Michael Franks; *Previously Unavailable* . . . . (DRG)
Born Yesterday
Everly Brothers; *Born Yesterday* . . . . (Mercury)
Boy In The Bubble
Paul Simon; *Graceland* . . . . (Warner Bros.)
Brenda's Got A Baby
Tupac; *2Pacalypse Now.* . . . . (Priority)
Brick
Ben Folds Five; *Whatever And Ever Amen.* . . . . (Caroline/550)
Careless Love
Dinah Washington; *Bessie Smith Songbook.* . . . . (Emarcy)
Pete Fountain; *Mr. New Orleans* . . . . (MCA)
Preservation Hall Jazz Band; *Best Of The Preservation Hall
Jazz Band* . . . . (Columbia)
New Orleans-#3-When The Saints Go Marchin' In . . . . (Columbia)
Child Is Born, A
Barbra Streisand; *Lazy Afternoon.* . . . . (Columbia)
Kenny Burrell; *Fire Into Music-Best Of Impulse!-#2-C* . . . (MCA/Impulse)
God Bless The Child . . . . (CBS Associated)
Heritage . . . . (Voss)
Toots Thielemans; *East Coast West Coast* . . . . (Private Music)
Come Back As A Flower
Stevie Wonder; *Journey Through The Secret Life Of Plants* . . . (Motown)
Country Bumpkin
Cal Smith; *16 Top Country Hits-#1-C* . . . . (MCA)
Country's Greatest Hits-#2-C . . . . (MCA Special Prod.)
Grand Ole Opry-75 Years-#2-C . . . . (MCA)
Cradle Of Love
Billy Idol; *Charmed Life* . . . . (Chrysalis)
ST/Adventures Of Ford Fairlane. . . . . (Elektra)
Cradle Of Love
Johnny Preston; *Running Bear* . . . . (Collectables)
Crazy Babies
Ozzy Osbourne; *The Ozzman Cometh* . . . . (Epic)
Crossing Muddy Waters
John Hiatt; *Crossing Muddy Waters.* . . . . (Vanguard)

Cry Baby Cry
Beatles; *The Beatles (White Album)* . . . . (Capitol)
Cry Baby Cry
Aldo Nova; *Subject...Aldo Nova* . . . . (Portrait)
Cry Baby Cry
Angels; *My Boyfriend's Back* . . . . (Collectables)
   Super Oldies Of The '60s-#4-C . . . .(Audio Fidelity)
   WCBS FM 101 History Of Rock-'60s-#5-C . . . . (Collectables)
Cry Baby Cry
Judy Garland; *Judy Garland-Collector's Items-1936-1945* . . . .(MCA)
Cry Like A Baby
Box Tops; *Billboard Top Rock 'N' Roll Hits-1968-C* . . . . (Rhino)
   Box Tops' Greatest Hits . . . . (Rhino)
   Super Hits-#5-C . . . . (Gusto)
   WCBS FM 101 History Of Rock-'60s-#4-C . . . . (Collectables)
Cry Like A Baby
A Flock Of Seagulls; *Dream Come True* . . . . (Jive)
Cry Like A Baby
Bourgeois Tagg; *Yoyo* . . . . (Island)
Danny's Song
Anne Murray; *Anne Murray-Country* . . . . (Capitol)
   Anne Murray's Greatest Hits . . . . (Capitol)
   Danny's Song . . . . (Capitol)
Loggins & Messina; *Loggins & Messina-On Stage* . . . . (Columbia)
   Sittin' In . . . . (Columbia)
   The Best Of Friends . . . . (Columbia)
Dead Babies
Alice Cooper; *Killer* . . . .(Warner Bros.)
Didn't Leave Nobody But The Baby
Emmylou Harris/Alison Krauss/Gillian Welch; *ST/O Brother, Where Art
Thou?* . . . . (Mercury)
Don't Take The Girl
Tim McGraw; *Not A Moment Too Soon* . . . . (Curb)
   Tim McGraw's Greatest Hits . . . . (Curb)
Every Night When The Sun Goes In
Jo Stafford; *Jo Plus Blues* . . . .(Corinthian)
Feet Up (Pat Him On The Po-Po)
Guy Mitchell; *Definitive Guy Mitchell* . . . . (Collector's Choice)
Free
Phish; *Billy Breathes* . . . . (Elektra)
Get Born Again
Alice In Chains; *Nothing Safe* . . . . (Columbia)
Goodnight Moon
Shivaree; *I Oughtta Give You A Shot* . . . . (Capitol)
Hand That Rocks The Cradle
Glen Campbell; *Country Classics-#10-1987-C* . . . . (Universal)
   Still Within The Sound Of My Voice . . . .(MCA)
Hand That Rocks The Cradle
Smiths; *Smiths* . . . . (Sire)
He Would Be Sixteen
Michelle Wright; *Now & Then* . . . . (Arista)
Hero Of The Day
Metallica; *Load* . . . . (Elektra)
High Hopes And Empty Pockets
McBride & The Ride; *McBride & The Ride* . . . .(MCA)
I Was Born
Kenny Rankin; *Like A Seed* . . . .(Little David)
I Was Born A Dreamer
Mickey Gilley; *Live At Gilley's* . . . .(Epic)
   ST/Tough Enough . . . . (Liberty)
I Was Born About Ten Thousand Years Ago
Elvis Presley; *Elvis Now* . . . . (RCA)
Odetta; *Odetta-Live* . . . . (Fantasy)
I Was Born When You Kissed Me
Whispers; *Excellence* . . . .(Allegiance)
   Shhhh . . . . (Dore)
I Wasn't Born Yesterday
Daryl Hall; *Three Hearts In The Happy Ending Machine* . . . . (RCA)
I Wasn't Born Yesterday
Allan Clarke; *I Wasn't Born Yesterday* . . . .(Atlantic)
I Wasn't Born Yesterday
Safire; *I Wasn't Born Yesterday* . . . . (Mercury)
If I Were A Carpenter
Bobby Darin; *Live At The Desert Inn* . . . . (Motown)
Four Tops; *Compact Command Performances-Four Tops* . . . . (Motown)
   Four Tops Reach Out . . . . (Motown)
   Four Tops-Anthology . . . . (Motown)
Johnny Cash & June Carter; *The Man In Black-His Greatest Hits* . . . . . (Legacy)
Tim Hardin; *Memorial Album* . . . . (Polydor)
If You Don't Wanna Get Pregnant
U.T.F.O.; *Bag It & Bone It* . . . . (Jive)
Isn't She Lovely
Keb' Mo'; *Big Wide Grin* . . . . (Sony Wonder)
Lee Ritenour; *Best Of Lee Ritenour* . . . .(Epic)
Stevie Wonder; *Original Musiquarium* . . . . (Motown)
   Songs In The Key Of Life . . . . (Motown)
It's A Boy
Who; *Tommy* . . . .(MCA)

Jaded
Aerosmith; *Just Push Play* . . . . (Columbia)
   Now That's What I Call Music!-#7-C . . . .(Virgin)
Jungle, The
Kiss; *Carnival Of Souls: The Final Sessions* . . . . (Mercury)
Just The Two Of Us
Will Smith; *Big Willie Style* . . . . (Columbia)
Lightning Crashes
Live; *Throwing Copper* . . . . (Radioactive/MCA)
Lullaby
Tom Rush; *Tom Rush* . . . . (Columbia)
Lullaby For The First Born
Jesse Winchester; *3rd Down 110 To Go* . . . . Rhino)
Mammas Don't Let Your Babies Grow Up To Be Cowboys
Gibson/Miller Band; *Cowboy Super Hits-C* . . . . (Columbia)
   ST/The Cowboy Way . . . . (Epic)
Waylon Jennings & Willie Nelson; *Waylon & Willie* . . . . (RCA)
   Waylon Jennings & Willie Nelson's Greatest Hits . . . . (RCA)
Willie Nelson; *Greatest Hits (& Some That Will Be)* . . . . (Columbia)
   ST/The Electric Horseman . . . . (Columbia)
   Willie & Family Live . . . . (Columbia)
Mockingbird
Carly Simon & James Taylor; *Best Of Carly Simon & James Taylor* . . . (Elektra)
   Hotcakes . . . . (Elektra)
Inez Foxx with Charlie Foxx; *Billboard Top R&B Hits-1963-C* . . . . . (Original Sound)
   Oldies But Goodies-#8-C . . . .(Original Sound)
   Super Oldies Of The '60s-#4-C . . . . (Audio Fidelity)
Peter, Paul & Mary; *Peter, Paul & Mommy* . . . . (Warner Bros.)
My Baby Needs A Shepherd
Emmylou Harris; *Red Dirt Girl* . . . .(Nonesuch)
My Baby You
Marc Anthony; *Marc Anthony* . . . . (Columbia)
My Baby's Arms
John Steel; *Music From The New York Stage (1890-1920)-#4-1917-
1920-C* . . . .(Pearl)
Newborn Friend
Seal; *Seal 2* . . . .(Sire)
Oklahoma Hills
Arlo Guthrie; *Tribute To Woody Guthrie-C* . . . . (Warner Bros.)
Hank Thompson; *Hank Thompson's All-Time Greatest Hits* . . . .(Curb)
Jack Guthrie and his Oklahomans; *Birth Of A Dream-Capitol's Early
Hits-C* . . . . (Capitol)
   Great Records Of The Decade-'40s-Country-C . . . . (Curb)
Kay Starr; *Kay Starr-Country* . . . .(Crescendo)
Oldest Baby In The World
John Prine; *Aimless Love* . . . .(Oh Boy)
   Great Days-Anthology . . . . (Rhino)
   John Prine-Live . . . . (Oh Boy)
One's On The Way (Here In Topeka)
Loretta Lynn; *Loretta Lynn-20 Greatest Hits* . . . . (MCA)
   Loretta Lynn-Greatest Hits Live . . . . (K-Tel)
   Loretta Lynn's Greatest Hits-#2 . . . . (MCA)
   The Country Music Hall Of Fame-Loretta Lynn . . . . (MCA)
Other Side Of The Game
Erykah Badu; *Baduizm* . . . . (Kedar Entert./Universal)
Papa Don't Preach
Madonna; *Immaculate Collection* . . . .(Sire)
   Royal Box . . . .(Sire)
   True Blue . . . .(Sire)
Pill, The
Loretta Lynn; *Loretta Lynn-20 Greatest Hits* . . . . (MCA)
   The Country Music Hall Of Fame-Loretta Lynn . . . . (MCA)
Pregnant Again
Loretta Lynn; *45-#41185* . . . . (MCA)
Pretty Baby
Al Jolson; *The Al Jolson Story-#2* . . . . (MCA)
Leon Redbone; *Sugar* . . . .(Private Music)
Pretty Baby
Five Satins; *Five Satins Sing Their Greatest Hits* . . . . (Collectables)
Pretty Baby
Kool & The Gang; *As One* . . . .(De-Lite)
Ready Or Not
Jackson Browne; *For Everyman* . . . .(Asylum)
Rebecca Lynn
Bryan White; *Bryan White* . . . .(Asylum)
Rock A Bye Your Baby With A Dixie Melody
Al Jolson; *Best Of Al Jolson* . . . . (MCA)
   Jolson Sang 'Em . . . .(Biograph)
   Music From The New York Stage (1890-1920)-#4-1917-1920-C . . . . . .(Pearl)
   The Al Jolson Story-#1 . . . . (MCA)
Jerry Lewis; *Just Sings* . . . . (Razor & Tie)
Judy Garland; *Judy Garland-At Carnegie Hall* . . . . (Capitol)
   Miss Show Business . . . . (Capitol)
   One & Only . . . . (Capitol)
Scream Like A Baby
David Bowie; *Scary Monsters* . . . . (Rykodisc)
Shimmer
Shawn Mullins; *Songs From Dawson's Creek* . . . . (Sony Music Soundtrax)

Soul's Core . . . . (Columbia)

Shortenin' Bread
Andrews Sisters; *50th Anniversary Collection-#2*. . . . . (MCA)
Original Soundtrack; *Children's Favorites* . . . . (Kid Rhino/Rhino 4 Kids)
Sam McNeil/Dent Wimmer/Others; *Old Originals-#2* . . . . (Rounder)
Sonny Terry; *Folkways Years-1944-1963* . . . .(Smithsonian Folkways)

So Much To Say
Dave Matthews Band; *Crash* . . . . (RCA)

Something In Red
Lorrie Morgan; *Lorrie Morgan's Greatest Hits* . . . .(BNA)
Something In Red . . . . (RCA)
To Get To You-Greatest Hits Collection . . . . (BNA)

Space Baby
Tubes; *Tubes* . . . . (A&M)

Spirit Of A Boy, Wisdom Of A Man
Randy Travis; *Big Country Hits '99-C* . . . . (K-Tel)
You And You Alone . . . . (DreamWorks/SKG)

Sweet Baby James
James Taylor; *James Taylor's Greatest Hits* . . . . (Warner Bros.)
Sweet Baby James . . . . (Warner Bros.)

Sweet Baby James
Highway 101; *Paint The Town* . . . . (Warner Bros.)

Take Me There
Blackstreet & Mya featuring Mase & Blinky Blink;
Finally . . . . (Lil' Man/Interscope)
Now That's What I Call Music!-#2-C . . . .(Virgin)
ST/Rugrats . . . . (Interscope)

Tennessee Born & Bred
Eddie Rabbitt; *Jersey Boy* . . . . (Capitol)

Test Tube Babies
Skids; *Scared To Dance* . . . .(Blue Plate)

The Day (That You Gave Me A Son)
Babyface; *The Day* . . . . (Epic)

There Is A Sucker Born Ev'ry Minute
Cy Coleman; *Presents Barnum* . . . . (Bainbridge)

This Woman's Work
Kate Bush; *Sensual World* . . . .(Columbia)
ST/She's Having A Baby . . . . (I.R.S.)

Three Bells, The
Browns; *Billboard Top Country Hits-1959-C* . . . . (Rhino)
Nipper's Greatest Hits Of The '50s-#1-C . . . . (RCA)

Tiger
Paula Cole; *This Fire* . . . . (Imago)

To Zion
Lauryn Hill featuring Carlos Santana; *The Miseducation Of
Lauryn Hill* . . . . (Ruffhouse/Columbia)

Triplets
Fred Astaire/Nanette Fabray/Jack Buchanan; *ST/Band Wagon* . . . . (MCA)
Original Cast; *Forbidden Broadway* . . . .(DRG)

Two People Fell In Love
Brad Paisley; *Brad Paisley-Part II* . . . .(Arista)

Two Teardrops
Steve Wariner; *Two Teardrops* . . . . (Capitol)

Unborn Heart
Dan Hill; *Real Love* . . . .(Columbia)

War Baby
''C'' Company & Terry Nelson; *Wake Up America* . . . .(Plantation)

War Baby Son Of Zorro
Daryl Hall & John Oates; *War Babies* . . . . (Atlantic)

When My Baby Smiles At Me
Pete Fountain; *Best Of Pete Fountain* . . . . (MCA)
Ted Lewis & His Orchestra; *Music From The New York Stage (1890-1920)-
#4-1917-1920-C* . . . . (Pearl)

While You Loved Me
Rascal Flatts; *Rascal Flatts* . . . . (Lyric Street)

Why Was I Born
Billie Holiday; *Quintessential-#3-1936-1937* . . . . (Columbia)
Elisabeth Welch; *Elisabeth Welch Sings Jerome Kern* . . . .(RCA)
Frank Sinatra; *Voice: The Columbia Years-1943-1952* . . . . (Columbia)
Lena Horne; *20 Golden Pieces Of Lena Horne* . . . . (Bulldog)
The Lady . . . . (Dunhill Compact Classics)

With Arms Wide Open
Creed; *Human Clay* . . . .(Wind-up)
Now That's What I Call Music!-#6-C . . . .(Virgin)

With You I'm Born Again
Billy Preston & Syreeta; *15 Of Motown's Greatest Love Songs* . . . . . (Motown)
Endless Love-Motown's Greatest Love Songs-C . . . . (Motown)
Hard-To-Find Motown Classics-#2-C . . . . (Motown)
Motown Story-First 25 Years-#3-C . . . . (Motown)

You Don't Have To Be A Baby To Cry
Caravelles; *Best Of The Girl Groups-#1-C* . . . . (Rhino)
Sensational '60s-#5-C . . . . (Dominion Entert.)
Tennessee Ernie Ford; *The Ultimate Tennessee Ernie Ford* . . . . . .(Razor & Tie)

You Must Have Been A Beautiful Baby
Bobby Darin; *Splish Splash-Best Of Bobby Darin-#1* . . . . (Atlantic)
Johnny Mercer; *Johnny Mercer Sings Johnny Mercer* . . . .(Everest)
Russ Morgan & His Orchestra; *Russ Morgan & His Orchestra Play 22
Original Big Band Recordings* . . . . (Hindsight)

See Also: **ALCOHOL: RECOVERING ALCOHOLIC, HAPPINESS,
HELP, LOVE (various), MOTIVATION, PAIN & HEALING**

(Your Love Keeps Lifting Me) Higher And Higher
Bette Midler; *Bette Midler* . . . . (Atlantic)
Bonnie Bramlett; *It's Time* . . . .(Capricorn)
Jackie Wilson; *Billboard Top R&B Hits-1967-C* . . . .(Rhino)
Jackie Wilson's Greatest Hits . . . . (Brunswick)
Jackie Wilson's Greatest Hits-#2 . . . .(Brunswick)
Reet Petite-Best Of Jackie Wilson . . . .(Columbia)
The Jackie Wilson Story . . . . (Epic)
Very Best Of Jackie Wilson . . . . (Rhino)
Rita Coolidge; *Anytime...Anywhere* . . . . (A&M)
Havana Jam . . . .(Columbia)
Rita Coolidge-Classics-#5 . . . . (A&M)
Rita Coolidge's Greatest Hits . . . . (A&M)

Almost Doesn't Count
Brandy; *Never Say Never* . . . . (Atlantic)
Totally Hits-#1-C . . . . (Arista)

Almost Over You
Sheena Easton; *Best Of Sheena Easton* . . . . (EMI)
Sheena Easton's Greatest Hits . . . .(EMI Special Markets)
The World Of Sheena Easton: The Singles Collection-C . . . . (EMI)

Alright Already
Larry Stewart; *Down The Road* . . . . (RCA)

Angeline Is Coming Home
Badlees; *River Songs* . . . .(Atlas)

Back On My Feet Again
Babys; *Babys-Anthology* . . . .(Chrysalis)
Union Jacks . . . .(Chrysalis)

Back On My Feet Again
Furry Lewis; *Back On My Feet Again* . . . . (Prestige)
Shake 'Em On Down . . . .(Fantasy)

Back On My Feet Again
Randy Newman; *Good Old Boys* . . . . (Reprise)

Back On Top
Van Morrison; *Back On Top* . . . . (Point Blank/Virgin)

Better Days
Bruce Springsteen; *Bruce Springsteen's Greatest Hits* . . . .(Columbia)
Lucky Town . . . .(Columbia)

BFD
Kathy Mattea; *The Innocent Years* . . . .(Mercury)

Bright Lights And Country Music
Bill Anderson; *Bill Anderson's Greatest Hits* . . . . (MCA)

Broken Wing
Martina McBride; *Evolution* . . . . (RCA)

Brokenhearted
Brandy featuring Wanya Morris; *Brandy* . . . . (Atlantic)

Burnin' Old Memories With A Brand New Flame
Kathy Mattea; *Country Hits 4: Sweet Country-C* . . . . (Priority)
Willow In The Wind . . . .(Mercury)

Did I Do That?
Mariah Carey; *Rainbow* . . . .(Columbia)

Don't Feel Like Cryin'
Abra Moore; *Strangest Places* . . . .(Arista Austin)

Down To My Last Teardrop
Tanya Tucker; *Tanya Tucker's Greatest Hits-1990-1992* . . . .(Capitol)
What Do I Do With Me . . . . (Capitol)

Downtime
Jo Dee Messina; *Burn* . . . . (Warner Bros.)

Downtown
B-52's; *B-52's* . . . . (Warner Bros.)
Frank Sinatra; *Strangers In The Night* . . . .(Reprise)
Petula Clark; *Dick Clark's 21 All-Time Hits-#2-C* . . . . (Original Sound)
Petula Clark's Greatest Hits . . . . (Crescendo)

Everyday Is A Winding Road
Sheryl Crow; *1998 Grammy Nominees-C* . . . . (MCA)
Sheryl Crow . . . .(A&M)

Eye Of The Tiger
Survivor; *Eye Of The Tiger* . . . .(Scotti Bros.)
Frankenstein & Other Rock Monsters-C . . . .(CBS Associated)
Rocky Story-C . . . . (Scotti Bros.)
ST/Rocky III . . . .(EMI)

Fast As You
Dwight Yoakam; *This Time* . . . . (Reprise)

Feelin' Good About Feelin' Bad
Patty Loveless; *When Fallen Angels Fly* . . . .(Epic)

Free Girl Now
Tom Petty And The Heartbreakers; *Echo* . . . .(Warner Bros.)

From The Ashes
Martina McBride; *Emotion* . . . . (RCA)

From The Ashes
Rosanne Cash; *The Wheel* . . . . (Columbia)

Girl's Gotta Do (What A Girl's Gotta Do)
Mindy McCready; *Ten Thousand Angels* . . . .(BNA)

Go On
George Strait; *George Strait* . . . .(MCA)
Gonna Find Me A Bluebird
Frank Ifield; *Best Of Frank Ifield* . . . . (Curb)
Marvin Rainwater; *Greatest Hits-1957-C* . . . . (Deluxe)
Only Country-1955-1959-C . . . . (JCI Assoc. Labels)
Royal Wade Kimes; *ST/Traveller* . . . . (Asylum)
Gonna Get Along Without Ya Now
Patience & Prudence; *Lost Hits Of The 50's-C* . . . . (EMI Special Markets)
Gonna Get Along Without You Now
Maureen McGovern; *Baby I'm Yours* . . . .(RCA Victor)
Skeeter Davis; *Essential Skeeter Davis* . . . . (RCA)
Halfway Down
Patty Loveless; *When Fallen Angels Fly* . . . .(Epic)
Happy Days Are Here Again
Barbra Streisand; *A Happening In Central Park* . . . . (Columbia)
Barbra Streisand's Greatest Hits . . . . (Columbia)
One Voice . . . . (Columbia)
The Barbra Streisand Album . . . . (Columbia)
Leo Reisman & His Orchestra; *Nipper's Greatest Hits Of The
'30s-#1-C* . . . . (RCA)
How Was I To Know
Reba McEntire; *Forever Reba* . . . . (Universal)
What If It's You . . . .(MCA)
I Can See Clearly Now
Gladys Knight & The Pips; *Gladys Knight & The Pips'
Greatest Hits* . . . . (Buddah)
Imagination . . . . (Right Stuff)
On & On . . . . (Fifty One West)
Johnny Nash; *Billboard Top Rock 'N' Roll Hits-1972-C* . . . . (Rhino)
Rock Artifacts-From The Vaults-#2-C . . . . (Legacy)
I Didn't Know My Own Strength
Lorrie Morgan; *Lorrie Morgan's Greatest Hits* . . . . (BNA)
Reflections-Limited Edition Greatest Hits . . . . (BNA)
I Wanna Be Free
Loretta Lynn; *Loretta Lynn's Greatest Hits-#2* . . . . (MCA)
I Will Love Again
Lara Fabian; *Lara Fabian* . . . . (Columbia)
I Will Survive
Gloria Gaynor; *Billboard Top Hits-1979-C* . . . . (Rhino)
I Am Woman-C . . . . (Nick At Nite)
Love Tracks . . . . (Polydor)
The Disco Years-#2-On The Beat-1978-1982-C . . . . (Rhino)
I Won't Cry Anymore
Etta James; *These Foolish Things-The Classic Balladry Of Etta James* . . .(MCA)
Marvin Gaye; *Romantically Yours* . . . . (Columbia)
I'll Stick Around
Foo Fighters; *Foo Fighters* . . . .(Roswell/RCA)
I'm Alright
Kim Richey; *Bitter Sweet* . . . . (Mercury)
I'm Still Alive
Trisha Yearwood; *Real Live Woman* . . . .(MCA)
I'm Still Standing
Elton John; *Elton John's Greatest Hits-1976-1986* . . . .(MCA)
Too Low For Zero . . . .(MCA)
It Wouldn't Hurt To Have Wings
Mark Chesnutt; *Wings* . . . . (Decca)
It's Not Right But It's Okay
Whitney Houston; *My Love Is Your Love* . . . . (Arista)
Just My Luck
Kim Richey; *Kim Richey* . . . . (Mercury)
Land Of The Living
Pam Tillis; *Pam Tillis' Greatest Hits* . . . . (Arista)
Letting Go
Sozzi; *Songs From Dawson's Creek* . . . . (Sony Music Soundtrax)
Life Goes On
Little Texas; *Little Texas' Greatest Hits* . . . .(Warner Bros.)
Like There Ain't No Yesterday
BlackHawk; *Strong Enough* . . . . (Arista)
The Hits-Love & Gravity . . . . (Arista)
Lonely
Britney Spears; *Britney* . . . . (Jive)
Lost In Love
Air Supply; *Air Supply's Greatest Hits* . . . . (Arista)
Air Supply-The Definitive Collection . . . . (Arista)
Lost In Love . . . . (Arista)
Lost In Love: Dream 2-C . . . . (Madacy)
Rock On 1980-C . . . . (Madacy)
Love Working On You
John Michael Montgomery; *Leave A Mark* . . . . (Atlantic)
Moment To Myself
Macy Gray; *On How Life Is* . . . .(Epic)
Mourning
Tantric; *Tantric* . . . .(Maverick)
Myself Without You
Reba McEntire; *Reba McEntire's Greatest Hits-#3: I'm A Survivor* . . . . .(MCA)
New Attitude
Patti LaBelle; *Classic Soul-C* . . . .(MCA)

I Am Woman-C . . . .(Nick At Nite)
Soundtrack Smashes-'80s & More-C . . . . (MCA)
ST/Beverly Hills Cop . . . . (MCA)
Plop, Plop, Fizz, Fizz (Alka-Seltzer)
Original Soundtrack; *TeeVee Toons-The Commercials-#1-C* . . . . (TVT)
Red Rubber Ball
Cyrkle; *Even More Nuggets-C* . . . . (Rhino)
Pop Classics Of The '60s-C . . . . (Columbia)
Red Rubber Ball (A Collection) . . . . (Columbia)
Second Wind
Darryl Worley; *Hard Rain Don't Last* . . . .(DreamWorks/SKG)
She Won't Be Lonely Long
Lee Roy Parnell; *Hits And Highways Ahead* . . . . (Arista)
She's Gonna Make It
Garth Brooks; *Sevens* . . . . (Capitol)
Shine
Amel Larrieux; *Infinite Possibilities* . . . . (Epic)
So Good
Destiny's Child; *The Writing's On The Wall* . . . . (Columbia)
Soon
LeAnn Rimes; *I Need You* . . . . (Curb)
Special
Garbage; *Now That's What I Call Music!-#3-C* . . . .(Virgin)
Version 2.0 . . . . (Almo Sounds)
Stronger
Britney Spears; *Now That's What I Call Music!-#6-C* . . . .(Virgin)
Oops!...I Did It Again. . . . .(Jive)
Survivor
Destiny's Child; *Now That's What I Call Music!-#7-C* . . . .(Virgin)
Survivor . . . . (Columbia)
That's Enough Of That
Mila Mason; *That's Enough Of That* . . . .(Atlantic)
That's The Way I Feel
Faron Young; *45-#4050* . . . . (Capitol)
'Til I Can Make It On My Own
Faith Hill; *Tammy Wynette...Remembered-C* . . . . (Asylum)
Kenny Rogers & Dottie West; *Kenny Rogers-Classics* . . . . (EMI)
Kenny Rogers-Twenty Greatest Hits . . . . (EMI)
Tammy Wynette; *Tammy Wynette's Greatest Hits-#4* . . . . (Epic)
Tears Of Fire-25th Anniversary Collection . . . . (Epic)
'Til I Can Make It On My Own . . . . (Epic)
Time Changes Everything
Bob Wills & His Texas Playboys; *Bob Wills & His Texas Playboys-
Anthology 1935-1973* . . . . (Rhino)
Columbia Country Classics-#1-Golden Age-C . . . . (Columbia)
Essential Bob Wills & His Texas Playboys-1935-1973 . . . . (Legacy)
Roy Rogers; *The Country Music Hall Of Fame-Roy Rogers* . . . . (MCA)
Too Gone Too Long
Randy Travis; *Always & Forever* . . . . (Warner Bros.)
Great Divorce Songs For Him-C . . . . (Warner Bros.)
Randy Travis' Greatest Hits-#1 . . . . (Warner Bros.)
Where Were You When I Needed You
Bangles; *Bangles' Greatest Hits* . . . . (Columbia)
Grass Roots; *Grass Roots-All-Time Greatest Hits* . . . . (MCA)
Grass Roots-Anthology (1966-1975) . . . . (Rhino)
Whiskey Under The Bridge
Brooks & Dunn; *Brooks & Dunn-The Greatest Hits Collection* . . . . . . (Arista)
Waitin' On Sundown . . . . (Arista)
Without You
Audrey Hepburn; *ST/My Fair Lady* . . . . (Columbia)
Julie Andrews/Original Cast; *My Fair Lady* . . . . (Columbia)
Original Cast; *My Fair Lady* . . . .(London)
You Can Feel Bad
Patty Loveless; *Patty Loveless-Classics* . . . . (Epic)
Super Hits Of 1996-C . . . . (Epic)
The Trouble With The Truth . . . . (Epic)

BAD, Being Bad, Evil, Mean, Misbehavior, Sin, Terrible
*See Also: ANGER, DANGER & DISASTER, DEVILS, GOOD, HATE,
HELL, MISTAKES, MISTREATMENT, SLEAZY, TROUBLE*

7 Deadly Sins
Traveling Wilburys; *Traveling Wilburys-Vol. 3* . . . . (Wilbury/Warner Bros.)
7 Deadly Sins
Mary's Danish; *Circa* . . . . (Morgan Creek)
Ac-Cent-Tchu-Ate The Positive
Andrews Sisters; *Andrews Sisters Greatest Hits* . . . .(Curb)
Bing Crosby; *Bing Crosby's Greatest Hits* . . . . (MCA)
Original Soundtrack; *ST/Bugsy* . . . . (Epic)
American Bad Ass
Kid Rock; *History Of Rock* . . . . (Top Dog/Lava/Atlantic)
Angels Love Bad Men
Barbara Mandrell; *Sure Feels Good* . . . . (EMI)
Barbara Mandrell & Waylon Jennings; *Country Duets Two By
Two-C* . . . . (Capitol)

Awful
Hole; *Celebrity Skin*....................................(David Geffen Co.)
Baby Did A Bad Thing
Chris Isaak; *Forever Blue* ....(Reprise)
ST/Eyes Wide Shut ....(Reprise)
Bad
Michael Jackson; *Bad* .... (Epic)
Bad America
Gun Club; *Las Vegas Story* ....(I.R.S.)
Bad Bad Sign
Joe Cocker; *One Night Of Sin* ....(Capitol)
Bad Blood
Neil Sedaka; *Billboard Top Rock 'N' Roll Hits-1975-C* ....(Rhino)
Bad Blood
Babylon A.D.; *Nothing Sacred* ....(Arista)
Bad Blood
Exile; *Still Standing*..(Arista)
Bad Boy
Beatles; *Beatles VI*..(Capitol)
Beatles-Box Set...(Capitol)
Past Masters-Volume One ....(Parlophone)
Rock 'N' Roll Music ....(Capitol)
Bad Boy
Eddie Taylor; *Antone's Bringing You The Best In Blues* .... (Antone's)
Bad Boy
Ringo Starr; *Bad Boy* .... (Epic)
Bad Boy
Eric Clapton; *Eric Clapton* ....(Polydor)
Bad Boy
Eddie Money; *Nothing To Lose* ....(Columbia)
Bad Boy
Miami Sound Machine; *Primitive Love*.........................(Epic)
Bad Boy
Ray Parker Jr.; *Ray Parker Jr.'s Greatest Hits* ....(Arista)
Bad Boy For Life
P. Diddy & The Bad Boy Family; *The Saga Continues* .... (Bad Boy/Arista)
Totally Hits 2001-C ....(Arista)
Bad Boy/Having A Party
Luther Vandross; *Best Of Luther Vandross...The Best Of Love*.......... (Epic)
Forever For Always For Love................................ (Epic)
Bad Boys
Inner Circle; *Bad Boys*.....................................(Big Beat)
Bad Boys Running Wild
Scorpions; *Love At First Sting* ....(Mercury)
Wold Wide Live ....(Mercury)
Bad Boyz
Crosby, Stills & Nash; *After The Storm*.....................(Atlantic)
Bad Boyz
Shyne featuring Levy, Barrington; *Shyne* .... (Bad Boy/Arista)
Bad Brahma Bull
Chris LeDoux; *Old Cowboy Classics* ....(Capitol)
Sing Me A Song Mr. Rodeo Man..............................(Capitol)
Tex Ritter; *An American Legend* ....(Capitol)
Best Of Tex Ritter ....(Capitol)
Bad Brakes
Cat Stevens; *Back To Earth* ....(A&M)
Bad Case Of Lovin' You
Robert Palmer; *Addictions-#1* ....(Island)
Secrets ....(Island)
Bad Day
Fuel; *Now That's What I Call Music!-#8-C*...................(Virgin)
Something Like Human....................................(Epic)
Bad Friday
Eek-A-Mouse; *Assassinator* .... (Real Authentic Sound)
Bad Girl
Jon B.; *Cool Relax*.....................................(Yab Yum/550)
Bad Girls
Donna Summer; *Bad Girls* ....(Casablanca)
Dance Collection ....(Casablanca)
On The Radio-Greatest Hits-Volumes I & II.................(Casablanca)
Summer Collection ....(Mercury)
Walk Away-Best Of Donna Summer-1977-1980.................(Casablanca)
Bad Habits & Infections
Daryl Hall & John Oates; *Beauty On A Back Street* ....(RCA)
Bad Loser
Joy Lynn White; *Wild Love* ....(Columbia)
Bad Love
Eric Clapton; *24 Nights* ....(Duck/Reprise)
Journeyman ....(Duck/Reprise)
Bad Luck
Harold Melvin And The Blue Notes; *Harold Melvin And The Blue Notes-*
Collector's Item.....................................(Philadelphia Int'l)
Harold Melvin And The Blue Notes-Vol. 12 ....(Philadelphia Int'l)
Philadelphia Classics-C ....(Philadelphia Int'l)
Bad Luck
B.B. King; *B.B. King-16 Original Big Hits* ....(Fantasy)
Bad Luck Streak In Dancing School
Warren Zevon; *Bad Luck Streak In Dancing School* .... (Asylum)

Bad Magik
Godsmack; *Awake* .... (Republic/Universal)
Bad Man
R. Kelly; *I Wish (import EP)* ....(Jive)
Bad Medicine
Bon Jovi; *New Jersey*.....................................(Jambco)
Bad Moon Rising
Creedence Clearwater Revival; *1969*.........................(Fantasy)
Creedence Clearwater Revival-Chronicle ....(Fantasy)
Creedence Clearwater Revival-Gold ....(Fantasy)
Green River..(Fantasy)
Live In Europe ....(Fantasy)
Bad News
Johnny Winter; *About Blues*.................................(Janus)
Before The Storm..(Janus)
Bad News
Emmylou Harris; *Ballad Of Sally Rose* ....(Warner Bros.)
Bad Of The Heart
George LaMond; *Bad Of The Heart*...........................(Columbia)
Bad Religion
Godsmack; *Godsmack* .... (Republic/Universal)
Bad Shark
Rick Dees And His Cast Of Idiots; *Original Disco Duck*.............(RSO)
Bad Side Of The Moon
Elton John; *11-17-70* .... (Polydor)
Bad Sneakers
Steely Dan; *Katy Lied*.....................................(MCA)
Steely Dan's Greatest Hits ....(MCA)
Bad Thing
Cry Of Love; *Brother*.....................................(Columbia)
Bad To Me
Billy J. Kramer With The Dakotas; *History Of British Rock-#1-C*......(Rhino)
Rock Is Dead But It Won't Lie Down-C....................(Gold Rush)
Bad To The Bone
George Thorogood & The Destroyers; *Bad To The Bone*..............(EMI)
Bad Whiskey
Lightnin' Hopkins; *Low Down Dirty Blues* ....(Mainstream)
Bad, Bad Leroy Brown
Jim Croce; *Billboard Top Rock 'N' Roll Hits-1973-C*...............(Rhino)
Down The Highway.......................................(Atlantic)
Life & Times ....(Lifesong)
Photographs & Memories/His Greatest Hits ....(Atlantic)
Behind Blue Eyes
Who; *Hooligans*...(MCA)
Join Together ....(MCA)
Who's Last...(MCA)
Who's next...(MCA)
Best I Ever Had (Grey Sky Morning)
Vertical Horizon; *Everything You Want*......................(RCA)
Betty's Bein' Bad
Sawyer Brown; *Best Of Country Rock-C*......................(K-Tel)
Sawyer Brown's Greatest Hits ....(Curb)
Shakin' ....(Curb)
Big Bad Bill Is Sweet William Now
Ry Cooder; *Jazz* ....(Warner Bros.)
Big Bad John
Jimmy Dean; *American Originals-Jimmy Dean* ....(Columbia)
Billboard Top Country Hits-1961-C ....(Rhino)
Columbia Country Classics-#3-Americana-C ....(Columbia)
Jimmy Dean's Greatest Hits ....(Columbia)
Billy Got Some Bad News Today
Tom Paxton; *It Ain't Easy* ....(Flying Fish)
Bitch
Rolling Stones; *Made In The Shade*.......................(Rolling Stones)
Sticky Fingers ....(Virgin)
Bittersweet
Fuel; *Sunburn*..(550 Music)
Black Is Black
Los Bravos; *History Of British Rock-#7-C*...................(Rhino)
London Collector-Rock Invasion-C ....(London)
Born To Be Bad
George Thorogood & The Destroyers; *Born To Be Bad*..........(Gold Rush)
ST/Bull Durham ....(Capitol)
Born To Be Bad
Runaways; *Best Of The Runaways*..........................(Mercury)
Born Under A Bad Sign
Albert King; *Atlantic Blues-Guitar-C* ....(Atlantic)
Best Blues Album In The World...Ever!-C...................(Virgin)
Masterworks ....(Atlantic)
Stax Blues Masters-Blue Monday-C ....(Stax)
Booker T. & The M.G.s; *Best Of Booker T. & The M.G.s* ....(Atlantic)
Cream; *Strange Brew-Very Best Of Cream* ....(Polydor)
Wheels Of Fire ....(Polydor)
Jimi Hendrix; *Blues* ....(MCA)
Koko Taylor & Buddy Guy; *Force Of Nature* ....(Alligator)
Paul Butterfield Blues Band; *Paul Butterfield Blues Band-Live*.......(Elektra)
Rita Coolidge; *Rita Coolidge* ....(A&M)
Rita Coolidge's Greatest Hits ....(A&M)
Simpsons; *Simpsons Sing The Blues* ....(Geffen)

Bully, The
May Irwin; *Music From The New York Stage (1890-1920)-#1-1890-1908-C* . . . . (Pearl)
Cannibals
Mark Knopfler; *Golden Heart* . . . .(Warner Bros.)
Captain Hook's Waltz
Original Cast/Cyril Ritchard; *Peter Pan-The 1954 Broadway Production* . . . .(RCA Victor)
Church Of Logic, Sin & Love
Men; *The Men*. . . . . (Polydor)
Criminal
Fiona Apple; *1998 Grammy Nominees-C* . . . .(MCA)
Tidal. . . . .(Clean Slate/Work)
Cruel Little Number
Jeff Healey Band; *Feel This* . . . . (Arista)
Cruel Summer
Ace Of Base; *Cruel Summer*. . . . . (Arista)
Bananarama; *Bananarama* . . . . (London)
Cruel To Be Kind
Nick Lowe; *Basher: Best Of* . . . . (Columbia)
Labour Of Lust. . . . . (Columbia)
Cry For The Bad Man
Lynyrd Skynyrd; *Best Of Lynyrd Skynyrd* . . . . (MCA Special Prod.)
Gimme Back My Bullets. . . . . (MCA)
Delia's Gone
Johnny Cash; *American Recordings* . . . . (American)
Do Right
Jimmie's Chicken Shack; *Bring Your Own Stereo* . . . .(Rocket)
Don't Give Me Bad News
Bobby Caldwell; *Stuck On You*. . . . . (Sin-Drome)
Don't Say Nothing Bad About My Baby
Cookies; *Golden Girl Groups-C*. . . . . (K-Tel)
Original Rock 'N' Roll Hits Of The '60s-C. . . . . (Roulette)
Don't Treat Me Bad
Firehouse; *Firehouse* . . . .(Epic)
Even The Bad Times Are Good
Tremeloes; *Best Of The Tremeloes* . . . . (Rhino)
Evil On Your Mind
Jan Howard; *Grand Ladies Of The Opry-C* . . . . (Deluxe)
Evil Ways
Santana; *Best Of Santana* . . . . (Legacy)
Santana . . . . (Columbia)
Santana's Greatest Hits . . . . (Columbia)
Viva Santana! . . . . (Columbia)
Evil Wind
Bad Company; *Desolation Angels* . . . . (Swan Song)
Evil Woman
Electric Light Orchestra; *Afterglow* . . . .(Epic)
Electric Light Orchestra's Greatest Hits . . . . (Jet)
Face The Music . . . . (Jet)
Ole ELO . . . . (Jet)
Evil Woman
Doobie Brothers; *Captain & Me* . . . .(Warner Bros.)
Failed Christian
Nick Lowe; *Dig My Mood* . . . . (Upstart)
Falling In Love (Is Hard On The Knees)
Aerosmith; *A Little South Of Sanity* . . . .(Geffen)
Nine Lives . . . . (Columbia)
Fat Lip
Sum 41; *All Killer No Filler* . . . . (Island/IDJMG)
Now That's What I Call Music!-#8-C . . . . (Virgin)
Feel So Numb
Rob Zombie; *Sinister Urge*. . . . .(Geffen)
Feelin' Good About Feelin' Bad
Patty Loveless; *When Fallen Angels Fly* . . . .(Epic)
Goin' Down The Road Feeling Bad
Delaney & Bonnie; *Best Of Delaney & Bonnie* . . . . (Rhino)
Doc Watson; *Elementary Doctor Watson*. . . . . (Poppy)
Essential Doc Watson . . . . (Vanguard)
Grateful Dead; *Grateful Dead (Skull & Roses)*. . . . . .(Warner Bros.)
One From The Vault. (Grateful Dead)
Good Girls Go To Heaven
Charlie Floyd; *Charlie Floyd* . . . . (Liberty)
Good News, Bad News
Eddy Raven; *Eddy Raven-Greatest Country Hits* . . . . (Curb)
Good Run Of Bad Luck
Clint Black; *No Time To Kill*. . . . . (RCA)
Good Times Bad Times
Led Zeppelin; *Led Zeppelin* . . . . (Atlantic)
Good Times, Bad Times
Rolling Stones; *12 X 5*. . . . . (Abkco)
Big Hits (High Tide & Green Grass) . . . . (Abkco)
More Hot Rocks (big hits & fazed cookies) . . . . (Abkco)
Singles Collection-The London Years . . . . (Abkco)
Grown Up Wrong
Rolling Stones; *12 X 5*. . . . . (Abkco)
Hard Luck Stories
Richard & Linda Thompson; *Pour Down Like Silver* . . . . (Hannibal)

Hard Luck Story
Elton John; *Rock Of The Westies* . . . . (Polydor)
Hard Luck Woman
Garth Brooks; *Kiss My Ass-C* . . . . (Mercury)
Kiss; *Alive II* . . . . (Casablanca)
Double Platinum . . . . (Mercury)
Rock & Roll Over . . . . (Casablanca)
Hard Rock Bottom Of Your Heart
Randy Travis; *No Holdin' Back* . . . . (Warner Bros.)
Heaven's Just A Sin Away
Kelly Willis; *Hot Country-C* . . . . (MCA Special Prod.)
Kelly Willis . . . . (MCA)
Kendalls; *Best Of The Kendalls* . . . . (Curb)
Kendalls-20 Greatest Hits . . . . (Deluxe)
Hell Ain't A Bad Place To Be
AC/DC; *If You Want Blood You've Got It* . . . . (Atlantic)
Let There Be Rock. . . . . (Atco)
Hey Jude
Beatles; *Beatles 1* . . . . (Capitol)
Beatles-20 Greatest Hits . . . . (Capitol)
Past Masters-Volume Two . . . . (Parlophone)
The Beatles/1967-1970. . . . . (Capitol)
Paul McCartney; *Knebworth-The Album-C* . . . . (Polydor)
Wilson Pickett; *Wilson Pickett's Greatest Hits* . . . . (Atlantic)
Hollywood (Down On Your Luck)
Thin Lizzy; *Lizzy Lives! (1976-1984)* . . . . (Gland Slamm)
Renegade . . . . (Warner Bros.)
Hot & Nasty
Humble Pie; *Best Of Humble Pie*. . . . . (A&M)
Humble Pie-Classics-#14 . . . . (A&M)
Rockin' '60s-C . . . . (Priority)
Smokin'. . . . . (A&M)
Hot & Nasty
Black Oak Arkansas; *Best Of Black Oak Arkansas* . . . . (Atco)
Black Oak Arkansas . . . . (Atco)
Raunch 'N' Roll . . . . (Atco)
House Of The Rising Sun
Animals; *Animals Greatest Hits* . . . . (Allegiance)
Best Of The Animals . . . . (Abkco)
Greatest Hits Live!-Rip It To Shreds. . . . . (I.R.S.)
Hank Williams, Jr.; *Hank Williams, Jr. "Live"* . . . . (WB/Curb)
Ronnie Milsap; *Ronnie Milsap-16 Greatest Hits-#2* . . . .(Trip)
Hurt So Bad
Lettermen; *The Lettermen's All-Time Greatest Hits* . . . . . . (Capitol)
Linda Ronstadt; *Linda Ronstadt's Greatest Hits, Volume Two* . . . . . .(Asylum)
Mad Love . . . . (Elektra)
Little Anthony And The Imperials; *Best Of Little Anthony And The Imperials* . . . . (Rhino)
Best Of Little Anthony And The Imperials . . . . (EMI)
I Don't Worry About A Thing
Mose Allison; *Best Of Mose Allison* . . . . (Rhino)
I Don't Worry About A Thing . . . . (Rhino)
I Feel So Bad
Elvis Presley; *Elvis' Golden Records, Volume 3* . . . .(RCA)
Reconsider Baby. . . . . (RCA)
The Top Ten Hits . . . . (RCA)
Worldwide 50 Gold Award Hits, Vol. 1, Parts 1 & 2 . . . . . . (RCA)
I Got It Bad & That Ain't Good
Duke Ellington; *All Star Road Band* . . . .(Doctor Jazz)
Intimate . . . . (Pablo)
This Is Duke Ellington . . . . (RCA)
Johnny Mathis; *In A Sentimental Mood-Johnny Mathis Sings Ellington* . . . . (Columbia)
I Saved The World Today
Eurythmics; *Peace* . . . . (Arista)
I Wanna Be Bad
Willa Ford; *Totally Hits 2001-C* . . . . (Arista)
Willa Was Here . . . . (Lava)
I Wanna Love Him So Bad
Jelly Beans; *Best Of The Girl Groups-#1-C* . . . . (Rhino)
I Want You Bad (And That Ain't Good)
Collin Raye; *In This Life* . . . . (Epic)
If The Good Die Young
Tracy Lawrence; *Alibis* . . . .(Atlantic)
I'm A Bad, Bad Man
Ethel Merman/Bruce Yarnell/Original Cast; *Annie Get Your Gun* . . . . (RCA Victor)
I'm Bad, I'm Nationwide
ZZ Top; *Deguello* . . . . (Warner Bros.)
I'm Good At Being Bad
TLC; *Fanmail* . . . . (LaFace)
It Goes Like It Goes (Theme From "Norma Rae")
Jennifer Warnes; *Best Of Jennifer Warnes* . . . . (Arista)
The Envelope Please-Academy Award Winning Songs-#4 (1970-1981)-C . . . . (Rhino)
It's A Sin
George Thorogood & The Destroyers; *Bad To The Bone* . . . . . . (EMI)
It's A Sin
Marty Robbins; *Marty Robbins' All-Time Greatest Hits*. . . . . . (Columbia)

It's A Sin
Pet Shop Boys; *Actually* . . . . (EMI)
It's Bad You Know
R.L. Burnside; *The Sopranos-Music From The HBO Original Series* . . . . (Sony Music Soundtrax)
It's No Good
Depeche Mode; *Ultra* . . . . (Mute/Reprise)
It's Not Love (But It's Not Bad)
Merle Haggard & The Strangers; *For The Record: Merle Haggard-43 Legendary Hits* . . . . (BNA)
Jeremy
Pearl Jam; *Ten* . . . . (Epic Portrait Assoc.)
Johnny Too Bad
Slickers; *ST/The Harder They Come* . . . . (Mango)
Taj Mahal; *Best Of Taj Mahal* . . . . (Columbia)
Mo' Roots . . . . (Legacy)
UB40; *Labour Of Love* . . . . (A&M)
Live In Moscow . . . . (A&M)
Just Like Anyone
Soul Asylum; *Let Your Dim Light Shine* . . . . (Columbia)
Let's Roll
Neil Young; *Let's Roll-CD Single* . . . . (Reprise)
Little Old Lady (From Pasadena)
Beach Boys; *Concert/'69-Live In London* . . . . (Capitol)
Jan & Dean; *Best Of Jan & Dean* . . . . (EMI)
Billboard Top Rock 'N' Roll Hits-1964-C . . . . (Rhino)
Dead Man's Curve . . . . (EMI)
Surf City-Best Of Jan & Dean . . . . (EMI)
Living In Sin
Bon Jovi; *New Jersey* . . . . (Jambco)
Lookin' Good But Feelin' Bad
Original Cast; *Ain't Misbehavin'* . . . . (RCA)
Macon Georgia Bad Girl
Jeannie C. Riley; *Jeannie C. Riley & Fancy Friends* . . . . (Plantation)
Make Me Bad
Korn; *Issues* . . . . (Immortal/Epic)
Mama, He Treats Your Daughter Mean
Susan Tedeschi; *Just Won't Burn* . . . . (Tone Cool)
Mean Mama Blues
Bob Wills; *Stay A Little Longer-The Original Columbia Recordings* . . . . (Roswell/RCA)
Mean Mr. Mustard
Beatles; *Abbey Road* . . . . (Parlophone)
Mean Old Frisco
Eric Clapton; *Slowhand* . . . . (Polydor)
Jimmy Witherspoon; *Best Of Jimmy Witherspoon* . . . . . (Prestige)
Mean Old Frisco . . . . (Prestige)
Mean Old World
Bobby Bland & B.B. King; *Together Again Live* . . . . (MCA)
Climax Blues Band; *Climax Chicago Blues Band* . . . . (Sire)
Duane Allman & Eric Clapton; *Duane Allman-An Anthology* . . . . . (Capricorn)
Eric Clapton-Crossroads-C . . . . (Polydor)
Robert Palmer; *Secrets* . . . . (Island)
Missionary Man
Eurythmics; *Eurythmics' Greatest Hits* . . . . (Arista)
Revenge . . . . (RCA)
Nasty
Janet Jackson; *Control* . . . . (A&M)
Nasty Dogs & Funky Kings
ZZ Top; *Fandango* . . . . (Warner Bros.)
Six Pack . . . . (Warner Bros.)
Naughty Girls Need Love Too
Samantha Fox; *Samantha Fox* . . . . (Jive)
Oh Happy Day
Edwin Hawkins Singers; *Didn't It Blow Your Mind: Soul Hits Of The '70s-#1-C* . . . . (Rhino)
Super Hits-#3-C . . . . (Gusto)
Five Satins; *Five Satins Sing Their Greatest Hits* . . . . (Collectables)
One Bad Apple
Osmonds; *Billboard Top Rock 'N' Roll Hits-1971-C* . . . . (Rhino)
One Bad Elephant
Brian Slawson; *Distant Drums* . . . . (Columbia)
Only The Good Die Young
Billy Joel; *Billy Joel-Greatest Hits, Volume I & Volume II* . . . . . (Columbia)
KOHUEPT . . . . (Columbia)
The Stranger . . . . (Columbia)
Perpetual Blues Machine
Keb' Mo'; *Just Like You* . . . . (Okeh)
Rock 'N' Roll Is A Vicious Game
April Wine; *First Glance* . . . . (Capitol)
Saint Of Me
Rolling Stones; *Bridges To Babylon* . . . . (Virgin)
No Security . . . . (Virgin)
Scandalous!
Prince; *ST/Batman* . . . . (Warner Bros.)
Seven Deadly Sins
Bryan Ferry; *Bete Noire* . . . . (Reprise)

She's A Bad Mama Jama
Carl Carlton; *Carl Carlton* . . . . (20th Century Fox)
Sin Wagon
Dixie Chicks; *Fly* . . . . (Monument)
Sincere
Original Cast; *ST/The Music Man* . . . . (Warner Bros.)
Sing A Mean Tune Kid
Chicago; *Chicago At Carnegie Hall* . . . . (Chicago)
Chicago III . . . . (Chicago)
Sinner
Neil Finn; *Try Whistling This* . . . . (Work)
So Sad (To Watch Good Love Go Bad)
Everly Brothers; *The Reunion Concert-Live At Albert Hall 1983* . . . . (Mercury)
Walk Right Back: The Everly Brothers On Warner Bros.-1960-1969 . . . . (Warner Archives)
Frank Ifield; *Best Of Frank Ifield* . . . . (Curb)
Sweethearts Of The Rodeo; *Columbia Country Classics-#5-A New Tradition-C* . . . . (Columbia)
Some Change
Boz Scaggs; *My Time: A Boz Scaggs Anthology-1969-1997* . . . . . (Legacy)
Some Change . . . . (Virgin)
Son Of A Rotten Gambler
Anne Murray; *Anne Murray-Country* . . . . (Capitol)
Anne Murray-Country Hits . . . . (Capitol)
Love Song . . . . (Capitol)
Emmylou Harris; *Cimarron* . . . . (Warner Bros.)
Stone Cold Drag
James Brown; *People* . . . . (Polydor)
Swim
Madonna; *Ray Of Light* . . . . (Maverick)
Thankyou
Dido; *No Angel* . . . . (Arista)
Totally Hits 2001-C . . . . (Arista)
That's The Worst Jello
Chordiac Arrest; *1990 Top 20 Barbershop Quartets: Coney Island Baby-C* . . . . (ISD/Intersound)
This Bitter Earth
Aretha Franklin; *Aretha Franklin Sings The Blues* . . . . . . (Columbia)
Jazz To Soul . . . . (Columbia)
Dinah Washington; *Essential Dinah Washington-The Great Songs* . . . . (Verve)
The Unforgettable Dinah Washington . . . . (Mercury)
Two Out Of Three Ain't Bad
Meat Loaf; *Bat Out Of Hell* . . . . (Epic)
Hits Out Of Hell . . . . (Epic)
Want You Bad
Offspring; *Conspiracy Of One* . . . . (Columbia)
When It Hurts So Bad
Lauryn Hill; *The Miseducation Of Lauryn Hill* . . . . (Ruffhouse/Columbia)
Who's Afraid Of The Big Bad Wolf
Barbra Streisand; *Just For The Record* . . . . (Columbia)
The Barbra Streisand Album . . . . (Columbia)
L.L. Cool J; *Simply Mad About The Mouse-C* . . . . (Columbia)
Mormon Tabernacle Choir & Columbia Symphony Orchestra; *When You Wish Upon A Star-A Tribute To Walt Disney* . . . . . . (CBS Masterworks)
Why Does It Hurt So Bad
Whitney Houston; *ST/Waiting To Exhale* . . . . (Arista)
Wicked As It Seems
Keith Richards; *Main Offender* . . . . (Virgin)
Wicked Game
Chris Isaak; *Heart Shaped World* . . . . (Reprise)
ST/Wild At Heart . . . . (Polydor)
Wicked Garden
Stone Temple Pilots; *Core* . . . . (Atlantic)
Wicked Path
Bill Monroe & His Blue Grass Boys; *Essential Bill Monroe-1945-1949* . . . . (Columbia)
Jim & Jesse; *Music Among Friends* . . . . (Rounder)
New Grass Revival; *Commonwealth* . . . . (Flying Fish)
Wicked Rain
Los Lobos; *Just Another Band From East L.A.* . . . . (Slash)
Kiko . . . . (Slash)
Wicked Ways
Patty Loveless; *Patty Loveless* . . . . (MCA)
Wicked World
Rick Parker; *Wicked World* . . . . (Geffen)
Wicked World
Black Sabbath; *Black Sabbath* . . . . (Warner Bros.)
Wicked World
Jimmy Nail; *Growing Up In Public* . . . . (Atlantic)
Winning Ugly
Rolling Stones; *Dirty Work* . . . . (Virgin)
Wiser Time
Black Crowes; *Amorica* . . . . (American)
Worst, The
Rolling Stones; *Voodoo Lounge* . . . . (Virgin)
You Can Feel Bad
Patty Loveless; *Patty Loveless-Classics* . . . . (Epic)
Super Hits Of 1996-C . . . . (Epic)

The Trouble With The Truth..................(Epic)
You Give Love A Bad Name
Bon Jovi; *7800 Degrees Fahrenheit*.................... (Mercury)
Cross Road-14 Classic Grooves................. (Mercury)
You Make Me Feel Bad
Wood; *Songs From Stamford Hill*....................... (Columbia)
Your Good Girl's Gonna Go Bad
Billie Jo Spears; *Best Of Billie Jo Spears*........... (CEMA Special Prod.)
Best Of Billie Jo Spears..................... (Razor & Tie)
K.T. Oslin; *Tammy Wynette...Remembered-C*...................(Asylum)
Tammy Wynette; *Tammy Wynette-Anniversary-20 Years Of Hits*.......(Epic)
Tammy Wynette's Greatest Hits...................(Epic)
Your Good Girl's Gonna Go Bad.................. (Legacy)
Your Selfish Heart
Stanley Brothers & The Clinch Mountain Boys; *Stanley Brothers & The Clinch Mountain Boys*............................... (King)
You've Got It Bad Girl
Quincy Jones; *Best Of Quincy Jones-#2*.......................... (A&M)
Quincy Jones-Classics-#3...................... (A&M)
Stevie Wonder; *Talking Book*............................. (Motown)

BAGGAGE & WEIGHT, Burden, Heavy, Suitcases
See Also: *TRAVELING, TROUBLE*

(Pack Your) Suitcase Blues
Karrin Allyson; *I Didn't Know About You*..................(Concord Jazz)
800 Pound Jesus
Sawyer Brown; *Drive Me Wild*..................................... (Curb)
Bag Lady
Todd Rundgren; *Hermit Of Mink Hollow*..................... (Rhino)
Bag Lady
Erykah Badu; *Mama's Gun*............................... (Motown)
Bag Lady
Robby Krieger; *Versions/Robby Krieger*.....................(One Way)
Baggage
L7; *Hungry For Stink*............................... (Slash)
Baggage
Graham Parker; *Acid Bubblegum*..................... (Razor & Tie)
Baggage Claim
Chip Taylor; *The Port Huron Statement: Home Recordings-1997-1999*............................... (Powerhouse)
Baggage Coach Ahead
Mac Wiseman; *Great American Train Songs-C*...............(C.M.H. Prod.)
The Mac Wiseman Story........................(C.M.H. Prod.)
Wabash Cannonball: 20 Classic Train Songs-C........(C.M.H. Prod.)
Beast Of Burden
Bette Midler; *No Frills*............................. (Atlantic)
Rolling Stones; *Rewind (1971-1984)*..................(Rolling Stones)
Some Girls............................. (Virgin)
Sucking In The Seventies........................(Rolling Stones)
Big Bad John
Jimmy Dean; *American Originals-Jimmy Dean*............... (Columbia)
Billboard Top Country Hits-1961-C.................. (Rhino)
Columbia Country Classics-#3-Americana-C............. (Columbia)
Jimmy Dean's Greatest Hits................. (Columbia)
Brick
Ben Folds Five; *Whatever And Ever Amen*................. (Caroline/550)
Burden In My Hand
Soundgarden; *Down On The Upside*.................... (A&M)
Bushel And A Peck
Andrews Sisters; *Best Of The Andrews Sisters-#2*.................. (MCA)
Original Cast; *Guys & Dolls*..................... (MCA)
Bye Bye Blackbird
Dean Martin; *Swingin' Down Yonder*..................... (Capitol)
Joe Cocker; *With A Little Help From My Friends*.............. (A&M)
Liza Minnelli; *ST/Liza With A ''Z''*..................... (Columbia)
Miles Davis; *Ballads*......................... (Columbia)
Miles Davis Quintet/Jazz Sampler #2.............. (Columbia)
Miles Davis Quintet; *Round About Midnight*.............. (Columbia)
Candy By The Pound
Elton John; *Ice On Fire*.............................(MCA)
Carry That Weight
Beatles; *Abbey Road*............................. (Parlophone)
Carrying Your Love With Me
George Strait; *Carrying Your Love With Me*.................(MCA)
Latest Greatest Straitest Hits.....................(MCA)
Cold Day In July
Dixie Chicks; *Fly*............................. (Monument)
Joy White; *Between Midnight & Hindsight*.................. (Columbia)
Ray Price; *For The Good Times/I Won't Mention It Again*........ (Columbia)
Suzy Bogguss; *Voices In The Wind*......................... (Liberty)
Cumbersome
Seven Mary Three; *American Standard*..................... (Mammoth)
Happy Wanderer
Frank Weir & His Orchestra; *Hits To Remember-C* ... (PolyGram Special Prod.)

Joey Miskulin; *Hooked On Polkas*....................... (K-Tel)
Original Soundtrack; *Disney Travel Songs-C*.................. (Disney)
He Ain't Heavy, He's My Brother
Hollies; *Best Of The Hollies*..................... (EMI)
Best Of The Hollies-#2............................. (EMI)
Chicken Soup For The Soul: I'll Be There For You-Songs Of Friendship, Brotherhood And Sisterhood-C......................(Rhino)
Hollies-Epic Anthology From The Original Master Tapes.......... (Epic)
The Hollies' Greatest Hits..................... (Epic)
Neil Diamond; *Glory Road-1968-1972*.................... (MCA)
Tap Root Manuscript..................... (MCA)
Heavy
Collective Soul; *Dosage*..............................(Atlantic)
Heavy Things
Phish; *Farmhouse*............................. (Elektra)
Hey Jude
Beatles; *Beatles 1*............................. (Capitol)
Beatles-20 Greatest Hits..................... (Capitol)
Past Masters-Volume Two..................... (Parlophone)
The Beatles/1967-1970..................... (Capitol)
Paul McCartney; *Knebworth-The Album-C*................. (Polydor)
Wilson Pickett; *Wilson Pickett's Greatest Hits*..............(Atlantic)
Homeward Bound
Paul Simon; *Paul Simon In Concert/Live Rhymin'*............. (Columbia)
Paul Simon & George Harrison; *Nobody's Child-Romanian Angel Appeal-C*......................... (Warner Bros.)
Simon & Garfunkel; *Collected Works*.................... (Columbia)
Parsley Sage Rosemary & Thyme.................. (Columbia)
Simon & Garfunkel's Greatest Hits.................. (Columbia)
The Concert In Central Park..................... (Warner Bros.)
Willie Nelson & Waylon Jennings; *Take It To The Limit*......... (Columbia)
I Packed My Suitcase, Started To The Train
Memphis Jug Band; *The Story-1927-1934*...................... (EPM)
It's Not My Cross To Bear
Allman Brothers Band; *Allman Brothers Band*.....................(Polydor)
Beginnings.....................(Polydor)
Dreams.....................(Polydor)
Gregg Allman Band; *I'm No Angel*..................... (Epic)
Just Can't Last
Natalie Merchant; *Motherland*..................... (Elektra)
Lay Down Your Burden
Paul Winter; *Common Ground*..................... (A&M)
Lay Down Your Weary Tune
Ashley Hutchings; *The Guv'nor*.....................(Wildcat)
Bob Dylan; *Biograph*..................... (Columbia)
Byrds; *The Byrds*..................... (Columbia)
Turn! Turn! Turn!..................... (Legacy)
Tim O'Brien; *Red On Blonde*.....................(Sugar Hill)
Lay My Burden Down
David ''Honeyboy'' Edwards; *White Windows*......... (Evidence Music)
Furry Lewis; *Blues Magician*.....................(Lucky Seven)
Little Black Backpack
Stroke9; *Nasty Little Thoughts*.....................(Cherry/Universal)
Make The World Go Away
Eddy Arnold; *Best Of Eddy Arnold*..................... (RCA)
Billboard Top Country Hits-1965-C..................... (Rhino)
Eddy Arnold-Pure Gold..................... (RCA)
Nipper's Greatest Hits Of The '60s-#1-C..................... (RCA)
World Of Hits..................... (MGM)
Ray Price; *Ray Price-16 Biggest Hits*..................... (Legacy)
Ray Price-20 Hits..................... (Tee Vee)
Maybe We Should Just Sleep On It
Tim McGraw; *All I Want*..................... (Curb)
Tim McGraw's Greatest Hits..................... (Curb)
One After 909
Beatles; *Let It Be*..................... (Capitol)
The Beatles-Anthology-#1..................... (Capitol)
Pack Up Her Trunk Blues
Tommy Bradley; *Complete Recorded Works-1928-1932*.........(Document)
Pack Up Your Sins And Go To The Devil
Dorothy Loudon; *Broadway Baby*.....................(DRG)
Ella Fitzgerald & Chick Webb; *The Early Years-#1: With Chick Webb & His Orchestra-1935-1938*......................... (GRP)
Pack Up Your Sorrows
Joan Baez; *Best Of Joan Baez*..................... (Vanguard)
Judy Collins; *Judy Collins' Fifth Album*..................... (Elektra)
Mimi & Richard Farina; *Best Of Mimi & Richard Farina*...... (Vanguard)
Greatest Folksingers Of The '60s-C..................... (Vanguard)
Mimi Farina; *Celebrations For A Grey Day*.............. (Vanguard)
Peter, Paul & Mary; *Peter, Paul and Mary Album*.......... (Warner Bros.)
Pack Up Your Troubles In Your Old Kit Bag (And Smile, Smile, Smile)
James F. Harrison & Knickerbocker Quartet; *78-#2181*.......... (Columbia)
Pack Your Lies And Go
Celinda Pink; *Victimized*.....................(Step One)
Pack'd My Bags
Rufus; *Rufusized*..................... (MCA)
Stompin' At The Savoy..................... (Warner Bros.)
Packed Up And Left
Mac McAnally; *Mac McAnally*.....................(DreamWorks/SKG)

Packed Up And Took My Mind
Little Milton; *Tin Pan Alley* . . . . (Stax)
Packin' Trunk Blues
Leadbelly; *King Of The 12-String Guitar* . . . .(Legacy)
   Leadbelly . . . .(Columbia)
   The Slide Guitar-Bottles Knives & Steel-C . . . .(Legacy)
Sixteen Tons
Cactus Brothers; *Cactus Brothers* . . . .(Liberty)
Tennessee Ernie Ford; *Best Of Tennessee Ernie Ford-16 Tons Of
   Boogie* . . . . (Rhino)
   Capitol Collectors Series-Tennessee Ernie Ford . . . . (Capitol)
   When AM Was King-C . . . .(Capitol)
Weavers; *Weavers' Greatest Hits* . . . .(Vanguard)
Sixteen Tons
Stevie Wonder; *Down To Earth* . . . . (Motown)
Stairway To Heaven
O'Jays; *Family Reunion* . . . .(Philadelphia Int'l)
   O'Jays' Greatest Hits . . . .(Philadelphia Int'l)
   O'Jays-Collector's Item . . . .(Philadelphia Int'l)
Suitcase
Badfinger; *Best Of Badfinger* . . . .(Capitol)
   Straight Up . . . . (Apple)
Suitcase
Justin Hayward; *Night Flight* . . . . (Polydor)
Suitcase Blues
Jesse "Monkey Joe" Coleman; *Complete Recorded Works-#2-1939-
   1940* . . . . (Document)
Little Brother Montgomery; *At Home* . . . . (Earwig Music Co.)
Sippie Wallace; *Complete Recorded Works-#2-1925-1945* . . . (Document)
Suitcase Blues
Albert Ammons; *The First Day* . . . .(Blue Note)
Suitcase Blues
Triumph; *Just A Game* . . . .(RCA)
Suitcase Full Of Blues
Tommy Castro; *Can't Keep A Good Man Down* . . . . (Blind Pig)
Suitcase Of Leather
Delevantes; *Postcards From Along The Way* . . . .(Capitol)
Suitcases
Super Deluxe; *Famous* . . . . (Revolution)
Ten Pound Hammer
Aaron Tippin; *Tool Box* . . . . (RCA)
Theme From "Felix The Cat"
Original Soundtrack; *Television's Greatest Hits-#1-C* . . . . (TVT)
Thy Burdens Are Greater Than Mine
Hank Williams; *Alone With His Guitar* . . . .(Mercury)
Too Little Too Late
Barenaked Ladies; *Maroon* . . . . (Reprise)
Travelin' Light
Eric Clapton; *Reptile* . . . . (Duck/Reprise)
Walk On
U2; *America: A Tribute To Heroes-C* . . . . (Interscope)
   Now That's What I Call Music!-#8-C . . . .(Virgin)
Weight Of The World
Ringo Starr; *Time Takes Time* . . . .(Private Music)
Weight, The
Band; *Best Of The Band* . . . . (Capitol)
   Music From Big Pink . . . .(Capitol)
   Rock Of Ages . . . .(Capitol)
   The Last Waltz . . . . (Warner Bros.)
Staple Singers; *Soul Folk In Action* . . . . (Stax)
Staple Singers & Marty Stuart; *Rhythm Country And Blues-C* . . . . (MCA)
You Gotta Love That
Neal McCoy; *Neal McCoy's Greatest Hits* . . . . (Atlantic)
   Today's Country Love-C . . . . (K-Tel)
   You Gotta Love That! . . . . (Atlantic)
You've Got To Talk To Me
Lee Ann Womack; *Lee Ann Womack* . . . . (Decca)
Zip-Lock
Lit; *A Place In The Sun* . . . . (RCA)

BALLET, Ballerina

See Also: DANCE

At The Ballet
Original Cast; *A Chorus Line* . . . .(Columbia)
Bad Luck Streak In Dancing School
Warren Zevon; *Bad Luck Streak In Dancing School* . . . .(Asylum)
Ballerina
Van Morrison; *Astral Weeks* . . . . (Warner Bros.)
Ballerina
Nat "King" Cole; *Best Of Nat "King" Cole* . . . . (EMI Special Markets)
Ballerina Girl
Lionel Richie; *Dancing On The Ceiling* . . . . (Motown)
Ballerina Out Of Control
Ocean Blue; *Cerulean* . . . . (Reprise)

Ballet For A Rainy Day
XTC; *Skylarking* . . . . (Geffen)
Becky Is Back In The Ballet
Fanny Brice; *Music From The New York Stage (1890-1920)-#4-1917-
   1920-C* . . . . (Pearl)
Dance Of The Sugar Plum Fairy
Boston Pops Orchestra; *Encores-Boston Pops
   Orchestra* . . . .(Deutsche Grammophon)
   Sleigh Ride!-Classic Christmas Favorites-C . . . .(RCA)
Carpenters; *Christmas Collection* . . . .(A&M)
My Little Ballerina
Brent Mason; *Hot Wired* . . . .(Mercury)
Nina, Pretty Ballerina
Abba; *Ring Ring* . . . . (Polydor)
Pretty Ballerina
Left Banke; *History Of The Left Banke* . . . .(Rhino)
   Nuggets-#11-Pop-Part 4-C . . . .(Rhino)

BARS, Honky Tonks, Nightclubs

See Also: ALCOHOL, DANCE, JUKEBOX, MUSIC, PARTY, RESTAURANTS, WAITRESSES

All I Wanna Do
Sheryl Crow; *Tuesday Night Music Club* . . . .(A&M)
All The Rage In Paris
Derailers; *Here Come The Derailers* . . . .(Lucky Dog)
American Honky-Tonk Bar Association
Garth Brooks; *In Pieces* . . . .(Liberty)
Another Honky Tonk Night On Broadway
David Frizzell & Shelly West; *Golden Duets* . . . .(Viva)
   The David Frizzell & Shelly West Album . . . . (Warner Bros.)
Arkansas Road House Blues
Memphis Slim; *Traveling With The Blues* . . . .(Storyville)
Back To The Barrooms Again
Merle Haggard; *Back To The Barrooms Again* . . . .(MCA)
   Merle Haggard-His Best . . . .(MCA)
Bar Exam
Derailers; *Here Come The Derailers* . . . .(Lucky Dog)
Bar Room Buddies
Merle Haggard & Clint Eastwood; *ST/Bronco Billy* . . . .(Elektra)
Barroom Country Singer
Roger Whittaker; *Roger Whittaker Greatest Hits* . . . . (RCA)
Barstool Mountain
Moe Bandy; *Moe Bandy's Greatest Hits* . . . .(Columbia)
Wayne Carson; *45-#45358* . . . .(Elektra)
Beautiful Brown Eyes
Rosemary Clooney; *Songs From The Girl Singer-A Musical
   Autobiography* . . . .(Concord Jazz)
Beer And Bones
John Michael Montgomery; *John Michael Montgomery's
   Greatest Hits* . . . . (Atlantic)
   Life's A Dance . . . . (Atlantic)
Belly Up To The Bar, Boys
Debbie Reynolds; *ST/The Unsinkable Molly Brown* . . . .(MCA)
Original Cast; *The Unsinkable Molly Brown* . . . . (EMI-Angel)
Between An Old Memory And Me
Keith Whitley; *I Wonder Do You Think Of Me* . . . .(RCA)
Travis Tritt; *Ten Feet Tall And Bulletproof* . . . . (Warner Bros.)
Boy Named Sue
Johnny Cash; *Columbia Country Classics-#3-Americana-C* . . . .(Columbia)
   Johnny Cash's Biggest Hits . . . .(Columbia)
   Johnny Cash's Greatest Hits-#2 . . . .(Columbia)
   The Man In Black-His Greatest Hits . . . .(Legacy)
Bright Lights And Country Music
Bill Anderson; *Bill Anderson's Greatest Hits* . . . .(MCA)
Broadway
Goo Goo Dolls; *Dizzy Up The Girl* . . . . (Warner Sunset/Reprise)
Burnin' The Roadhouse Down
Steve Wariner & Garth Brooks; *Burnin' The Roadhouse Down* . . . . . .(Capitol)
Cabaret
Original Cast; *Cabaret* . . . .(Columbia)
Carol
Chuck Berry; *Berry Is On Top* . . . .(Chess)
   Chuck Berry-Golden Hits . . . .(Mercury)
   Chuck Berry's Greatest Hits . . . .(Everest)
   Roll Over Beethoven . . . .(Allegiance)
Rolling Stones; *England's Newest Hit Makers/The Rolling Stones* . . . . .(Abkco)
   Get Yer Ya-Ya's Out! . . . .(Abkco)
Chair, The
George Strait; *Country Classics-#5-1985-1986-C* . . . .(Universal)
   George Strait's Greatest Hits-#2 . . . .(MCA)
   MCA #1 Hits Of The '80s-#1-C . . . .(MCA Special Prod.)
   Something Special . . . .(MCA)
   Strait Out Of The Box . . . .(MCA)
Charleston Railroad Tavern
Bobby Bare; *This Is Bobby Bare* . . . .(RCA)

Chasin' That Neon Rainbow
Alan Jackson; *Here In The Real World* . . . . (Arista)
Close Up The Honky Tonks
Radney Foster; *Red Hot + Country-C* . . . . (Mercury)
Closing Time
Semisonic; *Feeling Strangely Fine* . . . . (MCA)
Now That's What I Call Music!-#2-C . . . . (Virgin)
Club At The End Of The Street
Elton John; *Sleeping With The Past* . . . . (MCA)
Copacabana (At The Copa)
Barry Manilow; *Barry Manilow's Greatest Hits-#2* . . . . (Arista)
Even Now . . . . (Arista)
ST/Foul Play . . . . (Arista)
The Manilow Collection-Twenty Classic Hits . . . . (Arista)
Columbia Ballroom Orchestra; *Let's Dance-#6* . . . . (Denon)
Country Bumpkin
Cal Smith; *16 Top Country Hits-#1-C* . . . . (MCA)
Country's Greatest Hits-#2-C . . . . (MCA Special Prod.)
Grand Ole Opry-75 Years-#2-C . . . . (MCA)
Country Club
Travis Tritt; *Country Club* . . . . (Warner Bros.)
Dear John Letter Lounge
Jerry Jeff Walker; *It's A Good Night For Singin'* . . . . (MCA)
Dim Lights Thick Smoke & Loud Loud Music
Flatt & Scruggs; *Golden Era* . . . . (Rounder)
Flying Burrito Brothers; *Close Encounters To The West Coast* . . . . (Relix)
Farther Along-Best Of The Flying Burrito Brothers . . . . . (A&M)
Ricky Skaggs and Kentucky Thunder; *History Of The Future* . . (Skaggs Family)
Don't The Girls All Get Prettier At Closing Time
Mickey Gilley; *Make It Like The First Time* . . . . (ISD/Intersound)
Don't Think I'm Not
Kandi; *Hey Kandi* . . . . (So So Def/Columbia)
Now That's What I Call Music!-#5-C . . . . (Virgin)
Down To The Night Club
Tower Of Power; *Bump City* . . . . (Warner Bros.)
Live & In Living Color . . . . (Warner Bros.)
Downtown
Neil Young; *Mirror Ball* . . . . (Reprise)
Drinkin' My Baby (Off My Mind)
Eddie Rabbitt; *Best Of Eddie Rabbitt/Greatest Hits-II* . . . . (Warner Bros.)
Great Divorce Songs For Him-C . . . . (Warner Bros.)
Number 1's . . . . (Warner Bros.)
Rocky Mountain Music . . . . (Elektra)
El Macho
Mark Knopfler; *Sailing To Philadelphia* . . . . (Warner Bros.)
El Paso
Grateful Dead; *Steal Your Face* . . . . (Grateful Dead)
Marty Robbins; *Billboard Top Country Hits-1960-C* . . . . (Rhino)
Gunfighter Ballads & Trail Songs . . . . (Legacy)
Marty Robbins' Biggest Hits . . . . (Columbia)
Radio Classics Of The '50s-C . . . . (Columbia)
Texas Super Hits-C . . . . (Columbia)
Gettin' Jiggy Wit It
Will Smith; *Big Willie Style* . . . . (Columbia)
Go Deep
Janet Jackson; *Velvet Rope* . . . . (Virgin)
Guantanamera
Wyclef Jean featuring Celia Cruz & Jeni Fujita; *Presents The Carnival F/*
Refugee Allstars . . . . (Ruffhouse/Columbia)
Hernando's Hideaway
Original Cast; *Pajama Game* . . . . (Columbia)
ST/Pajama Game . . . . (Collectables)
Hey Bartender
Blues Brothers; *Briefcase Full Of Blues* . . . . (Atlantic)
Johnny Lee; *Hey Bartender* . . . . (Warner Bros.)
Honky Tonk Country-C . . . . (Warner Bros.)
Johnny Lee's Greatest Hits . . . . (Full Moon/Asylum)
Koko Taylor; *Blues Delux* . . . . (Alligator)
Earthshaker . . . . (Alligator)
Hong Kong Bar
Tim Buckley; *Greetings From L.A.* . . . . (Bizarre/Straight)
Honky Tonk
Bill Doggett; *21 Number One Hits-C* . . . . (Original Sound)
Cruisin'-1956-C . . . . (Increase)
Rock & Roll Show-C . . . . (Gusto)
Honky Tonk Amnesia
Moe Bandy; *Best Of Moe Bandy-Vol. 1* . . . . (Columbia)
Honky Tonk Attitude
Joe Diffie; *Honky Tonk Attitude* . . . . (Epic)
Honky Tonk Blues
Charley Pride; *Charley Pride's Greatest Hits* . . . . (RCA)
Hank Williams With His Drifting Cowboys; *24 Of Hank Williams'*
Greatest Hits . . . . (Polydor)
Hank Williams-40 Greatest Hits . . . . (Polydor)
Let's Turn Back The Years-1951-1953 . . . . (Polydor)
Rare Takes & Radio Cuts . . . . (Polydor)
Huey Lewis and the News; *Sports* . . . . (Chrysalis)
Nitty Gritty Dirt Band; *Will The Circle Be Unbroken* . . . . (EMI)

Honky Tonk Crowd
Rick Trevino; *Rick Trevino* . . . . (Columbia)
Honky Tonk Heart
Highway 101; *Highway 101's Greatest Hits* . . . . (Warner Bros.)
One-O-One . . . . (Warner Bros.)
Jim Owen; *45-#1164* . . . . (Sun)
Keith Whitley; *Don't Close Your Eyes* . . . . (RCA)
Honky Tonk Internet
Savannah Taylor; *Savannah Taylor* . . . . (Ichiban Int'l)
Honky Tonk Man
Dwight Yoakam; *Guitars, Cadillacs, Etc., Etc.* . . . . (Reprise)
Just Lookin' For A Hit . . . . (Reprise)
Johnny Horton; *All Time Legends Of Country Music-C* . . . . . (Legacy)
Columbia Country Classics-#2-Honky Tonk Heroes-C . . (Columbia)
Marty Robbins; *Greatest Country Hits From The Movies-C* . . . . (Epic)
Honky Tonk Merry Go Round
Patsy Cline; *20 Golden Pieces Of Patsy Cline* . . . . (Bulldog)
Patsy Cline . . . . (Audio Fidelity)
Today Tomorrow & Forever . . . . (MCA)
Try Again . . . . (Quicksilver)
Walkin' Dreams-Her First Recordings-#1 . . . . (Rhino)
Honky Tonk Moon
Randy Travis; *Old 8 X 10* . . . . (Warner Bros.)
Randy Travis' Greatest Hits-#1 . . . . (Warner Bros.)
Rosie Flores; *Once More With Feeling* . . . . (Hightone)
Honky Tonk Night Time Man
Lynyrd Skynyrd; *Street Survivors* . . . . (MCA)
Merle Haggard & The Strangers; *Presents His 30th Album* . . . . (Capitol)
Songs I'll Always Sing . . . . (Capitol)
Honky Tonk Superman
Aaron Tippin; *Call Of The Wild* . . . . (RCA)
Honky Tonk Toys
John Conlee; *Friday Night Blues* . . . . (MCA)
Honky Tonk Truth
Brooks & Dunn; *Brooks & Dunn-The Greatest Hits Collection* . . (Arista)
Honky Tonk Women
Elton John; *11-17-70* . . . . (Polydor)
Humble Pie; *Best Of Humble Pie* . . . . (A&M)
Eat It . . . . (A&M)
Humble Pie-Classics-#14 . . . . (A&M)
Ike & Tina Turner; *Best Of Ike & Tina Turner* . . . . (EMI)
Get Back . . . . (Liberty)
Joe Cocker; *Mad Dogs & Englishmen* . . . . (A&M)
Rolling Stones; *Get Yer Ya-Ya's Out!* . . . . (Abkco)
Hot Rocks 1964-1971 . . . . (Abkco)
Love You Live . . . . (Virgin)
Through The Past, Darkly (Big Hits Vol. 2) . . . . (Abkco)
Willie Nelson & Leon Russell; *Half Nelson-C* . . . . (Columbia)
Honky Tonk Women Love Redneck Men
Ronnie McDowell; *American Music* . . . . (Curb)
Honky Tonkin'
Hank Williams; *24 Of Hank Williams' Greatest Hits* . . . . . . (Polydor)
I Ain't Got Nothin' But Time-1946-1947 . . . . (Polydor)
Lovesick Blues . . . . (Polydor)
Rare Takes & Radio Cuts . . . . (Polydor)
Hank Williams, Jr.; *Hank Williams, Jr.'s Greatest Hits-#2* . . . (WB/Curb)
High Notes . . . . (WB/Curb)
New Tradition Sings The Old Tradition-C . . . . (Warner Bros.)
Honky Tonkin' Fool
Doug Supernaw; *Red And Rio Grande* . . . . (BNA)
The Encore Collection . . . . (BMG Special Prod.)
Honky Tonkin's What I Do Best
Marty Stuart & Travis Tritt; *Grand Ole Opry-75 Years-#2-C* . . . (MCA)
Honky-Tonk Crazy
Gene Watson; *Honky-Tonk Crazy* . . . . (Epic)
George Strait; *Strait From The Heart* . . . . (MCA)
Honky-Tonk Crowd
John Anderson; *John Anderson's Greatest Hits-#2* . . . . . (Warner Bros.)
Honky-Tonk Heroes
Billy Joe Shaver; *Rebels, Renegades & Ramblers-C* . . . . . . (Polydor)
Waylon Jennings; *Outlaws* . . . . (RCA)
Waylon Jennings' Greatest Hits . . . . (RCA)
Hot Hot Hot
Buster Poindexter; *Buster Poindexter* . . . . (RCA)
I Don't Even Know Your Name
Alan Jackson; *Alan Jackson-The Greatest Hits Collection* . . . (Arista)
Who I Am . . . . (Arista)
I Know A Place
Petula Clark; *History Of British Rock-#7-C* . . . . (Rhino)
Petula Clark's Greatest Hits . . . . (Crescendo)
I Like It Like That, Part 1
Chris Kenner; *Billboard Top Rock 'N' Roll Hits-1961-C* . . . . (Rhino)
ST/Full Metal Jacket . . . . (Warner Bros.)
I Think I'll Just Stay Here And Drink
Merle Haggard; *For The Record: Merle Haggard-43 Legendary Hits* . . (BNA)
If You've Got The Money I've Got The Time
Lefty Frizzell; *American Originals-Lefty Frizzell* . . . . (Columbia)
Columbia Country Classics-#2-Honky Tonk Heroes-C . . (Columbia)
Lefty Frizzell's Greatest Hits . . . . (Columbia)

Willie Nelson; *Greatest Hits (& Some That Will Be)* . . . . (Columbia)
  Sound In Your Mind . . . . (Columbia)
  Willie & Family Live . . . . (Columbia)
I'm A Honky Tonk Girl
Loretta Lynn; *The Country Music Hall Of Fame-Loretta Lynn* . . . (MCA)
I'm Just Talkin' About Tonight
Toby Keith; *Pull My Chain* . . . . (DreamWorks/SKG)
It Wasn't God Who Made Honky Tonk Angels
Kitty Wells; *Grand Ole Opry-75 Years-#1-C* . . . . (MCA)
  Kitty Wells' Greatest Hits . . . . (Step One)
  The Kitty Wells Story . . . . (MCA)
Jumpin, Jumpin
Destiny's Child; *Now That's What I Call Music!-#5-C* . . . . (Virgin)
  The Writing's On The Wall . . . . (Columbia)
Kindly Keep It Country
Vince Gill; *The Key* . . . . (MCA)
Kiss This
Aaron Tippin; *People Like Us* . . . . (Lyric Street)
L.A. Song
Beth Hart; *Screamin' For My Supper* . . . . (143/Lava/Atlantic)
Last Night Of The World
Bruce Cockburn; *Breakfast In New Orleans, Dinner In Timbuktu* . . . . (Rykodisc)
Letter, The (That Johnny Walker Read)
Asleep At The Wheel; *Very Best Of Asleep At The Wheel
  Since 1970* . . . . (Relentless/Madacy)
Little Miss Honky Tonk
Brooks & Dunn; *Waitin' On Sundown* . . . . (Arista)
Little Old Wine Drinker Me
Dean Martin; *Dean Martin's Greatest Hits-#2* . . . . (Reprise)
  Welcome To My World . . . . (Reprise)
Mel Tillis; *Best Of Mel Tillis* . . . . (MCA)
Lonesome, I Know You Too Well
Shawn Mullins; *Beneath The Velvet Sun* . . . . (Columbia)
Louie Louie
Kingsmen; *Best Of The Kingsmen* . . . . (Rhino)
  Billboard Top Rock 'N' Roll Hits-1963-C . . . . (Rhino)
  Cruisin'-1963-C . . . . (Increase)
  Frat Rock!-C . . . . (Rhino)
  Oldies But Goodies-#11-C . . . . (Original Sound)
  Rock & Roll Is Here To Stay-C . . . . (Gusto)
  ST/Quadrophenia . . . . (MCA)
  WCBS FM 101 History Of Rock-'60s-#1-C . . . . (Collectables)
Love Or Something Like It
Kenny Rogers; *Kenny Rogers-Twenty Greatest Hits* . . . . (EMI)
Misery And Gin
Merle Haggard; *Back To The Barrooms* . . . . (MCA)
  Merle Haggard's Greatest Hits . . . . (MCA)
  Rainbow Stew-Live At Anaheim Stadium . . . . (MCA)
Mr. Shorty
Marty Robbins; *The Drifter* . . . . (Koch International)
My Next Broken Heart
Brooks & Dunn; *Brand New Man* . . . . (Arista)
My Second Home
Tracy Lawrence; *Alibis* . . . . (Atlantic)
Neon Moon
Brooks & Dunn; *Brand New Man* . . . . (Arista)
Old Enough To Know Better
Wade Hayes; *Country Dance Hits-C* . . . . (Columbia)
  Old Enough To Know Better . . . . (Columbia)
  Steppin' Country-#2-C . . . . (Columbia)
  Super Hits Of 1994-C . . . . (Columbia)
On The Verge
Collin Raye; *I Think About You* . . . . (Epic)
O'Reilly At The Bar
Dan Hicks & His Hot Licks; *Striking It Rich!* . . . . (MCA)
Over At Herbie's Juke Joint
Donald Brown; *People Music* . . . . (Muse)
People Like Us
Aaron Tippin; *People Like Us* . . . . (Lyric Street)
Piano Has Been Drinking
Tom Waits; *Small Change* . . . . (Asylum)
  Tom Waits-Anthology . . . . (Asylum)
Piano Man
Billy Joel; *Billy Joel-Greatest Hits, Volume I & Volume II* . . . . (Columbia)
  Piano Man . . . . (Columbia)
  Rock Classics Of The '70s-C . . . . (Columbia)
Picture Postcards From L.A.
Joshua Kadison; *Painted Desert Serenade* . . . . (SBK)
Pop A Top
Alan Jackson; *Under The Influence* . . . . (Arista)
Jim Ed Brown; *Essential Jim Ed Brown* . . . . (RCA)
Pour Me
Trick Pony; *Trick Pony* . . . . (H2E/Warner Bros.)
Prop Me Up Beside The Jukebox (If I Die)
Joe Diffie; *Honky Tonk Attitude* . . . . (Epic)
Raised On Robbery
Joni Mitchell; *Court & Spark* . . . . (Asylum)

Rednecks, White Socks And Blue Ribbon Beer
Johnny Russell; *Beer Redneck Mothers* . . . . (RCA)
  Country Legends-C . . . . (Madacy)
  Country's Greatest Drinking Songs-C . . . . (All-Star Music)
  Rednecks, White Socks & Blue Ribbon Beer . . . . (RCA)
Road Goes On Forever, The
Joe Ely; *Love & Danger* . . . . (MCA)
Roadhouse Blues
Doors; *Best Of The Doors* . . . . (Elektra)
  Doors 13 . . . . (Elektra)
  Doors' Greatest Hits . . . . (Elektra)
  Doors-Classics . . . . (Elektra)
  Morrison Hotel/Hard Rock Cafe . . . . (Elektra)
  ST/The Doors . . . . (Elektra)
Rocky Raccoon
Beatles; *Beatles-Box Set* . . . . (Capitol)
  The Beatles (White Album) . . . . (Capitol)
Sam's Place
Buck Owens & The Buckaroos; *Billboard Top Country Hits-1967-C* . . . . (Rhino)
Seaside Bar Song
Bruce Springsteen; *Tracks* . . . . (Columbia)
Little Bob Story; *One Step Up/Two Steps Back-The Songs Of Bruce
  Springsteen-C* . . . . (Right Stuff)
She's Got The Rhythm (And I Got The Blues)
Alan Jackson; *A Lot About Livin' (And A Little 'Bout Love)* . . . . (Arista)
Ships That Don't Come In
Joe Diffie; *Regular Joe* . . . . (Epic)
Six Pack To Go, A
Hank Thompson and His Brazos Valley Boys; *Best Of The Best Of Hank
  Thompson* . . . . (Gusto)
  Capitol Collectors Series-Hank Thompson . . . . (Capitol)
  Country Comes To Carnegie Hall-C . . . . (MCA)
  Hank Thompson . . . . (Dot)
  Hank Thompson's Greatest Hits-#2 . . . . (Step One)
Somebody Buy This Cowgirl A Beer
Tanya Tucker; *Tanya Tucker Live* . . . . (MCA Special Prod.)
Song From Moulin Rouge (Where Is Your Heart)
Percy Faith & His Orchestra; *Percy Faith & His Orchestra's All-Time
  Greatest Hits* . . . . (Columbia)
Sparrow In The Treetop
Guy Mitchell; *Guy Mitchell-16 Most Requested Songs* . . . . (Legacy)
Straight Tequila Night
John Anderson; *Seminole Wind* . . . . (BNA)
  Today's Hot Country-C . . . . (K-Tel)
Swing My Way
K.P. & Envyi; *ST/Can't Hardly Wait* . . . . (Elektra)
Swinging Doors
George Jones; *20 Golden Pieces Of George Jones* . . . . (Bulldog)
Merle Haggard; *Capitol Collectors Series-Merle Haggard* . . . . (Capitol)
Merle Haggard & The Strangers; *Best Of Merle Haggard & The
  Strangers* . . . . (Capitol)
  For The Record: Merle Haggard-43 Legendary Hits . . . . (BNA)
  Okie From Muskogee . . . . (Capitol)
  Songs I'll Always Sing . . . . (Capitol)
Take Me To Your World
George Jones; *Tammy Wynette...Remembered-C* . . . . (Asylum)
Tammy Wynette; *Tammy Wynette-16 Biggest Hits* . . . . (Legacy)
  Tammy Wynette's Greatest Hits . . . . (Epic)
Tattoos & Scars
Montgomery Gentry; *Tattoos & Scars* . . . . (Columbia)
Tequila Talkin'
Lonestar; *Lonestar* . . . . (BNA)
Texas Honky Tonk
David Houston; *David Houston Sings Texas Honky Tonk* . . . . (Delmark)
  Texas Country . . . . (Delmark)
Texas Rhythm Club
Joe McBride; *Texas Rhythm Club* . . . . (Heads Up Records Int'l)
That Girl Who Waits On Tables
Ronnie Milsap; *Collector's Series-Ronnie Milsap* . . . . (RCA)
  Where My Heart Is . . . . (RCA)
Theme From "Cheers"
Gary Portnoy; *Tube Tunes-#3-The '70s & '80s-C* . . . . (Rhino)
Original Soundtrack; *Television's Greatest Hits-#3-1970s & 1980s-C* . . . . (TVT)
There Is A Tavern In The Town
Four Aces; *Four Aces-More Greatest Hits* . . . . (Varese Vintage)
Mitch Miller; *Sing Along With Mitch* . . . . (Columbia)
Stan Wolowic & The Polka Chips; *Million-Seller Polkas* . . . . (Capitol)
There'll Always Be A Honky Tonk Somewhere
Randy Travis; *Honky Tonk Country-C* . . . . (Warner Bros.)
  Storms Of Life . . . . (Warner Bros.)
There'll Always Be Honky Tonks In Texas
Darrell McCall & Johnny Bush; *Hot Texas Country* . . . . (Step One)
To Beat The Devil
Johnny Cash; *Johnny Cash-16 Biggest Hits-#2* . . . . (Legacy)
Top Hat Bar & Grille
Jim Croce; *50th Anniversary Collection* . . . . (Saja)
We Be Clubbin'
Ice Cube; *ST/The Player's Club* . . . . (Heavyweight/A&M)

We Danced
Brad Paisley; *Who Needs Pictures* . . . . (Arista)
What It Is
Mark Knopfler; *Sailing To Philadelphia*. . . . .(Warner Bros.)
What'd You Come Here For?
Trina & Tamara; *Trina & Tamara* . . . . (C2/Columbia)
Whatever
Ideal; *Ideal* . . . . (Noontime/Virgin)
What's Made Milwaukee Famous (Has Made A Loser Out Of Me)
Jerry Lee Lewis; *Heartbreak* . . . . (Tomato)
Milestones . . . . (Rhino)
Rod Stewart; *Best Of Rod Stewart* . . . . (Mercury)
Storyteller/The Complete Anthology: 1964-1990 . . . .(Warner Bros.)
Where It's At
Beck; *Odelay* . . . . (David Geffen Co.)
Why Baby Why
Charley Pride; *Charley Pride's Greatest Hits-#2* . . . . (RCA)
George Jones; *George Jones' All-Time Greatest Hits* . . . . (Epic)
George Jones-Super Hits . . . . (Epic)
Red Sovine & Webb Pierce; *Greatest Country Duets Of All Time-C* . . . .(MCA Special Prod.)
Webb Pierce; *Webb Pierce-Golden Hits-#2* . . . . (Plantation)
Willie Nelson & Waylon Jennings; *Take It To The Limit* . . . . (Columbia)
Wine Me Up
Faron Young; *Faron Young-Golden Hits* . . . . (Mercury)
Faron Young-The Hits . . . . (Mercury)
Y'All Come Back Saloon
Oak Ridge Boys; *Oak Ridge Boys' Greatest Hits* . . . .(MCA)
Oak Ridge Boys-Collection . . . .(MCA)
Y'All Come Back Saloon . . . .(MCA)
Your Good Girl's Gonna Go Bad
Billie Jo Spears; *Best Of Billie Jo Spears* . . . . (CEMA Special Prod.)
Best Of Billie Jo Spears . . . . (Razor & Tie)
K.T. Oslin; *Tammy Wynette-Remembered-C* . . . . (Asylum)
Tammy Wynette; *Tammy Wynette-Anniversary-20 Years Of Hits* . . . . . .(Epic)
Tammy Wynette's Greatest Hits. . . . .(Epic)
Your Good Girl's Gonna Go Bad. . . . . (Legacy)

BATHROOMS, Bathtubs, Sinks, Toilet Functions, Toilets
See Also: CLEAN

30 Years In The Bathroom
Wonderstuff; *Hup!* . . . . (Polydor)
Armatage Shanks
Green Day; *Insomniac* . . . . (Reprise)
Away Go Troubles Down The Drain
Lenny White; *Venusian Summer* . . . . (Nemperor)
Bathin' In Love Waters
Paul Kelly; *Stand On The Positive Side* . . . .(Warner Bros.)
Bathroom Wall
Faster Pussycat; *Decline Of Western Civilization-#2* . . . . (Capitol)
Faster Pussycat . . . . (Elektra)
Bathtub
Snoop Doggy Dogg; *Doggystyle* . . . . (Death Row)
Bird Bathroom
Surf Punks; *My Beach* . . . .(Epic)
Constipated Duck
Jeff Beck; *Blow By Blow* . . . .(Epic)
Constipated Monkey
Kain; *The Blue Guerilla* . . . . (Collectables)
Constipation Blues
Screamin' Jay Hawkins; *Voodoo Jive: Best Of Screamin' Jay Hawkins* . . . . (Rhino)
Dancing In The Bathtub
John Hartford; *All In The Name Of Love*. . . . . (Flying Fish)
Digital Bath
Deftones; *White Pony* . . . .(Maverick)
Don't Eat The Yellow Snow
Frank Zappa; *Apostrophe/Overnite Sensation* . . . .(Rykodisc)
Enema Party
Buck Naked & The Bare Bottom Boys; *Buck Naked & The Bare Bottom Boys* . . . . (Heyday)
Enema Picnic
Dead Youth; *Intense Brutality* . . . . (Grind Core Int'l)
Fart Of The Bumblebee (and other similar songs)
Original Soundtrack; *Pull My Finger!-C* . . . .(Orchard)
Fat Man In The Bathtub
Little Feat; *Dixie Chicken* . . . .(Warner Bros.)
Waiting For Columbus. . . . .(Warner Bros.)
Germans At The Spa
Original London Cast; *Nine* . . . . (RCA)
I Do My Bawling In The Bathroom
David Peel & The Lower East Side; *Have A Marijuana* . . . . (Elektra)
I'm Gonna Wash That Man Right Outta My Hair
Mitzi Gaynor; *ST/South Pacific* . . . . (RCA)

Original Cast; *South Pacific* . . . . (CBS Masterworks)
Weather Girls; *Success* . . . . (Columbia)
In The Girls' Room
Rick James; *Wonderful* . . . .(Reprise)
Just Like Anyone
Soul Asylum; *Let Your Dim Light Shine* . . . . (Columbia)
Let's Talk It Over In The Ladies Room
Curtie & The Boom Box; *Black Kisses* . . . .(RCA)
Meeting In The Ladies Room
Klymaxx; *Meeting In The Ladies Room* . . . . (Constellation)
ST/Secret Admirer . . . . (MCA)
Men's Room L.A.
Kinky Friedman; *Lasso From El Paso* . . . . (Epic)
Mirror In The Bathroom
English Beat; *I Just Can't Stop It*. . . . . (I.R.S.)
ST/Dance Craze . . . . (Chrysalis)
What Is Beat . . . . (I.R.S.)
Molly
Sponge; *Rotting Pinata* . . . . (Work)
Norwegian Wood (This Bird Has Flown)
Beatles; *Beatles-Box Set* . . . . (Capitol)
Beatles-Love Songs . . . . (Capitol)
Rubber Soul . . . . (Capitol)
The Beatles/1962-1966 . . . . (Capitol)
Outhouse Quake
Bootsauce; *Bull* . . . . (Island)
Paper Toilet
Henry Threadgill; *Too Much Sugar For A Dime* . . . . (Axiom)
Piss On The Wall
J. Geils Band; *Freeze-Frame*. . . . . (EMI)
Pissin' In The Wind
Jerry Jeff Walker; *Ridin' High* . . . . (MCA)
Pissin' On A Skunk (No Need)
Saffire-Uppity Blues Women; *Hot Flash* . . . .(Alligator)
Pissing In A River
Patti Smith Group; *Radio Ethiopia* . . . . (Arista)
Potty Train 'Em
Poet Society; *Q.D. III Soundlab* . . . . (Qwest)
Pretty
Korn; *Follow The Leader* . . . . (Immortal/Epic)
Shaving Cream
Benny Bell & Paul Wynn; *Dr. Demento Presents The Greatest Novelty Records-#1-1940s & Before-C* . . . . (Rhino)
Dr. Demento's Dementia Royale-C . . . . (Rhino)
She Came In Through The Bathroom Window
Beatles; *Abbey Road* . . . . (Parlophone)
Beatles-Box Set. . . . . (Capitol)
Joe Cocker; *Joe Cocker Live* . . . . (Capitol)
Joe Cocker! . . . . (A&M)
Joe Cocker-Classics-#4 . . . . (A&M)
Mad Dogs & Englishmen . . . . (A&M)
Shit House Shuffle
Aerosmith; *Pandora's Box* . . . . (Columbia)
Smokin' In The Boy's Room
Brownsville Station; *Hit Singles-1958-1977-C* . . . .(Atlantic)
Legends Of Rock Guitar-'70s-C . . . . (Rhino)
ST/Rock 'N' Roll High School . . . . (Sire)
Motley Crue; *Decade Of Decadence* . . . . (Elektra)
Theatre Of Pain . . . . (Elektra)
Splish Splash
Barbra Streisand; *Wet* . . . . (Columbia)
Bobby Darin; *Bobby Darin's Greatest Hits*. . . . . (Curb)
Oldies But Goodies-#8-C . . . . (Original Sound)
Splish Splash-Best Of Bobby Darin-#1. . . . .(Atlantic)
The Bobby Darin Story. . . . .(Atlantic)
Sha Na Na; *Having An Oldies Party With Sha Na Na* . . . . (K-Tel)
Strawberries
Smooth; *Reality*. . . . . (Perspective/A&M)
T.S.R. (Toilet Stool Rap)
Biz Markie; *I Need A Haircut* . . . . (Cold Chillin')
Toilet
Jeffrey Frederick & The Clamtones; *Spiders In The Moonlight* . . . . . . (Rounder)
Toilet
Guttermouth; *The Record Formerly Known As Full-Length*. . . . .(Nitro)
Toilet
Orange 9mm; *Driver Not Included* . . . . (East West)
Toilet Bowl Blues
McKenna Mendelson Blues; *McKenna Mendelson Blues* . . . .(Pacemaker Entert. Ltd.)
Toilet Licking Maggot
Hell On Earth; *Biomechanical Ejaculations Of The Damned* . . . . (Neptune)
Toilet Piece
Yoko Ono; *Fly*. . . . . (Rykodisc)
Toilet Seats Coming Down
Chixdiggit; *Chixdiggit*. . . . . (Sub Pop)
Toilet Song
Bouncing Souls; *Bouncing Souls*. . . . .(Epitaph)

Tracy In The Bathroom Killing Thrills
Mary's Danish; *Circa* . . . . (Morgan Creek)
Experience-Live + Foxey Lady . . . . (Chameleon)
Two Little Girls
Ani DiFranco; *Little Plastic Castle* . . . . (Righteous Babe)
You Left The Water Running
Huey Lewis and the News; *Four Chords & Several Years Ago* . . . . (Elektra)
Otis Redding; *Otis Redding Story* . . . . (Atlantic)
Your Farts Are Like Frankincense To Me
Capitol Punishment; *Messiah Complex* . . . . (We Bite America)

BEAUTY, Attractive, Beautiful, Handsome, Lovely, Pretty, Ugly

See Also: COMPLIMENTS, COSMETICS, LOVE (various)

(It's A) Beautiful Morning
Rascals; *Rascals' Greatest Hits* . . . . (Atlantic)
Abilene
George Hamilton IV; *Billboard Top Country Hits-1963-C* . . . . (Rhino)
Nipper's Greatest Hits Of The '60s-#2-C . . . .(RCA)
Sonny James; *American Originals-Sonny James* . . . . (Columbia)
Texas Super Hits-C . . . . (Columbia)
Waylon Jennings; *Outlaw Reunion-#1* . . . . (Aura)
Adalida
George Strait; *Latest Greatest Straitest Hits* . . . . (MCA)
Lead On . . . . (MCA)
Ah, Paree, Beautiful Girls
Millicent Martin; *Collector's Sondheim-C* . . . . (RCA)
Stephen Sondheim; *Collector's Sondheim-C* . . . . (RCA)
Amapola (Pretty Little Poppy)
Jimmy Dorsey & His Orchestra; *Best Of Jimmy Dorsey & His Orchestra* . . . . (Curb)
America The Beautiful
American Philharmonic Orchestra Orchestra & Chorus; *Stars And Stripes Forever-#2-C* . . . . (Volcano Entertainment)
Elvis Presley; *Elvis Aron Presley* . . . .(RCA)
Frank Sinatra; *God Bless America-C* . . . . (Columbia)
Keb' Mo'; *Big Wide Grin* . . . . (Sony Wonder)
Lee Greenwood; *American Patriot* . . . . (Capitol)
Mormon Tabernacle Choir; *God Bless America* . . . . . . (Sony Music Classical)
This Is My Country . . . . (Columbia)
Original Soundtrack; *School Days-Kids Classics* . . . . (Benson)
Ray Charles; *Ray Charles' Greatest Hits-#2* . . . . (Rhino)
Ray Charles-His Greatest Hits-#2 . . . . (Dunhill Compact Classics)
Star Spangled Band; *Red, White & Bluegrass-C* . . . . (C.M.H. Prod.)
Willie Nelson; *America: A Tribute To Heroes-C* . . . . (Interscope)
American Beauty Rose
Frank Sinatra; *Come Swing With Me!* . . . . (Capitol)
Sentimental Journey . . . . (Capitol)
At Seventeen
Janis Ian; *Between The Lines* . . . . (Columbia)
Super Hits Of The '70s-Have A Nice Day-#15-C . . . . (Rhino)
Attractive Female Wanted
Rod Stewart; *Blondes Have More Fun* . . . . (Warner Bros.)
Baby Face
Al Jolson; *The Al Jolson Story-#3* . . . . (MCA)
World's Greatest . . . . (MCA)
Kinks; *Everybody's In Show-Biz* . . . . (Rhino)
Baby Makes Her Blue Jeans Talk
Dr. Hook; *Players In The Dark* . . . . (Casablanca)
Baby You're A Rich Man
Beatles; *Beatles-Box Set* . . . . (Capitol)
Magical Mystery Tour . . . . (Capitol)
Ballerina Girl
Lionel Richie; *Dancing On The Ceiling* . . . . (Motown)
Beautiful
Mary J. Blige; *ST/How Stella Got Her Groove Back* . . . . (Flyte Tyme/MCA)
Beautiful
Carole King; *Tapestry* . . . . (Epic)
Beautiful Black Girl
Quincy Jones; *Mellow Madness* . . . . (A&M)
Beautiful Boy
John Lennon; *Double Fantasy* . . . . (Capitol)
Beautiful Brown Eyes
Rosemary Clooney; *Songs From The Girl Singer-A Musical Autobiography* . . . . (Concord Jazz)
Beautiful Child
Fleetwood Mac; *25 Years-The Chain* . . . . (Warner Bros.)
Tusk . . . . (Warner Bros.)
Beautiful Child
Blow Monkeys; *She Was Only The Grocer's Daughter* . . . . (RCA)
Beautiful Day
U2; *All That You Can't Leave Behind* . . . . (Interscope)
Now That's What I Call Music!-#6-C . . . . (Virgin)
Beautiful Disaster
311; *Live!* . . . . (Capricorn)

Transistor . . . .(Capricorn)
Beautiful Downtown Burbank
Jeannie C. Riley; *Country Gold-Jeannie C. Riley* . . . . (Plantation)
Beautiful Dreamer
Mormon Tabernacle Choir; *Beautiful Dreamer* . . . .(Columbia)
Mormon Tabernacle Choir's Greatest Hits . . . .(Columbia)
The Mormon Tabernacle Choir Album . . . .(Columbia)
This Land Is Your Land . . . . (Columbia)
Beautiful Friendship
Nat "King" Cole; *Nat "King" Cole Sings/George Shearing Plays* . . . .(Capitol)
Beautiful Friendships
Loretta Lynn & Ernest Tubb; *The Ernest Tubb/Loretta Lynn Story* . . . . . . (MCA)
Beautiful Friendships
Lou Rawls; *Best From Lou Rawls* . . . .(Capitol)
Beautiful Hawaii
Magic Organ; *Around The World* . . . . (Ranwood)
Beautiful Hills Of Galilee
Hazel Dickens; *Old-Timey Gospel Music* . . . .(Rounder)
Beautiful Homes
Chris Isaak; *San Francisco Days* . . . . (Reprise)
Beautiful In My Eyes
Joshua Kadison; *Painted Desert Serenade* . . . .(SBK)
Beautiful Ireland
Anne & Francie Brolly; *Ireland My Home* . . . . (Rego Irish)
Beautiful Lies
Kenny Rogers & Dottie West; *Every Time Two Fools Collide* . . . . (EMI)
Beautiful Life
Ace Of Base; *Bridge* . . . .(Arista)
MTV Party To Go-#9-C . . . . (Tommy Boy)
Beautiful Noise
Neil Diamond; *12 Greatest Hits-#2* . . . .(Columbia)
Beautiful Noise . . . .(Columbia)
Love At The Greek . . . .(Columbia)
Beautiful Ones
Mariah Carey; *Butterfly* . . . . (Columbia)
Beautiful People
Marilyn Manson; *Antichrist Superstar* . . . . (Interscope)
Beautiful People
Bobby Vee; *Very Best Of Bobby Vee* . . . .(Collectables)
Beautiful People Of Denver
Original Cast; *The Unsinkable Molly Brown* . . . . (EMI-Angel)
Beautiful Story
Sonny & Cher; *Beat Goes On.* . . . .(Atco)
Best Of Sonny & Cher . . . .(Atco)
Beautiful Stranger
Madonna; *GHV2* . . . . (Warner Bros.)
ST/Austin Powers-The Spy Who Shagged Me . . . .(Maverick)
Totally Hits-#2-C . . . . (Elektra)
Beautiful Sunday
Daniel Boone; *Back To The '70s-#2-C.* . . . .(Dominion Entert.)
Super Hits Of The '70s-Have A Nice Day-#9-C . . . . (Rhino)
Roy Drusky; *English Gold* . . . . (Plantation)
Beautiful Texas
Leon Rausch; *Deep In The Heart Of Texas* . . . . (Southland)
Beautiful You
Oak Ridge Boys; *Together* . . . .(MCA)
Beauty And The Beast
Celine Dion & Peabo Bryson; *All The Way...A Decade Of Song* . . . . (550 Music)
Celine Dion . . . . (Epic)
ST/Beauty And The Beast . . . . (Disney)
Beauty Is Only Skin Deep
Temptations; *Good Feeling Music Of The Big Chill Generation-#1-C* . . . .(Motown)
Motown Story-First 25 Years-C . . . .(Motown)
Motown's Mustang-A Motown Video-C . . . .(Motown)
Temptations-Anthology-The Best Of The Temptations . . . .(Motown)
Beauty Of Nature
Edmund Sylvers; *Have You Heard.* . . . . (Casablanca)
Beauty Queen
Roxy Music; *For Your Pleasure.* . . . . (Reprise)
Beauty School Dropout
Original Broadway Cast; *Grease* . . . . (Polydor)
Beauty Secrets
Be Bop Deluxe; *Sunburst Finish* . . . .(Capitol)
Believe Me If All Those Endearing Young Charms
Bronn Journey; *Celtic Journey.* . . . . (Phileo)
Mitch Miller; *Favorite Irish Sing-Alongs.* . . . .(Legacy)
Roger Whittaker; *Danny Boy & Other Irish Favorites.* . . . .(RCA Victor)
Bird Of Beauty
Stevie Wonder; *Fulfillingness' First Finale.* . . . .(Motown)
Blistered
Johnny Cash; *Johnny Cash-16 Biggest Hits-#2* . . . .(Legacy)
Blue Autumn
Bobby Goldsboro; *10th Anniversary Album-#1* . . . . (EMI)
Bobby Goldsboro's Greatest Hits . . . .(Liberty)
Honey-Best Of Bobby Goldsboro . . . . (EMI)
Brown Eyed Handsome Man
Buddy Holly; *Buddy Holly-20 Golden Greats* . . . . (MCA)

For The First Time Anywhere . . . . (MCA)
Rock & Roll Collection . . . . (MCA)
Chuck Berry; *Best Of The Best Of Chuck Berry* . . . . (International Mktg. Group)
Roll Over Beethoven . . . .(Allegiance)
The Chess Box-Chuck Berry . . . . (Chess)
Waylon Jennings; *Essential Waylon Jennings* . . . . (RCA)
Waylon Jennings-Super Hits . . . . (RCA)
Californication
Red Hot Chili Peppers; *Californication* . . . .(Warner Bros.)
Can't Take My Eyes Off You
Frankie Valli; *25th Anniversary Collection* . . . . (Rhino)
Frankie Valli-Anthology . . . . (Rhino)
Very Best Of Frankie Valli . . . . (MCA)
Lauryn Hill; *The Miseducation Of Lauryn Hill* . . . . (Ruffhouse/Columbia)
Carlene
Phil Vassar; *Phil Vassar* . . . . (Arista)
Cherry, Cherry Coupe
Beach Boys; *Little Deuce Coupe/All Summer Long* . . . . (Capitol)
Christmas Shoes
Newsong; *Sheltering Tree* . . . . (Benson/Jive)
Claudette
Dwight Yoakam; *Under The Covers* . . . . (Reprise)
Everly Brothers; *Everly Brothers' Greatest Hits* . . . . (Delta)
Everly Brothers-Cadence Classics-Their 20 Greatest Hits . . . . . . (Rhino)
Roy Orbison; *Roy Orbison-The Sun Years* . . . . (Rhino)
Very Best Of Roy Orbison . . . . (Virgin)
Cockles & Mussels
Emily Mitchell; *The Irish Album* . . . . (RCA)
Cynthia
Bruce Springsteen; *Tracks* . . . . (Columbia)
Daddy's Money
Ricochet; *Ricochet* . . . . (Columbia)
Dance: Ten; Looks: Three
Original Cast; *A Chorus Line* . . . . (Columbia)
Darling Pretty
Mark Knopfler; *Golden Heart* . . . .(Warner Bros.)
Die Young, Stay Pretty
Blondie; *Eat To The Beat* . . . . (Chrysalis)
Do I Love You Because You're Beautiful
Julie Andrews & Jon Cypher; *Cinderella-The CBS Television
Production* . . . . (Columbia)
Rodgers & Hammerstein Songbook . . . . (Sony Music Classical)
Mel Torme; *Mel Torme-16 Most Requested Songs* . . . . (Columbia)
Stuart Damon & Lesley Ann Warren; *Cinderella-The CBS Television
Network Production* . . . . (Columbia)
Don't Put A Tax On The Beautiful Girls
Eddie Cantor; *Rare Early Recordings-1919-1921* . . . . (Biograph)
Don't The Girls All Get Prettier At Closing Time
Mickey Gilley; *Make It Like The First Time* . . . . (ISD/Intersound)
Everybody's Free (To Wear Sunscreen)
Baz Luhrmann; *Now That's What I Call Music!-#2-C* . . . . (Virgin)
Something For Everybody . . . . (Capitol)
Everything Is Beautiful
Ray Stevens; *Everything Is Beautiful* . . . . (MCA Special Prod.)
Five Foot Two, Eyes Of Blue
Mom & Dads; *Very Best Of The Mom & Dads* . . . . (Crescendo)
Flower Is A Lovesome Thing
Ella Fitzgerald; *Jazz 'Round Midnight Again* . . . . (Verve)
Frank Morgan; *Lush Life-Billy Strayhorn Songbook* . . . . (Verve)
Vince Guaraldi; *Jazz Impressions* . . . . (Original Jazz Classics)
For The Beauty Of The Earth
Paul Winter Consort; *Missa Gaia (Earth Mass)* . . . .(Living Music)
Fresno Beauties
Broadway Cast; *Most Happy Fella* . . . . (RCA)
Girl From Ipanema
Antonio Carlos Jobim; *Antonio Carlos Jobim* . . . .(Warner Bros.)
Compact Jazz-Antonio Carlos Jobim . . . . (Verve)
Ella Fitzgerald; *Ella A Nice* . . . . (Pablo)
Montreux '75 . . . . (Pablo)
Pablo Today-Ella Embraces Antonio Carlos Jobim . . . . (Pablo)
Stan Getz & Astrud Gilberto; *Cruisin'-1964-C* . . . . (Increase)
Getz/Gilberto . . . . (Verve)
God Blessed Texas
Little Texas; *Big Time* . . . .(Warner Bros.)
God Don't Make Lonely Girls
Wallflowers; *Bringing Down The Horse* . . . . (Interscope)
Good Morning Beautiful
Steve Holy; *Blue Moon* . . . . (Curb)
Have You Seen Her
Chi-Lites; *Chi-Lites' Greatest Hits* . . . . (Rhino)
Hammer; *Please Hammer Don't Hurt 'Em* . . . . (Capitol)
Hearts Are Gonna Roll
Hal Ketchum; *Sure Love* . . . . (Curb)
Hey Pretty
Poe; *Haunted* . . . . (FEI/Atlantic)
Hey, Good Lookin'
Hank Williams With His Drifting Cowboys; *24 Of Hank Williams'
Greatest Hits* . . . . (Polydor)

Hank Williams-40 Greatest Hits . . . . (Polydor)
Hey, Good Lookin'-December 1950-July 1951 . . . . (Polydor)
Loretta Lynn & Conway Twitty; *Hey, Good Lookin'* . . . . . (MCA Special Prod.)
Holdin' Heaven
Tracy Byrd; *Tracy Byrd* . . . . (MCA)
Hollywood Perfume
Pretenders; *Last Of The Independents* . . . . (Sire)
How Beautiful The Days
Original Broadway Cast; *The Most Happy Fella* . . . . (Sony Music Classical)
I Dream Of Women Like You
Ronnie McDowell; *Country Boy's Heart* . . . . (Epic)
Older Women & Other Greatest Hits . . . . (Epic)
I Feel Pretty
Julie Andrews; *A Little Bit Of Broadway* . . . . (Columbia)
Little Richard; *The Songs Of West Side Story* . . . . (RCA Victor)
Original Cast; *ST/West Side Story* . . . . (Sony Broadway)
I Had A Beautiful Time
Merle Haggard; *19 Hot Country Requests-#3-C* . . . . (Epic)
Friend In California . . . . (Epic)
Greatest Country Hits Of The '80s-1986-C . . . . (Columbia)
I Saw Her Standing There
Beatles; *Introducing...The Beatles* . . . . (Vee-Jay)
Meet The Beatles! . . . . (Capitol)
Please Please Me . . . . (Parlophone)
Rock 'N' Roll Music . . . . (Capitol)
The Beatles-Anthology-#1 . . . . (Capitol)
Paul McCartney; *Tripping The Live Fantastic-Highlights!* . . . . . . (Capitol)
I Saw Him Standing There
Tiffany; *Tiffany* . . . . (MCA)
Tiffany's Greatest Hits . . . . (Hip-O)
I.G.Y. (What A Beautiful World)
Donald Fagen; *The Nightfly* . . . . (Warner Bros.)
If You Wanna Be Happy
Jimmy Soul; *Best Of Jimmy Soul* . . . . (Rhino)
Dick Bartley's One-Hit Wonders Of The '60s-#1-C . . . . (Rhino)
Son Of Frat Rock!-C . . . . (Rhino)
ST/Mermaids . . . . (Geffen)
ST/My Best Friend's Wedding . . . . (Work/Epic)
Ini
Amel Larrieux; *Infinite Possibilities* . . . . (Epic)
Isn't She Lovely
Keb' Mo'; *Big Wide Grin* . . . . (Sony Wonder)
Lee Ritenour; *Best Of Lee Ritenour* . . . . (Epic)
Stevie Wonder; *Original Musiquarium* . . . . (Motown)
Songs In The Key Of Life . . . . (Motown)
Isn't This A Lovely Day
Ella Fitzgerald; *The Irving Berlin Songbook-#2* . . . . (Verve)
Fred Astaire; *Fred Astaire Sings* . . . . (MCA)
Irving Berlin Songbook . . . . (Verve)
Starring Fred Astaire . . . . (Columbia)
Itchycoo Park
Small Faces; *Baby Boomer Classics-British Sixties-C* . . . . (JCI Assoc. Labels)
It's A Lovely Lovely World
Gail Davies; *Gail Davies' Greatest Hits* . . . . (Little Chickadee)
It's Your Love
Tim McGraw with Faith Hill; *Everywhere* . . . . (Curb)
Tim McGraw's Greatest Hits . . . . (Curb)
Jolene
Dolly Parton; *Best Of Dolly Parton* . . . . (RCA)
Best There Is . . . . (RCA)
Jolene . . . . (RCA)
RCA Years-1967-1986 . . . . (RCA)
Sherrie Austin; *Followin' A Feelin'* . . . . (We/Madacy)
Keep Young And Beautiful
Annie Lennox; *Diva* . . . . (Arista)
La Isla Bonita
Madonna; *True Blue* . . . . (Sire)
Life Is Beautiful
Amy Correia; *Carnival Love* . . . . (Capitol)
Little Bitty Pretty One
Huey Lewis and the News; *Four Chords & Several Years Ago* . . . . . (Elektra)
Jackson 5; *Jackson 5-16 Greatest Hits* . . . . (Motown)
Jackson 5-Anthology . . . . (Motown)
Lookin' Through The Windows . . . . (Motown)
Motown Legends-Jackson 5 . . . . (Motown)
Top 10 With A Bullet-Motown Male Groups-C . . . . (Motown)
Thurston Harris; *Billboard Top R&B Hits-1957-C* . . . . (Rhino)
Collectables Presents The History Of Rock-#2-C . . . . (Collectables)
Love Is A Beautiful Thing
Tina Turner; *Diana, Princess Of Wales-Tribute-C* . . . . (Columbia)
Love So Beautiful, A
Michael Bolton; *Michael Bolton's Greatest Hits-1985-1995* . . . . (Columbia)
Roy Orbison; *Mystery Girl* . . . . (Virgin)
ST/Indecent Proposal . . . . (MCA)
Lovely Rita
Beatles; *Sgt. Pepper's Lonely Hearts Club Band* . . . . (Capitol)
Lucky
Britney Spears; *Now That's What I Call Music!-#5-C* . . . . (Virgin)
Oops!...I Did It Again . . . . (Jive)

Mary In The Morning
Al Martino; *Al Martino's Greatest Hits* . . . . (EMI Special Markets)
Memory Remains
Metallica; *Reload* . . . . (Elektra)
Mental Illness Can Be Beautiful
John Trubee & The Ugly Janitors Of America; *Naked Teenage Girls In Outer Space* . . . . (Enigma)
More Pretty Girls Than One
Tom Rush; *Blues Songs & Ballads* . . . . (Fantasy)
Woody Guthrie; *One Of A Kind* . . . . (Pair)
Most Beautiful Girl
Charlie Rich; *Behind Closed Doors* . . . . (Epic)
Charlie Rich's Greatest Hits . . . . (Epic)
Columbia Country Classics-#4-Nashville Sound-C . . . . (Columbia)
Most Beautiful Girl In The World
Frank Sinatra; *Strangers In The Night* . . . . (Reprise)
Tony Bennett; *Rodgers & Hart Songbook* . . . . (DRG)
Tony Bennett Sings More Great Rodgers & Hart . . . . (Improv)
Most Beautiful Girl In The World
Prince; *The Gold Experience* . . . . (NPG)
Most Beautiful World In The World
Nilsson; *Son Of Schmilsson* . . . . (RCA)
Mrs. Brown You've Got A Lovely Daughter
Herman's Hermits; *Herman's Hermits-Their Greatest Hits* . . . . (Abkco)
Something Good Again . . . . (Abkco)
Mrs. Steven Rudy
Mark McGuinn; *Mark McGuinn* . . . . (VFR)
My Beautiful Irish Maid
Chauncey Olcott; *Music From The New York Stage (1890-1920)-#1-1890-1908-C* . . . . (Pearl)
My Beautiful Reward
Bruce Springsteen; *Lucky Town* . . . . (Columbia)
My Little Miss America
Gary U.S. Bonds; *45-#1034* . . . . (LeGrand)
My Lovely Lady
Jimmy Buffett; *White Sport Coat & A Pink Crustacean* . . . . (MCA)
My Russia, You Are Beautiful
Ivan Rebroff; *Memories Of Russia* . . . . (Columbia)
My Truly, Truly Fair
Guy Mitchell; *Guy Mitchell-16 Most Requested Songs* . . . . (Legacy)
Oh You Beautiful Doll
Guy Lombardo & His Royal Canadians; *Dance To Songs Everybody Knows* . . . . (MCA)
Oh, Pretty Woman
2 Live Crew; *As Clean As They Wanna Be* . . . . (Luke)
Al Green; *Al Green's Greatest Hits-#2* . . . . (Motown)
I'm Still In Love With You . . . . (Right Stuff)
Ricky Van Shelton; *RVS III* . . . . (Columbia)
Roy Orbison; *In Dreams-Greatest Hits* . . . . (Orbison)
Roy Orbison's All-Time Greatest Hits-#1 & 2 . . . . (Monument)
ST/Pretty Woman . . . . (EMI)
Van Halen; *Diver Down* . . . . (Warner Bros.)
Oh, Pretty Woman
Gary Moore; *Blues Alive* . . . . (Virgin)
Still Got The Blues . . . . (Charisma)
Oh, Pretty Woman (Can't Make You Love Me)
Albert King; *The Ultimate Collection-Albert King* . . . . (Rhino)
Oh, What A Beautiful Morning
Original Broadway Cast; *Oklahoma!* . . . . (RCA)
Original Cast; *Oklahoma!* . . . . (MCA)
Outside
Staind; *Break The Cycle* . . . . (Flip/Elektra)
Paint Your Pretty Picture
Carmen McRae; *At The Great American Music Hall* . . . . (Blue Note)
Pearl Of The Quarter
Steely Dan; *Countdown To Ecstasy* . . . . (MCA)
Peggy Sue
Buddy Holly; *Billboard Top Rock 'N' Roll Hits-1957-C* . . . . (Rhino)
Buddy Holly . . . . (MCA)
Buddy Holly-20 Golden Greats . . . . (MCA)
Buddy Holly's Greatest Hits . . . . (MCA)
More American Graffiti-C . . . . (MCA)
Oldies But Goodies-#4-C . . . . (Original Sound)
Rock & Roll Collection . . . . (MCA)
Prettiest Eyes In California
B.W. Stevenson; *Rainbow Down The Road* . . . . (Amazing)
Prettiest Star
David Bowie; *Aladdin Sane* . . . . (Rykodisc)
Sound + Vision . . . . (Rykodisc)
Pretty
Korn; *Follow The Leader* . . . . (Immortal/Epic)
Pretty As You Feel
Jefferson Airplane; *2400 Fulton Street-An Anthology* . . . . (RCA)
Loves You . . . . (RCA)
Pretty Baby
Al Jolson; *The Al Jolson Story-#2* . . . . (MCA)
Leon Redbone; *Sugar* . . . . (Private Music)
Pretty Baby
Five Satins; *Five Satins Sing Their Greatest Hits* . . . . (Collectables)

Pretty Baby
Kool & The Gang; *As One* . . . . (De-Lite)
Pretty Ballerina
Left Banke; *History Of The Left Banke* . . . . (Rhino)
Nuggets-#11-Pop-Part 4-C . . . . (Rhino)
Pretty Blue Eyes
Steve Lawrence; *Best Of Steve Lawrence* . . . . (Taragon)
Pretty Boy Floyd
Arlo Guthrie & Pete Seeger; *Precious Friend* . . . . (Warner Bros.)
Bob Dylan; *Folkways: A Vision Shared-C* . . . . (Columbia)
Byrds; *Sweetheart Of The Rodeo* . . . . (Columbia)
The Byrds . . . . (Columbia)
Joan Baez; *Greatest Songs Of Woody Guthrie-C* . . . . (Vanguard)
Woody Guthrie; *Dust Bowl Ballads* . . . . (Rounder)
Legendary Woody Guthrie . . . . (Tradition)
Struggle . . . . (Smithsonian Folkways)
Woody Guthrie . . . . (Everest)
Worried Man Blues-Golden Classics-#1 . . . . (Collectables)
Pretty Donna
Collective Soul; *Hints, Allegations And Things Left Unsaid* . . . . (Atlantic)
Pretty Flamingo
Manfred Mann; *Best Of Manfred Mann* . . . . (EMI Special Markets)
History Of British Rock-#4-C . . . . (Rhino)
Rod Stewart; *Night On The Town* . . . . (Warner Bros.)
Pretty Fuck Look
Pussy Galore; *Corpse Love-The First Year* . . . . (Caroline)
Pretty Girl
Jon B.; *Bonafide* . . . . (Yab Yum/550)
Pretty Girl Is Like A Melody, A
John Steel; *Music From The New York Stage (1890-1920)-#4-1917-1920-C* . . . . (Pearl)
Pretty Girl Milking A Cow
Judy Garland; *Best Of Judy Garland* . . . . (MCA)
One & Only . . . . (Capitol)
Pretty Girls And Cadillacs
Nighthawks; *Backtrack* . . . . (Varrick)
Pretty Girls Don't Cry
Chris Isaak; *Silvertone* . . . . (Warner Bros.)
Pretty Girls Everywhere
Eugene Church & The Fellows; *Spotlite Series-Class Records-#1-C* . . . . (Collectables)
Pretty Girls In Chicago Polka
Li'l Wally; *Brings Happiness To You* . . . . (Jay Jay)
Pretty Girls Make Graves
Smiths; *Smiths* . . . . (Sire)
Pretty Green Island
George Tucker; *George Tucker* . . . . (Rounder)
Pretty In Pink
Psychedelic Furs; *All Of This & Nothing* . . . . (Columbia)
ST/Pretty In Pink . . . . (A&M)
Talk Talk Talk . . . . (Columbia)
Pretty Lady
Original Broadway Cast; *Pacific Overtures* . . . . (RCA)
Pretty Litle Lady From Beaumont, Texas
George Jones; *One Woman Man* . . . . (Epic)
Texas Super Hits-C . . . . (Columbia)
Pretty Little Adriana
Vince Gill; *High Lonesome Sound* . . . . (MCA)
Pretty Little Angel
Stevie Wonder; *Uptight (Everything's Alright)* . . . . (Motown)
Pretty Little Angel
Crests; *Crests Greatest Hits* . . . . (Collectables)
Pretty Little Angel Eyes
Curtis Lee; *Million-Dollar Memories-#2-C* . . . . (RCA)
Oldies But Goodies-#2-C . . . . (Original Sound)
Phil Spector-Back To Mono 1958-1969-C . . . . (Abkco)
Phil Spector-The Early Years-1958-1961-C . . . . (Rhino)
Rock & Roll U.S.A.-21 Rock & Roll Favorites-#2-C . . . . . . (Laurie)
Pretty Little Dogies
Skip Gorman; *A Cowboy's Wild Song To His Herd* . . . . (Rounder)
Pretty Little Indian
Dan Crary; *Lady's Fancy* . . . . (Rounder)
Pretty Little Miss
Patty Loveless; *Mountain Soul* . . . . (Epic)
Pretty Little Picture
Original Cast; *A Funny Thing Happened On The Way To The Forum* . . . (Angel)
Stephen Sondheim; *Collector's Sondheim-C* . . . . (RCA)
Pretty Little Pink
Doc Watson; *Old Timey Concert* . . . . (Vanguard)
Pretty Mouse
Fluid; *Glue* . . . . (Sub Pop)
Pretty Noose
Soundgarden; *Down On The Upside* . . . . (A&M)
Pretty Penny
Stone Temple Pilots; *Purple* . . . . (Atlantic)
Pretty Pink Rose
Adrian Belew; *Young Lions* . . . . (Atlantic)

Pretty Polly
Judy Collins; *Who Knows Where The Time Goes* . . . . (Elektra)
Stanley Brothers; *Complete Columbia Stanley Brothers* . . . . (Legacy)
   Folk Classics: Roots Of American Folk Music-C . . . . (Columbia)
   Long Journey Home . . . . (Rebel)
Pretty Princess
Loggins & Messina; *Native Sons* . . . . (Columbia)
Pretty Woman
Duke Ellington & His Orchestra; *Duke Ellington & His Orchestra Play 22*
   Original Big Band Recordings . . . . (Hindsight)
Pretty Women
Original Cast; *Sweeney Todd* . . . . (RCA)
Pretty Women/Ladies Who Lunch
Barbra Streisand; *The Broadway Album* . . . . (Columbia)
Pretty Words
Vince Gill; *I Still Believe In You* . . . .(MCA)
Pretty World
Sergio Mendes & Brasil '66; *Sergio Mendes & Brasil '66's*
   Greatest Hits . . . . (A&M)
   Sergio Mendes-Classics-#18 . . . . (A&M)
Pretty Wreath For Mother's Grave
Reno & Smiley; *1983 Collector's Edition-#9* . . . . . . (International Mktg. Group)
Ravishing Ruby
Tom T. Hall; *Essential Tom T. Hall-20th Anniversary Collection* . . . . (Mercury)
   Tom T. Hall's Greatest Hits-#2 . . . . (Mercury)
Santa Fe/Beautiful Obsession
Van Morrison; *Wavelength* . . . .(Warner Bros.)
Save It, Pretty Mama
Lionel Hampton & His Orchestra; *Tempo & Swing* . . . . (Bluebird)
Louis Armstrong; *1940s-Small Band Sides-C* . . . . (Bluebird)
   Louis Armstrong-1928-1931 . . . . (Nimbus)
Louis Armstrong & Earl Hines; *Louis Armstrong-Vol. 4-In*
   New York . . . . (Columbia)
Teddy Buckner; *Salute To Louis Armstrong* . . . . (Crescendo)
Sharp Dressed Man
ZZ Top; *Eliminator* . . . .(Warner Bros.)
   ZZ Top's Greatest Hits . . . .(Warner Bros.)
She Don't Know She's Beautiful
Sammy Kershaw; *Haunted Heart* . . . . (Mercury)
Sheila
Tommy Roe; *Billboard Top Rock 'N' Roll Hits-1962-C* . . . . (Rhino)
   Golden Years-1962-C . . . . (Dominion Entert.)
   Original Rock 'N' Roll Hits Of The '60s-C . . . . (Roulette)
   Sheila . . . . (Accord)
   Tommy Roe's Greatest Hits . . . . (MCA)
She's A Rainbow
Rolling Stones; *Get Yer Ya-Ya's Out!* . . . . (Abkco)
   More Hot Rocks (big hits & fazed cookies) . . . . (Abkco)
   Singles Collection-The London Years . . . . (Abkco)
   Their Satanic Majesties Request . . . . (Abkco)
   Through The Past, Darkly (Big Hits Vol. 2) . . . . (Abkco)
She's Lookin' Good
Rodger Collins; *Soul Shots-#2-The "In" Crowd-Sweet Soul-C* . . . . . . (Rhino)
Wilson Pickett; *Very Best Of Wilson Pickett* . . . . (Rhino)
   Wilson Pickett's Greatest Hits . . . . (Atlantic)
Shine
Jon B.; *Cool Relax* . . . . (Yab Yum/550)
Sick & Beautiful
Artificial Joy Club; *Melt* . . . . (Interscope)
Sick Of Myself
Matthew Sweet; *100% Fun* . . . . (Zoo)
Simply Irresistible
Robert Palmer; *Super Nova* . . . . (Island)
Sleeping Beauty Waltz
101 Strings Orchestra; *Million-Seller Themes From Tchaikovsky* . . . . (Alshire)
Smile Like Yours
Natalie Cole; *ST/A Smile Like Yours* . . . . (Elektra)
So Fine
Fiestas; *Baby Boomer Classics-Party Time Fifties-C* . . . . . . (JCI Assoc. Labels)
   Baby Boomer's Best-Jumpin' Jive 50's-C . . . . (Priority)
Some Beautiful Morning
Al Jolson; *Music From The New York Stage (1890-1920)-#4-1917-*
   1920-C . . . . (Pearl)
Someone Else's Dream
Faith Hill; *It Matters To Me* . . . .(Warner Bros.)
Something Beautiful Remains
Tina Turner; *Wildest Dreams* . . . . (Virgin)
Sweet And Lovely
Bing Crosby; *Pennies From Heaven* . . . . (Pro-Arte)
Thelonius Monk; *Monk's Dream* . . . . (Columbia)
Woody Herman; *Essential Big Bands-C* . . . . (Verve)
Teenage Cutie
Eddie Cochran; *Eddie Cochran-Legendary Masters* . . . .(EMI)
Thank You Pretty Baby
Brook Benton; *Brook Benton-At His Best* . . . . (Pair)
   It's Just A Matter Of Time-His Greatest Hits . . . . (Mercury)
Professor Longhair; *'Fess-Anthology* . . . . (Rhino)
Thanks For The Beautiful Land On The Delta
Duke Ellington; *New Orleans Suite* . . . . (Atlantic)

Theme From "The Miss America Pageant" (There She Is, Miss America)
Bert Parks; *Television's Greatest Hits-#4-Black & White Classics-C* . . . . (TVT)
Too Beautiful To Cry
Roger Whittaker; *Roger Whittaker Greatest Hits* . . . . (RCA)
   Wind Beneath My Wings . . . . (RCA)
T-R-O-U-B-L-E
Elvis Presley; *A Touch Of Platinum-#2* . . . . (RCA)
Travis Tritt; *Travis Tritt's Greatest Hits-From The Beginning* . . . (Warner Bros.)
   T-R-O-U-B-L-E . . . . (Warner Bros.)
True Colors
Cyndi Lauper; *She's So Unusual/True Colors/Hat Full Of Stars (Box)* . . . (Epic)
   True Colors . . . . (Portrait)
   Twelve Deadly Cyns...And Then Some . . . . (Epic)
Phil Collins; *Phil Collins-Hits* . . . .(Atlantic)
Try Not To Look So Pretty
Dwight Yoakam; *This Time* . . . . (Reprise)
Ugly
Fishbone; *Fishbone* . . . . (Columbia)
   Rhythm Come Forward: Volume II-C . . . . (Columbia)
Ugly
Saigon Kick; *Saigon Kick* . . . .(Third Stone)
Ugly Girl
Fleming & John; *The Way We Are* . . . . (Universal)
Universal Heart-Beat
Juliana Hatfield; *Box Presents Big Ones Of Alternative*
   Rock-#1-C . . . . (Box Tunes)
   Only Everything . . . .(Mammoth)
Unpretty
TLC; *Fanmail* . . . . (LaFace)
Up, Up & Away
5th Dimension; *5th Dimension-Anthology 1967-1973* . . . . (Rhino)
   Greatest Hits On Earth . . . . (Arista)
Vermont Is Afire In The Autumn
Lui Collins; *Made In New England* . . . . (Green Linnet)
Video
India.Arie; *Acoustic Soul* . . . . (Motown)
Warm & Beautiful
Wings; *Wings At The Speed Of Sound* . . . . (Capitol)
Way You Look Tonight, The
Billie Holiday; *Quintessential-#2-1936* . . . . (Columbia)
Erroll Garner; *Body And Soul* . . . . (Legacy)
Frank Sinatra; *Days Of Wine And Roses, Moon River, And Other Academy*
   Award Winners . . . . (Reprise)
   Sinatra Reprise-The Very Good Years . . . . (Reprise)
   The Reprise Collection . . . . (Reprise)
Fred Astaire; *Steppin' Out-Astaire Sings* . . . . (Verve)
Lettermen; *Best Of The Lettermen-All Original Recordings* . . . . (Curb)
   Capitol Collectors Series-The Lettermen . . . . (Capitol)
   The Lettermen's All-Time Greatest Hits . . . . (Capitol)
Tony Bennett; *ST/My Best Friend's Wedding* . . . . (Work/Epic)
Wendy
Original Cast/Mary Martin; *Peter Pan-The 1954 Broadway*
   Production . . . . (RCA Victor)
Why'd You Come In Here Lookin' Like That
Dolly Parton; *White Limozeen* . . . . (Columbia)
Woman In Me
Jessica Simpson featuring Destiny's Child; *Sweet Kisses* . . . . (Columbia)
Wonderful World, Beautiful People
Jimmy Cliff; *In Concert-Best Of Jimmy Cliff* . . . . (Reprise)
   Reggae Spectacular-C . . . . (A&M)
   Wonderful World, Beautiful People . . . . (A&M)
Yellow
Coldplay; *Now That's What I Call Music!-#6-C* . . . . (Virgin)
   Parachutes . . . . (Nettwerk/Capitol)
You Are So Beautiful
Joe Cocker; *Chicken Soup For The Soul: Love And Inspiration-C* . . . . (Rhino)
   Joe Cocker-Super Hits . . . . (Legacy)
   Organic . . . . (550 Music)
Kenny Rogers; *Timepiece* . . . . (Atlantic)
You Decorated My Life
Kenny Rogers; *Kenny Rogers' Greatest Hits* . . . . (EMI)
   Kenny Rogers-20 Great Years . . . . (Reprise)
   Kenny Rogers-Twenty Greatest Hits . . . . (EMI)
You Must Have Been A Beautiful Baby
Bobby Darin; *Splish Splash-Best Of Bobby Darin-#1* . . . . (Atlantic)
Johnny Mercer; *Johnny Mercer Sings Johnny Mercer* . . . . (Everest)
Russ Morgan & His Orchestra; *Russ Morgan & His Orchestra Play 22*
   Original Big Band Recordings . . . . (Hindsight)
You Walked In
Lonestar; *Crazy Nights* . . . . (BNA)
Young And Beautiful
Elvis Presley; *A Valentine Gift For You* . . . . (RCA)
   Heart & Soul . . . . (RCA)
   The Other Sides-Worldwide Gold Award Hits, Vol. 2 . . . . (RCA)
Young And Beautiful
Peter And Gordon; *Woman/Lady Godiva* . . . . (Collectables)
You're Sixteen
Johnny Burnette; *ST/American Graffiti* . . . . (MCA)

Ringo Starr; *Blast From Your Past* . . . . (Gold Rush)
   Ringo . . . . (Capitol)
You're The Reason Our Kids Are Ugly
Loretta Lynn & Conway Twitty; *Conway Twittty-20 Greatest Hits* . . . . . (MCA)
   Very Best Of Loretta Lynn & Conway Twitty . . . . (MCA)

BEGINNINGS, Discovery

See Also: **BABY, LOVE: FALLING IN LOVE, MARRIAGE,**
MORNING, NEW, NUMBERS: 1, SEASONS: SPRING

(Just Like) Starting Over
John Lennon & Yoko Ono; *Double Fantasy* . . . . (Capitol)
   ST/Imagine: John Lennon . . . . (Capitol)
And The Beat Goes On
Whispers; *Club Epic-#1-C* . . . . (Legacy)
Aquarius
Original Broadway Cast; *Hair* . . . . (RCA)
Aquarius/Let The Sunshine In Medley
5th Dimension; *Billboard Top Rock 'N' Roll Hits-1969-C* . . . . (Rhino)
   Greatest Hits On Earth . . . . (Arista)
   ST/1969 . . . . (Polydor)
   ST/Forrest Gump . . . . (Epic/Sony Music Soundtrax)
At The Beginning
Richard Marx & Donna Lewis; *ST/Anastasia-Music From The Motion*
   Picture . . . . (Atlantic)
Back Where It All Begins
Allman Brothers Band; *Where It All Begins* . . . . (Epic)
Begin The Beguine
Art Tatum; *Solos-1940* . . . . (MCA)
Ella Fitzgerald; *Cole Porter Songbook* . . . . (Verve)
Johnny Mathis; *Best Days Of My Life* . . . . (Columbia)
   First 25 Years-Silver Anniversary Album . . . . (Columbia)
   Johnny Mathis-Live . . . . (Columbia)
Tony Bennett; *Forty Years-The Artistry Of Tony Bennett* . . . . (Columbia)
Beginning, The
Keb' Mo'; *The Door* . . . . (550/Epic/Okeh)
Beyond The Blue Horizon
Jeanette MacDonald; *Hollywood Sings-C* . . . . (Living Era)
Lou Christie; *ST/Rain Man* . . . . (Capitol)
Brand New Day
Sting; *Brand New Day* . . . . (A&M)
Bus Stop
Hollies; *Best Of The Hollies* . . . . (EMI)
   History Of British Rock-#3-C . . . . (Rhino)
   The Hollies' Greatest Hits . . . . (Epic)
Can I Change My Mind
Tyrone Davis; *Soul Shots-#2-The "In" Crowd-Sweet Soul-C* . . . . . . (Rhino)
   Tyrone Davis' Greatest Hits . . . . (Rhino)
Can't Stand It
Wilco; *Summer Teeth* . . . . (Reprise)
Closing Time
Semisonic; *Feeling Strangely Fine* . . . . (MCA)
   Now That's What I Call Music!-#2-C . . . . (Virgin)
Coming Out Of The Dark
Gloria Estefan; *Gloria Estefan's Greatest Hits* . . . . (Epic)
   God Bless America-C . . . . (Columbia)
   Hot #1 Hits-C . . . . (Foundation)
   Into The Light . . . . (Epic)
Could I Be
Wood; *Songs From Stamford Hill* . . . . (Columbia)
Don't Get Me Started
Rhett Akins; *Somebody New* . . . . (Decca)
Embryonic Journey
Hot Tuna; *Splashdown* . . . . (Relix)
Jefferson Airplane; *2400 Fulton Street-An Anthology* . . . . (RCA)
   Surrealistic Pillow . . . . (RCA)
   The Worst Of Jefferson Airplane . . . . (RCA)
End Is The Beginning Is The End
Smashing Pumpkins; *ST/Batman & Robin-Music From And Inspired By The*
   Motion Picture . . . . (Jive)
Everything's Coming Up Roses
Ethel Merman; *Broadway Magic-The 1960s-C* . . . . (Columbia)
Original Cast; *Gypsy* . . . . (Columbia)
Original London Cast; *Gypsy* . . . . (RCA)
From The Beginning
Emerson, Lake & Palmer; *Best Of Emerson, Lake & Palmer* . . . . . . (Rhino)
   Trilogy . . . . (Atlantic)
From This Moment On
Shania Twain & Bryan White; *Come On Over* . . . . (Mercury)
Get The Party Started
Pink; *Missundaztood* . . . . (Arista)
Halfway Down
Patty Loveless; *When Fallen Angels Fly* . . . . (Epic)
Hey Jude
Beatles; *Beatles 1* . . . . (Capitol)

Beatles-20 Greatest Hits . . . . (Capitol)
Past Masters-Volume Two . . . . (Parlophone)
The Beatles/1967-1970 . . . . (Capitol)
Paul McCartney; *Knebworth-The Album-C* . . . . (Polydor)
Wilson Pickett; *Wilson Pickett's Greatest Hits* . . . . (Atlantic)
I Can't Get Started
Anita O'Day; *Jazz 'Round Midnight-Anita O'Day* . . . . (Verve)
Bunny Berigan & His Orchestra; *An Evening At Rao's: Songs From An*
   Italian Restaurant-C . . . . (Legacy)
   Idiot's Guide To Jazz-C . . . . (RCA Victor)
   The Pied Piper . . . . (Bluebird)
   The Swingingest Sounds Ever Heard-C . . . . (Hip-O)
Ella Fitzgerald; *Compact Jazz-Ella Fitzgerald* . . . . (Verve)
Lester Young; *Best Of Lester Young* . . . . (Pablo)
I Finally Found Someone
Barbra Streisand & Bryan Adams; *ST/The Mirror Has Two Faces* . . . (Columbia)
I Only Want To Be With You
Bay City Rollers; *Bay City Rollers' Greatest Hits* . . . . (Arista)
Dusty Springfield; *Dusty Springfield-Anthology* . . . . (Mercury)
   Dusty Springfield-Golden Hits . . . . (Mercury)
Vonda Shepard; *ST/Songs From "Ally McBeal" Featuring Vonda*
   Shepard . . . . (550/Epic)
I Started A Joke
Bee Gees; *Best Of The Bee Gees-#1* . . . . (Polydor)
   Here At Last...Bee Gees...Live . . . . (Polydor)
   One Night Only . . . . (Polydor)
Wallflowers; *ST/Zoolander* . . . . (Hollywood)
If I Never Stop Loving You
David Kersh; *If I Never Stop Loving You* . . . . (Curb)
It's Not Where You Start (It's Where You Finish)
Barbara Cook; *Dorothy Fields-Close As Pages In A Book* . . . . (DRG)
Original Broadway Cast; *See Saw* . . . . (DRG)
I've Got Beginner's Luck
Fred Astaire; *Top Hat, White Tie And Tails* . . . . (ASV)
Gregory Hines & Patti Austin; *Hollywood Bowl Orchestra's Greatest*
   Hits-C . . . . (Philips)
Let's Get Started
Gota; *Let's Get Started* . . . . (Instinct)
Life Has Just Begun
Spirit; *12 Dreams Of Dr. Sardonicus* . . . . (Epic)
Lock And Load
Bob Seger; *It's A Mystery* . . . . (Capitol)
Love Story
Tanita Tikaram; *Sweet Keeper* . . . . (Reprise)
Memory
Original Broadway Cast; *Cats* . . . . (Geffen)
My First Night With You
Mya; *Mya* . . . . (University/Interscope)
New Beginning
Tracy Chapman; *New Beginning* . . . . (Elektra)
New Beginning
Stir; *Holy Dogs* . . . . (Capitol)
New World Rising
Electric Light Orchestra; *On The Third Day* . . . . (Jet)
Pick Yourself Up
Diana King; *When I Look In Your Eyes* . . . . (GRP)
Frank Sinatra; *Sinatra and Swingin' Brass* . . . . (Reprise)
Fred Astaire; *Starring Fred Astaire* . . . . (Columbia)
   That's Dancing . . . . (EMI)
Promise Of A New Day
Paula Abdul; *Spellbound* . . . . (Captive)
Sinner
Neil Finn; *Try Whistling This* . . . . (Work)
Sittin' On Go
Bryan White; *Between Now And Forever* . . . . (Asylum)
Someday Out Of The Blue
Elton John; *ST/The Road To El Dorado* . . . . (DreamWorks/SKG)
Start A New Life
REO Speedwagon; *Ridin' The Storm Out* . . . . (Epic)
Start All Over Again
Desert Rose Band; *Pages Of Life* . . . . (Curb)
Start Me Up
Rolling Stones; *"Still Life" (American Concert 1981)* . . . . (Virgin)
   Flashpoint . . . . (Virgin)
   Tattoo You . . . . (Virgin)
Start The Commotion
Wiseguys; *Now That's What I Call Music!-#8-C* . . . . (Virgin)
   The Antidote . . . . (Mammoth)
Starting A New Life
Van Morrison; *Tupelo Honey* . . . . (Polydor)
Starting All Over Again
Daryl Hall & John Oates; *Change Of Season* . . . . (Arista)
Mel & Tim; *15 Original Big Hits-#1-C* . . . . (Stax)
   Top Of The Stax-Twenty Greatest Hits-C . . . . (Stax)
Starting Over Again
Steve Wariner; *Best Of Steve Wariner* . . . . (MCA Special Prod.)
   Country Classics-#7-1986-1987-C . . . . (Universal)
   Life's Highway . . . . (MCA)

Steve Wariner's Greatest Hits . . . . (MCA)
Starting Over Again
Dolly Parton; *Dolly Dolly Dolly* . . . . (RCA)
   Dolly Parton-Super Hits-#2 . . . . (RCA)
   Essential Dolly Parton . . . . (RCA)
Reba McEntire; *Starting Over* . . . . (MCA)
Starting Over Again
Natalie Cole; *Good To Be Back* . . . . (Elektra)
Starting To Fall
Marilyn Scott; *Avenues Of Love* . . . .(Warner Bros.)
Strike It Up
Black Box; *Dreamland* . . . . (RCA)
   Mixedup! . . . . (RCA)
That's How A Heartache Begins
Patsy Cline; *Songwriter's Tribute* . . . . (MCA)
That's When Your Heartaches Begin
Elvis Presley; *Elvis' Golden Records* . . . . (RCA)
   Million-Dollar Quartet . . . . (RCA)
   Worldwide 50 Gold Award Hits, Vol. 1, Parts 1 & 2 . . . . . (RCA)
Theme From "Love Story"
Andy Williams; *Andy Williams' Greatest Hits-#2* . . . . (Columbia)
   Love Story . . . . (Columbia)
Cincinnati Pops Orchestra/Erich Kunzel; *Hollywood's Greatest
   Hits-#1* . . . . (Telarc)
Francis Lai; *ST/Love Story* . . . .(MCA)
Johnny Mathis; *Johnny Mathis' All-Time Greatest Hits* . . . . . . (Columbia)
   Johnny Mathis-16 Most Requested Songs . . . . (Columbia)
Peter Nero; *Peter Nero's Greatest Hits* . . . . (Columbia)
Today I Started Loving You Again
Blue Ridge Rangers; *Blue Ridge Rangers* . . . . (Fantasy)
Merle Haggard; *Best Of The Best Of Merle Haggard* . . . . (Liberty)
   Merle Haggard-Super Hits-#2 . . . .(Epic)
Tomorrow Never Knows
Beatles; *Beatles-Box Set* . . . . (Capitol)
   Revolver . . . . (Capitol)
Phil Collins; *Face Value* . . . . (Atlantic)
Under African Skies
Paul Simon; *Graceland* . . . .(Warner Bros.)
Wanna Be Startin' Somethin'
Michael Jackson; *HIStory: Past, Present And Future-Book 1-C* . . . .(Epic)
   Thriller . . . .(Epic)
We're Off To See The Wizard
Jewel/Jackson Browne/Ry Cooder; *The Wizard Of Oz In Concert: Dreams
   Come True-C* . . . . (Rhino)
Judy Garland; *A&E Biography: A Musical Anthology* . . . . (Capitol)
Original Cast; *The Wizard Of Oz* . . . . (TVT)
Original Soundtrack; *The Wizard Of Oz-Selections From The Original Motion
   Picture Soundtrack* . . . . (Turner Classic Movies)
We've Only Just Begun
Barbra Streisand; *Just For The Record* . . . . (Columbia)
Carpenters; *Carpenters-Classics-#2* . . . . (A&M)
   Carpenters-The Singles 1969-1973 . . . . (A&M)
   Close To You . . . . (A&M)
   From The Top . . . . (A&M)
   Yesterday Once More . . . . (A&M)
You're Beginning To Get To Me
Clay Walker; *Clay Walker's Greatest Hits* . . . . (Giant)

BELLS

A-Ting A Ling
Stan Kenton; *Lighter Side* . . . . (Creative World)
Banjo Boy Chimes
White Brothers & New Kentucky Colonels; *Live In Sweden* . . . . . . (Rounder)
Bells Are Ringing
Original Cast; *Bells Are Ringing* . . . . (Columbia)
Bells Of St. Mary's, The
Bing Crosby; *My Favorite Hymns* . . . . (Universal Special Mkts.)
Bells Of St. Paul
Linda Eder; *Another Rosie Christmas-C* . . . . (Columbia)
Carol Of The Bells
4 Seasons; *4 Seasons Christmas Album* . . . . (Rhino)
Barry Manilow; *Because It's Christmas* . . . . (Arista)
Carpenters; *Carpenters Christmas Portrait* . . . . (A&M)
   Christmas Collection . . . . (A&M)
David Benoit; *GRP Christmas Collection-C* . . . . (GRP)
David Rose; *Best Of Christmas-C* . . . . (Capitol)
Forester Sisters; *Forester Sisters' Christmas Card* . . . . . .(Warner Bros.)
Johnny Mathis; *Christmas With Johnny Mathis* . . . . (Columbia)
   For Christmas . . . . (Columbia)
Kenny Rogers; *Kenny Rogers-Christmas* . . . . (EMI)
O'Jays; *Home For Christmas* . . . .(EMI)
Ronnie Milsap; *Christmas With Ronnie Milsap* . . . . (RCA)
Soundtrack; *Home Alone* . . . . (Columbia)
Steven Curtis Chapman; *Music Of Christmas, The* . . . . (Sparrow)
Chime Bells
Elton Britt; *The RCA Years* . . . . (Collector's Choice)

Jody King; *Photographs & Memories* . . . . (Capricorn)
Chimes Of Freedom
Bob Dylan; *Another Side Of Bob Dylan* . . . . (Columbia)
Bruce Springsteen; *Chimes Of Freedom* . . . . (Columbia)
Byrds; *The Byrds* . . . . (Columbia)
   The Byrds' Greatest Hits . . . . (Columbia)
Church Bells May Ring
Diamonds; *Best Of The Diamonds* . . . . (Rhino)
Willows; *Rockin' & Rollin' Wedding Songs-#1-C* . . . . (Rhino)
ST/A Rage In Harlem . . . . (MCA Special Prod.)
WCBS FM 101 History Of Rock-'50s-#2-C . . . . (Collectables)
Crazy Bells
Marcels; *Best Of The Marcels* . . . . (Rhino)
Ding Dong
Echoes; *Spotlite Series-Gee Records-#1-C* . . . . (Collectables)
Ding Dong The Witch Is Dead
Fifth Estate; *Dick Bartley's One-Hit Wonders Of The '60s-#2-C* . . . . . . (Rhino)
Meco; *The Wizard Of Oz* . . . .(Millennium)
MGM Studio Orchestra; *ST/The Wizard Of Oz* . . . . . (Sony Music Special Prod.)
Do You Hear Wedding Bells
Jive Five; *Jive Five-Their Greatest Hits* . . . . (Collectables)
Frere Jacques
Original Soundtrack; *Toddler Favorites* . . . . (Kid Rhino/Rhino 4 Kids)
Hells Bells
AC/DC; *Back In Black* . . . . (Atco)
   Who Made Who . . . .(Atlantic)
I Hear Those Bells
Kings; *45-#1018* . . . . (Collectables)
I Heard The Bells On Christmas Day
Bing Crosby; *That Christmas Feeling* . . . . (MCA Special Prod.)
Eddy Arnold; *Christmas With Eddy Arnold* . . . . (RCA)
Harry Belafonte; *To Wish You A Merry Christmas* . . . . (RCA)
Johnny Cash; *Christmas Spirit* . . . . (Columbia)
   Classic Christmas . . . . (Sony Music Special Prod.)
Michael Martin Murphey; *Cowboy Christmas* . . . . (Warner Bros.)
Travis Tritt; *Christmas-Loving Time Of The Year* . . . . . . (Warner Bros.)
If I Had A Hammer (The Hammer Song)
Pete Seeger; *Sing-A-Long-Live At Sanders
   Theatre 1980* . . . .(Smithsonian Folkways)
Peter, Paul & Mary; *10 Years Together/The Best Of Peter, Paul
   and Mary* . . . . (Warner Bros.)
   Peter, Paul and Mary . . . . (Warner Bros.)
   Peter, Paul and Mary In Concert . . . . (Warner Bros.)
Trini Lopez; *Best Of Trini Lopez* . . . . (Exact)
Weavers; *Weavers' Greatest Hits* . . . . (Vanguard)
If I Were A Bell
Original Cast; *Guys & Dolls* . . . . (MCA)
If I Were A Bell
Teena Marie; *Ivory* . . . . (Epic)
I'm Gonna Knock On Your Door
Eddie Hodges; *History Of Cadence Records-#1-C* . . . .(Varese Vintage)
I'm In Love Again
George Morgan; *Room Full Of Roses-The George Morgan
   Collection* . . . . (Razor & Tie)
Jingle Bell Rock
Bobby Helms; *Billboard's Great Country Christmas Hits-C* . . . . (Rhino)
   Christmas Classics-C . . . . (Rhino)
   Now That's What I Call Christmas!-C . . . . (UTV)
   ST/Home Alone 2-Lost In New York . . . . (Fox/Arista)
Booker T. & The M.G.s; *Cool Yule-C* . . . . (Rhino)
Brenda Lee; *All-Time Christmas Favorites-#4-C* . . . . (MCA Special Prod.)
Chet Atkins; *East Tennessee Christmas* . . . . (Columbia)
Jambalaya Cajun Band; *Alligator Stomp-#4-Cajun Christmas-C* . . . . . . (Rhino)
Johnny Mathis; *For Christmas* . . . . (Columbia)
Lenny Dee; *Best Of Lenny Dee* . . . . (MCA)
Neil Diamond; *Neil Diamond Christmas Album* . . . . (Columbia)
Randy Travis; *Very Special Christmas-#2-C* . . . . (A&M)
Rick Orozco; *Tejano Country Christmas-C* . . . . (Arista)
Wild Rose; *Christmas For The '90s-#1-C* . . . . (Liberty)
Ka-Ding Dong
Diamonds; *Best Of The Diamonds-The Mercury Years* . . . . (Mercury)
Oh Baby Doll
Chuck Berry; *The Chess Box-Chuck Berry* . . . . (Chess)
One Less Bell To Answer
5th Dimension; *5th Dimension-Anthology 1967-1973* . . . . (Rhino)
   Greatest Hits On Earth . . . . (Arista)
Barbra Streisand; *Barbra Joan Streisand* . . . . (Columbia)
Gladys Knight & The Pips; *Gladys Knight & The Pips-Anthology* . . . . (Motown)
   If I Were Your Woman . . . . (Motown)
Opera Of The Bells
Destiny's Child; *8 Days Of Christmas* . . . . (Columbia)
Platinum Bells
Destiny's Child; *8 Days Of Christmas* . . . . (Columbia)
Ring My Bell
Anita Ward; *Billboard Top Dance Hits-1979-C* . . . . (Rhino)
   Billboard Top Rock 'N' Roll Hits-1979-C . . . . (Rhino)
   Get Down Tonight! Best Of T.K. Records-C . . . . (Rhino)
   Mega Hits Dance Classics-#1-C . . . . (Priority)
   Songs Of Love . . . . (Juana)

Sweet Surrender . . . . (Juana)
Ring-A-Ling-A-Ling
　Isley Brothers; *Shout* . . . . (Collectables)
Silver Bells
　Atlantic Starr; *ST/Home Alone 2-Lost In New York* . . . . (Fox/Arista)
　Bob Wills; *Fiddle* . . . . (Country Music Foundation)
　Booker T. & The M.G.s; *Soul Christmas-C* . . . . (Atlantic)
　Brady Bunch Kids; *Christmas With The Brady Bunch* . . . . (MCA Special Prod.)
　Brenda Lee; *Brenda Lee-Christmas* . . . . (Warner Bros.)
　Diana Ross & The Supremes; *Merry Christmas* . . . . (Motown)
　Dwight Yoakam; *Come On Christmas* . . . . (Reprise)
　Earl Grant; *Winter Wonderland* . . . . (MCA Special Prod.)
　Elvis Presley; *If Every Day Was Like Christmas* . . . . (RCA)
　　Memories Of Christmas . . . . (RCA)
　Fats Domino; *Christmas Is A Special Day* . . . . (Right Stuff)
　Gary Morris; *Every Christmas* . . . . (Liberty)
　John Denver; *Rocky Mountain Christmas* . . . . (RCA)
　Johnny Mathis & Percy Faith and his Orchestra; *Merry Christmas* . . . (Columbia)
　Judds; *Christmas Time With The Judds* . . . . (RCA)
　Kenny Rogers; *Christmas In America* . . . . (Reprise)
　Kevin Eubanks; *GRP Christmas Collection-C* . . . . (GRP)
　Lacy J. Dalton; *Christmas For The '90s-#1-C* . . . . (Liberty)
　Liberace; *That Old Christmas Feeling* . . . . (MCA Special Prod.)
　Loretta Lynn; *Christmas Without Daddy* . . . . (MCA Special Prod.)
　Margaret Whiting & Jimmy Wakely; *Christmas On The Range-Cowboy*
　　Classics-C . . . . (Capitol)
　Merle Haggard; *Merle Haggard-Christmas Gift* . . . . (Curb)
　Miracles; *Christmas With The Miracles* . . . . (Motown)
　Mormon Tabernacle Choir; *White Christmas* . . . . (Columbia)
　Oak Ridge Boys; *Oak Ridge Boys-Christmas* . . . . . . (MCA Special Prod.)
　Perry Como; *I Wish It Could Be Christmas Forever* . . . . (RCA)
　Ray Price; *Christmas Gift For You From Ray Price* . . . . (Step One)
　Roches; *We Three Kings* . . . . (Rykodisc)
　Ronnie Milsap; *Christmas With Ronnie Milsap* . . . . (RCA)
　Rosie O'Donnell & Sugar Ray; *Another Rosie Christmas-C* . . . . . . (Columbia)
　Stevie Wonder; *Someday At Christmas* . . . . (Motown)
　Travis Tritt; *Christmas-Loving Time Of The Year* . . . . (Warner Bros.)
Silver Bells (That Ring In The Night)
　Bob Wills; *Best Of Bob Wills & His Texas Playboys* . . . . (MCA)
　　Best Of Bob Wills-#2 . . . . (MCA)
　　Bob Wills-Anthology . . . . (Sony Music Special Prod.)
Sleigh Bells
　Gene Autry; *Christmas Cowboy, The* . . . . (Laserlight)
Submarine Bells
　Chills; *Submarine Bells* . . . . (Slash)
That's Amore
　Dean Martin; *Best Of Dean Martin* . . . . (CEMA Special Prod.)
　　Dean Martin's All Time Greatest Hits . . . . (Curb)
　　Dean Martin's Greatest Hits . . . . (EMI)
　　The Capitol Years-Dean Martin . . . . (Capitol)
Three Bells, The
　Browns; *Billboard Top Country Hits-1959-C* . . . . (Rhino)
　　Nipper's Greatest Hits Of The '50s-#1-C . . . . (RCA)
Till There Was You
　Beatles; *Beatles-Box Set* . . . . (Capitol)
　　Meet The Beatles! . . . . (Capitol)
　　With The Beatles . . . . (Parlophone)
　Original Cast; *ST/The Music Man* . . . . (Warner Bros.)
Ting-A-Ling
　Clovers; *Down In The Alley* . . . . (Rhino)
Trolley Song
　Judy Garland; *Best Of Judy Garland* . . . . (MCA)
　　Judy Garland's All-Time Greatest Hits . . . . (Curb)
　Original Broadway Cast; *Meet Me In St. Louis* . . . . (DRG)
Wedding Bell Blues
　5th Dimension; *Greatest Hits On Earth* . . . . (Arista)
　　Rockin' & Rollin' Wedding Songs-#1-C . . . . (Rhino)
　　ST/My Girl . . . . (Epic)
Wedding Bells
　Hank Williams With His Drifting Cowboys; *24 Of Hank Williams'*
　　Greatest Hits . . . . (Polydor)
　　Hank Williams-40 Greatest Hits . . . . (Polydor)
Wedding Bells (Are Breaking Up That Old Gang Of Mine)
　Four Aces; *Best Of The Four Aces* . . . . (MCA)
Winter Wonderland
　Air Supply; *Air Supply Christmas Album* . . . . (Arista)
　　White Christmas . . . . (Word)
　Alexander O'Neal; *My Gift To You* . . . . (Tabu)
　Amy Grant; *Home For Christmas* . . . . (A&M)
　Andrews Sisters; *Andrews Sisters-Christmas* . . . . (MCA Special Prod.)
　Anne Murray; *Best Of The Season* . . . . (EMI America)
　Aretha Franklin; *Rock 'N' Roll Christmas*
　　Classics-C . . . . (Music For Little People)
　Barbara Mandrell; *Christmas At Our House* . . . . (MCA Special Prod.)
　　Tennessee Christmas-C . . . . (MCA)
　Bing Crosby; *Bing Crosby Christmas Classics* . . . . (Capitol)
　Blue Notes; *Rhythm & Blues Christmas-#1-C* . . . . (Collectables)
　Brenda Lee; *Jingle Bell Rock* . . . . (MCA Special Prod.)
　Carnie & Wendy Wilson; *Hey Santa!* . . . . (SBK)
　Darlene Love; *Christmas Gift For You From Phil Spector-C* . . . . . . (Rhino)

Phil Spector-Back To Mono 1958-1969-C . . . . (Abkco)
Phil Spector's Christmas Album-C . . . . (Passport)
Eddy Arnold; *Christmas With Eddy Arnold* . . . . (RCA)
Elvis Presley; *If Every Day Was Like Christmas* . . . . (RCA)
Eurythmics; *Very Special Christmas-C* . . . . (A&M)
Faron Young; *Country Christmas* . . . . (Step One)
Frank Sinatra; *Christmas Songs By Sinatra* . . . . (Legacy)
George Strait; *Merry Christmas Strait To You* . . . . (MCA Special Prod.)
Hank Crawford; *We Got A Good Thing Going* . . . . (Kudo)
Johnny Mercer & The Pied Pipers; *Merry Christmas Baby-Romance &*
　Reindeer-C . . . . (Capitol)
Kathie Lee Gifford; *It's Christmas Time* . . . . (Warner Bros.)
Kenny Rogers; *Christmas In America* . . . . (Reprise)
London Symphony Orchestra; *Christmas Traditions* . . . . (Special Music Co.)
Merle Haggard; *Merle Haggard-Christmas Gift* . . . . (Curb)
Patti LaBelle & The Blue Belles; *A Soulful Christmas-C* . . . . (Collectables)
Randy Travis; *An Old Time Christmas* . . . . (Warner Bros.)
Robert Goulet; *Essence Of Christmas* . . . . (A&M)
Rosie O'Donnell & Macy Gray; *Another Rosie Christmas-C* . . . . . (Columbia)
Tanya Tucker; *Christmas For The '90s-#1-C* . . . . (Liberty)
Tony Bennett; *Now That's What I Call Christmas!-C* . . . . (UTV)
Travis Tritt; *Christmas-Loving Time Of The Year* . . . . (Warner Bros.)
Yellow Woman's Door Bells
　Leadbelly; *Leadbelly* . . . . (Fantasy)
　　Leadbelly . . . . (Everest)

BEST, Excellence, Favorite, Ideal, Perfection, Quality, Superiority, Superlatives

　See Also: *COMPLIMENTS, EXTREMES, GOOD, LOVE: MY IDEAL, SPECIAL*

Ain't Got Nothin' On Us
　John Michael Montgomery; *What I Do The Best* . . . . (Atlantic)
Ain't No Woman (Like The One I Got)
　Four Tops; *Ain't No Woman (Like The One I Got)* . . . . . . (MCA Special Prod.)
　　Four Tops' Greatest Hits (1972-1976) . . . . (MCA)
Alexander's Ragtime Band
　Al Jolson & Bing Crosby; *Al Jolson Story-#1* . . . . (MCA)
　　Immortal Al Jolson . . . . (MCA)
All Or Nothing
　O-Town; *O-Town* . . . . (J)
　　Totally Hits 2001-C . . . . (Arista)
All Star
　Smash Mouth; *Astro Lounge* . . . . (Interscope)
　　Now That's What I Call Music!-#3-C . . . . (Virgin)
All The Things You Are
　Ella Fitzgerald; *Complete Jerome Kern* . . . . (Verve)
　Mario Lanza; *Be My Love-Greatest Performances* . . . . (Rhino)
　Willie Nelson; *Healing Hands Of Time* . . . . (Liberty)
Amazed
　Lonestar; *Lonely Grill* . . . . (BNA)
　　Totally Hits-#2-C . . . . (Elektra)
Ascension (Don't Ever Wonder)
　Maxwell; *Maxwell's Urban Hang Suite* . . . . (Columbia)
Auctioneer, The
　Leroy Van Dyke; *Deep In The Heart Of Country-C* . . . . (Drive)
Bargain
　Who; *Who's next* . . . . (MCA)
Best Day
　George Strait; *Latest Greatest Straitest Hits* . . . . (MCA)
Best Days Of My Life
　Johnny Mathis; *Best Days Of My Life* . . . . (Columbia)
　　Best Of Johnny Mathis 1975-1980 . . . . (Columbia)
Best Days Of My Life
　Rod Stewart; *Blondes Have More Fun* . . . . (Warner Bros.)
Best Friend
　English Beat; *I Just Can't Stop It* . . . . (I.R.S.)
　　What Is Beat . . . . (I.R.S.)
Best Friend
　Toni Braxton; *Toni Braxton* . . . . (LaFace)
Best Friend
　Brandy; *Brandy* . . . . (Atlantic)
Best Friends
　ET (Eddie Towns); *45-#2433* . . . . (Total Experience)
Best Friends
　Basia; *London Warsaw New York* . . . . (Epic)
Best I Ever Had (Grey Sky Morning)
　Vertical Horizon; *Everything You Want* . . . . (RCA)
Best Is Yet To Come
　Grover Washington, Jr.; *Grover Washington, Jr.-Anthology* . . . . . (Elektra)
　Grover Washington, Jr. & Patti LaBelle; *Best Is Yet To Come* . . . . (Elektra)
Best Is Yet To Come
　Frank Sinatra; *It Might As Well Be Swing* . . . . (Reprise)
　　Sinatra Reprise-The Very Good Years . . . . (Reprise)
　Johnny Mathis; *I'll Buy You A Star* . . . . (Legacy)

Rosemary Clooney; *Girl Singer* . . . .(Concord Jazz)
Tony Bennett; *I Left My Heart In San Francisco* . . . . (Columbia)
  The Ultimate Tony Bennett . . . . (Legacy)

Best Man I Can Be
Ginuwine, R.L., Tyrese, Case; *ST/The Best Man* . . . . . . (Sony Music Soundtrax)

Best Of All Possible Worlds
Leonard Bernstein; *Bernstein Songbook* . . . . (Columbia)
Original Cast; *Candide* . . . . (Columbia)

Best Of Both Worlds
Midnight Oil; *Red Sails In The Sunset* . . . . (Columbia)

Best Of Both Worlds
Van Halen; *5150* . . . .(Warner Bros.)

Best Of Both Worlds
Robert Palmer; *Double Fun* . . . . (Island)

Best Of Friends
Peter, Paul & Mary; *Reunion* . . . .(Warner Bros.)

Best Of Friends
Dangerous Toys; *Hellacious Acres* . . . . (Columbia)

Best Of Intentions
Travis Tritt; *Down The Road I Go* . . . . (Columbia)

Best Of Love, The
Michael Bolton; *All That Matters* . . . . (Columbia)

Best Of Me
Mya featuring Jadakiss; *Fear Of Flying* . . . . (University/Interscope)

Best Of My Love
Emotions; *Club Columbia-C* . . . . (Columbia)
  Rejoice . . . . (Columbia)
  ST/Queen's Logic . . . .(Epic)

Best Of My Love
Brooks & Dunn; *Common Thread-Songs Of The Eagles-C* . . . . (Giant)
Eagles; *Eagles/Their Greatest Hits 1971-1975* . . . . (Asylum)
  On The Border . . . . (Elektra)

Best Old Friend
Bonnie Raitt; *The Glow* . . . .(Warner Bros.)

Best Thing
Savage Garden; *Affirmation* . . . . (Columbia)

Best Things
Filter; *Title Of Record* . . . . (Reprise)

Best Things In Life Are Free
June Allyson; *ST/Good News* . . . .(Sony Music Special Prod.)
Luther Vandross & Janet Jackson; *ST/Mo' Money* . . . . (Bluebird)
Mel Torme; *Easy To Remember* . . . . (Glendale)
Sam Cooke; *Sam Cooke-At The Copa* . . . . (RCA)

Best Year Of My Life
Eddie Rabbitt; *Number 1's* . . . .(Warner Bros.)
  The Best Year Of My Life . . . .(Warner Bros.)

Blessed
Elton John; *Elton John-Love Songs* . . . .(MCA)
  Made In England . . . .(Rocket)

C'est Moi
Original Cast; *ST/Camelot* . . . .(Warner Bros.)
Robert Goulet; *Camelot* . . . . (Columbia)

Chocolate Mood
Marc Nelson; *chocolate mood* . . . . (Columbia)

Close Enough To Perfect
Alabama; *Alabama-Super Hits-#2* . . . . (RCA)
  Essential Alabama . . . . (RCA)
  Mountain Music . . . . (RCA)

Daddy's Little Girl
Al Martino; *Best Of Al Martino* . . . . (Capitol)
Mills Brothers; *50th Anniversary* . . . .(Ranwood)
  All Occasions Album . . . .(Gateway)
  Best Of The Mills Brothers . . . .(MCA)
  The Mills Brothers Story . . . .(Ranwood)

Dinah
Bing Crosby; *Bing Crosby-16 Most Requested Songs* . . . . (Legacy)
Cab Calloway; *Best Of The Big Bands-C* . . . . (Columbia)
Cliff Edwards; *Singin' In The Rain* . . . . (ASV)
Count Basie & Ethel Waters; *Tribute To Black Entertainers-C* . . . . (Columbia)
Duke Ellington; *Jubilee Stomp* . . . . (Bluebird)
Ethel Waters; *Am I Blue?* . . . . (ASV)
Fats Waller; *Ain't Misbehavin': 25 Greatest Hits* . . . . (Living Era)
Lionel Hampton & His Orchestra; *Tempo & Swing* . . . . . (Bluebird)
Louis Armstrong; *Louis Armstrong-Vol. 6-St. Louis Blues* . . . . . (Columbia)
Mills Brothers; *50th Anniversary* . . . .(Ranwood)

Finer Things, The
Steve Winwood; *Back In The High Life* . . . . (Island)

Giving You The Best That I Got
Anita Baker; *Giving You The Best That I Got* . . . . (Elektra)

God Must Have Spent A Little More Time On You
Alabama Featuring 'N Sync; *Twentieth Century* . . . . (RCA)
'N Sync; *'N Sync* . . . . (RCA)
  Totally Hits-#1-C . . . . (Arista)

Greatest Love Of All
George Benson; *George Benson-Collection* . . . .(Warner Bros.)
  ST/The Greatest . . . . (Arista)
  Weekend In L.A. . . . .(Warner Bros.)
Whitney Houston; *Whitney Houston* . . . . (Arista)

  Whitney Houston's Greatest Hits . . . . (Arista)

Greatest, The
Kenny Rogers; *She Rides Wild Horses* . . . .(Dreamcatcher)

Honky Tonkin's What I Do Best
Marty Stuart & Travis Tritt; *Grand Ole Opry-75 Years-#2-C* . . . . (MCA)

I Learned From The Best
Whitney Houston; *My Love Is Your Love* . . . . (Arista)

I Wanna Be A Cowboy's Sweetheart
Patsy Montana & The Prairie Ramblers; *All Time Legends Of Country
  Music-C* . . . . (Legacy)
  Respect: A History Of Women In Music-C . . . . (Rhino)

I'd Like To Teach The World To Sing (In Perfect Harmony)
New Seekers; *Chicken Soup For The Soul-Celebrating Life-C* . . . . (Rhino)

In A Perfect World
Lorrie Morgan; *Shakin' Things Up* . . . .(BNA)

It's A Perfect Relationship
Judy Holliday/Original Cast; *Bells Are Ringing* . . . . (Columbia)

I've Got My Eyes On You
Jessica Simpson; *Sweet Kisses* . . . . (Columbia)

Johnny B. Goode
Chuck Berry; *Chuck Berry's Greatest Hits* . . . . (Everest)
  Classic Rock-#2-C . . . . (MCA)
  Roll Over Beethoven . . . . (Allegiance)
  ST/American Graffiti . . . . (MCA)
  The Chess Box-Chuck Berry . . . . (Chess)
Elvis Presley; *Elvis In Concert* . . . . (RCA)
  From Memphis To Vegas/From Vegas To Memphis . . . .(RCA)
Grateful Dead; *Bill Graham Presents The Last Days Of The
  Fillmore-C* . . . . (Epic Portrait Assoc.)
Johnny Winter; *Live/Johnny Winter And* . . . . (Columbia)
  Second Winter . . . . (Columbia)

Juke Box Baby
Perry Como; *Perry Como's Greatest Hits* . . . . (RCA)

Kate
Ben Folds Five; *Whatever And Ever Amen* . . . .(Caroline/550)

Love Of My Life
Brian McKnight; *Superhero* . . . . (Motown)

Magnolia
J.J. Cale; *Naturally* . . . . (MCA)

Mint Car
Cure; *Wild Mood Swings* . . . . (Elektra)

More (Than)
Perry Como; *Perry Como's Greatest Hits* . . . . (RCA)

Most Beautiful Girl
Charlie Rich; *Behind Closed Doors* . . . . (Epic)
  Charlie Rich's Greatest Hits . . . . (Epic)
  Columbia Country Classics-#4-Nashville Sound-C . . . . (Columbia)

Most Beautiful Girl In The World
Frank Sinatra; *Strangers In The Night* . . . . (Reprise)
Tony Bennett; *Rodgers & Hart Songbook* . . . .(DRG)
  Tony Bennett Sings More Great Rodgers & Hart . . . . (Improv)

Most Beautiful World In The World
Nilsson; *Son Of Schmilsson* . . . . (RCA)

Mr. Too Damn Good
Gerald Levert; *G* . . . . (East West)

My Best Friend
Jefferson Airplane; *2400 Fulton Street-An Anthology* . . . . (RCA)
  Surrealistic Pillow . . . . (RCA)

My Best Friend
Tim McGraw; *A Place In The Sun* . . . . (Curb)
  Tim McGraw's Greatest Hits . . . . (Curb)

My Best Friend
Air Supply; *Lost In Love* . . . . (Arista)

My Best Friend
Marshall Tucker Band; *Running Like The Wind* . . . . (Warner Bros.)

My Best Was Never Good Enough
Bruce Springsteen; *The Ghost Of Tom Joad* . . . . (Columbia)

My Favorite Girl
Dave Hollister; *Ghetto Hymns* . . . . (Def Squad/DreamWorks)

My Favorite Headache
Geddy Lee; *My Favorite Headache* . . . .(Anthem/Atlantic)

My Favorite Lies
George Jones; *George Jones' All-Time Greatest Hits* . . . . (Epic)

My Favorite Memory
Merle Haggard; *For The Record: Merle Haggard-43 Legendary Hits* . . . .(BNA)

My Favorite Mistake
Sheryl Crow; *Now That's What I Call Music!-#2-C* . . . .(Virgin)
  The Globe Sessions . . . . (A&M)

My Favorite Spring
Tom Paxton; *Live For The Record* . . . .(Sugar Hill)

My Favorite Things
Andy Williams; *Merry Christmas* . . . . (Columbia)
Barbra Streisand; *Barbra Streisand Christmas Album* . . . . . . (Columbia)
Betty Carter; *Compact Jazz-Betty Carter* . . . . (Verve)
Diana Ross & The Supremes; *Merry Christmas* . . . . (Motown)
  Motown Christmas Album-C . . . . (Motown)
Herb Alpert & The Tijuana Brass; *Herb Alpert & The Tijuana Brass
  Christmas Album* . . . . (A&M)

John Coltrane; *Best Of John Coltrane* . . . . (Atlantic)
Johnny Mathis; *Give Me Your Love For Christmas* . . . . (Columbia)
Julie Andrews; *ST/The Sound Of Music* . . . . (RCA)
Kenny Rogers; *Kenny Rogers-Christmas* . . . . (EMI)
Lorrie Morgan; *Merry Christmas From London* . . . . (BNA)

My Favorite Town Osaka
Shonen Knife; *712* . . . . (Rockville)

My Guy
Mary Wells; *Mary Wells' Greatest Hits* . . . . (Motown)
My Guy . . . . (Motown)
Oldies But Goodies-#11-C . . . . (Original Sound)

My Love Is The Shhh!
Somethin' For The People; *This Time It's Personal* . . . . (Warner Bros.)

Naturally
Marty Stuart; *Country Goes Raffi-C* . . . . (Rounder)

New Favorite
Alison Krauss & Union Station; *New Favorite* . . . . (Rounder)

Nobody Does It Better
Carly Simon; *13 Original James Bond Themes-C* . . . . (EMI)
Carly Simon-Greatest Hits Live . . . . (Arista)
ST/The Spy Who Loved Me . . . . (EMI)

Nobody I Know
Peter And Gordon; *History Of British Rock-#1-C* . . . . (Rhino)

Off The Hook
Jody Watley; *12'' Maxi Single* . . . . (Atlantic)

Old Master Painter
Peggy Lee; *Capitol Collectors Series-Peggy Lee-#1-Early Years* . . . . . . (Capitol)

Only One You
T.G. Sheppard; *Best Of T.G. Sheppard* . . . . (Curb)
T.G. Sheppard's All-Time Greatest Hits . . . . (Warner Bros.)

Optimistic
Radiohead; *Kid A* . . . . (Capitol)

Painted Perfect
One Way Ride; *Strait Up!* . . . . (Refuge/MCA)

Perfect
Smashing Pumpkins; *Adore* . . . . (Virgin)

Perfect Day
Collective Soul; *Blender* . . . . (Atlantic)

Perfect Drug
Nine Inch Nails; *ST/Lost Highway* . . . . (Interscope)

Perfect Love
Trisha Yearwood; *Songbook-A Collection Of Hits* . . . . (MCA)

Poetry In Motion
Johnny Tillotson; *10 Top Ten Hits-#1* . . . . (Laurie)
American Graffiti-#3-C . . . . (MCA)
Jukebox Classics-#1-C . . . . (Rhino)
Mellow '60s-C . . . . (Priority)
Million-Dollar Memories-#2-C . . . . (RCA)

Reach
Gloria Estefan; *Destiny* . . . . (Epic)

Reunited
Peaches & Herb; *Best Of Peaches & Herb* . . . . (Polydor)
Chicken Soup For The Couples Soul-C . . . . (Rhino)
Didn't It Blow Your Mind: Soul Hits Of The '70s-#20-C . . . . . . (Rhino)
Only Love-1975-1979-C . . . . (JCI Assoc. Labels)

Right On The Money
Alan Jackson; *Big Country Hits '99-C* . . . . (K-Tel)
High Mileage . . . . (Arista)

Salt Of The Earth
Mick Jagger & Keith Richards; *The Concert For New York City-C* . . (Columbia)
Rolling Stones; *Beggars Banquet* . . . . (Abkco)

Save The Best For Last
Vanessa Williams; *Grammy's Greatest Moments-#2-C* . . . . (Atlantic)
The Comfort Zone . . . . (Wing)
Women For Women-C . . . . (Mercury)

Sexy Sadie
Beatles; *Beatles-Box Set* . . . . (Capitol)
The Beatles (White Album) . . . . (Capitol)

Simply The Best
Irma Thomas; *Simply The Best-Live!* . . . . (Rounder)

So Fine
Fiestas; *Baby Boomer Classics-Party Time Fifties-C* . . . (JCI Assoc. Labels)
Baby Boomer's Best-Jumpin' Jive 50's-C . . . . (Priority)

Stellar
Incubus; *Make Yourself* . . . . (Immortal/Epic)

Summer Of '69
Bryan Adams; *Reckless* . . . . (A&M)

Thankyou
Dido; *No Angel* . . . . (Arista)
Totally Hits 2001-C . . . . (Arista)

Theme From "Father Knows Best"
Original Soundtrack; *Television's Greatest Hits-#4-Black & White
Classics-C* . . . . (TVT)

Theme From "The Courtship Of Eddie's Father" (Best Friend)
Nilsson; *Television's Greatest Hits-#2-C* . . . . (TVT)

**Theme From "The Miss America Pageant" (There She Is, Miss
America)**
Bert Parks; *Television's Greatest Hits-#4-Black & White Classics-C* . . . . (TVT)

This Kiss
Faith Hill; *Faith* . . . . (Warner Bros.)
Totally Hits-#1-C . . . . (Arista)

To Me
South Sixty Five; *South Sixty Five* . . . . (Atlantic)

Truly Madly Deeply
Savage Garden; *Savage Garden* . . . . (Columbia)

Well Respected Man
Kinks; *History Of British Rock-#4-C* . . . . (Rhino)
Kinks' Greatest Hits . . . . (Rhino)
Kinks-Size Kinkdom . . . . (Rhino)

We're Off To See The Wizard
Jewel/Jackson Browne/Ry Cooder; *The Wizard Of Oz In Concert: Dreams
Come True-C* . . . . (Rhino)
Judy Garland; *A&E Biography: A Musical Anthology* . . . . (Capitol)
Original Cast; *The Wizard Of Oz* . . . . (TVT)
Original Soundtrack; *The Wizard Of Oz-Selections From The Original Motion
Picture Soundtrack* . . . . (Turner Classic Movies)

When You Say Nothing At All
Alison Krauss & Union Station; *Kieth Whitley-A Tribute Album* . . . . . . (BNA)
Now That I've Found You: A Collection . . . . (Rounder)
ST/Switchback . . . . (RCA)
Keith Whitley; *Billboard Top Country Hits-1988-C* . . . . (Rhino)
Country Wedding Album-C . . . . (Scotti Bros.)
Don't Close Your Eyes . . . . (RCA)
Essential Keith Whitley . . . . (RCA)
Keith Whitley's Greatest Hits . . . . (RCA)

World's Greatest Lover
Bellamy Brothers; *Bellamy Brothers' Greatest Hits-#2* . . . . (MCA)
Bellamy Brothers' Greatest Hits-#2 . . . . (Curb)

World's Greatest, The
R. Kelly; *ST/Ali* . . . . (Interscope)

You Are
Lionel Richie; *Lionel Richie* . . . . (Motown)

You Brought A New Kind Of Love To Me
Ella Fitzgerald; *Ella Swings Lightly* . . . . (Verve)

Younger Than Springtime
Original Cast; *South Pacific* . . . . (CBS Masterworks)

You're The Top
Cole Porter; *Nipper's Greatest Hits Of The '30s-#1-C* . . . . (RCA)
Ella Fitzgerald; *Cole Porter Songbook* . . . . (Verve)
Ethel Merman; *Lovely Ladies Of Stage & Screen-C* . . . . (Legacy)
Frank Sinatra; *Good Man Is Hard To Find* . . . . (Pilz America)
Louis Armstrong; *American Songbook* . . . . (Verve)

BIG, Huge, Large, Tall

Bed's Too Big Without You
Police; *Regatta De Blanc* . . . . (A&M)

Big Apple
Tommy Dorsey & His Clambake Seven; *Nipper's Greatest Hits Of The
'30s-#2-C* . . . . (RCA)
Tommy Dorsey & His Orchestra; *Seventeen Number Ones* . . . . . . (RCA)

Big Bad Bill Is Sweet William Now
Ry Cooder; *Jazz* . . . . (Warner Bros.)

Big Bad John
Jimmy Dean; *American Originals-Jimmy Dean* . . . . (Columbia)
Billboard Top Country Hits-1961-C . . . . (Rhino)
Columbia Country Classics-#3-Americana-C . . . . (Columbia)
Jimmy Dean's Greatest Hits . . . . (Columbia)

Big Balls
AC/DC; *Dirty Deeds Done Dirt Cheap* . . . . (Atlantic)

Big Ball's In Cowtown
Asleep At The Wheel; *Very Best Of Asleep At The Wheel
Since 1970* . . . . (Relentless/Madacy)
Asleep At The Wheel featuring George Strait; *Tribute To The Music Of Bob
Wills And The Texas Playboys-C* . . . . (Liberty)
Bob Wills & His Texas Playboys; *Best Of Bob Wills & His Texas
Playboys* . . . . (MCA)
For The Last Time . . . . (Capitol)

Big Bang Baby
Stone Temple Pilots; *Tiny Music...Songs From The Vatican
Gift Shop* . . . . (Atlantic)

Big Black Cadillac Blues
Lightnin' Hopkins; *Drinkin' In The Blues-Golden Classics-#1* . . . . (Collectables)
Lightnin' Hopkins . . . . (Everest)

Big Black Smoke
Kinks; *Kink Kronikles* . . . . (Reprise)

Big Boss Man
B.B. King; *Six Silver Strings* . . . . (MCA)
Elvis Presley; *ST/Clambake* . . . . (RCA)
Grateful Dead; *Grateful Dead (Skull & Roses)* . . . . (Warner Bros.)
Jimmy Reed; *Best Of Jimmy Reed* . . . . (Crescendo)
Oldies But Goodies-#1-C . . . . (Original Sound)
John Hammond; *Best Of John Hammond* . . . . (Vanguard)
So Many Roads . . . . (Vanguard)

Big Boys Don't Cry
Extreme; *Extreme* . . . . (A&M)
Big Bright Green Pleasure Machine
Simon & Garfunkel; *Collected Works* . . . . (Columbia)
  Parsley Sage Rosemary & Thyme . . . . (Columbia)
  ST/The Graduate . . . . (Columbia)
Big Butt
Bobby Jimmy & The Critters; *West Coast Rap-First Dynasty-#3-C* . . . (Rhino)
Big Butter And Egg Man
Louis Armstrong; *Best Of Louis Armstrong* . . . . (Audio Fidelity)
  Hot Fives & Hot Sevens-#2 . . . . (Columbia)
Merle Haggard; *Kern River* . . . . (Epic)
  Walking The Line . . . . (Epic)
Big Chested Girls
Prince Charles & The City Beat Band; *Stone Killers!* . . . . . (Roir)
Big Chief
Dr. John; *Dr. John's Gumbo* . . . . (Alligator)
Neville Brothers; *Live At Tipitina's-#1-Nevillization* . . . . (Spindletop)
Professor Longhair; *Crawfish Fiesta* . . . . (Alligator)
  Mardi Gras Party . . . . (Rounder)
  New Orleans Party Classics-C . . . . (Rhino)
Big Chief From New Orleans
Mike Bloomfield; *Between The Hard Place & The Ground* . . . . (Takoma)
Big City
Merle Haggard; *For The Record: Merle Haggard-43 Legendary Hits* . . . . (BNA)
Big City Miss Ruth Ann
Gallery; *Super Hits Of The '70s-Have A Nice Day-#11-C* . . . . (Rhino)
Big City Nights
Scorpions; *Best Of Rockers 'N' Ballads* . . . . (Mercury)
  Love At First Sting . . . . (Mercury)
  World Wide Live . . . . (Mercury)
Big D
Broadway Cast; *Most Happy Fella* . . . . (RCA)
Original Broadway Cast; *Most Happy Fella* . . . . (Sony Music Classical)
Big Dreams In A Small Town
Restless Heart; *Big Dreams In A Small Town* . . . . (RCA)
Big Electric Cat
Adrian Belew; *Desire Of The Rhino King* . . . . (Island)
Big Empty
Stone Temple Pilots; *Purple* . . . . (Atlantic)
Big Fat Daddy
Jeannie & Jimmy Cheatham; *Midnight Mama* . . . . (Concord Jazz)
Big Fat Funky Booty
Spin Doctors; *Up For Grabs...Live* . . . . (Epic Portrait Assoc.)
Big Fat Ham
Jelly Roll Morton; *Immortal Jelly Roll Morton* . . . . (Milestone)
Big Fat Lady
George Benson; *Cookbook* . . . . (Columbia)
Big Fat Mama
Fred McDowell; *Long Way From Home* . . . . (Milestone)
Big Fat Mama
Big Joe Williams; *Legacy Of The Blues-#6* . . . . (Crescendo)
Big Fat Woman
Leadbelly; *Bourgeois Blues-Golden Classics-#1* . . . . . . (Collectables)
Tom Rush; *Blues Songs & Ballads* . . . . (Fantasy)
Big Fish, Little Fish
Original Broadway Cast; *Purlie* . . . . (RCA)
Big Four Poster Bed
Brenda Lee; *Brenda Lee-Anthology-#1 & #2* . . . . (MCA)
Big Fun
Scatterbrain; *Scamboogery* . . . . (Elektra)
Big Fun
Kool & The Gang; *As One* . . . . (De-Lite)
Big Girls Don't Cry
4 Seasons; *4 Seasons' Greatest Hits-#1* . . . . (Rhino)
  4 Seasons-Anthology . . . . (Rhino)
  Billboard Top Rock 'N' Roll Hits-1962-C . . . . (Rhino)
  More Dirty Dancing-C . . . . (RCA)
Big Goodbye
Great White; *Psycho City* . . . . (Capitol)
Big Gun
AC/DC; *ST/Last Action Hero* . . . . (Columbia)
Big Guns
Skid Row; *Skid Row* . . . . (Atlantic)
Big Guns
Heatwave; *Heatwave's Greatest Hits* . . . . (Epic)
Big Hotel
Big Pig; *Bonk* . . . . (A&M)
Big In America
Stranglers; *Dreamtime* . . . . (Epic)
  Stranglers' Greatest Hits-1977-1990 . . . . (Epic)
Big In Japan
Alphaville; *Alphaville-The Singles Collection* . . . . (Atlantic)
  Forever Young . . . . (Atlantic)
Big In Vegas
Buck Owens; *Buck Owens' All-Time Greatest Hits-#1* . . . . (Curb)
  Buck Owens Collection-1959-1990 . . . . (Rhino)
  Great Records Of The Decade-'70s Hits-Country-C . . . . (Curb)

Big Iron
Marty Robbins; *Columbia Country Classics-#3-Americana-C* . . . . (Columbia)
  Gunfighter Ballads & Trail Songs . . . . (Legacy)
  Marty Robbins' All-Time Greatest Hits . . . . (Columbia)
  Marty Robbins-More Greatest Hits . . . . (Columbia)
Big Jesus Trash Can
Birthday Party; *Best & Rarest* . . . . (Missing Link)
  Birthday Party-Collection . . . . (Missing Link)
Big Joe & Phantom 309
Tom Waits; *Double Live* . . . . (Asylum)
  Nighthawks At The Diner . . . . (Asylum)
Big John
Shirelles; *Shirelles-16 Greatest Hits* . . . . (Trip)
  Shirelles-Anthology 1959-1964 . . . . (Rhino)
  Shirelles-Classics . . . . (Bac-Trac)
  Super Oldies Of The '60s-#10-C . . . . (Audio Fidelity)
Big Log
Robert Plant; *Principle Of Moments* . . . . (Es Paranza)
Big Love
Fleetwood Mac; *25 Years-The Chain* . . . . (Warner Bros.)
  Fleetwood Mac's Greatest Hits . . . . (Warner Bros.)
  Tango In The Night . . . . (Warner Bros.)
Big Love
Tracy Byrd; *Big Love* . . . . (MCA)
Big Love
Delevantes; *Long About That Time* . . . . (Rounder)
Big Love
Bellamy Brothers; *Bellamy Brothers' Greatest Hits-#3* . . . . (MCA)
  Rebels Without A Clue . . . . (MCA)
Big Man
Charlie Daniels Band; *Uneasy Rider* . . . . (Epic)
Big Man In Town
4 Seasons; *4 Seasons' Greatest Hits-#1* . . . . (Rhino)
  4 Seasons-Anthology . . . . (Rhino)
Big Me
Foo Fighters; *Foo Fighters* . . . . (Roswell/RCA)
Big Mexican Dinner
Kentucky HeadHunters; *Electric Barnyard* . . . . (Mercury)
Big Money
Rush; *Power Windows* . . . . (Mercury)
  Show Of Hands . . . . (Mercury)
Big Money
Garth Brooks; *Scarecrow* . . . . (Capitol)
Big Mouth Blues
Gram Parsons; *G.P./Grievous Angel* . . . . (Reprise)
  Gram Parsons/Fallen Angels Live-1973 . . . . (Sierra)
Big Muddy
Bruce Springsteen; *Lucky Town* . . . . (Columbia)
Big Music
Waterboys; *Pagan Place* . . . . (Chrysalis)
Big Noise From Winnetka
Bette Midler; *Divine Madness* . . . . (Atlantic)
  Thighs And Whispers . . . . (Atlantic)
Bob Crosby & His Bob Cats; *Best Of Bob Crosby & His Bob Cats* . . . . (MCA)
Bob Crosby & His Orchestra; *Bob Crosby & His Orchestra Play 22 Original
  Big Band Hits* . . . . (Hindsight)
Big Ole Brew
Mel McDaniel; *Mel McDaniel's Greatest Hits* . . . . (Capitol)
  Take Me To The Country . . . . (Capitol)
Big Pimpin'
Jay-Z; *Vol. 3-Life & Times of S. Carter* . . . . (Roc-A-Fella/DJMG)
Big Poppa
Notorious B.I.G.; *MTV Party To Go-#8-C* . . . . (Tommy Boy)
  Ready To Die . . . . (Bad Boy/Arista)
Big Railroad Blues
Grateful Dead; *Grateful Dead (Skull & Roses)* . . . . . . (Warner Bros.)
Big Rig
Jimmy Buffett; *Havana Daydreamin'* . . . . (MCA)
Big Rig Rolling Man
Billy Larkin; *Blue Ribbon Country-#2-C* . . . . (Accord)
Johnny Dollar; *Truck Driver Boogie Big Rig Hits-1939-1969-C* . . . . (Audium)
Big River
Grateful Dead; *One From The Vault* . . . . (Grateful Dead)
  Steal Your Face . . . . (Grateful Dead)
Johnny Cash; *Johnny Cash-Legend* . . . . (Sun)
  Johnny Cash's Greatest Hits-#2 . . . . (Columbia)
  Johnny Cash-Sun Years . . . . (Rhino)
  Superbilly . . . . (Sun)
  The Man In Black-His Greatest Hits . . . . (Legacy)
Rosanne Cash; *Right Or Wrong* . . . . (Columbia)
Big River
Bob Seger System; *Mongrel* . . . . (Capitol)
Big River
Beat Farmers; *The Pursuit Of Happiness* . . . . (Curb)
Big River, Big Man
Claude King; *American Originals-Claude King* . . . . (Columbia)
  Best Of Claude King . . . . (Gusto)
Big Rock Candy Mountain
Burl Ives; *Burl Ives' Greatest Hits* . . . . (MCA)

Poor Wayfaring Stranger . . . .(Flapper)
Harry McClintock; *ST/O Brother, Where Art Thou?* . . . . (Mercury)
John Hartford; *ST/Down From The Mountain* . . . . (Lost Highway/IDJMG)
Pete Seeger; *20 Golden Pieces Of Pete Seeger* . . . . (Bulldog)
Tex Ritter; *Capitol Collectors Series-Tex Ritter* . . . . (Capitol)

Big Shot
Billy Joel; *52nd Street* . . . . (Columbia)
Billy Joel-Greatest Hits, Volume I & Volume II . . . . (Columbia)
KOHUEPT . . . . (Columbia)

Big Sky
Kate Bush; *Hounds Of Love* . . . . (EMI)

Big Sleep
Simple Minds; *New Gold Dream* . . . . (A&M)
Simple Minds Live: In The City Of Light . . . . (A&M)

Big Spender (Muriel Cigars)
Original Soundtrack; *TeeVee Toons-The Commercials-#1-C* . . . . (TVT)

Big Texas
Jimmy C. Newman; *Happy Cajun* . . . . (Plantation)

Big Time
Neil Young & Crazy Horse; *Broken Arrow* . . . . (Reprise)
Year Of The Horse . . . . (Reprise)

Big Train From Memphis
John Fogerty; *Centerfield* . . . . (Warner Bros.)

Big Trash
Thompson Twins; *Big Trash* . . . . (Red Eye)

Big Tulsa Tillie
Donnie Rohrs; *Country Music USA* . . . . (Pacific Challenger)

Big Wednesday
Surf M.C.'s; *Surf Or Die* . . . . (Profile)

Big Wheels In The Moonlight
Dan Seals; *Dan Seals' Greatest Hits* . . . . (Liberty)
Dan Seals-Classics Collection-#2 . . . . (Liberty)
Rage On . . . . (Capitol)

Big White Cloud
John Cale; *Vintage Violence* . . . . (Columbia)

Big Yellow Taxi
Amy Grant; *House Of Love* . . . . (A&M)
Joni Mitchell; *Ladies Of The Canyon* . . . . (Reprise)
Joni Mitchell with Tom Scott & The L.A. Express; *Miles Of Aisles* . . . (Asylum)

Bigger Than The Beatles
Joe Diffie; *Life's So Funny* . . . . (Epic)

Biggest Airport In The World
Moe Bandy; *Best Of Moe Bandy-Vol. 1* . . . . (Columbia)

Biggest Ball Of Twine In Minnesota
"Weird Al" Yankovic; *ST/UHF & Other Stuff* . . . . (Scotti Bros.)

Biggest Thing That Man Has Ever Done (Great Historical Bum)
Tom Paxton; *Tribute To Woody Guthrie-C* . . . . (Warner Bros.)

Caldonia (What Makes Your Big Head So Hard?)
Louis Jordan; *No Moe! Louis Jordan's Greatest Hits* . . . . (Verve)
Original Cast; *Five Guys Named Moe* . . . . (Columbia)
Woody Herman & His Orchestra; *Verve Jazz Masters 54* . . . . (Verve)

El Rancho Grande
Tune Wranglers; *Doughboys, Playboys And Cowboys: The Golden Years Of*
Western Swing-C . . . . (Proper)

Everybody's Making It Big But Me
Dr. Hook; *Bankrupt* . . . . (Capitol)

Eyes As Big As Dallas
Randy Wagner; *45-#236* . . . . (Door Knob)

Fool #1
Brenda Lee; *The Brenda Lee Story-Her Greatest Hits* . . . . (MCA)
Joe Stampley/The Uniques; *Joe Stampley-Golden Hits* . . . . (Paula)

Give Him A Great Big Kiss
Shangri-Las; *Best Of The Girl Groups-#1-C* . . . . (Rhino)
Remember The Shangri-Las At Their Best . . . . (Collectables)

Great Balls Of Fire
Jerry Lee Lewis; *Billboard Top Rock 'N' Roll Hits-1958-C* . . . . (Rhino)
Jerry Lee Lewis-Original Golden Hits-#1 . . . . (Sun)
Jerry Lee Lewis-Original Golden Hits-#1 . . . . (Sun)
Jerry Lee's Greatest! . . . . (Rhino)
Oldies But Goodies-#12-C . . . . (Original Sound)
Original Memphis Rock & Roll . . . . (Sun)
Rock & Roll Show-C . . . . (Gusto)
Twenty Classic Jerry Lee Lewis Hits . . . . (Original Sound)

Great Divide
Bruce Hornsby; *Spirit Trail* . . . . (RCA)

Great Speckled Bird
Roy Acuff; *Best Of Roy Acuff* . . . . (Liberty)
Bluegrass Super Hits-C . . . . (Columbia)
Roy Acuff's Greatest Hits . . . . (Columbia)

Heartache Big As Texas
Ricky Van Shelton; *Texas Super Hits-C* . . . . (Columbia)

I Like 'Em Big & Stupid
Julie Brown; *Trapped In The Body Of A White Girl* . . . . (Sire)

I Wish
Skee-Lo; *I Wish* . . . . (Sunshine/Scotti Bros.)
Stevie Wonder; *Original Musiquarium* . . . . (Motown)
Songs In The Key Of Life . . . . (Motown)

I'm In Love With A Big Blue Frog
Peter, Paul & Mary; *Album 1700* . . . . (Warner Bros.)

Kiss From A Rose
Seal; *Seal 2* . . . . (Sire)

Large Time
Atlanta Rhythm Section; *Are You Ready!* . . . . (Polydor)
Champagne Jam . . . . (Polydor)

Larger Than Life
Backstreet Boys; *Millennium* . . . . (Jive)
Now That's What I Call Music!-#4-C . . . . (Virgin)

Let's Go To Big Houston
Papa Link Davis; *Best Of Cajun Country-C* . . . . (Era)

Long White Cadillac
Blasters; *Blasters-Collection* . . . . (Slash)
Dave Alvin; *Romeo's Escape* . . . . (Epic)
Dwight Yoakam; *Just Lookin' For A Hit* . . . . (Reprise)

Love's The Only House
Martina McBride; *Emotion* . . . . (RCA)

Mr. Big Stuff
Jean Knight; *'70s Hit(s) Back Again-C* . . . . (Hip-O)
Have A Nice Decade-The '70s Pop Culture Box-C . . . . (Rhino)

My Big Iron Skillet
Wanda Jackson; *Rockin' In The Country-Best Of Wanda Jackson* . . . . . (Rhino)

Ode To Big Blue
Gordon Lightfoot; *Don Quixote* . . . . (Warner Archives)

Oh You Beautiful Doll
Guy Lombardo & His Royal Canadians; *Dance To Songs Everybody*
Knows . . . . (MCA)

One Big Love
Emmylou Harris; *Red Dirt Girl* . . . . (Nonesuch)
Patty Griffin; *Flaming Red* . . . . (A&M)

Return Of The Giant Hogweed
Genesis; *Genesis-Live* . . . . (Atlantic)
Nursery Cryme . . . . (Atlantic)

Roll On Big Mama
Joe Stampley; *Encore-Joe Stampley* . . . . (Epic)
Joe Stampley's Biggest Hits . . . . (Epic)
Joe Stampley's Greatest Hits . . . . (Epic)
Truckers' Jukebox-10 All-Time Radio Requests-C . . . . (Legacy)

Standin' At The Big Hotel
Joe Ely; *Down On The Drag* . . . . (MCA)

Taco Grande
"Weird Al" Yankovic; *Off The Deep End* . . . . (Scotti Bros.)
The Food Album . . . . (Scotti Bros.)

Tall Cool One
Robert Plant; *Knebworth-The Album-C* . . . . (Polydor)
Now And Zen . . . . (Es Paranza)

Tall Paul
Annette with the Afterbeats; *Best Of Annette Funicello* . . . . (Rhino)
Sherman Brothers . . . . (Disney)
Too Cute-C . . . . (Dunhill Compact Classics)

Tall Trees In Georgia
Buffy Sainte-Marie; *Best Of Buffy Sainte-Marie-#2* . . . . (Vanguard)
I'm Gonna Be A Country Girl Again . . . . (Vanguard)

Tall, Tall Trees
Alan Jackson; *Alan Jackson-The Greatest Hits Collection* . . . . (Arista)
George Jones; *Cup Of Loneliness-Classic Mercury Years* . . . . (Mercury)
George Jones-The Hits . . . . (Mercury)
Roger Miller; *King Of The Road-Genius Of Roger Miller* . . . . (Mercury)
Roger Miller-The Hits . . . . (Mercury)

Ten Feet Tall And Bulletproof
Travis Tritt; *Ten Feet Tall And Bulletproof* . . . . (Warner Bros.)

Ten Tall Giraffes
Liquid Pink; *Liquid Pink* . . . . (Atomic)

Texas Is Bigger Than It Used To Be
Mark Chesnutt; *Almost Goodbye* . . . . (MCA)
ST/8 Seconds . . . . (MCA)

Texas Size Heartache
Joe Diffie; *Joe Diffie's Greatest Hits* . . . . (Epic)

There Was A Tall Oak Tree
Dorsey Burnette; *Super Hits-#1-C* . . . . (International Mktg. Group)

Under The Big Black Sun
X; *Under The Big Black Sun* . . . . (Elektra)

Walls
Tom Petty And The Heartbreakers; *ST/She's The One* . . . . (Warner Bros.)

Wasp (Texas Radio & The Big Beat)
Doors; *Alive She Cried* . . . . (Elektra)
Doors-Classics . . . . (Elektra)
L.A. Woman . . . . (Elektra)
Weird Scenes Inside The Gold Mine . . . . (Elektra)

White Rabbit
Damned; *Best Of The Damned* . . . . (Roadracer)
Machine Gun Etiquette . . . . (Roadracer)
George Benson; *George Benson-Collection* . . . . (Warner Bros.)
White Rabbit . . . . (CBS Associated)
Jefferson Airplane; *2400 Fulton Street-An Anthology* . . . . (RCA)
Flight Log (1966-1976) . . . . (Grunt)
Loves You . . . . (RCA)
ST/Platoon . . . . (Atlantic)
Surrealistic Pillow . . . . (RCA)

The Worst Of Jefferson Airplane . . . . (RCA)

Who's Afraid Of The Big Bad Wolf
Barbra Streisand; *Just For The Record* . . . . (Columbia)
The Barbra Streisand Album . . . . (Columbia)
L.L. Cool J; *Simply Mad About The Mouse-C* . . . . (Columbia)
Mormon Tabernacle Choir & Columbia Symphony Orchestra; *When You Wish Upon A Star-A Tribute To Walt Disney* . . . . (CBS Masterworks)

Wynona's Big Brown Beaver
Primus; *Tales From The Punchbowl* . . . . (Interscope)

Your Feet's Too Big
Beatles; *45-#1503* . . . . (Collectables)
Fats Waller; *20 Golden Pieces Of Fats Waller* . . . . (Bulldog)
Ain't Misbehavin' . . . . (RCA)
Fats Waller-Legendary Performer . . . . (RCA)
Joint Is Jumpin' . . . . (Bluebird)
Original Cast; *Ain't Misbehavin'* . . . . (RCA)

BIRTHDAY, Happy Birthday

See Also: ***AGES (various), ANNIVERSARY, BABY, CHILDREN, FUN, PARTY, TEENAGERS***

16 Candles
Crests; *Alan Freed's Memory Lane-C* . . . . (MCA)
Billboard Top Rock 'N' Roll Hits-1959-C . . . . (Rhino)
Crests Greatest Hits . . . . (Collectables)
Cruisin'-1959-C . . . . (Increase)
Oldies But Goodies-#14-C . . . . (Original Sound)
Rock & Roll U.S.A.-21 Rock & Roll Favorites-#2-C . . . . (Laurie)
ST/American Graffiti . . . . (MCA)

Andy's Birthday
Original Soundtrack; *ST/Toy Story* . . . . (Disney)

Birthday
Beatles; *The Beatles (White Album)* . . . . (Capitol)
Daffy Duck; *Bugs & Friends Sing The Beatles* . . . . . . (Kid Rhino/Rhino 4 Kids)
Paul McCartney; *Tripping The Live Fantastic-Highlights!* . . . . (Capitol)
Texas Chainsaw Orchestra; *The Texas Chainsaw Orchestra* . . . . (Rhino)

Birthday
Sugarcubes; *Life's Too Good* . . . . (Elektra)
Modern Rock 1987-Hang The DJ-C . . . . (Rhino)
The Great Crossover Potential . . . . (Elektra)

Birthday
Meredith Brooks; *Blurring The Edges* . . . . (Capitol)

Birthday
Destiny's Child; *Destiny's Child* . . . . (Grass Roots/Columbia)

Birthday
Timbaland; *Tim's Bio* . . . . (BlackGround Enterp./Atlantic)

Birthday
Jesus & Mary Chain; *Munki* . . . . (Sub Pop)

Birthday
Dan Baird; *Buffalo Nickel* . . . . (American)

Birthday Blues
Bert Jansch; *Best Of Bert Jansch* . . . . (Shanachie)

Birthday Boy
Residents; *Duck Stab/Buster & Glenn/Goosebump* . . . . (East Side Digital)

Birthday Boy
Chicago; *Chicago XIV* . . . . (Chicago)

Birthday Carol
Todd Rundgren; *Runt* . . . . (Rhino)

Birthday Girl
Hi-Five; *Hi-Five's Greatest Hits* . . . . (Jive)

Birthday Party
Grandmaster Flash & The Furious Five; *Message From Beat Street-The Best Of-C* . . . . (Rhino)

Birthday Party
Pixies Three; *Growin' Up Too Fast-The Girl Group Anthology-C* . . . . (Mercury)

Birthday Present, The
Loudon Wainwright III; *Grown Man* . . . . (Virgin)

Birthday Song
Original Cast; *Fanny* . . . . (RCA Victor)

Birthday Song
Mac Davis; *Baby Don't Get Hooked On Me/Stop And Smell The Roses* . . . . (Collectables)

Birthday Waltz
Barbara Lamb; *Tonight I Feel Like Texas* . . . . (Sugar Hill)

Happy Birthday
Stevie Wonder; *Hotter Than July* . . . . (Motown)
ST/Our Friend Martin . . . . (Motown)

Happy Birthday
Original Cast; *Zorba* . . . . (RCA Victor)

Happy Birthday
Steppenwolf; *At Your Birthday Party* . . . . (MCA Special Prod.)

Happy Birthday
Altered Images; *Happy Birthday* . . . . (Portrait)
I Could Be Happy: The Best Of Altered Images . . . . (Epic)

Happy Birthday
New Kids On The Block; *Step By Step* . . . . (Columbia)

Happy Birthday
Carly Simon; *Clouds In My Coffee-1965-1995* . . . . (Arista)
Have You Seen Me Lately . . . . (Arista)

Happy Birthday
"Weird Al" Yankovic; *"Weird Al" Yankovic* . . . . (Volcano Entertainment)

Happy Birthday
Loretta Lynn; *Loretta Lynn's Greatest Hits* . . . . (MCA)

Happy Birthday 1975
Joni Mitchell; *Mingus* . . . . (Elektra)

Happy Birthday 2U
Lowen & Navarro; *Scratch At The Door* . . . . (ISD/Intersound)

Happy Birthday Baby
Claudine Clark; *Party Lights* . . . . (Collectables)

Happy Birthday Baby
B.B. King; *Take It Home* . . . . (MCA)

Happy Birthday Blues
Kathy Young with The Innocents; *More '60s Jukebox Favorites-C* . . . . . (K-Tel)

Happy Birthday Blues
B.B. King; *Take It Home* . . . . (MCA)

Happy Birthday Broken Heart
Rex Hobart; *Forever Always Ends* . . . . (Bloodshot)

Happy Birthday Caroline
Concrete Blonde; *Free* . . . . (Capitol)
Recollection: The Best Of Concrete Blonde . . . . (Capitol)

Happy Birthday Darlin'
Conway Twitty; *Conway Twitty Sings The Hits* . . . . . . (MCA Special Prod.)
Conway Twitty-Number Ones . . . . (MCA)

Happy Birthday Dear America/In 1776
Ella Jenkins; *We Are All America's Children* . . . . (Smithsonian Folkways)

Happy Birthday Dear Heartache
Barbara Mandrell; *Barbara Mandrell's Greatest Hits* . . . . (MCA)
Country Classics-#1-C . . . . (Universal)
Today's Country Classics-C . . . . (MCA Special Prod.)

Happy Birthday Elvis
Loudon Wainwright III; *Career Moves* . . . . (Virgin)

Happy Birthday Jamaica
Lee "Scratch" Perry; *The Upsetter & The Beat* . . . . (Heartbeat)

Happy Birthday Mr. President
Marilyn Monroe; *20 Golden Greatest Hits* . . . . (Stardance)
Marilyn Monroe-The Essential Recordings . . . . (Music Club)

Happy Birthday Mr. President
John Southworth; *Mars Pennsylvania* . . . . (Bar/None)

Happy Birthday To Little Sally Spingel Spungel Sporn
Dr. Seuss; *The Cat In The Hat Songbook* . . . . (RCA Special Prod.)

Happy Birthday To Me
Barney; *Barney's Big Surprise* . . . . (Lyrick Studios)

Happy Birthday To Me
Cracker; *Cracker* . . . . (Virgin)

Happy Birthday To Me
Hank Locklin; *45-#7921* . . . . (RCA)

Happy Birthday To You
Eddy Howard & His Orchestra; *Best Of Eddy Howard-The Mercury Years* . . . . (Mercury)
K-Tel's Original Party Music-#1-C . . . . (K-Tel)
Monkees; *ST/Head* . . . . (Rhino)
Various Artists; *Drew's Famous All Occasions Party Music-C* . . . . (Turn Up The Music)
Drew's Famous Kids Birthday Music-C . . . . (Turn Up The Music)
Music & Songs For All Occasions-C . . . . (Madacy)
Toddler Favorites . . . . (Kid Rhino/Rhino 4 Kids)

Happy Birthday To You And To You
Original Cast; *Side Show* . . . . (Sony Music Classical)

Happy Birthday, America
Li'l Wally; *Happy Birthday, America* . . . . (Jay Jay)

Happy Birthday, America
Paul Evans; *I Was Part Of The Fifties* . . . . (Original Cast)

Happy Birthday, Jesus
Original Sins; *Bethlehem* . . . . (Bar/None)

Happy Birthday, John (Happy Trails)
Janis Joplin; *Janis* . . . . (Legacy)

Happy Birthday, Mrs. J.J. Brown
Original Cast; *The Unsinkable Molly Brown* . . . . (EMI-Angel)

Happy Birthday, Sweet Sixteen
Neil Sedaka; *Neil Sedaka Sings His Greatest Hits* . . . . (RCA)
Neil Sedaka Sings The Hits . . . . (RCA)
Neil Sedaka's All-Time Greatest Hits . . . . (RCA)

Happy, Happy Birthday Baby
Ronnie Milsap; *Essential Ronnie Milsap* . . . . (RCA)
Sandy Posey; *45-#45703* . . . . (Columbia)
Tune Weavers; *Cruisin'-1957-C* . . . . (Increase)

It's My Party
Lesley Gore; *Billboard Top Rock 'N' Roll Hits-1963-C* . . . . (Rhino)
Golden Hits Of Lesley Gore . . . . (Mercury)
Good Time Rock 'N' Roll-C . . . . (MCA)
Lesley Gore-Anthology . . . . (Rhino)
Oldies But Goodies-#3-C . . . . (Original Sound)

Laurie (Strange Things Happen)
Dickey Lee; *Collector's Essentials-#1-1960s-C* . . . . (Varese Sarabande)

My Next Thirty Years
Tim McGraw; *A Place In The Sun* . . . . (Curb)
Tim McGraw's Greatest Hits . . . . (Curb)
Old
Paul Simon; *You're The One* . . . . (Warner Bros.)
Today Is Your Birthday
Solomon Burke; *Best Blues Album In The World...Ever!-C* . . . . (Virgin)
Washington's Birthday
Bob Hope; *Thanks For The Memories* . . . . (Collectables)

BITS & PIECES, Falling Apart

See Also: BREAK, LITTLE, SMALL

Absence Of The Heart
Deana Carter; *Everything's Gonna Be Alright* . . . . (Capitol)
All Of Me
Billie Holiday; *Billie Holiday-Love Songs* . . . . (Legacy)
Count Basie; *Compact Jazz-The Standards* . . . . (Verve)
Diana Ross; *ST/Lady Sings The Blues* . . . . (Motown)
Dinah Washington; *Compact Jazz-Dinah Washington* . . . . (Verve)
Duke Ellington; *Jazz Party* . . . . (Legacy)
Esquivel; *Music From A Sparkling Planet* . . . . (Bar/None)
Frank Sinatra; *Sinatra Sings His Greatest Hits* . . . . (Legacy)
Helen O'Connell; *Great Girl Singers Sing 22 Original*
Recordings-C . . . . (Hindsight)
Louis Armstrong; *Louis Armstrong's Greatest Hits* . . . . (Legacy)
Martha Tilton; *Sweet And Lovely: Capitol's Great Ladies Of Song-C* . . (Capitol)
Paul Whiteman & Mildred Bailey; *Those Wonderful Years: Happy Days Are*
Here Again-C . . . . (JCI Assoc. Labels)
Sarah Vaughan; *Essential Sarah Vaughan-The Great Songs* . . . . (Verve)
Willie Nelson; *Stardust* . . . . (Legacy)
Bent
Matchbox Twenty; *Mad Season By Matchbox Twenty* . . . . (Lava)
Totally Hits-#3-C . . . . (Atlantic)
Bits And Pieces
Dave Clark Five; *History Of The Dave Clark Five* . . . . (Hollywood)
Broken Down In Tiny Pieces
Billy "Crash" Craddock; *Crash's Smashes: The Hits Of Billy "Crash"*
Craddock . . . . (Razor & Tie)
Broken Pieces
Strato Vocalz; *Love Shouldn't Hurt-C* . . . . (Qwest)
Come A Little Bit Closer
Jay & The Americans; *Good Vibrations (Sounds Of Top 40 Radio: 1964-*
1967)-C . . . . (Capitol)
Jay & The Americans' All-Time Greatest Hits . . . . (Rhino)
Jay & The Americans' Greatest Hits . . . . (CEMA Special Prod.)
Come A Little Bit Closer
Fleetwood Mac; *25 Years-The Chain* . . . . (Warner Bros.)
Come A Little Bit Closer
Johnny Duncan & Janie Fricke; *Johnny Duncan & Janie Fricke's*
Greatest Hits . . . . (Columbia)
Nice 'N' Easy . . . . (Columbia)
Crazy
Alana Davis; *Blame It On Me* . . . . (Elektra)
Everything Falls Apart
Dog's Eye View; *Happy Nowhere* . . . . (Columbia)
Everything Is Broken
Kenny Wayne Shepherd; *Trouble Is...* . . . . (Revolution)
Everytime You Go Away
Daryl Hall & John Oates; *Best Of Daryl Hall & John Oates* . . . . (RCA)
Voices . . . . (RCA)
Paul Young; *From Time To Time-The Singles Collection* . . . . (Columbia)
Secret Of Association . . . . (Columbia)
T.J. Martell-Music For The Miracle-C . . . . (Epic Portrait Assoc.)
Falls Apart
Sugar Ray; *14:59* . . . . (Lava)
Totally Hits-#2-C . . . . (Elektra)
Gold Dust Woman
Fleetwood Mac; *25 Years-The Chain* . . . . (Warner Bros.)
Rumours . . . . (Warner Bros.)
Sister Hazel; *Legacy-A Tribute To Fleetwood Mac's Rumours-C* . . . . . (Lava)
I Fall To Pieces
Aaron Neville & Trisha Yearwood; *Rhythm Country And Blues-C* . . . . . (MCA)
Patsy Cline; *12 Greatest Hits* . . . . (MCA)
Always . . . . (MCA)
ST/Sweet Dreams . . . . (MCA)
The Patsy Cline Story . . . . (MCA)
I Go To Pieces
Del Shannon; *Rock On!* . . . . (Gone Gator)
Peter And Gordon; *Best Of Peter And Gordon* . . . . (Rhino)
History Of British Rock-#3-C . . . . (Rhino)
Southern Pacific; *County Line* . . . . (Warner Bros.)
Southern Pacific's Greatest Hits . . . . (Warner Bros.)
Itsy Bitsy Spider, The
Original Soundtrack; *Mother Goose Songs* . . . . (Madacy)
Itsy Bitsy Teenie Weenie Yellow Polkadot Bikini
Brian Hyland; *Brian Hyland's Greatest Hits* . . . . (Rhino)

Dr. Demento Presents The Greatest Novelty Records-#3-1960s-C . . . . (Rhino)
Vintage Music-#5-C . . . . (MCA)
Junkie Doll
Mark Knopfler; *Sailing To Philadelphia* . . . . (Warner Bros.)
Let's Fall To Pieces Together
George Strait; *George Strait's Greatest Hits* . . . . (MCA)
Right Or Wrong . . . . (MCA)
Strait Out Of The Box . . . . (MCA)
Little Bit Me, A Little Bit You
Monkees; *Monkees' Greatest Hits* . . . . (Rhino)
Little Bit Of Soul
Music Explosion; *Best Of Ohio Express & Other Bubblegum*
Smashes-#1-C . . . . (Rhino)
Cruisin'-1967-C . . . . (Increase)
Million-Dollar Memories #1-C . . . . (RCA)
Little Bit Of You
Lee Roy Parnell; *We All Get Lucky Sometimes* . . . . (Career)
Little Bits & Pieces
Jim Stafford; *45-#04339* . . . . (Columbia)
Little Bitty
Alan Jackson; *Everything I Love* . . . . (Arista)
Tom T. Hall; *Songs From Sopchoppy* . . . . (Mercury)
Tom T. Hall-The Hits . . . . (Mercury)
Little Bitty Pretty One
Huey Lewis and the News; *Four Chords & Several Years Ago* . . . . . . (Elektra)
Jackson 5; *Jackson 5-16 Greatest Hits* . . . . (Motown)
Jackson 5-Anthology . . . . (Motown)
Lookin' Through The Windows . . . . (Motown)
Motown Legends-Jackson 5 . . . . (Motown)
Top 10 With A Bullet-Motown Male Groups-C . . . . (Motown)
Thurston Harris; *Billboard Top R&B Hits-1957-C* . . . . (Rhino)
Collectables Presents The History Of Rock-#2-C . . . . (Collectables)
Little Bitty Tear
Burl Ives; *Best Of Burl Ives-#2* . . . . (MCA)
Burl Ives Live . . . . (MCA)
MCA Records 30 Years Of Hits-1958-1988-C . . . . (MCA)
Hank Cochran; *45-#47062* . . . . (Elektra)
Little By Little
Rolling Stones; *England's Newest Hit Makers/The Rolling Stones* . . . . . (Abkco)
Little By Little
James House; *Days Gone By* . . . . (Epic)
Little By Little
Dusty Springfield; *Dusty Springfield-Golden Hits* . . . . (Mercury)
Little By Little
Robert Plant; *Little By Little-Collector's Edition* . . . . (Es Paranza)
Shaken 'N' Stirred . . . . (Es Paranza)
Little By Little
Nighthawks; *Open All Nite* . . . . (Adelphi)
Little Dab'll Do Ya (Brylcreem)
Original Soundtrack; *TeeVee Toons-The Commercials-#1-C* . . . . (TVT)
New Beginning
Tracy Chapman; *New Beginning* . . . . (Elektra)
One Of These Days
Pink Floyd; *Collection Of Great Dance Songs* . . . . (Columbia)
Delicate Sound Of Thunder . . . . (Columbia)
Meddle . . . . (Capitol)
Pink Floyd-Gift Set . . . . (Capitol)
Works . . . . (Capitol)
One Piece At A Time
Johnny Cash; *The Man In Black-His Greatest Hits* . . . . (Legacy)
Ooh Aah...Just A Little Bit
Gina G; *Fresh!* . . . . (Eternal/Warner Bros.)
Piece Of My Heart
Big Brother & The Holding Company; *Cheap Thrills* . . . . (Columbia)
Rock Classics Of The '60s-C . . . . (Columbia)
Seems Like Yesterday-#6-Late '60s-C . . . . (K-Tel)
Bryan Ferry; *These Foolish Things* . . . . (Reprise)
Delaney & Bonnie; *Best Of Delaney & Bonnie* . . . . (Rhino)
Faith Hill; *Take Me As I Am* . . . . (Warner Bros.)
Janis Joplin; *Janis Joplin In Concert* . . . . (Columbia)
Janis Joplin's Greatest Hits . . . . (Columbia)
ST/Janis . . . . (Columbia)
Sammy Hagar; *Standing Hampton* . . . . (Geffen)
Piece Of My Heart
Tara Kemp; *Tara Kemp* . . . . (Giant)
Place To Fall Apart
Merle Haggard & Janie Fricke; *For The Record: Merle Haggard-43*
Legendary Hits . . . . (BNA)
Schism
Tool; *Lateralus* . . . . (Volcano Entertainment)
Slide
Goo Goo Dolls; *Dizzy Up The Girl* . . . . (Warner Sunset/Reprise)
Step By Step
Whitney Houston; *ST/The Preacher's Wife* . . . . (Arista)
Tearin' Up My Heart
'N Sync; *'N Sync* . . . . (RCA)
There Goes My Heart
Nat "King" Cole; *Let's Fall In Love* . . . . (Paisley Park)

Nat ''King'' Cole Sings For Two In Love-& More . . . . (Capitol)

Too Soon To Know
Don Gibson; *Oh Lonesome Me* . . . . (Collectables)
Roy Orbison; *The Classic Roy Orbison-1965-1968* . . . . (Rhino)

Un-Break My Heart
Toni Braxton; *Secrets* . . . . (LaFace)

Walking On Broken Glass
Annie Lennox; *Diva* . . . . (Arista)

You're The One
Paul Simon; *You're The One* . . . .(Warner Bros.)

BLOOD

See Also: **AIDS, ANATOMY (various), HEART, PAIN & HEALING**

Bad Blood
Neil Sedaka; *Billboard Top Rock 'N' Roll Hits-1975-C* . . . . (Rhino)

Bad Blood
Babylon A.D.; *Nothing Sacred* . . . . (Arista)

Bad Blood
Exile; *Still Standing* . . . . (Arista)

Bleed American
Jimmy Eat World; *Bleed American* . . . . (DreamWorks/SKG)

Bleed Together
Soundgarden; *A-Sides* . . . . (A&M)

Bleeders
Wallflowers; *Bringing Down The Horse* . . . . (Interscope)

Bleeding Me
Metallica; *Load* . . . . (Elektra)

Blood
Pearl Jam; *Vs.* . . . . (Epic Portrait Assoc.)

Blood Brothers
Bruce Springsteen; *Bruce Springsteen's Greatest Hits* . . . . (Columbia)

Blood Is Thicker Than Water
Wyclef Jean featuring G&B (The Product); *The Sopranos-Music From The
HBO Original Series* . . . . (Sony Music Soundtrax)

Blood Makes Noise
Suzanne Vega; *99.9 F* . . . . (A&M)

Blood On The Dance Floor
Michael Jackson; *Blood On The Dance Floor-HIStory*. . . . . . . (MJJ Music/Work)

Bloodshot Eyes
Wynonie Harris; *Bloodshot Eyes: The Best Of Wynonie Harris* . . . . (Rhino)
Good Rockin' Blues . . . . (Gusto)

Bloodshot Eyes
Asleep At The Wheel; *Bloodshot Eyes* . . . .(Epic)

Bloody Mary
Original Cast; *South Pacific* . . . .(CBS Masterworks)
Soundtrack; *South Pacific* . . . . (RCA)

Bloody Mary
Whitesnake; *Snakebite* . . . . (Geffen)

Bread & Blood
Air Supply; *The Earth Is...* . . . . (Giant)

California Bloodlines
John Stewart; *American Originals-John Stewart* . . . . (Capitol)
Shaw Brothers; *Shaw Brothers' Greatest Hits* . . . . (Folk Era)

Cold Blooded
Rick James; *Cold Blooded* . . . . (Motown)
Rick James' Greatest Hits . . . . (Motown)

Flesh And Blood
Roxy Music; *Flesh + Blood* . . . . (Atco)

Flesh And Blood
Johnny Cash; *Johnny Cash's Biggest Hits* . . . . (Columbia)
The Man In Black-His Greatest Hits . . . . (Legacy)

Give Blood
Pete Townshend; *White City* . . . . (Atco)

Hand Song, The
Nickel Creek; *Nickel Creek* . . . . (Sugar Hill)

Hemorrhage (In My Hands)
Fuel; *Now That's What I Call Music!-#6-C* . . . . (Virgin)
Something Like Human . . . .(Epic)

High Blood Pressure
Huey ''Piano'' Smith And The Clowns; *Serious Clownin'-History Of Huey
''Piano'' Smith And The Clowns.* . . . . (Rhino)

High Blood Pressure
Paula Lockheart & Peter Ecklund; *Paula Lockheart & Peter
Ecklund.* . . . . (Flying Fish)

Hot Blooded
Foreigner; *Double Vision* . . . .(Atlantic)
Records . . . .(Atlantic)
ST/Vision Quest . . . .(Geffen)

Human Beings
Seal; *Human Being* . . . .(Warner Bros.)

In The Blood
Better Than Ezra; *Deluxe* . . . . (Swell/Elektra)

Let It Bleed
Rolling Stones; *Let It Bleed* . . . . (Abkco)

More Hot Rocks (big hits & fazed cookies) . . . .(Abkco)

Life In The Bloodstream
Guess Who; *Best Of The Guess Who-#2* . . . . (RCA)

Mack The Knife
Bobby Darin; *Bobby Darin-At The Copa* . . . . (Bainbridge)
Hit Singles-1958-1977-C . . . .(Atlantic)
The Bobby Darin Story . . . .(Atlantic)
Frank Sinatra; *The Reprise Collection.* . . . .(Reprise)
Louis Armstrong; *Best Of Louis Armstrong* . . . . (Vanguard)

My Bleeding Heart
Elmore James; *Complete Fire & Enjoy Sessions-#2* . . . . (Collectables)

Night In My Veins
Pretenders; *Last Of The Independents* . . . .(Sire)

Night The Lights Went Out In Georgia
Lynn Anderson; *Top Of The World* . . . . (Columbia)
Reba McEntire; *For My Broken Heart* . . . . (MCA)
Reba McEntire's Greatest Hits-#3: I'm A Survivor . . . . (MCA)
Vicki Lawrence; *Super Hits Of The '70s-Have A Nice Day-#10-C* . . . . . . (Rhino)

Only Women Bleed
Alice Cooper; *The Alice Cooper Show* . . . . (Warner Bros.)
Welcome To My Nightmare . . . .(Atlantic)
Lita Ford; *Stiletto* . . . . (RCA)

Positive Bleeding
Urge Overkill; *Saturation* . . . . (Geffen)

Power In The Blood
Weary Hearts; *By Heart* . . . . (Flying Fish)

River Blood
Walkabouts; *Scavenger* . . . . (Sub Pop)

Rock Is In My Blood
Sammy Hagar; *VOA* . . . . (Geffen)

Sabbath, Bloody Sabbath
Anthrax; *I'm The Man* . . . . (Island)
Black Sabbath; *Sabbath Bloody Sabbath* . . . . (Warner Bros.)
We Sold Our Soul For Rock 'N' Roll . . . . (Warner Bros.)
Ozzy Osbourne; *Speak Of The Devil* . . . .(Jet)

Scum Of The Earth
Rob Zombie; *ST/Mission: Impossible 2* . . . . (Hollywood)

Suck On The Jugular
Rolling Stones; *Voodoo Lounge* . . . .(Virgin)

Sunday Bloody Sunday
U2; *Under A Blood Red Sky.* . . . . (Island)
War. . . . . (Island)

Sunday Bloody Sunday
John Lennon/Plastic Ono Band; *Sometime In New York City* . . . . (Capitol)

Thicker Than Blood
Garth Brooks; *Scarecrow* . . . . (Capitol)

Too Much Blood
Rolling Stones; *Undercover* . . . . (Rolling Stones)

Too Much Blood In My Alcohol System
Cold Shot; *Salt City Blues-C* . . . . (Blue Wave)

Transfusion
Nervous Norvus; *Dr. Demento Presents The Greatest Novelty Records-#2-
1950s-C* . . . . (Rhino)
Dr. Demento: 20th Anniversary Collection-C . . . . (Rhino)
Vintage Music-#3-C . . . . (MCA)
Wacky Weirdos-C . . . . (K-Tel)

Virginia's Bloody Soil
Tennessee Ernie Ford; *Tennessee Ernie Ford Sings Songs Of The
Civil War.* . . . . (Capitol)

Wash It Away
Black Lab; *Your Body Above Me.* . . . .(David Geffen Co.)

Watch Me Bleed
Tears For Fears; *The Hurting* . . . . (Mercury)

We Must Bleed
Terms; *M.I.A.* . . . .(Slash)

Will I Start To Bleed
Marty Willson-Piper; *Spirit Level* . . . . (Rykodisc)

Will Jesus Wash The Bloodstains From Your Hands
Bill Frisell; *Nashville* . . . . (Nonesuch)
Exene Cervenka; *Running Sacred* . . . . (Rhino)

Young Blood
Bad Company; *Run With The Pack* . . . . (Swan Song)
Coasters; *Coasters' Greatest Hits* . . . . (Atco)
Coasters-Their Greatest Recordings-Early Years . . . . (Atco)
The Ultimate Coasters . . . . (Warner Special Prod.)

Young Blood
Rickie Lee Jones; *Naked Songs Live And Acoustic* . . . . (Reprise)
Rickie Lee Jones . . . . (Warner Bros.)

BOOKS, Diary, Myths, Poetry, Reading, Stories, Writing

See Also: **COMMUNICATION (various), MAIL, NEWS, SCHOOL,
THINKING & KNOWING**

(Just Like) Romeo & Juliet
Reflections; *'60s Dance Party-C* . . . . (Dominion Entert.)

Sensational '60s-#1-C .... (Dominion Entert.)

Absolutely (Story Of A Girl)
Nine Days; *Maddening Crowd* .... (550 Music)
Now That's What I Call Music!-#5-C ....(Virgin)

All Around The World Or The Myth Of Fingerprints
Paul Simon; *Graceland* .... (Warner Bros.)

All I Can Do Is Write About It
Lynyrd Skynyrd; *Gimme Back My Bullets* .... (MCA)

Another Story
Ernest Tubb; *Ernest Tubb's Greatest Hits* .... (MCA)

Autobiography
Phoebe Snow; *It Looks Like Snow* .... (Columbia)

Autograph
John Denver; *John Denver's Greatest Hits-#3* ....(RCA)

Autumn Almanac
Kinks; *Kink Kronikles* ....(Reprise)

Avinu Malkeinu
Barbra Streisand; *Higher Ground* .... (Columbia)

Banjo Story
Elizabeth Cotten; *Elizabeth Cotten-Live* ....(Arhoolie)

Beautiful Story
Sonny & Cher; *Beat Goes On* .... (Atco)
Best Of Sonny & Cher .... (Atco)

Bedtime Story
Tammy Wynette; *First Lady Of Country Music* .... (Epic)
Tammy Wynette's Biggest Hits .... (Epic)
Tammy Wynette's Greatest Hits-#3 .... (Epic)

Bedtime Story
Madonna; *Bedtime Stories* .... (Maverick/Sire)
GHV2 .... (Warner Bros.)

Behind The Lines
Genesis; *Duke* .... (Atlantic)
Three Sides Live .... (Atlantic)
Phil Collins; *Face Value* .... (Atlantic)

Bible Tells Me So
Don Cornell; *Rock 'N Roll Reunion: Class Of '55-C* ..... (Madacy)

Book Of Dreams
Bruce Springsteen; *Lucky Town* .... (Columbia)

Book Of Love
Monotones; *Bedrock-Late '50s/'60s Rock 'N' Roll* .... (Allegiance)
Best Of Chess Rock 'N' Roll-#1-C .... (Chess)
Original Golden Rock Oldies-#1-C .... (Specialty)
ST/American Graffiti .... (MCA)
Super Oldies Of The '50s-#2-C. .... (Audio Fidelity)

Book Of Love
Fleetwood Mac; *Mirage* .... (Warner Bros.)

Book Of Love
Book Of Love; *Book Of Love* ....(Sire)

Book Of Miracles
Fleetwood Mac; *45-#7-28317* .... (Warner Bros.)

Book Of Rules
Heptones; *Night Food* .... (Island)
This Is Reggae Music-#1-C. .... (Island)

Book Of Saturday
King Crimson; *Lark's Tongues In Aspic* .... (Editions E.G.)

Book Song
Fairport Convention; *Fairport Convention* ....(A&M)
Fairport Convention-Chronicles ....(A&M)

Book, The
Sheryl Crow; *Sheryl Crow* ....(A&M)

Bookends
Joe Walsh; *The Smoker You Drink The Player You Get* .... (MCA)

Bookends
Simon & Garfunkel; *Bookends* .... (Columbia)
Collected Works .... (Columbia)
Simon & Garfunkel's Greatest Hits .... (Columbia)

Books I Read
Talking Heads; *'77* ....(Sire)

Both Sides Of The Story
Phil Collins; *Both Sides* .... (Atlantic)

Brush Up Your Shakespeare
Dick Hyman; *Cole Porter- All Through The Night* ....(Musicmasters)
Keenan Wynn & James Whitmore; *ST/Kiss Me Kate* .... (MCA)
Original Cast; *Kiss Me Kate* .... (Sony Music Classical)

Bubblegoose
Wyclef Jean; *Chef Aid-The South Park Album* ....(Columbia)
Wyclef Jean featuring Melky Sedeck; *Presents The Carnival F/Refugee Allstars.* .... (Ruffhouse/Columbia)

By The Book
Michael Peterson; *Michael Peterson* ....(Reprise)

Camelot
Original 1982 London Cast; *Camelot* ....(Varese Sarabande)
Original Cast; *Camelot* .... (Columbia)
Richard Burton; *Broadway Magic-The 1960s-C* .... (Columbia)
Richard Harris; *ST/Camelot.* .... (Warner Bros.)

Captain Nemo
Michael Schenker Group; *Built To Destroy.* .... (Chrysalis)
Rock Will Never Die .... (Chrysalis)

C'est Moi
Original Cast; *ST/Camelot* .... (Warner Bros.)
Robert Goulet; *Camelot* ....(Columbia)

Close As Pages In A Book
Benny Goodman; *Best Of The Big Bands-C* ....(Columbia)
Warren Vache; *Polished Brass.* ....(Concord Jazz)

Common Disaster
Cowboy Junkies; *Lay It Down* .... (Geffen)

Cover Of Rolling Stone
Dr. Hook & The Medicine Show; *Dr. Hook & The Medicine Show's Greatest Hits* ....(Capitol)
Revisited ....(Columbia)

Dear Diary
Moody Blues; *On The Threshold Of A Dream* .... (Polydor)
This Is The Moody Blues .... (Polydor)

Death Of An Unpopular Poet
Jimmy Buffett; *White Sport Coat & A Pink Crustacean.* .... (MCA)

Diary
Bread; *Baby I'm-A Want You* ....(Elektra)
Best Of Bread ....(Elektra)
Bread-Anthology. ....(Elektra)

Diary
Little Anthony And The Imperials; *Best Of Little Anthony And The Imperials* ....(Rhino)

Diary Of A Madman
Ozzy Osbourne; *Diary Of A Madman* .... (Jet)

Diary Of Horace Wimp
Electric Light Orchestra; *Discovery.* .... (Jet)

Diary Of My Mind
George Jones; *Alone Again* .... (Epic)

Diary, The
Neil Sedaka; *Neil Sedaka Sings His Greatest Hits* .... (RCA)
Neil Sedaka's All-Time Greatest Hits .... (RCA)
Nipper's Greatest Hits Of The '50s-#2-C .... (RCA)

Dolphin Story
Claudia Schmidt; *Midwestern Heart* .... (Flying Fish)

Don't Get Me Started
Rhett Akins; *Somebody New* ....(Decca)

Ecology Poem
Mutabaruka; *Blakk Wi Blak...k...k.* .... (Shanachie)

Editions Of You
Roxy Music; *For Your Pleasure.* .... (Reprise)
Heart Still Beating .... (Virgin)
Roxy Music's Greatest Hits ....(Atco)

Editorial
Paul Davis; *Singer Of Songs-Teller Of Tales* .... (Bang)
Southern Tracks & Fantasies .... (Bang)

Eight Line Poem
David Bowie; *Hunky Dory.* ....(Rykodisc)

Empty Pages
Traffic; *John Barleycorn Must Die.* ....(Island)

Empty Pages
Air Supply; *Love & Other Bruises* ....(Columbia)

Fairy Tale
Pointer Sisters; *Retrospect* .... (MCA)

Fairy Tale
Rita Remington; *Country Girl Gold.* .... (Plantation)

Fairy Tale
Elvis Presley; *Elvis In Concert* .... (RCA)

Fairy Tale High
Donna Summer; *Live & More* .... (Casablanca)
Once Upon A Time .... (Casablanca)

Fairy Tales
Anita Baker; *Compositions* .... (Elektra)

Fairy Tales
Style Council; *Cost Of Loving* .... (Polydor)

Fairy Tales
Rivingtons; *Liberty Years-Legends Of Rock & Roll.* ....(EMI)

Fairytale Of New York
Pogues; *Essential Pogues.* ....(Island)
If I Should Fall From Grace With God ....(Island)

Ghost Writer
Garland Jeffreys; *Ghost Writer* ....(A&M)

God's Coloring Book
Dolly Parton; *Here You Come Again* ....(Dunhill Compact Classics)

Goin' By The Book
Johnny Cash; *Mystery Of Life* ....(Mercury)

Goodbye Yellow Brick Road
Elton John; *Billboard Top Rock 'N' Roll Hits-1973-C* ....(Rhino)
Elton John's Greatest Hits .... (Polydor)
Goodbye Yellow Brick Road .... (Polydor)

Greatest Story Ever Told
Bob Weir; *Ace* .... (Grateful Dead)
Grateful Dead; *Dead Set.* ....(Arista)

Guenevere
Original Cast; *Camelot* ....(Columbia)
Original Soundtrack; *ST/Camelot* .... (Warner Bros.)

Hard Luck Stories
Richard & Linda Thompson; *Pour Down Like Silver* . . . . (Hannibal)
Hard Luck Stories
Neil Young; *Landing On Water* . . . .(Geffen)
Hard Luck Story
Elton John; *Rock Of The Westies* . . . . (Polydor)
Here's Where The Story Ends
Sundays; *Reading Writing & Arithmetic* . . . . (David Geffen Co.)
I Could Write A Book
Frank Sinatra; *Voice: The Columbia Years-1943-1952* . . . . (Columbia)
Original Cast; *Pal Joey* . . . . (Columbia)
Tony Bennett; *Rodgers & Hart Songbook* . . . . (DRG)
I Love A Murder Mystery
Jerry Lewis; *Capitol Collectors Series-Jerry Lewis* . . . . (Capitol)
I Thought I'd Write To Juliet
Elvis Costello; *The Juliet Letters* . . . .(Warner Bros.)
I Wrote The Book
Lauren Bacall; *Woman Of The Year* . . . . (Bay Cities)
If You Could Read My Mind
Gordon Lightfoot; *Gord's Gold* . . . . (Reprise)
If You Could Read My Mind . . . . (Reprise)
Sit Down Young Stranger . . . . (Reprise)
If You Leave Me Tonight I'll Cry
Jerry Wallace; *From The Vaults: Decca Country Classics-1934-
1973-C* . . . . (Decca)
Jerry Wallace's Greatest Hits . . . . (Curb)
It Ain't Necessarily So
Aretha Franklin; *The Great-First 12 Sides* . . . . (Columbia)
Cab Calloway; *Sullivan Years-Best Of Broadway* . . . . (TVT)
Cal Tjader; *Cal Tjader Plays/Mary Stallings Sings* . . . . (Fantasy)
Cher; *Glory Of Gershwin Featuring Larry Adler-C* . . . . (Mercury)
Ella Fitzgerald & Louis Armstrong; *Porgy & Bess* . . . . (Verve)
Miles Davis & His Orchestra; *Porgy & Bess* . . . . (Columbia)
It Was Written In The Stars
Ella Fitzgerald; *Harold Arlen Songbook-#2* . . . . (Verve)
It's In The Book (Parts 1 & 2)
Johnny Standley; *Dr. Demento Gooses Mother-C* . . . . (Kid Rhino/Rhino 4 Kids)
Johnny Can't Read
Don Henley; *I Can't Stand Still* . . . . (Asylum)
Lady Writer
Dire Straits; *Communique* . . . .(Warner Bros.)
Las Vegas Story
Gun Club; *Las Vegas Story* . . . . (I.R.S.)
Leech
Eve 6; *Eve 6* . . . . (RCA)
Life's Like Poetry
Lefty Frizzell; *Legendary Lefty Frizzell* . . . . (MCA)
Little Black Book
Jimmy Dean; *American Originals-Jimmy Dean* . . . . (Columbia)
Jimmy Dean's Greatest Hits . . . . (Columbia)
Longfellow Serenade
Neil Diamond; *12 Greatest Hits-#2* . . . . (Columbia)
Love At The Greek . . . . (Columbia)
On The Way To The Sky . . . . (Columbia)
Serenade . . . . (Columbia)
Love Story
Jethro Tull; *20 Years Of Jethro Tull* . . . .(Chrysalis)
Living In The Past . . . .(Chrysalis)
Love Story
Stephen Stills; *Stills* . . . . (Columbia)
Love Story
Tanita Tikaram; *Sweet Keeper* . . . . (Reprise)
Love, Me
Collin Raye; *All I Can Be* . . . .(Epic)
Greatest Country Hits Of The '90s-1992-C . . . . (Columbia)
Marian The Librarian
Original Broadway Cast; *The Music Man* . . . . (Angel)
Robert Preston; *ST/The Music Man* . . . .(Warner Bros.)
Murder Story
Simple Minds; *Life In A Day* . . . . (Virgin)
My Back Pages
Bob Dylan; *Another Side Of Bob Dylan* . . . . (Columbia)
Bob Dylan's Greatest Hits-#2 . . . . (Columbia)
Byrds; *20 Essential Tracks From The Box Set* . . . . (Columbia)
Byrds Play Dylan . . . . (Columbia)
The Byrds' Greatest Hits . . . . (Columbia)
Younger Than Yesterday . . . . (Columbia)
My Coloring Book
Barbra Streisand; *Barbra Streisand's Greatest Hits* . . . . (Columbia)
The Second Barbra Streisand Album . . . . (Columbia)
Perry Como; *This Is Perry Como-#2* . . . . (RCA)
My Little Brown Book
Duke Ellington; *Duke Ellington & John Coltrane* . . . .(MCA/Impulse)
John Coltrane; *The Gentle Side Of John Coltrane* . . . . (GRP)
My Little Red Book
Love; *Best Of Love* . . . . (Rhino)
Elektrock-Sixties-C . . . . (Elektra)
Nuggets-#2-Punk-C . . . . (Rhino)

My Mother's Bible
Warrior River Boys; *New Beginnings* . . . . (Rounder)
My True Story
Jive Five; *Back Seat Jams-C* . . . . (Dunhill Compact Classics)
Billboard Top R&B Hits-1961-C . . . . (Rhino)
Cruisin'-1961-C . . . . (Increase)
Jive Five-Their Greatest Hits . . . . (Collectables)
Oldies But Goodies-#4-C . . . .(Original Sound)
Neighborhood
Vonda Shepard; *ST/Songs From ''Ally McBeal'' Featuring Vonda
Shepard* . . . .(550/Epic)
Never Ending Story
Limahl; *ST/Never Ending Story* . . . . (EMI)
Nietzche's Eyes
Paula Cole; *This Fire* . . . .(Imago)
Once Upon A Time
Donna Summer; *Live & More* . . . . (Casablanca)
Once Upon A Time . . . . (Casablanca)
Once Upon A Time
Marvin Gaye & Mary Wells; *Marvin Gaye-Anthology* . . . . (Motown)
Together . . . . (Motown)
Once Upon A Time
Dan Fogelberg; *Nether Lands* . . . .(Full Moon)
Once Upon A Time
Simple Minds; *Once Upon A Time* . . . . (A&M)
Simple Minds Live: In The City Of Light . . . . (A&M)
Once Upon A Time
Frank Sinatra; *September Of My Years* . . . . (Reprise)
Tony Bennett; *I Left My Heart In San Francisco* . . . . (Columbia)
Open Up Your Eyes
Tonic; *Lemon Parade* . . . . (Polydor)
Pagan Poetry
Bjork; *Vespertine* . . . . (Elektra)
Page 43
Crosby, Stills & Nash; *CSN* . . . .(Atlantic)
David Crosby & Graham Nash; *David Crosby & Graham Nash* . . . . . .(Atlantic)
Pages Of My Mind
Ray Charles; *From The Pages Of My Mind* . . . . (Columbia)
Paperback Writer
Beatles; *Beatles 1* . . . . (Capitol)
Beatles-20 Greatest Hits . . . . (Capitol)
Beatles-Box Set . . . . (Capitol)
Hey Jude . . . . (Capitol)
Past Masters-Volume Two . . . .(Parlophone)
The Beatles/1962-1966 . . . . (Capitol)
Paul McCartney; *Paul Is Live* . . . . (Capitol)
Piano Lesson & If You Don't Mind My Saying So
Shirley Jones; *ST/The Music Man* . . . . (Warner Bros.)
Picture Book
Kinks; *Are The Village Green Preservation Society* . . . . (Reprise)
Picture Book
Simply Red; *Picture Book* . . . . (Elektra)
Poem 58
Chicago; *Chicago Transit Authority* . . . . (Chicago)
Group Portrait . . . . (Chicago)
Poem For The People
Chicago; *Chicago II* . . . . (Chicago)
Poem Of Summer
J.D. Robb; *Triptyque/Other Electronic Compositions* . .(Smithsonian Folkways)
Poem On The Underground Wall
Simon & Garfunkel; *Collected Works* . . . . (Columbia)
Parsley Sage Rosemary & Thyme . . . . (Columbia)
Poems, Prayers & Promises
John Denver; *Evening With John Denver* . . . . (RCA)
John Denver's Greatest Hits . . . . (RCA)
Poems, Prayers & Promises . . . . (RCA)
John Denver & The Muppets; *Rocky Mountain Holiday* . . . . (RCA)
Poetry In Motion
Johnny Tillotson; *10 Top Ten Hits-#1* . . . . (Laurie)
American Graffiti-#3-C . . . . (MCA)
Jukebox Classics-#1-C . . . . (Rhino)
Mellow '60s-C . . . . (Priority)
Million-Dollar Memories-#2-C . . . . (RCA)
Poetry Man
Phoebe Snow; *Best Of Phoebe Snow* . . . . (Columbia)
Phoebe Snow . . . . (MCA)
Poet's Heart
Kate Wolf; *Gold In California-Retrospective-1975-1985* . . . . . . (Kaleidoscope)
Poet's Heart . . . . (Kaleidoscope)
Poison Pen
Hoodoo Gurus; *Mars Needs Guitars* . . . . (Elektra)
Poison Pen
Molly Hatchet; *Beatin' The Odds* . . . .(Epic)
Read About It
Midnight Oil; *10-9-8-7-6-5-4-3-2-1* . . . . (Columbia)
Scream In Blue Live . . . . (Columbia)
Read Between The Lines
Aaron Tippin; *Read Between The Lines* . . . . (RCA)

Read It In Books
Echo & The Bunnymen; *Crocodiles* ....(Sire)

Rhymes & Reasons
John Denver; *Evening With John Denver* ....(RCA)
   John Denver's Greatest Hits.............................(RCA)
   Take Me Home, Country Roads & Other Hits............(RCA)

Rhythm In My Nursery Rhymes
Tommy Dorsey & His Clambake Seven; *Music Goes Round & Round*...(Bluebird)

Rime Of The Ancient Mariner
Iron Maiden; *Live After Death-World Slavery Tour* ....(Capitol)
   Powerslave..(Capitol)

Sad Story
Jack Scott; *Capitol Collectors Series-Jack Scott* ....(Capitol)

Same Old Story
Billie Holiday; *Fine & Mellow* ....(Collectables)
   Quintessential-#8-1939-1940..........................(Legacy)

Same Old Story
Stevie Wonder; *Journey Through The Secret Life Of Plants* ....(Motown)

Same Old Story
Garth Brooks; *No Fences*................................(Capitol)

Same Old Story
Ronna Reeves; *Only The Heart* ....(Mercury)

Same Script, Different Cast
Whitney Houston & Deborah Cox; *Whitney Houston's Greatest Hits* ... (Arista)

San Antonio Story
Stephen Woodfin & Joe Vickers; *Waco*.....................(Step One)

Serpentine Fire
Earth, Wind & Fire; *All 'N All* ....(Columbia)
   Best Of Earth, Wind & Fire-#2 ....(Columbia)
   Eternal Dance..(Columbia)

Shakespeare Stole My Baby
Eye To Eye; *Shakespeare Stole My Baby* .... (Warner Bros.)

Shakespeare's Sister
Smiths; *Louder Than Bombs* ....(Sire)

Shakespeare's Sonnet No. 18
Bryan Ferry; *Diana, Princess Of Wales-Tribute-C* ....(Columbia)

Sign Your Name
Terence Trent D'Arby; *Introducing The Hardline According To Terence Trent D'Arby* ....(Columbia)
   Slow Dancin'-C .... (K-Tel)

Skellig
Loreena McKennitt; *The Book Of Secrets* .... (Quinlan Rd./Warner Bros.)

Smoke
Ben Folds Five; *Whatever And Ever Amen* .... (Caroline/550)

Song Of The South (Gone With The Wind)
Alabama; *Alabama's Greatest Hits-#2* ....(RCA)
   Southern Star..(RCA)

Stories For Boys
U2; *Boy* .... (Island)

Stories I Tell
Toad The Wet Sprocket; *Fear* ....(Columbia)

Stories Of Old
Depeche Mode; *Some Great Reward*.........................(Sire)

Stories We Could Tell
Jimmy Buffett; *A1A* .... (MCA)
John Sebastian; *Best Of John Sebastian*..................(Rhino)
Tom Petty And The Heartbreakers; *Pack Up The Plantation-Live!*...... (MCA)

Story Behind The Story
Big Al Downing; *Story Behind The Story-45*.............. (Warner Bros.)

Story Book Of Love
Whispers; *Excellence* .... (Allegiance)
   Shhhh ....(Dore)

Story Goes On
Original Broadway Cast; *Baby* .... (Polydor)

Story In Your Eyes
Moody Blues; *Every Good Boy Deserves Favour* .... (Polydor)
   This Is The Moody Blues............................. (Polydor)

Story Of A Broken Heart
Johnny Cash; *Johnny Cash-Original Golden Hits-#3* ....(Sun)
   Original Johnny Cash.................................(Sun)
   Rough Cut King Of Country Music ....(Sun)
   The Man-The World-His Music ....(Sun)

Story Of A Teenager
America; *Hearts* .... (Warner Bros.)

Story Of Bo Diddley
Animals; *Best Of The Animals*........................... (Abkco)
Bo Diddley; *In The Spotlight* ....(Chess)

Story Of Love
Desert Rose Band; *Pages Of Life*..........................(Curb)

Story Of My Life
Don Williams; *Lovers & Best Friends*.......................(MCA)
   Yellow Moon...(MCA)
Marty Robbins; *Essential Marty Robbins-1951-1982*............(Columbia)
   Lifetime Of Song-1951-1982...........................(Columbia)
   Marty Robbins' Greatest Hits.........................(Columbia)

Story Of My Life
Neil Diamond; *Headed For The Future*.....................(Columbia)

Story Of My Life
Unrelated Segments; *Nuggets-#11-Pop-Part 4-C* ....(Rhino)

Story Of Rock & Roll
Turtles; *Best Of The Turtles-Golden Archive Series*...........(Rhino)
   Chalon Road ....(Rhino)
   Turtles-20 Greatest Hits ....(Rhino)

Story Untold
Nutmegs; *Back Seat Jams-C* ....(Dunhill Compact Classics)
   Cruisin'-1955-C ....(Increase)
   Nutmegs' Greatest Hits ....(Collectables)
   Oldies But Goodies-#2-C .... (Original Sound)

Storybook Children
Bette Midler; *Broken Blossom* .... (Atlantic)
Nancy Sinatra & Lee Hazlewood; *Fairy Tales & Fantasies-Best Of* .....(Rhino)

Storybook Love
Mark Knopfler & Willy DeVille; *ST/The Princess Bride*........ (Warner Bros.)

Storybook Of Love
Rozalla; *Everybody's Free* ....(Epic)

Story's Been Told
Third World; *The Story's Been Told* ....(Island)

Stranger Than Fiction
Killer Dwarfs; *Method To The Madness* ....(Epic)

Stranger Than Fiction
Belouis Some; *Belouis Some* ....(Capitol)

Stranger Than Fiction
Split Enz; *Mental Notes* .... (Chrysalis)

Summer I Read Collette, The
Rosanne Cash; *10 Song Demo* ....(Capitol)

Survival Handbook Vs. Global Extinction
Sister Souljah; *360 Degrees Of Power* ....(Epic)

Sweetheart
Jermaine Dupri & Mariah Carey; *Presents Life In 1472-Original Soundtrack* .... (So So Def/Columbia)
Mariah Carey featuring Jermaine Dupri; *Mariah Carey-#1's* ....(Columbia)

Tales From The Vienna Woods
101 Strings Orchestra; *Best Of Johann Strauss, Jr.* ....(Alshire)
Lawrence Welk; *22 Great Waltzes*........................ (Ranwood)

Tales Of Brave Ulysses
Cream; *Disraeli Gears* .... (Polydor)
   Eric Clapton-Crossroads-C .... (Polydor)
   Live Cream-#2.. (Polydor)

Tales Of Kilimanjaro
Carlos Santana; *Havana Moon*...........................(Columbia)
Santana; *Zebop!* ....(Columbia)

Tell Me A Bedtime Story
Norman Connors; *Remember Who You Are* ....(Mojazz)
Quincy Jones; *Sounds... And Stuff Like That!!* ....(A&M)

Telling Stories
Tracy Chapman; *Telling Stories*...........................(Elektra)

That Ain't In Any Catalog
Mustard & Gravy; *Long Gone Daddy-C* ....(Collectables)

That's My Story
Collin Raye; *Extremes* ....(Epic)

Them Poems
White Mountain Singers; *Memories-Live!*....................(Folk Era)

Theme From "Love Story"
Andy Williams; *Andy Williams' Greatest Hits-#2* ....(Columbia)
   Love Story..(Columbia)
Cincinnati Pops Orchestra/Erich Kunzel; *Hollywood's Greatest Hits-#1* .... (Telarc)
Francis Lai; *ST/Love Story* .... (MCA)
Johnny Mathis; *Johnny Mathis' All-Time Greatest Hits* ....(Columbia)
   Johnny Mathis-16 Most Requested Songs ....(Columbia)
Peter Nero; *Peter Nero's Greatest Hits* ....(Columbia)

Theme From "Murder, She Wrote"
Original Soundtrack; *CBS: The First 50 Years*.................(TVT)

Theme From "Out Of Africa"
John Barry; *ST/Out Of Africa* .... (MCA)

Tom Sawyer
Rush; *Exit...Stage Left*.................................(Mercury)
   Moving Pictures.....................................(Mercury)
   Rush-Chronicles.....................................(Mercury)

Tore Down A La Rimbaud
Van Morrison; *A Sense Of Wonder* ....(Mercury)

Trinidad
Eddie Money; *Playing For Keeps* ....(Columbia)
   Unplug It In ....(Columbia)

Turn Back The Pages
Crosby, Stills & Nash; *CSN* .... (Atlantic)
Stephen Stills; *Stills* ....(Columbia)

Turn The Page
Rush; *Hold Your Fire* ....(Mercury)
   Show Of Hands ....(Mercury)
Terence Trent D'Arby; *Symphony Or Damn* ....(Columbia)

Turn The Page
Metallica; *Garage Inc.* ....(Elektra)

Turn The Page
Aaliyah; *ST/Music Of The Heart* .... (Epic/Sony Music Soundtrax)

TV Movie
Bruce Springsteen; *Tracks* . . . . (Columbia)
Two Fairy Tales
Mark Lambert & Victoria Mallory; *Sondheim-A Musical Tribute* . . . . (RCA)
Original Cast; *Marry Me A Little* . . . . (RCA)
Two Story House
George Jones & Tammy Wynette; *George Jones & Tammy Wynette-16*
Biggest Hits . . . . (Epic/Legacy)
Typewriter, The
101 Strings Orchestra; *Strings Have Fun!* . . . . (Alshire)
Rochester Pops Orchestra; *Leroy Anderson's Greatest Hits*. . . . . (Pro-Arte)
Rochester Pops Orchestra & Erich Kunzel; *Syncopated Clock*. . . . . . (Pro-Arte)
U.F.O. Story
Flaming Lips; *Telepathic Surgery* . . . .(Restless)
Under African Skies
Paul Simon; *Graceland*. . . . .(Warner Bros.)
Virginia Woolf
Indigo Girls; *Rites Of Passage* . . . .(Epic)
Washable Ink
John Hiatt; *Slug Line*. . . . .(MCA)
Y'All Caught? Ones That Got Away, 1979-85 . . . . (Geffen)
Neville Brothers; *Love Gets Strange-Songs Of John Hiatt-C* . . . . (Rhino)
Treacherous: A History Of The Neville Brothers. . . . . (Rhino)
Whale Of A Tale
Original London Cast; *Moby Dick* . . . . (RCA)
Whaling Stories
Procol Harum; *Home* . . . . (A&M)
Procol Harum Live In Concert with the Edmonton Symphony. . . . . (A&M)
Procol Harum-Classics-#17 . . . . (A&M)
What It Is
Mark Knopfler; *Sailing To Philadelphia*. . . . .(Warner Bros.)
While You Loved Me
Rascal Flatts; *Rascal Flatts*. . . . . (Lyric Street)
Whiter Shade Of Pale
Annie Lennox; *Medusa*. . . . . (Arista)
Procol Harum; *Best Of Procol Harum* . . . . (A&M)
Billboard Top Pop Hits-1967-C. . . . . (Rhino)
History Of British Rock-#8-C . . . . (Rhino)
ST/Big Chill . . . . (Motown)
Whither Thou Goest
Les Paul & Mary Ford; *Best Of The Capitol Masters* . . . .(Gold Rush)
Les Paul's All-Time Greatest Hits . . . . (EMI Special Markets)
Wild Billy's Circus Story
Bruce Springsteen; *The Wild, The Innocent & The E Street Shuffle* . . (Columbia)
Wild Tales
Crosby, Stills & Nash; *CSN* . . . .(Atlantic)
Wondrous Stories
Yes; *Classic Yes* . . . .(Atlantic)
Going For The One . . . . (Atlantic)
Yesshows . . . . (Atlantic)
Write Your Own Songs (Mr. Record Executive)
Asleep At The Wheel; *Asleep At The Wheel* . . . .(MCA Special Prod.)
Waylon Jennings & Willie Nelson; *WWII* . . . . (RCA)
Willie Nelson; *Revolutions In Time-The Journey-1975-1993* . . . . . . (Legacy)
Willie Nelson & Kris Kristofferson; *Music From ''Songwriter''*. . . . (Columbia)
Writer
UFO; *Best Of The Rest Of UFO* . . . .(Chrysalis)
Mechanix . . . .(Chrysalis)
Writing
Elton John; *Captain Fantastic And The Brown Dirt Cowboy* . . . . (Polydor)
Saga; *Heads Or Tales* . . . . (Portrait)
Writing On The Wall
Lene Lovich; *Stateless...Plus* . . . . (Rhino)
Writing On The Wall
Cheap Trick; *Dream Police* . . . .(Epic)
Writing On The Wall
Ted Nugent; *Free For All* . . . .(Epic)
Writing On The Wall
Original Broadway Cast; *Mystery Of Edwin Drood* . . . . (Polydor)
Writing On The Wall
Triumph; *Never Surrender* . . . .(MCA)
Writing On The Wall
George Jones; *One Woman Man*. . . . .(Epic)
Written All Over Your Face
Rude Boys; *Rude Awakening* . . . . (Atlantic)
Written In Sand
Santana; *Beyond Appearances* . . . . (Columbia)
Written In Stone
Randy Travis; *Old 8 X 10* . . . .(Warner Bros.)
Written In The Stars
Elton John & LeAnn Rimes; *ST/Aida* . . . . (Island)
Written On The Wind
Four Aces; *Best Of The Four Aces* . . . . (MCA)
Four Aces' 20 Greatest Hits. . . . . (Everest)
Love Is A Many Splendored Thing . . . . (Accord)
You Can't Judge A Book By Its Cover
Stevie Wonder; *Signed Sealed & Delivered* . . . . (Motown)

You Can't Judge A Book By The Cover
Hank Williams, Jr.; *Montana Cafe* . . . . (WB/Curb)
Patti LaBelle; *Patti LaBelle*. . . . . (Epic)

BORED, Tired Of Things
See Also: RELAX, SLEEP, STUCK

Battle Of Who Could Care Less
Ben Folds Five; *Whatever And Ever Amen* . . . .(Caroline/550)
Beautiful Disaster
311; *Live!* . . . . (Capricorn)
Transistor. . . . . (Capricorn)
Better Things To Do
Terri Clark; *Terri Clark*. . . . . (Mercury)
Burnout
Green Day; *Dookie* . . . .(Reprise)
Dancing In The Dark
Bruce Springsteen; *Born In The U.S.A.* . . . . (Columbia)
Bruce Springsteen's Greatest Hits . . . . (Columbia)
Dis-Satisfied
Bill Anderson & Jan Howard; *More Great Country*
Duets-C . . . . (MCA Special Prod.)
Exquisitely Bored
Pete Townshend; *All The Best Cowboys Have Chinese Eyes* . . . . (Atco)
Flowers On The Wall
Eric Heatherly; *Swimming In Champagne* . . . . (Mercury)
Statler Brothers; *All Time Legends Of Country Music-C*. . . . . (Legacy)
Best Of The Statler Brothers . . . . (Mercury)
Billboard Top Country Hits-1966-C. . . . . (Rhino)
Columbia Country Classics-#3-Americana-C . . . . (Columbia)
Pop Classics Of The '60s-C . . . . (Columbia)
I Get A Kick Out Of You
Ethel Merman with Johnny Green & His Orchestra; *The Ethel Merman*
Collection . . . . (Razor & Tie)
This Is Art Deco-C . . . . (Columbia)
Frank Sinatra; *My One & Only Love* . . . . (Capitol)
Round #1 . . . . (Capitol)
Sinatra and Swingin' Brass . . . . (Reprise)
Sinatra-The Main Event Live . . . . (Reprise)
The Capitol Years. . . . . (Capitol)
The Reprise Collection . . . . (Reprise)
Original Cast; *Anything Goes* . . . . (Epic)
Paul Whiteman & His Orchestra; *78-#24769* . . . .(Victor)
I Love You (But You're Boring)
Beautiful South; *Welcome To The Beautiful South* . . . . (Elektra)
I'd Rather Have What We Had
Conway Twitty; *Two's A Party* . . . . (MCA Special Prod.)
Lee Ann Womack; *Some Things I Know*. . . . . (Decca)
I'll Never Get Tired Of You
Patty Loveless; *Honky Tonk Angel* . . . . (MCA)
I'm So Bored With The U.S.A.
Clash; *The Clash* . . . . (Epic)
Is There Life Out There
Reba McEntire; *For My Broken Heart* . . . . (MCA)
Reba McEntire's Greatest Hits Volume Two . . . . (MCA)
Rattlesnake
Live; *Secret Samadhi* . . . . (Radioactive/MCA)
Run
Collective Soul; *Dosage* . . . .(Atlantic)
Serve The Servants
Nirvana; *In Utero* . . . .(David Geffen Co.)
Sheep Go To Heaven
Cake; *Prolonging The Magic* . . . . (Capricorn)
Small Town Saturday Night
Hal Ketchum; *Past The Point Of Rescue* . . . . (Curb)
Then I'll Be Tired Of You
Coleman Hawkins; *Real Thing* . . . .(Prestige)
Jonathan Schwartz; *Alone Together* . . . .(Muse)
Paul Desmond; *Late Lament* . . . . (Bluebird)
Then What
Clay Walker; *Clay Walker's Greatest Hits* . . . .(Giant)
Turn The Page
Metallica; *Garage Inc.* . . . . (Elektra)

BOSSES, Captains, In Charge
See Also: FAMILY: FATHERS, FAMILY: MOTHERS, KINGS, PARENTS (various), POWER & CONTROL, QUEENS, POLITICS: POLITICS & GOVERNMENT, ROYALTY, SLAVERY, SOCIAL CLASS: GENERAL, WORK, WAR

Big Boss Man
B.B. King; *Six Silver Strings* . . . . (MCA)

Elvis Presley; *ST/Clambake*.............................(RCA)
Grateful Dead; *Grateful Dead (Skull & Roses)* .... (Warner Bros.)
Jimmy Reed; *Best Of Jimmy Reed*......................(Crescendo)
   Oldies But Goodies-#1-C ....(Original Sound)
John Hammond; *Best Of John Hammond* ....(Vanguard)
   So Many Roads ....(Vanguard)

Blue Tail Fly
Burl Ives; *Best Of Burl Ives* ....(MCA)
Pete Seeger; *20 Golden Pieces Of Pete Seeger* .... (Bulldog)

Boss
Diana Ross; *Boss* ....(Motown)
   Composer-Greatest By Ashford & Simpson .... (Motown)
   Diana Ross-Anthology ....(Motown)

Captain Of Her Heart
Double; *Blue* ....(A&M)
   Romantic Hits Of The '80s-C ....(K-Tel)

Dirty Business
New Riders Of The Purple Sage; *New Riders Of The Purple Sage* ... (Columbia)

Hallelujah, I'm A Bum
Al Jolson; *You Ain't Heard Nothin' Yet*......................(Legacy)
Bobby Short; *Bobby Short Celebrates Rodgers & Hart*............ (Atlantic)

Head Of The Table
Joan Armatrading; *Whatever's For Us* ....(A&M)

I Wanna Be A Boss
10 CC; *How Dare You!* ....(Mercury)

If I Ruled The World
Diana Ross & The Supremes; *Diana Ross & The Supremes-25th
   Anniversary* ....(Motown)

If I Ruled The World
NaS; *It Was Written* ....(Columbia)

If I Ruled The World
Tony Bennett; *Forty Years-The Artistry Of Tony Bennett* .... (Columbia)

If I Ruled The World
Stevie Wonder; *Looking Back* ....(Motown)

If I Ruled The World
Sammy Davis, Jr.; *Sammy Davis, Jr.'s Greatest Hits* ....(Reprise)

If I Ruled The World
James Brown; *Sex Machine*........................ (Polydor)

If Women Ruled The World
Joan Armatrading; *Square The Circle* ....(A&M)

I've Got My Captain Working For Me Now
Eddie Cantor; *Music From The New York Stage (1890-1920)-#4-1917-
   1920-C* ....(Pearl)

Mob Rules
Black Sabbath; *Live Evil* .... (Warner Bros.)
   Mob Rules .... (Warner Bros.)
   ST/Heavy Metal ....(Asylum)

Mrs. Clara Sullivan's Letter
Pete Seeger; *Best Of Broadside 1962-1968: Anthems Of The American
   Underground From The Pages Of Broadside
   Magazine-C*........................(Smithsonian Folkways)

No Can Do
Mark Knopfler; *Golden Heart* .... (Warner Bros.)

Oney
Johnny Cash; *Johnny Cash-16 Biggest Hits-#2* ....(Legacy)

Ride Captain Ride
Blues Image; *Back To The '70s-#3-C* .... (Dominion Entert.)
   Hit Singles-1958-1977-C ....(Atlantic)

Shadow Captain
Crosby, Stills & Nash; *Allies*.........................(Atlantic)
   CSN..................................(Atlantic)
   Replay................................(Atlantic)

Theme From "Who's The Boss"
Original Soundtrack; *Television's Greatest Hits-#6-Remote Control-C* ... (TVT)

Under My Thumb
Rolling Stones; *"Still Life" (American Concert 1981)*...........(Virgin)
   12 X 5 ....(Abkco)
   Aftermath ....(Abkco)
   got Live if you want it!.......................(Abkco)
   Hot Rocks 1964-1971 ....(Abkco)
Who; *Odds & Sods* .... (MCA)
   Who's Missing .... (MCA)

Women Will Rule The World
Ry Cooder; *Get Rhythm*...................... (Warner Bros.)

Working For The Man
Roy Orbison; *For The Lonely: A Roy Orbison Anthology 1959-1965*.... (Rhino)
   In Dreams-Greatest Hits........................(Orbison)
   Roy Orbison-More Greatest Hits ....(Monument)
   Roy Orbison's All-Time Greatest Hits-#1 & 2 ....(Monument)

BOTTLES, Buckets, Cups
See Also: ALCOHOL, FOOD & BEVERAGES: GENERAL

Bottle Of Blues
Beck; *Mutations* ....(David Geffen Co.)

Bottle Of Red Wine
Derek And The Dominos; *Live At The Fillmore*.................. (Polydor)
Eric Clapton; *Eric Clapton*......................... (Polydor)

Bottle Of Smoke
Pogues; *If I Should Fall From Grace With God* ....(Island)

Bottle Of Wine
Jimmy Gilmer And The Fireballs; *Frat Rock!-#4-C* ....(Rhino)
   Son Of Frat Rock!-C ....(Rhino)
   Super Hits-#1-C ....(Gusto)

Bottle Of Wine
Tom Paxton; *Best Of The Vanguard Years*.....................(Vanguard)

Broken Bottles
Bill Miller; *Art Of Survival*.........................(Vanguard)

Buckets Of Rain
Bob Dylan; *Blood On The Tracks*......................(Columbia)

Drink That Bottle Down
Brian Setzer Orchestra; *Brian Setzer Orchestra*..............(Hollywood)

Drinkin' Wine (Spo Dee O De)
"Stick" McGhee and His Buddies; *Atlantic Rhythm & Blues 1947-1974-#1
   (1947-1952)-C* ....(Atlantic)
   Soul Years-C ....(Atlantic)
Jerry Lee Lewis; *18 Original Sun Greatest Hits*...............(Rhino)
   Best Of Town & Country-#3-C ....(Gusto)
   I'm On Fire ....(Mercury)
   Milestones ....(Rhino)

Dust On The Bottle
David Lee Murphy; *Out With A Bang* ....(MCA)

Empty Bottle Blues
Jerry Ricks; *Deep In The Well* .... (Rooster Blues)

From The Bottle To The Bottom
Kris Kristofferson; *Singer Songwriter* .... (Sony Music Special Prod.)

Genie In A Bottle
Christina Aguilera; *Christina Aguilera* .... (RCA)
   Totally Hits-#2-C ....(Elektra)

Last Cup Of Sorrow
Faith No More; *Album Of The Year* .... (Reprise)

Lie Still Little Bottle
They Might Be Giants; *Lincoln* ....(Restless)

Little Brown Jug
Glenn Miller; *Best Of Glenn Miller* .... (RCA)
   Glenn Miller-A Legendary Performer-#1 & 2.............(Bluebird)
   The Glenn Miller Story .... (RCA)
Glenn Miller & His Orchestra; *Glenn Miller & His Orchestra-
   Pure Gold*..............................(Bluebird)
   The Unforgettable Glenn Miller & His Orchestra......... (RCA)

Longneck Bottle
Garth Brooks; *Sevens*..........................(Capitol)

Love Potion Number 9
Clovers; *ST/American Graffiti* ....(MCA)
   Super Oldies Of The '50s-#7-C .... (Audio Fidelity)
Herb Alpert & The Tijuana Brass; *Herb Alpert & The Tijuana Brass'
   Greatest Hits* ....(A&M)
   Herb Alpert & The Tijuana Brass-Classics-#1 ....(A&M)
Searchers; *History Of British Rock-#3-C* ....(Rhino)
   Searchers' Greatest Hits ....(Rhino)

Message In A Bottle
Police; *Every Breath You Take-The Classics* .... (A&M)
   Regatta De Blanc ....(A&M)
Sting; *The Secret Policeman's Other Ball/The Music* ....(Rhino)

My Bucket's Got A Hole In It
Hank Williams; *Complete Hank Williams* ....(Mercury)

My Cup Runneth Over
Ed Ames; *My Cup Runneth Over* .... (RCA)
   Nipper's Greatest Hits Of The '60s-#2-C .... (RCA)
George Jones; *Homecoming In Heaven* .... (Razor & Tie)
Jim Nabors; *Jim Nabors-16 Most Requested Songs* ....(Legacy)
Original Broadway Cast; *I Do! I Do!* .... (RCA Victor)

Nipple To The Bottle
Grace Jones; *Living My Life* ....(Island)
   Private Life-The Compass Point Sessions ....(Island)

Old Oaken Bucket, The
Old Homestead Double Quartet; *Music From The New York Stage (1890-
   1920)-#1-1890-1908-C* .... (Pearl)

One Million Bottlebags
Public Enemy; *Apocalypse 91...The Enemy Strikes Black* .. (Def Jam/Columbia)

Rocket From A Bottle
XTC; *Black Sea* .... (Geffen)

Secret Of The Bottle
Jackyl; *Push Comes To Shove* .... (Geffen)

Take This Bottle
Faith No More; *King For A Day-Fool For A Lifetime* .... (Slash)

Theme From "I Dream Of Jeannie"
Original Soundtrack; *Television's Greatest Hits-#1-C* ....(TVT)

Time In A Bottle
Jim Croce; *50th Anniversary Collection* .... (Saja)
   Photographs & Memories/His Greatest Hits .... (Atlantic)
   Time In A Bottle/Jim Croce's Greatest Love Songs............. (Atlantic)

Two More Bottles Of Wine
Delbert McClinton; *Honky Tonkin'-I Done Me Some* .... (Alligator)

Emmylou Harris; *Honky Tonk Country-C* . . . .(Warner Bros.)
   Profile/Best Of Emmylou Harris . . . .(Warner Bros.)
   Quarter Moon In A Ten Cent Town . . . .(Warner Bros.)
Martina McBride; *Wild Angels* . . . . (RCA)

Underneath The Bottle
Lou Reed; *Blue Mask* . . . . (RCA)

Whiskey Bottle
Uncle Tupelo; *No Depression*. . . . . (Rockville)

Whiskey In The Jar
Metallica; *Garage Inc.* . . . . (Elektra)

World In A Bottle
John Waite; *Essential John Waite*. . . . .(Chrysalis)

Yea! Heavy And A Bottle Of Bread
Bob Dylan And The Band; *Basement Tapes* . . . . (Columbia)

Yo Ho Ho And A Bottle Of Rum
Original Cast; *Rugrats Sing-Along* . . . . (Interscope)

BRAGGING

See Also: BEST, EGO, INSULTS, SPECIAL

#1
Nelly; *Soundtrack Single* . . . . (Priority)

#1 Stunna
Big Tymers; *I Got That Work* . . . .(Cash Money/Universal)

32 Flavors
Alana Davis; *Blame It On Me* . . . . (Elektra)
Ani DiFranco; *Living In Clip* . . . .(Righteous Babe)
   Not A Pretty Girl . . . .(Righteous Babe)

All The Fun
Paul Overstreet; *Best Of Paul Overstreet* . . . . (RCA)

American Made
Oak Ridge Boys; *American Made*. . . . . (MCA)
   Oak Ridge Boys' Greatest Hits 2 . . . . (MCA)

Anything You Can Do (I Can Do Better)
Betty Hutton & Howard Keel; *That's Entertainment! III-C* . . . . . . (Angel)
Ethel Merman/Bruce Yarnell/Original Cast; *Annie Get*
   Your Gun. . . . .(RCA Victor)
Ethel Merman/Ray Middleton/Original Cast; *Annie Get Your Gun* . . . . . .(MCA)
John Raitt & Bonnie Raitt; *Broadway Legend* . . . . (Angel)

Big Bad Mamma
Foxy Brown featuring Dru Hill; *Ill Na Na* . . . .(Violator)

Big Man
Four Preps; *Best Of The Four Preps* . . . . (Curb)
   Capitol Collectors Series-Four Preps . . . . (Collectables)

Big Pimpin'
Jay-Z; *Vol. 3-Life & Times of S. Carter*. . . . . (Roc-A-Fella/DJMG)

Big Shot
Billy Joel; *52nd Street*. . . . . (Columbia)
   Billy Joel-Greatest Hits, Volume I & Volume II. . . . . (Columbia)
   KOHUEPT. . . . . (Columbia)

Biggest Thing That Man Has Ever Done (Great Historical Bum)
Tom Paxton; *Tribute To Woody Guthrie-C*. . . . .(Warner Bros.)

Bitch Is Back
Elton John; *Caribou*. . . . .(Rocket)
   Elton John's Greatest Hits-#2 . . . . (Polydor)
   Here And There . . . .(Rocket)
Tina Turner; *Two Rooms-Celebrating The Songs Of Elton John & Bernie
   Taupin-C*. . . . . (Polydor)

Boombastic
Shaggy; *Boombastic*. . . . . (Virgin)

Bootylicious
Destiny's Child; *Now That's What I Call Music!-#8-C* . . . . (Virgin)
   Survivor. . . . . (Columbia)

Bragging Song (The Great Historical Bum)
Chad Mitchell Trio; *At The Bitter End* . . . . (Folk Era)

Can't Deny It
Fabolous featuring Nate Dogg; *Ghetto Fabolous* . . . (Desert Storm/Elektra/EEG)

Can't Nobody Hold Me Down
Puff Daddy; *No Way Out* . . . .(Bad Boy/Arista)

Captain Hook's Waltz
Original Cast/Cyril Ritchard; *Peter Pan-The 1954 Broadway
   Production* . . . .(RCA Victor)

C'est Moi
Original Cast; *ST/Camelot* . . . .(Warner Bros.)
Robert Goulet; *Camelot* . . . . (Columbia)

Cowboy
Kid Rock; *Devil Without A Cause*. . . . .(Top Dog/Lava/Atlantic)

Daddy's Money
Ricochet; *Ricochet* . . . . (Columbia)

Everybody (Backstreet's Back)
Backstreet Boys; *Backstreet Boys*. . . . . (Jive)

Everybody's Trying To Be My Baby
Beatles; *Beatles '65* . . . . (Capitol)
   For Sale . . . . (Capitol)
   The Beatles-Anthology-#2 . . . . (Capitol)

Carl Perkins; *Blue Suede Shoes: The Very Best Of Carl Perkins* . . . (Collectables)
   Carl Perkins' Greatest Hits/Finest Performances . . . . (Sun)
   Carl Perkins-Original Sun Greatest Hits . . . . (Rhino)

Falling In Love Again (Can''t Help It)
Billie Holiday; *Quintessential-#8-1939-1940* . . . . (Legacy)
Linda Ronstadt; *Lush Life* . . . .(Asylum)
Marlene Dietrich; *Best Of Marlene Dietrich* . . . . (Columbia)
   Falling In Love Again . . . . (MCA)
   Her Complete Decca Recordings . . . . (MCA)

Feel So Good
Mase; *Harlem World* . . . .(Bad Boy/Arista)

Feet Up (Pat Him On The Po-Po)
Guy Mitchell; *Definitive Guy Mitchell* . . . . (Collector's Choice)

Get Ur Freak On
Missy "Misdemeanor" Elliot; *Miss E...So
   Addictive* . . . . (Gold Mind/East West/EEG)
   Totally Hits 2001-C . . . . (Arista)

Handy Man
Del Shannon; *Del Shannon's Greatest Hits*. . . . . (Curb)
   Del Shannon's Greatest Hits . . . . (Rhino)
James Taylor; *James Taylor-Best Live* . . . . (Columbia)
   JT . . . . (Columbia)
Jimmy Jones; *Billboard Top Rock 'N' Roll Hits-1960-C* . . . . (Rhino)
   Hard To Find 45s On CD-#1-1955-1960-C . . . .(Eric)

Hey Leonardo (She Likes Me For Me)
Blessid Union Of Souls; *Now That's What I Call Music!-#3-C*. . . . . . .(Virgin)
   Walking Off The Buzz. . . . . (Push/V2)

Horse & Carriage
Cam'ron featuring Mase; *Confessions Of Fire* . . . . (Untertainment/Epic)

I'm A Man
Bo Diddley; *Bo Diddley-His Best* . . . . (Chess)
   Super Blues. . . . . (Chess)
   *The Sopranos-Music From The HBO Original
   Series*. . . . . (Sony Music Soundtrax)
Yardbirds; *Five Live Yardbirds* . . . . (Rhino)
   History Of British Rock-#3-C . . . . (Rhino)
   Yardbirds' Greatest Hits-#1 (1964-1966) . . . . (Rhino)

I'm Good At Being Bad
TLC; *Fanmail*. . . . . (LaFace)

I'm The Man Who Murdered Love
XTC; *Wasp Star (Apple Venus Volume 2)* . . . . (Idea/TVT)

I've Gotta Crow
Original Cast/Mary Martin; *Peter Pan-The 1954 Broadway
   Production* . . . .(RCA Victor)

Keep Their Heads Ringin'
Dr. Dre; *Hip Hop's Most Wanted-C* . . . .(Priority)
   ST/Friday . . . .(Priority)

Man Smart, Woman Smarter
Harry Belafonte; *Harry Belafonte-Pure Gold* . . . . (RCA)
Robert Palmer; *Some People Can Do What They Like* . . . . (Island)
Rosanne Cash; *I Am Woman-C* . . . .(Nick At Nite)
   Right Or Wrong . . . . (Columbia)

Mannish Boy
Muddy Waters; *Electric Mud* . . . . (Chess)
   King Of The Electric Blues. . . . . (Legacy)
   The Best Blues Album In The World...Ever!-C. . . . .(Virgin)

My Dog's Better Than Your Dog (Ken-L Ration Dog & Puppy Food)
Original Soundtrack; *TeeVee Toons-The Commercials-#1-C* . . . . (TVT)

One More Chance
Notorious B.I.G.; *Ready To Die* . . . .(Bad Boy/Arista)

One Piece At A Time
Johnny Cash; *The Man In Black-His Greatest Hits* . . . . (Legacy)

Popular
Nada Surf; *High/Low* . . . . (Elektra)

Pull Over
Trina; *Da Baddest B***h* . . . .(Slip 'N Slide)

Put Your Hands Where My Eyes Could See
Busta Rhymes; *When Disaster Strikes* . . . . (Elektra)

Real Slim Shady
Eminem; *The Marshall Mathers LP* . . . .(Aftermath/Interscope)

Red Hot
Billy Lee Riley & His Little Green Men; *Red Hot: The Very Best Of Billy
   Lee Riley* . . . . (Collectables)
   Rock This Town-Rockabilly Hits-#1-C . . . . (Rhino)
Robert Gordon; *Rock This Town-Rockabilly Hits-#2-C* . . . . (Rhino)
Robert Gordon & Link Wray; *Robert Gordon & Link Wray* . . . . (RCA)

Set It Off
Juvenile; *Project English* . . . .(Cash Money/Universal)

So Fresh, So Clean
Outkast; *Stankonia* . . . .(LaFace/Arista)
   Totally Hits 2001-C . . . . (Arista)

Stiff Upper Lip
AC/DC; *Stiff Upper Lip*. . . . . (East West)

Superwoman
Lil' Mo; *Based On A True Story* . . . . (Gold Mind/East West/EEG)

Surrey With The Fringe On Top
Ellis Marsalis; *Heart Of Gold* . . . . (Columbia)
Original Broadway Cast; *Oklahoma!* . . . . (RCA)

Original Cast; *Oklahoma!* . . . . (MCA)
Then You May Take Me To The Fair
Original Cast; *Camelot* . . . . (Columbia)
Vanessa Redgrave; *ST/Camelot* . . . . (Warner Bros.)
U Can't Touch This
Hammer; *Please Hammer Don't Hurt 'Em* . . . . (Capitol)
What'chu Like
Da Brat; *Unrestricted* . . . . (So So Def/Columbia)
Whoa
Black Rob; *Life Story* . . . . (Bad Boy/Arista)
X-Girlfriend
Mariah Carey; *Rainbow* . . . . (Columbia)

BREAK, Bend, Broken, Busted, Fragile, Ragged, Torn

*See Also: **BITS & PIECES, FIXING, HEART, LOVE: PAINFUL BREAK-UP, SADNESS***

Among My Souvenirs
Connie Francis; *Connie Francis' Greatest Hits* . . . . (Polydor)
Frank Sinatra; *Columbia Years-1943-1952-Complete Recordings* . . . . . (Legacy)
Marty Robbins; *Marty Robbins-Super Hits* . . . . (Columbia)
Sons Of The Pioneers; *Country & Western Memories* . . . . (Pair)
Bad Liver & A Broken Heart
Tom Waits; *Small Change* . . . . (Asylum)
Be Careful
Ricky Martin & Madonna; *Ricky Martin* . . . . (Columbia)
Bend It Until It Breaks
John Anderson; *John Anderson's Greatest Hits* . . . .(BNA)
Bend Me, Shape Me
American Breed; *The Ultimate History Of Rock 'N' Roll-#7-C* . . . . (K-Tel)
Bent
Matchbox Twenty; *Mad Season By Matchbox Twenty* . . . . (Lava)
Totally Hits-#3-C . . . . (Atlantic)
Born With A Broken Heart
Kenny Wayne Shepherd; *Ledbetter Heights* . . . . (Giant)
Boulevard Of Broken Dreams
Diana Krall; *All For You (A Dedication To The Nat "King" Cole Trio)* . . . .(Impulse!)
Tony Bennett; *Forty Years-The Artistry Of Tony Bennett* . . . . (Columbia)
Tony Bennett-16 Most Requested Songs . . . . (Legacy)
Tony Bennett's All-Time Greatest Hits . . . . (Columbia)
Break It To Me Gently
Brenda Lee; *Brenda Lee-Anthology-#1 & #2* . . . . (MCA)
The Brenda Lee Story-Her Greatest Hits . . . . (MCA)
Juice Newton; *Juice Newton's Greatest Country Hits* . . . . (Curb)
Juice Newton's Greatest Hits . . . . (Gold Rush)
Break Stuff
Limp Bizkit; *Significant Other* . . . .(Flip/Interscope)
Break Ya Neck
Busta Rhymes; *Genesis* . . . . (J)
Breakaway
ZZ Top; *Antenna* . . . . (RCA)
Breakdown
Queensryche; *Q2k* . . . . (Atlantic)
Breakdown
Tantric; *Tantric* . . . . (Maverick)
Breakin' Me
Jonny Lang; *Wander This World* . . . . (A&M)
Breaking All The Rules
She Moves; *Boom! 17 Explosive Hits-C* . . . . (Simitar)
Breaking All The Rules . . . . (Geffen)
Breakout
Swing Out Sister; *'80s-Hot Dance Trax-C* . . . . (K-Tel)
It's Better To Travel . . . . (Mercury)
Breakout
Foo Fighters; *There Is Nothing Left To Lose* . . . .(Roswell/RCA)
Broke Down Engine
Blind Willie McTell; *Between The Rails: America's Train Songs-C* . . . . (Crescendo)
Brokedown Palace
Grateful Dead; *American Beauty* . . . . (Warner Bros.)
Persuasions; *Might As Well...The Persuasions Sing Grateful Dead* . . . .(Grateful Dead)
Broken Arrow
Buffalo Springfield; *Buffalo Springfield Again* . . . . (Atco)
Buffalo Springfield-Retrospective . . . . (Atco)
Neil Young; *Decade* . . . .(Reprise)
Broken Arrow
Robbie Robertson; *Robbie Robertson* . . . . (Geffen)
Rod Stewart; *Vagabond Heart* . . . . (Warner Bros.)
Broken Arrow
Chuck Berry; *Rockin' At The Hops* . . . . (Chess)
Broken Barricades
Procol Harum; *Broken Barricades* . . . . (A&M)
Broken Bottles
Bill Miller; *Art Of Survival* . . . .(Vanguard)

Broken Bubble
Ten Foot Pole; *Rev* . . . . (Epitaph)
Broken Down In Tiny Pieces
Billy "Crash" Craddock; *Crash's Smashes: The Hits Of Billy "Crash" Craddock* . . . .(Razor & Tie)
Broken English
Marianne Faithfull; *Broken English* . . . .(Island)
The Island Story-1962-1987-25th Anniversary-C . . . .(Island)
Broken Hearted Savior
Big Head Todd & The Monsters; *Sister Sweetly* . . . . (Giant)
Broken Heartland
Don Williams; *One Good Well* . . . . (RCA)
Broken Heartland
Holly Dunn; *Heart Full Of Love* . . . . (Warner Bros.)
Broken Home
Papa Roach; *Infest* . . . . (DreamWorks/SKG)
Broken Pieces
Strato Vocalz; *Love Shouldn't Hurt-C* . . . . (Qwest)
Broken Promise Land
Mark Chesnutt; *Too Cold At Home* . . . . (MCA)
Broken Toys
Jerry Jeff Walker; *Mr. Bojangles* . . . .(Bainbridge)
Broken Toys
B.J. Thomas; *Throwin' Rocks At The Moon* . . . . (Columbia)
Broken Wing
Martina McBride; *Evolution* . . . . (RCA)
Broken Wings
Mr. Mister; *Nipper's Greatest Hits Of The '80s-C* . . . . (RCA)
Welcome To The Real World . . . . (RCA)
Broken Wings
Chris DeBurgh; *At The End Of A Perfect Day* . . . . (A&M)
Broken Yo-Yo
Texas Alexander; *Story Of The Blues-C* . . . .(Columbia)
Brokenhearted
Brandy featuring Wanya Morris; *Brandy* . . . . (Atlantic)
Brokenhearted Me
Anne Murray; *15 Of The Best* . . . .(Liberty)
Anne Murray's Greatest Hits . . . .(Capitol)
Broken-Hearted Melody
Sarah Vaughan; *Essential Sarah Vaughan-The Great Songs* . . . .(Verve)
Sarah Vaughan-Golden Hits . . . .(Mercury)
Busted
Harlan Howard; *All-Time Favorite Country Songwriter* . . . .(Koch International)
John Conlee; *John Conlee's Greatest Hits* . . . . (MCA)
Songs For The Working Man . . . . (MCA)
Johnny Cash; *Johnny Cash-16 Biggest Hits-#2* . . . . (Legacy)
Ray Charles; *Ray Charles' Greatest Hits* . . . . (Rhino)
Ray Charles-His Greatest Hits-#2 . . . . (Dunhill Compact Classics)
Cloudburst
Jon Hendricks; *Jon Hendricks* . . . . (Enja)
Lambert, Hendricks & Bavan; *Swingin' Till The Girls Come Home* . . .(Bluebird)
Lambert, Hendricks & Ross; *Best Of Lambert, Hendricks & Ross* . . . .(Columbia)
Lambert, Hendricks & Ross & Ike Isaacs Trio: Everybody's Boppin' . . . . (Columbia)
Pointer Sisters; *Retrospect* . . . . (MCA)
Communication Breakdown
Led Zeppelin; *Led Zeppelin* . . . . (Atlantic)
Led Zeppelin-Box Set . . . . (Atlantic)
Don't Go Breaking My Heart
Elton John & Kiki Dee; *Elton John's Greatest Hits-#2* . . . . (Polydor)
Down To My Last Broken Heart
Janie Fricke; *Greatest Country Hits Of The '80s-1980-C* . . .(Columbia)
Janie Fricke-17 Greatest Hits . . . . (Columbia)
Janie Fricke's Greatest Hits . . . . (Columbia)
Everything Is Broken
Kenny Wayne Shepherd; *Trouble Is...* . . . .(Revolution)
Final Heartbreak
Jessica Simpson; *Sweet Kisses* . . . . (Columbia)
Fragile
Sting; *...Nothing Like The Sun* . . . .(A&M)
America: A Tribute To Heroes-C . . . . (Interscope)
Fields Of Gold-The Best Of Sting 1984-1994 . . . .(A&M)
Goodbye Lament
Iommi; *Iommi* . . . . (Divine/Priority)
Great Beyond, The
R.E.M.; *Man On The Moon* . . . .(Warner Bros.)
Totally Hits-#2-C . . . .(Elektra)
Happy Birthday Broken Heart
Rex Hobart; *Forever Always Ends* . . . . (Bloodshot)
Heart Bowed Down, The
Henri Scott; *Music From The New York Stage (1890-1920)-#4-1917-1920-C* . . . . (Pearl)
Heartbreak Hotel
Albert King; *Blues For Elvis* . . . . (Stax)
Elvis Presley; *Elvis As Recorded At Madison Square Garden* . . . . (RCA)
Elvis' Golden Records . . . . (RCA)
Elvis-A Legendary Performer, Volume 1 . . . . (RCA)
Nipper's Greatest Hits Of The '50s-#1-C . . . . (RCA)
Worldwide 50 Gold Award Hits, Vol. 1, Parts 1 & 2 . . . . (RCA)

Stan Freberg; *Capitol Collectors Series-Stan Freberg* . . . . . (Capitol)
Willie Nelson; *Greatest Hits (& Some That Will Be)* . . . . . (Columbia)
Willie Nelson & Leon Russell: One For The Road . . . . . (Columbia)

Heartbreak Hotel
Whitney Houston Featuring Faith Evans & Kelly Price; *My Love Is Your Love* . . . . . (Arista)
Totally Hits-#1-C . . . . . (Arista)
Whitney Houston's Greatest Hits . . . . . (Arista)

Heartbreak U.S.A.
Kitty Wells; *I Love Country-Hits Of The '60s-#1-C* . . . . . (Priority)
Kitty Wells' Greatest Songs . . . . . (Curb)
The Country Music Hall Of Fame-Kitty Wells . . . . . (MCA Special Prod.)

Heartbreak, Tennessee
Johnny Paycheck; *This Is Country-C* . . . . . (Pegasus/Cleopatra)

Heartbreaker
Grand Funk Railroad; *Capitol Collectors Series-Grand Funk Railroad* . . . . . (Capitol)

Heartbreaker
Mariah Carey; *Rainbow* . . . . . (Columbia)

Heartbreaker
Tanya Tucker; *Love Me Like You Used To* . . . . . (Liberty)

Heartbreaker
Pat Benatar; *Best Shots* . . . . . (Chrysalis)
In The Heat Of The Night . . . . . (Chrysalis)
Live From Earth . . . . . (Chrysalis)

Heartbreaker
Led Zeppelin; *Led Zeppelin II* . . . . . (Atlantic)
Led Zeppelin-The Complete Studio Recordings . . . . . (Atlantic)

Heartbreaker
Dionne Warwick; *Heartbreaker* . . . . . (Arista)

Heartbreaker
Great White; *Hooked* . . . . . (Capitol)

Heartbreaker
Bee Gees; *One Night Only* . . . . . (Polydor)

Heartbroke
George Strait; *Strait From The Heart* . . . . . (MCA)
Strait Out Of The Box . . . . . (MCA)
Guy Clark; *Craftsman* . . . . . (Philo)
Keepers . . . . . (Sugar Hill)
Ricky Skaggs; *Country Gentleman: The Best Of Ricky Skaggs* . . . . . (Legacy)
Greatest Country Hits Of The '80s-#2-C . . . . . (Columbia)
Highways & Heartaches . . . . . (Epic)
Live In London . . . . . (Epic)
Ricky Skaggs-Super Hits . . . . . (Epic)
Rodney Crowell; *Rodney Crowell-Collection* . . . . . (Warner Bros.)

Heartbroke Every Day
Lonestar; *Lonestar* . . . . . (BNA)

Hero Of The Day
Metallica; *Load* . . . . . (Elektra)

How Can You Mend A Broken Heart
Al Green; *Al Green's Greatest Hits-#1* . . . . . (Motown)
Compact Command Performances-Al Green . . . . . (Motown)
Let's Stay Together . . . . . (Right Stuff)
Bee Gees; *Bee Gees-Gold* . . . . . (Polydor)
Here At Last...Bee Gees...Live . . . . . (Polydor)
Nobody's Child-Romanian Angel Appeal-C . . . . . (Warner Bros.)

How Could An Angel Break My Heart
Kenny G with Toni Braxton; *Kenny G's Greatest Hits* . . . . . (Arista)
Toni Braxton with Kenny G; *Diana, Princess Of Wales-Tribute-C* . . (Columbia)
Secrets . . . . . (LaFace)

How Do I Say I'm Sorry
Tami Davis; *Only You* . . . . . (Red Ant)

Husbands And Wives
Brooks & Dunn; *Big Country Hits '99-C* . . . . . (K-Tel)
If You See Her . . . . . (Arista)
Neil Diamond; *Neil Diamond-Love Songs* . . . . . (MCA)
Rainbow . . . . . (MCA)
Stones . . . . . (MCA)
Roger Miller; *Best Of Roger Miller* . . . . . (Mercury)
Best Of Roger Miller-His Greatest Songs . . . . . (Curb)
Roger Miller-Super Hits . . . . . (Epic)
Roger Miller-The Hits . . . . . (Mercury)

I Don't Make Promises (I Can't Break)
Shannon Curfman; *Loud Guitars Big Suspicions* . . . . . (Arista)

I Think I'm Paranoid
Garbage; *Now That's What I Call Music!-#2-C* . . . . . (Virgin)
Version 2.0 . . . . . (Almo Sounds)

I Will Love Again
Lara Fabian; *Lara Fabian* . . . . . (Columbia)

If He Should Break Your Heart
Journey; *Trial By Fire* . . . . . (Columbia)

I'll Never Break Your Heart
Backstreet Boys; *Backstreet Boys* . . . . . (Jive)
Now That's What I Call Music!-#2-C . . . . . (Virgin)

Iris
Goo Goo Dolls; *Dizzy Up The Girl* . . . . . (Warner Sunset/Reprise)
ST/City Of Angels . . . . . (Warner Sunset/Reprise)

Just Like A Woman
Bob Dylan; *Before The Flood* . . . . . (Columbia)
Biograph . . . . . (Columbia)
Blonde On Blonde . . . . . (Columbia)
Bob Dylan At Budokan . . . . . (Columbia)
Bob Dylan's Greatest Hits . . . . . (Columbia)
Byrds; *The Byrds* . . . . . (Columbia)

Knock Down Walls
Tonic; *Sugar* . . . . . (Universal)

Like Humans Do
David Byrne; *Look Into The Eyeball* . . . . . (Luaka Bop)

Long Goodbye, The
Brooks & Dunn; *Steers & Stripes* . . . . . (Arista)

Me And Bobby McGee
Grateful Dead; *Grateful Dead (Skull & Roses)* . . . . . (Warner Bros.)
Janis Joplin; *Janis* . . . . . (Legacy)
Janis Joplin's Greatest Hits . . . . . (Columbia)
Pearl . . . . . (Legacy)
Rock Classics Of The '70s-C . . . . . (Columbia)
Willie Nelson; *Willie Nelson Sings Kristofferson* . . . . . (Columbia)

My Love Is Your Love
Whitney Houston; *My Love Is Your Love* . . . . . (Arista)
Totally Hits-#2-C . . . . . (Elektra)

My Next Broken Heart
Brooks & Dunn; *Brand New Man* . . . . . (Arista)

Never Let You Go
Third Eye Blind; *Blue* . . . . . (Elektra)
Totally Hits-#2-C . . . . . (Elektra)

New Beginning
Tracy Chapman; *New Beginning* . . . . . (Elektra)

One Step Closer
Linkin Park; *Hybrid Theory* . . . . . (Warner Bros.)

One Way Track
Ricky Skaggs and Kentucky Thunder; *History Of The Future* . . (Skaggs Family)

Only Love Can Break A Heart
Gene Pitney; *Gene Pitney* . . . . . (Everest)
Gene Pitney-Anthology 1961-1968 . . . . . (Rhino)
Love Sixties-C . . . . . (JCI Assoc. Labels)
Pick Of Gene Pitney . . . . . (Fifty One West)

Original Prankster
Offspring; *Conspiracy Of One* . . . . . (Columbia)

Over The Rise
Bruce Springsteen; *Tracks* . . . . . (Columbia)

People That We Love, The
Bush; *Golden State* . . . . . (Atlantic)

Piece Of My Heart
Big Brother & The Holding Company; *Cheap Thrills* . . . . . (Columbia)
Rock Classics Of The '60s-C . . . . . (Columbia)
Seems Like Yesterday-#6-Late '60s-C . . . . . (K-Tel)
Bryan Ferry; *These Foolish Things* . . . . . (Reprise)
Delaney & Bonnie; *Best Of Delaney & Bonnie* . . . . . (Rhino)
Faith Hill; *Take Me As I Am* . . . . . (Warner Bros.)
Janis Joplin; *Janis Joplin In Concert* . . . . . (Columbia)
Janis Joplin's Greatest Hits . . . . . (Columbia)
ST/Janis . . . . . (Columbia)
Sammy Hagar; *Standing Hampton* . . . . . (Geffen)

Promises Broken
Soul Asylum; *Let Your Dim Light Shine* . . . . . (Columbia)

Ragged Old Flag
Johnny Cash; *Patriot* . . . . . (Columbia)
We The People-C . . . . . (Columbia)

Shake It And Break It
Big Joe Turner; *Things That I Used To Do* . . . . . (Pablo)
Charley Patton; *Founder Of The Delta Blues-1929-1934* . . . . . (Yazoo)
Preservation Hall Jazz Band; *Best Of The Preservation Hall Jazz Band* . . . . . (Columbia)

She's A Heartbreaker
ZZ Top; *Six Pack* . . . . . (Warner Bros.)
Tejas . . . . . (Warner Bros.)

So It Goes
Wes Cunningham; *12 Ways To Win People To Your Way Of Thinking* . . . . . (Warner Bros.)

Some Broken Hearts
Bellamy Brothers; *The Reggae Cowboys* . . . . . (Bellamy Bros./Intersound)

Some Broken Hearts Never Mend
Don Williams; *Best Of Don Williams-#2* . . . . . (MCA)
Don Williams-20 Greatest Hits . . . . . (MCA)
Some Broken Hearts Never Mend . . . . . (MCA Special Prod.)

Standing Outside A Broken Phone Booth With Money In My Hand
Primitive Radio Gods; *MTV Best Of The Buzz Bin-#2-C* . . . . . (Mammoth)
Rocket . . . . . (Ergo)

Stop Breaking Down
Rolling Stones; *Exile On Main Street* . . . . . (Virgin)

Thanks A Lot
Ernest Tubb; *The Country Music Hall Of Fame-Ernest Tubb* . . . . . (MCA)
IIIrd Time Out; *IIIrd Time Out* . . . . . (Rebel)
Ronnie & Rob McCoury; *Ronnie & Rob McCoury* . . . . . (Rounder)

There Goes My Heart
Mavericks; *Best Of The Mavericks-Super Colossal Smash Hits Of The '90s* . . . . . (Mercury)
What A Crying Shame . . . . . (MCA)

This Broken Heart
Mavericks; *From Hell To Paradise* . . . . (MCA)
Three Hearts In A Tangle
Roy Drusky; *45-#31193* . . . . (Decca)
Too Soon To Know
Don Gibson; *Oh Lonesome Me* . . . . (Collectables)
Roy Orbison; *The Classic Roy Orbison-1965-1968* . . . . (Rhino)
Torn
Natalie Imbruglia; *Left Of The Middle* . . . . (RCA)
Torn And Frayed
Rolling Stones; *Exile On Main Street* . . . . (Virgin)
Total Eclipse Of The Heart
Bonnie Tyler; *Billboard Top Hits-1983-C* . . . . (Rhino)
Faster Than The Speed Of Night . . . . (Columbia)
Seems Like Yesterday-#4-Early '80s-C . . . . (K-Tel)
Nicki French; *Dance Hits '96 Supermix-C* . . . . (Critique)
Secrets . . . . (Critique)
Un-Break My Heart
Toni Braxton; *Secrets* . . . . (LaFace)
Unbreakable
Michael Jackson; *Invincible* . . . . (Epic)
Victim Of A Broken Heart
Aldo Nova; *Portrait Of Aldo Nova* . . . . (Epic)
Subject...Aldo Nova . . . . (Portrait)
Walk On
U2; *America: A Tribute To Heroes-C* . . . . (Interscope)
Now That's What I Call Music!-#8-C . . . . (Virgin)
Way We Make A Broken Heart
Rosanne Cash; *30 Years Of #1 Hits-#16-C* . . . . (Columbia)
Greatest Country Hits Of The '80s-1987-C . . . . (Columbia)
King's Record Shop . . . . (Columbia)
Love Gets Strange-Songs Of John Hiatt-C . . . . (Rhino)
Rosanne Cash-Hits-1979-1989 . . . . (Columbia)
Ry Cooder; *Borderline* . . . . (Warner Bros.)
Wedding Bells (Are Breaking Up That Old Gang Of Mine)
Four Aces; *Best Of The Four Aces* . . . . (MCA)
What Becomes Of The Brokenhearted
Jimmy & David Ruffin; *Motown Superstar Series-#8-Jimmy & David
Ruffin* . . . . (Motown)
Jimmy Ruffin; *Motown Story-First 25 Years-C* . . . . (Motown)
Paul Young; *ST/Fried Green Tomatoes* . . . . (MCA)
Whatever
En Vogue; *Bass In Your Face: Essential Drum And Bass-C* . . . . (Elektra)
What's Love Got To Do With It
Tina Turner; *Live In Europe* . . . . (Capitol)
Private Dancer . . . . (Capitol)
Simply The Best . . . . (Capitol)
Where Do Broken Hearts Go
Whitney Houston; *Whitney* . . . . (Arista)
Whitney Houston's Greatest Hits . . . . (Arista)
Woman's Touch
Toby Keith; *Blue Moon* . . . . (Polydor Country)
You're Breaking My Heart
Nilsson; *Son Of Schmilsson* . . . . (RCA)
You're The One
Paul Simon; *You're The One* . . . . (Warner Bros.)

BRIDGES

See Also: RIVERS, ROAD

59th Street Bridge Song (Feelin' Groovy)
Harper's Bizarre; *Baby Boomer Classics-More Mellow
Sixties-C* . . . . (JCI Assoc. Labels)
Better Days-C . . . . (Rhino)
Simon & Garfunkel; *Collected Works* . . . . (Columbia)
Parsley Sage Rosemary & Thyme . . . . (Columbia)
Simon & Garfunkel's Greatest Hits . . . . (Columbia)
The Concert In Central Park . . . . (Warner Bros.)
Another Bridge To Burn
Mel Tillis; *Best Of Mel Tillis* . . . . (MCA)
Big Time
Neil Young & Crazy Horse; *Broken Arrow* . . . . (Reprise)
Year Of The Horse . . . . (Reprise)
Bridge
Sonny Rollins; *Bluebird Sampler-C* . . . . (Bluebird)
Sonny Rollins Quartets with Jim Hall . . . . (Bluebird)
Bridge
Queensryche; *Promised Land* . . . . (EMI)
Bridge Across Forever
Highway 101; *Highway 101* . . . . (Warner Bros.)
Bridge I'm Still Building On
Vern Gosdin; *Out Of My Heart* . . . . (Columbia)
Bridge Of Caulaincourt
Original Cast; *Irma La Douce* . . . . (Sony Music Special Prod.)
Bridge Of Sighs
Robin Trower; *Best Of Hard Rock-#2-C* . . . . (MCA Special Prod.)

Bridge Of Sighs . . . . (Chrysalis)
Bridge Of Spies
T'Pau; *Bridge Of Spies* . . . . (Virgin)
Bridge On The River Kwai
Magic Organ; *The Magic Organ Plays Movie Themes* . . . . (Ranwood)
Bridge Over Troubled Water
Aretha Franklin; *Aretha Franklin-30 Greatest Hits* . . . . (Rhino)
Aretha Franklin's Greatest Hits . . . . (Atlantic)
Live At Fillmore West . . . . (Atlantic)
Paul Simon; *America: A Tribute To Heroes-C* . . . . (Interscope)
Concert In The Park-August 15 1991 . . . . (Warner Bros.)
Paul Simon In Concert/Live Rhymin' . . . . (Columbia)
Simon & Garfunkel; *Bridge Over Troubled Water* . . . . . . (Columbia)
Collected Works . . . . (Columbia)
God Bless America-C . . . . (Columbia)
Simon & Garfunkel's Greatest Hits . . . . (Columbia)
The Concert In Central Park . . . . (Warner Bros.)
Bridge That Just Won't Burn
Conway Twitty; *Number Ones* . . . . (MCA)
Bridge Washed Out
Warner Mack; *Country's Greatest Hits-#3-C* . . . . (MCA)
MCA Records 30 Years Of Hits-1958-1988-C . . . . (MCA)
Bridges & Walls
Oak Ridge Boys; *Monongahela* . . . . (MCA)
Oak Ridge Boys' Greatest Hits 3 . . . . (MCA)
Bridges Burning
Mission U.K.; *God's Own Medicine* . . . . (Mercury)
Bridges Over Borders
Spoons; *Bridges Over Borders* . . . . (Mercury)
Brooklyn Bridge
Frank Sinatra; *Sinatra Sings His Greatest Hits* . . . . (Legacy)
Brothers Under The Bridges ('83)
Bruce Springsteen; *Tracks* . . . . (Columbia)
Burn Down The Bridges
Artch; *For The Sake Of Mankind* . . . . (Metal Blade)
Burn That Bridge
Jimmy Buffett; *Riddles In The Sand* . . . . (MCA)
Burning Bridges
Pink Floyd; *Pink Floyd-Gift Set* . . . . (Capitol)
ST/Obscured By Clouds . . . . (Capitol)
Burning Bridges
Naked Eyes; *Best Of Naked Eyes* . . . . (EMI)
Burning Bridges
38 Special; *Bone Against Steel* . . . . (Charisma)
Burning Bridges
Glen Campbell; *Glen Campbell's Greatest Hits* . . . . (Capitol)
Burning Bridges
Collective Soul; *Hints, Allegations And Things Left Unsaid* . . . . (Atlantic)
Burning Bridges
Jack Scott; *Capitol Collectors Series-Jack Scott* . . . . (Capitol)
Super Oldies Of The '60s-#6-C . . . . (Audio Fidelity)
Burning Bridges
Mike Curb Congregation; *Super Hits Of The '70s-Have A Nice
Day-#5-C* . . . . (Rhino)
Burning Bridges
Garth Brooks; *Ropin' The Wind* . . . . (Liberty)
Burning Bridges
Roger Miller; *King Of The Road* . . . . (Laserlight)
Burning Bridges
George Jones; *Jones Country* . . . . (Epic)
One Woman Man . . . . (Epic)
Chelsea Bridge
Duke Ellington; *Blanton-Webster Band* . . . . (Bluebird)
Concert In The Virgin Islands . . . . (Discovery)
Sarah Vaughan; *Duke Ellington Songbook Two* . . . . (Pablo)
Cross Over The Bridge
Patti Page; *Patti Page-Golden Hits* . . . . (Mercury)
Patti Page's Greatest Hits . . . . (Columbia)
Cross That Bridge
Status Quo; *Status Quo* . . . . (Mercury)
Gonna Burn Some Bridges
Ray Price; *For The Good Times/I Won't Mention It Again* . . . . (Columbia)
Kohoutek
R.E.M.; *Fables Of The Reconstruction* . . . . (I.R.S.)
London Bridge
Bread; *Best Of Bread-#2* . . . . (Elektra)
Bread . . . . (Elektra)
Bread-Anthology . . . . (Elektra)
London Bridge
Big Audio Dynamite; *Megatop Phoenix* . . . . (Columbia)
London Bridge
Original Soundtrack; *Children's Favorites* . . . . (Kid Rhino/Rhino 4 Kids)
London Bridge Is Falling Down
Count Basie; *Good Morning Blues* . . . . (MCA)
London Bridge Is Falling Down
Newtrament; *Word 2* . . . . (Jive)
Love Can Build A Bridge
Judds; *Love Can Build A Bridge* . . . . (MCA)

Nippon Bridge
Kim Robertson; *Angels In Disguise* . . . . (Invincible)
Ode To Billy Joe
Bobbi Gentry; *All-Time Country Classics-#1-C* . . . . (Capitol)
On London Bridge
Jo Stafford; *International Hits* . . . .(Corinthian)
One Lane Bridge
Kim Pensyl; *Eyes Of Wonder* . . . . (GRP)
Prayer For The Dying
Seal; *Diana, Princess Of Wales-Tribute-C* . . . . (Columbia)
Seal 2 . . . . (Sire)
Racin' Burnin' Bridges
Ranch Romance; *Blue Blazes* . . . . (Sugar Hill)
Ruck A Pit Bridge
Tuff; *What Comes Around Goes Around* . . . . (Atlantic)
Seven Bridges Road
Eagles; *Eagles Greatest Hits, Volume 2* . . . . (Asylum)
Eagles Live . . . . (Asylum)
Steve Young; *Seven Bridges Road* . . . . (Rounder)
Singing Bridge Of Memphis Tennessee
John Fahey; *Essential John Fahey* . . . . (Vanguard)
Some Bridges
Jackson Browne; *Looking East* . . . . (Elektra)
Swinging Bridge
Jerry Douglas; *Plant Early* . . . .(MCA)
Sampler '89-#1-C . . . .(MCA)
Under The Bridge
Red Hot Chili Peppers; *Blood Sugar Sex Magik* . . . .(Warner Bros.)
What Hits!? . . . .(EMI)
Under The Bridge
Merle Haggard; *Blue Jungle* . . . . (Curb)
Under The Bridges Of Paris
Michel Legrand; *Legrand Piano* . . . . (Columbia)
Walk Softly On The Bridge
Mel Street; *Mel Street's Greatest Hits* . . . . (GRT)
Water Under The Bridge
Dan Seals; *Dan Seals' Greatest Hits* . . . . (Liberty)
On Arrival . . . . (Capitol)
Olivia Newton-John; *Have You Never Been Mellow* . . . .(MCA)
We'll Burn That Bridge
Brooks & Dunn; *Hard Workin' Man* . . . . (Arista)
Which Bridge To Cross (Which Bridge To Burn)
Vince Gill; *When Love Finds You* . . . .(MCA)
Whiskey Under The Bridge
Brooks & Dunn; *Brooks & Dunn-The Greatest Hits Collection* . . . . (Arista)
Waitin' On Sundown . . . . (Arista)

BROTHERHOOD, Sisterhood

*See Also: FAMILY (various), FEMINISM, GOD, HELP, PEACE,
POLITICS: POLITICAL CLASSICS, PROTEST, TOGETHERNESS,
WORK (unions)*

Aquarius
Original Broadway Cast; *Hair* . . . . (RCA)
Aquarius/Let The Sunshine In Medley
5th Dimension; *Billboard Top Rock 'N' Roll Hits-1969-C* . . . . (Rhino)
Greatest Hits On Earth . . . . (Arista)
ST/1969 . . . . (Polydor)
ST/Forrest Gump . . . . (Epic/Sony Music Soundtrax)
Best Friend
Brandy; *Brandy* . . . . (Atlantic)
Brotherhood Of Man
New Broadway Cast; *How To Succeed In Business Without Really
Trying* . . . .(RCA Victor)
Original Cast; *How To Succeed In Business Without Really Trying* . . . . . . (RCA)
Dreamer
Ozzy Osbourne; *Down To Earth* . . . .(Epic)
From A Distance
Bette Midler; *Some People's Lives* . . . . (Atlantic)
Byrds; *20 Essential Tracks From The Box Set* . . . . (Columbia)
The Byrds . . . . (Columbia)
Judy Collins; *Fires Of Eden* . . . . (Columbia)
Kathy Mattea; *Time Passes By* . . . . (Mercury)
Nanci Griffith; *Lone Star State Of Mind* . . . .(MCA)
One Fair Summer Evening . . . .(MCA)
Get Together
Big Mountain; *Resistance* . . . . (Giant)
Youngbloods; *Best Of The Youngbloods* . . . . (RCA)
Billboard Top Rock 'N' Roll Hits-1969-C . . . . (Rhino)
*Chicken Soup For The Soul: I'll Be There For You-Songs Of Friendship,
Brotherhood And Sisterhood-C* . . . . (Rhino)
ST/Forrest Gump . . . . (Epic/Sony Music Soundtrax)
Summer Of Love-#1-C . . . . (Rhino)
He Ain't Heavy, He's My Brother
Hollies; *Best Of The Hollies* . . . .(EMI)
Best Of The Hollies-#2 . . . .(EMI)

*Chicken Soup For The Soul: I'll Be There For You-Songs Of Friendship,
Brotherhood And Sisterhood-C* . . . . (Rhino)
Hollies-Epic Anthology From The Original Master Tapes . . . . (Epic)
The Hollies' Greatest Hits . . . .(Epic)
Neil Diamond; *Glory Road-1968-1972* . . . .(MCA)
Tap Root Manuscript . . . .(MCA)
He Was My Brother
Simon & Garfunkel; *Wednesday Morning 3 A.M.* . . . . (Columbia)
Hello Brother
Louis Armstrong; *What A Wonderful World* . . . . (Decca Jazz)
Hollywood
Wallflowers; *The Wallflowers* . . . .(Virgin)
If I Had A Hammer (The Hammer Song)
Pete Seeger; *Sing-A-Long-Live At Sanders
Theatre 1980* . . . .(Smithsonian Folkways)
Peter, Paul & Mary; *10 Years Together/The Best Of Peter, Paul
and Mary* . . . . (Warner Bros.)
Peter, Paul and Mary . . . . (Warner Bros.)
Peter, Paul and Mary In Concert . . . . (Warner Bros.)
Trini Lopez; *Best Of Trini Lopez* . . . . (Exact)
Weavers; *Weavers' Greatest Hits* . . . . (Vanguard)
I'm Every Woman
Chaka Khan; *Chicken Soup For The Soul: I'll Be There For You-Songs Of
Friendship, Brotherhood And Sisterhood-C* . . . . (Rhino)
Epiphany: The Best Of Chaka Khan-#1 . . . .(Reprise)
I Am Woman-C . . . . (Nick At Nite)
Whitney Houston; *ST/The Bodyguard* . . . . (Arista)
Whitney Houston's Greatest Hits . . . . (Arista)
Imagine
Diana Ross; *Best Of The Beatles Songs-C* . . . . (Motown)
Diana Ross-Anthology . . . . (Motown)
Touch Me In The Morning . . . . (Motown)
Joan Baez; *Best Of Joan Baez* . . . . (A&M)
Come From The Shadows . . . . (A&M)
John Lennon; *Lennon* . . . . (Capitol)
Live In New York City . . . . (Capitol)
ST/Imagine: John Lennon . . . . (Capitol)
John Lennon & Yoko Ono; *The John Lennon Collection* . . . . (Capitol)
John Lennon/Plastic Ono Band; *Imagine* . . . . (Capitol)
Shaved Fish . . . . (Capitol)
Neil Young; *America: A Tribute To Heroes-C* . . . .(Interscope)
Joe Hill
Arlo Guthrie & Pete Seeger; *Together In Concert* . . . .(Reprise)
Joan Baez; *Carry It On* . . . . (Vanguard)
From Every Stage . . . . (A&M)
One Day At A Time . . . . (Vanguard)
ST/Woodstock . . . . (Atlantic)
Links On The Chain
Broadside Singers & Phil Ochs; *Best Of Broadside 1962-1968: Anthems
Of The American Underground From The Pages Of Broadside
Magazine-C* . . . .(Smithsonian Folkways)
Love Train
Keb' Mo'; *Big Wide Grin* . . . . (Sony Wonder)
O'Jays; *Billboard Top Rock 'N' Roll Hits-1973-C* . . . . (Rhino)
O'Jays' Greatest Hits . . . . (Philadelphia Int'l)
O'Jays-Collector's Item . . . . (Philadelphia Int'l)
Philadelphia Classics-C . . . . (Philadelphia Int'l)
Train Trax-C . . . . (Sony Music Special Prod.)
More Than One Way Home
Keb' Mo'; *Just Like You* . . . .(Okeh)
Put A Little Love In Your Heart
Annie Lennox & Al Green; *ST/Scrooged* . . . .(A&M)
Jackie DeShannon; *Chicken Soup For The Soul: I'll Be There For You-Songs
Of Friendship, Brotherhood And Sisterhood-C* . . . . (Rhino)
ST/Drugstore Cowboy . . . . (Novus)
Very Best Of Jackie DeShannon . . . .(EMI)
Reach Out Of The Darkness
Friend And Lover; *Chicken Soup For The Soul: I'll Be There For You-Songs
Of Friendship, Brotherhood And Sisterhood-C* . . . . (Rhino)
Flower Power-Psychedelic Rock Classics-C . . . . (K-Tel)
Right On
Marvin Gaye; *What's Going On* . . . . (Motown)
Simple Creed
Live; *V* . . . . (Radioactive/MCA)
Sisters Are Doin' It For Themselves
Ann Wilson/Nancy Wilson/Lisa Simpson; *Simpsons-The Yellow
Album* . . . . (Geffen)
Eurythmics & Aretha Franklin; *Be Yourself Tonight* . . . .(RCA)
*Chicken Soup For The Soul: I'll Be There For You-Songs Of Friendship,
Brotherhood And Sisterhood-C* . . . . (Rhino)
Eurythmics' Greatest Hits . . . . (Arista)
Who's Zoomin' Who? . . . . (Arista)
Stomp Dance (Unity)
Robbie Robertson featuring The Six Nations Women Singers; *Contact From
The Underworld of Redboy* . . . . (Capitol)
United We Stand
Brotherhood Of Man; *Chicken Soup For The Soul: I'll Be There For You-
Songs Of Friendship, Brotherhood And Sisterhood-C* . . . . (Rhino)
Super Hits Of The '70s-Have A Nice Day-#2-C . . . . (Rhino)

Mike Curb Congregation; *Mike Curb Congregation's Greatest Hits* . . . . . (Curb)
Visions
Commodores; *Natural High* . . . . (Motown)
Visions
Stevie Wonder; *Innervisions* . . . . (Motown)
Visions
Eagles; *One Of These Nights* . . . . (Asylum)
We Are Family
Sister Sledge; *Atlantic Records 50 Years-The Gold Anniversary*
Collection-C . . . . (Atlantic)
Best Of Sister Sledge-1973-1985 . . . . (Rhino)
Chicken Soup For The Soul: I'll Be There For You-Songs Of Friendship,
Brotherhood And Sisterhood-C . . . . (Rhino)
ST/The Full Monty . . . . (RCA Victor)
We Are Family . . . . (Rhino)
What's Going On
Cyndi Lauper; *True Colors* . . . . (Portrait)
Marvin Gaye; *20/20-C* . . . . (Motown)
Marvin Gaye Live At The London Palladium . . . . (Motown)
Marvin Gaye-Anthology . . . . (Motown)
Marvin Gaye's Greatest Hits/ . . . . (Motown)
More Songs From "The Big Chill" Soundtrack-C . . . . (Motown)
What's Going On . . . . (Motown)
Quincy Jones; *Quincy Jones-The Best* . . . . (A&M)
Wholy Holy
Aretha Franklin; *Aretha Franklin-30 Greatest Hits* . . . . (Rhino)
Marvin Gaye; *Musical Testament 1964-1984* . . . . (Motown)
What's Going On . . . . (Motown)
Windows Of The World
Burt Bacharach; *One Amazing Night* . . . . (N2K)
Dionne Warwick; *Dionne Warwick Collection-Her All-Time*
Greatest Hits . . . . (Rhino)
Dionne Warwick-Definitive Collection . . . . (Arista)
Isaac Hayes; *Live At The Sahara Tahoe* . . . . (Stax)
Mormon Tabernacle Choir; *Voices In Harmony* . . . . (CBS Masterworks)
Pretenders; *ST/1969.* . . . . (Polydor)
Woodstock
Crosby, Stills & Nash; *CSN.* . . . . (Atlantic)
Crosby, Stills, Nash & Young; *Deja Vu.* . . . . (Atlantic)
So Far. . . . . (Atlantic)
Joni Mitchell; *Ladies Of The Canyon* . . . . (Reprise)
Shadows & Light. . . . . (Asylum)
Joni Mitchell with Tom Scott & The L.A. Express; *Miles Of Aisles* . . . (Asylum)

BUBBLES

See Also: **ALCOHOL, CLEAN**

Boy In The Bubble
Paul Simon; *Graceland* . . . . (Warner Bros.)
Broken Bubble
Ten Foot Pole; *Rev.* . . . . (Epitaph)
Bubble
Red House Painters; *Red House Painters* . . . . (4AD)
Bubble Gum Years
Gomez; *Bring It On* . . . . (Virgin)
Bubblegoose
Wyclef Jean; *Chef Aid-The South Park Album* . . . . (Columbia)
Wyclef Jean featuring Melky Sedeck; *Presents The Carnival F/Refugee*
Allstars. . . . . (Ruffhouse/Columbia)
Bubblegum
Sonic Youth; *Evol* . . . . (SST)
Bubbles
Bush; *ST/Mallrats* . . . . (MCA)
Bubbles
Tricky; *Nearly God* . . . . (Island)
Bubbles In My Beer
Bob Wills; *Sounds Of Texas* . . . . (Capitol)
Bob Wills & His Texas Playboys; *Bob Wills & His Texas Playboys-24*
Great Hits . . . . (Polydor)
Bob Wills & His Texas Playboys-Anthology 1935-1973. . . . . (Rhino)
Willie Nelson; *Shotgun Willie* . . . . (Atlantic)
Bubbles In The Wine
Lawrence Welk; *Best Of Lawrence Welk-20 Great Hits* . . . . (Ranwood)
Lawrence Welk-16 Most Requested Songs . . . . (Columbia)
Original Soundtrack; *Television's Greatest Hits-#4-Black & White*
Classics-C . . . . (TVT)
I'm Forever Blowing Bubbles
Lawrence Welk; *I'm Forever Blowing Bubbles.* . . . . (Ranwood)
Live At Lake Tahoe . . . . (Ranwood)
Reminiscing-#1. . . . . (Ranwood)
North Sea Bubble
Billy Bragg; *Don't Try This At Home* . . . . (Elektra)
Pikebubble
Cardigans; *Emmerdale* . . . . (Mint)
Thinking About Your Troubles
Nilsson; *The Point* . . . . (RCA)

BUILDING & CONSTRUCTION

See Also: **BUSINESS & INDUSTRY, FIXING, HOUSES,**
TOOLS, WORK

25th Floor
Patti Smith Group; *Easter* . . . . (Arista)
Another Brick In The Wall, Part 2
Class Of '99; *ST/The Faculty* . . . . (Columbia)
Pink Floyd; *Collection Of Great Dance Songs* . . . . (Columbia)
Delicate Sound Of Thunder . . . . (Columbia)
The Wall . . . . (Columbia)
Roger Waters; *The Wall-Live In Berlin* . . . . (Mercury)
Baby, Now That I've Found You
Alison Krauss & Union Station; *Best Of Austin City Limits-Country Music's*
Finest Hour-C . . . . (Legacy)
Now That I've Found You: A Collection . . . . (Rounder)
Foundations; *Best Of Rock 'N Soul-C* . . . . (Priority)
History Of British Rock-#6-C . . . . (Rhino)
Bicycle Built For Two
Kidsongs; *Cars, Boats, Trains, Planes.* . . . . (Sony Wonder)
Original Soundtrack; *School Days-Kids Classics* . . . . (Benson)
Big Brother
David Bowie; *David Live* . . . . (Rykodisc)
Diamond Dogs . . . . (Rykodisc)
Sound + Vision . . . . (Rykodisc)
ST/Breaking Glass. . . . . (A&M)
Big Yellow Taxi
Amy Grant; *House Of Love* . . . . (A&M)
Joni Mitchell; *Ladies Of The Canyon.* . . . . (Reprise)
Joni Mitchell with Tom Scott & The L.A. Express; *Miles Of Aisles.* . . . (Asylum)
Brother, Can You Spare A Dime
Bing Crosby; *Bing Crosby-16 Most Requested Songs* . . . . (Legacy)
Odetta/Dr. John/John Campbell/Rufus Reid; *Strike A Deep Chord-Blues For*
The Homeless-C . . . . (Justice)
Peter, Paul & Mary; *See What Tomorrow Brings* . . . . (Warner Bros.)
Weavers; *Weavers' Greatest Hits* . . . . (Vanguard)
Build Me Up Buttercup
Foundations; *Billboard Top Rock 'N' Roll Hits-1969-C* . . . . (Rhino)
History Of British Rock-#9-C . . . . (Rhino)
ST/There's Something About Mary . . . . (Capitol)
Building A Mystery
Sarah McLachlan; *Lilith Fair-A Celebration Of Women In Music-C* . . . . (Arista)
Mirrorball . . . . (Arista)
Surfacing . . . . (Arista)
Don't Build Your World Around It
Jim Lauderdale; *Every Second Counts* . . . . (Atlantic)
God Must Have Spent A Little More Time On You
Alabama Featuring 'N Sync; *Twentieth Century* . . . . (RCA)
'N Sync; *'N Sync* . . . . (RCA)
Totally Hits-#1-C . . . . (Arista)
Home
Alan Jackson; *Alan Jackson-The Greatest Hits Collection* . . . . (Arista)
Here In The Real World. . . . . (Arista)
How Do You Raise A Barn?
Original Cast; *Plain And Fancy* . . . . (EMI-Angel)
Hundred Pounds Of Clay
Gene McDaniels; *Best Of Gene McDaniels-A Hundred Pounds*
Of Clay . . . . (Collectables)
Rock Is Dead But It Won't Lie Down-C . . . . (Gold Rush)
I Am Made Of You
Ricky Martin; *Ricky Martin* . . . . (Columbia)
If I Could Build My Whole World Around You
Marvin Gaye & Tammi Terrell; *Every Great Motown Hit Of*
Marvin Gaye. . . . . (Motown)
Marvin Gaye & Tammi Terrell's Greatest Hits. . . . . (Motown)
Marvin Gaye-Anthology . . . . (Motown)
Motown Superstar Series-#2-Marvin Gaye. . . . . (Motown)
United . . . . (Motown)
I'll Build A Stairway To Paradise
George Gershwin; *Manhattan* . . . . (Klavier)
Issy Van Randwyck; *Glory Of Gershwin Featuring Larry Adler-C.* . . . (Mercury)
Liza Minnelli; *Fascinatin' Rhythm-Capitol Sings Gershwin-C* . . . . (Capitol)
Let's Build A World Together
George Jones & Tammy Wynette; *George Jones & Tammy Wynette-16*
Biggest Hits . . . . (Epic/Legacy)
Life And How To Live It
R.E.M.; *Fables Of The Reconstruction* . . . . (I.R.S.)
Love In An Elevator
Aerosmith; *Pump* . . . . (Geffen)
One Piece At A Time
Johnny Cash; *The Man In Black-His Greatest Hits* . . . . (Legacy)
Silvertown Blues
Mark Knopfler; *Sailing To Philadelphia* . . . . (Warner Bros.)
So Long, Frank Lloyd Wright
Simon & Garfunkel; *Bridge Over Troubled Water* . . . . (Columbia)
Stairway To Heaven
Neil Sedaka; *Neil Sedaka Sings His Greatest Hits* . . . . (RCA)

Neil Sedaka's All-Time Greatest Hits . . . . (RCA)
Theme From ''Home Improvement''
  Original Soundtrack; *Television's Greatest Hits-#7-Cable Ready-C* . . . . . (TVT)
They're Moving Father's Grave To Build A Sewer
  Clancy Brothers & Tommy Makem; *Luck Of The Irish* . . . . (Columbia)
Warmth, The
  Incubus; *Make Yourself* . . . .(Immortal/Epic)
We Live In Two Different Worlds
  Auldridge/Bennett/Gaudreau; *This Old Town* . . . .(Rebel)
Wendy
  Original Cast/Mary Martin; *Peter Pan-The 1954 Broadway*
    Production . . . .(RCA Victor)

BUS

See Also: **CARS (various), GAS STATIONS, LEAVING,**
MOTORCYCLES, ROAD, ROAD ACCIDENTS, TAXI,
TRAVELING, TRUCKS

26 Cents
  Wilkinsons; *Nothing But Love* . . . . (Giant)
America
  David Bowie; *The Concert For New York City-C* . . . . (Columbia)
  Paul Simon; *Paul Simon In Concert/Live Rhymin'* . . . . (Columbia)
  Simon & Garfunkel; *Bookends* . . . . (Columbia)
    Collected Works . . . . (Columbia)
    Simon & Garfunkel's Greatest Hits . . . . (Columbia)
    The Concert In Central Park . . . .(Warner Bros.)
Another One Rides The Bus
  ''Weird Al'' Yankovic; *''Weird Al'' Yankovic* . . . .(Volcano Entertainment)
    Dr. Demento Presents The Greatest Novelty Records-#5-1980s-C . . . . (Rhino)
Bus Driver
  Muddy Waters; *Hard Again* . . . . (Blue Sky)
Bus Drivin' Woman
  Chicago Bob; *Hit & Run Lover* . . . . (Ichiban Int'l)
Bus Dust
  Count Basie; *Long Live The Chief* . . . . (Denon)
Bus Fare Home
  Spaniels; *Heart & Soul-#2-C* . . . . (Vee-Jay)
Bus Fare To Kentucky
  Skeeter Davis; *Best Of The Best Of Skeeter Davis* . . . . (Gusto)
Bus From Amarillo
  Original Cast; *Best Little Whorehouse In Texas* . . . .(MCA)
Bus Has Come
  Jai Uttal; *Footprints* . . . . (Triloka)
Bus Ride
  Original New York Cast; *Oil City Symphony* . . . . (DRG)
Bus Rider
  Guess Who; *Best Of The Guess Who* . . . . (RCA)
    Guess Who-At Their Best . . . . (RCA)
    Track Record-Collection . . . . (RCA)
Bus Rider Blues
  Blind Boy Fuller; *1935-1940* . . . . (Blues Classics)
Bus Song
  Tony Gable & 206; *Tony Gable & 206* . . . .(Heads Up Records Int'l)
Bus Station Blues
  John Lee Hooker; *Great Bluesmen At Newport-C* . . . . (Vanguard)
Bus Stations & Train Yards
  Gutterboy; *Gutterboy* . . . . (Mercury)
Bus Stop
  Hollies; *Best Of The Hollies* . . . .(EMI)
    History Of British Rock-#3-C . . . . (Rhino)
    The Hollies' Greatest Hits . . . .(Epic)
Bus Stop (Electric Slide)
  World Class Wreckin' Cru; *Best of Electric Slide* . . .(SOH Distributors Network)
Bus Stop Bench
  Darden Smith; *Native Soil* . . . . (Watermelon)
Bus Tours
  George Duke; *Snapshot* . . . .(Warner Bros.)
Bus With No Driver
  Thelonius Monster; *Beautiful Mess* . . . . (Capitol)
Busman's Holiday
  Chad & Jeremy; *Of Cabbages And Kings* . . . . (M.I.L. Multimedia)
  Ray Anthony; *Young Man With A Horn-1952-1954--22 Original Big Band*
    Recordings . . . . (Hindsight)
Does This Bus Stop At 82nd Street?
  Bruce Springsteen; *Greetings From Asbury Park, N.J.* . . . . (Columbia)
    Tracks . . . . (Columbia)
Emma Jean's Guitar
  Chely Wright; *Let Me In* . . . .(MCA)
Frisco Depot
  Mickey Newbury; *Frisco Mabel Joy* . . . . (Mountain Retreat)
Gimme A Quarter, 25 Cents For The Bus
  October Faction; *October Faction* . . . .(SST)
Heads Carolina, Tails California
  Jo Dee Messina; *Greatest Hits Of Country Dance-C* . . . . (Curb)

Jo Dee Messina . . . . (Curb)
I Kissed The Bus
  Geezinslaw Brothers; *Feelin' Good, Gittin' Up, Gittin' Down* . . . .(Step One)
I Missed The Bus
  Kris Kross; *Totally Krossed Out* . . . .(Ruffhouse)
I Ride This Bus
  4 P.M.; *Jackin' Boots* . . . . (Reprise)
Invitation To The Blues
  Holly Cole; *Temptation* . . . . (Metro Blue)
  Tom Waits; *Small Change* . . . .(Asylum)
Kiss Me On The Bus
  Replacements; *Tim* . . . .(Sire)
Lady Bus Driver
  Ultra Head; *Cement Truck* . . . . (Imperial Stab Chamber)
Leaving Town
  Dexter Freebish; *Life Of Saturdays* . . . . (Capitol)
Lodi
  Creedence Clearwater Revival; *1969* . . . .(Fantasy)
    Creedence Clearwater Revival-Chronicle . . . .(Fantasy)
    Creedence Country . . . .(Fantasy)
    Green River . . . . (Fantasy)
    Live In Europe . . . . (Fantasy)
    More Creedence Gold . . . . (Fantasy)
    Travelin' Band . . . . (Fantasy)
Magic Bus
  Who; *Live At Leeds* . . . . (MCA)
    Magic Bus-The Who On Tour . . . . (MCA)
    Meaty Beaty Big & Bouncy . . . . (MCA)
    ST/The Kids Are Alright . . . . (MCA)
    Who Greatest Hits . . . . (MCA)
    Who's Last . . . . (MCA)
Midnight Bus
  Jesse Winchester; *Third Down 110 To Go.* . . . . (Rhino)
New York State Of Mind
  Barbra Streisand; *Memories* . . . . (Columbia)
    Streisand Superman . . . . (Columbia)
  Billy Joel; *America: A Tribute To Heroes-C* . . . .(Interscope)
    Billy Joel-Greatest Hits, Volume I & Volume II . . . . (Columbia)
    The Concert For New York City-C . . . . (Columbia)
    Turnstiles . . . . (Columbia)
  Carmen McRae; *Ms. Magic* . . . . (Dunhill Compact Classics)
  Tony Bennett with Billy Joel; *Playin' With My Friends-Bennett Sings The*
    Blues-C . . . . (Columbia)
On A Bus To St. Cloud
  Gretchen Peters; *The Secret Of Life* . . . .(Purple Crayon Prod.)
  Trisha Yearwood; *Thinkin' About You* . . . . (MCA)
On A Lopsided Bus
  Original Cast; *Pipe Dream* . . . . (RCA)
One Way Bus
  New Birth; *Golden Classics-New Birth.* . . . . (Collectables)
Only Losers Take The Bus (Dump The Dead)
  Fatima Mansions; *Viva Dead Ponies.* . . . . (Radioactive/MCA)
Porcelin Bus
  Pajama Slave Dancers; *Blood Sweat & Beers* . . . . (Restless)
Pound For A Brown On The Bus
  Frank Zappa; *Electric Aunt Jemima* . . . . (Rhino)
    Uncle Meat. . . . . (Barking Pumpkin)
Promised Land
  Band; *Moondog Matinee* . . . . (Capitol)
  Chuck Berry; *Rock 'N' Roll Rarities-20 Magic Tracks* . . . . (Chess)
    The Chess Box-Chuck Berry . . . . (Chess)
  Elvis Presley; *Promised Land* . . . . (RCA)
    ST/This Is Elvis . . . . (RCA)
  Freddy Weller; *Country Music Classics-#11-Early '70s-C.* . . . . (K-Tel)
    Freddy Weller's Greatest Hits . . . . (Columbia)
  Gary Morris; *Full Moon Empty Heart.* . . . . (Liberty)
  Grateful Dead; *Steal Your Face* . . . .(Grateful Dead)
  James Taylor; *Walking Man* . . . . (Warner Bros.)
  Kingfish; *Kingfish/Alive In Eighty Five-Double Dose* . . . .(Relix)
Restless
  Carl Perkins; *Jive After Five-Best Of Carl Perkins-1959-1978.* . . . . (Rhino)
  Mark O'Connor; *Great Divorce Songs For Him-C* . . . . (Warner Bros.)
    The New Nashville Cats . . . . (Warner Bros.)
Rosa Parks
  Outkast; *Aquemini.* . . . .(LaFace/Arista)
She Came From Fort Worth
  Kathy Mattea; *Willow In The Wind* . . . . (Mercury)
  Pat Alger & Kathy Mattea; *True Love & Other Short Stories-C* . . . . .(Sugar Hill)
Sister Rosa
  Neville Brothers; *Yellow Moon* . . . . (A&M)
Slow Bus Movin' (Howard's Beach Party)
  Fishbone; *Truth & Soul* . . . . (Columbia)
Thank God & Greyhound
  Roy Clark; *Best Of Roy Clark* . . . . (MCA)
    Great Picks And New Tricks . . . .(ISD/Intersound)
    Roy Clark-Live . . . . (MCA)
    Roy Clark's Greatest Hits. . . . . (MCA)
Theme From ''The Honeymooners''
  Original Soundtrack; *Television's Greatest Hits-#2-C* . . . . (TVT)

Tie A Yellow Ribbon Round The Ole Oak Tree
Dawn Featuring Tony Orlando; *'70s Party Killers-C* . . . . (Rhino)
   Fantastic-#1-C . . . . (K-Tel)
Frank Sinatra; *Some Nice Things I've Missed* . . . . (Reprise)
Lawrence Welk; *Best Of Lawrence Welk-20 Great Hits* . . . . (Ranwood)
Sonny James & Karla Taylor; *Classic Country Duets-C* . . . . (Curb)
Turn The Page
Metallica; *Garage Inc.* . . . . (Elektra)
Waitin' For The Bus
ZZ Top; *Best Of ZZ Top* . . . . (Warner Bros.)
   Six Pack . . . . (Warner Bros.)
   Tres Hombres . . . . (Warner Bros.)

BUSINESS & INDUSTRY, Technology

See Also: BOSSES, BUILDING & CONSTRUCTION, COMPUTERS, MACHINES, MONEY, NATURE, PROTEST, RECORD BUSINESS, SHOPPING, SHOW BIZ, WORK

1913 Massacre
Arlo Guthrie; *Hobo's Lullaby* . . . . (Reprise)
Jack Elliot; *Tribute To Woody Guthrie-C* . . . . (Warner Bros.)
Ramblin' Jack Elliott; *Greatest Songs Of Woody Guthrie-C* . . . . (Vanguard)
Woody Guthrie; *Struggle.* . . . . (Smithsonian Folkways)
9 To 5
Dolly Parton; *9 To 5 And Odd Jobs* . . . . (RCA)
   Best There Is . . . . (RCA)
   Dolly Parton's Greatest Hits . . . . (RCA)
   I Am Woman-C . . . . (Nick At Nite)
   Nipper's Greatest Hits Of The '80s-C . . . . (RCA)
Ain't Nobody's Business
Billie Holiday; *From The Original Decca Masters* . . . . (MCA)
Bobby Bland; *Soul Of The Man* . . . . (MCA)
Jimmy Witherspoon; *Jazz Legacy* . . . . (Inner City)
   Monterey Jazz Festival . . . . (Everest)
   'Spoon Concerts . . . . (Fantasy)
Ashes In The Fall
Rage Against The Machine; *The Battle Of Los Angeles* . . . . (Epic)
Atlantic City
Bruce Springsteen; *Bruce Springsteen's Greatest Hits* . . . . (Columbia)
   Nebraska. . . . . (Columbia)
Back In Business
Liza Minnelli & Billy Stritch; *Sondheim-A Celebration At Carnegie Hall-C* . . . . (RCA Victor)
Back In Business
AC/DC; *Fly On The Wall* . . . . (Atco)
Back In Business
Madonna; *I'm Breathless-Music From Dick Tracy* . . . . (Sire)
Big Yellow Taxi
Amy Grant; *House Of Love* . . . . (A&M)
Joni Mitchell; *Ladies Of The Canyon* . . . . (Reprise)
Joni Mitchell with Tom Scott & The L.A. Express; *Miles Of Aisles* . . . (Asylum)
Birmingham
Amanda Marshall; *Amanda Marshall* . . . . (Epic)
Bizzness Ain't Dead
New World Singers; *Best Of Broadside 1962-1968: Anthems Of The American Underground From The Pages Of Broadside Magazine-C* . . . . (Smithsonian Folkways)
Boy In The Bubble
Paul Simon; *Graceland* . . . . (Warner Bros.)
Business
Pete Seeger; *Best Of Broadside 1962-1968: Anthems Of The American Underground From The Pages Of Broadside Magazine-C* . . . . (Smithsonian Folkways)
   God Bless The Grass. . . . . (Legacy)
Business
Brian May; *Another World* . . . . (Hollywood)
Business Ain't Nothin' But The Blues
Rahsaan Roland Kirk; *I Talk With The Spirits* . . . . (Verve)
Business As Usual
Blues Traveler; *Straight On Till Morning* . . . . (A&M)
Business As Usual
Expectations; *The Quill Records Story: The Best Of Chicago Garage Bands-C* . . . . (Collectables)
Business As Usual
Little Feat; *Let It Roll.* . . . . (Warner Bros.)
Business As Usual
Orleans; *Still The One* . . . . (Elektra)
Business Goes On As Usual
Roberta Flack; *Chapter Two* . . . . (Atlantic)
Business Of Love
Charlie Daniels; *The Door.* . . . . (Sparrow)
Business On The Street
Stephen Stills; *Down The Road* . . . . (Atlantic)
Business With My Baby
B.B. King; *King Of The Blues* . . . . (MCA)

Businessmen
Subhumans; *Worlds Apart* . . . . (Bluurg)
Businessmen Are Okay
Loud Family; *Days For Days* . . . . (Alias)
Businss You're Doin'
Lightnin' Hopkins; *Goin' Away* . . . . (Original Blues Classics)
Californication
Red Hot Chili Peppers; *Californication* . . . . (Warner Bros.)
Company Way, The
New Broadway Cast; *How To Succeed In Business Without Really Trying* . . . . (RCA Victor)
Original Cast; *How To Succeed In Business Without Really Trying* . . . . . . (RCA)
Cotton Mill Man
Jim & Jesse; *Old Dominion Masters* . . . . (Pinecastle)
Crushed By The Wheels Of Industry
Heaven 17; *Luxury Gap* . . . . (Caroline)
Daddy Won't Sell The Farm
Montgomery Gentry; *Tattoos & Scars* . . . . (Columbia)
Daysleeper
R.E.M.; *Up* . . . . (Warner Bros.)
Dirty Business
New Riders Of The Purple Sage; *New Riders Of The Purple Sage* . . . . (Columbia)
Dream Merchant
New Birth; *Smooth Grooves-A Sensual Collection-#5-C* . . . . (Rhino)
Everything's Changed
Lonestar; *Country Cares For Kids II-C* . . . . (BNA)
   Crazy Nights . . . . (BNA)
   Lonely Grill . . . . (BNA)
Exhuming McCarthy
R.E.M.; *Document* . . . . (EMI-Capitol Entert. Properties)
Factory
Bruce Springsteen; *Darkness On The Edge Of Town* . . . . (Columbia)
Factory Girl
Rolling Stones; *Beggars Banquet.* . . . . (Abkco)
Free Trade And A Misty Moon
Greek Evans & Ensemble; *Music From The New York Stage (1890-1920)-#4-1917-1920-C* . . . . (Pearl)
Grand Coulee Dam
Bob Dylan; *Tribute To Woody Guthrie-C* . . . . (Warner Bros.)
How To Succeed
New Broadway Cast; *How To Succeed In Business Without Really Trying* . . . . (RCA Victor)
Original Cast; *How To Succeed In Business Without Really Trying* . . . . . . (RCA)
Hula Hoop, The
Original Soundtrack; *ST/The Hudsucker Proxy* . . . . (Varese Sarabande)
Industrial Disease
Dire Straits; *Love Over Gold* . . . . (Warner Bros.)
Kansas City
Original Cast; *Oklahoma!* . . . . (MCA)
Keep The Customer Satisfied
Simon & Garfunkel; *Bridge Over Troubled Water* . . . . (Columbia)
   Collected Works . . . . (Columbia)
Little Man
Alan Jackson; *High Mileage* . . . . (Arista)
Lollipop Guild
Original Cast; *The Wizard Of Oz-Selections From The Original Motion Picture Soundtrack.* . . . . (Turner Classic Movies)
Montana
Frank Zappa; *You Can't Do That On Stage Anymore-#3* . . . . (Rykodisc)
Mothers Of Invention; *Apostrophe/Overnite Sensation* . . . . (Rykodisc)
Mr. Dream Merchant
Jerry Butler; *Best Of Jerry Butler* . . . . (Rhino)
   Soul Shots-#2-The "In" Crowd-Sweet Soul-C . . . . (Rhino)
My Hometown
Bruce Springsteen; *Born In The U.S.A.* . . . . (Columbia)
   Bruce Springsteen's Greatest Hits . . . . (Columbia)
Packing House Blues
Lillian Glinn; *Lillian Glinn-1927-1929* . . . . (Document)
Pajama Game/Racing With The Clock
Original Cast; *Pajama Game* . . . . (Columbia)
Roll On Columbia
Judy Collins; *Tribute To Woody Guthrie-C* . . . . (Warner Bros.)
Secretary Is Not A Toy
New Broadway Cast; *How To Succeed In Business Without Really Trying* . . . . (RCA Victor)
Original Cast; *How To Succeed In Business Without Really Trying* . . . . . . (RCA)
Sheep Go To Heaven
Cake; *Prolonging The Magic* . . . . (Capricorn)
Takin' Care Of Business
Bachman-Turner Overdrive; *Bachman-Turner Overdrive II* . . . . (Mercury)
   Best Of B.T.O.-So Far . . . . (Mercury)
Testify
Rage Against The Machine; *The Battle Of Los Angeles* . . . . (Epic)
Theme From "Dallas"
Original Soundtrack; *CBS: The First 50 Years* . . . . (TVT)
   Television's Greatest Hits-#3-1970s & 1980s-C . . . . (TVT)
   TV Classic Themes: 25th Anniversary Edition-C . . . . (Breakable)

Theme From "Sanford & Son"
Original Soundtrack; *Television's Greatest Hits-#3-1970s & 1980s-C* . . . (TVT)
There's No Business Like Show Business
Ethel Merman; *Irving Berlin 100th Anniversary Collection-C* . . . . (MCA)
   Merman Sings Merman . . . . (London)
Original Cast; *Annie Get Your Gun* . . . . (MCA)
Trademark
Mandy Barnett; *I've Got A Right To Cry* . . . . (Sire)
Union Maid
Judy Collins; *Tribute To Woody Guthrie-C* . . . . (Warner Bros.)
Welcome To The Occupation
R.E.M.; *Document* . . . . (EMI-Capitol Entert. Properties)
Workin' It
Don Henley; *Inside Job* . . . . (Warner Bros.)
Youngstown
Bruce Springsteen; *The Ghost Of Tom Joad* . . . . (Columbia)

BUSY

See Also: FAST, LATE, RELAX, TIME: GENERAL,
URGENT, WAITING

Busy Bee
Ugly Kid Joe; *America's Least Wanted* . . . . (Stardog)
Busy Being Blue
k.d. lang; *Shadowland.* . . . . (Sire)
Busy Bodies
Elvis Costello; *Armed Forces* . . . . (Rykodisc)
Busy Man
Billy Ray Cyrus; *Shot Full Of Love* . . . . (Mercury)
Devil's Been Busy, The
Traveling Wilburys; *Traveling Wilburys-Vol. 3* . . . . (Wilbury/Warner Bros.)
Does Anybody Really Know What Time It Is?
Chicago; *Chicago At Carnegie Hall* . . . .(Chicago)
   Chicago IX-Chicago's Greatest Hits . . . . (Chicago)
   Chicago Transit Authority . . . . (Chicago)
   If You Leave Me Now . . . . (Chicago)
Given More Time
Vince Gill; *High Lonesome Sound* . . . .(MCA)
If Your Heart Ain't Busy Tonight
Tanya Tucker; *What Do I Do With Me* . . . . (Capitol)
I'm In A Hurry (And Don't Know Why)
Alabama; *American Pride* . . . . (RCA)
Keepin' Up
Alabama; *For The Record: 41 Number One Hits* . . . . (RCA)
Look Through Any Window
Hollies; *History Of British Rock-#6-C* . . . . (Rhino)
   The Hollies' Greatest Hits . . . .(Epic)
Nadine (Is It You?)
Chuck Berry; *Rock & Roll Rarities* . . . . (Chess)
Never Too Busy
Kenny Lattimore; *Kenny Lattimore* . . . . (Columbia)
No Time
Guess Who; *American Woman* . . . . (RCA)
   Best Of The Guess Who . . . . (RCA)
   Greatest Of The Guess Who . . . . (RCA)
   Track Record-Collection . . . . (RCA)
Not Now James, We're Busy
Pop Will Eat Itself; *Tonin'; This Is The Day...This Is The Hour...* . . . . . . (RCA)
Pajama Game/Racing With The Clock
Original Cast; *Pajama Game* . . . . (Columbia)
Squeeze Me In
Garth Brooks; *Scarecrow* . . . . (Capitol)
They're Playin' Our Song
Neal McCoy; *Neal McCoy's Greatest Hits* . . . . (Atlantic)
   You Gotta Love That! . . . . (Atlantic)
Too Busy Being In Love
Doug Stone; *From The Heart* . . . .(Epic)
Too Busy Thinking About My Baby
Manhattan Transfer; *Tonin'* . . . . (Atlantic)
Marvin Gaye; *Every Great Motown Hit Of Marvin Gaye* . . . . (Motown)
   Superhits . . . . (Motown)
You Don't Have To Cry
Crosby, Stills & Nash; *Crosby, Stills & Nash* . . . . (Atlantic)
You Should Be Mine (Don't Waste Your Time)
Brian McKnight; *Anytime* . . . . (Motown)

CANDY, Chocolate, Lollipops

See Also: DRUGS (various), FOOD & BEVERAGES (various),
SWEET, WOMEN'S NAMES: C

1-2-3
Len Barry; *24 Of The Grooviest Hits Of All Time! The '60s Ultimate*
   Collection-#1-C . . . . (Sundazed Music)

Baby Ruth
John Prine; *Storm Windows* . . . .(Asylum)
Ballad Of A Teenage Queen
Johnny Cash; *Johnny Cash* . . . . (Sun)
   Johnny Cash-Original Golden Hits-#2. . . . . (Sun)
   Johnny Cash-Sun Years . . . . (Rhino)
   ST/Harper Valley PTA . . . . (Sun)
   The Legend . . . .(Plantation)
   The Man In Black-His Greatest Hits. . . . . (Legacy)
Big Rock Candy Mountain
Burl Ives; *Burl Ives' Greatest Hits* . . . . (MCA)
   Poor Wayfaring Stranger . . . . (Flapper)
Harry McClintock; *ST/O Brother, Where Art Thou?* . . . . (Mercury)
John Hartford; *ST/Down From The Mountain* . . . . (Lost Highway/IDJMG)
Pete Seeger; *20 Golden Pieces Of Pete Seeger* . . . . (Bulldog)
Tex Ritter; *Capitol Collectors Series-Tex Ritter* . . . . (Capitol)
Black Cow
Steely Dan; *Aja* . . . . (MCA)
   Steely Dan-Gold. . . . . (MCA)
Black Licorice
Grand Funk Railroad; *Caught In The Act* . . . . (Capitol)
   We're An American Band. . . . . (Capitol)
Candy
Cameo; *12'' Collection And More* . . . . (Mercury)
   Best Of Cameo . . . . (Mercury/Funk Essentials)
   Billboard Top R&B Hits-1987-C . . . . (Rhino)
   Greatest Hits . . . . (Chronicles)
Will Smith featuring Larry Blackmon; *Big Willie Style* . . . . (Columbia)
Candy
Ray Charles; *Ray Charles & Betty Carter-Dedicated To You* . . . . (Rhino)
Candy
Big Maybelle; *Blues, Candy & Big Maybelle* . . . . (Savoy)
Candy
Jessie Hill; *Golden Classics-Jessie Hill* . . . . (Collectables)
Candy
Morphine; *Cure For Pain* . . . . (Rykodisc)
Candy
Martin Sexton; *The American* . . . .(Atlantic)
Candy
Astors; *Astors Meet The Newcomers* . . . . (Stax)
   Funky Broadway-Stax Revue Live At The Ballroom . . . . (Stax)
Candy
Dinah Shore; *Best Of The Big Band Era-1945-C* . . . . (BMG Special Prod.)
   V-Disc Recordings-Dinah Shore . . . . (Collector's Choice)
Dr. John; *In A Sentimental Mood* . . . . (Warner Bros.)
Four Freshmen; *Capitol Collectors Series-Four Freshman* . . . . (Capitol)
Henry "Sweets" Edison; *In Copenhagen* . . . .(Mobile Fidelity Sound Lab)
Jo Stafford; *Coming Back Like A Song* . . . .(ASV)
   The "Big Band" Sound . . . . (Corinthian)
John Pizzarelli; *My Blue Heaven* . . . . (Chesky)
   One Night Without You-The John Pizzarelli Collection . . . . (Chesky)
Johnny Mercer; *Capitol Collectors Series-Johnny Mercer.* . . . . (Capitol)
Johnny Mercer, Jo Stafford & The Pied Pipers; *G.I. Jukebox-Songs From*
   World War II-C . . . .(Hip-O)
   Music Of The War Years-#2-C . . . . (Madacy)
Lennon Sisters; *Among Our Souvenirs* . . . . (Ranwood)
Manhattan Transfer; *Manhattan Transfer.* . . . . (Rhino)
   Manhattan Transfer-Anthology-Down In Birdland . . . . (Rhino)
   Very Best Of The Manhattan Transfer . . . . (Rhino)
Nat "King" Cole; *ST/Home For The Holidays.* . . . . (Mercury)
   V-Disc Recordings-Nat "King" Cole. . . . . (Collector's Choice)
Sammy Kaye & His Orchestra; *Sammy Kaye-22 Original Big Band*
   Recordings-1941-1944 . . . . (Hindsight)
Candy
Iggy Pop; *Best Of Iggy Pop* . . . . (Virgin)
   Brick By Brick . . . . (Virgin)
Candy
Solomon Burke; *Soul Of The Blues* . . . .(Black Top)
Candy
Byrds; *Dr. Byrds & Mr. Hyde* . . . . (Legacy)
Candy
Dag; *Righteous* . . . . (Columbia)
Candy
Con Funk Shun; *Best Of Con Funk Shun-#2* . . . . (Mercury/Funk Essentials)
Candy
Presidents Of The United States Of America; *Presidents Of The United States*
   Of America . . . . (Columbia)
Candy
L.L. Cool J; *Phenomenon* . . . . (Def Jam/Mercury)
Candy
Jackson Browne; *Lives In The Balance* . . . .(Asylum)
Candy
Talk Talk; *Party's Over.* . . . . (EMI)
Candy (Sugar Shoppe)
Brady Bunch Kids; *It's A Sunshine Day-Best Of The Brady*
   Bunch Kids . . . . (MCA)
Candy And A Currant Bun
Pink Floyd; *Saucerful Of Secrets.* . . . . (Capitol)
   Shine On . . . . (Columbia)

Candy And Cake
Mindy Carson; *Lost Female Hits Of The '50s-C* . . . . (Taragon)
Candy And Cake
Evelyn Knight; *Best Of Evelyn Knight.* . . . . (Collector's Choice)
Candy And Roses
Sue Thompson; *Sue Thompson's Greatest Hits.* . . . . (Curb)
Candy Bars For Elvis
Barry Tiffin; *A Tribute To Elvis.* . . . . (K-Tel)
Candy By The Pound
Elton John; *Ice On Fire* . . . . (MCA)
Candy Cain (1958)
Steve Miller; *Steve Miller-Box Set.* . . . . (Capitol)
Candy Cane Madness
Lowell George; *Lightning-Rod Man* . . . . (Rhino)
Candy Corn
Sponge; *Rotting Pinata* . . . . (Work)
Candy Everybody Wants
10,000 Maniacs; *MTV Unplugged-10,000 Maniacs* . . . . . . (Elektra)
Our Time In Eden . . . . (Elektra)
Candy Girl
4 Seasons; *25th Anniversary Collection* . . . . (Rhino)
4 Seasons-Anthology . . . . (Rhino)
Lil' Bit Of Gold 3'' CD Series-C. . . . . (Rhino)
Candy Kisses
Tony Bennett; *I Left My Heart In San Francisco* . . . . (Columbia)
Candy Kisses
Elton Britt; *The RCA Years* . . . . (Collector's Choice)
George Morgan; *Room Full Of Roses-The George Morgan
Collection* . . . . (Razor & Tie)
Lorrie Morgan; *Essential Lorrie Morgan* . . . . (RCA)
Roy Rogers; *Best Of Roy Rogers* . . . . (Curb)
Candy Man
Fred Neil; *Little Bit Of Rain.* . . . . (Elektra)
Mickey Gilley & Charly McClain; *It Takes Believers* . . . . (Epic)
Roy Orbison; *In Dreams-Greatest Hits* . . . . (Orbison)
Roy Orbison Greatest Hits . . . . (Monument)
Roy Orbison's All-Time Greatest Hits-#1 & 2 . . . . (Monument)
Very Best Of Roy Orbison . . . . (Monument)
Candy Man
Mississippi John Hurt; *Best Of Mississippi John Hurt.* . . . . (Vanguard)
Today!. . . . . (Vanguard)
Candy Man
Mary Jane Girls; *In My House: The Best Of The Mary Jane Girls* . . . . (Motown)
Mary Jane Girls . . . . (Motown)
Candy Man
Hot Tuna; *Best Of Hot Tuna* . . . . (RCA)
Classic Electric. . . . . (Relix)
First Pull Up, Then Pull Down . . . . (RCA)
John Fahey; *Return Of The Repressed: The John Fahey Anthology* . . . . (Rhino)
Jorma Kaukonen; *Magic Two* . . . . (Relix)
Reverend Gary Davis; *Pure Religion & Bad
Company* . . . . (Smithsonian Folkways)
Rising Sons; *Rising Sons Featuring Taj Mahal & Ry Cooder* . . . . (Legacy)
Taj Mahal; *Giant Step/De Ole Folks At Home* . . . . (Columbia)
Candy Man
Donovan; *Fairytale* . . . . (Sequel)
Candy Man, The
Mike Curb Congregation; *Mike Curb Congregation's Greatest Hits* . . . . (Curb)
Sammy Davis, Jr.; *Best Of Sammy Davis, Jr.* . . . . (Curb)
Sammy Davis, Jr.'s Greatest Songs . . . . (Curb)
Super Hits Of The '70s-Have A Nice Day-#8-C . . . . (Rhino)
Candy Man's Gone
Bruce Cockburn; *Trouble With Normal.* . . . . (Columbia)
Candy Perfume Girl
Madonna; *Ray Of Light* . . . . (Maverick)
Candy Rain
Soul For Real; *Candy Rain* . . . . (Uptown/MCA)
Candy Says
Velvet Underground; *Velvet Underground* . . . . (Polydor)
Candy Song
Masters Of Reality; *Masters Of Reality.* . . . . (Delicious Vinyl)
Candy Store Blues
Maria Muldaur; *Big Blues-C* . . . . (Music For Little People)
Candy Store Love
Valchords; *Legends Of Doo-Wop-#1-C.* . . . . (Juke Box Treasures)
Candy Store Rock
Led Zeppelin; *Led Zeppelin-Box Set* . . . . (Atlantic)
Presence . . . . (Swan Song)
Candy Yam
Lee Dorsey; *Wheelin' And Dealin': The Definitive Collection* . . . . . . (Arista)
Candy, Candy
Beau Hunks; *The Beau Hunks Play The Little Rascals
Music* . . . . (Koch International)
Candyman
Grateful Dead; *American Beauty* . . . . (Warner Bros.)
Dead Set . . . . (Arista)
Candyman
Siouxsie And The Banshees; *Tinderbox* . . . . (Geffen)

Twice Upon A Time-The Singles . . . . (Geffen)
Candyman Messiah
Army Of Lovers; *Massive Luxury Overdose* . . . . (Giant)
Candy-O
Cars; *Candy-O* . . . . (Elektra)
Just What I Needed: The Cars Anthology . . . . (Rhino)
Chocolate
Smothers Brothers; *Sibling Revelry-Best Of The Smothers Brothers* . . . . (Rhino)
Chocolate And Vanilla Pudding
Everything; *Labrador* . . . . (Capricorn)
Chocolate Brown Eyes
Millie Jackson; *Rock 'N' Roll Soul.* . . . . (Ichiban Int'l)
Chocolate Buttermilk
Kool & The Gang; *Best Of Kool & The Gang-1969-
1976* . . . . (Mercury/Funk Essentials)
Kool & The Gang . . . . (Mercury)
Live At The Sex Machine . . . . (Mercury)
Chocolate Cadillac
Red Mitchell; *Chocolate Cadillac* . . . . (Steeplechase)
Chocolate Cake
Crowded House; *Woodface* . . . . (Capitol)
Chocolate Chip
Isaac Hayes; *Chocolate Chip* . . . . (Stax)
Chocolate City
Roger Troutman & Shirley Murdock; *ST/A Thin Line Between Love
And Hate.* . . . . (Warner Bros.)
Zapp & Roger; *Compilation-Greatest Hits II And More* . . . . (Reprise)
Chocolate City
Parliament; *Best Of Parliament-Give Up The Funk* . . . . (Mercury)
Chocolate City. . . . . (Casablanca)
In Yo' Face!-History Of Funk-#2-C . . . . (Rhino)
Tear The Roof Off-1974-1980 . . . . (Mercury/Funk Essentials)
Chocolate City Groovin'
Marcus Johnson; *Chocolate City Groovin'* . . . . (N2K)
Chocolate Elvis
Tosca; *Trip Hop & Jazz-#2-Beats From The Underground-C* . . . . (Instinct)
Chocolate Fudge
Mannheim Steamroller; *Fresh Aire* . . . . (American Gramaphone)
Chocolate Girl
Whispers; *Greatest Slow Jams #1* . . . . (Right Stuff)
Open Up Your Love . . . . (Right Stuff)
Chocolate Girl
Keith Sweat; *Keith Sweat.* . . . . (Elektra)
Chocolate Havlah
Frank Zappa; *You Can't Do That On Stage Anymore-#5* . . . . (Rykodisc)
Chocolate Jesus
Tom Waits; *Mule Variations* . . . . (Epitaph)
Chocolate Mood
Marc Nelson; *chocolate mood* . . . . (Columbia)
Chocolate River
Seeds; *Travel With Your Mind* . . . . (Crescendo)
Chocolate Sauce
Rachel Portman; *ST/Chocolat* . . . . (Sony Music Soundtrax)
Chocolate Shake
Duke Ellington; *Wicked Swing-C.* . . . . (RCA Victor)
Chocolate Whip
Selecter; *Hairspray* . . . . (Triple X Entert.)
Chocolates
Aluminum Group; *Plano* . . . . (Mint)
Wonder Boy Plus . . . . (Mint)
Choo Choo Charlie (Good & Plenty)
Original Soundtrack; *TeeVee Toons-The Commercials-#1-C* . . . . (TVT)
Come On-A My House
Rosemary Clooney; *Rosemary Clooney-16 Most Requested Songs* . . . . (Legacy)
Sentimental Journey: Pop Vocal Classics-#3-C . . . . (Rhino)
Cotton Candy Land
Elvis Presley; *Elvis Sings For Children And Grownups Too!* . . . . (RCA)
Discotheque
U2; *Pop* . . . . (Island)
Fine & Dandy
Art Tatum; *Solo Masterpieces-#5* . . . . (Pablo)
Barbra Streisand; *People* . . . . (Columbia)
Chet Baker; *Out Of Nowhere* . . . . (Milestone)
Milt Jackson & Sonny Stitt; *Milt Jackson & Sonny Stitt-In The
Beginning* . . . . (Galaxy)
I Want Candy
Bow Wow Wow; *Best Of Bow Wow Wow* . . . . (RCA)
I Want Candy. . . . . (RCA)
Strangeloves; *Frat Rock!-#3-Grandson Of Frat Rock!-C* . . . . (Rhino)
Ice Cream
Sarah McLachlan; *Fumbling Towards Ecstasy* . . . . (Arista)
Incense And Peppermints
Strawberry Alarm Clock; *Billboard Top Rock 'N' Roll Hits-1967-C* . . . . (Rhino)
Cruisin'-1967-C . . . . (Increase)
Even More Nuggets-C . . . . (Rhino)
Nuggets-#8-Acid Rock-C. . . . . (Rhino)
Kitchenware And Candy Bars
Stone Temple Pilots; *Purple.* . . . . (Atlantic)

Lollipop
Chordettes; *Best Of The Chordettes* . . . . (Rhino)
  Chordettes Greatest Hits . . . . (Everest)
  Jukebox Classics-#2-C . . . . (Rhino)
  Lil' Bit Of Gold 3'' CD Series-C . . . . (Rhino)
  ST/Stand By Me . . . . (Atlantic)

Lollipop
Woody Herman; *Keeper Of The Flame: Complete Capitol*
  Recordings . . . . (Blue Note)

Lollipop (Candyman)
Aqua; *Aquarium* . . . .(MCA)

Lollipop Guild
Original Cast; *The Wizard Of Oz-Selections From The Original Motion*
  Picture Soundtrack . . . . (Turner Classic Movies)

Lollipop Lips
Connie Francis; *Connie Francis-Souvenirs* . . . . (Polydor)

Lollipop Train (You Never Had It So Good)
Grass Roots; *Grass Roots-Anthology (1966-1975)* . . . . (Rhino)
P.F. Sloan; *P.F. Sloan-Anthology* . . . .(One Way)

Lollipop Tree
Burl Ives; *A Twinkle In Your Eye* . . . . (Legacy)
Limeliters; *Through The Children's Eyes* . . . . (Folk Era)

Lollipops And Roses
Four Preps; *Best Of The Four Preps* . . . . (Curb)
Herb Alpert & The Tijuana Brass; *Herb Alpert & The Tijuana Brass-*
  Classics-#1 . . . . (A&M)
  Whipped Cream & Other Delights . . . . (A&M)
Jack Jones; *Jack Jones' Greatest Hits* . . . .(MCA)

Lolly Pop Mama
Wynonie Harris; *Risque Blues: Sixty Minute Man-C* . . . . (King)

Lollypop
Hunter And Jenkins; *Raunchy Business-Hot Nuts & Lollypops-C* . . . . . (Legacy)

Lollypop (Crazy 'Bout)
Louis Jordan; *At The Swing Cat's Ball* . . . .(MCA)

Lollypop Mama
Clarence Samuels; *Chess Blues Box-C* . . . . (Chess)

Love Looks Good On You (You're Candy Sweet)
Blood, Sweat & Tears; *Found Treasures* . . . . (Sony Music Special Prod.)

Melt In Your Mouth
Candyman; *Ain't No Shame In My Game* . . . .(Epic)

More
Trace Adkins; *More...* . . . . (Capitol)

Morphine And Chocolate
4 Non Blondes; *Bigger, Better, Faster, More!* . . . . (Interscope)

My Boy Lollipop
Millie Small; *The Island Story-1962-1987-25th Anniversary-C* . . . . . . (Island)

On The Good Ship Lollipop
4 Seasons; *Rarities-#1* . . . . (Rhino)
Firehouse Five Plus Two; *Goes To Sea* . . . . (Good Time Jazz)

Peppermint Man
Dick Dale And The Del-Tones; *Dick Dale And The Del-Tones'*
  Greatest Hits . . . . (Crescendo)

Peppermint Stick
Elchords; *Memories Of Times Square Record Shop-#1-C* . . . . . . (Collectables)

Peppermint Twist
Joey Dee & the Starliters; *Billboard Top Rock 'N' Roll Hits-1962-C* . . . . (Rhino)
  Hey Let's Twist! Best Of Joey Dee & The Starliters . . . . (Rhino)
  ST/American Graffiti . . . .(MCA)

Rock Candy
Bulletboys; *ST/Wayne's World* . . . . (Reprise)
Montrose; *Montrose* . . . .(Warner Bros.)

Rose And A Baby Ruth, A
George Hamilton IV; *At The Hop* . . . .(MCA)
  Vintage Music-#12-C . . . .(MCA)

Sex And Candy
Marcy Playground; *Marcy Playground* . . . . (Capitol)
  Now That's What I Call Music!-#1-C . . . . (Virgin)

So Like Candy
Elvis Costello; *Mighty Like A Rose* . . . .(Warner Bros.)

Sometimes You Feel Like A Nut (Mounds & Almond Joy Candy Bars)
Original Soundtrack; *TeeVee Toons-The Commercials-#1-C* . . . . (TVT)

Sugar, Sugar
Archies; *Billboard Top Rock 'N' Roll Hits-1969-C* . . . . (Rhino)

Sunshine & Chocolate
Semisonic; *All About Chemistry* . . . .(MCA)

Sunshine, Lollipops & Rainbows
Lesley Gore; *Golden Hits Of Lesley Gore* . . . . (Mercury)
  Lesley Gore-Anthology . . . . (Rhino)

Sweeter Than Chocolate
Burning Spear; *The World Should Know* . . . . (Heartbeat)

Take Me Out To The Ball Game
Bruce Springstone; *Baseball's Greatest Hits-C* . . . . (Rhino)
Doc & Merle Watson; *Baseball's Greatest Hits-C* . . . . (Rhino)
Frank Zappa; *You Can't Do That On Stage Anymore#4* . . . . (Rykodisc)

Taste Of Chocolate
Big Daddy Kane; *Taste Of Chocolate* . . . .(Cold Chillin')

There's Nothing Like The Face (Hershey's Chocolate Bars)
Original Soundtrack; *TeeVee Toons-The Commercials-#1-C* . . . . (TVT)

Three Boats Down From The Candy
Marillion; *Script For A Jester's Tear* . . . . (Capitol)

CAPITAL PUNISHMENT, Hanging

See Also: CRIME, DEATH, KILL, LAW & ORDER, POLITICS (various), PRISON, PROTEST, REBELS, STRINGS & ROPE

Another Execution
Above The Law; *Livin' Like Hustlers* . . . . (Ruthless)

Asswhippin'
Fishbone; *Reality Of My Surroundings* . . . . (Columbia)

At The Gallows End
Candlemass; *Candlemass-Live* . . . . (Metal Blade)

Crucified
Agnostic Front; *Best Of Agnostic Front* . . . . (Relativity)
  Last Warning . . . . (Relativity)

Crucified
Fixx; *Ink* . . . . (Impact)

Crucified
Army Of Lovers; *Massive Luxury Overdose* . . . .(Giant)

Dang Me
Roger Miller; *Billboard Top Rock 'N' Roll Hits-1964-C* . . . . (Rhino)
  Cruisin'-1964-C . . . . (Increase)
  Roger Miller-Golden Hits . . . . (Smash)

Death Row
David Allan Coe; *Penitentiary Blues* . . . . (SSS International)

Death Sentence
Capitol Punishment; *Livin' On The Edge Of A Razor* . . . . (Wrap/Ichiban)

Death Sentence
Big Daddy Kane; *Prince Of Darkness* . . . .(Cold Chillin')

Electric Chair
Sleepy John Estes & The Tennessee Jug Busters; *Broke & Hungry (Ragged*
  & Dirty Too) . . . . (Delmark)

Electric Chair
Prince; *ST/Batman* . . . .(Warner Bros.)

Electric Chair Blues
Guitar Welch; *Angola Prisoner's Blues* . . . . (Arhoolie)

Electric Chair, The
SNFU; *Last Of The Big Time Suspenders* . . . . (Cargo)

Ellis Unit One
Steve Earle; *Johnny Too Bad* . . . .(E Squared)
  ST/Dead Man Walking . . . . (Columbia)

Executioner Style
Awesome Dre & The Hardcore Committee; *You Can't Hold*
  Me Back . . . . (Priority)

Flip The Switch
Rolling Stones; *Bridges To Babylon* . . . .(Virgin)
  No Security . . . .(Virgin)

Gallows Pole
Leadbelly; *Leadbelly* . . . . (Everest)
Led Zeppelin; *Led Zeppelin III* . . . .(Atlantic)
Page & Plant; *Unledded* . . . .(Atlantic)

Gallows Song
Carl Sandburg; *Americana* . . . . (Everest)

Green Green Grass Of Home
Burl Ives; *Best Of Burl Ives-#2* . . . .(MCA)
Elvis Presley; *Elvis Presley Today* . . . .(RCA)
  Our Memories Of Elvis, Volume 2 . . . .(RCA)
George Jones; *20 Golden Pieces Of George Jones* . . . .(Bulldog)
Johnny Cash; *Johnny Cash-16 Biggest Hits-#2* . . . . (Legacy)
Tom Jones; *Country Side Of Tom Jones* . . . . (London)
  Things That Matter Most To Me . . . . (Mercury)
  Tom Jones-London Collector-Greatest Hits . . . . (London)

Guenevere
Original Cast; *Camelot* . . . . (Columbia)
Original Soundtrack; *ST/Camelot* . . . . (Warner Bros.)

Hang 'Em High
Booker T. & The M.G.s; *15 Original Big Hits-#4-C* . . . . (Stax)
  Booker T. & The M.G.s' Greatest Hits . . . . (Stax)
Van Halen; *Diver Down* . . . .(Warner Bros.)

Hanging Song
Fairport Convention; *Babbacombe Lee* . . . . (A&M)

Hangman
John Jacob Niles; *Best Of John Jacob Niles* . . . .(Tradition)
Peter, Paul & Mary; *See What Tomorrow Brings* . . . . (Warner Bros.)

Hangman & Papist
Strawbs; *From The Witchwood* . . . . (A&M)

Hangman Hang My Shell On A Tree
Spooky Tooth; *Spooky Two* . . . . (A&M)

Hangman Jury
Aerosmith; *Permanent Vacation* . . . . (Geffen)

Hangman's Boogie
Cowboy Copas; *Tragic Tales Of Love & Life* . . . .(King)

Hangman's Knee
Jeff Beck Group; *Beck-Ola* . . . . (Epic)

Heads Will Roll
Echo & The Bunnymen; *Porcupine*............................(Sire)
Heads Will Roll
Ted Nugent; *Intensities In 10 Cities*....................... (Epic)
I Cheat The Hangman
Doobie Brothers; *Stampede*..................... (Warner Bros.)
I'm Not That Man
10,000 Maniacs; *MTV Unplugged-10,000 Maniacs* ....(Elektra)
Our Time In Eden ....(Elektra)
It's Not My Cross To Bear
Allman Brothers Band; *Allman Brothers Band* ....(Polydor)
Beginnings ....(Polydor)
Dreams ....(Polydor)
Gregg Allman Band; *I'm No Angel* ....(Epic)
Joe Hill
Arlo Guthrie & Pete Seeger; *Together In Concert* ....(Reprise)
Joan Baez; *Carry It On* .... (Vanguard)
From Every Stage .... (A&M)
One Day At A Time .... (Vanguard)
ST/Woodstock...................................... (Atlantic)
John Barleycorn
Traffic; *John Barleycorn Must Die* .... (Island)
Last Meal
Asleep At The Wheel; *Very Best Of Asleep At The Wheel*
Since 1970 ....(Relentless/Madacy)
Life In Prison
Byrds; *Jailhouse Rock (Hits From The Big*
House)-C .... (Sony Music Special Prod.)
Sweetheart Of The Rodeo .... (Columbia)
Nebraska
Bruce Springsteen; *Nebraska* .... (Columbia)
Bruce Springsteen & The E Street Band; *Bruce Springsteen & The E Street*
Band Live/1975-85 .... (Legacy)
Night The Lights Went Out In Georgia
Lynn Anderson; *Top Of The World* .... (Columbia)
Reba McEntire; *For My Broken Heart* .... (MCA)
Reba McEntire's Greatest Hits-#3: I'm A Survivor .... (MCA)
Vicki Lawrence; *Super Hits Of The '70s-Have A Nice Day-#10-C* .....(Rhino)
Nobody Knows But Me
Jimmie Rodgers; *Riding High-1929-1930*...............(Rounder)
Merle Haggard & The Strangers; *Same Train Different Time* ....(Capitol)
Only A Hangman
Brownie Ford; *Stories From Mountains, Swamps & Honky-*
Tonks ....(Flying Fish)
Over Yonder (Jonathan's Song)
Steve Earle; *Transcendental Blues* .... (Artemis)
Pigs, Sheep & Wolves
Paul Simon; *You're The One* .... (Warner Bros.)
Poor Will & The Jolly Hangman
Richard Thompson; *Guitar/Vocal* .... (Hannibal)
Pretty Noose
Soundgarden; *Down On The Upside* .... (A&M)
Public Execution
Mouse & The Traps; *Nuggets-#2-Punk-C* .... (Rhino)
Quarterdrawing Of The Dog
Siouxsie And The Banshees; *Tinderbox* .... (Geffen)
Renegade
Styx; *Pieces Of Eight*................................. (A&M)
Styx-Classics-#15 .... (A&M)
Road Goes On Forever, The
Joe Ely; *Love & Danger* .... (MCA)
Send Me To The 'Lectric Chair
David Bromberg; *Out Of The Blues-Best Of David Bromberg* ...... (Columbia)
Wanted Dead Or Alive .... (Columbia)
Hoyt Axton; *Down & Out* .... (Allegiance)
Sing Me Back Home
Alabama; *Mama's Hungry Eyes-Merle Haggard Tribute-C* ....(Arista)
Flying Burrito Brothers; *Farther Along-Best Of The Flying Burrito*
Brothers .... (A&M)
Merle Haggard & The Strangers; *Best Of Merle Haggard & The*
Strangers ....(Capitol)
Capitol Collectors Series-Merle Haggard & The Strangers........(Capitol)
For The Record: Merle Haggard-43 Legendary Hits........(BNA)
Okie From Muskogee ....(Capitol)
Songs I'll Always Sing ....(Capitol)
Smackwater Jack
Carole King; *Carole King's Greatest Hits*.............. (Epic)
Tapestry .... (Epic)
Stray Cat Blues
Rolling Stones; *Beggars Banquet* .... (Abkco)
Get Yer Ya-Ya's Out! .... (Abkco)
They're Hanging Me Tonight
Marty Robbins; *Gunfighter Ballads & Trail Songs* .... (Legacy)
Tom Dooley
Doc Watson; *Doc Watson* ....(Vanguard)
Essential Doc Watson ....(Vanguard)
Out In The Country .... (Intermedia)
Kingston Trio; *Capitol Collectors Series-The Kingston Trio* .... (Capitol)

From The Hungry i ....(Capitol)
Kingston Trio's Greatest Hits ....(Curb)
Tom Dooley ....(Capitol)
Troubadours Of The Folk Era-#3-C ....(Rhino)
Tomb Of The Unknown Love
Cassell Webb; *Songs Of A Stranger* .... (Venture)
Kenny Rogers; *The Heart Of The Matter* .... (RCA)
Torture
Jacksons; *Victory* ....(Epic)
Torture
Replacements; *All Shook Down* .... (Sire)
Torture
Cure; *Kiss Me Kiss Me Kiss Me* ....(Elektra)
Twenty-Five Minutes To Go
Johnny Cash; *Essential Johnny Cash* ....(Columbia)
Johnny Cash At Folsom Prison & San Quentin...........(Columbia)
True West ....(Columbia)
Two Years Of Torture
Lou Rawls; *Lou Rawls-At Last* .... (Blue Note)
Percy Mayfield; *Please Send Me Someone To Love* .... (Intermedia)
Walking Down Death Row
Pete Seeger; *Dangerous Songs*....................(Out Of Print)
Waterloo
Stonewall Jackson; *American Originals-Stonewall Jackson* ....(Columbia)
Billboard Top Country Hits-1959-C ....(Rhino)
Columbia Country Classics-#3-Americana-C ....(Columbia)
Country Music Classics-#1-1950s-C ....(K-Tel)
When The Whip Comes Down
Rolling Stones; *Some Girls* .... (Virgin)
Sucking In The Seventies .... (Rolling Stones)
Whip
Eddie Kendricks; *Vintage '78* ....(Arista)
Whip It
Devo; *Best Of Devo-Greatest Hits* .... (Warner Bros.)
EZ Listening Disc ....(Rykodisc)
Freedom Of Choice ....(Warner Bros.)
Last American Virgin ....(Columbia)
Whipping Post
Allman Brothers Band; *Allman Brothers Band* .... (Polydor)
At Fillmore East .... (Capricorn)
Beginnings..................................... (Polydor)
Decade Of Hits-1969-1979 .... (Polydor)
Dreams .... (Polydor)
The Road Goes On Forever, A Collection Of Their Greatest
Recordings .... (Polydor)
Whipping Post
Frank Zappa; *Them Or Us* .... (Rykodisc)

CAREFREE, No Worries

See Also: **FEAR & COURAGE, FREEDOM, HAPPINESS, HELP, RELAX, TRAINS (hobos), TRAVELING**

(You're So Square) Baby I Don't Care
Elvis Presley; *A Date With Elvis* .... (RCA)
Joni Mitchell; *Wild Things Run Fast* .... (Geffen)
59th Street Bridge Song (Feelin' Groovy)
Harper's Bizarre; *Baby Boomer Classics-More Mellow*
Sixties-C .... (JCI Assoc. Labels)
Better Days-C ....(Rhino)
Simon & Garfunkel; *Collected Works* ....(Columbia)
Parsley Sage Rosemary & Thyme ....(Columbia)
Simon & Garfunkel's Greatest Hits.................(Columbia)
The Concert In Central Park ....(Warner Bros.)
All Night Long
Faith Evans featuring Puff Daddy; *Keep The Faith* .... (Bad Boy/Arista)
Animal Song
Savage Garden; *Affirmation*.......................(Columbia)
Anything Goes
Count Basie & Tony Bennett; *Anything Goes-Capitol Sings Cole*
Porter-C ....(Capitol)
Basie Swings Bennett Sings ....(Roulette)
Dionne Warwick; *Dionne Warwick Sings Cole Porter-C* ....(Arista)
Ella Fitzgerald; *Night & Day-Cole Porter Songbook-C*.............(Verve)
Frank Sinatra; *Frank Sinatra Sings The Select Cole Porter* ....(Capitol)
Mary Martin; *Mary Martin-16 Most Requested Songs*......(Columbia)
Original Cast; *Anything Goes*......................(Epic)
Paul Whiteman & His Orchestra; *78-#24770*............. (Victor)
Yo-Yo Ma; *Anything Goes-The Music Of Cole Porter* ....(Columbia)
Backroads
Ricky Van Shelton; *Backroads*.....................(Columbia)
Battle Of Who Could Care Less
Ben Folds Five; *Whatever And Ever Amen*............. (Caroline/550)
Beautiful Day
U2; *All That You Can't Leave Behind* .... (Interscope)
Now That's What I Call Music!-#6-C .... (Virgin)

Beer Barrel Polka
Andrews Sisters; *Andrews Sisters-16 Great Performances* . . . . (MCA)
   Best Of The Andrews Sisters . . . . (MCA)
Frankie Yankovic & His Yanks; *Frankie Yankovic & His Yanks'*
   Greatest Hits . . . . (Columbia)
Will Glahe; *This Is Will Glahe-Decade Of The '30s* . . . . (RCA)

Big Deal
LeAnn Rimes; *LeAnn Rimes* . . . . (Curb)

Bumming Around
''T'' Texas Tyler; *Only Country-1950-1954-C* . . . . . . (JCI Assoc. Labels)

Bye Bye Blackbird
Dean Martin; *Swingin' Down Yonder* . . . . (Capitol)
Joe Cocker; *With A Little Help From My Friends* . . . . (A&M)
Liza Minnelli; *ST/Liza With A ''Z''* . . . . (Columbia)
Miles Davis; *Ballads* . . . . (Columbia)
   Miles Davis Quintet/Jazz Sampler #2 . . . . (Columbia)
Miles Davis Quintet; *Round About Midnight* . . . . (Columbia)

Canned Heat
Jamiroquai; *Synkronized* . . . . (Work/Epic)

Carefree
Refreshments; *Fizzy Fuzzy Big & Buzzy* . . . . (Mercury)

Carefree Country Day
Buffalo Springfield; *Last Time Around* . . . . (Atco)

Careless
Go-Betweens; *Send Me A Lullaby* . . . . (Beggar's Banquet)

Careless
Replacements; *Sorry Ma, Forgot To Take Out The Trash* . . . . (Restless)

Careless Heart
Roy Orbison; *Mystery Girl* . . . . (Virgin)

Careless Memories
Duran Duran; *Arena* . . . . (Capitol)

Careless Whisper
Dave Koz featuring Montell Jordan; *Dance* . . . . (Capitol)
Wham! Featuring George Michael; *Make It Big* . . . . (Columbia)
   Music For The Miracle-C . . . . (Epic Portrait Assoc.)

Careless Whisper
Tamia; *Tamia* . . . . (Qwest)

Couldn't Care Less About
Evan And Jaron; *We've Never Heard Of You Either* . . . . (Island)

Devil May Care
Diana Krall; *When I Look In Your Eyes* . . . . (GRP)
Frank Sinatra; *What'll I Do* . . . . (RCA)
Tommy Dorsey & Frank Sinatra; *Sessions-#1-February 1, 1940-July*
   17, 1940 . . . . (RCA)

Does Anybody Out There Even Care
Lenny Kravitz; *Let Love Rule* . . . . (Virgin)

Don't Care
King's X; *Dogman* . . . . (Atlantic)

Don't Care
Victor; *Victor* . . . . (Atlantic)

Don't Let It Bother You
Fats Waller; *Have A Little Dream On Me* . . . . (Eclipse)

Don't Worry
B-52's; *Whammy* . . . . (Warner Bros.)

Don't Worry
Goo Goo Dolls; *Superstar Car Wash* . . . . (Metal Blade)

Don't Worry
Sister Double Happiness; *Sister Double Happiness* . . . . (SST)

Don't Worry About Me
Doris Day; *Doris Day Sings 22 Great Songs-Original Big Band* . . . . (Hindsight)
Ella Fitzgerald; *Classy Pair* . . . . (Pablo)
Ella Fitzgerald & Joe Pass; *Easy Living* . . . . (Pablo)

Don't Worry About The Government
Talking Heads; *'77* . . . . (Sire)
   Name Of This Band Is Talking Heads . . . . (Sire)
   Popular Favorites-1984-1992 . . . . (Sire)

Don't Worry 'bout Me
Frank Sinatra; *Capitol Collectors Series-Frank Sinatra* . . . . (Capitol)

Don't Worry, Be Happy
Bobby McFerrin; *Simple Pleasures* . . . . (EMI)
   ST/Cocktail . . . . (Elektra)

Don't You Care
Buckinghams; *Buckinghams' Greatest Hits* . . . . (Columbia)

Don't You Worry
Beloved; *Happiness* . . . . (Atlantic)

Don't You Worry 'bout A Thing
Incognito; *Tribes, Vibes & Scribes* . . . . (Verve)

Downtown
B-52's; *B-52's* . . . . (Warner Bros.)
Frank Sinatra; *Strangers In The Night* . . . . (Reprise)
Petula Clark; *Dick Clark's 21 All-Time Hits-#2-C* . . . . (Original Sound)
   Petula Clark's Greatest Hits . . . . (Crescendo)

Family Affair
Mary J. Blige; *No More Drama* . . . . (MCA)

First Week, Last Week Carefree
Talking Heads; *'77* . . . . (Sire)

Get Happy
Benny Goodman; *Benny Goodman's Greatest Hits* . . . . (RCA Victor)

   Ella Fitzgerald; *Harold Arlen Songbook-#2* . . . . (Verve)
Judy Garland; *Best Of Judy Garland In Hollywood* . . . . (Turner Classic Movies)
Nat Shilkret & The Victor Orchestra; *78-#22444* . . . . (Victor)

Good Day To Run
Darryl Worley; *Hard Rain Don't Last* . . . . (DreamWorks/SKG)

Hakuna Matata
Jimmy Cliff; *Disney's Greatest Pop Hits-C* . . . . (Disney)
Nathan Lane/Ernie Sabella/Jason Weaver/Joseph Williams; *ST/The*
   Lion King . . . . (Walt Disney)
Original Cast; *The Lion King* . . . . (Disney)
Rembrandts; *Disney's Music From The Park-C* . . . . (Disney)

Happiness Street
Georgia Gibbs; *Best Of Georgia Gibbs-The Mercury Years* . . . . (Chronicles)

Happy Days Are Here Again
Barbra Streisand; *A Happening In Central Park* . . . . (Columbia)
   Barbra Streisand's Greatest Hits . . . . (Columbia)
   One Voice . . . . (Columbia)
   The Barbra Streisand Album . . . . (Columbia)
Leo Reisman & His Orchestra; *Nipper's Greatest Hits Of The*
   '30s-#1-C . . . . (RCA)

Happy Girl
Beth Nielsen Chapman; *Sand And Water* . . . . (Reprise)
Martina McBride; *Evolution* . . . . (RCA)

Heads Carolina, Tails California
Jo Dee Messina; *Greatest Hits Of Country Dance-C* . . . . (Curb)
   Jo Dee Messina . . . . (Curb)

Heaven Right Here
Jeb Loy Nichols; *Just What Time It Is* . . . . (Rykodisc)

High Hopes
Doris Day; *The Envelope Please-Academy Award Winning Songs (1934-*
   1993)-C . . . . (Rhino)
Frank Sinatra; *Best Of The Capitol Years* . . . . (Capitol)
   ST/Sinatra-CBS Mini-Series . . . . (Reprise)

Honky Tonk Attitude
Joe Diffie; *Honky Tonk Attitude* . . . . (Epic)

Hoop-Dee-Doo
Perry Como; *Perry Como's Greatest Hits* . . . . (RCA)

How Your Love Makes Me Feel
Diamond Rio; *Diamond Rio's Greatest Hits* . . . . (Arista)

I Couldn't Care Less
Frank Sinatra; *The Capitol Years* . . . . (Capitol)

I Don't Care
Bad Company; *Holy Water* . . . . (Atco)

I Don't Care
Elton John & Gary Osborne; *A Single Man* . . . . (MCA)

I Don't Care
Magnapop; *Rubbing It Doesn't Help* . . . . (Play It Again Sam)

I Don't Care
Ramones; *Rocket To Russia* . . . . (Sire)

I Don't Care
Shakespear's Sister; *Hormonally Yours* . . . . (London)

I Don't Care About You
Fear; *The Record* . . . . (Slash)

I Don't Care About You
Guns N' Roses; *The Spaghetti Incident?* . . . . (Geffen)

I Don't Care Anymore
Phil Collins; *Hello, I Must Be Going* . . . . (Atlantic)

I Don't Care If The Sun Don't Shine
Elvis Presley; *A Golden Celebration* . . . . (RCA)
   The Sun Sessions . . . . (RCA)

I Don't Care Too Much For Raggae Dub
Sublime; *Robbin' The Hood* . . . . (Gasoline Alley)

I Don't Worry About A Thing
Mose Allison; *Best Of Mose Allison* . . . . (Rhino)
   I Don't Worry About A Thing . . . . (Rhino)

I Got Rhythm
Ella Fitzgerald; *George & Ira Gershwin Songbook* . . . . (Verve)
Ethel Waters; *I Got Rhythm: The Smithsonian George Gershwin*
   Collection-C . . . . (Smithsonian Collection)
Happenings; *'60s Rock Classics-#1-C* . . . . (Rhino)
Judy Garland; *Judy Garland-Collector's Items-1936-1945* . . . . (MCA)
Louis Armstrong; *Essential Louis Armstrong* . . . . (MCA)
Original Cast; *Girl Crazy* . . . . (Nonesuch)
Original London Cast; *Crazy For You* . . . . (RCA)
Robert Palmer; *Glory Of Gershwin Featuring Larry Adler-C* . . . . . . (Mercury)

I Just Don't Care
Moody Blues; *Other Side Of Life* . . . . (Polydor)

I Should Care
Frank Sinatra; *Best Of The Columbia Years-1943-1952* . . . . (Columbia)

I Used To Worry
Delbert McClinton; *Never Been Rocked Enough* . . . . (Curb)

I Wanna Go Too Far
Trisha Yearwood; *Thinkin' About You* . . . . (MCA)

I'm So Bad (Baby I Don't Care)
Motorhead; *1916* . . . . (WTG)

In The Summertime
Mungo Jerry; *In The Summertime-Best Of Mungo Jerry* . . . . (Rhino)
   Super Hits Of The '70s-Have A Nice Day-#3-C . . . . (Rhino)

Is It Wicked Not To Care?
Belle And Sebastion; *Boy With The Arab Strap* .... (Matador)
It Don't Matter To Me
Bread; *Bread-Anthology* .... (Elektra)
Bread-Retrospective .... (Rhino)
Just Ain't
Lester Flatt, Earl Scruggs & The Foggy Mountain Boys; *Essential Flatt & Scruggs-'Tis Sweet To Be Remembered* .... (Legacy)
Last Night On Earth
U2; *Pop* .... (Island)
Let's Live For Today
Grass Roots; *At The Hop* .... (MCA)
Grass Roots-All-Time Greatest Hits .... (MCA)
Let's Live For Today .... (MCA Special Prod.)
Summer Of Love-#1-C .... (Rhino)
Vintage Music-#10-C .... (MCA)
Life Is Just A Bowl Of Cherries
Ethel Merman; *The Ethel Merman Collection* .... (Razor & Tie)
Jaye P. Morgan; *The Jaye P. Morgan Story* .... (Simitar)
Original Cast; *Fosse* .... (RCA Victor)
Rudy Vallee & His Connecticut Yankees; *As Time Goes By* .... (Varese Sarabande)
Little Shoe Maker
Eddie Fisher; *Very Best Of Eddie Fisher* .... (Taragon)
Gaylords; *Choice Voices! Pop Vocal Group Gems Of The '50s-C* .... (Collector's Choice)
Lucky One
Alison Krauss & Union Station; *New Favorite* .... (Rounder)
Maryland
Vonda Shepard; *ST/Songs From "Ally McBeal" Featuring Vonda Shepard* .... (550/Epic)
Mexico
James Taylor; *Gorilla* .... (Warner Bros.)
James Taylor-Live .... (Columbia)
James Taylor's Greatest Hits .... (Warner Bros.)
Mellow Rock Hits Of The '70s-Summer Breeze-C .... (Rhino)
Jimmy Buffett; *Barometer Soup* .... (Margaritaville)
Most Beautiful Girl In The World
Frank Sinatra; *Strangers In The Night* .... (Reprise)
Tony Bennett; *Rodgers & Hart Songbook* .... (DRG)
Tony Bennett Sings More Great Rodgers & Hart .... (Improv)
Muddy Water
Keb' Mo'; *Slow Down* .... (550/Epic/Okeh)
My Sacrifice
Creed; *Weathered* .... (Wind-up)
New Attitude
Patti LaBelle; *Classic Soul-C* .... (MCA)
I Am Woman-C .... (Nick At Nite)
Soundtrack Smashes-'80s & More-C .... (MCA)
ST/Beverly Hills Cop .... (MCA)
Off The Wall
Jacksons; *Jacksons Live* .... (Epic)
Michael Jackson; *Off The Wall* .... (Epic)
Old Enough To Know Better
Wade Hayes; *Country Dance Hits-C* .... (Columbia)
Old Enough To Know Better .... (Columbia)
Steppin' Country-#2-C .... (Columbia)
Super Hits Of 1994-C .... (Columbia)
On The Sunny Side Of The Street
Diana Krall; *Stepping Out* .... (Justin Time)
Frank Sinatra; *Come Swing With Me!* .... (Capitol)
One More For The Road .... (Capitol)
Sentimental Journey .... (Capitol)
The Capitol Years .... (Capitol)
Judy Garland; *Best Of Judy Garland* .... (MCA)
Louis Armstrong; *Best Of Louis Armstrong* .... (MCA)
Chicago Concert 1956 .... (Columbia)
Jazz Club-Vocal .... (Verve)
Music Autobiography .... (MCA)
Ted Lewis & His Orchestra; *Charming Gents Of Stage & Screen-C* .... (Legacy)
Those Wonderful Years: Puttin' On The Ritz-C .... (JCI Assoc. Labels)
One Way Ticket (Because I Can)
LeAnn Rimes; *Blue* .... (MCG/Curb)
Out With A Bang
David Lee Murphy; *Out With A Bang* .... (MCA)
Peaceful World
John Mellencamp; *Cuttin' Heads* .... (Columbia)
God Bless America-C .... (Columbia)
The Concert For New York City-C .... (Columbia)
Pretending To Care
Jennifer Warnes; *The Hunter* .... (Private Music)
Todd Rundgren; *A Cappella* .... (Warner Bros.)
Pretending To Care
Daryl Braithwaite; *Edge* .... (Epic Portrait Assoc.)
Raindrops Keep Fallin' On My Head
B.J. Thomas; *'70s Greatest Rock Hits-#9-#1 Hits-C* .... (Priority)
B.J. Thomas' Greatest Hits .... (Rhino)
B.J. Thomas-16 Greatest Hits .... (Trip)
Best Of B.J. Thomas .... (Dominion Entert.)
ST/Butch Cassidy & The Sundance Kid .... (A&M)
ST/Forrest Gump .... (Epic/Sony Music Soundtrax)
Saddle Tramp
Marty Robbins; *Gunfighter Ballads & Trail Songs* .... (Legacy)
Marty Robbins-More Greatest Hits .... (Columbia)
Scary Kisses
Voice Of The Beehive; *Sex And Misery* .... (Discovery)
See If I Care
Martika; *Martika* .... (Columbia)
She Don't Care About Time
Byrds; *Original Singles-#1-1965-1967* .... (Columbia)
The Byrds .... (Columbia)
She Thinks I Still Care
Elvis Presley; *Moody Blue* .... (RCA)
George Jones; *Best Of George Jones-1955-1967* .... (Rhino)
Billboard Top Country Hits-1962-C .... (Rhino)
George Jones' All-Time Greatest Hits .... (Epic)
George Jones-Super Hits-#2 .... (Epic)
Silver, Sharp And Could Not Care
Residents; *God In Three Persons* .... (East Side Digital)
Sittin' On Top Of The World
Bob Dylan; *Good As I Been To You* .... (Columbia)
Bob Wills & His Texas Playboys; *Bob Wills & His Texas Playboys-24 Great Hits* .... (Polydor)
Bob Wills-Anthology .... (Sony Music Special Prod.)
Tiffany Transcriptions-#8-More Of The Best .... (Rhino)
Cream; *Wheels Of Fire* .... (Polydor)
Doc Watson; *Doc Watson* .... (Vanguard)
Greatest Folksingers Of The '60s-C .... (Vanguard)
Old Timey Concert .... (Vanguard)
Grateful Dead; *Grateful Dead (Skull & Roses)* .... (Warner Bros.)
Jerry Jeff Walker; *Will The Circle Be Unbroken-#2-C* .... (Uni)
Ray Charles; *20 Golden Pieces Of Ray Charles* .... (Bulldog)
Sweet Honey In The Rock; *Believe I'll Run On, See What The End's Gonna Be* .... (Redwood)
Stay (Wasting Time)
Dave Matthews Band; *Before These Crowded Streets* .... (RCA)
Summer Song
Chad & Jeremy; *Best Of Chad & Jeremy* .... (K-Tel)
Capitol Gold-Best Of Chad & Jeremy .... (Capitol)
History Of British Rock-#2-C .... (Rhino)
Tears Don't Care Who Cries Them
k.d. lang; *Shadowland* .... (Sire)
Theme From "The Monkees"
Monkees; *Monkees' Greatest Hits* .... (Rhino)
Original Soundtrack; *Television's Greatest Hits-#2-C* .... (TVT)
They Don't Care About Us
Michael Jackson; *HIStory: Past, Present And Future-Book 1-C* .... (Epic)
Things Have Changed
Bob Dylan; *Essential Bob Dylan* .... (Columbia)
ST/Wonder Boys .... (Columbia)
Too Cool To Care
Bobs; *Plugged* .... (Rounder)
Up On The Roof
Cryan' Shames; *Scratch In The Sky* .... (Columbia)
Drifters; *Cruisin'-1962-C* .... (Increase)
Drifters' Greatest Hits .... (Gusto)
Drifters-16 Greatest Hits .... (Trip)
Drifters-Golden Hits .... (Atlantic)
James Taylor; *Flag* .... (Columbia)
The Concert For New York City-C .... (Columbia)
Nylons; *Four On The Floor* .... (Scotti Bros.)
Up, Up & Away
5th Dimension; *5th Dimension-Anthology 1967-1973* .... (Rhino)
Greatest Hits On Earth .... (Arista)
We'll Sing In The Sunshine
Gale Garnett; *21 Country Rock & Love Songs Of The '50s & '60s-#1-C* .... (Laurie)
Nipper's Greatest Hits Of The '60s-#1-C .... (RCA)
What I Got
Sublime; *Now That's What I Call Music!-#2-C* .... (Virgin)
Sublime .... (Gasoline Alley)
When No One Cares
Frank Sinatra; *Concepts* .... (Capitol)
No One Cares .... (Capitol)
Who Cares Wins
Anthrax; *State Of Euphoria* .... (Island)
Who Cares?
Stan Getz; *Gershwin Jazz* .... (Legacy)
Why Should I Care
Toni Braxton; *Secrets* .... (LaFace)
Why Worry
Dire Straits; *Brothers In Arms* .... (Warner Bros.)
You Can Feel Bad
Patty Loveless; *Patty Loveless-Classics* .... (Epic)
Super Hits Of 1996-C .... (Epic)
The Trouble With The Truth .... (Epic)
You Don't Care About Us
Placebo; *Without You I'm Nothing* .... (Virgin)

You Don't Care Nothin'
Rancid; ...And Out Come The Wolves .... (Epitaph)
You Don't Have To Worry
En Vogue; Born To Sing .... (Atlantic)
You Don't Have To Worry
New Edition; Home Again .... (MCA)

CARNIVALS, Amusement Parks & Rides, Boardwalk, Circus, Clowns, Fairs, Mardi Gras, Parades
See Also: **CITIES: NEW ORLEANS, FUN, HAPPINESS**

1941
Nilsson; Pandemonium Shadow Show .... (RCA)
4th Of July, Asbury Park (Sandy)
Bruce Springsteen; The Wild, The Innocent & The E Street Shuffle .. (Columbia)
Bruce Springsteen & The E Street Band; Bruce Springsteen & The E Street Band Live/1975-85 .... (Legacy)
76 Trombones
Original Cast; The Music Man .... (Gold Rush)
Animal Fair
Original Soundtrack; School Days-Kids Classics .... (Benson)
Arcade Queen
Rubinoos; Back To The Drawing Board .... (Beserkley)
Assholes On Parade
Timbuk 3; Best Of Timbuk 3 .... (I.R.S.)
At The Chicago World's Fair
Original Cast; Show Boat .... (RCA Victor)
At The Fair In Pacanow
Myron Floren; Polka Party................................. (Ranwood)
Before The Parade Passes By
Carol Channing/Original Cast; Hello Dolly! .... (RCA)
Original Cast; Hello Dolly! .... (RCA)
Being For The Benefit Of Mr. Kite
Beatles; Beatles-Box Set .... (Capitol)
Sgt. Pepper's Lonely Hearts Club Band.................... (Capitol)
Bourbon Street Parade
Al Hirt; Best Of Al Hirt .... (RCA)
Dukes Of Dixieland; Digital Dixieland .... (Pro Jazz)
Pete Fountain; Best Of Pete Fountain-#2 .... (MCA)
Preservation Hall Jazz Band; New Orleans-#4 .... (Columbia)
Wynton Marsalis; Standard Time-#2-Intimacy Calling .... (Columbia)
Bulls On Parade
Rage Against The Machine; Evil Empire ....(Epic)
Cafe Carnival
Craig Chaquico; Panorama: The Best Of Craig Chaquico ...... (Higher Octave)
Carnaval
Santana; Festival .... (Columbia)
Moonflower .... (Columbia)
Sergio Mendes; Sergio Mendes .... (A&M)
Carney
Leon Russell; Carney .... (Right Stuff)
Carnival
Mose Allison; Down Home Piano ....(Prestige)
Mose Allison ....(Prestige)
Carnival
Natalie Merchant; Tigerlily................................ (Elektra)
Carnival
Stomu Yamashta & Others; Go Live From Paris .... (Island)
Carnival
Eric Clapton; No Reason To Cry............................. (RSO)
Carnival
Wyclef Jean featuring Sweet Mickey; Presents The Carnival F/Refugee Allstars .... (Ruffhouse/Columbia)
Carnival
Tito Puente; Puente Now! .... (Crescendo)
Carnival
Simple Minds; Real To Real Cacophony .... (Virgin)
Carnival In New Orleans
Professor Longhair; Last Mardi Gras........................ (Atlantic)
Carnival Is Over
Seekers; Best Of The Seekers .... (Capitol)
Carnival Of Sorts
R.E.M.; Dead Letter Office ....(I.R.S.)
Carnival Of Venice
Carmen Cavallaro; Best Of Carmen Cavallaro ....(MCA)
Mantovani; Mantovani's Italia........................... (Bainbridge)
Carnival Song
Tim Buckley; Best Of Tim Buckley......................... (Rhino)
Carousel
Original Cast; Jacques Brel Is Alive & Well And Living In New York City .... (Columbia)
Jacques Brel Is Alive & Well And Living In New York City .... (Atlantic)
Carousel
Siouxsie And The Banshees; Peepshow .... (Geffen)

Carousel Man
Cher; Cher's Greatest Hits .... (MCA)
Carousel Of Love
Jane Olivor; First Night .... (Columbia)
Jane Olivor In Concert .... (Columbia)
Carousel Waltz
Original Cast; Carousel.................................... (MCA)
Cathy's Clown
Everly Brothers; Billboard Top Rock 'N' Roll Hits-1960-C .... (Rhino)
Golden Hits Of The Everly Brothers..................... (Warner Bros.)
The Reunion Concert-Live At Albert Hall 1983 .... (Mercury)
Very Best Of The Everly Brothers .... (Warner Bros.)
Reba McEntire; Sweet Sixteen .... (MCA)
Children In The Carousel
Mabel Mercer & Bobby Short; At Town Hall ....(Atlantic)
Circle Game, The
Buffy Sainte-Marie; Best Of Buffy Sainte-Marie............. (Vanguard)
Fire & Fleet & Candlelight .... (Vanguard)
Ian & Sylvia; Ian & Sylvia's Greatest Hits .... (Vanguard)
Joni Mitchell; Ladies Of The Canyon .... (Reprise)
Joni Mitchell with Tom Scott & The L.A. Express; Miles Of Aisles .... (Asylum)
Tom Rush; Classic Rush .... (Elektra)
The Circle Game .... (Elektra)
Circus
Erasure; Circus ....(Sire)
Two Ring Circus ....(Sire)
Circus Girl
Gretchen Peters; The Secret Of Life............... (Purple Crayon Prod.)
Circus Of Heaven
Yes; Tormato..(Atlantic)
Circus Polka
Myron Floren; 22 Great Polkas .... (Ranwood)
Great Polka Hits .... (Ranwood)
Clown Woman
Montrose; Montrose .... (Warner Bros.)
Clown, The
Conway Twitty; Latest Greatest Hits-#1 .... (Warner Bros.)
Number One's: The Warner Bros. Years .... (Warner Bros.)
Southern Comfort.................................... (Warner Bros.)
Clown, The
Images; Master Series Sampler '89-C .... (Capitol)
Clowntime Is Over
Elvis Costello; Girls Girls Girls .... (Columbia)
Taking Liberties .... (Columbia)
Elvis Costello & The Attractions; Get Happy! .... (Rykodisc)
Coney Island Baby
Excellents; WCBS FM 101 History Of Rock-Doo-Wop-#1-C ..... (Collectables)
Lou Reed; City Lights .... (Arista)
Walk On The Wild Side-The Best Of Lou Reed .... (RCA)
Coney Island Washboard
Mills Brothers; 50th Anniversary .... (Ranwood)
Mills Brothers-22 Great Hits .... (Ranwood)
Cowboys & Clowns
Billy Strange; Great Western Themes ....(Crescendo)
Ronnie Milsap; ST/Bronco Billy .... (Elektra)
Death Of A Clown
Kinks; Kink Kronikles.................................... (Reprise)
Something Else .... (Reprise)
Disney Girls
Art Garfunkel; Breakaway .... (Columbia)
Beach Boys; Surf's Up ....(Caribou)
Captain & Tennille; Captain & Tennille's Greatest Hits .... (A&M)
Don't Cry Out Loud
Melissa Manchester; Melissa Manchester's Greatest Hits .... (Arista)
Peter Allen; At His Best .... (A&M)
I Could Have Been A Sailor .... (A&M)
It Is Time For Peter Allen .... (A&M)
Don't Rain On My Parade
Barbra Streisand; Barbra Streisand...and other musical instruments .... (Columbia)
Barbra Streisand's Greatest Hits .... (Columbia)
Live Concert At The Forum .... (Columbia)
Original Cast-Funny Girl .... (Capitol)
ST/Funny Girl.. (Columbia)
Easter Parade
Andy Russell; Puttin' On The Ritz-Capitol Sings Berlin-C .... (Capitol)
Bing Crosby; All Time Best Of Bing Crosby .... (Curb)
Judy Garland & Fred Astaire; ST/Easter Parade............. (Rhino)
Sarah Vaughan; Complete Sarah Vaughan On Mercury-#2 ..... (Mercury)
Elephant Day Parade
Beat Farmers; The Pursuit Of Happiness .... (Curb)
Elephant Trainer
Liz Story; Part Of Fortune ....(Novus)
Fourth Of July At A County Fair
Red Clay Ramblers; Chuckin' The Frizz .... (Flying Fish)
Funhouse
Kid 'N Play; Kid 'N Play's Funhouse .... (Select)
Go Let It Out
Oasis; Standing On The Shoulders Of Giants .... (Epic)

Goodbye Cruel World
James Darren; *Best Of James Darren* . . . . (Rhino)
   Billboard Top Rock 'N' Roll Hits-1961-C . . . . (Rhino)

Halloween Parade
Lou Reed; *New York* . . . . (Sire)

Here Comes The Big Parade
Harry Connick, Jr.; *She* . . . . (Columbia)

Highwire
Rolling Stones; *Flashpoint* . . . . (Virgin)

Honky Tonk Merry Go Round
Patsy Cline; *20 Golden Pieces Of Patsy Cline* . . . . (Bulldog)
   Patsy Cline . . . . (Audio Fidelity)
   Today Tomorrow & Forever . . . . (MCA)
   Try Again . . . . (Quicksilver)
   Walkin' Dreams-Her First Recordings-#1 . . . . (Rhino)

Hurdy Gurdy Man
Butthole Surfers; *ST/Dumb And Dumber* . . . . (RCA)
Donovan; *Donovan's Greatest Hits* . . . . (Epic)
   Hurdy Gurdy Man . . . . (Epic)

I Love A Parade
Cab Calloway; *Bessie Smith/Louis Armstrong/Cab Calloway* . . . . . . (Biograph)

I Remember Coney Island
Lounge Lizards; *Lounge Lizards* . . . . (Editions E.G.)

June Parade
Vic Shine; *Far & Distant Shore* . . . . (RCA)

Karn Evil 9
Emerson, Lake & Palmer; *Best Of Emerson, Lake & Palmer* . . . . (Rhino)
   Brain Salad Surgery . . . . (Rhino)
   Welcome back, my friends, to the show that never ends-Ladies and
   Gentlemen . . . . (Manticore)

Life Is A Carnival
Band; *Best Of The Band* . . . . (Capitol)
   Cahoots . . . . (Capitol)
   Rock Of Ages . . . . (Capitol)
   The Band-Anthology-#2 . . . . (Capitol)
   The Last Waltz . . . . (Warner Bros.)

Little Bitty Tear
Burl Ives; *Best Of Burl Ives-#2* . . . . (MCA)
   Burl Ives Live . . . . (MCA)
   MCA Records 30 Years Of Hits-1958-1988-C . . . . (MCA)
Hank Cochran; *45-#47062* . . . . (Elektra)

Love Parade
Dream Academy; *Dream Academy* . . . . (Warner Bros.)

Love Rollercoaster
Ohio Players; *Honey* . . . . (Mercury)
   Ohio Players-Gold . . . . (Mercury)
   The Jam . . . . (Mercury)
Red Hot Chili Peppers; *ST/Beavis & Butt-Head Do America* . . . . (Geffen)

Magical Mystery Tour
Beatles; *Magical Mystery Tour* . . . . (Capitol)
   Reel Music . . . . (Capitol)
   The Beatles/1967-1970 . . . . (Capitol)

Mardi Gras
Gino Vannelli; *Pauper In Paradise* . . . . (A&M)

Mardi Gras
Original Cast; *House Of Flowers* . . . . (Sony Music Special Prod.)

Mardi Gras Boogie
Clifton Chenier; *In New Orleans* . . . . (Crescendo)

Mardi Gras In New Orleans
Professor Longhair; *Atlantic Rhythm & Blues 1947-1974-#1 (1947-*
   1952)-C . . . . (Atlantic)
   New Orleans Jazz & Heritage Festival-1976-C . . . . (Rhino)
   New Orleans Piano-Blues Originals-#2 . . . . (Atlantic)
Rockin' Dopsie; *Alligator Stomp-#2-C* . . . . (Rhino)

Mardi Gras Mambo
Hawketts; *Treacherous: A History Of The Neville Brothers* . . . . (Rhino)

Meet Me In St. Louis, Louis
Judy Garland; *Best Of Judy Garland* . . . . (MCA)

Merry Go Round
Charlie Parker; *Bird/Savoy Recordings (Master Takes)* . . . . (Savoy)
   Bird/Savoy Recordings (Master Takes)-#2 . . . . (Savoy)
   Charlie Parker-Complete Savoy Studio Sessions . . . . (Savoy)
   Encores-Charlie Parker-#2 . . . . (Savoy)
J.B. Summers; *Big Band Blues* . . . . (Collectables)
   Collectables Blues Collection-#2-C . . . . (Collectables)
   J.B. Summers & The Blues Shouters . . . . (Collectables)

Merry Go Round
Replacements; *All Shook Down* . . . . (Sire)

Merry Go Round
Keith Sweat; *I'll Give All My Love To You* . . . . (Vintertainment)

Merry Go Round
Buffalo Springfield; *Last Time Around* . . . . (Atco)

Merry Go Round
Neil Diamond; *And The Singer Sings His Song* . . . . (MCA)
   Velvet Gloves & Spit . . . . (MCA Special Prod.)

Midnight Carnival
Chris Mars; *Horseshoes & Hand Grenades* . . . . (Smash)

Mrs. Potter's Lullaby
Counting Crows; *This Desert Life* . . . . (David Geffen Co.)

My Carnival
Wings; *Venus And Mars* . . . . (Capitol)

Night The Carousel Burned Down
Todd Rundgren; *Something/Anything?* . . . . (Rhino)

Nobody's Gonna Rain On Our Parade
Kathy Mattea; *Walking Away A Winner* . . . . (Mercury)

On A Carousel
Hollies; *Best Of The Hollies* . . . . (EMI)
   History Of British Rock-#6-C . . . . (Rhino)
   The Hollies' Greatest Hits . . . . (Epic)

Opryland In Paris
Andy Badale & The Beer Garden Band; *Nashville Beer Garden* . . . . . (Ranwood)

Paducah Parade
Bob Crosby; *The Uncollected Bob Crosby-#2-1952-1953* . . . . (Hindsight)

Palisades Park
Beach Boys; *15 Big Ones* . . . . (Brother)
Freddy Cannon; *14 Booming Hits* . . . . (Rhino)
   Billboard Top Rock 'N' Roll Hits-1962-C . . . . (Rhino)
   Freddy Cannon-His Latest & Greatest . . . . (Critique)
   Memories Of The Cow Palace . . . . (Rhino)
   Oldies But Goodies-#11-C . . . . (Original Sound)
Ramones; *Brain Drain* . . . . (Sire)

Pink Elephants On Parade
Barbara Cook; *Disney Album* . . . . (Disney)

Planet Of The Clowns
Bruce Cockburn; *Trouble With Normal* . . . . (Columbia)

Pocket Of A Clown
Dwight Yoakam; *This Time* . . . . (Reprise)

Psycho Circus
Kiss; *Psycho Circus* . . . . (Mercury)

Rollercoaster
Echo & The Bunnymen; *45-#7-28260* . . . . (Sire)
Fabulous Thunderbirds; *Walk That Walk Talk That Talk* . . . (Epic Portrait Assoc.)

Rollercoaster
Jesus & Mary Chain; *Honey's Dead* . . . . (Def American)

Rollercoaster
Mighty Lemon Drops; *Out Of Hand* . . . . (Sire)

Rollercoaster
Fabulous Thunderbirds; *Walk That Walk Talk That Talk* . . . (Epic Portrait Assoc.)

Roseville Fair
Nanci Griffith; *One Fair Summer Evening* . . . . (MCA)

See The Funny Little Clown
Bobby Goldsboro; *10th Anniversary Album-#1* . . . . (EMI)
   Bobby Goldsboro's Greatest Hits . . . . (Liberty)
   Honey-Best Of Bobby Goldsboro . . . . (EMI)

Send In The Clowns
Barbra Streisand; *The Broadway Album* . . . . (Columbia)
Carmen McRae; *Sarah-Dedicated To You* . . . . (Novus)
Frank Sinatra; *The Reprise Collection* . . . . (Reprise)
Judy Collins; *Judith* . . . . (Elektra)
   So Early In The Spring, The First 15 Years . . . . (Elektra)
Original Cast; *Little Night Music* . . . . (Columbia)

She Moved Through The Fair
Art Garfunkel; *Watermark* . . . . (Legacy)
James Galway & The Chieftains; *In Ireland* . . . . (RCA)

She's A Carnival
Siouxsie And The Banshees; *Kiss In The Dream House* . . . . (Geffen)

Side Show
Blue Magic; *Blue Magic* . . . . (Atco)
   Blue Magic Live . . . . (WMOT)
   Blue Magic's Greatest Hits . . . . (Omni)
   Didn't It Blow Your Mind: Soul Hits Of The '70s-#13-C . . . . (Rhino)
   Golden Age Of Black Music-1970-1975-C . . . . (Atlantic)
   Magic Of The Blue-Greatest Hits . . . . (Collectables)

Something Like That
Tim McGraw; *A Place In The Sun* . . . . (Curb)
   Tim McGraw's Greatest Hits . . . . (Curb)

Spanish Eyes
Ricky Martin; *Ricky Martin* . . . . (Columbia)

Spinning Wheel
Blood, Sweat & Tears; *Blood, Sweat & Tears* . . . . (Columbia)
   Blood, Sweat & Tears Greatest Hits . . . . (Columbia)
   Rock Classics Of The '60s-C . . . . (Columbia)

State Fair
Doug Supernaw; *Deep Thoughts From A Shallow Mind* . . . . (BNA)

Stayed Too Long At The Fair
Bonnie Raitt; *Give It Up* . . . . (Warner Bros.)

Stuck In The Middle With You
Stealers Wheel; *Super Hits Of The '70s-Have A Nice Day-#10-C* . . . . . . (Rhino)

Sweethearts On Parade
Guy Lombardo & His Royal Canadians; *Best Of Guy Lombardo* . . . . . (Curb)
   Best Of Guy Lombardo . . . . (MCA)
Louis Armstrong; *Louis Armstrong-Vol. 7-You're Driving Me*
   Crazy . . . . (Columbia)
Pete Fountain; *Pete Fountain's New Orleans* . . . . (MCA)
Roy Eldridge; *Happy Time* . . . . (Pablo)

Take Me To The Fair
Elvis Presley; *It Happened At The World's Fair* . . . . (RCA)

Original Soundtrack; *Camelot* . . . . (Warner Bros.)
Take Me To The Mardi Gras
Paul Simon; *There Goes Rhymin' Simon* . . . . (Columbia)
Tears Of A Clown
English Beat; *I Just Can't Stop It* . . . .(I.R.S.)
What Is Beat. . . . .(I.R.S.)
Smokey Robinson & The Miracles; *25 #1 Hits From 25 Years-C* . . . (Motown)
Billboard Top Rock 'N' Roll Hits-1970-C . . . . (Rhino)
Compact Command Performances-Smokey Robinson & The
Miracles . . . . (Motown)
Endless Love-Motown's Greatest Love Songs-C . . . . (Motown)
Smokey Robinson & The Miracles' Anthology. . . . . (Motown)
Tears Of A Clown. . . . . (Motown)
Thanks For The Ride On The MerryGoRound
Andy Badale & The Beer Garden Band; *Nashville Beer Garden* . . . . .(Ranwood)
That Song About The Midway
Bonnie Raitt; *Streetlights* . . . . (Warner Bros.)
Joni Mitchell; *Clouds* . . . . (Reprise)
Theme From "Jurassic Park"
John Williams; *ST/Jurassic Park* . . . .(MCA)
Theme From "Monty Python's Flying Circus"
Original Soundtrack; *Television's Greatest Hits-#2-C* . . . . (TVT)
Then You May Take Me To The Fair
Original Cast; *Camelot* . . . . (Columbia)
Vanessa Redgrave; *ST/Camelot* . . . .(Warner Bros.)
Things We Did Last Summer
Beach Boys; *Good Vibrations-Thirty Years Of The Beach Boys* . . . . (Capitol)
Frank Sinatra; *Sinatra Rarities-Columbia Years* . . . . (Columbia)
Michael Feinstein; *Michael Feinstein Sings The Jule Styne*
Songbook . . . . (Nonesuch)
Third Man Theme (Harry Lime Theme)
Band; *Moondog Matinee* . . . . (Capitol)
Dukes Of Dixieland; *Dukes Of Dixieland's Greatest Hits* . . . .(MCA)
Guy Lombardo & His Royal Canadians; *Best Of Guy Lombardo* . . . . . . (Curb)
This Ain't Disneyland
Forever Einstein; *Opportunity Crosses The Bridge* . . . .(Cuneiform)
Ticket To Ride
Beatles; *Beatles 1* . . . . (Capitol)
Beatles-20 Greatest Hits . . . . (Capitol)
Beatles-Box Set . . . . (Capitol)
Reel Music . . . . (Capitol)
ST/Help!. . . . . (Capitol)
The Beatles At The Hollywood Bowl . . . . (Capitol)
The Beatles/1962-1966 . . . . (Capitol)
Carpenters; *Carpenters-Classics-#2.* . . . . (A&M)
Carpenters-The Singles 1969-1973 . . . . (A&M)
From The Top . . . . (A&M)
Ticket To Ride . . . . (A&M)
Yesterday Once More. . . . . (A&M)
Vanilla Fudge; *Best Of Vanilla Fudge* . . . . (Atco)
Vanilla Fudge . . . . (Atco)
Tightrope
Stevie Ray Vaughan and Double Trouble; *In Step* . . . .(Epic)
Tightrope
Electric Light Orchestra; *Afterglow* . . . .(Epic)
Tightrope
Tracy Nelson; *Homemade Songs* . . . . (Flying Fish)
Tightrope
Bob Seger & The Silver Bullet Band; *Like A Rock* . . . . (Capitol)
Tightrope Walk
Damned; *Anything* . . . .(MCA)
Too Long At The Fair
Bonnie Raitt; *Give It Up* . . . .(Warner Bros.)
Tunnel Of Love
Dire Straits; *Live-Alchemy* . . . . (Warner Bros.)
Making Movies. . . . . (Warner Bros.)
Money For Nothing . . . . (Warner Bros.)
ST/An Officer And A Gentleman. . . . . (Island)
Tunnel Of Love
Byrds; *Byrdmaniax* . . . . (Columbia)
Tunnel Of Love
Bruce Springsteen; *Tunnel Of Love* . . . . (Columbia)
Under The Boardwalk
Bette Midler; *ST/Beaches* . . . . (Atlantic)
Bruce Willis; *Return Of Bruno* . . . . (Motown)
Drifters; *Atlantic Rhythm & Blues 1947-1974-#5 (1962-1966)-C* . . . . .(Atlantic)
Drifters-16 Greatest Hits. . . . . (Trip)
Drifters-Golden Hits . . . . (Atlantic)
Super Oldies Of The '60s-#5-C . . . . (Audio Fidelity)
John Mellencamp; *Rough Harvest* . . . . (Mercury)
Lynn Anderson; *What She Does Best* . . . . (Mercury)
Rickie Lee Jones; *Girl At Her Volcano* . . . .(Warner Bros.)
Rolling Stones; *12 X 5.* . . . . (Abkco)
Untouchables; *Agent Double O Soul.* . . . . (Restless)
Virgo Clowns
Van Morrison; *His Band And The Street Choir.* . . . .(Warner Bros.)
W.S. Walcott Medicine Show
Band; *Rock Of Ages* . . . . (Capitol)
Stage Fright. . . . . (Capitol)

To Kingdom Come-The Definitive Collection. . . . . (Capitol)
Watching The Wheels
John Lennon; *Lennon* . . . . (Capitol)
John Lennon & Yoko Ono; *Double Fantasy* . . . . (Capitol)
When The Circus Comes
Los Lobos; *Just Another Band From East L.A.* . . . .(Slash)
Kiko . . . .(Slash)
Wild Billy's Circus Story
Bruce Springsteen; *The Wild, The Innocent & The E Street Shuffle* . . . (Columbia)
Working Without A Net
Waylon Jennings; *Country Classics-#5-1985-1986-C* . . . . (Universal)
New Classic Waylon . . . . (MCA)
Today's Country Classics-#2-C . . . . (MCA)
Will The Wolf Survive. . . . . (MCA)
Wynona's Big Brown Beaver
Primus; *Tales From The Punchbowl* . . . . (Interscope)

CARS: CADILLAC

See Also: CARS: GENERAL, CARS: SPECIFIC MAKES & MODELS, MONEY

#1 Stunna
Big Tymers; *I Got That Work* . . . .(Cash Money/Universal)
1970 #1 Song Cadillac
Terry Radigan; *Pawnbroker's Daughter.* . . . .(Asylum)
Always Drive A Cadillac
Everly Brothers; *Mercury Years* . . . . (Mercury)
Baby's Got A Hold On Me
Nitty Gritty Dirt Band; *Hold On* . . . . (Warner Bros.)
Be Thankful For What You Got
William DeVaughn; *Didn't It Blow Your Mind: Soul Hits Of The*
'70s-#12-C. . . . . (Rhino)
Oldies But Goodies-#11-C. . . . . (Original Sound)
Beep Beep
Playmates; *Dr. Demento: 20th Anniversary Collection-C* . . . . (Rhino)
Big Black Cadillac Blues
Lightnin' Hopkins; *Drinkin' In The Blues-Golden Classics-#1* . . . (Collectables)
Lightnin' Hopkins. . . . . (Everest)
Big Daddy
Heavy D; *Waterbed Hev* . . . . (Universal)
Black Cadillac
Catfish Hodge Band; *Eyewitness Blues* . . . .(Adelphi)
Lightnin' Hopkins; *How Many More Years I Got* . . . .(Fantasy)
Brand New Cadillac
Clash; *London Calling* . . . . (Epic)
On Broadway . . . . (Epic)
Brand New Cadillac
Brian Setzer Orchestra; *Brian Setzer Orchestra* . . . . (Hollywood)
Brand New Cadillac
Clash; *London Calling* . . . . (Epic)
Bring That Cadillac Back
Harry Crafton; *Harry Crafton* . . . . (Collectables)
Buy The Bitch A Cadillac
Annie Moscow; *Wolves At My Door* . . . .(Melonball)
Cadillac
Bo Diddley; *Bo Diddley Is A Gunslinger.* . . . . (Chess)
Firm; *Mean Business.* . . . .(Atlantic)
Kinks; *Compleat Collection-20th Anniversary* . . . . (Compleat)
You Really Got Me . . . . (Rhino)
Steve Earle & The Dukes; *Early Tracks* . . . . (Epic)
Cadillac Assembly Line
Albert King; *Masterworks.* . . . .(Atlantic)
Truckload Of Lovin' . . . . (Tomato)
Cadillac Blues
Gary Primich; *Gary Primich* . . . .(Amazing)
T.N.T. Tribble; *Red Hot Boogie-#2-C* . . . . (Collectables)
T.N.T. Tribble. . . . . (Collectables)
Cadillac Car
Original Cast; *Dreamgirls.* . . . . (Geffen)
Cadillac Cowboy
Chris LeDoux; *Chris LeDoux & The Saddle Boogie Band* . . . . (Liberty)
Chris LeDoux-20 Greatest Hits . . . . (Capitol)
Cadillac Dreams
Kiss; *Hot In The Shade* . . . . (Mercury)
Cadillac Jack Fever
Clint Black; *Clint Black-The Greatest Hits.* . . . .(RCA)
Cadillac Of The Skies
American Boy Choir; *Spielberg/Williams Collaboration* . . . . (Columbia)
Cadillac Ranch
Bruce Springsteen; *Live 1975-1985* . . . . (Legacy)
The River . . . . (Legacy)
Bruce Springsteen & The E Street Band; *Bruce Springsteen & The E Street*
Band Live/1975-85 . . . . (Legacy)
Nitty Gritty Dirt Band; *More Great Dirt-Best Of-#3* . . . . (Warner Bros.)
Plain Dirt Fashion . . . . (Warner Bros.)

Cadillac Red
Judds; *Collection-1983-1990* . . . (RCA)
River Of Time . . . (RCA)
This Country's Rockin' . . . (RCA)
Cadillac Slim
Rick Braun; *Beat Street* . . . (Mesa/Bluemoon)
Cadillac Style
Sammy Kershaw; *Don't Go Near The Water* . . . (Mercury)
Cadillac Walk
Mink De Ville; *Mink De Ville* . . . (Capitol)
Savoire Faire . . . (Capitol)
Chocolate Cadillac
Red Mitchell; *Chocolate Cadillac* . . . (Steeplechase)
Cool Daddy In A Cadillac
Elvis Hitler; *Disgraceland* . . . (Restless)
Cowboy Cadillac
Garth Brooks; *Sevens* . . . (Capitol)
Daddy Never Was The Cadillac Kind
Confederate Railroad; *Notorious* . . . (Atlantic)
Dead Flowers
Rolling Stones; *Sticky Fingers* . . . (Virgin)
Steve Earle & The Dukes; *Shut Up And Die Like An Aviator* . . . (MCA)
Do-Wacka-Do
Roger Miller; *Best Of Roger Miller-His Greatest Songs* . . . (Curb)
Dumb Ditties-C . . . (K-Tel)
Eggs And Sausage (In A Cadillac With Susan Michelson)
Tom Waits; *Nighthawks At The Diner* . . . (Asylum)
Eldorado To The Moon
Michael Nesmith; *Newer Stuff* . . . (Rhino)
Fearless Boogie
ZZ Top; *XXX* . . . (RCA)
Freeway Of Love
Aretha Franklin; *Who's Zoomin' Who?* . . . (Arista)
Galaxie
Blind Melon; *Soup* . . . (Capitol)
Geronimo's Cadillac
Michael Martin Murphey; *Best Of Michael Martin Murphey* . . . (Liberty)
Guitars, Cadillacs
Dwight Yoakam; *Guitars, Cadillacs, Etc., Etc.* . . . (Reprise)
Just Lookin' For A Hit . . . (Reprise)
Horse & Carriage
Cam'ron featuring Mase; *Confessions Of Fire* . . . (Untertainment/Epic)
Hot Rod Lincoln
Asleep At The Wheel; *Western Standard Time* . . . (Epic)
Commander Cody & His Lost Planet Airmen; *Lost In The Ozone* . . . (MCA)
Super Hits Of The '70s-Have A Nice Day-#8-C . . . (Rhino)
Johnny Bond; *Best Of Johnny Bond* . . . (Starday)
If You Ain't Lovin' (You Ain't Livin')
Faron Young; *Heroes Of Country Music-#3-Legends Of Nashville-C* . . . (Rhino)
Live Fast, Love Hard: Original Capitol Recordings-1952-1962-C . . . (Country Music Foundation)
George Strait; *If You Ain't Lovin' You Ain't Livin'* . . . (MCA)
Ten Strait Hits . . . (MCA)
If You've Got The Money I've Got The Time
Lefty Frizzell; *American Originals-Lefty Frizzell* . . . (Columbia)
Columbia Country Classics-#2-Honky Tonk Heroes-C . . . (Columbia)
Lefty Frizzell's Greatest Hits . . . (Columbia)
Willie Nelson; *Greatest Hits (& Some That Will Be)* . . . (Columbia)
Sound In Your Mind . . . (Columbia)
Willie & Family Live . . . (Columbia)
I'm A Cadillac/El Camino Dolo Roso
Mott The Hoople; *Mott* . . . (Columbia)
Johnny Bye-Bye
Bruce Springsteen; *Tracks* . . . (Columbia)
Long White Cadillac
Blasters; *Blasters-Collection* . . . (Slash)
Dave Alvin; *Romeo's Escape* . . . (Epic)
Dwight Yoakam; *Just Lookin' For A Hit* . . . (Reprise)
Look At That Cadillac
Stray Cats; *Best Of Stray Cats-Rock This Town* . . . (EMI)
Looking Back To See
Goldie Hill & Justin Tubb; *Justin Tubb-Star Of The Grand Ole Opry* . . . (Starday)
Jim Ed Brown & Maxine Brown; *Essential Jim Ed Brown* . . . (RCA)
Maybelline
Chuck Berry; *Chuck Berry-Golden Hits* . . . (Mercury)
Chuck Berry's Greatest Hits . . . (Everest)
Cruisin'-1955-C . . . (Increase)
Oldies But Goodies-#11-C . . . (Original Sound)
Super Oldies Of The '50s-#5-C . . . (Audio Fidelity)
Johnny Rivers; *Johnny Rivers-Anthology 1964-1977* . . . (Rhino)
Very Best Of Johnny Rivers . . . (EMI)
My Black Cadillac
Lightnin' Hopkins; *Lightnin' Hopkins-Complete Prestige/Bluesville Recordings* . . . (Bluesville)
Next Episode
Dr. Dre; *Dr. Dre 2001* . . . (Aftermath/Interscope)
Night Of The Cadillacs
L.A. Guns; *Cuts* . . . (Polydor)
Northside Cadillac
James Cotton; *Mighty Long Time* . . . (Antone's)
Not Fade Away
Buddy Holly/The Crickets; *Buddy Holly-20 Golden Greats* . . . (MCA)
Buddy Holly's Greatest Hits . . . (MCA)
From The Original Master Tapes-Buddy Holly . . . (MCA)
Legend-From The Original Master Tapes . . . (MCA)
The Buddy Holly Collection . . . (MCA)
Grateful Dead; *Dick's Picks-#2* . . . (Arista)
Dozin' At The Knick . . . (Arista)
Rolling Stones; *Big Hits (High Tide & Green Grass)* . . . (Abkco)
England's Newest Hit Makers/The Rolling Stones . . . (Abkco)
got Live if you want it! . . . (Abkco)
More Hot Rocks (big hits & fazed cookies) . . . (Abkco)
Singles Collection-The London Years . . . (Abkco)
Stripped . . . (Virgin)
One Piece At A Time
Johnny Cash; *The Man In Black-His Greatest Hits* . . . (Legacy)
Pink Cadillac
Bruce Springsteen; *Tracks* . . . (Columbia)
Natalie Cole; *Everlasting* . . . (Elektra)
Gotta Have House-Best Of House Music-#2-C . . . (Profile)
Southern Pacific; *Killbilly Hill* . . . (Warner Bros.)
Rockin' Country-C . . . (Warner Bros.)
Southern Pacific's Greatest Hits . . . (Warner Bros.)
Pretty Girls And Cadillacs
Nighthawks; *Backtrack* . . . (Varrick)
Ragtop Cadillac
Lonestar; *Lonestar* . . . (BNA)
Rainbow's Cadillac
Bruce Hornsby; *Harbor Lights* . . . (RCA)
Ray's Dad Cadillac
Joni Mitchell; *Night Ride Home* . . . (Geffen)
Red Cadillac
Colin Winski; *Rock Therapy* . . . (Takoma)
Reverend Jack & His Roamin' Cadillac Church
Timbuk 3; *Eden Alley* . . . (I.R.S.)
Riding With The King
B.B. King & Eric Clapton; *Riding With The King* . . . (Duck/Reprise)
Sandpaper Cadillac
Joe Cocker; *With A Little Help From My Friends* . . . (A&M)
Santa Claus Is Back In Town
Dwight Yoakam; *Warner Bros. Christmas Tradition-C* . . . (Warner Bros.)
Elvis Presley; *Elvis' Christmas Album* . . . (RCA)
Elvis Presley Sings Leiber & Stoller . . . (RCA)
Memories Of Christmas . . . (RCA)
White Christmas . . . (RCA)
Trisha Yearwood; *The Sweetest Gift* . . . (MCA)
Satin Sheets
Jeannie Pruett; *16 Top Country Hits-#1-C* . . . (MCA)
Country Chart-Toppers . . . (Dominion Entert.)
Grand Ole Opry-75 Years-#2-C . . . (MCA)
MCA Records 30 Years Of Hits-1958-1988-C . . . (MCA)
Shawn Colvin; *Cover Girl* . . . (Columbia)
Seaside Bar Song
Bruce Springsteen; *Tracks* . . . (Columbia)
Little Bob Story; *One Step Up/Two Steps Back-The Songs Of Bruce Springsteen-C* . . . (Right Stuff)
She's My Cadillac
Santa Fe; *Santa Fe* . . . (Creative Indep. Artists)
Slick Black Cadillac
Quiet Riot; *Heavy Metal Memories-C* . . . (Rhino)
Metal Health . . . (Pasha)
Solid Gold Cadillac
Mitch Woods & The Rocket 88's; *Solid Gold Cadillac* . . . (Blind Pig)
Somebody Else's Money
Wallflowers; *The Wallflowers* . . . (Virgin)
Southern Hospitality
Ludacris; *Back For The First Time* . . . (Def Jam South/IDJMG)
Summer Days
Bob Dylan; *''Love And Theft''* . . . (Columbia)
Summer's Comin'
Clint Black; *Clint Black-The Greatest Hits* . . . (RCA)
One Emotion . . . (RCA)
Swing Low, Sweet Cadillac
Dizzy Gillespie; *Dizzy's Diamonds-Best Of The Verve Years* . . . (Verve)
Swingin'
Tom Petty And The Heartbreakers; *Echo* . . . (Warner Bros.)
Welfare Cadillac
Gary B.B. Coleman; *Too Much Weekend* . . . (Ichiban Int'l)
Why Brothers Drive Cadillacs
Robin Harris; *Be-Be's Kids* . . . (Wing)
You Win My Love
Shania Twain; *The Woman In Me* . . . (Mercury)

CARS: GENERAL, Driving, Limousines, Riding In Cars

See Also: **BUS, CARS: CADILLAC, CARS: SPECIFIC MAKES & MODELS, GAS STATIONS, MOTORCYCLES, ROAD, ROAD ACCIDENTS, SPORTS: CAR RACING, TAXI, TRAVELING, TRUCKS**

409
Beach Boys; *Beach Boys' Greatest Hits* . . . . (Gusto)
   Best Of The Beach Boys . . . . (Capitol)
   Made In The U.S.A. . . . . (Capitol)
   Spirit Of America . . . . (Capitol)
Angels Working Overtime
Deana Carter; *Everything's Gonna Be Alright* . . . . (Capitol)
Arrested For Driving While Blind
ZZ Top; *Six Pack* . . . .(Warner Bros.)
   Tejas . . . .(Warner Bros.)
Asleep At The Wheel
Wallflowers; *The Wallflowers* . . . . (Virgin)
At The Stars
Better Than Ezra; *How Does Your Garden Grow?* . . . . (Elektra)
Automatic Drive
Platinum Blonde; *Contact* . . . .(Epic)
Automobile
John Prine; *Great Days-Anthology* . . . . (Rhino)
   Pink Cadillac . . . . (Asylum)
Automobile
N.W.A.; *Efil4zaggin* . . . .(Ruthless/Priority)
Automobile Blues
Lightnin' Hopkins; *Early Recordings-#1* . . . . (Arhoolie)
   Lightnin' . . . . (Prestige)
   Low Down Dirty Blues . . . .(Mainstream)
Automobile Noise
Blue Nile; *Walk Across The Rooftops* . . . . (A&M)
Baby Driver
Simon & Garfunkel; *Bridge Over Troubled Water* . . . . (Columbia)
   Collected Works . . . . (Columbia)
Back Seat Of My Car
Paul And Linda McCartney; *RAM* . . . . (Capitol)
   Paul McCartney; *Paul McCartney-Gift Set* . . . . (Capitol)
Backroads
Ricky Van Shelton; *Backroads* . . . . (Columbia)
Bad Brakes
Cat Stevens; *Back To Earth* . . . . (A&M)
Big Log
Robert Plant; *Principle Of Moments* . . . .(Es Paranza)
Big Yellow Taxi
Amy Grant; *House Of Love* . . . . (A&M)
   Joni Mitchell; *Ladies Of The Canyon* . . . . (Reprise)
   Joni Mitchell with Tom Scott & The L.A. Express; *Miles Of Aisles* . . . . (Asylum)
Black Limousine
Rolling Stones; *Tattoo You* . . . . (Virgin)
Blondes In Black Cars
Autograph; *That's The Stuff* . . . . (RCA)
Brand New Car
Rolling Stones; *Voodoo Lounge* . . . . (Virgin)
Brand New Convertible Car
Die Warzau; *Big Electric Metal Bass Face* . . . . (Atlantic)
Brothers Under The Bridges ('83)
Bruce Springsteen; *Tracks* . . . . (Columbia)
Bug, The
Dire Straits; *On Every Street* . . . .(Warner Bros.)
   Mary Chapin Carpenter; *Come On Come On* . . . . (Columbia)
Burn Rubber On Me
Gap Band; *12'' Collection* . . . . (Mercury)
   Gap Gold/Best Of The Gap Band . . . . (Mercury)
   The Gap Band III . . . . (Mercury)
Buy, Buy This American Car
Charlie King; *Food Phone Gas Lodging* . . . . (Flying Fish)
Bye, Bye
Jo Dee Messina; *I'm Alright* . . . . (Curb)
Candy's Room
Bruce Springsteen; *Darkness On The Edge Of Town* . . . . (Columbia)
   Bruce Springsteen & The E Street Band; *Bruce Springsteen & The E Street Band Live/1975-85* . . . . (Legacy)
Car Bomb
Negativeland; *Escape From Noise* . . . .(SST)
Car On A Hill
Joni Mitchell; *Court & Spark* . . . . (Asylum)
Car Wash
Rose Royce; *Best Of Rose Royce* . . . .(Omni)
   Billboard Top Hits-1977-C . . . . (Rhino)
   Rose Royce's Greatest Hits . . . .(Whitfield)
   The Disco Years-#1-Turn The Beat Around-1974-1978-C . . . . (Rhino)
Car Wheels On A Gravel Road
Lucinda Williams; *Car Wheels On A Gravel Road* . . . . (Mercury)

Car, Car
Peter, Paul & Mary; *Peter, Paul and Mary In Concert* . . . . (Warner Bros.)
Car, The
Jeff Carson; *Jeff Carson* . . . .(Curb)
Cars
Fear Factory; *Obsolete* . . . .(Roadrunner)
   Gary Numan; *18 Modern Rock Classics From The '80s-C* . . . . (Rhino)
   Pleasure Principle . . . . (Atco)
Cars
Tom Wopat; *Little Bit Closer* . . . . (EMI)
Cars Hiss By My Window
Doors; *L.A. Woman* . . . . (Elektra)
Cherry Bomb
John Cougar Mellencamp; *Check It Out* . . . . (Mercury)
   The Lonesome Jubilee . . . . (Mercury)
Cherry, Cherry Coupe
Beach Boys; *Little Deuce Coupe/All Summer Long* . . . . (Capitol)
Counting Blue Cars
Dishwalla; *Pet Your Friends* . . . . (A&M)
Crosstown Traffic
Jimi Hendrix; *Kiss The Sky* . . . . (Reprise)
   Jimi Hendrix Experience; *Electric Ladyland* . . . . (Reprise)
   Essential Jimi Hendrix, Volume 2. . . . . (Reprise)
   Smash Hits . . . . (Reprise)
Cruisin'
Michael Nesmith; *Newer Stuff.* . . . . (Rhino)
Cruisin'
Alabama; *The Touch* . . . . (RCA)
Cruisin'
Ted Nugent; *Weekend Warriors* . . . . (Epic)
Custom Machine
Beach Boys; *Beach Boys-Gift Set* . . . . (Capitol)
   Little Deuce Coupe/All Summer Long . . . . (Capitol)
   Spirit Of America . . . . (Capitol)
D.U.I.
Drink Small; *Round Two* . . . . (Ichiban Int'l)
Dead Man's Curve
Jan & Dean; *21 Legendary Superstars-C* . . . .(Original Sound)
   Best Of Jan & Dean . . . . (EMI)
   Dead Man's Curve . . . . (EMI)
Death Alley Driver
Rainbow; *Straight Between The Eyes* . . . . (Mercury)
Detroit 442
Blondie; *Plastic Letters* . . . . (Chrysalis)
Detroit City
Ace Cannon; *Golden Favorites* . . . . (Ranwood)
   Bill Anderson; *Best Of Bill Anderson* . . . . (Curb)
   Bobby Bare; *Nipper's Greatest Hits Of The '60s-#2-C* . . . . (RCA)
   This Is Bobby Bare . . . . (RCA)
   Chet Atkins; *Country Gems.* . . . . (Pair)
   Flatt & Scruggs; *20 All-Time Great Recordings* . . . . (Columbia)
   Hank Williams, Jr.; *Live At Cobo Hall Detroit* . . . . (Polydor)
   Standing In The Shadows . . . .(Polydor)
   Mel Tillis; *Best Of Mel Tillis* . . . . (MCA)
   Live At The Sam Houston Coliseum . . . . (MGM)
   Solomon Burke; *Home In Your Heart-Best Of Solomon Burke* . . . . (Rhino)
Devil In A Fast Car
Sheena Easton; *Best Kept Secret* . . . . (EMI)
Diamonds On My Windshield
Tom Waits; *The Heart Of Saturday Night* . . . .(Asylum)
   Tom Waits-Anthology . . . . (Asylum)
Distance, The
Cake; *Fashion Nugget.* . . . . (Capricorn)
Don't Drink & Drive
James Cannings; *Music For All Seasons* . . . . (J.C.)
Don't Drive Drunk
Stevie Wonder; *ST/Woman In Red* . . . . (Motown)
Don't Look Back
Bruce Springsteen; *Tracks* . . . . (Columbia)
   Knack; *One Step Up/Two Steps Back-The Songs Of Bruce Springsteen-C* . . . . (Right Stuff)
   Retrospective-Best Of The Knack . . . . (Gold Rush)
Don't You Get It
Mark Knopfler; *Golden Heart* . . . .(Warner Bros.)
Drag City
Jan & Dean; *Beach Party Blasts* . . . . (EMI)
   Best Of Jan & Dean . . . . (EMI)
   Dead Man's Curve . . . . (EMI)
   One Summer Night-Live . . . . (Rhino)
Drinkin' & Drivin'
Johnny Paycheck; *Encore-Johnny Paycheck* . . . . (Epic)
   Everybody's Got a Family . . . . (Epic)
   Johnny Paycheck's Biggest Hits . . . . (Epic)
Drinking And Driving
Black Flag; *In My Head* . . . .(SST)
Drive (For Daddy Gene)
Alan Jackson; *Drive* . . . . (Arista)
Drive
Cars; *Heartbeat City* . . . . (Elektra)

MTV's Rock 'N' Roll To Go-C . . . . (Elektra)
The Cars' Greatest Hits . . . . (Elektra)
Drive
Incubus; *Make Yourself* . . . . (Immortal/Epic)
Now That's What I Call Music!-#6-C . . . . (Virgin)
Drive
R.E.M.; *Automatic For The People* . . . . (Warner Bros.)
Drive All Night
Bruce Springsteen; *The River* . . . . (Columbia)
Drive My Car
Beatles; *''Yesterday''...And Today* . . . . (Capitol)
Rock 'N' Roll Music . . . . (Capitol)
The Beatles/1962-1966 . . . . (Capitol)
Drive On
Johnny Cash; *American Recordings* . . . . (American)
Drive South
John Hiatt; *Slow Turning* . . . . (A&M)
Suzy Bogguss; *Voices In The Wind* . . . . (Liberty)
Drive-In
Beach Boys; *All Summer Long* . . . . (Capitol)
Spirit Of America . . . . (Capitol)
Drive-In Movies & Dashboard Lights
Nanci Griffith; *Storms* . . . . (MCA)
Driven
Rush; *Test For Echo* . . . . (Atlantic)
Driver's Seat
Sniff 'n' The Tears; *Fickle Heart* . . . . (Atlantic)
Drivin' & Cryin'
Steve Wariner; *Steve Wariner-Drive* . . . . (Arista)
Drivin' Around
Raspberries; *Best Of The Raspberries* . . . . (Capitol)
Capitol Collectors Series-The Raspberries . . . . (Capitol)
Drivin' My Life Away
Eddie Rabbitt; *Eddie Rabbitt's All-Time Greatest Hits* . . (Warner Bros.)
Eddie Rabbitt's Greatest Hits-#2 . . . . (Warner Bros.)
Horizon . . . . (Elektra)
Number 1's . . . . (Warner Bros.)
Ten Years Of Greatest Hits . . . . (Capitol)
Drivin' Wheel
Albert King; *Stax Blues Masters-Blue Monday-C* . . . . . (Stax)
Foghat; *Best Of Foghat* . . . . (Rhino)
Night Shift . . . . (Rhino)
Little Junior Parker; *Annie Get Your Yo Yo* . . . . . (MCA Special Prod.)
Best Of Little Junior Parker . . . . (MCA)
Soul Shots-#4-Urban Blues-C . . . . (Rhino)
Drivin' With Your Eyes Closed
Don Henley; *Building The Perfect Beast* . . . . (Geffen)
Driving Along
Nilsson; *Nilsson Schmilsson* . . . . (RCA)
Driving At Night
Delevantes; *Long About That Time* . . . . (Rounder)
Driving Rain
Paul McCartney; *Driving Rain* . . . . (Columbia)
Driving Sister
Mott The Hoople; *Mott* . . . . (Columbia)
Drop Top
Jeff Golub; *Dangerous Curves* . . . . (GRP/VMG)
Drunken Driver
Ricky Skaggs and Kentucky Thunder; *Bluegrass Rules!* . . . . (Rounder)
Easy Driver
Kenny Loggins; *Kenny Loggins Alive* . . . . (Columbia)
Nightwatch . . . . (Columbia)
Fast Car
Tracy Chapman; *Tracy Chapman* . . . . (Elektra)
Faster
George Harrison; *George Harrison* . . . . (Dark Horse)
Four Wheel Drive
C.W. McCall; *C.W. McCall's Greatest Hits* . . . . (Polydor)
Wolf Creek Pass . . . . (MGM)
Four Wheels
38 Special; *38 Special* . . . . (A&M)
Fuel
Metallica; *Reload* . . . . (Elektra)
Gas Station Woman
Phil Ochs; *The War Is Over-Best Of Phil Ochs* . . . . (A&M)
Gasoline Alley
Rod Stewart; *Absolutely Live* . . . . (Warner Bros.)
Best Of Rod Stewart . . . . (Mercury)
Gasoline Alley . . . . (Mercury)
Sing It Again, Rod . . . . (Mercury)
Storyteller/The Complete Anthology: 1964-1990 . . . . . . (Warner Bros.)
Get Outta My Dreams, Get Into My Car
Billy Ocean; *Billy Ocean's Greatest Hits* . . . . (Jive)
ST/License To Drive . . . . (MCA)
Going For A Drive
Tammy Rogers; *The Speed Of Love* . . . . (Dead Reckoning)
Going Mobile
Who; *Who's next* . . . . (MCA)

Good Day To Run
Darryl Worley; *Hard Rain Don't Last* . . . . (DreamWorks/SKG)
Grease Megamix
Grease Megamix; *Pure Disco* . . . . (A&M)
Great Filling Station Holdup
Jimmy Buffett; *White Sport Coat & A Pink Crustacean* . . . . (MCA)
Hang Up And Drive
Ray Stevens; *Osama-Yo' Mama* . . . . (Curb)
Hard Drivin' Man
J. Geils Band; *Full House* . . . . (Atlantic)
J. Geils Band . . . . (Atlantic)
Heaven In The Back Seat
Eddie Money; *Right Here* . . . . (Columbia)
Hey Little Minivan
Austin Lounge Lizards; *Employee Of The Month* . . . . . (Sugar Hill)
Hey Pretty
Poe; *Haunted* . . . . (FEI/Atlantic)
High-Tech Redneck
George Jones; *High-Tech Redneck* . . . . (MCA)
Hot Rod
Ray Charles; *Ray Charles-Live* . . . . (Atlantic)
Hot Rod Baby
Ronny & The Daytonas; *45-#19* . . . . (Flashback)
Hot Rod Hearts
Robbie Dupree; *Robbie Dupree* . . . . (Elektra)
How Bizarre
OMC; *How Bizarre* . . . . (Huh!/Mercury)
How Your Love Makes Me Feel
Diamond Rio; *Diamond Rio's Greatest Hits* . . . . (Arista)
I Can't Drive 55
Sammy Hagar; *VOA* . . . . (Geffen)
I Don't Know
Gretchen Peters; *Gretchen Peters* . . . . (Purple Crayon Prod.)
I Drove All Night
Cyndi Lauper; *Night To Remember* . . . . (Epic)
I Get Around
Beach Boys; *Best Of The Beach Boys* . . . . (Capitol)
Billboard Top Rock 'N' Roll Hits-1964-C . . . . (Rhino)
Endless Summer . . . . (Capitol)
Made In The U.S.A. . . . . (Capitol)
ST/Good Morning, Vietnam . . . . (A&M)
I'd Rather Ride Around With You
Reba McEntire; *What If It's You* . . . . (MCA)
If My Heart Had Wings
Faith Hill; *Breathe* . . . . (Warner Bros.)
I'll Be Your Chauffeur
David J; *Songs From Another Season* . . . . (RCA)
I'll Change Your Flat Tire, Merle
Pure Prairie League; *Two Lane Highway* . . . . (RCA)
I'm In Love With My Car
Queen; *A Night At The Opera* . . . . (Hollywood)
Live Killers . . . . (Hollywood)
In The Car
Barenaked Ladies; *Stunt* . . . . (Reprise)
In The Garage
Weezer; *Weezer* . . . . (David Geffen Co.)
It Must Be Love
Ty Herndon; *Big Hopes* . . . . (Epic)
It's Late
Ricky Nelson; *Lonesome Town* . . . . (CEMA Special Prod.)
Ricky Nelson Volume 1 . . . . (Gold Rush)
Johnny Needs A Fast Car
Chris Rea; *Espresso Logic* . . . . (East West)
Joy Ride
Rick Derringer; *All American Boy* . . . . (Blue Sky)
Joyride
Roxette; *Joyride* . . . . (EMI)
Junk Cars
Mac McAnally; *Live & Learn* . . . . (MCA)
Just Cruisin'
Will Smith; *ST/Men In Black* . . . . (Columbia)
Keep It Between The Lines
Ricky Van Shelton; *Backroads* . . . . (Columbia)
Kentucky Rain
Elvis Presley; *Elvis Presley-Pure Gold* . . . . (RCA)
Memphis Record . . . . (RCA)
Worldwide 50 Gold Award Hits, Vol. 1, Parts 1 & 2 . . . . . (RCA)
Kiss Me In The Car
John Berry; *John Berry* . . . . (Liberty)
L.A. Woman
Billy Idol; *Charmed Life* . . . . (Chrysalis)
Doors; *Best Of The Doors* . . . . (Elektra)
Doors' Greatest Hits . . . . (Elektra)
L.A. Woman . . . . (Elektra)
ST/The Doors . . . . (Elektra)
Weird Scenes Inside The Gold Mine . . . . (Elektra)
Laredo
Chris Cagle; *Play It Loud* . . . . (Capitol)

Last Chance Texaco
Rickie Lee Jones; *Naked Songs Live And Acoustic* . . . . (Reprise)
Rickie Lee Jones . . . .(Warner Bros.)

Last Chance To Turn Around
Gene Pitney; *Best Of Gene Pitney* . . . . (K-Tel)
Gene Pitney-Anthology 1961-1968 . . . . (Rhino)

Let It Roll
Little Feat; *Let It Roll* . . . .(Warner Bros.)

Let Me Be Your Car
Rod Stewart; *Best Of Rod Stewart* . . . . (Mercury)
Rod Stewart & Elton John; *Storyteller/The Complete Anthology: 1964-
1990* . . . .(Warner Bros.)

Let Me Drive
Greg Holland; *Greg Holland* . . . .(Warner Bros.)

Let Sally Drive
Sammy Hagar; *Ten 13* . . . . (Cabo Wabo/Beyond)

Let's Go Ridin' In The Car
Country Joe McDonald; *Goodbye Blues* . . . . (Fantasy)

Let's Take A Drive
Billy Burnette; *Soldier Of Love* . . . . (Curb)

Limousine Boogie (Hey Hey Mama)
Savoy Brown; *Make Me Sweat* . . . .(Crescendo)

Limousine Driver
James Taylor; *That's Why I'm Here* . . . . (Columbia)

Limousines
Robbie Nevil; *Robbie Nevil* . . . .(EMI)

Little Deuce Coupe
Beach Boys; *Best Of The Beach Boys* . . . . (Capitol)
Concert/'69-Live In London . . . . (Capitol)
Endless Summer . . . . (Capitol)
Good Vibrations-Thirty Years Of The Beach Boys . . . . (Capitol)
Summer Means Fun-California Surf Music-C . . . . (Capitol)

Little Gasoline, A
Terri Clark; *Fearless* . . . . (Mercury)

Little Old Lady (From Pasadena)
Beach Boys; *Concert/'69-Live In London* . . . . (Capitol)
Jan & Dean; *Best Of Jan & Dean* . . . .(EMI)
Billboard Top Rock 'N' Roll Hits-1964-C . . . . (Rhino)
Dead Man's Curve . . . .(EMI)
Surf City-Best Of Jan & Dean . . . .(EMI)

Little Past Little Rock
Lee Ann Womack; *Some Things I Know* . . . . (Decca)

London Traffic
Jam; *This Is The Modern World* . . . . (Polydor)

Long Black Limousine
Bobby Bare; *This Is Bobby Bare* . . . . (RCA)
Elvis Presley; *From Elvis In Memphis* . . . . (RCA)
Memphis Record . . . . (RCA)

Long White Car
Hipsway; *Hipsway* . . . . (Columbia)

Looking Back To See
Goldie Hill & Justin Tubb; *Justin Tubb-Star Of The Grand
Ole Opry* . . . . (Starday)
Jim Ed Brown & Maxine Brown; *Essential Jim Ed Brown* . . . . (RCA)

Lord, Mr. Ford
Jerry Reed; *Best Of A Great Year-#3-C* . . . . (RCA)
Jerry Reed In Concert . . . . (RCA)

Love Is A Stranger
Eurythmics; *Eurythmics' Greatest Hits* . . . . (Arista)
Sweet Dreams (Are Made Of This) . . . . (RCA)

Lucky Man
Bruce Springsteen; *Tracks* . . . . (Columbia)

Mach 5
Presidents Of The United States Of America; *Presidents Of The United States
Of America II* . . . . (Columbia)

Magic Jewelled Limousine
Nasa; *Insha-Allah!* . . . . (Sire)
ST/Wild Orchid . . . . (Sire)

Maybelline
Chuck Berry; *Chuck Berry-Golden Hits* . . . . (Mercury)
Chuck Berry's Greatest Hits . . . . (Everest)
Cruisin'-1955-C . . . .(Increase)
Oldies But Goodies-#11-C . . . . (Original Sound)
Super Oldies Of The '50s-#5-C . . . . (Audio Fidelity)
Johnny Rivers; *Johnny Rivers-Anthology 1964-1977* . . . . (Rhino)
Very Best Of Johnny Rivers . . . .(EMI)

Me And Bobby McGee
Grateful Dead; *Grateful Dead (Skull & Roses)* . . . .(Warner Bros.)
Janis Joplin; *Janis* . . . . (Legacy)
Janis Joplin's Greatest Hits . . . . (Columbia)
Pearl . . . . (Legacy)
Rock Classics Of The '70s-C . . . . (Columbia)
Willie Nelson; *Willie Nelson Sings Kristofferson* . . . . (Columbia)

MFC
Pearl Jam; *Yield* . . . .(Epic)

Moonlight Drive
Doors; *Alive She Cried* . . . . (Elektra)
Doors 13 . . . . (Elektra)

Strange Days . . . . (Elektra)

Moonlight Drive-In
Turner Nichols; *Moonlight Drive-In* . . . .(BNA)

Motoring
Martha Reeves; *Motown Milestones* . . . . (Motown)
The Ultimate Collection-Martha Reeves . . . . (Motown)

My Kingdom For A Car
Gene Parsons; *Melodies* . . . . (Sierra)

My Kingdom For A Car
Jason & The Scorchers; *Thunder & Fire* . . . . (A&M)

My Kingdom For A Car
Phil Ochs; *Phil Ochs' Greatest Hits* . . . . (A&M)

My Old Yellow Car
Dan Seals; *Best Of Dan Seals* . . . . (Capitol)
Dan Seals-Classics Collection-#1 . . . . (Capitol)
Early Dan Seals . . . . (Capitol)
San Antone . . . . EMI)
Lacy J. Dalton; *Blue Eyed Blues* . . . . (Columbia)
Dream Baby . . . . (Columbia)

Nadine (Is It You?)
Chuck Berry; *Rock & Roll Rarities* . . . . (Chess)

Night
Bruce Springsteen; *Born To Run* . . . . (Columbia)

No Can Do
Mark Knopfler; *Golden Heart* . . . . (Warner Bros.)

No Money Down
Chuck Berry; *The Chess Box-Chuck Berry* . . . . (Chess)
John Hammond; *Best Of John Hammond* . . . . (Vanguard)
Blues Explosion . . . .(Atlantic)

No Particular Place To Go
Chuck Berry; *Best Of The Best Of Chuck Berry* . . . . (International Mktg. Group)
The Chess Box-Chuck Berry . . . . (Chess)

No Scrubs
TLC; *Fanmail* . . . . (LaFace)
Totally Hits-#1-C . . . . (Arista)

Nothin' But The Taillights
Clint Black; *Nothin' But The Taillights* . . . . (RCA)

Nothin' But The Wheel
Patty Loveless; *Only What I Feel* . . . . (Epic)
Patty Loveless-Classics . . . . (Epic)

Objects In The Rear View Mirror May Appear Closer Than They Are
Meat Loaf; *Bat Out Of Hell II: Back Into Hell* . . . . (MCA)

Ol' '55
Eagles; *On The Border* . . . . (Elektra)
Tom Waits; *Tom Waits-Anthology* . . . .(Asylum)

Old Blue Car
Peter Case; *Peter Case* . . . . (Geffen)

On The Road Again
Tom Rush; *Classic Rush* . . . . (Elektra)
Tom Rush . . . . (Elektra)

One Headlight
Wallflowers; *Bringing Down The Horse* . . . .(Interscope)

One More Payment
Clint Black; *Put Yourself In My Shoes* . . . .(RCA)

Paradise By The Dashboard Light
Meat Loaf; *Bat Out Of Hell* . . . . (Epic)

Party In The Parking Lot
Johnny Van Zant; *Brickyard Road* . . . .(Atlantic)

Peaceful World
John Mellencamp; *Cuttin' Heads* . . . . (Columbia)
God Bless America-C . . . . (Columbia)
The Concert For New York City-C . . . . (Columbia)

Plastic Jesus
Ernie Marrs & The Marrs Family; *Best Of Broadside 1962-1968: Anthems
Of The American Underground From The Pages Of Broadside
Magazine-C* . . . .(Smithsonian Folkways)

Pontiac Blues
Sonny Boy Williamson; *King Biscuit Time* . . . .(Arhoolie)

Pop, Let Me Have The Car
Carl Perkins; *Restless-Columbia Recordings* . . . . (Columbia)
Whole Lotta Shakin' . . . . (Sony Music Special Prod.)

Power Windows
Billy Falcon; *Pretty Blue World* . . . . (Jambco)

Promised Land
Bruce Springsteen; *Darkness On The Edge Of Town* . . . . (Columbia)
Bruce Springsteen & The E Street Band; *Bruce Springsteen & The E Street
Band Live/1975-85* . . . . (Legacy)

Radar Gun
Bottle Rockets; *The Brooklyn Side* . . . .(East Side Digital)

Ramrod
Bruce Springsteen; *The River* . . . . (Columbia)

Rearviewmirror
Pearl Jam; *Vs.* . . . . (Epic Portrait Assoc.)

Rhythm From A Red Car
Hardline; *Double Eclipse* . . . . (MCA)

Ride My New Car With Me
Big Joe Williams; *Dark Muddy Bottom Blues-C* . . . .(Specialty)

Ride On Josephine
George Thorogood & The Destroyers; *George Thorogood & The Destroyers* . . . . (Rounder)
Ride To A Funeral In A V-8
Dan Pickett; *1949 Country Blues* . . . . (Collectables)
Ride Wit Me
Nelly; *Country Grammar* . . . . (Fo' Reel/Universal)
Now That's What I Call Music!-#7-C . . . . (Virgin)
Ridin'
Buckcherry; *Time Bomb* . . . . (DreamWorks/SKG)
Ridin' In My Car
NRBQ; *All Hopped Up* . . . . (Rounder)
At Yankee Stadium . . . . (Mercury)
Peek-A-Boo-Best Of-1969-1989 . . . . (Rhino)
Riding In My Car
Woody Guthrie; *Greatest Songs Of Woody Guthrie-C* . . . . (Vanguard)
Riding With A Movie Star
L7; *Hungry For Stink* . . . . (Slash)
Riding With Private Malone
David Ball; *Amigo* . . . . (Razor & Tie)
Riding With The King
B.B. King & Eric Clapton; *Riding With The King* . . . . (Duck/Reprise)
Road Beneath My Wheels
Dan Fogelberg; *Live-Greetings From The West* . . . . (Full Moon)
Rockin' In The Parkin' Lot
Razzy Bailey; *Country Classics-#6-1985-1986-C* . . . . (Universal)
Rollin' In My 5.0
Vanilla Ice; *Extremely Live* . . . . (SBK)
Rolls Royce
Virginia Liston; *Rare Blues Of The Twenties-1924-1929-C* . . . . (Historical)
Rumbleseat
John Cougar Mellencamp; *Scarecrow* . . . . (Riva)
Runnin' Away With My Heart
Lonestar; *Lonestar* . . . . (BNA)
Running On Empty
Jackson Browne; *Running On Empty* . . . . (Asylum)
Seven Little Girls Sitting In The Back Seat
Paul Evans; *Music To Remember-C* . . . . (Dominion Entert.)
Shade Tree Mechanic
Joe Louis Walker; *The Gift* . . . . (Hightone)
Z.Z. Hill; *I'm A Blues Man* . . . . (Malaco)
Z.Z. Hill's Greatest Hits . . . . (Malaco)
She Don't Have A License
Porter Wagoner; *45-#7-29772* . . . . (Warner Bros.)
She Has Funny Cars
Allman Brothers Band/Second Coming; *Dreams* . . . . (Polydor)
Jefferson Airplane; *2400 Fulton Street-An Anthology* . . . . (RCA)
Loves You . . . . (RCA)
Surrealistic Pillow . . . . (RCA)
She Loves My Automobile
ZZ Top; *Deguello* . . . . (Warner Bros.)
She Loves My Car
Ronnie Milsap; *One More Try For Love* . . . . (RCA)
She Loves My Car
Bobby Caldwell; *August Moon* . . . . (Sin-Drome)
She's My Girl
Turtles; *'60s Sound Explosion-C* . . . . (K-Tel)
Nuggets-#9-Acid Rock-C . . . . (Rhino)
Turtles-20 Greatest Hits . . . . (Rhino)
Shut Down
Beach Boys; *Absolute Best-#1* . . . . (Capitol)
Endless Summer . . . . (Capitol)
Little Deuce Coupe/All Summer Long . . . . (Capitol)
Monster Summer Hits-Drag City-C . . . . (Capitol)
Surfin' U.S.A. . . . . (Capitol)
Shut Up And Drive
Chely Wright; *Woman In The Moon* . . . . (Polydor Country)
Sin Wagon
Dixie Chicks; *Fly* . . . . (Monument)
Sitting At The Wheel
Moody Blues; *The Present* . . . . (Polydor)
Voices In The Sky-The Best Of The Moody Blues . . . . (Threshold)
Sleeping In My Car
Roxette; *Crash! Boom! Bang!* . . . . (EMI)
Slow Ride
Kenny Wayne Shepherd; *Trouble Is...* . . . . (Revolution)
Something In The Night
Bruce Springsteen; *Darkness On The Edge Of Town* . . . . (Columbia)
Southside
Moby featuring Gwen Stefani; *12" Maxi Single* . . . . (V2)
Play . . . . (V2)
Spirit Of America
Beach Boys; *Beach Boys-Gift Set* . . . . (Capitol)
Little Deuce Coupe/All Summer Long . . . . (Capitol)
Spirit Of America . . . . (Capitol)
Stand On It
Mel McDaniel; *Hot Rod-Hot Rod Cowboys-C* . . . . (Right Stuff)

Start The Car
Jude Cole; *Start The Car* . . . . (Reprise)
State Trooper
Bruce Springsteen; *Nebraska* . . . . (Columbia)
The Sopranos-Music From The HBO Original Series . . . . (Sony Music Soundtrax)
Stay The Night
IMx; *IMx* . . . . (MCA)
Stolen Car
Bruce Springsteen; *The River* . . . . (Columbia)
Tracks . . . . (Columbia)
Elliott Murphy; *One Step Up/Two Steps Back-The Songs Of Bruce Springsteen-C* . . . . (Right Stuff)
Stranded In A Limousine
Paul Simon; *Greatest Hits, Etc.* . . . . (Columbia)
Strangers In A Car
Marc Cohn; *Marc Cohn* . . . . (Atlantic)
Street Machine
Super Stocks; *Monster Summer Hits-Drag City-C* . . . . (Capitol)
Sunday Driving
Jerry Lewis; *Capitol Collectors Series-Jerry Lewis* . . . . (Capitol)
Dr. Demento Presents The Greatest Novelty Records-#2-1950s-C . . . . (Rhino)
Sweet Little '66
Steve Earle & The Dukes; *Exit 0* . . . . (MCA)
Taking Everything
Gerald Levert; *Love & Consequences* . . . . (East West)
Tennessee Plates
Charlie Sexton; *ST/Thelma & Louise* . . . . (MCA)
John Hiatt; *Slow Turning* . . . . (A&M)
Testarossa
Sir Mix-A-Lot; *Mack Daddy* . . . . (Def American)
Texaco Star Theme
Original Soundtrack; *TeeVee Toons-The Commercials-#1-C* . . . . (TVT)
Texas In My Rear View Mirror
Mac Davis; *Mac Davis-Very Best & More* . . . . (Casablanca)
Texas In My Rear View Mirror . . . . (Casablanca)
Theme From "Car 54, Where Are You?"
Original Soundtrack; *Television's Greatest Hits-#2-C* . . . . (TVT)
Theme From "My Mother The Car"
Original Soundtrack; *Television's Greatest Hits-#2-C* . . . . (TVT)
There Ain't Nothin' Wrong With The Radio
Aaron Tippin; *Read Between The Lines* . . . . (RCA)
Today's Hit Country-C . . . . (K-Tel)
This Car Of Mine
Beach Boys; *Beach Boys-Gift Set* . . . . (Capitol)
Shut Down, Volume 2 . . . . (Capitol)
Spirit Of America . . . . (Capitol)
Thousand Miles From Nowhere
Dwight Yoakam; *This Time* . . . . (Reprise)
Three Window Coupe
Rip Chords; *Rock Artifacts-From The Vaults-#4-C* . . . . (Columbia)
Thunder Road
Bruce Springsteen; *Born To Run* . . . . (Columbia)
Bruce Springsteen's Greatest Hits . . . . (Columbia)
Bruce Springsteen & The E Street Band; *Bruce Springsteen & The E Street Band Live/1975-85* . . . . (Legacy)
Too Many Drivers
Lightnin' Hopkins; *Soul Blues* . . . . (Prestige)
Paul Butterfield's Better Days; *It All Comes Back* . . . . (Rhino)
Traffic Jam
Artie Shaw; *Begin The Beguine* . . . . (Bluebird)
Ella Fitzgerald & Chick Webb; *Ella Sings/Chick Swings* . . . . (Olympic)
Traffic Jam
James Taylor; *JT* . . . . (Columbia)
Transfusion
Nervous Norvus; *Dr. Demento Presents The Greatest Novelty Records-#2-1950s-C* . . . . (Rhino)
Dr. Demento: 20th Anniversary Collection-C . . . . (Rhino)
Vintage Music-#3-C . . . . (MCA)
Wacky Weirdos-C . . . . (K-Tel)
Two-Car Garage
B.J. Thomas; *19 Hot Country Requests-#2-C* . . . . (Epic)
Great American Dream . . . . (Cleveland International)
Greatest Country Hits Of The '80s-1984-C . . . . (Columbia)
Under The Light Of The Texaco
Jeff Stevens & The Bullets; *Jeff Stevens & The Bullets* . . . . (Atlantic)
Lisa Stewart; *Lisa Stewart* . . . . (BNA)
Used Cars
Bruce Springsteen; *Nebraska* . . . . (Columbia)
Waiting For The Light To Turn Green
Gretchen Peters; *The Secret Of Life* . . . . (Purple Crayon Prod.)
Way, The
Fastball; *All The Pain Money Can Buy* . . . . (Hollywood)
Now That's What I Call Music!-#1-C . . . . (Virgin)
Wednesday Car
Johnny Cash; *Rambler* . . . . (Columbia)
Week In A County Jail, A
Tom T. Hall; *Storyteller, Poet, Philospher* . . . . (Mercury)

Tom T. Hall's Greatest Hits-#1 . . . . (Mercury)
What About Now
Lonestar; *Lonely Grill*. . . . . (BNA)
What I Need To Do
Kenny Chesney; *Everywhere We Go* . . . . (BNA)
Kenny Chesney's Greatest Hits . . . . (BNA)
White Car In Germany
Associates; *Popera-Singles Collection*. . . . . (Sire)
Whoever You Are
Geggy Tah; *Sacred Cow* . . . .(Luaka Bop)
Workin' At The Car Wash Blues
Jim Croce; *50th Anniversary Collection*. . . . . (Saja)
Greatest Character Songs . . . . (Lifesong)
I Got A Name . . . . (Lifesong)
Photographs & Memories/His Greatest Hits. . . . . (Atlantic)
You Already Drove Me There
Lisa Brokop; *Every Little Girl's Dream* . . . . (Patriot)
You Can't Catch Me
Chuck Berry; *Rock Rock Rock* . . . . (Chess)
The Chess Box-Chuck Berry . . . . (Chess)
George Thorogood & The Destroyers; *Born To Be Bad* . . . .(Gold Rush)
John Lennon; *Rock 'N' Roll* . . . . (Capitol)
Rolling Stones; *The Rolling Stones, Now!* . . . . (Abkco)
Stephen Stills; *Stephen Stills-Live* . . . . (Atlantic)
You Dream Flat Tires
Joni Mitchell; *Wild Things Run Fast*. . . . . (Geffen)
You Remind Me Of Something
R. Kelly; *R. Kelly* . . . . (Jive)
You Win My Love
Shania Twain; *The Woman In Me* . . . . (Mercury)
You're Still Not Safe In A Japanese Car
Jumpin' John Goldsmith; *45-#7-89686* . . . .(Atlantic)

CARS: SPECIFIC MAKES & MODELS

See Also: **CARS: CADILLAC, CARS: GENERAL, GAS STATIONS, MOTORCYCLES, ROAD, ROAD ACCIDENTS, TAXI, TRAVELING**

#1 Stunna (Lexus, Jaguar, Bentley, Prowler, Hummer, Rolls Royce, Monte Carlo, Yukon)
Big Tymers; *I Got That Work* . . . .(Cash Money/Universal)
(We're Not) The Jet Set (Chevrolet)
George Jones & Tammy Wynette; *George Jones & Tammy Wynette-16 Biggest Hits* . . . . (Epic/Legacy)
409
Beach Boys; *Beach Boys' Greatest Hits* . . . . (Gusto)
Best Of The Beach Boys . . . . (Capitol)
Made In The U.S.A. . . . . (Capitol)
Spirit Of America . . . . (Capitol)
455 Rocket (Oldsmobile, Chevrolet, Chevelle)
Kathy Mattea; *Love Travels* . . . . (Mercury)
59 Chevy
Geronimo Black; *Geronimo Black* . . . .(One Way)
Abigail Beecher (Jaguar)
Freddy Cannon; *14 Booming Hits*. . . . . (Rhino)
Big Blast From Boston: The Best Of Freddy "Boom Boom" Cannon . . . . (Rhino)
American Bad Ass ('65 Chevelle)
Kid Rock; *History Of Rock* . . . .(Top Dog/Lava/Atlantic)
American Pie (Chevrolet)
Don McLean; *American Pie* . . . .(EMI)
Best Of Don McLean . . . .(EMI)
Greatest Hits-Then & Now . . . .(EMI)
ST/Born On The Fourth Of July. . . . . (MCA)
Madonna; *ST/The Next Big Thing*. . . . . (Maverick)
Are The Good Times Really Over (I Wish A Buck Was Still Silver) (Chevy, Ford)
Merle Haggard; *Big City*. . . . .(Epic)
For The Record: Merle Haggard-43 Legendary Hits . . . . (BNA)
Greatest Country Hits Of The '80s-#2-C . . . . (Columbia)
His Epic Hits-First 11 To Be Continued-C . . . .(Epic)
Back When He Was Hungry (Chevrolet)
Bill Anderson; *A Lot Of Things Different* . . . . (Varese Sarabande)
Beep Beep (Nash Rambler)
Playmates; *Dr. Demento: 20th Anniversary Collection-C* . . . . (Rhino)
Best Day (Corvette)
George Strait; *Latest Greatest Straitest Hits* . . . .(MCA)
Big Blue Plymouth (Eyes Wide Open)
David Byrne; *The Catherine Wheel-Complete Broadway Score* . . . . (Sire)
Bitchin' Camaro
Dead Milkmen; *Big Lizard In My Backyard* . . . .(Restless)
Blue (Da Ba Dee) (Corvette)
Eiffel 65; *Europop* . . . .(Republic/Universal)
Now That's What I Call Music!-#4-C . . . . (Virgin)
Buick '55
Johnny & The Distractions; *My Desire*. (Burnside)

Buick '59
Vernon Green & The Medallions; *Best Vocal Group In Rhythm & Blues* . . . . (Dooto)
Vernon Green & The Medallions . . . . (Dooto)
Vernon Green & The Medallions-Golden Classics . . . . (Collectables)
Buick Mackane/Big Dumb Sex
Guns N' Roses; *The Spaghetti Incident?* . . . . (Geffen)
Buicks To The Moon
Alan Jackson; *Everything I Love* . . . . (Arista)
Car Wash (Mercedes, VWs)
Bruce Springsteen; *Tracks* . . . . (Columbia)
Case Of The Ex (Whatcha Gonna Do) (Mercedes)
Mya; *Fear Of Flying* . . . .(University/Interscope)
Now That's What I Call Music!-#5-C . . . . (Virgin)
Chain Of Love (Mercedes)
Clay Walker; *Live, Laugh, Love* . . . .(Giant)
Chevrolet
Jim Kweskin and His Jug Band; *Jim Kweskin and His Jug Band* . . . . (Vanguard)
Jim Kweskin and His Jug Band's Greatest Hits . . . . (Vanguard)
Chevrolet
Taj Mahal; *Best Of Taj Mahal* . . . . (Columbia)
Chevrolet
Foghat; *Stone Blue* . . . . (Rhino)
Chevrolet
ZZ Top; *Rio Grande Mud* . . . . (Warner Bros.)
Six Pack . . . . (Warner Bros.)
Chevy Van
Sammy Johns; *Super Hits Of The '70s-Have A Nice Day-#14-C* . . . . (Rhino)
Waylon Jennings; *Hangin' Tough*. . . . . (MCA)
Convoy (Kenworth)
C.W. McCall; *C.W. McCall's Greatest Hits* . . . .(Polydor)
ST/Convoy . . . .(Polydor)
Super Hits Of The '70s-Have A Nice Day-#15-C . . . . (Rhino)
Corvair
Jim White; *No Such Place* . . . .(Luaka Bop)
Country Club (Ford pickup)
Travis Tritt; *Country Club* . . . . (Warner Bros.)
Day That She Left Tulsa (In A Chevy)
Wade Hayes; *When The Wrong One Loves You Right* . . . . (Columbia/DKC)
Dead Man's Curve (Corvette and Jaguar)
Jan & Dean; *21 Legendary Superstars-C* . . . .(Original Sound)
Best Of Jan & Dean . . . . (EMI)
Dead Man's Curve . . . . (EMI)
Detroit 442
Blondie; *Plastic Letters* . . . . (Chrysalis)
Drive (For Daddy Gene) [Ford]
Alan Jackson; *Drive* . . . . (Arista)
Fall In Love (Chevrolet)
Kenny Chesney; *All I Need To Know* . . . .(BNA)
Kenny Chesney's Greatest Hits . . . .(BNA)
Fat Lip (El Camino)
Sum 41; *All Killer No Filler* . . . . (Island/IDJMG)
Now That's What I Call Music!-#8-C . . . .(Virgin)
Fearless Boogie (Pontiac)
ZZ Top; *XXX* . . . .(RCA)
Ford Econoline
Nanci Griffith; *Lone Star State Of Mind* . . . . (MCA)
The MCA Years-A Retrospective . . . . (MCA)
Ford Mustang
Serge Gainsbourg; *Comic Strip* . . . . (Mercury)
From A Buick 6
Bob Dylan; *Highway 61 Revisited*. . . . . (Columbia)
Fun, Fun, Fun (T-Bird)
Beach Boys; *Beach Boys-Gift Set* . . . . (Capitol)
Best Of The Beach Boys . . . . (Capitol)
Endless Summer . . . . (Capitol)
Made In The U.S.A. . . . . (Capitol)
The Beach Boys In Concert . . . . (Brother)
G.T.O.
Ronny & The Daytonas; *Beach Classics-All Original Recordings-C*. . . . . (Dunhill Compact Classics)
Galaxie
Blind Melon; *Soup* . . . . (Capitol)
Go Lil' Camaro Go
Ramones; *Halfway To Sanity* . . . . (Sire)
Hardin County Line (GTO)
Mark Collie; *Even The Man In The Moon Is Cryin'* . . . . (MCA)
Hardin County Line (Mustang)
Mark Collie; *Even The Man In The Moon Is Cryin'* . . . . (MCA)
He Will, She Knows (Chevrolet)
Kenny Rogers; *There You Go Again* . . . .(Dreamcatcher)
Heart Of Saturday Night, The (Looking For) (Oldsmobile)
Shawn Colvin; *Cover Girl* . . . . (Columbia)
Tom Waits; *The Heart Of Saturday Night* . . . .(Asylum)
Tom Waits-Anthology . . . .(Asylum)
Hit 'Em Up Style (Oops!) (BMW)
Blu Cantrell; *So Blu* . . . . (Arista)
Totally Hits 2001-C . . . . (Arista)

Hot Boyz ((Lexus, Lincoln, Mercedes Benz, Bentley, Rolls Royce)
Missy ''Misdemeanor'' Elliot; *Da Real World* . . . . (East West)
  Totally Hits-#2-C . . . . (Elektra)
Hot Rod Lincoln
Asleep At The Wheel; *Western Standard Time* . . . . (Epic)
Commander Cody & His Lost Planet Airmen; *Lost In The Ozone* . . . . . . (MCA)
  Super Hits Of The '70s-Have A Nice Day-#8-C . . . . . . (Rhino)
Johnny Bond; *Best Of Johnny Bond* . . . . (Starday)
How Bizarre ('69 Chevy)
OMC; *How Bizarre* . . . . (Huh!/Mercury)
How Forever Feels (Rambler)
Kenny Chesney; *Everywhere We Go* . . . . (BNA)
  Kenny Chesney's Greatest Hits . . . . (BNA)
I Don't Need Your Rockin' Chair (Corvette)
George Jones; *Platinum Country-C* . . . . (MCA)
  Walls Can Fall . . . . (MCA)
I Got 5 On It (Impala)
Luniz; *Operation Stackola* . . . . (Noo Trybe)
I Like Them Girls (Porsche, Mercedes-Benz)
Tyrese; *2000 Watts* . . . . (RCA)
I Walk The Line (Revisted) ('49 Ford)
Rodney Crowell; *The Houston Kid* . . . . (Sugar Hill)
I Wish (Impala)
Skee-Lo; *I Wish* . . . . (Sunshine/Scotti Bros.)
Stevie Wonder; *Original Musiquarium* . . . . (Motown)
  Songs In The Key Of Life . . . . (Motown)
I'm Changing My Name To Chrysler
Arlo Guthrie & Pete Seeger; *Precious Friend* . . . . (Warner Bros.)
Jeepster
T. Rex; *Electric Warrior* . . . . (Reprise)
Katie Wants A Fast One (Oldsmobile)
Steve Wariner & Garth Brooks; *Faith In You* . . . . (Capitol)
Let's Get Down (Chevrolet)
Tony Toni Tone; *House Of Music* . . . . (Mercury)
  Ultimate Hip Hop Party-1998-C . . . . (Arista)
Little Red Corvette
Prince; *1999* . . . . (Warner Bros.)
Little Red Rodeo
Collin Raye; *Best Of Collin Raye-Direct Hits* . . . . (Epic)
Love And Texaco (Pontiac)
Gretchen Peters; *Gretchen Peters* . . . . (Purple Crayon Prod.)
Lucky 4 You (Tonight I'm Just Me) (El Camino)
SHeDAISY; *The Whole Shebang* . . . . (Lyric Street)
Making Love In A Subaru
Damaskas; *Dr. Demento's Dementia Royale-C* . . . . (Rhino)
Maserati GT (I Ain't Got You)
Blue Oyster Cult; *On Your Feet Or On Your Knees* . . . . (Columbia)
Eric Clapton; *Eric Clapton-Crossroads-C* . . . . (Polydor)
Jimmy Reed; *Best Of Jimmy Reed* . . . . (Crescendo)
Yardbirds; *Yardbirds' Greatest Hits-#1 (1964-1966)* . . . . (Rhino)
Mercedes Benz
Janis Joplin; *Pearl* . . . . (Legacy)
  ST/Janis . . . . (Columbia)
Mercedes Boy
Pebbles; *Pebbles* . . . . (MCA)
Mercury Blues
Alan Jackson; *A Lot About Livin' (And A Little 'Bout Love)* . . . . . (Arista)
Steve Miller Band; *Fly Like An Eagle* . . . . (Capitol)
  Steve Miller Band-Live . . . . (Capitol)
Mustang Burn
Jack Ingram; *Hey You* . . . . (Lucky Dog)
Mustang Sally
Rascals; *Rascals' Greatest Hits* . . . . (Atlantic)
Wilson Pickett; *A Man & A Half-Best Of Wilson Pickett* . . . . . . (Rhino)
  Atlantic Rhythm & Blues 1947-1974-#6 (1966-1969)-C . . . (Atlantic)
  Best Of Wilson Pickett . . . . (Atlantic)
  Wilson Pickett's Greatest Hits . . . . (Atlantic)
  Wilson Pickett-Super Hits . . . . (Atlantic)
Young Rascals; *The Young Rascals* . . . . (Warner Special Prod.)
My Baby Drives A Buick
Sawyer Brown; *Buick* . . . . (Curb)
No One Said It Would Be Easy (Mercedes Benz)
Sheryl Crow; *Tuesday Night Music Club* . . . . (A&M)
Oh Marie (Camaro)
Sheryl Crow; *Sheryl Crow* . . . . (A&M)
One I Loved Back Then (Corvette Song)
George Jones; *19 Hot Country Requests-#3-C* . . . . (Epic)
  George Jones-Super Hits . . . . (Epic)
  Greatest Country Hits Of The '80s-1986-C . . . . (Columbia)
  Who's Gonna Fill Their Shoes . . . . (Epic)
Peaches And Cream (Bentley)
112; *Part III* . . . . (Bad Boy/Arista)
  Totally Hits 2001-C . . . . (Arista)
Pink Thunderbird
Jeff Beck; *Crazy Legs* . . . . (Epic)
Pontiac
Lyle Lovett; *Pontiac* . . . . (MCA)

Porsche
Seth Marsh; *Whole Lotta Noise* . . . . (JRS)
Powder Blue Mercedes Queen
Paul Revere And The Raiders; *Legend Of Paul Revere And The Raiders* . . . . (Columbia)
Racing In The Street (Camaro, Chevrolet)
Bruce Springsteen; *Darkness On The Edge Of Town* . . . . . . (Columbia)
Bruce Springsteen & The E Street Band; *Bruce Springsteen & The E Street Band Live/1975-85* . . . . (Legacy)
Radar Gun ('86 T-Bird)
Bottle Rockets; *The Brooklyn Side* . . . . (East Side Digital)
Ragtop Cadillac ('65 Chevy)
Lonestar; *Lonestar* . . . . (BNA)
Red Chevrolet
Jimmie Dale Gilmore; *Jimmie Dale Gilmore* . . . . (Hightone)
  Points West-New Horizons In Country-C . . . . (Hightone)
Riding With Private Malone ('66 Corvette)
David Ball; *Amigo* . . . . (Razor & Tie)
See The U.S.A. (Chevrolet)
Original Soundtrack; *TeeVee Toons-The Commercials-#1-C* . . . . (TVT)
She's In Love With The Boy (Chevrolet)
Trisha Yearwood; *Trisha Yearwood* . . . . (MCA)
Shut Out The Light (Ford)
Bruce Springsteen; *Tracks* . . . . (Columbia)
Shut Up (Rolls Royce, Volvo)
Trick Daddy; *Book Of Thugs-Chapter AK Verse 47* . . . . . . (Slip 'N Slide)
Silver Thunderbird
Jo Dee Messina; *I'm Alright* . . . . (Curb)
Marc Cohn; *Marc Cohn* . . . . (Atlantic)
Someday (' 67 Chevrolet)
Steve Earle & The Dukes; *Guitar Town* . . . . (MCA)
  Shut Up And Die Like An Aviator . . . . (MCA)
Song Of The South (Chevrolet)
Alabama; *Alabama's Greatest Hits-#2* . . . . (RCA)
  Southern Star . . . . (RCA)
Still A G Thang (Impala)
Snoop Dogg; *Da Game Is To Be Sold, Not To Be Told* . . . . . . (No Limit/Priority)
Studebaker
Riders In The Sky; *Riders Go Commercial* . . . . (MCA)
Summer's Comin' (Ford)
Clint Black; *Clint Black-The Greatest Hits* . . . . (RCA)
  One Emotion . . . . (RCA)
T-Bird To Vegas
Albert Lee; *Speechless* . . . . (MCA)
Theme From ''All In The Family'' (LaSalle)
Original Soundtrack; *CBS: The First 50 Years* . . . . (TVT)
  Television's Greatest Hits-#3-1970s & 1980s-C . . . . (TVT)
Three Marlenas (Rolls Royce, Chevrolet)
Wallflowers; *Bringing Down The Horse* . . . . (Interscope)
Thunder Road (Chevrolet)
Bruce Springsteen; *Born To Run* . . . . (Columbia)
  Bruce Springsteen's Greatest Hits . . . . (Columbia)
Bruce Springsteen & The E Street Band; *Bruce Springsteen & The E Street Band Live/1975-85* . . . . (Legacy)
Thunderbird
Quiet Riot; *Metal Health* . . . . (Pasha)
Thunderbird
ZZ Top; *Fandango* . . . . (Warner Bros.)
Trans Am
Neil Young & Crazy Horse; *Sleeps With Angels* . . . . (Reprise)
Wanna Be A Baller (Impala, Mercedes Benz, Expedition)
Lil' Troy; *Sittin' Fat Down South* . . . . . . (Short Stop/Republic/Universal)
When God Fearin' Women Get The Blues (Mustang)
Martina McBride; *Martina McBride's Greatest Hits* . . . . (RCA)
Where Have All The Cowboys Gone? ('56 Chevy)
Paula Cole; *This Fire* . . . . (Imago)
Wrong Side Of Memphis ('69 Tempest)
Matraca Berg; *Bittersweet Surrender* . . . . (RCA)
Trisha Yearwood; *Grand Ole Opry-75 Years-#1-C* . . . . (MCA)
  Hearts In Armor . . . . (MCA)
You Gotta Love That (Pontiac)
Neal McCoy; *Neal McCoy's Greatest Hits* . . . . (Atlantic)
  Today's Country Love-C . . . . (K-Tel)
  You Gotta Love That! . . . . (Atlantic)
You Win My Love ('55 Chevy)
Shania Twain; *The Woman In Me* . . . . (Mercury)

CARTOON CHARACTERS, Comic Book Characters

See Also: **BOOKS, HEROISM, STORYBOOK CHARACTERS, TELEVISION, TOYS & GAMES**

(Meet) The Flintstones
BC-52's; *ST/The Flintstones-The Music From Bedrock* . . . . (MCA)
Herb Ellis & Others; *After You've Gone* . . . . (Concord Jazz)
Herb Ellis & Ray Brown; *Soft Shoe* . . . . (Concord Jazz)

Alley-Oop
Hollywood Argyles; *American Graffiti-#3-C* . . . . (MCA)
Collectables Presents The History Of Rock-#5-C . . . . (Collectables)
M. Dung's Idiot Classics . . . . (Rhino)

Andy's Birthday
Original Soundtrack; *ST/Toy Story* . . . . (Disney)

Assorted Tracks
Carl Stallings Project; *Music From Warner Bros. Cartoons-
1936-58* . . . .(Warner Bros.)

Banana Splits Adventure Hour
Original Soundtrack; *Hanna-Barbera Pic-A-Nic Basket Of Cartoon
Classics* . . . . (Kid Rhino/Rhino 4 Kids)

Batdance
Prince; *ST/Batman* . . . .(Warner Bros.)

Bugs Bunny: Rhapsody Rabbit
Philadelphia Orchestra & Eugene Ormandy; *TV Classics-C* . . . . (RCA)

Captain Marvel
Arnold Bean; *Cosmic Bean.* . . . . (SSS International)
Chick Corea & Return To Forever; *Light As A Feather* . . . . (Polydor)

Charlie Brown's Parents
Dishwalla; *Pet Your Friends* . . . . (A&M)

Check Mr. Popeye
Eddie Bo; *Carnival Time-Best Of Ric Records-#1-C* . . . . (Rounder)
Check Mr. Popeye . . . . (Rounder)
Southside Johnny And The Asbury Jukes; *This Time It's For Real* . . . . . . (Epic)

Dick Tracy
Ice-T; *ST/Dick Tracy* . . . . (Sire)

Do The Bartman
Bart Simpson; *Simpsons Sing The Blues* . . . .(Geffen)

Hong Kong Phooey
Original Soundtrack; *Hanna-Barbera Pic-A-Nic Basket Of Cartoon
Classics* . . . . (Kid Rhino/Rhino 4 Kids)

Honky Tonk Superman
Aaron Tippin; *Call Of The Wild* . . . . (RCA)

House At Pooh Corner
Loggins & Messina; *Loggins & Messina-On Stage* . . . . (Columbia)
Sittin' In . . . . (Columbia)
The Best Of Friends . . . . (Columbia)
Nitty Gritty Dirt Band; *Best Of The Nitty Gritty Dirt Band.* . . . . (Liberty)
Best Of The Nitty Gritty Dirt Band. . . . . (Curb)
Dirt, Silver & Gold. . . . . (One Way)
Uncle Charlie And His Dog Teddy. . . . . (Liberty)

I Tawt I Taw A Puddy Tat
Mel Blanc; *From The Vaults-#7-The Movies...-C* . . . . (Capitol)

I Wanna Be A Flintstone
Screaming Blue Messiahs; *Bikini Red* . . . . (Elektra)

I'm Popeye The Sailor Man
Billy Costello; *Dr. Demento Presents The Greatest Novelty Records-#1-1940s
& Before-C* . . . . (Rhino)

It's Superman
Original Cast; *Superman.* . . . . (Sony Music Special Prod.)

Jimmy Olsen's Blues
Spin Doctors; *Pocket Full Of Kryptonite* . . . . (Epic Portrait Assoc.)

Kryptonite
3 Doors Down; *Better Life* . . . .(Republic/Universal)
Now That's What I Call Music!-#5-C . . . . (Virgin)

Linus & Lucy
Original Soundtrack; *Television's Greatest Hits-#2-C* . . . . (TVT)
Vince Guaraldi; *Charlie Brown Christmas.* . . . . (Fantasy)

Mickey Mouse
Sparks; *Angst In My Pants* . . . . (Atlantic)

Mickey Mouse Alma Mater
Mouseketeers; *Disney Collection-#1-C* . . . .(Disney)

Mickey Mouse March
Aaron Neville & Dr. John; *Stay Awake-Music Of Vintage Disney
Films-C* . . . . (A&M)
Mouseketeers; *Disney Collection-#1-C* . . . .(Disney)

Resignation Superman
Big Head Todd & The Monsters; *Beautiful World* . . . . (Revolution)
Live Monsters . . . . (Revolution)

Return Of The Red Baron
Royal Guardsmen; *Royal Guardsmen-Anthology.* . . . .(One Way)

Salsa Smurf
Special Request; *Tommy Boy's Greatest Beats-C.* . . . . (Tommy Boy)

Saturday Morning Cartoons
Sergio Salvatore; *Sergio Salvatore* . . . . (GRP)

Snoopy Vs. The Red Baron
Royal Guardsmen; *Best Of The Royal Guardsmen-#1* . . . . (Rhino)
Collectables Presents The History Of Rock-#9-C . . . . (Collectables)
Cruisin'-1967-C . . . .(Increase)
Million-Dollar Memories #1-C . . . . (RCA)
Super Oldies Of The '60s-#6-C . . . .(Audio Fidelity)

Snoopy's Christmas
Royal Guardsmen; *Snoopy & His Friends* . . . . (Laurie)

Space Ghost
Original Soundtrack; *Hanna-Barbera Pic-A-Nic Basket Of Cartoon
Classics.* . . . . (Kid Rhino/Rhino 4 Kids)

Sunshine Superman
Donovan; *Donovan's Greatest Hits* . . . . (Epic)
History Of British Rock-#5-C . . . .(Rhino)
Sunshine Superman . . . . (Epic)
Troubadour-Definitive Collection . . . . (Epic)

Superman
101 Strings Orchestra; *Superman-Music From & Other Space
Themes.* . . . . (Alshire)
Barbra Streisand; *Barbra Streisand's Greatest Hits, Volume 2* . . . . . (Columbia)
Streisand Superman . . . . (Columbia)
Robyn Hitchcock & The Egyptians; *Queen Elvis* . . . . (A&M)

Superman
R.E.M.; *Life's Rich Pageant* . . . . (EMI-Capitol Entert. Properties)

Superman (I Wish I Could Fly Like)
Kinks; *Come Dancing With The Kinks-Best Of The Kinks 1977-1986* . . . (Arista)
Low Budget. . . . . (Arista)

Superman (It's Not Easy)
Five For Fighting; *America Town* . . . . (Aware/C2/Columbia)
The Concert For New York City-C . . . . (Columbia)

Superman Inside
Eric Clapton; *Reptile* . . . .(Duck/Reprise)

Superman's Dead
Our Lady Peace; *Clumsy* . . . . (Columbia)

Superman's Ghost
Don McLean; *Greatest Hits Then & Now* . . . . (EMI)

Superman's Song
Crash Test Dummies; *Ghosts That Haunt Me* . . . . (Arista)

Superwoman
Karyn White; *Karyn White* . . . . (Warner Bros.)
Stevie Wonder; *Music Of My Mind* . . . . (Motown)
Original Musiquarium . . . . (Motown)

Superwoman
Lil' Mo; *Based On A True Story* . . . . (Gold Mind/East West/EEG)

Take Me There
Blackstreet & Mya featuring Mase & Blinky Blink;
Finally . . . . (Lil' Man/Interscope)
Now That's What I Call Music!-#2-C . . . . (Virgin)
ST/Rugrats . . . .(Interscope)

Theme From "Augie Doggie"
Original Soundtrack; *Hanna-Barbera Classics-#1-Original Recordings Of
The World's Most Famous Cartoon Themes &
Scores* . . . . (Kid Rhino/Rhino 4 Kids)
*Hanna-Barbera Pic-A-Nic Basket Of Cartoon
Classics* . . . . (Kid Rhino/Rhino 4 Kids)

Theme From "Batman"
Original Soundtrack; *Television's Greatest Hits-#1-C* . . . . (TVT)

Theme From "Casper The Friendly Ghost"
Original Soundtrack; *Television's Greatest Hits-#1-C* . . . . (TVT)

Theme From "Courageous Cat & Minute Mouse"
Original Soundtrack; *Television's Greatest Hits-#2-C* . . . . (TVT)

Theme From "Dastardly & Muttley In Their Flying Machine"
Original Soundtrack; *Hanna-Barbera Pic-A-Nic Basket Of Cartoon
Classics* . . . . (Kid Rhino/Rhino 4 Kids)
Television's Greatest Hits-#3-1970s & 1980s-C . . . . (TVT)

Theme From "Dudley-Do-Right"
Original Soundtrack; *Television's Greatest Hits-#3-1970s & 1980s-C* . . . (TVT)

Theme From "Fat Albert And The Cosby Kids"
Original Soundtrack; *Television's Greatest Hits-#3-1970s & 1980s-C* . . . (TVT)

Theme From "Felix The Cat"
Original Soundtrack; *Television's Greatest Hits-#1-C* . . . . (TVT)

Theme From "Fractured Fairy Tales"
Original Soundtrack; *Television's Greatest Hits-#3-1970s & 1980s-C* . . . (TVT)

Theme From "George Of The Jungle"
Original Soundtrack; *Television's Greatest Hits-#2-C* . . . . (TVT)

Theme From "Hokey Wolf"
Original Soundtrack; *Hanna-Barbera Classics-#1-Original Recordings Of
The World's Most Famous Cartoon Themes &
Scores* . . . .(Kid Rhino/Rhino 4 Kids)
*Hanna-Barbera Pic-A-Nic Basket Of Cartoon
Classics* . . . .(Kid Rhino/Rhino 4 Kids)

Theme From "Huckleberry Hound"
Original Soundtrack; *Hanna-Barbera Classics-#1-Original Recordings Of
The World's Most Famous Cartoon Themes &
Scores* . . . .(Kid Rhino/Rhino 4 Kids)
*Hanna-Barbera Pic-A-Nic Basket Of Cartoon
Classics* . . . .(Kid Rhino/Rhino 4 Kids)
Television's Greatest Hits-#2-C. . . . . (TVT)

Theme From "Johnny Quest"
Original Soundtrack; *Hanna-Barbera Pic-A-Nic Basket Of Cartoon
Classics* . . . .(Kid Rhino/Rhino 4 Kids)
Television's Greatest Hits-#2-C. . . . . (TVT)

Theme From "Josie & The Pussycats"
Original Soundtrack; *Hanna-Barbera Pic-A-Nic Basket Of Cartoon
Classics* . . . .(Kid Rhino/Rhino 4 Kids)
Television's Greatest Hits-#3-1970s & 1980s-C . . . . (TVT)

Theme From "Lippy The Lion & Hardy Har Har"
Original Soundtrack; *Hanna-Barbera Classics-#1-Original Recordings Of
The World's Most Famous Cartoon Themes &
Scores* . . . .(Kid Rhino/Rhino 4 Kids)

*Hanna-Barbera Pic-A-Nic Basket Of Cartoon
    Classics* . . . . (Kid Rhino/Rhino 4 Kids)
Theme From "Looney Tunes"
Original Soundtrack; *Television's Greatest Hits-#2-C* . . . . (TVT)
Theme From "Loopy De Loop"
Original Soundtrack; *Hanna-Barbera Classics-#1-Original Recordings Of
    The World's Most Famous Cartoon Themes &
    Scores* . . . . (Kid Rhino/Rhino 4 Kids)
*Hanna-Barbera Pic-A-Nic Basket Of Cartoon
    Classics* . . . . (Kid Rhino/Rhino 4 Kids)
Theme From "Magilla Gorilla"
Original Soundtrack; *Hanna-Barbera Classics-#1-Original Recordings Of
    The World's Most Famous Cartoon Themes &
    Scores* . . . . (Kid Rhino/Rhino 4 Kids)
*Hanna-Barbera Pic-A-Nic Basket Of Cartoon
    Classics* . . . . (Kid Rhino/Rhino 4 Kids)
Television's Greatest Hits-#1-C . . . . (TVT)
Theme From "Merrie Melodies"
Original Soundtrack; *Television's Greatest Hits-#2-C* . . . . (TVT)
Theme From "Mighty Mouse"
Original Soundtrack; *Television's Greatest Hits-#2-C* . . . . (TVT)
Theme From "Mr. Magoo"
Original Soundtrack; *Television's Greatest Hits-#3-1970s & 1980s-C* . . . . (TVT)
Theme From "Pebbles & Bamm-Bamm"
Original Soundtrack; *Hanna-Barbera Pic-A-Nic Basket Of Cartoon
    Classics* . . . . (Kid Rhino/Rhino 4 Kids)
Theme From "Peter Potamus"
Original Soundtrack; *Hanna-Barbera Classics-#1-Original Recordings Of
    The World's Most Famous Cartoon Themes &
    Scores* . . . . (Kid Rhino/Rhino 4 Kids)
*Hanna-Barbera Pic-A-Nic Basket Of Cartoon
    Classics* . . . . (Kid Rhino/Rhino 4 Kids)
Theme From "Pixie And Dixie"
Original Soundtrack; *Hanna-Barbera Classics-#1-Original Recordings Of
    The World's Most Famous Cartoon Themes &
    Scores* . . . . (Kid Rhino/Rhino 4 Kids)
*Hanna-Barbera Pic-A-Nic Basket Of Cartoon
    Classics* . . . . (Kid Rhino/Rhino 4 Kids)
Theme From "Quick Draw McGraw"
Original Soundtrack; *Hanna-Barbera Classics-#1-Original Recordings Of
    The World's Most Famous Cartoon Themes &
    Scores* . . . . (Kid Rhino/Rhino 4 Kids)
*Hanna-Barbera Pic-A-Nic Basket Of Cartoon
    Classics* . . . . (Kid Rhino/Rhino 4 Kids)
Theme From "Ren And Stimpy"
Original Soundtrack; *Television's Greatest Hits-#7-Cable Ready-C* . . . . . (TVT)
Theme From "Road Runner"
Original Soundtrack; *Television's Greatest Hits-#2-C* . . . . (TVT)
Theme From "Roger Ramjet"
Original Soundtrack; *Television's Greatest Hits-#4-Black & White
    Classics-C* . . . . (TVT)
Theme From "Ruff And Reddy"
Original Soundtrack; *Hanna-Barbera Classics-#1-Original Recordings Of
    The World's Most Famous Cartoon Themes &
    Scores* . . . . (Kid Rhino/Rhino 4 Kids)
*Hanna-Barbera Pic-A-Nic Basket Of Cartoon
    Classics* . . . . (Kid Rhino/Rhino 4 Kids)
Theme From "Scooby Doo, Where Are You?"
Original Soundtrack; *Hanna-Barbera Classics-#1-Original Recordings Of
    The World's Most Famous Cartoon Themes &
    Scores* . . . . (Kid Rhino/Rhino 4 Kids)
*Hanna-Barbera Pic-A-Nic Basket Of Cartoon
    Classics* . . . . (Kid Rhino/Rhino 4 Kids)
Television's Greatest Hits-#3-1970s & 1980s-C . . . . (TVT)
Theme From "Secret Squirrel"
Original Soundtrack; *Hanna-Barbera Pic-A-Nic Basket Of Cartoon
    Classics* . . . . (Kid Rhino/Rhino 4 Kids)
Television's Greatest Hits-#5-In Living Color-C . . . . (TVT)
Theme From "Snagglepuss"
Original Soundtrack; *Hanna-Barbera Classics-#1-Original Recordings Of
    The World's Most Famous Cartoon Themes &
    Scores* . . . . (Kid Rhino/Rhino 4 Kids)
*Hanna-Barbera Pic-A-Nic Basket Of Cartoon
    Classics* . . . . (Kid Rhino/Rhino 4 Kids)
*Toon Tunes: 50 Favorite Classic Cartoon
    Songs-C* . . . . (Kid Rhino/Rhino 4 Kids)
Theme From "Snooper & Blabber"
Original Soundtrack; *Hanna-Barbera Classics-#1-Original Recordings Of
    The World's Most Famous Cartoon Themes &
    Scores* . . . . (Kid Rhino/Rhino 4 Kids)
*Hanna-Barbera Pic-A-Nic Basket Of Cartoon
    Classics* . . . . (Kid Rhino/Rhino 4 Kids)
Theme From "Space Ghost Coast To Coast"
Original Soundtrack; *Television's Greatest Hits-#7-Cable Ready-C* . . . . . (TVT)
Theme From "Speed Racer"
Original Soundtrack; *Television's Greatest Hits-#3-1970s & 1980s-C* . . . . (TVT)
Theme From "Spiderman"
Original Soundtrack; *Television's Greatest Hits-#2-C* . . . . (TVT)

Theme From "Superman"
London Symphony Orchestra & John Williams; *ST/Superman-The
    Movie* . . . . (Warner Bros.)
Neil Norman; *Greatest Science Fiction Hits* . . . . (Crescendo)
Original Soundtrack; *Television's Greatest Hits-#1-C* . . . . (TVT)
Theme From "Tennessee Tuxedo"
Original Soundtrack; *Television's Greatest Hits-#4-Black & White
    Classics-C* . . . . (TVT)
Theme From "The Alvin Show"
Original Soundtrack; *Television's Greatest Hits-#3-1970s & 1980s-C* . . . . (TVT)
Theme From "The Archies"
Original Soundtrack; *Television's Greatest Hits-#3-1970s & 1980s-C* . . . . (TVT)
Theme From "The Atom Ant Show"
Original Soundtrack; *Hanna-Barbera Pic-A-Nic Basket Of Cartoon
    Classics* . . . . (Kid Rhino/Rhino 4 Kids)
Television's Greatest Hits-#5-In Living Color-C . . . . (TVT)
Theme From "The Beany & Cecil Show"
Original Soundtrack; *Television's Greatest Hits-#4-Black & White
    Classics-C* . . . . (TVT)
Theme From "The Brothers Grunt"
Original Soundtrack; *Television's Greatest Hits-#7-Cable Ready-C* . . . . . (TVT)
Theme From "The Flintstones"
Original Soundtrack; *Hanna-Barbera Classics-#1-Original Recordings Of
    The World's Most Famous Cartoon Themes &
    Scores* . . . . (Kid Rhino/Rhino 4 Kids)
*Hanna-Barbera Pic-A-Nic Basket Of Cartoon
    Classics* . . . . (Kid Rhino/Rhino 4 Kids)
Television's Greatest Hits-#1-C . . . . (TVT)
Steve Hobbs; *Escape* . . . . (Cexton)
Theme From "The Gumby Show"
Original Soundtrack; *Television's Greatest Hits-#4-Black & White
    Classics-C* . . . . (TVT)
Theme From "The Jetsons"
Original Soundtrack; *Hanna-Barbera Pic-A-Nic Basket Of Cartoon
    Classics* . . . . (Kid Rhino/Rhino 4 Kids)
Television's Greatest Hits-#1-C . . . . (TVT)
Stunners; *ST/Jetsons-The Movie* . . . . (MCA)
Theme From "The Mighty Hercules"
Original Soundtrack; *Television's Greatest Hits-#4-Black & White
    Classics-C* . . . . (TVT)
Theme From "The Pink Panther"
Henry Mancini; *Henry Mancini-Legendary Performer* . . . . (RCA)
Henry Mancini-Pure Gold . . . . (RCA)
Peter Gunn . . . . (RCA)
ST/Revenge Of The Pink Panther . . . . (EMI)
Television's Greatest Hits-#2-C . . . . (TVT)
Theme From "The Rocky & Bullwinkle Show"
Original Soundtrack; *Television's Greatest Hits-#2-C* . . . . (TVT)
Theme From "The Simpsons"
Original Soundtrack; *Television's Greatest Hits-#7-Cable Ready-C* . . . . . (TVT)
Theme From "The Smurfs"
Original Soundtrack; *Television's Greatest Hits-#3-1970s & 1980s-C* . . . . (TVT)
Theme From "Tom & Jerry"
Henry Mancini; *ST/Tom & Jerry-The Movie* . . . . (MCA)
Theme From "Top Cat"
Original Soundtrack; *Hanna-Barbera Pic-A-Nic Basket Of Cartoon
    Classics* . . . . (Kid Rhino/Rhino 4 Kids)
Television's Greatest Hits-#1-C . . . . (TVT)
Theme From "Touche Turtle"
Original Soundtrack; *Hanna-Barbera Classics-#1-Original Recordings Of
    The World's Most Famous Cartoon Themes &
    Scores* . . . . (Kid Rhino/Rhino 4 Kids)
*Hanna-Barbera Pic-A-Nic Basket Of Cartoon
    Classics* . . . . (Kid Rhino/Rhino 4 Kids)
Theme From "Underdog"
Original Soundtrack; *Television's Greatest Hits-#2-C* . . . . (TVT)
Theme From "Wally Gator"
Original Soundtrack; *Hanna-Barbera Classics-#1-Original Recordings Of
    The World's Most Famous Cartoon Themes &
    Scores* . . . . (Kid Rhino/Rhino 4 Kids)
*Hanna-Barbera Pic-A-Nic Basket Of Cartoon
    Classics* . . . . (Kid Rhino/Rhino 4 Kids)
Theme From "Yakky Doodle"
Original Soundtrack; *Hanna-Barbera Classics-#1-Original Recordings Of
    The World's Most Famous Cartoon Themes &
    Scores* . . . . (Kid Rhino/Rhino 4 Kids)
*Hanna-Barbera Pic-A-Nic Basket Of Cartoon
    Classics* . . . . (Kid Rhino/Rhino 4 Kids)
Theme From "Yogi Bear"
Original Soundtrack; *Hanna-Barbera Classics-#1-Original Recordings Of
    The World's Most Famous Cartoon Themes &
    Scores* . . . . (Kid Rhino/Rhino 4 Kids)
*Hanna-Barbera Pic-A-Nic Basket Of Cartoon
    Classics* . . . . (Kid Rhino/Rhino 4 Kids)
Television's Greatest Hits-#1-C . . . . (TVT)
Wheelie & The Chopper Bunch
Original Soundtrack; *Hanna-Barbera Pic-A-Nic Basket Of Cartoon
    Classics* . . . . (Kid Rhino/Rhino 4 Kids)

When The Flintstones Meet The President
Dirty Dozen Brass Band; *Louisiana Scrapbook-C* . . . .(Rykodisc)
Woody Woodpecker Song
Kay Kyser & His Orchestra; *Best Of The Big Bands-C* . . . . (Columbia)
Sentimental Favorites . . . . (Columbia)
Mel Blanc & The Sportsmen; *Small Fry-Capitol Sings Kids Songs For
Grownups-C* . . . . (Capitol)
You're A Good Man, Charlie Brown
Original Cast; *You're A Good Man, Charlie Brown* . . . . (Polydor)

CELEBRITIES: SPECIFIC, Famous People

See Also: ELVIS, MEN'S NAMES: A-Z, MOVIES, PRESIDENTS, SHOW BIZ, TELEVISION, WOMEN'S NAMES A-Z

#1 Stunna (James Bond, Jackie Chan, MacGyver)
Big Tymers; *I Got That Work* . . . .(Cash Money/Universal)
Abraham, Martin And John
Dion; *Collectables Presents The History Of Rock-#3-C* . . . . (Collectables)
Dion-24 Original Classics . . . . (Arista)
Songs Of Protest-C . . . . (Rhino)
WCBS FM 101 History Of Rock-'60s-#2-C . . . . (Collectables)
Harry Belafonte; *Harry Belafonte's All Time Greatest Hits-#1* . . . . . . (RCA)
Smokey Robinson & The Miracles; *Smokey Robinson & The Miracles'
Anthology* . . . . (Motown)
*Time Out For Smokey Robinson & The Miracles/Special
Occasion* . . . . (Motown)
Amelia Earhart
BTO; *Rock 'N' Roll Nights* . . . . (Mercury)
American Pie (Buddy Holly)
Don McLean; *American Pie* . . . .(EMI)
Best Of Don McLean . . . .(EMI)
Greatest Hits-Then & Now . . . .(EMI)
ST/Born On The Fourth Of July . . . . (MCA)
Madonna; *ST/The Next Big Thing* . . . .(Maverick)
Anne Frank Story
Human Sexual Response; *Fig. 15* . . . .(Eat)
Are You Sure Hank Done It This Way
Hank Williams, Jr.; *Rowdy* . . . . (WB/Curb)
Waylon Jennings; *Waylon Jennings' Greatest Hits* . . . . (RCA)
Bad Touch, The (Prince, Siskel & Ebert, Lyle Lovett)
Bloodhound Gang; *Hooray For Boobies* . . . .(Republic/Geffen)
Ballad Of Bonnie And Clyde
Georgie Fame; *History Of British Rock-#8-C* . . . . (Rhino)
Ballad Of John And Yoko
Beatles; *Beatles 1* . . . . (Capitol)
Beatles-Box Set . . . . (Capitol)
Hey Jude . . . . (Capitol)
Past Masters-Volume Two . . . .(Parlophone)
ST/Imagine: John Lennon . . . . (Capitol)
The Beatles/1967-1970 . . . . (Capitol)
Ballad Of Martin Luther King
Mike Millius; *Best Of Broadside 1962-1968: Anthems Of The American
Underground From The Pages Of Broadside
Magazine-C* . . . . (Smithsonian Folkways)
Bette Davis Eyes (Greta Garbo, Jean Harlow)
Kim Carnes; *Best Of Kim Carnes* . . . . (EMI Special Markets)
Billboard Top Hits-1981-C . . . . (Rhino)
Mistaken Identity . . . .(EMI)
Better Things To Do (Phil Donahue)
Terri Clark; *Terri Clark* . . . . (Mercury)
Bigger Than The Beatles
Joe Diffie; *Life's So Funny* . . . . (Epic)
Billy The Kid
Charlie Daniels Band; *High Lonesome* . . . . (Epic)
Billy The Kid
Marty Robbins; *Gunfighter Ballads & Trail Songs* . . . . (Legacy)
Billy The Kid
Ry Cooder; *Into The Purple Valley* . . . . (Reprise)
Bo Diddley
Bo Diddley; *Good Time Rock 'N' Roll-C* . . . .(MCA)
History Of Rock-#5-C . . . . (Collectables)
Oldies But Goodies-#10-C . . . . (Original Sound)
ST/Rage In Harlem . . . . (Sire)
Buddy Holly; *Buddy Holly-20 Golden Greats* . . . . (MCA)
For The First Time Anywhere . . . .(MCA)
Bob Wills Is Still The King
Clint Black & Asleep At The Wheel; *Ride With Bob-C* . . . . (DreamWorks/SKG)
Bobby Orr Breakaway
Kirk Elliott; *No Fixed Address* . . . . (Boot)
Brain Of J. (J.F.K.)
Pearl Jam; *Yield* . . . . (Epic)
Brian Wilson
Barenaked Ladies; *Gordon* . . . . (Reprise)
Rock Spectacle . . . . (Reprise)
Brush Up Your Shakespeare
Dick Hyman; *Cole Porter- All Through The Night* . . . . (Musicmasters)

Keenan Wynn & James Whitmore; *ST/Kiss Me Kate* . . . . (MCA)
Original Cast; *Kiss Me Kate* . . . . (Sony Music Classical)
Buddy Holly
Weezer; *Weezer* . . . .(David Geffen Co.)
Candle In The Wind (Norma Jean)
Elton John; *Goodbye Yellow Brick Road* . . . .(Polydor)
Live In Australia With The Melbourne Symphony Orchestra . . . . (MCA)
Your Songs . . . .(Polydor)
Candle In The Wind 1997 (Diana, Princess Of Wales)
Elton John; *Candle In The Wind 1997 (Diana, Princess Of Wales)
(Single)* . . . . (Rocket)
Chanukah Song, The
Adam Sandler; *What The Hell Happened To Me?* . . . . (Warner Bros.)
Clap For The Wolfman
Guess Who; *Only Dance 1970-1974-C* . . . . (Rhino)
Clint Eastwood
Gorillaz; *Gorillaz* . . . .#(Virgin)
Coca Cola Cowboy (Clint Eastwood, Robert Redford)
Mel Tillis; *Mel Tillis' Greatest Hits* . . . . (Curb)
Very Best Of Mel Tillis . . . . (MCA)
Colonel Buffalo Bill
Ethel Merman/Bruce Yarnell/Original Cast; *Annie Get
Your Gun* . . . . (RCA Victor)
Cowboy Heaven
Roy Rogers; *Peace In The Valley* . . . .(Pair)
Creeque Alley
Mamas & The Papas; *Best Of The Mamas & The Papas* . . . . (MCA)
Mamas & The Papas' Greatest Hits . . . . (MCA)
Mamas & The Papas-16 Of Their Greatest Hits . . . . (MCA)
David Duchovny
Bree Sharp; *Cheap & Evil Girl* . . . . (Trauma)
Dear Mrs. Roosevelt
Bob Dylan; *Tribute To Woody Guthrie-C* . . . . (Warner Bros.)
Did You See Jackie Robinson Hit That Ball?
Count Basie; *RCA Victor Blues & Rhythm Revue-C* . . . . (RCA)
Count Basie & His Orchestra; *Baseball's Greatest Hits-C* . . . . (Rhino)
Diddley Daddy
Bo Diddley; *Bo Diddley-His Best* . . . . (Chess)
Bo Knows Bo . . . . (MCA Special Prod.)
Chris Isaak; *Heart Shaped World* . . . . (Reprise)
D-O-D-G-E-R-S Song (Oh, Really? No, O'Malley)
Danny Kaye; *Baseball's Greatest Hits-C* . . . . (Rhino)
Done With Bonaparte
Mark Knopfler; *Golden Heart* . . . . (Warner Bros.)
Eddie's First Wife (Brigitte Bardot)
Gretchen Peters; *Gretchen Peters* . . . . (Purple Crayon Prod.)
Elvis & Marilyn
Leon Russell; *Americana* . . . . (Paradise)
Even Cowboys Like A Little Rock And Roll
Chris LeDoux; *Chris LeDoux-20 Greatest Hits* . . . . (Capitol)
Exhuming McCarthy
R.E.M.; *Document* . . . . (EMI-Capitol Entert. Properties)
F. Lee Bailey Blues
Sugar Ray & The Bluetones; *Don't Stand In My Way* . . . . (Bullseye Blues)
Forgot About Dre
Dr. Dre featuring Eminem; *Dr. Dre 2001* . . . .(Aftermath/Interscope)
Free Nelson Mandela
Special AKA; *In The Studio* . . . . (Chrysalis)
Goodbye England's Rose (Princess Diana)
Elton John; *Countdown Singers-England's Rose-C* . . . .(Madacy)
Got 'Til It's Gone (Joni Mitchell)
Janet featuring Q-Tip & Joni Mitchell; *Velvet Rope* . . . . (Virgin)
Happy Birthday Mr. President
Marilyn Monroe; *20 Golden Greatest Hits* . . . . (Stardance)
Marilyn Monroe-The Essential Recordings . . . .(Music Club)
Hey Leonardo (She Likes Me For Me)
Blessid Union Of Souls; *Now That's What I Call Music!-#3-C* . . . .(Virgin)
Walking Off The Buzz . . . .(Push/V2)
I Just Shot John Lennon
Cranberries; *To The Faithful Departed* . . . . (Island)
I Love Mickey
Mickey Mantle & Teresa Brewer; *Baseball's Greatest Hits-C* . . . . . . (Rhino)
If I Had A Boat (Roy Rogers, Dale Evans)
Lyle Lovett; *Pontiac* . . . . (MCA)
**If It Makes You Happy (Coltrane, Geronimo, Benny Goodman,
Marilyn Monroe)**
Sheryl Crow; *Sheryl Crow* . . . . (A&M)
I'll Be Missing You (Notorious B.I.G.)
Puff Daddy & Family & Faith Evans & 112; *No Way Out* . . . . .(Bad Boy/Arista)
Imelda
Mark Knopfler; *Golden Heart* . . . . (Warner Bros.)
Jackie Wilson Said (I'm In Heaven When You Smile)
Van Morrison; *Best Of Van Morrison* . . . .(Polydor)
St. Dominic's Preview . . . . (Warner Bros.)
ST/Queen's Logic . . . . (Epic)
James Dean
Eagles; *On The Border* . . . . (Elektra)

Jerry Springer
"Weird Al" Yankovic; *Running With Scissors*...... (Volcano Entertainment)
Joe DiMaggio Done It Again
Wilco; *Mermaid Avenue-#2*................................... (Elektra)
John Barleycorn
Traffic; *John Barleycorn Must Die* .... (Island)
Joltin' Joe DiMaggio
Les Brown & His Orchestra; *Baseball's Greatest Hits-C* .... (Rhino)
   Words & Music Of World War II-C .... (Columbia)
Keith Don't Go (Ode To The Glimmer Twin)
Nils Lofgren; *Best Of Nils Lofgren* .... (A&M)
   Night After Night.................................. (A&M)
   Nils Lofgren....................................... (Rykodisc)
   Nils Lofgren-Classics-#13 .... (A&M)
Kevorkian
Public Enemy; *There's A Poison Goin On*.................. (Atomic Pop)
Legend Of Bonnie And Clyde
Merle Haggard & The Strangers; *For The Record: Merle Haggard-43*
   Legendary Hits ....(BNA)
Life Is A Rock (But The Radio Rolled Me)
Reunion; *Super Hits Of The '70s-Have A Nice Day-#13-C* .... (Rhino)
Like A Rembrandt
Badlees; *Diamonds In The Coal* .... (Rite-Off)
Longfellow Serenade
Neil Diamond; *12 Greatest Hits-#2* .... (Columbia)
   Love At The Greek.................................. (Columbia)
   On The Way To The Sky............................. (Columbia)
   Serenade.. (Columbia)
Lookin' Out My Back Door (Buck Owens)
Creedence Clearwater Revival; *1970* ....(Fantasy)
   Cosmo's Factory................................... (Fantasy)
   Creedence Clearwater Revival-Chronicle .... (Fantasy)
   Creedence Country................................. (Fantasy)
   More Creedence Gold.............................. (Fantasy)
Lullaby
Shawn Mullins; *Soul's Core* .... (Columbia)
Man On The Moon (Andy Kaufman)
R.E.M.; *Automatic For The People* .... (Warner Bros.)
Maria Maria (Carlos Santana)
Santana; *Supernatural* .... (Arista)
   Totally Hits-#2-C .... (Elektra)
Miseducation Of Lauryn Hill
Lauryn Hill; *The Miseducation Of Lauryn Hill* .... (Ruffhouse/Columbia)
Mister Sandman (Liberace)
Chordettes; *Best Of The Chordettes*....................... (Rhino)
Emmylou Harris; *Evangeline* .... (Warner Bros.)
   Profile II-The Best Of Emmylou Harris .... (Warner Bros.)
Most Beautiful Girl In The World (Garbo, Dietrich)
Frank Sinatra; *Strangers In The Night*...................... (Reprise)
Tony Bennett; *Rodgers & Hart Songbook* ....(DRG)
   Tony Bennett Sings More Great Rodgers & Hart .... (Improv)
Mrs. Robinson (Joe DiMaggio)
Simon & Garfunkel; *Bookends* .... (Columbia)
   Collected Works .... (Columbia)
   Hollywood Magic-1960s-C .... (Columbia)
   Simon & Garfunkel's Greatest Hits .... (Columbia)
   ST/Forrest Gump .... (Epic/Sony Music Soundtrax)
   ST/The Graduate .... (Columbia)
   The Concert In Central Park........................ (Warner Bros.)
Murder On Music Row (Hank Williams, George Jones)
George Strait & Alan Jackson; *Latest Greatest Straitest Hits* .... (MCA)
Nietzche's Eyes
Paula Cole; *This Fire*....................................(Imago)
Nolan Ryan (He's A Hero To Us All)
Jerry Jeff Walker; *Navajo Rug*............................ (Rykodisc)
Old Count Basie Is Gone (Old Piney Brown Is Gone)
Tony Bennett; *Playin' With My Friends-Bennett Sings The*
   Blues-C .... (Columbia)
Operaman (Rudy Guiliani, Destiny's Child, Osama bin Laden)
Adam Sandler; *The Concert For New York City-C* .... (Columbia)
Osama, Yo' Mama
Ray Stevens; *Osama-Yo' Mama* .... (Curb)
Picasso's Last Words
Paul McCartney & Wings; *Band On The Run* .... (Capitol)
Wings; *Wings Over America*............................. (Capitol)
Pretty Fly (For A White Guy)
Offspring; *Americana* .... (Columbia)
Puttin' On The Ritz (Gary Cooper)
Ella Fitzgerald; *Silver Collection-Songbooks* .... (Verve)
Fred Astaire; *Irving Berlin Always-C* .... (Verve)
   Irving Berlin Always-C .... (Verve)
Harry Richman; *Hollywood Sings-C*................... (Living Era)
   Those Wonderful Years: Puttin' On The Ritz-C ....(JCI Assoc. Labels)
Judy Garland; *One & Only* .... (Capitol)
Mandy Patinkin; *Mandy Patinkin* .... (Columbia)
Taco; *After Eight* .... (RCA)
   Nipper's Greatest Hits Of The '80s-C............... (RCA)
Red Baron
David Benoit; *Here's To You Charlie Brown: 50th Great*........ (GRP/VMG)

Riding With The King
B.B. King & Eric Clapton; *Riding With The King* ....(Duck/Reprise)
Roll Over Beethoven
Beatles; *Beatles-Box Set*.................................(Capitol)
   Rock 'N' Roll Music ....(Capitol)
   The Beatles At The Hollywood Bowl ....(Capitol)
   The Beatles' Second Album ....(Capitol)
   With The Beatles .... (Parlophone)
Byrds; *The Byrds*...................................... (Columbia)
Chuck Berry; *Chuck Berry-Golden Hits* ....(Mercury)
   Chuck Berry's Greatest Hits ....(Everest)
   Cruisin'-1956-C ....(Increase)
   Oldies But Goodies-#10-C .... (Original Sound)
   The Chess Box-Chuck Berry ....(Chess)
Electric Light Orchestra; *Afterglow* ....(Epic)
   Ole ELO .... (Jet)
Rosa Parks
Outkast; *Aquemini* .... (LaFace/Arista)
Safe Sex (Magic Johnson)
Erick Sermon; *No Pressure* .... (Def Jam/IDJMG)
Say Hey (The Willie Mays Song)
Treniers; *Baseball's Greatest Hits-C*.......................(Rhino)
Set 'Em Up Joe
Vern Gosdin; *Chiseled In Stone* ....(Columbia)
   Greatest Country Hits Of The '80s-1988-C...........(Columbia)
Shakespeare Stole My Baby
Eye To Eye; *Shakespeare Stole My Baby*................. (Warner Bros.)
Shakespeare's Sister
Smiths; *Louder Than Bombs* .... (Sire)
Shakespeare's Sonnet No. 18
Bryan Ferry; *Diana, Princess Of Wales-Tribute-C* ....(Columbia)
Simple Desultory Phillipic, A (Or How I Was Robert McNamara'd Into
   Submission) (Various)
Simon & Garfunkel; *Parsley Sage Rosemary & Thyme* ....(Columbia)
Sir Duke
Stevie Wonder; *Original Musiquarium* ....(Motown)
   Songs In The Key Of Life...........................(Motown)
Sleepwalker (Sam Cooke)
Sam Cooke; *Breach* .... (Interscope)
So Long, Frank Lloyd Wright
Simon & Garfunkel; *Bridge Over Troubled Water* ....(Columbia)
Spider Web
Joan Osborne; *Relish* .... (Blue Gorilla/Mercury)
Story Of Bo Diddley
Animals; *Best Of The Animals* .... (Abkco)
Bo Diddley; *In The Spotlight* ....(Chess)
Summer I Read Collette, The
Rosanne Cash; *10 Song Demo* ....(Capitol)
Sweet Soul Music
Arthur Conley; *Atlantic Soul Classics-C* ....(Warner Special Prod.)
   Golden Age Of Black Music-1960-1970-C .... (Atlantic)
Swingin'
Tom Petty And The Heartbreakers; *Echo* .... (Warner Bros.)
Tears In Heaven
Eric Clapton; *Diana, Princess Of Wales-Tribute-C* .... (Columbia)
   Eric Clapton-Unplugged .... (Reprise)
   ST/Rush .... (Reprise)
Teenage Dirtbag (Iron Maiden)
Wheatus; *Wheatus* ....(Columbia)
That Don't Impress Me Much (Brad Pitt)
Shania Twain; *Come On Over* .... (Mercury)
There Goes The Neighborhood
Sheryl Crow; *The Globe Sessions* ....(A&M)
Van Gogh's Left Ear
Kenny Garrett; *Black Hope* .... (Warner Bros.)
Vincent
Don McLean; *American Pie*................................(EMI)
   Best Of Don McLean................................(EMI)
   Greatest Hits Then & Now ....(EMI)
Virginia Woolf
Indigo Girls; *Rites Of Passage*............................(Epic)
Visions Of Gaudi
Phil Woods; *Here's To My Lady* .... (Chesky)
We Didn't Start The Fire
Billy Joel; *Storm Front*..................................(Columbia)
When Smokey Sings
ABC; *Alphabet City* ....(Mercury)
Where Have All The Cowboys Gone? (John Wayne)
Paula Cole; *This Fire* ....(Imago)
Who Played Poker With Pocahontas?
Fannie Watson; *Music From The New York Stage (1890-1920)-#4-1917-*
   1920-C .... (Pearl)
Who's Gonna Fill Their Shoes
George Jones; *George Jones-Super Hits* ....(Epic)
   Greatest Country Hits Of The '80s-1985-C...........(Columbia)
   Who's Gonna Fill Their Shoes ....(Epic)
Willie, Mickey & The Duke (Talkin' Baseball)
Terry Cashman; *Baseball's Greatest Hits-C* ....(Rhino)

Yes, Yes Y'all
Will Smith; *Big Willie Style* . . . . (Columbia)
You Walked In (Cindy, Naomi, Madonna, Diana)
Lonestar; *Crazy Nights* . . . . (BNA)

CHANGES

See Also: **AGING, DECISIONS, LIFE, OPPOSITES**

10,000 Horses
Candlebox; *Happy Pills* . . . .(Maverick)
Across The Universe
Beatles; *Let It Be* . . . . (Capitol)
Past Masters-Volume Two . . . . (Parlophone)
Rarities . . . . (Capitol)
The Beatles/1967-1970 . . . . (Capitol)
David Bowie; *Young Americans* . . . .(Rykodisc)
After The Love Is Gone
Earth, Wind & Fire; *Best Of Earth, Wind & Fire-#2* . . . . (Columbia)
Earth, Wind & Fire-Greatest Hits-#1 . . . . (Legacy)
All I Need To Know
Kenny Chesney; *All I Need To Know* . . . . (BNA)
Kenny Chesney's Greatest Hits . . . . (BNA)
Am I Ever Going To Change
Extreme; *III Sides To Every Story* . . . . (A&M)
Another Way
Tevin Campbell; *Tevin Campbell* . . . . (Qwest)
Anything Goes
Count Basie & Tony Bennett; *Anything Goes-Capitol Sings Cole
Porter-C* . . . . (Capitol)
Basie Swings Bennett Sings . . . . (Roulette)
Dionne Warwick; *Dionne Warwick Sings Cole Porter* . . . . (Arista)
Ella Fitzgerald; *Night & Day-Cole Porter Songbook-C* . . . . (Verve)
Frank Sinatra; *Frank Sinatra Sings The Select Cole Porter* . . . . (Capitol)
Mary Martin; *Mary Martin-16 Most Requested Songs* . . . . (Columbia)
Original Cast; *Anything Goes* . . . .(Epic)
Paul Whiteman & His Orchestra; *78-#24770* . . . . (Victor)
Yo-Yo Ma; *Anything Goes-The Music Of Cole Porter* . . . . (Columbia)
Are The Good Times Really Over (I Wish A Buck Was Still Silver)
Merle Haggard; *Big City* . . . .(Epic)
For The Record: Merle Haggard-43 Legendary Hits . . . . (BNA)
Greatest Country Hits Of The '80s-1982-C . . . . (Columbia)
His Epic Hits-First 11 To Be Continued-C . . . .(Epic)
Back In The Day
Blues Traveler; *Bridge* . . . . (A&M)
Beat Goes On, The
Sonny & Cher; *Best Of Sonny & Cher* . . . . (Atco)
Hit Singles-1958-1977-C . . . . (Atlantic)
Sonny & Cher-Live . . . . (MCA)
The Beat Goes On-Best Of Sonny & Cher . . . . (Rhino)
Two Of Us . . . . (Atco)
Bitch
Meredith Brooks; *Blurring The Edges* . . . . (Capitol)
Bitter Sweet Symphony
Verve; *Urban Hymns* . . . . (Hut/Virgin)
Brain Of J.
Pearl Jam; *Yield* . . . .(Epic)
Brand New Me
Dusty Springfield; *Brand New Me* . . . . (Rhino)
Can't Find My Way Home
Blind Faith; *Blind Faith* . . . . (Polydor)
Eric Clapton-Crossroads-C . . . . (Polydor)
ST/1969 . . . . (Polydor)
Can't Stop Lovin' You
Van Halen; *Balance* . . . .(Warner Bros.)
Carmen
Paula Cole; *This Fire* . . . . (Imago)
Chameleon
Creedence Clearwater Revival; *1970* . . . . (Fantasy)
Pendulum . . . . (Fantasy)
Chameleon
Grover Washington, Jr.; *Love Affair-Music Of Ivan Lins-C* . . . . (Telarc)
Chameleon
Herbie Hancock; *Best Of Herbie Hancock* . . . . (Legacy)
Headhunters . . . . (Columbia)
Chameleon
Elton John; *Blue Moves* . . . .(MCA)
Chameleon
Labelle; *Chameleon* . . . .(Epic)
Change
Blind Melon; *Blind Melon* . . . . (Capitol)
Candlebox; *Candlebox* . . . .(Maverick)
Change
Sheryl Crow; *Sheryl Crow* . . . . (A&M)
Change
Keb' Mo'; *The Door* . . . . (550/Epic/Okeh)

Change (In The House Of Flies)
Deftones; *White Pony* . . . . (Maverick)
Change In Louise
Joe Cocker; *With A Little Help From My Friends* . . . . (A&M)
Change My Mind
John Berry; *Faces* . . . . (Capitol)
Change Of Heart
Judds; *Judds* . . . .(RCA)
Judds' Greatest Hits . . . . (MCA)
Change Of Heart
Eric Carmen; *Best Of Eric Carmen* . . . . (Arista)
Change Of Heart . . . . (Arista)
Change Of Heart
Toto; *Isolation* . . . . (Columbia)
Change Of Heart
Tom Petty And The Heartbreakers; *Long After Dark* . . . . (MCA)
Change Of Heart
Stray Cats; *Rock Therapy* . . . . (EMI)
Change Of Heart
Cyndi Lauper; *True Colors* . . . . (Portrait)
Change Partners
Rosanne Cash; *The Wheel* . . . . (Columbia)
Change The Locks
Tom Petty And The Heartbreakers; *ST/She's The One* . . . . (Warner Bros.)
Change The World
Eric Clapton; *ST/Phenomenon* . . . . (Reprise)
Change The World
Offspring; *Ixnay On The Hombre* . . . . (Columbia)
Change Your Mind
Neil Young & Crazy Horse; *Sleeps With Angels* . . . . (Reprise)
Change Your Mind
Sister Hazel; *Fortress* . . . . (Universal)
Changes
David Bowie; *The Singles-1969-1993* . . . . (Rykodisc)
Ozzy Osbourne; *Live & Loud* . . . . (Epic Portrait Assoc.)
Changes
2Pac; *2Pac Greatest Hits* . . . . (Amaru/Death Row/Interscope)
Changes
Phil Ochs; *Best Of Broadside 1962-1968: Anthems Of The American
Underground From The Pages Of Broadside
Magazine-C* . . . . (Smithsonian Folkways)
Changing Horses
Dan Fogelberg; *Dan Fogelberg-Souvenirs* . . . .(Full Moon)
Changing Partners
Bing Crosby; *Bing Crosby* . . . . (MCA Special Prod.)
Kay Starr; *Capitol Collectors Series-Kay Starr* . . . . (Capitol)
Patti Page; *Patti Page-Golden Hits* . . . . (Mercury)
Cool Change
Little River Band; *First Under The Wire* . . . . (Capitol)
Little River Band's Greatest Hits . . . . (Capitol)
Cross Over The Bridge
Patti Page; *Patti Page-Golden Hits* . . . . (Mercury)
Patti Page's Greatest Hits . . . . (Columbia)
Daddy Won't Sell The Farm
Montgomery Gentry; *Tattoos & Scars* . . . . (Columbia)
Difficult Kind, The
Sheryl Crow; *The Globe Sessions* . . . . (A&M)
Dis-Satisfied
Bill Anderson & Jan Howard; *More Great Country
Duets-C* . . . . (MCA Special Prod.)
Don't Change Horses
Tower Of Power; *Back To Oakland* . . . . (Warner Bros.)
Don't Wanna Change The World
Phyllis Hyman; *Prime Of My Life* . . . . (PIR)
Down Town, The
Days Of The New; *Days Of The New* . . . .(Outpost/Interscope)
Enemy
Days Of The New; *Days Of The New 2* . . . .(Outpost/Interscope)
Engineers Don't Wave From The Trains Anymore
Earl Scruggs & Tom T. Hall; *The Storyteller & The Banjo Man* . . . . . (Columbia)
Lynn Morris; *The Bramble And The Rose* . . . . (Rounder)
Epistle To Dippy
Donovan; *Donovan's Greatest Hits* . . . . (Epic)
Everything Must Change
Barbra Streisand; *Higher Ground* . . . . (Columbia)
Everything's Changed
Lonestar; *Country Cares For Kids II-C* . . . .(BNA)
Crazy Nights . . . .(BNA)
Lonely Grill . . . .(BNA)
Fast Changes
Seal; *Seal 2* . . . . (Sire)
For A Change
Neal McCoy; *You Gotta Love That!* . . . .(Atlantic)
Forty Six & 2
Tool; *Aenima* . . . . (Freeworld/Capitol)
Free Bird
Lynyrd Skynyrd; *Gold & Platinum* . . . . (MCA)
One More From The Road . . . . (MCA)

Pronounced Leh-nerd Skin-nerd . . . . (MCA)
Southern By The Grace Of God-Tribute '87 . . . . (MCA)
Wynonna; *Skynyrd Frynds-C* . . . . (MCA)
Gonna Get A Life
Mark Chesnutt; *Mark Chesnutt's Greatest Hits* . . . . (Decca)
What A Way To Live . . . . (Decca)
Graduation (Friends Forever)
Vitamin C; *Totally Hits-#3-C* . . . . (Atlantic)
Vitamin C . . . . (Elektra)
Have You Ever Been Lonely (Have You Ever Been Blue)
Ernest Tubb; *Best Of Ernest Tubb* . . . . (Curb)
The Country Music Hall Of Fame-Ernest Tubb . . . . (MCA)
Jim Reeves & Patsy Cline; *Jim Reeves' Greatest Hits* . . . . (RCA)
Patsy Cline; *Showcase-With The Jordanaires* . . . . (MCA)
Here In Your Bedroom
Goldfinger; *Richter* . . . . (Mojo Music/Universal)
Hold On (Change Is Comin')
Sounds Of Blackness; *Time For Healing* . . . . (Perspective/A&M)
How Can I Be Sure
Rascals; *Groovin'* . . . . (Warner Special Prod.)
Rascals-Anthology 1965-1972 . . . . (Rhino)
The Ultimate Rascals . . . . (Warner Special Prod.)
Very Best Of The Rascals . . . . (Rhino)
How Can I Help You Say Goodbye
Patty Loveless; *Only What I Feel* . . . . (Epic)
Patty Loveless-Classics . . . . (Epic)
Hymn To Her
Pretenders; *Diana, Princess Of Wales-Tribute-C* . . . . (Columbia)
Get Close . . . . (Sire)
The Isle Of View . . . . (Warner Bros.)
I'd Love To Change The World
Ten Years After; *A Space In Time* . . . . (Columbia)
Classic Performances Of Ten Years After . . . . (Columbia)
Universal . . . . (Chrysalis)
If I Was A Drinkin' Man
Neal McCoy; *Neal McCoy's Greatest Hits* . . . . (Atlantic)
Neal McCoy-Super Hits . . . . (Atlantic)
You Gotta Love That! . . . . (Atlantic)
If You Change Your Mind
Rosanne Cash; *King's Record Shop* . . . . (Columbia)
Rosanne Cash-Super Hits . . . . (Columbia)
If You Ever Change Your Mind
Crystal Gayle; *Crystal Gayle Greatest Hits* . . . . (Columbia)
These Days . . . . (Columbia)
I'm Gonna Change Everything
Mandy Barnett; *I've Got A Right To Cry* . . . . (Sire)
I'm Looking Through You
Beatles; *The Beatles-Anthology-#2* . . . . (Capitol)
Is There Life Out There
Reba McEntire; *For My Broken Heart* . . . . (MCA)
Reba McEntire's Greatest Hits Volume Two . . . . (MCA)
Istanbul (Not Constantinople)
Four Lads; *Four Lads-16 Most Requested Songs* . . . . (Legacy)
It's On!
Korn; *Follow The Leader* . . . . (Immortal/Epic)
It's The Same Old Song
Four Tops; *Billboard Top R&B Hits-1965-C* . . . . (Rhino)
Compact Command Performances-Four Tops . . . . (Motown)
Four Tops' Greatest Hits . . . . (Motown)
Four Tops-Anthology . . . . (Motown)
Just Like The Weather
Suzy Bogguss; *Something Up My Sleeve* . . . . (Liberty)
Just The Way You Are
Billy Joel; *Billy Joel-Greatest Hits, Volume I & Volume II* . . . . . (Columbia)
Pop Classics Of The '70s-C . . . . (Columbia)
The Stranger . . . . (Columbia)
Landslide
Fleetwood Mac; *25 Years-The Chain* . . . . (Warner Bros.)
Fleetwood Mac . . . . (Reprise)
Fleetwood Mac Live . . . . (Warner Bros.)
The Dance . . . . (Reprise)
Smashing Pumpkins; *Pisces Iscariot* . . . . (Virgin)
Laws Must Change
John Mayall; *Best Of John Mayall* . . . . (Polydor)
The Turning Point . . . . (Polydor)
John Mayall's Bluesbreakers; *Behind The Iron Curtain* . . . . . (Crescendo)
Let It Flow
Toni Braxton; *Secrets* . . . . (LaFace)
ST/Waiting To Exhale . . . . (Arista)
Life So Changed, A
James Horner; *ST/Titanic* . . . . (Sony Music Classical)
Look What Love Has Done
Patty Smyth; *ST/Junior* . . . . (MCA)
Lost You In The Canyon
Marc Cohn; *Burning The Daze* . . . . (Atlantic)
Love Changes Everything
Michael Crawford; *Michael Crawford Performs Andrew Lloyd*
Webber . . . . (Atlantic)

Lucky Man
Verve; *Urban Hymns* . . . . (Hut/Virgin)
Marry The Man Today
Original Cast; *ST/Guys & Dolls* . . . . (MCA)
Maybe Someday
Cure; *Bloodflowers* . . . . (Fiction/Elektra)
Music Must Change
Who; *Who Are You* . . . . (MCA)
Never Let You Go
Third Eye Blind; *Blue* . . . . (Elektra)
Totally Hits-#2-C . . . . (Elektra)
New Attitude
Patti LaBelle; *Classic Soul-C* . . . . (MCA)
I Am Woman-C . . . . (Nick At Nite)
Soundtrack Smashes-'80s & More-C . . . . (MCA)
ST/Beverly Hills Cop . . . . (MCA)
New Beginning
Tracy Chapman; *New Beginning* . . . . (Elektra)
Nobody's Supposed To Be Here
Deborah Cox; *One Wish* . . . . (Arista)
Totally Hits-#1-C . . . . (Arista)
One
Creed; *My Own Prison* . . . . (Wind-up)
One Woman Man
Dave Hollister; *Chicago '85 The Movie* . . . . (Def Squad/DreamWorks)
Open Your Eyes
Yes; *Open Your Eyes* . . . . (Beyond)
Planets Of The Universe
Stevie Nicks; *Trouble In Shangri-La* . . . . (Reprise)
Real Life (I Never Was The Same Again)
Jeff Carson; *Real Life* . . . . (Curb)
Re-Arranged
Limp Bizkit; *Significant Other* . . . . (Flip/Interscope)
Renegades Of Funk
Rage Against The Machine; *Renegades* . . . . (Epic)
Revolution
Beatles; *Beatles-Box Set* . . . . (Capitol)
Hey Jude . . . . (Capitol)
Past Masters-Volume Two . . . . (Parlophone)
Rock 'N' Roll Music . . . . (Capitol)
ST/Imagine: John Lennon . . . . (Capitol)
The Beatles/1967-1970 . . . . (Capitol)
Roll With The Changes
REO Speedwagon; *A Decade Of Rock And Roll 1970 To 1980* . . . (Epic)
REO Speedwagon-The Hits . . . . (Epic)
You Can Tune A Piano But You Can't Tuna Fish . . . . (Epic)
Ruby Tuesday
Rolling Stones; *Between The Buttons* . . . . (Abkco)
Flashpoint . . . . (Virgin)
Flowers . . . . (Abkco)
Hot Rocks 1964-1971 . . . . (Abkco)
Singles Collection-The London Years . . . . (Abkco)
Through The Past, Darkly (Big Hits Vol. 2) . . . . (Abkco)
Same Script, Different Cast
Whitney Houston & Deborah Cox; *Whitney Houston's Greatest Hits* . . . (Arista)
Seasons Change
Expose; *Exposure* . . . . (Arista)
Making Love-C . . . . (Priority)
Romantic Hits Of The '80s-C . . . . (K-Tel)
Seasons Change
Michael Murphey; *Swans Against The Sun* . . . . (Epic)
Season's No Reason To Change
Gap Band; *Gap Band IV* . . . . (Mercury)
Gap Gold/Best Of The Gap Band . . . . (Mercury)
See The Changes
Crosby, Stills & Nash; *CSN* . . . . (Atlantic)
CSN . . . . (Atlantic)
She Couldn't Change Me
Montgomery Gentry; *Carrying On* . . . . (Columbia)
She's A River
Simple Minds; *Good News From The Next World* . . . . (Virgin)
Signs That We Never Change
Hollies; *Evolution* . . . . (Epic)
Some Change
Boz Scaggs; *My Time: A Boz Scaggs Anthology-1969-1997* . . . (Legacy)
Some Change . . . . (Virgin)
Some Things Never Change
Tim McGraw; *A Place In The Sun* . . . . (Curb)
Somebody Done Changed The Lock On My Door
Louis Jordan; *Best Of Louis Jordan* . . . . (MCA)
Jazz Heritage-Greatest Hits-#2-1941-1947 . . . . (MCA)
State Of Mind
Clint Black; *No Time To Kill* . . . . (RCA)
Sunday Will Never Be The Same
Spanky & Our Gang; *Flower Power-Psychedelic Rock Classics-C* . . . (K-Tel)
Sweet Surrender
Sarah McLachlan; *Mirrorball* . . . . (Arista)
Surfacing . . . . (Arista)

There Is A Mountain
Donovan; *Donovan's Greatest Hits* . . . .(Epic)
Troubadour-Definitive Collection . . . .(Epic)
They Were Doin' The Mambo
Vaughn Monroe; *Very Best Of Vaughn Monroe* . . . .(Taragon)
Things Have Changed
Bob Dylan; *Essential Bob Dylan* . . . . (Columbia)
ST/Wonder Boys . . . . (Columbia)
Things That I Used To Do
Guitar Slim; *Blues Classics-C* . . . . (K-Tel)
Thinking About Leaving
Dwight Yoakam; *Last Chance For A Thousand Years-Greatest Hits From*
The '90s . . . . (Reprise)
Time Changes Everything
Bob Wills & His Texas Playboys; *Bob Wills & His Texas Playboys-*
Anthology 1935-1973 . . . . (Rhino)
Columbia Country Classics-#1-Golden Age-C . . . . (Columbia)
Essential Bob Wills & His Texas Playboys-1935-1973 . . . . (Legacy)
Roy Rogers; *The Country Music Hall Of Fame-Roy Rogers* . . . .(MCA)
Times Have Changed
Supertramp; *Indelibly Stamped.* . . . . (A&M)
Times They Are A-Changin'
Billy Joel; *KOHUEPT* . . . . (Columbia)
Bob Dylan; *Biograph* . . . . (Columbia)
Bob Dylan At Budokan. . . . . (Columbia)
Bob Dylan's Greatest Hits . . . . (Columbia)
The Bootleg Series-Volumes 1-3 [Rare & Unreleased] . . . . (Columbia)
The Times They Are A-Changin' . . . . (Columbia)
Byrds; *The Byrds* . . . . (Columbia)
Turn! Turn! Turn! . . . . (Legacy)
Peter, Paul & Mary; *Peter, Paul and Mary In Concert* . . . .(Warner Bros.)
Simon & Garfunkel; *Collected Works* . . . . (Columbia)
Wednesday Morning 3 A.M. . . . . (Columbia)
Twelve Thirty (Young Girls Are Coming To The Canyon)
Mamas & The Papas; *Best Of The Mamas & The Papas.* . . . .(MCA)
Mamas & The Papas-16 Of Their Greatest Hits . . . .(MCA)
The Papas & The Mamas. . . . .(MCA)
Two Headed Sex Change
Cramps; *Look Mom No Head!* . . . .(Restless)
Victim Of Changes
Judas Priest; *Best Of Judas Priest.* . . . . (RCA)
Sad Wings Of Destiny . . . . (RCA)
Waiting For The Light To Change
Tonic; *Sugar.* . . . . (Universal)
Walk Like I Do
William Topley; *Spanish Wells* . . . . (Mercury)
Way It Is
Bruce Hornsby & The Range; *Heart Of Rock-C* . . . . (Columbia)
Nipper's Greatest Hits Of The '80s-C . . . . (RCA)
The Way It Is . . . . (RCA)
We Can Change The World
Graham Nash; *Songs For Beginners.* . . . . (Atlantic)
We Can Change The World
Jacksons; *Victory* . . . .(Epic)
We Need A Resolution
Aaliyah; *Aaliyah.* . . . . (BlackGround Enterp./Atlantic)
We're Not Making Love No More
Dru Hill; *ST/Soul Food.* . . . . (LaFace)
What Do I Have To Do?
Stabbing Westward; *Wither Blister Burn & Peel* . . . . (Columbia)
Whatever Comes First
Sons Of The Desert; *Whatever Comes First* . . . .(Epic)
Why Do I Feel So Sad
Alicia Keys; *Songs In A Minor* . . . . (J)
Wind Of Change
Peter Frampton; *Comes Alive* . . . . (A&M)
Shine On-Collection . . . . (A&M)
Wind Of Change. . . . . (A&M)
Wind Of Change
Bee Gees; *Bee Gees' Greatest* . . . . (Polydor)
Main Course . . . . (RSO)
Wind Of Change
Scorpions; *Crazy World* . . . . (Mercury)
Winds Of Change
Jefferson Starship; *Winds Of Change* . . . .(Grunt)
Winds Of Change
Guadalcanal Diary; *2 X 4* . . . . (Elektra)
Winds Of Change
Cinderella; *Heartbreak Station.* . . . . (Mercury)
Woman's Got A Right To Change Her Mind
Rex Stewart & The Ellingtonians; *Rex Stewart & The*
Ellingtonians. . . . .(Riverside)
Won't Get Fooled Again
Van Halen; *LIVE: Right here, right now.* . . . .(Warner Bros.)
Who; *ST/The Kids Are Alright* . . . . (MCA)
The Concert For New York City-C. . . . . (Columbia)
Who Greatest Hits . . . . (MCA)
Who's Last . . . . (MCA)

Who's next . . . . (MCA)
World Is Changing Hands
Dave Davies; *Dave Davies* . . . . (RCA)
Your Life Is Now
John Mellencamp; *John Mellencamp* . . . . (Columbia)
You're Gonna Change (Or I'm Gonna Leave)
Hank Williams With His Drifting Cowboys; *Hank Williams-24 Greatest*
Hits-#2. . . . .(Polydor)
Hank Williams-40 Greatest Hits. . . . .(Polydor)
Health & Happiness Shows . . . . (Mercury)
Hank Williams, Jr.; *A Tribute To My Father* . . . . (Curb)
Tom Petty; *Timeless: Hank Williams Tribute-C* . . . . (Lost Highway/IDJMG)

CHARACTER & INTEGRITY, Be A Good Person, Decency, Honesty, Kind, Morality, Nice, Patience, Respect, Trustworthy, Values

> *See Also: BROTHERHOOD, CHEATING & LIES, FEAR & COURAGE, GENTLE, HELP, HEROISM, LOVE: DEVOTION, PATRIOTISM, PROMISE, TEACHING VALUES, STRONG, TRUTH, WORK*

(This Thing Called) Wantin' And Havin' It All
Sawyer Brown; *Greatest Hits Of Country Dance-C* . . . . (Curb)
This Thing Called Wantin' & Havin' It All. . . . . (Curb)
32 Flavors
Alana Davis; *Blame It On Me* . . . . (Elektra)
Ani DiFranco; *Living In Clip.* . . . . (Righteous Babe)
Not A Pretty Girl . . . . (Righteous Babe)
Alfie
Barbra Streisand; *What About Today* . . . . (Columbia)
Dionne Warwick; *Dionne Warwick Greatest Hits.* . . . . (Everest)
Dionne Warwick-Anthology 1962-1971 . . . . (Rhino)
Almost Grown
Chuck Berry; *Berry Is On Top.* . . . . (Chess)
Cruisin'-1959-C. . . . . (Increase)
Roll Over Beethoven. . . . . (Allegiance)
ST/American Graffiti . . . . (MCA)
The Chess Box-Chuck Berry. . . . . (Chess)
Apple Tree
Erykah Badu; *Baduizm* . . . . (Kedar Entert./Universal)
Are You That Somebody?
Aaliyah; *ST/Dr. Dolittle* . . . .(Atlantic)
Bang The Drum Slowly
Emmylou Harris; *Red Dirt Girl.* . . . . (Nonesuch)
Beauty Is Only Skin Deep
Temptations; *Good Feeling Music Of The Big Chill*
Generation-#1-C. . . . . (Motown)
Motown Story-First 25 Years-C. . . . . (Motown)
Motown's Mustang-A Motown Video-C. . . . . (Motown)
Temptations-Anthology-The Best Of The Temptations . . . . (Motown)
Best Of Intentions
Travis Tritt; *Down The Road I Go* . . . . (Columbia)
Bible Tells Me So
Don Cornell; *Rock 'N Roll Reunion: Class Of '55-C.* . . . .(Madacy)
Blood Is Thicker Than Water
Wyclef Jean featuring G&B (The Product); *The Sopranos-Music From The*
HBO Original Series . . . . (Sony Music Soundtrax)
Careful With That Mic...
Clutch; *Pure Rock Fury.* . . . .(Atlantic)
C'est Moi
Original Cast; *ST/Camelot* . . . . (Warner Bros.)
Robert Goulet; *Camelot* . . . . (Columbia)
Changes
2Pac; *2Pac Greatest Hits.* . . . . (Amaru/Death Row/Interscope)
Close My Eyes
Mariah Carey; *Butterfly.* . . . . (Columbia)
Country Is
Tom T. Hall; *Tom T. Hall's Greatest Hits-#2* . . . . (Mercury)
Tom T. Hall-The Hits . . . . (Mercury)
Dammit (Growing Up)
Blink-182; *Dude Ranch.* . . . . (Cargo)
Deep Inside
Mary J. Blige; *Mary* . . . . (MCA)
Distant Drums
Jim Reeves; *Best Of The Best Of Jim Reeves* . . . . (King)
Billboard Top Country Hits-1966-C. . . . . (Rhino)
Essential Jim Reeves . . . . (RCA)
Do You Really Want Me
Robyn; *Robyn Is Here* . . . . (RCA)
Don't Let Me Be Misunderstood
Animals; *Greatest Hits Live!-Rip It To Shreds* . . . . (I.R.S.)
Sullivan Years-British Invasion . . . . (TVT)
Joe Cocker; *With A Little Help From My Friends* . . . . (A&M)
Doo Wop (That Thing)
Lauryn Hill; *The Miseducation Of Lauryn Hill* . . . . (Ruffhouse/Columbia)

Everybody's Free (To Wear Sunscreen)
Baz Luhrmann; *Now That's What I Call Music!-#2-C* . . . .(Virgin)
Something For Everybody . . . . (Capitol)
Fancy Free
Oak Ridge Boys; *Fancy Free* . . . . (MCA)
Oak Ridge Boys' Greatest Hits 2 . . . . (MCA)
Feet Up (Pat Him On The Po-Po)
Guy Mitchell; *Definitive Guy Mitchell* . . . .(Collector's Choice)
Fill Her Up
Earl Scruggs & Sting; *Earl Scruggs And Friends-C* . . . . (MCA)
First Night
Monica; *The Boy Is Mine* . . . . (Arista)
Forgive Them Father
Lauryn Hill featuring Shelly Thunder; *The Miseducation Of
Lauryn Hill* . . . . (Ruffhouse/Columbia)
From Here To Eternity
Michael Peterson; *Michael Peterson* . . . . (Reprise)
Wedding Day Music-C . . . . (Reprise)
Go On With The Wedding
Patti Page; *Patti Page-Golden Celebration* . . . . (Mercury)
God's Gonna Get'cha (For That)
George Jones & Tammy Wynette; *George Jones & Tammy Wynette-16
Biggest Hits* . . . .(Epic/Legacy)
George Jones & Tammy Wynette's Greatest Hits . . . . (Epic)
Goodbye
Jagged Edge; *Jagged Little Thrill* . . . . (So So Def/Columbia)
Groovy People
Lou Rawls; *All Things In Time* . . . . (Right Stuff)
Lou Rawls-Live (Right Stuff) . . . . (Right Stuff)
Hand Song, The
Nickel Creek; *Nickel Creek* . . . .(Sugar Hill)
Hands
Jewel; *Spirit* . . . . (Atlantic)
Hands Of A Working Man
Ty Herndon; *Big Hopes* . . . . (Epic)
Hardest Thing
98 Degrees; *98 Degrees And Rising* . . . . (Universal)
Now That's What I Call Music!-#3-C . . . .(Virgin)
He Was Too Good To Me
Barbara Cook; *Barbara Cook-Live At Carnegie Hall* . . . .(Sony Music Classical)
Bette Midler; *Some People's Lives* . . . . (Atlantic)
Carmen McRae; *Carmen McRae Sings Great American
Songwriters* . . . . (Decca Jazz)
Helen Merrill; *Dream Of You* . . . .(Emarcy)
Jeri Southern; *The Very Thought Of You: The Decca Years-1951-1957* . . . (GRP)
Head Over Feet
Alanis Morissette; *Jagged Little Pill* . . . . (Maverick)
High Noon
Frankie Laine; *Billboard Top Movie Hits-1950-1954-C* . . . . (Rhino)
Tex Ritter; *Heroes Of Country Music-#4-Legends Of The West
Coast-C* . . . . (Rhino)
*The Envelope Please-Academy Award Winning Songs (1946-
1957)-C* . . . . (Rhino)
Higher Ground
Barbra Streisand; *Higher Ground* . . . . (Columbia)
Hollywood
Wallflowers; *The Wallflowers* . . . .(Virgin)
Honesty
Billy Joel; *52nd Street* . . . . (Columbia)
KOHUEPT . . . . (Columbia)
I Can't Wai To Meetchu
Macy Gray; *On How Life Is* . . . . (Epic)
I Hope You Dance
Lee Ann Womack; *I Hope You Dance* . . . . (MCA)
I Like It, I Love It
Tim McGraw; *All I Want* . . . .(Curb)
Tim McGraw's Greatest Hits . . . . (Curb)
In Harm's Way
Bebe Winans; *Bebe Winans* . . . . (Atlantic)
Iowa Stubborn
Original Cast; *The Music Man* . . . . (Gold Rush)
Robert Preston; *ST/The Music Man* . . . . (Warner Bros.)
I've Been Down That Road Before
Hank Williams; *Alone And Forsaken* . . . . (Mercury)
Beyond The Sunset . . . . (Polydor)
Just Between You And Me
DC Talk; *First Generation: 25 Years Of Virgin Records-C* . . . .(Virgin)
Jesus Freak . . . .(Virgin)
Just The Two Of Us
Will Smith; *Big Willie Style* . . . . (Columbia)
Just To See You Smile
Tim McGraw; *Everywhere* . . . .(Curb)
Tim McGraw's Greatest Hits . . . . (Curb)
Key To Life, The
Vince Gill; *The Key* . . . . (MCA)
Kind & Generous
Natalie Merchant; *Ophelia* . . . . (Elektra)

Last Kiss
J. Frank Wilson and The Cavaliers; *Billboard Top Rock 'N' Roll Hits-
1964-C* . . . .(Rhino)
Collectables Presents The History Of Rock-#2-C . . . .(Collectables)
Oldies But Goodies-#9-C . . . . (Original Sound)
Teenage Tragedies-C . . . . (Rhino)
Pearl Jam; *No Boundaries-Benefit For The Kosovar Refugees-C* . . . . (Epic)
Let's Roll
Neil Young; *Let's Roll-CD Single* . . . . (Reprise)
Let's Talk About Love
Celine Dion with The Bee Gees; *Let's Talk About Love-C* . . . . (550 Music)
Love Keep Us Together
Martin Sexton; *Black Sheep* . . . .(Eastern Front)
The American . . . . (Atlantic)
Lullaby
Tom Rush; *Tom Rush* . . . .(Columbia)
Maker Said Take Her
Alabama; *In Pictures* . . . . (RCA)
Man Ain't Supposed To Cry
Public Announcement; *Don't Hold Back* . . . . (RCA)
Man Of La Mancha
Original Cast; *Lost In The Stars* . . . . (MCA)
Original London Cast; *Man Of La Mancha* . . . . (MCA)
Next Lifetime
Erykah Badu; *Baduizm* . . . .(Kedar Entert./Universal)
No More (Baby I'ma Do Right)
3LW; *3LW* . . . .(Epic)
Now That's What I Call Music!-#6-C . . . . (Virgin)
Okie From Muskogee
Merle Haggard; *Friend In California* . . . .(Epic)
Merle Haggard & The Strangers; *Best Of Merle Haggard & The
Strangers* . . . .(Capitol)
Capitol Collectors Series-Merle Haggard & The Strangers . . . .(Capitol)
Country Music Classics-#3-1965-1970-C . . . . (K-Tel)
For The Record: Merle Haggard-43 Legendary Hits . . . . (BNA)
Songs I'll Always Sing . . . .(Capitol)
ST/Platoon . . . . (Atlantic)
On My Word Of Honor
Platters; *Enchanted-The Best Of The Platters* . . . .(Rhino)
One Night Stand
J-Shin featuring La Tocha Scott; *My Soul, My Life* . . . . (Atlantic)
Only Daddy That'll Walk The Line
Hank Williams, Jr.; *Family Tradition* . . . .(WB/Curb)
Kentucky HeadHunters; *Electric Barnyard* . . . . (Mercury)
Ricky Skaggs; *My Father's Son* . . . .(Epic)
Waylon Jennings; *Best Of Waylon Jennings* . . . . (RCA)
Waylon Jennings' Greatest Hits . . . . (RCA)
Waylon Jennings-Early Years . . . . (RCA)
Willie Nelson; *Willie & Family Live* . . . .(Columbia)
Only The Strong Survive
Elvis Presley; *From Elvis In Memphis* . . . . (RCA)
Memphis Record . . . . (RCA)
Jerry Butler; *Best Of Jerry Butler* . . . . (Mercury)
Best Of Jerry Butler . . . . (Rhino)
Open My Heart
Yolanda Adams; *Mountain High Valley Low* . . . .(Elektra)
Passin' Thru
Earl Scruggs & Don Henley & Johnny Cash; *Earl Scruggs And
Friends-C* . . . . (MCA)
Randy Scruggs; *Crown Of Jewels* . . . . (Reprise)
Randy Scruggs & Joan Osborne; *ST/Happy Texas* . . . .(Arista)
Rachel
Buddy & Julie Miller; *Buddy & Julie Miller* . . . . (Hightone)
Respect
Aretha Franklin; *Aretha Franklin-30 Greatest Hits* . . . .(Rhino)
Best Of Aretha Franklin . . . . (Atlantic)
I Am Woman-C . . . . (Nick At Nite)
I Never Loved A Man The Way I Love You . . . . (Atlantic)
Live At Fillmore West . . . . (Atlantic)
Soul Years-C . . . . (Atlantic)
ST/Forrest Gump . . . . (Epic/Sony Music Soundtrax)
Otis Redding; *History Of Otis Redding* . . . .(Atco)
Live In Europe . . . .(Atco)
Otis Blue-Sings Soul . . . .(Atco)
The Otis Redding Story . . . . (Atlantic)
Reba McEntire; *Reba* . . . . (MCA)
Respect Yourself
Bruce Willis; *Heart Of Soul-C* . . . .(Columbia)
Return Of Bruno . . . .(Motown)
Kane Gang; *Bad Guys* . . . . (Casablanca)
Lowdown . . . . (London)
Staple Singers; *15 Original Big Hits-#2-C* . . . . (Stax)
Staple Singers' Greatest Hits . . . . (Fantasy)
Staple Singers-Chronicle . . . . (Stax)
Top Of The Stax-Twenty Greatest Hits-C . . . . (Stax)
Stevie Wonder; *Motown Legends-Stevie Wonder* . . . .(Motown)
Sell Out
Reel Big Fish; *Turn The Radio Off* . . . . (Mojo Music/Universal)

Send Down An Angel
Allison Moorer; *The Hardest Part* . . . .(MCA)
She's Been Good To Me
Marc Anthony; *Marc Anthony* . . . . (Columbia)
Shimmer
Shawn Mullins; *Songs From Dawson's Creek* . . . . (Sony Music Soundtrax)
Soul's Core . . . . (Columbia)
Since I Lost My Baby
Temptations; *Temptations' Greatest Hits-#1* . . . . (Motown)
Temptations-Anthology-The Best Of The Temptations . . . . (Motown)
Temptations-The Ultimate Collection . . . . (Motown)
Sincere
Original Cast; *ST/The Music Man*. . . . .(Warner Bros.)
Skellig
Loreena McKennitt; *The Book Of Secrets*. . . . . (Quinlan Rd./Warner Bros.)
Slide
Goo Goo Dolls; *Dizzy Up The Girl* . . . .(Warner Sunset/Reprise)
Smile
Lonestar; *Lonely Grill*. . . . . (BNA)
Son Of Hickory Holler's Tramp
O.C. Smith; *Me And You* . . . . (Columbia Special Prod.)
Story Songs-C . . . . (K-Tel)
Special
Garbage; *Now That's What I Call Music!-#3-C* . . . . (Virgin)
Version 2.0. . . . . (Almo Sounds)
Spirit Of A Boy, Wisdom Of A Man
Randy Travis; *Big Country Hits '99-C* . . . . (K-Tel)
You And You Alone . . . .(DreamWorks/SKG)
Stand And Be Counted
Crosby, Stills, Nash & Young; *Looking Forward*. . . . . (Reprise)
Straight Lines
Wood; *Songs From Stamford Hill*. (Columbia)
Swinging On A Star
Bing Crosby; *All-Time Best* . . . . (Curb)
Best Of Bing Crosby. . . . .(MCA)
Dion And The Belmonts; *Dion And The Belmonts-Their Best* . . . . (Laurie)
Frank Sinatra; *Frank Sinatra Sings The Songs Of Van Heusen*
& Cahn . . . . (Reprise)
Take Good Care Of My Baby
Bobby Vee; *Best Of Bobby Vee*. . . . .(EMI)
Billboard Top Rock 'N' Roll Hits-1961-C . . . . (Rhino)
'Til My Dreamin' Comes True-C . . . . (Capitol)
Bobby Vinton; *Bobby Vinton-16 Most Requested Songs* . . . . (Legacy)
Dion; *Runaround Sue (Right Stuff)* . . . . (Right Stuff)
That's How You Know It's Love
Deana Carter; *Did I Shave My Legs For This?* . . . . (Capitol)
Theme From "Casper The Friendly Ghost"
Original Soundtrack; *Television's Greatest Hits-#1-C* . . . . (TVT)
Theme From "Dudley-Do-Right"
Original Soundtrack; *Television's Greatest Hits-#3-1970s & 1980s-C* . . . (TVT)
Theme From "The Lone Ranger" (William Tell Overture)
Boston Pops Orchestra; *TV Classics-C*. (RCA)
Boston Pops Orchestra/Arthur Fiedler; *Fiedler-Greatest Hits* . . . . (RCA)
Original Soundtrack; *Television's Greatest Hits-#7-Cable Ready-C* . . . . . (TVT)
Spike Jones & His City Slickers; *Best Of Spike Jones & His City*
Slickers . . . . (RCA)
There It Is
Ginuwine; *Life* . . . . (Epic)
These Are The Times
Dru Hill; *Enter The Dru* . . . . (Def Jam/RAL/Mercury/Island)
They Don't Know
Jon B.; *Cool Relax* . . . . (Yab Yum/550)
To Beat The Devil
Johnny Cash; *Johnny Cash-16 Biggest Hits-#2* . . . . (Legacy)
Tonight
Marc Nelson; *chocolate mood* . . . . (Columbia)
Too Little Too Late
Barenaked Ladies; *Maroon*. . . . . (Reprise)
Treat Her Like A Lady
Cornelius Brothers & Sister Rose; *Billboard Top Rock 'N' Roll Hits-*
1971-C . . . . (Rhino)
Didn't It Blow Your Mind: Soul Hits Of The '70s-#5-C . . . . (Rhino)
Johnny Lee; *Best Of Johnny Lee* . . . . (Curb)
Treat Her Like A Lady
Celine Dion; *Let's Talk About Love-C* . . . . (550 Music)
Treat Her Like A Lady
Joe; *My Name Is Joe* . . . . (Jive)
Undo
Bjork; *Vespertine* . . . . (Elektra)
Uptight (Everything's Alright)
Stevie Wonder; *16 #1 Hits From The Early '60s-C* . . . . (Motown)
Looking Back . . . . (Motown)
Motown Dance Party-#1-C . . . . (Motown)
Motown Legends-Stevie Wonder . . . . (Motown)
Stevie Wonder's Greatest Hits . . . . (Motown)
Uptight (Everything's Alright) . . . . (Motown)
Walk Like A Man
Bruce Springsteen; *Tunnel Of Love* . . . . (Columbia)

We Live In Two Different Worlds
Auldridge/Bennett/Gaudreau; *This Old Town*. . . . . (Rebel)
Well Respected Man
Kinks; *History Of British Rock-#4-C* . . . . (Rhino)
Kinks' Greatest Hits . . . . (Rhino)
Kinks-Size Kinkdom . . . . (Rhino)
What It's Like
Everlast; *Whitey Ford Sings The Blues* . . . .(Tommy Boy)
Where I Wanna Be
Donell Jones; *Where I Wanna Be* . . . . (LaFace)
Wood And Wire
George Jones; *The Rock: Stone Cold Country 2001* . . . .(BNA)
Workin' Man Blues
Diamond Rio/Lee Roy Parnell/Steve Wariner; *Mama's Hungry Eyes-Merle*
Haggard Tribute-C . . . . (Arista)
Gary Morris; *These Days*. . . . . (Capitol)
Merle Haggard & The Strangers; *Best Of Country Blues* . . . . (Curb)
Capitol Collectors Series-Merle Haggard & The Strangers . . . . (Capitol)
For The Record: Merle Haggard-43 Legendary Hits. . . . .(BNA)
Okie From Muskogee . . . . (Capitol)
Songs I'll Always Sing . . . . (Capitol)
Ricky Van Shelton; *Wild-Eyed Dream* . . . . (Columbia)
Working My Way Back To You
4 Seasons; *25th Anniversary Collection* . . . . (Rhino)
4 Seasons-Anthology . . . . (Rhino)
Working My Way Back To You/Forgive Me, Girl
Spinners; *Billboard Top Hits-1980-C* . . . . (Rhino)
One Of A Kind Love Affair-Anthology . . . . (Rhino)
Very Best Of The Spinners . . . . (Rhino)

CHASING

See Also: *FOLLOWING, TRAVELING*

Breakout
Foo Fighters; *There Is Nothing Left To Lose* . . . .(Roswell/RCA)
Catch Us If You Can
Dave Clark Five; *History Of The Dave Clark Five* . . . . (Hollywood)
Chasin' That Neon Rainbow
Alan Jackson; *Here In The Real World* . . . . (Arista)
Chasin' The Wind
Chicago; *Twenty 1* . . . .(Full Moon)
Chasing Forever
Will Smith; *Big Willie Style*. . . . . (Columbia)
Chasing Shadows
Kansas; *Vinyl Confessions* . . . . (Kirshner)
Chasing Shadows
Deep Purple; *Purple Passages* . . . . (Warner Bros.)
Chasing The Wind
Greg Karukas; *Nightshift*. . . . .(N-Coded)
Chestnut Mare
Byrds; *Best Of The Byrds-Greatest Hits-#2*. . . . . (Columbia)
Rock Classics Of The '70s-C . . . . (Columbia)
The Byrds . . . . (Columbia)
The Byrds (Untitled) . . . . (Legacy)
I'm Always Chasing Rainbows
Harry Fox; *Music From The New York Stage (1890-1920)-#4-1917-*
1920-C. . . . . (Pearl)
Judy Garland; *Best Of Judy Garland*. . . . . (MCA)
Judy Garland . . . . (Audio Fidelity)
Pick Of Judy Garland . . . .(Fifty One West)
Let's Chase Each Other Around The Room
Merle Haggard; *19 Hot Country Requests-#2-C* . . . . (Epic)
For The Record: Merle Haggard-43 Legendary Hits. . . . .(BNA)
It's All In The Game . . . . (Epic)
Little Red Rodeo
Collin Raye; *Best Of Collin Raye-Direct Hits* . . . . (Epic)
Midnight Rider
Allman Brothers Band; *Beginnings*. . . . .(Polydor)
Best Of The Allman Brothers Band. . . . .(Polydor)
Decade Of Hits-1969-1979 . . . .(Polydor)
Idlewild South. . . . .(Polydor)
The Road Goes On Forever, A Collection Of Their Greatest
Recordings. . . . .(Polydor)
Duane Allman; *Duane Allman-An Anthology-Vol. II* . . . . (Capricorn)
Gregg Allman; *Laid Back*. . . . .(Polydor)
South's Greatest Hits-C . . . .(Capricorn)
Willie Nelson; *ST/The Electric Horseman* . . . . (Columbia)
Ridge Running Roan
Skip Gorman; *A Cowboy's Wild Song To His Herd*. . . . . (Rounder)
There She Goes
Babyface; *Face 2 Face* . . . . (Arista)
Waterfalls
TLC; *1996 Grammy Nominees-C* . . . . (Columbia)
CrazySexyCool . . . . (LaFace)
What About Now
Lonestar; *Lonely Grill*. . . . .(BNA)

CHEATING & LIES, Deceit, Illicit Affairs, Unfaithful
See Also: FAKE, HIDING, LOVE (various), MISTREATMENT, PRETEND, SECRETS, TRUTH

(Eye) Hate U
"AFKAP"; *The Gold Experience* . . . . (NPG)
(Margie's At) The Lincoln Park Inn
Bobby Bare; *Ryman Country Homecoming 1-C* . . . . (Springhouse Music Grp./Chordant)
Acoustic #3
Goo Goo Dolls; *Dizzy Up The Girl* . . . . (Warner Sunset/Reprise)
After The Fire Is Gone
Loretta Lynn & Conway Twitty; *MCA Records 30 Years Of Hits-1958-1988-C* . . . . (MCA)
Very Best Of Loretta Lynn & Conway Twitty . . . . (MCA)
Ain't It The Life
Foo Fighters; *There Is Nothing Left To Lose* . . . . (Roswell/RCA)
Alibi
Teena Marie; *Starchild* . . . . (Epic)
Alibis
Sergio Mendes; *Sergio Mendes* . . . . (A&M)
Sergio Mendes-Classics-#18 . . . . (A&M)
Alibis
Tracy Lawrence; *Alibis* . . . . (Atlantic)
All About Me Intro
Xscape; *Traces Of My Lipstick* . . . . (So So Def/Columbia)
All Around The World Or The Myth Of Fingerprints
Paul Simon; *Graceland* . . . . (Warner Bros.)
All Cried Out
Allure; *Allure* . . . . (Track Masters/Crave)
Boom! 17 Explosive Hits-C . . . . (Simitar)
Lisa Lisa; *Lisa Lisa & Cult Jam With Full Force* . . . . (Columbia)
Lisa Lisa-Super Hits . . . . (Columbia)
Past, Present & Future . . . . (TMP)
All Eyes On Me
Goo Goo Dolls; *Dizzy Up The Girl* . . . . (Warner Sunset/Reprise)
All I Need
Temptations; *Temptations-Anthology-The Best Of The Temptations* . . (Motown)
All These Years
Sawyer Brown; *Cafe On The Corner* . . . . (Curb)
All Those Lies
Glenn Frey; *No Fun Aloud* . . . . (Asylum)
Almost
George Morgan; *Room Full Of Roses-The George Morgan Collection* . . . . (Razor & Tie)
The Late, Great George Morgan: 14 Greatest Hits . . . . (Power Play)
Almost Honest
Megadeth; *Cryptic Writings* . . . . (Capitol)
ST/Mortal Kombat 3: Annihilation . . . . (TVT)
Always True To You In My Fashion
Blossom Dearie; *Night & Day-Cole Porter Songbook-C* . . . . (Verve)
Original Cast; *Kiss Me Kate* . . . . (EMI-Angel)
Peggy Lee & George Shearing; *Anything Goes-Capitol Sings Cole Porter-C* . . . . (Capitol)
Angels Don't Lie
Jim Reeves; *Best Of Jim Reeves-#4* . . . . (RCA)
As We Lay
Kelly Price; *Mirror Mirror* . . . . (Def Soul/IDJMG)
Ashes By Now
Lee Ann Womack; *I Hope You Dance* . . . . (MCA)
Rodney Crowell; *Rodney Crowell-Collection* . . . . (Warner Bros.)
Avenging Annie
Andy Pratt; *Andy Pratt* . . . . (Columbia)
Roger Daltrey; *Best Bits* . . . . (MCA)
One Of The Boys . . . . (MCA)
Baby I Lied
Deborah Allen; *Best Of The '80s...So Far-C* . . . . (RCA)
Cheat The Night . . . . (RCA)
Baby It's You
Beatles; *Introducing...The Beatles* . . . . (Vee-Jay)
The Early Beatles . . . . (Capitol)
Baby's Got A Brand New Baby
S-K-O; *S-K-O* . . . . (MTM)
Back 2 Good
Matchbox Twenty; *Yourself Or Someone Like You* . . . . (Lava)
Back Stabbers
O'Jays; *Billboard Top Rock 'N' Roll Hits-1972-C* . . . . (Rhino)
Live In London . . . . (Philadelphia Int'l)
O'Jays-Collector's Item . . . . (Philadelphia Int'l)
Beautiful Lies
Kenny Rogers & Dottie West; *Every Time Two Fools Collide* . . . . (EMI)
Beep Me 911
Missy "Misdemeanor" Elliot; *Supa Dupa Fly* . . . . (East West)
Believe Me Baby (I Lied)
Trisha Yearwood; *Everybody Knows* . . . . (MCA)
Better Things To Do
Terri Clark; *Terri Clark* . . . . (Mercury)

Between Me And You
Ja Rule featuring Christina Milian; *Rule 3:36* . . . (Murder Inc./Def Jam/IDJMG)
Big Girls Don't Cry
4 Seasons; *4 Seasons' Greatest Hits-#1* . . . . (Rhino)
4 Seasons-Anthology . . . . (Rhino)
Billboard Top Rock 'N' Roll Hits-1962-C . . . . (Rhino)
More Dirty Dancing-C . . . . (RCA)
Billie Jean
Michael Jackson; *Thriller* . . . . (Epic)
Bizounce
Olivia; *Olivia* . . . . (J)
Blame It On Your Heart
Patty Loveless; *Only What I Feel* . . . . (Epic)
Patty Loveless-Classics . . . . (Epic)
Blue
LeAnn Rimes; *Blue* . . . . (MCG/Curb)
Blues In The Night
Benny Goodman; *Small Groups-1941-1945* . . . . (Columbia)
Bobby Bland; *Introspective Of The Early Years* . . . . (MCA)
Dinah Shore; *Nipper's Greatest Hits Of The '40s-#1-C* . . . . (RCA)
Doc Severinsen; *Best Of Doc Severinsen* . . . . (MCA)
Frank Sinatra; *Frank Sinatra sings for Only The Lonely* . . . . (Capitol)
Jimmie Lunceford & His Orchestra; *Warner Bros.' 75 Years Entertaining The World-Film Music-C* . . . . (Rhino)
Mel Torme; *Torme* . . . . (Verve)
Robins; *Best Of The Robins* . . . . (Crescendo)
Rosemary Clooney; *Rosemary Clooney-16 Most Requested Songs* . . . . . (Legacy)
Tony Bennett; *Playin' With My Friends-Bennett Sings The Blues-C* . . . . (Columbia)
Woody Herman; *Blues On Parade* . . . . (GRP)
Woody Herman-Best Of The Decca Years . . . . (Decca)
Woody Herman & His Orchestra; *Big Bands Greatest Hits-#3-C* . . . . (MCA Special Prod.)
Body Bumpin'
Mytown; *Mytown* . . . . (Cherry/Universal)
Born In The Dark
Doug Stone; *Faith In Me Faith In You* . . . . (Columbia)
Steppin' Country-#2-C . . . . (Columbia)
Borrowed Love
Earl Scruggs & Dwight Yoakam; *Earl Scruggs And Friends-C* . . . . (MCA)
Bread And Butter
Newbeats; *Billboard Top Rock 'N' Roll Hits-1964-C* . . . . (Rhino)
Collectables Presents The History Of Rock-#9-C . . . . (Collectables)
Oldies But Goodies-#2-C . . . . (Original Sound)
Breakdown
Mariah Carey featuring Bone Thugs-N-Harmony; *Butterfly* . . . . (Columbia)
Bring It On Home
Led Zeppelin; *Led Zeppelin II* . . . . (Atlantic)
Bring On The Night
Bruce Springsteen; *Tracks* . . . . (Columbia)
Broken Promise Land
Mark Chesnutt; *Too Cold At Home* . . . . (MCA)
Bye Bye Bye
'N Sync; *No Strings Attached* . . . . (Jive)
Now That's What I Call Music!-#6-C . . . . (Virgin)
Camera Never Lies
Elton John; *Reg Strikes Back* . . . . (MCA)
Camera Never Lies
Michael Franks; *Camera Never Lies* . . . . (Warner Bros.)
Can't Believe
Faith Evans featuring Carl Thomas; *12" Maxi Single* . . . . (Bad Boy/Arista)
Can't Get This Stuff No More
Van Halen; *Best Of Van Halen-#1* . . . . (Warner Bros.)
Can't Help It
Jon B.; *Cool Relax* . . . . (Yab Yum/550)
Can't Stay
Dave Hollister; *Ghetto Hymns* . . . . (Def Squad/DreamWorks)
Card Cheat
Clash; *London Calling* . . . . (Epic)
Carolyn
Merle Haggard & The Strangers; *For The Record: Merle Haggard-43 Legendary Hits* . . . . (BNA)
Carroll County Accident
Porter Wagoner; *Essential Porter Wagoner* . . . . (RCA)
Porter Wagoner-Greatest Songs . . . . (Curb)
Chain, The
Fleetwood Mac; *25 Years-The Chain* . . . . (Warner Bros.)
Rumours . . . . (Warner Bros.)
Shawn Colvin; *Legacy-A Tribute To Fleetwood Mac's Rumours-C* . . . . . (Lava)
Chair, The
George Strait; *Country Classics-#5-1985-1986-C* . . . . (Universal)
George Strait's Greatest Hits-#2 . . . . (MCA)
MCA #1 Hits Of The '80s-#1-C . . . . (MCA Special Prod.)
Something Special . . . . (MCA)
Strait Out Of The Box . . . . (MCA)
Cheat On You
Mase; *Harlem World* . . . . (Bad Boy/Arista)
Cheat The Night
Deborah Allen; *Cheat The Night* . . . . (RCA)

Cheated
English Beat; *Wha'ppen* . . . .(I.R.S.)
Cheater
Judas Priest; *Hero Hero* . . . . (RCA)
Rocka-Rolla . . . . (RCA)
Cheaters Never Win
Love Committee; *Beachbeat Shaggin'* . . . .(Dunhill Compact Classics)
Cheaters Never Win
Moe Bandy; *It's A Cheating Situation* . . . . (Columbia)
Cheater's Prayer
Kendalls; *Stickin' Together* . . . . (Mercury)
Thank God For The Radio (& All The Hits) . . . . (Mercury)
Cheater's Road
Lonestar; *Crazy Nights* . . . . (BNA)
Cheatin'
Gin Blossoms; *New Miserable Experience* . . . . (A&M)
Cheatin' Fire
Conway Twitty; *Mr. T* . . . . (MCA)
Cheatin' In School
Corey Hart; *First Offense* . . . .(EMI)
Cheatin' Is
Barbara Fairchild; *Biggest Hurt* . . . .(Audiograph)
Country Stars Country Nights . . . . (Fifty One West)
Glen Campbell; *Walkin' In The Sun* . . . . (Capitol)
Cheatin' On A Cheater
Loretta Lynn; *Lookin' Good* . . . .(MCA)
Cheatin' Woman
Lynyrd Skynyrd; *Best Of Lynyrd Skynyrd* . . . .(MCA Special Prod.)
Nuthin' Fancy . . . . (MCA)
Molly Hatchet; *Molly Hatchet* . . . .(Epic)
Cheatin's Only Cheatin'
Mel McDaniel & Oklahoma Wind; *Mel McDaniel & Oklahoma Wind* . . . . (Capitol)
Cleopatra, Queen Of Denial
Pam Tillis; *Homeward Looking Angel* . . . . (Arista)
C'mon Marianne
4 Seasons; *25th Anniversary Collection* . . . . (Rhino)
4 Seasons-Anthology . . . . (Rhino)
Cold Hard Facts Of Life, The
Porter Wagoner; *Essential Porter Wagoner* . . . . (RCA)
Porter Wagoner's Greatest Hits . . . . (Pair)
Confessions
Destiny's Child; *The Writing's On The Wall* . . . . (Columbia)
Contagious
Isley Brothers featuring Ronald Isley; *Eternal* . . . .(DreamWorks/SKG)
Corrina, Corrina
Asleep At The Wheel featuring Brooks & Dunn; *Tribute To The Music Of Bob Wills And The Texas Playboys-C* . . . . (Liberty)
Big Joe Turner; *Best Of Big Joe Turner* . . . .(Pablo)
Big Joe Turner's Greatest Hits . . . . (Atlantic)
Bob Dylan; *Freewheelin'* . . . . (Columbia)
Ray Peterson; *Good Old Rock & Roll-C* . . . . (International Mktg. Group)
Super Hits-#1-C . . . . (Gusto)
Steppenwolf; *Live Steppenwolf* . . . .(MCA)
Couldn't Last A Moment
Collin Raye; *Tracks* . . . .(Epic)
Creep
TLC; *CrazySexyCool* . . . . (LaFace)
Cupid
112; *112* . . . . (Bad Boy/Arista)
Dandelion
Rolling Stones; *More Hot Rocks (big hits & fazed cookies)* . . . . (Abkco)
Through The Past, Darkly (Big Hits Vol. 2) . . . . (Abkco)
Dark End Of The Street
Commitments; *ST/The Commitments* . . . .(MCA)
James Carr; *Essential James Carr* . . . . (Razor & Tie)
Linda Ronstadt; *Heart Like A Wheel* . . . . (Capitol)
Percy Sledge; *Best Of Percy Sledge* . . . . (Atlantic)
Day After Day
Def Leppard; *Euphoria* . . . . (Mercury)
Day Tripper
Beatles; *''Yesterday''...And Today* . . . . (Capitol)
Beatles 1 . . . . (Capitol)
Beatles-Box Set . . . . (Capitol)
Past Masters-Volume Two . . . . (Parlophone)
The Beatles/1962-1966 . . . . (Capitol)
Jimi Hendrix Experience; *Radio One* . . . . (Rykodisc)
Otis Redding; *Dictionary Of Soul* . . . .(Atco)
The Otis Redding Story . . . . (Atlantic)
Sergio Mendes & Brasil '66; *Sergio Mendes & Brasil '66's Greatest Hits* . . . . (A&M)
Deceiver
Judas Priest; *Best Of Judas Priest* . . . . (RCA)
Sad Wings Of Destiny . . . . (RCA)
Deceiver
Alarm; *Declaration* . . . .(I.R.S.)
Deceiver
Beat Farmers; *Van Go* . . . . (Curb)

Devil In Her Heart
Beatles; *The Beatles' Second Album* . . . . (Capitol)
With The Beatles . . . . (Parlophone)
Donays; *Beatles Originals* . . . . (Rhino)
Devil Woman
Marty Robbins; *Billboard Top Country Hits-1962-C* . . . . (Rhino)
Columbia Country Classics-#4-Nashville Sound-C . . . . (Columbia)
Lifetime Of Song-1951-1982 . . . . (Columbia)
Marty Robbins' Greatest Hits-#4 . . . . (Columbia)
Digging In The Dirt
Peter Gabriel; *Us* . . . . (Geffen)
Dirty Laundry
Don Henley; *I Can't Stand Still* . . . .(Asylum)
Do For Love
2Pac featuring Eric Williams; *R U Still Down (Remember Me)* . . . .(Amaru/Jive)
Do You Know Where Your Man Is
Pam Tillis; *Homeward Looking Angel* . . . . (Arista)
Do Your Thing
7 Mile; *7 Mile* . . . . (Crave)
Does He Love You
Reba McEntire & Linda Davis; *Reba McEntire's Greatest Hits Volume Two* . . . . (MCA)
Does My Ring Hurt Your Finger
Charley Pride; *Charley Pride-24 Greatest Hits* . . . . (Tee Vee)
Essential Charley Pride . . . . (RCA)
Don't Believe The Hype
Public Enemy; *It Takes A Nation Of Millions To Hold Us Back* . . . . . . (Def Jam)
Mr. Magic's Rap Attack-#4-C . . . .(Profile)
Don't Cheat In Our Hometown
Ricky Skaggs; *Don't Cheat In Our Hometown* . . . . (Epic)
Don't Make Love To Mary
Merle Travis; *Johnny Gimble's Texas Honky-Tonk Hits-C* . . . . . . (C.M.H. Prod.)
Don't Play That Song (You Lied)
Aretha Franklin; *Aretha Franklin-30 Greatest Hits* . . . . (Rhino)
Aretha Franklin's Greatest Hits . . . .(Atlantic)
Golden Age Of Black Music-1970-1975-C . . . .(Atlantic)
Don't Tell Me Lies
Breathe; *All That Jazz* . . . . (A&M)
Don't Think I'm Not
Kandi; *Hey Kandi* . . . . (So So Def/Columbia)
Now That's What I Call Music!-#5-C . . . .(Virgin)
Don't You Care
Buckinghams; *Buckinghams' Greatest Hits* . . . . (Columbia)
Don't You Lie To Me
Chuck Berry; *New Jukebox Hits-C* . . . . (Chess)
Flamin' Groovies; *Groovies' Greatest Grooves* . . . .(Sire)
Down Low (Nobody Has To Know)
R. Kelly; *R. Kelly* . . . .(Jive)
Drink, Swear, Steal & Lie
Michael Peterson; *Michael Peterson* . . . .(Reprise)
End Of The Lyin'
Alabama; *Roll On* . . . . (RCA)
Everything Is Everything
Lauryn Hill; *The Miseducation Of Lauryn Hill* . . . . (Ruffhouse/Columbia)
Fairweather Friend
John Cale; *Vintage Violence* . . . . (Columbia)
Fairweather Friend
Johnny Gill; *Johnny Gill* . . . . (Motown)
Faithfull
Pearl Jam; *Yield* . . . .(Epic)
Fake
Alexander O'Neal; *All Mixed Up* . . . . (Tabu)
Hearsay . . . . (Tabu)
Fear Of Falling
Badlees; *River Songs* . . . .(Atlas)
Fill Me In
Craig David; *Born To Do It* . . . .(Wildside/Atlantic)
Totally Hits 2001-C . . . . (Arista)
Fine
Whitney Houston; *Totally Hits-#3-C* . . . .(Atlantic)
Whitney Houston's Greatest Hits . . . . (Arista)
Fire
Bruce Springsteen & The E Street Band; *Bruce Springsteen & The E Street Band Live/1975-85* . . . . (Legacy)
Pointer Sisters; *Cover Me (Bruce Springsteen Tribute)-C* . . . . (Rhino)
Energy . . . . (Planet)
I Am Woman-C . . . . (Nick At Nite)
Flight 309 To Tennessee
Shelly West; *West By West* . . . . (Viva)
Flowers On The Wall
Eric Heatherly; *Swimming In Champagne* . . . . (Mercury)
Statler Brothers; *All Time Legends Of Country Music-C* . . . . (Legacy)
Best Of The Statler Brothers . . . . (Mercury)
Billboard Top Country Hits-1966-C . . . . (Rhino)
Columbia Country Classics-#3-Americana-C . . . . (Columbia)
Pop Classics Of The '60s-C . . . . (Columbia)
Follow Me
Uncle Kracker; *Double Wide* . . . . (Warner Bros.)

Totally Hits 2001-C .... (Arista)

For Your Love
Tevin Campbell; *Tevin Campbell* .... (Qwest)

Forgive Them Father
Lauryn Hill featuring Shelly Thunder; *The Miseducation Of
Lauryn Hill* .... (Ruffhouse/Columbia)

Friend Of Mine
Kelly Price; *Soul Of A Woman* .... (T-Neck/Island)

G.H.E.T.T.O.U.T.
Changing Faces; *All Day, All Night* .... (Big Beat/Atlantic)

Georgy Porgy
Eric Benet featuring Faith Evans; *A Day In The Life* .... (Warner Bros.)
Toto; *Past To Present 1977-1990* .... (Columbia)
Toto. .... (Columbia)

Gettin' In The Way
Jill Scott; *Who Is Jill Scott? Words And Sounds-#1* ...... (Hidden Beach/Epic)

Give It Up Or Let Me Go
Dixie Chicks; *Wide Open Spaces* .... (Monument)

Go On
George Strait; *George Strait* .... (MCA)

God Will
Holly Cole Trio; *Blame It On My Youth.* .... (Blue Note)
Lyle Lovett; *Lyle Lovett.* .... (MCA)
Lyle Lovett Anthology-#1-Cowboy Man .... (MCA)
Patty Loveless; *Up Against My Heart* .... (MCA)

God's Gonna Get'cha (For That)
George Jones & Tammy Wynette; *George Jones & Tammy Wynette-16
Biggest Hits* .... (Epic/Legacy)
George Jones & Tammy Wynette's Greatest Hits .... (Epic)

Golden Vanity
Pete Seeger & Arlo Guthrie; *Together In Concert* .... (Reprise)

Gonna Get Along Without Ya Now
Patience & Prudence; *Lost Hits Of The 50's-C* .... (EMI Special Markets)

Good Girls
Joe; *All That I Am* .... (Jive)

Got A Feelin'
Mamas & The Papas; *Best Of The Mamas & The Papas* .... (MCA)

Grapevyne
Brownstone; *Dancin' Divas-C* .... (Epic Dance)
From The Bottom Up .... (MJJ/Epic)

Great Deception
Van Morrison; *Hard Nose The Highway* .... (Polydor)

Great Pretender
Band; *Moondog Matinee* .... (Capitol)
Platters; *Billboard Top R&B Hits-1956-C* .... (Rhino)
Cruisin'-1956-C .... (Increase)
Encore Of Golden Hits-Platters .... (Mercury)
Platters-Anthology .... (Rhino)
ST/American Graffiti .... (MCA)
Super Oldies Of The '50s-#3-C .... (Audio Fidelity)
Roy Orbison; *Best Of Roy Orbison-Loved Standards* .... (Monument)
Stan Freberg; *Capitol Collectors Series-Stan Freberg* .... (Capitol)

Grey Cloudy Lies
George Harrison; *Extra Texture* .... (Capitol)

Hands In The Air
Bob Seger; *It's A Mystery* .... (Capitol)

Hardest Thing
98 Degrees; *98 Degrees And Rising.* .... (Universal)
Now That's What I Call Music!-#3-C .... (Virgin)

Harper Valley P.T.A.
Jeannie C. Riley; *Harper Valley P.T.A.* .... (Plantation)
Jeannie C. Riley's Greatest Hits .... (Plantation)
Oldies But Goodies-#4-C .... (Original Sound)
Souvenirs Of Music City U.S.A.-C .... (Plantation)

Hate This Place
Goo Goo Dolls; *Dizzy Up The Girl* .... (Warner Sunset/Reprise)

Heard It All Before
Sunshine Anderson; *Your Woman* .... (Soullife/Atlantic)

Heart Won't Lie, The
Reba McEntire & Vince Gill; *It's Your Call* .... (MCA)
Reba McEntire's Greatest Hits-#3: I'm A Survivor .... (MCA)

Heartbreak Hotel
Whitney Houston Featuring Faith Evans & Kelly Price; *My Love Is
Your Love.* .... (Arista)
Totally Hits-#1-C .... (Arista)
Whitney Houston's Greatest Hits .... (Arista)

Heaven's Just A Sin Away
Kelly Willis; *Hot Country-C* .... (MCA Special Prod.)
Kelly Willis .... (MCA)
Kendalls; *Best Of The Kendalls* .... (Curb)
Kendalls-20 Greatest Hits .... (Deluxe)

Heaven's What I Feel
Gloria Estefan; *Gloria!* .... (Epic)

Here I Am
Patty Loveless; *Patty Loveless-Classics* .... (Epic)
When Fallen Angels Fly .... (Epic)

Here We Go Again
Aretha Franklin; *A Rose Is Still A Rose* .... (Arista)

Here's A Quarter (Call Someone Who Cares)
Travis Tritt; *It's All About To Change* .... (Warner Bros.)

He's The Great Imposter
Fleetwoods; *ST/American Graffiti* .... (MCA)

Hey Hey What Can I Do
Hootie & The Blowfish; *Encomium: Tribute To Led Zeppelin-C* ...... (Atlantic)
Led Zeppelin; *Led Zeppelin-Box Set* .... (Atlantic)
Led Zeppelin-The Complete Studio Recordings .... (Atlantic)

Hey Joe
Jimi Hendrix; *Essential Jimi Hendrix, Volume 2* .... (Reprise)
Live At Winterland .... (Rykodisc)
Jimi Hendrix Experience; *Are You Experienced?* .... (Reprise)
Smash Hits. .... (Reprise)
Love; *Best Of Love.* .... (Rhino)

High Head Blues
Black Crowes; *Amorica* .... (American)

Hit 'Em Up Style (Oops!)
Blu Cantrell; *So Blu* .... (Arista)
Totally Hits 2001-C .... (Arista)

Honesty
Billy Joel; *52nd Street* .... (Columbia)
KOHUEPT .... (Columbia)

Honky Tonk Truth
Brooks & Dunn; *Brooks & Dunn-The Greatest Hits Collection.* .... (Arista)

House With No Curtains
Alan Jackson; *Everything I Love* .... (Arista)

How Deep Is Your Love
Dru Hill featuring Redman; *Enter The Dru* .... (Def Jam/RAL/Mercury/Island)
ST/Rush Hour .... (Def Jam)

How Long
Ace; *Lava Love-C* .... (K-Tel)
Super Hits Of The '70s-Have A Nice Day-#14-C .... (Rhino)

How's It Goin' Down
DMX; *It's Dark And Hell Is Hot* .... (Def Jam)

I Am Your Woman
Syleena Johnson; *Chapter One: Love, Pain & Forgiveness* .... (Jive)

I Can See For Miles
Who; *Hooligans* .... (MCA)
Join Together .... (MCA)
Meaty Beaty Big & Bouncy .... (MCA)
ST/The Kids Are Alright .... (MCA)
The Who Sell Out. .... (MCA)

I Can't Quit You Baby
Led Zeppelin; *Coda* .... (Atlantic)
Led Zeppelin .... (Atlantic)
Led Zeppelin-Box Set .... (Atlantic)

I Cheated Me Right Out Of You
Moe Bandy; *Moe Bandy's Greatest Hits* .... (Columbia)

I Could Have Told You
Frank Sinatra; *No One Cares* .... (Capitol)

I Do (Whatcha Say Boo)
Jon B.; *Cool Relax* .... (Yab Yum/550)

I Don't Ever Want To See You Again
Uncle Sam; *Uncle Sam.* .... (Stone Creek/Epic)

I Don't Need You
Kenny Rogers; *Kenny Rogers-Twenty Greatest Hits* .... (EMI)
Share Your Love .... (Liberty)

I Guess You Had To Be There
Lorrie Morgan; *To Get To You-Greatest Hits Collection* .... (BNA)
Watch Me .... (BNA)

I Let Her Lie
Daryle Singletary; *Daryle Singletary* .... (Giant)

I Lie
Loretta Lynn; *I Lie* .... (MCA)

I Miss You A Little
John Michael Montgomery; *John Michael Montgomery's
Greatest Hits* .... (Atlantic)

I Really Don't Need No Light
Jeffrey Osborne; *Jeffrey Osborne.* .... (A&M)

I Saw Her Again
Mamas & The Papas; *Best Of The Mamas & The Papas* .... (MCA)
Farewell To The First Golden Era .... (MCA)
Mamas & The Papas .... (MCA)

I Saw The Light
Wynonna; *Wynonna.* .... (MCA)

I Want To Come Over
Melissa Etheridge; *Your Little Secret.* .... (Island)

I Was The One
Elvis Presley; *Elvis' Golden Records.* .... (RCA)

I Was Wrong
Keb' Mo'; *Slow Down* .... (550/Epic/Okeh)

I Wasn't With It
Jesse Powell; *'Bout It.* .... (Silas)

I Will Lead You
Filter; *Title Of Record* .... (Reprise)

I Will Wait
Hootie & The Blowfish; *Musical Chairs* .... (Atlantic)

I Wish
Carl Thomas; *Emotional* . . . . (Bad Boy/Arista)
I Won't Let You Do That To Me
Luther Vandross; *One Night With You-The Best Of Love-#2* . . . . (LV/Epic)
I Wouldn't Lie
Yarbrough & Peoples; *Guilty* . . . . (Total Experience)
I'd Lie For You (And That's The Truth)
Meat Loaf; *Welcome To The Neighborhood* . . . . (MCA)
I'd Rather Have What We Had
Conway Twitty; *Two's A Party* . . . . (MCA Special Prod.)
Lee Ann Womack; *Some Things I Know* . . . . (Decca)
If You Had My Love
Jennifer Lopez; *On The 6* . . . . (Work)
If Your Girl Only Knew
Aaliyah; *MTV Party To Go '98-C* . . . . (Tommy Boy)
One In A Million . . . . (BlackGround Enterp./Atlantic)
I'll Lie Myself To Sleep
Shelby Lynne; *Greatest Country Hits Of The '90s-1990-C* . . . . (Columbia)
Tough All Over . . . . (Epic)
I'm A Little Liar
Kings; *45-#1019* . . . . (Collectables)
I'm Not At All In Love
Original Cast/Doris Day; *ST/Pajama Game* . . . . (Collectables)
I'm Not In Love
10 CC; *10 CC's Greatest Hits-1972-1978* . . . . (Polydor)
Super Hits Of The '70s-Have A Nice Day-#14-C . . . . (Rhino)
Will To Power; *Journey Home* . . . . (Epic)
I'm Over You
Keith Whitley; *I Wonder Do You Think Of Me* . . . . (RCA)
Keith Whitley's Greatest Hits . . . . (RCA)
I'm Still Alive
Trisha Yearwood; *Real Live Woman* . . . . (MCA)
I'm The Biggest Liar In Town
Reno & Smiley; *1983 Collector's Edition-#11* . . . . (Gusto)
I'm Tired Of Living This Lie
Bob Wills & His Texas Playboys; *Bob Wills & His Texas Playboys-24 Great Hits* . . . . (Polydor)
Imposter
Elvis Costello & The Attractions; *Get Happy!* . . . . (Rykodisc)
Kampuchea-C . . . . (Atlantic)
Oingo Boingo; *Only A Lad* . . . . (A&M)
In A Small Moment
Carly Simon; *Boys In The Trees* . . . . (Elektra)
In A Week Or Two
Diamond Rio; *Close To The Edge* . . . . (Arista)
Diamond Rio's Greatest Hits . . . . (Arista)
In My Bed
Dru Hill; *Dru Hill* . . . . (Island)
Innuendo
Queen; *Innuendo* . . . . (Hollywood)
Interstate Love Song
Stone Temple Pilots; *Purple* . . . . (Atlantic)
It Hurts Me Too
Keb' Mo'; *The Door* . . . . (550/Epic/Okeh)
It Wasn't God Who Made Honky Tonk Angels
Kitty Wells; *Grand Ole Opry-75 Years-#1-C* . . . . (MCA)
Kitty Wells' Greatest Hits . . . . (Step One)
The Kitty Wells Story . . . . (MCA)
It Wasn't Me
Shaggy; *Hotshot* . . . . (MCA)
Now That's What I Call Music!-#6-C . . . . (Virgin)
It's A Sin To Tell A Lie
Fats Waller; *20 Golden Pieces Of Fats Waller* . . . . (Bulldog)
Somethin' Smith & The Redheads; *45-#5-9093* . . . . (Epic)
It's About Time
Public Announcement; *All Work, No Play* . . . . (A&M)
It's All Over Now
Bobby Womack; *Lookin' For A Love-Best Of Bobby Womack-1968-1975* . . . . (Razor & Tie)
John Anderson; *Great Divorce Songs For Him-C* . . . . (Warner Bros.)
John Anderson's Greatest Hits-#2 . . . . (Warner Bros.)
Rod Stewart; *Best Of Rod Stewart* . . . . (Mercury)
Gasoline Alley . . . . (Mercury)
Vintage Rod Stewart . . . . (Mercury)
Rolling Stones; *12 X 5* . . . . (Abkco)
Big Hits (High Tide & Green Grass) . . . . (Abkco)
More Hot Rocks (big hits & fazed cookies) . . . . (Abkco)
Singles Collection-The London Years . . . . (Abkco)
Ry Cooder; *Paradise And Lunch* . . . . (Reprise)
It's Not Love (But It's Not Bad)
Merle Haggard & The Strangers; *For The Record: Merle Haggard-43 Legendary Hits* . . . . (BNA)
It's Not Right But It's Okay
Whitney Houston; *My Love Is Your Love* . . . . (Arista)
It's Over
Roy Orbison; *Roy Orbison's All-Time Greatest Hits-#1 & 2* . . . . . . (Monument)
Roy Orbison-Super Hits . . . . (Columbia)
Very Best Of Roy Orbison . . . . (Virgin)

It's Over Now
Deborah Cox; *One Wish* . . . . (Arista)
It's Over Now
112; *Part III* . . . . (Bad Boy/Arista)
I've Been Hurt
Bill Deal & The Rhondels; *Best Of Bill Deal & The Rhondels* . . . . (Rhino)
Oldies But Goodies-#7-C . . . . (Original Sound)
Soul Shots-#2-The ''In'' Crowd-Sweet Soul-C . . . . (Rhino)
Soul Shots-#6-Blue-Eyed Soul-C . . . . (Rhino)
I've Seen That Movie Too
Elton John; *Goodbye Yellow Brick Road* . . . . (Polydor)
Jack Daniels, You Lied To Me Again
Ray Stevens; *20 Comedy Hits Special Collection* . . . . (Curb)
Jackson
Johnny Cash & June Carter; *Johnny Cash's Greatest Hits* . . . . (Columbia)
The Man In Black-His Greatest Hits . . . . (Legacy)
Nancy Sinatra & Lee Hazlewood; *Nancy Sinatra-The Hit Years* . . . . . . (Rhino)
Jesus Children Of America
Stevie Wonder; *Innervisions* . . . . (Motown)
Jilted
Teresa Brewer; *Best Of Teresa Brewer* . . . . (MCA Jazz)
Jive Talkin'
Bee Gees; *Bee Gees' Greatest* . . . . (Polydor)
Main Course . . . . (RSO)
ST/Saturday Night Fever . . . . (Polydor)
Jumper
Third Eye Blind; *Third Eye Blind* . . . . (Elektra)
Totally Hits-#1-C . . . . (Arista)
Just Another Girl
Monica; *ST/Down To Earth* . . . . (Epic)
Just Be A Man About It
Toni Braxton; *The Heat* . . . . (LaFace)
Keep On Loving You
REO Speedwagon; *A Second Decade Of Rock And Roll 1981 To 1991* . . . (Epic)
Hi Infidelity . . . . (Epic)
REO Speedwagon-The Hits . . . . (Epic)
Kind Of A Drag
Buckinghams; *Kind Of A Drag* . . . . (Sundazed Music)
Mercy, Mercy, Mercy . . . . (Legacy Rock Artifacts Series)
Kiss Of Fire
Georgia Gibbs; *Best Of Georgia Gibbs-The Mercury Years* . . . . (Chronicles)
Tony Martin; *Best Of Tony Martin On RCA* . . . . (Collector's Choice)
Last Chance To Turn Around
Gene Pitney; *Best Of Gene Pitney* . . . . (K-Tel)
Gene Pitney-Anthology 1961-1968 . . . . (Rhino)
Last Cheater's Waltz
Emmylou Harris; *Cimarron* . . . . (Warner Bros.)
T.G. Sheppard; *T.G. Sheppard's All-Time Greatest Hits* . . . . (Warner Bros.)
T.G. Sheppard's Greatest Hits . . . . (Warner Bros./Curb)
Last Goodbye
Kenny Wayne Shepherd Band; *Live On* . . . . (Giant)
Lazy Eye
Goo Goo Dolls; *ST/Batman & Robin-Music From And Inspired By The Motion Picture* . . . . (Jive)
Learning The Game
Buddy Holly; *Complete Buddy Holly* . . . . (MCA)
The Buddy Holly Collection . . . . (MCA)
Leech
Eve 6; *Eve 6* . . . . (RCA)
Liar
Three Dog Night; *Best Of Three Dog Night* . . . . (MCA)
Joy To The World-Greatest Hits . . . . (MCA)
Liar
Profyle; *Nothin' But Drama* . . . . (Motown)
Liar
Argent; *Argent-Anthology-Collection Of Greatest Hits* . . . . (Epic)
Liar
Pandoras; *Live Nymphomania* . . . . (Restless)
Liar
Buckinghams; *Matter Of Time* . . . . (Red Label)
Liar
Sex Pistols; *Never Mind The Bollocks, Here's The Sex Pistols* . . . (Warner Bros.)
Liar
Bros; *Push* . . . . (Epic)
Liar
Queen; *Queen* . . . . (Hollywood)
Liar
Megadeth; *so far, so good...so what!* . . . . (Capitol)
Liar Liar
Castaways; *Frat Rock!-#3-Grandson Of Frat Rock!-C* . . . . (Rhino)
Oldies But Goodies-#9-C . . . . (Original Sound)
ST/Good Morning, Vietnam . . . . (A&M)
Liars A To E
Dexy's Midnight Runners; *Too-Rye-Ay* . . . . (Mercury)
Lie
Dream Theater; *Awake* . . . . (East West)
Lie Detector
Al Corley; *Square Rooms* . . . . (Mercury)

Lie For A Lie
Nick Mason & Rick Fenn; *Profiles* . . . . (Columbia)
Lie On Lie
Chalk Farm; *Notwithstanding* . . . .(Columbia)
Lie To Me
Jonny Lang; *Lie To Me* . . . . (A&M)
Lie To You For Your Love
Bellamy Brothers; *Howard & David* . . . . (MCA)
Lies
Knickerbockers; *Nuggets-#3-Pop-C* . . . . (Rhino)
   Oldies But Goodies-#9-C . . . .(Original Sound)
   Super Oldies Of The '60s-#9-C . . . . (Audio Fidelity)
Linda Ronstadt; *Get Closer* . . . . (Asylum)
Lies
En Vogue; *Born To Sing* . . . . (Atlantic)
Lies
J.J. Cale; *Really* . . . . (Mercury)
   Special Edition . . . . (Mercury)
Lies
Violent Femmes; *Violent Femmes 3* . . . . (Slash)
Lies
EMF; *Schubert Dip* . . . . (Capitol)
Lies
Rolling Stones; *Some Girls* . . . . (Virgin)
Life #9
Martina McBride; *The Way That I Am* . . . .(RCA)
Light My Fire
Doors; *Best Of The Doors* . . . . (Elektra)
   Doors . . . . (Elektra)
   Doors 13 . . . . (Elektra)
   Doors' Greatest Hits . . . . (Elektra)
   ST/The Doors . . . . (Elektra)
Jose Feliciano; *Encore-Jose Feliciano* . . . .(RCA)
   Jose Feliciano's All-Time Greatest Hits . . . .(RCA)
Lightnin' Strikes
Lou Christie; *Oldies But Goodies-#14-C* . . . .(Original Sound)
Linger
Jonatha Brooke; *Steady Pull* . . . . (Bad Dog)
Lipstick Don't Lie
Mark Collie; *Tennessee Plates* . . . . (Giant)
Lipstick Lies
Pat Benatar; *Live From Earth* . . . . (Chrysalis)
Lipstick On Your Collar
Connie Francis; *Very Best Of Connie Francis* . . . . (Polydor)
Lipstick Promises
George Ducas; *George Ducas* . . . . (Capitol)
   I Love Country-Hits Of The '90s-#4-C . . . . (Priority)
Little Lies
Fleetwood Mac; *Fleetwood Mac's Greatest Hits* . . . . (Warner Bros.)
   Tango In The Night . . . . (Warner Bros.)
Little Rock
Reba McEntire; *Whoever's In New England* . . . . (MCA)
   Woman To Woman-#2-C . . . . (MCA)
Little White Lie
Sammy Hagar; *Marching To Mars* . . . . (MCA)
Little White Lies
Dick Haymes with Gordon Jenkins & His Orchestra; *Sentimental Journey:*
   Pop Vocal Classics-#2-1947-1950-C . . . .(Rhino)
Dinah Shore; *Dinah Shore-16 Most Requested Songs-Encore!* . . . .(Legacy)
Fred Waring's Pennsylvanians featuring Clare Hanlon; *Very Best Of Fred*
   Waring & The Pennsylvanians . . . .(Reader's Digest Music)
Tommy Dorsey; *Best Of Tommy Dorsey* . . . . (Bluebird)
   Complete Tommy Dorsey-#6 . . . .(RCA)
Little White Lies
Romantics; *The Romantics* . . . . (Columbia)
Long Tall Sally
Beatles; *Past Masters-Volume One* . . . .(Parlophone)
   Rock 'N' Roll Music . . . . (Capitol)
   The Beatles At The Hollywood Bowl . . . . (Capitol)
   The Beatles' Second Album . . . . (Capitol)
Little Richard; *Billboard Top R&B Hits-1956-C* . . . . (Rhino)
   Here's Little Richard . . . . (Specialty)
   Little Richard-18 Greatest Hits . . . . (Rhino)
   Little Richard's Greatest Hits . . . . (Everest)
   Oldies But Goodies-#3-C . . . .(Original Sound)
   ST/Heaven Help Us . . . . (EMI)
   Super Oldies Of The '50s-#3-C . . . . (Audio Fidelity)
   Tutti Frutti . . . . (Accord)
Lookin' At Me
Mase Featuring Puff Daddy; *Harlem World* . . . . (Bad Boy/Arista)
Love Letters In The Sand
Mac Wiseman; *24 Greatest Bluegrass Hits-C* . . . . . . (C.M.H. Prod.)
Pat Boone; *Best Of Pat Boone* . . . . (MCA)
   Pat Boone-16 Great Performances . . . . (MCA)
   Vintage Music-#2-C . . . . (MCA)
Ted Black & His Orchestra; *78-#22799.* . . . .(Victor)
Lovefool
Cardigans; *First Band On The Moon* . . . . (Mercury)

   MTV Best Of The Buzz Bin-#2-C . . . . (Mammoth)
Lyin' Again
Kenny Rogers; *Daytime Friends* . . . . (EMI)
Mickey Gilley; *That's All That Matters To Me* . . . . (Epic)
Lyin' Ass Bitch
Fishbone; *Fishbone* . . . . (Columbia)
Lyin' Comes So Easy To Your Lips
David Allan Coe; *D.A.C.* . . . .(Columbia)
Lyin' Eyes
Eagles; *Eagles/Their Greatest Hits 1971-1975* . . . . (Asylum)
   One Of These Nights . . . . (Asylum)
   ST/Urban Cowboy. . . . . (Asylum)
Lyin' Jukebox
Hank Williams, Jr.; *Maverick.* . . . .(Capicorn)
Lying
Baxter, Baxter & Baxter; *45-#1167* . . . . (Sun)
Lying
Peter Frampton; *Premonition* . . . . (Atlantic)
Lying Here Lying
Mac Davis; *Forty 82.* . . . . (Casablanca)
Lying Time Again
Mel Tillis; *Mel Tillis' Greatest Hits* . . . .(Curb)
Lying To The Moon
Matraca Berg; *Lying To The Moon And Other Stories* . . . . (RCA)
Lying To Yourself
Asia; *Very Best Of Asia-Heat Of The Moment-1982-1990* . . . . (Geffen)
Make It Hot
Nicole; *Make It Hot* . . . .(Gold Mind/East West/EEG)
Mama Didn't Lie
Jan Bradley; *Best Of Chess Rhythm & Blues-#1-C.* . . . .(Chess)
   ST/Hairspray. . . . . (MCA Special Prod.)
Maybe I Deserve
Tank; *Force Of Nature* . . . .(BlackGround Enterp./Atlantic)
Maybe I Know
Lesley Gore; *Golden Hits Of Lesley Gore* . . . .(Mercury)
   Lesley Gore-Anthology . . . .(Rhino)
Maybelline
Chuck Berry; *Chuck Berry-Golden Hits* . . . .(Mercury)
   Chuck Berry's Greatest Hits . . . .(Everest)
   Cruisin'-1955-C . . . .(Increase)
   Oldies But Goodies-#11-C . . . .(Original Sound)
   Super Oldies Of The '50s-#5-C . . . .(Audio Fidelity)
Johnny Rivers; *Johnny Rivers-Anthology 1964-1977* . . . .(Rhino)
   Very Best Of Johnny Rivers . . . .(EMI)
Minnesota Man Claims Monkey Bowled Perfect Game
Jad Fair; *Strange But True* . . . . (Matador)
Misled
Kool & The Gang; *Emergency* . . . .(Mercury)
Misled
Celine Dion; *The Colour Of My Love* . . . . (550 Music)
Missing You
Brooks & Dunn; *Tight Rope* . . . .(Arista)
John Waite; *'80s Greatest Rock Hits-#1-Passion & Power-C* . . . . (Priority)
   Complete John Waite-#1-Falling Backwards . . . . (EMI)
   Essential John Waite-1976-1986 . . . . (Chrysalis)
Tina Turner; *Wildest Dreams* . . . . (Virgin)
Momma, Where's My Daddy
Keb' Mo'; *Just Like You.* . . . . (Okeh)
Mother Mother
Tracy Bonham; *Burdens Of Being Uprigh* . . . .(Island)
Move It On Over
Hank Williams; *Complete Hank Williams* . . . .(Mercury)
Movin' On
Mya featuring Silkk The Shocker; *Mya* . . . . (University/Interscope)
Mr. Man
Alicia Keys with Jimmy Cozier; *Songs In A Minor* . . . . (J)
Must To Avoid, A
Herman's Hermits; *Herman's Hermits-Their Greatest Hits* . . . . (Abkco)
My Daddy Was A Milkman
Kentucky HeadHunters; *Pickin' On Nashville.* . . . .(Mercury)
My Favorite Lies
George Jones; *George Jones' All-Time Greatest Hits* . . . .(Epic)
My Little Secret
Xscape; *Traces Of My Lipstick.* . . . . (So So Def/Columbia)
My Man
Barbra Streisand; *Barbra Streisand's Greatest Hits* . . . .(Columbia)
   Live Concert At The Forum . . . .(Columbia)
   My Name Is Barbra . . . .(Columbia)
   ST/Funny Girl . . . .(Columbia)
Billie Holiday; *Billie Holiday-Live* . . . .(Verve)
   Essential Billie Holiday-Carnegie Hall Concert. . . . . (Verve)
Diana Ross; *Evening With Diana Ross.* . . . .(Motown)
   ST/Lady Sings The Blues. . . . . (Motown)
Ella Fitzgerald & Tommy Flanagan Trio; *Montreux '77-C* . . . . (Pablo)
Peggy Lee; *Peggy Lee's All-Time Greatest Hits* . . . .(Curb)
Sarah Vaughan; *Jazz 'Round Midnight-Sarah Vaughan* . . . . (Verve)
My Way
Usher; *My Way.* . . . .(LaFace)

Never Ever
All Saints; *All Saints* . . . . (London)
   Now That's What I Call Music!-#1-C . . . . (Virgin)
Never Gonna Be Your Fool Again
Lisa Brokop; *Every Little Girl's Dream* . . . . (Patriot)
Never Is A Promise
Fiona Apple; *Tidal* . . . . (Clean Slate/Work)
Never Lie
Immature; *Playtyme Is Over* . . . .(MCA)
New Kid In Town (Johnny Come Lately)
Eagles; *Eagles Greatest Hits, Volume 2* . . . . (Asylum)
   Eagles Live . . . . (Asylum)
   Hotel California . . . . (Asylum)
Trisha Yearwood; *Common Thread-Songs Of The Eagles-C* . . . . . (Giant)
New Worried Mind
Bob Wills; *Stay A Little Longer-The Original Columbia*
   Recordings . . . . (Roswell/RCA)
Night Before
Beatles; *Beatles-Box Set* . . . . (Capitol)
   Rock 'N' Roll Music . . . . (Capitol)
   ST/Help! . . . . (Capitol)
Night Has A Thousand Eyes
Anita O'Day; *Night Has A Thousand Eyes* . . . . (Emily)
Bobby Vee; *Best Of Bobby Vee* . . . .(EMI)
   Bobby Vee-Legendary Masters . . . .(EMI)
   Golden Years-1962-C . . . . (Dominion Entert.)
Night Lights
Nat "King" Cole; *Night Lights* . . . . (Capitol/EMI)
Night The Lights Went Out In Georgia
Lynn Anderson; *Top Of The World* . . . . (Columbia)
Reba McEntire; *For My Broken Heart* . . . .(MCA)
   Reba McEntire's Greatest Hits-#3: I'm A Survivor . . . .(MCA)
Vicki Lawrence; *Super Hits Of The '70s-Have A Nice Day-#10-C* . . . . . . (Rhino)
No Lie
Buddy Guy; *Buddy Guy* . . . . (Chess)
   Buddy Guy-Complete Chess Studio Recordings . . . . (Chess)
   I Was Walkin' Through The Woods . . . . (Chess)
No Lies
Original Cast; *Best Little Whorehouse In Texas* . . . .(MCA)
No More
Ruff Endz; *Love Crimes* . . . .(Epic)
No More Lies
Michel'le; *Michel'le* . . . . (Ruthless)
No More Lies
Moody Blues; *Sur La Mer* . . . . (Polydor)
No Reply
Beatles; *Beatles '65* . . . . (Capitol)
   Beatles-Box Set . . . . (Capitol)
   For Sale . . . . (Capitol)
No Such Thing
John Mayer; *Room For Squares* . . . .(Aware/C2/Columbia)
Nobody Knows But Me
Jimmie Rodgers; *Riding High-1929-1930* . . . . (Rounder)
Merle Haggard & The Strangers; *Same Train Different Time* . . . . (Capitol)
Not An Addict
K's Choice; *Paradise In Me* . . . . (550 Music)
Not Gon' Cry
Mary J. Blige; *Share My World* . . . .(MCA)
Now I Lay Me Down To Cheat
David Allan Coe; *David Allan Coe-17 Greatest Hits* . . . . (Columbia)
   David Allan Coe's Biggest Hits . . . . (Legacy)
   For The Record-The First 10 Years . . . . (Columbia)
   Rough Rider . . . . (Columbia)
Ocean Front Property
George Strait; *Country Classics-#8-1986-1987-C* . . . . . . (Universal)
   George Strait's Greatest Hits-#2 . . . .(MCA)
   MCA Records 30 Years Of Hits-1958-1988-C . . . .(MCA)
   Ocean Front Property . . . .(MCA)
Off The Hook
Barenaked Ladies; *Maroon* . . . . (Reprise)
Old Man From The Mountain
Merle Haggard & The Strangers; *For The Record: Merle Haggard-43*
   Legendary Hits . . . . (BNA)
On The Down Low
Brian McKnight; *I Remember You* . . . . (Mercury)
One Day You'll Be Mine
Usher; *My Way* . . . . (LaFace)
One Love At A Time
Tanya Tucker; *Tanya Tucker's Greatest Hits* . . . . (Liberty)
One More Chance
Notorious B.I.G.; *Ready To Die* . . . .(Bad Boy/Arista)
One Night Stand
J-Shin featuring La Tocha Scott; *My Soul, My Life* . . . . (Atlantic)
Ooh Baby Baby
Linda Ronstadt; *Linda Ronstadt's Greatest Hits, Volume Two* . . . . (Asylum)
   Living In The USA . . . . (Asylum)
Miracles; *Best Of Smokey Robinson & The Miracles-Anthology* . . . . . (Motown)
   Smokey Robinson's Greatest Hits-#2 . . . . (Motown)

Pack Your Lies And Go
Celinda Pink; *Victimized* . . . .(Step One)
Pair Of Old Sneakers
George Jones; *George Jones & Tammy Wynette-16*
   Biggest Hits . . . . (Epic/Legacy)
Papa Loved Mama
Garth Brooks; *Garth Brooks-Double Live* . . . . (Capitol)
   Ropin' The Wind . . . . (Liberty)
Papa Was A Rollin' Stone
Temptations; *20/20-C* . . . . (Motown)
   25 #1 Hits From 25 Years-C . . . . (Motown)
   All The Million-Sellers . . . . (Motown)
   Billboard Top Rock 'N' Roll Hits-1972-C . . . . (Rhino)
   Compact Command Performances-Temptations . . . . (Motown)
   Temptations-Anthology-The Best Of The Temptations . . . . (Motown)
Party Time
T.G. Sheppard; *Great Divorce Songs For Him-C* . . . . . (Warner Bros.)
   T.G. Sheppard's All-Time Greatest Hits . . . . (Warner Bros.)
   T.G. Sheppard's Greatest Hits . . . .(Warner Bros./Curb)
Pictures Don't Lie
Billy Ray Cyrus; *Red Hot + Country-C* . . . . (Mercury)
Pocket Full Of Gold
Vince Gill; *Pocket Full Of Gold* . . . . (MCA)
Poor Little Fool
Rick Nelson; *Live In '85* . . . . (Rhino)
Ricky Nelson; *Best Of Ricky Nelson* . . . . (EMI)
   EMI Legends Of Rock & Roll-24 Greatest Hits-C . . . . (EMI)
   Ricky Nelson-Legendary Masters . . . . (EMI)
Promises
Cranberries; *Bury The Hatchet* . . . . (Island/IDJMG)
Promises Broken
Soul Asylum; *Let Your Dim Light Shine* . . . . (Columbia)
Propaganda Machine
1927; *...Ish* . . . .(Atlantic)
Quit Playing Games (With My Heart)
Backstreet Boys; *Backstreet Boys* . . . .(Jive)
   MTV Party To Go '98-C . . . . (Tommy Boy)
   The Concert For New York City-C . . . . (Columbia)
Reasons I Cheat
Randy Travis; *Storms Of Life* . . . . (Warner Bros.)
Release Me
Dolly Parton; *Country & Western* . . . . (Intercom Music)
Dolly Parton & Donna Fargo; *Queens Of Country* . . . . (Intermedia)
Elvis Presley; *On Stage-February, 1970* . . . . (RCA)
   Welcome To My World . . . . (RCA)
Engelbert Humperdinck; *Engelbert Humperdinck-His Greatest Hits* . . . . (Parrot)
   Live In Concert/All Of Me . . . . (Epic)
   Release Me . . . . (Mercury)
Esther Phillips; *Atlantic Rhythm & Blues 1947-1974-#5 (1962-*
   1966)-C . . . .(Atlantic)
   Billboard Top R&B Hits-1962-C . . . . (Rhino)
   Oldies But Goodies-#9-C . . . . (Original Sound)
Kitty Wells; *Kitty Wells' Greatest Hits* . . . . (MCA)
   The Kitty Wells Story . . . . (MCA)
Lefty Frizzell; *Lefty Frizzell's Greatest Hits* . . . . (Columbia)
Meli'sa Morgan; *Still In Love With You* . . . . (Pendulum)
Ray Price; *Ray Price's Greatest Hits* . . . . (Columbia)
   Ray Price's Greatest Hits-#1-3 . . . . (Step One)
Wilson Phillips; *Wilson Phillips* . . . . (SBK)
Return Of The Mack
Mark Morrison; *Return Of The Mack* . . . .(Atlantic)
Ricochet
Teresa Brewer; *Best Of Teresa Brewer* . . . .(MCA Jazz)
Ring On Her Finger, Time On Her Hands
Lee Greenwood; *Best Of Lee Greenwood-God Bless America* . . . . (Curb)
   Inside Out/You've Got A Good Love Comin' . . . . (MCA)
   Lee Greenwood's Greatest Hits . . . . (MCA)
   Lee Greenwood-Super Hits . . . . (Epic)
Reba McEntire; *Starting Over* . . . . (MCA)
River Of Deceit
Mad Season; *Above* . . . . (Columbia)
Roses In The Fire
Rosanne Cash; *The Wheel* . . . . (Columbia)
Run For Your Life
Beatles; *Beatles-Box Set* . . . . (Capitol)
   Rubber Soul . . . . (Capitol)
Run-Around
Blues Traveler; *Four* . . . . (A&M)
   ST/Crossroads-VH1 Television Program . . . .(Atlantic)
Runaround Sue
Dion; *Billboard Top Rock 'N' Roll Hits-1961-C* . . . . (Rhino)
   Everything You Always Wanted To Hear . . . .(Laurie)
   Million-Dollar Memories-#1-C . . . . (RCA)
   Oldies But Goodies-#7-C . . . . (Original Sound)
   ST/The Flamingo Kid . . . . (Motown)
   ST/The Wanderers . . . . (Warner Bros.)
Runaround, The
Xscape; *Traces Of My Lipstick* . . . . (So So Def/Columbia)

Sad Eyes
Bruce Springsteen; *Tracks* . . . . (Columbia)
Trisha Yearwood; *Real Live Woman* . . . . (MCA)

Saginaw, Michigan
Lefty Frizzell; *American Originals-Lefty Frizzell* . . . . (Columbia)
Billboard Top Country Hits-1964-C . . . . (Rhino)
Columbia Country Classics-#3-Americana-C . . . . (Columbia)
Lefty Frizzell's Greatest Hits . . . . (Columbia)

Said I Loved You...But I Lied
Michael Bolton; *The One Thing* . . . . (Columbia)

Sail Away
Linda Ronstadt; *Don't Cry Now* . . . . (Asylum)
Randy Newman; *Guilty: 30 Years Of Randy Newman* . . . . (Rhino)
Sail Away . . . . (Reprise)

Same Script, Different Cast
Whitney Houston & Deborah Cox; *Whitney Houston's Greatest Hits* . . . (Arista)

Say It Isn't So
Daryl Hall & John Oates; *MTV's Rock 'N' Roll To Go-C* . . . . (Elektra)
Rock 'N Soul, Part 1 . . . . (RCA)

Say It Isn't So
Outfield; *Play Deep* . . . . (Columbia)

Say It Isn't So Joe
Roger Daltrey; *Best Bits* . . . . (MCA)
One Of The Boys . . . . (MCA)

Say My Name
Destiny's Child; *The Writing's On The Wall* . . . . (Columbia)

Self Made Man
Montgomery Gentry; *Tattoos & Scars* . . . . (Columbia)

Separated
Avant; *My Thoughts* . . . . (MCA)

She Didn't Lie
Garland Jeffreys; *One-Eyed Jack* . . . . (A&M)

She Drew A Broken Heart
Patty Loveless; *The Trouble With The Truth* . . . . (Epic)

She Thinks I Still Care
Elvis Presley; *Moody Blue* . . . . (RCA)
George Jones; *Best Of George Jones-1955-1967* . . . . (Rhino)
Billboard Top Country Hits-1962-C . . . . (Rhino)
George Jones' All-Time Greatest Hits . . . . (Epic)
George Jones-Super Hits-#2 . . . . (Epic)

She's Lying
Lee Greenwood; *Inside Out/You've Got A Good Love Comin'* . . . . (MCA)
Lee Greenwood's Greatest Hits . . . . (MCA)

She's Not There
Santana; *Moonflower* . . . . (Columbia)
Viva Santana! . . . . (Columbia)
Vanilla Fudge; *Vanilla Fudge* . . . . (Atco)
Zombies; *Best & The Rest Of The Zombies* . . . . (Epic)
Billboard Top Rock 'N' Roll Hits-1964-C . . . . (Rhino)
History Of British Rock-#1-C . . . . (Rhino)
Time Of The Zombies . . . . (Bac-Trac)

Shit You Hear At Parties
Minutemen; *Ballot Result* . . . . (SST)

Silence Is Golden
4 Seasons; *25th Anniversary Collection* . . . . (Rhino)
4 Seasons-Anthology . . . . (Rhino)
Tremeloes; *Best Of The Tremeloes* . . . . (Rhino)
History Of British Rock-#7-C . . . . (Rhino)
Rock Artifacts-From The Vaults-#4-C . . . . (Columbia)

Silver Threads And Golden Needles
Honky Tonk Angels; *Honky Tonk Angels* . . . . (Columbia)
Linda Ronstadt; *Don't Cry Now* . . . . (Asylum)
Hand Sown Home Grown . . . . (Capitol)
Linda Ronstadt-Retrospective . . . . (Capitol)
Linda Ronstadt's Greatest Hits . . . . (Asylum)
Springfields; *Troubadours Of The Folk Era-#3-C* . . . . (Rhino)

Silver Tongue & Gold Plated Lies
Hotmud Family; *Meat & Potatoes (& Stuff Like That)* . . . . . (Flying Fish)

Slippin' And Slidin'
Little Richard; *Little Richard-18 Greatest Hits* . . . . (Rhino)

Slipping Around
Ernest Tubb; *45-#46173* . . . . (Decca)
Margaret Whiting & Jimmy Wakely; *45-#40224* . . . . (Capitol)

Smiling Faces Sometimes
Undisputed Truth; *Didn't It Blow Your Mind: Soul Hits Of The
'70s-#5-C* . . . . (Rhino)
Hard-To-Find Motown Classics-#2-C . . . . (Motown)

So Fine
Mint Condition; *From The Mint Factory* . . . . (Perspective/A&M)

Somebody's Crying
Chris Isaak; *Forever Blue* . . . . (Reprise)
VH-1 Crossroads-C . . . . (Atlantic)

Sorry I Lied
Cliff Thomas; *45-#63* . . . . (Sun)

South Of The Border (Down Mexico Way)
Bob Wills & His Texas Playboys; *Best Of Bob Wills & His Texas
Playboys* . . . . (MCA)
Bob Wills & His Texas Playboys-Greatest Hits . . . . (Curb)
Frank Sinatra; *Capitol Collectors Series-Frank Sinatra* . . . . (Capitol)

Come Fly With Me . . . . (Capitol)
Gene Autry; *The Country Music Hall Of Fame-Gene Autry-15 Of His All-
Time Greatest Hits* . . . . (Columbia)
Patsy Cline; *Always* . . . . (MCA)
The Patsy Cline Story . . . . (MCA)
Willie Nelson; *What A Wonderful World* . . . . (Columbia)

Space Between, The
Dave Matthews Band; *Everyday* . . . . (RCA)

Spark
Tori Amos; *From The Choirgirl Hotel* . . . . (Atlantic)

Spit Of Love
Bonnie Raitt; *Fundamental* . . . . (Capitol)
Lilith Fair-A Celebration Of Women In Music-#3-C . . . . (Arista)

Star 69
R.E.M.; *Monster* . . . . (Warner Bros.)

Stop! In The Name Of Love
Diana Ross & The Supremes; *16 #1 Hits From The Early '60s-C* . . . . . (Motown)
Diana Ross & The Supremes' Greatest Hits . . . . (Motown)
Diana Ross & The Supremes-Anthology (1962-1969) . . . . . . (Motown)
Evening With Diana Ross . . . . (Motown)
Girl Groups-Story Of A Sound-C . . . . (Rhino)
Motown Superstar Series-#1-Diana Ross & The Supremes . . . (Motown)
Hollies; *45-#89819* . . . . (Atlantic)
Supremes; *Billboard Top Pop Hits-1965-C* . . . . (Rhino)

Streets Of Fire
Bruce Springsteen; *Darkness On The Edge Of Town* . . . . (Columbia)

String Of Lies
Goo Goo Dolls; *Superstar Car Wash* . . . . (Metal Blade)

Strong Enough
Sheryl Crow; *Tuesday Night Music Club* . . . . (A&M)

Stutter
Joe featuring Mystikal; *My Name Is Joe* . . . . (Jive)
Now That's What I Call Music!-#8-C . . . . (Virgin)

Suspicion
Elvis Presley; *ST/Pot Luck* . . . . (RCA)
Terry Stafford; *Billboard Top Rock 'N' Roll Hits-1964-C* . . . . (Rhino)
Cruisin'-1964-C . . . . (Increase)
Oldies But Goodies-#8-C . . . . (Original Sound)

Suspicious Minds
Elvis Presley; *Aloha from Hawaii via Satellite* . . . . (RCA)
From Memphis To Vegas/From Vegas To Memphis . . . . (RCA)
Memphis Record . . . . (RCA)
Nipper's Greatest Hits Of The '60s-#2-C . . . . (RCA)
ST/This Is Elvis . . . . (RCA)

Sweet Misery
Amel Larrieux; *Infinite Possibilities* . . . . (Epic)

Take A Message To Mary
Bob Dylan; *Self Portrait* . . . . (Columbia)
Everly Brothers; *Everly Brothers-All-Time Original Hits* . . . . (Rhino)
Everly Brothers-Cadence Classics-Their 20 Greatest Hits . . . . . (Rhino)
Rockpile; *Seconds Of Pleasure* . . . . (Columbia)

Take It On The Run
REO Speedwagon; *A Second Decade Of Rock And Roll 1981 To 1991* . . . (Epic)
Hi Infidelity . . . . (Epic)
REO Speedwagon-The Hits . . . . (Epic)

Take That
Lisa Brokop; *Every Little Girl's Dream* . . . . (Patriot)

Take Time To Know Her
Percy Sledge; *Best Of Percy Sledge* . . . . (Atlantic)
It Tears Me Up-Best Of Percy Sledge . . . . (Rhino)

Talk Show Shhh!
Shae Jones; *Talk Show* . . . . (Universal)

Tell Me A Lie
Janie Fricke; *19 Hot Country Requests-C* . . . . (Epic)
Greatest Country Hits Of The '80s-1983-C . . . . (Columbia)
It Ain't Easy . . . . (Columbia)
Janie Fricke-17 Greatest Hits . . . . (Columbia)
Love Lies . . . . (Columbia)
Very Best Of Janie Fricke . . . . (Columbia)

Tell Me That It Isn't True
Bob Dylan; *Nashville Skyline* . . . . (Columbia)

Tell Me Why
Beatles; *Beatles-Box Set* . . . . (Capitol)
Something New . . . . (Capitol)
ST/A Hard Day's Night . . . . (Capitol)

Telling Me Lies
Dolly Parton/Emmylou Harris/Linda Ronstadt; *Trio* . . . . (Warner Bros.)

Telling Stories
Tracy Chapman; *Telling Stories* . . . . (Elektra)

Tender Lie
Restless Heart; *Best Of Restless Heart* . . . . (RCA)
Big Dreams In A Small Town . . . . (RCA)
Restless Heart's Greatest Hits . . . . (RCA)

Tequila Talkin'
Lonestar; *Lonestar* . . . . (BNA)

That Other Woman
Changing Faces; *Visit Me* . . . . (Atlantic)

That'll Be The Day
Buddy Holly; *ST/American Graffiti* . . . . (MCA)

Buddy Holly/The Crickets; *Buddy Holly-20 Golden Greats* .... (MCA)
Chirping Crickets .... (MCA)
Crickets; *Billboard Top Rock 'N' Roll Hits-1957-C* .... (Rhino)
Foghat; *Best Of Foghat-#2* .... (Rhino)
Energized .... (Rhino)
Linda Ronstadt; *Hasten Down The Wind* .... (Asylum)
Linda Ronstadt's Greatest Hits .... (Asylum)

That's My Story
Collin Raye; *Extremes* .... (Epic)

Then What
Clay Walker; *Clay Walker's Greatest Hits* .... (Giant)

There Are No Cats In America
Nehemiah Persoff/John Guarnieri/Warren Hays; *ST/An American Tail* ... (MCA)

There Is No Arizona
Jamie O'Neal; *Shiver* .... (Mercury)

There You Go
Johnny Cash; *The Man In Black-His Greatest Hits* .... (Legacy)

There You Go
Pink; *Can't Take Me Home* .... (LaFace)

These Eyes
Guess Who; *Best Of The Guess Who* .... (RCA)
Greatest Of The Guess Who .... (RCA)
Nipper's Greatest Hits Of The '60s-#1-C .... (RCA)
Track Record-Collection .... (RCA)

They Didn't Believe Me
Hal Mooney; *Heritage Of Broadway-Music Of Jerome Kern* .... (Bainbridge)
Joe Williams; *Joe Williams Sings* .... (Savoy Jazz)
Johnny Mercer; *Song Is You-Capitol Sings Jerome Kern* .... (Capitol)
Pearl Bailey; *Pearl Bailey-16 Most Requested Songs* .... (Legacy)
Tommy Dorsey; *Best Of Tommy Dorsey* .... (MCA)

They Don't Know
Jon B.; *Cool Relax* .... (Yab Yum/550)

Things That I Used To Do
Guitar Slim; *Blues Classics-C* .... (K-Tel)

Thinkin' 'Bout It
Gerald Levert; *Love & Consequences* .... (East West)

This Lonely Place
Goldfinger; *Hang-Ups* .... (Mojo Music/Universal)

This Night Won't Last Forever
Bill LaBounty; *The Right Direction* .... (Noteworthy)
This Night Won't Last Forever .... (Warner Bros.)
Michael Johnson; *Dialogue* .... (EMI)
Have A Nice Night-Romantic Hits Of The '70s-C .... (Rhino)
Radio Daze-Pop Hits Of The '80s-#1-C .... (Rhino)
Then & Now .... (ISD/Intersound)
Moe Bandy; *Many Mansions* .... (Curb)
Sawyer Brown; *Six Days On The Road* .... (Curb)

Thunder Rolls, The
Garth Brooks; *Garth Brooks-Double Live* .... (Capitol)
No Fences .... (Capitol)

Tired Of Your Jive
B.B. King; *Electric B.B. King-His Best* .... (MCA)
Great Moments With B.B. King .... (MCA)

Tomb Of The Unknown Love
Cassell Webb; *Songs Of A Stranger* .... (Venture)
Kenny Rogers; *The Heart Of The Matter* .... (RCA)

Too Good To Be True
Michael Peterson; *Michael Peterson* .... (Reprise)

Too Late, Too Soon
Jon Secada; *Secada* .... (Capitol)

Trouble In Paradise
Bruce Springsteen; *Tracks* .... (Columbia)

Trouble With The Truth
Patty Loveless; *The Trouble With The Truth* .... (Epic)

Trust
Megadeth; *Cryptic Writings* .... (Capitol)

Tryin' To Love Two
William Bell; *Coming Back For More* .... (Razor & Tie)

Tumble In The Rough
Stone Temple Pilots; *Tiny Music...Songs From The Vatican Gift Shop* .... (Atlantic)

Turn Back Time
Aqua; *Aquarium* .... (MCA)
ST/Sliding Doors .... (MCA)

Twenty-Four Hours From Tulsa
Burt Bacharach; *Walk On By* .... (MCA Special Prod.)
Gene Pitney; *Best Of Gene Pitney* .... (K-Tel)

Two-Timin' Me
Remingtons; *Blue Frontier* .... (BNA)

U Don't Love Me
Kumbia Kings; *Amor Familia Respeto* .... (EMI Latin)

Ugly Hour
David Bromberg; *Bandit In A Bathing Suit* .... (Fantasy)

Understanding
Candlebox; *Lucy* .... (Maverick)

Unfaithful Servant
Band; *Rock Of Ages* .... (Capitol)
The Band .... (Capitol)
The Band-Gift Set .... (Capitol)
To Kingdom Come-The Definitive Collection .... (Capitol)

Unfaithfully Yours (One Love)
Stephen Bishop; *Best Of Bish* .... (Rhino)

Upside Down
Diana Ross; *Billboard Top Dance Hits-1980-C* .... (Rhino)
Billboard Top Hits-1980-C .... (Rhino)
Diana .... (Motown)
Diana Ross-All The Great Hits .... (Motown)
Diana Ross-Anthology .... (Motown)

Use Me
Bill Withers; *Bill Withers' Greatest Hits* .... (Columbia)
Still Bill .... (Columbia)

Walk On By
Leroy Van Dyke; *Billboard Top Country Hits-1961-C* .... (Rhino)
Country Classics-C .... (Sun)
Country Music Classics-#2-1960-1965-C .... (K-Tel)
Souvenirs Of Music City U.S.A.-C .... (Plantation)

Walkaway Joe
Trisha Yearwood; *Hearts In Armor* .... (MCA)
Songbook-A Collection Of Hits .... (MCA)

Wandering Eyes
Ronnie McDowell; *Older Women & Other Greatest Hits* .... (Epic)

Wanted
Perry Como; *Perry Como's All-Time Greatest Hits-#1* .... (RCA)
Perry Como's Greatest Hits .... (RCA)

War Is Hell (On The Homefront Too)
T.G. Sheppard; *Perfect Stranger* .... (Warner Bros.)
T.G. Sheppard's All-Time Greatest Hits .... (Warner Bros.)
T.G. Sheppard's Greatest Hits .... (Warner Bros./Curb)

We Live In Two Different Worlds
Auldridge/Bennett/Gaudreau; *This Old Town* .... (Rebel)

We Loved It Away
George Jones & Tammy Wynette; *George Jones & Tammy Wynette-16 Biggest Hits* .... (Epic/Legacy)

We Tell Ourselves
Clint Black; *The Hard Way* .... (RCA)

What About Us
Total; *Kima, Keisha & Pam* .... (Bad Boy/Arista)
LaFace Records Presents The Platinum Collection-C .... (LaFace)
ST/Soul Food .... (LaFace)

What Goes On
Beatles; *"Yesterday"...And Today* .... (Capitol)

What I Meant To Say
Wade Hayes; *Old Enough To Know Better* .... (Columbia)

What Kind Of Man Would I Be
Mint Condition; *Definition Of A Band* .... (Perspective/A&M)

What You Want
DMX; *...And Then There Was X* .... (Ruff Ryders/IDJMG)

What You're Doing
Beatles; *For Sale* .... (Capitol)

When You Think Of Me
Eric Benet; *A Day In The Life* .... (Warner Bros.)

White Lies
Grin; *Rock Artifacts-From The Vaults-#1-C* .... (Columbia)
Nils Lofgren; *Grin* .... (Epic Portrait Assoc.)

Who Is He And What Is He To You
Me'Shell Ndegeocello; *Peace Beyond Passion* .... (Maverick)

Who Walks In When I Walk Out
Bob Wills; *Stay A Little Longer-The Original Columbia Recordings* .... (Roswell/RCA)

Who's Cheatin' Who
Charly McClain; *Charly McClain's Greatest Hits* .... (Epic)
Encore-Charly McClain .... (Epic)
Greatest Country Hits Of The '80s-1980-C .... (Columbia)
Greatest Hits From The Jukebox-C .... (Epic)
Ten Year Anniversary .... (Epic)

Who's Cheatin' Who
Alan Jackson; *Everything I Love* .... (Arista)

Who's Makin' Love
Blues Brothers; *Blues Brothers-The Definitive Collection* .... (Atlantic)
Made In America .... (Atlantic)
Johnnie Taylor; *Billboard Top R&B Hits-1965-1969-C* .... (Rhino)
Johnnie Taylor-Super Hits .... (Stax)
Oldies But Goodies-#5-C .... (Original Sound)
Top Of The Stax-Twenty Greatest Hits-C .... (Stax)

Whose Bed Have Your Boots Been Under?
Shania Twain; *The Woman In Me* .... (Mercury)

Why Oh Why
Celine Dion; *Let's Talk About Love-C* .... (550 Music)

Window Up Above
George Jones; *Cup Of Loneliness-Classic Mercury Years* .... (Mercury)
George Jones' All-Time Greatest Hits .... (Epic)
George Jones-Super Hits .... (Epic)
George Jones-Super Hits .... (Epic)
Hank Wilson; *Hank Wilson's Back, Vol. 1* .... (Right Stuff)
Hot Rize; *Red Knuckle-Hot Rize Live* .... (Flying Fish)
Johnny Cash; *Back To Back* .... (K-Tel)

Mickey Gilley; *Mickey Gilley's Greatest Hits-#1* . . . . (Epic)
Ten Years Of Hits . . . . (Epic)
Ralph Stanley; *Clinch Mountain Country* . . . . (Rebel)
Ricky Skaggs; *Ricky Skaggs-Country Boy* . . . . (Epic)
Wanda Jackson; *Wanda Jackson-Vintage Collection* . . . . (Capitol)

Windy
Association; *Association Greatest Hits* . . . . (Warner Bros.)
Billboard Top Rock 'N' Roll Hits-1967-C . . . . (Rhino)
Summer Of Love-#1-C . . . . (Rhino)
Vintage Association . . . . (Fifty One West)
Wes Montgomery; *A Day In The Life* . . . . (A&M)
Wes Montgomery-Classics-#22 . . . . (A&M)
Wes Montgomery's Greatest Hits . . . . (A&M)

With Me Part 1
Destiny's Child featuring JD; *Destiny's Child*. . . (Grass Roots/Columbia)

Woman To Woman
Tammy Wynette; *Tammy Wynette-Anniversary-20 Years Of Hits* . . . . . . (Epic)
Tammy Wynette's Greatest Hits-#3 . . . . (Epic)
Tears Of Fire-25th Anniversary Collection . . . . (Epic)
Wynonna; *Tammy Wynette...Remembered-C* . . . . (Asylum)

Woman, Woman
Union Gap Featuring Gary Puckett; *Best Of Gary
Puckett* . . . . (Hollywood/DNA-Rounder)
Gary Puckett And The Union Gap's Greatest Hits . . . . . (Columbia)

Women Who Cheat On The World
Tanita Tikaram; *Lovers In The City* . . . . (Reprise)

Wonderful
Everclear; *Now That's What I Call Music!-#5-C* . . . . (Virgin)
Songs From An American Movie-#1-Learning How To Smile . . . . . . (Capitol)

Won't Get Fooled Again
Van Halen; *LIVE: Right here, right now*. . . . . (Warner Bros.)
Who; *ST/The Kids Are Alright*. (MCA)
The Concert For New York City-C . . . . (Columbia)
Who Greatest Hits . . . . (MCA)
Who's Last . . . . (MCA)
Who's next . . . . (MCA)

Words
Bee Gees; *Bee Gees-Gold* . . . . (Polydor)
Here At Last...Bee Gees...Live . . . . (Polydor)
History Of British Rock-#9-C . . . . (Rhino)
Elvis Presley; *From Memphis To Vegas/From Vegas To Memphis* . . . . . . (RCA)
That's The Way It Is . . . . (RCA)
Joan Armatrading; *Shouting Stage* . . . . (A&M)
Rita Coolidge; *Anytime...Anywhere* . . . . (A&M)
Rita Coolidge-Classics-#5 . . . . (A&M)
Rita Coolidge's Greatest Hits . . . . (A&M)

Words
Monkees; *Missing Links-#2*. (Rhino)
Monkees' Greatest Hits . . . . (Rhino)
More Greatest Hits Of The Monkees . . . . (Arista)

Working For MCA
Hank Williams, Jr.; *Hank Williams, Jr. "Live"* . . . . (WB/Curb)
Lynyrd Skynyrd; *Best Of The Rest Of Lynyrd Skynyrd* . . . . . . (MCA)
One More From The Road . . . . (MCA)
Second Helping . . . . (MCA)

Worried Mind
Roy Acuff; *Night Train To Memphis*. . . . . . (Columbia River Entert. Group)

Would I Lie To You
Charles & Eddie; *Duophonic*. . . . . (Capitol)

Would I Lie To You
Eurythmics; *Be Yourself Tonight*. . . . . (RCA)
Eurythmics' Greatest Hits . . . . (Arista)

Would I Lie To You
Whitesnake; *Come An' Get It* . . . . (Geffen)

You Bring Me Up
K-Ci & JoJo; *Love Always*. (MCA)

You Caused It All By Telling Lies
Hank Williams; *Alone With His Guitar* . . . . (Mercury)
Complete Hank Williams . . . . (Mercury)

You Cheated
Shields; *Oldies But Goodies-#3-C*. . . . . (Original Sound)

You Lie
Reba McEntire; *Reba McEntire's Greatest Hits Volume Two* . . . . . . (MCA)
Rumor Has It. . . . . (MCA)

You Say You Will
Trisha Yearwood; *Hearts In Armor*. . . . . (MCA)

You Should Know Better
Kenny Wayne Shepherd Band; *Live On* . . . . (Giant)

You Were Mine
Dixie Chicks; *Big Country Hits '99-C*. . . . . (K-Tel)
Wide Open Spaces . . . . (Monument)

You Win Again
Hank Williams With His Drifting Cowboys; *24 Of Hank Williams'
Greatest Hits* . . . . (Polydor)
Hank Williams-40 Greatest Hits . . . . (Polydor)
Jerry Lee Lewis; *Heartbreak* . . . . (Tomato)
Memphis Country-C . . . . (Sun)
Rockin' My Life Away . . . . (Tomato)
Taste Of Country. . . . . (Sun)

The Golden Hits Of Jerry Lee Lewis . . . . (Smash)
Johnny Cash; *Johnny Cash-Original Golden Hits-#3* . . . . (Sun)
Keith Richards; *Timeless: Hank Williams Tribute-C* . . . .(Lost Highway/IDJMG)
Keith Whitley; *Kentucky Bluebird* . . . . (RCA)
Mary Chapin Carpenter; *Greatest Country Hits Of The '90s-#2-C* . . .(Columbia)
Tommy Edwards; *It's All In The Game-The Complete Hits Of Tommy
Edwards* . . . . (Eric)

Young Girl
Union Gap Featuring Gary Puckett; *Billboard Top Pop Hits-1968-C* . . . .(Rhino)

Your Cheatin' Heart
Beck; *Timeless: Hank Williams Tribute-C*. . . . . . .(Lost Highway/IDJMG)
Elvis Presley; *Elvis For Everyone!*. . . . . (RCA)
Welcome To My World . . . . (RCA)
Frankie Laine; *Frankie Laine's 16 Greatest Hits* . . . . (Trip)
Frankie Laine's Greatest Hits . . . . (Columbia)
Hank Williams With His Drifting Cowboys; *24 Of Hank Williams'
Greatest Hits* . . . . (Polydor)
Hank Williams-16 Great Hits . . . . (Everest)
Hank Williams-40 Greatest Hits . . . . (Polydor)
Hank Williams, Jr.; *Very Best Of Hank Williams, Jr.* . . . . . (Polydor)
Jerry Lee Lewis; *Live At The Star Club-Hamburg 1964.* . . . . . (Rhino)
The Golden Hits Of Jerry Lee Lewis . . . . (Smash)
Patsy Cline; *ST/Sweet Dreams* . . . . (MCA)
The Patsy Cline Story . . . . (MCA)
Ray Charles; *Ray Charles' Greatest Hits-#2* . . . . (Rhino)

Your Little Secret
Melissa Etheridge; *Your Little Secret*. . . . . (Island)

Your Secret Love
Luther Vandross; *Your Secret Love* . . . . (LV/Epic)

Your Selfish Heart
Stanley Brothers & The Clinch Mountain Boys; *Stanley Brothers & The
Clinch Mountain Boys* . . . . (King)

You're A God
Vertical Horizon; *Everything You Want* . . . . (RCA)

You're The One
SWV; *MTV Party To Go-#10-C* . . . . (Tommy Boy)
New Beginning . . . . (RCA)
SWV's Greatest Hits . . . . (Beast)

CHILDREN

See Also: *AGES (various), AGING, BABY, CHILDREN LEAVING
HOME, DOMESTIC ABUSE, FAMILY (various), ORPHANS,
PARENTS (various), PEOPLE, SCHOOL, SOCIAL OUTCASTS,
TEACHING VALUES, TEENAGERS, TOYS & GAMES, YOUNG*

1, 2, Buckle My Shoe
Bob McGrath; *The Baby Record* . . . .(Golden Boy Jazz/Optimism)

Adrian
Jewel; *Pieces Of You* . . . . (Atlantic)

All God's Chillun Got Rhythm
Judy Garland; *Judy Garland-Collector's Items-1936-1945* . . . . (MCA)

All I Want For Christmas (Is My Two Front Teeth)
David Seville & The Chipmunks; *Christmas With The Chipmunks-#2* . . . .(EMI)
Nat "King" Cole; *Let It Snow!-Cuddly Christmas Classics* . . . .(Capitol)
Spike Jones; *Dr. Demento Presents The Greatest Novelty Records-#6-
Christmas-C* . . . . (Rhino)
Spike Jones-Christmas . . . . (Rhino)

All The Children Sing
Todd Rundgren; *Hermit Of Mink Hollow*. . . . . (Rhino)
Todd Rundgren-Anthology 1968-1985 . . . .(Rhino)

All The Kids Are Right
Local H; *Pack Up The Cats* . . . . (Island)

All Through The Night
Judy Collins; *Baby's Bedtime*. . . . . (Lightyear)

Angel Child
Lightnin' Hopkins; *How Many More Years I Got* . . . . (Fantasy)
Lightnin' Hopkins' Greatest Hits . . . . (Prestige)

Anne Frank Story
Human Sexual Response; *Fig. 15* . . . . (Eat)

Another Brick In The Wall, Part 2
Class Of '99; *ST/The Faculty* . . . .(Columbia)
Pink Floyd; *Collection Of Great Dance Songs* . . . .(Columbia)
Delicate Sound Of Thunder. . . . .(Columbia)
The Wall . . . .(Columbia)
Roger Waters; *The Wall-Live In Berlin* . . . .(Mercury)

Artificial Flowers
Bobby Darin; *The Bobby Darin Story* . . . . (Atlantic)

As Tears Go By
Marianne Faithfull; *Marianne Faithfull's Greatest Hits* . . . . . . (Abkco)
Strange Weather . . . . (Island)
Rolling Stones; *Big Hits (High Tide & Green Grass)*. . . . . . (Abkco)
December's Children (and everybody's). . . . . (Abkco)
Hot Rocks 1964-1971 . . . . (Abkco)
Singles Collection-The London Years . . . . (Abkco)

At The Same Time
Barbra Streisand; *Higher Ground* . . . .(Columbia)

Autumn Of My Life
Bobby Goldsboro; *10th Anniversary Album-#1* ....(EMI)
Bobby Goldsboro's Greatest Hits ....(Liberty)

Baby Talk
Jan & Dean; *Best Of Jan & Dean* ....(EMI)
Collectables Presents The History Of Rock-#9-C .....(Collectables)
One Summer Night-Live.....................................(Rhino)

Bang Bang
Cher; *Cher* ....(Geffen)
EMI Legends Of Rock & Roll-24 Greatest Hits-C ....(EMI)

Beautiful Boy
John Lennon; *Double Fantasy* ....(Capitol)

Beautiful Child
Fleetwood Mac; *25 Years-The Chain* ....(Warner Bros.)
Tusk ....(Warner Bros.)

Beautiful Child
Blow Monkeys; *She Was Only The Grocer's Daughter* .... (RCA)

Belfast Child
Simple Minds; *Street Fighting Years* ....(A&M)

Billy The Kid (I Miss...)
Billy Dean; *Billy Dean* ....(Liberty)

Blessed
Elton John; *Elton John-Love Songs* ....(MCA)
Made In England ....(Rocket)

Boogie Child
Bee Gees; *Children Of The World* ....(RSO)
Here At Last...Bee Gees...Live ....(Polydor)

Boogie Chillun
John Lee Hooker; *Best Of John Lee Hooker* ....(Crescendo)
Best Of John Lee Hooker ....(Vee-Jay)
Boogie Chillun ....(Fantasy)
Hooked On The Blues ....(Everest)

Bookends
Joe Walsh; *The Smoker You Drink The Player You Get* ....(MCA)

Broken Home
Papa Roach; *Infest* ....(DreamWorks/SKG)

Butterfly Kisses
Bob Carlisle; *Butterfly Kisses (Shades Of Grace)*...............(DMG/Jive)

Carrie-Anne
Hollies; *Best Of The Hollies* ....(EMI)
Evolution ....(Epic)
Hollies-Epic Anthology From The Original Master Tapes .....(Epic)
The Hollies' Greatest Hits ....(Epic)

Check Yes Or No
George Strait; *Strait Out Of The Box* ....(MCA)

Child Apart
Ian & Sylvia; *Ian & Sylvia's Greatest Hits* .... (Vanguard)

Child In These Hills
Jackson Browne; *Jackson Browne* ....(Asylum)

Child In Time
Deep Purple; *Deepest Purple/The Very Best Of Deep Purple*.....(Warner Bros.)
In Rock...(Warner Bros.)
Made In Japan..(Warner Bros.)

Child Is Born, A
Barbra Streisand; *Lazy Afternoon*.......................(Columbia)
Kenny Burrell; *Fire Into Music-Best Of Impulse!-#2-C* ....(MCA/Impulse)
God Bless The Child ....(CBS Associated)
Heritage ....(Voss)
Toots Thielemans; *East Coast West Coast* .... (Private Music)

Child Is Coming
Paul Kantner/Jefferson Starship; *Blows Against The Empire* ....(RCA)

Child Is Gone
Fiona Apple; *Tidal* ....(Clean Slate/Work)

Child Of Babylon
Whitesnake; *Come An' Get It* ....(Geffen)

Child Of Clay
Jimmie Rodgers; *Best Of Jimmie Rodgers* ....(Rhino)

Child Of Innocence
Kansas; *Masque* ....(Kirshner)

Child Of Light
Deep Purple; *Deepest Purple/The Very Best Of Deep Purple*.....(Warner Bros.)
In Rock..(Warner Bros.)
Made In Japan...(Warner Bros.)

Child Of Mine
Fleetwood Mac; *Bare Trees* ....(Reprise)

Child Of Our Times
Barry McGuire; *Sixties Rule! Chapter Two-C* ....(One Way)

Child Of Poverty
Paul Martin; *Country Gold-Paul Martin*....................(Plantation)
Great Country Gold ....(Plantation)

Child Of The Fifties
Statler Brothers; *Legend Goes On*........................(Mercury)

Child Of The Moon
Rolling Stones; *More Hot Rocks (big hits & fazed cookies)* ....(Abkco)

Child Of The Wild Blue Yonder
John Hiatt; *Stolen Moments* ....(A&M)

Child Of Vision
Supertramp; *Breakfast In America* ....(A&M)

Child Should Live Forever (Theme For The Eddie Cantor Fund For Children With AIDS)
Original Off-Broadway Cast; *A Hard Time To Be Single* .... (Original Cast)

Child Support
Barbara Mandrell; *Sure Feels Good* ....(EMI)
Buck Owens; *Buck 'Em*................................ (Warner Bros.)

Childhood Hero
Bobby Bare; *Bare* ....(Columbia)

Children
Rex Allen, Jr.; *Country Cowboy* ....(Accord)
Today's Generation ....(SSS International)

Children
Robert Miles; *Platipus Records: Ultimate Dream Collection-C* .... (Avex-Critique)

Children
America; *America* .... (Warner Bros.)

Children
Joe South; *Best Of Joe South*...............................(Rhino)

Children
Jeannie C. Riley; *Jeannie* ....(Plantation)

Children
Burning Spear; *Man In The Hills*.........................(Island)

Children
Starship; *No Protection* ....(Grunt)

Children
EMF; *Schubert Dip* ....(Capitol)

Children And All That Jazz
Joan Baez; *Best Of Joan Baez* ....(A&M)
Diamonds & Rust ....(A&M)
Joan Baez-Classics-#8 ....(A&M)

Children And Art
Original Cast; *Sunday In The Park With George*.............. (RCA Victor)

Children Children
Wings; *London Town* ....(Capitol)

Children Go Where I Send Thee
Michael McDonald; *In The Spirit-A Christmas Album* .... (MCA)
Peter, Paul & Mary & The New York Choral Society; *Holiday Celebration* .... (Warner Bros.)
Weavers; *Weavers At Carnegie Hall*...................... (Vanguard)
White Mountain Singers; *Best Of The White Mountain Singers* ...... (Folk Era)

Children In The Carousel
Mabel Mercer & Bobby Short; *At Town Hall* ....(Atlantic)

Children Of Darkness
Joan Baez; *Contemporary Ballad Book*...................... (Vanguard)

Children Of Poland
Si Kahn; *Unfinished Portraits* .... (Flying Fish)

Children Of Production
Parliament; *Parliament Live/P. Funk Earth Tour* ....(Casablanca)
The Clones Of Dr. Funkenstein ....(Casablanca)

Children Of Sanchez
Chuck Mangione; *Best Of Chuck Mangione* ....(A&M)
Children Of Sanchez.......................................(A&M)
Chuck Mangione-Classics-#6 ....(A&M)
Evening Of Magic...(A&M)

Children Of The Damned
Iron Maiden; *Live After Death-World Slavery Tour* .... (Capitol)
Number Of The Beast ....(Capitol)

Children Of The Earth
Tower Of Power; *Bump City* .... (Warner Bros.)

Children Of The Future
Steve Miller Band; *Children Of The Future* ....(Capitol)

Children Of The Ghetto
Courtney Pine; *Journey To The Urge Within*.................(Antilles)

Children Of The Ghetto
Philip Bailey; *Chinese Wall*...............................(Columbia)

Children Of The Korn
Korn with Ice Cube; *Follow The Leader* ....(Immortal/Epic)

Children Of The Land
Styx; *45-#10492* ....(RCA)

Children Of The Night
Richard Marx; *Repeat Offender* ....(EMI)

Children Of The Revolution
Violent Femmes; *Blind Leading The Naked* ....(Slash)

Children Of The World
Bee Gees; *Bee Gees' Greatest*.............................(Polydor)
Children Of The World ....(RSO)

Children Of The World
Amy Grant; *House Of Love* ....(A&M)

Children Of The World
Wailers Band; *I.D.* ....(Atlantic)

Children Of The World
Third World; *Sense Of Purpose* ....(Columbia)

Children Of The World Unite
Angela Bofill; *Angie* ....(GRP)

Child's Claim To Fame
Buffalo Springfield; *Buffalo Springfield* ....(Atco)
Buffalo Springfield Again..................................(Atco)

China Boy
Benny Goodman; *Carnegie Hall Jazz Concert* . . . . (Columbia)
ST/The Benny Goodman Story . . . . (MCA)
The Benny Goodman Story . . . . (Capitol)
Clair
Gilbert O'Sullivan; *Super Hits Of The '70s-Have A Nice Day-#9-C* . . . . . (Rhino)
Close My Eyes
Mariah Carey; *Butterfly* . . . . (Columbia)
Coat Of Many Colors
Dolly Parton; *Best Of Dolly Parton* . . . . (RCA)
Dolly Parton-Super Hits . . . . (Columbia)
Essential Dolly Parton-#2 . . . . (RCA)
Emmylou Harris; *Pieces Of The Sky* . . . . (Reprise)
Count Your Blessings (Instead Of Sheep)
Bing Crosby; *45-#29251* . . . . (Decca)
Eddie Fisher; *Best Of Eddie Fisher* . . . . (MCA)
Rosemary Clooney; *Essence Of Rosemary Clooney* . . . . (Legacy)
Counting Blue Cars
Dishwalla; *Pet Your Friends* . . . . (A&M)
Daybreak (Storybook Children)
Cheryl Lynn; *Cheryl Lynn* . . . . (Columbia)
Dear Prudence
Beatles; *The Beatles (White Album)* . . . . (Capitol)
Siouxsie And The Banshees; *Hyaena* . . . . (Geffen)
Nocturne . . . . (Geffen)
Devil Comes Back To Georgia
Marc O'Connor; *Heroes* . . . . (Warner Bros.)
Difference, The
Wallflowers; *Bringing Down The Horse* . . . . (Interscope)
D-I-V-O-R-C-E
Rosanne Cash; *Tammy Wynette...Remembered-C* . . . . (Asylum)
Tammy Wynette; *Super Hits Of The '60s-C* . . . . (Epic)
Tammy Wynette-Anniversary-20 Years Of Hits . . . . (Epic)
Tammy Wynette's Biggest Hits . . . . (Epic)
Tammy Wynette's Greatest Hits . . . . (Epic)
Dogs Kids Love To Bite, The (Armour Hot Dogs)
Original Soundtrack; *TeeVee Toons-The Commercials-#1-C* . . . . (TVT)
Down By The Water
PJ Harvey; *ST/Basketball Diaries* . . . . (Island)
To Bring You My Love . . . . (Island)
Down The Road
Mac McAnally; *Knots* . . . . (MCA)
Down To The Valley
Nilsson; *Everybody's Talkin': The Encore Collection* . . . . (BMG Special Prod.)
Down With The Sickness
Disturbed; *The Sickness* . . . . (Giant)
End Of The Innocence
Don Henley; *The End Of The Innocence* . . . . (Geffen)
Endless Cycle
Lou Reed; *New York* . . . . (Sire)
Every Ghetto, Every City
Lauryn Hill; *The Miseducation Of Lauryn Hill* . . . . (Ruffhouse/Columbia)
Eyes Of A Child
Moody Blues; *This Is The Moody Blues* . . . . (Polydor)
To Our Children's Children's Children . . . . (Polydor)
Eyes Of A Child
Naked Eyes; *Best Of Naked Eyes* . . . . (EMI)
For A Child
Michael McDonald; *Love Shouldn't Hurt-C* . . . . (Qwest)
Free To Go
Folk Implosion; *One Part Lullaby* . . . . (Interscope)
Friday The 13th Child
David Clayton-Thomas; *Clayton* . . . . (MCA)
Funky London Childhood
Marc Bolan; *T. Rex Unchained: The Unreleased Recordings-#6* . . . (Chronicles)
Gabriel's Mother's Hiway Ballad 16 Blues
Arlo Guthrie; *Best Of Arlo Guthrie* . . . . (Warner Bros.)
Gemini Childe
Mamas & The Papas; *The Papas & The Mamas* . . . . (MCA)
Ghetto Child
Spinners; *Best Of The Spinners* . . . . (Atlantic)
Gimme Shelter
Goo Goo Dolls; *Jed* . . . . (Metal Blade)
Grand Funk Railroad; *Capitol Collectors Series-Grand Funk Railroad* . . . . (Capitol)
Caught In The Act . . . . (Capitol)
Rolling Stones; *Hot Rocks 1964-1971* . . . . (Abkco)
Let It Bleed . . . . (Abkco)
No Security . . . . (Virgin)
God Bless The Child
Billie Holiday; *Billie Holiday's Greatest Hits* . . . . (Decca Jazz)
Billie Holiday's Greatest Hits . . . . (Legacy)
From The Original Decca Masters . . . . (MCA)
Songbook . . . . (Verve)
The Billie Holiday Story-#2 . . . . (Columbia)
Blood, Sweat & Tears; *Blood, Sweat & Tears* . . . . (Columbia)
Blood, Sweat & Tears Greatest Hits . . . . (Columbia)
Diana Ross; *ST/Lady Sings The Blues* . . . . (Motown)
Liza Minnelli; *4-Sider* . . . . (Cypress)
ST/Liza With A "Z" . . . . (Columbia)
Lou Rawls; *Best From Lou Rawls* . . . . (Capitol)
God Bless The Children
Loretta Lynn; *Out Of My Head And Back In My Bed* . . . . (MCA)
God Bless The Children
Motley Crue; *Shout At The Devil* . . . . (Elektra)
God's Children
Kinks; *Kink Kronikles* . . . . (Reprise)
Goonies 'R' Good Enough
Cyndi Lauper; *ST/The Goonies* . . . . (Epic)
Got A Letter From My Kid Today
Asleep At The Wheel; *Tribute To The Music Of Bob Wills And The Texas Playboys-C* . . . . (Liberty)
Merle Haggard & The Strangers; *18 Rare Classics* . . . . (Curb)
Working Man Can't Get Nowhere Today . . . . (Capitol)
Greatest Discovery
Elton John; *Elton John* . . . . (Polydor)
Live In Australia With The Melbourne Symphony Orchestra . . . . (MCA)
Greatest Love Of All
George Benson; *George Benson-Collection* . . . . (Warner Bros.)
ST/The Greatest . . . . (Arista)
Weekend In L.A. . . . . (Warner Bros.)
Whitney Houston; *Whitney Houston* . . . . (Arista)
Whitney Houston's Greatest Hits . . . . (Arista)
Greatest, The
Kenny Rogers; *She Rides Wild Horses* . . . . (Dreamcatcher)
Happy Jack
Who; *Happy Jack* . . . . (MCA)
Meaty Beaty Big & Bouncy . . . . (MCA)
ST/The Kids Are Alright . . . . (MCA)
Who Greatest Hits . . . . (MCA)
He Didn't Have To Be
Brad Paisley; *Who Needs Pictures* . . . . (Arista)
Heaven Help Us All
Stevie Wonder; *Signed Sealed & Delivered* . . . . (Motown)
Stevie Wonder-Love Songs-20 Classic Hits . . . . (Motown)
Stevie Wonder's Greatest Hits-#2 . . . . (Motown)
Hell Is For Children
Pat Benatar; *Best Shots* . . . . (Chrysalis)
Crimes Of Passion . . . . (Chrysalis)
Live From Earth . . . . (Chrysalis)
MTV's Rock 'N' Roll To Go-C . . . . (Elektra)
ST/American Pop . . . . (MCA)
Hello Muddah, Hello Fadduh
Allan Sherman; *Dr. Demento Presents The Greatest Novelty Records-#3-1960s-C* . . . . (Rhino)
Dr. Demento Presents The Greatest Novelty Records-C . . . . (Rhino)
Heroes & Villains
Beach Boys; *Concert/'69-Live In London* . . . . (Capitol)
Endless Harmony . . . . (Capitol)
Good Vibrations-Thirty Years Of The Beach Boys . . . . (Capitol)
Made In The U.S.A. . . . . (Capitol)
Smiley Smile/Wild Honey . . . . (Capitol)
Sunshine Dream . . . . (Capitol)
Highway Child
Bob Seger System; *Mongrel* . . . . (Capitol)
Highway Chile
Jimi Hendrix Experience; *Are You Experienced?* . . . . (Reprise)
Holes In The Floor Of Heaven
Steve Wariner; *Burnin' The Roadhouse Down* . . . . (Capitol)
Honey Child
Bad Company; *Run With The Pack* . . . . (Swan Song)
Honey Chile
Martha Reeves & The Vandellas; *Compact Command Performances-Martha Reeves & The Vandellas* . . . . (Motown)
Martha Reeves & The Vandellas-Anthology . . . . (Motown)
Motown Superstar Series-#11-Martha Reeves & The Vandellas . . . . (Motown)
Hot Child In The City
Nick Gilder; *Billboard Top Hits-1978-C* . . . . (Rhino)
City Nights . . . . (Chrysalis)
House At Pooh Corner
Loggins & Messina; *Loggins & Messina-On Stage* . . . . (Columbia)
Sittin' In . . . . (Columbia)
The Best Of Friends . . . . (Columbia)
Nitty Gritty Dirt Band; *Best Of The Nitty Gritty Dirt Band* . . . . (Liberty)
Best Of The Nitty Gritty Dirt Band . . . . (Curb)
Dirt, Silver & Gold . . . . (One Way)
Uncle Charlie And His Dog Teddy . . . . (Liberty)
How Can I Help You Say Goodbye
Patty Loveless; *Only What I Feel* . . . . (Epic)
Patty Loveless-Classics . . . . (Epic)
I Am A Child
Buffalo Springfield; *Buffalo Springfield* . . . . (Atco)
Buffalo Springfield-Retrospective . . . . (Atco)
Classic Rock 1966-1988-C . . . . (Atlantic)
Last Time Around . . . . (Atco)
ST/Made In Heaven . . . . (Elektra)
Neil Young; *Crazy Horse/Live Rust* . . . . (Reprise)

Decade . . . . (Reprise)
I Don't Call Him Daddy
Doug Supernaw; *Pure Country-Best Of The '90s-C* . . . . (Priority)
Red And Rio Grande . . . . (BNA)
I Think About You
Collin Raye; *Best Of Collin Raye-Direct Hits* . . . . (Epic)
I Think About You . . . .(Epic)
I Thought I Was A Child
Bonnie Raitt; *Takin' My Time* . . . .(Warner Bros.)
Jackson Browne; *For Everyman* . . . . (Asylum)
I Wanna Grow Up To Be A Politician
Byrds; *20 Essential Tracks From The Box Set* . . . . (Columbia)
Best Of The Byrds-Greatest Hits-#2. . . . . (Columbia)
Byrdmaniax . . . . (Columbia)
The Byrds . . . . (Columbia)
I Want A Little Girl
Big Joe Turner; *Atlantic Jazz-Singers-C* . . . . (Atlantic)
Ray Charles; *Life In Music* . . . . (Atlantic)
I Was Made To Love Her
Stevie Wonder; *16 #1 Hits From The Late '60s-C* . . . . (Motown)
Stevie Wonder's Greatest Hits . . . . (Motown)
I Wish I Could Have Been There
John Anderson; *Solid Ground* . . . . (BNA)
I Won't Grow Up
Original Cast/Mary Martin; *Peter Pan-The 1954 Broadway
Production* . . . .(RCA Victor)
If I Could
Barbra Streisand; *Higher Ground* . . . . (Columbia)
I'm Already Taken
Steve Wariner; *Country Cares For Kids II-C* . . . . (BNA)
Two Teardrops . . . . (Capitol)
I'm Already There
Lonestar; *I'm Already There* . . . . (BNA)
I'm Just A Kid
Daryl Hall & John Oates; *Abandoned Luncheonette* . . . .(Atlantic)
Livetime . . . . (RCA)
In Pictures
Alabama; *Alabama-Super Hits* . . . . (RCA)
In Pictures . . . . (RCA)
Isn't She Lovely
Keb' Mo'; *Big Wide Grin* . . . . (Sony Wonder)
Lee Ritenour; *Best Of Lee Ritenour* . . . .(Epic)
Stevie Wonder; *Original Musiquarium* . . . . (Motown)
Songs In The Key Of Life . . . . (Motown)
Jeremy
Pearl Jam; *Ten* . . . . (Epic Portrait Assoc.)
Jesus Children Of America
Stevie Wonder; *Innervisions* . . . . (Motown)
Jesus To A Child
George Michael; *Ladies & Gentlemen: The Best Of George Michael* . . . . .(Epic)
Older . . . . (DreamWorks/SKG)
Just Like A Woman
Bob Dylan; *Before The Flood* . . . . (Columbia)
Biograph . . . . (Columbia)
Blonde On Blonde . . . . (Columbia)
Bob Dylan At Budokan . . . . (Columbia)
Bob Dylan's Greatest Hits . . . . (Columbia)
Byrds; *The Byrds* . . . . (Columbia)
Kid Who Hates Summer
John McCutcheon; *John McCutcheon's Four Seasons:
Summersongs* . . . . (Rounder)
Kids
Original Broadway Cast; *Bye Bye Birdie* . . . . (Columbia)
Paul Lynde; *ST/Bye Bye Birdie* . . . . (RCA)
Kids Aren't Alright
Offspring; *Americana* . . . . (Columbia)
Kids Of The Baby Boom
Bellamy Brothers; *Bellamy Brothers' Greatest Hits-#3* . . . . (MCA)
Country Rap . . . .(MCA)
MCA #1 Hits Of The '80s-#3-C . . . .(MCA Special Prod.)
Lady Madonna
Beatles; *Beatles 1* . . . . (Capitol)
Hey Jude . . . . (Capitol)
Past Masters-Volume Two . . . . (Parlophone)
The Beatles/1967-1970 . . . . (Capitol)
Wings; *Wings Over America* . . . . (Capitol)
Last Child
Aerosmith; *Aerosmith-Classics Live 2* . . . . (Columbia)
Aerosmith's Greatest Hits . . . . (Columbia)
Live! Bootleg . . . . (Columbia)
Rocks . . . . (Columbia)
Leaving October (Sara)
Sons Of The Desert; *Whatever Comes First* . . . .(Epic)
Let The Children Play
Santana; *Festival* . . . . (Columbia)
Moonflower . . . . (Columbia)
Let's Hear It For The Boy
Deniece Williams; *Billboard Top Hits-1984-C* . . . . (Rhino)

ST/Footloose . . . .(Columbia)
Little Child
Beatles; *Meet The Beatles!* . . . . (Capitol)
Little Children
Billy J. Kramer With The Dakotas; *History Of British Rock-#1-C* . . . . . . (Rhino)
Little Girl
Stephen Bishop; *Love Shouldn't Hurt-C* . . . .(Qwest)
Little Girl, The
John Michael Montgomery; *Brand New Me* . . . .(Atlantic)
Totally Hits-#3-C . . . .(Atlantic)
Little Green
Joni Mitchell; *Blue* . . . .(Reprise)
Little John Of God
Los Lobos; *The Neighborhood* . . . .(Slash)
Lonely Boy
Andrew Gold; *Listen To The Music-'70s California-C* . . . . (Rhino)
Super Hits Of The '70s-Have A Nice Day-#19-C . . . . (Rhino)
What's Wrong With This Picture? . . . .(Asylum)
Lonely Child
Styx; *Equinox* . . . . (A&M)
Lonely Children
Foreigner; *Double Vision* . . . .(Atlantic)
Lord Protect My Child
Bob Dylan; *The Bootleg Series-Volumes 1-3 [Rare & Unreleased]* . . (Columbia)
Lost Children, The
Michael Jackson; *Invincible* . . . . (Epic)
Love Child
Diana Ross & The Supremes; *Billboard Top Rock 'N' Roll Hits-
1968-C* . . . . (Rhino)
Diana Ross & The Supremes' Greatest Hits-#3 . . . . (Motown)
Diana Ross & The Supremes-Anthology (1962-1969) . . . . . . (Motown)
Every Great #1 Hit . . . . (Motown)
Motown Story-First 25 Years-C . . . . (Motown)
Motown's Biggest Pop Hits-C . . . . (Motown)
Sweet Sensation; *Love Child* . . . . (Atco)
Love Shouldn't Hurt
All Star Group; *Love Shouldn't Hurt-C* . . . .(Qwest)
Love Without End, Amen
George Strait; *Livin' It Up* . . . . (MCA)
Ten Strait Hits . . . . (MCA)
Luka
Suzanne Vega; *Solitude Standing* . . . . (A&M)
Lullaby
Take 6; *Join The Band-C* . . . .(Reprise)
Love Shouldn't Hurt-C . . . .(Qwest)
Mama Sang A Song
Bill Anderson; *Bill Anderson's Greatest Hits* . . . .(Varese Sarabande)
Country Music Classics-#17-C . . . . (K-Tel)
March Of The Siamese Children
Original Broadway Cast; *The King And I* . . . . (RCA Victor)
Original Cast; *The King And I* . . . . (MCA)
Memphis
Chuck Berry; *Chuck Berry* . . . . (Audio Fidelity)
Chuck Berry-Golden Hits . . . . (Mercury)
Chuck Berry's Greatest Hits . . . . (Everest)
St. Louis To Liverpool . . . . (Chess)
ST/Hail! Hail! Rock 'N' Roll . . . . (MCA)
The Chess Box-Chuck Berry . . . . (Chess)
Toronto Rock 'N' Roll Revival-#2-C . . . . (Accord)
John Cale; *IRS Greatest Hits-#2 & #3-C* . . . . (I.R.S.)
Johnny Rivers; *Best Of Johnny Rivers* . . . . (EMI)
Johnny Rivers-Anthology 1964-1977 . . . . (Rhino)
Lonnie Mack; *Rock Instrumental Classics-#2-'60s-C* . . . . (Rhino)
Teen Beat-Instrumental Rock-1957-1965-C . . . . (Capitol)
Mindless Child Of Motherhood
Kinks; *Kink Kronikles* . . . .(Reprise)
Monday's Child
Cambridge Singers; *Fancies* . . . .(Collegium)
Moonchild
King Crimson; *In The Court Of The Crimson King-An Observation By King
Crimson* . . . . (Editions E.G.)
Moonchild
Shakespear's Sister; *Hormonally Yours* . . . .(London)
Moonchild
Iron Maiden; *Seventh Son Of A Seventh Son* . . . . (Capitol)
Morning Side
Neil Diamond; *Hot August Night* . . . . (MCA)
Moods . . . . (MCA)
Mother And Child Reunion
Paul Simon; *Negotiations And Love Songs, 1971-1986* . . . . (Warner Bros.)
Paul Simon . . . . (Columbia)
Paul Simon In Concert/Live Rhymin' . . . . (Columbia)
Motherless Child
Steve Miller Band; *Steve Miller Band-Anthology* . . . . (Capitol)
Your Saving Grace . . . . (Capitol)
Motherless Children
Eric Clapton; *461 Ocean Boulevard* . . . .(Polydor)
Eric Clapton-Crossroads-C . . . .(Polydor)

From The Cradle .... (Duck/Reprise)

My Baby You
Marc Anthony; *Marc Anthony* .... (Columbia)

My Darling Child
Sinead O'Connor; *Universal Mother* .... (Ensign)

My Mammy
Al Jolson; *Best Of Al Jolson* .... (MCA)
Let Me Sing And I'm Happy .... (Turner Classic Movies)
The '20s-From Broadway To Hollywood-#3-C .... (Flapper)
Happenings; *Happenings-Golden Hits!* .... (B.T. Puppy)

Nature's Child
Triumph; *Progressions Of Power* .... (MCA)

Nobody's Child
Beatles With Tony Sheridan; *The Beatles featuring Tony Sheridan-In The Beginning (Circa 1960)* .... (Polydor)
Electric Light Orchestra; *Eldorado* .... (Jet)
Hank Williams, Jr.; *Best Of Hank Williams, Jr.-#1-Roots & Branches* .... (Mercury)
Maria McKee; *Maria McKee* .... (Geffen)
Traveling Wilburys; *Nobody's Child-Romanian Angel Appeal-C* .... (Warner Bros.)

North Carolina Tune/Child Of My Heart
Liz Carroll; *Friend Indeed* .... (Shanachie)

October's Child
Elvin Jones; *Brother John* .... (Palo Alto Jazz)

Ode To My Family
Cranberries; *No Need To Argue* .... (Island)

Old Dogs, Children & Watermelon Wine
Tom T. Hall; *Essential Tom T. Hall-20th Anniversary Collection* ..... (Mercury)
Tom T. Hall's Greatest Hits-#2 .... (Mercury)

One Child China
Ecoteur; *Decorated Life* .... (Dali)

One Voice
Billy Gilman; *One Voice* .... (Epic)

One's On The Way (Here In Topeka)
Loretta Lynn; *Loretta Lynn-20 Greatest Hits* .... (MCA)
Loretta Lynn-Greatest Hits Live .... (K-Tel)
Loretta Lynn's Greatest Hits-#2 .... (MCA)
The Country Music Hall Of Fame-Loretta Lynn .... (MCA)

Only 12 Years Old
Tony Adolescent & The Flower Leperds; *Dirges In The Dark* .... (Triple X Entert.)

Only A Lad
Oingo Boingo; *10th Anniversary-These People Are Nuts-C* .... (I.R.S.)
Best O' Boingo .... (MCA)
Boingo Alive .... (MCA)
Only A Lad .... (A&M)
Skeletons In The Closet: The Best Of Oingo Boingo .... (A&M)

Only Child
Jackson Browne; *The Pretender* .... (Asylum)

Ooh Child
Dino; *The Way I Am* .... (East West)

O-o-h Child
Five Stairsteps; *Didn't It Blow Your Mind: Soul Hits Of The '70s-#2-C* .... (Rhino)
Five Stairsteps' Greatest Hits .... (Collectables)
Radio Active Hits-#2-C .... (Accord)
Spinners; *Best Of The Spinners* .... (Motown)
Valerie Carter; *Just A Stone's Throw Away* .... (Columbia)
ST/Over The Edge .... (Warner Bros.)

Orphan Girl
Emmylou Harris; *Wrecking Ball* .... (Asylum)
Gillian Welch; *Revival* .... (Almo Sounds)
Tim O'Brien; *Away Out On The Mountain* .... (Sugar Hill)

Other Generation, The
Original Cast; *Flower Drum Song* .... (Angel)
Flower Drum Song .... (Sony Music Classical)

Poor Little Orphaned Boy
Carter Family; *Their Complete Victor Recordings-Gold Watch And Chain-1933-1934* .... (Rounder)

Pretty Little Adriana
Vince Gill; *High Lonesome Sound* .... (MCA)

Pretty Little Dogies
Skip Gorman; *A Cowboy's Wild Song To His Herd* .... (Rounder)

Problem Child
AC/DC; *Dirty Deeds Done Dirt Cheap* .... (Atlantic)
If You Want Blood You've Got It .... (Atlantic)
Let There Be Rock .... (Atco)

Problem Child
Royal Tramps; *Dangerous & Extremely Unhealthy* .... (Red Light)

Problem Child
3rd Bass; *Derelicts Of Dialect* .... (Def Jam)

Problem Child
Damned; *Light At The End Of The Tunnel* .... (MCA)

Problem Child
Mitch Malloy; *Mitch Malloy* .... (RCA)

Problem Child
Hanoi Rocks; *Self-Destruction Blues* .... (Geffen)

Problem Child
Graham Parker And The Rumour; *Stick To Me* .... (Mercury)

Puerto Rican Children
Hilton Ruiz; *Something Grand* .... (Novus)

Puff The Magic Dragon
Peter, Paul & Mary; *10 Years Together/The Best Of Peter, Paul and Mary* .... (Warner Bros.)
Moving .... (Warner Bros.)
Peter, Paul & Mommy .... (Warner Bros.)
Peter, Paul and Mary In Concert .... (Warner Bros.)

Rebecca Lynn
Bryan White; *Bryan White* .... (Asylum)

Remember The Children
Earth, Wind & Fire; *Last Days & Time* .... (Columbia)

Rock 'N' Roll Children
Dio; *Intermission* .... (Warner Bros.)
Sacred Heart .... (Warner Bros.)

Roll On Mississippi
Charley Pride; *Charley Pride's Greatest Hits* .... (RCA)

Roller Skating Child
Beach Boys; *Love You* .... (Caribou)
Ten Years In Harmony .... (Caribou)

Run Away Child, Running Wild
Temptations; *All The Million-Sellers* .... (Motown)
Cloud Nine .... (Motown)
Compact Command Performances-Temptations .... (Motown)
Temptations' Greatest Hits-#2 .... (Motown)
Temptations-Anthology-The Best Of The Temptations .... (Motown)

Russians
Sting; *Dream Of The Blue Turtles* .... (A&M)
Fields Of Gold-The Best Of Sting 1984-1994 .... (A&M)

Saturday's Child
Monkees; *Listen To The Band* .... (Rhino)
More Greatest Hits Of The Monkees .... (Arista)

Saturday's Kids
Jam; *Setting Sons* .... (Polydor)

Save The Children
Diana Ross; *Diana Ross-Anthology* .... (Motown)
Touch Me In The Morning .... (Motown)
Gil Scott-Heron; *Gil Scott-Heron* .... (Bluebird)
Revolution Will Not Be Televised .... (Flying Dutchman)
Marvin Gaye; *Marvin Gaye Live At The London Palladium* .... (Motown)
Marvin Gaye-Anthology .... (Motown)
Musical Testament 1964-1984 .... (Motown)
What's Going On .... (Motown)

Save The Life Of My Child
Simon & Garfunkel; *Bookends* .... (Columbia)
Collected Works .... (Columbia)

Scarlet Ribbons (For Her Hair)
Harry Belafonte; *Harry Belafonte-Legendary Performer* .... (RCA)
Harry Belafonte's All Time Greatest Hits-#1 .... (RCA)
This Is Harry Belafonte .... (RCA)
Jim Ed Brown & Maxine Brown; *Essential Jim Ed Brown* .... (RCA)
Kingston Trio; *At Large/Here We Go Again!* .... (Capitol)
Capitol Collectors Series-The Kingston Trio .... (Capitol)
Lennon Sisters; *Best Of The Lennon Sisters* .... (Ranwood)
Les Paul; *Legend & The Legacy-#1-4* .... (Capitol)
NRBQ; *Diggin' Uncle Q* .... (Rounder)
Patti Page; *Patti Page-16 Most Requested Songs* .... (Legacy)
Roger Whittaker; *Roger Whittaker-Classics Collection-#2* .... (Liberty)

See Emily Play
David Bowie; *Bowie Pin Ups* .... (Rykodisc)
Pink Floyd; *Relics* .... (Capitol)
Works .... (Capitol)

Seein' My Father In Me
Paul Overstreet; *Sowin' Love* .... (RCA)

Simple Days
Babyface; *The Day* .... (Epic)

Sing Child
Heart; *Dreamboat Annie* .... (Capitol)

Six O'Clock News
John Prine; *John Prine* .... (Atlantic)
John Prine-Souvenirs .... (Oh Boy)

Small Fry
Georgie Fame/Annie Ross/Hoagy Carmichael; *In Hoagland* .... (DRG)
June Christy; *Small Fry-Capitol Sings Kids Songs For Grownups-C* ... (Capitol)

Society's Child (Baby I've Been Thinking)
Janis Ian; *Songs Of Protest-C* .... (Rhino)
The Bottom Line Encore Collection .... (Bottom Line)
Lou Gramm; *A Foreigner In His Own Land: Best Of Early Years* .... (Collectables)
Past Times Behind Rock & Roll-C .... (Intermedia)

Solitude
Edwin McCain; *Honor Among Thieves* .... (Lava)
Edwin McCain & Darius Rucker; *VH-1 Crossroads-C* .... (Atlantic)

Somebody Should Leave
Reba McEntire; *Grand Ole Opry-75 Years-#2-C* .... (MCA)
MCA #1 Hits Of The '80s-#2-C .... (MCA Special Prod.)
My Kind Of Country .... (MCA)

Reba McEntire's Greatest Hits ....(MCA)
Sometimes I Feel Like A Motherless Child
Dave Van Ronk; *Folksinger* ....(Prestige)
Inside Dave Van Ronk ....(Fantasy)
Grant Green; *Feelin' The Spirit* ....(Blue Note)
Iron City ....(Muse)
Jerry Butler; *Jerry Butler-Gold*................(Vee-Jay)
Mormon Tabernacle Choir; *Songs Of The Civil War And Stephen Foster Favorites* ....(Sony Music Classical)
O.V. Wright; *O.V. Wright*.........................(MCA)
Odetta; *Essential Odetta* ....(Vanguard)
Peter, Paul & Mary; *The Song Will Rise* .....(Warner Bros.)
Van Morrison; *Poetic Champions Compose*........(Mercury)
Son Of Hickory Holler's Tramp
O.C. Smith; *Me And You*.........(Columbia Special Prod.)
Story Songs-C ....(K-Tel)
Soul Of My Soul
Michael Bolton; *Love Shouldn't Hurt-C*.........(Qwest)
Space Child
UFO; *Phenomenon* ....(Chrysalis)
Space Child
Spirit; *12 Dreams Of Dr. Sardonicus* ....(Epic)
Spirit Of A Boy, Wisdom Of A Man
Randy Travis; *Big Country Hits '99-C*..........(K-Tel)
You And You Alone ....(DreamWorks/SKG)
Starchild
Teena Marie; *Starchild*...........................(Epic)
Stay Together For The Kids
Blink-182; *Take Off Your Pants And Jacket* .....(MCA)
Storybook Children
Bette Midler; *Broken Blossom* ....(Atlantic)
Nancy Sinatra & Lee Hazlewood; *Fairy Tales & Fantasies-Best Of* ....(Rhino)
Sugar Mountain
Neil Young; *Decade* ....(Reprise)
Neil Young & Crazy Horse; *Live Rust* ....(Reprise)
Suicide Child
Nuns; *Best Of Rodney On The 'ROQ* ....(Posh Boy)
Posh Hits-#1-C ....(Posh Boy)
Sweet Child O' Mine
Guns N' Roses; *Appetite For Destruction* ....(Geffen)
Sweet Little Rock & Roller
Chuck Berry; *Chuck Berry Is On Top* ....(Chess)
The Chess Box-Chuck Berry ....(Chess)
Richard Thompson; *Guitar/Vocal* ....(Hannibal)
Rod Stewart; *Absolutely Live* ....(Warner Bros.)
Best Of Rod Stewart ....(Mercury)
Storyteller/The Complete Anthology: 1964-1990 ...(Warner Bros.)
Sweet Summer
Diamond Rio; *One More Day*......................(Arista)
Take Me There
Blackstreet & Mya featuring Mase & Blinky Blink; *Finally*.................(Lil' Man/Interscope)
Now That's What I Call Music!-#2-C ....(Virgin)
ST/Rugrats.................................(Interscope)
Teach The Gifted Children
Lou Reed; *Between Thought & Expression-Anthology*.............(RCA)
Teach Your Children
Crosby, Stills & Nash; *CSN* ....(Atlantic)
Crosby, Stills, Nash & Young; *4 Way Street* ...(Atlantic)
Deja Vu ....(Atlantic)
So Far ....(Atlantic)
ST/The Wonder Years-Music From The Show & Era...(Atlantic)
Suzy Bogguss/Alison Krauss/Kathy Mattea/Crosby, Stills & Nash; *Red Hot + Country-C*.................(Mercury)
Tears In Heaven
Eric Clapton; *Diana, Princess Of Wales-Tribute-C* .....(Columbia)
Eric Clapton-Unplugged ....(Reprise)
ST/Rush..(Reprise)
Tender Shepherd
Original Cast; *Peter Pan-The 1954 Broadway Production*.......(RCA Victor)
Texas Girl At The Funeral Of Her Father
Randy Newman; *Little Criminals*............(Warner Bros.)
Thank God For Kids
Oak Ridge Boys; *Christmas For The '90s-#1-C* ...(Liberty)
Oak Ridge Boys' Greatest Hits 2 ....(MCA)
Oak Ridge Boys-Christmas ....(MCA Special Prod.)
Oak Ridge Boys-Collection ....(MCA)
Thank Heaven For Little Girls
Maurice Chevalier; *ST/Gigi* ....(Sony Music Special Prod.)
Merle Haggard & Janie Fricke; *It's All In The Game* ......(Epic)
That's My Boy
Stan Freberg; *Capitol Collectors Series-Stan Freberg* ...(Capitol)
Theme From "All My Children"
Original Soundtrack; *Television's Greatest Hits-#5-In Living Color-C*...(TVT)
Theme From "Charles In Charge"
Shandi; *Television's Greatest Hits-#6-Remote Control-C* ....(TVT)
Tube Tunes-#3-The '70s & '80s-C................(Rhino)
Theme From "Dennis The Menace"
Original Soundtrack; *Television's Greatest Hits-#1-C*.........(TVT)

Theme From "Eight Is Enough"
Original Soundtrack; *Television's Greatest Hits-#6-Remote Control-C*...(TVT)
Theme From "Fat Albert And The Cosby Kids"
Original Soundtrack; *Television's Greatest Hits-#3-1970s & 1980s-C* ...(TVT)
Theme From "Howdy Doody"
Original Soundtrack; *Television's Greatest Hits-#1-C* ....(TVT)
Theme From "Leave It To Beaver"
Original Soundtrack; *CBS: The First 50 Years* ....(TVT)
Television's Greatest Hits-#1-C.................(TVT)
Theme From "Little Rascals"
Original Soundtrack; *Television's Greatest Hits-#1-C*.........(TVT)
Theme From "Mr. Rogers' Neighborhood"
Original Soundtrack; *Television's Greatest Hits-#2-C*.........(TVT)
Theme From "Nanny And The Professor"
Original Soundtrack; *Television's Greatest Hits-#5-In Living Color-C*...(TVT)
Theme From "Sesame Street"
Original Soundtrack; *Television's Greatest Hits-#3-1970s & 1980s-C* ...(TVT)
Theme From "Silver Spoons"
Original Soundtrack; *Television's Greatest Hits-#6-Remote Control-C*...(TVT)
Theme From "The Alvin Show"
Original Soundtrack; *Television's Greatest Hits-#3-1970s & 1980s-C* ...(TVT)
Theme From "The Brady Bunch"
Brady Bunch Kids; *It's A Sunshine Day-Best Of The Brady Bunch Kids* ....(MCA)
Television's Greatest Hits-#2-C.................(TVT)
Theme From "The Nanny"
Original Soundtrack; *Television's Greatest Hits-#7-Cable Ready-C* .....(TVT)
Theme From "Webster" (Then Came You)
Original Soundtrack; *Television's Greatest Hits-#6-Remote Control-C*...(TVT)
Things Will Grow
Sweethearts Of The Rodeo; *Rodeo Waltz* ......(Sugar Hill)
Third World Child
Johnny Clegg & Savuka; *Sounds Of Soweto* ......(Capitol)
Third World Child ....(Capitol)
This Child Needs Its Father
Gladys Knight & The Pips; *Neither One Of Us* ...(Motown)
This One's For The Children
New Kids On The Block; *Hangin' Tough*..........(Columbia)
Thursday's Child
Abbey Lincoln; *Abbey Is Blue* ....(Riverside)
Anthony Davis; *Trio 2*.......................(Gramavision)
Barbara Lea; *Barbara Lea*......................(Prestige)
Bev Kelly; *Love Locked Out* ....(Riverside)
Chameleons UK; *Script Of The Bridge* ....(MCA)
Tanita Tikaram; *Sweet Keeper* ....(Reprise)
Time Bomb
Rancid; *...And Out Come The Wolves* ....(Epitaph)
Toys Are Made For Children
Joe Stampley/The Uniques; *Joe Stampley-Golden Hits* ....(Paula)
Tranquillo (Melt My Heart)
Carly Simon; *Boys In The Trees* ....(Elektra)
Trouble Child
Joni Mitchell; *Court & Spark* ....(Asylum)
Tuesday's Child
Trouble; *Run To The Light* ....(Metal Blade)
Twelve Year Old Boy
Elmore James; *Collectables Blues Collection-#1-C* ....(Collectables)
Golden Classics-Elmore James ....(Collectables)
The Sky Is Crying-History Of Elmore James ......(Rhino)
Two Of A Kind, Workin' On A Full House
Garth Brooks; *No Fences* ....(Capitol)
Two-Bit Man Child
Neil Diamond; *Glory Road-1968-1972*..............(MCA)
Velvet Gloves & Spit................(MCA Special Prod.)
Vision Of A Child
Steve Young; *Honky Tonk Man* ....(Rounder)
Voodoo Child
Voodoo Child; *Best Of Techno-#1-C* ....(Profile)
Voodoo Chile
Jimi Hendrix; *Concerts* ....(Reprise)
Essential Jimi Hendrix ....(Reprise)
Kiss The Sky ....(Reprise)
Lifelines/Jimi Hendrix Story ....(Reprise)
Jimi Hendrix Experience; *Electric Ladyland* .....(Reprise)
Stevie Ray Vaughan; *Couldn't Stand The Weather* ...(Epic)
Stevie Ray Vaughan and Double Trouble; *Live Alive* ...(Epic)
War Child
Jethro Tull; *Repeat-The Best Of Jethro Tull, Vol. II* ...(Chrysalis)
Too Old To Rock 'N' Roll: Too Young To Die! ...(Chrysalis)
Way Down The Line
Offspring; *Ixnay On The Hombre* ....(Columbia)
We Are The World
USA For Africa; *We Are The World-C* ....(Columbia)
What Children Believe
Shenandoah; *Shenandoah 2000* ....(Free Falls Entert.)
When I Grow Up (To Be A Man)
Beach Boys; *Absolute Best-#1*....................(Capitol)
Beach Boys-Gift Set.............................(Capitol)

Dance Dance Dance .... (Capitol)
Made In The U.S.A. .... (Capitol)
Spirit Of America .... (Capitol)
When The Children Are Asleep
Original Broadway Cast; *Carousel* .... (Angel)
Original Cast; *Carousel* .... (MCA)
When The Children Cry
White Lion; *Best Of White Lion* .... (Atlantic)
Pride .... (Atlantic)
When The Kids Get Married
Original Broadway Cast; *I Do! I Do!* .... (RCA Victor)
Where Do The Children Play
Cat Stevens; *Cat Stevens-Classics-#24* .... (A&M)
Footsteps In The Dark-Greatest Hits-#2. .... (A&M)
Tea For The Tillerman .... (A&M)
Wild Child
W.A.S.P.; *Head Banging Metal-C.* .... (Priority)
Last Command .... (Capitol)
Live...In The Raw .... (Capitol)
Wild Child
Heart; *Brigade* .... (Capitol)
Rock The House "Live" .... (Capitol)
Wild Child
Doors; *Doors 13* .... (Elektra)
Doors-Classics .... (Elektra)
Soft Parade .... (Elektra)
Wild Child
Lou Reed; *Walk On The Wild Side-The Best Of Lou Reed* .... (RCA)
Wild Child
Untouchables; *Wild Child* .... (MCA)
Wild Children
Van Morrison; *Hard Nose The Highway* .... (Polydor)
It's Too Late To Stop Now. .... (Warner Bros.)
Wild Kids
David Benoit; *Urban Daydreams* .... (GRP)
Wonderful
Everclear; *Now That's What I Call Music!-#5-C.* .... (Virgin)
Songs From An American Movie-#1-Learning How To Smile ...... (Capitol)
You Better Sit Down Kids
Cher; *Bang, Bang The Early Years* .... (Capitol)
You Must Have Been A Beautiful Baby
Bobby Darin; *Splish Splash-Best Of Bobby Darin-#1* .... (Atlantic)
Johnny Mercer; *Johnny Mercer Sings Johnny Mercer* .... (Everest)
Russ Morgan & His Orchestra; *Russ Morgan & His Orchestra Play 22*
Original Big Band Recordings .... (Hindsight)
You Were Mine
Dixie Chicks; *Big Country Hits '99-C* .... (K-Tel)
Wide Open Spaces .... (Monument)
You Won't Be An Orphan For Long
Original Broadway Cast; *Annie* .... (Columbia)
You're The Reason Our Kids Are Ugly
Loretta Lynn & Conway Twitty; *Conway Twittty-20 Greatest Hits* ..... (MCA)
Very Best Of Loretta Lynn & Conway Twitty .... (MCA)
Youth Of The Nation
P.O.D.; *Satellite* .... (Atlantic)

CHILDREN LEAVING HOME

See Also: AGING, CHILDREN, FAMILY (various), HOME,
LEAVING, PARENTS (various), REBELS, SOCIAL OUTCASTS,
TEENAGERS, TRAVELING

26 Cents
Wilkinsons; *Nothing But Love* .... (Giant)
500 Miles Away From Home
Bobby Bare; *500 Miles Away From Home* .... (RCA)
Foy Willing; *Cowboy/The New Sound Of American Folk* .... (DRG)
Reba McEntire; *Starting Over* .... (MCA)
Adios
Jimmy Webb; *Suspending Disbelief* .... (Elektra)
Linda Ronstadt; *Cry Like A Rainstorm-Howl Like The Wind* .... (Elektra)
At The Stars
Better Than Ezra; *How Does Your Garden Grow?* .... (Elektra)
Ballad Of A Teenage Queen
Johnny Cash; *Johnny Cash* .... (Sun)
Johnny Cash-Original Golden Hits-#2. .... (Sun)
Johnny Cash-Sun Years .... (Rhino)
ST/Harper Valley PTA .... (Sun)
The Legend .... (Plantation)
The Man In Black-His Greatest Hits .... (Legacy)
Born To Fly
Sara Evans; *Born To Fly* .... (RCA)
Child's Song
Tom Rush; *Best Of Tom Rush: No Regrets* .... (Legacy)
Tom Rush .... (Columbia)
Come Back To Us Barbara Lewis Hare Krisha Beauregard
John Prine; *Common Sense* .... (Atlantic)

Great Days-Anthology .... (Rhino)
Prime Prine-The Best Of John Prine .... (Atlantic)
Fields Have Turned Brown
Stanley Brothers & The Clinch Mountain Boys; *Bluegrass Super*
Hits-C. .... (Columbia)
I Wonder How The Old Folks Are At Home
Doc & Merle Watson; *Home Sweet Home* .... (Sugar Hill)
Independence Day
Martina McBride; *The Way That I Am* .... (RCA)
Letting Go
Suzy Bogguss; *Aces* .... (Liberty)
Voices In The Wind .... (Liberty)
Mommy Can I Come Home
Keb' Mo'; *The Door.* .... (550/Epic/Okeh)
My Mammy
Al Jolson; *Best Of Al Jolson* .... (MCA)
Let Me Sing And I'm Happy. .... (Turner Classic Movies)
The '20s-From Broadway To Hollywood-#3-C. .... (Flapper)
Happenings; *Happenings-Golden Hits!* .... (B.T. Puppy)
She's Leaving Home
Al Jarreau; *All Fly Home* .... (Warner Bros.)
Beatles; *Beatles-Box Set.* .... (Capitol)
Beatles-Love Songs .... (Capitol)
Sgt. Pepper's Lonely Hearts Club Band .... (Capitol)
Tenth Avenue Freeze-Out
Bruce Springsteen; *Born To Run* .... (Columbia)
Bruce Springsteen & The E Street Band; *Bruce Springsteen & The E Street*
Band Live/1975-85 .... (Legacy)
That's Not Me
Beach Boys; *Pet Sounds.* .... (Capitol)
The Pet Sounds Sessions: A 30th Anniversary Collection ..... (Capitol)
Theme From "The Mary Tyler Moore Show"
Original Soundtrack-Sonny Curtis; *CBS: The First 50 Years* ..... (TVT)
Television's Greatest Hits-#2-C .... (TVT)
When You Come Back Down
Nickel Creek; *Nickel Creek* .... (Sugar Hill)
Wide Open Spaces
Dixie Chicks; *Big Country Hits '99-C* .... (K-Tel)
Wide Open Spaces .... (Monument)
You Can't Lose Me
Faith Hill; *It Matters To Me* .... (Warner Bros.)
You Gotta Love That
Neal McCoy; *Neal McCoy's Greatest Hits* .... (Atlantic)
Today's Country Love-C. .... (K-Tel)
You Gotta Love That! .... (Atlantic)

CHRISTMAS, New Year's, Santa Claus

See Also: COLD, GOD, MONTHS & DATES: DECEMBER,
SEASONS: WINTER, SNOW

12 Gays Of Christmas, The
Venus Envy; *I'll Be Homo For Christmas* .... (Venus Envy)
1913 Massacre
Arlo Guthrie; *Hobo's Lullaby* .... (Reprise)
Jack Elliot; *Tribute To Woody Guthrie-C.* .... (Warner Bros.)
Ramblin' Jack Elliott; *Greatest Songs Of Woody Guthrie-C* ... (Vanguard)
Woody Guthrie; *Struggle* .... (Smithsonian Folkways)
2000 Miles
Pretenders; *Martha Stewart Living: Home For The Holidays-C* ... (Rhino)
25th Day Of Last December
Roberta Flack; *Blue Lights In The Basement* .... (Atlantic)
Christmas Album, The .... (Angel)
25th Of December
Bonnie Koloc; *You're Gonna Love Yourself In The Morning* ..... (Ovation)
8 Days Of Christmas
Destiny's Child; *8 Days Of Christmas* .... (Columbia)
Adeste Fideles (O Come All Ye Faithful)
Anne Murray; *Anne Murray Christmas* .... (Liberty)
Bing Crosby & The Andrews Sisters; *Merry Christmas* ... (MCA Special Prod.)
Boys Choir Of Vienna Woods; *Christmas Voices & Bells* ... (Special Music Co.)
Connie Francis; *Christmas In My Heart.* .... (Polydor)
Don Williams; *Home For The Holidays-C.* .... (RCA)
Donna Summer; *Christmas Spirit* .... (Mercury)
Ella Fitzgerald; *Ella Fitzgerald-Christmas* .... (Capitol)
Elvis Presley; *If Every Day Was Like Christmas* .... (RCA)
Memories Of Christmas .... (RCA)
Jackie Wilson; *Merry Christmas From Jackie Wilson* .... (Rhino)
Joel Nava; *Tejano Country Christmas-C* .... (Arista)
Johnny Cash; *Classic Christmas* .... (Sony Music Special Prod.)
Judy Collins; *Christmas At The Biltmore Estate* .... (Elektra)
Luther Vandross; *Now That's What I Call Christmas!-C.* .... (UTV)
Nat "King" Cole; *Nat "King" Cole Christmas Gift Set* .... (Capitol)
Philadelphia Orchestra & Eugene Ormandy; *Joy To The World* .... (RCA)
Yuletide Cheer-C. .... (Columbia)
Ricky Skaggs; *Voices Of The Season-A Capella-C* .... (Epic)
Take 6; *He Is Christmas* .... (Reprise)
Vienna Boys Choir; *Christmas Festival-C.* .... (RCA)

Wynton Marsalis & Marcus Roberts; *Acoustic Christmas* (Columbia)

After December Slips Away
Donny Osmond; *Christmas At Home* (Legacy)

Alfie, The Christmas Tree
John Denver & The Muppets; *Christmas Together* (RCA)

All I Want For Christmas
Ray Charles; *Spirit Of Christmas* (Columbia)

All I Want For Christmas (Is My Girl)
New Edition; *Christmas All Over The World* (MCA)

All I Want For Christmas (Is My Two Front Teeth)
David Seville & The Chipmunks; *Christmas With The Chipmunks-#2* (EMI)
Nat ''King'' Cole; *Let It Snow!-Cuddly Christmas Classics* (Capitol)
Spike Jones; *Dr. Demento Presents The Greatest Novelty Records-#6-Christmas-C* (Rhino)
Spike Jones-Christmas (Rhino)

All I Want For Christmas Dear Is You
Buck Owens; *Christmas With Buck Owens* (Curb)
Travis Tritt; *Christmas-Loving Time Of The Year* (Warner Bros.)

All I Want For Christmas Is You
Foghat; *Billboard Rock 'N Roll Christmas-C* (Rhino)
Christmas Party With Eddie G.-C (Columbia)

All I Want For Christmas Is You
Carla Thomas; *Soul Christmas-C* (Atlantic)

All I Want For Christmas Is You
Doug Stone; *First Christmas* (Epic)

All I Want For Christmas Is You
Vince Vance & The Valiants; *All I Want For Christmas Is You* (Waldoxy)

All On A Wintry Night
Judy Collins; *Christmas At The Biltmore Estate* (Elektra)

All We Need Is Love (Christmas In The Yard)
Shaggy; *Now That's What I Call Christmas!-C* (UTV)

Alone On New Year's Eve
Manhattans; *A Soulful Christmas-C* (Collectables)
For You & Yours-Golden Carnival-#2 (Collectables)

Amigos Del Mundo (Happy Christmas)
La Diferenzia; *Tejano Country Christmas-C* (Arista)

And The Glory Of The Lord
Dianne Reeves; *Handel's Messiah-Soulful Celebration-C* (Warner Bros.)

Angel Eyes
Emmylou Harris; *Light Of The Stable* (Warner Bros.)

Angel Like You
Doug Stone; *First Christmas* (Epic)

Angel Song (Glory To God In The Highest)
Lynn Anderson & Butch Baker; *Christmas On The General Jackson-C* (Mercury)

Angels Cried
Alan Jackson; *A Country Superstar Christmas-C* (Hip-O)
Honky Tonk Christmas (Arista)

Angels We Have Heard On High
Amy Grant; *Amy Grant Christmas Album* (Word)
Andy Williams; *Andy Williams Christmas Present* (Columbia)
Charlie Byrd; *Charlie Byrd Christmas Album* (Concord Jazz)
Collin Raye; *Christmas-The Gift* (Epic)
Commodores; *Commodores-Christmas* (Commodores)
Joan Baez; *Noel* (Vanguard)
Joan Sutherland; *Christmas Stars-C* (London)
Joy Of Christmas (London)
Michael McDonald; *In The Spirit-A Christmas Album* (MCA)
Roches; *We Three Kings* (Rykodisc)
Roger Williams; *Christmas Time* (MCA)
Golden Christmas (Special Music Co.)
Tennessee Ernie Ford; *Heart Of Christmas* (Capitol)

Another Christmas Song
Jethro Tull; *Rock Island* (Chrysalis)

As Long As There's Christmas
Peabo Bryson; *Peace On Earth* (Angel)
Peabo Bryson & Roberta Flack; *Disney's Beauty And The Beast-The Enchanted Christmas* (Disney)
Roberta Flack; *Christmas Album, The* (Angel)

At Christmas Time
Luther Vandross; *A Soulful Christmas-C* (Collectables)

At The Christmas Ball
Bessie Smith; *Bessie Smith-The Complete Recordings-#2* (Legacy)
Jingle Blues-C (House Of Blues)
Nobody's Blues But Mine (Columbia)

Ave Maria
Barbra Streisand; *Barbra Streisand Christmas Album* (Columbia)
Christmas Memories (Columbia)
Carpenters; *Carpenters Christmas Portrait* (A&M)
Harry Connick, Jr.; *When My Heart Finds Christmas* (Columbia)
James Galway & The Royal Philharmonic; *James Galway's Christmas Carol* (RCA)
Luciano Pavarotti; *O Holy Night* (London)
Mario Lanza; *Christmas With Mario Lanza* (RCA)
Michael Bolton; *Diana, Princess Of Wales-Tribute-C* (Columbia)
Perry Como; *I Wish It Could Be Christmas Forever* (RCA)
Renata Tebaldi; *Christmas Stars-C* (London)
Stevie Wonder; *Motown Christmas Album-C* (Motown)
Someday At Christmas (Motown)

Away In A Manger
Andy Williams; *Andy Williams Christmas Album* (Columbia)
Anne Murray; *Christmas Wishes* (Capitol)
Ed Ames; *This Is Christmas-C* (RCA)
Emmylou Harris; *Light Of The Stable* (Warner Bros.)
Joan Baez; *Noel* (Vanguard)
Judds; *Christmas Time With The Judds* (RCA)
Julie Andrews & Andre Previn; *Christmas Treasure* (RCA)
Lacy J. Dalton; *Christmas For The '90s-#2-C* (Liberty)
Loretta Lynn; *Country Christmas* (MCA)
Mannheim Steamroller; *Now That's What I Call Christmas!-C* (UTV)
Nat ''King'' Cole; *Nat ''King'' Cole Christmas Gift Set* (Capitol)
Philadelphia Orchestra & Eugene Ormandy; *Joy To The World* (RCA)
Reba McEntire; *Merry Christmas To You* (MCA Special Prod.)
Tennessee Christmas-C (MCA)
Trisha Yearwood; *The Sweetest Gift* (MCA)

Ay, Ay, Ay It's Christmas
Rosie O'Donnell & Ricky Martin; *Another Rosie Christmas-C* (Columbia)

Back Door Santa
Clarence Carter; *Christmas Classics-C* (Rhino)
Snatching It Back-The Best Of Clarence Carter (Rhino)
Soul Christmas-C (Atlantic)

Back Door Santa
Bon Jovi; *Very Special Christmas-C* (A&M)

Ballad Of The Harp Weaver, The
Johnny Cash; *Country Holidays-C* (Sony Music Special Prod.)

Because It's Chrismastime
Buck Owens; *Christmas With Buck Owens* (Curb)

Because It's Christmas (For All The Children)
Rosie O'Donnell & Barry Manilow; *Another Rosie Christmas-C* (Columbia)

Bells Of St. Paul
Linda Eder; *Another Rosie Christmas-C* (Columbia)

Bethlehem Tonight
Brian McKnight; *Bethlehem* (Motown)

Better Do It Right
Smash Mouth; *ST/How The Grinch Stole Christmas* (Interscope)

Blanca Navidad (White Christmas)
Freddy Fender; *Tejano Country Christmas-C* (Arista)

Blue Christmas
Anne Wilson & Nancy Wilson; *Very Special Christmas-#2-C* (A&M)
Beach Boys; *Beach Boys Christmas Album* (Capitol)
Ultimate Christmas (Capitol)
Booker T. & The M.G.s; *In The Christmas Spirit* (Rhino)
Earl Thomas Conley; *Best Of Christmas-C* (RCA)
Eddy Raven; *Warner Bros. Christmas Tradition-C* (Warner Bros.)
Elvis Presley; *Blue Christmas* (RCA)
Elvis' Christmas Album (RCA)
Memories Of Christmas (RCA)
Now That's What I Call Christmas!-C (UTV)
Ernest Tubb; *Billboard's Greatest Christmas Hits-C* (Rhino)
Freddy Fender; *Christmas Time In The Valley* (MCA Special Prod.)
Highway 101; *Warner Bros. Christmas Tradition-#2-C* (Warner Bros.)
Jim Reeves; *12 Songs Of Christmas* (RCA)
Sawyer Brown; *Christmas Country Classics-#1-C* (Curb)
Christmas For The '90s-#1-C (Liberty)

Blue Xmas (To Whom It May Concern)
Miles Davis; *Hipster's Holiday-Vocal Jazz & R&B-C* (Rhino)

Bobby Wants A Puppy For Christmas
Merle Haggard; *A Christmas Present* (Curb)

Boogie Woogie Santa Claus
Mabel Scott; *Hipster's Holiday-Vocal Jazz & R&B-C* (Rhino)

Brahm's Bethlehem Lullaby
Nat ''King'' Cole; *Cole Christmas & Kids* (Capitol)
Roger Whittaker; *Roger Whittaker-Christmas Album* (RCA)
Statler Brothers; *Statler Brothers Christmas Present* (Mercury)

Breath Of Heaven
Melissa Manchester; *Colors Of Christmas, The-C* (Windham Hill)

Breath Of Heaven
Donna Summer; *Christmas Spirit* (Mercury)

Breath Of Heaven
Amy Grant; *Home For Christmas* (A&M)

Bring Christmas Home
Lee Greenwood; *Lee Greenwood-Christmas To Christmas* (MCA Special Prod.)

Bring The Torch
Eric Tingstad & Nancy Rumbel; *The Gift* (Sona Gaia)

C.H.R.I.S.T.M.A.S.
Ricky Van Shelton; *Sings Christmas* (Columbia)

California Christmas
Hillary Kanter; *Country Christmas-#4-C* (RCA)

Call Me Claus
Garth Brooks; *The Magic Of Christmas: Songs From Call Me Claus* (Capitol)

Candle In The Window
Alabama; *Alabama-Christmas* (RCA)

Canticle Noel
Carpenters; *Carpenters Christmas Portrait* (A&M)
Eric Tingstad & Nancy Rumbel; *The Gift* (Sona Gaia)
Glenn Miller; *In The Christmas Mood* (Laserlight)
John Denver; *Rocky Mountain Christmas* (RCA)

Johnny Mathis; *Merry Christmas* . . . .(Columbia)
Mariah Carey; *Merry Christmas* . . . .(Columbia)
Michael Bolton; *This Is The Time-The Christmas Album* . . . .(Columbia)
Mormon Tabernacle Choir; *It's Christmas* . . . . (Sony Music Special Prod.)
Oak Ridge Boys; *Christmas* . . . . (MCA Special Prod.)
Patti LaBelle; *This Christmas* . . . . (MCA)

Carol Of The Bells
4 Seasons; *4 Seasons Christmas Album* . . . . (Rhino)
Barry Manilow; *Because It's Christmas* . . . . (Arista)
Carpenters; *Carpenters Christmas Portrait*. . . . .(A&M)
Christmas Collection . . . .(A&M)
David Benoit; *GRP Christmas Collection-C* . . . .(GRP)
David Rose; *Best Of Christmas-C* . . . . (Capitol)
Forester Sisters; *Forester Sisters' Christmas Card* . . . . (Warner Bros.)
Johnny Mathis; *Christmas With Johnny Mathis* . . . . (Columbia)
For Christmas . . . . (Columbia)
Kenny Rogers; *Kenny Rogers-Christmas* . . . . (EMI)
O'Jays; *Home For Christmas* . . . . (EMI)
Ronnie Milsap; *Christmas With Ronnie Milsap*. . . . . (RCA)
Soundtrack; *Home Alone* . . . . (Columbia)
Steven Curtis Chapman; *Music Of Christmas, The* . . . . (Sparrow)

Celebrate
RuPaul; *Ho Ho Ho* . . . . (Rhino)

Child Of The King, A
Mahalia Jackson; *Silent Night-Gospel Christmas With Mahalia Jackson* . . . . (Laserlight)

Child Of Winter
Beach Boys; *Child Of Winter-45* . . . . (Reprise)

Children Go Where I Send Thee
Michael McDonald; *In The Spirit-A Christmas Album* . . . . (MCA)
Peter, Paul & Mary & The New York Choral Society; *Holiday Celebration* . . . . (Warner Bros.)
Weavers; *Weavers At Carnegie Hall*. . . . .(Vanguard)
White Mountain Singers; *Best Of The White Mountain Singers* . . . . . (Folk Era)

Children's Christmas Song
Diana Ross & The Supremes; *Merry Christmas* . . . . (Motown)
Motown Christmas Album-C . . . . (Motown)

Chipmunk Song
Chipmunks; *Christmas With The Chipmunks-#1*. . . . . (EMI)
David Seville & The Chipmunks; *Billboard's Greatest Christmas Hits-C* . . . . (Rhino)
Dr. Demento's Greatest Christmas CD-C . . . . (Rhino)

Christ Child's Lullaby
Kathy Mattea; *Good News*. . . . . (Mercury)

Christ Is Born
Carpenters; *Carpenters Christmas Portrait*. . . . .(A&M)
From The Top . . . .(A&M)
Perry Como; *I Wish It Could Be Christmas Forever* . . . .(RCA)
Perry Como Christmas Album . . . .(RCA)

Christ Time Is Here
Vince Guaraldi; *Charlie Brown Christmas* . . . . (Fantasy)

Christmas
Chuck Berry; *Back Home* . . . . (Chess)
Clarence ''Gatemouth'' Brown; *Alligator Records Christmas Collection-C* . . . . (Alligator)
Elmo & Patsy; *Grandma Got Run Over By A Reindeer* . . . . (Epic)
Jim Reeves; *12 Songs Of Christmas* . . . . (RCA)
Who; *Tommy*. . . . . (MCA)

C-H-R-I-S-T-M-A-S
Eddy Arnold; *Billboard's Greatest Christmas Hits-C* . . . . (Rhino)
Perry Como; *Perry Como Sings Merry Christmas Music* . . . (Special Music Co.)

Christmas (Baby, Please Come Home)
Crystals; *Christmas Gift For You From Phil Spector-C* . . . . (Rhino)
Darlene Love; *Phil Spector-Back To Mono 1958-1969-C* . . . . (Abkco)
Phil Spector's Christmas Album-C. . . . . (Passport)
Hanson; *Snowed In* . . . . (Mercury)
Mariah Carey; *Merry Christmas* . . . . (Columbia)
U2; *Very Special Christmas-C*. . . . .(A&M)

Christmas Ain't Christmas, New Year's Ain't New Year's Without The One You Love
Ebonys; *Slow Jams-Christmas-#2-C* . . . . (Right Stuff)
O'Jays; *A Soulful Christmas-C* . . . . (Collectables)
Have A Merry Chess Christmas-C . . . . (MCA Special Prod.)
Rhythm & Blues Christmas-C . . . . (MCA Special Prod.)

Christmas Alphabet
McGuire Sisters; *McGuire Sisters' Greatest Hits* . . . . (MCA)

Christmas As I Knew It
Johnny Cash; *Christmas Spirit* . . . . (Columbia)

Christmas At Ground Zero
''Weird Al'' Yankovic; *Billboard Rock 'N Roll Christmas-C*. . . . . . . (Rhino)

Christmas At Our House
Barbara Mandrell; *Christmas At Our House* . . . . (MCA Special Prod.)
Christmas In The Country-C. . . . . (MCA Special Prod.)

Christmas Auld Lang Syne
Marc Anthony; *Another Rosie Christmas-C* . . . . (Columbia)

Christmas Blues
Canned Heat; *Blue Yule-Christmas Blues & R&B Classics-C* . . . . (Rhino)
Dean Martin; *Winter Romance* . . . . (Capitol)
Willie Nelson; *Pretty Paper* . . . . (Columbia)

Christmas Card From A Hooker In Minneapolis
Tom Waits; *Blue Valentine* . . . . (Asylum)

Christmas Carol
Oak Ridge Boys; *Oak Ridge Boys-Christmas* . . . . (MCA Special Prod.)
Skip Ewing; *Following Yonder Star*. . . . . (MCA Special Prod.)
Tom Lehrer; *Dr. Demento Presents The Greatest Novelty Records-#6-Christmas-C* . . . .(Rhino)
Dr. Demento's Greatest Christmas CD-C. . . . . (Rhino)
Evening Wasted With Tom Lehrer . . . . (Reprise)

Christmas Celebration
B.B. King; *The Best Christmas Ever-C* . . . . (Virgin)

Christmas Collage
Kathy Mattea; *Now That's What I Call Christmas!-C* . . . . (UTV)

Christmas Cookies
George Strait; *Christmas Cookies-C* . . . . (MCA)

Christmas Country Style
Statler Brothers; *Statler Brothers Christmas Present*. . . . .(Mercury)

Christmas Cowboy Style
Michael Martin Murphey; *Cowboy Christmas*. . . . . (Warner Bros.)

Christmas Day
Beach Boys; *Beach Boys Christmas Album* . . . .(Capitol)
Detroit Junior; *Blue Yule-Christmas Blues & R&B Classics-C* . . . . . .(Rhino)
Squeeze; *Just In Time For Christmas-C*. . . . . (I.R.S.)

Christmas Eve
Billy Eckstine; *Have Yourself A Jazzy Little Christmas-C* . . . .(Verve)
Maureen McGovern; *Christmas With Maureen McGovern* . . . .(Columbia)

Christmas Eve In My Home Town
Bobby Vinton; *Country Christmas-C*. . . . . (Epic)
Jim Nabors; *Christmas Album* . . . .(Columbia)
Kate Smith; *Kate Smith Christmas Album* . . . . (RCA)

Christmas Everyday
Kenny Rogers; *Kenny Rogers-Christmas*. . . . . (EMI)
Miracles; *Christmas With The Miracles*. . . . . (Motown)
Smokey Robinson & The Miracles; *Christmas Hits-C*. . . . . (MCA Special Prod.)
Temptations; *Christmas Card/Give Love At Christmas*. . . . . (Motown)

Christmas For Cowboys
John Denver; *Rocky Mountain Christmas* . . . . (RCA)

Christmas In Dixie
Alabama; *Alabama-Christmas*. . . . . (RCA)
Best Of Christmas-C . . . . (RCA)
Country Christmas-#3-C. . . . . (RCA)

Christmas In My Heart
Jets; *Christmas With The Jets* . . . . (MCA Special Prod.)
Ray Charles; *The Spirit Of Christmas* . . . .(Rhino)

Christmas In My Soul
Laura Nyro; *Christmas & The Beads Of Sweat* . . . .(Columbia)

Christmas In Prison
John Prine; *John Prine Christmas* . . . . (Oh Boy)
John Prine-Souvenirs . . . . (Oh Boy)
Sweet Revenge . . . . (Atlantic)

Christmas In The Caribbean
Jimmy Buffett; *Boats Beaches Bars & Ballads* . . . . (Margaritaville)
Tennessee Christmas-C . . . . (MCA)

Christmas In Vietnam
Johnny & Jon; *45-#776* . . . . (Jewel)

Christmas Is A Birthday
Burl Ives; *Have A Holly Jolly Christmas* . . . . (MCA Special Prod.)

Christmas Is For Children
Glen Campbell; *Best Of Christmas-C* . . . .(Capitol)
Merry Christmas . . . .(Liberty)

Christmas Is Here
Donna Summer; *Christmas Spirit* . . . .(Mercury)

Christmas Is Paintin' The Town
Oak Ridge Boys; *Oak Ridge Boys-Christmas* . . . . (MCA Special Prod.)
Tennessee Christmas-C . . . . (MCA)

Christmas Is The Time To Say I Love You
Billy Squier; *Billboard Rock 'N Roll Christmas-C*. . . . .(Rhino)

Christmas Island
Andrews Sisters & Guy Lombardo; *Billboard's Greatest Christmas Hits-C* . . . .(Rhino)
Jackie Gleason; *All I Want For Christmas* . . . . (Capitol)
Jimmy Buffett; *Christmas Island* . . . . (MCA)
Leon Redbone; *Christmas Island* . . . . (Private Music)

Christmas Letter
Keith Whitley; *Country Christmas-#4-C* . . . . (RCA)
Season's Greetings-C . . . . (RCA)
Reba McEntire; *Merry Christmas To You* . . . . (MCA Special Prod.)

Christmas Love Song, A
Barbra Streisand; *Christmas Memories* . . . . (Columbia)

Christmas Lullaby
Barbra Streisand; *Christmas Memories* . . . . (Columbia)

Christmas Memories
Alabama; *Alabama-Christmas*. . . . . (RCA)
Steve Wariner; *Steve Wariner Christmas Memories* . . . . (MCA Special Prod.)

Christmas Mem'ries
Barbra Streisand; *Christmas Message* . . . .(Lection)

Christmas Must Be Tonight
Band; *Islands* . . . . (Capitol)
To Kingdom Come-The Definitive Collection . . . . (Capitol)

Robbie Robertson; *ST/Scrooged*. (A&M)
Christmas Night In Harlem
  Louis Armstrong & His All-Stars; *Hipster's Holiday-Vocal Jazz &*
   R&B-C . . . . (Rhino)
Christmas Nite
  RuPaul; *Ho Ho Ho* . . . . (Rhino)
Christmas Only Once A Year
  Chaka Khan; *12 Soulful Nights Of Christmas-C* . . . . (So So Def/Columbia)
Christmas Prayer
  Marty Robbins; *Christmas With Marty Robbins* . . . . (Columbia)
Christmas Rock
  Toby Keith; *Christmas To Christmas* . . . . (Polydor Country)
Christmas Shoes
  Newsong; *Sheltering Tree* . . . . (Benson/Jive)
Christmas Shopping
  Buck Owens & The Buckaroos; *Merry Hee Haw Christmas* . . (Capitol)
Christmas Song
  Jethro Tull; *Living In The Past* . . . . (Chrysalis)
Christmas Song, The (Chestnuts Roasting On An Open Fire-Merry Christmas To You)
  Amy Grant; *Amy Grant Christmas Album* . . . . (Word)
  Anne Murray; *Anne Murray Christmas* . . . . (Liberty)
  Barbra Streisand; *Barbra Streisand Christmas Album* . . . . (Columbia)
  Bing Crosby; *Bing Crosby Sings Christmas Songs* . . . . . . (MCA Special Prod.)
  Brenda Lee; *Tennessee Christmas-C* . . . . (MCA)
  Buddy Emmons; *Christmas Sounds Of The Steel Guitar* . . . . (Step One)
  Carpenters; *Carpenters Christmas Portrait* . . . . (A&M)
  Celine Dion; *All-Star Christmas-C* . . . . (Epic)
  Charlie Daniels; *Christmas Time Down South* . . . . (Epic)
  Crystal Gayle; *Crystal Christmas* . . . . (Warner Bros.)
  Don McLean; *Christmas Dreams* . . . . (Hip-O)
  Donna Summer; *Christmas Spirit* . . . . (Mercury)
  Drifters; *Soul Christmas-C* . . . . (Atlantic)
  Dwight Yoakam; *Come On Christmas* . . . . (Reprise)
  Frank Sinatra; *Jolly Christmas from Frank Sinatra* . . . . . . (Capitol)
  Glen Campbell; *Merry Christmas* . . . . (Liberty)
  Herb Alpert & The Tijuana Brass; *Herb Alpert & The Tijuana Brass*
   Christmas Album . . . . (A&M)
  James Brown; *Funky Christmas* . . . . (Polydor)
   Santa's Got A Brand New Bag . . . . (Rhino)
  John Denver; *Rocky Mountain Christmas* . . . . (RCA)
  Kathy Mattea; *Home For Christmas* . . . . (Warner Bros.)
  Kenny Rogers & Dolly Parton; *Once Upon A Christmas* . . . (RCA)
  Lee Greenwood; *Lee Greenwood-Christmas To*
   Christmas . . . . (MCA Special Prod.)
  Lou Rawls; *Merry Christmas Ho! Ho! Ho!* . . . . (Capitol)
  Luther Vandross; *Very Special Christmas-#2-C* . . . . (A&M)
  Manhattan Transfer; *Manhattan Transfer-The Christmas Album* . . . (Columbia)
  Mel Torme; *Have Yourself A Jazzy Little Christmas-C* . . . . (Verve)
  Miracles; *Christmas With The Miracles* . . . . (Motown)
  Nat "King" Cole; *Best Of Christmas-C* . . . . (Capitol)
   Billboard's Greatest Christmas Hits-C . . . . (Rhino)
   Now That's What I Call Christmas!-C . . . . (UTV)
  Neil Diamond; *The Christmas Album* . . . . (Columbia)
  O'Jays; *Home For Christmas* . . . . (EMI)
  Perry Como; *Season's Greetings-C* . . . . (RCA)
  Randy Travis; *Old Time Christmas* . . . . (Warner Bros.)
  Reba McEntire; *Merry Christmas To You* . . . . (MCA Special Prod.)
  Roger Whittaker; *Christmas With Roger Whittaker* . . . . . . (RCA)
  Roger Williams; *Golden Christmas* . . . . (Special Music Co.)
  Rosemary Clooney; *Magic Of Christmas* . . . . (Special Music Co.)
  Smokey Robinson & Temptations; *Motown Christmas Album-C* . . . . (Motown)
  Stevie Wonder; *Someday At Christmas* . . . . (Motown)
  Stylistics; *Stylistics-Christmas* . . . . (Amherst)
  Temprees; *A Soulful Christmas-C* . . . . (Collectables)
  Temptations; *Give Love At Christmas* . . . . (Motown)
  Tony Bennett; *Tony Bennett Christmas Album* . . . . (Columbia)
  Trisha Yearwood; *The Sweetest Gift* . . . . (MCA)
  Vince Guaraldi; *Charlie Brown Christmas* . . . . (Fantasy)
Christmas Spirit
  Donna Summer; *All-Star Christmas-C* . . . . (Epic)
   Christmas Spirit . . . . (Mercury)
  Julia Lee And Her Boy Friends; *Hipster's Holiday-Vocal Jazz &*
   R&B-C . . . . (Rhino)
  Wailers; *Bummed Out Christmas-C* . . . . (Rhino)
   Rockin' Christmas-The '60s-C . . . . (Rhino)
Christmas Star
  CeCe Winans; *His Gift* . . . . (PMG/Atlantic)
Christmas Started With A Child
  Ed Bruce; *Country Christmas-#4-C* . . . . (RCA)
Christmas Through Your Eyes
  Gloria Estefan; *All-Star Christmas-C* . . . . (Epic)
Christmas Time
  Bryan Adams; *45-#8651* . . . . (A&M)
  Gary Morris; *Every Christmas* . . . . (Liberty)
  Ray Charles; *Spirit Of Christmas* . . . . (Columbia)
Christmas Time
  Hanson; *Snowed In* . . . . (Mercury)
Christmas Time In The Motor City
  Was (Not Was); *Was (Not Was) Christmas Record* . . . . . . (Passport)

Christmas Time Is Here
  Brian McKnight; *Bethlehem* . . . . (Motown)
  Mel Torme; *Christmas Songs* . . . . (Telarc)
  Rosemary Clooney; *White Christmas* . . . . (Concord Jazz)
Christmas To Christmas
  Lee Greenwood; *Christmas In The Country-C* . . . . (MCA Special Prod.)
   Christmas To Christmas . . . . (MCA Special Prod.)
  Toby Keith; *Christmas To Christmas* . . . . (Polydor Country)
Christmas Trail
  Michael Martin Murphey; *Cowboy Christmas* . . . . (Warner Bros.)
Christmas Waltz
  Carpenters; *Carpenters Christmas Portrait* . . . . (A&M)
  Frank Sinatra; *Jolly Christmas from Frank Sinatra* . . . . . . (Capitol)
  Johnny Mathis; *Christmas Eve With Johnny Mathis* . . . . . (Columbia)
  Lettermen; *For Christmas This Year* . . . . (Capitol)
  Nancy Wilson; *Best Of Christmas-C* . . . . (Capitol)
   Merry Christmas Baby-Romance & Reindeer-C . . . . (Capitol)
  Peggy Lee; *Christmas Carousel* . . . . (Capitol)
Christmas Without Daddy
  Loretta Lynn; *Christmas Without Daddy* . . . . (MCA Special Prod.)
Christmas Without Mary
  Charley Pride; *Country Christmas-#4-C* . . . . (RCA)
Christmas Yodel
  Riders In The Sky; *Christmas The Country Way* . . . . (Rounder)
Closer
  Barbra Streisand; *Christmas Memories* . . . . (Columbia)
Closing Of The Year
  Musical Cast Of Toys f/Wendy & Lisa; *Just Say Noel-C* . . . (Geffen)
  Wendy & Lisa; *ST/Toys* . . . . (Geffen)
Cool Yule
  Louis Armstrong & The Commanders; *Hipster's Holiday-Vocal Jazz &*
   R&B-C . . . . (Rhino)
Corn, Water And Wood
  Riders In The Sky; *Christmas The Country Way* . . . . (Rounder)
Coventry Carol
  Alison Moyet; *Very Special Christmas-C* . . . . (A&M)
  Anne Murray; *Anne Murray Christmas* . . . . (Liberty)
   Best Of The Season . . . . (EMI America)
  Joan Baez; *Noel* . . . . (Vanguard)
  John Denver; *Rocky Mountain Christmas* . . . . (RCA)
  Kenny Loggins; *December* . . . . (Columbia)
  Royal College Of Music Chamber Choir; *Carols For Christmas-#1*
   & 2 . . . . (Rykodisc)
Cowboy Christmas Ball
  Michael Martin Murphey; *Cowboy Christmas* . . . . (Warner Bros.)
Daddy Stuff
  Sammy Kershaw; *Christmas Time's A Comin'* . . . . (Mercury)
Daddy Won't Be Home Again For Christmas
  Merle Haggard; *Goin' Home For Christmas* . . . . (Sony Music Special Prod.)
Daddy's Drinking Up Our Christmas
  Commander Cody; *Hillbilly Holiday-C* . . . . (Rhino)
Dance Of The Sugar Plum Fairy
  Boston Pops Orchestra; *Encores-Boston Pops*
   Orchestra . . . . (Deutsche Grammophon)
   Sleigh Ride!-Classic Christmas Favorites-C . . . . (RCA)
  Carpenters; *Christmas Collection* . . . . (A&M)
Dead By X-Mas
  Hanoi Rocks; *Self-Destruction Blues* . . . . (Geffen)
Dear Santa-Bring Me A Man This Christmas
  Weather Girls; *Success* . . . . (Columbia)
Deck The Halls
  Bing Crosby; *Christmas With Bing & Frank* . . . . (Eclipse)
  Bobby Vinton; *Great Songs Of Christmas* . . . . (Curb)
  Christmas Children's Chorus; *Christmas Children's Chorus-*
   Vol. 2 . . . . (Special Music Co.)
  David Seville & The Chipmunks; *Christmas With The Chipmunks-#2* . . . . (EMI)
  Jackie Wilson; *Merry Christmas From Jackie Wilson* . . . . . (Rhino)
  John Denver; *A Christmas Together* . . . . (Laserlight)
  Mannheim Steamroller; *Christmas Angel, The* . . . . (American Gramaphone)
  Mantovani; *Christmas Favorites* . . . . (London)
  Mario Lanza; *Christmas With Mario Lanza* . . . . (RCA)
  Mormon Tabernacle Choir; *Mormon Tabernacle Choir Christmas*
   Album . . . . (Columbia)
  Nat "King" Cole; *Nat "King" Cole Christmas Gift Set* . . . . (Capitol)
  Ottmar Liebert; *Now That's What I Call Christmas!-C* . . . . (UTV)
  Roger Williams; *Christmas Time* . . . . (MCA)
  SHeDAISY; *Mickey's Once Upon A Christmas* . . . . (Lyric Street)
  Shirley & Squirrely; *Christmas With Shirley & Squirrely* . . . (GRT)
  Trapp Family Singers; *Christmas With The Trapp Family*
   Singers . . . . (MCA Special Prod.)
Deck Us All With Boston Charlie
  Lambert, Hendricks & Ross; *Hipster's Holiday-Vocal Jazz & R&B-C* . . . (Rhino)
Dig That Crazy Santa Claus
  Oscar McLollie And His Honey Jumpers; *Hipster's Holiday-Vocal Jazz &*
   R&B-C . . . . (Rhino)
Do They Know
  Boyz II Men; *Christmas Interpretations* . . . . (Motown)
Do They Know It's Christmas
  Band Aid; *Now That's What I Call Christmas!-C* . . . . (UTV)

Do You Hear What I Hear
Bing Crosby; *Best Of Christmas-C* . . . . (Capitol)
   Christmas With Bing . . . . (CEMA Special Prod.)
Chet Atkins; *East Tennessee Christmas* . . . . (Columbia)
   Nashville's Greatest Christmas Hits-C . . . . (Columbia)
Commodores; *Commodores-Christmas* . . . . (Commodores)
Connie Scott; *Christmas In Your Heart* . . . . (Word)
Destiny's Child; *8 Days Of Christmas* . . . . (Columbia)
Gladys Knight & The Pips; *Bless The House* . . . . (Motown)
Jim Nabors; *A Personal Christmas Collection* . . . . (Legacy)
Mahalia Jackson; *Christmas With Mahalia Jackson* . . . . . . (Columbia)
Sonny James; *It's Christmas Time* . . . . (Liberty)
Steve Wariner; *Steve Wariner Christmas Memories* . . . . (MCA Special Prod.)
Vince Gill; *Let There Be Peace On Earth* . . . . (MCA)
Whitney Houston; *Very Special Christmas-C* . . . . (A&M)

Don't Believe In Christmas
Sonics; *Bummed Out Christmas-C* . . . . (Rhino)

Don't Save It All For Christmas Day
Celine Dion; *Now That's What I Call Christmas!-C* . . . . (UTV)

Early Christmas Morning
Cyndi Lauper; *All-Star Christmas-C* . . . . (Epic)

Every Time Christmas Comes Around
Michael McDonald; *In The Spirit-A Christmas Album* . . . . . . (MCA)

Every Year, Every Christmas
Luther Vandross; *All-Star Christmas-C* . . . . (Epic)

Everybody Knows The Clause
Hanson; *Snowed In* . . . . (Mercury)

Eyes Of A Child, The
Air Supply; *Air Supply Christmas Album* . . . . (Arista)

Face Of Love
Rosie O'Donnell & Jewel; *Another Rosie Christmas-C* . . . . (Columbia)

Father Christmas
Kinks; *Billboard Rock 'N Roll Christmas-C* . . . . (Rhino)
   Come Dancing With The Kinks-Best Of The Kinks 1977-1986 . . . . (Arista)

Feliz Navidad
Asleep At The Wheel; *Merry Texas Christmas, Y'all* . . . . . . (High Street)
Holly Dunn; *A Christmas Tradition* . . . . (Warner Bros.)
Jose Feliciano; *15 Especiales De* . . . . (Globo)
   Jose Feliciano's Greatest Hits . . . . (RCA)

Figgy Pudding
Johnny Cash; *Country Christmas* . . . . (Laserlight)

Fight On Christmas Fight On
John Fahey; *Essential John Fahey* . . . . (Vanguard)
   John Fahey . . . . (Vanguard)

Finest Gift, The
Clint Black; *Looking For Christmas* . . . . (RCA)

First Noel
Air Supply; *Air Supply Christmas Album* . . . . (Arista)
BeBe & CeCe Winans; *First Christmas* . . . . (Capitol)
Bing Crosby; *Bing Crosby Sings Christmas Songs* . . . (MCA Special Prod.)
Connie Francis; *Christmas In My Heart* . . . . (Polydor)
Crash Test Dummies; *Lump Of Coal* . . . . (First Warning)
Dolly Parton; *Home For Christmas* . . . . (Columbia)
Ella Fitzgerald; *Ella Fitzgerald-Christmas* . . . . (Capitol)
Elvis Presley; *Blue Christmas* . . . . (RCA)
   If Every Day Was Like Christmas . . . . (RCA)
Emmylou Harris; *Light Of The Stable* . . . . (Warner Bros.)
   Martha Stewart Living: Home For The Holidays-C . . . . (Rhino)
George Howard; *GRP Christmas Collection-#2-C* . . . . (GRP)
Joe Williams; *That Holiday Feelin'* . . . . (Verve)
John Tesh; *Romantic Christmas* . . . . (GTS)
Johnny Mathis & Percy Faith and his Orchestra; *Merry Christmas* . . . (Columbia)
Kenny Rogers; *Christmas In America* . . . . (Reprise)
Loretta Lynn; *Tennessee Christmas-C* . . . . (MCA)
Lou Rawls; *Christmas Is The Time* . . . . (Manhattan)
Mitch Miller; *Christmas Sing Along With Mitch* . . . . (Columbia)
Nat "King" Cole; *Nat "King" Cole Christmas Gift Set* . . . . . (Capitol)
Neil Diamond; *Christmas Album-II* . . . . (Columbia)
Pete Seeger; *Traditional Christmas Carols* . . . . . . (Smithsonian Folkways)
Philadelphia Orchestra & Eugene Ormandy; *Joy To The World* . . . . (RCA)
Roger Whittaker; *Christmas With Roger Whittaker* . . . . . . (Liberty)
Suzy Bogguss; *Christmas For The '90s-#2-C* . . . . (Liberty)
Vanessa Williams; *Star Bright* . . . . (Mercury)

Five Pound Box Of Money
Pearl Bailey; *Hipster's Holiday-Vocal Jazz & R&B-C* . . . . . . (Rhino)

For Momma
Statler Brothers; *Statler Brothers Christmas Present* . . . . . . (Mercury)

For Unto Us A Child Is Born
BeBe & CeCe Winans; *First Christmas* . . . . (Capitol)
Roches; *We Three Kings* . . . . (Rykodisc)

Forgive Me Santa
Jimmie Davis; *Best Of Jimmie Davis* . . . . (MCA)
   Canaan Country Christmas . . . . (Canaan)
Shirley Caesar; *Christmasing* . . . . (Word)

Friendly Beasts
Garth Brooks; *Beyond The Season* . . . . (Liberty)
Peter, Paul & Mary & The New York Choral Society; *Holiday Celebration* . . . . (Warner Bros.)
Riders In The Sky; *Christmas The Country Way* . . . . (Rounder)

Frosty The Snowman
Beach Boys; *Beach Boys Christmas Album* . . . . (Capitol)
   Ultimate Christmas . . . . (Capitol)
Bing Crosby; *Bing Crosby Christmas Classics* . . . . (Capitol)
Conway Twitty; *Merry Twismas From C.T. & Little Friends* . . . (Warner Bros.)
Flaco Jimenez/Freddie Fender; *Tejano Country Christmas-C* . . . (Arista)
Gene Autry; *16 Most Requested Songs Of Christmas-C* . . . . . (Legacy)
   Gene Autry Christmas . . . . (Legacy)
George Strait; *Merry Christmas Strait To You* . . . . . (MCA Special Prod.)
Jackson 5; *Jackson 5-Christmas Album* . . . . (Motown)
Jan & Dean; *Legends Of Christmas Past-Rock & R&B-C* . . . . . (EMI)
Loretta Lynn; *Christmas Without Daddy* . . . . (MCA Special Prod.)
Ray Conniff; *Yuletide Cheer-C* . . . . (Columbia)
Ronettes; *Phil Spector's Christmas Album-C* . . . . (Passport)

Funky Christmas
Whispers; *Happy Holidays To You* . . . . (Solar)

Funky New Year
Eagles; *45-#45555* . . . . (Asylum)

Ghetto Santa
Spyder-D; *Christmas Rap* . . . . (Profile)

Gift Of Magi
Squirrel Nut Zippers; *Christmas Caravan* . . . . (Mammoth)

Gift, The
Jim Brickman with Ashton & Raye; *The Gift* . . . . (Windham Hill)
   Visions Of Love . . . . (Windham Hill)

Give Love On Christmas Day
Jackson 5; *Jackson 5-Christmas Album* . . . . (Motown)
Johnny Gill; *Motown Christmas Album-C* . . . . (Motown)
New Edition; *Christmas All Over The World* . . . . (MCA)
Temptations; *Give Love At Christmas* . . . . (Motown)

Give Me Your Love For Christmas
Johnny Mathis; *Give Me Your Love For Christmas* . . . . . . (Columbia)

Go Tell It On The Mountain
Bobby Darin; *Bobby Darin-25th Day Of December* . . . . (Atco)
Bruce Cockburn; *Christmas* . . . . (Columbia)
Dolly Parton; *Home For Christmas* . . . . (Columbia)
Don McLean; *Christmas* . . . . (Curb)
Garth Brooks; *Beyond The Season* . . . . (Liberty)
Simon & Garfunkel; *Collected Works* . . . . (Columbia)
   Wednesday Morning 3 A.M. . . . . (Columbia)
Weavers; *On Tour* . . . . (Vanguard)

God Rest Ye Merry Gentlemen
Bing Crosby; *Bing Crosby Sings Christmas Songs* . . . . . (MCA Special Prod.)
   Merry Christmas . . . . (MCA Special Prod.)
   Voice Of Christmas-The Complete Decca Christmas Songbook . . . . (Decca)
Bobby Vinton; *Christmas All-Time Greatest Records-#2-C* . . . . (Curb)
Ella Fitzgerald; *Best Of Christmas-C* . . . . (Capitol)
Garth Brooks; *Beyond The Season* . . . . (Liberty)
   Christmas For The '90s-#1-C . . . . (Liberty)
Jackie Wilson; *Merry Christmas From Jackie Wilson* . . . . . . (Rhino)
Kenny Rogers; *Christmas In America* . . . . (Reprise)
Leontyne Price; *Christmas Songs* . . . . (London)
Mannheim Steamroller; *Christmas Live* . . . . (American Gramaphone)
Mel Torme; *Christmas Songs* . . . . (Telarc)
Nat "King" Cole; *Cole Christmas & Kids* . . . . (Capitol)
Neil Diamond; *Neil Diamond Christmas Album* . . . . (Columbia)
Perry Como; *Season's Greetings From Perry Como* . . . . (RCA)
Randy Travis; *An Old Time Christmas* . . . . (Warner Bros.)
Roger Whittaker; *Tidings Of Comfort & Joy* . . . . (Liberty)
Smokey Robinson & The Miracles; *Season For Miracles* . . . . . (Motown)
Steve Wariner; *Steve Wariner Christmas Memories* . . . . (MCA Special Prod.)
T Bone Burnett; *Acoustic Christmas* . . . . (Columbia)
Take 6 & The Yellowjackets; *He Is Christmas* . . . . (Reprise)

Good King Wenceslas
E. Power Biggs; *Music For A Merry Christmas* . . . . . (Sony Music Special Prod.)
E. Power Biggs/Gregg Smith Singers; *We Wish You A Merry Christmas* . . . . (Columbia)
Eric Tingstad & Nancy Rumbel; *The Gift* . . . . (Sona Gaia)
Joan Baez; *Noel* . . . . (Vanguard)
Mel Torme; *Christmas Songs* . . . . (Telarc)
Philadelphia Orchestra & Eugene Ormandy; *Joy To The World* . . . . (RCA)
Roches; *We Three Kings* . . . . (Rykodisc)
Stan Kenton; *Merry Christmas From The Creative World Of Stan Kenton* . . . . (Capitol)

Grandma Got Run Over By A Reindeer
Elmo & Patsy; *Billboard's Greatest Christmas Hits-C* . . . . (Rhino)
   Dr. Demento Presents The Greatest Novelty Records-#6-Christmas-C . . . . (Rhino)
   Dr. Demento Presents The Greatest Novelty Records-C . . . . (Rhino)
   Grandma Got Run Over By A Reindeer . . . . (Epic)
   Greatest Children's Christmas Hits-C . . . . (Columbia)
   Now That's What I Call Christmas!-C . . . . (UTV)

Grandma's Killer Fruitcake
Elmo Shropshire; *Dr. Elmo's Twisted Christmas* . . . . . (Laughing Stock)

Grandpa's Gonna Sue The Pants Off Of Santa
Elmo Shropshire; *Dr. Elmo's Twisted Christmas* . . . . . . (Laughing Stock)

Greatest Gift Of All
Kenny Rogers & Dolly Parton; *Once Upon A Christmas* . . . . . . (RCA)
Lee Greenwood; *Lee Greenwood-Christmas To Christmas* . . . . (MCA Special Prod.)

Greatest Little Christmas Ever Wuz
Ray Stevens; *Country Christmas To Remember-C* (MCA Special Prod.)
Tennessee Christmas-C (MCA)

Green Christmas
Stan Freberg; *Capitol Collectors Series-Stan Freberg* (Capitol)
Christmas Comedy Classics-C (Priority)
Dr. Demento Presents The Greatest Novelty Records-#6-Christmas-C (Rhino)
Dr. Demento's Greatest Christmas CD-C (Rhino)

Green Christmas
Barenaked Ladies; *ST/How The Grinch Stole Christmas* (Interscope)

Greensleeves
Jeff Beck Group; *Truth* (Epic)
Olivia Newton-John; *Come On Over* (MCA)
Ray Conniff Singers; *Ray Conniff Singers-Christmas* (Columbia)
Vienna Boys Choir; *Christmas Festival-C* (RCA)

Grown-Up Christmas
David Foster; *River Of Love* (Atlantic)

Grown-Up Christmas List
Barbra Streisand; *Christmas Memories* (Columbia)

Happy Birthday
Loretta Lynn; *Loretta Lynn's Greatest Hits* (MCA)

Happy Birthday Jesus (I'll Open This One For You)
Reba McEntire; *Merry Christmas To You* (MCA Special Prod.)

Happy Birthday, Jesus
Original Sins; *Bethlehem* (Bar/None)

Happy Christmas
Toots & The Maytals; *Natty And Nice: A Reggae Christmas* (Rhino)

Happy Holidays
Alabama; *Alabama-Christmas* (RCA)
Bing Crosby & Norman Luboff Choir; *Christmas Sing With Bing* (MCA Special Prod.)

Happy Kwanza
Teddy Pendergrass; *This Christmas (I'd Rather Have Love)* (Surefire)

Happy New Year
Judy Garland; *Alone* (Capitol)

Happy New Year
Lightnin' Hopkins; *Blue Yule-Christmas Blues & R&B Classics-C* (Rhino)

Happy New Year
Abba; *Super Trouper* (Atlantic)

Happy Xmas (War Is Over)
Andy Williams; *I Still Believe In Santa Claus* (Curb)
Jimmy Buffett; *Christmas Island* (MCA)
John Lennon; *Lennon* (Capitol)
John Lennon/Plastic Ono Band; *Shaved Fish* (Capitol)
John Lennon/Plastic Ono Band/Harlem Community Choir; *Now That's What I Call Christmas!-C* (UTV)
Neil Diamond; *Neil Diamond Christmas Album* (Columbia)

Hard Candy Christmas
Dolly Parton; *Best Of Christmas-C* (RCA)
Country Christmas-#2-C (RCA)
Dolly Parton's Greatest Hits (RCA)
Season's Greetings-C (RCA)
ST/Best Little Whorehouse In Texas (MCA)
Original Cast; *Best Little Whorehouse In Texas* (MCA)
RuPaul; *Ho Ho Ho* (Rhino)

Hark! The Herald Angels Sing
Amy Grant; *Amy Grant Christmas Album* (Word)
Bing Crosby; *Bing Crosby Christmas Classics* (Capitol)
Guy Lombardo & His Royal Canadians; *Best Of Christmas-C* (Capitol)
James Cleveland; *Merry Christmas* (Savoy)
Johnny Cash; *Classic Christmas* (Sony Music Special Prod.)
Jose Feliciano; *This Is Christmas-C* (RCA)
Mariah Carey; *Merry Christmas* (Columbia)
Marty Robbins; *Christmas Greetings From Nashville* (Columbia)
Country Christmas Favorites (Columbia)
Nashville's Greatest Christmas Hits-C (Columbia)
Mormon Tabernacle Choir; *It's Christmas* (Sony Music Special Prod.)
Joy To The World (Columbia)
Spirit Of Christmas (Columbia)
National Philharmonic Orchestra & Chorus; *50 Songs Of Christmas* (Sparrow)
Philadelphia Orchestra & Eugene Ormandy; *Joy To The World* (RCA)

Have Yourself A Merry Little Christmas
Amy Grant; *Home For Christmas* (A&M)
Babyface; *All-Star Christmas-C* (Epic)
Barbra Streisand; *Barbra Streisand Christmas Album* (Columbia)
Bing Crosby; *Bing Crosby Christmas Classics* (Capitol)
Brian McKnight; *Bethlehem* (Motown)
Buddy Emmons; *Christmas Sounds Of The Steel Guitar* (Step One)
Canadian Brass; *Christmas Celebration-C* (Columbia)
Crystal Gayle; *Crystal Christmas* (Warner Bros.)
Warner Bros. Christmas Tradition-C (Warner Bros.)
David Seville & The Chipmunks; *Christmas With The Chipmunks-#2* (EMI)
Eddie Rabbitt; *Christmas For The '90s-#2-C* (Liberty)
Frank Sinatra; *Christmas Songs By Sinatra* (Legacy)
Jolly Christmas from Frank Sinatra (Capitol)
Now That's What I Call Christmas!-C (UTV)
Jackson 5; *Jackson 5-Christmas Album* (Motown)
John Scofield; *Christmas Guitars-C* (Green Linnet)
Johnny Mathis; *Christmas With Johnny Mathis* (Columbia)
Judy Garland; *Best Of Judy Garland* (MCA)
Kenny Rogers; *Christmas In America* (Reprise)
Kiri Te Kanawa; *Christmas With Kiri Te Kanawa* (London)
Lou Rawls; *Merry Christmas Baby-Romance & Reindeer-C* (Capitol)
Luther Vandross; *This Is Christmas* (Epic)
Manhattan Transfer; *Manhattan Transfer-The Christmas Album* (Columbia)
Martina McBride; *White Christmas* (RCA)
Maureen McGovern; *Christmas With Maureen McGovern* (Columbia)
Mel Torme; *ST/Home Alone* (Columbia)
O'Jays; *Home For Christmas* (EMI)
Pretenders; *Very Special Christmas-C* (A&M)
Tom Scott; *GRP Christmas Collection-C* (GRP)
Vanessa Williams; *Christmas Message* (Lection)

Head Crushing Yuletide Sing-A-Long
Mojo Nixon & The Toadliquors; *Horny Holidays!* (Triple X Entert.)

Hello Mr. New Year
Coolbreezers; *Hipster's Holiday-Vocal Jazz & R&B-C* (Rhino)

Here Comes Santa Claus (Right Down Santa Claus Lane)
Asleep At The Wheel; *Merry Texas Christmas, Y'all* (High Street)
Bob B. Soxx/Blue Jeans; *Christmas Gift For You From Phil Spector-C* (Rhino)
Phil Spector-Back To Mono 1958-1969-C (Abkco)
Phil Spector's Christmas Album-C (Passport)
Doris Day; *16 Most Requested Songs Of Christmas-C* (Legacy)
Dwight Yoakam; *Come On Christmas* (Reprise)
Elvis Presley; *Elvis' Christmas Album* (RCA)
Gene Autry; *Billboard's Greatest Christmas Hits-C* (Rhino)
Christmas Cowboy, The (Laserlight)
His Christmas Album (Everest)
Season's Greetings From Nashville-C (Columbia)
Kitty Wells; *Christmas Day* (MCA Special Prod.)
Ramsey Lewis Trio; *Sound Of Christmas* (MCA Special Prod.)
Riders In The Sky; *Merry Christmas From Harmony Ranch* (Columbia)
Spike Jones; *It's A Spike Jones Christmas* (Rhino)

Here We Come A-Wassailing
Atlanta Gay Men's Chorus; *Carols, Revels And Holiday Cheer* (Diversecity)
Mannheim Steamroller; *Mannheim Steamroller-Christmas* (American Gramaphone)
Players; *Players-Christmas* (Rykodisc)

His Will Was Done
Lee Ann Womack; *Country Christmas '98* (MCA Special Prod.)

Ho Ho Ho-Who'd Be A Turkey At Christmas
Elton John; *Rockin' Christmas-C* (MCA Special Prod.)

Holidaze (S'cuze Me, I've Got Gifts To Buy)
Bob Rivers; *More Twisted Christmas* (Atlantic)

Holly & The Ivy
Bing Crosby; *Bing Crosby Christmas Classics* (Capitol)
Charlie Byrd; *Charlie Byrd Christmas Album* (Concord Jazz)
Emily Mitchell; *Holly & The Ivy* (RCA)
Empire Brass; *Joy To The World-Music Of Christmas* (Angel)
Joan Sutherland; *Joy Of Christmas* (London)
Jon Anderson; *3 Ships* (Elektra)
Players; *Players-Christmas* (Rykodisc)

Holly Jolly Christmas, A
Alan Jackson; *Honky Tonk Christmas* (Arista)
ST/Home Alone 2-Lost In New York (Fox/Arista)
Burl Ives; *Christmas Hits-C* (MCA Special Prod.)
Have A Holly Jolly Christmas (MCA Special Prod.)
Now That's What I Call Christmas!-C (UTV)
Rudolph The Red-Nosed Reindeer (MCA Special Prod.)

Holly Leaves & Christmas Trees
Elvis Presley; *If Every Day Was Like Christmas* (RCA)

Home To Texas For Christmas
Mickey Gilley; *Christmas At Gilley's* (Sony Music Special Prod.)

Homecoming Christmas
Alabama; *Alabama-Christmas* (RCA)

Honky Tonk Christmas
Alan Jackson; *Honky Tonk Christmas* (Arista)
Mickey Gilley; *Christmas At Gilley's* (Sony Music Special Prod.)

Hot Christmas
Squirrel Nut Zippers; *Christmas Caravan* (Mammoth)

Hot Rod Sleigh
Toby Keith; *Christmas To Christmas* (Polydor Country)

House Full Of Love
Michael McDonald; *In The Spirit-A Christmas Album* (MCA)

How Do I Wrap My Heart For Christmas
Randy Travis; *An Old Time Christmas* (Warner Bros.)

Howdy Doody Christmas
Howdy Doody & Fontane Sisters; *TV Family Christmas-C* (Scotti Bros.)

I Believe In Father Christmas
Greg Lake; *Emerson Lake & Palmer-Works-#2* (Atlantic)

I Believe In Santa Claus
Kenny Rogers & Dolly Parton; *Once Upon A Christmas* (RCA)

I Believe In Santa's Cause
Statler Brothers; *Statler Brothers Christmas Present* (Mercury)

I Don't Believe You
Sinead O'Connor; *Very Special Christmas-#2-C* (A&M)

I Found The Brains Of Santa Claus
Jason & The Straptones; *Demento's Mementos* . . . . (PVC)

I Hate The Holidays
Venus Envy; *I'll Be Homo For Christmas* . . . . (Venus Envy)

I Heard The Bells On Christmas Day
Bing Crosby; *That Christmas Feeling* . . . . (MCA Special Prod.)
Eddy Arnold; *Christmas With Eddy Arnold*. . . . .(RCA)
Harry Belafonte; *To Wish You A Merry Christmas* . . . . (RCA)
Johnny Cash; *Christmas Spirit* . . . . (Columbia)
  Classic Christmas . . . . (Sony Music Special Prod.)
Michael Martin Murphey; *Cowboy Christmas* . . . . (Warner Bros.)
Travis Tritt; *Christmas-Loving Time Of The Year* . . . . (Warner Bros.)

I Like A Sleighride
Peggy Lee; *Best Of Christmas-C* . . . . (Capitol)
  Christmas Carousel . . . . (Capitol)

I Love The Winter Weather
Tony Bennett; *Snowfall: The Tony Bennett Christmas Album* . . . (Columbia)

I Only Want You For Christmas
Alan Jackson; *Honky Tonk Christmas* . . . . (Arista)

I Pray On Christmas
Harry Connick, Jr.; *When My Heart Finds Christmas* . . . . (Columbia)

I Remember
Barbra Streisand; *Christmas Memories* . . . . (Columbia)

I Saw Daddy Kissing Santa Clause
RuPaul; *Ho Ho Ho* . . . . (Rhino)

I Saw Mommy Kissing Santa Claus
Andy Williams; *I Still Believe In Santa Claus* . . . . (Curb)
Impressions; *Funky Christmas* . . . . (Cotillion)
Jackie Gleason; *All I Want For Christmas* . . . . (Capitol)
Jackson 5; *Jackson 5-Christmas Album*. . . . . (Motown)
  Motown Christmas Album-C . . . . (Motown)
Jimmy Boyd; *Billboard's Great Country Christmas Hits-C* . . . . (Rhino)
  Billboard's Greatest Christmas Hits-C . . . . (Rhino)
John Cougar Mellencamp; *Very Special Christmas-C* . . . . . . (A&M)
Mitch Miller; *Holiday Sing Along With Mitch* . . . . (Columbia)
Ronettes; *Christmas Gift For You From Phil Spector-C* . . . . . . (Rhino)
  Phil Spector-Back To Mono 1958-1969-C . . . . (Abkco)
  Phil Spector's Christmas Album-C. . . . . (Passport)
Tiny Tim; *Tiny Tim's Christmas Album* . . . . (Rounder)

I Saw Three Ships Come Sailing In
Mannheim Steamroller; *Mannheim Steamroller-
  Christmas.* . . . . (American Gramaphone)
Mario Lanza; *Christmas With Mario Lanza* . . . . (RCA)
Nat "King" Cole; *Nat "King" Cole Christmas Gift Set.* . . . . . (Capitol)

I Tan't Wait Till Quithmuth Day
Mel Blanc; *Christmas Comedy Classics-C* . . . . (Priority)

I Wanna Spend Christmas With You
Lowell Fulsom; *The Best Christmas Ever-C* . . . .(Virgin)

I Want A Hippopotamus For Christmas
Gayla Peevey; *Dr. Demento Presents The Greatest Novelty Records-#6-
  Christmas-C.* . . . . (Rhino)
  Dr. Demento's Greatest Christmas CD-C . . . . (Rhino)
Three Stooges; *Christmas Time With The Three Stooges* . . . . (Rhino)

I Want Elvis For Christmas
Holly Twins & Eddie Cochran; *Legends Of Christmas Past-Rock &
  R&B-C.* . . . . (EMI)

I Wish It Could Be Christmas Forever
Perry Como; *I Wish It Could Be Christmas Forever* . . . . (RCA)

I Wonder As I Wander
Barbra Streisand; *Barbra Streisand Christmas Album* . . . . (Columbia)
Gary Morris; *Every Christmas*. . . . . (Liberty)
Grover Washington, Jr.; *Breath Of Heaven-A Holiday Collection* . . . (Columbia)
Joan Baez; *Noel* . . . . (Vanguard)
Julie Andrews; *Christmas With Julie Andrews* . . . . (Columbia)
Mormon Tabernacle Choir; *This Land Is Your Land* . . . . . . (Columbia)
Peter, Paul & Mary; *Holiday Celebration* . . . . (Warner Bros.)
Philadelphia Orchestra & Eugene Ormandy; *Sleigh Ride!-Classic Christmas
  Favorites-C.* . . . . (RCA)
Sandi Patty; *Gift Goes On* . . . . (Word)
Vanessa Williams; *Star Bright* . . . . (Mercury)

I Yust Go Nuts At Christmas
Yogi Yorgesson; *Christmas Kisses-Capitol's Early Years-C* . . . . . (Capitol)
  *Dr. Demento Presents The Greatest Novelty Records-#6-
  Christmas-C.* . . . . (Rhino)
  Dr. Demento's Greatest Christmas CD-C . . . . (Rhino)

I'd Like To Hitch A Ride With Santa
Andrews Sisters; *All-Time Christmas Favorites-#3-C* . . . . (MCA Special Prod.)
  Christmas . . . . (MCA Special Prod.)

If Every Day Was Like Christmas
Elvis Presley; *If Every Day Was Like Christmas* . . . .(RCA)
  Memories Of Christmas . . . . (RCA)

If I Get Home On Christmas Day
Elvis Presley; *If Every Day Was Like Christmas* . . . .(RCA)

If We Make It Through December
Merle Haggard; *A Christmas Present* . . . . (Curb)
  Eleven Winners . . . . (Capitol)
  Goin' Home For Christmas . . . . (Sony Music Special Prod.)
  Merle Haggard-Christmas Gift . . . . (Curb)
  Very Best Of Merle Haggard . . . . (Capitol)

If You Don't Wanna See Santa Claus Cry
Alan Jackson; *Honky Tonk Christmas* . . . .(Arista)

I'll Be A Homo For Christmas
Venus Envy; *I'll Be Homo For Christmas* . . . .(Venus Envy)

I'll Be Gnome For Christmas
Jethros; *Dark Side Of The Xmas Tree-C* . . . . (Performance)

I'll Be Home For Christmas
Al Green; *All-Star Christmas-C* . . . .(Epic)
  White Christmas . . . . (Word)
Amy Grant; *Home For Christmas* . . . .(A&M)
Anne Murray; *Christmas Wishes* . . . . (Capitol)
Barbara Mandrell; *Christmas At Our House* . . . . . (MCA Special Prod.)
Barbra Streisand; *Christmas Memories* . . . .(Columbia)
Beach Boys; *Beach Boys Christmas Album* . . . . (Capitol)
Carpenters; *Carpenters Christmas Portrait* . . . .(A&M)
Crystal Gayle; *Crystal Christmas*. . . . .(Warner Bros.)
Dean Martin; *Making Spirits Bright* . . . . (Capitol)
Dolly Parton; *Home For Christmas* . . . .(Columbia)
Donna Summer; *Christmas Spirit* . . . . (Mercury)
Duke Ellington & His Orchestra; *Take The Holiday Train.* . . . (Special Music Co.)
Elvis Presley; *Elvis' Christmas Album*. . . . . (RCA)
Floyd Cramer; *We Wish You A Merry Christmas* . . . . (RCA)
Forester Sisters; *Forester Sisters' Christmas Card* . . . . . . (Warner Bros.)
Frank Sinatra; *Jolly Christmas from Frank Sinatra* . . . . . . (Capitol)
Glen Campbell; *Merry Christmas Baby-Romance & Reindeer-C* . . . . (Capitol)
Gloria Estefan; *Christmas Through Your Eyes* . . . . (Epic)
Kenny Rogers; *Christmas In America* . . . . (Reprise)
Lee Greenwood; *Lee Greenwood-Christmas To
  Christmas* . . . . (MCA Special Prod.)
Mickey Gilley; *Christmas At Gilley's* . . . . (Sony Music Special Prod.)
  Nashville's Greatest Christmas Hits-#2-C . . . .(Columbia)
Pat Boone; *White Christmas.* . . . . (MCA Special Prod.)
Percy Faith & His Orchestra; *Christmas Is Percy Faith & His
  Orchestra* . . . .(Columbia)
  Christmas Melodies. . . . .(Columbia)
Reba McEntire; *Christmas In The Country-C* . . . . . (MCA Special Prod.)
  Merry Christmas To You . . . . (MCA Special Prod.)
Ronnie Milsap; *Christmas With Ronnie Milsap* . . . . (RCA)
Spyro Gyra; *GRP Christmas Collection-#2-C* . . . .(GRP)
Statler Brothers; *Statler Brothers Christmas Present.* . . . . . (Mercury)
Suzy Bogguss; *Christmas For The '90s-#1-C* . . . . (Liberty)
  Family Christmas Treasury-C. . . . . (Liberty)
Tony Bennett; *Snowfall: The Tony Bennett Christmas Album* . . . . . (Columbia)
Vince Gill; *Let There Be Peace On Earth* . . . . (MCA)
Wayne Newton; *Christmas All-Time Greatest Records-#2-C* . . . . .(Curb)

I'll Be Walking The Floor This Christmas
Ernest Tubb; *Hillbilly Holiday-C.* . . . .(Rhino)

I'll Be Your Santa, Baby
Rufus Thomas; *It's Christmas Time Again-C* . . . . (Stax)

I'll Make Everyday Christmas
Joe Tex; *Soul Christmas-C.* . . . . (Atlantic)

I'll Place My Order Early
Johnny Paycheck; *45-#55* . . . . (Little Darlin')

I'm A Christmas Tree
Wild Man Fischer & Dr. Demento; *Dr. Demento's Greatest
  Christmas CD-C.* . . . .(Rhino)

I'm A Pleasure To Shop For
Ogden Nash; *Christmas With Ogden Nash* . . . .(Caedmon)

I'm Christmasing With You
Patti LaBelle; *Starlight Christmas* . . . . (MCA)

I'm Gonna E-Mail Santa
Rosie O'Donnell & Billy Gilman; *Another Rosie Christmas-C* . . . . .(Columbia)

I'm Gonna Lasso Santa Claus
Brenda Lee; *Hillbilly Holiday-C* . . . .(Rhino)
  Rockin' Little Christmas-C . . . . (MCA)

I'm Spending Christmas With You
Mickey Gilley; *Christmas At Gilley's* . . . . (Sony Music Special Prod.)

In A Humble Place
Jim Nabors; *Christmas Album* . . . .(Columbia)

In Dulci Jubilo
Michael Hedges; *Winter's Solstice III-C* . . . . (Windham Hill)
Players; *Players-Christmas* . . . . (Rykodisc)
Virgil Fox; *Virgil Fox Christmas Album* . . . .(Bainbridge)

Indian Giver
Squirrel Nut Zippers; *Christmas Caravan* . . . . (Mammoth)

It Came Upon A Midnight Clear
Anne Murray; *Anne Murray Christmas* . . . .(Liberty)
Beausoleil; *Alligator Stomp-#4-Cajun Christmas-C* . . . .(Rhino)
Burl Ives; *Christmas Eve* . . . . (MCA)
Don McLean; *Christmas Dreams.* . . . . (Hip-O)
Frank Sinatra; *Jolly Christmas from Frank Sinatra* . . . . . . (Capitol)
Guy Lombardo & His Royal Canadians; *Peace On Earth* . . . . .(Capitol)
Highway 101; *Warner Bros. Christmas Tradition-C* . . . . . . (Warner Bros.)
John Tesh; *Romantic Christmas.* . . . . (GTS)
Julie Andrews & Andre Previn; *Christmas Treasure* . . . . (RCA)
Mahalia Jackson; *Christmas With Mahalia Jackson* . . . . . .(Columbia)
Manhattan Transfer; *Manhattan Transfer-The Christmas Album* . . . .(Columbia)
Mitch Miller; *Christmas Sing Along With Mitch* . . . .(Columbia)
Rosanne Cash; *Acoustic Christmas* . . . .(Columbia)
Tammy Wynette; *Country Christmas-C* . . . . (Epic)

Nashville's Greatest Christmas Hits-#2-C . . . . (Columbia)
Voices Of The Season-A Capella-C . . . .(Epic)

It Doesn't Have To Be That Way
Jim Croce; *Life & Times* . . . . (Lifesong)

It Is His Birthday
Oak Ridge Boys; *Christmas* . . . .(MCA Special Prod.)

It Must Have Been The Mistletoe
Barbra Streisand; *Christmas Memories* . . . . (Columbia)

It Wasn't His Child
Skip Ewing; *Following Yonder Star* . . . .(MCA Special Prod.)
Trisha Yearwood; *The Sweetest Gift* . . . .(MCA)

It Won't Be The Same This Year
Vince Gill; *Let There Be Peace On Earth* . . . .(MCA)

It's Beginning To Look A Lot Like Christmas
Bing Crosby; *All-Time Christmas Favorites-#4-C* . . . . .(MCA Special Prod.)
Bing Crosby Sings Christmas Songs . . . .(MCA Special Prod.)
Duke Ellington & His Orchestra; *Take The Holiday Train* . . .(Special Music Co.)
Johnny Mathis; *ST/Home Alone 2-Lost In New York* . . . . .(Fox/Arista)
Osmonds; *Christmas* . . . . (Curb)

It's Christmas
John Schneider; *White Christmas* . . . . (Scotti Bros.)
Ronnie Milsap; *Best Of Christmas-C* . . . . (RCA)
Christmas With Ronnie Milsap . . . . (RCA)
Country Christmas-#3-C . . . . (RCA)

It's Christmas Time
Carpenters; *Carpenters Christmas Portrait* . . . . (A&M)
Castelles; *Rhythm & Blues Christmas-#1-C* . . . . (Collectables)
Sweet Sounds Of The Castelles . . . . (Collectables)
Clifton Chenier; *King Of The Bayous* . . . . (Arhoolie)
Five Keys; *Doo-Wop Christmas-C* . . . . (Rhino)
Legends Of Christmas Past-Rock & R&B-C . . . . (EMI)
Marvin & Johnny; *Legends Of Christmas Past-Rock & R&B-C* . . . . . .(EMI)
Rockin' Christmas-'50s-C . . . . (Rhino)
Smokey Robinson & The Miracles; *Motown Christmas Album-C* . . . .(Motown)
Season For Miracles . . . . (Motown)

It's Christmastime In Louisiana
Johnnie Allan; *Alligator Stomp-#4-Cajun Christmas-C* . . . . . . (Rhino)

It's Gonna Be a Punk Rock Christmas
Ravers; *45-#7683* . . . . (Zombie)

It's Just Another New Year's Eve
Barry Manilow; *Barry Manilow/Live* . . . . (Arista)

It's That Time Of The Year
Manhattans; *A Soulful Christmas-C* . . . . (Collectables)

It's The Most Fattening Time Of The Year
Bob Rivers; *More Twisted Christmas* . . . . (Atlantic)

I've Got What You Want For Christmas
Louise Mandrell; *Country Christmas-#2-C* . . . . (RCA)

Jesu, Joy Of Man's Desiring
Eric Tingstad & Nancy Rumbel; *The Gift* . . . . (Sona Gaia)
John Tesh; *Romantic Christmas* . . . . (GTS)

Jesus Born On This Day
Mariah Carey; *Merry Christmas* . . . . (Columbia)

Jesus Gets Jealous Of Santa Claus
Toby Keith; *Christmas To Christmas* . . . . (Polydor Country)

Jesus, Jesus, Rest Your Head
Trapp Family Singers; *Christmas With The Trapp Family
Singers* . . . .(MCA Special Prod.)

Jingle Bell Boogie
Big Jack Johnson; *Blue Yule-Christmas Blues & R&B Classics-C* . . . . . (Rhino)

Jingle Bell Jamboree
Keb' Mo'; *All-Star Christmas-C* . . . .(Epic)

Jingle Bell Rock
Bobby Helms; *Billboard's Great Country Christmas Hits-C* . . . . (Rhino)
Christmas Classics-C . . . . (Rhino)
Now That's What I Call Christmas!-C . . . . (UTV)
ST/Home Alone 2-Lost In New York . . . .(Fox/Arista)
Booker T. & The M.G.s; *Cool Yule-C* . . . . (Rhino)
Brenda Lee; *All-Time Christmas Favorites-#4-C* . . . .(MCA Special Prod.)
Chet Atkins; *East Tennessee Christmas* . . . . (Columbia)
Jambalaya Cajun Band; *Alligator Stomp-#4-Cajun Christmas-C* . . . . . . (Rhino)
Johnny Mathis; *For Christmas* . . . . (Columbia)
Lenny Dee; *Best Of Lenny Dee* . . . .(MCA)
Neil Diamond; *Neil Diamond Christmas Album* . . . . (Columbia)
Randy Travis; *Very Special Christmas-#2-C* . . . . (A&M)
Rick Orozco; *Tejano Country Christmas-C* . . . . (Arista)
Wild Rose; *Christmas For The '90s-#1-C* . . . . (Liberty)

Jingle Bells
4 Seasons; *4 Seasons Christmas Album* . . . . (Rhino)
Al Green; *White Christmas* . . . . (Word)
Barbra Streisand; *Barbra Streisand Christmas Album* . . . . (Columbia)
Bing Crosby & The Andrews Sisters; *Christmas All-Time Greatest
Records-C* . . . . (Curb)
Booker T. & The M.G.s; *In The Christmas Spirit* . . . . (Rhino)
Brian Setzer Orchestra; *Merry Axemas-A Guitar Christmas* . . . . (Epic)
Buck Owens; *Christmas With Buck Owens* . . . . (Curb)
Carpenters; *Carpenters Christmas Portrait* . . . . (A&M)
Count Basie; *Yule Struttin'-C* . . . . (Blue Note)
Diana Krall; *Now That's What I Call Christmas!-C* . . . . (UTV)
Dolly Parton; *Home For Christmas* . . . . (Columbia)

Flaco Jimenez/Freddie Fender/Others; *Tejano Country Christmas-C* . . . . (Arista)
Frank Sinatra & Bing Crosby; *Happy Holiday* . . . . (Special Music Co.)
Gladys Knight & The Pips; *That Special Time Of Year* . . . . (Columbia)
Jim Nabors; *Christmas Album* . . . . (Columbia)
Judy Collins; *Christmas At The Biltmore Estate* . . . . (Elektra)
Leo Watson; *Hipster's Holiday-Vocal Jazz & R&B-C* . . . . (Rhino)
Les Paul; *Christmas Kisses-Capitol's Early Years-C* . . . . (Capitol)
Mannheim Steamroller; *Christmas In The Aire* . . . . . . (American Gramaphone)
Mitch Miller; *Holiday Sing Along With Mitch* . . . . (Columbia)
Roger Wagner; *Caroles* . . . . (Capitol)
Roy Rogers; *Christmas On The Range-Cowboy Classics-C* . . . . (Capitol)
Spike Jones; *It's A Spike Jones Christmas* . . . . (Rhino)
Statler Brothers; *Statler Brothers Christmas Present* . . . . (Mercury)
Tony Bennett; *Snowfall: The Tony Bennett Christmas Album* . . . . . (Columbia)
Ventures; *Ventures' Christmas Album* . . . . (EMI)
Willie Nelson; *Pretty Paper* . . . . (Columbia)
Wynton Marsalis; *Crescent City Christmas Card* . . . . (Columbia)

Jingle Cats Medley
Jingle Cats; *Christmas Comedy Classics-#2-C* . . . . (Priority)

Jingle Hell
Space Negros; *Dark Side Of The Xmas Tree-C* . . . .(Performance)

Jingle Jangle
Archies; *Grooviest Hits Of The Archies* . . . .(Bac-Trac)
Penguins; *Doo-Wop Christmas-C* . . . . (Rhino)

Johnny Ace Christmas, A
Squirrel Nut Zippers; *Christmas Caravan* . . . .(Mammoth)

Jolly Old Saint Nicholas
Boots Randolph; *Boots And Stockings* . . . . . . (Sony Music Special Prod.)
Eddy Arnold; *Christmas With Eddy Arnold* . . . .(RCA)
Michael Martin Murphey; *Cowboy Christmas* . . . . (Warner Bros.)

Joseph And Mary's Boy
Alabama; *Alabama-Christmas* . . . . (RCA)

Joy To The World (Christmas)
Anne Murray; *Christmas Wishes* . . . . (Capitol)
Aretha Franklin; *Christmas Of Hope-C* . . . . (Columbia)
Billy Vaughn; *Christmas With Billy Vaughn* . . . . (Eclipse)
Traditional Christmas Classics . . . . (MCA Special Prod.)
Bob Rivers Comedy Corp.; *Twisted Christmas* . . . . (Critique)
Boston Pops Orchestra/Arthur Fiedler; *Christmas
Festival* . . . . (Deutsche Grammophon)
Brenda Lee; *Brenda Lee Christmas* . . . . (Warner Bros.)
Empire Brass; *Joy To The World-Music Of Christmas* . . . . (Angel)
Johnny Cash; *Nashville's Greatest Christmas Hits-C* . . . . (Columbia)
Kenny Rogers; *Christmas In America* . . . . (Reprise)
Larry Carlton; *Christmas At My House* . . . . (MCA)
Larry Gatlin & The Gatlin Brothers Band; *Christmas With Larry Gatlin &
The Gatlin Brothers* . . . . (Capitol)
Larry Groce & Disney Chorus; *Family Christmas* . . . . (Disney)
Liberace; *Liberace-Christmas* . . . . (MCA Special Prod.)
Mariah Carey; *Merry Christmas* . . . . (Columbia)
Mormon Tabernacle Choir; *Joy To The World* . . . . (Columbia)
Pat Boone; *White Christmas* . . . . (MCA Special Prod.)
Ronnie Milsap; *Christmas With Ronnie Milsap* . . . . (RCA)
Slim Whitman; *Country Christmas Classics* . . . . (Liberty)

Junk Bond Christmas Blues
Elmo Shropshire; *Dr. Elmo's Twisted Christmas* . . . . (Laughing Stock)

Just Put A Ribbon In Your Hair
Riders In The Sky; *Christmas The Country Way* . . . . (Rounder)

Kling, Glockshen
Mannheim Steamroller; *Christmas In The Aire* . . . . . . (American Gramaphone)

Lamb Of God
Donna Summer; *Christmas Spirit* . . . . (Mercury)

Last Christmas
Wham!; *All-Star Christmas-C* . . . . (Epic)

Leroy The Redneck Reindeer
Joe Diffie; *Country Christmas-#2-C* . . . . (Collectables)

Lesbians We Have Heard On High
Venus Envy; *I'll Be Homo For Christmas* . . . . (Venus Envy)

Let It Snow! Let It Snow! Let It Snow!
Asleep At The Wheel; *Merry Texas Christmas, Y'all* . . . . (High Street)
Bing Crosby; *Bing Crosby Christmas Classics* . . . . (Capitol)
Boys Choir Of Harlem; *Christmas Carols & Sacred Songs* . . . . (Blue Note)
Carpenters; *Carpenters Christmas Portrait* . . . . (A&M)
Charley Pride; *Country Christmas-#1-C* . . . . (RCA)
Dean Martin; *Now That's What I Call Christmas!-C* . . . . (UTV)
Winter Romance . . . . (Capitol)
Herb Alpert & The Tijuana Brass; *Herb Alpert & The Tijuana Brass
Christmas Album* . . . . (A&M)
Jackie Gleason; *'Tis The Season* . . . . (Capitol)
Joe Williams; *That Holiday Feelin'* . . . . (Verve)
Lee Greenwood; *Christmas In The Country-C* . . . . (MCA Special Prod.)
Country Christmas To Remember-C . . . . (MCA Special Prod.)
Lee Greenwood-Christmas To Christmas . . . . (MCA Special Prod.)
Manhattan Transfer; *Manhattan Transfer-The Christmas Album* . . . . (Columbia)
Marcus Roberts; *Merry Jazzmus* . . . . (Novus)
Marie Osmond; *Christmas Country Classics-#1-C* . . . . (Curb)
Miracles; *Christmas With The Miracles* . . . . (Motown)
Mitch Miller; *Yuletide Cheer-C* . . . . (Columbia)
Steve Wariner; *Steve Wariner Christmas Memories* . . . . . (MCA Special Prod.)
Temptations; *Christmas Card/Give Love At Christmas* . . . . (Motown)

Christmas Card/Give Love At Christmas . . . . (Motown)
Trisha Yearwood; *The Sweetest Gift* . . . . (MCA)
Vaughn Monroe; *Billboard's Greatest Christmas Hits-C* . . . . (Rhino)
Wynton Marsalis; *Crescent City Christmas Card* . . . . (Columbia)

Let's Make Christmas Mean Something This Year
James Brown; *Rockin' Christmas-The '60s-C* . . . . (Rhino)
  Santa's Got A Brand New Bag . . . . (Rhino)

Let's Make Christmas Merry, Baby
Amos Milburn; *Billboard's Greatest R&B Christmas Hits-C* . . . . (Rhino)
  Legends Of Christmas Past-Rock & R&B-C . . . . (EMI)

Let's Put The 'X' Back In Christmas
Pinkard & Bowden; *P.G. 13* . . . . (Warner Bros.)

Let's Unite The Whole World At Christmas
James Brown; *Santa's Got A Brand New Bag* . . . . (Rhino)

Light Of The Stable
Emmylou Harris; *Light Of The Stable* . . . . (Warner Bros.)
  Warner Bros. Christmas Tradition-C . . . . (Warner Bros.)
Judds; *Best Of Christmas-C* . . . . (RCA)
  Country Christmas-#3-C . . . . (RCA)
  Season's Greetings-C . . . . (RCA)

Linus & Lucy
Original Soundtrack; *Television's Greatest Hits-#2-C* . . . . (TVT)
Vince Guaraldi; *Charlie Brown Christmas* . . . . (Fantasy)

Little Alter Boy
Carpenters; *Carpenters Christmas Portrait* . . . . (A&M)

Little Boy That Santa Forgot
Nat "King" Cole; *Cole Christmas & Kids* . . . . (Capitol)
  Nat "King" Cole Christmas Gift Set . . . . (Capitol)

Little Bummer Boy
Jethros; *Dark Side Of The Xmas Tree-C* . . . .(Performance)

Little Christmas Tree
Michael Jackson; *Motown Christmas Album-C* . . . . (Motown)

Little Drum Machine Boy, The
Beck; *Just Say Noel-C* . . . . (Geffen)

Little Drummer Boy, The
4 Seasons; *4 Seasons Christmas Album* . . . . (Rhino)
Air Supply; *Air Supply Christmas Album* . . . . (Arista)
Alexander O'Neal; *My Gift To You* . . . . (Tabu)
Anne Murray; *Christmas Wishes* . . . . (Capitol)
Bob Seger & The Silver Bullet Band; *Very Special Christmas-C* . (A&M)
Boston Pops Orchestra/Arthur Fiedler; *Christmas Festival-C* . . . (RCA)
Brady Bunch Kids; *Christmas With The Brady Bunch* . . . . (MCA Special Prod.)
Burl Ives; *Have A Holly Jolly Christmas* . . . . (MCA Special Prod.)
Charlotte Church; *All-Star Christmas-C* . . . . (Epic)
David Bowie & Bing Crosby; *Bowie-The Singles-1969-1993* . . . . (Rykodisc)
  Now That's What I Call Christmas!-C . . . . (UTV)
Destiny's Child; *8 Days Of Christmas* . . . . (Columbia)
Diana Ross & The Supremes; *Merry Christmas* . . . . (Motown)
Dino; *Dino-Christmas Gift* . . . . (Benson)
Dolly Parton; *Home For Christmas* . . . . (Columbia)
Elvin Bishop; *Alligator Records Christmas Collection-C* . . . . . (Alligator)
Emmylou Harris; *Light Of The Stable* . . . . (Warner Bros.)
Four Tops; *Christmas Here With You* . . . . (Motown)
Hank Williams, Jr.; *Christmas Country Classics-#1-C* . . . . (Curb)
Harry Simeone Chorale; *Best Of Christmas-C* . . . . . . (Special Music Co.)
  Billboard's Greatest Christmas Hits-C . . . . (Rhino)
  Little Drummer Boy . . . . (Special Music Co.)
Henry Mancini; *Merry Mancini Christmas* . . . . (RCA)
Jackson 5; *Jackson 5-Christmas Album* . . . . (Motown)
Joan Jett & The Blackhearts; *I Love Rock 'n' Roll* . . . . . . (Blackheart)
Johnny Cash; *Billboard's Great Country Christmas Hits-C* . . . . (Rhino)
Larry Carlton; *Christmas At My House* . . . . (MCA)
Larry Gatlin & The Gatlin Brothers Band; *Christmas For The
  '90s-#1-C* . . . . (Liberty)
Lettermen; *For Christmas This Year* . . . . (Capitol)
Lou Rawls; *A Soulful Christmas-C* . . . . (Collectables)
Marlene Dietrich; *Best Of Christmas-C* . . . . (Capitol)
  Marlene . . . . (Capitol)
Mormon Tabernacle Choir; *White Christmas* . . . . (Columbia)
Neil Diamond; *Neil Diamond Christmas Album* . . . . (Columbia)
Peggy Lee; *Christmas Carousel* . . . . (Capitol)
Restless Heart; *Home For The Holidays-C* . . . . (RCA)
Stevie Wonder; *Someday At Christmas* . . . . (Motown)
Stylistics; *Stylistics-Christmas* . . . . (Amherst)
Temptations; *Christmas Card/Give Love At Christmas* . . . . . . (Motown)
  Give Love At Christmas . . . . (Motown)
  Motown Christmas Album-C . . . . (Motown)
Wynton Marsalis; *Crescent City Christmas Card* . . . . (Columbia)

Little Jack Frost Get Lost
Bing Crosby; *Voice Of Christmas-The Complete Decca Christmas
  Songbook* . . . . (Decca)

Little Saint Nick
Beach Boys; *Beach Boys Christmas Album* . . . . (Capitol)
  Billboard Rock 'N Roll Christmas-C . . . . (Rhino)
  Christmas All-Time Greatest Records-C . . . . (Curb)
  Legends Of Christmas Past-Rock & R&B-C . . . . (EMI)
  Now That's What I Call Christmas!-C . . . . (UTV)
  Party!/Stack-O-Tracks . . . . (Capitol)

Little Toy Trains
Forester Sisters; *Forester Sisters' Christmas Card* . . . . (Warner Bros.)

Lo, How A Rose E'er Blooming
Beane Music; *Christmas Classics From Around The World* . . . . (Critique)
John Fahey; *Christmas Guitar-#1* . . . . (Varrick)
New York City Gay Men's Chorus; *Christmas Comes Anew* . . . . (Virgin)
Pete Seeger; *Traditional Christmas Carols* . . . . (Smithsonian Folkways)
Philadelphia Brass Ensemble & Eugene Ormandy; *Festival Of Carols In
  Brass* . . . .(Columbia)
Trapp Family Singers; *Christmas With The Trapp Family
  Singers* . . . . (MCA Special Prod.)
Vienna Boys Choir; *Christmas Festival-C* . . . . (RCA)
Vienna Boys Choir & Hermann Prey; *Christmas With The Vienna Boys Choir
  & Hermann Prey* . . . . (RCA)

Log Cabin Home In The Sky
Michael Martin Murphey; *Cowboy Christmas* . . . . (Warner Bros.)

Lone Star Christmas
Lee Greenwood; *Lee Greenwood-Christmas To
  Christmas* . . . . (MCA Special Prod.)

Lonely Christmas
Ferlin Husky; *Christmas On The Range-Cowboy Classics-C* . . . . (Capitol)
Sonny Til & The Orioles; *Rhythm & Blues Christmas-#1-C* . . .(Collectables)
  Sonny Til & The Orioles' Greatest Hits . . . .(Collectables)

Lonely Christmas Eve
Ben Folds; *ST/How The Grinch Stole Christmas* . . . . (Interscope)

Lonely Night
Merle Haggard; *Goin' Home For Christmas* . . . . (Sony Music Special Prod.)

Looking For Christmas
Clint Black; *Looking For Christmas* . . . . (RCA)

Louisiana Christmas Day
Aaron Neville; *Soulful Christmas* . . . . (A&M)

Love Comes With Christmas
Temptations; *Give Love At Christmas* . . . . (Motown)

Love On Layaway
Gloria Estefan; *All-Star Christmas-C* . . . . (Epic)
  Now That's What I Call Christmas!-C . . . . (UTV)

Lullaby On Christmas Eve
Garrison Keillor; *Now It Is Christmas Again* . . . . (Angel)

Mama's Boy
Joel Nava; *Tejano Country Christmas-C* . . . . (Arista)

Man With All The Toys
Beach Boys; *Beach Boys Christmas Album* . . . . (Capitol)
  Ultimate Christmas . . . . (Capitol)

Mary, Did You Know?
Donny Osmond; *Christmas At Home* . . . . (Legacy)
Kathy Mattea; *Good News* . . . . (Mercury)

Mary's Boy Child
Andy Williams; *Merry Christmas* . . . . (Columbia)
Anne Murray; *Anne Murray Christmas* . . . . (Liberty)
Harry Belafonte; *Billboard's Greatest Christmas Hits-C* . . . . . . (Rhino)
  This Is Christmas-C . . . . (RCA)
Kiri Te Kanawa; *Christmas With Kiri Te Kanawa* . . . . (London)

Mary's Sweet Smile
Statler Brothers; *Statler Brothers Christmas Present* . . . . (Mercury)

Meet Me Under The Mistletoe
Randy Travis; *An Old Time Christmas* . . . . (Warner Bros.)

Mele Kalikimaka
Beach Boys; *Ultimate Christmas* . . . . (Capitol)
Bing Crosby; *Voice Of Christmas-The Complete Decca Christmas
  Songbook* . . . . (Decca)
Jimmy Buffett; *Christmas Island* . . . . (MCA)

Merry Christmas (I Don't Want To Fight Tonight)
Ramones; *Hey! Ho! Let's Go: The Anthology* . . . . (Rhino)

Merry Christmas Baby
Bonnie Raitt & Charles Brown; *Very Special Christmas-#2-C* . . . . . . (A&M)
Booker T. & The M.G.s; *Soul Christmas-C* . . . . (Atlantic)
Bruce Springsteen; *Very Special Christmas-C* . . . . (A&M)
Charles Brown; *Christmas Classics-C* . . . . (Rhino)
Chuck Berry; *Christmas Hits-C* . . . . (MCA Special Prod.)
  Cool Yule-C . . . . (Rhino)
  Have A Merry Chess Christmas-C . . . . (MCA Special Prod.)
  Rockin' Little Christmas-C . . . . (MCA)
  The Chess Box-Chuck Berry . . . . (Chess)
Elvis Presley; *If Every Day Was Like Christmas* . . . . (RCA)
  Memories Of Christmas . . . . (RCA)
  Reconsider Baby . . . . (RCA)
Ike & Tina Turner; *Best Of Cool Yule-C* . . . . (Rhino)
Johnny Moore's 3 Blazers; *Billboard's Greatest R&B Christmas
  Hits-C* . . . . (Rhino)
Lionel Hampton & His Orchestra; *Hipster's Holiday-Vocal Jazz &
  R&B-C* . . . . (Rhino)
Otis Redding; *The Otis Redding Story* . . . . (Atlantic)
Poets; *Rockin' Christmas-The '60s-C* . . . . (Rhino)

Merry Christmas From The Family
Rosie O'Donnell & Dixie Chicks; *Another Rosie Christmas-C* . . . . .(Columbia)

Merry Christmas I Love You
James Brown; *Funky Christmas* . . . . (Polydor)

Merry Christmas To You From Me
Marty Robbins; *Christmas With Marty Robbins* . . . . (Columbia)

Merry Christmas, Alabama
Jimmy Buffett; *Christmas Island* . . . . (MCA)

Merry Christmas, Baby
Beach Boys; *Beach Boys Christmas Album* .... (Capitol)
Merry Christmas, Darling
Carpenters; *Carpenters Christmas Portrait* .... (A&M)
From The Top .... (A&M)
Now That's What I Call Christmas!-C .... (UTV)
Dino; *Christmas...A Time For Peace* .... (Benson)
Fabulous Thunderbirds; *Christmas Party With Eddie G.-C* .... (Columbia)
Poppa Hop & His Orchestra; *Blue Yule-Christmas Blues & R&B Classics-C* .... (Rhino)
Uniques; *Doo-Wop Christmas-C* .... (Rhino)
Merry Texas Christmas You All
Ernest Tubb; *Christmas* .... (MCA Special Prod.)
Michael Martin Murphey; *Cowboy Christmas* .... (Warner Bros.)
Miss You Most (At Christmas Time)
Mariah Carey; *Merry Christmas* .... (Columbia)
Mistletoe And Me, The
Isaac Hayes; *A Soulful Christmas-C* .... (Collectables)
Monster's Holiday
Bobby "Boris" Pickett & The Crypt-Kickers; *Elvira Presents Revenge Of The Monster Hits-C* .... (Rhino)
Buck Owens; *Buck Owens Collection-1959-1990* .... (Rhino)
Lon Chaney; *Christmas Comedy Classics-C* .... (Priority)
Legends Of Christmas Past-Rock & R&B-C .... (EMI)
Most Wonderful Time Of The Year, The
Amy Grant; *Home For Christmas* .... (A&M)
Andy Williams; *Andy Williams Christmas Album* .... (Columbia)
Johnny Mathis; *Christmas Eve With Johnny Mathis* .... (Columbia)
Now That's What I Call Christmas!-C .... (UTV)
Rosemary Clooney; *White Christmas* .... (Concord Jazz)
Mr. Mistletoe
Lynn Anderson; *Lynn Anderson-Christmas Album* .... (Columbia)
Mr. Santa Claus
Nathaniel Mayer; *Rockin' Christmas-The '60s-C* .... (Rhino)
Mrs. Santa Claus
Nat "King" Cole; *Cole Christmas & Kids* .... (Capitol)
Mrs. Santa Claus
Skip Ewing; *Following Yonder Star* .... (MCA Special Prod.)
My Birthday Comes On Christmas
Spike Jones; *It's A Spike Jones Christmas* .... (Rhino)
Let's Sing A Song Of Christmas .... (Verve)
My Christmas Tree
Diana Ross & The Supremes; *Merry Christmas* .... (Motown)
Home Alone Children's Choir; *ST/Home Alone 2-Lost In New York* .... (Fox/Arista)
Temptations; *Christmas Card/Give Love At Christmas* .... (Motown)
My Favorite Things
Andy Williams; *Merry Christmas* .... (Columbia)
Barbra Streisand; *Barbra Streisand Christmas Album* .... (Columbia)
Betty Carter; *Compact Jazz-Betty Carter* .... (Verve)
Diana Ross & The Supremes; *Merry Christmas* .... (Motown)
Motown Christmas Album-C .... (Motown)
Herb Alpert & The Tijuana Brass; *Herb Alpert & The Tijuana Brass Christmas Album* .... (A&M)
John Coltrane; *Best Of John Coltrane* .... (Atlantic)
Johnny Mathis; *Give Me Your Love For Christmas* .... (Columbia)
Julie Andrews; *ST/The Sound Of Music* .... (RCA)
Kenny Rogers; *Kenny Rogers-Christmas* .... (EMI)
Lorrie Morgan; *Merry Christmas From London* .... (BNA)
My Mom And Santa Claus
George Jones; *Hillbilly Holiday-C* .... (Rhino)
My Only Wish (This Year)
Britney Spears; *Now That's What I Call Christmas!-C* .... (UTV)
Natividad Song
Freddy Fender; *Country Christmas To Remember-C* ...... (MCA Special Prod.)
Nestor, The Long Eared Christmas Donkey
Marty Robbins; *Christmas Remembered* .... (Sony Music Special Prod.)
New Deal For Christmas
Original Broadway Cast; *Annie* .... (Columbia)
New Year's Day
U2; *Under A Blood Red Sky* .... (Island)
War .... (Island)
Night Before Christmas
Amy Grant; *Home For Christmas* .... (A&M)
Carly Simon; *ST/This Is My Life* .... (Qwest)
Chipmunks; *Christmas With The Chipmunks-#2* .... (Gold Rush)
Gladys Knight & The Pips; *Bless This House* .... (Buddah)
Glen Campbell; *Merry Christmas* .... (Liberty)
Judy Collins; *Christmas At The Biltmore Estate* .... (Elektra)
Stan Freberg; *Christmas Kisses-Capitol's Early Years-C* .... (Capitol)
White Mountain Singers; *Folk Era Christmas* .... (Folk Era)
Night Before Christmas Song, The
Gene Autry; *Sing Cowboy Sing: The Gene Autry Collection* .... (Rhino)
No Christmas In Kentucky
Phil Ochs; *Toast To Those Who Are Gone* .... (Rhino)
No More Blue Christmas
Natalie Cole; *Holly & Ivy* .... (Elektra)
No Presents For Christmas
King Diamond; *Dark Sides* .... (Roadrunner)
King Diamond In Concert-1987-Abigail .... (Roadrunner)
No Reservation At The Inn
Statler Brothers; *Statler Brothers Christmas Present* .... (Mercury)
No Room At The Inn
Anne Murray; *Anne Murray Christmas* .... (Liberty)
James Cleveland; *Merry Christmas* .... (Savoy)
Mahalia Jackson; *Christmas With Mahalia Jackson* .... (Columbia)
Staple Singers; *Staple Singers-25th Day Of December* .... (Fantasy)
Nothing But A Child
Kathy Mattea; *Good News* .... (Mercury)
Nuttin' For Christmas
Barry Gordon; *Billboard's Greatest Christmas Hits-C* .... (Rhino)
Rosie O'Donnell & Smash Mouth; *Another Rosie Christmas-C* ..... (Columbia)
Stan Freberg; *Christmas Comedy Classics-C* .... (Priority)
Dr. Demento Presents The Greatest Novelty Records-#6-Christmas-C .... (Rhino)
Dr. Demento's Greatest Christmas CD-C .... (Rhino)
O Come All Ye Grateful Dead Heads
Bob Rivers; *Twisted Christmas* .... (Atlantic)
O Come, O Come, Emmanuel
Bryan Duncan; *Our Christmas-C* .... (Word)
Carpenters; *Carpenters Christmas Portrait* .... (A&M)
Eric Tingstad & Nancy Rumbel; *The Gift* .... (Sona Gaia)
Joan Baez; *Noel* .... (Vanguard)
Mike Reid; *Voices Of The Season-A Capella-C* .... (Epic)
Mormon Tabernacle Choir; *Joy To The World* .... (Columbia)
Mormon Tabernacle Choir Sings .... (Columbia)
New York Choral Artists; *O Come All Ye Faithful* .... (Angel)
Peter, Paul & Mary & The New York Choral Society; *Holiday Celebration* .... (Warner Bros.)
Philadelphia Orchestra & Eugene Ormandy; *Glorious Sound Of Christmas* .... (Columbia)
Riders In The Sky; *Christmas The Country Way* .... (Rounder)
O Holy Night
Al Green; *White Christmas* .... (Word)
Al Hirt; *Sound Of Christmas* .... (RCA)
Anne Murray; *Christmas Wishes* .... (Capitol)
Bing Crosby; *Bing Crosby Christmas Classics* .... (Capitol)
Carpenters; *Christmas Collection* .... (A&M)
Old Fashioned Christmas .... (A&M)
Destiny's Child; *8 Days Of Christmas* .... (Columbia)
Dino; *Dino-Christmas Gift* .... (Benson)
Donna Summer; *Christmas Spirit* .... (Mercury)
Ella Fitzgerald; *Ella Fitzgerald-Christmas* .... (Capitol)
Glen Campbell; *Christmas For The '90s-#2-C* .... (Liberty)
Jerry Butler; *A Soulful Christmas-C* .... (Collectables)
Jewel; *Joy: A Holiday Collection* .... (Atlantic)
Joan Baez; *Noel* .... (Vanguard)
John Denver; *Rocky Mountain Christmas* .... (RCA)
Larry Gatlin & The Gatlin Brothers Band; *Christmas With Larry Gatlin & The Gatlin Brothers* .... (Capitol)
Lee Greenwood; *Lee Greenwood-Christmas To Christmas* .... (MCA Special Prod.)
Lettermen; *For Christmas This Year* .... (Capitol)
Luciano Pavarotti; *O Holy Night* .... (London)
Miracles; *Christmas With The Miracles* .... (Motown)
Mormon Tabernacle Choir; *Holly & The Ivy* .... (Columbia)
Joy To The World .... (Columbia)
Mormon Tabernacle Choir Sings .... (Columbia)
Nat "King" Cole; *Nat "King" Cole Christmas Gift Set* .... (Capitol)
Neil Diamond; *Neil Diamond Christmas Album* .... (Columbia)
Patti LaBelle; *This Christmas* .... (MCA)
Peabo Bryson; *Peace On Earth* .... (Angel)
Reba McEntire; *Christmas In The Country-C* .... (MCA Special Prod.)
Merry Christmas To You .... (MCA Special Prod.)
Ronnie Milsap; *Christmas With Ronnie Milsap* .... (RCA)
Tracy Chapman; *Very Special Christmas-#3-C* .... (A&M)
O Little Town Of Bethlehem
Bing Crosby & Others; *Christmas Sing With Bing* .... (MCA Special Prod.)
Bobby Vinton; *Great Songs Of Christmas* .... (Curb)
Dino; *Christmas...A Time For Peace* .... (Benson)
Dolly Parton; *Home For Christmas* .... (Columbia)
Elvis Presley; *If Every Day Was Like Christmas* .... (RCA)
Emmylou Harris; *Light Of The Stable* .... (Warner Bros.)
Frank Sinatra; *Jolly Christmas from Frank Sinatra* .... (Capitol)
Gene Autry; *Christmas Cowboy, The* .... (Laserlight)
Julie Andrews; *Christmas With Julie Andrews* .... (Columbia)
Kenny Rogers; *Christmas In America* .... (Reprise)
King's College Choir; *Carols From King's College Choir* .... (Angel)
Mario Lanza; *Christmas With Mario Lanza* .... (RCA)
Mormon Tabernacle Choir; *Joy Of Christmas* .... (Columbia)
Spirit Of Christmas .... (Columbia)
Nat "King" Cole; *Peace On Earth* .... (Capitol)
Philadelphia Orchestra & Eugene Ormandy; *Greatest Christmas Hits* .... (Columbia)
Ray Price; *Nashville's Greatest Christmas Hits-C* .... (Columbia)
Roger Williams; *All-Time Christmas Favorites-#3-C* ..... (MCA Special Prod.)
Oh Christmas Tree (O Tannenbaum)
Chipmunks; *Christmas With The Chipmunks-#2* .... (Gold Rush)
David Benoit; *Christmastime* .... (Blue Moon)

Glenn Miller; *In The Christmas Mood* . . . . (Laserlight)
Jim Brickman; *The Gift* . . . . (Windham Hill)
Kevin Gibbs Trio; *Christmas Presence* . . . . (Concord Jazz)
Leontyne Price; *Christmas Songs* . . . . (London)
Michael W. Smith; *Christmastime* . . . . (Reunion)
Mormon Tabernacle Choir; *Joy To The World* . . . . (Columbia)
Nat "King" Cole; *Nat "King" Cole Christmas Gift Set* . . . . (Capitol)
Richard Clayderman; *Christmas Celebration-C* . . . . (Columbia)
Roger Wagner; *Caroles* . . . . (Capitol)
Wynton Marsalis; *Crescent City Christmas Card* . . . . (Columbia)

Oh! He Is Christmas
Take 6; *He Is Christmas* . . . . (Reprise)

Old Christmas Card
Forester Sisters; *Forester Sisters' Christmas Card* . . . . (Warner Bros.)
Jim Reeves; *Twelve Songs Of Christmas* . . . . (RCA)
Mickey Gilley; *Christmas At Gilley's* . . . . (Sony Music Special Prod.)

Old Fashioned Christmas
Jimmie Rodgers; *Christmas With Jimmie* . . . . (MCA Special Prod.)
Statler Brothers; *Statler Brothers Christmas Present* . . . . (Mercury)

Old Fashioned Christmas Polka
Riders In The Sky; *Christmas The Country Way* . . . . (Rounder)

Old Toy Trains
Billy Strange; *Railroad Man* . . . . (Crescendo)
Glen Campbell; *All-Star Country Christmas-C* . . . . (Capitol)
That Christmas Feeling . . . . (Capitol)
Statler Brothers; *Statler Brothers Christmas Present* . . . . (Mercury)

Old Year Is Gone
Johnny Paycheck; *45-#55* . . . . (Little Darlin')

On A Snowy Christmas Night
Elvis Presley; *Elvis Sings The Wonderful World Of Christmas* . . . (RCA)
If Every Day Was Like Christmas . . . . (RCA)

On Christmas Eve
John Hartford; *Headin' Down Into The Mystery Below* . . . . (Flying Fish)
Me Oh My-How The Time Does Fly-Anthology . . . . (Flying Fish)

On Christmas Morning
Michael McDonald; *In The Spirit-A Christmas Album* . . . . . (MCA)

On This Christmas Night
B.J. Thomas; *On This Christmas Night* . . . . (Liberty)

On This Night
Michael McDonald; *In The Spirit-A Christmas Album* . . . . . (MCA)

One Bright Star
John Jarvis; *Sounds Of The Season* . . . . (MCA Special Prod.)
Nicolette Larson; *Have Yourself A Merry Little Christmas-C* . . . . (Rhino)
Tennessee Christmas-C . . . . (MCA)
Vince Gill; *Let There Be Peace On Earth* . . . . (MCA)

One Christmas Tree
Nitty Gritty Dirt Band; *Christmas Album, The* . . . . (Rising Tide)

One Gift
Michael McDonald; *In The Spirit-A Christmas Album* . . . . . (MCA)

One God
Barbra Streisand; *Christmas Memories* . . . . (Columbia)

One Little Christmas Tree
Stevie Wonder; *Motown Christmas Album-C* . . . . (Motown)

Opera Of The Bells
Destiny's Child; *8 Days Of Christmas* . . . . (Columbia)

Our Love Is Like A Holiday
Michael Bolton; *Now That's What I Call Christmas!-C* . . . . (UTV)

Parade Of The Wooden Soldiers
Boston Pops Orchestra/Arthur Fiedler; *Christmas At The Pops* . . . . (RCA)
Harry Connick, Jr.; *When My Heart Finds Christmas* . . . . (Columbia)

Peace
Michael McDonald; *In The Spirit-A Christmas Album* . . . . . (MCA)

Pearls In The Snow
Michael Martin Murphey; *Cowboy Christmas* . . . . (Warner Bros.)

Percy, The Puny Poinsettia
Elmo & Patsy; *Grandma Got Run Over By A Reindeer* . . . . (Epic)

Pink Christmas
Leo Kottke; *Regards From Chuck Pink* . . . . (Private Music)

Platinum Bells
Destiny's Child; *8 Days Of Christmas* . . . . (Columbia)

Please Come Home For Christmas
Aaron Neville; *Soulful Christmas* . . . . (A&M)
Bon Jovi; *Very Special Christmas-#2-C* . . . . (A&M)
Charles Brown; *Billboard's Greatest Christmas Hits-C* . . . . (Rhino)
Eagles; *45-#45555* . . . . (Asylum)
Fats Domino; *Christmas Is A Special Day* . . . . (Right Stuff)
Freddy Fender; *Country Christmas To Remember-C* . . . . . (MCA Special Prod.)
Merry Christmas From Freddy Fender . . . . (MCA Special Prod.)
Tejano Country Christmas-C . . . . (Arista)
James Brown; *Santa's Got A Brand New Bag* . . . . (Rhino)
John Schneider; *Tennessee Christmas-C* . . . . (MCA)
Leon Rausch; *Rausch Touch* . . . . (Southland)
Little Johnny Taylor; *It's Christmas Time Again-C* . . . . (Stax)
Sawyer Brown; *Christmas For The '90s-#2-C* . . . . (Liberty)
Family Christmas Treasury-C . . . . (Liberty)

Poppa Santa Claus, (The Toys Gave A Party For)
Andrews Sisters; *Christmas* . . . . (CMC Special Prod.)

Postpone Christmas
Mutabaruka; *High Times All-Star Explosion* . . . . (Alligator)

Prarie Dog Christmas Ball, The
Riders In The Sky; *Christmas The Country Way* . . . . (Rounder)

Pretty Paper
Asleep At The Wheel; *Merry Texas Christmas, Y'all* . . . . (High Street)
Don McLean; *Christmas Country Classics-#1-C* . . . . (Curb)
Don McLean-Christmas . . . . (Curb)
Freddy Fender; *Country Christmas To Remember-C* . . . . . (MCA Special Prod.)
Glen Campbell; *Merry Christmas* . . . . (Liberty)
Randy Travis; *Old Time Christmas* . . . . (Warner Bros.)
Roy Orbison; *Legendary Roy Orbison* . . . . (Sony Music Special Prod.)
Roy Orbison's All-Time Greatest Hits-#1 & 2 . . . . (Monument)
Willie Nelson; *Best Of Christmas-C* . . . . (RCA)
Country Christmas-#1-C . . . . (RCA)
Hillbilly Holiday-C . . . . (Rhino)
Nashville's Greatest Christmas Hits-#2-C . . . . (Columbia)
What A Wonderful World . . . . (Columbia)

Prince Of Peace
Trans-Siberian Orchestra featuring Marlene Danielle; *Another Rosie*
Christmas-C . . . . (Columbia)

Reason For The Season
Patti LaBelle; *This Christmas* . . . . (MCA)

Redneck 12 Days Of Christmas
Jeff Foxworthy; *Crank It Up: The Music Album* . . . . (Warner Bros.)
Jeff Foxworthy's Greatest Bits . . . . (Warner Bros.)

Reindeer Boogie
Trisha Yearwood; *The Sweetest Gift* . . . . (MCA)

Reindeer Boogie
Hank Snow; *Hillbilly Holiday-C* . . . . (Rhino)

Remember (Christmas)
Nilsson; *Son Of Schmilsson* . . . . (RCA)

Ridin' Home On Christmas Eve
Michael Martin Murphey; *Cowboy Christmas* . . . . (Warner Bros.)

Rock And Roll Christmas
George Thorogood & The Destroyers; *Billboard Rock 'N Roll*
Christmas-C . . . . (Rhino)

Rockin' "J" Bells
Bobby Rey; *45-#4529* . . . . (Original Sound)

Rockin' Around The Christmas Tree
Amy Grant; *Home For Christmas* . . . . (A&M)
Bill Haley & His Comets; *Legends Of Christmas Past-Rock & R&B-C* . . . (EMI)
Brenda Lee; *Billboard's Greatest Christmas Hits-C* . . . . (Rhino)
Christmas Classics-C . . . . (Rhino)
Country Christmas To Remember-C . . . . (MCA Special Prod.)
Now That's What I Call Christmas!-C . . . . (UTV)
Yuletide Soiree-C . . . . (Rhino)
Cajun Gold; *Alligator Stomp-#4-Cajun Christmas-C* . . . . (Rhino)
Eddie Rabbitt; *Christmas For The '90s-#1-C* . . . . (Liberty)
Forester Sisters; *Forester Sisters' Christmas Card* . . . . (Warner Bros.)
Lynn Anderson; *Greatest Children's Christmas Hits-C* . . . . . . (Columbia)
Ronnie Spector & Darlene Love; *Very Special Christmas-C* . . . . (A&M)
Rosie O'Donnell & Jessica Simpson; *Another Rosie Christmas-C* . . . (Columbia)

Rockin' Little Christmas
Deborah Allen; *Country Christmas-#3-C* . . . . (RCA)
Season's Greetings-C . . . . (RCA)

Rosie Christmas
Donna Summer; *Another Rosie Christmas-C* . . . . (Columbia)

Round & Round The Christmas Tree
Frank Sinatra; *Christmas Sing With Frank And Bing* . . . . (Laserlight)

Ruby
Ray Charles; *Love Songs* . . . . (Rhino)

Rudolph The Reggae Reindeer
Bolivar; *Natty And Nice: A Reggae Christmas* . . . . (Rhino)

Rudolph, The Red Nosed Reindeer
Al Hirt; *Sound Of Christmas* . . . . (RCA)
Bing Crosby; *Bing Crosby Sings Christmas Songs* . . . . (MCA Special Prod.)
Brady Bunch Kids; *Christmas With The Brady Bunch* . . . . (MCA Special Prod.)
Burl Ives; *Have A Holly Jolly Christmas* . . . . (MCA Special Prod.)
Cadillacs; *Billboard's Greatest R&B Christmas Hits-C* . . . . (Rhino)
Conway Twitty; *Merry Twismas From C.T. & Little Friends* . . . . (Warner Bros.)
Crystals; *Christmas Gift For You From Phil Spector-C* . . . . (Rhino)
Phil Spector-Back To Mono 1958-1969-C . . . . (Abkco)
Phil Spector's Christmas Album-C . . . . (Passport)
Dean Martin; *Best Of Christmas-C* . . . . (Capitol)
Christmas All-Time Greatest Records-C . . . . (Curb)
Dolly Parton; *Home For Christmas* . . . . (Columbia)
Ernest Tubb; *Country Christmas To Remember-C* . . . . (MCA Special Prod.)
Gene Autry; *16 Most Requested Songs Of Christmas-C* . . . . (Legacy)
Billboard's Greatest Christmas Hits-C . . . . (Rhino)
Greatest Children's Christmas Hits-C . . . . (Columbia)
Now That's What I Call Christmas!-C . . . . (UTV)
Yuletide Soiree-C . . . . (Rhino)
Hank Thompson and His Brazos Valley Boys; *Christmas On The Range-*
Cowboy Classics-C . . . . (Capitol)
Jackson 5; *Jackson 5-Christmas Album* . . . . (Motown)
Johnny Mathis; *Christmas With Johnny Mathis* . . . . (Columbia)
Lena Horne; *Merry Christmas Baby-Romance & Reindeer-C* . . . . . . (Capitol)
Lynyrd Skynyrd; *Christmas Time Again* . . . . (CMC Int'l)
Merle Haggard; *Goin' Home For Christmas* . . . . (Sony Music Special Prod.)
Riders In The Sky; *Merry Christmas From Harmony Ranch* . . . . (Columbia)

Spike Jones; *It's A Spike Jones Christmas* (Rhino)
Stephanie Mills; *Stephanie Mills-Christmas* (MCA)
Temptations; *Christmas Card/Give Love At Christmas* (Motown)
Motown Christmas Album-C (Motown)

Run Rudolph Run
Bryan Adams; *Very Special Christmas-C* (A&M)
Chuck Berry; *Billboard's Greatest R&B Christmas Hits-C* (Rhino)
Rhythm & Blues Christmas-#1-C (Collectables)
The Chess Box-Chuck Berry (Chess)
Yuletide Soiree-C (Rhino)
Jimmy Buffett; *Christmas Island* (MCA)
Southern Pacific; *Warner Bros. Christmas Tradition-C* (Warner Bros.)

Sailing Home For Christmas
Doug Stone; *First Christmas* (Epic)

Sailor's Christmas
Jimmy Buffett; *Christmas Island* (MCA)

Same Old Lang Syne
Dan Fogelberg; *Dan Fogelberg/Greatest Hits* (Full Moon)
Innocent Age (Full Moon)
Live-Greetings From The West (Full Moon)

Santa & The Kids
Charley Pride; *Country Christmas-#3-C* (RCA)

Santa And The Satellite
Dickie Goodman; *Dr. Demento Presents The Greatest Novelty Records-#6-Christmas-C* (Rhino)

Santa Baby
Charmaine Neville; *Christmas In New Orleans-R&B Jazz Gospel* (Mardi Gras)
Eartha Kitt; *Billboard's Greatest Christmas Hits-C* (Rhino)
Hipster's Holiday-Vocal Jazz & R&B-C (Rhino)
Madonna; *Very Special Christmas-C* (A&M)
RuPaul; *Ho Ho Ho* (Rhino)

Santa Claus
Throwing Muses; *Hunkpapa* (Sire)

Santa Claus & His Old Lady
Cheech & Chong; *Dr. Demento Presents The Greatest Novelty Records-#6-Christmas-C* (Rhino)
Dr. Demento's Greatest Christmas CD-C (Rhino)

Santa Claus (I Still Believe In You)
Alabama; *Alabama-Christmas* (RCA)
Season's Greetings-C (RCA)

Santa Claus (It Must Have Been Ol')
Harry Connick, Jr.; *Now That's What I Call Christmas!-C* (UTV)
When My Heart Finds Christmas (Columbia)

Santa Claus And Popcorn
Merle Haggard; *Goin' Home For Christmas* (Sony Music Special Prod.)
Merle Haggard-Christmas Gift (Curb)

Santa Claus Blues
Louis Armstrong & King Oliver; *Louis Armstrong & King Oliver* (Milestone)
Walter Davis; *Cripple Clarence Lofton & Walter Davis* (Yazoo)

Santa Claus Came In The Spring
Benny Goodman; *Birth Of Swing* (Bluebird)

Santa Claus' Daughter
Charlie Rich; *Charlie Rich-Complete Smash Sessions* (Mercury)

Santa Claus Goes Straight To The Ghetto
James Brown; *Christmas Classics-C* (Rhino)
Cool Yule-C (Rhino)
Funky Christmas (Polydor)
Santa's Got A Brand New Bag (Rhino)

Santa Claus Is Back In Town
Dwight Yoakam; *Warner Bros. Christmas Tradition-C* (Warner Bros.)
Elvis Presley; *Elvis' Christmas Album* (RCA)
Elvis Presley Sings Leiber & Stoller (RCA)
Memories Of Christmas (RCA)
White Christmas (RCA)
Trisha Yearwood; *The Sweetest Gift* (MCA)

Santa Claus Is Comin' To Town
Andrews Sisters; *Christmas* (MCA Special Prod.)
Beach Boys; *Beach Boys Christmas Album* (Capitol)
Bing Crosby & The Andrews Sisters; *Merry Christmas* (MCA Special Prod.)
Booker T. & The M.G.s; *In The Christmas Spirit* (Rhino)
Boston Pops Orchestra/Arthur Fiedler; *Pop Goes Christmas* (RCA)
This Is Christmas-C (RCA)
Bruce Springsteen; *In Harmony 2-C* (Columbia)
Now That's What I Call Christmas!-C (UTV)
Chipmunks; *Christmas With The Chipmunks-#1* (EMI)
Crystals; *Phil Spector-Back To Mono 1958-1969-C* (Abkco)
Phil Spector's Christmas Album-C (Passport)
David Grisman; *Acoustic Christmas* (Rounder)
Dolly Parton; *Home For Christmas* (Columbia)
Eddie Fisher; *Christmas With Eddie Fisher* (MCA Special Prod.)
Eddy Arnold; *Christmas With Eddy Arnold* (RCA)
George Strait; *Christmas In The Country-C* (MCA Special Prod.)
Merry Christmas Strait To You (MCA Special Prod.)
Hank Thompson and His Brazos Valley Boys; *Christmas On The Range-Cowboy Classics-C* (Capitol)
Jackson 5; *Billboard's Greatest R&B Christmas Hits-C* (Rhino)
Johnny Mercer; *Christmas Kisses-Capitol's Early Years-C* (Capitol)
Judy Collins; *Christmas At The Biltmore Estate* (Elektra)
Loretta Lynn; *Christmas Without Daddy* (MCA Special Prod.)
Louis Armstrong & Pete Fountain; *Christmas In New Orleans* (MCA Special Prod.)
Michael Martin Murphey; *Warner Bros. Christmas Tradition-#2-C* (Warner Bros.)
Neil Diamond; *Neil Diamond Christmas Album* (Columbia)
Patti Page; *16 Most Requested Songs Of Christmas-C* (Legacy)
Pointer Sisters; *Very Special Christmas-C* (A&M)
Randy Travis; *An Old Time Christmas* (Warner Bros.)
Temptations; *Christmas Card/Give Love At Christmas* (Motown)
Ventures; *Ventures' Christmas Album* (EMI)
Whispers; *Happy Holidays To You* (Solar)

Santa Claus Is Coming For Christmas
Eddy Raven; *Country Christmas-#4-C* (RCA)

Santa Claus Is Skaing To Town
Granville Williams Orchestra; *Natty And Nice: A Reggae Christmas* (Rhino)

Santa Claus Schottische
Michael Martin Murphey; *Cowboy Christmas* (Warner Bros.)

Santa Claus Wants Some Lovin'
Albert King; *It's Christmas Time Again-C* (Stax)
Mack Rice; *It's Christmas Time Again-C* (Stax)

Santa Doesn't Cop Out On Dope
Martin Mull; *Mulling It Over: A Musical Oeuvre View* (Razor & Tie)
Sonic Youth; *Just Say Noel-C* (Geffen)

Santa Done Got Hip
Marquees; *Cool Yule-C* (Rhino)
Hipster's Holiday-Vocal Jazz & R&B-C (Rhino)

Santa I'm Right Here
Toby Keith; *Christmas To Christmas* (Polydor Country)

Santa Looked A Lot Like Daddy
Buck Owens; *All-Star Country Christmas-C* (Capitol)
Billboard's Great Country Christmas Hits-C (Rhino)
Christmas With Buck Owens (Curb)
Hillbilly Holiday-C (Rhino)
Buck Owens & The Buckaroos; *Merry Hee Haw Christmas* (Capitol)
Garth Brooks; *Beyond The Season* (Liberty)
Tractors; *Have Yourself A Tractors Christmas* (Arista)
Travis Tritt; *Christmas-Loving Time Of The Year* (Warner Bros.)
Travis Tritt Christmas (Warner Bros.)

Santa Must Be Polish
Bobby Vinton; *Great Songs Of Christmas* (Curb)

Santa, Are You Coming To Atlanta
Pake McEntire; *Country Christmas-#4-C* (RCA)
Season's Greetings-C (RCA)

Santafly
Martin Mull; *Mulling It Over: A Musical Oeuvre View* (Razor & Tie)

Santa's Beard
Beach Boys; *Beach Boys Christmas Album* (Capitol)

Santa's Gonna Take It All Back
Toby Keith; *Christmas To Christmas* (Polydor Country)

Santa's Got A Brand New Bag
Murphy's Law; *Best Of Times* (Relativity)

Secret Of Christmas
Johnny Mathis; *Christmas With Johnny Mathis* (Columbia)
Julie Andrews; *Christmas With Julie Andrews* (Columbia)

Senor Santa Claus
Elmo & Patsy; *Grandma Got Run Over By A Reindeer* (Epic)
Jim Reeves; *Twelve Songs Of Christmas* (RCA)

Sidemeat's Christmas Stew
Riders In The Sky; *Christmas The Country Way* (Rounder)

Silent Night
Aaron Neville; *Soulful Christmas* (A&M)
Anne Murray; *Christmas Wishes* (Capitol)
Asleep At The Wheel; *Merry Texas Christmas, Y'all* (High Street)
B.J. Thomas; *All Is Calm All Is Bright* (Columbia)
Baby Washington; *A Soulful Christmas-C* (Collectables)
Legends Of Christmas Past-Rock & R&B-C (EMI)
Only Those In Love (Collectables)
Barbra Streisand; *A Happening In Central Park* (Columbia)
Barbra Streisand Christmas Album (Columbia)
Just For The Record (Columbia)
BeBe & CeCe Winans; *BeBe & CeCe Winans-Christmas* (Sparrow)
Bing Crosby; *Christmas Sing With Bing* (MCA Special Prod.)
Boston Pops Orchestra/Arthur Fiedler; *Christmas Festival-C* (RCA)
Pop Goes Christmas (RCA)
Boyz II Men; *Now That's What I Call Christmas!-C* (UTV)
Connie Francis; *Christmas In My Heart* (Polydor)
Cristy Lane; *White Christmas* (Arrival)
Destiny's Child; *8 Days Of Christmas* (Columbia)
Dinah Washington; *Have Yourself A Jazzy Little Christmas-C* (Verve)
Dr. John; *Have Yourself A Merry Little Christmas-C* (Rhino)
Ella Fitzgerald; *Ella Fitzgerald-Christmas* (Capitol)
Elmo & Patsy; *Grandma Got Run Over By A Reindeer* (Epic)
Elvis Presley; *Blue Christmas* (RCA)
Elvis' Christmas Album (RCA)
Emmylou Harris; *Light Of The Stable* (Warner Bros.)
Engelbert Humperdinck; *Merry Christmas With Engelbert Humperdinck* (Epic)
Four Tops; *Christmas Here With You* (Motown)
Frank Sinatra; *Jolly Christmas from Frank Sinatra* (Capitol)

Garth Brooks; *Beyond The Season* .... (Liberty)
Christmas For The '90s#2-C .... (Liberty)
Family Christmas Treasury-C .... (Liberty)
Gary Morris; *Every Christmas* .... (Liberty)
Glen Campbell; *Merry Christmas* .... (Liberty)
Huey "Piano" Smith And The Clowns; *Best Of Cool Yule-C* ... (Rhino)
Impressions; *Funky Christmas* .... (Cotillion)
James Galway & The Royal Philharmonic; *James Galway's Christmas
Carol* .... (RCA)
Jerry Butler; *A Soulful Christmas-C* .... (Collectables)
Jim Hendricks; *Handcrafted Christmas* .... (Benson)
Joan Baez; *Noel* .... (Vanguard)
John Denver; *Rocky Mountain Christmas* .... (RCA)
John Schneider; *White Christmas* .... (Scotti Bros.)
Johnny Cash; *Christmas Spirit* .... (Columbia)
Classic Christmas .... (Sony Music Special Prod.)
Judds; *Christmas Time With The Judds* .... (RCA)
Julie Andrews; *Christmas With Julie Andrews* .... (Columbia)
Kenny Rogers & Dolly Parton; *Once Upon A Christmas* .... (RCA)
La Diferenzia; *Tejano Country Christmas-C* .... (Arista)
Mahalia Jackson; *Best Of Mahalia Jackson* .... (Kenwood)
Christmas With Mahalia Jackson .... (Special Music Co.)
Manhattan Transfer; *Manhattan Transfer-The Christmas Album* .. (Columbia)
Mannheim Steamroller; *Mannheim Steamroller-
Christmas* .... (American Gramaphone)
Mariah Carey; *Merry Christmas* .... (Columbia)
Merle Haggard; *Merle Haggard-Christmas Gift* .... (Curb)
Michael W. Smith; *Smith* .... (Word)
Mormon Tabernacle Choir; *Joy To The World* .... (Columbia)
Mormon Tabernacle Choir Sings .... (Columbia)
Nat "King" Cole; *Nat "King" Cole Christmas Gift Set* ...... (Capitol)
Neil Diamond; *Neil Diamond Christmas Album* .... (Columbia)
Oak Ridge Boys; *Oak Ridge Boys-Christmas* ...... (MCA Special Prod.)
Phil Spector & Artists; *Phil Spector-Back To Mono 1958-1969-C* ... (Abkco)
Philadelphia Orchestra & Eugene Ormandy; *Joy To The World* ... (RCA)
Reba McEntire; *Merry Christmas To You* .... (MCA Special Prod.)
Ronnie Milsap; *Christmas With Ronnie Milsap* .... (RCA)
Sister Rosetta Tharpe; *Billboard's Greatest R&B Christmas Hits-C* ... (Rhino)
Special EFX; *GRP Christmas Collection-C* .... (GRP)
Stanley Jordan; *Standards-#1* .... (Blue Note)
Yule Struttin'-C .... (Blue Note)
Stevie Nicks; *Very Special Christmas-C* .... (A&M)
Take 6; *He Is Christmas* .... (Reprise)
Tanya Tucker; *Country Christmas Favorites* .... (Columbia)
Jingle All The Way-C .... (Sony Music Special Prod.)
Temptations; *Christmas Card/Give Love At Christmas* ...... (Motown)
Motown Christmas Album-C .... (Motown)
Tim Fuller Experience; *Hipster's Holiday-Vocal Jazz & R&B-C* ... (Rhino)
Vienna Boys Choir; *Vienna Boys Choir* .... (RCA)
Waylon Jennings & Jessi Colter; *Best Of Christmas-C* .... (RCA)
Wayne Newton; *Best Of Christmas* .... (Capitol)
Wilson Phillips; *Very Special Christmas-#2-C* .... (A&M)
Zaca Creek; *Voices Of The Season-A Capella-C* .... (Epic)

Silver And Gold
Burl Ives; *Christmas Songs-C* .... (Sony Wonder)

Silver Bells
Atlantic Starr; *ST/Home Alone 2-Lost In New York* ...... (Fox/Arista)
Bob Wills; *Fiddle* .... (Country Music Foundation)
Booker T. & The M.G.s; *Soul Christmas-C* .... (Atlantic)
Brady Bunch Kids; *Christmas With The Brady Bunch* .... (MCA Special Prod.)
Brenda Lee; *Brenda Lee-Christmas* .... (Warner Bros.)
Diana Ross & The Supremes; *Merry Christmas* .... (Motown)
Dwight Yoakam; *Come On Christmas* .... (Reprise)
Earl Grant; *Winter Wonderland* .... (MCA Special Prod.)
Elvis Presley; *If Every Day Was Like Christmas* .... (RCA)
Memories Of Christmas .... (RCA)
Fats Domino; *Christmas Is A Special Day* .... (Right Stuff)
Gary Morris; *Every Christmas* .... (Liberty)
John Denver; *Rocky Mountain Christmas* .... (RCA)
Johnny Mathis & Percy Faith and his Orchestra; *Merry Christmas* ... (Columbia)
Judds; *Christmas Time With The Judds* .... (RCA)
Kenny Rogers; *Christmas In America* .... (Reprise)
Kevin Eubanks; *GRP Christmas Collection-C* .... (GRP)
Lacy J. Dalton; *Christmas For The '90s-#1-C* .... (Liberty)
Liberace; *That Old Christmas Feeling* .... (MCA Special Prod.)
Loretta Lynn; *Christmas Without Daddy* .... (MCA Special Prod.)
Margaret Whiting & Jimmy Wakely; *Christmas On The Range-Cowboy
Classics-C* .... (Capitol)
Merle Haggard; *Merle Haggard-Christmas Gift* .... (Curb)
Miracles; *Christmas With The Miracles* .... (Motown)
Mormon Tabernacle Choir; *White Christmas* .... (Columbia)
Oak Ridge Boys; *Oak Ridge Boys-Christmas* ...... (MCA Special Prod.)
Perry Como; *I Wish It Could Be Christmas Forever* .... (RCA)
Ray Price; *Christmas Gift For You From Ray Price* .... (Step One)
Roches; *We Three Kings* .... (Rykodisc)
Ronnie Milsap; *Christmas With Ronnie Milsap* .... (RCA)
Rosie O'Donnell & Sugar Ray; *Another Rosie Christmas-C* ... (Columbia)
Stevie Wonder; *Someday At Christmas* .... (Motown)
Travis Tritt; *Christmas-Loving Time Of The Year* ..... (Warner Bros.)

Sleep Well, Little Children
Rosemary Clooney; *White Christmas* .... (Concord Jazz)

Vanessa Williams; *Star Bright* .... (Mercury)

Sleigh Bells
Gene Autry; *Christmas Cowboy, The* .... (Laserlight)

Sleigh Ride
Amy Grant; *Amy Grant Christmas Album* .... (Word)
Andy Williams; *16 Most Requested Songs Of Christmas-C* ..... (Legacy)
A-Strings; *Home For Christmas* .... (Warner Bros.)
Bing Crosby; *Voice Of Christmas-The Complete Decca Christmas
Songbook* .... (Decca)
Boston Pops Orchestra/Arthur Fiedler; *Christmas
Festival* .... (Deutsche Grammophon)
Pops Go Christmas .... (RCA)
Carpenters; *Carpenters Christmas Portrait* .... (A&M)
Chipmunks; *Rockin' Through The Decades* .... (EMI)
Commodores; *Commodores-Christmas* .... (Commodores)
Debbie Gibson; *Very Special Christmas-#2-C* .... (A&M)
Doc Severinsen & The Tonight Show Orchestra; *Merry Christmas From Doc
Severinsen & The Tonight Show Orchestra* .... (Amherst)
Eddie Daniels; *GRP Christmas Collection-C* .... (GRP)
Ella Fitzgerald; *Now That's What I Call Christmas!-C* .... (UTV)
Garth Brooks; *The Magic Of Christmas: Songs From Call Me Claus* ... (Capitol)
Jack Jones; *Christmas All-Time Greatest Records-#2-C* .... (Curb)
London Symphony Orchestra; *Christmas Traditions* ... (Special Music Co.)
Mel Torme; *Christmas Songs* .... (Telarc)
Ronettes; *Christmas Gift For You From Phil Spector-C* ...... (Rhino)
Phil Spector-Back To Mono 1958-1969-C .... (Abkco)
Phil Spector's Christmas Album-C .... (Passport)
Squirrel Nut Zippers; *Christmas Caravan* .... (Mammoth)

Sleigh Ride Serenade
Bing Crosby; *Voice Of Christmas-The Complete Decca Christmas
Songbook* .... (Decca)
Clint Black; *Looking For Christmas* .... (RCA)

Snoopy's Christmas
Royal Guardsmen; *Snoopy & His Friends* .... (Laurie)

Snowbound
Barbra Streisand; *Christmas Memories* .... (Columbia)

Sock It To Me Santa
Bud Logan; *Cool Yule-C* .... (Rhino)

Some Children See Him
Dave Grusin; *GRP Christmas Collection-C* .... (GRP)
Debby Boone; *Home For Christmas* .... (Benson)
Evie Tornquist; *Come On Ring Those Bells* .... (Word)
Kenny Loggins; *December* .... (Columbia)
Tennessee Ernie Ford; *Star Carol* .... (Capitol)

Somebody Talkin' About Jesus
Kathy Mattea; *Good News* .... (Mercury)

Someday At Christmas
Jackson 5; *Jackson 5-Christmas Album* .... (Motown)
Stevie Wonder; *Christmas Classics-C* .... (Rhino)
Christmas Hits-C .... (MCA Special Prod.)
Motown Christmas Album-C .... (Motown)
Uptight (Everything's Alright) .... (Motown)
Temptations; *Christmas Card/Give Love At Christmas* ...... (Motown)

Soulful Christmas
James Brown; *Funky Christmas* .... (Polydor)

Sounds Of Christmas
Johnny Mathis; *Christmas With Johnny Mathis* .... (Columbia)

Special Gift
Isley Brothers; *Now That's What I Call Christmas!-C* .... (UTV)

Spending Christmas With The Blues
Floyd Miles; *Mountain To Climb* .... (Kingsnake)

Spread A Little Love On Christmas Day
Destiny's Child; *8 Days Of Christmas* .... (Columbia)
Another Rosie Christmas-C .... (Columbia)

Star Bright
Vanessa Williams; *Star Bright* .... (Mercury)

Step Into Christmas
Elton John; *Christmas Of Hope-C* .... (Columbia)
Rockin' Christmas-C .... (MCA Special Prod.)

Sweet Little Baby Boy
James Brown; *Funky Christmas* .... (Polydor)

Sweet Little Jesus Boy
Anne Murray; *Anne Murray Christmas* .... (Liberty)
Booker T. & The M.G.s; *In The Christmas Spirit* .... (Rhino)
Boys Choir Of Harlem; *Christmas Carols & Sacred Songs* ... (Blue Note)
Trisha Yearwood; *The Sweetest Gift* .... (MCA)

Sweetest Gift, The
Trisha Yearwood; *The Sweetest Gift* .... (MCA)

Swingin' Silent Nite
Asleep At The Wheel; *Merry Texas Christmas, Y'all* ...... (High Street)

Take A Walk Through Bethlehem
Trisha Yearwood; *The Sweetest Gift* .... (MCA)

Tennessee Christmas
Alabama; *Alabama-Christmas* .... (RCA)
Amy Grant; *Amy Grant Christmas Album* .... (Word)
Lee Greenwood; *Lee Greenwood-Christmas To
Christmas* .... (MCA Special Prod.)
Steve Wariner; *Country Christmas To Remember-C* ... (MCA Special Prod.)
Tennessee Christmas-C .... (MCA)

Thank God For Kids
Oak Ridge Boys; *Christmas For The '90s-#1-C* (Liberty)
Oak Ridge Boys' Greatest Hits 2 (MCA)
Oak Ridge Boys-Christmas (MCA Special Prod.)
Oak Ridge Boys-Collection (MCA)

Thank God It's Christmas
Queen; *Billboard Rock 'N Roll Christmas-C* (Rhino)
Queen Collection (Hollywood)

There Ain't No Santa Claus On The Evenin' Stage
Captain Beefheart; *The Spotlight Kid* (Reprise)

There's A New Kid In Town
Alan Jackson; *Honky Tonk Christmas* (Arista)
Kathy Mattea; *Good News* (Mercury)
Trisha Yearwood; *The Sweetest Gift* (MCA)

There's No Place Like Home For The Holidays
Perry Como; *Now That's What I Call Christmas!-C* (UTV)
Perry Como's Greatest Hits (RCA)

This Christmas
Alexander O'Neal; *My Gift To You* (Tabu)
Destiny's Child; *8 Days Of Christmas* (Columbia)
Donny Hathaway; *A Soulful Christmas-C* (Collectables)
Best Of Donny Hathaway (Atco)
Soul Christmas-C (Atlantic)
Gloria Estefan; *Christmas Through Your Eyes* (Epic)
Jets; *Christmas With The Jets* (MCA Special Prod.)
Joe; *Now That's What I Call Christmas!-C* (UTV)
Patti LaBelle; *This Christmas* (MCA)
Rula Brown; *Reggae Christmas-C* (Profile)
Stephanie Mills; *Stephanie Mills-Christmas* (MCA)
Temptations; *Give Love At Christmas* (Motown)
Yutaka; *GRP Christmas Collection-C* (GRP)

This Is The Way Christmas Ought To Be
Disney Players; *Christmas Carol-C* (Disney)

Thistlehair The Christmas Bear
Alabama; *Alabama-Christmas* (RCA)

Three Wise Men
Jim Nabors; *Christmas Album* (Columbia)

To Heck With Ole Santa Claus
Loretta Lynn; *Country Christmas* (MCA)
Hillbilly Holiday-C (Rhino)

To Make A Miracle
Michael McDonald; *In The Spirit-A Christmas Album* (MCA)

Tonight Is Christmas
Alabama; *Alabama-Christmas* (RCA)

Toyland
Dr. John; *Have Yourself A Merry Little Christmas-C* (Rhino)
Johnny Mathis; *Christmas Eve With Johnny Mathis* (Columbia)
Perry Como; *I Wish It Could Be Christmas Forever* (RCA)

Twas Da Nite
Take 6; *He Is Christmas* (Reprise)

'Twas The Night Before Christmas
Chipmunks; *TV Family Christmas-C* (Scotti Bros.)
Liberace; *Best Of Music* (Special Music Co.)
Peter, Paul & Mary & The New York Choral Society; *Holiday Celebration* (Warner Bros.)
Wynton Marsalis; *Crescent City Christmas Card* (Columbia)

Twelve Days Of Christmas
Allan Sherman; *Christmas Comedy Classics-#2-C* (Priority)
Dr. Demento Presents The Greatest Novelty Records-#6-Christmas-C (Rhino)
Andrews Sisters; *Andrews Sisters-Christmas* (MCA Special Prod.)
Bing Crosby; *That Christmas Feeling* (MCA Special Prod.)
Bob & Doug McKenzie; *Dr. Demento's Greatest Christmas CD-C* (Rhino)
David Seville & The Chipmunks; *Christmas With The Chipmunks-#2* (EMI)
Frank Sinatra; *Sinatra Christmas Album* (Reprise)
Fred Waring's Pennsylvanians; *Now Is The Caroling Season* (Capitol)
Garrison Keillor; *Now It Is Christmas Again* (Angel)
Harry Belafonte; *Christmas Classics-#2* (RCA)
Joan Sutherland; *Christmas Stars-C* (London)
John Denver; *A Christmas Together* (Laserlight)
Kiri Te Kanawa; *Christmas With Kiri Te Kanawa* (London)
Ray Conniff; *Christmas Wonderland* (Sony Music Special Prod.)

Twelve Days Of Cowboy Christmas, The
Riders In The Sky; *Christmas The Country Way* (Rounder)

Twelve Days To Christmas
Original Cast; *She Loves Me* (Polydor)

Twelve Gifts Of Christmas
Bob & Doug McKenzie; *Dr. Demento Presents The Greatest Christmas Novelty CD Of All Time-C* (Rhino)

Twelve Pains Of Christmas
Bob Rivers Comedy Corp.; *Twisted Christmas* (Critique)

Under The Mistletoe
Clint Black; *Looking For Christmas* (RCA)

Up On The House Top
Jimmy Buffett; *Christmas Island* (MCA)
Michael Jackson & The Jackson 5; *Jackson 5-Christmas Album* (Motown)

Various Tracks
Alligator Records; *Christmas Collection* (Alligator)

Virgen Maria (Why Are You Weeping?)
Riders In The Sky; *Christmas The Country Way* (Rounder)

We Have Love
Mickey Mouse (As Bob Cratchit); *Christmas Carol-C* (Disney)

We Need A Little Christmas
Angela Lansbury; *16 Most Requested Songs Of Christmas-C* (Legacy)
Johnny Mathis; *Christmas Music With Johnny Mathis-Personal Collection* (Columbia)
Original Cast; *Mame* (Columbia)
Percy Faith & His Orchestra; *Yuletide Cheer-C* (Columbia)

We Three Kings Of Orient Are
Adrian Belew; *Christmas Guitars-C* (Green Linnet)
Barbara Higbie; *Winter's Solstice-C* (Windham Hill)
Beach Boys; *Beach Boys Christmas Album* (Capitol)
Booker T. & The M.G.s; *In The Christmas Spirit* (Rhino)
Gary Morris; *Every Christmas* (Liberty)
Leontyne Price; *Christmas Stars-C* (London)
Mannheim Steamroller; *Mannheim Steamroller-Christmas* (American Gramaphone)
Michael W. Smith; *Christmastime* (Reunion)
Mojo Nixon & The Toadliquors; *Horny Holidays!* (Triple X Entert.)
Philadelphia Orchestra & Eugene Ormandy; *Greatest Christmas Hits* (Columbia)
Greatest Hits Of Christmas (RCA)
Robert Shaw Chorale; *Festival Of Carols* (RCA)
Teddy Pendergrass; *This Christmas (I'd Rather Have Love)* (Surefire)
Wynton Marsalis; *Crescent City Christmas Card* (Columbia)

We Want To See Santa Do The Mambo
Big John Greer; *Hipster's Holiday-Vocal Jazz & R&B-C* (Rhino)

We Wish You A Merry Christmas
Booker T. & The M.G.s; *In The Christmas Spirit* (Rhino)
David Grisman; *Acoustic Christmas* (Rounder)
Floyd Cramer; *We Wish You A Merry Christmas* (RCA)
Mormon Tabernacle Choir; *Joy To The World* (Columbia)
Perry Como; *I Wish It Could Be Christmas Forever* (RCA)
Peter, Paul & Mary & The New York Choral Society; *Holiday Celebration* (Warner Bros.)
Raffi; *Raffi Christmas Album* (Shoreline)
Tony Bennett; *Snowfall: The Tony Bennett Christmas Album* (Columbia)
Weavers; *We Wish You A Merry Christmas* (MCA Special Prod.)

We Wish You The Merriest
Frank Sinatra; *Sinatra Christmas Album* (Reprise)

We're A Couple Of Misfits
Burl Ives; *Rudolph The Red-Nosed Reindeer* (MCA Special Prod.)

What A Merry Christmas It Would Be
Ray Price; *Christmas Gift For You From Ray Price* (Step One)

What Are You Doing New Year's Eve
Andy Williams; *I Still Believe In Santa Claus* (Curb)
Barbra Streisand; *Christmas Memories* (Columbia)
Carpenters; *Old Fashioned Christmas* (A&M)
Gladys Knight & The Pips; *That Special Time Of Year* (Columbia)
Harry Connick, Jr.; *When My Heart Finds Christmas* (Columbia)
Joe Williams; *The Ultimate Joe Williams* (Verve)
Kay Kyser & His Orchestra; *Best Of The Big Bands: Christmas On The Bandstand-C* (Legacy)
King Curtis; *Soul Christmas-C* (Atlantic)
Lena Horne; *Happy Holidays-Capitol Sings Christmas-C* (Capitol)
Lou Rawls; *Merry Christmas Ho! Ho! Ho!* (Capitol)
Nancy Wilson; *A Soulful Christmas-C* (Collectables)
Yesterday's Love Songs...Today's Blues (Blue Note)
Orioles; *A Soulful Christmas-C* (Collectables)
Sonny Til & The Orioles; *Doo-Wop Christmas-C* (Rhino)
Rhythm & Blues Christmas-#1-C (Collectables)

What Can I Give
Mahalia Jackson; *Mahalia Sings Songs Of Christmas* (Legacy)

What Child Is This
Al Martino; *Best Of Christmas-C* (Capitol)
Bing Crosby; *Bing Crosby Christmas Classics* (Capitol)
Boston Pops Orchestra/Arthur Fiedler; *Pop Goes Christmas* (RCA)
David Benoit; *Christmastime* (Blue Moon)
Garth Brooks; *Beyond The Season* (Liberty)
Glen Campbell; *Home For The Holidays* (Benson)
Glenn Medeiros; *Glenn Medeiros-Christmas Album* (Amherst)
Harry Connick, Jr.; *When My Heart Finds Christmas* (Columbia)
Joan Baez; *Noel* (Vanguard)
John Anderson; *Sounds Of The Season* (BNA)
John Denver; *Rocky Mountain Christmas* (RCA)
Johnny Mathis; *Merry Christmas* (Columbia)
Judds; *Christmas Time With The Judds* (RCA)
Kathie Lee Gifford; *It's Christmas Time* (Warner Bros.)
Larry Coryell; *Christmas Guitars-C* (Green Linnet)
Martina McBride; *White Christmas* (RCA)
Mitch Miller; *Christmas Sing Along With Mitch* (Columbia)
Mormon Tabernacle Choir; *Holly & The Ivy* (Columbia)
Mormon Tabernacle Choir Sings (Columbia)
Roberta Flack; *Our Christmas-C* (Word)
Tanya Tucker; *Christmas For The '90s-#2-C* (Liberty)
Family Christmas Treasury-C (Liberty)
Vanessa Williams; *Very Special Christmas-#2-C* (A&M)
Vince Gill; *Let There Be Peace On Earth* (MCA)

Vince Guaraldi; *Charlie Brown Christmas* (Fantasy)
What Christmas Means To Me
Al Green; *White Christmas* (Myrrh)
Bing Crosby; *Christmas Sing With Bing* (MCA Special Prod.)
Hanson; *Snowed In* (Mercury)
Paul Young; *Very Special Christmas-C* (A&M)
Stevie Wonder; *Motown Christmas Album-C* (Motown)
Someday At Christmas (Motown)
What Do The Lonely Do At Christmas
Emotions; *A Soulful Christmas-C* (Collectables)
It's Christmas Time Again-C (Stax)
When It's Christmas Time In Texas
Rick Orozco; *Tejano Country Christmas-C* (Arista)
When My Heart Finds Christmas
Harry Connick, Jr.; *When My Heart Finds Christmas* (Columbia)
When The Rain Turns To Snow
Lee Greenwood; *Lee Greenwood-Christmas To Christmas* (MCA Special Prod.)
When The Stars Come Out For Christmas
Commodores; *Commodores-Christmas* (Commodores)
Where Are You Christmas
Faith Hill; *ST/How The Grinch Stole Christmas* (Interscope)
While Shepherds Watched Their Flocks
Fred Bock; *25 Piano Christmas Carols* (Benson)
Jim Hendricks; *20 Appalachian Christmas Carols* (Benson)
Mormon Tabernacle Choir; *Holly & The Ivy* (Columbia)
Spirit Of Christmas (Columbia)
White Christmas
Aaron Neville; *Soulful Christmas* (A&M)
Al Green; *White Christmas* (Word)
Andy Williams; *New Andy Williams Christmas Album* (Laserlight)
Baby Washington; *A Soulful Christmas-C* (Collectables)
Only Those In Love (Collectables)
Barbra Streisand; *Barbra Streisand Christmas Album* (Columbia)
Beach Boys; *Beach Boys Christmas Album* (Capitol)
Billy Squier; *45-#5037* (Capitol)
Bing Crosby; *Billboard's Greatest Christmas Hits-C* (Rhino)
Bing Crosby Sings Christmas Songs (MCA Special Prod.)
Now That's What I Call Christmas!-C (UTV)
Boston Pops Orchestra/Arthur Fiedler; *Christmas Treasures* (RCA)
Carpenters; *From The Top* (A&M)
Darlene Love; *Christmas Gift For You From Phil Spector-C* (Rhino)
Phil Spector-Back To Mono 1958-1969-C (Abkco)
Phil Spector's Christmas Album-C (Passport)
Dean Martin; *Making Spirits Bright* (Capitol)
Destiny's Child; *8 Days Of Christmas* (Columbia)
Diana Ross & The Supremes; *Merry Christmas* (Motown)
Dion; *Rock & Roll Christmas* (Right Stuff)
Dolly Parton; *Christmas Classics-#1* (RCA)
Don McLean; *Don McLean-Christmas* (Curb)
Donna Summer; *Christmas Spirit* (Mercury)
Drifters; *A Soulful Christmas-C* (Collectables)
Billboard's Greatest Christmas Hits-C (Rhino)
Christmas Classics-C (Rhino)
Drifters-Their Greatest Recordings (Atco)
ST/Home Alone (Columbia)
Earl Thomas Conley; *Season's Greetings-C* (RCA)
Elvis Presley; *Elvis' Christmas Album* (RCA)
Ernest Tubb; *Billboard's Great Country Christmas Hits-C* (Rhino)
Faron Young; *Country Christmas* (Step One)
Frank Sinatra; *Frank Sinatra Christmas Album* (Columbia)
Garth Brooks; *Beyond The Season* (Liberty)
George Strait; *Christmas In The Country-C* (MCA Special Prod.)
Merry Christmas Strait To You (MCA Special Prod.)
Glen Campbell; *Merry Christmas* (Liberty)
Gloria Estefan; *Christmas Through Your Eyes* (Epic)
Henry Mancini; *Merry Mancini Christmas* (RCA)
Jackie Wilson; *Merry Christmas From Jackie Wilson* (Rhino)
Jerry Jeff Walker; *Christmas Gonzo Style* (Rykodisc)
Jimmy Smith; *Christmas Cookin'* (Verve)
Jo Stafford; *Puttin' On The Ritz-Capitol Sings Berlin-C* (Capitol)
John Denver; *Rocky Mountain Christmas* (RCA)
Johnny Mathis; *Christmas Music With Johnny Mathis-Personal Collection* (Columbia)
Jose Carreras/Placido Domingo/Luciano Pavarotti; *Christmas Favorites From The World's Tenors* (Sony Music Classical)
Kathie Lee Gifford; *It's Christmas Time* (Warner Bros.)
Kenny Loggins; *December* (Columbia)
Kenny Rogers; *Kenny Rogers-Christmas* (EMI)
Lee Ritenour; *GRP Christmas Collection-C* (GRP)
Lena Horne; *Merry From Lena* (EMI)
Loretta Lynn; *Christmas Without Daddy* (MCA Special Prod.)
Country Christmas (MCA)
Mel Tillis; *Christmas On The General Jackson-C* (Mercury)
Merle Haggard; *Merle Haggard-Christmas Gift* (Curb)
Michael Bolton; *Timeless-Classics* (Columbia)
Very Special Christmas-#2-C (A&M)
Neil Diamond; *Neil Diamond Christmas Album* (Columbia)
Oak Ridge Boys; *Oak Ridge Boys-Christmas* (MCA Special Prod.)
Otis Redding; *A Soulful Christmas-C* (Collectables)
The Otis Redding Story (Atlantic)
The Ultimate R&B Christmas-C (Right Stuff)
Reba McEntire; *Merry Christmas To You* (MCA Special Prod.)
Roger Williams; *Golden Christmas* (Special Music Co.)
Statues; *Doo-Wop Christmas-C* (Rhino)
Stephanie Mills; *Stephanie Mills-Christmas* (MCA)
Tony Bennett; *16 Most Requested Songs Of Christmas-C* (Legacy)
Essence Of Christmas (Columbia)
Vince Gill; *Let There Be Peace On Earth* (MCA)
Wayne Newton; *Merry Christmas From Wayne Newton* (Curb)
Wesley Tuttle; *Christmas On The Range-Cowboy Classics-C* (Capitol)
White Christmas Makes Me Blue
Randy Travis; *An Old Time Christmas* (Warner Bros.)
Christmas Tradition (Warner Bros.)
Who Do You Think
Statler Brothers; *Statler Brothers Christmas Present* (Mercury)
Who Is This Babe
Judds; *Christmas Time With The Judds* (RCA)
Country Christmas-#4-C (RCA)
Who Took The Merry Out Of Christmas
Staple Singers; *A Soulful Christmas-C* (Collectables)
Bummed Out Christmas-C (Rhino)
Complete Stax/Volt Soul Singles-#2-C (Stax)
It's Christmas Time Again-C (Stax)
Who Would Have Thought
Boyz II Men; *Christmas Interpretations* (Motown)
Whose Birthday Is Christmas
Statler Brothers; *Statler Brothers Christmas Present* (Mercury)
Why Christmas
Boyz II Men; *Christmas Interpretations* (Motown)
Why Do The Nations So Furiously Rage
Al Jarreau; *Handel's Messiah-Soulful Celebration-C* (Warner Bros.)
Will 2K
Will Smith; *Willenium* (Columbia)
Winter Paradise
Destiny's Child; *8 Days Of Christmas* (Columbia)
Winter Wonderland
Air Supply; *Air Supply Christmas Album* (Arista)
White Christmas (Word)
Alexander O'Neal; *My Gift To You* (Tabu)
Amy Grant; *Home For Christmas* (A&M)
Andrews Sisters; *Andrews Sisters-Christmas* (MCA Special Prod.)
Anne Murray; *Best Of The Season* (EMI America)
Aretha Franklin; *Rock 'N' Roll Christmas Classics-C* (Music For Little People)
Barbara Mandrell; *Christmas At Our House* (MCA Special Prod.)
Tennessee Christmas-C (MCA)
Bing Crosby; *Bing Crosby Christmas Classics* (Capitol)
Blue Notes; *Rhythm & Blues Christmas-#1-C* (Collectables)
Brenda Lee; *Jingle Bell Rock* (MCA Special Prod.)
Carnie & Wendy Wilson; *Hey Santa!* (SBK)
Darlene Love; *Christmas Gift For You From Phil Spector-C* (Rhino)
Phil Spector-Back To Mono 1958-1969-C (Abkco)
Phil Spector's Christmas Album-C (Passport)
Eddy Arnold; *Christmas With Eddy Arnold* (RCA)
Elvis Presley; *If Every Day Was Like Christmas* (RCA)
Eurythmics; *Very Special Christmas-C* (A&M)
Faron Young; *Country Christmas* (Step One)
Frank Sinatra; *Christmas Songs By Sinatra* (Legacy)
George Strait; *Merry Christmas Strait To You* (MCA Special Prod.)
Hank Crawford; *We Got A Good Thing Going* (Kudo)
Johnny Mercer & The Pied Pipers; *Merry Christmas Baby-Romance & Reindeer-C* (Capitol)
Kathie Lee Gifford; *It's Christmas Time* (Warner Bros.)
Kenny Rogers; *Christmas In America* (Reprise)
London Symphony Orchestra; *Christmas Traditions* (Special Music Co.)
Merle Haggard; *Merle Haggard-Christmas Gift* (Curb)
Patti LaBelle & The Blue Belles; *A Soulful Christmas-C* (Collectables)
Randy Travis; *An Old Time Christmas* (Warner Bros.)
Robert Goulet; *Essence Of Christmas* (A&M)
Rosie O'Donnell & Macy Gray; *Another Rosie Christmas-C* (Columbia)
Tanya Tucker; *Christmas For The '90s-#1-C* (Liberty)
Tony Bennett; *Now That's What I Call Christmas!-C* (UTV)
Travis Tritt; *Christmas-Loving Time Of The Year* (Warner Bros.)
With A Christmas Heart
Luther Vandross; *This Is Christmas* (Epic)
With Christmas Near
Ray Price; *Christmas Gift For You From Ray Price* (Step One)
Wonderful Christmastime
Paul McCartney; *Now That's What I Call Christmas!-C* (UTV)
Superstars Of Christmas 1995 (Capitol)
Wings; *Back To The Egg* (Capitol)
Wonderful World Of Christmas
Elvis Presley; *If Every Day Was Like Christmas* (RCA)
World Out Of A Dream
Michael McDonald; *In The Spirit-A Christmas Album* (MCA)
Wreck The Halls With Boughs Of Holly
Three Stooges; *Christmas Time With The Three Stooges* (Rhino)
Dr. Demento Presents The Greatest Novelty Records-#6-Christmas-C (Rhino)

X-Mas Shopping Blues
Christmas Jug Band; *Mistletoe Jam* . . . . (Relix)
Yah Das Ist Ein Christmas Tree
Mel Blanc; *Christmas Comedy Classics-#2-C* . . . . (Priority)
Christmas Kisses-Capitol's Early Years-C . . . . (Capitol)
Yingle Bells
Yogi Yorgesson; *45-#3904* . . . . (Capitol)
Yo Ho Ho
Klark Kent; *Just In Time For Christmas-C* . . . .(I.R.S.)
You Are My Christmas
Bobby Bland; *You've Got Me Loving You* . . . . (Universal)
You Don't Have To Be Alone
'N Sync; *ST/How The Grinch Stole Christmas* . . . . (Interscope)
You Don't Have To Be Alone (On Christmas)
'N Sync; *Now That's What I Call Christmas!-C* . . . . (UTV)
You Make It Feel Like Christmas
Neil Diamond; *Neil Diamond Christmas Album* . . . . (Columbia)
Primitive . . . . (Columbia)
You're A Mean One, Mr. Grinch
Thurl Ravenscroft; *Yuletide Soiree-C* . . . . (Rhino)
You're All I Want For Christmas
Al Martino; *Merry Christmas Baby-Romance & Reindeer-C* . . . . (Capitol)
Bing Crosby; *Bing Crosby Sings Christmas Songs* . . . . (MCA Special Prod.)
That Christmas Feeling . . . . (MCA Special Prod.)
Brook Benton; *Best Of Christmas-C* . . . .(Special Music Co.)
Merry Christmas . . . . (Special Music Co.)
Jackie Gleason; *'Tis The Season* . . . . (Capitol)
'Zat You, Santa Claus?
Louis Armstrong & The Commanders; *Hipster's Holiday-Vocal Jazz &*
R&B-C . . . . (Rhino)
Soul Of Christmas-#2-C . . . . (Malaco)
What A Wonderful Christmas . . . . (Hip-O)

CIGARETTES, Ashtrays, Cigars, Smoking, Tobacco
See Also: DRUGS: GENERAL (addictions), FIRE

90 Minute Cigarette
John Hart; *Blue Guitar* . . . . (Blue Note)
Another Cup Of Coffee & A Cigarette
Robbin Thompson; *Robbin Thompson* . . . . (Nemperor)
Another Pack Of Cigarettes...
Marty Robbins; *The Performer* . . . . (Columbia)
Ashtray Blues
Papa Charlie Jackson; *Papa Charlie Jackson* . . . . (Biograph)
Ashtray Heart
Captain Beefheart; *Doc At The Radar Station* . . . . (Blue Plate)
Ashtray Taxi
Sam Chatmon; *Sam Chatmon's Advice* . . . . (Rounder)
Big Spender (Muriel Cigars)
Original Soundtrack; *TeeVee Toons-The Commercials-#1-C* . . . . (TVT)
Can I Have A Smoke, Dude?
Mary's Danish; *Edge Of Rock-C* . . . . (Era)
There Goes The Wondertruck . . . . (Chameleon)
Cigarette
Ben Folds Five; *Whatever And Ever Amen* . . . .(Caroline/550)
Smithereens; *Especially For You* . . . . (Enigma)
Cigarette Motel
Leaving Trains; *Kill Tunes* . . . .(SST)
Cigarette Of A Single Man
Squeeze; *Babylon & On* . . . . (A&M)
Cigarettes
City Boy; *Book Early* . . . . (Mercury)
Cigarettes & Alcohol
Oasis; *Definitely Maybe* . . . .(Epic)
Rod Stewart; *When We Were The New Boys* . . . .(Warner Bros.)
Cigarettes & Coffee
Otis Redding; *Best Of Otis Redding* . . . . (Atco)
Best Of Otis Redding . . . . (Atlantic)
The Otis Redding Story . . . . (Atlantic)
Cowboy Serenade (While I'm Rollin' My Last Cigarette)
Glenn Miller & His Orchestra; *Complete Glenn Miller & His*
Orchestra . . . . (Bluebird)
Dim Lights Thick Smoke & Loud Loud Music
Flatt & Scruggs; *Golden Era* . . . . (Rounder)
Flying Burrito Brothers; *Close Encounters To The West Coast* . . . . (Relix)
Farther Along-Best Of The Flying Burrito Brothers . . . . (A&M)
Ricky Skaggs and Kentucky Thunder; *History Of The Future* . . (Skaggs Family)
Don't Smoke In Bed
Nina Simone; *Finest Of* . . . .(Bethlehem)
Nina Simone In Concert/I Put A Spell On You . . . . (Mercury)
Peggy Lee; *Capitol Collectors Series-Peggy Lee-#1-Early Years* . . . . . (Capitol)
Peggy Lee's Greatest Hits . . . . (Capitol)
Flowers On The Wall
Eric Heatherly; *Swimming In Champagne* . . . . (Mercury)
Statler Brothers; *All Time Legends Of Country Music-C* . . . . (Legacy)

Best Of The Statler Brothers . . . . (Mercury)
Billboard Top Country Hits-1966-C . . . . (Rhino)
Columbia Country Classics-#3-Americana-C . . . . (Columbia)
Pop Classics Of The '60s-C . . . . (Columbia)
Fool About A Cigarette
Tom Ball & Kenny Sultan; *Bloodshot Eyes* . . . . (Flying Fish)
Fool For A Cigarette
Ry Cooder; *Paradise And Lunch* . . . .(Reprise)
Have A Cigar
Pink Floyd; *Wish You Were Here* . . . . (Columbia)
I'm Down To My Last Cigarette
k.d. lang; *Shadowland* . . . .(Sire)
King Of The Road
R.E.M.; *Dead Letter Office* . . . . (I.R.S.)
Roger Miller; *Billboard Top Country Hits-1965-C* . . . . (Rhino)
Cruisin'-1965-C . . . . (Increase)
Roger Miller-Golden Hits . . . .(Smash)
Last Cigarette
Dramarama; *Live At The China Club* . . . . (Chameleon)
Stuck In Wonderamaland . . . . (Chameleon)
Lipstick Traces (On A Cigarette)
Amazing Rhythm Aces; *Amazing Rhythm Aces* . . . . (MCA)
Benny Spellman; *Fortune Teller-Golden Classics* . . . . (Collectables)
History Of New Orleans R&B-#3-1962-1970-C . . . . (Rhino)
It Will Stand-Minit Records-1960-1963-C . . . . (EMI)
Delbert McClinton; *Live From Austin* . . . . (Alligator)
Plain From The Heart-Classics-#2 . . . . (Curb)
O'Jays; *Beg, Scream & Shout! The Big Ol' Box Of '60s Soul-C* . . . . . . (Rhino)
Soul Shots-#10-More Sweet Soul-C . . . . (Rhino)
Ringo Starr; *Bad Boy* . . . . (Epic)
Long Drag Off A Cigarette
Joe Cocker; *Civilized Man* . . . . (Capitol)
Love Is Like A Cigarette
Duke Ellington; *Rockin' In Rhythm* . . . . (ASV)
Man From The South, The
Ted Weems & His Orchestra; *78-#22238* . . . . (Victor)
Marlboro Song, The (Theme From "Magnificent 7")
Original Soundtrack; *TeeVee Toons-The Commercials-#1-C* . . . . (TVT)
Miles Is A Cigarette
Chris Rea; *Espresso Logic* . . . .(East West)
Nicotine Stain
Siouxsie And The Banshees; *The Scream* . . . . (Geffen)
Old King Cole
Original Soundtrack; *Children's Favorites* . . . .(Kid Rhino/Rhino 4 Kids)
One Paper Kid
Emmylou Harris; *Quarter Moon In A Ten Cent Town* . . . . (Warner Bros.)
Pack Of Pall Malls
Joe LoCascio; *Marionette* . . . . (Chase Music Group)
Pack Of Winstons
Green & Checkers; *Green & Checkers* . . . .(Trip)
Papa Rolled His Own
Tommy James And The Shondells; *Crimson & Clover/Cellophane*
Symphony . . . . (Rhino)
Papirossen (Cigarettes)
Gordon Jenkins; *Soul Of A People* . . . . (Bainbridge)
Peace Pipe
Cry Of Love; *Brother* . . . . (Columbia)
Peace Pipe
Edgar Winter; *Entrance* . . . . (Epic)
Pick One Up And Smoke It Sometime (Muriel Cigars)
Original Soundtrack; *TeeVee Toons-The Commercials-#1-C* . . . . (TVT)
Pope On A Rope (Cigarette Butt)
Squirrels; *What Gives?* . . . .(Pop Llama Prod.)
Roll Your Own
Hoyt Axton; *Southbound* . . . . (A&M)
Smoke (La Vie En Fumer)
Tubes; *Tubes Now* . . . . (A&M)
What Do You Want From Live . . . . (A&M)
Smoke Dreams (Chesterfield Supper Club)
Benny Goodman; *Complete Benny Goodman-#3* . . . . (RCA)
This Is Benny Goodman-#2 . . . . (RCA)
Mildred Bailey; *Her Greatest* . . . . (Columbia)
Smoke From Your Cigarette
Belmonts; *Lost Treasures* . . . .(Relic)
Fabulous; *Harlem Holiday-New York Rhythm & Blues-#7-C* . . . . (Collectables)
Mellows; *Yesterday's Memories* . . . .(Relic)
Smoke Rings
Django Reinhardt Quintet; *Django 1935* . . . .(Crescendo)
Glen Gray; *Best Of The Big Bands-C* . . . . (Columbia)
Glen Gray & The Casa Loma Orchestra; *ST/Wild At Heart* . . . . (Polydor)
Les Paul; *Legend & The Legacy-#1-4* . . . . (Capitol)
Smoke Rings In The Dark
Gary Allan; *Smoke Rings In The Dark* . . . . (MCA)
Smoke! Smoke! Smoke!
Commander Cody & His Lost Planet Airmen; *Country Casanova* . . . . . (MCA)
Too Much Fun-Best Of Commander Cody & His Lost Planet Airmen . . (MCA)
We've Got A Live One Here! . . . . (Warner Bros.)
Doc Watson; *Red Rocking Chair* . . . .(Flying Fish)

Johnny Bond & His Red River Valley Boys; *All Time Legends Of Country Music-C* .... (Legacy)
Merle Travis; *Johnny Gimble's Texas Honky-Tonk Hits-C* ...... (C.M.H. Prod.)
Tex Williams; *Birth Of A Dream-Capitol's Early Hits-C* .... (Capitol)
  Dr. Demento Presents The Greatest Novelty Records-#1-1940s & Before-C .... (Rhino)
Smoke-Off
Shel Silverstein; *Songs & Stories* .... (Parachute)
Smokin' Cigarettes & Drinkin' Coffee Blues
David Ball; *David Ball* .... (BMG Special Prod.)
Marty Robbins; *Essential Marty Robbins-1951-1982* .... (Columbia)
Smokin' In The Boy's Room
Brownsville Station; *Hit Singles-1958-1977-C* .... (Atlantic)
  Legends Of Rock Guitar-'70s-C .... (Rhino)
  ST/Rock 'N' Roll High School. .... (Sire)
Motley Crue; *Decade Of Decadence* .... (Elektra)
  Theatre Of Pain .... (Elektra)
Smokin' Room
Randy Brown; *Check It Out.* .... (Stax)
Ronnie Milsap; *Star Spangled Country-C* .... (RCA)
Rufus; *Rags To Rufus* .... (MCA)
Some Broken Hearts Never Mend
Don Williams; *Best Of Don Williams-#2.* .... (MCA)
  Don Williams-20 Greatest Hits. .... (MCA)
  Some Broken Hearts Never Mend. .... (MCA Special Prod.)
Spark
Tori Amos; *From The Choirgirl Hotel* .... (Atlantic)
Talking Cancer Blues
Dave Van Ronk; *Inside Dave Van Ronk* .... (Fantasy)
  Van Ronk .... (Fantasy)
Three Cigarettes In An Ashtray
k.d. lang; *New Tradition Sings The Old Tradition-C* .... (Warner Bros.)
k.d. lang and The Reclines; *Angel With A Lariat* .... (Sire)
Patsy Cline; *20 Golden Pieces Of Patsy Cline* .... (Bulldog)
  Patsy Cline .... (MCA)
  Stop Look & Listen .... (MCA)
  Walkin' Dreams-Her First Recordings-#1 .... (Rhino)
To A Smoker It's A Kent
Original Soundtrack; *TeeVee Toons-The Commercials-#1-C* ...... (TVT)
Tobacco Box
Cumberland Three; *Songs Of The Civil War-C* .... (Rhino)
Tobacco Road
Dan Seals; *Won't Be Blue Anymore* .... (EMI)
David Lee Roth; *Eat 'Em & Smile* .... (Warner Bros.)
Edgar Winter; *Edgar Winter Group-Collection* .... (Rhino)
  Entrance .... (Epic)
Edgar Winter's White Trash; *Roadwork* .... (Epic)
Eric Burdon; *Eric Burdon Sings The Animals' Greatest Hits* .... (Rhino)
Jefferson Airplane; *Loves You* .... (RCA)
  Takes Off. .... (RCA)
John D. Loudermilk; *Rockabilly Stars-#3-C* .... (Epic)
Junior Wells; *Best Of The Chicago Blues-C* .... (Vanguard)
  Comin' At You. .... (Vanguard)
Lou Rawls; *Best From Lou Rawls* .... (Capitol)
  Legendary Lou Rawls .... (Blue Note)
  Lou Rawls' Greatest Hits .... (Curb)
  Lou Rawls-Live. .... (Capitol)
Nashville Teens; *London Collector-Rock Invasion-C* .... (London)
Rare Earth; *Get Ready.* .... (Motown)
Steve Young; *Redneck Mothers-C.* .... (RCA)
  Solo/Live. .... (Watermelon)
Two Cigarettes In The Dark
Alberta Hunter; *Legendary Alberta Hunter-London Sessions* .... (DRG)
Betty Carter; *'Round Midnight* .... (Atlantic)
When You Wish Upon A Fag
Leon Russell & Marc Benno; *Asylum Choir II* .... (MCA)
Winston Tastes Good (Winston Cigarettes)
Original Soundtrack; *TeeVee Toons-The Commercials-#1-C* ...... (TVT)
You Can Take Salem Out Of The Country
Original Soundtrack; *TeeVee Toons-The Commercials-#1-C* .... (TVT)

CIRCLES, Deja Vu, Karma, Repeat, Round, Turning, Wheels

See Also: ASTROLOGY, LIFE, RETURNING, TRAVELING

(Just Like) Starting Over
John Lennon & Yoko Ono; *Double Fantasy* .... (Capitol)
  ST/Imagine: John Lennon. .... (Capitol)
808
Blaque; *Blaque* .... (Track Masters/Columbia)
Adam Raised A Cain
Bruce Springsteen; *Darkness On The Edge Of Town.* .... (Columbia)
Affirmation
Savage Garden; *Affirmation.* .... (Columbia)
All For You
Sister Hazel; *...Somewhere More Familiar* .... (Universal)

Sister Hazel .... (Universal)
All That You Are (x3)
Econoline Crush; *Devil You Know* .... (Restless)
Always Come Back To You
Natasha's Brother; *Always Come Back To You* .... (Atlantic)
And On And On
Janet Jackson; *Any Time Any Place* .... (Virgin)
And When I Die
Blood, Sweat & Tears; *Blood, Sweat & Tears* .... (Columbia)
  Blood, Sweat & Tears Greatest Hits .... (Columbia)
  Blood, Sweat & Tears In Concert .... (Columbia)
Laura Nyro; *First Songs* .... (Columbia)
  Live At The Bottom Line .... (Cypress)
Around & Around
38 Special; *38 Special* .... (A&M)
Animals; *Best Of The Animals* .... (Abkco)
Chuck Berry; *Berry Is On Top* .... (Chess)
  ST/Hail! Hail! Rock 'N' Roll .... (MCA)
  The Chess Box-Chuck Berry .... (Chess)
Grateful Dead; *One From The Vault* .... (Grateful Dead)
  Steal Your Face .... (Grateful Dead)
Rolling Stones; *12 X 5* .... (Abkco)
  Love You Live .... (Virgin)
Around The World
Bing Crosby; *Heart Beats-Closer Than A Kiss-Crooner Classics-C* ..... (Rhino)
Frank Sinatra; *Come Fly With Me* .... (Capitol)
McGuire Sisters; *McGuire Sisters-Anthology* .... (MCA)
Around The World (La La La...)
ATC; *Now That's What I Call Music!-#6-C.* .... (Virgin)
  Planet Pop. .... (Republic/Universal)
Atlantic City
Bruce Springsteen; *Bruce Springsteen's Greatest Hits* .... (Columbia)
  Nebraska. .... (Columbia)
Back On Earth
Ozzy Osbourne; *The Ozzman Cometh* .... (Epic)
Back Where I Started
Box Of Frogs; *Box Of Frogs* .... (Epic)
Bang The Drum Slowly
Emmylou Harris; *Red Dirt Girl* .... (Nonesuch)
Been There
Clint Black with Steve Wariner; *D'lectrified* .... (RCA)
Beginning, The
Keb' Mo'; *The Door.* .... (550/Epic/Okeh)
Big Wheels In The Moonlight
Dan Seals; *Dan Seals' Greatest Hits* .... (Liberty)
  Dan Seals-Classics Collection-#2. .... (Liberty)
  Rage On. .... (Capitol)
California Here I Come
Al Jolson; *Best Of Al Jolson* .... (MCA)
Chain Of Love
Clay Walker; *Live, Laugh, Love.* .... (Giant)
Circle
Sarah McLachlan; *Fumbling Towards Ecstasy* .... (Arista)
Circle
Barbra Streisand; *Higher Ground* .... (Columbia)
Circle
Big Head Todd & The Monsters; *Sister Sweetly* .... (Giant)
Circle Dance
Bonnie Raitt; *Longing In Their Hearts.* .... (Capitol)
Circle Game, The
Buffy Sainte-Marie; *Best Of Buffy Sainte-Marie* .... (Vanguard)
  Fire & Fleet & Candlelight. .... (Vanguard)
Ian & Sylvia; *Ian & Sylvia's Greatest Hits.* .... (Vanguard)
Joni Mitchell; *Ladies Of The Canyon.* .... (Reprise)
Joni Mitchell with Tom Scott & The L.A. Express; *Miles Of Aisles.* .... (Asylum)
Tom Rush; *Classic Rush* .... (Elektra)
  The Circle Game .... (Elektra)
Circle In The Sand
Belinda Carlisle; *Heaven On Earth* .... (MCA)
Circle Is Small
Gordon Lightfoot; *Back Here On Earth* .... (United Artists)
  Endless Wire .... (Warner Bros.)
Circle Of Friends
Ray Pillow; *20 Great Hits-C* .... (Plantation)
  People Music. .... (Plantation)
Circle Of Hands
Uriah Heep; *Demons And Wizards.* .... (Mercury)
  Uriah Heep-Live. .... (Mercury)
Circle Of Life
Elton John; *Elton John-Love Songs* .... (MCA)
  ST/The Lion King. .... (Walt Disney)
Original Cast; *The Lion King.* .... (Disney)
Circle Of One
Oleta Adams; *Circle Of One* .... (Fontana)
Circle Of Steel
Gordon Lightfoot; *Gord's Gold.* .... (Reprise)
  Sundown .... (Reprise)
Circle Of Your Arms
Louis Armstrong; *Louis Armstrong* .... (Everest)

Circles
Atlantic Starr; *Atlantic Starr-Classics-#10* . . . . (A&M)
Secret Lovers: Best Of Atlantic Starr . . . . (A&M)
Circles
Soul Coughing; *El Oso* . . . . (Slash)
Circles
Captain & Tennille; *Captain & Tennille's Greatest Hits* . . . . (A&M)
Circles
Arlo Guthrie & Pete Seeger; *Precious Friend* . . . . (Warner Bros.)
Circles
Harry Chapin; *Sniper & Other Love Songs* . . . . (Elektra)
Circles
Pete Townshend; *Scoop* . . . . (Atco)
Who; *Two's Missing* . . . . (MCA)
Coming Around Again
Carly Simon; *Coming Around Again* . . . . (Arista)
Crazy Circles
Bad Company; *Desolation Angels* . . . . (Swan Song)
Cycles
Frank Sinatra; *Cycles* . . . . (Reprise)
Frank Sinatra's Greatest Hits-#2 . . . . (Reprise)
Daddy Sang Bass
Johnny Cash; *Columbia Country Classics-#5-A New Tradition-C* . . . (Columbia)
Johnny Cash's Greatest Hits-#2 . . . . (Columbia)
The Man In Black-His Greatest Hits . . . . (Legacy)
Day After Day
Def Leppard; *Euphoria* . . . . (Mercury)
Days Of The Week
Stone Temple Pilots; *Shangri-La-Dee-Da* . . . . (Atlantic)
Dear Prudence
Beatles; *The Beatles (White Album)* . . . . (Capitol)
Siouxsie And The Banshees; *Hyaena* . . . . (Geffen)
Nocturne . . . . (Geffen)
Deja Vu
Teena Marie; *Compact Command Performances-Teena Marie* . . . . . . (Motown)
Teena Marie's Greatest Hits . . . . (Motown)
Wild & Peaceful . . . . (Motown)
Deja Vu
Crosby, Stills, Nash & Young; *Deja Vu* . . . . (Atlantic)
So Far . . . . (Atlantic)
Deja Vu
Dionne Warwick; *Dionne* . . . . (Arista)
Perfect 10 III . . . . (Arista)
Deja Vu
Statler Brothers; *Maple Street Memories* . . . . (Mercury)
Deja Vu
Iron Maiden; *Somewhere In Time* . . . . (Capitol)
Do It Again
Steely Dan; *Can't Buy A Thrill* . . . . (MCA)
Classic Rock-#1-C . . . . (MCA)
ST/FM . . . . (MCA)
Steely Dan's Greatest Hits . . . . (MCA)
Do It Again
Kinks; *Come Dancing With The Kinks-Best Of The Kinks 1977-1986* . . . (Arista)
Word Of Mouth . . . . (Arista)
Do It Again
New Birth; *Golden Classics-New Birth* . . . . (Collectables)
Do It Again
Judy Garland; *Judy Garland-At Carnegie Hall* . . . . (Capitol)
Sarah Vaughan; *Sarah Vaughan Sings George Gershwin Songbook,
Vol. 1* . . . . (Emarcy)
Don't Stop To Watch The Wheels
Doobie Brothers; *Minute By Minute* . . . . (Warner Bros.)
Dream On
Depeche Mode; *Exciter* . . . . (Mute/Reprise)
Drivin' Wheel
Albert King; *Stax Blues Masters-Blue Monday-C* . . . . (Stax)
Foghat; *Best Of Foghat* . . . . (Rhino)
Night Shift . . . . (Rhino)
Little Junior Parker; *Annie Get Your Yo Yo* . . . . (MCA Special Prod.)
Best Of Little Junior Parker . . . . (MCA)
Soul Shots-#4-Urban Blues-C . . . . (Rhino)
End Is The Beginning Is The End
Smashing Pumpkins; *ST/Batman & Robin-Music From And Inspired By The
Motion Picture* . . . . (Jive)
End, The
Beatles; *Abbey Road* . . . . (Parlophone)
Eternal Circle
Bob Dylan; *The Bootleg Series-Volumes 1-3 [Rare & Unreleased]* . . (Columbia)
Everybody's Everything
Santana; *Santana* . . . . (Columbia)
Santana's Greatest Hits . . . . (Columbia)
Viva Santana! . . . . (Columbia)
Everything Falls Apart
Dog's Eye View; *Happy Nowhere* . . . . (Columbia)
Everything Zen
Bush; *MTV Buzz Bin-C* . . . . (Mammoth)
Sixteen Stone . . . . (Trauma)

Fakin' It
Simon & Garfunkel; *Bookends* . . . . (Columbia)
Collected Works . . . . (Columbia)
Falling Again
Don Williams; *Don Williams' Greatest Hits* . . . . (MCA)
Especially For You . . . . (MCA)
I Believe In You . . . . (MCA)
Falling In Love (Uh-Oh)
Miami Sound Machine; *Primitive Love* . . . . (Epic)
Feel It Again
Honeymoon Suite; *Big Prize* . . . . (Warner Bros.)
Fool On The Hill
Beatles; *Beatles-Box Set* . . . . (Capitol)
Magical Mystery Tour . . . . (Capitol)
The Beatles/1967-1970 . . . . (Capitol)
Full Circle
Jeff Healey Band; *Hell To Pay* . . . . (Arista)
Full Circle
Aerosmith; *Nine Lives* . . . . (Columbia)
Get Born Again
Alice In Chains; *Nothing Safe* . . . . (Columbia)
Going In Circles
Friends Of Distinction; *Didn't It Blow Your Mind: Soul Hits Of The
'70s-#1-C* . . . . (Rhino)
Friends Of Distinction-Golden Classics . . . . (Collectables)
Gap Band; *Gap Band VII* . . . . (Total Experience)
Luther Vandross; *Songs* . . . . (Epic)
Golden Ring
Emmylou Harris/Linda Ronstadt/Anna & Kate McGarrigle; *Tammy
Wynette...Remembered-C* . . . . (Asylum)
George Jones & Tammy Wynette; *George Jones & Tammy Wynette-16
Biggest Hits* . . . . (Epic/Legacy)
Tammy Wynette & George Jones; *Encore-Tammy Wynette & George
Jones* . . . . (Epic)
Tammy Wynette & George Jones' Greatest Hits . . . . (Epic)
Tammy Wynette-Anniversary-20 Years Of Hits . . . . (Epic)
Hard Times Come Easy
Richie Sambora; *Undiscovered Soul* . . . . (Mercury)
Heart Like A Wheel
Steve Miller Band; *Circle Of Love* . . . . (Capitol)
Heart Like A Wheel
Linda Ronstadt; *Heart Like A Wheel* . . . . (Capitol)
Here I Go Again
Hollies; *The Hollies' Greatest Hits* . . . . (Imperial)
The Hollies' Greatest Hits . . . . (Epic)
Here I Go Again
Smokey Robinson & The Miracles; *Smokey Robinson & The Miracles'
Anthology* . . . . (Motown)
*Time Out For Smokey Robinson & The Miracles/Special
Occasion* . . . . (Motown)
Here I Go Again
Robbie Nevil; *A Place Like This* . . . . (EMI)
Here I Go Again
Force MD's; *Chillin'* . . . . (Tommy Boy)
Here I Go Again
Whitesnake; *Saints & Sinners* . . . . (Geffen)
Whitesnake . . . . (Geffen)
Here We Go Again
Aretha Franklin; *A Rose Is Still A Rose* . . . . (Arista)
Here We Go Again!
Portrait; *Portrait* . . . . (Capitol)
Higher Ground
Stevie Wonder; *Innervisions* . . . . (Motown)
Original Musiquarium . . . . (Motown)
Highwayman
Glen Campbell; *Highwayman* . . . . (Capitol)
Johnny Cash with Waylon Jennings, Kris Kristofferson, Willie Nelson; *The
Man In Black-His Greatest Hits* . . . . (Legacy)
Waylon Jennings, Willie Nelson, Johnny Cash, Kris Kristofferson; *Columbia
Country Classics-#3-Americana-C* . . . . (Columbia)
Johnny Cash-16 Biggest Hits-#2 . . . . (Legacy)
Willie Nelson; *Greatest Country Hits Of The '80s-1985-C* . . . . (Columbia)
Hokey Pokey
Original Soundtrack; *Children's Favorites* . . . . (Kid Rhino/Rhino 4 Kids)
School Days-Kids Classics . . . . (Benson)
Ray Anthony; *Capitol Collectors Series-Ray Anthony* . . . . (Capitol)
Human Wheels
John Mellencamp; *Human Wheels* . . . . (Mercury)
Hush Hush Hush
Paula Cole; *This Fire* . . . . (Imago)
I Get Around
Beach Boys; *Best Of The Beach Boys* . . . . (Capitol)
Billboard Top Rock 'N' Roll Hits-1964-C . . . . (Rhino)
Endless Summer . . . . (Capitol)
Made In The U.S.A. . . . . (Capitol)
ST/Good Morning, Vietnam . . . . (A&M)
I Started A Joke
Bee Gees; *Best Of The Bee Gees-#1* . . . . (Polydor)
Here At Last...Bee Gees...Live . . . . (Polydor)

One Night Only. . . . . (Polydor)
Wallflowers; *ST/Zoolander* . . . .(Hollywood)
I Want To Make The World Turn Around
Steve Miller Band; *Living In The 20th Century* . . . .(Capitol)
I Will Still Be Laughing
Soul Asylum; *Candy From A Stranger* . . . .(Columbia)
ST/Basketball . . . .(Mojo Music/Universal)
I'd Love You All Over Again
Alan Jackson; *Here In The Real World* . . . . (Arista)
I'll Come Back As Another Woman
Tanya Tucker; *Girls Like Me* . . . .(Capitol)
Tanya Tucker's Greatest Hits . . . . (Liberty)
I'm Gonna Be A Wheel Someday
Fats Domino; *Best Of Fats Domino* . . . . (EMI)
Fats Domino's Greatest Hits . . . . (MCA)
Fats Domino's Greatest Hits . . . . (Everest)
My Blue Heaven . . . .(Gold Rush)
My Blue Heaven-Best Of Fats Domino-#1 . . . . (EMI)
Los Lobos; *Fine Mess* . . . .(Motown)
Instant Karma
John Lennon; *Lennon* . . . .(Capitol)
Live In New York City . . . .(Capitol)
John Lennon/Plastic Ono Band; *Shaved Fish* . . . .(Capitol)
Instant Replay
Dan Hartman; *Instant Replay* . . . .(Blue Sky)
Night At Studio 54-C . . . .(Casablanca)
It Comes Around
Jude Cole; *Start The Car* . . . . (Reprise)
It's All Been Done
Barenaked Ladies; *Stunt* . . . . (Reprise)
It's All Coming Back
Keb' Mo'; *The Door* . . . .(550/Epic/Okeh)
It's Inevitable
Charlie; *Charlie* . . . .(Mirage)
I've Been In Love Before
Cutting Crew; *Broadcast* . . . . (Virgin)
I've Been This Way Before
Neil Diamond; *Love At The Greek* . . . .(Columbia)
Serenade . . . .(Columbia)
Just A Little Bit Of Love
Celine Dion; *Let's Talk About Love-C* . . . . (550 Music)
Karma Chameleon
Culture Club; *Colour By Numbers* . . . .(Virgin)
Keep Coming Back
Edie Brickell & New Bohemians; *Shooting Rubberbands At The
Stars* . . . . (Geffen)
Keep Coming Back
Richard Marx; *Rush Street* . . . .(Capitol)
Keep Me Turning
Pete Townshend & Ronnie Lane; *Rough Mix* . . . . (Atlantic)
King Of The Wheels
Bobby Fuller Four; *Best Of The Bobby Fuller Four* . . . .(Rhino)
Learn To Be Still
Eagles; *Hell Freezes Over* . . . . (Geffen)
Leech
Eve 6; *Eve 6* . . . .(RCA)
Let's See How Far You Get
BR549; *This Is BR549* . . . . (Lucky Dog)
Let's Start All Over Again
Paragons; *Best Of The Paragons* . . . .(Collectables)
Harlem Holiday-New York Rhythm & Blues-#4-C . . . .(Collectables)
Super Oldies Of The '50s-#4-C . . . .(Audio Fidelity)
Let's Start Love Over
Miles Jaye; *Miles* . . . . (Island)
Life Goes On
Little Texas; *Little Texas' Greatest Hits* . . . . (Warner Bros.)
Lightning Crashes
Live; *Throwing Copper* . . . . (Radioactive/MCA)
Little Old Fashioned Karma
Willie Nelson; *Tougher Than Leather* . . . .(Columbia)
Little Wheel
John Lee Hooker; *Best Of John Lee Hooker* . . . . (Crescendo)
Best Of John Lee Hooker . . . .(Vee-Jay)
John Lee Hooker . . . .(Everest)
Little Wheel Spin & Spin
Buffy Sainte-Marie; *Best Of Buffy Sainte-Marie* . . . .(Vanguard)
Little Wheel Spin & Spin . . . .(Vanguard)
Native North American Child . . . .(Vanguard)
Little White Lie
Sammy Hagar; *Marching To Mars* . . . . (MCA)
Living Loving Maid
Led Zeppelin; *Led Zeppelin II* . . . .(Atlantic)
Lotus
R.E.M.; *Up* . . . . (Warner Bros.)
Love Is All
Marc Anthony; *Marc Anthony* . . . .(Columbia)
Love Makes The World Go Round
Deon Jackson; *Deon Jackson-Golden Classics* . . . .(Collectables)

Oldies But Goodies-#15-C . . . . (Original Sound)
Soul Shots-#2-The ''In'' Crowd-Sweet Soul-C . . . .(Rhino)
Super Oldies Of The '60s-#7-C . . . .(Audio Fidelity)
Love Makes The World Go Round
Madonna; *True Blue* . . . . (Sire)
Love Makes The World Go Round
Jo Basile; *Hit Broadway Musicals* . . . .(Audio Fidelity)
Original Broadway Cast; *Me & My Girl* . . . . (MCA)
Original Cast; *Me & My Girl* . . . . (EMI)
Love Me Over Again
Don Williams; *Best Of Don Williams-#3* . . . . (MCA)
Don Williams' Greatest Hits . . . . (MCA)
Lovers & Best Friends . . . . (MCA)
Love Will Lead You Back
Taylor Dayne; *Can't Fight Fate* . . . .(Arista)
Chicken Soup For The Woman's Soul-C . . . .(Rhino)
Love Will Turn You Around
Kenny Rogers; *Kenny Rogers-Twenty Greatest Hits* . . . . (EMI)
Love Will Turn You Around . . . . (EMI)
May Be A Price To Pay
Alan Parsons Project; *Turn Of A Friendly Card* . . . .(Arista)
Never Again, Again
Lee Ann Womack; *Lee Ann Womack* . . . .(Decca)
Never Let You Go
Third Eye Blind; *Blue* . . . .(Elektra)
Totally Hits-#2-C . . . .(Elektra)
Next Lifetime
Erykah Badu; *Baduizm*. . . . .(Kedar Entert./Universal)
Nothin' But The Wheel
Patty Loveless; *Only What I Feel* . . . . (Epic)
Patty Loveless-Classics . . . . (Epic)
On A Carousel
Hollies; *Best Of The Hollies* . . . . (EMI)
History Of British Rock-#6-C . . . .(Rhino)
The Hollies' Greatest Hits . . . . (Epic)
On And On
Stephen Bishop; *Best Of Bish* . . . .(Rhino)
Only God Knows Why
Kid Rock; *Devil Without A Cause* . . . . (Top Dog/Lava/Atlantic)
Outside Of A Small Circle Of Friends
Phil Ochs; *The War Is Over-Best Of Phil Ochs* . . . .(A&M)
There & Now-Live In Vancouver-1968 . . . .(Rhino)
Over & Over
Bobby Day; *Oldies But Goodies-#9-C* . . . . (Original Sound)
Rockin' Robin . . . .(Collectables)
Super Oldies Of The '50s-#3-C . . . .(Audio Fidelity)
Over & Over
Babys; *Babys* . . . .(Chrysalis)
Over & Over
Joe Walsh; *But Seriously Folks* . . . .(Asylum)
Over & Over
Chicago; *Chicago 18* . . . . (Full Moon/Warner Bros.)
Over & Over
Fleetwood Mac; *Fleetwood Mac Live* . . . .(Warner Bros.)
Tusk . . . .(Warner Bros.)
Over & Over
Georgia Satellites; *Georgia Satellites* . . . .(Elektra)
Over & Over
Madonna; *Like A Virgin* . . . . (Sire)
You Can Dance . . . . (Sire)
Over & Over
Angel; *Live Without A Net* . . . .(Casablanca)
White Hot . . . .(Casablanca)
Over & Over
Black Sabbath; *Mob Rules* . . . .(Warner Bros.)
Over & Over
Neil Young & Crazy Horse; *Ragged Glory* . . . . (Reprise)
Over & Over
Railway Children; *Recurrence* . . . . (Virgin)
Over & Over
Wilson Phillips; *Wilson Phillips* . . . .(SBK)
Over And Over
Pajama Party; *Freestyle's Greatest Hits* . . . .(Turnstyle)
Up All Night . . . .(Atlantic)
Over Now
Alice In Chains; *Alice In Chains* . . . .(Columbia)
Payback
Choice; *Explicit Rap-C* . . . .(Priority)
James Brown; *In Yo' Face!-History Of Funk-#4-C* . . . .(Rhino)
Payback Is A Mutha
Luke; *I Got Sumthin' On My Mind* . . . . (Luke)
Payback Is Hell
Candy Fresh; *Just The Way I Like It* . . . .(Wrap/Ichiban)
Payback's A Mutha
King Tee; *Act A Fool* . . . .(Capitol)
Rap Beginnings-#2-C . . . .(K-Tel)

Perfect Circle
  R.E.M.; *Murmur* . . . .(I.R.S.)
Piccadilly Circus
  Stiff Little Fingers; *See You Up There!* . . . . (Caroline)
Price You Pay
  Bruce Springsteen; *The River* . . . . (Columbia)
Repetitive Regret
  Eddie Rabbitt; *Rabbit Trax* . . . . (RCA)
Ring Of Fire
  Country Joe McDonald; *Best Of Country Joe McDonald-The Vanguard*
    Years-1969-1975 . . . . (Vanguard)
  Tonight I'm Singing Just For You . . . . (Vanguard)
  Dwight Yoakam; *Guitars, Cadillacs, Etc., Etc.* . . . . (Reprise)
  Earl Scruggs & Billy Bob Thornton; *Earl Scruggs And Friends-C* . . . . . .(MCA)
  Johnny Cash; *All Time Legends Of Country Music-C* . . . . (Legacy)
    Billboard Top Country Hits-1963-C . . . . (Rhino)
    Classic Cash-Hall Of Fame Series . . . . (Mercury)
    Johnny Cash's Greatest Hits . . . . (Columbia)
    The Man In Black-His Greatest Hits . . . . (Legacy)
  Stan Ridgway & Wall Of Voodoo; *Best Of Stan Ridgway & Wall Of*
    Voodoo . . . .(I.R.S.)
  Wall Of Voodoo; *Ugly Americans In Australia* . . . .(I.R.S.)
Road Beneath My Wheels
  Dan Fogelberg; *Live-Greetings From The West* . . . . (Full Moon)
Road You Leave Behind
  David Lee Murphy; *Gettin' Out The Good Stuff* . . . .(MCA)
Round & Round
  Edgar Winter Group; *Edgar Winter Group-Collection* . . . . (Rhino)
    They Only Come Out At Night . . . . (Epic)
Round About Way
  George Strait; *Carrying Your Love With Me* . . . .(MCA)
    Latest Greatest Straitest Hits . . . .(MCA)
Round And Round
  Ratt; *Classic Rock 1966-1988-C* . . . . (Atlantic)
    Out Of The Cellar . . . . (Atlantic)
    Ratt & Roll 8191 . . . . (Atlantic)
Round And Round
  Perry Como; *Como's Golden Records* . . . . (RCA)
    Perry Como's All-Time Greatest Hits-#1 . . . . (RCA)
    This Is Perry Como . . . . (RCA)
Round And Round
  4 P.M.; *Jackin' Boots* . . . . (Reprise)
Round And Round
  Aerosmith; *Gems* . . . . (Columbia)
    Pandora's Box . . . . (Columbia)
    Toys In The Attic . . . . (Columbia)
Round And Round
  Strawbs; *Best Of The Strawbs* . . . . (A&M)
    Here & Heroine . . . . (A&M)
Round And Round
  Neil Young & Crazy Horse; *Everybody Knows This Is Nowhere* . . . . . . (Reprise)
Round And Round
  Original Cast; *Fantasticks* . . . . (Polydor)
Round And Round
  Lionel Richie; *Lionel Richie* . . . . (Motown)
Round And Round
  David Bowie; *Sound + Vision* . . . .(Rykodisc)
Round And Round
  Tevin Campbell; *ST/Graffiti Bridge* . . . . (Paisley Park)
    T.E.V.I.N. . . . . (Qwest)
Round And Round
  New Order; *Technique* . . . . (Qwest)
Roundabout
  Yes; *Fragile* . . . . (Atlantic)
    Yessongs . . . . (Atlantic)
    Yesyears . . . . (Atco)
Sex On Wheelz
  My Life With The Thrill Kill Kult; *Sexplosion!* . . . .(Rykodisc)
Silver Wheels
  Heart; *Bebe Le Strange* . . . . (Epic)
    Heart's Greatest Hits/Live . . . . (Epic)
Silver Wheels
  Bruce Cockburn; *Waiting For A Miracle-Singles 1970-1987* . . . . . .(Gold Castle)
So It Goes
  Nick Lowe; *Basher: Best Of* . . . . (Columbia)
    Pure Pop For Now People . . . . (Columbia)
    ST/Rock 'N' Roll High School . . . . (Sire)
Something In Red
  Lorrie Morgan; *Lorrie Morgan's Greatest Hits* . . . . (BNA)
    Something In Red . . . . (RCA)
    To Get To You-Greatest Hits Collection . . . . (BNA)
Spaceman
  Nilsson; *Son Of Schmilsson* . . . . (RCA)
    Songwriter . . . . (RCA)
Spinning Around Over You
  Lenny Kravitz; *Spinning Around Over You* . . . . (Virgin)

Spinning Wheel
  Blood, Sweat & Tears; *Blood, Sweat & Tears* . . . . (Columbia)
    Blood, Sweat & Tears Greatest Hits . . . . (Columbia)
    Rock Classics Of The '60s-C . . . . (Columbia)
Starting All Over Again
  Daryl Hall & John Oates; *Change Of Season* . . . . (Arista)
  Mel & Tim; *15 Original Big Hits-#1-C* . . . . (Stax)
    Top Of The Stax-Twenty Greatest Hits-C . . . . (Stax)
Starting Over Again
  Steve Wariner; *Best Of Steve Wariner* . . . . (MCA Special Prod.)
    Country Classics-#7-1986-1987-C . . . . (Universal)
    Life's Highway . . . .(MCA)
    Steve Wariner's Greatest Hits . . . .(MCA)
Summer's Coming Around Again
  Carly Simon; *Anticipation* . . . . (Elektra)
Surrounded
  Chantal Kreviazuk; *Under These Rocks And Stones* . . . . (Columbia)
Tattva
  Kula Shaker; *K* . . . . (Columbia)
Thank U
  Alanis Morissette; *Supposed Former Infatuation Junkie* . . . . (Maverick)
Then The Morning Comes
  Smash Mouth; *Astro Lounge* . . . .(Interscope)
    Now That's What I Call Music!-#4-C . . . .(Virgin)
Thinking About Your Troubles
  Nilsson; *The Point* . . . .(RCA)
This Song Has No Title
  Elton John; *Goodbye Yellow Brick Road* . . . .(Polydor)
This Wheel's On Fire
  Band; *Music From Big Pink* . . . . (Capitol)
    Rock Of Ages . . . . (Capitol)
    The Band-Anthology-#1 . . . . (Capitol)
  Bob Dylan And The Band; *Basement Tapes* . . . . (Columbia)
  Byrds; *The Byrds* . . . . (Columbia)
  Ian & Sylvia; *Ian & Sylvia's Greatest Hits* . . . . (Vanguard)
  Siouxsie And The Banshees; *Through The Looking Glass* . . . . (Geffen)
    Twice Upon A Time-The Singles . . . . (Geffen)
Three Bells, The
  Browns; *Billboard Top Country Hits-1959-C* . . . . (Rhino)
    Nipper's Greatest Hits Of The '50s-#1-C . . . . (RCA)
Turn! Turn! Turn! (To Everything There Is A Season)
  Byrds; *Billboard Top Rock 'N' Roll Hits-1965-C* . . . . (Rhino)
    Original Singles-#1-1965-1967 . . . . (Columbia)
    ST/Forrest Gump . . . .(Epic/Sony Music Soundtrax)
    The Byrds . . . . (Columbia)
    The Byrds' Greatest Hits . . . . (Columbia)
    Turn! Turn! Turn! . . . . (Legacy)
  Pete Seeger; *Pete Seeger's Greatest Hits* . . . . (Columbia)
    Troubadours Of The Folk Era-#2-C . . . . (Rhino)
Turning Circles
  Judas Priest; *Point Of Entry* . . . . (Columbia)
Two Teardrops
  Steve Wariner; *Two Teardrops* . . . . (Capitol)
Under My Wheels
  Alice Cooper; *Alice Cooper's Greatest Hits* . . . . (Warner Bros.)
    Killer . . . . (Warner Bros.)
    The Alice Cooper Show . . . . (Warner Bros.)
Until Your Love Comes Back Around
  RTZ; *Return To Zero* . . . .(Giant)
Voodoo
  Godsmack; *Godsmack* . . . . (Republic/Universal)
Waiting For The Tide To Turn
  Robert Cray Band; *Bad Influence* . . . .(Hightone)
Watching The Wheels
  John Lennon; *Lennon* . . . . (Capitol)
  John Lennon & Yoko Ono; *Double Fantasy* . . . . (Capitol)
Waterwheel
  Daryl Hall & John Oates; *Whole Oats* . . . .(Atlantic)
Way Down The Line
  Offspring; *Ixnay On The Hombre* . . . . (Columbia)
What Goes Around
  Regina Belle; *Stay With Me* . . . . (Columbia)
What Goes Around
  Jerry Garcia; *Compliments* . . . . (Grateful Dead)
What Goes Around
  Gloria Estefan; *Into The Light* . . . . (Epic)
What Goes Around
  Ringo Starr; *Time Takes Time* . . . . (Private Music)
What I Got
  Sublime; *Now That's What I Call Music!-#2-C* . . . . (Virgin)
    Sublime . . . . (Gasoline Alley)
Wheel In The Sky
  Journey; *Infinity* . . . . (Columbia)
    Journey-Captured . . . . (Columbia)
    Journey's Greatest Hits . . . . (Columbia)
Wheel Of Fortune
  Cardinals; *Atlantic Rhythm & Blues 1947-1974-box-C* . . . .(Atlantic)

Kay Starr; *Capitol Collectors Series-Kay Starr* . . . . (Capitol)

Wheel Of Life
Rance Allen; *Straight From The Heart* . . . . (Stax)

Wheel, The
Utopia; *Another Live* . . . . (Rhino)
Utopia-Anthology 1974-1985 . . . . (Rhino)

Wheel, The
Rosanne Cash; *The Wheel* . . . . (Columbia)

Wheel, The
Jerry Garcia; *Garcia* . . . .(Grateful Dead)

Wheel, The
Jefferson Airplane; *Jefferson Airplane* . . . . (Epic)

Wheel, The
Edie Brickell & New Bohemians; *Shooting Rubberbands At The
    Stars* . . . . (Geffen)

Wheel, The
Asleep At The Wheel; *Wheel* . . . . (Capitol)

Wheels
Flying Burrito Brothers; *Cabin Fever* . . . . (Relix)
Close Up The Honky Tonks . . . . (A&M)
Farther Along-Best Of The Flying Burrito Brothers . . . . (A&M)
Gilded Palace Of Sin . . . . (A&M)

Wheels
Billy Vaughn; *Billy Vaughn's Greatest Hits* . . . . (Curb)

Wheels
Emmylou Harris; *Elite Hotel* . . . .(Reprise)

Wheels
Chet Atkins; *Best Of Chet Atkins* . . . .(RCA)
On The Road Live . . . .(RCA)

Wheels
Restless Heart; *Best Of Restless Heart* . . . .(RCA)
Wheels . . . .(RCA)

Wheels
Lone Justice; *Shelter* . . . . (Geffen)

Wheels Of Fortune
Doobie Brothers; *Takin' It To The Streets* . . . . (Warner Bros.)

Wheels Of Life
Gino Vannelli; *Best Of Gino Vannelli* . . . . (A&M)
Brother To Brother . . . . (A&M)
Gino Vannelli-Classics-#7 . . . . (A&M)

When It All Goes Wrong Again
Everclear; *Songs From An American Movie-#2-Good Time For A Bad
    Attitude* . . . . (Capitol)

When You Come Back To Me Again
Garth Brooks; *Scarecrow* . . . . (Capitol)

Width Of A Circle
David Bowie; *David Live* . . . . (Rykodisc)
Man Who Sold The World . . . . (Rykodisc)
ST/Ziggy Stardust-The Motion Picture . . . . (Rykodisc)

Will It Go Round In Circles
Billy Preston; *Best Of Billy Preston* . . . . (A&M)
Billboard Top Rock 'N' Roll Hits-1973-C . . . . (Rhino)
Didn't It Blow Your Mind: Soul Hits Of The '70s-#11-C . . . . (Rhino)

Will The Circle Be Unbroken
Charlie Daniels Band & Friends; *Volunteer Jam 3 & 4* . . . . (Epic)
Joan Baez; *Country Music Album* . . . . (Vanguard)
The First 10 Years . . . . (Vanguard)
Nitty Gritty Dirt Band; *Will The Circle Be Unbroken* . . . . (EMI)
Roy Acuff; *Best Of Roy Acuff* . . . . (Liberty)
Willie Nelson; *Willie & Family Live* . . . . (Columbia)

Won't Get Fooled Again
Van Halen; *LIVE: Right here, right now..* . . . . (Warner Bros.)
Who; *ST/The Kids Are Alright* . . . . (MCA)
The Concert For New York City-C . . . . (Columbia)
Who Greatest Hits . . . . (MCA)
Who's Last . . . . (MCA)
Who's next . . . . (MCA)

World Keeps Spinning
Behan Johnson; *Behan Johnson* . . . .(RCA)

World Turning
Fleetwood Mac; *Fleetwood Mac* . . . .(Reprise)

Yesterday Once More
Carpenters; *Carpenters-Classics-#2* . . . . (A&M)
Carpenters-The Singles 1969-1973 . . . . (A&M)
Now & Then . . . . (A&M)
Yesterday Once More . . . . (A&M)

You Can Make History (Young Again)
Elton John; *Elton John-Love Songs* . . . . (MCA)

You Shouldn't Kiss Me Like This
Toby Keith; *How Do You Like Me Now?!* . . . . (DreamWorks/SKG)

You Spin Me Around (Like A Record)
Dead Or Alive; *Rip It Up* . . . . (Epic)
Youthquake . . . . (Epic)

You're My Driving Wheel
Diana Ross & The Supremes; *Diana Ross & The Supremes' Greatest Hits &
    Rare Classics* . . . . (Motown)

CITIES: A

See Also: **CITIES: AMSTERDAM, CITIES: ATLANTA, CITIES:
GENERAL, COUNTRIES: A-Z, STATES: A-Z**

''E'' Street Shuffle (Asbury Park)
Bruce Springsteen; *The Wild, The Innocent & The E Street Shuffle* . . .(Columbia)

4th Of July, Asbury Park (Sandy)
Bruce Springsteen; *The Wild, The Innocent & The E Street Shuffle* . . .(Columbia)
Bruce Springsteen & The E Street Band; *Bruce Springsteen & The E Street
    Band Live/1975-85* . . . .(Legacy)

Aberdeen
Kenny Wayne Shepherd; *Ledbetter Heights* . . . . (Giant)

Abilene
George Hamilton IV; *Billboard Top Country Hits-1963-C* . . . .(Rhino)
Nipper's Greatest Hits Of The '60s-#2-C . . . . (RCA)
Sonny James; *American Originals-Sonny James* . . . .(Columbia)
Texas Super Hits-C . . . .(Columbia)
Waylon Jennings; *Outlaw Reunion-#1* . . . .(Aura)

Acapulco
Neil Diamond; *Jazz Singer* . . . .(Capitol)

Acapulco 1922
Herb Alpert & The Tijuana Brass; *Lonely Bull* . . . . (A&M)
Solid Brass . . . . (A&M)

Acapulco Gold
Rainy Daze; *Acapulco Gold* . . . .(Out Of Print)

Acid Annapolis
Leon Russell; *Carney* . . . .(Right Stuff)

Albuquerque
Neil Young; *Tonight's The Night* . . . . (Reprise)

Alexandria, VA
Bill Jennings; *Stompin' With Bill* . . . .(Collectables)

All Alone In Austin
Marty Mitchell; *You Are The Sunshine Of My Life* . . . . (MC)

Allentown
Billy Joel; *Billy Joel-Greatest Hits, Volume I & Volume II* . . . .(Columbia)
KOHUEPT . . . .(Columbia)
Nylon Curtain . . . .(Columbia)

Allentown Jail
Jo Stafford; *International Hits* . . . .(Corinthian)
Kingston Trio; *Rediscovering The Kingston Trio* . . . .(Folk Era)

Alleys Of Austin
Michael Murphey; *Cosmic Cowboy Souvenir* . . . . (A&M)

Amarillo
Emmylou Harris; *Elite Hotel* . . . . (Reprise)

Amarillo (Is This The Way To)
Neil Sedaka; *A Song* . . . . (Reprise)

Amarillo By Morning
George Strait; *George Strait's Greatest Hits* . . . . (MCA)
Strait From The Heart . . . . (MCA)

Amarillo Waltz
Skip Gorman; *A Cowboy's Wild Song To His Herd* . . . .(Rounder)

Amy's Back In Austin
Little Texas; *Kick A Little* . . . .(Warner Bros.)
Little Texas' Greatest Hits . . . .(Warner Bros.)

Anaheim, Azusa & Cucamonga Sewing Circle
Jan & Dean; *Best Of Jan & Dean* . . . . (EMI)
Jan & Dean-Legendary Masters . . . . (EMI)

Ann Arbor
John Fahey; *John Fahey Visits Washington D.C.* . . . . (Takoma)

Ann Arbor Polka
Michigan Dutchmen; *More New Polkas* . . . .(Jay Jay)

Arlington Girl
Shivaree; *I Oughtta Give You A Shot...* . . . .(Capitol)

Aspen
Dan Fogelberg; *Captured Angel* . . . . (Full Moon)

Atlantic City
Randy Newman; *ST/Ragtime* . . . .(Elektra)

Atlantic City
Bruce Springsteen; *Bruce Springsteen's Greatest Hits* . . . .(Columbia)
Nebraska . . . .(Columbia)

Atlantic City
Paul Anka; *ST/Atlantic City* . . . . (DRG)

Atlantic City Gambler
Grace Jones; *Muse* . . . .(Island)

Atlantis
Steve Kilbey; *Earthed* . . . .(Rykodisc)
Steal This Disc 2-C . . . .(Rykodisc)

Atlantis
Donovan; *Barbarajagal* . . . .(Epic)

Attica State
John Lennon/Plastic Ono Band; *Sometime In New York City* . . . .(Capitol)

Austin
Jeff Palmer; *Laser Wizard* . . . .(Statiras)

Austin
Blake Shelton; *Blake Shelton* . . . . (Giant)

Avalon
Al Jolson; *Best Of Al Jolson* . . . . (MCA)

Jolson Sang 'Em . . . . (Biograph)
The Al Jolson Story-#2 . . . . (MCA)
Avalon
Roxy Music; *Avalon* . . . . (Warner Bros.)
Heart Still Beating . . . . (Virgin)
Street Life-20 Great Hits . . . . (Reprise)
Avalon My Home Town
Mississippi John Hurt; *Best Of Mississippi John Hurt* . . . . (Vanguard)
Bob Wills Is Still The King (Austin)
Clint Black & Asleep At The Wheel; *Ride With Bob-C* . . . . (DreamWorks/SKG)
Bus From Amarillo
Original Cast; *Best Little Whorehouse In Texas* . . . . (MCA)
By The Time I Get To Phoenix (Albuquerque)
Glen Campbell; *All-Time Country Classics-#1-C* . . . . (Capitol)
Glen Campbell-Classics Collection . . . . (Capitol)
Glen Campbell-Live . . . . (Capitol)
Glen Campbell's Greatest Hits . . . . (Capitol)
Reba McEntire; *Starting Over* . . . . (MCA)
Charlie Dunn (Austin TX)
Jerry Jeff Walker; *Gypsy Songman* . . . . (Rykodisc)
Jerry Jeff Walker . . . . (MCA)
Everywhere (Albuquerque)
Tim McGraw; *Everywhere* . . . . (Curb)
Goin' To Acapulco
Bob Dylan And The Band; *Basement Tapes* . . . . (Columbia)
I'm Leavin' Abilene Tonight
Dede Upchurch; *45-#050* . . . . (Little Giant)
It's A Long Way From Detroit...To Austin
Buddy Harris; *45-#148* . . . . (Plantation)
Just To See You Smile (Amarillo)
Tim McGraw; *Everywhere* . . . . (Curb)
Midnight In Old Amarillo
Buddy Emmons & Ray Pennington; *Swing & Other Things* . . . . (Step One)
She Loves Austin
Johnny Rodriguez; *Gracias* . . . . (Capitol)
Tennessee Flat Top Box (Austin)
Johnny Cash; *Classic Cash-Hall Of Fame Series* . . . . (Mercury)
Columbia Country Classics-#3-Americana-C . . . . (Columbia)
Essential Johnny Cash . . . . (Columbia)
Rosanne Cash; *30 Years Of #1 Hits-#17-C* . . . . (Columbia)
Hits-1979-1989 . . . . (Columbia)
King's Record Shop . . . . (Columbia)
That Acapulco Gold
Rainy Daze; *Summer Of Love-#2-Turn On-Mind Expansion & Signs Of The Times-C* . . . . (Rhino)
Theme From "The Miss America Pageant" (There She Is, Miss America) (Atlantic City)
Bert Parks; *Television's Greatest Hits-#4-Black & White Classics-C* . . . . (TVT)
Timon Of The Athens March
Duke Ellington & Boston Pops Orchestra; *Duke At Tanglewood* . . . . (RCA)
Train For Auschwitz
Tom Paxton; *Best Of Broadside 1962-1968: Anthems Of The American Underground From The Pages Of Broadside Magazine-C* . . . . (Smithsonian Folkways)
Walkaway Joe (Abilene)
Trisha Yearwood; *Hearts In Armor* . . . . (MCA)
Songbook-A Collection Of Hits . . . . (MCA)
Way Out In Abilene
Lightnin' Hopkins; *Legacy Of The Blues-#12* . . . . (Crescendo)
When You Leave Amarillo
Bob Wills & His Texas Playboys; *For The Last Time* . . . . (Capitol)

CITIES: AMSTERDAM
See Also: *COUNTRIES: NETHERLANDS*

Amsterdam
Original Cast; *Jacques Brel Is Alive & Well And Living In New York City* . . . . (Columbia)
Amsterdam
Van Halen; *Balance* . . . . (Warner Bros.)
Amsterdam
Joan Baez; *Play Me Backwards* . . . . (Virgin)
Amsterdam
John Denver; *Take Me To Tomorrow* . . . . (RCA)
Amsterdam Dog Shit Blues
Mojo Nixon & Skid Roper; *Enigma Variations-#2-C* . . . . . (Enigma Capitol)
Ballad Of John And Yoko
Beatles; *Beatles 1* . . . . (Capitol)
Beatles-Box Set . . . . (Capitol)
Hey Jude . . . . (Capitol)
Past Masters-Volume Two . . . . (Parlophone)
ST/Imagine: John Lennon . . . . (Capitol)
The Beatles/1967-1970 . . . . (Capitol)
Girls Of Amsterdam
Shaw Brothers; *Best Of The Shaw Brothers* . . . . (Folk Era)

Shaw Brothers-Collection . . . . (Folk Era)
Goodbye San Francisco, Hello Amsterdam
Doug Sahm; *SDQ '98* . . . . (Watermelon)
Kicking Back In Amsterdam
Kevin Welch; *Life Down Here On Earth* . . . . (Dead Reckoning)
New Amsterdam
Elvis Costello; *Girls Girls Girls* . . . . (Columbia)
Elvis Costello & The Attractions; *Get Happy!* . . . . (Rykodisc)

CITIES: ATLANTA
See Also: *STATES: GEORGIA*

Angel From Atlanta
Reddog; *Reddog* . . . . (Survival)
Angels Of Atlanta
Marvin "Hannibal" Peterson; *Angels Of Atlanta* . . . . (Enja)
Atlanta
Stanley Clarke & George Duke; *Project 2* . . . . (Epic)
Atlanta
Wagoneers; *Good Fortune* . . . . (A&M)
Atlanta Blue
Statler Brothers; *14 Country Favorites-C* . . . . (Mercury)
Atlanta Blue . . . . (Mercury)
Statler Brothers' Greatest Hits . . . . (Mercury)
Atlanta Burned Again Last Night
Atlanta; *Pictures* . . . . (MCA)
Atlanta Georgia Stray
Johnny Duncan; *Johnny Duncan* . . . . (Columbia)
Johnny Duncan's Greatest Hits . . . . (Columbia)
Nice 'N' Easy . . . . (Columbia)
Atlanta June
Pablo Cruise; *A Place In The Sun* . . . . (A&M)
Atlanta Lady
Marty Balin; *Balin* . . . . (EMI)
Balince-A Collection . . . . (Rhino)
Atlanta Song
David Allan Coe; *Mysterious Rhinestone Cowboy* . . . . (Columbia)
Atlanta Special
Bukka White; *Legacy Of The Blues-#1* . . . . (Crescendo)
Mississippi Blues . . . . (Takoma)
Atlanta Town
Chasey Collins; *Jug Jook & Washboard Bands* . . . . (Blues Classics)
Atlanta, GA
Sammy Kaye & His Orchestra; *Dance To My Golden Favorites* . . . . (MCA)
Woody Herman; *Best Of The Big Bands-C* . . . . (Columbia)
Atlanta's Burning Down
Dickey Betts & Great Southern; *Dickey Betts & Great Southern* . . . . (Arista)
Randy Howard; *All-American Redneck* . . . . (Warner Bros.)
Back To Atlanta
David Allan Coe; *I've Got Something To Say* . . . . (Columbia)
Battle Of Atlanta
Reno & Smiley; *1983 Collector's Edition-#2* . . . . (Gusto)
Burning Of Atlanta
Claude King; *American Originals-Claude King* . . . . (Columbia)
Dark Side Of Atlanta
Dan Hill; *Best Of Dan Hill* . . . . (20th Century Fox)
Frozen In The Night . . . . (20th Century Fox)
Girl From Atlanta
Benny Carter All-Star Sax Ensemble; *Over The Rainbow* . . . . . . (Musicmasters)
Hot 'Lanta
Allman Brothers Band; *At Fillmore East* . . . . (Capricorn)
The Road Goes On Forever, A Collection Of Their Greatest Recordings . . . . (Polydor)
Hot 'Lanta
38 Special; *Rock & Roll Strategy* . . . . (A&M)
Meant To Be
Sammy Kershaw; *Politics Religion & Her* . . . . (Mercury)
Oh Atlanta
Bad Company; *Desolation Angels* . . . . (Swan Song)
Charlie Daniels Band; *Simple Man* . . . . (Epic)
Little Feat; *Feats Don't Fail Me Now* . . . . (Warner Bros.)
Waiting For Columbus . . . . (Warner Bros.)
Sue Medley; *Sue Medley* . . . . (Mercury)
Partyin' Gal
Charlie Daniels Band; *Windows* . . . . (Epic)
Portrait In Atlanta
House Of Love; *Audience With The Mind* . . . . (Fontana)
Santa, Are You Coming To Atlanta
Pake McEntire; *Country Christmas-#4-C* . . . . (RCA)
Season's Greetings-C . . . . (RCA)
Theme From "Designing Women" (Georgia On My Mind)
Original Soundtrack; *Television's Greatest Hits-#7-Cable Ready-C* . . . . . (TVT)

CITIES: B

See Also: CITIES: BALTIMORE, BERLIN, BIRMINGHAM, BOSTON, CITIES: GENERAL, COUNTRIES: A-Z, STATES: A-Z

26 Cents (Beaumont)
Wilkinsons; *Nothing But Love* . . . . (Giant)
3 A.M. Somewhere Out Of Beaumont
KLF; *Chill Out* . . . . (Wax Trax)
Babylon
David Gray; *White Ladder* . . . . (ATO/RCA)
Back To Bologna
Milt Jackson & The Gold Medal Winners; *Brother Jim* . . . . (Pablo)
Baghdad Ragman
Karen Alexander; *Isn't It Always Love* . . . . (Asylum)
Ballad Of Jed Clampett (Beverly Hills)
Flatt & Scruggs; *Columbia Country Classics-#3-Americana-C* . . . . . (Columbia)
On Foggy Mountain . . . . (Fifty One West)
Bangkok Attorney
Doves; *Affinity* . . . . (Elektra)
Bangkok Cockfight
Martin Denny; *Exotica-Best Of Martin Denny* . . . . (Rhino)
Bangkok Rain
Cult; *Ceremony* . . . . (Sire)
Barcelona
Original Cast; *Company* . . . . (Columbia)
Barcelona
Nomad; *Changing Cabins* . . . . (Capitol)
Barcelona
Juan Carlos Quintero; *Juan Carlos Quintero* . . . . (Nova)
Barcelona
Spies; *Music Of Espionage* . . . . (Telarc)
Barefoot In Beverly Hills
Grace Jones; *Inside Story* . . . . (Manhattan)
Barrytown
Steely Dan; *Pretzel Logic* . . . . (MCA)
Barstow Blue Eyes
Jo Jo Gunne; *Jo Jo Gunne* . . . . (Asylum)
Baton Rouge
Bill Medley; *Sweet Thunder* . . . . (United Artists)
Baton Rouge
Nixons; *The Nixons* . . . . (MCA)
Beaumont Rag
Bob Wills; *Best Of Bob Wills-#2* . . . . (MCA)
Tiffany Transcriptions-#4-You're From Texas . . . . (Rhino)
Bob Wills & His Texas Playboys; *Bob Wills & His Texas Playboys-In Concert* . . . . (Capitol)
Beautiful Downtown Burbank
Jeannie C. Riley; *Country Gold-Jeannie C. Riley* . . . . (Plantation)
Beirut
Steps Ahead; *Magnetic* . . . . (Elektra)
Belfast
Orbital; *Orbital* . . . . (Full Frequency Range)
Belfast
Energy Orchard; *Energy Orchard* . . . . (MCA)
Belfast
Richard Pinhas; *L'Ethique* . . . . (Cuneiform)
Belfast Child
Simple Minds; *Street Fighting Years* . . . . (A&M)
Belfast Cowboys
Pretty Things; *Silk Torpedo* . . . . (Swan Song)
Belfast Hornpipe
James Galway; *James Galway's Greatest Hits* . . . . (RCA)
Berkeley Woman
John Denver; *Farewell Andromeda* . . . . (RCA)
John Denver . . . . (RCA)
Bicyclettes De Belsize
Engelbert Humperdinck; *Engelbert* . . . . (Parrot)
Engelbert Humperdinck-His Greatest Hits . . . . (Parrot)
Live In Concert/All Of Me . . . . (Epic)
Biloxi
Ian Matthews; *Some Days You Eat The Bear* . . . . (Elektra)
Jesse Winchester; *Best Of Jesse Winchester* . . . . (Rhino)
Jesse Winchester . . . . (Rhino)
Jimmy Buffett; *Changes In Latitudes, Changes In Attitudes* . . . . (MCA)
Bimbombey
Jimmie Rodgers; *Best Of Jimmie Rodgers* . . . . (Rhino)
Best Of Jimmie Rodgers . . . . (Curb)
Bombay
Golden Earring; *Mad Love* . . . . (MCA)
Bombay
Lawrence Welk; *Calcutta* . . . . (Ranwood)
Bowling Green
Everly Brothers; *Walk Right Back: The Everly Brothers On Warner Bros.- 1960-1969* . . . . (Warner Archives)
Bristol Stomp
Dovells; *Echoes Of A Rock Era-Middle Years-C* . . . . (Roulette)

Let's Dance . . . . (Gusto)
Rock-O-Rama-#1-C . . . . (Abkco)
Brownsville Blues
Hammie Nixon; *Tappin' That Thing* . . . . (High Water)
Brownsville Girl
Bob Dylan; *Knocked Out Loaded* . . . . (Columbia)
Brownsville Road
Peter Lang; *Prime Cuts* . . . . (Waterhouse)
Brownsville Turnaround On The Tex-Mex Border
KLF; *Chill Out* . . . . (Wax Trax)
Budapest
Jethro Tull; *Crest Of A Knave* . . . . (Chrysalis)
Budapest By Blimp
Thomas Dolby; *Aliens Ate My Buick* . . . . (EMI)
Buenos Aires
Original Cast; *Evita* . . . . (MCA)
Callin' Baton Rouge
Garth Brooks; *In Pieces* . . . . (Liberty)
New Grass Revival; *New Grass Revival-Anthology* . . . . (Liberty)
Oak Ridge Boys; *Room Service* . . . . (MCA Special Prod.)
Child Of Babylon
Whitesnake; *Come An' Get It* . . . . (Geffen)
Goin' To Brownsville
Ron Thompson & The Resistors with Rollo Smith; *Treat Her Like Gold/No Band Days* . . . . (Takoma)
Ry Cooder; *Ry Cooder* . . . . (Reprise)
Going Back To Big Sur
Johnny Rivers; *Johnny Rivers-Anthology 1964-1977* . . . . (Rhino)
Touch Of Gold . . . . (Imperial)
Honeymoon In Beirut
Rick Springfield; *Rock Of Life* . . . . (RCA)
I'm Going To Brownsville
Furry Lewis; *Back On My Feet Again* . . . . (Prestige)
Shake 'Em On Down . . . . (Fantasy)
Ladies Night In Buffalo
David Lee Roth; *Eat 'Em & Smile* . . . . (Warner Bros.)
Long Gone John From Bowling Green
Red Knuckles & The Trailblazers; *Red Knuckles & The Trailblazers* . . . . (Flying Fish)
Long Legged Hannah (From Butte, Montana)
Jesse Hunter; *A Man Like Me* . . . . (BNA)
Louisiana Rain (Baton Rouge)
Tom Petty; *Playback* . . . . (MCA)
Tom Petty And The Heartbreakers; *Damn The Torpedoes* . . . . (MCA)
Man From Bowling Green
Johnny Paycheck; *Johnny Paycheck Hits Home* . . . . . (Columbia Special Prod.)
Take This Job And Shove It . . . . (Epic)
Mary's Boy Child (Bethlehem)
Andy Williams; *Merry Christmas* . . . . (Columbia)
Anne Murray; *Anne Murray Christmas* . . . . (Liberty)
Harry Belafonte; *Billboard's Greatest Christmas Hits-C* . . . . (Rhino)
This Is Christmas-C . . . . (RCA)
Kiri Te Kanawa; *Christmas With Kiri Te Kanawa* . . . . (London)
Me And Bobby McGee (Baton Rouge)
Grateful Dead; *Grateful Dead (Skull & Roses)* . . . . (Warner Bros.)
Janis Joplin; *Janis* . . . . (Legacy)
Janis Joplin's Greatest Hits . . . . (Columbia)
Pearl . . . . (Legacy)
Rock Classics Of The '70s-C . . . . (Columbia)
Willie Nelson; *Willie Nelson Sings Kristofferson* . . . . (Columbia)
Melancholy Blue (Biloxi)
Trisha Yearwood; *Inside Out* . . . . (MCA)
Next Stop Brattleboro
NRBQ; *Freight Train Blues-Classic Railroad Songs-#4-C* . . . . (Rounder)
Night In Buenos Aires
101 Strings Orchestra; *Best Of Latin* . . . . (Alshire)
Off To Buffalo
Fletcher Henderson & The Dixie Stompers; *Fletcher Henderson & The Dixie Stompers-1925-1928* . . . . (Disques Swing)
Miroslav Vitous; *Guardian Angels* . . . . (Evidence Music)
One Night In Bangkok
Murray Head; *Chess Pieces* . . . . (RCA)
Original Broadway Cast; *Chess* . . . . (RCA)
Passage To Bangkok
Rush; *2112* . . . . (Mercury)
Exit...Stage Left . . . . (Mercury)
Rush-Chronicles . . . . (Mercury)
Pretty Little Lady From Beaumont, Texas
George Jones; *One Woman Man* . . . . (Epic)
Texas Super Hits-C . . . . (Columbia)
Richest Man In Bogota
Gil Melle; *Mindscape* . . . . (Blue Note)
Riflemen Of Bennington
Jim Burroughs; *Songs Of Rebellion* . . . . (Audio Fidelity)
Rivers Of Babylon
Boney M; *Nightflight To Venus* . . . . (Sire)
Linda Ronstadt; *Hasten Down The Wind* . . . . (Asylum)
Melodians; *Grooveyard-C* . . . . (Mango)

ST/The Harder They Come . . . .(Mango)
Road To Bangor
Northeast Winds; *Songs Of Ireland & The Sea* . . . . (Folk Era)
She Came From Fort Worth (Boulder)
Kathy Mattea; *Willow In The Wind* . . . . (Mercury)
Pat Alger & Kathy Mattea; *True Love & Other Short Stories-C* . . . . . (Sugar Hill)
Shuffle Off To Buffalo
Hal Kemp; *Best Of The Big Bands-C* . . . . (Columbia)
Original Broadway Cast; *42nd Street* . . . .(RCA Victor)
Star Of Bethlehem
Emmylou Harris & Neil Young; *Duets-C* . . . . (Reprise)
Neil Young; *Decade* . . . . (Reprise)
Neil Young, Crazy Horse & The Bullets; *American Stars 'N Bars* . . . . . (Reprise)
Streets Of Bakersfield
Buck Owens; *Buck Owens' All-Time Greatest Hits-#1* . . . . (Curb)
Buck Owens Collection-1959-1990 . . . . (Rhino)
Dwight Yoakam; *Buenas Noches From A Lonely Room* . . . . (Reprise)
Just Lookin' For A Hit . . . . (Reprise)
Dwight Yoakam & Buck Owens; *Country's Greatest Hits-#9-'80s Duets-C* . . . . (Priority)
Streets Of Belfast
Celtic Thunder; *Light Of Other Days* . . . .(Green Linnet)
Theme From ''Beverly Hills 90210''
John Davis; *Beverly Hills 90210: Songs From The Peach Pit* . . . . (Rhino)
ST/Beverly Hills, 90210-College Years . . . . (Giant)
Television's Greatest Hits-#7-Cable Ready-C . . . . (TVT)
Theme From ''Fresh Prince Of Bel-Air''
Original Soundtrack; *Television's Greatest Hits-#7-Cable Ready-C* . . . . . (TVT)
Theme From ''The Beverly Hillbillies''
Original Soundtrack; *CBS: The First 50 Years* . . . . (TVT)
Television's Greatest Hits-#1-C . . . . (TVT)
Theme From ''The Flintstones'' (Bedrock)
Original Soundtrack; *Hanna-Barbera Classics-#1-Original Recordings Of The World's Most Famous Cartoon Themes & Scores* . . . . (Kid Rhino/Rhino 4 Kids)
Hanna-Barbera Pic-A-Nic Basket Of Cartoon Classics . . . . (Kid Rhino/Rhino 4 Kids)
Television's Greatest Hits-#1-C . . . . (TVT)
Steve Hobbs; *Escape* . . . . (Cexton)
There Ain't No Beverly Hills In Tennessee
Shenandoah; *Long Time Comin'* . . . . (RCA)
Tiananmen Square (Beijing)
Blazing Redheads; *Crazed Women* . . . . (Reference)
Tiger (Bethlehem)
Paula Cole; *This Fire* . . . . (Imago)
Train To Bombay
Christopher Max; *More Than Physical* . . . .(EMI)
Tree Grows In Burbank
Harry James; *The Uncollected Harry James-#5-1943-1953* . . . . (Hindsight)
What Mattered Most (Baton Rouge)
Ty Herndon; *Super Hits Of 1995-C* . . . .(Epic)
What Mattered Most . . . .(Epic)

CITIES: BALTIMORE

*See Also: **STATES: MARYLAND***

Baltimore
Nina Simone; *Let It Be Me* . . . . (Verve)
Randy Newman; *Little Criminals* . . . .(Warner Bros.)
Baltimore
Drifters; *1959-1965-All-Time Greatest Hits And More* . . . . (Atlantic)
Baltimore
Lyle Lovett; *Joshua Judges Ruth* . . . . (Curb/MCA)
Baltimore Oriole
George Harrison; *Somewhere In England* . . . . (Dark Horse)
Baltimore Oriole
Carmen McRae; *Greatest Of Carmen McRae* . . . .(MCA)
Barefoot In Baltimore
Strawberry Alarm Clock; *Best Of The Strawberry Alarm Clock-#1* . . .(Bac-Trac)
Engine Engine #9
Roger Miller; *Best Of Roger Miller-#2-King Of The Road* . . . . (Mercury)
Best Of Roger Miller-His Greatest Songs . . . . (Curb)
King Of The Road-Genius Of Roger Miller . . . . (Mercury)
Roger Miller-Golden Hits . . . . (Smash)
Roger Miller-The Hits . . . . (Mercury)
Train Trax-C . . . . (Sony Music Special Prod.)
From Baltimore To Paris
Go West; *Dancing On The Couch* . . . . (Chrysalis)
Girl From Baltimore
Fleshtones; *Living Legends* . . . .(I.R.S.)
Hungry Heart
Bruce Springsteen; *Bruce Springsteen's Greatest Hits* . . . . (Columbia)
The River . . . . (Columbia)
Bruce Springsteen & The E Street Band; *Bruce Springsteen & The E Street Band Live/1975-85* . . . . (Legacy)

Lady Came From Baltimore
Joan Baez; *Contemporary Ballad Book* . . . . (Vanguard)
Joan . . . . (Vanguard)
John Stewart; *Neon Beach* . . . . (Homecoming)
Johnny Cash; *Johnny Cash-16 Biggest Hits-#2* . . . . (Legacy)
Tim Hardin; *Hang On To A Dream-Verve Recordings* . . . .(Polydor)
Port Of Baltimore
Gerry Mulligan & Scott Hamilton; *Soft Lights And Sweet Music* . . . . (Concord Jazz)
Raining In Baltimore
Counting Crows; *August And Everything After* . . . . (David Geffen Co.)
Streets Of Baltimore, The
Bobby Bare; *This Is Bobby Bare* . . . . (RCA)
Flying Burrito Brothers; *Live From Europe* . . . .(Relix)
Gram Parsons; *GP/Grievous Angel* . . . . (Reprise)
Gram Parsons/Fallen Angels Live-1973 . . . . (Sierra)
Tomorrow Night In Baltimore
Roger Miller; *Best Of Roger Miller* . . . . (Mercury)
More Golden Hits . . . .(Smash)
What's New In Baltimore?
Frank Zappa; *Meets The Mothers Of Prevention* . . . . (Rykodisc)
You Can't Do That On Stage Anymore-#5 . . . . (Rykodisc)

CITIES: BERLIN

*See Also: **COUNTRIES: GERMANY***

Berlin
Marillion; *Seasons End* . . . . (Capitol)
Berlin
Lou Reed; *Berlin* . . . .(RCA)
Berlin To Memphis
Elvis Hitler; *Disgraceland* . . . . (Restless)
Berlin Tonight
Bruce Cockburn; *World Of Wonders* . . . . (Columbia)
Berlin Wall
Johnny Clegg & Savuka; *Third World Child* . . . . (Capitol)
City Of Night (Berlin)
Peter Schilling; *Different Story (World Of Lust & Crime)* . . . . (Elektra)
Dancing In Berlin
Berlin; *Love Life* . . . . (Geffen)
Doing The Best That I Can (Escape From Berlin)
Stevie Nicks; *Other Side Of The Mirror* . . . .(Modern)
First We Take Manhattan
Jennifer Warnes; *Critics Choice-C* . . . .(Cypress)
Famous Blue Raincoat . . . . (Private Music)
Leonard Cohen; *I'm Your Man* . . . . (Columbia)
R.E.M.; *I'm Your Fan-Songs Of Leonard Cohen* . . . .(Atlantic)
Party At The Berlin Wall
Root Boy Slim & The Sex Change Band; *Root 6* . . . . (Naked Language)
Road Movie To Berlin
They Might Be Giants; *Flood* . . . . (Elektra)
Rudiger
Mark Knopfler; *Golden Heart* . . . . (Warner Bros.)
Summer In Berlin
Alphaville; *Forever Young* . . . .(Atlantic)
There'll Be A Hot Time In The Old Town Tonight (Berlin)
Bessie Smith; *Bessie Smith-The Complete Recordings-#3* . . . . (Legacy)
Louis Armstrong; *Best Of Louis Armstrong* . . . . (Audio Fidelity)
Turk Murphy's San Francisco Jazz Band; *Turk Murphy's San Francisco Jazz Band* . . . . (Good Time Jazz)
Woody Herman; *The Uncollected Woody Herman & His First Herd* . . . . (Hindsight)

CITIES: BIRMINGHAM

*See Also: **COUNTRIES: ENGLAND, STATES: ALABAMA***

96 Miles To Birmingham
Dick Silveras; *Negro Folk Songs & Ballads* . . . . (Stinson)
All The Way To Birmingham/Roaring Mary
Celtic Thunder; *Celtic Thunder* . . . . (Green Linnet)
Birmingham
Randy Newman; *Good Old Boys* . . . .(Reprise)
Birmingham
Jeannie Kendall; *45-#17513* . . . . (Dot)
Birmingham
Amanda Marshall; *Amanda Marshall* . . . . (Epic)
Birmingham Alabama
Harry Belafonte; *Harry Belafonte's All-Time Greatest Hits-#3* . . . . (RCA)
Birmingham Blues
Charlie Daniels Band; *Night Rider* . . . . (Epic)
Volunteer Jam-C . . . . (Capricorn)
Birmingham Blues
Electric Light Orchestra; *Out Of The Blue* . . . .(Jet)

Birmingham Bounce
Red Foley; *45-#46234* . . . .(Decca)
Tommy Dorsey & His Orchestra; *Swing Vocalists Greatest Hits-C* . . . . (RCA Victor)
The Post-War Era . . . .(Bluebird)
Birmingham Jail
Leadbelly; *Last Sessions* . . . .(Smithsonian Folkways)
Michael Martin Murphey; *Cowboy Songs-#3-Rhymes Of The Renegades* . . . .(Warner Western)
Birmingham Jail
Peggy Lee; *Peggy Lee Sings The Blues* . . . .(Musicmasters)
Birmingham Sunday
Joan Baez; *Contemporary Ballad Book* . . . .(Vanguard)
Joan Baez/5 . . . .(Vanguard)
Richard Farina; *Best Of Broadside 1962-1968: Anthems Of The American Underground From The Pages Of Broadside Magazine-C* . . . .(Smithsonian Folkways)
Boulder To Birmingham
Emmylou Harris; *Pieces Of The Sky* . . . .(Reprise)
Profile/Best Of Emmylou Harris . . . .(Warner Bros.)
Down And Out In Birmingham
Pirates Of The Mississippi; *Pirates Of The Mississippi* . . . .(Liberty)
Fifteen Miles To Birmingham
Happy & Artie Traum/Others; *Mud Acres* . . . .(Rounder)
From Cotton To Satin
Gene Watson; *This Dream's On Me* . . . . (MCA)
Johnny Paycheck; *Take This Job And Shove It* . . . . Epic)
Going Back To Birmingham
Ten Years After; *Universal* . . . . (Chrysalis)
My Elusive Dreams
Bobby Vinton; *Autumn Memories* . . . . (Epic)
Bobby Vinton's All-Time Greatest Hits . . . . (Epic)
Charlie Rich; *Charlie Rich-16 Biggest Hits* . . . . (Legacy)
Charlie Rich's Greatest Hits . . . . (Epic)
Charlie Rich-Super Hits . . . . (Epic)
David Houston & Tammy Wynette; *Best Of David Houston* . . . .(Collector's Choice)
Billboard Top Country Hits-1967-C . . . .(Rhino)
Tammy Wynette's Greatest Hits . . . . (Epic)
Promised Land
Band; *Moondog Matinee* . . . .(Capitol)
Chuck Berry; *Rock 'N' Roll Rarities-20 Magic Tracks* . . . . (Chess)
The Chess Box-Chuck Berry . . . . (Chess)
Elvis Presley; *Promised Land* . . . . (RCA)
ST/This Is Elvis . . . . (RCA)
Freddy Weller; *Country Music Classics-#11-Early '70s-C* . . . . (K-Tel)
Freddy Weller's Greatest Hits . . . .(Columbia)
Gary Morris; *Full Moon Empty Heart* . . . . (Liberty)
Grateful Dead; *Steal Your Face* . . . .(Grateful Dead)
James Taylor; *Walking Man* . . . . (Warner Bros.)
Kingfish; *Kingfish/Alive In Eighty Five-Double Dose* . . . . (Relix)
Train To Birmingham
Kevin Welch & The Overtones; *Western Beat* . . . .(Reprise)
When Jesus Left Birmingham
John Mellencamp & Sounds Of Blackness; *Human Wheels* . . . . (Mercury)

CITIES: BOSTON

See Also: **STATES: MASSACHUSETTS**

Boston
Byrds; *...In The Beginning* . . . .(Rhino)
Gene Clark; *Echoes* . . . .(Columbia)
Boston
Lori Lieberman; *Letting Go* . . . . (Millennium)
Boston Lady
John Stewart; *Fire In The Wind* . . . .(RSO)
Boston Rag
Steely Dan; *Countdown To Ecstasy* . . . . (MCA)
Dirty Water
Standells; *Best Of The Standells* . . . .(Rhino)
Nuggets-Classic Collection From The Psychedelic '60s-C . . . . (Rhino)
Super Oldies Of The '60s-#10-C . . . . (Audio Fidelity)
Hey Nineteen
Steely Dan; *Gaucho* . . . . (MCA)
Steely Dan-Gold . . . . (MCA)
M.T.A.
Kingston Trio; *25 Years Non-Stop* . . . . (Xeres)
Best Of The Kingston Trio . . . .(Capitol)
Capitol Collectors Series-The Kingston Trio . . . .(Capitol)
Scarlet Ribbons . . . .(Capitol)
Very Best Of The Kingston Trio . . . .(Capitol)
Please Come To Boston
Dave Loggins; *Apprentice (In A Musical Workshop)* . . . . Epic)
Rock Artifacts-From The Vaults-#2-C . . . .(Legacy)
Super Hits Of The '70s-Have A Nice Day-#13-C . . . .(Rhino)
David Allan Coe; *David Allan Coe-17 Greatest Hits* . . . .(Columbia)

For The Record-The First 10 Years . . . .(Columbia)
Joan Baez; *Best Of Joan Baez* . . . . (A&M)
Joan Baez-Classics-#8 . . . . (A&M)
Reba McEntire; *Starting Over* . . . . (MCA)
Railroad Lady
J.D. Crowe and the New South; *My Home Ain't In The Hall Of Fame* . . . . (Rounder)
Jerry Jeff Walker; *A Man Must Carry On.* . . . . (MCA)
Gypsy Songman . . . . (Rykodisc)
Jimmy Buffett; *White Sport Coat & A Pink Crustacean.* . . . . (MCA)
Willie Nelson; *Greatest Hits (& Some That Will Be)* . . . . (Columbia)
To Lefty From Willie . . . . (Columbia)
Red Moon Over Boston
Romanovsky & Phillips; *Be Political Not Polite* . . . .(Fresh Fruit)
Sandy MacIntyre's Trip To Boston
John Campbell; *Cape Breton Violin Music* . . . .(Rounder)
Theresa & Marie MacLellan; *Trip To Mabou Ridge* . . . .(Rounder)
Twilight In Boston
Jonathan Richman; *I Jonathan* . . . .(Rounder)

CITIES: C

See Also: **CITIES: CHICAGO, CITIES: CINCINNATI, CITIES: GENERAL, COUNTRIES: A-Z, STATES: A-Z**

1-900-2-COMPTON
N.W.A.; *Efil4zaggin.* . . . .(Ruthless/Priority)
Anaheim, Azusa & Cucamonga Sewing Circle
Jan & Dean; *Best Of Jan & Dean* . . . .(EMI)
Jan & Dean-Legendary Masters . . . .(EMI)
April In Cambridge
Peter Walker; *Rainy Day Raga.* . . . .(Vanguard)
Beaches Of Cheyenne
Garth Brooks; *Fresh Horses* . . . .(Capitol)
Limited Series Box. . . . .(Capitol)
Big Ball's In Cowtown
Asleep At The Wheel; *Very Best Of Asleep At The Wheel Since 1970* . . . .(Relentless/Madacy)
Asleep At The Wheel featuring George Strait; *Tribute To The Music Of Bob Wills And The Texas Playboys-C* . . . .(Liberty)
Bob Wills & His Texas Playboys; *Best Of Bob Wills & His Texas Playboys* . . . . (MCA)
For The Last Time . . . .(Capitol)
Born And Raised In Compton
DJ Quik; *Quik Is The Name* . . . . (Profile)
Boyz-N-The-Hood (Compton)
Dynamite Hack; *Superfast* . . . . (Farm Club/Universal)
Burn On (Cleveland)
Randy Newman; *Sail Away* . . . . (Reprise)
Calcutta
Lawrence Welk; *Best Of Lawrence Welk-20 Great Hits* . . . .(Ranwood)
Calcutta. . . . .(Ranwood)
Camarillo Brillo
Mothers; *Apostrophe/Overnite Sensation* . . . .(Rykodisc)
Carmel By The Sea
Kitty Wells; *45-#31123* . . . .(Decca)
Casey, Illinois
Erica Wheeler; *Three Wishes* . . . .(Signature)
Charleston
Paul Whiteman & His Orchestra; *Nipper's Greatest Hits Of The '20s-C* . . . . (RCA)
Charleston Rag
Eubie Blake; *Greatest Ragtime Of The Century-C* . . . . (Biograph)
Charleston Railroad Tavern
Bobby Bare; *This Is Bobby Bare* . . . . (RCA)
Charlotte's In North Carolina
Ronnie McDowell; *Country Boy's Heart* . . . . (Epic)
Chattanooga Choo Choo
Asleep At The Wheel; *Train Trax-C* . . . . (Sony Music Special Prod.)
Billy Strange; *Railroad Man* . . . . (Crescendo)
Boston Pops Orchestra/Arthur Fiedler; *Boston Pops Orchestra/Arthur Fiedler* . . . . (RCA)
Greatest Hits Of The '40s . . . . (RCA)
Glenn Miller; *Best Of Glenn Miller* . . . . (RCA)
Decade Of The '40s-C . . . . (RCA)
Glenn Miller-A Legendary Performer-#1 & 2. . . . .(Bluebird)
Memorial 1944-1969 . . . .(Bluebird)
Nipper's Greatest Hits Of The '40s-#1-C . . . . (RCA)
Glenn Miller & His Orchestra; *Glenn Miller & His Orchestra-Pure Gold.* . . . .(Bluebird)
Tuxedo Junction; *Best Of Butterfly Records-C* . . . .(Hot Prod.)
Tuxedo Junction . . . .(Butterfly)
Chattanoogie Shoe Shine Boy
Freddy Cannon; *14 Booming Hits* . . . .(Rhino)
Red Foley; *Red Foley: The Country Music Hall Of Fame* . . . . (MCA Special Prod.)
The Nashville Sound: Owen Bradley-C . . . .(Decca)

Chelsea Bridge
Duke Ellington; *Blanton-Webster Band* . . . . (Bluebird)
Concert In The Virgin Islands . . . . (Discovery)
Sarah Vaughan; *Duke Ellington Songbook Two* . . . .(Pablo)

Chelsea Morning
Joni Mitchell; *Clouds* . . . . (Reprise)
Judy Collins; *New York Songs-C* . . . . (Rhino)
Neil Diamond; *Rainbow* . . . .(MCA)
Stones . . . .(MCA)

Cherry Hill Park
Billy Joe Royal; *Billy Joe Royal's Greatest Hits*. . . . . (Columbia)
Super Hits Of The '70s-Have A Nice Day-#1-C . . . . (Rhino)

Cheyenne
Bluegrass Album Band; *Bluegrass Compact Disc* . . . . (Rounder)
Bo Diddley; *Bo Diddley Is A Gunslinger* . . . . (Chess)
Hanoi Rocks; *Bangkok Shocks Saigon Shakes Hanoi Rocks*. . . . .(Geffen)
Ricky Lynn Gregg; *Ricky Lynn Gregg* . . . . (Liberty)
Sons Of The Pioneers; *Sunset On The Range* . . . . (Pair)

Cheyenne Autumn
Kansas; *Leftoverture*. . . . . (Kirshner)

China Grove
Doobie Brothers; *Best Of The Doobies*. . . . .(Warner Bros.)
Captain & Me . . . .(Warner Bros.)
Farewell Tour . . . .(Warner Bros.)

Chinatown
Joe Jackson; *Night & Day* . . . . (A&M)

Chinatown
Chaka Khan; *I Feel For You* . . . .(Warner Bros.)

Chinatown
Doobie Brothers; *Livin' On The Fault Line* . . . .(Warner Bros.)

Chinatown
Greg Kihn; *Next Of Kihn* . . . . (Beserkley)

Chinatown My Chinatown
Al Jolson; *The Al Jolson Story-#1* . . . .(MCA)
Louis Armstrong; *Armstrong #2* . . . . (Everest)
Stardust . . . . (Portrait)

Cleveland
Martin Mull; *Sex & Violins* . . . .(MCA)

Cleveland Polka
Li'l Wally; *Thanks For A Wonderful Evening* . . . .(Jay Jay)

Cleveland Rocks
Ian Hunter; *ST/Light Of Day*. . . . . (CBS Associated)
You're Never Alone With A Schizophrenic. . . . . (Razor & Tie)

Clovis, New Mexico
Hank Williams, Jr.; *Hank Williams, Jr. & Friends* . . . . (Polydor)

Cold Irons Bound
Bob Dylan; *Time Out Of Mind* . . . . (Columbia)

C-O-N-S-T-A-N-T-I-N-O-P-L-E
Paul Whiteman & His Orchestra; *78-#1402* . . . . (Columbia)

Cooperstown
Terry Cashman; *Passin' It On-America's Baseball Heritage In Song* . . (Legacy)

Copenhagen
Artie Shaw; *Best Of The Big Bands-#3* . . . . (Columbia)
Bix Beiderbecke & His Chicago Cornets; *Bix Beiderbecke & His Chicago Cornets* . . . . (Milestone)
Chris LeDoux; *Songs Of Rodeo Life* . . . . (Capitol)

Copenhagen Junkie
Chris LeDoux; *Melodies & Memories* . . . . (Liberty)

Cowtown
George Strait; *George Strait-Number 7* . . . .(MCA)
Webb Pierce; *Webb Pierce-Golden Hits-#2* . . . . (Plantation)

Cowtown
Carly Simon; *Another Passenger* . . . . (Elektra)

Down In Chihuahua
Stan Kenton; *Lighter Side*. . . . . (Creative World)

Evening In Casablanca
Art Farmer Quintet; *Art Farmer Quintet*. . . . .(Prestige)

Fall Of Charleston
Tennessee Ernie Ford; *Tennessee Ernie Ford Sings Songs Of The Civil War*. . . . . (Capitol)

Fire In Cairo
Cure; *Boys Don't Cry* . . . . (Elektra)

Fuck Compton
Tim Dog; *Penicillin On Wax*. . . . . (Ruffhouse)

Goin' To Cairo
Joel Mabus; *Settin' The Woods On Fire* . . . . (Flying Fish)

Goin' To Chattanooga
Ralph Willis; *East Coast Blues* . . . . (Collectables)

Grant Avenue
Original Cast; *Flower Drum Song* . . . . (Sony Music Classical)

I Can Still Make Cheyenne
George Strait; *Blue Clear Sky* . . . .(MCA)
Latest Greatest Straitest Hits . . . .(MCA)

I'm Gonna Charleston Back To Charleston
Firehouse Five Plus Two; *Goes South* . . . . (Good Time Jazz)

Istanbul (Not Constantinople)
Four Lads; *Four Lads-16 Most Requested Songs* . . . . (Legacy)

It's A Compton Thang
Compton's Most Wanted; *It's A Compton Thang* . . . . (Orpheus)

Last Train To Clarksville
Monkees; *Monkees* . . . . (Arista)
Monkees' Greatest Hits . . . . (Rhino)
Monkees-Live-1967 . . . . (Rhino)
Then & Now...The Best Of The Monkees . . . . (Arista)

Look Out Cleveland
Band; *The Band*. . . . . (Capitol)

Night Boat To Cairo
Madness; *One Step Beyond* . . . .(Sire)
ST/Dance Craze . . . . (Chrysalis)

On The Road To Calais
Al Jolson; *Music From The New York Stage (1890-1920)-#4-1917-1920-C*. . . . . (Pearl)

Pancho And Lefty (Cleveland)
Merle Haggard & Willie Nelson; *19 Hot Country Requests-C* . . . . (Epic)
Columbia Country Classics-#3-Americana-C . . . . (Columbia)
For The Record: Merle Haggard-43 Legendary Hits . . . . (BNA)
His Epic Hits-First 11 To Be Continued-C . . . . (Epic)
Pancho And Lefty . . . . (Epic)
Townes Van Zandt; *Live & Obscure* . . . . (Sugar Hill)

Pride Of Cucamonga
Grateful Dead; *From The Mars Hotel* . . . . (Grateful Dead)

Purple Rose Of Cairo
New Orleans Ragtime Orchestra; *New Orleans Jazz-C*. . . . . (Arhoolie)

Raised In Compton
Compton's Most Wanted; *Straight Checkn 'Em* . . . . (Orpheus)

Relaxin' At Camarillo
Charlie Parker; *Very Best Of Bird* . . . . (Warner Bros.)
Joe Henderson; *Relaxin' At Camarillo* . . . . (Contemporary)
Joe Pass; *Appassionato* . . . . (Pablo)

Road To Columbus
Sally Van Meter; *All In Good Time* . . . . (Sugar Hill)

Sail Away (Charleston Bay)
Linda Ronstadt; *Don't Cry Now* . . . . (Asylum)
Randy Newman; *Sail Away*. . . . . (Reprise)

Shipmates In Cheyenne
Bobby Darin; *1936-1973*. . . . . (Motown)

Shoot Out In Chinatown
Band; *Cahoots*. . . . . (Capitol)

Straight Outta Compton
N.W.A.; *Straight Outta Compton* . . . . (Ruthless/Priority)

Streets Of Calgary
Kate Wolf; *Wind Blows Wild*. (Kaleidoscope)

This Is Compton
Compton's Most Wanted; *It's A Compton Thang* . . . . (Orpheus)

UFO Over Cairo
Nasa; *Insha-Allah!* . . . .(Sire)

Welcome To Chinatown
John Cougar; *John Cougar* . . . . (Riva)

When The Swallows Come Back To Capistrano
Glenn Miller; *In The Mood* . . . . (Pro-Arte)
Ink Spots; *Best Of The Ink Spots* . . . .(MCA)
Ink Spots' Greatest Hits-Original Recordings-1939-1946 . . . . (MCA)

Wild Horses (Cheyenne)
Garth Brooks; *No Fences* . . . . (Capitol)

Wonderful Copenhagen
Danny Kaye; *Hans Christian Andersen* . . . .(MCA)
Dave Brubeck; *I Like Jazz-Essence Of Dave Brubeck*. . . . . (Columbia)
Dave Brubeck Quartet; *Concerts-Amsterdam/Copenhagen/Carnegie* . . . . (Columbia)
Jazz Masters-27 Classic Performances-C . . . . (Columbia)

CITIES: CHICAGO

See Also: *STATES: ILLINOIS*

2120 South Michigan Avenue
Rolling Stones; *12 X 5* . . . .(Abkco)

At The Chicago World's Fair
Original Cast; *Show Boat* . . . . (RCA Victor)

Back To Chicago
Styx; *Edge of The Century*. . . . . (A&M)

Back To Chicago
Duke Tumatoe; *Dukes Up* . . . . (Blind Pig)

Bad, Bad Leroy Brown
Jim Croce; *Billboard Top Rock 'N' Roll Hits-1973-C* . . . . (Rhino)
Down The Highway . . . . (Atlantic)
Life & Times . . . . (Lifesong)
Photographs & Memories/His Greatest Hits . . . .(Atlantic)

Band From Chicago
Max Creek; *Windows* . . . .(Relix)

Born In Chicago
George Thorogood & The Destroyers; *Boogie People* . . . . (EMI)
Paul Butterfield Blues Band; *Golden Butter* . . . . (Elektra)

Paul Butterfield Blues Band . . . . (Elektra)
Born In Chicago
Pixies; *Rubaiyat-Elektra's 40th Anniversary-C* . . . . (Elektra)
Chicago
Al Jolson; *Immortal Al Jolson* . . . . (MCA)
Judy Garland; *Hits Of Judy Garland* . . . . (Capitol)
Judy Garland-At Carnegie Hall . . . . (Capitol)
Tony Bennett & Count Basie; *Echoes Of An Era-Count Basie Vocal
Years* . . . . (Roulette)
Chicago
Doobie Brothers; *Doobie Brothers* . . . . (Warner Bros.)
Chicago
Crosby, Stills, Nash & Young; *4 Way Street* . . . . (Atlantic)
David Crosby & Graham Nash; *Best Of David Crosby &
Graham Nash* . . . . (MCA)
Graham Nash; *Songs For Beginners* . . . . (Atlantic)
Chicago Breakdown
Louis Armstrong; *Genius Of Louis Armstrong* . . . . (Columbia)
The Louis Armstrong Story-#2 . . . . (Columbia)
Louis Armstrong & Earl Hines; *Louis Armstrong-Vol. 4-In
New York* . . . . (Columbia)
Chicago Institute
Manfred Mann's Earth Band; *Watch* . . . . (Warner Bros.)
Chicago Send Her Home
Thelma Houston & Jerry Butler; *Two To One* . . . . (Motown)
Chicago Song
David Sanborn; *Change Of Heart* . . . . (Warner Bros.)
City Of Chicago
Christy Moore; *Christy Moore* . . . . (Atlantic)
Ride On . . . . (Green Linnet)
Cold Windy City Of Chicago
Boxcar Willie; *Best Of Boxcar Willie-#1* . . . . (Mainstreet)
Comin' Back To South Chicago
Jeannie & Jimmy Cheatham; *Luv In The Afternoon* . . . . (Concord Jazz)
Eggplant That Ate Chicago
Dr. West's Medicine Show & Junk Band; *Dr. Demento Presents The
Greatest Novelty Records-#3-1960s-C* . . . . (Rhino)
Going To Chicago Blues
Count Basie; *Essential Count Basie-#1* . . . . (Columbia)
Jimmy Rushing; *Essential Jimmy Rushing* . . . . (Vanguard)
Joe Williams; *Jazz Singers* . . . . (Prestige)
Lambert, Hendricks & Ross; *Twisted-Best Of Lambert, Hendricks
& Ross* . . . . (Rhino)
Lowell Fulsom; *Let's Go Get Stoned* . . . . (Kent)
Golden Ring
Emmylou Harris/Linda Ronstadt/Anna & Kate McGarrigle; *Tammy
Wynette...Remembered-C* . . . . (Asylum)
George Jones & Tammy Wynette; *George Jones & Tammy Wynette-16
Biggest Hits* . . . . (Epic/Legacy)
Tammy Wynette & George Jones; *Encore-Tammy Wynette & George
Jones* . . . . (Epic)
Tammy Wynette & George Jones' Greatest Hits . . . . (Epic)
Tammy Wynette-Anniversary-20 Years Of Hits . . . . (Epic)
I Wish I Was In Chicago
Original Cast; *Charlie Sent Me* . . . . (Glendale)
I'm Leaving Chicago
Luther "Guitar Jr." Johnson & His Magic Rockers; *I Want To Groove
With You* . . . . (Bullseye Blues)
In Chicago's Forest Preserve
Li'l Wally; *Polish Feelings* . . . . (Jay Jay)
In The Ghetto
Elvis Presley; *Elvis Presley-Pure Gold* . . . . (RCA)
From Elvis In Memphis . . . . (RCA)
From Memphis To Vegas/From Vegas To Memphis . . . . (RCA)
The Top Ten Hits . . . . (RCA)
Worldwide 50 Gold Award Hits, Vol. 1, Parts 1 & 2 . . . . (RCA)
Mac Davis; *Mac Davis' Greatest Hits* . . . . (Columbia)
Is Chicago, Is Not Chicago
Soul Coughing; *Ruby Vroom* . . . . (Slash)
ST/Tommy Boy . . . . (Warner Bros.)
Jesus Just Left Chicago
ZZ Top; *Best Of ZZ Top* . . . . (Warner Bros.)
Six Pack . . . . (Warner Bros.)
Tres Hombres . . . . (Warner Bros.)
Land Of Wrigley, The
Stormy Weather; *Baseball's Greatest Hits-C* . . . . (Rhino)
Little Chicago Fire
Count Basie & His Orchestra; *Live At El Morocco* . . . . (Telarc)
Little Joe From Chicago
Mary Lou Williams; *Best Of Mary Lou Williams* . . . . (Pablo)
Nat "King" Cole; *Straighten Up And Fly Right* . . . . (Pro-Arte)
Mama Chicago
Bonnie Koloc; *With You On My Side* . . . . (Flying Fish)
Man From The South, The
Ted Weems & His Orchestra; *78-#22238* . . . . (Victor)
My Kind Of Town
Frank Sinatra; *At The Sands* . . . . (Reprise)
Sinatra Reprise-The Very Good Years . . . . (Reprise)

Sinatra: A Man And His Music . . . . (Reprise)
Sinatra-The Main Event Live . . . . (Reprise)
The Reprise Collection . . . . (Reprise)
Night Chicago Died
Paper Lace; *Back To The '70s-#3-C* . . . . (Dominion Entert.)
Super Hits Of The '70s-Have A Nice Day-#13-C . . . . (Rhino)
On The Southside Of Chicago
Vic Damone; *Best Of Vic Damone* . . . . (RCA)
Only In Chicago
Barry Manilow; *Barry* . . . . (Arista)
Phone Call From Chicago
Peter Himmelman; *From Strength To Strength* . . . . (Epic)
Pretty Girls In Chicago Polka
Li'l Wally; *Brings Happiness To You* . . . . (Jay Jay)
Sheik Of Chicago
Joe Stampley; *Joe Stampley's Greatest Hits* . . . . (Epic)
Streets Of Old Chicago
Carl Martin/Ted Bogan/Howard Armstrong; *That Old Gang
Of Mine* . . . . (Flying Fish)
Sweet Chicago Home
David Bromberg; *How Late'll Ya Play 'Til?* . . . . (Fantasy)
Sweet Home Chicago
Blues Brothers; *ST/The Blues Brothers* . . . . (Atlantic)
Foghat; *Best Of Foghat-#2* . . . . (Rhino)
Stone Blue . . . . (Rhino)
Junior Parker; *Best Of Junior Parker* . . . . (MCA)
Leon Russell & Marc Benno; *Asylum Choir II* . . . . (MCA)
Magic Sam; *Magic Sam-Live* . . . . (Delmark)
Robert Johnson; *King Of The Delta Blues Singers-#2* . . . . (Columbia)
Robert Johnson-Complete Recordings . . . . (Columbia)
Taj Mahal; *Recycling The Blues & Other Related Stuff* . . . . . . (Columbia)
Urban Knights; *Urban Knights 3* . . . . (Narada)
Take Me Back To Chicago
Chicago; *Chicago XI* . . . . (Chicago)
Chicago's Greatest Hits-#2 (1974-81) . . . . (Chicago)
Group Portrait . . . . (Chicago)
Take Me Back To Chicago . . . . (Columbia)
Theme From "Chicago Hope"
Original Soundtrack; *CBS: The First 50 Years* . . . . (TVT)
Tight In Chicago
Mozelle Alderson; *Barrelhouse Mamas: Born In The Alley, Raised In The
Slums-C* . . . . (Yazoo)
Two Years In Chicago
Robin Trower; *1st Dibs* . . . . (Flying Fish)
When The Levee Breaks
Led Zeppelin; *Led Zeppelin IV* . . . . (Atlantic)
Led Zeppelin-Box Set . . . . (Atlantic)

CITIES: CINCINNATI
See Also: **STATES: OHIO**

Cincinnati Blues
Jesse Fuller; *Brother Lowdown* . . . . (Fantasy)
Favorites-Jesse Fuller . . . . (Prestige)
Frisco Bound . . . . (Arhoolie)
Ray Pennington & Buddy Emmons; *Swingin' From The '40s Through
The '80s* . . . . (Step One)
Cincinnati Daddy
Duke Ellington; *Jazz Heritage-Rockin' In Rhythm-#3-C* . . . (MCA Special Prod.)
Jungle Band-Brunswick Era-#2 . . . . (Decca)
Cincinnati Fatback
Roogalator; *Stiff Records Box Set* . . . . (Rhino)
Cincinnati Fireball
Johnny Burnette; *Best Of Johnny Burnette-You're Sixteen* . . . . . . (Gold Rush)
Cincinnati Jail
Lonnie Mack; *Attack Of The Killer V* . . . . (Alligator)
Second Sight . . . . (Alligator)
Cincinnati Lou
Merle Travis; *Best Of Merle Travis* . . . . (Rhino)
Cincinnati Rag
Jerry Douglas; *Fluxedo* . . . . (Rounder)
Cincinnati Stomp
Big Joe Duskin; *Cincinnati Stomp* . . . . (Arhoolie)
Cincinnati Underworld Woman
Bob Coleman & The Cincinnati Jug Band; *Cincinnati Blues-1928-
1936* . . . . (Sony Broadway)
Cincinnati, Ohio
Bill Anderson; *The Bill Anderson Story* . . . . (MCA)
Connie Smith; *Best Of Connie Smith* . . . . (Dominion Entert.)
Connie Smith's Greatest Hits-#1 . . . . (RCA)
Osborne Brothers; *Red, White & Bluegrass-C* . . . . (C.M.H. Prod.)
Cockroach That Ate Cincinnati
Possum; *Dr. Demento's Delights-C* . . . . (Warner Bros.)
Rose & The Arrangement; *Dr. Demento Presents The Greatest Novelty
Records-#4-1970s-C* . . . . (Rhino)

Sam's Place
 Buck Owens & The Buckaroos; *Billboard Top Country Hits-1967-C* . . . (Rhino)
South Of Cincinnati
 Dwight Yoakam; *Guitars, Cadillacs, Etc., Etc.* . . . . (Reprise)
Susie Cincinnati
 Beach Boys; *15 Big Ones* . . . . (Brother)
Theme From "WKRP In Cincinnati"
 Original Soundtrack; *CBS: The First 50 Years* . . . . (TVT)
 Television's Greatest Hits-#3-1970s & 1980s-C . . . . (TVT)
 Steve Carlisle; *Steve Carlisle Sings WKRP* . . . .(MCA)

CITIES: D

 See Also: **CITIES: DALLAS, DENVER, DETROIT, DUBLIN, CITIES: GENERAL, COUNTRIES: A-Z, STATES: A-Z**

Back Home In Derry
 Christy Moore; *Ride On* . . . .(Green Linnet)
 Spirit Of Freedom . . . .(Green Linnet)
Cliffs Of Dover
 Eric Johnson; *Ah Via Musicom* . . . . (Capitol)
Davenport Blues
 Bix Beiderbecke & His Chicago Cornets; *Bix Beiderbecke & His Chicago Cornets* . . . . (Milestone)
 Ry Cooder; *Jazz* . . . .(Warner Bros.)
Dayton Ohio 1903
 Randy Newman; *Sail Away* . . . . (Reprise)
Deadwood, South Dakota
 Nanci Griffith; *One Fair Summer Evening* . . . .(MCA)
Doraville
 Atlanta Rhythm Section; *Are You Ready!* . . . . (Polydor)
 South's Greatest Hits-C . . . . (Capricorn)
 Third Annual Pipe Dream . . . . (Polydor)
Drag City
 Jan & Dean; *Beach Party Blasts* . . . .(EMI)
 Best Of Jan & Dean . . . .(EMI)
 Dead Man's Curve . . . .(EMI)
 One Summer Night-Live . . . . (Rhino)
Dry Cleaner From Des Moines
 Joni Mitchell; *Mingus* . . . . (Elektra)
 Shadows & Light . . . . (Asylum)
Dubuque, Crazy Creek, & Goldrush
 Robin Flower; *Green Sneakers* . . . . (Flying Fish)
Duke Of Dubuque
 Manhattan Transfer; *Bop doo-wopp* . . . .(Atlantic)
 Manhattan Transfer-Live . . . .(Atlantic)
Eight'r From Decatur
 Bob Wills; *Best Of Bob Wills-#2* . . . .(MCA)
It's A Long Way To Daytona
 Mel Tillis; *45-#47412* . . . . (Elektra)
Ramona From Daytona
 Dave Holladay; *Ramona From Daytona* . . . . (Step One)
Romance In Durango
 Bob Dylan; *Biograph* . . . . (Columbia)
 Desire . . . . (Columbia)
Streets Of Derry
 Andy Irvine & Paul Brady; *Andy Irvine & Paul Brady* . . . .(Green Linnet)
There'll Be Bluebirds Over The White Cliffs Of Dover
 Kay Kyser & His Orchestra; *Best Of The Big Bands-C* . . . . (Columbia)
White Cliffs Of Dover
 Kay Kyser & His Orchestra; *16 Most Requested Songs Of The '40s-#1-C* . . . . (Legacy)
 Lee Andrews And The Hearts; *Lee Andrews And The Hearts' Biggest Hits* . . . .(Collectables)
 Mystics; *Mystics-16 Golden Classics* . . . .(Collectables)
 Righteous Brothers; *Righteous Brothers' Greatest Hits* . . . . (Verve)
 Righteous Brothers-Anthology 1962-1974 . . . . (Rhino)
 Rosemary Clooney; *For The Duration* . . . .(Concord Jazz)

CITIES: DALLAS

 See Also: **STATES: TEXAS**

Alice You've Made Dallas (Paradise)
 Lee Ferrell; *Hard Times* . . . . (TMS)
All The Rage In Paris
 Derailers; *Here Come The Derailers* . . . . (Lucky Dog)
Backside Of Dallas
 Jeannie C. Riley; *Jeannie C. Riley's Greatest Hits* . . . . (Plantation)
 Things Go Better With Love . . . . (Plantation)
Big D
 Broadway Cast; *Most Happy Fella* . . . . (RCA)
 Original Broadway Cast; *Most Happy Fella* . . . . (Sony Music Classical)
Cowboy Hat In Dallas
 Charlie Daniels Band; *Homesick Heroes* . . . .(Epic)

Dallas
 Joe Ely; *Must Notta Gotta Lotta* . . . . (MCA)
Dallas
 Jimmy Buffett; *A1A* . . . . (MCA)
Dallas
 Poco; *Head Over Heels* . . . . (MCA)
Dallas
 Jimmie Dale Gilmore; *Jimmie Dale Gilmore* . . . .(Hightone)
Dallas
 Johnny Winter; *Johnny Winter* . . . . (Columbia)
Dallas Alice
 Doug Sahm; *She's About A Mover: The Best Of Doug Sahm* . . . .(Edsel)
 Sir Douglas Quintet; *The Crazy Cajun Recordings* . . . .(Edsel)
Dallas Blues
 Louis Armstrong & His Orchestra; *Louis Armstrong & The Big Bands* . . . . (Disques Swing)
Dallas Cowboys
 Charley Pride; *45-#11736* . . . .(RCA)
Dallas Delight
 Buck Clayton & Buddy Tate; *Kansas City Nights* . . . .(Prestige)
Dallas Doings
 Duke Ellington; *Jubilee Stomp* . . . . (Bluebird)
Dallas Rag
 Dallas String Band; *The Greatest In Country Blues (1927-1936)-#2-C* . . . . (Sony Broadway)
 New Lost City Ramblers; *New Lost City Ramblers-Early Years-1958-1962* . . . .(Smithsonian Folkways)
Dallas Rag/Maple Leaf Rag
 David Bromberg; *How Late'll Ya Play 'Til?* . . . .(Fantasy)
Dallas To Odessa
 Lyn Childress; *Different Shade Of Country* . . . .(Step One)
Dallas We Come From
 Nemesis; *Munchies For Your Bass* . . . .(Profile)
Dallas, Texas
 Austin Lounge Lizards; *Highway Cafe Of The Damned* . . . . (Watermelon)
Down Dallas Alley
 Buckwheat Zydeco; *Taking It Home* . . . . (Island)
Eyes As Big As Dallas
 Randy Wagner; *45-#236* . . . . (Door Knob)
Forth Worth & Dallas Blues
 Leadbelly; *King Of The Twelve-String Guitar* . . . . (Columbia)
 Legends Of The Blues-#1-C . . . . (Columbia)
Goin' Through The Big D
 Mark Chesnutt; *What A Way To Live* . . . . (Decca)
Goin' To Dallas To See My Pony Run
 Lightnin' Hopkins; *Blues In My Bottle* . . . . (Bluesville)
 Drinkin' In The Blues-Golden Classics-#1 . . . . (Collectables)
 Lightnin' Hopkins . . . . (Everest)
Goodnight Dallas
 Carlene Carter; *I Fell In Love* . . . . (Reprise)
Hot Nite In Dallas
 Moon Martin; *Shots From A Cold Nightmare* . . . . (Capitol)
If You're Ever Down In Dallas
 Lee Ann Womack; *Some Things I Know* . . . . (Decca)
Little Past Little Rock
 Lee Ann Womack; *Some Things I Know* . . . . (Decca)
Out Of Dallas
 Jerry Giddens; *Devil's Front Door* . . . .(Dr. Dream Music Group)
Raining In Dallas
 Kelly Schoppa; *Amarillo By Morning* . . . .(Bellaire)
Run
 George Strait; *The Road Goes On Forever, A Collection Of Their Greatest Recordings* . . . .(Polydor)
Saturday Night In Dallas
 Kenny Seratt; *45-#1003* . . . . (MDJ)
South Dallas Drop
 Ron "C"; *"C" Ya* . . . .(Profile)
Spirit Of A Boy, Wisdom Of A Man
 Randy Travis; *Big Country Hits '99-C* . . . . (K-Tel)
 You And You Alone . . . .(DreamWorks/SKG)
Theme From "Dallas"
 Original Soundtrack; *CBS: The First 50 Years* . . . . (TVT)
 Television's Greatest Hits-#3-1970s & 1980s-C . . . . (TVT)
 TV Classic Themes: 25th Anniversary Edition-C . . . . (Breakable)
This Ain't Dallas
 Hank Williams, Jr.; *Five-O* . . . . (WB/Curb)
 Hank Williams, Jr.'s Greatest Hits III . . . . (Curb)
Trouble In Dallas
 Regulators; *Regulators* . . . .(Polydor)

CITIES: DENVER

 See Also: **STATES: COLORADO**

Almost Dawn In Denver
 Faron Young; *Faron Young's Greatest Hits-#3* . . . .(Step One)

Beautiful People Of Denver
 Original Cast; *The Unsinkable Molly Brown* . . . .(EMI-Angel)
Coming Down From Denver
 Byron Berline; *Dad's Favorites* . . . . (Rounder)
Cover You In Kisses
 John Michael Montgomery; *Leave A Mark* . . . . (Atlantic)
Denver
 Larry Gatlin & The Gatlin Brothers Band; *Houston To Denver* . . . . . (Columbia)
 Larry Gatlin & The Gatlin Brothers-17 Greatest Hits . . . . (Columbia)
 The Gatlin Brothers' Biggest Hits . . . .(Columbia)
 Ronnie Milsap; *Denver* . . . .(Fifty One West)
 There Goes My Heart . . . .(Fifty One West)
 Willie Nelson; *Red Headed Stranger* . . . . (Columbia)
Denver Blues
 Tampa Red; *Great Blues Guitarists-String Dazzlers-C* . . . . (Columbia)
Fort Worth And Denver Blues
 Bessie Tucker; *Barrelhouse Mamas: Born In The Alley, Raised In The
  Slums-C* . . . .(Yazoo)
Get Out Of Denver
 Bob Seger; *Live Bullet* . . . .(Capitol)
 Dave Edmunds; *Get It* . . . . (Swan Song)
Gone To Denver
 Waylon Jennings; *Lonesome On're & Mean* . . . .(RCA)
I Won't Go Back To Denver
 Lynn Anderson; *What A Man My Man Is.* . . . . (Columbia)
Kid From Denver
 Paul Quinichette; *Kid From Denver* . . . . (Biograph)
Lone Star State Of Mind
 Don Williams; *Currents* . . . .(RCA)
 Nanci Griffith; *Country Classics-#8-1986-1987-C* . . . . (Universal)
 Lone Star State Of Mind . . . . (MCA)
 Pat Alger/Nanci Griffith/Trisha Yearwood; *True Love & Other Short
  Stories-C* . . . .(Sugar Hill)
O.D.'d In Denver
 Hank Williams, Jr.; *Whiskey Bent & Hell Bound.* . . . .(WB/Curb)
Please Come To Boston
 Dave Loggins; *Apprentice (In A Musical Workshop)* . . . . (Epic)
 Rock Artifacts-From The Vaults-#2-C . . . . (Legacy)
 Super Hits Of The '70s-Have A Nice Day-#13-C . . . .(Rhino)
 David Allan Coe; *David Allan Coe-17 Greatest Hits* . . . .(Columbia)
 For The Record-The First 10 Years . . . . (Columbia)
 Joan Baez; *Best Of Joan Baez* . . . .(A&M)
 Joan Baez-Classics-#8 . . . . (A&M)
 Reba McEntire; *Starting Over* . . . . (MCA)
Theme From "Dynasty"
 Original Soundtrack; *Television's Greatest Hits-#3-1970s & 1980s-C* . . . . (TVT)
Things To Do In Denver When You're Dead
 Warren Zevon; *Mr. Bad Example* . . . . (Giant)
This Ain't The Denver I Remember
 Pirates Of The Mississippi; *Walk The Plank* . . . . (Liberty)

CITIES: DETROIT

See Also: CARS (various), STATES: MICHIGAN

Born In Detroit
 Rockets; *Rocket Roll* . . . . (Elektra)
 Rockets-Live . . . . (Capitol)
Christmas Time In The Motor City
 Was (Not Was); *Was (Not Was) Christmas Record* . . . . (Passport)
Cry Baby
 Enchanters; *Billboard Top R&B Hits-1963-C* . . . .(Rhino)
 Soul Shots-#5-La-La Means I Love You-C . . . . (Rhino)
 Garnet Mimms; *18 Soulful Ballads-C* . . . . (Rhino)
 Beg, Scream & Shout! The Big Ol' Box Of '60s Soul-C . . . . (Rhino)
 Janis Joplin; *Janis Joplin's Greatest Hits* . . . . (Columbia)
 Pearl . . . .(Legacy)
 ST/Janis . . . . (Columbia)
Detroit
 J To The D; *Living On The Edge* . . . .(Wrap/Ichiban)
Detroit
 Almighty; *Blood Fire & Love* . . . . (Polydor)
Detroit 442
 Blondie; *Plastic Letters* . . . . (Chrysalis)
Detroit Blues
 Blind James Campbell; *Blind James Campbell & His Nashville
  Street Band* . . . .(Arhoolie)
Detroit Breakdown
 J. Geils Band; *Best Of The J. Geils Band* . . . . (Atlantic)
 Blow Your Face Out . . . . (Rhino)
 Nightmares . . . . (Atlantic)
Detroit City
 Ace Cannon; *Golden Favorites* . . . . (Ranwood)
 Bill Anderson; *Best Of Bill Anderson* . . . .(Curb)
 Bobby Bare; *Nipper's Greatest Hits Of The '60s-#2-C* . . . .(RCA)
 This Is Bobby Bare . . . .(RCA)
 Chet Atkins; *Country Gems* . . . .(Pair)

Flatt & Scruggs; *20 All-Time Great Recordings.* . . . .(Columbia)
Hank Williams, Jr.; *Live At Cobo Hall Detroit.* . . . .(Polydor)
 Standing In The Shadows . . . . (Polydor)
Mel Tillis; *Best Of Mel Tillis* . . . .(MCA)
 Live At The Sam Houston Coliseum. . . . .(MGM)
Solomon Burke; *Home In Your Heart-Best Of Solomon Burke* . . . .(Rhino)
Detroit Diesel
 Alvin Lee; *Detroit Diesel.* . . . .(21)
Detroit Girls
 Starz; *Live In Action.* . . . .(Metal Blade)
 Starz . . . .(Metal Blade)
Detroit Oberek
 Li'l Wally; *Here Comes Li'l Wally* . . . . (Jay Jay)
Detroit Rock City
 Kiss; *Alive II.* . . . . (Casablanca)
 Destroyer. . . . . (Casablanca)
 Double Platinum . . . .(Mercury)
 Smashes, Thrashes & Hits. . . . .(Mercury)
Detroit Snackbar Dreamer
 Edgar Froese; *Stuntman* . . . . (Blue Plate)
Detroit Special
 Big Bill Broonzy; *Unissued Test Pressings* . . . .(Milan)
Going Back To Detroit
 Platters; *Double Gold-The Platters* . . . .(Mustcor)
It's A Long Way From Detroit...To Austin
 Buddy Harris; *45-#148.* . . . . (Plantation)
Last Time I Saw Richard
 Joni Mitchell; *Blue.* . . . . (Reprise)
Motor City
 Randy Weeks; *Madeline* . . . . (Hightone)
Motor City Madhouse
 Ted Nugent; *Double Live Gonzo* . . . . (Epic)
 Ted Nugent . . . .(Epic)
Motownphilly
 Boyz II Men; *Cooleyhighharmony.* . . . .(Motown)
One Piece At A Time
 Johnny Cash; *The Man In Black-His Greatest Hits* . . . .(Legacy)
Panic In Detroit
 David Bowie; *Aladdin Sane* . . . . (Rykodisc)
 Scary Monsters . . . . (Rykodisc)
 Sound + Vision . . . . (Rykodisc)
Passport To Detroit
 Joe Strummer; *Earthquake Weather* . . . . (Epic)
Three Girls From Detroit
 Will & The Bushmen; *Will & The Bushmen.* . . . .(SBK)

CITIES: DUBLIN

See Also: COUNTRIES: IRELAND

Cockles & Mussels
 Emily Mitchell; *The Irish Album* . . . . (RCA)
Dublin In My Tears
 Fureys & Dave Arthur; *Dublin Songs-C* . . . . (AJK Music)
Dublin In The Rare Old Times
 Garrison Brothers; *Songs & Stories* . . . .(Boot)
Dublin Lady
 Andy M. Stewart & Manus Lunny; *Dublin Lady* . . . . (Green Linnet)
Dublin My Dublin
 Paddy Reilly; *Dublin Songs-C* . . . . (AJK Music)
Dublin Saunter
 Paddy Reilly; *Dublin Songs-C* . . . . (AJK Music)
Dublin Town
 Brendan Grace; *Dublin Songs-C* . . . . (AJK Music)
Going Back To Dublin
 Eric Bogle; *Something Of Value.* . . . . (Philo)
Off To Dublin In The Green
 Dubliners; *Best Of The Dubliners-Irish Favorites* . . . . (Tradition)
Rocky Road To Dublin
 Dubliners; *Dublin Songs-C* . . . . (AJK Music)
 Skip Gorman; *A Cowboy's Wild Song To His Herd* . . . .(Rounder)
Saturday Night In Dublin
 Michael "Jesse" Owens; *Across The Sea To Ireland* . . . . (Rego Irish)
Summer In Dublin
 James Last & His Orchestra; *James Last & His Orchestra Play The Rose Of
  Tralee* . . . . (Rego Irish)
 Jim McCann; *Dublin Songs-C* . . . . (AJK Music)

CITIES: E

See Also: CITIES: GENERAL, COUNTRIES: A-Z, STATES: A-Z

All The Way From East St. Louis
 Mississippi Fred McDowell; *Mississippi Fred McDowell* . . . .(Rounder)

Asshole From El Paso
Kinky Friedman; *Lasso From El Paso* . . . . (Epic)
Kinky Friedman & His Texas Jewboys; *Old Testaments & New Revelations* . . . . (Fruit Of The Tune)

East St. Louis Toodle oo
Duke Ellington; *Bethlehem Years-#1* . . . . (Bethlehem)
Brunswick Era-#1-1926-1929 . . . . (MCA)
Era . . . . (Columbia)
Jazz Heritage-Beginning 1926-1928 . . . . (MCA)
Steely Dan; *Pretzel Logic* . . . . (MCA)
Steely Dan's Greatest Hits . . . . (MCA)

El Paso
Grateful Dead; *Steal Your Face* . . . . (Grateful Dead)
Marty Robbins; *Billboard Top Country Hits-1960-C* . . . . (Rhino)
Gunfighter Ballads & Trail Songs . . . . (Legacy)
Marty Robbins' Biggest Hits . . . . (Columbia)
Radio Classics Of The '50s-C . . . . (Columbia)
Texas Super Hits-C . . . . (Columbia)

El Paso Blues
Phillip Walker; *Someday You'll Have These Blues* . . . . (Alligator)

El Paso City
Marty Robbins; *El Paso City* . . . . (Columbia)
Greatest Country Hits Of The '70s-C . . . . (Columbia)
Lifetime Of Song-1951-1982 . . . . (Columbia)
Marty Robbins' Greatest Hits-#4 . . . . (Columbia)

I Left My Wallet In El Segundo
Tribe Called Quest; *People's Instinctive Travels And The Paths Of Rhythm* . . . . (Jive)
Rap: Most Valuable Players-C . . . . (K-Tel)

New East St. Louis Toodle-oo
Duke Ellington; *Reminiscing In Tempo* . . . . (Columbia)

CITIES: F

See Also: CITIES: GENERAL, COUNTRIES: A-Z, STATES: A-Z

August In Forest City
Carol Montag; *Song For Carrie* . . . . (Salek)

Does Fort Worth Ever Cross Your Mind
George Strait; *Country Classics-#3-1984-1985-C* . . . . (Universal)
Does Fort Worth Ever Cross Your Mind . . . . (MCA)
George Strait's Greatest Hits-#2 . . . . (MCA)
MCA #1 Hits Of The '80s-#1-C . . . . (MCA Special Prod.)

Fist City
Loretta Lynn; *Loretta Lynn-20 Greatest Hits* . . . . (MCA)
Loretta Lynn-Greatest Hits Live . . . . (K-Tel)
Loretta Lynn's Greatest Hits-#2 . . . . (MCA)
The Country Music Hall Of Fame-Loretta Lynn . . . . (MCA)

Folsom Prison Blues
Brooks & Dunn with Johnny Cash; *Red Hot + Country-C* . . . . (Mercury)
Johnny Cash; *Billboard Top Country Hits-1968-C* . . . . (Rhino)
Classic Cash-Hall Of Fame Series . . . . (Mercury)
Hot Tracks-Train Super Hits-C . . . . (Epic)
Jailhouse Rock (Hits From The Big House)-C . . . . . (Sony Music Special Prod.)
Johnny Cash At Folsom Prison & San Quentin . . . . (Columbia)
Johnny Cash-Original Golden Hits-#1 . . . . (Sun)
Johnny Cash's Greatest Hits-#2 . . . . (Columbia)
Superbilly . . . . (Sun)
The Man In Black-His Greatest Hits . . . . (Legacy)

Fort Lauderdale
Cannonball Adderley; *Compact Jazz-Cannonball Adderley* . . . . (Emarcy)
Impacts; *Wipe Out* . . . . (Oceana)

Fort Lauderdale Chamber Of Commerce
Elvis Presley; *ST/Girl Happy* . . . . (RCA)

Fort Smith
Oswald Brothers & Charlie Collins; *That's Country* . . . . (Rounder)

Fort Worth
Joe Lovano; *From The Soul* . . . . (Blue Note)

Fort Worth And Denver Blues
Bessie Tucker; *Barrelhouse Mamas: Born In The Alley, Raised In The Slums-C* . . . . (Yazoo)

Fort Worth Blues
Guy Clark; *Cold Dog Soup* . . . . (Sugar Hill)

Fort Worth Hambone Blues
Johnny Gimble & The Texas Swing Pioneers; *Johnny Gimble's Texas Honky-Tonk Hits-C* . . . . (C.M.H. Prod.)

Fort Worth Jail
Tex Ritter; *Hillbilly Music-Thank God!-#1-C* . . . . (Bug)

Forth Worth & Dallas Blues
Leadbelly; *King Of The Twelve-String Guitar* . . . . (Columbia)
Legends Of The Blues-#1-C . . . . (Columbia)

Fresno Beauties
Broadway Cast; *Most Happy Fella* . . . . (RCA)

Ft. Worth Featherbed
Donnie Rohrs; *Country Music USA* . . . . (Pacific Challenger)

She Came From Fort Worth
Kathy Mattea; *Willow In The Wind* . . . . (Mercury)
Pat Alger & Kathy Mattea; *True Love & Other Short Stories-C* . . . . . (Sugar Hill)

Trip To Flagstaff
Kornos; *On Seven Winds* . . . . (Green Linnet)

CITIES: G

See Also: CITIES: GENERAL, COUNTRIES: A-Z, STATES: A-Z

Bring Me A Shawl From Galway
Mary O'Hara; *At The Royal Festival Hall* . . . . (Shanachie)
Song For Ireland . . . . (Shanachie)

Galveston
Glen Campbell; *Glen Campbell-Classics Collection* . . . . (Capitol)
Glen Campbell's Greatest Hits . . . . (Capitol)
Very Best Of Glen Campbell . . . . (Capitol)

Galveston Bay
Bruce Springsteen; *The Ghost Of Tom Joad* . . . . (Columbia)

Galveston Flood
Tom Rush; *Best Of Tom Rush: No Regrets* . . . . (Legacy)

Gary, Indiana
Original Cast; *ST/The Music Man* . . . . (Gold Rush)

Glendale Train
New Riders Of The Purple Sage; *Best Of New Riders Of The Purple Sage* . . . . (Columbia)
New Riders Of The Purple Sage . . . . (Columbia)

Gotham City
R. Kelly; *ST/Batman & Robin-Music From And Inspired By The Motion Picture* . . . . (Jive)

Granada
Frankie Laine; *Frankie Laine's Greatest Hits* . . . . (Columbia)

Guadalajara
Desi Arnaz; *Best Of Desi Arnaz-The Mambo King* . . . . (RCA)

Guantanamera
Sandpipers; *Mellow '60s-C* . . . . (Priority)
Sandpipers' Greatest Hits . . . . (A&M)

How Are Things In Glocca Mora
Julie Andrews; *A Little Bit Of Broadway* . . . . (Columbia)
Original Cast; *Finian's Rainbow* . . . . (RCA)
Rosemary Clooney; *Show Tunes* . . . . (Concord Jazz)

I Belong To Glasgow
Jack Elliot; *Essential Jack Elliott* . . . . (Prestige)
Jack Elliot . . . . (Vanguard)
Ramblin' Jack Elliott; *Hard Travelin'* . . . . (Fantasy)

North Gulfport Boogie
Roosevelt Sykes; *Hard Drivin' Blues* . . . . (Delmark)

Sunday In Genoa
101 Strings Orchestra; *101 Strings Orchestra-30th Anniversary* . . . . . . (Alshire)

CITIES: GENERAL, City, Downtown, Multiple Cities, Town, Village

See Also: CITIES: A-Z, COUNTRIES: A-Z, SMALL TOWN LIFE, STATES: A-Z, STREETS: GENERAL, STREETS: SPECIFIC

Abandon City
Utopia; *Oops! Wrong Planet* . . . . (Rhino)

American City Suite
Cashman & West; *Super Hits Of The '70s-Have A Nice Day-#9-C* . . . . . (Rhino)

Angel Of The City
Robert Tepper; *No Easy Way Out* . . . . (Scotti Bros.)
ST/Cobra . . . . (Scotti Bros.)

Area Codes
Ludacris; *Word Of Mouf* . . . . (Murder Inc./Def Jam/IDJMG)

Armenia City In The Sky
Who; *The Who Sell Out* . . . . (MCA)

Big City
Merle Haggard; *For The Record: Merle Haggard-43 Legendary Hits* . . . . (BNA)

Big City Miss Ruth Ann
Gallery; *Super Hits Of The '70s-Have A Nice Day-#11-C* . . . . (Rhino)

Big City Nights
Scorpions; *Best Of Rockers 'N' Ballads* . . . . (Mercury)
Love At First Sting . . . . (Mercury)
World Wide Live . . . . (Mercury)

Big Dreams In A Small Town
Restless Heart; *Big Dreams In A Small Town* . . . . (RCA)

Big Man In Town
4 Seasons; *4 Seasons' Greatest Hits-#1* . . . . (Rhino)
4 Seasons-Anthology . . . . (Rhino)

Blue Side Of Town
Patty Loveless; *Honky Tonk Angel* . . . . (MCA)
Patty Loveless' Greatest Hits . . . . (MCA)

Bob Away My Blues
Clint Black; *D'lectrified* . . . . (RCA)

Boogie Back To Texas
Asleep At The Wheel; *Asleep At The Wheel-10* . . . . (Epic)
Swinging Best Of Asleep At The Wheel . . . . (Epic)

Texas Super Hits-C . . . . (Columbia)
Very Best Of Asleep At The Wheel Since 1970 . . . .(Relentless/Madacy)
Boys Are Back In Town
Bon Jovi; *ST/Navy Seals* . . . . (Atlantic)
Thin Lizzy; *'70s Greatest Rock Hits-#14-King Of Rock-C* . . . .(Priority)
Dedication-Very Best Of Thin Lizzy . . . . (Mercury)
Jailbreak . . . . (Mercury)
Live And Dangerous . . . . (Warner Bros.)
Boys Are Back In Town
Gap Band; *The Gap Band II* . . . .(Mercury)
Cellulite City
Redd Kross; *Born Innocent* . . . . (Frontier)
Cheap Seats, The
Alabama; *Cheap Seats* . . . .(RCA)
Chocolate City
Roger Troutman & Shirley Murdock; *ST/A Thin Line Between Love
And Hate* . . . . (Warner Bros.)
Zapp & Roger; *Compilation-Greatest Hits II And More* . . . . (Reprise)
Chocolate City
Parliament; *Best Of Parliament-Give Up The Funk* . . . .(Mercury)
Chocolate City . . . .(Casablanca)
In Yo' Face!-History Of Funk-#2-C . . . . (Rhino)
Tear The Roof Off-1974-1980 . . . . (Mercury/Funk Essentials)
Chocolate City Groovin'
Marcus Johnson; *Chocolate City Groovin'* . . . . (N2K)
Cities Are Burning, The
Jimmy Collier & Rev. F.D. Kirkpatrick; *Best Of Broadside 1962-1968:
Anthems Of The American Underground From The Pages Of Broadside
Magazine-C* . . . .(Smithsonian Folkways)
Cities On Flame With Rock & Roll
Blue Oyster Cult; *Blue Oyster Cult* . . . .(Columbia)
Career Of Evil . . . .(Columbia)
Extraterrestrial Live . . . .(Columbia)
On Your Feet Or On Your Knees . . . .(Columbia)
City Of Angels
10,000 Maniacs; *In My Tribe* . . . . (Elektra)
City Of God
Rubber Rodeo; *Scenic Views* . . . . (Mercury)
City Put The Country Back In Me
Neal McCoy; *No Doubt About It* . . . . (Atlantic)
City's Burning
Heart; *Private Audition* . . . .(Epic)
Clash City Rockers
Clash; *The Clash* . . . .(Epic)
The Story Of The Clash, Volume 1 . . . .(Epic)
Concrete Jungle
Bob Marley & The Wailers; *Babylon By Bus* . . . . (Tuff Gong)
Catch A Fire . . . . (Tuff Gong)
Reggae Roots-C . . . . (Garland)
This Is Reggae Music-#1-C . . . . (Island)
Concrete Jungle
Anvil; *Best Of Metal Blade-#3-C* . . . . (Metal Blade)
Strength Of Steel . . . . (Metal Blade)
Concrete Jungle
Specials; *Specials* . . . . (Chrysalis)
ST/Dance Craze . . . . (Chrysalis)
Crime In The City
Neil Young & Crazy Horse; *WELD* . . . .(Reprise)
Cryin' For The Carolines
Fred Waring's Pennsylvanians; *Fred Waring's
Greatest Hits* . . . .(Collector's Choice)
Dancing In The Street
David Bowie & Mick Jagger; *Bowie-The Singles-1969-1993* . . . . (Rykodisc)
Grateful Dead; *Terrapin Station* . . . .(Arista)
Martha & The Vandellas; *20 Greatest Songs In Motown History-C* . . . (Motown)
*Compact Command Performances-Martha Reeves & The
Vandellas* . . . . (Motown)
Motown Story-First 25 Years-C . . . . (Motown)
Oldies But Goodies-#14-C . . . .(Original Sound)
Van Halen; *Diver Down* . . . . (Warner Bros.)
Darkness On The Edge Of Town
Bruce Springsteen; *Darkness On The Edge Of Town* . . . . (Columbia)
Bruce Springsteen & The E Street Band; *Bruce Springsteen & The E Street
Band Live/1975-85* . . . .(Legacy)
Deserted Cities Of The Heart
Cream; *Cream-Live-#2* . . . . (Polydor)
Wheels Of Fire . . . . (Polydor)
Don't Take Your Guns To Town
Johnny Cash; *Billboard Top Country Hits-1959-C* . . . .(Rhino)
Columbia Country Classics-#3-Americana-C . . . . (Columbia)
Johnny Cash-16 Biggest Hits-#2 . . . . (Legacy)
Johnny Cash's Greatest Hits . . . . (Columbia)
The Man In Black-His Greatest Hits . . . . (Legacy)
Down Home Town
Electric Light Orchestra; *Face The Music* . . . .(Jet)
Down Town, The
Days Of The New; *Days Of The New* . . . .(Outpost/Interscope)
Downtown
B-52's; *B-52's* . . . . (Warner Bros.)

Frank Sinatra; *Strangers In The Night* . . . . (Reprise)
Petula Clark; *Dick Clark's 21 All-Time Hits-#2-C* . . . . (Original Sound)
Petula Clark's Greatest Hits . . . . (Crescendo)
Downtown
Neil Young; *Mirror Ball* . . . . (Reprise)
Downtown Train
Patty Smyth; *Train Trax-C* . . . . (Sony Music Special Prod.)
Rod Stewart; *Downtown Train-Selections From The Storyteller
Anthology* . . . .(Warner Bros.)
Storyteller/The Complete Anthology: 1964-1990 . . . . (Warner Bros.)
Downtown Train
Mary Chapin Carpenter; *Hometown Girl* . . . .(Columbia)
Elderly Woman Behind The Counter In A Small Town
Pearl Jam; *Vs.* . . . .(Epic Portrait Assoc.)
Erotik City
Emoja; *ST/Men In Black* . . . .(Columbia)
Every Ghetto, Every City
Lauryn Hill; *The Miseducation Of Lauryn Hill* . . . .(Ruffhouse/Columbia)
Everything's Got 'Em
Nilsson; *The Point* . . . . (RCA)
Fool For The City
Foghat; *Best Of Foghat* . . . .(Rhino)
Best Of Hard Rock-#1-C . . . . (MCA Special Prod.)
Foghat-Live . . . .(Rhino)
Fool For The City . . . . (Rhino)
Fox, The
Nickel Creek; *Nickel Creek* . . . . (Sugar Hill)
Friday On My Mind
David Bowie; *Bowie Pin Ups* . . . .(Rykodisc)
Easybeats; *Best Of The Easybeats* . . . . (Rhino)
Nuggets-Classic Collection From The Psychedelic '60s-C . . .(Rhino)
Garden City
Orchestral Manoeuvres In The Dark; *Junk Culture* . . . .(A&M)
Gotta Travel On
Bill Monroe & His Blue Grass Boys; *20th Century Masters-The Millennium
Collection-The Best Of Bill Monroe* . . . . (MCA)
Country's Greatest Hits-#1-C . . . . (MCA Special Prod.)
Guitar Town
Steve Earle & The Dukes; *Country Classics-#8-1986-1987-C* . . . . .(Universal)
Guitar Town . . . .(MCA)
Hanginaround
Counting Crows; *This Desert Life* . . . . (David Geffen Co.)
Heartbreak Town
Dixie Chicks; *Fly* . . . .(Monument)
Heroes & Villains
Beach Boys; *Concert/'69-Live In London* . . . .(Capitol)
Endless Harmony . . . .(Capitol)
Good Vibrations-Thirty Years Of The Beach Boys . . . .(Capitol)
Made In The U.S.A. . . . . (Capitol)
Smiley Smile/Wild Honey . . . . (Capitol)
Sunshine Dream . . . .(Capitol)
High School U.S.A.
Tommy Facenda; *45-#51 to #78* . . . . (Atlantic)
Hometown Blues
Tom Petty And The Heartbreakers; *Tom Petty &The
Heartbreakers* . . . . (Gone Gator)
Hometown Blues
Rosanne Cash; *Seven Year Ache* . . . .(Columbia)
Hot Child In The City
Nick Gilder; *Billboard Top Hits-1978-C* . . . .(Rhino)
City Nights . . . . (Chrysalis)
I Can Hear Music
Beach Boys; *Friends-20/20* . . . .(Capitol)
Sunshine Dream . . . .(Capitol)
Beach Boys & Kathy Troccoli; *Stars And Stripes-#1* . . . . (River North)
I Got A Woman
Ray Charles; *Ray Charles' Greatest Hits* . . . .(Rhino)
Ray Charles-Anthology . . . .(Rhino)
If You Can Do Anything Else
George Strait; *George Strait* . . . . (MCA)
I'm Looking High And Low For My Baby
Ernest Tubb; *Ernest Tubb's Greatest Hits* . . . . (MCA)
In A Little Spanish Town
Ray Charles; *Ray Charles-Live* . . . .(Atlantic)
In A Turkish Town
Ritchie Valens; *Best Of Ritchie Valens* . . . .(Rhino)
History Of Ritchie Valens . . . . (Rhino)
Ritchie Valens . . . . (Rhino)
In City Dreams
Robin Trower; *In City Dreams* . . . . (Chrysalis)
Invisible City
Wallflowers; *Bringing Down The Horse* . . . . (Interscope)
It's A Lonesome Old Town (When You're Not Around)
Ben Bernie & His Orchestra featuring Donald Saxon; *78-#4943* . . . .(Brunswick)
Frank Sinatra; *Sings For Only The Lonely* . . . . . (EMI-Capitol Entert. Properties)
Lena Horne; *Love Is The Thing* . . . . (RCA)
Les Paul; *Les Paul's Greatest Hits* . . . .(Pair)
Sting; *ST/Leaving Las Vegas* . . . .(Pangaea)

It's Hard To Be A Saint In The City
Bruce Springsteen; *Greetings From Asbury Park, N.J.* . . . . (Columbia)
Live 1975-1985 . . . . (Legacy)
Tracks . . . . (Columbia)
David Bowie; *One Step Up/Two Steps Back-The Songs Of Bruce
Springsteen-C* . . . . (Right Stuff)

It's The Talk Of The Town
Art Tatum; *Art Tatum-Complete Capitol Recordings-#2* . . . . (Capitol)
Hank Jones; *Live At Maybeck Recital Hall-#16* . . . . (Concord Jazz)
Ray Conniff Singers; *It's The Talk Of The Town* . . . . (Columbia)

I've Been Everywhere
Johnny Cash; *Unchained* . . . . (American)

Jet City Woman
Queensryche; *Empire* . . . . (EMI)

Kill City
Iggy Pop & James Williamson; *Kill City* . . . . (Bomp)

Leaving This Town
Beach Boys; *Holland* . . . . (Brother)
The Beach Boys In Concert . . . . (Brother)

Leaving Town
Dexter Freebish; *Life Of Saturdays* . . . . (Capitol)

Legend Of A Cowgirl
Imani Coppola; *Chupacapra* . . . . (Columbia)

Life In A Northern Town
Dream Academy; *Dream Academy* . . . . (Warner Bros.)

Little Dutch Town
Mac Davis; *Mac Davis With Love* . . . . (Accord)
Volume XC . . . . (Allegiance)

Living For The City
Stevie Wonder; *Innervisions* . . . . (Motown)
Original Musiquarium . . . . (Motown)

Lonesome Town
Ricky Nelson; *Best Of Ricky Nelson* . . . . (Curb)

Lucky Town
Bruce Springsteen; *Lucky Town* . . . . (Columbia)

Man From Out Of Town
Bill Morrissey; *Inside* . . . . (Rounder)

Metropolis
Motorhead; *No Sleep At All.* . . . . (Roadracer)
No Sleep 'Til Hammersmith . . . . (Castle Music America)

Metropolis
Manhattan Transfer; *Brasil.* . . . . (Atlantic)

Metropolis
Church; *Gold Afternoon Fix* . . . . (Arista)

Metropolis
Pogues; *If I Should Fall From Grace With God* . . . . (Island)

Mississippi Delta City Blues
Chicago; *Chicago XI.* . . . . (Chicago)
Group Portrait. . . . . (Chicago)

My City Of Ruin
Bruce Springsteen; *America: A Tribute To Heroes-C* . . . . (Interscope)

My City Was Gone
Pretenders; *Learning To Crawl.* . . . . (Sire)

My Hometown
Bruce Springsteen; *Born In The U.S.A.* . . . . (Columbia)
Bruce Springsteen's Greatest Hits . . . . (Columbia)

My Little Town
Paul Simon; *Still Crazy After All These Years.* . . . . (Columbia)

Neon Rainbow
Box Tops; *Box Tops' Greatest Hits* . . . . (Rhino)

New Career In A New Town
David Bowie; *Low* . . . . (Rykodisc)

New Kid In Town (Johnny Come Lately)
Eagles; *Eagles Greatest Hits, Volume 2* . . . . (Asylum)
Eagles Live . . . . (Asylum)
Hotel California. . . . . (Asylum)
Trisha Yearwood; *Common Thread-Songs Of The Eagles-C* . . . . . . (Giant)

Night In The City
Joni Mitchell; *Joni Mitchell* . . . . (Reprise)

Night On The Town
Bruce Hornsby & The Range; *Night On The Town.* . . . . (RCA)

Old Coyote Town
Don Williams; *Traces.* . . . . (Capitol)

One Horse Town
Bobby Bland; *Introspective Of The Early Years* . . . . (MCA)
Touch Of The Blues . . . . (MCA)

One Horse Town
Elton John; *Blue Moves* . . . . (MCA)

One Horse Town
David Frishberg; *Live At Vine Street.* . . . . (Original Jazz Classics)

One Horse Town
Rembrandts; *Untitled* . . . . (Atco)

Orange City
Laszlo Gardony; *Legend Of Tsumi* . . . . (Antilles)

Orinoco Flow (Sail Away)
Enya; *Watermark* . . . . (Reprise)

Our Town
Iris DeMent; *Infamous Angel* . . . . (Warner Bros.)

Outskirts Of Town
Sawyer Brown; *Outskirts Of Town* . . . . (Curb)

Partytown
Glenn Frey; *No Fun Aloud* . . . . (Asylum)

Perfect Blue Buildings
Counting Crows; *August And Everything After* . . . . (David Geffen Co.)

Phat City
Chieli Minucci; *Jewels* . . . . (JVC Musical Industries)

Poor Side Of Town
Johnny Rivers; *Best Of Johnny Rivers.* . . . . (EMI)
Changes/Rewind. . . . . (EMI)
Johnny Rivers-Anthology 1964-1977 . . . . (Rhino)
Very Best Of Johnny Rivers . . . . (EMI)

Quiche Woman In A Barbecue Town
Tarwater Band; *Walking Across Egypt* . . . . (Flying Fish)

Ramblin' Round Your City
Linda Ronstadt; *Linda Ronstadt* . . . . (Capitol)
Linda Ronstadt-Retrospective . . . . (Capitol)
Odetta; *Greatest Songs Of Woody Guthrie-C* . . . . (Vanguard)
Tribute To Woody Guthrie-C . . . . (Warner Bros.)

Rock City
Damn Yankees; *Damn Yankees.* . . . . (Warner Bros.)

Rock This Town
Stray Cats; *Best Of Stray Cats-Rock This Town* . . . . (EMI)
Built For Speed. . . . . (EMI)
Reelin' In The Years-#1-C . . . . (Sandstone Music)
Rock This Town-Rockabilly Hits-#2-C . . . . (Rhino)

Route 66
Asleep At The Wheel; *Served Live* . . . . (Capitol)
Very Best Of Asleep At The Wheel Since 1970 . . . . . (Relentless/Madacy)
Wheelin' & Dealin' . . . . (Capitol)
Depeche Mode; *ST/Earth Girls Are Easy* . . . . (Sire)
George Maharis; *45-#15-2227* . . . . (Epic)
Manhattan Transfer; *Bop doo-wopp* . . . . (Atlantic)
Nat ''King'' Cole; *Capitol Collectors Series-Nat ''King'' Cole* . . . . . . (Capitol)
The Nat ''King'' Cole Story . . . . (Capitol)
Natalie Cole; *Unforgettable With Love* . . . . (Elektra)
Rolling Stones; *December's Children (and everybody's)* . . . . (Abkco)
England's Newest Hit Makers/The Rolling Stones . . . . (Abkco)

Ruby, Don't Take Your Love To Town
Kenny Rogers; *Kenny Rogers-20 Great Years* . . . . (Reprise)
Kenny Rogers-Twenty Greatest Hits . . . . (EMI)
Ten Years Of Gold . . . . (EMI)
Kenny Rogers And The First Edition; *Hits & Pieces.* . . . . (MCA)
Kenny Rogers And The First Edition's Greatest Hits . . . . (K-Tel)
Mel Tillis; *Best Of Mel Tillis.* . . . . (MCA)
Mel Tillis & The Statesiders; *Mel Tillis & The Statesiders-24
Great Hits* . . . . (MGM)
M-M-Mel Live . . . . (MCA)

Seventh Avenue
Rosanne Cash; *The Wheel* . . . . (Columbia)

Silver City
Joe Ely; *Lord Of The Highway* . . . . (Hightone)
Mance Lipscomb; *Texas Songwriter-#2* . . . . (Arhoolie)

Skyscraper
David Lee Roth; *Skyscraper* . . . . (Warner Bros.)

Small Town
John Cougar Mellencamp; *Scarecrow.* . . . . (Riva)

Small Town Saturday Night
Hal Ketchum; *Past The Point Of Rescue* . . . . (Curb)

So Young And In Love
Bruce Springsteen; *Tracks* . . . . (Columbia)

Softest Touch In Town
Bobby G. Rice; *45-#031* . . . . (Republic/Universal)

Some Bridges
Jackson Browne; *Looking East* . . . . (Elektra)

South City Midnight Lady
Doobie Brothers; *Best Of The Doobies* . . . . (Warner Bros.)
Captain & Me. . . . . (Warner Bros.)

Southern Loving
Jim Ed Brown; *Essential Jim Ed Brown* . . . . (RCA)

Spanish Town
Garland Jeffreys; *Ghost Writer* . . . . (A&M)
Matador & More . . . . (A&M)

Speedway At Nazareth
Mark Knopfler; *Sailing To Philadelphia* . . . . (Warner Bros.)

Steven's Last Night In Town
Ben Folds Five; *Whatever And Ever Amen* . . . . (Caroline/550)

Suffragette City
David Bowie; *The Singles-1969-1993.* . . . . (Rykodisc)

Summer In The City
Lovin' Spoonful; *Billboard Top Rock 'N' Roll Hits-1966-C* . . . . (Rhino)
Lovin' Spoonful-Anthology . . . . (Rhino)
Rockin' '60s-C . . . . (Priority)

Summertime In The City
Manhattans; *45-#13-33330* . . . . (Columbia)

Sunday Morning Coming Down
Johnny Cash; *Classic Cash-Hall Of Fame Series* . . . . (Mercury)

Johnny Cash's Greatest Hits-#2 . . . . (Columbia)
The Man In Black-His Greatest Hits . . . . (Legacy)
Kris Kristofferson; *Me & Bobby McGee* . . . . (Columbia)
Songs Of Kris Kristofferson . . . . (Columbia)
Vikki Carr; *Best Of Vikki Carr.* . . . . (EMI)
Willie Nelson; *Willie* . . . . (RCA)
Willie Nelson Sings Kristofferson . . . . (Columbia)
Surf City
Jan & Dean; *Billboard Top Rock 'N' Roll Hits-1963-C* . . . . (Rhino)
Monster Summer Hits-Wild Surf-C . . . . (Capitol)
Surf City-Best Of Jan & Dean . . . . (EMI)
Sweet City Woman
Stampeders; *'70s Smash Hits-#5-C* . . . . (Rhino)
Super Hits Of The '70s-Have A Nice Day-#6-C . . . . . . (Rhino)
Sweet Little Sixteen
Beatles; *45-#1502* . . . . (Collectables)
Chuck Berry; *Best Of The Best Of Chuck Berry.* . . . . . (International Mktg. Group)
Chuck Berry-Golden Hits . . . . (Mercury)
Chuck Berry-Greatest Hits Live . . . . (Quicksilver)
Cruisin'-1965-C . . . . (Increase)
Oldies But Goodies-#12-C . . . . (Original Sound)
Jerry Lee Lewis; *Jerry Lee Lewis-Original Golden Hits-#3* . . . . (Sun)
Jerry Lee Lewis & Friends; *Jerry Lee Lewis & Friends-Duets* . . . . (Sun)
John Lennon; *Lennon* . . . . (Capitol)
Rock 'N' Roll . . . . (Capitol)
Talk Of The Town
Pretenders; *Pretenders II* . . . . (Sire)
Pretenders-The Singles. . . . . (Sire)
Talk Of The Town
Lightnin' Hopkins; *Nothin' But The Blues-Golden Classics-#4* . . . (Collectables)
Terror On The Town
Lizzy Borden; *Menace To Society* . . . . (Metal Blade)
Theme From ''Asphalt Jungle''
Original Soundtrack; *Television's Greatest Hits-#4-Black & White Classics-C* . . . . (TVT)
Theme From ''Midnight Cowboy''
Cincinnati Pops Orchestra/Erich Kunzel; *Hollywood's Greatest Hits-#2* . . . . (Telarc)
There Is A Tavern In The Town
Four Aces; *Four Aces-More Greatest Hits* . . . . (Varese Vintage)
Mitch Miller; *Sing Along With Mitch.* . . . . (Columbia)
Stan Wolowic & The Polka Chips; *Million-Seller Polkas* . . . . . . (Capitol)
There'll Be A Hot Time In The Old Town Tonight
Bessie Smith; *Bessie Smith-The Complete Recordings-#3* . . . . . (Legacy)
Louis Armstrong; *Best Of Louis Armstrong* . . . . . . (Audio Fidelity)
Turk Murphy's San Francisco Jazz Band; *Turk Murphy's San Francisco Jazz Band* . . . . (Good Time Jazz)
Woody Herman; *The Uncollected Woody Herman & His First Herd* . . . . (Hindsight)
This Part Of Town
Widespread Panic; *Don't Tell The Band* . . . . (Widespread/SRG)
This Town Ain't Big Enough For The Both Of Us
Siouxsie And The Banshees; *Through The Looking Glass* . . . (Geffen)
Sparks; *Profile-The Ultimate Sparks Collection* . . . . (Rhino)
The Island Story-1962-1987-25th Anniversary-C . . . . (Island)
Titty City
Nasty Niggas; *Banned From The Planet* . . . . (Critique)
Town Without Pity
Gene Pitney; *Gene Pitney-Anthology 1961-1968* . . . . (Rhino)
ST/Hairspray . . . . (MCA Special Prod.)
WCBS FM 101 History Of Rock-'60s-#3-C . . . . (Collectables)
Train That Carried My Girl From Town, The
Doc Watson; *Essential Doc Watson* . . . . (Vanguard)
Watson Family; *Watson Family* . . . . (Smithsonian Folkways)
Trash Can City
Bob Florence; *Jewels.* . . . . (Discovery)
Trash City
Kik Tracee; *No Rules.* . . . . (RCA)
Upstairs Downtown
Toby Keith; *Boomtown* . . . . (Polydor Country)
Uptown Girl
Billy Joel; *An Innocent Man* . . . . (Columbia)
Billy Joel-Greatest Hits, Volume I & Volume II . . . . . (Columbia)
KOHUEPT . . . . (Columbia)
Voodoo Village
Bola Sete; *Incomparable* . . . . (Fantasy)
We Built This City
Starship; *Greatest Hits-Ten Years & Change-1979-1991* . . . . . (RCA)
Knee Deep In The Hoopla. . . . . (Grunt)
Nipper's Greatest Hits Of The '80s-C . . . . (RCA)
What It Is
Mark Knopfler; *Sailing To Philadelphia* . . . . (Warner Bros.)
When Country Comes To Town
Toby Keith; *How Do You Like Me Now?!* . . . . . . (DreamWorks/SKG)
Where Corn Don't Grow
Travis Tritt; *The Restless Kind* . . . . (Warner Bros.)
You Belong To The City
Glenn Frey; *'80s Greatest Rock Hits-#1-Passion & Power-C* . . . . (Priority)
Soundtrack Smashes-'80s & More-C . . . . (MCA)

ST/Miami Vice. . . . . (MCA)
Young Blood
Rickie Lee Jones; *Naked Songs Live And Acoustic* . . . . (Reprise)
Rickie Lee Jones . . . . (Warner Bros.)
Your Body's Here With Me
O'Jays; *My Favorite Person.* . . . . (Philadelphia Int'l)

CITIES: H

See Also: **CITIES: GENERAL, CITIES: HAVANA, CITIES: HOUSTON, COUNTRIES: A-Z, STATES: A-Z**

Back Home In Huntsville Again
Bobby Bare; *20 Great Country Hits-C* . . . . (RCA)
20 Greatest Country Hits-C . . . . (RCA)
Blues For The Hague
Joe Pass & Niels Henning Orsted Pederson; *North Sea Nights* . . . . . (Pablo)
Brush Fire In Hoboken
Chris Stamey; *It's A Wonderful Life.* . . . . (DB)
Girl From Hiroshima
Third World; *Sense Of Purpose* . . . . (Columbia)
Harrisburg
Midnight Oil; *Red Sails In The Sunset* . . . . (Columbia)
Hippietown
Ugly Americans; *Boom Boom Baby* . . . . (Capricorn)
Hiroshima
Todd Rundgren's Utopia; *Ra* . . . . (Rhino)
Hiroshima Hole
Barefoot Jerry; *Barefootin'* . . . . (Monument)
Hiroshima, Nagasaki Russian Roulette
Jim Page; *Best Of Broadside 1962-1968: Anthems Of The American Underground From The Pages Of Broadside Magazine-C* . . . . (Smithsonian Folkways)
Honolulu
Michael Murphey; *Cosmic Cowboy Souvenir* . . . . (A&M)
Honolulu Lulu
Jan & Dean; *Dead Man's Curve.* . . . . (EMI)
Jan & Dean-Legendary Masters . . . . (EMI)
One Summer Night-Live . . . . (Rhino)
Surf City-Best Of Jan & Dean . . . . (EMI)
Hot Springs, Arkansas
Bukka White; *Three Shades Of Blues-C* . . . . (Biograph)
New Huntsville Jail
Joe Evans & John Dilleshaw; *Early Country Music* . . . . . . (Historical)
Rush Hour In Hong Kong
Gil Melle; *Primitive Modern* . . . . (Prestige)
Sheriff Of Hong Kong
Captain Beefheart; *Doc At The Radar Station* . . . . (Blue Plate)
Shoeless Joe From Hannibal, Mo.
Original Broadway Cast; *Damn Yankees* . . . . (RCA)
Swingtime In Honolulu
Duke Ellington/Cootie Williams/R. Cutters; *Duke's Men-Small Groups-#2-C* . . . . (Columbia)
Theme From ''The Dukes Of Hazzard''
Waylon Jennings; *Only Daddy That'll Walk The Line-The RCA Years* . . . (RCA)
Television's Greatest Hits-#6-Remote Control-C . . . . (TVT)
Waylon Jennings' Greatest Hits-#2. . . . . (RCA)
West Helena Blues
Jimmy Cotton; *Chicago/The Blues Today* . . . . (Vanguard)

CITIES: HAVANA

See Also: **COUNTRIES: CUBA**

Back To Havana
Michael Pluznick; *Cradle Of The Sun* . . . . (Sona Gaia)
Blues From Havana
Cal Tjader; *Latin Kick* . . . . (Fantasy)
Havana
Kenny G; *Kenny G's Greatest Hits* . . . . (Arista)
The Moment. . . . . (Arista)
Havana Affair
Ramones; *All The Stuff & More-#1* . . . . (Sire)
Ramones . . . . (Sire)
Havana Daydreamin'
Jimmy Buffett; *Havana Daydreamin'* . . . . (MCA)
You Had To Be There . . . . (MCA)
Havana For A Night
Mae West; *Fabulous Mae West* . . . . (MCA)
Havana Moon
Carlos Santana; *Havana Moon.* . . . . (Columbia)
Chuck Berry; *After School Session.* . . . . (Chess)
Rockit . . . . (Atco)
The Chess Box-Chuck Berry . . . . (Chess)

Holiday In Havana
Desi Arnaz; *Best Of Desi Arnaz-The Mambo King* . . . . (RCA)
Sister Havana
Urge Overkill; *Saturation* . . . .(Geffen)
This Ain't Havana
Ramones; *End Of The Century* . . . . (Sire)

CITIES: HOUSTON
See Also: *STATES: TEXAS*

Amarillo By Morning
George Strait; *George Strait's Greatest Hits* . . . .(MCA)
Strait From The Heart . . . .(MCA)
Angel Loose In Houston
Larry Gatlin & The Gatlin Brothers Band; *Cookin' Up A Storm.* . . . . . . (Capitol)
Flood In Houston
Savoy Brown; *Getting To The Point* . . . . (Rebound)
Fly (The Angel Song)
Wilkinsons; *Nothing But Love* . . . .(Giant)
God Bless The USA
Lee Greenwood; *American Patriot* . . . . (Capitol)
God Bless America-C . . . . (Columbia)
God Bless The USA . . . .(MCA Special Prod.)
Inside Out/You've Got A Good Love Comin' . . . .(MCA)
Lee Greenwood's Greatest Hits . . . .(MCA)
Lee Greenwood's Greatest Hits-#2 . . . .(MCA)
Today's Country Classics-C . . . .(MCA Special Prod.)
Heaven, Hell Or Houston
ZZ Top; *El Loco* . . . .(Warner Bros.)
Six Pack . . . .(Warner Bros.)
Houston
Dean Martin; *Dean Martin's Greatest Hits* . . . . (Reprise)
Glen Campbell; *Best Of Glen Campbell* . . . . (Capitol)
Johnny Copeland; *Ain't Nothin' But A Party* . . . . (Rounder)
Texas Twister . . . . (Rounder)
Houston (Means I'm One Day Closer To You)
Larry Gatlin & The Gatlin Brothers Band; *19 Hot Country Requests-C* . . . .(Epic)
Greatest Country Hits Of The '80s-1983-C . . . . (Columbia)
Larry Gatlin & The Gatlin Brothers' Greatest Hits-Encore . . . . . (Capitol)
Larry Gatlin & The Gatlin Brothers-17 Greatest Hits . . . . (Columbia)
Houston Solution
Ronnie Milsap; *Stranger Things Have Happened* . . . . (RCA)
Houston, Treat My Lady Good
Joe Stampley; *Red Wine & Blue Memories*. . . . .(Epic)
If You Ain't Been To Houston
Lonesome Sundown; *Been Gone Too Long* . . . .(Hightone)
If You Ever Get To Houston
Mickey Newbury; *Sweet Memories* . . . .(MCA)
Let's Go To Big Houston
Papa Link Davis; *Best Of Cajun Country-C* . . . . (Era)
Midnight Special
Creedence Clearwater Revival; *1969* . . . . (Fantasy)
Creedence Clearwater Revival-Chronicle-#2 . . . . (Fantasy)
Creedence Clearwater Revival-Gold . . . . (Fantasy)
Movie Album . . . . (Fantasy)
Willy & The Poor Boys . . . . (Fantasy)
Johnny Rivers; *Johnny Rivers-Anthology 1964-1977* . . . . (Rhino)
Very Best Of Johnny Rivers . . . .(EMI)
Spend Another Night In Houston
Sonny James; *Sonny's Side Of The Street* . . . . (Monument)
Struggle Here In Houston
Juke Boy Bonner; *Life Gave Me A Dirty Deal* . . . . (Arhoolie)
The Struggle . . . . (Arhoolie)

CITIES: I
See Also: *CITIES: GENERAL, COUNTRIES: A-Z, STATES: A-Z*

Girl From Ipanema
Antonio Carlos Jobim; *Antonio Carlos Jobim* . . . .(Warner Bros.)
Compact Jazz-Antonio Carlos Jobim. . . . . (Verve)
Ella Fitzgerald; *Ella A Nice*. . . . .(Pablo)
Montreux '75 . . . .(Pablo)
Pablo Today-Ella Embraces Antonio Carlos Jobim . . . .(Pablo)
Stan Getz & Astrud Gilberto; *Cruisin'-1964-C* . . . .(Increase)
Getz/Gilberto . . . . (Verve)
Going Back To Iuka
Albert King; *Lovejoy* . . . .(Stax)
Koko Taylor & Her Blues Machine; *Live From Chicago-With The
Queen* . . . . (Alligator)
Indianapolis Blues
David Lahm; *Freal Jazz For The Folks Who Feel Jazz*. . . . . (Palo Alto Jazz)
Istanbul (Not Constantinople)
Four Lads; *Four Lads-16 Most Requested Songs* . . . . (Legacy)

Little Green Apples (Indianapolis)
O.C. Smith; *Pop Classics Of The '60s-C*. . . . . (Columbia)
Telephone Call From Istanbul
Tom Waits; *Big Time.* . . . . (Island)
Frank's Wild Years-Un Operachi Romantico . . . . (Island)

CITIES: J
See Also: *CITIES: GENERAL, COUNTRIES: A-Z, STATES: A-Z*

Back To Johnson City
J.E. Mainer's Crazy Mountaineers; *J.E. Mainer's Crazy Mountaineers-
Vol. 2* . . . . (Old Timey)
Don't You Hear Jerusalem Moan
Nitty Gritty Dirt Band; *Will The Circle Be Unbroken-#2-C* . . . . (Uni)
Freedom Riders (Jackson, MS)
Phil Ochs; *Best Of Broadside 1962-1968: Anthems Of The American
Underground From The Pages Of Broadside
Magazine-C* . . . .(Smithsonian Folkways)
From Jerusalem To Jericho
Uncle Dave Macon; *Laugh Your Blues Away* . . . . (Rounder)
Funkin' For Jamaica (NY)
Tom Browne; *Love Approach* . . . . (GRP)
Honky Tonk Women (Jackson)
Elton John; *11-17-70* . . . .(Polydor)
Humble Pie; *Best Of Humble Pie.* . . . . (A&M)
Eat It. . . . . (A&M)
Humble Pie-Classics-#14 . . . . (A&M)
Ike & Tina Turner; *Best Of Ike & Tina Turner* . . . . (EMI)
Get Back. . . . . (Liberty)
Joe Cocker; *Mad Dogs & Englishmen.* . . . . (A&M)
Rolling Stones; *Get Yer Ya-Ya's Out!* . . . .(Abkco)
Hot Rocks 1964-1971 . . . .(Abkco)
Love You Live . . . . (Virgin)
Through The Past, Darkly (Big Hits Vol. 2) . . . .(Abkco)
Willie Nelson & Leon Russell; *Half Nelson-C* . . . . (Columbia)
Jackson
Johnny Cash & June Carter; *Johnny Cash's Greatest Hits* . . . . (Columbia)
The Man In Black-His Greatest Hits. . . . . (Legacy)
Nancy Sinatra & Lee Hazlewood; *Nancy Sinatra-The Hit Years* . . . . . . (Rhino)
Jackson Ain't A Very Big Town
Tammy Wynette; *My World* . . . .(Fifty One West)
Jerusalem On The Jukebox
Richard Thompson; *Amnesia* . . . . (Capitol)
Johannesburg Woman
David Rudder; *1990* . . . .(Sire)
Johnsburg, Illinois
Tom Waits; *Beautiful Maladies: The Island Years* . . . . (Island)
Swordfishtrombones . . . . (Island)
Joshua Fought The Battle Of Jericho
Elvis Presley; *His Hand In Mine* . . . . (RCA)
Jordanaires; *Tribute To Elvis' Favorite Spirituals* . . . .(Step One)
New Messengers Of Happiness; *Swinging Gospel* . . . . (Alshire)
Pete Seeger; *20 Golden Pieces Of Pete Seeger* . . . .(Bulldog)
Sister Rosetta Tharpe; *Live At The Hot Club De France* . . . . (Milan)
New Jerusalem
Word Of Mouth Chorus; *Rivers Of Delight* . . . .(Nonesuch)
New Jerusalem
Tom Gavornik; *High Places* . . . . (August Prod.)
Road To Jakarta
Steve Hunter; *The Deacon.* . . . .(I.R.S./No Speak)
Run, Come See Jerusalem
Arlo Guthrie & Pete Seeger; *Precious Friend* . . . . (Warner Bros.)
Train To Johannesburg
Original Cast; *Lost In The Stars* . . . . (MCA)
Walkin' In Jerusalem
Bill Monroe; *The Country Music Hall Of Fame-Bill Monroe* . . . . (MCA)
Doc Watson; *Old Timey Concert.* . . . . (Vanguard)
Ricky Skaggs; *Love's Gonna Get Ya*. . . . .(Epic)

CITIES: K
See Also: *CITIES: GENERAL, CITIES: KANSAS CITY, COUNTRIES: A-Z, STATES: A-Z*

Funky Kingston
Toots & The Maytals; *Funky Kingston* . . . . (Island)
The Island Story-1962-1987-25th Anniversary-C . . . . (Island)
Toots & The Maytals-Live . . . . (Mango)
Girl From Key Biscayne
Diego Modena & Jean Philippe Audin; *Ocarina* . . . .(Private Music)
Girl From Knoxville
Dave Loggins; *Apprentice (In A Musical Workshop)* . . . . (Epic)
Hungry Heart (Kingston)
Bruce Springsteen; *Bruce Springsteen's Greatest Hits* . . . . (Columbia)

The River .... (Columbia)
Bruce Springsteen & The E Street Band; *Bruce Springsteen's
  Greatest Hits* .... (Columbia)

I've Got A Gal In Kalamazoo
Glenn Miller; *Best Of Glenn Miller* .... (RCA)
  Decade Of The '40s-C .... (RCA)
  Glenn Miller-A Legendary Performer-#1 & 2 ...... (Bluebird)
  Memorial-1944-1969 .... (Bluebird)
  The Glenn Miller Story .... (RCA)
Glenn Miller & His Orchestra; *Glenn Miller & His Orchestra-
  Pure Gold* .... (Bluebird)
  The Unforgettable Glenn Miller & His Orchestra .... (RCA)

Jamaica Farewell
Harry Belafonte; *Calypso* .... (RCA)
  Harry Belafonte-Legendary Performer .... (RCA)
  Harry Belafonte-Pure Gold .... (RCA)
  Harry Belafonte's All Time Greatest Hits-#1 .... (RCA)
  This Is Harry Belafonte .... (RCA)

Kaplan Waltz
Nathan Abshire; *Kaplan Waltz & Other Cajun Gems* .... (Arhoolie)

Katmandu
Bob Seger; *Beautiful Loser* .... (Capitol)
  Live Bullet .... (Capitol)
Cat Stevens; *Cat Stevens-Classics-#24* .... (A&M)
  Footsteps In The Dark-Greatest Hits-#2. .... (A&M)
  Mona Bone Jakon .... (A&M)

Knoxville Blues
Toulouse Engelhardt; *Toullusions* .... (Briar)

Knoxville Courthouse Blues
Hank Williams, Jr.; *Major Moves* .... (WB/Curb)

Knoxville Girl
Cathy Fink & Duck Donald; *Cathy Fink & Duck Donald* .... (Flying Fish)
Jimmy Martin; *Me 'N Ole Pete* .... (International Mktg. Group)
Stanley Brothers; *Stanley Series-Vol. 1-#1* .... (Copper Creek)

Knoxville Rag
Etta Baker; *One-Dime Blues* .... (Rounder)

One Sad Night In Kerrville
Tom Kell; *Sad Night* .... (Warner Bros.)

Satan Is Busy In Knoxville
Leola Manning; *Barrelhouse Mamas: Born In The Alley, Raised In The
  Slums-C* .... (Yazoo)

Theme From "Knots Landing"
Original Soundtrack; *CBS: The First 50 Years* .... (TVT)
  Television's Greatest Hits-#3-1970s & 1980s-C .... (TVT)

CITIES: KANSAS CITY

See Also: STATES: KANSAS, STATES: MISSOURI

Blue Monday At Kansas City Red's
Cary Bell; *Blues Harp* .... (Delmark)

Eternal Kansas City
Van Morrison; *Period Of Transition* .... (Warner Bros.)

From K.C. To L.A.
Max Groove; *Maximum Groove* .... (Optimism)

Goin' To Kansas City
Furry Lewis; *Shake 'Em On Down* .... (Fantasy)
Jimmy Witherspoon; *'Spoon Concerts* .... (Fantasy)

I'm Goin' To Kansas City
Frances Faye; *Caught In The Act-Thunderbird* .... (Crescendo)

Kansas City
Beatles; *Beatles VI.* .... (Capitol)
  Beatles-Box Set. .... (Capitol)
  Rock 'N' Roll Music .... (Capitol)
  Super Oldies Of The '60s-#10-C. .... (Audio Fidelity)
Bill Haley & His Comets; *Bill Haley & His Comets' Greatest Hits.* ..... (Everest)
Fats Domino; *Fats Domino's Greatest Hits.* .... (Everest)
Wilbert Harrison; *American Graffiti-#3-C* .... (MCA)
  Billboard Top Rock 'N' Roll Hits-1959-C .... (Rhino)
  Cruisin'-1959-C. .... (Increase)
  Echoes Of A Rock Era-Middle Years-C .... (Roulette)
  Super Oldies Of The '50s-#2-C. .... (Audio Fidelity)

Kansas City Blues
Big Joe Turner; *Turns On The Blues* .... (Kent)
Janis Joplin; *ST/Janis.* .... (Columbia)
Jo Stafford; *Jo Plus Blues* .... (Corinthian)
Joe Williams; *Everyday I Have The Blues.* .... (Savoy)

Kansas City Bomber
Phil Ochs; *The War Is Over-Best Of Phil Ochs* .... (A&M)

Kansas City Lights
Steve Wariner; *Steve Wariner* .... (RCA)
  Steve Wariner's Greatest Hits .... (RCA)

Kansas City Papa
Leadbelly; *King Of The Twelve-String Guitar.* .... (Columbia)
  Leadbelly .... (Columbia)

Kansas City Railroad Blues
Nashville Bluegrass Band; *Waitin' For The Hard Times To Go* ..... (Sugar Hill)

Kansas City Song
Buck Owens; *Buck Owens Collection-1959-1990* .... (Rhino)

Kansas City Southern
Pure Prairie League; *Freight Train Blues-Classic Railroad
  Songs-#4-C.* .... (Rounder)
  Takin' The Stage .... (RCA)
  Two Lane Highway .... (RCA)

Kansas City Star
Roger Miller; *Best Of Roger Miller-His Greatest Songs* ..... (Curb)
  Roger Miller-Golden Hits .... (Smash)

Kansas City Stomp
Jelly Roll Morton; *1923-1924* .... (Milestone)
  Jelly Roll Morton. .... (Bluebird)

Kansas City Tango
Bud Shank & Shorty Rogers; *California Concert* .... (Contemporary)

Kansas City Woman
Little Charlie & The Nightcats; *Big Break!* .... (Alligator)

Kansas City Wrinkle
Count Basie & His Orchestra; *ST/Listen Up-The Lives Of Quincy
  Jones.* .... (Qwest)

Leaving Kansas City
George Jackson; *Sweet Down Home Delta Blues* .... (Amblin')

Mobile & K.C. Line
Robert Shaw; *Ma Grinder* .... (Arhoolie)

Powder River/Carrie's Gone To Kansas City
Bill Shute & Lisa Null; *American Primitive* .... (Green Linnet)

Running Gun
Marty Robbins; *Gunfighter Ballads & Trail Songs* .... (Legacy)

Train From Kansas City
Shangri-Las; *Golden Hits Of The Shangri-Las* .... (Mercury)

We Gonna Move To Kansas City
Walter Horton; *Fine Cuts* .... (Blind Pig)

CITIES: L

See Also: CITIES: GENERAL, CITIES: LAS VEGAS, LONDON, LOS ANGELES, COUNTRIES: A-Z, STATES: A-Z

Big Bad Bill Is Sweet William Now (Louisville)
Ry Cooder; *Jazz* .... (Warner Bros.)

Deportee (Plane Wreck At Los Gatos)
Arlo Guthrie & Pete Seeger; *Together In Concert* .... (Reprise)
Byrds; *The Byrds* .... (Columbia)
Cisco Houston; *Greatest Songs Of Woody Guthrie-C* ..... (Vanguard)
Gene Clark & Carla Olson; *So Rebellious A Lover* .... (Rhino)
Judy Collins; *Tribute To Woody Guthrie-C* .... (Warner Bros.)
Waylon Jennings, Willie Nelson, Johnny Cash, Kris Kristofferson;
  Highwayman .... (Columbia)

Eight More Miles To Louisville
Eric Weissberg; *Dueling Banjos From "Deliverance"* .... (Warner Bros.)
Grandpa Jones; *Truckin' On-C.* .... (Hollywood)
Mike Auldridge; *Dobro/Blues & Bluegrass* .... (Takoma)
Reno & Smiley; *1983 Collector's Edition-#3* .... (Gusto)
  Best Of Reno & Smiley .... (Starday)

Girl From Lodi
Bola Sete; *Incomparable* .... (Fantasy)

Goin' Down To Laurel
Steve Forbert; *Alive On Arrival* .... (Nemperor)

Going Back To Liverpool
Jackie Lomax; *Is This What You Want?* .... (Capitol)

Going Down To Liverpool
Bangles; *All Over The Place* .... (Columbia)
  Bangles' Greatest Hits .... (Columbia)

How Far To Little Rock
Stanley Brothers; *Stanley Series-Vol. 1-#2* .... (Copper Creek)

Laredo
Chris Cagle; *Play It Loud* .... (Capitol)

Leaving Lexington
Fiction Brothers; *Things Are Coming My Way* .... (Flying Fish)

Leaving Of Liverpool
Clancy Brothers; *Clancy Brothers Greatest Hits* .... (Vanguard)

Leningrad
Billy Joel; *Storm Front.* .... (Columbia)

Lisbon Antigua
Nelson Riddle & His Orchestra; *Memories Are Made Of This-C* ..... (Capitol)

Little Girl From Little Rock
Original Cast; *Gentlemen Prefer Blondes* .... (Sony Music Special Prod.)

Little Past Little Rock
Lee Ann Womack; *Some Things I Know* .... (Decca)

Little Rock
Collin Raye; *Extremes* .... (Epic)

Livingston Saturday Night
Jimmy Buffett; *Son Of A Son Of A Sailor* .... (MCA)
  ST/FM. .... (MCA)

Lodi
Creedence Clearwater Revival; *1969.* .... (Fantasy)

Creedence Clearwater Revival-Chronicle . . . . (Fantasy)
Creedence Country . . . . (Fantasy)
Green River . . . . (Fantasy)
Live In Europe . . . . (Fantasy)
More Creedence Gold . . . . (Fantasy)
Travelin' Band . . . . (Fantasy)
Lonesome Town
Ricky Nelson; *Best Of Ricky Nelson* . . . . (Curb)
Louisville
Jann Browne; *Tell Me Why* . . . . (Curb)
Louisville Lou
Johnny Mercer; *The Uncollected Johnny Mercer-1944* . . . . (Hindsight)
Lovetown
Peter Gabriel; *ST/Philadelphia* . . . . (Epic/Sony Music Soundtrax)
Luckenbach Texas (Back To The Basics Of Love)
Waylon Jennings; *Ol' Waylon* . . . . (RCA)
Stars Are Out In Texas-C . . . . (RCA)
Waylon Jennings' Greatest Hits . . . . (RCA)
Man Of La Mancha (La Mancha)
Original Cast; *Lost In The Stars* . . . . (MCA)
Original London Cast; *Man Of La Mancha* . . . . (MCA)
Streets Of Laredo
Buck Owens & The Buckaroos; *Buck Owens & The Buckaroos-Live At Carnegie Hall* . . . . (Country Music Foundation)
Marty Robbins; *Cowboy Super Hits-C* . . . . (Columbia)
Marty Robbins' All-Time Greatest Hits . . . . (Columbia)
Marty Robbins-More Greatest Hits . . . . (Columbia)
More Gunfighter Ballads & Trail Songs . . . . (Columbia)
Rex Allen; *Great American Singing Cowboys-C* . . . . . (Republic/Universal)
Sunrise In La Jolla
Kilauea; *Antigua Blue* . . . . (Brainchild)
Theme From "The Lawman" (Laramie)
Original Soundtrack; *Television's Greatest Hits-#4-Black & White Classics-C* . . . . (TVT)

CITIES: LAS VEGAS

See Also: **GAMBLING, LUCK, STATES: NEVADA**

Big In Vegas
Buck Owens; *Buck Owens' All-Time Greatest Hits-#1* . . . . (Curb)
Buck Owens Collection-1959-1990 . . . . (Rhino)
Great Records Of The Decade-'70s Hits-Country-C . . . . (Curb)
Goin' To Las Vegas
Suicide; *1/2 Alive* . . . . (Roir)
Heaven Or Las Vegas
Cocteau Twins; *Heaven Or Las Vegas* . . . . (Capitol)
Las Vegas Basement
Julian Cope; *Peggy Suicide* . . . . (Island)
Las Vegas Blues
Don Malena; *City Boy* . . . . (Accent)
Las Vegas Oberek
Cavaliers; *Have Polka Will Travel* . . . . (Accent)
Las Vegas Ramble
Happy Polkateers; *Happy Polkateers* . . . . (Crescendo)
Las Vegas Story
Gun Club; *Las Vegas Story* . . . . (I.R.S.)
Las Vegas Tango
Gil Evans; *Individualism Of Gil Evans* . . . . (Verve)
Las Vegas Turnaround
Daryl Hall & John Oates; *Abandoned Luncheonette* . . . . (Atlantic)
No Goodbyes . . . . (Atlantic)
Leaving Las Vegas
Sheryl Crow; *Tuesday Night Music Club* . . . . (A&M)
Let's Go To Vegas
Faith Hill; *It Matters To Me* . . . . (Warner Bros.)
Mambo Las Vegas
Howard Rumsey's Lighthouse All-Stars; *Music For Lighthousekeeping* . . . . (Contemporary)
Ooh Las Vegas
Emmylou Harris; *Elite Hotel* . . . . (Reprise)
Gram Parsons; *Grievous Angel* . . . . (Reprise)
Queen Of Las Vegas
B-52's; *Whammy* . . . . (Warner Bros.)
Sands Of Nevada
Mark Knopfler; *Sailing To Philadelphia* . . . . (Warner Bros.)
T-Bird To Vegas
Albert Lee; *Speechless* . . . . (MCA)
That Night In Las Vegas
Ennio Morricone; *ST/Bugsy* . . . . (Epic)
Theme From "Vegas"
Original Soundtrack; *Television's Greatest Hits-#6-Remote Control-C* . . (TVT)
Vegas Weekend
Thelonius Monster; *Beautiful Mess* . . . . (Capitol)
Viva Las Vegas
Elvis Presley; *ST/This Is Elvis* . . . . (RCA)

Worldwide 50 Gold Award Hits, Vol. 1, Parts 1 & 2 . . . . (RCA)

CITIES: LONDON

See Also: **COUNTRIES: ENGLAND**

Autumn In London Town
Norrie Paramor; *Autumn* . . . . (Angel)
Babylon
David Gray; *White Ladder* . . . . (ATO/RCA)
Dark Streets Of London
Greater Than One; *Duty & Trust* . . . . (Roir)
Dead Girls Of London
Frank Zappa; *You Can't Do That On Stage Anymore-#5* . . . . (Rykodisc)
Foggy Day
Billie Holiday; *All Or Nothing At All* . . . . (Verve)
Dick Hyman; *Music Of 1937-Maybeck Recital Hall-#3* . . . (Concord Jazz)
Ella Fitzgerald; *Ella In Rome-Birthday Concert* . . . . (Verve)
George & Ira Gershwin Songbook . . . . (Verve)
Ella Fitzgerald & Joe Pass; *Take Love Easy* . . . . (Pablo)
Ella Fitzgerald & Louis Armstrong; *Ella & Louis* . . . . (Verve)
Frank Sinatra; *Songs For Young Lovers & Swing Easy* . . . . (Capitol)
Fred Astaire; *Fred Astaire Sings* . . . . (MCA)
Starring Fred Astaire . . . . (Columbia)
Judy Garland; *Judy Garland-At Carnegie Hall* . . . . (Capitol)
Wynton Marsalis; *Marsalis Standard Time-#1* . . . . (Columbia)
Foggy Streets Of London
Special EFX; *Special EFX* . . . . (GRP)
Funky London Childhood
Marc Bolan; *T. Rex Unchained: The Unreleased Recordings-#6* . . . (Chronicles)
I Love London
Tommy Page; *Tommy Page* . . . . (Sire)
Inner London Violence
Bad Manners; *ST/Dance Craze* . . . . (Chrysalis)
Last Train To London
Electric Light Orchestra; *Box Of Their Best* . . . . (Jet)
Discovery . . . . (Jet)
Leaving London
Tom Paxton; *Compleat Tom Paxton* . . . . (Elektra)
Outward Bound . . . . (Elektra)
Life In London
Pat Travers; *Boom Boom...The Best Of* . . . . (Polydor)
Putting It Straight . . . . (Polydor)
Little London Boys
Johnny Thunders; *Stations Of The Cross* . . . . (Roir)
London
Queensryche; *Rage For Order* . . . . (EMI)
Smiths; *Louder Than Bombs* . . . . (Sire)
Rank . . . . (Sire)
London After Midnight
Wrathchild America; *Climbin' The Walls* . . . . (Atlantic)
London Belongs To Me
Saint Etienne; *Foxbase Alpha* . . . . (Warner Bros.)
London Blues (Shoe Shiner's Drag)
Jelly Roll Morton; *1923-1924* . . . . (Milestone)
London Boys
David Bowie; *David Bowie-London Collector-Starting Point* . . . . . (London)
Love You Till Tuesday . . . . (London)
London Bridge
Bread; *Best Of Bread-#2* . . . . (Elektra)
Bread . . . . (Elektra)
Bread-Anthology . . . . (Elektra)
London Bridge
Big Audio Dynamite; *Megatop Phoenix* . . . . (Columbia)
London Bridge
Original Soundtrack; *Children's Favorites* . . . . (Kid Rhino/Rhino 4 Kids)
London Bridge Is Falling Down
Count Basie; *Good Morning Blues* . . . . (MCA)
London Bridge Is Falling Down
Newtrament; *Word 2* . . . . (Jive)
London By Night
Frank Sinatra; *Come Fly With Me* . . . . (Capitol)
Sinatra Rarities-Columbia Years . . . . (Columbia)
London Bye Ta-Ta
David Bowie; *Sound + Vision* . . . . (Rykodisc)
London Calling
Clash; *London Calling* . . . . (Epic)
On Broadway . . . . (Epic)
The Story Of The Clash, Volume 1 . . . . (Epic)
London Gets Ready
Oscar Peterson; *Royal Wedding Suite* . . . . (Pablo)
London Girl
Jam; *This Is The Modern World* . . . . (Polydor)
London Girls
Vibrators; *Pure Mania* . . . . (Columbia)
London Homesick Blues
David Allan Coe; *David Allan Coe's Biggest Hits* . . . . (Legacy)

Jerry Jeff Walker; *Great Gonzos* . . . . (MCA)
 Viva Terlingua . . . . (MCA)
London In July
 Corky Hale; *Corky Hale Plays George Gershwin & Vernon Duke* . . (Crescendo)
London Lady
 Stranglers; *All Live & All Of The Night* . . . . (Epic)
 Rattus Norvegicus . . . . (A&M)
London Leatherboys
 Accept; *Balls To The Wall* . . . . (Portrait)
 Compilation . . . . (Portrait)
London Life
 Ian & Sylvia; *Ian & Sylvia's Greatest Hits* . . . . (Vanguard)
 Nashville . . . . (Vanguard)
London Lowdown
 Ronny Jordan; *Brighter Day* . . . . (Blue Note)
London Luck & Love
 Daryl Hall & John Oates; *Bigger Than Both Of Us* . . . . (RCA)
London Pride
 John Williams; *Echoes Of London* . . . . (Columbia)
London Rain (Nothing Heals Like You Do)
 Heather Nova; *Siren* . . . . (Big Cat)
 Songs From Dawson's Creek . . . . (Sony Music Soundtrax)
London Skyline
 Acoustic Alchemy; *New Edge* . . . . (GRP)
London Song
 Seatrain; *Marblehead Messenger* . . . . (One Way)
London Suite
 Fats Waller; *Fats Waller In London* . . . . (Disques Swing)
London Town
 Donovan; *Troubadour-Definitive Collection* . . . . (Epic)
 James Taylor; *Dad Loves His Work* . . . . (Columbia)
 Wings; *London Town* . . . . (Capitol)
London Traffic
 Jam; *This Is The Modern World* . . . . (Polydor)
London You're A Lady
 Pogues; *Peace & Love* . . . . (Island)
London/Old Welsh Song
 Joan Baez; *First Ten Years* . . . . (Vanguard)
Londonderry Air
 Mormon Tabernacle Choir; *Lord's Prayer* . . . . (Columbia)
 Mormon Tabernacle Choir's Greatest Hits-#2 . . . . (Columbia)
 The Mormon Tabernacle Choir Album . . . . (Columbia)
London's Burning
 Clash; *On Broadway* . . . . (Epic)
 The Clash . . . . (Epic)
 The Story Of The Clash, Volume 1 . . . . (Epic)
Modern Girl
 Sheena Easton; *Best Of Sheena Easton* . . . . (EMI)
 Sheena Easton . . . . (EMI)
 Sheena Easton's Greatest Hits . . . . (EMI Special Markets)
 The World Of Sheena Easton: The Singles Collection-C . . . . (EMI)
Next Plane To London
 Rose Garden; *Only Love-1965-1969-C* . . . . (JCI Assoc. Labels)
Night In London
 Poncho Sanchez; *Chile Con Soul* . . . . (Concord Picante Jazz)
Nightingale Sang In Berkeley Square
 Harry Connick, Jr.; *We Are In Love* . . . . (Columbia)
 Manhattan Transfer; *Best Of The Manhattan Transfer* . . . . (Atlantic)
 Mecca For Moderns . . . . (Atlantic)
 Tony Bennett; *Perfectly Frank* . . . . (Columbia)
No Place Like London
 Original Cast/Angela Lansbury; *Sweeney Todd* . . . . (RCA)
On London Bridge
 Jo Stafford; *International Hits* . . . . (Corinthian)
Piccadilly
 Squeeze; *East Side Story* . . . . (A&M)
Piccadilly Circus
 Stiff Little Fingers; *See You Up There!* . . . . (Caroline)
Piccadilly Palare
 Morrissey; *Bona Drag* . . . . (Sire)
 Kill Uncle . . . . (Sire)
Port London Early
 Robin Williamson & His Merry Band; *American Stonehenge* . . . . . (Flying Fish)
Rainy Day In London
 Boulevard; *Into The Street* . . . . (MCA)
She Wears Red Feathers
 Guy Mitchell; *Guy Mitchell-16 Most Requested Songs* . . . . (Legacy)
Souvenir Of London
 Cleo Laine; *Born On A Friday* . . . . (RCA)
 Return To Carnegie . . . . (RCA)
Souvenir Of London (V.D.)
 Procol Harum; *Grand Hotel* . . . . (Chrysalis)
Street Fighting Man
 Rod Stewart; *Best Of Rod Stewart* . . . . (Mercury)
 Sing It Again, Rod . . . . (Mercury)
 Storyteller/The Complete Anthology: 1964-1990 . . . . (Warner Bros.)
 Rolling Stones; *Beggars Banquet* . . . . (Abkco)
 Get Yer Ya-Ya's Out! . . . . (Abkco)

Hot Rocks 1964-1971 . . . . (Abkco)
 Singles Collection-The London Years . . . . (Abkco)
 Through The Past, Darkly (Big Hits Vol. 2) . . . . (Abkco)
Streets Of London
 Mary Hopkin; *Earth Song/Ocean Song* . . . . (Capitol)
This Amazing London Town
 Original Broadway Cast; *The Rothschilds* . . . . (Sony Music Classical)
Tower Of London
 ABC; *How To Be A Zillionaire* . . . . (Mercury)
Werewolves Of London
 Warren Zevon; *Excitable Boy* . . . . (Asylum)
 Quiet Normal Life-Best Of Warren Zevon . . . . (Asylum)
 ST/Color Of Money . . . . (MCA)
 Stand In The Fire . . . . (Asylum)
West End Girls
 Pet Shop Boys; *Disco* . . . . (EMI)
 Discography-Complete Singles Collection . . . . (EMI)
 Please . . . . (EMI)
Wild West End
 Dire Straits; *Dire Straits* . . . . (Warner Bros.)
Worst Pies In London
 Original Cast; *Sweeney Todd* . . . . (RCA)

CITIES: LOS ANGELES, L.A. Suburbs

See Also: *CELEBRITIES: SPECIFIC, HOLLYWOOD, MOVIES, SHOW BIZ, STATES: CALIFORNIA*

1-900-2-COMPTON
 N.W.A.; *Efil4zaggin* . . . . (Ruthless/Priority)
Ain't Nobody Straight In L.A.
 Miracles; *City Of Angels* . . . . (Tamla)
All I Wanna Do
 Sheryl Crow; *Tuesday Night Music Club* . . . . (A&M)
Anaheim, Azusa & Cucamonga Sewing Circle
 Jan & Dean; *Best Of Jan & Dean* . . . . (EMI)
 Jan & Dean-Legendary Masters . . . . (EMI)
Another Nice Day In L.A.
 Eddie Money; *Right Here* . . . . (Columbia)
Back In L.A.
 B.B. King; *There Is Always One More Time* . . . . (MCA)
Back In L.A.
 Neil Diamond; *Hot August Night II* . . . . (Columbia)
Beautiful Downtown Burbank
 Jeannie C. Riley; *Country Gold-Jeannie C. Riley* . . . . (Plantation)
Blue Jay Way
 Beatles; *Beatles-Box Set* . . . . (Capitol)
 Magical Mystery Tour . . . . (Capitol)
Born And Raised In Compton
 DJ Quik; *Quik Is The Name* . . . . (Profile)
Born In East L.A.
 Cheech & Chong; *Get Out Of My Room* . . . . (MCA)
Boyz-N-The-Hood (Compton)
 Dynamite Hack; *Superfast* . . . . (Farm Club/Universal)
Burnin' In L.A.
 Lightnin' Hopkins; *Lightnin' Sam Hopkins* . . . . (Arhoolie)
California Dreamin'
 Beach Boys; *Made In The U.S.A.* . . . . (Capitol)
 Mamas & The Papas; *At The Hop* . . . . (MCA)
 Good Feeling Music Of The Big Chill Generation-#1-C . . . . (Motown)
 Mamas & The Papas-20 Golden Hits . . . . * . . . . . (MCA)
 ST/Air America . . . . (MCA)
 ST/American Pop . . . . (MCA)
 ST/Forrest Gump . . . . (Epic/Sony Music Soundtrax)
California Love
 2Pac featuring Dr. Dre; *All Eyez On Me* . . . . (Death Row)
 MTV Party To Go-#10-C . . . . (Tommy Boy)
Century City
 Tom Petty And The Heartbreakers; *Damn The Torpedoes* . . . . (MCA)
City Of Angels
 Jay Ferguson; *Real Life Ain't This Way* . . . . (Asylum)
City Of Angels
 Miracles; *City Of Angels* . . . . (Tamla)
City Of The Angels
 Wang Chung; *ST/To Live And Die In L.A.* . . . . (Geffen)
City Of The Angels
 Journey; *Evolution* . . . . (Columbia)
Coming Into Los Angeles
 Arlo Guthrie; *Best Of Arlo Guthrie* . . . . (Warner Bros.)
 Running Down The Road . . . . (Reprise)
 ST/Woodstock . . . . (Atlantic)
Country Boy (You Got Your Feet In L.A.)
 Glen Campbell; *Best Of Glen Campbell* . . . . (Capitol)
 Glen Campbell-Classics Collection . . . . (Capitol)
 Glen Campbell's Greatest Hits . . . . (Capitol)
Cowboy
 Kid Rock; *Devil Without A Cause* . . . . (Top Dog/Lava/Atlantic)

Creeque Alley
Mamas & The Papas; *Best Of The Mamas & The Papas* . . . . (MCA)
   Mamas & The Papas' Greatest Hits . . . . (MCA)
   Mamas & The Papas-16 Of Their Greatest Hits . . . . (MCA)
Do America
Mark Knopfler; *Sailing To Philadelphia* . . . .(Warner Bros.)
Do You Know The Way To San Jose
Dionne Warwick; *Dionne Warwick Greatest Hits* . . . . (Everest)
   Dionne Warwick-Anthology 1962-1971 . . . . (Rhino)
   Hot! Live & Otherwise . . . . (Arista)
Electric L.A. Sunset
Al Stewart; *Al Stewart-Early Years* . . . . (Janus)
Electrolite
Michael Stipe/Mike Mills; *Tibetan Freedom Concert* . . . . (Capitol)
R.E.M.; *New Adventures In Hi-Fi* . . . .(Warner Bros.)
Free Fallin'
Tom Petty; *Full Moon Fever* . . . .(MCA)
From K.C. To L.A.
Max Groove; *Maximum Groove* . . . . (Optimism)
Going To Live In L.A.
Roger Waters; *45-#38-07180* . . . . (Columbia)
Honey Don't Leave L.A.
James Taylor; *JT* . . . . (Columbia)
Hot Rod Lincoln
Asleep At The Wheel; *Western Standard Time* . . . .(Epic)
Commander Cody & His Lost Planet Airmen; *Lost In The Ozone* . . . . . .(MCA)
   Super Hits Of The '70s-Have A Nice Day-#8-C . . . . (Rhino)
Johnny Bond; *Best Of Johnny Bond* . . . . (Starday)
How Much Is It Worth To Live In L.A.
Waylon Jennings; *New Classic Waylon* . . . .(MCA)
I Am...I Said
Neil Diamond; *Hot August Night* . . . .(MCA)
   Hot August Night II . . . . (Columbia)
   Neil Diamond-His 12 Greatest Hits . . . . (MCA)
   Stones . . . .(MCA)
I Love L.A.
Randy Newman; *Trouble In Paradise* . . . .(Warner Bros.)
It's A Compton Thang
Compton's Most Wanted; *It's A Compton Thang* . . . . (Orpheus)
Join Me In L.A.
Warren Zevon; *Warren Zevon* . . . . (Asylum)
L.A.
Neil Young; *Time Fades Away* . . . . (Reprise)
L.A. (My Town)
Four Tops; *Still Waters Run Deep* . . . . (Motown)
L.A. Breakdown
Helen Reddy; *I Don't Know How To Love Him* . . . . (Capitol)
L.A. Connection
Rainbow; *Long Live Rock 'n' Roll* . . . . (Polydor)
L.A. Dreams
Charlie; *Lines* . . . .(Janus)
L.A. Freeway
Guy Clark; *Old No. 1* . . . . (Sugar Hill)
Jerry Jeff Walker; *Best Of Jerry Jeff Walker* . . . .(MCA)
   Great Gonzos . . . . (MCA)
L.A. Girls
Nazareth; *Play'n' The Game* . . . . (A&M)
L.A. International Airport
Susan Raye; *Best Of Susan Raye* . . . . (Capitol)
L.A. Lady
New Riders Of The Purple Sage; *Adventures Of Panama Red* . . . . . . (Columbia)
L.A. Mama
Jim Stafford; *Jim Stafford* . . . . (Polydor)
L.A. Serenade
Livingston Taylor; *3-Way Mirror* . . . .(Epic)
L.A. Sunshine
War; *Platinum Jazz* . . . . (Blue Note)
L.A. Woman
Billy Idol; *Charmed Life* . . . .(Chrysalis)
Doors; *Best Of The Doors* . . . . (Elektra)
   Doors' Greatest Hits . . . . (Elektra)
   L.A. Woman . . . . (Elektra)
   ST/The Doors . . . . (Elektra)
   Weird Scenes Inside The Gold Mine . . . . (Elektra)
Ladies Of The Canyon
Joni Mitchell; *Ladies Of The Canyon* . . . . (Reprise)
Letter To L.A.
Joe Ely; *Live At Liberty Lunch* . . . .(MCA)
   Lord Of The Highway . . . . (Hightone)
Life Beyond L.A.
Ambrosia; *Life Beyond L.A.* . . . .(Warner Bros.)
Little Old Lady (From Pasadena)
Beach Boys; *Concert/'69-Live In London* . . . . (Capitol)
Jan & Dean; *Best Of Jan & Dean* . . . .(EMI)
   Billboard Top Rock 'N' Roll Hits-1964-C . . . . (Rhino)
   Dead Man's Curve . . . .(EMI)
   Surf City-Best Of Jan & Dean . . . .(EMI)

Livin' In South Central L.A.
South Central Posse; *We're All In The Same Gang-C* . . . . (Warner Bros.)
Lonesome L.A. Cowboy
New Riders Of The Purple Sage; *Adventures Of Panama Red* . . . . . (Columbia)
   Midnight Moonlight . . . .(Relix)
Long December
Counting Crows; *Recovering The Satellites* . . . .(David Geffen Co.)
Los Angelenos
Billy Joel; *Songs In The Attic* . . . . (Columbia)
   Streetlife Serenade . . . . (Columbia)
Los Angeles
X; *Dangerous-#1* . . . . (Frontier)
   Live At The Whisky A Go-Go . . . . (Elektra)
   Los Angeles/Wild Gift . . . .(Slash)
   Los Angeles/Wild Gift . . . .(Slash)
Los Angeles
F. Machine; *Here Comes The 21st Century* . . . . (Reprise)
Los Angeles
Circus Of Power; *Vices* . . . . (RCA)
Los Angeles Blues
Lightnin' Hopkins; *Los Angeles Blues* . . . . (Rhino)
Los Angeles Boogie
Lightnin' Hopkins; *Los Angeles Blues* . . . . (Rhino)
Lullaby
Shawn Mullins; *Soul's Core* . . . . (Columbia)
MacArthur Park
Andy Williams; *Andy Williams' Greatest Hits-#2* . . . . (Columbia)
Donna Summer; *Live & More* . . . .(Casablanca)
   On The Radio-Greatest Hits-Volumes I & II . . . . (Casablanca)
   Summer Collection . . . . (Mercury)
   Walk Away-Best Of Donna Summer-1977-1980 . . . . (Casablanca)
Richard Harris; *Love Album* . . . . (MCA)
   Richard Harris-His Greatest Performances . . . . (MCA)
   Tramp Shining . . . . (MCA)
   Vintage Music-#13-C . . . . (MCA)
Waylon Jennings; *Are You Ready For The Country* . . . . (RCA)
   Best Of Waylon Jennings . . . . (RCA)
Magic
Cars; *Heartbeat City* . . . . (Elektra)
   The Cars' Greatest Hits . . . . (Elektra)
Maria Maria
Santana; *Supernatural* . . . . (Arista)
   Totally Hits-#2-C . . . . (Elektra)
Marina Del Rey
George Strait; *George Strait's Greatest Hits* . . . . (MCA)
   Strait From The Heart . . . . (MCA)
Men's Room L.A.
Kinky Friedman; *Lasso From El Paso* . . . . (Epic)
Midnight Train To Georgia
Gladys Knight & The Pips; *Billboard Top Rock 'N' Roll Hits-1973-C* . . . (Rhino)
   Gladys Knight & The Pips' Greatest Hits . . . .(Buddah)
   Imagination . . . . (Right Stuff)
   On & On . . . . (Fifty One West)
   Radio Active Hits-C . . . . (Accord)
   Train Trax-C . . . . (Sony Music Special Prod.)
   Very Best Of Gladys Knight & The Pips . . . .(Buddah)
Next Episode
Dr. Dre; *Dr. Dre 2001* . . . .(Aftermath/Interscope)
Out In L.A.
Red Hot Chili Peppers; *Red Hot Chili Peppers* . . . . (EMI)
Pasadena
Al Jolson; *Lullaby Of Broadway-Music Of H. Warren* . . . . (Pearl Flapper)
Please Come To Boston
Dave Loggins; *Apprentice (In A Musical Workshop)* . . . . (Epic)
   Rock Artifacts-From The Vaults-#2-C . . . . (Legacy)
   Super Hits Of The '70s-Have A Nice Day-#13-C . . . . (Rhino)
David Allan Coe; *David Allan Coe-17 Greatest Hits* . . . . (Columbia)
   For The Record-The First 10 Years . . . . (Columbia)
Joan Baez; *Best Of Joan Baez* . . . . (A&M)
   Joan Baez-Classics-#8 . . . . (A&M)
Reba McEntire; *Starting Over* . . . . (MCA)
Pride Of Cucamonga
Grateful Dead; *From The Mars Hotel* . . . .(Grateful Dead)
Promised Land
Band; *Moondog Matinee* . . . . (Capitol)
Chuck Berry; *Rock 'N' Roll Rarities-20 Magic Tracks* . . . . (Chess)
   The Chess Box-Chuck Berry . . . . (Chess)
Elvis Presley; *Promised Land* . . . . (RCA)
   ST/This Is Elvis . . . . (RCA)
Freddy Weller; *Country Music Classics-#11-Early '70s-C* . . . . (K-Tel)
   Freddy Weller's Greatest Hits . . . . (Columbia)
Gary Morris; *Full Moon Empty Heart* . . . . (Liberty)
Grateful Dead; *Steal Your Face* . . . .(Grateful Dead)
James Taylor; *Walking Man* . . . . (Warner Bros.)
Kingfish; *Kingfish/Alive In Eighty Five-Double Dose* . . . . (Relix)
Raised In Compton
Compton's Most Wanted; *Straight Checkn 'Em* . . . . (Orpheus)
Redondo Beach
Patti Smith; *Horses* . . . . (Arista)

Sam's Place (Pasadena)
Buck Owens & The Buckaroos; *Billboard Top Country Hits-1967-C* . . . . (Rhino)
San Fernando
Mary McCaslin; *Sunny California* . . . . (Mercury)
Roy Orbison; *Legendary Roy Orbison* . . . . (Sony Music Special Prod.)
Rare Orbison II . . . . (Monument)
Santa Ana
Willi Jones; *Willi Jones* . . . . (Geffen)
Santa Ana Woman
Bobs; *Songs For Tomorrow Morning* . . . . (Kaleidoscope)
Santa Monica
Savage Garden; *Savage Garden* . . . . (Columbia)
Santa Monica (Watch The World Die)
Everclear; *Sparkle And Fade* . . . . (Capitol)
Santa Monica Pier
Christine Lavin; *Good Thing He Can't Read My Mind* . . . . (Philo)
Holly Near; *Live Album* . . . . (Redwood)
Nitty Gritty Dirt Band; *Dream* . . . . (United Artists)
She's Gone To L.A. Again
Oak Ridge Boys; *Fancy Free* . . . . (MCA)
So L.A.
Motels; *All Four One* . . . . (Capitol)
Best Of The Motels-No Vacancy . . . . (Capitol)
Sons Of Westwood
Original Soundtrack; *College Fight Songs: The Pac Ten-C* . . . . (K-Tel)
The Greatest College Fight Songs . . . . (Laserlight)
South Central L.A.
Broken Homes; *Wing & A Prayer* . . . . (MCA)
Straight Outta Compton
N.W.A.; *Straight Outta Compton* . . . . (Ruthless/Priority)
Sunday Night In San Fernando
Mel Torme & The Mel-Tones; *California Suite* . . . . (Discovery)
Take Me To Los Angeles
Jimmy Soul; *Best Of Jimmy Soul* . . . . (Rhino)
That's How We Do It In L.A.
Lindsey Buckingham; *Law And Order* . . . . (Asylum)
Theme From "77 Sunset Strip"
Original Soundtrack; *Television's Greatest Hits-#1-C* . . . . (TVT)
TV Classic Themes: 25th Anniversary Edition-C . . . . (Breakable)
Theme From "Beverly Hills 90210"
John Davis; *Beverly Hills 90210: Songs From The Peach Pit* . . . . (Rhino)
ST/Beverly Hills, 90210-College Years . . . . (Giant)
Television's Greatest Hits-#7-Cable Ready-C . . . . (TVT)
Theme From "Burke's Law"
Original Soundtrack; *Television's Greatest Hits-#4-Black & White Classics-C* . . . . (TVT)
Theme From "Chico And The Man"
Original Soundtrack; *Television's Greatest Hits-#5-In Living Color-C* . . . (TVT)
Theme From "Dragnet"
Original Soundtrack; *Television's Greatest Hits-#1-C* . . . . (TVT)
Theme From "Fresh Prince Of Bel-Air"
Original Soundtrack; *Television's Greatest Hits-#7-Cable Ready-C* . . . . (TVT)
Theme From "Hunter"
Original Soundtrack; *Television's Greatest Hits-#6-Remote Control-C* . . . (TVT)
Theme From "L.A. Law"
Original Soundtrack; *Television's Greatest Hits-#3-1970s & 1980s-C* . . . . (TVT)
Theme From "Melrose Place"
Original Soundtrack; *Television's Greatest Hits-#7-Cable Ready-C* . . . . (TVT)
Theme From "The Beverly Hillbillies"
Original Soundtrack; *CBS: The First 50 Years* . . . . (TVT)
Television's Greatest Hits-#1-C . . . . (TVT)
This Is Compton
Compton's Most Wanted; *It's A Compton Thang* . . . . (Orpheus)
To Live And Die In L.A.
Wang Chung; *ST/To Live And Die In L.A.* . . . . (Geffen)
Too Dumb For New York City
Waylon Jennings; *Too Dumb For New York City, Too Ugly For L.A.* . . . . . (Epic)
Tree Grows In Burbank
Harry James; *The Uncollected Harry James-#5-1943-1953* . . . . (Hindsight)
Twelve Thirty (Young Girls Are Coming To The Canyon)
Mamas & The Papas; *Best Of The Mamas & The Papas* . . . . (MCA)
Mamas & The Papas-16 Of Their Greatest Hits . . . . (MCA)
The Papas & The Mamas . . . . (MCA)
Uptown L.A.
Beau Coup; *Born & Raised (On Rock & Roll)* . . . . (Amherst)
Walking In L.A.
Missing Persons; *Best Of Missing Persons* . . . . (Capitol)
West L.A. Fadeaway
Grateful Dead; *In The Dark* . . . . (Arista)
Westside
TQ; *They Never Saw Me Coming* . . . . (ClockWork/Epic)
You're Not In Kansas Anymore
Jo Dee Messina; *Jo Dee Messina* . . . . (Curb)
You're The Reason God Made Oklahoma
David Frizzell & Shelly West; *Carryin' On The Family Names* . . . . (Warner Bros.)
Country's Greatest Hits-#9-'80s Duets-C . . . . (Priority)
Golden Duets . . . . (Viva)

CITIES: M

See Also: **CITIES: GENERAL, CITIES: MEMPHIS, MIAMI, MOBILE, MOSCOW, NEW YORK (Manhattan)**

Angel From Montgomery
Bonnie Raitt; *Streetlights* . . . . (Warner Bros.)
Bonnie Raitt & John Prine; *Bonnie Raitt-Collection* . . . . (Warner Bros.)
John Prine; *John Prine* . . . . (Atlantic)
John Prine-Souvenirs . . . . (Oh Boy)
By The Waters Of Lake Minnetonka (Minneapolis)
Glenn Miller; *Best Of Glenn Miller-#2* . . . . (RCA)
Glenn Miller & His Orchestra; *Complete Glenn Miller & His Orchestra* . . . . (Bluebird)
Christmas Card From A Hooker In Minneapolis
Tom Waits; *Blue Valentine* . . . . (Asylum)
Coast Of Marseilles
Jimmy Buffett; *Son Of A Son Of A Sailor* . . . . (MCA)
Dixie Road (Montgomery, Alabama)
Lee Greenwood; *Country Classics-#3-1984-1985-C* . . . . (Universal)
Lee Greenwood's Greatest Hits . . . . (MCA)
MCA #1 Hits Of The '80s-#2-C . . . . (MCA Special Prod.)
Everywhere (Monterey)
Tim McGraw; *Everywhere* . . . . (Curb)
Fog In Monterey
Mary Black; *No Frontiers* . . . . (Gift Horse)
Girl From Mill Valley
Jeff Beck Group; *Beck-Ola* . . . . (Epic)
Girls Of Montreal
Artie Traum; *Life On Earth* . . . . (Rounder)
Goin' Down To Muskogee
Jim Pepper; *Comin' & Goin'* . . . . (Antilles)
Going To Malibu
Malibooz; *Malibooz Rule* . . . . (Rhino)
Hotter Than Mojave In My Heart
Iris DeMent; *Infamous Angel* . . . . (Warner Bros.)
I Just Wanna Stop (Montreal)
Gino Vannelli; *Best Of Gino Vannelli* . . . . (A&M)
Brother To Brother . . . . (A&M)
Gino Vannelli-Classics-#7 . . . . (A&M)
It Happened In Monterey
Frank Sinatra & Nelson Riddle Orchestra; *songs for swingin' Lovers!* . . . . (Capitol)
Mel Torme & The Mel-Tones; *Back In Town* . . . . (Verve)
Lady Marmalade
Christina Aguilera, Lil' Kim, Mya & Pink; *ST/Moulin Rouge* . . . . . . (Interscope)
Labelle; *Nightbirds* . . . . (Epic)
Patti LaBelle; *Best Of Patti LaBelle* . . . . (Epic)
Sheila E.; *Sex Cymbal* . . . . (Warner Bros.)
Little Red Rodeo (Monterey)
Collin Raye; *Best Of Collin Raye-Direct Hits* . . . . (Epic)
Macon Georgia Bad Girl
Jeannie C. Riley; *Jeannie C. Riley & Fancy Friends* . . . . (Plantation)
Macon Hambone Blues
Wet Willie; *Drippin' Wet/Live!* . . . . (Capricorn)
Madison Blues
George Thorogood & The Destroyers; *George Thorogood & The Destroyers* . . . . (Rounder)
George Thorogood & The Destroyers-Live . . . . (EMI)
Steal This Disc-C . . . . (Rykodisc)
Nighthawks; *Best Of The Blues* . . . . (Adelphi)
Open All Nite . . . . (Adelphi)
Malibu
Hole; *Celebrity Skin* . . . . (David Geffen Co.)
Man From Madrid
John Barry; *The EMI Years-#2-1961* . . . . (Scamp)
Man From Milwaukee
Hanson; *Live From Albertane* . . . . (Mercury)
Middle Of Nowhere . . . . (Mercury)
Manchester England
Original Broadway Cast; *Hair* . . . . (RCA)
Marching Through Madrid
Herb Alpert & The Tijuana Brass; *Featuring Herb Alpert-#2* . . . . (A&M)
Herb Alpert & The Tijuana Brass-Classics-#1 . . . . (A&M)
Marina Del Rey
George Strait; *George Strait's Greatest Hits* . . . . (MCA)
Strait From The Heart . . . . (MCA)
Marrakesh Express
Crosby, Stills & Nash; *Crosby, Stills & Nash* . . . . (Atlantic)
CSN . . . . (Atlantic)
Replay . . . . (Atlantic)
Woodstock Two . . . . (Atlantic)
Memories Of Madrid
Herb Alpert & The Tijuana Brass; *Herb Alpert & The Tijuana Brass-Classics-#1* . . . . (A&M)
Mendocino
Sir Douglas Quintet; *Best Of The Sir Douglas Quintet* . . . . (Takoma)

Mexicali Blues
Bob Weir; *Ace*. . . . . (Grateful Dead)
Grateful Dead; *Best Of The Grateful Dead-Skeletons From The*
Closet . . . .(Warner Bros.)

Mexicali Rose
Bing Crosby; *Best Of Bing Crosby* . . . .(Sony Music Special Prod.)
Bob Wills; *Bob Wills-Anthology*. . . . .(Sony Music Special Prod.)

Midnight In Montgomery
Alan Jackson; *Don't Rock The Jukebox* . . . . (Arista)

Milwaukee
Al Jarreau; *Glow*. . . . . (Reprise)

Milwaukee Blues
Red Clay Ramblers; *Merchant's Lunch* . . . . (Flying Fish)
Steve James; *Two Track Mind* . . . . (Antone's)

Milwaukee Polka
Frankie Yankovic & His Yanks; *America's Favorites* . . . . (Smash)
Frankie Yankovic & His Yanks' Greatest Hits . . . . (Columbia)

Milwaukee Waltz
Michigan Dutchmen; *W.J.R.T. TV All-Time Polkas* . . . .(Jay Jay)

Milwaukee's Favorite Waltz
Li'l Wally; *America's Favorite* . . . .(Jay Jay)

Minneapolis
ABC; *Alphabet City* . . . . (Mercury)

Minneapolis
That Dog; *Retreat From The Sun* . . . . (David Geffen Co.)

Minneapolis
MPLS; *1-800-New-Funk* . . . . (Bellmark)

Minneapolis
Tom Daily; *Happily Deceiving Culture* . . . .(Thick)

Minneapolis Girls
Joel Johnson; *City Music* . . . .(Blue Loon)

Minneapolis Twirl
Li'l Wally; *Here Comes Li'l Wally*. . . . .(Jay Jay)

Montego Bay
Amazulu; *The Island Story-1962-1987-25th Anniversary-C* . . . . . . (Island)
Bobby Bloom; *Super Hits Of The '70s-Have A Nice Day-#3-C* . . . . (Rhino)

Monterey
Eric Burdon & The Animals; *Eric Burdon & The Animals'*
Greatest Hits. . . . . (MGM)

Monterey
Danny Gottlieb; *Aquamarine* . . . . (Atlantic)

Monterey
Tim Buckley; *Starsailor* . . . . (Bizarre/Straight)

Monterey Mist
Modern Jazz Quartet; *Blues At Carnegie Hall* . . . .(Atlantic)

Monterrey Pen
Marc Benno; *Lost In Austin* . . . . (A&M)

Montevideo
Monty Alexander Quintet; *Ivory & Steel* . . . . (Concord Picante Jazz)

Montgomery In The Rain
Hank Williams, Jr.; *Hank Williams, Jr.-Early Years* . . . . (WB/Curb)
Steve Young; *No Place To Fall* . . . . (RCA)
Seven Bridges Road . . . . (Rounder)

Montreal
Lucie Blue Tremblay; *Tendresse* . . . . (Olivia)

Montreal
Bruce Cockburn; *Further Adventures Of Bruce Cockburn*. . . . . (Island)

Montreal
Adam Ant; *Strip* . . . .(Epic)

Montreal Blues
Big Joe Williams; *Shake Your Boogie* . . . .(Arhoolie)

Montreux
Azymuth; *Rapid Transit* . . . . (Milestone)

Montreux Blues
Roy Eldridge/Dizzy Gillespie/Clark Terry; *Trumpet Kings At*
Montreux '75 . . . .(Pablo)

Montreux Ramble
Adrian Legg; *Guitars & Other Cathedrals* . . . .(Relativity)

Moonlight In Marrakesh
Otto Cesana; *Otto Cesana-Vol. 2* . . . .(Tudor)

Moonlight Montreal
Peter White; *Reveillez-Vous* . . . . (Chase Music Group)

Morning Morgantown
Joni Mitchell; *Ladies Of The Canyon* . . . . (Reprise)

Munich Beer Garden
Michigan Dutchmen; *German Polka Favorites* . . . .(Jay Jay)

My Cousin In Milwaukee
Ella Fitzgerald; *George & Ira Gershwin Songbook* . . . . (Verve)

Night Train To Madrid
Bertram Levy; *That Old Gut Feeling* . . . . (Flying Fish)

Okie From Muskogee
Merle Haggard; *Friend In California* . . . .(Epic)
Merle Haggard & The Strangers; *Best Of Merle Haggard & The*
Strangers. . . . . (Capitol)
Capitol Collectors Series-Merle Haggard & The Strangers . . . . (Capitol)
Country Music Classics-#3-1965-1970-C . . . . (K-Tel)
For The Record: Merle Haggard-43 Legendary Hits . . . . (BNA)
Songs I'll Always Sing . . . . (Capitol)

ST/Platoon . . . .(Atlantic)

On The Road To Mandalay
Count Basie; *Compact Jazz-The Standards*. . . . . (Verve)
Frank Sinatra; *Come Fly With Me* . . . . (Capitol)

Punch Out At Malibu
Surf Punks; *My Beach* . . . . (Epic)

Rainy Day In Monterey
Joe Sample; *Carmel* . . . . (MCA)
Joe Sample-Collection . . . . (GRP)

Red Dirt Girl (Meridian)
Emmylou Harris; *Red Dirt Girl*. . . . .(Nonesuch)

Rose Of Old Monterey
Happy Polkateers; *Happy Polkateers* . . . .(Crescendo)

Sabu Visits The Twin Cities Alone
John Prine; *Bruised Orange* . . . .(Oh Boy)

Somewhere South Of Macon
Marshall Chapman; *Me I'm Feeling Free* . . . . (Epic)

Sweet Milwaukee Rose
Andy Badale & The Beer Garden Band; *Nashville Beer Garden* . . . . (Ranwood)

Theme From "Laverne & Shirley" (Milwaukee)
Original Soundtrack; *Television's Greatest Hits-#3-1970s & 1980s-C* . . . (TVT)

What's Made Milwaukee Famous (Has Made A Loser Out Of Me)
Jerry Lee Lewis; *Heartbreak*. . . . .(Tomato)
Milestones . . . .(Rhino)
Rod Stewart; *Best Of Rod Stewart*. . . . . (Mercury)
Storyteller/The Complete Anthology: 1964-1990. . . . . (Warner Bros.)

Winter In Madrid
Stan Kenton & Ann Richards; *By Request-#5-1953-1960*. . . . . .(Creative World)

Wintry Feeling (Montreal)
Anne Murray; *Country Collection*. . . . . (Capitol)
I'll Always Love You. . . . . (Capitol)
Jesse Winchester; *Touch On The Rainy Side* . . . . (Rhino)

CITIES: MEMPHIS

See Also: **STATES: TENNESSEE**

18 Miles To Memphis
Stray Cats; *Rant 'N' Rave With The Stray Cats* . . . . (EMI)

All The Way From Memphis
Mott The Hoople; *Mott* . . . . (Columbia)
Mott The Hoople-Live . . . .(Columbia)
Mott The Hoople's Greatest Hits . . . . (Columbia)
The Ballad Of Mott: A Retrospective . . . . (Columbia)

All The Way From Memphis
Contraband; *Contraband*. . . . . (Impact)

Back To Memphis
Band; *To Kingdom Come-The Definitive Collection* . . . . (Capitol)

Berlin To Memphis
Elvis Hitler; *Disgraceland* . . . . (Restless)

Big Train From Memphis
John Fogerty; *Centerfield* . . . . (Warner Bros.)

Black Velvet
Alannah Myles; *Alannah Myles* . . . .(Atlantic)
Robin Lee; *Black Velvet* . . . .(Atlantic)

City Of New Orleans
Arlo Guthrie; *Best Of Arlo Guthrie* . . . . (Warner Bros.)
Hobo's Lullaby . . . .(Reprise)
Together In Concert . . . .(Reprise)
HARP; *HARP* . . . . (Redwood)
Willie Nelson; *19 Hot Country Requests-#2-C* . . . . (Epic)
City Of New Orleans. . . . . (Columbia)
Greatest Country Hits Of The '80s-#4-C . . . . (Columbia)
Hot Tracks-Train Super Hits-C . . . . (Epic)
Train Trax-C . . . . (Sony Music Special Prod.)

Dallas
Alan Jackson; *Don't Rock The Jukebox*. (Arista)

Dixie Chicken
Little Feat; *Dixie Chicken* . . . . (Warner Bros.)
Waiting For Columbus . . . . (Warner Bros.)

Goin' To Memphis
Carl Perkins; *Best Of Carl Perkins-Jive After 5-1958-1978* . . . . (Rhino)

Going Back To Memphis
Muddy Waters; *Muddy Brass & Blues* . . . . (Chess)

Graceland
Paul Simon; *Graceland* . . . . (Warner Bros.)

Honky Tonk Women
Elton John; *11-17-70*. . . . .(Polydor)
Humble Pie; *Best Of Humble Pie*. . . . . (A&M)
Eat It. . . . . (A&M)
Humble Pie-Classics-#14. . . . . (A&M)
Ike & Tina Turner; *Best Of Ike & Tina Turner* . . . . (EMI)
Get Back. . . . .(Liberty)
Joe Cocker; *Mad Dogs & Englishmen*. . . . . (A&M)
Rolling Stones; *Get Yer Ya-Ya's Out!* . . . . (Abkco)
Hot Rocks 1964-1971 . . . .(Abkco)

Love You Live . . . .(Virgin)
Through The Past, Darkly (Big Hits Vol. 2) . . . . (Abkco)
Willie Nelson & Leon Russell; *Half Nelson-C* . . . . (Columbia)

How I Got To Memphis
Bobby Bare; *This Is Bare Country* . . . . (Mercury)
Otis Williams & The Midnight Cowboys; *From Where I Stand: The Black Experience In Country Music-C* . . . . (Warner Bros.)

I Lost My Gal From Memphis
New Sunshine Jazz Band; *Too Much Mustard* . . . . (Biograph)
Tex Williams; *Tex Williams-Vintage Collections* . . . . (Capitol)

Johnny Bye-Bye
Bruce Springsteen; *Tracks* . . . . (Columbia)

Katie Left Memphis
Tangle Eye; *Roots Of The Blues* . . . . (Nightwork)

Leavin' Memphis, Frisco Bound
Jesse Fuller; *Frisco Bound* . . . .(Arhoolie)
Lone Cat . . . . (Good Time Jazz)

Long Way From Memphis
Lonnie Mack; *Strike Like Lightning* . . . .(Alligator)

Maybe It Was Memphis
Pam Tillis; *Pam Tillis' Greatest Hits* . . . . (Arista)
Pam Tillis-Collection . . . . (Warner Bros.)
Put Yourself In My Place . . . . (Arista)

Meet Me In Memphis
Jimmy Buffett; *Floridays* . . . . (MCA)

Memphis
Chuck Berry; *Chuck Berry* . . . . (Audio Fidelity)
Chuck Berry-Golden Hits . . . . (Mercury)
Chuck Berry's Greatest Hits . . . . (Everest)
St. Louis To Liverpool . . . . (Chess)
ST/Hail! Hail! Rock 'N' Roll . . . . (MCA)
The Chess Box-Chuck Berry . . . . (Chess)
Toronto Rock 'N' Roll Revival-#2-C . . . . (Accord)
John Cale; *IRS Greatest Hits-#2 & #3-C* . . . . (I.R.S.)
Johnny Rivers; *Best Of Johnny Rivers* . . . . (EMI)
Johnny Rivers-Anthology 1964-1977 . . . . (Rhino)
Lonnie Mack; *Rock Instrumental Classics-#2-'60s-C* . . . . . (Rhino)
Teen Beat-Instrumental Rock-1957-1965-C . . . . (Capitol)

Memphis
Joe Jackson; *ST/Mike's Murder* . . . . (A&M)
Steppin' Out: The Very Best Of Joe Jackson . . . . (A&M)

Memphis
John Cale; *IRS Greatest Hits-#2 & #3-C* . . . . (I.R.S.)

Memphis #999
Graveyard Train; *Graveyard Train* . . . . (Geffen)

Memphis Belle
Hank Williams, Jr.; *Pure Hank* . . . . (WB/Curb)

Memphis B-K
Sonny Little; *Black & Blue* . . . . (Stax)

Memphis Blues
Duke Ellington; *Black, Brown & Beige: 1944-1946 Band Recordings* . . . . (Bluebird)
Eubie Blake; *Memories Of You* . . . . (Biograph)
Nat "King" Cole; *ST/St. Louis Blues* . . . . (Capitol)
Wild Bill Davison; *Giants Of Traditional Jazz* . . . . (Savoy)

Memphis Boogie
Dr. Isaiah Ross; *Boogie Disease* . . . . (Arhoolie)

Memphis Flyer
Neil Diamond; *You Don't Bring Me Flowers* . . . . (Columbia)

Memphis Hip Shake
Cult; *Electric* . . . .(Sire)

Memphis In June
Eddie Miller & His Orchestra; *The Uncollected Eddie Miller & His Orchestra-1944-1945* . . . . (Hindsight)
Hoagy Carmichael; *Hoagy Sings Carmichael* . . . . (Pausa)
Hoagy Sings Carmichael . . . . (EMI)

Memphis In The Meantime
John Hiatt; *Bring The Family* . . . . (A&M)

Memphis Jellyroll
Stefan Grossman; *Yazoo Basin Boogie* . . . . (Shanachie)

Memphis Mail
Eli Owens; *Roosevelt Holts & His Friends* . . . . (Arhoolie)

Memphis Pearl
Lucinda Williams; *Sweet Old World* . . . .(Chameleon)

Memphis Queen
Southern Pacific; *County Line* . . . . (Warner Bros.)

Memphis Rendezvous
Jim Horn; *Work It Out* . . . . (Warner Bros.)

Memphis Shakedown
Trapezoid; *Three Forks Of Cheat* . . . . (Rounder)

Memphis Slim U.S.A.
Memphis Slim; *Blue This Evening* . . . . (Black Lion)

Memphis Soul Stew
King Curtis; *Atlantic Jazz-Soul-C* . . . . (Atlantic)
Atlantic Rhythm & Blues 1947-1974-#6 (1966-1969)-C . . . . (Atlantic)
Best Of King Curtis . . . . (Atlantic)
Golden Soul-C . . . . (Atlantic)
Live At The Fillmore West . . . . (Atlantic)

Memphis Streets
Neil Diamond; *Glory Road-1968-1972* . . . . (MCA)
Sweet Caroline . . . . (MCA)

Memphis Sun
Orion; *Rockabilly* . . . . (Sun)

Memphis Thing
Rob Jungklas; *Closer To The Flame* . . . . (Manhattan)

Memphis Underground
Herbie Mann; *Best Of Herbie Mann* . . . . (Atlantic)
Great Moments In Jazz-C . . . . (Atlantic)
Memphis Underground . . . . (Atlantic)

Memphis Yodel
Jimmie Rodgers; *First Sessions-1927-1928-#1* . . . .(Rounder)

Memphis, Tennessee Hot Rock
Gordon Terry; *Tennessee Hot Rock* . . . . (Plantation)

Midnight In Memphis
Bette Midler; *ST/The Rose* . . . . (Atlantic)
Hoyt Axton; *Where Did The Money Go* . . . . (Jeremiah)
Meri Wilson; *First Take* . . . .(GRT)

Music Makin' Mama From Memphis
Hank Snow; *Best Of Hank Snow* . . . . (RCA)

My Elusive Dreams
Bobby Vinton; *Autumn Memories* . . . . (Epic)
Bobby Vinton's All-Time Greatest Hits . . . . (Epic)
Charlie Rich; *Charlie Rich-16 Biggest Hits* . . . .(Legacy)
Charlie Rich's Greatest Hits . . . . (Epic)
Charlie Rich-Super Hits . . . . (Epic)
David Houston & Tammy Wynette; *Best Of David Houston* . . . .(Collector's Choice)
Billboard Top Country Hits-1967-C . . . .(Rhino)
Tammy Wynette's Greatest Hits . . . . (Epic)

My Memphis Baby
Johnny Wiggs; *Jazz Fest Masters-Traditionalists* . . . . (Jazz Masters)

Night Train To Memphis
Jerry Lee Lewis; *Rare Tracks* . . . .(Rhino)
Taste Of Country . . . . (Sun)
Joe Maphis; *Great American Train Songs-C* . . . .(C.M.H. Prod.)
Roy Acuff; *Best Of Roy Acuff* . . . .(Liberty)
Essential Roy Acuff-1936-1949 . . . .(Legacy)
Roy Acuff's Greatest Hits . . . . (Columbia)

One Way Ticket To Memphis
Bobby King & Terry Evans; *Rhythm Blues Soul & Grooves* . . . .(Rounder)

Queen Of Memphis
Confederate Railroad; *Confederate Railroad* . . . . (Atlantic)

Singing Bridge Of Memphis Tennessee
John Fahey; *Essential John Fahey* . . . .(Vanguard)

Slow Train To Memphis
Jim Horn; *Work It Out* . . . . (Warner Bros.)

Stuck Inside Of Mobile With The Memphis Blues Again
Bob Dylan; *Blonde On Blonde* . . . .(Columbia)
Bob Dylan's Greatest Hits-#2 . . . .(Columbia)
Hard Rain . . . .(Columbia)

That's How I Got To Memphis
Rosanne Cash; *Somewhere In The Stars* . . . .(Columbia)
Tom T. Hall; *Storyteller, Poet, Philospher* . . . .(Mercury)
Tom T. Hall's Greatest Hits-#1 . . . .(Mercury)
Tom T. Hall-The Hits . . . .(Mercury)

Walking In Memphis
Marc Cohn; *Marc Cohn* . . . . (Atlantic)

West Memphis Blues
Sonny Boy Williamson; *King Biscuit Time* . . . . (Arhoolie)

Wrong Side Of Memphis
Matraca Berg; *Bittersweet Surrender* . . . . (RCA)
Trisha Yearwood; *Grand Ole Opry-75 Years-#1-C* . . . . . . (MCA)
Hearts In Armor . . . . (MCA)

You Don't Have To Go To Memphis
Asleep At The Wheel; *Keepin' Me Up Nights* . . . . (Arista)

CITIES: MIAMI

See Also: STATES: FLORIDA

Dateline Miami
Judy Nylon & Crucial; *Pal Judy* . . . . (Roir)

Going Back To Miami
Blues Brothers; *Best Of The Blues Brothers* . . . . (Atlantic)
Made In America . . . . (Atlantic)
Wayne Cochran; *Soul Shots-#6-Blue-Eyed Soul-C* . . . .(Rhino)

Mambo In Miami
Peggy Lee & George Shearing; *Beauty & The Beat!* . . . . (Blue Note)

Miami
Randy Newman; *Trouble In Paradise* . . . .(Warner Bros.)

Miami
Will Smith; *Big Willie Style* . . . .(Columbia)

Miami
John Cougar; *John Cougar* . . . .(Riva)

Miami 2017
  Billy Joel; *Songs In The Attic* .... (Columbia)
    The Concert For New York City-C .... (Columbia)
    Turnstiles .... (Columbia)
Miami Beach
  Garland Jeffreys; *Escape Artist* ....(Epic)
Miami, My Amy
  Keith Whitley; *Keith Whitley's Greatest Hits* .... (RCA)
    L.A. To Miami .... (RCA)
    Star Spangled Country-C .... (RCA)
Moon Over Miami
  Bourbon Street Stompers; *I Like Dixieland* .... (Bainbridge)
  Vaughn Monroe; *This Is Vaughn Monroe/Decade Of The '40s* .... (RCA)
Only In Miami
  Bette Midler; *Experience The Divine-Greatest Hits* ....(Atlantic)
    No Frills .... (Atlantic)
Theme From "Miami Vice"
  Jan Hammer; *Escape From Television* .... (MCA)
    Soundtrack Smashes-'80s & More-C ....(MCA)
    ST/Miami Vice ....(MCA)
  Original Soundtrack; *Television's Greatest Hits-#3-1970s & 1980s-C* ... (TVT)
Theme From "Surfside 6"
  Original Soundtrack; *Television's Greatest Hits-#1-C* .... (TVT)

CITIES: MOBILE

See Also: STATES: ALABAMA

Donna From Mobile
  Anne Hills; *Don't Panic (Panic Is On/Don't Explain)* .... (Hogeye)
Mobile
  Marcia Ball; *Gartorrhythms* .... (Rounder)
Mobile & K.C. Line
  Robert Shaw; *Ma Grinder* .... (Arhoolie)
Mobile Bay
  Hank Crawford; *Night Beat* .... (Milestone)
  Rex Stewart; *RCA Victor Jazz: First Half-Century-C* .... (RCA)
Mobile Bay (Magnolia Blossoms)
  Cal Smith; *Stories Of Life By Cal Smith* .... (Step One)
  Johnny Cash; *Johnny Cash's Biggest Hits* .... (Columbia)
  Merle Haggard & George Jones; *Taste Of Yesterday's Wine* ....(Epic)
Mobile Boogie
  Hank Williams, Jr.; *Hank Williams, Jr.-Early Years* .... (WB/Curb)
    One Night Stands ....(Warner Bros.)
Mobile Line
  Jim Kweskin and His Jug Band; *Jim Kweskin and His Jug Band* .... (Vanguard)
    Jim Kweskin and His Jug Band's Greatest Hits .... (Vanguard)
    Troubadours Of The Folk Era-#3-C .... (Rhino)
Mobile/Texas Line
  Tom Rush; *Blues Songs & Ballads* .... (Fantasy)
    Mind Ramblin' .... (Prestige)
    Tom Rush .... (Fantasy)
Stuck Inside Of Mobile With The Memphis Blues Again
  Bob Dylan; *Blonde On Blonde* .... (Columbia)
    Bob Dylan's Greatest Hits-#2 .... (Columbia)
    Hard Rain .... (Columbia)
Thirty Nine Miles To Mobile
  Charlie Daniels Band; *Charlie Daniels Band* .... (Capitol)

CITIES: MOSCOW

See Also: COUNTRIES: RUSSIA

Born In Moscow
  Vasily Shumov; *My District* .... (Gold Castle)
Midnight In Moscow
  Dukes Of Dixieland; *Dixieland's Greatest Hits* ....(MCA)
  Kenny Ball; *Billboard Top Pop Hits-1962-C* .... (Rhino)
Mission To Moscow
  Benny Goodman; *All The Cats Join In* .... (Columbia)
  Glenn Miller; *Glenn Miller-A Legendary Performer-#3* .... (Bluebird)
  Glenn Miller & His Army/Air Force Band; *This Is Glenn Miller & His Army/
    Air Force Band* .... (RCA)
Moscow
  Chris Cutler & Fred Frith; *Live In Moscow, Prague &
    Washington* ....(Cuneiform)
Moscow Blues
  Paul Horn; *Inside The Cathedral (Inside Russia)* .... (Kuckuck)
Moscow Diskow
  Telex; *Moscow Diskow-12''* .... (Sire)
Moscow Farewell
  Ennio Morricone; *Film Music-#1* .... (Virgin Movie Music)
Moscow Nights
  Feelies; *Crazy Rhythms* .... (A&M)
Radio Free Moscow
  Jethro Tull; *Under Wraps* ....(Chrysalis)

Roads To Moscow
  Al Stewart; *Past, Present & Future* .... (Rhino)
Suburbs Of Moscow
  Kim Wilde; *Teases & Dares* .... (MCA)

CITIES: N

See Also: CITIES: GENERAL, CITIES: NASHVILLE, NEW ORLEANS, NEW YORK, COUNTRIES: A-Z, STATES: A-Z

All The Fuckers Live In Newport Beach
  Fluf; *The Classic Years* ....(Headhunter)
Funky Nassau
  Beginning Of The End; *Atlantic Rhythm & Blues 1947-1974-#7 (1969-
    1974)-C* ....(Atlantic)
    Didn't It Blow Your Mind: Soul Hits Of The '70s-#5-C .... (Rhino)
Going To Newport
  Frankie Laine; *Frankie Laine's 16 Greatest Hits* ....(Trip)
Hiroshima, Nagasaki Russian Roulette
  Jim Page; *Best Of Broadside 1962-1968: Anthems Of The American
    Underground From The Pages Of Broadside
    Magazine-C* ....(Smithsonian Folkways)
Last Train To Nuremberg
  Pete Seeger; *A Link In The Chain* .... (Legacy)
Moon Over Naples
  Billy Vaughn; *Best Of Billy Vaughn* .... (MCA)
Nagasaki
  Cab Calloway; *Hi De Ho Man* .... (Columbia)
  Fletcher Henderson & His Orchestra; *Fletcher Henderson & His
    Orchestra* .... (ASV Living Era)
Nevada City
  Lonesome Romeos; *Lonesome Romeos* .... (Curb)
New Delhi
  Cannonball Adderley; *Plus* .... (Riverside)
New Delhi Freight Train
  Little Feat; *Time Loves A Hero* .... (Warner Bros.)
Norfolk Ferry
  Panama Francis; *Panama Francis & The Savoy Sultans* .... (Classic Jazz)
Norfolk Girls
  John Townley & The Press Gang; *Chesapeake Sailor's Companion* ...(Adelphi)
Northfield, The Disaster
  Charlie Daniels Band; *Legend Of Jesse James-C* .... (A&M)
Northfield, The Plan
  Levon Helm; *Legend Of Jesse James-C* .... (A&M)
Nutbush City Limits
  Bob Seger; *Beautiful Loser* .... (Capitol)
    Live Bullet .... (Capitol)
  Ike & Tina Turner; *Best Of Ike & Tina Turner* .... (EMI)
    Proud Mary-Best Of Ike & Tina Turner .... (EMI)
  Tina Turner; *Live In Europe* .... (Capitol)
    Simply The Best .... (Capitol)
Promised Land
  Band; *Moondog Matinee* .... (Capitol)
  Chuck Berry; *Rock 'N' Roll Rarities-20 Magic Tracks* .... (Chess)
    The Chess Box-Chuck Berry .... (Chess)
  Elvis Presley; *Promised Land* ....(RCA)
    ST/This Is Elvis ....(RCA)
  Freddy Weller; *Country Music Classics-#11-Early '70s-C* .... (K-Tel)
    Freddy Weller's Greatest Hits .... (Columbia)
  Gary Morris; *Full Moon Empty Heart* .... (Liberty)
  Grateful Dead; *Steal Your Face* ....(Grateful Dead)
  James Taylor; *Walking Man* .... (Warner Bros.)
  Kingfish; *Kingfish/Alive In Eighty Five-Double Dose* ....(Relix)
Shaw Of Newark
  Bobby Watson; *The Inventor* .... (Blue Note)
Speedway At Nazareth
  Mark Knopfler; *Sailing To Philadelphia* .... (Warner Bros.)
That's Amore (Naples)
  Dean Martin; *Best Of Dean Martin* .... (CEMA Special Prod.)
    Dean Martin's All Time Greatest Hits .... (Curb)
    Dean Martin's Greatest Hits .... (EMI)
    The Capitol Years-Dean Martin .... (Capitol)
Whaler Out Of New Bedford
  Musical Film Score; *Whaler Out Of New Bedford* .....(Smithsonian Folkways)

CITIES: NASHVILLE

See Also: MUSIC, RECORD BUSINESS, STATES: TENNESSEE

16th Avenue
  Lacy J. Dalton; *19 Hot Country Requests-#2-C* .... (Epic)
    Greatest Country Hits Of The '80s-1982-C .... (Columbia)
    Lacy J. Dalton's Greatest Hits .... (Columbia)
Are You Sure Hank Done It This Way
  Hank Williams, Jr.; *Rowdy* .... (WB/Curb)
  Waylon Jennings; *Waylon Jennings' Greatest Hits* .... (RCA)

Down In Nashville, Tennessee
Reno & Smiley; *1983 Collector's Edition-#2* . . . . (Gusto)
Emma Jean's Guitar
Chely Wright; *Let Me In* . . . . (MCA)
Flood, The (Wish I Was In Nashville)
Don Williams; *I've Got A Winner In You* . . . . (Universal)
God Don't Live In Nashville, Tennessee
Randy Howard; *All-American Redneck* . . . . (Warner Bros.)
Heavy Traffic Ahead
Bill Monroe & His Blue Grass Boys; *The Father Of Bluegrass: The Early
Years-1940-1947* . . . . (ASV)
Ricky Skaggs with Steve Wariner; *Big Mon: The Songs Of Bill
Monroe-C* . . . . (Skaggs Family)
I Wish I Was In Nashville
Mel McDaniel; *Take Me To The Country* . . . . (Capitol)
Missin' You
Little Feat; *Time Loves A Hero* . . . . (Warner Bros.)
Murder On Music Row
George Strait & Alan Jackson; *Latest Greatest Straitest Hits* . . . . (MCA)
My Elusive Dreams
Bobby Vinton; *Autumn Memories* . . . . (Epic)
Bobby Vinton's All-Time Greatest Hits . . . . (Epic)
Charlie Rich; *Charlie Rich-16 Biggest Hits* . . . . (Legacy)
Charlie Rich's Greatest Hits . . . . (Epic)
Charlie Rich-Super Hits . . . . (Epic)
David Houston & Tammy Wynette; *Best Of David
Houston* . . . . (Collector's Choice)
Billboard Top Country Hits-1967-C . . . . (Rhino)
Tammy Wynette's Greatest Hits . . . . (Epic)
Nashville
Ray Stevens; *Best Of Ray Stevens* . . . . (Rhino)
Nashville . . . . (Barnaby)
Nashville
Mason Williams; *Anthology Of The 12-String Guitar* . . . . (Tradition)
Nashville
Indigo Girls; *Rites Of Passage* . . . . (Epic)
Nashville
Hoyt Axton; *Southbound* . . . . (A&M)
Nashville
Wind Machine; *Wind Machine-featuring Steve Mesple* . . . . . (Silver Wave)
Nashville 1 A.M.
Harvey Mandel; *Cristo Redentor* . . . . (Editions E.G.)
Nashville Beer Garden
Andy Badale & The Beer Garden Band; *Nashville Beer Garden* . . . . (Ranwood)
Nashville Blues
Doc Watson; *Doc Watson* . . . . (Vanguard)
J.D. Crowe; *J.D. Crowe/New South* . . . . (Rounder)
Nitty Gritty Dirt Band; *Will The Circle Be Unbroken* . . . . (EMI)
Nashville Cats
Del McCoury Band; *The Family* . . . . (Ceili Music)
Lovin' Spoonful; *Lovin' Spoonful-Anthology* . . . . (Rhino)
Nashville Connection
Rodney Lay & Wild West; *Rockabilly Nuggets-C* . . . . (Sun)
Nashville In The Rain
Ginger Boatwright; *Fertile Ground* . . . . (Flying Fish)
Nashville Moon
Charlie Daniels Band; *Windows* . . . . (Epic)
Ronnie Milsap; *Lost In The Fifties Tonight* . . . . (RCA)
Nashville Nightengale
Royal Society Jazz Orchestra; *Harlem To Hollywood* . . . . (Klavier)
Nashville Nights/Redneck Blues
Pirates Of The Mississippi; *Walk The Plank* . . . . (Liberty)
Nashville Pickin'
Doc Watson; *Southbound* . . . . (Vanguard)
Nashville Scene
Hank Williams, Jr.; *Five-O* . . . . (WB/Curb)
Nashville Shuffle Boogie
Mark O'Connor; *New Nashville Cats* . . . . (Warner Bros.)
Nashville Skyline Rag
Bob Dylan; *Nashville Skyline* . . . . (Columbia)
Nashville West
Byrds; *Dr. Byrds & Mr. Hyde* . . . . (Legacy)
Legends Of Country Guitar-#1-C . . . . (Rhino)
The Byrds . . . . (Columbia)
The Byrds (Untitled) . . . . (Legacy)
Nashville West; *Nashville West* . . . . (Sierra)
Nashville Women's Blues
Bessie Smith; *Bessie Smith-The Complete Recordings-#2* . . . . (Legacy)
Nashville, Tenn. Blues
Washboard Sam; *Blues Classics By.* . . . . (Blues Classics)
Nashville, Tennessee
Troy Cory; *Real Country* . . . . (Video Record Albums)
Nobody Eats At Linebaugh's Anymore
John Hartford; *Me Oh My-How The Time Does Fly-Anthology* . . . . . (Flying Fish)
Old Nashville Cowboys
Hank Williams, Jr.; *Whiskey Bent & Hell Bound* . . . . (WB/Curb)
Outside The Nashville City Limits
Joan Baez; *Blessed Are* . . . . (Vanguard)

Country Music Album . . . . (Vanguard)
Paddy Goes To Nashville
Adrian Legg; *Mrs. Crowe's Blue Waltz* . . . . (Relativity)
Song A Day In Nashville
John Sebastian; *Welcome Back* . . . . (Reprise)
Steal My Kisses
Ben Harper; *Burn To Shine* . . . . (Virgin)
Now That's What I Call Music!-#4-C . . . . (Virgin)
Straight Through To Nashville
Agitpop; *Open Seasons* . . . . (Twin-Tone)
That Was The Day
Marianne Faithfull; *Faithless* . . . . (Sony Music Special Prod.)
To Beat The Devil
Johnny Cash; *Johnny Cash-16 Biggest Hits-#2* . . . . (Legacy)
Trains Don't Run From Nashville
Kate Campbell; *Freight Train Blues-Classic Railroad Songs-#4-C* . . . (Rounder)
West Nashville Boogie
Steve Earle & The Dukes; *Shut Up And Die Like An Aviator* . . . . (MCA)
The Hard Way . . . . (MCA)
West Nashville Grand Ballroom Gown
Jimmy Buffett; *Living & Dying In 3/4 Time* . . . . (MCA)
Wrong Side Of Memphis
Matraca Berg; *Bittersweet Surrender* . . . . (RCA)
Trisha Yearwood; *Grand Ole Opry-75 Years-#1-C* . . . . (MCA)
Hearts In Armor . . . . (MCA)

CITIES: NEW ORLEANS

See Also: CARNIVALS, STATES: LOUISIANA

Aberdeen
Kenny Wayne Shepherd; *Ledbetter Heights* . . . . (Giant)
Back To New Orleans
Lightnin' Hopkins; *Lightnin'* . . . . (Bluesville)
Lightnin' Hopkins' Greatest Hits . . . . (Prestige)
Sonny Terry & Brownie McGhee; *Back To New Orleans* . . . . (Fantasy)
Basin Street Blues
Louis Armstrong; *Best Of Louis Armstrong* . . . . (MCA)
Jazz Heritage-Old Favorites-C . . . . (MCA)
Satchmo-Musical Autobiography-#2 . . . . (MCA)
Young Louis Armstrong . . . . (RCA)
Battle Of New Orleans
Chet Atkins & The Boston Pops; *Best Of Chet Atkins & The
Boston Pops* . . . . (RCA)
Johnny Horton; *American Originals-Johnny Horton* . . . . (Columbia)
Johnny Horton's Greatest Hits . . . . (Columbia)
Radio Classics Of The '50s-C . . . . (Columbia)
Nitty Gritty Dirt Band; *Dirt, Silver & Gold* . . . . (One Way)
Dream . . . . (United Artists)
Stars And Stripes Forever . . . . (Capitol)
Big Chief From New Orleans
Mike Bloomfield; *Between The Hard Place & The Ground* . . . . (Takoma)
Bourbon Street
Elvin Bishop; *Let It Flow* . . . . (Capricorn)
Bourbon Street Parade
Al Hirt; *Best Of Al Hirt* . . . . (RCA)
Dukes Of Dixieland; *Digital Dixieland* . . . . (Pro Jazz)
Pete Fountain; *Best Of Pete Fountain-#2* . . . . (MCA)
Preservation Hall Jazz Band; *New Orleans-#4* . . . . (Columbia)
Wynton Marsalis; *Standard Time-#2-Intimacy Calling* . . . . (Columbia)
Carnival In New Orleans
Professor Longhair; *Last Mardi Gras* . . . . (Atlantic)
City Of New Orleans
Arlo Guthrie; *Best Of Arlo Guthrie* . . . . (Warner Bros.)
Hobo's Lullaby . . . . (Reprise)
Together In Concert . . . . (Reprise)
HARP; *HARP* . . . . (Redwood)
Willie Nelson; *19 Hot Country Requests-#2-C* . . . . (Epic)
City Of New Orleans . . . . (Columbia)
Greatest Country Hits Of The '80s-#4-C . . . . (Columbia)
Hot Tracks-Train Super Hits-C . . . . (Epic)
Train Trax-C . . . . (Sony Music Special Prod.)
Crescent City Crawl
Wynton Marsalis; *ST/Tune In Tomorrow...* . . . . (Columbia)
Dixie Chicken
Little Feat; *Dixie Chicken* . . . . (Warner Bros.)
Waiting For Columbus . . . . (Warner Bros.)
Do You Know What It Means To Miss New Orleans
Billie Holiday; *Sing 2* . . . . (Kent)
Harry Connick, Jr.; *Twenty* . . . . (Columbia)
Louis Armstrong; *Chicago Concert 1956* . . . . (Columbia)
Mostly Blues . . . . (Olympic)
Pops . . . . (Bluebird)
Pete Fountain; *Best Of Pete Fountain* . . . . (MCA)
Down Home In New Orleans
Magic Organ; *Traveling With The Magic Organ* . . . . (Ranwood)

Down South In New Orleans
Van Morrison & The Band; *The Last Waltz* . . . .(Warner Bros.)
Down To New Orleans
Vince Gill; *Country Superstar Hits-C*. . . . . (Hip-O)
High Lonesome Sound . . . .(MCA)
Fancy
Bobbi Gentry; *All-Time Country Classics-#1-C* . . . . (Capitol)
Reba McEntire; *Rumor Has It*. . . . .(MCA)
Go To The Mardi Gras
Professor Longhair; *New Orleans Party Classics-C* . . . . (Rhino)
Goin' To New Orleans
Rockin' Tabby Thomas; *Rockin' With The Blues* . . . . (Maison De Soul)
Going Back To New Orleans
Dr. John; *Going Back To New Orleans* . . . .(Warner Bros.)
Heart Of The Night
Poco; *Backtracks* . . . .(MCA)
Poco-Legend . . . .(MCA)
Home To New Orleans
Queen Ida; *Caught In The Act*. . . . .(Crescendo)
Hometown New Orleans
Champion Jack Dupree; *Forever & Ever* . . . . (Bullseye Blues)
House Of The Rising Sun
Animals; *Animals Greatest Hits* . . . .(Allegiance)
Best Of The Animals . . . .(Abkco)
Greatest Hits Live!-Rip It To Shreds . . . .(I.R.S.)
Hank Williams, Jr.; *Hank Williams, Jr. "Live"* . . . . (WB/Curb)
Ronnie Milsap; *Ronnie Milsap-16 Greatest Hits-#2*. . . . .(Trip)
I Love New Orleans Music
Ronnie Milsap; *Inside Ronnie Milsap* . . . . (RCA)
I Wish I Was In New Orleans
Tom Waits; *Small Change* . . . . (Asylum)
I'm Going Down To Bourbon Street
Waylon Thibodeaux; *Jimmy Buffett's Margaritaville Cafe: New
Orleans-C* . . . .(Margaritaville)
Johnny B. Goode
Chuck Berry; *Chuck Berry's Greatest Hits*. . . . . (Everest)
Classic Rock-#2-C . . . .(MCA)
Roll Over Beethoven . . . .(Allegiance)
ST/American Graffiti . . . .(MCA)
The Chess Box-Chuck Berry . . . . (Chess)
Elvis Presley; *Elvis In Concert* . . . . (RCA)
From Memphis To Vegas/From Vegas To Memphis . . . . (RCA)
Grateful Dead; *Bill Graham Presents The Last Days Of The
Fillmore-C* . . . . (Epic Portrait Assoc.)
Johnny Winter; *Live/Johnny Winter And* . . . . (Columbia)
Second Winter . . . . (Columbia)
King Creole
Elvis Presley; *Hits Like Never Before-Essential-#3* . . . . (RCA)
ST/King Creole . . . . (RCA)
The Great Performances . . . . (RCA)
The Other Sides-Worldwide Gold Award Hits, Vol. 2 . . . . . . (RCA)
King Of New Orleans
Better Than Ezra; *Friction, Baby* . . . . (Swell/Elektra)
Magnolia
J.J. Cale; *Naturally* . . . .(MCA)
Man From New Orleans
Swampwater; *Swampwater* . . . .(One Way)
Mardi Gras
Gino Vannelli; *Pauper In Paradise* . . . . (A&M)
Mardi Gras
Original Cast; *House Of Flowers* . . . .(Sony Music Special Prod.)
Mardi Gras Boogie
Clifton Chenier; *In New Orleans* . . . .(Crescendo)
Mardi Gras In New Orleans
Professor Longhair; *Atlantic Rhythm & Blues 1947-1974-#1 (1947-
1952)-C*. . . . .(Atlantic)
New Orleans Jazz & Heritage Festival-1976-C . . . . (Rhino)
New Orleans Piano-Blues Originals-#2 . . . . (Atlantic)
Rockin' Dopsie; *Alligator Stomp-#2-C* . . . . (Rhino)
Mardi Gras Mambo
Hawketts; *Treacherous: A History Of The Neville Brothers* . . . (Rhino)
Message To Michael
Dionne Warwick; *Dionne Warwick* . . . . (Everest)
Dionne Warwick Greatest Hits . . . . (Everest)
Dionne Warwick-Anthology 1962-1971 . . . . (Rhino)
Hot! Live & Otherwise . . . . (Arista)
Original Rock 'N' Roll Hits Of The '60s-C . . . . (Roulette)
Moon Over Bourbon Street
Sting; *Bring On The Night* . . . . (A&M)
Dream Of The Blue Turtles . . . . (A&M)
My Little Home Down In New Orleans
Jimmie Rodgers; *Jimmie Rodgers-Early Years-1928-1929* . . . . (Rounder)
New Orleans
Elvis Presley; *ST/King Creole* . . . . (RCA)
Gary U.S. Bonds; *Gary U.S. Bonds-Golden Hits* . . . .(Laurie)
Oldies But Goodies-#7-C . . . .(Original Sound)
School Of Rock 'N' Roll-Best Of Gary U.S. Bonds . . . . (Rhino)
Hank Williams, Jr.; *Five-O* . . . .(WB/Curb)

Neil Diamond; *Double Gold-Neil Diamond* . . . .(Bang)
Neil Diamond's Greatest Hits . . . . (Bang)
The Feel Of Neil Diamond . . . . (Bang)
Wynton Marsalis; *Marsalis Standard Time-#1* . . . . (Columbia)
New Orleans Blues
Marcus Roberts; *Alone With Three Giants* . . . .(Novus)
New Orleans Bump
Jelly Roll Morton; *Jazz Classics In Digital Stereo* . . . . (ABC)
New Orleans Ceremony
Dukes Of Dixieland; *Best Of Dukes Of Dixieland*. . . . . (Columbia)
New Orleans Function
Louis Armstrong; *Louis Armstrong Of New Orleans* . . . . (MCA)
New Orleans Hop Scop Blues
Bessie Smith; *Bessie Smith-The Complete Recordings-#4* . . . . (Legacy)
New Orleans Instrumental No. 1
R.E.M.; *Automatic For The People* . . . . (Warner Bros.)
New Orleans Is Sinking
Tragically Hip; *Up To Here* . . . . (MCA)
New Orleans Joys
Butch Thompson; *New Orleans Joys* . . . . (Daring)
New Orleans Ladies
Louisiana's Le Roux; *'70s Greatest Rock Hits-#4-C* . . . .(Priority)
Louisiana's Le Roux . . . . (Capitol)
New Orleans Low-Down
Duke Ellington & His Orchestra; *Brunswick Era-#1-1926-1929* . . . . . . (MCA)
New Orleans Shuffle
Johnny Otis; *Original Johnny Otis Show* . . . .(Savoy)
New Orleans Stomp
Johnny Dodds; *South Side Chicago Jazz*. . . . . (MCA)
New Orleans Streamline
Bukka White; *Legacy Of The Blues-#1* . . . .(Crescendo)
New Orleans Street Beat
Marlon Jordan; *The Undaunted* . . . . (Columbia)
New Orleans Waltz
Nathan Abshire; *French Blues* . . . . (Arhoolie)
New Orleans Wins The War
Randy Newman; *Land Of Dreams* . . . . (Reprise)
Pearl Of The Quarter
Steely Dan; *Countdown To Ecstasy*. . . . . (MCA)
Planet Of New Orleans
Dire Straits; *On Every Street* . . . . (Warner Bros.)
Promised Land
Band; *Moondog Matinee* . . . . (Capitol)
Chuck Berry; *Rock 'N' Roll Rarities-20 Magic Tracks* . . . . . . (Chess)
The Chess Box-Chuck Berry . . . . (Chess)
Elvis Presley; *Promised Land* . . . . (RCA)
ST/This Is Elvis . . . . (RCA)
Freddy Weller; *Country Music Classics-#11-Early '70s-C*. . . . . (K-Tel)
Freddy Weller's Greatest Hits . . . . (Columbia)
Gary Morris; *Full Moon Empty Heart* . . . .(Liberty)
Grateful Dead; *Steal Your Face*. . . . .(Grateful Dead)
James Taylor; *Walking Man* . . . . (Warner Bros.)
Kingfish; *Kingfish/Alive In Eighty Five-Double Dose* . . . . (Relix)
Proud Mary
Creedence Clearwater Revival; *1968-1969* . . . . (Fantasy)
Bayou Country . . . . (Fantasy)
Creedence Clearwater Revival-Chronicle . . . . (Fantasy)
Creedence Clearwater Revival-Gold . . . . (Fantasy)
Live In Europe . . . . (Fantasy)
George Jones & Johnny Paycheck; *My Very Special Guests* . . . . (Epic)
Ike & Tina Turner; *Best Of Ike & Tina Turner* . . . . (EMI)
Didn't It Blow Your Mind: Soul Hits Of The '70s-#4-C . . . . (Rhino)
EMI Legends Of Rock & Roll-24 Greatest Hits-C . . . . (EMI)
Ike & Tina Turner's Greatest Hits . . . . (Curb)
Rock Island Line
Johnny Cash; *Johnny Cash-Sun Years* . . . . (Rhino)
Story Songs Of The Trains & Rivers . . . . (Sun)
Vintage Years-1955-1963 . . . . (Rhino)
Sonny Terry & Brownie McGhee; *Hootin'* . . . .(Muse)
Jazz Heritage . . . . (MCA)
Weavers; *Best Of The Weavers* . . . . (MCA)
Weavers At Carnegie Hall . . . . (Vanguard)
Weavers' Greatest Hits . . . . (Vanguard)
Roll On Mississippi
Charley Pride; *Charley Pride's Greatest Hits* . . . .(RCA)
Royal Orleans
Led Zeppelin; *Presence*. . . . . (Swan Song)
Suite Home New Orleans
Dr. John; *Brightest Smile In Town* . . . . (Clean Cuts)
Take Me Back To New Orleans
Chris Barber & Dr. John; *Take Me Back To New Orleans*. . . . . . . (Black Lion)
Gary U.S. Bonds; *School Of Rock 'N' Roll-Best Of Gary U.S. Bonds* . . . . (Rhino)
Take Me To The Mardi Gras
Paul Simon; *There Goes Rhymin' Simon* . . . . (Columbia)
Walking To New Orleans
Fats Domino; *Fats Domino's All Time Greatest Hits* . . . . (Curb)
Fats Domino's Greatest Hits . . . . (CEMA Special Prod.)
Fats Domino's Greatest Hits . . . . (MCA)

My Blue Heaven-Best Of Fats Domino-#1 . . . . (EMI)
They Call Me The Fat Man . . . . (EMI)

Way Down Yonder In New Orleans
Freddy Cannon; *14 Booming Hits* . . . . (Rhino)
Rockin' '50s-C . . . . (Priority)
Louis Armstrong; *20 Golden Pieces Of Louis Armstrong & Friends* . . (Bulldog)
I Like Jazz-Essence Of Louis Armstrong . . . . (Columbia)
Louis Armstrong's Greatest Hits . . . . (Curb)
Mostly Blues . . . . (Olympic)

When The Saints Go Marching In
Al Hirt; *Best Of Al Hirt* . . . . (RCA)
Our Man-In New Orleans . . . . (Novus)
Jerry Lee Lewis; *Jerry Lee Lewis* . . . . (Rhino)
Louis Armstrong; *At The Crescendo* . . . . (MCA)
Big Bands Of The Swinging Years-#1-C . . . . (Collectables)
C'Est Si Bon . . . . (Rhino)
Essential Louis Armstrong . . . . (Vanguard)
Louis Armstrong Of New Orleans . . . . (MCA)
Original Soundtrack; *Children's Favorites* . . . . (Kid Rhino/Rhino 4 Kids)
Pete Fountain; *Best Of Pete Fountain* . . . . (MCA)
Down On Rampart Street . . . . (Intermedia)
Pete Fountain's New Orleans . . . . (MCA)
Preservation Hall Jazz Band; *Best Of The Preservation Hall
Jazz Band* . . . . (Columbia)

Where The Blues Were Born In New Orleans
Louis Armstrong; *Louis Armstrong Sings The Blues* . . . . (Bluebird)
Pops: 1940s Small Band Sides . . . . (Bluebird)

CITIES: NEW YORK, Broadway, Bronx, Brooklyn, Harlem, Manhattan, Queens (N.Y.C.), Staten Island
See Also: SHOW BIZ, STATES: NEW YORK, STREETS: SPECIFIC

42nd Street
Diana Krall; *Stepping Out* . . . . (Justin Time)
Hal Kemp; *Best Of The Big Bands-C* . . . . (Columbia)
Mel Torme; *Cocktail Mix-#3-Swingin' Singles-C* . . . . (Rhino)
Original Broadway Cast; *42nd Street* . . . . (RCA Victor)

59th Street Bridge Song (Feelin' Groovy)
Harper's Bizarre; *Baby Boomer Classics-More Mellow
Sixties-C* . . . . (JCI Assoc. Labels)
Better Days-C . . . . (Rhino)
Simon & Garfunkel; *Collected Works* . . . . (Columbia)
Parsley Sage Rosemary & Thyme . . . . (Columbia)
Simon & Garfunkel's Greatest Hits . . . . (Columbia)
The Concert In Central Park . . . . (Warner Bros.)

All The Critics Love U In New York
Prince; *1999* . . . . (Warner Bros.)

Am I Ever Gonna Fall In Love In New York
Grace Jones; *Fame* . . . . (Island)

Angel Of Harlem
U2; *Rattle And Hum* . . . . (Island)

Another Night In The Bronx
Donald D; *Notorious* . . . . (Epic)

Another Rainy Day In New York City
Chicago; *Chicago X* . . . . (Chicago)
If You Leave Me Now . . . . (Chicago)

Arrival In New York
Joe Zawinul; *Zawinul* . . . . (Atlantic)

Arthur's Theme (Best That You Can Do)
Christopher Cross; *ST/Arthur* . . . . (Warner Bros.)

Autumn In New York
Frank Sinatra; *Come Fly With Me* . . . . (Capitol)
Round #1 . . . . (Capitol)
Sinatra-The Main Event Live . . . . (Reprise)
The Capitol Years . . . . (Capitol)
Mel Torme; *Songs Of New York* . . . . (Rhino)
Sarah Vaughan; *Complete Sarah Vaughan On Mercury-#2* . . . . . . (Mercury)
Sarah Vaughan-Golden Hits . . . . (Mercury)

Back To Brooklyn
Prince Markie Dee & The Soul Convention; *Free* . . . . (Columbia)

Back To The Apple
Count Basie & His Orchestra; *ST/Hannah & Her Sisters* . . . . (MCA)

Back To The Island
Leon Russell; *Best Of Leon Russell* . . . . (MCA)
Rock Of The '70s-C . . . . (MCA Special Prod.)
Will O' The Wisp . . . . (MCA)

Bavarian In New York
Triumvirat; *A LaCarte* . . . . (Capitol)

Big Apple
Tommy Dorsey & His Clambake Seven; *Nipper's Greatest Hits Of The
'30s-#2-C* . . . . (RCA)
Tommy Dorsey & His Orchestra; *Seventeen Number Ones* . . . . (RCA)

Birdland
Manhattan Transfer; *Atlantic Jazz Vocal Classics-C* . . . . (Rhino)
Best Of The Manhattan Transfer . . . . (Atlantic)
Billboard Top Contemporary Jazz Vocals-C . . . . (Rhino)

Extensions . . . . (Rhino)
Quincy Jones; *Back On The Block* . . . . (Qwest)
Weather Report; *8:30* . . . . (Legacy)
Heavy Weather . . . . (Legacy)

Blame It On New York City
Dramatics; *Positive State Of Mind* . . . . (Volt)

Boogaloo Down Broadway
Fantastic Johnny C; *Dick Bartley Presents On The Radio-#7-C* . . . . . . (VSI)

Boxer, The
Simon & Garfunkel; *Bridge Over Troubled Water* . . . . (Columbia)
Collected Works . . . . (Columbia)
Simon & Garfunkel's Greatest Hits . . . . (Columbia)
The Concert In Central Park . . . . (Warner Bros.)

Boy From New York City
Ad-Libs; *Jewels-#1-C* . . . . (SSS International)
Oldies But Goodies-#6-C . . . . (Original Sound)
Original Golden Hits Of The Great Groups-#1-C . . . . (SSS International)
Original New York Rock & Roll-#1-C . . . . (SSS International)
Manhattan Transfer; *Best Of The Manhattan Transfer* . . . . (Atlantic)
Mecca For Moderns . . . . (Atlantic)

Broadway
Count Basie; *Essential Count Basie-#3* . . . . (Columbia)
Count Basie & His Orchestra; *Best Of Count Basie & His Orchestra-The
Roulette Years* . . . . (Roulette)

Broadway
Jack McDuff & Friends; *Color Me Blue* . . . . (Concord Jazz)

Broadway
Mel Torme; *Songs Of New York* . . . . (Rhino)

Broadway
Clash; *On Broadway* . . . . (Epic)
Sandinista . . . . (Epic)

Broadway Baby
Julia McKenzie; *Collector's Sondheim-C* . . . . (RCA)
Original Broadway Cast; *Follies* . . . . (Capitol)

Broadway Ballet
Gene Kelly/Chorus; *ST/Singin' In The Rain* . . . . . . (Sony Music Special Prod.)

Broadway Fools
Branford Marsalis; *Random Abstract* . . . . (Columbia)

Broadway Hotel
Al Stewart; *Year Of The Cat* . . . . (Arista)

Broadway My Street
Original Broadway Cast; *70 Girls 70* . . . . (Sony Music Classical)

Brooklyn
Cody Jameson; *45-#7073* . . . . (Atco)

Brooklyn
Steely Dan; *Can't Buy A Thrill* . . . . (MCA)

Brooklyn Bridge
Frank Sinatra; *Sinatra Sings His Greatest Hits* . . . . (Legacy)

Brooklyn Roads
Neil Diamond; *And The Singer Sings His Song* . . . . (MCA)
Neil Diamond-His 12 Greatest Hits . . . . (MCA)
Velvet Gloves & Spit . . . . (MCA Special Prod.)

Cathedrals
Jump, Little Children; *Magazine* . . . . (Breaking/Atlantic)

Chelsea Morning
Joni Mitchell; *Clouds* . . . . (Reprise)
Judy Collins; *New York Songs-C* . . . . (Rhino)
Neil Diamond; *Rainbow* . . . . (MCA)
Stones . . . . (MCA)

City
Fleetwood Mac; *Mystery To Me* . . . . (Reprise)

Cold Hands From New York
Gordon Lightfoot; *United Artists Collection* . . . . (EMI)

Come Back To Brooklyn
Jimmy Roselli; *Saloon Songs-#3* . . . . (M&R)

Crack In New York
Culture; *Nuff Crisis!* . . . . (Shanachie)

Crazy Downtown
Allan Sherman; *New York Songs-C* . . . . (Rhino)

Daddy Don't Live In That New York City No More
Steely Dan; *Katy Lied* . . . . (MCA)

Deja Vu (Uptown Baby)
Lord Tariq & Peter Gunz; *Deja Vu* . . . . (Codeine/Columbia)

Do America
Mark Knopfler; *Sailing To Philadelphia* . . . . (Warner Bros.)

Do Like You Do In New York
Boz Scaggs; *Middle Man* . . . . (Columbia)

Does This Bus Stop At 82nd Street?
Bruce Springsteen; *Greetings From Asbury Park, N.J.* . . . . (Columbia)
Tracks . . . . (Columbia)

Drop Me Off In Harlem
David Frishberg; *Can't Take You Nowhere* . . . . (Fantasy)
Duke Ellington; *I Like Jazz-Essence Of Duke Ellington* . . . . (Columbia)
Ella Fitzgerald; *Essential Ella Fitzgerald-The Great Songs* . . . . (Verve)
Louis Armstrong & Duke Ellington; *Louis Armstrong & Duke Ellington-
Complete Sessions* . . . . (Roulette)

Easter Parade
Andy Russell; *Puttin' On The Ritz-Capitol Sings Berlin-C* . . . . (Capitol)

Bing Crosby; *All Time Best Of Bing Crosby* ... (Curb)
Judy Garland & Fred Astaire; *ST/Easter Parade* ... (Rhino)
Sarah Vaughan; *Complete Sarah Vaughan On Mercury-#2* ... (Mercury)

Echoes Of Harlem
Clark Terry Five; *Memories Of Duke* ... (Pablo)
Claude Bolling; *Claude Bollling Plays Ellington-#1* ... (Columbia)
Cootie Williams; *Jazz Sampler-#3-C* ... (Columbia)
Duke Ellington; *Mood Indigo* ... (Pro-Arte)

Englishman In New York
Sting; *...Nothing Like The Sun* ... (A&M)
Fields Of Gold-The Best Of Sting 1984-1994 ... (A&M)

Ev'ry Street's A Boulevard In Old N.Y.
Norrie Paramor; *Autumn* ... (Angel)

Eyes Of A New York Woman
B.J. Thomas; *B.J. Thomas' Greatest Hits* ... (Rhino)
B.J. Thomas-16 Greatest Hits ... (Trip)

Fairytale Of New York
Pogues; *Essential Pogues* ... (Island)
If I Should Fall From Grace With God ... (Island)

First We Take Manhattan
Jennifer Warnes; *Critics Choice-C* ... (Cypress)
Famous Blue Raincoat ... (Private Music)
Leonard Cohen; *I'm Your Man* ... (Columbia)
R.E.M.; *I'm Your Fan-Songs Of Leonard Cohen* ... (Atlantic)

Forty-Five Minutes From Broadway
Mickey Finn; *Caught In The Act* ... (Crescendo)

From Cotton To Satin
Gene Watson; *This Dream's On Me* ... (MCA)
Johnny Paycheck; *Take This Job And Shove It* ... (Epic)

Funky Broadway
Dyke & The Blasers; *Dyke & The Blasers' Greatest Hits* ... (Original Sound)
Soul Shots-C ... (Rhino)
Wilson Pickett; *Atlantic Rhythm & Blues 1947-1974-#6 (1966-1969)-C* ... (Atlantic)
Best Of Wilson Pickett ... (Atlantic)
Oldies But Goodies-#14-C ... (Original Sound)
Wilson Pickett's Greatest Hits ... (Atlantic)

Girl From New York City
Beach Boys; *Today/Summer Days (& Summer Nights!)* ... (Capitol)

Give It Back To The Indians (New York)
Ella Fitzgerald; *Rodgers & Hart Songbook* ... (Verve)

Give My Regards To Broadway
Barry Manilow; *Showstoppers* ... (Arista)
Joel Grey; *Broadway Magic-The 1960s-C* ... (Columbia)
Original Cast; *George M.* ... (Columbia)

Go Brooklyn
Hostyle; *Get Off* ... (Atlantic)

God Bless The USA
Lee Greenwood; *American Patriot* ... (Capitol)
God Bless America-C ... (Columbia)
God Bless The USA ... (MCA Special Prod.)
Inside Out/You've Got A Good Love Comin' ... (MCA)
Lee Greenwood's Greatest Hits ... (MCA)
Lee Greenwood's Greatest Hits-#2 ... (MCA)
Today's Country Classics-C ... (MCA Special Prod.)

Going To New York
Climax Blues Band; *FM/Live* ... (Sire)
Jimmy Reed; *Best Of Jimmy Reed* ... (Crescendo)
Jimmy Reed-At Carnegie Hall ... (Vee-Jay)
Jimmy Reed's Greatest Hits-#2 ... (Kent)
Legend-The Man ... (Vee-Jay)
Siegel-Schwall Band; *Best Of The Siegel-Schwall Band* ... (Vanguard)
Siegel-Schwall Band ... (Vanguard)

Grey Cloud Over New York
Philip Glass; *1000 Airplanes On The Roof* ... (Virgin)

Ground Zero Brooklyn
Carnivore; *Retaliation* ... (Roadrunner)

Harlem
Bill Withers; *Best Of Bill Withers* ... (Columbia)
Just As I Am ... (Columbia)
Suicide; *1/2 Alive* ... (Roir)
Ghost Riders ... (Roir)

Harlem Blues
Cynda Williams; *ST/Mo' Better Blues* ... (Columbia)
Nat "King" Cole; *ST/St. Louis Blues* ... (Capitol)

Harlem Camp Meeting
Cab Calloway; *Cab Calloway & Co.* ... (RCA)
Wicked Swing-C ... (RCA Victor)

Harlem Nocturne
Mel Torme; *Songs Of New York* ... (Rhino)
Viscounts; *Soul Shots-#3-Soul Twist-C* ... (Rhino)

Harlem On My Mind
Ethel Waters; *Irving Berlin 100th Anniversary Collection-C* ... (MCA)

Harlem On My Mind
Tim Curry; *Read By Lips* ... (A&M)

Harlem Shuffle
Bill Deal & The Rhondels; *Best Of Bill Deal & The Rhondels* ... (Rhino)
Bob & Earl; *Cruisin'-1964-C* ... (Increase)
Tell It Like It Is: 60's Soul-C ... (K-Tel)

Johnny & Edgar Winter; *Together* ... (Blue Sky)
Rolling Stones; *Dirty Work* ... (Virgin)

Heart In New York
Art Garfunkel; *Garfunkel* ... (Columbia)
Scissors Cut ... (Columbia)
Simon & Garfunkel; *The Concert In Central Park* ... (Warner Bros.)

Heat In Harlem
Graham Parker; *Pourin' It All Out-Mercury Years* ... (Mercury)
Graham Parker And The Rumour; *Stick To Me* ... (Mercury)
The Parkerilla ... (Mercury)

Hot Night In New York City
Bonnie Koloc; *With You On My Side* ... (Flying Fish)

I Am...I Said
Neil Diamond; *Hot August Night* ... (MCA)
Hot August Night II ... (Columbia)
Neil Diamond-His 12 Greatest Hits ... (MCA)
Stones ... (MCA)

I Guess The Lord Must Be In New York City
Nilsson; *Harry* ... (Dunhill Compact Classics)
Nilsson's Greatest Hits ... (RCA)

I Happen To Like New York
Bobby Short; *Live At The Cafe Carlyle* ... (Atlantic)

I Hate New York
Ann Jillian; *In The Middle Of Love-The Songs Of Steve Allen* ... (Aero Space)

I Love New York
Bernadette Peters; *Song & Dance* ... (RCA)

I Remember Harlem
Roy Eldridge; *Roy Eldridge* ... (Crescendo)

I'll Take New York
Tom Waits; *Frank's Wild Years-Un Operachi Romantico* ... (Island)

In A New York Minute
Ronnie McDowell; *19 Hot Country Requests-#3-C* ... (Epic)
In A New York Minute ... (Epic)
Older Women & Other Greatest Hits ... (Epic)

In Brooklyn
Al Stewart; *Love Chronicles* ... (Epic)

In Old New York
Victor Herbert; *Victor Herbert* ... (Alshire)

Incident On 57th Street
Bruce Springsteen; *The Wild, The Innocent & The E Street Shuffle* ... (Columbia)

Istanbul (Not Constantinople)
Four Lads; *Four Lads-16 Most Requested Songs* ... (Legacy)

Italian From New York
Chicago; *Chicago VII* ... (Chicago)

Jungleland
Bruce Springsteen; *Born To Run* ... (Columbia)

Just Another Death In NYC
Judy Small; *One Voice In The Crowd* ... (Redwood)

King Of New York
Schoolly D; *How A Black Man Feels* ... (Capitol)

King Of The New York Streets
Dion; *Yo Frankie* ... (Arista)

Last Chance To Turn Around
Gene Pitney; *Best Of Gene Pitney* ... (K-Tel)
Gene Pitney-Anthology 1961-1968 ... (Rhino)

Latin From Manhattan
Al Jolson; *Best Of Al Jolson* ... (MCA)
Immortal Al Jolson ... (MCA)

Let Me Off Uptown
Anita O'Day; *Let Me Off Uptown* ... (Legacy)
Gene Krupa; *Drummer Man* ... (Verve)
Gene Krupa Orchestra; *Uptown Saturday Night-C* ... (Rebound)

Life Is Beautiful
Amy Correia; *Carnival Love* ... (Capitol)

Livin' La Vida Loca
Ricky Martin; *Ricky Martin* ... (Columbia)

Living For The City
Stevie Wonder; *Innervisions* ... (Motown)
Original Musiquarium ... (Motown)

Lost In The Lights Of Broadway
Bernie Shanahan; *Bernie Shanahan* ... (Atlantic)

Lullaby Of Birdland
Ella Fitzgerald; *Best Of Ella Fitzgerald-#2* ... (MCA)
Ella Fitzgerald With Billie Holiday ... (MCA)
Four Freshmen; *Greatest Hits-Four Freshman* ... (Curb)
Mel Torme; *Songs Of New York* ... (Rhino)
Sarah Vaughan; *Sarah Vaughan-Golden Hits* ... (Mercury)
Tito Puente & His Latin Ensemble; *Mambo Diablo* ... (Concord Jazz)

Lullaby Of Broadway
Andrews Sisters; *Best Of The Andrews Sisters-#2* ... (MCA)
Bette Midler; *Bette Midler* ... (Atlantic)
Live At Last ... (Atlantic)
Original Broadway Cast; *42nd Street* ... (RCA Victor)
Tony Bennett; *Jazz* ... (Columbia)

Man From Harlem
Cab Calloway & His Orchestra; *Cab Calloway-1932* ... (Classics)
Tribute To Black Entertainers-C ... (Columbia)

Manhattan
Ella Fitzgerald; *Rodgers & Hart Songbook* ... (Verve)

Mel Torme; *Songs Of New York* ....(Rhino)
Tony Bennett; *Rodgers & Hart Songbook* ....(DRG)
Tony Bennett Sings 10 Rodgers & Hart Songs ....(Improv)
Manhattan Island Serenade
Leon Russell; *Carney* ....(Right Stuff)
Manhattan Project
Rush; *Power Windows* ....(Mercury)
Show Of Hands ....(Mercury)
Manhattan Rumble
Electric Light Orchestra; *No Answer* ....(Jet)
Manhattan Serenade
Dinah Shore; *Some Of The Best-Dinah Shore* ....(Laserlight)
Manhattan Skyline
David Shire; *ST/Saturday Night Fever* ....(Polydor)
Manhattan Skyline
Julia Fordham; *New York Songs-C* ....(Rhino)
Porcelain ....(Virgin)
The Julia Fordham Collection ....(Virgin)
Manhattan Spiritual
Reg Owen; *Hard To Find Pop Instrumentals-C* ....(Eric)
Maria Maria
Santana; *Supernatural* ....(Arista)
Totally Hits-#2-C ....(Elektra)
Me And Julio Down By The Schoolyard
Paul Simon; *Greatest Hits, Etc.* ....(Columbia)
Negotiations And Love Songs, 1971-1986 .... (Warner Bros.)
Paul Simon ....(Columbia)
Paul Simon In Concert/Live Rhymin' ....(Columbia)
Simon & Garfunkel; *The Concert In Central Park* ....(Warner Bros.)
Miami 2017
Billy Joel; *Songs In The Attic* ....(Columbia)
The Concert For New York City-C ....(Columbia)
Turnstiles ....(Columbia)
Mona Lisas And Mad Hatters
Elton John; *Honky Chateau* ....(Rocket)
Reg Strikes Back ....(MCA)
The Concert For New York City-C ....(Columbia)
Moon Over Brooklyn
Anne Murray; *Somebody's Waiting* ....(Capitol)
My Time Of Day
Mel Torme; *Songs Of New York* ....(Rhino)
Original Cast; *Guys & Dolls* ....(RCA Victor)
Guys & Dolls ....(MCA)
N.Y.C.
Weather Report; *Weather Report* ....(Columbia)
N.Y.C.
Original Broadway Cast; *Annie* ....(Columbia)
N.Y.C.
Charles & Eddie; *Duophonic* ....(Capitol)
N.Y.C.
Human Radio; *Human Radio* ....(Columbia)
Native New Yorker
Esther Phillips; *All About* ....(Mercury)
Odyssey; *Nipper's Greatest Hits Of The '70s-C* ....(RCA)
New Amsterdam
Elvis Costello; *Girls Girls Girls* ....(Columbia)
Elvis Costello & The Attractions; *Get Happy!* ....(Rykodisc)
New York
Sex Pistols; *Live At Chelmsford Top Security Prison* ....(Restless)
Never Mind The Bollocks, Here's The Sex Pistols .....(Warner Bros.)
New York
Dreams; *Dreams* ....(Columbia)
New York
Nuggetts; *N.Y.* ....(Mercury)
New York Boy
Neil Diamond; *Glory Road-1968-1972* ....(MCA)
Touching You Touching Me ....(MCA)
New York Broken Toy
Nazareth; *Expect No Mercy* ....(A&M)
New York City
John Lennon; *Lennon* ....(Capitol)
Live In New York City ....(Capitol)
John Lennon/Plastic Ono Band; *Sometime In New York City* ....(Capitol)
New York City
Statler Brothers; *Best Of The Statler Brothers* ....(Mercury)
New York City
Manhattans; *Love Talk* ....(Columbia)
New York City Blues
Bonnie Koloc; *After All This Time* ....(Ovation)
Bonnie Koloc-At Her Best ....(Ovation)
Duke Ellington & His Orchestra; *Carnegie Hall Concerts-
December 1947* ....(Prestige)
Jimmy Witherspoon; *Midnight Lady Called The Blues* ....(Muse)
Yardbirds; *Best Of British Rock-C* ....(Pair)
New York City King Size Rosewood Bed
Charlie Daniels Band; *Fire On The Mountain* ....(Epic)
John Grease & Wolfman ....(Epic)
New York City Rhythm
Barry Manilow; *Barry Manilow/Live* ....(Arista)

Barry Manilow's Greatest Hits-#1 ....(Arista)
Tryin' To Get The Feeling ....(Arista)
New York City Serenade
Bruce Springsteen; *The Wild, The Innocent & The E Street Shuffle* ...(Columbia)
New York City Song
Mighty High; *Mighty High* ....(MCA)
New York Girls
Kingston Trio; *Kingston Trio/From The Hungry i* ....(Capitol)
New York Groove
Ace Frehley; *Ace Frehley* ....(Casablanca)
New York Hippodrome
Detroit Concert Band; *Sousa American Bicentennial Collection* ....(H&L)
New York Interlude
Original Broadway Cast; *Crazy For You* ....(Angel)
New York J-D Blues
Pete Seeger; *Best Of Broadside 1962-1968: Anthems Of The American
Underground From The Pages Of Broadside
Magazine-C* .... (Smithsonian Folkways)
New York Lady
Burt Bacharach; *Burt Bacharach-Classics-#23* ....(A&M)
New York Mining Disaster 1941 (Mr. Jones)
Bee Gees; *Bee Gees-Gold* ....(Polydor)
Here At Last...Bee Gees...Live ....(Polydor)
History Of British Rock-#8-C ....(Rhino)
New York Minute
Don Henley; *End Of The Innocence* ....(Geffen)
New York On My Mind
John McLaughlin; *Electric Guitarist* ....(Columbia)
New York Rhapsody
Hollywood Bowl Orchestra/Gregory Hines/Patti Austin; *Gershwins In
Hollywood* ....(Philips)
New York Shuffle
Graham Parker And The Rumour; *Stick To Me* ....(Mercury)
The Parkerilla ....(Mercury)
New York Skyline
Garland Jeffreys; *Ghost Writer* ....(A&M)
Matador & More ....(A&M)
New York State Of Mind
Barbra Streisand; *Memories* ....(Columbia)
Streisand Superman ....(Columbia)
Billy Joel; *America: A Tribute To Heroes-C* ....(Interscope)
Billy Joel-Greatest Hits, Volume I & Volume II ....(Columbia)
The Concert For New York City-C ....(Columbia)
Turnstiles ....(Columbia)
Carmen McRae; *Ms. Magic* ....(Dunhill Compact Classics)
Tony Bennett with Billy Joel; *Playin' With My Friends-Bennett Sings The
Blues-C* ....(Columbia)
New York Telephone Conversation
Lou Reed; *Transformer* ....(RCA)
Walk On The Wild Side-The Best Of Lou Reed ....(RCA)
New York Tendaberry
Laura Nyro; *New York Tendaberry* ....(Columbia)
New York Willies
Barbra Streisand; *ST/Prince Of Tides* ....(Columbia)
New York, I Don't Know About You
Peter Allen; *Taught By Experts* ....(A&M)
New York, New York
Frank Sinatra; *Sinatra Reprise-The Very Good Years* ....(Reprise)
The Reprise Collection ....(Reprise)
Trilogy: Pasts, Present, Future ....(Reprise)
Frank Sinatra & Tony Bennett; *Frank Sinatra-Duets-C* ....(Capitol)
Leonard Bernstein; *Bernstein Songbook* ....(Columbia)
Mel Torme; *Songs Of New York* ....(Rhino)
New York, New York
Ryan Adams; *Gold* ....(Lost Highway/IDJMG)
New York, New York/Sailors On The Town
Original Broadway Cast; *Jerome Robbins' Broadway* ....(RCA)
New York's A Lonely Town
Tradewinds; *Beach Classics-All Original
Recordings-C* .... (Dunhill Compact Classics)
Original Golden Hits Of The Great Groups-#1-C ....(SSS International)
Surfin' Hits-C ....(Rhino)
New York's My Home
Ray Charles; *The Genius Hits The Road* ....(Rhino)
Sammy Davis, Jr.; *New York Songs-C* ....(Rhino)
New York's Not My Home
Jim Croce; *Photographs & Memories/His Greatest Hits* ....(Atlantic)
New York's Not My Home
Kid Rock; *Grits Sandwiches For Breakfast* ....(Jive)
Nights In Harlem
Luther Vandross; *I Know* ....(LV/Virgin)
Nights On Broadway
Bee Gees; *Bee Gees' Greatest* ....(Polydor)
Here At Last...Bee Gees...Live ....(Polydor)
Main Course ....(RSO)
No Sleep Till Brooklyn
Beastie Boys; *Licensed To Ill* ....(Def Jam)
Oldest Established (Permanent Floating Crap Game In New York)
Original Cast; *ST/Guys & Dolls* ....(MCA)

On Broadway
Drifters; *Drifters-16 Greatest Hits* .... (Trip)
Drifters-Golden Hits .... (Atlantic)
George Benson; *George Benson-Collection* .... (Warner Bros.)
ST/All That Jazz .... (Casablanca)
Weekend In L.A. .... (Warner Bros.)
On The Other Side Of Harlem
David Munyon; *Code Name: Jumper* .... (Los Hermanos)
Only Living Boy In New York
Simon & Garfunkel; *Bridge Over Troubled Water* .... (Columbia)
Collected Works .... (Columbia)
Only One You
T.G. Sheppard; *Best Of T.G. Sheppard* .... (Curb)
T.G. Sheppard's All-Time Greatest Hits .... (Warner Bros.)
Operaman
Adam Sandler; *The Concert For New York City-C* .... (Columbia)
Peace To New York
Doug E. Fresh & The Get Fresh Crew; *Doin' What I Gotta Do* .... (Bust It)
Positively 4th Street
Bob Dylan; *Biograph* .... (Columbia)
Bob Dylan's Greatest Hits .... (Columbia)
Byrds; *The Byrds* .... (Columbia)
The Byrds (Untitled) .... (Legacy)
Posse On Broadway
Sir Mix-A-Lot; *Rap Straight Outta The Ghetto-C* .... (K-Tel)
Swass .... (Nastymix)
Puttin' On The Ritz
Ella Fitzgerald; *Silver Collection-Songbooks* .... (Verve)
Fred Astaire; *Irving Berlin Always-C* .... (Verve)
Irving Berlin Songbook .... (Verve)
Harry Richman; *Hollywood Sings-C* .... (Living Era)
Those Wonderful Years: Puttin' On The Ritz-C .... (JCI Assoc. Labels)
Judy Garland; *One & Only* .... (Capitol)
Mandy Patinkin; *Mandy Patinkin* .... (Columbia)
Taco; *After Eight* .... (RCA)
Nipper's Greatest Hits Of The '80s-C .... (RCA)
Rage In Harlem
Little Jimmy Scott & The Expressions; *ST/Rage In Harlem* .... (Sire)
Red Cab To Manhattan
Stephen Bishop; *Best Of Bish* .... (Rhino)
Reggae On Broadway
Bob Marley; *Chances Are* .... (Cotillion)
Robinson Crusoe In New York
Silencers; *Dance To The Holy Man* .... (RCA)
Rockin' Around In N.Y.C.
Marshall Crenshaw; *Marshall Crenshaw* .... (Rhino)
Royal Scam
Steely Dan; *The Royal Scam* .... (MCA)
Safe In New York City
AC/DC; *Stiff Upper Lip* .... (East West)
Saga Of New York
Rascals; *Rascals-Anthology 1965-1972* .... (Rhino)
Searching For Ecstasy-Rest Of The Rascals-1969-1972 .... (Rhino)
Sally's Got A Friend In New York City
Larry McCray; *Ambition* .... (Charisma)
She's A Latin From Manhattan
Al Jolson; *Lullaby Of Broadway-Music Of H. Warren* .... (Pearl Flapper)
Sidewalks Of New York
Cannonball Adderley & Milt Jackson; *Things Are Getting Better* .... (Riverside)
Mel Torme; *Songs Of New York* .... (Rhino)
Son Of A New York Gun
Gino Vannelli; *Powerful People* .... (A&M)
South Bronx
Boogie Down Productions; *Live Hardcore Worldwide-Paris-London-NYC* .... (Jive)
Spanish Harlem
Aretha Franklin; *Aretha Franklin-30 Greatest Hits* .... (Rhino)
Best Of Aretha Franklin .... (Atlantic)
Ten Years Of Gold .... (Atlantic)
Ben E. King; *Ben E. King's Greatest Hits* .... (Atco)
Phil Spector-Back To Mono 1958-1969-C .... (Abkco)
Crusaders; *Crusaders-At Their Best* .... (Motown)
Drifters; *Drifters' Greatest Hits* .... (Gusto)
Spanish Harlem Incident
Bob Dylan; *Another Side Of Bob Dylan* .... (Columbia)
Byrds; *Mr. Tambourine Man* .... (Columbia)
The Byrds .... (Columbia)
Stayin' Alive
Bee Gees; *Bee Gees' Greatest* .... (Polydor)
ST/Saturday Night Fever .... (Polydor)
ST/Stayin' Alive .... (Polydor)
Stranger Than You
Joe Jackson; *Steppin' Out: The Very Best Of Joe Jackson* .... (A&M)
Street Of Dreams
Ella Fitzgerald; *Best Of Ella Fitzgerald* .... (Pablo)
Frank Sinatra; *The Reprise Collection* .... (Reprise)
Frank Sinatra with Count Basie & The Orchestra; *Sinatra At The Sands* .... (Reprise)
Ink Spots; *Best Of The Ink Spots* .... (MCA)
Ink Spots' Greatest Hits-Original Recordings-1939-1946 .... (MCA)
Nia Peeples; *Nia Peeples* .... (Charisma)
Ray Brown Trio; *Red Hot Ray Brown Trio* .... (Concord Jazz)
Tommy Dorsey & Frank Sinatra; *Tommy Dorsey & Frank Sinatra's All-Time Greatest Hits-#1* .... (Bluebird)
Tony Bennett; *Jazz* .... (Columbia)
Streets Of New York
Kool G Rap & D.J. Polo; *Wanted: Dead Or Alive* .... (Cold Chillin')
Streets Of New York
Carmel Quinn/Anna McGoldrick/Paddy Noonan/Others; *Let's Have An Irish Party* .... (Rego Irish)
Sunday In New York
Mel Torme; *Songs Of New York* .... (Rhino)
Sunday School To Broadway
Sammi Smith; *45-#45334* .... (Elektra)
Surfin' In Harlem
Swamp Dogg; *Surfin' In Harlem* .... (Volt)
Take Me Back To Manhattan
Original Cast; *Anything Goes* .... (Epic)
Take Me Back To New York City
Si Kahn; *Unfinished Portraits* .... (Flying Fish)
Take The "A" Train
Bobby McFerrin; *The Voice* .... (Elektra)
Dave Brubeck Quartet; *Jazz Goes To College* .... (Columbia)
Duke Ellington; *20 Golden Pieces Of Duke Ellington* .... (Bulldog)
Greatest Jazz Concert In The World .... (Pablo)
Sophisticated Lady .... (Bluebird)
Duke Ellington & Betty Roche; *Uptown* .... (Columbia)
Duke Ellington & Billy Strayhorn; *Great Times* .... (Riverside)
Duke Ellington & Count Basie Orchestra; *First Time!-Count Meets The Duke* .... (Columbia)
Glenn Miller; *Best Of Glenn Miller-#2* .... (RCA)
Glenn Miller-A Legendary Performer-#1 & 2 .... (Bluebird)
Glenn Miller & His Orchestra; *Complete Glenn Miller & His Orchestra-#6* .... (Bluebird)
Harry James; *Golden Trumpet Of Harry James* .... (London)
Mel Torme; *Duke Ellington & Count Basie Songbook* .... (Verve)
Sarah Vaughan; *Jazz Club-Vocal* .... (Verve)
Talkin' New York
Bob Dylan; *Bob Dylan* .... (Columbia)
The Times They Are A-Changin' .... (Columbia)
That Man From New York City
Lightnin' Hopkins; *Lost Texas Tapes-#1* .... (Collectables)
That's The Way We Do Things In New York
Original Cast; *Jelly's Last Jam* .... (Mercury)
Theme From "Car 54, Where Are You?"
Original Soundtrack; *Television's Greatest Hits-#2-C* .... (TVT)
Theme From "Fame"
Original Soundtrack; *Television's Greatest Hits-#5-In Living Color-C* .... (TVT)
Theme From "N.Y.P.D. Blue"
Original Soundtrack; *Television's Greatest Hits-#7-Cable Ready-C* .... (TVT)
Theme From "Seinfeld"
Original Soundtrack; *Television's Greatest Hits-#7-Cable Ready-C* .... (TVT)
Theme From "Taxi"
Original Soundtrack; *Television's Greatest Hits-#3-1970s & 1980s-C* .... (TVT)
Theme From "The Days And Nights Of Molly Dodd"
Original Soundtrack; *Television's Greatest Hits-#7-Cable Ready-C* .... (TVT)
Theme From "The Nanny"
Original Soundtrack; *Television's Greatest Hits-#7-Cable Ready-C* .... (TVT)
Theme From "The Odd Couple"
Original Soundtrack; *Television's Greatest Hits-#7-Cable Ready-C* .... (TVT)
There's A Boat Dat's Leavin' Soon For New York
Ella Fitzgerald & Louis Armstrong; *Porgy & Bess* .... (Verve)
Original Cast; *Porgy & Bess* .... (MCA)
There's A Broken Heart For Every Light On Broadway
Mel Torme; *Songs Of New York* .... (Rhino)
Times Square
Marianne Faithfull; *Blazing Away* .... (Island)
Too Dumb For New York City
Waylon Jennings; *Too Dumb For New York City, Too Ugly For L.A.* .... (Epic)
Twelve Thirty (Young Girls Are Coming To The Canyon)
Mamas & The Papas; *Best Of The Mamas & The Papas* .... (MCA)
Mamas & The Papas-16 Of Their Greatest Hits .... (MCA)
The Papas & The Mamas .... (MCA)
U.M.M.G. (Upper Manhattan Medical Group)
Art Farmer Quartet; *Warm Valley* .... (Concord Jazz)
Branford Marsalis; *Trio Jeepy* .... (Columbia)
Duke Ellington & Dizzy Gillespie; *Jazz Party* .... (Legacy)
Under The Harlem Moon
Fletcher Henderson & His Orchestra; *Fletcher Henderson & His Orchestra* .... (ASV)
Underneath The Harlem Moon
Randy Newman; *12 Songs* .... (Reprise)
Unique New York
John Scofield; *Grace Under Pressure* .... (Blue Note)
Uptown Manhattan
Budd Johnson; *Let's Swing* .... (Prestige)

Michel Camilo; *On Fire* . . . . (Epic)
Wings Over Manhattan
Charlie Barnet; *1941* . . . . (Circle)
World I Know, The
Collective Soul; *Collective Soul* . . . . (Atlantic)

CITIES: O

See Also: CITIES: GENERAL, COUNTRIES: A-Z, STATES: A-Z

Dallas To Odessa
Lyn Childress; *Different Shade Of Country* . . . .(Step One)
Goin' Back To Oakland
Isaac Scott; *San Francisco Blues Festival-#2-C* . . . .(Solid Smoke)
Tom McFarland; *Travelin' With The Blues* . . . . (Arhoolie)
Going Back To Okinawa
Ry Cooder; *Get Rhythm* . . . . (Warner Bros.)
My Favorite Town Osaka
Shonen Knife; *712* . . . . (Rockville)
Oakland
Pooh-Man; *Life Of A Criminal* . . . .(Jive)
Oakland Blues
Conjure; *Music For The Texts Of Ishmael Reed* . . . . (Pangaea)
Oscar Peterson & The Trumpet Kings; *Jousts* . . . . (Pablo)
Oakland Jungle
Wild Boyz; *It Had To Be Done* . . . . (Volt)
Oakland Stroke
Tony Toni Tone; *Revival* . . . . (Wing)
Oakland Stroke
Tower Of Power; *Back To Oakland* . . . . (Warner Bros.)
Oklahoma City Times
Limeliters; *Harmony!* . . . .(Folk Era)
Omaha
Golden Palominos; *History-1982-1986* . . . .(Metrotone)
Moby Grape; *Very Best Of Moby Grape-Vintage* . . . .(Columbia)
Omaha
Waylon Jennings; *Taker/Tulsa & Honky Tonk
Heroes* . . . . (Mobile Fidelity Sound Lab)
Omaha
Counting Crows; *August And Everything After* . . . .(David Geffen Co.)
Omaha Blues
Big Joe Williams; *Piney Woods Blues* . . . .(Delmark)
Omaha Celebration
Pat Metheny; *Bright Size Life* . . . . (ECM)
Omaha Polka
Li'l Wally; *Here Comes Li'l Wally* . . . . (Jay Jay)
Omaha, Nebraska
Doug Mathews; *Legacy II* . . . .(High Street)
Onion Town
John Delafose & The Eunice Playboys; *Stomp Down Zydeco-C* . . . . . .(Rounder)
Osaka
John Hicks & Elise Wood; *Luminous* . . . . (Evidence Music)
Osaka Castle
Peter Erskine; *Transition* . . . . (Denon)
Osaka Rocka
Jeff Watson; *Lone Ranger* . . . .(Shrapnel)
West Oakland Strut
Ed Kelly & Pharoah Sanders; *Ed Kelly & Pharoah Sanders* . . . (Evidence Music)
Wild Night In Odessa
Klezmorim; *Metropolis* . . . .(Flying Fish)

CITIES: P

See Also: CITIES: GENERAL, CITIES: PARIS, CITIES: PHILADELPHIA, COUNTRIES: A-Z, STATES: A-Z

All The Rage In Paris (Texas)
Derailers; *Here Come The Derailers* . . . .(Lucky Dog)
At The Fair In Pacanow
Myron Floren; *Polka Party* . . . .(Ranwood)
By The Time I Get To Phoenix
Glen Campbell; *All-Time Country Classics-#1-C* . . . .(Capitol)
Glen Campbell-Classics Collection . . . .(Capitol)
Glen Campbell-Live . . . .(Capitol)
Glen Campbell's Greatest Hits . . . .(Capitol)
Very Best Of Glen Campbell . . . . (Capitol)
Reba McEntire; *Starting Over* . . . . (MCA)
Come To The Supermarket (In Old Peking)
Barbra Streisand; *The Barbra Streisand Album* . . . .(Columbia)
Good Man Is Hard To Find (Pittsburgh)
Bruce Springsteen; *Tracks* . . . .(Columbia)
I Wish I Was In Peoria
Max Morath; *Max Morath & His Ragtime Stompers* . . . .(Vanguard)
Little Old Lady (From Pasadena)
Beach Boys; *Concert/'69-Live In London* . . . .(Capitol)

Jan & Dean; *Best Of Jan & Dean* . . . .(EMI)
Billboard Top Rock 'N' Roll Hits-1964-C . . . .(Rhino)
Dead Man's Curve . . . .(EMI)
Surf City-Best Of Jan & Dean . . . .(EMI)
Marching To Pretoria
Weavers; *Weavers At Carnegie Hall, Vol. 2* . . . .(Vanguard)
My Niece From Pittsburgh In 1992
PFS; *Illustrative Problems* . . . .(Cuneiform)
Night Life In Pompeii
Earl ''Fatha'' Hines; *Earl ''Fatha'' Hines* . . . . (Crescendo)
Night Ride Out Of Phoenix
Gillan; *Future Shock* . . . .(Metal Blade)
O'er The Town Of Pedro
Firehouse; *Flyin' The Flannel* . . . . (Columbia)
Paducah
George Thomas; *Chocolate Dandies (1928-1933)* . . . .(Disques Swing)
Paducah Parade
Bob Crosby; *The Uncollected Bob Crosby-#2-1952-1953* . . . .(Hindsight)
Palm Springs
Marc Antoine; *Universal Language* . . . .(GRP/NMG)
Palm Springs Jump
Flat Foot Floogie Boys & Slim Gaillard; *1940s-The Singers-C* . . . . .(Columbia)
Palo Alto
Lee Konitz; *Subconscious-Lee* . . . . (Prestige)
Palo Alto Cowboy
Reilly & Maloney; *Profiles* . . . .(Freckle)
Paradise City
Guns N' Roses; *Appetite For Destruction* . . . .(Geffen)
Parsons, Kansas Blues
Bob Scobey's Frisco Band & Clancy Hayes; *Bob Scobey's Frisco Band &
Clancy Hayes* . . . .(Good Time Jazz)
Pasadena
Al Jolson; *Lullaby Of Broadway-Music Of H. Warren* . . . . (Pearl Flapper)
Pascagoula Run
Jimmy Buffett; *Boats Beaches Bars & Ballads* . . . . (Margaritaville)
Off To See The Lizard . . . .(MCA)
Peking Doll
Kazumi Watanabe & Resonance Vox; *Pandora* . . . .(Gramavision)
Peking Fling
Vassar Clements; *Vassar* . . . .(Flying Fish)
Peking Theme (So Little Time)
Andy Williams; *ST/55 Days At Peking* . . . . (Varese Sarabande)
Pensacola
Joan Osborne; *Relish* . . . . (Blue Gorilla/Mercury)
Pensacola Joy
Kellis Ethridge; *Tomorrow Sky* . . . .(Inner City)
Phoenix City
Skatalites; *Original Club Ska* . . . .(Heartbeat)
Pinkville Helicopter
Thom Parrott; *Best Of Broadside 1962-1968: Anthems Of The American
Underground From The Pages Of Broadside
Magazine-C* . . . . (Smithsonian Folkways)
Pittsburgh
Ahmad Jamal; *Pittsburgh* . . . .(Atlantic)
Pittsburgh 1901
Mark Isham; *Sampler '86-C* . . . . (Windham Hill)
Windham Hill-First Ten Years-C . . . . (Windham Hill)
Pittsburgh Stealers
Kendalls; *Kendalls-20 Favorites* . . . .(Epic)
Pittsburgh Town
Pete Seeger; *American Industrial Ballads* . . . . (Smithsonian Folkways)
Pittsburgh, Pennsylvania
101 Strings Orchestra; *Million-Seller Hits From Mexico* . . . .(Alshire)
Guy Mitchell; *Guy Mitchell-16 Most Requested Songs* . . . .(Legacy)
Plano Texas Girl
Steve Wariner; *I Got Dreams* . . . .(MCA)
Playa Del Rey
Warne Marsh Quartet; *Music For Prancing* . . . .(V.S.O.P.)
Pompeii
Peter Hammill; *Nadir's Big Chance* . . . . (Blue Plate)
Port Arthur Blues
Eric Thompson; *Flatpicking Guitar Festival-C* . . . . (Shanachie)
Savoy-Doucet Cajun Band; *Harias-Home Music* . . . . (Arhoolie)
Port Arthur Waltz
Harry Choates; *Fiddle King Of Cajun Swing* . . . . (Arhoolie)
Porterville
Creedence Clearwater Revival; *1968-1969* . . . .(Fantasy)
Creedence Clearwater Revival . . . .(Fantasy)
More Creedence Gold . . . .(Fantasy)
Portland Town
Joan Baez; *Joan Baez In Concert, Part 2* . . . .(Vanguard)
Ramblin' Jack Elliott; *Essential Ramblin' Jack Elliott* . . . .(Vanguard)
Portland Woman
New Riders Of The Purple Sage; *New Riders Of The Purple Sage* . . . .(Columbia)
Vintage NRPS . . . . (Relix)
Prague
Chris Cutler & Fred Frith; *Live In Moscow, Prague &
Washington* . . . .(Cuneiform)

Prague In March
Hendrik Meurkens; *Sambahia* . . . . (Concord Picante Jazz)
Prague Spring
Legendary Pink Dots; *Shadow Weaver* . . . . (Play It Again Sam)
Puerto Vallarta
101 Strings Orchestra; *Million-Seller Hits From Mexico* . . . . (Alshire)
Music From Mexico . . . . (Alshire)
Saddle Tramp (Phoenix)
Marty Robbins; *Gunfighter Ballads & Trail Songs* . . . . (Legacy)
Marty Robbins-More Greatest Hits . . . . (Columbia)
Sam's Place (Pasadena)
Buck Owens & The Buckaroos; *Billboard Top Country Hits-1967-C* . . . (Rhino)
Theme From "Petticoat Junction"
Flatt & Scruggs; *20 All-Time Great Recordings* . . . . (Columbia)
Original Soundtrack; *Television's Greatest Hits-#1-C* . . . . (TVT)
TV Theme Sing-Along Album . . . . (Rhino)
Theme From "Peyton Place"
Original Soundtrack; *Television's Greatest Hits-#5-In Living Color-C* . . . (TVT)
There's A Fella Waitin' In Poughkeepsie
Pied Pipers; *Capitol Collectors Series-Pied Pipers* . . . . (Capitol)
To Portsmouth
John Townley & The Press Gang; *Chesapeake Sailor's Companion* . . . (Adelphi)
Town Called Paradise
Van Morrison; *No Guru No Method No Teacher* . . . . (Mercury)
View From Pony, Montana
Philip Aaberg; *Upright* . . . . (Windham Hill)

CITIES: PARIS

See Also: *COUNTRIES: FRANCE*

Afternoon In Paris
Sonny Stitt; *Genesis* . . . . (Prestige)
Stitt/Bud Powell/J.J. Johnson . . . . (Prestige)
Afternoon In Paris
Anita O'Day; *Night Has A Thousand Eyes* . . . . (Emily)
Ah, Paree, Beautiful Girls
Millicent Martin; *Collector's Sondheim-C* . . . . (RCA)
Stephen Sondheim; *Collector's Sondheim-C* . . . . (RCA)
Alone In Paris
Alphonse Mouzon; *Best Of Alphonse Mouzon* . . . . (Black Sun)
Early Spring . . . . (Tenacious)
American In Paris, An
Atlantic Brass Quintet; *By George! Gershwin's Greatest Hits* . . . (Musicmasters)
George Gershwin; *Rhapsody In Blue* . . . . (Biograph)
April In Paris
Charlie Parker; *Charlie Parker With Strings* . . . . (Verve)
Verve Years-1950-1951 . . . . (Verve)
Ella Fitzgerald & Oscar Peterson; *Ella & Oscar* . . . . (Pablo)
Frank Sinatra; *Come Fly With Me* . . . . (Capitol)
Mel Torme; *Mel Torme* . . . . (Glendale)
Sarah Vaughan; *Complete Sarah Vaughan On Mercury-#1-Great Jazz Years-1954-1956* . . . . (Mercury)
Sarah Vaughan . . . . (Emarcy)
Wynton Marsalis; *Marsalis Standard Time-#1* . . . . (Columbia)
Perspectives: Columbia Jazz Sampler . . . . (Columbia)
Au Revoir, Paris
Andy Williams; *Under Paris Skies* . . . . (Varese Vintage)
Azure-Te (Paris Blues)
Frank Sinatra; *Hello Young Lovers* . . . . (Columbia)
Louis Jordan; *Five Guys Named Moe-Original Decca Recordings-#2* . . . . (MCA)
Nat "King" Cole; *Nat "King" Cole (Box Set)* . . . . (Capitol)
Original Cast; *Five Guys Named Moe* . . . . (Columbia)
Original London Cast; *Five Guys Named Moe* . . . . (Relativity)
Ballad Of John And Yoko
Beatles; *Beatles 1* . . . . (Capitol)
Beatles-Box Set . . . . (Capitol)
Hey Jude . . . . (Capitol)
Past Masters-Volume Two . . . . (Parlophone)
ST/Imagine: John Lennon . . . . (Capitol)
The Beatles/1967-1970 . . . . (Capitol)
Belles Of Paris
Beach Boys; *M.I.U. Album* . . . . (Brother)
Crimes Of Paris
Elvis Costello; *Girls Girls Girls* . . . . (Columbia)
Elvis Costello & The Attractions; *Blood & Chocolate* . . . . (Columbia)
Evening In Paris
Stan Getz; *Artistry Of-Stan Getz-Best Of Verve Years-#1* . . . . (Verve)
Free Man In Paris
Joni Mitchell; *Court & Spark* . . . . (Asylum)
Shadows & Light . . . . (Asylum)
From Baltimore To Paris
Go West; *Dancing On The Couch* . . . . (Chrysalis)
Goin' Back To Paris
Bill Collins; *Charmin' Billy* . . . . (Chestnut)
Going To Paris
Champion Jack Dupree; *Tricks* . . . . (Crescendo)

He Went To Paris
Jimmy Buffett; *Songs You Know By Heart-Jimmy Buffett's Greatest Hit(s)* . . . . (MCA)
White Sport Coat & A Pink Crustacean . . . . (MCA)
You Had To Be There . . . . (MCA)
How Ya Gonna Keep 'Em Down On The Farm
Eddie Cantor; *Memories* . . . . (MCA)
I Love Paris
Frank Sinatra; *Frank Sinatra Sings The Select Cole Porter* . . . . (Capitol)
Sinatra Sings...of love and things . . . . (Capitol)
It Wasn't Paris, It Was You
Nancy Holloway; *Songbirds* . . . . (Bainbridge)
King Of Paris
Jo Stafford; *By Request* . . . . (Corinthian)
Last Mango In Paris
Jimmy Buffett; *Feeding Frenzy* . . . . (MCA)
Last Mango In Paris . . . . (MCA)
Last Tango In Paris
Herb Alpert & The Tijuana Brass; *Four Sider* . . . . (A&M)
Herb Alpert & The Tijuana Brass-Greatest Hits-#2 . . . . (A&M)
Last Time I Saw Paris
Dinah Shore; *That's Entertainment-The Ultimate Anthology Of MGM Musicals-C* . . . . (Turner Classic Movies)
Jonathan & Darlene Edwards; *In Paris* . . . . (Corinthian)
Jonathan & Darlene Edwards' Greatest Hits . . . . (Corinthian)
Memories Of Paris
Michel Petrucciani; *Music* . . . . (Blue Note)
Midnight In Paris
Michael Hurley & The Unholy Modal Rounders; *Have Moicy* . . . . . . (Rounder)
Midnight In Paris
Stephen Stills; *Illegal Stills* . . . . (Columbia)
Morning In Paris
John Lewis; *Private Concert* . . . . (Emarcy)
On The Roofs Of Paris
Ennio Morricone; *ST/Frantic* . . . . (Elektra)
One Night In Paris
John Boswell; *Count Me In* . . . . (Hearts Of Space)
Only One You
T.G. Sheppard; *Best Of T.G. Sheppard* . . . . (Curb)
T.G. Sheppard's All-Time Greatest Hits . . . . (Warner Bros.)
Opryland In Paris
Andy Badale & The Beer Garden Band; *Nashville Beer Garden* . . . . (Ranwood)
Paris
Figures On A Beach; *Standing On Ceremony* . . . . (Sire)
Paris
Elton John; *Leather Jackets* . . . . (MCA)
Paris
Nicki Richards; *Naked (To The World)* . . . . (Atlantic)
Paris
Shawn Lane; *Powers Of Ten* . . . . (Reprise)
Paris Blues
Duke Ellington & His Orchestra; *Featuring Paul Gonsalves* . . . . (Fantasy)
Milt Jackson; *Statements* . . . . (GRP)
Paris Calling
Shark Island; *Law Of The Order* . . . . (Epic)
Paris Finale
Santana; *Viva Santana!* . . . . (Columbia)
Paris In The Spring
Michel Legrand; *Legrand Piano* . . . . (Columbia)
Paris Is Burning
Dokken; *Breaking The Chains* . . . . (Elektra)
Paris Is Paris Again
Original Cast; *Gigi* . . . . (RCA Victor)
Paris Loves Lovers
Don Ameche & Hildelgard Neff; *Cole Porter-A Centennial Celebration-C* . . . . (RCA)
Paris Summer
Nancy Sinatra & Lee Hazlewood; *Fairy Tales & Fantasies-Best Of* . . . . (Rhino)
Paris, Tennessee
Dennis Robbins; *Man With A Plan* . . . . (Giant)
Kenny Chesney; *All I Need To Know* . . . . (BNA)
Tracy Lawrence; *Sticks & Stones* . . . . (Atlantic)
Parisian Thoroughfare
Bud Powell; *Amazing-#2* . . . . (Blue Note)
Genius Of Bud Powell . . . . (Verve)
Clifford Brown/Max Roach/Harold Land; *Compact Jazz-Clifford Brown* . . . . (Verve)
Stephane Grappelli; *Parisian Thoroughfare* . . . . (Black Lion)
Play The Paris Blues
Dr. John; *It's In The Air* . . . . (Sumertone)
Poor People Of Paris
Les Baxter & His Orchestra; *Memories Are Made Of This-C* . . . . (Capitol)
Postcard From Paris
Jimmy Webb; *Suspending Disbelief* . . . . (Elektra)
Sleeping In Paris
Rosanne Cash; *The Wheel* . . . . (Columbia)
Summer I Read Collette, The
Rosanne Cash; *10 Song Demo* . . . . (Capitol)

Tango In Paris
Regina Belle; *Passion* . . . . (Columbia)
There Is Only One Paris For That
Original Cast; *Irma La Douce* . . . . (Sony Music Special Prod.)
There's A Place Called Paris
Mae Barnes; *Mae Barnes*. . . . . (Disques Swing)
Under Paris Skies
Arthur Murray & His Orchestra; *Music For Dancing-Waltz* . . . .(RCA)
Gordon Jenkins; *France* . . . . (Bainbridge)
Under The Bridges Of Paris
Michel Legrand; *Legrand Piano* . . . . (Columbia)
Whores Of Paris
Bernie Taupin; *He Who Rides The Tiger* . . . . (Asylum)

CITIES: PHILADELPHIA

See Also: **STATES: PENNSYLVANIA**

Baby Do The Philly Dog
Olympics; *Official Record Album Of The Olympics* . . . . (Rhino)
Bristol Stomp
Dovells; *Echoes Of A Rock Era-Middle Years-C*. . . . . (Roulette)
Let's Dance. . . . . (Gusto)
Rock-O-Rama-#1-C . . . . (Abkco)
Fall In Philadelphia
Daryl Hall & John Oates; *Whole Oats* . . . . (Atlantic)
Motownphilly
Boyz II Men; *Cooleyhighharmony* . . . . (Motown)
Off To Philadelphia
Robert White & The Monte Carlo Philharmonic; *Favorite Irish Songs Of
Princess Grace*. . . . . (Vanguard Classics)
Oh! How I Hate To Get Up In The Morning
Irving Berlin; *American Songbook Series-Irving
Berlin*. . . . . (Smithsonian Collection)
War Years-C. . . . . (ISD/Intersound)
Soundtrack; *American Musical Theater-#2*. . . . . (Smithsonian Collection)
On The Road Again
Tom Rush; *Classic Rush* . . . . (Elektra)
Tom Rush . . . . (Elektra)
Philadelphia
Neil Young; *ST/Philadelphia* . . . . (Epic/Sony Music Soundtrax)
Philadelphia
Magazine; *Correct Use Of Soap* . . . .(Blue Plate)
Philadelphia
Mongo Santamaria; *Live At Jazz Alley*. . . . .(Concord Picante Jazz)
Philadelphia
John O'Connor; *Songs For Our Times* . . . .(Flying Fish)
Philadelphia Baby
Charlie Rich; *Charlie Rich-20 Golden Hits* . . . .(Sun)
Original Charlie Rich . . . .(Sun)
Philadelphia Boogie
Len McCall; *Philadelphia Boogie* . . . .(Collectables)
Philadelphia Fillies
Del Reeves; *Super Country Hits Of The '70s-C* . . . . (Gusto)
Philadelphia Freedom
Daryl Hall & John Oates; *Two Rooms-Celebrating The Songs Of Elton John
& Bernie Taupin-C* . . . . (Polydor)
Elton John; *Billboard Top Rock 'N' Roll Hits-1975-C* . . . . (Rhino)
Elton John's Greatest Hits-#2 . . . . (Polydor)
Philadelphia Hop
Li'l Wally; *Here Comes Li'l Wally* . . . . (Jay Jay)
Philadelphia Lawyer
Rose Maddox; *Rose Of The West Coast Country*. . . . .(Arhoolie)
Super Country Hits Of The '40s-C . . . . (Gusto)
Willie Nelson; *Tribute To Woody Guthrie And Leadbelly-C* . . . . (Columbia)
Woody Guthrie; *Cowboy Songs On Folkways-C*. . . . . .(Smithsonian Folkways)
Philadelphia Mambo
Cal Tjader; *Black Orchid*. . . . .(Fantasy)
Philly Dog
Mar-Keys; *Back To Back: Mar-Keys & Booker T. & The M.G.s* . . . . . . (Atlantic)
Great Memphis Sound . . . . (Atlantic)
Stax/Volt Revue-#1-Live In London-C . . . . (Atlantic)
Super Hits-#1-C . . . . (Atlantic)
Philly Freeze
Alvin Cash & The Registers; *45-#176*. . . . . (Eric)
Philly Rag
Dan Hicks & His Hot Licks; *Striking It Rich!* . . . . (MCA)
Sailing To Philadelphia
Mark Knopfler; *Sailing To Philadelphia* . . . . (Warner Bros.)
Streets Of Philadelphia
Bruce Springsteen; *Bruce Springsteen's Greatest Hits* . . . . (Columbia)
Diana, Princess Of Wales-Tribute-C . . . . (Columbia)
ST/Philadelphia . . . . (Epic/Sony Music Soundtrax)

T.S.O.P. (The Sound Of Philadelphia)
MFSB; *Ten Years Of #1 Hits-C* . . . .(Philadelphia Int'l)
MFSB & The Three Degrees; *Didn't It Blow Your Mind: Soul Hits Of The
'70s-#12-C* . . . . (Rhino)
Philadelphia Classics-C . . . .(Philadelphia Int'l)
Trees In Philadelphia
Patti Page; *Touch Of Country*. . . . . (Fifty One West)
Trimble's Compliments To The City Of Philadelphia
Gerald Trimble; *Crosscurrents* . . . . (Green Linnet)

CITIES: R

See Also: **CITIES: GENERAL, CITIES: RIO DE JANEIRO,
COUNTRIES: A-Z, STATES: A-Z**

All The Way To Reno (You're Gonna Be A Star)
R.E.M.; *Reveal*. . . . .(Warner Bros.)
All The Way To Richmond
Roger Whittaker; *Reflections Of Love* . . . . (RCA)
Dancing In Rackville, Maryland
Fred Frith; *Gravity*. . . . .(Ralph)
Folsom Prison Blues (Reno)
Johnny Cash; *Billboard Top Country Hits-1968-C* . . . .(Rhino)
Classic Cash-Hall Of Fame Series . . . .(Mercury)
Jailhouse Rock (Hits From The Big House)-C . . . . (Sony Music Special Prod.)
Johnny Cash At Folsom Prison & San Quentin . . . . (Columbia)
Johnny Cash-Original Golden Hits-#1 . . . . (Sun)
Johnny Cash's Greatest Hits-#2 . . . . (Columbia)
Superbilly . . . . (Sun)
Guitar Picker From Rody, Wyoming
Joey Davis; *45-#2248*. . . . . (MRC)
Raywood Texas
Queen Ida; *Caught In The Act* . . . .(Crescendo)
Queen Ida & Her Bon Temps Zydeco Band; *In San Francisco* . . . . . (Crescendo)
Redondo Beach
Patti Smith; *Horses* . . . .(Arista)
Reno
Doug Supernaw; *Red And Rio Grande* . . . . (BNA)
Reno And Me
T.G. Sheppard; *Perfect Stranger* . . . . (Warner Bros.)
Waylon Jennings; *The Eagle* . . . .(Epic)
Reno Bound
Southern Pacific; *Southern Pacific* . . . . (Warner Bros.)
Southern Pacific's Greatest Hits . . . . (Warner Bros.)
ST/Pink Cadillac . . . . (Warner Bros.)
Reno Burrito
Tom Collier; *Pacific Aire* . . . .(Nebula)
Reno Waltz
Marc Savoy; *Oh What A Night* . . . . (Arhoolie)
Reno, Nevada
Ian Matthews; *Circle Dance-Hokey Pokey Charity-C* . . . . (Green Linnet)
Mimi & Richard Farina; *Best Of Mimi & Richard Farina* . . . .(Vanguard)
Celebrations For A Grey Day . . . .(Vanguard)
Troubadours Of The Folk Era-#1-C . . . . (Rhino)
Richland Woman Blues
Mississippi John Hurt; *Best Of Mississippi John Hurt* . . . .(Vanguard)
Richmond Cotillion
Delaware Water Gap; *Fox Follow String Band* . . . . (Biograph)
Roanoke
Blaine Sprouse; *Summertime* . . . .(Rounder)
Vassar Clements & Others; *Nashville Jam*. . . . . (Flying Fish)
Rock Island
Soundtrack; *ST/The Music Man* . . . .(Warner Bros.)
Rock Island Line
Johnny Cash; *Johnny Cash-Sun Years* . . . .(Rhino)
Story Songs Of The Trains & Rivers . . . . (Sun)
Vintage Years-1955-1963 . . . .(Rhino)
Sonny Terry & Brownie McGhee; *Hootin'* . . . . (Muse)
Jazz Heritage. . . . .(MCA)
Weavers; *Best Of The Weavers* . . . . (MCA)
Weavers At Carnegie Hall . . . .(Vanguard)
Weavers' Greatest Hits . . . .(Vanguard)
Rock Island Rocket
Tom Scott; *Best Of Tom Scott* . . . .(Columbia)
Tom Scott & The L.A. Express; *Tom Cat*. . . . . (Epic Ode)
Rockport Sunday
Tom Rush; *The Circle Game* . . . .(Elektra)
Rockville (Don't Go Back To)
R.E.M.; *Eponymous* . . . . (I.R.S.)
Reckoning . . . . (I.R.S.)
Roseville Fair
Nanci Griffith; *One Fair Summer Evening*. . . . . (MCA)
Rotterdam Blues
Dave Brubeck; *We're All Together Again* . . . . (Atlantic)
Ruins Of Richmond
Norman Blake; *Fields Of November* . . . . (Flying Fish)

Walking Back To Richmond
Dry Brance Fire Squad; *Fannin' The Flames* . . . . (Rounder)

Veni-Vidi-Vici (I Came, I Saw, I Conquered)
Gaylords; *Best Of The Gaylords* . . . . (Chronicles)

CITIES: RIO DE JANEIRO

See Also: **COUNTRIES: BRAZIL**

Fiesta In Rio
Bette Midler; *Live At Last* . . . . (Atlantic)
Flying Down To Rio
Bobby Short; *Ertegun's New York, N.Y. Cabaret Music-#5-C* . . . . (Atlantic)
Holiday In Rio
Barney Kessel; *Barney Plays Kessel*. . . . . (Concord Jazz)
I Go To Rio
Pablo Cruise; *Worlds Away* . . . . (A&M)
Peter Allen; *At His Best*. . . . . (A&M)
It Is Time For Peter Allen. . . . . (A&M)
Taught By Experts . . . . (A&M)
Only A Dream In Rio
James Taylor; *That's Why I'm Here* . . . . (Columbia)
Rainy Night In Rio
Susannah McCorkle; *Thanks For The Memory* . . . . (Pausa)
Return To Rio
Oscar Castro-Neves; *Brazilian Scandals* . . . . (JVC Musical Industries)
Riding To Rio
William Orbit; *Strange Cargo* . . . . (I.R.S./No Speak)
Rio
Duran Duran; *Decade* . . . . (Capitol)
Rio . . . . (Capitol)
Rio
Doobie Brothers; *Takin' It To The Streets* . . . . (Warner Bros.)
Rio
Michael Nesmith; *From A Radio Engine To The Photon Wing*. . . . . (Pacific Arts)
Newer Stuff . . . . (Rhino)
Rio De Janeiro
Barry White; *Beware!*. . . . . (Unlimited Gold)
Rio De Janeiro Blue
Nicolette Larson; *In The Nick Of Time* . . . . (Warner Bros.)
Randy Crawford; *Secret Combination* . . . . (Warner Bros.)
See You In Rio
Joyce; *Music Inside*. . . . . (Verve/Forecast)
Spanish Eyes
Ricky Martin; *Ricky Martin* . . . . (Columbia)

CITIES: ROME

See Also: **COUNTRIES: ITALY**

All Roads Lead To Rome
Stranglers; *Feline* . . . . (Epic)
Arrivederci Roma
Jerry Vale; *Jerry Vale Sings The Great Italian Hits* . . . . (Columbia)
Jerry Vale-17 Most Requested Songs. . . . . (Legacy)
Mario Lanza; *Best Of Mario Lanza*. . . . . (RCA)
Legendary Tenor . . . . (RCA)
Mario Lanza-Legendary Performer. . . . . (RCA)
Back To The Days Of The Romans
Lou Christie; *Enlightnin'ment-Best Of Lou Christie* . . . . (Rhino)
Book, The (Rome)
Sheryl Crow; *Sheryl Crow* . . . . (A&M)
Cathedrals
Jump, Little Children; *Magazine* . . . . (Breaking/Atlantic)
Road To Rome
PFS; *279* . . . . (Cuneiform)
Rome Is A Song
Jimmy Roselli; *More I See You*. . . . . (M&R)
Rome Wasn't Built In A Day
Sam Cooke; *The Man And His Music* . . . . (RCA)
Rome Will Never Leave You
Richard Chamberlain; *The Reel Burt Bacharach-C* . . . . (Hip-O)
Three Coins In The Fountain
Andy Williams; *Moon River & Other Great Movie Themes* . . . . (Columbia)
Doris Day & Frank De Vol Orchestra; *Hooray For
Hollywood-#2-C* . . . . (Columbia)
Four Aces; *Billboard Top Movie Hits-1950-1954-C* . . . . (Rhino)
Four Aces' Greatest Hits . . . . (MCA)
Frank Sinatra; *At The Movies* . . . . (Capitol)
Capitol Collectors Series-Frank Sinatra . . . . (Capitol)
Harry James; *Harry James Plays The Songs That Sold A Million* . . . . (Columbia)
Julius LaRosa; *The Envelope Please-Academy Award Winning Songs-#2
(1946-1957)-C* . . . . (Rhino)

CITIES: S

See Also: **CITIES: GENERAL, CITIES: SAN ANTONIO, SAN
FRANCISCO, SANTA FE, SAVANNAH, ST. LOUIS, COUNTRIES:
A-Z, STATES: A-Z**

Balboa Park (San Diego)
Bruce Springsteen; *The Ghost Of Tom Joad* . . . . (Columbia)
Bosnia (Sarajevo)
Cranberries; *To The Faithful Departed* . . . . (Island)
Chains (Seattle)
Patty Loveless; *Honky Tonk Angel* . . . . (MCA)
Patty Loveless' Greatest Hits . . . . (MCA)
Come Back To Sorrento
Dean Martin; *Dean Martin's All Time Greatest Hits*. . . . . (Curb)
Frank Sinatra; *Columbia Years-1943-1952-Complete Recordings* . . . . (Legacy)
Dancing In Sunrise, Switzerland
Muffins; *Open City* . . . . (Cuneiform)
Dear Old Stockholm
Miles Davis; *Best Of Miles Davis: The Capitol And Blue Note
Years* . . . . (Blue Note)
Miles Davis Quintet; *Round About Midnight* . . . . (Columbia)
Terence Blanchard; *Simply Stated*. . . . . (Columbia)
Toots Thielemans; *East Coast West Coast* . . . . (Private Music)
Dear Old Syracuse
Original New York Cast; *Boys From Syracuse* . . . . (Angel)
Do You Know The Way To San Jose
Dionne Warwick; *Dionne Warwick Greatest Hits*. . . . . (Everest)
Dionne Warwick-Anthology 1962-1971. . . . . (Rhino)
Hot! Live & Otherwise . . . . (Arista)
Don Jose Of Sevilla
W.H. MacDonald & Jessie Bartlett Davis; *Music From The New York Stage
(1890-1920)-#1-1890-1908-C*. . . . . (Pearl)
Fall Of Saigon
Original London Cast; *Miss Saigon*. . . . . (Geffen)
Frances Farmer Will Have Her Revenge On Seattle
Nirvana; *In Utero* . . . . (David Geffen Co.)
From Silver Lake
Jackson Browne; *Jackson Browne* . . . . (Asylum)
Get 'Em Outta Here (San Diego)
Sprung Monkey; *Mr. Funny Face* . . . . (Surfdog/Hollywood)
Goodnight Saigon
Billy Joel; *Billy Joel-Greatest Hits, Volume I & Volume II* . . . . (Columbia)
KOHUEPT. . . . . (Columbia)
Nylon Curtain. . . . . (Columbia)
Heat Is On Is Saigon
Original London Cast; *Miss Saigon*. . . . . (Geffen)
I Left My Flannel In Seattle
Butt Trumpet; *Primitive Enema* . . . . (Chrysalis)
I Lost My Sugar In Salt Lake City
Johnny Mercer; *Capitol Collectors Series-Johnny Mercer* . . . . (Capitol)
It Happened In Sun Valley
Glenn Miller & His Orchestra; *Complete Glenn Miller & His
Orchestra*. . . . . (Bluebird)
Kill Surf City
Jesus & Mary Chain; *Barbed Wire Kisses*. . . . . (Warner Bros.)
Leaving Sedona
Don Harriss; *Elevations* . . . . (Sonic Atmospheres)
Like A Sunday In Salem
Gene Cotton; *No Strings Attached*. . . . . (Ariola America)
Save The Dancer . . . . (Ariola America)
Little Bit South Of Saskatoon
Sonny James; *American Originals-Sonny James* . . . . (Columbia)
Midnight In San Juan
Earl Klugh; *Midnight In San Juan*. (Warner Bros.)
Miss Sarajevo
Passengers; *Diana, Princess Of Wales-Tribute-C*. . . . . (Columbia)
My Antonia (Santa Maria)
Emmylou Harris; *Red Dirt Girl*. . . . . (Nonesuch)
Old San Juan
Spyro Gyra; *Access All Areas* . . . . (MCA)
Incognito . . . . (MCA)
Spyro Gyra-Collection . . . . (GRP)
On A Bus To St. Cloud
Gretchen Peters; *The Secret Of Life*. . . . . (Purple Crayon Prod.)
Trisha Yearwood; *Thinkin' About You* . . . . (MCA)
Queen Of Sydney
Oregon; *Crossing* . . . . (ECM)
Road To Santa Rosa
Frank Chacksfield; *Mirrors*. . . . . (Starborn)
Road To Spencer
Ricky Skaggs and Kentucky Thunder; *History Of The Future* . . (Skaggs Family)

Runnin' Back To Saskatoon
Guess Who; *Track Record-Collection* . . . .(RCA)
Sacramento
Chrysanthemum Ragtime Band; *Chrysanthemum Ragtime Band-#1* . . . (Omega)
Saginaw, Michigan
Lefty Frizzell; *American Originals-Lefty Frizzell* . . . .(Columbia)
  Billboard Top Country Hits-1964-C . . . .(Rhino)
  Columbia Country Classics-#3-Americana-C . . . .(Columbia)
  Lefty Frizzell's Greatest Hits . . . .(Columbia)
Saigon
John Prine; *Pink Cadillac* . . . .(Asylum)
Saigon Bride
Joan Baez; *Contemporary Ballad Book* . . . .(Vanguard)
Saigon Warrior
Saul Broudy & Robin Thomas; *In Country-Americans In The*
  Vietnam War . . . .(Flying Fish)
Salt Lake City
Beach Boys; *Beach Boys-Gift Set* . . . .(Capitol)
  California Girls . . . .(Capitol)
  Spirit Of America . . . .(Capitol)
Bob Weir; *Heaven Help The Fool* . . . . (Arista)
Salt Lake City Blues
Eric Thompson & Alan Senauke; *Two Guitars* . . . .(Flying Fish)
Salt Pork, West Virginia
Louis Jordan; *Jazz Heritage-Greatest Hits-#2-1941-1947* . . . . (MCA)
Salzburg
Jean Stapleton & Eddie Lawrence; *Bells Are Ringing* . . . .(Columbia)
San Angelo
Marty Robbins; *All Around Cowboy* . . . .(Columbia)
  Essential Marty Robbins-1951-1982 . . . .(Columbia)
  More Gunfighter Ballads & Trail Songs . . . .(Columbia)
San Ber'dino
Frank Zappa/Mothers Of Invention; *One Size Fits All* . . . . (Rykodisc)
San Carlos
Don Grusin; *No Borders* . . . . (GRP)
San Diego Serenade
Nanci Griffith; *Late Night Grande Hotel* . . . . (MCA)
Tom Waits; *The Heart Of Saturday Night* . . . .(Asylum)
  Tom Waits-Anthology . . . .(Asylum)
San Fernando
Mary McCaslin; *Sunny California* . . . .(Mercury)
Roy Orbison; *Legendary Roy Orbison* . . . . (Sony Music Special Prod.)
  Rare Orbison II . . . .(Monument)
San Jacinto
Peter Gabriel; *Security* . . . . (Geffen)
  Shaking The Tree-Sixteen Golden Greats . . . . (Geffen)
San Jose
Blind Snooks Eaglin; *Down Yonder (Snooks Eaglin Today)* . . . .(Crescendo)
San Miguel
Beach Boys; *10 Years Of Harmony* . . . .(Caribou)
San Tropez
Pink Floyd; *Meddle* . . . .(Capitol)
  Pink Floyd-Gift Set . . . .(Capitol)
Santa Ana
Willi Jones; *Willi Jones* . . . . (Geffen)
Santa Ana Woman
Bobs; *Songs For Tomorrow Morning* . . . .(Kaleidoscope)
Santa Barbara
David Benoit; *This Side Up* . . . .(Spindletop)
Santa Barbara
Ronnie Milsap; *Only One Love In My Life* . . . .(RCA)
Santa Cruz
Dirty Dozen Brass Band; *Voodoo* . . . .(Columbia)
Ray Barretto; *Handprints* . . . .(Concord Picante Jazz)
Santa Lucia
Elvis Presley; *Elvis For Everyone!* . . . .(RCA)
Mario Lanza; *Legendary Tenor* . . . .(RCA)
Santa Monica
Savage Garden; *Savage Garden* . . . .(Columbia)
Santa Monica (Watch The World Die)
Everclear; *Sparkle And Fade* . . . .(Capitol)
Santa Monica Pier
Christine Lavin; *Good Thing He Can't Read My Mind* . . . .(Philo)
Holly Near; *Live Album* . . . .(Redwood)
Nitty Gritty Dirt Band; *Dream* . . . .(United Artists)
Santa Rosa
Gino Vannelli; *Nightwalker* . . . . (Arista)
Sao Paulo
Dan Moretti; *Point Of Entry* . . . . (Parc)
David Amram; *No More Walls* . . . .(Flying Fish)
David Benoit; *Every Step Of The Way* . . . . (GRP)
Freddie Hubbard & Woody Shaw; *Eternal Triangle* . . . .(Blue Note)
Sausalito
Mark Murphy; *Bridging A Gap* . . . . (Muse)
  September Ballads . . . .(Milestone)
Sausalito
Ashra; *Belle Alliance* . . . .(Blue Plate)

Sausalito
SOS All-Stars; *Greetings From New York* . . . .(Chase Music Group)
Sausalito
Grover Washington, Jr.; *Live At The Bijou* . . . .(Motown)
Sausalito Summernight
Diesel; *Watts In A Tank* . . . .(Regency/Atco)
Scarborough Fair/Canticle
Simon & Garfunkel; *Collected Works* . . . .(Columbia)
  Parsley Sage Rosemary & Thyme . . . .(Columbia)
  Simon & Garfunkel's Greatest Hits . . . .(Columbia)
  ST/The Graduate . . . .(Columbia)
  The Concert In Central Park . . . .(Warner Bros.)
Seattle
Bobby Sherman; *Very Best Of Bobby Sherman* . . . .(Restless)
Perry Como; *This Is Perry Como* . . . .(RCA)
Seattle
Public Image Ltd.; *Greatest Hits So Far* . . . . (Virgin)
  Happy? . . . . (Virgin)
Seattle Afternoon
Reilly & Maloney; *Reilly & Maloney-At Last* . . . .(Freckle)
Seattle Ain't Bullshittin'
Sir Mix-A-Lot; *Mack Daddy* . . . .(Def American)
Seattle Hunch
Jelly Roll Morton; *Centennial-Complete Victor Recordings* . . . .(Bluebird)
Seattle Morning
David Benoit; *Urban Daydreams* . . . .(GRP)
Sedona
Freeway Philharmonic; *Car Tunes* . . . .(Spindletop)
Shanghai Breezes
John Denver; *John Denver's Greatest Hits-#3* . . . . (RCA)
  Seasons Of The Heart . . . . (RCA)
Shanghai Lil
Guy Lombardo & His Royal Canadians; *Guy Lombardo-16 Most Requested*
  Songs . . . .(Legacy)
Shanghai Noodle Factory
Traffic; *Last Exit* . . . .(Island)
Shanghai Shuffle
Bunny Berigan & His Orchestra; *Bunny Berigan & His Orchestra-1937-*
  1938 . . . .(Hindsight)
Fletcher Henderson & His Orchestra; *1924-1941* . . . .(Biograph)
Silverton
C.W. McCall; *C.W. McCall's Greatest Hits* . . . . (Polydor)
Silvertown Blues
Mark Knopfler; *Sailing To Philadelphia* . . . .(Warner Bros.)
Sioux City Sue
Bob Wills & His Texas Playboys; *Tiffany Transcriptions-#8-More Of*
  The Best . . . .(Rhino)
Gene Autry; *The Country Music Hall Of Fame-Gene Autry-15 Of His All-*
  Time Greatest Hits . . . .(Columbia)
Jimmy C. Newman; *Cajun Cowboy* . . . .(Plantation)
Mom & Dads; *In The Good Old Summertime* . . . .(Crescendo)
Willie Nelson & Leon Russell; *One For The Road* . . . .(Columbia)
Skatetown U.S.A.
Dave Mason; *Skatetown U.S.A.-C* . . . .(Columbia)
Snow In San Anselmo
Van Morrison; *Hard Nose The Highway* . . . . (Polydor)
Southampton
James Horner; *ST/Titanic* . . . .(Sony Music Classical)
Starkville City Jail
Johnny Cash; *Johnny Cash At Folsom Prison & San Quentin* . . . .(Columbia)
Statesboro Blues
Allman Brothers Band; *At Fillmore East* . . . .(Capricorn)
  Best Of The Allman Brothers Band . . . . (Polydor)
  Decade Of Hits-1969-1979 . . . . (Polydor)
  Dreams . . . . (Polydor)
  The Road Goes On Forever, A Collection Of Their Greatest
   Recordings . . . . (Polydor)
Blind Willie McTell; *Blind Willie McTell-Early Years-1927-1932* . . . . . (Yazoo)
Charlie Daniels Band & Friends; *Volunteer Jam 3 & 4* . . . . (Epic)
Duane Allman; *Duane Allman-An Anthology* . . . .(Capricorn)
Pat Travers; *Makin' Magic* . . . . (Polydor)
Taj Mahal; *Taj's Blues* . . . .(Columbia)
Still In Saigon
Charlie Daniels Band; *A Decade Of Hits* . . . . (Epic)
  Windows . . . . (Epic)
Stockholm
Django Reinhardt; *Immortal Django Reinhardt* . . . .(Crescendo)
Stockholm
New Fast Automatic Daffodils; *Body Exit Mind* . . . .(Mute/Reprise)
Stockholm
Dave Edmunds; *Closer To The Flame* . . . .(Capitol)
Stockholm Stomp
California Ramblers; *Miss Annabelle Lee-#1* . . . .(Biograph)
Stockholm Sweetnin'
Al Jarreau; *1965* . . . .(Bainbridge)
Cannonball Adderley & His Orchestra; *African Waltz* . . .(Original Jazz Classics)
Clifford Brown; *Memorial* . . . .(Prestige)
Jon Hendricks; *Jazz Club-Vocal* . . . .(Verve)

Patti Austin; *Real Me* .... (Qwest)
Sugar Town
Nancy Sinatra; *Nancy's Greatest Hits* .... (Reprise)
   Sugar .... (Sundazed Music)
   The Hit Years .... (Rhino)
Sun City
Artists United Against Apartheid; *Sun City-C* .... (Manhattan)
Sunday Night In San Fernando
Mel Torme & The Mel-Tones; *California Suite* .... (Discovery)
Sweetwater Nights
Dave Grusin; *Out Of The Shadows* .... (GRP)
Sweetwater, Texas
Charlie Daniels Band; *Saddle Tramp* ....(Epic)
Sydney By Night
James Morrison; *Postcards From Down Under* .... (Atlantic)
Sydney From A 727
Paul Kelly & The Messengers; *Comedy* .... (Dr. Dream Music Group)
Syracuse
Jean Sablon; *1932-1962* .... (DRG)
Syracuse Oberek
Li'l Wally; *Here Comes Li'l Wally* ....(Jay Jay)
Theme From "Santa Barbara"
Original Soundtrack; *Soap Opera's Greatest Love Themes* .... (Scotti Bros.)
Theme From "Simon And Simon" (San Diego)
Original Soundtrack; *Television's Greatest Hits-#3-1970s & 1980s-C* ... (TVT)
There Is No Arizona (Sedona)
Jamie O'Neal; *Shiver* .... (Mercury)
Would They Love Him Down In Shreveport
George Jones; *Hallelujah Weekend* ....(Epic)
Oak Ridge Boys; *Bobbie Sue* ....(MCA)

CITIES: SAN ANTONIO

See Also: **AMERICAN WEST, COWBOYS, STATES: TEXAS**

Across The Alley From The Alamo
Asleep At The Wheel featuring Johnny Rodriguez; *Tribute To The Music Of*
   Bob Wills And The Texas Playboys-C .... (Liberty)
Bob Wills & His Texas Playboys; *Best Of Bob Wills & His Texas*
   Playboys ....(MCA)
   Tiffany Transcriptions-#4-You're From Texas .... (Rhino)
Ain't No Fun To Be Alone In San Antone
Gene Watson; *Mack In The Fire* ....(Warner Bros.)
All The Rage In Paris
Derailers; *Here Come The Derailers* .... (Lucky Dog)
Amarillo By Morning
George Strait; *George Strait's Greatest Hits* ....(MCA)
   Strait From The Heart ....(MCA)
China Grove
Doobie Brothers; *Best Of The Doobies* ....(Warner Bros.)
   Captain & Me ....(Warner Bros.)
   Farewell Tour ....(Warner Bros.)
Folsom Prison Blues
Brooks & Dunn with Johnny Cash; *Red Hot + Country-C* .... (Mercury)
Johnny Cash; *Billboard Top Country Hits-1968-C* .... (Rhino)
   Classic Cash-Hall Of Fame Series .... (Mercury)
   Hot Tracks-Train Super Hits-C ....(Epic)
   Jailhouse Rock (Hits From The Big House)-C ..... (Sony Music Special Prod.)
   Johnny Cash At Folsom Prison & San Quentin .... (Columbia)
   Johnny Cash-Original Golden Hits-#1 .... (Sun)
   Johnny Cash's Greatest Hits-#2 .... (Columbia)
   Superbilly .... (Sun)
   The Man In Black-His Greatest Hits .... (Legacy)
Home In San Antone
Bob Wills & His Texas Playboys; *Tiffany Transcriptions-#4-You're From*
   Texas .... (Rhino)
George Strait; *The Chill Of An Early Fall* ....(MCA)
Texas Playboys & Leon McAuliffe; *Greatest Hits Of Texas-C* .... (Rhino)
   San Antonio Rose Story .... (Delmark)
Honky Tonk Moon (San Antonio)
Rosie Flores; *Once More With Feeling* ....(Hightone)
In San Antone
Dan Seals; *Early Dan Seals* .... (Capitol)
   San Antone ....(EMI)
My Sweetheart Lives In San Antonio
Ray Duncan; *45-#232* .... (Door Knob)
New San Antonio Rose
Bob Wills & His Texas Playboys; *Bob Wills & His Texas Playboys-*
   Greatest Hits .... (Curb)
   Columbia Country Classics-#1-Golden Age-C .... (Columbia)
   Essential Bob Wills & His Texas Playboys-1935-1973 .... (Legacy)
Dwight Yoakam & Asleep At The Wheel; *Ride With*
   Bob-C .... (DreamWorks/SKG)
Put Me On A Train Back To Texas
Waylon Jennings & Willie Nelson; *Clean Shirt* ....(Epic)
   Hot Tracks-Train Super Hits-C ....(Epic)
Rosa De San Antonio
Santiago Jimenez, Jr.; *Mero Mero De San Antonio* .... (Arhoolie)

Rose Of San Antone
Bashful Brother Oswald; *Don't Say Aloha* .... (Rounder)
San Anton'
Thomas "Fats" Waller; *Fats Waller & His Rhythm-1936-1938* ..... (Bluebird)
San Antonio Champagne
Troy Cory; *Real Country*...................... (Video Record Albums)
San Antonio Girl
Steve Earle & The Dukes; *Exit 0* .... (MCA)
San Antonio Girl
Lyle Lovett; *Lyle Lovett Anthology-#1-Cowboy Man* .... (MCA)
San Antonio Nights
Eddy Raven; *Eddy Raven's Greatest Hits* .... (Warner Bros.)
San Antonio Rose
Asleep At The Wheel; *Western Standard Time* .... (Epic)
Bob Wills; *Best Of Bob Wills-#2* .... (MCA)
   Sounds Of Texas .... (Capitol)
   Texas State Of Mind-C .... (Capitol)
Floyd Cramer; *Billboard Top Country Hits-1961-C* .... (Rhino)
   Country Love .... (Step One)
Patsy Cline; *The Patsy Cline Story* .... (MCA)
Ricky Skaggs; *Comin' Home To Stay* .... (Epic)
Willie Nelson; *What A Wonderful World* .... (Columbia)
San Antonio Rose To You
Rick Trevino; *Texas Super Hits-C* .... (Columbia)
San Antonio Shout
Bob Crosby & His Orchestra; *Bob Crosby & His Orchestra Play 22 Original*
   Big Band Hits .... (Hindsight)
San Antonio Story
Stephen Woodfin & Joe Vickers; *Waco* ....(Step One)
San Antonio Stroll
Tanya Tucker; *MCA Records 30 Years Of Hits-1958-1988-C* .... (MCA)
   Tanya Tucker-Greatest Hits Encore .... (Gold Rush)
   Tanya Tucker's Greatest Country Hits .... (Curb)
   Tanya Tucker's Greatest Hits .... (MCA)
   The Tanya Tucker Collection .... (MCA)
Walkin' Back To San Antonio
Hank Thompson; *Here's To Country Music* ....(Step One)
What The Cowgirls Do
Vince Gill; *When Love Finds You* .... (MCA)
Wild Horses
Garth Brooks; *No Fences* .... (Capitol)

CITIES: SAN FRANCISCO, San Francisco Suburbs

See Also: **BRIDGES, HIPPIES, STATES: CALIFORNIA**

(Sittin' On) The Dock Of The Bay
Michael Bolton; *The Hunger* .... (Columbia)
Otis Redding; *(Sittin' On) The Dock Of The Bay*................... (Atco)
   Best Of Otis Redding .... (Atco)
   Golden Age Of Black Music-1960-1970-C ....(Atlantic)
   Golden Soul-C ....(Atlantic)
   Soul Years-C ....(Atlantic)
   The Otis Redding Story ....(Atlantic)
Arizona
Mark Lindsay; *Super Hits Of The '70s-Have A Nice Day-#1-C* ..... (Rhino)
Big Time
Neil Young & Crazy Horse; *Broken Arrow* .... (Reprise)
   Year Of The Horse .... (Reprise)
Blame It On Texas
Mark Chesnutt; *Mark Chesnutt's Greatest Hits* .... (Decca)
   Too Cold At Home .... (MCA)
Do You Know The Way To San Jose
Dionne Warwick; *Dionne Warwick Greatest Hits*.................. (Everest)
   Dionne Warwick-Anthology 1962-1971 .... (Rhino)
   Hot! Live & Otherwise .... (Arista)
Frisco Blues
John Lee Hooker; *Hooked On The Blues* .... (Everest)
   The Ultimate Collection-1948-1990 ....
Lesley Riddle; *Step By Step: Lesley Riddle Meets The Carter Family: Blues,*
   Country & Sacred Songs .... (Rounder)
Frisco Depot
Mickey Newbury; *Frisco Mabel Joy*.................. (Mountain Retreat)
Frisco Lines
Fred McDowell; *Blues Roots*.................................(Tomato)
Goodbye San Francisco, Hello Amsterdam
Doug Sahm; *SDQ '98* .... (Watermelon)
Grant Avenue
Original Cast; *Flower Drum Song*................. (Sony Music Classical)
Here In Frisco
Merle Haggard; *18 Rare Classics* .... (Curb)
I Left My Heart In San Francisco
Tony Bennett; *I Left My Heart In San Francisco*................. (Columbia)
   Pop Classics Of The '60s-C .... (Columbia)
   Tony Bennett's All-Time Greatest Hits .... (Columbia)
In San Francisco
Dinah Washington; *Echoes Of An Era-Dinah Washington* .... (Roulette)

Earl ''Fatha'' Hines; *Another Monday Date* . . . . (Prestige)
Leavin' Memphis, Frisco Bound
Jesse Fuller; *Frisco Bound* . . . .(Arhoolie)
Lone Cat . . . . (Good Time Jazz)
Lights
Journey; *Infinity* . . . . (Columbia)
Journey-Captured . . . . (Columbia)
Mean Old Frisco
Eric Clapton; *Slowhand* . . . . (Polydor)
Jimmy Witherspoon; *Best Of Jimmy Witherspoon* . . . . (Prestige)
Mean Old Frisco . . . . (Prestige)
New Frisco Train
Washington White; *Mississippi Moaners-1927-1942* . . . . (Yazoo)
Road To Santa Rosa
Frank Chacksfield; *Mirrors* . . . . (Starborn)
San Carlos
Don Grusin; *No Borders* . . . . (GRP)
San Franciscan Nights
Eric Burdon & The Animals; *Eric Burdon & The Animals'*
Greatest Hits . . . .(MGM)
History Of British Rock-#8-C . . . . (Rhino)
San Francisco
Judy Garland; *America's Treasure* . . . . (Dunhill Compact Classics)
Judy Garland-At Carnegie Hall . . . . (Capitol)
One & Only . . . . (Capitol)
Vikki Carr; *Best Of Vikki Carr* . . . . (EMI)
San Francisco (Be Sure To Wear Some Flowers In Your Hair)
Scott McKenzie; *Nuggets-#10-Folk Rock-C* . . . . (Rhino)
Rock Artifacts-From The Vaults-#3-C . . . . (Columbia)
ST/Forrest Gump . . . . (Epic/Sony Music Soundtrax)
Summer Of Love-#1-C . . . . (Rhino)
San Francisco (You've Got Me)
Village People; *Billboard Top Dance Hits-1977-C* . . . . (Rhino)
Live & Sleazy . . . . (Casablanca)
Village People . . . . (Casablanca)
Village People's Greatest Hits . . . . (Rhino)
San Francisco Bay Blues
Eric Clapton; *Eric Clapton-Unplugged* . . . . (Reprise)
Janis Joplin; *ST/Janis* . . . . (Columbia)
Jesse Fuller; *Brother Lowdown* . . . . (Fantasy)
Great Blues Men-C . . . . (Vanguard)
San Francisco Bay Blues . . . . (Good Time Jazz)
Paul McCartney; *Unplugged (The Official Bootleg)* . . . . (Capitol)
Ramblin' Jack Elliott; *Bread & Roses Festival Of Acoustic*
Music-#1-C . . . . (Fantasy)
Essential Ramblin' Jack Elliott . . . . (Vanguard)
Hard Travelin' . . . . (Fantasy)
Troubadours Of The Folk Era-#1-C . . . . (Rhino)
San Francisco Blues
Quincy Jones; *P's & Q's* . . . . (Capitol)
San Francisco Days
Chris Isaak; *San Francisco Days* . . . . (Reprise)
San Francisco Fan
Cab Calloway; *Hi De Ho Man* . . . . (Columbia)
Joe Jackson; *Jumpin' Jive* . . . . (A&M)
San Francisco Girls
Fever Tree; *Best Of Fever Tree* . . . . (Bac-Trac)
Nuggets-#11-Pop-Part 4-C . . . . (Rhino)
Sixties Rule! Chapter 1-C . . . . (One Way)
San Francisco Holiday (Worry Later)
Thelonius Monk; *In Person* . . . . (Milestone)
San Francisco Is A Lonely Town
Orion; *Sunrise* . . . . (Sun)
San Francisco Mabel Joy
Joan Baez; *Country Music Album* . . . . (Vanguard)
John Denver; *Some Days Are Diamonds* . . . . (RCA)
Kenny Rogers; *The Gambler* . . . . (EMI)
Mickey Newbury; *Bread & Roses Festival Of Acoustic Music-#1-C* . . (Fantasy)
Heaven Help The Child . . . . (Elektra)
Live At Montezuma Hall . . . . (Elektra)
San Francisco Treat, The (Rice-A-Roni)
Original Soundtrack; *TeeVee Toons-The Commercials-#1-C* . . . . . . (TVT)
San Jose
Blind Snooks Eaglin; *Down Yonder (Snooks Eaglin Today)* . . . . . (Crescendo)
Santa Rosa
Gino Vannelli; *Nightwalker* . . . . (Arista)
Sausalito
Mark Murphy; *Bridging A Gap* . . . . (Muse)
September Ballads . . . . (Milestone)
Sausalito
Ashra; *Belle Alliance* . . . . (Blue Plate)
Sausalito
SOS All-Stars; *Greetings From New York* . . . . (Chase Music Group)
Sausalito
Grover Washington, Jr.; *Live At The Bijou* . . . . (Motown)
Sausalito Summernight
Diesel; *Watts In A Tank* . . . . (Regency/Atco)
Snow In San Anselmo
Van Morrison; *Hard Nose The Highway* . . . . (Polydor)

Song For Frisco
Quicksilver Messenger Service; *Quicksilver* . . . .(Capitol)
Streets Of San Francisco
Statler Brothers; *Carry Me Back* . . . .(Mercury)
Summer In San Francisco
Hendrik Meurkens; *Sambahia* . . . .(Concord Picante Jazz)
Theme From ''The Streets Of San Francisco''
Original Soundtrack; *Television's Greatest Hits-#3-1970s & 1980s-C* . . . .(TVT)
TV Cop Show Theme Songs . . . . (Laserlight)
Union Square
Cal Tjader; *San Francisco Moods* . . . . (Fantasy)
We Built This City
Starship; *Greatest Hits-Ten Years & Change-1979-1991* . . . . . . (RCA)
Knee Deep In The Hoopla . . . .(Grunt)
Nipper's Greatest Hits Of The '80s-C . . . . (RCA)

CITIES: SANTA FE

See Also: **AMERICAN WEST, COWBOYS, STATES: NEW MEXICO**

Along The Santa Fe Trail
Glenn Miller; *Original Live Recordings* . . . . (Pair)
Sons Of The Pioneers; *Sunset On The Range* . . . . (Pair)
Amarillo By Morning
George Strait; *George Strait's Greatest Hits* . . . . (MCA)
Strait From The Heart . . . . (MCA)
Back To Santa Fe
Cee Cee Chapman; *Twist Of Fate* . . . .(Curb)
Back To Santa Fe
Lee Hunter; *Texas Blues-Gold Star Sessions* . . . . (Arhoolie)
Blame It On Texas
Mark Chesnutt; *Mark Chesnutt's Greatest Hits* . . . .(Decca)
Too Cold At Home . . . . (MCA)
Girls Of Santa Fe
Bill Morrissey; *Standing Eight* . . . . (Philo)
Memories Of Old Santa Fe
Randy Travis; *Wind In The Wire* . . . . (Warner Bros.)
Midnight Flyer
Eagles; *On The Border* . . . . (Elektra)
Osborne Brothers; *Essential Bluegrass Album* . . . .(C.M.H. Prod.)
Osborne Brothers & Mac Wiseman; *Great American Train*
Songs-C . . . .(C.M.H. Prod.)
My One And Only Heart
Perry Como; *Sing Just For You* . . . . (RCA)
Over The Santa Fe Trail
Sons Of The Pioneers; *Empty Saddles* . . . . (MCA)
Tumbling Tumbleweeds . . . . (MCA Special Prod.)
Santa Fe
Little Brother Montgomery; *Tasty Blues* . . . . (Prestige)
Roosevelt Sykes & L. Brother Montgomery; *Urban Blues* . . . . . . (Fantasy)
Santa Fe
Bellamy Brothers; *Bellamy Brothers' Greatest Hits-#3* . . . . (MCA)
Crazy From The Heart . . . . (MCA)
Santa Fe
Bon Jovi; *Blaze Of Glory-ST/Young Guns II* . . . .(Mercury)
Santa Fe
Bob Dylan; *The Bootleg Series-Volumes 1-3 [Rare & Unreleased]* . .(Columbia)
Santa Fe Blues
Lightnin' Hopkins; *Nothin' But The Blues-Golden Classics-#4* . . .(Collectables)
Lil' Son Jackson; *Blues Come To Texas* . . . . (Arhoolie)
Pee Wee Hughes; *Sugar Mama Blues (1949)* . . . . (Biograph)
Santa Fe/Beautiful Obsession
Van Morrison; *Wavelength* . . . . (Warner Bros.)
South Of Santa Fe
Brooks & Dunn; *If You See Her* . . . .(Arista)
They Were Doin' The Mambo
Vaughn Monroe; *Very Best Of Vaughn Monroe* . . . . (Taragon)
Wild Horses
Garth Brooks; *No Fences* . . . .(Capitol)

CITIES: SAVANNAH

See Also: **STATES: GEORGIA**

One More Sunday In Savannah
Nina Simone; *The Tomato Collection* . . . . (Tomato)
Savannah
Gary Brooker; *No More Fear Of Flying* . . . . (Chrysalis)
Savannah
Tommy Wiggins; *Cool Saturdays* . . . . (Nouveau)
Savannah
Eternal Wind; *Eternal Wind* . . . . (Flying Fish)
Savannah
Kurt Riemann; *Gaia* . . . .(Nightwork)
Savannah Awakes
Barbra Streisand; *ST/Prince Of Tides* . . . .(Columbia)

Savannah Blues
Thomas ''Fats'' Waller; *Fats & His Buddies-1927-1929* . . . . (Bluebird)
Savannah Dance
Michael Pluznick; *Where The Rain Is Born* . . . . (Sona Gaia)
Savannah Mama
Blind Willie McTell; *Blind Willie McTell-Early Years-1927-1932* . . . . . (Yazoo)
Three Shades Of Blues-C . . . . (Biograph)
Blind Willie McTell & Memphis Minnie; *Love Changin' Blues* . . . . . (Biograph)
Paul Geremia; *My Kinda Place* . . . . (Flying Fish)
Savannah Nights
Tom Johnston; *Everything You've Heard Is True* . . . . (Warner Bros.)
Savannah Russet/Jete The Dancing Cat
Jeanne Newhall; *Novice* . . . . (Marzipan Music)
Savannah The Serene
Billy Cobham; *Crosswinds* . . . . (Atlantic)
Savannah Woman
Tommy Bolin; *Teaser* . . . . (Columbia)
Savannah Woman
Brother Noland; *Pacific Bad Boy* . . . . (Mountain Apple)
Sweet Savannah Sue
Fats Waller; *Turn On The Heat-Fats Waller Piano Solos* . . . . (Bluebird)
Louis Armstrong; *Louis Armstrong-Vol. 5-In New York* . . . . (Columbia)

CITIES: ST. LOUIS

See Also: **STATES: MISSOURI**

Dancing In St. Louis
Li'l Wally; *Here Comes Li'l Wally* . . . . (Jay Jay)
East St. Louis Toodle oo
Duke Ellington; *Bethlehem Years-#1* . . . . (Bethlehem)
Brunswick Era-#1-1926-1929 . . . . (MCA)
Era . . . . (Columbia)
Jazz Heritage-Beginning 1926-1928 . . . . (MCA)
Steely Dan; *Pretzel Logic* . . . . (MCA)
Steely Dan's Greatest Hits . . . . (MCA)
Going To St. Louis
Yank Rachell & Others; *Chicago Style* . . . . (Delmark)
Meet Me In St. Louis, Louis
Judy Garland; *Best Of Judy Garland* . . . . (MCA)
New East St. Louis Toodle-oo
Duke Ellington; *Reminiscing In Tempo* . . . . (Columbia)
New St. Louis Blues
Johnny Dodds; *South Side Chicago Jazz* . . . . (MCA)
Shim, Sham Shimmy On The St. Louis Blues
Dizzy Gillespie; *Best Of Dizzy Gillespie* . . . . (Pablo)
Spirits Of St. Louis
Johnny Paycheck; *Take This Job And Shove It* . . . . (Epic)
St. Louis Blues
Bessie Smith; *Beauty Of The Blues* . . . . (Columbia)
Bessie Smith-The Collection . . . . (Legacy)
Big Joe Turner; *Boss Of The Blues* . . . . (Atlantic)
Billie Holiday; *Quintessential-#9-1940-1942* . . . . (Columbia)
The Billie Holiday Story-#3 . . . . (Columbia)
Bob Wills & His Texas Playboys; *Bob Wills & His Texas Playboys-24
Great Hits* . . . . (Polydor)
Cleo Laine; *Jazz* . . . . (RCA)
Dave Brubeck Quartet; *25th Anniversary Reunion* . . . . (A&M)
Dave Brubeck Quartet-At Carnegie Hall . . . . (Columbia)
Paper Moon . . . . (Concord Jazz)
Duke Ellington; *1953 Pasadena Concert* . . . . (Crescendo)
Ella Fitzgerald; *These Are The Blues* . . . . (Verve)
Louis Armstrong; *At The Crescendo* . . . . (MCA)
Louis Armstrong-Legendary Performer . . . . (RCA)
Louis Armstrong-Vol. 6-St. Louis Blues . . . . (Columbia)
Nipper's Greatest Hits Of The '30s-#2-C . . . . (RCA)
Merle Haggard & Asleep At The Wheel; *Ride With
Bob-C* . . . . (DreamWorks/SKG)
Original Broadway Cast; *Black & Blue* . . . . (DRG)
Pete Fountain; *Best Of Pete Fountain* . . . . (MCA)
Preservation Hall Jazz Band; *Best Of The Preservation Hall
Jazz Band* . . . . (Columbia)
New Orleans-#2 . . . . (Columbia)
Stranded In St. Louis
Omar Sharif; *The Raven* . . . . (Arhoolie)
You Came A Long Way From St. Louis
Peggy Lee & George Shearing; *Beauty & The Beat!* . . . . (Blue Note)
Perry Como; *This Is Perry Como-#2* . . . . (RCA)

CITIES: T

See Also: **CITIES: GENERAL, CITIES: TOKYO, CITIES: TULSA,
COUNTRIES: A-Z, STATES: A-Z**

Battle Of Trenton
Jim Burroughs; *Songs Of Rebellion* . . . . (Audio Fidelity)

Boy From Tupelo
Emmylou Harris; *Red Dirt Girl* . . . . (Nonesuch)
Further It Is From Tipperary, The
Jack Norworth; *Music From The New York Stage (1890-1920)-#4-1917-
1920-C* . . . . (Pearl)
Get Back (Tucson)
Beatles; *Beatles 1* . . . . (Capitol)
Beatles-20 Greatest Hits . . . . (Capitol)
Beatles-Box Set . . . . (Capitol)
Let It Be . . . . (Capitol)
Past Masters-Volume Two . . . . (Parlophone)
Reel Music . . . . (Capitol)
Rock 'N' Roll Music . . . . (Capitol)
The Beatles/1967-1970 . . . . (Capitol)
Goin' Down To Tampa
Jeff Warner & Jeff Davis; *Wilder Joy-Traditional American Folk
Songs* . . . . (Flying Fish)
Going Back To Tampa
Roy Bookbinder; *Going Back To Tampa* . . . . (Flying Fish)
Old Tucson
Youssou N'Dour; *The Lion* . . . . (Virgin)
One's On The Way (Here In Topeka)
Loretta Lynn; *Loretta Lynn-20 Greatest Hits* . . . . (MCA)
Loretta Lynn-Greatest Hits Live . . . . (K-Tel)
Loretta Lynn's Greatest Hits-#2 . . . . (MCA)
The Country Music Hall Of Fame-Loretta Lynn . . . . (MCA)
Send Me Down To Tucson
Mel Tillis; *Very Best Of Mel Tillis* . . . . (MCA)
Tacoma Trailer
Leonard Cohen; *The Future* . . . . (Columbia)
Tallahassee
Country Gazette; *Hello Operator...This Is Country Gazette* . . . . . . (Flying Fish)
Tallahassee Lassie
Freddy Cannon; *14 Booming Hits* . . . . (Rhino)
Freddy Cannon-His Latest & Greatest . . . . (Critique)
Partytime '50s-C . . . . (Priority)
Tampico
Stan Kenton & June Christy; *Birth Of A Dream-Capitol's Early
Hits-C* . . . . (Capitol)
Tampico Trauma
Jimmy Buffett; *Boats Beaches Bars & Ballads* . . . . (Margaritaville)
Changes In Latitudes, Changes In Attitudes . . . . (MCA)
You Had To Be There . . . . (MCA)
Taos
Oregon; *Oregon* . . . . (ECM)
Taos To Tennessee
Tish Hinojosa; *Taos To Tennessee* . . . . (Watermelon)
Ten O'Clock In Toronto
Christine Lavin; *Compass* . . . . (Philo)
Texarkana
R.E.M.; *Out Of Time* . . . . (Warner Bros.)
Texarkana Baby
Billy Hardwick, Jr.; *Too Country* . . . . (JRS)
Eddy Arnold; *Eddy Arnold-Super Hits* . . . . (RCA)
Kenny Wayne; *Borned With The Blues & Raised On Rock* . . . . (Candy)
Thomasville
Stanley Turrentine; *More Than A Mood* . . . . (Musicmasters)
Tiburon
Stan Kenton & His Orchestra; *Kenton '76* . . . . (Creative World)
Tijuana
Memphis Slim; *Memphis Slim* . . . . (Chess)
Real Folk Blues-C . . . . (Chess)
Tijuana Jail
Gilby Clarke; *Pawnshop Guitars* . . . . (Virgin)
Kingston Trio; *25 Years Non-Stop* . . . . (Xeres)
Best Of The Kingston Trio . . . . (Capitol)
Capitol Collectors Series-The Kingston Trio . . . . (Capitol)
Kingston Trio's Greatest Hits . . . . (Curb)
Tijuana Moon
Tim Buckley; *Look At The Fool* . . . . (Bizarre/Straight)
Tijuana Sauerkraut
Herb Alpert & The Tijuana Brass; *Lonely Bull* . . . . (A&M)
Tijuana Taxi
Herb Alpert & The Tijuana Brass; *Four Sider* . . . . (A&M)
Herb Alpert & The Tijuana Brass' Greatest Hits . . . . (A&M)
Herb Alpert & The Tijuana Brass-Classics-#1 . . . . (A&M)
Tipperary Far Away
Clancy Brothers & Tommy Makem; *Irish Songs Of Drinking &
Rebellion* . . . . (Bescol, Ltd.)
Tipperary Town
Larry Cunningham; *Golden Irish Favorites* . . . . (Gateway)
Toledo
John Denver; *Evening With John Denver* . . . . (RCA)
Tomb Of The Unknown Love (Taos, New Mexico)
Cassell Webb; *Songs Of A Stranger* . . . . (Venture)
Kenny Rogers; *The Heart Of The Matter* . . . . (RCA)
Toronto
Lenny Breau; *Five O'Clock Bells* . . . . (Adelphi)

Toytown
Walking Wounded; *New West* . . . . (Charisma)
Toytown People
Fabulous Poodles; *Mirror Stars* . . . . (Epic)
Trenchtown Rock
Bob Marley & The Wailers; *Bob Marley & The Wailers-Live* . . . . . (Tuff Gong)
Confrontation . . . . (Tuff Gong)
More Of The Mighty . . . . (Tuff Gong)
Songs Of Freedom . . . . (Tuff Gong)
Tucson, Arizona
Dan Fogelberg; *Windows & Walls* . . . . (Full Moon)
Tupelo
John Lee Hooker; *Best Of John Lee Hooker* . . . . (Crescendo)
Great Bluesmen At Newport-C . . . . (Vanguard)
Steve Cropper/Albert King/Pops Staples; *The Stax Blues Brothers-C* . . . . (Stax)
Subdudes; *Subdudes* . . . . (Atlantic)
Tupelo County Jail
Mel Tillis; *American Originals-Mel Tillis* . . . . (Columbia)
Webb Pierce; *Webb Pierce-Golden Hits* . . . . (Plantation)
Tupelo Honey
Van Morrison; *Van Morrison* . . . . (Warner Bros.)
Tupelo Mississippi Flash
Jerry Reed; *Best Of Jerry Reed* . . . . (RCA)
Wild Goose Grasses In Tarrytown
Weavers; *Weavers' Greatest Hits* . . . . (Vanguard)
Weavers-Classics . . . . (Vanguard)

CITIES: TOKYO

See Also: COUNTRIES: JAPAN

All Right Tokyo!!
Adrenalin O.D.; *Ishtar* . . . . (Restless)
Calling From Tokyo
Ryuichi Sakamoto; *Beauty* . . . . (Virgin)
Love From Tokyo
Rita Coolidge; *Rita Coolidge-Classics-#5* . . . . (A&M)
Midnight In Tokyo
Y & T; *Best Of '81 To '85* . . . . (A&M)
Mean Streak . . . . (A&M)
Yesterday & Today Live . . . . (Metal Blade)
Rainy Night In Tokyo
Michael Franks; *Passionfruit* . . . . (Warner Bros.)
Storm Over Tokyo Bay
Jessie Allen Cooper; *Soft Wave* . . . . (Sona Gaia)
Tokyo
Brothers Johnson; *Brothers Johnson-Classics-#11* . . . . (A&M)
Tokyo
10 CC; *Bloody Tourists* . . . . (Polydor)
Tokyo
Bruce Cockburn; *Humans* . . . . (Columbia)
Tokyo
Donna Summer; *She Works Hard For The Money* . . . . (Mercury)
Tokyo Joe
Bryan Ferry; *In Your Mind* . . . . (Reprise)
Tokyo Nights
Bee Gees; *One* . . . . (Warner Bros.)
Tokyo Nights
Rob Mullins; *Tokyo Nights* . . . . (Nova)
Tokyo Road
Bon Jovi; *7800 Degrees Fahrenheit* . . . . (Mercury)
Tokyo Rose
Van Dyke Parks; *Tokyo Rose* . . . . (Warner Bros.)
Tokyo Rose
Shok Paris; *Steel & Starlight* . . . . (I.R.S.)
Tokyo Storm Warning
Elvis Costello; *Girls Girls Girls* . . . . (Columbia)
Elvis Costello & The Attractions; *Blood & Chocolate* . . . . (Columbia)
Tokyo, Oklahoma
John Anderson; *John Anderson's Greatest Hits-#2* . . . . (Warner Bros.)
Vacation In Tokyo
Urge Overkill; *Supersonic Storybook* . . . . (Touch & Go)
When It's Cherry Time In Tokio
James P. Johnson; *Rare Piano Roll Solos-#2-1917* . . . . (Biograph)
Woman From Tokyo
Deep Purple; *Deepest Purple/The Very Best Of Deep Purple* . . . . (Warner Bros.)
Nobody's Perfect . . . . (Mercury)
When We Rock We Rock & When We Roll We Roll . . . . (Warner Bros.)
Who Do You Think We Are . . . . (Warner Bros.)

CITIES: TULSA

See Also: STATES: OKLAHOMA

24 Hours From Tulsa
Gene Pitney; *45-#3015* . . . . (Collectables)

Double Gold-Gene Pitney . . . . (Mustcor)
Ian & Sylvia; *Best Of Ian & Sylvia* . . . . (Vanguard)
Ian & Sylvia's Greatest Hits . . . . (Vanguard)
Play One More . . . . (Vanguard)
Almost Of Tulsa
Red Rhodes; *Steel Guitar Favorites* . . . . (Alshire)
Big Tulsa Tillie
Donnie Rohrs; *Country Music USA* . . . . (Pacific Challenger)
Day That She Left Tulsa (In A Chevy)
Wade Hayes; *When The Wrong One Loves You Right* . . . . (Columbia/DKC)
Last Trip To Tulsa
Neil Young; *Neil Young* . . . . (Reprise)
Take Me Back To Tulsa
Asleep At The Wheel; *Route 66* . . . . (Liberty)
Very Best Of Asleep At The Wheel Since 1970 . . . . (Relentless/Macady)
Bob Wills & His Texas Playboys; *All Time Legends Of Country*
Music-C . . . . (Legacy)
Bob Wills-Anthology . . . . (Sony Music Special Prod.)
Columbia Country Classics-#1-Golden Age-C . . . . (Columbia)
Tiffany Transcriptions-#2-Best Of The Tiffanys . . . . (Rhino)
Clay Walker & Asleep At The Wheel; *Ride With Bob-C* . . . (DreamWorks/SKG)
Tulsa (Don't Let The Sun Set On You)
Waylon Jennings; *Taker/Tulsa & Honky Tonk*
Heroes . . . . (Mobile Fidelity Sound Lab)
Tulsa County
Byrds; *The Byrds* . . . . (Columbia)
Tulsa Queen
Emmylou Harris; *Luxury Liner* . . . . (Warner Bros.)
T-U-L-S-A Straight Ahead
Asleep At The Wheel; *Asleep At The Wheel-10* . . . . (Epic)
Swinging Best Of Asleep At The Wheel . . . . (Epic)
Texas Playboys; *Texas Playboys Today* . . . . (Capitol)
Tulsa Time
Don Williams; *Best Of Don Williams-#2* . . . . (MCA)
Country's Greatest Hits-#6-Superstars-C . . . . (Priority)
Don Williams-Legends . . . . (MCA)
Expressions . . . . (MCA)
Eric Clapton; *Backless* . . . . (Polydor)
Just One Night . . . . (Polydor)
Tulsa Turnaround
Kenny Rogers And The First Edition; *Country Songs* . . . . . (MCA Special Prod.)
Kenny Rogers And The First Edition's All-Time Greatest
Hits-#2 . . . . (MCA Special Prod.)
Twenty-Four Hours From Tulsa
Burt Bacharach; *Walk On By* . . . . (MCA Special Prod.)
Gene Pitney; *Best Of Gene Pitney* . . . . (K-Tel)

CITIES: U

See Also: CITIES: GENERAL, COUNTRIES: A-Z, STATES: A-Z

Ukiah
Doobie Brothers; *Captain & Me* . . . . (Warner Bros.)

CITIES: V

See Also: CITIES: GENERAL, CITIES: VIENNA, COUNTRIES: A-Z, STATES: A-Z

Bobby's In Vicksburg
Sylvia; *Snapshot* . . . . (RCA)
Carnival Of Venice
Carmen Cavallaro; *Best Of Carmen Cavallaro* . . . . (MCA)
Mantovani; *Mantovani's Italia* . . . . (Bainbridge)
Moon Over Venice
Thom Rotella; *Home Again* . . . . (Digital Music Prod.)
Send Me Down To Vicksburg
John Mayall's Bluesbreakers; *Sense Of Place* . . . . (Island)
Valdosta Blues
Larry Willis; *Steal Away* . . . . (Audioquest)
Van Nuys Jam
Alex Acuna & The Unknowns; *Alex Acuna & The*
Unknowns . . . . (JVC Musical Industries)
Vancouver
Andrew Calhoun; *Gates Of Love* . . . . (Flying Fish)
Vancouver Shakedown
Nazareth; *Close Enough For Rock 'N' Roll* . . . . (A&M)
Hot Tracks . . . . (A&M)
Venice
Love Tractor; *Themes From Venus* . . . . (DB)
Modern Jazz Quartet; *One Never Knows* . . . . (Atlantic)
Venice Blue
Bobby Darin; *Capitol Collectors Series-Bobby Darin* . . . . (Capitol)
Venice Drowning
Duran Duran; *Liberty* . . . . (Capitol)

Venice U.S.A.
Van Morrison; *Wavelength*. . . . .(Warner Bros.)
Vera Cruz
Warren Zevon; *Excitable Boy*. . . . . (Asylum)
Vicksburg Blues
Little Brother Montgomery; *Atlantic Blues-Piano-C* . . . .(Atlantic)
Tasty Blues. . . . . (Prestige)
We Open In Venice
Original Cast; *Kiss Me Kate* . . . .(MCA)

CITIES: VIENNA
See Also: COUNTRIES: A

Ballad Of John And Yoko
Beatles; *Beatles 1* . . . . (Capitol)
Beatles-Box Set . . . . (Capitol)
Hey Jude . . . . (Capitol)
Past Masters-Volume Two . . . . (Parlophone)
ST/Imagine: John Lennon . . . . (Capitol)
The Beatles/1967-1970 . . . . (Capitol)
Do You Ever Dream Of Vienna
Original Cast; *Little Mary Sunshine* . . . . (Out Of Print)
Goodnight Vienna
Ringo Starr; *Goodnight Vienna* . . . . (Capitol)
Non-Viennese Waltz Blues
Joe Gordon; *Lookin' Good!* . . . .(Contemporary)
One Night In Vienna
Schoenerz & Scott; *One Night In Vienna* . . . . (Windham Hill)
Summer In Vienna
Mantovani; *Mantovani-Golden Hits*. (London)
Tales From The Vienna Woods
101 Strings Orchestra; *Best Of Johann Strauss, Jr.*. . . . . (Alshire)
Lawrence Welk; *22 Great Waltzes* . . . .(Ranwood)
Third Man Theme (Harry Lime Theme)
Band; *Moondog Matinee* . . . . (Capitol)
Dukes Of Dixieland; *Dukes Of Dixieland's Greatest Hits* . . . .(MCA)
Guy Lombardo & His Royal Canadians; *Best Of Guy Lombardo* . . . . (Curb)
Vienna
Ultravox; *If I Was-Very Best Of Midge Ure &* . . . .(Chrysalis)
Ultravox-Collection. . . . .(Chrysalis)
Vienna . . . .(Chrysalis)
Vienna
Billy Joel; *The Stranger* . . . . (Columbia)
Vienna
Rippingtons; *Weekend in Monaco* . . . . (GRP)
Vienna Calling
Falco; *Falco 3* . . . . (A&M)
Remix Hit Collection . . . . (Sire)
Vienna Echoes
Lawrence Welk; *Lawrence Welk Celebrates 50 Years In Music*. . . . .(Ranwood)
Vienna Life
Lawrence Welk; *22 All-Time Favorite Waltzes* . . . .(Ranwood)

CITIES: W
See Also: CITIES: GENERAL, COUNTRIES: A-Z, STATES: A-Z

"Way" Cross Georgia
David Sanborn; *Takin' Off* . . . .(Warner Bros.)
As Falls Wichita, So Falls Wichita Falls
Pat Metheny & Lyle Mays; *As Falls Wichita, So Falls Wichita Falls* . . . . .(ECM)
Big Noise From Winnetka
Bette Midler; *Divine Madness* . . . . (Atlantic)
Thighs And Whispers . . . . (Atlantic)
Bob Crosby & His Bob Cats; *Best Of Bob Crosby & His Bob Cats* . . . . . .(MCA)
Bob Crosby & His Orchestra; *Bob Crosby & His Orchestra Play 22 Original
Big Band Hits* . . . .(Hindsight)
Cross The Brazos At Waco
Billy Walker; *Columbia Country Classics-#3-Americana-C* . . . . (Columbia)
Super Country Hits Of The '60s-C . . . . (Gusto)
Goin' To D.C.
Sonny Stitt; *Soul Classics* . . . .(Prestige)
Guerrilla Radio (Washington, D.C.)
Rage Against The Machine; *The Battle Of Los Angeles* . . . .(Epic)
Hail Wichita
Wichita State University Marching Band; *Wichita State University
Marching Band* . . . .(Fidelity Sound)
Jack Straw (Wichita)
Bruce Hornsby & The Range; *Deadicated-C* . . . . (Arista)
Grateful Dead; *Europe '72* . . . .(Warner Bros.)
*What A Long Strange Trip It's Been: The Best Of The
Grateful Dead* . . . .(Warner Bros.)
Not Being In Warsaw
Colin Newman; *It Seems*. . . . .(Restless)

Nothing As Original As You (Washington, D.C.)
Statler Brothers; *The Originals* . . . . (Mercury)
Pearl From Warsaw
Klezmer Conservatory Band; *Jumpin' Night In The Garden
Of Eden* . . . . (Rounder)
Warsaw
Joy Division; *Substance* . . . .(Qwest)
Warsaw 1943 (I Never Betrayed The Revolution)
Johnny Clegg & Savuka; *Cruel, Crazy, Beautiful World* . . . . (Capitol)
Warsaw Concerto
Roger Williams; *Moments To Remember* . . . . (MCA Special Prod.)
Washington Bullets
Clash; *On Broadway* . . . . (Epic)
Sandinista . . . . (Epic)
Washington March/Waiting For Nancy
Bertram Levy; *That Old Gut Feeling* . . . .(Flying Fish)
Washington Post
John Philip Sousa; *The March King: John Philip Sousa Conducts His Own
Marches And Other Favorites* . . . . (Legacy International)
Mormon Tabernacle Choir; *Stars And Stripes Forever! The Mormon
Tabernacle Choir Sings March Favorites And College
Songs* . . . .(Sony Music Classical)
Washington We're Watching You
Staple Singers; *45-#1060* . . . . (Stax)
Washington, D.C.
Magnetic Fields; *69 Love Songs-#2*. . . . .(Merge)
Washington, D.C. Hospital Center Blues
Skip James; *Greatest Of The Delta Blues Singers* . . . .(Biograph)
Skip James Today . . . . (Vanguard)
Waterloo
Stonewall Jackson; *American Originals-Stonewall Jackson*. . . . . . . (Columbia)
Billboard Top Country Hits-1959-C. . . . . (Rhino)
Columbia Country Classics-#3-Americana-C . . . . (Columbia)
Country Music Classics-#1-1950s-C . . . . (K-Tel)
Waterloo
Abba; *Abba's Greatest Hits*. . . . .(Atlantic)
Waterloo. . . . .(Atlantic)
Waterloo Sunset
Kinks; *Kink Kronikles* . . . .(Reprise)
Something Else . . . .(Reprise)
Wichita
Peter Buffett; *Yonnondio* . . . . (Narada)
Wichita
Jayhawks; *Hollywood Town Hall* . . . .(Def American)
Wichita Cross Winds
John Stewart; *Centennial* . . . . (Homecoming)
Wichita Jail
Charlie Daniels Band; *Banded Together-C* . . . . (Epic)
Saddle Tramp . . . . (Epic)
Wichita Lineman
Dwight Yoakam; *Under The Covers* . . . .(Reprise)
Glen Campbell; *Best Of Glen Campbell* . . . . (Capitol)
Country Music Classics-#3-1965-1970-C . . . . (K-Tel)
Glen Campbell-Classics Collection . . . . (Capitol)
Glen Campbell-Live . . . . (Capitol)
Glen Campbell's Greatest Hits. . . . . (Capitol)
Jimmy Webb Collection . . . . (Columbia)
Winnipeg
Tom Russell; *Hurricane Season* . . . .(Philo)
Winter In Winnipeg
Rob McConnell & His Boss Brass; *Brass Is Back*. . . . . (Concord Jazz)
Woodstock
Crosby, Stills & Nash; *CSN*. . . . .(Atlantic)
Crosby, Stills, Nash & Young; *Deja Vu* . . . .(Atlantic)
So Far. . . . .(Atlantic)
Joni Mitchell; *Ladies Of The Canyon* . . . .(Reprise)
Shadows & Light . . . .(Asylum)
Joni Mitchell with Tom Scott & The L.A. Express; *Miles Of Aisles* . . . .(Asylum)

CITIES: Y
See Also: CITIES: GENERAL, COUNTRIES: A-Z, STATES: A-Z

Youngstown
Bruce Springsteen; *The Ghost Of Tom Joad* . . . . (Columbia)

CLEAN, Laundry, Soap, Wash
See Also: BATHROOMS, DIRT, TRASH

(I Was Born In A) Laundromat
Camper Van Beethoven; *Key Lime Pie* . . . .(Virgin)
All Night Laundromat Blues
Joe Walsh; *So What* . . . .(MCA)

All Washed Up
Urge; *Receiving The Gift Of Flavor*. . . . . (Immortal/Epic)
Brainwash
Rick Danko; *Rick Danko* . . . . (Arista)
Brainwash
Telex; *Sex* . . . . (PVC)
Brainwashed
Kinks; *Arthur Or The Decline And Fall Of The British Empire* . . . .(Reprise)
Everybody's In Show-Biz . . . . (Rhino)
Brainwashed
Nuclear Assault; *Survive* . . . . (I.R.S.)
Buddle-Uddle-Um-Dum (The Washing Song)
Original Cast; *Walt Disney's Snow White And The Seven Dwarfs-Classic
Soundtrack Series* . . . . (Disney)
Car Wash
Rose Royce; *Best Of Rose Royce* . . . . (Omni)
Billboard Top Hits-1977-C. . . . . (Rhino)
Rose Royce's Greatest Hits. . . . . (Whitfield)
The Disco Years-#1-Turn The Beat Around-1974-1978-C. . . . .(Rhino)
Car Wash
Bruce Springsteen; *Tracks*. . . . . (Columbia)
Clean
Depeche Mode; *Violator* . . . .(Sire)
Clean Break
Verve Pipe; *I've Suffered A Head Injury* . . . . (RCA)
Clean Heart
Sade; *Stronger Than Pride* . . . . (Epic)
Clean My Wounds
Corrosion Of Conformity; *Deliverance*. . . . .(Columbia)
Clean Steve
Robyn Hitchcock; *Eye*. . . . . (Rhino)
Clean Up Woman
Betty Wright; *Atlantic Rhythm & Blues 1947-1974-#6 (1966-
1969)-C* . . . . (Atlantic)
Betty Wright Live . . . . (Atlantic)
Golden Classics-Betty Wright. . . . . (Collectables)
Soul Years-C. . . . . (Atlantic)
Clean Up Your Own Backyard
Elvis Presley; *Elvis' Gold Records, Volume 5* . . . .(RCA)
Cleaning Windows
Van Morrison; *Beautiful Vision*. . . . . (Warner Bros.)
Best Of Van Morrison . . . . (Polydor)
Cleanse The Soul
Slayer; *South Of Heaven* . . . . (American)
Cleansed By Fire
Alice Cooper; *Last Temptation* . . . . (Epic)
Cleanup Time
John Lennon; *Double Fantasy*. . . . . (Capitol)
Coming Clean
Green Day; *Dookie* . . . . (Reprise)
Definitely Clean
Dream Syndicate; *Days Of Wine & Roses* . . . . (Slash)
Dirty Laundry
Don Henley; *I Can't Stand Still* . . . . (Asylum)
Do It Clean
Echo & The Bunnymen; *Crocodiles* . . . .(Sire)
Dreams
Corrs; *Legacy-A Tribute To Fleetwood Mac's Rumours-C* . . . .(Lava)
Fleetwood Mac; *25 Years-The Chain* . . . . (Warner Bros.)
Fleetwood Mac Live . . . . (Warner Bros.)
Fleetwood Mac's Greatest Hits. . . . . (Warner Bros.)
Rumours . . . . (Warner Bros.)
Dry Cleaner From Des Moines
Joni Mitchell; *Mingus* . . . . (Elektra)
Shadows & Light. . . . . (Asylum)
Dust My Broom
Canned Heat; *Uncanned!-Best Of
Canned Heat* . . . . (EMI Legends Of Rock 'N' Roll)
Elmore James; *Best Blues Album In The World...Ever!-C*. . . . .(Virgin)
Elmore James-Complete Fire & Enjoy Sessions-#1 . . . . (Collectables)
King Of The Slide Guitar . . . . (Capricorn)
Ike & Tina Turner; *Bold Soul Sister-Best Of The Blue Thumb
Recordings* . . . . (Hip-O)
Robert Johnson; *King Of The Delta Blues Singers-#2* . . . . (Columbia)
ZZ Top; *Deguello* . . . . (Warner Bros.)
Good Clean Fun
Allman Brothers Band; *Seven Turns* . . . . (Epic)
Good Clean Fun
Monkees; *Present* . . . . (Rhino)
I Use The Soap
Bread; *Bread-Retrospective* . . . . (Rhino)
I Washed My Hands In Muddy Water
Elvis Presley; *Elvis Country ("I'm 10,000 Years Old")* . . . .(RCA)
If The Washing Don't Get You, The Rinsing Will
Albert King; *Years Gone By* . . . . (Stax)
I'm Gonna Wash That Man Right Outta My Hair
Mitzi Gaynor; *ST/South Pacific*. (RCA)
Original Cast; *South Pacific*. . . . . (CBS Masterworks)

**Weather Girls; *Success*. . . . . (Columbia)
It's In The Book (Parts 1 & 2)
Johnny Standley; *Dr. Demento Gooses Mother-C* . . . . (Kid Rhino/Rhino 4 Kids)
Laundromat Blues
Albert King; *Masterworks* . . . . (Atlantic)
Laundromat Monday
Joe Jackson; *ST/Mike's Murder* . . . .(A&M)
Laundromat Song
Dead Milkmen; *Big Lizard In My Backyard*. . . . . (Restless)
Laundry Man
Fenton Robinson; *Genuine Houserockin' Music-C* . . . . (Alligator)
Nightflight . . . . (Alligator)
Leader Of The Laundromat
Detergents; *Silly Songs-C*. . . . . (K-Tel)
Lick Your Fingers Clean
Jethro Tull; *20 Years Of Jethro Tull* . . . . (Chrysalis)
Little Bit Of Soap
Jarmels; *Collectables Presents The History Of Rock-#7-C* . . . . . .(Collectables)
Jarmels-Golden Classics. . . . . (Collectables)
Laurie Golden Oldies . . . . (Laurie)
Million-Dollar Memories #1-C . . . . (RCA)
Pick Hits Of The Radio Good Guys-C . . . . (Laurie)
Paul Davis; *Best Of Paul Davis* . . . . (Bang)
Little Bit Of Paul Davis . . . . (Bang)
Monkey Wash Donkey Rinse
Warren Zevon; *Mutineer* . . . . (Giant)
Mr. Clean
Frank Zappa; *Cucamonga* . . . .(Del Fi)
Mr. Clean, Mr. Clean
Original Soundtrack; *TeeVee Toons-The Commercials-#1-C* . . . .(TVT)
No Can Do
Mark Knopfler; *Golden Heart* . . . . (Warner Bros.)
Oh Fab, I'm Glad (Fab Laundry Detergent)
Original Soundtrack; *TeeVee Toons-The Commercials-#1-C* . . . .(TVT)
Oh Happy Day
Edwin Hawkins Singers; *Didn't It Blow Your Mind: Soul Hits Of The
'70s-#1-C*. . . . .(Rhino)
Super Hits-#3-C . . . . (Gusto)
Five Satins; *Five Satins Sing Their Greatest Hits*. . . . .(Collectables)
Peace Tonight
Indigo Girls; *Come On Now Social* . . . . (Epic)
Pills And Soap
Elvis Costello & The Attractions; *Punch The Clock* . . . . (Rykodisc)
Rag Mop
Ames Brothers; *Best Of The Ames Brothers*. . . . . (Pair)
Reality Whitewash
Crass; *Christ: The Album/Well Forked But Not Dead* . . . . (Crass)
See That My Grave Is Kept Clean
Blind Lemon Jefferson; *Blind Lemon Jefferson-Vol. 1-1926-1929* . . . (Biograph)
Bob Dylan; *Bob Dylan* . . . .(Columbia)
The Times They Are A-Changin' . . . .(Columbia)
Dream Syndicate; *Ghost Stories*. . . . . (Restless)
So Fresh, So Clean
Outkast; *Stankonia* . . . . (LaFace/Arista)
Totally Hits 2001-C. . . . .(Arista)
Soap Box Preacher
Robbie Robertson; *Storyville* . . . . (Geffen)
Soap Star Joe
Liz Phair; *Exile In Guyville* . . . .(Matador)
Soapbox Opera
Supertramp; *Crisis? What Crisis?* . . . .(A&M)
Stronger Than Dirt (Ajax)
Original Soundtrack; *TeeVee Toons-The Commercials-#1-C* . . . .(TVT)
Theme From "Mr. Belvedere" (According To Our New Arrivals)
Leon Redbone; *Television's Greatest Hits-#6-Remote Control-C* . . . .(TVT)
Theme From "The Odd Couple"
Original Soundtrack; *Television's Greatest Hits-#7-Cable Ready-C* . . . . .(TVT)
Trouble In Paradise
Bruce Springsteen; *Tracks* . . . .(Columbia)
Unwashed & Somewhat Slightly Dazed
David Bowie; *Space Oddity* . . . . (Rykodisc)
Use Ajax The Foaming Cleanser
Original Soundtrack; *TeeVee Toons-The Commercials-#1-C* . . . .(TVT)
Wash
Pearl Jam; *Live 9/5/2000-Pittsburgh, PA* . . . .(Epic)
Wash It Away
Black Lab; *Your Body Above Me* . . . . (David Geffen Co.)
Wash Me Clean
k.d. lang; *Ingenue*. . . . . (Sire)
Wash 'n Dry (There's A Cat In The Dryer)
Loudmouths; *Loudmouths*. . . . .(New Red Archives)
Washed Away
Tom Cochrane; *Mad Mad World* . . . .(Capitol)
Washing Machine
Sonic Youth; *Washing Machine*. . . . . (David Geffen Co.)
Washing Of The Water
Peter Gabriel; *Us* . . . . (Geffen)

White, Clean And Neat
Robert Plant; *Now And Zen* ....(Es Paranza)
Whitewash
Gin Blossoms; *Congratulations I'm Sorry* .... (A&M)
Workin' At The Car Wash Blues
Jim Croce; *50th Anniversary Collection* ....(Saja)
Greatest Character Songs .... (Lifesong)
I Got A Name .... (Lifesong)
Photographs & Memories/His Greatest Hits ....(Atlantic)

CLIMBING, Ladders, Stairs

See Also: ***DISTANCE, MOTIVATION, MOUNTAINS, TRAVELING***

Ain't No Mountain High Enough
Diana Ross; *20/20-C* .... (Motown)
25 #1 Hits From 25 Years-C .... (Motown)
Diana Ross .... (Motown)
Diana Ross-The Ultimate Collection .... (Motown)
Every Great Motown Song-First 25 Years-C .... (Motown)
Greatest Songs By Ashford & Simpson .... (Motown)
Motown Legends-Diana Ross .... (Motown)
Motown Story-First 25 Years-C .... (Motown)
Motown's Biggest Pop Hits-C .... (Motown)
TV ST/Diana-C .... (Motown)
Marvin Gaye & Tammi Terrell; *20 Greatest Songs In Motown History-C* .... (Motown)
Classic Duets-Marvin Gaye & His Women-C .... (Motown)
Marvin Gaye & Tammi Terrell's Greatest Hits .... (Motown)
Marvin Gaye Live At The London Palladium .... (Motown)
Motown Grammy R&B Performances Of The '60s & '70s-C .... (Motown)
Performances Of The '60s & '70s-C .... (Motown)
United .... (Motown)
Climb Ev'ry Mountain
Mormon Tabernacle Choir; *Climb Ev'ry Mountain* .... (Columbia)
Original Cast/Mary Martin; *The Sound Of Music* ....(Sony Broadway)
Trapp Family Singers; *The Sound Of Music* ....(Warner Bros.)
Climb That Hill
Tom Petty And The Heartbreakers; *ST/She's The One* ....(Warner Bros.)
I'll Build A Stairway To Paradise
George Gershwin; *Manhattan* .... (Klavier)
Issy Van Randwyck; *Glory Of Gershwin Featuring Larry Adler-C* ... (Mercury)
Liza Minnelli; *Fascinatin' Rhythm-Capitol Sings Gershwin-C* .... (Capitol)
Itsy Bitsy Spider, The
Original Soundtrack; *Mother Goose Songs* ....(Madacy)
Jacob's Ladder
Rush; *Exit...Stage Left* .... (Mercury)
Permanent Waves .... (Mercury)
Jacob's Ladder
Mark Wills; *Mark Wills* .... (Mercury)
Jacob's Ladder
Huey Lewis and the News; *Fore!* ....(Chrysalis)
Jacob's Ladder
Bruce Hornsby & The Range; *Scenes From The Southside* .... (RCA)
Just To Hear You Say That You Love Me
Faith Hill & Tim McGraw; *Faith* ....(Warner Bros.)
Ladder
Joan Osborne; *Lilith Fair-A Celebration Of Women In Music-C* .... (Arista)
Relish .... (Blue Gorilla/Mercury)
No Place That Far
Sara Evans; *No Place That Far* .... (RCA)
Reach
Gloria Estefan; *Destiny* ....(Epic)
Room At The Top Of The Stairs
David Grisman; *Retrograss* .... (Acoustic Disc)
Leo Kottke; *Leo Kottke-Live* .... (Private Music)
Peculiaroso .... (Private Music)
Stanley Brothers & The Clinch Mountain Boys; *Ralph Stanley-50th Anniversary* ....(Rebel)
Stella Parton; *Stella Parton-Anthology* .... (Renaissance)
Stairway To Heaven
O'Jays; *Family Reunion* .... (Philadelphia Int'l)
O'Jays' Greatest Hits .... (Philadelphia Int'l)
O'Jays-Collector's Item .... (Philadelphia Int'l)
Stairway To Heaven
Led Zeppelin; *Led Zeppelin IV* ....(Atlantic)
Led Zeppelin-Box Set ....(Atlantic)
Remasters ....(Atlantic)
ST/The Song Remains The Same .... (Swan Song)
Stanley Jordan; *Best Of Stanley Jordan* .... (Blue Note)
Flying Home ....(EMI)
Stairway To Heaven
Neil Sedaka; *Neil Sedaka Sings His Greatest Hits* .... (RCA)
Neil Sedaka's All-Time Greatest Hits .... (RCA)
Stairway To The Stars
Ella Fitzgerald; *Best Of Ella Fitzgerald* ....(MCA)
Ella Fitzgerald In Hollywood .... (Verve)
Glenn Miller & Ray Eberle; *Chattanooga Choo Choo-#1 Hits* .... (Bluebird)
Memorial-1944-1969 .... (Bluebird)
Milt Jackson & Wes Montgomery; *Bags Meets Wes!* .... (Riverside)
Stairway To The Stars
Blue Oyster Cult; *Blue Oyster Cult* .... (Columbia)
To Be Loved By You
Wynonna; *Revelations* .... (Curb/MCA)
Wynonna-Collection .... (Curb)
Tonight I Climbed The Wall
Alan Jackson; *A Lot About Livin' (And A Little 'Bout Love)* .... (Arista)
Wolverton Mountain
Claude King; *American Originals-Claude King* .... (Columbia)
Best Of Claude King .... (Gusto)
Billboard Top Country Hits-1962-C .... (Rhino)
Super Hits Of The '60s-C .... (Epic)

CLOTHES, Blue Jeans, Fashion, Swimsuits

See Also: ***CLEAN (laundry), FABRICS, HATS, RIBBONS, SHOES, SHOPPING***

Absolutely (Story Of A Girl)
Nine Days; *Maddening Crowd* ....(550 Music)
Now That's What I Call Music!-#5-C ....(Virgin)
Alice Blue Gown
Edith Day; *Music From The New York Stage (1890-1920)-#4-1917-1920-C* .... (Pearl)
Nipper's Greatest Hits Of The '20s-C .... (RCA)
All Dressed Up & Lonely
Jim Reeves; *Touch Of Velvet* .... (RCA)
Ants In My Pants
Bo Carter; *Rare Blues Of The Twenties-1927-1930-C* .... (Historical)
Baby Don't You Tear My Clothes
Lightnin' Hopkins; *Lost Texas Tapes-#4* .... (Collectables)
Baby Makes Her Blue Jeans Talk
Dr. Hook; *Players In The Dark* .... (Casablanca)
Baby's Got Her Blue Jeans On
Mel McDaniel; *All-Time Country Classics-#2-C* .... (Capitol)
Let It Roll .... (Capitol)
Mel McDaniel's Greatest Hits .... (Capitol)
Bandit In A Bathing Suit
David Bromberg; *Bandit In A Bathing Suit* .... (Fantasy)
Baubles, Bangles And Beads
Frank Sinatra & Antonio Carlos Jobim; *Francis Albert Sinatra & Antonio Carlos Jobim* .... (Reprise)
Marlene Dietrich; *Marlene Dietrich-Live* .... (Columbia)
Original Cast; *Kismet* .... (Columbia)
Peggy Lee; *Best Of Peggy Lee* .... (MCA)
Percy Faith & His Orchestra; *Percy Faith & His Orchestra's All-Time Greatest Hits* .... (Columbia)
Beggar In Blue Jeans
Rowans; *Rowans* .... (Asylum)
Bell Bottom Blues
Derek And The Dominos; *Layla* .... (Polydor)
Eric Clapton; *24 Nights* .... (Duck/Reprise)
Bell Bottom Pants
Loudon Wainwright III; *Attempted Mustache* .... (Legacy)
Between Blue Eyes And Jeans
Conway Twitty; *Don't Call Him A Cowboy* .... (Warner Bros.)
Bikini Girls With Machine Guns
Cramps; *Stay Sick!* .... (Enigma Capitol)
Birthday Suit
Johnny Kemp; *ST/Sing* .... (Columbia)
Black Denim Trousers & Motorcycle Boots
Cheers; *Monster Summer Hits-Drag City-C* .... (Capitol)
Black Slacks
Joe Bennett; *Vintage Music-#16-C* .... (MCA)
Robert Gordon; *Rock Billy Boogie* .... (RCA)
Sparkletones; *Black Slacks* .... (MCA)
Blue Collar
Bachman-Turner Overdrive; *Best Of B.T.O.-So Far* .... (Mercury)
Blue Collar Man
Styx; *Caught In The Act* .... (A&M)
Pieces Of Eight .... (A&M)
Styx-Classics-#15 .... (A&M)
Blue Jean Blues
Hank Williams, Jr.; *Strong Stuff* .... (Warner Bros.)
ZZ Top; *Best Of ZZ Top* .... (Warner Bros.)
Fandango .... (Warner Bros.)
Six Pack .... (Warner Bros.)
Blue Jean Boy
Michael Stanley Band; *Ladies' Choice* .... (Epic)
Blue Jeans
Chocolate Milk; *Greatest Grooves Of Chocolate Milk-Ice Cold Funk* .... (Razor & Tie)
Blue Skirt Waltz
Frankie Yankovic & His Yanks; *Frankie Yankovic & His Yanks' Greatest Hits* .... (Columbia)

Mom & Dads; *Best Of The Mom & Dads*. (Crescendo)
Blue Canadian Rockies. . . . . (Crescendo)

Blue Velvet
Bobby Vinton; *Bobby Vinton-16 Most Requested Songs*. . . . . (Legacy)
Bobby Vinton's All-Time Greatest Hits. . . . . (Epic)
Bobby Vinton's Greatest Hits/Greatest Hits Of Love. . . . . (Columbia)

Bluejean Bop
Gene Vincent and His Blue Caps; *Capitol Collectors Series-Gene Vincent
and His Blue Caps*. . . . . (Gold Rush)
Gene Vincent and His Blue Caps' Greatest Hits. . . . . (Curb)
*The Screaming End-The Best Of Gene Vincent and His
Blue Caps*. . . . . (Razor & Tie)

Bobby Sox To Stockings
Frankie Avalon; *Best Of Frankie Avalon*. . . . . (MCA)
Collectables Presents The History Of Rock-#3-C. . . . . (Collectables)
Frankie Avalon's Greatest Hits. . . . . (Everest)
Greatest Of Fabian and Frankie Avalon. . . . . (MCA)
Pick Of Frankie Avalon. . . . . (Fifty One West)
Super Oldies Of The '50s-#7-C. (Audio Fidelity)

Bring Me A Shawl From Galway
Mary O'Hara; *At The Royal Festival Hall*. . . . .(Shanachie)
Song For Ireland. . . . .(Shanachie)

Button Off My Shirt
Ronnie Milsap; *Heart & Soul*. . . . . (RCA)
Ronnie Milsap's Greatest Hits-#3. . . . . (RCA)

Button Up Your Overcoat
Rose Murphy; *Rose Murphy Sings Again*. (MCA)
Sarah Vaughan; *Sarah Vaughan*. . . . . (Everest)

Buttons And Bows
Dinah Shore; *16 Most Requested Songs Of The '40s-#1-C*. . . . . (Legacy)
Golden Hits Of The '40s-C. . . . . (Columbia Special Prod.)
Gene Autry; *Ridin' West-#2-C*. . . . . (Crescendo)
Songs Of The West-#3-Gene Autry & Roy Rogers-C. . . . . (Rhino)

Chantilly Lace
Big Bopper; *45s On CD-#1-1956-1959-C*. . . . . (Mercury)
Cruisin'-1958-C. . . . . (Increase)
Oldies But Goodies-#4-C. . . . .(Original Sound)
ST/American Graffiti. . . . . (MCA)
Jerry Lee Lewis; *''Killer'' Rocks On*. . . . . (Mercury)
Best Of Jerry Lee Lewis-#2. . . . . (Mercury)

Chick-A-Boom (Don't Ya Jes' Love It)
Daddy Dewdrop; *'70s Smash Hits-#4-C*. . . . . (Rhino)
Super Hits Of The '70s-Have A Nice Day-#5-C. . . . . (Rhino)

Clothesline Saga
Bob Dylan And The Band; *Basement Tapes*. . . . . (Columbia)

Coat Of Many Colors
Dolly Parton; *Best Of Dolly Parton*. . . . . (RCA)
Dolly Parton-Super Hits. . . . . (Columbia)
Essential Dolly Parton-#2. . . . . (RCA)
Emmylou Harris; *Pieces Of The Sky*. . . . . (Reprise)

Country In My Jeans
Loretta Lynn; *Still Country*. . . . . (Audium)

Cowboy In The Continental Suit
Chris LeDoux; *Rodeo & Living Free*. (Liberty)
Marty Robbins; *American Originals-Marty Robbins*. . . . . (Columbia)

Dance Naked
John Mellencamp; *Dance Naked*. . . . . (Mercury)

Dance With A Dolly (Hole In Her Stocking)
Bill Haley & His Comets; *King Of Rock & Roll*. . . . . (Alshire)
Rockin' & Rollin'. . . . . (Accord)

Dedicated Follower Of Fashion
Kinks; *Kinks' Greatest Hits*. . . . . (Rhino)
Kinks-Size Kinkdom. . . . . (Rhino)

Devil With A Blue Dress On & Good Golly Miss Molly
Bruce Springsteen; *ST/No Nukes-Muse Concerts*. . . . . (Asylum)
Mitch Ryder And The Detroit Wheels; *Frat Rock!-#4-C*. . . . . . (Rhino)
Rev Up-Best Of Mitch Ryder. . . . . (Rhino)
Son Of Frat Rock!-C. . . . . (Rhino)
Toga Rock-C. . . . . (Dunhill Compact Classics)

Dress Me Up As A Robber
Paul McCartney; *Tug Of War*. . . . . (Gold Rush)

Dress You Up
Madonna; *Like A Virgin*. . . . .(Sire)

Dressed For Success
Roxette; *Look Sharp!*. . . . . (EMI)

Dressed In Black
Hoodoo Gurus; *Kinky*. . . . .(RCA)

Dressed In Black
Depeche Mode; *Black Celebration*. . . . .(Sire)

Dressed To Kill
Nazareth; *Fool Circle*. . . . . (A&M)
Nazareth-Classics-#16. . . . . (A&M)
'Snaz. . . . . (A&M)

Dressed To Kill
Lita Ford; *Dancin' On The Edge*. . . . . (Mercury)

Dresses Too Short
Syl Johnson; *Twilight & Twinight-Masters Collection*. . . . . (Collectables)

Drinkin' In My Sunday Dress
Maria McKee; *Maria McKee*. . . . . (Geffen)

Dry Cleaner From Des Moines
Joni Mitchell; *Mingus*. . . . .(Elektra)
Shadows & Light. . . . .(Asylum)

Eat My Shorts
Rick Dees; *45-#89601*. . . . . (Atlantic)

Emperor's New Clothes
Sinead O'Connor; *I Do Not Want What I Haven't Got*. . . . . (Ensign)

Fashion
David Bowie; *Changesbowie*. . . . . (Rykodisc)
Changestwobowie. . . . . (RCA)
Scary Monsters. . . . . (Rykodisc)
The Singles-1969-1993. . . . . (Rykodisc)

Fashion For Me
Brooklyn Dreams; *Sleepless Nights*. . . . . (Casablanca)

Fashion Victim
Green Day; *Warning*. . . . . (Reprise)

Fool For Your Stockings
ZZ Top; *Deguello*. . . . .(Warner Bros.)

Forever In Blue Jeans
Neil Diamond; *12 Greatest Hits-#2*. . . . .(Columbia)
Hot August Night II. . . . .(Columbia)
You Don't Bring Me Flowers. . . . .(Columbia)

From The Indies To The Andies In His Undies
Hoosier Hot Shots; *All Time Legends Of Country Music-C*. . . . .(Legacy)

Gel
Collective Soul; *Collective Soul*. . . . .(Atlantic)
ST/Jerky Boys. . . . . (Atlantic)

German Overalls
Peter Hammill; *Chameleon In The Shadow Of The Night*. . . . . (Blue Plate)

Girl In A T-Shirt
ZZ Top; *Antenna*. . . . . (RCA)

Gold-Tipped Boots, Black Jacket And Tie
Jethro Tull; *Catfish Rising*. . . . . (Chrysalis)

Got A Bran' New Suit
Louis Armstrong; *Jazz Heritage-Back In New York*. . . . . (MCA)

Green Shirt
Elvis Costello; *Girls Girls Girls*. . . . .(Columbia)
Elvis Costello & The Attractions; *Armed Forces*. . . . .(Rykodisc)

Hand In My Pocket
Alanis Morissette; *Jagged Little Pill*. . . . . (Maverick)

Harper Valley P.T.A.
Jeannie C. Riley; *Harper Valley P.T.A.*. . . . . (Plantation)
Jeannie C. Riley's Greatest Hits. . . . . (Plantation)
Oldies But Goodies-#4-C. . . . .(Original Sound)
Souvenirs Of Music City U.S.A.-C. . . . . (Plantation)

High Fashion Queen
Flying Burrito Brothers; *Last Of The Red Hot Burritos*. . . . .(A&M)

Honey Can I Put On Your Clothes
Barbra Streisand; *Songbird*. . . . .(Columbia)

Hot Pants
James Brown; *In The Jungle Groove*. . . . . (Polydor)
Revolution Of The Mind. . . . . (Polydor)

Hot Pants In The Summertime
Dramatics; *Whatcha See Is Whatcha Get*. . . . . (Stax)

I Can't Dance
Genesis; *We Can't Dance*. . . . . (Atlantic)

I Got Stripes
Johnny Cash; *Johnny Cash-16 Biggest Hits-#2*. . . . .(Legacy)

I Left My Flannel In Seattle
Butt Trumpet; *Primitive Enema*. . . . . (Chrysalis)

If The Love Fits Wear It
Leslie Pearl; *Words & Music*. . . . . (RCA)

I'll Go On Loving You
Alan Jackson; *High Mileage*. . . . .(Arista)

I'm Going Back
Judy Holliday/Original Cast; *Bells Are Ringing*. . . . .(Columbia)

I'm Still Wearing Your Name
Ann Nesby; *I'm Here For You*. . . . . (Perspective/A&M)

In The Raw
Whispers; *Love Is Where You Find It*. . . . . (Solar)

Itsy Bitsy Teenie Weenie Yellow Polkadot Bikini
Brian Hyland; *Brian Hyland's Greatest Hits*. . . . .(Rhino)
Dr. Demento Presents The Greatest Novelty Records-#3-1960s-C. . . . (Rhino)
Vintage Music-#5-C. . . . . (MCA)

Jeans On
David Dundas; *David Dundas*. . . . . (Chrysalis)

King Is Half-Undressed
Jellyfish; *Bellybutton*. . . . . (Charisma)

Kiss Me
Sixpence None The Richer; *Sixpence None The Richer*. . . . . . (Squint/Columbia)
Songs From Dawson's Creek. . . . . (Sony Music Soundtrax)

Lady Came From Baltimore
Joan Baez; *Contemporary Ballad Book*. . . . .(Vanguard)
Joan. . . . .(Vanguard)
John Stewart; *Neon Beach*. . . . . (Homecoming)
Johnny Cash; *Johnny Cash-16 Biggest Hits-#2*. . . . . (Legacy)
Tim Hardin; *Hang On To A Dream-Verve Recordings*. . . . . (Polydor)

Laurie (Strange Things Happen)
Dickey Lee; *Collector's Essentials-#1-1960s-C* . . . . (Varese Sarabande)
Leather & Lace
Stevie Nicks & Don Henley; *Bella Donna* . . . . (Modern)
Leather Britches
John Hartford; *Aereo-Plain* . . . . (Warner Bros.)
Pete Sutherland; *Poor Man's Dream* . . . . (Flying Fish)
Leather Jacket
Mick Taylor; *Mick Taylor* . . . . (Columbia)
Leopard Skin Pillbox Hat
Bob Dylan; *Blonde On Blonde* . . . . (Columbia)
Lipstick And Leather
Y & T; *Best Of Y & T 81-85* . . . . (A&M)
Lipstick On Your Collar
Connie Francis; *Very Best Of Connie Francis* . . . . (Polydor)
London Leatherboys
Accept; *Balls To The Wall* . . . . (Portrait)
Compilation . . . . (Portrait)
Long Cool Woman In A Black Dress
Hollies; *Best Of The Hollies* . . . .(EMI)
Best Of The Hollies-#2 . . . .(EMI)
Billboard Top Rock 'N' Roll Hits-1972-C . . . . (Rhino)
Distant Light . . . .(Epic)
Hollies-Epic Anthology From The Original Master Tapes . . . .(Epic)
The Hollies' Greatest Hits . . . .(Epic)
Love You For A Day
Ricky Martin; *Ricky Martin* . . . . (Columbia)
Low Spark Of High Heeled Boys
Traffic; *On The Road* . . . . (Island)
The Low Spark Of High Heeled Boys . . . . (Island)
Makeup & Faded Blue Jeans
Merle Haggard; *Back To The Barrooms* . . . .(MCA)
Country Classics-#4-1984-1985-C . . . . (Universal)
Merle Haggard-His Best . . . .(MCA)
Mama Don't Get Dressed Up For Nothing
Brooks & Dunn; *Borderline* . . . . (Arista)
Mama Don't You Tear My Clothes
Blind Snooks Eaglin; *Rural Blues* . . . . (Fantasy)
Man In Black
Johnny Cash; *Essential Johnny Cash* . . . . (Columbia)
Patriot . . . . (Columbia)
The Man In Black-His Greatest Hits . . . . (Legacy)
Man In The Long Black Coat
Joan Osborne; *Relish* . . . . (Blue Gorilla/Mercury)
Mary Jane's Last Dance
Tom Petty And The Heartbreakers; *Playback* . . . .(MCA)
Tom Petty And The Heartbreakers' Greatest Hits . . . .(MCA)
Matchbox
Beatles; *Past Masters-Volume Two* . . . . (Parlophone)
Rock 'N' Roll Music . . . . (Capitol)
Something New . . . . (Capitol)
Mini Dress
Luther Johnson & Muddy Waters; *Chicken Shack* . . . . (Muse)
Miniskirt Minnie
Wilson Pickett; *A Man & A Half-Best Of Wilson Pickett* . . . . . . (Rhino)
Most Beautiful Girl In The World
Frank Sinatra; *Strangers In The Night* . . . . (Reprise)
Tony Bennett; *Rodgers & Hart Songbook* . . . . (DRG)
Tony Bennett Sings More Great Rodgers & Hart . . . . (Improv)
New Attitude
Patti LaBelle; *Classic Soul-C* . . . .(MCA)
I Am Woman-C . . . . (Nick At Nite)
Soundtrack Smashes-'80s & More-C . . . .(MCA)
ST/Beverly Hills Cop . . . .(MCA)
Nobody Knows But Me
Jimmie Rodgers; *Riding High-1929-1930* . . . . (Rounder)
Merle Haggard & The Strangers; *Same Train Different Time* . . . . (Capitol)
On The Sunny Side Of The Street
Diana Krall; *Stepping Out* . . . . (Justin Time)
Frank Sinatra; *Come Swing With Me!* . . . . (Capitol)
One More For The Road . . . . (Capitol)
Sentimental Journey . . . . (Capitol)
The Capitol Years . . . . (Capitol)
Judy Garland; *Best Of Judy Garland* . . . .(MCA)
Louis Armstrong; *Best Of Louis Armstrong* . . . .(MCA)
Chicago Concert 1956 . . . . (Columbia)
Jazz Club-Vocal . . . . (Verve)
Music Autobiography . . . . (Verve)
Ted Lewis & His Orchestra; *Charming Gents Of Stage & Screen-C* . . . (Legacy)
Those Wonderful Years: Puttin' On The Ritz-C . . . . (JCI Assoc. Labels)
One Shirt, Soulless Shoes
Latimore; *I'll Do Anything For You* . . . . (Malaco)
Only Thing That Looks Good On Me Is You
Bryan Adams; *18 Til I Die* . . . . (A&M)
Orange Was The Color Of Her Dress
Charles Mingus; *Changes Two* . . . . (Atlantic)
Charles Mingus In Europe-#2 . . . . (Enja)
Gil Evans; *Live At Sweet Basil-#1* . . . . (Evidence Music)

Gil Evans & Laurent Cugny Big Band; *Golden Hair* . . . . (Emarcy)
Out Of The Wardrobe
Kinks; *Misfits* . . . . (Arista)
Overcoats
John Hiatt; *Overcoats* . . . . (Epic)
Paddy McGinty's Coat
Pat Harrington; *St. Patrick's Day Celebration* . . . . (Columbia)
Pajama Game/Racing With The Clock
Original Cast; *Pajama Game* . . . . (Columbia)
Penny Loafers & Bobby Socks
Joe Bennett and The Sparkletones; *Rock This Town-Rockabilly Hits-#2-C* . . . . (Rhino)
Perfume And Pink Chiffon
Sonny Lester & His Orchestra; *Take It Off: Striptease Classics-C* . . . . . . (Rhino)
Pink Cashmere
Prince; *The Hits 1* . . . . (Paisley Park)
The Hits/The B-Sides . . . . (Paisley Park)
Pink Pedal Pushers
Carl Perkins; *Best Of Carl Perkins-Jive After 5-1958-1978* . . . . . . (Rhino)
Restless-Columbia Recordings . . . . (Columbia)
Jerry Lee Lewis; *Monsters* . . . . (Sun)
Pink Petticoats
Big Bopper; *Chantilly Lace Starring The Big Bopper* . . . . . . (Mercury)
Hellooo Baby! Best Of The Big Bopper-1954-1959 . . . . (Rhino)
Pizza In My Shorts
Da Yoopers; *Yoopy Do Wah* . . . . (You Guys)
Polythene Pam
Beatles; *Abbey Road* . . . . (Parlophone)
Beatles-Box Set . . . . (Capitol)
Pop Ya Collar
Usher; *All About U* . . . . (LaFace)
Pseudo Silk Kimono
Marillion; *Misplaced Childhood* . . . . (Capitol)
Put On Your Old Grey Bonnet
Jimmy Dean; *Jimmy Dean's Greatest Hits* . . . . (Columbia)
Pete Fountain; *Best Of Pete Fountain* . . . .(MCA)
Mr. New Orleans . . . .(MCA)
Put On Your Sunday Clothes
Carol Channing/Original Cast; *Hello Dolly!* . . . .(RCA)
Put Your Cat Clothes On
Carl Perkins; *Carl Perkins-Original Sun Greatest Hits* . . . . . . (Rhino)
Legends Of Rock Guitar-'50s-#1-C . . . . (Rhino)
Put Your Clothes Back On
Joe Stampley; *Encore-Joe Stampley* . . . . (Epic)
Joe Stampley's Biggest Hits . . . . (Epic)
Puttin' On My Sunday Best
Dick & Mel Tunney; *Let The Dreamers Dream* . . . . . . (Warner Bros.)
Puttin' On The Ritz
Ella Fitzgerald; *Silver Collection-Songbooks* . . . . (Verve)
Fred Astaire; *Irving Berlin Always-C* . . . . (Verve)
Irving Berlin Songbook . . . . (Verve)
Harry Richman; *Hollywood Sings-C* . . . . (Living Era)
Those Wonderful Years: Puttin' On The Ritz-C . . . . (JCI Assoc. Labels)
Judy Garland; *One & Only* . . . . (Capitol)
Mandy Patinkin; *Mandy Patinkin* . . . . (Columbia)
Taco; *After Eight* . . . . (RCA)
Nipper's Greatest Hits Of The '80s-C . . . . (RCA)
Red Bandana
Merle Haggard; *Merle Haggard's Greatest Hits* . . . .(MCA)
More Of The Best . . . . (Rhino)
Serving 190 Proof . . . .(MCA)
Red Sex Dress
Alfonia Tims & The Flying Tigers; *Future Funk/Uncut!* . . . . (Roir)
Rednecks, White Socks And Blue Ribbon Beer
Johnny Russell; *Beer Redneck Mothers* . . . . (RCA)
Country Legends-C . . . .(Madacy)
Country's Greatest Drinking Songs-C . . . . (All-Star Music)
Rednecks, White Socks & Blue Ribbon Beer . . . . (RCA)
Rose Colored Glasses
John Conlee; *Backstage At The Grand Ole Opry-C* . . . . (RCA)
Grand Ole Opry-75 Years-#1-C . . . .(MCA)
John Conlee-Legends . . . .(MCA)
John Conlee's Greatest Hits . . . .(MCA)
MCA Records 30 Years Of Hits-1958-1988-C . . . .(MCA)
Rose Colored Glasses . . . . (Universal)
Sam, You Made The Pants Too Long
Barbra Streisand; *Barbra Streisand's Greatest Hits* . . . . (Columbia)
Color Me Barbra . . . . (Columbia)
Satin Sheets
Jeannie Pruett; *16 Top Country Hits-#1-C* . . . .(MCA)
Country Chart-Toppers . . . . (Dominion Entert.)
Grand Ole Opry-75 Years-#2-C . . . .(MCA)
MCA Records 30 Years Of Hits-1958-1988-C . . . .(MCA)
Shawn Colvin; *Cover Girl* . . . . (Columbia)
Saturday Clothes
Gordon Lightfoot; *If You Could Read My Mind* . . . . (Reprise)
Saturday Suit
Art Garfunkel; *Watermark* . . . . (Legacy)

Save That Dress
T. Graham Brown; *Brilliant Conversationalist* . . . . (Capitol)
Second Hand Rose
Barbra Streisand; *A Happening In Central Park* . . . . (Columbia)
  Barbra Streisand...and other musical instruments . . . . (Columbia)
  Barbra Streisand's Greatest Hits . . . . (Columbia)
  Just For The Record . . . . (Columbia)
  My Name Is Barbra, Two . . . . (Columbia)
Shake Your Pants
Cameo; *Cameosis* . . . . (Casablanca)
Sharp Dressed Man
ZZ Top; *Eliminator* . . . . (Warner Bros.)
  ZZ Top's Greatest Hits . . . . (Warner Bros.)
She Got Me (When She Got Her Dress On)
Masters Of Reality; *Sunrise On The Sufferbus* . . . . (Chrysalis)
She Wears Red Feathers
Guy Mitchell; *Guy Mitchell-16 Most Requested Songs* . . . . (Legacy)
She's A Hum Dum Dinger
Jimmie Davis; *The Roots Of Rap-Classic Recordings-C* . . . . (Yazoo)
Shine
Ry Cooder; *Jazz* . . . . (Warner Bros.)
Shiny Stockings
Count Basie; *April In Paris* . . . . (Verve)
  Basie In London . . . . (Verve)
  Dedication-#11 . . . . (MCA)
  The Deacon . . . . (Intermedia)
Jon Hendricks; *Compact Jazz-Best Of The Compact Jazz Vocalists-C* . . (Verve)
  Recorded In Person At The Trident . . . . (Smash)
Shirt
Bonzo Dog Band; *Best Of The Bonzo Dog Band* . . . . (Rhino)
  Tadpoles . . . . (Liberty)
Shopping For Clothes
Coasters; *Coasters-Their Greatest Recordings-Early Years* . . . . (Atco)
Short Shorts
Royal Teens; *Cruisin'-1958-C* . . . . (Increase)
  Goofy Greats-C . . . . (K-Tel)
  Short Shorts . . . . (MCA)
Short Skirt/Long Jacket
Cake; *Comfort Eagle* . . . . (Columbia)
Silver Threads Among The Gold
Mike Auldridge; *Dobro/Blues & Bluegrass* . . . . (Takoma)
Slit Skirts
Pete Townshend; *All The Best Cowboys Have Chinese Eyes* . . . . (Atco)
Something In Red
Lorrie Morgan; *Lorrie Morgan's Greatest Hits* . . . . (BNA)
  Something In Red . . . . (RCA)
  To Get To You-Greatest Hits Collection . . . . (BNA)
Something Like That (white T-shirt)
Tim McGraw; *A Place In The Sun* . . . . (Curb)
  Tim McGraw's Greatest Hits . . . . (Curb)
Steppin' Out With My Baby
Fred Astaire; *Cheek To Cheek: The Irving Berlin Songbook-C* . . . . . (Verve)
  Fred Astaire At MGM . . . . (Rhino)
  ST/Easter Parade . . . . (Rhino)
  Steppin' Out-Astaire Sings . . . . (Verve)
Tony Bennett; *MTV Unplugged-Tony Bennett* . . . . (Columbia)
  Steppin' Out . . . . (Columbia)
Streak, The
Ray Stevens; *Ray Stevens' Greatest Hits* . . . . (RCA)
  Ray Stevens' Greatest Hits . . . . (MCA)
  Ray Stevens-All-Time Greatest Comic Hits . . . . (Curb)
  Super Hits Of The '70s-Have A Nice Day-#12-C . . . . (Rhino)
Strip Polka
Andrews Sisters; *Best Of The Andrews Sisters* . . . . (MCA)
Bobby Vinton; *Greatest Polka Hits Of All-Time* . . . . (Curb)
Stripper
David Rose; *Dick Bartley's One-Hit Wonders Of The '60s-#1-C* . . . . . (Rhino)
Style Kills
Robert Palmer; *Addictions-#1* . . . . (Island)
Sucker In A 3-Piece Suit
Van Halen; *OU812* . . . . (Warner Bros.)
Suedehead
Morrissey; *Bona Drag* . . . . (Sire)
  Viva Hate . . . . (Sire)
Suit Of Lights
Costello Show (Featuring Elvis Costello); *King Of America* . . . . (Columbia)
Summer Girls
LFO; *Summer Girls-CD Single* . . . . (Logic)
  Totally Hits-#1-C . . . . (Arista)
Sundress
Phat Cat Players featuring Coco Brown; *Make It Phat Baby* . . . . . . (Parlane)
Sunglasses At Night
Corey Hart; *First Offense* . . . . (EMI)
  The Singles . . . . (EMI)
Take Off That Dress
Ray Charles; *Love & Peace* . . . . (Atlantic)
Take Off Your Uniform
John Hiatt; *Slug Line* . . . . (MCA)

Take Your Clothes Off When You Dance
Frank Zappa; *You Can't Do That On Stage Anymore-#6* . . . . (Rykodisc)
Mothers Of Invention; *We're Only In It For The Money* . . . . (Rykodisc)
Terrorist Trousers
Jim Carroll Band; *Praying Mantis* . . . . (Giant)
Theme From "Petticoat Junction"
Flatt & Scruggs; *20 All-Time Great Recordings* . . . . (Columbia)
Original Soundtrack; *Television's Greatest Hits-#1-C* . . . . (TVT)
  TV Theme Sing-Along Album . . . . (Rhino)
Thong Song
Sisqo; *Unleash The Dragon* . . . . (Dragon/Def Soul/IDJMG)
Tiger In A Dress
Dan Reed Network; *Slam* . . . . (Mercury)
Tight Fittin' Jeans
Conway Twitty; *Classic Conway* . . . . (MCA)
  Conway Twitty-Legends . . . . (MCA)
  Mister T. . . . . (MCA)
Top Hat Bar & Grille
Jim Croce; *50th Anniversary Collection* . . . . (Saja)
Top Hat, White Tie And Tails
Fred Astaire; *Irving Berlin Songbook* . . . . (Verve)
Torn And Frayed
Rolling Stones; *Exile On Main Street* . . . . (Virgin)
Totally Nude
Talking Heads; *Naked* . . . . (Fly/Sire)
Wallets; *Take It* . . . . (Twin-Tone)
Trouser Press
Bonzo Dog Band; *Best Of The Bonzo Dog Band* . . . . (Rhino)
Tuxedo Junction
Boston Pops Orchestra/Arthur Fiedler; *Greatest Hits Of The '40s-#2* . . (RCA)
Ella Fitzgerald; *Things Ain't What They Used To Be* . . . . (Bainbridge)
Glenn Miller; *Best Of Glenn Miller* . . . . (Bluebird)
  Glenn Miller-A Legendary Performer-#1 & 2 . . . . (Bluebird)
  Memorial-1944-1969 . . . . (Bluebird)
  ST/The Glenn Miller Story . . . . (MCA)
Glenn Miller & His Orchestra; *Glenn Miller & His Orchestra-*
  Pure Gold . . . . (Bluebird)
  The Unforgettable Glenn Miller & His Orchestra . . . . (RCA)
Harry James Sextet; *1940s-Small Groups-C* . . . . (Columbia)
Joe Jackson; *Jumpin' Jive* . . . . (A&M)
Manhattan Transfer; *Best Of The Manhattan Transfer* . . . . (Atlantic)
  Manhattan Transfer-Anthology-Down In Birdland . . . . (Rhino)
  The Manhattan Transfer . . . . (Rhino)
New York City Gay Men's Chorus; *Love Lives On* . . . . (Virgin)
Undone-The Sweater
Weezer; *Weezer* . . . . (David Geffen Co.)
Velcro Fly
ZZ Top; *Afterburner* . . . . (Warner Bros.)
Velvet Green Whistler
Jethro Tull; *Songs From The Wood* . . . . (Chrysalis)
Venom Wearin' Denim
Junior Brown; *Semi Crazy* . . . . (Curb)
Venus In Blue Jeans
Jimmy Clanton; *All-Star Chartbusters* . . . . (Intermedia)
  Golden Years-1962-C . . . . (Dominion Entert.)
Vicar In A Tutu
Smiths; *Rank* . . . . (Sire)
  The Queen Is Dead . . . . (Sire)
Violets For Your Furs
Frank Sinatra; *Concepts* . . . . (Capitol)
  Frank Sinatra-Gift Set . . . . (Capitol)
  Songs For Young Lovers & Swing Easy . . . . (Capitol)
Jesse Davis; *Horn Of Passion* . . . . (Concord Jazz)
John Coltrane; *Prestige Recordings* . . . . (Prestige)
Tommy Dorsey & Frank Sinatra; *Sessions-#1-February 1, 1940-July*
  17, 1940 . . . . (RCA)
Vogue
Madonna; *I'm Breathless-Music From Dick Tracy* . . . . (Sire)
  Immaculate Collection . . . . (Sire)
  Royal Box . . . . (Sire)
Watching The Clothes
Pretenders; *Learning To Crawl* . . . . (Sire)
We Don't Have To Take Our Clothes Off
Jermaine Stewart; *Frantic Romantic* . . . . (Arista)
Wear Your Love Like Heaven
Donovan; *Donovan's Greatest Hits* . . . . (Epic)
  Gift From A Flower To A Garden . . . . (Epic)
  Summer Of Love-#1-C . . . . (Rhino)
  Troubadour-Definitive Collection . . . . (Epic)
Sarah McLachlan; *Solace* . . . . (Arista)
Welcome To The Occupation
R.E.M.; *Document* . . . . (EMI-Capitol Entert. Properties)
West Nashville Grand Ballroom Gown
Jimmy Buffett; *Living & Dying In 3/4 Time* . . . . (MCA)
When You Wore A Tulip
Judy Garland; *Best Of Judy Garland* . . . . (MCA)
Where Do My Socks Go?
Ray Stevens; *Lend Me Your Ears* . . . . (Curb)

White Sport Coat (And A Pink Carnation)
Marty Robbins; *16 Most Requested Songs Of The '50s-#2-C* . . . . (Legacy)
Lifetime Of Song-1951-1982 . . . . (Columbia)
Marty Robbins' Greatest Hits . . . . (Columbia)

Who Threw The Overalls In Mrs. Murphy's Chowder
Bing Crosby; *Shillelaghs & Shamrocks* . . . .(MCA)

Words By Heart
Billy Ray Cyrus; *It Won't Be The Last* . . . . (Mercury)

Yellow Roses On Her Gown
Johnny Mathis; *I Only Have Eyes For You* . . . . (Columbia)

Yes It Is
Beatles; *Beatles VI* . . . . (Capitol)
Beatles-Box Set . . . . (Capitol)
Beatles-Love Songs . . . . (Capitol)
Past Masters-Volume One . . . . (Parlophone)

You Can Feel Bad
Patty Loveless; *Patty Loveless-Classics* . . . .(Epic)
Super Hits Of 1996-C . . . .(Epic)
The Trouble With The Truth . . . .(Epic)

You Make My Pants Want To Get Up & Dance
Dr. Hook; *Pleasure & Pain* . . . . (Capitol)

You Wear It Well
DeBarge; *DeBarge's Greatest Hits* . . . . (Motown)
Rhythm Of The Night . . . . (Motown)
Rod Stewart; *Best Of Rod Stewart* . . . . (Mercury)
Sing It Again, Rod . . . . (Mercury)
Storyteller/The Complete Anthology: 1964-1990 . . . .(Warner Bros.)

You're Never Fully Dressed Without A Smile
Original Broadway Cast; *Annie* . . . . (Columbia)

Zoot Suit Riot
Cherry Poppin' Daddies; *Now That's What I Call Music!-#1-C* . . . . (Virgin)
Zoot Suit Riot-The Swingin' Hits Of The Cherry Poppin'
Daddies . . . . (Mojo Music/Universal)

COLD, Freezing, Frost, Frozen, Ice

See Also: CHRISTMAS, COOL, MONTHS & DATES (various), SEASONS: WINTER, SNOW

500 Miles Away From Home
Bobby Bare; *500 Miles Away From Home* . . . . (RCA)
Foy Willing; *Cowboy/The New Sound Of American Folk.* . . . . (DRG)
Reba McEntire; *Starting Over* . . . .(MCA)

911
Wyclef Jean featuring Mary J. Blige; *The Ecleftic-2 Sides II*
A Book . . . . (Ruffhouse/Columbia)

August Freeze
Grace Pool; *Where We Live* . . . . (Reprise)

Autumn's Not That Cold
Lorrie Morgan; *Something In Red.* . . . . (RCA)
Skip Ewing; *Coast Of Colorado* . . . .(MCA)

Baby Ice Dog
Blue Oyster Cult; *Tyranny & Mutation.* . . . . (Columbia)

Baby, It's Cold Outside
Pearl Bailey; *Pearl Bailey-16 Most Requested Songs* . . . . (Legacy)
Ray Charles; *Ray Charles-His Greatest Hits-#2* . . . . .(Dunhill Compact Classics)

Black Balloon
Goo Goo Dolls; *Dizzy Up The Girl* . . . . (Warner Sunset/Reprise)

Black Jesus
Everlast; *Eat At Whitey's* . . . . (Tommy Boy)

Chill Of An Early Fall
George Strait; *The Chill Of An Early Fall.* . . . .(MCA)

Cold As Ice
Foreigner; *Foreigner* . . . . (Atlantic)
Records . . . . (Atlantic)
ST/FM . . . .(MCA)

Cold Blooded
Rick James; *Cold Blooded* . . . . (Motown)
Rick James' Greatest Hits . . . . (Motown)

Cold Blue Steel & Sweet Fire
Joni Mitchell; *For The Roses* . . . . (Asylum)
Joni Mitchell with Tom Scott & The L.A. Express; *Miles Of Aisles* . . . . (Asylum)

Cold Cold Heart
Hank Williams; *Complete Hank Williams* . . . . (Mercury)
Hank Williams With His Drifting Cowboys; *24 Of Hank Williams'*
Greatest Hits . . . . (Polydor)
Hank Williams . . . . (MGM)
Hank Williams-40 Greatest Hits . . . . (Polydor)
Live At Opry . . . . (MGM)
Long Gone Lonesome Blues . . . . (Polydor)
Jerry Lee Lewis; *Duets* . . . . (Sun)
Golden Cream Of Jerry Lee Lewis . . . . (Sun)
Jerry Lee Lewis & Friends-Duets . . . . (Sun)
Lucinda Williams; *Timeless: Hank Williams*
Tribute-C . . . . (Lost Highway/IDJMG)
Tony Bennett; *Tony Bennett-16 Most Requested Songs* . . . . (Legacy)

Cold Cold World
Teddy Pendergrass; *Life Is A Song Worth Singing* . . . . (Philadelphia Int'l)

Cold Contagious
Bush; *Razorblade Suitcase* . . . .(Trauma)

Cold Day In December
George Jones; *You Oughta Be Here With Me* . . . . (Epic)

Cold Day In Hell
Gary Moore; *After Hours* . . . . (Charisma)

Cold Day In July
Dixie Chicks; *Fly* . . . . (Monument)
Joy White; *Between Midnight & Hindsight.* . . . . (Columbia)
Ray Price; *For The Good Times/I Won't Mention It Again* . . . . (Columbia)
Suzy Bogguss; *Voices In The Wind.* . . . . (Liberty)

Cold Day In Tennessee
Rob Crosby; *Another Time & Place* . . . . (Arista)

Cold December
Mike Auldridge; *Mike Auldridge & Old Dog* . . . . (Flying Fish)

Cold Fever
Models; *Out Of Mind Out Of Sight* . . . . (Geffen)

Cold Fire
Rush; *Counterparts* . . . .(Atlantic)

Cold Hands From New York
Gordon Lightfoot; *United Artists Collection* . . . . (EMI)

Cold Hard Cash
Greg Kihn; *Next Of Kihn* . . . . (Beserkley)

Cold Hard Facts Of Life, The
Porter Wagoner; *Essential Porter Wagoner* . . . . (RCA)
Porter Wagoner's Greatest Hits. . . . .(Pair)

Cold Hard Truth, The
George Jones; *Cold Hard Truth* . . . .(Asylum)
Jamie O'Hara; *Rise Above It* . . . . (RCA)

Cold Hearted
Paula Abdul; *Forever Your Girl* . . . .(Virgin)
Get Up & Dance-Dance Mixes. . . . .(Virgin)

Cold Irons Bound
Bob Dylan; *Time Out Of Mind* . . . . (Columbia)

Cold Love
Donna Summer; *The Wanderer.* . . . . (Geffen)

Cold November
John O'Connor; *Songs For Our Times* . . . . (Flying Fish)

Cold On The Shoulder
Gordon Lightfoot; *Cold On The Shoulder.* . . . .(Reprise)
Gord's Gold . . . .(Reprise)

Cold Rain
Crosby, Stills & Nash; *CSN.* . . . .(Atlantic)

Cold Rain And Snow
Grateful Dead; *Grateful Dead (Skull & Roses)* . . . . (Warner Bros.)
Steal Your Face . . . .(Grateful Dead)

Cold Rain In Kansas
Don Lange; *Natural Born Heathen* . . . . (Flying Fish)

Cold Rock A Party
MC Lyte; *Bad As I Wanna B* . . . . (East West)

Cold Shot
Johnny Otis; *Cold Shot* . . . . (Kent)
Stevie Ray Vaughan; *Couldn't Stand The Weather.* . . . . (Epic)
Live Alive . . . . (Epic)

Cold Sky
Cyndi Lauper; *Music Speaks Louder Than Words-C* . . . . (Epic)

Cold Summer Day In Georgia
Gene Watson; *Memories To Burn* . . . . (Epic)

Cold Sweat
James Brown; *Billboard Top R&B Hits-1967-C* . . . . (Rhino)
Can Your Heart Stand It . . . .(Solid Smoke)
James Brown's Greatest Hits . . . . (Rhino)
Live At The Apollo-Vol. 2-Part 1 . . . . (Rhino)

Cold Sweat
Warrant; *Dirty Rotten Filthy Stinking Rich* . . . . (Columbia)

Cold Wind In August
Van Morrison; *Period Of Transition* . . . . (Warner Bros.)

Cold Windy City Of Chicago
Boxcar Willie; *Best Of Boxcar Willie-#1.* . . . . (Mainstreet)

Cold Winter Day
Blind Willie McTell; *Doing That Atlanta Strut-1927-1935* . . . .(Yazoo)

Cold Winter's Day
BoDeans; *Go Slow Down* . . . .(Slash)

Cold, Cold, Cold
Little Feat; *Feats Don't Fail Me Now* . . . . (Warner Bros.)
Sailin' Shoes . . . . (Warner Bros.)

Colder Are My Nights
Isley Brothers; *45-#28860.* . . . . (Warner Bros.)

Colder Than Winter
Vince Gill; *Things That Matter* . . . . (RCA)

Cool Breeze
Jeremy Spencer Band; *Flee* . . . .(Atlantic)

Cool Change
Little River Band; *First Under The Wire* . . . . (Capitol)
Little River Band's Greatest Hits . . . . (Capitol)

Cool Cool Water
Beach Boys; *10 Years Of Harmony* . . . . (Caribou)
Sunflower . . . . (Caribou)
Cool Down
Triumph; *Thunder Seven* . . . . (MCA)
Cool It Down
Velvet Underground; *Loaded* . . . . (Warner Special Prod.)
Cool It Now
New Edition; *New Edition* . . . . (MCA)
New Edition's Greatest Hits, Vol. 1 . . . . (MCA)
Cool Love
Wanda Jackson; *Rockin' In The Country-Best Of Wanda Jackson* . . . . . . (Rhino)
Cool Love
Pablo Cruise; *Reflector* . . . . (A&M)
Cool Love
Sheena Easton; *The Lover In Me* . . . . (MCA)
Cool Night
Paul Davis; *Cool Night* . . . . (Arista)
Cool The Engines
Boston; *Third Stage* . . . . (MCA)
Cool Water
Bob Nolan; *Sound Of A Pioneer* . . . . (Elektra)
Frankie Laine; *Frankie Laine-16 Most Requested Songs* . . . . (Legacy)
Jack Scott; *Capitol Collectors Series-Jack Scott* . . . . (Capitol)
Joni Mitchell; *Chalk Mark In A Rain Storm* . . . . (Geffen)
Marty Robbins; *Gunfighter Ballads & Trail Songs* . . . . (Legacy)
Sons Of The Pioneers; *60 Years Of Country Music-C* . . . . (RCA)
Best Of The Sons Of The Pioneers . . . . (RCA)
Cool Water . . . . (RCA)
Western Country . . . . (Granite)
Cool Water
Talking Heads; *Naked* . . . . (Fly/Sire)
Cool, Clear Water
Bonnie Raitt; *Longing In Their Hearts* . . . . (Capitol)
Could've Been
Tiffany; *Tiffany* . . . . (MCA)
Tiffany's Greatest Hits . . . . (Hip-O)
Darlin' Corey
Ricky Skaggs with Bruce Hornsby; *Big Mon: The Songs Of Bill
Monroe-C* . . . . (Skaggs Family)
Deep Freeze
Judas Priest; *Hero Hero* . . . . (RCA)
Rocka-Rolla . . . . (RCA)
Electron Cold
Sea Level; *On The Edge* . . . . (Capricorn)
Fire And Ice
Pat Benatar; *Best Shots* . . . . (Chrysalis)
Live From Earth . . . . (Chrysalis)
Precious Time . . . . (Chrysalis)
Flip The Switch
Rolling Stones; *Bridges To Babylon* . . . . (Virgin)
No Security . . . . (Virgin)
Freezing
Nick Lowe; *Dig My Mood* . . . . (Upstart)
Frozen
Madonna; *GHV2* . . . . (Warner Bros.)
Ray Of Light . . . . (Maverick)
Funky Cold Medina
Tone Loc; *Loc-ed After Dark* . . . . (Delicious Vinyl)
Gone Away
Offspring; *Ixnay On The Hombre* . . . . (Columbia)
Hey Get Your Cold Beer (Ballantine Premium Beer)
Original Soundtrack; *TeeVee Toons-The Commercials-#1-C* . . . . . (TVT)
Hot Corn, Cold Corn
Flatt & Scruggs; *Flatt & Scruggs At Carnegie Hall!* . . . . (Koch International)
Hot Love Cold World
Bob Welch; *French Kiss* . . . . (Capitol)
Ice
Sarah McLachlan; *Fumbling Towards Ecstasy* . . . . (Arista)
Ice Ice Baby
Vanilla Ice; *To The Extreme* . . . . (SBK)
Icehouse
Icehouse; *Icehouse* . . . . (Chrysalis)
Iceman
Bruce Springsteen; *Tracks* . . . . (Columbia)
Icicle
Tori Amos; *Under The Pink* . . . . (Atlantic)
If I Fall You're Going Down With Me
Dixie Chicks; *Fly* . . . . (Monument)
If We Make It Through December
Merle Haggard; *A Christmas Present* . . . . (Curb)
Eleven Winners . . . . (Capitol)
Goin' Home For Christmas . . . . (Sony Music Special Prod.)
Merle Haggard-Christmas Gift . . . . (Curb)
Very Best Of Merle Haggard . . . . (Capitol)
In The Cool, Cool, Cool Of The Evening
Bing Crosby; *Best Of Bing Crosby* . . . . (MCA)

Frank Sinatra; *Days Of Wine And Roses, Moon River, And Other Academy
Award Winners* . . . . (Reprise)
Rosemary Clooney; *Rosemary Clooney-16 Most Requested Songs* . . . . .(Legacy)
Is It Cold In Here
Joe Diffie; *Regular Joe* . . . . (Epic)
Keep Me From The Cold
Curtis Stigers; *Time Was* . . . .(Arista)
Let's Chill
Guy; *Future* . . . . (Uptown/MCA)
Long Cold Winter
Pure Prairie League; *If The Shoe Fits* . . . . (RCA)
Love In The Ice Age
Pat Benatar; *Tropico* . . . . (Chrysalis)
Nine Below Zero
Muddy Waters; *King Of The Electric Blues* . . . .(Legacy)
Snooky Pryor; *Blind Pig Sampler: Prime Chops-#1-C* . . . . (Blind Pig)
Sonny Boy Williamson; *More Real Folk Blues-Sonny Boy Williamson*. . .(Chess)
October & The Frost Is Early
Dusing Singers; *Cool Of The Day-Music Of Jean Ritchie* . . . . (Green Hays)
Out In The Cold
Judas Priest; *Priest...Live!* . . . .(Columbia)
Turbo . . . .(Columbia)
Out In The Cold
Tom Petty And The Heartbreakers; *Into The Great Wide Open* . . . . . (MCA)
Out In The Cold
George Howard; *When Summer Comes* . . . .(GRP)
Peas, Porridge Hot
Original Soundtrack; *Toddler Favorites* . . . . (Kid Rhino/Rhino 4 Kids)
Ring Of Ice
Jennifer Rush; *Jennifer Rush* . . . . (Epic)
Running On Ice
Billy Joel; *The Bridge* . . . .(Columbia)
Selfless, Cold And Composed
Ben Folds Five; *Whatever And Ever Amen* . . . . (Caroline/550)
She's Coming Back Some Cold Rainy Day
Georgia Cotton Pickers; *The Greatest In Country Blues (1929-
1956)-#3-C* . . . . (Sony Broadway)
She's So Cold
Rolling Stones; *Emotional Rescue* . . . . (Rolling Stones)
Shiver
Coldplay; *Parachutes* . . . .(Nettwerk/Capitol)
Skating On Thin Ice
Tower Of Power; *Bump City* . . . . (Warner Bros.)
Soul On Ice
Graham Parker And The Rumour; *Stick To Me* . . . . (Mercury)
Stone Cold
Rainbow; *Finyl Vinyl* . . . .(Mercury)
Straight Between The Eyes . . . .(Mercury)
Stone Cold Country
Gibson/Miller Band; *Where There's Smoke* . . . . (Epic)
Stone Cold Crazy
Queen; *Classic Queen* . . . .(Hollywood)
Sheer Heart Attack . . . .(Hollywood)
ST/Encino Man . . . .(Hollywood)
Stone Cold Dead In The Market
Ella Fitzgerald; *Best Of Ella Fitzgerald-#2* . . . . (MCA)
Stone Cold Drag
James Brown; *People* . . . . (Polydor)
Stone Cold Fever
Humble Pie; *Best Of Humble Pie* . . . .(A&M)
Humble Pie-Classics-#14 . . . .(A&M)
Performance-Rockin' The Fillmore . . . .(A&M)
Rock On . . . .(A&M)
Stone Cold Gentleman
Ralph Tresvant; *Ralph Tresvant* . . . . (MCA)
Stone Cold Sober
Rod Stewart; *Atlantic Crossing* . . . . (Warner Bros.)
Storyteller/The Complete Anthology: 1964-1990 . . . . (Warner Bros.)
Sugarfoot
Wallflowers; *The Wallflowers* . . . . (Virgin)
Summer Chill
Grover Washington, Jr.; *Next Exit* . . . .(Columbia)
Summer In Dixie
Confederate Railroad; *Notorious* . . . . (Atlantic)
Sure Got Cold After The Rain
ZZ Top; *Rio Grande Mud* . . . . (Warner Bros.)
Six Pack . . . . (Warner Bros.)
Ten Degrees & Gettin' Colder
Nanci Griffith; *Other Voices Other Rooms* . . . . (Elektra)
Tenth Avenue Freeze-Out
Bruce Springsteen; *Born To Run* . . . .(Columbia)
Bruce Springsteen & The E Street Band; *Bruce Springsteen & The E Street
Band Live/1975-85* . . . .(Legacy)
There Goes My Baby
Trisha Yearwood; *Where Your Road Leads* . . . . (MCA)
Thin Ice
Pink Floyd; *Shine On* . . . .(Columbia)
The Wall . . . .(Columbia)

Roger Waters; *The Wall-Live In Berlin* . . . . (Mercury)

Thin Ice
Daryl Hall & John Oates; *H2O* . . . . (RCA)

Thin Ice
Ozark Mountain Daredevils; *Car Over The Lake Album* . . . . (A&M)

Thin Ice
Robin Trower & Jack Bruce; *Truce* . . . . (Chrysalis)

This Cold War With You
Floyd Tillman; *Columbia Country Classics-#2-Honky Tonk
Heroes-C* . . . . (Columbia)
John Prine; *Pink Cadillac* . . . . (Asylum)
Merle Haggard; *Friend In California* . . . . (Epic)
Ray Price; *Ray Price's Greatest Hits-#4-By Request* . . . . (Step One)
Willie Nelson; *San Antonio Rose* . . . . (Columbia)

Too Cold At Home
Mark Chesnutt; *Too Cold At Home* . . . . (MCA)

Too Cold In The Winter
Cry Of Love; *Brother* . . . . (Columbia)

Torn
Natalie Imbruglia; *Left Of The Middle* . . . . (RCA)

Tourette's
Nirvana; *In Utero* . . . . (David Geffen Co.)

Under Ice
Kate Bush; *Hounds Of Love* . . . . (EMI)

Warm Beer & Cold Women
Tom Waits; *Nighthawks At The Diner* . . . . (Asylum)

Warmth, The
Incubus; *Make Yourself* . . . . (Immortal/Epic)

What It Is
Mark Knopfler; *Sailing To Philadelphia* . . . . (Warner Bros.)

When It's Springtime In Alaska
Johnny Horton; *American Originals-Johnny Horton* . . . . (Columbia)
Johnny Horton's Greatest Hits . . . . (Columbia)

World Is So Cold
Ginuwine; *The Bachelor* . . . . (550 Music)

COLORS: BLACK, Ebony

See Also: COLORS (various)

1952 Vincent Black Lightning
Richard Thompson; *Richard Thompson-Best Of Capitol Years* . . . . (Capitol)

6th Avenue Heartache
Wallflowers; *Best Of Rockline-C* . . . . (Priority)
Bringing It All Back Home . . . . (Columbia)

After The Blackbird Sings
Wallflowers; *The Wallflowers* . . . . (Virgin)

Baa Baa Black Sheep
Original Soundtrack; *Toddler Favorites* . . . . (Kid Rhino/Rhino 4 Kids)

Baby's In Black
Beatles; *Beatles '65* . . . . (Capitol)
Beatles-Box Set . . . . (Capitol)
For Sale . . . . (Capitol)

Back In Black
AC/DC; *AC/DC Live* . . . . (Atco)
Atlantic Rock & Roll-C . . . . (Atlantic)
Back In Black . . . . (Atco)

Be Real Black For Me
Roberta Flack & Donny Hathaway; *Roberta Flack & Donny
Hathaway* . . . . (Atlantic)

Beautiful Black Girl
Quincy Jones; *Mellow Madness* . . . . (A&M)

Beyond The Black
Metal Church; *Metal Church* . . . . (Elektra)

Big Black Cadillac Blues
Lightnin' Hopkins; *Drinkin' In The Blues-Golden Classics-#1* . . . (Collectables)
Lightnin' Hopkins . . . . (Everest)

Big Black Smoke
Kinks; *Kink Kronikles* . . . . (Reprise)

Black
Pearl Jam; *Ten* . . . . (Epic Portrait Assoc.)

Black & Blue
Louis Armstrong; *Louis Armstrong's Greatest Hits* . . . . (Legacy)
Louis Armstrong-Vol. 5-In New York . . . . (Columbia)
Satchmo At Symphony Hall . . . . (Columbia)
Louis Armstrong & His Orchestra; *Louis Armstrong & The Big
Bands* . . . . (Disques Swing)
Original Cast; *Ain't Misbehavin'* . . . . (RCA)

Black & Tan Fantasy
Duke Ellington; *Beginning* . . . . (MCA)
Carnegie Hall Concert . . . . (Prestige)
Carnegie Hall Concert -December 11, 1943 . . . . (Everest)
Continuum . . . . (Fantasy)
Duke Ellington-Pure Gold . . . . (RCA)
Duke Ellington's Greatest Hits . . . . (Reprise)
Echoes Of An Era-Duke Ellington & Louis Armstrong . . . . (Roulette)

Duke Ellington & Mercer Ellington; *Duke Ellington & Mercer
Ellington* . . . . (Fantasy)

Black & White
Three Dog Night; *Best Of Three Dog Night* . . . . (MCA)
Billboard Top Rock 'N' Roll Hits-1972-C . . . . (Rhino)
Joy To The World-Greatest Hits . . . . (MCA)

Black & White
Todd Rundgren; *Back To The Bars* . . . . (Rhino)
Faithful . . . . (Rhino)
Todd Rundgren-Anthology 1968-1985 . . . . (Rhino)

Black & White
Rosanne Cash; *Rosanne Cash-Hits-1979-1989* . . . . (Columbia)

Black & White
Jackson Browne; *Lives In The Balance* . . . . (Asylum)

Black & White
INXS; *Dekadance* . . . . (Atco)
Shabooh Shoobah . . . . (Atco)

Black Africa
Devonsquare; *Walking On Ice* . . . . (Atlantic)

Black And Blue
Van Halen; *OU812* . . . . (Warner Bros.)

Black And White Television
Ian Anderson; *Walk Into Light* . . . . (Chrysalis)

Black Autumn
Roy Buchanan; *Sweet Dreams-The Anthology* . . . . (Polydor)

Black Balloon
Goo Goo Dolls; *Dizzy Up The Girl* . . . . (Warner Sunset/Reprise)

Black Bayou
Charlie Daniels Band; *Midnight Wind* . . . . (Epic)

Black Bear Road
C.W. McCall; *C.W. McCall's Greatest Hits* . . . . (Polydor)

Black Blade
Blue Oyster Cult; *Career Of Evil* . . . . (Columbia)
Cultosaurus Erectus . . . . (Columbia)
Extraterrestrial Live . . . . (Columbia)

Black Bottom
Johnny Hamp's Kentucky Serenaders; *Nipper's Greatest Hits Of The
'20s-C* . . . . (RCA)

Black Bottom
Eddie Condon; *Best Of Eddie Condon* . . . . (MCA)

Black Boys On The Corner
Thin Lizzy; *Thin Lizzy-London Collector* . . . . (London)

Black Boys, White Boys
Original Broadway Cast; *Hair* . . . . (RCA)

Black Butterfly
Deniece Williams; *Let's Hear It For The Boy* . . . . (Columbia)

Black Butterfly
Duke Ellington; *Best Of Duke Ellington* . . . . (Pablo)

Black Cadillac
Catfish Hodge Band; *Eyewitness Blues* . . . . (Adelphi)
Lightnin' Hopkins; *How Many More Years I Got* . . . . (Fantasy)

Black Cat
Janet Jackson; *Janet Jackson's Rhythm Nation 1814* . . . . (A&M)

Black Cat
Chris Daniels & The Kings; *In Your Face* . . . . (Flying Fish)

Black Cat Blues
John Lee Hooker; *...Alone* . . . . (Specialty)
Memphis Minnie; *Hoodoo Lady-1933-1937* . . . . (Columbia)

Black Cat Bone
Albert Collins & Johnny Copeland; *Alligator Records 20th Anniversary
Collection-C* . . . . (Alligator)
Johnny Winter; *Progressive Blues Experiment* . . . . (One Way)
Lightnin' Hopkins; *Dark Muddy Bottom Blues-C* . . . . (Specialty)
Mojo Hand-Anthology . . . . (Rhino)
Lonesome Sundown; *Been Gone Too Long* . . . . (Hightone)
Roy Rogers; *Blues On The Range* . . . . (Blind Pig)

Black Cat Moan
Beck, Bogert & Appice; *Beck, Bogert & Appice* . . . . (Epic)
Beckology-C . . . . (Epic)

Black Cat Shuffle
Al DiMeola; *Electric Rendezvous* . . . . (Columbia)

Black Chick, White Guy
Kid Rock; *Devil Without A Cause* . . . . (Top Dog/Lava/Atlantic)

Black Coffee
k.d. lang; *Just Say Yo-#2 Of Just Say Yes-C* . . . . (Sire)
Shadowland . . . . (Sire)

Black Coffee
Humble Pie; *Best Of Humble Pie* . . . . (A&M)
Eat It . . . . (A&M)

Black Coffee
Peggy Lee; *Best Of Peggy Lee* . . . . (MCA)

Black Coffee
Lacy J. Dalton; *Lacy J.* . . . . (Capitol)

Black Coffee
Black Flag; *Slip It In* . . . . (SST)

Black Coffee In Bed
Squeeze; *Sweets From A Stranger* . . . . (A&M)

Black Country Rock
David Bowie; *Man Who Sold The World* . . . . (Rykodisc)
Sound + Vision . . . . (Rykodisc)
Black Country Woman
Led Zeppelin; *Physical Graffiti* . . . . (Swan Song)
Black Cow
Steely Dan; *Aja* . . . . (MCA)
Steely Dan-Gold . . . . (MCA)
Black Crow
Joni Mitchell; *Hejira* . . . . (Asylum)
Shadows & Light . . . . (Asylum)
Black Crow Blues
Bob Dylan; *Another Side Of Bob Dylan* . . . . (Columbia)
Black Day In July
Gordon Lightfoot; *Best Of Gordon Lightfoot* . . . . (EMI)
Did She Mention My Name . . . . (United Artists)
Lightfoot . . . . (EMI)
Black Denim Trousers & Motorcycle Boots
Cheers; *Monster Summer Hits-Drag City-C* . . . . (Capitol)
Black Diamond
Kiss; *Alive!* . . . . (Mercury)
Double Platinum . . . . (Mercury)
Kiss . . . . (Casablanca)
The Originals . . . . (Casablanca)
Black Diamond Bay
Bob Dylan; *Desire* . . . . (Columbia)
Black Dog
Led Zeppelin; *Led Zeppelin IV* . . . . (Atlantic)
Led Zeppelin-Box Set . . . . (Atlantic)
Black Flag
King's X; *King's X* . . . . (Atlantic)
Black Friday
Steely Dan; *Katy Lied* . . . . (MCA)
Steely Dan's Greatest Hits . . . . (MCA)
Black Friday
Splinter; *Two Man Band* . . . . (MCA)
Black Gold
Soul Asylum; *Grace Dancers Union* . . . . (Columbia)
Black Hearted Woman
Allman Brothers Band; *Allman Brothers Band* . . . . (Polydor)
Beginnings . . . . (Polydor)
The Road Goes On Forever, A Collection Of Their Greatest
Recordings . . . . (Polydor)
Black Hole Sun
Soundgarden; *Superunknown* . . . . (A&M)
Black Honey
Graham Parker; *Heart Treatment* . . . . (Mercury)
Live! Alone In America . . . . (RCA)
Black Is Black
Los Bravos; *History Of British Rock-#7-C* . . . . (Rhino)
London Collector-Rock Invasion-C . . . . (London)
Black Is The Color Of My True Love's Hair
Joan Baez; *Best Of Joan Baez* . . . . (A&M)
Joan Baez In Concert . . . . (Vanguard)
The Joan Baez Ballad Book . . . . (Vanguard)
Black Is The Night
Sandy Posey; *45-#49104* . . . . (Warner Bros.)
Black Jack Blues
Fleetwood Mac; *In Chicago* . . . . (Sire)
Gabriel Brown; *Country Blues Classics-#4* . . . . (Blues Classics)
Black Jack County Chain
Henson Cargill; *Jailhouse Rock (Hits From The Big*
House)-C . . . . (Sony Music Special Prod.)
Black Jack David
Alice Stuart; *All The Good Times* . . . . (Arhoolie)
Steeleye Span; *All Around My Hat* . . . . (Chrysalis)
The Steeleye Span Story . . . . (Chrysalis)
Warren Smith; *45-#11* . . . . (Sun)
Black Jesus
Everlast; *Eat At Whitey's* . . . . (Tommy Boy)
Black Land Farmer
Sleepy LaBeef; *Bull's Night Out* . . . . (Sun)
Souvenirs Of Music City U.S.A.-C . . . . (Plantation)
Black Land Farmer
Frankie Miller; *45-#2101* . . . . (Gusto)
Black Licorice
Grand Funk Railroad; *Caught In The Act* . . . . (Capitol)
We're An American Band . . . . (Capitol)
Black Limousine
Rolling Stones; *Tattoo You* . . . . (Virgin)
Black Magic Woman
Fleetwood Mac; *25 Years-The Chain* . . . . (Warner Bros.)
Vintage Years . . . . (Sire)
Santana; *Abraxas* . . . . (Columbia)
Moonflower . . . . (Columbia)
Rock Classics Of The '70s-C . . . . (Columbia)
Santana's Greatest Hits . . . . (Columbia)
Viva Santana! . . . . (Columbia)

Black Man
Stevie Wonder; *Songs In The Key Of Life* . . . . (Motown)
Black Man
Alberta Hunter; *Look For The Silver Lining* . . . . (Columbia)
Black Man Can't Get A Cab
U.T.F.O.; *Bag It & Bone It* . . . . (Jive)
Black Maria
Todd Rundgren; *Back To The Bars* . . . . (Rhino)
Something/Anything? . . . . (Rhino)
Black Messiah
Kinks; *Misfits* . . . . (Arista)
Black Money
Vinnie James; *All-American Boy* . . . . (RCA)
Black Moonlight
Bing Crosby; *Pennies From Heaven* . . . . (Pro-Arte)
Black Mountain Blues
Bessie Smith; *Bessie Smith-The Collection* . . . . (Legacy)
Janis Joplin; *ST/Janis* . . . . (Columbia)
Black Mountain Breakdown
Youngbloods; *Youngbloods* . . . . (RCA)
Black Mountain Rag
Doc Watson; *Doc Watson* . . . . (Vanguard)
Essential Doc Watson-#2 . . . . (Vanguard)
Newport Country Music & Blues . . . . (Vanguard)
Doc Watson/Hot Rize/Dan Crary/Peter Rowan; *Tellulive* . . . . (Flying Fish)
Nitty Gritty Dirt Band; *Will The Circle Be Unbroken* . . . . (EMI)
Black Mountain Side
Led Zeppelin; *Led Zeppelin* . . . . (Atlantic)
Led Zeppelin-Box Set . . . . (Atlantic)
Black Night
Deep Purple; *Deepest Purple/The Very Best Of Deep Purple* . . . . (Warner Bros.)
Nobody's Perfect . . . . (Mercury)
Black Night
Bob Seger; *Beautiful Loser* . . . . (Capitol)
Black Night
Dr. John; *In A Sentimental Mood* . . . . (Warner Bros.)
Black Night
Muddy Waters; *The Chess Box-Muddy Waters* . . . . (Chess)
Black Nights
Bobby Bland; *Ain't Nothing You Can Do* . . . . (MCA)
Introspective Of The Early Years . . . . (MCA)
Black Nights
Charles Brown; *Best Of Charles Brown-Driftin' Blues* . . . . . (Collectables)
Black Notes
David Crosby & Graham Nash; *David Crosby & Graham Nash* . . . . . (Atlantic)
Black Or White
Michael Jackson; *Dangerous* . . . . (Epic)
Black Orpheus
Roger Williams; *Best Of Roger Williams* . . . . (MCA)
Vince Guaraldi & Bola Sete; *Live At El Matador* . . . . (Fantasy)
Black Pearl
Sonny Charles; *Soul Shots-#2-The "In" Crowd-Sweet Soul-C* . . . . (Rhino)
Sonny Charles and The Checkmates, Ltd.; *Soul Shots-C* . . . . . (Rhino)
Black Peter
Grateful Dead; *History Of The Grateful Dead-Vol. 1 (Bear's*
Choice) . . . . (Warner Bros.)
What A Long Strange Trip It's Been: The Best Of The
Grateful Dead . . . . (Warner Bros.)
Workingman's Dead . . . . (Warner Bros.)
Black Polished Chrome
Doors; *An American Prayer-Jim Morrison* . . . . (Elektra)
Black Queen
Crosby, Stills & Nash; *CSN* . . . . (Atlantic)
Stephen Stills; *Stephen Stills* . . . . (Atlantic)
Black Queen
Jimmy Cliff; *Unlimited* . . . . (Reprise)
Black Rose
Waylon Jennings; *Honky Tonk Heroes* . . . . (RCA)
Willie Nelson; *Me & Paul* . . . . (Columbia)
Black Rose
Eric Clapton; *Another Ticket* . . . . (RSO)
Black Rose
J.D. Souther; *Black Rose* . . . . (Asylum)
Black Rose
Sad Cafe; *Misplaced Ideals* . . . . (A&M)
Black Sabbath
Black Sabbath; *Black Sabbath* . . . . (Warner Bros.)
Live Evil . . . . (Warner Bros.)
We Sold Our Soul For Rock 'N' Roll . . . . (Warner Bros.)
Ozzy Osbourne; *Speak Of The Devil* . . . . (Jet)
The Ozzman Cometh . . . . (Epic)
Black Satin Dancer
Jethro Tull; *Minstrel In The Gallery* . . . . (Chrysalis)
Black Sheep
John Anderson; *All The People Are Talkin'* . . . . (Warner Bros.)
John Anderson's Greatest Hits . . . . (Warner Bros.)
Black Sheep
Sam The Sham and The Pharaohs; *Pharaohization! (Best Of)* . . . . (Rhino)

Black Sheep Boy
Tim Hardin; *Memorial Album* . . . . (Polydor)
Black Sheep Of The Family
Blackmore's Rainbow; *Ritchie Blackmore's R-A-I-N-B-O-W* . . . . (Polydor)
Black Skies
Rex Allen, Jr.; *Today's Generation* . . . . (SSS International)
Black Sky
Ozark Mountain Daredevils; *It's Alive* . . . . (A&M)
Ozark Mountain Daredevils. . . . . (A&M)
Black Slacks
Joe Bennett; *Vintage Music-#16-C* . . . . (MCA)
Robert Gordon; *Rock Billy Boogie* . . . . (RCA)
Sparkletones; *Black Slacks* . . . . (MCA)
Black Snake
John Lee Hooker; *Country Blues Of John Lee Hooker* . . . . (Riverside)
Ramblin' Jack Elliott; *Essential Ramblin' Jack Elliott* . . . . (Vanguard)
Black Snake Blues
Clifton Chenier; *Sixty Minutes With The King Of Zydeco* . . . . (Arhoolie)
Black Snake Dream Blues
Blind Lemon Jefferson; *Master Of The Blues-#2-1926-1929* . . . . (Biograph)
Black Snake Moan
Blind Lemon Jefferson; *Great Blues Guitarists-String Dazzlers-C* . . (Columbia)
Leadbelly; *Leadbelly* . . . . (Columbia)
Black Soul
Burning Spear; *Burning Spear-Live* . . . . (Island)
Man In The Hills . . . . (Island)
Black Summer Rain
Eric Clapton; *No Reason To Cry* . . . . (RSO)
Black Sunday
Skatalites; *Ska Bonanza-Studio One Ska Years-C* . . . . (Heartbeat)
Black Sunday
Jethro Tull; *A* . . . . (Chrysalis)
Black Sunshine
White Zombie; *La Sexorcisto-Devil Music-#1* . . . . (Geffen)
Black Throated Wind
Bob Weir; *Ace* . . . . (Grateful Dead)
Grateful Dead; *Steal Your Face* . . . . (Grateful Dead)
Black Train
Montrose; *Montrose* . . . . (Warner Bros.)
Black Uncle Remus
Loudon Wainwright III; *Loudon Wainwright III* . . . . (Atlantic)
Black Valentine
Scott Thomas Band; *California* . . . . (Elektra)
Black Velvet
Alannah Myles; *Alannah Myles* . . . . (Atlantic)
Robin Lee; *Black Velvet* . . . . (Atlantic)
Black Water
Doobie Brothers; *Best Of The Doobies* . . . . (Warner Bros.)
What Were Once Vices Are Now Habits. . . . . (Warner Bros.)
Black Widow
Alice Cooper; *The Alice Cooper Show* . . . . (Warner Bros.)
Welcome To My Nightmare . . . . (Atlantic)
Black Widow
Lita Ford; *Dangerous Curves* . . . . (RCA)
Black Widow
Jefferson Starship; *Winds Of Change* . . . . (Grunt)
Blackbird
Beatles; *Beatles-Box Set* . . . . (Capitol)
The Beatles (White Album) . . . . (Capitol)
Crosby, Stills & Nash; *CSN* . . . . (Atlantic)
Paul McCartney; *Unplugged (The Official Bootleg)* . . . . (Capitol)
Wings; *Wings Over America* . . . . (Capitol)
Black-Eyed Blues
Joe Cocker; *Joe Cocker* . . . . (A&M)
Joe Cocker's Greatest Hits . . . . (A&M)
Black-Eyed Susan
Esther Phillips; *Best Of Esther Phillips.* . . . . (CBS Associated)
Blackleg Miner
Steeleye Span; *Hark The Village Wait* . . . . (Chrysalis)
The Steeleye Span Story . . . . (Chrysalis)
Blackmail
Robert Palmer; *Sneakin' Sally Through The Alley* . . . . (Island)
Blackmail
10 CC; *Original Soundtrack* . . . . (Mercury)
Blackout
David Bowie; *Heroes* . . . . (Rykodisc)
Stage . . . . (Rykodisc)
Blackout
Scorpions; *Blackout* . . . . (Mercury)
World Wide Live . . . . (Mercury)
Blacks Are Giving Me The Blues
Martin Mull; *No Hits Four Errors* . . . . (Capricorn)
Normal. . . . . (Capricorn)
Blondes In Black Cars
Autograph; *That's The Stuff* . . . . (RCA)
Blue On Black
Kenny Wayne Shepherd; *Trouble Is...* . . . . (Revolution)

Bye Bye Blackbird
Dean Martin; *Swingin' Down Yonder* . . . . (Capitol)
Joe Cocker; *With A Little Help From My Friends* . . . . (A&M)
Liza Minnelli; *ST/Liza With A ''Z''*. (Columbia)
Miles Davis; *Ballads* . . . . (Columbia)
Miles Davis Quintet/Jazz Sampler #2 . . . . (Columbia)
Miles Davis Quintet; *Round About Midnight* . . . . (Columbia)
Collard Greens & Black-Eyed Peas
Bud Powell; *Best Of Bud Powell* . . . . (Blue Note)
Creature From The Black Lagoon
Dave Edmunds; *Best Of Dave Edmunds* . . . . (Swan Song)
Elvira Presents Haunted Hits-C . . . . (Rhino)
Repeat When Necessary . . . . (Swan Song)
Dressed In Black
Hoodoo Gurus; *Kinky* . . . . (RCA)
Dressed In Black
Depeche Mode; *Black Celebration* . . . . (Sire)
Ebony And Ivory
Paul McCartney & Stevie Wonder; *All The Best!* . . . . (Capitol)
Tug Of War. . . . . (Gold Rush)
Ebony Eyes
Everly Brothers; *Golden Hits Of The Everly Brothers* . . . . (Warner Bros.)
Very Best Of The Everly Brothers. . . . . (Warner Bros.)
Ebony Eyes
Rick James Featuring Smokey Robinson; *Cold Blooded* . . . . (Motown)
Rick James' Greatest Hits . . . . (Motown)
Ebony Eyes
Bob Welch; *French Kiss* . . . . (Capitol)
Ebony Eyes
Stevie Wonder; *Songs In The Key Of Life* . . . . (Motown)
Endless Black Ribbon
Red Simpson; *Trucks,Trains & Airplanes-C* . . . . . . (International Mktg. Group)
Red Sovine/Willis Bros./Reno & Smiley; *Heavy Haulers* . . . . (Power Pak)
Fear Of A Black Planet
Public Enemy; *Fear Of A Black Planet* . . . . (Def Jam)
Feel So Numb
Rob Zombie; *Sinister Urge* . . . . (Geffen)
Fell On Black Days
Soundgarden; *Superunknown* . . . . (A&M)
Girl I Love
Led Zeppelin; *BBC Sessions* . . . . (Atlantic)
Gold-Tipped Boots, Black Jacket And Tie
Jethro Tull; *Catfish Rising* . . . . (Chrysalis)
Lateralus
Tool; *Lateralus* . . . . (Volcano Entertainment)
Let's Make The Water Turn Black
Mothers Of Invention; *Lumpy Gravy* . . . . (Rykodisc)
Light In The Black
Blackmore's Rainbow; *Rainbow Rising* . . . . (Polydor)
Little Black Backpack
Stroke9; *Nasty Little Thoughts* . . . . (Cherry/Universal)
Little Black Book
Jimmy Dean; *American Originals-Jimmy Dean* . . . . (Columbia)
Jimmy Dean's Greatest Hits . . . . (Columbia)
Long Black Limousine
Bobby Bare; *This Is Bobby Bare* . . . . (RCA)
Elvis Presley; *From Elvis In Memphis.* . . . . (RCA)
Memphis Record. . . . . (RCA)
Long Black Veil
Band; *Music From Big Pink* . . . . (Capitol)
To Kingdom Come-The Definitive Collection. . . . . (Capitol)
Joan Baez; *Joan Baez In Concert, Part 2.* . . . . (Vanguard)
One Day At A Time . . . . (Vanguard)
Johnny Cash; *Classic Cash-Hall Of Fame Series* . . . . (Mercury)
Johnny Cash At Folsom Prison & San Quentin . . . . (Columbia)
Lefty Frizzell; *American Originals-Lefty Frizzell.* . . . . (Columbia)
Columbia Country Classics-#3-Americana-C . . . . (Columbia)
Long Cool Woman In A Black Dress
Hollies; *Best Of The Hollies* . . . . (EMI)
Best Of The Hollies-#2 . . . . (EMI)
Billboard Top Rock 'N' Roll Hits-1972-C . . . . (Rhino)
Distant Light. . . . . (Epic)
Hollies-Epic Anthology From The Original Master Tapes. . . . . (Epic)
The Hollies' Greatest Hits . . . . (Epic)
Losing Lisa
Ben Folds; *Rockin' The Suburbs* . . . . (Epic)
Man In Black
Johnny Cash; *Essential Johnny Cash* . . . . (Columbia)
Patriot . . . . (Columbia)
The Man In Black-His Greatest Hits. . . . . (Legacy)
Man In The Long Black Coat
Joan Osborne; *Relish.* . . . . (Blue Gorilla/Mercury)
Men In Black
Will Smith; *Big Willie Style* . . . . (Columbia)
ST/Men In Black . . . . (Columbia)
Mexican Blackbird
ZZ Top; *Fandango* . . . . (Warner Bros.)
Six Pack . . . . (Warner Bros.)

My Black Cadillac
Lightnin' Hopkins; *Lightnin' Hopkins-Complete Prestige/Bluesville Recordings* ....(Bluesville)

My TV Went Black & White On Me
Young Black Teenagers; *Young Black Teenagers* ....(S.O.U.L.)

Old Black Choo Choo
Rose Maddox; *Rose Of The West Coast Country* ....(Arhoolie)

One Piece At A Time
Johnny Cash; *The Man In Black-His Greatest Hits* ....(Legacy)

Paint It, Black
Eric Burdon; *Eric Burdon Sings The Animals' Greatest Hits* ...(Rhino)
Rolling Stones; *Aftermath* ....(Abkco)
    Flashpoint ....(Virgin)
    Hot Rocks 1964-1971 ....(Abkco)
    Singles Collection-The London Years ....(Abkco)
    Through The Past, Darkly (Big Hits Vol. 2) ....(Abkco)

Pink And Black
Robert Plant; *Shaken 'N' Stirred* ....(Es Paranza)

Proud To Be Black
Young Black Teenagers; *Young Black Teenagers* ....(S.O.U.L.)

Proud To Be Black
Run-D.M.C.; *Raising Hell* ....(Profile)

Red & Black
Original Broadway Cast; *Les Miserables* ....(Geffen)

Red And The Black
Blue Oyster Cult; *Career Of Evil* ....(Columbia)
    Extraterrestrial Live ....(Columbia)
    On Your Feet Or On Your Knees ....(Columbia)
    Tyranny & Mutation ....(Columbia)

Reverend Mr. Black
Johnny Cash; *Johnny Cash's Biggest Hits* ....(Columbia)
Kingston Trio; *Capitol Collectors Series-The Kingston Trio* ....(Capitol)

Say It Loud I'm Black & I'm Proud
Afrika Bambaataa; *Decade Of Darkness* ....(EMI)
James Brown; *Billboard Top R&B Hits-1965-1969-C* ...(Rhino)

Sing A Song Of Sixpence
Original Soundtrack; *Children's Favorites* .... (Kid Rhino/Rhino 4 Kids)

Slick Black Cadillac
Quiet Riot; *Heavy Metal Memories-C* ....(Rhino)
    Metal Health ....(Pasha)

Sweet Black Angel
Rolling Stones; *Exile On Main Street* ....(Virgin)

Sweet Black Girl
Buddy Guy & Junior Wells; *Alone & Acoustic* ....(Alligator)

That Black Snake Moan
Blind Lemon Jefferson; *Blind Lemon Jefferson* ....(Milestone)

That Old Black Magic
Ella Fitzgerald; *Best Of Ella Fitzgerald* ....(MCA)
    Big Bands Of The Swinging Years-C ....(Everest)
    In Rome-Birthday Concert ....(Verve)
Frank Sinatra; *Come Swing With Me!* ....(Capitol)
Glenn Miller & His Orchestra; *Chattanooga Choo Choo-#1 Hits* .....(Bluebird)
Judy Garland; *Best Of Judy Garland* ....(MCA)
Louis Prima & Keely Smith; *Memories Are Made Of This-C* ....(Capitol)
Marcels; *Best Of The Marcels* ....(Rhino)
Sammy Davis, Jr.; *Hey There-At His Dynamite Greatest* ......(MCA)
Spike Jones; *Best Of Spike Jones-#2* ....(RCA)

This Black Cat Has 9 Lives
Louis Armstrong; *What A Wonderful World* ....(Bluebird)

Under The Big Black Sun
X; *Under The Big Black Sun* ....(Elektra)

We Work The Black Seam
Sting; *Bring On The Night* ....(A&M)
    Dream Of The Blue Turtles ....(A&M)

White Man/Black Man
James Gang; *James Gang-16 Greatest Hits* ....(MCA)
    Thirds ....(One Way)

Wish I Were You
Patty Smyth; *ST/Armageddon-The Album* ....(Columbia)

COLORS: BLUE

See Also: COLORS (various), LOVE (various), SADNESS

(They Long To Be) Close To You
Carpenters; *Carpenters-Classics-#2* ....(A&M)
    Carpenters-Love Songs ....(A&M)
    Carpenters-The Singles 1969-1973 ....(A&M)
    From The Top ....(A&M)

Afro Blue
Cal Tjader; *Cal Tjader-Concert By The Sea* ....(Fantasy)
    Cal Tjader's Greatest Hits ....(Fantasy)
    Monterey Concerts ....(Prestige)
John Coltrane; *Afro Blue Impressions* ....(Pablo)
    Best Of John Coltrane ....(Pablo)
    Best Of John Coltrane-His Greatest Years ....(MCA)
Mongo Santamaria; *Afro-Roots* ....(Prestige)

Mongo Santamaria's Greatest Hits ....(Fantasy)

Alice Blue Gown
Edith Day; *Music From The New York Stage (1890-1920)-#4-1917-1920-C* ....(Pearl)
    Nipper's Greatest Hits Of The '20s-C ....(RCA)

Am I Blue
George Strait; *Country Classics-#11-1987-1988-C* ....(Universal)
    George Strait's Greatest Hits-#2 ....(MCA)
    MCA #1 Hits Of The '80s-#3-C ....(MCA Special Prod.)
    Ocean Front Property ....(MCA)

Am I Blue
Barbra Streisand; *ST/Funny Lady* ....(Arista)
Billie Holiday; *God Bless The Child* ....(Columbia)
Ray Charles; *Genius Of Ray Charles* ....(Atlantic)

Angel In Blue
J. Geils Band; *Freeze-Frame* ....(EMI)

Atlanta Blue
Statler Brothers; *14 Country Favorites-C* ....(Mercury)
    Atlanta Blue ....(Mercury)
    Statler Brothers' Greatest Hits ....(Mercury)

Aunt Hagar's Blues
Art Tatum; *Solo Masterpieces-#4* ....(Pablo)
Kid Ory's Creole Jazz Band; *This Kid's The Greatest* .....(Good Time Jazz)

Baby Blue
Gene Vincent and His Blue Caps; *Capitol Collectors Series-Gene Vincent and His Blue Caps* ....(Gold Rush)

Baby Blue
George Strait; *If You Ain't Lovin' You Ain't Livin'* ....(MCA)

Baby Blue
Beach Boys; *L.A.-The Light Album* ....(Caribou)

Baby Blue
Paul Butterfield Blues Band; *North South* ....(Rhino)

Baby Blue
Echoes; *Super Oldies Of The '60s-#5-C* ....(Audio Fidelity)

Baby's Got Her Blue Jeans On
Mel McDaniel; *All-Time Country Classics-#2-C* ....(Capitol)
    Let It Roll ....(Capitol)
    Mel McDaniel's Greatest Hits ....(Capitol)

Barstow Blue Eyes
Jo Jo Gunne; *Jo Jo Gunne* ....(Asylum)

Be Like The Bluebird
Cole Porter; *Cole Porter-A Centennial Celebration-C* .....(RCA)

Beautiful Brown Eyes
Rosemary Clooney; *Songs From The Girl Singer-A Musical Autobiography* ....(Concord Jazz)

Behind Blue Eyes
Who; *Hooligans* ....(MCA)
    Join Together ....(MCA)
    Who's Last ....(MCA)
    Who's next ....(MCA)

Between Blue Eyes And Jeans
Conway Twitty; *Don't Call Him A Cowboy* ....(Warner Bros.)

Between The Devil And The Deep Blue Sea
Cab Calloway; *Jazz Heritage: Mr. Hi-De-Ho* ....(MCA)
Chris Rea; *Espresso Logic* ....(East West)
Diana Krall; *Stepping Out* ....(Justin Time)
Ella Fitzgerald; *Harold Arlen Songbook-#1* ....(Verve)

Beyond The Blue Horizon
Jeanette MacDonald; *Hollywood Sings-C* ....(Living Era)
Lou Christie; *ST/Rain Man* ....(Capitol)

Black & Blue
Louis Armstrong; *Louis Armstrong's Greatest Hits* .....(Legacy)
    Louis Armstrong-Vol. 5-In New York ....(Columbia)
    Satchmo At Symphony Hall ....(Columbia)
Louis Armstrong & His Orchestra; *Louis Armstrong & The Big Bands* ....(Disques Swing)
Original Cast; *Ain't Misbehavin'* ....(RCA)

Black And Blue
Van Halen; *OU812* ....(Warner Bros.)

Black Is Black
Los Bravos; *History Of British Rock-#7-C* ....(Rhino)
    London Collector-Rock Invasion-C ....(London)

Blonde Ambition
Billy Burnette; *Soldier Of Love* ....(Curb)

Blue
Joni Mitchell; *Blue* ....(Reprise)
Joni Mitchell with Tom Scott & The L.A. Express; *Miles Of Aisles* ....(Asylum)

Blue
LeAnn Rimes; *Blue* ....(MCG/Curb)

Blue
Emotional Fish; *Emotional Fish* ....(Atlantic)

Blue
Fine Young Cannibals; *Fine Young Cannibals* ....(I.R.S.)

Blue
Peter, Paul & Mary; *Peter, Paul and Mary In Concert* ....(Warner Bros.)

Blue (Da Ba Dee)
Eiffel 65; *Europop* ....(Republic/Universal)
    Now That's What I Call Music!-#4-C ....(Virgin)

Blue And Sentimental
Tony Bennett with Kay Starr; *Playin' With My Friends-Bennett Sings The Blues-C* . . . . (Columbia)

Blue Angel
Roy Orbison; *For The Lonely: 18 Greatest Hits* . . . . (Rhino)
In Dreams-Greatest Hits . . . . (Orbison)
Roy Orbison Greatest Hits . . . . (Monument)
Roy Orbison's All-Time Greatest Hits-#1 & 2 . . . . (Monument)
Very Best Of Roy Orbison . . . . (Monument)

Blue Angel Suite
Strawbs; *Best Of The Strawbs* . . . . (A&M)

Blue Autumn
Bobby Goldsboro; *10th Anniversary Album-#1* . . . . (EMI)
Bobby Goldsboro's Greatest Hits . . . . (Liberty)
Honey-Best Of Bobby Goldsboro . . . . (EMI)

Blue Avenue
Elton John; *Sleeping With The Past* . . . . (MCA)

Blue Bayou
Linda Ronstadt; *Linda Ronstadt's Greatest Hits, Volume Two* . . . . . . (Asylum)
Simple Dreams . . . . (Asylum)
Roy Orbison; *For The Lonely: A Roy Orbison Anthology 1959-1965* . . . (Rhino)
In Dreams-Greatest Hits . . . . (Orbison)
Roy Orbison-More Greatest Hits . . . . (Monument)
Roy Orbison's All-Time Greatest Hits-#1 & 2 . . . . (Monument)
Roy Orbison & Friends; *Black & White Night-Live* . . . . (Virgin)

Blue Boy
Jim Reeves; *Best Of Jim Reeves* . . . . (RCA)
Live At The Opry . . . . (Country Music Foundation)

Blue Boy
Joni Mitchell; *Ladies Of The Canyon* . . . . (Reprise)

Blue Canadian Rockies
Byrds; *Sweetheart Of The Rodeo* . . . . (Columbia)
Gene Autry; *50th Anniversary* . . . . (Republic/Universal)
Live From Madison Square Garden . . . . (Republic/Universal)
Jimmy C. Newman; *Cajun Cowboy* . . . . (Plantation)

Blue Champagne
Manhattan Transfer; *The Manhattan Transfer* . . . . (Rhino)

Blue Clear Sky
George Strait; *Blue Clear Sky* . . . . (MCA)
Latest Greatest Straitest Hits . . . . (MCA)

Blue Collar
Bachman-Turner Overdrive; *Best Of B.T.O.-So Far* . . . . (Mercury)

Blue Collar Man
Styx; *Caught In The Act* . . . . (A&M)
Pieces Of Eight . . . . (A&M)
Styx-Classics-#15 . . . . (A&M)

Blue Darlin'
Jimmy C. Newman; *Jimmy C. Newman's Greatest Hits* . . . . (Plantation)

Blue Eden
Neil Young & Crazy Horse; *Sleeps With Angels* . . . . (Reprise)

Blue Eyes
Elton John; *Elton John's Greatest Hits-1976-1986* . . . . (MCA)
Jump Up! . . . . (MCA)

Blue Eyes Blue
Eric Clapton; *Clapton Chronicles-The Best Of Eric Clapton 1981-1999* . . . . (Reprise)
ST/Runaway Bride . . . . (Sony Music Soundtrax)

Blue Eyes Crying In The Rain
Roy Acuff; *Roy Acuff's Greatest Hits* . . . . (Elektra)
Roy Acuff and his Smoky Mountain Boys; *Columbia Country Classics-#1-Golden Age-C* . . . . (Columbia)
Willie Nelson; *Columbia Country Classics-#5-A New Tradition-C* . . (Columbia)
Greatest Hits (& Some That Will Be) . . . . (Columbia)
Red Headed Stranger . . . . (Columbia)
ST/Honeysuckle Rose . . . . (Columbia)

Blue Gardenia
Nat "King" Cole; *The Nat "King" Cole Story* . . . . (Capitol)

Blue Hawaii
Billy Vaughn; *Best Of Billy Vaughn* . . . . (MCA)
Billy Vaughn-16 Great Performances . . . . (MCA)
Billy Vaughn-Golden Hits . . . . (MCA)
Billy Vaughn & His Orchestra; *Billy Vaughn & His Orchestra Play 22 Of His Greatest Hits* . . . . (Ranwood)
Elvis Presley; *Elvis-A Legendary Performer, Volume 2* . . . . (RCA)
ST/Blue Hawaii . . . . (RCA)

Blue Jay Way
Beatles; *Beatles-Box Set* . . . . (Capitol)
Magical Mystery Tour . . . . (Capitol)

Blue Jean
David Bowie; *Changesbowie* . . . . (Rykodisc)
The Singles-1969-1993 . . . . (Rykodisc)
Tonight . . . . (EMI)

Blue Jean Blues
Hank Williams, Jr.; *Strong Stuff* . . . . (Warner Bros.)
ZZ Top; *Best Of ZZ Top* . . . . (Warner Bros.)
Fandango . . . . (Warner Bros.)
Six Pack . . . . (Warner Bros.)

Blue Jean Boy
Michael Stanley Band; *Ladies' Choice* . . . . (Epic)

Blue Jeans
Chocolate Milk; *Greatest Grooves Of Chocolate Milk-Ice Cold Funk* . . . . (Razor & Tie)

Blue Kentucky Girl
Emmylou Harris; *Blue Kentucky Girl* . . . . (Warner Bros.)
Profile II-The Best Of Emmylou Harris . . . . (Warner Bros.)
Loretta Lynn; *Loretta Lynn's Greatest Hits* . . . . (MCA)

Blue Kiss
Jane Wiedlin; *Jane Wiedlin* . . . . (I.R.S.)

Blue Kiss
Chuck Loeb; *Listen* . . . . (Shanachie)

Blue Lamp
Stevie Nicks; *ST/Heavy Metal* . . . . (Asylum)

Blue Letter
Fleetwood Mac; *Fleetwood Mac* . . . . (Reprise)

Blue Lou
Benny Carter; *1933* . . . . (Prestige)
Ella Fitzgerald; *Best Of Ella Fitzgerald-#2* . . . . (MCA)
Ella Sings/Chick Swings . . . . (Olympic)

Blue Memories
Patty Loveless; *On Down The Line* . . . . (MCA)

Blue Monday
Bobby Darin; *Darin 1963-1973* . . . . (Motown)
Fats Domino; *At Montreux* . . . . (Atlantic)
Fats Domino's All Time Greatest Hits . . . . (Curb)
Fats Domino's Greatest Hits . . . . (Everest)
Fats Domino's Greatest Hits . . . . (MCA)
My Blue Heaven . . . . (Gold Rush)
Super Oldies Of The '50s-#5-C . . . . (Audio Fidelity)
Huey Lewis and the News; *Four Chords & Several Years Ago* . . . . (Elektra)
Kingsnakes; *19 Lucky Strikes* . . . . (Blue Wave)
Hardlife Boogie . . . . (Blue Wave)

Blue Monday
Orgy; *Candyass* . . . . (Elementree/Reprise)

Blue Monday At Kansas City Red's
Cary Bell; *Blues Harp* . . . . (Delmark)

Blue Monday People
Curtis Mayfield; *America Today* . . . . (Curtom)

Blue Money
Van Morrison; *His Band And The Street Choir* . . . . (Warner Bros.)

Blue Monk
Bill Evans; *Conversations With Myself* . . . . (Verve)
Thelonius Monk; *Alone In San Francisco* . . . . (Riverside)
Thelonius Monk-Composer . . . . (Columbia)

Blue Moon
Billie Holiday; *Billie's Blues* . . . . (Blue Note)
First Verve Sessions . . . . (Verve)
History Of Billie Holiday . . . . (Verve)
Elvis Presley; *Elvis Presley* . . . . (RCA)
The Sun Sessions . . . . (RCA)
Marcels; *Best Of The Marcels* . . . . (Rhino)
Billboard Top Rock 'N' Roll Hits-1961-C . . . . (Rhino)

Blue Moon Of Kentucky
Bill Monroe; *American Originals-Bill Monroe* . . . . (Columbia)
Bean Blossom . . . . (MCA)
Best Of Bill Monroe & His Blue Grass Boys . . . . (MCA)
Bill Monroe & His Blue Grass Boys; *Bluegrass Super Hits-C* . . . . . (Columbia)
Elvis Presley; *A Date With Elvis* . . . . (RCA)
A Golden Celebration . . . . (RCA)
The Sun Sessions . . . . (RCA)

Blue Moon With Heartache
Rosanne Cash; *19 Hot Country Requests-#2-C* . . . . (Epic)
Rosanne Cash-Hits-1979-1989 . . . . (Columbia)
Seven Year Ache . . . . (Columbia)

Blue Morning Blue Day
Foreigner; *Double Vision* . . . . (Atlantic)

Blue Motel Room
Joni Mitchell; *Hejira* . . . . (Asylum)

Blue Motorcycle Eyes
Havana 3 A.M.; *Havana 3 A.M.* . . . . (I.R.S.)

Blue Must Be The Color Of The Blues
Willie Nelson; *There'll Be No Teardrops Tonight* . . . . (United Artists)

Blue On Black
Kenny Wayne Shepherd; *Trouble Is...* . . . . (Revolution)

Blue On Blue
Bobby Vinton; *Autumn Memories* . . . . (Epic)
Bobby Vinton-16 Most Requested Songs . . . . (Legacy)
Bobby Vinton's All-Time Greatest Hits . . . . (Epic)

Blue Oyster Cult
Blue Oyster Cult; *Imaginos* . . . . (Columbia)

Blue Railroad Train
Doc Watson; *Doc Watson & Merle Watson: Southbound* . . . . (Vanguard)
Essential Doc Watson . . . . (Vanguard)
Lonesome Road . . . . (United Artists)

Blue Red & Grey
Who; *By Numbers* . . . . (MCA)

Blue Ridge Mountain Blues
Blue Ridge Rangers; *Blue Ridge Rangers* . . . . (Fantasy)

Doc Watson; *Essential Doc Watson* . . . . (Vanguard)
Earl Scruggs & John Fogerty; *Earl Scruggs And Friends-C* . . . . (MCA)
Norman Blake; *Directions*. . . . . (Takoma)

Blue Ridge Mountain Sky
Marshall Tucker Band; *New Life* . . . . (AJK Music)

Blue Ridge Mountains Turnin' Green
Charley Pride; *Amazing Love* . . . . (RCA)

Blue River
Elvis Presley; *Lost Album* . . . . (RCA)
ST/Double Trouble . . . . (RCA)

Blue Rock Montana/Red Headed Stranger
Willie Nelson; *Red Headed Stranger* . . . . (Columbia)

Blue Room
Ella Fitzgerald; *Rodgers & Hart Songbook* . . . . (Verve)

Blue Room
Diana Ross; *Diana Ross & The Supremes-25th Anniversary*. . . . . . . (Motown)

Blue Rose Is
Pam Tillis; *Put Yourself In My Place* . . . . (Arista)

Blue Rose Of Texas
Holly Dunn; *Blue Rose Of Texas* . . . . (Warner Bros.)

Blue Shadows
B.B. King; *B.B. King Greatest Hits* . . . . (Kent)
From The Beginning . . . . (Kent)
The Jungle . . . . (Kent)

Blue Shadows
Blasters; *ST/Streets Of Fire* . . . . (MCA)

Blue Shadows On The Trail
Sons Of The Pioneers; *Cool Water* . . . . (RCA)

Blue Side
Crystal Gayle; *Crystal Gayle Greatest Hits*. . . . . (Capitol)
Miss The Mississippi. . . . . (Capitol)

Blue Side Of Lonesome
George Jones; *George Jones Sings The Great Songs Of Leon
Payne* . . . . (Hollywood/DNA-Rounder)
Jim Reeves; *Best Of Jim Reeves-#4* . . . .(RCA)

Blue Side Of Town
Patty Loveless; *Honky Tonk Angel* . . . . (MCA)
Patty Loveless' Greatest Hits . . . . (MCA)

Blue Skies
Benny Goodman; *Benny Goodman Today* . . . .(London)
Carnegie Hall Jazz Concert . . . . (Columbia)
The Birth Of Swing (1935-1936). (Bluebird)
This Is Benny Goodman . . . . (RCA)
Bing Crosby; *Bing Crosby's Greatest Hits* . . . . (MCA)
Duke Ellington; *Carnegie Hall Concert* . . . . (Prestige)
Golden Duke . . . . (Prestige)
Willie Nelson; *Stardust* . . . . (Legacy)

Blue Skirt Waltz
Frankie Yankovic & His Yanks; *Frankie Yankovic & His Yanks'
Greatest Hits* . . . . (Columbia)
Mom & Dads; *Best Of The Mom & Dads* . . . . (Crescendo)
Blue Canadian Rockies. . . . . (Crescendo)

Blue Sky
Allman Brothers Band; *An Evening With The Allman Brothers Band-
First Set* . . . . (Epic)
Best Of The Allman Brothers Band. . . . . (Polydor)
Decade Of Hits-1969-1979. . . . . (Polydor)
Dreams . . . . (Polydor)
Eat A Peach . . . . (Polydor)
*The Road Goes On Forever, A Collection Of Their Greatest
Recordings* . . . . (Polydor)

Blue Sky
Sweethearts Of The Rodeo; *Buffalo Zone* . . . . (Columbia)

Blue Sky
Patty Griffin; *Flaming Red* . . . . (A&M)

Blue Sky Mine
Midnight Oil; *Blue Sky Mining* . . . . (Columbia)

Blue Sky Shinin'
Marie Osmond; *There's No Stopping Your Heart* . . . . (Curb)
Mickey Newbury; *Sailor* . . . . (MCA)

Blue Spruce Woman
Foghat; *Rock & Roll Outlaws* . . . . (Rhino)

Blue Star
Mystics; *Mystics-16 Golden Classics* . . . . (Collectables)

Blue Star
Blue Notes; *Blue Notes-Early Years* . . . . (Collectables)

Blue Star
Charlie Daniels Band; *Million Mile Reflections*. . . . . (Epic)

Blue Suede Shoes
Carl Perkins; *Blue Suede Shoes* . . . . (Sun)
Carl Perkins-Original Sun Greatest Hits . . . . (Rhino)
Cruisin'-1956-1957-C . . . . (Dunhill Compact Classics)
Oldies But Goodies-#4-C . . . .(Original Sound)
Elvis Presley; *Aloha from Hawaii via Satellite* . . . . (RCA)
Elvis Presley . . . . (RCA)
Elvis-A Legendary Performer, Volume 2 . . . . (RCA)
From Memphis To Vegas/From Vegas To Memphis . . . . (RCA)
ST/G.I. Blues. . . . . (RCA)

Blue Sunday
Doors; *Morrison Hotel/Hard Rock Cafe* . . . . (Elektra)

Blue Tail Fly
Burl Ives; *Best Of Burl Ives* . . . . (MCA)
Pete Seeger; *20 Golden Pieces Of Pete Seeger*. . . . . (Bulldog)

Blue Tango
Billy Vaughn; *String Of Pearls-Greatest Hits* . . . .(Pro-Arte)
Leroy Anderson; *Best Of Leroy Anderson-Sleigh Ride* . . . . (Decca)

Blue Texas Waltz
Billy Joe Shaver; *Taste Of Texas-Songs 'Bout Texas By Texans-C* . . .(Columbia)

Blue Thursday
Franz Jackson Original All-Stars; *Featuring Bob Shoffner* . . . . (Riverside)

Blue Train
Johnny Cash; *Classic Cash-Hall Of Fame Series*. . . . .(Mercury)
Original Johnny Cash . . . . (Sun)
Story Songs Of The Trains & Rivers . . . . (Sun)
The Man-The World-His Music. . . . . (Sun)
Marty Stuart; *Freight Train Blues-Classic Railroad Songs-#4-C* . . .(Rounder)

Blue Train
John Coltrane; *Best Of Blue Note-#1-C* . . . . (Blue Note)
Blue Train . . . . (Blue Note)

Blue Train, The
Linda Ronstadt; *Feels Like Home* . . . . (Elektra)
Maura O'Connell; *Blue Is The Colour Of Hope* . . . . (Warner Bros.)

Blue Turning Grey Over You
Billie Holiday; *Billie's Blues* . . . . (Blue Note)
Louis Armstrong & Luis Russell & Orchestra; *Satchmo Style* . . .(Disques Swing)
Ringo Starr; *Sentimental Journey*. . . . .(Capitol)

Blue Turns To Grey
Rolling Stones; *December's Children (and everybody's)* . . . . (Abkco)

Blue Umbrella
John Prine; *Sweet Revenge* . . . . (Atlantic)

Blue Umbrella
Ed Bruce; *Ed Bruce* . . . . (MCA)

Blue Valentine
Tom Waits; *The Heart Of Saturday Night* . . . . (Asylum)

Blue Velvet
Bobby Vinton; *Bobby Vinton-16 Most Requested Songs* . . . .(Legacy)
Bobby Vinton's All-Time Greatest Hits . . . . (Epic)
Bobby Vinton's Greatest Hits/Greatest Hits Of Love . . . . (Columbia)

Blue Water
Poco; *Crazy Eyes* . . . . (Epic)
Ride The Country . . . . (Epic)

Blue White Planet
Raffi; *Country Goes Raffi-C* . . . . (Rounder)

Blue Yodel #1
Bob Wills; *Bob Wills-Anthology* . . . . (Sony Music Special Prod.)
Lynyrd Skynyrd; *Best Of The Rest Of Lynyrd Skynyrd*. . . . . (MCA)
One More From The Road. . . . . (MCA)

Blue Yodel #4 (California Blues)
Bill Monroe; *Columbia Historic Edition-Bill Monroe* . . . .(Columbia)
Jimmie Rodgers; *Jimmie Rodgers-Early Years-1928-1929* . . . .(Rounder)
Never No Mo' Blues . . . . (RCA)
This Is Jimmie Rodgers . . . . (RCA)
Merle Haggard & The Strangers; *Train Whistle Blues* . . . .(Rounder)

Blueberry Hill
Elvis Presley; *Elvis Recorded Live On Stage In Memphis* . . . . (RCA)
Loving You . . . . (RCA)
Fats Domino; *Fats Domino's Greatest Hits* . . . .(Everest)
Fats Domino's Greatest Hits. . . . . (MCA)
My Blue Heaven-Best Of Fats Domino-#1 . . . . (EMI)
Little Richard; *Big Hits* . . . . (Crescendo)
Louis Armstrong; *Best Of Louis Armstrong*. . . . . (MCA)
Essential Louis Armstrong . . . . (Vanguard)
I Like Jazz-Essence Of Louis Armstrong . . . . (Columbia)

Bluebird
Buffalo Springfield; *Buffalo Springfield Again* . . . .(Atco)
Buffalo Springfield-Retrospective . . . .(Atco)
Classic Rock 1966-1988-C . . . . (Atlantic)

Bluebird
Paul McCartney & Wings; *Band On The Run* . . . .(Capitol)
Wings; *Wings Over America* . . . .(Capitol)

Bluebird
Robin Trower; *In City Dreams* . . . . (Chrysalis)

Bluebird
Electric Light Orchestra; *Secret Messages*. . . . . (Jet)

Bluebird
Helen Reddy; *Live In London*. . . . .(Capitol)
No Way To Treat A Lady . . . .(Capitol)

Bluebird
Leon Russell; *Best Of Leon Russell* . . . . (MCA)
Will O' The Wisp . . . . (MCA)

Bluebird Is Dead
Electric Light Orchestra; *Afterglow* . . . . (Epic)
On The Third Day . . . . (Jet)

Bluebird Of Happiness
Lee Andrews And The Hearts; *Gotham Recording Sessions* . . . . . .(Collectables)
Lee Andrews And The Hearts' Biggest Hits. . . . .(Collectables)

Bluebirds Over the Mountain
Beach Boys; *Absolute Best-#2* . . . . (Capitol)
  Beach Boys '69 (The Beach Boys Live In London) . . . . (Capitol)
  Friends-20/20 . . . . (Capitol)
  Sunshine Dream . . . . (Capitol)
Ritchie Valens; *Best Of Ritchie Valens* . . . . (Rhino)
  History Of Ritchie Valens . . . . (Rhino)
  Ritchie Valens . . . . (Rhino)

Blueboy
John Fogerty; *Blue Moon Swamp* . . . .(Warner Bros.)

Bluejean Bop
Gene Vincent and His Blue Caps; *Capitol Collectors Series-Gene Vincent
  and His Blue Caps* . . . . (Gold Rush)
  Gene Vincent and His Blue Caps' Greatest Hits . . . . (Curb)
  *The Screaming End-The Best Of Gene Vincent and His
  Blue Caps* . . . . (Razor & Tie)

Bluer Than Blue
Michael Johnson; *The Michael Johnson Album* . . . .(EMI)
  Then & Now . . . . (ISD/Intersound)

Bluest Eyes In Texas
Restless Heart; *Big Dreams In A Small Town* . . . . (RCA)

Born To Be Blue
George Shearing & Mel Torme; *Evening With George Shearing & Mel
  Torme* . . . .(Concord Jazz)
Judds; *Judds' Greatest Hits-#2* . . . .(MCA)
  Love Can Build A Bridge . . . .(MCA)
Mel Torme; *Mel Torme-Compact Jazz* . . . . (Verve)
Steve Miller; *Born 2 B Blue* . . . . (Gold Rush)

Boy Blue
Electric Light Orchestra; *Afterglow* . . . .(Epic)
  Eldorado . . . . (Jet)
  Ole ELO . . . . (Jet)

Boy Blue
Cyndi Lauper; *True Colors* . . . . (Portrait)

Brown To Blue
Elvis Costello & The Attractions; *Almost Blue* . . . . (Columbia)

Bullet The Blue Sky
U2; *Joshua Tree* . . . . (Island)
  Rattle And Hum . . . . (Island)

California Blue
Herb Alpert; *Fandango* . . . . (A&M)

California Blue
Roy Orbison; *Mystery Girl* . . . . (Virgin)

Carolina Blue
Annie McGowan; *Rattlesnakes & Rusty Water* . . . . (Rattlesnake)

Chicken Cordon Blues
Steve Goodman; *Somebody Else's Troubles* . . . . (Buddah)

Child Of The Wild Blue Yonder
John Hiatt; *Stolen Moments* . . . . (A&M)

Clear Blue Skies
Crosby, Stills, Nash & Young; *American Dream* . . . .(Atlantic)

Cold Blue Steel & Sweet Fire
Joni Mitchell; *For The Roses* . . . . (Asylum)
Joni Mitchell with Tom Scott & The L.A. Express; *Miles Of Aisles* . . . . (Asylum)

Computer Blue
Prince and the Revolution; *ST/Purple Rain* . . . .(Warner Bros.)

Counting Blue Cars
Dishwalla; *Pet Your Friends* . . . . (A&M)

Crystal Blue Persuasion
Tommy James And The Shondells; *Best Of Tommy James And The
  Shondells* . . . . (Roulette)
  Tommy James And The Shondells-Anthology . . . . (Rhino)

Deacon Blues
Steely Dan; *Aja* . . . .(MCA)
  Steely Dan-Gold . . . .(MCA)

Devil With A Blue Dress On & Good Golly Miss Molly
Bruce Springsteen; *ST/No Nukes-Muse Concerts* . . . . (Asylum)
Mitch Ryder And The Detroit Wheels; *Frat Rock!-#4-C* . . . . (Rhino)
  Rev Up-Best Of Mitch Ryder . . . . (Rhino)
  Son Of Frat Rock!-C . . . . (Rhino)
  Toga Rock-C . . . .(Dunhill Compact Classics)

Does That Blue Moon Ever Shine On You
Toby Keith; *Blue Moon* . . . . (Polydor Country)
  Toby Keith's Greatest Hits, Volume One . . . . (Mercury)

Dog Blue
Mimi & Richard Farina; *Best Of Mimi & Richard Farina* . . . . (Vanguard)

Don't It Make My Brown Eyes Blue
Crystal Gayle; *Classic Crystal* . . . .(EMI)
  Heartbreak Hotel-C . . . .(EMI)
  ST/Convoy . . . . (Polydor)
  We Must Believe In Magic . . . . (United Artists)

Down By The Water
PJ Harvey; *ST/Basketball Diaries* . . . . (Island)
  To Bring You My Love . . . . (Island)

Dream Of The Blue Turtles
Sting; *Dream Of The Blue Turtles* . . . . (A&M)

Drunken Blue Rooster
Todd Rundgren; *Todd* . . . . (Rhino)

Easy On The Pain
Michael Martin Murphey; *Cowboy Songs Four* . . . .(Valley Entert.)

Electric Blue
Icehouse; *Man Of Colours* . . . . (Chrysalis)

Eskimo Blue Day
Jefferson Airplane; *2400 Fulton Street-An Anthology* . . . . (RCA)
  Volunteers . . . . (RCA)
  Woodstock Two . . . .(Atlantic)

Everyday (I Have The Blues)
Tony Bennett with Stevie Wonder; *Playin' With My Friends-Bennett Sings
  The Blues-C* . . . . (Columbia)

Eyes Of Blue
Paul Carrack; *Blue Views* . . . . (Ark 21)

First Year Blues
Hank Williams; *Alone With His Guitar* . . . . (Mercury)

Five Foot Two, Eyes Of Blue
Mom & Dads; *Very Best Of The Mom & Dads* . . . .(Crescendo)

For You Blue
Beatles; *Beatles-Box Set* . . . . (Capitol)
  Let It Be . . . . (Capitol)
George Harrison; *Best Of George Harrison* . . . . (Capitol)

Forever In Blue
Journey; *Trial By Fire* . . . . (Columbia)

Forever In Blue Jeans
Neil Diamond; *12 Greatest Hits-#2* . . . . (Columbia)
  Hot August Night II . . . . (Columbia)
  You Don't Bring Me Flowers . . . . (Columbia)

Gonna Find Me A Bluebird
Frank Ifield; *Best Of Frank Ifield* . . . . (Curb)
Marvin Rainwater; *Greatest Hits-1957-C* . . . . (Deluxe)
  Only Country-1955-1959-C . . . .(JCI Assoc. Labels)
Royal Wade Kimes; *ST/Traveller* . . . . (Asylum)

Goodbye Blue Monday
City Boy; *Dinner At The Ritz* . . . . (Mercury)

Goodbye Blue Sky
Pink Floyd; *The Wall* . . . . (Columbia)
Roger Waters; *The Wall-Live In Berlin* . . . . (Mercury)

Goodbye Blue Sky
Daryl Braithwaite; *Higher Than Hope* . . . . (Epic Portrait Assoc.)
  Rise . . . . (Epic Portrait Assoc.)

Have You Ever Been Lonely (Have You Ever Been Blue)
Ernest Tubb; *Best Of Ernest Tubb* . . . . (Curb)
  The Country Music Hall Of Fame-Ernest Tubb . . . . (MCA)
Jim Reeves & Patsy Cline; *Jim Reeves' Greatest Hits* . . . . (RCA)
Patsy Cline; *Showcase-With The Jordanaires* . . . . (MCA)

Hey, Mr. Bluebird
Ernest Tubb & Wilburn Brothers; *More Great Country
  Duets-C* . . . . (MCA Special Prod.)

Hot, Blue & Righteous
ZZ Top; *Six Pack* . . . . (Warner Bros.)
  Tres Hombres . . . . (Warner Bros.)

House Of Blue Lights
Andrews Sisters; *Best Of The Andrews Sisters-#2* . . . . (MCA)
Asleep At The Wheel; *Asleep At The Wheel-10* . . . . (Epic)
  Greatest Country Hits Of The '80s-1987-C . . . . (Columbia)
  More Hot Country Requests-#2-C . . . . (Epic)
  Trucker's Jukebox-#2-C . . . . (Legacy)
  Very Best Of Asleep At The Wheel Since 1970 . . . .(Relentless/Madacy)
Canned Heat; *Canned Heat & John Lee Hooker: Live At The Fox
  Venice* . . . . (Rhino)
  Human Conditions . . . . (Takoma)
Chuck Berry; *More Rock 'N' Roll Rarities-Golden Era* . . . . (Chess)
  The Chess Box-Chuck Berry . . . . (Chess)
Chuck Miller; *Hard To Find 45s On CD-#1-1955-1960-C* . . . .(Eric)

House Of Blue Lovers
James O'Gwynn; *James O'Gwynn's Greatest Hits* . . . . (Plantation)
  Souvenirs Of Music City U.S.A.-C . . . . (Plantation)

How Blue
Reba McEntire; *MCA #1 Hits Of The '80s-#1-C* . . . . . . (MCA Special Prod.)
  My Kind Of Country . . . . (MCA)
  Reba McEntire's Greatest Hits . . . . (MCA)

How Blue Can You Get
B.B. King; *Best Of B.B. King* . . . . (MCA)
  Live At The Regal . . . . (MCA)
  Live In Cook County Jail . . . . (MCA)

If You Could Only See
Tonic; *Lemon Parade* . . . .(Polydor)
  Now That's What I Call Music!-#1-C . . . .(Virgin)

I'm Blue (The Gong-Gong Song)
Ikettes; *Great R&B Female Groups-Hits Of The '60s-C* . . . . (K-Tel)

I'm In Love With A Big Blue Frog
Peter, Paul & Mary; *Album 1700* . . . . (Warner Bros.)

I'm Thinking Tonight Of My Blue Eyes
Gene Autry; *All Time Legends Of Country Music-C* . . . . (Legacy)

Indescribably Blue
Elvis Presley; *Elvis' Gold Records, Volume 4* . . . . (RCA)
  From Nashville To Memphis-The Essential '60s Masters . . . . (RCA)

It Would Be You
Gary Allan; *It Would Be You* . . . .(Decca)

It's All Over Now, Baby Blue
Bob Dylan; *Biograph*.................................(Columbia)
Bob Dylan's Greatest Hits-#2..................(Columbia)
Bringing It All Back Home.....................(Columbia)
Byrds; *Ballad Of Easy Rider*...................(Columbia)
The Byrds....................................(Columbia)

I've Got A Right To Sing The Blues
Tony Bennett with Bonnie Raitt; *Playin' With My Friends-Bennett Sings The Blues-C*...........(Columbia)

Jackie Blue
Ozark Mountain Daredevils; *Best Of The Ozark Mountain Daredevils*...(A&M)
Billboard Top Hits-1975-C.....................(Rhino)
It'll Shine When It Shines....................(A&M)
It's Alive....................................(A&M)
Super Hits Of The '70s-Have A Nice Day-#14-C..(Rhino)

Jaded
Aerosmith; *Just Push Play*.....................(Columbia)
Now That's What I Call Music!-#7-C............(Virgin)

Lady Blue
George Benson; *Weekend In L.A.*................(Warner Bros.)
Leon Russell; *Best Of Leon Russell*...........(MCA)
Will O' The Wisp.............................(MCA)

Little Blue Man
Betty Johnson; *45-#13146*......................(Atlantic)

Little Blue Whale
Country Joe McDonald; *Goodbye Blues*...........(Fantasy)

Little Boy Blue
Elegants; *Best Of The Elegants*...............(Collectables)

Little Girl Blue
Ella Fitzgerald; *Rodgers & Hart Songbook*......(Verve)

Lonely Blue Boy
Conway Twitty; *Conway Twitty's Greatest Hits*..(Curb)
Very Best Of Conway Twitty....................(MCA)

Love Is Blue
Andre Kostelanetz; *Andre Kostelanetz-16 Most Requested Songs*..(Columbia)
Paul Mauriat; *Love Is Blue*....................(Mercury)
Sandpipers; *Softly*............................(A&M)

Makeup & Faded Blue Jeans
Merle Haggard; *Back To The Barrooms*..........(MCA)
Country Classics-#4-1984-1985-C...............(Universal)
Merle Haggard-His Best.......................(MCA)

Melancholy Blue
Trisha Yearwood; *Inside Out*..................(MCA)

Midnight Blue
Melissa Manchester; *Melissa*...................(Arista)
Melissa Manchester's Greatest Hits...........(Arista)

Midnight Blue
Electric Light Orchestra; *Afterglow*..........(Epic)
Discovery....................................(Jet)

Midnight Blue
King Curtis; *Enjoy...Best Of*.................(Collectables)
Soul Twist & Other Golden Classics...........(Collectables)

Midnight Blue
Lou Gramm; *Ready or Not*......................(Atlantic)

Midnight Blue
Johnny Mathis; *Feelings*......................(Columbia)

Midnight Blue
Louise Tucker; *Midnight Blue*.................(Arista)

Midnight Blue
Seals & Crofts; *Takin' It Easy*...............(Warner Bros.)

Midnight Blue
Foreigner; *Jukebox Heroes-Anthology*..........(Rhino)

Midnight Blues
Charlie Daniels Band; *Original Charlie Daniels Band*...(Sun)
Time For Tears-C.............................(Sun)

Midnight Blues
Allman Brothers Band; *An Evening With The Allman Brothers Band-First Set*...(Epic)

Midnight Blues
Bessie Smith; *Bessie Smith-The Complete Recordings-#1*..........(Legacy)

Midnight Blues
Gary Moore; *Still Got The Blues*..............(Charisma)

Midnight Blues
Memphis Slim; *Traveling With The Blues*.......(Storyville)

Miss Blue
Filter; *Title Of Record*.......................(Reprise)

Misty Blue
Dorothy Moore; *Blues Is Alright*..............(Malaco)
Misty Blue...................................(Malaco)
Sexy Soul-C..................................(K-Tel)
Eddy Arnold; *Best Of Eddy Arnold-#2*.....(Dunhill Compact Classics)
Country Gold-Eddy Arnold.....................(RCA)
This Is Eddy Arnold..........................(RCA)
Wilma Burgess; *From The Vaults: Decca Country Classics-1934-1973-C*...(Decca)

Mood Indigo
Duke Ellington; *1954 Los Angeles Concert*.....(Crescendo)
Black, Brown & Beige: 1944-1946 Band Recordings.....(Bluebird)
Carnegie Hall Concert-January 23, 1943.........(Prestige)

Ellington Indigos............................(Columbia)
Sophisticated Ellington......................(RCA)
Ella Fitzgerald; *Ella A Nice*.................(Pablo)
Ella Fitzgerald Sings-#2......................(Verve)
Four Freshmen; *Capitol Collectors Series-Four Freshman*...(Capitol)
Frank Sinatra; *In The Wee Small Hours*.........(Capitol)
Jimmie Lunceford & His Orchestra; *Stomp It Off-#1-1934-1935*.......(GRP)
Preservation Hall Jazz Band; *Best Of The Preservation Hall Jazz Band*...(Columbia)
New Orleans-#4...............................(Columbia)

Mr. Blue
Fleetwoods; *Best Of The Fleetwoods*...........(Rhino)
Timmy & The Tulips; *ST/American Hot Wax*......(A&M)

Mr. Blue
Garth Brooks; *No Fences*......................(Capitol)

Mr. Blue
Michael Franks; *Art Of Tea*...................(Reprise)

Mr. Blue Sky
Electric Light Orchestra; *Afterglow*..........(Epic)
Electric Light Orchestra's Greatest Hits.....(Jet)
Out Of The Blue.............................(Jet)

My Blue Angel
Aaron Tippin; *Read Between The Lines*.........(RCA)

My Blue Heaven
Artie Shaw; *Complete Artie Shaw-#4*...........(RCA)
This Is Artie Shaw...........................(Bluebird)
Fats Domino; *Fats Domino-Legendary Masters*...(United Artists)
Fats Domino's Greatest Hits..................(Everest)
My Blue Heaven-Best Of Fats Domino-#1........(EMI)
Oldies But Goodies-#10-C.....................(Original Sound)
Frank Sinatra; *Frank Sinatra-Gift Set*........(Capitol)
Sinatra's Swingin' Session!!!................(Capitol)

New Blue Moon
Traveling Wilburys; *Traveling Wilburys-Vol. 3*.......(Wilbury/Warner Bros.)

New Shade Of Blue
Bobby Fuller Four; *Best Of The Bobby Fuller Four*.......(Rhino)
Tapes-#1....................................(Rhino)
Southern Pacific; *Country Love Songs-C*.......(Warner Bros.)
Southern Pacific's Greatest Hits.............(Warner Bros.)
Zuma..(Warner Bros.)

Ode To Big Blue
Gordon Lightfoot; *Don Quixote*................(Warner Archives)

Old Blue
Byrds; *The Byrds*.............................(Columbia)
Furry Lewis; *Back On My Feet Again*...........(Prestige)
Shake 'Em On Down............................(Fantasy)
Joan Baez; *Joan Baez, Vol. 2*.................(Vanguard)
The Joan Baez Ballad Book....................(Vanguard)

Old Blue Car
Peter Case; *Peter Case*.......................(Geffen)

Once In A Blue Moon
Earl Thomas Conley; *Earl Thomas Conley's Greatest Hits*...........(RCA)
Hits Of '86-C...............................(RCA)

Once In A Very Blue Moon
Nanci Griffith; *One Fair Summer Evening*......(MCA)
Steal This Disc-C...........................(Rykodisc)
Pat Alger; *True Love & Other Short Stories-C*.................(Sugar Hill)

Orange Was The Color Of Her Dress
Charles Mingus; *Changes Two*..................(Atlantic)
Charles Mingus In Europe-#2..................(Enja)
Gil Evans; *Live At Sweet Basil-#1*............(Evidence Music)
Gil Evans & Laurent Cugny Big Band; *Golden Hair*..............(Emarcy)

Out Of The Blue
Roxy Music; *Country Life*.....................(Atco)
Heart Still Beating..........................(Virgin)
Roxy Music's Greatest Hits...................(Atco)
Viva! Roxy Music.............................(Reprise)

Out Of The Blue
George Harrison; *All Things Must Pass*........(Parlophone)

Out Of The Blue
Elton John; *Blue Moves*.......................(MCA)

Out Of The Blue
Foreigner; *Inside Information*................(Atlantic)

Out Of The Blue
John Lennon; *Lennon*..........................(Capitol)
Mind Games...................................(Capitol)

Out Of The Blue
Debbie Gibson; *Out Of The Blue*...............(Atlantic)

Out Of The Blue
Didier Lockwood; *Out Of The Blue*.............(Gramavision)

Out Of The Blue
Band; *The Last Waltz*.........................(Warner Bros.)

Out Of The Blue
Tommy James And The Shondells; *Tommy James And The Shondells-Anthology*.........(Rhino)

Out Of The Blue
Reba McEntire; *Unlimited*.....................(Mercury)

Perfect Blue Buildings
Counting Crows; *August And Everything After*..........(David Geffen Co.)

Pink Cocktail For A Blue Lady
Glenn Miller & His Orchestra; *Complete Glenn Miller & His Orchestra* .... (Bluebird)
Complete Glenn Miller & His Orchestra-#9 .... (Bluebird)

Pink Turns To Blue
Husker Du; *Zen Arcade* ....(SST)

Powder Blue Mercedes Queen
Paul Revere And The Raiders; *Legend Of Paul Revere And The Raiders* .... (Columbia)

Pretty Blue Eyes
Steve Lawrence; *Best Of Steve Lawrence* ....(Taragon)

Red Roses For A Blue Lady
Al Martino; *Best Of Al Martino* .... (Capitol)
Capitol Collectors Series-Al Martino .... (Capitol)
Andy Williams; *Andy Williams-16 Most Requested Songs*.......... (Legacy)
Mom & Dads; *Best Of The Mom & Dads* ....(Crescendo)
Roger Whittaker; *All-Time Heart-Touching Favorites* .... (Capitol)
Roger Whittaker-Classics Collection-#1 .... (Capitol)
Vaughn Monroe; *Best Of Vaughn Monroe* .... (RCA)

Red Wine & Blue Memories
Joe Stampley; *Joe Stampley's Biggest Hits* ....(Epic)

Rednecks, White Socks And Blue Ribbon Beer
Johnny Russell; *Beer Redneck Mothers* .... (RCA)
Country Legends-C ....(Madacy)
Country's Greatest Drinking Songs-C .... (All-Star Music)
Rednecks, White Socks & Blue Ribbon Beer .... (RCA)

Rhapsody In Blue
Boston Pops Orchestra/Arthur Fiedler; *Gershwin-Greatest Hits* .... (RCA)
Columbia Jazz Band with Michael Tilson Thomas; *Classic Gershwin*.. (Columbia)
Freddy Martin & His Orchestra; *Fascinatin' Rhythm-Capitol Sings Gershwin-C*....................................... (Capitol)
George Gershwin; *Rhapsody In Blue* .... (Biograph)
George Gershwin & Paul Whiteman & His Orchestra; *Nipper's Greatest Hits Of The '20s-C* .... (RCA)
Larry Adler & George Martin; *Glory Of Gershwin Featuring Larry Adler-C* .... (Mercury)

Rio De Janeiro Blue
Nicolette Larson; *In The Nick Of Time* ....(Warner Bros.)
Randy Crawford; *Secret Combination* ....(Warner Bros.)

Runnin' Blue
Doors; *Soft Parade* .... (Elektra)
Weird Scenes Inside The Gold Mine .... (Elektra)

September Blue
Chris Rea; *Dancing With The Strangers*.................... (Motown)

Serenade In Blue
Glenn Miller; *Best Of Glenn Miller-#2* .... (RCA)
Glenn Miller-A Legendary Performer-#1 & 2.............. (Bluebird)
Memorial-1944-1969. .... (Bluebird)
Glenn Miller & His Orchestra; *Complete Glenn Miller & His Orchestra-#8.* .... (Bluebird)
The Unforgettable Glenn Miller & His Orchestra................ (RCA)
Gloria Lynne; *Gloria Lynne-Golden Classics* .... (Collectables)
Tonight Show Band featuring Doc Severinsen; *Tonight Show Band featuring Doc Severinsen-#2* .... (Amherst)

Seventh Avenue
Rosanne Cash; *The Wheel.* .... (Columbia)

Shades Of Blue
Desert Rose Band; *True Love* .... (Curb/MCA)

She's A Rainbow
Rolling Stones; *Get Yer Ya-Ya's Out!* ....(Abkco)
More Hot Rocks (big hits & fazed cookies) .... (Abkco)
Singles Collection-The London Years .... (Abkco)
Their Satanic Majesties Request .... (Abkco)
Through The Past, Darkly (Big Hits Vol. 2) .... (Abkco)

Silver Blue
Linda Ronstadt; *Prisoner In Disguise.* .... (Asylum)

Silver Stars, Purple Sage, Eyes Of Blue
Roy Rogers & Sons Of The Pioneers; *Roy Rogers & Sons Of The Pioneers* .... (Varese Sarabande)

Silver, Blue & Gold
Bad Company; *Run With The Pack.* .... (Swan Song)

Soldier Blue
Buffy Sainte-Marie; *Native North American Child* .... (Vanguard)
She Used To Wanna Be A Ballerina .... (Vanguard)

Soldier Blue
Julian Cope; *Peggy Suicide.* .... (Island)

Soldier Blue
Cult; *Sonic Temple* .... (Sire)

Someday Out Of The Blue
Elton John; *ST/The Road To El Dorado* .... (DreamWorks/SKG)

Something In Red
Lorrie Morgan; *Lorrie Morgan's Greatest Hits* .... (BNA)
Something In Red .... (RCA)
To Get To You-Greatest Hits Collection .... (BNA)

Song Sung Blue
Neil Diamond; *Glory Road-1968-1972* .... (MCA)
Hot August Night. ....(MCA)
Love At The Greek .... (Columbia)

Moods. .... (MCA)
Neil Diamond-His 12 Greatest Hits .... (MCA)

Soulful Shade Of Blue
Buffy Sainte-Marie; *Best Of Buffy Sainte-Marie* .... (Vanguard)
I'm Gonna Be A Country Girl Again .... (Vanguard)

Stella Blue
Grateful Dead; *Steal Your Face.* ....(Grateful Dead)
Wake Of The Flood. ....(Grateful Dead)
Robert Hunter; *Box Of Rain* .... (Rykodisc)

Stone Blue
Foghat; *Best Of Foghat* .... (Rhino)
Stone Blue. .... (Rhino)

Suite Madame Blue
Styx; *Caught In The Act* .... (A&M)
Equinox .... (A&M)
Styx-Classics-#15. .... (A&M)

Suite: Judy Blue Eyes
Crosby, Stills & Nash; *Crosby, Stills & Nash* ....(Atlantic)
CSN ....(Atlantic)
ST/Woodstock. ....(Atlantic)
Crosby, Stills, Nash & Young; *So Far.* ....(Atlantic)

Sullen Girl
Fiona Apple; *Tidal* ....(Clean Slate/Work)

Sweet Little Bullet From A Pretty Blue Gun
Tom Waits; *Blue Valentine* ....(Asylum)

Sweet Little Miss Blue Eyes
Jim & Jesse/The Virginia Boys; *Appalachian Stomp: More Bluegrass Classics-C* .... (Rhino)

Sweet Summer Blue And Gold
Stone Poneys Featuring Linda Ronstadt; *The Stone Poneys Featuring Linda Ronstadt.* .... (EMI)

Tangled Up In Blue
Bob Dylan; *Biograph* .... (Columbia)
Blood On The Tracks .... (Columbia)
Real Live .... (Columbia)
The Bootleg Series-Volumes 1-3 [Rare & Unreleased] .... (Columbia)

Theme From "N.Y.P.D. Blue"
Original Soundtrack; *Television's Greatest Hits-#7-Cable Ready-C* ..... (TVT)

There'll Be Bluebirds Over The White Cliffs Of Dover
Kay Kyser & His Orchestra; *Best Of The Big Bands-C* .... (Columbia)

There's A Blue Sky Way Out Yonder
Riders In The Sky; *Riders Go Commercial* .... (MCA)
Saturday Morning With Riders In The Sky .... (MCA)

Tired Of Midnight Blue
George Harrison; *Extra Texture* .... (Capitol)

Truck Driver Blues
Cliff Bruner And His Boys; *Truck Driver Boogie Big Rig Hits-1939-1969-C.* .... (Audium)

Truck Driver's Blues
Johnny Gimble & The Texas Swing Pioneers; *Johnny Gimble's Texas Honky-Tonk Hits-C* .... (C.M.H. Prod.)

Truck Drivers Night Run Blues
Joe "Cannonball" Lewis; *Truck Driver Boogie Big Rig Hits-1939-1969-C.* .... (Audium)

True Blue
Rod Stewart; *Best Of Rod Stewart-#2* .... (Mercury)
Storyteller/The Complete Anthology: 1964-1990. .... (Warner Bros.)

True Blue
Madonna; *True Blue* ....(Sire)

Undecided Blues
Tony Bennett; *Playin' With My Friends-Bennett Sings The Blues-C* .... (Columbia)

Under Blue Canadian Skies
Glenn Miller & His Orchestra; *Complete Glenn Miller & His Orchestra.* .... (Bluebird)

Used To Blue
Sawyer Brown; *Sawyer Brown* .... (Curb)
Sawyer Brown's Greatest Hits .... (Curb)

Venice Blue
Bobby Darin; *Capitol Collectors Series-Bobby Darin* .... (Capitol)

Venus In Blue Jeans
Jimmy Clanton; *All-Star Chartbusters* .... (Intermedia)
Golden Years-1962-C. .... (Dominion Entert.)

Visions In Blue
Ultravox; *Ultravox-Collection* .... (Chrysalis)

When My Blue Moon Turns To Gold Again
Elvis Presley; *A Golden Celebration.* ....(RCA)
Elvis ....(RCA)
The Other Sides-Worldwide Gold Award Hits, Vol. 2 ....(RCA)
Merle Haggard; *Merle Haggard-His Best* .... (MCA)
Ramblin' Fever. .... (MCA)

When Sunny Gets Blue
Barbra Streisand; *Simply Streisand* .... (Columbia)
Johnny Mathis; *First 25 Years-Silver Anniversary Album* .... (Columbia)
Johnny Mathis' All-Time Greatest Hits .... (Columbia)
Johnny Mathis' Greatest Hits .... (Columbia)
Johnny Mathis-Love Songs .... (Columbia)
Kenny Rankin; *The Kenny Rankin Album* .... (Little David)

Steve Miller; *Born 2 B Blue* .... (Gold Rush)
Where The Blue Of The Night Meets The Gold Of The Day
Bing Crosby; *All-Time Best Of* .... (Curb)
   Best Of Bing Crosby .... (MCA)
   Where The Blue Of The Night Meets The Gold Of The Day .... (Biograph)
White Sport Coat (And A Pink Carnation)
Marty Robbins; *16 Most Requested Songs Of The '50s-#2-C* .... (Legacy)
   Lifetime Of Song-1951-1982 .... (Columbia)
   Marty Robbins' Greatest Hits .... (Columbia)
Wild & Blue
Hank Williams, Jr.; *Major Moves* .... (WB/Curb)
John Anderson; *John Anderson's Greatest Hits* .... (Warner Bros.)
   Wild & Blue .... (Warner Bros.)
Wish I Were You
Patty Smyth; *ST/Armageddon-The Album* .... (Columbia)
Woke Up This Morning
A3; *Exile On Coldharbour Lane* .... (C2/Columbia)
   The Sopranos-Music From The HBO Original
    Series .... (Sony Music Soundtrax)
Wrong Number
Cure; *Galore-The Singles-1987-1997* .... (Fiction/Elektra)
You Gotta Love That
Neal McCoy; *Neal McCoy's Greatest Hits* .... (Atlantic)
   Today's Country Love-C .... (K-Tel)
   You Gotta Love That! .... (Atlantic)
You Put The Blue In Me
Whites; *Old Familiar Feeling* .... (Elektra/Curb)
   Whites' Greatest Hits .... (Curb)

COLORS: BROWN, Tan

See Also: **ANATOMY: HAIR (brunette), COLORS (various)**

Beautiful Brown Eyes
Rosemary Clooney; *Songs From The Girl Singer-A Musical*
  Autobiography .... (Concord Jazz)
Black & Tan Fantasy
Duke Ellington; *Beginning* .... (MCA)
   Carnegie Hall Concert .... (Prestige)
   Carnegie Hall Concert -December 11, 1943 .... (Everest)
   Continuum .... (Fantasy)
   Duke Ellington-Pure Gold .... (RCA)
   Duke Ellington's Greatest Hits .... (Reprise)
   Echoes Of An Era-Duke Ellington & Louis Armstrong ..... (Roulette)
Duke Ellington & Mercer Ellington; *Duke Ellington & Mercer*
  Ellington .... (Fantasy)
Blonde Hair, Brown Nose
Dweezil Zappa; *Havin' A Bad Day* .... (Rykodisc)
Brown Earth
Laura Nyro; *Christmas & The Beads Of Sweat* .... (Columbia)
Brown Eyed Girl
Isley Brothers; *Live It Up* .... (T-Neck/Columbia)
Jimmy Buffett; *One Particular Harbour* .... (MCA)
Van Morrison; *Bang Masters* .... (Epic)
   Best Of Van Morrison .... (Polydor)
   ST/Born On The Fourth Of July .... (MCA)
   ST/Sleeping With The Enemy .... (Columbia)
   Wonder Years-Music From Emmy Shows/Era-C .... (Atlantic)
Brown Eyed Handsome Man
Buddy Holly; *Buddy Holly-20 Golden Greats* .... (MCA)
   For The First Time Anywhere .... (MCA)
   Rock & Roll Collection .... (MCA)
Chuck Berry; *Best Of The Best Of Chuck Berry* ... (International Mktg. Group)
   Roll Over Beethoven .... (Allegiance)
   The Chess Box-Chuck Berry .... (Chess)
Waylon Jennings; *Essential Waylon Jennings* .... (RCA)
   Waylon Jennings-Super Hits .... (RCA)
Brown Eyed Woman
Grateful Dead; *Europe '72* .... (Warner Bros.)
   What A Long Strange Trip It's Been: The Best Of The
    Grateful Dead .... (Warner Bros.)
Brown Eyes
Fleetwood Mac; *25 Years-The Chain* .... (Warner Bros.)
   Tusk .... (Warner Bros.)
Brown Eyes
Jimmy Cliff; *Cliff Hanger* .... (Columbia)
Brown Girl In The Ring
Boney M; *Nightflight To Venus* .... (Sire)
Brown Man Do
Small Faces; *78 In The Shade* .... (Atlantic)
Brown Skin
India.Arie; *Acoustic Soul* .... (Motown)
Brown Skin Gal
Bob Wills; *Best Of Bob Wills & His Texas Playboys* .... (MCA)
Brown Skin Girl
Jesse Fuller; *Brother Lowdown* .... (Fantasy)
   San Francisco Bay Blues .... (Good Time Jazz)

Brown Sugar
Rolling Stones; *Classic Rock 1966-1988-C* .... (Atlantic)
   Hot Rocks 1964-1971 .... (Abkco)
   Made In The Shade .... (Rolling Stones)
   Sticky Fingers .... (Virgin)
Brown Sugar
D'Angelo; *Brown Sugar* .... (EMI)
Brown Sugar
ZZ Top; *Six Pack* .... (Warner Bros.)
   ZZ Top .... (Warner Bros.)
Brown To Blue
Elvis Costello & The Attractions; *Almost Blue* .... (Columbia)
California Dreamin'
Beach Boys; *Made In The U.S.A.* .... (Capitol)
Mamas & The Papas; *At The Hop* .... (MCA)
   Good Feeling Music Of The Big Chill Generation-#1-C ..... (Motown)
   Mamas & The Papas-20 Golden Hits .... (MCA)
   ST/Air America .... (MCA)
   ST/American Pop .... (MCA)
   ST/Forrest Gump .... (Epic/Sony Music Soundtrax)
Captain Fantastic And The Brown Dirt Cowboy
Elton John; *Captain Fantastic And The Brown Dirt Cowboy* .... (Polydor)
Chocolate Brown Eyes
Millie Jackson; *Rock 'N' Roll Soul* .... (Ichiban Int'l)
Crossing Muddy Waters
John Hiatt; *Crossing Muddy Waters* .... (Vanguard)
Don't It Make My Brown Eyes Blue
Crystal Gayle; *Classic Crystal* .... (EMI)
   Heartbreak Hotel-C .... (EMI)
   ST/Convoy .... (Polydor)
   We Must Believe In Magic .... (United Artists)
Every Time I Get Around You
David Lee Murphy; *Gettin' Out The Good Stuff* .... (MCA)
Fields Have Turned Brown
Stanley Brothers & The Clinch Mountain Boys; *Bluegrass Super*
  Hits-C .... (Columbia)
Good Times Bad Times
Led Zeppelin; *Led Zeppelin* .... (Atlantic)
Hazy Shade Of Winter
Bangles; *Bangles' Greatest Hits* .... (Columbia)
   ST/Less Than Zero .... (Def Jam)
Simon & Garfunkel; *Bookends* .... (Columbia)
   Collected Works .... (Columbia)
I Dream Of Jeanie With Light Brown Hair
Al Jolson; *The Al Jolson Story-#5* .... (MCA)
Joan Baez; *Diamonds & Rust* .... (A&M)
Mormon Tabernacle Choir; *Beautiful Dreamer* .... (Columbia)
   Mormon Tabernacle Choir's Greatest Hits-#3 .... (Columbia)
   Old Beloved Songs .... (Columbia)
Little Brown Bird
Elvin Bishop; *Live! Raisin' Hell* .... (Capricorn)
Little Brown Dog
Judy Collins; *Golden Apples Of The Sun* .... (Elektra)
Little Brown Jug
Glenn Miller; *Best Of Glenn Miller* .... (RCA)
   Glenn Miller-A Legendary Performer-#1 & 2 .... (Bluebird)
   The Glenn Miller Story .... (RCA)
Glenn Miller & His Orchestra; *Glenn Miller & His Orchestra-*
  Pure Gold .... (Bluebird)
   The Unforgettable Glenn Miller & His Orchestra .... (RCA)
Livin' La Vida Loca
Ricky Martin; *Ricky Martin* .... (Columbia)
Mrs. Brown You've Got A Lovely Daughter
Herman's Hermits; *Herman's Hermits-Their Greatest Hits* ... (Abkco)
   Something Good Again .... (Abkco)
My Brown Eyed Texas Rose
Tex Ritter; *Arizona Days* .... (MCA Special Prod.)
   The Country Music Hall Of Fame-Tex Ritter .... (MCA)
My Little Brown Book
Duke Ellington; *Duke Ellington & John Coltrane* .... (MCA/Impulse)
John Coltrane; *The Gentle Side Of John Coltrane* .... (GRP)
Old Brown Shoe
Beatles; *Beatles-Box Set* .... (Capitol)
   Hey Jude .... (Capitol)
   Past Masters-Volume Two .... (Parlophone)
One Brown Mouse
Jethro Tull; *Bursting Out* .... (Chrysalis)
   Heavy Horses .... (Chrysalis)
Orange, Brown & Green
Herb Ellis & Freddie Green; *Rhythm Willie* .... (Concord Jazz)
Plain Brown Wrapper
Gary Morris; *Gary Morris' Greatest Hits-#2* .... (Warner Bros.)
   Plain Brown Wrapper .... (Warner Bros.)
Plain Brown Wrapper
Count Basie; *I Told You So* .... (Pablo)
Pound For A Brown On The Bus
Frank Zappa; *Electric Aunt Jemima* .... (Rhino)
   Uncle Meat .... (Barking Pumpkin)

Sparkling Brown Eyes
Webb Pierce with the Wilburn Brothers; *King Of The Honky-Tonk: From The Original Decca Masters-1952-1959* . . . . (Country Music Foundation)
Webb Pierce-Greatest Hits/Finest Performances . . . . (Sun)

Sweet Georgia Brown
Anita O'Day; *Compact Jazz-Best Of The Compact Jazz Vocalists-C* . . . . (Verve)
Beatles; *The Beatles featuring Tony Sheridan-In The Beginning (Circa 1960).* . . . . (Polydor)
Ben Bernie & His Orchestra; *78-#15002* . . . . (Vocalion)
Bing Crosby; *Bing Crosby-16 Most Requested Songs* . . . . (Legacy)
Coasters; *Coasters' Greatest Hits* . . . . (Atco)
Django Reinhardt; *Djangologie USA-#1* . . . . (Disques Swing)
Quintet Of The Hot Club Of France . . . . (Prestige)
Ella Fitzgerald; *Ella Fitzgerald In London* . . . . (Pablo)
Whisper Not . . . . (Verve)
Ella Fitzgerald & Count Basie; *Perfect Match* . . . . (Pablo)
Original Broadway Cast; *Bubbling Brown Sugar* . . . . (Amherst)
Stephane Grappelli; *Live In London* . . . . (Black Lion)
Tito Puente; *Out Of This World* . . . . (Concord Picante Jazz)

Sweet Marijuana Brown
Paula Lockheart; *It Ain't The End Of The World* . . . . (Flying Fish)

Two Hits And The Joint Turned Brown
Pfaff Family Dog; *Marijuana's Greatest Hits Revisited-C* . . . . (Rehash)
Rodney & Doug Dillard and John Hartford; *Glitter Grass From The Nashwood Hollyville Strings & Permanent Wave.* . . . . (Flying Fish)

Wynona's Big Brown Beaver
Primus; *Tales From The Punchbowl.* . . . . (Interscope)

COLORS: GENERAL, Multiple Colors

See Also: COLORS (various), RAINBOWS

All Together Now
Beatles; *Yellow Submarine* . . . . (Capitol)
Muppets; *Kermit Unpigged* . . . . (Jim Henson)

An Acceptable Level Of Ecstasy (The Wedding Song)
Lyle Lovett; *Lyle Lovett* . . . . (MCA)

Any Color You Like
Pink Floyd; *Dark Side Of The Moon.* . . . . (Capitol)

Blue Autumn
Bobby Goldsboro; *10th Anniversary Album-#1* . . . . (EMI)
Bobby Goldsboro's Greatest Hits . . . . (Liberty)
Honey-Best Of Bobby Goldsboro. . . . . (EMI)

Coat Of Many Colors
Dolly Parton; *Best Of Dolly Parton* . . . . (RCA)
Dolly Parton-Super Hits . . . . (Columbia)
Essential Dolly Parton-#2 . . . . (RCA)
Emmylou Harris; *Pieces Of The Sky* . . . . (Reprise)

Color Him Father
Linda Martell; *20 Great Hits-C.* . . . . (Plantation)
Color Me Country . . . . (Plantation)

Color Me Impressed
Replacements; *Hootenanny* . . . . (Chameleon)

Color Me Once
Violent Femmes; *ST/The Crow.* . . . . (Interscope)

Color My World
Petula Clark; *Petula Clark's Greatest Hits.* . . . . (Crescendo)

Color Of Right
Rush; *Test For Echo.* . . . . (Atlantic)

Color Of Roses
Beth Nielsen Chapman; *Sand And Water* . . . . (Reprise)

Color Of The Mood
Dave Loggins; *One Way Ticket To Paradise* . . . . (Epic)

Color Of The Night
Lauren Christy; *ST/Color Of Night* . . . . (Mercury)

Colored People
DC Talk; *Jesus Freak* . . . . (Virgin)

Colored Spade
Original Broadway Cast; *Hair* . . . . (RCA)

Colors
Ted Nugent & The Amboy Dukes; *Ted Nugent & The Amboy Dukes* . . . . (Mainstream)

Colors
Angst; *Mystery Spot* . . . . (SST)

Colors
Ice-T; *ST/Colors.* . . . . (Warner Bros.)

Colors
Minutemen; *What Makes A Man Start Fires.* . . . . (SST)

Colors Of The Spirit
Journey; *Trial By Fire.* . . . . (Columbia)

Colors Of The Sun
Bonnie Koloc; *Bonnie Koloc-At Her Best.* . . . . (Ovation)
You're Gonna Love Yourself In The Morning . . . . (Ovation)
Jackson Browne; *For Everyman.* . . . . (Asylum)

Colors Of The Wind
Judy Kuhn; *Princess Collection* . . . . (Disney)

Vanessa Williams; *ST/Pocahontas* . . . . (Hollywood)
Vanessa Williams' Greatest Hits-The First Ten Years . . . . (Mercury)

Colour My World
Chicago; *Chicago At Carnegie Hall* . . . . (Chicago)
Chicago II. . . . . (Chicago)
Chicago IX-Chicago's Greatest Hits . . . . (Chicago)

Colour Of Love
Billy Ocean; *Billy Ocean's Greatest Hits* . . . . (Jive)
Tear Down These Walls . . . . (Jive)

Coloured Rain
Traffic; *Best Of Traffic.* . . . . (Island)
Mr. Fantasy . . . . (Island)

Colours
Donovan; *Catch The Wind* . . . . (Garland)
Donovan's Greatest Hits . . . . (Epic)
History Of British Rock-#3-C. . . . . (Rhino)

Colours
Phil Collins; *...But Seriously* . . . . (Atlantic)

Colours
Sisters Of Mercy; *Floodland.* . . . . (Elektra)

Fancy Colours
Chicago; *Chicago At Carnegie Hall* . . . . (Chicago)
Chicago II. . . . . (Chicago)
Group Portrait. . . . . (Chicago)

Flying Colours
Jethro Tull; *The Broadsword And The Beast.* . . . . (Chrysalis)

Gel
Collective Soul; *Collective Soul* . . . . (Atlantic)
ST/Jerky Boys. . . . . (Atlantic)

Great Speckled Bird
Roy Acuff; *Best Of Roy Acuff* . . . . (Liberty)
Bluegrass Super Hits-C . . . . (Columbia)
Roy Acuff's Greatest Hits . . . . (Columbia)

I Used To Be Color Blind
Anita O'Day; *Blue Skies: The Irving Berlin Songbook-C* . . . . (Verve)
Fred Astaire; *The Irving Berlin Songbook.* . . . . (Verve)

I Wish I Felt Nothing
Wallflowers; *Bringing Down The Horse.* . . . . (Interscope)

Joseph's Coat (Coat Of Many Colors)
Original Cast; *Joseph & The Amazing Technicolor Dreamcoat* . . . . (Polydor)

Kodachrome
Paul Simon; *Greatest Hits, Etc.* . . . . (Columbia)
Negotiations And Love Songs, 1971-1986 . . . . (Warner Bros.)
There Goes Rhymin' Simon . . . . (Columbia)
Simon & Garfunkel; *The Concert In Central Park* . . . . (Warner Bros.)

Love Colours
Pretenders; *Last Of The Independents* . . . . (Sire)

Lucy In The Sky With Diamonds
Beatles; *Sgt. Pepper's Lonely Hearts Club Band* . . . . (Capitol)
The Beatles/1967-1970. . . . . (Capitol)
Yellow Submarine. . . . . (Capitol)
Elton John; *All This & World War 2* . . . . (20th Century Fox)
Elton John's Greatest Hits-#2 . . . . (Polydor)
John Lennon; *Lennon* . . . . (Capitol)

May This Be Love
Emmylou Harris; *Wrecking Ball* . . . . (Asylum)
Jimi Hendrix; *Are You Experienced?* . . . . (Reprise)

Multi Colored Lady
Gregg Allman; *Laid Back* . . . . (Polydor)

My Coloring Book
Barbra Streisand; *Barbra Streisand's Greatest Hits* . . . . (Columbia)
The Second Barbra Streisand Album . . . . (Columbia)
Perry Como; *This Is Perry Como-#2.* . . . . (RCA)

Old Master Painter
Peggy Lee; *Capitol Collectors Series-Peggy Lee-#1-Early Years* . . . . . (Capitol)

She Comes In Colors
Hooters; *Nervous Night.* . . . . (Columbia)

She Comes In Colors
Love; *Best Of Love* . . . . (Rhino)

She's A Rainbow
Rolling Stones; *Get Yer Ya-Ya's Out!* . . . . (Abkco)
More Hot Rocks (big hits & fazed cookies). . . . . (Abkco)
Singles Collection-The London Years . . . . (Abkco)
Their Satanic Majesties Request. . . . . (Abkco)
Through The Past, Darkly (Big Hits Vol. 2) . . . . (Abkco)

Theme From "Walt Disney's Wonderful World Of Color"
Original Soundtrack; *Television's Greatest Hits-#4-Black & White Classics-C* . . . . (TVT)

Tie Dye On The Highway
Robert Plant; *Manic Nirvana.* . . . . (Es Paranza)

True Colors
Cyndi Lauper; *She's So Unusual/True Colors/Hat Full Of Stars (Box)* . . . (Epic)
True Colors . . . . (Portrait)
Twelve Deadly Cyns...And Then Some. . . . . (Epic)
Phil Collins; *Phil Collins-Hits.* . . . . (Atlantic)

True Colors
Asia; *Alpha* . . . . (Geffen)

Wear Your Love Like Heaven
Donovan; *Donovan's Greatest Hits* . . . . (Epic)

Gift From A Flower To A Garden .... (Epic)
Summer Of Love-#1-C .... (Rhino)
Troubadour-Definitive Collection .... (Epic)
Sarah McLachlan; *Solace* .... (Arista)
When I Fall In Love
Celine Dion; *The Colour Of My Love* .... (550 Music)
Doris Day; *Doris Day-16 Most Requested Songs-Encore!* .... (Columbia)
Where The Colors Don't Go
Sam Phillips; *Cruel Intentions* .... (Virgin)
Wish I Were You
Patty Smyth; *ST/Armageddon-The Album* .... (Columbia)

COLORS: GREEN

See Also: **COLORS (various)**

"Star Is Born" (Evergreen), Love Theme From "A Star Is Born"
Barbra Streisand; *Barbra Streisand's Greatest Hits* .... (Columbia)
Barbra Streisand's Greatest Hits, Volume 2. .... (Columbia)
Diana, Princess Of Wales-Tribute-C .... (Columbia)
Memories .... (Columbia)
ST/A Star Is Born .... (Columbia)
Luther Vandross; *Songs* .... (Epic)
Paul Williams; *Paul Williams-Classics* .... (A&M)
A Tisket, A Tasket
Ella Fitzgerald; *Best Of Ella Fitzgerald* .... (MCA)
Ella Fitzgerald .... (Laserlight)
Glenn Miller & His Army/Air Force Band; *Glenn Miller & His Army/Air
Force Band* .... (Laserlight)
Tommy Dorsey; *Complete Tommy Dorsey-#7* .... (RCA)
All In Green Went My Love Riding
Joan Baez; *Love Song Album* .... (Vanguard)
Almost Green
John Bergamo; *On The Edge* .... (Creative Music Prod.)
Another Green World
Brian Eno; *Another Green World* .... (Editions E.G.)
Avocado Green
Johnny Winter; *About Blues* .... (Janus)
Before The Storm .... (Janus)
Ballad Of The Green Berets
Barry Sadler; *Cruisin'-1966-C* .... (Increase)
Hits Of The Sixties-C .... (Intercom Music)
More American Graffiti-#4-C .... (MCA)
Nipper's Greatest Hits Of The '60s-#2-C .... (RCA)
Super Hits-#3-C .... (Gusto)
Bein' Green
Frank Sinatra; *Frank Sinatra's Greatest Hits-#2* .... (Reprise)
Frank Sinatra & Antonio Carlos Jobim; *Sinatra & Company* .... (Reprise)
Muppets with Kermit The Frog; *Muppet Show* .... (Arista)
Van Morrison; *Hard Nose The Highway* .... (Polydor)
Big Bright Green Pleasure Machine
Simon & Garfunkel; *Collected Works* .... (Columbia)
Parsley Sage Rosemary & Thyme .... (Columbia)
ST/The Graduate .... (Columbia)
Blue Ridge Mountains Turnin' Green
Charley Pride; *Amazing Love* .... (RCA)
Cabbage Greens
Champion Jack Dupree; *New Orleans Barrelhouse Boogie-
Complete* .... (Columbia)
Collard Greens & Black-Eyed Peas
Bud Powell; *Best Of Bud Powell* .... (Blue Note)
Green Christmas
Stan Freberg; *Capitol Collectors Series-Stan Freberg* .... (Capitol)
Christmas Comedy Classics-C .... (Priority)
Dr. Demento Presents The Greatest Novelty Records-#6-
Christmas-C. .... (Rhino)
Dr. Demento's Greatest Christmas CD-C .... (Rhino)
Green Door
Jim Lowe; *Billboard Top Rock 'N' Roll Hits-1956-C* .... (Rhino)
Super Hits-#4-C .... (Gusto)
Green Earrings
Steely Dan; *Steely Dan-Gold.* .... (MCA)
The Royal Scam .... (MCA)
Green Eyed Lady
Sugarloaf; *Sugarloaf-Spaceship Earth* .... (Collectables)
Green Eyes
Jimmy Dorsey & His Orchestra; *Best Of Jimmy Dorsey* .... (MCA)
Jimmy Dorsey & His Orchestra's Greatest Hits. .... (MCA)
Green Eyes
Husker Du; *Flip Your Wig* .... (SST)
Green Fields Of America
Paddy Tunney; *Stone Fiddle* .... (Green Linnet)
Green Fields Of Canada
Eric Schoenberg; *Acoustic Guitar* .... (Rounder)
Green Fields Of France
Phil Coulter; *Forgotten Dreams* .... (Shanachie)

Green Finch & Linnet Bird
Original Cast/Angela Lansbury/Len Cariou; *Sweeney Todd* .... (RCA)
Green Gorilla
Spirit; *Time Circle* .... (Epic)
Green Grass & High Tides
Outlaws; *Bring It Back Alive* .... (Arista)
Outlaws .... (Arista)
Green Green Grass Of Home
Burl Ives; *Best Of Burl Ives-#2.* .... (MCA)
Elvis Presley; *Elvis Presley Today.* .... (RCA)
Our Memories Of Elvis, Volume 2. .... (RCA)
George Jones; *20 Golden Pieces Of George Jones.* .... (Bulldog)
Johnny Cash; *Johnny Cash-16 Biggest Hits-#2* .... (Legacy)
Tom Jones; *Country Side Of Tom Jones.* .... (London)
Things That Matter Most To Me .... (Mercury)
Tom Jones-London Collector-Greatest Hits .... (London)
Green Grow The Lilacs
Tex Ritter; *An American Legend* .... (Capitol)
Best Of Tex Ritter .... (Capitol)
Best Of Town & Country-#3-C .... (Gusto)
Hillbilly Heaven .... (Capitol)
Green Grow The Rushes, Ho
Chieftains; *Bonaparte's Retreat.* .... (Shanachie)
Green Kentucky Eyes
Pal Rakes; *Midnight Rain.* .... (Atlantic America)
Green Leaves Of Summer
Brothers Four; *Brothers Four-Greatest Hits* .... (Columbia)
Greenfields & Other Gold .... (First Warning)
Hollywood Magic-1950s-C .... (Columbia)
Green Light
Sonic Youth; *Evol* .... (SST)
Green Light
Cliff Richard; *Green Light* .... (Rocket)
Green Lights
Bonnie Raitt; *Green Light* .... (Warner Bros.)
NRBQ; *At Yankee Stadium.* .... (Mercury)
Peek-A-Boo-Best Of-1969-1989 .... (Rhino)
Green Manalishi
Fleetwood Mac; *25 Years-The Chain.* .... (Warner Bros.)
Judas Priest; *Hell Bent For Leather* .... (Columbia)
Unleashed In The East. .... (Columbia)
Green Onions
Booker T. & The M.G.s; *Best Of Booker T. & The M.G.s* .... (Atlantic)
Billboard Top R&B Hits-1962-C. .... (Rhino)
Green Onions .... (Atlantic)
ST/American Graffiti .... (MCA)
ST/Quadrophenia .... (MCA)
Green River
Alabama; *Mountain Music.* .... (RCA)
Creedence Clearwater Revival; *1969.* .... (Fantasy)
Creedence Clearwater Revival-Chronicle .... (Fantasy)
Green River. .... (Fantasy)
Live In Europe. .... (Fantasy)
Royal Albert Hall Concert. .... (Fantasy)
ST/1969. .... (Polydor)
Green River Ramble
Skip Gorman; *A Cowboy's Wild Song To His Herd* .... (Rounder)
Green Rocky Road
Dave Van Ronk; *In The Tradition.* .... (Prestige)
Tim Hardin; *Memorial Album* .... (Polydor)
Green Shirt
Elvis Costello; *Girls Girls Girls.* .... (Columbia)
Elvis Costello & The Attractions; *Armed Forces* .... (Rykodisc)
Green Tambourine
Lemon Pipers; *Best Of Ohio Express & Other Bubblegum
Smashes-#1-C.* .... (Rhino)
Billboard Top Rock 'N' Roll Hits-1968-C. .... (Rhino)
Bubblegum's Greatest Hits-#3-C. .... (Accord)
Fabulous Bubblegum Years-C .... (Fifty One West)
Green, Green
New Christy Minstrels; *New Christy Minstrels' Greatest Hits* ...... (Columbia)
Greenback Dollar
Kingston Trio; *Best Of The Best Of The Kingston Trio* .... (Pro-Arte)
Capitol Collectors Series-The Kingston Trio .... (Capitol)
Very Best Of The Kingston Trio. .... (Capitol)
Greenfields
Brothers Four; *Tokyo Tapes* .... (Folk Era)
Vogues; *Vogues' Greatest Hits* .... (Rhino)
Greensleeves
Jeff Beck Group; *Truth.* .... (Epic)
Olivia Newton-John; *Come On Over.* .... (MCA)
Ray Conniff Singers; *Ray Conniff Singers-Christmas* .... (Columbia)
Vienna Boys Choir; *Christmas Festival-C.* .... (RCA)
Greenwood Creek
Doobie Brothers; *Doobie Brothers.* .... (Warner Bros.)
Grey To Green
Stephen Stills; *Right By You.* .... (Atlantic)
Guinnevere
Crosby, Stills & Nash; *Crosby, Stills & Nash.* .... (Atlantic)

CSN . . . . (Atlantic)
Crosby, Stills, Nash & Young; *So Far* . . . . (Atlantic)
   Woodstock Two . . . . (Atlantic)
His Green Eyes
  Barbara Fairchild; *Standing In Your Line* . . . . (Columbia)
John Deere Green
  Joe Diffie; *Honky Tonk Attitude* . . . .(Epic)
   Joe Diffie's Greatest Hits . . . .(Epic)
Leaves That Are Green
  Country Gentlemen; *Country Gentlemen* . . . . (Vanguard)
  Simon & Garfunkel; *Collected Works* . . . . (Columbia)
   Sounds Of Silence . . . . (Columbia)
Little Bit Of Green
  Elvis Presley; *Back In Memphis* . . . . (RCA)
   From Memphis To Vegas/From Vegas To Memphis . . . . (RCA)
Little Green
  Joni Mitchell; *Blue* . . . . (Reprise)
Little Green Apples
  O.C. Smith; *Pop Classics Of The '60s-C* . . . . (Columbia)
Little Green Valley
  Marty Robbins; *Gunfighter Ballads & Trail Songs* . . . . (Legacy)
Long Green
  Kingsmen; *Best Of The Kingsmen* . . . . (Rhino)
Lucy In The Sky With Diamonds
  Beatles; *Sgt. Pepper's Lonely Hearts Club Band* . . . . (Capitol)
   The Beatles/1967-1970 . . . . (Capitol)
   Yellow Submarine . . . . (Capitol)
  Elton John; *All This & World War 2* . . . . (20th Century Fox)
   Elton John's Greatest Hits-#2 . . . . (Polydor)
  John Lennon; *Lennon* . . . . (Capitol)
Mountain Greenery
  Ella Fitzgerald; *Rodgers & Hart Songbook* . . . . (Verve)
  Tony Bennett; *Rodgers & Hart Songbook* . . . . (DRG)
   Tony Bennett Sings More Great Rodgers & Hart. . . . . (Improv)
New Greenback Dollar
  Roy Acuff; *Columbia Historic Edition-Roy Acuff* . . . . (Columbia)
Off To Dublin In The Green
  Dubliners; *Best Of The Dubliners-Irish Favorites* . . . . (Tradition)
On Green Dolphin Street
  Anita O'Day; *Anita O'Day* . . . . (Glendale)
  Carmen McRae; *At The Great American Music Hall* . . . . (Blue Note)
  Miles Davis; *Basic Miles* . . . . (Columbia)
  Red Garland; *Saying Something* . . . . (Prestige)
On The Greener Side
  Michelle Shocked; *Captain Swing* . . . . (Mercury)
Orange And The Green
  Irish Rovers; *Irish Rovers' Greatest Hits* . . . . (MCA)
   The Unicorn . . . .(MCA)
  Northeast Winds; *Folk Era's Live Sampler* . . . . (Folk Era)
   Ireland By Sail . . . . (Folk Era)
Orange, Brown & Green
  Herb Ellis & Freddie Green; *Rhythm Willie* . . . .(Concord Jazz)
Other Man's Grass Is Always Greener
  Petula Clark; *Petula Clark's Greatest Hits* . . . . (Crescendo)
Paddy's Green Shamrock Shore
  Chieftains; *Another Country* . . . . (RCA)
Pale Green Stars
  Everclear; *Sparkle And Fade* . . . . (Capitol)
Pretty Green Island
  George Tucker; *George Tucker* . . . . (Rounder)
Redwood Evergreen
  Lorraine Duisit; *Hawks & Herons* . . . . (Flying Fish)
Shades Of Green (Pt. II)
  Mission U.K.; *Masque* . . . . (Mercury)
She's More
  Andy Griggs; *You Won't Ever Be Lonely* . . . . (RCA)
Six O'Clock Train & A Girl With Green Eyes
  John Hartford; *All In The Name Of Love* . . . . (Flying Fish)
Something In Red
  Lorrie Morgan; *Lorrie Morgan's Greatest Hits* . . . . (BNA)
   Something In Red . . . . (RCA)
   To Get To You-Greatest Hits Collection . . . . (BNA)
Sure The Boy Was Green
  Horslips; *Aliens* . . . . (DJM)
Theme From "Green Acres"
  Eddie Albert & Eva Gabor; *ST/Son In Law* . . . . (Hollywood)
  Original Soundtrack; *CBS: The First 50 Years* . . . . (TVT)
   Television's Greatest Hits-#1-C . . . . (TVT)
Theme From "The Green Hornet"
  Original Soundtrack; *Television's Greatest Hits-#2-C* . . . . (TVT)
Third Stone From The Sun
  Jimi Hendrix; *Essential Jimi Hendrix* . . . . (Reprise)
   Kiss The Sky . . . . (Reprise)
  Jimi Hendrix Experience; *Are You Experienced?* . . . . (Reprise)
Velvet Green Whistler
  Jethro Tull; *Songs From The Wood* . . . . (Chrysalis)
Village Green Preservation Society
  Kinks; *Are The Village Green Preservation Society* . . . . (Reprise)

   Kink Kronikles . . . . (Reprise)
When The Wind Was Green
  Frank Sinatra; *September Of My Years* . . . . (Reprise)
Where The Green Grass Grows
  Tim McGraw; *Big Country Hits '99-C* . . . . (K-Tel)
   Everywhere. . . . . (Curb)
   Tim McGraw's Greatest Hits . . . . (Curb)
Wrong Number
  Cure; *Galore-The Singles-1987-1997* . . . . (Fiction/Elektra)

COLORS: GREY

*See Also: **COLORS (various)***

Another Grey Morning
  James Taylor; *JT* . . . . (Columbia)
As The Seasons Grey
  Testament; *The Ritual* . . . .(Atlantic)
Best I Ever Had (Grey Sky Morning)
  Vertical Horizon; *Everything You Want* . . . . (RCA)
Black Is Black
  Los Bravos; *History Of British Rock-#7-C* . . . . (Rhino)
   London Collector-Rock Invasion-C . . . . (London)
Blue Red & Grey
  Who; *By Numbers* . . . . (MCA)
Blue Turning Grey Over You
  Billie Holiday; *Billie's Blues* . . . . (Blue Note)
  Louis Armstrong & Luis Russell & Orchestra; *Satchmo Style* . . (Disques Swing)
  Ringo Starr; *Sentimental Journey* . . . . (Capitol)
Blue Turns To Grey
  Rolling Stones; *December's Children (and everybody's)* . . . .(Abkco)
California Dreamin'
  Beach Boys; *Made In The U.S.A.* . . . . (Capitol)
  Mamas & The Papas; *At The Hop* . . . . (MCA)
   Good Feeling Music Of The Big Chill Generation-#1-C . . . . (Motown)
   Mamas & The Papas-20 Golden Hits . . . . (MCA)
   ST/Air America. . . . . (MCA)
   ST/American Pop . . . . (MCA)
   ST/Forrest Gump . . . . (Epic/Sony Music Soundtrax)
Celebration For A Grey Day
  Mimi & Richard Farina; *Best Of Mimi & Richard Farina* . . . . (Vanguard)
   Celebrations For A Grey Day. . . . . (Vanguard)
   Memories . . . . (Vanguard)
Daddy's Gone Grey
  Lonesome Strangers; *Lonesome Strangers* . . . .(Hightone)
Daysleeper
  R.E.M.; *Up* . . . . (Warner Bros.)
Everything Turns Grey
  Agent Orange; *Living In Darkness* . . . . (Posh Boy)
   Real Live Sound . . . . (Restless)
Gray Eagle
  Taylor's Kentucky Boys; *Traditional Country Classics 1927-1929* . . (Historical)
Gray Haired Young Man
  Don Potter; *Over The Rainbow* . . . .(Mirror)
Grey Cloud Over New York
  Philip Glass; *1000 Airplanes On The Roof* . . . . (Virgin)
Grey Cloudy Lies
  George Harrison; *Extra Texture* . . . . (Capitol)
Grey Day
  Madness; *Madness* . . . . (Geffen)
Grey Ghost
  Henry Paul Band; *Grey Ghost* . . . .(Atlantic)
Grey Goose/Sixpenny Money
  Joe Burke; *Traditional Music Of Ireland* . . . . (Green Linnet)
Grey Lagoons
  Roxy Music; *For Your Pleasure...* . . . . (Reprise)
Grey Matter
  Oingo Boingo; *Boingo Alive* . . . . (MCA)
   Nothing To Fear . . . . (A&M)
   Skeletons In The Closet: The Best Of Oingo Boingo . . . . (A&M)
Grey Matter
  An Emotional Fish; *An Emotional Fish* . . . .(Atlantic)
Grey October Clouds
  Tommy Makem & Liam Clancy; *Two For The Early Dew* . . . .(Shanachie)
Grey Seal
  Elton John; *Goodbye Yellow Brick Road.* . . . . (Polydor)
Grey Talk
  Francis X & The Bushmen; *Scream-The Compilation* . . . . (Geffen)
Grey To Green
  Stephen Stills; *Right By You* . . . .(Atlantic)
Grey Victory
  10,000 Maniacs; *Hope Chest-Fredonia Recordings-1982-1983* . . . . . . (Elektra)
   Wishing Chair . . . . (Elektra)
Greystoke
  Soundtrack; *Greystoke-Legend Of Tarzan* . . . . (Warner Bros.)
It's Gray
  T.S.O.L.; *Change Today* . . . .(Enigma)

Kiss From A Rose
Seal; *Seal 2* ....(Sire)
Morse Moose & The Grey Goose
Wings; *London Town*. ....(Capitol)
New Grey Bonnet
Johnny Gimble; *Still Fiddlin' Around* .... (MCA)
Old Gray Mare, The
Original Soundtrack; *School Days-Kids Classics* ....(Benson)
Pearl Grey
Adam Makowicz; *The Name Is Makowicz*. .... (Sheffield Lab)
Put On Your Old Grey Bonnet
Jimmy Dean; *Jimmy Dean's Greatest Hits* ....(Columbia)
Pete Fountain; *Best Of Pete Fountain* ....(MCA)
Mr. New Orleans ....(MCA)
Saddle Up The Grey
New Lost City Ramblers; *20 Years Of Concert Performances* .....(Flying Fish)
Shade Of Grey
Bob Weir; *Heaven Help The Fool* ....(Arista)
Shades Of Gray
Billy Barber; *Shades Of Gray* .... (Digital Music Prod.)
Monkees; *10th Anniversary Tour-1986*. ....(Rhino)
Listen To The Band ....(Rhino)
Monkees' Greatest Hits ....(Rhino)
Shades Of Grey
Al B. Sure!; *Private Times & The Whole 9* .... (Warner Bros.)
Thoughts On A Grey Day
Fleetwood Mac; *Bare Trees*. ....(Reprise)
Touch Of Grey
Grateful Dead; *Heart Of Rock-C* ....(Columbia)
In The Dark. ....(Arista)
Worlds Apart
Vince Gill; *High Lonesome Sound* .... (MCA)

COLORS: ORANGE

See Also: COLORS (various), FOOD & BEVERAGES: FRUIT

Apples & Oranges
Pink Floyd; *Shine On*. ....(Columbia)
Bright Orange Spot
Dharma Bums; *Welcome* .... (Frontier)
Orange
10,000 Maniacs; *Hope Chest-Fredonia Recordings-1982-1983* ...... (Elektra)
Orange
Miles Davis; *Aura* ....(Columbia)
Orange
Romeo Void; *Benefactor*. ....(Columbia)
Orange
Frank Sinatra; *Conducts Tone Poems Of Color* ....(Capitol)
Orange And The Green
Irish Rovers; *Irish Rovers' Greatest Hits*. .... (MCA)
The Unicorn .... (MCA)
Northeast Winds; *Folk Era's Live Sampler* ....(Folk Era)
Ireland By Sail ....(Folk Era)
Orange Blossom Lane
Glenn Miller & His Orchestra; *Complete Glenn Miller & His
Orchestra*. ....(Bluebird)
Complete Glenn Miller & His Orchestra-#7. ....(Bluebird)
Orange Blossom Mandolin
Northeast Winds; *Northeast Winds In Concert* .... (Folk Era)
Orange Blossom Special
Bill Monroe; *Bean Blossom*. .... (MCA)
Bill Monroe and His Blue Grass Boys-60 Years Of Country. ....(RCA)
Stars Of The Grand Ole Opry-1926-1974-C. ....(RCA)
Charlie Daniels Band; *Fire On The Mountain* ....(Epic)
ST/Urban Cowboy 2 .... (Epic)
Flatt & Scruggs; *Hear The Whistles Blow* .... (International Mktg. Group)
Gordon Terry; *Disco Country*. ....(Plantation)
Gordon Terry-20 Golden Souvenirs ....(Plantation)
Johnny Cash; *Columbia Records-1958-1986* ....(Columbia)
Essential Johnny Cash ....(Columbia)
Johnny Cash-16 Biggest Hits-#2 ....(Legacy)
Johnny Cash's Greatest Hits ....(Columbia)
The Man In Black-His Greatest Hits. ....(Legacy)
Train Trax-C. ....(Sony Music Special Prod.)
Johnson Mountain Boys; *Steel Rails-Classic Railroad Songs-#1-C* ... (Rounder)
Nitty Gritty Dirt Band; *Will The Circle Be Unbroken* .... (EMI)
Orange Blossom Time
Bing Crosby; *Crooner-Columbia Years-1928-1934* ....(Columbia)
Orange City
Laszlo Gardony; *Legend Of Tsumi* .... (Antilles)
Orange Claw Hammer
Captain Beefheart & His Magic Band; *Trout Mask Replica* ....(Reprise)
Orange Colored Sky
Johnny Mathis; *Johnny Mathis-Live* ....(Columbia)
Nat ''King'' Cole; *The Nat ''King'' Cole Story*. ....(Capitol)

Natalie Cole; *Unforgettable With Love* ....(Elektra)
Orange Crush
R.E.M.; *Best Of MTV's 120 Minutes-#2-C*. ....(Rhino)
Green. ....(Warner Bros.)
Orange Express
Miami Sound Machine; *Eyes Of Innocence* ....(Epic)
Orange Guitars
Jimmy Haslip; *Arc* ....(GRP)
Orange Juice Blues
Bob Dylan And The Band; *Basement Tapes* ....(Columbia)
Orange King
Cafe Noir; *Window To The Sea* ....(Carpe Diem)
Orange Lady
Weather Report; *Weather Report*. ....(Columbia)
Orange Sherbert
Count Basie; *Basie Big Band*. .... (Pablo)
Orange Skies
Love; *Best Of Love*. ....(Rhino)
Orange Was The Color Of Her Dress
Charles Mingus; *Changes Two*. .... (Atlantic)
Charles Mingus In Europe-#2. ....(Enja)
Gil Evans; *Live At Sweet Basil-#1* ....(Evidence Music)
Gil Evans & Laurent Cugny Big Band; *Golden Hair* .... (Emarcy)
Orange, Brown & Green
Herb Ellis & Freddie Green; *Rhythm Willie* ....(Concord Jazz)
Why Is A Carrot More Orange Than An Orange
Amboy Dukes; *Journey To The Center Of The Mind* .... (Mainstream)
Wrong Number
Cure; *Galore-The Singles-1987-1997* ....(Fiction/Elektra)

COLORS: PINK

See Also: COLORS (various)

Cherry Pink And Apple Blossom White
Fabulous Thunderbirds; *Butt Rockin'*. ....(Chrysalis)
Perez Prado & His Orchestra; *This Is Perez Prado-Decade Of
The '50s* .... (RCA)
Freeway Of Love
Aretha Franklin; *Who's Zoomin' Who?* ....(Arista)
Hot Pink
Meat Puppets; *Up On The Sun* .... (SST)
Hot Pink
Eddy Raven; *Right For The Flight* ....(Liberty)
Little Pink Mack
Kay Adams; *Truck Driver Boogie Big Rig Hits-1939-1969-C*. .... (Audium)
Perfume And Pink Chiffon
Sonny Lester & His Orchestra; *Take It Off: Striptease Classics-C*. ......(Rhino)
Pink
Aerosmith; *Nine Lives* ....(Columbia)
Pink And Black
Robert Plant; *Shaken 'N' Stirred* ....(Es Paranza)
Pink And Velvet
Berlin; *Count Three & Pray*. .... (Geffen)
Pink Bedroom
John Hiatt; *Y'All Caught? Ones That Got Away, 1979-85* .... (Geffen)
Rosanne Cash; *Rhythm & Romance*. ....(Columbia)
Pink Cadillac
Bruce Springsteen; *Tracks*. ....(Columbia)
Natalie Cole; *Everlasting*. ....(Elektra)
Gotta Have House-Best Of House Music-#2-C. ....(Profile)
Southern Pacific; *Killbilly Hill* .... (Warner Bros.)
Rockin' Country-C. ....(Warner Bros.)
Southern Pacific's Greatest Hits ....(Warner Bros.)
Pink Cashmere
Prince; *The Hits 1*. ....(Paisley Park)
The Hits/The B-Sides. ....(Paisley Park)
Pink Christmas
Leo Kottke; *Regards From Chuck Pink* .... (Private Music)
Pink Cocktail For A Blue Lady
Glenn Miller & His Orchestra; *Complete Glenn Miller & His
Orchestra*. ....(Bluebird)
Complete Glenn Miller & His Orchestra-#9. ....(Bluebird)
Pink Elephants
Eddie Lang Blue Five & Joe Venuti; *Jazz In The Thirties-C* ....(Disques Swing)
Pink Elephants On Parade
Barbara Cook; *Disney Album*. .... (Disney)
Pink Flamingos
Rickie Lee Jones; *Traffic From Paradise*. ....(Geffen)
Pink Houses
John Cougar Mellencamp; *Rock For Amnesty-C* ....(Mercury)
Uh-Huh. ....(Riva)
John Mellencamp featuring Kid Rock; *The Concert For New York
City-C*. ....(Columbia)
Pink Pedal Pushers
Carl Perkins; *Best Of Carl Perkins-Jive After 5-1958-1978*. ....(Rhino)

Restless-Columbia Recordings . . . . (Columbia)
Jerry Lee Lewis; *Monsters* . . . . (Sun)

Pink Petticoats
Big Bopper; *Chantilly Lace Starring The Big Bopper* . . . . (Mercury)
Hellooo Baby! Best Of The Big Bopper-1954-1959 . . . . (Rhino)

Pink Pussycat
Devo; *Duty Now For The Future* . . . .(Warner Bros.)
Rest Of Devo-Greatest Misses . . . .(Warner Bros.)

Pink Shoe Laces
Dodie Stevens; *Original Classic Oldies Of The '50s & '60s-#18-C* . . . . .(MCA)

Pink Thunderbird
Jeff Beck; *Crazy Legs* . . . .(Epic)

Pink Turns To Blue
Husker Du; *Zen Arcade* . . . . (SST)

Pink-Eyed Pussycat
Bill Haley & His Comets; *Rock Around The Country* . . . .(Crescendo)
Rockin' & Rollin' . . . . (Accord)

Pinky
Elton John; *Caribou* . . . .(Rocket)

Pretty In Pink
Psychedelic Furs; *All Of This & Nothing* . . . . (Columbia)
ST/Pretty In Pink . . . . (A&M)
Talk Talk Talk . . . . (Columbia)

Pretty Little Pink
Doc Watson; *Old Timey Concert* . . . . (Vanguard)

Pretty Pink Rose
Adrian Belew; *Young Lions* . . . . (Atlantic)

Theme From ''The Pink Panther''
Henry Mancini; *Henry Mancini-Legendary Performer* . . . . (RCA)
Henry Mancini-Pure Gold . . . . (RCA)
Peter Gunn . . . . (RCA)
ST/Revenge Of The Pink Panther . . . . (EMI)
Television's Greatest Hits-#2-C . . . . (TVT)

White Sport Coat (And A Pink Carnation)
Marty Robbins; *16 Most Requested Songs Of The '50s-#2-C* . . . . . (Legacy)
Lifetime Of Song-1951-1982 . . . . (Columbia)
Marty Robbins' Greatest Hits . . . . (Columbia)

COLORS: PURPLE

See Also: COLORS (various)

Approaching Lavender
Gordon Lightfoot; *If You Could Read My Mind* . . . . (Reprise)

Deep Purple
Art Tatum; *Group Masterpieces-#2* . . . .(Pablo)
Masterpieces . . . .(MCA)
Solo Masterpieces-#3. . . . .(Pablo)
Johnny Mathis; *First 25 Years-Silver Anniversary Album* . . . . (Columbia)
Nino Tempo & April Stevens; *Hit Singles-1958-1977-C* . . . .(Atlantic)
Sarah Vaughan; *After Hours* . . . .(Sony Music Special Prod.)
Divine Sarah Vaughan-Columbia Years-1949-1953 . . . . (Columbia)

Mood Indigo
Duke Ellington; *1954 Los Angeles Concert* . . . .(Crescendo)
Black, Brown & Beige: 1944-1946 Band Recordings . . . . (Bluebird)
Carnegie Hall Concert-January 23, 1943 . . . . (Prestige)
Ellington Indigos . . . . (Columbia)
Sophisticated Ellington . . . . (RCA)
Ella Fitzgerald; *Ella A Nice.* . . . . (Pablo)
Ella Fitzgerald Sings-#2 . . . . (Verve)
Four Freshmen; *Capitol Collectors Series-Four Freshman* . . . . (Capitol)
Frank Sinatra; *In The Wee Small Hours* . . . . (Capitol)
Jimmie Lunceford & His Orchestra; *Stomp It Off-#1-1934-1935* . . . . (GRP)
Preservation Hall Jazz Band; *Best Of The Preservation Hall*
Jazz Band . . . . (Columbia)
New Orleans-#4 . . . . (Columbia)

Pilots Of Purple Twilight
Tangerine Dream; *Exit* . . . . (Elektra)

Purple Avenue
Holly Cole Trio; *Blame It On My Youth* . . . . (Blue Note)

Purple Haze
Cure; *Stone Free: A Tribute To Jimi Hendrix-C* . . . . (Reprise)
Jimi Hendrix; *Kiss The Sky.* . . . . (Reprise)
ST/Jimi Hendrix. . . . . (Reprise)
Jimi Hendrix Experience; *Are You Experienced?.* . . . . (Reprise)
Essential Jimi Hendrix. . . . . (Reprise)
Radio One . . . .(Rykodisc)
Smash Hits . . . . (Reprise)
Winger; *Winger* . . . .(Atlantic)

Purple Heart
David Allan Coe; *Invictus Means Unconquered.* . . . . (Columbia)

Purple Heart
T Bone Burnett; *Talking Animals* . . . . (Columbia)

Purple Heather
Van Morrison; *Hard Nose The Highway* . . . .(Polydor)

Purple Mountain
Scott Cossu; *Wind Dance* . . . . (Windham Hill)

Windham Hill Retrospective-C. . . . .(Windham Hill)

Purple People Eater
Sheb Wooley; *45s On CD-#1-1956-1959-C* . . . . (Mercury)
Dr. Demento: 20th Anniversary Collection-C . . . . (Rhino)
Halloween Hits-C. . . . . (Rhino)
Horror Rock Classics-#2-C . . . . (Rhino)
Super Hits-#4-C . . . . (Gusto)

Purple People Eater Meets The Witch Doctor
Big Bopper; *Hellooo Baby! Best Of The Big Bopper-1954-1959* . . . . (Rhino)

Purple Pills
D12; *Devil's Night* . . . . (Shady/Interscope)

Purple Rain
Prince and the Revolution; *ST/Purple Rain.* . . . . (Warner Bros.)

Purple Rivers
Swimming Pool Q's; *Swimming Pool Q's.* . . . .(A&M)

Purple Rose Of Cairo
New Orleans Ragtime Orchestra; *New Orleans Jazz-C.* . . . .(Arhoolie)

Purple Shades
Troggs; *Archeology-1967-1977* . . . .(Polydor)

Purple Sky
Gillan; *Magic* . . . . (Metal Blade)

Purples
Chicago; *Toronto Rock & Roll Revival 1969-#1-C* . . . . (Accord)

Silver Stars, Purple Sage, Eyes Of Blue
Roy Rogers & Sons Of The Pioneers; *Roy Rogers & Sons Of The*
Pioneers. . . . .(Varese Sarabande)

Southern California Purples
Chicago; *Chicago At Carnegie Hall* . . . . (Chicago)
Chicago Transit Authority . . . . (Chicago)

Twilight Time
Platters; *Pick Of The Platters* . . . . (Fifty One West)
Platters . . . . (Everest)
Platters-16 Greatest Hits . . . .(Trip)
Platters-Anthology . . . . (Rhino)
Sold Out . . . . (Fifty One West)
Willie Nelson; *What A Wonderful World* . . . . (Columbia)

Two Purple Shadows
Jerry Vale; *Jerry Vale-17 Most Requested Songs* . . . . (Legacy)
Jerry Vale's All-Time Greatest Hits . . . . (Columbia)

Violet
Hole; *Ask For It* . . . . (Caroline)
Live Through This . . . .(David Geffen Co.)

Violet
Savage Garden; *Savage Garden* . . . . (Columbia)

COLORS: RED, Crimson, Scarlet

See Also: ANATOMY: HAIR (redhead), COLORS (various)

(Only Angels Wanna Wear My) Red Shoes
Elvis Costello; *Girls Girls Girls* . . . . (Columbia)
My Aim Is True . . . . (Columbia)
Elvis Costello & The Attractions; *Best Of Elvis Costello & The*
Attractions . . . . (Columbia)

99 Luftballons (99 Red Balloons)
Nena; *99 Luftballons* . . . . (Epic)

Blue Monday At Kansas City Red's
Cary Bell; *Blues Harp* . . . .(Delmark)

Blue Red & Grey
Who; *By Numbers* . . . . (MCA)

Blue Rock Montana/Red Headed Stranger
Willie Nelson; *Red Headed Stranger* . . . . (Columbia)

Bongo Red
Gladiators; *Best Of Reggae Sunsplash-C* . . . .(Genes CD Co.)
Gladiators & Israel Vibration Live! . . . .(Genes CD Co.)

Bottle Of Red Wine
Derek And The Dominos; *Live At The Fillmore* . . . .(Polydor)
Eric Clapton; *Eric Clapton* . . . .(Polydor)

Cadillac Red
Judds; *Collection-1983-1990* . . . .(RCA)
River Of Time . . . .(RCA)
This Country's Rockin'. . . . .(RCA)

Cherry Red
Big Joe Turner; *Atlantic Blues-Piano-C* . . . .(Atlantic)
Boss Of The Blues. . . . .(Atlantic)
Count Basie & Big Joe Turner; *Bosses* . . . . (Pablo)
Ella Fitzgerald; *These Are The Blues.* . . . . (Verve)
Esther Phillips; *Confessin' The Blues-Jazzlore-#41* . . . . (Rhino)

Cherry Red
Lime Spiders; *Beethoven's Fist* . . . . (Caroline)

Cherry Red
Little Richard; *Big Hits* . . . .(Crescendo)

Country Ham & Red Gravy
Hotmud Family; *Live As We Know It* . . . . (Flying Fish)

Court Of The Crimson King-Part 1
King Crimson; *In The Court Of The Crimson King-An Observation By King*
Crimson. . . . . (Editions E.G.)

Cowboy Love Song (Red River Valley)
Skip Gorman; *A Cowboy's Wild Song To His Herd* . . . . (Rounder)
Crimson And Clover
Joan Jett & The Blackhearts; *I Love Rock 'n' Roll* . . . . (Blackheart)
Tommy James And The Shondells; *Best Of Tommy James And The
Shondells* . . . . (Roulette)
Billboard Top Rock 'N' Roll Hits-1969-C . . . . (Rhino)
Jewels-#1-C . . . . (SSS International)
Tommy James And The Shondells-Anthology . . . . (Rhino)
Cuyahoga
R.E.M.; *Life's Rich Pageant* . . . . (EMI-Capitol Entert. Properties)
East Texas Red
Arlo Guthrie; *Tribute To Woody Guthrie And Leadbelly-C* . . . . (Columbia)
Flowers Are Red
Harry Chapin; *Legends Of The Lost & Found* . . . . (Elektra)
Living Room Suite . . . . (Elektra)
House Burning Down
Jimi Hendrix; *Essential Jimi Hendrix* . . . . (Reprise)
Jimi Hendrix Experience; *Electric Ladyland* . . . . (Reprise)
I Saw Red
Warrant; *Cherry Pie* . . . . (Columbia)
Ida Red
Asleep At The Wheel featuring Jody Nix, Huey Lewis & Willie Nelson;
Tribute To The Music Of Bob Wills And The Texas Playboys-C . . . . (Liberty)
Bob Wills & His Texas Playboys; *Bob Wills & His Texas Playboys-
Greatest Hits* . . . . (Curb)
Tiffany Transcriptions-#2-Best Of The Tiffanys . . . . (Rhino)
I'm In Love With My Little Red Tricycle
Napoleon XIV; *The Second Coming* . . . . (Rhino)
Indian Red
Wild Tchoupitoulas; *Wild Tchoupitoulas* . . . . (Island)
Lady In Red
Charlie Daniels Band; *Windows* . . . . (Epic)
Lady In Red
Joan Jett & The Blackhearts; *I Love Rock 'n' Roll* . . . . (Blackheart)
Lady In Red
Chris DeBurgh; *Into The Light* . . . . (A&M)
Lady In Red
Stan Getz; *Stan Getz's Greatest Hits* . . . . (Prestige)
Lateralus
Tool; *Lateralus* . . . . (Volcano Entertainment)
Li'l Red Riding Hood
Sam The Sham and The Pharaohs; *Best Of Sam The Sham and The
Pharaohs* . . . . (Polydor)
Cruisin'-1966-C . . . . (Increase)
Pharaohization! (Best Of) . . . . (Rhino)
Little Red Corvette
Prince; *1999* . . . . (Warner Bros.)
Little Red Hen
Johnny Otis; *Original Johnny Otis Show* . . . . (Savoy)
Little Red Lights
Todd Rundgren; *Something/Anything?* . . . . (Rhino)
Little Red Rodeo
Collin Raye; *Best Of Collin Raye-Direct Hits* . . . . (Epic)
Little Red Rooster
B.B. King/Muddy Waters/Big Mama Thornton; *Live At Newport* . . . (Intermedia)
Big Mama Thornton; *Jail* . . . . (Vanguard)
Rolling Stones; *Love You Live* . . . . (Virgin)
The Rolling Stones, Now! . . . . (Abkco)
Sam Cooke; *Having A Party* . . . . (RCA)
This Is Sam Cooke . . . . (RCA)
Lonely
Tracy Lawrence; *Lessons Learned* . . . . (Atlantic)
My Little Red Book
Love; *Best Of Love* . . . . (Rhino)
Elektrock-Sixties-C . . . . (Elektra)
Nuggets-#2-Punk-C . . . . (Rhino)
Ol' Red
Blake Shelton; *Blake Shelton* . . . . (Giant)
One Color Red
G.G.F.H.; *Eclipse/Reality* . . . . (Dreamtime)
One Red Rose
John Prine; *Great Days-Anthology* . . . . (Rhino)
Storm Windows . . . . (Asylum)
Panama Red
New Riders Of The Purple Sage; *Adventures Of Panama Red* . . . . . (Columbia)
Best Of New Riders Of The Purple Sage . . . . (Columbia)
Rock Classics Of The '70s-C . . . . (Columbia)
Poor Red Georgia Dirt
Robin & Linda Williams; *Close As We Can Get* . . . . (Flying Fish)
Promise
Eve 6; *Horrorscope* . . . . (RCA)
Red
Sammy Hagar; *All Night Long* . . . . (One Way)
Sammy Hagar . . . . (Capitol)
Red
Bette Midler; *Broken Blossom* . . . . (Atlantic)

Red
Chris Rea; *Espresso Logic* . . . . (East West)
Red
XTC; *Go 2* . . . . (Geffen)
Red
King Crimson; *Red* . . . . (Editions E.G.)
Red & Black
Original Broadway Cast; *Les Miserables* . . . . (Geffen)
Red Alert
Saxon; *Destiny* . . . . (Enigma)
Red Alert
Quiet Riot; *Condition Critical* . . . . (Epic Portrait Assoc.)
Red Alert
Red Garland; *Red Alert* . . . . (Galaxy)
Red And Rio Grande
Doug Supernaw; *Red And Rio Grande* . . . . (BNA)
Red And The Black
Blue Oyster Cult; *Career Of Evil* . . . . (Columbia)
Extraterrestrial Live . . . . (Columbia)
On Your Feet Or On Your Knees . . . . (Columbia)
Tyranny & Mutation . . . . (Columbia)
Red Army Blues
Waterboys; *Pagan Place* . . . . (Chrysalis)
Red Bandana
Merle Haggard; *Merle Haggard's Greatest Hits* . . . . (MCA)
More Of The Best . . . . (Rhino)
Serving 190 Proof . . . . (MCA)
Red Barchetta
Rush; *Exit...Stage Left* . . . . (Mercury)
Moving Pictures . . . . (Mercury)
Rush-Chronicles . . . . (Mercury)
Red Baron
David Benoit; *Here's To You Charlie Brown: 50th Great* . . . . (GRP/VMG)
Red Beans
Coleman Hawkins & Red Garland Trio; *Coleman Hawkins & Red
Garland Trio* . . . . (Prestige)
Kingsnakes; *19 Lucky Strikes* . . . . (Blue Wave)
Professor Longhair; *Crawfish Fiesta* . . . . (Alligator)
Red Beans And Rice
Booker T. & The M.G.s; *Back To Back: Mar-Keys & Booker T. & The
M.G.s* . . . . (Atlantic)
Best Of Booker T. & The M.G.s . . . . (Atlantic)
Legends Of Rock Guitar-'60s-#1-C . . . . (Rhino)
Red Bird Tennessee Waltz
Clark Kessinger & Gene Meade; *Clark Kessinger & Gene Meade* . . . (Rounder)
Red Cab To Manhattan
Stephen Bishop; *Best Of Bish* . . . . (Rhino)
Red Cadillac
Colin Winski; *Rock Therapy* . . . . (Takoma)
Red Chevrolet
Jimmie Dale Gilmore; *Jimmie Dale Gilmore* . . . . (Hightone)
Points West-New Horizons In Country-C . . . . (Hightone)
Red Dirt Girl
Emmylou Harris; *Red Dirt Girl* . . . . (Nonesuch)
Red Eye
Joe Beck; *Beck & Sanborn* . . . . (CBS Associated)
Fire Into Music-Best Of Impulse!-#2-C . . . . (MCA/Impulse)
Red Eye
Devo; *Duty Now For The Future* . . . . (Warner Bros.)
Red Eye
Nicky Thomas & Dolares; *Explosive Rock Steady-Amalgamated
Label* . . . . (Heartbeat)
Red Football
Sinead O'Connor; *Universal Mother* . . . . (Ensign)
Red Headed Irishman
J.P. Fraley & Annadeene; *Wild Rose Of The Mountain* . . . . (Rounder)
Red Headed Stranger
Willie Nelson; *Red Headed Stranger* . . . . (Columbia)
What A Wonderful World . . . . (Columbia)
Red Hot
Billy Lee Riley & His Little Green Men; *Red Hot: The Very Best Of Billy
Lee Riley* . . . . (Collectables)
Rock This Town-Rockabilly Hits-#1-C . . . . (Rhino)
Robert Gordon; *Rock This Town-Rockabilly Hits-#2-C* . . . . (Rhino)
Robert Gordon & Link Wray; *Robert Gordon & Link Wray* . . . . . . (RCA)
Red Hot Chicken
Wet Willie; *Drippin' Wet/Live!* . . . . (Capricorn)
Wet Willie's Greatest Hits . . . . (Polydor)
Red Hot Poker
Rufus; *Numbers* . . . . (MCA)
Red House
Jimi Hendrix; *Concerts* . . . . (Reprise)
Kiss The Sky . . . . (Reprise)
Lifelines/Jimi Hendrix Story . . . . (Reprise)
Live At Winterland . . . . (Rykodisc)
ST/Jimi Hendrix . . . . (Reprise)
Jimi Hendrix Experience; *Are You Experienced?* . . . . (Reprise)
Smash Hits . . . . (Reprise)

Red House
Great White; *Recovery-Live!* . . . .(Enigma Capitol)
Red House
David Byrne; *The Catherine Wheel-Complete Broadway Score* . . . . (Sire)
Red Light Mama Red Hot
Humble Pie; *Humble Pie* . . . . (A&M)
Red Light Special
TLC; *CrazySexyCool* . . . . (LaFace)
Red Money
David Bowie; *Lodger* . . . . (Rykodisc)
Red Moon Over Boston
Romanovsky & Phillips; *Be Political Not Polite* . . . .(Fresh Fruit)
Red Neck Friend
Jackson Browne; *For Everyman* . . . . (Asylum)
Red Neckin' Love Makin' Night
Conway Twitty; *Classic Conway* . . . .(MCA)
  Conway Twitty-Legends . . . .(MCA)
  Mr. T . . . .(MCA)
  Night With Conway Twitty . . . .(MCA)
Red Plains
Bruce Hornsby & The Range; *The Way It Is* . . . . (RCA)
Red Rain
Peter Gabriel; *Greenpeace/Rainbow Warriors-C* . . . .(Geffen)
  Secret World Live . . . .(Geffen)
  Shaking The Tree-Sixteen Golden Greats . . . .(Geffen)
  So . . . .(Geffen)
Red Red Rose
Dave Mallett; *Vital Signs* . . . . (Flying Fish)
Emmylou Harris; *Brand New Dance* . . . . (Reprise)
Red Red Sun
INXS; *Listen Like Thieves* . . . .(Atlantic)
Red Red Wine
Neil Diamond; *Double Gold-Neil Diamond* . . . .(Bang)
  Hot August Night . . . .(MCA)
  Neil Diamond-Classics (Early Years) . . . . (Columbia)
  Neil Diamond's Greatest Hits . . . .(Bang)
Replacements; *Pleased To Meet Me* . . . . (Sire)
UB40; *Labour Of Love* . . . . (A&M)
Red River
Alabama; *Alabama-Live* . . . . (RCA)
  Closer You Get . . . . (RCA)
Red River
BoDeans; *Home* . . . . (Slash)
Red River
Leadbelly; *Leadbelly* . . . . (Columbia)
  Midnight Special . . . . (Rounder)
Red River Blues
Jesse Fuller; *Jesse Fuller's Favorites* . . . . (Prestige)
Sonny Terry; *Sonny Terry* . . . . (Everest)
  Sonny Terry With Brownie McGhee-Midnight Special . . . . (Fantasy)
Red River Rock
Johnny And The Hurricanes; *Echoes Of A Rock Era-Middle*
  Years-C . . . .(Roulette)
  History Of Rock Instrumentals-#1-C . . . . (Rhino)
Red River Valley
Gene Autry; *Cowboy Hall Of Fame* . . . .(Republic/Universal)
  The Country Music Hall Of Fame-Gene Autry-15 Of His All-Time
    Greatest Hits . . . . (Columbia)
  Western Classics . . . . (Columbia)
Pete Seeger; *American Favorite Ballads-#5* . . . . (Smithsonian Folkways)
Red Rocking Chair
Jody Stecher & Kate Brislin; *Song That Will Linger* . . . . (Rounder)
Red Rooster
Howlin' Wolf; *The Chess Box-Howlin' Wolf* . . . . (Chess)
Paula Lockheart; *It Ain't The End Of The World* . . . . (Flying Fish)
Red Rose
Alphaville; *Afternoons In Utopia* . . . .(Atlantic)
  Alphaville-The Singles Collection . . . .(Atlantic)
Red Roses
Midnight Star; *Work It Out* . . . . (Solar)
Red Roses (Won't Work Now)
Reba McEntire; *Have I Got A Deal For You* . . . .(MCA)
Red Roses For A Blue Lady
Al Martino; *Best Of Al Martino* . . . . (Capitol)
  Capitol Collectors Series-Al Martino . . . . (Capitol)
Andy Williams; *Andy Williams-16 Most Requested Songs* . . . . (Legacy)
Mom & Dads; *Best Of The Mom & Dads* . . . . (Crescendo)
Roger Whittaker; *All-Time Heart-Touching Favorites* . . . . (Capitol)
  Roger Whittaker-Classics Collection-#1 . . . . (Capitol)
Vaughn Monroe; *Best Of Vaughn Monroe* . . . . (RCA)
Red Rubber Ball
Cyrkle; *Even More Nuggets-C* . . . . (Rhino)
  Pop Classics Of The '60s-C . . . .(Columbia)
  Red Rubber Ball (A Collection) . . . .(Columbia)
Red Sails
David Bowie; *Lodger* . . . . (Rykodisc)
  Sound + Vision . . . . (Rykodisc)
Red Sails In The Sunset
Big Joe Turner; *Nobody In Mind* . . . . (Pablo)

Dinah Washington; *Echoes Of An Era-Dinah Washington* . . . . (Roulette)
Jarmels; *Jarmels-Golden Classics* . . . . (Collectables)
Nat ''King'' Cole; *Unforgettable* . . . . (Capitol)
Platters; *Platters Greatest Hits* . . . . (Everest)
Red Sector A
Rush; *Grace Under Pressure* . . . .(Mercury)
  Rush-Chronicles . . . .(Mercury)
  Show Of Hands . . . .(Mercury)
Red Sex Dress
Alfonia Tims & The Flying Tigers; *Future Funk/Uncut!* . . . . (Roir)
Red Sharks
Crimson Glory; *Transcendance* . . . . (MCA)
Red Shoes
Tom Waits; *Big Time* . . . . (Island)
Red Shoes
Chris Rea; *Auberge* . . . . (Atco)
Red Shoes By The Drugstore
Tom Waits; *Blue Valentine* . . . .(Asylum)
Red Skies
Fixx; *One Thing Leads To Another-Greatest Hits* . . . . (MCA)
  React . . . . (MCA)
  Shuttered Room . . . . (MCA)
Red Skies Over Georgia
Charlie Walker; *45-#172* . . . . (Plantation)
Red Sky
Michael Schenker Group; *Built To Destroy* . . . .(Chrysalis)
Red Sky
Status Quo; *Status Quo* . . . . (Mercury)
Red Streamliner
Little Feat; *Hoy-Hoy!* . . . . (Warner Bros.)
  Time Loves A Hero . . . . (Warner Bros.)
Red Telephone
Love; *Forever Changes* . . . . (Elektra)
Red Tide
Rush; *Presto* . . . .(Atlantic)
Red Wine & Blue Memories
Joe Stampley; *Joe Stampley's Biggest Hits* . . . . (Epic)
Rednecks, White Socks And Blue Ribbon Beer
Johnny Russell; *Beer Redneck Mothers* . . . .(RCA)
  Country Legends-C . . . .(Madacy)
  Country's Greatest Drinking Songs-C . . . . (All-Star Music)
  Rednecks, White Socks & Blue Ribbon Beer . . . .(RCA)
Redwood Evergreen
Lorraine Duisit; *Hawks & Herons* . . . . (Flying Fish)
Redwood Tree
Van Morrison; *St. Dominic's Preview* . . . . (Warner Bros.)
Rev On The Red Line
Foreigner; *Head Games* . . . .(Atlantic)
Rhode Island Red
Brew Moore; *Brew Moore* . . . . (Fantasy)
Rhythm From A Red Car
Hardline; *Double Eclipse* . . . . (MCA)
River Runs Red
Midnight Oil; *Blue Sky Mining* . . . .(Columbia)
Rose Colored Glasses
John Conlee; *Backstage At The Grand Ole Opry-C* . . . . (RCA)
  Grand Ole Opry-75 Years-#1-C . . . . (MCA)
  John Conlee-Legends . . . . (MCA)
  John Conlee's Greatest Hits . . . . (MCA)
  MCA Records 30 Years Of Hits-1958-1988-C . . . . (MCA)
  Rose Colored Glasses . . . .(Universal)
Roses Ain't Red
Diane Pfeifer; *Diane Pfeifer* . . . . (Capitol)
Roses Are Red
Bobby Vinton; *Bobby Vinton-16 Most Requested Songs* . . . . (Legacy)
  Bobby Vinton's All-Time Greatest Hits . . . . (Epic)
  Spring Sensations . . . . (Epic)
Ruby Red
Kingston Trio; *Hidden Treasures* . . . . (Folk Era)
  Treasure Chest . . . . (Folk Era)
Run Red Run
Coasters; *The Ultimate Coasters* . . . . (Warner Special Prod.)
Sad Old Red
Simply Red; *Picture Book* . . . . (Elektra)
Scarlet Begonias
Grateful Dead; *From The Mars Hotel* . . . .(Grateful Dead)
Scarlet Fever
Kenny Rogers; *We've Got Tonight* . . . . (Razor & Tie)
Scarlet Ribbons (For Her Hair)
Harry Belafonte; *Harry Belafonte-Legendary Performer* . . . . (RCA)
  Harry Belafonte's All Time Greatest Hits-#1 . . . . (RCA)
  This Is Harry Belafonte . . . . (RCA)
Jim Ed Brown & Maxine Brown; *Essential Jim Ed Brown* . . . . (RCA)
Kingston Trio; *At Large/Here We Go Again!* . . . . (Capitol)
  Capitol Collectors Series-The Kingston Trio . . . . (Capitol)
Lennon Sisters; *Best Of The Lennon Sisters* . . . . (Ranwood)
Les Paul; *Legend & The Legacy-#1-4* . . . . (Capitol)
NRBQ; *Diggin' Uncle Q* . . . .(Rounder)

Patti Page; *Patti Page-16 Most Requested Songs* . . . . (Legacy)
Roger Whittaker; *Roger Whittaker-Classics Collection-#2* . . . . (Liberty)

Scarlet Water
Johnny Duncan; *Best Of Johnny Duncan* . . . . (Columbia)
   Johnny Duncan's Greatest Hits . . . . (Columbia)

She Drew A Broken Heart
Patty Loveless; *The Trouble With The Truth* . . . . (Epic)

She Wears Red Feathers
Guy Mitchell; *Guy Mitchell-16 Most Requested Songs* . . . . (Legacy)

Smith's Red Apple Rag
Skip Gorman; *A Cowboy's Wild Song To His Herd* . . . . (Rounder)

Snoopy Vs. The Red Baron
Royal Guardsmen; *Best Of The Royal Guardsmen-#1* . . . . (Rhino)
   Collectables Presents The History Of Rock-#9-C . . . . (Collectables)
   Cruisin'-1967-C . . . . (Increase)
   Million-Dollar Memories #1-C . . . . (RCA)
   Super Oldies Of The '60s-#6-C . . . . (Audio Fidelity)

Something In Red
Lorrie Morgan; *Lorrie Morgan's Greatest Hits* . . . . (BNA)
   Something In Red . . . . (RCA)
   To Get To You-Greatest Hits Collection . . . . (BNA)

Strawberry Roan
Marty Robbins; *Gunfighter Ballads & Trail Songs* . . . . (Legacy)

Sweet Rhode Island Red
Ike & Tina Turner; *Proud Mary-Best Of Ike & Tina Turner* . . . . (EMI)

Take A Red
New Riders Of The Purple Sage; *Alive & Kicking* . . . . (MCA Special Prod.)
   Marin County Line . . . . (MCA)

Texas Red
Strength In Numbers; *Telluride Sessions* . . . . (MCA)

They're Red Hot
Red Hot Chili Peppers; *Blood Sugar Sex Magik* . . . . (Warner Bros.)
Robert Johnson; *Robert Johnson-Complete Recordings* . . . . (Columbia)

Thin Red Line
Cretones; *Cretones* . . . . (Planet)

Under The Red Sky
Bob Dylan; *Under The Red Sky* . . . . (Columbia)

Utah Carol
Harry K. McClintock; *Cowboy Songs On
   Folkways-C* . . . . (Smithsonian Folkways)
Marty Robbins; *Gunfighter Ballads & Trail Songs* . . . . (Legacy)

When The Red, Red Robin
Al Jolson; *Best Of Al Jolson* . . . . (MCA)
   The Al Jolson Story-#3 . . . . (MCA)
Louis Armstrong; *I Like Jazz-Essence Of Louis Armstrong* . . . . . . (Columbia)
Mitch Miller; *Mitch Miller-16 Most Requested Songs* . . . . (Columbia)

White Heat, Red Hot
Judas Priest; *Stained Class* . . . . (Columbia)

Wish I Were You
Patty Smyth; *ST/Armageddon-The Album* . . . . (Columbia)

Wrong Number
Cure; *Galore-The Singles-1987-1997* . . . . (Fiction/Elektra)

Yes It Is
Beatles; *Beatles VI* . . . . (Capitol)
   Beatles-Box Set . . . . (Capitol)
   Beatles-Love Songs . . . . (Capitol)
   Past Masters-Volume One . . . . (Parlophone)

COLORS: WHITE, Ivory, Pale

See Also: COLORS (various)

Big White Cloud
John Cale; *Vintage Violence* . . . . (Columbia)

Black & White
Three Dog Night; *Best Of Three Dog Night* . . . . (MCA)
   Billboard Top Rock 'N' Roll Hits-1972-C . . . . (Rhino)
   Joy To The World-Greatest Hits . . . . (MCA)

Black & White
Todd Rundgren; *Back To The Bars* . . . . (Rhino)
   Faithful . . . . (Rhino)
   Todd Rundgren-Anthology 1968-1985 . . . . (Rhino)

Black & White
Rosanne Cash; *Rosanne Cash-Hits-1979-1989* . . . . (Columbia)

Black & White
Jackson Browne; *Lives In The Balance* . . . . (Asylum)

Black & White
INXS; *Dekadance* . . . . (Atco)
   Shabooh Shoobah . . . . (Atco)

Black And White Television
Ian Anderson; *Walk Into Light* . . . . (Chrysalis)

Black Boys, White Boys
Original Broadway Cast; *Hair* . . . . (RCA)

Black Chick, White Guy
Kid Rock; *Devil Without A Cause* . . . . (Top Dog/Lava/Atlantic)

Black Jesus
Everlast; *Eat At Whitey's* . . . . (Tommy Boy)

Black Or White
Michael Jackson; *Dangerous* . . . . (Epic)

Blanca Navidad (White Christmas)
Freddy Fender; *Tejano Country Christmas-C* . . . . (Arista)

Blue White Planet
Raffi; *Country Goes Raffi-C* . . . . (Rounder)

Cherry Pink And Apple Blossom White
Fabulous Thunderbirds; *Butt Rockin'* . . . . (Chrysalis)
Perez Prado & His Orchestra; *This Is Perez Prado-Decade Of
   The '50s* . . . . (RCA)

China White
Scorpions; *Blackout* . . . . (Mercury)

China White
Little Feat; *Hoy-Hoy!* . . . . (Warner Bros.)

Dirty White Boy
Foreigner; *Head Games* . . . . (Atlantic)
   Records . . . . (Atlantic)

Ebony And Ivory
Paul McCartney & Stevie Wonder; *All The Best!* . . . . (Capitol)
   Tug Of War . . . . (Gold Rush)

Edelweiss
Original Cast/Mary Martin; *The Sound Of Music* . . . . (Sony Broadway)

Extra Pale
Goo Goo Dolls; *Dizzy Up The Girl* . . . . (Warner Sunset/Reprise)

Great White Buffalo
Ted Nugent; *Double Live Gonzo* . . . . (Epic)

Great White Hope
Styx; *Pieces Of Eight* . . . . (A&M)

Great White Horse
Guy & Ralna; *22 Golden Country Classics* . . . . (Ranwood)
   Guy & Ralna-Country . . . . (Ranwood)

Great White Line
Point Blank; *On A Roll* . . . . (MCA)

Lateralus
Tool; *Lateralus* . . . . (Volcano Entertainment)

Little White Cloud That Cried
Johnnie Ray; *Best Of Johnnie Ray* . . . . (Columbia)
   Best Of Johnnie Ray . . . . (Exact)
   Johnnie Ray's Greatest Hits . . . . (Sony Music Special Prod.)

Little White Lie
Sammy Hagar; *Marching To Mars* . . . . (MCA)

Little White Lies
Dick Haymes with Gordon Jenkins & His Orchestra; *Sentimental Journey:
   Pop Vocal Classics-#2-1947-1950-C* . . . . (Rhino)
Dinah Shore; *Dinah Shore-16 Most Requested Songs-Encore!* . . . . . (Legacy)
Fred Waring's Pennsylvanians featuring Clare Hanlon; *Very Best Of Fred
   Waring & The Pennsylvanians* . . . . (Reader's Digest Music)
Tommy Dorsey; *Best Of Tommy Dorsey* . . . . (Bluebird)
   Complete Tommy Dorsey-#6 . . . . (RCA)

Little White Lies
Romantics; *The Romantics* . . . . (Columbia)

Long White Cadillac
Blasters; *Blasters-Collection* . . . . (Slash)
Dave Alvin; *Romeo's Escape* . . . . (Epic)
Dwight Yoakam; *Just Lookin' For A Hit* . . . . (Reprise)

Long White Car
Hipsway; *Hipsway* . . . . (Columbia)

My TV Went Black & White On Me
Young Black Teenagers; *Young Black Teenagers* . . . . (S.O.U.L.)

My White Bicycle
Nazareth; *Hot Tracks* . . . . (A&M)
   Nazareth-Classics-#16 . . . . (A&M)

My White Devil
Echo & The Bunnymen; *Porcupine* . . . . (Sire)

My White Knight
Original Broadway Cast; *The Music Man* . . . . (Angel)
Original Cast; *The Music Man* . . . . (Gold Rush)

Nights In White Satin
Moody Blues; *Billboard Top Rock 'N' Roll Hits-1972-C* . . . . (Rhino)
   Caught Live Plus Five . . . . (Polydor)
   Days Of Future Passed . . . . (Polydor)
   History Of British Rock-#8-C . . . . (Rhino)
   This Is The Moody Blues . . . . (Polydor)

Northern White Clouds
Bill Monroe; *Live From Mountain Stage* . . . . (Blue Plate)

One Big Love
Emmylou Harris; *Red Dirt Girl* . . . . (Nonesuch)
Patty Griffin; *Flaming Red* . . . . (A&M)

Pale September
Fiona Apple; *Tidal* . . . . (Clean Slate/Work)

Please
Bing Crosby; *Bing Crosby-16 Most Requested Songs* . . . . (Legacy)

Po' White Trash
White Trash; *White Trash* . . . . (Elektra)

Poor White Hound Dog
Merry Clayton; *ST/Performance* . . . . (Warner Bros.)

Pretty Fly (For A White Guy)
Offspring; *Americana* . . . . (Columbia)

Promise
Eve 6; *Horrorscope* . . . . (RCA)

Rednecks, White Socks And Blue Ribbon Beer
Johnny Russell; *Beer Redneck Mothers* . . . . (RCA)
   Country Legends-C . . . . (Madacy)
   Country's Greatest Drinking Songs-C . . . . (All-Star Music)
   Rednecks, White Socks & Blue Ribbon Beer . . . . (RCA)

Sail On White Moon
Boz Scaggs; *Slow Dancer* . . . . (Columbia)

She'll Be Coming 'Round The Mountain
Four Freshmen & Stan Kenton & Orchestra; *Live At Butler*
   University . . . . (Creative World)
Mormon Tabernacle Choir; *This Land Is Your Land* . . . . (Columbia)
Original Soundtrack; *Children's Favorites* . . . . (Kid Rhino/Rhino 4 Kids)
   School Days-Kids Classics . . . . (Benson)

Some Folks Is Even Whiter Than Me
Todd Rundgren; *Something/Anything?* . . . . (Rhino)

Something In Red
Lorrie Morgan; *Lorrie Morgan's Greatest Hits* . . . . (BNA)
   Something In Red . . . . (RCA)
   To Get To You-Greatest Hits Collection . . . . (BNA)

There'll Be Bluebirds Over The White Cliffs Of Dover
Kay Kyser & His Orchestra; *Best Of The Big Bands-C* . . . . (Columbia)

Top Hat, White Tie And Tails
Fred Astaire; *Irving Berlin Songbook* . . . . (Verve)

Trapped In The Body Of A White Girl
Julie Brown; *Trapped In The Body Of A White Girl* . . . . (Sire)

Two White Horses
John Lee Hooker; *That's Where It's At* . . . . (Stax)

When The White Lilacs Bloom Again
Billy Vaughn; *Best Of Billy Vaughn* . . . . (MCA)
   Billy Vaughn's Greatest Hits . . . . (Curb)

White Bird
It's A Beautiful Day; *Bill Graham Presents The Last Days Of The*
   Fillmore-C . . . . (Epic Portrait Assoc.)
   It's A Beautiful Day . . . . (Columbia)

White Boys
Original Cast; *ST/Hair* . . . . (RCA)

White Car In Germany
Associates; *Popera-Singles Collection* . . . . (Sire)

White Cliffs Of Dover
Kay Kyser & His Orchestra; *16 Most Requested Songs Of The*
   '40s-#1-C . . . . (Legacy)
Lee Andrews And The Hearts; *Lee Andrews And The Hearts'*
   Biggest Hits . . . . (Collectables)
Mystics; *Mystics-16 Golden Classics* . . . . (Collectables)
Righteous Brothers; *Righteous Brothers' Greatest Hits* . . . . (Verve)
   Righteous Brothers-Anthology 1962-1974 . . . . (Rhino)
Rosemary Clooney; *For The Duration* . . . . (Concord Jazz)

White Dove
Lynyrd Skynyrd; *First & Last* . . . . (MCA)

White Fishes
John Renbourn; *Sir Jon Alot Of Merrie Englanders* . . . . (Reprise)

White Freightliner Blues
Jimmie Dale Gilmore; *Fair & Square* . . . . (Hightone)
New Grass Revival; *When The Storm Is Over* . . . . (Flying Fish)
Townes Van Zandt; *Live & Obscure* . . . . (Sugar Hill)

White Heat, Red Hot
Judas Priest; *Stained Class* . . . . (Columbia)

White Honey
Graham Parker; *Howlin' Wind* . . . . (Mercury)

White Horse
Laid Back; *Castles In The Sand* . . . . (Sire)
   For The Record . . . . (Sire)
   Greatest Hits Of The Street-C . . . . (Priority)
   Keep Smiling . . . . (Sire)

White Horses
Outlaws; *Ghost Riders* . . . . (Arista)

White Hot
Black Flag; *In My Head* . . . . (SST)

White Hot
Red Rider; *Don't Fight It* . . . . (Capitol)

White House Blues
Doc Watson; *Essential Doc Watson* . . . . (Vanguard)
Doc Watson & Family; *Treasures Untold-C* . . . . (Vanguard)
Stanley Brothers; *Shadows Of The Past* . . . . (Copper Creek)

White Houses
Eric Burdon & The Animals; *Eric Burdon & The Animals'*
   Greatest Hits . . . . (MGM)

White Knuckles
Elvis Costello & The Attractions; *Trust* . . . . (Rykodisc)

White Lies
Grin; *Rock Artifacts-From The Vaults-#1-C* . . . . (Columbia)
Nils Lofgren; *Grin* . . . . (Epic Portrait Assoc.)

White Light
Gene Clark; *White Light* . . . . (A&M)

White Light/White Heat
David Bowie; *Sound + Vision* . . . . (Rykodisc)
   ST/Ziggy Stardust-The Motion Picture . . . . (Rykodisc)

Lou Reed; *Rock N Roll Animal* . . . . (RCA)
   Walk On The Wild Side-The Best Of Lou Reed . . . . (RCA)
Velvet Underground; *1969: Velvet Underground Live* . . . . (Mercury)
   White Light/White Heat . . . . (Verve)

White Lightning
Angel; *Live Without A Net* . . . . (Casablanca)
   On Earth As It Is In Heaven . . . . (Casablanca)

White Lightning
Big Bopper; *Helloo Baby! Best Of The Big Bopper-1954-1959* . . . . . . (Rhino)
George Jones; *Best Of George Jones-1955-1967* . . . . (Rhino)
   Billboard Top Country Hits-1959-C . . . . (Rhino)
   George Jones' All-Time Greatest Hits . . . . (Epic)
   The Bradley Barn Sessions . . . . (MCA)
Hank Williams, Jr.; *Whiskey Bent & Hell Bound* . . . . (WB/Curb)

White Lightning
Def Leppard; *Adrenalize* . . . . (Mercury)

White Lightning
Furry Lewis; *Back On My Feet Again* . . . . (Prestige)
   Shake 'Em On Down . . . . (Fantasy)

White Lightning
Babys; *Head First* . . . . (Chrysalis)

White Lightning & Wine
Heart; *Dreamboat Annie* . . . . (Capitol)

White Line
Emmylou Harris; *Ballad Of Sally Rose* . . . . (Warner Bros.)
Neil Young & Crazy Horse; *Ragged Glory* . . . . (Reprise)

White Line Fever
Flying Burrito Brothers; *Close Encounters To The West Coast* . . . . (Relix)
Merle Haggard; *More Of The Best* . . . . (Rhino)
Merle Haggard & The Strangers; *Okie From Muskogee* . . . . (Capitol)

White Lines (Don't Do It)
Grandmaster Flash & Melle Mel; *Hip Hop Greats-Classic Raps-C* . . . . (Rhino)

White Man
Queen; *Day At The Races* . . . . (Hollywood)

White Man In Hammersmith Palais
Clash; *On Broadway* . . . . (Epic)
   The Clash . . . . (Epic)
   The Story Of The Clash, Volume 1 . . . . (Epic)

White Man/Black Man
James Gang; *James Gang-16 Greatest Hits* . . . . (MCA)
   Thirds . . . . (One Way)

White Minority
Black Flag; *First Four Years* . . . . (SST)
   ST/Decline Of Western Civilization . . . . (Slash)

White Mountain
Genesis; *Trespass* . . . . (MCA)

White Nigger
Big Boys; *The Fat Elvis* . . . . (Touch & Go)

White Noise
Jay Ferguson; *White Noise* . . . . (Capitol)

White Palace
Clay Walker; *Clay Walker* . . . . (Giant)

White Punks On Dope
Tubes; *T.R.A.S.H. (Tubes Rarities And Smash Hits)* . . . . (A&M)
   Tubes . . . . (A&M)
   What Do You Want From Live . . . . (A&M)

White Queen (As It Began)
Queen; *Queen II* . . . . (Hollywood)

White Rabbit
Damned; *Best Of The Damned* . . . . (Roadracer)
   Machine Gun Etiquette . . . . (Roadracer)
George Benson; *George Benson-Collection* . . . . (Warner Bros.)
   White Rabbit . . . . (CBS Associated)
Jefferson Airplane; *2400 Fulton Street-An Anthology* . . . . (RCA)
   Flight Log (1966-1976) . . . . (Grunt)
   Loves You . . . . (RCA)
   ST/Platoon . . . . (Atlantic)
   Surrealistic Pillow . . . . (RCA)
   The Worst Of Jefferson Airplane . . . . (RCA)

White Rhythm & Blues
J.D. Souther; *You're Only Lonely* . . . . (Legacy)
Linda Ronstadt; *Living In The USA* . . . . (Asylum)

White Riot
Clash; *On Broadway* . . . . (Epic)
   The Clash . . . . (Epic)
   The Story Of The Clash, Volume 1 . . . . (Epic)

White Room
Cream; *Cream-Live-#2* . . . . (Polydor)
   History Of British Rock-#9-C . . . . (Rhino)
   Strange Brew-Very Best Of Cream . . . . (Polydor)
   Wheels Of Fire . . . . (Polydor)
Eric Clapton; *24 Nights* . . . . (Duck/Reprise)
   Eric Clapton-Crossroads-C . . . . (Polydor)

White Russia
Dirt Band; *Dirt Band* . . . . (United Artists)

White Shadow
Peter Gabriel; *Peter Gabriel* . . . . (Atlantic)

White Ship
H.P. Lovecraft; *H.P. Lovecraft* . . . . (Out Of Print)

White Silver Sands
Ace Cannon; *Golden Classics-Ace Cannon* . . . . (Gusto)
Ray Anthony; *Great Golden Hits* . . . . (Ranwood)
Sonny James; *45-#4-45706* . . . . (Columbia)
White Sport Coat (And A Pink Carnation)
Marty Robbins; *16 Most Requested Songs Of The '50s-#2-C* . . . . (Legacy)
Lifetime Of Song-1951-1982. . . . . (Columbia)
Marty Robbins' Greatest Hits. . . . . (Columbia)
White Sugar
Peter Frampton; *Frampton's Camel* . . . . (A&M)
White Sun
Doobie Brothers; *Toulouse Street* . . . . (Warner Bros.)
White Tornado
R.E.M.; *Dead Letter Office* . . . . (I.R.S.)
White Trash
Orchestral Manoeuvres In The Dark; *Junk Culture* . . . . (A&M)
White Trash
Redd Kross; *Born Innocent* . . . . (Frontier)
White Trash
Bellamy Brothers; *Crazy From The Heart.* . . . . (MCA)
White Trash
Bad Religion; *How Could Hell Be Any Worse* . . . . (Epitaph)
White Trash
Steve Cash; *White Mansions* . . . . (A&M)
White Trash Song
Steve Young; *Honky-Tonk Man* . . . . (Rounder)
Solo/Live . . . . (Watermelon)
White Trash Wife
Exene Cervenka; *Old Wives' Tales* . . . . (Rhino)
White Trash With Cash
Southgang; *Group Therapy* . . . . (Charisma)
White Wall
Bob Seger System; *Ramblin' Gamblin' Man.* . . . . (Capitol)
White Wedding
Billy Idol; *Billy Idol.* . . . . (Chrysalis)
ST/The Wedding Singer . . . . (Maverick)
Vital Idol. . . . . (Chrysalis)
White, Discussion
Live; *ST/Virtuosity* . . . . (Radioactive/MCA)
Throwing Copper . . . . (Radioactive/MCA)
Whiter Shade Of Pale
Annie Lennox; *Medusa* . . . . (Arista)
Procol Harum; *Best Of Procol Harum* . . . . (A&M)
Billboard Top Pop Hits-1967-C . . . . (Rhino)
History Of British Rock-#8-C . . . . (Rhino)
ST/Big Chill . . . . (Motown)
Wings Of A Dove
Bob Marley & The Wailers; *Birth Of A Legend 1963-1966.* . . . . (Epic Portrait Assoc.)
Ferlin Husky; *Billboard Top Country Hits-1960-C* . . . . (Rhino)
Country Music Classics-#2-1960-1965-C . . . . (K-Tel)
Ferlin Husky's Greatest Hits . . . . (Curb)
Winterwhite
Nitty Gritty Dirt Band; *Dream.* . . . . (United Artists)
Wrong Number
Cure; *Galore-The Singles-1987-1997* . . . . (Fiction/Elektra)

COLORS: YELLOW

See Also: ANATOMY: HAIR (blonde), COLORS (various)

A Tisket, A Tasket
Ella Fitzgerald; *Best Of Ella Fitzgerald.* . . . . (MCA)
Ella Fitzgerald . . . . (Laserlight)
Glenn Miller & His Army/Air Force Band; *Glenn Miller & His Army/Air Force Band* . . . . (Laserlight)
Tommy Dorsey; *Complete Tommy Dorsey-#7* . . . . (RCA)
Band Played On, The
Guy Lombardo & His Royal Canadians; *Guy Lombardo-All Time Favorites* . . . . (MCA Special Prod.)
Big Yellow Taxi
Amy Grant; *House Of Love* . . . . (A&M)
Joni Mitchell; *Ladies Of The Canyon* . . . . (Reprise)
Joni Mitchell with Tom Scott & The L.A. Express; *Miles Of Aisles* . . . (Asylum)
Don't Eat The Yellow Snow
Frank Zappa; *Apostrophe/Overnite Sensation* . . . . (Rykodisc)
Goodbye Yellow Brick Road
Elton John; *Billboard Top Rock 'N' Roll Hits-1973-C* . . . . (Rhino)
Elton John's Greatest Hits . . . . (Polydor)
Goodbye Yellow Brick Road . . . . (Polydor)
Itsy Bitsy Teenie Weenie Yellow Polkadot Bikini
Brian Hyland; *Brian Hyland's Greatest Hits.* . . . . (Rhino)
Dr. Demento Presents The Greatest Novelty Records-#3-1960s-C . . . . (Rhino)
Vintage Music-#5-C . . . . (MCA)
Lateralus
Tool; *Lateralus* . . . . (Volcano Entertainment)

Lucy In The Sky With Diamonds
Beatles; *Sgt. Pepper's Lonely Hearts Club Band* . . . . (Capitol)
The Beatles/1967-1970 . . . . (Capitol)
Yellow Submarine . . . . (Capitol)
Elton John; *All This & World War 2.* . . . . (20th Century Fox)
Elton John's Greatest Hits-#2 . . . . (Polydor)
John Lennon; *Lennon.* . . . . (Capitol)
Mellow Yellow
Donovan; *Donovan's Greatest Hits* . . . . (Epic)
Seems Like Yesterday-#5-Mid '60s-C . . . . (K-Tel)
Moon Was Yellow
Frank Sinatra; *Moonlight Sinatra.* . . . . (Reprise)
Mother's Little Helper
Rolling Stones; *Flowers.* . . . . (Abkco)
Hot Rocks 1964-1971 . . . . (Abkco)
Through The Past, Darkly (Big Hits Vol. 2) . . . . (Abkco)
Tesla; *Five Man Acoustical Jam* . . . . (Geffen)
My Canary Is Yellow
Chesterfield Kings; *Stop.* . . . . (Mirror)
My Old Yellow Car
Dan Seals; *Best Of Dan Seals.* . . . . (Capitol)
Dan Seals-Classics Collection-#1 . . . . (Capitol)
Early Dan Seals. . . . . (Capitol)
San Antone . . . . (EMI)
Lacy J. Dalton; *Blue Eyed Blues.* . . . . (Columbia)
Dream Baby . . . . (Columbia)
She Wore A Yellow Ribbon
Mitch Miller; *Sing Along With Mitch* . . . . (Columbia)
Shy Of The Moon
Wallflowers; *The Wallflowers* . . . . (Virgin)
Tie A Yellow Ribbon Round The Ole Oak Tree
Dawn Featuring Tony Orlando; *'70s Party Killers-C* . . . . (Rhino)
Fantastic-#1-C . . . . (K-Tel)
Frank Sinatra; *Some Nice Things I've Missed* . . . . (Reprise)
Lawrence Welk; *Best Of Lawrence Welk-20 Great Hits* . . . . (Ranwood)
Sonny James & Karla Taylor; *Classic Country Duets-C* . . . . (Curb)
Yellow
Coldplay; *Now That's What I Call Music!-#6-C* . . . . (Virgin)
Parachutes . . . . (Nettwerk/Capitol)
Yellow Beach Umbrella
Bette Midler; *Broken Blossom* . . . . (Atlantic)
Yellow Bird
Brothers Four; *Brothers Four-Greatest Hits* . . . . (Columbia)
Lawrence Welk; *Best Of Lawrence Welk-20 Great Hits* . . . . (Ranwood)
Mills Brothers; *Cab Driver* . . . . (Ranwood)
Mills Brothers-16 Great Performances . . . . (MCA)
Mills Brothers-22 Great Hits. . . . . (Ranwood)
Roger Whittaker; *Roger Whittaker Greatest Hits* . . . . (RCA)
Yellow Cat
John Denver; *Rhymes & Reasons.* . . . . (RCA)
Yellow Days
Frank Sinatra & Duke Ellington; *Francis A. & Edward K.* . . . . (Reprise)
Yellow Dog Blues
Bessie Smith; *Bessie Smith-The Complete Recordings-#2.* . . . . (Legacy)
Eddie Condon; *Best Of Eddie Condon* . . . . (MCA)
Yellow Gal
Leadbelly; *Leadbelly* . . . . (Fantasy)
Legend Of Leadbelly . . . . (Tradition)
Memorial-#2 . . . . (Stinson)
Take This Hammer . . . . (Smithsonian Folkways)
Yellow Magic
Yellow Magic Orchestra; *Yellow Magic Orchestra* . . . . (A&M)
Yellow Man
Randy Newman; *12 Songs* . . . . (Reprise)
Randy Newman/Live . . . . (Warner Archives)
Yellow Raven
Scorpions; *Best Of The Ballads Hot & Slow-C.* . . . . (RCA)
Virgin Killer . . . . (RCA)
Yellow River
Christie; *Rock Artifacts-From The Vaults-#1-C.* . . . . (Columbia)
Super Hits Of The '70s-Have A Nice Day-#4-C . . . . (Rhino)
Yellow Rose
Johnny Lee & Lane Brody; *'Til The Bars Burn Down* . . . . (Full Moon/Warner Bros.)
You & I-Classic Country Duets-C . . . . (Warner Bros.)
Yellow Rose Of Texas
Hoyt Axton; *Songs Of The Civil War-C* . . . . (Columbia)
Michael Martin Murphey; *Cowboy Songs* . . . . (Warner Western)
Mitch Miller; *Mitch Miller-16 Most Requested Songs* . . . . (Columbia)
Roy Rogers; *Great American Singing Cowboys-C* . . . . . . (Republic/Universal)
Yellow Roses
Dolly Parton; *Greatest Country Hits Of The '80s-1989-C* . . . . (Columbia)
White Limozeen . . . . (Columbia)
Yellow Roses
Ry Cooder; *Chicken Skin Music* . . . . (Reprise)
Yellow Roses On Her Gown
Johnny Mathis; *I Only Have Eyes For You.* . . . . (Columbia)
Yellow Star
Donovan; *Essence To Essence* . . . . (Epic)

Yellow Submarine
Beatles; *Beatles 1* . . . . (Capitol)
Beatles-Box Set . . . . (Capitol)
Reel Music . . . . (Capitol)
Revolver . . . . (Capitol)
The Beatles/1962-1966 . . . . (Capitol)
Yellow Woman's Door Bells
Leadbelly; *Leadbelly* . . . . (Fantasy)
Leadbelly . . . . (Everest)

COMMUNICATION: CONVERSATION,
Discussion, Voices
See Also: COMMUNICATION (various), GOSSIP

Brilliant Conversationalist
T. Graham Brown; *Brilliant Conversationalist* . . . . (Capitol)
T. Graham Brown's Greatest Hits . . . . (Capitol)
Computer Voice
Robert Schroeder; *Computer Voice* . . . .(Racket)
Conversation
Waylon Jennings; *Waylon And Company* . . . . (RCA)
Waylon Jennings' Greatest Hits-#2 . . . . (RCA)
You & I-Classic Country Duets-C . . . .(Warner Bros.)
Conversation
Hank Williams, Jr.; *Hank Williams, Jr. "Live"* . . . . (WB/Curb)
Whiskey Bent & Hell Bound . . . . (WB/Curb)
Conversation
Joni Mitchell; *Ladies Of The Canyon* . . . . (Reprise)
Conversation
Joan Armatrading; *Whatever's For Us* . . . . (A&M)
Conversations
Saga; *Worlds Apart* . . . . (Portrait)
Conversations
Journey; *Journey* . . . . (Columbia)
Dangling Conversation
Simon & Garfunkel; *Parsley Sage Rosemary & Thyme* . . . . (Columbia)
Fear The Voices
Alice In Chains; *Music Bank* . . . . (Columbia)
Go On
George Strait; *George Strait* . . . .(MCA)
Heirloom
Bjork; *Vespertine* . . . . (Elektra)
I Don't Want To Discuss It
Delaney & Bonnie; *Best Of Delaney & Bonnie* . . . . (Rhino)
Delaney & Bonnie & Friends On Tour With Eric Clapton . . . . (Rhino)
I Hear Your Voice
Lionel Richie; *Time* . . . . (Mercury)
I Wish I Felt Nothing
Wallflowers; *Bringing Down The Horse* . . . . (Interscope)
Is That A Tear
Tracy Lawrence; *Best Of Tracy Lawrence* . . . .(Atlantic)
Time Marches On . . . .(Atlantic)
Master's Call
Marty Robbins; *Gunfighter Ballads & Trail Songs* . . . . (Legacy)
Moment To Myself
Macy Gray; *On How Life Is* . . . .(Epic)
New York Telephone Conversation
Lou Reed; *Transformer* . . . . (RCA)
Walk On The Wild Side-The Best Of Lou Reed . . . . (RCA)
Next Voice You Hear
Jackson Browne; *The Next Voice You Hear-Best Of Jackson Browne* . . (Elektra)
Private Conversation
Lyle Lovett; *The Road To Ensenada* . . . .(MCA)
Sound Of Your Voice
38 Special; *Bone Against Steel* . . . .(Charisma)
Spanish Is The Loving Tongue
Bob Dylan; *Dylan* . . . . (Columbia)
Emmylou Harris; *Cimarron* . . . .(Warner Bros.)
Evangeline . . . .(Warner Bros.)
Ian & Sylvia; *Four Strong Winds* . . . . (Vanguard)
Ian & Sylvia's Greatest Hits . . . . (Vanguard)
Michael Martin Murphey; *Cowboy Songs* . . . . (Warner Western)
Stutter
Joe featuring Mystikal; *My Name Is Joe* . . . . (Jive)
Now That's What I Call Music!-#8-C . . . . (Virgin)
Voice Of America
Asia; *Astra* . . . .(Geffen)
Then & Now . . . .(Geffen)
Voice Of America
Little Steven; *Voice Of America* . . . . (Razor & Tie)
Voice Of America's Son
John Cafferty And The Beaver Brown Band; *ST/Cobra* . . . .(Scotti Bros.)
Tough All Over . . . .(Scotti Bros.)
Voice Of Harold
R.E.M.; *Dead Letter Office* . . . .(I.R.S.)

Voice Of The Eagle
Robbie Basho; *Voice Of The Eagle* . . . . (Vanguard)
Voice Of The Heart
Diana Ross; *Take Me Higher* . . . . (Motown)
Voice On Tape
Laurie Anderson; *United States Live* . . . . (Warner Bros.)
Voice On The Radio
Andre Cymone; *Livin' In The New Wave* . . . . (Columbia)
Voice On The Radio
Sheena Easton; *Sheena Easton* . . . . (EMI)
Voice, The
Ultravox; *Rage In Eden* . . . . (Chrysalis)
Ultravox-Collection . . . . (Chrysalis)
Voice, The
Alan Parsons Project; *I Robot* . . . . (Arista)
Voice, The
Moody Blues; *Long Distance Voyager* . . . .(Polydor)
Voices
Cheap Trick; *Cheap Trick's Greatest Hits* . . . . (Epic)
Dream Police . . . . (Epic)
Voices
Disturbed; *The Sickness* . . . .(Giant)
Voices
Russ Ballard; *Russ Ballard* . . . . (EMI)
Voices Carry
'Til Tuesday; *Voices Carry* . . . . (Epic)
Voices In My Head
Naked Eyes; *Best Of Naked Eyes* . . . . (EMI)
Voices In The Rain
Joe Sample; *Voices In The Rain* . . . . (MCA)
Voices In The Sky
Moody Blues; *In Search Of The Lost Chord* . . . .(Polydor)
Voices In The Wind
Little Feat; *Let It Roll* . . . . (Warner Bros.)
Voices Inside My Head
Police; *Zenyatta Mondatta* . . . . (A&M)
Voices Of Babylon
Outfield; *Voices Of Babylon* . . . . (Columbia)
Voices Of Freedom
Jackson Browne/Peter Gabriel/Youssou N'Dour/Lou Reed; *Secret
Policeman's Third Ball-The Music-C* . . . .(Virgin)
Lou Reed; *Between Thought & Expression-Anthology* . . . .(RCA)
Voices Of Old People
Simon & Garfunkel; *Bookends* . . . . (Columbia)
Collected Works . . . . (Columbia)
Voices That Care
Voices That Care; *Voices That Care* . . . .(Giant)
Vox Humana
Kenny Loggins; *Vox Humana* . . . . (Columbia)
What Is Truth
Johnny Cash; *The Man In Black-His Greatest Hits* . . . . (Legacy)
When Love Starts Talkin'
Wynonna; *The Other Side* . . . .(Curb/MCA)
When You Come Back To Me Again
Garth Brooks; *Scarecrow* . . . . (Capitol)
Where Are You Now
Trisha Yearwood; *Real Live Woman* . . . . (MCA)
White, Discussion
Live; *ST/Virtuosity* . . . . (Radioactive/MCA)
Throwing Copper . . . . (Radioactive/MCA)
Within You Without You
Beatles; *Beatles-Box Set* . . . . (Capitol)
Sgt. Pepper's Lonely Hearts Club Band . . . . (Capitol)

COMMUNICATION: SAY, Calling Out
See Also: COMMUNICATION (various), GOSSIP

"Murder", He Says
Roy Eldridge/Gene Krupa Orchestra/Anita O'Day; *Uptown* . . . . (Columbia)
(Who Says) You Can't Have It All
Alan Jackson; *A Lot About Livin' (And A Little 'Bout Love)* . . . . (Arista)
A World Without Love
Peter And Gordon; *Billboard Top Pop Hits-1964-C* . . . . (Rhino)
All That I Can Say
Mary J. Blige; *Mary* . . . . (MCA)
All The Small Things
Blink-182; *Enema Of The State* . . . . (MCA)
Now That's What I Call Music!-#4-C . . . .(Virgin)
All The Things She Said
Simple Minds; *Once Upon A Time* . . . . (A&M)
As You Said
Cream; *Wheels Of Fire* . . . .(Polydor)
Baby You Got It
Brenton Wood; *18 Best-Brenton Wood* . . . .(Original Sound)
Bad Goodbye, A
Clint Black with Wynonna; *Clint Black-The Greatest Hits* . . . . (RCA)

Grammy's Greatest Country Moments-#1-C . . . . (Atlantic)
No Time To Kill. . . . .(RCA)

Believe
Cher; *Believe* . . . . (Warner Bros.)
Totally Hits-#1-C . . . . (Arista)

Believe What You Say
Rick Nelson; *Rick Nelson In Concert-Troubadour 1969*. . . . . (MCA)
Ricky Nelson; *Ricky Nelson Volume 1*. . . . . (Gold Rush)
Ricky Nelson's All Time Greatest Hits . . . . (Curb)
Rock This Town-Rockabilly Hits-#1-C . . . . (Rhino)

Betcha Say That
Gloria Estefan and Miami Sound Machine; *Let It Loose* . . . . (Epic)

Big Poppa
Notorious B.I.G.; *MTV Party To Go-#8-C* . . . .(Tommy Boy)
Ready To Die . . . . (Bad Boy/Arista)

Break Stuff
Limp Bizkit; *Significant Other* . . . .(Flip/Interscope)

By A Waterfall
Ruby Keeler & Dick Powell; *Lullaby Of Broadway-The Best Of Busby*
Berkeley At Warner Brothers. . . . . (Rhino)
Sammy Fain; *Sammy Sings Fain* . . . . (Living Era)

Can'tcha Say (You Believe In Me)
Boston; *Third Stage* . . . . (MCA)

C'est Si Bon (It's So Good)
Eartha Kitt; *Lost Female Hits Of The '50s-C* . . . . (Taragon)

De Doo Doo Doo, De Da Da Da
Police; *Every Breath You Take-The Classics* . . . . (A&M)
Zenyatta Mondatta . . . . (A&M)

Declaration Of Love
Celine Dion; *Falling Into You* . . . . (550 Music)

Do I Have To Come Right Out & Say It
Buffalo Springfield; *Buffalo Springfield* . . . . (Atco)

Do I Have To Say The Words?
Bryan Adams; *Waking Up The Neighbours*. . . . . (A&M)

Don't Say
Jon B.; *Cool Relax* . . . .(Yab Yum/550)

Don't Say Goodnight
Valentines; *Original Rock 'N' Roll Hits Of The '50s-C* . . . . (Roulette)

Don't Say No Tonight
Eugene Wilde; *The Glory Of Love-'80s Sweet & Soulful Love*
Songs-C . . . .(Hip-O)

Don't Say Nothing Bad About My Baby
Cookies; *Golden Girl Groups-C* . . . . (K-Tel)
Original Rock 'N' Roll Hits Of The '60s-C . . . . (Roulette)

Don't Say Things You Don't Mean
Lynn Anderson; *Lynn Anderson's Greatest Hits* . . . . (Columbia)

Don't Say You Love Me
Crickets; *Liberty Years* . . . . (EMI)

Don't Say You Love Me
Freddie Jackson; *Do Me Again* . . . . (Capitol)

Don't Say You Love Me
Billy Squier; *Hear & Now* . . . . (Capitol)

Down By The Bay
Eric Heatherly; *Country Goes Raffi-C* . . . . (Rounder)

Easier Said Than Done
Radney Foster; *Del Rio, TX 1959* . . . . (Arista)

Easier Said Than Done
Essex; *Best Of The Girl Groups-#2-C* . . . . (Rhino)
Billboard Top Rock 'N' Roll Hits-1963-C . . . . (Rhino)
Original Rock 'N' Roll Hits Of The '60s-C . . . . (Roulette)

Easy For You To Say
Emmylou Harris; *Brand New Dance* . . . . (Reprise)
Linda Ronstadt; *Get Closer* . . . . (Asylum)

Fa Fa (Never Be The Same Again)
Guster; *Lost & Gone Forever* . . . . (Hybrid/Sire)

Give Peace A Chance
John Lennon; *Lennon* . . . . (Capitol)
Live In New York City . . . . (Capitol)
ST/Imagine: John Lennon. . . . . (Capitol)
The John Lennon Collection . . . . (Capitol)
John Lennon/Plastic Ono Band; *Shaved Fish* . . . . (Capitol)
Plastic Ono Band; *Plastic Ono Band-Live Peace In Toronto 1969* . . . . . (Capitol)

Goodbye Says It All
BlackHawk; *BlackHawk* . . . . (Arista)

Goodnight Tonight (Don't Say It)
Paul McCartney & Wings; *All The Best!* . . . . (Capitol)

Hard To Say
Sawyer Brown; *Outskirts Of Town* . . . . (Curb)

Hard To Say Goodbye, My Love
Original Cast; *Dreamgirls* . . . . (Geffen)

Hard To Say I'm Sorry
Az Yet; *Az Yet* . . . .(LaFace)
Chicago; *Chicago 16* . . . . (Full Moon/Warner Bros.)

Hear Say
Soul Children; *15 Original Big Hits-#3-C* . . . . (Stax)
Soul Children-Chronicle . . . . (Stax)

Hello Goodbye
Beatles; *Beatles 1*. . . . . (Capitol)

Beatles-20 Greatest Hits . . . .(Capitol)
Beatles-Box Set . . . .(Capitol)
Magical Mystery Tour . . . .(Capitol)
The Beatles/1967-1970 . . . .(Capitol)

Hope You Love Me Like You Say You Do
Huey Lewis and the News; *Picture This*. . . . . (Chrysalis)

How A Cowgirl Says Goodbye
Tracy Lawrence; *The Coast Is Clear* . . . . (Atlantic)

How Can I Help You Say Goodbye
Patty Loveless; *Only What I Feel* . . . . (Epic)
Patty Loveless-Classics. . . . . (Epic)

How Do You Say Auf Wiedersehen
George Shearing & Mel Torme; *Top Drawer* . . . . (Concord Jazz)

I Am…I Said
Neil Diamond; *Hot August Night* . . . . (MCA)
Hot August Night II . . . . (Columbia)
Neil Diamond-His 12 Greatest Hits . . . . (MCA)
Stones . . . . (MCA)

I Cain't Say No
Original Broadway Cast; *Oklahoma!* . . . . (RCA)
Original Cast; *Oklahoma!* . . . . (MCA)

I Can't Say It On The Radio
Susie Allanson; *45-#75001* . . . . (Enigma)

I Can't Say It On The Radio
Girls Next Door; *Girls Next Door* . . . .(MTM)

I Can't Say No
Natalie Cole; *Inseparable* . . . . (Capitol)
Natalie Cole-Collection . . . . (Capitol)
Reaching For The Sky-Towering Soul From The '70s-C. . . . .(Capitol)

I Declare
Lee Roy Parnell with Keb' Mo'; *Tell The Truth*. . . . .(Vanguard)

I Do (Whatcha Say Boo)
Jon B.; *Cool Relax* . . . . (Yab Yum/550)

I Feel Fine
Beatles; *Beatles 1* . . . .(Capitol)
Beatles '65. . . . .(Capitol)
Beatles-20 Greatest Hits . . . .(Capitol)
Past Masters-Volume One . . . . (Parlophone)
The Beatles/1962-1966 . . . .(Capitol)
Sweethearts Of The Rodeo; *One Time One Night* . . . .(Columbia)

I Just Called To Say I Love You
Aretha Franklin; *Aretha Franklin's Greatest Hits* . . . . (Atlantic)
Aretha's Gold . . . . (Atlantic)
Best Of Aretha Franklin . . . . (Atlantic)
Stevie Wonder; *ST/Lady In Red* . . . .(Motown)

I Meant Every Word He Said
Ricky Van Shelton; *Greatest Country Hits Of The '90s-#2-C* . . . . . .(Columbia)
RVS III. . . . .(Columbia)

I Only Want To Say (Gethsemane)
Original London Cast; *Jesus Christ Superstar* . . . . (MCA)
Soundtrack; *Jesus Christ Superstar* . . . . (MCA)

I Said A Prayer
Pam Tillis; *Every Time*. . . . .(Arista)

I Said I Love You
Babyface; *The Day*. . . . . (Epic)

I Say A Little Prayer
Aretha Franklin; *Aretha Franklin's Greatest Hits* . . . . (Atlantic)
Aretha's Gold . . . . (Atlantic)
Best Of Aretha Franklin . . . . (Atlantic)
Burt Bacharach; *Burt Bacharach-Classics-#23* . . . . (A&M)
Burt Bacharach's Greatest Hits . . . . (A&M)
Reach Out . . . . (A&M)
Diana King; *ST/My Best Friend's Wedding* . . . . (Work/Epic)
Dionne Warwick; *Dionne Warwick* . . . . (Everest)
Dionne Warwick Greatest Hits . . . . (Everest)
Dionne Warwick-Anthology 1962-1971 . . . .(Rhino)
Original Rock 'N' Roll Hits Of The '60s-C . . . . (Roulette)

I Think We're Alone Now
Tiffany; *Tiffany* . . . . (MCA)
Tiffany's Greatest Hits . . . . (Hip-O)
Tommy James And The Shondells; *Best Of Tommy James And The*
Shondells . . . . (Roulette)
Billboard Top Rock 'N' Roll Hits-1967-C . . . .(Rhino)
Tommy James And The Shondells-Anthology . . . .(Rhino)

I Wanna Say Yes
Louise Mandrell; *Maybe My Baby* . . . . (RCA)

I Wasn't With It
Jesse Powell; *'Bout It* . . . .(Silas)

I Wonder Why She Kept On Saying "Si-Si-Si-Si Senor"
Al Jolson; *Music From The New York Stage (1890-1920)-#4-1917-*
1920-C . . . . (Pearl)

I Won't Mention It Again
Ray Price; *Ray Price's Greatest Hits-#1-3*. . . . . (Step One)
Ray Price-Super Hits. . . . .(Columbia)
Reba McEntire; *Starting Over* . . . . (MCA)

I'd Still Say Yes
Klymaxx; *Klymaxx*. . . . . (Constellation)

If I Say Yes
Five Star; *Silk & Steel*. . . . . (RCA)

If This Is It
Huey Lewis and the News; *Sports* . . . . (Chrysalis)
  The Heart Of Rock & Roll-The Best Of Huey Lewis and
    the News . . . . (Chrysalis)
  Time Flies...Best Of Huey Lewis and the News . . . . (Elektra)

I'll Have To Say I Love You In A Song
Jim Croce; *Baby Boomer Classics-Love Seventies-C* . . . . . . (JCI Assoc. Labels)
  Billboard Top Soft Rock Hits-1974-C . . . . (Rhino)
  Dim The Lights-C . . . . (K-Tel)

I'll Never Say No
Harve Presnell; *ST/The Unsinkable Molly Brown* . . . . (MCA)

I'll Say She Does
Al Jolson; *Music From The New York Stage (1890-1920)-#4-1917-*
  1920-C . . . . (Pearl)

I'm Already Taken
Steve Wariner; *Country Cares For Kids II-C* . . . . (BNA)
  Two Teardrops . . . . (Capitol)

I'm Not Strong Enough To Say No
BlackHawk; *Strong Enough* . . . . (Arista)

It's In Your Eyes (Any Time At All)
Phil Collins; *Dance Into The Light* . . . . (Atlantic)

It's No Good
Depeche Mode; *Ultra* . . . . (Mute/Reprise)

It's Not For Me To Say
Johnny Mathis; *First 25 Years-Silver Anniversary Album* . . . . (Columbia)
  Johnny Mathis' All-Time Greatest Hits . . . . (Columbia)
  Johnny Mathis' Greatest Hits . . . . (Columbia)
  Johnny Mathis-16 Most Requested Songs . . . . (Columbia)

It's So Hard To Say Goodbye To Yesterday
Boyz II Men; *Cooleyhighharmony* . . . . (Motown)
G.C. Cameron; *Motown Memories-#3-C* . . . . (Motown)

Jackie Wilson Said (I'm In Heaven When You Smile)
Van Morrison; *Best Of Van Morrison* . . . . (Polydor)
  St. Dominic's Preview . . . . (Warner Bros.)
  ST/Queen's Logic . . . . (Epic)

Jenny Says
Cowboy Mouth; *Are You With Me?* . . . . (MCA)
  Word Of Mouth . . . . (Monkey Hill)

Just Between You And Me
DC Talk; *First Generation: 25 Years Of Virgin Records-C* . . . . (Virgin)
  Jesus Freak . . . . (Virgin)

Just To Hear You Say That You Love Me
Faith Hill & Tim McGraw; *Faith* . . . . (Warner Bros.)

Kiss And Say Goodbye
Manhattans; *Best Of The Manhattans-Kiss And Say Goodbye* . . . . (Legacy)
  Manhattans Greatest Hits . . . . (Columbia)

Lean On Me
Bill Withers; *Bill Withers' Greatest Hits* . . . . (Columbia)
  Chicken Soup For The Soul: I'll Be There For You-Songs Of Friendship,
    Brotherhood And Sisterhood-C . . . . (Rhino)
  God Bless America-C . . . . (Columbia)
  Still Bill . . . . (Columbia)
Club Nouveau; *Life Love & Pain* . . . . (Warner Bros.)
Grover Washington, Jr.; *Greatest Performances-Grover*
  Washington, Jr. . . . . (Motown)

Leave Me Alone
Jerry Cantrell; *ST/The Cable Guy* . . . . (Work)

Leavin' And Sayin' Goodbye
Faron Young; *Faron Young-Golden Hits* . . . . (Mercury)
  Faron Young's Greatest Hits-#1-3 . . . . (Step One)

Let 'Er Rip
Dixie Chicks; *Wide Open Spaces* . . . . (Monument)

Let's Build A World Together
George Jones & Tammy Wynette; *George Jones & Tammy Wynette-16*
  Biggest Hits . . . . (Epic/Legacy)

Letting The Cables Sleep
Bush; *Science Of Things* . . . . (Trauma)

Little White Lie
Sammy Hagar; *Marching To Mars* . . . . (MCA)

Maggie May
Rod Stewart; *Absolutely Live* . . . . (Warner Bros.)
  Best Of Rod Stewart . . . . (Mercury)
  Billboard Top Rock 'N' Roll Hits-1971-C . . . . (Rhino)
  Every Picture Tells A Story . . . . (Mercury)
  Rod Stewart's Greatest Hits . . . . (Warner Bros.)
  Sing It Again, Rod . . . . (Mercury)
  Storyteller/The Complete Anthology: 1964-1990 . . . . (Warner Bros.)

Make The World Go Away
Eddy Arnold; *Best Of Eddy Arnold* . . . . (RCA)
  Billboard Top Country Hits-1965-C . . . . (Rhino)
  Eddy Arnold-Pure Gold . . . . (RCA)
  Nipper's Greatest Hits Of The '60s-#1-C . . . . (RCA)
  World Of Hits . . . . (MGM)
Ray Price; *Ray Price-16 Biggest Hits* . . . . (Legacy)
  Ray Price-20 Hits . . . . (Tee Vee)

Maker Said Take Her
Alabama; *In Pictures* . . . . (RCA)

Mama Said
Shirelles; *Original Rock 'N' Roll Hits Of The '60s-C* . . . . (Roulette)

  Shirelles' Greatest Hits . . . . (Everest)
  Shirelles-Anthology 1959-1964 . . . . (Rhino)
  Shirelles-Classics . . . . (Bac-Trac)
  Super Oldies Of The '60s-#3-C . . . . (Audio Fidelity)

Mama Say
Heptones; *Night Food* . . . . (Island)

Mama Used To Say
Junior; *Jr.* . . . . (Mercury)
  Sophisticated Street . . . . (London)

Man Of My Word
Collin Raye; *Extremes* . . . . (Epic)

Martha Say
John Cougar Mellencamp; *Big Daddy* . . . . (Mercury)

Miles From Our Home
Cowboy Junkies; *Miles From Our Home* . . . . (Geffen)

More Than I Can Say
Dolly Parton; *Rainbow* . . . . (Columbia)

More Than I Can Say
Leo Sayer; *Have You Ever Been In Love* . . . . (Warner Bros.)

More Than I Can Say
Bobby Vee; *Bobby Vee-Golden Greats* . . . . (Liberty)
  Bobby Vee-Legendary Masters . . . . (EMI)

More Than That
Backstreet Boys; *Black & Blue* . . . . (Jive)
  Now That's What I Call Music!-#8-C . . . . (Virgin)

More Than Words Can Say
Alias; *Alias* . . . . (EMI)

Mother Says
Joe Walsh; *Barnstorm* . . . . (Mobile Fidelity Sound Lab)
  Best Of Joe Walsh . . . . (MCA)

My Baby Left Me
Arthur "Big Boy" Crudup; *That's All Right (Mama)* . . . . (Bluebird)
Creedence Clearwater Revival; *Cosmo's Factory* . . . . (Fantasy)
  Creedence Country . . . . (Fantasy)
Elvis Presley; *Elvis Recorded Live On Stage In Memphis* . . . . (RCA)

Neither One Of Us (Wants To Be First To Say Goodbye)
Gladys Knight & The Pips; *Gladys Knight & The Pips-All The*
  Great Hits . . . . (Motown)
  Gladys Knight & The Pips-Anthology . . . . (Motown)
  Gladys Knight & The Pips-Superstars Series-#13 . . . . (Motown)
  Motown Grammy R&B Performances Of The '60s & '70s-C . . . . . . (Motown)
  Neither One Of Us . . . . (Motown)

Never Can Say Goodbye
Jackson 5; *Jackson 5's Greatest Hits* . . . . (Motown)
  Jackson 5-The Ultimate Collection . . . . (Motown)

Never Did Say Goodbye
Lisa Brokop; *Every Little Girl's Dream* . . . . (Patriot)

Never Say Die
Dixie Chicks; *Wide Open Spaces* . . . . (Monument)

Never Say Never
T. Graham Brown; *Best Of T. Graham Brown* . . . . (Liberty)
  Come As You Were . . . . (Capitol)

Never Say Never
Romeo Void; *Benefactor* . . . . (Columbia)
  Never Say Never . . . . (Columbia)
  Warm In Your Coat . . . . (Columbia)

Never Say Never
Styx; *Cornerstone* . . . . (A&M)

Never Say Never
Mr. Big; *Lean Into It* . . . . (Atlantic)

Never Say Never
Third World; *Serious Business* . . . . (Mercury)

Never Say Never
Christopher Plummer & Phillip Glasser; *ST/An American Tail* . . . . (MCA)

Never Say Never
Triumph; *Surveillance* . . . . (MCA)

Never Say Never
Deniece Williams; *Water Under The Bridge* . . . . (Columbia)

Never Say No
Steve Miller Band; *Abracadabra* . . . . (Capitol)
  Steve Miller Band-Gift Set . . . . (Capitol)

Never Say No
Paul Butterfield Blues Band; *East-West* . . . . (Elektra)

Never Say No
Original Cast; *Fantasticks* . . . . (Polydor)

No Matter What They Say
Lil' Kim; *Notorious K.I.M.* . . . . (Queen Bee/Undeas/Atlantic)

No One Said It Would Be Easy
Sheryl Crow; *Tuesday Night Music Club* . . . . (A&M)

Nothing To Say
Jethro Tull; *Benefit* . . . . (Chrysalis)

One Step Closer
Linkin Park; *Hybrid Theory* . . . . (Warner Bros.)

Only Time
Enya; *A Day Without Rain* . . . . (Reprise)

Over And Over
Dave Clark Five; *History Of The Dave Clark Five* . . . . (Hollywood)
  The Dave Clark Five's Greatest Hits . . . . (Epic)

People Say
Dixie Cups; *Girl Groups-Story Of A Sound-C* . . . . (Rhino)
  Original Golden Hits Of The Great Groups-#1-C . . . . (SSS International)
  Wonder Women-History Of Girl Group Sound-C . . . . (Rhino)
People Will Say We're In Love
Frank Sinatra; *A Lovely Way To Spend An Evening* . . . . (ASV)
Original Broadway Cast; *Oklahoma!* . . . . (RCA)
Spaniels; *Spaniels' Golden Hits* . . . . (Juke Box Treasures)
  The Acapella Collection . . . . (Juke Box Treasures)
Please
Bing Crosby; *Bing Crosby-16 Most Requested Songs* . . . . (Legacy)
Pretty
Korn; *Follow The Leader* . . . . (Immortal/Epic)
Push
Matchbox Twenty; *Yourself Or Someone Like You* . . . . (Lava)
Radiation Vibe
Fountains Of Wayne; *Fountains Of Wayne* . . . .(Tag/Atlantic)
Rhythm Divine
Enrique Iglesias; *Enrique* . . . . (Overbrook/Interscope)
Said I Loved You…But I Lied
Michael Bolton; *The One Thing* . . . . (Columbia)
Say Goodbye To Hollywood
Bette Midler; *Broken Blossom* . . . . (Atlantic)
Billy Joel; *Billy Joel-Greatest Hits, Volume I & Volume II* . . . . (Columbia)
  Songs In The Attic . . . . (Columbia)
  Turnstiles . . . . (Columbia)
Say Hello
Breathe; *Peace Of Mind* . . . . (A&M)
Say Hello
April Wine; *Harder…Faster* . . . . (Capitol)
Say Hello
Heart; *Little Queen* . . . . (Portrait)
Say Hello To Heaven
Temple Of The Dog; *Temple Of The Dog* . . . . (A&M)
Say Hey (The Willie Mays Song)
Treniers; *Baseball's Greatest Hits-C* . . . . (Rhino)
Say I Am
Tommy James And The Shondells; *Tommy James And The Shondells-*
  Anthology . . . . (Rhino)
Say I'm Your Number One
Princess; *45-#50035* . . . . (Next Plateau/London/Island)
Say It
Voices Of Theory; *Voices Of Theory* . . . . (H.O.L.A./Red Ant)
Say It Again
Don Williams; *Best Of Don Williams-#2* . . . . (MCA)
Say It Again
Santana; *Beyond Appearances* . . . . (Columbia)
Say It Ain't So
Weezer; *Weezer* . . . . (David Geffen Co.)
Say It Isn't So
Dinah Washington; *Irving Berlin Always-C* . . . . (Verve)
Michael Feinstein; *Remember-Michael Feinstein Sings Irving Berlin* . . (Elektra)
Nat "King" Cole; *Spotlight On Nat "King" Cole* . . . . (Capitol)
Ray Conniff; *'S Awful Nice* . . . . (Columbia)
Say It Isn't So
Daryl Hall & John Oates; *MTV's Rock 'N' Roll To Go-C* . . . . (Elektra)
  Rock 'N Soul, Part 1 . . . . (RCA)
Say It Isn't So
Outfield; *Play Deep* . . . . (Columbia)
Say It Isn't So Joe
Roger Daltrey; *Best Bits* . . . . (MCA)
  One Of The Boys . . . . (MCA)
Say It Loud I'm Black & I'm Proud
Afrika Bambaataa; *Decade Of Darkness* . . . . (EMI)
James Brown; *Billboard Top R&B Hits-1965-1969-C* . . . . (Rhino)
Say It With A Kiss
Billie Holiday; *Quintessential-#6-1938* . . . . (Columbia)
  The Billie Holiday Story-#3 . . . . (Columbia)
Say It With Trumpets
Maynard Ferguson; *Birdland Dreamband* . . . . (Bluebird)
Say It's Alright Joe
Genesis; *And Then There Were Three* . . . . (Atlantic)
Say Man
Bo Diddley; *Bo Diddley-His Best* . . . . (Chess)
  Cruisin'-1959-C . . . . (Increase)
Say My Name
Destiny's Child; *The Writing's On The Wall* . . . . (Columbia)
Say Say Say
Paul McCartney & Michael Jackson; *All The Best!* . . . . (Capitol)
  Pipes Of Peace . . . . (Capitol)
Say What
Stevie Ray Vaughan and Double Trouble; *Live Alive* . . . . (Epic)
  Soul To Soul . . . . (Epic)
Say What
Jesse Winchester; *Best Of Jesse Winchester* . . . . (Rhino)
Say What
Erasure; *Wonderland* . . . . (Sire)

Say What U Got To Say (Mix It Up)
Dan Reed Network; *Say What U Want-Rock The Vote-C* . . . . (Mercury)
Say What's In My Heart
Aaron Neville; *To Make You Who I Am* . . . . (A&M)
Say When
Lonestar; *Crazy Nights* . . . . (BNA)
Say Yeah
Commodores; *All The Great Love Songs-Commodores* . . . . (Motown)
  Natural High . . . . (Motown)
Say You Love Me
Fleetwood Mac; *25 Years-The Chain* . . . . (Warner Bros.)
  Fleetwood Mac . . . . (Reprise)
  Fleetwood Mac Live . . . . (Warner Bros.)
  Fleetwood Mac's Greatest Hits . . . . (Warner Bros.)
Say You Love Me
Jo-el Sonnier; *Come On Joe* . . . . (RCA)
Say You Love Me
Ce Ce Rogers; *Never Give Up* . . . . (Atlantic)
Say You Love Me Or Say Goodbye
REO Speedwagon; *A Decade Of Rock And Roll 1970 To 1980* . . . . (Epic)
  You Can Tune A Piano But You Can't Tuna Fish . . . . (Epic)
Say You Will
Gregory Abbott; *Shake You Down* . . . . (Columbia)
Say You Will
Bridge 2 Far; *Bridge 2 Far* . . . . (WTG)
Say You Will
Isley Brothers; *Go All The Way* . . . . (T-Neck/Columbia)
Say You Will
Foreigner; *Inside Information* . . . . (Atlantic)
Say You Will
Dan Siegel; *Late One Night* . . . . (Epic Portrait Assoc.)
Say You Will
BoDeans; *Love & Hope & Sex & Dreams* . . . . (Slash)
Say You Will
Al Hudson & One Way; *New Beginning* . . . . (Capitol)
Say You Will
Robert Palmer; *Pride* . . . . (Island)
Say You Will
Mick Jagger; *Primitive Cool* . . . . (Columbia)
Say You, Say Me
Lionel Richie; *Back To Front* . . . . (Motown)
  Dancing On The Ceiling . . . . (Motown)
Say You'll Be Mine
Amy Grant; *House Of Love* . . . . (A&M)
Say You'll Be Mine
Christopher Cross; *Christopher Cross* . . . . (Warner Bros.)
Say You'll Be There
Spice Girls; *Now That's What I Call Music!-#1-C* . . . . (Virgin)
  Spice . . . . (Virgin)
Say You're Wrong
Julian Lennon; *Valotte* . . . . (Atlantic)
Saying Goodbye To A Friend
Suzy Bogguss; *Give Me Some Wheels* . . . . (Capitol)
Saying Hello, Saying I Love You, Saying Goodbye
Jim Ed Brown & Helen Cornelius; *Jim Ed Brown & Helen Cornelius'*
  Greatest Hits . . . . (RCA)
She Can't Say I Didn't Cry
Rick Trevino; *Rick Trevino* . . . . (Columbia)
She Can't Say That Anymore
John Conlee; *Friday Night Blues* . . . . (MCA)
  John Conlee's Greatest Hits . . . . (MCA)
She Said
Collective Soul; *Dosage* . . . . (Atlantic)
  ST/Scream 2 . . . . (Dimension/Capitol)
She Said She Said
Beatles; *Beatles-Box Set* . . . . (Capitol)
  Revolver . . . . (Capitol)
She Said The Same Things To Me
John Hiatt; *Warming Up To The Ice Age* . . . . (Geffen)
  Y'All Caught? Ones That Got Away, 1979-85 . . . . (Geffen)
She Said Yeah
Rolling Stones; *December's Children (and everybody's)* . . . . (Abkco)
Wilson Pickett; *A Man & A Half-Best Of Wilson Pickett* . . . . (Rhino)
She Said Yes
Rhett Akins; *A Thousand Memories* . . . . (Decca)
She Say (Oom Dooby Doom)
Diamonds; *Best Of The Diamonds* . . . . (Rhino)
She's About A Mover
Sir Douglas Quintet; *Best Of The Sir Douglas Quintet* . . . . (Takoma)
  Texas Music-#3-Garage Bands & Psychedelia-C . . . . (Rhino)
Shout
Beatles; *The Beatles-Anthology-#1* . . . . (Capitol)
Isley Brothers; *Nipper's Greatest Hits Of The '50s-#2-C* . . . . (RCA)
  Shout . . . . (Collectables)
  ST/The Wanderers . . . . (Warner Bros.)
Joey Dee & the Starliters; *Echoes Of A Rock Era-Later Years-C* . . . . . (Roulette)
  Hey Let's Twist! Best Of Joey Dee & The Starliters . . . . (Rhino)
  Live At The Peppermint Lounge . . . . (Accord)

Original Rock 'N' Roll Hits Of The '60s-C .... (Roulette)
Sock Hoppin' Sixties-C .... (JCI Assoc. Labels)
Otis Day & The Knights; *Shout* .... (MCA)
ST/Animal House .... (MCA)
Tom Petty And The Heartbreakers; *Pack Up The Plantation-Live!* ...... (MCA)

Simply Said
Kenny Garrett; *Simply Said* .... (Warner Bros.)

Smells Like Teen Spirit
Nirvana; *Nevermind* .... (David Geffen Co.)

So Much To Say
Dave Matthews Band; *Crash* .... (RCA)

So Much To Say So Much To Give
Chicago; *Chicago At Carnegie Hall* .... (Chicago)
Chicago II .... (Chicago)
Group Portrait .... (Chicago)

So Sad To Say
Mighty Mighty Bosstones; *Pay Attention* .... (Big Rig/DJMG)

Some Things Are Better Left Unsaid
Daryl Hall & John Oates; *Big Bam Boom* .... (RCA)

Somebody To Love
Jefferson Airplane; *2400 Fulton Street-An Anthology* .... (RCA)
Loves You .... (RCA)
Nipper's Greatest Hits Of The '60s-#1-C .... (RCA)
Surrealistic Pillow .... (RCA)
The Worst Of Jefferson Airplane .... (RCA)

Somebody's Always Saying Goodbye
Anne Murray; *Anne Murray-Country Hits* .... (Capitol)
Hottest Night Of The Year .... (Capitol)

Somethin' Stupid
Frank & Nancy Sinatra; *Frank Sinatra's Greatest Hits!* .... (Reprise)
The World We Knew .... (Reprise)
Nancy Sinatra & Frank Sinatra; *Boots-Nancy Sinatra's Greatest Hits* ... (Rhino)

Stay The Night
IMx; *IMx* .... (MCA)

Tell Me I Was Dreaming
Travis Tritt; *Ten Feet Tall And Bulletproof* .... (Warner Bros.)
Travis Tritt's Greatest Hits-From The Beginning .... (Warner Bros.)

That's What He Said
Reba McEntire; *My Kind Of Country* .... (MCA)

That's What I Said
M.C. Hammer; *Let's Get It Started* .... (Capitol)
ST/Rocky V .... (Bust It)

There You Have It
BlackHawk; *Big Country Hits '99-C* .... (K-Tel)
The Sky's The Limit .... (Arista)

There! I've Said It Again
Bobby Vinton; *Bobby Vinton's All-Time Greatest Hits* .... (Epic)
Bobby Vinton's Greatest Hits/Greatest Hits Of Love .... (Columbia)
Johnny Mathis; *First 25 Years-Silver Anniversary Album* .... (Columbia)
Vaughn Monroe; *Best Of Vaughn Monroe* .... (MCA)
Nipper's Greatest Hits Of The '40s-#1-C .... (RCA)

These Lips Don't Know How To Say Goodbye
Doug Stone; *Doug Stone* .... (Epic)
Greatest Country Hits Of The '90s-1991-C .... (Columbia)
Forester Sisters; *Sincerely* .... (Warner Bros.)

They Say It's Spring
Bobby Short; *Swing That Music* .... (Telarc)

They Say It's Wonderful
Frank Sinatra; *The Voice-Columbia Years-1943-1952* .... (Columbia)
Johnny Mathis; *Heavenly* .... (Columbia)
Original Cast; *Annie Get Your Gun* .... (RCA Victor)
Sarah Vaughan; *Irving Berlin Always-C* .... (Verve)

They Say That Falling In Love Is Wonderful
Mark Shane & Terry Blaine; *With Thee I Swing!* .... (Nagel-Heyer)

Things I Should Have Said
Grass Roots; *Grass Roots-All-Time Greatest Hits* .... (MCA)
Grass Roots-Anthology (1966-1975) .... (Rhino)

Things We Said Today
Beatles; *Beatles-Box Set* .... (Capitol)
Something New .... (Capitol)
The Beatles At The Hollywood Bowl .... (Capitol)
Paul McCartney; *Tripping The Live Fantastic-Highlights!* .... (Capitol)

To Make You Love Me (What Can I Say)
Alexander O'Neal; *All Mixed Up* .... (Tabu)
Hearsay .... (Tabu)

To The Moon And Back
Savage Garden; *Savage Garden* .... (Columbia)

Too Shy To Say
Stevie Wonder; *Fulfillingness' First Finale* .... (Motown)

Voice Your Choice
Radiants; *Best Of Chess Rhythm & Blues-#2-C* .... (Chess)

Waffle
Sevendust; *Home* .... (TVT)

We Can Work It Out
Beatles; *"Yesterday"...And Today* .... (Capitol)
Beatles 1 .... (Capitol)
Beatles-20 Greatest Hits .... (Capitol)
Beatles-Box Set .... (Capitol)
Past Masters-Volume Two .... (Parlophone)
The Beatles/1962-1966 .... (Capitol)
Paul McCartney; *Unplugged (The Official Bootleg)* .... (Capitol)
Stevie Wonder; *Beatles Songs By Greatest Stars* .... (Motown)
Signed Sealed & Delivered .... (Motown)
Stevie Wonder's Greatest Hits-#2 .... (Motown)
Top 10 With A Bullet-Motown Solo Stars-C .... (Motown)

We Don't Have To Do It
Tanya Tucker; *Soon* .... (Liberty)

What Do You Say To That
George Strait; *Always Never The Same* .... (MCA)

What I Meant To Say
Wade Hayes; *Old Enough To Know Better* .... (Columbia)

What I Really Meant To Say
Cyndi Thomson; *My World* .... (Capitol)

What If I Said
Anita Cochran & Steve Wariner; *Back To You* .... (Warner Bros.)
Steve Wariner & Anita Cochran; *Burnin' The Roadhouse Down* ...... (Capitol)

What She Said
Smiths; *Meat Is Murder* .... (Sire)
Rank .... (Sire)

What The President Meant To Say
Leaving Trains; *Fuck* .... (SST)

What Will My Mary Say
Jay & The Americans; *Come A Little Bit Closer-Best Of Jay & The Americans* .... (Gold Rush)
Johnny Mathis; *Johnny Mathis' All-Time Greatest Hits* .... (Columbia)
Johnny Mathis-16 Most Requested Songs .... (Columbia)

What Would You Say
Dave Matthews Band; *MTV Buzz Bin-C* .... (Mammoth)
Under The Table And Dreaming .... (RCA)

What'd I Say
Elvis Presley; *Collector's Gold* .... (RCA)
Elvis' Gold Records, Volume 4 .... (RCA)
Elvis In Concert .... (RCA)
Elvis-Greatest Hits, Volume One .... (RCA)
Jerry Lee Lewis; *Jerry Lee Lewis-Original Golden Hits-#2* .... (Sun)
Jerry Lee Lewis-Original Golden Hits-#2 .... (Sun)
Milestones .... (Rhino)
Rocket 88 .... (Tomato)
Rockin' My Life Away .... (Tomato)
John Mayall's Bluesbreakers with Eric Clapton; *John Mayall's Bluesbreakers with Eric Clapton* .... (Deram)
Ray Charles; *Atlantic Rhythm & Blues 1947-1974-#4 (1958-1962)-C* .. (Atlantic)
Atlantic Soul Classics-C .... (Warner Special Prod.)
Frat Rock!-#3-Grandson Of Frat Rock!-C .... (Rhino)
Life In Music .... (Atlantic)
Ray Charles-Anthology .... (Rhino)

Whatever You Say
Martina McBride; *Evolution* .... (RCA)

What's My Age Again?
Blink-182; *Enema Of The State* .... (MCA)
Now That's What I Call Music!-#3-C .... (Virgin)

When All Is Said And Done
Abba; *Forever Gold* .... (Polydor)

When I Call Your Name
Vince Gill; *When I Call Your Name* .... (MCA)

When I Said I Do
Clint Black & Lisa Hartman Black; *D'lectrified* .... (RCA)

When You Say Bud (Budweiser Beer)
Original Soundtrack; *TeeVee Toons-The Commercials-#1-C* .... (TVT)

When You Say Nothing At All
Alison Krauss & Union Station; *Kieth Whitley-A Tribute Album* .... (BNA)
Now That I've Found You: A Collection .... (Rounder)
ST/Switchback .... (RCA)
Keith Whitley; *Billboard Top Country Hits-1988-C* .... (Rhino)
Country Wedding Album-C .... (Scotti Bros.)
Don't Close Your Eyes .... (RCA)
Essential Keith Whitley .... (RCA)
Keith Whitley's Greatest Hits .... (RCA)

Whore Said It's Yours
Threat; *Sickinnahead* .... (Mercury)

Why Would I Say Goodbye
Brooks & Dunn; *Borderline* .... (Arista)

Yes!
Chad Brock; *Yes!* .... (Warner Bros.)

You Can't Hurry Love
Diana Ross; *Diana Ross-The Ultimate Collection* .... (Motown)
Diana Ross & The Supremes; *16 #1 Hits From The Early '60s-C* ..... (Motown)
Phil Collins; *Hello, I Must Be Going* .... (Atlantic)

You Don't Have To Say You Love Me
Dusty Springfield; *Dusty Springfield-Golden Hits* .... (Mercury)
History Of British Rock-#7-C .... (Rhino)
Elvis Presley; *Elvis As Recorded At Madison Square Garden* .... (RCA)
That's The Way It Is .... (RCA)
The Other Sides-Worldwide Gold Award Hits, Vol. 2 .... (RCA)
Vikki Carr; *Best Of Vikki Carr* .... (EMI)

You Get The Best From Me (Say, Say, Say)
Alicia Myers; *I Appreciate* .... (MCA)

You Make It So Hard (To Say No)
Boz Scaggs; *Hits!* . . . . (Columbia)
Slow Dancer . . . . (Columbia)
You Said The Words
Wood; *Songs From Stamford Hill* . . . . (Columbia)
You Say Yes
Judas Priest; *Point Of Entry* . . . . (Columbia)
You Say You Will
Trisha Yearwood; *Hearts In Armor* . . . . (MCA)
You've Got A Friend
Barbra Streisand; *Barbra Joan Streisand* . . . . (Columbia)
Carole King; *Tapestry* . . . . (Epic)
Donny Hathaway & Roberta Flack; *Best Of Donny Hathaway* . . . . (Atco)
Jamaica Boys; *J Boys* . . . . (Reprise)
James Taylor; *James Taylor's Greatest Hits* . . . . (Warner Bros.)
Mud Slide Slim And The Blue Horizon . . . . (Warner Bros.)
Michael Jackson; *Got To Be There* . . . . (Motown)
Original Soul Of Michael Jackson . . . . (Motown)
Roberta Flack & Donny Hathaway; *Best Of Roberta Flack* . . . . (Atlantic)
Roberta Flack & Donny Hathaway. . . . . (Atlantic)

COMMUNICATION: SCREAM, Howl

See Also: **COMMUNICATION (various)**

7 Screaming Diz Busters
Blue Oyster Cult; *On Your Feet Or On Your Knees* . . . . (Columbia)
Tyranny & Mutation . . . . (Columbia)
And Even The Vegetables Screamed
Legendary Pink Dots; *Golden Age* . . . . (Play It Again Sam)
At The Stars
Better Than Ezra; *How Does Your Garden Grow?* . . . . (Elektra)
Baby, Let Me Scream At You
Adam Ant; *Strip.* . . . . (Epic)
Blue On Black
Kenny Wayne Shepherd; *Trouble Is...* . . . . (Revolution)
From A Whisper To A Scream
Esther Phillips; *Best Of Esther Phillips* . . . . (CBS Associated)
From A Whisper To A Scream. . . . . (CBS Associated)
From A Whisper To A Scream
Allen Toussaint; *The Allen Toussaint Collection.* . . . . (Reprise)
Robert Palmer; *Sneakin' Sally Through The Alley.* . . . . (Island)
From A Whisper To A Scream
Elvis Costello & The Attractions; *Trust.* . . . . (Rykodisc)
Hear The Wind Howl
Leo Kottke; *Mudlark* . . . . (Capitol)
My Feet Are Smiling . . . . (Capitol)
Howlin' At The Moon
Hank Williams; *Hank Williams-24 Greatest Hits-#2* . . . . (Polydor)
Hank Williams-40 Greatest Hits. . . . . (Polydor)
Hey Good Lookin' (December 1950-July 1951). . . . . (Polydor)
Howlin' At The Moon
Chenille Sisters; *Haute Chenille: A Retrospective.* . . . . (Red House)
House On Fire: An Urban Folk Collection-C . . . . (Red House)
Howlin' Wind
Graham Parker; *Howlin' Wind* . . . . (Mercury)
Pourin' It All Out-Mercury Years. . . . . (Mercury)
I Shall Scream
Original Broadway Cast; *Oliver!* . . . . (RCA Victor)
Original London Cast; *Oliver!.* . . . . (EMI-Angel)
Meet Virginia
Train; *Now That's What I Call Music!-#4-C* . . . . (Virgin)
Train. . . . . (Aware/C2/Columbia)
Pinch Me
Barenaked Ladies; *Maroon* . . . . (Reprise)
Totally Hits-#3-C . . . . (Atlantic)
Primal Scream
Maynard Ferguson; *Essence Of Maynard Ferguson* . . . . (Columbia)
Motley Crue; *Decade Of Decadence* . . . . (Elektra)
Scream
Collective Soul; *Hints, Allegations And Things Left Unsaid* . . . . (Atlantic)
Scream
Michael Jackson with Janet Jackson; *HIStory: Past, Present And Future-Book 1-C* . . . . (Epic)
Scream & Shout
Quiet Riot; *Condition Critical* . . . . (Epic Portrait Assoc.)
Winners Take All. . . . . (Sony Music Special Prod.)
Scream Like A Baby
David Bowie; *Scary Monsters* . . . . (Rykodisc)
Screaming
Payolas; *No Stranger To Danger* . . . . (A&M)
Screaming
Bronski Beat; *Age Of Consent* . . . . (MCA)
Screaming For A Lovebite
Accept; *Metal Heart* . . . . (Portrait)
Staying A Life . . . . (Epic)

Screaming For Vengeance
Judas Priest; *Metal Giants-C* . . . . (Columbia)
Screaming For Vengeance . . . . (Columbia)
Screaming In The Night
Krokus; *Headhunter.* . . . . (Arista)
Stayed Awake All Night-Best Of Krokus . . . . (Arista)
Screaming Night Hog
Steppenwolf; *Steppenwolf-16 Greatest Hits* . . . . (MCA)
Screaming Skull
Fleshtones; *Living Legends* . . . . (I.R.S.)
Screaming Slave
Nine Inch Nails; *Fixed* . . . . (Nothing)
Screams
Blue Oyster Cult; *Blue Oyster Cult* . . . . (Columbia)
Screams Of Passion
Family; *Family.* . . . . (Warner Bros.)
Scum Of The Earth
Rob Zombie; *ST/Mission: Impossible 2* . . . . (Hollywood)
Sidewalk Annie
Wallflowers; *The Wallflowers* . . . . (Virgin)
What's Up
4 Non Blondes; *Bigger, Better, Faster, More!* . . . . (Interscope)
DJ Miko; *ESPN Presents Jock Jams-#2-C* . . . . (Tommy Boy)
Whisper To A Scream (Birds Fly)
Icicle Works; *Icicle Works* . . . . (Arista)

COMMUNICATION: SHOUT, Crying Out

See Also: **COMMUNICATION (various)**

Carolina Shout
Fats Waller; *Piano Solos-1929-1941* . . . . (RCA)
Holler & Shout
Elvin Bishop; *Struttin' My Stuff* . . . . (Capricorn)
I Got The Hook Up
Master P featuring Sons Of Funk; *ST/I Got The Hook Up* . . . . (No Limit/Priority)
Sons Of Funk; *The Game Of Funk* . . . . (No Limit/Priority)
I Want To Sing That Rock And Roll
Gillian Welch; *Time (The Revelator)* . . . . (Acony)
Inner City Blues (Make Me Wanna Holler)
Marvin Gaye; *What's Going On.* . . . . (Motown)
It's All Over But The Shoutin'
Joe Cocker; *Jamaica Say You Will* . . . . (A&M)
Jump Jive An' Wail
Brian Setzer Orchestra; *Dirty Boogie* . . . . (Interscope)
Now That's What I Call Music!-#1-C . . . . (Virgin)
Louis Prima; *Capitol Collectors Series-Louis Prima* . . . . (Capitol)
Ultra-Lounge-#5-Wild, Cool & Swingin'-C . . . . (Capitol)
Nowhere To Go
Melissa Etheridge; *Your Little Secret.* . . . . (Island)
Pearl, The
Emmylou Harris; *Red Dirt Girl* . . . . (Nonesuch)
Precious Declaration
Collective Soul; *Disciplined Breakdown* . . . . (Atlantic)
Ready To Go
Republica; *Republica.* . . . . (RCA)
Rebel Yell
Billy Idol; *MTV's Rock 'N' Roll To Go-C* . . . . (Elektra)
Rebel Yell . . . . (Chrysalis)
Roar Of The Masses Could Be Farts
Minutemen; *Double Nickels On The Dime.* . . . . (SST)
Rock And Roll All Nite
Kiss; *Alive!.* . . . . (Mercury)
Double Platinum . . . . (Mercury)
Dressed To Kill . . . . (Mercury)
Heavy Metal Memories-C . . . . (Rhino)
Smashes, Thrashes & Hits. . . . . (Mercury)
The Originals . . . . (Casablanca)
San Antonio Shout
Bob Crosby & His Orchestra; *Bob Crosby & His Orchestra Play 22 Original Big Band Hits* . . . . (Hindsight)
Shout
Beatles; *The Beatles-Anthology-#1* . . . . (Capitol)
Isley Brothers; *Nipper's Greatest Hits Of The '50s-#2-C* . . . . (RCA)
Shout . . . . (Collectables)
ST/The Wanderers. . . . . (Warner Bros.)
Joey Dee & the Starliters; *Echoes Of A Rock Era-Later Years-C* . . . . . . (Roulette)
Hey Let's Twist! Best Of Joey Dee & The Starliters . . . . (Rhino)
Live At The Peppermint Lounge . . . . (Accord)
Original Rock 'N' Roll Hits Of The '60s-C . . . . (Roulette)
Sock Hoppin' Sixties-C . . . . (JCI Assoc. Labels)
Otis Day & The Knights; *Shout* . . . . (MCA)
ST/Animal House. . . . . (MCA)
Tom Petty And The Heartbreakers; *Pack Up The Plantation-Live!* . . . . . (MCA)

Shout
Tears For Fears; *Billboard Top Hits-1985-C* . . . . (Rhino)
   Songs From The Big Chair . . . . (Mercury)
   Tears Roll Down-The-Hits-1982-1992 . . . . (Fontana)

Shout And Shimmy
Who; *Who's Missing* . . . .(MCA)

Shout At The Devil
Motley Crue; *Decade Of Decadence* . . . . (Elektra)
   Shout At The Devil . . . . (Elektra)

Shout Bamalama
Mickey Murray; *Jewels-#2-C* . . . . (SSS International)
   Soul Gold-#1 . . . . (SSS International)
Wet Willie; *Southern Rock* . . . . (K-Tel)
   Wet Willie's Greatest Hits . . . . (Polydor)

Shout It Out
Slaughter; *ST/Bill & Ted's Bogus Journey* . . . . (Interscope)

Shout It Out
Burning Spear; *Dry & Heavy* . . . .(Mango)

Shout It Out
Kingdom Come; *Kingdom Come* . . . . (Polydor)

Shout It Out
Patrice Rushen; *Let There Be Funk* . . . . (Prestige)

Shout It Out Loud
Kiss; *Alive II* . . . . (Casablanca)
   Destroyer . . . . (Casablanca)
   Smashes, Thrashes & Hits . . . . (Mercury)

Shout Shout
Ernie Maresca; *22 Leaders Of The Pack-#1-C* . . . . (Laurie)
   Classic Old & Gold-C . . . . (Laurie)
   Collectables Presents The History Of Rock-#10-C . . . . (Collectables)
   Million-Dollar Memories-#2-C . . . . (RCA)
   Son Of Frat Rock!-C . . . . (Rhino)

Shout To The Devil
Alarm; *Declaration* . . . . (I.R.S.)

Shout To The Top
Style Council; *Internationalists* . . . .(Geffen)
   ST/Vision Quest . . . .(Geffen)

Shouting Out Love
Emotions; *15 Original Big Hits-#2-C* . . . .(Stax)
   Sunshine . . . .(Stax)
   The Emotions-Chronicle . . . .(Stax)

Stand Up & Shout
Tubes; *What Do You Want From Live* . . . . (A&M)
   Young And Rich . . . . (A&M)

Stand Up & Shout
Dio; *Holy Diver* . . . .(Warner Bros.)

Stein Song (University Of Maine)
Rudy Vallee & His Connecticut Yankees; *Billboard Pop Memories-The*
   1930s-C . . . . (Rhino)
   Heigh-Ho Everybody: This Is Rudy Vallee . . . . (Living Era)
   Those Wonderful Years: Puttin' On The Ritz-C . . . . (JCI Assoc. Labels)
University Of Michigan Band; *Greatest College Football Marches* . (Vanguard)

Twist And Shout
Beatles; *Beatles-Box Set* . . . . (Capitol)
   Please Please Me . . . . (Parlophone)
   Rock 'N' Roll Music . . . . (Capitol)
   ST/Imagine: John Lennon . . . . (Capitol)
   The Beatles At The Hollywood Bowl . . . . (Capitol)
   The Early Beatles . . . . (Capitol)
Buck Owens & The Buckaroos; *Buck Owens & The Buckaroos-Live At*
   Carnegie Hall . . . .(Country Music Foundation)
Isley Brothers; *Best Of The Isley Brothers* . . . . (Curb)
   Cruisin'-1963-C . . . .(Increase)
   Frat Rock!-C . . . . (Rhino)
   Oldies But Goodies-#10-C . . . . (Original Sound)
   Solid Gold Music-WCBS FM 101-'60s-#1-C . . . . (Collectables)
   Toga Rock-C . . . .(Dunhill Compact Classics)
Mamas & The Papas; *Best Of The Mamas & The Papas* . . . . (MCA)
Who; *Who's Last* . . . . (MCA)

When Doves Cry
Ginuwine; *The Bachelor* . . . . (550 Music)
Prince and the Revolution; *ST/Purple Rain* . . . . (Warner Bros.)

When Johnny Comes Marching Home
Marilyn Horne; *Beautiful Dreamer-Great American Songbook* . . . . (London)
Mormon Tabernacle Choir; *Songs Of The Civil War And Stephen Foster*
   Favorites . . . . (Sony Music Classical)
United States Military Academy Band; *Songs Of The Civil War-C* . . (Columbia)

Wind Cries Mary
Jimi Hendrix; *Essential Jimi Hendrix, Volume 2* . . . . (Reprise)
Jimi Hendrix Experience; *Are You Experienced?* . . . . (Reprise)
   Smash Hits . . . . (Reprise)

You Cried Wolf
Todd Rundgren; *Hermit Of Mink Hollow* . . . . (Rhino)
   Todd Rundgren-Anthology 1968-1985 . . . . (Rhino)

You Were Mine
Dixie Chicks; *Big Country Hits '99-C* . . . . (K-Tel)
   Wide Open Spaces . . . . (Monument)

COMMUNICATION: TALK, Speak
See Also: COMMUNICATION (various), GOSSIP

Ain't Talkin' 'Bout Love
Van Halen; *Van Halen* . . . . (Warner Bros.)

All I Do
Somethin' For The People; *This Time It's Personal* . . . . (Warner Bros.)

Animal Speaks
Golden Palominos; *Visions Of Excess* . . . .(Celluloid)

Another Saturday Night
Cat Stevens; *Cat Stevens Greatest Hits* . . . . (A&M)
Jimmy Buffett; *Margaritaville Cafe Late Night Menu* . . . .(Margaritaville)
Sam Cooke; *The Man And His Music* . . . . (RCA)
   This Is Sam Cooke . . . . (RCA)

Baby Makes Her Blue Jeans Talk
Dr. Hook; *Players In The Dark* . . . . (Casablanca)

Baby Talk
Jan & Dean; *Best Of Jan & Dean* . . . . (EMI)
   Collectables Presents The History Of Rock-#9-C . . . . . (Collectables)
   One Summer Night-Live . . . . (Rhino)

Baby Talk
Billy Idol; *Don't Stop* . . . . (Chrysalis)

Baby Talks Dirty
Knack; *But The Little Girls Understand* . . . . (Capitol)

Back Chat
Queen; *Hot Space* . . . . (Hollywood)

Big Boss Man
B.B. King; *Six Silver Strings* . . . . (MCA)
Elvis Presley; *ST/Clambake* . . . . (RCA)
Grateful Dead; *Grateful Dead (Skull & Roses)* . . . . (Warner Bros.)
Jimmy Reed; *Best Of Jimmy Reed* . . . .(Crescendo)
   Oldies But Goodies-#1-C . . . . (Original Sound)
John Hammond; *Best Of John Hammond* . . . . (Vanguard)
   So Many Roads . . . . (Vanguard)

Big Me
Foo Fighters; *Foo Fighters* . . . .(Roswell/RCA)

Big Time
Neil Young & Crazy Horse; *Broken Arrow* . . . .(Reprise)
   Year Of The Horse . . . . (Reprise)

Body Talk
Ratt; *Dancing Undercover* . . . .(Atlantic)
   Ratt & Roll 8191 . . . .(Atlantic)
   ST/The Golden Child . . . . (Capitol)

Body Talk
Deele; *Body Talk* . . . .(Solar)
   Street Beat . . . .(Solar)

Body Talk
Wallets; *Body Talk* . . . . (Twin-Tone)

Body Talk
Kix; *Cool Kids* . . . .(Atlantic)

Broken English
Marianne Faithfull; *Broken English* . . . . (Island)
   The Island Story-1962-1987-25th Anniversary-C . . . . (Island)

Calling You
Hank Williams; *I Saw The Light* . . . .(Polydor)

Can We Talk
Tevin Campbell; *I'm Ready* . . . .(Qwest)

Can't We Talk It Over?
Bing Crosby; *Bing Crosby-16 Most Requested Songs* . . . . (Legacy)
Helen O'Connell; *Great Girl Singers Sing 22 Original*
   Recordings-C . . . . (Hindsight)

Charlie Brown's Parents
Dishwalla; *Pet Your Friends* . . . . (A&M)

Darling Be Home Soon
Joe Cocker; *Joe Cocker!* . . . . (A&M)
   Joe Cocker-Classics-#4 . . . . (A&M)
   Joe Cocker's Greatest Hits . . . . (A&M)
Lovin' Spoonful; *Best Of The Lovin' Spoonful-#2* . . . . (Rhino)
   Lovin' '60s-C . . . . (Priority)
   Lovin' Spoonful-Anthology . . . . (Rhino)

Dialogue
Chicago; *Chicago V* . . . . (Chicago)
   Chicago's Greatest Hits-#2 (1974-81) . . . . (Chicago)

Diamonds On The Soles Of Her Shoes
Paul Simon; *Concert In The Park-August 15 1991* . . . . . . (Warner Bros.)
   Graceland . . . . (Warner Bros.)
   Negotiations And Love Songs, 1971-1986 . . . . (Warner Bros.)

Did You Ever See A Dream Walking
Bing Crosby; *Crosby Classics* . . . . (Columbia)
Hal Kemp & Skinnay Ennis; *The Uncollected Hal Kemp-#2 & #3* . . . (Hindsight)

Dirty Cash (Money Talks)
Adventures Of Stevie V; *Best Of '90s Dance Music-#1-Hip*
   House-C . . . . (PWL America)
   Dirty Cash (Money Talks) . . . . (Mercury)

Don't Get Me Started
Rhett Akins; *Somebody New* . . . . (Decca)

Don't Speak
No Doubt; *Tragic Kingdom* . . . .(Trauma)
Don't Start Me Talkin'
Doobie Brothers; *Farewell* . . . . (Warner Bros.)
Toulouse Street . . . . (Warner Bros.)
New York Dolls; *In Too Much Too Soon* . . . .(Mercury)
Sonny Boy Williamson; *Down & Out Blues* . . . . (Chess)
Superblues-#2-All-Time Classic Blues-C . . . . (Stax)
Don't Talk
Jon B.; *Pleasures You Like* . . . . (Edmonds/Epic)
Don't Talk (Put Your Head On My Shoulder)
Beach Boys; *Pet Sounds* . . . . (Capitol)
The Pet Sounds Sessions: A 30th Anniversary Collection . . . . (Capitol)
Linda Ronstadt; *Winter Light* . . . .(Elektra)
Don't Talk To Strangers
Rick Springfield; *Rick Springfield's Greatest Hits* . . . .(RCA)
Success Hasn't Spoiled Me Yet . . . .(RCA)
Don't Talk To Strangers
Beau Brummels; *Best Of The Beau Brummels* . . . . (Rhino)
Just A Little & Other Hits . . . . (Accord)
Don't Talk To Strangers
Dio; *Holy Diver* . . . . (Warner Bros.)
Don't Talk To Strangers
Roger Daltrey; *Under A Raging Moon* . . . . (Atlantic)
Don't Tell Me No
Cars; *Panorama* . . . .(Elektra)
Don't Tell Me You Love Me
Night Ranger; *Dawn Patrol* . . . .(Camel)
Night Ranger's Greatest Hits . . . .(Camel)
Elephant Talk
King Crimson; *Abbreviated* . . . . (Editions E.G.)
Compact . . . . (Editions E.G.)
Discipline . . . . (Editions E.G.)
Everybody's Talkin'
Nilsson; *Everybody's Talkin': The Encore Collection* . . . . (BMG Special Prod.)
ST/Forrest Gump . . . . (Epic/Sony Music Soundtrax)
ST/Midnight Cowboy . . . .(EMI)
Willie Nelson; *Best Of Willie* . . . .(RCA)
Sweet Memories . . . .(RCA)
Frankie
Bruce Springsteen; *Tracks* . . . . (Columbia)
Freedom
Paul McCartney; *Driving Rain* . . . . (Columbia)
The Concert For New York City-C . . . . (Columbia)
Freedom Overspill
Steve Winwood; *Back In The High Life* . . . . (Island)
Girl Talk
Betty Carter; *Finally* . . . .(Roulette)
Ella Fitzgerald & Joe Pass; *Speak Love* . . . . (Pablo)
Girls Talk
Dave Edmunds; *Best Of Dave Edmunds* . . . . (Swan Song)
Repeat When Necessary . . . . (Swan Song)
Dave Edmunds Band; *I Hear You Rockin'* . . . . (Columbia)
Elvis Costello; *Girls Girls Girls* . . . . (Columbia)
Taking Liberties . . . . (Columbia)
Linda Ronstadt; *Mad Love* . . . . (Elektra)
Give Peace A Chance
John Lennon; *Lennon* . . . . (Capitol)
Live In New York City . . . . (Capitol)
ST/Imagine: John Lennon . . . . (Capitol)
The John Lennon Collection . . . . (Capitol)
John Lennon/Plastic Ono Band; *Shaved Fish* . . . . (Capitol)
Plastic Ono Band; *Plastic Ono Band-Live Peace In Toronto 1969* . . . . . (Capitol)
Go On
George Strait; *George Strait* . . . . (MCA)
Good Morning
Gene Kelly/Debbie Reynolds/Donald O'Connor; *ST/Singin' In
The Rain* . . . . (Sony Music Special Prod.)
Grey Talk
Francis X & The Bushmen; *Scream-The Compilation* . . . . (Geffen)
Happy Talk
Original Cast; *South Pacific* . . . . (CBS Masterworks)
Have A Talk With God
Stevie Wonder; *Songs In The Key Of Life* . . . . (Motown)
He Talks To Me
Lorrie Morgan; *Leave The Light On* . . . .(RCA)
Lorrie Morgan's Greatest Hits . . . .(BNA)
Lorrie Morgan-Super Hits . . . .(RCA)
To Get To You-Greatest Hits Collection . . . .(BNA)
Heart To Heart Talk
Lee Ann Womack & Asleep At The Wheel; *Ride With
Bob-C* . . . . (DreamWorks/SKG)
Hearts Of Stone
Bruce Springsteen; *Tracks* . . . . (Columbia)
Southside Johnny And The Asbury Jukes; *Best Of Southside Johnny And The
Asbury Jukes* . . . . (Legacy)
Cover Me (Bruce Springsteen Tribute)-C . . . . (Rhino)
Hearts Of Stone . . . . (Epic)

Here Comes The Rain Again
Eurythmics; *Eurythmics' Greatest Hits* . . . .(Arista)
Eurythmics' Greatest Hits . . . .(Arista)
Hey Bulldog
Beatles; *Rock 'N' Roll Music* . . . .(Capitol)
Yellow Submarine . . . .(Capitol)
How Do You Speak To An Angel?
Etta James; *These Foolish Things-The Classic Balladry Of Etta James* . . . (MCA)
How Do You Talk To An Angel
Heights; *ST/Heights* . . . .(Capitol)
How Do You Talk To Girls
Rick Springfield; *Success Hasn't Spoiled Me Yet* . . . . (RCA)
Human Touch
Bruce Springsteen; *Bruce Springsteen's Greatest Hits* . . . .(Columbia)
Human Touch . . . .(Columbia)
I Don't Wanna Talk About It Now
Emmylou Harris; *Red Dirt Girl* . . . .(Nonesuch)
I Don't Want To Talk About It
Rita Coolidge; *Anytime...Anywhere* . . . .(A&M)
Rita Coolidge's Greatest Hits . . . .(A&M)
Rod Stewart; *Absolutely Live* . . . .(Warner Bros.)
Atlantic Crossing . . . .(Warner Bros.)
Downtown Train-Selections From The Storyteller Anthology. . (Warner Bros.)
Rod Stewart's Greatest Hits . . . . (Warner Bros.)
Storyteller/The Complete Anthology: 1964-1990 . . . . (Warner Bros.)
I Never Talk To Strangers
Bette Midler; *Broken Blossom* . . . . (Atlantic)
Tom Waits; *Foreign Affairs* . . . . (Asylum)
Tom Waits-Anthology . . . . (Asylum)
I Talk To The Trees
Al Hirt; *Al Hirt* . . . . (Dunhill Compact Classics)
Showtime . . . .(Allegiance)
Alan Jay Lerner; *Alan Jay Lerner Performs His Own Songs* . . . . (DRG)
Original Broadway Cast; *Paint Your Wagon* . . . . (RCA Victor)
I Talk To The Wind
King Crimson; *In The Court Of The Crimson King-An Observation By King
Crimson* . . . .(Editions E.G.)
If I Could Talk I'd Tell You
Lemonheads; *Car Button Cloth* . . . . (Tag/Atlantic)
If These Old Walls Could Speak
Nanci Griffith with Jimmy Webb; *Red Hot + Country-C* . . . .(Mercury)
If Walls Could Talk
Little Milton; *If Walls Could Talk* . . . .(Chess)
Little Milton's Greatest Hits . . . .(Chess)
Ry Cooder; *Paradise And Lunch* . . . . (Reprise)
If Walls Could Talk
Celine Dion; *All The Way...A Decade Of Song* . . . . (550 Music)
I'm Just Talkin' About Tonight
Toby Keith; *Pull My Chain* . . . . (DreamWorks/SKG)
It Matters To Me
Faith Hill; *It Matters To Me* . . . .(Warner Bros.)
It's The Talk Of The Town
Art Tatum; *Art Tatum-Complete Capitol Recordings-#2* . . . .(Capitol)
Hank Jones; *Live At Maybeck Recital Hall-#16* . . . .(Concord Jazz)
Ray Conniff Singers; *It's The Talk Of The Town* . . . .(Columbia)
Jackson
Johnny Cash & June Carter; *Johnny Cash's Greatest Hits* . . . .(Columbia)
The Man In Black-His Greatest Hits . . . .(Legacy)
Nancy Sinatra & Lee Hazlewood; *Nancy Sinatra-The Hit Years* . . . . (Rhino)
Jeremy
Pearl Jam; *Ten* . . . .(Epic Portrait Assoc.)
Jive Talkin'
Bee Gees; *Bee Gees' Greatest* . . . .(Polydor)
Main Course . . . .(RSO)
ST/Saturday Night Fever . . . . (Polydor)
Just A Little Talk With Jesus
Elvis Presley; *Million-Dollar Quartet* . . . . (RCA)
Keep Talking
Pink Floyd; *The Division Bell* . . . .(Columbia)
Lay Down Sally
Eric Clapton; *Eric Clapton-Crossroads-C* . . . . (Polydor)
Just One Night . . . . (Polydor)
Slowhand . . . . (Polydor)
Time Pieces-#1-The Best Of Eric Clapton . . . . (Polydor)
Let Me Talk
Earth, Wind & Fire; *Faces* . . . .(Columbia)
Let's Not Talk About It
Original Broadway Cast; *Romance/Romance* . . . . (MCA)
Let's Stop Talkin' About It
Janie Fricke; *Janie Fricke-17 Greatest Hits* . . . .(Columbia)
Love Lies . . . .(Columbia)
Very Best Of Janie Fricke . . . .(Columbia)
Let's Talk About Love
Celine Dion with the Bee Gees; *Let's Talk About Love-C* . . . . (550 Music)
Let's Talk About Me
Alan Parsons Project; *Best Of Alan Parsons Project-#2* . . . .(Arista)
Vulture Culture . . . .(Arista)
Let's Talk About Sex
Salt-N-Pepa; *Blacks' Magic* . . . . (Next Plateau/London/Island)

Blitz Of Salt-N-Pepa Hits . . . . (London)
MTV Party To Go-#2-C . . . . (Tommy Boy)
Let's Talk About Us
Jerry Lee Lewis; *Jerry Lee Lewis-Original Golden Hits-#3* . . . . (Sun)
Jerry Lee's Greatest! . . . . (Rhino)
Milestones . . . . (Rhino)
Let's Talk It Over
Vaneese Thomas; *Vaneese Thomas* . . . . (Geffen)
Let's Talk It Over In The Ladies Room
Curtie & The Boom Box; *Black Kisses* . . . . (RCA)
Letting The Cables Sleep
Bush; *Science Of Things* . . . . (Trauma)
Lip Service
Elvis Costello; *This Year's Model* . . . .(Rykodisc)
Lip Service
Michael Franks; *Camera Never Lies* . . . .(Warner Bros.)
Lip Service
John Astley; *Everyone Loves The Pilot Except The Crew* . . . . (Atlantic)
Lip Service
Jimmy Buffett; *Somewhere Over China* . . . .(MCA)
Little Black Backpack
Stroke9; *Nasty Little Thoughts* . . . . (Cherry/Universal)
Little Less Talk And A Lot More Action
Toby Keith; *Toby Keith* . . . . (Mercury)
Loose Talk
Carl Smith; *Very Special Love Song-C* . . . . (Fifty One West)
Patsy Cline; *Live At The Opry* . . . .(MCA)
Love Talks
Ronnie McDowell; *In A New York Minute* . . . .(Epic)
Older Women & Other Greatest Hits . . . . (Epic)
Lover In Me, The
Sheena Easton; *The Lover In Me* . . . .(MCA)
Meow Meow Meow Meow (Meow Mix Cat Food)
Original Soundtrack; *TeeVee Toons-The Commercials-#1-C* . . . . (TVT)
Money Talks
J.J. Cale; *Number 8* . . . . (Mercury)
Special Edition . . . . (Mercury)
Money Talks
Living Colour; *Biscuits* . . . .(Epic)
Money Talks
Gang Of Four; *Mall* . . . . (Polydor)
Money Talks
Bar-Kays; *Money Talks* . . . . (Stax)
Money Talks
Rick James; *Throwin' Down* . . . . (Motown)
Moneytalks
AC/DC; *Razor's Edge* . . . . (Atco)
Mothers Talk
Tears For Fears; *Songs From The Big Chair* . . . . (Mercury)
Tears Roll Down-The Hits-1982-1992 . . . . (Fontana)
Mrs. Potter's Lullaby
Counting Crows; *This Desert Life* . . . . (David Geffen Co.)
My Generation
Who; *Live At Leeds* . . . .(MCA)
Meaty Beaty Big & Bouncy . . . .(MCA)
ST/The Kids Are Alright . . . .(MCA)
The Who Sings ''My Generation'' . . . .(MCA)
Who Greatest Hits . . . .(MCA)
No Time For Talk
Christopher Cross; *Another Page* . . . .(Warner Bros.)
No, No, No
Destiny's Child; *Destiny's Child* . . . . (Grass Roots/Columbia)
Nobody's Talking
Exile; *Country's Greatest Hits-#3-C* . . . . (Priority)
Still Standing . . . . (Arista)
Now You're Talkin'
Dixiana; *Now You're Talkin'* . . . . (Epic)
Open My Heart
Yolanda Adams; *Mountain High Valley Low* . . . . (Elektra)
Our Lips Are Sealed
Go-Go's; *Beauty & The Beat* . . . .(I.R.S.)
Go-Go's Greatest . . . .(I.R.S.)
Physical
Olivia Newton-John; *Back To Basics-Essential Collection 1971-1992* . .(Geffen)
Olivia Newton-John's Greatest Hits-#2 . . . .(MCA)
Physical . . . .(MCA)
Pick-A-Little, Talk-A-Little
Hermione Gingold & Biddys; *ST/The Music Man* . . . .(Warner Bros.)
Original Cast; *The Music Man* . . . . (Gold Rush)
Pillow Talk
Sylvia; *All Platinum Gold* . . . . (All Platinum)
Super Bad Is Back-Soul Love-C . . . . (K-Tel)
Please Don't Talk About Me When I'm Gone
Ann-Margret; *Let Me Entertain You* . . . . (RCA)
Arlo Guthrie & Pete Seeger; *Precious Friend* . . . .(Warner Bros.)
Billie Holiday; *Compact Jazz-Billie Holiday* . . . . (Verve)
Music For Torching: Billie Holiday Story-#5 . . . . (Verve)
The Ultimate Billie Holiday . . . . (Verve)

Ella Fitzgerald & Count Basie; *Perfect Match* . . . . (Pablo)
Frank Sinatra; *Swing Along With Me* . . . . (Reprise)
Gene Austin; *The Voice Of The Southland* . . . . (Living Era)
Harry Connick, Jr.; *20* . . . . (Columbia)
Leon Redbone; *Champagne Charlie* . . . . (Warner Bros.)
Ray Price; *Portrait Of A Singer* . . . .(Step One)
Practice What I Preach
Hank Williams, Jr.; *America (The Way I See It)* . . . . (WB/Curb)
Born To Boogie . . . . (WB/Curb)
Practice What You Preach
Santana; *Borboletta* . . . . (Columbia)
Practice What You Preach
Barry White; *The Icon Is Love* . . . . (A&M)
Practice What You Preach
American Girls; *American Girls* . . . . (I.R.S.)
Practice What You Preach
Proven Innocent; *And Then There Were 2* . . . .(First Priority)
Practice What You Preach
Alex Taylor; *Dancing With The Devil* . . . . (Ichiban Int'l)
Practice What You Preach
Testament; *Practice What You Preach* . . . . (Megaforce)
Psychobabble
Alan Parsons Project; *Best Of The Alan Parsons Project* . . . . (Arista)
Eye In The Sky . . . . (Arista)
Rastaman Chant
Wailers; *Burnin'* . . . .(Tuff Gong)
Ronnie, Talk To Russia
Prince; *Controversy* . . . . (Warner Bros.)
Sex Me, Talk Me
Berlin; *Count Three & Pray* . . . . (Geffen)
Shaddap You Face
Joe Dolce; *45-#51053* . . . . (MCA)
She Don't Talk Like Us No More
K.T. Oslin; *This Woman* . . . . (RCA)
She Talks To Angels
Black Crowes; *Shake Your Money Maker* . . . .(Def American)
Shut Up And Drive
Chely Wright; *Woman In The Moon* . . . .(Polydor Country)
Shut Up And Kiss Me
Mary Chapin Carpenter; *Stones In The Road* . . . . (Columbia)
Sidewalk Annie
Wallflowers; *The Wallflowers* . . . .(Virgin)
Sidewalk Talk
Jellybean; *Dance Mix* . . . . (EMI)
Wotupski . . . . (EMI)
Sleep Talk
Alyson Williams; *Raw* . . . . (Def Jam)
Small Talk
Doris Day & John Raitt; *ST/Pajama Game* . . . . (Collectables)
Original Cast; *Pajama Game* . . . . (Columbia)
Something To Talk About
Bonnie Raitt; *Luck Of The Draw* . . . . (Capitol)
Speak Softly-You're Talking To My Heart
Gene Watson; *Gene Watson's Greatest Hits* . . . . (MCA)
Old Loves Never Die . . . . (MCA)
Stereo Chickens
Jerry Jeff Walker; *A Man Must Carry On* . . . . (MCA)
Street Corner Talking
Savoy Brown; *Savoy Brown-London Collector* . . . .(London)
Street Corner Talking . . . . (Deram)
Stutter
Elastica; *Elastica* . . . . (David Geffen Co.)
Sweet Talker
Richard Thompson; *ST/Sweet Talker* . . . . (Capitol)
Sweet Talkin' Guy
Chiffons; *Best Of The Chiffons* . . . .(Laurie)
Chiffons-Golden Classics . . . . (Collectables)
Collectables Presents The History Of Rock-#1-C . . . . (Collectables)
Everything You Always Wanted . . . .(Laurie)
Sweet Talking Woman
Electric Light Orchestra; *Afterglow* . . . . (Epic)
Box Of Their Best . . . . (Jet)
Electric Light Orchestra's Greatest Hits . . . . (Jet)
Out Of The Blue . . . . (Jet)
T.V. Talkin' Song
Bob Dylan; *Under The Red Sky* . . . . (Columbia)
Talk About Suffering
Doc Watson; *Doc Watson* . . . . (Vanguard)
Ricky Skaggs; *Family & Friends* . . . . (Rounder)
Live In London . . . . (Epic)
Talk About The Good Times
Elvis Presley; *Good Times* . . . . (RCA)
Talk Back Trembling Lips
Ernest Ashworth; *Best Of Ernest Ashworth* . . . . (Curb)
Johnny Tillotson; *Cruisin'-1964-C* . . . . (Increase)
Talk Dirty To Me
Poison; *Look What The Cat Dragged In* . . . . (Capitol)
Swallow This Live . . . . (Capitol)

Talk It Over
Grayson Hugh; *Blind To Reason* . . . . (RCA)
Pretty Girls Everywhere-Beach Classics-#1-C . . . . (RCA)
Talk Of The Town
Pretenders; *Pretenders II* . . . . (Sire)
Pretenders-The Singles . . . . (Sire)
Talk Of The Town
Lightnin' Hopkins; *Nothin' But The Blues-Golden Classics-#4* . . . (Collectables)
Talk Show Shhh!
Shae Jones; *Talk Show* . . . . (Universal)
Talk Talk
Talk Talk; *History Revisited* . . . . (EMI)
Party's Over . . . . (EMI)
Spinning Pups . . . . (EMI)
ST/Nightshift . . . . (Warner Bros.)
Very Best Of Talk Talk-Natural History . . . . (EMI)
Talk Talk
Music Machine; *Battle Of The Bands-C* . . . . (K-Tel)
Nuggets-#1-The Hits-C . . . . (Rhino)
Talk The Talk
Kombo; *Big Blast* . . . . (GRP/NMG)
Talk To Me
Mickey Gilley; *19 Hot Country Requests-C* . . . . (Epic)
Put Your Dreams Away . . . . (Epic)
Ten Years Of Hits . . . . (Epic)
Talk To Me
NRBQ; *At Yankee Stadium* . . . . (Mercury)
Talk To Me
Southside Johnny And The Asbury Jukes; *Best Of Southside Johnny And The
Asbury Jukes* . . . . (Legacy)
Havin' A Party With Southside Johnny And The Asbury Jukes . . . . (Epic)
Talk To Me
Chico DeBarge; *Chico DeBarge* . . . . (Motown)
Talk To Me
Anita Baker; *Compositions* . . . . (Elektra)
Talk To Me
Joni Mitchell; *Don Juan's Reckless Daughter* . . . . (Asylum)
Talk To Me
Fiona; *Fiona* . . . . (Atlantic)
Talk To Me
Bonnie Raitt; *Green Light* . . . . (Warner Bros.)
Talk To Me
Europe; *Prisoners In Paradise* . . . . (Epic)
Talk To Me
Stevie Nicks; *Rock A Little* . . . . (Modern)
TimeSpace-The Best Of Stevie Nicks . . . . (Modern)
Talk To Me
Chris Isaak; *Silvertone* . . . . (Warner Bros.)
Talk To Me
Babyface; *The Day* . . . . (Epic)
Talk To Me Baby
Frank Sinatra; *Softly, As I Leave You* . . . . (Reprise)
Talk To Me Baby
Elmore James; *Golden Classics-Elmore James* . . . . (Collectables)
Talk To Me Baby
Toni Tennille; *Never Let Me Go* . . . . (Bay Cities)
Talk To Me Daddy
Thelma Cooper/Boyfriends; *Collectables Blues Collection-#3-C* . . (Collectables)
Talk To Me Like The Sea
Everything But The Girl; *Worldwide* . . . . (Atlantic)
Talk To Me Lonesome Heart
James O'Gwynn; *James O'Gwynn's Greatest Hits* . . . . (Plantation)
Talk To Me Texas
Keith Whitley; *Keith Whitley's Greatest Hits* . . . . (RCA)
Tracy Byrd; *Tracy Byrd* . . . . (MCA)
Talk To The Animals
Sammy Davis, Jr.; *Sammy Davis, Jr.'s Greatest Songs* . . . . (Curb)
Talk To The Lawyer
David Lindley & El Rayo-X; *Win This Record* . . . . (Elektra)
Talk To Ya Later
Tubes; *Best Of The Tubes* . . . . (Gold Rush)
Completion Backward Principle . . . . (Capitol)
Rock The First-#4-C . . . . (Sandstone Music)
Talkin' About You
Animals; *Best Of The Animals* . . . . (Abkco)
Talkin' At The Texaco
James McMurtry; *Too Long In The Wasteland* . . . . (Columbia)
Talkin' 'Bout Love
Nazareth; *Malice In Wonderland* . . . . (A&M)
Talkin' 'Bout Women Obviously
Buddy Guy/Junior Mance/Junior Wells; *Buddy & The Juniors* . . . . (MCA)
Talkin' Fishin'
Ramblin' Jack Elliott; *Greatest Songs Of Woody Guthrie-C* . . . . . . (Vanguard)
Talkin' Hava Negeilah Blues
Bob Dylan; *The Bootleg Series-Volumes 1-3 [Rare & Unreleased]* . . (Columbia)
Talkin' New York
Bob Dylan; *Bob Dylan* . . . . (Columbia)
The Times They Are A-Changin' . . . . (Columbia)

Talkin' To Myself
Lonesome River Band; *Talkin' To Myself* . . . . (Sugar Hill)
Talkin' To The Moon
Gatlin Brothers; *Best Of The Gatlins-All The Gold In California* . . . . . . (Legacy)
Larry Gatlin & The Gatlin Brothers Band; *Live At 8:00* . . . . (Capitol)
More Hot Country Requests-#2-C . . . . (Epic)
Partners . . . . (Columbia)
The Gatlin Brothers' Biggest Hits . . . . (Columbia)
Talkin' To The Moon
Charlie Daniels Band; *Me & The Boys* . . . . (Epic)
Talkin' Trash
Tom Principato; *Smokin'* . . . . (Powerhouse)
Talkin' Trash
Chico Freeman; *Tradition In Transition* . . . . (Elektra)
Talking About My Baby
Curtis Mayfield & The Impressions; *Curtis Mayfield-The Anthology-1961-
1977* . . . . (MCA)
Impressions; *Impressions' Greatest Hits* . . . . (MCA)
Talking Airplane Disaster
Phil Ochs; *Original New Folks* . . . . (Vanguard)
Talking Back To The Night
Steve Winwood; *Steve Winwood-Chronicles* . . . . (Island)
Talking Back To The Night . . . . (Island)
Talking Blues
Bob Marley & The Wailers; *Natty Dread* . . . . (Tuff Gong)
Talking Cancer Blues
Dave Van Ronk; *Inside Dave Van Ronk* . . . . (Fantasy)
Van Ronk . . . . (Fantasy)
Talking Casey
Mississippi John Hurt; *Best Of Mississippi John Hurt* . . . . (Vanguard)
Candy Man . . . . (Intermedia)
Today! . . . . (Vanguard)
Talking In The Dark
Elvis Costello; *2 1/2 Years* . . . . (Rykodisc)
Elvis Costello & The Attractions; *Armed Forces* . . . . (Rykodisc)
Linda Ronstadt; *Mad Love* . . . . (Elektra)
Talking In Your Sleep
Crystal Gayle; *Classic Crystal* . . . . (EMI)
Country Gold-C . . . . (Priority)
Crystal Gayle's All-Time Greatest Hits . . . . (Curb)
When I Dream . . . . (Liberty)
Reba McEntire; *Starting Over* . . . . (MCA)
Talking In Your Sleep
Romantics; *Billboard Top Hits-1984-C* . . . . (Rhino)
In Heat . . . . (Epic Portrait Assoc.)
Rock Of The '80s-#3-C . . . . (Priority)
Talking Old Soldiers
Elton John; *Tumbleweed Connection* . . . . (Polydor)
Talking Pay T.V.
Phil Ochs; *Broadside Tapes-#1* . . . . (Smithsonian Folkways)
Talking To A Tennessee Moon
Candace Anderson; *Talking To A Tennessee Moon* . . . . (Adobe)
Talking To My Angel
Melissa Etheridge; *Yes I Am* . . . . (Island)
Talking To The Moon
Don Henley; *I Can't Stand Still* . . . . (Asylum)
Talking To Yourself
Original Broadway Cast; *Hallelujah Baby!* . . . . (Sony Music Classical)
Talking Union
Pete Seeger; *Pete Seeger's Greatest Hits* . . . . (Columbia)
Pete Seeger & Others; *Songs Of America's Working People* . . . . . . (Flying Fish)
Talking Vietnam Pot Luck Blues
Tom Paxton; *Morning After* . . . . (Elektra)
Talking Watergate
Tom Paxton; *New Songs From The Briarpatch* . . . . (Vanguard)
Talking World War III Blues
Bob Dylan; *Freewheelin'* . . . . (Columbia)
Tequila Talkin'
Lonestar; *Lonestar* . . . . (BNA)
Thank You For Talking To Me, Africa
Miki Howard; *Femme Fatale* . . . . (Giant)
Sly & The Family Stone; *Sly & The Family Stone-Anthology* . . . . (Epic)
There's A Riot Goin' On . . . . (Epic)
Theme From "Mr. Ed"
Original Soundtrack; *Television's Greatest Hits-#1-C* . . . . (TVT)
Then The Morning Comes
Smash Mouth; *Astro Lounge* . . . . (Interscope)
Now That's What I Call Music!-#4-C . . . . (Virgin)
Thinkin' Out Loud
Band; *Cahoots* . . . . (Capitol)
This Heart Speaks For Itself
Bobbie Cryner; *Bobbie Cryner* . . . . (Epic)
This Is Me
Randy Travis; *This Is Me* . . . . (Warner Bros.)
Trash Talkin'
Albert Collins; *Albert Collins-Complete Imperial Recordings* . . . . (EMI)
Walkin', Talkin'...Beatin' Broken Heart
Highway 101; *Country's Greatest Hits-#4-Sweet Country-C* . . . . (Priority)

Paint The Town . . . .(Warner Bros.)

We Better Talk This Over
Bob Dylan; *Street Legal* . . . . (Columbia)

We Can Talk
Band; *Music From Big Pink* . . . . (Capitol)

We Don't Have To Talk (About Love)
Peabo Bryson; *Don't Play With Fire* . . . . (Capitol)
The Peabo Bryson Collection . . . . (Capitol)

We Don't Talk Anymore
Cliff Richard; *We Don't Talk Anymore* . . . .(EMI)

What They're Talkin' About
Rhett Akins; *A Thousand Memories* . . . . (Decca)

When I Get Home
Beatles; *Beatles-Box Set* . . . . (Capitol)
Something New . . . . (Capitol)

When Love Starts Talkin'
Wynonna; *The Other Side* . . . . (Curb/MCA)

When The Generals Talk
Midnight Oil; *Red Sails In The Sunset* . . . . (Columbia)

When You Talk About Love
Patti LaBelle; *Flame* . . . .(MCA)
Live! One Night Only . . . .(MCA)

Within You Without You
Beatles; *Beatles-Box Set* . . . . (Capitol)
Sgt. Pepper's Lonely Hearts Club Band. . . . . (Capitol)

Wond'ring Aloud
Jethro Tull; *20 Years Of Jethro Tull* . . . .(Chrysalis)
Aqualung . . . .(Chrysalis)

Wouldn't It Be Nice
Beach Boys; *Absolutely Best-#2* . . . . (Capitol)
Made In The U.S.A. . . . . (Capitol)
Pet Sounds . . . . (Capitol)
Still Cruisin' . . . . (Capitol)

Yakety Yak
2 Live Crew; *ST/Twins* . . . .(WTG)
Coasters; *Atlantic Rhythm & Blues 1947-1974-#3 (1955-1958)-C* . . . . .(Atlantic)
Billboard Top Rock 'N' Roll Hits-1958-C . . . . (Rhino)
Coasters' Greatest Hits . . . . (Atco)
Cruisin'-1958-C . . . . (Increase)
ST/Stand By Me . . . . (Atlantic)

You Should Hear How She Talks About You
Melissa Manchester; *Hey Ricky* . . . . (Arista)
Melissa Manchester's Greatest Hits . . . . (Arista)

You Talk Too Much
Cheap Trick; *Next Position Please* . . . .(Epic)

You Talk Too Much
Joe Jones; *American Graffiti-#3-C* . . . .(MCA)
Billboard Top Rock 'N' Roll Hits-1960-C . . . . (Rhino)
Carnival Time-Best Of Ric Records-#1-C . . . . (Rounder)
Echoes Of A Rock Era-Middle Years-C . . . . (Roulette)
Original Rock 'N' Roll Hits Of The '60s-C . . . . (Roulette)

You Talk Too Much
George Thorogood & The Destroyers; *Born To Be Bad* . . . .(Gold Rush)

You Talk Too Much
Run-D.M.C.; *King Of Rock.* . . . . (Profile)

You've Got To Talk To Me
Lee Ann Womack; *Lee Ann Womack* . . . . (Decca)

COMMUNICATION: TELL
See Also: **COMMUNICATION (various), GOSSIP**

(Everything I Do) I Do It For You
Bryan Adams; *ST/Robin Hood: Prince Of Thieves* . . . .(Morgan Creek)
Waking Up The Neighbours . . . . (A&M)

(We've Been Told) Jesus Is Coming Soon
Eric Clapton; *There's One In Every Crowd* . . . . (Polydor)

Achy Breaky Heart
Billy Ray Cyrus; *Some Gave All* . . . . (Mercury)

And I Am Telling You I'm Not Going
Jennifer Holliday/Original Cast; *Dreamgirls* . . . .(Geffen)

Any Major Dude Will Tell You
Steely Dan; *Pretzel Logic* . . . .(MCA)
Steely Dan's Greatest Hits. . . . .(MCA)

Baby Won't You Tell Me
Johnny Hammond; *Big City Blues* . . . . (Vanguard)

Bible Tells Me So
Don Cornell; *Rock 'N Roll Reunion: Class Of '55-C* . . . . (Madacy)

Birds And The Bees
Jewel Akens; *American Graffiti-#3-C* . . . .(MCA)
Collectables Presents The History Of Rock-#4-C . . . . (Collectables)
Cruisin'-1965-C . . . . (Increase)
Oldies But Goodies-#9-C . . . . (Original Sound)
Super Hits-#3-C. . . . . (Gusto)

Blue Monday
Orgy; *Candyass* . . . . (Elementree/Reprise)

Blues In The Night
Benny Goodman; *Small Groups-1941-1945* . . . . (Columbia)
Bobby Bland; *Introspective Of The Early Years* . . . . (MCA)
Dinah Shore; *Nipper's Greatest Hits Of The '40s-#1-C* . . . .(RCA)
Doc Severinsen; *Best Of Doc Severinsen* . . . . (MCA)
Frank Sinatra; *Frank Sinatra sings for Only The Lonely* . . . . (Capitol)
Jimmie Lunceford & His Orchestra; *Warner Bros.' 75 Years Entertaining The World-Film Music-C.* . . . . (Rhino)
Mel Torme; *Torme* . . . . (Verve)
Robins; *Best Of The Robins.* . . . .(Crescendo)
Rosemary Clooney; *Rosemary Clooney-16 Most Requested Songs* . . . . (Legacy)
Tony Bennett; *Playin' With My Friends-Bennett Sings The Blues-C* . . . . (Columbia)
Woody Herman; *Blues On Parade* . . . . (GRP)
Woody Herman-Best Of The Decca Years . . . . (Decca)
Woody Herman & His Orchestra; *Big Bands Greatest Hits-#3-C.* . . . . (MCA Special Prod.)

But Anyway
Blues Traveler; *Blues Traveler* . . . . (A&M)
Live From The Fall. . . . . (A&M)

Can You Dance (Baby Tell Me)
Shanice Wilson; *Discovery* . . . . (A&M)

Darkness On The Edge Of Town
Bruce Springsteen; *Darkness On The Edge Of Town* . . . . (Columbia)
Bruce Springsteen & The E Street Band; *Bruce Springsteen & The E Street Band Live/1975-85* . . . . (Legacy)

Do Ya Think I'm Sexy?
Rod Stewart; *Absolutely Live* . . . . (Warner Bros.)
Blondes Have More Fun. . . . . (Warner Bros.)
Rod Stewart's Greatest Hits . . . . (Warner Bros.)

Don't Tell Me
Madonna; *GHV2* . . . . (Warner Bros.)
Music . . . . (Maverick)

Don't Tell Me Lies
Breathe; *All That Jazz* . . . . (A&M)

Don't Tell Me No
Cars; *Panorama* . . . . (Elektra)

Don't Tell Me What To Do
Pam Tillis; *Put Yourself In My Place* . . . . (Arista)

Don't Tell Me You Love Me
Night Ranger; *Dawn Patrol* . . . . (Camel)
Night Ranger's Greatest Hits . . . .(Camel)

Don't Tell Me Your Troubles
Doc Watson; *Memories* . . . . (Sugar Hill)
Don Gibson; *45-#7566* . . . .(RCA)
Ray Charles; *Greatest Country & Western Hits* . . . . (Dunhill Compact Classics)

Don't Tell Your Mama
Eddie Floyd; *Eddie Floyd-Chronicle* . . . . (Stax)

Don'tcha Tell Henry
Bob Dylan And The Band; *Basement Tapes* . . . . (Columbia)

Drops Of Jupiter (Tell Me)
Train; *Drops Of Jupiter* . . . . (Aware/C2/Columbia)

For Your Love
Stevie Wonder; *Conversation Peace* . . . . (Motown)
Natural Wonder . . . . (Motown)
Song Review-A Greatest Hits Collection . . . . (Motown)

Gel
Collective Soul; *Collective Soul* . . . .(Atlantic)
ST/Jerky Boys . . . .(Atlantic)

Girl Don't Tell Me
Beach Boys; *Beach Boys-Gift Set* . . . . (Capitol)
California Girls . . . . (Capitol)
Endless Summer . . . . (Capitol)

Give The Girl A Kiss
Bruce Springsteen; *Tracks* . . . . (Columbia)

Go Tell It On The Mountain
Bobby Darin; *Bobby Darin-25th Day Of December* . . . . (Atco)
Bruce Cockburn; *Christmas* . . . . (Columbia)
Dolly Parton; *Home For Christmas.* . . . . (Columbia)
Don McLean; *Christmas* . . . . (Curb)
Garth Brooks; *Beyond The Season* . . . . (Liberty)
Simon & Garfunkel; *Collected Works.* . . . . (Columbia)
Wednesday Morning 3 A.M. . . . . (Columbia)
Weavers; *On Tour.* . . . . (Vanguard)

Gotta Tell You
Samantha Mumba; *Gotta Tell You* . . . .(Wildcard/Polydor/Interscope)
Now That's What I Call Music!-#6-C . . . . (Virgin)

Grandma Told Grandpa
Lightnin' Hopkins; *Drinkin' In The Blues-Golden Classics-#1* . . . (Collectables)

Grandpa (Tell Me 'Bout The Good Old Days)
Judds; *Judds' Greatest Hits.* . . . .(MCA)
Rockin' With The Rhythm. . . . .(MCA)
Super 10-#2-C . . . .(RCA)

Have I Told You Lately
Rod Stewart; *Unplugged...And Seated* . . . . (Warner Bros.)
Vagabond Heart. . . . . (Warner Bros.)
Van Morrison; *Best Of Van Morrison.* . . . .(Polydor)

Have I Told You Lately?
Original Cast; *I Can Get It For You Wholesale* . . . . (Columbia)

Hello
Lionel Richie; *Back To Front* .... (Motown)
   Can't Slow Down .... (Motown)
   Truly-The Love Songs .... (Motown)
Luther Vandross; *Songs* .... (Epic)
Hold Me
Brian McKnight; *Anytime* .... (Motown)
Hold Me, Thrill Me, Kiss Me
Mel Carter; *Baby Boomer Classics-Love Sixties-C* .... (JCI Assoc. Labels)
How Do I Get There
Deana Carter; *Did I Shave My Legs For This?.* .... (Capitol)
How Do You Tell The One
After 7; *Reflections* .... (Virgin)
I Can't Tell You Why
Brownstone; *From The Bottom Up* .... (MJJ/Epic)
Eagles; *Eagles Greatest Hits, Volume 2* .... (Asylum)
   Eagles Live .... (Asylum)
   The Long Run .... (Asylum)
Vince Gill; *Common Thread-Songs Of The Eagles-C* .... (Giant)
I Could Have Told You
Frank Sinatra; *No One Cares* .... (Capitol)
I Feel Fine
Beatles; *Beatles 1.* .... (Capitol)
   Beatles '65. .... (Capitol)
   Beatles-20 Greatest Hits. .... (Capitol)
   Past Masters-Volume One .... (Parlophone)
   The Beatles/1962-1966. .... (Capitol)
Sweethearts Of The Rodeo; *One Time One Night* .... (Columbia)
I Heard It Through The Grapevine
Creedence Clearwater Revival; *Chooglin'* .... (Fantasy)
   Cosmo's Factory. .... (Fantasy)
   Creedence Clearwater Revival-Chronicle .... (Fantasy)
   Creedence Clearwater Revival-Gold .... (Fantasy)
   Movie Album. .... (Fantasy)
Gladys Knight & The Pips; *16 #1 Hits From The Late '60s-C* .... (Motown)
   Compact Command Performances-Gladys Knight & The Pips ..... (Motown)
   Every Great Motown Song-First 25 Years-C .... (Motown)
   Motown Grammy R&B Performances Of The '60s & '70s-C ...... (Motown)
   Motown Superstar Series-#13-Gladys Knight & The Pips ...... (Motown)
   Top 10 With A Bullet-Motown Girl Groups-C .... (Motown)
Marvin Gaye; *25 #1 Hits From 25 Years-C* .... (Motown)
   Every Great Motown Hit Of Marvin Gaye .... (Motown)
   Marvin Gaye Live At The London Palladium .... (Motown)
   Marvin Gaye-Anthology .... (Motown)
   Most Played Songs On America's Jukeboxes .... (Motown)
   Motown Story-First 25 Years-C .... (Motown)
I Tell It Like It Used To Be
T. Graham Brown; *45-#5524.* .... (Capitol)
I Think I'm In Love With You
Jessica Simpson; *Now That's What I Call Music!-#5-C* ...... (Virgin)
   Sweet Kisses .... (Columbia)
I Wanna Be Your Man
Beatles; *Meet The Beatles!* .... (Capitol)
   Rock 'N' Roll Music .... (Capitol)
I Want It That Way
Backstreet Boys; *Millennium.* .... (Jive)
I Want To Hold Your Hand
Beatles; *Beatles 1.* .... (Capitol)
   Beatles-20 Greatest Hits. .... (Capitol)
   Meet The Beatles! .... (Capitol)
   Past Masters-Volume One .... (Parlophone)
   The Beatles/1962-1966. .... (Capitol)
Lakeside; *Galactic Grooves/Best Of Lakeside* .... (Right Stuff)
   Your Wish Is My Command. .... (Solar)
I Want To Tell You
Beatles; *Revolver.* .... (Capitol)
If I Could Talk I'd Tell You
Lemonheads; *Car Button Cloth* .... (Tag/Atlantic)
If You Love Me (Let Me Know)
Olivia Newton-John; *Back To Basics-Essential Collection 1971-1992.* ... (Geffen)
   If You Love Me Let Me Know .... (MCA)
   Olivia Newton-John's Greatest Hits. .... (MCA)
If You Really Love Me
Stevie Wonder; *Stevie Wonder's Greatest Hits-#2* .... (Motown)
   Where I'm Coming From. .... (Motown)
If You See Him/If You See Her
Brooks & Dunn & Reba McEntire; *If You See Her* .... (Arista)
Reba McEntire & Brooks & Dunn; *If You See Him* .... (MCA)
   Reba McEntire's Greatest Hits-#3: I'm A Survivor ...... (MCA)
I'll Be
Edwin McCain; *Misguided Roses* .... (Lava)
I'm Telling You Now
Freddie And The Dreamers; *History Of British Rock-#1-C.* ..... (Rhino)
I'm Telling You Now
Keb' Mo'; *Slow Down* .... (550/Epic/Okeh)
In The Cool, Cool, Cool Of The Evening
Bing Crosby; *Best Of Bing Crosby* .... (MCA)
Frank Sinatra; *Days Of Wine And Roses, Moon River, And Other Academy*
   Award Winners .... (Reprise)

Rosemary Clooney; *Rosemary Clooney-16 Most Requested Songs* ..... (Legacy)
Informer
Snow; *12 Inches Of Snow.* .... (East West)
It's Bad You Know
R.L. Burnside; *The Sopranos-Music From The HBO Original*
   Series .... (Sony Music Soundtrax)
It's Your Thing
Isley Brothers; *Billboard Top R&B Hits-1969-C* .... (Rhino)
   The Isley Brothers Story-#2-The T-Neck Years-1969-1985. ..... (Rhino)
   Timeless. .... (T-Neck/Columbia)
I've Told Ev'ry Little Star
David Allyn; *David Allyn Sings Jerome Kern* .... (Discovery)
Linda Scott; *Billboard Top Pop Hits-1961-C.* .... (Rhino)
Just Tell Her Jim Said Hello
Elvis Presley; *Collector's Gold* .... (RCA)
   Elvis' Gold Records, Volume 4 .... (RCA)
   The Other Sides-Worldwide Gold Award Hits, Vol. 2 .... (RCA)
Lately
Tyrese; *Tyrese.* .... (RCA)
Leader Of Men
Nickelback; *State* .... (Roadrunner)
Leave Me Alone
Jerry Cantrell; *ST/The Cable Guy.* .... (Work)
Let Me Call You Sweetheart
Bette Midler; *ST/The Rose.* .... (Atlantic)
Billy Vaughn & His Orchestra; *Billy Vaughn & His Orchestra Play 22 Of*
   His Greatest Hits .... (Ranwood)
Bing Crosby; *Bing Crosby-Love Songs* .... (Universal)
Bob Ralston; *22 Great Organ Hits-#2* .... (Ranwood)
Gene Autry; *Gene Autry-Love Songs* .... (Varese Sarabande)
Lawrence Welk; *American Favorites.* .... (Ranwood)
Peerless Quartet; *78-#1057* .... (Columbia)
Let Me Tell You About Love
Judds; *River Of Time* .... (RCA)
Little Things
Tanya Tucker; *Complicated.* .... (Capitol)
Little White Lies
Dick Haymes with Gordon Jenkins & His Orchestra; *Sentimental Journey:*
   Pop Vocal Classics-#2-1947-1950-C. .... (Rhino)
Dinah Shore; *Dinah Shore-16 Most Requested Songs-Encore!* ..... (Legacy)
Fred Waring's Pennsylvanians featuring Clare Hanlon; *Very Best Of Fred*
   Waring & The Pennsylvanians .... (Reader's Digest Music)
Tommy Dorsey; *Best Of Tommy Dorsey* .... (Bluebird)
   Complete Tommy Dorsey-#6. .... (RCA)
Love Untold
Paul Westerberg; *Eventually* .... (Reprise)
Mama Done Told Me
Miracles; *Greatest Hits From The Beginning* .... (Motown)
Mama Told Me Not To Come
Randy Newman; *12 Songs* .... (Reprise)
   Randy Newman/Live .... (Warner Archives)
Three Dog Night; *Best Of Three Dog Night* .... (MCA)
   Billboard Top Rock 'N' Roll Hits-1970-C. .... (Rhino)
Wilson Pickett; *Wilson Pickett's Greatest Hits* .... (Atlantic)
Midnight Confessions
Grass Roots; *Grass Roots-Anthology (1966-1975)* .... (Rhino)
   Original Rock 'N' Roll Hits Of The '60s-C .... (Roulette)
   Vintage Music-#9-C .... (MCA)
Most Beautiful Girl
Charlie Rich; *Behind Closed Doors* .... (Epic)
   Charlie Rich's Greatest Hits .... (Epic)
   Columbia Country Classics-#4-Nashville Sound-C ...... (Columbia)
My Heart Can't Tell Me No
Rod Stewart; *Downtown Train-Selections From The Storyteller*
   Anthology. .... (Warner Bros.)
   Out Of Order. .... (Warner Bros.)
   Storyteller/The Complete Anthology: 1964-1990 .... (Warner Bros.)
My Heart Tells Me
Etta Jones; *Something Nice* .... (Original Jazz Classics)
Nat "King" Cole; *Very Thought Of You* .... (Capitol)
Never Ever
All Saints; *All Saints.* .... (London)
   Now That's What I Call Music!-#1-C .... (Virgin)
No Tell Lover
Chicago; *Chicago's Greatest Hits-#2 (1974-81)* .... (Chicago)
   Group Portrait .... (Chicago)
   Hot Streets. .... (Columbia)
   If You Leave Me Now. .... (Chicago)
Nobody Told Me
John Lennon; *Lennon.* .... (Capitol)
John Lennon & Yoko Ono; *Milk & Honey.* .... (Polydor)
Please
Bing Crosby; *Bing Crosby-16 Most Requested Songs* ...... (Legacy)
Please Don't Tell Her
Big Head Todd & The Monsters; *Beautiful World* .... (Revolution)
   Live Monsters. .... (Revolution)
Roll Over Beethoven
Beatles; *Beatles-Box Set.* .... (Capitol)
   Rock 'N' Roll Music. .... (Capitol)

The Beatles At The Hollywood Bowl . . . . (Capitol)
The Beatles' Second Album . . . . (Capitol)
With The Beatles . . . . (Parlophone)
Byrds; *The Byrds* . . . . (Columbia)
Chuck Berry; *Chuck Berry-Golden Hits* . . . . (Mercury)
Chuck Berry's Greatest Hits . . . . (Everest)
Cruisin'-1956-C . . . . (Increase)
Oldies But Goodies-#10-C . . . . (Original Sound)
The Chess Box-Chuck Berry . . . . (Chess)
Electric Light Orchestra; *Afterglow* . . . . (Epic)
Ole ELO . . . . (Jet)

Scarborough Fair/Canticle
Simon & Garfunkel; *Collected Works* . . . . (Columbia)
Parsley Sage Rosemary & Thyme . . . . (Columbia)
Simon & Garfunkel's Greatest Hits . . . . (Columbia)
ST/The Graduate . . . . (Columbia)
The Concert In Central Park . . . . (Warner Bros.)

Secrets Told
Kim Waters; *One Special Moment* . . . . (Shanachie)

She Came In Through The Bathroom Window
Beatles; *Abbey Road* . . . . (Parlophone)
Beatles-Box Set . . . . (Capitol)
Joe Cocker; *Joe Cocker Live* . . . . (A&M)
Joe Cocker! . . . . (A&M)
Joe Cocker-Classics-#4 . . . . (A&M)
Mad Dogs & Englishmen . . . . (A&M)

She Cried
Jay & The Americans; *Come A Little Bit Closer-Best Of Jay & The
Americans* . . . . (Gold Rush)
Jay & The Americans' All-Time Greatest Hits . . . . (Rhino)
Jay & The Americans' Greatest Hits . . . . (Curb)

She's Not There
Santana; *Moonflower* . . . . (Columbia)
Viva Santana! . . . . (Columbia)
Vanilla Fudge; *Vanilla Fudge* . . . . (Atco)
Zombies; *Best & The Rest Of The Zombies* . . . . (Epic)
Billboard Top Rock 'N' Roll Hits-1964-C . . . . (Rhino)
History Of British Rock-#1-C . . . . (Rhino)
Time Of The Zombies . . . . (Bac-Trac)

Shop Around
Captain & Tennille; *Captain & Tennille's Greatest Hits* . . . . (A&M)
Miracles; *Greatest Hits From The Beginning* . . . . (Motown)
Hi-We're The Miracles . . . . (Motown)
Smokey Robinson & The Miracles; *16 #1 Hits From The Early
'60s-C* . . . . (Motown)
Every Great Motown Song-First 25 Years-C . . . . (Motown)
Smokey Robinson & The Miracles' Anthology . . . . (Motown)

Show Don't Tell
Rush; *Presto* . . . . (Atlantic)
Rush-Chronicles . . . . (Mercury)

Show Me The Meaning Of Being Lonely
Backstreet Boys; *Millennium* . . . . (Jive)
Now That's What I Call Music!-#5-C . . . . (Virgin)

Sing Me A Love Song To Baby
Billy Walker; *45-#14422* . . . . (MGM)

Someone Should Tell Her
Mavericks; *Trampoline* . . . . (MCA)

Still...You Turn Me On
Emerson, Lake & Palmer; *Best Of Emerson, Lake & Palmer* . . . . . (Rhino)
Brain Salad Surgery . . . . (Rhino)
From The Beginning-The Greg Lake Retrospective . . . . (Rhino)

Stories I Tell
Toad The Wet Sprocket; *Fear* . . . . (Columbia)

Stories We Could Tell
Jimmy Buffett; *A1A* . . . . (MCA)
John Sebastian; *Best Of John Sebastian* . . . . (Rhino)
Tom Petty And The Heartbreakers; *Pack Up The Plantation-Live!* . . . (MCA)

Straight Up
Paula Abdul; *Disco Queens-The '80s-C* . . . . (Rhino)
First Generation: 25 Years Of Virgin Records-C . . . . (Virgin)
Forever Your Girl . . . . (Virgin)
Shut Up And Dance . . . . (Virgin)
Shut Up And Dance (The Dance Mixes) . . . . (Virgin)

Take It On Faith
Joshua Kadison; *Delilah Blue* . . . . (EMI)

Tell All The People
Doors; *Soft Parade* . . . . (Elektra)

Tell 'Em I'm Surfing
Fantastic Baggies; *Monster Summer Hits-Wild Surf-C* . . . . . . (Capitol)

Tell Her
Lonestar; *Lonely Grill* . . . . (BNA)

Tell Her About It
Billy Joel; *An Innocent Man* . . . . (Columbia)
Billy Joel-Greatest Hits, Volume I & Volume II . . . . (Columbia)

Tell Her No
Juice Newton; *Dirty Looks* . . . . (Capitol)
Juice Newton-Greatest Hits & More . . . . (Capitol)
Zombies; *Best Of The Rest Of The Zombies* . . . . (Bac-Trac)
History Of British Rock-#2-C . . . . (Rhino)

Live On The BBC . . . . (Rhino)
Time Of The Zombies . . . . (Bac-Trac)

Tell Him
Barbra Streisand & Celine Dion; *Higher Ground* . . . . (Columbia)
Celine Dion & Barbra Streisand; *Let's Talk About Love-C* . . . . (550 Music)

Tell Him No
Travis & Bob; *The History Of Dot-#2-Come Go
With Me-C* . . . . (Varese Sarabande)

Tell It Like It Is
Aaron Neville; *Classic Aaron Neville* . . . . (Rounder)
Soul Shots-#5-La-La Means I Love You-C . . . . (Rhino)
Super Oldies Of The '60s-#7-C . . . . (Audio Fidelity)
Tell It Like It Is . . . . (Curb)
Tell it Like It Is-Golden Classics . . . . (Collectables)
Treacherous: A History Of The Neville Brothers . . . . (Rhino)
Billy Joe Royal; *Billy Joe Royal's Greatest Hits* . . . . (Atlantic)
Tell It Like It Is . . . . (Atlantic)
George Benson; *Best Of George Benson* . . . . (A&M)
UB40; *Live In Moscow* . . . . (A&M)
Rat In The Kitchen . . . . (A&M)

Tell It To Carrie
Romantics; *The Romantics* . . . . (Columbia)
What I Like About You (And Other Romantic Hits) . . . . (Nemperor)

Tell It To My Heart
Taylor Dayne; *Rock The First-#6-C* . . . . (Sandstone Music)
Tell It To My Heart . . . . (Arista)

Tell It To The Judge
Monotones; *Best Of Chess Vocal Groups-C* . . . . (Chess)

Tell It To The Judge On Sunday
Long Ryders; *Native Sons* . . . . (Frontier)

Tell It To The Rain
4 Seasons; *4 Seasons' Greatest Hits-#2* . . . . (Rhino)
4 Seasons-Anthology . . . . (Rhino)

Tell Laura I Love Her
Ray Peterson; *Nipper's Greatest Hits Of The '60s-#1-C* . . . . . (RCA)
Teenage Tragedies-C . . . . (Rhino)

Tell Mama
Etta James; *Didn't It Blow Your Mind: Soul Hits Of The '70s-#1-C* . . . . (Rhino)
Essential Etta James . . . . (Chess)
Tell Mama . . . . (Chess)
Janis Joplin; *Janis* . . . . (Legacy)
Savoy Brown; *Savoy Brown-London Collector* . . . . (London)
Street Corner Talking . . . . (Deram)

Tell Me
Stevie Ray Vaughan and Double Trouble; *Stevie Ray Vaughan and Double
Trouble-In The Beginning* . . . . (Epic Portrait Assoc.)
Texas Flood . . . . (Epic)

Tell Me
Dru Hill; *ST/Eddie* . . . . (Island)

Tell Me
Groove Theory; *Groove Theory* . . . . (Epic)
MTV Party To Go-#9-C . . . . (Tommy Boy)

Tell Me
Bangles; *All Over The Place* . . . . (Columbia)

Tell Me
White Lion; *Best Of White Lion* . . . . (Atlantic)
Pride . . . . (Atlantic)

Tell Me
Al Jarreau; *High Crime* . . . . (Warner Bros.)

Tell Me
Kenny G; *Kenny G* . . . . (Arista)

Tell Me
Lionel Richie; *Lionel Richie* . . . . (Motown)

Tell Me
Bob Dylan; *The Bootleg Series-Volumes 1-3 [Rare & Unreleased]* . . (Columbia)

Tell Me
Howlin' Wolf; *The Chess Box-Howlin' Wolf* . . . . (Chess)

Tell Me
Fabulous Thunderbirds; *Tuff Enuff* . . . . (Epic Portrait Assoc.)

Tell Me (How It Feels)
52nd St.; *Children Of The Night* . . . . (MCA)

Tell Me (You're Coming Back)
Rolling Stones; *Big Hits (High Tide & Green Grass)* . . . . (Abkco)
England's Newest Hit Makers/The Rolling Stones . . . . (Abkco)
More Hot Rocks (big hits & fazed cookies) . . . . (Abkco)
Singles Collection-The London Years . . . . (Abkco)

Tell Me A Bedtime Story
Norman Connors; *Remember Who You Are* . . . . (Mojazz)
Quincy Jones; *Sounds... And Stuff Like That!!* . . . . (A&M)

Tell Me A Lie
Janie Fricke; *19 Hot Country Requests-C* . . . . (Epic)
Greatest Country Hits Of The '80s-1983-C . . . . (Columbia)
It Ain't Easy . . . . (Columbia)
Janie Fricke-17 Greatest Hits . . . . (Columbia)
Love Lies . . . . (Columbia)
Very Best Of Janie Fricke . . . . (Columbia)

Tell Me About It
Tanya Tucker & Delbert McClinton; *Can't Run From Yourself* . . . . . . (Liberty)

Tell Me All The Things You Do
Fleetwood Mac; *Kiln House* ....(Reprise)

Tell Me Do U Wanna
Ginuwine; *Ginuwine...The Bachelor*. .... (550 Music)

Tell Me I Was Dreaming
Travis Tritt; *Ten Feet Tall And Bulletproof*. . . . . (Warner Bros.)
Travis Tritt's Greatest Hits-From The Beginning. . . . . (Warner Bros.)

Tell Me If You Still Care
S.O.S. Band; *On The Rise* ....(Tabu)

Tell Me I'm Crazy
Shelby Lynne; *Temptation*. .... (Morgan Creek)

Tell Me I'm Not Dreamin'
Jermaine Jackson; *Jermaine Jackson* .... (Arista)

Tell Me I'm Not Dreaming
Robert Palmer; *Heavy Nova* ....(EMI)

Tell Me I'm October
Porn Orchard; *Urges & Angers* ....(C/Z)

Tell Me I'm Only Dreaming
Lorrie Morgan; *Lorrie Morgan-Classics*. ....(Curb)

Tell Me It's Real
K-Ci & JoJo; *It's Real* . . . . (Rock Land/Interscope)
Now That's What I Call Music!-#3-C ....(Virgin)

Tell Me On A Sunday
Marti Webb; *Premiere Collection-Best Of Andrew Lloyd Webber-C* .... (MCA)
Michael Crawford; *Michael Crawford Performs Andrew Lloyd Webber*. .... (Atlantic)

Tell Me Something Good
Rufus; *Rags To Rufus* ....(MCA)
Rufus Featuring Chaka Khan; *Classic Soul-C* ....(MCA)
Live-Stompin' At The Savoy .... (Warner Bros.)

Tell Me That It Isn't True
Bob Dylan; *Nashville Skyline* .... (Columbia)

Tell Me That You Love Me
Eric Clapton; *Backless*. ....(Polydor)

Tell Me The Truth
Midnight Oil; *Alternative NRG* ....(Hollywood)
Earth & Sun & Moon ....(Columbia)

Tell Me The Truth
Billy Stewart; *One More Time/Chess Years* .... (Chess)

Tell Me The Truth
Timothy B. Schmit; *Tell Me The Truth* .... (MCA)

Tell Me This Is A Dream
Delfonics; *Best Of The Delfonics*. ....(Arista)

Tell Me To My Face
Dan Fogelberg & Tim Weisberg; *Twin Sons Of Different Mothers* . ... (Full Moon)

Tell Me Tomorrow
Angela Bofill; *Angela Bofill*. ....(Arista)
Best Of Angela Bofill. ....(Arista)
Karyn White; *Karyn White* .... (Warner Bros.)
Smokey Robinson; *Blame It On Love & All The Great Hits* .... (Motown)

Tell Me What The Papers Say
Elton John; *Ice On Fire* ....(MCA)

Tell Me What You See
Beatles; *Beatles VI*. ....(Capitol)
Beatles-Box Set. ....(Capitol)
Beatles-Love Songs. ....(Capitol)

Tell Me What You Want
Doobie Brothers; *What Were Once Vices Are Now Habits* ...... (Warner Bros.)

Tell Me What You Want Me To Do
Tevin Campbell; *T.E.V.I.N.* ....(Qwest)

Tell Me When The Whistle Blows
Elton John; *Captain Fantastic And The Brown Dirt Cowboy* .... (Polydor)

Tell Me Why
Beatles; *Beatles-Box Set* ....(Capitol)
Something New ....(Capitol)
ST/A Hard Day's Night. ....(Capitol)

Tell Me Why
Sunbeams; *Harlem Holiday-New York Rhythm & Blues-#5-C* .... (Collectables)

Tell Me Why
Belmonts; *Classic Old & Gold-C* ....(Laurie)
I Got Rhythm-C. ....(K-Tel)

Tell Me Why
Mavericks; *Trampoline* . . . . (MCA)

Tell Me Why
Elvis Presley; *A Valentine Gift For You*. ....(RCA)
The King Of Rock 'N' Roll-The Complete 50's Masters ....(RCA)
The Other Sides-Worldwide Gold Award Hits, Vol. 2. ....(RCA)

Tell Me Why
Bobby Vinton; *Bobby Vinton-16 Most Requested Songs*............. (Legacy)
Bobby Vinton's Greatest Hits/Greatest Hits Of Love .... (Columbia)
Four Aces; *Four Aces' Greatest Hits*. ....(MCA)

Tell Me Why
Wynonna; *Tell Me Why* ....(MCA)

Tell Me Why
Neil Young; *After The Gold Rush* ....(Reprise)

Tell Me Why
Berlin; *Pleasure Victim* . ...(Geffen)

Tell Me Why
Jann Browne; *'Til A Tear Becomes A Rose* ....(Curb)

Tell Me Why
Genesis; *We Can't Dance*. ....(Atlantic)

Tell That To The Marines
Al Jolson; *Music From The New York Stage (1890-1920)-#4-1917-1920-C* . ... (Pearl)

Tell The Truth
Otis Redding; *Best Of Otis Redding* . . . .(Atco)
Tell The Truth . . . . (Rhino)
The Otis Redding Story .... (Atlantic)
Ray Charles; *Birth Of Soul-Complete Atlantic R&B 1952-1959-C* .... (Atlantic)

Tell The Truth
Derek And The Dominos; *Derek & The Dominos In Concert* .... (RSO)
Eric Clapton-Crossroads-C ....(Polydor)
Layla. ....(Polydor)

Tell The Truth
David Lee Roth; *A Little Ain't Enough*. .... (Warner Bros.)

Tell The Truth
Lee Roy Parnell; *Tell The Truth* ....(Vanguard)

Tell The World
Dells; *Harlem New York-Ballad Era-C* ....(Collectables)

Tell The World
Ratt; *Ratt & Roll 8191* .... (Atlantic)

Tell The World How I Feel About 'Cha Baby
Harold Melvin And The Blue Notes; *Wake Up Everybody* ...(Philadelphia Int'l)

Telling Me Lies
Dolly Parton/Emmylou Harris/Linda Ronstadt; *Trio* .... (Warner Bros.)

Telling Stories
Tracy Chapman; *Telling Stories*. ....(Elektra)

Tender Moment, A
Lee Roy Parnell; *Hits And Highways Ahead* ....(Arista)
Love Without Mercy ....(Arista)
Pure Country-Best Of The '90s-C ....(Priority)

Then You Can Tell Me Goodbye
Casinos; *Then You Can Tell Me Goodbye* .... (Varese Vintage)
Neal McCoy; *Neal McCoy's Greatest Hits* .... (Atlantic)

Thing Called Love
Bonnie Raitt; *Nick Of Time* ....(Capitol)

This Woman Needs
SHeDAISY; *The Whole Shebang*. .... (Lyric Street)

Tulip Or Turnip (Tell Me Dream Face)
Duke Ellington & Teresa Brewer; *It Don't Mean A Thing If It Ain't Got That Swing* . ...(Columbia)

We Tell Ourselves
Clint Black; *The Hard Way* .... (RCA)

What Can I Tell My Heart
Vanessa Williams; *The Comfort Zone* .... (Wing)

What You Won't Do For Love
Bobby Caldwell; *Love Shouldn't Hurt-C* .... (Qwest)
Go West; *Chicken Soup For The Woman's Soul-C* ....(Rhino)

When You Ask About Love
Crickets; *45-#9-55153* .... (Brunswick)

Whispering Pines
Johnny Horton; *Johnny Horton's Greatest Hits*................(Columbia)

Why
Annie Lennox; *Diva*. ....(Arista)

Wind Beneath My Wings
Bette Midler; *ST/Beaches*. .... (Atlantic)
Gary Morris; *Chicken Soup For The Soul: I'll Be There For You-Songs Of Friendship, Brotherhood And Sisterhood-C*. ....(Rhino)
Country Love Songs-C ....(Warner Bros.)
Gary Morris-Hits ....(Warner Bros.)
Why Lady Why. ....(Warner Bros.)
James Galway; *Wind Beneath My Wings* .... (RCA)
Lee Greenwood; *Somebody's Gonna Love You* ....(MCA)
Lou Rawls; *When The Night Comes* ....(Epic)
Roger Whittaker; *Roger Whittaker Greatest Hits* ....(RCA)
Wind Beneath My Wings. ....(RCA)
Willie Nelson; *City Of New Orleans* ....(Columbia)

Wonderful
Everclear; *Now That's What I Call Music!-#5-C* .... (Virgin)
Songs From An American Movie-#1-Learning How To Smile ....(Capitol)

You Belong To Me
Carly Simon; *Boys In The Trees* ....(Elektra)
Carly Simon-Greatest Hits Live ....(Arista)
Chicken Soup For The Woman's Soul-C ....(Rhino)
Doobie Brothers; *Best Of The Doobies, Volume II* . . . . (Warner Bros.)
Livin' On The Fault Line ....(Warner Bros.)

You Can Tell The World
Simon & Garfunkel; *Collected Works* ....(Columbia)
Wednesday Morning 3 A.M. ....(Columbia)

You Can't Do That
Beatles; *Beatles-Box Set* ....(Capitol)
Rock 'N' Roll Music . ...(Capitol)
The Beatles' Second Album. ....(Capitol)

You Caused It All By Telling Lies
Hank Williams; *Alone With His Guitar* ....(Mercury)

Complete Hank Williams . . . . (Mercury)
You Should've Told Me
    Kelly Price; *Mirror Mirror* . . . .(Def Soul/IDJMG)
You Tell Me
    Johnny Cash; *Original Johnny Cash.* . . . . (Sun)
    Tom Petty And The Heartbreakers; *Damn The Torpedoes* . . . .(MCA)

COMMUNICATION: WHISPER

See Also: **COMMUNICATION (various), GOSSIP**

(I Could Only) Whisper Your Name
    Harry Connick, Jr.; *She* . . . . (Columbia)
    ST/The Mask . . . . (Chaos)
Blue On Black
    Kenny Wayne Shepherd; *Trouble Is...* . . . . (Revolution)
Careless Whisper
    Dave Koz featuring Montell Jordan; *Dance* . . . . (Capitol)
    Wham! Featuring George Michael; *Make It Big* . . . . (Columbia)
    Music For The Miracle-C . . . . (Epic Portrait Assoc.)
Dedicated To The One I Love
    Mamas & The Papas; *Best Of The Mamas & The Papas.* . . . .(MCA)
    Farewell To The First Golden Era. . . . .(MCA)
    Original Classic Oldies Of The '50s & '60s-#13-C . . . .(MCA)
    Shirelles; *Oldies But Goodies-#10-C* . . . . (Original Sound)
    Shirelles' Greatest Hits . . . . (Everest)
    Shirelles-Anthology 1959-1964 . . . . (Rhino)
    Super Oldies Of The '50s-#4-C . . . .(Audio Fidelity)
Do You Want To Know A Secret
    Beatles; *Introducing...The Beatles* . . . . (Vee-Jay)
    Please Please Me . . . . (Parlophone)
    The Early Beatles. . . . . (Capitol)
From A Whisper To A Scream
    Esther Phillips; *Best Of Esther Phillips.* . . . . (CBS Associated)
    From A Whisper To A Scream . . . . (CBS Associated)
From A Whisper To A Scream
    Allen Toussaint; *The Allen Toussaint Collection* . . . . (Reprise)
    Robert Palmer; *Sneakin' Sally Through The Alley* . . . . (Island)
From A Whisper To A Scream
    Elvis Costello & The Attractions; *Trust* . . . .(Rykodisc)
Let It Be
    Aretha Franklin; *Aretha Franklin's Greatest Hits* . . . .(Atlantic)
    Beatles; *Beatles 1* . . . . (Capitol)
    Beatles-20 Greatest Hits . . . . (Capitol)
    Past Masters-Volume Two . . . . (Parlophone)
    Reel Music . . . . (Capitol)
    The Beatles/1967-1970 . . . . (Capitol)
    Paul McCartney; *The Concert For New York City-C* . . . . (Columbia)
    Tripping The Live Fantastic-Highlights! . . . . (Capitol)
    Rockestra; *Kampuchea-C* . . . .(Atlantic)
Louise
    Maurice Chevalier; *Louise* . . . . (ASV)
Shhh
    Tevin Campbell; *I'm Ready* . . . . (Qwest)
Shifting, Whispering Sands
    Billy Vaughn; *Melody Of Love-Best Of Billy Vaughn.* . . . . (Varese Vintage)
    Rusty Draper; *Rusty Draper's Greatest Hits* . . . . (Collector's Choice)
Sidewalk Annie
    Wallflowers; *The Wallflowers.* . . . . (Virgin)
Softly Whispering I Love You
    English Congregation; *Super Hits Of The '70s-Have A Nice Day-#7-C* . . (Rhino)
    Mike Curb Congregation; *Your Favorite Songs-C* . . . . (Curb)
    Paul Young; *From Time To Time-The Singles Collection.* . . . . (Columbia)
Speak Softly-You're Talking To My Heart
    Gene Watson; *Gene Watson's Greatest Hits* . . . .(MCA)
    Old Loves Never Die . . . .(MCA)
Summer Rain
    Carl Thomas; *Emotional.* . . . .(Bad Boy/Arista)
Whisper In The Dark
    Dionne Warwick; *Friends* . . . . (Arista)
Whisper My Name
    Randy Travis; *This Is Me* . . . .(Warner Bros.)
Whisper To A Scream (Birds Fly)
    Icicle Works; *Icicle Works* . . . . (Arista)
Whispering
    Jan Garber & His Orchestra; *Jan Garber & His Orchestra Play 22 Original*
    Big Band Favorites . . . . (Hindsight)
    Les Paul & Mary Ford; *Selections From "Legend & The Legacy"* . . . . (Capitol)
    Miles Davis; *Dig* . . . . (Prestige)
    Early Miles . . . . (Prestige)
    Miles Davis & Horns . . . . (Prestige)
    Miles Davis-Chronicle-Complete Prestige Recordings. . . . . (Prestige)
    Paul Whiteman & His Orchestra; *Nipper's Greatest Hits Of The*
    '20s-C . . . . (RCA)
    Wayne King & His Orchestra; *Best Of Wayne King* . . . .(MCA)
Whispering Breezes
    Al H. Wilson; *Music From The New York Stage (1890-1920)-#1-1890-*
    1908-C . . . . (Pearl)

Whispering Grass
    Hank Crawford; *Great Moments In Jazz-C* . . . .(Atlantic)
    Ink Spots; *Best Of The Ink Spots* . . . . (MCA)
    If I Didn't Care . . . . (Pro-Arte)
    Ink Spots' Greatest Hits-Original Recordings-1939-1946. . . . . (MCA)
    Ink Spots In London . . . . (Everest)
    Sandy Denny; *Who Knows Where The Time Goes* . . . .(Hannibal)
Whispering Heart
    Empires; *Harlem Holiday-New York Rhythm & Blues-#3-C* . . . . . . (Collectables)
Whispering Hope
    Jo Stafford; *Capitol Collectors Series-Jo Stafford* . . . . (Capitol)
Whispering Pines
    Johnny Horton; *Johnny Horton's Greatest Hits* . . . . (Columbia)
Whispering Pines
    Band; *The Band.* . . . . (Capitol)
Whispering Wind
    Mandy Barnett; *I've Got A Right To Cry* . . . .(Sire)
Words Of Love
    Beatles; *Beatles VI* . . . . (Capitol)
    Beatles-Box Set. . . . . (Capitol)
    Beatles-Love Songs . . . . (Capitol)
    For Sale . . . . (Capitol)
    Buddy Holly; *Buddy Holly* . . . . (MCA)
    Legend-From The Original Master Tapes . . . . (MCA)
    Rock & Roll Collection. . . . . (MCA)
    Buddy Holly/The Crickets; *Buddy Holly-20 Golden Greats* . . . . (MCA)

COMMUNICATION: WORDS, Language

See Also: **COMMUNICATION (various), GOSSIP, LOVE:**
    LOOKING FOR THE WORDS

32 Flavors
    Alana Davis; *Blame It On Me* . . . . (Elektra)
    Ani DiFranco; *Living In Clip.* . . . .(Righteous Babe)
    Not A Pretty Girl. . . . .(Righteous Babe)
Action! Not Words
    Def Leppard; *Pyromania.* . . . . (Mercury)
Cheerful Little Earful
    Ella Fitzgerald; *Swings Brightly With Nelson* . . . . (Verve)
Cherish
    Association; *Association Greatest Hits* . . . . (Warner Bros.)
    Billboard Top Pop Hits-1966-C . . . . (Rhino)
Come Down
    Toad The Wet Sprocket; *Coil* . . . . (Columbia)
Country Grammar (Hot Sh*t)
    Nelly; *Country Grammar* . . . .(Fo' Reel/Universal)
Don't Believe A Word
    Thin Lizzy; *'Life'-Live* . . . . (Warner Bros.)
    Live And Dangerous . . . . (Warner Bros.)
    Lizzy Lives! (1976-1984) . . . . (Gland Slamm)
Fill In The Words
    Robert Klein/Original Cast; *They're Playing Our Song* . . . . (Casablanca)
From The Word Go
    Michael Martin Murphey; *River Of Time* . . . . (Warner Bros.)
Guilty
    Def Leppard; *Euphoria* . . . . (Mercury)
He'll Have To Go
    Jim Reeves; *60 Years Of Country Music-C* . . . . (RCA)
    Best Of Jim Reeves . . . . (RCA)
    Billboard Top Country Hits-1960-C. . . . . (Rhino)
    Great Moments At The Grand Ole Opry-C . . . . (RCA)
    Jim Reeves' Greatest Hits. . . . . (RCA)
    Nipper's Greatest Hits Of The '50s-#1-C . . . . (RCA)
    Ry Cooder; *Chicken Skin Music* . . . . (Reprise)
Human Nature
    Madonna; *Bedtime Stories* . . . .(Maverick/Sire)
    GHV2 . . . . (Warner Bros.)
Hypnotize
    Notorious B.I.G.; *Life After Death* . . . .(Bad Boy/Arista)
If You Leave Me Tonight I'll Cry
    Jerry Wallace; *From The Vaults: Decca Country Classics-1934-*
    1973-C. . . . . (Decca)
    Jerry Wallace's Greatest Hits . . . . (Curb)
I'll Be There For You
    Bon Jovi; *New Jersey* . . . .(Jambco)
I'm Gonna Sit Right Down And Write Myself A Letter
    Billy Williams; *Stardust: The Classic Decca Hits & Standards*
    Collection-C . . . . (Decca)
    Fats Waller; *Fats Waller* . . . .(RCA Special Prod.)
    Frank Sinatra; *Sinatra-Basie.* . . . . (Reprise)
    Songs For Young Lovers & Swing Easy . . . . (Capitol)
    Nat "King" Cole; *Just One Of Those Things (& More)* . . . . (Capitol)
    Nat "King" Cole-Gift Set . . . . (Capitol)
    Original Cast; *Ain't Misbehavin'.* . . . . (RCA)
Language Of Love
    Dan Fogelberg; *Windows & Walls* . . . .(Full Moon)

Language Of Love
John D. Loudermilk; 45-#47-7938 . . . .(RCA)
Language Of Love
Steve Wariner; *I Got Dreams* . . . . (MCA)
Language Of Love
Orleans; *Grown-Up Children* . . . . (MCA)
Language Of Love
Intrigues; *Intrigues-Golden Classics* . . . .(Collectables)
Language Of Love
Heart; *Passionworks* . . . . (Epic)
Language Of The Kiss
Indigo Girls; *Swamp Ophelia* . . . . (Epic)
Las Palabras De Amor
Queen; *Hot Space* . . . . (Hollywood)
Last Word, The
Mary Chapin Carpenter; *Stones In The Road* . . . . (Columbia)
Let It Be
Aretha Franklin; *Aretha Franklin's Greatest Hits* . . . . (Atlantic)
Beatles; *Beatles 1* . . . . (Capitol)
  Beatles-20 Greatest Hits . . . . (Capitol)
  Past Masters-Volume Two . . . . (Parlophone)
  Reel Music . . . . (Capitol)
  The Beatles/1967-1970 . . . . (Capitol)
Paul McCartney; *The Concert For New York City-C* . . . . (Columbia)
  Tripping The Live Fantastic-Highlights! . . . . (Capitol)
Rockestra; *Kampuchea-C* . . . . (Atlantic)
Let's Call The Whole Thing Off
Fred Astaire; *Steppin' Out-Astaire Sings* . . . . (Verve)
Lost For Words
Pink Floyd; *The Division Bell* . . . . (Columbia)
Man Of My Word
Collin Raye; *Extremes* . . . . (Epic)
Michelle
Beatles; *Beatles-Love Songs* . . . . (Capitol)
  Rubber Soul . . . . (Capitol)
  The Beatles/1962-1966 . . . . (Capitol)
More Than Words
Extreme; *Best Of Extreme: An Accidental Collocation Of Atoms?* . . . . . . (A&M)
  Billboard Top Hits-1991-C . . . . (Rhino)
  Pornograffitti . . . . (A&M)
More Than Words Can Say
Alias; *Alias* . . . . (EMI)
My Baby Left Me
Arthur ''Big Boy'' Crudup; *That's All Right (Mama)* . . . . (Bluebird)
Creedence Clearwater Revival; *Cosmo's Factory* . . . .(Fantasy)
  Creedence Country . . . . (Fantasy)
Elvis Presley; *Elvis Recorded Live On Stage In Memphis* . . . . (RCA)
No More ''I Love You's''
Annie Lennox; *Medusa* . . . . (Arista)
Over There
Glenn Miller; *Original Recordings-#3-Army/Air Force Band* . . . .(Pair)
Glenn Miller & His Army/Air Force Band; *Glenn Miller-A Legendary
  Performer-#3* . . . . (Bluebird)
Mormon Tabernacle Choir; *God Bless America* . . . .(Sony Music Classical)
Peace Is Just A Word
Eurythmics; *Peace* . . . . (Arista)
Picasso's Last Words
Paul McCartney & Wings; *Band On The Run* . . . . (Capitol)
Wings; *Wings Over America* . . . . (Capitol)
Please Please Me
Beatles; *Beatles-Box Set* . . . . (Capitol)
  Please Please Me . . . .(Parlophone)
  The Beatles/1962-1966 . . . . (Capitol)
  The Early Beatles . . . . (Capitol)
Pretty Words
Vince Gill; *I Still Believe In You* . . . . (MCA)
Promise I Make
Dakota Moon; *Dakota Moon* . . . . (Elektra)
Promises
Cranberries; *Bury The Hatchet* . . . . (Island/IDJMG)
Promises Broken
Soul Asylum; *Let Your Dim Light Shine* . . . . (Columbia)
Revolutionary Words
Mutabaruka; *Mystery Unfolds* . . . .(Shanachie)
Show Me
Julie Andrews/Original Cast; *My Fair Lady* . . . . (Columbia)
Simple Little Words
Cristy Lane; *Cristy Lane-At Her Best* . . . . (EMI)
Sorry Seems To Be The Hardest Word
Elton John; *Blue Moves* . . . . (MCA)
  Elton John's Greatest Hits-#2 . . . . (Polydor)
  Live In Australia With The Melbourne Symphony Orchestra . . . . (MCA)
Joe Cocker; *Two Rooms-Celebrating The Songs Of Elton John & Bernie
  Taupin-C* . . . . (Polydor)
Sound Of Silence, The
Paul Simon; *Paul Simon In Concert/Live Rhymin'* . . . . (Columbia)
Simon & Garfunkel; *Collected Works* . . . . (Columbia)
  More American Graffiti-#4-C . . . . (MCA)

Simon & Garfunkel's Greatest Hits . . . .(Columbia)
  Sounds Of Silence . . . . (Columbia)
  ST/The Graduate . . . . (Columbia)
  The Concert In Central Park . . . . (Warner Bros.)
Strange Currencies
R.E.M.; *Monster* . . . . (Warner Bros.)
The Action
Keb' Mo'; *Just Like You* . . . . (Okeh)
Thousand Words, A
Savage Garden; *Savage Garden* . . . .(Columbia)
Three Little Words
Carmen McRae; *Great American Songbook* . . . . (Atlantic)
Duke Ellington & His Orchestra; *Nipper's Greatest Hits Of The
  '30s-#2-C* . . . . (RCA)
Nat ''King'' Cole; *L-O-V-E* . . . .(Capitol)
Time And A Word
Yes; *Time And A Word* . . . . (Atlantic)
  Yesshows . . . . (Atlantic)
  Yesterdays . . . . (Atlantic)
Too Marvelous For Words
Billie Holiday; *Lady Sings The Blues* . . . .(Verve)
Frank Sinatra; *Frank Sinatra-Gift Set* . . . .(Capitol)
  The Capitol Years . . . . (Capitol)
Nat ''King'' Cole; *Nat ''King'' Cole (Box Set)* . . . .(Capitol)
Too Young
Donny Osmond; *Donny Osmond's Greatest Hits* . . . .(Curb)
Nat ''King'' Cole; *Nat ''King'' Cole-Greatest Hits* . . . .(Capitol)
Wasted Words
Allman Brothers Band; *Brothers & Sisters* . . . . (Polydor)
  Decade Of Hits-1969-1979 . . . . (Polydor)
  Dreams . . . . (Polydor)
Gregg Allman; *Laid Back* . . . . (Polydor)
Why Can't The English
Rex Harrison; *ST/My Fair Lady* . . . .(Columbia)
Rex Harrison/Original Cast; *My Fair Lady* . . . .(Columbia)
Wonderful Guy, A
Original Cast; *South Pacific* . . . . (CBS Masterworks)
Word Games
Billy Walker; *45-#10205* . . . . (RCA)
  Lovin' and Losin' . . . . (RCA)
Word Up
Cameo; *Word Up* . . . . (Casablanca)
Word, The
Beatles; *Beatles-Box Set* . . . .(Capitol)
  Rubber Soul . . . . (Capitol)
Words
Bee Gees; *Bee Gees-Gold* . . . . (Polydor)
  Here At Last...Bee Gees...Live . . . . (Polydor)
  History Of British Rock-#9-C . . . .(Rhino)
Elvis Presley; *From Memphis To Vegas/From Vegas To Memphis* . . . . (RCA)
  That's The Way It Is . . . . (RCA)
Joan Armatrading; *Shouting Stage* . . . .(A&M)
Rita Coolidge; *Anytime...Anywhere* . . . .(A&M)
  Rita Coolidge-Classics-#5 . . . . (A&M)
  Rita Coolidge's Greatest Hits . . . . (A&M)
Words
Monkees; *Missing Links-#2* . . . .(Rhino)
  Monkees' Greatest Hits . . . . (Rhino)
  More Greatest Hits Of The Monkees . . . . (Arista)
Words
Solomon Burke; *Best Of Solomon Burke* . . . . (Atlantic)
  Home In Your Heart-Best Of Solomon Burke . . . .(Rhino)
Words
Missing Persons; *Best Of Missing Persons* . . . .(Capitol)
Words
F.R. David; *Words* . . . . (Carrere)
Words
Dwight Yoakam; *ST/South Of Heaven, West Of Hell* . . . . (Reprise)
Words By Heart
Billy Ray Cyrus; *It Won't Be The Last* . . . .(Mercury)
Words Get In The Way
Miami Sound Machine; *Primitive Love* . . . . (Epic)
Words Of Love
Beatles; *Beatles VI* . . . .(Capitol)
  Beatles-Box Set . . . . (Capitol)
  Beatles-Love Songs . . . . (Capitol)
  For Sale . . . . (Capitol)
Buddy Holly; *Buddy Holly* . . . . (MCA)
  Legend-From The Original Master Tapes . . . . (MCA)
  Rock & Roll Collection . . . . (MCA)
Buddy Holly/The Crickets; *Buddy Holly-20 Golden Greats* . . . . (MCA)
Words Of Love
Mamas & The Papas; *Best Of The Mamas & The Papas* . . . . (MCA)
  Farewell To The First Golden Era . . . . (MCA)
  Mamas & The Papas-16 Of Their Greatest Hits . . . . (MCA)
  Mama's Big Ones-Her Greatest Hits . . . . (MCA)
Words Of Wisdom
Wyclef Jean featuring The Refugee Allstars; *Presents The Carnival F/
  Refugee Allstars* . . . .(Ruffhouse/Columbia)

Words Of Wisdom
Christopher Cross; *Another Page* . . . .(Warner Bros.)
You Said The Words
Wood; *Songs From Stamford Hill.* . . . . (Columbia)
You Took The Words Right Out Of My Mouth
Meat Loaf; *Bat Out Of Hell.* . . . .(Epic)
You're A Man Of Words, I'm A Woman
Betty LaVette; *Lost Soul-#1-C* . . . .(Epic)

COMPLAINTS, Criticize

See Also: **ANGER, INSULTS, LOVE (various), SADNESS**

1040 Blues
Robert Cray Band; *Shame + Sin* . . . . (Mercury)
57 Channels (And Nothin' On)
Bruce Springsteen; *Human Touch* . . . . (Columbia)
Adelaide's Lament
Original Cast; *Guys & Dolls* . . . .(MCA)
Guys & Dolls . . . . (Motown)
Ain't My Bitch
Metallica; *Load* . . . . (Elektra)
Ain't That A Bitch
Aerosmith; *Nine Lives* . . . . (Columbia)
All I Want Is A Life
Tim McGraw; *All I Want* . . . . (Curb)
All The Fun
Paul Overstreet; *Best Of Paul Overstreet* . . . . (RCA)
All You Ever Do Is Bring Me Down
Mavericks; *Best Of The Mavericks-Super Colossal Smash Hits Of*
The '90s. . . . . (Mercury)
Country Superstar Hits-C . . . . (Hip-O)
Honky Tonk Boogie-C . . . . (Hip-O)
Music For All Occasions . . . .(MCA)
Anything But Down
Sheryl Crow; *The Globe Sessions* . . . . (A&M)
A-sleepin' At The Foot Of The Bed
"Little" Jimmy Dickens; *Bluegrass Super Hits-C* . . . . (Columbia)
Better Days (And The Bottom Drops Out)
Citizen King; *Mobile Estates* . . . .(Warner Bros.)
Big Boss Man
B.B. King; *Six Silver Strings.* . . . .(MCA)
Elvis Presley; *ST/Clambake* . . . . (RCA)
Grateful Dead; *Grateful Dead (Skull & Roses).* . . . . (Warner Bros.)
Jimmy Reed; *Best Of Jimmy Reed* . . . . (Crescendo)
Oldies But Goodies-#1-C . . . . (Original Sound)
John Hammond; *Best Of John Hammond* . . . . (Vanguard)
So Many Roads . . . . (Vanguard)
Bills, Bills, Bills
Destiny's Child; *The Writing's On The Wall* . . . . (Columbia)
Bittersweet Me
R.E.M.; *New Adventures In Hi-Fi.* . . . .(Warner Bros.)
Busted
Harlan Howard; *All-Time Favorite Country Songwriter* . . . (Koch International)
John Conlee; *John Conlee's Greatest Hits* . . . .(MCA)
Songs For The Working Man . . . .(MCA)
Johnny Cash; *Johnny Cash-16 Biggest Hits-#2* . . . . (Legacy)
Ray Charles; *Ray Charles' Greatest Hits* . . . . (Rhino)
Ray Charles-His Greatest Hits-#2 . . . .(Dunhill Compact Classics)
Chains
Patty Loveless; *Honky Tonk Angel* . . . .(MCA)
Patty Loveless' Greatest Hits. . . . .(MCA)
Computer Took My Job
Maurice John Vaughn; *Generic Blues Album* . . . . (Alligator)
Do Right
Jimmie's Chicken Shack; *Bring Your Own Stereo* . . . .(Rocket)
Don't Be Cruel
Cheap Trick; *Cheap Trick's Greatest Hits* . . . .(Epic)
Lap Of Luxury . . . . (Epic)
Elvis Presley; *Billboard Top Rock 'N' Roll Hits-1956-C* . . . .(Rhino)
Nipper's Greatest Hits Of The '50s-#2-C . . . . (RCA)
Number One Hits . . . . (RCA)
The Great Performances . . . . (RCA)
The Top Ten Hits . . . . (RCA)
Judds; *Heartland* . . . .(MCA)
Don't Be Cruel
Bobby Brown; *Chart Toppers-R&B Hits Of The '80s-C* . . . . (Priority)
He Treats Me Like A Dog
St. Louis Bessie; *Barrelhouse Mamas: Born In The Alley, Raised In The*
Slums-C. . . . . (Yazoo)
Heart-Shaped Box
Nirvana; *In Utero* . . . . (David Geffen Co.)
Heavy
Collective Soul; *Dosage* . . . . (Atlantic)
Honey, I'm Home
Shania Twain; *Come On Over* . . . . (Mercury)

I Wish You Didn't Love Me So Much
"Little" Jimmy Dickens; *All Time Legends Of Country Music-C* . . . . . (Legacy)
If You Think You're Lonely Now
Bobby Womack; *The Poet.* . . . . (Razor & Tie)
K-Ci Hailey; *ST/Jason's Lyric* . . . . (Mercury)
I'm Payin' Taxes, What Am I Buyin'
JB's; *Funky Good Time-The Anthology* . . . .(Polydor)
I've Had It
Danielle Brisebois; *Portable Life* . . . .(RCA)
Just A Girl
No Doubt; *Tragic Kingdom.* . . . . (Trauma)
Kids Of The Baby Boom
Bellamy Brothers; *Bellamy Brothers' Greatest Hits-#3* . . . . (MCA)
Country Rap . . . . (MCA)
MCA #1 Hits Of The '80s-#3-C . . . . (MCA Special Prod.)
Life's A Bitch
Shooter; *Songs From Dawson's Creek* . . . .(Sony Music Soundtrax)
Mo Money Mo Problems
Notorious B.I.G.; *Jock Jams-#4-C* . . . . (Tommy Boy)
Life After Death . . . .(Bad Boy/Arista)
The Ultimate Dance Party-1998-C. . . . . (Arista)
My Best Was Never Good Enough
Bruce Springsteen; *The Ghost Of Tom Joad* . . . . (Columbia)
Never There
Cake; *Now That's What I Call Music!-#2-C* . . . .(Virgin)
Prolonging The Magic . . . . (Capricorn)
Nobody
Ry Cooder; *Jazz* . . . . (Warner Bros.)
Oh! How I Hate To Get Up In The Morning
Irving Berlin; *American Songbook Series-Irving*
Berlin. . . . . (Smithsonian Collection)
War Years-C. . . . .(ISD/Intersound)
Soundtrack; *American Musical Theater-#2.* . . . . . . (Smithsonian Collection)
Ooh! My Feet!
Original Broadway Cast; *Most Happy Fella* . . . . (Sony Music Classical)
Please Please Me
Beatles; *Beatles-Box Set* . . . . (Capitol)
Please Please Me . . . . (Parlophone)
The Beatles/1962-1966. . . . . (Capitol)
The Early Beatles . . . . (Capitol)
Poor Poor Pitiful Me
Linda Ronstadt; *Linda Ronstadt's Greatest Hits, Volume Two* . . . . . . (Asylum)
Simple Dreams . . . . (Asylum)
Terri Clark; *Just The Same* . . . . (Mercury)
Warren Zevon; *A Quiet Normal Life-Best Of* . . . . (Asylum)
Stand In The Fire . . . . (Asylum)
Pop
'N Sync; *Celebrity.* . . . . (Jive)
Now That's What I Call Music!-#8-C . . . .(Virgin)
Satellite Blues
AC/DC; *Stiff Upper Lip.* . . . . (East West)
Shake, Rattle And Roll
Big Joe Turner; *Big Joe Turner's Greatest Hits* . . . .(Atlantic)
Every Day I Have The Blues . . . . (Pablo)
Oldies But Goodies-#2-C . . . .(Original Sound)
Soul Years-C. . . . .(Atlantic)
Bill Haley & His Comets; *Bill Haley & His Comets' Greatest Hits* . . . (MCA)
Bill Haley & His Comets-Golden Hits . . . . (MCA)
Elvis Presley; *For LP Fans Only.* . . . .(RCA)
Rocker . . . . (RCA)
ST/This Is Elvis . . . . (RCA)
Fats Domino; *Fats Domino's Greatest Hits* . . . . (MCA)
Huey Lewis and the News; *Four Chords & Several Years Ago.* . . . . . (Elektra)
NRBQ; *At Yankee Stadium* . . . . (Mercury)
Vern Gosdin; *Best Of Vern Gosdin* . . . . (Warner Bros.)
She's Got Issues
Offspring; *Americana* . . . . (Columbia)
Sick & Beautiful
Artificial Joy Club; *Melt* . . . .(Interscope)
Slow Poke
Ray Conniff; *Speak To Me Of Love* . . . . (Columbia)
Smashing Young Man
Collective Soul; *Collective Soul* . . . .(Atlantic)
Spaniard That Blighted My Life
Al Jolson; *Music From The New York Stage (1890-1920)-#3-1913-*
1917-C. . . . . (Pearl)
Steal My Kisses
Ben Harper; *Burn To Shine* . . . .(Virgin)
Now That's What I Call Music!-#4-C . . . .(Virgin)
Stepsisters' Lament
Barbara Ruick & Pat Carroll; *Cinderella-The CBS Television Network*
Production. . . . . (Columbia)
Original Cast; *Cinderella-The CBS Television Production.* . . . . . . (Columbia)
Stop Doggin' Me
Johnnie Taylor; *Chronicle: The 20 Greatest Hits* . . . . (Stax)
Little Bluebird . . . . (Stax)
Subway Ride
Sheryl Crow; *The Globe Sessions* . . . . (A&M)

Summertime Blues
Alan Jackson; *Who I Am* (Arista)
Blue Cheer; *Good Times Are So Hard To Find-History Of Blue Cheer* (Mercury)
Louder Than God-Best Of Blue Cheer (Rhino)
San Francisco Nights-C (Rhino)
Brian Setzer; *ST/La Bamba* (Slash)
Eddie Cochran; *Eddie Cochran-Legendary Masters* (EMI)
Eddie Cochran's Greatest Hits (Curb)
EMI Legends Of Rock & Roll-24 Greatest Hits-C (EMI)
Joan Jett & The Blackhearts; *I Love Rock 'n' Roll* (Blackheart)
Who; *Hooligans* (MCA)
Live At Leeds (MCA)
Who's Last (MCA)
Ten Cents A Dance
Eileen Farrell; *I Gotta Right To Sing The Blues* (Sony Music Classical)
Ella Fitzgerald; *Rodgers & Hart Songbook* (Verve)
There Ain't No Country Music On This Jukebox
Tom T. Hall; *Storyteller, Poet, Philospher* (Mercury)
There Is Nothin' Like A Dame
Original Cast; *South Pacific* (CBS Masterworks)
There It Is
Ginuwine; *Life* (Epic)
Too Much Monkey Business
Chuck Berry; *Classic Oldies From The '50s & '60s-#16-C* (MCA)
Roll Over Beethoven (Allegiance)
ST/Hail! Hail! Rock 'N' Roll (MCA)
Toronto Rock 'N' Roll Revival-#2-C (Accord)
Elvis Presley; *Guitar Man* (RCA)
Million-Dollar Quartet (RCA)
ST/This Is Elvis (RCA)
Yardbirds; *Five Live Yardbirds* (Rhino)
For Your Love (Accord)
Yardbirds' Greatest Hits-#1 (1964-1966) (Rhino)
Tryin' To Love Two
William Bell; *Coming Back For More* (Razor & Tie)
Turn The Page
Metallica; *Garage Inc.* (Elektra)
Tyrone
Erykah Badu; *Erykah Badu-Live* (Kedar Entert./Universal)
Up And Gone
McCarters; *Better Be Home Soon* (Warner Bros.)
Way I Am
Eminem; *The Marshall Mathers LP* (Aftermath/Interscope)
Wedding Bells (Are Breaking Up That Old Gang Of Mine)
Four Aces; *Best Of The Four Aces* (MCA)
Weight, The
Band; *Best Of The Band* (Capitol)
Music From Big Pink (Capitol)
Rock Of Ages (Capitol)
The Last Waltz (Warner Bros.)
Staple Singers; *Soul Folk In Action* (Stax)
Staple Singers & Marty Stuart; *Rhythm Country And Blues-C* (MCA)
Western Movies (My Baby Loves)
Olympics; *All-Time Greatest Hits Of Rock 'N' Roll-C* (Curb)
American Graffiti-#3-C (MCA)
Best Of The Olympics (Vee-Jay)
Jumpin' Jive '50s-C (Priority)
What'd You Come Here For?
Trina & Tamara; *Trina & Tamara* (C2/Columbia)
What's My Age Again?
Blink-182; *Enema Of The State* (MCA)
Now That's What I Call Music!-#3-C (Virgin)
Why Don't You Get A Job?
Offspring; *Americana* (Columbia)
X-Girlfriend
Mariah Carey; *Rainbow* (Columbia)
You Haven't Done Nothin'
Stevie Wonder; *Fulfillingness' First Finale* (Motown)
You Keep Me Hangin' On
Diana Ross; *Evening With Diana Ross* (Motown)
Diana Ross & The Supremes; *Diana Ross & The Supremes-Anthology (1962-1969)* (Motown)
Motown Story-First 25 Years-C (Motown)
Kim Wilde; *Another Step* (MCA)
Reba McEntire; *Starting Over* (MCA)
Supremes; *Billboard Top R&B Hits-1965-C* (Rhino)
Diana Ross & The Supremes' Greatest Hits-#2 (Motown)
Vanilla Fudge; *Best Of Vanilla Fudge* (Atco)
Vanilla Fudge (Atco)
Wilson Pickett; *A Man & A Half-Best Of Wilson Pickett* (Rhino)
Wilson Pickett's Greatest Hits (Atlantic)
You Never Give Me Your Money
Beatles; *Abbey Road* (Parlophone)
Beatles-Box Set (Capitol)
George Benson; *The Best* (Rebound)
You Talk Too Much
Cheap Trick; *Next Position Please* (Epic)
You Talk Too Much
Joe Jones; *American Graffiti-#3-C* (MCA)
Billboard Top Rock 'N' Roll Hits-1960-C (Rhino)
Carnival Time-Best Of Ric Records-#1-C (Rounder)
Echoes Of A Rock Era-Middle Years-C (Roulette)
Original Rock 'N' Roll Hits Of The '60s-C (Roulette)
You Talk Too Much
George Thorogood & The Destroyers; *Born To Be Bad* (Gold Rush)
You Talk Too Much
Run-D.M.C.; *King Of Rock* (Profile)

COMPLIMENTS, Praise

See Also: ***ANGELS, BEAUTY, BEST, LOVE (various), SPECIAL***

(You Make Me Feel Like) A Natural Woman
Aretha Franklin; *Aretha Franklin's Greatest Hits-1980-1994* (Arista)
Chicken Soup For The Woman's Soul-C (Rhino)
Carole King; *Tapestry* (Epic)
Celine Dion; *Tapestry Revisited: Tribute To Carole King-C* (Lava)
(You've Got) The Magic Touch
Platters; *Encore Of Golden Hits-Platters* (Mercury)
Adalida
George Strait; *Latest Greatest Straitest Hits* (MCA)
Lead On (MCA)
Ain't No Woman (Like The One I Got)
Four Tops; *Ain't No Woman (Like The One I Got)* (MCA Special Prod.)
Four Tops' Greatest Hits (1972-1976) (MCA)
Ain't She Sweet?
Beatles; *History Of British Rock-#5-C* (Rhino)
The Beatles-Anthology-#3 (Capitol)
Erroll Garner; *Body And Soul* (Legacy)
Frank Sinatra; *Sinatra and Swingin' Brass* (Reprise)
Pearl Bailey; *Pearl Bailey-16 Most Requested Songs* (Legacy)
All The Things You Are
Ella Fitzgerald; *Complete Jerome Kern* (Verve)
Mario Lanza; *Be My Love-Greatest Performances* (Rhino)
Willie Nelson; *Healing Hands Of Time* (Liberty)
American Made
Oak Ridge Boys; *American Made* (MCA)
Oak Ridge Boys' Greatest Hits 2 (MCA)
Angels Would Fall
Melissa Etheridge; *Breakdown* (Island)
Annie's Song
John Denver; *Back Home Again* (RCA)
Evening With John Denver (RCA)
John Denver's Greatest Hits-#2 (RCA)
Baby (You've Got What It Takes)
Brook Benton & Dinah Washington; *Cruisin'-1960-C* (Increase)
Endlessly-The Best Of Brook Benton (Rhino)
Baby Face
Al Jolson; *The Al Jolson Story-#3* (MCA)
World's Greatest (MCA)
Kinks; *Everybody's In Show-Biz* (Rhino)
Baby You Got It
Brenton Wood; *18 Best-Brenton Wood* (Original Sound)
Bang The Drum Slowly
Emmylou Harris; *Red Dirt Girl* (Nonesuch)
Beautiful People
Bobby Vee; *Very Best Of Bobby Vee* (Collectables)
Be-Bop-A-Lula
Everly Brothers; *Everly Brothers* (Rhino)
Gene Vincent and His Blue Caps; *Billboard Top Rock 'N' Roll Hits-1956-C* (Rhino)
ST/Wild At Heart (Polydor)
Jerry Lee Lewis; *Monsters* (Sun)
Trio Plus (Sun)
John Lennon; *Rock 'N' Roll* (Capitol)
Better Man
Warren Brothers; *Beautiful Day In The Cold Cruel World* (BNA)
Can't Take My Eyes Off You
Frankie Valli; *25th Anniversary Collection* (Rhino)
Frankie Valli-Anthology (Rhino)
Very Best Of Frankie Valli (MCA)
Lauryn Hill; *The Miseducation Of Lauryn Hill* (Ruffhouse/Columbia)
Close Enough To Perfect
Alabama; *Alabama-Super Hits-#2* (RCA)
Essential Alabama (RCA)
Mountain Music (RCA)
Cousin Dupree
Steely Dan; *Two Against Nature* (Giant)
Crazy Love
Brian McKnight; *Anytime* (Motown)
I Remember You (Mercury)
ST/Jason's Lyric (Mercury)
Van Morrison; *Moondance* (Warner Bros.)

Daddy's Money
Ricochet; *Ricochet* . . . . (Columbia)
Dinah
Bing Crosby; *Bing Crosby-16 Most Requested Songs* . . . . (Legacy)
Cab Calloway; *Best Of The Big Bands-C* . . . . (Columbia)
Cliff Edwards; *Singin' In The Rain* . . . . (ASV)
Count Basie & Ethel Waters; *Tribute To Black Entertainers-C* . . . . . (Columbia)
Duke Ellington; *Jubilee Stomp* . . . . (Bluebird)
Ethel Waters; *Am I Blue?* . . . . (ASV)
Fats Waller; *Ain't Misbehavin': 25 Greatest Hits* . . . . (Living Era)
Lionel Hampton & His Orchestra; *Tempo & Swing* . . . . (Bluebird)
Louis Armstrong; *Louis Armstrong-Vol. 6-St. Louis Blues* . . . . (Columbia)
Mills Brothers; *50th Anniversary* . . . .(Ranwood)
Do I Have To Come Right Out & Say It
Buffalo Springfield; *Buffalo Springfield* . . . . (Atco)
Easter Parade
Andy Russell; *Puttin' On The Ritz-Capitol Sings Berlin-C* . . . . (Capitol)
Bing Crosby; *All Time Best Of Bing Crosby* . . . . (Curb)
Judy Garland & Fred Astaire; *ST/Easter Parade* . . . . (Rhino)
Sarah Vaughan; *Complete Sarah Vaughan On Mercury-#2* . . . . (Mercury)
Easy Loving
Freddie Hart; *Best Of Freddie Hart* . . . . (CEMA Special Prod.)
Even The Bad Times Are Good
Tremeloes; *Best Of The Tremeloes* . . . . (Rhino)
Fabulous Character
Sarah Vaughan; *Complete Sarah Vaughan On Mercury-#1-Great Jazz Years-*
1954-1956 . . . . (Mercury)
Femininity
Eric Benet; *True To Myself* . . . . (Jac-Mac/Warner Bros.)
Fine
Whitney Houston; *Totally Hits-#3-C* . . . . (Atlantic)
Whitney Houston's Greatest Hits . . . . (Arista)
Friendly Persuasion
Pat Boone; *Best Of Pat Boone* . . . . (MCA)
Pat Boone-16 Great Performances . . . . (MCA)
Give Her Thorns & She'll Find The Roses
Roger Whittaker; *Wind Beneath My Wings* . . . . (RCA)
God Must Have Spent A Little More Time On You
Alabama Featuring 'N Sync; *Twentieth Century* . . . . (RCA)
'N Sync; *'N Sync* . . . . (RCA)
Totally Hits-#1-C . . . . (Arista)
Guantanamera
Wyclef Jean featuring Celia Cruz & Jeni Fujita; *Presents The Carnival F/*
Refugee Allstars . . . . (Ruffhouse/Columbia)
Happy Birthday, Sweet Sixteen
Neil Sedaka; *Neil Sedaka Sings His Greatest Hits* . . . . (RCA)
Neil Sedaka Sings The Hits . . . . (RCA)
Neil Sedaka's All-Time Greatest Hits . . . . (RCA)
He Didn't Have To Be
Brad Paisley; *Who Needs Pictures* . . . . (Arista)
He Left A Lot To Be Desired
Ricochet; *Blink Of An Eye* . . . . (Columbia)
He's So Fine
Chiffons; *Best Of The Girl Groups-#1-C* . . . . (Rhino)
Billboard Top Rock 'N' Roll Hits-1963-C . . . . (Rhino)
Chiffons Greatest Hits . . . . (Right Stuff)
Jody Miller; *Jody Miller's Greatest Hits* . . . . (Epic)
Hey, Good Lookin'
Hank Williams With His Drifting Cowboys; *24 Of Hank Williams'*
Greatest Hits . . . . (Polydor)
Hank Williams-40 Greatest Hits . . . . (Polydor)
Hey, Good Lookin'-December 1950-July 1951 . . . . (Polydor)
Loretta Lynn & Conway Twitty; *Hey, Good Lookin'* . . . . . . (MCA Special Prod.)
Honey Bun
Original Cast; *South Pacific* . . . .(CBS Masterworks)
Hot Boyz
Missy "Misdemeanor" Elliot; *Da Real World* . . . . (East West)
Totally Hits-#2-C . . . . (Elektra)
Hymn To Her
Pretenders; *Diana, Princess Of Wales-Tribute-C* . . . . (Columbia)
Get Close . . . . (Sire)
The Isle Of View . . . .(Warner Bros.)
Hypnotize The Moon
Clay Walker; *Hypnotize The Moon* . . . . (Giant)
I Can Hear Music
Beach Boys; *Friends-20/20* . . . . (Capitol)
Sunshine Dream . . . . (Capitol)
Beach Boys & Kathy Troccoli; *Stars And Stripes-#1* . . . .(River North)
I Like Ev'rybody
Original Broadway Cast; *The Most Happy Fella* . . . . (Sony Music Classical)
I May Be Wrong
Frankie Laine; *The Uncollected Frankie Laine* . . . . (Hindsight)
Ice Cream
Sarah McLachlan; *Fumbling Towards Ecstasy* . . . . (Arista)
I'll Be
Edwin McCain; *Misguided Roses* . . . . (Lava)
Isn't She Lovely
Keb' Mo'; *Big Wide Grin* . . . . (Sony Wonder)

Lee Ritenour; *Best Of Lee Ritenour* . . . . (Epic)
Stevie Wonder; *Original Musiquarium* . . . . (Motown)
Songs In The Key Of Life . . . . (Motown)
It's Your Song
Garth Brooks; *Big Country Hits '99-C* . . . . (K-Tel)
Garth Brooks-Double Live . . . . (Capitol)
Jolene
Dolly Parton; *Best Of Dolly Parton* . . . . (RCA)
Best There Is . . . . (RCA)
Jolene . . . . (RCA)
RCA Years-1967-1986 . . . . (RCA)
Sherrie Austin; *Followin' A Feelin'* . . . . (We/Madacy)
Josie
Steely Dan; *Aja* . . . . (MCA)
Steely Dan's Greatest Hits . . . . (MCA)
Juke Box Baby
Perry Como; *Perry Como's Greatest Hits* . . . . (RCA)
Just The Way You Are
Billy Joel; *Billy Joel-Greatest Hits, Volume I & Volume II* . . . . (Columbia)
Pop Classics Of The '70s-C . . . . (Columbia)
The Stranger . . . . (Columbia)
Kate
Ben Folds Five; *Whatever And Ever Amen* . . . .(Caroline/550)
Kentucky Woman
Deep Purple; *Purple Passages* . . . . (Warner Bros.)
When We Rock We Rock & When We Roll We Roll . . . . (Warner Bros.)
Gary Puckett And The Union Gap; *Gary Puckett And The Union Gap's*
Greatest Hits . . . .(Bac-Trac)
Neil Diamond; *Love At The Greek* . . . . (Columbia)
Neil Diamond-Classics (Early Years) . . . . (Columbia)
Neil Diamond-Gold . . . . (MCA)
Kind & Generous
Natalie Merchant; *Ophelia* . . . . (Elektra)
Lady (You Bring Me Up)
Commodores; *All The Great Love Songs-Commodores* . . . . (Motown)
Commodores-All The Great Hits . . . . (Motown)
Compact Command Performances-Commodores . . . . (Motown)
Larger Than Life
Backstreet Boys; *Millennium* . . . .(Jive)
Now That's What I Call Music!-#4-C . . . .(Virgin)
Let's Hear It For The Boy
Deniece Williams; *Billboard Top Hits-1984-C* . . . . (Rhino)
ST/Footloose . . . . (Columbia)
Little Bit Of You
Lee Roy Parnell; *We All Get Lucky Sometimes* . . . .(Career)
Magic Touch, (You've Got) The
Platters; *Enchanted-The Best Of The Platters* . . . . (Rhino)
Mary In The Morning
Al Martino; *Al Martino's Greatest Hits* . . . . (EMI Special Markets)
Mercy, Mercy, Mercy
Buckinghams; *Mercy, Mercy, Mercy* . . . . (Legacy Rock Artifacts Series)
Time & Charges-Portraits . . . .(Sundazed Music)
Most Beautiful Girl
Charlie Rich; *Behind Closed Doors* . . . . (Epic)
Charlie Rich's Greatest Hits . . . . (Epic)
Columbia Country Classics-#4-Nashville Sound-C . . . . (Columbia)
Most Beautiful Girl In The World
Frank Sinatra; *Strangers In The Night* . . . . (Reprise)
Tony Bennett; *Rodgers & Hart Songbook* . . . . (DRG)
Tony Bennett Sings More Great Rodgers & Hart . . . . (Improv)
Mr. Wonderful
Peggy Lee; *Best Of Peggy Lee* . . . . (MCA)
Mrs. Brown You've Got A Lovely Daughter
Herman's Hermits; *Herman's Hermits-Their Greatest Hits* . . . .(Abkco)
Something Good Again . . . .(Abkco)
My Baby Must Be A Magician
Marvelettes; *Marvelettes-The Ultimate Collection* . . . . (Motown)
My Baby You
Marc Anthony; *Marc Anthony* . . . . (Columbia)
My Kind Of Girl
Collin Raye; *Best Of Collin Raye-Direct Hits* . . . . (Epic)
Extremes . . . . (Epic)
Nashville Cats
Del McCoury Band; *The Family* . . . .(Ceili Music)
Lovin' Spoonful; *Lovin' Spoonful-Anthology* . . . . (Rhino)
No Diggity
Blackstreet; *Another Level* . . . .(Interscope)
Nobody Does It Better
Carly Simon; *13 Original James Bond Themes-C* . . . . (EMI)
Carly Simon-Greatest Hits Live . . . . (Arista)
ST/The Spy Who Loved Me . . . . (EMI)
Nothing As Original As You
Statler Brothers; *The Originals* . . . . (Mercury)
Oh How Happy
Shades Of Blue; *Oldies But Goodies-#2-C* . . . .(Original Sound)
Oh! My Papa
Eddie Fisher; *Eddie Fisher's All-Time Greatest Hits-#1* . . . . (RCA)
Hebrew National Kosher Classics-C . . . . (RCA)

Nipper's Greatest Hits Of The '50s-#2-C . . . . (RCA)
Old Flames Can't Hold A Candle To You
Dolly Parton; *Dolly Dolly Dolly* . . . . (RCA)
Dolly Parton's Greatest Hits . . . . (RCA)
Joe Sun; *Old Flames Can't Hold A Candle To You* . . . . (Ovation)
Merle Haggard; *Kern River* . . . . (Epic)
Old Master Painter
Peggy Lee; *Capitol Collectors Series-Peggy Lee-#1-Early Years* . . . . . . (Capitol)
One In A Million
Platters; *Magic Touch-An Anthology* . . . . (Mercury)
Only One You
T.G. Sheppard; *Best Of T.G. Sheppard* . . . . (Curb)
T.G. Sheppard's All-Time Greatest Hits . . . . (Warner Bros.)
Only You (And You Alone)
Platters; *Cruisin'-1955-C* . . . . (Increase)
Encore Of Golden Hits-Platters . . . . (Mercury)
Millennium Collection-20th Century Masters . . . . (Mercury)
Open Your Eyes
Yes; *Open Your Eyes* . . . . (Beyond)
Personality
Lloyd Price; *Lloyd Price's Greatest Hits* . . . . (MCA)
Lloyd Price's Greatest Hits . . . . (Curb)
Poetry In Motion
Johnny Tillotson; *10 Top Ten Hits-#1* . . . . (Laurie)
American Graffiti-#3-C . . . . (MCA)
Jukebox Classics-#1-C . . . . (Rhino)
Mellow '60s-C . . . . (Priority)
Million-Dollar Memories-#2-C . . . . (RCA)
Praise
Sevendust; *Animosity* . . . . (TVT)
Praise You
Fatboy Slim; *Now That's What I Call Music!-#2-C* . . . . (Virgin)
You've Come A Long Way, Baby . . . . (Skint)
Pretty Fly (For A White Guy)
Offspring; *Americana* . . . . (Columbia)
Right On The Money
Alan Jackson; *Big Country Hits '99-C* . . . . (K-Tel)
High Mileage . . . . (Arista)
She's A Hum Dum Dinger
Jimmie Davis; *The Roots Of Rap-Classic Recordings-C* . . . . (Yazoo)
She's Got A Way
Billy Joel; *Billy Joel-Greatest Hits, Volume I & Volume II* . . . . (Columbia)
Cold Spring Harbor . . . . (Columbia)
Songs In The Attic . . . . (Columbia)
She's Got It All
Kenny Chesney; *I Will Stand* . . . . (BNA)
Shine
Jon B.; *Cool Relax* . . . . (Yab Yum/550)
Shining Star
Manhattans; *After Midnight* . . . . (Columbia)
Manhattans Greatest Hits . . . . (Columbia)
Seems Like Yesterday-#4-Early '80s-C . . . . (K-Tel)
Smile Like Yours
Natalie Cole; *ST/A Smile Like Yours* . . . . (Elektra)
Smooth
Santana featuring Rob Thomas; *Supernatural* . . . . (Arista)
Totally Hits-#1-C . . . . (Arista)
So Fine
Fiestas; *Baby Boomer Classics-Party Time Fifties-C* . . . . . . (JCI Assoc. Labels)
Baby Boomer's Best-Jumpin' Jive 50's-C . . . . (Priority)
Something About The Way You Look Tonight
Elton John; *The Big Picture* . . . . (Rocket)
Stay As Sweet As You Are
Art Tatum; *Art Tatum Solo Masterpieces-#1* . . . . (Pablo)
Betty Carter; *It's Not About The Melody* . . . . (Verve)
Jimmie Grier & His Orchestra; *78-#7307* . . . . (Brunswick)
Nat "King" Cole; *Love Is The Thing* . . . . (Capitol)
Stay You
Wood; *Songs From Dawson's Creek* . . . . (Sony Music Soundtrax)
Songs From Stamford Hill . . . . (Columbia)
Stellar
Incubus; *Make Yourself* . . . . (Immortal/Epic)
Susie Q
Creedence Clearwater Revival; *1968-1969* . . . . (Fantasy)
Chooglin' . . . . (Fantasy)
Creedence Clearwater Revival . . . . (Fantasy)
Creedence Clearwater Revival-Chronicle . . . . (Fantasy)
Creedence Clearwater Revival-Gold . . . . (Fantasy)
Live In Europe . . . . (Fantasy)
Dale Dawkins; *Collectables Presents The History Of Rock-#3-C* . . (Collectables)
Legends Of Rock Guitar-'50s-#1-C . . . . (Rhino)
Rockin' Rebels-C . . . . (K-Tel)
Jose Feliciano; *Jose Feliciano's All-Time Greatest Hits* . . . . (RCA)
Three Times A Lady
Commodores; *All The Great Love Songs-Commodores* . . . . (Motown)
Commodores Greatest Hits . . . . (Motown)
Commodores-All The Great Hits . . . . (Motown)
Endless Love-Motown's Greatest Love Songs-C . . . . (Motown)
Natural High . . . . (Motown)

To Know Him, Is To Love Him
Dolly Parton/Emmylou Harris/Linda Ronstadt; *Trio* . . . . (Warner Bros.)
Teddy Bears; *At The Hop-'50s Rock 'N' Roll* . . . . (K-Tel)
Phil Spector-Back To Mono 1958-1969-C . . . . (Abkco)
Trimble's Compliments To The City Of Philadelphia
Gerald Trimble; *Crosscurrents* . . . . (Green Linnet)
Try Too Hard
Dave Clark Five; *History Of The Dave Clark Five* . . . . (Hollywood)
Tupelo Honey
Van Morrison; *Van Morrison* . . . . (Warner Bros.)
Tweedlee Dee
Ike & Tina Turner; *Ike & Tina Turner's Greatest Hits-#3* . . . . (Saja)
LaVern Baker; *20 Million-Dollar Memories-#1-C* . . . . (Laurie)
Billboard Top Rock 'N' Roll Hits-1955-C . . . . (Rhino)
Unbelievable
Diamond Rio; *Unbelievable* . . . . (Arista)
Unforgettable
Nat "King" Cole; *Capitol Collectors Series-Nat "King" Cole* . . . . . (Capitol)
The Nat "King" Cole Story . . . . (Capitol)
Unforgettable . . . . (Capitol)
Natalie Cole with Nat "King" Cole; *Unforgettable With Love* . . . . . (Elektra)
Venus In Blue Jeans
Jimmy Clanton; *All-Star Chartbusters* . . . . (Intermedia)
Golden Years-1962-C . . . . (Dominion Entert.)
Vivrant Thing
Q-Tip; *Amplified* . . . . (Def Jam/IDJMG)
Way She Loves Me
Richard Marx; *Paid Vacation* . . . . (Capitol)
Way That You Love, The
Vanessa Williams; *The Sweetest Days* . . . . (Uptown/MCA)
Way You Do The Things You Do
Rita Coolidge; *Rita Coolidge's Greatest Hits* . . . . (A&M)
Temptations; *Temptations' Greatest Hits-#1* . . . . (Motown)
Temptations-Anthology-The Best Of The Temptations . . . . (Motown)
Temptations-The Ultimate Collection . . . . (Motown)
UB40; *Labour Of Love II* . . . . (Virgin)
Way You Look Tonight, The
Billie Holiday; *Quintessential-#2-1936* . . . . (Columbia)
Erroll Garner; *Body And Soul* . . . . (Legacy)
Frank Sinatra; *Days Of Wine And Roses, Moon River, And Other Academy
Award Winners* . . . . (Reprise)
Sinatra Reprise-The Very Good Years . . . . (Reprise)
The Reprise Collection . . . . (Reprise)
Fred Astaire; *Steppin' Out-Astaire Sings* . . . . (Verve)
Lettermen; *Best Of The Lettermen-All Original Recordings* . . . . (Curb)
Capitol Collectors Series-The Lettermen . . . . (Capitol)
The Lettermen's All-Time Greatest Hits . . . . (Capitol)
Tony Bennett; *ST/My Best Friend's Wedding* . . . . (Work/Epic)
Way You Love Me, The
Faith Hill; *Breathe* . . . . (Warner Bros.)
Totally Hits-#3-C . . . . (Atlantic)
When Irish Eyes Are Smiling
Billy Shepherd Singers; *Irish Sing-Along* . . . . (MCA)
Bing Crosby; *When Irish Eyes Are Smiling* . . . . (MCA)
Dennis Day; *Irish Album* . . . . (RCA)
**When The World Is Running Down, You Make The Best Of What's
Still Around**
Police; *Zenyatta Mondatta* . . . . (A&M)
Wifey
Next; *Totally Hits-#3-C* . . . . (Atlantic)
Welcome To Nextacy . . . . (Arista)
Wind Beneath My Wings
Bette Midler; *ST/Beaches* . . . . (Atlantic)
Gary Morris; *Chicken Soup For The Soul: I'll Be There For You-Songs Of
Friendship, Brotherhood And Sisterhood-C* . . . . (Rhino)
Country Love Songs-C . . . . (Warner Bros.)
Gary Morris-Hits . . . . (Warner Bros.)
Why Lady Why . . . . (Warner Bros.)
James Galway; *Wind Beneath My Wings* . . . . (RCA)
Lee Greenwood; *Somebody's Gonna Love You* . . . . (MCA)
Lou Rawls; *When The Night Comes* . . . . (Epic)
Roger Whittaker; *Roger Whittaker Greatest Hits* . . . . (RCA)
Wind Beneath My Wings . . . . (RCA)
Willie Nelson; *City Of New Orleans* . . . . (Columbia)
Wonderful
Adam Ant; *Wonderful* . . . . (Capitol)
Wonderful Tonight
Eric Clapton; *24 Nights* . . . . (Duck/Reprise)
Eric Clapton-Crossroads-C . . . . (Polydor)
Just One Night . . . . (Polydor)
Slowhand . . . . (Polydor)
Time Pieces-#1-The Best Of Eric Clapton . . . . (Polydor)
Yellow
Coldplay; *Now That's What I Call Music!-#6-C* . . . . (Virgin)
Parachutes . . . . (Nettwerk/Capitol)
You
Jesse Powell; *'Bout It* . . . . (Silas)
You Are So Beautiful
Joe Cocker; *Chicken Soup For The Soul: Love And Inspiration-C* . . . . (Rhino)

Joe Cocker-Super Hits.................................... (Legacy)
Organic.. (550 Music)
Kenny Rogers; Timepiece.................................. (Atlantic)

You Got What It Takes
Dave Clark Five; History Of The Dave Clark Five .... (Hollywood)
Marv Johnson; All-Time Greatest Hits Of Rock 'N' Roll-C .... (Curb)

You Gotta Love That
Neal McCoy; Neal McCoy's Greatest Hits..................... (Atlantic)
Today's Country Love-C.................................. (K-Tel)
You Gotta Love That!................................... (Atlantic)

You Look So Good In Love
George Strait; George Strait's Greatest Hits .... (MCA)
Right Or Wrong.. (MCA)
Strait Out Of The Box................................... (MCA)

You Make My Dreams
Daryl Hall & John Oates; Rock 'N Soul, Part 1................. (RCA)
Voices.. (RCA)

You Must Have Been A Beautiful Baby
Bobby Darin; Splish Splash-Best Of Bobby Darin-#1 .... (Atlantic)
Johnny Mercer; Johnny Mercer Sings Johnny Mercer .... (Everest)
Russ Morgan & His Orchestra; Russ Morgan & His Orchestra Play 22
Original Big Band Recordings .... (Hindsight)

You Oughta Be In Pictures
Doris Day; Sentimental Journey.......................... (Hindsight)
Jackie Gleason; The Romantic Moods Of Jackie Gleason .... (Capitol)
Rudy Vallee & His Connecticut Yankees; 78-#24580 .... (Victor)

You'd Be So Nice To Come Home To
Dinah Shore; Songs That Got Us Through WWII-#2-C .... (Rhino)

Your Farts Are Like Frankincense To Me
Capitol Punishment; Messiah Complex .... (We Bite America)

Your Love Amazes Me
John Berry; John Berry................................. (Liberty)

You're The Best Break This Old Heart Ever Had
Ed Bruce; Ed Bruce's Greatest Hits .... (MCA)
One To One.. (MCA)

You're The Cream In My Coffee
Lawrence Welk; Lawrence Welk-16 Most Requested Songs .... (Columbia)
Les Brown & His Orchestra; Best Of Les Brown & His Orchestra ...... (MCA)

You're The Inspiration
Chicago; Chicago 17 .... (Warner Bros.)
Chicago's Greatest Hits-1982-1989 .... (Full Moon)
Peter Cetera featuring Az Yet; You're The Inspiration-A
Collection .... (River North)

You're The Top
Cole Porter; Nipper's Greatest Hits Of The '30s-#1-C .... (RCA)
Ella Fitzgerald; Cole Porter Songbook .... (Verve)
Ethel Merman; Lovely Ladies Of Stage & Screen-C.............. (Legacy)
Frank Sinatra; Good Man Is Hard To Find .... (Pilz America)
Louis Armstrong; American Songbook...................... (Verve)

You've Got A Way
Shania Twain; Come On Over .... (Mercury)
ST/Notting Hill...................................... (Mercury)

You've Made Me So Very Happy
Blood, Sweat & Tears; Blood, Sweat & Tears .... (Columbia)
Blood, Sweat & Tears Greatest Hits .... (Columbia)
Live & Improvised .... (Columbia)
Pop Classics Of The '60s-C .... (Columbia)

COMPUTERS, Digital, Internet
See Also: BUSINESS & INDUSTRY, MACHINES, TELEPHONES

Access To Data
Brand X; Masques .... (Blue Plate)

Age Of Information
Bill Bruford; Gradually Going Tornado.................. (Editions E.G.)

Byte-By-Byte
Software; Chip Meditation .... (Innovative Comm.)

Cheap Computer
Three Johns; 10 Roir Years-Anthology-C .... (Roir)
Deathrocker Scrapbook................................. (Roir)

Computer
Circuitry featuring Sam Bostic; Circuitry featuring Sam Bostic....... (Atlantic)

Computer
Bob Mintzer Big Band; Incredible Journey .... (Digital Music Prod.)

Computer "G"
Kenny Garrett; Black Hope......................... (Warner Bros.)

Computer Age
Neil Young; Trans .... (Geffen)
Sonic Youth; The Bridge: A Tribute To Neil Young-C .... (Caroline)

Computer Age (Push The Button)
Newcleus; Jam On Revenge .... (Sunnyview)
Street Jams-Electric Funk-#2-C .... (Rhino)

Computer Beeps
Original Soundtrack; The Outer Limits................... (Crescendo)

Computer Blue
Prince and the Revolution; ST/Purple Rain .... (Warner Bros.)

Computer Boogie
Valentine Brothers; Have A Good Time .... (A&M)

Computer Cowboy
Neil Young; Trans.................................... (Geffen)

Computer Data
Emerson, Lake & Palmer; King Biscuit Flower Hour Presents Emerson, Lake
& Palmer: Greatest Hits Live .... (King Biscuit Entert.)

Computer Dreams
187 Lockdown; Groove Radio Presents Speed Garage .... (Priority)

Computer Dub
Greater Than One; London .... (Wax Trax)

Computer Eyes
Carole King; Speeding Time .... (Atlantic)

Computer Games
Yellow Magic Orchestra; '80s New Wave-#2-Electronic '80s-C .... (Universal)
Kyoretsu Na Rhythm-Characters .... (Restless)

Computer Games
George Clinton; Computer Games .... (Capitol)

Computer Games
Mi Sex; Richard Blade's Flashback Favorites-#6-C .... (Oglio)
This Ain't No Disco (New Wave Dance Hits)-C .... (Risky Business)

Computer God
Black Sabbath; Dehumanizer .... (Reprise)

Computer In Love
Perrey & Kingsley; Essential Perrey & Kingsley .... (Vanguard)
The In Sound From Way Out! .... (Vanguard)

Computer Incantations For World Peace
Jean-Luc Ponty; Individual Choice .... (Rhino)
Le Voyage: The Jean-Luc Ponty Anthology .... (Rhino)

Computer Lady
Allen Toussaint; Connected .... (NYNO)

Computer Love
Kraftwerk; Computer World .... (Elektra)
The Mix.. (Elektra)

Computer Love
Zapp; Smooth Grooves-A Sensual Collection-#9-C .... (Rhino)
Zapp & Roger; All The Greatest Hits .... (Reprise)

Computer Love
Techmaster P.E.B.; Bass Computer .... (Newtown)

Computer Love
NKRU; Freaky To You .... (RCA)

Computer Minds
Leroy Jenkins; Live! .... (Black Saint)

Computer One
Dear Enemy; Ransom Notes .... (Capitol)

Computer Pilot
Jerry Clower; More Good 'Uns .... (MCA Special Prod.)

Computer Power
Jamie Jupitor; Electro Funk-#2-C .... (Priority)
Street Jams-Electric Funk-#4-C .... (Rhino)

Computer Sex And Self Help
Carl Reiner; The 2000-Year-Old Man In The Year 2000............. (Rhino)

Computer Song
Valerie & Walter Crockett; Unbutton Your Heart................. (Daring)

Computer Took My Job
Maurice John Vaughn; Generic Blues Album .... (Alligator)

Computer Voice
Robert Schroeder; Computer Voice........................ (Racket)

Computer Weekend
Jean-Michel Jarre; Images: The Best Of Jean-Michel Jarre .... (Dreyfus)

Computer World
Kraftwerk; Computer World .... (Elektra)

Computerize
Yellowman; Rambo. .... (Moving Target)

Computers Don't Blunder
Exploited; The Singles Collection .... (Cleopatra)

Computers That Breathe
Tanner; Ill-Gotten Gains .... (Caroline)

Data Bank
Time; Pandemonium .... (Paisley Park)

Data Control
Husker Du; Land Speed Record .... (SST)

Daysleeper
R.E.M.; Up .... (Warner Bros.)

Digital Bath
Deftones; White Pony .... (Maverick)

Digital Display
Ready For The World; Ready For The World .... (MCA)

Digital Dolphins
Dolphins; Malayan Breeze .... (Digital Music Prod.)

Digital Get Down
'N Sync; No Strings Attached .... (Jive)

Electrical Language
Be Bop Deluxe; Best Of Be Bop Deluxe-Raiding The Divine Archive... (Capitol)
Drastic Plastic .... (Capitol)

E-Mail My Heart
Britney Spears; ...Baby One More Time .... (Jive)

Fiction (Dreams In Digital)
Orgy; *Vapor Transmission* . . . . (Elementree/Reprise)
Hello
Poe; *Hello* . . . . (Modern)
Higher & Higher
Moody Blues; *To Our Children's Children's Children* . . . . (Polydor)
Homecomputer
Kraftwerk; *The Mix* . . . . (Elektra)
Honky Tonk Internet
Savannah Taylor; *Savannah Taylor.* . . . . (Ichiban Int'l)
Information
Dave Edmunds; *Information* . . . . (Columbia)
Eric Martin; *Eric Martin* . . . . (Capitol)
Potatoland; *Spirit.* . . . . (Rhino)
Rainmakers; *Rainmakers.* . . . . (Mercury)
Internet Is Gay
A.C.; *I Like It When You Die* . . . . (Earache)
Internet Worm
Paul K.; *Achilles Heel* . . . . (Thirsty Ear)
Pocket Calculator
Kraftwerk; *Computer World* . . . . (Elektra)
The Mix. . . . . (Elektra)
Seen Enough
Crosby, Stills, Nash & Young; *Looking Forward* . . . . (Reprise)
Silicon Valley
Peter Seiler; *Flying Frames* . . . . (Innovative Comm.)
Someone's Computer
Tom Paxton; *One Million Lawyers & Other Disasters* . . . . (Flying Fish)
Theme From "Max Headroom"
Original Soundtrack; *Television's Greatest Hits-#7-Cable Ready-C* . . . . . (TVT)
User Friendly
Ian Anderson; *Walk Into Light.* . . . . (Chrysalis)
Virtual Party (See_You@Party.net)
Peter, Paul & Mary; *Lifelines Live* . . . . (Warner Bros.)
Virtual Reality
Rusted Root; *Evil Ways* . . . . (Mercury)
Remember. . . . . (Mercury)
Virtual Reality
Original Soundtrack; *ST/Lois & Clark: The New Adventures Of*
Superman. . . . . (Sonic Images)
Workin' It
Don Henley; *Inside Job* . . . . (Warner Bros.)
www.Memory
Alan Jackson; *Under The Influence* . . . . (Arista)

COOL, Hip, Modern, Stylish, Trendy
See Also: CLOTHES (fashion), COLD

"In" Crowd, The
Dobie Gray; *Beg, Scream & Shout! The Big Ol' Box Of '60s Soul-C* . . . . (Rhino)
Dobie Gray Sings For In Crowders That Go "Go Go" . . . . (Collectables)
Ramsey Lewis; *Greatest Hits Of Ramsey Lewis* . . . . (Chess)
Party Super Hits-C . . . . (Columbia)
Ramsey Lewis' Greatest Hits . . . . (Columbia)
#1 Stunna
Big Tymers; *I Got That Work* . . . . (Cash Money/Universal)
Abigail Beecher
Freddy Cannon; *14 Booming Hits* . . . . (Rhino)
Big Blast From Boston: The Best Of Freddy "Boom Boom"
Cannon . . . . (Rhino)
Baby You're A Rich Man
Beatles; *Beatles-Box Set* . . . . (Capitol)
Magical Mystery Tour . . . . (Capitol)
Battle Of Who Could Care Less
Ben Folds Five; *Whatever And Ever Amen* . . . . (Caroline/550)
Be Cool
Joni Mitchell; *Wild Things Run Fast* . . . . (Geffen)
Big Willie Style
Will Smith featuring Left Eye; *Big Willie Style* . . . . (Columbia)
Bohemian Like You
Dandy Warhols; *Thirteen Tales From Urban Bohemia* . . . . (Capitol)
Cool
Original Cast; *ST/West Side Story* . . . . (Sony Broadway)
Time; *Time* . . . . (Warner Bros.)
Cool Cat
Queen; *Hot Space* . . . . (Hollywood)
Cool Daddy In A Cadillac
Elvis Hitler; *Disgraceland.* . . . . (Restless)
Cool For Cats
Squeeze; *Cool For Cats* . . . . (A&M)
Singles-45's and under . . . . (A&M)
Squeeze-Classics-#25. . . . . (A&M)
Cool Jerk
Capitols; *Atlantic Rhythm & Blues 1947-1974-#5 (1962-1966)-C* . . . . (Atlantic)
Billboard Top R&B Hits-1966-C . . . . (Rhino)
Capitols-Their Greatest Recordings. . . . . (Solid Smoke)

Collectables Presents The History Of Rock-#5-C . . . . (Collectables)
Son Of Frat Rock!-C . . . . (Rhino)
Super Oldies Of The '60s-#5-C . . . . (Audio Fidelity)
Cool Magic
Steve Miller Band; *Abracadabra* . . . . (Capitol)
Cool Pearl
Capitols; *Golden Classics-Capitols* . . . . (Collectables)
Cool Relax
Jon B.; *Cool Relax* . . . . (Yab Yum/550)
Cool To Hate
Offspring; *Ixnay On The Hombre.* . . . . (Columbia)
Cool, Calm, Collected
Atlantic Starr; *As The Band Turns* . . . . (A&M)
Daddy Cool
Boney M; *Love For Sale* . . . . (Atlantic)
Take The Heat Off Me . . . . (Atco)
Diamonds; *Best Of The Diamonds* . . . . (Rhino)
Dedicated Follower Of Fashion
Kinks; *Kinks' Greatest Hits* . . . . (Rhino)
Kinks-Size Kinkdom . . . . (Rhino)
Down
311; *311* . . . . (Capricorn)
Freak
Silverchair; *Freak Show* . . . . (Epic)
Groovy People
Lou Rawls; *All Things In Time* . . . . (Right Stuff)
Lou Rawls-Live (Right Stuff) . . . . (Right Stuff)
Help! I'm White And I Can't Get Down
Geezinslaws; *Feelin' Good, Gittin' Up, Gittin' Down* . . . . (Step One)
Hepcat's Advice, A
Elmore Nixon; *Best Of Duke-Peacock Blues-C* . . . . (MCA Special Prod.)
Hip To Be Square
Huey Lewis and the News; *Fore!* . . . . (Chrysalis)
I Was Country When Country Wasn't Cool
Barbara Mandrell; *Barbara Mandrell Live* . . . . (MCA)
Barbara Mandrell's Greatest Hits . . . . (MCA)
I'm The Coolest
Alice Cooper; *Goes To Hell* . . . . (Warner Bros.)
It Ain't Cool To Be Crazy About You
George Strait; *Country Classics-#7-1986-1987-C* . . . . (Universal)
George Strait-Number 7 . . . . (MCA)
George Strait's Greatest Hits-#2. . . . . (MCA)
MCA #1 Hits Of The '80s-#2-C . . . . (MCA Special Prod.)
Just Coolin'
Levert; *Just Coolin'* . . . . (Atlantic)
Kansas City
Original Cast; *Oklahoma!* . . . . (MCA)
King Cool
Donnie Iris; *King Cool* . . . . (MCA)
Le Freak
Chic; *Dance Dance Dance-Best Of* . . . . (Atlantic)
Little Superstar
Sheryl Crow; *Sheryl Crow* . . . . (A&M)
Long Cool Woman In A Black Dress
Hollies; *Best Of The Hollies* . . . . (EMI)
Best Of The Hollies-#2 . . . . (EMI)
Billboard Top Rock 'N' Roll Hits-1972-C . . . . (Rhino)
Distant Light . . . . (Epic)
Hollies-Epic Anthology From The Original Master Tapes . . . . (Epic)
The Hollies' Greatest Hits. . . . . (Epic)
Mellow Yellow
Donovan; *Donovan's Greatest Hits* . . . . (Epic)
Seems Like Yesterday-#5-Mid '60s-C . . . . (K-Tel)
Mohair Sam
Derailers; *Here Come The Derailers* . . . . (Lucky Dog)
One Piece At A Time
Johnny Cash; *The Man In Black-His Greatest Hits* . . . . (Legacy)
Peaceful World
John Mellencamp; *Cuttin' Heads.* . . . . (Columbia)
God Bless America-C . . . . (Columbia)
The Concert For New York City-C . . . . (Columbia)
Pink
Aerosmith; *Nine Lives* . . . . (Columbia)
Pretty Fly (For A White Guy)
Offspring; *Americana* . . . . (Columbia)
Pretty Fly For A Rabbi
"Weird Al" Yankovic; *Running With Scissors* . . . . . . (Volcano Entertainment)
San Francisco (Be Sure To Wear Some Flowers In Your Hair)
Scott McKenzie; *Nuggets-#10-Folk Rock-C* . . . . (Rhino)
Rock Artifacts-From The Vaults-#3-C . . . . (Columbia)
ST/Forrest Gump. . . . . (Epic/Sony Music Soundtrax)
Summer Of Love-#1-C. . . . . (Rhino)
Santa Monica
Savage Garden; *Savage Garden.* . . . . (Columbia)
So Hip It Hurts
ABC; *How To Be A Zillionaire* . . . . (Mercury)
Someone Who's Cool
Odds; *Nest* . . . . (Elektra)

Superfly
Curtis Mayfield; *Super Bad-C* .... (K-Tel)
  Superfly .... (Curtom)
Tall Cool One
Robert Plant; *Knebworth-The Album-C* .... (Polydor)
  Now And Zen .... (Es Paranza)
That's Cool, That's Trash
Kingsmen; *Best Of The Kingsmen* .... (Rhino)
Thee Cool Cats
Beatles; *The Beatles-Anthology-#1* .... (Capitol)
Theme From "Mod Squad"
Original Soundtrack; *Television's Greatest Hits-#1-C* .... (TVT)
Walkin' On The Sun
Smash Mouth; *Fush Yu Mang* .... (Interscope)
What Is Hip
Tower Of Power; *In Yo' Face!-History Of Funk-#2-C* .... (Rhino)
  Tower Of Power .... (Warner Bros.)
Who Dat
JT Money; *Pimpin' On Wax* .... (Tony Mercedes/Freeworld/Priority)
You're So Vain
Carly Simon; *'70s Greatest Rock Hits-#3-High Times-C* .... (Priority)
  Best Of Carly Simon .... (Elektra)
  Carly Simon-Greatest Hits Live .... (Arista)
  No Secrets .... (Elektra)

COSMETICS, Lipstick, Makeup, Perfume
See Also: **ANATOMY: FACE, ANATOMY: LIPS, BEAUTY, EYES**

(Now You See Me) Now You Don't
Lee Ann Womack; *Some Things I Know* .... (Decca)
All About Me Intro
Xscape; *Traces Of My Lipstick* .... (So So Def/Columbia)
Another You
David Kersh; *Goodnight Sweetheart* .... (Curb)
Atlantic City
Bruce Springsteen; *Bruce Springsteen's Greatest Hits* .... (Columbia)
  Nebraska .... (Columbia)
Bad Day
Fuel; *Now That's What I Call Music!-#8-C* .... (Virgin)
  Something Like Human .... (Epic)
Bubba Hyde
Diamond Rio; *Diamond Rio's Greatest Hits* .... (Arista)
  Love A Little Stronger .... (Arista)
Candy Perfume Girl
Madonna; *Ray Of Light* .... (Maverick)
Chanel No. Fever
De La Soul; *ST/Men In Black* .... (Columbia)
Chop Suey!
System Of A Down; *Toxicity* .... (American/Columbia)
Cosmetic Surgery
Dixie Carter; *Dixie Carter Sings John Wallowitch Live At The Carlyle* ... (DRG)
John Wallowitch; *My Manhattan* .... (DRG)
Crush With Eyeliner
R.E.M.; *Monster* .... (Warner Bros.)
Desert Rose
Sting; *Brand New Day* .... (A&M)
Devil With A Blue Dress On & Good Golly Miss Molly
Bruce Springsteen; *ST/No Nukes-Muse Concerts* .... (Asylum)
Mitch Ryder And The Detroit Wheels; *Frat Rock!-#4-C* .... (Rhino)
  Rev Up-Best Of Mitch Ryder .... (Rhino)
  Son Of Frat Rock!-C .... (Rhino)
  Toga Rock-C .... (Dunhill Compact Classics)
Dream Walkin'
Toby Keith; *Dream Walkin'* .... (Mercury)
  Toby Keith's Greatest Hits, Volume One .... (Mercury)
Everybody's Free (To Wear Sunscreen)
Baz Luhrmann; *Now That's What I Call Music!-#2-C* .... (Virgin)
  Something For Everybody .... (Capitol)
I Say A Little Prayer
Aretha Franklin; *Aretha Franklin's Greatest Hits* .... (Atlantic)
  Aretha's Gold .... (Atlantic)
  Best Of Aretha Franklin .... (Atlantic)
Burt Bacharach; *Burt Bacharach-Classics-#23* .... (A&M)
  Burt Bacharach's Greatest Hits .... (A&M)
  Reach Out .... (A&M)
Diana King; *ST/My Best Friend's Wedding* .... (Work/Epic)
Dionne Warwick; *Dionne Warwick* .... (Everest)
  Dionne Warwick Greatest Hits .... (Everest)
  Dionne Warwick-Anthology 1962-1971 .... (Rhino)
  Original Rock 'N' Roll Hits Of The '60s-C .... (Roulette)
Lipgloss
Pulp; *His 'N' Hers* .... (Island)
Lipstick
Suzi Quatro; *The Wild One-Classic Quatro* .... (Razor & Tie)
Lipstick
Buzzcocks; *Operators Manual (Buzzcocks Best)* .... (I.R.S.)

  Singles Going Steady .... (I.R.S.)
Lipstick And Bruises
Lit; *Atomic* .... (RCA)
Lipstick And Leather
Y & T; *Best Of Y & T 81-85* .... (A&M)
Lipstick Don't Lie
Mark Collie; *Tennessee Plates* .... (Giant)
Lipstick Lies
Pat Benatar; *Live From Earth* .... (Chrysalis)
Lipstick On A Fingertip
Victor Mecyssne; *Personal Mercury* .... (Sweetfish)
Lipstick On My Dick
Luke; *Luke's Greatest Hits* .... (Lil' Joe)
Lipstick On The Radio
Neal McCoy; *Life Of The Party* .... (Atlantic)
Lipstick On Your Collar
Connie Francis; *Very Best Of Connie Francis* .... (Polydor)
Lipstick Promises
George Ducas; *George Ducas* .... (Capitol)
  I Love Country-Hits Of The '90s-#4-C .... (Priority)
Lipstick Sunset
John Hiatt; *Bring The Family* .... (A&M)
  Hiatt Comes Alive At Budokan .... (A&M)
  John Hiatt's Greatest Hits-The A&M Years '87-'94 .... (A&M)
Lipstick Traces (On A Cigarette)
Amazing Rhythm Aces; *Amazing Rhythm Aces* .... (MCA)
Benny Spellman; *Fortune Teller-Golden Classics* .... (Collectables)
  History Of New Orleans R&B-#3-1962-1970-C .... (Rhino)
  It Will Stand-Minit Records-1960-1963-C .... (EMI)
Delbert McClinton; *Live From Austin* .... (Alligator)
  Plain From The Heart-Classics-#2 .... (Curb)
O'Jays; *Beg, Scream & Shout! The Big Ol' Box Of '60s Soul-C* ... (Rhino)
  Soul Shots-#10-More Sweet Soul-C .... (Rhino)
Ringo Starr; *Bad Boy* .... (Epic)
Lipstick Vogue
Elvis Costello; *2 1/2 Years* .... (Rykodisc)
  This Year's Model .... (Rykodisc)
Lipstick, Powder & Paint
Big Joe Turner; *Rhythm & Blues Years* .... (Rhino)
Delbert McClinton; *The Ultimate Collection-Delbert McClinton* ...... (Hip-O)
Little Bit Of Soap
Jarmels; *Collectables Presents The History Of Rock-#7-C* ...... (Collectables)
  Jarmels-Golden Classics .... (Collectables)
  Laurie Golden Oldies .... (Laurie)
  Million-Dollar Memories #1-C .... (RCA)
  Pick Hits Of The Radio Good Guys-C .... (Laurie)
Paul Davis; *Best Of Paul Davis* .... (Bang)
  Little Bit Of Paul Davis .... (Bang)
Makeup & Faded Blue Jeans
Merle Haggard; *Back To The Barrooms* .... (MCA)
  Country Classics-#4-1984-1985-C .... (Universal)
  Merle Haggard-His Best .... (MCA)
Perfume
Jesus & Mary Chain; *Munki* .... (Sub Pop)
Perfume And Pink Chiffon
Sonny Lester & His Orchestra; *Take It Off: Striptease Classics-C* ...... (Rhino)
Perfume, Powder And Lead
Lonesome River Band; *Finding The Way* .... (Sugar Hill)
Perfumed Garden of Gulliver Smith
Marc Bolan; *T. Rex Classics* .... (Cleopatra)
Powder Your Face With Sunshine (Smile!)
Guy Lombardo & His Royal Canadians; *Best Of Guy Lombardo* .... (Curb)
Sammy Kaye & His Orchestra; *Sammy Kaye & His Orchestra Play 22
  Original Big Band Recordings* .... (Hindsight)
Psycho Circus
Kiss; *Psycho Circus* .... (Mercury)
Scentless Apprentice
Nirvana; *In Utero* .... (David Geffen Co.)
She Drew A Broken Heart
Patty Loveless; *The Trouble With The Truth* .... (Epic)
Spilled Perfume
Pam Tillis; *Sweetheart's Dance* .... (Arista)
That Ain't No Way To Go
Brooks & Dunn; *Hard Workin' Man* .... (Arista)
Thunder Rolls, The
Garth Brooks; *Garth Brooks-Double Live* .... (Capitol)
  No Fences .... (Capitol)
Tracks Of My Tears, The
Bryan Ferry; *These Foolish Things* .... (Reprise)
Gladys Knight & The Pips; *Gladys Knight & The Pips-Anthology* .... (Motown)
Johnny Rivers; *Best Of Johnny Rivers* .... (EMI)
Linda Ronstadt; *Linda Ronstadt's Greatest Hits* .... (Asylum)
  Prisoner In Disguise .... (Asylum)
Smokey Robinson & The Miracles; *Billboard Top R&B Hits-1965-
  1969-C* .... (Rhino)
  Smokey Robinson & The Miracles' Anthology .... (Motown)
  Smokey Robinson & The Miracles' Greatest Hits-#2 .... (Motown)
  ST/Big Chill .... (Motown)

ST/Sound Of "Murphy Brown" . . . . (MCA)
Unpretty
 TLC; *Fanmail* . . . . (LaFace)
Vanishing Cream
 Hunger; *Devil Thumbs A Ride* . . . . (Universal)
Who Stole The Jukebox (From Lucy's Perfume Parlor)
 Johnny Bond; *Johnny Gimble's Texas Honky-Tonk Hits-C* . . . . . . (C.M.H. Prod.)
Young Blood
 Rickie Lee Jones; *Naked Songs Live And Acoustic* . . . . (Reprise)
 Rickie Lee Jones . . . . (Warner Bros.)
Your Farts Are Like Frankincense To Me
 Capitol Punishment; *Messiah Complex* . . . . (We Bite America)
Your Good Girl's Gonna Go Bad
 Billie Jo Spears; *Best Of Billie Jo Spears* . . . . (CEMA Special Prod.)
 Best Of Billie Jo Spears . . . . (Razor & Tie)
 K.T. Oslin; *Tammy Wynette...Remembered-C* . . . . (Asylum)
 Tammy Wynette; *Tammy Wynette-Anniversary-20 Years Of Hits* . . . . . . (Epic)
 Tammy Wynette's Greatest Hits . . . . (Epic)
 Your Good Girl's Gonna Go Bad . . . . (Legacy)

COUNTING SONGS

*See Also: **NUMBERS** (various), **SPELLING SONGS***

(We're Gonna) Rock Around The Clock
 Bill Haley & His Comets; *Bill Haley & His Comets' Greatest Hits* . . . . . . (MCA)
 Bill Haley & His Comets' Greatest Hits . . . . (Everest)
 Bill Haley & His Comets-Golden Hits . . . . (MCA)
 Billboard Top Rock 'N' Roll Hits-1955-C . . . . (Rhino)
 ST/American Graffiti . . . . (MCA)
1, 2, 3
 311; *Grassroots* . . . . (Capricorn)
1, 2, Buckle My Shoe
 Bob McGrath; *The Baby Record* . . . . (Golden Boy Jazz/Optimism)
1,2,3,4 (Sumpin' New)
 Coolio; *ESPN Presents Jock Jams-#2-C* . . . . (Tommy Boy)
 MTV Party To Go-#9-C . . . . (Tommy Boy)
 Tommy Boy's Greatest Beats-#2-C . . . . (Tommy Boy)
1-2-3
 Gloria Estefan; *Gloria Estefan's Greatest Hits* . . . . (Epic)
 Gloria Estefan and Miami Sound Machine; *Let It Loose* . . . . (Epic)
1-2-3
 Len Barry; *24 Of The Grooviest Hits Of All Time! The '60s Ultimate
   Collection-#1-C* . . . . (Sundazed Music)
5 Steps
 Dru Hill; *Dru Hill* . . . . (Island)
5-4-3-2 (Yo! Time Is Up)
 Jade; *Mind Body & Soul* . . . . (Giant)
ABC
 Jackson 5; *ABC* . . . . (Motown)
 Jackson 5-Anthology . . . . (Motown)
 Jackson 5's Greatest Hits . . . . (Motown)
All Together Now
 Beatles; *Yellow Submarine* . . . . (Capitol)
 Muppets; *Kermit Unpigged* . . . . (Jim Henson)
Ants Go Marching, The
 Original Soundtrack; *Mother Goose Songs, The* . . . . (Madacy)
Any Man Of Mine
 Shania Twain; *1996 Grammy Nominees-C* . . . . (Columbia)
 The Woman In Me . . . . (Mercury)
 Snoopy; *Snoopy's Country Classiks On Toys* . . . . (Lightyear)
Are You Ready?
 Creed; *Human Clay* . . . . (Wind-up)
Area Codes
 Ludacris; *Word Of Mouf* . . . . (Murder Inc./Def Jam/IDJMG)
Back At One
 Brian McKnight; *Back At One* . . . . (Motown)
 Mark Wills; *Permanently* . . . . (Mercury)
Backfield In Motion
 Mel & Tim; *Collectables Presents The History Of Rock-#4-C* . . . . (Collectables)
 Oldies But Goodies-#2-C . . . . (Original Sound)
 Soul Shots-#2-The "In" Crowd-Sweet Soul-C . . . . (Rhino)
 Super Oldies Of The '60s-#10-C . . . . (Audio Fidelity)
Barrel Of A Gun (4,3,2,1)
 Guster; *Lost & Gone Forever* . . . . (Hybrid/Sire)
Blue Suede Shoes
 Carl Perkins; *Blue Suede Shoes* . . . . (Sun)
 Carl Perkins-Original Sun Greatest Hits . . . . (Rhino)
 Cruisin'-1956-1957-C . . . . (Dunhill Compact Classics)
 Oldies But Goodies-#4-C . . . . (Original Sound)
 Elvis Presley; *Aloha from Hawaii via Satellite* . . . . (RCA)
 Elvis Presley . . . . (RCA)
 Elvis-A Legendary Performer, Volume 2 . . . . (RCA)
 From Memphis To Vegas/From Vegas To Memphis . . . . (RCA)
 ST/G.I. Blues . . . . (RCA)
Bodies
 Drowning Pool; *Sinner* . . . . (Wind-up)

Book Of Love
 Monotones; *Bedrock-Late '50s/'60s Rock 'N' Roll* . . . . (Allegiance)
 Best Of Chess Rock 'N' Roll-#1-C . . . . (Chess)
 Original Golden Rock Oldies-#1-C . . . . (Specialty)
 ST/American Graffiti . . . . (MCA)
 Super Oldies Of The '50s-#2-C . . . . (Audio Fidelity)
Bowling Song
 Asleep At The Wheel; *Country Goes Raffi-C* . . . . (Rounder)
Count Me In
 Gary Lewis And The Playboys; *Gary Lewis & The Playboys* . . . . . . (Gold Rush)
 Gary Lewis And The Playboys' Greatest Hits . . . . (Curb)
Count Your Blessings
 Ashford & Simpson; *Best Of Ashford & Simpson* . . . . . . (EMI Special Markets)
Count Your Blessings (Instead Of Sheep)
 Bing Crosby; *45-#29251* . . . . (Decca)
 Eddie Fisher; *Best Of Eddie Fisher* . . . . (MCA)
 Rosemary Clooney; *Essence Of Rosemary Clooney* . . . . (Legacy)
Counting Blue Cars
 Dishwalla; *Pet Your Friends* . . . . (A&M)
Days Of The Week
 Stone Temple Pilots; *Shangri-La-Dee-Da* . . . . (Atlantic)
Door #1
 LSG; *Levert-Sweat-Gill* . . . . (East West)
Five Feet High And Rising
 Johnny Cash; *The Man In Black-His Greatest Hits* . . . . (Legacy)
Good Lovin'
 Grateful Dead; *Shakedown Street* . . . . (Arista)
 Rascals; *Hit Singles-1958-1977-C* . . . . (Atlantic)
 Rascals' Greatest Hits . . . . (Atlantic)
 Rascals-Super Hits . . . . (Atlantic)
 ST/Big Chill . . . . (Motown)
Helplessly Hoping
 Crosby, Stills & Nash; *Crosby, Stills & Nash* . . . . (Atlantic)
 CSN . . . . (Atlantic)
 Crosby, Stills, Nash & Young; *So Far* . . . . (Atlantic)
Hitchin' A Ride
 Green Day; *Nimrod* . . . . (Reprise)
How Many Tears
 Bobby Vee; *Bobby Vee-Legendary Masters* . . . . (EMI)
I Count The Minutes
 Ricky Martin; *Ricky Martin* . . . . (Columbia)
I Saw Her Standing There
 Beatles; *Introducing...The Beatles* . . . . (Vee-Jay)
 Meet The Beatles! . . . . (Capitol)
 Please Please Me . . . . (Parlophone)
 Rock 'N' Roll Music . . . . (Capitol)
 The Beatles-Anthology-#1 . . . . (Capitol)
 Paul McCartney; *Tripping The Live Fantastic-Highlights!* . . . . (Capitol)
I Won't Let You Do That To Me
 Luther Vandross; *One Night With You-The Best Of Love-#2* . . . . . . (LV/Epic)
I-Feel-Like-I'm-Fixin'-To-Die Rag
 Country Joe & The Fish; *Country Joe & The Fish-Greatest Hits* . . . . . (Vanguard)
 Greatest '60s Folksingers-C . . . . (Vanguard)
 I-Feel-Like-I'm-Fixin'-To-Die . . . . (Vanguard)
 Life & Times Of Country Joe & The Fish . . . . (Vanguard)
 More American Graffiti-#4-C . . . . (MCA)
 Songs Of Protest-C . . . . (Rhino)
 ST/Woodstock . . . . (Atlantic)
Jerry Springer
 "Weird Al" Yankovic; *Running With Scissors* . . . . . . (Volcano Entertainment)
Kansas City
 Beatles; *Beatles VI* . . . . (Capitol)
 Beatles-Box Set . . . . (Capitol)
 Rock 'N' Roll Music . . . . (Capitol)
 Super Oldies Of The '60s-#10-C . . . . (Audio Fidelity)
 Bill Haley & His Comets; *Bill Haley & His Comets' Greatest Hits* . . . . . (Everest)
 Fats Domino; *Fats Domino's Greatest Hits* . . . . (Everest)
 Wilbert Harrison; *American Graffiti-#3-C* . . . . (MCA)
 Billboard Top Rock 'N' Roll Hits-1959-C . . . . (Rhino)
 Cruisin'-1959-C . . . . (Increase)
 Echoes Of A Rock Era-Middle Years-C . . . . (Roulette)
 Super Oldies Of The '50s-#2-C . . . . (Audio Fidelity)
Little Honda
 Beach Boys; *Absolute Best-#1* . . . . (Capitol)
 All Summer Long . . . . (Capitol)
 Best Of The Beach Boys . . . . (Capitol)
 Spirit Of America . . . . (Capitol)
 Hondells; *Beach Classics-All Original
   Recordings-C* . . . . (Dunhill Compact Classics)
 Cruisin'-1964-C . . . . (Increase)
Major Tom (Coming Home)
 Peter Schilling; *Different Story (World Of Lust & Crime)* . . . . (Elektra)
 Error In The System . . . . (Elektra)
Mas Tequila
 Sammy Hagar; *Red Voodoo* . . . . (MCA)
Mr. Lee
 Bobbettes; *Billboard Top R&B Hits-1957-C* . . . . (Rhino)
 ST/Stand By Me . . . . (Atlantic)
 Pointer Sisters; *Rock Rhythm & Blues-C* . . . . (Warner Bros.)

One Potato
Sesame Street; *The Count's Countdown* . . . . (Sony Wonder)
One Potato Two
Music Explosion; *Super K Kollection-#2-C* . . . . (Collectables)
One Potato, Two Potato
Westside Children's Singers; *Play Time: 25 Favorite Play And Party Songs* . . . . (EMI Special Markets)
One Step Closer
Doobie Brothers; *Best Of The Doobies, Volume II* . . . .(Warner Bros.)
One Step Closer . . . .(Warner Bros.)
Redneck 12 Days Of Christmas
Jeff Foxworthy; *Crank It Up: The Music Album* . . . .(Warner Bros.)
Jeff Foxworthy's Greatest Bits . . . .(Warner Bros.)
Rock And Roll Waltz
Kay Starr; *Capitol Collectors Series-Kay Starr* . . . . (Capitol)
Sixteen Reasons
Connie Stevens; *Only Rock 'N Roll-1960-1964-#1 Radio Hits-C* . . . . . . (Rhino)
So Many Ways
Braxtons; *So Many Ways* . . . .(Atlantic)
Stand And Be Counted
Crosby, Stills, Nash & Young; *Looking Forward* . . . . (Reprise)
Step By Step
Eddie Rabbitt; *Best Of Eddie Rabbitt/Greatest Hits-II* . . . .(Warner Bros.)
Number 1's . . . .(Warner Bros.)
Ten Little Indians
Nilsson; *Pandemonium Shadow Show* . . . . (RCA)
Ten Little Numbers
Hank Williams; *Complete Hank Williams* . . . . (Mercury)
Tender Shepherd
Original Cast; *Peter Pan-The 1954 Broadway Production* . . . .(RCA Victor)
This Old Man
Dana; *Dana's Best Sing & Play-Along Tunes!* . . . .(Real Music For Kidz)
Original Soundtrack; *Children's Favorites* . . . . (Kid Rhino/Rhino 4 Kids)
Three Marlenas
Wallflowers; *Bringing Down The Horse* . . . . (Interscope)
Three Times A Lady
Commodores; *All The Great Love Songs-Commodores* . . . . (Motown)
Commodores Greatest Hits . . . . (Motown)
Commodores-All The Great Hits . . . . (Motown)
Endless Love-Motown's Greatest Love Songs-C . . . . (Motown)
Natural High . . . . (Motown)
TV Movie
Bruce Springsteen; *Tracks* . . . . (Columbia)
Twelve Days Of Christmas
Allan Sherman; *Christmas Comedy Classics-#2-C* . . . . (Priority)
Dr. Demento Presents The Greatest Novelty Records-#6-Christmas-C . . . . (Rhino)
Andrews Sisters; *Andrews Sisters-Christmas* . . . .(MCA Special Prod.)
Bing Crosby; *That Christmas Feeling* . . . .(MCA Special Prod.)
Bob & Doug McKenzie; *Dr. Demento's Greatest Christmas CD-C* . . . . . (Rhino)
David Seville & The Chipmunks; *Christmas With The Chipmunks-#2* . . . .(EMI)
Frank Sinatra; *Sinatra Christmas Album* . . . . (Reprise)
Fred Waring's Pennsylvanians; *Now Is The Caroling Season* . . . . (Capitol)
Garrison Keillor; *Now It Is Christmas Again* . . . . (Angel)
Harry Belafonte; *Christmas Classics-#2* . . . . (RCA)
Joan Sutherland; *Christmas Stars-C* . . . . (London)
John Denver; *A Christmas Together* . . . . (Laserlight)
Kiri Te Kanawa; *Christmas With Kiri Te Kanawa* . . . . (London)
Ray Conniff; *Christmas Wonderland* . . . .(Sony Music Special Prod.)
Twenty-Five Miles
Edwin Starr; *Motown Superstar Series-#3-Edwin Starr* . . . . (Motown)
Michael Jackson; *Original Soul Of Michael Jackson* . . . . (Motown)
You Never Give Me Your Money
Beatles; *Abbey Road* . . . .(Parlophone)
Beatles-Box Set . . . . (Capitol)
George Benson; *The Best* . . . . (Rebound)
Your Little Secret
Melissa Etheridge; *Your Little Secret* . . . . (Island)

COUNTRIES: A

See Also: CITIES: A-Z, COUNTRIES: AMERICA, COUNTRIES: AUSTRALIA

4:37 AM (Arabs With Knives & West German Skies)
Roger Waters; *Pros & Cons Of Hitchhiking* . . . . (Columbia)
Ahab The Arab
Ray Stevens; *Best Of Ray Stevens* . . . . (Rhino)
Gitarzan . . . . (Barnaby)
Very Best Of Ray Stevens . . . . (Barnaby)
Air Algiers
Country Joe McDonald; *Hold On It's Coming* . . . . (Vanguard)
Albania National Anthem
Vienna State Opera Orchestra; *National Anthems Of The World* . . .(Bescol, Ltd.)
Algeria National Anthem
Swarovski Musik Wattens; *National Anthems Of The World* . . . . (Koch International)

Angola
Ry Cooder; *ST/Johnny Handsome* . . . . (Warner Bros.)
Angola
Ambrosia; *Live Beyond L.A.* . . . . (Warner Bros.)
Arabia
Art Blakey & His Jazz Messengers; *History Of Art Blakey/Jazz Messengers* . . . .(Blue Note)
Mosaic . . . .(Blue Note)
Arabia
Jerry Garcia & David Grisman; *Jerry Garcia & David Grisman* . . . .(Grateful Dead)
Arabian Knights
Siouxsie And The Banshees; *Juju* . . . . (Geffen)
Once Upon A Time-The Singles . . . . (Geffen)
Arabian Love Call
Art Neville; *That Old Time Rock 'N' Roll* . . . .(Specialty)
Arabian Lover
Duke Ellington; *Jungle Nights In Harlem* . . . . (Bluebird)
Arabian Nights
Bruce Adler; *ST/Aladdin* . . . . (Disney)
Argentina National Anthem (Libertad!)
Banda Sinfonica De Madrid; *National Anthems* . . . . (International Music)
Swarovski Musik Wattens; *National Anthems Of The World* . . . . (Koch International)
Armenia City In The Sky
Who; *The Who Sell Out* . . . . (MCA)
Armenia National Anthem
Swarovski Musik Wattens; *National Anthems Of The World* . . . . (Koch International)
Aruba
Tim Weisberg; *Outrageous Temptations* . . . .(Cypress)
Aruba
Jim Hall; *Circles* . . . . (Concord Jazz)
Aruba
Kenny Barron & Ted Dunbar; *In Tandem* . . . .(Muse)
Aruba!
Rippingtons; *Tourist In Paradise* . . . . (GRP)
Arubian Nights
Larry Coryell & Emily Remler; *Together* . . . . (Concord Jazz)
At An Arabian House Party
Raymond Scott; *Reckless Nights & Turkish Twilights* . . . . (Columbia)
Austria National Anthem (Österreichische Bendeshymne [Land Der Berge, Land Am Strome])
American Brass Band; *National Anthems* . . . .(Laserlight)
Vienna State Opera Orchestra; *National Anthems Of The World* . . (Bescol, Ltd.)
Austrian Anthill
Brian Ritchie; *The Blend* . . . .(SST)
Buenos Dias Argentina
Marty Robbins; *All Around Cowboy* . . . . (Columbia)
Encore-Marty Robbins . . . . (Columbia)
Don't Cry For Me Argentina
Madonna; *GHV2* . . . . (Warner Bros.)
ST/Evita-Music From The Motion Picture . . . . (Warner Bros.)
Original Cast; *Evita* . . . . (MCA)
Killing An Arab
Cure; *Boys Don't Cry* . . . . (Elektra)
Standing On A Beach-The Singles . . . . (Elektra)
New Argentina
Original Cast; *Evita* . . . . (MCA)
Secret Life Of Arabia
David Bowie; *Heroes* . . . . (Rykodisc)
Sheik Of Araby
Beatles; *The Beatles-Anthology-#1* . . . . (Capitol)
Benny Goodman; *Benny Goodman Sextet featuring Charlie Christian-1939-1941* . . . . (Columbia)
Django Reinhardt; *Djangologie USA-#1* . . . . (Disques Swing)
Fred Astaire; *Three Evenings With Fred Astaire* . . . .(DRG)
Leon Redbone; *Double Time* . . . . (Warner Bros.)
Theme From "Lawrence Of Arabia"
BBC Concert Orchestra; *Golden Cinema Classics-#1-The Adventure Film* . . . . (Bainbridge)
Cincinnati Pops Orchestra/Erich Kunzel; *Hollywood's Greatest Hits-#1* . . . . (Telarc)
Winter In Austria
L. Subramaniam; *Spanish Wave* . . . . (Milestone)

COUNTRIES: AMERICA

See Also: CITIES: A-Z, DRAFT, FREEDOM, MONTHS & DATES: JULY, PATRIOTISM, POLITICS (various), PRESIDENTS, PROTEST, STATES: A-Z, WAR

(You Can Still) Rock In America
Night Ranger; *Midnight Madness* . . . . (MCA)
4th Of July
U2; *Unforgettable Fire* . . . . (Island)

4th Of July, Asbury Park (Sandy)
Bruce Springsteen; *The Wild, The Innocent & The E Street Shuffle* . . . (Columbia)
Bruce Springsteen & The E Street Band; *Bruce Springsteen & The E Street Band Live/1975-85* . . . . (Legacy)

Abraham, Martin And John
Dion; *Collectables Presents The History Of Rock-#3-C* . . . . (Collectables)
Dion-24 Original Classics . . . . (Arista)
Songs Of Protest-C . . . . (Rhino)
WCBS FM 101 History Of Rock-'60s-#2-C . . . . (Collectables)
Harry Belafonte; *Harry Belafonte's All Time Greatest Hits-#1* . . . . (RCA)
Smokey Robinson & The Miracles; *Smokey Robinson & The Miracles' Anthology* . . . . (Motown)
Time Out For Smokey Robinson & The Miracles/Special Occasion . . . . (Motown)

All American
Original Cast/Sammy Davis, Jr.; *Stop The World I Want To Get Off* . . . . (Warner Bros.)

All American
Sammy Hagar; *Nine On A Ten Scale* . . . . (Capitol)

All American Boy
Bill Parsons; *History Of Rock-#10-C* . . . . (Collectables)

All American Boy
Statler Brothers; *Son Of The Motherland* . . . . (Mercury)

All American Girl
Daryl Hall & John Oates; *Big Bam Boom* . . . . (RCA)

All American Girl
Melissa Etheridge; *Yes I Am* . . . . (Island)

All American Girls
Sister Sledge; *Best Of Sister Sledge-1973-1985* . . . . (Rhino)

All American Man
Kiss; *Alive II* . . . . (Casablanca)

All American Redneck
Geezinslaw Brothers; *If You Think I'm Crazy Now* . . . . (Lone Star)

All The Way From America
Joan Armatrading; *Joan Armatrading-Classics-#21* . . . . (A&M)
Joan Armatrading's Greatest Hits . . . . (A&M)
Me Myself I . . . . (A&M)

America
Neil Diamond; *12 Greatest Hits-#2* . . . . (Columbia)
Hot August Night II . . . . (Columbia)
ST/The Jazz Singer . . . . (Capitol)

America
David Bowie; *The Concert For New York City-C* . . . . (Columbia)
Paul Simon; *Paul Simon In Concert/Live Rhymin'* . . . . (Columbia)
Simon & Garfunkel; *Bookends* . . . . (Columbia)
Collected Works . . . . (Columbia)
Simon & Garfunkel's Greatest Hits . . . . (Columbia)
The Concert In Central Park . . . . (Warner Bros.)

America
Kurtis Blow; *America* . . . . (Mercury)

America
Prince and the Revolution; *Around The World In A Day* . . . . (Paisley Park)

America
KBC Band; *KBC Band* . . . . (Arista)

America
Heart; *Private Audition* . . . . (Epic)

America
Original Cast; *ST/West Side Story* . . . . (Sony Broadway)

America
Waylon Jennings; *Waylon Jennings' Greatest Hits-#2* . . . . (RCA)

America (My Country 'Tis Of Thee)
Mormon Tabernacle Choir; *God Bless America* . . . . (Sony Music Classical)
Original Soundtrack; *School Days-Kids Classics* . . . . (Benson)
Pat Boone; *Star Spangled Banner* . . . . (Word)
Spirit Of Freedom Singers with Roland Shaw & His Orchestra; *Stars And Stripes Forever-#2-C* . . . . (Volcano Entertainment)

America Is My Home
James Brown; *Best Of James Brown* . . . . (Polydor)

America The Beautiful
American Philharmonic Orchestra Orchestra & Chorus; *Stars And Stripes Forever-#2-C* . . . . (Volcano Entertainment)
Elvis Presley; *Elvis Aron Presley* . . . . (RCA)
Frank Sinatra; *God Bless America-C* . . . . (Capitol)
Keb' Mo'; *Big Wide Grin* . . . . (Sony Wonder)
Lee Greenwood; *American Patriot* . . . . (Capitol)
Mormon Tabernacle Choir; *God Bless America* . . . . (Sony Music Classical)
This Is My Country . . . . (Columbia)
Original Soundtrack; *School Days-Kids Classics* . . . . (Benson)
Ray Charles; *Ray Charles' Greatest Hits-#2* . . . . (Rhino)
Ray Charles-His Greatest Hits-#2 . . . . (Dunhill Compact Classics)
Star Spangled Band; *Red, White & Bluegrass-C* . . . . (C.M.H. Prod.)
Willie Nelson; *America: A Tribute To Heroes-C* . . . . (Interscope)

America The Beautiful, 1976
Charlie Rich; *Charlie Rich's Greatest Hits* . . . . (Epic)

America Town
Five For Fighting; *America Town* . . . . (Aware/C2/Columbia)

America, I Believe In You
Charlie Daniels; *America, I Believe In You* . . . . (Liberty)

American Bad Ass
Kid Rock; *History Of Rock* . . . . (Top Dog/Lava/Atlantic)

American Beat '84
Fleshtones; *Living Legends* . . . . (I.R.S.)

American Beauty Rose
Frank Sinatra; *Come Swing With Me!* . . . . (Capitol)
Sentimental Journey . . . . (Capitol)

American Boy
Eddie Rabbitt; *American Music Greatest Hits-C* . . . . (Curb)
Eddie Rabbitt-Greatest Country Hits . . . . (Curb)
Jersey Boy . . . . (Capitol)

American Boys
Deborah Galli; *Radio Active* . . . . (Mercury)

American City Suite
Cashman & West; *Super Hits Of The '70s-Have A Nice Day-#9-C* . . . . . (Rhino)

American Dream
John Cougar Mellencamp; *Chestnut Street Incident* . . . . (Rhino)

American Dream
Crosby, Stills, Nash & Young; *American Dream* . . . . (Atlantic)

American Dream
Oak Ridge Boys; *American Dreams* . . . . (MCA)

American Dream
Chicago; *Chicago XIV* . . . . (Chicago)

American Dream
Original London Cast; *Miss Saigon* . . . . (Geffen)

American Dream
Nitty Gritty Dirt Band; *Twenty Years Of Dirt-Best Of The Nitty Gritty Dirt Band* . . . . (Warner Bros.)

American Girl
Goo Goo Dolls; *The Concert For New York City-C* . . . . (Columbia)
Tom Petty And The Heartbreakers; *Pack Up The Plantation-Live!* . . . . . (MCA)
Tom Petty & The Heartbreakers . . . . (Gone Gator)
You're Gonna Get It! . . . . (Gone Gator)

American Girls
Rick Springfield; *Success Hasn't Spoiled Me Yet* . . . . (RCA)

American Heartbeat
Survivor; *Eye Of The Tiger* . . . . (Scotti Bros.)

American Hearts
Air Supply; *Lost In Love* . . . . (Arista)

American Honky-Tonk Bar Association
Garth Brooks; *In Pieces* . . . . (Liberty)

American In Paris, An
Atlantic Brass Quintet; *By George! Gershwin's Greatest Hits* . . (Musicmasters)
George Gershwin; *Rhapsody In Blue* . . . . (Biograph)

American Made
Oak Ridge Boys; *American Made* . . . . (MCA)
Oak Ridge Boys' Greatest Hits 2 . . . . (MCA)

American Music
Blasters; *Blasters* . . . . (Slash)
Blasters-Collection . . . . (Slash)

American Music
Pointer Sisters; *So Excited* . . . . (Planet)

American Music
Violent Femmes; *Why Do Birds Sing?* . . . . (Slash)

American Patrol
Glenn Miller & His Orchestra; *Glenn Miller & His Orchestra-Pure Gold* . . . . (Bluebird)
Moonlight Serenade . . . . (Ranwood)
Stars And Stripes Forever-#2-C . . . . (Volcano Entertainment)
The Unforgettable Glenn Miller & His Orchestra . . . . (RCA)

American Pie
Don McLean; *American Pie* . . . . (EMI)
Best Of Don McLean . . . . (EMI)
Greatest Hits Then & Now . . . . (EMI)
ST/Born On The Fourth Of July . . . . (MCA)
Madonna; *ST/The Next Big Thing* . . . . (Maverick)

American Popular Song
Neil Diamond; *You Don't Bring Me Flowers* . . . . (Columbia)

American Prayer
Doors; *An American Prayer-Jim Morrison* . . . . (Elektra)

American Remains
Waylon Jennings, Willie Nelson, Johnny Cash, Kris Kristofferson; *Highwayman 2* . . . . (Columbia)

American Roulette
Robbie Robertson; *Robbie Robertson* . . . . (Geffen)

American Skin (41 Shots)
Bruce Springsteen & The E Street Band; *Live In New York City* . . . . . (Columbia)

American Squirm
Nick Lowe; *Basher: Best Of.* . . . . (Columbia)
Labour Of Lust . . . . (Columbia)

American Storm
Bob Seger & The Silver Bullet Band; *Like A Rock* . . . . (Capitol)

American Tune
Paul Simon; *Paul Simon In Concert/Live Rhymin'* . . . . (Columbia)
There Goes Rhymin' Simon . . . . (Columbia)
Simon & Garfunkel; *The Concert In Central Park* . . . . (Warner Bros.)

American Woman
Guess Who; *American Woman* . . . . (RCA)

Best Of The Guess Who . . . . (RCA)
Greatest Of The Guess Who . . . . (RCA)
Nipper's Greatest Hits Of The '70s-C . . . . (RCA)
Rock Classics-C . . . . (K-Tel)
Lenny Kravitz; *5.* . . . . (Virgin)
Now That's What I Call Music!-#3-C . . . . (Virgin)
ST/Austin Powers-The Spy Who Shagged Me . . . . (Maverick)

Americana
Moe Bandy; *Best Of Branson U.S.A.-#1-C* . . . . (Curb)
Country's Greatest Hits-American Pride-C . . . . (Priority)
Moe Bandy's Greatest Hits . . . . (Curb)

Americans
Tex Ritter; *An American Legend.* . . . . (Capitol)

Amerika
Trick Daddy; *Thugs Are Us* . . . . (Slip 'N Slide/Atlantic)

Amerikka's Most Wanted
Ice Cube; *AmeriKKKa's Most Wanted* . . . . (Priority)

Among The Americans
10,000 Maniacs; *Wishing Chair* . . . . (Elektra)

An American Trilogy
Elvis Presley; *Aloha from Hawaii via Satellite* . . . . (RCA)
Elvis Aron Presley . . . . (RCA)
Elvis Recorded Live On Stage In Memphis . . . . (RCA)
Madison Square Garden . . . . (RCA)
ST/This Is Elvis . . . . (RCA)
Mickey Newbury; *Frisco Mabel Joy* . . . . (Mountain Retreat)
Stars And Stripes Forever-#2-C. . . . . (Volcano Entertainment)

Any Bonds Today?
Andrews Sisters; *Swing Out To Victory: Songs Of World*
    War II-C . . . . (ISD/Intersound)
Barry Wood; *78-#27478.* . . . . (Victor)
Bing Crosby; *Original Soundtrack Sessions.* . . . . (Vintage Jazz Classics)

Back In The U.S.A.
Chuck Berry; *Chuck Berry-Golden Hits* . . . . (Mercury)
Chuck Berry's Greatest Hits . . . . (Everest)
Roll Over Beethoven . . . . (Allegiance)
The Chess Box-Chuck Berry . . . . (Chess)
Linda Ronstadt; *Linda Ronstadt's Greatest Hits, Volume Two* . . . . (Asylum)
Living In The USA . . . . (Asylum)

Bad America
Gun Club; *Las Vegas Story.* . . . . (I.R.S.)

Ballad Of William Worthy
Phil Ochs; *Best Of Broadside 1962-1968: Anthems Of The American*
    Underground From The Pages Of Broadside
    Magazine-C . . . . (Smithsonian Folkways)

Bang The Drum Slowly
Emmylou Harris; *Red Dirt Girl* . . . . (Nonesuch)

Banned In The U.S.A.
Luke Skyywalker; *Banned In The U.S.A.* . . . . (Luke)

Battle Hymn Of The Republic, The
Charlie Sexton; *Charlie Sexton.* . . . . (MCA)
Judy Collins; *Songs Of The Civil War-C.* . . . . (Columbia)
Mormon Tabernacle Choir; *God Bless America* . . . . (Sony Music Classical)
Stars And Stripes Forever . . . . (Columbia)
National Philharmonic Orchestra & Chorus; *Stars And Stripes*
    Forever-#2-C. . . . . (Volcano Entertainment)
Original Soundtrack; *School Days-Kids Classics.* . . . . (Benson)
Pat Boone; *Star Spangled Banner.* . . . . (Word)

Better In The USA
Glenn Frey; *The Allnighter.* . . . . (MCA)

Bicentennial
Loudon Wainwright III; *T-Shirt* . . . . (Arista)

Bicentennial Blues
Gil Scott-Heron; *It's Your World* . . . . (Arista)
Mind Of . . . . (Arista)

Big In America
Stranglers; *Dreamtime* . . . . (Epic)
Stranglers' Greatest Hits-1977-1990 . . . . (Epic)

Bleed American
Jimmy Eat World; *Bleed American.* . . . . (DreamWorks/SKG)

Born In America
Riot; *Born In America.* . . . . (Quality)

Born In The U.S.A.
Bruce Springsteen; *Born In The U.S.A.* . . . . (Columbia)
Bruce Springsteen's Greatest Hits . . . . (Columbia)
Tracks . . . . (Columbia)
Bruce Springsteen & The E Street Band; *Bruce Springsteen & The E Street*
    Band Live/1975-85 . . . . (Legacy)

Brand New Amerika
Poorboys; *Pardon Me* . . . . (Hollywood)

Breakfast In America
Supertramp; *Breakfast In America* . . . . (A&M)
Paris . . . . (A&M)
Supertramp-Classics-#9 . . . . (A&M)

Buy American
Tex Payer; *Work's Many Voices-#1 & 2-C* . . . . (Arhoolie)

Buy, Buy This American Car
Charlie King; *Food Phone Gas Lodging.* . . . . (Flying Fish)

Caissons Go Rolling Along
Leon Berry; *Best Of Theater Organ* . . . . (Audio Fidelity)
Giant Wurlitzer Pipe Organ-#3 . . . . (Audio Fidelity)
Robert Merrill & Mormon Tabernacle Choir; *Yankee Doodle*
    Dandies . . . . (Columbia)

California Girls
Beach Boys; *Beach Boys '69 (The Beach Boys Live In London)* . . . . (Capitol)
Best Of The Beach Boys-#2 . . . . (Capitol)
Endless Summer . . . . (Capitol)
Good Vibrations-Thirty Years Of The Beach Boys . . . . (Capitol)
The Beach Boys In Concert . . . . (Brother)
David Lee Roth; *Crazy From The Heat.* . . . . (Warner Bros.)
ST/Down & Out In Beverly Hills . . . . (Warner Bros.)

Calling America
Electric Light Orchestra; *Balance Of Power* . . . . (CBS Associated)

Cheap Seats, The
Alabama; *Cheap Seats* . . . . (RCA)

Chop Suey
Original Cast; *ST/Flower Drum Song* . . . . (Sony Music Classical)

City Of New Orleans
Arlo Guthrie; *Best Of Arlo Guthrie* . . . . (Warner Bros.)
Hobo's Lullaby. . . . . (Reprise)
Together In Concert . . . . (Reprise)
HARP; *HARP* . . . . (Redwood)
Willie Nelson; *19 Hot Country Requests-#2-C* . . . . (Epic)
City Of New Orleans . . . . (Columbia)
Greatest Country Hits Of The '80s-#4-C . . . . (Columbia)
Hot Tracks-Train Super Hits-C . . . . (Epic)
Train Trax-C . . . . (Sony Music Special Prod.)

Compared To What
Les McCann; *Atlantic Jazz-Soul-C* . . . . (Atlantic)
Les McCann & Eddie Harris; *Great Moments In Jazz-C.* . . . . . (Atlantic)
Jazz Years . . . . (Atlantic)
Swiss Movement . . . . (Atlantic)

Country's In The Best Of Hands
Original Cast; *Li'l Abner.* . . . . (Columbia)

Cowboy, You're America
Dave Dudley; *King Of The Road.* . . . . (Sun)

Crawling To The U.S.A.
Elvis Costello; *ST/Americathon* . . . . (Columbia)
Taking Liberties . . . . (Columbia)

Day We Lost The America's Cup
Tom Paxton; *One Million Lawyers & Other Disasters* . . . . (Flying Fish)

Deadline U.S.A.
Shalamar; *ST/D.C. Cab* . . . . (MCA)

Do America
Mark Knopfler; *Sailing To Philadelphia* . . . . (Warner Bros.)

Don't Give Us A Reason
Hank Williams, Jr.; *America (The Way I See It)* . . . . (WB/Curb)

Dreams In America
Luka Bloom; *Riverside* . . . . (Reprise)

Edge Of America
Duran Duran; *Big Thing* . . . . (Capitol)

Elvis Ate America
Passengers; *Original Soundtracks-1* . . . . (Island)

Elvis Presley And America
U2; *Unforgettable Fire* . . . . (Island)

Exhuming McCarthy
R.E.M.; *Document* . . . . (EMI-Capitol Entert. Properties)

Fightin' Side Of Me
Merle Haggard; *All American* . . . . (Capitol)
Best Of Merle Haggard . . . . (Capitol)
Capitol Collectors Series-Merle Haggard . . . . (Capitol)
The Fightin' Side Of Me . . . . (Capitol)
Merle Haggard & The Strangers; *Songs I'll Always Sing* . . . . . . (Capitol)

For America
Jackson Browne; *Lives In The Balance* . . . . (Asylum)

For Your Country And My Country
Frances Alda; *78-#64689* . . . . (Victor)
Peerless Quartet; *78-#2273* . . . . (Columbia)

Forty Hour Week (For A Livin')
Alabama; *Alabama's Greatest Hits.* . . . . (RCA)
Forty Hour Week . . . . (RCA)

Fourth Of July
X; *See How We Are* . . . . (Elektra)

Fourth Of July
Linda Waterfall; *Body English* . . . . (Flying Fish)

Fourth Of July
Rosalie Sorrels; *Lonesome Roving Wolves-Songs & Ballads Of*
    The West . . . . (Green Linnet)

Fourth Of July
Dave Alvin; *Romeo's Escape* . . . . (Epic)

Fourth Of July At A County Fair
Red Clay Ramblers; *Chuckin' The Frizz* . . . . (Flying Fish)

Freedom Train, The
Bing Crosby; *Bing Crosby-Complete Recordings.* . . . . (MCA)
Peggy Lee; *Peggy Lee-Complete Recordings-1941-1947.* . . . . . (Legacy)

Geek U.S.A.
Smashing Pumpkins; *Siamese Dream.* . . . . (Virgin)

Give Me Your Tired, Your Poor
Mormon Tabernacle Choir; *Around The World: A Musical Journey Of Best-Loved Favorites* ....(Sony Music Classical)

God Bless America
Anita Bryant; *Golden Classics-Anita Bryant*.................(Collectables)
Bill & Gloria Gaither; *Kennedy Center Homecoming: A Celebration Of Our Faith And Heritage* ....(Springhouse Music Grp./Chordant)
Celine Dion; *America: A Tribute To Heroes-C* .... (Interscope)
God Bless America-C ....(Columbia)
Drew Carey; *ST/The Drew Carey Show*.........................(Rhino)
Frank Zappa; *Uncle Meat* ....(Barking Pumpkin)
Kate Smith; *Best Of Kate Smith*...............................(RCA)
God Bless America ....(Pickwick)
Kate Smith-Legendary Performer..............................(RCA)
Nipper's Greatest Hits Of The '30s-#1-C ....(RCA)
Stars And Stripes Forever-#2-C .... (Volcano Entertainment)
LeAnn Rimes; *You Light Up My Life-Inspirational Songs* ....(Curb)
Lee Greenwood; *American Patriot* ....(Capitol)
Mormon Tabernacle Choir; *God Bless America* ......(Sony Music Classical)
Original Soundtrack; *ST/The Deer Hunter* ....(Capitol)
Peter Pan Kids; *I Love America Sing Along*....................(Compose)
Robert Shaw Chorale; *Battle Cry Of Freedom* ....(RCA)

God Bless America Again
Bobby Bare; *Best Of Bobby Bare*.......................(Razor & Tie)
Country Shots: God Bless America-C..........................(Rhino)
Loretta Lynn & Conway Twitty; *From Seven Till Ten* .... (MCA Special Prod.)
United Talent ....(MCA)
Very Best Of Loretta Lynn & Conway Twitty ....(MCA)

God Bless The USA
Lee Greenwood; *American Patriot* ....(Capitol)
God Bless America-C ....(Columbia)
God Bless The USA........................... (MCA Special Prod.)
Inside Out/You've Got A Good Love Comin' ....(MCA)
Lee Greenwood's Greatest Hits ....(MCA)
Lee Greenwood's Greatest Hits-#2 ....(MCA)
Today's Country Classics-C ....(MCA Special Prod.)

God Must Have Blessed America
Glen Campbell; *Country Shots: God Bless America-C* ....(Rhino)

Goin' By The Book
Johnny Cash; *Mystery Of Life* ....(Mercury)

Good Old American Guest
Merle Haggard; *Big City* ....(Epic)

Green Fields Of America
Paddy Tunney; *Stone Fiddle* ....(Green Linnet)

Happiest Girl In The Whole U.S.A.
Donna Fargo; *Best Of Donna Fargo* ....(Curb)
Jeanne Pruett; *Stand By Your Man*.......................(Allegiance)

Happy Birthday Dear America/In 1776
Ella Jenkins; *We Are All America's Children* ....(Smithsonian Folkways)

Happy Birthday, America
Li'l Wally; *Happy Birthday, America* ....(Jay Jay)

Happy Birthday, America
Paul Evans; *I Was Part Of The Fifties* ....(Original Cast)

Heartbreak U.S.A.
Kitty Wells; *I Love Country-Hits Of The '60s-#1-C* ....(Priority)
Kitty Wells' Greatest Songs ....(Curb)
The Country Music Hall Of Fame-Kitty Wells .... (MCA Special Prod.)

Hello America
Def Leppard; *On Through The Night*.......................(Mercury)

Here Comes The Freedom Train
Merle Haggard; *Capitol Collectors Series-Merle Haggard*.......... (Capitol)

House I Live In (That's America To Me)
Frank Sinatra; *Frank Sinatra-In The Beginning-1943-1951* ....(Columbia)
Portrait Of Sinatra-Columbia Classics ....(Legacy)
Sinatra: A Man And His Music ....(Reprise)
Sinatra-The Main Event Live ....(Reprise)

House Un-American Blues Activity Dream
Mimi & Richard Farina; *Best Of Mimi & Richard Farina* ....(Vanguard)
Memories ....(Vanguard)
Reflections In A Crystal Wind ....(Vanguard)

I Found My Girl In The Good Old U.S.A.
Jimmie Skinner; *45-#2095.* ....(Gusto)

I Like America
Noel Coward; *Live From Las Vegas & New York* ....(Columbia)

I Wanna Grow Up To Be A Politician
Byrds; *20 Essential Tracks From The Box Set* ....(Columbia)
Best Of The Byrds-Greatest Hits-#2 ....(Columbia)
Byrdmaniax ....(Columbia)
The Byrds ....(Columbia)

I Want To Hear A Yankee Doodle Tune
George M. Cohan; *Music From The New York Stage (1890-1920)-#1-1890-1908-C.* ....(Pearl)

I'm A Yankee Doodle Dandy
Robert Merrill & Mormon Tabernacle Choir; *Yankee Doodle Dandies* ....(Columbia)

I'm So Bored With The U.S.A.
Clash; *The Clash* ....(Epic)

In America
Charlie Daniels Band; *A Decade Of Hits* ....(Epic)

Full Moon ....(Epic)
Me & The Boys ....(Epic)

Independence Day
Bruce Springsteen; *The River*...............................(Columbia)
Bruce Springsteen & The E Street Band; *Bruce Springsteen & The E Street Band Live/1975-85* ....(Legacy)

Independence Day
Martina McBride; *The Way That I Am* .... (RCA)

It's Alright
Loggins & Messina; *Native Sons* ....(Columbia)

I've Been Everywhere
Johnny Cash; *Unchained* ....(American)

J.A.P. Rap
2 Live Jews; *As Kosher As They Wanna Be* ....(Kosher)

Jammin' In America
Gap Band; *V-Jammin'* ....(Polydor)

Jesus Children Of America
Stevie Wonder; *Innervisions* ....(Motown)

June 25 At The Fourth Of July
Shel Silverstein; *Great Conch Train Robbery* .... (Flying Fish)

Kid's American
Matthew Wilder; *I Don't Speak The Language* ....(Private I)

King & Queen Of America
Eurythmics; *Eurythmics' Greatest Hits* ....(Arista)
We Too Are One ....(Arista)

Last Cowboy Song
Ed Bruce; *16 Top Country Hits-#2-C* ....(MCA)
Ed Bruce's Greatest Hits ....(MCA)
Waylon Jennings, Willie Nelson, Johnny Cash, Kris Kristofferson; *Cowboy Super Hits-C* ....(Columbia)
Highwayman ....(Columbia)

Last Great American Whale
Lou Reed; *Greenpeace/Rainbow Warriors-C* .... (Geffen)
New York ....(Sire)

Letter From America
Proclaimers; *This Is The Story* ....(Chrysalis)

Letter To Americans
Albert Brooks; *Star Is Bought* ....(Asylum)

Little America
R.E.M.; *Reckoning* ....(I.R.S.)

Living In America
Aztec Two-Step; *See It Was Like This...Acoustic Retrospective* ... (Flying Fish)

Living In America
James Brown; *Gravity* ....(Scotti Bros.)
Rocky Story-C ....(Scotti Bros.)
ST/Rocky IV ....(Scotti Bros.)

Living In America
Donna Summer; *Donna Summer* ....(Geffen)

Living In America
Hiroshima; *East* ....(Epic)

Living In The Promiseland
Willie Nelson; *30 Years Of #1 Hits-#18-C* ....(Columbia)
Greatest Country Hits Of The '80s-1986-C ....(Columbia)
More Hot Country Requests-C ....(Epic)
The Promiseland ....(Columbia)

Living In The U.S.A.
Steve Miller Band; *Best Of Steve Miller 1968-1973.*................(Capitol)
On The Road Again-Rock's New Frontiers-C ....(Capitol)
Sailor. ....(Capitol)
Steve Miller Band-Anthology ....(Capitol)
Steve Miller Band-Live ....(Capitol)

Lost In America
Crack The Sky; *From The Greenhouse* ....(Grudge)

Me & Crippled Soldiers
Merle Haggard; *American Music Greatest Hits-C*.................(Curb)
Blue Jungle ....(Curb)

Meet Me In America
Lauren Christy; *Lauren Christy* ....(Mercury)

Memphis Slim U.S.A.
Memphis Slim; *Blue This Evening* ....(Black Lion)

Miss America
Styx; *Caught In The Act* ....(A&M)
Grand Illusion ....(A&M)
Styx-Classics-#15 ....(A&M)

Miss America
Mark Lindsay; *Mark Lindsey: Golden Classics* ....(Collectables)

Miss America
Big Dish; *Satellites.* ....(East West)

Mister Touchdown U.S.A.
Original Soundtrack; *Top Ten College Fight Songs*...............(K-Tel)
University Of Michigan Band; *Greatest College Football Marches* ..(Vanguard)

More Than A Name On The Wall
Statler Brothers; *Statler Brothers' Greatest Hits* ....(Mercury)

My America
Red Steagall & The Coleman County Cowboys; *For All Our Cowboy Friends* ....(MCA)

My America
Blow Monkeys; *Forbidden Fruit* ....(RCA)

My Country 'Tis Of Thee
David Crosby; *Oh Yes I Can* . . . . (A&M)
My Little Miss America
Gary U.S. Bonds; *45-#1034* . . . . (LeGrand)
My Love Is In America
Chieftains; *10--Cotton-Eyed Joe* . . . . (Shanachie)
My Own United States
William H. Thompson; *Music From The New York Stage (1890-1920)-#1-1890-1908-C* . . . . (Pearl)
National Emotion
Tommy Tutone; *National Emotion* . . . . (Columbia)
New Age In America
Larry Coryell; *American Odyssey* . . . . (DRG)
New America
Flim & The BB's; *Big Notes* . . . .(Digital Music Prod.)
Okie From Muskogee
Merle Haggard; *Friend In California* . . . .(Epic)
Merle Haggard & The Strangers; *Best Of Merle Haggard & The Strangers* . . . . (Capitol)
Capitol Collectors Series-Merle Haggard & The Strangers . . . . (Capitol)
Country Music Classics-#3-1965-1970-C . . . . (K-Tel)
For The Record: Merle Haggard-43 Legendary Hits . . . . (BNA)
Songs I'll Always Sing . . . . (Capitol)
ST/Platoon . . . . (Atlantic)
Oklahoma U.S.A.
Kinks; *Muswell Hillbillies* . . . . (VelVel)
Once Upon A Time In America
Dennio Morricone; *Film Music-#2* . . . . (Virgin)
One Time, One Night
Los Lobos; *By The Light Of The Moon* . . . . (Slash)
Only For Americans
Andrews Sisters; *Beat Me Daddy Eight To The Bar* . . . .(MCA Special Prod.)
Original Broadway Cast; *Miss Liberty* . . . . (Sony Music Classical)
Only In America
Jay & The Americans; *Come A Little Bit Closer-Best Of Jay & The Americans* . . . .(Gold Rush)
Jay & The Americans' All-Time Greatest Hits . . . . (Rhino)
Only In America
Brooks & Dunn; *Steers & Stripes* . . . . (Arista)
Over There
Glenn Miller; *Original Recordings-#3-Army/Air Force Band* . . . . (Pair)
Glenn Miller & His Army/Air Force Band; *Glenn Miller-A Legendary Performer-#3* . . . . (Bluebird)
Mormon Tabernacle Choir; *God Bless America* . . . . . . (Sony Music Classical)
Party Time U.S.A.
Oscar Peterson; *Silent Partner* . . . .(Pablo)
Patriot's Dream
Arlo Guthrie; *Amigo* . . . . (Koch International)
Gordon Lightfoot; *Don Quixote* . . . .(Warner Archives)
Pink Houses
John Cougar Mellencamp; *Rock For Amnesty-C* . . . . (Mercury)
Uh-Huh . . . . (Riva)
John Mellencamp featuring Kid Rock; *The Concert For New York City-C* . . . . (Columbia)
Pledge Of Allegiance
Lee Greenwood; *American Patriot* . . . . (Capitol)
Mormon Tabernacle Choir; *American Tribute* . . . . (Columbia)
Proud To Be An American
Li'l Wally; *Happy Birthday, America* . . . .(Jay Jay)
Proud To Be An American
Tubes; *Young And Rich* . . . . (A&M)
Queen Of The U.S.A.
Thompson Twins; *Big Trash* . . . .(Red Eye)
R.O.C.K. In The U.S.A.
John Cougar Mellencamp; *Scarecrow* . . . . (Riva)
Ragged Old Flag
Johnny Cash; *Patriot* . . . . (Columbia)
We The People-C . . . . (Folk Era)
Rally 'Round The Flag
Pico Payne; *ST/The Long Riders* . . . .(Warner Bros.)
Ry Cooder; *Boomer's Story* . . . . (Reprise)
White Mountain Singers; *Round The Bend* . . . . (Folk Era)
We The People-C . . . . (Folk Era)
Real American
Rick Derringer; *Wrestling Album* . . . .(Epic)
Real American Folk Song (Is A Rag)
Marni Nixon & Lincoln Mayorga; *Marni Nixon Sings Gershwin* . . . . (Reference)
Red White & Blue Medley
Chet Atkins; *My Country America* . . . . (RCA)
Redneck Is The Backbone Of America
John Schneider; *You Ain't Seen The Last Of Me* . . . .(MCA)
Rednecks, White Socks And Blue Ribbon Beer
Johnny Russell; *Beer Redneck Mothers* . . . . (RCA)
Country Legends-C . . . . (Madacy)
Country's Greatest Drinking Songs-C . . . . (All-Star Music)
Rednecks, White Socks & Blue Ribbon Beer . . . . (RCA)
Reggae In The U.S.A.
Bunny Wailer; *Rule Dance Hall* . . . . (Shanachie)

Revolution Will Not Be Televised
Gil Scott-Heron; *Gil Scott-Heron* . . . . (Bluebird)
Pieces Of A Man . . . . (Flying Dutchman)
Revolution Will Not Be Televised . . . . (Flying Dutchman)
Rhythm Nation
Janet Jackson; *Janet Jackson's Rhythm Nation 1814* . . . . (A&M)
Rip This Joint
Rolling Stones; *Exile On Main Street* . . . .(Virgin)
Made In The Shade . . . . (Rolling Stones)
Rock America
Afrika & Family Bambaataa; *Beware (The Funk Is Everywhere)* . . . . (Tommy Boy)
Rock America
Danger Danger; *Danger Danger* . . . . (Imagine)
Rock In America
Night Ranger; *Midnight Madness* . . . . (MCA)
Night Ranger's Greatest Hits . . . .(Camel)
Rock Of America
Bad Company; *Dangerous Age* . . . .(Atlantic)
Rock The Nation
Montrose; *Montrose* . . . . (Warner Bros.)
Rock This Country
Shania Twain; *Come On Over* . . . . (Mercury)
Rockin' In The Free World
Bon Jovi; *One Wild Night: Live 1985-2001* . . . . (Island)
Neil Young; *Freedom* . . . . (Reprise)
Neil Young & Crazy Horse; *WELD* . . . . (Reprise)
Pearl Jam; *8/12/00: Tampa, Florida* . . . . (Epic)
Rockin' In The U.S.A.
Kiss; *Alive II* . . . .(Casablanca)
Royal Scam
Steely Dan; *The Royal Scam* . . . . (MCA)
Russians & Americans
Al Stewart; *Russians & Americans* . . . . (Passport)
Sail Away
Linda Ronstadt; *Don't Cry Now* . . . .(Asylum)
Randy Newman; *Guilty: 30 Years Of Randy Newman* . . . . (Rhino)
Sail Away . . . . (Reprise)
Sailing To America
Saxon; *Crusader* . . . . (Carrere)
Sailing To Philadelphia
Mark Knopfler; *Sailing To Philadelphia* . . . . (Warner Bros.)
Saturday In The Park
Chicago; *Chicago IX-Chicago's Greatest Hits* . . . . (Chicago)
Chicago V . . . . (Chicago)
Chicken Soup For The Soul: I'll Be There For You-Songs Of Friendship, Brotherhood And Sisterhood-C . . . . (Rhino)
Group Portrait . . . . (Chicago)
If You Leave Me Now . . . . (Chicago)
ST/My Girl . . . . (Epic)
The Heart Of Chicago-1967-1997 . . . . (Reprise)
Saturday Night U.S.A.
Charlie Daniels Band; *Powder Keg* . . . . (Epic)
Save The Country
5th Dimension; *5th Dimension-Anthology 1967-1973* . . . . (Rhino)
Greatest Hits On Earth . . . . (Arista)
Bobby Darin; *Live At The Desert Inn* . . . . (Motown)
Laura Nyro; *New York Tendaberry* . . . . (Columbia)
See The U.S.A. (Chevrolet)
Original Soundtrack; *TeeVee Toons-The Commercials-#1-C* . . . . (TVT)
Skateboard Surfin' U.S.A.
Jan Berry; *45-#2020* . . . . (A&M)
Skatetown U.S.A.
Dave Mason; *Skatetown U.S.A.-C* . . . . (Columbia)
Song For America
Kansas; *Best Of Kansas* . . . . (CBS Associated)
Song For America . . . . (Kirshner)
Two For The Show . . . . (Kirshner)
Song Of Freedom
Bing Crosby; *Original Soundtrack Sessions* . . . .(Vintage Jazz Classics)
Song Of The Patriot
Johnny Cash; *Patriot* . . . . (Columbia)
Star Spangled Banner
American Brass Band; *National Anthems* . . . .(Laserlight)
Banda Sinfonica De Madrid; *National Anthems* . . . . (International Music)
Duke Ellington; *Carnegie Hall Concert-January 23, 1943* . . . .(Prestige)
Houston Symphony Orchestra; *Celebrate America* . . . . (Pro-Arte)
Jimi Hendrix; *Essential Jimi Hendrix, Volume 2* . . . . (Reprise)
Lifelines/Jimi Hendrix Story . . . . (Reprise)
ST/Jimi Hendrix . . . . (Reprise)
ST/Woodstock . . . . (Atlantic)
Lee Greenwood; *American Patriot* . . . . (Capitol)
Marvin Gaye; *Musical Testament 1964-1984* . . . . (Motown)
Mormon Tabernacle Choir; *God Bless America* . . . . . . (Sony Music Classical)
God Bless America-C . . . . (Columbia)
This Is My Country . . . . (Columbia)
Original Soundtrack; *The Greatest College Fight Songs* . . . . (Laserlight)
Sandi Patty; *Stars And Stripes Forever-#2-C* . . . . (Volcano Entertainment)
Vienna State Opera Orchestra; *National Anthems Of The World* . . (Bescol, Ltd.)

Vinnie Vincent Invasion; *Head Banging Metal-C* . . . . (Priority)
Whitney Houston; *Whitney Houston's Greatest Hits* . . . . (Arista)

Stars And Stripes Forever
Boston Pops Orchestra/Arthur Fiedler; *Boston Pops Orchestra/Arthur Fiedler-*
  Legendary Performer. . . . .(RCA)
Boston Pops Orchestra/Arthur Fiedler's Greatest Hits . . . . (Polydor)
Forever Fiedler . . . .(RCA)
Mister Music U.S.A. . . . . (Deutsche Grammophon)
Yankee Doodle Dandy . . . .(RCA)
Killer Cadet Band; *Stars And Stripes Forever-#2-C* . . . (Volcano Entertainment)
Mormon Tabernacle Choir; *God Bless America* . . . .(Sony Music Classical)
Stars And Stripes Forever. . . . . (Columbia)
Star Spangled Band; *Red, White & Bluegrass-C* . . . . (C.M.H. Prod.)

Stranded In The Jungle
Cadets; *Collectables Presents The History Of Rock-#2-C* . . . . (Collectables)
Cruisin'-1956-C . . . . (Increase)
Oldies But Goodies-#1-C . . . .(Original Sound)
Original Rock 'N' Roll Hits Of The '50s-C . . . . (Roulette)
New York Dolls; *In Too Much Too Soon.* . . . . (Mercury)
Live In NYC-1975 . . . . (Restless)

Strictly U.S.A.
Tom Hooper; *Tom Hooper Sings Great Songs From Movie*
  Musicals. . . . . (Hindsight)

Surfin' U.S.A.
Beach Boys; *Absolute Best-#1* . . . . (Capitol)
Best Of The Beach Boys . . . . (Capitol)
Billboard Top Rock 'N' Roll Hits-1963-C . . . . (Rhino)
Endless Summer . . . . (Capitol)
Made In The U.S.A. . . . . (Capitol)

Surfin' U.S.A.
Jesus & Mary Chain; *Barbed Wire Kisses* . . . . (Warner Bros.)

Sweet Young America
Roger Whittaker; *Wind Beneath My Wings* . . . .(RCA)

Take Pride In America
Oak Ridge Boys; *Oak Ridge Boys' Greatest Hits 3* . . . . (MCA)

That's America
Johnnie Taylor; *This Is Your Night* . . . . (Malaco)

Theme From "American Bandstand" (Bandstand Boogie)
Barry Manilow; *Barry Manilow's Greatest Hits-#1* . . . . (Arista)
Trying To Get The Feeling . . . . (Arista)
Original Soundtrack; *Television's Greatest Hits-#3-1970s & 1980s-C.* . . . . (TVT)

Theme From "America's Most Wanted"
Original Soundtrack; *Television's Greatest Hits-#7-Cable Ready-C* . . . . . (TVT)

Theme From "Greatest American Hero"
Joey Scarbury; *Television's Greatest Hits-#3-1970s & 1980s-C* . . . . (TVT)
Tube Tunes-#3-The '70s & '80s-C . . . . (Rhino)

Theme From "Love, American Style"
Original Soundtrack; *Television's Greatest Hits-#2-C* . . . . (TVT)
TV Classic Themes: 25th Anniversary Edition-C . . . .(Breakable)

Theme From "The Miss America Pageant" (There She Is, Miss America)
Bert Parks; *Television's Greatest Hits-#4-Black & White Classics-C* . . . . . (TVT)

There Are No Cats In America
Nehemiah Persoff/John Guarnieri/Warren Hays; *ST/An American Tail* . . (MCA)

There's A Star-Spangled Banner
Ray Stevens; *American Music Greatest Hits-C* . . . .(Curb)
Ray Stevens' Greatest Hits . . . .(Curb)

This Ain't No Rag, It's A Flag
Charlie Daniels Band; *This Ain't No Rag, It's A Flag-CD Single* . . . . . (Blue Hat)

This Is A Great Country
Original Cast; *Mr. President* . . . . (Sony Broadway)

This Is My Country
Mormon Tabernacle Choir; *God Bless America* . . . .(Sony Music Classical)
Mormon Tabernacle Choir's Greatest Hits . . . . (Columbia)
This Is My Country . . . . (Columbia)

This Is Not America
David Bowie & Pat Metheny Group; *ST/Falcon & The Snowman* . . . . (EMI)

This Land Is Your Land
Bruce Springsteen & The E Street Band; *Bruce Springsteen & The E Street*
  Band Live/1975-85 . . . . (Legacy)
Glen Campbell; *All American* . . . . (Liberty)
Lee Greenwood; *American Patriot* . . . . (Capitol)
Odetta, Arlo Guthrie & Company; *Tribute To Woody*
  Guthrie-C. . . . . (Warner Bros.)
Pete Seeger; *God Bless America-C* . . . . (Columbia)
Pete Seeger Sings Woody Guthrie. . . . .(Smithsonian Folkways)
Pete Seeger-Complete Carnegie Hall Concert-1963 . . . . (Columbia)
Weavers; *Weavers' Greatest Hits* . . . . (Vanguard)
Woody Guthrie; *Greatest Songs Of Woody Guthrie-C* . . . . (Vanguard)
Troubadours Of The Folk Era-#1-C . . . . (Rhino)
Woody Guthrie . . . . (Vanguard)

Together In America
King Errisson; *Global Music* . . . . (Ichiban Int'l)

Trader
Beach Boys; *10 Years Of Harmony* . . . . (Caribou)
Holland. . . . .(Brother)

U.S. Air Force
Mormon Tabernacle Choir; *Stars And Stripes Together* . . . . (Columbia)

U.S. Blues
Grateful Dead; *From The Mars Hotel* . . . . (Grateful Dead)
One From The Vault . . . . (Grateful Dead)
Steal Your Face . . . . (Grateful Dead)

U.S. Male
Jerry Reed; *Best Of Jerry Reed.* . . . . (RCA)

U.S. Of A.
Donna Fargo; *Best Of Donna Fargo* . . . . (MCA)
Country's Greatest Hits-American Pride-C . . . . (Priority)

U.S.A.
Beat; *Beat.* . . . .(Columbia)

U.S.A. Today
George Jones; *Too WIld Too Long* . . . . (Epic)
Hank Williams, Jr.; *America (The Way I See It)* . . . . (WB/Curb)
Lone Wolf . . . . (WB/Curb)

Venice U.S.A.
Van Morrison; *Wavelength* . . . . (Warner Bros.)

Vietnamerica
Stranglers; *Stranglers IV* . . . . (I.R.S.)

Voice Of America
Asia; *Astra* . . . . (Geffen)
Then & Now . . . . (Geffen)

Voice Of America
Little Steven; *Voice Of America.* . . . . (Razor & Tie)

Voice Of America's Son
John Cafferty And The Beaver Brown Band; *ST/Cobra* . . . . (Scotti Bros.)
Tough All Over . . . . (Scotti Bros.)

Volunteers
Jefferson Airplane; *"White Rabbit" & Other Hits* . . . . (RCA)
2400 Fulton Street-An Anthology . . . . (RCA)
Flight Log (1966-1976). . . . . (Grunt)
ST/Forrest Gump. . . . . (Epic/Sony Music Soundtrax)
ST/Woodstock . . . . (Atlantic)
The Worst Of Jefferson Airplane . . . . (RCA)
Volunteers . . . . (RCA)

Wabash Cannonball
Billy Strange; *Between The Rails: America's Train Songs-C* . . . . . . (Crescendo)
Nitty Gritty Dirt Band; *Will The Circle Be Unbroken* . . . .(EMI)
Roy Acuff; *All Time Legends Of Country Music-C* . . . . (Legacy)
Backstage At The Grand Ole Opry-C . . . . (RCA)
Best Of Roy Acuff. . . . . (Liberty)
Columbia Historic Edition-Roy Acuff . . . . (Columbia)
Essential Roy Acuff-1936-1949. . . . . (Legacy)
Hot Tracks-Train Super Hits-C . . . . (Epic)
Roy Acuff's Greatest Hits . . . . (Columbia)
Steel Rails-Classic Railroad Songs-#1-C . . . .(Rounder)

We Love U.S.A.
Li'l Wally; *Happy Birthday, America* . . . . (Jay Jay)

Welcome To The United States
Frank Zappa; *The Yellow Shark* . . . . (Rykodisc)

We're An American Band
Grand Funk Railroad; *Capitol Collectors Series-Grand Funk*
  Railroad . . . .(Capitol)
Caught In The Act . . . . (Capitol)
ST/Spirit Of '76 . . . . (Rhino)
We're An American Band . . . . (Capitol)
When AM Was King-C. . . . . (Capitol)

When It Rains In America
Sarah Brightman; *Dive.* . . . . (A&M)

Where Stars And Stripes And The Eagle Fly
Aaron Tippin; *CD Single-#164059* . . . . (Lyric Street)

Where Were You (When The World Stopped Turning)
Alan Jackson; *Alan Jackson-Drive.* . . . .(Arista)

Which Way To America
Living Colour; *Vivid* . . . . (Epic)

Wild America
Tora Tora; *Wild America* . . . . (A&M)

Winter In America
Gil Scott-Heron; *Best Of Gil Scott-Heron* . . . . (Arista)
First Minute Of a New Day . . . . (Arista)

Winter In America
Margaret Roadknight; *Living In The Land Of Oz* . . . .(Redwood)

With God On Our Side
Bob Dylan; *The Times They Are A-Changin'* . . . .(Columbia)
Joan Baez; *The First 10 Years* . . . . (Vanguard)
Manfred Mann; *Songs Of Protest-C* . . . . (Rhino)
Neville Brothers; *Uptown Rulin': The Best Of The Neville Brothers* . . . . . (A&M)
Yellow Moon . . . . (A&M)
Wire Train; *Best Of 415 Records-C* . . . . (Legacy)

Workin' It
Don Henley; *Inside Job* . . . . (Warner Bros.)

Wrong Number
Cure; *Galore-The Singles-1987-1997* . . . .(Fiction/Elektra)

XXX's And OOO's
Trisha Yearwood; *Thinkin' About You.* . . . . (MCA)

Yankee Doodle
Boston Pops Orchestra/Arthur Fiedler; *Fiedler's Favorite Marches* . . . . . (RCA)
Music For All Occasions . . . . (RCA)

Yankee Doodle Dandy
''C'' Company & Terry Nelson; *Wake Up America* . . . . (Plantation)
Houston Symphony Orchestra; *Top Of The Pops* . . . . (Pro-Arte)
Yankee Rose
David Lee Roth; *Eat 'Em & Smile* . . . .(Warner Bros.)
Young Americans
David Bowie; *Changesbowie* . . . .(Rykodisc)
Sound + Vision. . . . .(Rykodisc)
The Singles-1969-1993 . . . .(Rykodisc)
Young Americans . . . .(Rykodisc)
Your Flag Decal Won't Get You Into Heaven Anymore
John Prine; *John Prine* . . . . (Atlantic)
You're A Grand Old Flag
Marilyn Horne; *Beautiful Dreamer-Great American Songbook* . . . . (London)
Mormon Tabernacle Choir; *God Bless America* . . . . (Sony Music Classical)
Original Soundtrack; *School Days-Kids Classics* . . . . (Benson)
Robert Merrill & Mormon Tabernacle Choir; *Yankee Doodle*
Dandies . . . . (Columbia)
Youth Of The Nation
P.O.D.; *Satellite* . . . . (Atlantic)

COUNTRIES: AUSTRALIA

See Also: *ANIMALS: KANGAROOS, CITIES: A-Z*

Australia
Kinks; *Arthur Or The Decline And Fall Of The British Empire* . . . . (Reprise)
Australia
Steve Howe; *Beginnings* . . . . (Atco)
Australia National Anthem (Advance Australia Fair)
American Brass Band; *National Anthems* . . . . (Laserlight)
Swarovski Musik Wattens; *National Anthems Of The*
World . . . . (Koch International)
Didjerama
Jamiroquai; *Traveling Without Moving* . . . . (Work/Epic)
Do The Boomerang
Junior Walker & The All Stars; *Junior Walker & The All Stars-*
Anthology . . . . (Motown)
Shotgun . . . . (Motown)
Down Under
Men At Work; *Business As Usual* . . . . (Columbia)
Far Away In Australia
De Danann; *Ballroom* . . . . (Green Linnet)
Sail To Australia
New Grass Revival; *When The Storm Is Over* . . . . (Flying Fish)
South Australia
Northeast Winds; *Northeast Winds In Concert* . . . . (Folk Era)
Pogues; *If I Should Fall From Grace With God* . . . . (Island)
Theme From ''Skippy, The Bush Kangaroo''
Original Soundtrack; *Television's Greatest Hits-#5-In Living Color-C* . . . (TVT)
Tie Me Kangaroo Down, Sport
Rolf Harris; *45-#213* . . . . (Eric)
Tie Me Kangaroo Down, Sport & Sun Arise . . . .(Epic)
Waltzing Matilda
Burl Ives; *Best Of Burl Ives.* . . . .(MCA)
Fred Astaire; *Three Evenings With Fred Astaire* . . . . (DRG)
James Galway; *Pachebel Canon & Other Favorites* . . . . (RCA)
Original Soundtrack; *Children's Favorites* . . . . (Kid Rhino/Rhino 4 Kids)

COUNTRIES: B

See Also: *CITIES: A-Z, COUNTRIES: BRAZIL*

Bangladesh
George Harrison; *Best Of George Harrison* . . . . (Capitol)
Concert For Bangladesh-C . . . . (Capitol)
Barbados
Charlie Parker; *Bird At The Roost.* . . . . (Savoy)
Bird/Savoy Recordings (Master Takes) . . . . (Savoy)
Charlie Parker. . . . . (Savoy)
Encores-Charlie Parker-#2 . . . . (Savoy)
Barbados
Poco; *Poco-Legend.* . . . .(MCA)
Barbados
Jesse Colin Young; *Light Shine* . . . .(Warner Bros.)
Barbados National Anthem
Swarovski Musik Wattens; *National Anthems Of The*
World . . . . (Koch International)
Belgian Ballad
Connie Crothers & Lenny Popkin Quartet; *In Motion* . . . .(New Artists)
Belgian Team
Hal Michael Ketchum; *Threadbare Alibis* . . . . (Watermelon)
Belgian Tom's Hat Trick
Whitesnake; *Trouble* . . . .(Geffen)

Belgium National Anthem (La Brabanconne)
American Brass Band; *National Anthems* . . . .(Laserlight)
Vienna State Opera Orchestra; *National Anthems Of The World* . . (Bescol, Ltd.)
Belgium Stomp
American Jazz Orchestra & John Lewis; *Music Of Jimmie*
Lunceford . . . .(Musicmasters)
Bermuda
Roky Erickson; *Don't Slander Me* . . . . (Rust)
You're Gonna Miss Me-Best Of Roky Erickson . . . . (Restless)
Bermuda Triangle
Fleetwood Mac; *Heroes Are Hard To Find* . . . . (Reprise)
Bermuda Triangle Blues (Flight 45)
Blondie; *Plastic Letters.* . . . . (Chrysalis)
Bolivia National Anthem
Banda Sinfonica De Madrid; *National Anthems* . . . . (International Music)
Swarovski Musik Wattens; *National Anthems Of The*
World. . . . . (Koch International)
Bosnia
Cranberries; *To The Faithful Departed* . . . . (Island)
Bulgaria National Anthem (Dear Fatherland)
Swarovski Musik Wattens; *National Anthems Of The*
World. . . . . (Koch International)
Vienna State Opera Orchestra; *National Anthems Of The World* . . (Bescol, Ltd.)
Down In Bermuda
Del Vikings; *Del Vikings.* . . . . (Collectables)
Just Like Belgium
Elton John; *The Fox.* . . . . (MCA)
Mountains Of Burma
Midnight Oil; *Blue Sky Mining* . . . . (Columbia)
Song Of Bangladesh
Joan Baez; *Come From The Shadows* . . . . (A&M)

COUNTRIES: BRAZIL

See Also: *CITIES: A-Z, CITIES: RIO DE JANEIRO*

Bird Of Brazil
Joyce; *Music Inside.* . . . .(Verve/Forecast)
Brazil
Gato Barbieri; *Third World Revisited* . . . . (Bluebird)
Brazil
Jimmy Dorsey & His Orchestra; *Best Of Jimmy Dorsey* . . . . (MCA)
Brazil
Antonio Carlos Jobim; *Stone Flower* . . . . (CBS Associated)
Brazil
Chris DeBurgh; *The End Of A Perfect Name.* . . . . (A&M)
Brazil National Anthem (Hino Nacional)
Banda Sinfonica De Madrid; *National Anthems* . . . . (International Music)
Orlando Philharmonic Orchestra; *The National Anthems* . . . .(Madacy)
Swarovski Musik Wattens; *National Anthems Of The*
World. . . . . (Koch International)
Brazilian Memories
Grover Washington, Jr.; *Best Is Yet To Come* . . . . (Elektra)
Brazilian Stomp
George Benson & Earl Klugh; *Collaboration* . . . . (Warner Bros.)
Brazilian Ukelele
Buddy Merrill; *Best Of Buddy Merrill.* . . . . (Accord)
Latin Festival . . . . (Accord)
Coffee Song (They've Got An Awful Lot Of Coffee In Brazil)
Frank Sinatra; *Frank Sinatra-16 Most Requested Songs* . . . . (Columbia)
Frank Sinatra-In The Beginning-1943-1951 . . . . (Columbia)
Frank Sinatra & Johnny Mandel; *Ring-A-Ding Ding* . . . .(Reprise)
Down In Brazil
Michael Franks; *Sleeping Gypsy* . . . . (Warner Bros.)
Going To Brazil
Motorhead; *1916.* . . . . (WTG)
One Summer Night In Brazil
Rippingtons; *Tourist In Paradise* . . . . (GRP)
Take Me To Brazil
Dave MacKay & Lori Bell Sextet; *Take Me To Brazil* . . . . (Discovery)
Wild Sewerage Tickles Brazil
Squeeze; *Squeeze-Classics-#25* . . . . (A&M)

COUNTRIES: C

See Also: *CITIES: A-Z, COUNTRIES: CANADA, CHINA, CUBA*

Cameroon National Anthem
Swarovski Musik Wattens; *National Anthems Of The*
World. . . . . (Koch International)
Chile National Anthem
Banda Sinfonica De Madrid; *National Anthems* . . . . (International Music)
Colombia National Anthem
Banda Sinfonica De Madrid; *National Anthems* . . . . (International Music)

Swarovski Musik Wattens; *National Anthems Of The World*. . . . . (Koch International)
Congo
Genesis; *Calling All Stations*. . . . . (Atlantic)
Costa Rica National Anthem
Banda Sinfonica De Madrid; *National Anthems* . . . . (International Music)
Czech Republic National Anthem (Kde Domov Nuj?)
Orlando Philharmonic Orchestra; *The National Anthems* . . . . (Madacy)
Swarovski Musik Wattens; *National Anthems Of The World*. . . . . (Koch International)
Czechoslovakia
Michael McClure & Ray Manzarek; *Love Lion*. . . . . (Shanachie)
Holiday In Cambodia
Overlords; *Organic?*. . . . . (Antler Subway)
They Dance Alone (Cueca Solo) (Chile)
Sting; ...*Nothing Like The Sun*. (A&M)
Fields Of Gold-The Best Of Sting 1984-1994 . . . . (A&M)

COUNTRIES: CANADA
See Also: *CITIES: A-Z*

Acadian Driftwood
Band; *Northern Lights-Southern Cross*. (Capitol)
To Kingdom Come-The Definitive Collection . . . . (Capitol)
Alberta Bound
Gordon Lightfoot; *Don Quixote* . . . . (Warner Archives)
Gord's Gold-#2 . . . . (Warner Bros.)
Alberta Bound
Curly Chaker; *Nashville Sundown*. (Crescendo)
Alberta, My Alberta
Ray Griff; *Maple Leaf* . . . . (Boot)
Alone In Manitoba
Humphrey & The Dumptrucks; *Six Days Of Paper Ladies* . . . . (Boot)
Blue Canadian Rockies
Byrds; *Sweetheart Of The Rodeo* . . . . (Columbia)
Gene Autry; *50th Anniversary*. . . . . (Republic/Universal)
Live From Madison Square Garden . . . . (Republic/Universal)
Jimmy C. Newman; *Cajun Cowboy*. . . . . (Plantation)
Canada
Ray Griff; *Canada*. . . . . (Boot)
Ray Griff's Greatest Hits . . . . (Boot)
Canada National Anthem (O Canada)
Alan Mills; *Alan Mills Sings History Of Canada*. . . . . . . (Smithsonian Folkways)
American Brass Band; *National Anthems* . . . . (Laserlight)
Vienna State Opera Orchestra; *National Anthems Of The World*. . (Bescol, Ltd.)
Canadian Capers
Tommy Dorsey; *Complete Tommy Dorsey-#5* . . . . (RCA)
Canadian Errant
Ian & Sylvia; *Best Of Ian & Sylvia*. . . . . (Vanguard)
Ian & Sylvia . . . . (Vanguard)
Ian & Sylvia's Greatest Hits . . . . (Vanguard)
Newport Broadside: Newport Folk Festival-1963-C . . . . (Vanguard)
Canadian Lumber Jack
Stompin' Tom Connors; *Bud The Spud*. . . . . (EMI)
Canadian Pacific
Ray Griff; *Canada*. . . . . (Boot)
Canadian Railroad Trilogy
Gordon Lightfoot; *Best Of Gordon Lightfoot* . . . . (EMI)
Gord's Gold . . . . (Reprise)
Sunday Concert . . . . (EMI)
The Way I Feel . . . . (United Artists)
United Artists Collection . . . . (EMI)
Canadian Sunset
Andy Williams; *Andy Williams-16 Most Requested Songs* . . . . (Legacy)
Etta Jones; *Etta Jones' Greatest Hits*. . . . . (Prestige)
Something Nice . . . . (Original Jazz Classics)
Case Of You
Joni Mitchell; *Blue*. . . . . (Reprise)
Joni Mitchell with Tom Scott & The L.A. Express; *Miles Of Aisles* . . . (Asylum)
Cross Canada
Stompin' Tom Connors; *My Stompin' Concerts* . . . . (Boot)
Green Fields Of Canada
Eric Schoenberg; *Acoustic Guitar* . . . . (Rounder)
Justice In Ontario
Steve Earle & The Dukes; *The Hard Way* . . . . (MCA)
Song For Canada
Ian & Sylvia; *Ian & Sylvia*. . . . . (Vanguard)
Ian & Sylvia's Greatest Hits . . . . (Vanguard)
Thank You Canada
Frank Jones; *45-#4595*. . . . . (Soundwaves)
Theme From "Dudley-Do-Right"
Original Soundtrack; *Television's Greatest Hits-#3-1970s & 1980s-C*. . . . (TVT)
This Is My Country, Thank You Canada
Shelley Looney; *45-#76050*. . . . . (Mercury)

Under Blue Canadian Skies
Glenn Miller & His Orchestra; *Complete Glenn Miller & His Orchestra*. . . . . (Bluebird)
With Love From Alberta
Jim Post; *Shipshape* . . . . (Flying Fish)

COUNTRIES: CHINA
See Also: *CITIES: A-Z*

7 Chinese Bros.
R.E.M.; *Reckoning*. . . . . (I.R.S.)
All The Tea In China
Buck Owens; *Kickin'* . . . . (Curb)
Anita Goes To China
David Hayes; *Logos Through A Sideman*. . . . . (Gold Castle)
Apolitical Blues
Little Feat; *Last Record Album*. . . . . (Warner Bros.)
Sailin' Shoes. . . . . (Warner Bros.)
Waiting For Columbus . . . . (Warner Bros.)
Van Halen; *OU812*. . . . . (Warner Bros.)
Chin Chin Chinaman
James T. Powers; *Music From The New York Stage (1890-1920)-#1-1890-1908-C* . . . . (Pearl)
China
Bob Welch; *Three Hearts*. . . . . (Capitol)
China
Red Rockers; *Good As Gold*. . . . . (Columbia)
China
Bobby Caldwell; *Heart Of Mine* . . . . (Sin-Drome)
China
Sammy Hagar; *Nine On A Ten Scale*. . . . . (Capitol)
China
Paul Kantner/Grace Slick; *Sunfighter*. . . . . (Grunt)
China Boy
Benny Goodman; *Carnegie Hall Jazz Concert* . . . . (Columbia)
ST/The Benny Goodman Story. . . . . (MCA)
The Benny Goodman Story . . . . (Capitol)
China Cat Sunflower
Grateful Dead; *Aoxomoxoa* . . . . (Warner Bros.)
Europe '72. . . . . (Warner Bros.)
Without A Net . . . . (Arista)
China Doll
Slim Whitman; *15th Anniversary*. . . . . (Imperial)
Best Of Slim Whitman-Legendary Master Series. . . . . (EMI)
Paloma Blanca-Best Of Slim Whitman-Legendary Masters . . . . (EMI)
China Doll
Suzanne Vega; *Deadicated-C* . . . . (Arista)
China Doll
Grateful Dead; *From The Mars Hotel* . . . . (Grateful Dead)
Reckoning . . . . (Arista)
China Girl
David Bowie; *Changesbowie*. (Rykodisc)
Let's Dance . . . . (EMI)
The Singles-1969-1993 . . . . (Rykodisc)
China Girl
John Cougar; *American Fool* . . . . (Riva)
China Grove
Doobie Brothers; *Best Of The Doobies* . . . . (Warner Bros.)
Captain & Me . . . . (Warner Bros.)
Farewell Tour . . . . (Warner Bros.)
China Lady
Accept; *Accept*. . . . . (Portrait)
Midnight Highway. . . . . (PVC)
China National Anthem
Orlando Philharmonic Orchestra; *The National Anthems* . . . . (Madacy)
China White
Scorpions; *Blackout*. . . . . (Mercury)
China White
Little Feat; *Hoy-Hoy!*. . . . . (Warner Bros.)
Chinatown
Joe Jackson; *Night & Day* . . . . (A&M)
Chinatown
Chaka Khan; *I Feel For You*. . . . . (Warner Bros.)
Chinatown
Doobie Brothers; *Livin' On The Fault Line* . . . . (Warner Bros.)
Chinatown
Greg Kihn; *Next Of Kihn* . . . . (Beserkley)
Chinatown My Chinatown
Al Jolson; *The Al Jolson Story-#1* . . . . (MCA)
Louis Armstrong; *Armstrong #2* . . . . (Everest)
Stardust. . . . . (Portrait)
Chinese Arithmetic
Faith No More; *Introduce Yourself* . . . . (Slash)
Chinese Cafe
Joni Mitchell; *Wild Things Run Fast* . . . . (Geffen)

Chinese Checkers
Booker T. & The M.G.s; *Very Best Of Booker T. & The MG's* . . . . (Rhino)
Chinese Kitchen
Fleshtones; *Fleshtones* . . . .(I.R.S.)
Roman Gods . . . .(I.R.S.)
Chinese Mule Train
Spike Jones; *Best Of Spike Jones-#2* . . . . (RCA)
Everybody Works In China
Judy Collins; *Home Again* . . . . (Elektra)
Going Down The China Road
Peter Lang; *Back To The Wall* . . . .(Waterhouse)
Great Wall Of China
Christmas; *Ultraprophets Of Thee Psykick Revolution* . . . .(I.R.S.)
Great Wall Of China
Kitaro; *Silk Road 1* . . . . (Gramavision)
I Can Sail To China
John Conlee; *American Faces* . . . . (Columbia)
In China Or A Woman's Heart
Kate Wolf; *Poet's Heart* . . . . (Kaleidoscope)
Irishman In Chinatown
Luka Bloom; *Riverside* . . . . (Reprise)
Living In China
Men Without Hats; *Rhythm Of Youth* . . . .(MCA)
Mann's Chinese
Naked; *Naked* . . . .(Red Ant)
Many Chinas
Mark Isham; *Vapor Drawings* . . . . (Windham Hill)
Not In A Chinese Restaurant
Country Joe McDonald; *Child's Play* . . . . (Rag Baby)
On A Chinese Honeymoon
Mills Brothers; *The Mills Brothers Story* . . . .(Ranwood)
On A Slow Boat To China
Jimmy Buffett; *Somewhere Over China* . . . .(MCA)
Kay Kyser & His Orchestra; *16 Most Requested Songs Of The
'40s-#2-C* . . . . (Legacy)
Sentimental Favorites . . . . (Columbia)
Sonny Rollins; *First Recordings* . . . .(Prestige)
Vintage Sonny Rollins . . . . (Prestige)
One Child China
Ecoteur; *Decorated Life* . . . . (Dali)
Overtones Of China
Sun Ra; *Sun Ra Visits Planet Earth* . . . . (Evidence Music)
Rockin' Over China
Commander Cody; *Let's Rock* . . . .(Blind Pig)
Sketches Of China
Jefferson Airplane; *Flight Log (1966-1976)* . . . .(Grunt)
Paul Kantner, Grace Slick & David Freiberg; *Baron Von Tollbooth & The
Chrome Nun* . . . .(Grunt)
Slow Boat To China
Spike Robinson & Harry "Sweets" Edison; *Jusa Bit O' Blues-#1* . . . (Capri Ltd.)
Take Me Back To My Love In China
Durell Coleman; *Durell Coleman* . . . . (Island)
Two Chinese Songs
Pete Seeger; *Banks Of Marble* . . . . (Smithsonian Folkways)
Upstairs By A Chinese Lamp
Laura Nyro; *Christmas & The Beads Of Sweat* . . . . (Columbia)
Visions Of China
Japan; *Oil On Canvas* . . . . (Blue Plate)
Tin Drum . . . . (Blue Plate)

COUNTRIES: CUBA

See Also: CITIES: A-Z, CITIES: HAVANA

Another Cuba
U.K. Subs; *Japan Today* . . . .(Restless)
Ballad Of William Worthy
Phil Ochs; *Best Of Broadside 1962-1968: Anthems Of The American
Underground From The Pages Of Broadside
Magazine-C* . . . . (Smithsonian Folkways)
Cuba
Gibson Brothers; *The Island Story-1962-1987-25th Anniversary-C* . . . . (Island)
Cuba National Anthem
Banda Sinfonica De Madrid; *National Anthems* . . . .(International Music)
Swarovski Musik Wattens; *National Anthems Of The
World* . . . . (Koch International)
Cuban Connections
Outback; *Putumayo Presents Best Of World Music-#2-C* . . . . (Rhino)
Cuban Crime Of Passion
Jimmy Buffett; *Boats Beaches Bars & Ballads* . . . .(Margaritaville)
White Sport Coat & A Pink Crustacean . . . .(MCA)
Cuban Crisis
Phil Manzanera; *K-Scope* . . . .(Editions E.G.)
Cuban Fantasy
Cal Tjader; *Good Vibes* . . . . (Concord Picante Jazz)
Cuban Getaway
Sue Foley; *Young Girl Blues* . . . .(Antone's)

Cuban Love Song
George Shearing; *Best Of George Shearing* . . . .(Capitol)
Cuban Lullaby
Mario Bauza & His Afro-Cuban Jazz Orchestra; *Tanga* . . . .(Messidor)
Cuban Nightingale
Joe Holiday; *Mambo Jazz* . . . .(Prestige)
Cuban Slide
Pretenders; *Extended Play* . . . .(Sire)
Cubano Chant
Cal Tjader; *Cal Tjader's Greatest Hits* . . . .(Fantasy)
Latin Concert . . . .(Fantasy)
Live At The Funky Quarters . . . . (Fantasy)
Ritmos Calientes . . . .(Fantasy)
From Hell To Paradise
Mavericks; *From Hell To Paradise* . . . . (MCA)
Moon Over Cuba
Duke Ellington; *Duke Ellington & The Blanton-Webster Band* . . . . . .(Bluebird)
Running Down To Cuba
John Townley & The Press Gang; *Chesapeake Sailor's Companion* . . .(Adelphi)

COUNTRIES: D

See Also: CITIES: A-Z

Denmark Blues
Sleepy John Estes; *Sleepy John Estes In Europe* . . . . (Delmark)
Denmark National Anthem (Kong Kristian Stod Ved Hojen Mast)
American Brass Band; *National Anthems* . . . .(Laserlight)
Vienna State Opera Orchestra; *National Anthems Of The World* . . (Bescol, Ltd.)
Denmark Street
Kinks; *Lola Versus Powerman And The Moneygoround, Part One* . . . .(Reprise)
Dominican Republic National Anthem
Banda Sinfonica De Madrid; *National Anthems* . . . . (International Music)
On Danish Shore
Oscar Peterson Four; *If You Could See Me Now* . . . . (Pablo)

COUNTRIES: E

See Also: CITIES: A-Z, COUNTRIES: EGYPT, ENGLAND

Ecuador
Carlos Santana; *Havana Moon* . . . . (Columbia)
Ecuador
Stan Kenton; *Encores-Stan Kenton* . . . .(Creative World)
Ecuador National Anthem
Banda Sinfonica De Madrid; *National Anthems* . . . . (International Music)
Swarovski Musik Wattens; *National Anthems Of The
World* . . . . (Koch International)
Ecuadorean Memories
Butch Thompson; *New Orleans Joys* . . . . (Daring)
El Salvador National Anthem
Banda Sinfonica De Madrid; *National Anthems* . . . . (International Music)
Estonia National Anthem
Swarovski Musik Wattens; *National Anthems Of The
World* . . . . (Koch International)
Ethiopia
Joni Mitchell; *Dog Eat Dog* . . . . (Geffen)
Ethiopia National Anthem
Ethiopians; *Slave Call* . . . .(Heartbeat)
Ethiopia Rag
William Bolcom; *Heliotrope Bouquet Piano Rags-1900-1970* . . . . . .(Nonesuch)
Ethiopia Salaam
Judy Mowatt; *Working Wonders* . . . .(Shanachie)
Radio Ethiopia
Patti Smith Group; *Radio Ethiopia* . . . . (Arista)
Straight To Ethiopia
Augustus Pablo; *Rockers All-Star Explosion-C* . . . .(Alligator)

COUNTRIES: EGYPT

See Also: CITIES: A-Z

Cleopatra, Queen Of Denial
Pam Tillis; *Homeward Looking Angel* . . . . (Arista)
Cleopatra's Cat
Spin Doctors; *Turn It Upside Down* . . . . (Epic)
Egypt
Kate Bush; *Never For Ever* . . . . (EMI)
Egypt (The Chains Are On)
Dio; *Last In Line* . . . . (Warner Bros.)
Egypt National Anthem
Swarovski Musik Wattens; *National Anthems Of The
World* . . . . (Koch International)

Egypt Texas
Shadowy Men On A Shadowy Planet; *Savvy Show Stoppers* . . . . (Cargo)
Egypt, Egypt
Egyptian Lover; *Hip Hop Greats-Classic Raps-C* . . . . (Rhino)
West Coast Rap-First Dynasty-#1-C . . . . (Rhino)
Egyptian
Litter; *Distortions* . . . . (K-Tel)
Egyptian Cream
Robyn Hitchcock & The Egyptians; *Fegmania* . . . . (Slash)
Egyptian Danza
Al DiMeola; *Casino* . . . . (Columbia)
Tour De Force-Live . . . . (Columbia)
Egyptian Gardens
Kaleidoscope; *Egyptian Candy-Collection* . . . . (Epic)
Side Trips . . . . (Epic)
Egyptian Song
Rufus Featuring Chaka Khan; *Ask Rufus* . . . . (MCA)
Egypt's Revenge
Egyptian Lover; *West Coast Rap-Renegades-C* . . . . (Rhino)
Go Down Moses
Arlo Guthrie; *Arlo Guthrie* . . . . (Rising Son)
Fats Waller; *Ain't Misbehavin'* . . . . (Laserlight)
Paul Robeson; *Ballad For Americans* . . . . (Vanguard)
The Power & The Glory . . . . (Columbia)
Simon Estes; *Spirituals* . . . . (Philips)
Little Egypt
Coasters; *Atlantic Rhythm & Blues 1947-1974-#4 (1958-1962)-C* . . . . (Atlantic)
Coasters-Their Greatest Recordings-Early Years . . . . (Atco)
Elvis Presley; *Elvis Presley Sings Leiber & Stoller* . . . . (RCA)
Man Come Into Egypt
Peter, Paul & Mary; *Moving* . . . . (Warner Bros.)
Nights Over Egypt
Jones Girls; *Get As Much Love As You Can* . . . . (Philadelphia Int'l)
Nights Over Egypt
Rastine; *Afrodisiac* . . . . (Zoo)
Spirits Of Ancient Egypt
Wings; *Venus And Mars* . . . . (Capitol)
Wings Over America . . . . (Capitol)
Sue Egypt
Captain Beefheart; *Doc At The Radar Station* . . . . (Blue Plate)
Walk Like An Egyptian
Bangles; *Bangles' Greatest Hits* . . . . (Columbia)
Different Light . . . . (Columbia)
Modern A Cappella . . . . (Rhino)
Walking Across Egypt
Tarwater Band; *Walking Across Egypt* . . . . (Flying Fish)
You Belong To Me
Dean Martin; *Dean Martin's All Time Greatest Hits* . . . . (Curb)
Duprees; *13 Of The Best Doo Wop Love Songs-#2-C* . . . . (Original Sound)
Baby Boomer's Best-Mellow '60s-C . . . . (Priority)
Best Of The Duprees . . . . (Rhino)
Jo Stafford; *Billboard Pop Memories-1950-1954-C* . . . . (Rhino)
Jo Stafford's Greatest Hits . . . . (Curb)
Johnny Mathis; *In The Still Of The Night* . . . . (Columbia)
Patsy Cline; *Patsy Cline Sings Songs Of Love* . . . . (MCA Special Prod.)
Sentimentally Yours . . . . (MCA)
Vonda Shepard; *ST/Songs From "Ally McBeal" Featuring Vonda*
Shepard . . . . (550/Epic)

COUNTRIES: ENGLAND

**See Also: CITIES: A-Z, CITIES: BIRMINGHAM, LONDON,
COUNTRIES: SCOTLAND**

'A' Bomb In Waldour Street
Jam; *All Mad Cons* . . . . (Polydor)
Adventures In A Yorkshire Landscape
Be Bop Deluxe; *Best Of Be Bop Deluxe-Raiding The Divine Archive* . . . (Capitol)
Live! In The Air Age . . . . (Harvest)
An English Gentleman
Original Broadway Cast; *Me & My Girl* . . . . (MCA)
Anarchy In The U.K.
Megadeth; *so far, so good...so what!* . . . . (Capitol)
Sex Pistols; *Never Mind The Bollocks, Here's The Sex Pistols* . . . (Warner Bros.)
Ballad Of Mad Dogs & Englishmen
Ivan "Boogaloo Joe" Jones; *Black Whip* . . . . (Prestige)
Leon Russell; *Leon Russell & The Shelter People* . . . . (MCA)
Battle Of New Orleans
Chet Atkins & The Boston Pops; *Best Of Chet Atkins & The*
Boston Pops . . . . (RCA)
Johnny Horton; *American Originals-Johnny Horton* . . . . (Columbia)
Johnny Horton's Greatest Hits . . . . (Columbia)
Radio Classics Of The '50s-C . . . . (Columbia)
Nitty Gritty Dirt Band; *Dirt, Silver & Gold* . . . . (One Way)
Dream . . . . (United Artists)
Stars And Stripes Forever . . . . (Capitol)

Berkshire
Wha-Koo; *Berkshire* . . . . (MCA)
Berkshire Blues
Randy Weston; *Berkshire Blues* . . . . (Arista)
Self Portraits . . . . (Verve)
Berkshire Poppies
Traffic; *Mr. Fantasy* . . . . (Island)
British Grenadiers
Cambridge Singers; *The Lark In The Clear Air* . . . . (Collegium)
British Pharmaceuticals
Miss World; *Miss World* . . . . (Atlantic)
British Summertime
Everything But The Girl; *Worldwide* . . . . (Atlantic)
Candle In The Wind 1997
Elton John; *Candle In The Wind 1997 (Diana, Princess Of Wales)*
(Single) . . . . (Rocket)
England
Roger Whittaker; *Wind Beneath My Wings* . . . . (RCA)
England Rocks
Ian Hunter & Mott The Hoople; *Shades Of Ian Hunter* . . . . (Chrysalis)
England Swings
Roger Miller; *Best Of Roger Miller-#2-King Of The Road* . . . . (Mercury)
Roger Miller-Golden Hits . . . . (Smash)
England's Carol
Modern Jazz Quartet; *Art Of The Modern Jazz Quartet* . . . . (Atlantic)
Jazzlore-At Music Inn . . . . (Atlantic)
More From The Last Concert . . . . (Atlantic)
English Boys
Blondie; *The Hunter* . . . . (Chrysalis)
English Boys (With Guns)
Deaf School; *English Boys/Working Girls* . . . . (Warner Bros.)
English Civil War
Clash; *Give 'Em Enough Rope* . . . . (Epic)
The Story Of The Clash, Volume 1 . . . . (Epic)
English Dream
Generation X; *Valley Of The Dolls* . . . . (Chrysalis)
English Eyes
Toto; *Turn Back* . . . . (Columbia)
English Rose
Jam; *All Mad Cons* . . . . (Polydor)
Snap! . . . . (Polydor)
English Roses
Pretenders; *Pretenders II* . . . . (Sire)
English Roundabout
XTC; *English Settlement* . . . . (Geffen)
English Summer
Eurythmics; *In The Garden* . . . . (RCA)
Englishman In New York
Sting; *...Nothing Like The Sun* . . . . (A&M)
Fields Of Gold-The Best Of Sting 1984-1994 . . . . (A&M)
Garden Of England
Gerry Rafferty; *Right Down The Line-Best Of Gerry Rafferty* . . . . (EMI)
Goodbye England's Rose (Princess Diana)
Elton John; *Countdown Singers-England's Rose-C* . . . . (Madacy)
Great Britain National Anthem (God Save The Queen)
American Brass Band; *National Anthems* . . . . (Laserlight)
Swarovski Musik Wattens; *National Anthems Of The*
World . . . . (Koch International)
Vienna State Opera Orchestra; *National Anthems Of The World* . . . (Bescol, Ltd.)
Hard Times Of Old England
Steeleye Span; *All Around My Hat* . . . . (Chrysalis)
In Britain
Red Alert; *Punk & Disorderly* . . . . (Posh Boy)
King & Queen Of England
Sandy Denny; *Circle Dance-Hokey Pokey Charity-C* . . . . (Green Linnet)
Last God Of England
Pete Morton; *Frivolous Love* . . . . (Philo)
Little Old Church In England
Glenn Miller & His Orchestra; *Complete Glenn Miller & His*
Orchestra . . . . (Bluebird)
Long Haired Guys From England
Too Much Joy; *Cereal Killers* . . . . (Giant)
Mad Dogs & Englishmen
Noel Coward; *Live From Las Vegas & New York* . . . . (Columbia)
Made In England
Ian Anderson; *Walk Into Light* . . . . (Chrysalis)
Made In England
Elton John; *Made In England* . . . . (Rocket)
Old England
Waterboys; *This Is The Sea* . . . . (Chrysalis)
Picture Of England
Sun & The Moon; *Sun & The Moon* . . . . (Geffen)
Rose Of England
Nick Lowe; *Basher: Best Of* . . . . (Columbia)
Scarborough Fair/Canticle
Simon & Garfunkel; *Collected Works* . . . . (Columbia)
Parsley Sage Rosemary & Thyme . . . . (Columbia)
Simon & Garfunkel's Greatest Hits . . . . (Columbia)

ST/The Graduate . . . . (Columbia)
The Concert In Central Park . . . .(Warner Bros.)
Something About England
Clash; Sandinista . . . .(Epic)
Summertime In England
Van Morrison; Common One . . . .(Warner Bros.)
There'll Be Bluebirds Over The White Cliffs Of Dover
Kay Kyser & His Orchestra; Best Of The Big Bands-C . . . . (Columbia)
What It Is
Mark Knopfler; Sailing To Philadelphia. . . . .(Warner Bros.)
Why Can't The English
Rex Harrison; ST/My Fair Lady . . . . (Columbia)
Rex Harrison/Original Cast; My Fair Lady. . . . . (Columbia)

COUNTRIES: F

See Also: **CITIES: A-Z, COUNTRIES: FRANCE**

Finland National Anthem (Mamme)
American Brass Band; National Anthems. . . . . (Laserlight)
Vienna State Opera Orchestra; National Anthems Of The World . . .(Bescol, Ltd.)

COUNTRIES: FRANCE

See Also: **CITIES: A-Z, CITIES: PARIS**

1812 Overture
New York Philharmonic & Leonard Bernstein; Conducts
Tchaikovsky . . . . (Columbia)
Great Tchaikovsky . . . . (Columbia)
Overtures and Tone Poems . . . . (Columbia)
Tchaikovsky's Greatest Hits-#1 . . . . (Columbia)
Various Overtures . . . . (Columbia)
Ballad Of John And Yoko
Beatles; Beatles 1 . . . . (Capitol)
Beatles-Box Set . . . . (Capitol)
Hey Jude . . . . (Capitol)
Past Masters-Volume Two . . . . (Parlophone)
ST/Imagine: John Lennon . . . . (Capitol)
The Beatles/1967-1970 . . . . (Capitol)
C'est Si Bon (It's So Good)
Eartha Kitt; Lost Female Hits Of The '50s-C . . . .(Taragon)
Done With Bonaparte
Mark Knopfler; Golden Heart . . . .(Warner Bros.)
Fields Of France
Al Stewart; Last Days Of The Century . . . .(Enigma Capitol)
France
Grateful Dead; Shakedown Street . . . . (Arista)
France Chance
Ry Cooder; Ry Cooder . . . . (Reprise)
France National Anthem (La Marseillaise)
American Brass Band; National Anthems. . . . . (Laserlight)
Swarovski Musik Wattens; National Anthems Of The
World . . . . (Koch International)
Vienna State Opera Orchestra; National Anthems Of The World . . .(Bescol, Ltd.)
French Kiss
Lil Louis & His World; This Beat Is Hot-C . . . .(Epic)
French Song
Monkees; Present . . . . (Rhino)
French Waltz
Art Garfunkel; Scissors Cut . . . . (Columbia)
Green Fields Of France
Phil Coulter; Forgotten Dreams . . . . (Shanachie)
House In France
Doris Day & Andre Previn; Duet . . . . (DRG)
Sacha Distel; Amour Tout Court . . . . (DRG)
In France They Kiss On Main Street
Joni Mitchell; Hissing Of Summer Lawns. . . . .(Asylum)
Shadows & Light . . . . (Asylum)
La Marseillaise
Mormon Tabernacle Choir; This Is My Country . . . . (Columbia)
Made In France
Bireli Lagrene; Acoustic Moments . . . . (Bluebird)
Place In France
Death Squad; Split You At The Seams . . . . (Ever Rat)
Poor People Of Paris
Les Baxter & His Orchestra; Memories Are Made Of This-C . . . . (Capitol)
Summer I Read Collette, The
Rosanne Cash; 10 Song Demo . . . . (Capitol)
When He Takes You To France
Kevin Roth; Voyages . . . . (Flying Fish)

COUNTRIES: G

See Also: **CITIES: A-Z, COUNTRIES: GERMANY**

Almost Made It To Guam
Michael Gulezian; Distant Memories & Dreams . . . . (Timbreline)
Appointment In Ghana
Christopher Hollyday; Christopher Hollyday . . . .(Novus)
Jackie McLean; Jackie's Bag . . . . (Blue Note)
Flowers Of Guatemala
R.E.M.; Life's Rich Pageant . . . . (EMI-Capitol Entert. Properties)
Georgia National Anthem
Swarovski Musik Wattens; National Anthems Of The
World . . . . (Koch International)
Girl From Greenland
Chet Baker; Compact Jazz-Chet Baker . . . .(Emarcy)
Greece
George Harrison; Gone Troppo . . . .(Dark Horse)
Greece National Anthem (Segnorizo Apo Tin Kopsi)
American Brass Band; National Anthems . . . .(Laserlight)
Orlando Philharmonic Orchestra; The National Anthems . . . .(Madacy)
Greeks Don't Want No Freaks
Eagles; The Long Run . . . .(Asylum)
Greenland Fisheries
Pete Seeger; 20 Golden Pieces Of Pete Seeger . . . .(Bulldog)
Pete Seeger . . . . (Everest)
Pete Seeger Sings Folk Music Of The World . . . .(Tradition)
Greenland Whale Fisheries
Judy Collins & Theodore Bikel; Greatest Folksingers Of The
'60s-C . . . . (Vanguard)
Guatemala
Pete Sears & Others; Watchfire . . . . (Redwood)
Guatemala
Life Sex & Death; Silent Majority. . . . .(Reprise)
Guatemala Connection
Hubert Laws; Romeo & Juliet . . . . (Columbia)
Guatemala National Anthem
Banda Sinfonica De Madrid; National Anthems . . . . (International Music)
Payed Vacation: Greece
Camper Van Beethoven; Telephone Free Landslide Victory . . . . (I.R.S.)
Shaft In Greenland
Dead Milkmen; Soul Rotation . . . . (Hollywood)
Stranded In Greenland
For Against; December . . . . (Charisma)
Theme From "Zorba The Greek"
Cincinnati Pops Orchestra/Erich Kunzel; Hollywood's Greatest
Hits-#2 . . . . (Telarc)

COUNTRIES: GERMANY

See Also: **CITIES: A-Z, CITIES: BERLIN**

4:37 AM (Arabs With Knives & West German Skies)
Roger Waters; Pros & Cons Of Hitchhiking . . . . (Columbia)
Bavarian In New York
Triumvirat; A LaCarte. . . . . Capitol)
Der Kommisar
After The Fire; Club Epic-#5-C . . . . (Epic)
Different Germany
Ian Anderson; Walk Into Light . . . . (Chrysalis)
Fraulein
Bobby Helms; Pop-A-Dilly . . . . (MCA)
Super Country Hits Of The '50s-C . . . . (Gusto)
Mickey Gilley; Mickey Gilley's Greatest Hits-#1 . . . . (Epic)
German Kid
Dee Dee King; Standing In The Spotlight . . . . (Red Eye)
German Lunch
Frank Zappa; You Can't Do That On Stage Anymore-#5. . . . . (Rykodisc)
German Nun
Sex Gang Children; Ecstasy & Vendetta Over New York . . . . (Roir)
German Overalls
Peter Hammill; Chameleon In The Shadow Of The Night . . . .(Blue Plate)
German Special
Li'l Wally; All Around The World. . . . . (Jay Jay)
German Waltz Medley
Lawrence Welk; Come Waltz With Me . . . . (Ranwood)
Germans At The Spa
Original London Cast; Nine. . . . .(RCA)
Germany
Sloppy Seconds; First Seven Inches...& Then Some! . . . . (Taang!)
Stains; Stains . . . . (SST)
Germany National Anthem (Deutschlandlied)
American Brass Band; National Anthems . . . .(Laserlight)
Orlando Philharmonic Orchestra; The National Anthems . . . .(Madacy)
Vienna State Opera Orchestra; National Anthems Of The World . . (Bescol, Ltd.)

Girl From Germany
Sparks; *Profile-The Ultimate Sparks Collection* . . . . (Rhino)
Heartbreak U.S.A.
Kitty Wells; *I Love Country-Hits Of The '60s-#1-C* . . . .(Priority)
Kitty Wells' Greatest Songs . . . . (Curb)
The Country Music Hall Of Fame-Kitty Wells . . . . (MCA Special Prod.)
How Do You Say Auf Wiedersehen
George Shearing & Mel Torme; *Top Drawer* . . . . (Concord Jazz)
In Germany Before The War
Randy Newman; *Little Criminals* . . . . (Warner Bros.)
Lili Marlene
Marlene Dietrich; *Best Of Marlene Dietrich* . . . .(Columbia)
Essential Marlene Dietrich . . . .(Capitol)
Live At The Cafe De Paris . . . .(Columbia)
This Is Art Deco-C . . . .(Columbia)
Lost In Germany
King's X; *King's X* . . . . (Atlantic)
Man Who Put The Germ In Germany, The
Nora Bayes; *Music From The New York Stage (1890-1920)-#4-1917-
1920-C* . . . .(Pearl)
Snoopy Vs. The Red Baron
Royal Guardsmen; *Best Of The Royal Guardsmen-#1* . . . . (Rhino)
Collectables Presents The History Of Rock-#9-C . . . . (Collectables)
Cruisin'-1967-C . . . . (Increase)
Million-Dollar Memories #1-C . . . .(RCA)
Super Oldies Of The '60s-#6-C . . . . (Audio Fidelity)
Springtime For Hitler
Mel Brooks; *ST/High Anxiety* . . . . (Asylum)
Original Broadway Cast; *The Producers* . . . .(Sony Music Classical)
To Germany With Love
Alphaville; *Forever Young* . . . . (Atlantic)
Wars Of Germany
Clancy Brothers & Tommy Makem; *Luck Of The Irish* . . . . (Columbia)
West Germany
Minutemen; *Double Nickels On The Dime* . . . . (SST)
White Car In Germany
Associates; *Popera-Singles Collection* . . . .(Sire)

COUNTRIES: H

See Also: CITIES: A-Z

Cowboys In Hong Kong (As Far As Siam)
Red Rider; *As Far As Siam* . . . . (Capitol)
Haiti National Anthem
Banda Sinfonica De Madrid; *National Anthems* . . . . (International Music)
Haitian Divorce
Steely Dan; *Steely Dan's Greatest Hits* . . . . (MCA)
The Royal Scam . . . . (MCA)
Honduras National Anthem
Banda Sinfonica De Madrid; *National Anthems* . . . . (International Music)
Hong Kong
Quinns; *Harlem Holiday-New York Rhythm & Blues-#4-C* . . . . . .(Collectables)
Screamin' Jay Hawkins; *At Home With Screamin' Jay Hawkins* . . . . . (Columbia)
Cow Fingers & Mosquito Pie . . . . (Epic)
Hong Kong Bar
Tim Buckley; *Greetings From L.A.* . . . . (Bizarre/Straight)
Hong Kong Blues
George Harrison; *Somewhere In England* . . . .(Dark Horse)
Hoagy Carmichael; *Stardust Road* . . . . (MCA)
Hong Kong Fireworks
Henry Mancini; *ST/Revenge Of The Pink Panther* . . . . (EMI)
Hong Kong Garden
Siouxsie And The Banshees; *Once Upon A Time-The Singles* . . . . (Geffen)
Hungary National Anthem (Himnusz)
American Brass Band; *National Anthems* . . . .(Laserlight)
Vienna State Opera Orchestra; *National Anthems Of The World* . . . (Bescol, Ltd.)
I Left My Hat In Haiti
Fred Astaire; *Fred Astaire At MGM* . . . . (Rhino)
ST/Royal Wedding . . . . (Sony Music Special Prod.)
Road To Hong Kong
Billy May; *I Believe In You* . . . . (Bainbridge)

COUNTRIES: I

*See Also: CITIES: A-Z, COUNTRIES: INDIA, IRELAND,
ISRAEL, ITALY*

I Left My Heart In Iran
Forgotten Rebels; *Surfin' On Heroin* . . . . (Restless)
Iceland National Anthem
Swarovski Musik Wattens; *National Anthems Of The
World* . . . .(Koch International)
Iran National Anthem
Swarovski Musik Wattens; *National Anthems Of The
World* . . . .(Koch International)

Iraq National Anthem
Swarovski Musik Wattens; *National Anthems Of The
World* . . . .(Koch International)

COUNTRIES: INDIA

See Also: CITIES: A-Z

Hunting Tigers Out In India
Bonzo Dog Band; *Best Of The Bonzo Dog Band* . . . .(Rhino)
Tadpoles . . . .(Liberty)
India
John Coltrane; *Best Of John Coltrane-#2* . . . . (MCA)
John McLaughlin & Shakti; *Handful Of Beauty* . . . .(Columbia)
India
Roxy Music; *Avalon* . . . . (Warner Bros.)
Heart Still Beating . . . . (Virgin)
New Electric India
Shadowfax; *Shadow Dance* . . . . (Windham Hill)
What Goes Around-Best Of Shadowfax . . . . (Windham Hill)
Postcard From India
Rosalie Sorrels; *Travelin' Lady Rides Again* . . . . (Green Linnet)
Return From India
Jerry Holland; *Jerry Holland* . . . .(Rounder)
Song Of India
101 Strings Orchestra; *Big Band Hits-#1* . . . .(Alshire)
BBC Big Band; *Age Of Swing-#1* . . . .(Bainbridge)
Tommy Dorsey; *Best Of Tommy Dorsey* . . . .(Bluebird)
Stop, Look And Listen-1936-1939 . . . .(RCA Victor)
Tommy Dorsey & The David Rose String Orchestra . . . . (Laserlight)
Tommy Dorsey & Frank Sinatra; *Dorsey/Sinatra Radio Years-1940-
1942* . . . . (RCA)
Sweet Song Of India
McGuire Sisters; *Best Of The McGuire Sisters* . . . . (MCA)
Taste Of India
Aerosmith; *Nine Lives* . . . .(Columbia)
Thank U
Alanis Morissette; *Supposed Former Infatuation Junkie* . . . . (Maverick)

COUNTRIES: IRELAND

See Also: CITIES: A-Z, CITIES: DUBLIN

Beautiful Ireland
Anne & Francie Brolly; *Ireland My Home* . . . . (Rego Irish)
Come Back To Erin
Billy Shepherd Singers; *Irish Sing-Along* . . . . (MCA)
Did Your Mother Come From Ireland
Bing Crosby; *Shillelaghs & Shamrocks* . . . . (MCA)
Drink A Round To Ireland
Judy Collins; *Times Of Our Lives* . . . .(Elektra)
Farewell To Ireland
Phil Cunningham; *Airs & Graces* . . . . (Green Linnet)
Galway Bay
Bing Crosby; *Best Of Bing Crosby* . . . . (MCA)
When Irish Eyes Are Smiling . . . . (MCA)
Ireland
Flim & The BB's; *Further Adventures* . . . . (Digital Music Prod.)
Marianne Faithfull; *Child's Adventure* . . . . (Island)
Maura O'Connell; *Real Life Story* . . . . (Warner Bros.)
Ireland Mother Ireland
John McCormack; *Irish Minstrel* . . . .(RCA)
Louis Browne; *Evening In Ireland* . . . . (Rego Irish)
Ireland My Home
Anne & Francie Brolly; *Ireland My Home* . . . . (Rego Irish)
Barley Bree; *Speak Up For Old Ireland* . . . . (Shanachie)
Ireland National Anthem (Amthran Na Bh Flann)
American Brass Band; *National Anthems* . . . . (Laserlight)
Swarovski Musik Wattens; *National Anthems Of The
World* . . . .(Koch International)
Ireland We Know
Ed Reavy; *Ed Reavy* . . . .(Rounder)
Ireland, My Sireland
Vernon Stiles; *Music From The New York Stage (1890-1920)-#4-1917-
1920-C* . . . . (Pearl)
Ireland's 32
Paddy Noonan; *Happy Hours* . . . . (Rego Irish)
Irish
Buddy Merrill; *Holiday For Guitars* . . . . (Accent)
Irish Boy
Mark Knopfler; *CT/Cal* . . . .(Mercury)

Irish Have A Great Day Tonight, The
Vernon Stiles Quartet; *Music From The New York Stage (1890-1920)-#4-1917-1920-C* . . . . (Pearl)
Irish Heartbeat
Van Morrison; *Inarticulate Speech Of The Heart* . . . . (Warner Bros.)
Van Morrison & The Chieftains; *Irish Heartbeat* . . . . (Mercury)
Irish Jig (The Ball)
Original Broadway Cast; *Meet Me In St. Louis* . . . . (DRG)
Irish Jubilee
Pat Harrington; *St. Patrick's Day Celebration* . . . . (Columbia)
Irish Love Song
Mormon Tabernacle Choir; *Old Beloved Songs* . . . . (Columbia)
Irish Lullabye
Paddy Noonan; *Irish Party* . . . . (Rego Irish)
Irish March: March Of The Mayomen
Chieftains & The RTE Concert Orchestra; *Year Of The French* . . . . . (Shanachie)
Irish Rover
Clancy Brothers; *Clancy Brothers With Lou* . . . . (Vanguard)
Irish Rovers; *First Of The Irish Rovers* . . . . (MCA)
Irish Spring
Country Gentlemen; *Country Gentlemen With Ricky Skaggs* . . . . . . (Vanguard)
Irish Suite: Irish Washerwoman
Boston Pops Orchestra/Arthur Fiedler; *Irish Night At The Pops* . . . . . (RCA)
Irishman In Chinatown
Luka Bloom; *Riverside* . . . . (Reprise)
Luck Of The Irish
John Lennon/Plastic Ono Band; *Sometime In New York City* . . . . (Capitol)
Memories Of Ireland
Paddy Noonan; *Memories Of Ireland* . . . . (Rego Irish)
Minstrel Boy
Boston Pops Orchestra/Arthur Fiedler; *Irish Album* . . . . (RCA)
Irish Night At The Pops . . . . (RCA)
John McDermott; *Battlefields Of Green-Songs Of Love & Loss* . . . . (Angel)
My Beautiful Irish Maid
Chauncey Olcott; *Music From The New York Stage (1890-1920)-#1-1890-1908-C* . . . . (Pearl)
My Irish Molly-O
De Danann; *Best Of De Danann* . . . . (Shanachie)
My Wild Irish Rose
Magic Organ; *22 Great Organ Favorites* . . . . (Ranwood)
Mom & Dads; *One Dozen Roses* . . . . (Crescendo)
Paddy Doyle's Boots
Clancy Brothers & Tommy Makem; *Best Of Clancy Brothers & Tommy Makem* . . . . (Tradition)
Paddy Goes To Nashville
Adrian Legg; *Mrs. Crowe's Blue Waltz* . . . . (Relativity)
Paddy Kelly's Brew
Tommy Makem; *Evening With Tommy Makem* . . . . (Shanachie)
Paddy McGinty's Coat
Pat Harrington; *St. Patrick's Day Celebration* . . . . (Columbia)
Paddy On The Railway
Barley Bree; *Castles In The Air* . . . . (Shanachie)
Paddy Ryan's Dream
Matt Molloy; *Stony Steps* . . . . (Green Linnet)
Paddy Won't You Drink Some Cider
Red Clay Ramblers; *Chuckin' The Frizz* . . . . (Flying Fish)
Paddy's Green Shamrock Shore
Chieftains; *Another Country* . . . . (RCA)
Rambling Irishman
De Danann; *Best Of De Danann* . . . . (Shanachie)
Red Headed Irishman
J.P. Fraley & Annadeene; *Wild Rose Of The Mountain* . . . . (Rounder)
Rockin' Rockin' Leprechauns
Jonathan Richman & The Modern Lovers; *Rock 'N' Roll With Jonathan Richman & The Modern Lovers* . . . . (Rhino)
Rose Of Tralee
Bing Crosby; *When Irish Eyes Are Smiling* . . . . (MCA)
Patrick O'Hagan; *22 Golden Shamrocks* . . . . (Rego Irish)
Shall My Soul Pass Through Old Ireland
Pat Daly & Frank Fitzpatrick Band; *One Of The Old Brigade* . . . . . . (Rego Irish)
Small Hills Of Offaly
Irish Tradition; *Times We've Had* . . . . (Green Linnet)
There's A Little Bit Of Irish
Patrick O'Hagan; *22 Golden Shamrocks* . . . . (Rego Irish)
They Wounded Old Ireland
Andy M. Stewart; *By The Hush* . . . . (Green Linnet)
Too Ra Loo Ra Loo Ral
Band; *The Last Waltz* . . . . (Warner Bros.)
Bing Crosby; *Best Of Bing Crosby* . . . . (MCA)
When Irish Eyes Are Smiling . . . . (MCA)
When Irish Eyes Are Smiling
Billy Shepherd Singers; *Irish Sing-Along* . . . . (MCA)
Bing Crosby; *When Irish Eyes Are Smiling* . . . . (MCA)
Dennis Day; *Irish Album* . . . . (RCA)
Whiskey In The Jar
Metallica; *Garage Inc.* . . . . (Elektra)

COUNTRIES: ISRAEL
See Also: CITIES: A-Z

Beautiful Hills Of Galilee
Hazel Dickens; *Old-Timey Gospel Music* . . . . (Rounder)
Hatikvah
Barbra Streisand & Golda Meir; *Just For The Record* . . . . (Columbia)
Mormon Tabernacle Choir; *This Is My Country* . . . . (Columbia)
Israel
Bill Evans; *Bill Evans-Complete Riverside Recordings* . . . . (Riverside)
Miles Davis; *Birth Of The Cool* . . . . (Capitol)
Israel
Siouxsie And The Banshees; *Nocturne* . . . . (Geffen)
Once Upon A Time-The Singles . . . . (Geffen)
Israel In Our House
Al Jolson; *The Al Jolson Story-#5* . . . . (MCA)
Israel National Anthem (Hatikvah)
American Brass Band; *National Anthems* . . . . (Laserlight)
Vienna State Opera Orchestra; *National Anthems Of The World* . . (Bescol, Ltd.)
Israelis, Terrorists And Arabs
Jackie Mason; *ST/Brand New* . . . . (Sony Broadway)
Israelites (The)
Desmond Dekker & The Aces; *ST/Drugstore Cowboy* . . . . (Novus)
The Island Story-1962-1987-25th Anniversary-C . . . . (Island)
Man From Galilee
Billy Parker; *Average Man* . . . . (Sunshine Country)
Milk & Honey
Original Cast; *Milk & Honey* . . . . (RCA Victor)
Theme From ''Exodus''
101 Strings Orchestra; *Golden Movie Themes* . . . . (Alshire)
Boston Pops Orchestra/Arthur Fiedler; *Motion Picture Classics-#1* . . . . (RCA Victor)
Ferrante & Teicher; *Grand Pianos* . . . . (Pair)

COUNTRIES: ITALY
See Also: CITIES: A-Z, CITIES: ROME

Botcha-A-Me (Ba-Ba-Baciami Piccina)
Rosemary Clooney; *Rosemary Clooney-16 Most Requested Songs* . . . . (Legacy)
Funiculi, Funicula
Mario Lanza; *Legendary Tenor* . . . . (RCA)
Isle Of Capri
Billy Vaughn; *Billy Vaughn-22 Of His Greatest Hits* . . . . (Ranwood)
Frank Sinatra; *Come Fly With Me* . . . . (Capitol)
Italian From New York
Chicago; *Chicago VII* . . . . (Chicago)
Italian Girls
Daryl Hall & John Oates; *H2O* . . . . (RCA)
Soulful Sounds . . . . (RCA)
Italian Girls
Rod Stewart; *Best Of Rod Stewart-#2* . . . . (Mercury)
Italian Plastic
Crowded House; *Woodface* . . . . (Capitol)
Italian Shoes
Dynatones; *Shameless* . . . . (Warner Bros.)
Italy National Anthem (Inno Di Mameli)
American Brass Band; *National Anthems* . . . . (Laserlight)
Vienna State Opera Orchestra; *National Anthems Of The World* . . (Bescol, Ltd.)
Mambo Italiano
Rosemary Clooney; *Rosemary Clooney-16 Most Requested Songs* . . . . (Legacy)
Pepino The Italian Mouse
Lou Monte; *Pepino The Italian Mouse & Other Songs* . . . . (Reprise)
Scenes From An Italian Restaurant
Billy Joel; *The Stranger* . . . . (Columbia)
That's Amore
Dean Martin; *Best Of Dean Martin* . . . . (CEMA Special Prod.)
Dean Martin's All Time Greatest Hits . . . . (Curb)
Dean Martin's Greatest Hits . . . . (EMI)
The Capitol Years-Dean Martin . . . . (Capitol)
Theme From ''Cinema Paradiso''
Original Soundtrack; *Ennio Morricone With Love* . . . . (DRG)
Veni-Vidi-Vici (I Came, I Saw, I Conquered)
Gaylords; *Best Of The Gaylords* . . . . (Chronicles)

COUNTRIES: JAMAICA
See Also: CITIES: A-Z

Boogie On Reggae Woman
Stevie Wonder; *Fulfillingness' First Finale* . . . . (Motown)
Motown Time Capsule-#2-'70s-C . . . . (Motown)
Original Musiquarium . . . . (Motown)

Come Back To Jamaica
Yellowman; *Going To The Chapel* ....(Shanachie)
Coming Back, Jamaica
Lester Bowie's Brass Fantasy; *I Only Have Eyes For You* .... (ECM)
Happy Birthday Jamaica
Lee "Scratch" Perry; *The Upsetter & The Beat* .... (Heartbeat)
I've Committed Murder
Macy Gray; *On How Life Is* .... (Epic)
Jamaica
George Benson & Earl Klugh; *Collaboration* .... (Warner Bros.)
Jamaica
Lacy J. Dalton; *16th Avenue* ....(Columbia)
Jamaica
Bobby Caldwell; *Carry On* .... (Sin-Drome)
Jamaica
Caron Wheeler; *Uk Blak* .... (EMI)
Jamaica
Scott Cossu; *Wind Dance* .... (Windham Hill)
Jamaica Farewell
Harry Belafonte; *Calypso* ....(RCA)
Harry Belafonte-Legendary Performer ....(RCA)
Harry Belafonte-Pure Gold ....(RCA)
Harry Belafonte's All Time Greatest Hits-#1 ....(RCA)
This Is Harry Belafonte ....(RCA)
Jamaica In My Mind
McGuffey Lane; *Day By Day* .... (Atlantic America)
Jamaica Jerkoff
Elton John; *Goodbye Yellow Brick Road* .... (Polydor)
Jamaica Lady
Nitty Gritty Dirt Band; *Dirt, Silver & Gold* .... (One Way)
Jamaica Say You Will
Jackson Browne; *Jackson Browne* .... (Asylum)
Jamaica Ska
Annette Funicello; *Best Of Annette Funicello* .... (Rhino)
Jamaica Sunday Morning
Kim Carnes; *St. Vincent's Court* .... (Out Of Print)
Louie Louie
Kingsmen; *Best Of The Kingsmen* .... (Rhino)
Billboard Top Rock 'N' Roll Hits-1963-C .... (Rhino)
Cruisin'-1963-C .... (Increase)
Frat Rock!-C .... (Rhino)
Oldies But Goodies-#11-C ....(Original Sound)
Rock & Roll Is Here To Stay-C .... (Gusto)
ST/Quadrophenia .... (MCA)
WCBS FM 101 History Of Rock-'60s-#1-C .... (Collectables)
My Jamaican Guy
Grace Jones; *Island Life* .... (Island)
On And On
Stephen Bishop; *Best Of Bish* .... (Rhino)
On Jamaica
Country Joe McDonald; *Paradise With An Ocean View* .... (Fantasy)
Rastafari Is
Peter Tosh; *Captured Live* .... (EMI)
Wanted Dread & Alive .... (EMI)
Rastafari Liveth
Peter Broggs; *Rastafari Liveth*. .... (Real Authentic Sound)
Real Authentic Sampler-C .... (Real Authentic Sound)
Rastaman
Bunny Wailer; *Blackheart Man*. .... (Island)
Rastaman Chant
Wailers; *Burnin'* .... (Tuff Gong)
Rastaman Live Up
Bob Marley & The Wailers; *Confrontation* .... (Tuff Gong)
Reggae On Broadway
Bob Marley; *Chances Are* ....(Cotillion)
Reggae Radio Station
Third World; *Hold On To Love* .... (Columbia)
Reggae Revolution
Ziggy Marley & The Melody Makers; *Hey World!* .... (EMI)
Time Has Come...Best Of Ziggy Marley & The Melody Makers........ (EMI)
Roots Woman
Jimmy Cliff; *Power & The Glory* .... (Columbia)
Roots, Rock, Reggae
Bob Marley & The Wailers; *Rastaman Vibration* .... (Tuff Gong)
Rootsman Skanking
Bunny Wailer; *Rootsman Skanking*..........................(Shanachie)
Sweet Jamaica
Cat Stevens; *Izitso* .... (A&M)
Temple Jamaica
Peter Manning Robinson; *Phoenix Rising* .... (Chase Music Group)
Vahevala
Loggins & Messina; *Loggins & Messina-On Stage*............. (Columbia)
Sittin' In .... (Columbia)
The Best Of Friends .... (Columbia)
You're My Jamaica
Charley Pride; *Charley Pride Live* ....(RCA)
Charley Pride's Greatest Hits ....(RCA)

COUNTRIES: JAPAN
See Also: **CITIES: A-Z, CITIES: TOKYO**

Big In Japan
Alphaville; *Alphaville-The Singles Collection* .... (Atlantic)
Forever Young. .... (Atlantic)
Bird Of Japan
Joyce; *Music Inside* .... (Verve/Forecast)
Discovering Japan
Graham Parker And The Rumour; *Squeezing Out Sparks* .... (Arista)
Geisha Girl
Hank Locklin; *Hank Locklin-Golden Hits* .... (Plantation)
Heartbreak U.S.A.
Kitty Wells; *I Love Country-Hits Of The '60s-#1-C*. .... (Priority)
Kitty Wells' Greatest Songs. ....(Curb)
The Country Music Hall Of Fame-Kitty Wells. .... (MCA Special Prod.)
Japan
Be Bop Deluxe; *Best Of Be Bop Deluxe-Raiding The Divine Archive* ...(Capitol)
Japan
Oregon; *Our First Record* ....(Vanguard)
Japan National Anthem (Kimiga Yowa Chiyoni)
American Brass Band; *National Anthems* .... (Laserlight)
Vienna State Opera Orchestra; *National Anthems Of The World* ... (Bescol, Ltd.)
Japanese Drums
Kitaro; *Asia* .... (Geffen)
Japanese Sandman
Benny Goodman; *The Birth Of Swing (1935-1936)* ....(Bluebird)
Japanese Tears
Denny Laine; *Japanese Tears* .... (Takoma)
Living In Japan
Fun Fun; *33* ....(TSR)
Made In Japan
Buck Owens; *Buck Owens' All-Time Greatest Hits-#1* ....(Curb)
Buck Owens Collection-1959-1990.........................(Rhino)
Made In Japan
Kat; *Beethoven On Speed*............................ (Roadrunner)
Silent Eyes
Paul Simon; *Still Crazy After All These Years* ....(Columbia)
Turning Japanese
Vapors; *New Clear Days* .... (Liberty)
Rock Of The '80s-#3-C .... (Priority)
Working For The Japanese
Ray Stevens; *#1 With A Bullet* ....(Curb)
Top Ten Records ....(Curb)
You're Still Not Safe In A Japanese Car
Jumpin' John Goldsmith; *45-#7-89686* .... (Atlantic)

COUNTRIES: K
See Also: **CITIES: A-Z**

Kenya
J.J. Johnson; *Lt's Hang Out* ....(Verve)
Rippingtons; *Welcome To The St. James' Club* ....(GRP)
Sad News From Korea
Lightnin' Hopkins; *Houston's King of the Blues-1952-1953*.... (Blues Classics)

COUNTRIES: L
See Also: **CITIES: A-Z**

Latvia National Anthem
Swarovski Musik Wattens; *National Anthems Of The*
World ....(Koch International)
Lithuania National Anthem
Swarovski Musik Wattens; *National Anthems Of The World*...... (Bescol, Ltd.)
Luxembourg National Anthem (Ons Hemecht)
American Brass Band; *National Anthems* .... (Laserlight)
Swarovski Musik Wattens; *National Anthems Of The*
World ....(Koch International)

COUNTRIES: M
See Also: **CITIES: A-Z, COUNTRIES: MEXICO**

Club Morocco
Azymuth; *Cascades* ....(Milestone)
Dawn In Malaysia
Kitaro; *Asia* .... (Geffen)
El Morocco
Santana; *Moonflower* ....(Columbia)

Malta National Anthem
Swarovski Musik Wattens; *National Anthems Of The
World* . . . . (Koch International)
Marrakesh Express (Morocco)
Crosby, Stills & Nash; *Crosby, Stills & Nash* . . . . (Atlantic)
CSN . . . . (Atlantic)
So Far . . . . (Atlantic)
Woodstock Two . . . . (Atlantic)
Midnight In Morocco
Michael Powers; *Perpetual Motion* . . . . (Nastymix)
Moldova National Anthem
Swarovski Musik Wattens; *National Anthems Of The
World* . . . . (Koch International)
Monaco National Anthem
Swarovski Musik Wattens; *National Anthems Of The
World* . . . . (Koch International)
Mongolia National Anthem
Swarovski Musik Wattens; *National Anthems Of The
World* . . . . (Koch International)
Moroccan Nights
John Tropea; *NY Cats Direct* . . . . (Digital Music Prod.)
Morocco
Rippingtons; *Kilimanjaro* . . . . (GRP)
Morocco National Anthem
Swarovski Musik Wattens; *National Anthems Of The
World* . . . . (Koch International)
Mozambique
Bob Dylan; *Desire* . . . . (Columbia)
Emily Remler; *Emily Remler-Retrospective-#2-Compositions* . . . (Concord Jazz)
Mozambique National Anthem
Swarovski Musik Wattens; *National Anthems Of The
World* . . . . (Koch International)
She Drives Me Madagascar
Chi; *Jet Stream* . . . . (Sonic Atmospheres)
Something Fine (Morocco)
Jackson Browne; *Jackson Browne* . . . . (Asylum)

COUNTRIES: MEXICO

See Also: **CITIES: A-Z, COUNTRIES: SPAIN, HISPANIC**

Across The Border
Bruce Springsteen; *The Ghost Of Tom Joad* . . . . (Columbia)
Across The Borderline
Willie Nelson; *Across The Borderline* . . . . (Columbia)
Ain't No God In Mexico
Waylon Jennings; *Honky Tonk Heroes* . . . . (RCA)
Amukiriki
Les Paul; *Legend And The Legacy* . . . . (Gold Rush)
Banditos
Refreshments; *Fizzy Fuzzy Big & Buzzy* . . . . (Mercury)
Bay Of Mexico
Kingston Trio; *Folk Era Sampler-Digitally* . . . . (Folk Era)
Stereo Concert Plus . . . . (Folk Era)
Tom Dooley . . . . (Capitol)
Big Mexican Dinner
Kentucky HeadHunters; *Electric Barnyard* . . . . (Mercury)
Blame It On Mexico
George Strait; *Strait Country* . . . . (MCA)
Strait Out Of The Box . . . . (MCA)
Border, The
America; *America In Concert* . . . . (Capitol)
Encore-More Greatest Hits . . . . (Rhino)
Your Move . . . . (Capitol)
Brownsville Turnaround On The Tex-Mex Border
KLF; *Chill Out* . . . . (Wax Trax)
Deportee (Plane Wreck At Los Gatos)
Arlo Guthrie & Pete Seeger; *Together In Concert* . . . . (Reprise)
Byrds; *The Byrds* . . . . (Columbia)
Cisco Houston; *Greatest Songs Of Woody Guthrie-C* . . . . (Vanguard)
Gene Clark & Carla Olson; *So Rebellious A Lover* . . . . (Rhino)
Judy Collins; *Tribute To Woody Guthrie-C* . . . . (Warner Bros.)
Waylon Jennings, Willie Nelson, Johnny Cash, Kris Kristofferson;
Highwayman . . . . (Columbia)
Down In Mexico
Coasters; *Atlantic Rhythm & Blues 1947-1974-#3 (1955-1958)-C* . . . . (Atlantic)
Coasters' Greatest Hits . . . . (Atco)
Down To Mexico
Angie Meyer; *Texas Folk & Outlaw Music* . . . . (Adelphi)
Dreams Of Mexico
Arlen Roth; *Guitarist* . . . . (Rounder)
El Paso
Grateful Dead; *Steal Your Face* . . . . (Grateful Dead)
Marty Robbins; *Billboard Top Country Hits-1960-C* . . . . (Rhino)
Gunfighter Ballads & Trail Songs . . . . (Legacy)
Marty Robbins' Biggest Hits . . . . (Columbia)

Radio Classics Of The '50s-C . . . . (Columbia)
Texas Super Hits-C . . . . (Columbia)
Escape To Mexico
William Orbit; *Orbit* . . . . (I.R.S.)
From Maine To Mexico
Leon Russell; *Americana* . . . . (Paradise)
God Don't Make Lonely Girls
Wallflowers; *Bringing Down The Horse* . . . . (Interscope)
Going Down To Mexico
ZZ Top; *Six Pack* . . . . (Warner Bros.)
ZZ Top . . . . (Warner Bros.)
Going To Mexico
Steve Miller Band; *Best Of Steve Miller 1968-1973* . . . . (Capitol)
Steve Miller Band-Anthology . . . . (Capitol)
Steve Miller Band-Number 5 . . . . (Capitol)
He'll Have To Go
Jim Reeves; *60 Years Of Country Music-C* . . . . (RCA)
Best Of Jim Reeves . . . . (RCA)
Billboard Top Country Hits-1960-C . . . . (Rhino)
Great Moments At The Grand Ole Opry-C . . . . (RCA)
Jim Reeves' Greatest Hits . . . . (RCA)
Nipper's Greatest Hits Of The '50s-#1-C . . . . (RCA)
Ry Cooder; *Chicken Skin Music* . . . . (Reprise)
Henry
New Riders Of The Purple Sage; *Best Of New Riders Of The
Purple Sage* . . . . (Columbia)
*Bill Graham Presents The Last Days Of The
Fillmore-C* . . . . (Epic Portrait Assoc.)
Home Home On The Road . . . . (Columbia)
New Riders Of The Purple Sage . . . . (Columbia)
I Got Mexico
Eddy Raven; *14 #1 Country Hits-C* . . . . (RCA)
Best Of Eddy Raven . . . . (RCA)
I Could Use Another You . . . . (RCA)
Late Winter, Early Spring
John Denver; *Rocky Mountain High* . . . . (RCA)
Line, The
Bruce Springsteen; *The Ghost Of Tom Joad* . . . . (Columbia)
Lonely Rose Of Mexico
Sons Of The Pioneers; *Tumbleweed Trails* . . . . (MCA)
Lost In Mexico
Billy Joe Walker, Jr.; *Treehouse* . . . . (MCA)
Lost John Boogied His Way Into Mexico
Maddox Brothers & Rose; *On The Air-#1 & 2* . . . . (Arhoolie)
Love Letters From Old Mexico
Leslie Satcher; *Love Letters* . . . . (Warner Bros.)
Mas Tequila
Sammy Hagar; *Red Voodoo* . . . . (MCA)
Maybe Mexico
Jerry Jeff Walker; *Mr. Bojangles* . . . . (Bainbridge)
Mexican Blackbird
ZZ Top; *Fandango* . . . . (Warner Bros.)
Six Pack . . . . (Warner Bros.)
Mexican Connection
Billy Joel; *Streetlife Serenade* . . . . (Columbia)
Mexican Divorce
Drifters; *1959-1965-All-Time Greatest Hits And More* . . . . (Atlantic)
Nicolette Larson; *Nicolette* . . . . (Warner Bros.)
Ry Cooder; *Paradise And Lunch* . . . . (Reprise)
Mexican Hat Dance
Percy Faith & His Orchestra; *Percy Faith & His Orchestra's All-Time
Greatest Hits* . . . . (Columbia)
Mexican Minutes
Brooks & Dunn; *Hard Workin' Man* . . . . (Arista)
Mexican Radio
Wall Of Voodoo; *Call Of The West* . . . . (I.R.S.)
Ugly Americans In Australia . . . . (I.R.S.)
Wall Of Voodoo . . . . (I.R.S.)
Mexican Shuffle
Herb Alpert & The Tijuana Brass; *Herb Alpert & The Tijuana Brass'
Greatest Hits* . . . . (A&M)
Herb Alpert & The Tijuana Brass-Classics-#1 . . . . (A&M)
Tijuana Brass; *South Of The Border* . . . . (A&M)
Mexican, The
Jellybean; *Rocks The House* . . . . (Chrysalis)
Wotupski . . . . (EMI)
Mexico
Herb Alpert & The Tijuana Brass; *Lonely Bull* . . . . (A&M)
Mexico
James Taylor; *Gorilla* . . . . (Warner Bros.)
James Taylor-Live . . . . (Columbia)
James Taylor's Greatest Hits . . . . (Warner Bros.)
Mellow Rock Hits Of The '70s-Summer Breeze-C . . . . (Rhino)
Jimmy Buffett; *Barometer Soup* . . . . (Margaritaville)
Mexico
Bob Moore and His Orchestra; *Mexico* . . . . (Collectables)
The Monument Story-C . . . . (Sony Music Special Prod.)
Mexico
Grace Slick; *Best Of Grace Slick* . . . . (RCA)

Jefferson Airplane; *2400 Fulton Street-An Anthology* . . . . (RCA)
Early Flight . . . . (RCA)
Mexico
Katrina And The Waves; *Katrina And The Waves* . . . . (Capitol)
Katrina And The Waves-Anthology . . . . (One Way)
Mexico
Firefall; *Best Of Firefall* . . . . (Atlantic)
Firefall . . . . (Rhino)
Firefall's Greatest Hits . . . . (Rhino)
Mexico
Lee Dorsey; *Golden Classics-Lee Dorsey* . . . . (Collectables)
Mexico
Beck; *KCRW Rare On Air-#1-C* . . . . (Mammoth)
Mexico
Nazareth; *2XS* . . . . (A&M)
Mexico National Anthem (Himno Nacional)
American Brass Band; *National Anthems* . . . . (Laserlight)
Banda Sinfonica De Madrid; *National Anthems* . . . . (International Music)
Swarovski Musik Wattens; *National Anthems Of The
World* . . . . (Koch International)
Mexico Rain
Johnny Rodriguez; *Johnny Rodriguez's Biggest Hits* . . . . (Epic)
Old Mexico
Orion; *Fresh* . . . . (Sun)
Old Mexico
Bad Company; *Rough Diamonds* . . . . (Swan Song)
Pancho And Lefty
Merle Haggard; *For The Record: Merle Haggard-43 Legendary Hits* . . . . (BNA)
Merle Haggard & Willie Nelson; *19 Hot Country Requests-C* . . . . (Epic)
All Time Legends Of Country Music-C . . . . (Legacy)
Columbia Country Classics-#3-Americana-C . . . . (Columbia)
His Epic Hits-First 11 To Be Continued-C . . . . (Epic)
Pancho And Lefty . . . . (Epic)
Townes Van Zandt; *Live & Obscure* . . . . (Sugar Hill)
Refried Dreams
Tim McGraw; *Not A Moment Too Soon* . . . . (Curb)
Ride Like The Wind
Christopher Cross; *Christopher Cross* . . . . (Warner Bros.)
Riding My Thumb To Mexico
Johnny Rodriguez; *40 Years Of Country Music-#3-1970-1979-C* . . . . . (Mercury)
All I Ever Meant To Do . . . . (Mercury)
Desperado . . . . (Mercury)
Johnny Rodriguez's Greatest Hits . . . . (Mercury)
Rodeo Or Mexico
Garth Brooks; *Scarecrow* . . . . (Capitol)
Romance In Durango
Bob Dylan; *Biograph* . . . . (Columbia)
Desire . . . . (Columbia)
Run To Mexico
Babys; *Head First* . . . . (Chrysalis)
San Miguel
Beach Boys; *10 Years Of Harmony* . . . . (Caribou)
Seashores Of Old Mexico
Merle Haggard & Willie Nelson; *Seashores Of Old Mexico* . . . . (Epic)
Sexy Mexican Maid
Red Hot Chili Peppers; *Mother's Milk* . . . . (EMI)
Silence On The Line
Chris LeDoux; *Cowboy* . . . . (Capitol)
Sinaloa Cowboys
Bruce Springsteen; *The Ghost Of Tom Joad* . . . . (Columbia)
South Of The Border (Down Mexico Way)
Bob Wills & His Texas Playboys; *Best Of Bob Wills & His Texas
Playboys* . . . . (MCA)
Bob Wills & His Texas Playboys-Greatest Hits . . . . (Curb)
Frank Sinatra; *Capitol Collectors Series-Frank Sinatra* . . . . (Capitol)
Come Fly With Me . . . . (Capitol)
Gene Autry; *The Country Music Hall Of Fame-Gene Autry-15 Of His All-
Time Greatest Hits* . . . . (Columbia)
Patsy Cline; *Always* . . . . (MCA)
The Patsy Cline Story . . . . (MCA)
Willie Nelson; *What A Wonderful World* . . . . (Columbia)
Sunrise In Mexico
Clifford Jordan; *Starting Time* . . . . (Jazz Land)
Theme From "The Magnificent Seven"
BBC Concert Orchestra; *Golden Cinema Classics-#1-The
Adventure Film* . . . . (Bainbridge)
They All Went To Mexico
Carlos Santana; *Havana Moon* . . . . (Columbia)
Willie Nelson & Carlos Santana; *Half Nelson-C* . . . . (Columbia)
Thief In Mexico
Don Michael Sampson; *Coyote* . . . . (Revolver)
Think Of Tomorrow
Chris Isaak; *Baja Sessions* . . . . (Reprise)
This Is My Year For Mexico
Crystal Gayle; *Crystal Gayle* . . . . (United Artists)
Till It Snows In Mexico
Reba McEntire; *What Am I Gonna Do About You* . . . . (MCA)
Trail To Mexico
Peter La Farge; *Cowboy Songs On Folkways-C* . . . . . . (Smithsonian Folkways)

COUNTRIES: N
See Also: CITIES: A-Z, COUNTRIES: NETHERLANDS

Dream Home In New Zealand
English Beat; *Wha'ppen* . . . . (I.R.S.)
New Zealand National Anthem
Swarovski Musik Wattens; *National Anthems Of The
World* . . . . (Koch International)
Nicaragua
Bruce Cockburn; *Stealing Fire* . . . . (Columbia)
Nicaragua Blues
Gil Evans; *Bud & Bird* . . . . (Evidence Music)
Nicaragua National Anthem
Banda Sinfonica De Madrid; *National Anthems* . . . . (International Music)
Nicaragua Nicaraguita
Billy Bragg; *Internationale* . . . . (Elektra)
Nicaragua Night
Holly Near; *All-Ears Review-#7-Still
Amazing...-C* . . . . (Really Outstanding Music)
Nigerian Juju Hilife
Pharoah Sanders; *Rejoice* . . . . (Evidence Music)
Nigerian Marketplace
Oscar Peterson Trio; *Nigerian Marketplace* . . . . (Pablo)
Norway National Anthem (Ja Vi Elsker Dette Landet)
American Brass Band; *National Anthems* . . . . (Laserlight)
Orlando Philharmonic Orchestra; *The National Anthems* . . . . (Madacy)
Norwegian Aire
Magical Strings; *Crossing To Skellig* . . . . (Flying Fish)
Norwegian Dance
Stephane Grappelli; *Stephanova* . . . . (Concord Jazz)
Norwegian Dance No. 2
Django Reinhardt & Stephane Grappelli; *Django Reinhardt & Stephane
Grappelli* . . . . (Crescendo)
Norwegian Girl
Vernon Castle; *Polka Update* . . . . (Taggart)
Norwegian Waltz/Liza Lynn
Jackie Daly & Seamus & Manus McGuire; *Buttons & Bows* . . . . . (Green Linnet)
Norwegian Wood (This Bird Has Flown)
Beatles; *Beatles-Box Set* . . . . (Capitol)
Beatles-Love Songs . . . . (Capitol)
Rubber Soul . . . . (Capitol)
The Beatles/1962-1966 . . . . (Capitol)
Shipyards Of New Zealand
Midnight Oil; *Red Sails In The Sunset* . . . . (Columbia)
Surf Nicaragua
Sacred Reich; *Mega Metal-C* . . . . (K-Tel)

COUNTRIES: NETHERLANDS, Dutch, Holland
See Also: CITIES: A-Z, CITIES: AMSTERDAM

Ballad Of John And Yoko
Beatles; *Beatles 1* . . . . (Capitol)
Beatles-Box Set . . . . (Capitol)
Hey Jude . . . . (Capitol)
Past Masters-Volume Two . . . . (Parlophone)
ST/Imagine: John Lennon . . . . (Capitol)
The Beatles/1967-1970 . . . . (Capitol)
Dutch Morning
Phil Woods & Jim McNeely; *Flowers For Hodges* . . . . (Concord Jazz)
Dutch Treat
Rex Stewart; *Capitol Jazz 50th Anniversary Collection-C* . . . . (Blue Note)
Dutchman
Jerry Jeff Walker; *Hill Country Rain* . . . . (Rykodisc)
Tommy Makem & Liam Clancy; *Tommy Makem & Liam Clancy-
Collection* . . . . (Shanachie)
Dutchmen Bohemian Polka
Michigan Dutchmen; *Beer & Dutchmen Polkas* . . . . (Jay Jay)
Holland Park
John Williams; *Echoes Of London* . . . . (Columbia)
Little Dutch Girl
George Morgan; *American Originals-George Morgan* . . . . (Columbia)
Little Dutch Mill
Bing Crosby; *Crooner-Columbia Years-1928-1934* . . . . (Columbia)
Little Dutch Town
Mac Davis; *Mac Davis With Love* . . . . (Accord)
Volume XC . . . . (Allegiance)
Netherlands National Anthem (Wilelmus Van Nassouwe)
American Brass Band; *National Anthems* . . . . (Laserlight)
Swarovski Musik Wattens; *National Anthems Of The
World* . . . . (Koch International)
Vienna State Opera Orchestra; *National Anthems Of The World* . . . (Bescol, Ltd.)

Sail On Flying Dutchman
Nick Seeger; *Sail On Flying Dutchman* . . . . (Biograph)

COUNTRIES: O

See Also: **CITIES: A-Z**

Oman National Anthem
Swarovski Musik Wattens; *National Anthems Of The
World* . . . . (Koch International)

COUNTRIES: P

See Also: **CITIES: A-Z, COUNTRIES: POLAND**

Abril En Portugal
Julio Iglesias; *Libra* . . . . (Columbia)
April In Portugal
Eartha Kitt; *Best Of Eartha Kitt* . . . . (MCA)
In A Persian Market
Wilbur DeParis; *ST/New York Stories.* . . . . (Elektra)
Lost Paraguayos
Rod Stewart; *Best Of Rod Stewart-#2* . . . . (Mercury)
Sing It Again, Rod . . . . (Mercury)
Man From Pakistan
Flaming Lips; *Hear It Is* . . . . (Restless)
Midnight 'N Peru
Ken Tamplin; *Soul Survivor* . . . . (Intense)
My Paraguayan Song
Roberto Perera; *Erotica* . . . . (Epic)
Panama
Kid Ory's Creole Jazz Band; *Favorites!* . . . . (Good Time Jazz)
Louis Armstrong; *Best Of Louis Armstrong* . . . . (Audio Fidelity)
Louis Armstrong & His All-Stars . . . . (Laserlight)
Louis Armstrong Of New Orleans . . . . (MCA)
Louis Armstrong-Vol. 2 . . . . (Everest)
Preservation Hall Jazz Band; *New Orleans-#1* . . . . (Columbia)
Panama
Van Halen; *1984.* . . . .(Warner Bros.)
Panama
Crosby, Stills & Nash; *After The Storm* . . . . (Atlantic)
Panama National Anthem
Banda Sinfonica De Madrid; *National Anthems* . . .(International Music)
Panama Red
New Riders Of The Purple Sage; *Adventures Of Panama Red* . . . . . . (Columbia)
Best Of New Riders Of The Purple Sage . . . . (Columbia)
Rock Classics Of The '70s-C . . . . (Columbia)
Panama Tones/Nuevo Boogaloo
Iguanas; *Nuevo Boogaloo* . . . .(Margaritaville)
Paraguay National Anthem
Banda Sinfonica De Madrid; *National Anthems* . . . .(International Music)
Peru
Eric Tingstad & Nancy Rumbel; *Homeland* . . . . (Narada)
Marcos Loya; *Love Is The Reason* . . . .(Spindletop)
Peru National Anthem
Banda Sinfonica De Madrid; *National Anthems* . . . .(International Music)
Swarovski Musik Wattens; *National Anthems Of The
World* . . . . (Koch International)
Philippines National Anthem
Swarovski Musik Wattens; *National Anthems Of The
World* . . . . (Koch International)
Portugal National Anthem (A Portuguesa)
American Brass Band; *National Anthems.* . . . . (Laserlight)
Banda Sinfonica De Madrid; *National Anthems* . . . .(International Music)
Portuguese Love
Teena Marie; *It Must Be Magic.* . . . . (Motown)
Teena Marie's Greatest Hits . . . . (Motown)
Portuguese Washerwoman
Astrud Gilberto; *Look To The Rainbow* . . . . (Verve)
Buddy Merrill; *Holiday For Guitars.* . . . .(Accent)
Puerto Rican Children
Hilton Ruiz; *Something Grand* . . . . (Novus)
Puerto Rican Rhythms
Last Poets; *Right On!* . . . . (Collectables)
Puerto Rico
Charles Sepulveda & Turnaround; *Algo Nuestro* . . . . (Antilles)
Puerto Rico
Bobby Caldwell; *ST/Salsa* . . . . (MCA)
Puerto Rico National Anthem
Banda Sinfonica De Madrid; *National Anthems* . . . .(International Music)
Two Gentlemen Of Peru
Simon & Bard Group; *Enormous Radio* . . . . (Flying Fish)

Villa In Portugal
Pursuit Of Happiness; *Downward Road* . . . . (Mercury)

COUNTRIES: POLAND

See Also: **CITIES: A-Z**

Children Of Poland
Si Kahn; *Unfinished Portraits* . . . . (Flying Fish)
My Polish Girlfriend
Li'l Wally; *My Polish Girlfriend & Others* . . . . (Jay Jay)
Poland National Anthem (Mazurek Debrowskiego)
American Brass Band; *National Anthems* . . . . (Laserlight)
Vienna State Opera Orchestra; *National Anthems Of The World* . . (Bescol, Ltd.)
Poland Whole/Madam I'm Adam
Tubes; *Young And Rich* . . . . (A&M)
Polish Feelings
Li'l Wally; *Polish Feelings* . . . . (Jay Jay)
Polish Folk Song Medley
101 Strings Orchestra; *Greatest Hits Of The 101 Strings Orchestra* . . . . (Alshire)
Polish Hop Polka
Cavaliers; *Have Polka Will Travel* . . . . (Accent)
Polish Lullaby
Marvin Hamlisch; *ST/Sophie's Choice* . . . .(Southern Cross)
Polish Memories Waltz
New Yorkers; *Polka Smile* . . . . (Jay Jay)
Polish National Anthem
101 Strings Orchestra; *Soul Of Poland* . . . . (Alshire)
Polish Sausage Polka
Li'l Wally; *Li'l Wally* . . . . (Jay Jay)
Polish Song
Jimmy Sturr & His Orchestra; *Sturr-It-Up* . . . . (Ranwood)
Road To Poland
Mike Figgis; *ST/Stormy Monday.* . . . .(Virgin Movie Music)
Santa Must Be Polish
Bobby Vinton; *Great Songs Of Christmas* . . . . (Curb)

COUNTRIES: R

See Also: **CiTIES: A-Z, COUNTRIES: RUSSIA**

Romania National Anthem (Imnul De Stat)
Orlando Philharmonic Orchestra; *The National Anthems* . . . .(Madacy)
Vienna State Opera Orchestra; *National Anthems Of The World* . . (Bescol, Ltd.)

COUNTRIES: RUSSIA, Soviet Union

See Also: **CITIES: A-Z, CITIES: MOSCOW**

1812 Overture
New York Philharmonic & Leonard Bernstein; *Conducts
Tchaikovsky.* . . . . (Columbia)
Great Tchaikovsky . . . . (Columbia)
Overtures and Tone Poems. . . . . (Columbia)
Tchaikovsky's Greatest Hits-#1 . . . . (Columbia)
Various Overtures . . . . (Columbia)
Back In The U.S.S.R.
Beatles; *Beatles-Box Set* . . . . (Capitol)
Rock 'N' Roll Music . . . . (Capitol)
The Beatles (White Album) . . . . (Capitol)
The Beatles/1967-1970. . . . . (Capitol)
Billy Joel; *KOHUEPT.* . . . . (Columbia)
Bomb The Russians
Fear; *More Beer* . . . .(Enigma)
Done With Bonaparte
Mark Knopfler; *Golden Heart.* . . . . (Warner Bros.)
Dressed To Kill
Nazareth; *Fool Circle* . . . . (A&M)
Nazareth-Classics-#16 . . . . (A&M)
'Snaz. . . . . (A&M)
From Russia With Love
Matt Monro; *13 Original James Bond Themes-C* . . . . (EMI)
Glorious Russian
Original Broadway Cast; *Stop The World I Want To Get Off.* . . . .(Polydor)
Original Cast/Sammy Davis, Jr.; *Stop The World I Want To
Get Off.* . . . . (Warner Bros.)
Hymn To The Russian Earth
Paul Winter Consort; *Concert For The Earth-Live At The United
Nations* . . . . (Living Music)
In America
Charlie Daniels Band; *A Decade Of Hits.* . . . . (Epic)

Full Moon .... (Epic)
Me & The Boys .... (Epic)
Lawyers, Guns & Money
Warren Zevon; *Excitable Boy* .... (Asylum)
Quiet Normal Life-Best Of Warren Zevon .... (Asylum)
Stand In The Fire .... (Asylum)
Meadowlands
101 Strings Orchestra; *Soul Of Russia* .... (Madacy)
Jefferson Airplane; *Volunteers* .... (RCA)
Morrisey & The Russian Sailor
Tom Dahill; *Irish Music From St. Paul To Donegal* .... (Flying Fish)
Mother Russia
Renaissance; *Renaissance-Live At Carnegie Hall* .... (Sire)
Tales Of 1001 Nights-#1 .... (Sire)
Turn Of The Cards .... (Sire)
Mother Russia
Iron Maiden; *No Prayer For The Dying* .... (Epic)
My Russia, You Are Beautiful
Ivan Rebroff; *Memories Of Russia* .... (Columbia)
Nikita
Elton John; *Elton John's Greatest Hits-1976-1986* .... (MCA)
Ice On Fire .... (MCA)
Return To Russia
Kitaro; *Asia* .... (Geffen)
Silver Cloud .... (Geffen)
Rocking Over Russia
Elvis Hitler; *Disgraceland* .... (Restless)
Ronnie, Talk To Russia
Prince; *Controversy* .... (Warner Bros.)
Russia National Anthem (Hymn Of The Soviet Union)
American Brass Band; *National Anthems* .... (Laserlight)
Vienna State Opera Orchestra; *National Anthems Of The World* ... (Bescol, Ltd.)
Russian Bandstand
Spencer & Spencer; *Dr. Demento Presents The Greatest Novelty Records-#2-1950s-C* .... (Rhino)
Russian Imperial Anthem
Royal Scots Dragoon Guard; *Amazing Grace* ..... (RCA)
Russian Lady
Karen Alexander; *Isn't It Always Love* .... (Asylum)
Russian Lullaby
Jerry Garcia; *Compliments* .... (Grateful Dead)
Jerry Garcia & David Grisman; *Jerry Garcia & David Grisman* .... (Grateful Dead)
Russian Lullaby
John Coltrane; *Soultrane* .... (Prestige)
Russian Lullaby
Al Cohn; *Standards Of Excellence* .... (Concord Jazz)
Russian Radio
Red Flag; *Naive Art* .... (Enigma Capitol)
Russian Reggae
Nina Hagen; *In Ekstasy* .... (Columbia)
Russian Roulette
Lords Of The New Church; *Killer Lords* .... (I.R.S.)
Lords Of The New Church .... (I.R.S.)
Russian Roulette
Michelle Shocked; *Captain Swing* .... (Mercury)
Russian Roulette
Taxxi; *Expose* .... (MCA)
Russian Roulette
Hollies; *Hollies* .... (Epic)
Russian Roulette
Accept; *Russian Roulette* .... (Portrait)
Russian Roulette
Joan Armatrading; *Sleight Of Hand* .... (A&M)
Russian Winter
Krokus; *Headhunter* .... (Arista)
Russians
Sting; *Dream Of The Blue Turtles* .... (A&M)
Fields Of Gold-The Best Of Sting 1984-1994 ..... (A&M)
Russians & Americans
Al Stewart; *Russians & Americans* .... (Passport)
Siberian Khatru
Yes; *Close To The Edge* .... (Atlantic)
Yessongs .... (Atlantic)
Song Of Russia
Red Army Ensemble; *Red Army Ensemble* .... (Angel)
Surfin' U.S.S.R.
Ray Stevens; *Everything Is Beautiful* .... (MCA Special Prod.)
I Never Made A Record I Didn't Like .... (MCA)
Ray Stevens-Collection .... (MCA)
Visitors
Abba; *Visitors* .... (Atlantic)
Waiting For The Russians
Trees; *Forrest Fires* .... (Adelphi)
White Russia
Dirt Band; *Dirt Band* .... (United Artists)

Young 'N' Russian
Korgis; *Korgis* .... (Warner Bros.)

COUNTRIES: S

See Also: CITIES: A-Z, COUNTRIES: SCOTLAND, SPAIN, SWEDEN, SWITZERLAND

Man From Senegal
Mad Professor; *Psychedelic Dub* .... (Ariwa)
March Of The Siamese Children
Original Broadway Cast; *The King And I* ..... (RCA Victor)
Original Cast; *The King And I* .... (MCA)
On A Little Street In Singapore
Glenn Miller; *Original Recordings-#4* .... (Pair)
Harry James; *Two O'Clock Jump* .... (Pro-Arte)
Manhattan Transfer; *Manhattan Transfer-Anthology-Down In Birdland* .... (Rhino)
Party In Senegal
Wallets; *Take It* .... (Twin-Tone)
Queen Of Siam
Holy Moses; *Queen Of Siam* .... (GWR)
San Marino National Anthem
Swarovski Musik Wattens; *National Anthems Of The World* .... (Koch International)
Saudi Arabia National Anthem
Swarovski Musik Wattens; *National Anthems Of The World* .... (Koch International)
Senegal
Bireli Lagrene; *Foreign Affairs* .... (Blue Note)
Senegal Market Place
Sly Dunbar; *Sly Wicked & Slick* .... (Front Line)
Singapore National Anthem
Swarovski Musik Wattens; *National Anthems Of The World* .... (Koch International)
Slovak Republic National Anthem
Swarovski Musik Wattens; *National Anthems Of The World* .... (Koch International)
Slovenia National Anthem
Swarovski Musik Wattens; *National Anthems Of The World* .... (Koch International)
Summer In Siam
Pogues; *Essential Pogues* .... (Island)
Hell's Ditch .... (Island)
Syria
Psychefunkapus; *Skin* .... (Atlantic)
Syria National Anthem
Swarovski Musik Wattens; *National Anthems Of The World* .... (Koch International)

COUNTRIES: SCOTLAND

See Also: CITIES: A-Z, COUNTRIES: ENGLAND

Back To Scotland
Chris Proctor; *Delicate Dance* .... (Flying Fish)
Highlands
Bob Dylan; *Time Out Of Mind* .... (Columbia)
Misty Isles Of Scotland
Anne & Francie Brolly; *Ireland My Home* ...... (Rego Irish)
Roxanna Waltz & Scotland Calling Jesse
Jay Ungar & Others; *Fiddle Fever* .... (Flying Fish)
Scotland
Bill Monroe; *MCA Records 30 Years Of Hits-1958-1988-C* .... (MCA)
Emmylou Harris & The Nash Ramblers; *At The Ryman* .... (Reprise)
Scotland
King Missile; *The Way To Salvation* .... (Atlantic)
Scotland I
Larry Coryell; *Essential Larry Coryell* .... (Vanguard)
Scotland The Brave
Gordon Highlanders; *Scotland: Scottish Bagpipes & Drums-C* ..... (Laserlight)
Original Cast; *Forever Plaid* .... (RCA)
Original Soundtrack; *ST/More Music From Braveheart* .... (Philips)
Scotland/Big Mon
Richard Greene Band; *Blue Rondo* .... (Sierra)
Scotsman
Bryan Bowers; *Dr. Demento Presents The Greatest Novelty Records-#5-1980s-C* .... (Rhino)
Dr. Demento: 20th Anniversary Collection-C ..... (Rhino)
Home Home On The Road .... (Flying Fish)
Scotsman Over The Border
Eugene O'Donnell & Mickey Moloney; *Slow Airs & Set Dances* .... (Green Linnet)
Scottish Air
Carl MacKenzie; *Welcome To Your Feet Again* ..... (Rounder)

Scottish Medley
Pat Roper; *From The Shannon To The Clyde* . . . . (Rego Irish)
Scottish Rain
Silencers; *Blues For Buddha* . . . . (RCA)
Greenpeace/Rainbow Warriors-C . . . .(Geffen)
Scottish Settler's Lament
Tannahill Weavers; *Land Of Light* . . . . (Green Linnet)
Scottish Tea
Ted Nugent & The Amboy Dukes; *Greatest*
Collection Ever . . . .(Dunhill Compact Classics)
Skye Boat Song
King's Singers; *American Balladeer-Golden Classics-#1-C* . . . . . (Collectables)
Annie Laurie-Folk Songs Of British Isles . . . . (Angel)
Roger Whittaker; *Live In Concert* . . . . (RCA)
What It Is
Mark Knopfler; *Sailing To Philadelphia* . . . .(Warner Bros.)

COUNTRIES: SPAIN

See Also: **CITIES: A-Z, COUNTRIES: MEXICO, HISPANIC**

Echoes Of Spain
Django Reinhardt; *Djangologie USA-#2* . . . . (Disques Swing)
Granada
Frankie Laine; *Frankie Laine's Greatest Hits* . . . . (Columbia)
In A Little Spanish Town
Ray Charles; *Ray Charles-Live* . . . . (Atlantic)
Lady Of Spain
Bing Crosby; *The Radio Years: 20 Songs* . . . . (Crescendo)
Les Paul; *Legend & The Legacy-#1-4* . . . . (Capitol)
Muppets/Amazing Marvin Suggs/Muppaphone; *Muppet Hits* . . . . (Jim Henson)
Letter From Spain
Electric Light Orchestra; *Secret Messages* . . . . (Jet)
Little Spain
Lee Morgan Quintet; *Take Twelve* . . . . (Jazz Land)
Malaguena
Percy Faith & His Orchestra; *Percy Faith & His Orchestra's All-Time*
Greatest Hits . . . . (Columbia)
Placido Domingo; *Love Until The End Of Time-Greatest* . . . . (Columbia)
Ritchie Valens; *Best Of Ritchie Valens* . . . . (Rhino)
History Of Ritchie Valens . . . . (Rhino)
Roy Clark; *Best Of Roy Clark* . . . .(MCA)
Never Been To Spain
Elvis Presley; *Elvis As Recorded At Madison Square Garden* . . . . (RCA)
Hoyt Axton; *Never Been To Spain* . . . .(MCA Special Prod.)
Three Dog Night; *Best Of Three Dog Night* . . . .(MCA)
Joy To The World-Greatest Hits . . . .(MCA)
News From Spain
Al Stewart; *Al Stewart-Early Years* . . . . (Janus)
Rain In Spain
Original Cast; *Forbidden Broadway-#2* . . . . (DRG)
My Fair Lady . . . . (Columbia)
Rex Harrison & Audrey Hepburn; *ST/My Fair Lady* . . . . (Columbia)
Spain National Anthem (Marcha Real)
American Brass Band; *National Anthems* . . . . (Laserlight)
Banda Sinfonica De Madrid; *National Anthems* . . . .(International Music)
Vienna State Opera Orchestra; *National Anthems Of The World* . . .(Bescol, Ltd.)
Spaniard That Blighted My Life
Al Jolson; *Music From The New York Stage (1890-1920)-#3-1913-*
1917-C . . . . (Pearl)
Spanish Castle Magic
Jimi Hendrix; *Axis: Bold As Love* . . . . (Reprise)
Lifelines/Jimi Hendrix Story . . . . (Reprise)
Live At Winterland . . . .(Rykodisc)
Jimi Hendrix Experience; *Radio One* . . . .(Rykodisc)
Spanish Town
Garland Jeffreys; *Ghost Writer* . . . . (A&M)
Matador & More . . . . (A&M)

COUNTRIES: SWEDEN

See Also: **CITIES: A-Z**

Serenade To Sweden
Duke Ellington; *Duke Ellington-Vol. 4-Studio Sessions-New York-1963* . . . (Saja)
Sweden National Anthem (Due Gamia, du Fria)
American Brass Band; *National Anthems* . . . . (Laserlight)
Vienna State Opera Orchestra; *National Anthems Of The World* . . .(Bescol, Ltd.)
Swedish Carol
Paul Winter; *Wintersong* . . . .(Living Music)
Swedish Dance
Danny Thompson; *Instruments-Collection* . . . . (Hannibal)
Swedish Folk Song
Yvonne Roome & Toots Thielemans; *Something Cool* . . . . (DRG)

Swedish Jig
John Renbourn & Stefan Grossman; *Music Of Ireland* . . . . (Shanachie)
Swedish March
Pat Kilbride; *Rock & More Roses* . . . . (Temple)
Swedish Meatball
Steve Lyon; *There's No Place Like Mars* . . . . (Flying Fish)
Swedish Melody
Barry Hall; *Virtuoso 5-String Banjo* . . . .(Smithsonian Folkways)
Swedish Pastry
Bill Evans; *Time Remembered* . . . . (Milestone)
Bill Evans Trio; *At Shelly's Manne-Hole* . . . . (Riverside)
Bud Powell Trio; *Time Was* . . . . (Bluebird)
Swedish Rhapsody (Midsummer Vigil)
Chet Atkins; *RCA Years* . . . . (RCA)
Percy Faith & His Orchestra; *Percy Faith & His Orchestra's*
Greatest Hits . . . . (Columbia)
Swedish Schnapps
Charlie Parker; *Swedish Schnapps* . . . . (Verve)
Verve Years-1950-1951 . . . . (Verve)
Swedish Suite
Dizzy Gillespie; *Dizziest* . . . . (Bluebird)

COUNTRIES: SWITZERLAND

See Also: **CITIES: A-Z**

Dancing In Sunrise, Switzerland
Muffins; *Open City* . . . . (Cuneiform)
My Swiss Mountain Lullaby
Montana Slim; *60 Years Of Country Music-C* . . . . (RCA)
Swiss Army Girl
Scatterbrain; *Scamboogery* . . . . (Elektra)
Swiss Boy
Michigan Dutchmen; *German Polka Favorites* . . . . (Jay Jay)
Swiss Boy Waltz
Michigan Dutchmen; *German Polka Favorites* . . . . (Jay Jay)
Swiss Celebration
David Friedman; *Of The Wind's Eye* . . . . (Enja)
Swiss Lullaby
Roy Eldridge/Gene Krupa Orchestra/Anita O'Day; *Uptown* . . . . (Columbia)
Swiss Maid
Del Shannon; *Del Shannon-Legends* . . . .(Laurie)
Del Shannon's Greatest Hits . . . . (Rhino)
Swiss Miss
Fred Astaire; *Crazy Feet!* . . . . (ASV Living Era)
Swiss Retreat
Nat "King" Cole; *L-O-V-E* . . . . (Capitol)
Swiss Waltz
Ampol Aires; *Greatest Jay Jay Hits* . . . . (Jay Jay)
Switzerland National Anthem
American Brass Band; *National Anthems* . . . . (Laserlight)
Swarovski Musik Wattens; *National Anthems Of The*
World . . . . (Koch International)

COUNTRIES: T

See Also: **CITIES: A-Z**

Another Night In Tunisia
Bobby McFerrin; *Spontaneous Inventions* . . . . (Blue Note)
Manhattan Transfer; *Vocalese* . . . .(Atlantic)
In A Turkish Town
Ritchie Valens; *Best Of Ritchie Valens* . . . . (Rhino)
History Of Ritchie Valens . . . . (Rhino)
Ritchie Valens . . . . (Rhino)
Night In Tunisia
Charlie Parker; *Bird On 52nd St.* . . . .(Fantasy)
Charlie Parker . . . .(Prestige)
One Night In Birdland . . . .(Columbia)
Very Best Of Bird . . . . (Warner Bros.)
Dizzy Gillespie; *Electrifying Evening* . . . . (Verve)
Jazz At Massey Hall . . . .(Fantasy)
Musician Composer Raconteur . . . . (Pablo)
Nipper's Greatest Hits Of The '40s-#2-C . . . . (RCA)
Tuxedo Junction; *Take The "A" Train* . . . . (Butterfly)
One Night In Trinidad
Earl "Fatha" Hines; *Lionel Hampton Presents Earl "Fatha"*
Hines . . . . (Who's Who In Jazz)
Return Of The Tasmanian Tiger
John Fahey; *Live In Tasmania* . . . . (Takoma)
Tahiti
Milt Jackson; *Milt Jackson* . . . .(Blue Note)
Tahiti Condo
Michael Nesmith; *Newer Stuff* . . . . (Rhino)

Tahitian Moon
Michael Franks; *Objects Of Desire* . . . . (Warner Bros.)
Tahitian Moon
Porno For Pyros; *Good God's Urge*. . . . . (Warner Bros.)
Tahitian Skies
Chet Atkins & Mark Knopfler; *Neck And Neck* . . . . (Columbia)
Thailand National Anthem
Swarovski Musik Wattens; *National Anthems Of The
World* . . . . (Koch International)
Tibetan Side Of Town
Bruce Cockburn; *Big Circumstance* . . . . (Columbia)
Trinidad
Eddie Money; *Playing For Keeps* . . . . (Columbia)
Unplug It In. . . . . (Columbia)
Tunisia National Anthem
Swarovski Musik Wattens; *National Anthems Of The
World* . . . . (Koch International)
Tunnels Of Tunisia
Malaysian Pale; *Nature's Fantasies* . . . . (Fortuna)
Turkey National Anthem (Istiklal Marst)
American Brass Band; *National Anthems* . . . . (Laserlight)
Vienna State Opera Orchestra; *National Anthems Of The World* . . . (Bescol, Ltd.)
Turkish March
Boston Pops Orchestra/Arthur Fiedler; *Fiedler's Favorite Marches*. . . . . (RCA)
Turkish Song Of The Damned
Pogues; *Essential Pogues* . . . . (Island)
If I Should Fall From Grace With God . . . . (Island)
Twilight In Turkey
Raymond Scott; *Reckless Nights & Turkish Twilights*. . . . . (Columbia)
Young Turks
Rod Stewart; *Absolutely Live*. . . . . (Warner Bros.)
Downtown Train-Selections From The Storyteller Anthology . . (Warner Bros.)
Storyteller/The Complete Anthology: 1964-1990. . . . . (Warner Bros.)
Tonight I'm Yours. . . . . (Warner Bros.)

COUNTRIES: U

See Also: **CITIES: A-Z**

Girl From Uganda
Les Baxter & His Orchestra; *African Blue-Brazil Now* . . . . (Crescendo)
Ukraine National Anthem (Ukraine Is Still Alive)
Orlando Philharmonic Orchestra; *The National Anthems* . . . . (Madacy)
United Arab Emirates National Anthem
Swarovski Musik Wattens; *National Anthems Of The
World* . . . . (Koch International)
Uruguay National Anthem
Banda Sinfonica De Madrid; *National Anthems* . . . . (International Music)
Swarovski Musik Wattens; *National Anthems Of The
World* . . . . (Koch International)

COUNTRIES: V

See Also: **CITIES: A-Z, COUNTRIES: VIETNAM**

Sweetheart From Venezuela
Harry Belafonte; *Harry Belafonte-Pure Gold* . . . . (RCA)
Venezuela
Richard Dyer-Bennett; *Art Of Richard Dyer-Bennett* . . . . . . (Vanguard Classics)
Venezuela National Anthem (Gloria Al Bravo Pueblo)
Banda Sinfonica De Madrid; *National Anthems* . . . . (International Music)
Orlando Philharmonic Orchestra; *The National Anthems* . . . . (Madacy)

COUNTRIES: VIETNAM

See Also: **CITIES: A-Z, DRAFT, POLITICS (various),
PROTEST, WAR**

Born In The U.S.A.
Bruce Springsteen; *Born In The U.S.A.* . . . . (Columbia)
Bruce Springsteen's Greatest Hits . . . . (Columbia)
Tracks . . . . (Columbia)
Bruce Springsteen & The E Street Band; *Bruce Springsteen & The E Street
Band Live/1975-85* . . . . (Legacy)
Christmas In Vietnam
Johnny & Jon; *45-#776* . . . . (Jewel)
Galveston Bay
Bruce Springsteen; *The Ghost Of Tom Joad* . . . . (Columbia)
Hell No, I Ain't Gonna Go
Matt Jones & Elaine Laron; *Best Of Broadside 1962-1968: Anthems
Of The American Underground From The Pages Of Broadside
Magazine-C* . . . . (Smithsonian Folkways)

Hello Vietnam
Johnny Wright; *ST/Full Metal Jacket*. . . . . (Warner Bros.)
I-Feel-Like-I'm-Fixin'-To-Die Rag
Country Joe & The Fish; *Country Joe & The Fish-Greatest Hits* . . . . .(Vanguard)
Greatest '60s Folksingers-C . . . .(Vanguard)
I-Feel-Like-I'm-Fixin'-To-Die . . . .(Vanguard)
Life & Times Of Country Joe & The Fish . . . .(Vanguard)
More American Graffiti-#4-C . . . . (MCA)
Songs Of Protest-C . . . .(Rhino)
ST/Woodstock . . . .(Atlantic)
Pinkville Helicopter
Thom Parrott; *Best Of Broadside 1962-1968: Anthems Of The American
Underground From The Pages Of Broadside
Magazine-C* . . . . (Smithsonian Folkways)
Red Dirt Girl
Emmylou Harris; *Red Dirt Girl* . . . .(Nonesuch)
Talking Vietnam Pot Luck Blues
Tom Paxton; *Morning After*. . . . .(Elektra)
Viet Cong Blues
Junior Wells; *Best Of The Chicago Blues-C*. . . . .(Vanguard)
Chicago/The Blues Today . . . .(Vanguard)
Vanguard Collector's Edition-C . . . .(Vanguard)
Junior Wells & His Chicago Blues Band; *Legends Of Electric Blues
Guitar-#2-C* . . . .(Rhino)
Viet Cong Live Next Door
Left; *Last Train To Hagerstown*. . . . . (Green World)
Vietnam
Jimmy Cliff; *In Concert-Best Of Jimmy Cliff*. . . . . (Reprise)
Reggae Spectacular-C . . . .(A&M)
Wonderful World, Beautiful People . . . .(A&M)
Vietnam
Paul Kaplan; *Best Of Broadside 1962-1968: Anthems Of The American
Underground From The Pages Of Broadside
Magazine-C* . . . . (Smithsonian Folkways)
Vietnam Blues
Champion Jack Dupree; *Legacy Of The Blues-#3* . . . .(Crescendo)
Vietnam National Anthem
Swarovski Musik Wattens; *National Anthems Of The
World* . . . .(Koch International)
Vietnam Never Again
Country Joe McDonald; *Child's Play* . . . .(Rag Baby)
Vietnam Veteran Still Alive
Country Joe McDonald; *Into The Fray* . . . .(Rag Baby)
Vietnamerica
Stranglers; *Stranglers IV* . . . .(I.R.S.)

COUNTRIES: Y

See Also: **CITIES: A-Z**

Yugoslavia National Anthem
Vienna State Opera Orchestra; *National Anthems Of The World* . . . (Bescol, Ltd.)

COUNTRIES: Z

See Also: **CITIES: A-Z**

Zimbabwe National Anthem
Swarovski Musik Wattens; *National Anthems Of The
World* . . . .(Koch International)

COUNTRY, Country Music, Countryside, Prairie

See Also: **AMERICAN WEST, FARMS, MUSIC, NATURE, SMALL
TOWN LIFE, SOCIAL CLASS: RURAL**

Away Out On The Mountain
Jimmie Rodgers; *Best Of Jimmie Rodgers-Legendary Master Series* . . . . (RCA)
Essential Jimmie Rodgers . . . . (RCA)
First Sessions-1927-1928-#1 . . . . (Rounder)
My Rough & Rowdy Ways . . . . (RCA)
This Is Jimmie Rodgers . . . . (RCA)
Skip Gorman; *A Cowboy's Wild Song To His Herd* . . . . (Rounder)
Tim & Mollie O'Brien; *Away Out On The Mountain* . . . . (Sugar Hill)
Barroom Country Singer
Roger Whittaker; *Roger Whittaker Greatest Hits* . . . . (RCA)
Beer And Bones
John Michael Montgomery; *John Michael Montgomery's
Greatest Hits* . . . . (Atlantic)
Life's A Dance . . . . (Atlantic)
Black Country Rock
David Bowie; *Man Who Sold The World* . . . . (Rykodisc)
Sound + Vision . . . . (Rykodisc)

Black Country Woman
Led Zeppelin; *Physical Graffiti* . . . . (Swan Song)
Blue Kentucky Girl
Emmylou Harris; *Blue Kentucky Girl* . . . .(Warner Bros.)
   Profile II-The Best Of Emmylou Harris . . . . (Warner Bros.)
Loretta Lynn; *Loretta Lynn's Greatest Hits* . . . . (MCA)
Bob Away My Blues
Clint Black; *D'lectrified* . . . . (RCA)
Born Country
Alabama; *Alabama's Greatest Hits-#2* . . . . (RCA)
Brand New Country Star
Jimmy Buffett; *Living & Dying In 3/4 Time* . . . .(MCA)
Bright Lights And Country Music
Bill Anderson; *Bill Anderson's Greatest Hits* . . . .(MCA)
Buckaroo
Lee Ann Womack; *Lee Ann Womack* . . . . (Decca)
Bury Me Not On The Lone Prairie
Jimmy C. Newman; *Cajun Cowboy* . . . . (Plantation)
Carefree Country Day
Buffalo Springfield; *Last Time Around* . . . . (Atco)
City Put The Country Back In Me
Neal McCoy; *No Doubt About It* . . . .(Atlantic)
C-O-U-N-T-R-Y
Joe Diffie; *Life's So Funny* . . . .(Epic)
Country Air
Beach Boys; *Smiley Smile/Wild Honey* . . . . (Capitol)
Country Boy
"Little" Jimmy Dickens; *Columbia Country Classics-#2-Honky Tonk*
   Heroes-C . . . . (Columbia)
Johnny Cash; *Johnny Cash-Original Golden Hits-#3* . . . . (Sun)
   Superbilly . . . . (Sun)
   The Man-The World-His Music . . . . (Sun)
Ricky Skaggs; *19 Hot Country Requests-#3-C* . . . .(Epic)
   Greatest Country Hits Of The '80s-1985-C . . . . (Columbia)
   Live In London . . . .(Epic)
   Ricky Skaggs-Country Boy . . . .(Epic)
Country Boy (You Got Your Feet In L.A.)
Glen Campbell; *Best Of Glen Campbell* . . . . (Capitol)
   Glen Campbell-Classics Collection . . . . (Capitol)
   Glen Campbell's Greatest Hits . . . . (Capitol)
Country Boy Can Survive
Hank Williams, Jr.; *America (The Way I See It)* . . . . (WB/Curb)
   Hank Williams, Jr. "Live" . . . . (WB/Curb)
   Hank Williams, Jr.'s Greatest Hits . . . . (WB/Curb)
   ST/Pressure Is On . . . . (WB/Curb)
Country Boy's Tool Box
Aaron Tippin; *Tool Box* . . . . (RCA)
Country Bumpkin
Cal Smith; *16 Top Country Hits-#1-C* . . . .(MCA)
   Country's Greatest Hits-#2-C . . . .(MCA Special Prod.)
   Grand Ole Opry-75 Years-#2-C . . . .(MCA)
Country Club
Travis Tritt; *Country Club* . . . .(Warner Bros.)
Country Comfort
Earl Scruggs & Elton John; *Earl Scruggs And Friends-C* . . . .(MCA)
Elton John; *Tumbleweed Connection* . . . . (Polydor)
Rod Stewart; *Best Of Rod Stewart-#2* . . . . (Mercury)
   Gasoline Alley . . . . (Mercury)
   Sing It Again, Rod . . . . (Mercury)
Country Girl
Faron Young; *Billboard Top Country Hits-1959-C* . . . . (Rhino)
   Faron Young's Greatest Hits-#2 . . . . (Step One)
Country Girl
Barbara Mandrell; *Barbara Mandrell Live* . . . .(MCA)
Country Girl
Steve Earle & The Dukes; *The Hard Way* . . . .(MCA)
Country Girl
Ozark Mountain Daredevils; *Best Of The Ozark Mountain Daredevils* . . (A&M)
   Ozark Mountain Daredevils . . . . (A&M)
Country Girl
Jeannie C. Riley; *Country Girl* . . . . (Plantation)
   Jeannie C. Riley's Greatest Hits . . . . (Plantation)
Country Girls
John Schneider; *John Schneider's Greatest Hits* . . . .(MCA)
   MCA #1 Hits Of The '80s-#1-C . . . .(MCA Special Prod.)
   Today's Country Classics-C . . . . (MCA Special Prod.)
   Too Good To Stop Now . . . .(MCA)
Country Grammar (Hot Sh*t)
Nelly; *Country Grammar* . . . . (Fo' Reel/Universal)
Country Ham & Red Gravy
Hotmud Family; *Live As We Know It* . . . . (Flying Fish)
Country Honk
Rolling Stones; *Let It Bleed* . . . . (Abkco)
Country In My Jeans
Loretta Lynn; *Still Country* . . . .(Audium)
Country Is
Tom T. Hall; *Tom T. Hall's Greatest Hits-#2* . . . . (Mercury)
   Tom T. Hall-The Hits . . . . (Mercury)

Country Jail
Volumes; *I Love You-Golden Classics* . . . . (Collectables)
Country Jail Blues
Eric Clapton; *No Reason To Cry* . . . . (RSO)
John T. Smith; *Original Howling Wolf* . . . .(Yazoo)
Country Pie
Bob Dylan; *Nashville Skyline* . . . . (Columbia)
Country Road
James Taylor; *James Taylor's Greatest Hits* . . . . (Warner Bros.)
   Sweet Baby James . . . . (Warner Bros.)
Country Road
Dolly Parton; *Eagle When She Flies* . . . . (Columbia)
Country State Of Mind
Hank Williams, Jr.; *Hank Williams, Jr.'s Greatest Hits III* . . . . (Curb)
   Montana Cafe . . . . (WB/Curb)
Country Sunshine
Dottie West; *Collector's Dottie West* . . . .(RCA)
   Great Moments At The Grand Ole Opry-C . . . . (RCA)
Rita Remington; *Country Girl Gold* . . . . (Plantation)
Cowboy Take Me Away
Dixie Chicks; *Fly* . . . . (Monument)
Daddy's Money
Ricochet; *Ricochet* . . . . (Columbia)
Darlin' Corey
Ricky Skaggs with Bruce Hornsby; *Big Mon: The Songs Of Bill*
   Monroe-C . . . . (Skaggs Family)
Don't Fence Me In
Andrews Sisters; *Andrews Sisters' All-Time Greatest Hits* . . . . (Decca)
Bing Crosby; *Best Of Bing Crosby* . . . . (MCA)
David Byrne; *Red Hot + Blue-Tribute To Cole Porter-C* . . . . . . (Chrysalis)
Ella Fitzgerald; *Cole Porter Songbook* . . . . (Verve)
Lari White/Shelby Lynne/Trisha Yearwood; *Don't Fence Me In* . . . . (RCA)
Willie Nelson & Leon Russell; *Cowboy Super Hits-C* . . . . (Columbia)
Don't Rock The Jukebox
Alan Jackson; *Alan Jackson-The Greatest Hits Collection* . . . . (Arista)
   Don't Rock The Jukebox . . . . (Arista)
Drowning On Dry Land
Albert King; *Hard Bargain* . . . . (Stax)
   The Stax Blues Brothers-C . . . . (Stax)
   Years Gone By . . . . (Stax)
Roy Buchanan; *Dancing On The Edge* . . . . (Alligator)
Fast Lanes & Country Roads
Barbara Mandrell; *Country Classics-#2-Today's Country*
   Classics-C . . . . (Universal)
   Country Classics-#6-1985-1986-C . . . . (Universal)
   Get To The Heart . . . .(MCA)
Fields Of France
Al Stewart; *Last Days Of The Century* . . . . (Enigma Capitol)
Fields Of Illinois
Don Lange; *Natural Born Heathen* . . . . (Flying Fish)
Fishin' In The Dark
Nitty Gritty Dirt Band; *Billboard Top Country Hits-1987-C* . . . . (Rhino)
   Hold On . . . . (Warner Bros.)
   More Great Dirt-Best Of Nitty Gritty Dirt Band . . . . (Warner Bros.)
Georgia Pineywoods
Osborne Brothers; *Best Of The Osborne Brothers* . . . . (MCA)
   Country Bluegrass . . . . (MCA Special Prod.)
   Red, White & Bluegrass-C . . . . (C.M.H. Prod.)
Girl From The North Country
Bob Dylan; *Freewheelin'* . . . . (Columbia)
   Nashville Skyline . . . . (Columbia)
   Real Live . . . . (Columbia)
Joe Cocker; *Mad Dogs & Englishmen* . . . . (A&M)
Johnny Cash with Bob Dylan; *The Man In Black-His Greatest Hits* . . . . (Legacy)
God's Country
Al Jolson; *The Al Jolson Story-#4* . . . . (MCA)
God's Country
Kool & The Gang; *Forever* . . . . (Mercury)
Going To The Country
Steve Miller Band; *Best Of Steve Miller 1968-1973* . . . . (Capitol)
   Number 5 . . . . (Capitol)
   Steve Miller Band-Anthology . . . . (Capitol)
Going To The Country
Bruce Cockburn; *Waiting For A Miracle-Singles 1970-1987* . . . . .(Gold Castle)
Going Up The Country
Canned Heat; *Best Of Canned Heat* . . . . (EMI)
   ST/1969 . . . . (Polydor)
   ST/Woodstock . . . .(Atlantic)
   Summer Of Love-#1-C . . . . (Rhino)
Golden Country
REO Speedwagon; *A Decade Of Rock And Roll 1970 To 1980* . . . . . . (Epic)
   REO Speedwagon Live/You Get What You Play For . . . . (Epic)
Gone Country
Alan Jackson; *Who I Am* . . . . (Arista)
Green Fields Of America
Paddy Tunney; *Stone Fiddle* . . . . (Green Linnet)
Green Fields Of Canada
Eric Schoenberg; *Acoustic Guitar* . . . . (Rounder)

Green Fields Of France
Phil Coulter; *Forgotten Dreams* . . . .(Shanachie)
Greenfields
Brothers Four; *Tokyo Tapes*. . . . . (Folk Era)
Vogues; *Vogues' Greatest Hits* . . . . (Rhino)
Heartland
George Strait; *ST/Pure Country*. . . . . (MCA)
Heartland
Sawyer Brown; *Boys Are Back* . . . .(Curb)
Heartland
Steve Wariner; *Life's Highway* . . . . (MCA)
Heartland
U2; *Rattle And Hum*. . . . . (Island)
Hillbilly Rock
Marty Stuart; *Hillbilly Rock*. . . . . (MCA)
Marty Party Hit Pack . . . . (MCA)
Home On The Range
Bing Crosby; *Crooner-Columbia Years-1928-1934* . . . . (Columbia)
Boston Pops Orchestra/Arthur Fiedler; *Yankee Doodle Dandy* . . . .(RCA)
Gene Autry; *50th Anniversary* . . . . (Republic/Universal)
*The Country Music Hall Of Fame-Gene Autry-15 Of His All-Time
Greatest Hits* . . . . (Columbia)
Neil Young; *ST/Where The Buffalo Roam* . . . . (Backstreet)
House In The Country
Blood, Sweat & Tears; *Child Is Father To The Man* . . . . (Columbia)
How To Be A Country Star
Statler Brothers; *Best Of The Statler Brothers-Rides Again-#2* . . . . (Mercury)
Hundred And Sixty Acres
Marty Robbins; *Gunfighter Ballads & Trail Songs* . . . . (Legacy)
I Dreamed Of A Hillbilly Heaven
Tex Ritter; *An American Legend* . . . . (Capitol)
Best Of Tex Ritter . . . . (Capitol)
Hillbilly Heaven . . . . (Capitol)
Opry Legends-Tex Ritter . . . . (Capitol)
I Like Mountain Music
Roy Acuff; *Grand Ole Opry-75 Years-#1-C* . . . . (MCA)
I Was Country When Country Wasn't Cool
Barbara Mandrell; *Barbara Mandrell Live* . . . . (MCA)
Barbara Mandrell's Greatest Hits . . . . (MCA)
I'm From The Country
Tracy Byrd; *I'm From The Country*. . . . . (MCA)
I'm Just A Country Boy
Don Williams; *Best Of Don Williams-#2*. . . . . (MCA)
Don Williams-Country Boy. . . . . (MCA)
In God's Country
U2; *Joshua Tree*. . . . . (Island)
In The Country
Chicago; *Chicago At Carnegie Hall* . . . . (Chicago)
Chicago II. . . . . (Chicago)
Johnny B. Goode
Chuck Berry; *Chuck Berry's Greatest Hits* . . . .(Everest)
Classic Rock-#2-C . . . . (MCA)
Roll Over Beethoven . . . . (Allegiance)
ST/American Graffiti . . . . (MCA)
The Chess Box-Chuck Berry . . . . (Chess)
Elvis Presley; *Elvis In Concert* . . . . (RCA)
From Memphis To Vegas/From Vegas To Memphis. . . . . (RCA)
Grateful Dead; *Bill Graham Presents The Last Days Of The
Fillmore-C* . . . . (Epic Portrait Assoc.)
Johnny Winter; *Live/Johnny Winter And* . . . . (Columbia)
Second Winter. . . . . (Columbia)
Jukebox With A Country Song
Doug Stone; *I Thought It Was You*. . . . . (Epic)
Just A Country Dream
Eric Andersen; *Best Of Eric Andersen*. . . . . (Vanguard)
Country Dream. . . . . (Vanguard)
Kindly Keep It Country
Vince Gill; *The Key* . . . . (MCA)
Listen To A Country Song
Loggins & Messina; *Loggins & Messina-On Stage*. . . . . (Columbia)
Sittin' In . . . . (Columbia)
Lynn Anderson; *Country Chartbusters-#2* . . . . (Columbia)
Lynn Anderson's Greatest Hits . . . . (Columbia)
Long Haired Country Boy
Charlie Daniels Band; *A Decade Of Hits*. . . . . (Epic)
Fire On The Mountain . . . . (Epic)
Me & The Boys . . . . (Epic)
South's Greatest Hits-#2-C. . . . . (Capricorn)
Trucker's Jukebox-#2-C . . . . (Legacy)
Volunteer Jam 3 & 4 . . . . (Epic)
Lord Have Mercy On A Country Boy
Don Williams; *True Love* . . . .(RCA)
Louisiana Hayride
Boswell Sisters; *That's How Rhythm Was Born* . . . . (Legacy)
Luckenbach Texas (Back To The Basics Of Love)
Waylon Jennings; *Ol' Waylon* . . . .(RCA)
Stars Are Out In Texas-C . . . . (RCA)
Waylon Jennings' Greatest Hits . . . . (RCA)

Meanwhile Back At The Ranch
Clark Family Experience; *Meanwhile Back At The Ranch*. . . . .(Curb)
Montana Plains
Moonshine Kate & Others; *Banjo Pickin' Girls* . . . .(Rounder)
Mountain Of Love
Charley Pride; *Charley Pride's Greatest Hits-#2*. . . . . (RCA)
Solid Country Gold-C . . . . (RCA)
David Houston; *American Originals-David Houston* . . . . (Columbia)
Harold Dorman; *Collectables Presents The History Of
Rock-#10-C* . . . . (Collectables)
Johnny Rivers; *Best Of Johnny Rivers* . . . . (EMI)
Johnny Rivers-Anthology 1964-1977 . . . .(Rhino)
North Country Blues
Bob Dylan; *The Times They Are A-Changin'* . . . .(Columbia)
Joan Baez; *Any Day Now: Songs Of Bob Dylan* . . . .(Vanguard)
North Country Girl
Pete Townshend; *Pete Townshend Live* . . . . (Platinum Music)
Nothin' But The Wheel
Patty Loveless; *Only What I Feel* . . . .(Epic)
Patty Loveless-Classics . . . .(Epic)
Now That's Country
Marty Stuart; *This One's Gonna Hurt You*. . . . . (MCA)
October Country
October Country; *Nuggets-#3-Pop-C* . . . .(Rhino)
Oklahoma Country Girl
Elvin Bishop; *Big Fun* . . . . (Alligator)
Ol' Country
Mark Chesnutt; *Longnecks & Short Stories* . . . . (MCA)
Old Country Church
Hank Williams; *I Ain't Got Nothin' But Time-1946-1947* . . . . (Polydor)
Old Virginia Lowlands
John Townley & The Press Gang; *Chesapeake Sailor's Companion* . . . (Adelphi)
One Room Country Shack
Buddy Guy; *Man & The Blues* . . . .(Vanguard)
My Time After Awhile . . . .(Vanguard)
Mercy Dee Walton; *Mercy's Troubles*. . . . . (Arhoolie)
One Room Country Shack . . . . (Specialty)
Pity & A Shame . . . . (Prestige)
Mose Allison; *Mose Allison's Greatest Hits* . . . . (Prestige)
Out In The Country
Three Dog Night; *Best Of Three Dog Night* . . . . (MCA)
Out On The Texas Plains
Mom & Dads; *Golden Country* . . . . (Crescendo)
Outskirts Of Town
Sawyer Brown; *Outskirts Of Town*. . . . .(Curb)
Peaches
Presidents Of The United States Of America; *The Presidents Of The United
States Of America*. . . . .(Columbia)
Place In The Country
Adam Ant; *Antics In The Forbidden Zone* . . . . (Epic)
Friend Or Foe . . . . (Epic)
Place In The Country
George Jones; *One Woman Man* . . . . (Epic)
Plains Of Nebrasky-O
Eric Andersen & Phil Ochs; *Best Of Broadside 1962-1968: Anthems
Of The American Underground From The Pages Of Broadside
Magazine-C* . . . . (Smithsonian Folkways)
Prairie Rose
Roxy Music; *Country Life* . . . .(Atco)
Prairie Wedding
Mark Knopfler; *Sailing To Philadelphia* . . . .(Warner Bros.)
Prisoner For Life
Skip Gorman; *A Cowboy's Wild Song To His Herd* . . . .(Rounder)
Rebecca Lynn
Bryan White; *Bryan White*. . . . . (Asylum)
Red And Rio Grande
Doug Supernaw; *Red And Rio Grande*. . . . . (BNA)
Red Plains
Bruce Hornsby & The Range; *The Way It Is*. . . . . (RCA)
Rock My World (Little Country Girl)
Brooks & Dunn; *Hard Workin' Man* . . . .(Arista)
Silver Stars, Purple Sage, Eyes Of Blue
Roy Rogers & Sons Of The Pioneers; *Roy Rogers & Sons Of The
Pioneers* . . . . (Varese Sarabande)
Soft Lights And Hard Country Music
Moe Bandy; *Honky Tonk Amnesia-The Hard Country Sound Of Moe
Bandy* . . . . (Razor & Tie)
Stone Cold Country
Gibson/Miller Band; *Where There's Smoke* . . . . (Epic)
Strawberry Fields Forever
Beatles; *Beatles-Box Set*. . . . .(Capitol)
Magical Mystery Tour. . . . . (Capitol)
ST/Imagine: John Lennon. . . . . (Capitol)
The Beatles/1967-1970 . . . . (Capitol)
Sweet Country Music
Atlanta; *Pictures* . . . . (MCA)
Today's Country Classics-C . . . . (MCA Special Prod.)

Sweet Country Woman
Johnny Duncan; *Country Music Classics-#11-Early '70s-C* . . . . (K-Tel)
Johnny Duncan's Greatest Hits . . . . (Columbia)
Winnin' Country . . . . (Fifty One West)

Take Me Home, Country Roads
John Denver; *Evening With John Denver* . . . . (RCA)
John Denver's Greatest Hits . . . . (RCA)
Poems, Prayers & Promises . . . . (RCA)
Take Me Home, Country Roads & Other Hits . . . . (RCA)
Toots & The Maytals; *Brand New Second-Hand* . . . . (Rykodisc)

Take Me To The Country
Mel McDaniel; *Take Me To The Country* . . . . (Capitol)

Texas Plains
Riders In The Sky; *Cowboy Way* . . . .(MCA)
Saturday Morning With Riders In The Sky . . . .(MCA)
Stuart Hamblen; *Stuart Hamblen-A Man & His Music* . . . . (Lamb & Lion)

Thank God I'm A Country Boy
John Denver; *Back Home Again* . . . . (RCA)
Evening With John Denver . . . . (RCA)
John Denver's Greatest Hits-#2 . . . . (RCA)

Thanks For The Beautiful Land On The Delta
Duke Ellington; *New Orleans Suite* . . . .(Atlantic)

Theme From "Green Acres"
Eddie Albert & Eva Gabor; *ST/Son In Law* . . . . (Hollywood)
Original Soundtrack; *CBS: The First 50 Years* . . . . (TVT)
Television's Greatest Hits-#1-C . . . . (TVT)

Theme From "Little House On The Prairie"
Original Soundtrack; *Television's Greatest Hits-#3-1970s & 1980s-C* . . . (TVT)

Theme From "Petticoat Junction"
Flatt & Scruggs; *20 All-Time Great Recordings* . . . . (Columbia)
Original Soundtrack; *Television's Greatest Hits-#1-C* . . . . (TVT)
TV Theme Sing-Along Album . . . . (Rhino)

Theme From "The High Chapparal"
Original Soundtrack; *Television's Greatest Hits-#5-In Living Color-C* . . . (TVT)

Theme From "The Waltons"
Original Soundtrack; *CBS: The First 50 Years* . . . . (TVT)
Television's Greatest Hits-#3-1970s & 1980s-C . . . . (TVT)

There Ain't No Country Music On This Jukebox
Tom T. Hall; *Storyteller, Poet, Philospher* . . . . (Mercury)

There Won't Be No Country Music (There Won't Be No Rock 'N' Roll)
C.W. McCall; *C.W. McCall's Greatest Hits* . . . . (Polydor)

This Hard Land
Bruce Springsteen; *Bruce Springsteen's Greatest Hits* . . . . (Columbia)
Tracks . . . . (Columbia)

This Land Is Your Land
Bruce Springsteen & The E Street Band; *Bruce Springsteen & The E Street
Band Live/1975-85* . . . . (Legacy)
Glen Campbell; *All American* . . . . (Liberty)
Lee Greenwood; *American Patriot* . . . . (Capitol)
Odetta, Arlo Guthrie & Company; *Tribute To Woody
Guthrie-C* . . . . (Warner Bros.)
Pete Seeger; *God Bless America-C* . . . . (Columbia)
Pete Seeger Sings Woody Guthrie . . . . (Smithsonian Folkways)
Pete Seeger-Complete Carnegie Hall Concert-1963 . . . . (Columbia)
Weavers; *Weavers' Greatest Hits* . . . . (Vanguard)
Woody Guthrie; *Greatest Songs Of Woody Guthrie-C* . . . . (Vanguard)
Troubadours Of The Folk Era-#1-C . . . . (Rhino)
Woody Guthrie . . . . (Vanguard)

Two Of A Kind, Workin' On A Full House
Garth Brooks; *No Fences* . . . . (Capitol)

Warning Labels
Doug Stone; *From The Heart* . . . .(Epic)

Weekend In The Country
Original Cast; *A Little Night Music* . . . .: (Columbia)
Original London Cast; *A Little Night Music* . . . . (RCA)

West Texas Plains
Rosie Flores; *After The Farm* . . . .(Hightone)

When Country Comes To Town
Toby Keith; *How Do You Like Me Now?!* . . . . (DreamWorks/SKG)

When It All Goes South
Alabama; *When It All Goes South* . . . . (RCA)

Where Corn Don't Grow
Travis Tritt; *The Restless Kind* . . . .(Warner Bros.)

Where The Blacktop Ends
keith urban; *keith urban* . . . . (Capitol)

Where The Green Grass Grows
Tim McGraw; *Big Country Hits '99-C* . . . . (K-Tel)
Everywhere . . . . (Curb)
Tim McGraw's Greatest Hits . . . . (Curb)

Wild Frontier
Bruce Hornsby & The Range; *The Way It Is* . . . . (RCA)

Wild Frontier
Gary Moore; *Wild Frontier* . . . . (Virgin)

Wild In The Country
Elvis Presley; *The Other Sides-Worldwide Gold Award Hits, Vol. 2* . . . . . (RCA)

You Can Take Salem Out Of The Country
Original Soundtrack; *TeeVee Toons-The Commercials-#1-C* . . . . (TVT)

You Can't Take The Country Out Of Me
Alabama; *American Pride* . . . . (RCA)

You Know Me Better Than That
George Strait; *Strait Out Of The Box* . . . . (MCA)
The Chill Of An Early Fall . . . . (MCA)

You're Lookin' At Country
Loretta Lynn; *Loretta Lynn-20 Greatest Hits* . . . . (MCA)
Loretta Lynn-Greatest Hits Live . . . .(K-Tel)
Loretta Lynn's Greatest Hits-#2 . . . . (MCA)
The Country Music Hall Of Fame-Loretta Lynn . . . . (MCA)

COUPLES, Pairs

See Also: **FRIENDS, LOVE (various), MARRIAGE, NUMBERS: 2, TOGETHERNESS**

(Just Like) Romeo & Juliet
Reflections; *'60s Dance Party-C* . . . . (Dominion Entert.)
Sensational '60s-#1-C . . . . (Dominion Entert.)

And You And I
Yes; *Close To The Edge* . . . .(Atlantic)
Yessongs . . . .(Atlantic)

Ballad Of Bonnie And Clyde
Georgie Fame; *History Of British Rock-#8-C* . . . . (Rhino)

Barbie Girl
Aqua; *Aquarium* . . . . (MCA)
Now That's What I Call Music!-#1-C . . . .(Virgin)

Ben
Michael Jackson; *Best Of Michael Jackson* . . . . (Motown)
Jackson 5-16 Greatest Hits . . . . (Motown)
Jackson 5-Anthology . . . . (Motown)
Jacksons Live . . . . (Epic)
Michael Jackson-Anthology . . . . (Motown)
Motown Superstar Series-#7-Michael Jackson . . . . (Motown)

Born To Be With You
Chordettes; *Best Of The Chordettes* . . . . (Rhino)
Chordettes Greatest Hits . . . . (Everest)
Lil' Bit Of Gold 3" CD Series-C . . . . (Rhino)

Brand New Day
Sting; *Brand New Day* . . . . (A&M)

Brand New Key
Deana Carter; *Everything's Gonna Be Alright* . . . . (Capitol)
Melanie; *Best Of Melanie* . . . . (Rhino)
Super Hits Of The '70s-Have A Nice Day-#7-C . . . . (Rhino)

Daydream Believer
Anne Murray; *Anne Murray's Greatest Hits* . . . . (Capitol)
I'll Always Love You . . . . (Capitol)
Monkees; *Billboard Top Rock 'N' Roll Hits-1967-C* . . . . (Rhino)
Mellow '60s-C . . . . (Priority)
Monkees' Greatest Hits . . . . (Rhino)

Donald And Lydia
John Prine; *John Prine* . . . .(Atlantic)
John Prine-Souvenirs . . . .(Oh Boy)
Prime Prine-The Best Of John Prine . . . .(Atlantic)

For Your Love
Tevin Campbell; *Tevin Campbell* . . . .(Qwest)

He Will, She Knows
Kenny Rogers; *There You Go Again* . . . .(Dreamcatcher)

I Believe In You And Me
Whitney Houston; *ST/The Preacher's Wife* . . . . (Arista)

I Believe In You And Me
Four Tops; *Smooth Grooves-Weddings Songs-C* . . . . (Rhino)
When She Was My Girl . . . . (Casablanca)

I Only Want To Be With You
Bay City Rollers; *Bay City Rollers' Greatest Hits* . . . . (Arista)
Dusty Springfield; *Dusty Springfield-Anthology* . . . . (Mercury)
Dusty Springfield-Golden Hits . . . . (Mercury)
Vonda Shepard; *ST/Songs From "Ally McBeal" Featuring Vonda
Shepard* . . . .(550/Epic)

I'd Like That
XTC; *Homespun* . . . . (Idea/TVT)

If You See Him/If You See Her
Brooks & Dunn & Reba McEntire; *If You See Her* . . . . (Arista)
Reba McEntire & Brooks & Dunn; *If You See Him* . . . . (MCA)
Reba McEntire's Greatest Hits-#3: I'm A Survivor . . . . (MCA)

It Works
Alabama; *In Pictures* . . . . (RCA)

Jack & Diane
John Cougar; *American Fool* . . . . (Riva)

John Deere Green
Joe Diffie; *Honky Tonk Attitude* . . . . (Epic)
Joe Diffie's Greatest Hits . . . . (Epic)

Just The Two Of Us
Grover Washington, Jr. & Bill Withers; *Billboard Top R&B Hits-
1981-C* . . . . (Rhino)
Grover Washington, Jr.-Anthology . . . . (Elektra)
Grover Washington, Jr.-Winelight . . . .(Elektra)

Legend Of Bonnie And Clyde
Merle Haggard & The Strangers; *For The Record: Merle Haggard-43 Legendary Hits* ....(BNA)
Let's Fall To Pieces Together
George Strait; *George Strait's Greatest Hits* ....(MCA)
Right Or Wrong ....(MCA)
Strait Out Of The Box ....(MCA)
Make Me Whole
Amel Larrieux; *Infinite Possibilities* ....(Epic)
Me & My Old Lady
Offspring; *Ixnay On The Hombre* ....(Columbia)
Me And My Arrow
Nilsson; *Nilsson's Greatest Hits* ....(RCA)
The Point ....(RCA)
Motorcycle Cowboy
Merle Haggard; *Merle Haggard-Live At Billy Bob's* ....(Razor & Tie)
My Kind Of Girl
Collin Raye; *Best Of Collin Raye-Direct Hits* ....(Epic)
Extremes ....(Epic)
My Kind Of Woman, My Kind Of Man
Patty Loveless; *Patty Loveless-Classics* ....(Epic)
Vince Gill with Patty Loveless; *The Key* ....(MCA)
My Love Is Your Love
Whitney Houston; *My Love Is Your Love* ....(Arista)
Totally Hits-#2-C ....(Elektra)
Ob-La-Di, Ob-La-Da (Desmond & Molly Jones)
Beatles; *Beatles-Box Set* ....(Capitol)
The Beatles (White Album) ....(Capitol)
The Beatles/1967-1970 ....(Capitol)
Old Man And Me
Hootie & The Blowfish; *Fairweather Johnson* ....(Atlantic)
One
George Jones & Tammy Wynette; *George Jones Collection* ....(MCA)
Grand Ole Opry-75 Years-#2-C ....(MCA)
One ....(MCA)
One Boy, One Girl
Collin Raye; *Best Of Collin Raye-Direct Hits* ....(Epic)
I Think About You ....(Epic)
Pair Of Old Sneakers
George Jones; *George Jones & Tammy Wynette-16 Biggest Hits* ....(Epic/Legacy)
Papa Loves Mambo
Perry Como; *Como's Golden Records* ....(RCA)
Perry Como-Pure Gold ....(RCA)
Perry Como's All-Time Greatest Hits-#1 ....(RCA)
This Is Perry Como ....(RCA)
Picasso And Me
Gretchen Peters; *Gretchen Peters* ....(Purple Crayon Prod.)
Power Of Love
Celine Dion; *All The Way...A Decade Of Song* ....(550 Music)
The Colour Of My Love ....(550 Music)
Running Bear
Johnny Preston; *45s On CD-#1-1956-1959-C* ....(Mercury)
Billboard Top Rock 'N' Roll Hits-1960-C ....(Rhino)
Cruisin'-1960-C ....(Increase)
Sonny James; *All-Time Country Classics-#1-C* ....(Capitol)
Say You, Say Me
Lionel Richie; *Back To Front* ....(Motown)
Dancing On The Ceiling ....(Motown)
So Much In Love
Tymes; *20th Century Rocks-#9-'60's Vocal Groups-I Got Rhythm-C* ....(Dominion Entert.)
Theme From "Chico And The Man"
Original Soundtrack; *Television's Greatest Hits-#5-In Living Color-C* ...(TVT)
Theme From "Courageous Cat & Minute Mouse"
Original Soundtrack; *Television's Greatest Hits-#2-C* ....(TVT)
Theme From "Dastardly & Muttley In Their Flying Machine"
Original Soundtrack; *Hanna-Barbera Pic-A-Nic Basket Of Cartoon Classics* ....(Kid Rhino/Rhino 4 Kids)
Television's Greatest Hits-#3-1970s & 1980s-C ....(TVT)
Theme From "Laverne & Shirley"
Original Soundtrack; *Television's Greatest Hits-#3-1970s & 1980s-C* ....(TVT)
Theme From "Lippy The Lion & Hardy Har Har"
Original Soundtrack; *Hanna-Barbera Classics-#1-Original Recordings Of The World's Most Famous Cartoon Themes & Scores* ....(Kid Rhino/Rhino 4 Kids)
Hanna-Barbera Pic-A-Nic Basket Of Cartoon Classics ....(Kid Rhino/Rhino 4 Kids)
Theme From "Lois And Clark: The New Adventures Of Superman"
Original Soundtrack; *Television's Greatest Hits-#7-Cable Ready-C* .....(TVT)
Theme From "Mork & Mindy"
Original Soundtrack; *Television's Greatest Hits-#6-Remote Control-C* ...(TVT)
Theme From "Pixie And Dixie"
Original Soundtrack; *Hanna-Barbera Classics-#1-Original Recordings Of The World's Most Famous Cartoon Themes & Scores* ....(Kid Rhino/Rhino 4 Kids)
Hanna-Barbera Pic-A-Nic Basket Of Cartoon Classics ....(Kid Rhino/Rhino 4 Kids)

Theme From "Ruff And Reddy"
Original Soundtrack; *Hanna-Barbera Classics-#1-Original Recordings Of The World's Most Famous Cartoon Themes & Scores* ....(Kid Rhino/Rhino 4 Kids)
Hanna-Barbera Pic-A-Nic Basket Of Cartoon Classics ....(Kid Rhino/Rhino 4 Kids)
Theme From "Siskel And Ebert"
Original Soundtrack; *Television's Greatest Hits-#6-Remote Control-C* ...(TVT)
Theme From "The Beany & Cecil Show"
Original Soundtrack; *Television's Greatest Hits-#4-Black & White Classics-C* ....(TVT)
Theme From "The Lone Ranger" (William Tell Overture)
Boston Pops Orchestra; *TV Classics-C* ....(RCA)
Boston Pops Orchestra/Arthur Fiedler; *Fiedler-Greatest Hits* ....(RCA)
Original Soundtrack; *Television's Greatest Hits-#7-Cable Ready-C* .....(TVT)
Spike Jones & His City Slickers; *Best Of Spike Jones & His City Slickers* ....(RCA)
Theme From "The Odd Couple"
Original Soundtrack; *Television's Greatest Hits-#7-Cable Ready-C* .....(TVT)
This Woman And This Man
Clay Walker; *If I Could Make A Living* ....(Giant)
Tweedle Dee & Tweedle Dum
Bob Dylan; *"Love And Theft"* ....(Columbia)
Two Of A Kind, Workin' On A Full House
Garth Brooks; *No Fences* ....(Capitol)
Two Step
Dave Matthews Band; *Crash* ....(RCA)
Two Teardrops
Steve Wariner; *Two Teardrops* ....(Capitol)
Us
Celine Dion; *Let's Talk About Love-C* ....(550 Music)
Whither Thou Goest
Les Paul & Mary Ford; *Best Of The Capitol Masters* ....(Gold Rush)
Les Paul's All-Time Greatest Hits ....(EMI Special Markets)
You And I
Eddie Rabbitt & Crystal Gayle; *Best Of Eddie Rabbitt/Greatest Hits-II* ....(Warner Bros.)
Chicken Soup For The Couples Soul-C ....(Rhino)
You And Me
Lorrie Morgan; *Tammy Wynette...Remembered-C* ....(Asylum)
Tammy Wynette; *Tammy Wynette-16 Biggest Hits* ....(Legacy)
Tammy Wynette-Anniversary-20 Years Of Hits ....(Epic)
Tammy Wynette-Super Hits ....(Epic)
You And Me Against The World
Helen Reddy; *Helen Reddy's Greatest Hits* ....(Capitol)
You And Me Against The World
Roy Rogers; *Best Of Roy Rogers* ....(Curb)

COWBOYS, Cowgirls, Ranch

See Also: AMERICAN WEST, ANIMALS: COWS, ANIMALS: HORSES, CITIES: A-Z, COUNTRY, NATIVE AMERICANS, REBELS, RODEO, STATES: A-Z

(Ghost) Riders In The Sky
Gene Autry; *50th Anniversary* ....(Republic/Universal)
Cowboy Hall Of Fame ....(Republic/Universal)
Johnny Cash; *The Man In Black-His Greatest Hits* ....(Legacy)
Outlaws; *Ghost Riders* ....(Arista)
Roy Clark; *Roy Clark In Concert* ....(MCA)
Roy Clark's Greatest Hits ....(MCA)
Superpicker ....(MCA)
Vaughn Monroe; *Best Of Vaughn Monroe* ....(RCA)
This Is Vaughn Monroe/Decade Of The '40s ....(RCA)
(Man Who Shot) Liberty Valance
Gene Pitney; *Gene Pitney-Anthology 1961-1968* ....(Rhino)
Gene Pitney's Greatest Hits ....(Evergreen Music)
Super Oldies Of The '60s-#9-C ....(Audio Fidelity)
Greg Kihn; *Glass House Rock* ....(Beserkley)
All Around Cowboy
Marty Robbins; *All Around Cowboy* ....(Columbia)
Encore-Marty Robbins ....(Columbia)
All Lonesome Cowboys
Pure Prairie League; *Takin' The Stage* ....(RCA)
Along The Santa Fe Trail
Glenn Miller; *Original Live Recordings* ....(Pair)
Sons Of The Pioneers; *Sunset On The Range* ....(Pair)
Are There Any Cowboys Left (In The Good Ol' U.S.A.?)
Lacy J. Dalton; *Lacy J. Dalton* ....(Columbia)
Are There Any More Real Cowboys
Willie Nelson & Neil Young; *Half Nelson-C* ....(Columbia)
Asphalt Cowboy
Sleepy LaBeef; *Bull's Night Out* ....(Sun)
Back In The Saddle
Aerosmith; *Aerosmith-Classics Live 2* ....(Columbia)
Aerosmith's Greatest Hits ....(Columbia)

Live! Bootleg . . . . (Columbia)
Pandora's Box . . . . (Columbia)
Rocks . . . . (Columbia)

Back In The Saddle Again
Gene Autry; *50th Anniversary* . . . .(Republic/Universal)
Columbia Country Classics-#1-Golden Age-C . . . . (Columbia)
Cowboy Hall Of Fame . . . . (Republic/Universal)
Cowboy Super Hits-C . . . . (Columbia)
Great American Singing Cowboys-C . . . .(Republic/Universal)
South Of The Border . . . . (Republic/Universal)

Ballad Of A Well Known Gun
Elton John; *Tumbleweed Connection* . . . . (Polydor)

Beautiful Disaster
311; *Live!* . . . . (Capricorn)
Transistor . . . . (Capricorn)

Belfast Cowboys
Pretty Things; *Silk Torpedo* . . . . (Swan Song)

Big Iron
Marty Robbins; *Columbia Country Classics-#3-Americana-C* . . . . . (Columbia)
Gunfighter Ballads & Trail Songs . . . . (Legacy)
Marty Robbins' All-Time Greatest Hits . . . . (Columbia)
Marty Robbins-More Greatest Hits . . . . (Columbia)

Blanket On The Ground
Billie Jo Spears; *'70s Hits: Country-#1-C* . . . . (Curb)
Best Of Billie Jo Spears . . . . (Razor & Tie)
Country Hits Of The '70s-C . . . . (CEMA Special Prod.)

Blazing Saddles
Mel Brooks; *ST/High Anxiety* . . . . (Asylum)

Blue Shadows On The Trail
Sons Of The Pioneers; *Cool Water* . . . . (RCA)

Buckaroo
Lee Ann Womack; *Lee Ann Womack* . . . . (Decca)

Cadillac Cowboy
Chris LeDoux; *Chris LeDoux & The Saddle Boogie Band* . . . . (Liberty)
Chris LeDoux-20 Greatest Hits . . . . (Capitol)

Captain Fantastic And The Brown Dirt Cowboy
Elton John; *Captain Fantastic And The Brown Dirt Cowboy* . . . . (Polydor)

Cattle Call
Eddy Arnold; *Best Of Eddy Arnold* . . . . (RCA)
Cattle Call . . . . (RCA)
Eddy Arnold-Pure Gold . . . . (RCA)
Nipper's Greatest Hits Of The '50s-#1-C . . . . (RCA)
Riders In The Sky; *Riders Radio Theater* . . . .(MCA)

Coca Cola Cowboy
Mel Tillis; *Mel Tillis' Greatest Hits* . . . . (Curb)
Very Best Of Mel Tillis . . . .(MCA)

Computer Cowboy
Neil Young; *Trans* . . . .(Geffen)

Cosmic Cowboy
Michael Murphey; *Cosmic Cowboy Souvenir* . . . . (A&M)
Nitty Gritty Dirt Band; *Dirt, Silver & Gold* . . . .(One Way)
Stars And Stripes Forever . . . . (Capitol)

Cowboy
Johnny Rodriguez; *Rodriguez Was Here* . . . . (Mercury)

Cowboy
Kid Rock; *Devil Without A Cause* . . . .(Top Dog/Lava/Atlantic)

Cowboy
C.W. McCall; *C.W. McCall & Company* . . . . (Polydor)

Cowboy
Bow Wow Wow; *I Want Candy* . . . . (RCA)

Cowboy
Randy Newman; *Randy Newman/Live* . . . .(Warner Archives)

Cowboy & The Hippie
Chris LeDoux; *Gold Buckle Dreams* . . . . (Liberty)
He Rides The Wild Horses . . . . (Liberty)

Cowboy & The Lady
John Denver; *Some Days Are Diamonds* . . . . (RCA)

Cowboy & The Lady
Johnny Duncan; *Come A Little Bit Closer* . . . . (Columbia)

Cowboy Band
Billy Dean; *Men'll Be Boys* . . . . (Liberty)

Cowboy Bill
Garth Brooks; *Garth Brooks* . . . . (Liberty)

Cowboy Blues
Gene Autry; *Gene Autry-His Greatest Hits* . . . .(Tradition)
South Of The Border . . . .(Republic/Universal)

Cowboy Boogie
Randy Travis; *Wind In The Wire* . . . .(Warner Bros.)

Cowboy Boots
Dave Dudley; *Red Simpson/Red Sovine/Dave Dudley-C* . . . . (Gusto)

Cowboy Christmas Ball
Michael Martin Murphey; *Cowboy Christmas* . . . .(Warner Bros.)

Cowboy From Wyoming
Sammi Smith; *Better Than Ever* . . . . (Step One)

Cowboy Hat In Dallas
Charlie Daniels Band; *Homesick Heroes* . . . .(Epic)

Cowboy Heaven
Roy Rogers; *Peace In The Valley* . . . . (Pair)

Cowboy In Me, The
Tim McGraw; *Set This Circus Down* . . . .(Curb)

Cowboy In The Continental Suit
Chris LeDoux; *Rodeo & Living Free* . . . . (Liberty)
Marty Robbins; *American Originals-Marty Robbins* . . . . (Columbia)

Cowboy In The Jungle
Jimmy Buffett; *Son Of A Son Of A Sailor* . . . . (MCA)

Cowboy Lips
Bobs; *The Bobs* . . . . (Rhino)

Cowboy Love
John Michael Montgomery; *John Michael Montgomery* . . . .(Atlantic)
John Michael Montgomery's Greatest Hits . . . .(Atlantic)

Cowboy Love Song
Skip Gorman; *A Cowboy's Wild Song To His Herd* . . . . (Rounder)

Cowboy Man
Lyle Lovett; *Country Classics-#9-1984-1987-C* . . . . (Universal)
ST/Always . . . . (MCA)
Lyle Lovett and his Large Band; *Lyle Lovett and his
Large Band* . . . .(Curb/MCA)

Cowboy Movie
David Crosby; *If I Could Only Remember My Name* . . . .(Atlantic)

Cowboy Night Herd Song
Roy Rogers & Sons Of The Pioneers; *Cowboy Super Hits-C* . . . . (Columbia)

Cowboy Of Dreams
David Crosby & Graham Nash; *Wind On The Water* . . . . (MCA)

Cowboy Rides Away
George Strait; *Country Classics-#1-C* . . . . (Universal)
Does Fort Worth Ever Cross Your Mind . . . . (MCA)
George Strait's Greatest Hits-#2 . . . . (MCA)

Cowboy Romance
Natalie Merchant; *Tigerlily* . . . . (Elektra)

Cowboy Serenade (While I'm Rollin' My Last Cigarette)
Glenn Miller & His Orchestra; *Complete Glenn Miller & His
Orchestra* . . . . (Bluebird)

Cowboy Singer
Sonny Curtis; *Love Is All Around* . . . . (Elektra)
Sonny Curtis . . . . (Elektra)

Cowboy Song
Thin Lizzy; *Jailbreak* . . . .(Mercury)
Live And Dangerous . . . . (Warner Bros.)
Lizzy Lives! (1976-1984) . . . . (Gland Slamm)

Cowboy Take Me Away
Dixie Chicks; *Fly* . . . . (Monument)

Cowboy, You're America
Dave Dudley; *King Of The Road* . . . . (Sun)

Cowboys & Clowns
Billy Strange; *Great Western Themes* . . . .(Crescendo)
Ronnie Milsap; *ST/Bronco Billy* . . . . (Elektra)

Cowboys & Playboys
Moe Bandy; *Best Of Moe Bandy-Vol. 1* . . . . (Columbia)

Cowboys Ain't Supposed To Cry
Moe Bandy; *Cowboys Ain't Supposed To Cry* . . . . (Columbia)

Cowboys Don't Cry
Daron Norwood; *Daron Norwood* . . . .(Giant)
Dude Mowrey; *Honky Tonk* . . . . (Capitol)
Ian Tyson; *All-Ears Review-#7-Still Amazing…-C* . . (Really Outstanding Music)
1 Outgrew The Wagon . . . . (Vanguard)

Cowboys Don't Get Lucky All The Time
Gene Watson; *Beautiful Country* . . . . (Capitol)
ST/Convoy . . . .(Polydor)

Cowboys Don't Shoot Straight
Tammy Wynette; *Tammy Wynette's Biggest Hits* . . . . (Epic)
Tears Of Fire-25th Anniversary Collection . . . . (Epic)

Cowboy's Dream
Eddy Arnold; *Cattle Call* . . . . (RCA)
Jimmy C. Newman; *Cajun Cowboy* . . . . (Plantation)

Cowboy's Dream No. 19
Dan Hicks & His Hot Licks; *Last Train To Hicksville* . . . . (MCA)

Cowboys From Hollywood
Camper Van Beethoven; *Camper Van Beethoven II & III* . . . . (I.R.S.)

Cowboys In Africa
Bush Tetras; *Better Late Than Never* . . . . (Roir)

Cowboys In Hong Kong (As Far As Siam)
Red Rider; *As Far As Siam* . . . . (Capitol)

Cowboy's Lament
Sons Of The Pioneers; *Country-Western Songbook* . . . .(RCA)
Western Country . . . . (Granite)

Cowboy's Prayer
Goebel Reeves; *Songs Of The Old West* . . . .(Glendale)
Texas Drifter . . . . (Glendale)

Cowboys To Girls
Intruders; *Intruders-Super Hits* . . . . (Philadelphia Int'l)
Soul Shots-C . . . . (Rhino)

Cowboys Trademarks
Gene Autry; *Cowboy Hall Of Fame* . . . . (Republic/Universal)

Cowboy's Wild Song To His Herd
Skip Gorman; *A Cowboy's Wild Song To His Herd* . . . . (Rounder)

Cowgirl & The Dandy
Brenda Lee; *Brenda Lee-Greatest Country Hits* . . . . (MCA)
   Even Better . . . . (MCA)
Dolly Parton; *Here You Come Again* . . . . (Dunhill Compact Classics)

Cowgirl In The Sand
Crosby, Stills, Nash & Young; *4 Way Street* . . . . (Atlantic)
Neil Young; *Decade* . . . . (Reprise)
Neil Young & Crazy Horse; *Everybody Knows This Is Nowhere* . . . . . (Reprise)

Dallas Cowboys
Charley Pride; *45-#11736* . . . . (RCA)

Damn Good Cowboy
Charlie Daniels Band; *Cowboy Super Hits-C* . . . . (Columbia)
   Night Rider . . . . (Epic)

Dancin' Cowboys
Bellamy Brothers; *Bellamy Brothers' Greatest Hits* . . . . (MCA)
   You Can Get Crazy . . . . (WB/Curb)

Don't Call Him A Cowboy
Conway Twitty; *Don't Call Him A Cowboy* . . . . (Warner Bros.)
   Number One's: The Warner Bros. Years . . . . (Warner Bros.)

Don't Fence Me In
Andrews Sisters; *Andrews Sisters' All-Time Greatest Hits* . . . . (Decca)
Bing Crosby; *Best Of Bing Crosby* . . . . (MCA)
David Byrne; *Red Hot + Blue-Tribute To Cole Porter-C* . . . . (Chrysalis)
Ella Fitzgerald; *Cole Porter Songbook* . . . . (Verve)
Lari White/Shelby Lynne/Trisha Yearwood; *Don't Fence Me In* . . . . (RCA)
Willie Nelson & Leon Russell; *Cowboy Super Hits-C.* . . . . (Columbia)

Don't Take Your Guns To Town
Johnny Cash; *Billboard Top Country Hits-1959-C* . . . . (Rhino)
   Columbia Country Classics-#3-Americana-C . . . . (Columbia)
   Johnny Cash-16 Biggest Hits-#2 . . . . (Legacy)
   Johnny Cash's Greatest Hits . . . . (Columbia)
   The Man In Black-His Greatest Hits . . . . (Legacy)

Down At The Old Corral
Randy Travis; *Wind In The Wire* . . . . (Warner Bros.)

Drug Store Cowboy
Humble Pie; *Eat It* . . . . (A&M)

Dusty Skies
Asleep At The Wheel featuring Riders In The Sky; *Tribute To The Music Of*
   Bob Wills And The Texas Playboys-C . . . . (Liberty)
Bob Wills & His Texas Playboys; *Bob Wills & His Texas Playboys-Historic*
   Edition . . . . (Columbia)
   Don't Fence Me In-Western Music's Early Golden Era-C . . . . (Rounder)

El Paso
Grateful Dead; *Steal Your Face* . . . . (Grateful Dead)
Marty Robbins; *Billboard Top Country Hits-1960-C* . . . . (Rhino)
   Gunfighter Ballads & Trail Songs. . . . . (Legacy)
   Marty Robbins' Biggest Hits. . . . . (Columbia)
   Radio Classics Of The '50s-C . . . . (Columbia)
   Texas Super Hits-C . . . . (Columbia)

El Rancho Grande
Tune Wranglers; *Doughboys, Playboys And Cowboys: The Golden Years Of*
   Western Swing-C . . . . (Proper)

Even Cowgirls Get The Blues
Emmylou Harris; *Blue Kentucky Girl* . . . . (Warner Bros.)
Johnny Cash & Waylon Jennings; *Cowboy Super Hits-C* . . . . (Columbia)
   Heroes . . . . (Columbia)

For All Our Cowboy Friends
Red Steagall & The Coleman County Cowboys; *For All Our Cowboy*
   Friends. . . . . (MCA)

Get Along Little Dogies
Riders In The Sky; *Saddle Pals* . . . . (Rounder)
Tex Ritter; *Tex Ritter: Country Music Hall Of Fame* . . . . . (MCA Special Prod.)

God Must Be A Cowboy
Dan Seals; *Best Of Dan Seals* . . . . (Capitol)
   Dan Seals-Classics Collection-#1 . . . . (Capitol)
   Rebel Heart. . . . . (Liberty)

Gunsmoke
Molly Hatchet; *Flirtin' With Disaster* . . . . (Epic)
Outlaws; *Hurry Sundown* . . . . (Arista)

Happy Trails
Michael Martin Murphey; *Cowboy Songs* . . . . (Warner Western)
Original Soundtrack; *Television's Greatest Hits-#1-C* . . . . (TVT)
Quicksilver Messenger Service; *Sons Of Mercury* . . . . (Rhino)
Randy Travis & Roy Rogers; *Heroes And Friends* . . . . (Warner Bros.)
Riders In The Sky; *Cowboy Way* . . . . (MCA)
Roy Rogers/Dale Evans/Dusty Rogers; *Roy Rogers Tribute-C* . . . . . . (RCA)
Van Halen; *Diver Down* . . . . (Warner Bros.)

Home On The Range
Bing Crosby; *Crooner-Columbia Years-1928-1934* . . . . (Columbia)
Boston Pops Orchestra/Arthur Fiedler; *Yankee Doodle Dandy* . . . . . . (RCA)
Gene Autry; *50th Anniversary* . . . . (Republic/Universal)
   The Country Music Hall Of Fame-Gene Autry-15 Of His All-Time
   Greatest Hits . . . . (Columbia)
Neil Young; *ST/Where The Buffalo Roam* . . . . (Backstreet)

How A Cowgirl Says Goodbye
Tracy Lawrence; *The Coast Is Clear* . . . . (Atlantic)

I Can Still Make Cheyenne
George Strait; *Blue Clear Sky* . . . . (MCA)
   Latest Greatest Straitest Hits . . . . (MCA)

I Ride An Old Paint/Whoopee Ti-Yi-Yo/Git Along Little Doggies
Michael Martin Murphey; *Cowboy Songs* . . . . (Warner Western)

I Wanna Be A Cowboy
Boys Don't Cry; *Boys Don't Cry* . . . . (Profile)

I Wanna Be A Cowboy's Sweetheart
Patsy Montana & The Prairie Ramblers; *All Time Legends Of Country*
   Music-C . . . . (Legacy)
   Respect: A History Of Women In Music-C . . . . (Rhino)

I'd Like To Be A Cowboy
Cathy Fink; *Grandma Slid Down The Mountain* . . . . (Rounder)
Mary-Kate & Ashley Olsen; *Give Us A Mystery* . . . . (Zoom Express)

I'm An Old Cowhand
Bing Crosby; *Best Of Bing Crosby* . . . . (MCA)
Sons Of The Pioneers; *Empty Saddles* . . . . (MCA)

In The Valley
Marty Robbins; *Gunfighter Ballads & Trail Songs* . . . . (Legacy)

Isis
Bob Dylan; *Biograph* . . . . (Columbia)
   Desire . . . . (Columbia)

Jingle Jangle Jingle (I've Got Spurs)
Kay Kyser & His Orchestra; *Best Of The Big Bands-C* . . . . (Columbia)
   Golden Hits Of The '40s-C . . . . (Columbia Special Prod.)
   Sentimental Favorites . . . . (Columbia)
Tex Ritter; *Opry Legends-Tex Ritter* . . . . (Capitol)
   Out West-C . . . . (Capitol)

Just Like Gene Autry
Moby Grape; *Very Best Of Moby Grape-Vintage* . . . . (Columbia)

Just Like Jesse James
Cher; *Heart Of Stone* . . . . (Geffen)

King Of The Cowboys
Amazing Rhythm Aces; *Stacked Deck* . . . . (MCA)
Roy Rogers & Dusty Rogers; *Roy Rogers Tribute-C* . . . . (RCA)

Lady Takes The Cowboy Every Time
Larry Gatlin & The Gatlin Brothers Band; *Houston To Denver* . . . . . (Columbia)
   The Gatlin Brothers' Biggest Hits . . . . (Columbia)

Lasso The Moon
Gary Morris; *Gary Morris-Hits* . . . . (Warner Bros.)

Last Cowboy Song
Ed Bruce; *16 Top Country Hits-#2-C* . . . . (MCA)
   Ed Bruce's Greatest Hits . . . . (MCA)
Waylon Jennings, Willie Nelson, Johnny Cash, Kris Kristofferson; *Cowboy*
   Super Hits-C . . . . (Columbia)
   Highwayman . . . . (Columbia)

Last Of The Singing Cowboys
Marshall Tucker Band; *Running Like The Wind* . . . . (Warner Bros.)

Legend Of A Cowgirl
Imani Coppola; *Chupacapra* . . . . (Columbia)

Little Joe The Wrangler
Goebel Reeves; *Songs Of Old West* . . . . (Glendale)
   Texas Drifter . . . . (Glendale)

Little Joe The Wrangler's Sister Nell
Skip Gorman; *A Cowboy's Wild Song To His Herd* . . . . (Rounder)

Littlest Cowboy Rides Again
Chris LeDoux; *Songbook Of The American West.* . . . . (Liberty)
   Sounds Of The Western Country . . . . (Liberty)

Lone Star Trail
Dave Frederickson; *Cowboy Songs On Folkways-C* . . . (Smithsonian Folkways)
Ken Maynard; *All Time Legends Of Country Music-C* . . . . (Legacy)

Lonesome Cowboy
Elvis Presley; *Essential Elvis-The First Movies* . . . . (RCA)
   Loving You . . . . (RCA)

Lonesome L.A. Cowboy
New Riders Of The Purple Sage; *Adventures Of Panama Red* . . . . . (Columbia)
   Midnight Moonlight . . . . (Relix)

Lonesome Rodeo Cowboy
George Strait; *Livin' It Up* . . . . (MCA)

Long Tall Texan
Beach Boys; *Best Of The Beach Boys-#2* . . . . (Capitol)
   Concert/'69-Live In London . . . . (Capitol)
Murry Kellum; *20 Golden Souvenirs Of Music City U.S.A.-C* . . . . . (Plantation)
   Country Comedy-20 Country Comedy Hits . . . . (Plantation)

Mammas Don't Let Your Babies Grow Up To Be Cowboys
Gibson/Miller Band; *Cowboy Super Hits-C* . . . . (Columbia)
   ST/The Cowboy Way . . . . (Epic)
Waylon Jennings & Willie Nelson; *Waylon & Willie.* . . . . (RCA)
   Waylon Jennings & Willie Nelson's Greatest Hits . . . . (RCA)
Willie Nelson; *Greatest Hits (& Some That Will Be)* . . . . (Columbia)
   ST/The Electric Horseman . . . . (Columbia)
   Willie & Family Live . . . . (Columbia)

Marlboro Song, The (Theme From "Magnificent 7")
Original Soundtrack; *TeeVee Toons-The Commercials-#1-C* . . . . (TVT)

Meanwhile Back At The Ranch
Clark Family Experience; *Meanwhile Back At The Ranch* . . . . (Curb)

Modern Day Cowboy
Tesla; *Five Man Acoustical Jam* . . . . (Geffen)
   Mechanical Resonance . . . . (Geffen)

Montana Cowboy
Emmylou Harris & The Nash Ramblers; *At The Ryman.* . . . . (Reprise)

Hot Rize; *Traditional Ties* . . . . (Sugar Hill)
Motorcycle Cowboy
Merle Haggard; *Merle Haggard-Live At Billy Bob's* . . . . (Razor & Tie)
Mr. Shorty
Marty Robbins; *The Drifter* . . . . (Koch International)
My Cowboy's Getting Old
Tanya Tucker; *Lovin' & Learnin'* . . . .(MCA)
My Cowboy's Last Ride
Jessi Colter; *That's The Way A Cowboy Rocks & Rolls* . . . . (Capitol)
Johnny Cash; *Rambler* . . . . (Columbia)
My Heroes Have Always Been Cowboys
Willie Nelson; *All Time Legends Of Country Music-C* . . . . (Legacy)
Cowboy Super Hits-C . . . . (Columbia)
Greatest Country Hits Of The '80s-1980-C . . . . (Columbia)
Greatest Hits (& Some That Will Be) . . . . (Columbia)
ST/My Heroes Have Always Been Cowboys . . . . (RCA)
ST/The Electric Horseman . . . . (Columbia)
Night Rider's Lament
Chris LeDoux; *Chris LeDoux & The Saddle Boogie Band* . . . . (Liberty)
Old Cowboy Classics . . . . (Capitol)
Paint Me Back Home In Wyoming . . . . (Liberty)
Garth Brooks; *The Chase* . . . . (Liberty)
Jerry Jeff Walker; *Ridin' High* . . . . (MCA)
Nanci Griffith; *Other Voices Other Rooms* . . . . (Elektra)
Suzy Bogguss; *Somewhere Between.* . . . . (Capitol)
Oklahoma Hills
Arlo Guthrie; *Tribute To Woody Guthrie-C* . . . .(Warner Bros.)
Hank Thompson; *Hank Thompson's All-Time Greatest Hits* . . . . (Curb)
Jack Guthrie and his Oklahomans; *Birth Of A Dream-Capitol's Early
Hits-C* . . . . (Capitol)
Great Records Of The Decade-'40s-Country-C. . . . . (Curb)
Kay Starr; *Kay Starr-Country.* . . . .(Crescendo)
Old Chisholm Trail
Michael Martin Murphey; *Cowboy Songs* . . . . (Warner Western)
Randy Travis; *Wind In The Wire.* . . . .(Warner Bros.)
Old Nashville Cowboys
Hank Williams, Jr.; *Whiskey Bent & Hell Bound* . . . . (WB/Curb)
Old Paint
Chris LeDoux; *Old Cowboy Classics* . . . . (Capitol)
Western Tunesmith . . . . (Liberty)
Linda Ronstadt; *Simple Dreams* . . . . (Asylum)
Oregon Trail
Sons Of The Pioneers; *Sunset On The Range* . . . . (Pair)
Over The Santa Fe Trail
Sons Of The Pioneers; *Empty Saddles* . . . .(MCA)
Tumbling Tumbleweeds . . . .(MCA Special Prod.)
Palo Alto Cowboy
Reilly & Maloney; *Profiles.* . . . . (Freckle)
Plastic Saddle
Danny O'Keefe; *American Roulette* . . . .(Warner Bros.)
Prisoner For Life
Skip Gorman; *A Cowboy's Wild Song To His Herd* . . . . (Rounder)
Queen Of The Cowboy Cafe
Si Kahn; *Home* . . . . (Flying Fish)
Ragtime Cowboy Joe
Jo Stafford; *Capitol Collectors Series-Jo Stafford* . . . . (Capitol)
Spike Jones & His City Slickers; *King Of Corn* . . . . (Glendale)
Rhinestone Cowboy
Glen Campbell; *Country's Greatest Hits-#6-Superstars-C* . . . . (Priority)
Glen Campbell-Classics Collection. . . . . (Capitol)
Glen Campbell-Live. . . . . (Capitol)
Rhinestone Cowboy . . . . (Capitol)
Very Best Of Glen Campbell . . . . (Capitol)
Ride Concrete Cowboy, Ride
Roy Rogers & Sons Of The Pioneers; *ST/Smokey And The Bandit* . . . .(MCA)
Ride 'Em Cowboy
Roy Rogers & Sons Of The Pioneers; *Roy Rogers & Sons Of The
Pioneers* . . . . (Varese Sarabande)
Ride 'Em Cowboy
Paul Davis; *Ride 'Em Cowboy* . . . . (Bang)
Ride On Cowboy
Alvin Lee/Ten Years Later; *Ride On* . . . . (RSO)
Ridin' Down The Canyon
Gene Autry; *Columbia Historic Edition-Gene Autry* . . . . (Columbia)
Western Classics . . . . (Columbia)
Riders In The Sky; *Cowboy Way* . . . .(MCA)
Willie Nelson & Leon Russell; *One For The Road.* . . . . (Columbia)
Ro Deo Deo Cowboy
Jerry Jeff Walker; *A Man Must Carry On* . . . .(MCA)
Roamin' Wyoming
Randy Travis; *Wind In The Wire.* . . . .(Warner Bros.)
Rodeo Cowboys
Lynn Anderson; *Lynn Anderson's Greatest Hits-#2.* . . . . (Columbia)
Rope The Moon
John Michael Montgomery; *Kickin' It Up* . . . . (Atlantic)
Roy Rogers
Elton John; *Goodbye Yellow Brick Road* . . . . (Polydor)
Saddle The Cow
Dr. John; *Brightest Smile In Town* . . . .(Clean Cuts)

She Couldn't Change Me
Montgomery Gentry; *Carrying On* . . . . (Columbia)
Should've Been A Cowboy
Toby Keith; *Toby Keith.* . . . . (Mercury)
Slim Carter
Nitty Gritty Dirt Band; *All The Good Times* . . . .(United Artists)
So You Think You're A Cowboy
Emmylou Harris; *ST/Honeysuckle Rose* . . . . (Columbia)
ST/The Electric Horseman . . . . (Columbia)
So You Want To Be A Cowboy
Chris LeDoux; *Gold Buckle Dreams* . . . . (Liberty)
He Rides The Wild Horses . . . . (Liberty)
Radio & Rodeo Hits . . . . (Liberty)
Somebody Buy This Cowgirl A Beer
Tanya Tucker; *Tanya Tucker Live.* . . . . (MCA Special Prod.)
Someday Soon
Chris LeDoux; *Rodeo Songs Old & New.* . . . . (Liberty)
Ian & Sylvia; *Ian & Sylvia's Greatest Hits* . . . . (Vanguard)
Northern Journey. . . . . (Vanguard)
Judy Collins; *Colors Of The Day-The Best Of Judy Collins* . . . . (Elektra)
Who Knows Where The Time Goes. . . . . (Elektra)
Moe Bandy; *Moe Bandy's Greatest Hits* . . . . (Columbia)
Rodeo Romeo . . . . (Columbia)
Suzy Bogguss; *Aces* . . . . (Liberty)
Suzy Bogguss' Greatest Hits. . . . . (Liberty)
Song Of A Cowboy
Skip Gorman; *A Cowboy's Wild Song To His Herd.* . . . . (Rounder)
Space Cowboy
Steve Miller Band; *Best Of Steve Miller 1968-1973* . . . . (Capitol)
Steve Miller Band-Anthology. . . . . (Capitol)
Space Cowboy (Yippie-Yi-Yay)
'N Sync featuring Lisa "Left Eye" Lopes; *No Strings Attached* . . . . . .(Jive)
Stampede
Chris LeDoux; *Chris LeDoux-20 Greatest Hits* . . . . (Capitol)
Still They Ride
Journey; *Escape* . . . . (Columbia)
Strawberry Roan
Marty Robbins; *Gunfighter Ballads & Trail Songs* . . . . (Legacy)
Streets Of Laredo
Buck Owens & The Buckaroos; *Buck Owens & The Buckaroos-Live At
Carnegie Hall* . . . . (Country Music Foundation)
Marty Robbins; *Cowboy Super Hits-C* . . . . (Columbia)
Marty Robbins' All-Time Greatest Hits . . . . (Columbia)
Marty Robbins-More Greatest Hits . . . . (Columbia)
More Gunfighter Ballads & Trail Songs. . . . . (Columbia)
Rex Allen; *Great American Singing Cowboys-C* . . . . (Republic/Universal)
Sweet Baby James
James Taylor; *James Taylor's Greatest Hits* . . . . (Warner Bros.)
Sweet Baby James . . . . (Warner Bros.)
Take Me Back To My Boots & Saddle
Gene Autry; *Essential Gene Autry* . . . . (Columbia)
Texas Cowboy
Luther "Guitar Jr." Johnson & His Magic Rockers; *I Want To Groove
With You* . . . .(Bullseye Blues)
Theme From "Bonanza"
Al Caiola & His Orchestra; *Songs Of The West-#4-Movie & Television
Themes-C.* . . . . (Rhino)
Cincinnati Pops Orchestra/Erich Kunzel; *Round-Up* . . . .(Telarc)
Original Soundtrack; *Television's Greatest Hits-#1-C* . . . . (TVT)
TV Classic Themes: 25th Anniversary Edition-C . . . .(Breakable)
Theme From "Branded"
Original Soundtrack; *Television's Greatest Hits-#1-C* . . . . (TVT)
Theme From "Have Gun Will Travel" (Ballad Of Paladin)
Duane Eddy; *Duane Eddy-Pure Gold* . . . .(RCA)
Johnny Western; *Columbia Country Classics-#3-Americana-C.* . . . . . (Columbia)
Television's Greatest Hits-#7-Cable Ready-C . . . . (TVT)
Theme From "Midnight Cowboy"
Cincinnati Pops Orchestra/Erich Kunzel; *Hollywood's Greatest
Hits-#2.* . . . .(Telarc)
Theme From "Rawhide"
Blues Brothers; *Original Soundtrack* . . . .(Atlantic)
Frankie Laine; *CBS: The First 50 Years* . . . . (TVT)
Cowboy Super Hits-C . . . . (Columbia)
Television's Greatest Hits-#2-C. . . . . (TVT)
Riders In The Sky; *Cowboy Way* . . . . (Rounder)
Theme From "The High Chapparal"
Original Soundtrack; *Television's Greatest Hits-#5-In Living Color-C* . . . (TVT)
Theme From "The Lone Ranger" (William Tell Overture)
Boston Pops Orchestra; *TV Classics-C* . . . .(RCA)
Boston Pops Orchestra/Arthur Fiedler; *Fiedler-Greatest Hits* . . . .(RCA)
Original Soundtrack; *Television's Greatest Hits-#7-Cable Ready-C* . . . (TVT)
Spike Jones & His City Slickers; *Best Of Spike Jones & His City
Slickers* . . . .(RCA)
This Cowboy Song
Sting; *Fields Of Gold-The Best Of Sting 1984-1994* . . . . (A&M)
This Ol' Cowboy
Marshall Tucker Band; *Marshall Tucker Band's Greatest Hits* . . . . . (Capricorn)
Where We All Belong . . . . (AJK Music)

True Western Movie
Chris LeDoux; *Songs Of Rodeo & Country* . . . . (Liberty)
Tumbling Tumbleweeds
Billy Vaughn; *Billy Vaughn's Greatest Hits* . . . .(Curb)
Gene Autry; *Essential Gene Autry* . . . . (Columbia)
Meat Puppets; *Meat Puppets* . . . . (SST)
Michael Martin Murphey; *Cowboy Songs* . . . . (Warner Western)
Roy Rogers/K.T. Oslin/Restless Heart; *Roy Rogers Tribute-C* . . . . (RCA)
Sons Of The Pioneers; *The Country Music Hall Of Fame-Sons Of The
    Pioneers* . . . . (MCA)
Twilight On The Trail
Michael Nesmith; *Tropical Campfires* . . . .(Pacific Arts)
Utah Carol
Harry K. McClintock; *Cowboy Songs On
    Folkways-C* . . . .(Smithsonian Folkways)
Marty Robbins; *Gunfighter Ballads & Trail Songs* . . . . (Legacy)
Utah Carroll
Skip Gorman; *A Cowboy's Wild Song To His Herd* . . . . (Rounder)
Wanted Dead Or Alive
Bon Jovi; *Slippery When Wet* . . . . (Jambco)
The Concert For New York City-C . . . . (Columbia)
What The Cowgirls Do
Vince Gill; *When Love Finds You* . . . . (MCA)
Whatcha Gonna Do With A Cowboy
Chris LeDoux & Garth Brooks; *Whatcha Gonna Do With A Cowboy* . . . (Liberty)
When I Camped Under The Stars
Roy Rogers; *Songs Of The West-#3-Gene Autry & Roy Rogers-C* . . . . . . (Rhino)
Where Have All The Cowboys Gone?
Paula Cole; *This Fire* . . . . (Imago)
Whoopee Ti Yi Yo
Burl Ives; *Best Of Burl Ives* . . . . (MCA)
David Bromberg; *How Late'll Ya Play 'Til?* . . . .(Fantasy)
Roy Rogers & Sons Of The Pioneers; *Roy Rogers & Sons Of The
    Pioneers* . . . .(Varese Sarabande)
Woody Guthrie & Cisco Houston; *Cowboy Songs On
    Folkways-C* . . . .(Smithsonian Folkways)
Wind In The Wire
Randy Travis; *Wind In The Wire* . . . . (Warner Bros.)
Your Friend In The Cowboy Hat (The Viagra Song)
Croatan; *Violent Passion Surrogate* . . . . (Man's Ruin)

**CRAZY, Anxious, Confused, Dizzy, Insanity, Mental Illness,
Nervous, Neurosis, Psychiatry, Spaced Out, Stress, Tense**
    See Also: **ALCOHOL, BREAK, DESPAIR, LOVE (various), LOW
    SELF-ESTEEM, PAIN & HEALING, SADNESS, STUCK, THINKING
    & KNOWING**

(You Drive Me) Crazy
Britney Spears; *...Baby One More Time* . . . . (Jive)
Now That's What I Call Music!-#4-C . . . .(Virgin)
19th Nervous Breakdown
Rolling Stones; *Big Hits (High Tide & Green Grass)* . . . . (Abkco)
got Live if you want it! . . . . (Abkco)
Hot Rocks 1964-1971 . . . . (Abkco)
Singles Collection-The London Years . . . . (Abkco)
Absent-Minded Me
Barbra Streisand; *People* . . . . (Columbia)
Acute Schizophrenia Paranoia Blues
Kinks; *Everybody's In Show-Biz* . . . . (Rhino)
Muswell Hillbillies . . . . (VelVel)
Afraid
Motley Crue; *Generation Swine* . . . .(Beyond)
Motley Crue's Greatest Hits . . . .(Beyond)
Ain't It Crazy
Lightnin' Hopkins; *Hootin' The Blues* . . . . (Prestige)
Lightnin' . . . . (Arhoolie)
Ain't It Great To Be Crazy
Wonder Kids; *Really Silly Songs* . . . . (Madacy)
Aladdin Sane
David Bowie; *Aladdin Sane* . . . . (Rykodisc)
Changestwobowie . . . .(RCA)
David Live . . . . (Rykodisc)
All For You
Sister Hazel; *...Somewhere More Familiar* . . . . (Universal)
Sister Hazel . . . . (Universal)
All Lovers Are Deranged
David Gilmour; *About Face* . . . . (Columbia)
All Mixed Up
Tom Petty And The Heartbreakers; *Let Me Up (I've Had Enough)* . . . . . . (MCA)
All Mixed Up
311; *311* . . . . (Capricorn)
All Mixed Up
Cars; *The Cars* . . . . (Elektra)
All Shook Up
Elvis Presley; *Elvis Aron Presley* . . . . (RCA)
Elvis As Recorded At Madison Square Garden . . . .(RCA)

Elvis' Golden Records . . . . (RCA)
Elvis Presley-Pure Gold . . . . (RCA)
From Memphis To Vegas/From Vegas To Memphis . . . . (RCA)
All The Madmen
David Bowie; *Man Who Sold The World* . . . . (Rykodisc)
Am I Going Crazy
Korn; *Issues* . . . . (Immortal/Epic)
Are You Crazy
Freddie McGregor; *Come On Over* . . . . (Real Authentic Sound)
Armed & Crazy
Johnny Paycheck; *Armed & Crazy* . . . . (Epic)
At My Front Door
Nilsson; *Son Of Schmilsson* . . . . (RCA)
Baby Drives Me Crazy
Thin Lizzy; *Live And Dangerous* . . . . (Warner Bros.)
Babydoll
Mariah Carey; *Butterfly* . . . .(Columbia)
Back 2 Good
Matchbox Twenty; *Yourself Or Someone Like You* . . . .(Lava)
Back At The Funny Farm
Motorhead; *Another Perfect Day* . . . .(Mercury)
Bad Religion
Godsmack; *Godsmack* . . . . (Republic/Universal)
Ball Of Confusion (That's What The World Is Today)
Temptations; *All The Million-Sellers* . . . .(Motown)
Compact Command Performances-Temptations . . . . (Motown)
Songs Of Protest-C . . . .(Rhino)
Temptations' Greatest Hits-#2 . . . . (Motown)
Temptations-Anthology-The Best Of The Temptations . . . . (Motown)
Top 10 With A Bullet-Motown Male Groups-C . . . . (Motown)
Ballad Of Lucy Jordan
Marianne Faithfull; *Blazing Away* . . . .(Island)
Collection Of Her Best Recordings . . . . (Island)
Basket Case
Green Day; *Dookie* . . . . (Reprise)
Beautiful Disaster
311; *Live!* . . . .(Capricorn)
Transistor . . . . (Capricorn)
Beep A Freak
Gap Band; *Gap Band VI* . . . . (Total Experience)
Bewitched
Anita O'Day; *Anita Sings The Most* . . . . (Verve)
Barbra Streisand; *Third Album* . . . . (Columbia)
Doris Day; *Doris Day's Greatest Hits* . . . . (Columbia)
Original Cast; *Pal Joey* . . . . (Columbia)
Bitter Sweet Symphony
Verve; *Urban Hymns* . . . .(Hut/Virgin)
Blame It On Texas
Mark Chesnutt; *Mark Chesnutt's Greatest Hits* . . . .(Decca)
Too Cold At Home . . . . (MCA)
Bleed Together
Soundgarden; *A-Sides* . . . . (A&M)
Blow Top Blues
Esther Phillips; *Confessin' The Blues-Jazzlore-#41* . . . .(Rhino)
Etta James & Huston Person; *Sugar* . . . . (Muse)
Koko Taylor; *From The Heart Of A Woman* . . . . (Alligator)
Blue Love
O'Kanes; *Tired Of The Runnin'* . . . . (Columbia)
Blurry
Puddle Of Mudd; *Come Clean* . . . .(Flawless/Geffen/Interscope)
Borderline
Madonna; *Immaculate Collection* . . . . (Sire)
Madonna . . . . (Sire)
Royal Box . . . . (Sire)
Boy Crazy
Tubes; *Tubes* . . . . (A&M)
What Do You Want From Live . . . . (A&M)
Brain Damage
Pink Floyd; *Dark Side Of The Moon* . . . .(Capitol)
Pink Floyd-Gift Set . . . .(Capitol)
Works . . . .(Capitol)
Brain Stew
Green Day; *Insomniac* . . . . (Reprise)
Breakdown
Mariah Carey featuring Bone Thugs-N-Harmony; *Butterfly* . . . .(Columbia)
Breakdown
Queensryche; *Q2k* . . . . (Atlantic)
Breakdown
Tantric; *Tantric* . . . . (Maverick)
Breakout
Foo Fighters; *There Is Nothing Left To Lose* . . . . (Roswell/RCA)
Brian Wilson
Barenaked Ladies; *Gordon* . . . . (Reprise)
Rock Spectacle . . . . (Reprise)
Burnout
Green Day; *Dookie* . . . . (Reprise)
Call Me Irresponsible
Frank Sinatra; *Sinatra: A Man And His Music* . . . . (Reprise)

Sinatra's Sinatra . . . . (Reprise)
Jackie Gleason; *Best Of Jackie Gleason & His Orchestra* . . . . (Curb)
Robert Goulet; *Robert Goulet-16 Most Requested Songs* . . . . (Columbia)
Rosemary Clooney; *Rosemary Clooney Sings The Music Of Jimmy Van
  Heusen* . . . .(Concord Jazz)

Candy Cane Madness
Lowell George; *Lightning-Rod Man* . . . . (Rhino)

Can't Help It
Jon B.; *Cool Relax* . . . . (Yab Yum/550)

Can't Wait
Bob Dylan; *Time Out Of Mind* . . . . (Columbia)

Chantilly Lace
Big Bopper; *45s On CD-#1-1956-1959-C* . . . . (Mercury)
  Cruisin'-1958-C . . . .(Increase)
  Oldies But Goodies-#4-C . . . . (Original Sound)
  ST/American Graffiti . . . . (MCA)
Jerry Lee Lewis; ''Killer'' Rocks On* . . . . (Mercury)
  Best Of Jerry Lee Lewis-#2 . . . . (Mercury)

Church Of The Poison Mind
Culture Club; *At Worst...The Best Of Boy George And Culture Club* . . . . . (SBK)
  Colour By Numbers . . . . (Virgin)

Cockeyed Optimist
Mitzi Gaynor; *ST/South Pacific* . . . . (RCA)
Original Cast; *South Pacific* . . . .(CBS Masterworks)

Come Undone
Duran Duran; *Duran Duran (The Wedding Album)* . . . . (Capitol)

Communication Breakdown
Led Zeppelin; *Led Zeppelin* . . . .(Atlantic)
  Led Zeppelin-Box Set . . . .(Atlantic)

Complicated
Carolyn Dawn Johnson; *Room With A View* . . . . (Arista)

Confusion
New Order; *Substance* . . . . (Qwest)

Confusion
Electric Light Orchestra; *Discovery* . . . . (Jet)

Cracking Up
Nick Lowe; *Basher: Best Of* . . . . (Columbia)
  Labour Of Lust . . . . (Columbia)
Rolling Stones; *Love You Live* . . . . (Virgin)

Crawling
Linkin Park; *Hybrid Theory* . . . .(Warner Bros.)

Crazay
Jesse Johnson & Sly Stone; *Shockadelica*. . . . . (A&M)

Crazed Weasel
Ricky Peterson; *Night Watch* . . . .(Warner Bros.)

Crazy
Boys; *The Boys* . . . . (Motown)

Crazy
Alana Davis; *Blame It On Me* . . . . (Elektra)

Crazy
Jimmie Dale Gilmore with Willie Nelson; *Red Hot + Country-C* . . . . (Mercury)
Kenny Rogers; *Kenny Rogers' Greatest Hits* . . . . (RCA)
  What About Me? . . . . (RCA)
Linda Ronstadt; *Hasten Down The Wind* . . . . (Asylum)
Patsy Cline; *Songwriter's Tribute* . . . .(MCA)
  ST/Sweet Dreams . . . .(MCA)
  The Patsy Cline Story . . . .(MCA)
Ray Price; *Ray Price's Greatest Hits-#2*. . . . . (Step One)
Willie Nelson; *Best Of Willie* . . . . (RCA)
  Healing Hands Of Time . . . . (Liberty)
  Nite Life-Greatest Hits & Rare Tracks . . . . (Rhino)
  Willie & Family Live . . . . (Columbia)

Crazy
K-Ci & JoJo; *Now That's What I Call Music!-#6-C* . . . . (Virgin)
  X. . . . .(MCA)

Crazy
Kay Starr; *Capitol Collectors Series-Kay Starr* . . . . (Capitol)

Crazy
R.E.M.; *Dead Letter Office* . . . .(I.R.S.)

Crazy
Supertramp; *Famous Last Words* . . . . (A&M)

Crazy
Manhattans; *Forever By Your Side* . . . . (Columbia)

Crazy
Aerosmith; *Get A Grip* . . . .(Geffen)

Crazy
Meat Puppets; *Huevos* . . . .(SST)

Crazy
Georgia Satellites; *In The Land Of Salvation & Sin* . . . . (Elektra)

Crazy
Miki Howard; *Love Confessions*. . . . .(Atlantic)

Crazy
Icehouse; *Man Of Colours* . . . . (Chrysalis)

Crazy
Neil Diamond; *Primitive* . . . . (Columbia)

Crazy
Seal; *Seal* . . . . (Sire)

Crazy About Her
Rod Stewart; *Out Of Order* . . . .(Warner Bros.)

Storyteller/The Complete Anthology: 1964-1990 . . . . (Warner Bros.)

Crazy Arms
Chuck Berry; *The Chess Box-Chuck Berry* . . . . (Chess)
Jerry Lee Lewis; *18 Original Sun Greatest Hits* . . . . (Rhino)
  Jerry Lee Lewis . . . . (Rhino)
  The Golden Hits Of Jerry Lee Lewis . . . .(Smash)
Linda Ronstadt; *Linda Ronstadt-Retrospective* . . . . (Capitol)
Patsy Cline; *Last Sessions* . . . . (MCA)
  Portrait Of Patsy Cline . . . . (MCA)
Ray Price; *Columbia Country Classics-#2-Honky Tonk Heroes-C* . . . (Columbia)
  Ray Price's Greatest Hits . . . . (Columbia)
  Ray Price's Greatest Hits-#1-3 . . . .(Step One)
Willie Nelson; *San Antonio Rose* . . . . (Columbia)

Crazy Babies
Ozzy Osbourne; *The Ozzman Cometh* . . . . (Epic)

Crazy Baby
Doug Sahm; *Juke Box Music* . . . .(Antone's)

Crazy Baby
Rodney Crowell; *Diamonds & Dirt* . . . . (Columbia)

Crazy Baldhead
Bob Marley & The Wailers; *Rastaman Vibration* . . . .(Tuff Gong)
  Rebel Music . . . .(Tuff Gong)
  Songs Of Freedom . . . .(Tuff Gong)

Crazy Bells
Marcels; *Best Of The Marcels* . . . . (Rhino)

Crazy 'Bout That Married Woman
Rockin' Dopsie; *Saturday Night Zydeco* . . . . (Maison De Soul)

Crazy Circles
Bad Company; *Desolation Angels*. . . . . (Swan Song)

Crazy Downtown
Allan Sherman; *New York Songs-C* . . . . (Rhino)

Crazy Eyes
Daryl Hall & John Oates; *Bigger Than Both Of Us* . . . . (RCA)

Crazy Faith
Alison Krauss & Union Station; *New Favorite* . . . . (Rounder)

Crazy Feelin'
Jefferson Starship; *Earth*. (Grunt)

Crazy For This Girl
Evan And Jaron; *Evan And Jaron* . . . . (Columbia)
  Now That's What I Call Music!-#6-C . . . .(Virgin)

Crazy For You
Madonna; *Immaculate Collection* . . . . (Sire)
  Royal Box . . . . (Sire)
  Something To Remember . . . .(Maverick/Sire)
  ST/Vision Quest . . . . (Geffen)

Crazy For You
Eboni Foster; *Just What You Want* . . . . (Nightbird/MCA)

Crazy For You
Heartbeats; *Best Of The Heartbeats* . . . . (Rhino)

Crazy For Your Love
Exile; *Exile's Greatest Hits* . . . . (Epic)
  Greatest Country Hits Of The '80s-1985-C . . . . (Columbia)
  Kentucky Hearts . . . . (Epic)

Crazy For Your Love
Bee Gees; *E-S-P* . . . . (Warner Bros.)

Crazy From The Heart
Bellamy Brothers; *Bellamy Brothers' Greatest Hits-#3* . . . . (MCA)
  Crazy From The Heart . . . . (MCA)

Crazy Heart
Forester Sisters; *Forester Sisters* . . . . (Warner Bros.)
Hank Williams With His Drifting Cowboys; *Hank Williams-24 Greatest
  Hits-#2*. . . . .(Polydor)
  Hank Williams-40 Greatest Hits. . . . .(Polydor)
  Hey Good Lookin' (December 1950-July 1951). . . . .(Polydor)
  Rare Takes & Radio Cuts . . . .(Polydor)

Crazy In Love
Kenny Rogers; *Love Is Strange* . . . . (Reprise)

Crazy In Love
Joe Cocker; *Civilized Man*. . . . . (Capitol)

Crazy Little Mama
Eldorados; *Greatest Groups Of The '50s-#2-C* . . . . (Collectables)
  Sock Hop-C . . . . (Dunhill Compact Classics)

Crazy Little Thing Called Love
Dwight Yoakam; *Last Chance For A Thousand Years-Greatest Hits From
  The '90s* . . . .(Reprise)
Queen; *Queen's Greatest Hits I & II* . . . . (Hollywood)
  The Game . . . . (Hollywood)

Crazy Love
Paul Anka; *Best Of Paul Anka* . . . . (Rhino)
  Paul Anka's 21 Golden Hits . . . . (RCA)
  Vintage Years '57-'61 . . . . (Sire)

Crazy Love
Brian McKnight; *Anytime* . . . . (Motown)
  I Remember You . . . . (Mercury)
  ST/Jason's Lyric. . . . . (Mercury)
Van Morrison; *Moondance* . . . . (Warner Bros.)

Crazy Love
Poco; *Backtracks*. . . . . (MCA)

Poco-Legend. . . . . (MCA)

Crazy Love
Allman Brothers Band; *Decade Of Hits-1969-1979* . . . . (Polydor)

Crazy Love
Joey Dee & the Starliters; *Hey Let's Twist! Best Of Joey Dee & The
Starliters* . . . . (Rhino)

Crazy Love
Buddy Guy; *Left My Blues In San Francisco* . . . . (Chess)

Crazy Love
Rita Coolidge; *Rita Coolidge-Classics-#5*. . . . . (A&M)

Crazy Love
Aaron Neville Featuring Robbie Robertson; *ST/Phenomenon* . . . . (Reprise)

Crazy Love
Bryan Ferry; *ST/She's Having A Baby*. . . . . (I.R.S.)

Crazy Love, Vol. II
Paul Simon; *Graceland* . . . . (Warner Bros.)

Crazy Mama
Rolling Stones; *Black And Blue* . . . . (Rolling Stones)
Sucking In The Seventies. . . . . (Rolling Stones)

Crazy Mama
J.J. Cale; *Naturally* . . . . (MCA)

Crazy Man Crazy
Bill Haley; *Still Rockin' Around The Clock* . . . . (BMG Special Prod.)

Crazy Man Michael
Fairport Convention; *Fairport Convention-Chronicles* . . . . (A&M)
In Real Time-Live '87 . . . . (Island)
Liege & Lief . . . . (A&M)

Crazy On You
Heart; *Dreamboat Annie* . . . . (Capitol)
Heart's Greatest Hits/Live . . . . (Epic)

Crazy Over You
Foster & Lloyd; *Crazy Over You* . . . . (RCA)
Foster & Lloyd . . . . (RCA)
Ricky Van Shelton; *Wild-Eyed Dream* . . . . (Columbia)

Crazy Over You
Maureen Gray; *45-#1163*. . . . . (Collectables)

Crazy She Calls Me
Abbey Lincoln; *Blue Series-Female Vocals-C* . . . . (Blue Note)
Aretha Franklin; *Aretha's Jazz* . . . . (Rhino)
Billie Holiday; *From The Original Decca Masters* . . . . (MCA)
Joe Mooney; *Erteguns' New York, N.Y. Cabaret Music-C* . . . . (Atlantic)
Linda Ronstadt; *What's New* . . . . (Asylum)
Lurlean Hunter; *Atlantic Jazz-Singers-C* . . . . (Atlantic)

Crazy Things I Do
Sammie; *From The Bottom To The Top* . . . . (Freeworld/Capitol)

Crazy Train
Ozzy Osbourne; *Blizzard Of Ozz* . . . .(Jet)
The Ozzman Cometh . . . . (Epic)
Tribute . . . . (Epic)

Crazy Water
Elton John; *Blue Moves* . . . . (MCA)

Crazy Woman
Juluka; *Stand Your Ground* . . . . (Warner Bros.)

Crush
Dave Matthews Band; *Before These Crowded Streets*. . . . .(RCA)

Dance With Me
Debelah Morgan; *Dance With Me* . . . . (Atlantic)
Totally Hits-#3-C . . . . (Atlantic)

Daysleeper
R.E.M.; *Up* . . . . (Warner Bros.)

Dazed And Confused
Led Zeppelin; *Classic Rock 1966-1988-C* . . . . (Atlantic)
Led Zeppelin . . . . (Atlantic)
Led Zeppelin-Box Set . . . . (Atlantic)
ST/The Song Remains The Same . . . . (Swan Song)

Dazed And Confused
Jake Holmes; *Nuggets-#10-Folk Rock-C* . . . . (Rhino)

Deja Voodoo
Kenny Wayne Shepherd; *Ledbetter Heights* . . . . (Giant)

Delirious
ZZ Top; *Afterburner* . . . . (Warner Bros.)

Delirious
Prince; *1999*. . . . . (Warner Bros.)

Delirium
Euphoria; *Euphoria*. . . . . (Six Degrees)

Devil Or Angel
Bobby Vee; *Best Of Bobby Vee* . . . . (EMI)
Bobby Vee-Golden Greats . . . . (Liberty)
Bobby Vee-Legendary Masters . . . . (EMI)
Clovers; *Atlantic Rhythm & Blues 1947-1974-#3 (1955-1958)-C* . . . . (Atlantic)
Oldies But Goodies-#2-C . . . . (Original Sound)
Very Best Of The Clovers . . . . (Rhino)

Diamonds On The Soles Of Her Shoes
Paul Simon; *Concert In The Park-August 15 1991* . . . . (Warner Bros.)
Graceland. . . . . (Warner Bros.)
Negotiations And Love Songs, 1971-1986 . . . . (Warner Bros.)

Diary Of A Madman
Ozzy Osbourne; *Diary Of A Madman* . . . .(Jet)

Dizzy
Tommy Roe; *Original Classic Oldies Of The '60s-#10-C* . . . . (MCA)
Super Hits-#1-C . . . .(Gusto)
Tommy Roe's Greatest Hits. . . . . (MCA)

Dizzy
Goo Goo Dolls; *Dizzy Up The Girl*. . . . . (Warner Sunset/Reprise)

Dizzy Atmosphere
Dizzy Gillespie; *Dizzy's Diamonds-Best Of The Verve Years* . . . .(Verve)
Oscar Peterson & Dizzy Gillespie; *Oscar Peterson & Dizzy Gillespie* . . . (Pablo)

Dizzy Miss Lizzy
Beatles; *Beatles VI* . . . .(Capitol)
Rock 'N' Roll Music . . . .(Capitol)
The Beatles At The Hollywood Bowl . . . .(Capitol)
Ronnie Hawkins and The Hawks; *Best Of Ronnie Hawkins and The
Hawks*. . . . .(Rhino)

Don't Leave Me
Blackstreet; *Another Level* . . . . (Interscope)

Don't Stop
Wade Hayes; *Old Enough To Know Better* . . . .(Columbia)
Steppin' Country-#2-C . . . .(Columbia)
Super Hits Of 1995-C . . . . (Epic)

Down With The Sickness
Disturbed; *The Sickness* . . . . (Giant)

East Tennessee Blues/Goin' Crazy
Stepping Stones; *Fresh Old Time String Band Music* . . . .(Rounder)

Every Time I Get Around You
David Lee Murphy; *Gettin' Out The Good Stuff* . . . . (MCA)

Everything For Free
K's Choice; *Cocoon Choice* . . . . (550 Music)

Excitable Boy
Warren Zevon; *Excitable Boy* . . . . (Asylum)
Quiet Normal Life-Best Of Warren Zevon . . . . (Asylum)
Stand In The Fire . . . . (Asylum)

Ex-Factor
Lauryn Hill; *The Miseducation Of Lauryn Hill* . . . . (Ruffhouse/Columbia)

Fire Escape
Fastball; *All The Pain Money Can Buy*. . . . .(Hollywood)

Flagpole Sitta
Harvey Danger; *Now That's What I Call Music!-#1-C* . . . . (Virgin)
Where Have All The Merrymakers Gone . . . . (Slash)

Foggy Mental Breakdown
Steppenwolf; *Steppenwolf 7*. . . . . (MCA)

Freak A Zoid
Midnight Star; *Midnight Star's Greatest Hits* . . . . (Solar)
No Parking On The Dance Floor. . . . . (Solar)

Freak Me
Silk; *Lose Control* . . . . (Elektra)

Freak Of The Week
Marvelous 3; *Hey Album* . . . . (HiFi/Elektra)

Freak On A Leash
Korn; *Follow The Leader*. . . . . (Immortal/Epic)

Freak Out
Chic; *LeFreak* . . . . (Atlantic)

Freak-A-Ristic
Atlantic Starr; *As The Band Turns* . . . . (A&M)
Atlantic Starr-Classics-#10. . . . . (A&M)
Secret Lovers: Best Of Atlantic Starr. . . . . (A&M)

Gimme All Your Lovin' Or I Will Kill You
Macy Gray; *The Id* . . . . (Epic)

Give It Up Or Let Me Go
Dixie Chicks; *Wide Open Spaces*. . . . . (Monument)

Givin' Water To A Drowning Man
Lee Roy Parnell; *We All Get Lucky Sometimes* . . . . (Career)

Go Away
Lorrie Morgan; *Lorrie Morgan-Super Hits* . . . . (RCA)
Shakin' Things Up . . . . (BNA)
To Get To You-Greatest Hits Collection . . . . (BNA)

Go Insane
Lindsey Buckingham; *Go Insane*. . . . . (Warner Bros.)

God Was Drunk When He Made Me
Jim White; *No Such Place* . . . . (Luaka Bop)

Goin' Crazy
David Lee Roth; *Eat 'Em & Smile* . . . . (Warner Bros.)

Goin' Down
Greg Guidry; *Over The Line*. . . . . (Badland)

Goin' Out Of My Head
Lettermen; *Best Of The Lettermen-#2* . . . .(Capitol)
The Lettermen's All-Time Greatest Hits . . . .(Capitol)
Little Anthony And The Imperials; *Best Of Little Anthony And The
Imperials* . . . .(Rhino)
EMI Legends Of Rock & Roll-24 Greatest Hits-C . . . . (EMI)

Going Out Of My Mind
McBride & The Ride; *Sacred Ground* . . . . (MCA)

Gone Crazy
Alan Jackson; *High Mileage* . . . .(Arista)

Good Intentions
Toad The Wet Sprocket; *ST/Friends-Music From The TV Series* . . . . . (Reprise)

Gotta Get Away
Offspring; *Smash* . . . . (Epitaph)
Great Balls Of Fire
Jerry Lee Lewis; *Billboard Top Rock 'N' Roll Hits-1958-C* . . . . (Rhino)
Jerry Lee Lewis-Original Golden Hits-#1 . . . . (Sun)
Jerry Lee Lewis-Original Golden Hits-#1 . . . . (Sun)
Jerry Lee's Greatest! . . . . (Rhino)
Oldies But Goodies-#12-C . . . . (Original Sound)
Original Memphis Rock & Roll . . . . (Sun)
Rock & Roll Show-C . . . . (Gusto)
Twenty Classic Jerry Lee Lewis Hits . . . . (Original Sound)
Helter Skelter
Aerosmith; *Pandora's Box* . . . . (Columbia)
Beatles; *Beatles-Box Set* . . . . (Capitol)
Rarities . . . . (Capitol)
Rock 'N' Roll Music . . . . (Capitol)
The Beatles (White Album) . . . . (Capitol)
Motley Crue; *Shout At The Devil* . . . . (Elektra)
Pat Benatar; *Precious Time* . . . .(Chrysalis)
Siouxsie And The Banshees; *Nocturne* . . . . (Geffen)
The Scream . . . . (Geffen)
U2; *Rattle And Hum* . . . . (Island)
Honky-Tonk Crazy
Gene Watson; *Honky-Tonk Crazy* . . . .(Epic)
George Strait; *Strait From The Heart* . . . .(MCA)
Hot! Wild! Unrestricted! Crazy Love
Millie Jackson; *Imitation Of Love* . . . . (Jive)
How Bizarre
OMC; *How Bizarre* . . . .(Huh!/Mercury)
Hypnotized
Fleetwood Mac; *25 Years-The Chain* . . . .(Warner Bros.)
I Almost Lost My Mind
Eddy Arnold; *World Of Hits* . . . . (MGM)
Fats Domino; *Fats Domino's Greatest Hits* . . . . (MCA)
Ivory Joe Hunter; *Since I Met You Baby* . . . . (Mercury)
Pat Boone; *Pat Boone's Greatest Hits* . . . . (Curb)
I Am
Train; *Train* . . . .(Aware/C2/Columbia)
I Belong To You (Every Time I See Your Face)
Rome; *Rome* . . . . (RCA)
I Don't Know
Gretchen Peters; *Gretchen Peters* . . . . (Purple Crayon Prod.)
I Don't Want To
Toni Braxton; *Secrets* . . . . (LaFace)
I Drive Myself Crazy
'N Sync; *'N Sync* . . . . (RCA)
Totally Hits-#2-C . . . . (Elektra)
I Go Crazy
Paul Davis; *Best Of Paul Davis* . . . . (Bang)
Billboard Top Hits-1978-C . . . . (Rhino)
Paul Davis' Greatest Hits . . . .(Epic)
Singer Of Songs-Teller Of Tales . . . . (Bang)
I Go To Pieces
Del Shannon; *Rock On!* . . . . (Gone Gator)
Peter And Gordon; *Best Of Peter And Gordon* . . . . (Rhino)
History Of British Rock-#3-C . . . . (Rhino)
Southern Pacific; *County Line* . . . .(Warner Bros.)
Southern Pacific's Greatest Hits . . . .(Warner Bros.)
I Go Wild
Rolling Stones; *Voodoo Lounge* . . . . (Virgin)
I Got Id
Pearl Jam; *Merkinball* . . . .(Epic)
I Guess I'm Crazy
Jim Reeves; *Billboard Top Country Hits-1964-C* . . . . (Rhino)
Essential Jim Reeves . . . . (RCA)
I Had The Craziest Dream
Frank Sinatra; *Trilogy: Pasts, Present, Future* . . . . (Reprise)
I Need A Lover
John Cougar; *John Cougar* . . . . (Riva)
Pat Benatar; *In The Heat Of The Night* . . . .(Chrysalis)
I Think I'm Paranoid
Garbage; *Now That's What I Call Music!-#2-C* . . . . (Virgin)
Version 2.0 . . . . (Almo Sounds)
I Think You've Got Your Fools Mixed Up
Brenton Wood; *Brenton Wood-18 Best* . . . . (Original Sound)
I Try To Think About Elvis
Patty Loveless; *Patty Loveless-Classics* . . . .(Epic)
When Fallen Angels Fly . . . .(Epic)
I'd Lie For You (And That's The Truth)
Meat Loaf; *Welcome To The Neighborhood* . . . .(MCA)
I'll Go Crazy
Andy Griggs; *You Won't Ever Be Lonely* . . . . (RCA)
I'm Freaky
O'Bryan; *You And I* . . . . (Capitol)
Impulsive
Wilson Phillips; *Wilson Phillips* . . . . (SBK)
Infatuation
Rod Stewart; *Camouflage* . . . .(Warner Bros.)
Downtown Train-Selections From The Storyteller Anthology . . .(Warner Bros.)

Storyteller/The Complete Anthology: 1964-1990 . . . . (Warner Bros.)
It Ain't Cool To Be Crazy About You
George Strait; *Country Classics-#7-1986-1987-C* . . . . (Universal)
George Strait-Number 7 . . . . (MCA)
George Strait's Greatest Hits-#2 . . . . (MCA)
MCA #1 Hits Of The '80s-#2-C . . . . (MCA Special Prod.)
It Hit Me Like A Hammer
Huey Lewis and the News; *Hard At Play* . . . . (EMI)
It's All In Your Head
Diamond Rio; *Diamond Rio IV* . . . . (Arista)
Diamond Rio's Greatest Hits . . . . (Arista)
I've Got My Eyes On You
Jessica Simpson; *Sweet Kisses* . . . . (Columbia)
Jane Doe
Alicia Keys; *Songs In A Minor* . . . . (J)
Jump Right In
Urge; *Master Of Styles* . . . . (Immortal/Epic)
Jungle Love
Steve Miller Band; *Book Of Dreams* . . . . (Capitol)
Steve Miller Band-Gift Set . . . . (Capitol)
Steve Miller Band-Live . . . . (Capitol)
Steve Miller Band's Greatest Hits-1974-78 . . . . (Capitol)
Just Another Nervous Wreck
Supertramp; *Breakfast In America* . . . . (A&M)
Just Crazy Love
Fleetwood Mac; *Mystery To Me* . . . . (Reprise)
Kryptonite
3 Doors Down; *Better Life* . . . . (Republic/Universal)
Now That's What I Call Music!-#5-C . . . . (Virgin)
Land Of Confusion
Genesis; *Invisible Touch* . . . .(Atlantic)
Last Resort
Papa Roach; *Infest* . . . .(DreamWorks/SKG)
Le Freak
Chic; *Dance Dance Dance-Best Of* . . . .(Atlantic)
Let's Go Crazy
Sly Fox; *Let's Go Crazy* . . . . (Capitol)
Let's Go Crazy
Prince and the Revolution; *ST/Purple Rain* . . . . (Warner Bros.)
Life In The Fast Lane
Eagles; *Eagles Live* . . . .(Asylum)
Hotel California . . . .(Asylum)
ST/FM . . . . (MCA)
Little Crazy
Fight; *War Of Words* . . . . (Epic)
Little Left Of Center
Randy Travis; *A Man Ain't Made Of Stone* . . . .(DreamWorks/SKG)
Livin' La Vida Loca
Ricky Martin; *Ricky Martin* . . . . (Columbia)
Loco
Iguanas; *Nuevo Boogaloo* . . . .(Margaritaville)
Lollypop (Crazy 'Bout)
Louis Jordan; *At The Swing Cat's Ball* . . . . (MCA)
Lonely Daze
Ginuwine; *The Bachelor* . . . .(550 Music)
Long Day
Matchbox Twenty; *Yourself Or Someone Like You* . . . . (Lava)
Losin' Your Mind
Pride & Glory; *Pride & Glory* . . . . (Geffen)
Losing My Mind
Bobby Short; *50 By Bobby Short* . . . .(Atlantic)
Cleo Laine; *Cleo Laine Sings Sondheim* . . . . (RCA)
Liza Minnelli; *Results* . . . .(Epic)
Original Broadway Cast; *Follies* . . . . (Capitol)
Original Cast; *ST/Follies-In Concert* . . . . (RCA Victor)
Love Bizarre
Sheila E.; *Romance 1600* . . . . (Paisley Park)
Love Her Madly
Doors; *Best Of The Doors* . . . . (Elektra)
Doors-Classics . . . . (Elektra)
L.A. Woman . . . . (Elektra)
Weird Scenes Inside The Gold Mine . . . . (Elektra)
Love Or Confusion
Jimi Hendrix Experience; *Are You Experienced?* . . . . (Reprise)
Lucky 4 You (Tonight I'm Just Me)
SHeDAISY; *The Whole Shebang* . . . .(Lyric Street)
Lunatic Fringe
Red Rider; *As Far As Siam* . . . . (Capitol)
Neruda + 3 . . . . (Capitol)
ST/Vision Quest . . . . (Geffen)
Mad About The Boy
Dinah Shore; *Dinah Shore-Love Songs* . . . . (Columbia)
Dinah Washington; *Dinah Washington-Golden Hits* . . . . (Mercury)
Mad About You
Belinda Carlisle; *Belinda* . . . . (I.R.S.)
Sting; *Soul Cages* . . . . (A&M)
Mad About You
Sting; *Soul Cages* . . . . (A&M)

Mad House
Robin Trower; *Victims Of The Fury* . . . . (Chrysalis)
Mad Love
Linda Ronstadt; *Different Drum* . . . . (Capitol)
Mad Season
Matchbox Twenty; *Mad Season By Matchbox Twenty* . . . . (Lava)
Madman Across The Water
Elton John; *Live In Australia With The Melbourne Symphony*
Orchestra. . . . . (MCA)
Madman Across The Water. . . . . (Polydor)
Madness
Elton John; *A Single Man* . . . . (MCA)
Madness
Madness; *One Step Beyond* . . . .(Sire)
Magnolia
J.J. Cale; *Naturally* . . . . (MCA)
Make Me Lose Control
Eric Carmen; *Best Of Eric Carmen* . . . . (Arista)
Dirty Dancing Live In Concert-C . . . .(RCA)
Mama He's Crazy
Judds; *Judds* . . . .(RCA)
Judds' Greatest Hits . . . . (MCA)
Why Not Me . . . . (MCA)
Mama Weer All Crazee Now
Quiet Riot; *Condition Critical* . . . . (Epic Portrait Assoc.)
Maniac
Michael Sembello; *Bossa Nova Hotel* . . . . (Warner Bros.)
ST/Flashdance . . . .(Casablanca)
Maniac
D.C. 3; *Program: Annihilator* . . . . (SST)
Manic Depression
Jeff Beck & Seal; *Stone Free: A Tribute To Jimi Hendrix-C* . . . .(Reprise)
Manic Depression
Jimi Hendrix Experience; *Are You Experienced?* . . . .(Reprise)
Manic Monday
Bangles; *Bangles' Greatest Hits* . . . .(Columbia)
Different Light . . . .(Columbia)
Memory Remains
Metallica; *Reload* . . . . (Elektra)
Mental Illness Can Be Beautiful
John Trubee & The Ugly Janitors Of America; *Naked Teenage Girls In Outer*
Space . . . .(Enigma)
Mi Vida Loca
Pam Tillis; *Sweetheart's Dance*. . . . . (Arista)
Midnight Madness
Clockwork; *Made In The U.S. Of Japan* . . . . (Mercury)
Midnight Madness
Foghat; *Stone Blue*. . . . .(Rhino)
Midnight Maniac
Krokus; *Blitz* . . . . (Arista)
Military Madness
Graham Nash; *Bread & Roses Festival Of Acoustic Music-#2-C* . . . . . .(Fantasy)
Songs For Beginners. . . . . (Atlantic)
Mimi
Maurice Chevalier; *Early Movie Hits* . . . .(DRG)
Nipper's Greatest Hits Of The '30s-#1-C . . . .(RCA)
ST/Pepe. . . . .(DRG)
Mind Blowin'
D.O.C.; *No One Can Do It Better* . . . . (Ruthless)
Mind Disaster
Initial Shock; *Nuggets-#8-Acid Rock-C*. . . . .(Rhino)
Miss You Like Crazy
Natalie Cole; *Good To Be Back* . . . . (Elektra)
Missing You
Mary J. Blige; *Share My World*. . . . . (MCA)
The Tour . . . . (MCA)
Mixed Up, Shook Up Girl
Mink De Ville; *Mink De Ville* . . . .(Capitol)
Motor City Madhouse
Ted Nugent; *Double Live Gonzo* . . . . (Epic)
Ted Nugent . . . . (Epic)
My Favorite Headache
Geddy Lee; *My Favorite Headache*. . . . . (Anthem/Atlantic)
My Own Worst Enemy
Lit; *A Place In The Sun* . . . .(RCA)
Negasonic Teenage Warhead
Monster Magnet; *Dopes To Infinity* . . . . (A&M)
Never Ever
All Saints; *All Saints* . . . . (London)
Now That's What I Call Music!-#1-C . . . .(Virgin)
New Beginning
Stir; *Holy Dogs* . . . . (Capitol)
No Control
Eddie Money; *Eddie Money's Greatest Hits-Sound Of Money* . . . . . .(Columbia)
No Control . . . .(Columbia)
No More "I Love You's"
Annie Lennox; *Medusa* . . . . (Arista)

Nobody In His Right Mind Would've Left Her
George Strait; *Country Classics-#6-1985-1986-C*. . . . . (Universal)
George Strait-Number 7 . . . . (MCA)
George Strait's Greatest Hits-#2. . . . . (MCA)
Obsession
Fem 2 Fem; *Woman To Woman* . . . . (Critique)
Obsession
Animotion; *Animotion* . . . .(Mercury)
Obsession-Best Of Animotion . . . .(Mercury)
VH-1 More Of The Big '80s-C. . . . .(Rhino)
Obvious
Christina Aguilera; *Christina Aguilera* . . . . (RCA)
Oh You Crazy Moon
Frank Sinatra; *Frank Sinatra Sings The Songs Of Van Heusen*
& Cahn . . . . (Reprise)
Moonlight Sinatra . . . . (Reprise)
Mark Murphy; *Mark Murphy Sings Nat's Choice-Nat "King" Cole*
Songbook-#1. . . . . (Muse)
One I Gave My Heart To
Aaliyah; *One In A Million* . . . .(BlackGround Enterp./Atlantic)
One Night Stand
J-Shin featuring La Tocha Scott; *My Soul, My Life* . . . . (Atlantic)
One Step Closer
Linkin Park; *Hybrid Theory* . . . . (Warner Bros.)
O'Sanity
John Lennon & Yoko Ono; *Milk & Honey* . . . . (Polydor)
Out Of Control
Jefferson Starship; *Winds Of Change*. . . . . (Grunt)
Out Of Control
U2; *Boy* . . . .(Island)
Out Of Control
Judy Collins; *Bread & Roses* . . . . (Elektra)
Out Of Control
Ted Nugent; *Cat Scratch Fever* . . . . (Epic)
Out Of Control
Saxon; *Denim & Leather* . . . . (Capitol)
Out Of Control
Eagles; *Desperado* . . . . (Asylum)
Out Of Control
Todd Rundgren; *Hermit Of Mink Hollow* . . . .(Rhino)
Out Of Control
Tribe After Tribe; *Tribe After Tribe* . . . . (Megaforce)
Out Of Control
Squeeze; *U.K. Squeeze*. . . . . (A&M)
Out Of Control
George Jones; *Very Best Of George Jones* . . . . (Epic)
Out Of My Mind
Buffalo Springfield; *Buffalo Springfield*. . . . .(Atco)
Over My Head
Fleetwood Mac; *25 Years-The Chain* . . . . (Warner Bros.)
Fleetwood Mac . . . . (Reprise)
Fleetwood Mac Live . . . . (Warner Bros.)
Fleetwood Mac's Greatest Hits . . . . (Warner Bros.)
Over You
Gary Puckett And The Union Gap; *Best Of Gary*
Puckett . . . . (Hollywood/DNA-Rounder)
Gary Puckett-Super Hits . . . .(Legacy)
Pac-Man Fever
Buckner & Garcia; *Pac Man Fever* . . . .(Columbia)
Party Up
DMX; *...And Then There Was X* . . . . (Ruff Ryders/IDJMG)
Poisoned Heart & A Twisted Memory
Richard Thompson; *Hand Of Kindness* . . . . (Hannibal)
Pop Pop Pop Goes My Mind
Levert; *Bloodline* . . . . (Atlantic)
Golden Age Of Black Music-1977-1988-C . . . . (Atlantic)
Porcelain
Moby; *Play*. . . . . (V2)
ST/Playing By Heart . . . .(Capitol)
ST/The Beach . . . . (Sire)
Possession Obsession
Daryl Hall & John Oates; *Big Bam Boom*. . . . . (RCA)
Daryl Hall & John Oates & Others; *Live At The Apollo* . . . . (RCA)
Pretty Vacant
Joan Jett; *The Hit List* . . . . (Epic)
Sex Pistols; *Live At Chelmsford Top Security Prison* . . . .(Restless)
Never Mind The Bollocks, Here's The Sex Pistols. . . . .(Warner Bros.)
Psycho Circus
Kiss; *Psycho Circus* . . . .(Mercury)
Psycho Dyke
Dead Serios; *Possessed By Polka*. (Long Song)
Psycho Killer
Talking Heads; *'77* . . . . (Sire)
Name Of This Band Is Talking Heads . . . . (Sire)
ST/Stop Making Sense . . . . (Sire)
Psycho Man
Black Sabbath; *Reunion* . . . . (Epic)

Psychotic Reaction
 Count Five; *Collectables Presents The History Of Rock-#6-C* . . . . (Collectables)
  Cruisin'-1966-C . . . .(Increase)
  Nuggets-#1-The Hits-C . . . . (Rhino)
  Nuggets-Classic Collection From The Psychedelic '60s-C . . . . (Rhino)
  Rockin' '60s-C . . . . (Priority)

Purple Haze
 Cure; *Stone Free: A Tribute To Jimi Hendrix-C* . . . . (Reprise)
 Jimi Hendrix; *Kiss The Sky* . . . . (Reprise)
  ST/Jimi Hendrix . . . . (Reprise)
 Jimi Hendrix Experience; *Are You Experienced?* . . . . (Reprise)
  Essential Jimi Hendrix . . . . (Reprise)
  Radio One . . . .(Rykodisc)
  Smash Hits . . . . (Reprise)
 Winger; *Winger* . . . . (Atlantic)

Push It
 Garbage; *Version 2.0* . . . . (Almo Sounds)

Questioning My Sanity
 L7; *Hungry For Stink* . . . . (Slash)

Radio Spot/Nervous Breakdown
 Bobby Fuller Four; *Tapes-#1* . . . . (Rhino)

Rattlesnake
 Live; *Secret Samadhi* . . . .(Radioactive/MCA)

Rave On
 Buddy Holly; *Buddy Holly* . . . . (MCA)
  Buddy Holly-20 Golden Greats . . . . (MCA)
  Legend-From The Original Master Tapes . . . . (MCA)
  Rock & Roll Collection . . . . (MCA)
  ST/American Graffiti . . . . (MCA)
 Gary Busey; *ST/Buddy Holly Story* . . . . (Epic)
 John Mellencamp; *ST/Cocktail* . . . . (Elektra)

Relating To A Psychopath
 Macy Gray; *The Id* . . . . (Epic)

Rhymes Fo Da Funny Farm
 The Jaz; *Ya Don't Stop* . . . .(EMI)

Roads To Madness
 Queensryche; *The Warning* . . . . (EMI)

Rock & Roll Crazies
 Stephen Stills; *Manassas* . . . . (Atlantic)
  Still Stills . . . . (Atlantic)

Rock That Boogie
 Commander Cody & His Lost Planet Airmen; *Country Casanova* . . . . . .(MCA)
  Too Much Fun-Best Of Commander Cody & His Lost Planet Airmen . . .(MCA)

Run To The Water
 Live; *The Distance To Here* . . . .(Radioactive/MCA)

Saint Joe On The School Bus
 Marcy Playground; *Marcy Playground* . . . . (Capitol)

Save The Best For Last
 Vanessa Williams; *Grammy's Greatest Moments-#2-C* . . . .(Atlantic)
  The Comfort Zone . . . . (Wing)
  Women For Women-C . . . . (Mercury)

Scatterbrain
 Jeff Beck; *Blow By Blow* . . . .(Epic)

Scatterbrain
 Erroll Garner; *Best Of Erroll Garner* . . . . (Mercury)

Schizophrenia
 Descendants; *All* . . . .(SST)

Schizophrenia
 Sonic Youth; *Sister* . . . .(SST)

Sea Of Madness
 Crosby, Stills, Nash & Young; *ST/Woodstock* . . . . (Atlantic)

Self Control
 Laura Branigan; *Hit Singles-1980-1988-C* . . . .(Atlantic)
  Self Control . . . . (Atlantic)

Seven Angels
 Bruce Springsteen; *Tracks* . . . . (Columbia)

Sex Fiend
 Awesome Dre & The Hardcore Committee; *Explicit Rap-C* . . . . (Priority)
  You Can't Hold Me Back . . . . (Priority)

Sex Maniac
 Bobby Nunn; *Private Party* . . . . (Motown)

Shape I'm In, The
 Band; *Best Of The Band* . . . . (Capitol)
  Rock Of Ages . . . . (Capitol)
  Stage Fright . . . . (Capitol)
  The Band-Anthology-#1 . . . . (Capitol)
  The Last Waltz . . . .(Warner Bros.)
  To Kingdom Come-The Definitive Collection . . . . (Capitol)
 Bob Dylan And The Band; *Before The Flood* . . . . (Columbia)

Shape I'm In, The
 Marty Stuart; *Marty Stuart* . . . . (Columbia)

She Don't Have A License
 Porter Wagoner; *45-#7-29772* . . . .(Warner Bros.)

She Drives Me Crazy
 Fine Young Cannibals; *Raw & The Cooked* . . . .(I.R.S.)
  Raw & The Remix . . . . (MCA)
  Rock The First-#1-C . . . .(Sandstone Music)

She's All I Got
 Jimmy Cozier; *Jimmy Cozier* . . . . (J)

She's Crazy For Leavin'
 Rodney Crowell; *30 Years Of #1 Hits-#19-C* . . . . (Columbia)
  Diamonds & Dirt . . . . (Columbia)
  Greatest Country Hits Of The '80s-1989-C . . . . (Columbia)
 Steve Wariner; *Life's Highway* . . . . (MCA)

She's Funny That Way (I Got A Woman Crazy For Me)
 Art Tatum; *Solo Masterpieces-#8* . . . . (Pablo)
 Count Basie Jam; *Montreux '77-C* . . . . (Pablo)
 Frank Sinatra; *At The Movies* . . . . (Capitol)
  Nice 'N' Easy . . . . (Capitol)
 Jackie Gleason; *Lush Moods* . . . .(Pair)
 Nat "King" Cole; *Big Band Cole* . . . . (Blue Note)

She's Got Issues
 Offspring; *Americana* . . . . (Columbia)

Shimmer
 Fuel; *Sunburn* . . . .(550 Music)

Shine On You Crazy Diamond
 Pink Floyd; *Collection Of Great Dance Songs* . . . . (Columbia)
  Delicate Sound Of Thunder . . . . (Columbia)
  Wish You Were Here . . . . (Columbia)

Silly
 Deniece Williams; *My Melody* . . . . (Columbia)

Sing Me A Love Song To Baby
 Billy Walker; *45-#14422* . . . . (MGM)

So Anxious
 Ginuwine; *100 Percent Ginuwine* . . . .(550 Music)

Some Girls Do
 Sawyer Brown; *Dirt Road* . . . . (Curb)

Someday, Someway
 Marshall Crenshaw; *Marshall Crenshaw* . . . . (Rhino)
  ST/Nightshift . . . . (Warner Bros.)

Song 2
 Blur; *Blur* . . . . (Virgin)

Spooky
 Atlanta Rhythm Section; *Underdog* . . . . (Polydor)
 Classics IV; *Ghastly Grooves-C* . . . . (K-Tel)
  Good Vibrations (Sounds Of Top 40 Radio: 1964-1967)-C . . . . (Capitol)
  Spooky . . . . (Liberty)
  Very Best Of The Classics IV . . . . (EMI)

Stars
 Hum; *You'd Prefer An Astronaut* . . . . (RCA)

State Of Shock
 Jacksons; *Victory* . . . . (Epic)

State Of Shock
 Ted Nugent; *State Of Shock* . . . . (Epic)

Step Out Of Your Mind
 American Breed; *Bend Me, Shape Me-Best Of The American
  Breed* . . . .(Varese Vintage)

Still Crazy After All These Years
 Paul Simon; *Greatest Hits, Etc.* . . . . (Columbia)
  Negotiations And Love Songs, 1971-1986 . . . . (Warner Bros.)
  Still Crazy After All These Years . . . . (Columbia)
 Simon & Garfunkel; *The Concert In Central Park* . . . . (Warner Bros.)

Stone Cold Crazy
 Queen; *Classic Queen* . . . . (Hollywood)
  Sheer Heart Attack . . . . (Hollywood)
  ST/Encino Man . . . . (Hollywood)

Stress In Marriage
 Negativeland; *Escape From Noise* . . . .(SST)

Stupify
 Disturbed; *The Sickness* . . . . (Giant)

Stutter
 Elastica; *Elastica* . . . . (David Geffen Co.)

Suicidal Mania
 Suicidal Tendencies; *How Will I Laugh Tomorrow When I Can't Even Smile
  Today* . . . . (Epic)

Suicidal Maniac
 Suicidal Tendencies; *Join The Army* . . . . (Caroline)

Suicide Madness
 Germs; *Germicide-Live At The Whisky-1977* . . . . (Roir)

Sunny Came Home
 Shawn Colvin; *1998 Grammy Nominees-C* . . . . (MCA)
  A Few Small Repairs . . . . (Columbia)

Super Freak
 Rick James; *Mega Hits Dance Classics-#7-C* . . . . (Priority)
  Rick James' Greatest Hits . . . . (Motown)

Sweet Daddy (Your Mama's Done Gone Mad)
 Little Brother Montgomery; *Chicago-Living Legends-South Side
  Blues* . . . . (Riverside)

Sweet Daze
 Pete.; *Pete.* . . . . (Warner Bros.)

Sweet Little Girl
 Stevie Wonder; *Music Of My Mind* . . . . (Motown)

Teenage Lobotomy
 Ramones; *All The Stuff & More-#2* . . . . (Sire)
  Ramones Mania . . . . (Sire)
  Rocket To Russia . . . . (Sire)

Teenage Nervous Breakdown
 Little Feat; *Hoy-Hoy!* . . . . (Warner Bros.)

Sailin' Shoes .... (Warner Bros.)

Tell Me I Was Dreaming
Travis Tritt; *Ten Feet Tall And Bulletproof* .... (Warner Bros.)
Travis Tritt's Greatest Hits-From The Beginning. .... (Warner Bros.)

Tell Me I'm Crazy
Shelby Lynne; *Temptation.* .... (Morgan Creek)

That Song Is Driving Me Crazy
Tom T. Hall; *Tom T. Hall's Greatest Hits-#2* .... (Mercury)

Theme From "Fractured Fairy Tales"
Original Soundtrack; *Television's Greatest Hits-#3-1970s & 1980s-C* .... (TVT)

Theme From "Looney Tunes"
Original Soundtrack; *Television's Greatest Hits-#2-C* .... (TVT)

Theme From "Mad About You"
Original Soundtrack; *Television's Greatest Hits-#7-Cable Ready-C* ..... (TVT)

They're Coming To Take Me Away, Ha Haaa!
Napoleon XIV; *Dr. Demento Presents The Greatest Novelty Records-#3-1960s-C* .... (Rhino)
Silly Songs-C .... (K-Tel)
The Second Coming .... (Rhino)

Things Have Changed
Bob Dylan; *Essential Bob Dylan* .... (Columbia)
ST/Wonder Boys .... (Columbia)

Things We Do For Love
10 CC; *Deceptive Bends* .... (Mercury)
Super Hits Of The '70s-Have A Nice Day-#19-C ...... (Rhino)
Amy Grant; *ST/Mr. Wrong* .... (Hollywood)

This Crazy Love
Oak Ridge Boys; *Country Classics-#10-1987-C* .... (Universal)
Oak Ridge Boys' Greatest Hits 3 .... (MCA)
This Crazy Love .... (MCA Special Prod.)
Where The Fast Lane Ends .... (MCA)

Those Lazy Hazy Crazy Days Of Summer
Nat "King" Cole; *Best Of Nat "King" Cole-Vol. 1* .... (Capitol)
Capitol Collectors Series-Nat "King" Cole. .... (Capitol)

'Til I Gain Control Again
Crystal Gayle; *Best Of Crystal Gayle* .... (Warner Bros.)
True Love .... (Elektra)
Emmylou Harris; *Elite Hotel.* .... (Reprise)
Rodney Crowell; *Rodney Crowell* .... (Warner Bros.)
Rodney Crowell-Collection .... (Warner Bros.)
Willie Nelson; *Greatest Hits (& Some That Will Be)* .... (Columbia)
Willie Nelson & Waylon Jennings; *Take It To The Limit* ..... (Columbia)
Willie & Family Live. .... (Columbia)
Willie Nelson & Waylon Jennings' Greatest Hits .... (Columbia)

Tonight I Climbed The Wall
Alan Jackson; *A Lot About Livin' (And A Little 'Bout Love)* .... (Arista)

Too Lazy To Work, Too Nervous To Steal
BR549; *This Is BR549* .... (Lucky Dog)

Total Eclipse Of The Heart
Bonnie Tyler; *Billboard Top Hits-1983-C* .... (Rhino)
Faster Than The Speed Of Night. .... (Columbia)
Seems Like Yesterday-#4-Early '80s-C .... (K-Tel)
Nicki French; *Dance Hits '96 Supermix-C* .... (Critique)
Secrets .... (Critique)

Touch & Go Crazy
Lee Greenwood; *Country Classics-#12-1987-1988-C* ..... (Universal)
Lee Greenwood's Greatest Hits-#2 .... (MCA)

Touch Of Madness
Night Ranger; *Midnight Madness* .... (MCA)

Treat Her Like A Lady
Celine Dion; *Let's Talk About Love-C* .... (550 Music)

Tremble For My Beloved
Collective Soul; *Dosage* .... (Atlantic)

Truly Madly Deeply
Savage Garden; *Savage Garden* .... (Columbia)

Twenty-First Century Schizoid Man
King Crimson; *Abbreviated.* .... (Editions E.G.)
Compact .... (Editions E.G.)
In The Court Of The Crimson King-An Observation By King Crimson .... (Editions E.G.)

Twisted
Bette Midler; *Bette Midler.* .... (Atlantic)
Joni Mitchell; *Court & Spark* .... (Asylum)
Lambert, Hendricks & Ross; *Twisted-Best Of Lambert, Hendricks & Ross* .... (Rhino)

Twisted
Keith Sweat; *Keith Sweat.* .... (Elektra)

U Bring The Freak Out
Rick James; *Cold Blooded.* .... (Motown)

Undun
Guess Who; *American Woman, These Eyes & Other Hits* .... (RCA)
Best Of The Guess Who. .... (RCA)

Unglued
Stone Temple Pilots; *Purple* .... (Atlantic)

Untanglin' My Mind
Clint Black; *One Emotion* .... (RCA)

Unwashed & Somewhat Slightly Dazed
David Bowie; *Space Oddity.* .... (Rykodisc)

Upside Down
Diana Ross; *Billboard Top Dance Hits-1980-C* .... (Rhino)
Billboard Top Hits-1980-C .... (Rhino)
Diana. .... (Motown)
Diana Ross-All The Great Hits .... (Motown)
Diana Ross-Anthology .... (Motown)

Victim Of The Insane
Trouble; *Psalm 9* .... (Metal Blade)

Virtual Insanity
Jamiroquai; *Traveling Without Moving* .... (Work/Epic)

Voices
Disturbed; *The Sickness* .... (Giant)

Walk Right In
Rooftop Singers; *Best Of The Rooftop Singers* .... (Vanguard)
Cruisin'-1963-C .... (Increase)
Greatest Folksingers Of The '60s-C .... (Vanguard)
ST/Forrest Gump. .... (Epic/Sony Music Soundtrax)
Troubadours Of The Folk Era-#3-C .... (Rhino)

Warm Summer Daze
Vybe; *Vybe* .... (Island)

Warped
Red Hot Chili Peppers; *One Hot Minute* .... (Warner Bros.)

Was
Kenny Wayne Shepherd Band; *Live On.* .... (Giant)

We Must Have Been Out Of Our Minds
George Jones; *George Jones-Greatest Country Hits* .... (Curb)
George Jones & Melba Montgomery; *Best Of George Jones-1955-1967* .... (Rhino)
Party Pickin' .... (International Mktg. Group)

Whammer Jammer
J. Geils Band; *Best Of The J. Geils Band* .... (Atlantic)
Full House. .... (Atlantic)

Whatever Comes First
Sons Of The Desert; *Whatever Comes First.* .... (Epic)

When A Man Loves A Woman
Bette Midler; *ST/The Rose* .... (Atlantic)
Michael Bolton; *Time, Love & Tenderness* .... (Columbia)
Percy Sledge; *Atlantic Rhythm & Blues 1947-1974-#5 (1962-1966)-C* .... (Atlantic)
Atlantic Soul Classics-C .... (Warner Special Prod.)
Best Of Percy Sledge .... (Atlantic)
Golden Age Of Black Music-1960-1970-C .... (Atlantic)
ST/Platoon .... (Atlantic)

Whenever You Come Around
Vince Gill; *When Love Finds You* .... (MCA)

Where Was I
Ricky Van Shelton; *Bridge I Didn't Burn* .... (Columbia)

White Room
Cream; *Cream-Live-#2* .... (Polydor)
History Of British Rock-#9-C .... (Rhino)
Strange Brew-Very Best Of Cream .... (Polydor)
Wheels Of Fire .... (Polydor)
Eric Clapton; *24 Nights* .... (Duck/Reprise)
Eric Clapton-Crossroads-C .... (Polydor)

Whole Lot To Think About
Wood; *Songs From Stamford Hill* .... (Columbia)

Wild & Crazy Love
Mary Jane Girls; *Only Four You* .... (Motown)

Wild Nights, Hot & Crazy Days
Judas Priest; *Metal Works-1973-1993* .... (Columbia)
Turbo. .... (Columbia)

Wildest Times Of The World
Vonda Shepard; *ST/Songs From "Ally McBeal" Featuring Vonda Shepard* .... (550/Epic)

Will You Marry Me?
Vonda Shepard; *ST/Songs From "Ally McBeal" Featuring Vonda Shepard* .... (550/Epic)

Winner Of Your Heart
Johnnie & Jack & Their Tennessee Mountain Boys; *45-Out of print* ..... (RCA)

You Could Drive A Person Crazy
Original Cast; *Company.* .... (Columbia)

You Go To My Head
Billie Holiday; *At Storyville* .... (Black Lion)
First Verve Sessions .... (Verve)
Bing Crosby; *The Radio Years: 20 Songs.* .... (Crescendo)
Frank Sinatra; *Nice 'N' Easy* .... (Capitol)
Round #1 .... (Capitol)
Voice: The Columbia Years-1943-1952 .... (Columbia)
Linda Ronstadt; *For Sentimental Reasons.* .... (Asylum)

You Make Me Crazy
Sammy Hagar; *Musical Chairs* .... (Capitol)
Three Decades Of Rock ('60s, '70s, '80s)-C .... (Priority)

You Make Me Crazy
Utopia; *Adventures In Utopia.* .... (Rhino)
Utopia-Anthology 1974-1985 .... (Rhino)

You Make Me Feel Bad
Wood; *Songs From Stamford Hill* .... (Columbia)

You May Be Right
Billy Joel; *Billy Joel-Greatest Hits, Volume I & Volume II* .... (Columbia)

Glass Houses . . . . (Columbia)
You Might Think
Cars; *Heartbeat City* . . . . (Elektra)
The Cars' Greatest Hits . . . . (Elektra)
You Nearly Lose Your Mind
Ernest Tubb/Willie Nelson/Waylon Jennings; *Ernest Tubb Collection-C* . . . . (Step One)
Merle Haggard & Janie Fricke; *It's All In The Game* . . . . (Epic)
You Really Got Me
Kinks; *Come Dancing With The Kinks-Best Of The Kinks 1977-1986* . . . (Arista)
History Of British Rock-#1-C . . . . (Rhino)
Kinks' Greatest Hits . . . . (Rhino)
Kinks-Live . . . . (Reprise)
Van Halen; *ST/Over The Edge* . . . . (Warner Bros.)
Van Halen . . . . (Warner Bros.)
You're Driving Me Crazy
Art Pepper; *Return Of Art Pepper-Complete Aladdin Recordings-#1* . . . . (Blue Note)
Big Joe Turner; *Boss Of The Blues* . . . . (Atlantic)
Dinah Shore; *Love & Kisses Dinah.* . . . . (RCA)
Frank Sinatra; *Strangers In The Night* . . . . (Reprise)
Louis Armstrong; *Louis Armstrong-Vol. 7-You're Driving Me Crazy.* . . . . (Columbia)
You're Insane
Rod Stewart; *Footloose & Fancy Free* . . . . (Warner Bros.)
Zombie
Cranberries; *No Need To Argue* . . . . (Island)
Zombie Jamboree
Kingston Trio; *25 Years Non-Stop* . . . . (Xeres)
From The Hungry i . . . . (Capitol)

CRIME, Steal

See Also: CAPITAL PUNISHMENT, CHEATING & LIES, DOMESTIC ABUSE, FIGHT, GUNS, KILL, LAW & ORDER, MISTAKES, MISTREATMENT, PIRATES, POLICE, PRISON, REBELS

911
Wyclef Jean featuring Mary J. Blige; *The Ecleftic-2 Sides II A Book.* . . . . (Ruffhouse/Columbia)
After The Rain Has Fallen
Sting; *Brand New Day* . . . . (A&M)
Ain't No Crime
Billy Joel; *Piano Man* . . . . (Columbia)
Alice's Restaurant Massacree
Arlo Guthrie; *Alice's Restaurant* . . . . (Reprise)
Best Of Arlo Guthrie . . . . (Warner Bros.)
Almost Illegal
Rod Stewart; *Out Of Order.* . . . . (Warner Bros.)
Arrested For Driving While Blind
ZZ Top; *Six Pack* . . . . (Warner Bros.)
Tejas . . . . (Warner Bros.)
Assault & Battery
Howard Jones; *Animal Liberation-C* . . . . (Wax Trax)
Dream Into Action . . . . (Elektra)
Atlantic City
Bruce Springsteen; *Bruce Springsteen's Greatest Hits.* . . . . (Columbia)
Nebraska . . . . (Columbia)
Balboa Park
Bruce Springsteen; *The Ghost Of Tom Joad* . . . . (Columbia)
Bandit
Jerry Reed; *ST/Smokey And The Bandit* . . . . (MCA)
Bandit In A Bathing Suit
David Bromberg; *Bandit In A Bathing Suit.* . . . . (Fantasy)
Banditos
Refreshments; *Fizzy Fuzzy Big & Buzzy* . . . . (Mercury)
Bankrobber
Clash; *On Broadway.* . . . . (Epic)
The Story Of The Clash, Volume 1 . . . . (Epic)
Bankrobber/Robber Dub
Clash; *Black Market Clash* . . . . (Epic)
Rhythm Come Forward: Volume III-C . . . . (Columbia)
Been Caught Stealing
Jane's Addiction; *Kettle Whistle.* . . . . (Warner Bros.)
Before You Accuse Me
Bo Diddley; *Bo Diddley.* . . . . (Chess)
Creedence Clearwater Revival; *1970* . . . . (Fantasy)
Cosmo's Factory . . . . (Fantasy)
Creedence Clearwater Revival-Chronicle-#2 . . . . (Fantasy)
Creedence Country . . . . (Fantasy)
Eric Clapton; *Eric Clapton-Unplugged* . . . . (Duck/Reprise)
Journeyman . . . . (Duck/Reprise)
Black Money
Vinnie James; *All-American Boy* . . . . (RCA)
Blackmail
Robert Palmer; *Sneakin' Sally Through The Alley* . . . . (Island)

Blackmail
10 CC; *Original Soundtrack* . . . . (Mercury)
Blood Is Thicker Than Water
Wyclef Jean featuring G&B (The Product); *The Sopranos-Music From The HBO Original Series* . . . . (Sony Music Soundtrax)
Bubba Shot The Jukebox
Mark Chesnutt; *Longnecks & Short Stories* . . . . (MCA)
Bubblegoose
Wyclef Jean; *Chef Aid-The South Park Album* . . . . (Columbia)
Wyclef Jean featuring Melky Sedeck; *Presents The Carnival F/Refugee Allstars* . . . . (Ruffhouse/Columbia)
Burnin' & Lootin'
Bob Marley & The Wailers; *Bob Marley & The Wailers-Live* . . . . . (Tuff Gong)
Wailers; *Burnin'* . . . . (Tuff Gong)
Commit A Crime
Howlin' Wolf; *The Chess Box-Howlin' Wolf* . . . . (Chess)
Complicated Shadows
Elvis Costello & The Attractions; *The Sopranos-Music From The HBO Original Series* . . . . (Sony Music Soundtrax)
Conspiracy
Black Crowes; *Amorica* . . . . (American)
Coward Of The County
Kenny Rogers; *Kenny* . . . . (Liberty)
Kenny Rogers' Greatest Hits . . . . (EMI)
Kenny Rogers-Twenty Greatest Hits . . . . (EMI)
Crime & Punishment
Agony Column; *Brave Words & Bloody Knuckles* . . . . (Big Chief)
Crime Don't Pay
Joe Jackson Band; *Beat Crazy* . . . . (A&M)
Crime In The City
Neil Young & Crazy Horse; *WELD.* . . . . (Reprise)
Crime Of Passion
Ricky Van Shelton; *More Hot Country Requests-#2-C* . . . . (Epic)
Wild-Eyed Dream. . . . . (Columbia)
Crime Of Passion
Diana Ross; *Eaten Alive* . . . . (RCA)
Crime Of Passion
Bonnie Raitt; *Nine Lives* . . . . (Warner Bros.)
Crime Of Passion
Rita Coolidge; *Satisfied.* . . . . (A&M)
Crime Of Passion
Loudon Wainwright III; *Unrequited* . . . . (Columbia)
Crime Of The Century
Supertramp; *Crime Of The Century.* . . . . (A&M)
Paris . . . . (A&M)
Supertramp-Classics-#9. . . . . (A&M)
Crime Wave
Prism; *See Forever Eyes* . . . . (Ariola America)
Crimes Of Paris
Elvis Costello; *Girls Girls Girls* . . . . (Columbia)
Elvis Costello & The Attractions; *Blood & Chocolate* . . . . (Columbia)
Criminal
Fiona Apple; *1998 Grammy Nominees-C* . . . . (MCA)
Tidal. . . . . (Clean Slate/Work)
Criminal Kind
Tom Petty And The Heartbreakers; *Hard Promises* . . . . (MCA)
Criminal World
David Bowie; *Let's Dance* . . . . (EMI)
Cuban Crime Of Passion
Jimmy Buffett; *Boats Beaches Bars & Ballads* . . . . (Margaritaville)
White Sport Coat & A Pink Crustacean . . . . (MCA)
Date Rape
Tribe Called Quest; *Low End Theory* . . . . (Jive)
Desperados Waiting For A Train
Guy Clark; *Old No. 1.* . . . . (Sugar Hill)
Jerry Jeff Walker; *Best Of Jerry Jeff Walker* . . . . (MCA)
Great Gonzos . . . . (MCA)
Viva Terlingua . . . . (MCA)
Waylon Jennings, Willie Nelson, Johnny Cash, Kris Kristofferson; *Highwayman* . . . . (Columbia)
Hot Tracks-Train Super Hits-C . . . . (Epic)
Did You Steal My Money
Who; *Face Dances* . . . . (MCA)
Dirty Deeds Done Dirt Cheap
AC/DC; *Dirty Deeds Done Dirt Cheap.* . . . . (Atlantic)
Don't Rob Another Man's Castle
Ernest Tubb; *The Ernest Tubb Story* . . . . (MCA)
Don't Take The Girl
Tim McGraw; *Not A Moment Too Soon* . . . . (Curb)
Tim McGraw's Greatest Hits . . . . (Curb)
Dress Me Up As A Robber
Paul McCartney; *Tug Of War* . . . . (Gold Rush)
Drink, Swear, Steal & Lie
Michael Peterson; *Michael Peterson.* . . . . (Reprise)
Drunken Driver
Ricky Skaggs and Kentucky Thunder; *Bluegrass Rules!* . . . . (Rounder)
Ends
Everlast; *Whitey Ford Sings The Blues* . . . . (Tommy Boy)

Fill Her Up
Earl Scruggs & Sting; *Earl Scruggs And Friends-C* . . . . (MCA)
Fingerprint File
Rolling Stones; *It's Only Rock 'N Roll* . . . . (Rolling Stones)
Love You Live . . . . (Virgin)
Forbidden Fruit
Band; *Northern Lights-Southern Cross* . . . . (Capitol)
Framed
Cheech & Chong; *ST/Up In Smoke* . . . . (Warner Bros.)
Little Feat; *Hoy-Hoy!* . . . . (Warner Bros.)
Los Lobos; *ST/La Bamba* . . . . (Slash)
Ritchie Valens; *History Of Ritchie Valens* . . . . (Rhino)
Ritchie Valens . . . . (Rhino)
Fugitive
Indigo Girls; *Swamp Ophelia* . . . . (Epic)
Ghost Of You And Me
BBMak; *Sooner Or Later* . . . . (Hollywood)
Glendale Train
New Riders Of The Purple Sage; *Best Of New Riders Of The*
Purple Sage . . . . (Columbia)
New Riders Of The Purple Sage . . . . (Columbia)
Goldfinger
Shirley Bassey; *13 Original James Bond Themes-C* . . . . (EMI)
Best Of Shirley Bassey . . . . (EMI)
Great Performances . . . . (Liberty)
Shirley Bassey-Live At Carnegie Hall . . . . (United Artists)
Shirley Bassey's Greatest Hits . . . . (EMI)
ST/Goldfinger . . . . (United Artists)
Gone Till November
Wyclef Jean featuring The Refugee Allstars; *Presents The Carnival F/*
Refugee Allstars . . . . (Ruffhouse/Columbia)
Great Filling Station Holdup
Jimmy Buffett; *White Sport Coat & A Pink Crustacean* . . . . (MCA)
Hail Mary
Makaveli; *The Don Killuminati: The 7 Day Theory*
Album . . . . (Death Row/Interscope)
Halfway Home Cafe
Ricky Skaggs and Kentucky Thunder; *History Of The Future* . . (Skaggs Family)
Hanging Tree
Marty Robbins; *Gunfighter Ballads & Trail Songs* . . . . (Legacy)
Hollywood Magic-1950s-C . . . . (Columbia)
Lifetime Of Song-1951-1982 . . . . (Columbia)
Marty Robbins' All-Time Greatest Hits . . . . (Columbia)
Have Mercy Judge
Chuck Berry; *Jailhouse Rock (Hits From The Big*
House)-C . . . . (Sony Music Special Prod.)
Have Mercy On The Criminal
Elton John; *Don't Shoot Me I'm Only The Piano Player* . . . . (Polydor)
Live In Australia With The Melbourne Symphony Orchestra . . . . (MCA)
Highway 29
Bruce Springsteen; *The Ghost Of Tom Joad* . . . . (Columbia)
Highway Robbery
Tanya Tucker; *Strong Enough To Bend* . . . . (Liberty)
House Arrest
Bryan Adams; *Waking Up The Neighbours* . . . . (A&M)
Hurricane
Bob Dylan; *Desire* . . . . (Columbia)
Husband Stealer
Barbara Mandrell; *This Is Barbara Mandrell* . . . . (MCA)
I Did It
Dave Matthews Band; *Everyday* . . . . (RCA)
I Fought The Law
Bobby Fuller Four; *Best Of The Bobby Fuller Four* . . . . (Rhino)
Heart & Soul Of Rock 'N' Roll-#1-C . . . . (Rhino)
Jailhouse Rock (Hits From The Big House)-C . . . . (Sony Music Special Prod.)
Oldies But Goodies-#9-C . . . . (Original Sound)
Super Oldies Of The '60s-#7-C . . . . (Audio Fidelity)
Clash; *The Clash* . . . . (Epic)
The Story Of The Clash, Volume 1 . . . . (Epic)
I Love Robbing Banks
Greg Austin Band; *Midnight Driver* . . . . (Xeres)
I Wonder If Heaven Got A Ghetto
2Pac; *R U Still Down (Remember Me)* . . . . (Amaru/Jive)
Illegal Smile
John Prine; *John Prine* . . . . (Atlantic)
Prime Prine-The Best Of John Prine . . . . (Atlantic)
I'm A Lonesome Fugitive
Merle Haggard; *Merle Haggard-16 Biggest Hits* . . . . (Legacy)
Merle Haggard & The Strangers; *Best Of Merle Haggard & The*
Strangers . . . . (Capitol)
Capitol Collectors Series-Merle Haggard & The Strangers . . . . . . (Capitol)
Songs I'll Always Sing . . . . (Capitol)
Roy Buchanan; *Roy Buchanan* . . . . (Polydor)
I'm A Thug
Trick Daddy; *Thugs Are Us* . . . . (Slip 'N Slide/Atlantic)
Is It A Crime
Sade; *Promise* . . . . (Portrait)
Is It A Crime
Judy Holliday/Original Cast; *Bells Are Ringing* . . . . (Columbia)

It's Not A Crime
Nils Lofgren; *Best Of Nils Lofgren* . . . . (A&M)
Cry Tough . . . . (A&M)
Nils Lofgren-Classics-#13 . . . . (A&M)
I've Committed Murder
Macy Gray; *On How Life Is* . . . . (Epic)
Joe Hill
Arlo Guthrie & Pete Seeger; *Together In Concert* . . . . (Reprise)
Joan Baez; *Carry It On* . . . . (Vanguard)
From Every Stage . . . . (A&M)
One Day At A Time . . . . (Vanguard)
ST/Woodstock . . . . (Atlantic)
Johnny 99
Bruce Springsteen; *Nebraska* . . . . (Columbia)
Bruce Springsteen & The E Street Band; *Bruce Springsteen & The E Street*
Band Live/1975-85 . . . . (Legacy)
Johnny Cash; *Cover Me (Bruce Springsteen Tribute)-C* . . . . . . (Rhino)
Johnny Porter
Persuasions; *Chirpin'* . . . . (Elektra)
Ry Cooder; *Borderline* . . . . (Warner Bros.)
Johnny Too Bad
Slickers; *ST/The Harder They Come* . . . . (Mango)
Taj Mahal; *Best Of Taj Mahal* . . . . (Columbia)
Mo' Roots . . . . (Legacy)
UB40; *Labour Of Love* . . . . (A&M)
Live In Moscow . . . . (A&M)
Jungleland
Bruce Springsteen; *Born To Run* . . . . (Columbia)
Lady Came From Baltimore
Joan Baez; *Contemporary Ballad Book* . . . . (Vanguard)
Joan . . . . (Vanguard)
John Stewart; *Neon Beach* . . . . (Homecoming)
Johnny Cash; *Johnny Cash-16 Biggest Hits-#2* . . . . (Legacy)
Tim Hardin; *Hang On To A Dream-Verve Recordings* . . . . . . (Polydor)
Lee Harvey Oswald
Skatalites; *Stretching Out* . . . . (Roir)
Legend Of Bonnie And Clyde
Merle Haggard & The Strangers; *For The Record: Merle Haggard-43*
Legendary Hits . . . . (BNA)
Lilies Of The Field
Gretchen Peters; *Gretchen Peters* . . . . (Purple Crayon Prod.)
Lily, Rosemary And The Jack Of Hearts
Bob Dylan; *Blood On The Tracks* . . . . (Columbia)
Listen Like Thieves
INXS; *Listen Like Thieves* . . . . (Atlantic)
Little Criminals
Randy Newman; *Little Criminals* . . . . (Warner Bros.)
Love In The First Degree
Alabama; *Alabama-Live* . . . . (RCA)
Alabama's Greatest Hits . . . . (RCA)
Feels So Right . . . . (RCA)
Nipper's Greatest Hits Of The '80s-C . . . . (RCA)
Love Is So Good When You're Stealing It
Z.Z. Hill; *Lost Soul-#3-C* . . . . (Epic)
Machine Gun Kelly
James Taylor; *Mud Slide Slim And The Blue Horizon* . . . . . . (Warner Bros.)
Mack The Knife
Bobby Darin; *Bobby Darin-At The Copa* . . . . (Bainbridge)
Hit Singles-1958-1977-C . . . . (Atlantic)
The Bobby Darin Story . . . . (Atlantic)
Frank Sinatra; *The Reprise Collection* . . . . (Reprise)
Louis Armstrong; *Best Of Louis Armstrong* . . . . (Vanguard)
Maggie Mae
Beatles; *Let It Be* . . . . (Capitol)
Manslaughter
EPMD; *Business As Usual* . . . . (Def Jam)
Master's Call
Marty Robbins; *Gunfighter Ballads & Trail Songs* . . . . (Legacy)
Maxwell's Silver Hammer
Beatles; *Abbey Road* . . . . (Parlophone)
Me & A Gun
Tori Amos; *Little Earthquakes* . . . . (Atlantic)
Me And Julio Down By The Schoolyard
Paul Simon; *Greatest Hits, Etc.* . . . . (Columbia)
Negotiations And Love Songs, 1971-1986 . . . . (Warner Bros.)
Paul Simon . . . . (Columbia)
Paul Simon In Concert/Live Rhymin' . . . . (Columbia)
Simon & Garfunkel; *The Concert In Central Park* . . . . (Warner Bros.)
Meeting Across The River
Bruce Springsteen; *Born To Run* . . . . (Columbia)
Movin' Violation
Skyy; *Skyyjammer* . . . . (Salsoul)
Murder Gonna Be My Crime
Sippie Wallace; *Women Be Wise* . . . . (Alligator)
Murder Incorporated
Bruce Springsteen; *Bruce Springsteen's Greatest Hits* . . . . . (Columbia)
Night The Lights Went Out In Georgia
Lynn Anderson; *Top Of The World* . . . . (Columbia)

Reba McEntire; *For My Broken Heart* ....(MCA)
   Reba McEntire's Greatest Hits-#3: I'm A Survivor ....(MCA)
Vicki Lawrence; *Super Hits Of The '70s-Have A Nice Day-#10-C* ......(Rhino)

No Sense Of Crime
Iggy Pop & James Williamson; *Kill City* ....(Bomp)

Oldest Established (Permanent Floating Crap Game In New York)
Original Cast; *ST/Guys & Dolls* ....(MCA)

One Piece At A Time
Johnny Cash; *The Man In Black-His Greatest Hits* ....(Legacy)

Original Prankster
Offspring; *Conspiracy Of One* ....(Columbia)

Other Side Of The Game
Erykah Badu; *Baduizm* ....(Kedar Entert./Universal)

Papa Was A Rollin' Stone
Temptations; *20/20-C* ....(Motown)
   25 #1 Hits From 25 Years-C ....(Motown)
   All The Million-Sellers ....(Motown)
   Billboard Top Rock 'N' Roll Hits-1972-C ....(Rhino)
   Compact Command Performances-Temptations ....(Motown)
   Temptations-Anthology-The Best Of The Temptations ....(Motown)

Perfect Crime
Guns N' Roses; *Use Your Illusion I* ....(Geffen)

Perry Mason
Ozzy Osbourne; *Ozzmosis* ....(Epic)

Pigs, Sheep & Wolves
Paul Simon; *You're The One* ....(Warner Bros.)

Pinkville Helicopter
Thom Parrott; *Best Of Broadside 1962-1968: Anthems Of The American Underground From The Pages Of Broadside Magazine-C* ....(Smithsonian Folkways)

Pittsburgh Stealers
Kendalls; *Kendalls-20 Favorites* ....(Epic)

Police And Thieves
Clash; *On Broadway* ....(Epic)
   The Clash ....(Epic)
   The Story Of The Clash, Volume 1 ....(Epic)
Junior Murvin; *Jammin'* ....(Mango)
   Police And Thieves ....(Mango)
   ST/Rockers ....(Mango)
   This Is Reggae Music #3-C ....(Island)

Pretty
Korn; *Follow The Leader* ....(Immortal/Epic)

Pretty Boy Floyd
Arlo Guthrie & Pete Seeger; *Precious Friend* ....(Warner Bros.)
Bob Dylan; *Folkways: A Vision Shared-C* ....(Columbia)
Byrds; *Sweetheart Of The Rodeo* ....(Columbia)
   The Byrds ....(Columbia)
Joan Baez; *Greatest Songs Of Woody Guthrie-C* ....(Vanguard)
Woody Guthrie; *Dust Bowl Ballads* ....(Rounder)
   Legendary Woody Guthrie ....(Tradition)
   Struggle ....(Smithsonian Folkways)
   Woody Guthrie ....(Everest)
   Worried Man Blues-Golden Classics-#1 ....(Collectables)

Punishment Fits The Crime
Ramones; *Brain Drain* ....(Sire)

Radar Gun
Bottle Rockets; *The Brooklyn Side* ....(East Side Digital)

Ragin' Cajun
Charlie Daniels Band; *Windows* ....(Epic)

Raised On Robbery
Joni Mitchell; *Court & Spark* ....(Asylum)

Ready Or Not
Fugees; *The Score* ....(Ruffhouse)
   The Score-Edit ....(Columbia)

Rex Bob Lowenstein
Mark Germino; *Rank & File* ....(Winter Harvest Entert.)

Road Goes On Forever, The
Joe Ely; *Love & Danger* ....(MCA)

Robber
Bram Tchaikovsky; *Strange Man, Changed Man* ....(Polydor)

Robbery Assault & Battery
Genesis; *Seconds Out* ....(Atlantic)
   Trick Of The Tail ....(Atco)

Robbery With Violins
Steeleye Span; *Parcel Of Rogues* ....(Chrysalis)

Rock And Roll Crook
Nils Lofgren; *Best Of Nils Lofgren* ....(A&M)
   Night After Night ....(A&M)
   Nils Lofgren ....(Rykodisc)
   Nils Lofgren-Classics-#13 ....(A&M)

Rockaway The Days
Bruce Springsteen; *Tracks* ....(Columbia)

Run Like A Thief
Bonnie Raitt; *Home Plate* ....(Warner Bros.)
J.D. Souther; *J.D. Souther* ....(Asylum)

Runaway Train
Soul Asylum; *Grave Dancers Union* ....(Columbia)

Scene Of A Perfect Crime
Concrete Blonde; *Free* ....(Capitol)

Scene Of The Crime
Lime Spiders; *Beethoven's Fist* ....(Caroline)

Scooby Snacks
Fun Lovin' Criminals; *Come Find Yourself* ....(EMI)

Seven Eleven
Commander Cody; *Midnight Man* ....(Out Of Print)

Sex Crime
Eurythmics; *Eurythmics' Greatest Hits* ....(Arista)

Sexual Harassment In The Workplace
Frank Zappa; *Guitar* ....(Rykodisc)

Shakespeare Stole My Baby
Eye To Eye; *Shakespeare Stole My Baby* ....(Warner Bros.)

Shame Shame Shame Shame
Mark Collie; *Mark Collie* ....(MCA)

Silent Fury
Gary Wright; *Light Of Smiles* ....(Warner Bros.)

Sing You Sinners
Sammy Davis, Jr./Original Cast; *Mr. Wonderful* ....(MCA)
Tony Bennett; *Forty Years-The Artistry Of Tony Bennett* ....(Columbia)
   Tony Bennett At Carnegie Hall ....(Sony Music Special Prod.)
   Tony Bennett's All-Time Greatest Hits ....(Columbia)

Smackwater Jack
Carole King; *Carole King's Greatest Hits* ....(Epic)
   Tapestry ....(Epic)

Smooth Criminal
Alien Ant Farm; *Alien Ant Farm-Anthology* ....(DreamWorks/SKG)
Michael Jackson; *Bad* ....(Epic)

Smuggler's Blues
Glenn Frey; *Allnighter* ....(MCA)
   Rock The First-#2-C ....(Sandstone Music)
   ST/Miami Vice ....(MCA)

Sneaky Private Lee
Paice/Ashton/Lord; *Malice In Wonderland* ....(Warner Bros.)

So You Want To Be A Gangster
Too Short; *Shorty The Player* ....(Jive)

Solitude
Edwin McCain; *Honor Among Thieves* ....(Lava)
Edwin McCain & Darius Rucker; *VH-1 Crossroads-C* ....(Atlantic)

Somebody Stole My Gal
Benny Goodman; *B.G. In Hi-Fi* ....(Blue Note)
   Best Of The Big Bands-C ....(Columbia)

Star 69
R.E.M.; *Monster* ....(Warner Bros.)

Steal Away
Johnnie Taylor; *Chronicle: The 20 Greatest Hits* ....(Stax)
   Johnnie Taylor-Super Hits ....(Stax)

Steal Away
Billy Joe Royal; *Billy Joe Royal's Greatest Hits* ....(Columbia)

Steal Away
Joy; *Joy* ....(Fantasy)

Steal Away
Robbie Dupree; *Robbie Dupree* ....(Elektra)

Steal Away
Poco; *Rose Of Cimarron* ....(MCA)

Steal Away
Whitesnake; *Snakebite* ....(Geffen)

Steal Away
Nils Lofgren; *Nils* ....(A&M)
   Nils Lofgren-Classics-#13 ....(A&M)

Steal My Kisses
Ben Harper; *Burn To Shine* ....(Virgin)
   Now That's What I Call Music!-#4-C ....(Virgin)

Steal My Sunshine
Len; *You Can't Stop The Bum Rush* ....(Work)

Steal Your Heart Away
Bonnie Raitt; *Longing In Their Hearts* ....(Capitol)

Steal Your Love
Lucinda Williams; *Essence* ....(Lost Highway/IDJMG)

Stealer
Free; *Best Of Free* ....(A&M)
   Highway ....(A&M)

Stealin'
Max Romeo & The Upsetters; *War In Babylon* ....(Island)

Stealin'
Jacky Ward; *Best Of Jacky Ward* ....(Mercury)
   Lover's Question ....(Mercury)

Stealin'
David Bromberg; *Reckless Abandon* ....(Fantasy)

Stealin'
Janis Joplin; *ST/Janis* ....(Columbia)

Stealin'
Uriah Heep; *Sweet Freedom* ....(Chrysalis)

Stealin' Con
Merle Haggard & The Strangers; *The Fightin' Side Of Me* ....(Capitol)

Stealin' Each Other Blind
Chip Taylor; *45-#4840* ....(Capitol)

Stealin' Feelin'
Mike Lunsford; *Mike Lunsford* ....(Gusto)

CRYING, Tears

See Also: **BREAK, DESPAIR, DIVORCE, EYES, HAPPINESS,
HEART, LOVE (various), PAIN & HEALING, RAIN, SADNESS**

After The Rain Has Fallen
Sting; *Brand New Day* . . . . (A&M)
Ain't Nobody Cryin' But Me
Tasty Licks; *Anchored To The Shore* . . . . (Rounder)
Ain't That A Shame
4 Seasons; *25th Anniversary Collection* . . . . (Rhino)
Cheap Trick; *Cheap Trick At Budokan* . . . .(Epic)
Fats Domino; *Best Of Fats Domino* . . . .(EMI)
  Fats Domino's Greatest Hits . . . . (Everest)
  Fats Domino's Greatest Hits . . . . (MCA)
  ST/American Graffiti . . . .(MCA)
Hank Williams, Jr.; *Hank Williams, Jr.-14 Greatest Hits* . . . (Polydor)
  Standing In The Shadows . . . . (Polydor)
John Lennon; *Lennon* . . . . (Capitol)
  Rock 'N' Roll . . . . (Capitol)
All Choked Up
Original Broadway Cast; *Grease* . . . . (Polydor)
All Cried Out
Dusty Springfield; *Dusty Springfield-Anthology* . . . . (Mercury)
  Dusty Springfield-Golden Greats . . . . (Philips)
  Dusty Springfield-Golden Hits . . . . (Mercury)
All Cried Out
Allure; *Allure* . . . .(Track Masters/Crave)
  Boom! 17 Explosive Hits-C . . . . (Simitar)
Lisa Lisa; *Lisa Lisa & Cult Jam With Full Force* . . . . (Columbia)
  Lisa Lisa-Super Hits . . . . (Columbia)
  Past, Present & Future . . . . (TMP)
All Cried Out
Alison Moyet; *Alf* . . . . (Columbia)
  Alison Moyet-The Singles . . . . (Columbia)
All I Can Do Is Cry
Arthur Prysock; *Here's To Good Friends* . . . .(MCA)
All Out Of Tears/Lovin' Tears Suite
French Kiss; *Panic* . . . . (Polydor)
All The Crying In The World
Jody Miller; *45-#2398* . . . . (Capitol)
And Her Tears Flowed Like Wine
Stan Kenton; *Lighter Side* . . . .(Creative World)
  Stan Kenton's Greatest Hits . . . . (Capitol)
Stan Kenton & Anita O'Day; *Comprehensive Kenton* . . . . (Capitol)
And The Baby Never Cries
Harry Chapin; *Sniper & Other Love Songs* . . . . (Elektra)
And The Heavens Cried
Anthony Newley; *Genuis Of Anthony Newley* . . . . (London)
Angels Don't Cry
Psychedelic Furs; *Midnight To Midnight* . . . . (Columbia)
Are U Still Down?
Jon B.; *Cool Relax* . . . . (Yab Yum/550)
Are You Weepin'
Gary Wright; *Light Of Smiles* . . . .(Warner Bros.)
As Tears Go By
Marianne Faithfull; *Marianne Faithfull's Greatest Hits* . . . . (Abkco)
  Strange Weather . . . . (Island)
Rolling Stones; *Big Hits (High Tide & Green Grass)* . . . . . . (Abkco)
  December's Children (and everybody's) . . . . (Abkco)
  Hot Rocks 1964-1971 . . . . (Abkco)
  Singles Collection-The London Years . . . . (Abkco)
Baby Did A Bad Thing
Chris Isaak; *Forever Blue* . . . . (Reprise)
  ST/Eyes Wide Shut . . . . (Reprise)
Baby Don't You Cry
Alvin Lee; *Rocket Fuel* . . . . (RSO)
Baby Don't You Cry
Ray Charles; *Ray Charles-His Greatest Hits-#1* . . . . .(Dunhill Compact Classics)
Baby Stop Crying
Bob Dylan; *Street Legal* . . . . (Columbia)
Baby, Baby Don't Cry
Miracles; *Motown Story-First 25 Years-C* . . . . (Motown)
  *Time Out For Smokey Robinson & The Miracles/Special
    Occasion* . . . . (Motown)
Smokey Robinson; *Top 10 With A Bullet-Motown Male Groups-C* . . . (Motown)
Smokey Robinson & The Miracles; *Compact Command Performances-
    Smokey Robinson & The Miracles* . . . . (Motown)
  Smokey Robinson & The Miracles' Anthology . . . . (Motown)
Baby, I Don't Cry Over You
Billie Holiday; *Billie Holiday & Ella Fitzgerald* . . . .(MCA)
Back Doors Crying
Peter Allen; *Taught By Experts* . . . . (A&M)
Battle Of Glass Tears
King Crimson; *Lizard* . . . .(Editions E.G.)
Before The Next Teardrop Falls
Freddy Fender; *Before The Next Teardrop Falls* . . . . (Universal)
  Best Of Freddy Fender . . . .(MCA)
  Oldies But Goodies-#2-C . . . . (Original Sound)
  Super Hits Of The '70s-Have A Nice Day-#17-C . . . . (Rhino)
Ray Anthony; *Great Golden Hits* . . . . (Ranwood)
Beggin' & Cryin'
Sonny Terry & Brownie McGhee; *Midnight Special* . . . . (Fantasy)

Betcha Can't Cry Just One
David Frizzell & Shelly West; *In Session* . . . . (Viva)
Big Boys Don't Cry
Extreme; *Extreme* . . . . (A&M)
Big Girls Don't Cry
4 Seasons; *4 Seasons' Greatest Hits-#1* . . . . (Rhino)
  4 Seasons-Anthology . . . . (Rhino)
  Billboard Top Rock 'N' Roll Hits-1962-C . . . . (Rhino)
  More Dirty Dancing-C . . . .(RCA)
Big River
Grateful Dead; *One From The Vault* . . . .(Grateful Dead)
  Steal Your Face . . . .(Grateful Dead)
Johnny Cash; *Johnny Cash-Legend* . . . . (Sun)
  Johnny Cash's Greatest Hits-#2 . . . . (Columbia)
  Johnny Cash-Sun Years . . . . (Rhino)
  Superbilly . . . . (Sun)
  The Man In Black-His Greatest Hits . . . . (Legacy)
Rosanne Cash; *Right Or Wrong* . . . . (Columbia)
Bits And Pieces
Dave Clark Five; *History Of The Dave Clark Five* . . . . (Hollywood)
Bitter Tears
INXS; *X* . . . .(Atlantic)
Blue Eyes Crying In The Rain
Roy Acuff; *Roy Acuff's Greatest Hits* . . . . (Elektra)
Roy Acuff and his Smoky Mountain Boys; *Columbia Country Classics-#1-
    Golden Age-C* . . . . (Columbia)
Willie Nelson; *Columbia Country Classics-#5-A New Tradition-C* . . (Columbia)
  Greatest Hits (& Some That Will Be) . . . . (Columbia)
  Red Headed Stranger . . . . (Columbia)
  ST/Honeysuckle Rose . . . . (Columbia)
Blue On Black
Kenny Wayne Shepherd; *Trouble Is...* . . . . (Revolution)
Boo-Hoo-Hoo-Hoo
Little Richard; *Grooviest 17 Original Hits* . . . .(Specialty)
  Little Richard-His Biggest Hits . . . .(Specialty)
Born To Cry
Dion And The Belmonts; *Dion And The Belmonts-20 Golden
    Classics* . . . . (Collectables)
  Dion-24 Original Classics . . . . (Arista)
  Everything You've Always Wanted . . . .(Laurie)
  More Great Hits . . . . (Laurie)
Boy In The Bubble
Paul Simon; *Graceland* . . . . (Warner Bros.)
Boys Cry Tough
Bad Company; *Holy Water* . . . . (Atco)
Broken Home
Papa Roach; *Infest* . . . .(DreamWorks/SKG)
Brown Eyed Handsome Man
Buddy Holly; *Buddy Holly-20 Golden Greats* . . . . (MCA)
  For The First Time Anywhere . . . . (MCA)
  Rock & Roll Collection . . . . (MCA)
Chuck Berry; *Best Of The Best Of Chuck Berry* . . . . (International Mktg. Group)
  Roll Over Beethoven . . . . (Allegiance)
  The Chess Box-Chuck Berry . . . . (Chess)
Waylon Jennings; *Essential Waylon Jennings* . . . . (RCA)
  Waylon Jennings-Super Hits . . . . (RCA)
Brush Those Tears From Your Eyes
Li'l Wally; *Unforgettable Hits* . . . . (Jay Jay)
Bubba Shot The Jukebox
Mark Chesnutt; *Longnecks & Short Stories* . . . . (MCA)
Bury Me Beneath The Willow
Jimmie Davis; *Best Of Jimmie Davis* . . . . (MCA)
Ricky Skaggs; *Skaggs & Rice-The Essential Old-Time Country Duet
    Recordings* . . . . (Sugar Hill)
Wilma Lee Cooper; *Wilma Lee Cooper* . . . . (Rounder)
Woody Guthrie; *Woody Guthrie-#1 & 2* . . . . (Collectables)
Bye Bye Love
Everly Brothers; *Everly Brothers' All-Time Greatest Hits* . . . . (Curb)
  Everly Brothers-Cadence Classics-Their 20 Greatest Hits . . . . . . (Rhino)
  Very Best Of The Everly Brothers . . . . (Warner Bros.)
Simon & Garfunkel; *Bridge Over Troubled Water* . . . . (Columbia)
Can't Cry Anymore
Sheryl Crow; *MTV Party To Go-#8-C* . . . . (Tommy Boy)
  Tuesday Night Music Club . . . . (A&M)
Can't Cry Anymore
Kansas; *Power* . . . . (MCA)
Can't Cry Hard Enough
Williams Brothers; *Williams Brothers* . . . . (Warner Bros.)
Check Your Tears At The Door
Drivin' N' Cryin'; *Whisper Tames The Lion* . . . . (Island)
Cloudy, With A Chance Of Tears
Manhattans; *After Midnight* . . . . (Columbia)
Come Cryin' To Me
Lonestar; *Crazy Nights* . . . .(BNA)
Come See About Me
Diana Ross & The Supremes; *16 #1 Hits From The Early '60s-C* . . . . (Motown)
  Diana Ross & The Supremes' Greatest Hits . . . . (Motown)
  Diana Ross & The Supremes-Anthology (1962-1969) . . . . (Motown)
  Diana Ross & The Supremes-At The Copa . . . . (Motown)

Every Great #1 Hit . . . . (Motown)
Girl Groups-Story Of A Sound-C . . . . (Rhino)
Motown Story-First 25 Years-C . . . . (Motown)
Motown Superstar Series-#1-Diana Ross & The Supremes . . . . (Motown)

Cowboys Ain't Supposed To Cry
Moe Bandy; *Cowboys Ain't Supposed To Cry* . . . . (Columbia)

Cowboys Don't Cry
Daron Norwood; *Daron Norwood* . . . . (Giant)
Dude Mowrey; *Honky Tonk* . . . . (Capitol)
Ian Tyson; *All-Ears Review-#7-Still Amazing...-C* . . (Really Outstanding Music)
I Outgrew The Wagon . . . . (Vanguard)

Crazy
Jimmie Dale Gilmore with Willie Nelson; *Red Hot + Country-C* . . . . . (Mercury)
Kenny Rogers; *Kenny Rogers' Greatest Hits* . . . . (RCA)
What About Me? . . . . (RCA)
Linda Ronstadt; *Hasten Down The Wind* . . . . (Asylum)
Patsy Cline; *Songwriter's Tribute* . . . . (MCA)
ST/Sweet Dreams . . . . (MCA)
The Patsy Cline Story . . . . (MCA)
Ray Price; *Ray Price's Greatest Hits-#2* . . . . (Step One)
Willie Nelson; *Best Of Willie* . . . . (RCA)
Healing Hands Of Time . . . . (Liberty)
Nite Life-Greatest Hits & Rare Tracks . . . . (Rhino)
Willie & Family Live . . . . (Columbia)

Cry
Crystal Gayle; *Best Of Crystal Gayle* . . . . (Warner Bros.)
Janie Fricke; *Celebration* . . . . (Columbia)
I'll Need To Hold Someone When I Cry . . . . (Columbia)
Johnnie Ray; *Best Of Johnnie Ray* . . . . (Exact)
Johnnie Ray-16 Most Requested Songs . . . . (Legacy)
Radio Classics Of The '50s-C . . . . (Columbia)
Lynn Anderson; *Lynn Anderson's Greatest Hits* . . . . (Columbia)
Ray Charles; *Ray Charles' Greatest Hits-#2* . . . . (Rhino)
Ray Charles-Anthology . . . . (Rhino)

Cry
Roxette; *Look Sharp!* . . . . (EMI)

Cry A While
Bob Dylan; *"Love And Theft"* . . . . (Columbia)

Cry Baby
Madonna; *I'm Breathless-Music From Dick Tracy* . . . . (Sire)

Cry Baby
Enchanters; *Billboard Top R&B Hits-1963-C* . . . . (Rhino)
Soul Shots-#5-La-La Means I Love You-C . . . . (Rhino)
Garnet Mimms; *18 Soulful Ballads-C* . . . . (Rhino)
Beg, Scream & Shout! The Big Ol' Box Of '60s Soul-C . . . . . . (Rhino)
Janis Joplin; *Janis Joplin's Greatest Hits* . . . . (Columbia)
Pearl . . . . (Legacy)
ST/Janis . . . . (Columbia)

Cry Baby
Percy Mayfield; *Best Of Percy Mayfield* . . . . (Specialty)

Cry Baby
Mad Lads; *Best Of The Mad Lads* . . . . (Stax)

Cry Baby
Scarlets; *Golden Classics-Scarlets* . . . . (Collectables)

Cry Baby
Quincy Jones; *Mellow Madness* . . . . (A&M)

Cry Baby
Kix; *Midnite Dynamite* . . . . (Atlantic)

Cry Baby
Johnny Otis; *Original Johnny Otis Show* . . . . (Savoy)

Cry Baby
Sheila E.; *Sex Cymbal* . . . . (Warner Bros.)

Cry Baby Cry
Beatles; *The Beatles (White Album)* . . . . (Capitol)

Cry Baby Cry
Aldo Nova; *Subject...Aldo Nova* . . . . (Portrait)

Cry Baby Cry
Angels; *My Boyfriend's Back* . . . . (Collectables)
Super Oldies Of The '60s-#4-C . . . . (Audio Fidelity)
WCBS FM 101 History Of Rock-'60s-#5-C . . . . (Collectables)

Cry Baby Cry
Judy Garland; *Judy Garland-Collector's Items-1936-1945* . . . . (MCA)

Cry Cry
Cheap Trick; *Cheap Trick* . . . . (Epic)

Cry Cry Darlin'
Jimmy C. Newman; *Jimmy C. Newman's Greatest Hits* . . . . (Plantation)

Cry For A Shadow
Beatles; *Beatles* . . . . (Audio Fidelity)
The Beatles featuring Tony Sheridan-In The Beginning (Circa 1960) . . . . (Polydor)

Cry For Freedom
White Lion; *Big Game* . . . . (Atlantic)

Cry For Help
Rick Astley; *Free* . . . . (RCA)

Cry For Home
Van Morrison; *Inarticulate Speech Of The Heart* . . . . (Warner Bros.)

Cry For Love
Iggy Pop; *Blah Blah Blah* . . . . (A&M)

Cry For Me
Blasters; *Blasters-Collection* . . . . (Slash)

Cry For Me Baby
Elmore James/Jimmy Reed/Eddie Taylor; *Street Talkin'* . . . . (Muse)

Cry For Mercy
Raindogs; *Lost Souls* . . . . (Atco)

Cry For The Bad Man
Lynyrd Skynyrd; *Best Of Lynyrd Skynyrd* . . . . (MCA Special Prod.)
Gimme Back My Bullets . . . . (MCA)

Cry For The Nations
Michael Schenker Group; *Michael Schenker Group* . . . . (Chrysalis)
One Night At Budokan . . . . (Chrysalis)

Cry For You
Jodeci; *Diary Of A Mad Band* . . . . (Uptown)

Cry Freedom
Dave Matthews Band; *Crash* . . . . (RCA)

Cry If You Want
Who; *It's Hard* . . . . (MCA)

Cry Just A Little
Marie Osmond; *I Only Wanted You* . . . . (Capitol)

Cry Just A Little Bit
Sylvia; *Sylvia's Greatest Hits* . . . . (RCA)

Cry Like A Baby
Box Tops; *Billboard Top Rock 'N' Roll Hits-1968-C* . . . . (Rhino)
Box Tops' Greatest Hits . . . . (Rhino)
Super Hits-#5-C . . . . (Gusto)
WCBS FM 101 History Of Rock-'60s-#4-C . . . . (Collectables)

Cry Like A Baby
A Flock Of Seagulls; *Dream Come True* . . . . (Jive)

Cry Like A Baby
Bourgeois Tagg; *Yoyo* . . . . (Island)

Cry Like A Rainstorm
Bonnie Raitt; *Takin' My Time* . . . . (Warner Bros.)
Linda Ronstadt; *Cry Like A Rainstorm-Howl Like The Wind* . . . . (Elektra)

Cry Love
John Hiatt; *Walk On* . . . . (Capitol)

Cry Me A River
Aerosmith; *Rock In A Hard Place* . . . . (Columbia)
Barbra Streisand; *A Happening In Central Park* . . . . (Columbia)
The Barbra Streisand Album . . . . (Columbia)
Diana Krall; *The Look Of Love* . . . . (Impulse!)
Joe Cocker; *Joe Cocker-Classics-#4* . . . . (A&M)
Joe Cocker's Greatest Hits . . . . (A&M)
Mad Dogs & Englishmen . . . . (A&M)

Cry Me A River
Crystal Gayle; *When I Dream* . . . . (Liberty)

Cry Myself To Sleep
Judds; *Collector's Series-The Judds* . . . . (RCA)
Hits Of '87-C . . . . (RCA)
Judds' Greatest Hits . . . . (MCA)
Rockin' With The Rhythm . . . . (MCA)

Cry Myself To Sleep
4 Seasons; *Rarities-#1* . . . . (Rhino)

Cry Myself To Sleep
Del Shannon; *Runaway Hits!* . . . . (Rhino)

Cry No More
Outlaws; *Outlaws* . . . . (Arista)

Cry No More
L.A. Guns; *L.A. Guns* . . . . (Vertigo)

Cry Not For Me
Patsy Cline; *Hungry For Love-Her First Recordings-#2* . . . . (Rhino)
Patsy Cline . . . . (Audio Fidelity)

Cry Of The Gypsy
Dokken; *Back For The Attack* . . . . (Elektra)

Cry Of The Wild Goose
Frankie Laine; *Frankie Laine-Golden Hits* . . . . (Mercury)

Cry On
Irma Thomas; *New Orleans Jazz & Heritage Festival-1976-C* . . . . (Rhino)

Cry On
Little Texas; *First Time For Everything* . . . . (Warner Bros.)
Great Divorce Songs For Him-C . . . . (Warner Bros.)

Cry On My Shoulder
Bonnie Raitt; *Nick Of Time* . . . . (Capitol)

Cry On Your Own Shoulder
General Public; *Hand To Mouth* . . . . (I.R.S.)

Cry One More Time
Gram Parsons; *GP/Grievous Angel* . . . . (Reprise)
Gram Parsons/Fallen Angels Live-1973 . . . . (Sierra)

Cry One More Time
J. Geils Band; *Best Of The J. Geils Band* . . . . (Atlantic)

Cry Ophelia
Adam Cohen; *Songs From Dawson's Creek* . . . . (Sony Music Soundtrax)

Cry So Easy
Erasure; *Wonderland* . . . . (Sire)

Cry Softly Lonely One
Roy Orbison; *Classic (1965-1968)* . . . . (Rhino)

Cry To Me
Betty Harris; *Soul Shots-#11-More Ballads-C* . . . . (Rhino)

Super Oldies Of The '60s-#3-C . . . . (Audio Fidelity)
Bob Marley & The Wailers; *Rastaman Vibration* . . . . (Tuff Gong)
Contours; *Dirty Dancing Live In Concert-C* . . . . (RCA)
Professor Longhair; *Crawfish Fiesta* . . . . (Alligator)
Last Mardi Gras . . . . (Atlantic)
Rolling Stones; *Out Of Our Heads* . . . . (Abkco)
Solomon Burke; *Atlantic Rhythm & Blues 1947-1974-#4 (1958-*
1962)-C . . . . (Atlantic)
Best Of Solomon Burke . . . . (Atlantic)
More Dirty Dancing-C . . . . (RCA)

Cry To Me
Heart; *Little Queen* . . . . (Portrait)

Cry Tough
Nils Lofgren; *Best Of Nils Lofgren* . . . . (A&M)
Nils Lofgren-Classics-#13 . . . . (A&M)

Cry Tough
Poison; *Look What The Cat Dragged In* . . . . (Capitol)

Cry Wolf
Laura Branigan; *Touch* . . . . (Atlantic)
Stevie Nicks; *Other Side Of The Mirror* . . . . (Modern)

Cry Wolf
Victoria Shaw; *In Full View* . . . . (Reprise)

Cry Darling
Ricky Skaggs with Dolly Parton; *Big Mon: The Songs Of Bill*
Monroe-C . . . . (Skaggs Family)

Cry, Cry, Cry
Highway 101; *Highway 101* . . . . (Warner Bros.)
Highway 101's Greatest Hits . . . . (Warner Bros.)
Johnny Cash; *Classic Cash-Hall Of Fame Series* . . . . (Mercury)
Johnny Cash-Legend . . . . (Sun)
Johnny Cash-Original Golden Hits-#1 . . . . (Sun)
Show Time . . . . (Sun)
Superbilly . . . . (Sun)

Cry, Cry, Cry
Bobby Bland; *Best Of Bobby Bland* . . . . (MCA)
Two Steps From The Blues . . . . (MCA)

Cry, Cry, Cry
Jack Scott; *Capitol Collectors Series-Jack Scott* . . . . (Capitol)

Cry, Cry, Cry
Pere Ubu; *Worlds In Collision* . . . . (Fontana)

Cry, Cry, Cry
Ritchie Valens; *History Of Ritchie Valens* . . . . (Rhino)
Ritchie Valens . . . . (Rhino)

Cry, Cry, Cry
Roxy Music; *Manifesto* . . . . (Atco)

Crybaby
Utopia; *Utopia-Anthology 1974-1985* . . . . (Rhino)

Crybaby
Mariah Carey featuring Snoop Dogg; *Rainbow* . . . . (Columbia)

Cryin'
Aerosmith; *Get A Grip* . . . . (Geffen)

Cryin' Eyes
Don Williams; *One Good Well* . . . . (RCA)

Cryin' For The Carolines
Fred Waring's Pennsylvanians; *Fred Waring's*
Greatest Hits . . . . (Collector's Choice)

Cryin' In The Streets
Lou Christie; *Enlightnin'ment-Best Of Lou Christie* . . . . (Rhino)

Cryin' Shame
Lyle Lovett and his Large Band; *Lyle Lovett and his*
Large Band . . . . (Curb/MCA)

Cryin' Shame
Faster Pussycat; *Wake Me When It's Over* . . . . (Elektra)

Cryin' Through The Night
Stevie Wonder; *Characters* . . . . (Motown)

Cryin' Time
Julio Iglesias; *Starry Night* . . . . (Columbia)

Cryin' Time
Barbra Streisand; *Butterfly* . . . . (Columbia)

Cryin' Time
Kendalls; *Kendalls-20 Favorites* . . . . (Epic)

Cryin' To Be Heard
Traffic; *Traffic* . . . . (Island)

Crying
Don McLean; *Best Of Don McLean* . . . . (EMI)
Greatest Hits Then & Now . . . . (EMI)
Roy Orbison; *For The Lonely: 18 Greatest Hits* . . . . (Rhino)
For The Lonely: A Roy Orbison Anthology 1959-1965 . . . . . . (Rhino)
In Dreams-Greatest Hits . . . . (Orbison)
Roy Orbison's All-Time Greatest Hits-#1 & 2 . . . . (Monument)

Crying & Laughing
Chris DeBurgh; *The Getaway* . . . . (A&M)

Crying Again
Oak Ridge Boys; *Oak Ridge Boys' Greatest Hits* . . . . (MCA)
Room Service . . . . (MCA Special Prod.)

Crying Days
Scorpions; *Best Of The Scorpions-#2* . . . . (RCA)
Virgin Killer . . . . (RCA)

Crying Game
Boy George; *At Worst...The Best Of Boy George And Culture Club* . . . . . (SBK)

Crying In The Chapel
Elvis Presley; *Elvis-A Legendary Performer, Volume 3* . . . . (RCA)
How Great Thou Art . . . . (RCA)
The Top Ten Hits . . . . (RCA)
Worldwide 50 Gold Award Hits, Vol. 1, Parts 1 & 2 . . . . (RCA)
June Valli; *Nipper's Greatest Hits Of The '50s-#2-C* . . . . (RCA)
Little Richard; *Shut Up-Collection Of Rare Tracks-1951-1964* . . . . (Rhino)
Orioles; *Super Oldies Of The '50s-#1-C* . . . . (Audio Fidelity)
Rex Allen; *Only Country-1950-1954-C* . . . . (JCI Assoc. Labels)
Sonny Til & The Orioles; *Echoes Of A Rock Era-Early Years-C* . . . . . (Roulette)
Sonny Til & The Orioles' Greatest Hits . . . . (Collectables)
ST/American Graffiti . . . . (MCA)

Crying In The Morning
Billy Tate; *Crying In The Morning-Anthology Of Postwar Blues* . . . . . (Muse)
Southern Blues . . . . (Savoy)

Crying In The Night
Melba Moore; *Soul Exposed* . . . . (Capitol)

Crying In The Rain
Art Garfunkel & James Taylor; *Up 'Til Now* . . . . (Columbia)
Dave Edmunds & Nick Lowe; *Dave Edmunds-Anthology-1968-1990* . . . (Rhino)
Everly Brothers; *Everly Brothers' All-Time Greatest Hits* . . . . (Curb)
Golden Hits Of The Everly Brothers . . . . (Warner Bros.)
Very Best Of The Everly Brothers . . . . (Warner Bros.)
Londonbeat; *In The Blood* . . . . (Radioactive/MCA)
Rockpile; *Seconds Of Pleasure* . . . . (Columbia)
Tammy Wynette; *Tammy Wynette's Biggest Hits* . . . . (Epic)
Tears Of Fire-25th Anniversary Collection . . . . (Epic)

Crying In The Rain
A-Ha; *East Of The Sun-West Of The Moon* . . . . (Warner Bros.)
Moments In Love-C . . . . (EMI)

Crying In The Rain
Whitesnake; *Saints & Sinners* . . . . (Geffen)
Whitesnake . . . . (Geffen)

Crying In The Shadows
Gary Moore; *Wild Frontier* . . . . (Virgin)

Crying My Heart Out For You
Diana Ross; *All The Great Love Songs-Diana Ross* . . . . (Motown)
Diana Ross-Anthology . . . . (Motown)

Crying My Heart Out For You
Doris Day; *Doris Day Sings 22 Great Songs-Original Big Band* . . . . (Hindsight)
The Uncollected Doris Day with The Page Cavanaugh Trio-#2 . . . (Hindsight)

Crying My Heart Out Over You
Ricky Skaggs; *Greatest Country Hits Of The '80s-1981-C* . . . . . . (Columbia)
Waiting For The Sun To Shine . . . . (Epic)

Crying On Your Shoulder Again
Doug Stone; *Doug Stone* . . . . (Epic)

Crying Overtime
Alexander O'Neal; *Hearsay* . . . . (Tabu)

Crying Scene
Aztec Camera; *Stray* . . . . (Sire)

Crying Shame
Michael Johnson; *Best Of Michael Johnson* . . . . (RCA)
That's That . . . . (RCA)

Crying Shame
Kate Wolf; *Evening In Austin* . . . . (Kaleidoscope)
Poet's Heart . . . . (Kaleidoscope)

Crying Song
Pink Floyd; *ST/More* . . . . (Capitol)

Crying Steel
Chuck Berry; *The Chess Box-Chuck Berry* . . . . (Chess)

Crying Time
Buck Owens & Emmylou Harris; *Act Naturally* . . . . (Capitol)
Ray Charles; *Ray Charles' Greatest Hits* . . . . (Rhino)
Ray Charles-Anthology . . . . (Rhino)
Ray Charles-His Greatest Hits-#1 . . . . (Dunhill Compact Classics)

Crying, Waiting, Hoping
Buddy Holly; *Buddy Holly Collection* . . . . (MCA)
Marshall Crenshaw; *ST/La Bamba* . . . . (Slash)

Dancing With Tears In My Eyes
Ray Conniff; *Young At Heart* . . . . (Columbia)

Dandelion
Rolling Stones; *More Hot Rocks (big hits & fazed cookies)* . . . . (Abkco)
Through The Past, Darkly (Big Hits Vol. 2) . . . . (Abkco)

Devil Woman
Marty Robbins; *Billboard Top Country Hits-1962-C* . . . . (Rhino)
Columbia Country Classics-#4-Nashville Sound-C . . . . (Columbia)
Lifetime Of Song-1951-1982 . . . . (Columbia)
Marty Robbins' Greatest Hits-#4 . . . . (Columbia)

Do You Really Want To Hurt Me
Culture Club; *Billboard Top Hits-1983-C* . . . . (Rhino)
Kissing To Be Clever . . . . (Virgin)

Don't Cry
Asia; *Alpha* . . . . (Geffen)
Then & Now . . . . (Geffen)

Don't Cry
Seal; *Seal 2* . . . . (Sire)

Don't Cry
Neil Young; *Freedom* . . . . (Reprise)
Don't Cry
Guns N' Roses; *Use Your Illusion I* . . . . (Geffen)
Don't Cry
Edith Piaf; *Vie En Rose* . . . . (Columbia)
Don't Cry Baby
Bob Wills & His Texas Playboys; *Tiffany Transcriptions-#5-Fun Dancing To* . . . . (Rhino)
Don't Cry Baby
Aretha Franklin; *Aretha After Hours* . . . . (Columbia)
Don't Cry Baby
Tony Bennett; *Playin' With My Friends-Bennett Sings The Blues-C* . . . . (Columbia)
Don't Cry Cherie
Glenn Miller & His Orchestra; *Complete Glenn Miller & His Orchestra-#6* . . . . (Bluebird)
Don't Cry Daddy
Elvis Presley; *Always On My Mind* . . . . (RCA)
Memphis Record . . . . (RCA)
The Top Ten Hits . . . . (RCA)
Worldwide 50 Gold Award Hits, Vol. 1, Parts 1 & 2 . . . . (RCA)
Don't Cry For Me Argentina
Madonna; *GHV2* . . . . (Warner Bros.)
ST/Evita-Music From The Motion Picture . . . . (Warner Bros.)
Original Cast; *Evita* . . . . (MCA)
Don't Cry Joe (Let Her Go, Let Her Go)
Frank Sinatra; *Sinatra Swings* . . . . (Reprise)
Don't Cry Joni
Conway Twitty; *Conway Twitty-Number Ones-#1* . . . . (Liberty)
Conway Twitty's Greatest Hits-#1 . . . . (MCA)
Very Best Of Conway Twitty . . . . (MCA)
Don't Cry My Lady Love
Quicksilver Messenger Service; *Quicksilver Messenger Service-Anthology* . . . . (Capitol)
Don't Cry No More
Bobby Bland; *Two Steps From The Blues* . . . . (MCA)
Vintage Music-#13-C . . . . (MCA)
Bobby Bland & B.B. King; *Together For The First Time* . . . . (MCA)
Don't Cry No Tears
Neil Young & Crazy Horse; *Zuma* . . . . (Reprise)
Don't Cry Now
Linda Ronstadt; *Different Drum* . . . . (Capitol)
Don't Cry Out Loud
Melissa Manchester; *Melissa Manchester's Greatest Hits* . . . . (Arista)
Peter Allen; *At His Best* . . . . (A&M)
I Could Have Been A Sailor . . . . (A&M)
It Is Time For Peter Allen . . . . (A&M)
Don't Cry, I'll Be Back Before You Know It Baby
Ted Nugent; *Scream Dream* . . . . (Epic)
Don't Feel Like Cryin'
Abra Moore; *Strangest Places* . . . . (Arista Austin)
Don't Forget To Cry
Mandy Barnett; *I've Got A Right To Cry* . . . . (Sire)
Don't Let The Sun Catch You Crying
Gerry And The Pacemakers; *Best Of Gerry And The Pacemakers* . . . . . . (EMI)
Gerry And The Pacemakers' Greatest Hits . . . . (Laurie)
History Of British Rock-#1-C . . . . (Rhino)
Super Oldies Of The '60s-#5-C . . . . (Audio Fidelity)
Louis Jordan; *Best Of Louis Jordan* . . . . (MCA)
Ray Charles; *Genius Of Ray Charles* . . . . (Atlantic)
Rickie Lee Jones; *Flying Cowboys* . . . . (Geffen)
Don't Pull Your Love
Hamilton, Joe Frank & Reynolds; *'70s Biggest Hits-C* . . . . (MCA Special Prod.)
Hamilton, Joe Frank & Reynolds' Greatest Hits . . . . . (MCA Special Prod.)
Rock Around The Oldies-#4-C . . . . (MCA Special Prod.)
Don't You Hear Jerusalem Moan
Nitty Gritty Dirt Band; *Will The Circle Be Unbroken-#2-C* . . . . (Uni)
Down To My Last Teardrop
Tanya Tucker; *Tanya Tucker's Greatest Hits-1990-1992* . . . . (Capitol)
What Do I Do With Me . . . . (Capitol)
Drive All Night
Bruce Springsteen; *The River* . . . . (Columbia)
Driven To Tears
Police; *ST/Urgh! A Music War* . . . . (A&M)
Zenyatta Mondatta . . . . (A&M)
Sting; *Bring On The Night* . . . . (A&M)
Drivin' & Cryin'
Steve Wariner; *Steve Wariner-Drive* . . . . (Arista)
Drown In My Own Tears
Aretha Franklin; *The Delta Meets Detroit: Aretha's Blues* . . . . (Rhino)
Floyd Cramer; *Essential Floyd Cramer* . . . . (RCA)
Ray Charles; *Best Of Ray Charles: The Atlantic Years* . . . . (Rhino)
Sweet & Soul Tears . . . . (Rhino)
Richie Havens; *Resume: The Best Of Richie Havens* . . . . (Rhino)
Drown In My Own Tears
Smithereens; *Blown To Smithereens: Best Of The Smithereens* . . . . . (Capitol)
Drown In My Own Tears
Joe Cocker; *Mad Dogs & Englishmen* . . . . (A&M)

Dublin In My Tears
Fureys & Dave Arthur; *Dublin Songs-C* . . . . (AJK Music)
Emotion
Destiny's Child; *Survivor* . . . . (Columbia)
The Concert For New York City-C . . . . (Columbia)
Even The Man In The Moon Is Crying
Mark Collie; *Mark Collie* . . . . (MCA)
Every Day I Have To Cry
Steve Alaimo; *Vintage Music-#8-C* . . . . (MCA)
Every Night When The Sun Goes In
Jo Stafford; *Jo Plus Blues* . . . . (Corinthian)
Few More Memories
Dolly Parton; *The Grass Is Blue* . . . . (Sugar Hill)
Finders Keepers, Losers Weepers
Soul Children; *Lost Soul-#1-C* . . . . (Epic)
Finders Keepers, Losers Weepers
Elvis Presley; *Elvis For Everyone!* . . . . (RCA)
Flying
Chris Isaak; *Speak Of The Devil* . . . . (Reprise)
Folsom Prison Blues
Brooks & Dunn with Johnny Cash; *Red Hot + Country-C* . . . . . . (Mercury)
Johnny Cash; *Billboard Top Country Hits-1968-C* . . . . (Rhino)
Classic Cash-Hall Of Fame Series . . . . (Mercury)
Hot Tracks-Train Super Hits-C . . . . (Epic)
Jailhouse Rock (Hits From The Big House)-C . . . . (Sony Music Special Prod.)
Johnny Cash At Folsom Prison & San Quentin . . . . (Columbia)
Johnny Cash-Original Golden Hits-#1 . . . . (Sun)
Johnny Cash's Greatest Hits-#2 . . . . (Columbia)
Superbilly . . . . (Sun)
The Man In Black-His Greatest Hits . . . . (Legacy)
Fool #1
Mavericks; *Trampoline* . . . . (MCA)
Fool To Cry
Rolling Stones; *Black And Blue* . . . . (Rolling Stones)
Rewind (1971-1984) . . . . (Rolling Stones)
Sucking In The Seventies . . . . (Rolling Stones)
For Crying Out Loud
Anita Cochran; *Anita* . . . . (Warner Bros.)
Davis Daniel; *Fighting Fire With Fire* . . . . (Mercury)
For No One
Beatles; *Beatles-Box Set* . . . . (Capitol)
Beatles-Love Songs . . . . (Capitol)
Revolver . . . . (Capitol)
Emmylou Harris; *Pieces Of The Sky* . . . . (Reprise)
Freshmen, The
Verve Pipe; *Villains* . . . . (RCA)
Georgy Porgy
Eric Benet featuring Faith Evans; *A Day In The Life* . . . . . (Warner Bros.)
Toto; *Past To Present 1977-1990* . . . . (Columbia)
Toto . . . . (Columbia)
Go Now!
Moody Blues; *History Of British Rock-#5-C* . . . . (Rhino)
Moody Blues-Anthology . . . . (Polydor)
Wings; *Wings Over America* . . . . (Capitol)
Gold Dust Woman
Fleetwood Mac; *25 Years-The Chain* . . . . (Warner Bros.)
Rumours . . . . (Warner Bros.)
Sister Hazel; *Legacy-A Tribute To Fleetwood Mac's Rumours-C* . . . . (Lava)
Golden Memories And Silver Tears
Jim Reeves; *Best Of Jim Reeves* . . . . (RCA)
Great Moments With Jim Reeves . . . . (RCA)
Jim Reeves' Greatest Hits . . . . (RCA)
Gonna Cry 'Til My Tears Run Dry
Irma Thomas; *Louisiana Scrapbook-C* . . . . (Rykodisc)
Grown Men Don't Cry
Tim McGraw; *Set This Circus Down* . . . . (Curb)
Guess I'll Hang My Tears Out To Dry
Diane Schuur; *In Tribute* . . . . (GRP)
Frank Sinatra; *The Capitol Years* . . . . (Capitol)
Frank Sinatra & Carly Simon; *Frank Sinatra-Duets-C* . . . . (Capitol)
Linda Ronstadt; *What's New* . . . . (Asylum)
Harbor Lights
Boz Scaggs; *Silk Degrees* . . . . (Columbia)
Dinah Washington; *Complete Dinah Washington On Mercury-#2-1950-1952* . . . . (Mercury)
Dinah Washington-Golden Hits . . . . (Mercury)
For Lonely Lovers . . . . (Mercury)
This Is My Story . . . . (Mercury)
Platters; *Super Oldies Of The '60s-#9-C* . . . . (Audio Fidelity)
Heat Wave
Linda Ronstadt; *Linda Ronstadt's Greatest Hits* . . . . (Asylum)
Prisoner In Disguise . . . . (Asylum)
Martha & The Vandellas; *Billboard Top R&B Hits-1963-C* . . . . . . (Rhino)
Martha Reeves & The Vandellas' Greatest Hits . . . . (Motown)
More American Graffiti-#4-C . . . . (MCA)
Motown Story-First 25 Years . . . . (Motown)
Who; *A Quick One (Happy Jack)/Sell Out* . . . . (MCA)
Two's Missing . . . . (MCA)

Hello Walls
Faron Young; *Billboard Top Country Hits-1961-C* . . . . (Rhino)
Willie Nelson; *Essential Willie Nelson* . . . . (RCA)
Willie Nelson-Greatest Songs . . . . (Curb)
Hey, Baby
Marty Stuart; *This One's Gonna Hurt You* . . . .(MCA)
Hey, Mr. Bluebird
Ernest Tubb & Wilburn Brothers; *More Great Country
Duets-C* . . . .(MCA Special Prod.)
Holding Back The Years
Simply Red; *Picture Book* . . . . (Elektra)
Simply Red's Greatest Hits . . . . (East West)
Holes In The Floor Of Heaven
Steve Wariner; *Burnin' The Roadhouse Down* . . . . (Capitol)
Hound Dog
Elvis Presley; *Aloha from Hawaii via Satellite* . . . . (RCA)
Elvis Aron Presley . . . . (RCA)
Elvis As Recorded At Madison Square Garden . . . . (RCA)
Elvis' Golden Records . . . . (RCA)
Elvis In Concert . . . . (RCA)
Elvis Recorded Live On Stage In Memphis . . . . (RCA)
Elvis-A Legendary Performer, Volume 3 . . . . (RCA)
From Memphis To Vegas/From Vegas To Memphis . . . . (RCA)
Number One Hits . . . . (RCA)
ST/Forrest Gump . . . .(Epic/Sony Music Soundtrax)
How Can I Help You Say Goodbye
Patty Loveless; *Only What I Feel* . . . .(Epic)
Patty Loveless-Classics . . . .(Epic)
How Many Tears
Bobby Vee; *Bobby Vee-Legendary Masters* . . . .(EMI)
Hushabye
Mystics; *Doo-Wop Uptempo-#2-C* . . . . (Rhino)
Million-Dollar Memories #1-C . . . . (RCA)
Mystics-16 Golden Classics . . . . (Collectables)
I Ain't Gonna Cry
Little Angels; *Young Gods* . . . . (Polydor)
I Ain't Gonna Cry No More
Penguins; *Golden Classics-Penguins* . . . . (Collectables)
Ronnie Milsap; *Back To The Grindstone* . . . . (RCA)
I Ain't Gonna Cry Tonight
Barbra Streisand; *Wet* . . . . (Columbia)
I Almost Lost My Mind
Eddy Arnold; *World Of Hits* . . . . (MGM)
Fats Domino; *Fats Domino's Greatest Hits* . . . . (MCA)
Ivory Joe Hunter; *Since I Met You Baby* . . . . (Mercury)
Pat Boone; *Pat Boone's Greatest Hits* . . . . (Curb)
I Am Made Of You
Ricky Martin; *Ricky Martin* . . . . (Columbia)
I Call Your Name
Beatles; *Past Masters-Volume One* . . . . (Parlophone)
Rock 'N' Roll Music . . . . (Capitol)
The Beatles' Second Album . . . . (Capitol)
I Can't Stop Crying
Ronnie Milsap; *Ronnie Milsap-16 Greatest Hits-#2* . . . .(Trip)
I Couldn't Keep From Crying
Marty Robbins; *Columbia Country Classics-#2-Honky Tonk
Heroes-C* . . . . (Columbia)
Essential Marty Robbins-1951-1982 . . . . (Columbia)
I Cried
Patti Page; *Patti Page's Greatest Hits-Finest Performances* . . . . (Sun)
I Cried A Tear
LaVern Baker; *Atlantic Rhythm & Blues 1947-1974-#4 (1958-
1962)-C* . . . . (Atlantic)
Billboard Top R&B Hits-1959-C . . . . (Rhino)
I Cried All The Way To The Altar
Patsy Cline; *20 Golden Pieces Of Patsy Cline* . . . .(Bulldog)
Patsy Cline . . . .(Audio Fidelity)
Walkin' Dreams-Her First Recordings-#1 . . . . (Rhino)
I Cried For You
Billie Holiday; *Essential Billie Holiday-Carnegie Hall Concert* . . . . (Verve)
Ella Fitzgerald; *The Intimate Ella* . . . . (Verve)
I Cried For You (Now It's Your Turn To Cry)
Billie Holiday; *First Verve Sessions* . . . . (Verve)
Quintessential-#2-1936 . . . . (Columbia)
Songbook . . . . (Verve)
Sarah Vaughan; *Complete Sarah Vaughan On Mercury-#2* . . . . . . (Mercury)
Divine Sarah Vaughan-Columbia Years-1949-1953 . . . . (Columbia)
Roulette Years . . . . (Roulette)
I Cried Last Night
Charles Brown; *One More For The Road* . . . .(Allegiance)
I Cry
Smokey Robinson & The Miracles; *Miracles' Greatest Hits* . . . . (Motown)
I Cry
Ja Rule; *Rule 3:36* . . . . (Murder Inc./Def Jam/IDJMG)
I Cry For You
Willie Dixon; *Hidden Charms* . . . . (Bug)
I Cry Just A Little Bit
Shakin' Stevens; *Greatest Hits Of The '80s-Get Into The
Greed-C* . . . . (Risky Business)

I Do My Bawling In The Bathroom
David Peel & The Lower East Side; *Have A Marijuana* . . . . (Elektra)
I Don't Make Promises (I Can't Break)
Shannon Curfman; *Loud Guitars Big Suspicions* . . . . (Arista)
I Don't Wanna Cry
Larry Gatlin & The Gatlin Brothers Band; *Larry Gatlin & The Gatlin
Brothers' Greatest Hits* . . . . (Columbia)
Larry Gatlin & The Gatlin Brothers' Greatest Hits-Encore . . . . (Capitol)
Larry Gatlin & The Gatlin Brothers-17 Greatest Hits . . . . (Columbia)
Mariah Carey; *Mariah Carey* . . . . (Columbia)
I Don't Wanna Play House
Sara Evans; *Tammy Wynette...Remembered-C* . . . .(Asylum)
Tammy Wynette; *Tammy Wynette-Anniversary-20 Years Of Hits* . . . . (Epic)
Tammy Wynette's Greatest Hits . . . . (Epic)
Tammy Wynette-Super Hits . . . . (Epic)
I Go To Pieces
Del Shannon; *Rock On!* . . . .(Gone Gator)
Peter And Gordon; *Best Of Peter And Gordon* . . . . (Rhino)
History Of British Rock-#3-C . . . . (Rhino)
Southern Pacific; *County Line* . . . . (Warner Bros.)
Southern Pacific's Greatest Hits . . . . (Warner Bros.)
I Love To Cry At Weddings
Original Cast; *Sweet Charity* . . . . (Columbia)
I Love You Drops
Bill Anderson; *Bill Anderson's Greatest Hits* . . . .(Varese Sarabande)
I Started A Joke
Bee Gees; *Best Of The Bee Gees-#1* . . . .(Polydor)
Here At Last...Bee Gees...Live . . . .(Polydor)
One Night Only . . . .(Polydor)
Wallflowers; *ST/Zoolander* . . . . (Hollywood)
I Take It Back
Sandy Posey; *Best Of Sandy Posey* . . . . (Collectables)
Best Of Sandy Posey-With Skeeter Davis . . . . (Gusto)
I Went To Your Wedding
Patti Page; *Patti Page-Golden Hits* . . . . (Mercury)
I Will Remember You
Sarah McLachlan; *Mirrorball* . . . . (Arista)
ST/Brothers McMullen . . . . (Arista)
Surfacing . . . . (Arista)
Totally Hits-#2-C . . . . (Elektra)
I Wish It Would Rain
Temptations; *16 #1 Hits From The Late '60s-C* . . . . (Motown)
All The Million-Sellers . . . . (Motown)
Billboard Top R&B Hits-1968-C . . . . (Rhino)
Compact Command Performances-Temptations . . . . (Motown)
Motown Story-First 25 Years-C . . . . (Motown)
Temptations-Anthology-The Best Of The Temptations . . . . (Motown)
I Wish It Would Rain
Nanci Griffith; *Little Love Affairs* . . . . (MCA)
I Won't Cry Anymore
Etta James; *These Foolish Things-The Classic Balladry Of Etta James* . . (MCA)
Marvin Gaye; *Romantically Yours* . . . . (Columbia)
If I Was To Start Crying
Oak Ridge Boys; *American Dreams* . . . . (MCA)
If The Jukebox Took Teardrops
Billy Joe Royal; *Out Of The Shadows* . . . .(Atlantic)
Mike Henderson; *Country Music Made Me Do It* . . . .(RCA)
If You Leave Me Tonight I'll Cry
Jerry Wallace; *From The Vaults: Decca Country Classics-1934-
1973-C* . . . .(Decca)
Jerry Wallace's Greatest Hits . . . . (Curb)
I'll Cry Instead
Beatles; *Beatles-Box Set* . . . . (Capitol)
Something New . . . . (Capitol)
ST/A Hard Day's Night . . . . (Capitol)
I'm Going To Sit Right Down And Cry Over You
Elvis Presley; *Elvis Presley* . . . . (RCA)
I'm Gonna Make You Love Me
Jayhawks; *Smile* . . . .(American/Columbia)
I'm Not In Love
10 CC; *10 CC's Greatest Hits-1972-1978* . . . .(Polydor)
Super Hits Of The '70s-Have A Nice Day-#14-C . . . . (Rhino)
Will To Power; Journey Home . . . . (Epic)
I'm So Happy I Can't Stop Crying
Sting; *Mercury Falling* . . . . (A&M)
Toby Keith with Sting; *Dream Walkin'* . . . . (Mercury)
Toby Keith's Greatest Hits, Volume One . . . . (Mercury)
I'm So Lonesome I Could Cry
B.J. Thomas; *B.J. Thomas' Greatest Hits* . . . . (Rhino)
Cowboy Junkies; *Trinity Session* . . . . (RCA)
Hank Williams; *24 Of Hank Williams' Greatest Hits* . . . .(Polydor)
Hank Williams-40 Greatest Hits . . . .(Polydor)
I'm So Lonesome I Could Cry-1949 . . . .(Polydor)
Hank Williams, Jr.; *Very Best Of Hank Williams, Jr.* . . . .(Polydor)
Jim Rooney; *One Day At A Time* . . . . (Rounder)
Johnny Cash; *Hank Williams Songbook-C* . . . . (Columbia)
Keb' Mo'; *Timeless: Hank Williams Tribute-C* . . . . . . (Lost Highway/IDJMG)
Imitation Of Life
R.E.M.; *Reveal* . . . .(Warner Bros.)

In The Valley
Marty Robbins; *Gunfighter Ballads & Trail Songs* (Legacy)
Into Each Life Some Rain Must Fall
Ella Fitzgerald; *Ella & Friends* (Decca Jazz)
Ink Spots; *Encore Of Golden Hits-Ink Spots* (Juke Box Treasures)
Is That A Tear
Tracy Lawrence; *Best Of Tracy Lawrence* (Atlantic)
Time Marches On (Atlantic)
It Only Hurts When I Cry
Dwight Yoakam; *If There Was A Way* (Reprise)
It Takes A Lot To Laugh, It Takes A Train To Cry
Bob Dylan; *Highway 61 Revisited* (Columbia)
The Bootleg Series-Volumes 1-3 [Rare & Unreleased] (Columbia)
Mike Bloomfield/Al Kooper/Stephen Stills; *Super Session* (Columbia)
Itchycoo Park
Small Faces; *Baby Boomer Classics-British Sixties-C* (JCI Assoc. Labels)
It's All Over But The Crying
Hank Williams, Jr.; *Hank Williams, Jr.-14 Greatest Hits* (Polydor)
It's All Over Now
Bobby Womack; *Lookin' For A Love-Best Of Bobby Womack-1968-1975* (Razor & Tie)
John Anderson; *Great Divorce Songs For Him-C* (Warner Bros.)
John Anderson's Greatest Hits-#2 (Warner Bros.)
Rod Stewart; *Best Of Rod Stewart* (Mercury)
Gasoline Alley (Mercury)
Vintage Rod Stewart (Mercury)
Rolling Stones; *12 X 5* (Abkco)
Big Hits (High Tide & Green Grass) (Abkco)
More Hot Rocks (big hits & fazed cookies) (Abkco)
Singles Collection-The London Years (Abkco)
Ry Cooder; *Paradise And Lunch* (Reprise)
It's My Party
Lesley Gore; *Billboard Top Rock 'N' Roll Hits-1963-C* (Rhino)
Golden Hits Of Lesley Gore (Mercury)
Good Time Rock 'N' Roll-C (MCA)
Lesley Gore-Anthology (Rhino)
Oldies But Goodies-#3-C (Original Sound)
I've Cried My Last Tear For You
Ricky Van Shelton; *Greatest Country Hits Of The '90s-1990-C* (Columbia)
RVS III (Columbia)
I've Got A Right To Cry
Mandy Barnett; *I've Got A Right To Cry* (Sire)
Japanese Tears
Denny Laine; *Japanese Tears* (Takoma)
Joy Inside My Tears
Stevie Wonder; *Songs In The Key Of Life* (Motown)
Judy's Turn To Cry
Lesley Gore; *'60s Dance Party-#2-C* (Dominion Entert.)
Golden Hits Of Lesley Gore (Mercury)
Lesley Gore-Anthology (Rhino)
Just Like A Woman
Bob Dylan; *Before The Flood* (Columbia)
Biograph (Columbia)
Blonde On Blonde (Columbia)
Bob Dylan At Budokan (Columbia)
Bob Dylan's Greatest Hits (Columbia)
Byrds; *The Byrds* (Columbia)
Keep Me Cryin'
Al Green; *Al Green's Greatest Hits-#2* (Motown)
Last Resort
Papa Roach; *Infest* (DreamWorks/SKG)
Layla
Derek And The Dominos; *Classic Rock 1966-1988-C* (Atlantic)
Eric Clapton-Crossroads-C (Polydor)
Layla (Polydor)
ST/Goodfellas (Atlantic)
Eric Clapton; *Eric Clapton-Unplugged* (Reprise)
Let 'Er Rip
Dixie Chicks; *Wide Open Spaces* (Monument)
Let Her Cry
Hootie & The Blowfish; *1996 Grammy Nominees-C* (Columbia)
Cracked Rear View (Atlantic)
Letter Full Of Tears
Gladys Knight & The Pips; *Echoes Down The Hall-16 Original Doo-Wop Hits-C* (Arista)
Gladys Knight & The Pips' Greatest Hits (Curb)
Gladys Knight & The Pips-Anthology (Motown)
Life Is Sweet
Natalie Merchant; *Ophelia* (Elektra)
Life Turned Her That Way
''Little'' Jimmy Dickens; *I'm Little, But I'm Loud-The ''Little'' Jimmy Dickens Collection* (Razor & Tie)
Mel Tillis; *Best Of Mel Tillis* (MCA)
Mel Tillis' Greatest Hits (Universal)
Ricky Van Shelton; *Ricky Van Shelton-16 Biggest Hits* (Legacy)
Wild-Eyed Dream (Columbia)
Little Bit Of Soap
Jarmels; *Collectables Presents The History Of Rock-#7-C* (Collectables)
Jarmels-Golden Classics (Collectables)
Laurie Golden Oldies (Laurie)
Million-Dollar Memories #1-C (RCA)
Pick Hits Of The Radio Good Guys-C (Laurie)
Paul Davis; *Best Of Paul Davis* (Bang)
Little Bit Of Paul Davis (Bang)
Little Bitty Tear
Burl Ives; *Best Of Burl Ives-#2* (MCA)
Burl Ives Live (MCA)
MCA Records 30 Years Of Hits-1958-1988-C (MCA)
Hank Cochran; *45-#47062* (Elektra)
Little Old Wine Drinker Me
Dean Martin; *Dean Martin's Greatest Hits-#2* (Reprise)
Welcome To My World (Reprise)
Mel Tillis; *Best Of Mel Tillis* (MCA)
Little White Cloud That Cried
Johnnie Ray; *Best Of Johnnie Ray* (Columbia)
Best Of Johnnie Ray (Exact)
Johnnie Ray's Greatest Hits (Sony Music Special Prod.)
Lonely Teardrops
Jackie Wilson; *Billboard Top R&B Hits-1958-C* (Rhino)
Reet Petite-Best Of Jackie Wilson (Columbia)
The Jackie Wilson Story (Epic)
The Jackie Wilson Story-#2 (Epic)
Lonesome Road
4 Seasons; *25th Anniversary Collection* (Rhino)
Anita O'Day; *Rules Of The Road* (Pablo)
Frank Sinatra; *The Capitol Years* (Capitol)
Preservation Hall Jazz Band; *New Orleans-#4* (Columbia)
Tommy Dorsey; *Sentimental Memories* (Pair)
Lonesome Town
Ricky Nelson; *Best Of Ricky Nelson* (Curb)
Long And Winding Road, The
Beatles; *Beatles 1* (Capitol)
Beatles-20 Greatest Hits (Capitol)
Beatles-Love Songs (Capitol)
Let It Be (Capitol)
Reel Music (Capitol)
The Beatles/1967-1970 (Capitol)
Paul McCartney; *Tripping The Live Fantastic-Highlights!* (Capitol)
Wings; *Wings Over America* (Capitol)
Losing Lisa
Ben Folds; *Rockin' The Suburbs* (Epic)
Love Letters From Old Mexico
Leslie Satcher; *Love Letters* (Warner Bros.)
Lucky
Britney Spears; *Now That's What I Call Music!-#5-C* (Virgin)
Oops!...I Did It Again (Jive)
Man Ain't Supposed To Cry
Public Announcement; *Don't Hold Back* (RCA)
Man Who Couldn't Cry
Johnny Cash; *American Recordings* (American)
Marie
Tommy Dorsey & His Orchestra; *Seventeen Number Ones* (RCA)
Misty
Erroll Garner; *Other Voices* (Columbia)
Johnny Mathis; *First 25 Years-Silver Anniversary Album* (Columbia)
Heavenly (Columbia)
Johnny Mathis' All-Time Greatest Hits (Columbia)
Johnny Mathis-Live (Columbia)
Sarah Vaughan; *Sarah Vaughan-Golden Hits* (Mercury)
Momma Cried
Alison Krauss & Union Station; *New Favorite* (Rounder)
Monday Monday
Mamas & The Papas; *Best Of The Mamas & The Papas* (MCA)
Billboard Top Rock 'N' Roll Hits-1966-C (Rhino)
Farewell To The First Golden Era (MCA)
Gathering Of The Flowers (Dunhill Compact Classics)
ST/Stardust (Dunhill Compact Classics)
Vintage Music-#9-C (MCA)
Neil Diamond; *Double Gold-Neil Diamond* (Bang)
Gang At Bang (Bang)
Shilo (Bang)
The Feel Of Neil Diamond (Bang)
Moon Tears
Nils Lofgren; *Best Of Grin* (Epic)
Grin (Epic Portrait Assoc.)
Night After Night (A&M)
Nils Lofgren-Classics-#13 (A&M)
Most Beautiful Girl
Charlie Rich; *Behind Closed Doors* (Epic)
Charlie Rich's Greatest Hits (Epic)
Columbia Country Classics-#4-Nashville Sound-C (Columbia)
Ms. Jackson
Outkast; *Stankonia* (LaFace/Arista)
My Baby Left Me
Arthur ''Big Boy'' Crudup; *That's All Right (Mama)* (Bluebird)
Creedence Clearwater Revival; *Cosmo's Factory* (Fantasy)
Creedence Country (Fantasy)
Elvis Presley; *Elvis Recorded Live On Stage In Memphis* (RCA)

My First Night With You
Mya; *Mya* . . . . (University/Interscope)
My Heart Cries For You
Charlie Rich; *Charlie Rich-20 Golden Hits* . . . . (Sun)
Time For Tears-C . . . . (Sun)
Dinah Shore; *Nipper's Greatest Hits Of The '50s-#1-C* . . . . (RCA)
Guy Mitchell; *Guy Mitchell-16 Most Requested Songs* . . . . (Legacy)
My Sacrifice
Creed; *Weathered* . . . . (Wind-up)
My True Story
Jive Five; *Back Seat Jams-C* . . . .(Dunhill Compact Classics)
Billboard Top R&B Hits-1961-C . . . . (Rhino)
Cruisin'-1961-C . . . . (Increase)
Jive Five-Their Greatest Hits . . . . (Collectables)
Oldies But Goodies-#4-C . . . . (Original Sound)
Na Na Hey Hey Kiss Him Goodbye
Steam; *Billboard Top Rock 'N' Roll Hits-1969-C* . . . . (Rhino)
Super Hits Of The '70s-Have A Nice Day-#1-C . . . . (Rhino)
Toga Rock-C . . . .(Dunhill Compact Classics)
Needles And Pins
Jackie DeShannon; *Very Best Of Jackie DeShannon* . . . .(EMI)
Searchers; *History Of British Rock-#1-C* . . . . (Rhino)
Searchers' Greatest Hits . . . . (Rhino)
Tom Petty And The Heartbreakers; *Pack Up The Plantation-Live!* . . . . . .(MCA)
New Beginning
Stir; *Holy Dogs* . . . . (Capitol)
Night Time Is Cry Time
Jimmy C. Newman; *Jimmy C. Newman's Greatest Hits* . . . . (Plantation)
Nights
Ed Bruce; *Night Things* . . . . (RCA)
No More Drama
Mary J. Blige; *No More Drama* . . . .(MCA)
No More Tears
Ozzy Osbourne; *No More Tears* . . . . (Epic Portrait Assoc.)
The Ozzman Cometh . . . .(Epic)
No More Tears (Enough Is Enough)
Barbra Streisand & Donna Summer; *Memories* . . . . (Columbia)
Wet . . . . (Columbia)
Donna Summer; *Dance Collection* . . . . (Casablanca)
On The Radio-Greatest Hits-Volumes I & II . . . . (Casablanca)
No One Has To Cry
Fixx; *Ink* . . . .(Impact)
No Tears Left
Crosby, Stills, Nash & Young; *Looking Forward*. . . . . (Reprise)
No Woman, No Cry
Bob Marley; *Bob Marley & The Wailers-Live* . . . .(Tuff Gong)
Bob Marley & The Wailers; *Legend: The Best Of Bob Marley & The
Wailers* . . . . (Island)
Natty Dread . . . .(Tuff Gong)
Songs Of Freedom . . . .(Tuff Gong)
Londonbeat; *In The Blood* . . . .(Radioactive/MCA)
Nobody Wants To Be Lonely
Ricky Martin; *Sound Loaded* . . . . (Columbia)
Not Gon' Cry
Mary J. Blige; *Share My World* . . . .(MCA)
Nothing But A Heartache
Flirtations; *Soul Shots-#2-The ''In'' Crowd-Sweet Soul-C* . . . . (Rhino)
Ocean I'll Cry
Jackie Wilson; *Soul Time* . . . .(Brunswick)
Oh How The Years Go By
Vanessa Williams; *NBA At 50-A Musical Celebration-C* . . . . (Mercury)
Oh Mary Don't You Weep
Pete Seeger; *Live At Newport* . . . . (Vanguard)
Oh Me, Oh My, Sweet Baby
Diamond Rio; *Close To The Edge* . . . . (Arista)
George Strait; *Beyond The Blue Neon*. . . . .(MCA)
Oh, Susanna
Disneyland Cast; *Children's Favorite Songs-#1* . . . . (Disney)
James Taylor; *Sweet Baby James* . . . .(Warner Bros.)
Myron Floren; *Best Of The Wurstfest* . . . .(Ranwood)
Myron Floren . . . .(Ranwood)
One Last Cry
Brian McKnight; *Brian McKnight* . . . . (Mercury)
One Less Bell To Answer
5th Dimension; *5th Dimension-Anthology 1967-1973* . . . . (Rhino)
Greatest Hits On Earth . . . . (Arista)
Barbra Streisand; *Barbra Joan Streisand* . . . . (Columbia)
Gladys Knight & The Pips; *Gladys Knight & The Pips-Anthology* . . . . (Motown)
If I Were Your Woman . . . . (Motown)
Only The Lonely (Know The Way I Feel)
Roy Orbison; *For The Lonely: A Roy Orbison Anthology 1959-1965* . . . (Rhino)
In Dreams-Greatest Hits . . . . (Orbison)
Roy Orbison's All-Time Greatest Hits-#1 & 2 . . . . (Monument)
Ooh Baby Baby
Linda Ronstadt; *Linda Ronstadt's Greatest Hits, Volume Two* . . . . (Asylum)
Living In The USA . . . . (Asylum)
Miracles; *Best Of Smokey Robinson & The Miracles-Anthology* . . . . (Motown)
Smokey Robinson's Greatest Hits-#2 . . . . (Motown)

Out Of Tears
Rolling Stones; *Voodoo Lounge* . . . .(Virgin)
Pass You By
Boyz II Men; *Nathan Michael Shawn Wanya* . . . . (Universal)
Piano In The Dark
Brenda Russell; *Brenda Russell's Greatest Hits* . . . . (A&M)
Get Here . . . . (A&M)
Making Love-C. . . . . (Priority)
Slow Dancin'-C . . . . (K-Tel)
Piece Of My Heart
Big Brother & The Holding Company; *Cheap Thrills*. . . . . (Columbia)
Rock Classics Of The '60s-C . . . . (Columbia)
Seems Like Yesterday-#6-Late '60s-C . . . . (K-Tel)
Bryan Ferry; *These Foolish Things* . . . .(Reprise)
Delaney & Bonnie; *Best Of Delaney & Bonnie* . . . . (Rhino)
Faith Hill; *Take Me As I Am*. (Warner Bros.)
Janis Joplin; *Janis Joplin In Concert* . . . . (Columbia)
Janis Joplin's Greatest Hits . . . . (Columbia)
ST/Janis . . . . (Columbia)
Sammy Hagar; *Standing Hampton* . . . . (Geffen)
Possession
Sarah McLachlan; *Fumbling Towards Ecstasy*. . . . . (Arista)
Pretty Girls Don't Cry
Chris Isaak; *Silvertone* . . . . (Warner Bros.)
Price Of Love
Bryan Ferry; *Let's Stick Together* . . . .(Virgin)
Cactus Brothers; *Cactus Brothers* . . . . (Liberty)
Everly Brothers; *The Reunion Concert-Live At Albert Hall 1983* . . . . . (Mercury)
*Walk Right Back: The Everly Brothers On Warner Bros.-1960-
1969* . . . . (Warner Archives)
Poco; *Crazy Loving-Best Of Poco-1975-1982* . . . . (MCA)
Puke & Cry
Dinosaur Jr.; *Green Mind* . . . .(Sire)
Just Say Anything-#5 Of Just Say Yes-C . . . .(Sire)
Queen Of Tears
Gladys Knight & The Pips; *Every Beat Of My Heart-
Greatest Hits* . . . . (Chameleon)
Raining In My Heart
Anne Murray; *New Kind Of Feeling* . . . . (Capitol)
Buddy Holly; *Buddy Holly-20 Golden Greats*. . . . . (MCA)
The Buddy Holly Collection . . . . (MCA)
Vintage Music-#6-C . . . . (MCA)
Jo-el Sonnier; *Come On Joe* . . . .(RCA)
Leo Sayer; *Leo Sayer*. . . . . (Warner Bros.)
Razorblades
Chris Stills; *100 Year Thing* . . . .(Atlantic)
Read 'Em & Weep
Barry Manilow; *Barry Manilow's Greatest Hits-#3* . . . . (Arista)
Reason To Cry
Lucinda Williams; *Essence* . . . . (Lost Highway/IDJMG)
Reflections
Diana Ross & The Supremes; *Diana Ross & The Supremes' Greatest
Hits-#3* . . . . (Motown)
Diana Ross & The Supremes-25th Anniversary . . . . (Motown)
Diana Ross & The Supremes-Anthology (1962-1969) . . . . (Motown)
Motown Story-First 25 Years-C . . . . (Motown)
Four Tops; *Four Tops-Anthology* . . . . (Motown)
Still Waters Run Deep . . . . (Motown)
Until You Love Someone: More Of The Best (1965-1970) . . . . (Rhino)
Luther Vandross; *Songs* . . . . (Epic)
Richard Cory Cries
Midnight Reign; *Mountain Of Metal*. . . . . (Mountain)
Ridiculous Thoughts
Cranberries; *No Need To Argue*. . . . . (Island)
River Of Tears
York Brothers; *Super Country Hits Of The '40s-C* . . . . (Gusto)
River Of Tears
Highway 101; *Bing Bang Boom* . . . . (Warner Bros.)
River Of Tears
Bonnie Raitt; *Green Light* . . . . (Warner Bros.)
Round About Way
George Strait; *Carrying Your Love With Me* . . . . (MCA)
Latest Greatest Straitest Hits . . . . (MCA)
Run From Tears
Crosby, Stills & Nash; *CSN*. . . . .(Atlantic)
Sad Movies (Make Me Cry)
Sue Thompson; *Collectables Presents The History Of
Rock-#10-C* . . . . (Collectables)
Sue Thompson's Greatest Hits . . . . (Curb)
Sailing Down The Tears
Hanoi Rocks; *Back To Mystery City* . . . . (Geffen)
Senorita With A Necklace Of Tears
Paul Simon; *You're The One* . . . . (Warner Bros.)
She Can't Say I Didn't Cry
Rick Trevino; *Rick Trevino* . . . . (Columbia)
She Cried
Jay & The Americans; *Come A Little Bit Closer-Best Of Jay & The
Americans* . . . . (Gold Rush)
Jay & The Americans' All-Time Greatest Hits . . . . (Rhino)

Jay & The Americans' *Greatest Hits* . . . .(Curb)

She Cried
Toad The Wet Sprocket; *Pale* . . . . (Columbia)

She Doesn't Cry Anymore
Shenandoah; *Road Not Taken* . . . . (Columbia)
Shenandoah . . . . (Columbia)

She Needs Someone To Hold Her (When She Cries)
Conway Twitty; *Best Of Conway Twitty-#2* . . . . (MCA Special Prod.)
Conway Twitty's Greatest Hits-#2 . . . . (MCA)

She's Crying For Me
New Orleans Rhythm Kings; *RCA Victor Jazz: First Half-Century-C* . . . .(RCA)

She's Long, She's Tall, She Weeps Like A Willow Tree
John Lee Hooker; *Black Snake* . . . .(Fantasy)
Country Blues Of John Lee Hooker . . . . (Riverside)

She's Not Cryin' Anymore
Billy Ray Cyrus; *Some Gave All* . . . . (Mercury)

Sister Don't Cry
Collective Soul; *Hints, Allegations And Things Left Unsaid* . . . (Atlantic)

Sky Is Crying
Albert King; *I'm In A Phone Booth Baby* . . . . (Stax)
Years Gone By . . . . (Stax)
Elmore James; *Elmore James-Complete Fire & Enjoy
Sessions-#1* . . . . (Collectables)
Red Hot Blues . . . . (Intermedia)
Eric Clapton; *Eric Clapton-Crossroads-C* . . . . (Polydor)
George Thorogood & The Destroyers; *George Thorogood & The Destroyers-
Live* . . . . (EMI)
Move It On Over . . . . (Rounder)
Stevie Ray Vaughan and Double Trouble; *The Sky Is Crying* . . . . (Epic)

Smoke Gets In Your Eyes
Bryan Ferry; *Another Time Another Place* . . . . (Reprise)
Street Life-20 Great Hits . . . . (Reprise)
Dinah Washington; *Golden Classics-Dinah Washington* . . . . (Collectables)
Lawrence Welk; *Musical Memories With Lawrence Welk* . . . . (Ranwood)
Patti Austin; *Real Me* . . . . (Qwest)
Platters; *Encore Of Golden Hits-Platters* . . . . (Mercury)
Oldies But Goodies-#14-C . . . .(Original Sound)
Platters Greatest Hits . . . . (Everest)
ST/Always . . . . (MCA)
ST/American Graffiti . . . . (MCA)
Super Oldies Of The '50s-#5-C . . . . (Audio Fidelity)

Some Broken Hearts
Bellamy Brothers; *The Reggae Cowboys* . . . . (Bellamy Bros./Intersound)

Some Broken Hearts Never Mend
Don Williams; *Best Of Don Williams-#2* . . . . (MCA)
Don Williams-20 Greatest Hits . . . . (MCA)
Some Broken Hearts Never Mend . . . . (MCA Special Prod.)

Somebody's Crying
Chris Isaak; *Forever Blue* . . . . (Reprise)
VH-1 Crossroads-C . . . . (Atlantic)

Somehow Tonight
Ricky Skaggs and Kentucky Thunder; *Bluegrass Rules!* . . . . (Rounder)

Someone's Gotta Cry
Jean Shepard; *45-#5392* . . . . (Capitol)

Something Beautiful Remains
Tina Turner; *Wildest Dreams* . . . .(Virgin)

Spilled Perfume
Pam Tillis; *Sweetheart's Dance* . . . . (Arista)

Stacked Actors
Foo Fighters; *There Is Nothing Left To Lose* . . . .(Roswell/RCA)

Standin' Round Crying
Eric Clapton; *From The Cradle* . . . . (Duck/Reprise)

Standing In The Doorway
Bob Dylan; *Time Out Of Mind* . . . . (Columbia)

Start Me Up
Rolling Stones; *"Still Life" (American Concert 1981)* . . . .(Virgin)
Flashpoint . . . .(Virgin)
Tattoo You . . . .(Virgin)

Still She Cries
Journey; *Trial By Fire* . . . . (Columbia)

Stop Your Sobbing
Kinks; *Kinks' Greatest Hits* . . . . (Rhino)
One For The Road . . . . (Arista)
You Really Got Me . . . . (Rhino)
Pretenders; *Pretenders* . . . . (Sire)
Pretenders-The Singles . . . . (Sire)

Sue Me
Original Cast; *Guys & Dolls* . . . . (MCA)
Guys & Dolls . . . . (Motown)

Sullivan
Caroline's Spine; *Monsoon* . . . . (Hollywood)

Summer Kisses, Winter Tears
Elvis Presley; *Collector's Gold* . . . .(RCA)

Summertime
Billy Stewart; *Best Of Chess Rhythm & Blues-#1-C* . . . . (Chess)
Summer & Sun-C . . . . (Rhino)
Booker T. & The M.G.s; *Best Of Booker T. & The M.G.s* . . . . . (Atlantic)
Carmen McRae; *Greatest Of Carmen McRae* . . . . (MCA)

Chet Baker; *My Favourite Songs-#1-Last Great Concert* . . . .(Enja)
Courtney Pine; *Glory Of Gershwin Featuring Larry Adler-C* . . . .(Mercury)
Ella Fitzgerald & Louis Armstrong; *Porgy & Bess* . . . .(Verve)
George Benson; *Best Of George Benson* . . . .(CBS Associated)
Janis Joplin; *Janis Joplin's Greatest Hits* . . . . (Columbia)
ST/Janis . . . . (Columbia)
Lambert, Hendricks & Ross; *Best Of Lambert, Hendricks & Ross* . . . .(Columbia)
Miles Davis & His Orchestra; *Porgy & Bess* . . . . (Columbia)
Original Cast; *Porgy & Bess* . . . . (MCA)
Peter Gabriel; *Glory Of Gershwin Featuring Larry Adler-C* . . . . . .(Mercury)
Rick Nelson; *Best Of Rick Nelson-#2* . . . . (EMI)
Sam Cooke; *Best Of Sam Cooke* . . . . (RCA)
Sarah Vaughan; *1940s-The Singers-C* . . . . (Columbia)
Divine Sarah Vaughan-Columbia Years-1949-1953 . . . . (Columbia)
Stan Getz; *Compact Jazz-Stan Getz* . . . .(Verve)
Willie Nelson & Leon Russell; *One For The Road* . . . . (Columbia)

Sure Gonna Miss Her
Gary Lewis And The Playboys; *Gary Lewis And The Playboys'
Greatest Hits* . . . .(Curb)
Gary Lewis And The Playboys-Legendary Masters Series . . . . . (EMI)

Talk Back Trembling Lips
Ernest Ashworth; *Best Of Ernest Ashworth* . . . .(Curb)
Johnny Tillotson; *Cruisin'-1964-C* . . . . (Increase)

Tear Drops
Elton John & k.d. lang; *Duets-C* . . . . (MCA)
Jonathan Butler; *Deliverance* . . . . (Jive)

Tear Fell, A
Teresa Brewer; *Best Of Teresa Brewer* . . . . (MCA Jazz)

Tear For Tear
Walter Jackson; *Walter Jackson's Greatest Hits* . . . .(Epic)

Tear For The Girl
Martha Reeves & The Vandellas; *Live Wire! Singles-1962-1972* . . . . .(Motown)

Tear In Your Hand
Tori Amos; *Little Earthquakes* . . . . (Atlantic)

Tear Stained Letter
Jo-el Sonnier; *Best Of Country Rock-C* . . . .(K-Tel)
Come On Joe . . . . (RCA)
Richard Thompson; *Hand Of Kindness* . . . . (Hannibal)

Teardrop Collector
Love And Rockets; *Love And Rockets* . . . . (Beggar's Banquet)

Teardrop On A Rose
Hank Williams; *Alone With His Guitar* . . . .(Mercury)
Let's Turn Back The Years-1951-1953 . . . . (Polydor)

Teardrops
Lee Andrews And The Hearts; *Best Of Chess Rock 'N' Roll-#1-C* . . . . . .(Chess)
Lee Andrews And The Hearts' Biggest Hits . . . .(Collectables)
WCBS FM 101 History Of Rock-For Lovers-#1-C . . . .(Collectables)
WOGL Oldies 98-History Of Rock-#2-C . . . .(Collectables)

Teardrops
George Ducas; *George Ducas* . . . .(Capitol)

Teardrops
George Harrison; *Somewhere In England* . . . . (Dark Horse)

Teardrops
Rick James; *Throwin' Down* . . . .(Motown)

Teardrops From My Eyes
Ruth Brown; *Miss Rhythm-Greatest Hits & More* . . . .(Rhino)

Teardrops In My Eyes
David Grisman; *Home Is Where The Heart Is* . . . . (Rounder)
New Riders Of The Purple Sage; *Adventures Of Panama Red* . . . .(Columbia)

Teardrops In My Heart
Marty Robbins; *Marty Robbins' Biggest Hits* . . . . (Columbia)
Sons Of The Pioneers; *Cool Water* . . . . (RCA)

Teardrops Will Fall
Ry Cooder; *Into The Purple Valley* . . . . (Reprise)
Wilson Pickett; *In The Midnight Hour* . . . .(Rhino)

Tears
Chet Atkins & Mark Knopfler; *Neck And Neck* . . . .(Columbia)
Django Reinhardt & Stephane Grappelli; *Django Reinhardt & Stephane
Grappelli* . . . . (Crescendo)

Tears
Isley Brothers; *Mission To Please* . . . . (T-Neck/Island)

Tears
Rush; *2112* . . . .(Mercury)

Tears
Missing Persons; *Best Of Missing Persons* . . . .(Capitol)
Spring Session M . . . .(Capitol)

Tears
Chris Isaak; *Silvertone* . . . . (Warner Bros.)

Tears
Bobby Vinton; *More Of Bobby's Greatest Hits* . . . .(Epic)

Tears
Persuaders; *Harlem Holiday-New York Rhythm & Blues-#4-C* . . . .(Collectables)

Tears Are Just For Fools
Starlites; *Harlem Holiday-New York Rhythm & Blues-#7-C* . . . . . .(Collectables)

Tears Before Bedtime
Elvis Costello & The Attractions; *Imperial Bedroom* . . . . (Columbia)

Tears Came Rollin' Down
John Mayall's Bluesbreakers; *Chicago Line* . . . .(Island)

Tears Don't Care Who Cries Them
k.d. lang; *Shadowland*. . . . . (Sire)

Tears Falling Down
Rosanne Cash; *The Wheel*. . . . . (Columbia)

Tears For You
Judds; *Collection-1983-1990* . . . . (RCA)
  Collector's Series-The Judds . . . . (RCA)
  Rockin' With The Rhythm . . . . (MCA)

Tears In Heaven
Eric Clapton; *Diana, Princess Of Wales-Tribute-C* . . . . (Columbia)
  Eric Clapton-Unplugged . . . . (Reprise)
  ST/Rush . . . . (Reprise)

Tears In My Eyes
Baltineers; *For Collectors Only-#1-The Rarities-C* . . . . (Collectables)
  Great Groups Of The '50s-#2-C . . . . (Collectables)
Dreamers; *Harlem New York-Ballad Era-C* . . . . . . (Collectables)
Joan Baez; *Very Early Joan Baez* . . . . (Vanguard)

Tears In The Morning
Beach Boys; *Sunflower* . . . . (Caribou)

Tears In The Rain
Triumph; *Sport Of Kings* . . . . (MCA)
  Triumph-Classics . . . . (MCA)

Tears Keep On Falling
Jerry Vale; *Jerry Vale-17 Most Requested Songs* . . . . (Legacy)
  Jerry Vale's All-Time Greatest Hits . . . . (Columbia)

Tears Of A Clown
English Beat; *I Just Can't Stop It* . . . . (I.R.S.)
  What Is Beat . . . . (I.R.S.)
Smokey Robinson & The Miracles; *25 #1 Hits From 25 Years-C* . . . . (Motown)
  Billboard Top Rock 'N' Roll Hits-1970-C . . . . . . (Rhino)
  Compact Command Performances-Smokey Robinson & The
   Miracles . . . . (Motown)
  Endless Love-Motown's Greatest Love Songs-C . . . . . . (Motown)
  Smokey Robinson & The Miracles' Anthology . . . . (Motown)
  Tears Of A Clown . . . . (Motown)

Tears Of Pearls
Savage Garden; *Savage Garden* . . . . (Columbia)

Tears Of Rage
Band; *Best Of The Band* . . . . (Capitol)
  Music From Big Pink . . . . (Capitol)
  To Kingdom Come-The Definitive Collection . . . . (Capitol)
Bob Dylan And The Band; *Basement Tapes* . . . . (Columbia)

Tears Of Sahara
Tony MacAlpine; *Maximum Security* . . . . (Mercury)

Tears Of The Dragon
Bruce Dickinson; *Balls To Picasso* . . . . (Mercury)

Tears Of The Lonely
Mickey Gilley; *Mickey Gilley's Biggest Hits* . . . .(Epic)
  Ten Years Of Love . . . . (Epic)

Tears On My Pillow
Chimes; *Golden Groups-C* . . . . (Specialty)
  Original Rock Oldies-Golden Hits-#2-C . . . . (Specialty)
Kylie Minogue; *Enjoy Yourself* . . . .(Geffen)
Little Anthony And The Imperials; *Best Of Little Anthony And The*
  Imperials . . . .(EMI)
  Best Of Little Anthony And The Imperials . . . . . . (Rhino)
  Billboard Top R&B Hits-1958-C . . . . (Rhino)
  Good Time Rock 'N' Roll-C . . . . (MCA)
Lorrie Morgan; *Something In Red* . . . . (RCA)
New Edition & Little Anthony; *Under The Blue Moon* . . . . (MCA)
Reba McEntire; *Feel The Fire* . . . . (Mercury)
Sha Na Na; *ST/Grease* . . . . (Polydor)

Tears Will Be The Chaser For Your Wine
Wanda Jackson; *Rockin' In The Country-Best Of Wanda Jackson* . . . . . . (Rhino)
  Wanda Jackson's Greatest Hits . . . . (Gusto)

Tell Me Why
Beatles; *Beatles-Box Set* . . . . (Capitol)
  Something New . . . . (Capitol)
  ST/A Hard Day's Night . . . . (Capitol)

Ten Thousand Angels Cried
LeAnn Rimes; *You Light Up My Life-Inspirational Songs* . . . . (Curb)

Texas
Merle Haggard; *Friend In California* . . . .(Epic)
Merle Haggard & Freddy Powers; *Texas Super Hits-C* . . . . . . (Columbia)

Thanks A Lot
Ernest Tubb; *The Country Music Hall Of Fame-Ernest Tubb* . . . . . . (MCA)
IIIrd Time Out; *IIIrd Time Out* . . . .(Rebel)
Ronnie & Rob McCoury; *Ronnie & Rob McCoury*. . . . . (Rounder)

That's Why I'm Crying
Ivy League; *History Of British Rock-#2-C* . . . . (Rhino)
Koko Taylor; *I Got What It Takes* . . . . (Alligator)

There Goes My Heart
Mavericks; *Best Of The Mavericks-Super Colossal Smash Hits Of*
  The '90s. . . . . (Mercury)
  What A Crying Shame . . . . (MCA)

There'll Be No Teardrops Tonight
Anita Carter; *Hank Williams Songbook-C* . . . . (Columbia)

Hank Williams; *24 Of Hank Williams' Greatest Hits* . . . .(Polydor)
  Hank Williams' Greatest Hits. . . . .(Polydor)

There'll Be Sad Songs (To Make You Cry)
Billy Ocean; *Billy Ocean's Greatest Hits* . . . .(Jive)
  Love Zone. . . . .(Jive)

There's A Tear In My Beer
Hank Williams, Jr. & Hank Williams, Sr.; *Complete Hank Williams* . . (Mercury)
  Hank Williams, Jr.'s Greatest Hits III . . . . (Curb)

These Eyes
Guess Who; *Best Of The Guess Who* . . . . (RCA)
  Greatest Of The Guess Who . . . . (RCA)
  Nipper's Greatest Hits Of The '60s-#1-C . . . . . . (RCA)
  Track Record-Collection . . . .(RCA)

Thinking About Your Troubles
Nilsson; *The Point*. . . . .(RCA)

Thirty Years Of Tears
John Hiatt; *Stolen Moments*. . . . . (A&M)

This Ain't A Love Song
Bon Jovi; *These Days* . . . . (Mercury)

'Til A Tear Becomes A Rose
Jann Browne; *Tell Me Why* . . . . (Curb)
  'Til A Tear Becomes A Rose . . . . (Curb)
Keith Whitley; *Keith Whitley's Greatest Hits* . . . . . (RCA)
Lorrie Morgan; *Lorrie Morgan's Greatest Hits* . . . . (BNA)

Time To Cry
Paul Anka; *Paul Anka's 21 Golden Hits* . . . . (RCA)

To Cry You A Song
Jethro Tull; *Benefit* . . . . (Chrysalis)
  Repeat-The Best Of Jethro Tull, Vol. II. . . . . . . (Chrysalis)

To See My Angel Cry
Conway Twitty; *Conway Twitty-Number Ones-#1* . . . . (Liberty)
  Conway Twitty's Greatest Hits-#1 . . . . (MCA)

Today I Started Loving You Again
Blue Ridge Rangers; *Blue Ridge Rangers* . . . . (Fantasy)
Merle Haggard; *Best Of The Best Of Merle Haggard* . . . . . . (Liberty)
  Merle Haggard-Super Hits-#2 . . . . (Epic)

Today's Teardrops
Rick Nelson; *Best Of Rick Nelson-#2* . . . . (EMI)
Roy Orbison; *Rare Orbison*. . . . . (Monument)

Together Again
Buck Owens; *Buck Owens' All-Time Greatest Hits-#1* . . . . . . (Curb)
  Very Best Of Buck Owens-#1 . . . . (Rhino)
Emmylou Harris; *Elite Hotel*. . . . . (Reprise)
  Profile/Best Of Emmylou Harris. . . . . (Warner Bros.)

Tomb Of The Unknown Love
Cassell Webb; *Songs Of A Stranger* . . . .(Venture)
Kenny Rogers; *The Heart Of The Matter* . . . . (RCA)

Too Beautiful To Cry
Roger Whittaker; *Roger Whittaker Greatest Hits* . . . . (RCA)
  Wind Beneath My Wings. . . . . (RCA)

Toot Toot Tootsie (Goo'Bye)
Al Jolson; *Al Jolson-Best Of The Decca Years* . . . . . (MCA)
  Best Of Al Jolson . . . . (MCA)
Liza Minnelli; *Liza Minnelli-At Carnegie Hall* . . . . . (Telarc)

Tracks Of My Tears, The
Bryan Ferry; *These Foolish Things* . . . . (Reprise)
Gladys Knight & The Pips; *Gladys Knight & The Pips-Anthology* . . . . (Motown)
Johnny Rivers; *Best Of Johnny Rivers* . . . . (EMI)
Linda Ronstadt; *Linda Ronstadt's Greatest Hits* . . . .(Asylum)
  Prisoner In Disguise . . . . (Asylum)
Smokey Robinson & The Miracles; *Billboard Top R&B Hits-1965-*
  1969-C . . . . (Rhino)
  Smokey Robinson & The Miracles' Anthology . . . . (Motown)
  Smokey Robinson & The Miracles' Greatest Hits-#2 . . . . (Motown)
  ST/Big Chill . . . . (Motown)
  ST/Sound Of "Murphy Brown" . . . . (MCA)

Trail Of Tears
Southern Pacific; *Southern Pacific's Greatest Hits* . . . . . . (Warner Bros.)
  Zuma. . . . . (Warner Bros.)

Trail Of Tears
John Denver; *Dreamland Express* . . . . (RCA)

Trail Of Tears
Guadalcanal Diary; *Walking In The Shadow Of The Big Man* . . . . (Elektra)

Trail Of Tears
Tanya Tucker; *What Do I Do With Me* . . . . (Capitol)

True Love Never Dies
Earl Scruggs & Gary Scruggs & Travis Tritt; *Earl Scruggs And*
  Friends-C . . . . (MCA)
Kevin Welch; *Kevin Welch* . . . . (Reprise)

True Love, True Love (If You Can Cry)
Drifters; *1959-1965-All-Time Greatest Hits And More*. . . . .(Atlantic)
  Drifters-Golden Hits . . . .(Atlantic)

Two Faces Have I
Lou Christie; *Back To The '60s-#4-C* . . . . (Dominion Entert.)
  Enlighten'ment-Best Of Lou Christie . . . . (Rhino)

Two Kinds Of Teardrops
Del Shannon; *Del Shannon's Greatest Hits*. . . . . . . (Rhino)

Two Teardrops
Steve Wariner; *Two Teardrops* (Capitol)
Un-Break My Heart
Toni Braxton; *Secrets* (LaFace)
Until My Dreams Come True
Jack Greene; *Until My Dreams Come True* (Decca)
Valley Of Tears
Buddy Holly; *Buddy Holly* (MCA)
Fats Domino; *Antoine "Fats" Domino* (Rhino)
My Blue Heaven-Best Of Fats Domino-#1 (EMI)
Vidalia
Sammy Kershaw; *Politics Religion & Her* (Mercury)
Wailing Of The Willow
Nilsson; *Aerial Ballet* (RCA)
Walk Away Renee
Four Tops; *Compact Command Performances-Four Tops* (Motown)
Four Tops Reach Out (Motown)
Four Tops-Anthology (Motown)
Left Banke; *Cruisin'-1966-C.* (Increase)
History Of The Left Banke (Rhino)
Vonda Shepard; *ST/Songs From "Ally McBeal" Featuring Vonda Shepard* (550/Epic)
Walk On By
Dionne Warwick; *Dionne Warwick-Anthology 1962-1971* (Rhino)
Hot! Live & Otherwise (Arista)
I Am Woman-C (Nick At Nite)
Oldies But Goodies-#15-C (Original Sound)
Scepter Records Story-C (Capricorn)
Isaac Hayes; *Isaac Hayes' Greatest Hit Singles* (Stax)
Melissa Manchester; *Romantic Hits Of The '80s-C* (K-Tel)
Tribute (Polydor)
Sybil; *Sybil* (Next Plateau/London/Island)
Walk Softly
Billy "Crash" Craddock; *Billy "Crash" Craddock Live* (MCA)
Billy "Crash" Craddock Sings His Greatest Hits (MCA)
Easy As Pie (MCA)
Walkin', Talkin'...Beatin' Broken Heart
Highway 101; *Country's Greatest Hits-#4-Sweet Country-C* (Priority)
Paint The Town (Warner Bros.)
Wall Of Tears
K.T. Oslin; *80's Ladies* (RCA)
New Faces Of Country-C (K-Tel)
We're All Alone
Boz Scaggs; *Boz Scaggs-Hits!* (Columbia)
Slow Dancer (Columbia)
Rita Coolidge; *Rita Coolidge's Greatest Hits* (A&M)
Whales Weep Not (Overture)
Paul Winter Consort; *Whales Alive* (Living Music)
Paul Winter Consort & Paul Halley; *Living Music Collection II* (Living Music)
What A Crying Shame
Mavericks; *Best Of The Mavericks-Super Colossal Smash Hits Of The '90s* (Mercury)
What A Crying Shame (MCA)
What Would You Do?
City High; *City High* (Interscope)
Now That's What I Call Music!-#7-C (Virgin)
ST/Life (Rock Land/Interscope)
When Doves Cry
Ginuwine; *The Bachelor* (550 Music)
Prince and the Revolution; *ST/Purple Rain* (Warner Bros.)
When I Close My Eyes
Shanice; *Shanice* (LaFace)
When She Cries
Restless Heart; *Big Iron Horses* (RCA)
Restless Heart's Greatest Hits (RCA)
Today's Number One Country-C (K-Tel)
When The Children Cry
White Lion; *Best Of White Lion* (Atlantic)
Pride (Atlantic)
When U Cry I Cry
Jesse; *Never Let You Go* (Underworld/Capitol)
When You Ask About Love
Crickets; *45-#9-55153* (Brunswick)
When You See The Tears From My Eyes
Buddy Guy; *Very Best Of Buddy Guy* (Rhino)
Buddy Guy & Junior Wells; *Drinkin' TNT 'N' Smokin' Dynamite* (Blind Pig)
While My Guitar Gently Weeps
Beatles; *Beatles-Box Set* (Capitol)
The Beatles (White Album) (Capitol)
The Beatles/1967-1970 (Capitol)
George Harrison; *Best Of George Harrison* (Capitol)
Concert For Bangladesh-C (Capitol)
Live In Japan (Dark Horse)
Who's Crying Now
Journey; *Escape* (Columbia)
Journey-Greatest Hits Live (Columbia)
Journey's Greatest Hits (Columbia)
Time Cubed (Box) (Columbia)
Who's Sorry Now
Benny Goodman; *Stompin'* (Drive)
Big Bill Broonzy; *Black, Brown & White* (Evidence Music)
Bob Crosby; *Bob Crosby & His Orchestra* (EPM)
Connie Francis; *Dick Clark's 21 All-Time Hits-#1-C* (Original Sound)
Very Best Of Connie Francis (Polydor)
Ella Fitzgerald; *The Intimate Ella* (Verve)
Esquivel; *Space-Age Bachelor Pad Music* (Bar/None)
Glen Gray; *Moonglow: 1930-1936* (Aero Space)
Nat "King" Cole; *The Billy May Sessions* (Capitol)
Ray Anthony; *Swing Back To The '40s* (Aero Space)
Whose Shoulder Will You Cry On
Kitty Wells; *Kitty Wells' Greatest Hits* (Step One)
Why Baby Why
Charley Pride; *Charley Pride's Greatest Hits-#2* (RCA)
George Jones; *George Jones' All-Time Greatest Hits* (Epic)
George Jones-Super Hits (Epic)
Red Sovine & Webb Pierce; *Greatest Country Duets Of All Time-C* (MCA Special Prod.)
Webb Pierce; *Webb Pierce-Golden Hits-#2* (Plantation)
Willie Nelson & Waylon Jennings; *Take It To The Limit* (Columbia)
Why Should I Cry For You?
Sting; *Fields Of Gold-The Best Of Sting 1984-1994* (A&M)
Soul Cages (A&M)
Willow Weep For Me
Art Tatum; *Best Of Art Tatum* (Pablo)
Solo Masterpieces-#1 (Pablo)
Billie Holiday; *Billie Holiday-Live* (Verve)
Billie's Blues (Blue Note)
Lady Sings The Blues (Verve)
Stormy Blues (Verve)
Chad & Jeremy; *Best Of Chad & Jeremy* (Capitol)
History Of British Rock-#3-C (Rhino)
Super Oldies Of The '60s-#11-C (Audio Fidelity)
Dinah Shore; *Dinah Shore-16 Most Requested Songs* (Legacy)
Lou Rawls; *Legendary Lou Rawls* (Blue Note)
Roy Eldridge; *Best Of Roy Eldridge* (Pablo)
Steve Miller; *Born 2 B Blue* (Gold Rush)
Wine Me Up
Faron Young; *Faron Young-Golden Hits* (Mercury)
Faron Young-The Hits (Mercury)
Working My Way Back To You
4 Seasons; *25th Anniversary Collection* (Rhino)
4 Seasons-Anthology (Rhino)
Working My Way Back To You/Forgive Me, Girl
Spinners; *Billboard Top Hits-1980-C* (Rhino)
One Of A Kind Love Affair-Anthology (Rhino)
Very Best Of The Spinners (Rhino)
World I Know, The
Collective Soul; *Collective Soul* (Atlantic)
You Can't Lose Me
Faith Hill; *It Matters To Me* (Warner Bros.)
You Don't Have To Be A Baby To Cry
Caravelles; *Best Of The Girl Groups-#1-C* (Rhino)
Sensational '60s-#5-C (Dominion Entert.)
Tennessee Ernie Ford; *The Ultimate Tennessee Ernie Ford* (Razor & Tie)
You Don't Have To Cry
Crosby, Stills & Nash; *Crosby, Stills & Nash* (Atlantic)
You Were Mine
Dixie Chicks; *Big Country Hits '99-C* (K-Tel)
Wide Open Spaces (Monument)
You Won't See Me Cry
Wilson Phillips; *Shadows & Light* (SBK)
Your Cheatin' Heart
Beck; *Timeless: Hank Williams Tribute-C* (Lost Highway/IDJMG)
Elvis Presley; *Elvis For Everyone!* (RCA)
Welcome To My World (RCA)
Frankie Laine; *Frankie Laine's 16 Greatest Hits* (Trip)
Frankie Laine's Greatest Hits (Columbia)
Hank Williams With His Drifting Cowboys; *24 Of Hank Williams' Greatest Hits* (Polydor)
Hank Williams-16 Great Hits (Everest)
Hank Williams-40 Greatest Hits (Polydor)
Hank Williams, Jr.; *Very Best Of Hank Williams, Jr.* (Polydor)
Jerry Lee Lewis; *Live At The Star Club-Hamburg 1964* (Rhino)
The Golden Hits Of Jerry Lee Lewis (Smash)
Patsy Cline; *ST/Sweet Dreams* (MCA)
The Patsy Cline Story (MCA)
Ray Charles; *Ray Charles' Greatest Hits-#2* (Rhino)
You're Only Lonely
J.D. Souther; *Radio Daze-Pop Hits Of The '80s-#1-C* (Rhino)
You're Only Lonely (Legacy)
You're The One
Paul Simon; *You're The One* (Warner Bros.)
Zoomin'
Lionel Richie; *Time* (Mercury)

DANCE, Boogie, Dance Styles, Shaking, Shuffle
See Also: BALLET, FUN, MUSIC, PARTY, RHYTHM, ROCK

"E" Street Shuffle
Bruce Springsteen; *The Wild, The Innocent & The E Street Shuffle* . . (Columbia)
(I've Had) The Time Of My Life
Bill Medley; *Best Of Bill Medley* . . . . (Curb)
Bill Medley & Jennifer Warnes; *Dirty Dancing Live In Concert-C* . . . . . . (RCA)
ST/Dirty Dancing . . . . (RCA)
(When You Fall In Love) Everything's A Waltz
Ed Bruce; *One To One* . . . .(MCA)
1,2,3,4 (Sumpin' New)
Coolio; *ESPN Presents Jock Jams-#2-C* . . . . (Tommy Boy)
MTV Party To Go-#9-C . . . . (Tommy Boy)
Tommy Boy's Greatest Beats-#2-C . . . . (Tommy Boy)
42nd Street
Diana Krall; *Stepping Out* . . . . (Justin Time)
Hal Kemp; *Best Of The Big Bands-C* . . . . (Columbia)
Mel Torme; *Cocktail Mix-#3-Swingin' Singles-C* . . . . (Rhino)
Original Broadway Cast; *42nd Street* . . . .(RCA Victor)
Adalida
George Strait; *Latest Greatest Straitest Hits* . . . .(MCA)
Lead On . . . .(MCA)
African Dance
Soul II Soul; *Keep On Movin'* . . . . (Virgin)
After The Ball
Barbara Cook/Original Cast; *Show Boat* . . . . (Columbia)
After The Dance
Marvin Gaye; *I Heard It Through The Grapevine/I Want You* . . . . . . (Motown)
I Want You . . . . (Motown)
Marvin Gaye's Greatest Hits . . . . (Motown)
Musical Testament 1964-1984 . . . . (Motown)
After The Lights Go Down Low
Al Hibbler; *After The Lights Go Down Low* . . . . (Atlantic)
Air Dance
Black Sabbath; *Never Say Die* . . . .(Warner Bros.)
All Night Long
Faith Evans featuring Puff Daddy; *Keep The Faith* . . . . . (Bad Boy/Arista)
All Night Long
Montgomery Gentry; *Tattoos & Scars* . . . . (Columbia)
All Night Long (All Night)
Lionel Richie; *Can't Slow Down* . . . . (Motown)
Motown Story-First 25 Years-C . . . . (Motown)
All She Wants To Do Is Dance
Don Henley; *Building The Perfect Beast* . . . .(Geffen)
And We Danced
Hooters; *Nervous Night* . . . . (Columbia)
Anniversary Song
Al Jolson; *Al Jolson-Best Of The Decca Years* . . . .(MCA)
Cocktail Hour . . . . (Columbia River Entert. Group)
Dinah Shore; *Buttons & Bows* . . . . (ASV)
Dinah Shore-16 Most Requested Songs-Encore! . . . . (Legacy)
Django Reinhardt; *Verve Jazz Masters 38* . . . .(Verve)
Eva Cassidy; *Time After Time* . . . .(Blix Street)
Guy Lombardo & His Royal Canadians; *Enjoy Yourself, The Hits Of Guy
Lombardo* . . . .(MCA)
Apache Dance
Woody Herman & His Orchestra; *The Uncollected Woody Herman & His
Orchestra* . . . . (Hindsight)
Apeman Hop
Ramones; *Animal Boy* . . . . (Sire)
April Waltz
Critton Hollow; *Great Dreams* . . . . (Flying Fish)
Aqua Boogie (A Pscychoalphadiscobetabioaquadoloop)
Parliament; *Motor-Booty Affair* . . . . (Casablanca)
Parliament's Greatest Hits . . . . (Casablanca)
At The Ballet
Original Cast; *A Chorus Line* . . . . (Columbia)
At The Hop
Danny & The Juniors; *Billboard Top Rock 'N' Roll Hits-1958-C* . . . . . . (Rhino)
Cruisin'-1958-C . . . .(Increase)
Oldies But Goodies-#2-C . . . . (Original Sound)
Rockin' With Danny & The Juniors . . . .(MCA Special Prod.)
Super Oldies Of The '50s-#6-C . . . . (Audio Fidelity)
Sha Na Na; *ST/Woodstock* . . . . (Atlantic)
At The Mambo Inn
George Benson; *Tenderly* . . . .(Warner Bros.)
Baby Do The Philly Dog
Olympics; *Official Record Album Of The Olympics* . . . . (Rhino)
Bad Luck Streak In Dancing School
Warren Zevon; *Bad Luck Streak In Dancing School* . . . . (Asylum)
Bailamos
Enrique Iglesias; *Bailamos Greatest Hits* . . . .(Overbrook/Interscope)
Enrique . . . .(Overbrook/Interscope)
Now That's What I Call Music!-#3-C . . . . (Virgin)
Ballerina Girl
Lionel Richie; *Dancing On The Ceiling* . . . . (Motown)

Ballroom Dancing
Paul McCartney; *ST/Give my regards to Broad Street* . . . . (Columbia)
Tug Of War . . . . (Gold Rush)
Band Played On, The
Guy Lombardo & His Royal Canadians; *Guy Lombardo-All Time
Favorites* . . . . (MCA Special Prod.)
Barbara Ann
Beach Boys; *Beach Boys '69 (The Beach Boys Live In London)* . . . . (Capitol)
Beach Boys-Gift Set . . . . (Capitol)
Best Of The Beach Boys-#2 . . . . (Capitol)
Frat Rock!-C . . . . (Rhino)
Spirit Of America . . . . (Capitol)
Regents; *Cruisin'-1961-C* . . . . (Increase)
Original Rock 'N' Roll Hits Of The '60s-C . . . . (Roulette)
ST/American Graffiti . . . . (MCA)
Who; *Who's Missing* . . . . (MCA)
Batdance
Prince; *ST/Batman* . . . . (Warner Bros.)
Beck's Bolero
Jeff Beck; *Beckology-C* . . . . (Epic)
Legends Of Rock Guitar-'60s-#2-C . . . . (Rhino)
Jeff Beck Group; *Truth* . . . . (Epic)
Begin The Beguine
Art Tatum; *Solos-1940* . . . . (MCA)
Ella Fitzgerald; *Cole Porter Songbook* . . . . (Verve)
Johnny Mathis; *Best Days Of My Life* . . . . (Columbia)
First 25 Years-Silver Anniversary Album . . . . (Columbia)
Johnny Mathis-Live . . . . (Columbia)
Tony Bennett; *Forty Years-The Artistry Of Tony Bennett* . . . . . (Columbia)
Big Ball's In Cowtown
Asleep At The Wheel; *Very Best Of Asleep At The Wheel
Since 1970* . . . .(Relentless/Madacy)
Asleep At The Wheel featuring George Strait; *Tribute To The Music Of Bob
Wills And The Texas Playboys-C* . . . . (Liberty)
Bob Wills & His Texas Playboys; *Best Of Bob Wills & His Texas
Playboys* . . . . (MCA)
For The Last Time . . . . (Capitol)
Birmingham Bounce
Red Foley; *45-#46234* . . . . (Decca)
Tommy Dorsey & His Orchestra; *Swing Vocalists Greatest
Hits-C* . . . . (RCA Victor)
The Post-War Era . . . . (Bluebird)
Birthday
Beatles; *The Beatles (White Album)* . . . . (Capitol)
Daffy Duck; *Bugs & Friends Sing The Beatles* . . . .(Kid Rhino/Rhino 4 Kids)
Paul McCartney; *Tripping The Live Fantastic-Highlights!* . . . . (Capitol)
Texas Chainsaw Orchestra; *The Texas Chainsaw Orchestra* . . . . (Rhino)
Birthday Waltz
Barbara Lamb; *Tonight I Feel Like Texas* . . . .(Sugar Hill)
Bishop Danced
Bruce Springsteen; *Tracks* . . . . (Columbia)
Black Cat Shuffle
Al DiMeola; *Electric Rendezvous* . . . . (Columbia)
Black Satin Dancer
Jethro Tull; *Minstrel In The Gallery* . . . . (Chrysalis)
Blame It On The Bossa Nova
Eydie Gorme; *45-#42661* . . . . (Columbia)
Blood On The Dance Floor
Michael Jackson; *Blood On The Dance Floor-HIStory...* . . . . . (MJJ Music/Work)
Blue Tango
Billy Vaughn; *String Of Pearls-Greatest Hits* . . . .(Pro-Arte)
Leroy Anderson; *Best Of Leroy Anderson-Sleigh Ride* . . . . (Decca)
Blue Texas Waltz
Billy Joe Shaver; *Taste Of Texas-Songs 'Bout Texas By Texans-C* . . . (Columbia)
Bluejean Bop
Gene Vincent and His Blue Caps; *Capitol Collectors Series-Gene Vincent
and His Blue Caps* . . . . (Gold Rush)
Gene Vincent and His Blue Caps' Greatest Hits . . . . (Curb)
*The Screaming End-The Best Of Gene Vincent and His
Blue Caps* . . . . (Razor & Tie)
Body Bumpin'-Yippie-Yi-Yo
Public Announcement; *All Work, No Play* . . . . (A&M)
Boogaloo Down Broadway
Fantastic Johnny C; *Dick Bartley Presents On The Radio-#7-C* . . . .(VSI)
Boogie Ala Georgia
Peggy Gilbert; *Dixieland Jazz* . . . . (Cambria)
Boogie Child
Bee Gees; *Children Of The World* . . . . (RSO)
Here At Last...Bee Gees...Live . . . .(Polydor)
Boogie Chillun
John Lee Hooker; *Best Of John Lee Hooker* . . . .(Crescendo)
Best Of John Lee Hooker . . . . (Vee-Jay)
Boogie Chillun . . . . (Fantasy)
Hooked On The Blues . . . . (Everest)
Boogie Down
Eddie Kendricks; *Billboard Top Rock 'N' Roll Hits-1974-C* . . . . (Rhino)
Eddie Kendricks-At His Best . . . . (Motown)
Eddie Kendricks-The Ultimate Collection . . . . (Motown)

Boogie In Your Butt
Eddie Murphy; *Eddie Murphy* . . . . (Columbia)
Boogie Nights
Heatwave; *Heatwave's Greatest Hits* . . . . (Epic)
Skatetown U.S.A.-C . . . . (Columbia)
Too Hot To Handle . . . . (Epic)
Boogie On Reggae Woman
Stevie Wonder; *Fulfillingness' First Finale* . . . . (Motown)
Motown Time Capsule-#2-'70s-C . . . . (Motown)
Original Musiquarium . . . . (Motown)
Boogie Oogie Oogie
Taste Of Honey; *Taste Of Honey* . . . . (Capitol)
The Disco Years-#1-Turn The Beat Around-1974-1978-C . . . (Rhino)
Boogie Wonderland
Earth, Wind & Fire; *Best Of Earth, Wind & Fire-#2* . . . . (Columbia)
I Am . . . . (Columbia)
Roller Boogie-C . . . . (Casablanca)
Skatetown U.S.A.-C . . . . (Columbia)
Boot Scootin' Boogie
Brooks & Dunn; *Brand New Man* . . . . (Arista)
Bootylicious
Destiny's Child; *Now That's What I Call Music!-#8-C* . . . . (Virgin)
Survivor . . . . (Columbia)
Bop
Dan Seals; *Best Of Dan Seals* . . . . (Capitol)
Dan Seals' Greatest Hits . . . . (Liberty)
Won't Be Blue Anymore . . . . (EMI)
Bop 'Til You Drop
Rick Springfield; *Rick Springfield's Greatest Hits* . . . . (RCA)
ST/Hard To Hold . . . . (RCA)
Bop 'Til You Drop
Ramones; *Halfway To Sanity* . . . . (Sire)
Mania . . . . (Sire)
Born To Boogie
Hank Williams, Jr.; *Born To Boogie* . . . . (WB/Curb)
Hank Williams, Jr.'s Greatest Hits III . . . . (Curb)
Born To Boogie
T. Rex; *T. Rextasy: Best Of T. Rex 1970-1973* . . . . . . (Warner Bros.)
Born To Hand-Jive
Original Broadway Cast; *Grease* . . . . (Polydor)
Sha Na Na; *ST/Grease* . . . . (Polydor)
Bossanovanight
Judson Spence; *I Guess I Love It* . . . . (Pioneer)
Bounce With Me
Lil Bow Wow; *Beware Of Dog* . . . . (So So Def/Columbia)
ST/Big Momma's House . . . . (So So Def/Columbia)
Brand New Dance
Emmylou Harris; *Brand New Dance* . . . . (Reprise)
Brand New Tennessee Waltz
Jesse Winchester; *Best Of Jesse Winchester* . . . . (Rhino)
Jesse Winchester . . . . (Rhino)
Joan Baez; *Country Music Album* . . . . (Vanguard)
Brazilian Stomp
George Benson & Earl Klugh; *Collaboration* . . . . (Warner Bros.)
Breakdance
Irene Cara; *What A Feelin'* . . . . (Geffen)
Breakin' (There's No Stoppin' Us)
Ollie & Jerry; *ST/Breakin'* . . . . (Mercury)
Bring On The Dancing Horses
Echo & The Bunnymen; *Songs To Learn & Sing-The Hits* . . . . . (Sire)
ST/Pretty In Pink . . . . (A&M)
Bristol Stomp
Dovells; *Echoes Of A Rock Era-Middle Years-C* . . . . . . (Roulette)
Let's Dance . . . . (Gusto)
Rock-O-Rama-#1-C . . . . (Abkco)
Bumble Bee Stomp
Benny Goodman; *On The Air-1937-1938* . . . . (Columbia)
Bump & Grind
R. Kelly; *12 Play* . . . . (Jive)
Burn This Disco Out
Michael Jackson; *Off The Wall* . . . . (Epic)
Burning The Ballroom Down
Amazing Rhythm Aces; *Burning The Ballroom Down* . . . . . . (MCA)
Buttermilk Biscuits (Keep On Square Dancin')
Sir Mix-A-Lot; *Swass* . . . . (Nastymix)
Can You Dance (Baby Tell Me)
Shanice Wilson; *Discovery* . . . . (A&M)
Canned Heat
Jamiroquai; *Synkronized* . . . . (Work/Epic)
Can't Stop Dancin'
Captain & Tennille; *Captain & Tennille's Greatest Hits* . . . . . . (A&M)
Can't Stop Dancing
Sylvester; *Living Proof* . . . . (Fantasy)
Sylvester's Greatest Hits . . . . (Fantasy)
Careless Whisper
Dave Koz featuring Montell Jordan; *Dance* . . . . (Capitol)
Wham! Featuring George Michael; *Make It Big* . . . . (Columbia)
Music For The Miracle-C . . . . (Epic Portrait Assoc.)

Carioca
Artie Shaw; *Artie Shaw Plays 22 Original Big Band Recordings-1938-1939* . . . . (Hindsight)
Begin The Beguine . . . . (Bluebird)
Gloomy Sunday . . . . (Pickwick)
This Is Artie Shaw-#2 . . . . (RCA)
Carol
Chuck Berry; *Berry Is On Top* . . . . (Chess)
Chuck Berry-Golden Hits . . . . (Mercury)
Chuck Berry's Greatest Hits . . . . (Everest)
Roll Over Beethoven . . . . (Allegiance)
Rolling Stones; *England's Newest Hit Makers/The Rolling Stones* . . . . (Abkco)
Get Yer Ya-Ya's Out! . . . . (Abkco)
Carry On Dancing
Savage Garden; *Savage Garden* . . . . (Columbia)
Chanel No. Fever
De La Soul; *ST/Men In Black* . . . . (Columbia)
Change Partners
Rosanne Cash; *The Wheel* . . . . (Columbia)
Changing Partners
Bing Crosby; *Bing Crosby* . . . . (MCA Special Prod.)
Kay Starr; *Capitol Collectors Series-Kay Starr* . . . . (Capitol)
Patti Page; *Patti Page-Golden Hits* . . . . (Mercury)
Charleston
Paul Whiteman & His Orchestra; *Nipper's Greatest Hits Of The '20s-C* . . . . (RCA)
Cheap Sunglasses
ZZ Top; *Deguello* . . . . (Warner Bros.)
ST/Teachers . . . . (Capitol)
Cheek To Cheek
Ella Fitzgerald; *Silver Collection-Songbooks* . . . . (Verve)
Frank Sinatra; *Come Dance With Me!* . . . . (Capitol)
Fred Astaire; *Cheek To Cheek* . . . . (Pro-Arte)
Irving Berlin Songbook . . . . (Verve)
Mundell Lowe; *Mundell Lowe Quartet* . . . . (Riverside)
Pete Fountain; *Cheek To Cheek* . . . . (Ranwood)
Tommy Dorsey; *Irving Berlin 100th Anniversary Collection-C* . . . . . (MCA)
Tony Bennett; *Bennett/Berlin* . . . . (Columbia)
Choo Choo Ch'Boogie (Jack)
Asleep At The Wheel; *All Time Legends Of Country Music-C* . . . . (Legacy)
Asleep At The Wheel . . . . (Epic)
Hot Tracks-Train Super Hits-C . . . . (Epic)
Served Live . . . . (Capitol)
Very Best Of Asleep At The Wheel Since 1970 . . . . . (Relentless/Madacy)
Beach Boys; *Ten Years Of Harmony* . . . . (Caribou)
Clifton Chenier; *Alligator Stomp-#2-C* . . . . (Rhino)
Louis Jordan; *Best Of Louis Jordan* . . . . (MCA)
Quincy Jones; *Birth Of A Band-#2* . . . . (Mercury)
Cincinnati Stomp
Big Joe Duskin; *Cincinnati Stomp* . . . . (Arhoolie)
Circle Dance
Bonnie Raitt; *Longing In Their Hearts* . . . . (Capitol)
Cloud Dancing
Roches; *Speak* . . . . (MCA)
Come Dancing
Kinks; *Come Dancing With The Kinks-Best Of The Kinks 1977-1986* . . . . (Arista)
State Of Confusion . . . . (Arista)
The Road . . . . (MCA)
Come From The Heart
Don Williams; *Traces* . . . . (Capitol)
Kathy Mattea; *Willow In The Wind* . . . . (Mercury)
Come On Do The Jerk
Smokey Robinson & The Miracles; *Smokey Robinson & The Miracles' Anthology* . . . . (Motown)
Smokey Robinson & The Miracles' Greatest Hits-#2 . . . . . . (Motown)
Come On Little Angel
Belmonts; *Lost Treasures* . . . . (Relic)
Conga
Leonard Bernstein; *Songbook* . . . . (Columbia)
Conga
Miami Sound Machine; *Primitive Love* . . . . (Epic)
Cool Jerk
Capitols; *Atlantic Rhythm & Blues 1947-1974-#5 (1962-1966)-C* . . . . (Atlantic)
Billboard Top R&B Hits-1966-C . . . . (Rhino)
Capitols-Their Greatest Recordings . . . . (Solid Smoke)
Collectables Presents The History Of Rock-#5-C . . . . . . (Collectables)
Son Of Frat Rock!-C . . . . (Rhino)
Super Oldies Of The '60s-#5-C . . . . (Audio Fidelity)
Copacabana (At The Copa)
Barry Manilow; *Barry Manilow's Greatest Hits-#2* . . . . (Arista)
Even Now . . . . (Arista)
ST/Foul Play . . . . (Arista)
The Manilow Collection-Twenty Classic Hits . . . . (Arista)
Columbia Ballroom Orchestra; *Let's Dance-#6* . . . . (Denon)
Could I Have This Dance?
Anne Murray; *Anne Murray's Greatest Hits* . . . . (Capitol)
ST/Urban Cowboy . . . . (Asylum)
Cow Cow Boogie
Ella Fitzgerald; *Best Of Ella Fitzgerald-#2* . . . . (MCA)

Freddie Slack & Ella Mae Morse; *Jukebox Saturday Night-Great Vocal Hits-C* .... (Capitol)
Judds; *Heartland* .... (MCA)
Cowboy Boogie
Randy Travis; *Wind In The Wire* .... (Warner Bros.)
Crazy Man Crazy
Bill Haley; *Still Rockin' Around The Clock* .... (BMG Special Prod.)
Crocodile Rock
Elton John; *Billboard Top Rock 'N' Roll Hits-1973-C* .... (Rhino)
Don't Shoot Me I'm Only The Piano Player .... (Polydor)
Elton John's Greatest Hits .... (Polydor)
Here And There .... (Rocket)
Crush
Dave Matthews Band; *Before These Crowded Streets* .... (RCA)
Cuban Slide
Pretenders; *Extended Play* .... (Sire)
Curly Shuffle
Jump 'N The Saddle Band; *Dr. Demento Presents The Greatest Novelty Records-#5-1980s-C* .... (Rhino)
Da Dip
Freak Nasty; *Controversee...That's Life...And That's The Way It Is* .... (Power)
Dance By The Light Of The Moon
Olympics; *Meet The Marathons* .... (Collectables)
Dance Dance Dance
Beach Boys; *Absolute Best-#1* .... (Capitol)
Beach Boys' Greatest Hits .... (Bovema)
Good Vibrations-Thirty Years Of The Beach Boys ..... (Capitol)
Made In The U.S.A. .... (Capitol)
Spirit Of America .... (Capitol)
Dance Dance Dance
Steve Miller Band; *Fly Like An Eagle* .... (Capitol)
Steve Miller Band's Greatest Hits-1974-78 .... (Capitol)
Dance Dance Dance
Clarence Clemons; *Night With Mr. C* .... (Columbia)
Dance Electric
Andre Cymone; *A.C.* .... (Columbia)
Pointer Sisters; *Break Out* .... (Planet)
Dance Floor
Zapp; *Zapp II* .... (Warner Bros.)
Dance Hall Days
Wang Chung; *Points On The Curve* .... (Geffen)
Dance Into The Light
Phil Collins; *Dance Into The Light* .... (Atlantic)
Dance Little Jean
Nitty Gritty Dirt Band; *Let's Go* .... (Warner Bros.)
Twenty Years Of Dirt-Best Of The Nitty Gritty Dirt Band ..... (Warner Bros.)
Dance Little Sister
Rolling Stones; *It's Only Rock 'N Roll* .... (Rolling Stones)
Made In The Shade .... (Rolling Stones)
Dance Little Sister
Terence Trent D'Arby; *Introducing The Hardline According To Terence Trent D'Arby* .... (Columbia)
Dance Naked
John Mellencamp; *Dance Naked* .... (Mercury)
Dance Of Electricity
Laurie Anderson; *United States Live* .... (Warner Bros.)
Dance Of The Imbeciles
D.C. 3; *This Is The Dream* .... (SST)
Dance Of The Sugar Plum Fairy
Boston Pops Orchestra; *Encores-Boston Pops Orchestra* .... (Deutsche Grammophon)
Sleigh Ride!-Classic Christmas Favorites-C .... (RCA)
Carpenters; *Christmas Collection* .... (A&M)
Dance On A Volcano
Genesis; *Seconds Out* .... (Atlantic)
Trick Of The Tail .... (Atco)
Dance On Little Girl
Paul Anka; *Best Of Paul Anka* .... (Rhino)
Paul Anka Sings His Big 15, Vol. 2 .... (RCA)
Paul Anka-30th Anniversary Anthology .... (Rhino)
Paul Anka's 21 Golden Hits .... (RCA)
She's A Lady .... (RCA)
Dance Only With Me
Blossom Dearie; *Blossoms On Broadway* .... (DRG)
Maxine Sullivan & Keith Ingham Sextet; *Together (Maxine Sings Jules Styne)* .... (Atlantic)
Dance The Night Away
Van Halen; *Van Halen II* .... (Warner Bros.)
Dance The Night Away
Mavericks; *Trampoline* .... (MCA)
Dance The Night Away
Cream; *Disraeli Gears* .... (Polydor)
Dance The Night Away
Europe; *Wings Of Tomorrow* .... (Epic)
Dance Time In Texas
George Strait; *Something Special* .... (MCA)
Dance To The Music
Sly & The Family Stone; *Frat Rock!-#2-C* .... (Rhino)

Frat Rock!-C .... (Rhino)
Sly & The Family Stone-Anthology .... (Epic)
Sly & The Family Stone's Greatest Hits .... (Epic)
Dance Tonight
Lucy Pearl; *Lucy Pearl* .... (Overbrook/Pookie/Beyond)
Dance Wit Me
Rufus Featuring Chaka Khan; *Live-Stompin' At The Savoy* .... (Warner Bros.)
Rufus featuring Chaka Khan .... (MCA)
Dance Wit' Me-Part 1
Rick James; *Reflections-Greatest Hits* .... (Motown)
Throwin' Down .... (Motown)
Dance With A Dolly (Hole In Her Stocking)
Bill Haley & His Comets; *King Of Rock & Roll* ...... (Alshire)
Rockin' & Rollin' .... (Accord)
Dance With Me
Orleans; *Dance With Me* .... (Rhino)
Still The One .... (Elektra)
Dance With Me
Drifters; *Drifters-16 Greatest Hits* .... (Deluxe)
Dance With Me
Debelah Morgan; *Dance With Me* .... (Atlantic)
Totally Hits-#3-C .... (Atlantic)
Dance With Me
112; *Part III* .... (Bad Boy/Arista)
Dance With The Dragon
Jefferson Starship; *Spitfire* .... (Grunt)
Dance With The One That Brought You
Shania Twain; *Shania Twain* .... (Mercury)
Dance With Who Brung Ya
Asleep At The Wheel; *Very Best Of Asleep At The Wheel Since 1970* .... (Relentless/Madacy)
Dance Your Ass Off
Bohannon; *Dance Your Ass Off* .... (Dakar)
Dance, The
Garth Brooks; *Garth Brooks* .... (Liberty)
Garth Brooks-Double Live .... (Capitol)
Dance: Ten; Looks: Three
Original Cast; *A Chorus Line* .... (Columbia)
Dancin'
Guy; *Guy-III* .... (MCA)
Dancin' Cowboys
Bellamy Brothers; *Bellamy Brothers' Greatest Hits* .... (MCA)
You Can Get Crazy .... (WB/Curb)
Dancin' Feet
Montrose; *Montrose* .... (Warner Bros.)
Dancin' Fool
Frank Zappa; *Sheik Yerbouti* .... (Zappa)
Dancin' Fool
Guess Who; *Greatest Of The Guess Who* .... (RCA)
Dancin' In The Ruins
Blue Oyster Cult; *Club Ninja* .... (Columbia)
Dancin' With Elvis
Gina Jeffreys; *Somebody's Daughter* .... (EMI)
Dancin', Shaggin' On The Boulevard
Alabama; *Dancin' On The Boulevard* .... (RCA)
Dancing
Carol Channing/Original Cast; *Hello Dolly!* .... (RCA)
Original Cast; *Hello Dolly!* .... (RCA)
Dancing Bumble Bee
Neil Diamond; *You Don't Bring Me Flowers* .... (Columbia)
Dancing Days
Led Zeppelin; *Houses Of The Holy* .... (Atlantic)
Stone Temple Pilots; *Encomium: Tribute To Led Zeppelin-C* .... (Atlantic)
Dancing In Berlin
Berlin; *Love Life* .... (Geffen)
Dancing In Rackville, Maryland
Fred Frith; *Gravity* .... (Ralph)
Dancing In St. Louis
Li'l Wally; *Here Comes Li'l Wally* .... (Jay Jay)
Dancing In Sunrise, Switzerland
Muffins; *Open City* .... (Cuneiform)
Dancing In The Bathtub
John Hartford; *All In The Name Of Love* .... (Flying Fish)
Dancing In The Dark
Barbara Cook; *Barbara Cook-Live At Carnegie Hall* .... (Sony Music Classical)
Diana Krall; *The Look Of Love* .... (Impulse!)
Fred Waring's Pennsylvanians; *78-#22708* .... (Victor)
Tony Bennett; *Forty Years-The Artistry Of Tony Bennett* ..... (Columbia)
Jazz .... (Columbia)
Dancing In The Dark
Bruce Springsteen; *Born In The U.S.A.* .... (Columbia)
Bruce Springsteen's Greatest Hits .... (Columbia)
Dancing In The Key Of Life
Steve Arrington; *Dance Traxx-C* .... (Atlantic)
Dancing In The Key Of Life .... (Atlantic)
Dancing In The Moonlight
Thin Lizzy; *Bad Reputation* .... (Mercury)
Live And Dangerous .... (Warner Bros.)

Dancing In The Moonlight
King Harvest; *Have A Nice Night-Romantic Hits Of The '70s-C* . . . . . . (Rhino)
   Super Hits Of The '70s-Have A Nice Day-#17-C . . . . (Rhino)
Dancing In The Moonlight
Be Bop Deluxe; *Modern Music* . . . . (Capitol)
Dancing In The Moonlight
Liza Minnelli; *Singer* . . . . (Columbia)
Dancing In The Sheets
Shalamar; *Shalamar's Greatest Hits* . . . .(Solar)
   ST/Footloose . . . . (Columbia)
Dancing In The Street
David Bowie & Mick Jagger; *Bowie-The Singles-1969-1993* . . . . . . (Rykodisc)
Grateful Dead; *Terrapin Station* . . . . (Arista)
Martha & The Vandellas; *20 Greatest Songs In Motown History-C* . . . (Motown)
   Compact Command Performances-Martha Reeves & The
     Vandellas . . . . (Motown)
   Motown Story-First 25 Years-C . . . . (Motown)
   Oldies But Goodies-#14-C . . . .(Original Sound)
Van Halen; *Diver Down* . . . . (Warner Bros.)
Dancing Machine
Jackson 5; *14 Greatest Hits* . . . . (Motown)
   Billboard Top Rock 'N' Roll Hits-1974-C . . . . (Rhino)
   Get It Together . . . . (Motown)
   Jackson 5-Anthology . . . . (Motown)
   Motown Dance Party-#2-C . . . . (Motown)
   Motown Story-First 25 Years-C . . . . (Motown)
   Motown Superstar Series-#12-Jackson 5 . . . . (Motown)
   Top 10 With A Bullet-Motown Dance Songs-C . . . . (Motown)
Dancing On Ground Zero
Carol Nethen; *Narada Mystique Sampler One-C* . . . . (Narada)
   View From The Bridge . . . . (Narada)
Dancing On The Ceiling
Chet Baker; *Chet Baker Sings It Could Happen*
   To You . . . . (Original Jazz Classics)
Ella Fitzgerald; *Rodgers & Hart Songbook* . . . . (Verve)
Frank Sinatra; *In The Wee Small Hours* . . . . (Capitol)
Dancing On The Ceiling
Lionel Richie; *Dancing On The Ceiling* . . . . (Motown)
Dancing Queen
Abba; *Abba Live* . . . . (Atlantic)
   Abba's Greatest Hits-#2 . . . . (Atlantic)
   Arrival . . . . (Polydor)
   Gold-Greatest Hits . . . . (Polydor)
   The Singles-First 10 Years . . . . (Atlantic)
Dancing Shoes
Bob Marley & The Wailers; *Birth Of A Legend 1963-*
   1966 . . . . (Epic Portrait Assoc.)
   Early Music . . . .(Calla)
Dancing Shoes
Dan Fogelberg; *Nether Lands* . . . . (Full Moon)
Dancing Shoes
Side Effect; *Side Effect's Greatest Hits* . . . .(Fantasy)
Dancing With Mr. D
Rolling Stones; *Goats Head Soup* . . . . (Rolling Stones)
Dancing With Tears In My Eyes
Ray Conniff; *Young At Heart* . . . . (Columbia)
Dancing Your Memory Away
Charly McClain; *Charly McClain's Biggest Hits* . . . . (Epic)
   Ten Year Anniversary . . . . (Epic)
   Too Good To Hurry . . . . (Epic)
Dear Lady Twist
Gary U.S. Bonds; *Best Of Gary U.S. Bonds* . . . . (Rhino)
Death Disco
Public Image Ltd.; *Greatest Hits So Far* . . . .(Virgin)
Death Of A Disco Dancer
Smiths; *Strangeways Here We Come* . . . . (Sire)
Did You Ever See A Dream Walking
Bing Crosby; *Crosby Classics* . . . . (Columbia)
Hal Kemp & Skinnay Ennis; *The Uncollected Hal Kemp-#2 & #3* . . . (Hindsight)
Disco Apocalypse
Jackson Browne; *Hold Out* . . . . (Asylum)
Disco Doctor
Robert Parker; *Golden Classics-Barefootin'* . . . . (Collectables)
Disco Duck
Rick Dees And His Cast Of Idiots; *Original Disco Duck* . . . . (RSO)
Disco Inferno
Trammps; *Best Of The Trammps* . . . . (Atlantic)
   Disco Inferno . . . . (Atlantic)
   ST/Saturday Night Fever . . . . (Polydor)
   The Disco Years-#1-Turn The Beat Around-1974-1978-C . . . . (Rhino)
Disco Lady
Johnnie Taylor; *Mega Hits Disco Explosion-#4-C* . . . .(Priority)
   Rated X-Traordinaire-Best Of Johnnie Taylor . . . . (Legacy)
Disco Strangler
Eagles; *Long Run* . . . . (Asylum)
Disco's Out, Murder's In
Suicidal Tendencies; *Lights...Camera...Revolution* . . . . (Epic)

Discotheque
U2; *Pop* . . . . (Island)
Dizzy Miss Lizzy
Beatles; *Beatles VI* . . . . (Capitol)
   Rock 'N' Roll Music . . . . (Capitol)
   The Beatles At The Hollywood Bowl . . . . (Capitol)
Ronnie Hawkins and The Hawks; *Best Of Ronnie Hawkins and The*
   Hawks . . . . (Rhino)
Do I Hear A Waltz?
Elizabeth Allen; *Broadway Magic-The 1960s-C* . . . .(Columbia)
Original Broadway Cast; *Do I Hear A Waltz?* . . . . (Sony Music Classical)
Do It (Let Me See You Shake)
Bar-Kays; *Propositions* . . . .(Mercury)
Do The Bartman
Bart Simpson; *Simpsons Sing The Blues* . . . . (Geffen)
Do The Bird
Dee Dee Sharp; *Let's Dance* . . . . (Gusto)
   Rock-O-Rama-#2-C . . . . (Abkco)
Do The Boomerang
Junior Walker & The All Stars; *Junior Walker & The All Stars-*
   Anthology . . . .(Motown)
   Shotgun . . . . (Motown)
Do The Freddy
Chubby Checker; *Chubby Checker's Greatest Hits* . . . . (Abkco)
Do The Funky Chicken
Rufus Thomas; *15 Original Big Hits-#3-C* . . . . (Stax)
   Let's Dance . . . . (Gusto)
   Rufus Thomas-Chronicle . . . . (Stax)
Do The Funky Penguin
Rufus Thomas; *15 Original Big Hits-#3-C* . . . . (Stax)
   Rufus Thomas . . . . (Gusto)
   Rufus Thomas-Chronicle . . . . (Stax)
Do The Strand
Roxy Music; *For Your Pleasure....* . . . . (Reprise)
   Roxy Music-Atlantic Years 1973-1980 . . . . (Atco)
   Street Life-20 Great Hits . . . . (Reprise)
   Viva! Roxy Music . . . . (Reprise)
Do You Love Me (Now That I Can Dance?)
Contours; *Frat Rock!-C* . . . . (Rhino)
   Greatest Movie Rock Hits-C . . . . (Rhino)
   Oldies But Goodies-#12-C . . . . (Original Sound)
   ST/More Dirty Dancing . . . . (RCA)
   ST/The Wanderers . . . . (Warner Bros.)
Dave Clark Five; *History Of The Dave Clark Five* . . . .(Hollywood)
Do You Wanna Dance?
Beach Boys; *Absolute Best-#1* . . . . (Capitol)
   Spirit Of America . . . . (Capitol)
Bette Midler; *Divine Miss M* . . . . (Atlantic)
   Live At Last . . . . (Atlantic)
Bobby Freeman; *ST/American Graffiti* . . . . (MCA)
Doin' The Do
Betty Boo; *Boomania* . . . . (Rhythm King)
Dolphin Dance
Herbie Hancock; *Best Of Herbie Hancock-The Blue Note Years* . . . . (Blue Note)
   Maiden Voyage . . . . (Blue Note)
Domino Dancing
Pet Shop Boys; *Introspective* . . . . (EMI)
Don't Stop Dancing
Bar-Kays; *Gotta Groove* . . . . (Stax)
Don't Stop The Dance
Bryan Ferry; *Boys & Girls* . . . . (Warner Bros.)
   Greenpeace/Rainbow Warriors-C . . . . (Geffen)
Down At The Twist And Shout
Mary Chapin Carpenter; *Greatest Country Hits Of The '90s-*
   1992-C . . . . (Columbia)
   Hitchhiker Examplar 2-C . . . . (Columbia)
   Shooting Straight In The Dark . . . . (Columbia)
   Today's Hot Country-C . . . . (K-Tel)
Down To The Night Club
Tower Of Power; *Bump City* . . . . (Warner Bros.)
   Live & In Living Color . . . . (Warner Bros.)
Downtown
Neil Young; *Mirror Ball* . . . . (Reprise)
Dracula's Dance
Flip Phillips; *Flipenstein* . . . . (Progressive)
Dream Dancing
Ella Fitzgerald; *Dream Dancing* . . . . (Pablo)
Duck, The
Jackie Lee; *Only Dance 1965-1969-C* . . . . (JCI Assoc. Labels)
   Sock Hop-C . . . . (Dunhill Compact Classics)
   Super Oldies Of The '60s-#6-C . . . . (Audio Fidelity)
Olympics; *Best Of The Olympics* . . . . (Vee-Jay)
Eighth Avenue Shuffle
Doobie Brothers; *Takin' It To The Streets* . . . . (Warner Bros.)
El Paso
Grateful Dead; *Steal Your Face* . . . . (Grateful Dead)
Marty Robbins; *Billboard Top Country Hits-1960-C* . . . . (Rhino)
   Gunfighter Ballads & Trail Songs . . . . (Legacy)
   Marty Robbins' Biggest Hits . . . .(Columbia)

Radio Classics Of The '50s-C .... (Columbia)
Texas Super Hits-C .... (Columbia)
Euthanasia Waltz
  Brand X; *Livestock* .... (Blue Plate)
  Unorthodox Behaviour .... (Blue Plate)
Everybody (Backstreet's Back)
  Backstreet Boys; *Backstreet Boys* .... (Jive)
Everybody Dance
  Ta Mara & The Seen; *Ta Mara & The Seen* .... (A&M)
Everybody's Doin' It
  Commander Cody & His Lost Planet Airmen; *Country Casanova* ...... (MCA)
Face Dances, Part 2
  Pete Townshend; *All The Best Cowboys Have Chinese Eyes* .... (Atco)
Family Affair
  Mary J. Blige; *No More Drama* .... (MCA)
Fancy Dancer
  Commodores; *Commodores Greatest Hits* .... (Motown)
  Commodores-Live .... (Motown)
  Compact Command Performances-Commodores .... (Motown)
  Hot On The Tracks .... (Motown)
Fancy Dancer
  Bread; *Best Of Bread-#2* .... (Elektra)
  Bread-Anthology .... (Elektra)
Fearless Boogie
  ZZ Top; *XXX* .... (RCA)
Flashdance...What A Feeling
  Irene Cara; *ST/Flashdance* .... (Casablanca)
Footloose
  Kenny Loggins; *ST/Footloose* .... (Columbia)
Freak Show On The Dance Floor
  Bar-Kays; *Dangerous* .... (Mercury)
  ST/Breakin' .... (Mercury)
Freaky Dancin'
  Cameo; *Knights Of The Sound Table* .... (Chocolate City)
Freedom Dance (Get Free!)
  Vanessa Williams; *The Comfort Zone* .... (Wing)
Freight Train Boogie
  Delmore Brothers; *45-#2077* .... (Gusto)
  Johnny Otis; *Original Johnny Otis Show-#2* .... (Savoy)
German Waltz Medley
  Lawrence Welk; *Come Waltz With Me* .... (Ranwood)
Get Down On It
  Kool & The Gang; *Something Special* .... (De-Lite)
Get Down Tonight
  KC And The Sunshine Band; *Best Of KC And The Sunshine Band* ...... (Rhino)
  Billboard Top Hits-1975-C .... (Rhino)
  Get Down Tonight! Best Of T.K. Records-C .... (Rhino)
Get Off Your Ass And Jam
  Parliament; *Parliament Live/P. Funk Earth Tour* ...... (Casablanca)
Get On Up
  Jodeci; *The Show, The After-Party, The Hotel* .... (Uptown/MCA)
Get Up! (Before The Night Is Over)
  Technotronic; *Pump Up The Jam-The Album* .... (SBK)
Gettin' Jiggy Wit It
  Will Smith; *Big Willie Style* .... (Columbia)
Getto Jam
  Domino; *Domino* .... (OutBurst)
Ghost Dance
  Patti Smith Group; *Easter* .... (Arista)
God Blessed Texas
  Little Texas; *Big Time* .... (Warner Bros.)
Going To A Go-Go
  Miracles; *Billboard Top R&B Hits-1966-C* .... (Rhino)
  Rolling Stones; *"Still Life" (American Concert 1981)* .... (Virgin)
  Smokey Robinson & The Miracles; *Compact Command Performances-Smokey Robinson & The Miracles* .... (Motown)
  Smokey Robinson & The Miracles' Anthology .... (Motown)
  Smokey Robinson & The Miracles' Greatest Hits-#2 .... (Motown)
Gonna Make You Sweat (Everybody Dance Now)
  C & C Music Factory; *Gonna Make You Sweat* .... (Columbia)
  Hot #1 Hits-C .... (Foundation)
Good Golly, Miss Molly
  Creedence Clearwater Revival; *1968-1969* .... (Fantasy)
  Bayou Country .... (Fantasy)
  Creedence Clearwater Revival-Chronicle-#2 .... (Fantasy)
  Little Richard; *Big Hits* .... (Crescendo)
  Cruisin'-1958-C .... (Increase)
  Greatest Hits Recorded Live .... (Epic)
  Little Richard-18 Greatest Hits .... (Rhino)
  Little Richard-His Greatest Hits .... (Vee-Jay)
  ST/The Flamingo Kid .... (Motown)
  Super Oldies Of The '50s-#2-C .... (Audio Fidelity)
Good Vibrations
  Marky Mark And The Funky Bunch; *Music For The People* ...... (Interscope)
Got The Life
  Korn; *Follow The Leader* .... (Immortal/Epic)
Groove Line, The
  Heatwave; *Club Epic-#1-C* .... (Legacy)

Disco Super Hits-C .... (Epic Dance)
The Funky Sounds Of The Soul '70s-C .... (Sony Music Special Prod.)
Harlem Shuffle
  Bill Deal & The Rhondels; *Best Of Bill Deal & The Rhondels* .... (Rhino)
  Bob & Earl; *Cruisin'-1964-C* .... (Increase)
  Tell It Like It Is: 60's Soul-C .... (K-Tel)
  Johnny & Edgar Winter; *Together* .... (Blue Sky)
  Rolling Stones; *Dirty Work* .... (Virgin)
Having A Party
  Norma Jean; *Norma Jean* .... (Bearsville)
  Pointer Sisters; *Having A Party* .... (MCA)
  Rod Stewart & Ronnie Wood; *Unplugged...And Seated* ..... (Warner Bros.)
  Sam Cooke; *Best Of Sam Cooke* .... (RCA)
  Feel It .... (RCA)
  Live At The Harlem Square Club .... (RCA)
  This Is Sam Cooke .... (RCA)
  Southside Johnny And The Asbury Jukes; *Havin' A Party With Southside Johnny And The Asbury Jukes* .... (Epic)
Hearts Of Stone
  Bruce Springsteen; *Tracks* .... (Columbia)
  Southside Johnny And The Asbury Jukes; *Best Of Southside Johnny And The Asbury Jukes* .... (Legacy)
  Cover Me (Bruce Springsteen Tribute)-C .... (Rhino)
  Hearts Of Stone .... (Epic)
Henry's Got Flat Feet (Can't Dance No More)
  Hank Ballard And The Midnighters; *Sexy Ways: The Best Of Hank Ballard & The Midnighters* .... (Rhino)
Hip Shake
  Rolling Stones; *Exile On Main Street* .... (Virgin)
Hip Sway
  Chris Standing; *Hip Sway* .... (Instinct)
Hippy Hippy Shake
  Chan Romero; *Del-Fi Record Hop-C* .... (Del Fi)
  Georgia Satellites; *Let It Rock-The Best Of The Georgia Satellites* ..... (Elektra)
  ST/Cocktail .... (Elektra)
  Swinging Blue Jeans; *Hippy Hippy Shake-The Definition Collection* ..... (EMI)
Hokey Pokey
  Original Soundtrack; *Children's Favorites* .... (Kid Rhino/Rhino 4 Kids)
  School Days-Kids Classics .... (Benson)
  Ray Anthony; *Capitol Collectors Series-Ray Anthony* .... (Capitol)
Holdin' Heaven
  Tracy Byrd; *Tracy Byrd* .... (MCA)
Hollywood Waltz
  Eagles; *One Of These Nights* .... (Asylum)
Honky Tonk Attitude
  Joe Diffie; *Honky Tonk Attitude* .... (Epic)
Honky Tonk Man
  Dwight Yoakam; *Guitars, Cadillacs, Etc., Etc.* .... (Reprise)
  Just Lookin' For A Hit .... (Reprise)
  Johnny Horton; *All Time Legends Of Country Music-C* .... (Legacy)
  Columbia Country Classics-#2-Honky Tonk Heroes-C .... (Columbia)
  Marty Robbins; *Greatest Country Hits From The Movies-C* .... (Epic)
Hoop-Dee-Doo
  Perry Como; *Perry Como's Greatest Hits* .... (RCA)
House Arrest
  Bryan Adams; *Waking Up The Neighbours* .... (A&M)
How To Dance
  Bingoboys; *Best Of Bingoboys* .... (Atlantic)
Humpin' Around
  Bobby Brown; *Bobby* .... (MCA)
Humpty Dance
  Digital Underground; *Sex Packets* .... (Tommy Boy)
Hustle, The
  Van McCoy & The Soul City Symphony; *21 #1 Hits-C* ...... (Original Sound)
  21 Oldies But Goodies-C .... (Original Sound)
  The Disco Years-#1-Turn The Beat Around-1974-1978-C .... (Rhino)
I Came To Dance
  Nils Lofgren; *Best Of Nils Lofgren* .... (A&M)
  Cry Tough .... (A&M)
  Nils Lofgren-Classics-#13 .... (A&M)
I Can Make You Dance
  Zapp; *Zapp III* .... (Warner Bros.)
I Can Tell By The Way You Dance
  Vern Gosdin; *10 Years Of Greatest Hits Newly Recorded* .... (Columbia)
  There Is A Season .... (Compleat)
I Can't Dance
  Genesis; *We Can't Dance* .... (Atlantic)
I Can't Stop Dancing
  Archie Bell; *Greatest Hits 1970-C* .... (Deluxe)
I Could Have Danced All Night
  Frank Sinatra; *Concepts* .... (Capitol)
  Julie Andrews/Original Cast; *My Fair Lady* .... (Columbia)
  Rosemary Clooney; *Rosemary Clooney-16 Most Requested Songs* .... (Legacy)
I Hope You Dance
  Lee Ann Womack; *I Hope You Dance* .... (MCA)
I Just Came Here To Dance
  David Frizzell & Shelly West; *David Frizzell & Shelly West Album* ...... (Viva)
  Golden Duets .... (Viva)

Peabo Bryson & Roberta Flack; *Born To Love* .... (Capitol)
The Peabo Bryson Collection .... (Capitol)

I Just Want To Dance With You
George Strait; *One Step At A Time* .... (MCA)

I Love Rock 'N Roll
Britney Spears; *Britney* .... (Jive)
Joan Jett & The Blackhearts; *I Love Rock 'n' Roll* .... (Blackheart)
ST/Wayne's World 2 .... (Reprise)

I Saw Her Standing There
Beatles; *Introducing...The Beatles* .... (Vee-Jay)
Meet The Beatles! .... (Capitol)
Please Please Me .... (Parlophone)
Rock 'N' Roll Music .... (Capitol)
The Beatles-Anthology-#1 .... (Capitol)
Paul McCartney; *Tripping The Live Fantastic-Highlights!* .... (Capitol)

I Saw Him Standing There
Tiffany; *Tiffany* .... (MCA)
Tiffany's Greatest Hits .... (Hip-O)

I Saw You Dancing
Yaki-Da; *Pride* .... (London)

I Still Believe In Waltzes
Conway Twitty & Loretta Lynn; *16 Top Country Hits-#4-C* .... (MCA)

I Wanna Dance With Somebody (Who Loves Me)
Whitney Houston; *Whitney* .... (Arista)
Whitney Houston's Greatest Hits .... (Arista)

I Want To Be A Dancin' Man
Fred Astaire; *That's Entertainment-The Ultimate Anthology Of MGM Musicals-C* .... (Turner Classic Movies)

I Won't Dance
Frank Sinatra; *Sinatra-Basie* .... (Reprise)
Original Cast; *Roberta* .... (Sony Music Special Prod.)

If Bubba Can Dance (I Can Too)
Shenandoah; *Under The Kudzu* .... (RCA)

If I Could Only Dance With You
Jim Glaser; *Man In The Mirror* .... (Noble Vision)

If The Devil Danced (In Empty Pockets)
Joe Diffie; *A Thousand Winding Roads* .... (Epic)

If U Can't Dance
Spice Girls; *Spice* .... (Virgin)

I'm A Slave 4 U
Britney Spears; *Britney* .... (Jive)

I'm Gonna Charleston Back To Charleston
Firehouse Five Plus Two; *Goes South* .... (Good Time Jazz)

I'm Happy Just To Dance With You
Anne Murray; *Somebody's Waiting* .... (Capitol)
Beatles; *Something New* .... (Capitol)
ST/A Hard Day's Night .... (Capitol)

I'm Into Something Good
Herman's Hermits; *Herman's Hermits-Their Greatest Hits* .... (Abkco)

In Between Dances
Pam Tillis; *Pam Tillis' Greatest Hits* .... (Arista)
Sweetheart's Dance .... (Arista)

In The Mood
Andrews Sisters; *Andrews Sisters-16 Great Performances* .... (MCA)
Boogie Woogie Bugle Girls .... (MCA)
Chesterfield Broadcasts-#1 .... (RCA Victor)
Bette Midler; *Bette Midler* .... (Atlantic)
Live At Last .... (Atlantic)
Glenn Miller; *Best Of Glenn Miller* .... (RCA)
Glenn Miller-A Legendary Performer-#1 & 2 .... (Bluebird)
The Glenn Miller Story .... (RCA)
Glenn Miller & His Orchestra; *Glenn Miller & His Orchestra-Pure Gold* .... (Bluebird)
The Unforgettable Glenn Miller & His Orchestra .... (RCA)

Irish Jig (The Ball)
Original Broadway Cast; *Meet Me In St. Louis* .... (DRG)

It's 3 O'Clock In The Morning
Mom & Dads; *Blue Hawaii* .... (Crescendo)

Jazzie's Groove
Soul II Soul; *Keep On Movin'* .... (Virgin)

Jerk Out
Time; *Pandemonium* .... (Paisley Park)

Jersey Bounce
Benny Goodman; *Benny Goodman-Live At Carnegie Hall* .... (London)
Hits Of Benny Goodman .... (Capitol)

John I'm Only Dancing
David Bowie; *Changesbowie* .... (Rykodisc)
Sound + Vision .... (Rykodisc)
The Singles-1969-1993 .... (Rykodisc)

Juke Box Baby
Perry Como; *Perry Como's Greatest Hits* .... (RCA)

Juke Joint Jump
Elvin Bishop; *Juke Joint Jump* .... (Capricorn)
Live! Raisin' Hell .... (Capricorn)

Jump
Kris Kross; *Billboard Top Hits-1992-C* .... (Rhino)
Totally Krossed Out .... (Ruffhouse)

Jump Jive An' Wail
Brian Setzer Orchestra; *Dirty Boogie* .... (Interscope)
Now That's What I Call Music!-#1-C .... (Virgin)
Louis Prima; *Capitol Collectors Series-Louis Prima* .... (Capitol)
Ultra-Lounge-#5-Wild, Cool & Swingin'-C .... (Capitol)

Jungle Boogie
Kool & The Gang; *Didn't It Blow Your Mind: Soul Hits Of The '70s-#12-C* .... (Rhino)
Everything Is-Greatest Hits .... (Mercury)
Kool & The Gang Spin Their Top Hits .... (De-Lite)

Jungle Hop
Cramps; *Psychedelic Jungle/Gravest Hits* .... (I.R.S.)

Just Like Gene Autry
Moby Grape; *Very Best Of Moby Grape-Vintage* .... (Columbia)

Kansas City Stomp
Jelly Roll Morton; *1923-1924* .... (Milestone)
Jelly Roll Morton .... (Bluebird)

Kentucky Waltz
Bill Monroe; *Columbia Historic Edition-Bill Monroe* .... (Columbia)
Bill Monroe & Emmylou Harris; *Bill Monroe & Friends* .... (MCA)

Killer Joe
Rocky Fellers; *Scepter Records Story-C* .... (Capricorn)

Kiss Me
Sixpence None The Richer; *Sixpence None The Richer* .... (Squint/Columbia)
Songs From Dawson's Creek .... (Sony Music Soundtrax)

La Bamba
Jose Feliciano; *Greatest '60s Folksingers-C* .... (Vanguard)
Newport Folk Music Festival-1964-C .... (Vanguard)
Los Lobos; *ST/La Bamba* .... (Slash)
Ritchie Valens; *American Graffiti-#3-C* .... (MCA)
Oldies But Goodies-#8-C .... (Original Sound)
Xavier Cugat; *Best Of Xavier Cugat* .... (MCA)
Xavier Cugat-Pure Gold .... (RCA)

Lambada
Kaoma; *World Beat* .... (Epic)

Lambeth Walk
Original Broadway Cast; *Me & My Girl* .... (MCA)
Original Cast; *Me & My Girl* .... (EMI)

Land Of 1000 Dances
Cannibal & The Headhunters; *History Of Latino Rock-#1-C* .... (Rhino)
Super Oldies Of The '60s-#8-C .... (Audio Fidelity)
Toga Rock-C .... (Dunhill Compact Classics)
Wilson Pickett; *Atlantic Rhythm & Blues 1947-1974-#6 (1966-1969)-C* .... (Atlantic)
Best Of Wilson Pickett .... (Atlantic)
ST/Forrest Gump .... (Epic/Sony Music Soundtrax)
Wilson Pickett's Greatest Hits .... (Atlantic)

Last Cheater's Waltz
Emmylou Harris; *Cimarron* .... (Warner Bros.)
T.G. Sheppard; *T.G. Sheppard's All-Time Greatest Hits* .... (Warner Bros.)
T.G. Sheppard's Greatest Hits .... (Warner Bros./Curb)

Last Dance
Donna Summer; *Dance Collection* .... (Casablanca)
Donna Summer's Greatest Hits .... (Casablanca)
Live & More .... (Casablanca)
On The Radio-Greatest Hits-Volumes I & II .... (Casablanca)
Studio 54 .... (Casablanca)
Summer Collection .... (Mercury)
Walk Away-Best Of Donna Summer-1977-1980 .... (Casablanca)

Last Dance
Frank Sinatra; *Come Dance With Me!* .... (Capitol)
Sinatra Reprise-The Very Good Years .... (Reprise)
The Reprise Collection .... (Reprise)

Last Dance
George Clinton; *Best Of George Clinton* .... (Capitol)

Last Tango In Paris
Herb Alpert & The Tijuana Brass; *Four Sider* .... (A&M)
Herb Alpert & The Tijuana Brass-Greatest Hits-#2 .... (A&M)

Last Waltz, The
Engelbert Humperdinck; *Engelbert Humperdinck-16 Most Requested Songs* .... (Epic)

Le Freak
Chic; *Dance Dance Dance-Best Of* .... (Atlantic)

Let It Whip
Dazz Band; *Dazz Band's Greatest Hits* .... (Motown)
Funkology-#1-Got To Give It Up-C .... (Motown)

Let Me In
Bonnie Raitt; *Takin' My Time* .... (Warner Bros.)
Sensations; *Billboard Top R&B Hits-1962-C* .... (Rhino)
Chess Rhythm & Roll Box-C .... (Chess)
Cruisin'-1962-1963-C .... (Dunhill Compact Classics)
Vintage Music-#6-C .... (MCA)

Let's Dance
Benny Goodman; *Benny Goodman-Live At Carnegie Hall* .... (London)
Benny Goodman's All-Time Greatest Hits .... (Columbia)
Big Band-Let's Dance .... (Columbia)
Big Bands Of The Swinging Years-#1-C .... (Collectables)
Swing's The Thing-C .... (Capitol)

Let's Dance
Beatles; *The Beatles featuring Tony Sheridan-In The Beginning (Circa 1960)* .... (Polydor)

Let's Dance
David Bowie; *Changesbowie* .... (Rykodisc)
   Let's Dance .... (EMI)
   The Singles-1969-1993 .... (Rykodisc)

Let's Face The Music And Dance
Diana Krall; *When I Look In Your Eyes* .... (GRP)
Ella Fitzgerald; *Irving Berlin Always-C* .... (Verve)
Tony Bennett; *Bennett/Berlin* .... (Columbia)
   Jazz .... (Columbia)

Let's Go Dancin'
Kool & The Gang; *As One* .... (De-Lite)

Let's Groove
Earth, Wind & Fire; *Best Of Earth, Wind & Fire-#1* .... (Legacy)
   Raise .... (Columbia)

Let's Twist Again
Chubby Checker; *Chubby Checker's Greatest Hits* .... (Everest)
   Chubby Checker's Greatest Hits .... (Abkco)
   Good Time Rock 'N' Roll-C .... (MCA)
   Hits Of The Sixties-C .... (Intercom Music)

Letters From The Wasteland
Wallflowers; *Breach* .... (Interscope)

Life's A Dance
John Michael Montgomery; *Life's A Dance* .... (Atlantic)

Limbo Rock
Chubby Checker; *Chubby Checker's Greatest Hits* .... (Everest)
   Moonlighting .... (MCA)
   Rock-O-Rama-#2-C .... (Abkco)

Limousine Boogie (Hey Hey Mama)
Savoy Brown; *Make Me Sweat* .... (Crescendo)

Little Child
Beatles; *Meet The Beatles!* .... (Capitol)

Little Night Dancin'
John Cougar; *John Cougar* .... (Riva)

Little Shoe Maker
Eddie Fisher; *Very Best Of Eddie Fisher* .... (Taragon)
Gaylords; *Choice Voices! Pop Vocal Group Gems Of The
   '50s-C* .... (Collector's Choice)

Loco-Motion
Grand Funk Railroad; *Billboard Top Rock 'N' Roll Hits-1974-C* .... (Rhino)
   Caught In The Act .... (Capitol)
   Grand Funk Railroad-Hits .... (Capitol)
Kylie Minogue; *Kylie* .... (Geffen)
Little Eva; *Billboard Top Rock 'N' Roll Hits-1962-C* .... (Rhino)
   Groove 'N' Grind-'50s & '60s Dance Hits-C .... (Rhino)
   More American Graffiti-C .... (MCA)

Los Angeles Boogie
Lightnin' Hopkins; *Los Angeles Blues* .... (Rhino)

Louisiana Saturday Night
Don Williams; *Best Of Cajun Country-C* .... (Era)
   Best Of Don Williams-#4 .... (MCA)
   Don Williams-Country Boy .... (MCA)
Jimmy C. Newman; *From The Vaults: Decca Country Classics-1934-
   1973-C* .... (Decca)
   Grand Ole Opry-75 Years-#2-C .... (MCA)
   Progressive CC .... (Plantation)
Mel McDaniel; *Mel McDaniel's Greatest Hits* .... (Capitol)

Louisiana Stomp
Clifton Chenier; *Zydeco-#1-The Early Years (1961-1962)-C* .... (Arhoolie)

Louisiana Two-Step
Clifton Chenier; *King Of Zydeco Live At Montreux* .... (Arhoolie)
   Out West .... (Arhoolie)

Lynda
Steve Wariner; *Country Classics-#11-1987-1988-C* .... (Universal)
   It's A Crazy World .... (MCA)
   MCA #1 Hits Of The '80s-#3-C .... (MCA Special Prod.)
   Steve Wariner's Greatest Hits .... (MCA)

Macarena
Los Del Rio; *Club Cutz* .... (RCA)
   Macarena Mix .... (Ariola America)

Make Believe Ballroom Time
Glenn Miller; *Glenn Miller-A Legendary Performer-#1 & 2* .... (Bluebird)
Glenn Miller & His Orchestra; *Complete Glenn Miller & His
   Orchestra-#5* .... (Bluebird)

Malaguena
Percy Faith & His Orchestra; *Percy Faith & His Orchestra's All-Time
   Greatest Hits* .... (Columbia)
Placido Domingo; *Love Until The End Of Time-Greatest.* .... (Columbia)
Ritchie Valens; *Best Of Ritchie Valens* .... (Rhino)
   History Of Ritchie Valens .... (Rhino)
Roy Clark; *Best Of Roy Clark* .... (MCA)

Mambo In Miami
Peggy Lee & George Shearing; *Beauty & The Beat!* .... (Blue Note)

Mambo Italiano
Rosemary Clooney; *Rosemary Clooney-16 Most Requested Songs* .... (Legacy)

Mambo Las Vegas
Howard Rumsey's Lighthouse All-Stars; *Music For
   Lighthousekeeping* .... (Contemporary)

Mambo No. 5 (A Little Bit Of...)
Lou Bega; *A Little Bit Of Mambo* .... (RCA)

   Totally Hits-#2-C .... (Elektra)

Mardi Gras Mambo
Hawketts; *Treacherous: A History Of The Neville Brothers* .... (Rhino)

Margaret's Waltz
Buttons & Bows; *The Celts Rise Again-C* .... (Green Linnet)

Martian Boogie
Brownsville Station; *Brownsville Station* .... (Private Stock)

Martian Hop
Ran-Dells; *Dr. Demento Presents The Greatest Novelty Records-#3-
   1960s-C* .... (Rhino)
   Elvira Presents Haunted Hits-C .... (Rhino)
   Halloween Hits-C .... (Rhino)

Mary Jane's Last Dance
Tom Petty And The Heartbreakers; *Playback* .... (MCA)
   Tom Petty And The Heartbreakers' Greatest Hits .... (MCA)

Mashed Potato Time
Dee Dee Sharp; *21 Oldies But Goodies-C* .... (Original Sound)
   Big Bad Bossa Beat .... (Original Sound)
   Oldies But Goodies-#6-C .... (Original Sound)

Masochism Tango
Tom Lehrer; *Dr. Demento Presents The Greatest Novelty Records-#2-
   1950s-C* .... (Rhino)
   Evening Wasted With Tom Lehrer .... (Reprise)

Memphis Boogie
Dr. Isaiah Ross; *Boogie Disease* .... (Arhoolie)

Memphis Hip Shake
Cult; *Electric* .... (Sire)

Mexican Hat Dance
Percy Faith & His Orchestra; *Percy Faith & His Orchestra's All-Time
   Greatest Hits* .... (Columbia)

Mexican Shuffle
Herb Alpert & The Tijuana Brass; *Herb Alpert & The Tijuana Brass'
   Greatest Hits* .... (A&M)
   Herb Alpert & The Tijuana Brass-Classics-#1 .... (A&M)
Tijuana Brass; *South Of The Border* .... (A&M)

Milk Cow Blues Boogie
Elvis Presley; *A Date With Elvis* .... (RCA)
   The Sun Sessions .... (RCA)
Rick Nelson; *Live In '85* .... (Rhino)

Milwaukee Waltz
Michigan Dutchmen; *W.J.R.T. TV All-Time Polkas* .... (Jay Jay)

Milwaukee's Favorite Waltz
Li'l Wally; *America's Favorite* .... (Jay Jay)

Mobile Waltz
Hank Williams, Jr.; *Hank Williams, Jr.-Early Years* .... (WB/Curb)
   One Night Stands .... (Warner Bros.)

Monday's Dance
Ira Sullivan; *Ira Sullivan* .... (Flying Fish)
Red Rodney & Ira Sullivan; *Alive In New York* .... (Muse)

Monkey Time
Major Lance; *Back To The '60s-#3-C* .... (Dominion Entert.)
   Groove 'N' Grind-'50s Dance Hits-C .... (Rhino)
   Soul Shots-#2-The "In" Crowd-Sweet Soul-C .... (Rhino)
Tubes; *Best Of The Tubes* .... (Gold Rush)

Monster Mash
Beach Boys; *Concert/'69-Live In London* .... (Capitol)
Big O; *ST/Return Of The Living Dead, Part 2* .... (Island)
Bobby "Boris" Pickett & The Crypt-Kickers; *Dr. Demento Presents The
   Greatest Novelty Records-#3-1960s-C* .... (Rhino)
   Dr. Demento: 20th Anniversary Collection-C .... (Rhino)
   Halloween Hits-C .... (Rhino)
   Horror Rock Classics-#2-C .... (Rhino)

Moondance
Van Morrison; *Best Of Van Morrison* .... (Polydor)
   Moondance .... (Warner Bros.)

Morning Dance
Spyro Gyra; *Access All Areas* .... (MCA)
   Morning Dance .... (MCA)
   Spyro Gyra-Collection .... (GRP)

Moscow Diskow
Telex; *Moscow Diskow-12''* .... (Sire)

Most Girls
Pink; *Can't Take Me Home* .... (LaFace)
   Totally Hits-#3-C .... (Atlantic)

Mr. Bojangles
David Bromberg; *Out Of The Blues-Best Of David Bromberg* ...... (Columbia)
Jerry Jeff Walker; *A Man Must Carry On* .... (MCA)
   Best Of Jerry Jeff Walker .... (MCA)
   Gypsy Songman .... (Rykodisc)
   Mr. Bojangles .... (Bainbridge)
Nitty Gritty Dirt Band; *Best Of The Nitty Gritty Dirt Band* ...... (Liberty)
   On The Road Again .... (Capitol)
   Super Hits Of The '70s-Have A Nice Day-#4-C .... (Rhino)
   Twenty Years Of Dirt-Best Of The Nitty Gritty Dirt Band ..... (Warner Bros.)
   Uncle Charlie And His Dog Teddy .... (Liberty)

Mummer's Dance
Loreena McKennitt; *The Book Of Secrets* .... (Quinlan Rd./Warner Bros.)

Music
Madonna; *GHV2* .... (Warner Bros.)

Music .... (Maverick)
Totally Hits-#3-C .... (Atlantic)
Music That Makes Me Dance
Barbra Streisand/Original Cast; *Funny Girl* ....(Capitol)
Michael Feinstein & Jule Styne; *M. Feinstein Sings Jule Styne*
Songbook .... (Elektra)
Mystery Dance
Elvis Costello; *Girls Girls Girls* ....(Columbia)
My Aim Is True .... (Columbia)
Neal's Fandango
Doobie Brothers; *Stampede* .... (Warner Bros.)
Neutron Dance
Pointer Sisters; *Break Out* ....(Planet)
Pointer Sisters' Greatest Hits ....(RCA)
ST/Beverly Hills Cop ....(MCA)
Never Felt Like Dancing
Teddy Pendergrass; *Workin' It Back* .... (Asylum)
New Hawaiian Boogie
George Thorogood & The Destroyers; *Move It On Over* ....(Rounder)
New Jack Swing
Wreckx-N-Effect; *Rap: On The Lighter Tip-C* ....(K-Tel)
Wreckx-N-Effect .... (Motown)
New Orleans Bump
Jelly Roll Morton; *Jazz Classics In Digital Stereo* ....(ABC)
New Orleans Shuffle
Johnny Otis; *Original Johnny Otis Show* ....(Savoy)
New Orleans Waltz
Nathan Abshire; *French Blues* ....(Arhoolie)
New Spanish Two-Step
Bob Wills & His Texas Playboys; *Country Music Classics-#14-*
1940s-C ....(K-Tel)
Essential Bob Wills & His Texas Playboys-1935-1973 ....(Legacy)
New York Shuffle
Graham Parker And The Rumour; *Stick To Me* ....(Mercury)
The Parkerilla ....(Mercury)
Nights In Harlem
Luther Vandross; *I Know* .... (LV/Virgin)
Nobody But Me
Human Beinz; *Flower Power-Psychedelic Rock Classics-C* ....(K-Tel)
Frat Rock!-C ....(Rhino)
Isley Brothers; *Isley Brothers-16 Greatest Hits* ....(Deluxe)
The Isley Brothers Story-#1-Rockin' Soul-1959-1968 ....(Rhino)
Non-Viennese Waltz Blues
Joe Gordon; *Lookin' Good!* .... (Contemporary)
North Gulfport Boogie
Roosevelt Sykes; *Hard Drivin' Blues* ....(Delmark)
Norwegian Dance
Stephane Grappelli; *Stephanova* ....(Concord Jazz)
Norwegian Dance No. 2
Django Reinhardt & Stephane Grappelli; *Django Reinhardt & Stephane*
Grappelli ....(Crescendo)
Norwegian Waltz/Liza Lynn
Jackie Daly & Seamus & Manus McGuire; *Buttons & Bows* ..... (Green Linnet)
Nowhere To Go
Melissa Etheridge; *Your Little Secret* ....(Island)
Oh, What A Night For Dancing
Barry White; *Barry White Sings For Someone You Love* .....(20th Century Fox)
Barry White's All-Time Greatest Hits ....(Mercury)
Oklahoma Dancer
Monkees; *Monkees Present* ....(Rhino)
Oklahoma Stomp
Duke Ellington; *Hot In Harlem* .... (MCA)
Jazz Heritage-Vocalion Rarities-C .... (MCA)
Spade Cooley; *Columbia Historic Edition-Spade Cooley* ....(Columbia)
Spade Cooley & His Orchestra; *Legends Of Country Guitar-#1-C* ......(Rhino)
Oklahoma Swing
Vince Gill & Reba McEntire; *When I Call Your Name* .... (MCA)
Oklahoma Waltz
Cavaliers; *Have Polka Will Travel* ....(Accent)
Old Folks Boogie
Little Feat; *Time Loves A Hero* .... (Warner Bros.)
Waiting For Columbus .... (Warner Bros.)
Old Maid Boogie
Eddie "Cleanhead" Vinson; *Late Show* ....(Fantasy)
On The Verge
Collin Raye; *I Think About You* ....(Epic)
Our Waltz
David Rose & His Orchestra; *David Rose & His Orchestra* ....(Laserlight)
Sarah Vaughan; *Complete Sarah Vaughan On Mercury-#3* ....(Mercury)
Over And Over
Dave Clark Five; *History Of The Dave Clark Five* ....(Hollywood)
The Dave Clark Five's Greatest Hits ....(Epic)
Palm Springs Jump
Flat Foot Floogie Boys & Slim Gaillard; *1940s-The Singers-C* ......(Columbia)
Papa Loves Mambo
Perry Como; *Como's Golden Records* ....(RCA)
Perry Como-Pure Gold ....(RCA)
Perry Como's All-Time Greatest Hits-#1 ....(RCA)

This Is Perry Como ....(RCA)
Papa's Got A Brand New Bag
James Brown; *21 Legendary Superstars-C* .... (Original Sound)
Everybody's Doin' The Hustle & Dead On The Double Bump ...... (Polydor)
James Brown's Greatest Hits ....(Rhino)
Live-Hot On The One .... (Polydor)
Otis Redding; *The Otis Redding Story* ....(Atlantic)
Unlimited! ....(Reprise)
Pata Pata
Miriam Makeba; *Planet Africa: World Of African Music-C* .... (Priority)
Welela ....(Verve)
Peach Tree Shuffle
Panama Francis; *All-Stars 1949* ....(Collectables)
Peppermint Twist
Joey Dee & the Starliters; *Billboard Top Rock 'N' Roll Hits-1962-C* ....(Rhino)
Hey Let's Twist! Best Of Joey Dee & The Starliters ....(Rhino)
ST/American Graffiti ....(MCA)
Philadelphia Boogie
Len McCall; *Philadelphia Boogie* ....(Collectables)
Philadelphia Hop
Li'l Wally; *Here Comes Li'l Wally* ....(Jay Jay)
Philadelphia Mambo
Cal Tjader; *Black Orchid* .... (Fantasy)
Philly Dog
Mar-Keys; *Back To Back: Mar-Keys & Booker T. & The M.G.s* ... (Atlantic)
Great Memphis Sound .... (Atlantic)
Stax/Volt Revue-#1-Live In London-C .... (Atlantic)
Super Hits-#1-C .... (Atlantic)
Philly Freeze
Alvin Cash & The Registers; *45-#176* .... (Eric)
Play
Jennifer Lopez; *J. Lo* ....(Epic)
Now That's What I Call Music!-#7-C ....(Virgin)
Play Me The Waltz Of The Angels
Derailers featuring Buck Owens; *Full Western Dress* .... (Sire)
Poetry In Motion
Johnny Tillotson; *10 Top Ten Hits-#1* .... (Laurie)
American Graffiti-#3-C ....(MCA)
Jukebox Classics-#1-C ....(Rhino)
Mellow '60s-C .... (Priority)
Million-Dollar Memories-#2-C ....(RCA)
Polish Memories Waltz
New Yorkers; *Polka Smile* ....(Jay Jay)
Pony Time
Chubby Checker; *Chubby Checker's Greatest Hits* .... (Abkco)
Good Time Rock 'N' Roll-C ....(MCA)
Let's Dance .... (Gusto)
Poor Boy Shuffle
Creedence Clearwater Revival; *1969* ....(Fantasy)
Willy & The Poor Boys .... (Fantasy)
Pop Pop Pop-Pie
Sherrys; *Golden Age Of American Rock-C* .... (Ace)
Popcorn, Pretzels & Beer Waltz
Michigan Dutchmen; *Beer & Dutchmen Polkas* ....(Jay Jay)
Port Arthur Waltz
Harry Choates; *Fiddle King Of Cajun Swing* ....(Arhoolie)
Pretty Ballerina
Left Banke; *History Of The Left Banke* ....(Rhino)
Nuggets-#11-Pop-Part 4-C ....(Rhino)
Private Dancer
Tina Turner; *Live In Europe* ....(Capitol)
Private Dancer ....(Capitol)
Simply The Best ....(Capitol)
Pump Up The Jam
Technotronic; *Pump Up The Jam-The Album* ....(SBK)
Rock The First-#3-C .... (Priority)
Puppets' Dance
Jean-Luc Ponty; *Cosmic Messenger* ....(Rhino)
Quarter To Three
Gary U.S. Bonds; *Best Of Gary U.S. Bonds* ....(Rhino)
Best Of Gary U.S. Bonds ....(EMI Legends Of Rock 'N' Roll)
Queen Of The Hop
Bobby Darin; *The Bobby Darin Story* ....(Atlantic)
Dave Edmunds; *ST/Porky's Revenge!* ....(Columbia)
Dion; *Dion Sings The Hits Of The '50s & '60s* .... (Laurie)
Ragtime Dance
Jean-Pierre Rampal; *Jean-Pierre Rampal Plays Scott Joplin* ....(Columbia)
Richard Zimmerman; *Scott Joplin-His Greatest Hits* ....(Everest)
Scott Joplin; *The Entertainer* ....(Biograph)
Ready Teddy
Buddy Holly; *Buddy Holly* .... (MCA)
Rock & Roll Collection .... (MCA)
Elvis Presley; *Elvis* ....(RCA)
Rocker ....(RCA)
The Great Performances ....(RCA)
Little Richard; *Georgia Peach* .... (Specialty)
Grooviest 17 Original Hits .... (Specialty)
More American Graffiti-C .... (MCA)

Redneck Stomp
Jeff Foxworthy; *America's Country: Good Time Country-C* . . . . (Madacy)
   Crank It Up: The Music Album . . . .(Warner Bros.)
   Jeff Foxworthy's Greatest Bits. . . . .(Warner Bros.)

Rhumba Girl
Nicolette Larson; *Nicolette*. . . . .(Warner Bros.)

Riverboat Shuffle
Hoagy Carmichael; *Stardust Road* . . . . (MCA)

Rock & Roll Waltz
Kay Starr; *Capitol Collectors Series-Kay Starr* . . . . (Capitol)
   Nipper's Greatest Hits Of The '50s-#1-C . . . . (RCA)

Rock A Beatin' Boogie
Bill Haley & His Comets; *Bill Haley & His Comets' Greatest Hits* . . . . (Everest)
   Bill Haley & His Comets-Golden Hits . . . .(MCA)
   Legends Of Rock Guitar-'50s-#2-C . . . . (Rhino)

Rock And Roll Music
Beach Boys; *15 Big Ones* . . . . (Brother)
   Beach Boys-Gift Set . . . . (Capitol)
   Made In The U.S.A. . . . . (Capitol)
   Ten Years Of Harmony . . . .(Caribou)
Beatles; *Beatles '65* . . . . (Capitol)
   Beatles-Box Set . . . . (Capitol)
   For Sale . . . . (Capitol)
   Rock 'N' Roll Music . . . . (Capitol)
Chuck Berry; *Chuck Berry-Golden Hits* . . . . (Mercury)
   Chuck Berry's Greatest Hits . . . . (Everest)
   Cruisin'-1958-C . . . .(Increase)
   The Chess Box-Chuck Berry . . . . (Chess)
REO Speedwagon; *Nine Lives* . . . .(Epic)

Rock And Roll Waltz
Kay Starr; *Capitol Collectors Series-Kay Starr* . . . . (Capitol)

Rock Billy Boogie
Robert Gordon; *Rock Billy Boogie* . . . . (RCA)

Rock That Boogie
Commander Cody & His Lost Planet Airmen; *Country Casanova*. . . . . . (MCA)
   Too Much Fun-Best Of Commander Cody & His Lost Planet Airmen . . .(MCA)

Rock With You
Jacksons; *Jacksons Live* . . . .(Epic)
Michael Jackson; *Off The Wall* . . . . (Epic)

Rockin' Boogie
Fleetwood Mac; *In Chicago* . . . . (Sire)

Roxanna Waltz & Scotland Calling Jesse
Jay Ungar & Others; *Fiddle Fever* . . . . (Flying Fish)

Rump Shaker
Wreckx-N-Effect; *Hard Or Smooth* . . . . (MCA)

Sad Pig Dance
Chris Proctor; *Delicate Dance* . . . . (Flying Fish)

Safety Dance
Men Without Hats; *Rhythm Of Youth* . . . .(MCA)

Sally Can't Dance
Lou Reed; *Sally Can't Dance* . . . . (RCA)
   Walk On The Wild Side-The Best Of Lou Reed. . . . . (RCA)

Salsa Smurf
Special Request; *Tommy Boy's Greatest Beats-C*. . . . . (Tommy Boy)

Same Old Song & Dance
Aerosmith; *Aerosmith-Classics Live 2* . . . . (Columbia)
   Aerosmith's Greatest Hits . . . . (Columbia)
   Get Your Wings . . . . (Columbia)
   Pandora's Box . . . . (Columbia)

San Antonio Stroll
Tanya Tucker; *MCA Records 30 Years Of Hits-1958-1988-C* . . . . (MCA)
   Tanya Tucker-Greatest Hits Encore . . . .(Gold Rush)
   Tanya Tucker's Greatest Country Hits . . . . (Curb)
   Tanya Tucker's Greatest Hits . . . . (MCA)
   The Tanya Tucker Collection. . . . . (MCA)

Saturday Dance
Bob Cooper; *Coop! Music Of* . . . .(Contemporary)

Saturday Night Boogie
Harry Crafton; *Harry Crafton*. . . . . (Collectables)

Saturday Night Stomp
Eddie "Blues Man" Kirkland; *It's The Blues Man!* . . . .(Tru-Sound)

Savannah Dance
Michael Pluznick; *Where The Rain Is Born* . . . . (Sona Gaia)

Savannah Russet/Jete The Dancing Cat
Jeanne Newhall; *Novice* . . . . (Marzipan Music)

Save The Last Dance For Me
Buck Owens; *Buck Owens Collection-1959-1990* . . . . (Rhino)
Dolly Parton; *Best Of Dolly Parton-#3*. . . . . (RCA)
   Great Pretender . . . . (RCA)
Drifters; *20 Top 10 Hits Of The '50s & '60s-C* . . . . (Laurie)
   Atlantic Rhythm & Blues 1947-1974-#4 (1958-1962)-C . . . .(Atlantic)
   Billboard Top Rock 'N' Roll Hits-1960-C . . . . (Rhino)
   Cruisin'-1960-C . . . .(Increase)
   Drifters-Golden Hits . . . .(Atlantic)
Emmylou Harris; *Blue Kentucky Girl*. . . . . (Warner Bros.)
   Profile II-The Best Of Emmylou Harris . . . . (Warner Bros.)
Jerry Lee Lewis; *20 Classic Jerry Lee Lewis Hits* . . . . (Original Sound)
   Duets . . . . (Sun)
   Jerry Lee Lewis-Original Golden Hits-#2 . . . . (Sun)

Monsters. . . . .(Sun)

Save Your Heart For Me
Gary Lewis And The Playboys; *Gary Lewis & The Playboys* . . . . . (Gold Rush)
   Gary Lewis And The Playboys' Greatest Hits . . . . (Curb)

School Days
Chuck Berry; *Best Of Chuck Berry* . . . . (Gusto)
   Billboard Top Rock 'N' Roll Hits-1957-C . . . .(Rhino)
   Chuck Berry-Golden Hits . . . . (Mercury)
   ST/Rock 'N' Roll High School . . . .(Sire)

September
Earth, Wind & Fire; *Best Of Earth, Wind & Fire-#1* . . . .(Legacy)
   Eternal Dance . . . . (Columbia)
   Mega Hits Dance Classics-#7-C . . . .(Priority)

Sexy Dancer
Prince; *Prince* . . . . (Warner Bros.)

Shackles (Praise You)
Mary Mary; *Thankful* . . . . (C2/Columbia)

Shadow Dancing
Andy Gibb; *Andy Gibb's Greatest Hits*. . . . . (RSO)
   Collection Of His Greatest Hits . . . .(Polydor)
   Shadow Dancing . . . . (RSO)

Shake
Ike & Tina Turner; *Ike & Tina Turner's Greatest Hits* . . . . . . (Saja)
Otis Redding; *Best Of Otis Redding* . . . . (Atco)
   History Of Otis Redding . . . . (Atco)
   Live In Europe . . . . (Atco)
   The Otis Redding Story. . . . .(Atlantic)
Rod Stewart with Brian Auger & The Trinity; *Storyteller/The Complete
   Anthology: 1964-1990* . . . . (Warner Bros.)
Sam Cooke; *The Man And His Music* . . . . (RCA)
Supremes; *We Remember Sam Cooke* . . . . (Motown)

Shake A Tail Feather
Five Du-Tones; *Toga Rock-#2-C* . . . . (Dunhill Compact Classics)
James & Bobby Purify; *Frat Rock!-#3-Grandson Of Frat Rock!-C* . . . . . (Rhino)

Shake And Fingerpop
Junior Walker & The All Stars; *Junior Walker & The All Stars'
   Greatest Hits* . . . . (Motown)
   Junior Walker & The All Stars-All The Great Hits . . . . (Motown)
   Junior Walker & The All Stars-Anthology . . . . (Motown)
   Shotgun . . . . (Motown)

Shake Down
Evelyn "Champagne" King; *Face To Face* . . . . (RCA)

Shake It
Ian Matthews; *Stealin' Home* . . . . (Mushroom)

Shake It And Break It
Big Joe Turner; *Things That I Used To Do* . . . . (Pablo)
Charley Patton; *Founder Of The Delta Blues-1929-1934* . . . .(Yazoo)
Preservation Hall Jazz Band; *Best Of The Preservation Hall
   Jazz Band* . . . . (Columbia)

Shake It Like A White Girl
E.U.; *Livin' Large* . . . . (Virgin)

Shake It Up
Bad Company; *Dangerous Age* . . . .(Atlantic)
Cars; *Shake It Up* . . . . (Elektra)
   The Cars' Greatest Hits . . . . (Elektra)

Shake It Up Tonight
Cheryl Lynn; *Club Columbia-C* . . . . (Columbia)
   In The Night . . . . (Columbia)

Shake It Up!
Jamaica Boys; *J Boys* . . . . (Reprise)

Shake Me I Rattle
Cristy Lane; *Cristy Lane Is The Name* . . . . (Laughing Stock)
   Cristy Lane-At Her Best . . . . (EMI)

Shake Shake Shake
Jackie Wilson; *Baby Workout* . . . . (Brunswick)
   Jackie Wilson's Greatest Hits. (Brunswick)
   Mr. Excitement . . . . (Rhino)
   My Golden Favorites . . . . (Brunswick)

Shake That Fat
Jo Jo Gunne; *Jo Jo Gunne* . . . . (Asylum)

Shake Your Ass!
Blowfly; *Twisted World Of Blowfly*. . . . .(Oops)

Shake Your Body (Down To The Ground)
Jacksons; *Destiny* . . . . (Epic)
   Jacksons Live . . . . (Epic)
   ST/Skatetown USA . . . . (Columbia)

Shake Your Booty
KC And The Sunshine Band; *Best Of KC And The Sunshine Band* . . . . . (Rhino)
   KC And The Sunshine Band's Greatest Hits. . . . . (TK)
   Mega Hits Dance Classics-#4-C . . . .(Priority)
   Part 3 . . . . (TK)

Shake Your Groove Thing
Peaches & Herb; *2 Hot* . . . .(Polydor)
   Billboard Top Dance Hits-1978-C . . . . (Rhino)
   Mega Hits Dance Classics-#2-C . . . .(Priority)
   Night At Studio 54-C . . . .(Casablanca)
   Polydor Dance Classics-C . . . .(Polydor)
   The Disco Years-#1-Turn The Beat Around-1974-1978-C . . . .(Rhino)

Shake Your Hips
Love Sculpture; *Blues Helping* .... (EMI)
Rolling Stones; *Exile On Main Street* ....(Virgin)
Slim Harpo; *Best Of Slim Harpo* .... (Rhino)
Shake Your Love
Debbie Gibson; *Out Of The Blue* .... (Atlantic)
Shake Your Love
Climax Blues Band; *FM/Live* ....(Sire)
Shake Your Money Maker
Elmore James; *King Of The Slide Guitar* ....(Capricorn)
Fleetwood Mac; *Vintage Years* ....(Sire)
George Thorogood & The Destroyers; *Born To Be Bad* .... (Gold Rush)
Paul Butterfield Blues Band; *Golden Butter* ....(Elektra)
Paul Butterfield Blues Band ....(Elektra)
Shake Your Pants
Cameo; *Cameosis* ....(Casablanca)
Shake Your Tailfeather
Blues Brothers & Ray Charles; *ST/The Blues Brothers* .... (Atlantic)
Shake, Rattle And Roll
Big Joe Turner; *Big Joe Turner's Greatest Hits* .... (Atlantic)
Every Day I Have The Blues .... (Pablo)
Oldies But Goodies-#2-C ....(Original Sound)
Soul Years-C .... (Atlantic)
Bill Haley & His Comets; *Bill Haley & His Comets' Greatest Hits* ...... (MCA)
Bill Haley & His Comets-Golden Hits .... (MCA)
Elvis Presley; *For LP Fans Only* ....(RCA)
Rocker...(RCA)
ST/This Is Elvis ....(RCA)
Fats Domino; *Fats Domino's Greatest Hits*...................... (MCA)
Huey Lewis and the News; *Four Chords & Several Years Ago* .... (Elektra)
NRBQ; *At Yankee Stadium* .... (Mercury)
Vern Gosdin; *Best Of Vern Gosdin* .... (Warner Bros.)
Shake, The
Neal McCoy; *Be Good At It* .... (Atlantic)
Neal McCoy's Greatest Hits............................ (Atlantic)
Shakin'
Eddie Money; *Eddie Money's Greatest Hits-Sound Of Money* ...... (Columbia)
No Control ....(Columbia)
Sawyer Brown; *Sawyer Brown's Greatest Hits* ....(Curb)
Shakin' ....(Curb)
Shakin' All Over
Guess Who; *Frat Rock!-#3-Grandson Of Frat Rock!-C* .... (Rhino)
Greatest Of The Guess Who ....(RCA)
Pirates; *Out Of Their Skulls* .... (Warner Bros.)
Skull Wars .... (Warner Bros.)
Who; *Live At Leeds* .... (MCA)
Shakin' Shakin' Shakes
Los Lobos; *By The Light Of The Moon* .... (Slash)
Shall We Dance
Original Broadway Cast; *The King And I* .... (RCA Victor)
Original Cast; *The King And I* .... (MCA)
Shall We Dance
Ella Fitzgerald; *George & Ira Gershwin Songbook*................. (Verve)
Shanghai Shuffle
Bunny Berigan & His Orchestra; *Bunny Berigan & His Orchestra-1937-1938*.. (Hindsight)
Fletcher Henderson & His Orchestra; *1924-1941* .... (Biograph)
She Said Yes
Rhett Akins; *A Thousand Memories* .... (Decca)
She Wants To Dance With Me
Rick Astley; *Hold Me In Your Arms* .... (RCA)
She's Got The Rhythm (And I Got The Blues)
Alan Jackson; *A Lot About Livin' (And A Little 'Bout Love)* .... (Arista)
She's Only Happy When She's Dancin'
Bryan Adams; *Reckless* .... (A&M)
Shim Sham Shimmy
Dorsey Brothers; *Best Of The Big Bands-C* .... (Columbia)
I'm Getting Sentimental Over You .... (Pro-Arte)
Shim, Sham Shimmy On The St. Louis Blues
Dizzy Gillespie; *Best Of Dizzy Gillespie* .... (Pablo)
Shimmy Like Kate
Olympics; *Meet The Marathons* .... (Collectables)
Official Record Album Of The Olympics...................... (Rhino)
Shimmy Shake
Beatles; *45-#1512* .... (Collectables)
Shimmy Shakin' Daddy
Maddox Brothers & Rose; *1946-1951-#2* ....(Arhoolie)
America's Most Colorful Hillbilly Band......................(Arhoolie)
Shimmy Shimmy
Bobby Freeman; *Let's Dance* .... (Gusto)
Shit House Shuffle
Aerosmith; *Pandora's Box* .... (Columbia)
Shout And Shimmy
Who; *Who's Missing* .... (MCA)
Shut Up And Dance
Pointer Sisters; *Serious Slammin'* ....(RCA)
Simon Smith & His Amazing Dancing Bear
Randy Newman; *Sail Away* .... (Reprise)

Skip To My Lou
Cathy Fink; *When The Rain Comes Down* ....(Rounder)
Leadbelly; *Defense Blues-Golden Classics-#2* ....(Collectables)
Original Soundtrack; *School Days-Kids Classics* .... (Benson)
Pete Seeger; *American Favorite Ballads-#1* .... (Smithsonian Folkways)
Skip To My Lu
Lisa Lisa; *Lisa Lisa 77* .... (Pendulum)
Sleeping Beauty Waltz
101 Strings Orchestra; *Million-Seller Themes From Tchaikovsky* ......(Alshire)
Slow Burn
T.G. Sheppard; *T.G. Sheppard's All-Time Greatest Hits* .... (Warner Bros.)
Slow Dance
R. Kelly & Public Announcement; *Born Into The '90s* .... (Jive)
Slow Dancer
Boz Scaggs; *Boz Scaggs-Hits!* ....(Columbia)
Slow Dancer ....(Columbia)
Robert Plant; *Pictures At Eleven* ....(Swan Song)
Slow Twistin'
Chubby Checker with Dee Dee Sharp; *Chubby Checker's Dance Party*...(K-Tel)
Let's Twist!-C ....(K-Tel)
Smoky Places
Corsairs; *Best Of Chess Rhythm & Blues-#1-C* ....(Chess)
Hard To Find Hits Of Rock 'N Roll-#1-C ....(Curb)
So Young And In Love
Bruce Springsteen; *Tracks* ....(Columbia)
Soft Shoe
Gerry Mulligan; *Gerry Mulligan's Greatest Hits* .... (RCA Victor)
Some Days You Gotta Dance
Dixie Chicks; *Fly* ....(Monument)
Spanish Dance
John Fahey; *Death Chants, Breakdowns & Military Waltzes*......... (Takoma)
Spanish Dancer
Steve Winwood; *Arc Of A Diver* ....(Island)
Steve Winwood-Chronicles ....(Island)
Spanish Eyes
Ricky Martin; *Ricky Martin* ....(Columbia)
Spanish Fandango
Chet Atkins; *Pickin' My Way-In Hollywood Alone* .... (Mobile Fidelity Sound Lab)
Mississippi John Hurt; *Best Of Mississippi John Hurt* ....(Vanguard)
Spanish Fandango
Bob Wills & His Texas Playboys; *Bob Wills & His Texas Playboys-24 Great Hits*.. (Polydor)
Spanish Two Step
Bob Wills; *Bob Wills-Anthology* .... (Sony Music Special Prod.)
Stay All Night (Stay A Little Longer)
Backwoods Banjo; *Jes' Fine* ....(Rounder)
Mark Chesnutt & Asleep At The Wheel; *Ride With Bob-C* .... (DreamWorks/SKG)
Willie Nelson; *Willie & Family Live* ....(Columbia)
Stayin' Alive
Bee Gees; *Bee Gees' Greatest* .... (Polydor)
ST/Saturday Night Fever............................... (Polydor)
ST/Stayin' Alive .... (Polydor)
Step That Step
Sawyer Brown; *New Faces Of Country-C* ....(K-Tel)
Sawyer Brown ....(Curb)
Sawyer Brown's Greatest Hits ....(Curb)
Still Dancin' With You
Wade Hayes; *Old Enough To Know Better* ....(Columbia)
Stockholm Stomp
California Ramblers; *Miss Annabelle Lee-#1*................. (Biograph)
Stomp
Brothers Johnson; *Billboard Top Dance Hits-1980-C* ....(Rhino)
Brothers Johnson-Classics-#11 ....(A&M)
Light Up The Night ....(A&M)
Stomp
God's Property; *MTV Jams-C* ....(Kedar Entert./Universal)
Stomp Dance (Unity)
Robbie Robertson featuring The Six Nations Women Singers; *Contact From The Underworld of Redboy*................................(Capitol)
Stompin' At The Savoy
Benny Goodman; *Benny Goodman-Pure Gold* .... (RCA)
Benny Goodman's All-Time Greatest Hits ....(Columbia)
Carnegie Hall Jazz Concert ....(Columbia)
Stompin' At The Savoy ....(Bluebird)
Doc Severinsen; *Facets* ....(Amherst)
Ella Fitzgerald & Louis Armstrong; *Ella & Louis* ....(Verve)
Louis Armstrong; *Essential Louis Armstrong* ....(Vanguard)
Stompin' In The '90s
Yo-Yo; *Make Way For The Motherlode* ....(East West)
Stop, Stop, Stop
Hollies; *Best Of The Hollies* ....(EMI)
Hollies' Greatest Hits ....(Epic)
The Hollies' Greatest Hits.............................(Epic)
Stray Cat Strut
Stray Cats; *Best Of Stray Cats-Rock This Town* ....(EMI)
Built For Speed ....(EMI)

Rock The First-#4-C . . . . (Sandstone Music)

Strike It Up
Black Box; *Dreamland* . . . . (RCA)
Mixedup! . . . . (RCA)

Stroll, The
Diamonds; *Groove 'N' Grind-'50s & '60s Dance Hits-C* . . . . (Rhino)
Partytime '50s-C . . . . (Priority)
ST/American Graffiti . . . . (MCA)

Sugarfoot Rag
Asleep At The Wheel; *Very Best Of Asleep At The Wheel
    Since 1970.* . . . . (Relentless/Madacy)
Bill Keith; *Something Auld, Something Newgrass, Something Borrowed,
    Something Bluegrass.* . . . . (Rounder)
Porter Wagoner; *Grand Ole Opry-75 Years-#2-C* . . . . (MCA)

Sundance
Kitaro; *Light Of The Spirit* . . . . (Geffen)

Sundance
Danny Joe Brown Band; *Danny Joe Brown Band.* . . . . (Epic)

Sundancing (For The Hopi/Navajo Energy)
Jon Anderson; *In The City Of Angels* . . . . (Columbia)

Super Bowl Shuffle
Chicago Bears Shufflin' Crew; *45-#71012* . . . . (Red Label)

Sway
Bobby Rydell; *Born With A Smile.* . . . . (Plum)
Dean Martin; *Best Of Dean Martin.* . . . . (CEMA Special Prod.)
Dean Martin's All Time Greatest Hits . . . . (Curb)
That's Amore: The Best Of Dean Martin . . . . (Capitol)

Swayin' To The Music
Johnny Rivers; *Johnny Rivers-Anthology 1964-1977.* . . . . (Rhino)

Swedish Dance
Danny Thompson; *Instruments-Collection.* . . . . (Hannibal)

Swedish Jig
John Renbourn & Stefan Grossman; *Music Of Ireland.* . . . . (Shanachie)

Sweet Dreams
La Bouche; *Sweet Dreams* . . . . (RCA)
The Ultimate Dance Party-1998-C . . . . (Arista)

Sweet Little Sixteen
Beatles; *45-#1502.* . . . . (Collectables)
Chuck Berry; *Best Of The Best Of Chuck Berry* . . . . (International Mktg. Group)
Chuck Berry-Golden Hits . . . . (Mercury)
Chuck Berry-Greatest Hits Live . . . . (Quicksilver)
Cruisin'-1965-C . . . . (Increase)
Oldies But Goodies-#12-C . . . . (Original Sound)
Jerry Lee Lewis; *Jerry Lee Lewis-Original Golden Hits-#3* . . . . (Sun)
Jerry Lee Lewis & Friends; *Jerry Lee Lewis & Friends-Duets* . . . . (Sun)
John Lennon; *Lennon* . . . . (Capitol)
Rock 'N' Roll . . . . (Capitol)

Sweet Pea
Tommy Roe; *Best Of Tommy Roe.* . . . . (Curb)
Cruisin'-1966-C . . . . (Increase)
Tommy Roe's Greatest Hits . . . . (MCA)

Take Your Clothes Off When You Dance
Frank Zappa; *You Can't Do That On Stage Anymore-#6* . . . . . . (Rykodisc)
Mothers Of Invention; *We're Only In It For The Money.* . . . . (Rykodisc)

Tango In Paris
Regina Belle; *Passion.* . . . . (Columbia)

Tango In The Night
Fleetwood Mac; *Tango In The Night* . . . . (Warner Bros.)

Taxi Dancer
John Cougar; *John Cougar.* . . . . (Riva)

Taxi War Dance
Count Basie; *Essential Count Basie-#1* . . . . (Columbia)
I Like Jazz-Essence Of Count Basie . . . . (Columbia)

Teach Me (The "Philly" Dog)
Manhattans; *Dedicated To You-Golden Classics-#1* . . . . (Collectables)

Teach Me How To Shimmy
Calamities; *Calamities.* . . . . (Posh Boy)

Ten Cents A Dance
Eileen Farrell; *I Gotta Right To Sing The Blues* . . . . (Sony Music Classical)
Ella Fitzgerald; *Rodgers & Hart Songbook* . . . . (Verve)

Tennessee Two Step
Charlie Daniels; *America, I Believe In You* . . . . (Liberty)

Tennessee Waltz
Cowboy Copas; *45-#696* . . . . (King)
Emmylou Harris; *Cimarron* . . . . (Warner Bros.)
Country's Greatest Hits-#5-C . . . . (Warner Bros.)
New Tradition Sings The Old Tradition-C . . . . (Warner Bros.)
Guy Lombardo & His Royal Canadians; *Best Of Guy Lombardo* . . . . (Curb)
Hank Williams, Jr.; *Living Proof-MGM Recordings 1963-1975* . . . . . (Mercury)
Lacy J. Dalton; *Lacy J. Dalton's Greatest Hits* . . . . (Columbia)
Les Paul & Mary Ford; *Les Paul-Selections From Legend & Legacy.* . . . (Capitol)
Patti Page; *Patti Page-Golden Hits* . . . . (Mercury)
Patti Page's Greatest Hits . . . . (Columbia)
Roy Acuff; *Essential Roy Acuff-1936-1949* . . . . (Legacy)
Roy Acuff's Greatest Hits . . . . (Columbia)
Roy Rogers; *Best Of Roy Rogers* . . . . (Curb)
Sammy Kaye & His Orchestra; *Best Of The Big Bands-C* . . . . . . (Columbia)
Spike Jones & His City Slickers; *Best Of Spike Jones & His City
    Slickers* . . . . (RCA)

Terrific Band & A Real Nice Crowd
Original Broadway Cast; *Ballroom* . . . . (Sony Music Classical)

Texas Jump
Ozzie Nelson & His Orchestra; *The Uncollected Ozzie Nelson & His
    Orchestra-1940-1942* . . . . (Hindsight)

Texas Shuffle
Count Basie; *Basie Reunions.* . . . . (Prestige)
Best Of Count Basie . . . . (MCA)
Houston Person; *Heavy Juice* . . . . (Muse)

Texas Sidestep
Deanna Cox; *Country Jukebox Greatest Hits-#2-C* . . . . (Warner Bros.)

Texas Two Step
Bob Wills; *The Country Music Hall Of Fame-Bob Wills.* . . . . . . (Universal)

That Boy Could Dance
"Weird Al" Yankovic; *In 3-D* . . . . (Scotti Bros.)

That Girl Wants To Dance With Me
Gregory Hines; *Gregory Hines* . . . . (Epic)

That Ol' Texas Two-Step
Charlie Walker; *Charlie Walker* . . . . (Dot)

Theme From "Dances With Wolves"
John Barry; *Moviola* . . . . (Epic)

Theme From "Solid Gold"
Original Soundtrack; *Television's Greatest Hits-#3-1970s & 1980s-C* . . . (TVT)

There's Going To Be A Party
Bob Wills; *Stay A Little Longer-The Original Columbia
    Recordings.* . . . . (Roswell/RCA)

They Dance Alone (Cueca Solo)
Sting; *...Nothing Like The Sun* . . . . (A&M)
Fields Of Gold-The Best Of Sting 1984-1994 . . . . (A&M)

They Don't Dance Like Carmen No More
Jimmy Buffett; *Boats Beaches Bars & Ballads* . . . . (Margaritaville)
White Sport Coat & A Pink Crustacean . . . . (MCA)

They Were Doin' The Mambo
Vaughn Monroe; *Very Best Of Vaughn Monroe* . . . . (Taragon)

They're Playin' Our Song
Neal McCoy; *Neal McCoy's Greatest Hits* . . . . (Atlantic)
You Gotta Love That! . . . . (Atlantic)

Thorazine Shuffle
Gov't Mule; *Live With A Little Help From Our Friends-Collector's
    Edition.* . . . . (Capricorn)
Savatage; *Gutter Ballet* . . . . (Atlantic)

Thundercrack
Bruce Springsteen; *Tracks* . . . . (Columbia)

Till I Waltz Again With You
Teresa Brewer; *Best Of Teresa Brewer* . . . . (MCA Jazz)

Tiny Dancer
Elton John; *Live In Australia With The Melbourne Symphony
    Orchestra.* . . . . (MCA)
Madman Across The Water . . . . (Polydor)

Too Close
Next; *Rated Next* . . . . (Divine Mill/Arista)

Toucan's Dance
Sergio Mendes; *Arara* . . . . (A&M)

Touch Me When We're Dancing
Alabama; *The Touch* . . . . (RCA)
Carpenters; *Carpenters-Classics-#2* . . . . (A&M)
Made In America . . . . (A&M)
Yesterday Once More . . . . (A&M)

Trance Dance
D-Mob; *Little Bit Of This Little Bit Of That.* . . . . (London)

Tripe Face Boogie
Little Feat; *Feats Don't Fail Me Now* . . . . (Warner Bros.)
Sailin' Shoes . . . . (Warner Bros.)
Waiting For Columbus . . . . (Warner Bros.)

Truck Drivers Boogie
Milo Twins; *Truck Driver Boogie Big Rig Hits-1939-1969-C* . . . . (Audium)

Trumpet Boogie
Ray Anthony; *Young Man With A Horn-1952-1954--22 Original Big Band
    Recordings.* . . . . (Hindsight)

Tubesnake Boogie
ZZ Top; *El Loco* . . . . (Warner Bros.)
Six Pack . . . . (Warner Bros.)
ZZ Top's Greatest Hits . . . . (Warner Bros.)

Twist And Shout
Beatles; *Beatles-Box Set* . . . . (Capitol)
Please Please Me . . . . (Parlophone)
Rock 'N' Roll Music . . . . (Capitol)
ST/Imagine: John Lennon . . . . (Capitol)
The Beatles At The Hollywood Bowl. . . . . (Capitol)
The Early Beatles . . . . (Capitol)
Buck Owens & The Buckaroos; *Buck Owens & The Buckaroos-Live At
    Carnegie Hall* . . . . (Country Music Foundation)
Isley Brothers; *Best Of The Isley Brothers.* . . . . (Curb)
Cruisin'-1963-C. . . . . (Increase)
Frat Rock!-C . . . . (Rhino)
Oldies But Goodies-#10-C . . . . (Original Sound)
Solid Gold Music-WCBS FM 101-'60s-#1-C . . . . (Collectables)
Toga Rock-C. . . . . (Dunhill Compact Classics)

Mamas & The Papas; *Best Of The Mamas & The Papas* (MCA)
Who; *Who's Last* (MCA)

Twist, The
Chubby Checker; *Billboard Top Rock 'N' Roll Hits-1960-C* (Rhino)
Chubby Checker's Greatest Hits (Abkco)
Let's Dance (Gusto)

Twist, Twist Senora
Gary U.S. Bonds; *Best Of Gary U.S. Bonds* (Rhino)
Let's Twist!-C (K-Tel)
School Of Rock 'N' Roll-Best Of Gary U.S. Bonds (Rhino)

Twistin' Postman
Marvelettes; *Compact Command Performances-Marvelettes* (Motown)
Marvelettes' Greatest Hits (Motown)
Marvelettes-Anthology (Motown)

Twistin' The Night Away
Rod Stewart; *Best Of Rod Stewart-#2* (Mercury)
Never A Dull Moment (Mercury)
Sing It Again, Rod (Mercury)
Storyteller/The Complete Anthology: 1964-1990 (Warner Bros.)
Sam Cooke; *Best Of Sam Cooke* (RCA)
Dance Music (RCA)
Nipper's Greatest Hits Of The '60s-#2-C (RCA)
Sam Cooke-At The Copa (RCA)
ST/Animal House (MCA)
The Man And His Music (RCA)

Twistin' With Linda
Isley Brothers; *Scepter Records Story-C* (Capricorn)
The Isley Brothers Story-#1-Rockin' Soul-1959-1968 (Rhino)

Two O'Clock Jump
Harry James; *All-Time Favorites By Harry James* (Sony Music Special Prod.)
Harry James' Greatest Hits (Columbia)
Two O'Clock Jump (Pro-Arte)

Two To Tango
Bing Crosby; *The Radio Years: 20 Songs* (Crescendo)

Unskinny Bop
Poison; *Flesh & Blood* (Capitol)
Swallow This Live (Capitol)

Varsity Drag
Jonathan & Darlene Edwards; *Songs For Shieks & Flappers* (Corinthian)
Les Elgart; *Best Of The Big Bands-#2* (Columbia)

Wag The Dog
Mark Knopfler; *ST/Wag The Dog* (Mercury)

Wah Watusi
Orlons; *Rock-O-Rama-#1-C* (Abkco)

Walk, The
Cure; *Japanese Whispers-The Singles* (Sire)
Mixed Up (Elektra)
Standing On A Beach-The Singles (Elektra)
Walk, The (Sire)

Walk, The
Eurythmics; *Sweet Dreams (Are Made Of This)* (RCA)

Walk, The
Rufus Thomas; *That Woman Is Poison!* (Alligator)

Walk, The
Jimmy McCracklin; *Best Of Chess Rhythm & Blues-#1-C* (Chess)
Groove 'N' Grind-'50s & '60s Dance Hits-C (Rhino)
Super Oldies Of The '50s-#7-C (Audio Fidelity)

Walk, The
Time; *What Time Is It?* (Warner Bros.)

Walk, The
Sawyer Brown; *Buick* (Curb)
Dirt Road (Curb)

Wall Street Shuffle
10 CC; *10 CC's Greatest Hits-1972-1978* (Polydor)
Live & Let Live (Mercury)

Wallflower, The
Etta James and "The Peaches"; *Collectables Presents The History Of Rock-#1-C* (Collectables)
Oldies But Goodies-#1-C (Original Sound)

Waltz Across Texas
Ernest Tubb; *Ernest Tubb's Greatest Hits* (MCA)
The Country Music Hall Of Fame-Ernest Tubb (MCA)
Ernest Tubb & Willie Nelson; *Ernest Tubb Collection-C* (Step One)

Waltz For A Ball
Television Cast; *Cinderella-The CBS Television Network Production* (Columbia)

Waltz For Debby
Bill Evans; *Bill Evans-Complete Riverside Recordings* (Riverside)
New Jazz Conceptions (Riverside)
Bill Evans & Cannonball Adderley; *Know What I Mean?* (Riverside)
Tony Bennett; *Forty Years-The Artistry Of Tony Bennett* (Columbia)
Tony Bennett & Bill Evans; *Tony Bennett & Bill Evans* (Fantasy)
Toots Thielemans; *East Coast West Coast* (Private Music)

Waltz Me Around Again Willie
Joan Morris & William Bolcom; *After The Ball* (Nonesuch)

Waltz Me To Heaven
Waylon Jennings; *Waylon Jennings' Greatest Hits-#2* (RCA)

Waltz Of The Flowers
Lawrence Welk; *22 All-Time Favorite Waltzes* (Ranwood)

Waltz Of The Wind
Hank Williams; *I'm So Lonesome I Could Cry-1949* (Polydor)
Roy Acuff; *Best Of Roy Acuff* (Liberty)
Essential Roy Acuff-1936-1949 (Legacy)

Waltz You Saved For Me
Bob Wills; *Bob Wills-Anthology* (Sony Music Special Prod.)
Lawrence Welk; *22 All-Time Big Band Favorites* (Ranwood)
Mom & Dads; *Mom & Dads-20 Favorite Waltzes* (Crescendo)
Wayne King & His Orchestra; *Best Of Wayne King* (MCA)

Waltzing Back
Cranberries; *Everybody Else Is Doing It, So Why Can't We?* (Island)

Waltzing Matilda
Burl Ives; *Best Of Burl Ives* (MCA)
Fred Astaire; *Three Evenings With Fred Astaire* (DRG)
James Galway; *Pachebel Canon & Other Favorites* (RCA)
Original Soundtrack; *Children's Favorites* (Kid Rhino/Rhino 4 Kids)

Wango Tango
Ted Nugent; *Scream Dream* (Epic)

Watermelon Crawl
Tracy Byrd; *No Ordinary Man* (MCA)

Watusi
Vibrations; *Best Of Chess Rhythm & Blues-#1-C* (Chess)

We Danced
Brad Paisley; *Who Needs Pictures* (Arista)

We Danced Anyway
Deana Carter; *Did I Shave My Legs For This?* (Capitol)

We Really Shouldn't Be Doing This
George Strait; *Latest Greatest Straitest Hits* (MCA)
One Step At A Time (MCA)

West Nashville Boogie
Steve Earle & The Dukes; *Shut Up And Die Like An Aviator* (MCA)
The Hard Way (MCA)

West Nashville Grand Ballroom Gown
Jimmy Buffett; *Living & Dying In 3/4 Time* (MCA)

West Oakland Strut
Ed Kelly & Pharoah Sanders; *Ed Kelly & Pharoah Sanders* (Evidence Music)

West Texas Waltz
Butch Hancock; *Own & Own* (Sugar Hill)

What Do The Simple Folk Do?
Julie Andrews; *Best Of Julie Andrews* (Rhino)
Julie Andrews & Richard Burton; *Camelot* (Columbia)
Original Soundtrack; *Camelot* (Warner Bros.)

What'd You Come Here For?
Trina & Tamara; *Trina & Tamara* (C2/Columbia)

What's It Gonna Be
Busta Rhymes Featuring Janet Jackson; *E.L.E.* (Elektra)

When We Dance
Sting; *All This Time* (Starwave)
Fields Of Gold-The Best Of Sting 1984-1994 (A&M)

When You Dance I Can Really Love
Neil Young; *After The Gold Rush* (Reprise)
Neil Young & Crazy Horse; *Live Rust* (Reprise)

Where You Are
Jessica Simpson featuring Nick Lachey; *Sweet Kisses* (Columbia)

White Sport Coat (And A Pink Carnation)
Marty Robbins; *16 Most Requested Songs Of The '50s-#2-C* (Legacy)
Lifetime Of Song-1951-1982 (Columbia)
Marty Robbins' Greatest Hits (Columbia)

Whole Lot Of Shakin' Going On
Elvis Presley; *Elvis Recorded Live On Stage In Memphis* (RCA)
Jerry Lee Lewis; *Cruisin'-1957-C* (Increase)
Oldies But Goodies-#4-C (Original Sound)
Original Memphis Rock & Roll (Sun)
Sun Story-C (Rhino)
Sun's Greatest Hits-C (RCA)
The Golden Hits Of Jerry Lee Lewis (Smash)

Wiggle It
2 In A Room; *Cutting's Dance Express 3-C* (Cutting)

With A Girl Like You
Troggs; *Best Of The Troggs* (Rhino)
History Of British Rock-#4-C (Rhino)

Wobble Wobble
504 Boyz; *Goodfellas* (No Limit/Priority)

Wooly Bully
Sam The Sham and The Pharaohs; *Best Of Sam The Sham and The Pharaohs* (Polydor)
Billboard Top Rock 'N' Roll Hits-1965-C (Rhino)
Cruisin'-1965-C (Increase)
Oldies But Goodies-#10-C (Original Sound)
ST/Full Metal Jacket (Warner Bros.)
Smithereens; *ST/Encino Man* (Hollywood)

Word Up
Cameo; *Word Up* (Casablanca)

You Make Me Feel Like Dancing
Leo Sayer; *Billboard Top Rock 'N' Roll Hits-1977-C* (Rhino)
Endless Flight (Chrysalis)
Mega Hits Dance Classics-#3-C (Priority)

You Make My Pants Want To Get Up & Dance
Dr. Hook; *Pleasure & Pain* (Capitol)

You Should Be Dancing
Bee Gees; *Bee Gees' Greatest* . . . . (Polydor)
Billboard Top Dance Hits-1976-C . . . . (Rhino)
Children Of The World . . . . (RSO)
Here At Last...Bee Gees...Live . . . . (Polydor)
ST/Saturday Night Fever . . . . (Polydor)
You Shouldn't Kiss Me Like This
Toby Keith; *How Do You Like Me Now?!*. . . . . (DreamWorks/SKG)
Your Mama Don't Dance
Loggins & Messina; *Loggins & Messina-On Stage* . . . . (Columbia)
Loggins And Messina. . . . . (Columbia)
Pop Classics Of The '70s-C . . . . (Columbia)
The Best Of Friends . . . . (Columbia)
Poison; *Open Up And Say...Ahh!* . . . . (Capitol)
Swallow This Live . . . . (Capitol)
You're Easy To Dance With
Fred Astaire; *Irving Berlin Songbook* . . . . (Verve)
Zoot Suit Riot
Cherry Poppin' Daddies; *Now That's What I Call Music!-#1-C* . . . . (Virgin)
*Zoot Suit Riot-The Swingin' Hits Of The Cherry Poppin'
Daddies* . . . . (Mojo Music/Universal)

DANGER & DISASTER, Catastrophe, Chaos, Destruction, Emergency, Explosions, Impending Doom, Terrorist Attacks

See Also: DROWN, EARTHQUAKE, FEAR & COURAGE, FIRE, FLOOD, HELP, LAW & ORDER, LIGHTHOUSES, NUCLEAR ENERGY, ROAD ACCIDENTS, SHIPS, TROUBLE, WAR, WARNINGS

(Just Like) Romeo & Juliet
Reflections; *'60s Dance Party-C* . . . . (Dominion Entert.)
Sensational '60s-#1-C . . . . (Dominion Entert.)
1913 Massacre
Arlo Guthrie; *Hobo's Lullaby*. . . . . (Reprise)
Jack Elliot; *Tribute To Woody Guthrie-C* . . . .(Warner Bros.)
Ramblin' Jack Elliott; *Greatest Songs Of Woody Guthrie-C* . . . . (Vanguard)
Woody Guthrie; *Struggle* . . . . (Smithsonian Folkways)
1999
Prince; *1999* . . . .(Warner Bros.)
911
Wyclef Jean featuring Mary J. Blige; *The Ecleftic-2 Sides II
A Book*. . . . . (Ruffhouse/Columbia)
Abandon City
Utopia; *Oops! Wrong Planet* . . . . (Rhino)
Aberfan Coal Tip Tragedy
Thom Parrott; *Best Of Broadside 1962-1968: Anthems Of The American
Underground From The Pages Of Broadside
Magazine-C* . . . . (Smithsonian Folkways)
Accidents Will Happen
Elvis Costello; *Girls Girls Girls* . . . . (Columbia)
Elvis Costello & The Attractions; *Armed Forces* . . . .(Rykodisc)
Best Of Elvis Costello & The Attractions . . . . (Columbia)
Accidents Will Happen
Frank Sinatra; *Rarities-Columbia Years* . . . . (Columbia)
Adrian
Jewel; *Pieces Of You*. . . . .(Atlantic)
Air Crash Museum
Dead Milkmen; *Eat Your Paisley* . . . . (Restless)
Air Disaster
Albert Hammond; *45-#6030*. . . . . (Mums)
All Along The Watchtower
Bob Dylan; *Before The Flood* . . . . (Columbia)
Biograph . . . . (Columbia)
Bob Dylan At Budokan. . . . . (Columbia)
Bob Dylan's Greatest Hits-#2 . . . . (Columbia)
John Wesley Harding. . . . . (Columbia)
Jimi Hendrix; *Kiss The Sky* . . . . (Reprise)
Lifelines/Jimi Hendrix Story . . . . (Reprise)
Jimi Hendrix Experience; *Electric Ladyland* . . . . (Reprise)
Essential Jimi Hendrix. . . . . (Reprise)
Smash Hits . . . . (Reprise)
U2; *Rattle And Hum* . . . . (Island)
Anarchy Divine
Fates Warning; *Best Of Metal Blade-#3-C* . . . .(Metal Blade)
No Exit . . . .(Metal Blade)
Anarchy In The U.K.
Megadeth; *so far, so good...so what!* . . . . (Capitol)
Sex Pistols; *Never Mind The Bollocks, Here's The Sex Pistols*. . . .(Warner Bros.)
Anarchy-X
Queensryche; *Operation: Mindcrime* . . . .(EMI)
Angel Without A Prayer
Deana Carter; *Love Shouldn't Hurt-C* . . . . (Qwest)
Angel's Eye
Aerosmith; *ST/Charlie's Angels* . . . . (Columbia)

Anything But Down
Sheryl Crow; *The Globe Sessions* . . . . (A&M)
April The 14th, Part 1
Gillian Welch; *Time (The Revelator)* . . . .(Acony)
Are You Jimmy Ray?
Jimmy Ray; *Jimmy Ray* . . . . (Epic)
Armageddon
Aldo Nova; *Subject...Aldo Nova* . . . . (Portrait)
Armageddon
Rush; *Hemispheres* . . . . (Mercury)
Armageddon
Planet P Project; *Planet P Project* . . . . (Geffen)
Armageddon It
Def Leppard; *Hysteria*. . . . . (Mercury)
Armageddon Man
Black Flag; *Family Man* . . . .(SST)
Armagideon Time
Clash; *Black Market Clash* . . . . (Epic)
The Story Of The Clash, Volume 1 . . . . (Epic)
Bad Moon Rising
Creedence Clearwater Revival; *1969* . . . .(Fantasy)
Creedence Clearwater Revival-Chronicle . . . .(Fantasy)
Creedence Clearwater Revival-Gold . . . .(Fantasy)
Green River . . . .(Fantasy)
Live In Europe . . . .(Fantasy)
Badlands
Bruce Springsteen; *Bruce Springsteen's Greatest Hits* . . . . (Columbia)
Darkness On The Edge Of Town. . . . . (Columbia)
Bruce Springsteen & The E Street Band; *Bruce Springsteen & The E Street
Band Live/1975-85* . . . . (Legacy)
Ball Of Confusion (That's What The World Is Today)
Temptations; *All The Million-Sellers* . . . . (Motown)
Compact Command Performances-Temptations . . . . (Motown)
Songs Of Protest-C . . . . (Rhino)
Temptations' Greatest Hits-#2 . . . . (Motown)
Temptations-Anthology-The Best Of The Temptations . . . . (Motown)
Top 10 With A Bullet-Motown Male Groups-C . . . . (Motown)
Barrel Of A Gun
Depeche Mode; *The Singles-1986-1998* . . . . (Mute/Reprise)
Ultra . . . . (Mute/Reprise)
Beautiful Disaster
311; *Live!* . . . . (Capricorn)
Transistor . . . . (Capricorn)
Bend It Until It Breaks
John Anderson; *John Anderson's Greatest Hits* . . . .(BNA)
Big Bad John
Jimmy Dean; *American Originals-Jimmy Dean* . . . . (Columbia)
Billboard Top Country Hits-1961-C . . . . (Rhino)
Columbia Country Classics-#3-Americana-C . . . . (Columbia)
Jimmy Dean's Greatest Hits . . . . (Columbia)
Big Bang Baby
Stone Temple Pilots; *Tiny Music...Songs From The Vatican
Gift Shop* . . . .(Atlantic)
Big Brother
David Bowie; *David Live* . . . . (Rykodisc)
Diamond Dogs . . . . (Rykodisc)
Sound + Vision . . . . (Rykodisc)
ST/Breaking Glass . . . . (A&M)
Big Money
Garth Brooks; *Scarecrow* . . . . (Capitol)
Blow Up The Outside World
Soundgarden; *A-Sides* . . . . (A&M)
Down On The Upside . . . . (A&M)
Breakdown
Queensryche; *Q2k* . . . .(Atlantic)
Breakdown
Tantric; *Tantric* . . . . (Maverick)
Breakdown Dead Ahead
Boz Scaggs; *Boz Scaggs-Hits!*. . . . . (Columbia)
Middle Man . . . . (Columbia)
California Mudslide
Lightnin' Hopkins; *Los Angeles Blues* . . . . (Rhino)
Casey Jones
Grateful Dead; *Best Of The Grateful Dead-Skeletons From The
Closet*. . . . . (Warner Bros.)
Bill Graham Presents The Last Days Of The
Fillmore-C . . . . (Epic Portrait Assoc.)
Workingman's Dead. . . . . (Warner Bros.)
Jerry Garcia Acoustic Band; *Almost Acoustic* . . . .(Grateful Dead)
Causing A Commotion
Madonna; *ST/Who's That Girl* . . . .(Sire)
Champagne Supernova
Oasis; *What's The Story Morning Glory?* . . . . (Epic)
Circles
Soul Coughing; *El Oso* . . . .(Slash)
City
Fleetwood Mac; *Mystery To Me* . . . . (Reprise)
Common Disaster
Cowboy Junkies; *Lay It Down*. . . . . (Geffen)

Crash And Burn
Sheryl Crow; *The Globe Sessions* . . . . (A&M)
Crumblin' Down
John Cougar Mellencamp; *Uh-Huh* . . . . (Riva)
Dance Electric
Andre Cymone; *A.C.* . . . . (Columbia)
Pointer Sisters; *Break Out* . . . . (Planet)
Danger
Selecter; *Too Much Pressure* . . . . (Chrysalis)
Danger
Kiss; *Creatures Of The Night* . . . . (Casablanca)
Danger
AC/DC; *Fly On The Wall* . . . . (Atco)
Danger
Gorky Park; *Gorky Park* . . . . (Mercury)
Danger
Pylon; *Pylon-Hits* . . . . (DB)
Danger
Motley Crue; *Shout At The Devil* . . . . (Elektra)
Danger (Been So Long)
Mystikal; *Now That's What I Call Music!-#7-C* . . . . (Virgin)
Mystikal featuring Nivea; *Let's Get Ready* . . . . (Jive)
Danger Ahead
Electric Light Orchestra; *Secret Messages* . . . . (Jet)
Danger Ahead
Tanya Tucker; *Can't Run From Yourself* . . . . (Liberty)
Danger At My Door
Mark Chesnutt; *Too Cold At Home* . . . . (MCA)
Danger Heartbreak Dead Ahead
Bonnie Raitt; *Bonnie Raitt* . . . . (Warner Bros.)
Marvelettes; *Marvelettes' Greatest Hits* . . . . (Motown)
Marvelettes-Anthology . . . . (Motown)
ST/Good Morning, Vietnam . . . . (A&M)
Danger List
John Cougar; *American Fool* . . . . (Riva)
Danger Man
David Bromberg; *Wanted Dead Or Alive* . . . . (Columbia)
Danger Stranger
Drivin' N' Cryin'; *Scarred But Smarter* . . . . (Island)
Danger Waters (Hold Me Tight)
Joan Baez; *Joan Baez In Concert* . . . . (Vanguard)
Lovesong Album . . . . (Vanguard)
Danger Zone
Ramones; *Too Tough To Die* . . . . (Sire)
Danger Zone
Kenny Loggins; *ST/Top Gun* . . . . (Columbia)
Danger Zone
Klymaxx; *Klymaxx* . . . . (Constellation)
Danger Zone
Crystal Gayle; *Miss The Mississippi* . . . . (Capitol)
Danger Zone
Planet Patrol; *Planet Patrol* . . . . (Tommy Boy)
Tommy Boy's Greatest Beats-#2-C . . . . (Tommy Boy)
Danger Zone
Shirley Murdock; *Shirley Murdock* . . . . (Elektra)
Danger Zone
L.A. Posse; *They Come In All Colors* . . . . (Atlantic)
Danger! She's A Stranger
Five Stairsteps; *Five Stairsteps' Greatest Hits* . . . . (Collectables)
Dangerous
Roxette; *Look Sharp!* . . . . (EMI)
Rock The First-#6-C . . . . (Sandstone Music)
Dangerous
Busta Rhymes; *When Disaster Strikes* . . . . (Elektra)
Dangerous
Doobie Brothers; *Brotherhood* . . . . (Capitol)
Dangerous
Natalie Cole; *Dangerous* . . . . (Modern)
Dangerous
Michael Jackson; *Dangerous* . . . . (Epic)
Dangerous
Who; *It's Hard* . . . . (MCA)
Dangerous
L.L. Cool J; *Radio* . . . . (Def Jam/Columbia)
Dangerous
Monalisa Young; *ST/Allnighter* . . . . (Chameleon)
Dangerous
Heaven 17; *Teddy Bear Duke & Psycho* . . . . (Caroline)
Dangerous Age
Gerry Rafferty; *Right Down The Line-Best Of Gerry Rafferty* . . . . (EMI)
Dangerous Age
Bad Company; *Dangerous Age* . . . . (Atlantic)
Dangerous Drug
Electric Angels; *Electric Angels* . . . . (Atlantic)
Dangerous Fun
Jesse Winchester; *Best Of Jesse Winchester* . . . . (Rhino)
Third Down 110 To Go . . . . (Rhino)

Dangerous Jade
Original Cast; *Evita* . . . . (MCA)
Dangerous Man
Dwight Yoakam; *If There Was A Way* . . . . (Reprise)
Dangerous Times
Cher; *Cher* . . . . (Geffen)
Dangerous Type
Cars; *Candy-O* . . . . (Elektra)
Dangerous Woman
Mississippi Jook Band; *Good Time Blues* . . . . (Columbia)
Dangerously Lonely
Johnny Lee; *Best Of Johnny Lee* . . . . (Curb)
Darkness On The Edge Of Town
Bruce Springsteen; *Darkness On The Edge Of Town* . . . . (Columbia)
Bruce Springsteen & The E Street Band; *Bruce Springsteen & The E Street Band/1975-85* . . . . (Legacy)
Death Of Titanic
James Horner; *ST/Titanic* . . . . (Sony Music Classical)
Deportee (Plane Wreck At Los Gatos)
Arlo Guthrie & Pete Seeger; *Together In Concert* . . . . (Reprise)
Byrds; *The Byrds* . . . . (Columbia)
Cisco Houston; *Greatest Songs Of Woody Guthrie-C* . . . . (Vanguard)
Gene Clark & Carla Olson; *So Rebellious A Lover* . . . . (Rhino)
Judy Collins; *Tribute To Woody Guthrie-C* . . . . (Warner Bros.)
Waylon Jennings, Willie Nelson, Johnny Cash, Kris Kristofferson; *Highwayman* . . . . (Columbia)
Dirty Business
New Riders Of The Purple Sage; *New Riders Of The Purple Sage* . . . . (Columbia)
Disco Apocalypse
Jackson Browne; *Hold Out* . . . . (Asylum)
Distant Early Warning
Rush; *Grace Under Pressure* . . . . (Mercury)
Hear 'N Aid-C . . . . (Mercury)
Show Of Hands . . . . (Mercury)
Dollhouse
Bruce Springsteen; *Tracks* . . . . (Columbia)
Driven
Rush; *Test For Echo* . . . . (Atlantic)
End Of The World
Skeeter Davis; *Best Of Skeeter Davis* . . . . (Gusto)
Billboard Top Country Hits-1963-C . . . . (Rhino)
Nipper's Greatest Hits Of The '60s-#1-C . . . . (RCA)
Stars Of The Grand Ole Opry-1926-1974-C . . . . (RCA)
Super Country Hits Of The '60s-C . . . . (Gusto)
End Of The World
Cold; *13 Ways To Bleed On Stage* . . . . (Flip/Geffen/Interscope)
Eve Of Destruction
Barry McGuire; *Billboard Top Rock 'N' Roll Hits-1965-C* . . . . (Rhino)
Cruisin'-1965-C . . . . (Increase)
Good Feeling Music Of The Big Chill Generation-#3-C . . . . . (Motown)
Songs Of Protest-C . . . . (Rhino)
Vintage Music-#9 & 10-C . . . . (MCA)
Dickies; *Great Dictations (Definitive Collection)* . . . . (A&M)
Incredible Shrinking Dickies . . . . (A&M)
Turtles; *Turtle Wax-Best Of The Turtles-#2* . . . . (Rhino)
Turtlesized . . . . (Rhino)
Everything Falls Apart
Dog's Eye View; *Happy Nowhere* . . . . (Columbia)
Explosion In The Fairmount Mines
Blind Alfred Reed; *How Can A Poor Man Stand Such Times And Live?* . . . . (Rounder)
Flood
Jars Of Clay; *Jars Of Clay* . . . . (Silvertone)
Where Music Meets Film: Live From The Sundance Film Festival-C . . . . (Beyond)
Follow You Down
Gin Blossoms; *Congratulations I'm Sorry* . . . . (A&M)
Fragile
Sting; *...Nothing Like The Sun* . . . . (A&M)
America: A Tribute To Heroes-C . . . . (Interscope)
Fields Of Gold-The Best Of Sting 1984-1994 . . . . (A&M)
Full Speed Ahead
John Mayall; *Best Of John Mayall* . . . . (Polydor)
Geek Stink Breath
Green Day; *Insomniac* . . . . (Reprise)
Going Up Against Chaos
Bruce Cockburn; *Trouble With Normal* . . . . (Columbia)
Great Joe Bob (A Regional Tragedy)
Country Gazette; *Hello Operator...This Is Country Gazette* . . . . . . (Flying Fish)
Groundzero (In Our Hearts You Remain)
Cash & Computa; *Groundzero (In Our Hearts You Remain)-CD Single* . . . . (Select)
Hands In The Air
Bob Seger; *It's A Mystery* . . . . (Capitol)
Hard Rain's Gonna Fall
Bob Dylan; *Bob Dylan's Greatest Hits-#2* . . . . (Columbia)
Concert For Bangladesh-C . . . . (Capitol)
Freewheelin' . . . . (Columbia)
Bryan Ferry; *Street Life-20 Great Hits* . . . . (Reprise)

These Foolish Things . . . . (Reprise)
Edie Brickell & New Bohemians; *ST/Born On The Fourth Of July* . . . . . (MCA)
Joan Baez; *Farewell Angelina* . . . . (Vanguard)
The First 10 Years . . . . (Vanguard)

Hellzapoppin'
Louis Armstrong; *What A Wonderful World* . . . . (Decca Jazz)

Helter Skelter
Aerosmith; *Pandora's Box* . . . . (Columbia)
Beatles; *Beatles-Box Set* . . . . (Capitol)
Rarities . . . . (Capitol)
Rock 'N' Roll Music . . . . (Capitol)
The Beatles (White Album) . . . . (Capitol)
Motley Crue; *Shout At The Devil* . . . . (Elektra)
Pat Benatar; *Precious Time* . . . . (Chrysalis)
Siouxsie And The Banshees; *Nocturne* . . . . (Geffen)
The Scream . . . . (Geffen)
U2; *Rattle And Hum* . . . . (Island)

Here Comes The Flood
Peter Gabriel; *Peter Gabriel* . . . . (Atco)
Revisited . . . . (Atlantic)
Shaking The Tree-Sixteen Golden Greats . . . . (Geffen)

Hero Of The Day
Metallica; *Load* . . . . (Elektra)

Higher Place
Tom Petty; *Wildflowers* . . . . (Warner Bros.)

House Burning Down
Jimi Hendrix; *Essential Jimi Hendrix* . . . . (Reprise)
Jimi Hendrix Experience; *Electric Ladyland* . . . . (Reprise)

Hurt By Love
BoDeans; *Blend* . . . . (Reprise)

I Ain't Goin' Down
Nashville Bluegrass Band; *Waitin' For The Hard Times To Go* . . . . . (Sugar Hill)

I Alone
Live; *Throwing Copper* . . . . (Radioactive/MCA)

If I Had A Hammer (The Hammer Song)
Pete Seeger; *Sing-A-Long-Live At Sanders
Theatre 1980* . . . . (Smithsonian Folkways)
Peter, Paul & Mary; *10 Years Together/The Best Of Peter, Paul
and Mary* . . . . (Warner Bros.)
Peter, Paul and Mary . . . . (Warner Bros.)
Peter, Paul and Mary In Concert . . . . (Warner Bros.)
Trini Lopez; *Best Of Trini Lopez* . . . . (Exact)
Weavers; *Weavers' Greatest Hits* . . . . (Vanguard)

Ike's Rap
Isaac Hayes; *The Ultimate Collection-Isaac Hayes* . . . . (Hip-O)

I'm Not Gonna Let It Bother Me Tonight
Atlanta Rhythm Section; *Are You Ready!* . . . . (Polydor)
Champagne Jam . . . . (Polydor)

In Harm's Way
Bebe Winans; *Bebe Winans* . . . . (Atlantic)

In The Year 2525 (Exordium & Terminus)
Zager & Evans; *Nipper's Greatest Hits Of The '60s-#2-C* . . . . . (RCA)

It's Alright
Loggins & Messina; *Native Sons* . . . . (Columbia)

Just In Case
Jaheim; *Ghetto Love* . . . . (Divine Mill/Warner Bros.)

Keep Smiling At Trouble
Al Jolson; *Rainbow 'Round My Shoulder* . . . . (MCA Special Prod.)
Tony Bennett; *Forty Years-The Artistry Of Tony Bennett* . . . . . . (Columbia)

Knock On Wood
Amii Stewart; *Double Smash Hits-C* . . . . (Volcano Entertainment)
Buddy Guy; *This Is Buddy Guy* . . . . (Vanguard)
Eddie Floyd; *15 Original Big Hits-#3-C* . . . . (Stax)
Atlantic Rhythm & Blues 1947-1974-#6 (1966-1969)-C . . . . . (Atlantic)
Best Of Wattstax-C . . . . (Stax)
Super Oldies Of The '60s-#11-C . . . . (Audio Fidelity)
Eric Clapton; *Behind The Sun* . . . . (Duck/Reprise)
Ike & Tina Turner; *Ike & Tina Turner's Greatest Hits-#3* . . . . (Saja)

Landslide
Fleetwood Mac; *25 Years-The Chain* . . . . (Warner Bros.)
Fleetwood Mac . . . . (Reprise)
Fleetwood Mac Live . . . . (Warner Bros.)
The Dance . . . . (Reprise)
Smashing Pumpkins; *Pisces Iscariot* . . . . (Virgin)

Landslide
AC/DC; *Flick Of The Switch* . . . . (Atlantic)

Last Night On Earth
U2; *Pop* . . . . (Island)

Lazy Eye
Goo Goo Dolls; *ST/Batman & Robin-Music From And Inspired By The
Motion Picture* . . . . (Jive)

Let's Roll
Neil Young; *Let's Roll-CD Single* . . . . (Reprise)

Lighthouse's Tale
Nickel Creek; *Nickel Creek* . . . . (Sugar Hill)

Li'l Red Riding Hood
Sam The Sham and The Pharaohs; *Best Of Sam The Sham and The
Pharaohs* . . . . (Polydor)
Cruisin'-1966-C . . . . (Increase)

Pharaohization! (Best Of) . . . . (Rhino)

Little Chicago Fire
Count Basie & His Orchestra; *Live At El Morocco* . . . . (Telarc)

Living In Danger
Ace Of Base; *The Sign* . . . . (Arista)

Locked & Loaded
Jackyl; *Cut The Crap-C* . . . . (Epic)

London Bridge Is Falling Down
Count Basie; *Good Morning Blues* . . . . (MCA)

London Bridge Is Falling Down
Newtrament; *Word 2* . . . . (Jive)

Loose Ends
Bruce Springsteen; *Tracks* . . . . (Columbia)

Louisiana Flood
Paul Butterfield's Better Days; *It All Comes Back* . . . . (Rhino)

Love Is Dangerous
Fleetwood Mac; *25 Years-The Chain* . . . . (Warner Bros.)

Love You For A Day
Ricky Martin; *Ricky Martin* . . . . (Columbia)

Man Overboard
Blink-182; *The Mark, Tom & Travis Show-The Enema Strikes Back* . . . . (MCA)

Meanwhile Back At The Ranch
Clark Family Experience; *Meanwhile Back At The Ranch* . . . . (Curb)

Miami 2017
Billy Joel; *Songs In The Attic* . . . . (Columbia)
The Concert For New York City-C . . . . (Columbia)
Turnstiles . . . . (Columbia)

Mind Disaster
Initial Shock; *Nuggets-#8-Acid Rock-C* . . . . (Rhino)

More Human Than Human
White Zombie; *Astro-Creep: 2000 Songs Of Love* . . . . (Geffen)

More Trouble Every Day
Zappa/Mothers; *Roxy & Elsewhere* . . . . (Rykodisc)

Most Precarious
Blues Traveler; *Straight On Till Morning* . . . . (A&M)

Murder (Or A Heart Attack)
Old 97's; *Fight Songs* . . . . (Elektra)

Murder Incorporated
Bruce Springsteen; *Bruce Springsteen's Greatest Hits* . . . . (Columbia)

My Baby Needs A Shepherd
Emmylou Harris; *Red Dirt Girl* . . . . (Nonesuch)

My City Of Ruin
Bruce Springsteen; *America: A Tribute To Heroes-C* . . . . (Interscope)

My Love Is Your Love
Whitney Houston; *My Love Is Your Love* . . . . (Arista)
Totally Hits-#2-C . . . . (Elektra)

My Oklahoma Home (It Blowed Away)
Sis Cunningham; *Best Of Broadside 1962-1968: Anthems Of The American
Underground From The Pages Of Broadside
Magazine-C* . . . . (Smithsonian Folkways)

My Wife
Who; *ST/The Kids Are Alright* . . . . (MCA)
Two's Missing . . . . (MCA)
Who Greatest Hits . . . . (MCA)
Who's next . . . . (MCA)

Nature's Way
Spirit; *12 Dreams Of Dr. Sardonicus* . . . . (Epic)
Best Of Spirit . . . . (Epic)
Time Circle . . . . (Epic)

Never Is A Promise
Fiona Apple; *Tidal* . . . . (Clean Slate/Work)

New Orleans Is Sinking
Tragically Hip; *Up To Here* . . . . (MCA)

New York Mining Disaster 1941 (Mr. Jones)
Bee Gees; *Bee Gees-Gold* . . . . (Polydor)
Here At Last...Bee Gees...Live . . . . (Polydor)
History Of British Rock-#8-C . . . . (Rhino)

New York Minute
Don Henley; *End Of The Innocence* . . . . (Geffen)

No Depression
Johnson Mountain Boys; *Goin' Up Copper Creek-C* . . . . . . (Copper Creek)
Uncle Tupelo; *No Depression* . . . . (Rockville)

No Leaf Clover
Metallica; *S&M* . . . . (Elektra)

Ordinary Morning
Sheryl Crow; *Sheryl Crow* . . . . (A&M)

Osama, Yo' Mama
Ray Stevens; *Osama-Yo' Mama* . . . . (Curb)

Panic In Detroit
David Bowie; *Aladdin Sane* . . . . (Rykodisc)
Scary Monsters . . . . (Rykodisc)
Sound + Vision . . . . (Rykodisc)

Panic In The World
Be Bop Deluxe; *Best Of And The Rest Of Be Bop Deluxe* . . . . . (Capitol)
Best Of Be Bop Deluxe-Raiding The Divine Archive . . . . (Capitol)
Drastic Plastic . . . . (Capitol)

Preservation
Kinks; *Preservation Act 2* . . . . (Rhino)

Prologue (Tradition)
Original Cast; *Fiddler On The Roof* . . . . (RCA Victor)
Promised Land
Bruce Springsteen; *Darkness On The Edge Of Town* . . . . (Columbia)
Bruce Springsteen & The E Street Band; *Bruce Springsteen & The E Street Band Live/1975-85* . . . . (Legacy)
Queen Of The Hours
Electric Light Orchestra; *No Answer* . . . .(Jet)
Quicksand
Martha & The Vandellas; *Motown Milestones* . . . . (Motown)
The Ultimate Collection-Martha Reeves . . . . (Motown)
Quicksand Jesus
Skid Row; *Slave To The Grind* . . . . (Atlantic)
Rampage
EPMD; *Business As Usual* . . . . (Def Jam)
Razorblades
Chris Stills; *100 Year Thing* . . . . (Atlantic)
Red Alert
Saxon; *Destiny* . . . .(Enigma)
Red Alert
Quiet Riot; *Condition Critical* . . . . (Epic Portrait Assoc.)
Red Alert
Red Garland; *Red Alert* . . . . (Galaxy)
Redneck Rampage
Mojo Nixon; *The Real Sock-Ray-Blue* . . . .(Yazoo)
Redneck Riot
Countrypolitans; *Full Tank-#1-C* . . . . (Jackass)
River, Stay 'Way From My Door
Guy Lombardo & His Royal Canadians; *Auld Lang Syne* . . . . (Pro-Arte)
Roulette
Bruce Springsteen; *Tracks* . . . . (Columbia)
Ruination Day, Part 2
Gillian Welch; *Time (The Revelator)* . . . . (Acony)
Runaway Train
Elton John featuring Eric Clapton; *The One* . . . . (MCA)
Runaway Train
Soul Asylum; *Grave Dancers Union* . . . . (Columbia)
Runaway Train
Rosanne Cash; *Greatest Country Hits Of The '80s-1988-C* . . . . (Columbia)
Hot Tracks-Train Super Hits-C . . . . (Epic)
King's Record Shop . . . . (Columbia)
Rosanne Cash-Retrospective . . . . (Columbia)
Runaway Train
Dawn Sears; *Nothin' But Good* . . . . (Decca)
Runaway Train
John Stewart; *Punch The Big Guy* . . . . (Cypress)
Runaway Trains
Tom Petty And The Heartbreakers; *Let Me Up (I've Had Enough)* . . . . . . (MCA)
Science Gone Too Far
Dictators; *Live-F..k 'Em If They Can't Take A Joke* . . . . (Roir)
Manifest Destiny . . . . (Asylum)
Secret Agent Man
Devo; *Duty Now For The Future* . . . . (Warner Bros.)
Johnny Rivers; *Best Of Johnny Rivers* . . . . (EMI)
Johnny Rivers-Anthology 1964-1977 . . . . (Rhino)
Television's Greatest Hits-#1-C . . . . (TVT)
Very Best Of Johnny Rivers . . . . (EMI)
Serious Juju
Sammy Hagar; *Ten 13* . . . . (Cabo Wabo/Beyond)
Shadowboxer
Fiona Apple; *Tidal* . . . . (Clean Slate/Work)
Shark Attack
Split Enz; *True Colours* . . . . (A&M)
Shark Attack
Wailing Souls; *All Over The World* . . . . (Chaos)
She's Got Issues
Offspring; *Americana* . . . . (Columbia)
Ship Titanic
Pink Anderson; *Gospel Blues & Street Songs* . . . . (Riverside)
Sinkin' In The Sea
Barefoot Jerry; *You Can't Get Off With Your Shoes On* . . . . (Monument)
Sinking, The
James Horner; *ST/Titanic* . . . . (Sony Music Classical)
Sky Is Falling
Daryl Hall & John Oates; *Marigold Sky* . . . . (Push)
Smooth Criminal
Alien Ant Farm; *Alien Ant Farm-Anthology* . . . . (DreamWorks/SKG)
Michael Jackson; *Bad* . . . . (Epic)
Space Lord
Monster Magnet; *Powertrip* . . . . (A&M)
State Trooper
Bruce Springsteen; *Nebraska* . . . . (Columbia)
The Sopranos-Music From The HBO Original Series . . . . (Sony Music Soundtrax)
Stupify
Disturbed; *The Sickness* . . . . (Giant)
Surfin' Tragedy
Bob Vaught & The Renegaids; *Original Surfin' Hits* . . . . (Crescendo)

Breakers; *World's Worst Records-C* . . . .(Rhino)
Swim
Madonna; *Ray Of Light* . . . . (Maverick)
Talking Airplane Disaster
Phil Ochs; *Original New Folks* . . . .(Vanguard)
Tenth Avenue Freeze-Out
Bruce Springsteen; *Born To Run* . . . .(Columbia)
Bruce Springsteen & The E Street Band; *Bruce Springsteen & The E Street Band Live/1975-85* . . . .(Legacy)
Terrorist Trousers
Jim Carroll Band; *Praying Mantis* . . . . (Giant)
Terrorist's Life
D.I.; *What Good Is Grief To A God* . . . . (Triple X Entert.)
Theme From "Armageddon"
Trevor Rabin; *ST/Armageddon-The Album* . . . .(Columbia)
Third Rock From The Sun
Joe Diffie; *A Thousand Winding Roads* . . . . (Epic)
This Time Around
Michael Jackson; *HIStory: Past, Present And Future-Book 1-C* . . . .(Epic)
This Wheel's On Fire
Band; *Music From Big Pink* . . . .(Capitol)
Rock Of Ages . . . .(Capitol)
The Band-Anthology-#1 . . . .(Capitol)
Bob Dylan And The Band; *Basement Tapes* . . . .(Columbia)
Byrds; *The Byrds* . . . . (Columbia)
Ian & Sylvia; *Ian & Sylvia's Greatest Hits* . . . . (Vanguard)
Siouxsie And The Banshees; *Through The Looking Glass* . . . . (Geffen)
Twice Upon A Time-The Singles . . . . (Geffen)
Three Mile Island
Pinkard & Bowden; *Writers In Disguise* . . . . (Warner Bros.)
Three Mile Smile
Aerosmith; *Night In The Ruts* . . . .(Columbia)
Pandora's Box . . . .(Columbia)
Thunder Rolls, The
Garth Brooks; *Garth Brooks-Double Live* . . . .(Capitol)
No Fences . . . .(Capitol)
Tidal Wave
Sugarcubes; *Here Today, Tomorrow Next Week!* . . . .(Elektra)
Til I Hear It From You
Gin Blossoms; *ST/Crossroads-VH1 Television Program* . . . . (Atlantic)
ST/Empire Records . . . . (A&M)
Time Bomb
Rancid; *...And Out Come The Wolves* . . . . (Epitaph)
Time Is Running Out
Steve Winwood; *Steve Winwood* . . . .(Island)
Titanic, The
John Townley & The Press Gang; *Chesapeake Sailor's Companion* . . . (Adelphi)
Tragedy
Bee Gees; *Bee Gees' Greatest* . . . . (Polydor)
Mega Hits Dance Classics-#8-C . . . . (Priority)
Spirits Having Flown . . . . (Polydor)
Train Wreck On Prom Night
Pajama Slave Dancers; *Blood Sweat & Beers* . . . . (Restless)
Trainwreck Of Emotion
Lorrie Morgan; *Essential Lorrie Morgan* . . . . (RCA)
Leave The Light On . . . . (RCA)
To Get To You-Greatest Hits Collection . . . . (BNA)
Tremble For My Beloved
Collective Soul; *Dosage* . . . . (Atlantic)
Trouble's Comin' Like A Train
Mark Collie; *Mark Collie* . . . . (MCA)
Utah Carroll
Skip Gorman; *A Cowboy's Wild Song To His Herd* . . . . (Rounder)
Utter Chaos
Gerry Mulligan & Paul Desmond; *Gerry Mulligan & Paul Desmond* . . (Fantasy)
Volcano
Jimmy Buffett; *Boats Beaches Bars & Ballads* . . . . (Margaritaville)
Songs You Know By Heart-Jimmy Buffett's Greatest Hit(s) . . . .(MCA)
Volcano . . . .(MCA)
Volcano
Band; *Cahoots* . . . . (Capitol)
Volcano
Count Basie; *Essential Count Basie-#2* . . . . (Columbia)
Volcano
Rupture; *Hardness Of The World* . . . . (Cotillion)
Slave . . . . (Cotillion)
Waiting For The End Of The World
Elvis Costello; *My Aim Is True* . . . . (Columbia)
Walkaway Joe
Trisha Yearwood; *Hearts In Armor* . . . . (MCA)
Songbook-A Collection Of Hits . . . . (MCA)
West Virginia Mine Disaster
Betsy Rutherford; *Betsy Rutherford* . . . . (Biograph)
Cindy Mangsen; *Long Time Traveling* . . . . (Hogeye)
When The Coyotes Come Near
Sons Of The Pioneers; *Horses, Cattle And Coyotes* . . . . (Shanachie)
When The Shit Hits The Fan
Circle Jerks; *Gig* . . . .(Relativity)

ST/Repo Man . . . . (MCA)

When You're Falling
Afro Celt Sound System featuring Peter Gabriel; *Vol. 3: Further
In Time* . . . . (Real World/Virgin)

Where Were You (When The World Stopped Turning)
Alan Jackson; *Alan Jackson-Drive* . . . . (Arista)

White Riot
Clash; *On Broadway* . . . .(Epic)
The Clash . . . .(Epic)
The Story Of The Clash, Volume 1 . . . . (Epic)

Who Let The Dogs Out
Baha Men; *Who Let The Dogs Out* . . . .(S-Curve)

Will You Marry Me?
Vonda Shepard; *ST/Songs From ''Ally McBeal'' Featuring Vonda
Shepard* . . . . (550/Epic)

Wolves
Garth Brooks; *No Fences* . . . . (Capitol)

World Is Upside Down
Joe Higgs; *This Is Reggae Music-#1-C* . . . . (Island)

Wreck Of The Edmund Fitzgerald
Gordon Lightfoot; *Gord's Gold-#2* . . . .(Warner Bros.)
Summertime Dream . . . . (Reprise)

Wreck Of The Old '97
Johnny Cash; *Johnny Cash At Folsom Prison & San Quentin* . . . . . . (Columbia)
Johnny Cash-Original Golden Hits-#3 . . . . (Sun)
Story Songs Of The Trains & Rivers . . . . (Sun)
Superbilly . . . . (Sun)
The Man-The World-His Music . . . . (Sun)

You Wreck Me
Tom Petty; *Wildflowers* . . . .(Warner Bros.)

Zoot Suit Riot
Cherry Poppin' Daddies; *Now That's What I Call Music!-#1-C* . . . . (Virgin)
*Zoot Suit Riot-The Swingin' Hits Of The Cherry Poppin'
Daddies* . . . . (Mojo Music/Universal)

DAYS OF THE WEEK: FRIDAY

*See Also: **DAYS: GENERAL, MONTHS & DATES (various), TIME:
GENERAL, TIME: SPECIFIC, WEEKEND***

Babylon
David Gray; *White Ladder* . . . . (ATO/RCA)

Bad Friday
Eek-A-Mouse; *Assassinator* . . . . (Real Authentic Sound)

Black Friday
Steely Dan; *Katy Lied* . . . .(MCA)
Steely Dan's Greatest Hits . . . .(MCA)

Black Friday
Splinter; *Two Man Band* . . . . (MCA)

Born On A Friday
Cleo Laine; *Born On A Friday* . . . . (RCA)
Return To Carnegie . . . . (RCA)
Linda Hopkins; *How Blue Can You Get* . . . . (Quicksilver)

Bristol Stomp
Dovells; *Echoes Of A Rock Era-Middle Years-C* . . . . (Roulette)
Let's Dance . . . . (Gusto)
Rock-O-Rama-#1-C . . . . (Abkco)

Chattahoochee
Alan Jackson; *A Lot About Livin' (And A Little 'Bout Love)* . . . . (Arista)

Dancing Queen
Abba; *Abba Live* . . . .(Atlantic)
Abba's Greatest Hits-#2 . . . . (Atlantic)
Arrival . . . . (Polydor)
Gold-Greatest Hits . . . . (Polydor)
The Singles-First 10 Years . . . . (Atlantic)

Finally Friday
George Jones; *Walls Can Fall* . . . .(MCA)
Working Man's Blues-C . . . . (Hip-O)

Friday
J.J. Cale; *5* . . . .(Sheher)
Joe Jackson; *I'm The Man* . . . . (A&M)

Friday I'm In Love
Cure; *Wish* . . . . (Elektra)

Friday Night
Loverboy; *Lovin' Every Minute Of It* . . . . (Columbia)
Roy Orbison; *Laminar Flow* . . . . (Asylum)

Friday Night Blues
John Conlee; *John Conlee-Live At Billy Bob's* . . . . (Razor & Tie)
John Conlee's Greatest Hits . . . .(MCA)
Sonny Throckmorton; *45-#57018.* . . . . (Mercury)

Friday On My Mind
David Bowie; *Bowie Pin Ups* . . . .(Rykodisc)
Easybeats; *Best Of The Easybeats.* . . . . (Rhino)
Nuggets-Classic Collection From The Psychedelic '60s-C . . . . . . (Rhino)

Friday The 13th
Alvin Lee; *Rocket Fuel* . . . . (RSO)

Friday The 13th Child
David Clayton-Thomas; *Clayton* . . . . (MCA)

Friday's Angels
Generation X; *Valley Of The Dolls* . . . . (Chrysalis)

Full Forever
Goo Goo Dolls; *Dizzy Up The Girl* . . . .(Warner Sunset/Reprise)

Get 'Em Out By Friday
Genesis; *Foxtrot* . . . .(Atlantic)

Good Friday
Cowboy Junkies; *Miles From Our Home* . . . . (Geffen)

Good Friday
Black Crowes; *Sho' Nuff* . . . . (American)
Three Snakes And One Charm . . . . (American)

Good Friday
Crust; *Crust* . . . . (Trance Syndicate)

Good Friday
Saints; *Howling* . . . . (Triple X Entert.)

Honky Tonk Attitude
Joe Diffie; *Honky Tonk Attitude* . . . . (Epic)

Just Got Paid
'N Sync; *No Strings Attached* . . . .(Jive)

Lady Madonna
Beatles; *Beatles 1* . . . .(Capitol)
Hey Jude . . . . (Capitol)
Past Masters-Volume Two . . . . (Parlophone)
The Beatles/1967-1970. . . . . (Capitol)
Wings; *Wings Over America* . . . . (Capitol)

Livin' For The Weekend
O'Jays; *Family Reunion* . . . . (Philadelphia Int'l)
O'Jays-Collector's Item . . . . (Philadelphia Int'l)

Livin' It Up (Friday Night)
Bell & James; *Bell & James* . . . . (A&M)

Monday Thru' Friday
Cliff Richard; *We Don't Talk Anymore* . . . . (EMI)

Never On Friday
Willie Smith; *Best Of Willie Smith* . . . .(Crescendo)

Pata Pata
Miriam Makeba; *Planet Africa: World Of African Music-C* . . . . (Priority)
Welela. . . . . (Verve)

Quiet Friday
Stan Kenton & His Orchestra; *Fire, Fury And Fun* . . . . (Creative World)

Redneck Rhythm & Blues
Brooks & Dunn; *Borderline* . . . . (Arista)

Reminiscing
Little River Band; *'70's Super Groups-C* . . . . (Rhino)
Reminiscing: The Twentieth Anniversary Collection . . . . (Rhino)

Thank God It's Friday
Love And Kisses; *ST/Thank God It's Friday.* . . . . (Casablanca)

Thank Goodness It's Friday
Moe Bandy & Joe Stampley; *Just Good Ol' Boys* . . . . (Columbia)
Moe Bandy & Joe Stampley's Greatest Hits. . . . . (Columbia)

We Were In Love
Toby Keith; *Dream Walkin'* . . . . (Mercury)
Toby Keith's Greatest Hits, Volume One . . . . (Mercury)

Workin' For The Weekend
Ken Mellons; *Ken Mellons* . . . . (Epic)
Steppin' Country-#2-C . . . . (Columbia)

DAYS OF THE WEEK: MONDAY

*See Also: **DAYS: GENERAL, MONTHS & DATES (various), TIME:
GENERAL, TIME: SPECIFIC, WEEKEND***

48 Hours Till Monday
Sawyer Brown; *Buick* . . . . (Curb)

Another Monday
John Renbourn; *John Renbourn* . . . . (Reprise)

Atlantic Monday
Nick Heyward; *North Of A Miracle.* . . . . (Arista)

Blue Monday
Bobby Darin; *Darin 1963-1973* . . . . (Motown)
Fats Domino; *At Montreux* . . . .(Atlantic)
Fats Domino's All Time Greatest Hits . . . . (Curb)
Fats Domino's Greatest Hits . . . . (Everest)
Fats Domino's Greatest Hits . . . . (MCA)
My Blue Heaven . . . . (Gold Rush)
Super Oldies Of The '50s-#5-C . . . . (Audio Fidelity)
Huey Lewis and the News; *Four Chords & Several Years Ago* . . . . . (Elektra)
Kingsnakes; *19 Lucky Strikes* . . . . (Blue Wave)
Hardlife Boogie . . . . (Blue Wave)

Blue Monday
Orgy; *Candyass.* . . . . (Elementree/Reprise)

Blue Monday At Kansas City Red's
Cary Bell; *Blues Harp* . . . . (Delmark)

Blue Monday People
Curtis Mayfield; *America Today* . . . .(Curtom)

Born On A Monday
Michael Quatro; *Bottom Line* . . . . (Spector)
Chelsea Monday
Marillion; *Script For A Jester's Tear.* . . . . (Capitol)
Thieving Magpie . . . . (Capitol)
Come Monday
Jimmy Buffett; *Living & Dying In 3/4 Time* . . . . (MCA)
Songs You Know By Heart-Jimmy Buffett's Greatest Hit(s) . . . . (MCA)
You Had To Be There . . . . (MCA)
Da Doo Ron Ron (When He Walked Me Home)
Crystals; *Best Of The Crystals* . . . . (Abkco)
Good Time Rock 'N' Roll-C . . . . (MCA)
Hits Of The Sixties-C . . . . (Intercom Music)
Phil Spector's Greatest Hits-C . . . . (Spector)
Shaun Cassidy; *Shaun Cassidy's Greatest Hits* . . . . (Curb)
Except For Monday
Lorrie Morgan; *Lorrie Morgan's Greatest Hits* . . . . (BNA)
Something In Red . . . . (RCA)
Friday On My Mind
David Bowie; *Bowie Pin Ups* . . . . (Rykodisc)
Easybeats; *Best Of The Easybeats* . . . . (Rhino)
Nuggets-Classic Collection From The Psychedelic '60s-C . . . . (Rhino)
From Monday On
Bix Beiderbecke; *The Indispensable Bix Beiderbecke-1924-1930* . . . . (RCA)
Paul Whiteman & His Orchestra; *78-#21274* . . . . (Victor)
Gloomy Monday
Jimi Hendrix & Curtis Knight; *Get That Feeling.* . . . . (Fifty One West)
Go To Work On Monday
Si Kahn; *Doing My Job* . . . . (Flying Fish)
Gonna Go To Work On Monday One More Time
Fiction Brothers; *Things Are Coming My Way* . . . . . . (Flying Fish)
Goodbye Blue Monday
City Boy; *Dinner At The Ritz.* . . . . (Mercury)
Goodbye Monday Blues
Si Kahn; *Home.* . . . . (Flying Fish)
I Don't Like Mondays
Bob Geldof & Johnny Fingers; *The Secret Policeman's Other Ball/The Music* . . . . (Rhino)
Boomtown Rats; *Fine Art Of Surfacing.* . . . . (Columbia)
If We're Not Back In Love By Monday
Merle Haggard; *MCA Records 30 Years Of Hits-1958-1988-C.* . . . . . . (MCA)
Merle Haggard-Legends . . . . (MCA)
Merle Haggard's Greatest Hits . . . . (MCA)
More Of The Best . . . . (MCA)
Ramblin' Fever. . . . . (MCA)
It Sure Is Monday
Mark Chesnutt; *Almost Goodbye.* . . . . (MCA)
Jam On Monday Morning
Buddy Guy; *Man & The Blues* . . . . (Vanguard)
Lady Madonna
Beatles; *Beatles 1.* . . . . (Capitol)
Hey Jude. . . . . (Capitol)
Past Masters-Volume Two . . . . (Parlophone)
The Beatles/1967-1970. . . . . (Capitol)
Wings; *Wings Over America* . . . . (Capitol)
Laundromat Monday
Joe Jackson; *ST/Mike's Murder.* . . . . (A&M)
Manic Monday
Bangles; *Bangles' Greatest Hits* . . . . (Columbia)
Different Light . . . . (Columbia)
Monday
Sonny & Cher; *Two Of Us* . . . . (Atco)
Monday Date
Earl "Fatha" Hines; *Hot Hazz 1928-30* . . . . (Nimbus)
Monday Date . . . . (Riverside)
Piano Giants . . . . (Prestige)
Louis Armstrong; *Hot Fives & Hot Sevens-#3* . . . . . . (Columbia)
Satchmo-Musical Autobiography. . . . . (MCA)
Monday Love
Tara Kemp; *Tara Kemp* . . . . (Giant)
Monday Monday
Mamas & The Papas; *Best Of The Mamas & The Papas* . . . . . (MCA)
Billboard Top Rock 'N' Roll Hits-1966-C . . . . (Rhino)
Farewell To The First Golden Era . . . . (MCA)
Gathering Of The Flowers . . . . (Dunhill Compact Classics)
ST/Stardust . . . . (Dunhill Compact Classics)
Vintage Music-#9-C . . . . (MCA)
Neil Diamond; *Double Gold-Neil Diamond* . . . . (Bang)
Gang At Bang . . . . (Bang)
Shilo . . . . (Bang)
The Feel Of Neil Diamond . . . . (Bang)
Monday Mornin' Keep A Hurtin' Blues
Sonny James; *Little Bit Of Saskatoon* . . . . (Columbia)
Monday Morning
Fleetwood Mac; *25 Years-The Chain* . . . . (Warner Bros.)
Fleetwood Mac. . . . . (Reprise)
Fleetwood Mac Live . . . . (Warner Bros.)
Monday Morning
Church; *Gold Afternoon Fix* . . . . (Arista)

Monday Morning
Peter, Paul & Mary; *Song Will Rise* . . . . (Warner Bros.)
Monday Morning Blues
Mississippi John Hurt; *Best Of Mississippi John Hurt* . . . . . . (Vanguard)
Candy Man . . . . (Intermedia)
Monday Morning Blues
Breathe; *All That Jazz.* . . . . (A&M)
Monday Morning In Paradise
Tom Paxton; *One Million Lawyers & Other Disasters* . . . . . . (Flying Fish)
Monday Morning Quarterback
Frank Sinatra; *She Shot Me Down* . . . . (Reprise)
Monday Morning Rock
Marshall Crenshaw; *Field Day.* . . . . (Warner Bros.)
Monday Morning Secretary
Statler Brothers; *Statler Brothers* . . . . (Mercury)
Monday Night
Golden Palominos; *Golden Palominos* . . . . (Celluloid)
History-1982-1986 . . . . (Metrotone)
Monday Night
Pere Ubu; *Cloudland* . . . . (Fontana)
Monday Struggle
Albert Ammons; *King Of Boogie Woogie-1939-1949* . . . . . (Blues Classics)
Monday Through Sunday
Gigi Gryce; *Rat Race Blues* . . . . (New Jazz)
Monday Thru' Friday
Cliff Richard; *We Don't Talk Anymore* . . . . (EMI)
Monday We'll Be Together
Nikki D; *Daddy's Little Girl* . . . . (Def Jam/Columbia)
Monday Will Never Be The Same
Husker Du; *Zen Arcade* . . . . (SST)
Monday's Child
Cambridge Singers; *Fancies* . . . . (Collegium)
Monday's Dance
Ira Sullivan; *Ira Sullivan* . . . . (Flying Fish)
Red Rodney & Ira Sullivan; *Alive In New York* . . . . . . (Muse)
Month Of Mondays
Jermaine Stewart; *Word Is Out.* . . . . (Arista)
Moody Monday
Mustard's Retreat; *All-Ears Review-#4-More Hot New Sounds-C* . . . . (Really Outstanding Music)
My Monday Date
Earl "Fatha" Hines; *Way Down Yonder In New Orleans* . . . . . (Biograph)
Louis Armstrong; *Jazz Masters-27 Classic Performances-C* . . . . . (Columbia)
Never On Monday
Diving For Pearls; *Diving For Pearls* . . . . (Epic)
New Moon On Monday
Duran Duran; *After The Hurricane* . . . . (Chrysalis)
Seven And The Ragged Tiger. . . . . (Capitol)
On A Monday
Arlo Guthrie & Others; *Tribute To Leadbelly* . . . . (Tomato)
Arlo Guthrie & Pete Seeger; *Together In Concert* . . . . . . (Reprise)
Leadbelly; *Defense Blues-Golden Classics-#2* . . . . . . (Collectables)
Ry Cooder; *Into The Purple Valley* . . . . (Reprise)
Our Monday Date
Earl "Fatha" Hines & His Band; *Our Monday Date* . . . . . (Riverside)
Louis Armstrong; *Hot Fives & Hot Sevens-#3* . . . . . . (Columbia)
Payday/Mine 'Til Monday
Original Broadway Cast; *Tree Grows In Brooklyn.* . . . . . (Sony Music Classical)
Rainy Days & Mondays
Carpenters; *Carpenters.* . . . . (A&M)
Carpenters-Classics-#2. . . . . (A&M)
Carpenters-The Singles 1969-1973. . . . . (A&M)
Yesterday Once More . . . . (A&M)
Paul Williams; *Classics-Here Comes Inspiration* . . . . (A&M)
She Came In Through The Bathroom Window
Beatles; *Abbey Road* . . . . (Parlophone)
Beatles-Box Set. . . . . (Capitol)
Joe Cocker; *Joe Cocker Live* . . . . (Capitol)
Joe Cocker! . . . . (A&M)
Joe Cocker-Classics-#4. . . . . (A&M)
Mad Dogs & Englishmen . . . . (A&M)
Stormy Monday (They Call It)
Allman Brothers Band; *At Fillmore East* . . . . (Capricorn)
The Road Goes On Forever, A Collection Of Their Greatest Recordings . . . . (Polydor)
Big Joe Turner; *Stormy Monday.* . . . . (Pablo)
Bobby Bland; *Best Of Bobby Bland* . . . . (MCA)
Here's The Man. . . . . (MCA)
Legends Of Electric Blues Guitar-#1-C . . . . (Rhino)
Tuesday's Just As Bad. . . . . (K-Tel)
Buddy Guy; *My Time After Awhile* . . . . (Vanguard)
Little Milton; *Best Of Chess Blues-C* . . . . (Chess)
Lou Rawls; *Legendary Lou Rawls* . . . . (Blue Note)
T-Bone Walker; *Best Of Blues-#2-C* . . . . (MCA Special Prod.)
Jazz Heritage-Dirty Mistreater . . . . (MCA)
Sunday Monday Or Always
Frank Sinatra; *Frank Sinatra-In The Beginning-1943-1951* . . . . . (Columbia)
Hello Young Lovers. . . . . (Columbia)

Sunday Mondays
Vanessa Paradis; *Vanessa Paradis* . . . . (Polydor)
Sunny Monday
Booker T. & The M.G.s; *Melting Pot* . . . .(Stax)
Thank God It's Monday
Dene Anton; *Texas Soul* . . . . (JRS)
Theme From "Monday Night Football"
Original Soundtrack; *Television's Greatest Hits-#6-Remote Control-C* . . (TVT)
Will You Be Staying After Sunday
Peppermint Rainbow; *Bubble Gum Classics-C* . . . .(MCA Special Prod.)
Workin' For The Weekend
Ken Mellons; *Ken Mellons* . . . .(Epic)
Steppin' Country-#2-C . . . . (Columbia)

DAYS OF THE WEEK: SATURDAY, Saturday Night

*See Also: DANCE, DAYS: GENERAL, MONTHS & DATES
(various), PARTY, FUN, TIME: GENERAL, TIME:
SPECIFIC, WEEKEND*

10:15 Saturday Night
Cure; *Boys Don't Cry* . . . . (Elektra)
Standing On A Beach-The Singles . . . . (Elektra)
All Night Long
Asleep At The Wheel featuring Leon Rausch; *Tribute To The Music Of Bob
Wills And The Texas Playboys-C* . . . . (Liberty)
Almost Saturday Night
Dave Edmunds; *Best Of Dave Edmunds* . . . . (Swan Song)
Dave Edmunds-Anthology-1968-1990 . . . . (Rhino)
Twangin' . . . . (Swan Song)
Gene Clark & Carla Olson; *So Rebellious A Lover* . . . . (Rhino)
Georgia Satellites; *Let It Rock-The Best Of The Georgia Satellites* . . . . (Elektra)
Rick Nelson; *Stay Young-Epic Recordings* . . . .(Epic)
Always Saturday
Guadalcanal Diary; *Flip-Flop* . . . . (Elektra)
Another Lonely Saturday Night
Greg Kihn Band; *With The Naked Eye* . . . . (Beserkley)
Another Saturday Night
Cat Stevens; *Cat Stevens Greatest Hits.* . . . . (A&M)
Jimmy Buffett; *Margaritaville Cafe Late Night Menu* . . . . (Margaritaville)
Sam Cooke; *The Man And His Music* . . . . (RCA)
This Is Sam Cooke . . . . (RCA)
Anything's Better Than Feelin' The Blues
Martina McBride; *Emotion* . . . . (RCA)
Babylon
David Gray; *White Ladder* . . . . (ATO/RCA)
Book Of Saturday
King Crimson; *Lark's Tongues In Aspic* . . . .(Editions E.G.)
Burnin' The Roadhouse Down
Steve Wariner & Garth Brooks; *Burnin' The Roadhouse Down* . . . . (Capitol)
Catfish Fry
Red Meat; *Alameda County Line* . . . .(Ranchero)
Clock Strikes Ten
Cheap Trick; *Cheap Trick At Budokan* . . . .(Epic)
In Color . . . .(Epic)
Come Dancing
Kinks; *Come Dancing With The Kinks-Best Of The Kinks 1977-1986* . . . (Arista)
State Of Confusion . . . . (Arista)
The Road . . . . (MCA)
Come Saturday Morning
Sandpipers; *Four Sider* . . . . (A&M)
Super Hits Of The '70s-Have A Nice Day-#1-C . . . . (Rhino)
Donald And Lydia
John Prine; *John Prine* . . . . (Atlantic)
John Prine-Souvenirs . . . . (Oh Boy)
Prime Prine-The Best Of John Prine . . . . (Atlantic)
Down To The Night Club
Tower Of Power; *Bump City* . . . .(Warner Bros.)
Live & In Living Color . . . .(Warner Bros.)
Drive In Saturday
David Bowie; *Aladdin Sane* . . . . (Rykodisc)
Sound + Vision . . . . (Rykodisc)
The Singles-1969-1993 . . . . (Rykodisc)
Every Saturday Night
Young's Creole Band; *Chicago Jazz (1923-1929)-C* . . . . (Biograph)
Everybody Loves Saturday Night
New Christy Minstrels; *New Christy Minstrels' Greatest Hits* . . . . . . (Columbia)
Everyday/Saturday
Greg Kihn Band; *Kihntinued* . . . . (Beserkley)
Heart Of Saturday Night, The (Looking For)
Shawn Colvin; *Cover Girl* . . . . (Columbia)
Tom Waits; *The Heart Of Saturday Night* . . . . (Asylum)
Tom Waits-Anthology . . . . (Asylum)
Homegrown Western Saturday Night
Chris LeDoux; *Powder River* . . . . (Liberty)
I'll Be Home
Flamingos; *Alan Freed's Memory Lane-C* . . . .(MCA)

Best Of The Flamingos . . . . (Rhino)
Super Oldies Of The '50s-#6-C . . . . (Audio Fidelity)
Platters; *Platters Greatest Hits-#2.* . . . .(Curb)
It Always Rains On Saturday
Reba McEntire; *Sweet Sixteen.* . . . . (MCA)
It's Going On Saturday
Aztec Two-Step; *See It Was Like This...Acoustic Retrospective* . . . . (Flying Fish)
I've Got Five Dollars And It's Saturday Night
Faron Young; *Faron Young's Greatest Hits* . . . . (CEMA Special Prod.)
George & Gene; *Gene Pitney-Anthology 1961-1968* . . . . (Rhino)
George Jones; *Best Of George Jones-1955-1967* . . . . (Rhino)
Juke Box Saturday Night
Glenn Miller; *Best Of Glenn Miller.* . . . . (RCA)
Glenn Miller-A Legendary Performer-#1 & 2 . . . . (Bluebird)
Memorial-1944-1969. . . . . (Bluebird)
This Is Glenn Miller . . . . (RCA)
Modernaires; *Big Bands' Greatest Hits-#1-C* . . . . (Columbia)
Juke Box Saturday Night
Roy Clark; *The Ultimate Roy Clark* . . . .(Bransounds)
Livingston Saturday Night
Jimmy Buffett; *Son Of A Son Of A Sailor* . . . . (MCA)
ST/FM. . . . . (MCA)
Louisiana Saturday Night
Don Williams; *Best Of Cajun Country-C* . . . . (Era)
Best Of Don Williams-#4 . . . . (MCA)
Don Williams-Country Boy . . . . (MCA)
Jimmy C. Newman; *From The Vaults: Decca Country Classics-1934-
1973-C* . . . . (Decca)
Grand Ole Opry-75 Years-#2-C . . . . (MCA)
Progressive CC . . . . (Plantation)
Mel McDaniel; *Mel McDaniel's Greatest Hits* . . . . (Capitol)
On A Saturday Night
Journey; *Journey-In The Beginning* . . . . (Columbia)
Look Into The Future . . . . (Columbia)
Queen Ida & Her Bon Temps Zydeco Band; *On A Saturday
Night* . . . . (Crescendo)
On Saturday Afternoons In 1963
Rickie Lee Jones; *Rickie Lee Jones* . . . . (Warner Bros.)
One More Saturday Night
Bob Weir; *Ace* . . . .(Grateful Dead)
Grateful Dead; *Best Of/Skeletons From The Closet.* . . . . (Warner Bros.)
Europe '72 . . . . (Warner Bros.)
Without A Net . . . . (Arista)
Painless Saturday
Broken Homes; *Broken Homes* . . . . (MCA)
Pata Pata
Miriam Makeba; *Planet Africa: World Of African Music-C* . . . . (Priority)
Welela . . . . (Verve)
Piano Man
Billy Joel; *Billy Joel-Greatest Hits, Volume I & Volume II* . . . . (Columbia)
Piano Man . . . . (Columbia)
Rock Classics Of The '70s-C . . . . (Columbia)
Ready For Saturday Night
Joanna Dean; *Misbehavin'* . . . .(Polydor)
Rip It Up
Elvis Presley; *Elvis* . . . . (RCA)
Rocker . . . . (RCA)
Little Richard; *Big Hits* . . . .(Crescendo)
Grooviest 17 Original Hits . . . .(Specialty)
Little Richard-18 Greatest Hits . . . . (Rhino)
Little Richard's Greatest Hits. . . . . (Everest)
Rockin' On A Saturday Night
Jason D. Williams; *Tore Up* . . . . (RCA)
Sabbath Prayer
Herschel Bernardi; *ST/Fiddler On The Roof* . . . . (Columbia)
Original Cast; *Fiddler On The Roof* . . . . (RCA Victor)
Same Old Saturday Night
Frank Sinatra; *Capitol Collectors Series-Frank Sinatra* . . . . (Capitol)
Saturday
Sarah Vaughan; *Complete Sarah Vaughan On Mercury-#1-Great Jazz Years-
1954-1956* . . . . (Mercury)
Saturday
Carpenters; *Carpenters* . . . . (A&M)
Saturday
Andre Previn Trio; *Like Previn* . . . . (Contemporary)
Saturday
Mose Allison; *Back Country Suite* . . . .(Prestige)
Saturday
Judybeats; *Down In The Shacks Where The Satellite Dishes Grow* . . . . (Sire)
Saturday
Original Sins; *Move.* . . . .(Psonic)
Saturday
Deltones; *Oddball Boy* . . . . (Roir)
Saturday & Sunday
Jackie McLean; *One Step Beyond* . . . . (Blue Note)
Saturday Afternoon
Jefferson Airplane; *After Bathing At Baxters* . . . . (RCA)
Flight Log (1966-1976) . . . . (Grunt)

Woodstock Two. . . . . (Atlantic)

Saturday Afternoon
Thelonius Monk; *Next Saturday Afternoon* . . . . (Relativity)

Saturday Afternoon
Cassell Webb; *Thief Of Sadness* . . . . (Venture)

Saturday Asylum
Rain Parade; *Best Of The Radio Tokyo Tapes* . . . . (Charisma)

Saturday At Midnight
Cheap Trick; *One On One* . . . . (Epic)

Saturday Blues
Ishman Bracey; *Canned Heat Blues-Masters Of Delta Blues* . . . . (Bluebird)

Saturday Boy
Billy Bragg; *Back To Basics* . . . . (Elektra)

Saturday Clothes
Gordon Lightfoot; *If You Could Read My Mind*. . . . .(Reprise)

Saturday Dance
Bob Cooper; *Coop! Music Of* . . . . (Contemporary)

Saturday Evening
Ronnie Laws; *Best Of Ronnie Laws*. . . . .(Blue Note)

Saturday Evening Blues
Larry Johnson; *Country Blues* . . . . (Biograph)

Saturday Freedom
Blue Cheer; *Good Times Are So Hard To Find-History Of Blue*
Cheer. . . . . (Mercury)

Saturday Gigs
Mott The Hoople; *Mott The Hoople's Greatest Hits* . . . . (Columbia)
The Ballad Of Mott: A Retrospective . . . . (Columbia)

Saturday In The Park
Chicago; *Chicago IX-Chicago's Greatest Hits* . . . . (Chicago)
Chicago V . . . . (Chicago)
Chicken Soup For The Soul: I'll Be There For You-Songs Of Friendship,
Brotherhood And Sisterhood-C . . . . (Rhino)
Group Portrait . . . . (Chicago)
If You Leave Me Now . . . . (Chicago)
ST/My Girl . . . . (Epic)
The Heart Of Chicago-1967-1997 . . . .(Reprise)

Saturday Love
Cherrelle & Alexander O'Neal; *Club Epic-#1-C*. . . . . (Legacy)
High Priority . . . . (Tabu)

Saturday Matinee
Gordon Brisker; *About Charlie* . . . .(Discovery)

Saturday Miles
Miles Davis; *Miles Davis At Fillmore* . . . . (Columbia)

Saturday Morning
Harry Chapin; *Greatest Stories-Live* . . . . (Elektra)

Saturday Morning
Joe Higgs; *Black Man Know Yourself* . . . .(Shanachie)

Saturday Morning
Tom Chapin; *In The City Of Mercy* . . . .(Spector)

Saturday Morning
Meat Puppets; *Meat Puppets* . . . . (SST)

Saturday Morning Cartoons
Sergio Salvatore; *Sergio Salvatore* . . . . (GRP)

Saturday Morning Confusion
Bobby Russell; *Super Hits Of The '70s-Have A Nice Day-#6-C* . . . . (Rhino)

Saturday Morning Fever
Loudon Wainwright III; *Fame & Wealth*. . . . .(Rounder)

Saturday Morning Movies
Bonnie Koloc; *Bonnie Koloc* . . . . (Ovation)
Bonnie Koloc-At Her Best. . . . . (Ovation)

Saturday Night
Bay City Rollers; *Bay City Rollers* . . . . (Arista)
Bay City Rollers' Greatest Hits. . . . . (Arista)
Billboard Top Rock 'N' Roll Hits-1976-C . . . . (Rhino)
Super Hits Of The '70s-Have A Nice Day-#15-C . . . . (Rhino)

Saturday Night
Ten Years After; *About Time* . . . . (Chrysalis)

Saturday Night
Schoolly D; *Adventures Of Schoolly D* . . . . (Rykodisc)

Saturday Night
Eagles; *Desperado*. . . . . (Asylum)
Eagles Live . . . . (Asylum)

Saturday Night
Bobby Fuller Four; *Best Of The Bobby Fuller Four* . . . . (Rhino)

Saturday Night
Count Basie; *Compact Jazz-Count Basie-Standards*. . . . .(Verve)

Saturday Night
Red Norvo Quintet; *Forward Look* . . . . (Reference)

Saturday Night
Herman Brood; *Herman Brood & His Wild Romance* . . . . (Ariola America)

Saturday Night
Commodores; *In The Pocket* . . . . (Motown)

Saturday Night
Original Cast; *Marry Me A Little* . . . . (RCA)

Saturday Night
Bunny Wailer; *Rule Dance Hall* . . . .(Shanachie)

Saturday Night
John Waite; *No Brakes* . . . . (EMI)

Saturday Night
Maynard Ferguson; *Maynard '61*. . . . . (Roulette)

Saturday Night
Kay Starr; *Kay Starr-Country* . . . . (Crescendo)

Saturday Night
Blue Nile; *Hats*. . . . .(A&M)

Saturday Night
Buddy Blue; *Guttersnipes 'N' Zealots* . . . .(Rhino)

Saturday Night
Bobby King & Terry Evans; *Live & Let Live* . . . .(Rounder)

Saturday Night & Sunday Morning
Phil Collins; *...But Seriously* . . . . (Atlantic)

Saturday Night (I Get All My Lovin')
Billy Strange; *Best Of Billy Strange*. . . . . (Crescendo)

Saturday Night (Is The Loneliest Night In The Week)
Frank Sinatra; *Come Dance With Me!* . . . .(Capitol)
Frank Sinatra-16 Most Requested Songs . . . .(Columbia)
Frank Sinatra-In The Beginning-1943-1951 . . . .(Columbia)
Portrait Of Sinatra-Columbia Classics . . . .(Legacy)
The Capitol Years . . . .(Capitol)

Saturday Night At Sea
John Townley & The Press Gang; *Chesapeake Sailor's Companion* . . . (Adelphi)

Saturday Night At The General Store
Margo Smith; *Happiness* . . . . (Warner Bros.)

Saturday Night At The Movies
Drifters; *1959-1965-All-Time Greatest Hits And More* . . . . (Atlantic)
Drifters-16 Greatest Hits . . . . (Trip)
Drifters-Golden Hits . . . . (Atlantic)
Save The Last Dance For Me. . . . . (Fifty One West)

Saturday Night At The World
Mason Williams; *Music-1968-1971*. . . . .(Vanguard)
Mason Williams & Mannheim Steamroller;
Classical Gas . . . . (American Gramaphone)

Saturday Night Blues
Kenny Burrell; *Midnight Blue* . . . . (Blue Note)

Saturday Night Boogie
Harry Crafton; *Harry Crafton* . . . .(Collectables)

Saturday Night Down South
Charlie Daniels Band; *Simple Man* . . . . (Epic)

Saturday Night Fish Fry
Louis Jordan; *Best Of Louis Jordan* . . . . (MCA)
No Moe! Louis Jordan's Greatest Hits . . . .(Verve)
Pearl Bailey; *Pearl Bailey-16 Most Requested Songs* . . . .(Legacy)

Saturday Night Fish Fry Drag
Joe Robichaux & The New Orleans Boys; *Joe Robichaux & The New*
Orleans Boys-1933. . . . . (Folklyric)

Saturday Night Function
Duke Ellington; *Okeh Ellington* . . . .(Columbia)

Saturday Night In Dallas
Kenny Seratt; *45-#1003* . . . .(MDJ)

Saturday Night In Dublin
Michael ''Jesse'' Owens; *Across The Sea To Ireland* . . . . (Rego Irish)

Saturday Night Jag
Clarence Williams & His Orchestra; *Clarence Williams & His Orchestra-#1*
(1927-1929) . . . . (Biograph)

Saturday Night Rub
Big Bill Broonzy; *Young Big Bill Broonzy-1928-1935* . . . . (Yazoo)

Saturday Night Special
Lynyrd Skynyrd; *Gold & Platinum* . . . . (MCA)
Nuthin' Fancy . . . . (MCA)
One More From The Road. . . . . (MCA)
Skynyrd's Innards-Their Greatest Hits . . . . (MCA)
McBride & The Ride; *Skynyrd Frynds-C* . . . . (MCA)

Saturday Night Stomp
Eddie ''Blues Man'' Kirkland; *It's The Blues Man!* . . . . (Tru-Sound)

Saturday Night U.S.A.
Charlie Daniels Band; *Powder Keg* . . . . (Epic)

Saturday Night, Sunday Morning
Thelma Houston; *Motown Superstar Series-#20-Thelma Houston* . . . .(Motown)
Ride To The Rainbow . . . .(Motown)

Saturday Night's Alright For Fighting
Elton John; *Elton John's Greatest Hits* . . . . (Polydor)
Goodbye Yellow Brick Road . . . . (Polydor)
Knebworth-The Album-C . . . . (Polydor)
Rock Classics-C . . . .(K-Tel)
Who; *Two Rooms-Celebrating The Songs Of Elton John & Bernie*
Taupin-C . . . . (Polydor)

Saturday Nite
Earth, Wind & Fire; *Best Of Earth, Wind & Fire-#2* . . . .(Columbia)
Eternal Dance . . . .(Columbia)
Spirit . . . .(Columbia)

Saturday Nite Is Dead
Graham Parker And The Rumour; *Squeezing Out Sparks* . . . .(Arista)

Saturday Nite Live
Masta Ace Incorporated; *SlaughtaHouse*. . . . . (Delicious Vinyl)

Saturday Sailing
James Morrison; *Postcards From Down Under*. . . . . (Atlantic)

Saturday Suit
Art Garfunkel; *Watermark* . . . . (Legacy)
Saturday Sun
Nick Drake; *Five Leaves Left* . . . . (Hannibal)
Saturdays
David Benoit; *Every Step Of The Way* . . . . (GRP)
Saturday's Child
Monkees; *Listen To The Band* . . . . (Rhino)
More Greatest Hits Of The Monkees . . . . (Arista)
Saturday's Father
4 Seasons; *25th Anniversary Collection* . . . . (Rhino)
Saturday's Heroes
Business; *Business-1979-1989* . . . . (Blackout!)
Saturday's Kids
Jam; *Setting Sons* . . . . (Polydor)
She's My Saturday Night Special
Ronnie McDowell; *Unchained Melody* . . . . (Curb)
Wayne Newton; *Best Of Wayne Newton-Now* . . . . (Curb)
Small Town Saturday Night
Hal Ketchum; *Past The Point Of Rescue* . . . . (Curb)
Standing On The Corner
Broadway Cast; *Most Happy Fella* . . . . (RCA)
Dean Martin; *Best Of Dean Martin* . . . . (CEMA Special Prod.)
Four Lads; *Four Lads-16 Most Requested Songs* . . . . (Legacy)
Original Broadway Cast; *Most Happy Fella* . . . . (Sony Music Classical)
Sugar Hill Saturday Night
Charlie Daniels Band; *Midnight Wind* . . . . (Epic)
Sunless Saturday
Fishbone; *Reality Of My Surroundings* . . . . (Columbia)
Sunshine Saturday Morning
Jim Aikin; *Light's Broken Speech Revived* . . . . (Linden)
Tennessee Saturday Night
Ella Mae Morse; *Capitol Collectors Series-Ella Mae Morse* . . . . (Capitol)
Red Foley; *Heroes Of Country Music-#2-Legends Of Honky Tonk-C* . . . (Rhino)
Red Foley: The Country Music Hall Of Fame . . . . (MCA Special Prod.)
Tennessee Saturday Nite
Commander Cody & His Lost Planet Airmen; *Aces High* . . . . (Relix)
Texas On A Saturday Night
Willie Nelson; *Taste Of Texas-Songs 'Bout Texas By Texans-C* . . . . (Columbia)
Willie Nelson & Mel Tillis; *Half Nelson-C* . . . . (Columbia)
Theme From "Saturday Night Live"
Original Soundtrack; *Television's Greatest Hits-#3-1970s & 1980s-C* . . . (TVT)
Saturday Night Live Band; *Jazz...The Digital Age* . . . . (Pro Jazz)
There Goes The Neighborhood
Sheryl Crow; *The Globe Sessions* . . . . (A&M)
Whatever Happened To Saturday Night
Tim Curry; *ST/Rocky Horror Picture Show* . . . . (Rhino)
Tim Curry & Original Roxy Cast; *Rocky Horror Show* . . . . (Rhino)
Where Did Robinson Crusoe Go With Friday On Saturday Night
Ian Whitcomb; *You Turn Me On-The Very Best Of Ian
Whitcomb* . . . . (Varese Sarabande)
Wildwood Days
Bobby Rydell; *Bobby Rydell* . . . . (Big Top)

DAYS OF THE WEEK: SUNDAY

*See Also: DAYS: GENERAL, MONTHS & DATES (various), TIME:
GENERAL, TIME: SPECIFIC, WEEKEND*

Always On A Sunday
Frank Anderson & Tommy McCook; *Ska Bonanza-Studio One Ska
Years-C* . . . . (Heartbeat)
Angel's Sunday
Jim Ed Brown; *Best Of Jim Ed Brown* . . . . (RCA)
Another Kind Of Sunday
Gerry Mulligan; *Little Big Horn* . . . . (GRP)
Another Park, Another Sunday
Doobie Brothers; *What Were Once Vices Are Now Habits* . . . . . . (Warner Bros.)
As Long As There's A Sunday
Sammi Smith; *As Long As There's A Sunday* . . . . (Elektra)
Austin
Blake Shelton; *Blake Shelton* . . . . (Giant)
Babylon
David Gray; *White Ladder* . . . . (ATO/RCA)
Beautiful Sunday
Daniel Boone; *Back To The '70s-#2-C* . . . . (Dominion Entert.)
Super Hits Of The '70s-Have A Nice Day-#9-C . . . . (Rhino)
Roy Drusky; *English Gold* . . . . (Plantation)
Birmingham Sunday
Joan Baez; *Contemporary Ballad Book* . . . . (Vanguard)
Joan Baez/5 . . . . (Vanguard)
Richard Farina; *Best Of Broadside 1962-1968: Anthems Of The American
Underground From The Pages Of Broadside
Magazine-C* . . . . (Smithsonian Folkways)
Black Sabbath
Black Sabbath; *Black Sabbath* . . . . (Warner Bros.)

Live Evil . . . . (Warner Bros.)
We Sold Our Soul For Rock 'N' Roll . . . . (Warner Bros.)
Ozzy Osbourne; *Speak Of The Devil* . . . . (Jet)
The Ozzman Cometh . . . . (Epic)
Black Sunday
Skatalites; *Ska Bonanza-Studio One Ska Years-C* . . . . (Heartbeat)
Black Sunday
Jethro Tull; *A* . . . . (Chrysalis)
Blue Sunday
Doors; *Morrison Hotel/Hard Rock Cafe* . . . . (Elektra)
Come Sunday
Jennifer Holliday; *Say You Love Me* . . . . (Geffen)
Johnny Mathis; *In A Sentimental Mood-Johnny Mathis Sings
Ellington* . . . . (Columbia)
Dayton Ohio 1903
Randy Newman; *Sail Away* . . . . (Reprise)
Don't Take My Sunday Paper
Holly Near & Jeff Langley; *You Can Know All I Am* . . . . (Redwood)
Down
Stone Temple Pilots; *No. 4* . . . . (Atlantic)
Drinkin' In My Sunday Dress
Maria McKee; *Maria McKee* . . . . (Geffen)
Eastern Sundays
Moraz & Bruford; *Music For Piano & Drums* . . . . (Editions E.G.)
Easy
Commodores; *20 Greatest Songs In Motown History-C* . . . . (Motown)
All The Great Love Songs-Commodores . . . . (Motown)
Commodores . . . . (Motown)
Commodores Greatest Hits . . . . (Motown)
Compact Command Performances-Commodores . . . . (Motown)
Composer-Great Love Songs By Lionel Richie . . . . (Motown)
Lionel Richie; *Back To Front* . . . . (Motown)
Every Day Is Like Sunday
Morrissey; *Best Of MTV's 120 Minutes-#2-C* . . . . (Rhino)
Bona Drag . . . . (Sire)
Viva Hate . . . . (Sire)
Every Day Seems Like Sunday
Buddy Moss; *Rediscovery* . . . . (Biograph)
Every Day Will Be Sunday By And By
Standard Quartette; *The Earliest Negro Vocals-#2-C* . . . . (Document)
Statler Brothers; *Innerview* . . . . (Mercury)
Every Sunday Afternoon
Bobby Short; *Bobby Short Celebrates Rodgers & Hart* . . . . (Atlantic)
Far Away Eyes
Rolling Stones; *Some Girls* . . . . (Virgin)
Food (Till Sunday) (No)
Click Click; *Wet Skin & Curious Eye* . . . . (Play It Again Sam)
Gloomy Sunday
Billie Holiday; *Billie Holiday's Greatest Hits* . . . . (Legacy)
Legacy Box-1933-1958 . . . . (Columbia)
Goodbye Sunday
Everything But The Girl; *Idlewild* . . . . (Sire)
Groovin'
Aretha Franklin; *Lady Soul* . . . . (Atlantic)
Booker T. & The M.G.s; *Best Of Booker T. & The M.G.s* . . . . (Atlantic)
Soul Shots-#3-Soul Twist-C . . . . (Rhino)
Rascals; *Groovin'* . . . . (Warner Special Prod.)
Hit Singles-1958-1977-C . . . . (Atlantic)
Rascals' Greatest Hits . . . . (Atlantic)
ST/Platoon . . . . (Atlantic)
Hymn For A Sunday Evening
Original Cast; *Bye Bye Birdie* . . . . (Columbia)
I Met Him On A Sunday
Shirelles; *Shirelles' Greatest Hits* . . . . (Everest)
Shirelles-16 Greatest Hits . . . . (Trip)
Shirelles-Anthology 1959-1964 . . . . (Rhino)
Shirelles-Classics . . . . (Bac-Trac)
I'll Be Back A-Sunday
"Little" Jimmy Dickens; *Columbia Historic Edition-"Little" Jimmy
Dickens* . . . . (Columbia)
Interstate Love Song
Stone Temple Pilots; *Purple* . . . . (Atlantic)
It Always Rains On Sundays
Box; *Pleasure & The Pain* . . . . (Capitol)
It Must Be Sunday
Phoebe Snow; *Phoebe Snow* . . . . (MCA)
It's A Shame To Ship Your Wife On Sunday
Fiddlin' John Carson; *The Old Hen Cackled (& The Rooster's Going To
Crow)* . . . . (Rounder)
It's Sunday
Frank Sinatra; *The Reprise Collection* . . . . (Reprise)
Jamaica Sunday Morning
Kim Carnes; *St. Vincent's Court* . . . . (Out Of Print)
Just Another Sunday
George Benson & Jack McDuff; *George Benson & Jack McDuff* . . . . (Prestige)
Just Another Sunday
Blasters; *Hard Line* . . . . (Slash)
Lazy Day
Moody Blues; *On The Threshold Of A Dream* . . . . (Polydor)

Lazy Sunday
Small Faces; *Immediate Singles Collection-#2-C* . . . (Sony Music Special Prod.)
Ogdens' Nut Gone Flake . . . . (Abkco)
Like A Sunday In Salem
Gene Cotton; *No Strings Attached* . . . . (Ariola America)
Save The Dancer . . . . (Ariola America)
Like Sunday
Cut; *Songs For The Radio* . . . . (Win)
Listen To The Bells
Doyle Lawson & Quicksilver; *Just Over In Heaven* . . . . (Sugar Hill)
Louisiana Sunday Afternoon
Diane Schuur; *Diane Schuur-Collection* . . . . (GRP)
Talkin' 'Bout You . . . . (GRP)
Loving You Sunday Morning
Scorpions; *Lovedrive* . . . . (Mercury)
World Wide Live . . . . (Mercury)
Monday Through Sunday
Gigi Gryce; *Rat Race Blues* . . . . (New Jazz)
Month Of Sundays
Church; *Remote Luxury* . . . . (Arista)
Month Of Sundays
Vern Gosdin; *Out Of My Heart* . . . . (Columbia)
Month Of Sundays
Saigon Kick; *Saigon Kick* . . . . (Third Stone)
Month Of Sundays
Ernest Tubb; *Walking The Floor Over You* . . . . (Laserlight)
Mr. Sunday
Simon Townshend; *Sweet Sound* . . . . (21)
My Girl Sunday
Chieli Minucci; *Sweet On You* . . . . (Shanachie)
My Sunday Feeling
Jethro Tull; *This Was* . . . . (Chrysalis)
My Sunday Gal
Duke Ellington; *Great Ellington Units* . . . . (Bluebird)
Mystic Eyes
Them featuring Van Morrison; *Here Comes The Night* . . . . (Out Of Print)
History Of British Rock-#6-C . . . . (Rhino)
*The Sopranos-Music From The HBO Original
Series* . . . . (Sony Music Soundtrax)
Naked Sunday
Stone Temple Pilots; *Core* . . . . (Atlantic)
Never On Sunday
Andy Williams; *Moon River & Other Great Movie Themes* . . . . (Columbia)
Boston Pops Orchestra/Arthur Fiedler; *Greatest Hits Of The '60s* . . . . . (RCA)
Motion Picture Classics-#1 . . . . (RCA Victor)
Boston Pops Orchestra/John Williams; *Digital Jukebox* . . . . (Philips)
Chordettes; *Chordettes Greatest Hits* . . . . (Everest)
No Plane On Sunday
Jimmy Buffett; *Floridays* . . . . (MCA)
On A Sunday Afternoon
Lighter Shade Of Brown & Huggy Boy; *Brown & Proud* . . . . (Pump)
On A Sunday By The Sea
Original Broadway Cast; *Jerome Robbins' Broadway* . . . . (RCA)
On Sunday
'Til Tuesday; *Welcome Home* . . . . (Epic)
On Sunday Afternoon
Harptones; *Echoes Of A Rock Era-The Harptones* . . . . (Roulette)
One Million Billionth Of A Millisecond On A Sunday Morning
Flaming Lips; *Oh My Gawd The Flaming Lips* . . . . (Restless)
One More Sunday In Savannah
Nina Simone; *The Tomato Collection* . . . . (Tomato)
Our Sunday Morning
Yoshio "Chin" Suzuki; *Morning Picture* . . . . (JVC Musical Industries)
Palm Sunday
Jerry Garcia; *Cats Under The Stars* . . . . (Arista)
Pleasant Valley Sunday
Monkees; *Listen To The Band* . . . . (Rhino)
Monkees' Greatest Hits . . . . (Rhino)
Nuggets-Classic Collection From The Psychedelic '60s-C . . . . . . (Rhino)
Put On Your Sunday Clothes
Carol Channing/Original Cast; *Hello Dolly!* . . . . (RCA)
Puttin' On My Sunday Best
Dick & Mel Tunney; *Let The Dreamers Dream* . . . . (Warner Bros.)
Rockport Sunday
Tom Rush; *The Circle Game* . . . . (Elektra)
Sabbath, Bloody Sabbath
Anthrax; *I'm The Man* . . . . (Island)
Black Sabbath; *Sabbath Bloody Sabbath* . . . . (Warner Bros.)
We Sold Our Soul For Rock 'N' Roll . . . . (Warner Bros.)
Ozzy Osbourne; *Speak Of The Devil* . . . . (Jet)
Sad Rush on Sunday
Dylans; *Dylans* . . . . (Beggar's Banquet)
Saturday & Sunday
Jackie McLean; *One Step Beyond* . . . . (Blue Note)
Saturday Night & Sunday Morning
Phil Collins; *...But Seriously* . . . . (Atlantic)
Saturday Night, Sunday Morning
Thelma Houston; *Motown Superstar Series-#20-Thelma Houston* . . . . (Motown)

Ride To The Rainbow . . . . (Motown)
Second Sunday In August
Weather Report; *I Sing The Body Electric* . . . . (Columbia)
Seven Days Come Sunday
Rodney Lay; *Silent Partners* . . . . (Sun)
Seven Sundays
Extreme; *III Sides To Every Story* . . . . (A&M)
Seventeen Come Sunday
John Wright & Catherine Perrier; *Traditional Music Of
Ireland* . . . . (Green Linnet)
She Came In Through The Bathroom Window
Beatles; *Abbey Road* . . . . (Parlophone)
Beatles-Box Set . . . . (Capitol)
Joe Cocker; *Joe Cocker Live* . . . . (Capitol)
Joe Cocker! . . . . (A&M)
Joe Cocker-Classics-#4 . . . . (A&M)
Mad Dogs & Englishmen . . . . (A&M)
She Misses Him On Sunday The Most
Diamond Rio; *Diamond Rio IV* . . . . (Arista)
Diamond Rio's Greatest Hits . . . . (Arista)
She Used To Sing On Sunday
Larry Gatlin & The Gatlin Brothers Band; *Larry Gatlin & The Gatlin
Brothers' Greatest Hits-#2* . . . . (Columbia)
Larry Gatlin & The Gatlin Brothers-17 Greatest Hits . . . . (Columbia)
Six-Thirty Sunday Morning
Peter Allen; *Taught By Experts* . . . . (A&M)
Sugar On Sunday
Tommy James And The Shondells; *Best Of Tommy James And The
Shondells* . . . . (Roulette)
Crimson & Clover/Cellophane Symphony . . . . (Rhino)
Tommy James And The Shondells-Anthology . . . . (Rhino)
Sunday
Carmen McRae; *Blue Note Meets The L. A. Philharmonic* . . . . (Blue Note)
Great American Songbook . . . . (Atlantic)
In Person . . . . (Mainstream)
Cranberries; *Everybody Else Is Doing It, So Why Can't We?* . . . . . . (Island)
Frank Sinatra; *Songs For Young Lovers & Swing Easy* . . . . (Capitol)
Michael Feinstein; *Michael Feinstein Sings The Jule Styne
Songbook* . . . . (Nonesuch)
Original Cast; *ST/Flower Drum Song* . . . . (Sony Music Classical)
Sunday In The Park With George . . . . (RCA Victor)
Sunday
Andreas Vollenweider; *Behind The Gardens, Behind The
Walls* . . . . (CBS Masterworks)
The Trilogy . . . . (Columbia)
Sunday & Me
Jay & The Americans; *Come A Little Bit Closer-Best Of Jay & The
Americans* . . . . (Gold Rush)
Jay & The Americans' All-Time Greatest Hits . . . . (Rhino)
Teen Rock Singles-1956-1966-C . . . . (EMI)
Sunday Afternoon
Candy Dulfer; *Sax-A-Go-Go* . . . . (RCA)
Sunday Afternoon In The Park
Van Halen; *Fair Warning* . . . . (Warner Bros.)
Sunday Bloody Sunday
U2; *Under A Blood Red Sky* . . . . (Island)
War . . . . (Island)
Sunday Bloody Sunday
John Lennon/Plastic Ono Band; *Sometime In New York City* . . . . (Capitol)
Sunday Down In Tennessee
Red Foley; *45-#46197* . . . . (Decca)
Sunday Driving
Jerry Lewis; *Capitol Collectors Series-Jerry Lewis* . . . . (Capitol)
Dr. Demento Presents The Greatest Novelty Records-#2-1950s-C . . . (Rhino)
Sunday For Tea
Peter And Gordon; *Best Of Peter And Gordon* . . . . (Rhino)
Sunday Girl
Blondie; *Best Of Blondie* . . . . (Chrysalis)
Parallel Lines . . . . (Chrysalis)
Sunday In Genoa
101 Strings Orchestra; *101 Strings Orchestra-30th Anniversary* . . . . . (Alshire)
Sunday In New York
Mel Torme; *Songs Of New York* . . . . (Rhino)
Sunday In The Park With George
Original Cast; *Sunday In The Park With George* . . . . (RCA Victor)
Sunday In The South
Shenandoah; *30 Years Of #1 Hits-#19-C* . . . . (Columbia)
Road Not Taken . . . . (Columbia)
Shenandoah's Greatest Hits . . . . (Columbia)
Sunday Kind Of Love
Ben Sidran; *That's Life I Guess* . . . . (Bluebird)
Ella Fitzgerald; *Best Of Ella Fitzgerald-#2* . . . . (MCA)
Harptones; *Collectables Presents The History Of Rock-#6-C* . . . (Collectables)
Kenny Rankin; *Inside Kenny Rankin* . . . . (Little David)
Reba McEntire; *Reba* . . . . (MCA)
Sunday Kind Of Woman
Charlie Rich; *Behind Closed Doors* . . . . (Epic)
Sunday Monday Or Always
Frank Sinatra; *Frank Sinatra-In The Beginning-1943-1951* . . . . (Columbia)

Hello Young Lovers . . . . (Columbia)
Sunday Mondays
Vanessa Paradis; *Vanessa Paradis* . . . . (Polydor)
Sunday Morning
Velvet Underground; *Live At Max's Kansas City* . . . . (Collectables)
Sunday Morning Blues
Big Joe Turner; *Big Joe Is Here* . . . . (Savoy)
Have No Fear Big Joe Is Here . . . . (Savoy)
Sunday Morning Coming Down
Johnny Cash; *Classic Cash-Hall Of Fame Series* . . . . (Mercury)
Johnny Cash's Greatest Hits-#2 . . . . (Columbia)
The Man In Black-His Greatest Hits . . . . (Legacy)
Kris Kristofferson; *Me & Bobby McGee.* . . . . (Columbia)
Songs Of Kris Kristofferson . . . . (Columbia)
Vikki Carr; *Best Of Vikki Carr* . . . . (EMI)
Willie Nelson; *Willie* . . . . (RCA)
Willie Nelson Sings Kristofferson . . . . (Columbia)
Sunday Morning Fool
Michael Dinner; *Great Pretenders* . . . . (Fantasy)
Sunday Morning Movies
Bonnie Koloc; *Bonnie Koloc* . . . . (Ovation)
Bonnie Koloc-At Her Best . . . . (Ovation)
Sunday Morning Radio
Sha Na Na; *Sh-Boom* . . . . (Accord)
Sunday Morning Sunshine
Harry Chapin; *Harry Chapin-Anthology* . . . . (Elektra)
Sunday Night In San Fernando
Mel Torme & The Mel-Tones; *California Suite* . . . . (Discovery)
Sunday Papers
Joe Jackson; *Live 1980/86* . . . . (A&M)
Look Sharp! . . . . (A&M)
No Wave. . . . . (A&M)
Sunday Rider
David Gates; *First.* . . . . (Elektra)
Goodbye Girl . . . . (Elektra)
Sunday School To Broadway
Sammi Smith; *45-#45334* . . . . (Elektra)
Sunday Song
Courtney Pine; *Journey To The Urge Within* . . . . (Antilles)
Sunday Sun
Neil Diamond; *Glory Road-1968-1972* . . . . (MCA)
Velvet Gloves & Spit . . . . (MCA Special Prod.)
Sunday Sunrise
Brenda Lee; *Brenda Lee-Greatest Country Hits.* . . . . (MCA)
Sunday Will Never Be The Same
Spanky & Our Gang; *Flower Power-Psychedelic Rock Classics-C* . . . . . (K-Tel)
Sunday's Best
Elvis Costello; *Girls Girls Girls* . . . . (Columbia)
Taking Liberties. . . . . (Columbia)
Sweet Sunday Kinda Love
Honeys; *Capitol Collectors Series-The Honeys* . . . . (Capitol)
Tell It To The Judge On Sunday
Long Ryders; *Native Sons.* . . . . (Frontier)
Tell Me On A Sunday
Marti Webb; *Premiere Collection-Best Of Andrew Lloyd Webber-C* . . . . (MCA)
Michael Crawford; *Michael Crawford Performs Andrew Lloyd
Webber* . . . . (Atlantic)
That Sunday, That Summer
Betty Carter; *Compact Jazz-Best Of The Compact Jazz Vocalists-C* . . . . (Verve)
Nat "King" Cole; *Nat "King" Cole (Box Set)* . . . . (Capitol)
Unforgettable. . . . . (Capitol)
Natalie Cole; *Unforgettable With Love.* . . . . (Elektra)
Theme For Sunday
Stan Kenton; *Jazz Compositions Of Stan Kenton* . . . . (Creative World)
Retrospective-Capitol Years . . . . (Blue Note)
Tippin' Home From Sunday School
Oliver Jones; *Class Act.* . . . . (Justin Time)
Ugly Sunday
Mark Lanegan; *Grunge Years.* . . . . (Sub Pop)
Winding Sheet . . . . (Sub Pop)
Warm Sunday
Conrad Herwig Quintet; *The Amulet.* . . . . (Ken)
Whiskey On A Sunday (Puppet Song)
Irish Rovers; *Irish Rovers' Greatest Hits* . . . . (MCA)
Will You Be Staying After Sunday
Peppermint Rainbow; *Bubble Gum Classics-C* . . . . (MCA Special Prod.)

DAYS OF THE WEEK: THURSDAY

*See Also: **DAYS: GENERAL, MONTHS & DATES (various), TIME:
GENERAL, TIME: SPECIFIC***

3:10 Smokey Thursday
Danny O'Keefe; *Seattle Tapes* . . . . (First Warning)
Blue Thursday
Franz Jackson Original All-Stars; *Featuring Bob Shoffner* . . . . (Riverside)

He Met Me On A Thursday Morning
Johnie Lewis; *Alabama Slide Guitar.* . . . . (Arhoolie)
Holy Thursday
Greg Brown; *Songs Of Innocence & Experience.* . . . . (Red House)
Lady Madonna
Beatles; *Beatles 1* . . . . (Capitol)
Hey Jude. . . . . (Capitol)
Past Masters-Volume Two . . . . (Parlophone)
The Beatles/1967-1970. . . . . (Capitol)
Wings; *Wings Over America* . . . . (Capitol)
Like A Summer Thursday
Townes Van Zandt; *Our Mother The Mountain* . . . . (Tomato)
Misty Thursday
Duke Jordan; *Misty Thursday* . . . . (Inner City)
Sweet Thursday
Sweet Thursday; *Sweet Thursday* . . . . (Out Of Print)
Sweet Thursday
Icicle Works; *If You Want To Defeat Your Enemy....* . . . . (Beggar's Banquet)
Sweet Thursday
Helen Traubel/Original Cast; *Pipe Dream* . . . . (RCA)
Thursday
Jim Croce; *50th Anniversary Collection* . . . . (Saja)
I Got A Name . . . . (Lifesong)
Time In A Bottle/Jim Croce's Greatest Love Songs . . . . (Atlantic)
Thursday
Count Basie; *Good Morning Blues* . . . . (MCA)
Thursday
Country Joe & The Fish; *I-Feel-Like-I'm-Fixin'-To-Die* . . . . (Vanguard)
Thursday
Mike Auldridge & Old Dog; *Mike Auldridge & Old Dog* . . . . (Flying Fish)
Thursday
Cranes; *Wings Of Joy* . . . . (Dedicated)
Thursday Afternoon
Brian Eno; *Thursday Afternoon.* . . . . (Editions E.G.)
Thursday Club
Truth; *Playground.* . . . . (I.R.S.)
Thursday Miles
Miles Davis; *Miles Davis At Fillmore* . . . . (Columbia)
Thursday Morning Garden Club
Buddy Winfield; *45-#167* . . . . (Nationwide Sound Distrib.)
Thursday Night Fever
Legendary Pink Dots; *Legendary Pink Dots* . . . . (Play It Again Sam)
Thursday's Child
Abbey Lincoln; *Abbey Is Blue.* . . . . (Riverside)
Anthony Davis; *Trio 2.* . . . . (Gramavision)
Barbara Lea; *Barbara Lea.* . . . . (Prestige)
Bev Kelly; *Love Locked Out* . . . . (Riverside)
Chameleons UK; *Script Of The Bridge* . . . . (MCA)
Tanita Tikaram; *Sweet Keeper* . . . . (Reprise)

DAYS OF THE WEEK: TUESDAY

*See Also: **DAYS: GENERAL, MONTHS & DATES (various), TIME:
GENERAL, TIME: SPECIFIC***

Everything's Tuesday
Chairmen Of The Board; *Didn't It Blow Your Mind: Soul Hits Of The
'70s-#3-C.* . . . . (Rhino)
Lady Madonna
Beatles; *Beatles 1* . . . . (Capitol)
Hey Jude. . . . . (Capitol)
Past Masters-Volume Two . . . . (Parlophone)
The Beatles/1967-1970. . . . . (Capitol)
Wings; *Wings Over America.* . . . . (Capitol)
Love You Til Tuesday
David Bowie; *David Bowie-London Collector-Starting Point* . . . . . . (London)
Love You Till Tuesday . . . . (London)
No More Booze (On Tuesdays)
Freewheelers; *Freewheelers* . . . . (David Geffen Co.)
Ruby Tuesday
Rolling Stones; *Between The Buttons* . . . . (Abkco)
Flashpoint . . . . (Virgin)
Flowers. . . . . (Abkco)
Hot Rocks 1964-1971. . . . . (Abkco)
Singles Collection-The London Years . . . . (Abkco)
Through The Past, Darkly (Big Hits Vol. 2) . . . . (Abkco)
She Came In Through The Bathroom Window
Beatles; *Abbey Road* . . . . (Parlophone)
Beatles-Box Set. . . . . (Capitol)
Joe Cocker; *Joe Cocker Live* . . . . (Capitol)
Joe Cocker! . . . . (A&M)
Joe Cocker-Classics-#4 . . . . (A&M)
Mad Dogs & Englishmen . . . . (A&M)
Sun Comes Up, It's Tuesday
Cowboy Junkies; *Caution Horses* . . . . (RCA)
Sweet Tuesday Morning
Badfinger; *Straight Up* . . . . (Apple)

Tuesday Afternoon
Moody Blues; *Caught Live Plus Five* .... (Polydor)
Days Of Future Passed .... (Polydor)
ST/1969 .... (Polydor)
This Is The Moody Blues .... (Polydor)
Tuesday At Ten
Count Basie; *Essential Count Basie-#3* .... (Columbia)
Tuesday Heartbreak
Stevie Wonder; *Talking Book* .... (Motown)
Tuesday Next
Stan Getz; *Billy Highstreet Samba* .... (Emarcy)
Tuesday Wednesday
Woodentops; *Wooden Foot Cops On The Highway* .... (Columbia)
Tuesday's Child
Trouble; *Run To The Light* .... (Metal Blade)
Tuesday's Dead
Cat Stevens; *Cat Stevens-Classics-#24* .... (A&M)
Teaser And The Firecat .... (A&M)
Tuesday's Gone
Hank Williams, Jr.; *Skynyrd Frynds-C* .... (MCA)
Wild Streak .... (WB/Curb)
Lynyrd Skynyrd; *Gold & Platinum* .... (MCA)
One More From The Road .... (MCA)
Pronounced Leh-nerd Skin-nerd. .... (MCA)

DAYS OF THE WEEK: WEDNESDAY

See Also: **DAYS: GENERAL, MONTHS & DATES (various), TIME: GENERAL, TIME: SPECIFIC**

Ash Wednesday
Shivaree; *I Oughtta Give You A Shot...* .... (Capitol)
Big Wednesday
Surf M.C.'s; *Surf Or Die* .... (Profile)
Full Forever
Goo Goo Dolls; *Dizzy Up The Girl* .... (Warner Sunset/Reprise)
Lady Madonna
Beatles; *Beatles 1* .... (Capitol)
Hey Jude .... (Capitol)
Past Masters-Volume Two .... (Parlophone)
The Beatles/1967-1970 .... (Capitol)
Wings; *Wings Over America* .... (Capitol)
She's Leaving Home
Al Jarreau; *All Fly Home* .... (Warner Bros.)
Beatles; *Beatles-Box Set* .... (Capitol)
Beatles-Love Songs .... (Capitol)
Sgt. Pepper's Lonely Hearts Club Band .... (Capitol)
Tuesday Wednesday
Woodentops; *Wooden Foot Cops On The Highway* .... (Columbia)
Wednesday
Detroit Emeralds; *Feel The Need* .... (Westbound)
Wednesday Car
Johnny Cash; *Rambler* .... (Columbia)
Wednesday Evening Blues
John Lee Hooker; *Black Snake* .... (Fantasy)
John Lee Hooker .... (Everest)
That's My Story .... (Riverside)
World's Greatest Blues Singer .... (Vee-Jay)
Wednesday Morning, 3 AM
Simon & Garfunkel; *Collected Works* .... (Columbia)
Wednesday Morning 3 A.M. .... (Columbia)

DAYS: GENERAL, Daytime, Multiple Days

See Also: **AFTERNOON, DAYS OF THE WEEK (various), MONTHS & DATES (various), MORNING, NIGHT, TIME: GENERAL, TIME: SPECIFIC, WEEKEND**

24-7 Man
Robert Cray Band; *Take Your Shoes Off* .... (Rykodisc)
6, 8, 12
Brian McKnight; *Back At One* .... (Motown)
All Day And All Of The Night
Kinks; *British Rock-#1-C* .... (Original Sound)
God Save The Kinks! .... (Castle Music America)
History Of British Rock-#2-C .... (Rhino)
All Those Yesterdays
Pearl Jam; *Yield* .... (Epic)
American Pie
Don McLean; *American Pie* .... (EMI)
Best Of Don McLean. .... (EMI)
Greatest Hits Then & Now .... (EMI)
ST/Born On The Fourth Of July .... (MCA)
Madonna; *ST/The Next Big Thing* .... (Maverick)

Another Day Goes By
Dakota Moon; *Dakota Moon* .... (Elektra)
Bad Day
Fuel; *Now That's What I Call Music!-#8-C* .... (Virgin)
Something Like Human .... (Epic)
Banana Boat (Day-O)
Harry Belafonte; *Belafonte '89* .... (EMI)
Nipper's Greatest Hits Of The '50s-#1-C .... (RCA)
Kinks; *Everybody's In Show-Biz* .... (Rhino)
Be Like That
3 Doors Down; *Better Life* .... (Republic/Universal)
Now That's What I Call Music!-#8-C .... (Virgin)
Beautiful Day
U2; *All That You Can't Leave Behind* .... (Interscope)
Now That's What I Call Music!-#6-C .... (Virgin)
Best Day
George Strait; *Latest Greatest Straitest Hits* ...... (MCA)
Better Days
Bruce Springsteen; *Bruce Springsteen's Greatest Hits* .... (Columbia)
Lucky Town .... (Columbia)
Better Days (And The Bottom Drops Out)
Citizen King; *Mobile Estates* .... (Warner Bros.)
Boy In The Bubble
Paul Simon; *Graceland* .... (Warner Bros.)
Brand New Day
Sting; *Brand New Day* .... (A&M)
Cold Day In July
Dixie Chicks; *Fly* .... (Monument)
Joy White; *Between Midnight & Hindsight* .... (Columbia)
Ray Price; *For The Good Times/I Won't Mention It Again* .... (Columbia)
Suzy Bogguss; *Voices In The Wind* .... (Liberty)
Dancing Days
Led Zeppelin; *Houses Of The Holy* .... (Atlantic)
Stone Temple Pilots; *Encomium: Tribute To Led Zeppelin-C* .... (Atlantic)
Day After Day
Pretenders; *Pretenders II* .... (Sire)
Pretenders-The Singles .... (Sire)
Day After Day
Alan Parsons Project; *I Robot* .... (Arista)
Day After Day
China Crisis; *Diary Of A Hollow Horse* .... (A&M)
Day After Day
Def Leppard; *Euphoria* .... (Mercury)
Day I Tried To Live, The
Soundgarden; *A-Sides* .... (A&M)
Superunknown. .... (A&M)
Day In The Life, A
Beatles; *Sgt. Pepper's Lonely Hearts Club Band* ..... (Capitol)
ST/Imagine: John Lennon .... (Capitol)
The Beatles/1967-1970 .... (Capitol)
Day In, Day Out
David Kersh; *Goodnight Sweetheart* .... (Curb)
Daylight Fading
Counting Crows; *Recovering The Satellites* ...... (David Geffen Co.)
Days Of Our Livez
Bone Thugs-N-Harmony; *The Collection-#1* .... (Ruthless)
Days Of The Week
Stone Temple Pilots; *Shangri-La-Dee-Da* .... (Atlantic)
Daysleeper
R.E.M.; *Up* .... (Warner Bros.)
Dear Prudence
Beatles; *The Beatles (White Album)* .... (Capitol)
Siouxsie And The Banshees; *Hyaena.* .... (Geffen)
Nocturne .... (Geffen)
Don't Take It Personal (Just One Of Dem Days)
Monica; *Miss Thang.* .... (Rowdy/Arista)
Doo-Wah Days
Mickey Gilley; *Back To Basics* .... (Epic)
More Hot Country Requests-C .... (Epic)
One & Only .... (Epic)
Eight Days A Week
Beatles; *Beatles 1* .... (Capitol)
Beatles VI .... (Capitol)
Beatles-20 Greatest Hits .... (Capitol)
The Beatles/1962-1966 .... (Capitol)
Every Day
Stevie Nicks; *Trouble In Shangri-La* .... (Reprise)
Every Day Of My Life
McGuire Sisters; *McGuire Sisters' Greatest Hits* .... (MCA)
McGuire Sisters-Anthology. .... (MCA)
Every Day Of The Week
Jade; *Mind, Body & Song* .... (Giant)
ST/Beverly Hills, 90210-College Years .... (Giant)
Everyday
Dave Matthews Band; *America: A Tribute To Heroes-C* .... (Interscope)
Everyday .... (RCA)

Everyday (I Have The Blues)
Tony Bennett with Stevie Wonder; *Playin' With My Friends-Bennett Sings The Blues-C* . . . . . (Columbia)
Everyday Is A Winding Road
Sheryl Crow; *1998 Grammy Nominees-C* . . . . . (MCA)
Sheryl Crow . . . . . (A&M)
Flying
Chris Isaak; *Speak Of The Devil* . . . . . (Reprise)
Foggy Day
Billie Holiday; *All Or Nothing At All* . . . . . (Verve)
Dick Hyman; *Music Of 1937-Maybeck Recital Hall-#3* . . . . . (Concord Jazz)
Ella Fitzgerald; *Ella In Rome-Birthday Concert* . . . . . (Verve)
George & Ira Gershwin Songbook . . . . . (Verve)
Ella Fitzgerald & Joe Pass; *Take Love Easy* . . . . . (Pablo)
Ella Fitzgerald & Louis Armstrong; *Ella & Louis* . . . . . (Verve)
Frank Sinatra; *Songs For Young Lovers & Swing Easy* . . . . . (Capitol)
Fred Astaire; *Fred Astaire Sings* . . . . . (MCA)
Starring Fred Astaire . . . . . (Columbia)
Judy Garland; *Judy Garland-At Carnegie Hall* . . . . . (Capitol)
Wynton Marsalis; *Marsalis Standard Time-#1* . . . . . (Columbia)
Friday On My Mind
David Bowie; *Bowie Pin Ups* . . . . . (Rykodisc)
Easybeats; *Best Of The Easybeats* . . . . . (Rhino)
Nuggets-Classic Collection From The Psychedelic '60s-C . . . . . (Rhino)
Get Born Again
Alice In Chains; *Nothing Safe* . . . . . (Columbia)
Gloria: The Enchantment Medley
Jesse Powell; *Jesse Powell* . . . . . (Silas)
Glycerine
Bush; *Sixteen Stone* . . . . . (Trauma)
Good Day Sunshine
Beatles; *Beatles-Box Set* . . . . . (Capitol)
Revolver . . . . . (Capitol)
Good Day To Run
Darryl Worley; *Hard Rain Don't Last* . . . . . (DreamWorks/SKG)
Happy Days Are Here Again
Barbra Streisand; *A Happening In Central Park* . . . . . (Columbia)
Barbra Streisand's Greatest Hits . . . . . (Columbia)
One Voice . . . . . (Columbia)
The Barbra Streisand Album . . . . . (Columbia)
Leo Reisman & His Orchestra; *Nipper's Greatest Hits Of The '30s-#1-C* . . . . . (RCA)
Hard Day's Night, A
Beatles; *Beatles 1* . . . . . (Capitol)
Beatles-20 Greatest Hits . . . . . (Capitol)
ST/A Hard Day's Night . . . . . (Capitol)
The Beatles At The Hollywood Bowl . . . . . (Capitol)
The Beatles/1962-1966 . . . . . (Capitol)
Heartbroke Every Day
Lonestar; *Lonestar* . . . . . (BNA)
Here's That Rainy Day
Frank Sinatra; *The Capitol Years* . . . . . (Capitol)
Gene Ammons; *The Boss Is Back* . . . . . (Prestige)
Kenny Rankin; *Kenny Rankin Album* . . . . . (Little David)
Rosemary Clooney; *Rosemary Clooney Sings Ballads* . . . . . (Concord Jazz)
Tony Bennett; *Perfectly Frank* . . . . . (Columbia)
Hero Of The Day
Metallica; *Load* . . . . . (Elektra)
Heroes
David Bowie; *Bridge School Concerts-#1* . . . . . (Reprise)
Changesbowie . . . . . (Rykodisc)
The Concert For New York City-C . . . . . (Columbia)
The Singles-1969-1993 . . . . . (Rykodisc)
Heroes
Wallflowers; *ST/Godzilla-The Album* . . . . . (Epic/Sony Music Soundtrax)
How Beautiful The Days
Original Broadway Cast; *The Most Happy Fella* . . . . . (Sony Music Classical)
I Can See Clearly Now
Gladys Knight & The Pips; *Gladys Knight & The Pips' Greatest Hits* . . . . . (Buddah)
Imagination . . . . . (Right Stuff)
On & On . . . . . (Fifty One West)
Johnny Nash; *Billboard Top Rock 'N' Roll Hits-1972-C* . . . . . (Rhino)
Rock Artifacts-From The Vaults-#2-C . . . . . (Legacy)
I Got Stripes
Johnny Cash; *Johnny Cash-16 Biggest Hits-#2* . . . . . (Legacy)
I'm Waiting For The Day
Beach Boys; *Pet Sounds* . . . . . (Capitol)
The Pet Sounds Sessions: A 30th Anniversary Collection . . . . . (Capitol)
Irish Have A Great Day Tonight, The
Vernon Stiles Quartet; *Music From The New York Stage (1890-1920)-#4-1917-1920-C* . . . . . (Pearl)
It's A Great Day To Be Alive
Travis Tritt; *Down The Road I Go* . . . . . (Columbia)
It's A Hap-Hap-Happy Day
Dick Todd; *Dick Todd: The Canadian Crosby-His Greatest Recordings* . . . . . (Living Era)
Just Another Day
John Mellencamp; *Mr. Happy Go Lucky* . . . . . (Mercury)
Just Another Day In Paradise
Phil Vassar; *Phil Vassar* . . . . . (Arista)
Ladder
Joan Osborne; *Lilith Fair-A Celebration Of Women In Music-C* . . . . . (Arista)
Relish . . . . . (Blue Gorilla/Mercury)
Last Day, The
Marilyn Scott; *Avenues Of Love* . . . . . (Warner Bros.)
Lately
Divine; *Fairy Tales* . . . . . (Pendulum)
Lazy Day
Spanky & Our Gang; *Best Of Spanky & Our Gang* . . . . . (Rhino)
Lazy Days
Enya; *A Day Without Rain* . . . . . (Reprise)
London Rain (Nothing Heals Like You Do)
Heather Nova; *Siren* . . . . . (Big Cat)
Songs From Dawson's Creek . . . . . (Sony Music Soundtrax)
Lonely Days
Bee Gees; *Bee Gees-Gold* . . . . . (Polydor)
Here At Last...Bee Gees...Live . . . . . (Polydor)
One Night Only . . . . . (Polydor)
Lonesome Day Blues
Bob Dylan; *''Love And Theft''* . . . . . (Columbia)
Long Day
Matchbox Twenty; *Yourself Or Someone Like You* . . . . . (Lava)
Long December
Counting Crows; *Recovering The Satellites* . . . . . (David Geffen Co.)
Longest Day
Arthur Fiedler; *Motion Picture Classics-#2* . . . . . (RCA Victor)
Mitch Miller; *Mitch Miller-The Gang & Orchestra-Greatest Hits* . . . (Columbia)
Paul Anka; *Paul Anka's 21 Golden Hits* . . . . . (RCA)
Lord I Hope This Day Is Good
Don Williams; *Best Of Don Williams-#3* . . . . . (MCA)
Especially For You . . . . . (MCA)
Lee Ann Womack; *Grand Ole Opry-75 Years-#1-C* . . . . . (MCA)
Love Will Be Waiting
Kevon Edmonds; *24/7* . . . . . (RCA)
Love You For A Day
Ricky Martin; *Ricky Martin* . . . . . (Columbia)
Mama Said
Shirelles; *Original Rock 'N' Roll Hits Of The '60s-C* . . . . . (Roulette)
Shirelles' Greatest Hits . . . . . (Everest)
Shirelles-Anthology 1959-1964 . . . . . (Rhino)
Shirelles-Classics . . . . . (Bac-Trac)
Super Oldies Of The '60s-#3-C . . . . . (Audio Fidelity)
Many A New Day
Original Cast; *Oklahoma!* . . . . . (MCA)
Memory
Original Broadway Cast; *Cats* . . . . . (Geffen)
New Day Yesterday, A
Jethro Tull; *Best Of Jethro Tull-The Anniversary Collection* . . . . . (Chrysalis)
Stand Up . . . . . (Chrysalis)
Night And Day
Bette Midler; *Some People's Lives* . . . . . (Atlantic)
Billie Holiday; *Legacy Box-1933-1958* . . . . . (Columbia)
Ella Fitzgerald; *Cole Porter Songbook* . . . . . (Verve)
Frank Sinatra; *Nipper's Greatest Hits Of The '40s-#1-C* . . . . . (RCA)
Sinatra & Strings . . . . . (Reprise)
Sinatra Reprise-The Very Good Years . . . . . (Reprise)
Sinatra: A Man And His Music . . . . . (Reprise)
The Capitol Years . . . . . (Capitol)
The Reprise Collection . . . . . (Reprise)
Fred Astaire; *Cheek To Cheek* . . . . . (Pro-Arte)
Steppin' Out-Astaire Sings . . . . . (Verve)
Tony Bennett; *Perfectly Frank* . . . . . (Columbia)
U2; *Red Hot + Blue-Tribute To Cole Porter-C* . . . . . (Chrysalis)
Night We Called It A Day
Diana Krall; *The Look Of Love* . . . . . (Impulse!)
Frank Sinatra; *Night We Called It A Day* . . . . . (Capitol)
Where Are You? . . . . . (Capitol)
Tommy Dorsey & Frank Sinatra; *Radio Years 1940-1942* . . . . . (RCA)
Oh Happy Day
Edwin Hawkins Singers; *Didn't It Blow Your Mind: Soul Hits Of The '70s-#1-C* . . . . . (Rhino)
Super Hits-#3-C . . . . . (Gusto)
Five Satins; *Five Satins Sing Their Greatest Hits* . . . . . (Collectables)
Oh Happy Day
Lawrence Welk; *Champagne Music Of Lawrence Welk* . . . . . (Universal)
Old Days/Old Ways
Ronnie Laws; *Dream A Little* . . . . . (HDH)
Once A Day
Connie Smith; *Billboard Top Country Hits-1964-C* . . . . . (Rhino)
Connie Smith-Super Hits . . . . . (RCA)
Essential Connie Smith . . . . . (RCA)
Once-A-Year Day!
Original Cast; *ST/Pajama Game* . . . . . (Collectables)
One Fine Day
Carpenters; *From The Top* . . . . . (A&M)
Now & Then . . . . . (A&M)

Chiffons; *Best Of The Chiffons* ....(Laurie)
Chiffons-Golden Classics ....(Collectables)
Collectables Presents The History Of Rock-#9-C ....(Collectables)
Oldies But Goodies-#12-C ....(Original Sound)

One More Day
New Edition; *Home Again* ....(MCA)

One More Day
Diamond Rio; *One More Day* ....(Arista)

One Sweet Day
Mariah Carey; *Daydream* ....(Columbia)
Mariah Carey & Boyz II Men; *1996 Grammy Nominees-C* ....(Columbia)

One Week
Barenaked Ladies; *Stunt* ....(Reprise)
Totally Hits-#1-C ....(Arista)

Only On Days That End In "Y"
Clay Walker; *Hypnotize The Moon* ....(Giant)

Perfect Day
Collective Soul; *Blender* ....(Atlantic)

Precious Time
Van Morrison; *Back On Top* ....(Point Blank/Virgin)

Rainy Day, Dream Away
Jimi Hendrix Experience; *Electric Ladyland* ....(Reprise)

Reason, The
Celine Dion with Carole King; *Let's Talk About Love-C* .... (550 Music)

Rest Of My Days
Indigenous; *Circle* ....(Pachyderm)

Rock And Roll All Nite
Kiss; *Alive!* ....(Mercury)
Double Platinum ....(Mercury)
Dressed To Kill ....(Mercury)
Heavy Metal Memories-C ....(Rhino)
Smashes, Thrashes & Hits ....(Mercury)
The Originals ....(Casablanca)

Rockaway The Days
Bruce Springsteen; *Tracks* ....(Columbia)

San Francisco Days
Chris Isaak; *San Francisco Days* ....(Reprise)

School Days
Chuck Berry; *Best Of Chuck Berry* ....(Gusto)
Billboard Top Rock 'N' Roll Hits-1957-C ....(Rhino)
Chuck Berry-Golden Hits ....(Mercury)
ST/Rock 'N' Roll High School ....(Sire)

School Days
Original Soundtrack; *School Days-Kids Classics* ....(Benson)

See Saw
Moonglows; *Moonglows-Their Greatest Hits* ....(Chess)

Seven Days
Mary J. Blige; *Share My World* ....(MCA)
The Tour ....(MCA)

Simple Days
Babyface; *The Day* ....(Epic)

Some Days You Gotta Dance
Dixie Chicks; *Fly* ....(Monument)

Some Of These Days
Cab Calloway; *Masters Of Jazz-#6-Male Vocal Classics-C* ....(Rhino)
Leon Redbone; *On The Track* ....(Warner Bros.)
Louis Armstrong; *Louis Armstrong And The Big Bands-1928-1930* .....(DRG)
Mills Brothers; *Close Harmony* ....(Ranwood)
Sophie Tucker; *Legendary Entertainers* ....(Pro-Arte)
Those Wonderful Years-Roaring '20s-C ....(JCI Assoc. Labels)

Sour Girl
Stone Temple Pilots; *No. 4* ....(Atlantic)

Southside
Moby featuring Gwen Stefani; *12'' Maxi Single* ....(V2)
Play ....(V2)

Summer Days
Roger Whittaker; *Best Of Roger Whittaker* ....(RCA)
Reflections Of Love ....(RCA)

Summer Days
Partridge Family; *Partridge Family's Greatest Hits* ....(Arista)

Summer Days
Bob Dylan; *''Love And Theft''* ....(Columbia)

Summer Of '69
Bryan Adams; *Reckless* ....(A&M)

Sweetest Days
Vanessa Williams; *The Sweetest Days* .... (Uptown/MCA)

Thank The Lord For The Night Time
Neil Diamond; *Glory Road-1968-1972* ....(MCA)
Hot August Night II ....(Columbia)
Neil Diamond-Classics (Early Years) ....(Columbia)
Neil Diamond-Gold ....(MCA)
Neil Diamond's Greatest Hits-1966-1992 ....(Columbia)

Thankyou
Dido; *No Angel* ....(Arista)
Totally Hits 2001-C ....(Arista)

Theme From "Happy Days"
Original Soundtrack; *Television's Greatest Hits-#3-1970s & 1980s-C* ....(TVT)

Theme From "One Day At A Time"
Original Soundtrack; *CBS: The First 50 Years* ....(TVT)

Theme From "The Days And Nights Of Molly Dodd"
Original Soundtrack; *Television's Greatest Hits-#7-Cable Ready-C* .....(TVT)

There Will Come A Day
Faith Hill; *America: A Tribute To Heroes-C* .... (Interscope)
Breathe ....(Warner Bros.)

Thirty Days In The Hole
Gov't Mule; *Live With A Little Help From Our Friends-Collector's
Edition* ....(Capricorn)
Humble Pie; *Best Of Humble Pie* ....(A&M)
Humble Pie-Classics-#14 ....(A&M)
Rock This Way Live-#1-C ....(BMG Special Prod.)
Smokin' ....(A&M)
Mr. Big; *Mr. Big* ....(Atlantic)

This Everyday Love
Rascal Flatts; *Rascal Flatts* ....(Lyric Street)

This Weekend
Ann Nesby; *I'm Here For You* ....(Perspective/A&M)

Wasted Days And Wasted Nights
Freddy Fender; *Before The Next Teardrop Falls* ....(Universal)
Best Of Freddy Fender ....(MCA)
Country Comes To Carnegie Hall-C ....(MCA)
Happy Trails ....(United Artists)
Texas Country ....(United Artists)
The Freddy Fender Collection ....(MCA)

What A Diff'rence A Day Makes
Dinah Washington; *What A Diff'rence A Day Makes* ....(Mercury)

Where The Blue Of The Night Meets The Gold Of The Day
Bing Crosby; *All-Time Best Of* ....(Curb)
Best Of Bing Crosby ....(MCA)
Where The Blue Of The Night Meets The Gold Of The Day .... (Biograph)

Wiser Time
Black Crowes; *Amorica* ....(American)

DEATH, Bury, Cemetery, Funerals, Graves
See Also: ANGELS, CAPITAL PUNISHMENT, DANGER &
DISASTER, DEVILS, DROWN, FLOOD, GOD, HEAVEN, HELL,
KILL, LEAVING, LIFE, LOSING & LOSS, PAIN & HEALING, ROAD
ACCIDENTS, SADNESS, SPIRITS, SUICIDE, WAR

(Don't Fear) The Reaper
Blue Oyster Cult; *Agents Of Fortune* ....(Columbia)
Extraterrestrial Live ....(Columbia)
Metalmania-C ....(Columbia)
Some Enchanted Evening ....(Columbia)

(I Just) Died In Your Arms
Cutting Crew; *Broadcast* ....(Virgin)
Chicken Soup For The Woman's Soul-C ....(Rhino)
MTV-VH1 Powerplayers-C ....(EMI)

18 Til I Die
Bryan Adams; *18 Til I Die* ....(A&M)

1979
Smashing Pumpkins; *Mellon Collie And The Infinite Sadness* .... (Virgin)
The Aeroplane Flies High ....(Virgin)

50,000 Names
George Jones; *The Rock: Stone Cold Country 2001* .... (BNA)

6 Underground
Sneaker Pimps; *Becoming X* ....(Virgin)

7 Deadly Sins
Traveling Wilburys; *Traveling Wilburys-Vol. 3* ....(Wilbury/Warner Bros.)

7 Deadly Sins
Mary's Danish; *Circa* ....(Morgan Creek)

Aberfan Coal Tip Tragedy
Thom Parrott; *Best Of Broadside 1962-1968: Anthems Of The American
Underground From The Pages Of Broadside
Magazine-C* .... (Smithsonian Folkways)

About To Die
Procol Harum; *Home* ....(A&M)

Ain't No Grave Can Hold My Body Down
Odetta; *Essential Odetta* ....(Vanguard)
One Grain Of Sand ....(Vanguard)

All Dead All Dead
Queen; *News Of The World* ....(Hollywood)

Alone Again (Naturally)
Gilbert O'Sullivan; *Best Of Gilbert O'Sullivan* ....(Rhino)
Billboard Top Rock 'N' Roll Hits-1972-C ....(Rhino)

American Pie
Don McLean; *American Pie* ....(EMI)
Best Of Don McLean ....(EMI)
Greatest Hits Then & Now ....(EMI)
ST/Born On The Fourth Of July ....(MCA)
Madonna; *ST/The Next Big Thing* ....(Maverick)

Amigone
Goo Goo Dolls; *Dizzy Up The Girl* .... (Warner Sunset/Reprise)

And When I Die
Blood, Sweat & Tears; *Blood, Sweat & Tears* ....(Columbia)

Blood, Sweat & Tears Greatest Hits . . . . (Columbia)
Blood, Sweat & Tears In Concert. . . . . (Columbia)
Laura Nyro; First Songs . . . . (Columbia)
Live At The Bottom Line . . . . (Cypress)

Angel
Jimi Hendrix; Cry Of Love . . . . (Reprise)
Experience Hendrix: The Best Of Jimi Hendrix . . . . (MCA)
First Rays Of The New Rising Sun . . . .(MCA)
Rod Stewart; Best Of Rod Stewart . . . . (Mercury)

Angel Band
Emmylou Harris; Angel Band . . . .(Warner Bros.)
Stanley Brothers; ST/O Brother, Where Art Thou?. . . . . (Mercury)
Stanley Brothers & The Clinch Mountain Boys; Best Of Bluegrass-#1-
Standards-C . . . . (Mercury)

Angel's Eye
Aerosmith; ST/Charlie's Angels . . . . (Columbia)

Angels In Waiting
Tammy Cochran; Tammy Cochran. . . . .(Epic)

Angel's Son
Strait Up featuring Lajon of Sevendust; Strait Up-C . . . . (Immortal/Virgin)

Another Man Done Gone
Pete Seeger/Memphis Slim/Willie Dixon; Pete Seeger At The
Village Gate . . . . (Smithsonian Folkways)

Another Man Done Gone
Jorma Kaukonen & Tom Hobson; Quah. . . . . (Relix)

Another One Bites The Dust
Queen; Queen's Greatest Hits I & II . . . . (Hollywood)
The Game. . . . . (Hollywood)

Art Of Dying
George Harrison; All Things Must Pass . . . . (Parlophone)

At My Funeral
Crash Test Dummies; The Ghosts That Haunt Me . . . . (Arista)

Atlantic City
Bruce Springsteen; Bruce Springsteen's Greatest Hits. . . . . (Columbia)
Nebraska . . . . (Columbia)

Axe Victim
Be Bop Deluxe; Axe Victim. . . . . (Capitol)
Best Of And The Rest Of Be Bop Deluxe . . . . (Capitol)

Baby's In Black
Beatles; Beatles '65 . . . . (Capitol)
Beatles-Box Set . . . . (Capitol)
For Sale . . . . (Capitol)

Bad Boyz
Shyne featuring Levy, Barrington; Shyne . . . . (Bad Boy/Arista)

Ballad Of Bonnie And Clyde
Georgie Fame; History Of British Rock-#8-C. . . . . (Rhino)

Ballad Of The Green Berets
Barry Sadler; Cruisin'-1966-C . . . .(Increase)
Hits Of The Sixties-C . . . . (Intercom Music)
More American Graffiti-#4-C . . . . (MCA)
Nipper's Greatest Hits Of The '60s-#2-C . . . . (RCA)
Super Hits-#3-C . . . . (Gusto)

Bang The Drum Slowly
Emmylou Harris; Red Dirt Girl . . . . (Nonesuch)

Bang, You're Dead
Bette Midler; Live At Last . . . . (Atlantic)

Barbara Allen
Joan Baez; Ballad Book-#2 . . . . (Vanguard)
Joan Baez, Vol. 2 . . . . (Vanguard)
The Joan Baez Ballad Book . . . . (Vanguard)
Tom Rush; Blues Songs & Ballads . . . . (Fantasy)
Tom Rush . . . . (Fantasy)

Beaches Of Cheyenne
Garth Brooks; Fresh Horses . . . . (Capitol)
Limited Series Box . . . . (Capitol)

Beginning, The
Keb' Mo'; The Door . . . . (550/Epic/Okeh)

Better Off Dead
Elton John; Captain Fantastic And The Brown Dirt Cowboy . . . . (Polydor)

Better Off Dead
Ice Cube; AmeriKKKa's Most Wanted . . . . (Priority)

Big Bad John
Jimmy Dean; American Originals-Jimmy Dean . . . . (Columbia)
Billboard Top Country Hits-1961-C . . . . (Rhino)
Columbia Country Classics-#3-Americana-C . . . . (Columbia)
Jimmy Dean's Greatest Hits . . . . (Columbia)

Big Money
Garth Brooks; Scarecrow . . . . (Capitol)

Billy Don't Be A Hero
Bo Donaldson & The Heywoods; Super Hits Of The '70s-Have A Nice
Day-#13-C . . . . (Rhino)

Blue Tail Fly
Burl Ives; Best Of Burl Ives. . . . .(MCA)
Pete Seeger; 20 Golden Pieces Of Pete Seeger . . . . (Bulldog)

Bluebird Is Dead
Electric Light Orchestra; Afterglow . . . .(Epic)
On The Third Day . . . . (Jet)

Body Count
Ice-T; Body Count. . . . .(Warner Bros.)

Body To Dust
Joan Armatrading; Back To The Night. . . . . (A&M)

Bohemian Rhapsody
Braids; Here We Come . . . . (Big Beat)
ST/High School High . . . . (Big Beat)
Queen; A Night At The Opera . . . . (Hollywood)
Classic Queen . . . . (Hollywood)
Live At Wembley '86 . . . . (Hollywood)
ST/Wayne's World . . . . (Reprise)

Brick
Ben Folds Five; Whatever And Ever Amen . . . .(Caroline/550)

Broadway
Goo Goo Dolls; Dizzy Up The Girl . . . .(Warner Sunset/Reprise)

Burden In My Hand
Soundgarden; Down On The Upside . . . . (A&M)

Bury Me Beneath The Willow
Jimmie Davis; Best Of Jimmie Davis. . . . . (MCA)
Ricky Skaggs; Skaggs & Rice-The Essential Old-Time Country Duet
Recordings. . . . . (Sugar Hill)
Wilma Lee Cooper; Wilma Lee Cooper. . . . . (Rounder)
Woody Guthrie; Woody Guthrie-#1 & 2 . . . . (Collectables)

Bury Me Not On The Lone Prairie
Jimmy C. Newman; Cajun Cowboy . . . .(Plantation)

Bury My Body
Animals; Best Of The Animals. . . . .(Abkco)

But I Might Die Tonight
Cat Stevens; Tea For The Tillerman . . . . (A&M)

Cadillac Ranch
Bruce Springsteen; Live 1975-1985 . . . . (Legacy)
The River . . . . (Columbia)
Bruce Springsteen & The E Street Band; Bruce Springsteen & The E Street
Band Live/1975-85 . . . . (Legacy)
Nitty Gritty Dirt Band; More Great Dirt-Best Of-#3 . . . . (Warner Bros.)
Plain Dirt Fashion . . . . (Warner Bros.)

Candle In The Wind
Elton John; Goodbye Yellow Brick Road. . . . .(Polydor)
Live In Australia With The Melbourne Symphony Orchestra . . . . (MCA)
Your Songs . . . .(Polydor)

Candle In The Wind 1997
Elton John; Candle In The Wind 1997 (Diana, Princess Of Wales)
(Single) . . . . (Rocket)

Careful With That Axe Eugene
Pink Floyd; Relics . . . . (Capitol)
Ummagumma . . . . (Capitol)

Carrion
Fiona Apple; Tidal . . . .(Clean Slate/Work)

Christmas Shoes
Newsong; Sheltering Tree . . . . (Benson/Jive)

Clementine
Bobby Darin; Bobby Darin-At The Copa . . . . (Bainbridge)
The Bobby Darin Story . . . .(Atlantic)
Original Soundtrack; Children's Favorites . . . .(Kid Rhino/Rhino 4 Kids)

Cockles & Mussels
Emily Mitchell; The Irish Album. . . . . (RCA)

Coffee, Donuts & Death
Paris; Sleeping With The Enemy . . . . (Scarface)

D.O.A.
Bloodrock; Heavy Metal Memories-C. . . . . (Rhino)

D.O.A.
Loverboy; Loverboy . . . . (Columbia)

D.O.A.
Van Halen; Van Halen II . . . . (Warner Bros.)

Daddy Never Was The Cadillac Kind
Confederate Railroad; Notorious . . . .(Atlantic)

Daddy's Last Letter (Private First Class John H. McCormick)
Tex Ritter; 45-#1267 . . . . (Capitol)

Darlin' Corey
Ricky Skaggs with Bruce Hornsby; Big Mon: The Songs Of Bill
Monroe-C . . . . (Skaggs Family)

Darling Lorraine
Paul Simon; You're The One . . . . (Warner Bros.)

Dead & Alive
Dead Boys; We Have Come For Your Children . . . . (Sire)

Dead & Bloated
Stone Temple Pilots; Core. . . . .(Atlantic)

Dead Babies
Alice Cooper; Killer . . . . (Warner Bros.)

Dead Bodies Everywhere
Korn; Follow The Leader . . . . (Immortal/Epic)

Dead By X-Mas
Hanoi Rocks; Self-Destruction Blues . . . . (Geffen)

Dead Cat
Shelleyan Orphan; Humroot . . . . (Columbia)

Dead Cat Alley
Dirty White Boy; Bad Reputation . . . . (Polydor)

Dead Cat On The Line
Lucky Peterson; Lucky Strikes! . . . . (Alligator)

Dead Flowers
Rolling Stones; *Sticky Fingers*. . . . .(Virgin)
Steve Earle & The Dukes; *Shut Up And Die Like An Aviator* . . . . (MCA)
Dead Girls Of London
Frank Zappa; *You Can't Do That On Stage Anymore-#5*. . . . . (Rykodisc)
Dead Is A Risin'
Loretta Lynn; *Out Of My Head And Back In My Bed*. . . . . (MCA)
Dead Man
Asleep At The Wheel; *Asleep At The Wheel* . . . . (Epic)
Dead Man's Curve
Jan & Dean; *21 Legendary Superstars-C*. . . . .(Original Sound)
Best Of Jan & Dean . . . . (EMI)
Dead Man's Curve . . . . (EMI)
Dead Man's Hill
Indigo Girls; *Swamp Ophelia* . . . . (Epic)
Dead Next Door
Billy Idol; *Rebel Yell* . . . . (Chrysalis)
Dead Of The Night
Shawn Colvin; *Steady On* . . . . (Columbia)
Dead Of The Night
Bad Company; *Holy Water* . . . . (Atco)
Dead On Arrival
Trees; *Forrest Fires*. . . . . (Adelphi)
Dead On Arrival
Billy Idol; *Billy Idol*. . . . . (Chrysalis)
Dead Or Alive
Oingo Boingo; *Boingo Alive* . . . . (MCA)
Good For Your Soul . . . . (A&M)
Dead Or Alive
Journey; *Escape*. . . . . (Columbia)
Dead Or Alive
Deep Purple; *Nobody's Perfect* . . . . (Mercury)
Dead Or Alive
Too $hort; *Short Dog's In The House* . . . . (Jive)
Dead Puppies
Ogden Edsl; *Dr. Demento Presents The Greatest Novelty Records-#4-
1970s-C* . . . . (Rhino)
Dr. Demento Presents The Greatest Novelty Records-C . . . . (Rhino)
Dead Skunk
Loudon Wainwright III; *Dr. Demento Presents The Greatest Novelty
Records-#4-1970s-C* . . . . (Rhino)
Super Hits Of The '70s-Have A Nice Day-#10-C . . . . (Rhino)
Dear Brother
Hank Williams; *I Saw The Light* . . . . (Polydor)
Dear Uncle Sam
Loretta Lynn; *Honky Tonk Girl: The Loretta Lynn Collection* . . . . (MCA)
Loretta Lynn's Greatest Hits . . . . (MCA)
Death Alley Driver
Rainbow; *Straight Between The Eyes* . . . . (Mercury)
Death At One's Elbow
Smiths; *Strangeways Here We Come* . . . .(Sire)
Death By Misadventure
John Hiatt; *Riding With The King* . . . . (Geffen)
Death By Misadventure
Ted Nugent; *Cat Scratch Fever* . . . . (Epic)
Death Defying
Hoodoo Gurus; *Mars Needs Guitars* . . . . (Elektra)
Death Disco
Public Image Ltd.; *Greatest Hits So Far* . . . .(Virgin)
Death Don't Have No Mercy
Grateful Dead; *Live/Dead* . . . . (Warner Bros.)
Hot Tuna; *Hot Tuna*. . . . .(RCA)
Reverend Gary Davis; *Great Bluesmen At Newport-C* . . . . (Vanguard)
Death From Your TV Screen
Voice Of Destruction; *Steamroller Tactics* . . . . (Cleopatra)
Death In The Autumn Air
Michael McDermott; *620 W. Surf* . . . . (Giant)
Death Letter Blues
Leadbelly; *King Of The Twelve-String Guitar*. . . . . (Columbia)
Leadbelly . . . . (Columbia)
Death March
Faith No More; *Introduce Yourself* . . . . (Slash)
Death Of A Clown
Kinks; *Kink Kronikles* . . . . (Reprise)
Something Else . . . . (Reprise)
Death Of A Disco Dancer
Smiths; *Strangeways Here We Come* . . . .(Sire)
Death Of A Ladies' Man
Leonard Cohen; *Death Of A Ladies' Man* . . . . (Columbia)
Death Of A Salesman
Steve Goodman; *Words We Can Dance To* . . . . (Asylum)
Death Of An Unpopular Poet
Jimmy Buffett; *White Sport Coat & A Pink Crustacean* . . . . (MCA)
Death Of Hank Williams
Jack Cardwell; *Super Country Hits Of The '50s-C* . . . . (Gusto)
Death Of Harry Simms
Pete Seeger; *Essential Pete Seeger* . . . . (Vanguard)

Death Of Louis
Champion Jack Dupree; *Happy To Be Free* . . . . (Crescendo)
Death Of Mother Nature
Kansas; *Kansas* . . . .(Kirshner)
Death Of Queen Jane
Joan Baez; *Joan Baez/5* . . . .(Vanguard)
Love Song Album . . . .(Vanguard)
Death Of Titanic
James Horner; *ST/Titanic*. . . . . (Sony Music Classical)
Death On Two Legs
Queen; *A Night At The Opera*. . . . .(Hollywood)
Live Killers . . . .(Hollywood)
Death or Glory
Clash; *London Calling* . . . .(Epic)
Death Row #172
Pacific Gas & Electric; *Jailhouse Rock (Hits From The Big
House)-C* . . . . (Sony Music Special Prod.)
Death Sentence
Capitol Punishment; *Livin' On The Edge Of A Razor*. . . . .(Wrap/Ichiban)
Death Sentence
Big Daddy Kane; *Prince Of Darkness* . . . . (Cold Chillin')
Death Sound Blues
Country Joe & The Fish; *Life & Times Of Country Joe &
The Fish* . . . .(Vanguard)
Death Train
Beat Farmers; *Glad 'N' Greasy* . . . .(Rhino)
Deathwish
Police; *Regatta De Blanc* . . . .(A&M)
Die By The Sword
Slayer; *Slayer-Live-Decade Of Aggression* . . . . (Def American)
Die Nigger Die
Schoolly D; *How A Black Man Feels* . . . .(Capitol)
Die With Your Boots On
Iron Maiden; *Live After Death-World Slavery Tour* . . . .(Capitol)
Piece Of Mind . . . .(Capitol)
Die Young, Stay Pretty
Blondie; *Eat To The Beat* . . . . (Chrysalis)
Died For Love
Richard & Linda Thompson; *First Light* . . . . (Chrysalis)
Diggin' Up Bones
Randy Travis; *Storms Of Life* . . . . (Warner Bros.)
Ding Dong The Witch Is Dead
Fifth Estate; *Dick Bartley's One-Hit Wonders Of The '60s-#2-C* . . . . . .(Rhino)
Meco; *The Wizard Of Oz* . . . . (Millennium)
MGM Studio Orchestra; *ST/The Wizard Of Oz* . . . . . (Sony Music Special Prod.)
Do It Or Die
Atlanta Rhythm Section; *Underdog* . . . . (Polydor)
Do Or Die
Grace Jones; *Fame*. . . . . (Island)
Island Life . . . . (Island)
Do Or Die
Human League; *Dare*. . . . .(A&M)
Do Or Die
Captain Beyond; *Dawn Explosion* . . . . (Warner Bros.)
Doin' It To Death
James Brown; *Doin' It To Death* . . . . (Polydor)
Philly Cream; *Philly Cream* . . . . (WMOT)
Don't Take Me Alive
Steely Dan; *The Royal Scam* . . . . (MCA)
Don't Take The Girl
Tim McGraw; *Not A Moment Too Soon*. . . . .(Curb)
Tim McGraw's Greatest Hits . . . .(Curb)
Don't Take Your Guns To Town
Johnny Cash; *Billboard Top Country Hits-1959-C* . . . .(Rhino)
Columbia Country Classics-#3-Americana-C . . . .(Columbia)
Johnny Cash-16 Biggest Hits-#2 . . . .(Legacy)
Johnny Cash's Greatest Hits . . . .(Columbia)
The Man In Black-His Greatest Hits . . . .(Legacy)
Dream On
Depeche Mode; *Exciter* . . . . (Mute/Reprise)
Dreams Die Hard
Gary Morris; *Gary Morris* . . . . (Warner Bros.)
Gary Morris' Greatest Hits-#2 . . . . (Warner Bros.)
Drunk Is Better Than Dead
Push Stars; *ST/Malcolm In The Middle* . . . . (Restless)
Dyin' Crapshooter's Blues
Blind Willie McTell; *Atlanta Twelve-String* . . . . (Atlantic)
David Bromberg; *How Late'll Ya Play 'Til?* . . . . (Fantasy)
Dyin' Gambler
Blind James Campbell; *Blind James Campbell & His Nashville
Street Band*. . . . . (Arhoolie)
Dyin' Gambler's Blues
Bessie Smith; *Bessie Smith-The Complete Recordings-#2* . . . .(Legacy)
Dying Cub Fan's Last Request
Steve Goodman; *Baseball's Greatest Hits-C*. . . . .(Rhino)
Dying Miner
Woody Guthrie; *Struggle* . . . . (Smithsonian Folkways)

Dying Soldier
Christy Moore; *Christy Moore* . . . . (Atlantic)
Dying To Meet You
Judas Priest; *Best Of Judas Priest* . . . . (RCA)
   Hero Hero . . . . (RCA)
   Rocka-Rolla . . . . (RCA)
El Paso
Grateful Dead; *Steal Your Face* . . . . (Grateful Dead)
Marty Robbins; *Billboard Top Country Hits-1960-C* . . . . (Rhino)
   Gunfighter Ballads & Trail Songs . . . . (Legacy)
   Marty Robbins' Biggest Hits . . . . (Columbia)
   Radio Classics Of The '50s-C . . . . (Columbia)
   Texas Super Hits-C . . . . (Columbia)
Elephant's Graveyard
Boomtown Rats; *Boomtown Rats' Greatest Hits* . . . . (Columbia)
   Mondo Bongo . . . . (Columbia)
Elvis Is Dead
Forgotten Rebels; *Surfin' On Heroin* . . . . (Restless)
Living Colour; *Super Hits* . . . .(Epic)
End Of The Road
Boyz II Men; *Cooleyhighharmony* . . . . (Motown)
Endless Sleep
Jody Reynolds; *American Graffiti-#3-C* . . . .(MCA)
   Teenage Tragedies-C . . . . (Rhino)
Endless Sleep
Babys; *Babys* . . . .(Chrysalis)
Everlasting Glaze
Smashing Pumpkins; *Machina: The Machines Of God* . . . . (Virgin)
Every Day A Little Death
Original Cast; *Little Night Music* . . . . (Columbia)
Original London Cast; *Little Night Music* . . . . (RCA)
Everybody Gotta Go
Atlanta Rhythm Section; *Rock & Roll Alternative* . . . . (Polydor)
Farther Along
Byrds; *The Byrds* . . . . (Columbia)
Elvis Presley; *Million-Dollar Quartet* . . . . (RCA)
Flying Burrito Brothers; *Farther Along-Best Of The Flying Burrito*
   Brothers . . . . (A&M)
Rose Maddox; *Rose Of The West Coast Country* . . . . (Arhoolie)
Fields Have Turned Brown
Stanley Brothers & The Clinch Mountain Boys; *Bluegrass Super*
   Hits-C . . . . (Columbia)
Flight Of Icarus
Iron Maiden; *Live After Death-World Slavery Tour* . . . . (Capitol)
   Piece Of Mind . . . . (Capitol)
Flip The Switch
Rolling Stones; *Bridges To Babylon* . . . . (Virgin)
   No Security . . . . (Virgin)
Foggy, Foggy Dew
Burl Ives; *Best Of Burl Ives* . . . .(MCA)
Freddie's Dead
Curtis Mayfield; *Very Best Of Curtis Mayfield* . . . . (Rhino)
Fishbone; *Truth & Soul* . . . . (Columbia)
From A Buick 6
Bob Dylan; *Highway 61 Revisited* . . . . (Columbia)
Funeral For A Friend
Elton John; *Goodbye Yellow Brick Road* . . . . (Polydor)
   Here And There . . . .(Rocket)
Genocide
Judas Priest; *Hero Hero* . . . . (RCA)
   Sad Wings Of Destiny . . . . (RCA)
   Unleashed In The East . . . . (Columbia)
Get Born Again
Alice In Chains; *Nothing Safe* . . . . (Columbia)
Ghost Of You
Richard Thompson; *Richard Thompson-Best Of Capitol Years* . . . . (Capitol)
Give My Love To Rose
George Jones; *George Jones Sings The Hits Of His Country*
   Cousins . . . . (Razor & Tie)
Johnny Cash; *Johnny Cash-Sun Years* . . . . (Rhino)
Go Rest High On That Mountain
Vince Gill; *When Love Finds You* . . . .(MCA)
Golden Vanity
Pete Seeger & Arlo Guthrie; *Together In Concert* . . . . (Reprise)
Gone Away
Offspring; *Ixnay On The Hombre* . . . . (Columbia)
Goodbye Earl
Dixie Chicks; *Fly* . . . . (Monument)
Grave
Don McLean; *American Pie* . . . .(EMI)
Graveyard
Public Image Ltd.; *Second Edition* . . . . (Island)
Graveyard Blues
John Lee Hooker; *Alone* . . . . (Specialty)
Graveyard People
Traffic; *When The Eagle Flies* . . . . (Asylum)
Graveyard Shift
Sawyer Brown; *Out Goin' Cattin'* . . . . (Capitol)

Graveyard Shift
Bobby "Boris" Pickett & The Crypt-Kickers; *Monster Mash* . . . . (Out Of Print)
Graveyard Train
Creedence Clearwater Revival; *1968-1969* . . . .(Fantasy)
   Bayou Country . . . .(Fantasy)
Greatest Man I Never Knew
Reba McEntire; *For My Broken Heart* . . . . (MCA)
   Reba McEntire's Greatest Hits Volume Two . . . . (MCA)
Green Green Grass Of Home
Burl Ives; *Best Of Burl Ives-#2* . . . . (MCA)
Elvis Presley; *Elvis Presley Today* . . . . (RCA)
   Our Memories Of Elvis, Volume 2 . . . . (RCA)
George Jones; *20 Golden Pieces Of George Jones* . . . .(Bulldog)
Johnny Cash; *Johnny Cash-16 Biggest Hits-#2* . . . . (Legacy)
Tom Jones; *Country Side Of Tom Jones* . . . .(London)
   Things That Matter Most To Me . . . . (Mercury)
   Tom Jones-London Collector-Greatest Hits. . . . . (London)
Grim Reaper
Detective; *Detective* . . . . (Swan Song)
Grind
Alice In Chains; *Alice In Chains* . . . . (Columbia)
Ground Beneath Her Feet, The
U2; *ST/The Million Dollar Hotel* . . . .(Interscope)
Hand Song, The
Nickel Creek; *Nickel Creek* . . . .(Sugar Hill)
He Stopped Loving Her Today
George Jones; *All Time Legends Of Country Music-C* . . . . (Legacy)
   First Time Live! . . . . (Epic)
   George Jones-Anniversary-Ten Years Of Hits . . . . (Epic)
   Greatest Country Hits Of The '80s-1980-C . . . . (Columbia)
   Greatest Hits From The Jukebox-C . . . . (Epic)
   I Am What I Am. . . . . (Epic)
Heartbreak Hotel
Albert King; *Blues For Elvis* . . . . (Stax)
Elvis Presley; *Elvis As Recorded At Madison Square Garden.* . . . . (RCA)
   Elvis' Golden Records . . . . (RCA)
   Elvis-A Legendary Performer, Volume 1 . . . . (RCA)
   Nipper's Greatest Hits Of The '50s-#1-C . . . . (RCA)
   Worldwide 50 Gold Award Hits, Vol. 1, Parts 1 & 2 . . . . (RCA)
Stan Freberg; *Capitol Collectors Series-Stan Freberg* . . . . (Capitol)
Willie Nelson; *Greatest Hits (& Some That Will Be).* . . . . (Columbia)
   Willie Nelson & Leon Russell: One For The Road . . . . (Columbia)
Heroes Die Young
Sleeze Beez; *Screwed Blued & Tattooed.* . . . .(Atlantic)
Heroes Die Young
Waysted; *Save Your Prayers* . . . . (Capitol)
Highwayman
Glen Campbell; *Highwayman* . . . . (Capitol)
Johnny Cash with Waylon Jennings, Kris Kristofferson, Willie Nelson; *The*
   Man In Black-His Greatest Hits . . . . (Legacy)
Waylon Jennings, Willie Nelson, Johnny Cash, Kris Kristofferson; *Columbia*
   Country Classics-#3-Americana-C . . . . (Columbia)
   Johnny Cash-16 Biggest Hits-#2 . . . . (Legacy)
Willie Nelson; *Greatest Country Hits Of The '80s-1985-C.* . . . . (Columbia)
Holes In The Floor Of Heaven
Steve Wariner; *Burnin' The Roadhouse Down* . . . . (Capitol)
Honey
Bobby Goldsboro; *Billboard Top Pop Hits-1968-C* . . . . (Rhino)
   Cruisin'-1968-C. . . . . (Increase)
How Can I Help You Say Goodbye
Patty Loveless; *Only What I Feel* . . . . (Epic)
   Patty Loveless-Classics . . . . (Epic)
Howard's Dead & Gone
Weavers; *Weavers-Classics* . . . . (Vanguard)
Human Beings
Seal; *Human Being* . . . . (Warner Bros.)
Hush Hush Hush
Paula Cole; *This Fire* . . . .(Imago)
I Ain't Livin' Long Like This
Emmylou Harris; *Quarter Moon In A Ten Cent Town* . . . . (Warner Bros.)
Rodney Crowell; *I Ain't Livin' Long Like This* . . . . (Warner Bros.)
   Rodney Crowell-Collection . . . . (Warner Bros.)
Waylon Jennings; *Waylon Jennings' Greatest Hits-#2* . . . . (RCA)
   What Goes Around Comes Around . . . . (RCA)
I Am Weary (Let Me Rest)
Cox Family; *ST/O Brother, Where Art Thou?* . . . . (Mercury)
I Disappear
Metallica; *ST/Mission: Impossible 2* . . . . (Hollywood)
I Got A Mind To Give Up Living
Paul Butterfield Blues Band; *East-West* . . . . (Elektra)
I Know An Old Lady Who Swallowed A Fly
Original Soundtrack; *More Silly Songs* . . . . (Disney)
Peter, Paul & Mary; *Peter, Paul & Mommy, Too* . . . . (Warner Bros.)
I Love The Dead
Alice Cooper; *Billion Dollar Babies* . . . . (Warner Bros.)
   The Alice Cooper Show . . . . (Warner Bros.)
I Miss My Homies
Master P; *Ghetto D* . . . . (No Limit/Priority)

I Want My Baby Back
Jimmy Cross; *Teenage Tragedies-C* . . . . (Rhino)
World's Worst Records-C . . . . (Rhino)
I Wish
R. Kelly; *Now That's What I Call Music!-#6-C* . . . . (Virgin)
TP-2.com . . . . (Jive)
I Wish You Were Here
Holly Near; *Sky Dances* . . . . (Redwood)
I Would Die 4 U
Prince and the Revolution; *ST/Purple Rain* . . . . (Warner Bros.)
I'd Be Better Off (In A Pine Box)
Doug Stone; *Doug Stone* . . . . (Epic)
Greatest Country Hits Of The '90s-1990-C . . . . (Columbia)
I'd Die Without You
PM Dawn; *Bliss Album...?* . . . . (Gee Street)
I'd Rather Be Dead
Nilsson; *Son Of Schmilsson* . . . . (RCA)
If I Should Die Tonight
Marvin Gaye; *Let's Get It On* . . . . (Motown)
Musical Testament 1964-1984 . . . . (Motown)
If The Good Die Young
Tracy Lawrence; *Alibis* . . . . (Atlantic)
If Tomorrow Never Comes
Garth Brooks; *Garth Brooks* . . . . (Liberty)
Limited Series-Box . . . . (Capitol)
Joose; *Joose* . . . . (Flavor Unit)
If You Love Me, Baby
Beatles; *In The Beginning-The Early Tapes* . . . . (Polydor)
I-Feel-Like-I'm-Fixin'-To-Die Rag
Country Joe & The Fish; *Country Joe & The Fish-Greatest Hits* . . . . (Vanguard)
Greatest '60s Folksingers-C . . . . (Vanguard)
I-Feel-Like-I'm-Fixin'-To-Die . . . . (Vanguard)
Life & Times Of Country Joe & The Fish . . . . (Vanguard)
More American Graffiti-#4-C . . . . (MCA)
Songs Of Protest-C . . . . (Rhino)
ST/Woodstock . . . . (Atlantic)
I'll Be Glad When You're Dead (You Rascal You)
Cab Calloway; *Jazz Heritage: Mr. Hi-De-Ho* . . . . (MCA)
I'll Be Missing You
Puff Daddy & Family & Faith Evans & 112; *No Way Out* . . . . . (Bad Boy/Arista)
I'll Fly Away
Gillian Welch & Alison Krauss; *ST/O Brother, Where Art Thou?* . . . . (Mercury)
In My Time Of Dyin'
Bob Dylan; *Bob Dylan* . . . . (Columbia)
The Times They Are A-Changin' . . . . (Columbia)
In My Time Of Dying
Led Zeppelin; *Physical Graffiti* . . . . (Swan Song)
Islands Of The Dead
Be Bop Deluxe; *Drastic Plastic* . . . . (Capitol)
It Must Be Him
Vikki Carr; *Greatest Hits* . . . . (Curb)
Jack You're Dead
Joe Jackson; *Jumpin' Jive* . . . . (A&M)
Louis Jordan; *Jazz Heritage-Greatest Hits-#2-1941-1947* . . . . . . (MCA)
Joe Hill
Arlo Guthrie & Pete Seeger; *Together In Concert* . . . . (Reprise)
Joan Baez; *Carry It On* . . . . (Vanguard)
From Every Stage . . . . (A&M)
One Day At A Time . . . . (Vanguard)
ST/Woodstock . . . . (Atlantic)
John Brown's Body
Pete Seeger; *American Favorite Ballads-#3* . . . . (Smithsonian Folkways)
Sonny Terry & Brownie McGhee; *Every Tone A Testimony-C* . . . . (Smithsonian Folkways)
John Doe No. 24
Mary Chapin Carpenter; *Stones In The Road* . . . . (Columbia)
John Henry
"Little" Jimmy Dickens; *Columbia Historic Edition-"Little" Jimmy Dickens* . . . . (Columbia)
Harry Belafonte; *Harry Belafonte-At Carnegie Hall* . . . . (RCA)
Harry Belafonte-Legendary Performer . . . . (RCA)
Harry Belafonte's All Time Greatest Hits-#1 . . . . (RCA)
Merle Travis; *Great American Train Songs-C* . . . . (C.M.H. Prod.)
Odetta; *Essential Odetta* . . . . (Vanguard)
Greatest Folksingers Of The '60s-C . . . . (Vanguard)
Woody Guthrie; *Immortal Woody Guthrie-Golden Classics-#2* . . . (Collectables)
Legendary Woody Guthrie . . . . (Tradition)
John Peel
Hermes Nye; *Anglo-American Songs* . . . . (Smithsonian Folkways)
Johnny Bye-Bye
Bruce Springsteen; *Tracks* . . . . (Columbia)
Jungle, The
Kiss; *Carnival Of Souls: The Final Sessions* . . . . (Mercury)
Just Another Death In NYC
Judy Small; *One Voice In The Crowd* . . . . (Redwood)
Keep It Between The Lines
Ricky Van Shelton; *Backroads* . . . . (Columbia)
Kern River
Merle Haggard; *For The Record: Merle Haggard-43 Legendary Hits* . . . (BNA)

Kern River . . . . (Epic)
Kevorkian
Public Enemy; *There's A Poison Goin On* . . . . (Atomic Pop)
Kid's Last Fight
Frankie Laine; *Frankie Laine-16 Most Requested Songs* . . . . (Legacy)
King Must Die
Elton John; *Elton John* . . . . (Polydor)
Live In Australia With The Melbourne Symphony Orchestra . . . . . (MCA)
Kiss Me Deadly
Lita Ford; *Best Of Lita Ford* . . . . (Dreamland)
Lita . . . . (Dreamland)
Kiss The World Goodbye
Kris Kristofferson; *Border Lord* . . . . (Columbia)
Lake Of Fire
Nirvana; *MTV Unplugged In New York* . . . . (David Geffen Co.)
Last Kiss
J. Frank Wilson and The Cavaliers; *Billboard Top Rock 'N' Roll Hits-1964-C* . . . . (Rhino)
Collectables Presents The History Of Rock-#2-C . . . . (Collectables)
Oldies But Goodies-#9-C . . . . (Original Sound)
Teenage Tragedies-C . . . . (Rhino)
Pearl Jam; *No Boundaries-Benefit For The Kosovar Refugees-C* . . . . (Epic)
Last Song
Elton John; *The One* . . . . (MCA)
Laurie (Strange Things Happen)
Dickey Lee; *Collector's Essentials-#1-1960s-C* . . . . (Varese Sarabande)
Leader Of The Pack
Bette Midler; *Divine Miss M* . . . . (Atlantic)
ST/Divine Madness . . . . (Atlantic)
Original Cast; *Leader Of The Pack* . . . . (Elektra)
Shangri-Las; *21 Number One Hits-C* . . . . (Original Sound)
Billboard Top Rock 'N' Roll Hits-1964-C . . . . (Rhino)
Girl Groups-Story Of A Sound-C . . . . (Rhino)
Golden Hits Of The Shangri-Las . . . . (Mercury)
Oldies But Goodies-#15-C . . . . (Original Sound)
Radio Active Hits-#2-C . . . . (Accord)
Remember The Shangri-Las At Their Best . . . . (Collectables)
Leaving October
Sons Of The Desert; *Whatever Comes First* . . . . (Epic)
Let The Mystery Be
10,000 Maniacs; *Few & Far Between* . . . . (Elektra)
Iris DeMent; *Infamous Angel* . . . . (Warner Bros.)
Light Years
Pearl Jam; *Binaural* . . . . (Epic)
Lighthouse's Tale
Nickel Creek; *Nickel Creek* . . . . (Sugar Hill)
Lightning Crashes
Live; *Throwing Copper* . . . . (Radioactive/MCA)
Little Girl, The
John Michael Montgomery; *Brand New Me* . . . . (Atlantic)
Totally Hits-#3-C . . . . (Atlantic)
Little Joe The Wrangler's Sister Nell
Skip Gorman; *A Cowboy's Wild Song To His Herd* . . . . (Rounder)
Little Things
Bush; *Sixteen Stone* . . . . (Trauma)
Live And Let Die
Paul McCartney; *13 Original James Bond Themes-C* . . . . (EMI)
All The Best! . . . . (Capitol)
Wings; *ST/Live And Let Die* . . . . (EMI)
Wings Greatest . . . . (Capitol)
Wings Over America . . . . (Capitol)
Live Until I Die
Clay Walker; *Clay Walker* . . . . (Giant)
Living Dead Girl
Rob Zombie; *Hellbilly Deluxe* . . . . (Geffen)
Living In A Moment
Ty Herndon; *Living In A Moment* . . . . (Epic)
Super Hits Of 1996-C . . . . (Epic)
Lonesome Valley
Fairfield Four; *ST/O Brother, Where Art Thou?* . . . . (Mercury)
Longest Day
Arthur Fiedler; *Motion Picture Classics-#2* . . . . (RCA Victor)
Mitch Miller; *Mitch Miller-The Gang & Orchestra-Greatest Hits* . . . (Columbia)
Paul Anka; *Paul Anka's 21 Golden Hits* . . . . (RCA)
Love Story
Randy Newman; *Randy Newman* . . . . (Warner Archives)
Love, Me
Collin Raye; *All I Can Be* . . . . (Epic)
Greatest Country Hits Of The '90s-1992-C . . . . (Columbia)
Maker Said Take Her
Alabama; *In Pictures* . . . . (RCA)
Man Of My Word
Collin Raye; *Extremes* . . . . (Epic)
Man Who Sold The World
David Bowie; *Man Who Sold The World* . . . . (Rykodisc)
Sound + Vision . . . . (Rykodisc)
Nirvana; *MTV Unplugged In New York* . . . . (David Geffen Co.)
Melancholy Blue
Trisha Yearwood; *Inside Out* . . . . (MCA)

Memory Remains
Metallica; *Reload* . . . . (Elektra)
Mer Girl
Madonna; *Ray Of Light*. . . . .(Maverick)
Mighty K.C.
For Squirrels; *Example* . . . . (550 Music)
Misery
Soul Asylum; *Let Your Dim Light Shine* . . . . (Columbia)
More Than A Name On The Wall
Statler Brothers; *Statler Brothers' Greatest Hits* . . . . (Mercury)
Mother's Only Sleeping
Ricky Skaggs and Kentucky Thunder; *History Of The Future* . . (Skaggs Family)
Mummy
Bob McFadden & Dor; *Dr. Demento Presents The Greatest Novelty Records-*
#2-1950s-C . . . . (Rhino)
Vintage Music-#15-C . . . . (MCA)
Murder On Music Row
George Strait & Alan Jackson; *Latest Greatest Straitest Hits* . . . .(MCA)
My Antonia
Emmylou Harris; *Red Dirt Girl* . . . . (Nonesuch)
My Dead Dog Rover
Hank, Stu, Dave & Hank; *Dr. Demento Presents The Greatest Novelty*
Records-#4-1970s-C . . . . (Rhino)
My Heart Will Go On (Love Theme from "Titanic")
Celine Dion; *All The Way...A Decade Of Song* . . . .(550 Music)
ST/Titanic . . . . (Sony Music Classical)
Celine Dion with The Bee Gees; *Let's Talk About Love-C* . . . . (550 Music)
Kenny G; *Kenny G's Greatest Hits* . . . . (Arista)
My Mummy's Dead
John Lennon; *Lennon* . . . . (Capitol)
John Lennon/Plastic Ono Band; *John Lennon/Plastic Ono Band* . . . . . . (Capitol)
My Wife & My Dead Wife
Robyn Hitchcock & The Egyptians; *Fegmania* . . . . (Slash)
Mystic Eyes
Them featuring Van Morrison; *Here Comes The Night* . . . . (Out Of Print)
History Of British Rock-#6-C . . . . (Rhino)
The Sopranos-Music From The HBO Original
Series . . . . (Sony Music Soundtrax)
Needle Of Death
Ian & Sylvia; *Best Of Ian & Sylvia* . . . . (Vanguard)
Never Say Die
Dixie Chicks; *Wide Open Spaces* . . . . (Monument)
Night Chicago Died
Paper Lace; *Back To The '70s-#3-C* . . . . (Dominion Entert.)
Super Hits Of The '70s-Have A Nice Day-#13-C . . . . (Rhino)
Night Game
Paul Simon; *Still Crazy After All These Years* . . . . (Columbia)
Nightshift
Commodores; *Nightshift*. . . . . (Motown)
Nothing Short Of Dying
Travis Tritt; *It's All About To Change* . . . .(Warner Bros.)
Nuclear Funeral
D.I.; *Team Goon* . . . .(Triple X Entert.)
O Bury Me Not On The Lone Prairie
Michael Martin Murphey; *Cowboy Songs* . . . . (Warner Western)
Sons Of The Pioneers; *Sunset On The Range* . . . . (Pair)
O Death
Ralph Stanley; *ST/O Brother, Where Art Thou?* . . . . (Mercury)
Oh Bury Me Not
Johnny Cash; *American Recordings* . . . . (American)
One Headlight
Wallflowers; *Bringing Down The Horse* . . . . (Interscope)
One Sweet Day
Mariah Carey; *Daydream* . . . . (Columbia)
Mariah Carey & Boyz II Men; *1996 Grammy Nominees-C* . . . . (Columbia)
Only Losers Take The Bus (Dump The Dead)
Fatima Mansions; *Viva Dead Ponies* . . . .(Radioactive/MCA)
Only The Good Die Young
Billy Joel; *Billy Joel-Greatest Hits, Volume I & Volume II.* . . . . . . (Columbia)
KOHUEPT . . . . (Columbia)
The Stranger . . . . (Columbia)
Open Casket
Death; *Best Of Death* . . . . (Relativity)
Order Of Death
Public Image Ltd.; *ST/Hardware* . . . . (Varese Sarabande)
Over The Next Hill
Johnny Cash with The Carter Family; *Johnny Cash-16 Biggest*
Hits-#2 . . . . (Legacy)
Papa Loved Mama
Garth Brooks; *Garth Brooks-Double Live* . . . . (Capitol)
Ropin' The Wind . . . . (Liberty)
Papa Was A Rollin' Stone
Temptations; *20/20-C* . . . . (Motown)
25 #1 Hits From 25 Years-C . . . . (Motown)
All The Million-Sellers . . . . (Motown)
Billboard Top Rock 'N' Roll Hits-1972-C . . . . (Rhino)
Compact Command Performances-Temptations . . . . (Motown)
Temptations-Anthology-The Best Of The Temptations . . . . (Motown)

Party In The Graveyard
Haunted Garage; *Possession Park*. . . . . (Metal Blade)
Passing Of The Graveyard
Eddie Money; *No Control* . . . . (Columbia)
Pepper
Butthole Surfers; *Electriclarryland*. . . . . (Capitol)
Pimp Or Die
Father M.C.; *ST/Who's The Man?* . . . .(Uptown)
Please Don't Bury Me
John Prine; *Prime Prine-The Best Of John Prine* . . . .(Atlantic)
Sweet Revenge . . . .(Atlantic)
Po Lazarus
James Carter & The Prisoners; *ST/O Brother, Where Art Thou?* . . . . . . (Mercury)
Pocket Full Of Gold
Vince Gill; *Pocket Full Of Gold* . . . . (MCA)
Pore Jud Is Daid
Original Cast; *Oklahoma!* . . . . (MCA)
Postmortem
Slayer; *Reign In Blood*. . . . . (American)
Slayer-Live-Decade Of Aggression . . . .(Def American)
Prayer For The Dying
Seal; *Diana, Princess Of Wales-Tribute-C* . . . . (Columbia)
Seal 2 . . . . (Sire)
Pretty Girls Make Graves
Smiths; *Smiths* . . . . (Sire)
Pretty Wreath For Mother's Grave
Reno & Smiley; *1983 Collector's Edition-#9* . . . . . (International Mktg. Group)
Prop Me Up Beside The Jukebox (If I Die)
Joe Diffie; *Honky Tonk Attitude* . . . . (Epic)
Psycho Man
Black Sabbath; *Reunion* . . . . (Epic)
Punks Not Dead
Exploited; *Apocalypse '77* . . . . (Relativity)
Pure Massacre
Silverchair; *Frogstomp* . . . . (Epic)
Push Me, Pull Me
Pearl Jam; *Yield*. . . . . (Epic)
Pushing Up Daisies
Garth Brooks; *Scarecrow* . . . . (Capitol)
Question Everything
8Stops7; *In Moderation*. . . . . (Reprise)
R&B Skeletons (In The Closet)
George Clinton; *R&B Skeletons (In The Closet)* . . . . (Capitol)
R.I.P.
Blood Feast; *Face Fate* . . . . (New Renaissance)
Kill For Pleasure . . . . (New Renaissance)
Rachel
Buddy & Julie Miller; *Buddy & Julie Miller* . . . .(Hightone)
Real Niggaz Don't Die
N.W.A.; *Efil4zaggin* . . . . (Ruthless/Priority)
Reason For Breathing
Babyface; *Collection Of His Greatest Hits* . . . .(Arista/Epic)
Rest In Peace
Extreme; *III Sides To Every Story* . . . . (A&M)
Rest Of Mine, The
Trace Adkins; *Big Time*. . . . . (Capitol)
Revolution
Pretenders; *Last Of The Independents*. . . . . (Sire)
Ride To A Funeral In A V-8
Dan Pickett; *1949 Country Blues* . . . . (Collectables)
Riding With Private Malone
David Ball; *Amigo* . . . . (Razor & Tie)
Rigor Mortis
Split-Second; *Split-Second* . . . . (Wax Trax)
Road To Dead
Paula Cole; *This Fire* . . . . (Imago)
Rock & Roll Widow
Wishbone Ash; *Live Dates* . . . . (MCA)
Wishbone Four. . . . . (MCA)
Rock And Roll Is Dead
Lenny Kravitz; *Circus*. . . . .(Virgin)
Rock Me 'Till I Die
Grim Reaper; *Rock You To Hell* . . . . (RCA)
Rock Will Never Die
Michael Schenker Group; *Built To Destroy*. . . . . (Chrysalis)
Rock Will Never Die . . . . (Chrysalis)
Rockaway The Days
Bruce Springsteen; *Tracks* . . . . (Columbia)
Roll Over & Play Dead
Lizzy Borden; *Master Of Disguise* . . . . (Metal Blade)
Room With A View
Carolyn Dawn Johnson; *Room With A View* . . . . (Arista)
Rosewood Casket
Dolly Parton/Emmylou Harris/Linda Ronstadt; *Trio* . . . (Warner Bros.)
Running Bear
Johnny Preston; *45s On CD-#1-1956-1959-C* . . . . (Mercury)
Billboard Top Rock 'N' Roll Hits-1960-C . . . . (Rhino)

Cruisin'-1960-C . . . . (Increase)
Sonny James; *All-Time Country Classics-#1-C* . . . . (Capitol)

Running Gun
Marty Robbins; *Gunfighter Ballads & Trail Songs* . . . . (Legacy)

Santa Monica (Watch The World Die)
Everclear; *Sparkle And Fade* . . . . (Capitol)

See That My Grave Is Kept Clean
Blind Lemon Jefferson; *Blind Lemon Jefferson-Vol. 1-1926-1929* . . . (Biograph)
Bob Dylan; *Bob Dylan* . . . . (Columbia)
The Times They Are A-Changin' . . . . (Columbia)
Dream Syndicate; *Ghost Stories* . . . . (Restless)

See You On The Other Side
Ozzy Osbourne; *Ozzmosis* . . . . (Epic)

Service For A Vacant Coffin
Autopsy; *Severed Survival* . . . . (Futurist)

Set Adrift On Memory Bliss
PM Dawn; *MTV Party To Go-#2-C* . . . . (Tommy Boy)
Red Hot + Dance-C . . . . (Columbia)

Seven Deadly Sins
Bryan Ferry; *Bete Noire* . . . . (Reprise)

Seven Deadly Virtues
Original Cast; *Camelot* . . . . (Columbia)

Sex And Dying In High Society
X; *Los Angeles/Wild Gift* . . . . (Slash)

She Misses Him On Sunday The Most
Diamond Rio; *Diamond Rio IV* . . . . (Arista)
Diamond Rio's Greatest Hits . . . . (Arista)

She Said She Said
Beatles; *Beatles-Box Set* . . . . (Capitol)
Revolver . . . . (Capitol)

She Thinks His Name Was John
Reba McEntire; *Read My Mind* . . . . (MCA)
Reba McEntire's Greatest Hits-#3: I'm A Survivor . . . . (MCA)

Sheer Heart Attack
Queen; *Live Killers* . . . . (Hollywood)
News Of The World . . . . (Hollywood)

She's Not Dead
Suede; *Suede* . . . . (Columbia)

Sinaloa Cowboys
Bruce Springsteen; *The Ghost Of Tom Joad* . . . . (Columbia)

Sing Me Back Home
Alabama; *Mama's Hungry Eyes-Merle Haggard Tribute-C* . . . . (Arista)
Flying Burrito Brothers; *Farther Along-Best Of The Flying Burrito Brothers* . . . . (A&M)
Merle Haggard & The Strangers; *Best Of Merle Haggard & The Strangers* . . . . (Capitol)
Capitol Collectors Series-Merle Haggard & The Strangers . . . . (Capitol)
For The Record: Merle Haggard-43 Legendary Hits . . . . (BNA)
Okie From Muskogee . . . . (Capitol)
Songs I'll Always Sing . . . . (Capitol)

Skeletons
Stevie Wonder; *Characters* . . . . (Motown)
MTV-VH1 Powerplayers-C . . . . (EMI)

Skeletons
Rickie Lee Jones; *Pirates* . . . . (Warner Bros.)

Smoke! Smoke! Smoke!
Commander Cody & His Lost Planet Airmen; *Country Casanova* . . . . . (MCA)
Too Much Fun-Best Of Commander Cody & His Lost Planet Airmen . . (MCA)
We've Got A Live One Here! . . . . (Warner Bros.)
Doc Watson; *Red Rocking Chair* . . . . (Flying Fish)
Johnny Bond & His Red River Valley Boys; *All Time Legends Of Country Music-C* . . . . (Legacy)
Merle Travis; *Johnny Gimble's Texas Honky-Tonk Hits-C* . . . . . (C.M.H. Prod.)
Tex Williams; *Birth Of A Dream-Capitol's Early Hits-C* . . . . (Capitol)
Dr. Demento Presents The Greatest Novelty Records-#1-1940s & Before-C . . . . (Rhino)

Some Gave All
Billy Ray Cyrus; *Some Gave All* . . . . (Mercury)

Some Memories Just Won't Die
Marty Robbins; *American Originals-Marty Robbins* . . . . (Columbia)
Come Back To Me . . . . (Columbia)
Lifetime Of Song-1951-1982 . . . . (Columbia)
Some Memories Just Won't Die . . . . (Columbia)

Souls Of The Departed
Bruce Springsteen; *Lucky Town* . . . . (Columbia)

Spirit In The Sky
Kentucky HeadHunters; *Electric Barnyard* . . . . (Mercury)
Norman Greenbaum; *Billboard Top Rock 'N' Roll Hits-1970-C* . . . . . (Rhino)
Super Hits Of The '70s-Have A Nice Day-#2-C . . . . (Rhino)

St. James Infirmary Blues
Benny Goodman; *Yale Recordings-#5-Private Collection* . . . . (Musicmasters)
Cab Calloway; *Cab Calloway* . . . . (Glendale)
Jack Teagarden; *Hundred Years From Today* . . . . (Grudge)
Joe Cocker; *Joe Cocker* . . . . (A&M)
Lou Rawls; *Best From Lou Rawls* . . . . (Capitol)
Louis Armstrong; *Best Of Louis Armstrong-Story-#3* . . . . . . (Audio Fidelity)
Essential Louis Armstrong . . . . (Vanguard)
Pops: 1940s Small Band Sides . . . . (Bluebird)
Volume IV-Louis Armstrong And Earl Hines . . . . (Columbia)

Louis Armstrong & Earl Hines; *Louis Armstrong-Vol. 4-In New York* . . . . (Columbia)
Preservation Hall Jazz Band; *New Orleans-#4* . . . . (Columbia)

Stacked Actors
Foo Fighters; *There Is Nothing Left To Lose* . . . . (Roswell/RCA)

Stairway To Heaven
Led Zeppelin; *Led Zeppelin IV* . . . . (Atlantic)
Led Zeppelin-Box Set . . . . (Atlantic)
Remasters . . . . (Atlantic)
ST/The Song Remains The Same . . . . (Swan Song)
Stanley Jordan; *Best Of Stanley Jordan* . . . . (Blue Note)
Flying Home . . . . (EMI)

Standing Knee Deep In A River (Dying Of Thirst)
Kathy Mattea; *Lonesome Standard Time* . . . . (Mercury)

Stone Cold Dead In The Market
Ella Fitzgerald; *Best Of Ella Fitzgerald-#2* . . . . (MCA)

Stop Dead
Cure; *Standing On A Beach-The Singles* . . . . (Elektra)

Streets Of Laredo
Buck Owens & The Buckaroos; *Buck Owens & The Buckaroos-Live At Carnegie Hall* . . . . (Country Music Foundation)
Marty Robbins; *Cowboy Super Hits-C* . . . . (Columbia)
Marty Robbins' All-Time Greatest Hits . . . . (Columbia)
Marty Robbins-More Greatest Hits . . . . (Columbia)
More Gunfighter Ballads & Trail Songs . . . . (Columbia)
Rex Allen; *Great American Singing Cowboys-C* . . . . . . (Republic/Universal)

Streets Of Philadelphia
Bruce Springsteen; *Bruce Springsteen's Greatest Hits* . . . . (Columbia)
Diana, Princess Of Wales-Tribute-C . . . . (Columbia)
ST/Philadelphia . . . . (Epic/Sony Music Soundtrax)

Sullivan
Caroline's Spine; *Monsoon* . . . . (Hollywood)

Superman's Dead
Our Lady Peace; *Clumsy* . . . . (Columbia)

Surprise! You're Dead!
Faith No More; *The Real Thing* . . . . (Slash)

Survival Handbook Vs. Global Extinction
Sister Souljah; *360 Degrees Of Power* . . . . (Epic)

Tears In Heaven
Eric Clapton; *Diana, Princess Of Wales-Tribute-C* . . . . (Columbia)
Eric Clapton-Unplugged . . . . (Reprise)
ST/Rush . . . . (Reprise)

Teen Angel
Dion And The Belmonts; *Everything You Always Wanted* . . . . . . (Laurie)
Rock & Roll U.S.A.-21 Rock & Roll Favorites-#2-C . . . . (Laurie)
Mark Dinning; *Golden Years-1959-C* . . . . (Dominion Entert.)
Oldies But Goodies-#7-C . . . . (Original Sound)
ST/American Graffiti . . . . (MCA)
Teenage Tragedies-C . . . . (Rhino)

Texas (When I Die)
Tanya Tucker; *Best Of Tanya Tucker* . . . . (MCA)
ST/Hard Country . . . . (Epic)
Tanya Tucker Live . . . . (MCA Special Prod.)
Tanya Tucker-Greatest Hits Encore . . . . (Gold Rush)
The Tanya Tucker Collection . . . . (MCA)

Texas Girl At The Funeral Of Her Father
Randy Newman; *Little Criminals* . . . . (Warner Bros.)

Tha Crossroads
Bone Thugs-N-Harmony; *Club Mix '97* . . . . (Cold Front)
MTV Party To Go-#10-C . . . . (Tommy Boy)

That'll Be The Day
Buddy Holly; *ST/American Graffiti* . . . . (MCA)
Buddy Holly/The Crickets; *Buddy Holly-20 Golden Greats* . . . . (MCA)
Chirping Crickets . . . . (MCA)
Crickets; *Billboard Top Rock 'N' Roll Hits-1957-C* . . . . (Rhino)
Foghat; *Best Of Foghat-#2* . . . . (Rhino)
Energized . . . . (Rhino)
Linda Ronstadt; *Hasten Down The Wind* . . . . (Asylum)
Linda Ronstadt's Greatest Hits . . . . (Asylum)

They'll Never Take Her Love From Me
Emmylou Harris; *Blue Kentucky Girl* . . . . (Warner Bros.)
George Jones; *George Jones Sings The Great Songs Of Leon Payne* . . . . (Hollywood/DNA-Rounder)
Hank Williams With His Drifting Cowboys; *Hank Williams-24 Greatest Hits-#2* . . . . (Polydor)
Hank Williams-40 Greatest Hits . . . . (Polydor)

They're Moving Father's Grave To Build A Sewer
Clancy Brothers & Tommy Makem; *Luck Of The Irish* . . . . (Columbia)

Things To Do In Denver When You're Dead
Warren Zevon; *Mr. Bad Example* . . . . (Giant)

This Jesus Must Die
Original London Cast; *Jesus Christ Superstar* . . . . (MCA)

This Ole House
Rosemary Clooney; *Rosemary Clooney-16 Most Requested Songs* . . . . (Legacy)
Statler Brothers; *The World Of The Statler Brothers* . . . . (Columbia)
Stuart Hamblen; *Stuart Hamblen-A Man & His Music* . . . . . (Lamb & Lion)

Thought I'd Died & Gone To Heaven
Bryan Adams; *Waking Up The Neighbours* . . . . (A&M)

Three Bells, The
Browns; *Billboard Top Country Hits-1959-C.* . . . . (Rhino)
Nipper's Greatest Hits Of The '50s-#1-C . . . . (RCA)
'Til I Die
Beach Boys; *10 Years Of Harmony* . . . . (Caribou)
Surf's Up . . . . (Caribou)
Till Death Do Us Part
Madonna; *Like A Prayer* . . . . (Sire)
Till I'm Too Old To Die Young
Moe Bandy; *Great Records Of The Decade-'80s Hits-Country-C* . . . . . . (Curb)
Moe Bandy's Greatest Hits . . . . (Curb)
To Live And Die In L.A.
Wang Chung; *ST/To Live And Die In L.A.* . . . .(Geffen)
To Live Is To Die
Metallica; *...And Justice For All.* . . . . (Elektra)
Tomb Of The Unknown Love
Cassell Webb; *Songs Of A Stranger* . . . . (Venture)
Kenny Rogers; *The Heart Of The Matter* . . . . (RCA)
Tombstone
Pogues; *Peace & Love* . . . . (Island)
Tombstone
Crowded House; *Crowded House.* . . . . (Capitol)
Tombstone Blues
Bob Dylan; *Biograph* . . . . (Columbia)
Highway 61 Revisited . . . . (Columbia)
Real Live . . . . (Columbia)
Tombstone Every Mile
Dave Dudley; *Interstate Gold.* . . . . (Sun)
Dick Curless; *Truck Driver Boogie Big Rig Hits-1939-1969-C* . . . .(Audium)
Tombstone Shadow
Creedence Clearwater Revival; *1969* . . . . (Fantasy)
Creedence Clearwater Revival-Chronicle-#2 . . . . (Fantasy)
Green River . . . . (Fantasy)
The Concert . . . . (Fantasy)
Too Old To Rock 'N' Roll: Too Young To Die
Jethro Tull; *Bursting Out* . . . .(Chrysalis)
Classic Case with the London Symphony Orchestra . . . . (RCA)
Original Masters . . . .(Chrysalis)
Repeat-The Best Of Jethro Tull, Vol. II . . . .(Chrysalis)
Travelin' Soldier
Bruce Robison; *Bruce Robison.* . . . .(Vireo)
Trippin' On A Hole In A Paper Heart
Stone Temple Pilots; *Tiny Music...Songs From The Vatican
Gift Shop* . . . . (Atlantic)
True Love Never Dies
Earl Scruggs & Gary Scruggs & Travis Tritt; *Earl Scruggs And
Friends-C* . . . . (MCA)
Kevin Welch; *Kevin Welch.* . . . . (Reprise)
Tryin' To Get Over You
Vince Gill; *I Still Believe In You* . . . . (MCA)
Tuesday's Dead
Cat Stevens; *Cat Stevens-Classics-#24.* . . . . (A&M)
Teaser And The Firecat . . . . (A&M)
TV Movie
Bruce Springsteen; *Tracks* . . . . (Columbia)
Two Teardrops
Steve Wariner; *Two Teardrops.* . . . . (Capitol)
Utah Carol
Harry K. McClintock; *Cowboy Songs On
Folkways-C.* . . . . (Smithsonian Folkways)
Marty Robbins; *Gunfighter Ballads & Trail Songs.* . . . . (Legacy)
Utah Carroll
Skip Gorman; *A Cowboy's Wild Song To His Herd* . . . . (Rounder)
Victim To The Tomb
Country Gentlemen; *Folk Songs & Bluegrass* . . . . (Smithsonian Folkways)
Voices
Disturbed; *The Sickness* . . . . (Giant)
Vulcan Death Grip
Ugly Americans; *Stereophonic Spanish Fly* . . . . (Mercury)
Waiting For The Worms
Pink Floyd; *The Wall* . . . . (Columbia)
Roger Waters; *The Wall-Live In Berlin.* . . . . (Mercury)
Walk Softly On This Heart Of Mine
Bill Monroe; *The Country Music Hall Of Fame-Bill Monroe* . . . .(MCA)
Joey Welz; *Lovin' My Country* . . . . (Capricorn)
Kentucky HeadHunters; *Best Of The Kentucky HeadHunters-Still
Pickin'.* . . . . (Mercury)
Pickin' On Nashville . . . . (Mercury)
Ricky Skaggs and the Dixie Chicks; *Ricky Skaggs & Friends-Big Mon: Songs
Of Bill Monroe* . . . . (Skaggs Family)
Wall Of Death
Richard & Linda Thompson; *Shoot Out The Lights* . . . . (Hannibal)
Richard Thompson; *Watching The Dark-History Of Richard
Thompson* . . . .(Rykodisc)
Wanted Dead Or Alive
Bon Jovi; *Slippery When Wet* . . . . (Jambco)
The Concert For New York City-C. . . . . (Columbia)
War Widow
Country Joe McDonald; *War War War.* . . . . (Vanguard)

Washed Up & Left For Dead
Selecter; *Celebrate The Bullet.* . . . . (Chrysalis)
Selected Selections . . . .(Chrysalis)
Waterfalls
TLC; *1996 Grammy Nominees-C* . . . . (Columbia)
CrazySexyCool . . . . (LaFace)
Waterloo
Stonewall Jackson; *American Originals-Stonewall Jackson.* . . . . (Columbia)
Billboard Top Country Hits-1959-C. . . . . (Rhino)
Columbia Country Classics-#3-Americana-C . . . . (Columbia)
Country Music Classics-#1-1950s-C . . . . (K-Tel)
We Are The Dead
David Bowie; *Diamond Dogs* . . . . (Rykodisc)
We Die Young
Alice In Chains; *Facelift.* . . . . (Columbia)
What A Way To Go
Ray Kennedy; *What A Way To Go* . . . .(Atlantic)
When I Die
Watson Family; *Watson Family* . . . .(Smithsonian Folkways)
Wherever You Will Go
Calling; *Camino Palmero* . . . . (RCA)
While You Loved Me
Rascal Flatts; *Rascal Flatts* . . . .(Lyric Street)
Who Wants To Live Forever
Queen; *A Kind Of Magic* . . . . (Hollywood)
Classic Queen. . . . . (Hollywood)
Diana, Princess Of Wales-Tribute-C . . . . (Columbia)
Wicker Man
Iron Maiden; *Brave New World.* . . . . (Portrait)
Widow's Walk
Suzanne Vega; *Songs In Red & Gray* . . . . (A&M)
Will The Circle Be Unbroken
Charlie Daniels Band & Friends; *Volunteer Jam 3 & 4* . . . . (Epic)
Joan Baez; *Country Music Album* . . . . (Vanguard)
The First 10 Years . . . . (Vanguard)
Nitty Gritty Dirt Band; *Will The Circle Be Unbroken* . . . . (EMI)
Roy Acuff; *Best Of Roy Acuff* . . . . (Liberty)
Willie Nelson; *Willie & Family Live* . . . . (Columbia)
Wish You Were Here
Mark Wills; *Wish You Were Here* . . . . (Mercury)
Work That Sucker To Death
Xavier; *Point Of Pleasure* . . . . (Liberty)
Yer Blues
Beatles; *The Beatles (White Album)* . . . . (Capitol)
Yo Ho Ho And A Bottle Of Rum
Original Cast; *Rugrats Sing-Along* . . . . (Interscope)
Youth Of The Nation
P.O.D.; *Satellite* . . . .(Atlantic)

DECISIONS, Choices

*See Also: CRAZY, LOVE: COMMITTED OR NOT?, OPPOSITES,
QUESTIONS & ANSWERS, STUCK, THINKING & KNOWING*

10 Days Late
Third Eye Blind; *Blue* . . . . (Elektra)
49 Bye-Byes
Crosby, Stills & Nash; *Crosby, Stills & Nash* . . . .(Atlantic)
Against The Wind
Bob Seger & The Silver Bullet Band; *Against The Wind.* . . . . (Capitol)
Nine Tonight . . . . (Capitol)
ST/Forrest Gump . . . .(Epic/Sony Music Soundtrax)
All Er Nothin'
Original Broadway Cast; *Oklahoma!* . . . .(RCA)
Original Cast; *Oklahoma!* . . . . (MCA)
All Or Nothing
O-Town; *O-Town* . . . . (J)
Totally Hits 2001-C . . . . (Arista)
Am I Dreaming
Ol Skool featuring Keith Sweat & Xscape; *Ol Skool.* . . . .(Keia/Universal)
Apple Tree
Erykah Badu; *Baduizm* . . . . (Kedar Entert./Universal)
As Any Fool Can See
Tracy Lawrence; *I See It Now* . . . . (Atlantic)
Live & Unplugged . . . .(Atlantic)
Barely Breathing
Duncan Sheik; *Duncan Sheik* . . . . (Atlantic)
Between The Devil And Me
Alan Jackson; *Everything I Love* . . . . (Arista)
Bicycle Built For Two
Kidsongs; *Cars, Boats, Trains, Planes* . . . . (Sony Wonder)
Original Soundtrack; *School Days-Kids Classics* . . . . (Benson)
Blood Is Thicker Than Water
Wyclef Jean featuring G&B (The Product); *The Sopranos-Music From The
HBO Original Series* . . . . (Sony Music Soundtrax)
Can I Change My Mind
Tyrone Davis; *Soul Shots-#2-The ''In'' Crowd-Sweet Soul-C* . . . . (Rhino)

Tyrone Davis' Greatest Hits . . . . (Rhino)

Can't Decide
Black Flag; *My War* . . . . (SST)

Chains Of Love
Big Joe Turner; *Big Joe Turner's Greatest Hits* . . . . (Atlantic)
In The Evening . . . . (Pablo)
Turns On The Blues . . . . (Kent)
Bobby Bland; *Introspective Of The Early Years* . . . . (MCA)
Spotlighting The Man . . . . (MCA)
Mickey Gilley; *First Class* . . . . (Playboy)
Mickey Gilley's Biggest Hits . . . . (Epic)

Check Yes Or No
George Strait; *Strait Out Of The Box* . . . . (MCA)

Choice In The Matter
Aimee Mann; *I'm With Stupid* . . . . (Geffen)

Choice Is Yours, The
Paula Abdul; *Head Over Heels* . . . . (Captive/Virgin)

Choices
Uriah Heep; *Innocent Victim* . . . . (Castle Music America)

Choose
Color Me Badd; *Time And Chance* . . . . (Giant)

Choose Any Memory
Firehose; *Ragin' Full On* . . . . (SST)

Choosey Lover (Old School, New School)
Aaliyah; *One In A Million* . . . . (BlackGround Enterp./Atlantic)

Cocaine Decisions
Frank Zappa; *Man From Utopia* . . . . (Barking Pumpkin)

Come With Me
Shai; *Blackface* . . . . (Gasoline Alley)

Complicated
Carolyn Dawn Johnson; *Room With A View* . . . . (Arista)

Count Me In
Deana Carter; *Did I Shave My Legs For This?* . . . . (Capitol)

Cry Of The Wild Goose
Frankie Laine; *Frankie Laine-Golden Hits* . . . . (Mercury)

Darned If I Don't (Danged If I Do)
Shenandoah; *In The Vicinity Of The Heart* . . . . (Capitol)

Decision Or Collision
ZZ Top; *Recycler* . . . . (Warner Bros.)

Did We Not Choose Each Other
Sophie B. Hawkins; *Whaler* . . . . (Columbia)

Did You Ever Have To Make Up Your Mind?
Lovin' Spoonful; *Best Of The Lovin' Spoonful* . . . . (Rhino)
Lovin' Spoonful-Anthology . . . . (Rhino)

Didn't Cha Know
Erykah Badu; *Mama's Gun* . . . . (Motown)

Do For Love
2Pac featuring Eric Williams; *R U Still Down (Remember Me)* . . . . (Amaru/Jive)

Don't Say
Jon B.; *Cool Relax* . . . . (Yab Yum/550)

Don't Stop
Wade Hayes; *Old Enough To Know Better* . . . . (Columbia)
Steppin' Country-#2-C . . . . (Columbia)
Super Hits Of 1995-C . . . . (Epic)

Don't Tell Me (What Love Can Do)
Van Halen; *Balance* . . . . (Warner Bros.)

Door #1
LSG; *Levert-Sweat-Gill* . . . . (East West)

Fate Decides
Bob Welch; *Man Overboard* . . . . (Edsel)

First Night
Monica; *The Boy Is Mine* . . . . (Arista)

Five Minutes
Lorrie Morgan; *Lorrie Morgan's Greatest Hits* . . . . (BNA)
Lorrie Morgan-Super Hits . . . . (RCA)
Pam Tillis; *Pam Tillis-Collection* . . . . (Warner Bros.)

Forty Six & 2
Tool; *Aenima* . . . . (Freeworld/Capitol)

Free To Decide
Cranberries; *To The Faithful Departed* . . . . (Island)

Freedom Of Choice
Devo; *Freedom Of Choice* . . . . (Warner Bros.)

Give It Up Or Let Me Go
Dixie Chicks; *Wide Open Spaces* . . . . (Monument)

Go Away
Lorrie Morgan; *Lorrie Morgan-Super Hits* . . . . (RCA)
Shakin' Things Up . . . . (BNA)
To Get To You-Greatest Hits Collection . . . . (BNA)

Go On With The Wedding
Patti Page; *Patti Page-Golden Celebration* . . . . (Mercury)

Go Your Own Way
Cranberries; *Legacy-A Tribute To Fleetwood Mac's Rumours-C* . . . . . . (Lava)
Fleetwood Mac; *25 Years-The Chain* . . . . (Warner Bros.)
Fleetwood Mac Live . . . . (Warner Bros.)
Fleetwood Mac's Greatest Hits . . . . (Warner Bros.)
Rumours . . . . (Warner Bros.)

Goodbye Yellow Brick Road
Elton John; *Billboard Top Rock 'N' Roll Hits-1973-C* . . . . (Rhino)

Elton John's Greatest Hits . . . . (Polydor)
Goodbye Yellow Brick Road . . . . (Polydor)

Got To Choose
Kiss; *Alive!* . . . . (Mercury)
Hotter Than Hell . . . . (Mercury)

Half Way Up
Clint Black; *Clint Black-The Greatest Hits* . . . . (RCA)

Hardest Thing
98 Degrees; *98 Degrees And Rising* . . . . (Universal)
Now That's What I Call Music!-#3-C . . . . (Virgin)

He Decides
Ace Of Base; *Cruel Summer* . . . . (Arista)

Headache Tomorrow (Or A Heartache Tonight)
Mickey Gilley; *Mickey Gilley's Biggest Hits* . . . . (Epic)
Ten Years Of Hits . . . . (Epic)
That's All That Matters To Me . . . . (Epic)

Heads Carolina, Tails California
Jo Dee Messina; *Greatest Hits Of Country Dance-C* . . . . (Curb)
Jo Dee Messina . . . . (Curb)

High Noon
Frankie Laine; *Billboard Top Movie Hits-1950-1954-C* . . . . (Rhino)
Tex Ritter; *Heroes Of Country Music-#4-Legends Of The West Coast-C* . . . . (Rhino)
The Envelope Please-Academy Award Winning Songs (1946-1957)-C . . . . (Rhino)

Him Or Me, What's It Going To Be
Paul Revere And The Raiders; *Essential Ride-'63-'67* . . . . (Legacy)

Hold On
Xscape; *Traces Of My Lipstick* . . . . (So So Def/Columbia)

How Deep Is Your Love
Dru Hill featuring Redman; *Enter The Dru* (Def Jam/RAL/Mercury/Island)
ST/Rush Hour . . . . (Def Jam)

I Am Not Hiding
Kenny Loggins; *The Unimaginable Life* . . . . (Columbia)

I Can't Stop Loving You
Don Gibson; *60 Years Of Country Music-C* . . . . (RCA)
Collector's Series-Don Gibson . . . . (RCA)
Stars Of The Grand Ole Opry-1926-1974-C . . . . (RCA)
Elvis Presley; *Aloha from Hawaii via Satellite* . . . . (RCA)
Elvis As Recorded At Madison Square Garden . . . . (RCA)
Elvis Recorded Live On Stage In Memphis . . . . (RCA)
From Memphis To Vegas/From Vegas To Memphis . . . . . . (RCA)
Ray Charles; *Ray Charles' Greatest Hits-#2* . . . . (Rhino)
Ray Charles-Anthology . . . . (Rhino)
Roy Orbison; *Best Of Roy Orbison-Loved Standards* . . . . . (Monument)
Legendary Roy Orbison . . . . (Sony Music Special Prod.)

I Choose
Offspring; *Ixnay On The Hombre* . . . . (Columbia)

I Choose You
Tears For Fears; *Raoul And The Kings Of Spain* . . . . (Columbia)

I Could Fall In Love
Selena; *Dreaming Of You* . . . . (EMI Latin)

I Have Decided
Amy Grant; *Age To Age* . . . . (RCA)

I Saw Her Again
Mamas & The Papas; *Best Of The Mamas & The Papas* . . . . (MCA)
Farewell To The First Golden Era . . . . (MCA)
Mamas & The Papas . . . . (MCA)

I Used To Love Him
Lauryn Hill featuring Mary J. Blige; *The Miseducation Of Lauryn Hill* . . . . (Ruffhouse/Columbia)

If You Asked Me To
Celine Dion; *All The Way...A Decade Of Song* . . . . (550 Music)
Celine Dion . . . . (Epic)
Patti LaBelle; *Be Yourself* . . . . (MCA)
Soundtrack Smashes-'80s & More-C . . . . (MCA)
ST/License To Kill . . . . (MCA)

If You Can Do Anything Else
George Strait; *George Strait* . . . . (MCA)

If You Change Your Mind
Rosanne Cash; *King's Record Shop* . . . . (Columbia)
Rosanne Cash-Super Hits . . . . (Columbia)

If You Really Love Me
Stevie Wonder; *Stevie Wonder's Greatest Hits-#2* . . . . (Motown)
Where I'm Coming From . . . . (Motown)

Immortality
Pearl Jam; *Vitalogy* . . . . (Epic)

In The Heat Of The Night
Pat Benatar; *In The Heat Of The Night* . . . . (Chrysalis)

Indecision
Eagle-Eye Cherry; *Desireless* . . . . (Work)

Indecision Time
Husker Du; *Zen Arcade* . . . . (SST)

Invitation To The Blues
Holly Cole; *Temptation* . . . . (Metro Blue)
Tom Waits; *Small Change* . . . . (Asylum)

It's Your Call
Reba McEntire; *It's Your Call* . . . . (MCA)

Jump Right In
Urge; *Master Of Styles* . . . .(Immortal/Epic)
Life Is Sweet
Natalie Merchant; *Ophelia* . . . . (Elektra)
Lifetime
Maxwell; *Now* . . . . (Columbia)
Little Woman
Bobby Sherman; *Bobby Sherman's Greatest Hits* . . . . (K-Tel)
   Bubblegum Classics-#3-C . . . . (Varese Vintage)
Lonely Teenager
Dion; *Collectables Presents The History Of Rock-#4-C* . . . . (Collectables)
   Dion-His Best . . . . (Laurie)
   Everything You Always Wanted To Hear By . . . . (Laurie)
   The Wanderer . . . . (Laurie)
Love Chooses You
Kathy Mattea; *Willow In The Wind* . . . . (Mercury)
Mahogany (Do You Know Where You're Going To), Theme From "Mahogany"
Diana Ross; *20/20-C* . . . . (Motown)
   Diana Ross . . . . (Motown)
   Diana Ross-Anthology . . . . (Motown)
   Diana Ross-The Ultimate Collection . . . . (Motown)
   Evening With Diana Ross . . . . (Motown)
Maybe Someday
Cure; *Bloodflowers* . . . . (Fiction/Elektra)
Maybe We Should Just Sleep On It
Tim McGraw; *All I Want* . . . . (Curb)
   Tim McGraw's Greatest Hits . . . . (Curb)
Miseducation Of Lauryn Hill
Lauryn Hill; *The Miseducation Of Lauryn Hill* . . . . (Ruffhouse/Columbia)
Mr. Man
Alicia Keys with Jimmy Cozier; *Songs In A Minor* . . . . (J)
Next Lifetime
Erykah Badu; *Baduizm* . . . . (Kedar Entert./Universal)
No More (Baby I'ma Do Right)
3LW; *3LW* . . . .(Epic)
   Now That's What I Call Music!-#6-C . . . . (Virgin)
One Choice
Texas; *Southside* . . . . (Mercury)
One Love At A Time
Tanya Tucker; *Tanya Tucker's Greatest Hits* . . . . (Liberty)
One Night Stand
J-Shin featuring La Tocha Scott; *My Soul, My Life* . . . . (Atlantic)
Open My Heart
Yolanda Adams; *Mountain High Valley Low* . . . . (Elektra)
Pass You By
Boyz II Men; *Nathan Michael Shawn Wanya* . . . . (Universal)
Right Where I Need To Be
Gary Allan; *Smoke Rings In The Dark* . . . .(MCA)
Ripple
Grateful Dead; *American Beauty* . . . .(Warner Bros.)
   Reckoning . . . . (Arista)
   What A Long Strange Trip It's Been: The Best Of The Grateful Dead . . . .(Warner Bros.)
   Jane's Addiction; *Deadicated-C* . . . . (Arista)
River Of Deceit
Mad Season; *Above* . . . . (Columbia)
Roll Me Away
Bob Seger & The Silver Bullet Band; *ST/Armageddon-The Album* . . (Columbia)
Running Scared
Roy Orbison; *For The Lonely: A Roy Orbison Anthology 1959-1965* . . . (Rhino)
   In Dreams-Greatest Hits . . . . (Orbison)
   Roy Orbison & Friends: Black & White Night-Live . . . . (Virgin)
   Roy Orbison's All-Time Greatest Hits-#1 & 2 . . . . (Monument)
Seven Days
Mary J. Blige; *Share My World* . . . . (MCA)
   The Tour . . . . (MCA)
Should I Stay Or Should I Go
Clash; *Clash On Broadway* . . . . (Legacy)
   Combat Rock . . . .(Epic)
Silence Is Golden
4 Seasons; *25th Anniversary Collection* . . . . (Rhino)
   4 Seasons-Anthology . . . . (Rhino)
   Tremeloes; *Best Of The Tremeloes* . . . . (Rhino)
   History Of British Rock-#7-C . . . . (Rhino)
   Rock Artifacts-From The Vaults-#4-C . . . . (Columbia)
Somebody Like Me
Silkk The Shocker Featuring Mya; *Made Man* . . . . (No Limit/Priority)
Spirit Of A Boy, Wisdom Of A Man
Randy Travis; *Big Country Hits '99-C* . . . . (K-Tel)
   You And You Alone . . . . (DreamWorks/SKG)
Split Decision
Steve Winwood; *Back In The High Life* . . . . (Island)
Stairway To Heaven
Led Zeppelin; *Led Zeppelin IV* . . . . (Atlantic)
   Led Zeppelin-Box Set . . . . (Atlantic)
   Remasters . . . . (Atlantic)
   ST/The Song Remains The Same . . . . (Swan Song)

Stanley Jordan; *Best Of Stanley Jordan* . . . . (Blue Note)
   Flying Home . . . . (EMI)
Standing On The Edge Of Goodbye
John Berry; *Standing On The Edge* . . . . (Capitol)
Stay Or Let It Go
Brian McKnight; *Back At One* . . . . (Motown)
Stop! In The Name Of Love
Diana Ross & The Supremes; *16 #1 Hits From The Early '60s-C* . . . . (Motown)
   Diana Ross & The Supremes' Greatest Hits . . . . (Motown)
   Diana Ross & The Supremes-Anthology (1962-1969) . . . . (Motown)
   Evening With Diana Ross . . . . (Motown)
   Girl Groups-Story Of A Sound-C . . . . (Rhino)
   Motown Superstar Series-#1-Diana Ross & The Supremes . . . . . (Motown)
   Hollies; *45-#89819* . . . . (Atlantic)
   Supremes; *Billboard Top Pop Hits-1965-C* . . . . (Rhino)
Straight Time
Bruce Springsteen; *The Ghost Of Tom Joad* . . . . (Columbia)
Tell Him
Barbra Streisand & Celine Dion; *Higher Ground* . . . . (Columbia)
   Celine Dion & Barbra Streisand; *Let's Talk About Love-C* . . . . . (550 Music)
Tentative Decisions
Talking Heads; *'77* . . . . (Sire)
Then We Are Decided
Soundtrack; *Jesus Christ Superstar* . . . . (MCA)
There Only Was One Choice
Harry Chapin; *Dance Band On The Titanic* . . . . (Elektra)
This Door Swings Both Ways
Herman's Hermits; *Herman's Hermits-Their Greatest Hits* . . . . (Abkco)
This Lonely Place
Goldfinger; *Hang-Ups* . . . . (Mojo Music/Universal)
Three Hearts In A Tangle
Roy Drusky; *45-#31193* . . . . (Decca)
To Zion
Lauryn Hill featuring Carlos Santana; *The Miseducation Of Lauryn Hill* . . . .(Ruffhouse/Columbia)
Tryin' To Love Two
William Bell; *Coming Back For More* . . . . (Razor & Tie)
Trying To Love Two Women
Oak Ridge Boys; *Oak Ridge Boys' Greatest Hits* . . . . (MCA)
   Oak Ridge Boys-Collection . . . . (MCA)
   Together . . . . (MCA)
Undecided
Silverchair; *Frogstomp* . . . . (Epic)
Undecided Blues
Tony Bennett; *Playin' With My Friends-Bennett Sings The Blues-C* . . . . (Columbia)
Waiting For You To Decide
Chicago; *Chicago 16* . . . . (Full Moon/Warner Bros.)
We Need A Resolution
Aaliyah; *Aaliyah* . . . . (BlackGround Enterp./Atlantic)
Whatever Comes First
Sons Of The Desert; *Whatever Comes First* . . . . (Epic)
What's It Gonna Be
Dusty Springfield; *Dusty Springfield-Anthology* . . . . (Mercury)
Where I Wanna Be
Donell Jones; *Where I Wanna Be* . . . . (LaFace)
Which Bridge To Cross (Which Bridge To Burn)
Vince Gill; *When Love Finds You* . . . . (MCA)
Why Oh Why
Celine Dion; *Let's Talk About Love-C* . . . .(550 Music)
Will You Marry Me?
Vonda Shepard; *ST/Songs From "Ally McBeal" Featuring Vonda Shepard* . . . .(550/Epic)
Woke Up This Morning
A3; *Exile On Coldharbour Lane* . . . . (C2/Columbia)
   The Sopranos-Music From The HBO Original Series . . . . (Sony Music Soundtrax)
You Make Me Wanna…
Usher; *My Way* . . . . (LaFace)
   Totally Hits-#1-C . . . . (Arista)
You Were Mine
Dixie Chicks; *Big Country Hits '99-C* . . . . (K-Tel)
   Wide Open Spaces . . . . (Monument)

DESERT

See Also: **COUNTRY, NATURE, WATER**

After The Rain Has Fallen
Sting; *Brand New Day* . . . . (A&M)
Another Pyramid
Sting; *ST/Aida* . . . . (Island)
Asleep In The Desert
ZZ Top; *Six Pack* . . . . (Warner Bros.)
   Tejas . . . . (Warner Bros.)
Ballad Of Ira Hayes, The
Johnny Cash; *The Man In Black-His Greatest Hits* . . . . (Legacy)

Peter La Farge; *Best Of Broadside 1962-1968: Anthems Of The American Underground From The Pages Of Broadside Magazine-C* . . . . (Smithsonian Folkways)

Caravan
Duke Ellington; *Best Of Duke Ellington* . . . . (Capitol)
  Money Jungle . . . . (Blue Note)
Ella Fitzgerald; *Montreux '75* . . . . (Pablo)
Johnny Mathis; *In A Sentimental Mood-Johnny Mathis Sings Ellington* . . . . (Columbia)
Wynton Marsalis; *Marsalis Standard Time-#1* . . . . (Columbia)

Cool Water
Bob Nolan; *Sound Of A Pioneer* . . . . (Elektra)
Frankie Laine; *Frankie Laine-16 Most Requested Songs* . . . . (Legacy)
Jack Scott; *Capitol Collectors Series-Jack Scott* . . . . (Capitol)
Joni Mitchell; *Chalk Mark In A Rain Storm* . . . . (Geffen)
Marty Robbins; *Gunfighter Ballads & Trail Songs* . . . . (Legacy)
Sons Of The Pioneers; *60 Years Of Country Music-C* . . . . (RCA)
  Best Of The Sons Of The Pioneers . . . . (RCA)
  Cool Water . . . . (RCA)
  Western Country . . . . (Granite)

Desert Moon
Great White; *Hooked* . . . . (Capitol)

Desert Moon
Dennis DeYoung; *Desert Moon* . . . . (A&M)

Desert Rose
Chris Hillman; *Desert Rose* . . . . (Sugar Hill)
Desert Rose Band; *Pages Of Life* . . . . (Curb)

Desert Rose
Eric Johnson; *Ah Via Musicom* . . . . (Capitol)

Desert Rose
Sting; *Brand New Day* . . . . (A&M)

Desert Song
Def Leppard; *Retro Active* . . . . (Mercury)

Goin' Cali
Bruce Springsteen; *Tracks* . . . . (Columbia)

Horse With No Name
America; *America* . . . . (Warner Bros.)
  America Live . . . . (Warner Bros.)
  Billboard Top Rock 'N' Roll Hits-1972-C . . . . (Rhino)
  History-Greatest Hits . . . . (Warner Bros.)

Hotter Than Mojave In My Heart
Iris DeMent; *Infamous Angel* . . . . (Warner Bros.)

Midnight At The Oasis
Maria Muldaur; *Maria Muldaur* . . . . (Reprise)
  Super Hits Of The '70s-Have A Nice Day-#13-C . . . . (Rhino)

Missing
Everything But The Girl; *Amplified Heart* . . . . (Atlantic)
  MTV Party To Go-#9-C . . . . (Tommy Boy)
  The Absolute Hits-C . . . . (Atlantic)
  The Ultimate Dance Party-1997-C . . . . (Arista)

On A Desert Island With You
Original Cast; *Sitting Pretty* . . . . (Nightwork)

Sahara
Esther Walker; *Music From The New York Stage (1890-1920)-#4-1917-1920-C* . . . . (Pearl)

Sands Of Nevada
Mark Knopfler; *Sailing To Philadelphia* . . . . (Warner Bros.)

Shifting, Whispering Sands
Billy Vaughn; *Melody Of Love-Best Of Billy Vaughn* . . . . . . (Varese Vintage)
Rusty Draper; *Rusty Draper's Greatest Hits* . . . . (Collector's Choice)

Snow On The Sahara
Anggun; *Anggun* . . . . (Epic)

Take Me
George Jones; *George Jones' Greatest Hits* . . . . (Epic)
George Jones & Tammy Wynette; *George Jones & Tammy Wynette-16 Biggest Hits* . . . . (Epic/Legacy)

Tea In The Sahara
Police; *Message In A Box-Complete Recordings* . . . . (A&M)
  Synchronicity . . . . (A&M)
Sting; *Bring On The Night* . . . . (A&M)

Tears Of Sahara
Tony MacAlpine; *Maximum Security* . . . . (Mercury)

There Is No Arizona
Jamie O'Neal; *Shiver* . . . . (Mercury)

DESIRE, Ask For, Beg, Crave, Longing, Need, Please, Requests & Favors, Want

See Also: *FOOD & BEVERAGES: GENERAL (hunger, thirst), HELP, LOVE (various), MOTIVATION, PRETEND, QUESTIONS & ANSWERS, URGENT, WAITING*

(It's Just) Desire
Nelson; *After The Rain* . . . . (David Geffen Co.)

(Let Me Be Your) Teddy Bear
Elvis Presley; *Elvis' Golden Records* . . . . (RCA)
  Elvis In Concert . . . . (RCA)

  Number One Hits . . . . (RCA)
  ST/Loving You . . . . (RCA)
  The Top Ten Hits . . . . (RCA)

(They Long To Be) Close To You
Carpenters; *Carpenters-Classics-#2* . . . . (A&M)
  Carpenters-Love Songs . . . . (A&M)
  Carpenters-The Singles 1969-1973 . . . . (A&M)
  From The Top . . . . (A&M)

(This Thing Called) Wantin' And Havin' It All
Sawyer Brown; *Greatest Hits Of Country Dance-C* . . . . (Curb)
  This Thing Called Wantin' & Havin' It All . . . . (Curb)

(Turn Out The Light And) Love Me Tonight
Don Williams; *Best Of Don Williams-#2* . . . . (MCA)
  Don Williams-20 Greatest Hits . . . . (MCA)

(Your Love Keeps Lifting Me) Higher And Higher
Bette Midler; *Bette Midler* . . . . (Atlantic)
Bonnie Bramlett; *It's Time* . . . . (Capricorn)
Jackie Wilson; *Billboard Top R&B Hits-1967-C* . . . . (Rhino)
  Jackie Wilson's Greatest Hits . . . . (Brunswick)
  Jackie Wilson's Greatest Hits-#2 . . . . (Brunswick)
  Reet Petite-Best Of Jackie Wilson . . . . (Columbia)
  The Jackie Wilson Story . . . . (Epic)
  Very Best Of Jackie Wilson . . . . (Rhino)
Rita Coolidge; *Anytime...Anywhere* . . . . (A&M)
  Havana Jam . . . . (Columbia)
  Rita Coolidge-Classics-#5 . . . . (A&M)
  Rita Coolidge's Greatest Hits . . . . (A&M)

...Baby One More Time
Britney Spears; *...Baby One More Time* . . . . (Jive)
  Now That's What I Call Music!-#2-C . . . . (Virgin)

2 Become 1
Spice Girls; *Spice* . . . . (Virgin)

49 Bye-Byes
Crosby, Stills & Nash; *Crosby, Stills & Nash* . . . . (Atlantic)

A Friend I Call Desire
Ultravox; *Lament* . . . . (One Way)

Ah! Sweet Mystery Of Life
Bing Crosby; *Little Bit Of Irish* . . . . (Atlantic)
Nelson Eddy; *Through The Years* . . . . (Living Era)

Ain't Too Proud To Beg
Rolling Stones; *It's Only Rock 'N Roll* . . . . (Rolling Stones)
Temptations; *Motown Story-First 25 Years-C* . . . . (Motown)
  ST/Big Chill . . . . (Motown)
  Temptations' Greatest Hits-#1 . . . . (Motown)
  Temptations-25th Anniversary . . . . (Motown)
  Temptations-Anthology-The Best Of The Temptations . . . . (Motown)

Air That I Breathe
Hollies; *Best Of The Hollies-#2* . . . . (EMI)
  Hollies . . . . (Epic)
  Hollies-Epic Anthology From The Original Master Tapes . . . . . . (Epic)

All At Once You Love Her
Perry Como; *Perry Como's Greatest Hits* . . . . (RCA)

All Day And All Of The Night
Kinks; *British Rock-#1-C* . . . . (Original Sound)
  God Save The Kinks! . . . . (Castle Music America)
  History Of British Rock-#2-C . . . . (Rhino)

All For You
Janet; *All For You* . . . . (Virgin)
  Now That's What I Call Music!-#7-C . . . . (Virgin)

All I Ask
Crowded House; *Woodface* . . . . (Capitol)

All I Ask Of You
Michael Crawford; *Michael Crawford Performs Andrew Lloyd Webber* . . . . (Atlantic)

All I Ask Of You
Barbra Streisand; *Till I Loved You* . . . . (Columbia)

All I Do
Somethin' For The People; *This Time It's Personal* . . . . (Warner Bros.)

All I Have To Do Is Dream
Everly Brothers; *All They Had To Do Was Dream* . . . . (Rhino)
  Best Of The Everly Brothers . . . . (Rhino)
  Fabulous Style Of The Everly Brothers . . . . (Rhino)
  Heartaches 'N' Harmonies . . . . (Rhino)
  Oldies But Goodies-#12-C . . . . (Original Sound)
  ST/Stealing Home . . . . (Atlantic)
  Very Best Of The Everly Brothers . . . . (Warner Bros.)
Nitty Gritty Dirt Band; *Best Of The Nitty Gritty Dirt Band* . . . . . . (Liberty)
  Heartbreak Hotel-C . . . . (EMI)

All I Have To Give
Backstreet Boys; *Backstreet Boys* . . . . (Jive)
  Now That's What I Call Music!-#3-C . . . . (Virgin)

All I Need
Forester Sisters; *All I Need* . . . . (Warner Bros.)

All I Need
Xscape; *Traces Of My Lipstick* . . . . (So So Def/Columbia)

All I Need
Temptations; *Temptations-Anthology-The Best Of The Temptations* . . . (Motown)

All I Need
Jack Wagner; *All I Need* . . . . (Qwest)

All I Really Want
Alanis Morissette; *Jagged Little Pill*. . . . .(Maverick)
All I Really Want To Do
Bob Dylan; *Another Side Of Bob Dylan* . . . . (Columbia)
  Bob Dylan At Budokan. . . . . (Columbia)
  Bob Dylan's Greatest Hits-#2 . . . . (Columbia)
Byrds; *Original Singles-#1-1965-1967* . . . . (Columbia)
  Play Dylan . . . . (Columbia)
  The Byrds . . . . (Columbia)
  The Byrds' Greatest Hits . . . . (Columbia)
Cher; *Best Of Cher* . . . .(EMI)
All I Wanna Do
Sheryl Crow; *Tuesday Night Music Club* . . . . (A&M)
All I Want
Joni Mitchell; *Blue* . . . . (Reprise)
Joni Mitchell with Tom Scott & The L.A. Express; *Miles Of Aisles* . . . . (Asylum)
All I Want
Offspring; *Ixnay On The Hombre* . . . . (Columbia)
All I Want
Toad The Wet Sprocket; *Fear*. . . . . (Columbia)
  P.S. (A Toad Retrospective) . . . . (Columbia)
All I Want For Christmas (Is My Two Front Teeth)
David Seville & The Chipmunks; *Christmas With The Chipmunks-#2* . . . .(EMI)
Nat "King" Cole; *Let It Snow!-Cuddly Christmas Classics* . . . . (Capitol)
Spike Jones; *Dr. Demento Presents The Greatest Novelty Records-#6-Christmas-C* . . . . (Rhino)
  Spike Jones-Christmas. . . . . (Rhino)
All I Want Is A Life
Tim McGraw; *All I Want* . . . . (Curb)
All I've Got To Do
Beatles; *Meet The Beatles!* . . . . (Capitol)
All That She Wants
Ace Of Base; *All That She Wants* . . . . (Arista)
All The Fun
Paul Overstreet; *Best Of Paul Overstreet* . . . . (RCA)
All The Man That I Need
Whitney Houston; *I'm Your Baby Tonight* . . . . (Arista)
  Whitney Houston's Greatest Hits. (Arista)
All The Places (I Will Kiss You)
Aaron Hall; *Inside Of You*. . . . .(MCA)
All The Things You Are
Ella Fitzgerald; *Complete Jerome Kern* . . . . (Verve)
Mario Lanza; *Be My Love-Greatest Performances*. . . . . (Rhino)
Willie Nelson; *Healing Hands Of Time* . . . . (Liberty)
All You Need Is Love
Beatles; *Beatles 1* . . . . (Capitol)
  Compact Disc Singles Collection. (Capitol)
  Magical Mystery Tour . . . . (Capitol)
  The Beatles/1967-1970 . . . . (Capitol)
  Yellow Submarine . . . . (Capitol)
Always Wanting You
Merle Haggard & The Strangers; *For The Record: Merle Haggard-43 Legendary Hits* . . . . (BNA)
An Echo, A Stain
Bjork; *Vespertine* . . . . (Elektra)
Ana's Song (Open Fire)
Silverchair; *Neon Ballroom* . . . .(Epic)
And Fools Shine On
Brother Cane; *Best Of Rockline-C* . . . . (Priority)
  Essential Southern Rock-C . . . .(House Of Blues)
  Seeds . . . . (Virgin)
Anema E Core
Eddie Fisher; *Very Best Of Eddie Fisher* . . . .(Taragon)
Angels
Earl Scruggs & Melissa Etheridge; *Earl Scruggs And Friends-C* . . . .(MCA)
Angels Would Fall
Melissa Etheridge; *Breakdown* . . . . (Island)
Animal Song
Savage Garden; *Affirmation* . . . . (Columbia)
Another Nine Minutes
Yankee Grey; *Untamed* . . . . (Monument)
Another Saturday Night
Cat Stevens; *Cat Stevens Greatest Hits*. . . . . (A&M)
Jimmy Buffett; *Margaritaville Cafe Late Night Menu* . . . . (Margaritaville)
Sam Cooke; *The Man And His Music* . . . . (RCA)
  This Is Sam Cooke . . . . (RCA)
Anticipation
Carly Simon; *Anticipation* . . . . (Elektra)
  Best Of Carly Simon. . . . . (Elektra)
Anyday
Derek And The Dominos; *Layla*. . . . . (Polydor)
Anyway You Want Me
Elvis Presley; *Elvis' Golden Records* . . . . (RCA)
Are You That Somebody?
Aaliyah; *ST/Dr. Dolittle* . . . .(Atlantic)
Ask
Go-Betweens; *Before Hollywood* . . . . (Beggar's Banquet)
Ask
Smiths; *Louder Than Bombs*. . . . . (Sire)

  Rank . . . .(Sire)
Ask Any Girl
Diana Ross & The Supremes; *Diana Ross & The Supremes' Greatest Hits* . . . . (Motown)
Supremes; *Where Did Our Love Go* . . . . (Motown)
Ask For Answers
Placebo; *Without You I'm Nothing* . . . .(Virgin)
Ask Me
Amy Grant; *Heart In Motion*. . . . . (A&M)
Ask Me
Elvis Presley; *Elvis' Gold Records, Volume 4* . . . .(RCA)
Ask Me 'bout Nothin' (But The Blues)
Boz Scaggs; *Come On Home*. . . . .(Virgin)
Ask Me How I Feel
Tina Turner; *Foreign Affair*. . . . . (Capitol)
Ask Me Jon
Ocean Blue; *Ocean Blue* . . . . (Reprise)
Ask Me Why
Beatles; *Please Please Me*. . . . . (Parlophone)
Ask Of You
Raphael Saadiq; *ST/Higher Learning* . . . .(550 Music)
Ask The Lonely
Vonda Shepard; *ST/Songs From "Ally McBeal" Featuring Vonda Shepard* . . . .(550/Epic)
Ask The Lonely
Journey; *Journey's Greatest Hits* . . . . (Columbia)
Ask The Magic 8 Ball
Less Than Jake; *Losing Streak* . . . . (Capitol)
Ask The Mountains
Vangelis; *Voices* . . . .(Atlantic)
Asking For It
Hole; *Live Through This* . . . . (David Geffen Co.)
Asking Me Lies
Replacements; *Don't Tell A Soul*. . . . . (Sire)
Asking Too Much
Ani DiFranco; *Not A Pretty Girl* . . . . (Righteous Babe)
Asking Us To Dance
Kathy Mattea; *Time Passes By* . . . . (Mercury)
At The Stars
Better Than Ezra; *How Does Your Garden Grow?* . . . . (Elektra)
At This Moment
Billy Vera & The Beaters; *Billboard Top Hits-1987-C* . . . . (Rhino)
  By Request: Best Of Billy Vera & The Beaters . . . . (Rhino)
Baby Come Back
Player; *Billboard Top Hits-1978-C* . . . . (Rhino)
  Mellow Rock Hits Of The '70s-Ventura Highway-C. . . . . . . (Rhino)
  Super Hits Of The '70s-Have A Nice Day-#21-C . . . . (Rhino)
Baby Got Back
Sir Mix-A-Lot; *Mack Daddy*. . . . .(Def American)
Baby I Need Your Loving
Four Tops; *Four Tops' Greatest Hits* . . . . (Motown)
  Four Tops-Anthology . . . . (Motown)
  The Ultimate Collection-Four Tops . . . . (Motown)
Johnny Rivers; *Johnny Rivers' Greatest Hits* . . . . (Capitol)
  Johnny Rivers-Anthology 1964-1977 . . . . (Rhino)
Baby I'm-A Want You
Bread; *Baby I'm-A Want You* . . . . (Elektra)
  Best Of Bread . . . . (Elektra)
  Bread-Anthology . . . . (Elektra)
Baby Love
Diana Ross; *Diana Ross-The Ultimate Collection* . . . . (Motown)
Supremes; *Motown Classic Hits-#5-C* . . . . (Motown)
Temptations; *ST/My Girl 2* . . . . (Epic)
Baby, Come Over (This Is Our Night)
Samantha Mumba; *Gotta Tell You* . . . .(Wildcard/Polydor/Interscope)
Baby, I Love You
Aretha Franklin; *Aretha Franklin-30 Greatest Hits* . . . . (Rhino)
Baby, Now That I've Found You
Alison Krauss & Union Station; *Best Of Austin City Limits-Country Music's Finest Hour-C* . . . . (Legacy)
  Now That I've Found You: A Collection. . . . . (Rounder)
Foundations; *Best Of Rock 'N Soul-C* . . . . (Priority)
  History Of British Rock-#6-C . . . . (Rhino)
Babydoll
Mariah Carey; *Butterfly* . . . . (Columbia)
Babylon
David Gray; *White Ladder* . . . . (ATO/RCA)
Back For Good
Take That; *Nobody Else* . . . . (Arista)
Back Here
BBMak; *Now That's What I Call Music!-#5-C* . . . .(Virgin)
  Sooner Or Later . . . . (Hollywood)
Back In Your Arms
Bruce Springsteen; *Tracks* . . . . (Columbia)
Back To The World
Tevin Campbell; *Back To The World* . . . . (Qwest)
Bad Girl
Jon B.; *Cool Relax* . . . .(Yab Yum/550)

Bad Touch, The
Bloodhound Gang; *Hooray For Boobies* . . . . (Republic/Geffen)
Bailamos
Enrique Iglesias; *Bailamos Greatest Hits* . . . . (Overbrook/Interscope)
Enrique . . . . (Overbrook/Interscope)
Now That's What I Call Music!-#3-C . . . .(Virgin)
Bali Ha'i
Original Cast; *South Pacific* . . . . (CBS Masterworks)
Band Of Gold
Don Cherry; *Very Best Of Don Cherry* . . . . (Collector's Choice)
Bang Bang
Stevie Wonder; *Down To Earth* . . . . (Motown)
Be Careful
Ricky Martin & Madonna; *Ricky Martin* . . . . (Columbia)
Be Like That
3 Doors Down; *Better Life* . . . . (Republic/Universal)
Now That's What I Call Music!-#8-C . . . .(Virgin)
Be My Baby Tonight
John Michael Montgomery; *John Michael Montgomery's
Greatest Hits* . . . . (Atlantic)
Kickin' It Up . . . . (Atlantic)
Beggars At The Feast
Original Broadway Cast; *Les Miserables* . . . . (Geffen)
Beggar's Day
Skid Row; *Slave To The Grind* . . . . (Atlantic)
Beggar's Farm
Dan Fogelberg; *This Was* . . . . (Chrysalis)
Beggar's Game
Dan Fogelberg; *Phoenix* . . . . (Full Moon)
Beggars On A Beach Of Gold
Mike & The Mechanics; *Beggar On A Beach Of Gold* . . . . (Atlantic)
Begging To You
Marty Robbins; *Essential Marty Robbins-1951-1982* . . . . (Columbia)
Marty Robbins-16 Biggest Hits . . . . (Legacy)
Bell Bottom Blues
Derek And The Dominos; *Layla* . . . . (Polydor)
Eric Clapton; *24 Nights* . . . . (Duck/Reprise)
Bend Me, Shape Me
American Breed; *The Ultimate History Of Rock 'N' Roll-#7-C* . . . . . (K-Tel)
Bernadette
Four Tops; *Compact Command Performances-Four Tops* . . . . (Motown)
Four Tops' Greatest Hits . . . . (Motown)
Four Tops Reach Out . . . . (Motown)
Four Tops-Anthology . . . . (Motown)
Motown Superstar Series-#14-Four Tops . . . . (Motown)
Bette Davis Eyes
Kim Carnes; *Best Of Kim Carnes* . . . . (EMI Special Markets)
Billboard Top Hits-1981-C . . . . (Rhino)
Mistaken Identity . . . . (EMI)
Better Man
Warren Brothers; *Beautiful Day In The Cold Cruel World* . . . .(BNA)
Big Spender
Original Cast; *Sweet Charity* . . . . (Columbia)
Billy Don't Be A Hero
Bo Donaldson & The Heywoods; *Super Hits Of The '70s-Have A Nice
Day-#13-C* . . . . (Rhino)
Black Magic Woman
Fleetwood Mac; *25 Years-The Chain* . . . . (Warner Bros.)
Vintage Years . . . .(Sire)
Santana; *Abraxas* . . . . (Columbia)
Moonflower . . . . (Columbia)
Rock Classics Of The '70s-C . . . . (Columbia)
Santana's Greatest Hits . . . . (Columbia)
Viva Santana! . . . . (Columbia)
Bobby's Girl
Marcie Blaine; *Collectables Presents The History Of Rock-#5-C* . . (Collectables)
Million-Dollar Memories-#2-C . . . .(RCA)
WCBS FM 101 History Of Rock-'60s-#5-C . . . . (Collectables)
Body And Soul
Benny Goodman & His Orchestra; *Benny Goodman's
Greatest Hits* . . . . (RCA Victor)
Benny Goodman Trio; *Ken Burns Jazz Collection-The Benny
Goodman Trio* . . . . (Legacy)
Billie Holiday; *Billie Holiday-16 Most Requested Songs* . . . . (Legacy)
Body And Soul . . . . (Verve)
The Billie Holiday Story-#2 . . . . (Columbia)
This Is Jazz #32: Billie Holiday Sings Standards . . . . (Columbia)
Verve Jazz Masters 47-Billie Holiday Sings Standards . . . . (Verve)
Carly Simon; *Torch* . . . . (Warner Bros.)
Coleman Hawkins; *Coleman Hawkins' Greatest Hits* . . . . (RCA Victor)
Verve Jazz Masters 34 . . . . (Verve)
Diana Krall; *Stepping Out* . . . .(Justin Time)
Eddie Jefferson; *Body And Soul* . . . . (Original Jazz Classics)
Letter From Home . . . . (Original Jazz Classics)
Main Man . . . . (Inner City)
The Jazz Singer . . . . (Evidence Music)
Louis Armstrong; *Essential Louis Armstrong* . . . . (Legacy)
Louis Armstrong-Love Songs . . . . (Legacy)
Musical Autobiography-#2 . . . . (MCA)

Satchmo At Symphony Hall . . . . (Decca Jazz)
Verve Jazz Masters 1 . . . .(Verve)
Manhattan Transfer; *Best Of The Manhattan Transfer* . . . . (Atlantic)
Extensions . . . .(Rhino)
Manhattan Transfer-Anthology-Down In Birdland . . . . (Rhino)
Paul Whiteman & His Orchestra; 78-#2297 . . . .(Columbia)
Sarah Vaughan; *How Long Has This Been Going On?* . . . . (Pablo)
One Night Stand-The Town Hall Concert-1947 . . . . (Blue Note)
Sarah Vaughan . . . .(Everest)
Body Bumpin'-Yippie-Yi-Yo
Public Announcement; *All Work, No Play* . . . .(A&M)
Borrowed Love
Earl Scruggs & Dwight Yoakam; *Earl Scruggs And Friends-C* . . . . (MCA)
Bounce With Me
Lil Bow Wow; *Beware Of Dog* . . . . (So So Def/Columbia)
ST/Big Momma's House . . . . (So So Def/Columbia)
Breakin' Me
Jonny Lang; *Wander This World* . . . .(A&M)
Breathless
Corrs; *In Blue* . . . . (143/Lava/Atlantic)
Totally Hits-#3-C . . . . (Atlantic)
Bring Him Home
Original Broadway Cast; *Les Miserables* . . . . (Geffen)
Bring It Down To My House
Asleep At The Wheel; *Tribute To The Music Of Bob Wills And The Texas
Playboys-C* . . . .(Liberty)
Merle Haggard; *Country Swing Essentials-C* . . . . (Hip-O)
Bring It On
Keith Washington; *KW* . . . .(Silas)
Brother, Can You Spare A Dime
Bing Crosby; *Bing Crosby-16 Most Requested Songs* . . . .(Legacy)
Odetta/Dr. John/John Campbell/Rufus Reid; *Strike A Deep Chord-Blues For
The Homeless-C* . . . . (Justice)
Peter, Paul & Mary; *See What Tomorrow Brings* . . . . (Warner Bros.)
Weavers; *Weavers' Greatest Hits* . . . . (Vanguard)
Brown Eyed Handsome Man
Buddy Holly; *Buddy Holly-20 Golden Greats* . . . . (MCA)
For The First Time Anywhere . . . . (MCA)
Rock & Roll Collection . . . . (MCA)
Chuck Berry; *Best Of The Best Of Chuck Berry* . . . . .(International Mktg. Group)
Roll Over Beethoven . . . . (Allegiance)
The Chess Box-Chuck Berry . . . . (Chess)
Waylon Jennings; *Essential Waylon Jennings* . . . . (RCA)
Waylon Jennings-Super Hits . . . . (RCA)
Brown Sugar
D'Angelo; *Brown Sugar* . . . . (EMI)
Build Me Up Buttercup
Foundations; *Billboard Top Rock 'N' Roll Hits-1969-C* . . . . (Rhino)
History Of British Rock-#9-C . . . .(Rhino)
ST/There's Something About Mary . . . .(Capitol)
Burn
Jo Dee Messina; *Burn* . . . .(Curb)
Burn Me Down
Marty Stuart; *Tempted* . . . . (MCA)
Butta Love
Next; *Rated Next* . . . . (Divine Mill/Arista)
Butterflies
Michael Jackson; *Invincible* . . . . (Epic)
Cabin On The Hill
Flatt & Scruggs; *Columbia Historic Edition-Flatt & Scruggs* . . . . . .(Columbia)
Lester Flatt & Earl Scruggs; *Bluegrass Super Hits-C* . . . .(Columbia)
Call Me
Blondie; *Best Of Blondie* . . . . (Chrysalis)
ST/American Gigolo . . . . (Chrysalis)
Can I Change My Mind
Tyrone Davis; *Soul Shots-#2-The "In" Crowd-Sweet Soul-C* . . . . (Rhino)
Tyrone Davis' Greatest Hits . . . . (Rhino)
Can We
SWV; *Release Some Tension* . . . . (RCA)
Can You See Me
Jimi Hendrix; *ST/Jimi Plays Monterey* . . . . (Reprise)
Jimi Hendrix Experience; *Are You Experienced?* . . . . (Reprise)
Smash Hits . . . . (Reprise)
Candy Everybody Wants
10,000 Maniacs; *MTV Unplugged-10,000 Maniacs* . . . . (Elektra)
Our Time In Eden . . . . (Elektra)
Candy Perfume Girl
Madonna; *Ray Of Light* . . . . (Maverick)
Candy's Room
Bruce Springsteen; *Darkness On The Edge Of Town* . . . .(Columbia)
Bruce Springsteen & The E Street Band; *Bruce Springsteen & The E Street
Band Live/1975-85* . . . . (Legacy)
Can't Get Enough
Kenny Lattimore; *ST/Love Jones* . . . . (Columbia)
Can't Get Enough
Patty Loveless; *Patty Loveless-Classics* . . . . (Epic)
Can't Take My Eyes Off You
Frankie Valli; *25th Anniversary Collection* . . . .(Rhino)

Frankie Valli-Anthology . . . . (Rhino)
Very Best Of Frankie Valli . . . .(MCA)
Lauryn Hill; *The Miseducation Of Lauryn Hill* . . . . (Ruffhouse/Columbia)

Careering (Don't Ask Me)
Peter Hammill; *Ph7* . . . . (Blue Plate)

Case Of You
Joni Mitchell; *Blue* . . . . (Reprise)
Joni Mitchell with Tom Scott & The L.A. Express; *Miles Of Aisles* . . . . (Asylum)

Caught A Lite Sneeze
Tori Amos; *Boys For Pele* . . . . (Atlantic)

Cecilia
Simon & Garfunkel; *Bridge Over Troubled Water* . . . . (Columbia)
Collected Works . . . . (Columbia)
Simon & Garfunkel's Greatest Hits . . . . (Columbia)

Cherish
Association; *Association Greatest Hits* . . . .(Warner Bros.)
Billboard Top Pop Hits-1966-C . . . . (Rhino)

Church Bells May Ring
Diamonds; *Best Of The Diamonds* . . . . (Rhino)
Willows; *Rockin' & Rollin' Wedding Songs-#1-C* . . . . (Rhino)
ST/A Rage In Harlem . . . .(MCA Special Prod.)
WCBS FM 101 History Of Rock-'50s-#2-C . . . . (Collectables)

Church Of Desire
Richie Sambora; *Stranger In This Town* . . . . (Mercury)

Closer To Free
BoDeans; *Chicago Bulls Greatest Hits-#3-C* . . . .(Atlantic)
Go Slow Down . . . . (Slash)
Joe Dirt Car . . . . (Reprise)
ST/Party Of Five . . . . (Reprise)

Closing Time
Semisonic; *Feeling Strangely Fine* . . . . (MCA)
Now That's What I Call Music!-#2-C . . . . (Virgin)

C'mon Marianne
4 Seasons; *25th Anniversary Collection* . . . . (Rhino)
4 Seasons-Anthology . . . . (Rhino)

Come A Little Bit Closer
Fleetwood Mac; *25 Years-The Chain* . . . .(Warner Bros.)

Come And Get It
Badfinger; *Best Of Badfinger* . . . . (Capitol)
Beatles; *The Beatles-Anthology-#3* . . . . (Capitol)

Come On
Billy Lawrence; *12" Maxi Single* . . . . (East West)

Come On Down To My Boat
Every Mother's Son; *Battle Of The Bands-#3-C* . . . . (K-Tel)

Come On Over (All I Want Is You)
Christina Aguilera; *Christina Aguilera* . . . . (RCA)

Come On-A My House
Rosemary Clooney; *Rosemary Clooney-16 Most Requested Songs* . . . . (Legacy)
Sentimental Journey: Pop Vocal Classics-#3-C . . . . (Rhino)

Come Over To My Place
Davina; *Best Of Both Worlds* . . . . (Loud/RCA)

Come See Me
112; *112* . . . . (Bad Boy/Arista)

Come Softly To Me
Fleetwoods; *Come Softly To Me: The Very Best Of The Fleetwoods* . . . . . .(EMI)
Only Love-1955-1959-C . . . . (Rhino)

Come To My Window
Melissa Etheridge; *The Concert For New York City-C* . . . . (Columbia)
Yes I Am . . . . (Island)

Come With Me
Shai; *Blackface* . . . . (Gasoline Alley)

Come With Me
Keith Sweat featuring Ronald Isley; *Keith Sweat* . . . . (Elektra)

Coming Back Home
Bebe Winans featuring Brian McKnight & Joe; *Love & Freedom* . . . . (Motown)

Common Disaster
Cowboy Junkies; *Lay It Down* . . . .(Geffen)

Constant Craving
k.d. lang; *Ingenue* . . . . (Sire)

Control
Puddle Of Mudd; *Come Clean* . . . . (Flawless/Geffen/Interscope)

Cool Water
Bob Nolan; *Sound Of A Pioneer* . . . . (Elektra)
Frankie Laine; *Frankie Laine-16 Most Requested Songs* . . . . (Legacy)
Jack Scott; *Capitol Collectors Series-Jack Scott* . . . . (Capitol)
Joni Mitchell; *Chalk Mark In A Rain Storm* . . . . (Geffen)
Marty Robbins; *Gunfighter Ballads & Trail Songs* . . . . (Legacy)
Sons Of The Pioneers; *60 Years Of Country Music-C* . . . . (RCA)
Best Of The Sons Of The Pioneers . . . . (RCA)
Cool Water . . . . (RCA)
Western Country . . . . (Granite)

Could I Have This Kiss Forever
Whitney Houston & Enrique Iglesias; *Whitney Houston's
Greatest Hits* . . . . (Arista)

Cowboy Take Me Away
Dixie Chicks; *Fly* . . . . (Monument)

Crash Into Me
Dave Matthews Band; *Crash* . . . . (RCA)

Crazy For You
Eboni Foster; *Just What You Want* . . . . (Nightbird/MCA)

Cup Of Life
Ricky Martin; *Ricky Martin* . . . . (Columbia)

Cupid
Sam Cooke; *Best Of Sam Cooke* . . . .(RCA)
The Man And His Music . . . . (RCA)
Spinners; *Love Trippin'* . . . . (Atlantic)

Cynthia
Bruce Springsteen; *Tracks* . . . . (Columbia)

Dance Tonight
Lucy Pearl; *Lucy Pearl* . . . . (Overbrook/Pookie/Beyond)

Dance With Me
Drifters; *Drifters-16 Greatest Hits* . . . . (Deluxe)

Dance With Me
Debelah Morgan; *Dance With Me* . . . .(Atlantic)
Totally Hits-#3-C . . . .(Atlantic)

Dancin'
Guy; *Guy-III* . . . . (MCA)

Dancing In The Dark
Bruce Springsteen; *Born In The U.S.A.* . . . . (Columbia)
Bruce Springsteen's Greatest Hits . . . . (Columbia)

Darkness On The Edge Of Town
Bruce Springsteen; *Darkness On The Edge Of Town* . . . . (Columbia)
Bruce Springsteen & The E Street Band; *Bruce Springsteen & The E Street
Band Live/1975-85* . . . . (Legacy)

Dazed And Confused
Led Zeppelin; *Classic Rock 1966-1988-C* . . . .(Atlantic)
Led Zeppelin . . . .(Atlantic)
Led Zeppelin-Box Set . . . .(Atlantic)
ST/The Song Remains The Same . . . . (Swan Song)

Dead Bodies Everywhere
Korn; *Follow The Leader* . . . . (Immortal/Epic)

Dedicated To The One I Love
Mamas & The Papas; *Best Of The Mamas & The Papas* . . . . (MCA)
Farewell To The First Golden Era . . . . (MCA)
Original Classic Oldies Of The '50s & '60s-#13-C . . . . (MCA)
Shirelles; *Oldies But Goodies-#10-C* . . . .(Original Sound)
Shirelles' Greatest Hits . . . . (Everest)
Shirelles-Anthology 1959-1964 . . . . (Rhino)
Super Oldies Of The '50s-#4-C . . . . (Audio Fidelity)

Desert Rose
Sting; *Brand New Day* . . . . (A&M)

Desire
2 Unlimited; *Get Ready* . . . . (Critique)

Desire
Andy Gibb; *After Dark* . . . .(Polydor)

Desire
Heart; *Desire Walks On* . . . . (Capitol)

Desire
Slayer; *Diabolus In Musica* . . . . (American)

Desire
Ozzy Osbourne; *Live & Loud* . . . . (Epic Portrait Assoc.)

Desire
Talk Talk; *Very Best Of Talk Talk-Natural History* . . . . (EMI)

Desire
Toad The Wet Sprocket; *Coil* . . . . (Columbia)

Desire
Yello; *Stella* . . . . (Mercury)

Desire
U2; *Rattle And Hum* . . . . (Island)

Desire Walks On
Heart; *Desire Walks On* . . . . (Capitol)

Desperately Wanting
Better Than Ezra; *Friction, Baby* . . . . (Swell/Elektra)

Detroit City
Ace Cannon; *Golden Favorites* . . . . (Ranwood)
Bill Anderson; *Best Of Bill Anderson* . . . . (Curb)
Bobby Bare; *Nipper's Greatest Hits Of The '60s-#2-C* . . . . (RCA)
This Is Bobby Bare . . . . (RCA)
Chet Atkins; *Country Gems* . . . .(Pair)
Flatt & Scruggs; *20 All-Time Great Recordings* . . . . (Columbia)
Hank Williams, Jr.; *Live At Cobo Hall Detroit* . . . .(Polydor)
Standing In The Shadows . . . .(Polydor)
Mel Tillis; *Best Of Mel Tillis* . . . . (MCA)
Live At The Sam Houston Coliseum . . . . (MGM)
Solomon Burke; *Home In Your Heart-Best Of Solomon Burke* . . . . (Rhino)

Devil Or Angel
Bobby Vee; *Best Of Bobby Vee* . . . . (EMI)
Bobby Vee-Golden Greats . . . . (Liberty)
Bobby Vee-Legendary Masters . . . . (EMI)
Clovers; *Atlantic Rhythm & Blues 1947-1974-#3 (1955-1958)-C* . . . . . .(Atlantic)
Oldies But Goodies-#2-C . . . . (Original Sound)
Very Best Of The Clovers . . . . (Rhino)

Devil Woman
Marty Robbins; *Billboard Top Country Hits-1962-C* . . . . (Rhino)
Columbia Country Classics-#4-Nashville Sound-C . . . . (Columbia)
Lifetime Of Song-1951-1982 . . . . (Columbia)

Marty Robbins' Greatest Hits-#4 . . . .(Columbia)

Dig A Pony
Beatles; *Let It Be* . . . . (Capitol)
The Beatles-Anthology-#3 . . . . (Capitol)

Digital Bath
Deftones; *White Pony* . . . . (Maverick)

Dim, Dim The Lights (I Want Some Atmosphere)
Bill Haley; *From The Original Master Tapes-Bill Haley* . . . . (MCA)

Discotheque
U2; *Pop* . . . . (Island)

Dizzy Miss Lizzy
Beatles; *Beatles VI* . . . . (Capitol)
Rock 'N' Roll Music . . . . (Capitol)
The Beatles At The Hollywood Bowl . . . . (Capitol)
Ronnie Hawkins and The Hawks; *Best Of Ronnie Hawkins and The
Hawks* . . . . (Rhino)

Do It Again A Little Bit Slower
Jon, Robin & The In Crowd; *Dick Bartley's One-Hit Wonders Of The
'60s-#1-C* . . . . (Rhino)

Do Not Ask For Love
Monkees; *Missing Links-#2* . . . . (Rhino)

Do You Really Want Me
Robyn; *Robyn Is Here* . . . . (RCA)

Don't Ask A Friend
Olivia Newton-John; *Making A Good Thing Better* . . . . (MCA)

Don't Ask Me
A Flock Of Seagulls; *A Flock Of Seagulls* . . . .(Jive)

Don't Ask Me No Questions
Lynyrd Skynyrd; *Second Helping* . . . . (MCA)

Don't Ask Me Why
Eurythmics; *We Too Are One* . . . . (Arista)

Don't Ask Me Why
Billy Joel; *Glass Houses* . . . . (Columbia)

Don't Ask Me Why
Elvis Presley; *King Creole* . . . . (RCA)

Don't Ask Why
Replacements; *Sorry Ma, Forgot To Take Out The Trash* . . . . (Restless)

Don't Go Away
Oasis; *Be Here Now* . . . . (Epic)

Don't Go Breaking My Heart
Elton John & Kiki Dee; *Elton John's Greatest Hits-#2* . . . . (Polydor)

Don't Leave Me
Blackstreet; *Another Level*. . . . . (Interscope)

Don't Let Go
Regina Belle; *Believe In Me* . . . . (MCA)

Don't Let Me Leave
Marc Anthony; *Marc Anthony*. . . . . (Columbia)

Don't Let The Stars Get In Your Eyes
Perry Como; *Como's Golden Records*. . . . .(RCA)
Perry Como-Pure Gold. . . . .(RCA)
Perry Como's All-Time Greatest Hits-#1 . . . . (RCA)
This Is Perry Como . . . . (RCA)

Don't Pull Your Love
Hamilton, Joe Frank & Reynolds; *'70s Biggest Hits-C* . . . . (MCA Special Prod.)
Hamilton, Joe Frank & Reynolds' Greatest Hits . . . . (MCA Special Prod.)
Rock Around The Oldies-#4-C . . . . (MCA Special Prod.)

Don't Take Your Love From Me
Etta James; *These Foolish Things-The Classic Balladry Of Etta James* . . (MCA)
King Sisters; *Spotlight On The King Sisters* . . . . (Capitol)
Three Suns; *Very Best Of The Three Suns* . . . . (Taragon)

Don't You Know
Keb' Mo'; *The Door* . . . .(550/Epic/Okeh)

Don't You Want Me
Jody Watley; *Jody Watley*. . . . . (MCA)
Jody Watley's Greatest Hits . . . . (MCA)
You Wanna Dance With Me? . . . . (MCA)

Down On My Knees
Beth Nielsen Chapman; *Beth Nielsen Chapman* . . . . (Reprise)
Trisha Yearwood; *Hearts In Armor* . . . . (MCA)

Dream Merchant
New Birth; *Smooth Grooves-A Sensual Collection-#5-C* . . . . (Rhino)

Drift Away
Dobie Gray; *Classic Rock-#1-C* . . . . (MCA)
Oldies But Goodies-#10-C . . . . (Original Sound)
Oldies But Goodies-#3-C . . . . (Original Sound)
Super Hits Of The '70s-Have A Nice Day-#10-C . . . . (Rhino)
Michael Bolton; *Timeless-Classics* . . . . (Columbia)
Rod Stewart; *Atlantic Crossing* . . . . (Warner Bros.)

Drops Of Jupiter (Tell Me)
Train; *Drops Of Jupiter* . . . . (Aware/C2/Columbia)

Eight Days A Week
Beatles; *Beatles 1* . . . . (Capitol)
Beatles VI . . . . (Capitol)
Beatles-20 Greatest Hits . . . . (Capitol)
The Beatles/1962-1966 . . . . (Capitol)

Elegantly Wasted
INXS; *Elegantly Wasted* . . . . (Mercury)

Eloise
Damned; *Light At The End Of The Tunnel* . . . . (MCA)

Embraceable You
Billie Holiday; *Body And Soul* . . . .(Verve)
Frank Sinatra; *The Capitol Years* . . . .(Capitol)
MGM Studio Orchestra; *ST/American In Paris* . . . . . (Sony Music Special Prod.)
Oleta Adams; *Glory Of Gershwin Featuring Larry Adler-C* . . . .(Mercury)
Sarah Vaughan; *Complete Sarah Vaughan On Mercury-#1-Great Jazz Years-
1954-1956* . . . .(Mercury)

Essence
Lucinda Williams; *Essence* . . . .(Lost Highway/IDJMG)

Everlasting Glaze
Smashing Pumpkins; *Machina: The Machines Of God* . . . . (Virgin)

Everlong
Foo Fighters; *The Colour And The Shape* . . . . (Roswell/RCA)

Every Breath You Take
Police; *Every Breath You Take-The Classics* . . . .(A&M)
Synchronicity . . . . (A&M)
Tammy Wynette & Sting; *Without Walls-C* . . . . (Epic)

Every Day
Stevie Nicks; *Trouble In Shangri-La* . . . . (Reprise)

Every Light In The House
Trace Adkins; *Dreamin' Out Loud*. . . . .(Capitol)

Everybody Needs Somebody To Love
Blues Brothers; *Best Of The Blues Brothers* . . . . (Atlantic)

Everybody's Trying To Be My Baby
Beatles; *Beatles '65* . . . . (Capitol)
For Sale . . . . (Capitol)
The Beatles-Anthology-#2 . . . . (Capitol)
Carl Perkins; *Blue Suede Shoes: The Very Best Of Carl Perkins* . . .(Collectables)
Carl Perkins' Greatest Hits/Finest Performances . . . . (Sun)
Carl Perkins-Original Sun Greatest Hits . . . . (Rhino)

Everyday
Dave Matthews Band; *America: A Tribute To Heroes-C* . . . . (Interscope)
Everyday . . . . (RCA)

Everything I Own
Bread; *Baby I'm-A Want You* . . . . (Elektra)
Best Of Bread . . . . (Elektra)
Bread-Anthology . . . . (Elektra)

Everything She Wants
Wham! Featuring George Michael; *'80s Greatest Rock Hits-#1-Passion &
Power-C* . . . . (Priority)
Make It Happen . . . .(Columbia)

Everything Your Heart Desires
Daryl Hall & John Oates; *ooh yeah!* . . . .(Arista)

Excuse Me Mr.
No Doubt; *Tragic Kingdom* . . . . (Trauma)

Eye
Smashing Pumpkins; *ST/Lost Highway* . . . . (Interscope)

Fall In Love
Kenny Chesney; *All I Need To Know* . . . . (BNA)
Kenny Chesney's Greatest Hits . . . . (BNA)

Falling In Love (Is Hard On The Knees)
Aerosmith; *A Little South Of Sanity* . . . . (Geffen)
Nine Lives . . . .(Columbia)

Falling In Love Again (Can't Help It)
Billie Holiday; *Quintessential-#8-1939-1940* . . . .(Legacy)
Linda Ronstadt; *Lush Life* . . . .(Asylum)
Marlene Dietrich; *Best Of Marlene Dietrich* . . . . (Columbia)
Falling In Love Again . . . . (MCA)
Her Complete Decca Recordings . . . . (MCA)

Feels So Good (Show Me Your Love)
Lina Santiago; *Best Of Dance Hits Supermix-#1 & 2-C* . . . .(Warlock)
Dance Mix USA-#5-C . . . .(Warlock)

Fever
Buddy Guy; *This Is Buddy Guy* . . . .(Vanguard)
Elvis Presley; *A Valentine Gift For You* . . . .(RCA)
Aloha from Hawaii via Satellite . . . . (RCA)
Elvis Presley-Pure Gold . . . . (RCA)
Little Willie John; *Best Of Little Willie John-Fever* . . . .(Rhino)
Peggy Lee; *Memories Are Made Of This-C* . . . . (Capitol)
Rita Coolidge; *Rita Coolidge-Classics-#5* . . . .(A&M)
Rita Coolidge's Greatest Hits . . . . (A&M)

Fire
Bruce Springsteen & The E Street Band; *Bruce Springsteen & The E Street
Band Live/1975-85* . . . . (Legacy)
Pointer Sisters; *Cover Me (Bruce Springsteen Tribute)-C* . . . .(Rhino)
Energy . . . . (Planet)
I Am Woman-C . . . . (Nick At Nite)

First Taste
Fiona Apple; *Tidal* . . . . (Clean Slate/Work)

Flavor Of The Weak
American Hi-Fi; *American Hi-Fi*. . . . .(Island)
Now That's What I Call Music!-#7-C . . . . (Virgin)

Flesh And Blood
Johnny Cash; *Johnny Cash's Biggest Hits* . . . .(Columbia)
The Man In Black-His Greatest Hits . . . . (Legacy)

Fly Like An Eagle
Seal; *ST/Space Jam* . . . . (Warner Sunset)

Steve Miller; *Fly Like An Eagle* (Capitol)
ST/FM (MCA)
Steve Miller Band-Gift Set (Capitol)
Steve Miller Band-Live (Capitol)
Steve Miller Band's Greatest Hits-1974-78 (Capitol)

Fool For Your Love
Mickey Gilley; *19 Hot Country Requests-C* (Epic)
Fool For Your Love (Epic)

Fools Rush In (Where Angels Fear To Tread)
Brook Benton; *Super Oldies Of The '60s-#10-C* (Audio Fidelity)
Tommy Dorsey & Frank Sinatra; *Sessions-#1-February 1, 1940-July 17, 1940* (RCA)

For Once In My Life
Gladys Knight & The Pips; *Gladys Knight & The Pips-Anthology* (Motown)
Motown Superstar Series-#13-Gladys Knight & The Pips (Motown)
Neither One Of Us (Motown)
Stevie Wonder; *Motown Story-First 25 Years-C* (Motown)
Stevie Wonder-Love Songs-20 Classic Hits (Motown)
Stevie Wonder's Greatest Hits-#2 (Motown)
Tony Bennett; *Tony Bennett's All-Time Greatest Hits* (Columbia)
Vikki Carr; *Best Of Vikki Carr* (EMI)

For Your Precious Love
Jerry Butler; *Best Of Jerry Butler* (Rhino)

Forever Tonight
Peter Cetera & Crystal Bernard; *One Clear Voice* (River North)

Foxey Lady
Jimi Hendrix; *Essential Jimi Hendrix, Volume 2* (Reprise)
ST/Jimi Plays Monterey (Reprise)
ST/Wayne's World (Reprise)
Jimi Hendrix Experience; *Are You Experienced?* (Reprise)
Smash Hits (Reprise)
Mary's Danish; *Circa* (Morgan Creek)

Freak Like Me
Adina Howard; *Do You Wanna Ride?* (East West)
MTV Party To Go-#7-C (Tommy Boy)

Free
Mya; *ST/Bait* (Warner Bros.)

Freek'n You
Jodeci; *MTV Party To Go-#7-C* (Tommy Boy)
The Show, The After-Party, The Hotel (Uptown/MCA)

From Me To You
Beatles; *Beatles 1* (Capitol)
Past Masters-Volume One (Parlophone)
The Beatles/1962-1966 (Capitol)
The Beatles-Anthology-#1 (Capitol)

Fuel
Metallica; *Reload* (Elektra)

Gel
Collective Soul; *Collective Soul* (Atlantic)
ST/Jerky Boys (Atlantic)

Genie In A Bottle
Christina Aguilera; *Christina Aguilera* (RCA)
Totally Hits-#2-C (Elektra)

Get Me Home
Foxy Brown; *Ill Na Na* (Violator)

Gimme Gimme Good Lovin'
Crazy Elephant; *Dick Bartley's One-Hit Wonders Of The '60s-#2-C* (Rhino)

Girl
Beatles; *Beatles-Box Set* (Capitol)
Beatles-Love Songs (Capitol)
Rubber Soul (Capitol)
The Beatles/1962-1966 (Capitol)

Girl Like You
Edwyn Collins; *Gorgeous George* (Bar/None)
ST/Empire Records (A&M)

Girls Dem Sugar
Beenie Man; *Art And Life* (Virgin)

Give It To You
Jordan Knight; *Jordan Knight* (Interscope)

Give Me Just One Night (Una Noche)
98 Degrees; *Now That's What I Call Music!-#5-C* (Virgin)
Revelation (Universal)

Give Me You
Mary J. Blige; *Mary* (MCA)

Give My Love To Rose
George Jones; *George Jones Sings The Hits Of His Country Cousins* (Razor & Tie)
Johnny Cash; *Johnny Cash-Sun Years* (Rhino)

Give My Regards To Broadway
Barry Manilow; *Showstoppers* (Arista)
Joel Grey; *Broadway Magic-The 1960s-C* (Columbia)
Original Cast; *George M.* (Columbia)

Give You What You Want
Chico DeBarge; *Game* (Motown)

Given More Time
Vince Gill; *High Lonesome Sound* (MCA)

Gliding Through My Memoree
Original Cast; *ST/Flower Drum Song* (Sony Music Classical)

Glycerine
Bush; *Sixteen Stone* (Trauma)

Go Where You Wanna Go
Mamas & The Papas; *Best Of The Mamas & The Papas* (MCA)
Farewell To The First Golden Era (MCA)
If You Can Believe Your Eyes & Ears (MCA)
Mamas & The Papas-16 Of Their Greatest Hits (MCA)

God Gave Me Everything
Mick Jagger; *Goddess In The Doorway* (Virgin)

Good Lovin'
Grateful Dead; *Shakedown Street* (Arista)
Rascals; *Hit Singles-1958-1977-C* (Atlantic)
Rascals' Greatest Hits (Atlantic)
Rascals-Super Hits (Atlantic)
ST/Big Chill (Motown)

Got Me Wrong
Alice In Chains; *Alice In Chains-MTV Unplugged* (Columbia)
ST/Clerks (Chaos)

Got To Get It
Sisqo; *Got To Get It (single)* (Dragon/Def Soul/IDJMG)

Got To Get You Into My Life
Beatles; *Beatles-Box Set* (Capitol)
Revolver (Capitol)
Rock 'N' Roll Music (Capitol)
The Beatles-Anthology-#2 (Capitol)
Earth, Wind & Fire; *Best Of Earth, Wind & Fire-#1* (Legacy)
ST/Sgt. Pepper's Lonely Hearts Club Band (RSO)
Paul McCartney & Wings; *Kampuchea-C* (Atlantic)

Gotta Tell You
Samantha Mumba; *Gotta Tell You* (Wildcard/Polydor/Interscope)
Now That's What I Call Music!-#6-C (Virgin)

Grease Megamix
Grease Megamix; *Pure Disco* (A&M)

Have You Ever Loved A Woman
Derek And The Dominos; *Layla* (Polydor)

Have You Ever?
Brandy; *Never Say Never* (Atlantic)

He Left A Lot To Be Desired
Ricochet; *Blink Of An Eye* (Columbia)

Head Over Heels
Allure; *The Greatest Dance Album In The World-C* (Epic)
Allure featuring NAS; *Allure* (Track Masters/Crave)

Heart Is A Lonely Hunter
Reba McEntire; *Read My Mind* (MCA)
Reba McEntire's Greatest Hits-#3: I'm A Survivor (MCA)

Heart's Desire
Lee Roy Parnell; *We All Get Lucky Sometimes* (Career)

Heaven
Nu Flavor; *110% Hits-C* (Simitar)
Nu Flavor (Reprise)

Heaven And Hot Rods
Stone Temple Pilots; *No. 4* (Atlantic)

Hello Brother
Louis Armstrong; *What A Wonderful World* (Decca Jazz)

Help!
Beatles; *Beatles 1* (Capitol)
Beatles-20 Greatest Hits (Capitol)
Rarities (Capitol)
Reel Music (Capitol)
ST/Help! (Capitol)
The Beatles At The Hollywood Bowl (Capitol)
The Beatles/1962-1966 (Capitol)

Hemorrhage (In My Hands)
Fuel; *Now That's What I Call Music!-#6-C* (Virgin)
Something Like Human (Epic)

Her Man
Gary Allan; *Cryin' Lyin' Lovin' & Leavin'-C* (Universal)
Used Heart For Sale (Decca)
Waylon Jennings; *The Eagle* (Epic)

Here
Tony Martin; *Best Of Tony Martin On RCA* (Collector's Choice)

Here In My Heart
Al Martino; *Capitol Collectors Series-Al Martino* (Capitol)

Here, There & Everywhere
Beatles; *Beatles-Box Set* (Capitol)
Beatles-Love Songs (Capitol)
Revolver (Capitol)
Kenny Loggins; *Kenny Loggins Alive* (Columbia)

Hero
Verve Pipe; *The Verve Pipe* (RCA)

He's Only A Prayer Away (I Asked The Lord)
Elvis Presley; *A Golden Celebration* (RCA)

He's So Fine
Chiffons; *Best Of The Girl Groups-#1-C* (Rhino)
Billboard Top Rock 'N' Roll Hits-1963-C (Rhino)
Chiffons Greatest Hits (Right Stuff)
Jody Miller; *Jody Miller's Greatest Hits* (Epic)

Hey Girl
Billy Joel; *Billy Joel's Greatest Hits-#3* (Columbia)

Freddie Scott; *Freddie Scott Sings And Sings And Sings* . . . . (Collectables)
Michael McDonald; *Best Of Smooth Jazz-#2-Under The Covers-C* . . . . (Warner Bros.)
Blink Of An Eye . . . . (Reprise)
Righteous Brothers; *Best Of The Righteous Brothers-#2* . . . . (Curb)

High Noon
Frankie Laine; *Billboard Top Movie Hits-1950-1954-C* . . . . (Rhino)
Tex Ritter; *Heroes Of Country Music-#4-Legends Of The West Coast-C* . . . . (Rhino)
The Envelope Please-Academy Award Winning Songs (1946-1957)-C . . . . (Rhino)

Hollow, The
A Perfect Circle; *Mer De Noms* . . . . (Virgin)

Hot Boyz
Missy "Misdemeanor" Elliot; *Da Real World* . . . . (East West)
Totally Hits-#2-C . . . . (Elektra)

How Can I Be Sure
Rascals; *Groovin'* . . . . (Warner Special Prod.)
Rascals-Anthology 1965-1972 . . . . (Rhino)
The Ultimate Rascals . . . . (Warner Special Prod.)
Very Best Of The Rascals . . . . (Rhino)

How Do I Get There
Deana Carter; *Did I Shave My Legs For This?* . . . . (Capitol)

How Forever Feels
Kenny Chesney; *Everywhere We Go* . . . . (BNA)
Kenny Chesney's Greatest Hits . . . . (BNA)

How Was I To Know
John Michael Montgomery; *What I Do The Best* . . . . (Atlantic)

How'd You Like To Be My Daddy?
Farber Sisters; *Music From The New York Stage (1890-1920)-#4-1917-1920-C* . . . . (Pearl)

Hunger
Waylon Jennings; *Ramblin' Man* . . . . (RCA)

Hunger Strike
Temple Of The Dog; *Temple Of The Dog* . . . . (A&M)

Hungry
Winger; *Winger* . . . . (Atlantic)

Hungry
Coasters; *It Ain't Sanitary* . . . . (Trip)

Hungry
Sammy Hagar; *Sammy Hagar* . . . . (Capitol)

Hungry (For Those Good Things)
Paul Revere And The Raiders; *Best Of Paul Revere And The Raiders-#1* . . . . (Bac-Trac)
Frat Rock!-C . . . . (Rhino)
Legend Of Paul Revere And The Raiders . . . . (Columbia)
Paul Revere And The Raiders' Greatest Hits . . . . (Columbia)

Hungry Eyes
Eric Carmen; *Best Of Eric Carmen* . . . . (Arista)
Dirty Dancing Live In Concert-C . . . . (RCA)
ST/Dirty Dancing . . . . (RCA)

Hungry Eyes
Emmylou Harris; *Mama's Hungry Eyes-Merle Haggard Tribute-C* . . . . . (Arista)
Merle Haggard; *For The Record: Merle Haggard-43 Legendary Hits* . . . . (BNA)

Hungry For Love
Patsy Cline; *20 Golden Pieces Of Patsy Cline* . . . . (Bulldog)
Hungry For Love-Her First Recordings-#2 . . . . (Rhino)
Patsy Cline . . . . (MCA)

Hungry For Love
Todd Rundgren; *A Wizard A True Star* . . . . (Rhino)

Hungry For Your Love
Van Morrison; *ST/An Officer And A Gentleman* . . . . (Island)
Wavelength . . . . (Warner Bros.)

Hungry Heart
Bruce Springsteen; *Bruce Springsteen's Greatest Hits* . . . . (Columbia)
The River . . . . (Columbia)
Bruce Springsteen & The E Street Band; *Bruce Springsteen & The E Street Band Live/1975-85* . . . . (Legacy)

Hurts So Good
John Cougar; *American Fool* . . . . (Riva)

I Asked For Water (He Gave Me Gasoline)
Lucinda Williams; *Lucinda Williams* . . . . (Koch International)

I Beg Of You
Elvis Presley; *50,000,000 Elvis Fans Can't Be Wrong-Elvis' Gold Records-Volume 2* . . . . (RCA)
The King Of Rock 'N' Roll-The Complete 50's Masters . . . . (RCA)
The Top Ten Hits . . . . (RCA)
Worldwide 50 Gold Award Hits, Vol. 1, Parts 1 & 2 . . . . (RCA)

I Cain't Say No
Original Broadway Cast; *Oklahoma!* . . . . (RCA)
Original Cast; *Oklahoma!* . . . . (MCA)

I Can't Help Myself (Sugar Pie Honey Bunch)
Four Tops; *16 #1 Hits From The Early '60s-C* . . . . (Motown)
Billboard Top R&B Hits-1965-C . . . . (Rhino)
Four Tops' Greatest Hits . . . . (Motown)
Four Tops-Anthology . . . . (Motown)
Good Feeling Music Of The Big Chill Generation-#1-C . . . . (Motown)
Motown Story-First 25 Years-C . . . . (Motown)
Motown Superstar Series-#14-Four Tops . . . . (Motown)
ST/Forrest Gump . . . . (Epic/Sony Music Soundtrax)
ST/Heaven Help Us . . . . (EMI)
ST/Into The Night . . . . (MCA)
ST/Where The Buffalo Roam . . . . (Backstreet)

I Can't Quit You Baby
Led Zeppelin; *Coda* . . . . (Atlantic)
Led Zeppelin . . . . (Atlantic)
Led Zeppelin-Box Set . . . . (Atlantic)

I Could Have Danced All Night
Frank Sinatra; *Concepts* . . . . (Capitol)
Julie Andrews/Original Cast; *My Fair Lady* . . . . (Columbia)
Rosemary Clooney; *Rosemary Clooney-16 Most Requested Songs* . . . . (Legacy)

I Could Use Another You
Eddy Raven; *Best Of Eddy Raven* . . . . (Curtom)

I Desire
Devo; *Oh No! It's Devo* . . . . (Warner Bros.)

I Didn't Ask And She Didn't Say
Tim McGraw; *All I Want* . . . . (Curb)

I Dig A Pony
Beatles; *Let It Be* . . . . (Capitol)

I Do
Toya; *Totally Hits 2001-C* . . . . (Arista)
Toya . . . . (Arista)

I Do Love You
Billy Stewart; *Best Of Chess Rhythm & Blues-#2-C* . . . . (Chess)
I Do Love You . . . . (MCA Special Prod.)
One More Time . . . . (Chess)
Smooth Grooves-The '60s-#2-C . . . . (Rhino)
GQ; *Didn't It Blow Your Mind: Soul Hits Of The '70s-#20-C* . . . . (Rhino)
Smooth Grooves-A Sensual Collection-#5-C . . . . (Rhino)

I Don't Know Why You Don't Want Me
Rosanne Cash; *Rosanne Cash-Hits-1979-1989* . . . . (Columbia)
Rosanne Cash-Super Hits . . . . (Columbia)

I Don't Sleep, I Dream
R.E.M.; *Monster* . . . . (Warner Bros.)

I Don't Wanna Talk About It Now
Emmylou Harris; *Red Dirt Girl* . . . . (Nonesuch)

I Don't Want To Miss A Thing
Aerosmith; *ST/Armageddon-The Album* . . . . (Columbia)
Mark Chesnutt; *I Don't Want To Miss A Thing* . . . . (MCA)

I Don't Want To Set The World On Fire
Ink Spots; *Best Of The Ink Spots* . . . . (MCA)

I Got A Love Jones For You
Refugee Camp All-Stars; *ST/Love Jones* . . . . (Columbia)

I Got Rhythm
Ella Fitzgerald; *George & Ira Gershwin Songbook* . . . . (Verve)
Ethel Waters; *I Got Rhythm: The Smithsonian George Gershwin Collection-C* . . . . (Smithsonian Collection)
Happenings; *'60s Rock Classics-#1-C* . . . . (Rhino)
Judy Garland; *Judy Garland-Collector's Items-1936-1945* . . . . (MCA)
Louis Armstrong; *Essential Louis Armstrong* . . . . (Verve)
Original Cast; *Girl Crazy* . . . . (Nonesuch)
Original London Cast; *Crazy For You* . . . . (RCA)
Robert Palmer; *Glory Of Gershwin Featuring Larry Adler-C* . . . . (Mercury)

I Hope You Want Me Too
Mavericks; *Trampoline* . . . . (MCA)

I Just Wanna Be Loved By You
Patty Loveless; *Patty Loveless-Classics* . . . . (Epic)

I Just Wanna Love U (Give It 2 Me)
Jay-Z; *Dynasty-Roc La Familia 2000* . . . . (Roc-A-Fella/DJMG)

I Just Want To Be Your Everything
Andy Gibb; *Andy Gibb-A Collection Of His Greatest Hits* . . . . (Polydor)

I Just Want To Dance With You
George Strait; *One Step At A Time* . . . . (MCA)

I Just Want You
Ozzy Osbourne; *Ozzmosis* . . . . (Epic)
The Ozzman Cometh . . . . (Epic)

I Know What Boys Like
Waitresses; *Best Of The Waitresses* . . . . (Polydor)
Just Can't Get Enough: New Wave Hits Of The '80s-#5-C . . . . (Rhino)

I Like It, I Love It
Tim McGraw; *All I Want* . . . . (Curb)
Tim McGraw's Greatest Hits . . . . (Curb)

I Like Them Girls
Tyrese; *2000 Watts* . . . . (RCA)

I Need A Hot Girl
Hot Boys; *Guerrilla Warfare* . . . . (Cash Money/Universal)

I Need A Lover
John Cougar; *John Cougar* . . . . (Riva)
Pat Benatar; *In The Heat Of The Night* . . . . (Chrysalis)

I Need A Man To Love
Big Brother & The Holding Company; *Cheap Thrills* . . . . (Columbia)

I Need To Know
Marc Anthony; *Marc Anthony* . . . . (Columbia)
Now That's What I Call Music!-#4-C . . . . (Virgin)

I Need You
Beatles; *ST/Help!* . . . . (Capitol)

I Need You
LeAnn Rimes; *ST/Jesus-The Epic Mini-Series* . . . . (Sparrow/Curb/Capitol)

I Need You Now
Eddie Fisher; *Very Best Of Eddie Fisher* . . . .(MCA)

I Need Your Love Tonight
Elvis Presley; *50,000,000 Elvis Fans Can't Be Wrong-Elvis' Gold Records-Volume 2* . . . . (RCA)
The Top Ten Hits . . . . (RCA)

I Never Asked To Be Your Mountain
Tim Buckley; *Goodbye And Hello* . . . . (Elektra)

I Only Want To Be With You
Bay City Rollers; *Bay City Rollers' Greatest Hits* . . . . (Arista)
Dusty Springfield; *Dusty Springfield-Anthology* . . . . (Mercury)
Dusty Springfield-Golden Hits . . . . (Mercury)
Vonda Shepard; *ST/Songs From ''Ally McBeal'' Featuring Vonda Shepard* . . . . (550/Epic)

I Think I Know
Reno; *Reno* . . . . (Curb)

I Wanna B With U
Fun Factory; *Close To You* . . . . (Curb)
Fun-Tastic . . . . (Curb)

I Wanna Be A Cowboy's Sweetheart
Patsy Montana & The Prairie Ramblers; *All Time Legends Of Country Music-C* . . . . (Legacy)
Respect: A History Of Women In Music-C . . . . (Rhino)

I Wanna Be A Drug-Sniffing Dog
Lard; *Pure Chewing Satisfaction* . . . . (Alternative Tentacles)
The Virus That Would Not Die!-C . . . . (Alternative Tentacles)

I Wanna Be Bad
Willa Ford; *Totally Hits 2001-C* . . . . (Arista)
Willa Was Here . . . . (Lava)

I Wanna Be Down
Brandy; *Brandy* . . . .(Atlantic)
MTV Party To Go-#7-C . . . . (Tommy Boy)

I Wanna Be Free
Loretta Lynn; *Loretta Lynn's Greatest Hits-#2* . . . .(MCA)

I Wanna Be Loved
Andrews Sisters; *Best Of The Andrews Sisters* . . . .(MCA)

I Wanna Be Loved By You
Helen Kane; *Nipper's Greatest Hits Of The '20s-#1-C* . . . . . (RCA)

I Wanna Be With You
Mandy Moore; *I Wanna Be With You* . . . . (550 Music)
Now That's What I Call Music!-#5-C . . . . (Virgin)

I Wanna Be Your Lover
Prince; *Prince* . . . .(Warner Bros.)

I Wanna Be Your Lover
Bob Dylan; *Biograph* . . . . (Columbia)

I Wanna Be Your Man
Beatles; *Meet The Beatles!* . . . . (Capitol)
Rock 'N' Roll Music . . . . (Capitol)

I Wanna Dance With Somebody (Who Loves Me)
Whitney Houston; *Whitney* . . . . (Arista)
Whitney Houston's Greatest Hits . . . . (Arista)

I Wanna Fall In Love
Lila McCann; *Lila* . . . . (Asylum)

I Wanna Feel That Way Again
Tracy Byrd; *I'm From The Country* . . . .(MCA)

I Wanna Get Next To You
Rose Royce; *Mellow Classics-C* . . . .(MCA Special Prod.)
Rose Royce's Greatest Hits . . . . (Whitfield)
ST/Car Wash . . . .(MCA)

I Wanna Go Too Far
Trisha Yearwood; *Thinkin' About You* . . . .(MCA)

I Wanna Know
Joe; *My Name Is Joe* . . . . (Jive)
Now That's What I Call Music!-#4-C . . . . (Virgin)

I Wanna Love Him So Bad
Jelly Beans; *Best Of The Girl Groups-#1-C* . . . . (Rhino)

I Wanna Love Like That
Tony Thompson; *Sexsational* . . . .(Giant/Warner Bros.)

I Wanna Love You Forever
Jessica Simpson; *Sweet Kisses* . . . . (Columbia)

I Wanna Marry A Lighthouse Keeper
Erika Eigen; *ST/A Clockwork Orange* . . . .(Warner Bros.)

I Wanna Remember This
Linda Davis; *I'm Yours* . . . .(DreamWorks/SKG)
ST/Black Dog . . . . (Decca)

I Want A Girl (Just Like The Girl)
Al Jolson; *The Al Jolson Story-#1* . . . .(MCA)
Spike Jones & His City Slickers; *King Of Corn* . . . . (Glendale)

I Want A New Duck
''Weird Al'' Yankovic; *Dare To Be Stupid* . . . .(Scotti Bros.)

I Want It That Way
Backstreet Boys; *Millennium* . . . . (Jive)

I Want My Baby Back
Jimmy Cross; *Teenage Tragedies-C* . . . . (Rhino)
World's Worst Records-C . . . . (Rhino)

I Want My Goodbye Back
Ty Herndon; *What Mattered Most* . . . .(Epic)

I Want To Be A Lady
Katie Barry; *Music From The New York Stage (1890-1920)-#1-1890-1908-C* . . . .(Pearl)

I Want To Be In Love
Melissa Etheridge; *Skin* . . . . (Island/IDJMG)

I Want To Be Loved Like That
Shenandoah; *Best Of Shenandoah* . . . .(RCA)

I Want To Be The One
Lonestar; *I'm Already There* . . . .(BNA)

I Want To Be Your Man
Roger; *Unlimited!* . . . . (Reprise)

I Want To Come Over
Melissa Etheridge; *Your Little Secret* . . . . (Island)

I Want To Hold Your Hand
Beatles; *Beatles 1* . . . . (Capitol)
Beatles-20 Greatest Hits . . . . (Capitol)
Meet The Beatles! . . . . (Capitol)
Past Masters-Volume One . . . .(Parlophone)
The Beatles/1962-1966 . . . . (Capitol)
Lakeside; *Galactic Grooves/Best Of Lakeside* . . . . (Right Stuff)
Your Wish Is My Command . . . . (Solar)

I Want To Spread A Little Sunshine
Jack Norworth; *Music From The New York Stage (1890-1920)-#4-1917-1920-C* . . . .(Pearl)

I Want To Touch You
Catherine Wheel; *Ferment* . . . .(Fontana)

I Want You
Juliet Roberts; *Natural Thing* . . . . (Reprise)

I Want You
Savage Garden; *Best Of Savage Garden* . . . . (Columbia)
Savage Garden . . . . (Columbia)

I Want You
Bob Dylan; *Blonde On Blonde* . . . . (Columbia)

I Want You Back
Jackson 5; *Billboard Top Rock 'N' Roll Hits-1970-C* . . . . . (Rhino)
Jackson 5's Greatest Hits . . . . (Motown)
Jackson 5-The Ultimate Collection . . . . (Motown)

I Want You Back
'N Sync; *'N Sync* . . . .(RCA)

I Want You Bad (And That Ain't Good)
Collin Raye; *In This Life* . . . . (Epic)

I Want You To Want Me
Cheap Trick; *Cheap Trick At Budokan* . . . . (Epic)
Cheap Trick's Greatest Hits . . . . (Epic)
In Color . . . . (Epic)
ST/Private Parts . . . .(Warner Bros.)

I Want You, I Need You, I Love You
Elvis Presley; *Heart & Soul* . . . .(RCA)

I'd Like That
XTC; *Homespun* . . . . (Idea/TVT)

I'd Like To Be In Texas
Don Edwards; *Saddle Songs* . . . .(Shanachie)
Skip Gorman; *Lonesome Prairie Love* . . . . (Rounder)

I'd Rather Have What We Had
Conway Twitty; *Two's A Party* . . . . (MCA Special Prod.)
Lee Ann Womack; *Some Things I Know* . . . . (Decca)

If Ever I Would Leave You
Richard Harris; *ST/Camelot* . . . . (Warner Bros.)
Robert Goulet; *Robert Goulet's Greatest Hits.* . . . . . . (Columbia)
Robert Goulet/Original Cast; *Camelot* . . . . (Columbia)

If I Could Only Win Your Love
Emmylou Harris; *Pieces Of The Sky* . . . . (Reprise)
Profile/Best Of Emmylou Harris. . . . .(Warner Bros.)

If I Could Turn Back The Hands Of Time
R. Kelly; *Now That's What I Call Music!-#3-C.* . . . . . . (Virgin)
R. . . . .(Jive)

If I Lose
Ricky Skaggs and Kentucky Thunder; *Bluegrass Rules!* . . . . (Rounder)

If I Needed Someone
Beatles; *Rubber Soul* . . . . (Capitol)

If I Only Had A Brain
Harry Connick, Jr.; *20* . . . . (Columbia)
Kay Kyser & His Orchestra; *Best Of The Big Bands-C* . . . (Columbia)
Original Soundtrack; *The Wizard Of Oz-The Deluxe Edition* . . (Rhino)
The Wizard Of Oz-The Story And Songs . . . . (Rhino)

If I Only Had A Heart
Jack Haley; *ST/The Wizard Of Oz* . . . . (Sony Music Special Prod.)
Original Soundtrack; *The Wizard Of Oz-The Deluxe Edition* . . (Rhino)
The Wizard Of Oz-The Story And Songs . . . . (Rhino)

If I Wanted To
Melissa Etheridge; *Yes I Am* . . . . (Island)

If I Was A Drinkin' Man
Neal McCoy; *Neal McCoy's Greatest Hits* . . . .(Atlantic)
Neal McCoy-Super Hits . . . .(Atlantic)
You Gotta Love That! . . . .(Atlantic)

If My Heart Had Wings
Faith Hill; *Breathe* . . . . (Warner Bros.)

If You Ask Me I Won't Say No
Pete Shelley; *Homosapien* . . . . (Razor & Tie)

If You Asked Me To
Celine Dion; *All The Way...A Decade Of Song* . . . . (550 Music)
  Celine Dion. . . . .(Epic)
Patti LaBelle; *Be Yourself* . . . .(MCA)
  Soundtrack Smashes-'80s & More-C . . . .(MCA)
  ST/License To Kill. . . . .(MCA)

If You Have To Ask
Red Hot Chili Peppers; *Blood Sugar Sex Magik* . . . . (Warner Bros.)

If You Want Me To Stay
Red Hot Chili Peppers; *Freaky Styley* . . . . (EMI)
  Out In L.A. . . . .(EMI)
  What Hits!?. . . . .(EMI)
Sly & The Family Stone; *Fresh* . . . .(Legacy)
  Sly & The Family Stone-Anthology. . . . .(Epic)

If You're Gone
Matchbox Twenty; *Mad Season By Matchbox Twenty* . . . .(Lava)

I'll Be
Edwin McCain; *Misguided Roses* . . . .(Lava)

I'll Make Love To You
Boyz II Men; *Boyz II Men II* . . . . (Motown)

I'll Never Break Your Heart
Backstreet Boys; *Backstreet Boys* . . . .(Jive)
  Now That's What I Call Music!-#2-C . . . .(Virgin)

I'm Happy Just To Dance With You
Anne Murray; *Somebody's Waiting* . . . . (Capitol)
Beatles; *Something New* . . . . (Capitol)
  ST/A Hard Day's Night. . . . . (Capitol)

I'm So Tired
Beatles; *The Beatles (White Album)* . . . . (Capitol)

In The Blood
Better Than Ezra; *Deluxe.* . . . . (Swell/Elektra)

In The Chapel In The Moonlight
Kitty Kallen; *Those Wonderful Years: Music! Music!*
  Music!-C . . . .(JCI Assoc. Labels)
Patti Page; *Patti Page-16 Most Requested Songs* . . . .(Legacy)
Shep Fields & His Rippling Rhythm Orchestra; *78-#6640* . . . .(Bluebird)

In The Mood
Robert Plant; *Principle Of Moments* . . . . (Es Paranza)

In Your Wildest Dreams
Tina Turner & Barry White; *Wildest Dreams* . . . .(Virgin)

Iris
Goo Goo Dolls; *Dizzy Up The Girl* . . . . (Warner Sunset/Reprise)
  ST/City Of Angels . . . . (Warner Sunset/Reprise)

Irresistible
Jessica Simpson; *Irresistible* . . . .(Columbia)

Is This Desire?
P.J. Harvey; *Is This Desire?* . . . . (Island)

It's All About Me
Mya featuring Sisqo of Dru Hill; *Mya* . . . . (University/Interscope)

It's On!
Korn; *Follow The Leader* . . . .(Immortal/Epic)

It's Your Body
Johnny Gill; *Let's Get The Mood Right* . . . . (Motown)

I've Got My Eyes On You
Jessica Simpson; *Sweet Kisses.* . . . .(Columbia)

Jack-Ass
Beck; *Odelay.* . . . .(David Geffen Co.)

J'ai Fait Tout
Emmylou Harris; *Red Dirt Girl* . . . .(Nonesuch)

January Friend
Goo Goo Dolls; *Dizzy Up The Girl* . . . . (Warner Sunset/Reprise)

Jesu, Joy Of Man's Desiring
Eric Tingstad & Nancy Rumbel; *The Gift* . . . .(Sona Gaia)
John Tesh; *Romantic Christmas* . . . .(GTS)

Jimmy Mack
Martha & The Vandellas; *Billboard Top R&B Hits-1967-C* . . . .(Rhino)
  Compact Command Performances-Martha Reeves & The
  Vandellas. . . . . (Motown)
  Martha Reeves & The Vandellas-Anthology. . . . . (Motown)
  Motown Story-First 25 Years-C . . . . (Motown)
  Motown Superstar Series-#11-Martha Reeves & The Vandellas . . . .(Motown)
  Top 10 With A Bullet-Motown Girl Groups-C . . . . (Motown)

Johnny Angel
Shelley Fabares; *Billboard Top Rock 'N' Roll Hits-1962-C* . . . .(Rhino)
  ST/Mermaids. . . . . (Geffen)

Johnny's Garden
Stephen Stills; *Manassas.* . . . .(Atlantic)

Jolene
Dolly Parton; *Best Of Dolly Parton* . . . .(RCA)
  Best There Is. . . . .(RCA)
  Jolene. . . . .(RCA)
  RCA Years-1967-1986 . . . .(RCA)
Sherrie Austin; *Followin' A Feelin'* . . . . (We/Madacy)

Josephine
Wallflowers; *Bringing Down The Horse* . . . .(Interscope)

Jumper
Third Eye Blind; *Third Eye Blind* . . . .(Elektra)
  Totally Hits-#1-C . . . .(Arista)

Just Once In My Life
Righteous Brothers; *Best Of The Righteous Brothers.* . . . .(Curb)
  Phil Spector-Back To Mono 1958-1969-C . . . .(Abkco)
  Righteous Brothers-Anthology 1962-1974 . . . .(Rhino)
  Unchained Melody-Very Best Of The Righteous Brothers . . . .(Polydor)

Just To Be Close To You
Commodores; *20th Century Masters-The Millennium Collection-The Best Of*
  The Commodores. . . . . (Motown)
  All The Great Love Songs-Commodores . . . . (Motown)
Lionel Richie; *Truly-The Love Songs* . . . . (Motown)

Just To See You Smile
Tim McGraw; *Everywhere.* . . . .(Curb)
  Tim McGraw's Greatest Hits . . . .(Curb)

Kindly Keep It Country
Vince Gill; *The Key* . . . .(MCA)

King Nothing
Metallica; *Load* . . . .(Elektra)

Kiss Of Fire
Georgia Gibbs; *Best Of Georgia Gibbs-The Mercury Years* . . . .(Chronicles)
Tony Martin; *Best Of Tony Martin On RCA* . . . .(Collector's Choice)

Kiss The Rain
Billie Myers; *A Taste Of '98-C* . . . .(Universal)
  Growing Pains . . . .(Universal)

Kiss You All Over
Exile; *Best Of Exile* . . . .(MCA)
  Exile's Greatest Hits. . . . .(MCA)
  Mixed Emotions. . . . .(MCA)

Kissin' You
Total; *Total.* . . . .(Bad Boy/Arista)

Knock Down Walls
Tonic; *Sugar.* . . . .(Universal)

Lady Lay Down
John Conlee; *Rose Colored Glasses.* . . . .(Universal)

Lady Marmalade
Christina Aguilera, Lil' Kim, Mya & Pink; *ST/Moulin Rouge* . . . . . (Interscope)
Labelle; *Nightbirds.* . . . .(Epic)
Patti LaBelle; *Best Of Patti LaBelle* . . . .(Epic)
Sheila E.; *Sex Cymbal* . . . . (Warner Bros.)

Lakini's Juice
Live; *Secret Samadhi* . . . .(Radioactive/MCA)

Last Chance Texaco
Rickie Lee Jones; *Naked Songs Live And Acoustic* . . . .(Reprise)
  Rickie Lee Jones. . . . . (Warner Bros.)

Last Goodbye
Jeff Buckley; *Grace.* . . . .(Columbia)

Last Train To Clarksville
Monkees; *Monkees.* . . . .(Arista)
  Monkees' Greatest Hits. . . . .(Rhino)
  Monkees-Live-1967. . . . .(Rhino)
  Then & Now...The Best Of The Monkees. . . . .(Arista)

Layla
Derek And The Dominos; *Classic Rock 1966-1988-C* . . . . (Atlantic)
  Eric Clapton-Crossroads-C . . . .(Polydor)
  Layla . . . .(Polydor)
  ST/Goodfellas . . . .(Atlantic)
Eric Clapton; *Eric Clapton-Unplugged* . . . .(Reprise)

Let Me In
Bonnie Raitt; *Takin' My Time* . . . . (Warner Bros.)
Sensations; *Billboard Top R&B Hits-1962-C* . . . .(Rhino)
  Chess Rhythm & Roll Box-C . . . .(Chess)
  Cruisin'-1962-1963-C. . . . .(Dunhill Compact Classics)
  Vintage Music-#6-C . . . .(MCA)

Let Me Let Go
Faith Hill; *Faith* . . . . (Warner Bros.)

Let The Good Times Roll
Barbra Streisand; *Butterfly* . . . .(Columbia)
Betty Everett & Jerry Butler; *Delicious Together* . . . . (Vee-Jay)
  Starring Betty Everett . . . .(Tradition)
Bobby Bland & B.B. King; *Together Again Live* . . . .(MCA)
Jerry Lee Lewis; *Golden Rock & Roll* . . . .(Sun)
Louis Jordan; *Best Of Louis Jordan* . . . .(MCA)
Molly Hatchet; *Flirtin' With Disaster* . . . .(Epic)
Nilsson; *Nilsson Schmilsson* . . . .(RCA)
Phoebe Snow; *Phoebe Snow* . . . .(MCA)
Ray Charles; *Genius Of Ray Charles* . . . .(Atlantic)
Shirley & Lee; *Billboard Top R&B Hits-1956-C* . . . .(Rhino)
  History Of New Orleans R&B-#1-1950-1958-C . . . .(Rhino)
  ST/Stand By Me. . . . .(Atlantic)
  Super Oldies Of The '50s-#4-C. . . . .(Audio Fidelity)
Tony Bennett with B.B. King; *Playin' With My Friends-Bennett Sings The*
  Blues-C. . . . .(Columbia)

Let's Build A World Together
George Jones & Tammy Wynette; *George Jones & Tammy Wynette-16*
  Biggest Hits . . . .(Epic/Legacy)

Let's Get It On
Marvin Gaye; *Billboard Top Rock 'N' Roll Hits-1973-C* . . . .(Rhino)
  Let's Get It On. . . . .(Motown)
  Marvin Gaye's Greatest Hits. . . . .(Motown)

Let's Get It On
By All Means; *Beyond A Dream* . . . . (Island)
Let's Get Married
Jagged Edge; *J.E. Heartbreak* . . . . (So So Def/Columbia)
Let's Hang On!
4 Seasons; *Four Seasons' Greatest Hits-#2* . . . . (Rhino)
Let's Lock The Door (And Throw Away The Key)
Jay & The Americans; *Jay & The Americans' All-Time Greatest Hits* . . . (Rhino)
Let's Make Love
Faith Hill & Tim McGraw; *Breathe* . . . .(Warner Bros.)
Tim McGraw & Faith Hill; *Tim McGraw's Greatest Hits* . . . . (Curb)
Let's Ride
Montell Jordan; *Let's Ride* . . . .(Def Jam/RAL/Mercury)
MTV Jams-C . . . . (Kedar Entert./Universal)
MTV Party To Go '99-C . . . . (Tommy Boy)
Letter, The
Macy Gray; *On How Life Is* . . . .(Epic)
Light My Fire
Doors; *Best Of The Doors* . . . . (Elektra)
Doors . . . . (Elektra)
Doors 13 . . . . (Elektra)
Doors' Greatest Hits . . . . (Elektra)
ST/The Doors . . . . (Elektra)
Jose Feliciano; *Encore-Jose Feliciano* . . . . (RCA)
Jose Feliciano's All-Time Greatest Hits . . . . (RCA)
Li'l Red Riding Hood
Sam The Sham and The Pharaohs; *Best Of Sam The Sham and The*
Pharaohs . . . . (Polydor)
Cruisin'-1966-C . . . . (Increase)
Pharaohization! (Best Of) . . . . (Rhino)
Lipstick And Bruises
Lit; *Atomic* . . . . (RCA)
Little Beggar Girl
Richard & Linda Thompson; *I Want To See The Bright Lights*
Tonight . . . . (Hannibal)
Little More Time With You
James Taylor; *Hourglass* . . . . (Columbia)
Little Sister
Elvis Presley; *Elvis' Golden Records, Volume 3* . . . . (RCA)
Elvis In Concert . . . . (RCA)
I Was The One . . . . (RCA)
The Top Ten Hits . . . . (RCA)
Worldwide 50 Gold Award Hits, Vol. 1, Parts 1 & 2 . . . . (RCA)
Lonely Teenager
Dion; *Collectables Presents The History Of Rock-#4-C* . . . . (Collectables)
Dion-His Best . . . . (Laurie)
Everything You Always Wanted To Hear By . . . . (Laurie)
The Wanderer . . . . (Laurie)
Loola Loo
Keb' Mo'; *The Door* . . . . (550/Epic/Okeh)
Lord I Hope This Day Is Good
Don Williams; *Best Of Don Williams-#3* . . . .(MCA)
Especially For You . . . .(MCA)
Lee Ann Womack; *Grand Ole Opry-75 Years-#1-C* . . . .(MCA)
Love
Kenny Loggins; *Love Shouldn't Hurt-C* . . . . (Qwest)
Love
Paul Simon; *You're The One* . . . .(Warner Bros.)
Love Doesn't Ask Why
Celine Dion; *The Colour Of My Love* . . . . (550 Music)
Love Is A Stranger
Eurythmics; *Eurythmics' Greatest Hits* . . . . (Arista)
Sweet Dreams (Are Made Of This) . . . . (RCA)
Love Is All We Need
Mary J. Blige; *Share My World* . . . . (MCA)
Love Is Like An Itching In My Heart
Diana Ross & The Supremes; *Beg, Scream & Shout! The Big Ol' Box Of*
'60s Soul-C . . . . (Rhino)
Love Is Stronger Than Pride
Ricochet; *Ricochet* . . . . (Columbia)
Love Me
Elvis Presley; *24 Karat Hits!* . . . .(Dunhill Compact Classics)
Love Me
112 Featuring Mase; *Room 112* . . . . (Bad Boy/Arista)
Love You Down
INOJ; *So So Def Bass All-Stars-#2-C* . . . . (So So Def/Columbia)
Total Dance Explosion-C . . . . (Columbia)
Love You For A Day
Ricky Martin; *Ricky Martin* . . . . (Columbia)
Loved Too Much
Ty Herndon; *Living In A Moment* . . . .(Epic)
Lovefool
Cardigans; *First Band On The Moon* . . . . (Mercury)
MTV Best Of The Buzz Bin-#2-C . . . . (Mammoth)
Love's In Need Of Love Today
Stevie Wonder featuring Take 6; *America: A Tribute To*
Heroes-C . . . . (Interscope)
Love's Train
Con Funk Shun; *Love's Train-C* . . . . (Mercury)

Smooth Grooves-A Sensual Collection-#1-C . . . . (Rhino)
To The Max . . . . (Mercury)
Luck Be A Lady
Frank Sinatra; *Sinatra Reprise-The Very Good Years* . . . .(Reprise)
The Reprise Collection . . . . (Reprise)
Original Cast; *Guys & Dolls* . . . . (MCA)
Mad Season
Matchbox Twenty; *Mad Season By Matchbox Twenty* . . . . (Lava)
Make It Hot
Nicole; *Make It Hot* . . . . (Gold Mind/East West/EEG)
Make Love To Me
Jo Stafford; *America's Most Versatile Singing Star* . . . . (Corinthian)
Make Me Bad
Korn; *Issues* . . . . (Immortal/Epic)
Make Me Yours
Bettye Swann; *Make Me Yours-Golden Classics* . . . . (Collectables)
Make Yourself Comfortable
Sarah Vaughan; *Essential Sarah Vaughan-The Great Songs* . . . . (Verve)
Man At The Top
Bruce Springsteen; *Tracks* . . . . (Columbia)
Man Loves His Money
Angie Stone; *Black Diamond* . . . . (Arista)
Man This Lonely, A
Brooks & Dunn; *Borderline* . . . . (Arista)
Maria
Blondie; *No Exit* . . . .(Beyond)
Me
Paula Cole; *This Fire* . . . . (Imago)
Me And Those Dreamin' Eyes Of Mine
D'Angelo; *Brown Sugar* . . . . (EMI)
Meeting In My Bedroom
Silk; *Tonight* . . . . (Elektra)
Michelle
Beatles; *Beatles-Love Songs* . . . . (Capitol)
Rubber Soul . . . . (Capitol)
The Beatles/1962-1966 . . . . (Capitol)
Minority
Green Day; *Warning* . . . .(Reprise)
Mister Sandman
Chordettes; *Best Of The Chordettes* . . . . (Rhino)
Emmylou Harris; *Evangeline* . . . . (Warner Bros.)
Profile II-The Best Of Emmylou Harris . . . . (Warner Bros.)
Money (That's What I Want)
Barrett Strong; *Motown Story-First 25 Years-C* . . . . (Motown)
Oldies But Goodies-#4-C . . . .(Original Sound)
Beatles; *Beatles-Box Set* . . . . (Capitol)
Rock 'N' Roll Music . . . . (Capitol)
The Beatles' Second Album . . . . (Capitol)
Buddy Guy; *Man & The Blues* . . . . (Vanguard)
Diana Ross & The Supremes; *Diana Ross & The Supremes Sing*
Motown . . . . (Motown)
Jerry Lee Lewis; *Jerry Lee's Greatest!* . . . . (Rhino)
John Lennon; *Lennon* . . . . (Capitol)
Junior Walker & The All Stars; *Junior Walker & The All Stars'*
Greatest Hits . . . . (S.O.U.L.)
Junior Walker & The All Stars-Anthology . . . . (Motown)
Rolling Stones; *More Hot Rocks (big hits & fazed cookies)* . . . .(Abkco)
Ronnie Milsap; *Lost In The Fifties Tonight* . . . . (RCA)
Todd Rundgren; *Something/Anything?* . . . . (Rhino)
More
Trace Adkins; *More* . . . . (Capitol)
Most Girls
Pink; *Can't Take Me Home* . . . . (LaFace)
Totally Hits-#3-C . . . .(Atlantic)
Mr. Dream Merchant
Jerry Butler; *Best Of Jerry Butler* . . . . (Rhino)
Soul Shots-#2-The "In" Crowd-Sweet Soul-C . . . . (Rhino)
Mr. Moonlight
Beatles; *Beatles '65* . . . . (Capitol)
Beatles-Box Set . . . . (Capitol)
For Sale . . . . (Capitol)
Mr. Spaceman
Byrds; *Original Singles-#1-1965-1967* . . . . (Columbia)
The Byrds . . . . (Columbia)
The Byrds (Untitled) . . . . (Legacy)
The Byrds' Greatest Hits . . . . (Columbia)
Mr. Too Damn Good
Gerald Levert; *G* . . . . (East West)
Mrs. Brown You've Got A Lovely Daughter
Herman's Hermits; *Herman's Hermits-Their Greatest Hits* . . . .(Abkco)
Something Good Again . . . .(Abkco)
My Baby Needs A Shepherd
Emmylou Harris; *Red Dirt Girl* . . . . (Nonesuch)
My Everything
98 Degrees; *Revelation* . . . . (Universal)
My Heart Cries For You
Charlie Rich; *Charlie Rich-20 Golden Hits* . . . .(Sun)
Time For Tears-C . . . .(Sun)

Dinah Shore; *Nipper's Greatest Hits Of The '50s-#1-C* (RCA)
Guy Mitchell; *Guy Mitchell-16 Most Requested Songs* (Legacy)
My One Desire (Vampir's Lullaby)
Willy Deville; *Loup Garou* (Discovery)
My Own Worst Enemy
Lit; *A Place In The Sun* (RCA)
My World Is Empty Without You
Diana Ross; *Diana Ross-Anthology* (Motown)
Evening With Diana Ross (Motown)
Stevie Wonder; *Down To Earth* (Motown)
Need A Little Sugar In My Bowl
Hadda Brooks; *Best Blues Album In The World...Ever!-C* (Virgin)
Needles And Pins
Jackie DeShannon; *Very Best Of Jackie DeShannon* (EMI)
Searchers; *History Of British Rock-#1-C* (Rhino)
Searchers' Greatest Hits (Rhino)
Tom Petty And The Heartbreakers; *Pack Up The Plantation-Live!* (MCA)
Never Enough
Groove Theory; *ST/Love Jones* (Columbia)
Never Ever
All Saints; *All Saints* (London)
Now That's What I Call Music!-#1-C (Virgin)
Never Gonna Let You Go
Faith Evans; *Keep The Faith* (Bad Boy/Arista)
New
No Doubt; *Return Of Saturn* (Interscope)
ST/Go (Work/Epic)
Night And Day
Bette Midler; *Some People's Lives* (Atlantic)
Billie Holiday; *Legacy Box-1933-1958* (Columbia)
Ella Fitzgerald; *Cole Porter Songbook* (Verve)
Frank Sinatra; *Nipper's Greatest Hits Of The '40s-#1-C* (RCA)
Sinatra & Strings (Reprise)
Sinatra Reprise-The Very Good Years (Reprise)
Sinatra: A Man And His Music (Reprise)
The Capitol Years (Capitol)
The Reprise Collection (Reprise)
Fred Astaire; *Cheek To Cheek* (Pro-Arte)
Steppin' Out-Astaire Sings (Verve)
Tony Bennett; *Perfectly Frank* (Columbia)
U2; *Red Hot + Blue-Tribute To Cole Porter-C* (Chrysalis)
Night To Remember
Joe Diffie; *A Night To Remember* (Epic)
No Diggity
Blackstreet; *Another Level* (Interscope)
No Questions Asked
Fleetwood Mac; *Fleetwood Mac's Greatest Hits* (Warner Bros.)
No, No, No
Destiny's Child; *Destiny's Child* (Grass Roots/Columbia)
Nobody Wants To Be Lonely
Ricky Martin; *Sound Loaded* (Columbia)
Norma Jean Riley
Diamond Rio; *Diamond Rio* (Arista)
Diamond Rio's Greatest Hits (Arista)
Not Too Much To Ask
Mary Chapin Carpenter & Joe Diffie; *Come On Come On* (Columbia)
Nothing As It Seems
Pearl Jam; *Binaural* (Epic)
O Death
Ralph Stanley; *ST/O Brother, Where Art Thou?* (Mercury)
Octopus's Garden
Beatles; *Abbey Road* (Parlophone)
Beatles-Box Set (Capitol)
The Beatles/1967-1970 (Capitol)
Oh, Baby Mine (I Get So Lonely)
Chet Atkins; *Tennessee Guitar Man* (Pair)
Four Knights; *Those Wonderful Years: Mr. Sandman-C* (JCI Assoc. Labels)
On A Night Like This
Trick Pony; *Trick Pony* (H2E/Warner Bros.)
On Bended Knee
Boyz II Men; *Boyz II Men II* (Motown)
Once In A While
Dishwalla; *And You Think You Know What Life's About* (A&M)
One Hit Wonder
Everclear; *So Much For The Afterglow* (Capitol)
One More Day
Diamond Rio; *One More Day* (Arista)
One Of Those Love Songs
Xscape; *Traces Of My Lipstick* (So So Def/Columbia)
One Of Those Nights Tonight
Lorrie Morgan; *Shakin' Things Up* (BNA)
To Get To You-Greatest Hits Collection (BNA)
One Small Miracle
Bryan White; *The Right Place* (Asylum)
One, The
Elton John; *Elton John-Love Songs* (MCA)
The One (MCA)
Only One For Me, The
Brian McKnight; *Anytime* (Motown)
Only Wanna Be With You
Hootie & The Blowfish; *Cracked Rear View* (Atlantic)
Ooh Aah...Just A Little Bit
Gina G; *Fresh!* (Eternal/Warner Bros.)
Out Of The Woods
Nickel Creek; *Nickel Creek* (Sugar Hill)
Pagan Poetry
Bjork; *Vespertine* (Elektra)
Papa Can You Hear Me?
Barbra Streisand; *One Voice* (Columbia)
ST/Yentl (Columbia)
Paper In Fire
John Cougar Mellencamp; *The Lonesome Jubilee* (Mercury)
John Mellencamp; *Best That I Could Do-1978-1988* (Mercury)
Parachute Woman
Rolling Stones; *Beggars Banquet* (Abkco)
Paradise
Nat ''King'' Cole; *Nat ''King'' Cole-Gift Set* (Capitol)
The Nat ''King'' Cole Story (Capitol)
Ray Conniff; *'S Awful Nice* (Columbia)
Russ Colombo; *Nipper's Greatest Hits Of The '30s-#2-C* (RCA)
Pardon Me
Incubus; *Make Yourself* (Immortal/Epic)
Party Doll
Buddy Knox; *Best Of Buddy Knox* (Rhino)
Billboard Top Rock 'N' Roll Hits-1957-C (Rhino)
ST/American Graffiti (MCA)
Peaches And Cream
112; *Part III* (Bad Boy/Arista)
Totally Hits 2001-C (Arista)
People Asking Why
Seal; *Seal 2* (Sire)
Perfect Drug
Nine Inch Nails; *ST/Lost Highway* (Interscope)
Physical
Olivia Newton-John; *Back To Basics-Essential Collection 1971-1992* (Geffen)
Olivia Newton-John's Greatest Hits-#2 (MCA)
Physical (MCA)
Please
Kinleys; *Just Between You And Me* (Epic)
Please
Chris Isaak; *Speak Of The Devil* (Reprise)
Please
Bing Crosby; *Bing Crosby-16 Most Requested Songs* (Legacy)
Please Call Home
Allman Brothers Band; *Beginnings* (Polydor)
Idlewild South (Polydor)
Gregg Allman; *Laid Back* (Polydor)
Please Call Me, Baby
Tom Waits; *The Heart Of Saturday Night* (Asylum)
Please Come To Boston
Dave Loggins; *Apprentice (In A Musical Workshop)* (Epic)
Rock Artifacts-From The Vaults-#2-C (Legacy)
Super Hits Of The '70s-Have A Nice Day-#13-C (Rhino)
David Allan Coe; *David Allan Coe-17 Greatest Hits* (Columbia)
For The Record-The First 10 Years (Columbia)
Joan Baez; *Best Of Joan Baez* (A&M)
Joan Baez-Classics-#8 (A&M)
Reba McEntire; *Starting Over* (MCA)
Please Don't Ask
Genesis; *Duke* (Atlantic)
Please Don't Ask About Barbara
Bobby Vee; *Best Of Bobby Vee* (EMI)
Bobby Vee-Golden Greats (Liberty)
Bobby Vee-Legendary Masters (EMI)
Very Best Of Bobby Vee (Collectables)
Please Don't Bury Me
John Prine; *Prime Prine-The Best Of John Prine* (Atlantic)
Sweet Revenge (Atlantic)
Please Don't Eat The Daisies
Doris Day; *Doris Day-16 Most Requested Songs-Encore!* (Columbia)
Please Don't Squeeze Da Banana
Louis Prima; *V-Disc Recordings-Louis Prima* (Collector's Choice)
Please Don't Tell Her
Big Head Todd & The Monsters; *Beautiful World* (Revolution)
Live Monsters (Revolution)
Please Love Me Forever
Bobby Vinton; *Bobby Vinton-16 Most Requested Songs* (Legacy)
Bobby Vinton's All-Time Greatest Hits (Epic)
Please Love Me Forever (Epic)
Please Mister Postman
Beatles; *Beatles-Box Set* (Capitol)
The Beatles' Second Album (Capitol)
With The Beatles (Parlophone)
Carpenters; *Carpenters-Classics-#2* (A&M)
Horizon (A&M)
Yesterday Once More (A&M)
Marvelettes; *Billboard Top Rock 'N' Roll Hits-1961-C* (Rhino)

Marvelettes' Greatest Hits................................. (Motown)
Marvelettes-Anthology .... (Motown)
Motown Story-First 25 Years-C .... (Motown)

Please Mr. Please
Olivia Newton-John; *Back To Basics-Essential Collection 1971-1992* . . (Geffen)

Please Mr. Sun
Johnny Ray; *Back To The Early '50s* .... (Dominion Entert.)
Johnnie Ray-16 Most Requested Songs .... (Legacy)
Vogues; *Vogues' Greatest Hits* .... (Rhino)

Please Please Me
Beatles; *Beatles-Box Set* .... (Capitol)
Please Please Me.. (Parlophone)
The Beatles/1962-1966 .... (Capitol)
The Early Beatles .... (Capitol)

Possession
Sarah McLachlan; *Fumbling Towards Ecstasy.* .... (Arista)

Pretty Girl
Jon B.; *Bonafide* .... (Yab Yum/550)

Privacy
Michael Jackson; *Invincible* ....(Epic)

Promise
Jagged Edge; *J.E. Heartbreak* .... (So So Def/Columbia)

Prove It All Night
Bruce Springsteen; *Darkness On The Edge Of Town* .... (Columbia)

Quit Playing Games (With My Heart)
Backstreet Boys; *Backstreet Boys.* .... (Jive)
MTV Party To Go '98-C.................................... (Tommy Boy)
The Concert For New York City-C .... (Columbia)

Rags To Riches
Tony Bennett; *Tony Bennett-16 Most Requested Songs* .... (Legacy)
Tony Bennett's All-Time Greatest Hits .... (Columbia)
Tony Bennett & Percy Faith & His Orchestra; *Radio Classics Of The*
'50s-C .... (Columbia)

Ragtop Cadillac
Lonestar; *Lonestar* .... (BNA)

Ready, Willing And Able
Lari White; *Best Of Lari White* .... (RCA)
Don't Fence Me In .... (RCA)

Real World
Matchbox Twenty; *Yourself Or Someone Like You* .... (Lava)

Reason For Breathing
Babyface; *Collection Of His Greatest Hits* .... (Arista/Epic)

Release Me
Angelina; *Angelina.* ....(Upstairs)

Request Line
Zhane'; *Saturday Night.* .... (Motown)

Rhythm Of The Night
Corona; *Hot Luv-Ultimate Dance Songs Collection-C* ....(EMI)
Rhythm Of The Night .... (East West)
DeBarge; *DeBarge's Greatest Hits* .... (Motown)
Motown Story-First 25 Years-C .... (Motown)
Rhythm Of The Night .... (Motown)

Right Here Right Now
Charlie Major & Joy Lynn White; *444* .... (Dead Reckoning)

Right In Time
Lucinda Williams; *Car Wheels On A Gravel Road.* .... (Mercury)

River, Stay 'Way From My Door
Guy Lombardo & His Royal Canadians; *Auld Lang Syne.* ...... (Pro-Arte)

Rock And Roll All Nite
Kiss; *Alive!* .... (Mercury)
Double Platinum .... (Mercury)
Dressed To Kill .... (Mercury)
Heavy Metal Memories-C .... (Rhino)
Smashes, Thrashes & Hits .... (Mercury)
The Originals .... (Casablanca)

Roof, The
Mariah Carey; *Butterfly* .... (Columbia)

Roses In The Fire
Rosanne Cash; *The Wheel.* .... (Columbia)

Ruby
Ray Charles; *Love Songs* .... (Rhino)

Run
George Strait; *The Road Goes On Forever, A Collection Of Their Greatest*
Recordings .... (Polydor)

Rush Rush
Paula Abdul; *Spellbound* .... (Captive)

Saints Rock 'n Roll, The
Bill Haley & His Comets; *Twentieth Century Masters-Millenium Collection-*
Bill Haley & His Comets. ....(MCA)

Salvation
Cranberries; *To The Faithful Departed.* .... (Island)

San Francisco Days
Chris Isaak; *San Francisco Days* .... (Reprise)

Save The Last Dance For Me
Buck Owens; *Buck Owens Collection-1959-1990* .... (Rhino)
Dolly Parton; *Best Of Dolly Parton-#3* .... (RCA)
Great Pretender .... (RCA)
Drifters; *20 Top 10 Hits Of The '50s & '60s-C* .... (Laurie)
Atlantic Rhythm & Blues 1947-1974-#4 (1958-1962)-C ....(Atlantic)

Billboard Top Rock 'N' Roll Hits-1960-C .... (Rhino)
Cruisin'-1960-C .... (Increase)
Drifters-Golden Hits ....(Atlantic)
Emmylou Harris; *Blue Kentucky Girl* .... (Warner Bros.)
Profile II-The Best Of Emmylou Harris .... (Warner Bros.)
Jerry Lee Lewis; *20 Classic Jerry Lee Lewis Hits* .... (Original Sound)
Duets .... (Sun)
Jerry Lee Lewis-Original Golden Hits-#2 .... (Sun)
Monsters.. (Sun)

Save Your Heart For Me
Gary Lewis And The Playboys; *Gary Lewis & The Playboys* ...... (Gold Rush)
Gary Lewis And The Playboys' Greatest Hits .... (Curb)

Say It Isn't So
Dinah Washington; *Irving Berlin Always-C* .... (Verve)
Michael Feinstein; *Remember-Michael Feinstein Sings Irving Berlin* . . (Elektra)
Nat "King" Cole; *Spotlight On Nat "King" Cole* .... (Capitol)
Ray Conniff; *'S Awful Nice* .... (Columbia)

Scary Kisses
Voice Of The Beehive; *Sex And Misery* .... (Discovery)

Sea Cruise
Billy "Crash" Craddock; *Billy "Crash" Craddock's Greatest Hits* ... (Capitol)
Changes .... (Capitol)
Frankie Ford; *American Hot Wax* .... (A&M)
Best Of New Orleans Rhythm & Blues-#2-C .... (Rhino)
Oldies But Goodies-#3-C ....(Original Sound)
Rock & Roll Show-C .... (Gusto)
Glenn Frey; *No Fun Aloud* .... (Asylum)
Johnny Rivers; *Johnny Rivers-Anthology 1964-1977* .... (Rhino)
Nighthawks; *Best Of The Nighthawks* ....(Genes CD Co.)
Robert Gordon & Link Wray; *Fresh Fish Special.* .... (RCA)

Semi-Charmed Life
Third Eye Blind; *Jock Rock 2000-C* .... (Tommy Boy)
Third Eye Blind .... (Elektra)

Sentimental Journey
Dinah Shore; *Sentimental Journey: Capitol's Great Ladies Of*
Song-C .... (Gold Rush)
Doris Day; *Doris Day Sings 22 Great Songs-Original Big Band* .... (Hindsight)
Hal McIntyre & His Orchestra; *Nipper's Greatest Hits Of The*
'40s-#2-C .... (RCA)
Les Brown & His Orchestra; *Best Of The Big Bands-C* ...... (Columbia)

Seven Rooms Of Gloom
Four Tops; *Four Tops' Greatest Hits* .... (Motown)
Four Tops Reach Out .... (Motown)
Four Tops-Anthology .... (Motown)

Sexual Healing
Marvin Gaye; *Last Concert Tour* ....(Giant)
Midnight Love .... (Columbia)
Seems Like Yesterday-#4-Early '80s-C .... (K-Tel)
Tribute To Black Entertainers-C .... (Columbia)
Max-A-Million; *Take Your Time.* .... (S.O.S./Zoo)

Shake Your Bon-Bon
Ricky Martin; *Ricky Martin.* .... (Columbia)

She Doesn't Need Me Anymore
Peter Cetera; *You're The Inspiration-A Collection* .... (River North)

She Is His Only Need
Wynonna; *Wynonna* .... (MCA)
Wynonna-Collection.. (Curb)

She Walks This Earth
Sting; *Love Affair-Music Of Ivan Lins-C.* .... (Telarc)

She Wants You
Billie; *Honey To The B* ....(Virgin)

She Was Asking For It
Cannibal Corpse; *The Bleeding.* .... (Metal Blade)

Sherry
4 Seasons; *4 Seasons' Greatest Hits-#1.* .... (Rhino)
4 Seasons-Anthology .... (Rhino)
ST/The Wanderers .... (Warner Bros.)

She's All I Ever Had
Ricky Martin; *Ricky Martin.* .... (Columbia)

Shy Guy
Diana King; *ST/Bad Boys* .... (Work)
Tougher Than Love .... (Work)

Silver Future
Monster Magnet; *ST/Heavy Metal 2000* .... (Restless)

Single Girl
Sandy Posey; *Greatest Hits Of 1966-C* .... (Deluxe)

Skin
Madonna; *Ray Of Light* .... (Maverick)

Sleep Now In The Fire
Rage Against The Machine; *The Battle Of Los Angeles* .... (Epic)

Slip Away
Clarence Carter; *Billboard Top Pop Hits-1968-C* .... (Rhino)
Snatching It Back-The Best Of Clarence Carter. .... (Rhino)

Sloop John B
Beach Boys; *Absolute Best-#2.* .... (Capitol)
Beach Boys '69 (The Beach Boys Live In London) .... (Capitol)
Beach Boys-Gift Set .... (Capitol)
Best Of (Good Vibrations) .... (Reprise)
Made In The U.S.A. .... (Capitol)

Pet Sounds . . . . (Capitol)
ST/Forrest Gump . . . . (Epic/Sony Music Soundtrax)
The Pet Sounds Sessions: A 30th Anniversary Collection . . . . (Capitol)

Slow Burn
T.G. Sheppard; *T.G. Sheppard's All-Time Greatest Hits* . . . . (Warner Bros.)

Slow Down
Beatles; *Past Masters-Volume One* . . . . (Parlophone)

Slow Ride
Kenny Wayne Shepherd; *Trouble Is...* . . . . (Revolution)

Smooth
Santana featuring Rob Thomas; *Supernatural* . . . . (Arista)
Totally Hits-#1-C . . . . (Arista)

So Anxious
Ginuwine; *100 Percent Ginuwine* . . . . (550 Music)

So You Want To Be A Rock 'N' Roll Star
Byrds; *Original Singles-#1-1965-1967* . . . . (Columbia)
Rock Classics Of The '60s-C . . . . (Columbia)
The Byrds . . . . (Columbia)
The Byrds (Untitled) . . . . (Legacy)
The Byrds' Greatest Hits . . . . (Columbia)
Patti Smith Group; *Wave* . . . . (Arista)
Tom Petty And The Heartbreakers; *Pack Up The Plantation-Live!* . . . . . . (MCA)
The Ultimate Rock Album-C . . . . (Foundation)

Sock It 2 Me
Missy ''Misdemeanor'' Elliot; *Supa Dupa Fly* . . . . (East West)

Somebody
Bryan Adams; *Greenpeace/Rainbow Warriors-C* . . . . (Geffen)
Reckless . . . . (A&M)
So Far So Good . . . . (A&M)

Somebody Somewhere
Original Broadway Cast; *The Most Happy Fella* . . . . (Sony Music Classical)

Somebody To Love
Jefferson Airplane; *2400 Fulton Street-An Anthology* . . . . (RCA)
Loves You . . . . (RCA)
Nipper's Greatest Hits Of The '60s-#1-C . . . . (RCA)
Surrealistic Pillow . . . . (RCA)
The Worst Of Jefferson Airplane . . . . (RCA)

Somebody's Somebody
''AFKAP''; *Emancipation* . . . . (NPG)

Someone Should Tell Her
Mavericks; *Trampoline* . . . . (MCA)

Song For The Asking
Simon & Garfunkel; *Bridge Over Troubled Water* . . . . (Columbia)

Sorry You Asked?
Dwight Yoakam; *Gone* . . . . (Reprise)

Spark
Tori Amos; *From The Choirgirl Hotel* . . . . (Atlantic)

Spend My Life With You
Eric Benet; *A Day In The Life* . . . . (Warner Bros.)

Stand Beside Me
Jo Dee Messina; *Big Country Hits '99-C* . . . . (K-Tel)
I'm Alright . . . . (Curb)

Stand By Me
Ben E. King; *Atlantic Soul Classics-C* . . . . (Warner Special Prod.)
Ben E. King's Greatest Hits . . . . (Atco)
Golden Age Of Black Music-1960-1970-C . . . . (Atlantic)
ST/Stand By Me . . . . (Atlantic)
Stand By Me-Best Of Ben E. King . . . . (Atlantic)
Drifters; *Drifters' Greatest Hits* . . . . (Gusto)
John Lennon; *Rock 'N' Roll* . . . . (Capitol)
ST/Imagine: John Lennon . . . . (Capitol)
The John Lennon Collection . . . . (Capitol)
Maurice White; *Maurice White* . . . . (Columbia)
Mickey Gilley; *Greatest Country Hits From The Movies-C* . . . . (Epic)
Mickey Gilley's Biggest Hits . . . . (Epic)
ST/Urban Cowboy . . . . (Asylum)
Ten Years Of Hits . . . . (Epic)
Ry Cooder; *Chicken Skin Music* . . . . (Reprise)

Standing In The Shadows Of Love
Barry White; *Barry White's Greatest Hits* . . . . (20th Century Fox)
I've Got So Much To Give . . . . (20th Century Fox)
Four Tops; *Four Tops' Greatest Hits* . . . . (Motown)
Four Tops Reach Out . . . . (Motown)
Four Tops-Anthology . . . . (Motown)
Motown Story-First 25 Years-C . . . . (Motown)
Motown Superstar Series-#14-Four Tops . . . . (Motown)
Rod Stewart; *Blondes Have More Fun* . . . . (Warner Bros.)

Starlight, Starbright
Linda Scott; *45-#133* . . . . (Eric)

Start Me Up
Rolling Stones; *''Still Life'' (American Concert 1981)* . . . . (Virgin)
Flashpoint . . . . (Virgin)
Tattoo You . . . . (Virgin)

State Trooper
Bruce Springsteen; *Nebraska* . . . . (Columbia)
*The Sopranos-Music From The HBO Original
Series* . . . . (Sony Music Soundtrax)

Stay
4 Seasons; *4 Seasons' Greatest Hits-#1* . . . . (Rhino)

Jackson Browne; *Running On Empty* . . . . (Asylum)
Maurice Williams & The Zodiacs; *Best Of Maurice Williams & The
Zodiacs* . . . . (Collectables)
Billboard Top Rock 'N' Roll Hits-1960-C . . . . (Rhino)
Cruisin'-1960-C . . . . (Increase)
Rock & Roll Is Here To Stay-C . . . . (Gusto)
ST/Dirty Dancing . . . . (RCA)

Stay
Destiny's Child; *The Writing's On The Wall* . . . . (Columbia)

Stay
Temptations; *Phoenix Rising* . . . . (Motown)

Stay Forever
Hal Ketchum; *Every Little Word* . . . . (Curb)
From Nashville With Love-C . . . . (Curb)
Hal Ketchum-The Hits . . . . (MCG/Curb)

Stay The Night
IMx; *IMx* . . . . (MCA)

Stay You
Wood; *Songs From Dawson's Creek* . . . . (Sony Music Soundtrax)
Songs From Stamford Hill . . . . (Columbia)

Steal Your Love
Lucinda Williams; *Essence* . . . . (Lost Highway/IDJMG)

Steam Heat
Carol Haney; *ST/Pajama Game* . . . . (Collectables)
Janis Paige/John Raitt/Original Cast; *Pajama Game* . . . . (Columbia)

Step Inside Love
Beatles; *The Beatles-Anthology-#3* . . . . (Capitol)

Still...You Turn Me On
Emerson, Lake & Palmer; *Best Of Emerson, Lake & Palmer* . . . . (Rhino)
Brain Salad Surgery . . . . (Rhino)
From The Beginning-The Greg Lake Retrospective . . . . (Rhino)

Stinkfist
Tool; *Aenima* . . . . (Freeworld/Capitol)

Strange Currencies
R.E.M.; *Monster* . . . . (Warner Bros.)

Strange Desire
INXS; *All* . . . . (Atlantic)

Stranger In Paradise
Arthur Lyman; *Pearly Shells* . . . . (Crescendo)
Bing Crosby; *The Radio Years: 20 Songs* . . . . (Crescendo)
Original Cast; *Kismet* . . . . (Columbia)
Tony Bennett; *Tony Bennett-16 Most Requested Songs* . . . . (Legacy)
Tony Bennett's All-Time Greatest Hits . . . . (Columbia)

Strawberries
Smooth; *Reality* . . . . (Perspective/A&M)

Such A Night
Elvis Presley; *From Nashville To Memphis-The Essential '60s Masters* . . (RCA)

Sugar, Sugar
Archies; *Billboard Top Rock 'N' Roll Hits-1969-C* . . . . (Rhino)

Sugarfoot
Wallflowers; *The Wallflowers* . . . . (Virgin)

Sweet Kisses
Jessica Simpson; *Sweet Kisses* . . . . (Columbia)

Sweet Sexy Thing
Nu Flavor; *Nu Flavor* . . . . (Reprise)

Sweet Virginia
Rolling Stones; *Exile On Main Street* . . . . (Virgin)

Take 54
Nilsson; *Son Of Schmilsson* . . . . (RCA)

Tearin' Up My Heart
'N Sync; *'N Sync* . . . . (RCA)

Tell Me Do U Wanna
Ginuwine; *Ginuwine...The Bachelor* . . . . (550 Music)

Temple
Jane Siberry; *Lesbian Favorites-Women Like Us-C* . . . . (Rhino)

Temptation
Bing Crosby; *Bing Crosby-16 Most Requested Songs* . . . . (Legacy)
Bing Crosby-Love Songs . . . . (Universal)
Perry Como; *Perry Como-Pure Gold* . . . . (RCA)
Perry Como's All-Time Greatest Hits-#1 . . . . (RCA)
Perry Como's Greatest Hits . . . . (RCA)

That Other Woman
Changing Faces; *Visit Me* . . . . (Atlantic)

That's All I Want From You
Jaye P. Morgan; *The Jaye P. Morgan Story* . . . . (Simitar)

That's Right (You're Not From Texas)
Lyle Lovett; *Live In Texas* . . . . (MCA)
The Road To Ensenada . . . . (MCA)

That's The Way Love Goes
Janet Jackson; *janet.* . . . . (Virgin)

The 13th
Cure; *Wild Mood Swings* . . . . (Elektra)

There Is Nothin' Like A Dame
Original Cast; *South Pacific* . . . . (CBS Masterworks)

There She Goes
Babyface; *Face 2 Face* . . . . (Arista)

This Is All I Ask
Frank Sinatra; *The Reprise Collection* . . . . (Reprise)

This Woman Needs
SHeDAISY; *The Whole Shebang* . . . . (Lyric Street)
Three Coins In The Fountain
Andy Williams; *Moon River & Other Great Movie Themes* . . . (Columbia)
Doris Day & Frank De Vol Orchestra; *Hooray For*
Hollywood-#2-C . . . . (Columbia)
Four Aces; *Billboard Top Movie Hits-1950-1954-C* . . . . (Rhino)
Four Aces' Greatest Hits . . . .(MCA)
Frank Sinatra; *At The Movies* . . . . (Capitol)
Capitol Collectors Series-Frank Sinatra . . . . (Capitol)
Harry James; *Harry James Plays The Songs That Sold A Million* . . . . (Columbia)
Julius LaRosa; *The Envelope Please-Academy Award Winning Songs-#2*
(1946-1957)-C . . . . (Rhino)
Three Little Words
Carmen McRae; *Great American Songbook* . . . . (Atlantic)
Duke Ellington & His Orchestra; *Nipper's Greatest Hits Of The*
'30s-#2-C . . . . (RCA)
Nat "King" Cole; *L-O-V-E* . . . . (Capitol)
Time In A Bottle
Jim Croce; *50th Anniversary Collection* . . . .(Saja)
Photographs & Memories/His Greatest Hits . . . . (Atlantic)
Time In A Bottle/Jim Croce's Greatest Love Songs . . . . (Atlantic)
To Love You More
Celine Dion with The Bee Gees; *All The Way...A Decade*
Of Song . . . . (550 Music)
Let's Talk About Love-C . . . . (550 Music)
Too Close
Next; *Rated Next* . . . .(Divine Mill/Arista)
Too Much
Dave Matthews Band; *Crash* . . . . (RCA)
Too Much To Ask
Bad Religion; *Generator* . . . . (Epitaph)
Total Eclipse Of The Heart
Bonnie Tyler; *Billboard Top Hits-1983-C* . . . . (Rhino)
Faster Than The Speed Of Night . . . . (Columbia)
Seems Like Yesterday-#4-Early '80s-C . . . . (K-Tel)
Nicki French; *Dance Hits '96 Supermix-C* . . . . (Critique)
Secrets . . . .(Critique)
Touch It
Monifah; *Mo'hogany* . . . . (Uptown)
Touch Me Tease Me
Case Featuring Foxy Brown; *Case* . . . .(Def Jam/RAL/Mercury)
Def Jam Greatest Hits-C . . . .(Def Jam)
ST/The Nutty Professor . . . .(Def Jam)
Ultimate Hip Hop Party-1998-C . . . . (Arista)
Touch, Peel, And Stand
Days Of The New; *Days Of The New* . . . . (Outpost/Interscope)
X Games-#3-Music From The X Games-C . . . . (Mammoth)
Trust
Megadeth; *Cryptic Writings* . . . . (Capitol)
Try A Little Tenderness
Aretha Franklin; *Sweet Bitter Love* . . . . (Columbia)
David Sanborn; *ST/The Mirror Has Two Faces* . . . . (Columbia)
Otis Redding; *Best Of Otis Redding* . . . . (Atco)
Best Of Otis Redding . . . . (Atlantic)
Live In Europe . . . . (Atco)
The Otis Redding Story . . . . (Atlantic)
Very Best Of Otis Redding . . . . (Rhino)
Three Dog Night; *Best Of Three Dog Night* . . . .(MCA)
Turn Me On "Mr. Deadman"
Union Underground; *...An Education In Rebellion* . . . . (Portrait)
Turn On Your Love Light
Bobby Bland; *Bobby Bland's Greatest Hits-#1* . . . . (MCA)
Psychedelic '60s-#6-C . . . . (Collectables)
Turn On Your Love Light-The Duke Recordings-#2 . . . . (MCA)
Grateful Dead; *Best Of The Grateful Dead-Skeletons From The*
Closet . . . . (Warner Bros.)
Fillmore East-2/11/69 . . . . (Arista)
Live/Dead . . . .(Warner Bros.)
Two From The Vault . . . . (Grateful Dead)
Twinkle, Twinkle Lucky Star
Merle Haggard; *Chill Factor* . . . .(Epic)
Greatest Country Hits Of The '80s-1988-C . . . . (Columbia)
U Know What's Up
Donell Jones; *Totally Hits-#2-C* . . . . (Elektra)
Where I Wanna Be . . . . (LaFace)
Unable To Stay, Unwilling To Leave
James Horner; *ST/Titanic* . . . . (Sony Music Classical)
Unbound
Robbie Robertson; *Contact From The Underworld of Redboy* . . . . (Capitol)
Un-Break My Heart
Toni Braxton; *Secrets* . . . . (LaFace)
Unchained Melody
Elvis Presley; *Always On My Mind* . . . . (RCA)
Moody Blue . . . . (RCA)
The Great Performances . . . . (RCA)
George Benson; *Livin' Inside Your Love* . . . . (Warner Bros.)
LeAnn Rimes; *LeAnn Rimes-Early Years-Unchained Melody* . . . . . (MCG/Curb)
Platters; *Platters Greatest Hits* . . . . (Everest)

Red Sails In The Sunset . . . . (Allegiance)
Richard Clayderman; *Richard Clayderman Plays Love Songs Of The*
World . . . . (Columbia)
Righteous Brothers; *Righteous Brothers' Greatest Hits* . . . . (Verve)
ST/Ghost . . . .(Varese Sarabande)
Willie Nelson; *Stardust* . . . . (Legacy)
Uninvited
Alanis Morissette; *ST/City Of Angels* . . . .(Warner Sunset/Reprise)
Up, Up & Away
5th Dimension; *5th Dimension-Anthology 1967-1973* . . . . (Rhino)
Greatest Hits On Earth . . . . (Arista)
Useless Begging
Todd Rundgren; *Todd* . . . . (Rhino)
Venus
Frankie Avalon; *21 Oldies But Goodies-C* . . . . (Original Sound)
'50s Sock Hop-C . . . . (K-Tel)
Billboard Top Rock 'N' Roll Hits-1959-C . . . . (Rhino)
Oldies But Goodies-#10-C . . . .(Original Sound)
Very Thought Of You, The
Diane Schuur; *A Time For Love: Priceless Jazz-C* . . . . (GRP)
Ray Noble & His Orchestra; *The Sweetest Sounds Ever Heard-C* . . . . . .(Hip-O)
Those Wonderful Years: Puttin' On The Ritz-C . . . .(JCI Assoc. Labels)
Wynton Marsalis; *The Very Thought Of You: Jazz For Lovers-C* . . . . . . (Legacy)
Violet
Hole; *Ask For It* . . . . (Caroline)
Live Through This . . . .(David Geffen Co.)
Wait
Huffamoose; *We've Been Had Again* . . . .(Interscope)
Walking In A Hurricane
John Fogerty; *Blue Moon Swamp* . . . . (Warner Bros.)
Wanderlust
Mark Knopfler; *Sailing To Philadelphia* . . . . (Warner Bros.)
Wannabe
Spice Girls; *First Generation: 25 Years Of Virgin Records-C* . . . .(Virgin)
MTV The Grind-#1-C . . . . (Tommy Boy)
Spice . . . .(Virgin)
Want You Bad
Offspring; *Conspiracy Of One* . . . . (Columbia)
Wanted
Perry Como; *Perry Como's All-Time Greatest Hits-#1* . . . . (RCA)
Perry Como's Greatest Hits . . . . (RCA)
We Can Work It Out
Beatles; *"Yesterday"...And Today* . . . . (Capitol)
Beatles 1 . . . . (Capitol)
Beatles-20 Greatest Hits . . . . (Capitol)
Beatles-Box Set . . . . (Capitol)
Past Masters-Volume Two . . . . (Parlophone)
The Beatles/1962-1966 . . . . (Capitol)
Paul McCartney; *Unplugged (The Official Bootleg)* . . . . (Capitol)
Stevie Wonder; *Beatles Songs By Greatest Stars* . . . . (Motown)
Signed Sealed & Delivered . . . . (Motown)
Stevie Wonder's Greatest Hits-#2 . . . . (Motown)
Top 10 With A Bullet-Motown Solo Stars-C . . . . (Motown)
What A Girl Wants
Christina Aguilera; *Christina Aguilera* . . . . (RCA)
Totally Hits-#3-C . . . .(Atlantic)
What About Now
Lonestar; *Lonely Grill* . . . . (BNA)
What Do You Want From Me
Pink Floyd; *The Division Bell* . . . . (Columbia)
What I'll Give You Since You've Asked
Judy Collins; *Colors Of The Day-The Best Of Judy Collins* . . . . (Elektra)
What The Heart Wants
Collin Raye; *Best Of Collin Raye-Direct Hits* . . . . (Epic)
What The Soul Desires
Donovan; *Troubadour-Definitive Collection* . . . . (Epic)
What Would Happen
Meredith Brooks; *Blurring The Edges* . . . . (Capitol)
What Ya Want
Ruff Ryders Featuring Eve & Nokio; *Ruff Ryders: Ride Or*
Die-#1 . . . .(Ruff Ryders/IDJMG)
What You Want
Mase Featuring Total; *Harlem World* . . . .(Bad Boy/Arista)
What You Want
DMX; *...And Then There Was X* . . . .(Ruff Ryders/IDJMG)
What'chu Like
Da Brat; *Unrestricted* . . . . (So So Def/Columbia)
What'd I Say
Elvis Presley; *Collector's Gold* . . . . (RCA)
Elvis' Gold Records, Volume 4 . . . . (RCA)
Elvis In Concert . . . . (RCA)
Elvis-Greatest Hits, Volume One . . . . (RCA)
Jerry Lee Lewis; *Jerry Lee Lewis-Original Golden Hits-#2* . . . . (Sun)
Jerry Lee Lewis-Original Golden Hits-#2 . . . . (Sun)
Milestones . . . . (Rhino)
Rocket 88 . . . . (Tomato)
Rockin' My Life Away . . . . (Tomato)
John Mayall's Bluesbreakers with Eric Clapton; *John Mayall's Bluesbreakers*
with Eric Clapton . . . .(Deram)

Ray Charles; *Atlantic Rhythm & Blues 1947-1974-#4 (1958-1962)-C* . (Atlantic)
Atlantic Soul Classics-C . . . . (Warner Special Prod.)
Frat Rock!-#3-Grandson Of Frat Rock!-C . . . . (Rhino)
Life In Music . . . . (Atlantic)
Ray Charles-Anthology . . . . (Rhino)

Whatever
Ideal; *Ideal* . . . . (Noontime/Virgin)

Whatever
En Vogue; *Bass In Your Face: Essential Drum And Bass-C* . . . . (Elektra)

Whatever Your Heart Desires
Donna Summer; *Another Place And Time* . . . . (Casablanca)

What's Love Got To Do With It
Tina Turner; *Live In Europe* . . . . (Capitol)
Private Dancer . . . . (Capitol)
Simply The Best . . . . (Capitol)

Wheel Of Fortune
Cardinals; *Atlantic Rhythm & Blues 1947-1974-box-C* . . . . (Atlantic)
Kay Starr; *Capitol Collectors Series-Kay Starr* . . . . (Capitol)

When I Need You
Celine Dion; *Let's Talk About Love-C* . . . . (550 Music)
Leo Sayer; *'70s Greatest Rock Hits-#5-Kickin' Back-C* . . . . (Priority)
Show Must Go On-Anthology . . . . (Rhino)

When It Hurts So Bad
Lauryn Hill; *The Miseducation Of Lauryn Hill* . . . . (Ruffhouse/Columbia)

When The Saints Go Marching In
Al Hirt; *Best Of Al Hirt* . . . . (RCA)
Our Man-In New Orleans . . . . (Novus)
Jerry Lee Lewis; *Jerry Lee Lewis* . . . . (Rhino)
Louis Armstrong; *At The Crescendo* . . . . (MCA)
Big Bands Of The Swinging Years-#1-C . . . . (Collectables)
C'Est Si Bon . . . . (Vanguard)
Essential Louis Armstrong . . . . (Vanguard)
Louis Armstrong Of New Orleans . . . . (MCA)
Original Soundtrack; *Children's Favorites* . . . . . . (Kid Rhino/Rhino 4 Kids)
Pete Fountain; *Best Of Pete Fountain* . . . . (MCA)
Down On Rampart Street . . . . (Intermedia)
Pete Fountain's New Orleans . . . . (MCA)
Preservation Hall Jazz Band; *Best Of The Preservation Hall
Jazz Band* . . . . (Columbia)

When You Need Me
Bruce Springsteen; *Tracks* . . . . (Columbia)

When You Need Me
Will Downing featuring Chante Moore; *All The Man You Need* . . . . . (Motown)

When You Need My Love
Darryl Worley; *Hard Rain Don't Last* . . . . (DreamWorks/SKG)

Whenever Wherever Whatever
Maxwell; *Maxwell's Urban Hang Suite* . . . . (Columbia)

Who Are You
Who; *Hooligans* . . . . (MCA)
The Concert For New York City-C . . . . (Columbia)
Who Are You . . . . (MCA)
Who Greatest Hits . . . . (MCA)
Who's Last . . . . (MCA)

Who Do U Love
Deborah Cox; *Deborah Cox* . . . . (Arista)
Ultimate Dance Party-1997-C . . . . (Arista)

Who Needs You Baby
Clay Walker; *Hypnotize The Moon* . . . . (Giant)

Who Wants To Live Forever
Queen; *A Kind Of Magic* . . . . (Hollywood)
Classic Queen . . . . (Hollywood)
Diana, Princess Of Wales-Tribute-C . . . . (Columbia)

Whole Lotta Love
Led Zeppelin; *Led Zeppelin II* . . . . (Atlantic)
Led Zeppelin-Box Set . . . . (Atlantic)
Remasters . . . . (Atlantic)
ST/The Song Remains The Same . . . . (Swan Song)

Wichita Lineman
Dwight Yoakam; *Under The Covers* . . . . (Reprise)
Glen Campbell; *Best Of Glen Campbell* . . . . (Capitol)
Country Music Classics-#3-1965-1970-C . . . . (K-Tel)
Glen Campbell-Classics Collection . . . . (Capitol)
Glen Campbell-Live . . . . (Capitol)
Glen Campbell's Greatest Hits . . . . (Capitol)
Jimmy Webb Collection . . . . (Columbia)

Wild Horses
Rolling Stones; *Hot Rocks 1964-1971* . . . . (Abkco)
Made In The Shade . . . . (Rolling Stones)
Singles Collection-The London Years . . . . (Abkco)
Sticky Fingers . . . . (Virgin)

Winner Of Your Heart
Johnnie & Jack & Their Tennessee Mountain Boys; *45-Out of print* . . . .(RCA)

Wishing Well
Terence Trent D'Arby; *Introducing The Hardline According To Terence
Trent D'Arby* . . . . (Columbia)

Wobble Wobble
504 Boyz; *Goodfellas* . . . . (No Limit/Priority)

Woman
Peter And Gordon; *Best Of Peter And Gordon* . . . . (Rhino)

History Of British Rock-#4-C . . . .(Rhino)

Woman In Me (Needs The Man In You)
Shania Twain; *Woman In Me* . . . .(Mercury)

Woman's Touch
Toby Keith; *Blue Moon* . . . . (Polydor Country)

Wouldn't It Be Nice
Beach Boys; *Absolutely Best-#2* . . . .(Capitol)
Made In The U.S.A. . . . .(Capitol)
Pet Sounds . . . .(Capitol)
Still Cruisin' . . . .(Capitol)

Wrapped Up In You
Garth Brooks; *Scarecrow* . . . .(Capitol)

Yearning (Just For You)
Asleep At The Wheel featuring Vince Gill; *Tribute To The Music Of Bob
Wills And The Texas Playboys-C* . . . . (Liberty)
Bob Wills & His Texas Playboys; *For The Last Time* . . . . (Capitol)

You Are My Sunshine
Bing Crosby; *Best Of Bing Crosby* . . . . (MCA)
Bing Crosby's Greatest Hits . . . . (MCA)
Jimmie Davis; *20 Golden Souvenirs Of Music City U.S.A.-C* . . . . . (Plantation)
Best Of Jimmie Davis . . . . (MCA)
Jimmie Davis-Golden Hits . . . . (Plantation)
The Country Music Hall Of Fame-Jimmie Davis . . . . (MCA)
Mississippi John Hurt; *Best Of Mississippi John Hurt* . . . . (Vanguard)
Mitch Miller; *Mitch Miller-16 Most Requested Songs* . . . . (Columbia)
Norman Blake; *ST/O Brother, Where Art Thou?* . . . . (Mercury)
Ray Charles; *Ray Charles-Anthology* . . . . (Rhino)
Ray Charles-His Greatest Hits-#2 . . . . (Dunhill Compact Classics)
Willie Nelson & Leon Russell; *One For The Road* . . . . (Columbia)

You Asked Me To
Elvis Presley; *Guitar Man* . . . . (RCA)

You Blew Me Off
Bare Jr.; *Boo-Tay* . . . . (Immortal/Epic)
ST/Cruel Intentions . . . . (Virgin)

You Can Get It If You Really Want
Jimmy Cliff; *In Concert-Best Of Jimmy Cliff* . . . . (Reprise)
ST/The Harder They Come . . . . (Mango)

You Cheated
Shields; *Oldies But Goodies-#3-C* . . . . (Original Sound)

You Don't Know What You've Got (Until You Lose It)
Ral Donner; *You Don't Know What You've Got (Until You
Lose It)* . . . . (Collectables)

You Got To Me
Neil Diamond; *Neil Diamond's Greatest Hits-1966-1992* . . . .(Columbia)

You Gotta Love That
Neal McCoy; *Neal McCoy's Greatest Hits* . . . . (Atlantic)
Today's Country Love-C . . . . (K-Tel)
You Gotta Love That! . . . . (Atlantic)

You Keep Me Hangin' On
Diana Ross; *Evening With Diana Ross* . . . .(Motown)
Diana Ross & The Supremes; *Diana Ross & The Supremes-Anthology (1962-
1969)* . . . .(Motown)
Motown Story-First 25 Years-C . . . .(Motown)
Kim Wilde; *Another Step* . . . . (MCA)
Reba McEntire; *Starting Over* . . . . (MCA)
Supremes; *Billboard Top R&B Hits-1965-C* . . . .(Rhino)
Diana Ross & The Supremes' Greatest Hits-#2 . . . .(Motown)
Vanilla Fudge; *Best Of Vanilla Fudge* . . . . (Atco)
Vanilla Fudge . . . . (Atco)
Wilson Pickett; *A Man & A Half-Best Of Wilson Pickett* . . . .(Rhino)
Wilson Pickett's Greatest Hits . . . .(Atlantic)

You Made Me Love You
Judy Garland; *Best Of Judy Garland* . . . . (MCA)
Judy Garland's All-Time Greatest Hits . . . .(Curb)
Patsy Cline; *Sentimentally Yours* . . . . (MCA)

You Make Me Sick
Pink; *Can't Take Me Home* . . . .(LaFace)

You Make Me Wanna…
Usher; *My Way* . . . .(LaFace)
Totally Hits-#1-C . . . .(Arista)

You Must Love Me
Madonna; *ST/Evita-Music From The Motion Picture* . . . . (Warner Bros.)

You Need To Be With Me
Susan Tedeschi; *Just Won't Burn* . . . . (Tone Cool)

You Send Me
Aretha Franklin; *Aretha's Gold* . . . .(Atlantic)
Manhattans; *Too Hot To Stop It* . . . .(Columbia)
Michael Bolton; *Timeless-Classics* . . . .(Columbia)
Sam Cooke; *Best Of Sam Cooke* . . . . (RCA)
ST/American Pop . . . . (MCA)
The Man And His Music . . . . (RCA)

You Should Be Mine (Don't Waste Your Time)
Brian McKnight; *Anytime* . . . .(Motown)

You Want This
Janet Jackson; *janet.* . . . . (Virgin)

You Won't Be Lonely Now
Billy Ray Cyrus; *Southern Rain* . . . .(Monument)

You Wreck Me
Tom Petty; *Wildflowers* . . . . (Warner Bros.)

Young Lust
Pink Floyd; *1980-1981 Wall Live-Is There Anybody Out There* . . . . . (Columbia)
The Wall. . . . . (Columbia)
Roger Waters & Bryan Adams; *The Wall-Live In Berlin* . . . . (Mercury)

Your Everything
keith urban; *keith urban* . . . . (Capitol)

You're Still A Young Man
Tower Of Power; *Bump City*. . . . .(Warner Bros.)
Live & In Living Color. . . . .(Warner Bros.)

You're Still The One
Shania Twain; *Come On Over* . . . . (Mercury)

You're The Inspiration
Chicago; *Chicago 17* . . . .(Warner Bros.)
Chicago's Greatest Hits-1982-1989 . . . .(Full Moon)
Peter Cetera featuring Az Yet; *You're The Inspiration-A*
Collection . . . .(River North)

You've Really Got A Hold On Me
Beatles; *The Beatles-Anthology-#1*. (Capitol)
Smokey Robinson & The Miracles; *Best Of Smokey Robinson & The*
Miracles-Anthology . . . . (Motown)
Great Songs & Performances That Inspired The Motown 25th Anniversary
Television Special-C. . . . . (Motown)
Smokey Robinson-The Ultimate Collection . . . . (Motown)

Zip-Lock
Lit; *A Place In The Sun* . . . . (RCA)

DESPAIR, Down & Out, Existential Angst, Hopelessness, Mental Anguish
See Also: *LOW SELF-ESTEEM, SADNESS, SUICIDE*

(Sittin' On) The Dock Of The Bay
Michael Bolton; *The Hunger* . . . . (Columbia)
Otis Redding; *(Sittin' On) The Dock Of The Bay* . . . . (Atco)
Best Of Otis Redding . . . . (Atco)
Golden Age Of Black Music-1960-1970-C . . . . (Atlantic)
Golden Soul-C . . . . (Atlantic)
Soul Years-C . . . . (Atlantic)
The Otis Redding Story . . . . (Atlantic)

Acoustic #3
Goo Goo Dolls; *Dizzy Up The Girl* . . . . (Warner Sunset/Reprise)

Alcohol
Kinks; *Everybody's In Show-Biz* . . . . (Rhino)
Muswell Hillbillies . . . . (VelVel)
The Kinks' Greatest-Celluloid Heroes . . . . (RCA)

Alone Again (Naturally)
Gilbert O'Sullivan; *Best Of Gilbert O'Sullivan* . . . . (Rhino)
Billboard Top Rock 'N' Roll Hits-1972-C . . . . (Rhino)

Am I The Only One (Who's Ever Felt This Way)
Dixie Chicks; *Wide Open Spaces* . . . . (Monument)

Amazed
Offspring; *Ixnay On The Hombre* . . . . (Columbia)

Angel
Sarah McLachlan; *Mirrorball*. . . . . (Arista)
ST/City Of Angels. . . . .(Warner Sunset/Reprise)
Surfacing . . . . (Arista)
Totally Hits-#1-C . . . . (Arista)

Angel Without A Prayer
Deana Carter; *Love Shouldn't Hurt-C*. . . . . (Qwest)

Artificial Flowers
Bobby Darin; *The Bobby Darin Story*. . . . . (Atlantic)

Better Days (And The Bottom Drops Out)
Citizen King; *Mobile Estates* . . . .(Warner Bros.)

Bittersweet
Fuel; *Sunburn* . . . . (550 Music)

Bohemian Rhapsody
Braids; *Here We Come* . . . . (Big Beat)
ST/High School High . . . . (Big Beat)
Queen; *A Night At The Opera* . . . . (Hollywood)
Classic Queen . . . . (Hollywood)
Live At Wembley '86 . . . . (Hollywood)
ST/Wayne's World . . . . (Reprise)

Bound For The Floor
Local H; *As Good As Dead* . . . . (Island)

Bridge Over Troubled Water
Aretha Franklin; *Aretha Franklin-30 Greatest Hits* . . . . (Rhino)
Aretha Franklin's Greatest Hits . . . . (Atlantic)
Live At Fillmore West . . . . (Atlantic)
Paul Simon; *America: A Tribute To Heroes-C* . . . . (Interscope)
Concert In The Park-August 15 1991. . . . .(Warner Bros.)
Paul Simon In Concert/Live Rhymin' . . . . (Columbia)
Simon & Garfunkel; *Bridge Over Troubled Water* . . . . (Columbia)
Collected Works. . . . . (Columbia)
God Bless America-C . . . . (Columbia)
Simon & Garfunkel's Greatest Hits . . . . (Columbia)
The Concert In Central Park . . . .(Warner Bros.)

Can't Cry Anymore
Sheryl Crow; *MTV Party To Go-#8-C*. . . . . (Tommy Boy)
Tuesday Night Music Club . . . . (A&M)

Can't Stand It
Wilco; *Summer Teeth* . . . . (Reprise)

Changes
2Pac; *2Pac Greatest Hits*. . . . . (Amaru/Death Row/Interscope)

Clean My Wounds
Corrosion Of Conformity; *Deliverance*. . . . . (Columbia)

Crash And Burn
Savage Garden; *Affirmation* . . . . (Columbia)

Day After Day
Def Leppard; *Euphoria* . . . . (Mercury)

Day I Tried To Live, The
Soundgarden; *A-Sides* . . . . (A&M)
Superunknown . . . . (A&M)

Desolation Row
Bob Dylan; *Highway 61 Revisited*. (Columbia)

Desperately Wanting
Better Than Ezra; *Friction, Baby*. . . . . (Swell/Elektra)

Don't Let The Sun Go Down On Me
Elton John; *Caribou* . . . . (Rocket)
Elton John's Greatest Hits . . . . (Polydor)
Live In Australia With The Melbourne Symphony Orchestra . . . . (MCA)
Elton John & George Michael; *Duets-C* . . . . (MCA)
George Michael & Elton John; *Two Rooms-Celebrating The Songs Of Elton*
John & Bernie Taupin-C . . . . (Polydor)

Download (I Will)
Expanding Man; *Head To The Ground* . . . . (Columbia)
ST/The Cable Guy . . . . (Work)

Drunk Is Better Than Dead
Push Stars; *ST/Malcolm In The Middle* . . . . (Restless)

Everybody Hurts
R.E.M.; *Automatic For The People* . . . . (Warner Bros.)
Diana, Princess Of Wales-Tribute-C . . . . (Columbia)

Fa Fa (Never Be The Same Again)
Guster; *Lost & Gone Forever* . . . .(Hybrid/Sire)

Falling Away From Me
Korn; *Issues*. . . . . (Immortal/Epic)

Freak On A Leash
Korn; *Follow The Leader* . . . . (Immortal/Epic)

Friends
John Michael Montgomery; *John Michael Montgomery's*
Greatest Hits . . . .(Atlantic)
What I Do The Best. . . . .(Atlantic)

Get Born Again
Alice In Chains; *Nothing Safe* . . . . (Columbia)

Giving In
Adema; *Adema* . . . . (Arista)

Godless
U.P.O.; *No Pleasantries* . . . . (Epic)

Gone Away
Offspring; *Ixnay On The Hombre* . . . . (Columbia)

Hear Me In The Harmony
Harry Connick, Jr.; *Star Turtle* . . . . (Columbia)

Here Comes The Rain
Mavericks; *Music For All Occasions* . . . . (MCA)

Hopeless
Dionne Farris; *ST/Love Jones* . . . . (Columbia)

Human Beings
Seal; *Human Being* . . . . (Warner Bros.)

Hurt
Nine Inch Nails; *The Downward Spiral* . . . .(Interscope)

I Don't Live Today
Jimi Hendrix; *Concerts* . . . . (Reprise)
Essential Jimi Hendrix, Volume 2. . . . .(Reprise)
Kiss The Sky . . . .(Reprise)
Jimi Hendrix Experience; *Are You Experienced?* . . . .(Reprise)

I Got Id
Pearl Jam; *Merkinball* . . . . (Epic)

I Heard It Through The Grapevine
Creedence Clearwater Revival; *Chooglin'* . . . .(Fantasy)
Cosmo's Factory . . . .(Fantasy)
Creedence Clearwater Revival-Chronicle . . . .(Fantasy)
Creedence Clearwater Revival-Gold . . . .(Fantasy)
Movie Album . . . .(Fantasy)
Gladys Knight & The Pips; *16 #1 Hits From The Late '60s-C* . . . . . . (Motown)
Compact Command Performances-Gladys Knight & The Pips . . . . . (Motown)
Every Great Motown Song-First 25 Years-C . . . . (Motown)
Motown Grammy R&B Performances Of The '60s & '70s-C. . . . . . (Motown)
Motown Superstar Series-#13-Gladys Knight & The Pips . . . . . . (Motown)
Top 10 With A Bullet-Motown Girl Groups-C . . . . (Motown)
Marvin Gaye; *25 #1 Hits From 25 Years-C*. . . . . (Motown)
Every Great Motown Hit Of Marvin Gaye . . . . (Motown)
Marvin Gaye Live At The London Palladium . . . . (Motown)
Marvin Gaye-Anthology. . . . . (Motown)
Most Played Songs On America's Jukeboxes . . . . (Motown)
Motown Story-First 25 Years-C . . . . (Motown)

I Wonder If Heaven Got A Ghetto
2Pac; *R U Still Down (Remember Me)* . . . . (Amaru/Jive)
If There's A God On My Side
Rosanne Cash; *The Wheel* . . . . (Columbia)
Innocent
Fuel; *Something Like Human* . . . . (Epic)
I've Tried Everything
Eurythmics; *The Sopranos-Music From The HBO Original
Series* . . . . (Sony Music Soundtrax)
Jumper
Third Eye Blind; *Third Eye Blind* . . . . (Elektra)
Totally Hits-#1-C . . . . (Arista)
Kids Aren't Alright
Offspring; *Americana* . . . . (Columbia)
Last Resort
Papa Roach; *Infest* . . . . (DreamWorks/SKG)
Layla
Derek And The Dominos; *Classic Rock 1966-1988-C* . . . . (Atlantic)
Eric Clapton-Crossroads-C . . . . (Polydor)
Layla . . . . (Polydor)
ST/Goodfellas . . . . (Atlantic)
Eric Clapton; *Eric Clapton-Unplugged* . . . . (Reprise)
Letting The Cables Sleep
Bush; *Science Of Things* . . . . (Trauma)
Life, The
Alicia Keys; *Songs In A Minor* . . . . (J)
Listen
Collective Soul; *Disciplined Breakdown* . . . . (Atlantic)
Long Day
Matchbox Twenty; *Yourself Or Someone Like You* . . . . (Lava)
Long Long Time
Linda Ronstadt; *Different Drum* . . . . (Capitol)
Linda Ronstadt-Retrospective . . . . (Capitol)
Linda Ronstadt's Greatest Hits . . . . (Asylum)
Silk Purse . . . . (Capitol)
Long Way Down
Goo Goo Dolls; *A Boy Named Goo* . . . . (Metal Blade)
Looking East
Jackson Browne; *Looking East* . . . . (Elektra)
Loser
3 Doors Down; *Better Life* . . . . (Republic/Universal)
Mad Season
Matchbox Twenty; *Mad Season By Matchbox Twenty* . . . . (Lava)
Malibu
Hole; *Celebrity Skin* . . . . (David Geffen Co.)
Man Overboard
Blink-182; *The Mark, Tom & Travis Show-The Enema Strikes Back* . . . . (MCA)
Me
Staind; *Dysfunction* . . . . (Flip/Elektra)
Mood Indigo
Duke Ellington; *1954 Los Angeles Concert* . . . . (Crescendo)
Black, Brown & Beige: 1944-1946 Band Recordings . . . . (Bluebird)
Carnegie Hall Concert-January 23, 1943 . . . . (Prestige)
Ellington Indigos . . . . (Columbia)
Sophisticated Ellington . . . . (RCA)
Ella Fitzgerald; *Ella A Nice* . . . . (Pablo)
Ella Fitzgerald Sings-#2 . . . . (Verve)
Four Freshmen; *Capitol Collectors Series-Four Freshman* . . . . (Capitol)
Frank Sinatra; *In The Wee Small Hours* . . . . (Capitol)
Jimmie Lunceford & His Orchestra; *Stomp It Off-#1-1934-1935* . . . . (GRP)
Preservation Hall Jazz Band; *Best Of The Preservation Hall
Jazz Band* . . . . (Columbia)
New Orleans-#4 . . . . (Columbia)
My Baby Needs A Shepherd
Emmylou Harris; *Red Dirt Girl* . . . . (Nonesuch)
My Favorite Headache
Geddy Lee; *My Favorite Headache* . . . . (Anthem/Atlantic)
My Friends
Red Hot Chili Peppers; *One Hot Minute* . . . . (Warner Bros.)
Naked
Goo Goo Dolls; *A Boy Named Goo* . . . . (Metal Blade)
No One
Cold; *13 Ways To Bleed On Stage* . . . . (Flip/Geffen/Interscope)
No Way Out
Stone Temple Pilots; *No. 4* . . . . (Atlantic)
Not Dark Yet
Bob Dylan; *Time Out Of Mind* . . . . (Columbia)
Nothing As It Seems
Pearl Jam; *Binaural* . . . . (Epic)
Novocaine For The Soul
Eels; *Beautiful Freak* . . . . (DreamWorks/SKG)
One Headlight
Wallflowers; *Bringing Down The Horse* . . . . (Interscope)
One Less Bell To Answer
5th Dimension; *5th Dimension-Anthology 1967-1973* . . . . (Rhino)
Greatest Hits On Earth . . . . (Arista)
Barbra Streisand; *Barbra Joan Streisand* . . . . (Columbia)
Gladys Knight & The Pips; *Gladys Knight & The Pips-Anthology* . . . . (Motown)

If I Were Your Woman . . . . (Motown)
Only Love (The Ballad Of Sleeping Beauty)
Sophie B. Hawkins; *Whaler* . . . . (Columbia)
Paint It, Black
Eric Burdon; *Eric Burdon Sings The Animals' Greatest Hits* . . . . (Rhino)
Rolling Stones; *Aftermath* . . . . (Abkco)
Flashpoint . . . . (Virgin)
Hot Rocks 1964-1971 . . . . (Abkco)
Singles Collection-The London Years . . . . (Abkco)
Through The Past, Darkly (Big Hits Vol. 2) . . . . (Abkco)
Pardon Me
Incubus; *Make Yourself* . . . . (Immortal/Epic)
Pearl, The
Emmylou Harris; *Red Dirt Girl* . . . . (Nonesuch)
Plowed
Sponge; *Rotting Pinata* . . . . (Work)
Promises Broken
Soul Asylum; *Let Your Dim Light Shine* . . . . (Columbia)
Red Dirt Girl
Emmylou Harris; *Red Dirt Girl* . . . . (Nonesuch)
River Of Deceit
Mad Season; *Above* . . . . (Columbia)
Roll To Me
Del Amitri; *ST/Crossroads-VH1 Television Program* . . . . (Atlantic)
Twisted . . . . (A&M)
Save Yourself
Stabbing Westward; *Darkest Days* . . . . (Columbia)
Scream
Michael Jackson with Janet Jackson; *HIStory: Past, Present And Future-
Book 1-C* . . . . (Epic)
Semi-Charmed Life
Third Eye Blind; *Jock Rock 2000-C* . . . . (Tommy Boy)
Third Eye Blind . . . . (Elektra)
Shut Out The Light
Bruce Springsteen; *Tracks* . . . . (Columbia)
Something In The Night
Bruce Springsteen; *Darkness On The Edge Of Town* . . . . (Columbia)
Stan
Eminem; *The Marshall Mathers LP* . . . . (Aftermath/Interscope)
Streets Of Fire
Bruce Springsteen; *Darkness On The Edge Of Town* . . . . (Columbia)
Streets Of Philadelphia
Bruce Springsteen; *Bruce Springsteen's Greatest Hits* . . . . (Columbia)
Diana, Princess Of Wales-Tribute-C . . . . (Columbia)
ST/Philadelphia . . . . (Epic/Sony Music Soundtrax)
This Is A Call
Foo Fighters; *Foo Fighters* . . . . (Roswell/RCA)
'Til I Fell In Love With You
Bob Dylan; *Time Out Of Mind* . . . . (Columbia)
Today My World Slipped Away
George Strait; *Carrying Your Love With Me* . . . . (MCA)
Latest Greatest Straitest Hits . . . . (MCA)
Vern Gosdin; *10 Years Of Greatest Hits Newly Recorded* . . . . (Columbia)
Legends Of The Silver Eagle-C . . . . (King Biscuit Entert.)
Today My World Slipped Away . . . . (AMI)
Torn
Natalie Imbruglia; *Left Of The Middle* . . . . (RCA)
Trouble In Mind
Bob Wills; *Stay A Little Longer-The Original Columbia
Recordings* . . . . (Roswell/RCA)
Vanishing Cream
Hunger; *Devil Thumbs A Ride* . . . . (Universal)
Waffle
Sevendust; *Home* . . . . (TVT)
What Becomes Of The Brokenhearted
Jimmy & David Ruffin; *Motown Superstar Series-#8-Jimmy & David
Ruffin* . . . . (Motown)
Jimmy Ruffin; *Motown Story-First 25 Years-C* . . . . (Motown)
Paul Young; *ST/Fried Green Tomatoes* . . . . (MCA)
What's This Life For
Creed; *My Own Prison* . . . . (Wind-up)
Yer Blues
Beatles; *The Beatles (White Album)* . . . . (Capitol)

DEVILS, Satan

See Also: **ANGELS, BAD, GOD, HEAVEN, HELL,
MONSTERS, SPIRITS**

(You're The) Devil In Disguise
Elvis Presley; *Elvis' Gold Records, Volume 4* . . . . (RCA)
The Top Ten Hits . . . . (RCA)
Alcohol
Kinks; *Everybody's In Show-Biz* . . . . (Rhino)
Muswell Hillbillies . . . . (VelVel)
The Kinks' Greatest-Celluloid Heroes . . . . (RCA)

Beat The Devil
Blow Up; *ST/Up The Academy* . . . . (Capitol)
Between The Devil And Me
Alan Jackson; *Everything I Love*. . . . . (Arista)
Between The Devil And The Deep Blue Sea
Cab Calloway; *Jazz Heritage: Mr. Hi-De-Ho* . . . .(MCA)
Chris Rea; *Espresso Logic* . . . . (East West)
Diana Krall; *Stepping Out*. . . . . (Justin Time)
Ella Fitzgerald; *Harold Arlen Songbook-#1* . . . . (Verve)
Black Sabbath
Black Sabbath; *Black Sabbath* . . . .(Warner Bros.)
Live Evil . . . .(Warner Bros.)
We Sold Our Soul For Rock 'N' Roll . . . .(Warner Bros.)
Ozzy Osbourne; *Speak Of The Devil*. . . . . (Jet)
The Ozzman Cometh . . . .(Epic)
Caballo Diablo
Charlie Daniels Band; *Fire On The Mountain* . . . .(Epic)
Detour (Devil Took A)
Patti Page; *Patti Page-Golden Hits*. . . . . (Mercury)
Devil
Hoyt Axton; *Bread & Roses Festival Of Acoustic Music-#2-C* . . . . (Fantasy)
Fearless . . . . (A&M)
Urban Dance Squad; *Mental Floss For The Globe* . . . . (Arista)
Devil Ain't A Lonely Woman's Friend
Red Steagall; *45-#2824*. . . . .(MCA)
Devil Came From Kansas
Procol Harum; *A Salty Dog* . . . . (A&M)
Devil Comes Back To Georgia
Marc O'Connor; *Heroes* . . . .(Warner Bros.)
Devil Delight
Heart; *Magazine* . . . . (Capitol)
Devil In A Fast Car
Sheena Easton; *Best Kept Secret*. . . . .(EMI)
Devil In Disguise
J.J. Cale; *Grasshopper* . . . . (Mercury)
Special Edition. . . . . (Mercury)
Devil In Her Heart
Beatles; *The Beatles' Second Album*. . . . . (Capitol)
With The Beatles . . . . (Parlophone)
Donays; *Beatles Originals* . . . . (Rhino)
Devil In The Bottle
T.G. Sheppard; *T.G. Sheppard's Greatest Hits-#2* . . . . (WB/Curb)
Devil In The Cane Field
Mose Allison; *Down Home Piano* . . . . (Prestige)
Ol' Devil Mose. . . . . (Prestige)
Devil Inside
INXS; *Kick* . . . .(Atlantic)
Pop Will Eat Itself; *Now For A Feast!* . . . .(Rough Trade)
Devil Is Dope
Dramatics; *Best Of The Dramatics* . . . .(Stax)
Dramatic Experience . . . .(Stax)
Devil Jumped The Blackman
Lightnin' Hopkins; *Best Of Lightnin' Hopkins* . . . . (Prestige)
How Many More Years I Got . . . . (Fantasy)
Devil Lives In Dallas, The
Rusty Weir Pettit; *Taste Of Texas-Songs 'Bout Texas By Texans-C* . . (Columbia)
Devil Loose In Georgia
Orrin Star & Gary Mehalick; *Premium Blend*. . . . . (Flying Fish)
Devil May Care
Diana Krall; *When I Look In Your Eyes* . . . . (GRP)
Frank Sinatra; *What'll I Do*. . . . . (RCA)
Tommy Dorsey & Frank Sinatra; *Sessions-#1-February 1, 1940-July 17, 1940* . . . . (RCA)
Devil Or Angel
Bobby Vee; *Best Of Bobby Vee*. . . . .(EMI)
Bobby Vee-Golden Greats . . . . (Liberty)
Bobby Vee-Legendary Masters . . . .(EMI)
Clovers; *Atlantic Rhythm & Blues 1947-1974-#3 (1955-1958)-C* . . . . . (Atlantic)
Oldies But Goodies-#2-C. . . . . (Original Sound)
Very Best Of The Clovers . . . . (Rhino)
Devil Went Down To Georgia
Charlie Daniels Band; *A Decade Of Hits* . . . .(Epic)
Billboard Top Hits-1979-C . . . . (Rhino)
Me & The Boys. . . . .(Epic)
Million Mile Reflections . . . .(Epic)
ST/Urban Cowboy . . . . (Asylum)
Devil Wind
Bob Welch; *Three Hearts* . . . . (Capitol)
Devil With A Blue Dress On & Good Golly Miss Molly
Bruce Springsteen; *ST/No Nukes-Muse Concerts* . . . . (Asylum)
Mitch Ryder And The Detroit Wheels; *Frat Rock!-#4-C* . . . . (Rhino)
Rev Up-Best Of Mitch Ryder . . . . (Rhino)
Son Of Frat Rock!-C . . . . (Rhino)
Toga Rock-C . . . .(Dunhill Compact Classics)
Devil Woman
Marty Robbins; *Billboard Top Country Hits-1962-C* . . . . (Rhino)
Columbia Country Classics-#4-Nashville Sound-C. . . . . (Columbia)
Lifetime Of Song-1951-1982 . . . . (Columbia)

Marty Robbins' Greatest Hits-#4 . . . . (Columbia)
Devil Woman
Buddy Knox; *Best Of Buddy Knox* . . . . (Rhino)
Devil Woman
Hanoi Rocks; *Oriental Beat* . . . . (Geffen)
Devil's Food
Alice Cooper; *The Alice Cooper Show* . . . . (Warner Bros.)
Welcome To My Nightmare . . . .(Atlantic)
Devil's Radio
George Harrison; *Cloud Nine* . . . .(Dark Horse)
Live In Japan . . . .(Dark Horse)
Devil's Right Hand
Steve Earle; *Essential Steve Earle*. . . . . (MCA)
Steve Earle & The Dukes; *Early Tracks* . . . . (Epic)
Shut Up And Die Like An Aviator . . . . (MCA)
Waylon Jennings; *Will The Wolf Survive*. . . . . (MCA)
Devil's Toy
Almighty; *Soul Destruction* . . . .(Polydor)
Devil's Train
Hank Williams; *Lovesick Blues*. . . . .(Polydor)
Roy Acuff; *Roy Acuff's Greatest Hits* . . . . (Columbia)
Devil's Whorehouse
Misfits; *Walk Among Us* . . . .(Ruby)
Downbound Train
Chuck Berry; *Chuck Berry-The Anthology* . . . . (MCA)
Friend Of The Devil
Grateful Dead; *American Beauty*. . . . . (Warner Bros.)
Best Of The Grateful Dead-Skeletons From The Closet . . . . . . (Warner Bros.)
Dead Set . . . . (Arista)
Lyle Lovett; *Deadicated-C* . . . . (Arista)
Garden Of Allah
Don Henley; *Actual Miles: Henley's Greatest Hits*. . . . . (Geffen)
Heaven's Just A Sin Away
Kelly Willis; *Hot Country-C* . . . . (MCA Special Prod.)
Kelly Willis . . . . (MCA)
Kendalls; *Best Of The Kendalls* . . . . (Curb)
Kendalls-20 Greatest Hits . . . . (Deluxe)
If The Devil Danced (In Empty Pockets)
Joe Diffie; *A Thousand Winding Roads* . . . . (Epic)
I'm Living With The 3-Foot Anti-Christ
Mojo Nixon; *Frenzy/Get Out Of My Way* . . . . (I.R.S.)
Jesus & Mama
Confederate Railroad; *Confederate Railroad* . . . .(Atlantic)
Mother In Law
Buddy Guy; *Left My Blues In San Francisco* . . . . (Chess)
Ernie K-Doe; *Best Of New Orleans Rhythm & Blues-#1-C* . . . . (Rhino)
Collectables Presents The History Of Rock-#7-C . . . . (Collectables)
New Orleans Jazz & Heritage Festival-1976-C . . . . (Rhino)
Huey Lewis and the News; *Four Chords & Several Years Ago* . . . . . . (Elektra)
My White Devil
Echo & The Bunnymen; *Porcupine* . . . .(Sire)
N.I.B.
Primus with Ozzy; *Nativity In Black II: Tribute To Black Sabbath-C* . . . . (Divine/Priority)
Old Devil Moon
Anita O'Day; *Anita Sings The Most* . . . . (Verve)
Frank Sinatra & Nelson Riddle Orchestra; *songs for Swingin' Lovers!*. . . . . (Capitol)
John Raitt; *Highlights Of Broadway-Under Open Skies* . . . . (Capitol)
Lena Horne; *The Lady*. . . . . (Dunhill Compact Classics)
Michael Feinstein; *Michael Feinstein Sings The Burton Lane Songbook-#1* . . . . (Nonesuch)
Miles Davis; *Blue Haze* . . . . (Prestige)
Original Cast; *Finian's Rainbow*. . . . . (Columbia)
Tony Bennett; *Forty Years-The Artistry Of Tony Bennett* . . . . (Columbia)
Pack Up Your Sins And Go To The Devil
Dorothy Loudon; *Broadway Baby* . . . .(DRG)
Ella Fitzgerald & Chick Webb; *The Early Years-#1: With Chick Webb & His Orchestra-1935-1938* . . . . (GRP)
Phone Call From The Devil
Jim Nesbitt; *Phone Call From The Devil*. . . . .(Scotti Bros.)
Po Lazarus
James Carter & The Prisoners; *ST/O Brother, Where Art Thou?*. . . . . (Mercury)
Praise
Sevendust; *Animosity* . . . . (TVT)
Preaching Blues (Up Jumped The Devil)
Robert Johnson; *King Of The Delta Blues Singers-#2* . . . . (Columbia)
Robert Johnson-Complete Recordings . . . . (Columbia)
Prince Of Darkness
Nylons; *Best Of The Nylons* . . . .(Open Air)
One Size Fits All . . . .(Open Air)
Prince Of Darkness
Indigo Girls; *Back On The Bus Y'All* . . . . (Epic)
Indigo Girls . . . . (Epic)
Prince Of Darkness
Big Daddy Kane; *Prince Of Darkness*. . . . . (Cold Chillin')
Prince Of Darkness
Alice Cooper; *Raise Your Fist And Yell*. (MCA)

Prince Of Darkness
Miles Davis; *Sorcerer* . . . . (Columbia)
Race With The Devil
Gene Vincent and His Blue Caps; *Capitol Collectors Series-Gene Vincent
and His Blue Caps* . . . . (Gold Rush)
Legends Of Rock Guitar-'50s-#1-C . . . . (Rhino)
Rainbow Demon
Uriah Heep; *Demons And Wizards* . . . . (Mercury)
Runnin' With The Devil
Van Halen; *Van Halen* . . . . (Warner Bros.)
Satan Is Busy In Knoxville
Leola Manning; *Barrelhouse Mamas: Born In The Alley, Raised In The
Slums-C* . . . . (Yazoo)
Satan Place
Jeannie C. Riley; *Harper Valley P.T.A.* . . . . (Plantation)
Satan Takes A Holiday
Ozzie Nelson & His Orchestra; *The Uncollected Ozzie Nelson & His
Orchestra-#2-1937* . . . . (Hindsight)
Tommy Dorsey; *Seventeen Number Ones* . . . . (RCA)
Tommy Vig & His Orchestra; *Space Race* . . . . (Discovery)
Satan's Choir
Red Clay Ramblers; *It Ain't Right* . . . . (Flying Fish)
Satan's Doll
Floyd Cramer; *Best Of Floyd Cramer* . . . . (RCA)
Satan's Jewel Crown
Emmylou Harris; *Elite Hotel* . . . . (Reprise)
Satan's Kingdom
Jimmy Cliff; *I Am The Living* . . . . (MCA)
Save A Prayer
Mavericks; *Trampoline* . . . . (MCA)
Shake The Devil
Tommy Bolin; *Metal Giants-C* . . . . (Columbia)
Metalmania-C . . . . (Columbia)
Private Eyes . . . . (Columbia)
The Ultimate Tommy Bolin . . . . (Geffen)
Shout At The Devil
Motley Crue; *Decade Of Decadence* . . . . (Elektra)
Shout At The Devil . . . . (Elektra)
Shout To The Devil
Alarm; *Declaration* . . . . (I.R.S.)
Sit Down, You're Rockin' The Boat
Don Henley; *ST/Leap Of Faith* . . . . (MCA)
Original Cast; *Guys & Dolls* . . . . (MCA)
Stupidly Happy
XTC; *Wasp Star (Apple Venus Volume 2)* . . . . (Idea/TVT)
Sway
Rolling Stones; *Sticky Fingers* . . . . (Virgin)
Sympathy For The Devil
Bryan Ferry; *These Foolish Things* . . . . (Reprise)
Jane's Addiction; *Jane's Addiction* . . . . (Triple X Entert.)
Rolling Stones; *Beggars Banquet* . . . . (Abkco)
Flashpoint . . . . (Virgin)
Get Yer Ya-Ya's Out! . . . . (Abkco)
Hot Rocks 1964-1971 . . . . (Abkco)
Love You Live . . . . (Virgin)
Take The Devil
Eagles; *Eagles* . . . . (Asylum)
That Old Devil Called Love
Chet Baker; *Baker's Holiday* . . . . (Verve)
Compact Jazz-Chet Baker . . . . (Verve)
Ella Fitzgerald; *All That Jazz* . . . . (Pablo)
Tie A Knot In The Devil's Tail
Chris LeDoux; *Old Cowboy Classics* . . . . (Capitol)
Rodeo & Living Free . . . . (Liberty)
To Beat The Devil
Johnny Cash; *Johnny Cash-16 Biggest Hits-#2* . . . . (Legacy)
To Hell With The Devil
Stryper; *Can't Stop The Rock: The Stryper Collection-1984-1991* . . (Hollywood)
To Hell With The Devil . . . . (Hollywood)
Tying Knots In The Devil's Tail
Michael Martin Murphey; *Cowboy Songs* . . . . (Warner Western)
Watch What Happens (Lola's Theme)
Frank Sinatra; *My Way* . . . . (Reprise)
Henry Mancini; *Mancini Magic* . . . . (Pair)
Sergio Mendes; *Foursider* . . . . (A&M)
Wrong Number
Cure; *Galore-The Singles-1987-1997* . . . . (Fiction/Elektra)
Yo Ho Ho And A Bottle Of Rum
Original Cast; *Rugrats Sing-Along* . . . . (Interscope)

DIFFICULT, Hard To Do

***See Also: DECISIONS, EASY, FEAR & COURAGE, MOTIVATION,
STUCK, TROUBLE***

(It's Hard) Letting You Go
Bon Jovi; *These Days* . . . . (Mercury)

10 Miles To Go On A 9 Mile Road
Jim White; *No Such Place* . . . . (Luaka Bop)
Against All Odds (Take A Look At Me Now)
Mariah Carey; *Rainbow* . . . . (Columbia)
Phil Collins; *Hit Singles-1980-1988-C* . . . . (Atlantic)
Serious Hits...Live! . . . . (Atlantic)
ST/Against All Odds . . . . (Atlantic)
Against The Wind
Bob Seger & The Silver Bullet Band; *Against The Wind* . . . . . . (Capitol)
Nine Tonight . . . . (Capitol)
ST/Forrest Gump . . . . (Epic/Sony Music Soundtrax)
Ballad Of John And Yoko
Beatles; *Beatles 1* . . . . (Capitol)
Beatles-Box Set . . . . (Capitol)
Hey Jude . . . . (Capitol)
Past Masters-Volume Two . . . . (Parlophone)
ST/Imagine: John Lennon . . . . (Capitol)
The Beatles/1967-1970 . . . . (Capitol)
Better Man, Better Off
Tracy Lawrence; *The Coast Is Clear* . . . . (Atlantic)
Boy Named Sue
Johnny Cash; *Columbia Country Classics-#3-Americana-C* . . (Columbia)
Johnny Cash's Biggest Hits . . . . (Columbia)
Johnny Cash's Greatest Hits-#2 . . . . (Columbia)
The Man In Black-His Greatest Hits . . . . (Legacy)
Breaking Up Is Hard To Do
Gloria Estefan; *Hold Me, Thrill Me, Kiss Me* . . . . (Epic)
Neil Sedaka; *Billboard Top Rock 'N' Roll Hits-1962-C* . . . . . . (Rhino)
Neil Sedaka's All-Time Greatest Hits . . . . (RCA)
Shelley Fabares; *Things We Did Last Summer* . . . . (Collectables)
Can't Get This Stuff No More
Van Halen; *Best Of Van Halen-#1* . . . . (Warner Bros.)
Catch The Wind
Donovan; *Donovan-Hits* . . . . (Epic)
Donovan's Greatest Hits . . . . (Epic)
History Of British Rock-#2-C . . . . (Rhino)
The Secret Policeman's Other Ball/The Music . . . . (Rhino)
Cold Hard Facts Of Life, The
Porter Wagoner; *Essential Porter Wagoner* . . . . (RCA)
Porter Wagoner's Greatest Hits . . . . (Pair)
Cold Hard Truth, The
George Jones; *Cold Hard Truth* . . . . (Asylum)
Jamie O'Hara; *Rise Above It* . . . . (RCA)
Complicated
Carolyn Dawn Johnson; *Room With A View* . . . . (Arista)
Complicated Shadows
Elvis Costello & The Attractions; *The Sopranos-Music From The HBO
Original Series* . . . . (Sony Music Soundtrax)
Difficult Kind, The
Sheryl Crow; *The Globe Sessions* . . . . (A&M)
Dirt Road, The
Sawyer Brown; *Dirt Road* . . . . (Curb)
Easier Said Than Done
Radney Foster; *Del Rio, TX 1959* . . . . (Arista)
Easier Said Than Done
Essex; *Best Of The Girl Groups-#2-C* . . . . (Rhino)
Billboard Top Rock 'N' Roll Hits-1963-C . . . . (Rhino)
Original Rock 'N' Roll Hits Of The '60s-C . . . . (Roulette)
Easy To Be Hard
Original Broadway Cast; *Hair* . . . . (RCA)
Original Cast; *ST/Hair* . . . . (RCA)
Three Dog Night; *Best Of Three Dog Night* . . . . (MCA)
Captured Live At The Forum . . . . (MCA)
Celebrate-The Three Dog Night Story . . . . (MCA)
Easy Tonight
Five For Fighting; *America Town* . . . . (Aware/C2/Columbia)
Ex-Factor
Lauryn Hill; *The Miseducation Of Lauryn Hill* . . . . . (Ruffhouse/Columbia)
Fallen On Hard Times
Jethro Tull; *20 Years Of Jethro Tull* . . . . (Chrysalis)
The Broadsword And The Beast . . . . (Chrysalis)
Falling In Love (Is Hard On The Knees)
Aerosmith; *A Little South Of Sanity* . . . . (Geffen)
Nine Lives . . . . (Columbia)
Good Man Is Hard To Find (Pittsburgh)
Bruce Springsteen; *Tracks* . . . . (Columbia)
Goodbye Comes Hard For Me
Mark Chesnutt; *Red Hot + Country-C* . . . . (Mercury)
Greed
Godsmack; *Awake* . . . . (Republic/Universal)
Growing Up The Hard Way
Foreigner; *Agent Provocateur* . . . . (Atlantic)
Hard Act To Follow
Brother Cane; *Brother Cane* . . . . (Virgin)
Hard Act To Follow
Split Enz; *History Never Repeats-Best Of Split Enz* . . . . . . (A&M)
Hard Day
George Michael; *Faith* . . . . (Columbia)

Hard Day's Night, A
Beatles; *Beatles 1* . . . . (Capitol)
  Beatles-20 Greatest Hits . . . . (Capitol)
  ST/A Hard Day's Night . . . . (Capitol)
  The Beatles At The Hollywood Bowl . . . . (Capitol)
  The Beatles/1962-1966 . . . . (Capitol)
Hard Enough Getting Over You
Cher; *Cher* . . . .(Geffen)
Hard Habit To Break
Chicago; *Chicago 17* . . . .(Warner Bros.)
  Chicago's Greatest Hits-1982-1989 . . . .(Full Moon)
Hard Headed Woman
Elvis Presley; *Billboard Top Rock 'N' Roll Hits-1958-C* . . . . (Rhino)
  Number One Hits . . . . (RCA)
  ST/King Creole . . . . (RCA)
  The Top Ten Hits . . . . (RCA)
  Worldwide 50 Gold Award Hits, Vol. 1, Parts 1 & 2 . . . . (RCA)
Hard Headed Woman
Cat Stevens; *Cat Stevens Greatest Hits*. . . . . (A&M)
  Tea For The Tillerman . . . . (A&M)
Hard Knock Life
Original Broadway Cast; *Annie* . . . . (Columbia)
Hard Knock Life (Ghetto Anthem)
Jay-Z; *Now That's What I Call Music!-#2-C* . . . . (Virgin)
  Vol. 2-Hard Knock Life . . . .(Def Jam)
Hard Life
Little River Band; *Backstage Pass* . . . . (Capitol)
  First Under The Wire . . . . (Capitol)
Hard Life
Roger Daltrey; *Daltrey* . . . .(MCA)
Hard Life To Love
Black Sabbath; *Eternal Idol* . . . .(Warner Bros.)
Hard Luck Stories
Richard & Linda Thompson; *Pour Down Like Silver* . . . . (Hannibal)
Hard Luck Stories
Neil Young; *Landing On Water* . . . . (Geffen)
Hard Luck Story
Elton John; *Rock Of The Westies* . . . . (Polydor)
Hard Monkeys
Ten Years After; *A Space In Time*. . . . . (Columbia)
Hard Nose The Highway
Van Morrison; *Hard Nose The Highway* . . . . (Polydor)
Hard On Me
Asia; *Astra* . . . .(Geffen)
Hard On Me
Tom Petty; *Wildflowers* . . . .(Warner Bros.)
Hard Promises To Keep
Trisha Yearwood; *The Song Remembers When* . . . .(MCA)
Hard Rain's Gonna Fall
Bob Dylan; *Bob Dylan's Greatest Hits-#2* . . . . (Columbia)
  Concert For Bangladesh-C . . . . (Capitol)
  Freewheelin' . . . . (Columbia)
Bryan Ferry; *Street Life-20 Great Hits* . . . . (Reprise)
  These Foolish Things . . . . (Reprise)
Edie Brickell & New Bohemians; *ST/Born On The Fourth Of July* . . . . . .(MCA)
Joan Baez; *Farewell Angelina* . . . . (Vanguard)
  The First 10 Years . . . . (Vanguard)
Hard Road
Deep Purple; *Purple Passages* . . . .(Warner Bros.)
  When We Rock We Rock & When We Roll We Roll . . . .(Warner Bros.)
Hard Road
Rod Stewart; *Best Of Rod Stewart-#2* . . . . (Mercury)
Hard Road
Joneses; *Hard* . . . .(Atlantic)
Hard Road
John Mayall's Bluesbreakers; *Hard Road* . . . . (London)
Hard Road
Black Sabbath; *Never Say Die* . . . .(Warner Bros.)
Hard Road
Triumph; *Progressions Of Power*. . . . .(MCA)
Hard Road To Travel
Jimmy Cliff; *Wonderful World, Beautiful People*. . . . . (A&M)
Hard Rock Bottom Of Your Heart
Randy Travis; *No Holdin' Back* . . . .(Warner Bros.)
Hard Time Killing Floor Blues
Chris Thomas King; *ST/O Brother, Where Art Thou?* . . . . (Mercury)
Hard Times
Boz Scaggs; *Down Two Then Left* . . . . (Columbia)
  Hits!. . . . . (Columbia)
Hard Times
Bob Dylan; *Good As I Been To You* . . . . (Columbia)
Hard Times
Kiss; *Dynasty-1979* . . . . (Mercury)
Hard Times
Chris LeDoux; *Powder River* . . . . (Liberty)
  Radio & Rodeo Hits . . . . (Liberty)
Hard Times
Ratt; *Detonator*. . . . .(Atlantic)

Hard Times
Sprung Monkey; *Mr. Funny Face* . . . .(Surfdog/Hollywood)
Hard Times
Emmylou Harris & The Nash Ramblers; *At The Ryman* . . . .(Reprise)
Hard Times
Eric Clapton; *24 Nights* . . . . (Duck/Reprise)
  Journeyman . . . . (Duck/Reprise)
Hard Times
Ray Charles; *Best Of Ray Charles* . . . .(Atlantic)
Hard Times
James Taylor; *Dad Loves His Work*. . . . . (Columbia)
Hard Times
Desert Rose Band; *Desert Rose Band* . . . . (MCA)
Hard Times
Houston Person; *Goodness* . . . .(Prestige)
Hard Times
Skip James; *Great Bluesmen At Newport-C* . . . . (Vanguard)
Hard Times
Red Clay Ramblers; *Hard Times* . . . .(Flying Fish)
Hard Times
Lacy J. Dalton; *Lacy J. Dalton's Greatest Hits* . . . . (Columbia)
Hard Times
Run-D.M.C.; *Run-D.M.C.* . . . .(Profile)
Hard Times Are Over
John Lennon; *Double Fantasy*. . . . . (Capitol)
Hard Times Come Again No More
Jennifer Warnes; *Shot Through The Heart* . . . . (Arista)
Mustard's Retreat; *Home By The Morning* . . . . (Red House)
Nanci Griffith; *Other Voices, Too (A Trip Back To Bountiful)* . . . . (Elektra)
Hard Times Come Easy
Richie Sambora; *Undiscovered Soul* . . . . (Mercury)
Hard Times For An Honest Man
John Cougar Mellencamp; *Lonesome Jubilee* . . . . (Mercury)
Hard Times In The Land Of Plenty
Omar & The Howlers; *Taste Of Texas-Songs 'Bout Texas By
  Texans-C* . . . . (Columbia)
Hard Times Of Old England
Steeleye Span; *All Around My Hat* . . . . (Chrysalis)
Hard To Be A Husband, Hard To Be A Wife
Chely Wright & Brad Paisley; *Grand Ole Opry-75 Years-#2-C* . . . . . . (MCA)
Hard To Be In Love With You
Daryl Hall & John Oates; *Voices*. . . . .(RCA)
Hard To Believe
Pat Benatar; *Precious Time* . . . . (Chrysalis)
Hard To Believe
Dokken; *Shadowlife* . . . .(CMC Int'l)
Hard To Believe
Monkees; *Pisces, Aquarius, Capricorn & Jones Ltd.* . . . . (Rhino)
Hard To Exist
Spin Doctors; *Pocket Full Of Kryptonite*. . . . . (Epic Portrait Assoc.)
Hard To Explain
Cowboy Junkies; *Pale Sun, Crescent Moon* . . . .(RCA)
Hard To Find The Words
Cinderella; *Still Climbing* . . . . (Mercury)
Hard To Handle
Black Crowes; *Shake Your Money Maker* . . . .(Def American)
Grateful Dead; *History Of The Grateful Dead-Vol. 1 (Bear's
  Choice)* . . . . (Warner Bros.)
Otis Redding; *Best Of Otis Redding* . . . .(Atlantic)
  The Otis Redding Story. . . . .(Atlantic)
  Very Best Of Otis Redding-#2 . . . . (Rhino)
Hard To Make A Stand
Sheryl Crow; *Sheryl Crow*. . . . . (A&M)
Hard To Say
Sawyer Brown; *Outskirts Of Town* . . . . (Curb)
Hard To Say
Dan Fogelberg; *Dan Fogelberg/Greatest Hits* . . . .(Full Moon)
  Innocent Age. . . . .(Full Moon)
Hard To Say Goodbye
Slaughter; *Revolution* . . . .(CMC Int'l)
Hard To Say Goodbye, My Love
Original Cast; *Dreamgirls*. . . . . (Geffen)
Hard To Say I'm Sorry
Az Yet; *Az Yet* . . . . (LaFace)
Chicago; *Chicago 16* . . . . (Full Moon/Warner Bros.)
Hard Way, The
Mary Chapin Carpenter; *Come On Come On* . . . . (Columbia)
Hard Way, The
Clint Black; *The Hard Way* . . . .(RCA)
Hard Way, The
Faith Hill; *Faith*. . . . . (Warner Bros.)
Hard Work
John Handy; *The ABC's Of Soul-#3-C* . . . . (Hip-O)
Hard Work
Passion Fodder; *Fat Tuesday*. . . . . (Island)
Hard Work & No Play
Country Joe McDonald; *Leisure Suite* . . . . (Fantasy)

Hard Workin' Man
Brooks & Dunn; *Hard Workin' Man* . . . . (Arista)
Hard Workin' Man
Jack Nitzsche; *ST/Blue Collar* . . . . (MCA)
Hard, Hard Winter
Strawbs; *Deep Cuts* . . . . (Oyster)
Harder Cards
Collin Raye; *Tracks* . . . . (Epic)
Hardest Part Is The Night, The
Bon Jovi; *7800 Degrees Fahrenheit* . . . . (Mercury)
Hardest Part, The
Blondie; *Eat To The Beat* . . . . (Chrysalis)
Hardest Part, The
Erasure; *Crackers International* . . . . (Reprise)
Hardest Thing
98 Degrees; *98 Degrees And Rising* . . . . (Universal)
Now That's What I Call Music!-#3-C . . . . (Virgin)
Hardest Thing In The World
Stone Roses; *Turns Into Stone* . . . . (Silvertone)
Heroes Are Hard To Find
Fleetwood Mac; *25 Years-The Chain* . . . . (Warner Bros.)
Heroes Are Hard To Find . . . . (Reprise)
I Wish I Felt Nothing
Wallflowers; *Bringing Down The Horse* . . . . (Interscope)
I'm Tryin'
Trace Adkins; *Chrome* . . . . (Capitol)
Invisible City
Wallflowers; *Bringing Down The Horse* . . . . (Interscope)
It Should Have Been Easy
Whites; *45-#52953* . . . . (Curb/MCA)
It's A Hard Life
Queen; *Queen's Greatest Hits I & II* . . . . (Hollywood)
The Works . . . . (Hollywood)
It's Hard
Who; *It's Hard* . . . . (MCA)
It's Hard To Be A Saint In The City
Bruce Springsteen; *Greetings From Asbury Park, N.J.* . . . . (Columbia)
Live 1975-1985 . . . . (Legacy)
Tracks . . . . (Columbia)
David Bowie; *One Step Up/Two Steps Back-The Songs Of Bruce
Springsteen-C* . . . . (Right Stuff)
It's Hard To Be Humble
Mac Davis; *It's Hard To Be Humble* . . . . (Casablanca)
Mac Davis' Greatest Hits . . . . (Columbia)
It's Hard To Find A Way
Accept; *Russian Roulette* . . . . (Portrait)
It's Hard To Say Goodbye
Paul Anka; *Body Of Work* . . . . (Epic)
It's Only Love
Beatles; *The Beatles-Anthology-#2* . . . . (Capitol)
It's So Hard
Anouk; *Together Alone* . . . . (Columbia)
It's So Hard
John Lennon; *Imagine* . . . . (Capitol)
It's So Hard To Say Goodbye To Yesterday
Boyz II Men; *Cooleyhighharmony* . . . . (Motown)
G.C. Cameron; *Motown Memories-#3-C* . . . . (Motown)
It's So Hard To Wait
Buffalo Springfield; *Last Time Around* . . . . (Atco)
Josephine
Wallflowers; *Bringing Down The Horse* . . . . (Interscope)
Leavin' And Sayin' Goodbye
Faron Young; *Faron Young-Golden Hits* . . . . (Mercury)
Faron Young's Greatest Hits-#1-3 . . . . (Step One)
Leaving Home Ain't Easy
Queen; *Jazz* . . . . (Hollywood)
Life Is Hard
Timbuk 3; *Greetings From Timbuk 3* . . . . (I.R.S.)
Life Is Hard, But Life Is Hardest When You're Dumb
Austin Lounge Lizards; *Small Minds* . . . . (Sugar Hill)
Little Bit Of Soul
Music Explosion; *Best Of Ohio Express & Other Bubblegum
Smashes-#1-C* . . . . (Rhino)
Cruisin'-1967-C . . . . (Increase)
Million-Dollar Memories #1-C . . . . (RCA)
Living In These Hard Times
Jethro Tull; *20 Years Of Jethro Tull* . . . . (Chrysalis)
Long Hard Road Out Of Hell, A
Marilyn Manson; *Spawn* . . . . (Epic)
Love Isn't Easy (But It Sure Is Hard Enough)
Abba; *Ring Ring* . . . . (Polydor)
Love's A Hard Game To Play
Stevie Nicks; *TimeSpace-The Best Of Stevie Nicks* . . . . (Modern)
Never Can Say Goodbye
Jackson 5; *Jackson 5's Greatest Hits* . . . . (Motown)
Jackson 5-The Ultimate Collection . . . . (Motown)
No Easy Goodbye
South Sixty Five; *South Sixty Five* . . . . (Atlantic)

No One Said It Would Be Easy
Sheryl Crow; *Tuesday Night Music Club* . . . . (A&M)
Old Habits Die Hard
Air Supply; *Lost In Love* . . . . (Arista)
Once You've Loved Somebody
Dixie Chicks; *Wide Open Spaces* . . . . (Monument)
One Love At A Time
Tanya Tucker; *Tanya Tucker's Greatest Hits* . . . . (Liberty)
Problems
Everly Brothers; *Everly Brothers' All-Time Greatest Hits* . . . . (Curb)
Everly Brothers-Cadence Classics-Their 20 Greatest Hits . . . . (Rhino)
Fabulous Style Of The Everly Brothers . . . . (Rhino)
Question Everything
8Stops7; *In Moderation* . . . . (Reprise)
Seems Hard
Cardigans; *Emmerdale* . . . . (Mint)
Shackles (Praise You)
Mary Mary; *Thankful* . . . . (C2/Columbia)
She Works Hard For The Money
Donna Summer; *I Am Woman-C* . . . . (Nick At Nite)
She Works Hard For The Money . . . . (Mercury)
Summer Collection . . . . (Mercury)
So Hard
Pet Shop Boys; *Behavior* . . . . (EMI)
So Very Hard To Go
Tower Of Power; *Didn't It Blow Your Mind: Soul Hits Of The
'70s-#17-C* . . . . (Rhino)
Tower Of Power . . . . (Warner Bros.)
Song 2
Blur; *Blur* . . . . (Virgin)
Sorry Seems To Be The Hardest Word
Elton John; *Blue Moves* . . . . (MCA)
Elton John's Greatest Hits-#2 . . . . (Polydor)
Live In Australia With The Melbourne Symphony Orchestra . . . . (MCA)
Joe Cocker; *Two Rooms-Celebrating The Songs Of Elton John & Bernie
Taupin-C* . . . . (Polydor)
Starseed
Our Lady Peace; *Naveed* . . . . (Relativity)
Stay You
Wood; *Songs From Dawson's Creek* . . . . (Sony Music Soundtrax)
Songs From Stamford Hill . . . . (Columbia)
Suite: Judy Blue Eyes
Crosby, Stills & Nash; *Crosby, Stills & Nash* . . . . (Atlantic)
CSN . . . . (Atlantic)
ST/Woodstock . . . . (Atlantic)
Crosby, Stills, Nash & Young; *So Far* . . . . (Atlantic)
Superman (It's Not Easy)
Five For Fighting; *America Town* . . . . (Aware/C2/Columbia)
The Concert For New York City-C . . . . (Columbia)
Taking It All To Heart
Genesis; *Genesis* . . . . (Atlantic)
Tales From The Hard Side
Biohazard; *State Of The World Address* . . . . (Warner Bros.)
That's The Way It Is
Celine Dion; *All The Way...A Decade Of Song* . . . . (550 Music)
Collector's Series-Celine Dion-#1 . . . . (550 Music)
Theme From "Mission: Impossible"
Adam Clayton & Larry Mullen; *ST/Mission: Impossible* . . . . (Mother/Island)
Lalo Schifrin; *The Reel Lalo Schifrin* . . . . (Hip-O)
Original Soundtrack; *CBS: The First 50 Years* . . . . (TVT)
Television's Greatest Hits-#1-C . . . . (TVT)
San Diego Symphony & Lalo Schifrin; *Hitchcock-Master Of
Mayhem* . . . . (Pro-Arte)
There Goes My Baby
Trisha Yearwood; *Where Your Road Leads* . . . . (MCA)
This Hard Land
Bruce Springsteen; *Bruce Springsteen's Greatest Hits* . . . . (Columbia)
Tracks . . . . (Columbia)
Tryin' To Love Two
William Bell; *Coming Back For More* . . . . (Razor & Tie)
Trying To Love Two Women
Oak Ridge Boys; *Oak Ridge Boys' Greatest Hits* . . . . (MCA)
Oak Ridge Boys-Collection . . . . (MCA)
Together . . . . (MCA)
Us
Celine Dion; *Let's Talk About Love-C* . . . . (550 Music)
Waiting For A Star To Fall
Boy Meets Girl; *Nipper's Greatest Hits Of The '80s-C* . . . . (RCA)
Reel Life . . . . (RCA)
Why's Is So Hard
Madonna; *Erotica* . . . . (Maverick/Sire)
Work Hard
Depeche Mode; *People Are People* . . . . (Reprise)
You're Easy On The Eyes
Terri Clark; *Big Country Hits '99-C* . . . . (K-Tel)
How I Feel . . . . (Mercury)

DIRECTIONS: EAST

See Also: ***CITIES: A-Z, COUNTRIES: A-Z, DIRECTIONS (various), PLACES, SEARCH, STATES: A-Z***

317 East 32nd
Lennie Tristano; *Continuity* . . . . (Jazz)
Live In Toronto 1952 . . . . (Jazz)
All Roads Lead To You
Chicago; *The Heart Of Chicago-1967-1988-#2* . . . . (Reprise)
Born In East L.A.
Cheech & Chong; *Get Out Of My Room* . . . . (MCA)
California Girls
Beach Boys; *Beach Boys '69 (The Beach Boys Live In London)* . . . . (Capitol)
Best Of The Beach Boys-#2 . . . . (Capitol)
Endless Summer . . . . (Capitol)
Good Vibrations-Thirty Years Of The Beach Boys . . . . (Capitol)
The Beach Boys In Concert . . . . (Brother)
David Lee Roth; *Crazy From The Heat* . . . . (Warner Bros.)
ST/Down & Out In Beverly Hills . . . . (Warner Bros.)
China Grove
Doobie Brothers; *Best Of The Doobies* . . . . (Warner Bros.)
Captain & Me . . . . (Warner Bros.)
Farewell Tour . . . . (Warner Bros.)
East Bound Train
Lester Flatt & Earl Scruggs; *Hear The
Whistles Blow* . . . . (International Mktg. Group)
East Kentucky Mountains
Anne Hills; *Don't Panic (Panic Is On/Don't Explain)* . . . . (Hogeye)
East Of Ginger Trees
Seals & Crofts; *Seals & Crofts' Greatest Hits* . . . . (Warner Bros.)
East Of The Sun & West Of The Moon
Al Cohn & Zoot Sims; *RCA Victor Jazz: First Half-Century-C* . . . . (RCA)
Billie Holiday; *Billie's Best* . . . . (Verve)
Diana Krall; *When I Look In Your Eyes* . . . . (GRP)
Tommy Dorsey & Frank Sinatra; *Stardust* . . . . (Bluebird)
East Tennessee Blues/Goin' Crazy
Stepping Stones; *Fresh Old Time String Band Music* . . . . (Rounder)
East Texas Red
Arlo Guthrie; *Tribute To Woody Guthrie And Leadbelly-C* . . . . (Columbia)
East Virginia
Joan Baez; *Greatest Folksingers Of The '60s-C* . . . . (Vanguard)
Joan Baez . . . . (Vanguard)
The Joan Baez Ballad Book . . . . (Vanguard)
Pete Seeger; *Essential Pete Seeger* . . . . (Vanguard)
Folk Classics: Roots Of American Folk Music-C . . . . (Columbia)
Greatest Folksingers Of The '60s-C . . . . (Vanguard)
Eastern Sundays
Moraz & Bruford; *Music For Piano & Drums* . . . . (Editions E.G.)
Far East Mississippi
Ohio Players; *Ohio Players-Gold* . . . . (Mercury)
I Shall Be Released
Band; *Music From Big Pink* . . . . (Capitol)
The Band-Anthology-#1 . . . . (Capitol)
The Last Waltz . . . . (Warner Bros.)
To Kingdom Come-The Definitive Collection . . . . (Capitol)
Bette Midler; *Bette Midler* . . . . (Atlantic)
ST/Divine Madness . . . . (Atlantic)
Bob Dylan; *Biograph* . . . . (Columbia)
Bob Dylan At Budokan . . . . (Columbia)
Bob Dylan's Greatest Hits-#2 . . . . (Columbia)
The Bootleg Series-Volumes 1-3 [Rare & Unreleased] . . . . (Columbia)
Bob Dylan And The Band; *Before The Flood* . . . . (Columbia)
Box Tops; *Box Tops' Greatest Hits* . . . . (Rhino)
Flying Burrito Brothers; *Farther Along-Best Of The Flying Burrito
Brothers* . . . . (A&M)
Joan Baez; *Any Day Now: Songs Of Bob Dylan* . . . . (Vanguard)
Carry It On . . . . (Vanguard)
From Every Stage . . . . (A&M)
Joe Cocker; *With A Little Help From My Friends* . . . . (A&M)
Nina Simone; *Best Of Nina Simone* . . . . (Verve)
Rick Nelson; *Rick Nelson In Concert-Troubadour 1969* . . . . (MCA)
Looking East
Jackson Browne; *Looking East* . . . . (Elektra)
Memories Of East Texas
Michelle Shocked; *Short Sharp Shocked* . . . . (Mercury)
New East St. Louis Toodle-oo
Duke Ellington; *Reminiscing In Tempo* . . . . (Columbia)
Northeast Texas Women
David Bromberg; *Bandit In A Bathing Suit* . . . . (Fantasy)
Jerry Jeff Walker; *Lone Wolf: The Best Of Jerry Jeff Walker Elektra
Sessions* . . . . (Warner Archives)
Willis Alan Ramsey; *Willis Alan Ramsey* . . . . (Dunhill Compact Classics)
Red Dirt Girl
Emmylou Harris; *Red Dirt Girl* . . . . (Nonesuch)
Southside
Moby featuring Gwen Stefani; *12'' Maxi Single* . . . . (V2)
Play . . . . (V2)

DIRECTIONS: NORTH, Yankee

See Also: ***CITIES: A-Z, COUNTRIES: A-Z, DIRECTIONS (various), PLACES, SEARCH, STATES: A-Z***

All Roads Lead To You
Chicago; *The Heart Of Chicago-1967-1988-#2* . . . . (Reprise)
California Girls
Beach Boys; *Beach Boys '69 (The Beach Boys Live In London)* . . . . . . (Capitol)
Best Of The Beach Boys-#2 . . . . (Capitol)
Endless Summer . . . . (Capitol)
Good Vibrations-Thirty Years Of The Beach Boys . . . . (Capitol)
The Beach Boys In Concert . . . . (Brother)
David Lee Roth; *Crazy From The Heat* . . . . (Warner Bros.)
ST/Down & Out In Beverly Hills . . . . (Warner Bros.)
Girl From The North Country
Bob Dylan; *Freewheelin'* . . . . (Columbia)
Nashville Skyline . . . . (Columbia)
Real Live . . . . (Columbia)
Joe Cocker; *Mad Dogs & Englishmen* . . . . (A&M)
Johnny Cash with Bob Dylan; *The Man In Black-His Greatest Hits* . . . . (Legacy)
Life In A Northern Town
Dream Academy; *Dream Academy* . . . . (Warner Bros.)
North
Joan Baez; *Joan* . . . . (Vanguard)
North Alabama
Cal Smith; *Stories Of Life By Cal Smith* . . . . (Step One)
North And South
Clash; *Cut The Crap* . . . . (Legacy)
North By Northgate
Stan Freberg; *Tip Of The Freberg: The Stan Freberg Collection-1951-
1998* . . . . (Rhino)
North By Northwest
Original Soundtrack; *Psycho: Great Hitchcock Movie Thrillers* . . . . (Decca)
The Lion's Roar: Classic MGM Film Scores-1935-1965 . . . . (Rhino)
North Carolina
Anne Romaine; *Take A Stand* . . . . (Flying Fish)
North Carolina
Poets Of Rhythm; *More Original Raw Soul-C* . . . . (Instinct)
North Carolina
Les McCann; *Talk To The People/River High, River Low* . . . . (Collectables)
North Carolina (Home In My Heart)
Claudia Church; *Claudia Church* . . . . (Reprise)
North Carolina Blues
Johnie Lewis; *Alabama Slide Guitar* . . . . (Arhoolie)
North Carolina Bound
Connie & Babe & The Backwoods Boys; *Backwoods Bluegrass* . . . . . (Rounder)
North Carolina Breakdown
Sammy Shelor; *Leading Roll* . . . . (Sugar Hill)
North Carolina Tune/Child Of My Heart
Liz Carroll; *Friend Indeed* . . . . (Shanachie)
North Country Blues
Bob Dylan; *The Times They Are A-Changin'* . . . . (Columbia)
Joan Baez; *Any Day Now: Songs Of Bob Dylan* . . . . (Vanguard)
North Country Girl
Pete Townshend; *Pete Townshend Live* . . . . (Platinum Music)
North Dakota
Lyle Lovett; *Joshua Judges Ruth* . . . . (Curb/MCA)
Live In Texas . . . . (MCA)
North Dakota
Thrush Hermit; *Sweet Homewrecker* . . . . (Elektra)
North Dakota Sunrise
Metamora; *Metamora* . . . . (Sugar Hill)
North Easter
Cusco; *Cusco 2000* . . . . (Higher Octave)
North Gulfport Boogie
Roosevelt Sykes; *Hard Drivin' Blues* . . . . (Delmark)
North Star Grassman And The Ravens
Sandy Denny; *Gold Dust: Live At The Royalty-The Final Concert* . . . . . (Island)
North Star Grassman And The Ravens . . . . (Hannibal)
North To Alaska
Dwight Yoakam; *Under The Covers* . . . . (Reprise)
Johnny Horton; *American Originals-Johnny Horton* . . . . (Columbia)
Billboard Top Country Hits-1961-C . . . . (Rhino)
Johnny Horton's Greatest Hits . . . . (Columbia)
Super Hits Of The '60s-C . . . . (Epic)
North Wind
Slim Whitman; *Slim Whitman's Greatest Hits* . . . . (Curb)
Slim Whitman-Vintage Collection . . . . (Capitol)
North Wind Blues
Big Joe Williams; *Complete Recorded Works-#1-1935-1941* . . . . . . (Document)
North Won The War Again Last Night, The
Cal Smith; *Cal Smith* . . . . (First Generation)
North, The
Elton John; *The One* . . . . (MCA)
Northbound-Southbound
Wynton Marsalis; *Big Train* . . . . (Columbia)

Northeast Texas Women
David Bromberg; *Bandit In A Bathing Suit* . . . .(Fantasy)
Jerry Jeff Walker; *Lone Wolf: The Best Of Jerry Jeff Walker Elektra*
Sessions . . . . (Warner Archives)
Willis Alan Ramsey; *Willis Alan Ramsey* . . . . (Dunhill Compact Classics)
Northern Lad
Tori Amos; *From The Choirgirl Hotel* . . . . (Atlantic)
Northern Lights
Val Gardena; *On The Bridge* . . . .(Mercury)
Northern Lights
Bruce Cockburn; *Dancing In The Dragon's Jaws* . . . . (Columbia)
Northern Lights
Duke Ellington; *The Ellington Suites* . . . . (Original Jazz Classics)
Northern Lights
Rippingtons; *Kilimanjaro* . . . . (GRP)
Northern Muse (Solid Ground)
Van Morrison; *Beautiful Vision* . . . . (Warner Bros.)
Live At The Grand Opera House Belfast . . . .(Polydor)
Northern White Clouds
Bill Monroe; *Live From Mountain Stage* . . . .(Blue Plate)
Northern Winds
Steve Earle; *Train A Comin'* . . . . (Warner Bros.)
Northside Cadillac
James Cotton; *Mighty Long Time* . . . . (Antone's)
Northwest 222
Harry Chapin; *Remember When The Music* . . . . (Dunhill Compact Classics)
Northwest Passage
Woody Herman & His Orchestra; *Best Of The Big Bands-Woody Herman &*
His Orchestra . . . . (Legacy)
This Is Jazz-#24: Woody Herman . . . .(Legacy)
Only A Northern Song
Beatles; *The Beatles-Anthology-#2* . . . .(Capitol)
Yellow Submarine . . . .(Capitol)
Sailing To Philadelphia
Mark Knopfler; *Sailing To Philadelphia* . . . . (Warner Bros.)
Southside
Moby featuring Gwen Stefani; *12'' Maxi Single* . . . . (V2)
Play . . . .(V2)
Swanee
Al Jolson; *Al Jolson-Best Of The Decca Years* . . . .(MCA)
Best Of Al Jolson . . . .(MCA)
Jolson Sang 'Em . . . .(Biograph)
Music From The New York Stage (1890-1920)-#4-1917-1920-C . . . . . .(Pearl)
George Gershwin; *Rhapsody In Blue* . . . .(Biograph)
Judy Garland; *Judy Garland-At Carnegie Hall* . . . . (Capitol)
Judy Garland's All-Time Greatest Hits . . . . (Curb)
Theme From "Northern Exposure"
David Schwartz; *ST/Music From "Northern Exposure"* . . . . (MCA)
Original Soundtrack; *CBS: The First 50 Years* . . . .(TVT)
Where I Come From
Alan Jackson; *When Somebody Loves You* . . . . (Arista)
Working For MCA
Hank Williams, Jr.; *Hank Williams, Jr. "Live"* . . . . (WB/Curb)
Lynyrd Skynyrd; *Best Of The Rest Of Lynyrd Skynyrd* . . . . (MCA)
One More From The Road . . . . (MCA)
Second Helping . . . .(MCA)

DIRECTIONS: SOUTH, Dixie

See Also: CITIES: A-Z, COUNTRIES: A-Z, DIRECTIONS (various),
PLACES, SEARCH, STATES: A-Z

2120 South Michigan Avenue
Rolling Stones; *12 X 5* . . . . (Abkco)
All Roads Lead To You
Chicago; *The Heart Of Chicago-1967-1988-#2* . . . .(Reprise)
At A Dixie Roadside Diner
Duke Ellington; *Duke Ellington & The Blanton-Webster Band* . . . . . .(Bluebird)
Blues For Dixie
Asleep At The Wheel featuring Lyle Lovett; *Tribute To The Music Of Bob*
Wills And The Texas Playboys-C . . . . (Liberty)
Barry & Holly Tashian; *Harmony* . . . . (Rounder)
Bob Wills & His Texas Playboys; *Bob Wills & His Texas Playboys-*
Anthology 1935-1973 . . . . (Rhino)
Tiffany Transcriptions-#8-More Of The Best . . . .(Rhino)
Merle Haggard & The Strangers; *Best Of Country Blues* . . . . (Curb)
Train Whistle Blues . . . .(Rounder)
Bright Sunny South
Alison Krauss & Union Station; *New Favorite* . . . .(Rounder)
California Girls
Beach Boys; *Beach Boys '69 (The Beach Boys Live In London)* . . . . . .(Capitol)
Best Of The Beach Boys-#2 . . . .(Capitol)
Endless Summer . . . . (Capitol)
Good Vibrations-Thirty Years Of The Beach Boys . . . . (Capitol)
The Beach Boys In Concert . . . . (Brother)
David Lee Roth; *Crazy From The Heat* . . . . (Warner Bros.)
ST/Down & Out In Beverly Hills . . . . (Warner Bros.)

Can't You See
Alabama; *Alabama-Live* . . . . (RCA)
Charlie Daniels Band; *Volunteer Jam VII-C* . . . .(Epic)
Hank Williams, Jr. & Friends . . . . (Polydor)
Rebels, Renegades & Ramblers-C . . . .(Polydor)
Standing In The Shadows . . . .(Polydor)
Marshall Tucker Band; *Marshall Tucker Band* . . . . (AJK Music)
Searchin' For A Rainbow . . . .(AJK Music)
Catfish John
Johnny Russell; *Johnny Russell's Greatest Hits* . . . . (Dominion Entert.)
Comin' Back To South Chicago
Jeannie & Jimmy Cheatham; *Luv In The Afternoon* . . . .(Concord Jazz)
Detroit City
Ace Cannon; *Golden Favorites* . . . .(Ranwood)
Bill Anderson; *Best Of Bill Anderson* . . . .(Curb)
Bobby Bare; *Nipper's Greatest Hits Of The '60s-#2-C* . . . .(RCA)
This Is Bobby Bare . . . . (RCA)
Chet Atkins; *Country Gems* . . . .(Pair)
Flatt & Scruggs; *20 All-Time Great Recordings* . . . . (Columbia)
Hank Williams, Jr.; *Live At Cobo Hall Detroit* . . . . (Polydor)
Standing In The Shadows . . . .(Polydor)
Mel Tillis; *Best Of Mel Tillis* . . . . (MCA)
Live At The Sam Houston Coliseum . . . .(MGM)
Solomon Burke; *Home In Your Heart-Best Of Solomon Burke* . . . .(Rhino)
Dixie
Black Oak Arkansas; *Best Of Black Oak Arkansas* . . . .(Atco)
Hot & Nasty-Best Of Black Oak Arkansas . . . .(Rhino)
Boston Pops Orchestra/Arthur Fiedler; *American Salute* . . . .(RCA)
Lee Greenwood; *American Patriot* . . . . (Capitol)
Mormon Tabernacle Choir; *Mormon Tabernacle Choir's Greatest*
Hits-#2 . . . .(Columbia)
Songs Of The Civil War And Stephen Foster
Favorites . . . . (Sony Music Classical)
Tennessee Ernie Ford; *Tennessee Ernie Ford Sings Songs Of The*
Civil War . . . .(Capitol)
Dixie Chicken
Little Feat; *Dixie Chicken* . . . . (Warner Bros.)
Waiting For Columbus . . . . (Warner Bros.)
Dixie Diner
Jimmy Buffett; *You Had To Be There* . . . . (MCA)
Dixie Dreamin'
Atlanta; *Pictures* . . . . (MCA)
Dixie In My Eye
Eddie Adcock Band; *Red, White & Bluegrass-C* . . . .(C.M.H. Prod.)
Dixie Road
Lee Greenwood; *Country Classics-#3-1984-1985-C* . . . .(Universal)
Lee Greenwood's Greatest Hits . . . .(MCA)
MCA #1 Hits Of The '80s-#2-C . . . . (MCA Special Prod.)
Dixieland Rock
Elvis Presley; *ST/King Creole* . . . .(RCA)
The Other Sides-Worldwide Gold Award Hits, Vol. 2 . . . .(RCA)
Down South In New Orleans
Van Morrison & The Band; *The Last Waltz* . . . . (Warner Bros.)
Drive South
John Hiatt; *Slow Turning* . . . .(A&M)
Suzy Bogguss; *Voices In The Wind* . . . .(Liberty)
Eight More Miles
Kieran Kane/Kevin Welch; *11/12/13: Live In Melbourne,*
Australia . . . . (Dead Reckoning)
Fight On, U.S.C.
Michigan University Band; *Kick Off, U.S.A.* . . . .(Vanguard)
Original Soundtrack; *College Fight Songs: The Pac Ten-C* . . . .(K-Tel)
The Greatest College Fight Songs . . . .(Laserlight)
Top Ten College Fight Songs . . . .(K-Tel)
First Train Heading South
Johnny Horton; *Between The Rails: America's Train Songs-C* . . . . . (Crescendo)
Freedom Riders
Phil Ochs; *Best Of Broadside 1962-1968: Anthems Of The American*
Underground From The Pages Of Broadside
Magazine-C . . . . (Smithsonian Folkways)
Highway Headin' South
Porter Wagoner; *Great Moments At The Grand Ole Opry-C* . . . . (RCA)
Hillbilly Rock
Marty Stuart; *Hillbilly Rock* . . . .(MCA)
Marty Party Hit Pack . . . .(MCA)
I Sang Dixie
Dwight Yoakam; *Buenas Noches From A Lonely Room* . . . . (Reprise)
Just Lookin' For A Hit . . . .(Reprise)
If The South Woulda Won
Hank Williams, Jr.; *Wild Streak* . . . .(WB/Curb)
Interstate Love Song
Stone Temple Pilots; *Purple* . . . .(Atlantic)
It Never Rains In Southern California
Albert Hammond; *Rock Artifacts-From The Vaults-#2-C* . . . .(Legacy)
Super Hits Of The '70s-Have A Nice Day-#10-C . . . .(Rhino)
Tony Toni Tone; *Revival* . . . .(Wing)
Just A Little Bit South Of North Carolina
Chuck Foster & Jimmy Castle; *The Uncollected Chuck Foster & His*
Orchestra-1940 . . . .(Hindsight)

Dean Martin; *Swingin' Down Yonder*. . . . . (Capitol)

Kansas City Southern
Pure Prairie League; *Freight Train Blues-Classic Railroad Songs-#4-C* . . . . (Rounder)
Takin' The Stage . . . . (RCA)
Two Lane Highway . . . . (RCA)

Katie, My Southern Rose
William H. Thompson; *Music From The New York Stage (1890-1920)-#1-1890-1908-C* . . . . (Pearl)

Little Bit South Of Saskatoon
Sonny James; *American Originals-Sonny James* . . . . (Columbia)

Livin' In South Central L.A.
South Central Posse; *We're All In The Same Gang-C* . . . .(Warner Bros.)

Lullaby Of The Leaves
Various Artists; *Birdlanders-#1-C* . . . .(Original Jazz Classics)

Man From The South, The
Ted Weems & His Orchestra; *78-#22238* . . . . (Victor)

Maybe It Was Memphis
Pam Tillis; *Pam Tillis' Greatest Hits* . . . . (Arista)
Pam Tillis-Collection . . . .(Warner Bros.)
Put Yourself In My Place . . . . (Arista)

Mississippi Goddam
Nina Simone; *Best Of Broadside 1962-1968: Anthems Of The American Underground From The Pages Of Broadside Magazine-C* . . . . (Smithsonian Folkways)

Night The Lights Went Out In Georgia
Lynn Anderson; *Top Of The World*. . . . . (Columbia)
Reba McEntire; *For My Broken Heart* . . . .(MCA)
Reba McEntire's Greatest Hits-#3: I'm A Survivor . . . .(MCA)
Vicki Lawrence; *Super Hits Of The '70s-Have A Nice Day-#10-C*. . . . . . (Rhino)

Night They Drove Old Dixie Down
Band; *Best Of The Band* . . . . (Capitol)
Rock Of Ages . . . . (Capitol)
The Band . . . . (Capitol)
The Band-Anthology-#1 . . . . (Capitol)
The Band-Gift Set . . . . (Capitol)
The Last Waltz . . . .(Warner Bros.)
Bob Dylan And The Band; *Before The Flood* . . . .(Columbia)
Joan Baez; *Country Music Album* . . . .(Vanguard)
From Every Stage . . . . (A&M)
Hits/Greatest & Others . . . .(Vanguard)
Joan Baez-Classics-#8 . . . . (A&M)

North And South
Clash; *Cut The Crap* . . . . (Legacy)

North Won The War Again Last Night, The
Cal Smith; *Cal Smith* . . . . (First Generation)

Northbound-Southbound
Wynton Marsalis; *Big Train* . . . .(Columbia)

On The Southside Of Chicago
Vic Damone; *Best Of Vic Damone* . . . . (RCA)

People Of The Southwind
Kansas; *Monolith* . . . . (Kirshner)

Red Dirt Girl
Emmylou Harris; *Red Dirt Girl* . . . . (Nonesuch)

Rock A Bye Your Baby With A Dixie Melody
Al Jolson; *Best Of Al Jolson* . . . .(MCA)
Jolson Sang 'Em . . . . (Biograph)
Music From The New York Stage (1890-1920)-#4-1917-1920-C . . . . . . (Pearl)
The Al Jolson Story-#1 . . . .(MCA)
Jerry Lewis; *Just Sings* . . . . (Razor & Tie)
Judy Garland; *Judy Garland-At Carnegie Hall* . . . . (Capitol)
Miss Show Business . . . . (Capitol)
One & Only . . . . (Capitol)

Sailing To Philadelphia
Mark Knopfler; *Sailing To Philadelphia*. . . . .(Warner Bros.)

Saturday Night Down South
Charlie Daniels Band; *Simple Man* . . . .(Epic)

Somewhere South Of Macon
Marshall Chapman; *Me I'm Feeling Free* . . . .(Epic)

Song Of The South
Alabama; *Alabama's Greatest Hits-#2* . . . . (RCA)
Southern Star . . . . (RCA)

South Africa
Sons Of Selassie; *Changes* . . . .(Rhythm Safari)

South Africa
Cadillac Tramps; *Cadillac Tramps*. . . . .(Dr. Dream Music Group)

South Africa
Zawinul Syndicate; *Lost Tribes* . . . . (Columbia)

South Africa
Gillan; *Magic* . . . .(Metal Blade)

South African Blues
Windy Rhythm Kings; *Chicago Jazz-#2 (1925-1929)-C* . . . .(Biograph)

South African Enlistment
Abyssinians; *Arise* . . . . (Front Line)

South Australia
Northeast Winds; *Northeast Winds In Concert* . . . . (Folk Era)
Pogues; *If I Should Fall From Grace With God* . . . . (Island)

South Bronx
Boogie Down Productions; *Live Hardcore Worldwide-Paris-London-NYC*. . . . .(Jive)

South By Southwest
Lee Roy Parnell with Delbert McClinton; *Tell The Truth* . . . . (Vanguard)

South Central L.A.
Broken Homes; *Wing & A Prayer* . . . . (MCA)

South City Midnight Lady
Doobie Brothers; *Best Of The Doobies* . . . . (Warner Bros.)
Captain & Me . . . . (Warner Bros.)

South Dallas Drop
Ron "C"; "C" Ya . . . .(Profile)

South Georgia Blues
Sonny Stitt & Sadik Hakim; *Sonny Stitt Meets Sadik Hakim* . . . .(Progressive)

South Of Cincinnati
Dwight Yoakam; *Guitars, Cadillacs, Etc., Etc.* . . . .(Reprise)

South Of Santa Fe
Brooks & Dunn; *If You See Her* . . . . (Arista)

South Of The Border (Down Mexico Way)
Bob Wills & His Texas Playboys; *Best Of Bob Wills & His Texas Playboys* . . . . (MCA)
Bob Wills & His Texas Playboys-Greatest Hits . . . .(Curb)
Frank Sinatra; *Capitol Collectors Series-Frank Sinatra* . . . . (Capitol)
Come Fly With Me . . . . (Capitol)
Gene Autry; *The Country Music Hall Of Fame-Gene Autry-15 Of His All-Time Greatest Hits*. . . . . (Columbia)
Patsy Cline; *Always* . . . . (MCA)
The Patsy Cline Story . . . . (MCA)
Willie Nelson; *What A Wonderful World* . . . .(Columbia)

South Saturn Delta
Jimi Hendrix; *Lifelines/Jimi Hendrix Story*. . . . . (Reprise)

Southbound
Allman Brothers Band; *An Evening With The Allman Brothers Band-First Set* . . . .(Epic)
Decade Of Hits-1969-1979 . . . .(Polydor)

Southbound Train
Julie Gold; *When October Goes: Autumn Love Songs-C* . . . .(Philo)
Nanci Griffith; *Flyer* . . . . (Elektra)

Southern California
George Jones & Tammy Wynette; *George Jones & Tammy Wynette-16 Biggest Hits* . . . .(Epic/Legacy)
Tammy Wynette & George Jones; *Encore-Tammy Wynette & George Jones* . . . . (Epic)
Tammy Wynette & George Jones' Greatest Hits . . . . (Epic)

Southern California Purples
Chicago; *Chicago At Carnegie Hall* . . . . (Chicago)
Chicago Transit Authority . . . . (Chicago)

Southern Cross
Ozark Mountain Daredevils; *Car Over The Lake Album*. . . . . (A&M)

Southern Hospitality
Ludacris; *Back For The First Time* . . . .(Def Jam South/IDJMG)

Southern Loving
Jim Ed Brown; *Essential Jim Ed Brown* . . . . (RCA)

Southern Nights
Chet Atkins & Allen Toussaint; *Rhythm Country And Blues-C*. . . . . . . (MCA)
Glen Campbell; *Best Of Glen Campbell* . . . . (Capitol)
Glen Campbell-Classics Collection . . . . (Capitol)
Glen Campbell-Live . . . . (Capitol)
Southern Nights . . . . (Capitol)
ST/Convoy . . . .(Polydor)

Southern Rains
Mel Tillis; *Mel Tillis' Greatest Hits* . . . .(Curb)

Southern Star
Alabama; *Southern Star* . . . . (RCA)

South's Gonna Do It Again
Charlie Daniels; *Charlie Daniels-Super Hits* . . . .(Columbia)
Charlie Daniels Band; *A Decade Of Hits* . . . . (Epic)
Fire On The Mountain . . . . (Epic)

Southside
Moby featuring Gwen Stefani; *12" Maxi Single*. . . . .(V2)
Play . . . .(V2)

Strange Fruit
Billie Holiday; *History Of The Real Billie Holiday* . . . . (Verve)
Lady Sings The Blues . . . . (Verve)
Songbook . . . . (Verve)
Nina Simone; *Compact Jazz-Nina Simone* . . . . (Verve)
Siouxsie And The Banshees; *Through The Looking Glass* . . . . (Geffen)

Summer In Dixie
Confederate Railroad; *Notorious* . . . .(Atlantic)

Sunday In The South
Shenandoah; *30 Years Of #1 Hits-#19-C* . . . .(Columbia)
Road Not Taken . . . . (Columbia)
Shenandoah's Greatest Hits . . . . (Columbia)

Swanee
Al Jolson; *Al Jolson-Best Of The Decca Years* . . . . (MCA)
Best Of Al Jolson . . . . (MCA)
Jolson Sang 'Em . . . .(Biograph)
Music From The New York Stage (1890-1920)-#4-1917-1920-C . . . .(Pearl)
George Gershwin; *Rhapsody In Blue* . . . .(Biograph)

Judy Garland; *Judy Garland-At Carnegie Hall* . . . . (Capitol)
  Judy Garland's All-Time Greatest Hits . . . .(Curb)
Theme From "Evening Shade"
  Original Soundtrack; *Television's Greatest Hits-#7-Cable Ready-C* . . . . .(TVT)
Theme From "Gone With The Wind"
  Toronto Festival Pops Orchestra; *Hooray For Hollywood* . . . .(Pro-Arte)
Theme From "I'll Fly Away"
  Original Soundtrack; *Television's Greatest Hits-#7-Cable Ready-C* . . . . .(TVT)
Theme From "In The Heat Of The Night"
  Original Soundtrack; *Television's Greatest Hits-#7-Cable Ready-C* . . . . .(TVT)
There's A Lump Of Sugar Down In Dixie
  Al Jolson; *Music From The New York Stage (1890-1920)-#4-1917-
  1920-C* . . . .(Pearl)
'Til I Fell In Love With You
  Bob Dylan; *Time Out Of Mind* . . . . (Columbia)
When It All Goes South
  Alabama; *When It All Goes South* . . . .(RCA)
When It's Sleepy Time Down South
  Billie Holiday; *Last Recordings* . . . . (Verve)
  Dizzy Gillespie; *20 Golden Pieces Of Dizzy GIllespie* . . . . (Bulldog)
  Louis Armstrong; *At The Crescendo* . . . . (MCA)
  Best Of Louis Armstrong . . . . (MCA)
  Best Of The Decca Years-#1-Hits!-C . . . . (Decca)
  Essential Louis Armstrong . . . . (Vanguard)
  I Like Jazz-Essence Of Louis Armstrong . . . . (Columbia)
  Louis Armstrong's Greatest Hits . . . .(Legacy)
  Satchmo-Musical Autobiography . . . . (MCA)
  Mel Torme; *Mel Torme* . . . .(Glendale)
  Wynton Marsalis; *Standard Time-#2-Intimacy Calling* . . . . (Columbia)
When The Sun Goes Down In The South
  Original Broadway Cast; *Big River-The Adventures Of
  Huckleberry Finn* . . . . (MCA)
Wild-Eyed Southern Boys
  38 Special; *Wild-Eyed Southern Boys* . . . .(A&M)
Working For MCA
  Hank Williams, Jr.; *Hank Williams, Jr. "Live"* . . . .(WB/Curb)
  Lynyrd Skynyrd; *Best Of The Rest Of Lynyrd Skynyrd* . . . . (MCA)
  One More From The Road . . . . (MCA)
  Second Helping . . . . (MCA)

DIRECTIONS: WEST

See Also: **AMERICAN WEST, CITIES: A-Z, COUNTRIES: A-Z,
DIRECTIONS (various), PLACES, SEARCH, STATES: A-Z**

4:37 AM (Arabs With Knives & West German Skies)
  Roger Waters; *Pros & Cons Of Hitchhiking* . . . . (Columbia)
All Roads Lead To You
  Chicago; *The Heart Of Chicago-1967-1988-#2* . . . .(Reprise)
Amelia
  Gretchen Peters; *Gretchen Peters* . . . .(Purple Crayon Prod.)
California Girls
  Beach Boys; *Beach Boys '69 (The Beach Boys Live In London)* . . . .(Capitol)
  Best Of The Beach Boys-#2 . . . . (Capitol)
  Endless Summer . . . . (Capitol)
  Good Vibrations-Thirty Years Of The Beach Boys . . . . (Capitol)
  The Beach Boys In Concert . . . . (Brother)
  David Lee Roth; *Crazy From The Heat* . . . . (Warner Bros.)
  ST/Down & Out In Beverly Hills . . . . (Warner Bros.)
California Golden West Waltz
  Golden West Singers & The Cavaliers; *45-#1378* . . . .(Accent)
Central Park West
  John Coltrane; *Art Of John Coltrane* . . . . (Atlantic)
  Best Of John Coltrane . . . . (Atlantic)
  Coltrane's Sound . . . . (Atlantic)
East Of The Sun & West Of The Moon
  Al Cohn & Zoot Sims; *RCA Victor Jazz: First Half-Century-C* . . . .(RCA)
  Billie Holiday; *Billie's Best* . . . . (Verve)
  Diana Krall; *When I Look In Your Eyes* . . . . (GRP)
  Tommy Dorsey & Frank Sinatra; *Stardust* . . . .(Bluebird)
Here At The Western World
  Steely Dan; *Steely Dan's Greatest Hits* . . . . (MCA)
Homegrown Western Saturday Night
  Chris LeDoux; *Powder River* . . . . (Liberty)
I Shall Be Released
  Band; *Music From Big Pink* . . . . (Capitol)
  The Band-Anthology-#1 . . . . (Capitol)
  The Last Waltz . . . . (Warner Bros.)
  To Kingdom Come-The Definitive Collection . . . . (Capitol)
  Bette Midler; *Bette Midler* . . . . (Atlantic)
  ST/Divine Madness . . . . (Atlantic)
  Bob Dylan; *Biograph* . . . . (Columbia)
  Bob Dylan At Budokan . . . . (Columbia)
  Bob Dylan's Greatest Hits-#2 . . . . (Columbia)
  The Bootleg Series-Volumes 1-3 [Rare & Unreleased] . . . . (Columbia)
  Bob Dylan And The Band; *Before The Flood* . . . . (Columbia)
  Box Tops; *Box Tops' Greatest Hits* . . . . (Rhino)

Flying Burrito Brothers; *Farther Along-Best Of The Flying Burrito
  Brothers* . . . .(A&M)
Joan Baez; *Any Day Now: Songs Of Bob Dylan* . . . . (Vanguard)
  Carry It On . . . .(Vanguard)
  From Every Stage . . . .(A&M)
Joe Cocker; *With A Little Help From My Friends* . . . .(A&M)
Nina Simone; *Best Of Nina Simone* . . . . (Verve)
Rick Nelson; *Rick Nelson In Concert-Troubadour 1969* . . . . (MCA)
Leaving West Virginia
  Kathy Mattea; *Walk The Way The Wind Blows* . . . . (Mercury)
Lily Of The West
  Joan Baez; *Joan Baez, Vol. 2* . . . .(Vanguard)
  The Joan Baez Ballad Book . . . .(Vanguard)
Little Gasoline, A
  Terri Clark; *Fearless* . . . . (Mercury)
Nashville West
  Byrds; *Dr. Byrds & Mr. Hyde* . . . .(Legacy)
  Legends Of Country Guitar-#1-C . . . . (Rhino)
  The Byrds . . . . (Columbia)
  The Byrds (Untitled) . . . .(Legacy)
  Nashville West; *Nashville West* . . . . (Sierra)
North By Northwest
  Original Soundtrack; *Psycho: Great Hitchcock Movie Thrillers* . . . .(Decca)
  The Lion's Roar: Classic MGM Film Scores-1935-1965 . . . . (Rhino)
Northwest 222
  Harry Chapin; *Remember When The Music* . . . . (Dunhill Compact Classics)
Northwest Passage
  Woody Herman & His Orchestra; *Best Of The Big Bands-Woody Herman &
  His Orchestra* . . . .(Legacy)
  This Is Jazz-#24: Woody Herman . . . .(Legacy)
One Way Ticket (Because I Can)
  LeAnn Rimes; *Blue* . . . . (MCG/Curb)
Red And Rio Grande
  Doug Supernaw; *Red And Rio Grande* . . . . (BNA)
She Couldn't Change Me
  Montgomery Gentry; *Carrying On* . . . .(Columbia)
South By Southwest
  Lee Roy Parnell with Delbert McClinton; *Tell The Truth* . . . .(Vanguard)
Southside
  Moby featuring Gwen Stefani; *12" Maxi Single* . . . . (V2)
  Play . . . . (V2)
Sweet Betsy From Pike
  Cisco Houston; *Cowboy Ballads* . . . . (Smithsonian Folkways)
  Mormon Tabernacle Choir; *This Land Is Your Land* . . . .(Columbia)
Theme From "Wild Wild West"
  Original Soundtrack; *CBS: The First 50 Years* . . . .(TVT)
  Television's Greatest Hits-#1-C . . . .(TVT)
Transatlantic Westbound Jet
  Hollies; *Hollies* . . . .(Epic)
Under Assistant West Coast Promotion Man
  Rolling Stones; *Out Of Our Heads* . . . . (Abkco)
  Singles Collection-The London Years . . . . (Abkco)
Way Out West In Kansas
  Nimrod Workman; *The Land Of Yahoe: Children's Entertainment From The
  Days Before Television-C* . . . .(Rounder)
Way Out West In Texas
  Don Edwards; *My Hero, Gene Autry: A Tribute* . . . . (Shanachie)
West Africa
  Willie Jackson; *West Africa* . . . . (Muse)
West Coast Sunset
  Billy Joe Walker, Jr.; *Life Is Good* . . . .(Liberty)
West Germany
  Minutemen; *Double Nickels On The Dime* . . . . (SST)
West Helena Blues
  Jimmy Cotton; *Chicago/The Blues Today* . . . .(Vanguard)
West L.A. Fadeaway
  Grateful Dead; *In The Dark* . . . . (Arista)
West Memphis Blues
  Sonny Boy Williamson; *King Biscuit Time* . . . . (Arhoolie)
West Nashville Boogie
  Steve Earle & The Dukes; *Shut Up And Die Like An Aviator* . . . . (MCA)
  The Hard Way . . . . (MCA)
West Nashville Grand Ballroom Gown
  Jimmy Buffett; *Living & Dying In 3/4 Time* . . . . (MCA)
West Oakland Strut
  Ed Kelly & Pharoah Sanders; *Ed Kelly & Pharoah Sanders* . . .(Evidence Music)
West Texas Highway & Me
  Gary Morris; *Faded Blue* . . . . (Warner Bros.)
West Texas Plains
  Rosie Flores; *After The Farm* . . . . (Hightone)
West Texas Waltz
  Butch Hancock; *Own & Own* . . . . (Sugar Hill)
West Texas Wind
  Joe Sun; *45-#1324* . . . . (AMI)
West Texas Women
  Whistlin' Alex Moore; *I'm Wild About My Lovin'-1928-1930* . . . . .(Historical)
Westbound Sign
  Green Day; *Insomniac* . . . .(Reprise)

Western Girls
Marty Stuart; *Hillbilly Rock* . . . . (MCA)
Western Hero
Neil Young & Crazy Horse; *Sleeps With Angels*. . . . . (Reprise)
Western Highway
Maura O'Connell; *Helpless Heart* . . . .(Warner Bros.)
Western Movies (My Baby Loves)
Olympics; *All-Time Greatest Hits Of Rock 'N' Roll-C* . . . . (Curb)
   American Graffiti-#3-C . . . . (MCA)
   Best Of The Olympics. . . . . (Vee-Jay)
   Jumpin' Jive '50s-C. . . . . (Priority)
Western Union
Five Americans; *Back To The '60s-Rock 'N' Roll-C* . . . . . . (Dominion Entert.)
   Nuggets-#1-The Hits-C . . . . (Rhino)
Western Union
Elvis Presley; *From Nashville To Memphis-The Essential '60s Masters* . . (RCA)
Westside
TQ; *They Never Saw Me Coming* . . . .(ClockWork/Epic)
Wide Open Spaces
Dixie Chicks; *Big Country Hits '99-C* . . . . (K-Tel)
   Wide Open Spaces . . . . (Monument)
Wild West End
Dire Straits; *Dire Straits* . . . .(Warner Bros.)
Wild West Hero
Electric Light Orchestra; *Out Of The Blue* . . . . (Jet)
Wild West Show
Darden Smith; *Native Soil* . . . . (Watermelon)
Wild West Show/Dog Act
Original Broadway Cast; *Will Rogers Follies* . . . . (Columbia)
Wild Wild West
Will Smith; *Willenium* . . . . (Columbia)
Wild, Wild West
Kool Moe Dee; *How Ya Like Me Now* . . . . (Jive)
   Jive Presents...Yo! MTV Raps-C . . . . (Jive)
   Kool Moe Dee's Greatest Hits . . . . (Jive)
   Mr. Magic's Rap Attack-#4-C . . . . (Profile)
Wild, Wild West
Escape Club; *Rock The First-#3-C* . . . . (Priority)
   Wild Wild West. . . . . (Atlantic)

DIRT, Dirty, Dust, Filth, Mud
See Also: *CLEAN, EARTH, SLEAZY, TRASH*

An Echo, A Stain
Bjork; *Vespertine* . . . . (Elektra)
Angel With A Dirty Face
Lou Gramm; *Long Hard Look* . . . .(Atlantic)
Angels With Dirty Faces
Tommy Dorsey; *Complete Tommy Dorsey-#8* . . . . (RCA)
Angels With Dirty Faces
Los Lobos; *Kiko* . . . . (Slash)
Another One Bites The Dust
Queen; *Queen's Greatest Hits I & II.* . . . . (Hollywood)
   The Game. . . . . (Hollywood)
Bang The Drum Slowly
Emmylou Harris; *Red Dirt Girl* . . . . (Nonesuch)
Big Muddy
Bruce Springsteen; *Lucky Town* . . . . (Columbia)
Black Muddy River
Grateful Dead; *In The Dark* . . . . (Arista)
Burning Dirt
My Life With The Thrill Kill Kult; *Confessions Of A Knife* . . . . (TVT)
Captain Fantastic And The Brown Dirt Cowboy
Elton John; *Captain Fantastic And The Brown Dirt Cowboy* . . . . (Polydor)
Chattahoochee
Alan Jackson; *A Lot About Livin' (And A Little 'Bout Love)*. . . . . (Arista)
Cities In Dust
Siouxsie And The Banshees; *Tinderbox*. . . . . (Geffen)
Crossing Muddy Waters
John Hiatt; *Crossing Muddy Waters* . . . . (Vanguard)
Crushed By The Wheels Of Industry
Heaven 17; *Luxury Gap* . . . . (Caroline)
Dear Sweet Filthy World
Elvis Costello; *Juliet Letters*. . . . .(Warner Bros.)
Detour (Devil Took A)
Patti Page; *Patti Page-Golden Hits* . . . . (Mercury)
Digging In The Dirt
Peter Gabriel; *Us.* . . . .(Geffen)
Dirt
Alice In Chains; *Dirt.* . . . . (Columbia)
Dirt
Lou Reed; *Street Hassle* . . . . (Out Of Print)
Dirt Bike
They Might Be Giants; *John Henry* . . . . (Elektra)

Dirt Gets Under The Fingernails
Harry Chapin; *Portrait Gallery*. . . . . (Elektra)
Dirt In The Ground
Tom Waits; *Bone Machine* . . . . (Island)
Dirt Road Blues
Bob Dylan; *Time Out Of Mind* . . . . (Columbia)
Dirt Road, The
Sawyer Brown; *Dirt Road* . . . .(Curb)
Dirty Black Hole
Steve Vai; *Sex And Religion* . . . . (Epic)
Dirty Black Summer
Danzig; *Danzig III-How The Gods Kill* . . . . (American)
Dirty Blvd.
Lou Reed; *New York* . . . .(Sire)
Dirty Boogie
Brian Setzer Orchestra; *Dirty Boogie* . . . .(Interscope)
Dirty Boots
Sonic Youth; *Goo* . . . . (Geffen)
Dirty Business
New Riders Of The Purple Sage; *New Riders Of The Purple Sage* . . . (Columbia)
Dirty Creature
Split Enz; *History Never Repeats-Best Of Split Enz* . . . . (A&M)
Dirty Dancing
Wu Tang Clan featuring Old Dirty Bastard; *ST/The Jerky Boys* . . . . (Select)
Dirty Day
U2; *Zooropa* . . . . (Island)
Dirty Deeds Done Dirt Cheap
AC/DC; *Dirty Deeds Done Dirt Cheap* . . . .(Atlantic)
Dirty Diana
Michael Jackson; *Bad* . . . . (Epic)
Dirty Dog
ZZ Top; *Eliminator* . . . . (Warner Bros.)
Dirty Dreams
Alice Cooper; *Hey Stoopid* . . . . (Epic)
Dirty Epic
Underworld; *Dubnobasswithmyheadman* . . . . (Wax Trax)
Dirty Eyes
AC/DC; *Bonfire.* . . . . (East West)
Dirty Jobs
Who; *ST/Quadrophenia* . . . . (MCA)
Dirty Laundry
Don Henley; *I Can't Stand Still* . . . .(Asylum)
Dirty Little Girl
Elton John; *Goodbye Yellow Brick Road* . . . .(Polydor)
Dirty Little Secrets
Pat Benatar; *Innamorata* . . . .(CMC Int'l)
Dirty Little Secrets
My Life With The Thrill Kill Kult; *13 Above The Night* . . . . (Rykodisc)
Dirty Livin'
Kiss; *Dynasty-1979.* . . . . (Mercury)
Dirty Luv
L.A. Guns; *Hollywood Vampires* . . . .(Polydor)
Dirty Magic
Offspring; *Ignition* . . . .(Epitaph)
Dirty Mind
Prince; *Dirty Mind.* . . . . (Warner Bros.)
Dirty Movies
Van Halen; *Fair Warning* . . . . (Warner Bros.)
Dirty Old Town
Liam Clancy; *Irish Troubadour* . . . . (Vanguard)
Dirty Old Town (Mapeye)
David Byrne; *Rei Momo* . . . . (Luaka Bop)
Dirty Summer's Day
Thompson Twins; *Big Trash*. . . . . (Red Eye)
Dirty Walls
Our Lady Peace; *Naveed* . . . . (Relativity)
Dirty Water
Standells; *Best Of The Standells* . . . . (Rhino)
   Nuggets-Classic Collection From The Psychedelic '60s-C . . . . (Rhino)
   Super Oldies Of The '60s-#10-C . . . . (Audio Fidelity)
Dirty Water
Jesus & Mary Chain; *Stoned And Dethroned* . . . . (American)
Dirty Water
Throwing Muses; *Red Heaven* . . . .(Sire)
Dirty Water Dog
Van Halen; *Van Halen 3* . . . . (Warner Bros.)
Dirty White Boy
Foreigner; *Head Games* . . . .(Atlantic)
   Records. . . . .(Atlantic)
Dirty Women
Black Sabbath; *Technical Ecstasy.* . . . . (Warner Bros.)
Dirty Work
Fabulous Thunderbirds; *What's The Word* . . . . (Chrysalis)
Dirty Work
Steely Dan; *Can't Buy A Thrill* . . . . (MCA)
Dirty Work
Rolling Stones; *Dirty Work* . . . .(Virgin)

Dirty World
Traveling Wilburys; *Traveling Wilburys-Volume One* . . (Wilbury/Warner Bros.)
Dirty, Dirty Feeling
Elvis Presley; *Elvis Is Back!* . . . . (RCA)
Dixie Road
Lee Greenwood; *Country Classics-#3-1984-1985-C* . . . . (Universal)
Lee Greenwood's Greatest Hits . . . . (MCA)
MCA #1 Hits Of The '80s-#2-C . . . . (MCA Special Prod.)
Don't Wanna Get It Dirty
38 Special; *Bone Against Steel* . . . . (Charisma)
Down And Dirty
Bad Company; *Company Of Strangers* . . . . (East West)
Down Into Muddy Water
Aaron Neville; *The Tattooed Heart* . . . . (A&M)
Down 'n Dirty
Kenny Loggins; *Nightwatch* . . . . (Columbia)
Downtown Dirt
Lou Reed; *Between Thought & Expression-Anthology* . . . . (RCA)
Dust
Steve Winwood; *Arc Of A Diver* . . . . (Island)
Dust
Fleetwood Mac; *Bare Trees* . . . . (Reprise)
Dust
Midnight Oil; *Midnight Oil* . . . . (Columbia)
Dust And Diesel
Bruce Cockburn; *Stealing Fire* . . . . (Columbia)
Dust Blows Forward 'n The Dust Blows Back
Captain Beefheart & His Magic Band; *Trout Mask Replica* . . . . (Reprise)
Dust Bowl
10,000 Maniacs; *Blind Man's Zoo* . . . . (Elektra)
Dust Devil
Butthole Surfers; *Independent Worm Saloon* . . . . (Capitol)
Dust Down A Country Road
John Hiatt; *Walk On* . . . . (Capitol)
Dust In The Wind
Kansas; *Best Of Kansas* . . . . (CBS Associated)
Point Of Know Return . . . . (Kirshner)
Two For The Show . . . . (Kirshner)
Dust In The Wind
Todd Rundgren; *Something/Anything?* . . . . (Rhino)
Dust My Broom
Canned Heat; *Uncanned!-Best Of*
Canned Heat . . . . (EMI Legends Of Rock 'N' Roll)
Elmore James; *Best Blues Album In The World...Ever!-C* . . . . (Virgin)
Elmore James-Complete Fire & Enjoy Sessions-#1 . . . . (Collectables)
King Of The Slide Guitar . . . . (Capricorn)
Ike & Tina Turner; *Bold Soul Sister-Best Of The Blue Thumb*
Recordings . . . . (Hip-O)
Robert Johnson; *King Of The Delta Blues Singers-#2* . . . . (Columbia)
ZZ Top; *Deguello* . . . . (Warner Bros.)
Dust N' Bones
Guns N' Roses; *Use Your Illusion I* . . . . (Geffen)
Dust On The Bottle
David Lee Murphy; *Out With A Bang* . . . . (MCA)
Dust Radio
Chris Whitley; *Living With The Law* . . . . (Columbia)
Dusty
Soundgarden; *Down On The Upside* . . . . (A&M)
Dusty Skies
Asleep At The Wheel featuring Riders In The Sky; *Tribute To The Music Of*
Bob Wills And The Texas Playboys-C . . . . (Liberty)
Bob Wills & His Texas Playboys; *Bob Wills & His Texas Playboys-Historic*
Edition . . . . (Columbia)
Don't Fence Me In-Western Music's Early Golden Era-C . . . . (Rounder)
Everyday
Dave Matthews Band; *America: A Tribute To Heroes-C* . . . . (Interscope)
Everyday . . . . (RCA)
Filthy Rich (I Don't Wanna Be)
PM Dawn; *Bliss Album...?* . . . . (Gee Street)
Filthy's Dance
Ren And Stimpy; *You Eadiot* . . . . (Rhino)
Frogs With Dirty Little Lips
Frank Zappa; *Them Or Us* . . . . (Rykodisc)
Full Moon Dirty Hearts
INXS; *All* . . . . (Atlantic)
Get Your Filthy Hands Off My Desert
Pink Floyd; *Final Cut* . . . . (Columbia)
Girl In The Dirty Shirt
Oasis; *Be Here Now* . . . . (Epic)
Gold Dust
Sandy Denny; *Rendezvous* . . . . (Hannibal)
Good As Gold (Stupid As Mud)
Beautiful South; *Best Of The Beautiful South-Carry On Up The*
Charts . . . . (Mercury)
Handful Of Dust
Patty Loveless; *When Fallen Angels Fly* . . . . (Epic)
High Speed Dirt
Megadeth; *Countdown To Extinction* . . . . (Capitol)

Hot Dusty Roads
Buffalo Springfield; *Buffalo Springfield* . . . . (Atco)
I Washed My Hands In Muddy Water
Elvis Presley; *Elvis Country ("I'm 10,000 Years Old")* . . . . (RCA)
If Dirt Were Dollars
Don Henley; *End Of The Innocence* . . . . (Geffen)
In The Gold Dust Rush
Cocteau Twins; *Head Over Heels* . . . . (Gold Rush)
Industrial Disease
Dire Straits; *Love Over Gold* . . . . (Warner Bros.)
Kiss The Dirt (Falling Down The Mountain)
INXS; *All* . . . . (Atlantic)
Lady Stardust
David Bowie; *Rise & Fall Of Ziggy Stardust And The Spiders*
From Mars . . . . (Rykodisc)
Little Dirty Blonde
Winger; *In The Heart Of The Young* . . . . (Atlantic)
Lovin' You's A Dirty Job
Ratt; *Detonator* . . . . (Atlantic)
Loving You's A Dirty Job But Somebody's Gotta Do It
Bonnie Tyler; *Secret Dreams And Forbidden Fire* . . . . (Columbia)
Mean Mr. Mustard
Beatles; *Abbey Road* . . . . (Parlophone)
Midnight On The Water/Dry And Dusty
Skip Gorman; *A Cowboy's Wild Song To His Herd* . . . . (Rounder)
Mud In Any Water
Tanita Tikaram; *Everybody's Angel* . . . . (Reprise)
Mud Shark, The
Mothers Of Invention; *Fillmore East-June 1971* . . . . (Reprise)
Mud Slide Slim
James Taylor; *Mud Slide Slim And The Blue Horizon* . . . . (Warner Bros.)
Muddy Jesus
Ian Moore; *Modernday Folklore* . . . . (Capricorn)
Muddy Mudskipper Theme
Ren And Stimpy; *You Eadiot* . . . . (Rhino)
Muddy River
Laurie Anderson; *Bright Red* . . . . (Warner Bros.)
Muddy Water
Clint Black; *Put Yourself In My Shoes* . . . . (RCA)
Muddy Water
Original Broadway Cast; *Big River-The Adventures Of*
Huckleberry Finn . . . . (MCA)
Muddy Water
Keb' Mo'; *Slow Down* . . . . (550/Epic/Okeh)
Mudflap Girl
Timbuk 3; *Best Of Timbuk 3* . . . . (I.R.S.)
Mudkicker
Skid Row; *Slave To The Grind* . . . . (Atlantic)
Must You Throw Dirt In My Face
Elvis Costello; *Kojak Variety* . . . . (Warner Bros.)
Louvin Brothers; *45-#4822* . . . . (Capitol)
My Name Is Mud
Primus; *Pork Soda* . . . . (Interscope)
On The Old Dirt Road
Leo Sayer; *Just A Boy* . . . . (Out Of Print)
Out With A Bang
David Lee Murphy; *Out With A Bang* . . . . (MCA)
Pay Dirt
k.d. lang and The Reclines; *Angel With A Lariat* . . . . (Sire)
Piece Of Dirt
They Might Be Giants; *Lincoln* . . . . (Restless)
Play Dirty
Poison; *Look What The Cat Dragged In* . . . . (Capitol)
Pop
'N Sync; *Celebrity* . . . . (Jive)
Now That's What I Call Music!-#8-C . . . . (Virgin)
Ragged And Dirty
Bob Dylan; *World Gone Wrong* . . . . (Columbia)
Red Dirt Girl
Emmylou Harris; *Red Dirt Girl* . . . . (Nonesuch)
Shooting Dirty Pool
Replacements; *Pleased To Meet Me* . . . . (Sire)
Stardust
Artie Shaw; *Begin The Beguine* . . . . (Bluebird)
Artie Shaw & His Orchestra; *22 Original Big Band Recordings-C* . . . (Hindsight)
Nipper's Greatest Hits Of The '40s-#1-C . . . . (RCA)
Benny Goodman; *Benny Goodman Sextet featuring Charlie Christian-1939-*
1941 . . . . (Columbia)
Benny Goodman-Live At Carnegie Hall . . . . (London)
Carly Simon; *Come Upstairs* . . . . (Warner Bros.)
Coleman Hawkins; *Hollywood Stampede* . . . . (Capitol)
Dave Brubeck; *Art Of Dave Brubeck* . . . . (Atlantic)
Greatest Hits From The Fantasy Years . . . . (Fantasy)
Dave Brubeck Quartet; *Jazz At Oberlin* . . . . (Fantasy)
Stardust . . . . (Fantasy)
Frank Sinatra; *Sinatra & Strings* . . . . (Reprise)
Harry Connick, Jr.; *25* . . . . (Columbia)
Hoagy Carmichael; *Nipper's Greatest Hits Of The '30s-#1-C* . . . . (RCA)

Stardust Road . . . . (MCA)
Johnny Mathis; *Feelings* . . . . (Columbia)
   First 25 Years-Silver Anniversary Album . . . . (Columbia)
Nat ''King'' Cole; *The Nat ''King'' Cole Story* . . . . (Capitol)
Rob Wasserman & Aaron Neville; *Duets-C* . . . . (MCA)
Roger Williams; *Best Of Roger Williams* . . . . (MCA)
Tommy Dorsey; *Best Of Tommy Dorsey* . . . . (Bluebird)
   This Is Tommy Dorsey . . . . (RCA)
Tommy Dorsey & Frank Sinatra; *Stardust* . . . . (Bluebird)
Wayne King & His Orchestra; *78-#22656* . . . . (Victor)

Stick In The Mud
Jayhawks; *Sound Of Lies* . . . . (American)

Straw Hat And Old Dirty Hank
Barenaked Ladies; *Born On A Pirate Ship* . . . . (Reprise)

Stronger Than Dirt (Ajax)
Original Soundtrack; *TeeVee Toons-The Commercials-#1-C* . . (TVT)

Tale Of Dusty And Pistol Pete
Smashing Pumpkins; *Adore* . . . . (Virgin)

Talk Dirty To Me
Poison; *Look What The Cat Dragged In* . . . . (Capitol)
   Swallow This Live . . . . (Capitol)

Talking Dust Bowl Blues
Woody Guthrie; *Dust Bowl Ballads* . . . . (Rounder)

Theme From ''The Odd Couple''
Original Soundtrack; *Television's Greatest Hits-#7-Cable Ready-C* . . (TVT)

Thirty Dirty Birds
Red Hot Chili Peppers; *Freaky Styley* . . . . (EMI)

Tracks In The Dust
Crosby, Stills & Nash; *CSN* . . . . (Atlantic)

Turn To Dust
Def Leppard; *Slang* . . . . (Mercury)

Until It Sleeps
Metallica; *Load* . . . . (Elektra)

Unwashed & Somewhat Slightly Dazed
David Bowie; *Space Oddity* . . . . (Rykodisc)

Walk The Dust
Texas; *Mothers Heaven* . . . . (Mercury)

Where The Blacktop Ends
keith urban; *keith urban* . . . . (Capitol)

Wrong Number
Cure; *Galore-The Singles-1987-1997* . . . . (Fiction/Elektra)

Young Blood
Rickie Lee Jones; *Naked Songs Live And Acoustic* . . . . (Reprise)
   Rickie Lee Jones . . . . (Warner Bros.)

Ziggy Stardust
David Bowie; *Changesbowie* . . . . (Rykodisc)
   Rise & Fall Of Ziggy Stardust And The Spiders From Mars . . (Rykodisc)
   Sound + Vision . . . . (Rykodisc)
   ST/Ziggy Stardust-The Motion Picture . . . . (Rykodisc)
   Stage . . . . (Rykodisc)
   The Singles-1969-1993 . . . . (Rykodisc)

DISTANCE, Close, Deeper, Far, Feet, Inches,
Measurements, Miles, Near
   See Also: **EXTREMES, LONELY, SEPARATION, TRAVELING**

(They Long To Be) Close To You
Carpenters; *Carpenters-Classics-#2* . . . . (A&M)
   Carpenters-Love Songs . . . . (A&M)
   Carpenters-The Singles 1969-1973 . . . . (A&M)
   From The Top . . . . (A&M)

10 Miles To Go On A 9 Mile Road
Jim White; *No Such Place* . . . . (Luaka Bop)

26 Miles
Four Preps; *True* . . . . (Capitol)

36 Inches High
Nick Lowe; *Pure Pop For Now People* . . . . (Columbia)

5 Miles To Empty
Brownstone; *Still Climbing* . . . . (MJJ Music/Work)

5 Steps
Dru Hill; *Dru Hill* . . . . (Island)

500 Miles Away From Home
Bobby Bare; *500 Miles Away From Home* . . . . (RCA)
Foy Willing; *Cowboy/The New Sound Of American Folk* . . . . . (DRG)
Reba McEntire; *Starting Over* . . . . (MCA)

A Step Too Far
John, Headley And Scott; *ST/Aida* . . . . (Island)

Ain't No Mountain High Enough
Diana Ross; *20/20-C* . . . . (Motown)
   25 #1 Hits From 25 Years-C . . . . (Motown)
   Diana Ross . . . . (Motown)
   Diana Ross-The Ultimate Collection . . . . (Motown)
   Every Great Motown Song-First 25 Years-C . . . . (Motown)
   Greatest Songs By Ashford & Simpson . . . . (Motown)
   Motown Legends-Diana Ross . . . . (Motown)

   Motown Story-First 25 Years-C . . . . (Motown)
   Motown's Biggest Pop Hits-C . . . . (Motown)
   TV ST/Diana-C . . . . (Motown)
Marvin Gaye & Tammi Terrell; *20 Greatest Songs In Motown*
   History-C . . . . (Motown)
   Classic Duets-Marvin Gaye & His Women-C . . . . (Motown)
   Marvin Gaye & Tammi Terrell's Greatest Hits . . . . (Motown)
   Marvin Gaye Live At The London Palladium . . . . (Motown)
   Motown Grammy R&B Performances Of The '60s & '70s-C . . (Motown)
   Performances Of The '60s & '70s-C . . . . (Motown)
   United . . . . (Motown)

Banana Boat (Day-O)
Harry Belafonte; *Belafonte '89* . . . . (EMI)
   Nipper's Greatest Hits Of The '50s-#1-C . . . . (RCA)
Kinks; *Everybody's In Show-Biz* . . . . (Rhino)

Be Near Me
ABC; *How To Be A Zillionaire* . . . . (Mercury)

Beautiful
Mary J. Blige; *ST/How Stella Got Her Groove Back* . . . . . . (Flyte Tyme/MCA)

Before I Go
John Hiatt; *Crossing Muddy Waters* . . . . (Vanguard)

Blue Train, The
Linda Ronstadt; *Feels Like Home* . . . . (Elektra)
Maura O'Connell; *Blue Is The Colour Of Hope* . . . . . (Warner Bros.)

Boogie Back To Texas
Asleep At The Wheel; *Asleep At The Wheel-10* . . . . (Epic)
   Swinging Best Of Asleep At The Wheel . . . . (Epic)
   Texas Super Hits-C . . . . (Columbia)
   Very Best Of Asleep At The Wheel Since 1970 . . . . . (Relentless/Madacy)

City Of New Orleans
Arlo Guthrie; *Best Of Arlo Guthrie* . . . . (Warner Bros.)
   Hobo's Lullaby . . . . (Reprise)
   Together In Concert . . . . (Reprise)
HARP; *HARP* . . . . (Redwood)
Willie Nelson; *19 Hot Country Requests-#2-C* . . . . (Epic)
   City Of New Orleans . . . . (Columbia)
   Greatest Country Hits Of The '80s-#4-C . . . . (Columbia)
   Hot Tracks-Train Super Hits-C . . . . (Epic)
   Train Trax-C . . . . (Sony Music Special Prod.)

Closer To Free
BoDeans; *Chicago Bulls Greatest Hits-#3-C* . . . . (Atlantic)
   Go Slow Down . . . . (Slash)
   Joe Dirt Car . . . . (Reprise)
   ST/Party Of Five . . . . (Reprise)

Closer To The Heart
Rush; *Exit...Stage Left* . . . . (Mercury)
   Farewell To Kings . . . . (Mercury)
   Rush-Chronicles . . . . (Mercury)
   Show Of Hands . . . . (Mercury)

Closer You Get, The
Alabama; *Alabama's Greatest Hits-#2* . . . . (RCA)
   For The Record: 41 Number One Hits . . . . (RCA)
   The Closer You Get . . . . (BMG Special Prod.)

Come A Little Bit Closer
Jay & The Americans; *Good Vibrations (Sounds Of Top 40 Radio: 1964-*
   1967)-C . . . . (Capitol)
   Jay & The Americans' All-Time Greatest Hits . . . . (Rhino)
   Jay & The Americans' Greatest Hits . . . . (CEMA Special Prod.)

Come A Little Bit Closer
Fleetwood Mac; *25 Years-The Chain* . . . . (Warner Bros.)

Come A Little Bit Closer
Johnny Duncan & Janie Fricke; *Johnny Duncan & Janie Fricke's*
   Greatest Hits . . . . (Columbia)
   Nice 'N' Easy . . . . (Columbia)

Cuddle Up A Little Closer
Jimmy Roselli; *When Your Old Wedding Ring Was* . . . . (M&R)

Dallas
Alan Jackson; *Don't Rock The Jukebox* . . . . (Arista)

Deep In The Heart Of Texas
Bing Crosby; *Bing Crosby's Greatest Hits* . . . . (MCA)
Bob Wills; *Best Of Bob Wills & His Texas Playboys* . . . . (MCA)
   Best Of Bob Wills-#2 . . . . (MCA)
Gene Autry; *Columbia Historic Edition-Gene Autry* . . . . . (Columbia)
   Texas Super Hits-C . . . . (Columbia)
Moe Bandy; *Taste Of Texas-Songs 'Bout Texas By Texans-C* . . (Columbia)

Deep Water
Asleep At The Wheel; *Asleep At The Wheel* . . . . (MCA Special Prod.)
Asleep At The Wheel featuring Garth Brooks; *Tribute To The Music Of Bob*
   Wills And The Texas Playboys-C . . . . (Liberty)
Bob Wills & His Texas Playboys; *Bob Wills & His Texas Playboys-*
   Anthology 1935-1973 . . . . (Rhino)
   Essential Bob Wills & His Texas Playboys-1935-1973 . . . . . (Legacy)
George Strait; *George Strait-Number 7.* . . . . (MCA)
Willie Nelson; *San Antonio Rose* . . . . (Columbia)

Deeper And Deeper
Madonna; *Erotica* . . . . (Maverick/Sire)
   GHV2 . . . . (Warner Bros.)

Deeper Than You Think
George Benson; *Absolute Benson* . . . . (GRP/VMG)

Distance Equals Rate Times Time
Pixies; *Trompe Le Monde* . . . . (Elektra)
Distance, The
Cake; *Fashion Nugget* . . . . (Capricorn)
Distant Drums
Jim Reeves; *Best Of The Best Of Jim Reeves* . . . . (King)
Billboard Top Country Hits-1966-C . . . . (Rhino)
Essential Jim Reeves . . . . (RCA)
Distant Melody
Original Cast/Mary Martin; *Peter Pan-The 1954 Broadway
Production* . . . . (RCA Victor)
Distant Memories
James Horner; *ST/Titanic* . . . . (Sony Music Classical)
Diving To Be Deeper
Sinead Lohan; *No Mermaid* . . . . (Grapevine)
Don't Let The Stars Get In Your Eyes
Perry Como; *Como's Golden Records* . . . . (RCA)
Perry Como-Pure Gold . . . . (RCA)
Perry Como's All-Time Greatest Hits-#1 . . . . (RCA)
This Is Perry Como . . . . (RCA)
Drag City
Jan & Dean; *Beach Party Blasts* . . . . (EMI)
Best Of Jan & Dean . . . . (EMI)
Dead Man's Curve . . . . (EMI)
One Summer Night-Live . . . . (Rhino)
Eight More Miles
Kieran Kane/Kevin Welch; *11/12/13: Live In Melbourne,
Australia* . . . . (Dead Reckoning)
Everyday Is A Winding Road
Sheryl Crow; *1998 Grammy Nominees-C* . . . . (MCA)
Sheryl Crow . . . . (A&M)
Father
Why Store; *The Why Store* . . . . (MCA)
Five Feet High And Rising
Johnny Cash; *The Man In Black-His Greatest Hits* . . . . . . (Legacy)
Fox, The
Nickel Creek; *Nickel Creek* . . . . (Sugar Hill)
Friends In The Distance
Poco; *Under The Gun* . . . . (MCA)
From A Distance
Bette Midler; *Some People's Lives* . . . . (Atlantic)
Byrds; *20 Essential Tracks From The Box Set* . . . . (Columbia)
The Byrds . . . . (Columbia)
Judy Collins; *Fires Of Eden* . . . . (Columbia)
Kathy Mattea; *Time Passes By* . . . . (Mercury)
Nanci Griffith; *Lone Star State Of Mind* . . . . (MCA)
One Fair Summer Evening . . . . (MCA)
From Hell To Paradise
Mavericks; *From Hell To Paradise* . . . . (MCA)
Further It Is From Tipperary, The
Jack Norworth; *Music From The New York Stage (1890-1920)-#4-1917-
1920-C* . . . . (Pearl)
Girl Next Door
Musiq Soulchild; *Aijuswanaseing* . . . . (Def Soul/IDJMG)
Go The Distance
Michael Bolton; *All That Matters* . . . . (Columbia)
Go The Distance
Faith Hill; *Take Me As I Am* . . . . (Warner Bros.)
Great Divide
Bruce Hornsby; *Spirit Trail* . . . . (RCA)
Half The World
Rush; *Test For Echo* . . . . (Atlantic)
Half Way Up
Clint Black; *Clint Black-The Greatest Hits* . . . . (RCA)
Halfway Down
Patty Loveless; *When Fallen Angels Fly* . . . . (Epic)
Heartache Big As Texas
Ricky Van Shelton; *Texas Super Hits-C* . . . . (Columbia)
Hello Goodbye
Beatles; *Beatles 1* . . . . (Capitol)
Beatles-20 Greatest Hits . . . . (Capitol)
Beatles-Box Set . . . . (Capitol)
Magical Mystery Tour . . . . (Capitol)
The Beatles/1967-1970 . . . . (Capitol)
Hey Bulldog
Beatles; *Rock 'N' Roll Music* . . . . (Capitol)
Yellow Submarine . . . . (Capitol)
Honey Bun
Original Cast; *South Pacific* . . . . (CBS Masterworks)
Honey Chile
Martha Reeves & The Vandellas; *Compact Command Performances-Martha
Reeves & The Vandellas* . . . . (Motown)
Martha Reeves & The Vandellas-Anthology . . . . (Motown)
Motown Superstar Series-#11-Martha Reeves & The Vandellas . . . . (Motown)
How Deep Is The Ocean? (How High Is The Sky?)
Diana Krall; *Love Scenes* . . . . (Impulse!)
Frank Sinatra; *Nice 'N' Easy* . . . . (Capitol)
Liza Minnelli; *Liza Minnelli-At Carnegie Hall* . . . . (Telarc)

How Deep Is Your Love
Bee Gees; *Bee Gees' Greatest* . . . . (Polydor)
ST/Saturday Night Fever . . . . (Polydor)
How Deep Is Your Love
Dru Hill featuring Redman; *Enter The Dru* . . . . (Def Jam/RAL/Mercury/Island)
ST/Rush Hour . . . . (Def Jam)
How Far Is Heaven
Kitty Wells; *Kitty Wells-20 Greatest Hits* . . . . (Tee Vee)
How High The Moon
Duke Ellington; *1954 Los Angeles Concert* . . . . (Crescendo)
Ella Fitzgerald; *Best Of Ella Fitzgerald* . . . . (MCA)
Les Paul & Mary Ford; *Memories Are Made Of This-C* . . . . . (Capitol)
Sarah Vaughan; *Compact Jazz-Best Of The Compact Jazz Vocalists-C* . . . (Verve)
Complete Sarah Vaughan On Mercury-#3 . . . . (Mercury)
Stephane Grappelli & Martin Taylor; *Just One Of Those Things* . . . . (Angel)
I Am Yours
Derek And The Dominos; *Layla* . . . . (Polydor)
I Can See For Miles
Who; *Hooligans* . . . . (MCA)
Join Together . . . . (MCA)
Meaty Beaty Big & Bouncy . . . . (MCA)
ST/The Kids Are Alright . . . . (MCA)
The Who Sell Out . . . . (MCA)
I Get Up I Get Down
Yes; *Close To The Edge* . . . . (Atlantic)
I Hear A Symphony
Diana Ross & The Supremes; *16 #1 Hits From The Early '60s-C* . . . . (Motown)
Diana Ross & The Supremes' Greatest Hits . . . . (Motown)
Diana Ross & The Supremes-25th Anniversary . . . . . . (Motown)
Diana Ross & The Supremes-Anthology (1962-1969) . . . . (Motown)
Evening With Diana Ross . . . . (Motown)
Every Great #1 Hit . . . . (Motown)
Good Feeling Music Of The Big Chill Generation-#2-C . . . (Motown)
Motown Story-First 25 Years-C . . . . (Motown)
Supremes; *I Hear A Symphony* . . . . (Motown)
I Love You Always Forever
Donna Lewis; *Now In A Minute* . . . . (Atlantic)
The Absolute Hits-C . . . . (Atlantic)
I May Never Get To Heaven
Conway Twitty; *Conway Twitty-20 Greatest Hits* . . . . (MCA)
Conway Twitty Sings The Hits . . . . (MCA Special Prod.)
I Wanna Get Next To You
Rose Royce; *Mellow Classics-C* . . . . (MCA Special Prod.)
Rose Royce's Greatest Hits . . . . (Whitfield)
ST/Car Wash . . . . (MCA)
I'll Walk Alone
Dinah Shore; *Dinah Shore's Greatest Hits* . . . . (Curtom)
I'm In The Mood For Love
McGuire Sisters; *Best Of The McGuire Sisters* . . . . (MCA)
Nat "King" Cole; *The Trio Recordings-#2* . . . . (Laserlight)
Ray Conniff; *Young At Heart* . . . . (Columbia)
Inchworm
Danny Kaye; *Billboard Presents Family Lullaby
Classics-C* . . . . (Kid Rhino/Rhino 4 Kids)
Victoria Jackson; *Child's Celebration Of Song-#2-C* . . (Music For Little People)
Keep Your Distance
Buddy & Julie Miller; *Buddy & Julie Miller* . . . . (Hightone)
Richard Thompson; *Rumor & Sigh* . . . . (Capitol)
Keeping My Distance
Martina McBride; *Evolution* . . . . (RCA)
Lay Down Your Arms
Chordettes; *Best Of The Chordettes* . . . . (Rhino)
Let's Build A World Together
George Jones & Tammy Wynette; *George Jones & Tammy Wynette-16
Biggest Hits* . . . . (Epic/Legacy)
Let's See How Far You Get
BR549; *This Is BR549* . . . . (Lucky Dog)
Let's Take The Long Way Home
Cab Calloway; *Cab Calloway-1942-1947* . . . . (Classics)
Rosemary Clooney; *Rosemary Clooney Sings The Music Of Harold
Arlen* . . . . (Concord Jazz)
Little Green Valley
Marty Robbins; *Gunfighter Ballads & Trail Songs* . . . . (Legacy)
Livin' On A Prayer
Bon Jovi; *America: A Tribute To Heroes-C* . . . . (Interscope)
Cross Road-14 Classic Grooves . . . . (Mercury)
Slippery When Wet . . . . (Jambco)
The Concert For New York City-C . . . . (Columbia)
Loneliness Of The Long Distance Runner
Iron Maiden; *Somewhere In Time* . . . . (Capitol)
Long Ago And Far Away
Erroll Garner; *Long Ago And Far Away* . . . . (Columbia)
Glenn Miller; *Glenn Miller-A Legendary Performer-#1 & 2* . . . (Bluebird)
Helen Forrest & Dick Haymes; *American Songbook Series-
Jerome Kern* . . . . (Smithsonian Collection)
Jo Stafford; *Capitol Collectors Series-Jo Stafford* . . . . . . (Capitol)
International Hits . . . . (Corinthian)
Jukebox Saturday Night-Great Vocal Hits-C . . . . (Capitol)
Songs That Got Us Through WWII-C . . . . (Rhino)

ST/*Bugsy* ....(Epic)
Johnny Mathis; *Hollywood Musicals* .... (Columbia)
Mantovani; *More Golden Hits* .... (London)
Perry Como; *Always In My Heart-Classic Songs Of World War II-#2* .... (RCA)
Rosemary Clooney; *Rosemary Clooney Sings The Lyrics Of Ira Gershwin*.....................................(Concord Jazz)

Long Distance Affair
38 Special; *Tour De Force* .... (A&M)

Long Distance Call
Muddy Waters; *Best Of Muddy Waters*..................... (Chess)
The Chess Box-Muddy Waters .... (Chess)
Muddy Waters Blues Band; *Mud In Your Ear* ....(Muse)

Long Distance Love
Little Feat; *Last Record Album* ....(Warner Bros.)

Long Distance Operator
Bob Dylan And The Band; *Basement Tapes* .... (Columbia)

Long Distance Runaround
Yes; *Classic Yes* ....(Atlantic)
Fragile ....(Atlantic)
Yessongs ....(Atlantic)

Long Distance Winner
Buckingham/Nicks; *Buckingham/Nicks*......................(Polydor)

Long Slow Distance
Michael Franks; *Blue Pacific* .... (Reprise)

Long Tall Sally
Beatles; *Past Masters-Volume One* .... (Parlophone)
Rock 'N' Roll Music ....(Capitol)
The Beatles At The Hollywood Bowl .... (Capitol)
The Beatles' Second Album .... (Capitol)
Little Richard; *Billboard Top R&B Hits-1956-C* ....(Rhino)
Here's Little Richard ....(Specialty)
Little Richard-18 Greatest Hits .... (Rhino)
Little Richard's Greatest Hits .... (Everest)
Oldies But Goodies-#3-C .... (Original Sound)
ST/*Heaven Help Us* ....(EMI)
Super Oldies Of The '50s-#3-C ....(Audio Fidelity)
Tutti Frutti ....(Accord)

Long Way From Home
Neil Diamond; *Double Gold-Neil Diamond* .... (Bang)
Just For You .... (Bang)

Long Way From Home
Whitesnake; *Love Hunter*.................................(Geffen)

Loser
3 Doors Down; *Better Life* ....(Republic/Universal)

Love A Little Stronger
Diamond Rio; *'90s Hot Country-C* .... (K-Tel)
Diamond Rio's Greatest Hits........................ (Arista)
Diamond Rio-Super Hits .... (Arista)
Hit Country '96-C .... (K-Tel)
Love A Little Stronger .... (Arista)

Love Travels
Kathy Mattea; *Love Travels* .... (Mercury)

Many A Mile To Freedom
Traffic; *The Low Spark Of High Heeled Boys*.......... (Island)

Many Rivers To Cross
Jimmy Cliff; *In Concert-Best Of Jimmy Cliff* .... (Reprise)
Reggae Spectacular-C............................... (A&M)
ST/*The Harder They Come* ....(Mango)
Wonderful World, Beautiful People....................(A&M)
Linda Ronstadt; *Prisoner In Disguise* ....(Asylum)
UB40; *Labour Of Love* .... (A&M)

Miles From Our Home
Cowboy Junkies; *Miles From Our Home* .... (Geffen)

Miles To Go (Before I Sleep)
Celine Dion; *Let's Talk About Love-C* ....(550 Music)

Million Miles
Bob Dylan; *Time Out Of Mind* .... (Columbia)

Moonlight Mile
Rolling Stones; *Sticky Fingers* .... (Virgin)

My Heart Will Go On (Love Theme from "Titanic")
Celine Dion; *All The Way...A Decade Of Song*................(550 Music)
ST/*Titanic* ....(Sony Music Classical)
Celine Dion with The Bee Gees; *Let's Talk About Love-C*........(550 Music)
Kenny G; *Kenny G's Greatest Hits*......................(Arista)

My Mammy
Al Jolson; *Best Of Al Jolson* ....(MCA)
Let Me Sing And I'm Happy .... (Turner Classic Movies)
The '20s-From Broadway To Hollywood-#3-C ...... (Flapper)
Happenings; *Happenings-Golden Hits!* .... (B.T. Puppy)

Near You
Francis Craig & His Orchestra; *Cigar Classics-#1-The Standards-C*.... (Hip-O)
George Jones & Tammy Wynette; *George Jones & Tammy Wynette-16 Biggest Hits* ....(Epic/Legacy)

Nearer, My God, To Thee
Mississippi John Hurt; *Best Of Mississippi John Hurt* ....(Vanguard)
Immortal Mississippi Hurt ....(Vanguard)
Richard Jose; *Music From The New York Stage (1890-1920)-#1-1890-1908-C* ....(Pearl)

Never Too Far
Mariah Carey; *Glitter* ....(Virgin)

Night And Day
Bette Midler; *Some People's Lives* ....(Atlantic)
Billie Holiday; *Legacy Box-1933-1958*................. (Columbia)
Ella Fitzgerald; *Cole Porter Songbook* .... (Verve)
Frank Sinatra; *Nipper's Greatest Hits Of The '40s-#1-C* .... (RCA)
Sinatra & Strings ....(Reprise)
Sinatra Reprise-The Very Good Years .... (Reprise)
Sinatra: A Man And His Music .... (Reprise)
The Capitol Years ....(Capitol)
The Reprise Collection .... (Reprise)
Fred Astaire; *Cheek To Cheek*....................... (Pro-Arte)
Steppin' Out-Astaire Sings .... (Verve)
Tony Bennett; *Perfectly Frank* .... (Columbia)
U2; *Red Hot + Blue-Tribute To Cole Porter-C* .... (Chrysalis)

One Belief Away
Bonnie Raitt; *Fundamental* .... (Capitol)

One Step Closer
Doobie Brothers; *Best Of The Doobies, Volume II* ...... (Warner Bros.)
One Step Closer .... (Warner Bros.)

One Step Closer
Linkin Park; *Hybrid Theory* .... (Warner Bros.)

Operator, Long Distance Please
Barbara Mandrell; *In Black & White* .... (MCA)

Silver Inches
Enya; *A Day Without Rain*............................. (Reprise)

Smoke From A Distant Fire
Sanford/Townsend Band; *Smoke From A Distant Fire* .... (Warner Bros.)

So Far Away
Carole King; *A Natural Woman: The Ode Collection-1968-1976* ..... (Legacy)
Tapestry ....(Epic)
Rod Stewart; *If We Fall In Love Tonight* .... (Warner Bros.)
Tapestry Revisited: Tribute To Carole King-C .... (Lava)

So Far Away
Stabbing Westward; *Stabbing Westward* .... (Koch International)

So Help Me Girl
Gary Barlow; *Open Road* .... (Arista)
Joe Diffie; *Third Rock From The Sun* .... (Epic)

Step By Step
Whitney Houston; ST/*The Preacher's Wife* .... (Arista)

Telefone (Long Distance Love Affair)
Sheena Easton; *Best Kept Secret* .... (EMI)
Sheena Easton's Greatest Hits ....(EMI Special Markets)
The World Of Sheena Easton: The Singles Collection-C .... (EMI)

Ten Feet Tall And Bulletproof
Travis Tritt; *Ten Feet Tall And Bulletproof*............... (Warner Bros.)

Texas Size Heartache
Joe Diffie; *Joe Diffie's Greatest Hits* .... (Epic)

Tips Of My Fingers
Bill Anderson; *Bill Anderson's Greatest Hits* .... (MCA)
The Bill Anderson Story .... (MCA)
Eddy Arnold; *Best Of Eddy Arnold-#2* .... (Dunhill Compact Classics)
Roy Clark; *Best Of Roy Clark* .... (MCA)
Roy Clark's Greatest Hits .... (MCA)
Yesterday When I Was Young .... (MCA)
Steve Wariner; *I Am Ready* .... (Arista)

Train In The Distance
Paul Simon; *Concert In The Park-August 15 1991* .... (Warner Bros.)
Hearts And Bones .... (Warner Bros.)
Negotiations And Love Songs, 1971-1986 ...... (Warner Bros.)

Twenty-Five Miles
Edwin Starr; *Motown Superstar Series-#3-Edwin Starr* ...... (Motown)
Michael Jackson; *Original Soul Of Michael Jackson* .... (Motown)

Waist Deep In The Big Muddy
Pete Seeger; *Best Of Broadside 1962-1968: Anthems Of The American Underground From The Pages Of Broadside Magazine-C* ....(Smithsonian Folkways)

Walk A Mile In My Shoes
Bryan Ferry; *Another Time Another Place* .... (Reprise)
Elvis Presley; *On Stage-February, 1970* .... (RCA)
Joe South; *Best Of Joe South* .... (Rhino)

What It's Like
Everlast; *Whitey Ford Sings The Blues* .... (Tommy Boy)

When The Coyotes Come Near
Sons Of The Pioneers; *Horses, Cattle And Coyotes* .... (Shanachie)

DIVORCE, Broken Marriage

See Also: **CHEATING & LIES, LOVE (various), MARRIAGE, PARENTS: SINGLE, STEP, ABSENT**

1941
Nilsson; *Pandemonium Shadow Show* .... (RCA)
50 Ways To Leave Your Lover
Paul Simon; *Greatest Hits, Etc.* .... (Columbia)

Negotiations And Love Songs, 1971-1986 . . . . (Warner Bros.)
Still Crazy After All These Years . . . . (Columbia)
Simon & Garfunkel; The Concert In Central Park . . . . (Warner Bros.)

Alimony
Ry Cooder; Ry Cooder. . . . . (Reprise)
Show Time . . . . (Warner Bros.)

Alimony
''Weird Al'' Yankovic; Even Worse . . . . (Scotti Bros.)

Alimony Blues
T-Bone Walker; T-Bone Walker . . . . (Blue Note)

All My Ex's Live In Texas
George Strait; Country Classics-#10-1987-C . . . . (Universal)
George Strait's Greatest Hits-#2 . . . . (MCA)
Ocean Front Property. . . . . (MCA)

Autumn Of My Life
Bobby Goldsboro; 10th Anniversary Album-#1 . . . . (EMI)
Bobby Goldsboro's Greatest Hits. . . . . (Liberty)

Band Of Gold
Freda Payne; Beachbeat Draggin'. . . . . (Dunhill Compact Classics)
Didn't It Blow Your Mind: Soul Hits Of The '70s-#2-C . . . . (Rhino)
Freda Payne's Greatest Hits . . . . (HDH)

Boats Against The Current
Eric Carmen; Best Of Eric Carmen . . . . (Arista)
Boats Against The Current . . . . (Arista)
Olivia Newton-John; Totally Hot . . . . (MCA)

Broken Home
Papa Roach; Infest . . . . (DreamWorks/SKG)

By The Book
Michael Peterson; Michael Peterson . . . . (Reprise)

Crazy Love, Vol. II
Paul Simon; Graceland . . . . (Warner Bros.)

Daddy's Song
Nilsson; Aerial Ballet . . . . (RCA)

Dallas
Alan Jackson; Don't Rock The Jukebox. . . . . (Arista)

D-I-V-O-R-C-E
Rosanne Cash; Tammy Wynette...Remembered-C . . . . (Asylum)
Tammy Wynette; Super Hits Of The '60s-C . . . . (Epic)
Tammy Wynette-Anniversary-20 Years Of Hits . . . . (Epic)
Tammy Wynette's Biggest Hits . . . . (Epic)
Tammy Wynette's Greatest Hits . . . . (Epic)

Drivin' & Cryin'
Steve Wariner; Steve Wariner-Drive . . . . (Arista)

Drivin' My Wife Away
Pinkard & Bowden; Great Divorce Songs For Him-C. . . . . (Warner Bros.)

Easy From Now On
Emmylou Harris; Profile/Best Of Emmylou Harris . . . . (Warner Bros.)
Quarter Moon In A Ten Cent Town. . . . . (Warner Bros.)

Everything You Did
Steely Dan; The Royal Scam . . . . (MCA)

Goin' Through The Big D
Mark Chesnutt; What A Way To Live . . . . (Decca)

Good As I Was To You
Lorrie Morgan; Greater Need . . . . (BNA)
Lorrie Morgan-Super Hits . . . . (RCA)
To Get To You-Greatest Hits Collection . . . . (BNA)

Good Man Is Hard To Find (Pittsburgh)
Bruce Springsteen; Tracks. . . . . (Columbia)

Grandpa (Tell Me 'Bout The Good Old Days)
Judds; Judds' Greatest Hits . . . . (MCA)
Rockin' With The Rhythm . . . . (MCA)
Super 10-#2-C . . . . (RCA)

Haitian Divorce
Steely Dan; Steely Dan's Greatest Hits . . . . (MCA)
The Royal Scam . . . . (MCA)

Have A Nice Rest Of Your Life
Randy Travis; Great Divorce Songs For Him-C . . . . (Warner Bros.)
No Holdin' Back . . . . (Warner Bros.)

He Thinks He'll Keep Her
Mary Chapin Carpenter; Come On Come On . . . . (Columbia)

Her Town Too
James Taylor & J.D. Souther; Dad Loves His Work . . . . (Columbia)

Here's A Quarter (Call Someone Who Cares)
Travis Tritt; It's All About To Change . . . . (Warner Bros.)

Hey Honey- I'm Packin' You In!
Bryan Adams; Waking Up The Neighbours . . . . (A&M)

Hey Jude
Beatles; Beatles 1. . . . . (Capitol)
Beatles-20 Greatest Hits . . . . (Capitol)
Past Masters-Volume Two . . . . (Parlophone)
The Beatles/1967-1970 . . . . (Capitol)
Paul McCartney; Knebworth-The Album-C. . . . . (Polydor)
Wilson Pickett; Wilson Pickett's Greatest Hits . . . . (Atlantic)

How Blue Can You Get
B.B. King; Best Of B.B. King. . . . . (MCA)
Live At The Regal . . . . (MCA)
Live In Cook County Jail. . . . . (MCA)

How Can I Help You Say Goodbye
Patty Loveless; Only What I Feel. . . . . (Epic)

Patty Loveless-Classics. . . . . (Epic)

Hungry Heart
Bruce Springsteen; Bruce Springsteen's Greatest Hits . . . . (Columbia)
The River . . . . (Columbia)
Bruce Springsteen & The E Street Band; Bruce Springsteen & The E Street
Band Live/1975-85 . . . . (Legacy)

Husband Stealer
Barbara Mandrell; This Is Barbara Mandrell. . . . . (MCA)

Husbands And Wives
Brooks & Dunn; Big Country Hits '99-C . . . . (K-Tel)
If You See Her . . . . (Arista)
Neil Diamond; Neil Diamond-Love Songs . . . . (MCA)
Rainbow . . . . (MCA)
Stones . . . . (MCA)
Roger Miller; Best Of Roger Miller . . . . (Mercury)
Best Of Roger Miller-His Greatest Songs . . . . (Curb)
Roger Miller-Super Hits . . . . (Epic)
Roger Miller-The Hits . . . . (Mercury)

I Don't Call Him Daddy
Doug Supernaw; Pure Country-Best Of The '90s-C. . . . . (Priority)
Red And Rio Grande . . . . (BNA)

I Don't Wanna Play House
Sara Evans; Tammy Wynette...Remembered-C . . . . (Asylum)
Tammy Wynette; Tammy Wynette-Anniversary-20 Years Of Hits . . . . (Epic)
Tammy Wynette's Greatest Hits . . . . (Epic)
Tammy Wynette-Super Hits . . . . (Epic)

I Just Came Home To Count The Memories
John Anderson; Honky-Tonk Country-Tender Lovin' Country . . . . . (Priority)
I Just Came Home To Count The Memories . . . . (Warner Bros.)
John Anderson's Greatest Hits . . . . (Warner Bros.)

I Wanna Be Free
Loretta Lynn; Loretta Lynn's Greatest Hits-#2 . . . . (MCA)

I'm Not Running Anymore
John Mellencamp; John Mellencamp. (Columbia)

I'm Not Supposed To Love You Anymore
Bryan White; Between Now And Forever . . . . (Asylum)

I'm So Happy I Can't Stop Crying
Sting; Mercury Falling. . . . . (A&M)
Toby Keith with Sting; Dream Walkin' . . . . (Mercury)
Toby Keith's Greatest Hits, Volume One. . . . . (Mercury)

I'm Still Wearing Your Name
Ann Nesby; I'm Here For You . . . . (Perspective/A&M)

I'm Tryin'
Trace Adkins; Chrome . . . . (Capitol)

Is It Over Yet
Wynonna; Tell Me Why . . . . (MCA)

Is It Still Over
Randy Travis; Old 8 X 10 . . . . (Warner Bros.)

It's A Little Too Late
Tanya Tucker; Can't Run From Yourself . . . . (Liberty)

Let That Pony Run
Pam Tillis; Homeward Looking Angel . . . . (Arista)

Liar
Profyle; Nothin' But Drama. . . . . (Motown)

Living Loving Maid
Led Zeppelin; Led Zeppelin II . . . . (Atlantic)

Marriage
Ted Nugent & The Amboy Dukes; Marriage On The Rocks . . . . (Polydor)
Rock Bottom . . . . (Polydor)

Marriage On Paper Only
Dramatics; Anytime Anyplace . . . . (MCA)

Married But Not To Each Other
Barbara Mandrell; Best Of Barbara Mandrell . . . . (MCA)
Lovers, Friends & Strangers . . . . (MCA)
Midnight Angel . . . . (MCA)

Married Man's A Fool
Blind Willie McTell; Last Session . . . . (Prestige)
Ry Cooder; Paradise And Lunch . . . . (Reprise)

Married Strangers
Johnny Russell; Perspectives . . . . (Mercury)

Me
Staind; Dysfunction . . . . (Flip/Elektra)

Memphis
Chuck Berry; Chuck Berry. . . . . (Audio Fidelity)
Chuck Berry-Golden Hits . . . . (Mercury)
Chuck Berry's Greatest Hits . . . . (Everest)
St. Louis To Liverpool . . . . (Chess)
St!/Hail! Hail! Rock 'N' Roll . . . . (MCA)
The Chess Box-Chuck Berry . . . . (Chess)
Toronto Rock 'N' Roll Revival-#2-C . . . . (Accord)
John Cale; IRS Greatest Hits-#2 & #3-C . . . . (I.R.S.)
Johnny Rivers; Best Of Johnny Rivers . . . . (EMI)
Johnny Rivers-Anthology 1964-1977 . . . . (Rhino)
Lonnie Mack; Rock Instrumental Classics-#2-'60s-C . . . . (Rhino)
Teen Beat-Instrumental Rock-1957-1965-C . . . . (Capitol)

Mexican Divorce
Drifters; 1959-1965-All-Time Greatest Hits And More . . . . (Atlantic)
Nicolette Larson; Nicolette . . . . (Warner Bros.)

Ry Cooder; *Paradise And Lunch* . . . . (Reprise)

Mommy Where's Daddy
Red Hot Chili Peppers; *Red Hot Chili Peppers* . . . .(EMI)

My Husband's Got No Courage In Him
Maddy Prior & June Tabor; *Silly Sisters* . . . . (Shanachie)

My Next Ex-Wife
Little Charlie & The Nightcats; *Night Vision* . . . . (Alligator)

My Second Home
Tracy Lawrence; *Alibis* . . . .(Atlantic)

My Son Calls Another Man Daddy
Hank Williams With His Drifting Cowboys; *Hank Williams-16*
  Great Hits . . . . (Everest)
  Hank Williams-40 Greatest Hits . . . . (Polydor)
  Rare Takes & Radio Cuts . . . . (Polydor)

Not Gon' Cry
Mary J. Blige; *Share My World* . . . .(MCA)

One More Last Chance
Vince Gill; *I Still Believe In You* . . . .(MCA)
  The Ultimate Country Party-C . . . . (Arista)
  Vince Gill-Souvenirs . . . .(MCA)

One Step Closer
Highway 101; *Highway 101* . . . .(Warner Bros.)

Paradise By The Dashboard Light
Meat Loaf; *Bat Out Of Hell* . . . .(Epic)

Pay Me Alimony
Maddox Brothers & Rose; *America's Most Colorful Hillbillly Band* . . (Arhoolie)

Please Don't Ask
Genesis; *Duke* . . . .(Atlantic)

Promises
Cranberries; *Bury The Hatchet* . . . .(Island/IDJMG)

Rose Bouquet
Phil Vassar; *Phil Vassar* . . . . (Arista)

Sad Lookin' Moon
Alabama; *Dancin' On The Boulevard* . . . . (RCA)
  For The Record: 41 Number One Hits . . . . (RCA)

Satin Sheets
Jeannie Pruett; *16 Top Country Hits-#1-C* . . . .(MCA)
  Country Chart-Toppers . . . . (Dominion Entert.)
  Grand Ole Opry-75 Years-#2-C . . . .(MCA)
  MCA Records 30 Years Of Hits-1958-1988-C . . . .(MCA)
Shawn Colvin; *Cover Girl* . . . . (Columbia)

Serve The Servants
Nirvana; *In Utero* . . . . (David Geffen Co.)

She Got The Goldmine (I Got The Shaft)
Jerry Reed; *14 #1 Country Hits-C* . . . . (RCA)
  Jerry Reed's Greatest Hits . . . . (RCA)
  Solid Country Gold-C . . . . (RCA)

She's Gone
Daryl Hall & John Oates; *Abandoned Luncheonette* . . . . (Atlantic)
  Rock 'N Soul, Part 1 . . . . (RCA)

She's Gone, Gone, Gone
Lefty Frizzell; *American Originals-Lefty Frizzell* . . . . (Columbia)
  Best Of Lefty Frizzell . . . . (Rhino)

She's Single Again
Janie Fricke; *19 Hot Country Requests-#3-C* . . . .(Epic)
  Greatest Country Hits Of The '80s-1985-C . . . . (Columbia)
  Janie Fricke-17 Greatest Hits . . . . (Columbia)
  Very Best Of Janie Fricke . . . . (Columbia)
Reba McEntire; *Have I Got A Deal For You* . . . .(MCA)

Starting Over Again
Dolly Parton; *Dolly Dolly Dolly* . . . . (RCA)
  Dolly Parton-Super Hits-#2 . . . . (RCA)
  Essential Dolly Parton . . . . (RCA)
Reba McEntire; *Starting Over* . . . .(MCA)

Stay Together For The Kids
Blink-182; *Take Off Your Pants And Jacket* . . . .(MCA)

Still Holding On
Clint Black & Martina McBride; *Nothin' But The Taillights* . . . . . (RCA)
Martina McBride & Clint Black; *Evolution* . . . . (RCA)

Take That
Lisa Brokop; *Every Little Girl's Dream* . . . . (Patriot)

Taking Everything
Gerald Levert; *Love & Consequences* . . . . (East West)

Theme From "One Day At A Time"
Original Soundtrack; *CBS: The First 50 Years* . . . . (TVT)

Theme From "The Days And Nights Of Molly Dodd"
Original Soundtrack; *Television's Greatest Hits-#7-Cable Ready-C* . . . . (TVT)

Theme From "The Odd Couple"
Original Soundtrack; *Television's Greatest Hits-#7-Cable Ready-C* . . . . (TVT)

There Goes My Everything
Elvis Presley; *Elvis Country ("I'm 10,000 Years Old")* . . . . (RCA)
Engelbert Humperdinck; *Engelbert Humperdinck-16 Most Requested
  Songs* . . . .(Epic)
Floyd Cramer; *Special Songs Of Love* . . . . (Step One)
Jack Greene; *Billboard Top Country Hits-1966-C* . . . . (Rhino)

These Eyes
Guess Who; *Best Of The Guess Who* . . . . (RCA)
  Greatest Of The Guess Who . . . . (RCA)

Nipper's *Greatest Hits Of The '60s-#1-C* . . . .(RCA)
  Track Record-Collection . . . . (RCA)

This Uncivil War
Martina McBride; *Emotion* . . . . (RCA)

Today My World Slipped Away
George Strait; *Carrying Your Love With Me* . . . . (MCA)
  Latest Greatest Straitest Hits . . . . (MCA)
Vern Gosdin; *10 Years Of Greatest Hits Newly Recorded* . . . . (Columbia)
  Legends Of The Silver Eagle-C . . . . (King Biscuit Entert.)
  Today My World Slipped Away . . . . (AMI)

Truck Driver Divorce
Frank Zappa; *Them Or Us* . . . . (Rykodisc)
  You Can't Do That On Stage Anymore-#4 . . . . (Rykodisc)

Tryin' To Get Over You
Vince Gill; *I Still Believe In You* . . . . (MCA)

Unconditional
Clay Davidson; *Unconditional* . . . . (Virgin)

Watch Me
Lorrie Morgan; *Lorrie Morgan's Greatest Hits* . . . . (BNA)
  Watch Me . . . . (BNA)

Who's That Man
Toby Keith; *Boomtown* . . . . (Polydor Country)

Wonderful
Everclear; *Now That's What I Call Music!-#5-C* . . . .(Virgin)
  Songs From An American Movie-#1-Learning How To Smile . . . . (Capitol)

Yard Sale
Sammy Kershaw; *Don't Go Near The Water* . . . . (Mercury)
  The Hits-Chapter 1 . . . . (Mercury)

Yes Yes Yes
Bill Cosby; *Bill Cosby Is Not Himself These Days* . . . . (Capitol)

You Already Drove Me There
Lisa Brokop; *Every Little Girl's Dream* . . . .(Patriot)

You Better Sit Down Kids
Cher; *Bang, Bang The Early Years* . . . . (Capitol)

You Make It Easy
James Taylor; *Gorilla* . . . . (Warner Bros.)

You Were Mine
Dixie Chicks; *Big Country Hits '99-C* . . . . (K-Tel)
  Wide Open Spaces . . . . (Monument)

You Wrecked My Happy Home
Various Artists; *Four Women Blues: Victor/Bluebird Recordings-C* . . (Bluebird)

DOMESTIC ABUSE, Domestic Violence

See Also: **ANGER, CRIME, FAMILY (various), FIGHT,
MISTREATMENT**

Abuse Me
Silverchair; *Freak Show* . . . . (Epic)

Bang Bang
Cher; *Cher* . . . . (Geffen)
  EMI Legends Of Rock & Roll-24 Greatest Hits-C . . . . (EMI)

Black Chick, White Guy
Kid Rock; *Devil Without A Cause* . . . . (Top Dog/Lava/Atlantic)

Boyz-N-The-Hood
Dynamite Hack; *Superfast* . . . . (Farm Club/Universal)

Brenda's Got A Baby
Tupac; *2Pacalypse Now* . . . . (Priority)

Broken Pieces
Strato Vocalz; *Love Shouldn't Hurt-C* . . . .(Qwest)

Chante's Got A Man
Chante Moore; *Now That's What I Call Music!-#3-C* . . . .(Virgin)
  This Moment Is Mine . . . . (Silas)

Do For Love
2Pac featuring Eric Williams; *R U Still Down (Remember Me)* . . . .(Amaru/Jive)

Don't Abuse Me
Joan Jett; *Bad Reputation* . . . . (Blackheart)

Down With The Sickness
Disturbed; *The Sickness* . . . .(Giant)

Father Of Mine
Everclear; *Now That's What I Call Music!-#2-C* . . . .(Virgin)
  So Much For The Afterglow . . . . (Capitol)

Freaks
Live; *Secret Samadhi* . . . . (Radioactive/MCA)

Free Girl Now
Tom Petty And The Heartbreakers; *Echo* . . . . (Warner Bros.)

Gave It A Name
Bruce Springsteen; *Tracks* . . . . (Columbia)

Goodbye Earl
Dixie Chicks; *Fly* . . . . (Monument)

Harder Cards
Collin Raye; *Tracks* . . . . (Epic)

Hey Joe
Jimi Hendrix; *Essential Jimi Hendrix, Volume 2* . . . . (Reprise)
  Live At Winterland . . . . (Rykodisc)
Jimi Hendrix Experience; *Are You Experienced?* . . . . (Reprise)

Smash Hits . . . .(Reprise)
Love; *Best Of Love* . . . . (Rhino)
How Come, How Long
Babyface & Stevie Wonder; *The Day* . . . . (Epic)
How's It Goin' Down
DMX; *It's Dark And Hell Is Hot* . . . . (Def Jam)
I Think About You
Collin Raye; *Best Of Collin Raye-Direct Hits* . . . . (Epic)
I Think About You . . . . (Epic)
I Wonder If Heaven Got A Ghetto
2Pac; *R U Still Down (Remember Me)* . . . . (Amaru/Jive)
Independence Day
Martina McBride; *The Way That I Am* . . . .(RCA)
Jeremy
Pearl Jam; *Ten* . . . . (Epic Portrait Assoc.)
Little Bit Of Abuse
Kinks; *Give The People What They Want* . . . . (Arista)
Little Girl
Stephen Bishop; *Love Shouldn't Hurt-C* . . . .(Qwest)
Little Girl, The
John Michael Montgomery; *Brand New Me* . . . . (Atlantic)
Totally Hits-#3-C . . . . (Atlantic)
Little Joe The Wrangler's Sister Nell
Skip Gorman; *A Cowboy's Wild Song To His Herd* . . . . (Rounder)
Louise, Louise
Pamela Rose; *Morpheus* . . . . (Grace)
Love Is Blind
Eve; *First Lady Of Ruff Ryders* . . . . (Ruff Ryders/IDJMG)
Love Shouldn't Hurt
All Star Group; *Love Shouldn't Hurt-C* . . . .(Qwest)
Luka
Suzanne Vega; *Solitude Standing* . . . . (A&M)
Mommy Can I Come Home
Keb' Mo'; *The Door* . . . .(550/Epic/Okeh)
My Man
Barbra Streisand; *Barbra Streisand's Greatest Hits* . . . . (Columbia)
Live Concert At The Forum . . . . (Columbia)
My Name Is Barbra . . . .(Columbia)
ST/Funny Girl . . . .(Columbia)
Billie Holiday; *Billie Holiday-Live* . . . . (Verve)
Essential Billie Holiday-Carnegie Hall Concert . . . . . . (Verve)
Diana Ross; *Evening With Diana Ross* . . . . (Motown)
ST/Lady Sings The Blues . . . . (Motown)
Ella Fitzgerald & Tommy Flanagan Trio; *Montreux '77-C* . . . .(Pablo)
Peggy Lee; *Peggy Lee's All-Time Greatest Hits* . . . .(Curb)
Sarah Vaughan; *Jazz 'Round Midnight-Sarah Vaughan* . . . .(Verve)
Oochie Wally
QB's Finest featuring Nas; *QB Finest* . . . . (Columbia)
Run For Your Life
Beatles; *Beatles-Box Set* . . . . (Capitol)
Rubber Soul . . . .(Capitol)
Seaside Bar Song
Bruce Springsteen; *Tracks* . . . . (Columbia)
Little Bob Story; *One Step Up/Two Steps Back-The Songs Of Bruce Springsteen-C* . . . . (Right Stuff)
Shake Ya Ass
Mystikal; *Let's Get Ready* . . . .(Jive)
Still
Macy Gray; *On How Life Is* . . . . (Epic)
Treat You Like A Queen
Rahsaan Patterson; *Love In Stereo* . . . . (MCA)
Used And Abused
Midnight Oil; *Midnight Oil* . . . . (Columbia)
Way Down The Line
Offspring; *Ixnay On The Hombre* . . . . (Columbia)
Wonderful
Adam Ant; *Wonderful* . . . . (Capitol)
Your Dictionary
XTC; *Homespun* . . . .(Idea/TVT)

DOORS, Gates, Keys, Locks
See Also: *HOUSES, LEAVING, SECRETS*

At My Front Door
Nilsson; *Son Of Schmilsson* . . . .(RCA)
Baby, I Knocked On Your Door
Sonny Terry & Brownie McGhee; *At Sugar Hill* . . . .(Fantasy)
Back Door Angels
Jethro Tull; *War Child* . . . . (Chrysalis)
Back Door Friend
Johnny Winter; *Johnny Winter* . . . . (Columbia)
Lightnin' Hopkins; *The Jewel/Paula Records Story* . . . . (Capricorn)
Back Door Man
Doors; *Doors* . . . . (Elektra)
Doors 13 . . . . (Elektra)

Howlin' Wolf; *Best Of Howlin' Wolf-Chess Blues* . . . .(Chess)
Willie Dixon; *I Am The Blues* . . . .(Columbia)
Back Door Man
John Hammond; *Best Of John Hammond* . . . .(Vanguard)
Back Door Santa
Clarence Carter; *Christmas Classics-C* . . . .(Rhino)
Snatching It Back-The Best Of Clarence Carter . . . .(Rhino)
Soul Christmas-C . . . .(Atlantic)
Back Door Santa
Bon Jovi; *Very Special Christmas-C* . . . .(A&M)
Back Doors Crying
Peter Allen; *Taught By Experts* . . . .(A&M)
Backdoor Love Affair
ZZ Top; *Best Of ZZ Top* . . . .(Warner Bros.)
Six Pack . . . . (Warner Bros.)
ZZ Top . . . . (Warner Bros.)
Banging The Door
Public Image Ltd.; *Flowers Of Romance* . . . .(Warner Bros.)
Live In Tokyo . . . .(Elektra)
Behind Closed Doors
Charlie Rich; *American Originals-Charlie Rich* . . . .(Columbia)
Behind Closed Doors . . . . (Epic)
Charlie Rich's Greatest Hits . . . .(Epic)
Columbia Country Classics-#4-Nashville Sound-C . . . . (Columbia)
Behind That Locked Door
George Harrison; *All Things Must Pass* . . . . (Parlophone)
Between The Devil And Me
Alan Jackson; *Everything I Love* . . . .(Arista)
Blue Love
O'Kanes; *Tired Of The Runnin'* . . . .(Columbia)
Bucket's Got A Hole In It, The
Preservation Hall Jazz Band; *Best Of The Preservation Hall Jazz Band* . . . .(Columbia)
Can't You Hear Me Knockin'
Rolling Stones; *Sticky Fingers* . . . . (Virgin)
Cars
Fear Factory; *Obsolete* . . . .(Roadrunner)
Gary Numan; *18 Modern Rock Classics From The '80s-C* . . . .(Rhino)
Pleasure Principle . . . .(Atco)
Change The Locks
Tom Petty And The Heartbreakers; *ST/She's The One* . . . .(Warner Bros.)
Check Your Tears At The Door
Drivin' N' Cryin'; *Whisper Tames The Lion* . . . .(Island)
Chop Suey!
System Of A Down; *Toxicity* . . . .(American/Columbia)
Close The Door
Teddy Pendergrass; *Best Of Teddy Pendergrass-Philadelphia International* . . . .(Philadelphia Int'l)
Life Is A Song Worth Singing . . . .(Philadelphia Int'l)
Philly Ballads-#2-C . . . .(Philadelphia Int'l)
Teddy Pendergrass-Live . . . .(Philadelphia Int'l)
Teddy Pendergrass's Greatest Hits . . . .(Philadelphia Int'l)
Ten Years Of #1 Hits-C . . . .(Philadelphia Int'l)
Come And Knock (On The Door Of My Heart)
Roy Acuff; *45-#1097* . . . . (Hickory)
Crack In Your Door
Little Feat; *Little Feat* . . . . (Warner Bros.)
Crazy Little Mama
Eldorados; *Greatest Groups Of The '50s-#2-C* . . . .(Collectables)
Sock Hop-C . . . .(Dunhill Compact Classics)
Danger At My Door
Mark Chesnutt; *Too Cold At Home* . . . .(MCA)
Dead Next Door
Billy Idol; *Rebel Yell* . . . .(Chrysalis)
Don't Answer The Door
B.B. King; *Back In The Alley* . . . . (MCA)
Blues 'N' Jazz/Electric B.B. King . . . . (MCA)
Electric B.B. King-His Best . . . . (MCA)
Live & Well . . . . (MCA)
Don't Bother To Knock
Barbara Mandrell; *Moods* . . . . (MCA)
Jim Ed Brown & Helen Cornelius; *Jim Ed Brown & Helen Cornelius' Greatest Hits* . . . . (RCA)
Don't Turn Me From Your Door
John Lee Hooker; *Don't Turn Me From Your Door* . . . .(Atlantic)
Door
George Jones; *Best Of George Jones* . . . .(Epic)
George Jones-Anniversary-Ten Years Of Hits . . . . (Epic)
Skip Ewing; *Will To Love* . . . . (MCA)
Door #1
LSG; *Levert-Sweat-Gill* . . . .(East West)
Door Is Always Open
Dave & Sugar; *Dave & Sugar's Greatest Hits* . . . . (RCA)
Door Is Still Open To My Heart
Dean Martin; *Dean Martin's Greatest Hits* . . . . (EMI)
Door Is Still Open To My Heart . . . .(Reprise)
Door Number Three
Jimmy Buffett; *A1A* . . . .(MCA)

Door Peep
Burning Spear; *Man In The Hills* .... (Island)
Door To Door
Creedence Clearwater Revival; *Live In Europe* .... (Fantasy)
Mardi Gras .... (Fantasy)
Door To Door
Cars; *Door To Door* .... (Elektra)
Door To Door Blues
Champion Jack Dupree; *Blues Roots-#6.* .... (Storyville)
Door You Closed To Me
Box Tops; *45-#38* .... (Flashback)
Door, The
Keb' Mo'; *The Door* .... (550/Epic/Okeh)
Doors Of Your Heart
English Beat; *Wha'ppen* .... (I.R.S.)
What Is Beat .... (I.R.S.)
Every Morning
Sugar Ray; *14:59* .... (Lava)
Everybody's Key Fits My Baby's Door
Rockin' Tabby Thomas; *King Of Swamp Blues* ...... (Maison De Soul)
Girl Next Door
Earl Lewis &The Channels; *Harlem Holiday-New York Rhythm &*
Blues-#2-C .... (Collectables)
New York's Finest .... (Collectables)
Girl Next Door
Johnny Crawford; *Best Of Johnny Crawford* .... (Rhino)
Girl Next Door
Frank Sinatra; *Frank Sinatra-Gift Set* .... (Capitol)
Girl Next Door
Bobby Brown; *Dance!...Ya Know It!* .... (MCA)
King Of Stage .... (MCA)
Green Door
Jim Lowe; *Billboard Top Rock 'N' Roll Hits-1956-C* ... (Rhino)
Super Hits-#4-C .... (Gusto)
Happiness Lives Next Door
Willie Nelson; *Diamonds In The Rough* .... (Delmark)
Legend Begins/Wild & Willie .... (Allegiance)
Honey (Open That Door)
Ricky Skaggs; *Don't Cheat In Our Hometown* .... (Epic)
Greatest Country Hits Of The '80s-1984-C .... (Columbia)
Live In London .... (Epic)
House Of Four Doors
Moody Blues; *In Search Of The Lost Chord* .... (Polydor)
I Hear You Knockin'
Smiley Lewis; *Billboard Top R&B Hits-1955-C* .... (Rhino)
Non-Stop Party Rock .... (EMI)
I Left My Heart At The Stage Door Canteen
Jo Stafford; *G.I. Jo* .... (Corinthian)
I'm Gonna Knock On Your Door
Eddie Hodges; *History Of Cadence Records-#1-C* .... (Varese Vintage)
I've Been Wrong Before
Deborah Allen; *Cheat The Night.* .... (RCA)
Keep A'Knocking
Wallace ''Cheese'' Read; *Cajun House Party ''C'ez Cheese''* ...... (Arhoolie)
Key To The Highway
David Bromberg; *You Should See The Rest Of The Band* ...... (Fantasy)
Derek And The Dominos; *Eric Clapton-Crossroads-C* .... (Polydor)
Layla .... (Polydor)
John Hammond; *Best Of John Hammond* .... (Vanguard)
Little Walter; *Best Of Little Walter-#2* .... (Chess)
Blues-#2-C .... (Chess)
Sonny Terry & Brownie McGhee; *Great Blues Men-C* ... (Vanguard)
Knockin' On Heaven's Door
Bob Dylan; *Biograph* .... (Columbia)
Bob Dylan At Budokan. .... (Columbia)
Rock Classics Of The '70s-C .... (Columbia)
ST/Pat Garrett & Billy The Kid .... (Columbia)
Bob Dylan & The Grateful Dead; *Dylan & The Dead.* .... (Columbia)
Bob Dylan And The Band; *Before The Flood* .... (Columbia)
Eric Clapton; *Eric Clapton-Crossroads-C* .... (Polydor)
Time Pieces-#1-The Best Of Eric Clapton .... (Polydor)
Guns N' Roses; *ST/Days Of Thunder* .... (David Geffen Co.)
Use Your Illusion II .... (Geffen)
Jerry Garcia; *Run For The Roses* .... (Arista)
Randy Crawford; *Rich & Poor* .... (Warner Bros.)
Knocking At Your Back Door
Deep Purple; *Nobody's Perfect.* .... (Mercury)
Perfect Strangers .... (Mercury)
Let 'Em In
Paul McCartney; *All The Best!* .... (Capitol)
Wings; *Wings At The Speed Of Sound* .... (Capitol)
Wings Greatest .... (Capitol)
Wings Over America .... (Capitol)
Let Me In
Bonnie Raitt; *Takin' My Time.* .... (Warner Bros.)
Sensations; *Billboard Top R&B Hits-1962-C* .... (Rhino)
Chess Rhythm & Roll Box-C .... (Chess)
Cruisin'-1962-1963-C .... (Dunhill Compact Classics)

Vintage Music-#6-C .... (MCA)
Let My Love Open The Door
Pete Townshend; *Empty Glass* .... (Atco)
Let's Lock The Door (And Throw Away The Key)
Jay & The Americans; *Jay & The Americans' All-Time Greatest Hits* ... (Rhino)
Long And Winding Road, The
Beatles; *Beatles 1* .... (Capitol)
Beatles-20 Greatest Hits .... (Capitol)
Beatles-Love Songs .... (Capitol)
Let It Be .... (Capitol)
Reel Music .... (Capitol)
The Beatles/1967-1970. .... (Capitol)
Paul McCartney; *Tripping The Live Fantastic-Highlights!.* ...... (Capitol)
Wings; *Wings Over America* .... (Capitol)
Lookin' Out My Back Door
Creedence Clearwater Revival; *1970* .... (Fantasy)
Cosmo's Factory. .... (Fantasy)
Creedence Clearwater Revival-Chronicle .... (Fantasy)
Creedence Country. .... (Fantasy)
More Creedence Gold .... (Fantasy)
Looking At The Front Door
Main Source; *Breaking Atoms.* .... (EMI)
Nasty Wax-C. .... (K-Tel)
Love Come Knocking
Staple Singers; *Hold Onto Your Dreams* .... (Out Of Print)
Murder (Or A Heart Attack)
Old 97's; *Fight Songs* .... (Elektra)
My Baby Done Changed The Lock On The Door
Sonny Terry & Brownie McGhee; *Great Bluesmen At Newport-C* ... (Vanguard)
My Back Door
Melissa Etheridge; *Brave & Crazy* .... (Island)
Next Door To An Angel
Neil Sedaka; *Neil Sedaka Sings His Greatest Hits* .... (RCA)
Neil Sedaka's All-Time Greatest Hits. .... (RCA)
No Reply
Beatles; *Beatles '65.* .... (Capitol)
Beatles-Box Set. .... (Capitol)
For Sale .... (Capitol)
Nobody's Supposed To Be Here
Deborah Cox; *One Wish* .... (Arista)
Totally Hits-#1-C. .... (Arista)
One Less Bell To Answer
5th Dimension; *5th Dimension-Anthology 1967-1973* .... (Rhino)
Greatest Hits On Earth. .... (Arista)
Barbra Streisand; *Barbra Joan Streisand* .... (Columbia)
Gladys Knight & The Pips; *Gladys Knight & The Pips-Anthology* ... (Motown)
If I Were Your Woman .... (Motown)
Open The Door
Royal Teens; *Short Shorts* .... (Collectables)
Open The Door
Michael McDonald; *Blue Obsession* .... (Ramp)
Open The Door
Otis Redding; *Dock Of The Bay.* .... (Atco)
Remember Me. .... (Stax)
Open The Door
Betty Carter; *Now It's My Turn.* .... (Roulette)
Open The Door To Your Heart
Little Milton; *Stax Blues Masters-Blue Monday-C* .... (Stax)
Walking The Back Streets. .... (Stax)
Open The Door, Homer
Bob Dylan And The Band; *Basement Tapes* .... (Columbia)
Thunderclap Newman; *Hollywood Dream* .... (MCA)
Open The Door, Richard
Louis Jordan; *Jazz Heritage-Greatest Hits-#2-1941-1947* ...... (MCA)
Open Up A New Door
John Mayall's Bluesbreakers; *Bare Wires.* .... (London)
Open Up Your Door
Romantics; *In Heat* .... (Epic Portrait Assoc.)
What I Like About You (And Other Romantic Hits) ...... (Nemperor)
Open Up Your Door
Steve Earle & The Dukes; *Early Tracks* .... (Epic)
Opened The Door
Journey; *Infinity.* .... (Columbia)
Out That Door
Hoodoo Gurus; *Blow Your Cool* .... (Elektra)
Please Take That Train From My Door
Wayne Horvitz; *This New Generation* .... (Elektra)
Question
Moody Blues; *A Night At Red Rocks With The Colorado Symphony*
Orchestra. .... (Polydor)
A Question Of Balance .... (Polydor)
This Is The Moody Blues. .... (Polydor)
Red House
Jimi Hendrix; *Concerts* .... (Reprise)
Kiss The Sky. .... (Reprise)
Lifelines/Jimi Hendrix Story. .... (Reprise)
Live At Winterland. .... (Rykodisc)
ST/Jimi Hendrix .... (Reprise)

Jimi Hendrix Experience; *Are You Experienced?* . . . . (Reprise)
   Smash Hits . . . . (Reprise)
River, Stay 'Way From My Door
Guy Lombardo & His Royal Canadians; *Auld Lang Syne* . . . . (Pro-Arte)
Seven Doors Hotel
Europe; *Europe* . . . . (Epic)
Shelf In The Room
Days Of The New; *Days Of The New.* . . . . (Outpost/Interscope)
Sleep's Dark & Silent Gate
Bonnie Raitt; *The Glow* . . . . (Warner Bros.)
Jackson Browne; *The Pretender* . . . . (Asylum)
Softest Place On Earth
Xscape; *Traces Of My Lipstick* . . . . (So So Def/Columbia)
Somebody
J. Geils Band; *Monkey Island* . . . . (Atlantic)
Somebody Done Changed The Lock On My Door
Louis Jordan; *Best Of Louis Jordan.* . . . . (MCA)
   Jazz Heritage-Greatest Hits-#2-1941-1947 . . . . (MCA)
Somebody Knockin'
Izzy Stradlin & Ju Ju Hounds; *Izzy Stradlin & Ju Ju Hounds* . . . . (Geffen)
Somebody's Knockin'
Terri Gibbs; *Best Of Terri Gibbs* . . . . (MCA)
   Country Gold-C . . . . (Priority)
   Country Music Classics-#6-1980-1985-C . . . . (K-Tel)
Stage Door
Justin Hayward; *Songwriter* . . . . (Deram)
Stagedoor Johnny
Donnie Iris; *Fortune 410* . . . . (MCA)
Standing In The Doorway
Bob Dylan; *Time Out Of Mind.* . . . . (Columbia)
Stone Outside Dan Murphy's Door
Anna McGoldrick; *Ireland On My Mind* . . . . (Rego Irish)
Storm, The
Garth Brooks; *Scarecrow* . . . . (Capitol)
Storming The Gates Of Hell
Riot; *Privilege Of Power* . . . . (Epic Portrait Assoc.)
Swing Wide Your Gate Of Love
Hank Thompson; *Hank Thompson's Greatest Hits* . . . . (Step One)
   The Country Music Hall Of Fame-Hank Thompson . . . . (MCA)
Swinging Doors
George Jones; *20 Golden Pieces Of George Jones* . . . . (Bulldog)
Merle Haggard; *Capitol Collectors Series-Merle Haggard.* . . . . (Capitol)
Merle Haggard & The Strangers; *Best Of Merle Haggard & The
   Strangers* . . . . (Capitol)
   For The Record: Merle Haggard-43 Legendary Hits . . . . (BNA)
   Okie From Muskogee . . . . (Capitol)
   Songs I'll Always Sing . . . . (Capitol)
Testify
Rage Against The Machine; *The Battle Of Los Angeles* . . . . (Epic)
There He Is (At My Door)
Martha Reeves & The Vandellas; *Live Wire! Singles-1962-1972* . . . . . (Motown)
   Martha Reeves & The Vandellas-Anthology. . . . . (Motown)
This Door Swings Both Ways
Herman's Hermits; *Herman's Hermits-Their Greatest Hits* . . . . (Abkco)
This Side Of The Door
Mark Chesnutt; *What A Way To Live.* . . . . (Decca)
To The Door Of The Sun
Al Martino; *Al Martino's Greatest Hits.* . . . . (Curb)
   Capitol Collectors Series-Al Martino . . . . (Capitol)
Tryin' To Get To Heaven
Bob Dylan; *Time Out Of Mind.* . . . . (Columbia)
Twenty-Nine Ways (To My Baby's Door)
Koko Taylor; *Koko Taylor.* . . . . (Chess)
   South Side Lady . . . . (Evidence Music)
Marc Cohn; *Marc Cohn.* . . . . (Atlantic)
Willie Dixon; *The Chess Box-Willie Dixon* . . . . (Chess)
Two Doors Down
Dolly Parton; *Collector's Series-Dolly Parton* . . . . (RCA)
   Dolly Parton's Greatest Hits . . . . (RCA)
   Here You Come Again . . . . (Dunhill Compact Classics)
Unforgiven II
Metallica; *Reload* . . . . (Elektra)
Walk Away
Cool For August; *Grand World* . . . . (Warner Bros.)
What If I Came Knocking
John Mellencamp; *Human Wheels* . . . . (Mercury)
Who Can It Be Now
Men At Work; *Billboard Top Hits-1982-C* . . . . (Rhino)
   Business As Usual. . . . . (Columbia)
Who's Behind The Door
Zebra; *Zebra* . . . . (Atlantic)
   Zebra-Live . . . . (Atlantic)
Who's That Knockin'
Genies; *WOGL Oldies 98-History Of Rock-#2-C* . . . . (Collectables)
Yellow Woman's Door Bells
Leadbelly; *Leadbelly.* . . . . (Fantasy)
   Leadbelly . . . . (Everest)

DRAFT, Draft Resistance, Enlistment

See Also: **COUNTRIES: AMERICA, PATRIOTISM, POLITICS
(various), PROTEST, WAR**

Alice's Restaurant Massacree
Arlo Guthrie; *Alice's Restaurant* . . . . (Reprise)
   Best Of Arlo Guthrie . . . . (Warner Bros.)
Boogie Woogie Bugle Boy
Andrews Sisters; *Andrews Sisters-16 Great Performances* . . . . (MCA)
   Best Of The Andrews Sisters . . . . (MCA)
   Boogie Woogie Bugle Girls . . . . (MCA)
   Rarities . . . . (MCA)
Bette Midler; *Divine Miss M* . . . . (Atlantic)
   Live At Last . . . . (Atlantic)
   ST/Divine Madness . . . . (Atlantic)
Call Up
Clash; *Sandinista* . . . . (Epic)
Draft Dodger Rag
Phil Ochs; *Chords Of Fame* . . . . (A&M)
   I Ain't Marching Anymore. . . . . (Carthage)
   Newport Folk Music Festival-1964-C . . . . (Vanguard)
   There But For Fortune . . . . (Elektra)
Draft Me If You Can
Joady Guthrie; *Spys On Wall Street* . . . . (Rag Baby)
Draft Morning
Byrds; *Notorious Byrd Brothers.* . . . . (Columbia)
   The Byrds . . . . (Columbia)
Draft Resister
Steppenwolf; *Live Steppenwolf* . . . . (MCA)
   Move Over. . . . . (MCA Special Prod.)
For Your Country And My Country
Frances Alda; *78-#64689.* . . . . (Victor)
Peerless Quartet; *78-#2273* . . . . (Columbia)
Gone With The Draft
Benny Goodman; *Benny Goodman Sextet featuring Charlie Christian-1939-
   1941* . . . . (Columbia)
Hell No, I Ain't Gonna Go
Matt Jones & Elaine Laron; *Best Of Broadside 1962-1968: Anthems
   Of The American Underground From The Pages Of Broadside
   Magazine-C* . . . . (Smithsonian Folkways)
Hey Mr. Draft Board
David Peel; *American Revolution* . . . . (Out Of Print)
I Don't Wanna Get Drafted
Frank Zappa; *The Lost Episodes* . . . . (Rykodisc)
I-Feel-Like-I'm-Fixin'-To-Die Rag
Country Joe & The Fish; *Country Joe & The Fish-Greatest Hits* . . . . . (Vanguard)
   Greatest '60s Folksingers-C . . . . (Vanguard)
   I-Feel-Like-I'm-Fixin'-To-Die . . . . (Vanguard)
   Life & Times Of Country Joe & The Fish . . . . (Vanguard)
   More American Graffiti-#4-C . . . . (MCA)
   Songs Of Protest-C . . . . (Rhino)
   ST/Woodstock . . . . (Atlantic)
I've Been Drafted
Chuck Foster & Jimmy Castle; *The Uncollected Chuck Foster & His
   Orchestra-1940* . . . . (Hindsight)
No No No To Draft & War
Minutemen; *Ballot Result* . . . . (SST)

DREAMS, Daydreaming, Nightmares

See Also: **DESIRE, FAITH, LOVE (various), MOTIVATION, NIGHT,
OPTIMISM, PRETEND, SLEEP**

35 Millimeter Dreams
Garland Jeffreys; *Ghost Rider* . . . . (A&M)
   Ghost Writer . . . . (A&M)
4:37 AM (Arabs With Knives & West German Skies)
Roger Waters; *Pros & Cons Of Hitchhiking* . . . . (Columbia)
African Dream
Stewart Copeland; *Rhythmatist* . . . . (A&M)
After The Goldrush
Emmylou Harris/Dolly Parton/Linda Ronstadt; *Trio II* . . . . (Asylum)
Neil Young; *After The Gold Rush* . . . . (Reprise)
   Decade . . . . (Reprise)
Neil Young & Crazy Horse; *Live Rust* . . . . (Reprise)
All I Do Is Dream Of You
Debbie Reynolds/The MGM Studio Chorus; *ST/Singin' In
   The Rain* . . . . (Turner Classic Movies)
Jan Garber & His Orchestra; *78-#24629* . . . . (Victor)
All I Have To Do Is Dream
Everly Brothers; *All They Had To Do Was Dream* . . . . (Rhino)
   Best Of The Everly Brothers . . . . (Rhino)
   Fabulous Style Of The Everly Brothers . . . . (Rhino)
   Heartaches 'N' Harmonies . . . . (Rhino)
   Oldies But Goodies-#12-C . . . . (Original Sound)

ST/*Stealing Home* ....(Atlantic)
Very Best Of The Everly Brothers ....(Warner Bros.)
Nitty Gritty Dirt Band; *Best Of The Nitty Gritty Dirt Band*....(Liberty)
Heartbreak Hotel-C................................(EMI)
All My Dreams
Pretenders; *Last Of The Independents*.................(Sire)
All That You Dream
Linda Ronstadt; *Living In The USA* ....(Asylum)
Little Feat; *Hoy-Hoy!* ....(Warner Bros.)
Last Record Album...........................(Warner Bros.)
ST/*Over The Edge* ....(Warner Bros.)
Waiting For Columbus ....(Warner Bros.)
All Through The Night
Original Broadway Cast; *Anything Goes* ....(RCA Victor)
Am I Dreamin'
Xscape; *Traces Of My Lipstick* ....(So So Def/Columbia)
Am I Dreaming
Ol Skool featuring Keith Sweat & Xscape; *Ol Skool* ....(Keia/Universal)
American Dream
John Cougar Mellencamp; *Chestnut Street Incident*...............(Rhino)
American Dream
Chicago; *Chicago XIV* ....(Chicago)
American Dream
Crosby, Stills, Nash & Young; *American Dream*...............(Atlantic)
American Dream
Oak Ridge Boys; *American Dreams*....................(MCA)
American Dream
Nitty Gritty Dirt Band; *Twenty Years Of Dirt-Best Of The Nitty Gritty Dirt Band* ....(Warner Bros.)
American Dream
Original London Cast; *Miss Saigon* ....(Geffen)
And Dream Of Sheep
Kate Bush; *Hounds Of Love* ....(EMI)
Anita, You're Dreaming
Waylon Jennings; *Best Of Waylon Jennings*.......(RCA)
Waylon Jennings-Early Years ....(RCA)
Another Night
Real McCoy; *Another Night*......................(Arista)
Another Nine Minutes
Yankee Grey; *Untamed* ....(Monument)
Any Dream Will Do
Michael Crawford; *Michael Crawford Performs Andrew Lloyd Webber*..................................(Atlantic)
Original Cast; *Joseph & The Amazing Technicolor Dreamcoat* ....(MCA)
Any Lucky Penny
Nikki Hassman; *Songs From Dawson's Creek* ....(Sony Music Soundtrax)
Appalachian Dream
Diamond Rio; *Love A Little Stronger* ....(Arista)
Are You Sitting Comfortably/The Dream
Moody Blues; *Caught Live Plus Five* ....(Polydor)
On The Threshold Of A Dream ....(Polydor)
This Is The Moody Blues ....(Polydor)
Army Dreamers
Kate Bush; *Never For Ever*.......................(EMI)
The Whole Story................................(EMI)
Au Revoir, Pleasant Dreams
Ben Bernie & His Orchestra; *78-#4943* ....(Brunswick)
Beautiful Dreamer
Mormon Tabernacle Choir; *Beautiful Dreamer* ....(Columbia)
Mormon Tabernacle Choir's Greatest Hits ....(Columbia)
The Mormon Tabernacle Choir Album ....(Columbia)
This Land Is Your Land ....(Columbia)
Been There
Clint Black with Steve Wariner; *D'lectrified* ......(RCA)
Big Dreams In A Small Town
Restless Heart; *Big Dreams In A Small Town* ......(RCA)
Big Time
Neil Young & Crazy Horse; *Broken Arrow* ....(Reprise)
Year Of The Horse ....(Reprise)
Black Snake Dream Blues
Blind Lemon Jefferson; *Master Of The Blues-#2-1926-1929*.......(Biograph)
Bob Dylan's 115th Dream
Bob Dylan; *Bringing It All Back Home* ....(Columbia)
Bob Dylan's Dream
Bob Dylan; *Freewheelin'* ....(Columbia)
Peter, Paul & Mary; *Album 1700* ....(Warner Bros.)
Book Of Dreams
Bruce Springsteen; *Lucky Town* ....(Columbia)
Boulevard Of Broken Dreams
Diana Krall; *All For You (A Dedication To The Nat "King" Cole Trio)* ....(Impulse!)
Tony Bennett; *Forty Years-The Artistry Of Tony Bennett*...(Columbia)
Tony Bennett-16 Most Requested Songs ....(Legacy)
Tony Bennett's All-Time Greatest Hits ....(Columbia)
Broken Wing
Martina McBride; *Evolution*.....................(RCA)
California Dreamin'
Beach Boys; *Made In The U.S.A.* ....(Capitol)

Mamas & The Papas; *At The Hop* ....(MCA)
Good Feeling Music Of The Big Chill Generation-#1-C ....(Motown)
Mamas & The Papas-20 Golden Hits...............(MCA)
ST/*Air America*................................(MCA)
ST/*American Pop*..............................(MCA)
ST/*Forrest Gump* ....(Epic/Sony Music Soundtrax)
Californication
Red Hot Chili Peppers; *Californication* ....(Warner Bros.)
Carolina Dreams
Ronnie Milsap; *Inside Ronnie Milsap* ....(RCA)
Castle Of Dreams
Dave Koz; *Dave Koz*..........................(Capitol)
Chasin' That Neon Rainbow
Alan Jackson; *Here In The Real World* ....(Arista)
Chick-A-Boom (Don't Ya Jes' Love It)
Daddy Dewdrop; *'70s Smash Hits-#4-C* ....(Rhino)
Super Hits Of The '70s-Have A Nice Day-#5-C ....(Rhino)
Color Of Roses
Beth Nielsen Chapman; *Sand And Water* ....(Reprise)
Computer Dreams
187 Lockdown; *Groove Radio Presents Speed Garage* ....(Priority)
Could've Been Me
Billy Ray Cyrus; *Some Gave All* ....(Mercury)
Cowboy Heaven
Roy Rogers; *Peace In The Valley* ....(Pair)
Cowboy Of Dreams
David Crosby & Graham Nash; *Wind On The Water* ....(MCA)
Cowboy's Dream
Eddy Arnold; *Cattle Call*........................(RCA)
Jimmy C. Newman; *Cajun Cowboy* ....(Plantation)
Cowboy's Dream No. 19
Dan Hicks & His Hot Licks; *Last Train To Hicksville* ....(MCA)
Creepin'
Kenny Rankin; *Inside Kenny Rankin*...........(Little David)
Luther Vandross; *Night I Fell In Love* ....(Epic)
Stevie Wonder; *Fulfillingness' First Finale* ....(Motown)
Cynthia
Bruce Springsteen; *Tracks* ....(Columbia)
Daddy's Dream
Vikki Carr; *Live At The Greek Theatre* ....(Columbia)
Dancy's Dream
Restless Heart; *Fast Moving Train* ....(RCA)
Day Dream
Duke Ellington; *And His Mother Called Him Bill* ....(Bluebird)
Carnegie Hall Concert ....(Prestige)
Greatest Jazz Concert In The World ....(Pablo)
Jazz Violin Session ....(Atlantic)
Day Dream
Journey; *Evolution* ....(Columbia)
Day Dream
Robin Trower; *Robin Trower-Live* ....(Chrysalis)
Twice Removed From Yesterday ....(Chrysalis)
Daydream
Lovin' Spoonful; *Lovin' Spoonful-Anthology*.............(Rhino)
Daydream Believer
Anne Murray; *Anne Murray's Greatest Hits*.........(Capitol)
I'll Always Love You...........................(Capitol)
Monkees; *Billboard Top Rock 'N' Roll Hits-1967-C* ....(Rhino)
Mellow '60s-C ....(Priority)
Monkees' Greatest Hits ....(Rhino)
Daydream Romance
Ray Stevens; *Feel The Music* ....(Warner Bros.)
Feeling's Not Right Again ....(Warner Bros.)
Daydreamin'
Tatyana Ali; *Kiss The Sky* ....(MJJ Music/Work)
Daydreaming
Aretha Franklin; *Ten Years Of Gold* ....(Atlantic)
Young, Gifted And Black ....(Atlantic & Atco Remasters)
Daydreams About Night Things
Ronnie Milsap; *Collector's Series-Ronnie Milsap* ....(RCA)
Night Things ....(RCA)
Ronnie Milsap-Live ....(RCA)
Ronnie Milsap's Greatest Hits ....(RCA)
Deep In A Dream
Artie Shaw; *This Is Artie Shaw* ....(Bluebird)
Frank Sinatra; *In The Wee Small Hours*............(Capitol)
Deep Purple
Art Tatum; *Group Masterpieces-#2* ....(Pablo)
Masterpieces ....(MCA)
Solo Masterpieces-#3 ....(Pablo)
Johnny Mathis; *First 25 Years-Silver Anniversary Album* ....(Columbia)
Nino Tempo & April Stevens; *Hit Singles-1958-1977-C* ....(Atlantic)
Sarah Vaughan; *After Hours* ....(Sony Music Special Prod.)
Divine Sarah Vaughan-Columbia Years-1949-1953 ....(Columbia)
Desert Rose
Sting; *Brand New Day*........................(A&M)
Detroit City
Ace Cannon; *Golden Favorites*..................(Ranwood)

Bill Anderson; *Best Of Bill Anderson* . . . . (Curb)
Bobby Bare; *Nipper's Greatest Hits Of The '60s-#2-C* . . . . (RCA)
  This Is Bobby Bare . . . . (RCA)
Chet Atkins; *Country Gems* . . . . (Pair)
Flatt & Scruggs; *20 All-Time Great Recordings* . . . . (Columbia)
Hank Williams, Jr.; *Live At Cobo Hall Detroit* . . . . (Polydor)
  Standing In The Shadows . . . . (Polydor)
Mel Tillis; *Best Of Mel Tillis* . . . . (MCA)
  Live At The Sam Houston Coliseum . . . . (MGM)
Solomon Burke; *Home In Your Heart-Best Of Solomon Burke* . . . . (Rhino)

Detroit Snackbar Dreamer
Edgar Froese; *Stuntman* . . . . (Blue Plate)

Did You Ever See A Dream Walking
Bing Crosby; *Crosby Classics* . . . . (Columbia)
Hal Kemp & Skinnay Ennis; *The Uncollected Hal Kemp-#2 & #3* . . . (Hindsight)

Dixie Dreamin'
Atlanta; *Pictures* . . . . (MCA)

Do You Ever Dream Of Vienna
Original Cast; *Little Mary Sunshine* . . . . (Out Of Print)

Dolphin Dreams
Lee Ritenour; *Captain Fingers* . . . . (Epic)
  Lee Ritenour-Collection . . . . (GRP)
  On The Line . . . . (GRP)

Don't Dream It's Over
Crowded House; *Crowded House* . . . . (Capitol)
Neil Finn; *Diana, Princess Of Wales-Tribute-C* . . . . (Columbia)

Don't Fall In Love With A Dreamer
Kenny Rogers; *Kenny Rogers-Twenty Greatest Hits* . . . . (EMI)
Kenny Rogers & Kim Carnes; *Gideon* . . . . (United Artists)
  Kenny Rogers' Greatest Hits . . . . (EMI)

Don't Make Me Dream About You
Chris Isaak; *Heart Shaped World* . . . . (Reprise)

Down The River Of Golden Dreams
Mom & Dads; *Down The River Of Golden Dreams* . . . . (Crescendo)
Slim Whitman; *Home On The Range* . . . . (United Artists)

Dream
Frank Sinatra; *Best Of The Columbia Years-1943-1952* . . . . (Columbia)
  Round #1 . . . . (Capitol)

Dream A Little Dream Of Me
Ella Fitzgerald; *All That Jazz* . . . . (Pablo)
Mama Cass; *Mama's Big Ones-Her Greatest Hits* . . . . (MCA)
Mama Cass With The Mamas & The Papas; *Best Of The Mamas & The*
  Papas . . . . (MCA)
  Mamas & The Papas-20 Golden Hits . . . . (MCA)
Wayne King & His Orchestra; *78-#22643* . . . . (Victor)

Dream About You
Stevie B; *Funky Melody* . . . . (Emporia West/Thump)

Dream All Day
Posies; *Frosting On The Beater* . . . . (David Geffen Co.)

Dream Baby (How Long Must I Dream)
Lacy J. Dalton; *Dream Baby* . . . . (Columbia)
  Greatest Country Hits Of The '80s-1983-C . . . . (Columbia)
  Lacy J. Dalton's Greatest Hits . . . . (Columbia)
Roy Orbison; *For The Lonely: 18 Greatest Hits* . . . . (Rhino)
  For The Lonely: A Roy Orbison Anthology 1959-1965 . . . . (Rhino)
  In Dreams-Greatest Hits . . . . (Orbison)
  Roy Orbison's All-Time Greatest Hits-#1 & 2 . . . . (Monument)

Dream Dancing
Ella Fitzgerald; *Dream Dancing* . . . . (Pablo)

Dream Gerrard
Traffic; *When The Eagle Flies* . . . . (Asylum)

Dream Girl
Stephen Bishop; *ST/Animal House* . . . . (MCA)

Dream Goes On Forever
Todd Rundgren; *Back To The Bars* . . . . (Rhino)
  ST/Rock 'N' Roll High School . . . . (Sire)
  Todd . . . . (Rhino)
  Todd Rundgren-Anthology 1968-1985 . . . . (Rhino)

Dream Home In New Zealand
English Beat; *Wha'ppen* . . . . (I.R.S.)

Dream In June
Tom Harrell; *Sail Away* . . . . (Contemporary)

Dream Is A Wish Your Heart Makes
Barbara Cook; *Disney Album* . . . . (Disney)
Linda Ronstadt; *Disney's Music From The Park-C* . . . . (Disney)
  Music Of Disney's Cinderella-C . . . . (Disney)
Michael Bolton; *Simply Mad About The Mouse-C* . . . . (Columbia)
Original Soundtrack; *ST/Cinderella* . . . . (Disney)

Dream Is Over
Van Halen; *For Unlawful Carnal Knowledge* . . . . (Warner Bros.)

Dream Is Still Alive
Wilson Phillips; *Wilson Phillips* . . . . (SBK)

Dream Lady
Bread; *Baby I'm-A Want You* . . . . (Elektra)
  Best Of Bread-#2 . . . . (Elektra)

Dream Lover
Bobby Darin; *Bobby Darin-At The Copa* . . . . (Bainbridge)
  The Bobby Darin Story . . . . (Atlantic)
Dion; *Runaround Sue* . . . . (Collectables)

Marshall Tucker Band; *Best Of Country Rock-C* . . . . (K-Tel)
  Together Forever . . . . (AJK Music)
Regina Belle; *Stay With Me* . . . . (Columbia)
Tanya Tucker & Glen Campbell; *Best Of Tanya Tucker* . . . . (MCA)

Dream Maker
Rick James; *Come Get It!* . . . . (Motown)

Dream Merchant
New Birth; *Smooth Grooves-A Sensual Collection-#5-C* . . . . (Rhino)

Dream Of Life
Billie Holiday; *Billie Holiday* . . . . (Columbia)
  The Billie Holiday Story-#1 . . . . (Columbia)
Carmen McRae; *Greatest Of Carmen McRae* . . . . (MCA)

Dream Of Life
Patti Smith; *Dream Of Life* . . . . (Arista)

Dream Of Me
Vern Gosdin; *Today My World Slipped Away* . . . . (AMI)

Dream Of The Blue Turtles
Sting; *Dream Of The Blue Turtles* . . . . (A&M)

Dream On
Oak Ridge Boys; *Oak Ridge Boys' Greatest Hits* . . . . (MCA)
  Oak Ridge Boys Have Arrived . . . . (MCA)

Dream On
Depeche Mode; *Exciter* . . . . (Mute/Reprise)

Dream On
Aerosmith; *Aerosmith* . . . . (Columbia)
  Aerosmith-Classics Live . . . . (Columbia)
  Aerosmith's Greatest Hits . . . . (Columbia)
  Live! Bootleg . . . . (Columbia)

Dream On
Mission U.K.; *Children* . . . . (Mercury)

Dream On
Southern Pacific; *Zuma* . . . . (Warner Bros.)

Dream On Dreamer
Brand New Heavies; *Brother Sister* . . . . (Delicious Vinyl)

Dream On Texas Ladies
John Michael Montgomery; *Life's A Dance* . . . . (Atlantic)
  ST/Maverick . . . . (Atlantic)

Dream Police
Cheap Trick; *Dream Police* . . . . (Epic)

Dream River
Mavericks; *Trampoline* . . . . (MCA)

Dream That Can Last
Neil Young & Crazy Horse; *Sleeps With Angels* . . . . (Reprise)

Dream Walkin'
Toby Keith; *Dream Walkin'* . . . . (Mercury)
  Toby Keith's Greatest Hits, Volume One . . . . (Mercury)

Dream Weaver
Gary Wright; *Billboard Top Hits-1976-C* . . . . (Rhino)
  Dream Weaver . . . . (Warner Bros.)

Dream With No Love
Gerald Levert; *ST/Bamboozled* . . . . (Motown)

Dream World
Jerry Butler; *Nothing Says I Love You Like I Love You* . . . . . . (Philadelphia Int'l)

Dreamboat Annie
Heart; *Dreamboat Annie* . . . . (Capitol)
  Heart's Greatest Hits/Live . . . . (Epic)

Dreamer
Supertramp; *Crime Of The Century* . . . . (A&M)
  Paris . . . . (A&M)
  Supertramp-Classics-#9 . . . . (A&M)

Dreamer
Foghat; *Rock & Roll Outlaws* . . . . (Rhino)

Dreamer
Toni Childs; *Union* . . . . (A&M)

Dreamer
Tommy Bolin; *Teaser* . . . . (Columbia)
  The Ultimate Tommy Bolin . . . . (Geffen)

Dreamer
Ozzy Osbourne; *Down To Earth* . . . . (Epic)

Dreamer's Ball
Queen; *Jazz* . . . . (Hollywood)
  Live Killers . . . . (Hollywood)

Dreamin'
Will To Power; *ST/Speed Zone* . . . . (Grudge)
  Will To Power . . . . (Epic)

Dreamin'
Vanessa Williams; *The Right Stuff* . . . . (Wing)

Dreamin'
Johnny Burnette; *Best Of Johnny Burnette-You're Sixteen* . . . . . (Gold Rush)
  Rock Is Dead But It Won't Lie Down-C . . . . (Gold Rush)

Dreamin' Again
Jim Croce; *Life & Times* . . . . (Lifesong)
  Time In A Bottle/Jim Croce's Greatest Love Songs . . . . (Atlantic)

Dreamin' Of You
Celine Dion; *Falling Into You* . . . . (550 Music)

Dreaming
Kate Bush; *Dreaming* . . . . (EMI)
  Whole Story . . . . (EMI)

Dreaming
Cliff Richard; *I'm No Hero* (EMI)
Dreaming
Blondie; *Best Of Blondie* (Chrysalis)
Eat To The Beat (Chrysalis)
Dreaming
Orchestral Manoeuvres In The Dark; *in the dark/the best of OMD* (A&M)
Dreaming A Dream
Crown Heights Affair; *Hustle Hits-C* (De-Lite)
Saturday Night Disco (De-Lite)
Dreaming From The Waist
Who; *By Numbers* (MCA)
Dreaming In Metaphors
Seal; *Seal 2* (Sire)
Dreaming My Dreams With You
Cowboy Junkies; *Trinity Session* (RCA)
Waylon Jennings; *Dreaming My Dreams* (RCA)
Dreaming Of You
Selena; *Dreaming Of You* (EMI Latin)
Dreaming While You Sleep
Genesis; *We Can't Dance* (Atlantic)
Dreaming With My Eyes Open
Clay Walker; *Clay Walker* (Giant)
Dreamland
Joni Mitchell; *Don Juan's Reckless Daughter* (Asylum)
Shadows & Light (Asylum)
Dreamland Express
John Denver; *Dreamland Express* (RCA)
Dreamline
Rush; *Roll The Bones* (Atlantic)
Dreamlover
Mariah Carey; *Music Box* (Columbia)
Dreams
BoDeans; *Outside Looking In* (Slash)
Dreams
Corrs; *Legacy-A Tribute To Fleetwood Mac's Rumours-C* (Lava)
Fleetwood Mac; *25 Years-The Chain* (Warner Bros.)
Fleetwood Mac Live (Warner Bros.)
Fleetwood Mac's Greatest Hits (Warner Bros.)
Rumours (Warner Bros.)
Dreams
Van Halen; *5150* (Warner Bros.)
Dreams
Cranberries; *Everybody Else Is Doing It, So Why Can't We?* (Island)
Dreams
Gabrielle; *Find Your Way* (Go! Discs)
Dreams (I'll Never See)
Allman Brothers Band; *Allman Brothers Band* (Polydor)
An Evening With The Allman Brothers Band-First Set (Epic)
Beginnings (Polydor)
Best Of The Allman Brothers Band (Polydor)
Decade Of Hits-1969-1979 (Polydor)
Gregg Allman Tour (Capricorn)
The Road Goes On Forever, A Collection Of Their Greatest Recordings (Polydor)
Molly Hatchet; *Molly Hatchet* (Epic)
Dreams A Dream
Soul II Soul; *Vol. II-1990-A New Decade* (Virgin)
Dreams Die Hard
Gary Morris; *Gary Morris* (Warner Bros.)
Gary Morris' Greatest Hits-#2 (Warner Bros.)
Dreams Go By
Harry Chapin; *Greatest Stories-Live* (Elektra)
Portrait Gallery (Elektra)
Dreams In America
Luka Bloom; *Riverside* (Reprise)
Dreams Of Mexico
Arlen Roth; *Guitarist* (Rounder)
Dreams Of The Everyday Housewife
Glen Campbell; *Glen Campbell-Classics Collection* (Capitol)
Glen Campbell-Live (Capitol)
Glen Campbell's Greatest Hits (Capitol)
Very Best Of Glen Campbell (Capitol)
Dreams Of Wounded Knee
Bill Miller; *The Red Road* (Warner Western)
Dreamsville
Henry Mancini; *Brass On Ivory* (RCA)
Henry Mancini With Doc Severinsen (RCA)
Peter Gunn (RCA)
This Is Henry Mancini (RCA)
Dreamtime
Daryl Hall; *Three Hearts In The Happy Ending Machine* (RCA)
Stranglers; *Dreamtime* (Epic)
Dreamy Georgiana Moon
Asa Martin; *Dr. Ginger Blue* (Rounder)
Drift Off To Dream
Travis Tritt; *Country Club* (Warner Bros.)
Drinkin' And Dreamin'
Waylon Jennings; *Best Of Waylon Jennings* (RCA)
Essential Waylon Jennings (RCA)
Turn The Page (RCA)
English Dream
Generation X; *Valley Of The Dolls* (Chrysalis)
Eric's Dream
Ken Navarro; *Brighter Days* (Positive)
Every Little Girl's Dream
Lisa Brokop; *Every Little Girl's Dream* (Patriot)
Fall From Grace
Amanda Marshall; *Amanda Marshall* (Epic)
Fast Car
Tracy Chapman; *Tracy Chapman* (Elektra)
Fiction (Dreams In Digital)
Orgy; *Vapor Transmission* (Elementree/Reprise)
Find A Dream
Crosby, Stills & Nash; *After The Storm* (Atlantic)
For Emily, Wherever I May Find Her
Simon & Garfunkel; *Collected Works* (Columbia)
Parsley Sage Rosemary & Thyme (Columbia)
Simon & Garfunkel's Greatest Hits (Columbia)
Gemini Dream
Moody Blues; *Long Distance Voyager* (Polydor)
Voices In The Sky-The Best Of The Moody Blues (Threshold)
Get Outta My Dreams, Get Into My Car
Billy Ocean; *Billy Ocean's Greatest Hits* (Jive)
ST/License To Drive (MCA)
Girl Of My Dreams
Bram Tchaikovsky; *D.I.Y.-#4-UK Pop II-Starry Eyes-1978-1979-C* (Rhino)
Strange Man, Changed Man (Polydor)
Girl Of My Dreams
Dizzy Gillespie & Stan Getz; *Diz & Getz* (Verve)
Girl Of My Dreams
Buddy Clark; *Buddy Clark-16 Most Requested Songs* (Columbia)
Going Away Party
Manhattan Transfer & Willie Nelson & Asleep At The Wheel; *Ride With Bob-C* (DreamWorks/SKG)
Goodnight
Beatles; *The Beatles (White Album)* (Capitol)
Goodnight Irene
Jim Reeves; *Jim Reeves-Pure Gold* (RCA)
Johnny Cash; *Rough Cut King Of Country Music* (Sun)
The Man-The World-His Music (Sun)
Ry Cooder; *Chicken Skin Music* (Reprise)
Weavers; *Best Of The Weavers* (MCA)
Weavers At Carnegie Hall (Vanguard)
Weavers' Greatest Hits (Vanguard)
Goodnight My Love (Pleasant Dreams)
Fleetwoods; *Best Of The Fleetwoods* (Rhino)
Fleetwoods' Greatest Hits (CEMA Special Prod.)
Jesse Belvin; *Collectables Presents The History Of Rock-#9-C* (Collectables)
Oldies But Goodies-#2-C (Original Sound)
Goodnight My Someone
Shirley Jones; *ST/The Music Man* (Warner Bros.)
Green Green Grass Of Home
Burl Ives; *Best Of Burl Ives-#2* (MCA)
Elvis Presley; *Elvis Presley Today* (RCA)
Our Memories Of Elvis, Volume 2 (RCA)
George Jones; *20 Golden Pieces Of George Jones* (Bulldog)
Johnny Cash; *Johnny Cash-16 Biggest Hits-#2* (Legacy)
Tom Jones; *Country Side Of Tom Jones* (London)
Things That Matter Most To Me (Mercury)
Tom Jones-London Collector-Greatest Hits (London)
Had A Dream (Sleeping With The Enemy)
Roger Hodgson; *In The Eye Of The Storm* (A&M)
Havana Daydreamin'
Jimmy Buffett; *Havana Daydreamin'* (MCA)
You Had To Be There (MCA)
He Will, She Knows
Kenny Rogers; *There You Go Again* (Dreamcatcher)
Heartbreaker
Pat Benatar; *Best Shots* (Chrysalis)
In The Heat Of The Night (Chrysalis)
Live From Earth (Chrysalis)
Heirloom
Bjork; *Vespertine* (Elektra)
Help You Dream
Blasters; *Blasters-Collection* (Slash)
Hard Line (Slash)
High Hopes And Empty Pockets
McBride & The Ride; *McBride & The Ride* (MCA)
Higher
Creed; *Human Clay* (Wind-up)
Hippie Dream
Neil Young; *Landing On Water* (Geffen)
Lucky Thirteen (Geffen)
Hold On Tight
Electric Light Orchestra; *Exposition* (Epic)

Time ....(Jet)
Hold On To Your Dream
Stevie Wonder; *Song Review-A Greatest Hits Collection* ....(Motown)
ST/The Adventures Of Pinocchio ....(London)
Hollywood Dream
James Gang; *Jesse Come Home*................................(Atco)
Hollywood Dream
Thunderclap Newman; *Hollywood Dream* .... (MCA)
Hollywood Dream
Steve Miller Band; *Italian X-Rays*.............................(Capitol)
Hollywood Dreaming
Father's Children; *Father's Children* ....(Mercury)
House Un-American Blues Activity Dream
Mimi & Richard Farina; *Best Of Mimi & Richard Farina*.........(Vanguard)
Memories ....(Vanguard)
Reflections In A Crystal Wind ....(Vanguard)
How Can We Hang Onto A Dream
Tim Hardin; *Memorial Album* .... (Polydor)
I Can Dream About You
Dan Hartman; *I Can Dream About You* .... (MCA)
Soundtrack Smashes-'80s & More-C .... (MCA)
ST/Streets Of Fire .... (MCA)
I Can Dream, Can't I?
Andrews Sisters; *Best Of The Andrews Sisters* .... (MCA)
I Don't Sleep, I Dream
R.E.M.; *Monster* .... (Warner Bros.)
I Dream Of Ice Cream
Bananas In Pajamas; *Bumping And A-Jumping*..................(Capitol)
I Dream Of Jeanie With Light Brown Hair
Al Jolson; *The Al Jolson Story-#5* .... (MCA)
Joan Baez; *Diamonds & Rust* ....(A&M)
Mormon Tabernacle Choir; *Beautiful Dreamer* ....(Columbia)
Mormon Tabernacle Choir's Greatest Hits-#3................(Columbia)
Old Beloved Songs ....(Columbia)
I Dream Of Women Like You
Ronnie Dove; *Country Boy's Heart* .... (Epic)
Older Women & Other Greatest Hits .... (Epic)
I Dreamed A Dream
Aretha Franklin; *Aretha Franklin's Greatest Hits-1980-1994* .... (Arista)
Michael Crawford; *With Love* .... (Atlantic)
Original Broadway Cast; *Les Miserables* .... (Geffen)
Patti LuPone; *Patti LuPone Live (Highlights)* .... (RCA Victor)
I Dreamed About Mama Last Night
Hank Williams; *Complete Hank Williams*.....................(Mercury)
Johnny Cash; *Timeless: Hank Williams Tribute-C* ..... (Lost Highway/IDJMG)
I Dreamed I Saw St. Augustine
Bob Dylan; *John Wesley Harding* ....(Columbia)
Joan Baez; *Any Day Now: Songs Of Bob Dylan*.................(Vanguard)
I Dreamed Of A Hillbilly Heaven
Tex Ritter; *An American Legend* ....(Capitol)
Best Of Tex Ritter ....(Capitol)
Hillbilly Heaven ....(Capitol)
Opry Legends-Tex Ritter.................................(Capitol)
I Found A Dream
Bob Wills; *Bob Wills-Anthology* .... (Sony Music Special Prod.)
I Got Dreams
Steve Wariner; *I Got Dreams* .... (MCA)
I Guess I Was Dreaming
Kingsmen; *Nuggets-#8-Acid Rock-C*..........................(Rhino)
I Had A Dream
John Sebastian; *ST/Woodstock* .... (Atlantic)
I Had A Dream
Paul Revere And The Raiders; *Legend Of Paul Revere*............. (Legacy)
I Had A Dream Last Night
Buddy Guy; *Best Of The Chicago Blues-C* ....(Vanguard)
This Is Buddy Guy.....................................(Vanguard)
I Had The Craziest Dream
Frank Sinatra; *Trilogy: Pasts, Present, Future* ....(Reprise)
I Had Too Much To Dream (Last Night)
Electric Prunes; *Even More Nuggets-C*........................(Rhino)
Nuggets-#1-The Hits-C .... (Rhino)
Summer Of Love-#1-C .... (Rhino)
I Have Dreamed
Barbra Streisand; *The Broadway Album* ....(Columbia)
Original Broadway Cast; *The King And I* .... (RCA Victor)
Original Cast; *The King And I* .... (MCA)
I Never Dreamed
Lynyrd Skynyrd; *Best Of The Rest Of Lynyrd Skynyrd* .... (MCA)
Street Survivors .... (MCA)
I Still Believe
Mariah Carey; *Mariah Carey-#1's* ....(Columbia)
MTV Unplugged-Mariah Carey...........................(Columbia)
I Touched A Dream
Dells; *Ear Candy-#2-C* .... (20th Century Fox)
I Touched A Dream....................... (20th Century Fox)
I Was Born A Dreamer
Mickey Gilley; *Live At Gilley's*..............................(Epic)
ST/Tough Enough....................................... (Liberty)

I Wish I Was Still In Your Dreams
Conway Twitty; *Still In Your Dreams* .... (MCA)
If I Can Dream
Elvis Presley; *Elvis-A Legendary Performer, Volume 2*............... (RCA)
The Great Performances................................. (RCA)
Worldwide 50 Gold Award Hits, Vol. 1, Parts 1 & 2 .... (RCA)
If My Heart Had Wings
Faith Hill; *Breathe* .... (Warner Bros.)
If There Were No Dreams
Neil Diamond; *Lovescape* ....(Columbia)
If You Are But A Dream
Frank Sinatra; *Portrait Of Sinatra-Columbia Classics* ....(Legacy)
Sarah Vaughan; *Slightly Classical* ....(Roulette)
I'll See You In My Dreams
Doris Day; *At The Movies* ....(Columbia)
Doris Day & Danny Thomas; *Calamity Jane/I'll See You In My
Dreams* .... (Sony Music Special Prod.)
I'll Tennessee You In My Dreams
Tanya Tucker; *Love Me Like You Used To* ....(Liberty)
I'm Dreamin'
Christopher Williams; *ST/New Jack City* .... (Giant)
I'm Getting Tired So I Can Sleep
Dinah Shore; *The Eddie Cantor Radio Show-1942-1943*........ (Original Cast)
Impossible Dream
Andy Williams; *Andy Williams' Greatest Hits-#2*...............(Columbia)
Andy Williams-16 Most Requested Songs ....(Legacy)
Impossible Dream ....(Columbia)
Ed Ames; *Best Of Ed Ames* .... (RCA)
Ed Ames-Pure Gold.................................... (RCA)
Impossible Dream .... (RCA)
This Is Ed Ames .... (RCA)
Jack Jones; *Best Of Jack Jones* .... (MCA)
Kate Smith; *Best Of Kate Smith* .... (RCA)
Kate Smith-Legendary Performer .... (RCA)
Luther Vandross; *Songs* ....(Epic)
Original London Cast; *Man Of La Mancha* .... (MCA)
Robert Goulet; *Robert Goulet's Greatest Hits* ....(Columbia)
In A Daydream
Freddy Jones Band; *Waiting For The Night* ....(Capricorn)
In City Dreams
Robin Trower; *In City Dreams*........................... (Chrysalis)
In Dreams
Roy Orbison; *For The Lonely: A Roy Orbison Anthology 1959-1965* ....(Rhino)
In Dreams-Greatest Hits .... (Orbison)
In My Dreams
REO Speedwagon; *Life As We Know It* .... (Epic)
REO Speedwagon-The Hits .... (Epic)
In My Dreams
Dokken; *Beast From The East* ....(Elektra)
Under Lock & Key.....................................(Elektra)
In My Dreams
Emmylou Harris; *White Shoes* .... (Warner Bros.)
In My Dreams
Crosby, Stills & Nash; *CSN* .... (Atlantic)
In My Dreams
Judds; *Love Can Build A Bridge* .... (MCA)
In My Dreams
Big Audio Dynamite II; *The Globe* ....(Columbia)
In My Dreams
Tracie Spencer; *Tracie Spencer* ....(Capitol)
In This Life
Collin Raye; *In This Life* .... (Epic)
In Your Wildest Dreams
Tina Turner & Barry White; *Wildest Dreams*.....................(Virgin)
It Takes Two
Marvin Gaye & Kim Weston; *Hitsville USA-The Motown Singles Collection-
1959-1971-C* ....(Motown)
It's Been A Long, Long Time
Bing Crosby; *Best Of Bing Crosby*........................... (MCA)
Harry James & His Orchestra; *Words & Music Of World
War II-C*...(Columbia)
Harry James & Kitty Kallen; *Best Of The Big Bands-C* ....(Columbia)
Jan Garber & His Orchestra; *Best Of Jan Garber*................. (MCA)
Louis Armstrong; *Hello Dolly! & Other Hits*................... (MCA)
It's Good To Be King
Tom Petty; *Wildflowers* .... (Warner Bros.)
It's Only Make Believe
Conway Twitty; *Conway Twitty-Number Ones-#1* ....(Liberty)
Conway Twitty's Greatest Hits-#2 ....(MCA)
Conway's #1 Classics-#2 .... (Warner Bros.)
Very Best Of Conway Twitty ....(MCA)
Glen Campbell; *Very Best Of Glen Campbell* ....(Capitol)
I've Got Dreams To Remember
Delbert McClinton; *Live From Austin* .... (Alligator)
Etta James; *Sticking To My Guns* ....(Island)
Otis Redding; *The Otis Redding Story* .... (Atlantic)
Just A Country Dream
Eric Andersen; *Best Of Eric Andersen* ....(Vanguard)

Country Dream . . . . (Vanguard)
Just A Dream
  Jimmy Clanton; *Good Old Rock & Roll-C* . . . . (International Mktg. Group)
  Lovin' '50s-C . . . . (Priority)
  Super Oldies Of The '50s-#1-C . . . .(Audio Fidelity)
Just Another Day In Paradise
  Phil Vassar; *Phil Vassar* . . . . (Arista)
Just Another Dream
  Cathy Dennis; *Move To This* . . . . (Polydor)
Keep On Dreamin'
  Alabama; *My Home's In Alabama* . . . . (RCA)
Kiss To Build A Dream On
  Louis Armstrong; *Best Of Louis Armstrong* . . . .(MCA)
  Essential Louis Armstrong . . . . (Vanguard)
  Hello Dolly! & Other Hits . . . .(MCA)
L.A. Dreams
  Charlie; *Lines* . . . .(Janus)
Land Of Hope And Dreams
  Bruce Springsteen & The E Street Band; *God Bless America-C* . . . . . (Columbia)
  Live In New York City . . . . (Columbia)
Last Night I Had A Dream
  Randy Newman; *Randy Newman/Live* . . . . (Warner Archives)
  Sail Away . . . . (Reprise)
Last Night I Had The Strangest Dream
  Simon & Garfunkel; *Collected Works* . . . . (Columbia)
  Wednesday Morning 3 A.M. . . . . (Columbia)
Lazarus Heart
  Sting; *...Nothing Like The Sun* . . . . (A&M)
Life Is But A Dream
  Harptones; *Echoes Of A Rock Era-The Harptones* . . . . (Roulette)
  ST/Goodfellas . . . . (Atlantic)
  Super Oldies Of The '50s-#4-C . . . .(Audio Fidelity)
Like Dreamers Do
  Beatles; *The Beatles-Anthology-#1* . . . . (Capitol)
Little Dreamer
  Van Halen; *Van Halen* . . . .(Warner Bros.)
Living In A Dream
  Band; *Islands* . . . . (Capitol)
  The Band-Anthology-#2 . . . . (Capitol)
Living In A Dream
  Arc Angels; *Arc Angels* . . . . (David Geffen Co.)
Living In A Dream
  Sea Level; *On The Edge* . . . . (Capricorn)
Long Ago And Far Away
  Erroll Garner; *Long Ago And Far Away* . . . . (Columbia)
  Glenn Miller; *Glenn Miller-A Legendary Performer-#1 & 2* . . . . (Bluebird)
  Helen Forrest & Dick Haymes; *American Songbook Series-*
    Jerome Kern . . . .(Smithsonian Collection)
  Jo Stafford; *Capitol Collectors Series-Jo Stafford* . . . . (Capitol)
  International Hits . . . . (Corinthian)
  Jukebox Saturday Night-Great Vocal Hits-C . . . . (Capitol)
  Songs That Got Us Through WWII-C . . . . (Rhino)
  ST/Bugsy . . . .(Epic)
  Johnny Mathis; *Hollywood Musicals* . . . . (Columbia)
  Mantovani; *More Golden Hits* . . . . (London)
  Perry Como; *Always In My Heart-Classic Songs Of World War II-#2* . . . . (RCA)
  Rosemary Clooney; *Rosemary Clooney Sings The Lyrics Of Ira*
    Gershwin . . . .(Concord Jazz)
Long Hard Road (Sharecropper's Dream)
  Nitty Gritty Dirt Band; *Live Two Five* . . . . (Capitol)
  Plain Dirt Fashion . . . .(Warner Bros.)
  Twenty Years Of Dirt-Best Of The Nitty Gritty Dirt Band . . . . .(Warner Bros.)
Lookin' Out My Back Door
  Creedence Clearwater Revival; *1970* . . . . (Fantasy)
  Cosmo's Factory . . . . (Fantasy)
  Creedence Clearwater Revival-Chronicle . . . . (Fantasy)
  Creedence Country . . . . (Fantasy)
  More Creedence Gold . . . . (Fantasy)
Lost In A Dream
  REO Speedwagon; *A Decade Of Rock And Roll 1970 To 1980* . . . .(Epic)
  Lost In A Dream . . . .(Epic)
Lost In A Dream
  Buster Brown; *New King Of The Blues* . . . . (Collectables)
Lost In A Dream
  Johnny Otis; *Roots Of Rock & Roll* . . . . (Savoy)
Lullaby
  Take 6; *Join The Band-C* . . . . (Reprise)
  Love Shouldn't Hurt-C . . . . (Qwest)
Maggie's Dream
  Don Williams; *Cafe Carolina* . . . .(MCA)
  Country Classics-#4-1984-1985-C . . . . (Universal)
Mary Lou
  Bruce Springsteen; *Tracks* . . . . (Columbia)
Me And Those Dreamin' Eyes Of Mine
  D'Angelo; *Brown Sugar* . . . .(EMI)
Michelangelo
  Emmylou Harris; *Red Dirt Girl* . . . . (Nonesuch)
Midnight Dreamer
  Journey; *Look Into The Future* . . . . (Columbia)

Mister Sandman
  Chordettes; *Best Of The Chordettes* . . . . (Rhino)
  Emmylou Harris; *Evangeline* . . . . (Warner Bros.)
  Profile II-The Best Of Emmylou Harris . . . . (Warner Bros.)
Moonage Daydream
  David Bowie; *David Live* . . . . (Rykodisc)
  Man Who Sold The World . . . . (Rykodisc)
  Rise & Fall Of Ziggy Stardust And The Spiders From Mars . . . . . . (Rykodisc)
  Sound + Vision . . . . (Rykodisc)
  ST/Ziggy Stardust-The Motion Picture . . . . (Rykodisc)
Morning Glory
  Oasis; *(What's The Story) Morning Glory* . . . . (Epic)
Mothers Dream
  Candlebox; *Candlebox* . . . . (Maverick)
Mr. Dream Merchant
  Jerry Butler; *Best Of Jerry Butler* . . . . (Rhino)
  Soul Shots-#2-The "In" Crowd-Sweet Soul-C . . . . (Rhino)
Music In Dreamland
  Be Bop Deluxe; *Best Of And The Rest Of Be Bop Deluxe* . . . . (Capitol)
  Best Of Be Bop Deluxe-Raiding The Divine Archive . . . . (Capitol)
  Futurama . . . .(Harvest)
My Elusive Dreams
  Bobby Vinton; *Autumn Memories* . . . . (Epic)
  Bobby Vinton's All-Time Greatest Hits . . . . (Epic)
  Charlie Rich; *Charlie Rich-16 Biggest Hits* . . . . (Legacy)
  Charlie Rich's Greatest Hits . . . . (Epic)
  Charlie Rich-Super Hits . . . . (Epic)
  David Houston & Tammy Wynette; *Best Of David*
    Houston . . . .(Collector's Choice)
  Billboard Top Country Hits-1967-C . . . . (Rhino)
  Tammy Wynette's Greatest Hits . . . . (Epic)
My Favorite Memory
  Merle Haggard; *For The Record: Merle Haggard-43 Legendary Hits* . . . .(BNA)
My Heroes Have Always Been Cowboys
  Willie Nelson; *All Time Legends Of Country Music-C* . . . . (Legacy)
  Cowboy Super Hits-C . . . . (Columbia)
  Greatest Country Hits Of The '80s-1980-C . . . . (Columbia)
  Greatest Hits (& Some That Will Be) . . . . (Columbia)
  ST/My Heroes Have Always Been Cowboys . . . . (RCA)
  ST/The Electric Horseman . . . . (Columbia)
My Reverie
  Ella Fitzgerald; *Clap Hands, Here Comes Charlie* . . . . (Verve)
  Ray Conniff; *Concert In Rhythm-#1* . . . . (Columbia)
  Sarah Vaughan; *Sarah Slightly Classical* . . . . (Rounder)
Neon Moon
  Brooks & Dunn; *Brand New Man* . . . . (Arista)
Never Dreamed You'd Leave In Summer
  Joan Baez; *Best Of Joan Baez* . . . . (A&M)
  Diamonds & Rust . . . . (A&M)
  Joan Baez-Classics-#8 . . . . (A&M)
  Stevie Wonder; *Looking Back* . . . . (Motown)
  Stevie Wonder-20 Classic Hits . . . . (Motown)
  Stevie Wonder's Greatest Hits-#2 . . . . (Motown)
  Where I'm Coming From . . . . (Motown)
Never Had A Dream Come True
  Stevie Wonder; *Signed Sealed & Delivered* . . . . (Motown)
  Stevie Wonder's Greatest Hits-#2 . . . . (Motown)
Never Had A Dream Come True
  S Club 7; *Now That's What I Call Music!-#7-C* . . . .(Virgin)
  S Club 7 . . . . (A&M)
New Gold Dream
  Simple Minds; *New Gold Dream* . . . . (A&M)
  Simple Minds Live: In The City Of Light . . . . (A&M)
New Gold Dream
  Utah Saints; *Utah Saints* . . . .(London)
Nickel Dreams
  Nanci Griffith; *Lone Star State Of Mind* . . . . (MCA)
Nightmare
  Artie Shaw; *Begin The Beguine* . . . . (Bluebird)
  Best Of The Big Bands-C . . . . (Columbia)
Nightmare
  Black Sabbath; *Eternal Idol* . . . . (Warner Bros.)
Nightmare
  Slaughterhouse; *Face Reality* . . . . (Metal Blade)
Nightmare
  Eddie Money; *Life For The Taking* . . . . (Columbia)
Nightmare
  Stevie Nicks; *Rock A Little* . . . .(Modern)
Nightmares
  A Flock Of Seagulls; *Best Of A Flock Of Seagulls* . . . .(Jive)
  Listen . . . .(Jive)
Nightmares
  J. Geils Band; *Nightmares* . . . .(Atlantic)
Nightmares
  Omen; *Nightmares* . . . . (Metal Blade)
Nightmares
  Dana Dane; *Rap Hall Of Fame-C* . . . . (K-Tel)
  With Fame . . . .(Profile)

Nightmares
Violent Femmes; *Violent Femmes 3* . . . . (Slash)
Number 9 Dream
John Lennon; *Lennon* . . . . (Capitol)
　The John Lennon Collection . . . . (Capitol)
　Walls And Bridges . . . . (Capitol)
John Lennon/Plastic Ono Band; *Shaved Fish* . . . . (Capitol)
Ocean Of Thoughts & Dreams
Dramatics; *Shake It Well* . . . . (MCA)
Oh, Baby Mine (I Get So Lonely)
Chet Atkins; *Tennessee Guitar Man* . . . . (Pair)
Four Knights; *Those Wonderful Years: Mr. Sandman-C* . . . . . (JCI Assoc. Labels)
Oklahoma Heartaches & California Dreams
Kris Carpenter; *45-#203* . . . . (Door Knob)
One Of Those Dreams
Michael Stanley Band; *MSB* . . . . (EMI)
One Summer Dream
Electric Light Orchestra; *Afterglow* . . . . (Epic)
　Face The Music . . . . (Jet)
Only A Dream In Rio
James Taylor; *That's Why I'm Here* . . . . (Columbia)
Only In America
Jay & The Americans; *Come A Little Bit Closer-Best Of Jay & The Americans* . . . . (Gold Rush)
　Jay & The Americans' All-Time Greatest Hits . . . . (Rhino)
Only In My Dreams
Debbie Gibson; *Out Of The Blue* . . . . (Atlantic)
Out Of My Dreams
Original Broadway Cast; *Oklahoma!* . . . . (RCA)
Original Cast; *Oklahoma!* . . . . (MCA)
Paddy Ryan's Dream
Matt Molloy; *Stony Steps* . . . . (Green Linnet)
Paper Sun
Def Leppard; *Euphoria* . . . . (Mercury)
Patriot's Dream
Arlo Guthrie; *Amigo* . . . . (Koch International)
Gordon Lightfoot; *Don Quixote* . . . . (Warner Archives)
Pilate's Dream
Original London Cast; *Jesus Christ Superstar* . . . . (MCA)
Pinch Me
Barenaked Ladies; *Maroon* . . . . (Reprise)
　Totally Hits-#3-C . . . . (Atlantic)
Pipe Dreams
Asleep At The Wheel; *Collision Course* . . . . (Capitol)
Planet Of My Dreams
Frank Zappa; *Them Or Us* . . . . (Rykodisc)
Porcelain
Moby; *Play* . . . . (V2)
　ST/Playing By Heart . . . . (Capitol)
　ST/The Beach . . . . (Sire)
Promised Land
Bruce Springsteen; *Darkness On The Edge Of Town* . . . . (Columbia)
Bruce Springsteen & The E Street Band; *Bruce Springsteen & The E Street Band Live/1975-85* . . . . (Legacy)
Psychobabble
Alan Parsons Project; *Best Of The Alan Parsons Project* . . . . (Arista)
　Eye In The Sky . . . . (Arista)
Puppy Song
Nilsson; *Harry* . . . . (Dunhill Compact Classics)
　ST/You've Got Mail . . . . (Atlantic)
Put Your Dreams Away (For Another Day)
Frank Sinatra; *Best Of The Columbia Years-1943-1952* . . . . (Columbia)
　Frank Sinatra-16 Most Requested Songs . . . . (Columbia)
　Sinatra: A Man And His Music . . . . (Reprise)
　The Capitol Years . . . . (Capitol)
Mickey Gilley; *Put Your Dreams Away* . . . . (Epic)
　Ten Years Of Hits . . . . (Epic)
Rachel's Dream
Benny Goodman; *I Like Jazz-Essence Of Benny Goodman* . . . (Columbia)
　Yale Recordings-#5-Private Collection . . . . (Musicmasters)
Radio Dream Girl
Roger Voudouris; *Radio Dream Girl* . . . . (Warner Bros.)
Rainbow Connection
Muppets with Kermit The Frog; *45-#3610* . . . . (Atlantic)
Rainy Day, Dream Away
Jimi Hendrix Experience; *Electric Ladyland* . . . . (Reprise)
Refried Dreams
Tim McGraw; *Not A Moment Too Soon* . . . . (Curb)
Remember (Christmas)
Nilsson; *Son Of Schmilsson* . . . . (RCA)
Rendezvous
Bruce Springsteen; *Tracks* . . . . (Columbia)
Gary U.S. Bonds; *Best Of Gary U.S. Bonds* . . . (EMI Legends Of Rock 'N' Roll)
Greg Kihn; *Kihnsolidation-Best Of Greg Kihn* . . . . (Rhino)
Greg Kihn Band; *Cover Me (Bruce Springsteen Tribute)-C* . . . . . (Rhino)
Rest Of The Dream
John Hiatt; *Stolen Moments* . . . . (A&M)
Nitty Gritty Dirt Band; *Rest Of The Dream* . . . . (MCA)

Restless Nights
Bruce Springsteen; *Tracks* . . . . (Columbia)
Rocking Chairs; *One Step Up/Two Steps Back-The Songs Of Bruce Springsteen-C* . . . . (Right Stuff)
Riding With Private Malone
David Ball; *Amigo* . . . . (Razor & Tie)
River Of Dreams
Billy Joel; *River Of Dreams* . . . . (Columbia)
Rock And Roll Dreams Come Through
Meat Loaf; *Bat Out Of Hell II: Back Into Hell* . . . . (MCA)
Rocks Off
Rolling Stones; *Exile On Main Street* . . . . (Virgin)
　Let There Be Drums!-#3-The '70s-C . . . . (Rhino)
Roll On Mississippi
Charley Pride; *Charley Pride's Greatest Hits* . . . . (RCA)
Row, Row, Row Your Boat
Bobby Darin/Johnny Mercer/Billy May Orchestra; *Two Of A Kind* . . . . (Atlantic)
Original Soundtrack; *Children's Favorites* . . . . (Kid Rhino/Rhino 4 Kids)
Spike Jones & His City Slickers; *King Of Corn* . . . . (Glendale)
Runnin' Down A Dream
Tom Petty; *Full Moon Fever* . . . . (MCA)
San Francisco Days
Chris Isaak; *San Francisco Days* . . . . (Reprise)
Scene From A Night's Dream
Genesis; *And Then There Were Three* . . . . (Atlantic)
Send Me The Pillow You Dream On
Browns; *45-#7804* . . . . (RCA)
Dwight Yoakam; *Buenas Noches From A Lonely Room* . . . . (Reprise)
Hank Locklin; *Hank Locklin-20 Golden Souvenirs* . . . . (RCA)
　Nipper's Greatest Hits Of The '50s-#1-C . . . . (RCA)
　Please Help Me I'm Falling . . . . (Collectables)
　Stars Of The Grand Ole Opry-1926-1974-C . . . . (RCA)
Johnny Tillotson; *Golden Classics-Johnny Tillotson* . . . . . . (Collectables)
Willie Nelson & Hank Snow; *Brand On My Heart* . . . . (Columbia)
Sewer Pipe Dream
Close Lobsters; *Foxheads Stalk This Land* . . . . (Enigma)
Sex And Candy
Marcy Playground; *Marcy Playground* . . . . (Capitol)
　Now That's What I Call Music!-#1-C . . . . (Virgin)
Shadow Dream Song
Tom Rush; *Classic Rush* . . . . (Elektra)
　The Circle Game . . . . (Elektra)
Shattered Dreams
Johnny Hates Jazz; *Turn Back The Clock* . . . . (Virgin)
Lowell Fulsom; *Blues Around Midnight* . . . . (Flair)
Sh-Boom
Chords; *Atlantic Rhythm & Blues 1947-1974-#2 (1952-1955)-C* . . . (Atlantic)
Crew-Cuts; *Partytime '50s-C* . . . . (Priority)
Stan Freberg; *Capitol Collectors Series-Stan Freberg* . . . . . . (Capitol)
She Dreams
Mark Chesnutt; *What A Way To Live* . . . . (Decca)
Ship Of Dreams
Nazareth; *Malice In Wonderland* . . . . (A&M)
Silver Dreams
Babys; *Broken Heart* . . . . (Chrysalis)
Simple Man Simple Dream
John David Souther; *Black Rose* . . . . (Asylum)
Linda Ronstadt; *Simple Dreams* . . . . (Asylum)
Singing In My Sleep
Semisonic; *Feeling Strangely Fine* . . . . (MCA)
Sleep
Little Willie John; *Best Of Little Willie John-Fever* . . . . (Rhino)
Sleep To Dream
Fiona Apple; *Tidal* . . . . (Clean Slate/Work)
Sleepwalker
Wallflowers; *Breach* . . . . (Interscope)
Smoke Dreams (Chesterfield Supper Club)
Benny Goodman; *Complete Benny Goodman-#3* . . . . (RCA)
　This Is Benny Goodman-#2 . . . . (RCA)
Mildred Bailey; *Her Greatest* . . . . (Columbia)
Someone Else's Dream
Faith Hill; *It Matters To Me* . . . . (Warner Bros.)
Somewhere Out There
James Ingram & Linda Ronstadt; *The Power Of Great Music* . . . (Warner Bros.)
Linda Ronstadt & James Ingram; *ST/An American Tail* . . . . . . (MCA)
Spanish Pipedream
John Prine; *John Prine* . . . . (Atlantic)
Straight Back
Fleetwood Mac; *Mirage* . . . . (Warner Bros.)
Street Of Dreams
Ella Fitzgerald; *Best Of Ella Fitzgerald* . . . . (Pablo)
Frank Sinatra; *The Reprise Collection* . . . . (Reprise)
Frank Sinatra with Count Basie & The Orchestra; *Sinatra At The Sands* . . . . (Reprise)
Ink Spots; *Best Of The Ink Spots* . . . . (MCA)
　Ink Spots' Greatest Hits-Original Recordings-1939-1946 . . . . . (MCA)
Nia Peeples; *Nia Peeples* . . . . (Charisma)
Ray Brown Trio; *Red Hot Ray Brown Trio* . . . . (Concord Jazz)

Tommy Dorsey & Frank Sinatra; *Tommy Dorsey & Frank Sinatra's All-Time Greatest Hits-#1* .... (Bluebird)
Tony Bennett; *Jazz* .... (Columbia)

Street Of Dreams
Rainbow; *Bent Out Of Shape* .... (Mercury)
Finyl Vinyl .... (Mercury)

Stuff That Dreams Are Made Of
Carly Simon; *Coming Around Again* .... (Arista)

Sugar Magnolia
Grateful Dead; *American Beauty* ....(Warner Bros.)
Best Of/Skeletons From The Closet ....(Warner Bros.)
Europe '72 ....(Warner Bros.)
Grateful Dead-Live-#1 ....(JCI Assoc. Labels)

Summertime Dream
Gordon Lightfoot; *Summertime Dream* .... (Reprise)

Sunset Dreams
Clannad; *Banba* ....(Atlantic)

Sweet Dream
Jethro Tull; *20 Years Of Jethro Tull* ....(Chrysalis)
Bursting Out ....(Chrysalis)
Living In The Past ....(Chrysalis)
Original Masters ....(Chrysalis)

Sweet Dreams
Air Supply; *Air Supply's Greatest Hits* .... (Arista)
The One That You Love .... (Arista)

Sweet Dreams
Yes; *Time And A Word* ....(Atlantic)
Yesterdays ....(Atlantic)

Sweet Dreams
La Bouche; *Sweet Dreams* .... (RCA)
The Ultimate Dance Party-1998-C .... (Arista)

Sweet Dreams (Are Made Of This)
Eurythmics; *Eurythmics' Greatest Hits* .... (Arista)
Sweet Dreams (Are Made Of This) .... (RCA)
Marilyn Manson; *Smells Like Children* .... (Interscope)

Sweet Dreams (Of You)
Chet Atkins & Mark Knopfler; *Neck And Neck.* .... (Columbia)
Don Gibson; *Don Gibson-18 Greatest Hits* .... (Curb)
Don Gibson's All-Time Greatest Hits .... (RCA)
Emmylou Harris; *Brand New Dance* .... (Reprise)
Elite Hotel .... (Reprise)
Profile/Best Of Emmylou Harris ....(Warner Bros.)
Jim Reeves; *Jim Reeves' Greatest Hits* .... (RCA)
Patsy Cline; *Patsy Cline's Greatest Hits* .... (MCA)
ST/Sweet Dreams .... (MCA)
The Patsy Cline Story .... (MCA)
Reba McEntire; *Out Of A Dream* .... (Mercury)

Talking In Your Sleep
Crystal Gayle; *Classic Crystal* .... (EMI)
Country Gold-C .... (Priority)
Crystal Gayle's All-Time Greatest Hits .... (Curb)
When I Dream .... (Liberty)
Reba McEntire; *Starting Over* .... (MCA)

Teacher, The
Paul Simon; *You're The One* ....(Warner Bros.)

Television Nightmare
Madrigal; *Madrigal* .... (SSS International)

Tell Me I Was Dreaming
Travis Tritt; *Ten Feet Tall And Bulletproof* ....(Warner Bros.)
Travis Tritt's Greatest Hits-From The Beginning ....(Warner Bros.)

Tell Me I'm Not Dreamin'
Jermaine Jackson; *Jermaine Jackson* .... (Arista)

Tell Me I'm Not Dreaming
Robert Palmer; *Heavy Nova* ....(EMI)

Tell Me I'm Only Dreaming
Lorrie Morgan; *Lorrie Morgan-Classics* .... (Curb)

Tell Me This Is A Dream
Delfonics; *Best Of The Delfonics* .... (Arista)

That's Not Me
Beach Boys; *Pet Sounds* .... (Capitol)
The Pet Sounds Sessions: A 30th Anniversary Collection .... (Capitol)

Theme From "I Dream Of Jeannie"
Original Soundtrack; *Television's Greatest Hits-#1-C* .... (TVT)

These Dreams
Jim Croce; *Photographs & Memories/His Greatest Hits* ......(Atlantic)
Time In A Bottle/Jim Croce's Greatest Love Songs ....(Atlantic)

These Dreams
Heart; *Heart* .... (Capitol)

These Dreams Of You
Van Morrison; *It's Too Late To Stop Now* ....(Warner Bros.)
Moondance ....(Warner Bros.)

This Dream's On Me
Gene Watson; *Gene Watson's Greatest Hits* ....(MCA)
MCA Records 30 Years Of Hits-1958-1988-C ....(MCA)

This Time The Dream's On Me
Annie Ross & Gerry Mulligan; *Annie Ross Sings A Song With Gerry Mulligan* ....(EMI)
Anthony Newley; *Great American Songwriters-#2-Johnny Mercer-C* .. (Rhino)
Charlie Parker; *Bebop & Bird-#2* .... (Rhino)

Ella Fitzgerald; *Harold Arlen Songbook-#1* .... (Verve)
Harry Connick, Jr.; *25* .... (Columbia)

Those Good Old Dreams
Carpenters; *Carpenters-Classics-#2* .... (A&M)
Yesterday Once More .... (A&M)

To Dream The Dream
Frankie Miller; *Standing On The Edge* .... (Capitol)

Tomorrow's Dreams
Black Sabbath; *Black Sabbath-Vol. 4* ....(Warner Bros.)
We Sold Our Soul For Rock 'N' Roll ....(Warner Bros.)

Trucker's Nightmare
Lawrence Hammond; *Coyote's Dream* .... (Takoma)
Critic's Choice-C .... (Takoma)

Truly Madly Deeply
Savage Garden; *Savage Garden* .... (Columbia)

Tulip Or Turnip (Tell Me Dream Face)
Duke Ellington & Teresa Brewer; *It Don't Mean A Thing If It Ain't Got That Swing* .... (Columbia)

TV Dreams
Charlie; *Fantasy Girls* .... (Columbia)

Until My Dreams Come True
Jack Greene; *Until My Dreams Come True* .... (Decca)

Wake Up Dreaming
Little Feat; *Down On The Farm* ....(Warner Bros.)

Waking & Dreaming
Orleans; *Waking & Dreaming* ....(Asylum)

Walking Dream
Patsy Cline; *Forever & Always* .... (Epic)
Here's Patsy Cline .... (MCA)

Way I Am
Merle Haggard; *Merle Haggard-Legends* .... (MCA)
Merle Haggard's Greatest Hits .... (MCA)

What A Dream
Conway Twitty; *Conway Twitty's Greatest Hits* .... (Curb)
Patti Page; *45-#70416* .... (Mercury)
Slim Harpo; *Raining In My Heart* .... (Hip-O)

When I Dream
Barbra Streisand; *Emotion* .... (Columbia)
Crystal Gayle; *Classic Crystal* .... (EMI)
Crystal Gayle's All-Time Greatest Hits .... (Curb)
Willie Nelson; *Partners* .... (Columbia)

When I Dream At Night
Marc Anthony; *Marc Anthony.* .... (Columbia)

When I Grow Too Old To Dream
Benny Goodman & His Orchestra; *Best Of Benny Goodman & His Orchestra.* .... (Curb)
Linda Ronstadt; *Living In The USA* ....(Asylum)
Louis Armstrong; *Essential Louis Armstrong* .... (Vanguard)

When I Stop Dreaming
Jim & Jesse; *All Time Legends Of Country Music-C* .... (Legacy)
Bluegrass Super Hits-C .... (Columbia)

When My Dreamboat Comes Home
Fats Domino; *My Blue Heaven* .... (Gold Rush)
Kay Starr; *Capitol Collectors Series-Kay Starr* .... (Capitol)

When My Ship Comes In
Clint Black; *The Hard Way* .... (RCA)

Wicked Game
Chris Isaak; *Heart Shaped World* .... (Reprise)
ST/Wild At Heart .... (Polydor)

Wide Awake In Dreamland
Pat Benatar; *Wide Awake In Dreamland* .... (Chrysalis)

Wildest Dreams
Asia; *Asia* .... (Geffen)
Then & Now .... (Geffen)

Wildest Dreams
Annie Haslam; *Annie Haslam* .... (Epic)

Wildest Dreams
Dolly Parton; *Eagle When She Flies* .... (Columbia)

Wild-Eyed Dream
Ricky Van Shelton; *Wild-Eyed Dream* .... (Columbia)

Wish I Were You
Patty Smyth; *ST/Armageddon-The Album.* .... (Columbia)

Wish, The
Bruce Springsteen; *Tracks* .... (Columbia)

With My Eyes Wide Open I'm Dreaming
Mandy Barnett; *I've Got A Right To Cry* .... (Sire)
Patti Page; *Patti Page-Golden Hits* .... (Mercury)
Patti Page's Greatest Hits .... (Columbia)

Yesterday's Dreams
Four Tops; *Four Tops-Anthology* .... (Motown)

You Are The Woman
Firefall; *Firefall.* .... (Rhino)
Firefall's Greatest Hits .... (Rhino)

You Can Dream Of Me
Steve Wariner; *Life's Highway* .... (MCA)
Steve Wariner's Greatest Hits .... (MCA)

You Dream Flat Tires
Joni Mitchell; *Wild Things Run Fast* .... (Geffen)

You Gotta Love That
Neal McCoy; *Neal McCoy's Greatest Hits* . . . . (Atlantic)
Today's Country Love-C . . . . (K-Tel)
You Gotta Love That! . . . . (Atlantic)
You Make My Dreams
Daryl Hall & John Oates; *Rock 'N Soul, Part 1* . . . .(RCA)
Voices . . . . (RCA)
You Never Give Me Your Money
Beatles; *Abbey Road* . . . .(Parlophone)
Beatles-Box Set . . . .(Capitol)
George Benson; *The Best* . . . .(Rebound)
You Stepped Out Of A Dream
Morgana King; *Higher Ground* . . . . (Muse)
Nat ''King'' Cole; *Nat ''King'' Cole Sings For Two In Love-*
   & More . . . . (Capitol)
Nat ''King'' Cole-Gift Set . . . . (Capitol)
Oscar Peterson; *Live At The North Sea Jazz Festival* . . . . (Pablo)
Sarah Vaughan; *Roulette Years* . . . . (Roulette)
You'll Be Back (Every Night In My Dreams)
Statler Brothers; *Years Ago* . . . . (Mercury)
Young Dreams
Elvis Presley; *ST/King Creole* . . . .(RCA)
The Other Sides-Worldwide Gold Award Hits, Vol. 2 . . . .(RCA)
Young Thing, Wild Dreams (Rock Me)
Red Rider; *Breaking Curfew* . . . . (Capitol)
Your Summer Dream
Beach Boys; *Surfer Girl* . . . . (Capitol)
Your Wildest Dreams
Moody Blues; *Other Side Of Life* . . . . (Polydor)

DROWN

See Also: **DANGER & DISASTER, DEATH, FLOOD, OCEAN,**
RIVERS, SHIPS, SWIMMING

Absolutely (Story Of A Girl)
Nine Days; *Maddening Crowd* . . . . (550 Music)
Now That's What I Call Music!-#5-C . . . .(Virgin)
Brick
Ben Folds Five; *Whatever And Ever Amen* . . . . (Caroline/550)
Bridge Washed Out
Warner Mack; *Country's Greatest Hits-#3-C* . . . . (MCA)
MCA Records 30 Years Of Hits-1958-1988-C . . . . (MCA)
Crossing Muddy Waters
John Hiatt; *Crossing Muddy Waters* . . . . (Vanguard)
Don't Pull Your Love
Hamilton, Joe Frank & Reynolds; *'70s Biggest Hits-C* . . . . (MCA Special Prod.)
Hamilton, Joe Frank & Reynolds' Greatest Hits . . . . (MCA Special Prod.)
Rock Around The Oldies-#4-C . . . . (MCA Special Prod.)
Drown
Son Volt; *Trace* . . . . (Warner Bros.)
Drown
Smashing Pumpkins; *ST/Singles* . . . . (Epic)
Drown In My Own Tears
Aretha Franklin; *The Delta Meets Detroit: Aretha's Blues* . . . . (Rhino)
Floyd Cramer; *Essential Floyd Cramer* . . . .(RCA)
Ray Charles; *Best Of Ray Charles: The Atlantic Years* . . . . (Rhino)
Sweet & Soul Tears . . . . (Rhino)
Richie Havens; *Resume: The Best Of Richie Havens* . . . . (Rhino)
Drown In My Own Tears
Smithereens; *Blown To Smithereens: Best Of The Smithereens* . . . . (Capitol)
Drown In My Own Tears
Joe Cocker; *Mad Dogs & Englishmen* . . . . (A&M)
Drown Soda
Hole; *Ask For It* . . . . (Caroline)
Drown Yourself
Staple Singers; *Be What You Are* . . . . (Stax)
Drowned
Who; *ST/Quadrophenia* . . . . (MCA)
Drowned
Candlebox; *Lucy* . . . . (Maverick)
Drowned World (My Substitute For Love)
Madonna; *GHV2* . . . . (Warner Bros.)
Ray Of Light . . . . (Maverick)
Drowners
Suede; *Suede* . . . . (Columbia)
Drownin'
Sponge; *Rotting Pinata* . . . . (Work)
Drowning
Hootie & The Blowfish; *Cracked Rear View* . . . . (Atlantic)
Drowning
Stabbing Westward; *Darkest Days* . . . . (Columbia)
Drowning
English Beat; *Wha'ppen* . . . . (I.R.S.)
Drowning
Cure; *Faith* . . . . (Elektra)

Drowning
Joe Jackson; *Laughter And Lust* . . . . (Virgin)
Drowning
Backstreet Boys; *The Hits-Chapter 1* . . . . (Jive)
Drowning At The Bottom
Luther Allison; *Reckless* . . . . (Alligator)
Drowning In Memories
T.G. Sheppard; *T.G. Sheppard's All-Time Greatest Hits* . . . .(Curb)
Drowning In The Sea Of Love
Boz Scaggs; *Live At The Beacon-C* . . . . (Giant)
Joe Simon; *Didn't It Blow Your Mind: Soul Hits Of The '70s-#7-C* . . . .(Rhino)
Music In My Bones: The Best Of Joe Simon . . . .(Rhino)
Ringo Starr; *Ringo The 4th* . . . . (Atlantic)
Drowning Man
Duran Duran; *Duran Duran (The Wedding Album)* . . . .(Capitol)
Drowning Man
U2; *War* . . . .(Island)
Drowning On Dry Land
Albert King; *Hard Bargain* . . . . (Stax)
The Stax Blues Brothers-C . . . . (Stax)
Years Gone By . . . . (Stax)
Roy Buchanan; *Dancing On The Edge* . . . . (Alligator)
Drowning Witch
Frank Zappa; *Ship arriving too late to save a drowning witch* . . . . (Rykodisc)
Givin' Water To A Drowning Man
Lee Roy Parnell; *We All Get Lucky Sometimes* . . . . (Career)
Higher Place
Tom Petty; *Wildflowers* . . . . (Warner Bros.)
In Too Deep
Sum 41; *All Killer No Filler* . . . . (Island/IDJMG)
Just You Wait
Julie Andrews/Original Cast; *My Fair Lady* . . . .(Columbia)
Kern River
Merle Haggard; *For The Record: Merle Haggard-43 Legendary Hits*. . . . (BNA)
Kern River . . . . (Epic)
Let Me Drown
Soundgarden; *Superunknown*. . . . .(A&M)
Lifeguard Sleeping, Girl Drowning
Morrissey; *Vauxhall And I* . . . . (Sire)
Man Overboard
Blink-182; *The Mark, Tom & Travis Show-The Enema Strikes Back* . . . . . (MCA)
Mississippi
Paula Cole; *This Fire* . . . . (Imago)
No Way Out
Stone Temple Pilots; *No. 4* . . . . (Atlantic)
Ready For Drowning
Manic Street Preachers; *This Is My Truth Tell Me Yours* . . . . (Virgin)
Running Bear
Johnny Preston; *45s On CD-#1-1956-1959-C* . . . .(Mercury)
Billboard Top Rock 'N' Roll Hits-1960-C . . . .(Rhino)
Cruisin'-1960-C . . . . (Increase)
Sonny James; *All-Time Country Classics-#1-C* . . . . (Capitol)
Sara
Fleetwood Mac; *25 Years-The Chain* . . . .(Warner Bros.)
Fleetwood Mac Live . . . .(Warner Bros.)
Fleetwood Mac's Greatest Hits . . . .(Warner Bros.)
Tusk . . . .(Warner Bros.)
Tahitian Moon
Porno For Pyros; *Good God's Urge* . . . .(Warner Bros.)
Waist Deep In The Big Muddy
Pete Seeger; *Best Of Broadside 1962-1968: Anthems Of The American*
   Underground From The Pages Of Broadside
   Magazine-C . . . . (Smithsonian Folkways)
Wasn't That A Mighty Storm
Eric Von Schmidt; *Troubadours Of The Folk Era-#1-C* . . . .(Rhino)

DRUGS: COCAINE, Crack

See Also: **DRUGS: GENERAL, DRUGS: MARIJUANA**

1st Of Tha Month
Bone Thugs-N-Harmony; *E. 1999 Eternal* . . . . (Ruthless/Relativity)
Balboa Park
Bruce Springsteen; *The Ghost Of Tom Joad* . . . .(Columbia)
Cabbies On Crack
Ramones; *Mondo Bizarro* . . . .(Radioactive/MCA)
Casey Jones
Grateful Dead; *Best Of The Grateful Dead-Skeletons From The*
   Closet . . . .(Warner Bros.)
Bill Graham Presents The Last Days Of The
   Fillmore-C . . . .(Epic Portrait Assoc.)
Workingman's Dead . . . .(Warner Bros.)
Jerry Garcia Acoustic Band; *Almost Acoustic* . . . . (Grateful Dead)
China White
Scorpions; *Blackout* . . . .(Mercury)
China White
Little Feat; *Hoy-Hoy!* . . . .(Warner Bros.)

Cigarettes & Alcohol
Oasis; *Definitely Maybe* ....(Epic)
Rod Stewart; *When We Were The New Boys* ....(Warner Bros.)
Cocaine
Eric Clapton; *Eric Clapton-Crossroads-C* ....(Polydor)
   Just One Night ....(Polydor)
   Slowhand ....(Polydor)
   Time Pieces-#1-The Best Of Eric Clapton ......(Polydor)
J.J. Cale; *Special Edition* ....(Mercury)
   Troubadour ....(MCA)
Cocaine
Tom Rush; *Blues Songs & Ballads* ....(Fantasy)
   Tom Rush ....(Fantasy)
Cocaine
Beautiful; *Storybook* ....(Giant)
Cocaine (Rock)
Country Joe McDonald; *Superstitious Blues* ....(Rykodisc)
Cocaine (Snow White)
Chris Thomas; *The Beginning* ....(Arhoolie)
Cocaine Blues
Dave Van Ronk; *Folksinger* ....(Prestige)
   Inside Dave Van Ronk ....(Fantasy)
   Troubadours Of The Folk Era-#1-C ....(Rhino)
David Bromberg; *My Own House* ....(Fantasy)
George Thorogood & The Destroyers; *Move It On Over* .(Rounder)
Jackson Browne; *Running On Empty* ....(Asylum)
Johnny Cash; *Essential Johnny Cash* ....(Columbia)
   Johnny Cash At Folsom Prison & San Quentin ....(Columbia)
   Silver ....(Columbia)
Lonnie Mack; *Road Houses & Dance Halls* ....(Epic)
Reverend Gary Davis; *From Blues To Gospel* ....(Biograph)
Cocaine Charlie
Atlanta Rhythm Section; *Boys From Doraville* ....(Polydor)
Cocaine Cocaine
Sly Dunbar; *Sly Wicked & Slick* ....(Front Line)
Cocaine Done Killed My Baby
Mance Lipscomb; *Texas Songwriter-#2* ....(Arhoolie)
Cocaine Drain
John Hall; *Power* ....(Columbia)
Cocaine Go Away
Warren Ceaser & Creole Zydeco Snap; *Zydeco Shootout At El Sid O's* ....(Rounder)
Cocaine Habit
Roy Bookbinder; *Going Back To Tampa* ....(Flying Fish)
Cocaine in My Brain
Dillinger; *Classic Reggae-#1-C* ....(Profile)
   Planet Reggae-World Of Reggae Music ....(Rhythm Safari)
Cocaine In The Back Of The Ride
UGK-Underground Kingz; *Too Hard To Swallow* ....(Jive)
Cocaine Lil
Mekons; *Rock 'N' Roll* ....(A&M)
Cocaine Or Me
Hamell On Trial; *Conviction* ....(Blue Wave)
Cocaine Train
Johnny Paycheck; *Banded Together-C* ....(Epic)
   Everybody's Got a Family ....(Epic)
Crack
Freddie Hubbard & Friends; *Solo Brothers & Professor Jive* ....(DRG)
Crack House Woman
George "Wild Child" Butler; *These Mean Old Blues* ....(Bullseye Blues)
Crack In New York
Culture; *Nuff Crisis!* ....(Shanachie)
Crack Killed Applejack
General Kane; *In Full Chill.* ....(Motown)
Crack Pipe (Burnin' My Hand)
Coolies; *Doug (A Rock Opera & Comic Book)* ....(DB)
Don't Sniff Coke
Pato Banton; *Never Give In.* ....(PMRC)
Ends
Everlast; *Whitey Ford Sings The Blues* ....(Tommy Boy)
Gimme No Crack
Shinehead; *Unity* ....(Elektra)
I Get A Kick Out Of You
Ethel Merman with Johnny Green & His Orchestra; *The Ethel Merman Collection* ....(Razor & Tie)
   This Is Art Deco-C ....(Columbia)
Frank Sinatra; *My One & Only Love* ....(Capitol)
   Round #1 ....(Capitol)
   Sinatra and Swingin' Brass ....(Reprise)
   Sinatra-The Main Event Live ....(Reprise)
   The Capitol Years ....(Capitol)
   The Reprise Collection. ....(Reprise)
Original Cast; *Anything Goes* ....(Epic)
Paul Whiteman & His Orchestra; *78-#24769* ....(Victor)
Ike's Rap
Isaac Hayes; *The Ultimate Collection-Isaac Hayes* ...(Hip-O)
In The Arms Of Cocaine
Hank Williams, Jr.; *Strong Stuff* ....(Warner Bros.)

Kid Charlemagne
Steely Dan; *Steely Dan's Greatest Hits* ....(MCA)
   The Royal Scam ....(MCA)
Let The Cocaine Be
Doc & Merle Watson; *Live & Pickin'* ....(United Artists)
Lit Up
Buckcherry; *Buckcherry* ....(DreamWorks/SKG)
Little Cocaine
Lee Clayton; *Naked City* ....(Capitol)
No Thing On Me (Cocaine Song)
Curtis Mayfield; *Superfly: Deluxe 25th Anniversary Edition* ....(Rhino)
Purple Pills
D12; *Devil's Night* ....(Shady/Interscope)
Rock And Roll Is Dead
Lenny Kravitz; *Circus* ....(Virgin)
Snowblind Friend
David Allan Coe; *Unchained* ....(Columbia)
Hoyt Axton; *Snowblind Friend* ....(MCA)
Steppenwolf; *Steppenwolf 7* ....(MCA)
   Steppenwolf-16 Greatest Hits ....(MCA)
Toy Soldiers
Martika; *Martika* ....(Columbia)
What Would You Do?
City High; *City High* ....(Interscope)
   Now That's What I Call Music!-#7-C ....(Virgin)
   ST/Life ....(Rock Land/Interscope)
White Lines (Don't Do It)
Grandmaster Flash & Melle Mel; *Hip Hop Greats-Classic Raps-C* .....(Rhino)

DRUGS: GENERAL, Addictions, Anti-drug Themes, Drug Abuse, Heroin, Pharmaceuticals, Prescriptions, Psychedelics

See Also: **AIDS, ALCOHOL, ALCOHOL: RECOVERING ALCOHOLIC, DRUGS: COCAINE, DRUGS: MARIJUANA, PAIN & HEALING**

21st Century Sha La La La Girl
Def Leppard; *Euphoria* ....(Mercury)
25th Floor
Patti Smith Group; *Easter* ....(Arista)
7 Things To Do On Speed
God's Acre; *Ten Gospel Greats* ....(Wax Trax)
Addicted
Dan Seals; *Dan Seals' Greatest Hits* ....(Liberty)
   Rage On ....(Capitol)
Addicted
Le Roux; *Last Safe Place* ....(RCA)
Addicted To Love
Robert Palmer; *Addictions-#1* ....(Island)
   Riptide ....(Island)
   The Island Story-1962-1987-25th Anniversary-C .(Island)
Tina Turner; *Live In Europe* ....(Capitol)
Addicted To Spuds
"Weird Al" Yankovic; *"Weird Al" Yankovic's Greatest Hits* ....(Scotti Bros.)
   The Food Album ....(Scotti Bros.)
Addictive Love
BeBe & CeCe Winans; *Different Lifestyles* ....(Capitol)
Aeroplane
Red Hot Chili Peppers; *One Hot Minute* ....(Warner Bros.)
Ain't It Strange
Patti Smith Group; *Radio Ethiopia* ....(Arista)
All Time High
Rita Coolidge; *13 Original James Bond Themes-C* .....(EMI)
   Rita Coolidge-Classics-#5 ....(A&M)
   ST/Octopussy ....(A&M)
Am I High
Asleep At The Wheel; *Served Live* ....(Capitol)
American Bad Ass (Rogaine)
Kid Rock; *History Of Rock* ....(Top Dog/Lava/Atlantic)
Amigone
Goo Goo Dolls; *Dizzy Up The Girl* ....(Warner Sunset/Reprise)
Amphetamine Annie
Canned Heat; *Best Of Canned Heat.* ....(EMI)
   Boogie With ....(Liberty)
And It Stoned Me
Van Morrison; *Best Of Van Morrison* ....(Polydor)
   Moondance. ....(Warner Bros.)
Angel Dust
Gil Scott-Heron & Brian Jackson; *Secrets.* ....(Arista)
Angel Dust
New Order; *Brotherhood* ....(Qwest)
Angeline Is Coming Home
Badlees; *River Songs.* ....(Atlas)
Are You Experienced?
Jimi Hendrix; *Kiss The Sky* ....(Reprise)

Jimi Hendrix Experience; *Are You Experienced?* . . . . (Reprise)
   Essential Jimi Hendrix . . . . (Reprise)
Aspirin Damage
   Alice Cooper; *Flush The Fashion* . . . . (Warner Bros.)
Beautiful Disaster
   311; *Live!* . . . . (Capricorn)
   Transistor . . . . (Capricorn)
Because I Got High
   Afroman; *Good Times* . . . . (Universal)
Been On A Train
   Laura Nyro; *Christmas & The Beads Of Sweat* . . . . (Columbia)
Billy Dee
   Kris Kristofferson; *The Silver Tongued Devil And I* . . . . . . (Columbia)
Bitter Pill
   Motley Crue; *Motley Crue's Greatest Hits* . . . . (Beyond)
Bittersweet
   Fuel; *Sunburn* . . . . (550 Music)
Black Balloon
   Goo Goo Dolls; *Dizzy Up The Girl* . . . . (Warner Sunset/Reprise)
Black Jesus
   Everlast; *Eat At Whitey's* . . . . (Tommy Boy)
Boys 'R A Drug
   Julie Brown; *Trapped In The Body Of A White Girl* . . . . (Sire)
Break It Up
   Patti Smith; *Horses* . . . . (Arista)
British Pharmaceuticals
   Miss World; *Miss World* . . . . (Atlantic)
Carmelita
   Linda Ronstadt; *Simple Dreams* . . . . (Asylum)
   Warren Zevon; *Warren Zevon* . . . . (Asylum)
Champagne Supernova
   Oasis; *What's The Story Morning Glory?* . . . . (Epic)
Changes
   2Pac; *2Pac Greatest Hits* . . . . (Amaru/Death Row/Interscope)
Cheap Shot
   John Cougar; *Nothin' Matters And What If It Did* . . . . (Riva)
   John Cougar Mellencamp; *John Cougar Mellencamp-Early Years* . . . . . (Rhino)
   Kid Inside . . . . (Rhino)
Children Of The Korn
   Korn with Ice Cube; *Follow The Leader* . . . . (Immortal/Epic)
Cigarette
   Ben Folds Five; *Whatever And Ever Amen* . . . . (Caroline/550)
Cloud Nine
   Temptations; *25 Years Of Grammy Greats-C* . . . . (Motown)
   Cloud Nine . . . . (Motown)
   Motown Grammy R&B Performances Of The '60s & '70s-C . . . . . . (Motown)
   Motown Story-First 25 Years-C . . . . (Motown)
   Temptations' Greatest Hits-#2 . . . . (Motown)
Cold Blue Steel & Sweet Fire
   Joni Mitchell; *For The Roses* . . . . (Asylum)
   Joni Mitchell with Tom Scott & The L.A. Express; *Miles Of Aisles* . . . (Asylum)
Cold Turkey
   John Lennon; *Live In New York City* . . . . (Capitol)
   John Lennon/Plastic Ono Band; *Shaved Fish* . . . . (Capitol)
   Some Time In New York City . . . . (Capitol)
   Plastic Ono Band; *Plastic Ono Band-Live Peace In Toronto 1969* . . . . (Capitol)
Comfortably Numb
   Pink Floyd; *Delicate Sound Of Thunder* . . . . (Columbia)
   Knebworth-The Album-C . . . . (Polydor)
   The Wall . . . . (Columbia)
   Roger Waters; *The Wall-Live In Berlin* . . . . (Mercury)
Coming Down (Drug Tongue)
   Cult; *The Cult* . . . . (Sire)
Copenhagen Junkie
   Chris LeDoux; *Melodies & Memories* . . . . (Liberty)
Crystal Ship
   Doors; *Best Of The Doors* . . . . (Elektra)
   Doors . . . . (Elektra)
   Doors 13 . . . . (Elektra)
   Doors-Classics . . . . (Elektra)
Cut You In
   Jerry Cantrell; *Boggy Depot* . . . . (Columbia)
Dangerous Drug
   Electric Angels; *Electric Angels* . . . . (Atlantic)
Dead Flowers
   Rolling Stones; *Sticky Fingers* . . . . (Virgin)
   Steve Earle & The Dukes; *Shut Up And Die Like An Aviator* . . . . . (MCA)
Dealer
   Traffic; *Mr. Fantasy* . . . . (Island)
Dealer
   Deep Purple; *Come Taste The Band* . . . . (Metal Blade)
Dealer
   Santana; *Inner Secrets* . . . . (Columbia)
Desperately Wanting
   Better Than Ezra; *Friction, Baby* . . . . (Swell/Elektra)
Devil Is Dope
   Dramatics; *Best Of The Dramatics* . . . . (Stax)
   Dramatic Experience . . . . (Stax)

Do Something
   Macy Gray; *On How Life Is* . . . . (Epic)
   ST/Music Of The Heart . . . . (Epic/Sony Music Soundtrax)
Dope Addict
   Sly Dunbar; *Sly Wicked & Slick* . . . . (Front Line)
Dope Head Blues
   Victoria Spivey; *News & The Blues-Telling It Like It Is-C* . . . . . (Columbia)
Doper Than Dope
   Salt-N-Pepa; *Blacks' Magic* . . . . (Next Plateau/London/Island)
Drug (It's Just A State Of Mind)
   Duran Duran; *Big Thing* . . . . (Capitol)
Drug Dealer
   Reggie Knighton Band; *Reggie Knighton Band* . . . . (Columbia)
Drug Squad
   Steel Pulse; *Reggae Fever (Caught You)* . . . . (Mango)
Drug Store Cowboy
   Humble Pie; *Eat It* . . . . (A&M)
Drug Store Truck Drivin' Man
   Byrds; *Best Of The Byrds-Greatest Hits-#2* . . . . (Columbia)
   Dr. Byrds & Mr. Hyde . . . . (Legacy)
   The Byrds . . . . (Columbia)
   Gram Parsons & Fallen Angels; *Live 1973* . . . . (Sierra)
   Joan Baez & Jeffrey Shurtleff; *ST/Woodstock* . . . . (Atlantic)
Drug Store Woman
   John Lee Hooker; *Best Of John Lee Hooker* . . . . (Vee-Jay)
   Best Of John Lee Hooker . . . . (Crescendo)
Drug Train
   Social Distortion; *Social Distortion* . . . . (Epic)
Drug Train
   Cramps; *Bad Music For Bad People* . . . . (I.R.S.)
Drugland Weekend
   Hounds; *Unleashed* . . . . (Columbia)
Drugs
   Lazy Cowgirls; *Lazy Cowgirls* . . . . (Restless)
   ST/Border Radio . . . . (Enigma)
Drugs
   Talking Heads; *Fear Of Music* . . . . (Sire)
   Name Of This Band Is Talking Heads . . . . (Sire)
Drugs Suck
   Steve Jones; *Mercy* . . . . (Gold Mountain)
Drug-Stabbing Time
   Clash; *Give 'Em Enough Rope* . . . . (Epic)
Dumb
   Nirvana; *In Utero* . . . . (David Geffen Co.)
   MTV Unplugged In New York . . . . (David Geffen Co.)
E-Bow The Letter
   R.E.M.; *New Adventures In Hi-Fi* . . . . (Warner Bros.)
Eight Miles High
   Byrds; *Fifth Dimension* . . . . (Columbia)
   Original Singles-#1-1965-1967 . . . . (Columbia)
   The Byrds . . . . (Columbia)
   The Byrds (Untitled) . . . . (Legacy)
   The Byrds' Greatest Hits . . . . (Columbia)
   Leo Kottke; *Best Of Leo Kottke* . . . . (Capitol)
   Mudlark . . . . (Capitol)
   Roxy Music; *Flesh + Blood* . . . . (Atco)
Elegantly Wasted
   INXS; *Elegantly Wasted* . . . . (Mercury)
Essence
   Lucinda Williams; *Essence* . . . . (Lost Highway/IDJMG)
Euphoria
   Youngbloods; *Best Of The Youngbloods* . . . . (RCA)
   This Is The Youngbloods . . . . (RCA)
Everyday Feels Like Another Drug
   Bill Nelson; *Vistamix* . . . . (Epic)
Feel So High
   Des'ree; *I Ain't Movin'* . . . . (550 Music)
   Mind Adventures . . . . (550 Music)
   Siren Song:Celebration Of Women In Music-C . . . . (550 Music)
Flavor Of The Weak
   American Hi-Fi; *American Hi-Fi* . . . . (Island)
   Now That's What I Call Music!-#7-C . . . . (Virgin)
Flyin' High In The Friendly Sky
   Marvin Gaye; *What's Going On* . . . . (Motown)
Freshmen, The
   Verve Pipe; *Villains* . . . . (RCA)
Friendly Neighborhood Narco Agent
   Jef Jaisun; *Dr. Demento's Delights-C* . . . . (Warner Bros.)
Fuel
   Metallica; *Reload* . . . . (Elektra)
Fu-gee-la
   Fugees; *The Score* . . . . (Ruffhouse)
   The Score-Edit . . . . (Columbia)
Geek Stink Breath
   Green Day; *Insomniac* . . . . (Reprise)
Get Born Again
   Alice In Chains; *Nothing Safe* . . . . (Columbia)

Get My Rocks Off
Dr. Hook & The Medicine Show; *Revisited* . . . . (Columbia)
   Sloppy Seconds . . . . (Columbia)
Ghost Dance
Patti Smith Group; *Easter* . . . . (Arista)
Give It 2 You
Da'Brat; *Funkdafied* . . . . (Chaos)
Gone Till November
Wyclef Jean featuring The Refugee Allstars; *Presents The Carnival F/*
   Refugee Allstars . . . . (Ruffhouse/Columbia)
Happiness Is A Warm Gun
Beatles; *The Beatles (White Album)* . . . . (Capitol)
Hard Habit To Break
Chicago; *Chicago 17* . . . .(Warner Bros.)
   Chicago's Greatest Hits-1982-1989 . . . . (Full Moon)
Hard Monkeys
Ten Years After; *A Space In Time* . . . . (Columbia)
Hash Pipe
Weezer; *Weezer 2001* . . . .(Geffen)
Heroin
Lou Reed; *Rock N Roll Animal* . . . . (RCA)
Velvet Underground; *1969: Velvet Underground Live* . . . . (Mercury)
   Live MCMXCIII . . . . (Sire)
   ST/The Doors . . . . (Elektra)
   The Velvet Underground & Nico . . . . (Verve)
Heroin Girl
Everclear; *Sparkle And Fade* . . . . (Capitol)
High
Jimmie's Chicken Shack; *Pushing The Salmanilla Envelope* . . . .(Rocket)
High On Drugs
Lou & Peter Berryman; *February March* . . . . (Cornbelt)
Home Is Where The Hatred Is
Esther Phillips; *Best Of Esther Phillips* . . . . (CBS Associated)
   From A Whisper To A Scream . . . . (CBS Associated)
Gil Scott-Heron; *Gil Scott-Heron* . . . . (Bluebird)
   It's Your World . . . . (Arista)
   Pieces Of A Man . . . . (Flying Dutchman)
Honey
Mariah Carey; *Butterfly* . . . . (Columbia)
Hooked On A Feeling
B.J. Thomas; *Best Of B.J. Thomas* . . . .(Hollywood/DNA-Rounder)
Vonda Shepard; *ST/Songs From "Ally McBeal" Featuring Vonda*
   Shepard . . . . (550/Epic)
Hurt
Nine Inch Nails; *The Downward Spiral* . . . . (Interscope)
I Believe
Blessid Union Of Souls; *Home* . . . .(EMI)
I Can Get Off On You
Waylon Jennings & Willie Nelson; *Waylon & Willie* . . . . (RCA)
Willie Nelson; *Willie & Family Live* . . . . (Columbia)
I Like Drugs
Simpletones; *Posh Hits-#1-C* . . . .(Posh Boy)
I Used To Love Him
Lauryn Hill featuring Mary J. Blige; *The Miseducation Of*
   Lauryn Hill . . . . (Ruffhouse/Columbia)
I Wanna Be A Drug-Sniffing Dog
Lard; *Pure Chewing Satisfaction* . . . . (Alternative Tentacles)
   The Virus That Would Not Die!-C . . . . (Alternative Tentacles)
I Wanna Be Sedated
Ramones; *Ramones Mania* . . . . (Sire)
   Road To Ruin . . . . (Sire)
I Want A New Drug
Huey Lewis and the News; *Sports* . . . .(Chrysalis)
I Wonder If Heaven Got A Ghetto
2Pac; *R U Still Down (Remember Me)* . . . . (Amaru/Jive)
If I Could Talk I'd Tell You (Zoloft)
Lemonheads; *Car Button Cloth* . . . . (Tag/Atlantic)
If I Ruled The World
NaS; *It Was Written* . . . . (Columbia)
Illegal Smile
John Prine; *John Prine* . . . .(Atlantic)
   Prime Prine-The Best Of John Prine . . . . (Atlantic)
I'm Waiting For The Man
Lou Reed; *Lou Reed Live* . . . . (RCA)
Velvet Underground; *Live MCMXCIII* . . . . (Sire)
   The Velvet Underground & Nico . . . . (Verve)
Immortality
Pearl Jam; *Vitalogy* . . . .(Epic)
In Praise Of Drugs & Alcohol
San Francisco Mime Troupe; *Steel Town* . . . . (Flying Fish)
It Ain't Nobody's Business
Billie Holiday; *History Of The Real Billie Holiday* . . . . (Verve)
Mississippi John Hurt; *Best Of Mississippi John Hurt* . . . . (Vanguard)
It's Been Awhile
Staind; *Break The Cycle* . . . . (Flip/Elektra)
Jack Of Speed
Steely Dan; *Two Against Nature* . . . . (Giant)

Johnny Bye-Bye
Bruce Springsteen; *Tracks* . . . . (Columbia)
Jukebox Junkie
Ken Mellons; *Ken Mellons* . . . . (Epic)
Julie's In The Drug Squad
Clash; *Give 'Em Enough Rope* . . . . (Epic)
Junker's Blues
King Curtis & Champion Jack Dupree; *Blues At Montreaux* . . . .(Atlantic)
Mike Bloomfield; *Best Of Mike Bloomfield* . . . . (Takoma)
   Cruisin' For A Bruisin' . . . . (Takoma)
Junkie
Dead Milkmen; *Big Lizard In My Backyard* . . . . (Restless)
Junkie Doll
Mark Knopfler; *Sailing To Philadelphia* . . . . (Warner Bros.)
Junkie For My Music
Lonnie Jordan; *Different Moods Of Me* . . . . (MCA)
Junkie For You
Ray Stevens; *Feel The Music* . . . . (Warner Bros.)
Junkie For Your Love
Cash McCall; *Omega Man* . . . .(Paula)
Junkie's Lament
James Taylor; *In The Pocket* . . . . (Warner Bros.)
Junkie's Prayer
Fishbone; *Reality Of My Surroundings* . . . . (Columbia)
Junkie's Prayer
Statler Brothers; *Bed Of Rose's* . . . . (Mercury)
Junkman
Danny O'Keefe; *Breezy Stories* . . . .(Atlantic)
Kicks
Paul Revere And The Raiders; *Legend Of Paul Revere And The*
   Raiders . . . . (Columbia)
   Midnight Ride . . . . (Columbia)
   Paul Revere And The Raiders' Greatest Hits . . . . (Columbia)
Kids Aren't Alright
Offspring; *Americana* . . . . (Columbia)
King Heroin
James Chance & The Contortions; *Live In New York* . . . . (Roir)
   New York Rockers-C . . . . (Roir)
   Soul Exorcism . . . . (Roir)
King Heroin
Jazzy Jeff; *On Fire* . . . .(Jive)
King Heroin
James Brown; *There It Is* . . . .(Polydor)
Kiss From A Rose
Seal; *Seal 2* . . . .(Sire)
Land
Patti Smith; *Horses* . . . . (Arista)
Let It Bleed
Rolling Stones; *Let It Bleed* . . . .(Abkco)
   More Hot Rocks (big hits & fazed cookies) . . . .(Abkco)
Life In The Fast Lane
Eagles; *Eagles Live* . . . .(Asylum)
   Hotel California . . . .(Asylum)
   ST/FM. . . . . (MCA)
Little Girl, The
John Michael Montgomery; *Brand New Me* . . . .(Atlantic)
   Totally Hits-#3-C . . . . (Atlantic)
Little More Time With You
James Taylor; *Hourglass* . . . . (Columbia)
Little Things
Bush; *Sixteen Stone* . . . .(Trauma)
Lively Up Yourself
Bob Marley & The Wailers; *Babylon By Bus* . . . .(Tuff Gong)
   Bob Marley & The Wailers-Live . . . . (Tuff Gong)
   Natty Dread . . . . (Tuff Gong)
Loser
3 Doors Down; *Better Life* . . . . (Republic/Universal)
Love Is A Drug
Gretchen Peters; *Gretchen Peters* . . . .(Purple Crayon Prod.)
Love Is The Drug
Grace Jones; *Island Life* . . . . (Island)
   Warm Leatherette . . . . (Island)
Roxy Music; *Heart Still Beating* . . . . (Virgin)
   Roxy Music-Atlantic Years 1973-1980 . . . . (Atco)
   Roxy Music's Greatest Hits . . . . (Atco)
   Siren . . . . (Atco)
   Street Life-20 Great Hits . . . . (Reprise)
Love Potion Number 9
Clovers; *ST/American Graffiti* . . . . (MCA)
   Super Oldies Of The '50s-#7-C . . . . (Audio Fidelity)
Herb Alpert & The Tijuana Brass; *Herb Alpert & The Tijuana Brass'*
   Greatest Hits . . . . (A&M)
   Herb Alpert & The Tijuana Brass-Classics-#1 . . . . (A&M)
Searchers; *History Of British Rock-#3-C* . . . . (Rhino)
   Searchers' Greatest Hits . . . . (Rhino)
LSD Fixation
Jerry Porter; *Don't Bother Me* . . . . (Mirror)

Lucy In The Sky With Diamonds
Beatles; *Sgt. Pepper's Lonely Hearts Club Band* . . . . (Capitol)
 The Beatles/1967-1970 . . . . (Capitol)
 Yellow Submarine . . . . (Capitol)
Elton John; *All This & World War 2* . . . . (20th Century Fox)
 Elton John's Greatest Hits-#2 . . . . (Polydor)
John Lennon; *Lennon* . . . . (Capitol)
Make It Hot
Nicole; *Make It Hot* . . . . (Gold Mind/East West/EEG)
Me
Staind; *Dysfunction* . . . . (Flip/Elektra)
Me & Baby Jane
Leon Russell; *Carney* . . . . (Right Stuff)
Meditation
Astrud Gilberto; *Compact Jazz-Astrud Gilberto* . . . . (Verve)
Billy Stritch; *Billy Stritch* . . . . (DRG)
Frank Sinatra & Antonio Carlos Jobim; *Francis Albert Sinatra & Antonio*
 Carlos Jobim . . . . (Reprise)
Lena Horne; *Goes Latin & Sings Your Requests* . . . . (DRG)
Original Cast; *Shenandoah* . . . . (RCA)
Meditation #2
Laraaji; *Day Of Radiance* . . . . (Editions E.G.)
Meditation: Psalm 1-6
Paul Horn; *Inside The Great Pyramid* . . . . (Kuckuck)
Monkey On Your Back
Aldo Nova; *Portrait Of Aldo Nova* . . . . (Epic)
 Subject...Aldo Nova . . . . (Portrait)
Morphine And Chocolate
4 Non Blondes; *Bigger, Better, Faster, More!* . . . . (Interscope)
Mother's Little Helper
Rolling Stones; *Flowers* . . . . (Abkco)
 Hot Rocks 1964-1971 . . . . (Abkco)
 Through The Past, Darkly (Big Hits Vol. 2) . . . . (Abkco)
Tesla; *Five Man Acoustical Jam* . . . . (Geffen)
Mr. Pharmacist
Other Half; *Nuggets-#12-Punk-#3-C* . . . . (Rhino)
Much Higher
Gary Wright; *Dream Weaver* . . . . (Warner Bros.)
My Drug Buddy
Lemonheads; *It's A Shame About Ray* . . . . (Atlantic)
Needle & Spoon
Savoy Brown; *Best Of Savoy Brown* . . . . (Parrot)
 Raw Sienna . . . . (Parrot)
 Savoy Brown-London Collector . . . . (London)
Needle & The Damage Done
Neil Young; *Decade* . . . . (Reprise)
 Harvest . . . . (Reprise)
Neil Young & Crazy Horse; *Live Rust* . . . . (Reprise)
Needle & The Spoon
Lynyrd Skynyrd; *One More From The Road* . . . . (MCA)
 Second Helping . . . . (MCA)
Needle Of Death
Ian & Sylvia; *Best Of Ian & Sylvia* . . . . (Vanguard)
New Amphetamine Shriek
Fugs; *Fugs 4 Rounders Score* . . . . (ESP Disk)
Nickel Bags
Digable Planets; *Reachin'-New Refutation Of Time & Space* . . . . . . (Pendulum)
No No Song
Ringo Starr; *Blast From Your Past* . . . . (Gold Rush)
 Goodnight Vienna . . . . (Capitol)
Not An Addict
K's Choice; *Paradise In Me* . . . . (550 Music)
Novocaine For The Soul
Eels; *Beautiful Freak* . . . . (DreamWorks/SKG)
Now I Wanna Sniff Some Glue
Ramones; *All The Stuff & More-#1* . . . . (Sire)
 Ramones . . . . (Sire)
Okie From Muskogee
Merle Haggard; *Friend In California* . . . . (Epic)
Merle Haggard & The Strangers; *Best Of Merle Haggard & The*
 Strangers . . . . (Capitol)
 Capitol Collectors Series-Merle Haggard & The Strangers . . . . (Capitol)
 Country Music Classics-#3-1965-1970-C . . . . (K-Tel)
 For The Record: Merle Haggard-43 Legendary Hits . . . . (BNA)
 Songs I'll Always Sing . . . . (Capitol)
 ST/Platoon . . . . (Atlantic)
Opiate
Tool; *Opiate* . . . . (Zoo)
Opiate Of The Masses
Heathen; *Victims Of Deception* . . . . (Roadracer)
Opiated
Tragically Hip; *Up To Here* . . . . (MCA)
Opium Bride
Annabouboula; *Greek Fire* . . . . (Shanachie)
Opium Dentine
Brothers & Systems; *Transcontinental Weekend* . . . . (Network)
Original Prankster (Prozac)
Offspring; *Conspiracy Of One* . . . . (Columbia)

Overdose
AC/DC; *Let There Be Rock* . . . . (Atco)
Pass The Valium (With Knobs On)
Adrian Legg; *Guitars & Other Cathedrals* . . . . (Relativity)
Passage To Bangkok
Rush; *2112* . . . . (Mercury)
 Exit...Stage Left . . . . (Mercury)
 Rush-Chronicles . . . . (Mercury)
Penicillin Penny
Dr. Hook; *Dr. Hook & The Medicine Show Revisited* . . . . (Columbia)
People That We Love, The
Bush; *Golden State* . . . . (Atlantic)
Perfect Drug
Nine Inch Nails; *ST/Lost Highway* . . . . (Interscope)
Pigs In Zen
Jane's Addiction; *Jane's Addiction* . . . . (Triple X Entert.)
 Nothing's Shocking . . . . (Warner Bros.)
Plop, Plop, Fizz, Fizz (Alka-Seltzer)
Original Soundtrack; *TeeVee Toons-The Commercials-#1-C* . . . . . (TVT)
Poppies
Buffy Sainte-Marie; *Best Of Buffy Sainte-Marie-#2* . . . . (Vanguard)
 Illuminations . . . . (Vanguard)
 Native North American Child . . . . (Vanguard)
Poppies
Patti Smith; *Radio Ethiopia* . . . . (Arista)
Post Toastee
Tommy Bolin; *Private Eyes* . . . . (Columbia)
Poverty Train
Laura Nyro; *Eli And The Thirteenth Confession* . . . . (Columbia)
Priests On Drugs
Paper Bag; *No Age-Compilation Of SST Instrumentals-C* . . . . (SST)
Prozac Baby
Broken Toys; *Shreds-#2: American Underground 1994-C* . . . (Shredder)
Psychedelic Sex Reaction
Babylon A.D.; *Nothing Sacred* . . . . (Arista)
Purple Haze
Cure; *Stone Free: A Tribute To Jimi Hendrix-C* . . . . (Reprise)
Jimi Hendrix; *Kiss The Sky* . . . . (Reprise)
 ST/Jimi Hendrix . . . . (Reprise)
Jimi Hendrix Experience; *Are You Experienced?* . . . . (Reprise)
 Essential Jimi Hendrix . . . . (Reprise)
 Radio One . . . . (Rykodisc)
 Smash Hits . . . . (Reprise)
Winger; *Winger* . . . . (Atlantic)
Purple Pills
D12; *Devil's Night* . . . . (Shady/Interscope)
Pusher, The
Steppenwolf; *Classic Rock-#2-C* . . . . (MCA)
 Live Steppenwolf . . . . (MCA)
 Steppenwolf . . . . (MCA)
 Steppenwolf Gold/Their Great Hits . . . . (MCA)
 Steppenwolf-16 Greatest Hits . . . . (MCA)
Pusherman
Curtis Mayfield; *Pimps, Players & Private Eyes-C* . . . . (Sire)
Radio Ethiopia
Patti Smith Group; *Radio Ethiopia* . . . . (Arista)
Rexall
Dave Navarro; *Trust No One* . . . . (Capitol)
Ridin'
Buckcherry; *Time Bomb* . . . . (DreamWorks/SKG)
Rock & Roll Junkie
Herman Brood; *Herman Brood & His Wild Romance* . . . . (Ariola America)
Rock & Roll Junkie
Back Street Crawler; *Band Plays On* . . . . (Atco)
Rock 'N' Roll Junkie
Motley Crue; *Decade Of Decadence* . . . . (Elektra)
Rolaids, Doan's Pills & Preparation H
Dave Dudley; *King Of The Road* . . . . (Sun)
Rollin' Stoned
Great White; *Can't Get There From Here* . . . . (Portrait)
Salvation
Cranberries; *To The Faithful Departed* . . . . (Island)
Sam Stone
John Prine; *John Prine* . . . . (Atlantic)
 John Prine-Souvenirs . . . . (Oh Boy)
 Prime Prine-The Best Of John Prine . . . . (Atlantic)
Santa Doesn't Cop Out On Dope
Martin Mull; *Mulling It Over: A Musical Oeuvre View* . . . . (Razor & Tie)
Sonic Youth; *Just Say Noel-C* . . . . (Geffen)
Say It Ain't So
Weezer; *Weezer* . . . . (David Geffen Co.)
Seeing Things
Black Crowes; *Shake Your Money Maker* . . . . (Def American)
Semi-Charmed Life
Third Eye Blind; *Jock Rock 2000-C* . . . . (Tommy Boy)
 Third Eye Blind . . . . (Elektra)
Sex, Drugs & Rock & Roll
Ian Dury; *New Boots & Panties* . . . . (Stiff)

Mantronix; *This Should Move Ya* .... (Capitol)
She Gets Too High
Rob Rule; *Rob Rule* .... (Mercury)
She's Like Heroin To Me
Gun Club; *Fire Of Love* .... (Slash)
Shootin' On Narcs
Pat Gangsta; *#1 Suspect* .... (Atlantic)
Sinaloa Cowboys
Bruce Springsteen; *The Ghost Of Tom Joad* .... (Columbia)
Sister Morphine
Marianne Faithfull; *Blazing Away* .... (Island)
Marianne Faithfull's Greatest Hits .... (Abkco)
Rolling Stones; *Sticky Fingers* .... (Virgin)
Smuggler's Blues
Glenn Frey; *Allnighter* .... (MCA)
Rock The First-#2-C .... (Sandstone Music)
ST/Miami Vice .... (MCA)
So High
Dave Mason; *Best Of Dave Mason* .... (Columbia)
Let It Flow .... (Columbia)
Soft Hearted Hana
George Harrison; *George Harrison* .... (Dark Horse)
Spanish Pipedream
John Prine; *John Prine* .... (Atlantic)
Speed Kills
Steve Gibbons Band; *Caught In The Act* .... (MCA)
Spiritual High
Moodswings; *Moodfood* .... (Arista)
Still
Macy Gray; *On How Life Is* .... (Epic)
Stop Breaking Down
Rolling Stones; *Exile On Main Street* .... (Virgin)
Suicidal Heroin
Ratos De Porao; *Brasil* .... (Roadracer)
Superfly
Curtis Mayfield; *Super Bad-C* .... (K-Tel)
Superfly .... (Curtom)
Surfin' On Heroin
Forgotten Rebels; *Surfin' On Heroin* .... (Restless)
Swing Street
Bruce Hornsby; *Hot House* .... (RCA)
T.M. Song
Beach Boys; *15 Big Ones* .... (Brother)
Take A Red
New Riders Of The Purple Sage; *Alive & Kicking* ...... (MCA Special Prod.)
Marin County Line .... (MCA)
Take A Whiff
Byrds; *The Byrds (Untitled)* .... (Legacy)
Cisco Houston; *Cisco Houston* .... (Everest)
Leadbelly; *Midnight Special* .... (Rounder)
Teenage Immigrant Welfare Mothers On Drugs
Austin Lounge Lizards; *Live Bait* .... (Sugar Hill)
Television, The Drug Of The Nation
Disposable Heroes Of Hiphoprisy; *Hypocrisy Is The Greatest Luxury* .... (4th & Broadway)
That Cat Is High
Manhattan Transfer; *Manhattan Transfer-Anthology-Down In Birdland* .... (Rhino)
The Manhattan Transfer .... (Rhino)
Them Downers
Hoyt Axton; *Free Sailin'* .... (MCA)
Theme From "Miami Vice"
Jan Hammer; *Escape From Television* .... (MCA)
Soundtrack Smashes-'80s & More-C .... (MCA)
ST/Miami Vice .... (MCA)
Original Soundtrack; *Television's Greatest Hits-#3-1970s & 1980s-C* ... (TVT)
There Goes The Neighborhood
Sheryl Crow; *The Globe Sessions* .... (A&M)
Thirty Days In The Hole
Gov't Mule; *Live With A Little Help From Our Friends-Collector's Edition* .... (Capricorn)
Humble Pie; *Best Of Humble Pie* .... (A&M)
Humble Pie-Classics-#14 .... (A&M)
Rock This Way Live-#1-C .... (BMG Special Prod.)
Smokin' .... (A&M)
Mr. Big; *Mr. Big* .... (Atlantic)
This Is A Call
Foo Fighters; *Foo Fighters* .... (Roswell/RCA)
Thorazine Shuffle
Gov't Mule; *Live With A Little Help From Our Friends-Collector's Edition* .... (Capricorn)
Savatage; *Gutter Ballet* .... (Atlantic)
Time Out Of Mind
Steely Dan; *Gaucho* .... (MCA)
Too High
Stevie Wonder; *Innervisions* .... (Motown)
Too Much Seconal
Johnny Winter; *Still Alive & Well* .... (Columbia)

Torn And Frayed
Rolling Stones; *Exile On Main Street* .... (Virgin)
Two Little Girls
Ani DiFranco; *Little Plastic Castle* .... (Righteous Babe)
Walkin' On The Sun
Smash Mouth; *Fush Yu Mang* .... (Interscope)
War On Drugs
2 Black 2 Strong MMG; *Doin' Hard Time On Planet Earth* .... (Clappers)
Welcome To The Boomtown
David & David; *Boomtown* .... (A&M)
What It's Like
Everlast; *Whitey Ford Sings The Blues* .... (Tommy Boy)
What Kind Of Love Are You On
Aerosmith; *ST/Armageddon-The Album* .... (Columbia)
White Punks On Dope
Tubes; *T.R.A.S.H. (Tubes Rarities And Smash Hits)* ...... (A&M)
Tubes .... (A&M)
What Do You Want From Live .... (A&M)
White Rabbit
Damned; *Best Of The Damned* .... (Roadracer)
Machine Gun Etiquette .... (Roadracer)
George Benson; *George Benson-Collection* ..... (Warner Bros.)
White Rabbit .... (CBS Associated)
Jefferson Airplane; *2400 Fulton Street-An Anthology* .... (RCA)
Flight Log (1966-1976) .... (Grunt)
Loves You .... (RCA)
ST/Platoon .... (Atlantic)
Surrealistic Pillow .... (RCA)
The Worst Of Jefferson Airplane .... (RCA)
White Ship
H.P. Lovecraft; *H.P. Lovecraft* .... (Out of Print)
Who Put The Benzedrine In Mrs. Murphy's Ovaltine?
Harry Gibson; *Dr. Demento's Delights-C* .... (Warner Bros.)
Whoa
Black Rob; *Life Story* .... (Bad Boy/Arista)
Willin'
Byrds; *The Byrds* .... (Columbia)
Linda Ronstadt; *Heart Like A Wheel* .... (Capitol)
Little Feat; *Little Feat* .... (Warner Bros.)
Sailin' Shoes .... (Warner Bros.)
Waiting For Columbus .... (Warner Bros.)
With A Little Help From My Friends
Beatles; *Beatles-Box Set* .... (Capitol)
Rarities .... (Capitol)
Sgt. Pepper's Lonely Hearts Club Band .... (Capitol)
The Beatles/1967-1970 .... (Capitol)
Joe Cocker; *History Of British Rock-#9-C* .... (Rhino)
Joe Cocker-Classics-#4 .... (A&M)
Joe Cocker's Greatest Hits .... (A&M)
ST/Woodstock .... (Atlantic)
With A Little Help From My Friends .... (A&M)
Ringo Starr & His All-Star Band; *Nobody's Child-Romanian Angel Appeal-C* .... (Warner Bros.)
Your Friend In The Cowboy Hat (The Viagra Song)
Croatan; *Violent Passion Surrogate* .... (Man's Ruin)
Your Mind Has Left Your Body
Paul Kantner, Grace Slick & David Freiberg; *Baron Von Tollbooth & The Chrome Nun* .... (Grunt)
You're Getting To Be A Habit With Me
Betty Carter; *I Can't Help It* .... (GRP)
Diana Krall; *Love Scenes* .... (Impulse!)
Doris Day; *Golden Girl: The Columbia Recordings-1944-1966* ...... (Legacy)
Frank Sinatra; *songs for Swingin' Lovers!* .... (Capitol)
Mel Torme; *Spotlight On Mel Torme* .... (Capitol)
Original Broadway Cast; *42nd Street* .... (RCA Victor)
Zak And Sara
Ben Folds; *Rockin' The Suburbs* .... (Epic)

DRUGS: MARIJUANA, Getting Stoned

See Also: DRUGS: COCAINE, DRUGS: GENERAL

1st Of Tha Month
Bone Thugs-N-Harmony; *E. 1999 Eternal* .... (Ruthless/Relativity)
Acapulco Gold
Rainy Daze; *Acapulco Gold* .... (Out Of Print)
Amsterdam
Van Halen; *Balance* .... (Warner Bros.)
Bag O' Weed
Nate Dogg; *G-Funk Classics-#1 & 2-C* .... (Breakaway)
Bush Doctor
Peter Tosh; *Bush Doctor* .... (Rolling Stones)
Captured Live .... (EMI)
The Toughest .... (Capitol)
Coming Into Los Angeles
Arlo Guthrie; *Best Of Arlo Guthrie* .... (Warner Bros.)

Running Down The Road ....(Reprise)
ST/Woodstock...(Atlantic)

Days Of Our Livez
Bone Thugs-N-Harmony; *The Collection-#1* ....(Ruthless)

Don't Bogart That Joint
Little Feat; *Last Record Album* ....(Warner Bros.)
Waiting For Columbus ....(Warner Bros.)

Don't Step On The Grass, Sam
Steppenwolf; *Live Steppenwolf* ....(MCA)
The Second ....(MCA)

Dope Sucks
Herman Brood; *Herman Brood & His Wild Romance* ....(Ariola America)

Down To Seeds & Stems Again Blues
Commander Cody & His Lost Planet Airmen; *Live From Deep In The Heart*
Of Texas ....(MCA)
Lost In The Ozone ....(MCA)

Funny Lookin' Eyes
Barefoot Jerry; *Watchin' TV* ....(Monument)

Get High
Sons Of Champlin; *Loosen Up Naturally* ....(Capitol)

Gone Till November
Wyclef Jean featuring The Refugee Allstars; *Presents The Carnival F/*
Refugee Allstars ....(Ruffhouse/Columbia)

Hemp Hemp Hooray (Relegalize Today)
Total Devastation; *Total Devastation* ....(PGA)

Hemp Rally
Total Devastation; *Total Devastation* ....(PGA)

Hempcake
Exit-13; *Smoking Songs*. ....(Relapse)

Hemphead
P.O.L.; *Parade Of Losers* ....(Giant)

Henry
New Riders Of The Purple Sage; *Best Of New Riders Of The*
Purple Sage ....(Columbia)
Bill Graham Presents The Last Days Of The
Fillmore-C ....(Epic Portrait Assoc.)
Home Home On The Road ....(Columbia)
New Riders Of The Purple Sage ....(Columbia)

Hey Nineteen
Steely Dan; *Gaucho*. ....(MCA)
Steely Dan-Gold ....(MCA)

I Got 5 On It
Luniz; *Operation Stackola*. ....(Noo Trybe)

I Got Stoned & I Missed It
Dr. Hook; *Bankrupt*. ....(Capitol)

I Like Marijuana
David Peel & The Lower East Side; *Have A Marijuana* ....(Elektra)

I Need A Joint
Basehead; *Not In Kansas Anymore* ....(Imago)

Illegal Smile
John Prine; *John Prine*. ....(Atlantic)
Prime Prine-The Best Of John Prine ....(Atlantic)

I've Got Some Grass
David Peel & The Lower East Side; *Have A Marijuana* ....(Elektra)

Late In The Evening
Paul Simon; *Negotiations And Love Songs, 1971-1986*. ....(Warner Bros.)
One-Trick Pony ....(Warner Bros.)
Simon & Garfunkel; *The Concert In Central Park* ....(Warner Bros.)

Legalize It
Peter Tosh; *Legalize It*. ....(Columbia)
Rhythm Come Forward: A Reggae Anthology-C ....(Columbia)

Let's Go Get Stoned
Joe Cocker; *Mad Dogs & Englishmen*. ....(A&M)
Ray Charles; *Ray Charles' Greatest Hits* ....(Rhino)
Ray Charles-Anthology ....(Rhino)
Ray Charles-His Greatest Hits-#1 ......(Dunhill Compact Classics)

Magnolia Blues
Paul Davis; *Southern Tracks & Fantasies* ....(Bang)

Marahuana
Bette Midler; *Songs For The New Depression*. ....(Atlantic)

Marijuana
Country Joe & The Fish; *Life & Times Of Country Joe &*
The Fish. ....(Vanguard)

Mariwana
Soul Syndicate; *Harvested*. ....(Out Of Print)

Mota
Offspring; *Ixnay On The Hombre* ....(Columbia)

Next Episode
Dr. Dre; *Dr. Dre 2001* ....(Aftermath/Interscope)

Okie From Muskogee
Merle Haggard; *Friend In California* ....(Epic)
Merle Haggard & The Strangers; *Best Of Merle Haggard & The*
Strangers ....(Capitol)
Capitol Collectors Series-Merle Haggard & The Strangers. ....(Capitol)
Country Music Classics-#3-1965-1970-C. ....(K-Tel)
For The Record: Merle Haggard-43 Legendary Hits. ....(BNA)
Songs I'll Always Sing ....(Capitol)
ST/Platoon ....(Atlantic)

Old Dope Peddler
Tom Lehrer; *Songs By Tom Lehrer* ....(Reprise)

On Jamaica
Country Joe McDonald; *Paradise With An Ocean View* ....(Fantasy)

One Toke Over The Line
Brewer & Shipley; *'70s Greatest Rock Hits-#10-C* ....(Priority)
Super Hits Of The '70s-Have A Nice Day-#4-C ....(Rhino)

Opium Trail
Thin Lizzy; *Bad Reputation* ....(Mercury)

Panama Red
New Riders Of The Purple Sage; *Adventures Of Panama Red*. ......(Columbia)
Best Of New Riders Of The Purple Sage ....(Columbia)
Rock Classics Of The '70s-C ....(Columbia)

Pass It On
Wailers; *Burnin'*. ....(Tuff Gong)

Pass The Joint
BFM; *City O' Dope* ....(Wrap/Ichiban)

Pipe Dreams
Asleep At The Wheel; *Collision Course* ....(Capitol)

Pot Smoker's Song
Neil Diamond; *Velvet Gloves & Spit* ....(MCA Special Prod.)

Purple Pills
D12; *Devil's Night* ....(Shady/Interscope)

Rain, The (Supa Dupa Fly)
Missy "Misdemeanor" Elliot; *Supa Dupa Fly* ....(East West)

Rainy Day Women #12 & 35
Bob Dylan; *Blonde On Blonde*. ....(Columbia)
Bob Dylan's Greatest Hits. ....(Columbia)
Rock Classics Of The '60s-C. ....(Columbia)
ST/Forrest Gump. ....(Epic/Sony Music Soundtrax)
Bob Dylan And The Band; *Before The Flood*. ....(Columbia)

Reefer Head Woman
Aerosmith; *Night In The Ruts*. ....(Columbia)

Reefer Song
Original Cast; *Ain't Misbehavin'* ....(RCA)

Rip This Joint
Rolling Stones; *Exile On Main Street*. ....(Virgin)
Made In The Shade ....(Rolling Stones)

Show Me The Way To Get Stoned
David Peel & The Lower East Side; *Have A Marijuana*. ....(Elektra)

Sinsemilla
Black Uhuru; *Sinsemilla* ....(Mango)
Tear It Up ....(Mango)
The Island Story-1962-1987-25th Anniversary-C. ....(Island)

Stoned
Orleans; *Before The Dance* ....(Elektra)

Stoned Out Of My Mind
Chi-Lites; *Chi-Lites*. ....(Brunswick)
Chi-Lites' Greatest Hits ....(Rhino)
Didn't It Blow Your Mind: Soul Hits Of The '70s-#12-C. ....(Rhino)

Sweet Marijuana Brown
Paula Lockheart; *It Ain't The End Of The World* ....(Flying Fish)

Sweet Sensimilla
Jimmy Riley; *Put The People First* ....(Shanachie)

Take One Toke
Atomic Rooster; *Atomic Rooster* ....(Elektra)

That Acapulco Gold
Rainy Daze; *Summer Of Love-#2-Turn On-Mind Expansion & Signs Of The*
Times-C. ....(Rhino)

To The Bone (Let's Get Stoned)
Children Of Judah; *Give 'Em Enough Dope-#1-C* ....(Mic Mac)

Tokin' Tickets
Barefoot Jerry; *Barefootin'* ....(Monument)

Two Hits And The Joint Turned Brown
Pfaff Family Dog; *Marijuana's Greatest Hits Revisited-C* ....(Rehash)
Rodney & Doug Dillard and John Hartford; *Glitter Grass From The*
Nashwood Hollyville Strings & Permanent Wave ....(Flying Fish)

Various Tracks
Various Artists; *Marijuana's Greatest Hits* ....(Rehash)

Way I Am
Eminem; *The Marshall Mathers LP*. ....(Aftermath/Interscope)

What If God Smoked Cannabis
Bob Rivers; *Best Of Twisted Tunes-#2*. ....(Atlantic)

Who's Got The Herb?
311; *Hempilation-C*. ....(Capricorn)

You Don't Know How It Feels
Tom Petty; *Wildflowers* ....(Warner Bros.)

EARTH

See Also: DIRT, NATURE, SPACE, STARS, WORLD

Back Down To Earth
Carly Simon; *Boys In The Trees* ....(Elektra)

Back On Earth
Ozzy Osbourne; *The Ozzman Cometh* ....(Epic)

Children Of The Earth
Tower Of Power; *Bump City*. . . . .(Warner Bros.)
Down To Earth
Stevie Wonder; *Looking Back* . . . . (Motown)
Uptight (Everything's Alright). (Motown)
Earth Angel
Elvis Presley; *A Golden Celebration* . . . . (RCA)
New Edition; *ST/Under The Blue Moon* . . . .(MCA)
Penguins; *Billboard Top Rock 'N' Roll Hits-1955-C* . . . .
Golden Classics-Penguins. . . . . (Collectables)
Oldies But Goodies-#1-C. . . . . (Original Sound)
ST/American Graffiti . . . .(MCA)
Earth Blues
Jimi Hendrix; *Rainbow Bridge* . . . . (Reprise)
Earth Crisis
Steel Pulse; *Earth Crisis* . . . . (Elektra)
Earth Girls Are Easy
Julie Brown; *Goddess In Progress* . . . . (Rhino)
Earth Mother
Paul Kantner/Grace Slick; *Sunfighter*. . . . .(Grunt)
Earth, The Sun, The Rain
Color Me Badd; *Now & Forever*. . . . . (Giant)
Eartheart
Kenny Rankin; *Like A Seed*. . . . .(Little David)
For The Beauty Of The Earth
Paul Winter Consort; *Missa Gaia (Earth Mass)* . . . .(Living Music)
Give Me Love (Give Me Peace On Earth)
George Harrison; *Best Of George Harrison* . . . . (Capitol)
Living In The Material World . . . . (Capitol)
Greatest Love On Earth
Chicago; *Hot Streets*. . . . . (Columbia)
Greatest Show On Earth
Michael Jackson; *2 Classic Albums: Got To Be There/Ben* . . . . (Motown)
Ben. . . . . (Motown)
Heaven Is A Place On Earth
Belinda Carlisle; *Greenpeace/Rainbow Warriors-C* . . . .(Geffen)
Heaven On Earth . . . .(MCA)
Heaven On Earth
Platters; *Encore Of Golden Hits-Platters* . . . . (Mercury)
Platters-16 Greatest Hits . . . .(Trip)
Platters-Anthology. . . . . (Rhino)
Red Sails In The Sunset . . . .(Allegiance)
Higher Ground
UB40; *Promises And Lies*. . . . . (Virgin)
Hymn To The Russian Earth
Paul Winter Consort; *Concert For The Earth-Live At The United Nations*. . . . .(Living Music)
Last Night On Earth
U2; *Pop*. . . . . (Island)
Letter From Earth
Black Sabbath; *Dehumanizer* . . . . (Reprise)
Mother Earth
Memphis Slim; *Memphis Slim* . . . . (Chess)
Real Folk Blues-C . . . . (Chess)
Mother Earth
Nitty Gritty Dirt Band; *Dirt, Silver & Gold* . . . .(One Way)
Mother Earth
Merry-Go-Round; *Best Of Merry-Go-Round* . . . . (Rhino)
Mother Earth
Tom Rush; *Best Of Tom Rush: No Regrets* . . . . (Legacy)
No One Else On Earth
Wynonna; *Wynonna* . . . .(MCA)
Not To Touch The Earth
Doors; *Doors' Greatest Hits* . . . . (Elektra)
Waiting For The Sun . . . . (Elektra)
One Voice
Billy Gilman; *One Voice*. . . . .(Epic)
Planet Earth
Duran Duran; *Arena* . . . . (Capitol)
Decade. . . . . (Capitol)
Duran Duran (The Wedding Album) . . . . (Capitol)
Planet Earth
Duncan Browne; *Wild Places* . . . . (Sire)
Roads Girdle The Globe
XTC; *Drums & Wires*. . . . .(Geffen)
Salt Of The Earth
Mick Jagger & Keith Richards; *The Concert For New York City-C* . . (Columbia)
Rolling Stones; *Beggars Banquet* . . . . (Abkco)
Savage Earth Heart
Waterboys; *Waterboys* . . . . (Ensign)
Save Mother Earth
Merl Saunders; *Heavy Turbulence* . . . . (Fantasy)
Merl Saunders & Friends; *Fire Up* . . . . (Fantasy)
Merl Saunders & The Rainforest Band; *Save The Planet* . . . .(Sumertone)
Save The Planet
Edgar Winter's White Trash; *Edgar Winter's White Trash* . . . .(Epic)

Roadwork . . . . (Epic)
Scum Of The Earth
Kinks; *Preservation Act 2* . . . . (Rhino)
Scum Of The Earth
Rob Zombie; *ST/Mission: Impossible 2* . . . . (Hollywood)
She Walks This Earth
Sting; *Love Affair-Music Of Ivan Lins-C*. . . . .(Telarc)
Sinner
Neil Finn; *Try Whistling This* . . . . (Work)
Softest Place On Earth
Xscape; *Traces Of My Lipstick* . . . . (So So Def/Columbia)
Sparrow
Simon & Garfunkel; *Wednesday Morning 3 A.M.*. . . . . (Columbia)
Third Rock From The Sun
Joe Diffie; *A Thousand Winding Roads*. . . . . (Epic)
Third Stone From The Sun
Jimi Hendrix; *Essential Jimi Hendrix* . . . .(Reprise)
Kiss The Sky . . . . (Reprise)
Jimi Hendrix Experience; *Are You Experienced?* . . . . (Reprise)
This Bitter Earth
Aretha Franklin; *Aretha Franklin Sings The Blues* . . . . (Columbia)
Jazz To Soul . . . . (Columbia)
Dinah Washington; *Essential Dinah Washington-The Great Songs* . . . . . (Verve)
The Unforgettable Dinah Washington . . . .(Mercury)
To The Ends Of The Earth
Nat "King" Cole; *The Nat "King" Cole Story* . . . . (Capitol)
You Make Your Own Heaven & Hell Right Here On Earth
Temptations; *Psychedelic Shack* . . . . (Motown)

EARTHQUAKE

See Also: DANCE (shaking), DANGER & DISASTER

California Earthquake
John Hartford; *Catalogue* . . . . (Flying Fish)
Rodney Crowell; *Ain't Living Long Like This*. . . . . (Warner Bros.)
Earth A Quake
Johnny Green & The Greenmen; *Seven Over From Mars* . . . .(American Variety)
Earthquake
Mickey Newbury; *Live At Montezuma Hall* . . . . (Elektra)
Ronnie Milsap; *Heart & Soul* . . . . (RCA)
Earthquake
Al Wilson; *Count The Days*. . . . .(Roadshow)
Earthquake
Triumvirat; *Pompeii* . . . . (Capitol)
Earthquake
Graham Central Station; *Now Do You U Wanta Dance*. . . . . (Warner Bros.)
Earthquake & Hurricane
Tina Turner; *Rough* . . . .(United Artists)
Willie Dixon; *Mighty Earthquake & Hurricane* . . . . (Pausa)
Fault
John Hall; *John Hall* . . . .(Asylum)
Housequake
Prince; *Sign "O" The Times*. (Paisley Park)
I Feel The Earth Move
Carole King; *Carole King's Greatest Hits* . . . . (Epic)
Tapestry . . . . (Epic)
Little Earthquakes
Tori Amos; *Little Earthquakes* . . . .(Atlantic)
Livin' On The Fault Line
Doobie Brothers; *Livin' On The Fault Line* . . . . (Warner Bros.)
Our Love Is On The Faultline
Crystal Gayle; *Best Of Crystal Gayle* . . . . (Warner Bros.)
True Love . . . . (Elektra)
Outhouse Quake
Bootsauce; *Bull* . . . . (Island)
Shakey Ground
Temptations; *A Song For You* . . . . (Motown)
Temptations-Anthology-The Best Of The Temptations. . . . . (Motown)
Shakey Ground
T. Graham Brown; *You Can't Take It With You* . . . . (Capitol)
Shakey Ground
Phoebe Snow; *Best Of Phoebe Snow*. . . . . (Columbia)
It Looks Like Snow . . . . (Columbia)
Shaky Ground
Lacy J. Dalton & Glen Campbell; *Country Duets Two By Two-C* . . . . . . (Capitol)
Lacy J. . . . . (Capitol)
That's How You Know (When You're In Love)
Lari White; *Best Of Lari White* . . . .(RCA)
Wishes . . . . (RCA)
When The Earth Moves Again
Jefferson Airplane; *30 Seconds Over Winterland* . . . . (RCA)
Loves You . . . . (RCA)

EASTER

See Also: GOD

Easter
Joe Henry; *Shuffletown* . . . . (A&M)
Marillion; *Seasons End* . . . . (Capitol)
  Six Of One-Half Dozen Of The Other . . . . (I.R.S.)
Easter
Love Battery; *Between The Eyes* . . . . (Sub Pop)
Easter
Patti Smith Group; *Easter* . . . . (Arista)
Easter
Joe Henry; *Shuffletown* . . . . (A&M)
Easter (Ballade)
Jasper Van't Hof & Others; *Eyeball* . . . . (Creative Music Prod.)
Easter '88
Urge Overkill; *Americruiser/Jesus Urge Superstar* . . . . (Touch & Go)
Easter Day
Robyn Archer; *Robyn Archer* . . . . (Angel)
Easter Dinner
Tribe; *Abort* . . . . (Slash)
Easter Everywhere
Julian Cope; *My Nation Underground* . . . . (Island)
Easter Island
Russ Freeman; *Nocturnal Playground* . . . . (Brainchild)
Easter Parade
Andy Russell; *Puttin' On The Ritz-Capitol Sings Berlin-C* . . . . (Capitol)
Bing Crosby; *All Time Best Of Bing Crosby* . . . . (Curb)
Judy Garland & Fred Astaire; *ST/Easter Parade* . . . . (Rhino)
Sarah Vaughan; *Complete Sarah Vaughan On Mercury-#2* . . . . (Mercury)
Easter Tree
June Tabor; *Ashes & Diamonds* . . . . (Green Linnet)
Easter Woman
Residents; *Commercial Album* . . . . (Ralph)
Hallelujah Chorus
Philadelphia Orchestra & Eugene Ormandy; *Ave Maria-Christmas*
  Favorites . . . . (RCA)
Robert Shaw Chorale; *Christmas Treasures* . . . . (RCA)
North Easter
Cusco; *Cusco 2000* . . . . (Higher Octave)
Watermelon In Easter Hay
Frank Zappa; *Guitar* . . . . (Rykodisc)
  Joe's Garage Acts I-III . . . . (Rykodisc)
Were You There (When They Crucified My Lord?)
Johnny Cash with The Carter Family; *The Man In Black-His*
  Greatest Hits . . . . (Legacy)

EASY, Basic, Simple

See Also: CAREFREE, DIFFICULT, RELAX

(It's Not Easy) Bein' Green
Don Henley; *Kermit Unpigged* . . . . (Jim Henson)
(Such An) Easy Question
Elvis Presley; *From Nashville To Memphis-The Essential '60s Masters* . . (RCA)
  Pot Luck With Elvis . . . . (RCA)
1-2-3
Gloria Estefan; *Gloria Estefan's Greatest Hits* . . . . (Epic)
Gloria Estefan and Miami Sound Machine; *Let It Loose* . . . . (Epic)
1-2-3
Len Barry; *24 Of The Grooviest Hits Of All Time! The '60s Ultimate*
  Collection-#1-C . . . . (Sundazed Music)
ABC
Jackson 5; *ABC* . . . . (Motown)
  Jackson 5-Anthology . . . . (Motown)
  Jackson 5's Greatest Hits . . . . (Motown)
After The Blackbird Sings
Wallflowers; *The Wallflowers* . . . . (Virgin)
All You Need Is Love
Beatles; *Beatles 1* . . . . (Capitol)
  Compact Disc Singles Collection . . . . (Capitol)
  Magical Mystery Tour . . . . (Capitol)
  The Beatles/1967-1970 . . . . (Capitol)
  Yellow Submarine . . . . (Capitol)
Alone And Easy Target
Foo Fighters; *Foo Fighters* . . . . (Roswell/RCA)
Am I That Easy To Forget
Carl Belew; *24 Hits: Best Of Country Stars On LP-C* . . . . (Tee Vee)
Debbie Reynolds; *Debbie Reynolds' Greatest Hits* . . . . (Curb)
Engelbert Humperdinck; *Engelbert Humperdinck-16 Most Requested*
  Songs . . . . (Epic)
Ballad Of Easy Rider
Byrds; *Ballad Of Easy Rider* . . . . (Columbia)

Bring On The Night
Bruce Springsteen; *Tracks* . . . . (Columbia)
Cry So Easy
Erasure; *Wonderland* . . . . (Sire)
Don't Let Me Down Easy
Kim Richey; *Bitter Sweet* . . . . (Mercury)
Don't Make It Easy For Me
Earl Thomas Conley; *Very Best Of Earl Thomas Conley* . . . . (RCA)
Earth Girls Are Easy
Julie Brown; *Goddess In Progress* . . . . (Rhino)
Easier Said Than Done
Radney Foster; *Del Rio, TX 1959* . . . . (Arista)
Easier Said Than Done
Essex; *Best Of The Girl Groups-#2-C* . . . . (Rhino)
  Billboard Top Rock 'N' Roll Hits-1963-C . . . . (Rhino)
  Original Rock 'N' Roll Hits Of The '60s-C . . . . (Roulette)
Easy
Commodores; *20 Greatest Songs In Motown History-C* . . . . (Motown)
  All The Great Love Songs-Commodores . . . . (Motown)
  Commodores . . . . (Motown)
  Commodores Greatest Hits . . . . (Motown)
  Compact Command Performances-Commodores . . . . (Motown)
  Composer-Great Love Songs By Lionel Richie . . . . (Motown)
Lionel Richie; *Back To Front* . . . . (Motown)
Easy
Faith No More; *Who Cares A Lot?-The Greatest Hits* . . . . (Slash)
Easy
Liz Phair; *Juvenilia* . . . . (Capitol)
Easy
Timbuk 3; *Eden Alley* . . . . (I.R.S.)
Easy
Matthew Sweet; *Earth* . . . . (A&M)
Easy And Slow
Clancy Brothers & Tommy Makem; *Luck Of The Irish* . . . . (Columbia)
Easy As It Seems
Kiss; *Unmasked* . . . . (Mercury)
Easy As Life
Tina Turner; *ST/Aida* . . . . (Island)
Easy Blues, The
John Martyn; *Solid Air* . . . . (Island)
Easy Come Easy Go
George Strait; *Easy Come Easy Go* . . . . (MCA)
Easy Come Easy Go
Cinderella; *Still Climbing* . . . . (Mercury)
Easy Come Easy Go
Elvis Presley; *Command Performances-Essential 60's Masters II* . . . . . . (RCA)
Easy Come Easy Go
Bobby Sherman; *Very Best Of Bobby Sherman* . . . . (Restless)
Easy Come Easy Go
Winger; *In The Heart Of The Young* . . . . (Atlantic)
Easy Does It
Supertramp; *Crisis? What Crisis?* . . . . (A&M)
Easy Driver
Kenny Loggins; *Kenny Loggins Alive* . . . . (Columbia)
  Nightwatch . . . . (Columbia)
Easy For You To Say
Emmylou Harris; *Brand New Dance* . . . . (Reprise)
Linda Ronstadt; *Get Closer* . . . . (Asylum)
Easy From Now On
Emmylou Harris; *Profile/Best Of Emmylou Harris* . . . . (Warner Bros.)
  Quarter Moon In A Ten Cent Town . . . . (Warner Bros.)
Easy Listening
Rutles; *Archaeology* . . . . (Virgin)
Easy Livin'
Uriah Heep; *Demons And Wizards* . . . . (Mercury)
Easy Living
Billie Holiday; *Quintessential-#4-1937* . . . . (Columbia)
Ella Fitzgerald & Joe Pass; *Easy Living* . . . . (Pablo)
Paul Desmond; *Easy Living* . . . . (Bluebird)
Easy Love
Bread; *On The Waters* . . . . (Elektra)
Easy Lover
Phil Collins; *Phil Collins-Hits* . . . . (Atlantic)
  Serious Hits...Live! . . . . (Atlantic)
Philip Bailey & Phil Collins; *Chinese Wall* . . . . (Columbia)
Easy Loving
Freddie Hart; *Best Of Freddie Hart* . . . . (CEMA Special Prod.)
Easy Money
Benny Carter; *The King* . . . . (Pablo)
Benny Carter All-Star Sax Ensemble; *Over The Rainbow* . . . . . . (Musicmasters)
Easy Money
King Crimson; *Lark's Tongues In Aspic* . . . . (Editions E.G.)
Easy Money
Billy Joel; *Innocent Man* . . . . (Columbia)
Easy Money
Rickie Lee Jones; *Rickie Lee Jones* . . . . (Warner Bros.)

Easy Money
James O'Gwynn; *James O'Gwynn's Greatest Hits* . . . . (Plantation)
Easy Money
REO Speedwagon; *Nine Lives* . . . .(Epic)
You Can Tune A Piano But You Can't Tuna Fish . . . .(Epic)
Easy Now
Eric Clapton; *Eric Clapton* . . . . (Polydor)
Easy Now
Hot Tuna; *Best Of Hot Tuna* . . . . (RCA)
Phosphorescent Rat . . . . (RCA)
Easy On The Eyes
Carly Simon; *Clouds In My Coffee-1965-1995.* . . . . (Arista)
Easy On The Pain
Michael Martin Murphey; *Cowboy Songs Four* . . . . (Valley Entert.)
Easy Read
Trash Can Sinatras; *I've Seen Everything* . . . . (Mercury)
Easy Ride
Doors; *Soft Parade* . . . . (Elektra)
Easy Rider
Janis Joplin; *Live At Winterland* . . . . (Legacy)
Easy Skanking
Bob Marley & The Wailers; *Kaya* . . . . (Tuff Gong)
Easy Target
Heart; *Bad Animals* . . . . (Capitol)
Easy There, Steady Now
Richard Thompson; *Mirror Blue* . . . . (Capitol)
Easy Thing
Peter Criss; *Peter Criss* . . . . (Mercury)
Easy To Be Hard
Original Broadway Cast; *Hair* . . . . (RCA)
Original Cast; *ST/Hair* . . . . (RCA)
Three Dog Night; *Best Of Three Dog Night* . . . .(MCA)
Captured Live At The Forum . . . .(MCA)
Celebrate-The Three Dog Night Story . . . .(MCA)
Easy To Fall
Journey; *Trial By Fire.* . . . . (Columbia)
Easy To Fall
Bob Welch; *French Kiss* . . . . (Capitol)
Easy To Forget
Rembrandts; *LP* . . . . (East West)
Easy To Ignore
Sixpence None The Richer; *Sixpence None The Richer* . . . . . .(Squint/Columbia)
Easy To Love
Cole Porter; *Cole Porter In The 1930's-#2-Easy To Love* . . (Koch International)
Easy To Love
Leo Sayer; *All The Best.* . . . . (Chrysalis)
Show Must Go On-Anthology . . . . (Rhino)
Easy To Slip
Little Feat; *Sailin' Shoes.* . . . .(Warner Bros.)
Easy Tonight
Five For Fighting; *America Town* . . . .(Aware/C2/Columbia)
Easy Winners
Itzhak Perlman & Andre Previn; *Easy Winners* . . . . (Angel)
Joshua Rifkin; *Digital Ragtime-Music Of Scott Joplin* . . . . (Angel)
Marvin Hamlisch; *ST/The Sting* . . . . (MCA)
Scott Joplin; *The Entertainer* . . . . (Biograph)
Easy, Come On
Kris Kristofferson; *Who's To Bless And Who's To Blame* . . . .(One Way)
Ecstasy Made Easy
Gordon Lightfoot; *East Of Midnight.* . . . .(Warner Bros.)
Go Down Easy
Dan Fogelberg; *High Country Snows* . . . .(Full Moon)
Go Down Easy
John Martyn; *Solid Air* . . . . (Island)
Go Easy
John Martyn; *Bless The Weather* . . . . (Island)
Good Lovin' Ain't Easy To Come By
Marvin Gaye; *Marvin Gaye-Anthology* . . . . (Motown)
Happiness Is Easy
Talk Talk; *Colour Of Spring* . . . .(EMI)
Hard Times Come Easy
Richie Sambora; *Undiscovered Soul* . . . . (Mercury)
High Road Easy
Sass Jordan; *Rats* . . . .(Impact)
Hurtin' Comes Easy
Alan Jackson; *High Mileage.* . . . . (Arista)
I Don't Fall In Love So Easy
Trisha Yearwood; *The Song Remembers When* . . . .(MCA)
If Leaving Me Is Easy
Phil Collins; *Face Value* . . . .(Atlantic)
I'll Keep You Satisfied
Billy J. Kramer With The Dakotas; *History Of British Rock-#2-C* . . . . . . (Rhino)
I'm Easy
David Lee Roth; *Eat 'Em & Smile* . . . .(Warner Bros.)
I'm Not That Easy To Forget
Lorrie Morgan; *Shakin' Things Up* . . . . (BNA)

It Ain't Easy
2Pac; *Me Against The World* . . . .(Interscope)
It Ain't Easy
David Bowie; *Rise & Fall Of Ziggy Stardust And The Spiders*
From Mars. . . . . (Rykodisc)
It Ain't Gonna Be Easy
Elton John; *A Single Man* . . . . (MCA)
It Don't Come Easy
Ringo Starr; *Blast From Your Past* . . . . (Gold Rush)
It Just Ain't Easy
Allman Brothers Band; *Enlightened Rogues* . . . .(Polydor)
It Was So Easy
Carly Simon; *No Secrets* . . . . (Elektra)
It's Easy
Boston; *Don't Look Back* . . . . (Epic)
It's Easy For You
Elvis Presley; *Moody Blue.* . . . .(RCA)
It's Not Easy
Suicidal Tendencies; *Controlled By Hatred/Feel Like Shit...Deja Vu* . . . . (Epic)
It's So Easy
Buddy Holly; *Buddy Holly's Greatest Hits* . . . . (MCA)
From The Original Master Tapes-Buddy Holly . . . . (MCA)
Linda Ronstadt; *Linda Ronstadt's Greatest Hits, Volume Two* . . . .(Asylum)
Simple Dreams . . . .(Asylum)
It's So Easy
Guns N' Roses; *Appetite For Destruction* . . . . (Geffen)
Leavin' And Sayin' Goodbye
Faron Young; *Faron Young-Golden Hits* . . . . (Mercury)
Faron Young's Greatest Hits-#1-3 . . . .(Step One)
Let Me Down Easy
Stranglers; *Aural Sculpture* . . . . (Epic)
Loco-Motion
Grand Funk Railroad; *Billboard Top Rock 'N' Roll Hits-1974-C* . . . . (Rhino)
Caught In The Act. . . . . (Capitol)
Grand Funk Railroad-Hits . . . . (Capitol)
Kylie Minogue; *Kylie* . . . . (Geffen)
Little Eva; *Billboard Top Rock 'N' Roll Hits-1962-C* . . . . (Rhino)
Groove 'N' Grind-'50s & '60s Dance Hits-C. . . . . (Rhino)
More American Graffiti-C . . . . (MCA)
Lou-Easy-Ann
J.J. Cale; *5* . . . . (Sheher)
Love Don't Come Easy
Paula Abdul; *Head Over Heels* . . . . (Captive/Virgin)
Love Don't Come Easy
White Lion; *Mane Attraction* . . . .(Atlantic)
Love Isn't Easy (But It Sure Is Hard Enough)
Abba; *Ring Ring* . . . .(Polydor)
Lovin' You Is Easy
Journey; *Evolution* . . . . (Columbia)
Loving You
Alicia Keys; *Songs In A Minor* . . . . (J)
Natural One
Folk Implosion; *MTV Best Of The Buzz Bin-#2-C* . . . .(Mammoth)
ST/Kids . . . . (London)
Never Easy
Boyzone; *Where We Belong* . . . . (Ravenous/Mercury/IDJMG)
Nice And Easy
Walter Beasley; *For Your Pleasure.* . . . .(Shanachie)
Nice 'N Easy
Frank Sinatra; *Best Of The Capitol Years* . . . . (Capitol)
Nighthawk Postcards
Tom Waits; *Nighthawks At The Diner.* . . . .(Asylum)
No Easy Goodbye
South Sixty Five; *South Sixty Five* . . . .(Atlantic)
No Easy Road
Wishbone Ash; *Wishbone Four.* . . . . (MCA)
No Easy Way
Seal; *Human Being* . . . . (Warner Bros.)
No Easy Way Out
Robert Tepper; *Rocky Story-C.* . . . .(Scotti Bros.)
ST/Rocky IV . . . .(Scotti Bros.)
No One Said It Would Be Easy
Sheryl Crow; *Tuesday Night Music Club* . . . . (A&M)
Nothing Is Easy
Jethro Tull; *Stand Up.* . . . . (Chrysalis)
Pure And Easy
Who; *Odds & Sods* . . . . (MCA)
Ready For A Fall
P.J. Olsson; *Songs From Dawson's Creek* . . . .(Sony Music Soundtrax)
Restless
Carl Perkins; *Jive After Five-Best Of Carl Perkins-1959-1978* . . . . (Rhino)
Mark O'Connor; *Great Divorce Songs For Him-C* . . . . (Warner Bros.)
The New Nashville Cats . . . . (Warner Bros.)
Ride Easy
Asia; *Very Best Of Asia-Heat Of The Moment-1982-1990* . . . . (Geffen)
Roll 'Em Easy
Linda Ronstadt; *Prisoner In Disguise* . . . .(Asylum)

Little Feat; *Dixie Chicken* . . . . (Warner Bros.)
Selfless, Cold And Composed
Ben Folds Five; *Whatever And Ever Amen* . . . . (Caroline/550)
Simple Creed
Live; *V* . . . . (Radioactive/MCA)
Simple Days
Babyface; *The Day* . . . . (Epic)
Simple Gifts
Original Soundtrack; *School Days-Kids Classics* . . . . (Benson)
Simple Joys Of Maidenhood
Julie Andrews; *Camelot*. . . . . (Columbia)
Various Artists; *ST/Camelot* . . . . (Warner Bros.)
Simple Lessons
Candlebox; *Lucy* . . . . (Maverick)
Simple Song Of Freedom
Tim Hardin; *Simple Songs Of Freedom: The Tim Hardin Collection* . . . (Legacy)
Simple Things
Jim Brickman & Rebecca Lynn Howard; *Simple Things*. . . . . . (Windham Hill)
Simple Twist Of Fate
Bob Dylan; *Blood On The Tracks* . . . . (Columbia)
 Bob Dylan At Budokan . . . . (Columbia)
Jerry Garcia Band; *Jerry Garcia Band* . . . . (Arista)
Joan Baez; *Best Of Joan Baez* . . . . (A&M)
 Diamonds & Rust . . . . (A&M)
Simple Twist Of Fate
Tim Curry; *Best Of Tim Curry*. . . . . (A&M)
Simply Said
Kenny Garrett; *Simply Said*. . . . . (Warner Bros.)
Sing Something Simple
June Christy; *The Misty Miss Christy* . . . . (Capitol)
Sleazy Come Easy Go
L.A. Guns; *Cocked And Loaded* . . . . (Polydor)
Slow Ride
Foghat; *Best Of Foghat* . . . . (Rhino)
 Best Of King Biscuit Live-#1-C . . . . (Sandstone Music)
 Foghat-Live . . . . (Rhino)
 Fool For The City . . . . (Rhino)
So Easy To Begin
Olivia Newton-John; *Making A Good Thing Better*. . . . . (MCA)
Some Folks Lives Roll Easy
Paul Simon; *Still Crazy After All These Years* . . . . (Columbia)
Song 2
Blur; *Blur*. . . . . (Virgin)
Stranded On Easy Street
Bruce Hornsby; *A Night On The Town* . . . . (RCA)
Take It Easy
Eagles; *Eagles* . . . . (Asylum)
 Eagles Live . . . . (Asylum)
 Eagles/Their Greatest Hits 1971-1975 . . . . (Asylum)
 Hell Freezes Over . . . . (Geffen)
Jackson Browne; *For Everyman* . . . . (Asylum)
Travis Tritt; *Common Thread-Songs Of The Eagles-C* . . . . (Giant)
Take It Easy
Duke Ellington; *Brunswick Era-#1-1926-1929* . . . . (MCA)
Take It Easy
Crystal Gayle; *Crystal Gayle Greatest Hits*. . . . . (Columbia)
 These Days . . . . (Columbia)
Takin' It Easy
Lacy J. Dalton; *Dream Baby* . . . . (Columbia)
 Lacy J. Dalton's Greatest Hits . . . . (Columbia)
Thousand Times A Day
Patty Loveless; *The Trouble With The Truth* . . . . (Epic)
Uneasy Rider
Charlie Daniels Band; *A Decade Of Hits* . . . . (Epic)
 Homesick Heroes . . . . (Epic)
 Super Hits Of The '70s-Have A Nice Day-#1-C . . . . (Rhino)
 Uneasy Rider . . . . (Epic)
When Somebody Loves You
Alan Jackson; *When Somebody Loves You* . . . . (Arista)
When You're Alone (It Ain't Easy)
Journey; *Evolution*. . . . . (Columbia)
You Make It Easy
James Taylor; *Gorilla* . . . . (Warner Bros.)
You Make It Seem So Easy
Kinleys; *Just Between You And Me* . . . . (Epic)
You Take It Nice And Easy, You Play It Safe Cause That's What People Do
George Strait; *One Step At A Time*. . . . . (MCA)
You'd Be So Easy To Love
Frank Sinatra; *Ring-A-Ding Ding* . . . . (Reprise)
 The Reprise Collection . . . . (Reprise)
You're Easy On The Eyes
Terri Clark; *Big Country Hits '99-C* . . . . (K-Tel)
 How I Feel . . . . (Mercury)
You're Easy To Dance With
Fred Astaire; *Irving Berlin Songbook* . . . . (Verve)

ECHOES, Traces
See Also: **HEAR, REFLECTIONS, SHADOWS**

An Echo, A Stain
Bjork; *Vespertine* . . . . (Elektra)
Echo Beach
Martha & The Muffins; *Metro Music* . . . . (Virgin)
Echo Valley 2-6809
Partridge Family; *Partridge Family's Greatest Hits* . . . . (Arista)
Echoes
Gene Clark; *Nuggets-#11-Pop-Part 4-C* . . . . (Rhino)
Echoes
Pink Floyd; *Meddle* . . . . (Capitol)
Echoes
New Riders Of The Purple Sage; *Marin County Line* . . . . (MCA)
Echoes Of Harlem
Clark Terry Five; *Memories Of Duke* . . . . (Pablo)
Claude Bolling; *Claude Bolling Plays Ellington-#1* . . . . (Columbia)
Cootie Williams; *Jazz Sampler-#3-C* . . . . (Columbia)
Duke Ellington; *Mood Indigo* . . . . (Pro-Arte)
Echoes Of Love
Doobie Brothers; *Best Of The Doobies, Volume II* . . . . (Warner Bros.)
 Livin' On The Fault Line . . . . (Warner Bros.)
Pointer Sisters; *Energy*. . . . . (Planet)
Echoes Of Love
Elvis Presley; *ST/Kissin' Cousins* . . . . (RCA)
Echoes Of Love
Kim Richey; *Kim Richey* . . . . (Mercury)
Echoes Of Spain
Django Reinhardt; *Djangologie USA-#2* . . . . (Disques Swing)
Echoes Of Spring
Willie ''The Lion'' Smith; *Echoes Of Spring*. . . . . (Milan)
Echoes Of The African Forest
Saka Acquaye Ensemble; *Voices Of Africa* . . . . (Nonesuch)
Echoes Of The Last Stampede
Norton Buffalo; *Desert Horizon*. . . . . (Capitol)
Everybody's Talkin'
Nilsson; *Everybody's Talkin': The Encore Collection* . . . . . (BMG Special Prod.)
 ST/Forrest Gump. . . . . (Epic/Sony Music Soundtrax)
 ST/Midnight Cowboy. . . . . (EMI)
Willie Nelson; *Best Of Willie* . . . . (RCA)
 Sweet Memories . . . . (RCA)
Faithfull
Pearl Jam; *Yield* . . . . (Epic)
Traces
Classics IV; *Very Best Of The Classics IV* . . . . (EMI)
Classics IV Featuring Dennis Yost; *Oldies But Goodies-#11-C* . . . . (Original Sound)
Ronnie Milsap; *Ronnie Milsap-16 Greatest Hits-#2* . . . . (Trip)
Traces/Memories
Lettermen; *Capitol Collectors Series-The Lettermen*. . . . . (Capitol)
 The Lettermen's All-Time Greatest Hits . . . . (Capitol)
Vienna Echoes
Lawrence Welk; *Lawrence Welk Celebrates 50 Years In Music* . . . . (Ranwood)

EGO, Attitude, Dignity, Identity, Pride, Self-centered, Selfishness, Self-respect, Taking A Stand, Vanity
See Also: **ADVICE, BRAGGING, CAREFREE, FEAR & COURAGE, FEMINISM, GREED, HAPPINESS, JEALOUSY, LIFE, LOW SELF-ESTEEM, MOTIVATION**

#1 Stunna
Big Tymers; *I Got That Work*. . . . . (Cash Money/Universal)
(It's Just) The Way That You Love Me
Paula Abdul; *Forever Your Girl*. . . . . (Virgin)
 Shut Up And Dance (The Dance Mixes) . . . . (Virgin)
(You Make Me Feel Like) A Natural Woman
Aretha Franklin; *Aretha Franklin's Greatest Hits-1980-1994* . . . . (Arista)
 Chicken Soup For The Woman's Soul-C . . . . (Rhino)
Carole King; *Tapestry* . . . . (Epic)
Celine Dion; *Tapestry Revisited: Tribute To Carole King-C* . . . . (Lava)
2 Legit 2 Quit
Hammer; *2 Legit 2 Quit* . . . . (Capitol)
32 Flavors
Alana Davis; *Blame It On Me*. . . . . (Elektra)
Ani DiFranco; *Living In Clip* . . . . (Righteous Babe)
 Not A Pretty Girl . . . . (Righteous Babe)
Ain't Too Proud To Beg
Rolling Stones; *It's Only Rock 'N Roll*. . . . . (Rolling Stones)
Temptations; *Motown Story-First 25 Years-C* . . . . (Motown)
 ST/Big Chill. . . . . (Motown)
 Temptations' Greatest Hits-#1 . . . . (Motown)
 Temptations-25th Anniversary . . . . (Motown)

Temptations-Anthology-The Best Of The Temptations . . . . (Motown)

Ain't Your Memory Got No Pride?
Merle Haggard; *Ramblin' Fever*. . . . .(MCA)

All I Need Is Me
Elaine & Ellen; *Elaine & Ellen*. . . . . (Mercury)

All I Want
Offspring; *Ixnay On The Hombre* . . . . (Columbia)

American Bad Ass
Kid Rock; *History Of Rock* . . . . (Top Dog/Lava/Atlantic)

Any Man Of Mine
Shania Twain; *1996 Grammy Nominees-C*. . . . . (Columbia)
The Woman In Me . . . . (Mercury)
Snoopy; *Snoopy's Country Classiks On Toys* . . . . (Lightyear)

Anything You Can Do (I Can Do Better)
Betty Hutton & Howard Keel; *That's Entertainment! III-C* . . . . (Angel)
Ethel Merman/Bruce Yarnell/Original Cast; *Annie Get
Your Gun*. . . . .(RCA Victor)
Ethel Merman/Ray Middleton/Original Cast; *Annie Get Your Gun* . . . . . .(MCA)
John Raitt & Bonnie Raitt; *Broadway Legend* . . . . (Angel)

Are We Ourselves
Fixx; *One Thing Leads To Another-Greatest Hits* . . . .(MCA)
React . . . .(MCA)

Are You Hung Up
Mothers Of Invention; *We're Only In It For The Money*. . . . .(Rykodisc)

Are You Jimmy Ray?
Jimmy Ray; *Jimmy Ray* . . . .(Epic)

Are You That Somebody?
Aaliyah; *ST/Dr. Dolittle* . . . . (Atlantic)

Baby You Ain't Nothin' Without Me
Karen Young; *Hot Shot*. . . . .(West End)

Back When He Was Hungry
Bill Anderson; *A Lot Of Things Different* . . . . (Varese Sarabande)

Bad
Michael Jackson; *Bad*. . . . .(Epic)

Bad Man
R. Kelly; *I Wish (import EP)* . . . . (Jive)

Be Good To Yourself
Journey; *Journey's Greatest Hits* . . . . (Columbia)
Raised On Radio . . . . (Columbia)

Be Good To Yourself
Frankie Miller; *Full House* . . . .(Chrysalis)

Be Somebody
Melissa Manchester; *Help Is On The Way* . . . . (Arista)

Be Thankful For What You Got
William DeVaughn; *Didn't It Blow Your Mind: Soul Hits Of The
'70s-#12-C* . . . . (Rhino)
Oldies But Goodies-#11-C. . . . . (Original Sound)

Be Your Own Best Friend
Ray Stevens; *Be Your Own Best Friend* . . . .(Warner Bros.)
Feeling's Not Right Again . . . .(Warner Bros.)

Be Yourself
Patti LaBelle; *Be Yourself*. . . . .(MCA)

Be Yourself
Cameo; *Alligator Woman* . . . . (Chocolate City)

Beep Beep
Playmates; *Dr. Demento: 20th Anniversary Collection-C* . . . . (Rhino)

Before I Go
John Hiatt; *Crossing Muddy Waters* . . . . (Vanguard)

Behind Closed Doors
Charlie Rich; *American Originals-Charlie Rich*. . . . . (Columbia)
Behind Closed Doors . . . .(Epic)
Charlie Rich's Greatest Hits . . . .(Epic)
Columbia Country Classics-#4-Nashville Sound-C. . . . . (Columbia)

Believe In Yourself
Lena Horne; *ST/The Wiz*. . . . . (MCA)

Believe Me Baby (I Lied)
Trisha Yearwood; *Everybody Knows* . . . .(MCA)

Bell Bottom Blues
Derek And The Dominos; *Layla*. . . . . (Polydor)
Eric Clapton; *24 Nights* . . . . (Duck/Reprise)

Better Than You
Metallica; *Reload* . . . . (Elektra)

Bidin' My Time
Original Cast; *Girl Crazy* . . . . (Sony Music Special Prod.)
Sarah Vaughan; *Sarah Vaughan Sings George Gershwin Songbook,
Vol. 1*. . . . . (Emarcy)

Big Boys Don't Cry
Extreme; *Extreme* . . . . (A&M)

Big Girls Don't Cry
4 Seasons; *4 Seasons' Greatest Hits-#1* . . . . (Rhino)
4 Seasons-Anthology . . . . (Rhino)
Billboard Top Rock 'N' Roll Hits-1962-C . . . . (Rhino)
More Dirty Dancing-C. . . . . (RCA)

Big Man
Charlie Daniels Band; *Uneasy Rider* . . . .(Epic)

Big Man
Four Preps; *Best Of The Four Preps* . . . . (Curb)
Capitol Collectors Series-Four Preps . . . . (Collectables)

Big Me
Foo Fighters; *Foo Fighters* . . . .(Roswell/RCA)

Big Shot
Billy Joel; *52nd Street* . . . . (Columbia)
Billy Joel-Greatest Hits, Volume I & Volume II . . . . (Columbia)
KOHUEPT. . . . . (Columbia)

Big Willie Style
Will Smith featuring Left Eye; *Big Willie Style*. . . . . (Columbia)

Bitch
Meredith Brooks; *Blurring The Edges* . . . . (Capitol)

Bitch Is Back
Elton John; *Caribou* . . . . (Rocket)
Elton John's Greatest Hits-#2 . . . . (Polydor)
Here And There . . . . (Rocket)
Tina Turner; *Two Rooms-Celebrating The Songs Of Elton John & Bernie
Taupin-C* . . . .(Polydor)

Bitter Sweet Symphony
Verve; *Urban Hymns* . . . . (Hut/Virgin)

Boombastic
Shaggy; *Boombastic*. . . . .(Virgin)

Bow Wow (That's My Name)
Lil Bow Wow; *Beware Of Dog* . . . . (So So Def/Columbia)

Boxer, The
Simon & Garfunkel; *Bridge Over Troubled Water* . . . . (Columbia)
Collected Works . . . . (Columbia)
Simon & Garfunkel's Greatest Hits . . . . (Columbia)
The Concert In Central Park . . . . (Warner Bros.)

Boys Are Back In Town
Bon Jovi; *ST/Navy Seals* . . . .(Atlantic)
Thin Lizzy; *'70s Greatest Rock Hits-#14-King Of Rock-C* . . . .(Priority)
Dedication-Very Best Of Thin Lizzy . . . . (Mercury)
Jailbreak. . . . . (Mercury)
Live And Dangerous. . . . . (Warner Bros.)

Branded Man
Merle Haggard & The Strangers; *For The Record: Merle Haggard-43
Legendary Hits* . . . .(BNA)

Brass In Pocket (I'm Special)
Pretenders; *Pretenders* . . . .(Sire)
Pretenders-The Singles . . . .(Sire)

Break My Stride
Matthew Wilder; *I Don't Speak The Language* . . . . (Private I)

Breakdown
Tantric; *Tantric* . . . . (Maverick)

Broken Wing
Martina McBride; *Evolution* . . . .(RCA)

Building A Mystery
Sarah McLachlan; *Lilith Fair-A Celebration Of Women In Music-C* . . . . (Arista)
Mirrorball . . . . (Arista)
Surfacing . . . . (Arista)

Bye, Bye
Jo Dee Messina; *I'm Alright* . . . . (Curb)

Camera One
Josh Joplin Group; *Useful Music*. . . . .(Artemis)

Can't Change Me
Chris Cornell; *Euphoria Morning* . . . . (A&M)

Can't Take That Away (Mariah's Theme)
Mariah Carey; *Rainbow* . . . . (Columbia)

Cathy's Clown
Everly Brothers; *Billboard Top Rock 'N' Roll Hits-1960-C* . . . . (Rhino)
Golden Hits Of The Everly Brothers. . . . . (Warner Bros.)
The Reunion Concert-Live At Albert Hall 1983 . . . .(Mercury)
Very Best Of The Everly Brothers. . . . . (Warner Bros.)
Reba McEntire; *Sweet Sixteen*. . . . . (MCA)

Cause I Can Do It Right
Big Daddy Kane; *Taste Of Chocolate* . . . . (Cold Chillin')

C'est Moi
Original Cast; *ST/Camelot* . . . . (Warner Bros.)
Robert Goulet; *Camelot* . . . . (Columbia)

Change The World
Offspring; *Ixnay On The Hombre* . . . . (Columbia)

Child Is Gone
Fiona Apple; *Tidal* . . . .(Clean Slate/Work)

Coal Miner's Daughter
Loretta Lynn; *Coal Miner's Daughter* . . . . (MCA)
Coal Miner's Daughter . . . . (MCA)
Loretta Lynn-20 Greatest Hits . . . . (MCA)
Loretta Lynn-Greatest Hits Live . . . . (K-Tel)
Loretta Lynn's Greatest Hits-#2 . . . . (MCA)
The Country Music Hall Of Fame-Loretta Lynn . . . . (MCA)

Coat Of Many Colors
Dolly Parton; *Best Of Dolly Parton* . . . . (RCA)
Dolly Parton-Super Hits. . . . . (Columbia)
Essential Dolly Parton-#2 . . . . (RCA)
Emmylou Harris; *Pieces Of The Sky* . . . . (Reprise)

Come On Over
Shania Twain; *Come On Over*. . . . . (Mercury)

Confident Rat
Ignorance; *Confident Rat*. . . . . (Metal Blade)

Cool
Original Cast; *ST/West Side Story* . . . . (Sony Broadway)
Time; *Time* . . . . (Warner Bros.)
C-O-U-N-T-R-Y
Joe Diffie; *Life's So Funny* . . . . (Epic)
Country Grammar (Hot Sh*t)
Nelly; *Country Grammar* . . . .(Fo' Reel/Universal)
Country In My Jeans
Loretta Lynn; *Still Country* . . . . (Audium)
Crazy
Alana Davis; *Blame It On Me* . . . . (Elektra)
Dawning Is The Day
Moody Blues; *A Question Of Balance* . . . . (Polydor)
Days Of Our Livez
Bone Thugs-N-Harmony; *The Collection-#1* . . . . (Ruthless)
Dedicated Follower Of Fashion
Kinks; *Kinks' Greatest Hits* . . . . (Rhino)
Kinks-Size Kinkdom . . . . (Rhino)
Deep Inside
Mary J. Blige; *Mary* . . . . (MCA)
Do Anything You Wanna Do
Eddie & The Hot Rods; *Life On The Line* . . . . (Island)
The Island Story-1962-1987-25th Anniversary-C . . . . (Island)
Do Anything You Want To
Thin Lizzy; *Black Rose/A Rock Legend* . . . . (Warner Bros.)
Do Something
Macy Gray; *On How Life Is* . . . . (Epic)
ST/Music Of The Heart . . . . (Epic/Sony Music Soundtrax)
Do The Evolution
Pearl Jam; *Yield* . . . . (Epic)
Do What You Do
Martina McBride; *Emotion* . . . . (RCA)
Do What You Feel
Deniece Williams; *I'm So Proud* . . . . (Columbia)
Doggy Dogg World
Snoop Doggy Dogg; *Doggystyle* . . . . (Death Row)
Donna The Prima Donna
Dion; *Bronx Blues-Columbia Recordings 1962-1965* . . . . (Columbia)
Dion-24 Original Classics . . . . (Arista)
Don't Cry Out Loud
Melissa Manchester; *Melissa Manchester's Greatest Hits* . . . . (Arista)
Peter Allen; *At His Best* . . . . (A&M)
I Could Have Been A Sailor . . . . (A&M)
It Is Time For Peter Allen . . . . (A&M)
Don't Give Up
Peter Gabriel; *Shaking The Tree-Sixteen Golden Greats* . . . . (Geffen)
So . . . . (Geffen)
Don't Make Me Over
Dionne Warwick; *Beg, Scream & Shout! The Big Ol' Box Of '60s*
Soul-C . . . . (Rhino)
Dionne Warwick Collection-Her All-Time Greatest Hits . . . . (Rhino)
Jennifer Warnes; *Shot Through The Heart* . . . . (Arista)
Don't Sleep In The Subway
Frank Sinatra; *Frank Sinatra* . . . . (Reprise)
Petula Clark; *Petula Clark's Greatest Hits* . . . . (Crescendo)
Summer Of Love-#1-C . . . . (Rhino)
Don't Tell Me (What Love Can Do)
Van Halen; *Balance* . . . . (Warner Bros.)
Doo Wop (That Thing)
Lauryn Hill; *The Miseducation Of Lauryn Hill* . . . . (Ruffhouse/Columbia)
Drive
Incubus; *Make Yourself* . . . . (Immortal/Epic)
Now That's What I Call Music!-#6-C . . . . (Virgin)
Drops Of Jupiter (Tell Me)
Train; *Drops Of Jupiter* . . . . (Aware/C2/Columbia)
Duck And Run
3 Doors Down; *Better Life* . . . . (Republic/Universal)
D'You Know What I Mean
Oasis; *Be Here Now* . . . . (Epic)
Ego
Betty Carter; *Family* . . . . (Roulette)
Elton John; *To Be Continued* . . . . (MCA)
Ego Tripper
Danny Kortchmar; *Innuendo* . . . . (Asylum)
Ego Tripping Out
Marvin Gaye; *Seek And You Shall Find-More Of The Best-1963-'81* . . . . (Rhino)
Erotica
Madonna; *Erotica* . . . . (Maverick/Sire)
GHV2 . . . . (Warner Bros.)
Everybody (Backstreet's Back)
Backstreet Boys; *Backstreet Boys* . . . . (Jive)
Everybody Be Yoself
Keb' Mo'; *Big Wide Grin* . . . . (Sony Wonder)
Everybody Else
Greg Kihn; *Next Of Kihn* . . . . (Beserkley)
Everybody Else Is Wrong
Utopia; *Deface The Music* . . . . (Rhino)

Everybody's A Star
Kinks; *Soap Opera* . . . . (Rhino)
Everybody's Trying To Be My Baby
Beatles; *Beatles '65* . . . . (Capitol)
For Sale . . . . (Capitol)
The Beatles-Anthology-#2 . . . . (Capitol)
Carl Perkins; *Blue Suede Shoes: The Very Best Of Carl Perkins* . . . (Collectables)
Carl Perkins' Greatest Hits/Finest Performances . . . . (Sun)
Carl Perkins-Original Sun Greatest Hits . . . . (Rhino)
Faith In Me, Faith In You
Doug Stone; *Country Lovin'-Songs From The Heart-C* . . . . (Rhino)
Faith In Me Faith In You . . . . (Columbia)
Super Hits Of 1995-C . . . . (Epic)
Feet Up (Pat Him On The Po-Po)
Guy Mitchell; *Definitive Guy Mitchell* . . . . (Collector's Choice)
Fire Escape
Fastball; *All The Pain Money Can Buy* . . . . (Hollywood)
Foolish Pride
Daryl Hall; *Three Hearts In The Happy Ending Machine* . . . . (RCA)
Joan Armatrading; *The Key* . . . . (A&M)
Foolish Pride
Travis Tritt; *Ten Feet Tall And Bulletproof* . . . . (Warner Bros.)
Free
Vast; *Music For People* . . . . (Elektra)
Free To Decide
Cranberries; *To The Faithful Departed* . . . . (Island)
Friends In Low Places
Garth Brooks; *Garth Brooks-Double Live* . . . . (Capitol)
No Fences . . . . (Capitol)
Gets Me Through
Ozzy Osbourne; *Down To Earth* . . . . (Epic)
Gettin' Jiggy Wit It
Will Smith; *Big Willie Style* . . . . (Columbia)
Girl's Gotta Do (What A Girl's Gotta Do)
Mindy McCready; *Ten Thousand Angels* . . . . (BNA)
Give It 2 You
Da'Brat; *Funkdafied* . . . . (Chaos)
Glory Of Love
Bette Midler; *ST/Beaches* . . . . (Atlantic)
Peter Cetera; *Solitude/Solitaire* . . . . (Full Moon)
ST/The Karate Kid Part II . . . . (EMI)
Go Your Own Way
Cranberries; *Legacy-A Tribute To Fleetwood Mac's Rumours-C* . . . . (Lava)
Fleetwood Mac; *25 Years-The Chain* . . . . (Warner Bros.)
Fleetwood Mac Live . . . . (Warner Bros.)
Fleetwood Mac's Greatest Hits . . . . (Warner Bros.)
Rumours . . . . (Warner Bros.)
Greatest Love Of All
George Benson; *George Benson-Collection* . . . . (Warner Bros.)
ST/The Greatest . . . . (Arista)
Weekend In L.A. . . . . (Warner Bros.)
Whitney Houston; *Whitney Houston* . . . . (Arista)
Whitney Houston's Greatest Hits . . . . (Arista)
Half The Man
Clint Black; *No Time To Kill* . . . . (RCA)
Halfway Down
Patty Loveless; *When Fallen Angels Fly* . . . . (Epic)
Happy
Sister Hazel; *...Somewhere More Familiar* . . . . (Universal)
Happy To Be Just Like I Am
Taj Mahal; *Happy To Be Just Like I Am* . . . . (Columbia)
Hard Way, The
Mary Chapin Carpenter; *Come On Come On* . . . . (Columbia)
Hero
Mariah Carey; *America: A Tribute To Heroes-C* . . . . (Interscope)
Diana, Princess Of Wales-Tribute-C . . . . (Columbia)
God Bless America-C . . . . (Columbia)
Mariah Carey-#1's . . . . (Columbia)
Music Box . . . . (Columbia)
Hey Leonardo (She Likes Me For Me)
Blessid Union Of Souls; *Now That's What I Call Music!-#3-C* . . . . (Virgin)
Walking Off The Buzz . . . . (Push/V2)
High Horse
Nitty Gritty Dirt Band; *Plain Dirt Fashion* . . . . (Warner Bros.)
Twenty Years Of Dirt-Best Of The Nitty Gritty Dirt Band . . . . (Warner Bros.)
High Horse
Evelyn "Champagne" King; *Best Of Evelyn "Champagne" King-Love*
Come Down . . . . (RCA)
Hold Your Head Up
Argent; *Argent-Anthology-Collection Of Greatest Hits* . . . . (Epic)
Encore-Argent . . . . (Epic)
Rock Artifacts-From The Vaults-#1-C . . . . (Columbia)
ST/Queen's Logic . . . . (Epic)
Home To Myself
Melissa Manchester; *Essence Of Melissa Manchester* . . . . (Arista)
Honor Bound
Earl Thomas Conley; *Treadin' Water* . . . . (RCA)
How Do You Like Me Now?!
Toby Keith; *How Do You Like Me Now?!* . . . . (DreamWorks/SKG)

Husbands And Wives
Brooks & Dunn; *Big Country Hits '99-C* . . . . (K-Tel)
   If You See Her . . . . (Arista)
Neil Diamond; *Neil Diamond-Love Songs* . . . . (MCA)
   Rainbow . . . .(MCA)
   Stones . . . .(MCA)
Roger Miller; *Best Of Roger Miller* . . . . (Mercury)
   Best Of Roger Miller-His Greatest Songs . . . . (Curb)
   Roger Miller-Super Hits . . . .(Epic)
   Roger Miller-The Hits . . . . (Mercury)

I Ain't Gonna Let You Break My Heart Again
Bonnie Raitt; *Nick Of Time* . . . . (Capitol)

I Alone
Live; *Throwing Copper* . . . .(Radioactive/MCA)

I Am A Simple Man
Ricky Van Shelton; *Backroads* . . . . (Columbia)

I Am That Man
Brooks & Dunn; *Borderline* . . . . (Arista)

I Am The Light Of This World
Jorma Kaukonen & Tom Hobson; *Quah.* . . . . (Relix)

I Am Woman
Helen Reddy; *Helen Reddy's Greatest Hits* . . . . (Capitol)
   I Am Woman. . . . . (Capitol)
   I Am Woman-C. . . . . (Nick At Nite)
   I Don't Know How To Love Him . . . . (Capitol)

I Am Your Woman
Syleena Johnson; *Chapter One: Love, Pain & Forgiveness* . . . . (Jive)

I Am...I Said
Neil Diamond; *Hot August Night* . . . . (MCA)
   Hot August Night II . . . . (Columbia)
   Neil Diamond-His 12 Greatest Hits . . . . (MCA)
   Stones. . . . .(MCA)

I Can't Do That Anymore
Faith Hill; *It Matters To Me* . . . .(Warner Bros.)

I Dare You
Black Rob; *Life Story* . . . .(Bad Boy/Arista)

I Declare
Lee Roy Parnell with Keb' Mo'; *Tell The Truth* . . . . (Vanguard)

I Didn't Know My Own Strength
Lorrie Morgan; *Lorrie Morgan's Greatest Hits* . . . . (BNA)
   Reflections-Limited Edition Greatest Hits . . . . (BNA)

I Don't Call Him Daddy
Doug Supernaw; *Pure Country-Best Of The '90s-C* . . . . (Priority)
   Red And Rio Grande . . . . (BNA)

I Don't Care Anymore
Phil Collins; *Hello, I Must Be Going.* . . . .(Atlantic)

I Don't Have To Crawl
Rodney Crowell; *Rodney Crowell-Collection* . . . .(Warner Bros.)
Rosanne Cash; *Hitchhiker Exampler-C* . . . . (Columbia)
   King's Record Shop . . . . (Columbia)

I Don't Need You
Kenny Rogers; *Kenny Rogers-Twenty Greatest Hits* . . . . (EMI)
   Share Your Love. . . . . (Liberty)

I Feel Pretty
Julie Andrews; *A Little Bit Of Broadway* . . . . (Columbia)
Little Richard; *The Songs Of West Side Story* . . . . (RCA Victor)
Original Cast; *ST/West Side Story.* . . . .(Sony Broadway)

I Got To Be Myself
Rance Allen; *15 Original Big Hits-#3-C.* . . . . (Stax)
Rufus Thomas; *I Ain't Getting Older I'm Getting Better* . . . . (American Variety)
   If There Were No Music . . . . (American Variety)

I Have Learned To Respect The Power Of Love
Angela Winbush; *Real Thing* . . . . (Mercury)
Stephanie Mills; *Stephanie Mills.* . . . .(MCA)

I Just Wanna Love U (Give It 2 Me)
Jay-Z; *Dynasty-Roc La Familia 2000* . . . . (Roc-A-Fella/DJMG)

I Me Mine
Beatles; *Let It Be.* . . . . (Capitol)
   The Beatles-Anthology-#3 . . . . (Capitol)

I Surrender Dear
Bing Crosby; *Pennies From Heaven.* . . . . (Pro-Arte)
   Where The Blue Of The Night Meets The Gold Of The Day . . . . (Biograph)
Count Basie; *Basie & Zoot* . . . .(Pablo)
   Jam-#3 . . . .(Pablo)
   Loose Walk . . . .(Pablo)
Count Basie & His Kansas City 3; *For The Second Time* . . . . (Pablo)
Gus Arnheim & His Orchestra featuring Bing Crosby; *78-#22618* . . . . . (Victor)
Mel Torme; *Smooth As Velvet.* . . . . (Pickwick)
Rosemary Clooney; *Rosemary Clooney Sings Bing* . . . .(Concord Jazz)

I Take A Lot Of Pride In What I Am
Clint Black; *Mama's Hungry Eyes-Merle Haggard Tribute-C* . . . . (Arista)
Merle Haggard; *Capitol Collectors Series-Merle Haggard* . . . . (Capitol)
   Merle Haggard's Greatest Hits . . . . (Curb)

I Used To Love Him
Lauryn Hill featuring Mary J. Blige; *The Miseducation Of Lauryn Hill* . . . . . . (Ruffhouse/Columbia)

I Was A Punk Before You Were A Punk
Tubes; *What Do You Want From Live* . . . . (A&M)

I Was Country When Country Wasn't Cool
Barbara Mandrell; *Barbara Mandrell Live* . . . . (MCA)
   Barbara Mandrell's Greatest Hits . . . . (MCA)

I Will Get There
Boyz II Men; *ST/The Prince Of Egypt-Inspirational.* . . . . . .(DreamWorks/SKG)

I Will Survive
Gloria Gaynor; *Billboard Top Hits-1979-C* . . . . (Rhino)
   I Am Woman-C. . . . .(Nick At Nite)
   Love Tracks . . . .(Polydor)
   The Disco Years-#2-On The Beat-1978-1982-C . . . . (Rhino)

I Won't Back Down
Tom Petty; *America: A Tribute To Heroes-C* . . . .(Interscope)
   Full Moon Fever. . . . . (MCA)

I'd Rather Be Dead
Nilsson; *Son Of Schmilsson.* . . . .(RCA)

If I Had My Way
Nancy Wilson; *If I Had My Way* . . . . (Columbia)
Willie Nelson; *Healing Hands Of Time* . . . . (Liberty)

If My Friends Could See Me Now
Original Cast/Gwen Verdon; *Sweet Charity* . . . . (Columbia)

If You Were Wondering
Peter Allen; *I Could Have Been A Sailor* . . . . (A&M)

I'll Be Your Everything
Tommy Page; *Paintings In My Mind.* . . . .(Sire)

I'm A Man
Bo Diddley; *Bo Diddley-His Best* . . . . (Chess)
   Super Blues. . . . . (Chess)
   The Sopranos-Music From The HBO Original Series. . . . . . . (Sony Music Soundtrax)
Yardbirds; *Five Live Yardbirds.* . . . . (Rhino)
   History Of British Rock-#3-C. . . . . (Rhino)
   Yardbirds' Greatest Hits-#1 (1964-1966) . . . . (Rhino)

I'm A Real Man
John Hiatt; *Warming Up To The Ice Age* . . . . (Geffen)

I'm A Survivor
Reba McEntire; *Reba McEntire's Greatest Hits-#3: I'm A Survivor.* . . . . . (MCA)

I'm A Woman
Maria Muldaur; *Waitress In The Donut Shop* . . . . . . (Warner Archives)
Peggy Lee; *I Am Woman-C* . . . .(Nick At Nite)
   Peggy Lee's All-Time Greatest Hits . . . . (Curb)
Reba McEntire; *Out Of A Dream.* . . . . (Mercury)

I'm Alright
Little Anthony And The Imperials; *Best Of Little Anthony And The Imperials* . . . . . . (Rhino)
   Forever Yours. . . . .(Roulette)
   Tears On My Pillow . . . .(Accord)

I'm Alright
Rolling Stones; *got Live if you want it!* . . . .(Abkco)
   Out Of Our Heads. . . . .(Abkco)

I'm Alright
Jo Dee Messina; *I'm Alright* . . . . (Curb)

I'm Alright
Kenny Loggins; *Kenny Loggins Alive* . . . . (Columbia)
   ST/Caddyshack. . . . .(Columbia)

I'm An Ordinary Man
Rex Harrison/Original Cast; *My Fair Lady* . . . . (Columbia)

I'm Bad, I'm Nationwide
ZZ Top; *Deguello.* . . . . (Warner Bros.)

I'm Coming Out
Diana Ross; *Diana* . . . . (Motown)
   Diana Ross-All The Great Hits. . . . . (Motown)
   Diana Ross-Anthology . . . . (Motown)

I'm Every Woman
Chaka Khan; *Chicken Soup For The Soul: I'll Be There For You-Songs Of Friendship, Brotherhood And Sisterhood-C* . . . . (Rhino)
   Epiphany: The Best Of Chaka Khan-#1 . . . . (Reprise)
   I Am Woman-C. . . . .(Nick At Nite)
Whitney Houston; *ST/The Bodyguard.* . . . . (Arista)
   Whitney Houston's Greatest Hits . . . . (Arista)

I'm Gonna Be Somebody
Travis Tritt; *Country Club.* . . . . (Warner Bros.)

I'm Gonna Sit Right Down And Write Myself A Letter
Billy Williams; *Stardust: The Classic Decca Hits & Standards Collection-C* . . . . (Decca)
Fats Waller; *Fats Waller.* . . . . (RCA Special Prod.)
Frank Sinatra; *Sinatra-Basie.* . . . . (Reprise)
   Songs For Young Lovers & Swing Easy . . . . (Capitol)
Nat "King" Cole; *Just One Of Those Things (& More)* . . . . (Capitol)
   Nat "King" Cole-Gift Set . . . . (Capitol)
Original Cast; *Ain't Misbehavin'.* . . . .(RCA)

I'm Good At Being Bad
TLC; *Fanmail.* . . . . (LaFace)

I'm Holding My Own
Lee Roy Parnell; *On The Road* . . . . (Arista)

I'm Just An Old Chunk Of Coal (But I'm Gonna Be A Diamond Someday)
Billy Joe Shaver; *Restless Wind-The Legendary Billy Joe Shaver-1973-1987.* . . . . (Razor & Tie)

John Anderson; *John Anderson's Greatest Hits* . . . . (Warner Bros.)

I'm Leaving
Aaron Tippin; *What This Country Needs* . . . . (Lyric Street)

I'm Not In Love
10 CC; *10 CC's Greatest Hits-1972-1978* . . . . (Polydor)
Super Hits Of The '70s-Have A Nice Day-#14-C . . . . (Rhino)
Will To Power; *Journey Home* . . . . (Epic)

I'm Not Running Anymore
John Mellencamp; *John Mellencamp* . . . . (Columbia)

I'm Real
Jennifer Lopez; *J. Lo* . . . . (Epic)
Now That's What I Call Music!-#8-C . . . .(Virgin)

I'm So Great I Don't Have To Brag
Shel Silverstein; *Crouchin'* . . . . (Out Of Print)

I'm So Proud
Impressions; *Impressions' Greatest Hits* . . . . (MCA)
Soul Shots-#11-More Ballads-C . . . . (Rhino)
Main Ingredient; *Golden Classics-Main Ingredient* . . . .(Collectables)
Todd Rundgren; *A Wizard A True Star* . . . . (Rhino)
Back To The Bars . . . . (Rhino)

I'm Still Standing
Elton John; *Elton John's Greatest Hits-1976-1986* . . . . (MCA)
Too Low For Zero . . . . (MCA)

I'm The Coolest
Alice Cooper; *Goes To Hell* . . . . (Warner Bros.)

I'm The Greatest
Ringo Starr; *Blast From Your Past* . . . . (Gold Rush)
Ringo . . . . (Capitol)

I'm The Greatest Star
Barbra Streisand; *ST/Funny Girl* . . . . (Columbia)
Diana Ross & The Supremes; *Diana Ross & The Supremes-Anthology (1962-1969)* . . . . (Motown)

I'm The Man Who Murdered Love
XTC; *Wasp Star (Apple Venus Volume 2)* . . . . (Idea/TVT)

I'm The One
Roberta Flack; *I'm The One* . . . . (Atlantic)

I'm The Only One
Melissa Etheridge; *Yes I Am* . . . . (Island)

I'm Too Sexy
Right Said Fred; *Up* . . . . (Charisma)

Imitation Of Life
R.E.M.; *Reveal* . . . . (Warner Bros.)

Impossible Dream
Andy Williams; *Andy Williams' Greatest Hits-#2* . . . . (Columbia)
Andy Williams-16 Most Requested Songs . . . .(Legacy)
Impossible Dream . . . . (Columbia)
Ed Ames; *Best Of Ed Ames* . . . .(RCA)
Ed Ames-Pure Gold . . . .(RCA)
Impossible Dream . . . .(RCA)
This Is Ed Ames . . . .(RCA)
Jack Jones; *Best Of Jack Jones* . . . .(MCA)
Kate Smith; *Best Of Kate Smith* . . . .(RCA)
Kate Smith-Legendary Performer . . . .(RCA)
Luther Vandross; *Songs* . . . . (Epic)
Original London Cast; *Man Of La Mancha* . . . .(MCA)
Robert Goulet; *Robert Goulet's Greatest Hits* . . . . (Columbia)

In Between Dances
Pam Tillis; *Pam Tillis' Greatest Hits* . . . . (Arista)
Sweetheart's Dance . . . . (Arista)

Indian Reservation (The Lament Of The Cherokee Reservation Indian)
Don Fardon; *45-#408* . . . .(GNP/Crescendo)
Raiders; *Billboard Top Rock 'N' Roll Hits-1971-C* . . . .(Rhino)
Legend Of Paul Revere And The Raiders . . . . (Columbia)
Pop Classics Of The '70s-C . . . . (Columbia)
Super Hits Of The '70s-Have A Nice Day-#5-C . . . . (Rhino)

Ini
Amel Larrieux; *Infinite Possibilities* . . . . (Epic)

It Ain't My Fault
Silkk The Shocker; *Charge It 2 Da Game* . . . . (No Limit/Priority)

It Won't Be Me
Tanya Tucker; *Tennessee Woman* . . . . (Capitol)

It's All About Me
Mya featuring Sisqo of Dru Hill; *Mya* . . . . (University/Interscope)

It's Hard To Be Humble
Mac Davis; *It's Hard To Be Humble* . . . . (Casablanca)
Mac Davis' Greatest Hits . . . . (Columbia)

It's Midnight Cinderella
Garth Brooks; *Fresh Horses* . . . . (Capitol)
Limited Series Box . . . . (Capitol)

It's My Life
Animals; *Animals Greatest Hits* . . . . (Allegiance)
Best Of The Animals . . . . (Abkco)

It's My Life
Bon Jovi; *Crush* . . . . (Island/IDJMG)
Now That's What I Call Music!-#5-C . . . .(Virgin)
The Concert For New York City-C . . . . (Columbia)

It's My Time
Martina McBride; *Emotion* . . . .(RCA)

It's My Turn
Diana Ross; *All The Great Love Songs-Diana Ross* . . . .(Motown)
Diana Ross-All The Great Hits . . . .(Motown)
Diana Ross-Anthology . . . .(Motown)
To Love Again . . . .(Motown)

I've Gotta Be Me
Sammy Davis, Jr.; *I've Gotta Be Me-Best Of Sammy Davis, Jr.-On Reprise* . . . . (Reprise)
Sammy Davis, Jr.'s Greatest Songs . . . .(Curb)

I've Gotta Crow
Original Cast/Mary Martin; *Peter Pan-The 1954 Broadway Production* . . . . (RCA Victor)

I've Never Been To Me
Charlene; *Endless Love-Motown's Greatest Love Songs-C* . . . .(Motown)
Hard-To-Find Motown Classics-#2-C . . . .(Motown)
I've Never Been To Me . . . .(Motown)
Motown Memories-#4-C . . . .(Motown)

Jigga My Nigga
Jay-Z; *Ruff Ryders: Ride Or Die-#1* . . . . (Ruff Ryders/IDJMG)

Joining You
Alanis Morissette; *Supposed Former Infatuation Junkie* . . . . (Maverick)

Just As I Am
Willie Nelson; *Red Headed Stranger* . . . .(Columbia)

Just Be Yourself
Cameo; *45-#3231* . . . .(Chocolate City)

Just Between You And Me
DC Talk; *First Generation: 25 Years Of Virgin Records-C* . . . . (Virgin)
Jesus Freak . . . . (Virgin)

Kate
Ben Folds Five; *Whatever And Ever Amen* . . . . (Caroline/550)

Keep Their Heads Ringin'
Dr. Dre; *Hip Hop's Most Wanted-C* . . . . (Priority)
ST/Friday . . . . (Priority)

Landslide
Fleetwood Mac; *25 Years-The Chain* . . . . (Warner Bros.)
Fleetwood Mac . . . . (Reprise)
Fleetwood Mac Live . . . . (Warner Bros.)
The Dance . . . . (Reprise)
Smashing Pumpkins; *Pisces Iscariot* . . . . (Virgin)

Legend In My Time
Don Gibson; *Don Gibson's All-Time Greatest Hits* . . . . (RCA)
Ronnie Milsap; *Lost In The Fifties Tonight* . . . . (RCA)
Ronnie Milsap-Live . . . . (RCA)
Ronnie Milsap's Greatest Hits . . . . (RCA)

Legend In Your Own Time
Carly Simon; *Anticipation* . . . . (Elektra)
Best Of Carly Simon . . . . (Elektra)

Lessons To Be Learned
Barbra Streisand; *Higher Ground* . . . . (Columbia)

Let It All Out (Let It All Hang Out)
Hombres; *Dick Bartley's One-Hit Wonders Of The '60s-#2-C* . . . .(Rhino)
Let It Out (Let It All Hang Out) . . . . (Verve/Forecast)
Summer Of Love-#2-Turn On-Mind Expansion & Signs Of The Times-C . . . .(Rhino)

Let Me Be
Britney Spears; *Britney* . . . . (Jive)

Level On The Inside
Dovetail Joint; *001* . . . . (Aware/C2/Columbia)

Life Is Sweet
Natalie Merchant; *Ophelia* . . . . (Elektra)

Like A Rolling Stone
Bob Dylan; *Biograph* . . . .(Columbia)
Bob Dylan At Budokan . . . .(Columbia)
Bob Dylan's Greatest Hits . . . .(Columbia)
Highway 61 Revisited . . . .(Columbia)
More American Graffiti-#4-C . . . .(MCA)
Self Portrait . . . .(Columbia)
Bob Dylan And The Band; *Before The Flood* . . . .(Columbia)
Jimi Hendrix; *ST/Jimi Plays Monterey* . . . . (Reprise)
Jimi Hendrix Experience; *Jimi Hendrix Experience* . . . . (Reprise)
Rolling Stones; *Stripped* . . . . (Virgin)

Little Respect, A
Erasure; *Innocents* . . . . (Sire)

Living Years, The
Mike & The Mechanics; *Living Years* . . . . (Atlantic)

London Pride
John Williams; *Echoes Of London* . . . .(Columbia)

Long Day
Matchbox Twenty; *Yourself Or Someone Like You* . . . .(Lava)

Look At Me I'm Wonderful
Bonzo Dog Band; *Best Of The Bonzo Dog Band* . . . .(Rhino)

Lookin' After #1
Boomtown Rats; *Boomtown Rats* . . . .(Mercury)

Lookin' Out For #1
Bachman-Turner Overdrive; *Best Of B.T.O.-So Far* . . . . (Mercury)
UFO; *Obsession* . . . . (Chrysalis)

Looking Out For Number One
Travis Tritt; *T-R-O-U-B-L-E* . . . . (Warner Bros.)

Love Is Stronger Than Pride
Ricochet; *Ricochet* . . . . (Columbia)
Lucky Man
Verve; *Urban Hymns* . . . . (Hut/Virgin)
Luxury: Cococure
Maxwell; *Embrya* . . . . (Columbia)
Man In The Mirror
Michael Jackson; *Bad* . . . .(Epic)
Man In The Mirror
Jim Glaser; *Man In The Mirror* . . . .(Noble Vision)
Man Of La Mancha
Original Cast; *Lost In The Stars* . . . . (MCA)
Original London Cast; *Man Of La Mancha* . . . . (MCA)
Man Of My Word
Collin Raye; *Extremes* . . . .(Epic)
Man! I Feel Like A Woman
Shania Twain; *Come On Over* . . . . (Mercury)
VH-1 Divas Live-C . . . .(Epic)
Mannish Boy
Muddy Waters; *Electric Mud* . . . . (Chess)
King Of The Electric Blues . . . . (Legacy)
The Best Blues Album In The World...Ever!-C . . . . (Virgin)
Many A Long & Lonesome Highway
Rodney Crowell; *Keys To The Highway* . . . . (Columbia)
Taste Of Texas-Songs 'Bout Texas By Texans-C . . . . . (Columbia)
Me
Paula Cole; *This Fire* . . . . (Imago)
Memory Remains
Metallica; *Reload* . . . . (Elektra)
Misfits
Kinks; *Come Dancing With The Kinks-Best Of The Kinks 1977-1986* . . . (Arista)
Misfits . . . . (Arista)
One For The Road . . . . (Arista)
Mississippi
Paula Cole; *This Fire* . . . . (Imago)
Mister Big Time
Jon Bon Jovi; *ST/Armageddon-The Album* . . . . (Columbia)
Moment To Myself
Macy Gray; *On How Life Is* . . . .(Epic)
Most Girls
Pink; *Can't Take Me Home* . . . . (LaFace)
Totally Hits-#3-C . . . . (Atlantic)
Mr. Big Stuff
Jean Knight; *'70s Hit(s) Back Again-C* . . . . (Hip-O)
Have A Nice Decade-The '70s Pop Culture Box-C . . . . (Rhino)
Mr. Vain
Culture Beat; *Serenity* . . . .(550 Music)
My Baby Loves Me
Martina McBride; *The Way That I Am* . . . . (RCA)
My Lady Loves Me (Just As I Am)
Leon Everette; *45-#13466* . . . . (RCA)
My Prerogative
Bobby Brown; *Dance!...Ya Know It!* . . . .(MCA)
Don't Be Cruel . . . .(MCA)
Rock The First-#1-C . . . . (Sandstone Music)
My Son Calls Another Man Daddy
Hank Williams With His Drifting Cowboys; *Hank Williams-16
Great Hits* . . . . (Everest)
Hank Williams-40 Greatest Hits . . . . (Polydor)
Rare Takes & Radio Cuts . . . . (Polydor)
My Way
Elvis Presley; *Aloha from Hawaii via Satellite* . . . . (RCA)
Canadian Tribute . . . . (RCA)
Elvis In Concert . . . . (RCA)
Frank Sinatra; *Frank Sinatra's Greatest Hits-#2* . . . . . (Reprise)
My Way . . . . (Reprise)
Sinatra Reprise-The Very Good Years . . . . (Reprise)
Sinatra-The Main Event Live . . . . (Reprise)
The Reprise Collection . . . . (Reprise)
Paul Anka; *Very Best Of Paul Anka* . . . . (Ranwood)
My Way
Usher; *My Way* . . . . (LaFace)
Myself Without You
Reba McEntire; *Reba McEntire's Greatest Hits-#3: I'm A Survivor* . . . . .(MCA)
Narcissus
City Boy; *Dinner At The Ritz* . . . . (Mercury)
Needles And Pins
Jackie DeShannon; *Very Best Of Jackie DeShannon* . . . .(EMI)
Searchers; *History Of British Rock-#1-C* . . . . (Rhino)
Searchers' Greatest Hits . . . . (Rhino)
Tom Petty And The Heartbreakers; *Pack Up The Plantation-Live!* . . . . . .(MCA)
Negasonic Teenage Warhead
Monster Magnet; *Dopes To Infinity* . . . . (A&M)
New Attitude
Patti LaBelle; *Classic Soul-C* . . . .(MCA)
I Am Woman-C . . . . (Nick At Nite)
Soundtrack Smashes-'80s & More-C . . . .(MCA)
ST/Beverly Hills Cop . . . .(MCA)

Next Voice You Hear
Jackson Browne; *The Next Voice You Hear-Best Of Jackson Browne* . . (Elektra)
No Matter What They Say
Lil' Kim; *Notorious K.I.M.* . . . .(Queen Bee/Undeas/Atlantic)
No Scrubs
TLC; *Fanmail* . . . .(LaFace)
Totally Hits-#1-C . . . . (Arista)
No Surrender
Bruce Springsteen; *Born In The U.S.A.* . . . . (Columbia)
Nobody But Me
Human Beinz; *Flower Power-Psychedelic Rock Classics-C* . . . . (K-Tel)
Frat Rock!-C . . . . (Rhino)
Isley Brothers; *Isley Brothers-16 Greatest Hits* . . . . (Deluxe)
The Isley Brothers Story-#1-Rockin' Soul-1959-1968 . . . . (Rhino)
November Rain
Guns N' Roses; *Use Your Illusion I* . . . . (Geffen)
Now I Know
Lari White; *Wishes* . . . .(RCA)
O.P.P.
Naughty By Nature; *MTV Party To Go-#2-C* . . . . (Tommy Boy)
Oh, Look At Me Now
Frank Sinatra; *a Swingin' Affair!* . . . . (Capitol)
Nancy Wilson; *But Beautiful* . . . .(Blue Note)
Sammy Kaye & His Orchestra; *Sammy Kaye & His Orchestra Play 22
Original Big Band Recordings* . . . . (Hindsight)
Tommy Dorsey; *Boogie Woogie* . . . .(Pro-Arte)
Tommy Dorsey & Frank Sinatra; *Tommy Dorsey & Frank Sinatra's All-Time
Greatest Hits-#1* . . . . (Bluebird)
Okie From Muskogee
Merle Haggard; *Friend In California* . . . . (Epic)
Merle Haggard & The Strangers; *Best Of Merle Haggard & The
Strangers* . . . . (Capitol)
Capitol Collectors Series-Merle Haggard & The Strangers . . . . . . (Capitol)
Country Music Classics-#3-1965-1970-C . . . . (K-Tel)
For The Record: Merle Haggard-43 Legendary Hits . . . . . (BNA)
Songs I'll Always Sing . . . . (Capitol)
ST/Platoon . . . .(Atlantic)
On Our Own
Bobby Brown; *Dance!...Ya Know It!* . . . . (MCA)
ST/Ghostbusters II . . . . (MCA)
One I Am
Dan Baird; *Love Songs For The Hearing Impaired* . . . .(Def American)
One Less Bell To Answer
5th Dimension; *5th Dimension-Anthology 1967-1973* . . . . . . (Rhino)
Greatest Hits On Earth . . . . (Arista)
Barbra Streisand; *Barbra Joan Streisand* . . . . (Columbia)
Gladys Knight & The Pips; *Gladys Knight & The Pips-Anthology* . . . (Motown)
If I Were Your Woman . . . . (Motown)
One Of These Days
Tim McGraw; *Everywhere* . . . .(Curb)
Only God Knows Why
Kid Rock; *Devil Without A Cause* . . . . (Top Dog/Lava/Atlantic)
Overprotected
Britney Spears; *Britney* . . . .(Jive)
Pick Yourself Up
Diana King; *When I Look In Your Eyes* . . . .(GRP)
Frank Sinatra; *Sinatra and Swingin' Brass* . . . . (Reprise)
Fred Astaire; *Starring Fred Astaire* . . . . (Columbia)
That's Dancing . . . . (EMI)
Pop
'N Sync; *Celebrity* . . . .(Jive)
Now That's What I Call Music!-#8-C . . . . (Virgin)
Popular
Nada Surf; *High/Low* . . . . (Elektra)
Power Trip
Defiance; *Beyond Recognition* . . . .(Roadrunner)
Pretty As You Feel
Jefferson Airplane; *2400 Fulton Street-An Anthology* . . . . (RCA)
Loves You . . . . (RCA)
Pretty Fly (For A White Guy)
Offspring; *Americana* . . . . (Columbia)
Pride
Earth, Wind & Fire; *Eternal Dance* . . . . (Columbia)
Faces . . . . (Columbia)
Pride
Robert Palmer; *Addictions-#1* . . . . (Island)
Pride . . . . (Island)
Pride
Husker Du; *Zen Arcade* . . . .(SST)
Pride
Echo & The Bunnymen; *Crocodiles* . . . . (Sire)
Pride
Ray Price; *Essential Ray Price-1951-1962* . . . . (Columbia)
Ray Price's Greatest Hits-#4-By Request . . . .(Step One)
Pride
Isley Brothers; *Go For Your Guns* . . . . (T-Neck/Columbia)
The Isley Brothers Story-#2-The T-Neck Years-1969-1985 . . . . (Rhino)
Pride
Robin Trower; *Long Misty Days* . . . . (Chrysalis)

Pride
Living Colour; *Time's Up* . . . (Epic)
Pride & Joy
Marvin Gaye; *Marvin Gaye Live At The London Palladium* . . . (Motown)
Marvin Gaye-Anthology . . . (Motown)
Marvin Gaye's Greatest Hits . . . (Motown)
Marvin Gaye-Super Hits . . . (Motown)
That Stubborn Kinda Fellow . . . (Motown)
Pride & Joy
Coverdale/Page; *Coverdale/Page* . . . (Geffen)
Pride & Joy
Lil' Ed & The Blues Imperials; *Genuine Houserockin' Music II-C* . . . (Alligator)
Roughhousin' . . . (Alligator)
Pride (In The Name Of Love)
Clivilles & Cole; *Greatest Remixes-#1* . . . (Columbia)
ST/Gladiator . . . (Columbia)
U2; *Greenpeace/Rainbow Warriors-C* . . . (Geffen)
Rattle And Hum . . . (Island)
Unforgettable Fire . . . (Island)
Pride Goes Before A Fall
Jim Reeves; *Best Of Jim Reeves* . . . (RCA)
Pride Of Franklin County
Tanya Tucker; *Lovin' & Learnin'* . . . (MCA)
Tanya Tucker's Greatest Hits . . . (MCA)
Pride Of Man
Quicksilver Messenger Service; *Quicksilver Messenger Service* . . . (Capitol)
Quicksilver Messenger Service-Anthology . . . (Capitol)
San Francisco Nights-C . . . (Rhino)
Sons Of Mercury . . . (Rhino)
Pride's Not Hard To Swallow
Hank Williams, Jr.; *Hank Williams, Jr.-14 Greatest Hits* . . . (Polydor)
Living Proof-MGM Recordings 1963-1975 . . . (Mercury)
Prima Donna
Jerry Vale; *Jerry Vale's All-Time Greatest Hits* . . . (Columbia)
Jerry Vale's Greatest Hits . . . (Columbia)
Project Chick/Project Bitch
Cash Money Millionaires; *12'' Maxi Single* . . . (Cash Money/Universal)
Promised Land
Bruce Springsteen; *Darkness On The Edge Of Town* . . . (Columbia)
Bruce Springsteen & The E Street Band; *Bruce Springsteen & The E Street Band Live/1975-85* . . . (Legacy)
Proud Mary
Creedence Clearwater Revival; *1968-1969* . . . (Fantasy)
Bayou Country . . . (Fantasy)
Creedence Clearwater Revival-Chronicle . . . (Fantasy)
Creedence Clearwater Revival-Gold . . . (Fantasy)
Live In Europe . . . (Fantasy)
George Jones & Johnny Paycheck; *My Very Special Guests* . . . (Epic)
Ike & Tina Turner; *Best Of Ike & Tina Turner* . . . (EMI)
Didn't It Blow Your Mind: Soul Hits Of The '70s-#4-C . . . (Rhino)
EMI Legends Of Rock & Roll-24 Greatest Hits-C . . . (EMI)
Ike & Tina Turner's Greatest Hits . . . (Curb)
Proud To Be An American
Li'l Wally; *Happy Birthday, America* . . . (Jay Jay)
Proud To Be An American
Tubes; *Young And Rich* . . . (A&M)
Proud To Be Black
Young Black Teenagers; *Young Black Teenagers* . . . (S.O.U.L.)
Proud To Be Black
Run-D.M.C.; *Raising Hell* . . . (Profile)
Proud To Fall
Ian McCulloch; *Candleland* . . . (Sire)
Question Everything
8Stops7; *In Moderation* . . . (Reprise)
Real Live Woman
Trisha Yearwood; *Real Live Woman* . . . (MCA)
Real Man
Todd Rundgren; *Back To The Bars* . . . (Rhino)
Todd Rundgren-Anthology 1968-1985 . . . (Rhino)
Real Man
Bruce Springsteen; *Human Touch* . . . (Columbia)
Real Man
Bonnie Raitt; *Nick Of Time* . . . (Capitol)
Real Niggaz
N.W.A.; *100 Miles & Runnin'* . . . (Ruthless/Priority)
Efil4zaggin . . . (Ruthless/Priority)
Real Niggaz Don't Die
N.W.A.; *Efil4zaggin* . . . (Ruthless/Priority)
Real Slim Shady
Eminem; *The Marshall Mathers LP* . . . (Aftermath/Interscope)
Reflection
Christina Aguilera; *Christina Aguilera* . . . (RCA)
ST/Mulan . . . (Walt Disney)
Respect
Aretha Franklin; *Aretha Franklin-30 Greatest Hits* . . . (Rhino)
Best Of Aretha Franklin . . . (Atlantic)
I Am Woman-C . . . (Nick At Nite)
I Never Loved A Man The Way I Love You . . . (Atlantic)
Live At Fillmore West . . . (Atlantic)
Soul Years-C . . . (Atlantic)
ST/Forrest Gump . . . (Epic/Sony Music Soundtrax)
Otis Redding; *History Of Otis Redding* . . . (Atco)
Live In Europe . . . (Atco)
Otis Blue-Sings Soul . . . (Atco)
The Otis Redding Story . . . (Atlantic)
Reba McEntire; *Reba* . . . (MCA)
Respect Yourself
Bruce Willis; *Heart Of Soul-C* . . . (Columbia)
Return Of Bruno . . . (Motown)
Kane Gang; *Bad Guys* . . . (Casablanca)
Lowdown . . . (London)
Staple Singers; *15 Original Big Hits-#2-C* . . . (Stax)
Staple Singers' Greatest Hits . . . (Fantasy)
Staple Singers-Chronicle . . . (Stax)
Top Of The Stax-Twenty Greatest Hits-C . . . (Stax)
Stevie Wonder; *Motown Legends-Stevie Wonder* . . . (Motown)
Respectable
Isley Brothers; *Shout* . . . (Collectables)
The Isley Brothers Story-#1-Rockin' Soul-1959-1968 . . . (Rhino)
Outsiders; *Best Of The Outsiders* . . . (Rhino)
Capitol Collectors Series-The Outsiders . . . (Capitol)
Rolling Stones; *Some Girls* . . . (Virgin)
Return Of The Mack
Mark Morrison; *Return Of The Mack* . . . (Atlantic)
Righteous
Eric Johnson; *Ah Via Musicom* . . . (Capitol)
Rock Bottom
Wynonna; *Tell Me Why* . . . (MCA)
Sacrifice
Elton John; *Sleeping With The Past* . . . (MCA)
Sinead O'Connor; *Two Rooms-Celebrating The Songs Of Elton John & Bernie Taupin-C* . . . (Polydor)
Sacrifice
Front 242; *Tyranny For You* . . . (Epic)
Sacrifice
Steve Miller Band; *Book Of Dreams* . . . (Capitol)
Steve Miller Band-Gift Set . . . (Capitol)
Sacrifice
Naked Eyes; *Best Of Naked Eyes* . . . (EMI)
Same Ol' G
Ginuwine; *ST/Dr. Dolittle* . . . (Atlantic)
Say It Loud I'm Black & I'm Proud
Afrika Bambaataa; *Decade Of Darkness* . . . (EMI)
James Brown; *Billboard Top R&B Hits-1965-1969-C* . . . (Rhino)
Secret
Madonna; *Bedtime Stories* . . . (Maverick/Sire)
GHV2 . . . (Warner Bros.)
Self Esteem
Offspring; *Smash* . . . (Epitaph)
Selfless, Cold And Composed
Ben Folds Five; *Whatever And Ever Amen* . . . (Caroline/550)
Set It Off
Juvenile; *Project English* . . . (Cash Money/Universal)
Sexual Revolution
Macy Gray; *The Id* . . . (Epic)
She Couldn't Change Me
Montgomery Gentry; *Carrying On* . . . (Columbia)
She Don't Know She's Beautiful
Sammy Kershaw; *Haunted Heart* . . . (Mercury)
She Works Hard For The Money
Donna Summer; *I Am Woman-C* . . . (Nick At Nite)
She Works Hard For The Money . . . (Mercury)
Summer Collection . . . (Mercury)
She'd Rather Be With Me
Turtles; *Best Of The Turtles-Golden Archive Series* . . . (Rhino)
Oldies But Goodies-#3-C . . . (Original Sound)
Turtles-20 Greatest Hits . . . (Rhino)
Shining Star
Earth, Wind & Fire; *Best Of Earth, Wind & Fire-#1* . . . (Legacy)
Eternal Dance . . . (Columbia)
Gratitude . . . (Legacy)
That's The Way Of The World . . . (Legacy)
Silly Ho
TLC; *Fanmail* . . . (LaFace)
Since I Don't Have To
Guns N' Roses; *The Spaghetti Incident?* . . . (Geffen)
Sisters Are Doin' It For Themselves
Ann Wilson/Nancy Wilson/Lisa Simpson; *Simpsons-The Yellow Album* . . . (Geffen)
Eurythmics & Aretha Franklin; *Be Yourself Tonight* . . . (RCA)
Chicken Soup For The Soul: I'll Be There For You-Songs Of Friendship, Brotherhood And Sisterhood-C . . . (Rhino)
Eurythmics' Greatest Hits . . . (Arista)
Who's Zoomin' Who? . . . (Arista)
Smells Like Teen Spirit
Nirvana; *Nevermind* . . . (David Geffen Co.)
Some Girls Do
Sawyer Brown; *Dirt Road* . . . (Curb)

Someone Else's Dream
Faith Hill; *It Matters To Me* . . . .(Warner Bros.)
Son Of A Gun (I Betcha You Think This Song's About You)
Janet (with Carly Simon); *All For You* . . . . (Virgin)
Son Of Hickory Holler's Tramp
O.C. Smith; *Me And You* . . . . (Columbia Special Prod.)
Story Songs-C . . . . (K-Tel)
Soul Man
Blues Brothers; *Best Of The Blues Brothers* . . . .(Atlantic)
Blues Brothers-The Definitive Collection . . . .(Atlantic)
Briefcase Full Of Blues . . . .(Atlantic)
Sam & Dave; *Best Of Sam & Dave* . . . .(Atlantic)
Golden Age Of Black Music-1960-1970-C . . . .(Atlantic)
Soul Men . . . . (Rhino)
South's Gonna Do It Again
Charlie Daniels; *Charlie Daniels-Super Hits* . . . . (Columbia)
Charlie Daniels Band; *A Decade Of Hits* . . . .(Epic)
Fire On The Mountain . . . .(Epic)
Stand
R.E.M.; *Green* . . . .(Warner Bros.)
Stand Back
Fleetwood Mac; *25 Years-The Chain* . . . .(Warner Bros.)
Stevie Nicks; *Dance Traxx-C* . . . .(Atlantic)
TimeSpace-The Best Of Stevie Nicks . . . .(Modern)
Wild Heart . . . . (Modern)
Stand Tall
Burton Cummings; *Burton Cummings* . . . . (Portrait)
Rock Artifacts-From The Vaults-#2-C . . . .(Legacy)
Seems Like Yesterday-#2-Mid '70s-C . . . . (K-Tel)
Stand Up
Mel McDaniel; *All-Time Country Classics-#2-C* . . . . (Capitol)
Mel McDaniel's Greatest Hits . . . . (Capitol)
Stand Up . . . . (Capitol)
Stand Up
AC/DC; *Fly On The Wall* . . . . (Atco)
Stand Up
Atlantic Starr; *Atlantic Starr-Classics-#10* . . . . (A&M)
Secret Lovers: Best Of Atlantic Starr . . . . (A&M)
Stand Up On Your Own Feet
Third World; *Arise In Harmony* . . . . (Island)
Standing Tall
Billie Jo Spears; *Best Of Billie Jo Spears* . . . . (CEMA Special Prod.)
Love Ain't Gonna Wait For Us . . . . (United Artists)
Standing Tall . . . . (United Artists)
Brenda Lee; *Brenda Lee* . . . .(Warner Bros.)
Standing Tall
Lorrie Morgan; *Lorrie Morgan's Greatest Hits* . . . . (BNA)
Struttin' My Stuff
Elvin Bishop; *'70s Greatest Rock Hits-#2-The South Rules-C* . . . . (Priority)
Live! Raisin' Hell . . . . (Capricorn)
Struttin' My Stuff . . . . (Capricorn)
Superman
R.E.M.; *Life's Rich Pageant* . . . .(EMI-Capitol Entert. Properties)
Superstar (Remember How You Got Where You Are)
Temptations; *Temptations-Anthology-The Best Of The Temptations* . . (Motown)
Take It Like A Man
Michelle Wright; *Now & Then* . . . . (Arista)
Today's Top Country-C . . . . (K-Tel)
Take Me As I Am
Faith Hill; *Take Me As I Am* . . . .(Warner Bros.)
Take Pride In America
Oak Ridge Boys; *Oak Ridge Boys' Greatest Hits 3* . . . .(MCA)
Tennessee Pride
Chet Atkins; *Country Gems* . . . . (Pair)
Testosterone
Bush; *Sixteen Stone* . . . . (Trauma)
Texas Strut
Gary Moore; *Still Got The Blues* . . . .(Charisma)
Thank You Falletin Me Be Mice Elf Again
Sly & The Family Stone; *In Yo' Face!-History Of Funk-#1-C* . . . . (Rhino)
Sly & The Family Stone-Anthology . . . .(Epic)
Sly & The Family Stone's Greatest Hits . . . .(Epic)
That Don't Impress Me Much
Shania Twain; *Come On Over* . . . . (Mercury)
That's Not Me
Beach Boys; *Pet Sounds* . . . . (Capitol)
The Pet Sounds Sessions: A 30th Anniversary Collection . . . . (Capitol)
Theme From "The Mary Tyler Moore Show"
Original Soundtrack-Sonny Curtis; *CBS: The First 50 Years* . . . . (TVT)
Television's Greatest Hits-#2-C . . . . (TVT)
They Can't Take That Away From Me
Billie Holiday; *God Bless The Child* . . . . (Pro-Arte)
I Like Jazz-Essence Of Billie Holiday . . . . (Columbia)
Diana Krall; *Love Scenes* . . . . (Impulse!)
Ella Fitzgerald; *Ella & Louis Again* . . . . (Verve)
Frank Sinatra; *My Kind Of Broadway* . . . . (Reprise)

Frank Sinatra & Natalie Cole; *Duets* . . . . (Capitol)
Fred Astaire; *Starring Fred Astaire* . . . . (Columbia)
Kate Smith; *Best Of Kate Smith* . . . . (Curb)
Lisa Stansfield; *Glory Of Gershwin Featuring Larry Adler-C* . . . . . . (Mercury)
Mary Lou Williams; *Mary Lou Williams In London* . . . .(Crescendo)
Original Broadway Cast; *Crazy For You* . . . . (Angel)
Original London Cast; *Crazy For You* . . . . (RCA)
Patti Austin; *The Real Me* . . . . (Qwest)
Sarah Vaughan; *Sarah Vaughan Sings George Gershwin Songbook,*
Vol. 1 . . . . (Emarcy)
Stanley Turrentine; *Blue Gershwin* . . . . (Blue Note)
Think For Yourself
Beatles; *Beatles-Box Set* . . . . (Capitol)
Rubber Soul . . . . (Capitol)
George Harrison; *Best Of George Harrison* . . . . (Capitol)
This Is Me
Randy Travis; *This Is Me* . . . .(Warner Bros.)
This Town Ain't Big Enough For The Both Of Us
Siouxsie And The Banshees; *Through The Looking Glass* . . . . (Geffen)
Sparks; *Profile-The Ultimate Sparks Collection* . . . . (Rhino)
The Island Story-1962-1987-25th Anniversary-C . . . . (Island)
Thorn In My Pride
Black Crowes; *Southern Harmony & Musical Companion* . . . . . .(Def American)
Tiger
Paula Cole; *This Fire* . . . . (Imago)
'Til I Can Make It On My Own
Faith Hill; *Tammy Wynette...Remembered-C* . . . .(Asylum)
Kenny Rogers & Dottie West; *Kenny Rogers-Classics* . . . . (EMI)
Kenny Rogers-Twenty Greatest Hits . . . . (EMI)
Tammy Wynette; *Tammy Wynette's Greatest Hits-#4* . . . .(Epic)
Tears Of Fire-25th Anniversary Collection . . . .(Epic)
'Til I Can Make It On My Own . . . .(Epic)
Time Is On My Side
Irma Thomas; *Best Of New Orleans Rhythm & Blues-#1-C* . . . . (Rhino)
Simply The Best-Live! . . . . (Rounder)
Keith Richards & The X-Pensive Winos; *Live At Hollywood Palladium-*
December 1988 . . . . (Virgin)
Rolling Stones; *"Still Life" (American Concert 1981)* . . . . (Virgin)
12 X 5 . . . . (Abkco)
Big Hits (High Tide & Green Grass) . . . . (Abkco)
got Live if you want it! . . . . (Abkco)
Hot Rocks 1964-1971 . . . . (Abkco)
Singles Collection-The London Years . . . . (Abkco)
To Beat The Devil
Johnny Cash; *Johnny Cash-16 Biggest Hits-#2* . . . . (Legacy)
To Each His Own
Eddy Howard & His Orchestra; *Big Band*
Treasures-#2-C . . . . (Dunhill Compact Classics)
The Uncollected Eddy Howard & His Orchestra-1946-1951 . . . . . . (Hindsight)
Ink Spots; *Best Of The Ink Spots* . . . . (MCA)
Ink Spots' Greatest Hits-Original Recordings-1939-1946 . . . . (MCA)
Platters; *More Encore Of Golden Hits* . . . . (Mercury)
Willie Nelson; *What A Wonderful World* . . . . (Columbia)
Without A Song . . . . (Columbia)
Too Legit To Quit
Hammer; *Too Legit To Quit* . . . . (Capitol)
True Colors
Cyndi Lauper; *She's So Unusual/True Colors/Hat Full Of Stars (Box)* . . . (Epic)
True Colors . . . . (Portrait)
Twelve Deadly Cyns...And Then Some . . . .(Epic)
Phil Collins; *Phil Collins-Hits* . . . .(Atlantic)
True Love Never Dies
Earl Scruggs & Gary Scruggs & Travis Tritt; *Earl Scruggs And*
Friends-C . . . . (MCA)
Kevin Welch; *Kevin Welch* . . . . (Reprise)
Tuff Enuff
Fabulous Thunderbirds; *Hot Stuff-Greatest Hits* . . . . (Epic Portrait Assoc.)
Rock The First-#2-C . . . . (Sandstone Music)
Tuff Enuff . . . . (Epic Portrait Assoc.)
TV Movie
Bruce Springsteen; *Tracks* . . . . (Columbia)
Two Faces Have I
Lou Christie; *Back To The '60s-#4-C* . . . . (Dominion Entert.)
Enlightnin'ment-Best Of Lou Christie . . . . (Rhino)
Unbreakable
Michael Jackson; *Invincible* . . . .(Epic)
Unpretty
TLC; *Fanmail* . . . . (LaFace)
Unselfish Lover
Full Force; *Full Force* . . . . (Columbia)
Very Ape
Nirvana; *In Utero* . . . . (David Geffen Co.)
Video
India.Arie; *Acoustic Soul* . . . . (Motown)
Walk Like A Man
4 Seasons; *4 Seasons' Greatest Hits-#1* . . . . (Rhino)
4 Seasons-Anthology . . . . (Rhino)
Billboard Top Rock 'N' Roll Hits-1963-C . . . . (Rhino)

ST/The Wanderers . . . . (Warner Bros.)

Walk On
U2; *America: A Tribute To Heroes-C* . . . . (Interscope)
Now That's What I Call Music!-#8-C . . . .(Virgin)

Walk Unafraid
R.E.M.; *Up* . . . . (Warner Bros.)

Watch Me
Lorrie Morgan; *Lorrie Morgan's Greatest Hits* . . . .(BNA)
Watch Me . . . .(BNA)

Watch Me Do My Thing
Immature; *ST/All That* . . . . (Loud/RCA)

Way I Am
Merle Haggard; *Merle Haggard-Legends* . . . . (MCA)
Merle Haggard's Greatest Hits . . . . (MCA)

Way I Am
Eminem; *The Marshall Mathers LP* . . . .(Aftermath/Interscope)

Well Respected Man
Kinks; *History Of British Rock-#4-C* . . . . (Rhino)
Kinks' Greatest Hits . . . . (Rhino)
Kinks-Size Kinkdom . . . . (Rhino)

What About Me
Anne Murray; *Anne Murray-Country* . . . . (Capitol)
Kenny Rogers with Kim Carnes & James Ingram; *What About Me?* . . . . . .(RCA)
Quicksilver Messenger Service; *Quicksilver Messenger Service-Anthology* . . . . (Capitol)
Sons Of Mercury . . . . (Rhino)

What Have You Done For Me Lately
Janet Jackson; *Control* . . . . (A&M)

What I Am
Edie Brickell & New Bohemians; *Shooting Rubberbands At The Stars* . . . . (Geffen)

What Makes You Think You're The One
Fleetwood Mac; *25 Years-The Chain* . . . . (Warner Bros.)

What Ya Want
Ruff Ryders Featuring Eve & Nokio; *Ruff Ryders: Ride Or Die-#1* . . . . (Ruff Ryders/IDJMG)

What You Want
Mase Featuring Total; *Harlem World* . . . . (Bad Boy/Arista)

What's It Gonna Be
Busta Rhymes Featuring Janet Jackson; *E.L.E.* . . . . (Elektra)

When I Paint My Masterpiece
Band; *Bob Dylan 30th Anniversary Concert* . . . . (Columbia)
To Kingdom Come-The Definitive Collection . . . . (Capitol)
Bob Dylan; *Bob Dylan's Greatest Hits-#2* . . . . (Columbia)

When You're Hot, You're Hot
Jerry Reed; *60 Years Of Country Music-C* . . . .(RCA)
Best Of Jerry Reed . . . .(RCA)
Super Hits Of The '70s-Have A Nice Day-#5-C . . . . (Rhino)
When You're Hot, You're Hot . . . .(RCA)

Who Am I (What's My Name)?
Snoop Doggy Dogg; *Doggystyle* . . . .(Death Row)

Who Do You Think You Are
Spice Girls; *Spice* . . . .(Virgin)

Who I Am
Jessica Andrews; *Who I Am* . . . . (DreamWorks/SKG)

Who You Are
Pearl Jam; *No Code* . . . . (Epic)

Whole Lotta Pride
Robert Cray Band; *I Was Warned* . . . . (Mercury)

Whole New You
Shawn Colvin; *Whole New You* . . . . (Columbia)

Who's That Girl
Eve; *Scorpion* . . . . (Ruff Ryders/IDJMG)

Wild Wild West
Will Smith; *Willenium* . . . . (Columbia)

Will Not Be Your Fool
David Bromberg; *How Late'll Ya Play 'Til?* . . . .(Fantasy)

Woman In Me
Jessica Simpson featuring Destiny's Child; *Sweet Kisses* . . . . (Columbia)

World Leader Pretend
R.E.M.; *Green* . . . . (Warner Bros.)

Yes, Yes Y'all
Will Smith; *Big Willie Style* . . . . (Columbia)

Yessir, That's My Baby
Frank Sinatra; *Strangers In The Night* . . . .(Reprise)
Milt Jackson; *Best Of Milt Jackson* . . . . (Pablo)
Mom & Dads; *Dance With The Mom & Dads* . . . . (Crescendo)
Very Best Of The Mom & Dads . . . . (Crescendo)

You Can Love Yourself
Keb' Mo'; *Just Like You* . . . . (Okeh)

You Don't Even Know Who I Am
Patty Loveless; *Patty Loveless-Classics* . . . . (Epic)
When Fallen Angels Fly . . . . (Epic)

You Don't Own Me
Joan Jett; *Bad Reputation* . . . . (Blackheart)
Lesley Gore; *Billboard Top Pop Hits-1964-C* . . . . (Rhino)

You Just Watch Me
Tanya Tucker; *Soon* . . . .(Liberty)

You Make Me Feel Like A Man
Ricky Skaggs; *Live In London* . . . . (Epic)

You Want This
Janet Jackson; *janet.* . . . . (Virgin)

Young Jews Be Proud
2 Live Jews; *As Kosher As They Wanna Be* . . . . (Kosher)

Young, Gifted And Black
Aretha Franklin; *Young, Gifted And Black* . . . . (Atlantic & Atco Remasters)
Bob & Marcia; *Archive Reggae-C* . . . .(Rialto)
Nina Simone; *The Tomato Collection* . . . . (Tomato)

You're Lookin' At Country
Loretta Lynn; *Loretta Lynn-20 Greatest Hits* . . . . (MCA)
Loretta Lynn-Greatest Hits Live . . . .(K-Tel)
Loretta Lynn's Greatest Hits-#2 . . . . (MCA)
The Country Music Hall Of Fame-Loretta Lynn . . . . (MCA)

You're So Vain
Carly Simon; *'70s Greatest Rock Hits-#3-High Times-C* . . . . (Priority)
Best Of Carly Simon . . . . (Elektra)
Carly Simon-Greatest Hits Live . . . .(Arista)
No Secrets . . . . (Elektra)

You're The Power
Kathy Mattea; *New Faces Of Country-C* . . . .(K-Tel)
Walk The Way The Wind Blows . . . .(Mercury)

You've Got To Stand For Something
Aaron Tippin; *You've Got To Stand For Something* . . . . (RCA)

ELVIS

See Also: CELEBRITIES: SPECIFIC, MUSIC, SHOW BIZ

Blue Moon Revisited (Song For Elvis)
Cowboy Junkies; *Trinity Session* . . . . (RCA)

Boy From Tupelo
Emmylou Harris; *Red Dirt Girl* . . . .(Nonesuch)

Bringing Out The Elvis
Faith Hill; *Breathe* . . . . (Warner Bros.)

Bubba Hyde
Diamond Rio; *Diamond Rio's Greatest Hits* . . . .(Arista)
Love A Little Stronger . . . .(Arista)

Calling Elvis
Dire Straits; *On Every Street* . . . . (Warner Bros.)

Candy Bars For Elvis
Barry Tiffin; *A Tribute To Elvis* . . . . (K-Tel)

Chocolate Elvis
Tosca; *Trip Hop & Jazz-#2-Beats From The Underground-C* . . .(Instinct)

Dancin' With Elvis
Gina Jeffreys; *Somebody's Daughter* . . . . (EMI)

Elvis
Kent; *Isola* . . . . (RCA)

Elvis
Longpigs; *Sun Is Often Out* . . . .(Island)

Elvis & Marilyn
Leon Russell; *Americana* . . . .(Paradise)

Elvis & Me
Jimmy Webb; *Suspending Disbelief.* . . . .(Elektra)

Elvis And Andy
Confederate Railroad; *Confederate Railroad's Greatest Hits* . . . . (Atlantic)
Notorious . . . . (Atlantic)

Elvis And His Boss
Residents; *Duck Stab/Buster & Glenn/Goosebump* . . . . (East Side Digital)

Elvis Ate America
Passengers; *Original Soundtracks-1* . . . .(Island)

Elvis Has Just Left The Building
Frank Zappa; *Broadway The Hard Way* . . . .(Rykodisc)

Elvis Impersonator-Black Pool Pier
Manic Street Preachers; *Everything Must Go* . . . . (Epic)

Elvis Is Dead
Forgotten Rebels; *Surfin' On Heroin* . . . .(Restless)
Living Colour; *Super Hits* . . . . (Epic)

Elvis Presley And America
U2; *Unforgettable Fire* . . . .(Island)

Elvis Presley Blues
Gillian Welch; *Time (The Revelator)* . . . . (Acony)

Everything Zen
Bush; *MTV Buzz Bin-C.* . . . .(Mammoth)
Sixteen Stone . . . . (Trauma)

Graceland
Paul Simon; *Graceland* . . . . (Warner Bros.)

Happy Birthday Elvis
Loudon Wainwright III; *Career Moves* . . . .(Virgin)

I Try To Think About Elvis
Patty Loveless; *Patty Loveless-Classics.* . . . . (Epic)

When Fallen Angels Fly . . . .(Epic)

I Want Elvis For Christmas
Holly Twins & Eddie Cochran; *Legends Of Christmas Past-Rock & R&B-C* . . . .(EMI)

Johnny Bye-Bye
Bruce Springsteen; *Tracks* . . . . (Columbia)

Man On The Moon
R.E.M.; *Automatic For The People* . . . .(Warner Bros.)

Me & Elvis
Human Radio; *Human Radio* . . . . (Columbia)

Queen Elvis
Robyn Hitchcock; *Eye* . . . . (Rhino)

Velvet Elvis
''Weird Al'' Yankovic; *Even Worse.* . . . . (Scotti Bros.)

EMPTY, Hollow, Open Space, Vacant

See Also: **DESERT, LONELY, LOSING & LOSS, LOST & MISPLACED, SADNESS**

5 Miles To Empty
Brownstone; *Still Climbing.* . . . . (MJJ Music/Work)

Absence Of The Heart
Deana Carter; *Everything's Gonna Be Alright* . . . . (Capitol)

Against All Odds (Take A Look At Me Now)
Mariah Carey; *Rainbow* . . . . (Columbia)
Phil Collins; *Hit Singles-1980-1988-C* . . . .(Atlantic)
Serious Hits...Live! . . . .(Atlantic)
ST/Against All Odds . . . .(Atlantic)

Armed With An Empty Gun
Dream Syndicate; *Medicine Show/This Is Not The New Album* . . . . (A&M)

Big Empty
Stone Temple Pilots; *Purple* . . . .(Atlantic)

Child Is Gone
Fiona Apple; *Tidal* . . . . (Clean Slate/Work)

Don't Fence Me In
Andrews Sisters; *Andrews Sisters' All-Time Greatest Hits* . . . . (Decca)
Bing Crosby; *Best Of Bing Crosby* . . . .(MCA)
David Byrne; *Red Hot + Blue-Tribute To Cole Porter-C* . . . .(Chrysalis)
Ella Fitzgerald; *Cole Porter Songbook* . . . . (Verve)
Lari White/Shelby Lynne/Trisha Yearwood; *Don't Fence Me In* . . . . (RCA)
Willie Nelson & Leon Russell; *Cowboy Super Hits-C* . . . . (Columbia)

Drink Yer Glasses Empty
Gordon Lightfoot; *Waiting For You* . . . . (Reprise)

Empty
Harry Chapin; *Heads & Tales.* . . . . (Elektra)

Empty
Cranberries; *No Need To Argue* . . . . (Island)

Empty
Del Amitri; *Waking Hours* . . . . (A&M)

Empty
Information Society; *InSoc Recombinant* . . . . (Cleopatra)

Empty
Janet Jackson; *Velvet Rope* . . . . (Virgin)

Empty Arms
Stevie Ray Vaughan and Double Trouble; *The Sky Is Crying* . . . .(Epic)

Empty Baseball Park
Whiskeytown; *Faithless Street* . . . .(Outpost/Interscope)

Empty Bed Blues
Bessie Smith; *Bessie Smith-The Collection* . . . . (Legacy)
Empty Bed Blues . . . . (Columbia)
Bette Midler; *Broken Blossom* . . . .(Atlantic)
LaVern Baker; *Atlantic Jazz-Singers-C* . . . .(Atlantic)
LaVern Baker Sings Bessie Smith . . . .(Atlantic)

Empty Box
Morphine; *Like Swimming* . . . .(DreamWorks/Rykodisc)

Empty Cages
Dan Fogelberg; *Innocent Age* . . . . (Full Moon)

Empty Causes
Bad Religion; *Gray Race* . . . .(Atlantic)

Empty Chairs At Empty Tables
Original Broadway Cast; *Les Miserables* . . . .(Geffen)

Empty City
Gentle Giant; *Interview.* . . . .(One Way)

Empty City
Jane Siberry; *Speckless Sky* . . . .(Open Air)

Empty Dancehall
All About Eve; *Scarlet And Other Stories* . . . . (Mercury)

Empty Garden (Hey Hey Johnny)
Elton John; *Elton John's Greatest Hits-1976-1986* . . . .(MCA)
Jump Up! . . . .(MCA)

Empty Glass
Pete Townshend; *Empty Glass* . . . . (Atco)

Empty Hands
Lenny Kravitz; *Let Love Rule* . . . .(Virgin)

Empty Heart
Rolling Stones; *12 X 5* . . . .(Abkco)

Empty Inside
Triumph; *Stages* . . . . (MCA)

Empty Lives
Graham Parker; *Passion Is No Ordinary Word-Graham Parker Anthology-1976-1991* . . . . (Rhino)
Up Escalator . . . . (Razor & Tie)

Empty Pages
Traffic; *John Barleycorn Must Die* . . . . (Island)

Empty Pages
Air Supply; *Love & Other Bruises* . . . . (Columbia)

Empty Pockets Filled With Love
Original Cast; *Mr. President* . . . . (Sony Broadway)

Empty Rooms
Gary Moore; *Ballads & Blues-1982-1994.* . . . . (Charisma)
Out In The Fields-The Very Best Of Gary Moore . . . .(Virgin)

Empty Sky
Elton John; *Empty Sky.* . . . .(Polydor)

Empty Spaces
Pink Floyd; *The Wall.* . . . . (Columbia)

Empty World
Cure; *Top.* . . . . (Sire)

Empty-Handed Heart
Warren Zevon; *Bad Luck Streak In Dancing School* . . . .(Asylum)

Ghost Town
Don Cherry; *Columbia & Monument Sides* . . . . (Collector's Choice)

Good
Better Than Ezra; *Deluxe* . . . . (Swell/Elektra)

Heart Half Empty
Ty Herndon; *What Mattered Most.* . . . . (Epic)

Heart Hotels
Dan Fogelberg; *Dan Fogelberg/Greatest Hits* . . . .(Full Moon)
Phoenix. . . . .(Full Moon)

Hello Walls
Faron Young; *Billboard Top Country Hits-1961-C* . . . . (Rhino)
Willie Nelson; *Essential Willie Nelson* . . . .(RCA)
Willie Nelson-Greatest Songs. . . . . (Curb)

Hollow
Pantera; *Vulgar Display Of Power* . . . . (Atco)

Hollow
Matthew Sweet; *Blue Sky On Mars* . . . . (Freeworld/Capitol)

Hollow Hills
Bauhaus; *Mask* . . . .(Beggar's Banquet)

Hollow Man
Cult; *Love* . . . .(Sire)

Hollow Man
Marillion; *Made Again* . . . . (Castle Music America)

Hollow Man (Part 2)
Kula Shaker; *K* . . . . (Columbia)

Hollow Men, The
Cocteau Twins; *Garlands* . . . .(Capitol)

Hollow, The
A Perfect Circle; *Mer De Noms.* . . . .(Virgin)

Hollowman
Econoline Crush; *Devil You Know* . . . . (Restless)

My Empty Room
Queensryche; *Operation: Mindcrime* . . . . (EMI)

My Friends
Red Hot Chili Peppers; *One Hot Minute* . . . . (Warner Bros.)

Pretty Vacant
Joan Jett; *The Hit List* . . . . (Epic)
Sex Pistols; *Live At Chelmsford Top Security Prison* . . . . (Restless)
Never Mind The Bollocks, Here's The Sex Pistols . . . . . . (Warner Bros.)

Running On Empty
Jackson Browne; *Running On Empty* . . . . (Asylum)

Season Of Hollow Soul
k.d. lang; *Ingenue* . . . .(Sire)

Seven Rooms Of Gloom
Four Tops; *Four Tops' Greatest Hits* . . . . (Motown)
Four Tops Reach Out . . . . (Motown)
Four Tops-Anthology . . . . (Motown)

Smokin' (Empty, Try Another)
Joni Mitchell; *Dog Eat Dog.* . . . . (Geffen)

These Empty Days
Crosby, Stills & Nash; *After The Storm.* . . . .(Atlantic)

This House Is Empty Now
Elvis Costello; *Painted From Memory* . . . . (Mercury)

Vacant Chair
Steve Winwood; *Steve Winwood.* . . . . (Island)
Steve Winwood-Chronicles . . . . (Island)

Walk Away Renee
Four Tops; *Compact Command Performances-Four Tops* . . . . (Motown)

Four Tops Reach Out .... (Motown)
Four Tops-Anthology .... (Motown)
Left Banke; *Cruisin'-1966-C.* .... (Increase)
  History Of The Left Banke .... (Rhino)
Vonda Shepard; *ST/Songs From ''Ally McBeal'' Featuring Vonda*
  Shepard ....(550/Epic)

Wide Open Spaces
Dixie Chicks; *Big Country Hits '99-C.* .... (K-Tel)
  Wide Open Spaces .... (Monument)

ENDINGS, Final, Last

See Also: **BEGINNINGS, CIRCLES, DEATH, DIVORCE, ETERNITY,
LEAVING, LOVE (various), LOSING & LOSS, STOP**

(Lost His Love) On Our Last Date
Emmylou Harris; *Profile II-The Best Of Emmylou Harris* .... (Warner Bros.)

5-4-3-2 (Yo! Time Is Up)
Jade; *Mind Body & Soul* .... (Giant)

All I Know
Art Garfunkel; *Angel Clare* .... (Columbia)
  Garfunkel .... (Columbia)

And The Beat Goes On
Whispers; *Club Epic-#1-C.* .... (Legacy)

Angel's Son
Strait Up featuring Lajon of Sevendust; *Strait Up-C* ....(Immortal/Virgin)

Another Bridge To Burn
Mel Tillis; *Best Of Mel Tillis* .... (MCA)

Are The Good Times Really Over (I Wish A Buck Was Still Silver)
Merle Haggard; *Big City* .... (Epic)
  For The Record: Merle Haggard-43 Legendary Hits ....(BNA)
  Greatest Country Hits Of The '80s-1982-C .... (Columbia)
  His Epic Hits-First 11 To Be Continued-C .... (Epic)

At The End Of A Rainbow
Earl Grant; *Best Of Earl Grant-Singin' And Swingin'* .... (MCA)
Jerry Wallace; *45-#006* .... (BMA)

Babe I'm Gonna Leave You
Led Zeppelin; *Led Zeppelin* .... (Atlantic)
  Led Zeppelin-Box Set .... (Atlantic)

Beginning, The
Keb' Mo'; *The Door* ....(550/Epic/Okeh)

Bobby Jean
Bruce Springsteen; *Born In The U.S.A.* .... (Columbia)
Bruce Springsteen & The E Street Band; *Bruce Springsteen & The E Street*
  Band Live/1975-85 .... (Legacy)

Boom! It Was Over
Robert Ellis Orrall; *Flying Colors* ....(RCA)

Break It To Me Gently
Brenda Lee; *Brenda Lee-Anthology-#1 & #2* .... (MCA)
  The Brenda Lee Story-Her Greatest Hits .... (MCA)
Juice Newton; *Juice Newton's Greatest Country Hits* .... (Curb)
  Juice Newton's Greatest Hits .... (Gold Rush)

But I Will
Faith Hill; *Take Me As I Am.* .... (Warner Bros.)

By The Time I Get To Phoenix
Glen Campbell; *All-Time Country Classics-#1-C* .... (Capitol)
  Glen Campbell-Classics Collection .... (Capitol)
  Glen Campbell-Live .... (Capitol)
  Glen Campbell's Greatest Hits .... (Capitol)
  Very Best Of Glen Campbell. .... (Capitol)
Reba McEntire; *Starting Over* .... (MCA)

Can't Really Be Gone
Tim McGraw; *All I Want* .... (Curb)

Can't Stand It
Wilco; *Summer Teeth* .... (Reprise)

Cara Mia
Jay & The Americans; *I Got Rhythm-C* .... (K-Tel)
  Jay & The Americans' Greatest Hits .... (CEMA Special Prod.)
  Jay & The Americans' Greatest Hits .... (Curb)

Casey's Last Ride
Johnny Cash; *Rainbow* .... (Columbia)

Chill Of An Early Fall
George Strait; *The Chill Of An Early Fall* .... (MCA)

Close Up The Honky Tonks
Radney Foster; *Red Hot + Country-C* .... (Mercury)

Closing Time
Semisonic; *Feeling Strangely Fine* .... (MCA)
  Now That's What I Call Music!-#2-C .... (Virgin)

Could I Be
Wood; *Songs From Stamford Hill* .... (Columbia)

Dance, The
Garth Brooks; *Garth Brooks* .... (Liberty)
  Garth Brooks-Double Live .... (Capitol)

Don't Dream It's Over
Crowded House; *Crowded House* .... (Capitol)
Neil Finn; *Diana, Princess Of Wales-Tribute-C* .... (Columbia)

Don't Let The Sun Go Down On Me
Elton John; *Caribou.* .... (Rocket)
  Elton John's Greatest Hits .... (Polydor)
  Live In Australia With The Melbourne Symphony Orchestra .... (MCA)
Elton John & George Michael; *Duets-C.* .... (MCA)
George Michael & Elton John; *Two Rooms-Celebrating The Songs Of Elton*
  John & Bernie Taupin-C .... (Polydor)

Don't Speak
No Doubt; *Tragic Kingdom* .... (Trauma)

Down So Long
Jewel; *Spirit* .... (Atlantic)

Down To My Last Broken Heart
Janie Fricke; *Greatest Country Hits Of The '80s-1980-C* ....(Columbia)
  Janie Fricke-17 Greatest Hits ....(Columbia)
  Janie Fricke's Greatest Hits ....(Columbia)

Down To My Last Teardrop
Tanya Tucker; *Tanya Tucker's Greatest Hits-1990-1992* ....(Capitol)
  What Do I Do With Me ....(Capitol)

Dream Is Over
Van Halen; *For Unlawful Carnal Knowledge* .... (Warner Bros.)

Emotional
Carl Thomas; *Emotional* .... (Bad Boy/Arista)

End Is The Beginning Is The End
Smashing Pumpkins; *ST/Batman & Robin-Music From And Inspired By The*
  Motion Picture .... (Jive)

End Of My Pirate Days
Mary Chapin Carpenter; *Stones In The Road* ....(Columbia)

End Of Our Road
Gladys Knight & The Pips; *Compact Command Performances-Gladys Knight*
  & The Pips ....(Motown)
  Gladys Knight & The Pips-All The Great Hits ....(Motown)
  Gladys Knight & The Pips-Anthology ....(Motown)
Jerry Lee Lewis; *Jerry Lee Lewis-Original Golden Hits-#1* ...... (Sun)
  Jerry Lee Lewis-Original Golden Hits-#1 .... (Sun)
Marvin Gaye; *Marvin Gaye-Anthology* ....(Motown)
  Marvin Gaye-Super Hits ....(Motown)
  Musical Testament 1964-1984 ....(Motown)

End Of Outside
Duncan Sheik; *Duncan Sheik.* .... (Atlantic)

End Of The Innocence
Don Henley; *The End Of The Innocence* .... (Geffen)

End Of The Line
Bob Wills & His Texas Playboys; *Bob Wills & His Texas Playboys-24*
  Great Hits ....(Polydor)
Buddy Emmons; *Buddy Emmons Sings Bob Wills* .... (Flying Fish)
Jason Roberts & Asleep At The Wheel; *Ride With Bob-C* .. (DreamWorks/SKG)

End Of The Line
Roxy Music; *Siren* .... (Atco)

End Of The Line
Robin Lee; *Heart On A Chain* .... (Atlantic)

End Of The Line
Traveling Wilburys; *The Traveling Wilburys.* ....(Wilbury/Warner Bros.)

End Of The Line
J.J. Cale; *Travel-Log* .... (Silvertone)

End Of The World
Allman Brothers Band; *Shades Of Two Worlds* ....(Epic)

End Of The World
Vonda Shepard; *ST/Songs From ''Ally McBeal'' Featuring Vonda*
  Shepard .... (550/Epic)

End Of The World
Cold; *13 Ways To Bleed On Stage* .... (Flip/Geffen/Interscope)

End, The
Beatles; *Abbey Road* .... (Parlophone)

Ex-Girlfriend
No Doubt; *Return Of Saturn.* .... (Interscope)

Fade
Staind; *Break The Cycle.* .... (Flip/Elektra)

Fancy Free
Oak Ridge Boys; *Fancy Free* .... (MCA)
  Oak Ridge Boys' Greatest Hits 2 .... (MCA)

Final Heartbreak
Jessica Simpson; *Sweet Kisses* ....(Columbia)

Fool (If You Think It's Over)
Chris Rea; *New Light Through Old Windows.* .... (Atlantic)
  Whatever Happened To Benny Santini .... (United Artists)

Forever Has Come To An End
Buddy & Julie Miller; *Buddy & Julie Miller* .... (Hightone)

Fred Jones Part 2
Ben Folds; *Rockin' The Suburbs* .... (Epic)

Get Out Of My Life, Woman
Lee Dorsey; *History Of New Orleans R&B-#3-1962-1970-C* ....(Rhino)
Paul Butterfield Blues Band; *East-West.* ....(Elektra)
  Golden Butter .... (Elektra)

Going Away Party
Manhattan Transfer & Willie Nelson & Asleep At The Wheel; *Ride With*
  Bob-C. .... (DreamWorks/SKG)

Graduation Day
Beach Boys; *Beach Boys-Gift Set.* ....(Capitol)
  Spirit Of America ....(Capitol)

Rover Boys; *Choice Voices! Pop Vocal Group Gems Of The '50s-C* .... (Collector's Choice)

Guns Of Love
Pamela Rose; *Morpheus* .... (Grace)

Hang Up My Rock & Roll Shoes
Band; *Rock Of Ages* .... (Capitol)
Chuck Willis; *Atlantic Rhythm & Blues 1947-1974-#3 (1955-1958)-C* .... (Atlantic)

Happy Endings
Liza Minnelli & Larry Kert; *ST/New York, New York* .... (EMI)

Hearts Of Stone
Bruce Springsteen; *Tracks* .... (Columbia)
Southside Johnny And The Asbury Jukes; *Best Of Southside Johnny And The Asbury Jukes* .... (Legacy)
Cover Me (Bruce Springsteen Tribute)-C .... (Rhino)
Hearts Of Stone .... (Epic)

Hit The Road Jack
Ray Charles; *Ray Charles' Greatest Hits* .... (Rhino)
Ray Charles-Anthology .... (Rhino)
Ray Charles-His Greatest Hits-#2 .... (Dunhill Compact Classics)

Hobo Bill's Last Ride
Merle Haggard & The Strangers; *Okie From Muskogee* .... (Capitol)
Same Train Different Time .... (Capitol)
Train Whistle Blues .... (Rounder)

House With No Curtains
Alan Jackson; *Everything I Love* .... (Arista)

I Don't Want To Wait
Paula Cole; *Live On Letterman-From The Late Show* .... (Reprise)
Songs From Dawson's Creek .... (Sony Music Soundtrax)
This Fire .... (Imago)

If It's The Last Thing I Do
Tammy Wynette; *Without Walls-C* .... (Epic)

I'll Get You
Beatles; *Past Masters-Volume One* .... (Parlophone)
The Beatles' Second Album .... (Capitol)

I'm Not Supposed To Love You Anymore
Bryan White; *Between Now And Forever* .... (Asylum)

In The End
Linkin Park; *Hybrid Theory* .... (Warner Bros.)

Is It Over Yet
Wynonna; *Tell Me Why* .... (MCA)

It Ain't Over 'Til It's Over
Lenny Kravitz; *Mama Said* .... (Virgin)

It Must Have Been Love
Roxette; *ST/Pretty Woman* .... (EMI)

It's All Over But The Shoutin'
Joe Cocker; *Jamaica Say You Will* .... (A&M)

It's All Over Now
Bobby Womack; *Lookin' For A Love-Best Of Bobby Womack-1968-1975* .... (Razor & Tie)
John Anderson; *Great Divorce Songs For Him-C* .... (Warner Bros.)
John Anderson's Greatest Hits-#2 .... (Warner Bros.)
Rod Stewart; *Best Of Rod Stewart* .... (Mercury)
Gasoline Alley .... (Mercury)
Vintage Rod Stewart .... (Mercury)
Rolling Stones; *12 X 5* .... (Abkco)
Big Hits (High Tide & Green Grass) .... (Abkco)
More Hot Rocks (big hits & fazed cookies) .... (Abkco)
Singles Collection-The London Years .... (Abkco)
Ry Cooder; *Paradise And Lunch* .... (Reprise)

It's All Over Now, Baby Blue
Bob Dylan; *Biograph* .... (Columbia)
Bob Dylan's Greatest Hits-#2 .... (Columbia)
Bringing It All Back Home .... (Columbia)
Byrds; *Ballad Of Easy Rider* .... (Columbia)
The Byrds .... (Columbia)

It's Not Where You Start (It's Where You Finish)
Barbara Cook; *Dorothy Fields-Close As Pages In A Book* .... (DRG)
Original Broadway Cast; *See Saw* .... (DRG)

It's Over
Roy Orbison; *Roy Orbison's All-Time Greatest Hits-#1 & 2* .... (Monument)
Roy Orbison-Super Hits .... (Columbia)
Very Best Of Roy Orbison .... (Virgin)

It's Over Now
Cause & Effect; *Trip* .... (Zoo)

It's Over Now
L.A. Guns; *Hollywood Vampires* .... (Polydor)

It's Over Now
112; *Part III* .... (Bad Boy/Arista)

It's The End Of The World As We Know It (And I Feel Fine)
R.E.M.; *Document* .... (EMI-Capitol Entert. Properties)

Just Friends
Charlie Parker; *Compact Jazz-Charlie Parker* .... (Verve)
Charlie Watts Quintet; *Tribute To Charlie Parker* .... (Continuum)
Frank Sinatra; *No One Cares* .... (Capitol)
Joe Pass; *I Remember Charlie Parker* .... (Pablo)
L.A. Four; *Just Friends* .... (Concord Jazz)
Sarah Vaughan; *Divine Sarah Vaughan-Columbia Years-1949-1953* .... (Columbia)

Tony Bennett; *Jazz* .... (Columbia)
Wynton Marsalis Quartet; *Live At Blues Alley* .... (Columbia)

Kiss The World Goodbye
Kris Kristofferson; *Border Lord* .... (Columbia)

Last Chance
John Mellencamp; *Whenever We Wanted* .... (Mercury)

Last Chance
Level 42; *Pursuit Of Accidents* .... (Polydor)

Last Chance
Bryan Adams; *You Want It, You Got It* .... (A&M)

Last Chance Texaco
Rickie Lee Jones; *Naked Songs Live And Acoustic* .... (Reprise)
Rickie Lee Jones .... (Warner Bros.)

Last Chance To Turn Around
Gene Pitney; *Best Of Gene Pitney* .... (K-Tel)
Gene Pitney-Anthology 1961-1968 .... (Rhino)

Last Cowboy Song
Ed Bruce; *16 Top Country Hits-#2-C* .... (MCA)
Ed Bruce's Greatest Hits .... (MCA)
Waylon Jennings, Willie Nelson, Johnny Cash, Kris Kristofferson; *Cowboy Super Hits-C* .... (Columbia)
Highwayman .... (Columbia)

Last Cup Of Sorrow
Faith No More; *Album Of The Year* .... (Reprise)

Last Date
Floyd Cramer; *Last Date/On The Rebound* .... (Collectables)

Last Day, The
Marilyn Scott; *Avenues Of Love* .... (Warner Bros.)

Last Goodbye
Jeff Buckley; *Grace* .... (Columbia)

Last Goodbye
Kenny Wayne Shepherd Band; *Live On* .... (Giant)

Last Great American Whale
Lou Reed; *Greenpeace/Rainbow Warriors-C* .... (Geffen)
New York .... (Sire)

Last Kiss
J. Frank Wilson and The Cavaliers; *Billboard Top Rock 'N' Roll Hits-1964-C* .... (Rhino)
Collectables Presents The History Of Rock-#2-C .... (Collectables)
Oldies But Goodies-#9-C .... (Original Sound)
Teenage Tragedies-C .... (Rhino)
Pearl Jam; *No Boundaries-Benefit For The Kosovar Refugees-C* .... (Epic)

Last Laugh
Mark Knopfler; *Sailing To Philadelphia* .... (Warner Bros.)

Last Letter
Jack Greene; *Jack Greene Sings His Best* .... (Step One)
Ray Price; *Heart Of Country Music* .... (Step One)

Last Night I Had The Strangest Dream
Simon & Garfunkel; *Collected Works* .... (Columbia)
Wednesday Morning 3 A.M. .... (Columbia)

Last Night Of The World
Bruce Cockburn; *Breakfast In New Orleans, Dinner In Timbuktu* .... (Rykodisc)

Last Night On Earth
U2; *Pop* .... (Island)

Last Resort
Papa Roach; *Infest* .... (DreamWorks/SKG)

Last Rose Of Summer
Boston Pops Orchestra/Arthur Fiedler; *Irish Album* .... (RCA)
James Galway & The Chieftains; *Over The Sea To Skye-Celtic Connection* .... (RCA)
Kiri Te Kanawa; *Come To The Fair* .... (Angel)
Phil Coulter; *Sea Of Tranquility* .... (Shanachie)

Last Rose Of Summer
Judas Priest; *Sin After Sin* .... (Columbia)

Last Song
Elton John; *The One* .... (MCA)

Last Steam Engine Train
John Fahey; *Best Of John Fahey: 1959-1977* .... (Takoma)
Dance Of Death & Other Plantation Faves .... (Takoma)
Leo Kottke; *Best Of Leo Kottke* .... (Capitol)
Greenhouse .... (Capitol)
Very Best Of Leo Kottke .... (Capitol)

Last Time
Rolling Stones; *Big Hits (High Tide & Green Grass)* .... (Abkco)
got Live if you want it! .... (Abkco)
More Hot Rocks (big hits & fazed cookies) .... (Abkco)
Out Of Our Heads .... (Abkco)
Singles Collection-The London Years .... (Abkco)

Last Train
Robin Trower & Jack Bruce; *Truce* .... (Chrysalis)

Last Train
Arlo Guthrie; *Best Of Arlo Guthrie* .... (Warner Bros.)

Last Train
Peter Rowan; *Steel Rails-Classic Railroad Songs-#1-C* .... (Rounder)

Last Train Done Gone Down
Marty Stuart; *Hot Tracks-Train Super Hits-C* .... (Epic)
Let There Be Country .... (Columbia)

Last Word, The
Mary Chapin Carpenter; *Stones In The Road* .... (Columbia)

Last Worthless Evening
Don Henley; *End Of The Innocence* . . . . (Geffen)
Long Road, The
Eddie Vedder; *America: A Tribute To Heroes-C* . . . . (Interscope)
Man Overboard
Blink-182; *The Mark, Tom & Travis Show-The Enema Strikes Back* . . . . (MCA)
Mary Jane's Last Dance
Tom Petty And The Heartbreakers; *Playback* . . . . (MCA)
Tom Petty And The Heartbreakers' Greatest Hits . . . . (MCA)
Memory
Original Broadway Cast; *Cats* . . . . (Geffen)
Miami 2017
Billy Joel; *Songs In The Attic* . . . .(Columbia)
The Concert For New York City-C . . . . (Columbia)
Turnstiles . . . . (Columbia)
My Man's Gone Now
Ella Fitzgerald & Louis Armstrong; *Porgy & Bess* . . . . (Verve)
Nina Simone; *Vocalists-Jazz Masters-C* . . . . (Bluebird)
Original Cast; *Porgy & Bess* . . . . (MCA)
Sarah Vaughan & L.A. Philharmonic; *Gershwin Live* . . . . (Columbia)
Sinead O'Connor; *Glory Of Gershwin Featuring Larry Adler-C* . . . . (Mercury)
My Whole World Ended (The Moment You Left Me)
David Ruffin; *David Ruffin-At His Best* . . . . (Motown)
Motown Year By Year-The Sound Of Young America-1969-C . . . . . . (Motown)
Spinners; *Best Of The Spinners* . . . . (Motown)
No More
Ruff Endz; *Love Crimes* . . . . (Epic)
No More ''I Love You's''
Annie Lennox; *Medusa* . . . . (Arista)
Not Dark Yet
Bob Dylan; *Time Out Of Mind* . . . . (Columbia)
Not Fade Away
Buddy Holly/The Crickets; *Buddy Holly-20 Golden Greats* . . . . (MCA)
Buddy Holly's Greatest Hits . . . . (MCA)
From The Original Master Tapes-Buddy Holly . . . . (MCA)
Legend-From The Original Master Tapes . . . . (MCA)
The Buddy Holly Collection . . . . (MCA)
Grateful Dead; *Dick's Picks-#2* . . . . (Arista)
Dozin' At The Knick . . . . (Arista)
Rolling Stones; *Big Hits (High Tide & Green Grass)* . . . . (Abkco)
England's Newest Hit Makers/The Rolling Stones . . . . (Abkco)
got Live if you want it! . . . . (Abkco)
More Hot Rocks (big hits & fazed cookies) . . . . (Abkco)
Singles Collection-The London Years . . . . (Abkco)
Stripped . . . . (Virgin)
Oh, The Last Rose Of Summer
Eddie Cantor; *Music From The New York Stage (1890-1920)-#4-1917-
1920-C* . . . . (Pearl)
Old Count Basie Is Gone (Old Piney Brown Is Gone)
Tony Bennett; *Playin' With My Friends-Bennett Sings The
Blues-C* . . . . (Columbia)
Out Of Time
Rolling Stones; *Flowers* . . . . (Abkco)
More Hot Rocks (big hits & fazed cookies) . . . . (Abkco)
Singles Collection-The London Years . . . . (Abkco)
Out Of Time
Sam Phillips; *Indescribable Wow* . . . . (Virgin)
Out Of Time
Divinyls; *Temperamental* . . . . (Chrysalis)
Over Now
Alice In Chains; *Alice In Chains* . . . . (Columbia)
Overs
Simon & Garfunkel; *Bookends* . . . . (Columbia)
Collected Works . . . . (Columbia)
Party's Over
Judy Garland; *One & Only* . . . . (Capitol)
Judy Holliday; *Broadway Magic-The 1960s-C* . . . . (Columbia)
Judy Holliday/Original Cast; *Bells Are Ringing* . . . . (Columbia)
Mel Torme; *Live At The Maisonette* . . . . (Atlantic)
Shirley Bassey; *Shirley Bassey-Live At Carnegie Hall* . . . . . . (United Artists)
Party's Over
Journey; *Journey-Captured* . . . . (Columbia)
Party's Over
Tesla; *Great Radio Controversy* . . . . (Geffen)
Party's Over
Raspberries; *Capitol Collectors Series-The Raspberries* . . . . (Capitol)
Party's Over
Willie Nelson; *Always On My Mind* . . . . (Columbia)
Party's Over
Marvin Gaye; *Hello Broadway* . . . . (Motown)
Please Don't Talk About Me When I'm Gone
Ann-Margret; *Let Me Entertain You* . . . . (RCA)
Arlo Guthrie & Pete Seeger; *Precious Friend* . . . . (Warner Bros.)
Billie Holiday; *Compact Jazz-Billie Holiday* . . . . (Verve)
Music For Torching: Billie Holiday Story-#5 . . . . (Verve)
The Ultimate Billie Holiday . . . . (Verve)
Ella Fitzgerald & Count Basie; *Perfect Match* . . . . (Pablo)
Frank Sinatra; *Swing Along With Me* . . . . (Reprise)
Gene Austin; *The Voice Of The Southland* . . . . (Living Era)

Harry Connick, Jr.; *20* . . . . (Columbia)
Leon Redbone; *Champagne Charlie* . . . . (Warner Bros.)
Ray Price; *Portrait Of A Singer* . . . . (Step One)
Quittin' Time
Mary Chapin Carpenter; *Greatest Country Hits Of The '90s-
1990-C* . . . . (Columbia)
State Of The Heart . . . . (Columbia)
Right Now
SR-71; *Now You See Inside* . . . . (RCA)
Running Out Of Time
Joan Osborne; *Righteous Love* . . . . (Interscope)
Saying Hello, Saying I Love You, Saying Goodbye
Jim Ed Brown & Helen Cornelius; *Jim Ed Brown & Helen Cornelius'
Greatest Hits* . . . . (RCA)
Second Sitting For The Last Supper
10 CC; *Live & Let Live* . . . . (Mercury)
She's Out Of My Life
Jacksons; *Jacksons Live* . . . . (Epic)
Michael Jackson; *Off The Wall* . . . . (Epic)
Soldier's Last Letter
Ernest Tubb; *Legend & The Legacy* . . . . (First Generation)
Living Legend . . . . (First Generation)
Ernest Tubb & Johnny Cash; *Ernest Tubb Collection-C* . . . . . (Step One)
George Jones; *20 Golden Pieces Of George Jones* . . . . (Bulldog)
Merle Haggard; *Capitol Collectors Series-Merle Haggard* . . . . . (Capitol)
Someone's Final Song
Elton John; *Blue Moves* . . . . (MCA)
Someone's Gotta Cry
Jean Shepard; *45-#5392* . . . . (Capitol)
Something Beautiful Remains
Tina Turner; *Wildest Dreams* . . . . (Virgin)
Song For The Dumped
Ben Folds Five; *Naked Baby Photos* . . . . (Caroline)
ST/Mr. Wrong . . . . (Hollywood)
Whatever And Ever Amen . . . . (Caroline/550)
Song Is Over
Who; *Hooligans* . . . . (MCA)
Who's next . . . . (MCA)
Spirit Slips Away
Thin Lizzy; *Fighting* . . . . (Mercury)
Standing In The Shadows Of Love
Barry White; *Barry White's Greatest Hits* . . . . (20th Century Fox)
I've Got So Much To Give . . . . (20th Century Fox)
Four Tops; *Four Tops' Greatest Hits* . . . . (Motown)
Four Tops Reach Out . . . . (Motown)
Four Tops-Anthology . . . . (Motown)
Motown Story-First 25 Years-C . . . . (Motown)
Motown Superstar Series-#14-Four Tops . . . . (Motown)
Rod Stewart; *Blondes Have More Fun* . . . . (Warner Bros.)
Stuck Inside Of Mobile With The Memphis Blues Again
Bob Dylan; *Blonde On Blonde* . . . . (Columbia)
Bob Dylan's Greatest Hits-#2 . . . . (Columbia)
Hard Rain . . . . (Columbia)
Summer Song
Chad & Jeremy; *Best Of Chad & Jeremy* . . . . (K-Tel)
Capitol Gold-Best Of Chad & Jeremy . . . . (Capitol)
History Of British Rock-#2-C . . . . (Rhino)
Summer's Almost Gone
Doors; *Waiting For The Sun* . . . . (Elektra)
Take This Job And Shove It
David Allan Coe; *David Allan Coe-17 Greatest Hits* . . . . (Columbia)
Johnny Paycheck; *Johnny Paycheck's Biggest Hits* . . . . (Epic)
Johnny Paycheck's Greatest Hits-#2 . . . . (Epic)
Take This Job And Shove It . . . . (Epic)
Truckers' Jukebox-10 All-Time Radio Requests-C . . . . (Legacy)
That Ain't No Way To Go
Brooks & Dunn; *Hard Workin' Man* . . . . (Arista)
That's All She Wrote
Rick Nelson; *Garden Party* . . . . (MCA Special Prod.)
Rick Nelson Sings ''For You'' . . . . (MCA)
That's All She Wrote
Ghetto Girlz; *Ain't Takin' No S@#T* . . . . (Heat Wave)
That's All She Wrote
Marty Robbins; *Come Back To Me* . . . . (Columbia)
That's All She Wrote
Conway Twitty; *Hello Darlin'* . . . . (MCA Special Prod.)
That's All She Wrote
Reba McEntire; *Rumor Has It* . . . . (MCA)
That's All There Is To That
Dinah Washington; *Complete Dinah Washington On Mercury-#6-1958-
1960* . . . . (Mercury)
Etta Jones; *Something Nice* . . . . (Original Jazz Classics)
Nat ''King'' Cole & The Four Knights; *From The Vaults-#6-Best
Of '56* . . . . (Capitol/EMI)
There Goes
Alan Jackson; *Everything I Love* . . . . (Arista)
Til The End
Vern Gosdin; *10 Years Of Greatest Hits Newly Recorded* . . . . . . (Columbia)

Best Of Vern Gosdin . . . . (Warner Bros.)
Til The End. . . . . (Elektra)

Till The End Of The World Rolls 'Round
Flatt & Scruggs; *Columbia Historic Edition-Flatt & Scruggs* . . . . . . (Columbia)
Golden Era . . . . (Rounder)

Till The End Of Time
Perry Como; *Como's Golden Records* . . . . (RCA)
Nipper's Greatest Hits Of The '40s-#2-C . . . . (RCA)
Perry Como-Pure Gold . . . . (RCA)
There Is Love-Wedding Songs-C . . . . (Scotti Bros.)

Till The End Of Time
Chicago; *Chicago XI.* . . . .(Chicago)

Time Of Your Life (Good Riddance)
Green Day; *Nimrod.* . . . . (Reprise)

Time's Up
Southern Pacific & Carlene Carter; *County Line* . . . .(Warner Bros.)
Favorite Country Duets-C . . . . (Warner Bros.)
Southern Pacific's Greatest Hits . . . . (Warner Bros.)

To Sir With Love
Lulu; *History Of British Rock-#6-C* . . . . (Rhino)
Hollywood Magic-1960s-C . . . . (Columbia)
Rock Artifacts-From The Vaults-#3-C . . . . (Columbia)

Today My World Slipped Away
George Strait; *Carrying Your Love With Me.* . . . .(MCA)
Latest Greatest Straitest Hits . . . .(MCA)
Vern Gosdin; *10 Years Of Greatest Hits Newly Recorded* . . . . (Columbia)
Legends Of The Silver Eagle-C . . . . (King Biscuit Entert.)
Today My World Slipped Away . . . . (AMI)

Took The Last Train
David Gates; *Goodbye Girl* . . . . (Elektra)

Tuesday's Gone
Hank Williams, Jr.; *Skynyrd Frynds-C* . . . .(MCA)
Wild Streak . . . . (WB/Curb)
Lynyrd Skynyrd; *Gold & Platinum.* . . . .(MCA)
One More From The Road. . . . .(MCA)
Pronounced Leh-nerd Skin-nerd . . . .(MCA)

Until The End Of The World
U2; *Achtung Baby.* . . . . (Island)
ST/Until The End Of The World . . . .(Warner Bros.)

Until The End Of Time
Guy & Ralna; *22 Golden Country Classics* . . . .(Ranwood)

Violet
Hole; *Ask For It* . . . . (Caroline)
Live Through This . . . . (David Geffen Co.)

Waiting For The End Of The World
Elvis Costello; *My Aim Is True* . . . . (Columbia)

War Is Over
Phil Ochs; *Chords Of Fame* . . . . (A&M)
Tape From California . . . . (A&M)
The War Is Over-Best Of Phil Ochs . . . . (A&M)

Washed Up & Left For Dead
Selecter; *Celebrate The Bullet* . . . .(Chrysalis)
Selected Selections . . . . (Chrysalis)

Watch Me
Lorrie Morgan; *Lorrie Morgan's Greatest Hits* . . . . (BNA)
Watch Me . . . . (BNA)

We Believe In Happy Endings
Earl Thomas Conley & Emmylou Harris; *Duets-C.* . . . . (Reprise)

Wedding's Over
Charlie Rich; *Charlie Rich-20 Golden Hits* . . . . (Sun)
Time For Tears-C . . . . (Sun)

What A Crying Shame
Mavericks; *Best Of The Mavericks-Super Colossal Smash Hits Of
The '90s.* . . . . (Mercury)
What A Crying Shame . . . .(MCA)

When All Is Said And Done
Abba; *Forever Gold* . . . . (Polydor)

When Day Is Done
Coleman Hawkins; *Body And Soul* . . . . (Bluebird)
Helen Humes; *Swingin' With Humes* . . . . (Contemporary)
Mormon Tabernacle Choir & Columbia Symphony Orchestra; *Songs America
Loves Best-Memories* . . . . (Columbia)

When It's Over
Sugar Ray; *Sugar Ray.* . . . . (Lava)
Totally Hits 2001-C . . . . (Arista)

Where The Blacktop Ends
keith urban; *keith urban* . . . . (Capitol)

You Stay With Me
Ricky Martin; *Ricky Martin* . . . . (Columbia)

ENERGY, Electricity, Solar Energy
See Also: **GAS STATIONS, MOTIVATION, NUCLEAR ENERGY, POWER & CONTROL**

A.C.D.C.
Sweet; *Desolation Boulevard* . . . . (Capitol)

Aneurysm
Nirvana; *From The Muddy Banks Of The Wishkah* . . . . (David Geffen Co.)

Are Friends Electric
Gary Numan & Tubeway Army; *Replicas.* . . . . (Atco)

Arkansas Coal
Nancy Sinatra & Lee Hazlewood; *Fairy Tales & Fantasies-Best Of.* . . . . (Rhino)

Back When Gas Was Thirty Cents A Gallon
Tom T. Hall; *Soldier Of Fortune* . . . . (RCA)

Ballad Of Jed Clampett
Flatt & Scruggs; *Columbia Country Classics-#3-Americana-C* . . . . . (Columbia)
On Foggy Mountain . . . . (Fifty One West)

Big Electric Cat
Adrian Belew; *Desire Of The Rhino King* . . . . (Island)

Body Electric
Rush; *Grace Under Pressure* . . . . (Mercury)

Dance Electric
Andre Cymone; *A.C.* . . . . (Columbia)
Pointer Sisters; *Break Out* . . . . (Planet)

Dance Of Electricity
Laurie Anderson; *United States Live* . . . . (Warner Bros.)

Electric
Church; *Seance* . . . . (Arista)
Olivia Newton-John; *45-#52686.* . . . . (MCA)

Electric Aunt Jemima
Frank Zappa; *Uncle Meat* . . . . (Barking Pumpkin)

Electric Avenue
Eddy Grant; *Killer On The Rampage.* . . . . (Portrait)

Electric Blue
Icehouse; *Man Of Colours.* . . . . (Chrysalis)

Electric Boogaloo
Ollie & Jerry; *Breakin' 2 Electric Boogaloo* . . . .(Polydor)

Electric Chair
Sleepy John Estes & The Tennessee Jug Busters; *Broke & Hungry (Ragged
& Dirty Too)* . . . .(Delmark)

Electric Chair
Prince; *ST/Batman.* . . . . (Warner Bros.)

Electric Chair Blues
Guitar Welch; *Angola Prisoner's Blues* . . . . (Arhoolie)

Electric Chair, The
SNFU; *Last Of The Big Time Suspenders* . . . . (Cargo)

Electric Co.
U2; *Boy* . . . . (Island)
Under A Blood Red Sky . . . . (Island)

Electric Eye
Judas Priest; *Priest...Live!* . . . . (Columbia)
Screaming For Vengeance . . . . (Columbia)

Electric Kingdom
Twilight 22; *Twilight 22* . . . . (Vanguard)

Electric L.A. Sunset
Al Stewart; *Al Stewart-Early Years* . . . .(Janus)

Electric Lady
Con Funk Shun; *Electric Lady* . . . . (Mercury)

Electric Land
Bad Company; *10 From 6* . . . .(Atlantic)
Rough Diamonds . . . . (Swan Song)

Electric Messengers
220 Volt; *Electric Messengers* . . . . (Epic)

Electric Youth
Debbie Gibson; *Electric Youth* . . . .(Atlantic)

Electrical Language
Be Bop Deluxe; *Best Of Be Bop Deluxe-Raiding The Divine Archive.* . . (Capitol)
Drastic Plastic . . . . (Capitol)

Electricity
Joni Mitchell; *For The Roses.* . . . .(Asylum)
Orchestral Manoeuvres In The Dark; *in the dark/the best of OMD* . . . . . (A&M)

Electricity
Midnight Star; *Midnight Star's Greatest Hits* . . . .(Solar)
No Parking On The Dance Floor . . . .(Solar)

Electrolite
Michael Stipe/Mike Mills; *Tibetan Freedom Concert* . . . . (Capitol)
R.E.M.; *New Adventures In Hi-Fi* . . . . (Warner Bros.)

Electron Cold
Sea Level; *On The Edge* . . . . (Capricorn)

Energy
Melissa Manchester; *Mathematics* . . . .(MCA)

Face The Fire
Dan Fogelberg; *Phoenix* . . . .(Full Moon)

Flip The Switch
Rolling Stones; *Bridges To Babylon* . . . .(Virgin)
No Security . . . .(Virgin)

Fuel
Metallica; *Reload* . . . . (Elektra)

Gallon Of Gas
Kinks; *Low Budget* . . . . (Arista)

Gasoline Alley
Rod Stewart; *Absolutely Live* . . . . (Warner Bros.)

Best Of Rod Stewart . . . . (Mercury)
Gasoline Alley . . . . (Mercury)
Sing It Again, Rod . . . . (Mercury)
Storyteller/The Complete Anthology: 1964-1990 . . . . (Warner Bros.)

Glow Worm
Mills Brothers; *Best Of The Mills Brothers* . . . . (MCA)
Cab Driver . . . . (Ranwood)
Mills Brothers' Greatest Hits . . . . (MCA)
Mills Brothers-16 Great Performances . . . . (MCA)

Have You Ever Been (To Electric Ladyland)
Jimi Hendrix Experience; *Electric Ladyland* . . . . (Reprise)

Heavy Fuel
Dire Straits; *On Every Street* . . . . (Warner Bros.)

High Voltage
AC/DC; *High Voltage* . . . . (Atco)
If You Want Blood You've Got It . . . . (Atlantic)

In Neon
Elton John; *Breaking Hearts* . . . . (MCA)

Jump Start
Natalie Cole; *Everlasting* . . . . (Elektra)
MTV & VH1 Powerplayers-C . . . . (EMI)

Lithium
Nirvana; *Nevermind* . . . . (David Geffen Co.)

Live Wire
AC/DC; *High Voltage* . . . . (Atco)
Martha & The Vandellas; *Compact Command Performances-Martha Reeves*
& The Vandellas . . . . (Motown)
Martha Reeves & The Vandellas' Greatest Hits . . . . (Motown)
Martha Reeves & The Vandellas-Anthology . . . . (Motown)

Lost In The Neon World
Be Bop Deluxe; *Modern Music* . . . . (Capitol)

Love Power
Dionne Warwick & Jeffrey Osborne; *Chicken Soup For The Couples*
Soul-C . . . . (Rhino)
Reservations For Two . . . . (Arista)

Luminous Energy
Yusef Lateef; *Nocturnes* . . . . (Atlantic)

Magnet And Steel
Walter Egan; *Rock Artifacts-From The Vaults-#2-C* . . . . (Legacy)

Magnetic
Earth, Wind & Fire; *Electric Universe* . . . . (Columbia)

Mining For Coal
Randy Travis; *No Holdin' Back* . . . . (Warner Bros.)

Neon Moon
Brooks & Dunn; *Brand New Man* . . . . (Arista)

Neon Moonlight
Rosco Martinez; *Neon Moonlight (Single)* . . . . (Zoo)

New Electric India
Shadowfax; *Shadow Dance* . . . . (Windham Hill)
What Goes Around-Best Of Shadowfax . . . . (Windham Hill)

Power
John Hall; *Power* . . . . (Columbia)
John Hall/Doobie Brothers/James Taylor; *No Nukes* . . . . (Asylum)

Power Windows
Billy Falcon; *Pretty Blue World* . . . . (Jambco)

Roll On Columbia
Judy Collins; *Tribute To Woody Guthrie-C* . . . . (Warner Bros.)

Sauerkraut 'N' Solar Energy
Norman Blake & Others; *Norman Blake/Others* . . . . (Flying Fish)

She's Got a 60 Cycle Brain
Paul Buff Organization; *45-#55* . . . . (Original Sound)

Shock The Monkey
Peter Gabriel; *Greenpeace-C* . . . . (A&M)
Peter Gabriel/Plays Live . . . . (Geffen)
Security . . . . (Geffen)
Shaking The Tree-Sixteen Golden Greats . . . . (Geffen)

Solar
Miles Davis; *Miles Davis' Greatest Hits* . . . . (Columbia)
Miles Davis-Chronicle-Complete Prestige Recordings . . . . (Prestige)
Walkin' . . . . (Columbia)

Solar Prestige A Gammon
Elton John; *Caribou* . . . . (Rocket)

Sparks Will Fly
Rolling Stones; *Voodoo Lounge* . . . . (Virgin)

Steam
Peter Gabriel; *Us* . . . . (Geffen)

Stereotomy
Alan Parsons Project; *Best Of Alan Parsons Project-#2* . . . . (Arista)
Stereotomy . . . . (Arista)

Suit Of Lights
Costello Show (Featuring Elvis Costello); *King Of America* . . . . . . (Columbia)

Sundancing (For The Hopi/Navajo Energy)
Jon Anderson; *In The City Of Angels* . . . . (Columbia)

Texas Tea
Dee Mullins; *20 Great Hits-C* . . . . (Plantation)
Dee Mullins . . . . (Plantation)

Train Running Low On Soul Coal
XTC; *Big Express* . . . . (Geffen)

T-U-R-T-L-E Power!
Partners In Kryme; *ST/Teenage Mutant Ninja Turtles* . . . . (SBK)

Twelve Volt Man
Jimmy Buffett; *Boats Beaches Bars & Ballads* . . . . (Margaritaville)
One Particular Harbour . . . . (MCA)

Wavelength
Van Morrison; *Wavelength* . . . . (Warner Bros.)

What's On Your Mind (Pure Energy)
Information Society; *Information Society* . . . . (Tommy Boy)

Wired All Night
Mick Jagger; *Wandering Spirit* . . . . (Atlantic)

Working In The Coal Mine
Devo; *Best Of Devo-Greatest Hits* . . . . (Warner Bros.)
Devo's Greatest Hits . . . . (Warner Bros.)
New Traditionalists . . . . (Warner Bros.)
Now It Can Be Told (Devo At The Palace) . . . . (Enigma)
ST/Heavy Metal . . . . (Asylum)
Judds; *Collection-1983-1990* . . . . (RCA)
Rockin' With The Rhythm . . . . (MCA)
Lee Dorsey; *Best Of New Orleans Rhythm & Blues-#2-C* . . . . . . (Rhino)
Golden Classics-Lee Dorsey . . . . (Collectables)
History Of New Orleans R&B-#3-1962-1970-C . . . . (Rhino)
Holy Cow . . . . (Arista)
New Orleans Jazz & Heritage Festival-1976-C . . . . (Rhino)

ESCAPE

*See Also: **FREEDOM, PRISON, REBELS, TRAVELING***

1983... (A Merman I Should Turn To Be)
Jimi Hendrix Experience; *Electric Ladyland* . . . . (Reprise)

All Along The Watchtower
Bob Dylan; *Before The Flood* . . . . (Columbia)
Biograph . . . . (Columbia)
Bob Dylan At Budokan . . . . (Columbia)
Bob Dylan's Greatest Hits-#2 . . . . (Columbia)
John Wesley Harding . . . . (Columbia)
Jimi Hendrix; *Kiss The Sky* . . . . (Reprise)
Lifelines/Jimi Hendrix Story . . . . (Reprise)
Jimi Hendrix Experience; *Electric Ladyland* . . . . (Reprise)
Essential Jimi Hendrix . . . . (Reprise)
Smash Hits . . . . (Reprise)
U2; *Rattle And Hum* . . . . (Island)

All I Know
Screaming Trees; *Dust* . . . . (Epic)

All Those Yesterdays
Pearl Jam; *Yield* . . . . (Epic)

Angel
Sarah McLachlan; *Mirrorball* . . . . (Arista)
ST/City Of Angels . . . . (Warner Sunset/Reprise)
Surfacing . . . . (Arista)
Totally Hits-#1-C . . . . (Arista)

Apples Peaches Pumpkin Pie
Jay And The Techniques; *Cruisin'-1967-C* . . . . (Increase)

Born To Run
Bruce Springsteen; *Born To Run* . . . . (Columbia)
Chimes Of Freedom . . . . (Columbia)
Bruce Springsteen & The E Street Band; *Bruce Springsteen & The E Street*
Band Live/1975-85 . . . . (Legacy)
Melissa Etheridge; *The Concert For New York City-C* . . . . . . (Columbia)

Darkness On The Edge Of Town
Bruce Springsteen; *Darkness On The Edge Of Town* . . . . . . (Columbia)
Bruce Springsteen & The E Street Band; *Bruce Springsteen & The E Street*
Band Live/1975-85 . . . . (Legacy)

Daylight Fading
Counting Crows; *Recovering The Satellites* . . . . (David Geffen Co.)

Doing The Best That I Can (Escape From Berlin)
Stevie Nicks; *Other Side Of The Mirror* . . . . (Modern)

Don't Look Back
Bruce Springsteen; *Tracks* . . . . (Columbia)
Knack; *One Step Up/Two Steps Back-The Songs Of Bruce*
Springsteen-C . . . . (Right Stuff)
Retrospective-Best Of The Knack . . . . (Gold Rush)

Dreamin' (Escape)
Lou Reed; *Magic And Loss* . . . . (Sire)

Drifter's Escape
Bob Dylan; *John Wesley Harding* . . . . (Columbia)
Jimi Hendrix; *Lifelines/Jimi Hendrix Story* . . . . (Reprise)

Escapade
Janet Jackson; *Design Of A Decade-1986/1996* . . . . (A&M)
Janet Jackson's Rhythm Nation 1814 . . . . (A&M)

Escape
Journey; *Escape* . . . . (Columbia)

Escape
Metallica; *Ride The Lightning* . . . . (Elektra)
Escape
Prince; *Lovesexy* . . . .(Warner Bros.)
The Hits/The B-Sides . . . . (Paisley Park)
Escape (Pina Colada Song)
Rupert Holmes; *Billboard Top Hits-1979-C* . . . . (Rhino)
Partners In Crime . . . .(MCA)
Escape From The Island Of Living Puke
Zoogz Rift; *Island Of Living Puke* . . . . (SST)
Escape From The Killing Fields
Ice-T; *O.G. Original Gangster* . . . . (Sire)
Escape From The Planet Of The Apes
They Might Be Giants; *Severe Tire Damage* . . . .(Restless)
Escape Is So Simple
Cowboy Junkies; *Caution Horses* . . . . (RCA)
Escape To Mexico
William Orbit; *Orbit* . . . .(I.R.S.)
Falls Apart
Sugar Ray; *14:59* . . . . (Lava)
Totally Hits-#2-C . . . . (Elektra)
Fire Escape
Fastball; *All The Pain Money Can Buy* . . . . (Hollywood)
Fly Away
Lenny Kravitz; *5* . . . . (Virgin)
Now That's What I Call Music!-#1-C . . . . (Virgin)
Free Girl Now
Tom Petty And The Heartbreakers; *Echo* . . . .(Warner Bros.)
Get Out Of This House
Shawn Colvin; *A Few Small Repairs* . . . . (Columbia)
Getaway
Kiss; *Dressed To Kill* . . . . (Mercury)
The Originals . . . . (Casablanca)
Rossington-Collins Band; *Anytime, Anyplace, Anywhere* . . . .(MCA)
Getaway
Earth, Wind & Fire; *Best Of Earth, Wind & Fire-#1* . . . . (Legacy)
Spirit . . . . (Columbia)
Getaway (February)
Jen Trynin; *Gun Shy Trigger Happy* . . . .(Squint/Columbia)
Good Day To Run
Darryl Worley; *Hard Rain Don't Last* . . . . (DreamWorks/SKG)
Gotta Get Away
Offspring; *Smash* . . . . (Epitaph)
Great Escape
Squeeze; *Ridiculous* . . . . (Ark 21)
Great Escape
Jamie Walters; *Ride* . . . . (Atlantic)
Great Escape, The
Marillion; *Made Again* . . . .(Castle Music America)
Guenevere
Original Cast; *Camelot* . . . . (Columbia)
Original Soundtrack; *ST/Camelot* . . . .(Warner Bros.)
Higher
Creed; *Human Clay* . . . . (Wind-up)
Highway 29
Bruce Springsteen; *The Ghost Of Tom Joad* . . . . (Columbia)
I Think We're Alone Now
Tiffany; *Tiffany* . . . .(MCA)
Tiffany's Greatest Hits . . . . (Hip-O)
Tommy James And The Shondells; *Best Of Tommy James And The
Shondells* . . . . (Roulette)
Billboard Top Rock 'N' Roll Hits-1967-C . . . . (Rhino)
Tommy James And The Shondells-Anthology . . . . (Rhino)
If I Had A Boat
Lyle Lovett; *Pontiac* . . . .(MCA)
If We're Not Back In Love By Monday
Merle Haggard; *MCA Records 30 Years Of Hits-1958-1988-C* . . . .(MCA)
Merle Haggard-Legends . . . .(MCA)
Merle Haggard's Greatest Hits . . . .(MCA)
More Of The Best . . . .(MCA)
Ramblin' Fever . . . .(MCA)
If You Leave
Destiny's Child; *The Writing's On The Wall* . . . . (Columbia)
I'm A Lonesome Fugitive
Merle Haggard; *Merle Haggard-16 Biggest Hits* . . . . (Legacy)
Merle Haggard & The Strangers; *Best Of Merle Haggard & The
Strangers* . . . . (Capitol)
Capitol Collectors Series-Merle Haggard & The Strangers . . . . . . (Capitol)
Songs I'll Always Sing . . . . (Capitol)
Roy Buchanan; *Roy Buchanan* . . . . (Polydor)
I've Committed Murder
Macy Gray; *On How Life Is* . . . .(Epic)
Life
K-Ci & JoJo; *It's Real* . . . .(Rock Land/Interscope)
Little Gasoline, A
Terri Clark; *Fearless* . . . . (Mercury)

Murder (Or A Heart Attack)
Old 97's; *Fight Songs* . . . . (Elektra)
My Wife
Who; *ST/The Kids Are Alright* . . . . (MCA)
Two's Missing . . . . (MCA)
Who Greatest Hits . . . . (MCA)
Who's next . . . . (MCA)
Narcolepsy
Ben Folds Five; *The Unauthorized Biography Of Reinhold
Messner* . . . .(550 Music)
Night
Bruce Springsteen; *Born To Run* . . . . (Columbia)
Nothin' But The Wheel
Patty Loveless; *Only What I Feel* . . . . (Epic)
Patty Loveless-Classics . . . . (Epic)
Ol' Red
Blake Shelton; *Blake Shelton* . . . .(Giant)
Pancho And Lefty
Merle Haggard; *For The Record: Merle Haggard-43 Legendary Hits* . . . .(BNA)
Merle Haggard & Willie Nelson; *19 Hot Country Requests-C* . . . . (Epic)
All Time Legends Of Country Music-C . . . . (Legacy)
Columbia Country Classics-#3-Americana-C . . . . (Columbia)
His Epic Hits-First 11 To Be Continued-C . . . . (Epic)
Pancho And Lefty . . . . (Epic)
Townes Van Zandt; *Live & Obscure* . . . . (Sugar Hill)
Paper Sun
Def Leppard; *Euphoria* . . . . (Mercury)
Parakeet
R.E.M.; *Up* . . . .(Warner Bros.)
Pinch Me
Barenaked Ladies; *Maroon* . . . . (Reprise)
Totally Hits-#3-C . . . .(Atlantic)
Razorblades
Chris Stills; *100 Year Thing* . . . .(Atlantic)
Roll Me Away
Bob Seger & The Silver Bullet Band; *ST/Armageddon-The Album* . . (Columbia)
Run
Collective Soul; *Dosage* . . . .(Atlantic)
Run Away
Real McCoy; *Another Night* . . . . (Arista)
Run Away (The Escape Song)
Oingo Boingo; *Dark At The End Of The Tunnel* . . . . (MCA Special Prod.)
Runaway
Lovemongers featuring Ann & Nancy Wilson; *Love Shouldn't Hurt-C* . . (Qwest)
Running Gun
Marty Robbins; *Gunfighter Ballads & Trail Songs* . . . . (Legacy)
Sailing
Christopher Cross; *Christopher Cross* . . . . (Warner Bros.)
Someday
Steve Earle & The Dukes; *Guitar Town* . . . . (MCA)
Shut Up And Die Like An Aviator . . . . (MCA)
Sullen Girl
Fiona Apple; *Tidal* . . . .(Clean Slate/Work)
Swingin'
Tom Petty And The Heartbreakers; *Echo* . . . .(Warner Bros.)
That's The Kind Of Mood I'm In
Patty Loveless; *Strong Heart* . . . . (Epic)
Theme From "The Fugitive"
Original Soundtrack; *Television's Greatest Hits-#4-Black & White
Classics-C* . . . . (TVT)
Tokyo Road
Bon Jovi; *7800 Degrees Fahrenheit* . . . . (Mercury)
Volare
Bobby Rydell; *'60s Rock 'N' Roll-#1-It's My Party-C* . . . . . (Dominion Entert.)
Way, The
Fastball; *All The Pain Money Can Buy* . . . . (Hollywood)
Now That's What I Call Music!-#1-C . . . .(Virgin)
What About Now
Lonestar; *Lonely Grill* . . . . (BNA)
Where The Green Grass Grows
Tim McGraw; *Big Country Hits '99-C* . . . . (K-Tel)
Everywhere . . . . (Curb)
Tim McGraw's Greatest Hits . . . . (Curb)
Wherever You Go
Clint Black; *Clint Black-The Greatest Hits* . . . . (RCA)
One Emotion . . . . (RCA)
Why Ain't I Running
Garth Brooks; *Scarecrow* . . . . (Capitol)
You'll Never Leave Harlan Alive
Patty Loveless; *Mountain Soul* . . . . (Epic)
Your Mama Don't Dance
Loggins & Messina; *Loggins & Messina-On Stage* . . . . (Columbia)
Loggins And Messina . . . . (Columbia)
Pop Classics Of The '70s-C . . . . (Columbia)
The Best Of Friends . . . . (Columbia)
Poison; *Open Up And Say...Ahh!* . . . . (Capitol)

Swallow This Live .... (Capitol)

ETERNITY, Always, Forever, Immortality
See Also: GOD, HEAVEN, HELL, LOVE: DEVOTION, TIME: GENERAL

"Star Is Born" (Evergreen), Love Theme From "A Star Is Born"
Barbra Streisand; *Barbra Streisand's Greatest Hits* .... (Columbia)
  Barbra Streisand's Greatest Hits, Volume 2 .... (Columbia)
  Diana, Princess Of Wales-Tribute-C .... (Columbia)
  Memories .... (Columbia)
  ST/A Star Is Born .... (Columbia)
Luther Vandross; *Songs* .... (Epic)
Paul Williams; *Paul Williams-Classics* .... (A&M)

24/7
Kevon Edmonds; *24/7* .... (RCA)

3 A.M. Eternal
KLF; *MTV Party To Go-#2-C* .... (Tommy Boy)
  The White Room .... (Arista)

5 Steps
Dru Hill; *Dru Hill* .... (Island)

All Day And All Of The Night
Kinks; *British Rock-#1-C* .... (Original Sound)
  God Save The Kinks! .... (Castle Music America)
  History Of British Rock-#2-C .... (Rhino)

All My Life
K-Ci & JoJo; *Love Always* .... (MCA)
  Now That's What I Call Music!-#1-C .... (Virgin)

Always
Bon Jovi; *Cross Road-14 Classic Grooves* .... (Mercury)

Always
Frank Sinatra; *I've Got A Crush On You* .... (Legacy)
Willie Nelson; *One For The Road* .... (Columbia)

Always And Forever
Heatwave; *Heatwave's Greatest Hits* .... (Epic)
  Too Hot To Handle .... (Epic)
Luther Vandross; *Songs* .... (Epic)
Whistle; *Always And Forever* .... (Select)

Always Be My Baby
Mariah Carey; *Daydream* .... (Columbia)

Always True To You In My Fashion
Blossom Dearie; *Night & Day-Cole Porter Songbook-C* .... (Verve)
Original Cast; *Kiss Me Kate* .... (EMI-Angel)
Peggy Lee & George Shearing; *Anything Goes-Capitol Sings Cole Porter-C* .... (Capitol)

Amazed
Lonestar; *Lonely Grill* .... (BNA)
  Totally Hits-#2-C .... (Elektra)

Amen Kind Of Love
Daryle Singletary; *All Because Of You* .... (Giant)
  Wedding Day Music-C .... (Reprise)

And I Love Her
Beatles; *ST/A Hard Day's Night* .... (Capitol)
  The Beatles/1962-1966 .... (Capitol)
  The Beatles-Anthology-#1 .... (Capitol)

Baby, I'm Yours
Barbara Lewis; *Hello Stranger-The Best Of Barbara Lewis* .... (Rhino)

Backstreets
Bruce Springsteen; *Born To Run* .... (Columbia)

Be My Baby
Linda Ronstadt; *Dedicated To The One I Love* .... (Elektra)
Melissa Etheridge; *Concert For The Rock & Roll Hall Of Fame-C* ... (Columbia)
Ronettes; *Best Of The Ronettes* .... (Abkco)
  Phil Spector-Back To Mono 1958-1969-C .... (Abkco)
  ST/Dirty Dancing .... (RCA)

Betcha By Golly, Wow
"AFKAP"; *Emancipation* .... (NPG)
Johnny Mathis; *First Time Ever I Saw Your Face* .... (Columbia)
Stylistics; *Best Of The Stylistics* .... (Amherst)

Better Than You
Metallica; *Reload* .... (Elektra)

Between Now And Forever
Bryan White; *Between Now And Forever* .... (Asylum)
  Wedding Day Music-C .... (Reprise)

Buicks To The Moon
Alan Jackson; *Everything I Love* .... (Arista)

By Heart
Jim Brickman; *By Heart* .... (Windham Hill)

Cara Mia
Jay & The Americans; *I Got Rhythm-C* .... (K-Tel)
  Jay & The Americans' Greatest Hits .... (CEMA Special Prod.)
  Jay & The Americans' Greatest Hits .... (Curb)

Child Should Live Forever (Theme For The Eddie Cantor Fund For Children With AIDS)
Original Off-Broadway Cast; *A Hard Time To Be Single* .... (Original Cast)

Close My Eyes Forever
Lita Ford & Ozzy Osbourne; *Lita* .... (Dreamland)

Cold Day In Hell
Gary Moore; *After Hours* .... (Charisma)

Commitment
LeAnn Rimes; *Big Country Hits '99-C* .... (K-Tel)
  Sittin' On Top Of The World .... (Curb)

Could I Have This Kiss Forever
Whitney Houston & Enrique Iglesias; *Whitney Houston's Greatest Hits* .... (Arista)

Crypts Of Eternity
Slayer; *Hell Awaits* .... (Metal Blade)

Diamonds Are Forever
Shirley Bassey; *13 Original James Bond Themes-C* .... (EMI)
  Best Of Shirley Bassey .... (EMI)
  Shirley Bassey's Greatest Hits .... (EMI)

Dream Goes On Forever
Todd Rundgren; *Back To The Bars* .... (Rhino)
  ST/Rock 'N' Roll High School .... (Sire)
  Todd .... (Rhino)
  Todd Rundgren-Anthology 1968-1985 .... (Rhino)

Endless Love
Diana Ross & Lionel Richie; *25 Years Of Grammy Greats-C* .... (Motown)
  All The Great Motown Love Song Duets-C .... (Motown)
  Motown Story-First 25 Years-C .... (Motown)
  ST/Endless Love .... (Mercury)
Luther Vandross & Mariah Carey; *Songs* .... (Epic)

Endless Summer Nights
Richard Marx; *Richard Marx* .... (Capitol)
  Richard Marx's Greatest Hits .... (Capitol)

Etenally Yours
2 Unlimited; *Get Ready* .... (Critique)

Eternal Circle
Bob Dylan; *The Bootleg Series-Volumes 1-3 [Rare & Unreleased]* .. (Columbia)

Eternal Flame
Bangles; *Bangles' Greatest Hits* .... (Columbia)
  Everything .... (Columbia)

Eternal Idol
Black Sabbath; *Eternal Idol* .... (Warner Bros.)

Eternal Kansas City
Van Morrison; *Period Of Transition* .... (Warner Bros.)

Eternal Legs
Yello; *Solid Pleasure* .... (Mercury)

Eternal Life
Jeff Buckley; *Grace* .... (Columbia)

Eternal Love
Todd Rundgren's Utopia; *Ra* .... (Rhino)

Eternity
Chaka Khan; *C.K.* .... (Warner Bros.)
Vikki Carr; *Best Of Vikki Carr* .... (EMI)

Eternity
Sheena Easton; *No Sound But A Heart* .... (One Way)
  The World Of Sheena Easton: The Singles Collection-C ..... (EMI)

Eternity
Richard Marx; *Flesh And Bone* .... (Capitol)

Eternity
Master P; *MP Da Last Don* .... (No Limit/Priority)

Eternity Road
Moody Blues; *To Our Children's Children's Children* .... (Polydor)

Ever True Evermore
Mandy Barnett; *I've Got A Right To Cry* .... (Sire)

Everlasting Glaze
Smashing Pumpkins; *Machina: The Machines Of God* .... (Virgin)

Everlasting Love
Carl Carlton; *Classic R&B Oldies Of The '70s-#2-C* ...... (MCA Special Prod.)
Gloria Estefan; *Hold Me, Thrill Me, Kiss Me* .... (Epic)
Robert Knight; *Everlasting Love* .... (Collectables)

Everlong
Foo Fighters; *The Colour And The Shape* .... (Roswell/RCA)

Ev'ry Day Of My Life
McGuire Sisters; *McGuire Sisters-Anthology* .... (MCA)

Fire I Can't Put Out
George Strait; *George Strait's Greatest Hits* .... (MCA)
  Strait From The Heart .... (MCA)

For You
Kenny Lattimore; *Kenny Lattimore* .... (Columbia)
  Modern Bride Presents The Wedding Album-C .... (Columbia)
  Songs From The Heart-C .... (Columbia)

Forever
Kiss; *Hot In The Shade* .... (Mercury)

Forever
Mariah Carey; *Daydream* .... (Columbia)

Forever
Kid Rock; *Cocky* .... (Top Dog/Lava/Atlantic)

Forever Has Come To An End
Buddy & Julie Miller; *Buddy & Julie Miller* .... (Hightone)

Forever In Blue
Journey; *Trial By Fire* .... (Columbia)

Forever In Blue Jeans
Neil Diamond; *12 Greatest Hits-#2* . . . . (Columbia)
  Hot August Night II . . . . (Columbia)
  You Don't Bring Me Flowers . . . . (Columbia)
Forever In Love
Kenny G; *Breathless* . . . . (Arista)
Forever Love
Reba McEntire; *If You See Him* . . . . (MCA)
  Reba McEntire's Greatest Hits-#3: I'm A Survivor . . . . (MCA)
Forever More
Puff Johnson; *Miracle* . . . . (Work)
Forever More (I'll Be The One)
James Ingram; *Forever More (Love Songs, Hits & Duets)* . . . . . . (Private Music)
John Tesh featuring James Ingram; *One World* . . . . (GTS)
Forever Together
Randy Travis; *High Lonesome* . . . . (Warner Bros.)
Forever Tonight
Peter Cetera & Crystal Bernard; *One Clear Voice* . . . . (River North)
Forever Young
Johnny Cash; *Red Hot + Country-C* . . . . (Mercury)
Forever Young
Chris Isaak; *Heart Shaped World* . . . . (Reprise)
Forever Young
Rod Stewart; *Downtown Train-Selections From The Storyteller*
  Anthology . . . . (Warner Bros.)
  If We Fall In Love Tonight . . . . (Warner Bros.)
  Storyteller/The Complete Anthology: 1964-1990 . . . . (Warner Bros.)
Forever Young
Alphaville; *Alphaville-The Singles Collection* . . . . (Atlantic)
  Forever Young . . . . (Atlantic)
Forever Young
Band; *Best Of The Band-#2* . . . . (Rhino)
  The Last Waltz . . . . (Warner Bros.)
Bob Dylan; *Biograph* . . . . (Columbia)
  Bob Dylan At Budokan . . . . (Columbia)
  Bob Dylan's Greatest Hits-#3 . . . . (Columbia)
  Planet Waves . . . . (Columbia)
Joan Baez; *From Every Stage* . . . . (A&M)
  Joan Baez's Greatest Hits . . . . (A&M)
Pretenders; *ST/Free Willy 2: The Adventure Home* . . . . . (MJJ Music/Work)
  ST/With Honors . . . . (Maverick)
Forever Your Girl
Paula Abdul; *Forever Your Girl* . . . . (Virgin)
  Shut Up And Dance (The Dance Mixes) . . . . (Virgin)
Forever's As Far As I'll Go
Alabama; *Alabama's Greatest Hits-#3* . . . . (RCA)
  Alabama-Super Hits . . . . (RCA)
  For The Record: 41 Number One Hits . . . . (RCA)
  Pass It On Down . . . . (BMG Special Prod.)
From Her To Eternity
Nick Cave; *Best Of Nick Cave & The Bad Seeds* . . . . (Reprise)
From Here To Eternity
Michael Peterson; *Michael Peterson* . . . . (Reprise)
  Wedding Day Music-C . . . . (Reprise)
From Here To Eternity
Frank Sinatra; *Capitol Collectors Series-Frank Sinatra* . . . . . . (Capitol)
From This Moment On
Shania Twain & Bryan White; *Come On Over* . . . . (Mercury)
Full Forever
Goo Goo Dolls; *Dizzy Up The Girl* . . . . (Warner Sunset/Reprise)
Give Me Forever (I Do)
John Tesh featuring James Ingram; *Grand Passion-C* . . . . (GTS)
Gotta Man
Eve; *First Lady Of Ruff Ryders* . . . . (Ruff Ryders/IDJMG)
Graduation (Friends Forever)
Vitamin C; *Totally Hits-#3-C* . . . . (Atlantic)
  Vitamin C . . . . (Elektra)
Guaranteed Eternal Sanctuary Man
Genesis; *Foxtrot* . . . . (Atlantic)
Here To Eternity
Rod Stewart; *Every Beat Of My Heart* . . . . (Warner Bros.)
How Forever Feels
Kenny Chesney; *Everywhere We Go* . . . . (BNA)
  Kenny Chesney's Greatest Hits . . . . (BNA)
I Ain't Never
Webb Pierce; *Billboard Top Country Hits-1959-C* . . . . (Rhino)
  Grand Ole Opry-75 Years-#2-C . . . . (MCA)
  Webb Pierce-Greatest Hits/Finest Performances . . . . (Sun)
I Believe In You And Me
Whitney Houston; *ST/The Preacher's Wife* . . . . (Arista)
I Can Love You Like That
All-4-One; *1996 Grammy Nominees-C* . . . . (Columbia)
  And The Music Speaks . . . . (Blitzz)
John Michael Montgomery; *John Michael Montgomery* . . . . (Atlantic)
I Love You Always Forever
Donna Lewis; *Now In A Minute* . . . . (Atlantic)
  The Absolute Hits-C . . . . (Atlantic)
I Say A Little Prayer
Aretha Franklin; *Aretha Franklin's Greatest Hits* . . . . (Atlantic)

  Aretha's Gold . . . . (Atlantic)
  Best Of Aretha Franklin . . . . (Atlantic)
Burt Bacharach; *Burt Bacharach-Classics-#23* . . . . (A&M)
  Burt Bacharach's Greatest Hits . . . . (A&M)
  Reach Out . . . . (A&M)
Diana King; *ST/My Best Friend's Wedding* . . . . (Work/Epic)
Dionne Warwick; *Dionne Warwick* . . . . (Everest)
  Dionne Warwick Greatest Hits . . . . (Everest)
  Dionne Warwick-Anthology 1962-1971 . . . . (Rhino)
  Original Rock 'N' Roll Hits Of The '60s-C . . . . (Roulette)
I Think I Know
Reno; *Reno* . . . . (Curb)
I Wanna Love You Forever
Jessica Simpson; *Sweet Kisses* . . . . (Columbia)
I Want To Spend My Lifetime Loving You
Marc Anthony & Tina Arena; *ST/Mask Of Zorro* . . . . (Sony Music Classical)
I Will
Beatles; *The Beatles (White Album)* . . . . (Capitol)
  The Beatles-Anthology-#3 . . . . (Capitol)
Ben Taylor; *ST/Bye Bye, Love* . . . . (Giant)
Dean Martin; *Dean Martin's Greatest Hits* . . . . (EMI)
I Will Always Love You
Dolly Parton; *Best Of Dolly Parton* . . . . (RCA)
  Best There Is . . . . (RCA)
  Chicken Soup For The Woman's Soul-C . . . . (Rhino)
  Dolly Parton's Greatest Hits . . . . (RCA)
  ST/Best Little Whorehouse In Texas . . . . (MCA)
Linda Ronstadt; *Prisoner In Disguise* . . . . (Asylum)
Whitney Houston; *ST/The Bodyguard* . . . . (Arista)
  Whitney Houston's Greatest Hits . . . . (Arista)
I Will Follow Him
Little Peggy March; *Nipper's Greatest Hits Of The '60s-#1-C* . . . . . . (RCA)
If I Never Stop Loving You
David Kersh; *If I Never Stop Loving You* . . . . (Curb)
If You Ever Have Forever In Mind
Vince Gill; *The Key* . . . . (MCA)
I'll Always Be Right There
Bryan Adams; *18 Til I Die* . . . . (A&M)
  MTV Unplugged-Bryan Adams . . . . (A&M)
I'll Go On Loving You
Alan Jackson; *High Mileage* . . . . (Arista)
I'll Still Be Loving You
Restless Heart; *Wheels* . . . . (RCA)
I'm Immortal
Trash Can Sinatras; *I've Seen Everything* . . . . (Mercury)
Imagine That
Diamond Rio; *Diamond Rio's Greatest Hits* . . . . (Arista)
Immortality
Pearl Jam; *Vitalogy* . . . . (Epic)
Immortality
Celine Dion with The Bee Gees; *Let's Talk About Love-C* . . . . . . (550 Music)
In The Chapel In The Moonlight
Kitty Kallen; *Those Wonderful Years: Music! Music!*
  Music!-C . . . . (JCI Assoc. Labels)
Patti Page; *Patti Page-16 Most Requested Songs* . . . . (Legacy)
Shep Fields & His Rippling Rhythm Orchestra; *78-#6640* . . . . (Bluebird)
Infinite Eyes
Keb' Mo'; *Big Wide Grin* . . . . (Sony Wonder)
Infinite Possibilities
Amel Larrieux; *Infinite Possibilities* . . . . (Epic)
Iris
Goo Goo Dolls; *Dizzy Up The Girl* . . . . (Warner Sunset/Reprise)
  ST/City Of Angels . . . . (Warner Sunset/Reprise)
It's No Good
Depeche Mode; *Ultra* . . . . (Mute/Reprise)
Last Waltz, The
Engelbert Humperdinck; *Engelbert Humperdinck-16 Most Requested*
  Songs . . . . (Epic)
Let Love Come Between Us
James & Bobby Purify; *Bubblegum Classics-#4-C* . . . . (Varese Vintage)
Life Is Eternal
Carly Simon; *Clouds In My Coffee-1965-1995* . . . . (Arista)
Live Forever
Oasis; *Definitely Maybe* . . . . (Epic)
Living Forever
Genesis; *We Can't Dance* . . . . (Atlantic)
Long As I Live
John Michael Montgomery; *John Michael Montgomery* . . . . (Atlantic)
Longer
Dan Fogelberg; *Dan Fogelberg/Greatest Hits* . . . . (Full Moon)
  Phoenix . . . . (Full Moon)
Love For All Seasons
Christina Aguilera; *Christina Aguilera* . . . . (RCA)
Love Me Tender
Elvis Presley; *Elvis* . . . . (RCA)
  Elvis Aron Presley . . . . (RCA)
  Elvis' Golden Records . . . . (RCA)
  Elvis-A Legendary Performer, Volume 1 . . . . (RCA)

Worldwide 50 Gold Award Hits, Vol. 1, Parts 1 & 2 . . . (RCA)
Love Now Till Eternity
Asia; *Astra* . . . (Geffen)
Mary's Boy Child
Andy Williams; *Merry Christmas* . . . (Columbia)
Anne Murray; *Anne Murray Christmas* . . . (Liberty)
Harry Belafonte; *Billboard's Greatest Christmas Hits-C* . . . (Rhino)
This Is Christmas-C . . . (RCA)
Kiri Te Kanawa; *Christmas With Kiri Te Kanawa* . . . (London)
More (Than)
Perry Como; *Perry Como's Greatest Hits* . . . (RCA)
My First Love
Avant; *My Thoughts* . . . (MCA)
My First Night With You
Mya; *Mya* . . . (University/Interscope)
My Heart Will Go On (Love Theme from "Titanic")
Celine Dion; *All The Way...A Decade Of Song* . . . (550 Music)
ST/Titanic . . . (Sony Music Classical)
Celine Dion with The Bee Gees; *Let's Talk About Love-C* . . . (550 Music)
Kenny G; *Kenny G's Greatest Hits* . . . (Arista)
My Love Goes On And On
Chris Cagle; *Play It Loud* . . . (Capitol)
My Love Is Your Love
Whitney Houston; *My Love Is Your Love* . . . (Arista)
Totally Hits-#2-C . . . (Elektra)
My Special Angel
Bobby Helms; *American Graffiti-#3-C* . . . (MCA)
Blue Ribbon Country-#3-C . . . (Accord)
Oldies But Goodies-#14-C . . . (Original Sound)
Pop A Billy . . . (MCA)
Vintage Music-#2-C . . . (MCA)
Vogues; *Vogues' Greatest Hits* . . . (Rhino)
Vogues' Greatest Hits/Finest Performances . . . (Sun)
N.I.B.
Primus with Ozzy; *Nativity In Black II: Tribute To Black Sabbath-C* . . . (Divine/Priority)
Near You
Francis Craig & His Orchestra; *Cigar Classics-#1-The Standards-C* . . . (Hip-O)
George Jones & Tammy Wynette; *George Jones & Tammy Wynette-16 Biggest Hits* . . . (Epic/Legacy)
Never A Time
Genesis; *We Can't Dance* . . . (Atlantic)
Never Be Anyone Else But You
Ricky Nelson; *Best Of Ricky Nelson* . . . (EMI)
Never Ending
Wood; *Songs From Stamford Hill* . . . (Columbia)
Never Ending Song Of Love
Conway Twitty & Loretta Lynn; *Lead Me On* . . . (MCA)
Delaney & Bonnie; *Best Of Delaney & Bonnie* . . . (Rhino)
Super Hits Of The '70s-Have A Nice Day-#16-C . . . (Rhino)
Never Enough
Groove Theory; *ST/Love Jones* . . . (Columbia)
Never Going Back Again
Fleetwood Mac; *25 Years-The Chain* . . . (Warner Bros.)
Fleetwood Mac Live . . . (Warner Bros.)
Rumours . . . (Warner Bros.)
Matchbox Twenty; *Legacy-A Tribute To Fleetwood Mac's Rumours-C* . . . (Lava)
Never Gonna Let You Go
Tina Moore; *Speed Garage Classics-C* . . . (Logic)
Never Gonna Let You Go
Faith Evans; *Keep The Faith* . . . (Bad Boy/Arista)
Never Is A Promise
Fiona Apple; *Tidal* . . . (Clean Slate/Work)
Never My Love
Association; *Association Greatest Hits* . . . (Warner Bros.)
Songs That Made Them Famous . . . (Pair)
There Is Still Love-Anniversary Songs-C . . . (Scotti Bros.)
Never Say Die
Dixie Chicks; *Wide Open Spaces* . . . (Monument)
Never There
Cake; *Now That's What I Call Music!-#2-C* . . . (Virgin)
Prolonging The Magic . . . (Capricorn)
No One
Marc Anthony; *Marc Anthony* . . . (Columbia)
Not On Your Love
Jeff Carson; *From Nashville With Love-C* . . . (Curb)
Jeff Carson . . . (Curb)
Now And Forever
Richard Marx; *Paid Vacation* . . . (Capitol)
Now And Forever (You And Me)
Anne Murray; *Anne Murray's Greatest Hits-#2* . . . (Capitol)
Something To Talk About . . . (Capitol)
Now 'Til Forever
Kirk Whalum; *Unconditional* . . . (Warner Bros.)
On & On
Erykah Badu; *Baduizm* . . . (Kedar Entert./Universal)
On A Clear Day (You Can See Forever)
Barbra Streisand; *Just For The Record* . . . (Columbia)
Live Concert At The Forum . . . (Columbia)
ST/On A Clear Day You Can See Forever . . . (Columbia Special Prod.)
The Concert . . . (Columbia)
Roger Williams; *Best Of Roger Williams* . . . (MCA)
Somewhere In Time . . . (Bainbridge)
Please Love Me Forever
Bobby Vinton; *Bobby Vinton-16 Most Requested Songs* . . . (Legacy)
Bobby Vinton's All-Time Greatest Hits . . . (Epic)
Please Love Me Forever . . . (Epic)
Real Love
Beatles; *The Beatles-Anthology-#2* . . . (Capitol)
John Lennon; *ST/Imagine: John Lennon* . . . (Capitol)
Road Goes On Forever, The
Joe Ely; *Love & Danger* . . . (MCA)
Running Bear
Johnny Preston; *45s On CD-#1-1956-1959-C* . . . (Mercury)
Billboard Top Rock 'N' Roll Hits-1960-C . . . (Rhino)
Cruisin'-1960-C . . . (Increase)
Sonny James; *All-Time Country Classics-#1-C* . . . (Capitol)
Sail On To The Eternal Reward
Cult; *Love* . . . (Sire)
Sara Smile
After 7; *Very Best Of After 7* . . . (Virgin)
Daryl Hall & John Oates; *Best Of Daryl Hall & John Oates* . . . (RCA)
Daryl Hall & John Oates . . . (RCA)
Livetime . . . (RCA)
Rock 'N Soul, Part 1 . . . (RCA)
Soulful Sounds . . . (RCA)
Saving Forever For You
Shanice; *ST/Beverly Hills, 90210-College Years* . . . (Giant)
Say You, Say Me
Lionel Richie; *Back To Front* . . . (Motown)
Dancing On The Ceiling . . . (Motown)
Sinner
Neil Finn; *Try Whistling This* . . . (Work)
Some Things Never Change
Tim McGraw; *A Place In The Sun* . . . (Curb)
Someday I'll Find You
Bobby Short; *Mad About Noel Coward* . . . (Atlantic)
Mary Martin & Noel Coward; *Together With Music* . . . (DRG)
Spend My Life With You
Eric Benet; *A Day In The Life* . . . (Warner Bros.)
Stars Over Texas
Tracy Lawrence; *Best Of Tracy Lawrence* . . . (Atlantic)
Time Marches On . . . (Atlantic)
Stay Forever
Hal Ketchum; *Every Little Word* . . . (Curb)
From Nashville With Love-C . . . (Curb)
Hal Ketchum-The Hits . . . (MCG/Curb)
Still
Commodores; *Best Of The Commodores-Anthology* . . . (Motown)
Commodores-All The Great Hits . . . (Motown)
Commodores-The Ultimate Collection . . . (Motown)
Lionel Richie; *Back To Front* . . . (Motown)
Truly-The Love Songs . . . (Motown)
Still
Bill Anderson; *Best Of Bill Anderson* . . . (Curb)
Bill Anderson's Greatest Hits . . . (Varese Sarabande)
Billboard Top Country Hits-1963-C . . . (Rhino)
From The Vaults: Decca Country Classics-1934-1973-C . . . (Decca)
Grand Ole Opry-75 Years-#2-C . . . (MCA)
Still In Love
Brian McKnight; *I Remember You* . . . (Mercury)
Strawberry Fields Forever
Beatles; *Beatles-Box Set* . . . (Capitol)
Magical Mystery Tour . . . (Capitol)
ST/Imagine: John Lennon . . . (Capitol)
The Beatles/1967-1970 . . . (Capitol)
Strong Enough To Bend
Tanya Tucker; *Strong Enough To Bend* . . . (Liberty)
Tanya Tucker's Greatest Hits . . . (Liberty)
Thank You Girl
Beatles; *Beatles-Box Set* . . . (Capitol)
Past Masters-Volume One . . . (Parlophone)
The Beatles' Second Album . . . (Capitol)
Then You Can Tell Me Goodbye
Casinos; *Then You Can Tell Me Goodbye* . . . (Varese Vintage)
Neal McCoy; *Neal McCoy's Greatest Hits* . . . (Atlantic)
Thirty-Three
Smashing Pumpkins; *Mellon Collie And The Infinite Sadness* . . . (Virgin)
This I Promise You
'N Sync; *No Strings Attached* . . . (Jive)
Now That's What I Call Music!-#7-C . . . (Virgin)
This Magic Moment
Drifters; *Drifters' Greatest Hits* . . . (Gusto)
Drifters-Golden Hits . . . (Atlantic)
Jay & The Americans; *Come A Little Bit Closer-Best Of Jay & The Americans* . . . (Gold Rush)
Jay & The Americans' All-Time Greatest Hits . . . (Rhino)
Marvin Gaye; *M.P.G.* . . . (Motown)

This Night Won't Last Forever
Bill LaBounty; *The Right Direction* . . . .(Noteworthy)
   This Night Won't Last Forever. . . . .(Warner Bros.)
Michael Johnson; *Dialogue* . . . .(EMI)
   Have A Nice Night-Romantic Hits Of The '70s-C . . . .(Rhino)
   Radio Daze-Pop Hits Of The '80s-#1-C. . . . .(Rhino)
   Then & Now . . . .(ISD/Intersound)
Moe Bandy; *Many Mansions* . . . .(Curb)
Sawyer Brown; *Six Days On The Road*. . . . .(Curb)
This Song Will Last Forever
Lou Rawls; *All Things In Time* . . . .(Right Stuff)
   Lou Rawls-Live (Right Stuff) . . . .(Right Stuff)
Til The End
Vern Gosdin; *10 Years Of Greatest Hits Newly Recorded* . . . .(Columbia)
   Best Of Vern Gosdin . . . .(Warner Bros.)
   Til The End . . . .(Elektra)
Till The End Of Time
Perry Como; *Como's Golden Records* . . . . (RCA)
   Nipper's Greatest Hits Of The '40s-#2-C . . . . (RCA)
   Perry Como-Pure Gold . . . . (RCA)
   There Is Love-Wedding Songs-C . . . .(Scotti Bros.)
Till The End Of Time
Chicago; *Chicago XI*. . . . .(Chicago)
Till The Rivers All Run Dry
Don Williams; *Best Of Don Williams-#2* . . . .(MCA)
   Country Comes To Carnegie Hall-C . . . .(MCA)
   Don Williams' Greatest Country Hits . . . . (Curb)
   Harmony-C . . . .(MCA Special Prod.)
   Till The Rivers All Run Dry . . . .(MCA Special Prod.)
Pete Townshend & Ronnie Lane; *Rough Mix* . . . .(Atlantic)
Time After Time
Cyndi Lauper; *Chicken Soup For The Woman's Soul-C*. . . . .(Rhino)
   She's So Unusual . . . .(Portrait)
   Twelve Deadly Cyns...And Then Some . . . .(Epic)
Everything But The Girl; *Acoustic* . . . .(Atlantic)
INOJ & So So Def Bass All-Stars; *Time After Time (Maxi
   Single)* . . . .(So So Def/Columbia)
Miles Davis; *Live Around The World* . . . .(Warner Bros.)
   You're Under Arrest . . . .(Columbia)
Time In A Bottle
Jim Croce; *50th Anniversary Collection* . . . . (Saja)
   Photographs & Memories/His Greatest Hits . . . .(Atlantic)
   Time In A Bottle/Jim Croce's Greatest Love Songs . . . .(Atlantic)
Timeless
Rick Derringer; *Guitars & Women* . . . .(Blue Sky)
Timeless & True Love
McCarters; *Country Love Songs-C* . . . .(Warner Bros.)
   The Gift . . . .(Warner Bros.)
Together Always
Porter Wagoner & Dolly Parton; *Lassoes N' Spurs* . . . . (RCA)
   Together Always . . . . (RCA)
Total Eclipse Of The Heart
Bonnie Tyler; *Billboard Top Hits-1983-C* . . . . (Rhino)
   Faster Than The Speed Of Night . . . .(Columbia)
   Seems Like Yesterday-#4-Early '80s-C . . . .(K-Tel)
Nicki French; *Dance Hits '96 Supermix-C* . . . .(Critique)
   Secrets . . . .(Critique)
True Love
Elton John & Kiki Dee; *Duets-C* . . . .(MCA)
Four Aces; *Best Of The Four Aces* . . . .(MCA)
Johnny Mathis & Henry Mancini; *Hollywood Musicals* . . . .(Columbia)
Patsy Cline; *Always* . . . .(MCA)
   The Patsy Cline Story. . . . .(MCA)
Roger Whittaker; *Best Loved Ballads-#2* . . . .(Liberty)
Truly Madly Deeply
Savage Garden; *Savage Garden* . . . .(Columbia)
Until The End Of Time
Guy & Ralna; *22 Golden Country Classics* . . . .(Ranwood)
Until The End Of Time
Foreigner; *Mr. Moonlight* . . . .(Generama/Rhythm Safari)
Valentine
Jim Brickman & Martina McBride; *Picture This* . . . .(Windham Hill)
   Smooth Sounds-C . . . .(Razor & Tie)
Martina McBride & Jim Brickman; *Evolution* . . . .(RCA)
Violet
Hole; *Ask For It* . . . .(Caroline)
   Live Through This . . . .(David Geffen Co.)
Walk Hand In Hand
Andy Williams; *I Like Your Kind Of Love-The Best Of The Cadence
   Years* . . . .(Varese Vintage)
We're All Alone
Boz Scaggs; *Boz Scaggs-Hits!* . . . .(Columbia)
   Slow Dancer . . . .(Columbia)
Rita Coolidge; *Rita Coolidge's Greatest Hits* . . . .(A&M)
What's Forever For
Michael Martin Murphey; *Best Of Michael Martin Murphey* . . . .(Liberty)
   What's Forever For . . . .(EMI Special Markets)
When I Fall In Love
Celine Dion; *The Colour Of My Love* . . . .(550 Music)

Doris Day; *Doris Day-16 Most Requested Songs-Encore!* . . . .(Columbia)
When You Love A Woman
Journey; *Trial By Fire* . . . .(Columbia)
Where Your Road Leads
Trisha Yearwood & Garth Brooks; *Where Your Road Leads* . . . .(MCA)
Who Wants To Live Forever
Queen; *A Kind Of Magic* . . . .(Hollywood)
   Classic Queen. . . . .(Hollywood)
   Diana, Princess Of Wales-Tribute-C . . . .(Columbia)
Why Don't You Believe Me?
Duprees; *Best Of The Duprees* . . . . (Rhino)
   Best Of The Duprees . . . .(Collectables)
Joni James; *Platinum & Gold Hits* . . . .(Taragon)
Patti Page; *Patti Page-Golden Celebration* . . . .(Mercury)
Wicker Man
Iron Maiden; *Brave New World*. . . . .(Portrait)
Wild One, Forever
Tom Petty And The Heartbreakers; *Tom Petty & The
   Heartbreakers* . . . .(Gone Gator)
Written In The Stars
Elton John & LeAnn Rimes; *ST/Aida* . . . . (Island)
Yesterday's Gone Forever
Little Texas; *Little Texas* . . . .(Warner Bros.)
   Little Texas-Super Hits. . . . .(Warner Bros.)
You & Forever & Me
Little Texas; *First Time For Everything* . . . .(Warner Bros.)
You Won't Ever Be Lonely
Andy Griggs; *Andy Griggs* . . . .(RCA)
You'll Always Be Loved By Me
Brooks & Dunn; *Tight Rope* . . . .(Arista)
You'll Be In My Heart
Phil Collins; *ST/Tarzan* . . . .(Hollywood)
You'll Never Never Know
Platters; *Magic Touch-An Anthology*. . . . .(Mercury)
   Very Best Of The Platters. . . . .(Mercury)

EXTREMES, Deepest, Highest
   See Also: **BEST**

Ain't No Mountain High Enough
Diana Ross; *20/20-C* . . . .(Motown)
   25 #1 Hits From 25 Years-C. . . . .(Motown)
   Diana Ross . . . .(Motown)
   Diana Ross-The Ultimate Collection . . . .(Motown)
   Every Great Motown Song-First 25 Years-C . . . .(Motown)
   Greatest Songs By Ashford & Simpson . . . .(Motown)
   Motown Legends-Diana Ross . . . .(Motown)
   Motown Story-First 25 Years-C . . . .(Motown)
   Motown's Biggest Pop Hits-C . . . .(Motown)
   TV ST/Diana-C . . . .(Motown)
Marvin Gaye & Tammi Terrell; *20 Greatest Songs In Motown
   History-C*. . . . .(Motown)
   Classic Duets-Marvin Gaye & His Women-C . . . .(Motown)
   Marvin Gaye & Tammi Terrell's Greatest Hits . . . .(Motown)
   Marvin Gaye Live At The London Palladium . . . .(Motown)
   Motown Grammy R&B Performances Of The '60s & '70s-C . . .(Motown)
   Performances Of The '60s & '70s-C . . . .(Motown)
   United . . . .(Motown)
Bitch
Meredith Brooks; *Blurring The Edges* . . . .(Capitol)
Both Sides Now
Sammy Hagar; *Marching To Mars* . . . .(MCA)
Captain Hook's Waltz
Original Cast/Cyril Ritchard; *Peter Pan-The 1954 Broadway
   Production* . . . .(RCA Victor)
Deeper Than The Holler
Randy Travis; *Randy Travis' Greatest #1 Hits* . . . .(Warner Bros.)
   Randy Travis' Greatest Hits-#1 . . . .(Warner Bros.)
Do You Love Me That Much?
Peter Cetera; *You're The Inspiration-A Collection* . . . .(River North)
Fortunate
Maxwell; *ST/Life*. . . . .(Rock Land/Interscope)
Freedom Overspill
Steve Winwood; *Back In The High Life* . . . . (Island)
Go Deep
Janet Jackson; *Velvet Rope* . . . .(Virgin)
Hard Rock Bottom Of Your Heart
Randy Travis; *No Holdin' Back* . . . .(Warner Bros.)
Have You Ever Loved A Woman
Derek And The Dominos; *Layla* . . . .(Polydor)
How Deep Is The Ocean? (How High Is The Sky?)
Diana Krall; *Love Scenes* . . . .(Impulse!)
Frank Sinatra; *Nice 'N' Easy* . . . .(Capitol)
Liza Minnelli; *Liza Minnelli-At Carnegie Hall* . . . .(Telarc)
I Go To Extremes
Billy Joel; *Storm Front* . . . .(Columbia)

I Wanna Go Too Far
Trisha Yearwood; *Thinkin' About You* . . . . (MCA)
I Will Follow Him
Little Peggy March; *Nipper's Greatest Hits Of The '60s-#1-C* . . . .(RCA)
Ice Cream
Sarah McLachlan; *Fumbling Towards Ecstasy* . . . . (Arista)
I'd Do Anything
Original Broadway Cast; *Oliver!* . . . . (RCA Victor)
Original London Cast; *Oliver!* . . . .(EMI-Angel)
If You Love Somebody
Kevin Sharp; *Measure Of A Man* . . . . (143/Asylum)
I'll Still Love You More
Trisha Yearwood; *Where Your Road Leads* . . . . (MCA)
In 2 Deep
Kenny Wayne Shepherd Band; *Live On* . . . . (Giant)
In Too Deep
Sum 41; *All Killer No Filler* . . . . (Island/IDJMG)
In Too Deep
Genesis; *Invisible Touch* . . . . (Atlantic)
Turn It On Again: The Hits . . . . (Atlantic)
In Your Wildest Dreams
Tina Turner & Barry White; *Wildest Dreams* . . . .(Virgin)
Indescribably Blue
Elvis Presley; *Elvis' Gold Records, Volume 4* . . . .(RCA)
From Nashville To Memphis-The Essential '60s Masters . . . .(RCA)
It Would Be You
Gary Allan; *It Would Be You* . . . . (Decca)
Jerry Springer
"Weird Al" Yankovic; *Running With Scissors* . . . . . . (Volcano Entertainment)
Just To Hear You Say That You Love Me
Faith Hill & Tim McGraw; *Faith* . . . . (Warner Bros.)
Let's Get Down
Tony Toni Tone; *House Of Music* . . . . (Mercury)
Tony Toni Tone-Hits . . . . (Mercury)
Ultimate Hip Hop Party-1998-C . . . . (Arista)
Love A Little Stronger
Diamond Rio; *'90s Hot Country-C* . . . . (K-Tel)
Diamond Rio's Greatest Hits . . . . (Arista)
Diamond Rio-Super Hits . . . . (Arista)
Hit Country '96-C . . . . (K-Tel)
Love A Little Stronger . . . . (Arista)
Meltdown
AC/DC; *Stiff Upper Lip* . . . . (East West)
More Than Words
Extreme; *Best Of Extreme: An Accidental Collocation Of Atoms?* . . . . . . (A&M)
Billboard Top Hits-1991-C . . . . (Rhino)
Pornograffitti . . . . (A&M)
More Than You'll Ever Know
Barbra Streisand; *Simply Streisand* . . . .(Columbia)
Billie Holiday; *Quintessential-#7-1938-1939* . . . .(Legacy)
Dinah Washington; *Jazz 'Round Midnight-Dinah Washington* . . . .(Verve)
Frank Sinatra; *Everything Happens To Me* . . . .(Reprise)
Johnny Mathis; *Heavenly* . . . .(Columbia)
Most Beautiful Girl
Charlie Rich; *Behind Closed Doors* . . . . (Epic)
Charlie Rich's Greatest Hits . . . . (Epic)
Columbia Country Classics-#4-Nashville Sound-C . . . . (Columbia)
Most High
Jimmy Page/Robert Plant; *Walking Into Clarksdale* . . . . (Atlantic)
Mr. Too Damn Good
Gerald Levert; *G* . . . . (East West)
My Love
Petula Clark; *History Of British Rock-#7-C* . . . .(Rhino)
Petula Clark's Greatest Hits . . . .(Crescendo)
My Own Worst Enemy
Lit; *A Place In The Sun* . . . . (RCA)
No Place That Far
Sara Evans; *No Place That Far* . . . . (RCA)
Nobody I Know
Peter And Gordon; *History Of British Rock-#1-C* . . . . (Rhino)
Queer
Garbage; *Garbage* . . . . (Almo Sounds)
Rock Bottom
Wynonna; *Tell Me Why* . . . . (MCA)
Sex-O-Matic Venus Freak
Macy Gray; *On How Life Is* . . . . (Epic)
Shallow End Of The Gene Pool
Austin Lounge Lizards; *Small Minds* . . . .(Sugar Hill)
Smile Like Yours
Natalie Cole; *ST/A Smile Like Yours* . . . . (Elektra)
Still Water Runs The Deepest
Asleep At The Wheel featuring Willie Nelson; *Tribute To The Music Of Bob
Wills And The Texas Playboys-C* . . . . (Liberty)
Teacher, The
Paul Simon; *You're The One* . . . . (Warner Bros.)
There Once Was A Man
Original Cast; *Pajama Game* . . . .(Columbia)
ST/Pajama Game . . . .(Collectables)

To Love Somebody
Bee Gees; *Bee Gees-Gold* . . . . (Polydor)
History Of British Rock-#7-C . . . .(Rhino)
Jimmy Somerville; *Jimmy Somerville-Singles Collection-1984-1990.* . (London)
Michael Bolton; *Timeless-Classics* . . . .(Columbia)
Too Close
Next; *Rated Next* . . . . (Divine Mill/Arista)
Too Close For Comfort
Eydie Gorme; *Eydie Gorme* . . . . (Taragon)
Too Gone Too Long
Randy Travis; *Always & Forever* . . . . (Warner Bros.)
Great Divorce Songs For Him-C . . . . (Warner Bros.)
Randy Travis' Greatest Hits-#1 . . . . (Warner Bros.)
Too High
Stevie Wonder; *Innervisions* . . . .(Motown)
Too Much
Dave Matthews Band; *Crash* . . . . (RCA)
True Companion
Marc Cohn; *Marc Cohn* . . . . (Atlantic)
Truly Madly Deeply
Savage Garden; *Savage Garden* . . . .(Columbia)
Two Dozen Roses
Shenandoah; *30 Years Of #1 Hits-#20-C* . . . .(Columbia)
Road Not Taken . . . .(Columbia)
Shenandoah's Greatest Hits . . . .(Columbia)
Warmth, The
Incubus; *Make Yourself* . . . .(Immortal/Epic)
Worst That Could Happen
Brooklyn Bridge; *Billboard Top Pop Hits-1969-C* . . . .(Rhino)
Brooklyn Bridge-Greatest Hits . . . .(Collectables)
You Talk Too Much
Cheap Trick; *Next Position Please* . . . .(Epic)
You Talk Too Much
Joe Jones; *American Graffiti-#3-C* . . . .(MCA)
Billboard Top Rock 'N' Roll Hits-1960-C . . . .(Rhino)
Carnival Time-Best Of Ric Records-#1-C . . . .(Rounder)
Echoes Of A Rock Era-Middle Years-C . . . .(Roulette)
Original Rock 'N' Roll Hits Of The '60s-C . . . .(Roulette)
You Talk Too Much
George Thorogood & The Destroyers; *Born To Be Bad* . . . . (Gold Rush)
You Talk Too Much
Run-D.M.C.; *King Of Rock* . . . . (Profile)

EYES, Eyeglasses, Sunglasses

See Also: **ANATOMY (various), FINDING, LOVE: SEARCHING
FOR LOVE, SEARCH, SEEING**

(They Long To Be) Close To You
Carpenters; *Carpenters-Classics-#2* . . . .(A&M)
Carpenters-Love Songs . . . .(A&M)
Carpenters-The Singles 1969-1973 . . . .(A&M)
From The Top . . . .(A&M)
20/20
George Benson; *20/20* . . . . (Warner Bros.)
3 Libras
A Perfect Circle; *Mer De Noms* . . . . (Virgin)
All Eyes On Me
Goo Goo Dolls; *Dizzy Up The Girl* . . . . (Warner Sunset/Reprise)
Amazing Grace
Jeff Beck; *All-Star Christmas-C* . . . .(Epic)
Judy Collins; *Colors Of The Day-The Best Of Judy Collins* . . . .(Elektra)
Whales & Nightingales . . . .(Elektra)
Maverick Choir; *ST/Maverick* . . . .(Atlantic)
Nitty Gritty Dirt Band; *Will The Circle Be Unbroken-#2-C* . . . .(Uni)
Tramaine Hawkins; *God Bless America-C* . . . .(Columbia)
Analyse
Cranberries; *Wake Up And Smell The Coffee* . . . . (MCA)
Angel Eyes
Frank Sinatra; *At The Sands* . . . . (Reprise)
Frank Sinatra sings for Only The Lonely. . . . .(Capitol)
Round #1 . . . .(Capitol)
Sinatra-The Main Event Live. . . . . (Reprise)
Angel Eyes
Jeff Healey Band; *See The Light* . . . .(Arista)
Angel Eyes
Jim Brickman; *By Heart* . . . . (Windham Hill)
Angel Eyes
Roxy Music; *Manifesto* . . . .(Atco)
Roxy Music-Atlantic Years 1973-1980 . . . .(Atco)
Angel Eyes
Abba; *Abba's Greatest Hits-#2* . . . . (Atlantic)
Voulez-Vous . . . . (Atlantic)
Angel Eyes
Ella Fitzgerald; *Best Of Ella Fitzgerald-#2* . . . . (MCA)

Angel In My Eyes
John Michael Montgomery; *John Michael Montgomery's Greatest Hits* . . . . (Atlantic)

Angel's Eye
Aerosmith; *ST/Charlie's Angels* . . . . (Columbia)

Angry Eyes
Loggins & Messina; *Best Of Friends* . . . . (Columbia)
Loggins & Messina-On Stage . . . . (Columbia)
Loggins And Messina . . . . (Columbia)

Apple Of Your Eye
Peter Frampton; *Frampton* . . . . (A&M)

Barney Google
Authentic Band Organ; *Catch The Brass Ring-Merry-Go-Round* . . . . . (Klavier)
Firehouse Five Plus Two; *Twenty Years Later* . . . . (Good Time Jazz)

Barstow Blue Eyes
Jo Jo Gunne; *Jo Jo Gunne* . . . . (Asylum)

Beautiful Brown Eyes
Rosemary Clooney; *Songs From The Girl Singer-A Musical Autobiography* . . . .(Concord Jazz)

Beautiful In My Eyes
Joshua Kadison; *Painted Desert Serenade* . . . . (SBK)

Bedroom Eyes
Evelyn ''Champagne'' King; *Sweet Delight* . . . . (RCA)

Bedroom Eyes
Eddie Rabbitt; *Radio Romance* . . . . (Elektra)

Behind Blue Eyes
Who; *Hooligans* . . . .(MCA)
Join Together . . . .(MCA)
Who's Last . . . .(MCA)
Who's next . . . .(MCA)

Bette Davis Eyes
Kim Carnes; *Best Of Kim Carnes* . . . . (EMI Special Markets)
Billboard Top Hits-1981-C . . . . (Rhino)
Mistaken Identity . . . .(EMI)

Between Blue Eyes And Jeans
Conway Twitty; *Don't Call Him A Cowboy* . . . .(Warner Bros.)

Black-Eyed Blues
Joe Cocker; *Joe Cocker* . . . . (A&M)
Joe Cocker's Greatest Hits . . . . (A&M)

Black-Eyed Blues
Esther Phillips; *Best Of Esther Phillips* . . . . (CBS Associated)

Blonde Ambition
Billy Burnette; *Soldier Of Love* . . . . (Curb)

Bloodshot Eyes
Wynonie Harris; *Bloodshot Eyes: The Best Of Wynonie Harris* . . . . (Rhino)
Good Rockin' Blues . . . . (Gusto)

Bloodshot Eyes
Asleep At The Wheel; *Bloodshot Eyes* . . . .(Epic)

Blue Eyes
Elton John; *Elton John's Greatest Hits-1976-1986* . . . .(MCA)
Jump Up! . . . .(MCA)

Blue Eyes Blue
Eric Clapton; *Clapton Chronicles-The Best Of Eric Clapton 1981-1999* . . . . (Reprise)
ST/Runaway Bride . . . . (Sony Music Soundtrax)

Blue Eyes Crying In The Rain
Roy Acuff; *Roy Acuff's Greatest Hits* . . . . (Elektra)
Roy Acuff and his Smoky Mountain Boys; *Columbia Country Classics-#1-Golden Age-C* . . . . (Columbia)
Willie Nelson; *Columbia Country Classics-#5-A New Tradition-C* . . (Columbia)
Greatest Hits (& Some That Will Be) . . . . (Columbia)
Red Headed Stranger . . . . (Columbia)
ST/Honeysuckle Rose . . . . (Columbia)

Blue Motorcycle Eyes
Havana 3 A.M.; *Havana 3 A.M.* . . . .(I.R.S.)

Bluest Eyes In Texas
Restless Heart; *Big Dreams In A Small Town* . . . . (RCA)

Born Cross-Eyed
Grateful Dead; *Anthem Of The Sun* . . . .(Warner Bros.)
What A Long Strange Trip It's Been: The Best Of The Grateful Dead . . . .(Warner Bros.)

Brilliant Disguise
Bruce Springsteen; *Bruce Springsteen's Greatest Hits* . . . . (Columbia)
Tunnel Of Love . . . . (Columbia)

Brown Eyed Girl
Isley Brothers; *Live It Up* . . . .(T-Neck/Columbia)
Jimmy Buffett; *One Particular Harbour* . . . .(MCA)
Van Morrison; *Bang Masters* . . . .(Epic)
Best Of Van Morrison . . . . (Polydor)
ST/Born On The Fourth Of July . . . .(MCA)
ST/Sleeping With The Enemy . . . . (Columbia)
Wonder Years-Music From Emmy Shows/Era-C . . . . (Atlantic)

Brown Eyed Handsome Man
Buddy Holly; *Buddy Holly-20 Golden Greats* . . . .(MCA)
For The First Time Anywhere . . . .(MCA)
Rock & Roll Collection . . . .(MCA)
Chuck Berry; *Best Of The Best Of Chuck Berry* . . . . (International Mktg. Group)
Roll Over Beethoven . . . .(Allegiance)

The Chess Box-Chuck Berry . . . . (Chess)
Waylon Jennings; *Essential Waylon Jennings* . . . . (RCA)
Waylon Jennings-Super Hits . . . . (RCA)

Brown Eyed Woman
Grateful Dead; *Europe '72* . . . . (Warner Bros.)
What A Long Strange Trip It's Been: The Best Of The Grateful Dead . . . .(Warner Bros.)

Brown Eyes
Fleetwood Mac; *25 Years-The Chain* . . . . (Warner Bros.)
Tusk . . . . (Warner Bros.)

Brown Eyes
Jimmy Cliff; *Cliff Hanger* . . . . (Columbia)

Brush Those Tears From Your Eyes
Li'l Wally; *Unforgettable Hits* . . . . (Jay Jay)

Butterfly Kisses
Bob Carlisle; *Butterfly Kisses (Shades Of Grace)* . . . .(DMG/Jive)

Camera Eye
Rush; *Moving Pictures* . . . . (Mercury)

Can't Take My Eyes Off You
Frankie Valli; *25th Anniversary Collection* . . . . (Rhino)
Frankie Valli-Anthology . . . . (Rhino)
Very Best Of Frankie Valli . . . . (MCA)
Lauryn Hill; *The Miseducation Of Lauryn Hill* . . . . (Ruffhouse/Columbia)

Carnival
Natalie Merchant; *Tigerlily* . . . . (Elektra)

Cheap Sunglasses
ZZ Top; *Deguello* . . . . (Warner Bros.)
ST/Teachers . . . . (Capitol)

Chocolate Brown Eyes
Millie Jackson; *Rock 'N' Roll Soul* . . . . (Ichiban Int'l)

Close My Eyes
Mariah Carey; *Butterfly* . . . . (Columbia)

Close My Eyes Forever
Lita Ford & Ozzy Osbourne; *Lita* . . . . (Dreamland)

Close Your Eyes
Ella Fitzgerald; *Like Someone In Love* . . . . (Verve)
Oscar Peterson & Dizzy Gillespie; *Oscar Peterson & Dizzy Gillespie* . . . (Pablo)
Tony Bennett; *Jazz* . . . . (Columbia)

Close Your Eyes
Peaches & Herb; *Love Is Strange-The Best Of Peaches & Herb* . . . . (Legacy)

Cockeyed Optimist
Mitzi Gaynor; *ST/South Pacific* . . . .(RCA)
Original Cast; *South Pacific* . . . . (CBS Masterworks)

Computer Eyes
Carole King; *Speeding Time* . . . .(Atlantic)

Cotton Eyed Joe
Bob Wills; *Columbia Historic Edition-Bob Wills* . . . . (Columbia)
Carlton Moody & The Moody Brothers; *Carlton Moody & The Moody Brothers* . . . . (Lamon)

Crazy Eyes
Daryl Hall & John Oates; *Bigger Than Both Of Us* . . . . (RCA)

Crush With Eyeliner
R.E.M.; *Monster* . . . . (Warner Bros.)

Cryin' Eyes
Don Williams; *One Good Well* . . . . (RCA)

Dark Eyes
Dizzy Gillespie & Stan Getz; *Diz & Getz* . . . . (Verve)
Tommy Dorsey; *Tommy Dorsey & The David Rose String Orchestra* . . . . (Laserlight)

Dark Eyes
Bob Dylan; *Empire Burlesque* . . . . (Columbia)

Dirty Eyes
AC/DC; *Bonfire* . . . . (East West)

Dirty Looks
Diana Ross; *Red Hot Rhythm & Blues-C* . . . .(RCA)

Dirty Looks
Juice Newton; *Juice Newton-Greatest Hits & More* . . . . (Capitol)

Doctor My Eyes
Jackson Browne; *Jackson Browne* . . . .(Asylum)

Don't Close Your Eyes
Keith Whitley; *Don't Close Your Eyes* . . . . (RCA)
Keith Whitley's Greatest Hits . . . . (RCA)

Don't It Make My Brown Eyes Blue
Crystal Gayle; *Classic Crystal* . . . . (EMI)
Heartbreak Hotel-C . . . . (EMI)
ST/Convoy . . . . (Polydor)
We Must Believe In Magic . . . . (United Artists)

Don't Let The Stars Get In Your Eyes
Perry Como; *Como's Golden Records* . . . . (RCA)
Perry Como-Pure Gold . . . . (RCA)
Perry Como's All-Time Greatest Hits-#1 . . . . (RCA)
This Is Perry Como . . . . (RCA)

Don't Let Your Eyes Go Shopping
Mark Murphy; *Mark Murphy Sings Nat's Choice-Nat ''King'' Cole Songbook-#2* . . . .(Muse)

Double Vision
Foreigner; *Double Vision* . . . . (Atlantic)
Records . . . .(Atlantic)

Down By The Water
PJ Harvey; *ST/Basketball Diaries* . . . . (Island)
To Bring You My Love . . . . (Island)
Dreaming With My Eyes Open
Clay Walker; *Clay Walker* . . . . (Giant)
Drink To Me Only With Thine Eyes
Paul Robeson; *Essential Paul Robeson* . . . . (Vanguard)
Roger Whittaker; *Folk Songs Of Our Time* . . . .(RCA)
Drivin' With Your Eyes Closed
Don Henley; *Building The Perfect Beast* . . . . (Geffen)
Earache My Eye featuring Alice Bowie
Cheech & Chong; *Dr. Demento: 20th Anniversary Collection-C* . . . . . . (Rhino)
Greatest Hit . . . . (Warner Bros.)
Wedding Album . . . . (Warner Bros.)
Ebony Eyes
Everly Brothers; *Golden Hits Of The Everly Brothers* . . . . (Warner Bros.)
Very Best Of The Everly Brothers . . . . (Warner Bros.)
Ebony Eyes
Rick James Featuring Smokey Robinson; *Cold Blooded*. . . . . (Motown)
Rick James' Greatest Hits . . . . (Motown)
Ebony Eyes
Bob Welch; *French Kiss* . . . . (Capitol)
Ebony Eyes
Stevie Wonder; *Songs In The Key Of Life* . . . . (Motown)
Electra Made Me Blind
Everclear; *Sparkle And Fade* . . . . (Capitol)
Electric Eye
Judas Priest; *Priest...Live!* . . . . (Columbia)
Screaming For Vengeance . . . . (Columbia)
Emerald Eyes
Eric Johnson; *Tones*. . . . .(Reprise)
Emerald Eyes
Fleetwood Mac; *Mystery To Me* . . . .(Reprise)
Emerald Eyes
Jimmy Page; *Outrider* . . . . (Geffen)
English Eyes
Toto; *Turn Back* . . . . (Columbia)
Epistle To Dippy
Donovan; *Donovan's Greatest Hits*. . . . . (Epic)
Every Time I Close My Eyes
Babyface; *The Day* . . . . (Epic)
Every Time I Get Around You
David Lee Murphy; *Gettin' Out The Good Stuff* . . . . (MCA)
Eye In The Sky
Alan Parsons Project; *Eye In The Sky* . . . . (Arista)
Turn Of A Friendly Card. . . . . (Arista)
Eye Of The Dragonfly
Friedemann; *Indian Summer* . . . . (Narada)
Eye Of The Tiger
Survivor; *Eye Of The Tiger* . . . . (Scotti Bros.)
Frankenstein & Other Rock Monsters-C . . . . (CBS Associated)
Rocky Story-C . . . . (Scotti Bros.)
ST/Rocky III . . . . (EMI)
Eye Of The Zombie
John Fogerty; *Eye Of The Zombie* . . . . (Warner Bros.)
Eyes As Big As Dallas
Randy Wagner; *45-#236* . . . . (Door Knob)
Eyes Like A Cat
Little Charlie & The Nightcats; *All The Way Crazy*. . . . .(Alligator)
Captured Live . . . .(Alligator)
Eyes Of A Child
Moody Blues; *This Is The Moody Blues* . . . . (Polydor)
To Our Children's Children's Children . . . . (Polydor)
Eyes Of A Child
Naked Eyes; *Best Of Naked Eyes*. . . . . (EMI)
Eyes Of A New York Woman
B.J. Thomas; *B.J. Thomas' Greatest Hits* . . . .(Rhino)
B.J. Thomas-16 Greatest Hits . . . . (Trip)
Eyes Of A Painter
Kate Wolf; *Close To You* . . . . (Kaleidoscope)
Evening In Austin . . . . (Kaleidoscope)
Gold In California-Retrospective-1975-1985. . . . . (Kaleidoscope)
Eyes Of Blue
Paul Carrack; *Blue Views* . . . . (Ark 21)
Eyes Of Silver
Doobie Brothers; *What Were Once Vices Are Now Habits* . . . . . . (Warner Bros.)
Eyes Of Texas
Michigan University Band; *Kick Off, U.S.A.* . . . . (Vanguard)
Sharkey & The Kings Of Dixieland; *Sharkey & The Kings Of
Dixieland.* . . . .(Southland)
Eyes Of Texas
Bill Boyd; *Western Swing-#1 & 2* . . . .(Arhoolie)
Eyes Of Texas
Masters Of Reality; *Masters Of Reality*. . . . . (Delicious Vinyl)
Eyes Of The World
Grateful Dead; *One From The Vault* . . . .(Grateful Dead)
Wake Of The Flood . . . .(Grateful Dead)
Without A Net . . . . (Arista)

Eyes Of The World
Fleetwood Mac; *25 Years-The Chain* . . . .(Warner Bros.)
Mirage . . . .(Warner Bros.)
Eyes That See In The Dark
Kenny Rogers & Dolly Parton; *Eyes That See In The Dark* . . . . (RCA)
Eyes Without A Face
Billy Idol; *Rebel Yell* . . . . (Chrysalis)
Flesheaters; *ST/Return Of The Living Dead* . . . . (Enigma)
Eyesight To The Blind
Pete Townshend; *Pete Townshend's Deep End Live!.* . . . .(Atco)
Who; *Join Together* . . . . (MCA)
Tommy. . . . . (MCA)
Far Away Eyes
Rolling Stones; *Some Girls* . . . . (Virgin)
Five Foot Two, Eyes Of Blue
Mom & Dads; *Very Best Of The Mom & Dads*. . . . . (Crescendo)
For Your Eyes Only
Sheena Easton; *13 Original James Bond Themes-C* . . . .(EMI)
ST/For Your Eyes Only . . . .(Liberty)
Frozen
Madonna; *GHV2* . . . . (Warner Bros.)
Ray Of Light . . . . (Maverick)
Funny Lookin' Eyes
Barefoot Jerry; *Watchin' TV.* . . . . (Monument)
Future's So Bright I Gotta Wear Shades
Timbuk 3; *Greetings From Timbuk 3.* . . . .(I.R.S.)
Gee Whiz (Look At His Eyes)
Carla Thomas; *Gee Whiz: The Best Of Carla Thomas* . . . .(Rhino)
Girl I Got My Eyes On You
Today; *Today.* . . . .(Motown)
Girl With April In Her Eyes
Chris DeBurgh; *Crusader* . . . .(A&M)
Girl With The Hungry Eyes
Jefferson Starship; *At Point Zero* . . . . (Grunt)
Gleam In Your Eyes
Earl Lewis &The Channels; *New York's Finest* . . . .(Collectables)
God Must Have Spent A Little More Time On You
Alabama Featuring 'N Sync; *Twentieth Century* . . . . (RCA)
'N Sync; *'N Sync* . . . . (RCA)
Totally Hits-#1-C . . . . (Arista)
Good Times Bad Times
Led Zeppelin; *Led Zeppelin* . . . . (Atlantic)
Green Eyed Lady
Sugarloaf; *Sugarloaf-Spaceship Earth.* . . . .(Collectables)
Green Eyes
Jimmy Dorsey & His Orchestra; *Best Of Jimmy Dorsey* . . . . (MCA)
Jimmy Dorsey & His Orchestra's Greatest Hits . . . . (MCA)
Green Eyes
Husker Du; *Flip Your Wig* . . . . (SST)
Green Kentucky Eyes
Pal Rakes; *Midnight Rain*. . . . .(Atlantic America)
Guinnevere
Crosby, Stills & Nash; *Crosby, Stills & Nash.* . . . . (Atlantic)
CSN . . . . (Atlantic)
Crosby, Stills, Nash & Young; *So Far* . . . . (Atlantic)
Woodstock Two . . . . (Atlantic)
Gypsy Eyes
Jimi Hendrix Experience; *Electric Ladyland* . . . . (Reprise)
Hands
Jewel; *Spirit* . . . . (Atlantic)
Heaven In Your Eyes
Loverboy; *Big Ones* . . . . (Columbia)
ST/Top Gun . . . .(Columbia)
His Eye Is On The Sparrow
Carmen McRae; *Greatest Of Carmen McRae* . . . . (MCA)
Marvin Gaye; *Musical Testament 1964-1984* . . . .(Motown)
Preservation Hall Jazz Band; *Best Of The Preservation Hall
Jazz Band* . . . .(Columbia)
Soundtrack; *Streetcar Named Desire.* . . . .(Allegiance)
His Green Eyes
Barbara Fairchild; *Standing In Your Line.* . . . .(Columbia)
Hit Between The Eyes
Scorpions; *Crazy World* . . . .(Mercury)
ST/Free Jack . . . . (Morgan Creek)
Hungry Eyes
Eric Carmen; *Best Of Eric Carmen* . . . .(Arista)
Dirty Dancing Live In Concert-C . . . . (RCA)
ST/Dirty Dancing . . . . (RCA)
Hungry Eyes
Emmylou Harris; *Mama's Hungry Eyes-Merle Haggard Tribute-C* . . . . .(Arista)
Merle Haggard; *For The Record: Merle Haggard-43 Legendary Hits.* . . . . (BNA)
Hurting Kind (I've Got My Eyes On You)
Robert Plant; *Manic Nirvana* . . . . (Es Paranza)
I Can See Forever In Your Eyes
Reba McEntire; *Feel The Fire* . . . . (Mercury)
I Count The Minutes
Ricky Martin; *Ricky Martin* . . . .(Columbia)

I Don't Want To Miss A Thing
Aerosmith; *ST/Armageddon-The Album* . . . . (Columbia)
Mark Chesnutt; *I Don't Want To Miss A Thing* . . . . (MCA)
I Got My Eyes On You
Buddy Guy; *This Is Buddy Guy* . . . . (Vanguard)
Peter Frampton; *Frampton's Camel* . . . . (A&M)
I Only Have Eyes For You
Art Garfunkel; *Breakaway* . . . . (Columbia)
Garfunkel . . . . (Columbia)
Flamingos; *Doo-Wop Ballads-#2-C* . . . . (Rhino)
Echoes Of A Rock Era-Middle Years-C . . . . (Roulette)
ST/American Graffiti . . . . (MCA)
I See The Lovelight In Your Eyes
Conway Twitty; *Number Ones* . . . . (MCA)
I See The Want In Your Eyes
Conway Twitty; *I'm Not Through Loving You Yet* . . . . (MCA)
Night With Conway Twitty . . . . (MCA)
Number Ones . . . . (MCA)
I Still Love You
Next; *Rated Next* . . . . (Divine Mill/Arista)
If You Could Only See
Tonic; *Lemon Parade* . . . . (Polydor)
Now That's What I Call Music!-#1-C . . . . (Virgin)
I'm Sorry
Brenda Lee; *Billboard Top Pop Hits-1960-C* . . . . (Rhino)
Brenda Lee-Anthology-#1 & #2 . . . . (MCA)
The Brenda Lee Story-Her Greatest Hits . . . . (MCA)
Platters; *Enchanted-The Best Of The Platters* . . . . (Rhino)
Magic Touch-An Anthology . . . . (Mercury)
I'm Thinking Tonight Of My Blue Eyes
Gene Autry; *All Time Legends Of Country Music-C* . . . . (Legacy)
In Another's Eyes
Trisha Yearwood & Garth Brooks; *Songbook-A Collection Of Hits* . . . . . (MCA)
In Buddy's Eyes
Jane Harvey; *Other Side Of Sondheim* . . . . (Atlantic)
In My Eyes
John Conlee; *Best Of John Conlee* . . . . (Curb)
In My Eyes . . . . (MCA)
John Conlee-20 Greatest Hits . . . . (MCA)
Lionel Cartwright; *Lionel Cartwright* . . . . (MCA)
In The Eye
Suzanne Vega; *Solitude Standing* . . . . (A&M)
In Your Eyes
Bucks Fizz; *45-#885040-7* . . . . (Polydor)
In Your Eyes
Boy Meets Girl; *Boy Meets Girl* . . . . (A&M)
In Your Eyes
Jeffrey Osborne; *Emotional* . . . . (A&M)
In Your Eyes
Billy Squier; *Emotions In Motion* . . . . (Capitol)
In Your Eyes
James "D Train" Williams; *In Your Eyes* . . . . (Columbia)
In Your Eyes
George Benson; *In Your Eyes* . . . . (Warner Bros.)
In Your Eyes
Shirley Murdock; *Let There Be Love!* . . . . (Elektra)
In Your Eyes
Reivers; *Saturday* . . . . (Capitol)
In Your Eyes
Peter Gabriel; *So* . . . . (Geffen)
In Your Eyes
Babys; *Union Jacks* . . . . (Chrysalis)
Infinite Eyes
Keb' Mo'; *Big Wide Grin* . . . . (Sony Wonder)
Invisible Man
98 Degrees; *98 Degrees* . . . . (Motown)
Is That A Tear
Tracy Lawrence; *Best Of Tracy Lawrence* . . . . (Atlantic)
Time Marches On . . . . (Atlantic)
Isabella's Eyes
Kenny Loggins; *Back To Avalon* . . . . (Columbia)
It's In Your Eyes (Any Time At All)
Phil Collins; *Dance Into The Light* . . . . (Atlantic)
I've Got My Eyes On You
Jessica Simpson; *Sweet Kisses* . . . . (Columbia)
Jeepers Creepers
Frank Sinatra; *Frank Sinatra-Gift Set* . . . . (Capitol)
Louis Armstrong; *20 Golden Pieces Of Louis Armstrong & Friends* . . . (Bulldog)
At The Crescendo . . . . (MCA)
Hello Dolly! & Other Hits . . . . (MCA)
Jewel Eyed Judy
Fleetwood Mac; *Kiln House* . . . . (Reprise)
John Doe No. 24
Mary Chapin Carpenter; *Stones In The Road* . . . . (Columbia)
Judy In Disguise (With Glasses)
John Fred & His Playboy Band; *Billboard Top Rock 'N' Roll Hits-
1968-C* . . . . (Rhino)
Cruisin'-1967-C . . . . (Increase)

ST/Drugstore Cowboy . . . . (Novus)
Super Oldies Of The '60s-#7-C . . . . (Audio Fidelity)
Keep Your Eye On Me
Herb Alpert; *Keep Your Eye On Me* . . . . (A&M)
Killer's Eyes
Kinks; *Give The People What They Want* . . . . (Arista)
Kiss From A Rose
Seal; *Seal 2* . . . . (Sire)
Last Game Of The Season (A Blind Man In The Bleachers)
David Geddes; *Super Hits Of The '70s-Have A Nice Day-#20-C* . . . . . (Rhino)
Last Resort
Papa Roach; *Infest* . . . . (DreamWorks/SKG)
Lazy Eye
Goo Goo Dolls; *ST/Batman & Robin-Music From And Inspired By The
Motion Picture* . . . . (Jive)
Leavin' Train
Bruce Springsteen; *Tracks* . . . . (Columbia)
Light In Your Eyes
Blessid Union Of Souls; *Blessid Union Of Souls* . . . . (Capitol)
Light In Your Eyes
LeAnn Rimes; *Blue* . . . . (MCG/Curb)
Linger
Jonatha Brooke; *Steady Pull* . . . . (Bad Dog)
Living Years, The
Mike & The Mechanics; *Living Years* . . . . (Atlantic)
Look Into My Eyes
Bone Thugs-N-Harmony; *Art Of War* . . . . (Ruthless/Relativity)
Look Of Love, The
Andy Williams; *Born Free-Love Andy* . . . . (Collectables)
Legend At His Best . . . . (Collectables)
Anita Baker; *Rhythm Of Love* . . . . (Atlantic)
Diana Krall; *The Look Of Love* . . . . (Impulse!)
Dionne Warwick; *Hidden Gems-Best Of Dionne Warwick-#2* . . . . . . (Rhino)
Neil Diamond; *As Time Goes By-The Movie Album* . . . . (Columbia)
Sergio Mendes & Brasil '66; *Sergio Mendes-Classics-#18* . . . . (A&M)
Look, The
Roxette; *Look Sharp!* . . . . (EMI)
Vanessa Williams; *45-#887781-7* . . . . (Wing)
Looking Through Patient Eyes
PM Dawn; *Bliss Album...?* . . . . (Gee Street)
Looking Through Your Eyes
LeAnn Rimes; *Sittin' On Top Of The World* . . . . (Curb)
ST/Quest For Camelot . . . . (Curb/Atlantic)
Lost In Your Eyes
Jeff Healey Band; *Feel This* . . . . (Arista)
Lost In Your Eyes
Debbie Gibson; *Electric Youth* . . . . (Atlantic)
Love Eyes
Nancy Sinatra; *Sugar* . . . . (Sundazed Music)
The Hit Years . . . . (Rhino)
Love In Your Eyes
Eddie Money; *Nothing To Lose* . . . . (Columbia)
Love Theme From "Eyes Of Laura Mars"
Barbra Streisand; *Barbra Streisand's Greatest Hits* . . . . (Columbia)
Lazy Afternoon . . . . (Columbia)
Loving You With My Eyes
Starland Vocal Band; *4 x 4* . . . . (Windsong)
Lyin' Eyes
Eagles; *Eagles/Their Greatest Hits 1971-1975* . . . . (Asylum)
One Of These Nights . . . . (Asylum)
ST/Urban Cowboy . . . . (Asylum)
Ma (She's) Making Eyes At Me
Eddie Cantor; *Memories* . . . . (MCA)
Mama's Never Seen Those Eyes
Forester Sisters; *Forester Sisters* . . . . (Warner Bros.)
Me And Those Dreamin' Eyes Of Mine
D'Angelo; *Brown Sugar* . . . . (EMI)
Moon-Faced, Starry-Eyed
Benny Goodman; *Jazz Collector Edition* . . . . (Laserlight)
Motel Eyes
Rick Springfield; *Living In Oz* . . . . (RCA)
Mother's Eyes
Matthews, Wright & King; *Power Of Love* . . . . (Columbia)
My Brown Eyed Texas Rose
Tex Ritter; *Arizona Days* . . . . (MCA Special Prod.)
The Country Music Hall Of Fame-Tex Ritter . . . . (MCA)
My Eyes Adored You
4 Seasons; *25th Anniversary Collection* . . . . (Rhino)
Frankie Valli; *4 Seasons' Greatest Hits-#2* . . . . (Rhino)
My Father's Eyes
Eric Clapton; *Pilgrim* . . . . (Duck/Reprise)
My Mother's Eyes
Bette Midler; *ST/Divine Madness* . . . . (Atlantic)
Forester Sisters; *You Again* . . . . (Warner Bros.)
My Mother's Eyes
Clovers; *Love Potion No. 9* . . . . (EMI)
My Shoes Keep Walking Back To You
Ray Price; *All Time Legends Of Country Music-C* . . . . (Legacy)

Essential Ray Price-1951-1962 . . . .(Columbia)
Ray Price's Greatest Hits . . . .(Columbia)

My Sweet Eyed Georgia Girl
Atlanta; *Atlanta* . . . . (MCA)

Mystic Eyes
Them featuring Van Morrison; *Here Comes The Night* . . . . (Out Of Print)
History Of British Rock-#6-C . . . .(Rhino)
*The Sopranos-Music From The HBO Original
Series* . . . . (Sony Music Soundtrax)

Nietzsche's Eyes
Paula Cole; *This Fire* . . . .(Imago)

Night Has A Thousand Eyes
Anita O'Day; *Night Has A Thousand Eyes* . . . . (Emily)
Bobby Vee; *Best Of Bobby Vee* . . . . (EMI)
Bobby Vee-Legendary Masters . . . . (EMI)
Golden Years-1962-C . . . . (Dominion Entert.)

Night Lights
Nat "King" Cole; *Night Lights* . . . .(Capitol/EMI)

One-Eyed Jack
Garland Jeffreys; *Matador & More* . . . . (A&M)
One-Eyed Jack . . . . (A&M)

Open Our Eyes
Earth, Wind & Fire; *Open Our Eyes* . . . . (Columbia)

Open Up Your Eyes
Tonic; *Lemon Parade* . . . . (Polydor)

Open Your Eyes
Black Box; *Dreamland* . . . .(RCA)

Open Your Eyes
Julian Lennon; *Mr. Jordan* . . . . (Atlantic)

Open Your Eyes
Bobby Caldwell; *Cat In The Hat* . . . . (Sin-Drome)

Open Your Eyes
Yes; *Open Your Eyes* . . . .(Beyond)

Open Your Eyes
Organized Konfusion; *Basic Beats Sampler-C* . . . . (Hollywood Basic)
Organized Konfusion . . . . (Hollywood Basic)

Open Your Eyes
Lords Of The New Church; *Lords Of The New Church* . . . . (I.R.S.)

Open Your Eyes
Doobie Brothers; *Minute By Minute* . . . . (Warner Bros.)

Open Your Eyes
Asia; *Alpha* . . . . (Geffen)
Live In Moscow . . . .(Rhino)

Open Your Eyes
Chiffons; *22 Leaders Of The Pack-#2-C* . . . .(Laurie)
Best Of The Chiffons . . . .(Laurie)
Chiffons-Golden Classics . . . . (Collectables)

Over Now
Alice In Chains; *Alice In Chains* . . . . (Columbia)

Pass You By
Boyz II Men; *Nathan Michael Shawn Wanya* . . . . (Universal)

Penny Lane
Beatles; *Beatles 1* . . . .(Capitol)
Magical Mystery Tour . . . .(Capitol)
The Beatles/1967-1970 . . . .(Capitol)
The Beatles-Anthology-#2 . . . .(Capitol)

Pink-Eyed Pussycat
Bill Haley & His Comets; *Rock Around The Country* . . . . (Crescendo)
Rockin' & Rollin' . . . . (Accord)

Possession
Sarah McLachlan; *Fumbling Towards Ecstasy* . . . . (Arista)

Prettiest Eyes In California
B.W. Stevenson; *Rainbow Down The Road* . . . . (Amazing)

Pretty Blue Eyes
Steve Lawrence; *Best Of Steve Lawrence* . . . . (Taragon)

Pretty Little Angel Eyes
Curtis Lee; *Million-Dollar Memories-#2-C* . . . . (RCA)
Oldies But Goodies-#2-C . . . .(Original Sound)
Phil Spector-Back To Mono 1958-1969-C . . . .(Abkco)
Phil Spector-The Early Years-1958-1961-C . . . .(Rhino)
Rock & Roll U.S.A.-21 Rock & Roll Favorites-#2-C . . . . .(Laurie)

Private Eyes
Daryl Hall & John Oates; *Private Eyes* . . . . (RCA)
Rock 'N Soul, Part 1 . . . . (RCA)

Put Your Hands Where My Eyes Could See
Busta Rhymes; *When Disaster Strikes* . . . .(Elektra)

Rainbow Eyes
Rainbow; *Long Live Rock 'n' Roll* . . . . (Polydor)

Rainbow In Your Eyes
Al Jarreau; *Glow* . . . .(Reprise)
Look To The Rainbow-Live In Europe . . . . (Warner Bros.)
Leon Russell; *Wedding Album* . . . . (Paradise)

Rat's Eyes
Black Flag; *Slip It In* . . . . (SST)

Red Eye
Joe Beck; *Beck & Sanborn* . . . . (CBS Associated)
Fire Into Music-Best Of Impulse!-#2-C . . . . (MCA/Impulse)

Red Eye
Devo; *Duty Now For The Future* . . . .(Warner Bros.)

Red Eye
Nicky Thomas & Dolares; *Explosive Rock Steady-Amalgamated
Label.* . . . .(Heartbeat)

Right Before Your Eyes
America; *Encore-More Greatest Hits* . . . .(Rhino)
View From The Ground . . . . (Capitol)

Rosalinda's Eyes
Billy Joel; *52nd Street* . . . .(Columbia)

Rose Colored Glasses
John Conlee; *Backstage At The Grand Ole Opry-C* . . . . (RCA)
Grand Ole Opry-75 Years-#1-C . . . .(MCA)
John Conlee-Legends . . . .(MCA)
John Conlee's Greatest Hits . . . . (MCA)
MCA Records 30 Years Of Hits-1958-1988-C . . . .(MCA)
Rose Colored Glasses . . . . (Universal)

Sad Eyed Lady Of The Lowlands
Bob Dylan; *Blonde On Blonde* . . . .(Columbia)
Joan Baez; *Any Day Now: Songs Of Bob Dylan* . . . .(Vanguard)
Lovesong Album . . . .(Vanguard)

Sad Eyes
Robert John; *Billboard Top Rock 'N' Roll Hits-1979-C* . . . . .(Rhino)
Robert John . . . . (EMI)

Sad Eyes
Bruce Springsteen; *Tracks* . . . .(Columbia)
Trisha Yearwood; *Real Live Woman* . . . . (MCA)

Sad Eyes
Robin Lee; *Black Velvet* . . . . (Atlantic)

Sad Eyes
Gary Wright; *Critics Choice-#2-C* . . . . (Cypress)
Who I Am . . . . (Cypress)

Searching With My Good Eye Closed
Soundgarden; *Badmotorfinger* . . . .(A&M)

See Me In Your Eyes
38 Special; *Tour De Force* . . . .(A&M)

Sexy Eyes
Dr. Hook; *Dr. Hook-Greatest Hits & More* . . . . (Capitol)
Sometimes You Win . . . .(Capitol)

She Blinded Me With Science
Thomas Dolby; *Golden Age Of Wireless* . . . . (Capitol)

She Closed Her Eyes
Chris Rea; *Espresso Logic* . . . .(East West)

She Has Eyes
L7; *Hungry For Stink* . . . . (Slash)

Shelter Of Your Eyes
Don Williams; *Don Williams' Greatest Hits* . . . . (MCA)

She's A River
Simple Minds; *Good News From The Next World* . . . . (Virgin)

She's Got That Look In Her Eyes
Alabama; *Dancin' On The Boulevard* . . . . (RCA)

She's More
Andy Griggs; *You Won't Ever Be Lonely* . . . .(RCA)

Silent Eyes
Paul Simon; *Still Crazy After All These Years* . . . . (Columbia)

Silver Stars, Purple Sage, Eyes Of Blue
Roy Rogers & Sons Of The Pioneers; *Roy Rogers & Sons Of The
Pioneers* . . . . (Varese Sarabande)

Six O'Clock Train & A Girl With Green Eyes
John Hartford; *All In The Name Of Love* . . . . (Flying Fish)

Smile Has Left Your Eyes
Asia; *Alpha.* . . . . (Geffen)
Live In Moscow . . . .(Rhino)
Then & Now . . . . (Geffen)

Smoke Gets In Your Eyes
Bryan Ferry; *Another Time Another Place* . . . . (Reprise)
Street Life-20 Great Hits . . . . (Reprise)
Dinah Washington; *Golden Classics-Dinah Washington* . . . .(Collectables)
Lawrence Welk; *Musical Memories With Lawrence Welk* . . . .(Ranwood)
Patti Austin; *Real Me* . . . . (Qwest)
Platters; *Encore Of Golden Hits-Platters* . . . .(Mercury)
Oldies But Goodies-#14-C . . . . (Original Sound)
Platters Greatest Hits . . . .(Everest)
ST/Always . . . . (MCA)
ST/American Graffiti . . . . (MCA)
Super Oldies Of The '50s-#5-C . . . . (Audio Fidelity)

Snake Eyes
Alan Parsons Project; *Turn Of A Friendly Card* . . . .(Arista)

Spanish Eyes
Ricky Martin; *Ricky Martin* . . . .(Columbia)

Spanish Eyes
Al Martino; *Best Of Al Martino* . . . .(Capitol)
Capitol Collectors Series-Al Martino . . . .(Capitol)
Spanish Eyes . . . . (Capitol)
Buddy Merrill; *Buddy Merrill's All-Time Hits* . . . .(Accent)
Engelbert Humperdinck; *Engelbert Humperdinck-16 Most Requested
Songs* . . . . (Epic)
Live In Concert/All Of Me . . . .(Epic)

Man Without Love . . . . (Mercury)

Spanish Eyes
U2; *Joshua Tree* . . . . (Island)

Sparkling Brown Eyes
Webb Pierce with the Wilburn Brothers; *King Of The Honky-Tonk: From The Original Decca Masters-1952-1959* . . . .(Country Music Foundation)
Webb Pierce-Greatest Hits/Finest Performances . . . . (Sun)

Star Eyes
Charlie Parker; *Bebop & Bird-#2* . . . . (Rhino)
Chet Baker; *RCA Victor Jazz: First Half-Century-#5-C* . . . . (RCA)
Sonny Rollins; *Rollins Plays For Bird* . . . . (Prestige)
Saxophone Colossus & More . . . . (Prestige)
Sonny Rollins-Complete Prestige Recordings . . . . (Prestige)
Stephane Grappelli; *Compact Jazz-Stephane Grappelli* . . . . (Verve)

Staring At The Sun
U2; *Pop* . . . . (Island)

Starry Eyes
Motley Crue; *Too Fast For Love* . . . . (Elektra)

Story In Your Eyes
Moody Blues; *Every Good Boy Deserves Favour* . . . . (Polydor)
This Is The Moody Blues . . . . (Polydor)

Suite: Judy Blue Eyes
Crosby, Stills & Nash; *Crosby, Stills & Nash* . . . .(Atlantic)
CSN . . . .(Atlantic)
ST/Woodstock . . . .(Atlantic)
Crosby, Stills, Nash & Young; *So Far* . . . .(Atlantic)

Sunglasses At Night
Corey Hart; *First Offense* . . . .(EMI)
The Singles . . . .(EMI)

Sunshine In Their Eyes
Stevie Wonder; *Where I'm Coming From* . . . . (Motown)

Sweet Little Miss Blue Eyes
Jim & Jesse/The Virginia Boys; *Appalachian Stomp: More Bluegrass Classics-C* . . . . (Rhino)

Sweet Sexy Eyes
Cristy Lane; *Country Classics* . . . . (Arrival)
Cristy Lane-At Her Best . . . .(EMI)

Teardrops From My Eyes
Ruth Brown; *Miss Rhythm-Greatest Hits & More* . . . . (Rhino)

Teardrops In My Eyes
David Grisman; *Home Is Where The Heart Is* . . . . (Rounder)
New Riders Of The Purple Sage; *Adventures Of Panama Red* . . . . . (Columbia)

Tears In My Eyes
Baltineers; *For Collectors Only-#1-The Rarities-C* . . . . (Collectables)
Great Groups Of The '50s-#2-C . . . . (Collectables)
Dreamers; *Harlem New York-Ballad Era-C* . . . . (Collectables)
Joan Baez; *Very Early Joan Baez* . . . . (Vanguard)

Teenage Eyes
Flash Cadillac & The Continental Kids; *Rock & Roll Forever* . . . .(Epic)

Television Eye
John Mayall; *Room To Move-1969-1974-Chronicle Series* . . . . (Polydor)

Tell Me What You See
Beatles; *Beatles VI* . . . . (Capitol)
Beatles-Box Set . . . . (Capitol)
Beatles-Love Songs . . . . (Capitol)

Temptation Eyes
Grass Roots; *Grass Roots-All-Time Greatest Hits* . . . .(MCA)
Grass Roots-Anthology (1966-1975) . . . . (Rhino)

Texas
Merle Haggard; *Friend In California* . . . .(Epic)
Merle Haggard & Freddy Powers; *Texas Super Hits-C* . . . . (Columbia)

Thank You For Loving Me
Bon Jovi; *Crush* . . . .(Island/IDJMG)

Them There Eyes
Anita O'Day; *Anita Sings The Most* . . . . (Verve)
Billie Holiday; *At Storyville* . . . . (Black Lion)
Billie's Blues . . . . (Blue Note)
From The Original Decca Masters . . . .(MCA)
Legacy Box-1933-1958 . . . . (Columbia)
Diane Schuur; *In Tribute* . . . . (GRP)
Gene Ammons; *The Gene Ammons Story-The 78 Era* . . . . (Prestige)
Rosemary Clooney; *Tribute To Billie Holiday* . . . .(Concord Jazz)
Sarah Vaughan; *Singles Sessions* . . . . (Roulette)

These Eyes
Guess Who; *Best Of The Guess Who* . . . . (RCA)
Greatest Of The Guess Who . . . . (RCA)
Nipper's Greatest Hits Of The '60s-#1-C . . . . (RCA)
Track Record-Collection . . . . (RCA)

These Eyes
Junior Walker & The All Stars; *Junior Walker & The All Stars-All The Great Hits* . . . . (Motown)
Junior Walker & The All Stars-Anthology . . . . (Motown)

Through The Eyes Of Love
Melissa Manchester; *Melissa Manchester's Greatest Hits* . . . . (Arista)
ST/Ice Castles . . . . (Arista)

Too Shy
Kajagoogoo; *White Feathers* . . . .(EMI)

Turn A Blind Eye
Call; *Modern Romans* . . . . (Mercury)

Walls Came Down-Best Of The Mercury Years . . . . (Mercury)

TV Eye
Iggy & The Stooges; *Legends Of Rock Guitar-'70s-C* . . . . (Rhino)
Stooges; *Elektrock-Sixties-C* . . . . (Elektra)
Fun House . . . . (Elektra)

U Got The Look
Prince; *Sign ''O'' The Times* . . . . (Paisley Park)

Under The Eye
Dennis Linde; *Under The Eye* . . . . (Monument)

Vintage Eyes
Second Coming; *Second Coming* . . . . (Capitol)

Vision Of Love
Mariah Carey; *Mariah Carey* . . . . (Columbia)
MTV Unplugged-Mariah Carey . . . . (Columbia)

Wandering Eyes
Ronnie McDowell; *Older Women & Other Greatest Hits* . . . . (Epic)

Warmth, The
Incubus; *Make Yourself* . . . . (Immortal/Epic)

Whatever It Takes
Sinead Lohan; *No Mermaid* . . . . (Grapevine)

When I Close My Eyes
Kenny Chesney; *Kenny Chesney's Greatest Hits* . . . .(BNA)
Me And You . . . .(BNA)

When I Close My Eyes
Shanice; *Shanice* . . . . (LaFace)

When I Look In Your Eyes
Romantics; *What I Like About You (And Other Romantic Hits)* . . . . . (Nemperor)

When I Look In Your Eyes
Diana Krall; *When I Look In Your Eyes* . . . . (GRP)

When I Look In Your Eyes
Jennifer Rush; *Passion* . . . . (Epic)

When I Look In Your Eyes
Gap Band; *The Gap Band III* . . . . (Mercury)

When I Look Into Your Eyes
Firehouse; *Hold Your Fire* . . . . (Epic)

When I Need You
Celine Dion; *Let's Talk About Love-C* . . . .(550 Music)
Leo Sayer; *'70s Greatest Rock Hits-#5-Kickin' Back-C* . . . . (Priority)
Show Must Go On-Anthology . . . . (Rhino)

When Irish Eyes Are Smiling
Billy Shepherd Singers; *Irish Sing-Along* . . . . (MCA)
Bing Crosby; *When Irish Eyes Are Smiling* . . . . (MCA)
Dennis Day; *Irish Album* . . . . (RCA)

When Sunny Gets Blue
Barbra Streisand; *Simply Streisand* . . . . (Columbia)
Johnny Mathis; *First 25 Years-Silver Anniversary Album* . . . . (Columbia)
Johnny Mathis' All-Time Greatest Hits . . . . (Columbia)
Johnny Mathis' Greatest Hits . . . . (Columbia)
Johnny Mathis-Love Songs . . . . (Columbia)
Kenny Rankin; *The Kenny Rankin Album* . . . . (Little David)
Steve Miller; *Born 2 B Blue* . . . . (Gold Rush)

When The Lovelight Starts Shining Through His Eyes
Diana Ross & The Supremes; *Diana Ross & The Supremes' Greatest Hits* . . . . (Motown)
Diana Ross & The Supremes-Anthology (1962-1969) . . . . (Motown)
Motown Superstar Series-#1-Diana Ross & The Supremes . . . . . . (Motown)
Supremes; *Where Did Our Love Go* . . . . (Motown)

When You Close Your Eyes
Night Ranger; *Midnight Madness* . . . . (MCA)
Night Ranger's Greatest Hits . . . .(Camel)

When You Close Your Eyes
Carly Simon; *No Secrets* . . . . (Elektra)

When You Love A Woman
Journey; *Trial By Fire* . . . . (Columbia)

When You See The Tears From My Eyes
Buddy Guy; *Very Best Of Buddy Guy* . . . . (Rhino)
Buddy Guy & Junior Wells; *Drinkin' TNT 'N' Smokin' Dynamite* . . (Blind Pig)

Where The Blue Of The Night Meets The Gold Of The Day
Bing Crosby; *All-Time Best Of* . . . . (Curb)
Best Of Bing Crosby . . . . (MCA)
Where The Blue Of The Night Meets The Gold Of The Day . . . .(Biograph)

Wild Eyed Boy From Freecloud
David Bowie; *Sound + Vision* . . . . (Rykodisc)
Space Oddity . . . . (Rykodisc)
ST/Ziggy Stardust-The Motion Picture . . . . (Rykodisc)

Wild-Eyed Dream
Ricky Van Shelton; *Wild-Eyed Dream* . . . . (Columbia)

Wild-Eyed Gypsies
John Hiatt; *Hangin' Around The Observatory* . . . . (Epic)

Wild-Eyed Southern Boys
38 Special; *Wild-Eyed Southern Boys* . . . . (A&M)

Windy
Association; *Association Greatest Hits* . . . . (Warner Bros.)
Billboard Top Rock 'N' Roll Hits-1967-C . . . . (Rhino)
Summer Of Love-#1-C . . . . (Rhino)
Vintage Association . . . . (Fifty One West)
Wes Montgomery; *A Day In The Life* . . . . (A&M)
Wes Montgomery-Classics-#22 . . . . (A&M)

Wes Montgomery's Greatest Hits . . . . (A&M)

Wink
Neal McCoy; *No Doubt About It* . . . . (Atlantic)

With Just One Look In Your Eyes
Charly McClain & Wayne Massey; *19 Hot Country Requests-#3-C* . . . . . (Epic)
   Charly McClain's Biggest Hits . . . . (Epic)
   Radio Heart . . . . (Epic)
   Ten Year Anniversary . . . . (Epic)

With My Eyes Wide Open I'm Dreaming
Mandy Barnett; *I've Got A Right To Cry* . . . . (Sire)
Patti Page; *Patti Page-Golden Hits* . . . . (Mercury)
   Patti Page's Greatest Hits . . . . (Columbia)

Woke Up This Morning
A3; *Exile On Coldharbour Lane* . . . . (C2/Columbia)
   *The Sopranos-Music From The HBO Original
   Series* . . . . (Sony Music Soundtrax)

World In My Eyes
Depeche Mode; *Violator* . . . . (Sire)

You Can Close Your Eyes
James Taylor; *Mud Slide Slim And The Blue Horizon* . . . . (Warner Bros.)
Linda Ronstadt; *Heart Like A Wheel* . . . . (Capitol)

You Sang To Me
Marc Anthony; *Marc Anthony* . . . . (Columbia)

Your Eyes
Xscape; *Traces Of My Lipstick* . . . . (So So Def/Columbia)

You're Easy On The Eyes
Terri Clark; *Big Country Hits '99-C* . . . . (K-Tel)
   How I Feel . . . . (Mercury)

FABRICS, Denim, Lace, Leather
See Also: CLOTHES, HATS, RIBBONS, SHOES

Baa Baa Black Sheep
Original Soundtrack; *Toddler Favorites* . . . . (Kid Rhino/Rhino 4 Kids)

Baby Makes Her Blue Jeans Talk
Dr. Hook; *Players In The Dark* . . . . (Casablanca)

Baby's Got Her Blue Jeans On
Mel McDaniel; *All-Time Country Classics-#2-C* . . . . (Capitol)
   Let It Roll . . . . (Capitol)
   Mel McDaniel's Greatest Hits . . . . (Capitol)

Beggar In Blue Jeans
Rowans; *Rowans* . . . . (Asylum)

Between Blue Eyes And Jeans
Conway Twitty; *Don't Call Him A Cowboy* . . . . (Warner Bros.)

Black Denim Trousers & Motorcycle Boots
Cheers; *Monster Summer Hits-Drag City-C* . . . . (Capitol)

Black Velvet
Alannah Myles; *Alannah Myles* . . . . (Atlantic)
Robin Lee; *Black Velvet* . . . . (Atlantic)

Blue Jean Blues
Hank Williams, Jr.; *Strong Stuff* . . . . (Warner Bros.)
ZZ Top; *Best Of ZZ Top* . . . . (Warner Bros.)
   Fandango . . . . (Warner Bros.)
   Six Pack . . . . (Warner Bros.)

Blue Jean Boy
Michael Stanley Band; *Ladies' Choice* . . . . (Epic)

Blue Jeans
Chocolate Milk; *Greatest Grooves Of Chocolate Milk-Ice
   Cold Funk* . . . . (Razor & Tie)

Blue Suede Shoes
Carl Perkins; *Blue Suede Shoes* . . . . (Sun)
   Carl Perkins-Original Sun Greatest Hits . . . . (Rhino)
   Cruisin'-1956-1957-C . . . . (Dunhill Compact Classics)
   Oldies But Goodies-#4-C . . . . (Original Sound)
Elvis Presley; *Aloha from Hawaii via Satellite* . . . . (RCA)
   Elvis Presley . . . . (RCA)
   Elvis-A Legendary Performer, Volume 2 . . . . (RCA)
   From Memphis To Vegas/From Vegas To Memphis . . . . . (RCA)
   ST/G.I. Blues . . . . (RCA)

Blue Velvet
Bobby Vinton; *Bobby Vinton-16 Most Requested Songs* . . . . . . (Legacy)
   Bobby Vinton's All-Time Greatest Hits . . . . (Epic)
   Bobby Vinton's Greatest Hits/Greatest Hits Of Love . . . (Columbia)

Bluejean Bop
Gene Vincent and His Blue Caps; *Capitol Collectors Series-Gene Vincent
   and His Blue Caps* . . . . (Gold Rush)
   Gene Vincent and His Blue Caps' Greatest Hits . . . . (Curb)
   *The Screaming End-The Best Of Gene Vincent and His
   Blue Caps* . . . . (Razor & Tie)

Boy From New York City (mohair)
Ad-Libs; *Jewels-#1-C* . . . . (SSS International)
   Oldies But Goodies-#6-C . . . . (Original Sound)
   Original Golden Hits Of The Great Groups-#1-C . . . (SSS International)
   Original New York Rock & Roll-#1-C . . . . (SSS International)
Manhattan Transfer; *Best Of The Manhattan Transfer* . . . . . . (Atlantic)
   Mecca For Moderns . . . . (Atlantic)

Chantilly Lace
Big Bopper; *45s On CD-#1-1956-1959-C* . . . . (Mercury)
   Cruisin'-1958-C . . . . (Increase)
   Oldies But Goodies-#4-C . . . . (Original Sound)
   ST/American Graffiti . . . . (MCA)
Jerry Lee Lewis; *"Killer" Rocks On* . . . . (Mercury)
   Best Of Jerry Lee Lewis-#2 . . . . (Mercury)

Coat Of Many Colors
Dolly Parton; *Best Of Dolly Parton* . . . . (RCA)
   Dolly Parton-Super Hits . . . . (Columbia)
   Essential Dolly Parton-#2 . . . . (RCA)
Emmylou Harris; *Pieces Of The Sky* . . . . (Reprise)

Cotton Eyed Joe
Bob Wills; *Columbia Historic Edition-Bob Wills* . . . . (Columbia)
Carlton Moody & The Moody Brothers; *Carlton Moody & The Moody
   Brothers* . . . . (Lamon)

Cotton Fields
Creedence Clearwater Revival; *1969* . . . . (Fantasy)
   Willy & The Poor Boys . . . . (Fantasy)

Cotton Fields
Highwaymen; *"Michael Row The Boat Ashore"-Best Of The
   Highwaymen* . . . . (EMI)

Cotton Fields
Beach Boys; *Absolute Best-#2* . . . . (Capitol)
   Friends-20/20 . . . . (Capitol)

Cotton Fields
Pogues; *Peace & Love* . . . . (Island)

Cotton Mill Man
Jim & Jesse; *Old Dominion Masters* . . . . (Pinecastle)

Cotton Tail
Duke Ellington; *Reminiscing In Tempo* . . . . (Columbia)
Duke Ellington & Ella Fitzgerald; *Compact Jazz-Best Of The Big
   Bands-C* . . . . (Verve)
Lambert, Hendricks & Ross; *Twisted-Best Of Lambert, Hendricks
   & Ross* . . . . (Rhino)
Wes Montgomery; *Artistry Of Wes Montgomery* . . . . . . (Riverside)

Country In My Jeans
Loretta Lynn; *Still Country* . . . . (Audium)

For Emily, Wherever I May Find Her (Organdy, Crinoline)
Simon & Garfunkel; *Collected Works* . . . . (Columbia)
   Parsley Sage Rosemary & Thyme . . . . (Columbia)
   Simon & Garfunkel's Greatest Hits . . . . (Columbia)

Forever In Blue Jeans
Neil Diamond; *12 Greatest Hits-#2* . . . . (Columbia)
   Hot August Night II . . . . (Columbia)
   You Don't Bring Me Flowers . . . . (Columbia)

Leather & Lace
Stevie Nicks & Don Henley; *Bella Donna* . . . . (Modern)

Leather Boots
Alice Cooper; *Flush The Fashion* . . . . (Warner Bros.)

Leather Britches
John Hartford; *Aereo-Plain* . . . . (Warner Bros.)
Pete Sutherland; *Poor Man's Dream* . . . . (Flying Fish)

Leather Jacket
Mick Taylor; *Mick Taylor* . . . . (Columbia)

Makeup & Faded Blue Jeans
Merle Haggard; *Back To The Barrooms* . . . . (MCA)
   Country Classics-#4-1984-1985-C . . . . (Universal)
   Merle Haggard-His Best . . . . (MCA)

Mohair Sam
Derailers; *Here Come The Derailers* . . . . (Lucky Dog)

Pink Cashmere
Prince; *The Hits 1* . . . . (Paisley Park)
   The Hits/The B-Sides . . . . (Paisley Park)

Satin Doll
Carmen McRae; *Great American Songbook* . . . . (Atlantic)
Count Basie & His Orchestra; *Warm Breeze* . . . . (Pablo)
Duke Ellington; *1954 Los Angeles Concert* . . . . (Crescendo)
   Jazz Party . . . . (Legacy)
Harry James; *Golden Trumpet Of Harry James* . . . . (London)
Stephane Grappelli & Jean-Luc Ponty; *Stephane Grappelli & Jean-Luc
   Ponty* . . . . (Accord)
Stylistics; *All-Time Classics* . . . . (Amherst)

Satin Sheets
Jeannie Pruett; *16 Top Country Hits-#1-C* . . . . (MCA)
   Country Chart-Toppers . . . . (Dominion Entert.)
   Grand Ole Opry-75 Years-#2-C . . . . (MCA)
   MCA Records 30 Years Of Hits-1958-1988-C . . . . . . (MCA)
Shawn Colvin; *Cover Girl* . . . . (Columbia)

Silk Stockings
Dave McKenna; *Piano Scene Of Dave Mckenna* . . . . (Koch International)

Silky Sam
Spirit; *Time Circle* . . . . (Epic)

Silky Soul
Maze featuring Frankie Beverly; *Silky Soul* . . . . (Warner Bros.)

Theme From "Rawhide"
Blues Brothers; *Original Soundtrack* . . . . (Atlantic)
Frankie Laine; *CBS: The First 50 Years* . . . . (TVT)
   Cowboy Super Hits-C . . . . (Columbia)

Television's Greatest Hits-#2-C . . . . (TVT)
Riders In The Sky; *Cowboy Songs* . . . . (Rounder)
Venom Wearin' Denim
Junior Brown; *Semi Crazy* . . . . (Curb)
Venus In Blue Jeans
Jimmy Clanton; *All-Star Chartbusters* . . . . (Intermedia)
Golden Years-1962-C . . . . (Dominion Entert.)
Winding Of The Yarn, The
Al H. Wilson; *Music From The New York Stage (1890-1920)-#1-1890-
1908-C* . . . . (Pearl)

FAITH, Believing, Hope, Trust

See Also: **CHARACTER & INTEGRITY, GOD, HEAVEN, LOVE:
DEVOTION, MOTIVATION, OPTIMISM, TEACHING
VALUES, TRUTH**

(I Believe) Our Time Is Gonna Come
REO Speedwagon; *A Decade Of Rock And Roll 1970 To 1980* . . . . (Epic)
R.E.O. . . . . (Epic)
REO Speedwagon Live/You Get What You Play For . . . . (Epic)
...Baby One More Time
Britney Spears; *...Baby One More Time* . . . . (Jive)
Now That's What I Call Music!-#2-C . . . . (Virgin)
800 Pound Jesus
Sawyer Brown; *Drive Me Wild* . . . . (Curb)
Affirmation
Savage Garden; *Affirmation* . . . . (Columbia)
Alfie
Barbra Streisand; *What About Today* . . . . (Columbia)
Dionne Warwick; *Dionne Warwick Greatest Hits* . . . . (Everest)
Dionne Warwick-Anthology 1962-1971 . . . . (Rhino)
All Things Must Pass
George Harrison; *All Things Must Pass* . . . . (Parlophone)
America, I Believe In You
Charlie Daniels; *America, I Believe In You* . . . . (Liberty)
Angel
Sarah McLachlan; *Mirrorball* . . . . (Arista)
ST/City Of Angels . . . . (Warner Sunset/Reprise)
Surfacing . . . . (Arista)
Totally Hits-#1-C . . . . (Arista)
Angels
Robbie Williams; *The Egg Has Landed* . . . . (Capitol)
At The Same Time
Barbra Streisand; *Higher Ground* . . . . (Columbia)
Away
Toadies; *Rubberneck* . . . . (Interscope)
Baby Hold On
Eddie Money; *Eddie Money* . . . . (Columbia)
Eddie Money's Greatest Hits-Sound Of Money . . . . (Columbia)
Badlands
Bruce Springsteen; *Bruce Springsteen's Greatest Hits* . . . . (Columbia)
Darkness On The Edge Of Town . . . . (Columbia)
Bruce Springsteen & The E Street Band; *Bruce Springsteen & The E Street
Band Live/1975-85* . . . . (Legacy)
Because You Loved Me
Celine Dion; *All The Way...A Decade Of Song* . . . . (550 Music)
Diana, Princess Of Wales-Tribute-C . . . . (Columbia)
Falling Into You . . . . (550 Music)
Believe
Lenny Kravitz; *Are You Gonna Go My Way* . . . . (Virgin)
Believe
Elton John; *Elton John-Love Songs* . . . . (MCA)
Made In England . . . . (Rocket)
Believe
Cher; *Believe* . . . . (Warner Bros.)
Totally Hits-#1-C . . . . (Arista)
Believe
Dig; *Dig* . . . . (Radioactive/MCA)
Believe In Me
Eric Clapton; *Reptile* . . . . (Duck/Reprise)
Believe In You
Jude Cole; *I Don't Know Why I Act This Way* . . . . (Island)
Believe In Yourself
Lena Horne; *ST/The Wiz* . . . . (MCA)
Believe What You Say
Rick Nelson; *Rick Nelson In Concert-Troubadour 1969* . . . . (MCA)
Ricky Nelson; *Ricky Nelson Volume I* . . . . (Gold Rush)
Ricky Nelson's All Time Greatest Hits . . . . (Curb)
Rock This Town-Rockabilly Hits-#1-C . . . . (Rhino)
Beyond The Blue Horizon
Jeanette MacDonald; *Hollywood Sings-C* . . . . (Living Era)
Lou Christie; *ST/Rain Man* . . . . (Capitol)
Blessed Are The Believers
Anne Murray; *Anne Murray-Country Hits* . . . . (Capitol)
Anne Murray's Greatest Hits-#2 . . . . (Capitol)

Camera One
Josh Joplin Group; *Useful Music* . . . . (Artemis)
Can I Count On You
McBride & The Ride; *Burnin' Up The Road* . . . . (MCA)
Can I Trust You With My Heart
Travis Tritt; *T-R-O-U-B-L-E* . . . . (Warner Bros.)
Can't Take That Away (Mariah's Theme)
Mariah Carey; *Rainbow* . . . . (Columbia)
Can'tcha Say (You Believe In Me)
Boston; *Third Stage* . . . . (MCA)
Caravan Of Love
Isley, Jasper, Isley; *Caravan Of Love* . . . . (CBS Associated)
**Child Should Live Forever (Theme For The Eddie Cantor Fund For
Children With AIDS)**
Original Off-Broadway Cast; *A Hard Time To Be Single* . . . . (Original Cast)
Circle Of Life
Elton John; *Elton John-Love Songs* . . . . (MCA)
ST/The Lion King . . . . (Walt Disney)
Original Cast; *The Lion King* . . . . (Disney)
Climb Ev'ry Mountain
Mormon Tabernacle Choir; *Climb Ev'ry Mountain* . . . . (Columbia)
Original Cast/Mary Martin; *The Sound Of Music* . . . . (Sony Broadway)
Trapp Family Singers; *The Sound Of Music* . . . . (Warner Bros.)
Cockeyed Optimist
Mitzi Gaynor; *ST/South Pacific* . . . . (RCA)
Original Cast; *South Pacific* . . . . (CBS Masterworks)
Comin' In On A Wing & A Prayer
Anita Ellis; *Songs That Won The War-C* . . . . . . (Columbia River Entert. Group)
Anne Shelton; *V-E Day 50th Anniversary-The Musical
Memories-C* . . . . (Living Era)
Four Vagabonds; *The Victory Collection: The Smithsonian Remembers When
America Went To War-C* . . . . (RCA)
Ry Cooder; *Boomer's Story* . . . . (Reprise)
Coming Out Of The Dark
Gloria Estefan; *Gloria Estefan's Greatest Hits* . . . . (Epic)
God Bless America-C . . . . (Columbia)
Hot #1 Hits-C . . . . (Foundation)
Into The Light . . . . (Epic)
Conviction Of The Heart
Kenny Loggins; *Leap Of Faith* . . . . (Columbia)
Outside: From The Redwoods . . . . (Columbia)
*Yesterday, Today, Tomorrow: The Greatest Hits Of Kenny
Loggins* . . . . (Columbia)
Count On Me
Whitney Houston and CeCe Winans; *ST/Waiting To Exhale* . . . . (Arista)
Crazy Faith
Alison Krauss & Union Station; *New Favorite* . . . . (Rounder)
Crying, Waiting, Hoping
Buddy Holly; *Buddy Holly Collection* . . . . (MCA)
Marshall Crenshaw; *ST/La Bamba* . . . . (Slash)
Cupid
112; *112.* . . . . (Bad Boy/Arista)
Dance Little Sister
Terence Trent D'Arby; *Introducing The Hardline According To Terence
Trent D'Arby* . . . . (Columbia)
Dance With The One That Brought You
Shania Twain; *Shania Twain* . . . . (Mercury)
Daydream Believer
Anne Murray; *Anne Murray's Greatest Hits* . . . . (Capitol)
I'll Always Love You . . . . (Capitol)
Monkees; *Billboard Top Rock 'N' Roll Hits-1967-C* . . . . (Rhino)
Mellow '60s-C . . . . (Priority)
Monkees' Greatest Hits . . . . (Rhino)
Dear God
XTC; *Best Of MTV's 120 Minutes-#1-C* . . . . (Rhino)
Skylarking . . . . (Geffen)
Upsy Daisy Assortment . . . . (Geffen)
Depend On Me
Bryan Adams; *Waking Up The Neighbours* . . . . (A&M)
Devil In Her Heart
Beatles; *The Beatles' Second Album* . . . . (Capitol)
With The Beatles . . . . (Parlophone)
Donays; *Beatles Originals* . . . . (Rhino)
Do You Believe In Magic
Lovin' Spoonful; *Lovin' Spoonful-Anthology* . . . . (Rhino)
Do You Believe In Us?
Jon Secada; *Jon Secada* . . . . (SBK)
Don't Believe A Word
Thin Lizzy; *'Life'-Live* . . . . (Warner Bros.)
Live And Dangerous . . . . (Warner Bros.)
Lizzy Lives! (1976-1984) . . . . (Gland Slamm)
Don't Give Up
Peter Gabriel; *Shaking The Tree-Sixteen Golden Greats* . . . . (Geffen)
So . . . . (Geffen)
Don't Go Breaking My Heart
Elton John & Kiki Dee; *Elton John's Greatest Hits-#2* . . . . (Polydor)
Don't Let Me Leave
Marc Anthony; *Marc Anthony* . . . . (Columbia)

Don't Let The Sun Catch You Crying
Gerry And The Pacemakers; *Best Of Gerry And The Pacemakers* . . . . (EMI)
Gerry And The Pacemakers' Greatest Hits . . . . (Laurie)
History Of British Rock-#1-C . . . . (Rhino)
Super Oldies Of The '60s-#5-C . . . . (Audio Fidelity)
Louis Jordan; *Best Of Louis Jordan* . . . . (MCA)
Ray Charles; *Genius Of Ray Charles* . . . . (Atlantic)
Rickie Lee Jones; *Flying Cowboys* . . . . (Geffen)
Don't Stop Believin'
Olivia Newton-John; *Olivia Newton-John's Greatest Hits* . . . . (MCA)
Physical . . . . (MCA)
Don't Stop Believin'
Journey; *Escape* . . . . (Columbia)
Journey's Greatest Hits . . . . (Columbia)
Down So Long
Jewel; *Spirit* . . . . (Atlantic)
Dream Is A Wish Your Heart Makes
Barbara Cook; *Disney Album* . . . . (Disney)
Linda Ronstadt; *Disney's Music From The Park-C* . . . . (Disney)
Music Of Disney's Cinderella-C . . . . (Disney)
Michael Bolton; *Simply Mad About The Mouse-C* . . . . (Columbia)
Original Soundtrack; *ST/Cinderella* . . . . (Disney)
Dreamer
Ozzy Osbourne; *Down To Earth* . . . . (Epic)
Eighteen Wheels And A Dozen Roses
Kathy Mattea; *Collection Of Hits* . . . . (Mercury)
Untasted Honey . . . . (Polydor Country)
Everyday
Buddy Holly; *Buddy Holly* . . . . (MCA)
Buddy Holly-20 Golden Greats . . . . (MCA)
Buddy Holly's Greatest Hits . . . . (MCA)
From The Original Master Tapes-Buddy Holly . . . . (MCA)
Legend-From The Original Master Tapes . . . . (MCA)
The Buddy Holly Collection . . . . (MCA)
Everywhere
Michelle Branch; *The Spirit Room* . . . . (Maverick)
Faith
George Michael; *Faith* . . . . (Columbia)
Faith In Me
Crosby, Stills, Nash & Young; *Looking Forward* . . . . (Reprise)
Faith In Me, Faith In You
Doug Stone; *Country Lovin'-Songs From The Heart-C* . . . . (Rhino)
Faith In Me Faith In You . . . . (Columbia)
Super Hits Of 1995-C . . . . (Epic)
Faith In You
Steve Wariner; *Faith In You* . . . . (Capitol)
Faith Of The Heart
Rod Stewart; *ST/Patch Adams* . . . . (Universal)
Faithful
Go West; *Indian Summer* . . . . (EMI)
Faithfull
Pearl Jam; *Yield* . . . . (Epic)
Fall From Grace
Amanda Marshall; *Amanda Marshall* . . . . (Epic)
Flood
Jars Of Clay; *Jars Of Clay* . . . . (Silvertone)
*Where Music Meets Film: Live From The Sundance Film
Festival-C* . . . . (Beyond)
Fly (The Angel Song)
Wilkinsons; *Nothing But Love* . . . . (Giant)
Free To Go
Folk Implosion; *One Part Lullaby* . . . . (Interscope)
From A Distance
Bette Midler; *Some People's Lives* . . . . (Atlantic)
Byrds; *20 Essential Tracks From The Box Set* . . . . (Columbia)
The Byrds . . . . (Columbia)
Judy Collins; *Fires Of Eden* . . . . (Columbia)
Kathy Mattea; *Time Passes By* . . . . (Mercury)
Nanci Griffith; *Lone Star State Of Mind* . . . . (MCA)
One Fair Summer Evening . . . . (MCA)
From The Ashes
Rosanne Cash; *The Wheel* . . . . (Columbia)
Give Me Wings
Michael Johnson; *Best Of Michael Johnson* . . . . (RCA)
Hits Of '86-C . . . . (RCA)
Wings . . . . (RCA)
Giving You The Benefit
Pebbles; *Always* . . . . (MCA)
Goodbye Lament
Iommi; *Iommi* . . . . (Divine/Priority)
Graceland
Paul Simon; *Graceland* . . . . (Warner Bros.)
Great White Hope
Styx; *Pieces Of Eight* . . . . (A&M)
Green, Green
New Christy Minstrels; *New Christy Minstrels' Greatest Hits* . . . (Columbia)
Hands
Jewel; *Spirit* . . . . (Atlantic)

Hard Way, The
Mary Chapin Carpenter; *Come On Come On* . . . . (Columbia)
Hatikvah
Barbra Streisand & Golda Meir; *Just For The Record* . . . . (Columbia)
Mormon Tabernacle Choir; *This Is My Country* . . . . (Columbia)
Help Me Hold On
Travis Tritt; *Country Club* . . . . (Warner Bros.)
Helplessly Hoping
Crosby, Stills & Nash; *Crosby, Stills & Nash* . . . . (Atlantic)
CSN . . . . (Atlantic)
Crosby, Stills, Nash & Young; *So Far* . . . . (Atlantic)
Higher
Creed; *Human Clay* . . . . (Wind-up)
Higher Ground
Barbra Streisand; *Higher Ground* . . . . (Columbia)
His Eye Is On The Sparrow
Carmen McRae; *Greatest Of Carmen McRae* . . . . (MCA)
Marvin Gaye; *Musical Testament 1964-1984* . . . . (Motown)
Preservation Hall Jazz Band; *Best Of The Preservation Hall
Jazz Band* . . . . (Columbia)
Soundtrack; *Streetcar Named Desire* . . . . (Allegiance)
Hold On
Triumph; *Just A Game* . . . . (RCA)
Stages . . . . (MCA)
Triumph-Classics . . . . (MCA)
Hold On
En Vogue; *Born To Sing* . . . . (Atlantic)
Hold On
John Lennon; *Lennon* . . . . (Capitol)
John Lennon/Plastic Ono Band; *John Lennon/Plastic Ono Band* . . . . . (Capitol)
Hold On
John Conlee; *Rose Colored Glasses* . . . . (Universal)
Hold On
Steve Winwood; *Steve Winwood* . . . . (Island)
Hold On
Wilson Phillips; *Wilson Phillips* . . . . (SBK)
Hold On (Change Is Comin')
Sounds Of Blackness; *Time For Healing* . . . . (Perspective/A&M)
Holdin'
Diamond Rio; *Diamond Rio IV* . . . . (Arista)
Diamond Rio's Greatest Hits . . . . (Arista)
Hollywood Hopeful
Loudon Wainwright III; *Live One* . . . . (Rounder)
T-Shirt . . . . (Arista)
Hooked On A Feeling
B.J. Thomas; *Best Of B.J. Thomas* . . . . (Hollywood/DNA-Rounder)
Vonda Shepard; *ST/Songs From "Ally McBeal" Featuring Vonda
Shepard* . . . . (550/Epic)
Hope In A Hopeless World
Widespread Panic; *Bombs & Butterflies* . . . . (Capricorn)
Hope You Love Me Like You Say You Do
Huey Lewis and the News; *Picture This* . . . . (Chrysalis)
House Of Love
Amy Grant & Vince Gill; *House Of Love* . . . . (A&M)
I Believe
Elvis Presley; *Amazing Grace-His Greatest Sacred Performances* . . . . . (RCA)
Frankie Laine; *Frankie Laine-16 Most Requested Songs* . . . . (Legacy)
Frankie Laine's Greatest Hits . . . . (Columbia)
Jo Stafford; *You'll Never Walk Alone* . . . . (CEMA Special Prod.)
I Believe
Blessid Union Of Souls; *Home* . . . . (EMI)
I Believe
Robert Plant; *Fate Of Nations* . . . . (Es Paranza)
I Believe I Can Fly
R. Kelly; *1998 Grammy Nominees-C* . . . . (MCA)
R. . . . . (Jive)
ST/Space Jam . . . . (Warner Sunset)
I Believe In Father Christmas
Greg Lake; *Emerson Lake & Palmer-Works-#2* . . . . (Atlantic)
I Believe In Love
Paula Cole Band; *Amen* . . . . (Warner Bros.)
I Believe In Love
Dixie Chicks; *America: A Tribute To Heroes-C* . . . . (Interscope)
I Believe In Santa's Cause
Statler Brothers; *Statler Brothers Christmas Present* . . . . (Mercury)
I Believe In You
Don Williams; *Best Of Don Williams-#3* . . . . (MCA)
Don Williams-Legends . . . . (MCA)
I Believe In You . . . . (MCA)
MCA Records 30 Years Of Hits-1958-1988-C . . . . (MCA)
Mel Tillis; *Very Best Of Mel Tillis* . . . . (MCA)
I Believe In You
Bob Dylan; *Biograph* . . . . (Columbia)
Slow Train Coming . . . . (Columbia)
I Believe In You
Original Cast; *How To Succeed In Business Without Really Trying* . . . . . (RCA)
I Believe In You And Me
Whitney Houston; *ST/The Preacher's Wife* . . . . (Arista)

I Believe In You And Me
Four Tops; *Smooth Grooves-Weddings Songs-C* . . . . (Rhino)
When She Was My Girl . . . . (Casablanca)
I Can't Wait To Meetchu
Macy Gray; *On How Life Is* . . . .(Epic)
I Cross My Heart
George Strait; *ST/Pure Country* . . . .(MCA)
I Disappear
Metallica; *ST/Mission: Impossible 2* . . . . (Hollywood)
I Don't Believe In Goodbye
Sawyer Brown; *Sawyer Brown's Greatest Hits 1990-1995* . . . . (Curb)
I Hope You Dance
Lee Ann Womack; *I Hope You Dance* . . . .(MCA)
I Need You
LeAnn Rimes; *ST/Jesus-The Epic Mini-Series* . . . . (Sparrow/Curb/Capitol)
I Shall Not Be Moved
Charley Patton; *King Of The Delta Blues: The Music Of Charley
    Patton* . . . . (Yazoo)
Mississippi John Hurt; *Best Of Mississippi John Hurt* . . . . (Vanguard)
Pops Staples; *Best Blues Album In The World...Ever!-C* . . . . (Virgin)
I Still Believe
Brenda K. Starr; *Brenda K. Starr* . . . .(MCA Special Prod.)
I Still Believe
Mariah Carey; *Mariah Carey-#1's* . . . . (Columbia)
MTV Unplugged-Mariah Carey . . . . (Columbia)
I Still Believe
Crystal Lewis & Kirk Franklin; *Touched By An Angel-The Christmas
    Album* . . . . (550 Music)
I Still Believe In Waltzes
Conway Twitty & Loretta Lynn; *16 Top Country Hits-#4-C* . . . .(MCA)
I Still Believe In You
Vince Gill; *I Still Believe In You* . . . .(MCA)
I Swear
All-4-One; *All-4-One* . . . . (Blitzz)
John Michael Montgomery; *John Michael Montgomery's
    Greatest Hits* . . . . (Atlantic)
Kickin' It Up . . . . (Atlantic)
I Will Get There
Boyz II Men; *ST/The Prince Of Egypt-Inspirational* . . . . . . (DreamWorks/SKG)
If I Ever Lose My Faith In You
Sting; *Fields Of Gold-The Best Of Sting 1984-1994* . . . . (A&M)
Ten Summoner's Tales . . . . (A&M)
If We Fall In Love Tonight
Rod Stewart; *If We Fall In Love Tonight* . . . .(Warner Bros.)
If You Believe
Jim Brickman; *By Heart-Piano Solos* . . . . (Windham Hill)
Windham Hill Records Sampler-96-C . . . . (Windham Hill)
If You've Got Love
John Michael Montgomery; *Kickin' It Up* . . . . (Atlantic)
I'll Be
Reba McEntire; *So Good Together* . . . .(MCA)
I'll Be All Right
Jorma Kaukonen & Tom Hobson; *Quah* . . . . (Relix)
I'll Be Missing You
Puff Daddy & Family & Faith Evans & 112; *No Way Out* . . . . . (Bad Boy/Arista)
I'll Stand By You
Pretenders; *Last Of The Independents* . . . . (Sire)
I'm A Believer
Monkees; *Billboard Top Rock 'N' Roll Hits-1966-C* . . . . (Rhino)
Monkees' Greatest Hits . . . . (Rhino)
More Of The Monkees . . . . (Rhino)
Oldies But Goodies-#3-C . . . . (Original Sound)
Neil Diamond; *Live In America* . . . . (Columbia)
Neil Diamond's Greatest Hits-1966-1992 . . . . (Columbia)
September Morn . . . . (Columbia)
Smash Mouth; *Now That's What I Call Music!-#8-C* . . . . (Virgin)
ST/Shrek . . . . (Interscope)
I'm On Your Side
Jennifer Holliday; *I'm On Your Side* . . . . (Arista)
I'm Putting All My Eggs In One Basket
Carmen McRae; *Greatest Of Carmen McRae* . . . .(MCA)
Fred Astaire; *Irving Berlin Songbook* . . . . (Verve)
Irving Berlin; *American Songbook Series-Irving
    Berlin* . . . .(Smithsonian Collection)
I'm Your Angel
Celine Dion & R. Kelly; *All The Way...A Decade Of Song* . . . . (550 Music)
These Are Special Times . . . . (550 Music)
R. Kelly & Celine Dion; *R.* . . . . (Jive)
Imagine That
Diamond Rio; *Diamond Rio's Greatest Hits* . . . . (Arista)
Impossible Dream
Andy Williams; *Andy Williams' Greatest Hits-#2* . . . . (Columbia)
Andy Williams-16 Most Requested Songs . . . . (Legacy)
Impossible Dream . . . . (Columbia)
Ed Ames; *Best Of Ed Ames* . . . . (RCA)
Ed Ames-Pure Gold . . . . (RCA)
Impossible Dream . . . . (RCA)
This Is Ed Ames . . . . (RCA)

Jack Jones; *Best Of Jack Jones* . . . . (MCA)
Kate Smith; *Best Of Kate Smith* . . . .(RCA)
Kate Smith-Legendary Performer . . . . (RCA)
Luther Vandross; *Songs* . . . . (Epic)
Original London Cast; *Man Of La Mancha* . . . . (MCA)
Robert Goulet; *Robert Goulet's Greatest Hits* . . . . (Columbia)
In The Heat Of The Night
Ray Charles; *Ray Charles-His Greatest Hits-#2* . . . . (Dunhill Compact Classics)
ST/In The Heat Of The Night . . . . (United Artists)
In The House Of Stone And Light
Martin Page; *In The House Of Stone And Light* . . . . (Mercury)
In Times Like These
Barbara Mandrell; *Barbara Mandrell's Greatest Hits* . . . . (MCA)
Spun Gold . . . . (MCA)
Infinite Eyes
Keb' Mo'; *Big Wide Grin* . . . . (Sony Wonder)
It's Only A Paper Moon
Art Blakey & His Jazz Messengers; *Big Beat* . . . .(Blue Note)
Bing Crosby; *The Radio Years-#2* . . . .(Crescendo)
David Rose & His Orchestra; *Music Of The 1930s-C* . . . . (MCA)
Ella Fitzgerald; *Harold Arlen Songbook-#2* . . . . (Verve)
Frank Sinatra; *Round #1* . . . . (Capitol)
Mystics; *Mystics-16 Golden Classics* . . . . (Collectables)
Nat ''King'' Cole; *Capitol Sings Harold Arlen: Over The
    Rainbow-C* . . . . (Gold Rush)
The Nat ''King'' Cole Story . . . . (Capitol)
Sammy Kaye & His Orchestra; *Sammy Kaye & His Orchestra Play 22
    Original Big Band Recordings* . . . . (Hindsight)
Just The Two Of Us
Grover Washington, Jr. & Bill Withers; *Billboard Top R&B Hits-
    1981-C* . . . . (Rhino)
Grover Washington, Jr.-*Anthology* . . . . (Elektra)
Grover Washington, Jr.-*Winelight* . . . . (Elektra)
Keep It Between The Lines
Ricky Van Shelton; *Backroads* . . . . (Columbia)
Keep It Together
Madonna; *Like A Prayer* . . . .(Sire)
Keep Smiling At Trouble
Al Jolson; *Rainbow 'Round My Shoulder* . . . .(MCA Special Prod.)
Tony Bennett; *Forty Years-The Artistry Of Tony Bennett* . . . . (Columbia)
Keep The Faith
Bon Jovi; *Keep The Faith* . . . . (Mercury)
Keep The Faith
Michael Jackson; *Dangerous* . . . . (Epic)
Keep The Faith, Baby
Tony Bennett with k.d. lang; *Playin' With My Friends-Bennett Sings The
    Blues-C* . . . . (Columbia)
Keep Tryin'
Groove Theory; *Groove Theory* . . . . (Epic)
Land Of Hope And Dreams
Bruce Springsteen & The E Street Band; *God Bless America-C* . . . . . (Columbia)
Live In New York City . . . . (Columbia)
Leading With Your Heart
Barbra Streisand; *Higher Ground* . . . . (Columbia)
Leap Of Faith
Bruce Springsteen; *Lucky Town* . . . . (Columbia)
Leap Of Faith
Lionel Cartwright; *Chasin' The Sun* . . . . (MCA)
Leap Of Faith
Kenny Loggins; *Leap Of Faith* . . . . (Columbia)
Lessons To Be Learned
Barbra Streisand; *Higher Ground* . . . . (Columbia)
Light In Your Eyes
LeAnn Rimes; *Blue* . . . . (MCG/Curb)
Like A River To The Sea
Steve Wariner; *I Am Ready* . . . . (Arista)
Little White Cloud That Cried
Johnnie Ray; *Best Of Johnnie Ray* . . . . (Columbia)
Best Of Johnnie Ray . . . . (Exact)
Johnnie Ray's Greatest Hits . . . . (Sony Music Special Prod.)
Livin' On A Prayer
Bon Jovi; *America: A Tribute To Heroes-C* . . . .(Interscope)
Cross Road-14 Classic Grooves . . . . (Mercury)
Slippery When Wet . . . . (Jambco)
The Concert For New York City-C . . . . (Columbia)
Long December
Counting Crows; *Recovering The Satellites* . . . . (David Geffen Co.)
Look For The Silver Lining
Alberta Hunter; *Look For The Silver Lining* . . . . (Columbia)
Chet Baker; *Let's Get Lost-Best Of Chet Baker Sings* . . . . (Blue Note)
Dave Brubeck Quartet; *Stardust* . . . . (Fantasy)
Judy Garland; *Best Of Judy Garland In Hollywood* . . . . (Turner Classic Movies)
Marion Harris; *78-#3367* . . . . (Columbia)
Look What Love Has Done
Patty Smyth; *ST/Junior* . . . . (MCA)
Lord I Hope This Day Is Good
Don Williams; *Best Of Don Williams-#3* . . . . (MCA)
Especially For You . . . . (MCA)
Lee Ann Womack; *Grand Ole Opry-75 Years-#1-C* . . . . (MCA)

Love Can Move Mountains
Celine Dion; *All The Way...A Decade Of Song* . . . . (550 Music)
Celine Dion . . . . (Epic)
Love Will Find A Way
Sam Cooke; *The Man And His Music* . . . . (RCA)
This Is Sam Cooke . . . . (RCA)
Love Will Find A Way
Lionel Richie; *Can't Slow Down* . . . . (Motown)
Love Will Find A Way
George Howard; *Dancing In The Sun* . . . . (GRP)
Love Will Find A Way
Pablo Cruise; *Worlds Away* . . . . (A&M)
Love Will Find A Way
Yes; *Big Generator* . . . . (Atco)
Love Will Find A Way
Christina Aguilera; *Christina Aguilera* . . . . (RCA)
Make Me Believe
Martina McBride; *Emotion* . . . . (RCA)
Make You A Believer
Sass Jordan; *Racine* . . . . (Impact)
Man Of My Word
Collin Raye; *Extremes* . . . . (Epic)
Man On The Moon
R.E.M.; *Automatic For The People* . . . . (Warner Bros.)
May It Be
Enya; *ST/The Lord Of The Rings* . . . . (Reprise)
May This Be Love
Emmylou Harris; *Wrecking Ball* . . . . (Asylum)
Jimi Hendrix; *Are You Experienced?* . . . . (Reprise)
Me Wise Magic
Van Halen; *Best Of Van Halen-#1* . . . . (Warner Bros.)
Mind Games
John Lennon; *Mind Games* . . . . (Capitol)
John Lennon/Plastic Ono Band; *Shaved Fish* . . . . (Capitol)
Miracle Of Love
Eileen Rodgers; *Hard To Find 45s On CD-#3-The Mid '50s-C* . . . . . . (Eric)
My Sacrifice
Creed; *Weathered* . . . . (Wind-up)
Never Gonna Let You Down
Surface; *3 Deep* . . . . (Columbia)
Best Of Surface...A Nice Time 4 Lovin' . . . . (Columbia)
Nice Work If You Can Get It
Billie Holiday; *Compact Jazz-Billie Holiday* . . . . (Verve)
Carmen McRae; *Greatest Of Carmen McRae* . . . . (MCA)
Ella Fitzgerald; *George & Ira Gershwin Songbook* . . . . (Verve)
Frank Sinatra; *My Kind Of Broadway* . . . . (Reprise)
Original Cast; *My One And Only* . . . . (Atlantic)
Sting; *Glory Of Gershwin Featuring Larry Adler-C* . . . . (Mercury)
No Fear
Terri Clark; *Fearless* . . . . (Mercury)
No More, No Less
Collective Soul; *Dosage* . . . . (Atlantic)
No One
Marc Anthony; *Marc Anthony* . . . . (Columbia)
None Of Ur Friends Business
Ginuwine; *100 Percent Ginuwine* . . . . (550 Music)
Obviously Five Believers
Bob Dylan; *Blonde On Blonde* . . . . (Columbia)
On The Side Of Angels
LeAnn Rimes; *You Light Up My Life-Inspirational Songs* . . . . (Curb)
One Belief Away
Bonnie Raitt; *Fundamental* . . . . (Capitol)
One More Try
George Michael; *Faith* . . . . (Columbia)
One Voice
Billy Gilman; *One Voice* . . . . (Epic)
Only Trust Your Heart
Diana Krall; *Only Trust Your Heart* . . . . (GRP)
Ooh Child
Dino; *The Way I Am* . . . . (East West)
Peace In The Valley
Elvis Presley; *A Golden Celebration* . . . . (RCA)
Elvis-A Legendary Performer, Volume 1 . . . . (RCA)
Million-Dollar Quartet . . . . (RCA)
Johnny Cash; *At San Quentin* . . . . (Columbia)
Classic Cash-Hall Of Fame Series . . . . (Mercury)
J.L. Lewis/Carl Perkins-The Survivors* . . . . (Columbia)
Red Foley; *Grand Ole Opry-75 Years-#1-C* . . . . (MCA)
Place In The Sun
Stevie Wonder; *Looking Back* . . . . (Motown)
Stevie Wonder's Greatest Hits . . . . (Motown)
Poor Side Of Town
Johnny Rivers; *Best Of Johnny Rivers* . . . . (EMI)
Changes/Rewind . . . . (EMI)
Johnny Rivers-Anthology 1964-1977 . . . . (Rhino)
Very Best Of Johnny Rivers . . . . (EMI)
Precious Declaration
Collective Soul; *Disciplined Breakdown* . . . . (Atlantic)

Prisoner Of Hope
Johnny Lee; *Johnny Lee's Greatest Hits* . . . . (Full Moon/Asylum)
Promise
Jagged Edge; *J.E. Heartbreak* . . . . (So So Def/Columbia)
Promised Land
Bruce Springsteen; *Darkness On The Edge Of Town* . . . . (Columbia)
Bruce Springsteen & The E Street Band; *Bruce Springsteen & The E Street
   Band Live/1975-85* . . . . (Legacy)
Put Your Hand In The Hand
Anne Murray; *Anne Murray-Country* . . . . (Capitol)
Danny's Song . . . . (Capitol)
Snowbird . . . . (Capitol)
Elvis Presley; *Canadian Tribute* . . . . (RCA)
Elvis Now . . . . (RCA)
Ocean; *Super Hits Of The '70s-Have A Nice Day-#4-C* . . . . (Rhino)
Rainbow (Interlude)
Mariah Carey; *Rainbow* . . . . (Columbia)
Reach Out I'll Be There
Four Tops; *Compact Command Performances-Four Tops* . . . . (Motown)
Four Tops' Greatest Hits . . . . (Motown)
Four Tops Reach Out . . . . (Motown)
Four Tops-Anthology . . . . (Motown)
Motown Dance Party-#2-C . . . . (Motown)
Reason To Believe
Rod Stewart; *Best Of Rod Stewart-#2* . . . . (Mercury)
Every Picture Tells A Story . . . . (Mercury)
Sing It Again, Rod . . . . (Mercury)
Storyteller/The Complete Anthology: 1964-1990 . . . . (Warner Bros.)
Unplugged...And Seated . . . . (Warner Bros.)
Reason To Believe
Bruce Springsteen; *Nebraska* . . . . (Columbia)
Bruce Springsteen & The E Street Band; *Bruce Springsteen & The E Street
   Band Live/1975-85* . . . . (Legacy)
Remember Me This Way
Jordan Hill; *Jordan Hill* . . . . (Atlantic)
ST/Casper . . . . (MCA)
Resignation Superman
Big Head Todd & The Monsters; *Beautiful World* . . . . (Revolution)
Live Monsters . . . . (Revolution)
Right Beside You
Sophie B. Hawkins; *Whaler* . . . . (Columbia)
Right Here Waiting
Richard Marx; *Chicken Soup For The Woman's Soul-C* . . . . (Rhino)
Repeat Offender . . . . (EMI)
Run Away
Real McCoy; *Another Night* . . . . (Arista)
Running On Faith
Eric Clapton; *Eric Clapton-Unplugged* . . . . (Reprise)
Seeing Is Believing
Three O'Clock; *Sixteen Tambourines* . . . . (Frontier)
Seeing Is Believing
Bobby King & Terry Evans; *Live & Let Live* . . . . (Rounder)
Seeing Is Believing
Mike & The Mechanics; *Living Years* . . . . (Atlantic)
She Believes In Me
Kenny Rogers; *Kenny Rogers-20 Great Years* . . . . (Reprise)
She Is His Only Need
Wynonna; *Wynonna* . . . . (MCA)
Wynonna-Collection . . . . (Curb)
Sick Of Myself
Matthew Sweet; *100% Fun* . . . . (Zoo)
Simple Creed
Live; *V* . . . . (Radioactive/MCA)
Sinner
Neil Finn; *Try Whistling This* . . . . (Work)
Sitting In Limbo
Jimmy Cliff; *ST/The Harder They Come* . . . . (Mango)
ST/The Harder They Come . . . . (Mango)
Somebody's Out There Watching
Kinleys; *Kinleys II* . . . . (Epic)
Someday
All-4-One; *ST/The Hunchback Of Notre Dame* . . . . (Disney)
Someday Out Of The Blue
Elton John; *ST/The Road To El Dorado* . . . . (DreamWorks/SKG)
Someday We'll All Be Free
Alicia Keys; *America: A Tribute To Heroes-C* . . . . (Interscope)
Donny Hathaway; *Best Of Donny Hathaway* . . . . (Atco)
James Ingram; *It's Real* . . . . (Warner Bros.)
Something
Beatles; *Abbey Road* . . . . (Parlophone)
Beatles 1 . . . . (Capitol)
The Beatles/1967-1970 . . . . (Capitol)
The Beatles-Anthology-#3 . . . . (Capitol)
Something To Believe In
Clannad; *Sirius* . . . . (RCA)
Clannad & Bruce Hornsby; *Past Present* . . . . (RCA)
Something To Believe In
Bangles; *Everything* . . . . (Columbia)

Something To Believe In
Hank Williams, Jr.; *Five-O* . . . . (WB/Curb)
Something To Believe In
Steve Miller Band; *The Joker* . . . . (Capitol)
Something To Believe In
Poison; *Flesh & Blood* . . . . (Capitol)
  Swallow This Live . . . . (Capitol)
Somewhere
Aretha Franklin; *Aretha's Jazz* . . . . (Rhino)
Barbra Streisand; *The Broadway Album* . . . . (Columbia)
Dave Brubeck; *Music From West Side Story* . . . . (Columbia)
Jose Carreras; *Amigos Para Siempre-Friends For Life* . . . . (Atlantic)
Original Cast; *ST/West Side Story* . . . . (Sony Broadway)
Tom Waits; *Tom Waits-Anthology* . . . . (Asylum)
Somewhere Out There
James Ingram & Linda Ronstadt; *The Power Of Great Music* . . . . (Warner Bros.)
Linda Ronstadt & James Ingram; *ST/An American Tail* . . . . (MCA)
Stand By Your Man
Elton John; *Tammy Wynette...Remembered-C* . . . . (Asylum)
Lyle Lovett and his Large Band; *Lyle Lovett and his Large Band* . . . . (Curb/MCA)
Tammy Wynette; *Columbia Country Classics-#4-Nashville Sound-C* . . . . (Columbia)
  ST/Sleepless In Seattle . . . . (Epic/Sony Music Soundtrax)
  Tammy Wynette's Biggest Hits . . . . (Epic)
  Tears Of Fire-25th Anniversary Collection . . . . (Epic)
Stick It Out
Rush; *Counterparts* . . . . (Atlantic)
Straight Lines
Wood; *Songs From Stamford Hill* . . . . (Columbia)
Stubborn Kind Of Fellow
Marvin Gaye; *Marvin Gaye-Anthology* . . . . (Motown)
  Marvin Gaye's Greatest Hits . . . . (Motown)
  Superhits . . . . (Motown)
Summertime
Billy Stewart; *Best Of Chess Rhythm & Blues-#1-C* . . . . (Chess)
  Summer & Sun-C . . . . (Rhino)
Booker T. & The M.G.s; *Best Of Booker T. & The M.G.s* . . . . . (Atlantic)
Carmen McRae; *Greatest Of Carmen McRae* . . . . (MCA)
Chet Baker; *My Favourite Songs-#1-Last Great Concert* . . . . (Enja)
Courtney Pine; *Glory Of Gershwin Featuring Larry Adler-C* . . . . (Mercury)
Ella Fitzgerald & Louis Armstrong; *Porgy & Bess* . . . . (Verve)
George Benson; *Best Of George Benson* . . . . (CBS Associated)
Janis Joplin; *Janis Joplin's Greatest Hits* . . . . (Columbia)
  ST/Janis . . . . (Columbia)
Lambert, Hendricks & Ross; *Best Of Lambert, Hendricks & Ross* . . . (Columbia)
Miles Davis & His Orchestra; *Porgy & Bess* . . . . (Columbia)
Original Cast; *Porgy & Bess* . . . . (MCA)
Peter Gabriel; *Glory Of Gershwin Featuring Larry Adler-C* . . . . (Mercury)
Rick Nelson; *Best Of Rick Nelson-#2* . . . . (EMI)
Sam Cooke; *Best Of Sam Cooke* . . . . (RCA)
Sarah Vaughan; *1940s-The Singers-C* . . . . (Columbia)
  Divine Sarah Vaughan-Columbia Years-1949-1953 . . . . . . (Columbia)
Stan Getz; *Compact Jazz-Stan Getz* . . . . (Verve)
Willie Nelson & Leon Russell; *One For The Road* . . . . (Columbia)
Superstition
Stevie Wonder; *20/20-C* . . . . (Motown)
  Original Musiquarium . . . . (Motown)
  Talking Book . . . . (Motown)
Take It On Faith
Joshua Kadison; *Delilah Blue* . . . . (EMI)
Thank God For Believers
Mark Chesnutt; *Thank God For Believers* . . . . (Decca)
That's The Way It Is
Celine Dion; *All The Way...A Decade Of Song* . . . . (550 Music)
  Collector's Series-Celine Dion-#1 . . . . (550 Music)
Theme From "Greatest American Hero"
Joey Scarbury; *Television's Greatest Hits-#3-1970s & 1980s-C* . . . . (TVT)
  Tube Tunes-#3-The '70s & '80s-C . . . . (Rhino)
Theme From "Promised Land"
Original Soundtrack; *CBS: The First 50 Years* . . . . (TVT)
There Are No Cats In America
Nehemiah Persoff/John Guarnieri/Warren Hays; *ST/An American Tail* . . . (MCA)
There Must Be A Better World Somewhere
B.B. King; *King Of The Blues* . . . . (MCA)
  There Must Be A Better World Somewhere . . . . (MCA)
There Will Come A Day
Faith Hill; *America: A Tribute To Heroes-C* . . . . (Interscope)
  Breathe . . . . (Warner Bros.)
There You Are
Martina McBride; *Emotion* . . . . (RCA)
They Didn't Believe Me
Hal Mooney; *Heritage Of Broadway-Music Of Jerome Kern* . . . . (Bainbridge)
Joe Williams; *Joe Williams Sings* . . . . (Savoy Jazz)
Johnny Mercer; *Song Is You-Capitol Sings Jerome Kern* . . . . . . (Capitol)
Pearl Bailey; *Pearl Bailey-16 Most Requested Songs* . . . . (Legacy)
Tommy Dorsey; *Best Of Tommy Dorsey* . . . . (MCA)
Thirty-Three
Smashing Pumpkins; *Mellon Collie And The Infinite Sadness* . . . . (Virgin)

This Little Light
Elizabeth Cook; *Country Goes Raffi-C* . . . . (Rounder)
Odetta; *Freedom Is A Constant Struggle-C* . . . . (Folk Era)
Paul Robeson; *American Balladeer-Golden Classics-#1-C* . . . . . (Collectables)
Raffi; *Rise And Shine* . . . . (Rounder)
Steeles; *ST/Corrina, Corrina* . . . . (RCA)
This Night Won't Last Forever
Bill LaBounty; *The Right Direction* . . . . (Noteworthy)
  This Night Won't Last Forever . . . . (Warner Bros.)
Michael Johnson; *Dialogue* . . . . (EMI)
  Have A Nice Night-Romantic Hits Of The '70s-C . . . . (Rhino)
  Radio Daze-Pop Hits Of The '80s-#1-C . . . . (Rhino)
  Then & Now . . . . (ISD/Intersound)
Moe Bandy; *Many Mansions* . . . . (Curb)
Sawyer Brown; *Six Days On The Road* . . . . (Curb)
Three Marlenas
Wallflowers; *Bringing Down The Horse* . . . . (Interscope)
To Be Loved By You
Wynonna; *Revelations* . . . . (Curb/MCA)
  Wynonna-Collection . . . . (Curb)
To Ev'ry Girl-To Ev'ry Boy (The Meaning Of Love)
Johnnie Ray; *45-#40252* . . . . (Columbia)
Tomorrow
Barbra Streisand; *Songbird* . . . . (Columbia)
Original Broadway Cast; *Annie* . . . . (Columbia)
Original Cast; *ST/Annie* . . . . (Columbia)
Tomorrow Never Knows
Beatles; *Beatles-Box Set* . . . . (Capitol)
  Revolver . . . . (Capitol)
Phil Collins; *Face Value* . . . . (Atlantic)
Tonight
Marc Nelson; *chocolate mood* . . . . (Columbia)
Tonight, Tonight
Smashing Pumpkins; *Mellon Collie And The Infinite Sadness* . . . . . . (Virgin)
Torn
Natalie Imbruglia; *Left Of The Middle* . . . . (RCA)
Trust
Megadeth; *Cryptic Writings* . . . . (Capitol)
Voice Of Harold
R.E.M.; *Dead Letter Office* . . . . (I.R.S.)
Walk Hand In Hand
Andy Williams; *I Like Your Kind Of Love-The Best Of The Cadence Years* . . . . (Varese Vintage)
Walk On Faith
Mike Reid; *Greatest Country Hits Of The '90s-1991-C* . . . . (Columbia)
  Turning For Home . . . . (Columbia)
We Believe In Happy Endings
Earl Thomas Conley & Emmylou Harris; *Duets-C* . . . . (Reprise)
We Shall Overcome
Bruce Springsteen; *Where Have All The Flowers Gone: The Songs Of Pete Seeger* . . . . (Appleseed)
James Cleveland & The Troubadors; *James Cleveland & The Troubadors* . . . . (Savoy)
Joan Baez; *Carry It On* . . . . (Vanguard)
  Joan Baez In Concert, Part 2 . . . . (Vanguard)
Mahalia Jackson; *God Bless America-C* . . . . (Columbia)
Pete Seeger; *Bitter & The Sweet* . . . . (Mobile Fidelity Sound Lab)
  Pete Seeger's Greatest Hits . . . . (Columbia)
We'll Meet Again
Vera Lynn; *ST/Dr. Strangelove: Music From The Films Of Stanley Kubrick* . . . . (Silva Classics)
  We'll Meet Again . . . . (Living Era)
Well, Alright!
CeCe Winans; *Everlasting Love* . . . . (PMG/Atlantic)
  Wow Gospel 1999-C . . . . (Verity/BMG)
Were You There (When They Crucified My Lord?)
Johnny Cash with The Carter Family; *The Man In Black-His Greatest Hits* . . . . (Legacy)
What A Fool Believes
Doobie Brothers; *Best Of The Doobies, Volume II* . . . . (Warner Bros.)
  Minute By Minute . . . . (Warner Bros.)
Kenny Loggins; *Kenny Loggins Alive* . . . . (Columbia)
  Nightwatch . . . . (Columbia)
What Children Believe
Shenandoah; *Shenandoah 2000* . . . . (Free Falls Entert.)
When You Believe
Mariah Carey & Whitney Houston; *Mariah Carey-#1's* . . . . (Columbia)
  ST/The Prince Of Egypt . . . . (DreamWorks/SKG)
Whitney Houston & Mariah Carey; *My Love Is Your Love* . . . . . (Arista)
Where Were You (When The World Stopped Turning)
Alan Jackson; *Alan Jackson-Drive* . . . . (Arista)
Where You Are
Jessica Simpson featuring Nick Lachey; *Sweet Kisses* . . . . (Columbia)
Whispering Hope
Jo Stafford; *Capitol Collectors Series-Jo Stafford* . . . . (Capitol)
White Cliffs Of Dover
Kay Kyser & His Orchestra; *16 Most Requested Songs Of The '40s-#1-C* . . . . (Legacy)

Lee Andrews And The Hearts; *Lee Andrews And The Hearts'*
  Biggest Hits . . . . (Collectables)
Mystics; *Mystics-16 Golden Classics* . . . . (Collectables)
Righteous Brothers; *Righteous Brothers' Greatest Hits* . . . . . (Verve)
  Righteous Brothers-Anthology 1962-1974 . . . . (Rhino)
Rosemary Clooney; *For The Duration* . . . . (Concord Jazz)

Who Can I Count On
Patsy Cline; *Portrait Of Patsy Cline* . . . . (MCA)

Who Do You Love, I Hope
Original Broadway Cast; *Annie Get Your Gun* . . . . (Angel)

Wichita Lineman
Dwight Yoakam; *Under The Covers* . . . . (Reprise)
Glen Campbell; *Best Of Glen Campbell* . . . . (Capitol)
  Country Music Classics-#3-1965-1970-C . . . . (K-Tel)
  Glen Campbell-Classics Collection . . . . (Capitol)
  Glen Campbell-Live . . . . (Capitol)
  Glen Campbell's Greatest Hits . . . . (Capitol)
  Jimmy Webb Collection . . . . (Columbia)

Will The Circle Be Unbroken
Charlie Daniels Band & Friends; *Volunteer Jam 3 & 4* . . . . (Epic)
Joan Baez; *Country Music Album* . . . . (Vanguard)
  The First 10 Years . . . . (Vanguard)
Nitty Gritty Dirt Band; *Will The Circle Be Unbroken* . . . . (EMI)
Roy Acuff; *Best Of Roy Acuff* . . . . (Liberty)
Willie Nelson; *Willie & Family Live* . . . . (Columbia)

Will You Be Loving Another Man
Bill Monroe & His Blue Grass Boys; *Essential Bill Monroe & His Blue*
  Grass Boys . . . . (Legacy)
  Essential Bill Monroe-1945-1949. . . . . (Columbia)

Wings Of A Dove
Bob Marley & The Wailers; *Birth Of A Legend 1963-*
  1966 . . . . (Epic Portrait Assoc.)
Ferlin Husky; *Billboard Top Country Hits-1960-C* . . . . (Rhino)
  Country Music Classics-#2-1960-1965-C . . . . (K-Tel)
  Ferlin Husky's Greatest Hits . . . . (Curb)

Woman Walk The Line
Emmylou Harris; *Ballad Of Sally Rose* . . . . (Warner Bros.)
Highway 101; *Featuring Paulette Carlson* . . . . (Warner Bros.)
Trisha Yearwood; *Hearts In Armor* . . . . (MCA)

Yes!
Chad Brock; *Yes!* . . . . (Warner Bros.)

Yesterday
Beatles; *"Yesterday"...And Today* . . . . (Capitol)
  Beatles 1 . . . . (Capitol)
  Beatles-20 Greatest Hits . . . . (Capitol)
  Beatles-Box Set . . . . (Capitol)
  Beatles-Love Songs . . . . (Capitol)
  Compact Disc Singles Collection . . . . (Capitol)
  The Beatles/1962-1966 . . . . (Capitol)
Elvis Presley; *On Stage-February, 1970* . . . . (RCA)
En Vogue; *Funky Divas* . . . . (East West)
Frank Sinatra; *My Way* . . . . (Reprise)
Paul McCartney; *The Concert For New York City-C* . . . . . . (Columbia)
Placido Domingo; *Domingo Songbook* . . . . (Sony Music Classical)
Ray Charles; *Ray Charles-His Greatest Hits-#1* . . . . (Dunhill Compact Classics)
Supremes; *I Hear A Symphony* . . . . (Motown)
Wings; *Wings Over America* . . . . (Capitol)

You Can Depend On Me
Brenda Lee; *The Brenda Lee Story-Her Greatest Hits.* . . . . . . (MCA)
Count Basie; *Best Of Count Basie* . . . . (MCA)
Louis Armstrong; *Stardust* . . . . (Portrait)
Manhattan Transfer; *The Manhattan Transfer* . . . . (Rhino)

You Can Depend On Me
Restless Heart; *Best Of Restless Heart.* . . . . (RCA)

You Can't Lose Me
Faith Hill; *It Matters To Me* . . . . (Warner Bros.)

You Don't Have To Say You Love Me
Dusty Springfield; *Dusty Springfield-Golden Hits* . . . . (Mercury)
  History Of British Rock-#7-C . . . . (Rhino)
Elvis Presley; *Elvis As Recorded At Madison Square Garden.* . . . . . (RCA)
  That's The Way It Is . . . . (RCA)
  The Other Sides-Worldwide Gold Award Hits, Vol. 2. . . . . (RCA)
Vikki Carr; *Best Of Vikki Carr* . . . . (EMI)

You Got Me
Roots featuring Erykah Badu; *Things Fall Apart* . . . . (MCA)

You Light Up My Life
Debby Boone; *Best Of Debby Boone.* . . . . (Curb)
  There Is Love-Wedding Songs-C . . . . (Scotti Bros.)
  You Light Up My Life . . . . (MCA)
LeAnn Rimes; *You Light Up My Life-Inspirational Songs* . . . . . . (Curb)

You Make Loving Fun
Fleetwood Mac; *25 Years-The Chain* . . . . (Warner Bros.)
  Fleetwood Mac's Greatest Hits . . . . (Warner Bros.)
  Rumours . . . . (Warner Bros.)
Jewel; *Legacy-A Tribute To Fleetwood Mac's Rumours-C* . . . . . (Lava)

You Still Believe In Me
Beach Boys; *Pet Sounds* . . . . (Capitol)

You'll Never Walk Alone
Andy Williams; *Unchained Melody-Greatest Songs* . . . . (Curb)

Jim Nabors; *Jim Nabors-16 Most Requested Songs* . . . . (Legacy)
Judy Garland; *Best Of The Capitol Masters-One & Only Box* . . . . (Capitol)
Mormon Tabernacle Choir; *Climb Ev'ry Mountain* . . . . (Columbia)
Original Broadway Cast; *Carousel* . . . . (Angel)
Original Cast; *Carousel* . . . . (MCA)
Pink Floyd; *Meddle* . . . . (Capitol)

Young, Gifted And Black
Aretha Franklin; *Young, Gifted And Black* . . . . (Atlantic & Atco Remasters)
Bob & Marcia; *Archive Reggae-C* . . . . (Rialto)
Nina Simone; *The Tomato Collection* . . . . (Tomato)

Your Faith In Me
Jessica Simpson; *Sweet Kisses* . . . . (Columbia)

You've Got To Talk To Me
Lee Ann Womack; *Lee Ann Womack* . . . . (Decca)

FAKE, Artificial, Man-made, Phony, Plastic
See Also: CHEATING & LIES, HIDING, PRETEND, SECRETS, TRUTH

Ain't It The Life
Foo Fighters; *There Is Nothing Left To Lose* . . . . (Roswell/RCA)

Ain't Nothing Like The Real Thing
Marvin Gaye & Tammi Terrell; *Every Great Motown Hit Of*
  Marvin Gaye. . . . . (Motown)
  Marvin Gaye's Greatest Hits. . . . . (Motown)
  Motown 40 Forever-C . . . . (Motown)
Vince Gill & Gladys Knight; *Rhythm Country And Blues-C* . . . . . . (MCA)

Artificial Flowers
Bobby Darin; *The Bobby Darin Story* . . . . (Atlantic)

Artificial Rose
Jimmy C. Newman; *Jimmy C. Newman's Greatest Hits* . . . . . (Plantation)

Barbie Girl
Aqua; *Aquarium.* . . . . (MCA)
  Now That's What I Call Music!-#1-C . . . . (Virgin)

Brilliant Disguise
Bruce Springsteen; *Bruce Springsteen's Greatest Hits* . . . . . (Columbia)
  Tunnel Of Love . . . . (Columbia)

Change
Sheryl Crow; *Sheryl Crow* . . . . (A&M)

Counterfeit Fake
They Might Be Giants; *Then-The Early Years* . . . . (Restless)

Crush With Eyeliner
R.E.M.; *Monster* . . . . (Warner Bros.)

Dance: Ten; Looks: Three
Original Cast; *A Chorus Line* . . . . (Columbia)

Dear Plastic
Sugarcubes; *Here Today, Tomorrow Next Week!.* . . . . (Elektra)

Dope Show
Marilyn Manson; *Mechanical Animals* . . . . (Nothing)

Fake
Alexander O'Neal; *All Mixed Up* . . . . (Tabu)
  Hearsay. . . . . (Tabu)

Fake
Brand New Heavies; *Brother Sister* . . . . (Delicious Vinyl)

Fake
Korn; *Korn.* . . . . (Immortal/Epic)

Fake Contest
Minutemen; *Introducing The Minutemen.* . . . . (SST)
  What Makes A Man Start Fires . . . . (SST)

Fake Friends
Joan Jett & The Blackhearts; *Joan Jett & The Blackhearts Album* . . . . (MCA)

Fake Healer
Metal Church; *Blessing In Disguise* . . . . (Elektra)

Fake It
Pete Townshend; *PsychoDerelict* . . . . (Atlantic)

Fake Plastic Trees
Radiohead; *Bends.* . . . . (Capitol)
  ST/Clueless . . . . (Capitol)

Fake Your Way To The Top
Original Cast; *Dreamgirls* . . . . (Geffen)

Fakin' It
Simon & Garfunkel; *Bookends.* . . . . (Columbia)
  Collected Works . . . . (Columbia)

Faking Love
T.G. Sheppard & Karen Brooks; *Perfect Stranger* . . . . . . (Warner Bros.)
  T.G. Sheppard's All-Time Greatest Hits . . . . (Warner Bros.)
  T.G. Sheppard's Greatest Hits-#2 . . . . (WB/Curb)
  You & I-Classic Country Duets-C . . . . (Warner Bros.)

Give Me Back My Wig
Luther Allison; *Live In Chicago* . . . . (Alligator)
Mike Henderson & The Bluebloods; *First Blood* . . . . . . (Dead Reckoning)
Stevie Ray Vaughan; *Couldn't Stand The Weather* . . . . (Epic)

Heart Of Glass
Blondie; *Best Of Blondie* . . . . (Chrysalis)
  Billboard Top Hits-1979-C . . . . (Rhino)

Parallel Lines . . . . (Chrysalis)
    The Disco Years-#2-On The Beat-1978-1982-C . . . . (Rhino)
I'm A Loser
    Beatles; *Beatles '65* . . . . (Capitol)
Invisible City
    Wallflowers; *Bringing Down The Horse*. . . . . (Interscope)
Italian Plastic
    Crowded House; *Woodface* . . . . (Capitol)
It's Only A Paper Moon
    Art Blakey & His Jazz Messengers; *Big Beat* . . . . (Blue Note)
    Bing Crosby; *The Radio Years-#2* . . . . (Crescendo)
    David Rose & His Orchestra; *Music Of The 1930s-C* . . . . (MCA)
    Ella Fitzgerald; *Harold Arlen Songbook-#2* . . . . (Verve)
    Frank Sinatra; *Round #1* . . . . (Capitol)
    Mystics; *Mystics-16 Golden Classics* . . . . (Collectables)
    Nat "King" Cole; *Capitol Sings Harold Arlen: Over The*
      Rainbow-C . . . . (Gold Rush)
    The Nat "King" Cole Story . . . . (Capitol)
    Sammy Kaye & His Orchestra; *Sammy Kaye & His Orchestra Play 22*
      Original Big Band Recordings . . . . (Hindsight)
Little Plastic Castle
    Ani DiFranco; *Little Plastic Castle* . . . . (Righteous Babe)
Living In The Plastic Age
    Buggles; *Age Of Plastic* . . . . (Island)
Muscle In Plastic
    Bauhaus; *Mask* . . . . (Beggar's Banquet)
One Man Army
    Our Lady Peace; *Happiness...Is Not A Fish That You Can Catch*. . . . (Columbia)
Paper Doll
    Bar-Kays; *Banging The Wall* . . . . (Mercury)
    Mills Brothers; *Best Of The Mills Brothers* . . . . (MCA)
    Billboard Pop Memories-1940-1944-C . . . . (Rhino)
    Mills Brothers' All Time Greatest Hits . . . . (MCA)
    Mills Brothers' Greatest Hits . . . . (MCA)
    Mills Brothers-22 Great Hits . . . . (Ranwood)
    Paper Doll . . . . (MCA)
    Sentimental Journey: Pop Vocal Classics-#1-1942-1946-C . . . . (Rhino)
    The Mills Brothers-Best Of The Decca Years. . . . . (Decca)
Paper Roses
    Kitty Wells; *Kitty Wells' Greatest Hits-#2* . . . . (Step One)
    Marie Osmond; *All Time Greatest Hits Of Country-C* . . . . (Curb)
    Marie Osmond-25 Hits-Special Collection . . . . (Curb)
Plastic
    PM Dawn; *Bliss Album...?* . . . . (Gee Street)
Plastic Fantastic Lover
    Jefferson Airplane; *Surrealistic Pillow* . . . . (RCA)
Plastic Jesus
    Ernie Marrs & The Marrs Family; *Best Of Broadside 1962-1968: Anthems*
    Of The American Underground From The Pages Of Broadside
    Magazine-C . . . . (Smithsonian Folkways)
Plastic Or Paper
    Bobs; *Songs For Tomorrow Morning* . . . . (Kaleidoscope)
Plastic Passion
    Cure; *Boys Don't Cry* . . . . (Elektra)
Plastic People
    Mothers Of Invention; *Absolutely Free* . . . . (Rykodisc)
Plastic Saddle
    Danny O'Keefe; *American Roulette* . . . . (Warner Bros.)
Plastic Surgery
    Adam & The Ants; *Fun Filth & Fury* . . . . (Blue Plate)
Polythene Pam
    Beatles; *Abbey Road* . . . . (Parlophone)
    Beatles-Box Set . . . . (Capitol)
Pull This Plastic Glider Higher
    Pink Floyd; *Saucerful Of Secrets* . . . . (Capitol)
Silicone Sally
    Slammin' Gladys; *Slammin' Gladys*. (Priority)
Souvenirs
    Gretchen Peters; *Gretchen Peters*. . . . . (Purple Crayon Prod.)
Stacked Actors
    Foo Fighters; *There Is Nothing Left To Lose* . . . . (Roswell/RCA)
Substitute
    Great White; *Great White* . . . . (EMI)
    Sex Pistols; *Live At Chelmsford Top Security Prison* . . . . (Restless)
    Who; *Live At Leeds* . . . . (MCA)
    Meaty Beaty Big & Bouncy . . . . (MCA)
    Who Greatest Hits . . . . (MCA)
    Who's Last . . . . (MCA)
Until The Real Thing Comes Along
    Andy Kirk; *Sweetest Sounds Ever Heard-C* . . . . (Hip-O)
    Billie Holiday; *God Bless The Child* . . . . (Columbia)
    Quintessential-#9-1940-1942 . . . . (Columbia)
    Dean Martin; *The Capitol Years-Dean Martin* . . . . (Capitol)
    Frank Sinatra & The Quincy Jones Orchestra; *Frank Sinatra-Complete*
      Reprise Studio Recordings . . . . (Reprise)
Vinyl
    Euge Groove; *Euge Groove* . . . . (Warner Bros.)
Wonderfully Colored Plastic War Toys
    Dead Milkmen; *Soul Rotation* . . . . (Hollywood)

Wrapped In Plastic
    Marilyn Manson; *Portrait Of An American Family*. . . . . (Interscope)

FALLING

See Also: LOVE: FALLING IN LOVE

6 Underground
    Sneaker Pimps; *Becoming X* . . . . (Virgin)
Absence Of The Heart
    Deana Carter; *Everything's Gonna Be Alright* . . . . (Capitol)
After The Rain Has Fallen
    Sting; *Brand New Day* . . . . (A&M)
Angels Would Fall
    Melissa Etheridge; *Breakdown* . . . . (Island)
Autumn Leaves
    Barbra Streisand; *Je m'appelle Barbra* . . . . (Columbia)
    Frank Sinatra; *Night We Called It A Day* . . . . (Capitol)
    Nat "King" Cole; *Blossom Fell* . . . . (Capitol)
    Roger Miller; *Music Of The 1950s-C* . . . . (MCA)
    Roger Williams; *Best Of Roger Williams* . . . . (MCA)
    Roger Williams-Golden Hits-#2. . . . . (MCA)
Before I Go
    John Hiatt; *Crossing Muddy Waters* . . . . (Vanguard)
Before The Next Teardrop Falls
    Freddy Fender; *Before The Next Teardrop Falls* . . . . (Universal)
    Best Of Freddy Fender . . . . (MCA)
    Oldies But Goodies-#2-C . . . . (Original Sound)
    Super Hits Of The '70s-Have A Nice Day-#17-C . . . . (Rhino)
    Ray Anthony; *Great Golden Hits* . . . . (Ranwood)
Big Me
    Foo Fighters; *Foo Fighters* . . . . (Roswell/RCA)
Black Balloon
    Goo Goo Dolls; *Dizzy Up The Girl* . . . . (Warner Sunset/Reprise)
Bomb! (These Sounds Fall Into My Mind)
    Bucketheads; *All In The Mind* . . . . (Big Beat/Atlantic)
Catch A Falling Star
    Perry Como; *Como's Golden Records* . . . . (RCA)
    Nipper's Greatest Hits Of The '50s-#1-C . . . . (RCA)
    Perry Como-Pure Gold . . . . (RCA)
    Perry Como's All-Time Greatest Hits-#1 . . . . (RCA)
    This Is Perry Como . . . . (RCA)
Closer You Get, The
    Alabama; *Alabama's Greatest Hits-#2* . . . . (RCA)
    For The Record: 41 Number One Hits . . . . (RCA)
    The Closer You Get. . . . . (BMG Special Prod.)
Do You Feel What I'm Feeling
    Warren Hill; *Truth*. . . . . (RCA)
Dollhouse
    Bruce Springsteen; *Tracks* . . . . (Columbia)
Easy To Fall
    Journey; *Trial By Fire* . . . . (Columbia)
Easy To Slip
    Little Feat; *Sailin' Shoes* . . . . (Warner Bros.)
Everything Falls Apart
    Dog's Eye View; *Happy Nowhere* . . . . (Columbia)
Fall From Grace
    Amanda Marshall; *Amanda Marshall* . . . . (Epic)
Fall, The
    Nixons; *The Nixons* . . . . (MCA)
Fallen Angels
    Kris Kristofferson; *Gift Of Song* . . . . (Polydor)
    Shake Hands With The Devil . . . . (Columbia)
Fallen Angels
    Aerosmith; *Nine Lives* . . . . (Columbia)
Fallen Angels
    Dio; *Sacred Heart* . . . . (Warner Bros.)
Fallen Embers
    Enya; *A Day Without Rain*. . . . . (Reprise)
Fallin'
    Connie Francis; *Very Best Of Connie Francis*. . . . . (Polydor)
Falling Away From Me
    Korn; *Issues*. . . . . (Immortal/Epic)
Falling For The First Time
    Barenaked Ladies; *Maroon* . . . . (Reprise)
Falling, Falling, Falling
    Mandy Barnett; *I've Got A Right To Cry* . . . . (Sire)
Fear Of Falling
    Badlees; *River Songs* . . . . (Atlas)
Fell On Black Days
    Soundgarden; *Superunknown* . . . . (A&M)
Godless
    U.P.O.; *No Pleasantries* . . . . (Epic)
Halfway Down
    Patty Loveless; *When Fallen Angels Fly* . . . . (Epic)
Hammer To Fall
    Queen; *Classic Queen* . . . . (Hollywood)

Live At Wembley '86 . . . . (Hollywood)
Queen's Greatest Hits I & II . . . . (Hollywood)
Queen-The Works . . . . (Hollywood)

Heavy
Collective Soul; *Dosage* . . . . (Atlantic)

Heavy Things
Phish; *Farmhouse* . . . . (Elektra)

Hemorrhage (In My Hands)
Fuel; *Now That's What I Call Music!-#6-C* . . . .(Virgin)
Something Like Human . . . . (Epic)

Hero Takes A Fall
Bangles; *All Over The Place* . . . .(Columbia)
Bangles' Greatest Hits . . . . (Columbia)
Bangles-Super Hits . . . . (Legacy)

I Choose
Offspring; *Ixnay On The Hombre* . . . . (Columbia)

I Fall To Pieces
Aaron Neville & Trisha Yearwood; *Rhythm Country And Blues-C* . . . . . . (MCA)
Patsy Cline; *12 Greatest Hits* . . . . (MCA)
Always . . . . (MCA)
ST/Sweet Dreams . . . . (MCA)
The Patsy Cline Story . . . . (MCA)

I Try
Macy Gray; *Now That's What I Call Music!-#4-C* . . . .(Virgin)
On How Life Is . . . . (Epic)

If I Fall You're Going Down With Me
Dixie Chicks; *Fly* . . . . (Monument)

I'm Always On A Mountain When I Fall
Merle Haggard; *For The Record: Merle Haggard-43 Legendary Hits* . . . .(BNA)

It Happened In Sun Valley
Glenn Miller & His Orchestra; *Complete Glenn Miller & His*
Orchestra . . . . (Bluebird)

It's OK
Tracy Chapman; *Telling Stories* . . . . (Elektra)

I've Just Seen A Face
Beatles; *Rubber Soul* . . . . (Capitol)
Paul McCartney; *Unplugged (The Official Bootleg)* . . . . (Capitol)
Wings; *Wings Over America* . . . . (Capitol)

Lean On Me
Kirk Franklin; *The Nu Nation Project* . . . . (Gospo Centric/Interscope)

Let Me Fall
Wood; *Songs From Stamford Hill* . . . . (Columbia)

Let's Fall To Pieces Together
George Strait; *George Strait's Greatest Hits* . . . . (MCA)
Right Or Wrong . . . . (MCA)
Strait Out Of The Box . . . . (MCA)

Like The Rain
Clint Black; *Clint Black-The Greatest Hits* . . . . (RCA)

Live Through This (Fifteen Stories)
Mighty Joe Plum; *Happiest Dogs* . . . . (Atlantic)

London Bridge
Original Soundtrack; *Children's Favorites* . . . . (Kid Rhino/Rhino 4 Kids)

Loser
3 Doors Down; *Better Life* . . . . (Republic/Universal)

Monkey Wrench
Foo Fighters; *The Colour And The Shape* . . . .(Roswell/RCA)

Most Likely You'll Go Your Way & I'll Go Mine
Bob Dylan; *Biograph* . . . . (Columbia)
Blonde On Blonde . . . . (Columbia)
Bob Dylan And The Band; *Before The Flood* . . . . (Columbia)

Night Is Fallin' In My Heart
Diamond Rio; *Diamond Rio's Greatest Hits* . . . . (Arista)
Love A Little Stronger . . . . (Arista)

On London Bridge
Jo Stafford; *International Hits* . . . . (Corinthian)

P.O.V. Waltz
Nilsson; *The Point* . . . . (RCA)

Place To Fall Apart
Merle Haggard & Janie Fricke; *For The Record: Merle Haggard-43*
Legendary Hits . . . .(BNA)

Ring Of Fire
Country Joe McDonald; *Best Of Country Joe McDonald-The Vanguard*
Years-1969-1975 . . . . (Vanguard)
Tonight I'm Singing Just For You . . . . (Vanguard)
Dwight Yoakam; *Guitars, Cadillacs, Etc., Etc.* . . . .(Reprise)
Earl Scruggs & Billy Bob Thornton; *Earl Scruggs And Friends-C* . . . . . . (MCA)
Johnny Cash; *All Time Legends Of Country Music-C* . . . . (Legacy)
Billboard Top Country Hits-1963-C . . . . (Rhino)
Classic Cash-Hall Of Fame Series . . . . (Mercury)
Johnny Cash's Greatest Hits . . . . (Columbia)
The Man In Black-His Greatest Hits . . . . (Legacy)
Stan Ridgway & Wall Of Voodoo; *Best Of Stan Ridgway & Wall Of*
Voodoo . . . . (I.R.S.)
Wall Of Voodoo; *Ugly Americans In Australia* . . . . (I.R.S.)

Safe In The Arms Of Love
Martina McBride; *ST/Switchback* . . . . (RCA)
Wild Angels . . . . (RCA)

Sky Is Falling
Daryl Hall & John Oates; *Marigold Sky* . . . . (Push)

Snow On The Sahara
Anggun; *Anggun* . . . . (Epic)

So Help Me Girl
Gary Barlow; *Open Road* . . . .(Arista)
Joe Diffie; *Third Rock From The Sun* . . . . (Epic)

Starting To Fall
Marilyn Scott; *Avenues Of Love* . . . . (Warner Bros.)

Tears Falling Down
Rosanne Cash; *The Wheel* . . . .(Columbia)

Theme From ''The Fall Guy''
Original Soundtrack; *Television's Greatest Hits-#6-Remote Control-C* . . .(TVT)

Trippin' On A Hole In A Paper Heart
Stone Temple Pilots; *Tiny Music...Songs From The Vatican*
Gift Shop . . . . (Atlantic)

Volcano Girls
Veruca Salt; *Eight Arms To Hold You* . . . . (Geffen)

Walk Unafraid
R.E.M.; *Up* . . . . (Warner Bros.)

Walls
Pamela Rose; *Morpheus* . . . .(Grace)

We Fall Down
Donnie McClurkin; *Live In London & More...* . . . . (Verity/BMG)

When The Fallen Angels Fly
Patty Loveless; *When Fallen Angels Fly* . . . . (Epic)

When The Golden Leaves Begin To Fall
Joe Val & The New England Bluegrass Boys; *Diamond Joe* . . . .(Rounder)
Joe Val & The New England Bluegrass Boys-Vol. 2 . . . .(Rounder)

When The Hammer Falls
Sammy Hagar; *I Never Said Goodbye* . . . . (Geffen)

When The Night Comes Falling From The Sky
Bob Dylan; *Empire Burlesque* . . . . (Columbia)
The Bootleg Series-Volumes 1-3 [Rare & Unreleased] . . . .(Columbia)
Jeff Healey Band; *ST/Road House* . . . .(Arista)

When You Come Back Down
Nickel Creek; *Nickel Creek* . . . . (Sugar Hill)

When You're Falling
Afro Celt Sound System featuring Peter Gabriel; *Vol. 3: Further*
In Time . . . .(Real World/Virgin)

Why They Call It Falling
Lee Ann Womack; *I Hope You Dance* . . . . (MCA)

FAMILY PLANNING, Abortion, Adoption, Birth Control, Teen Pregnancy, Unplanned Pregnancy, Unwed Parents
See Also: **BABY, FAMILY (various), PARENTS (various), SEX, SEX: RESISTING TEMPTATION**

10 Days Late
Third Eye Blind; *Blue* . . . .(Elektra)

Angels Working Overtime
Deana Carter; *Everything's Gonna Be Alright* . . . .(Capitol)

Babies Makin' Babies
Sly & The Family Stone; *Fresh* . . . . (Legacy)
Sly & The Family Stone-Anthology . . . . (Epic)

Birth Control
Lloyd Charmers; *Reggae Chartbusters-#2-C* . . . . (Metronome)
Wonderful World, Beautiful People-C . . . . (Recall)

Birth Control
Crass; *Christ: The Album/Well Forked But Not Dead* . . . . (Crass)

Blood On The Dance Floor
Michael Jackson; *Blood On The Dance Floor-HIStory...* . . . . .(MJJ Music/Work)

Brenda's Got A Baby
Tupac; *2Pacalypse Now* . . . . (Priority)

Brick
Ben Folds Five; *Whatever And Ever Amen* . . . . (Caroline/550)

Careless Love
Dinah Washington; *Bessie Smith Songbook* . . . . (Emarcy)
Pete Fountain; *Mr. New Orleans* . . . . (MCA)
Preservation Hall Jazz Band; *Best Of The Preservation Hall*
Jazz Band . . . .(Columbia)
New Orleans-#3-When The Saints Go Marchin' In . . . .(Columbia)

Got You (Where I Want You)
Flys; *Holiday Man* . . . . (Delicious Vinyl)
ST/Disturbing Behavior . . . . (Trauma)

Gypsies, Tramps And Thieves
Cher; *Half-Breed* . . . . (MCA Special Prod.)

Hard To Make A Stand
Sheryl Crow; *Sheryl Crow* . . . .(A&M)

He Would Be Sixteen
Michelle Wright; *Now & Then* . . . .(Arista)

I Am Your Mother Too
Keb' Mo' with Brenda Russell; *Big Wide Grin* . . . .(Sony Wonder)

I Don't Want To Have To Marry You
Jim Ed Brown & Helen Cornelius; *Jim Ed Brown & Helen Cornelius'*
Greatest Hits . . . . (RCA)

I Spent My Last Ten Dollars (On Birth Control And Beer)
Two Nice Girls; *Lesbian Favorites-Women Like Us-C* . . . . (Rhino)
Love Child
Diana Ross & The Supremes; *Billboard Top Rock 'N' Roll Hits-*
1968-C . . . . (Rhino)
Diana Ross & The Supremes' Greatest Hits-#3 . . . . (Motown)
Diana Ross & The Supremes-Anthology (1962-1969) . . . . (Motown)
Every Great #1 Hit . . . . (Motown)
Motown Story-First 25 Years-C . . . . (Motown)
Motown's Biggest Pop Hits-C . . . . (Motown)
Sweet Sensation; *Love Child* . . . . (Atco)
Love Keep Us Together
Martin Sexton; *Black Sheep* . . . .(Eastern Front)
The American . . . . (Atlantic)
No Condom, No Sex
Cruise Control; *No Condom, No Sex-12''* . . . . (Sire)
One Night Stand
J-Shin featuring La Tocha Scott; *My Soul, My Life* . . . . (Atlantic)
Papa Don't Preach
Madonna; *Immaculate Collection* . . . . (Sire)
Royal Box . . . . (Sire)
True Blue . . . . (Sire)
Pill, The
Loretta Lynn; *Loretta Lynn-20 Greatest Hits* . . . . (MCA)
The Country Music Hall Of Fame-Loretta Lynn . . . . (MCA)
River, The
Bruce Springsteen; *Bruce Springsteen's Greatest Hits* . . . . (Columbia)
The River . . . . (Columbia)
Bruce Springsteen & The E Street Band; *Bruce Springsteen & The E Street*
Band Live/1975-85 . . . . (Legacy)
RU 486
Pain Teens; *Destroy Me, Lover* . . . . (Trance Syndicate)
Safe Sex
Erick Sermon; *No Pressure* . . . . (Def Jam/IDJMG)
Slide
Goo Goo Dolls; *Dizzy Up The Girl* . . . . (Warner Sunset/Reprise)
Spirit Of A Boy, Wisdom Of A Man
Randy Travis; *Big Country Hits '99-C* . . . . (K-Tel)
You And You Alone . . . . (DreamWorks/SKG)
Sweet Sixteen
Destiny's Child; *The Writing's On The Wall* . . . . (Columbia)
Teenage Immigrant Welfare Mothers On Drugs
Austin Lounge Lizards; *Live Bait* . . . . (Sugar Hill)
To Zion
Lauryn Hill featuring Carlos Santana; *The Miseducation Of*
Lauryn Hill . . . . (Ruffhouse/Columbia)
Unwed Fathers
Gail Davies; *Best Of Gail Davies* . . . . (Capitol)
Tammy Wynette; *Best Loved Hits* . . . . (Epic)
Vasectomy
Limeliters; *Singing For The Fun* . . . . (Crescendo)
Way Down The Line
Offspring; *Ixnay On The Hombre* . . . . (Columbia)
What It's Like
Everlast; *Whitey Ford Sings The Blues* . . . . (Tommy Boy)

FAMILY: AUNTS

See Also: FAMILY (various), WOMEN: GENERAL, WOMEN'S
NAMES: A-Z

Aunt Alicia
Original Cast; *ST/Gigi* . . . . (Sony Music Special Prod.)
Aunt Avis
Widespread Panic; *Bombs & Butterflies* . . . . (Capricorn)
Aunt Bee
Andy Griffith; *The Andy Griffith Show* . . . . (EMI Special Markets)
Aunt Hagar's Blues
Art Tatum; *Solo Masterpieces-#4* . . . . (Pablo)
Kid Ory's Creole Jazz Band; *This Kid's The Greatest* . . . . . . (Good Time Jazz)
Aunt Rhody
Burl Ives; *Poor Wayfaring Stranger* . . . . (Flapper)
Aunt Thomasina
Sir Mix-A-Lot; *Return Of The Bumpasaurus* . . . . (American)
Auntie's Municipal Court
Monkees; *Birds Bees & The Monkees* . . . . (Rhino)
Electric Aunt Jemima
Frank Zappa; *Uncle Meat* . . . . (Barking Pumpkin)
Long Tall Sally
Beatles; *Past Masters-Volume One* . . . . (Parlophone)
Rock 'N' Roll Music . . . . (Capitol)
The Beatles At The Hollywood Bowl . . . . (Capitol)
The Beatles' Second Album . . . . (Capitol)
Little Richard; *Billboard Top R&B Hits-1956-C* . . . . (Rhino)
Here's Little Richard . . . . (Specialty)
Little Richard-18 Greatest Hits . . . . (Rhino)

Little Richard's Greatest Hits . . . . (Everest)
Oldies But Goodies-#3-C . . . . (Original Sound)
ST/Heaven Help Us . . . . (EMI)
Super Oldies Of The '50s-#3-C . . . . (Audio Fidelity)
Tutti Frutti . . . . (Accord)
Saint Joe On The School Bus
Marcy Playground; *Marcy Playground* . . . . (Capitol)
Theme From "Fresh Prince Of Bel-Air"
Original Soundtrack; *Television's Greatest Hits-#7-Cable Ready-C* . . . . . (TVT)

FAMILY: BROTHERS

See Also: BROTHERHOOD, FAMILY (various), MEN: GENERAL,
MEN'S NAMES: A-Z

7 Chinese Bros.
R.E.M.; *Reckoning* . . . . (I.R.S.)
Angels In Waiting
Tammy Cochran; *Tammy Cochran* . . . . (Epic)
Best Man I Can Be
Ginuwine, R.L., Tyrese, Case; *ST/The Best Man* . . . . . (Sony Music Soundtrax)
Blood Brothers
Bruce Springsteen; *Bruce Springsteen's Greatest Hits* . . . . (Columbia)
Brotha
Angie Stone; *Mahogany Soul* . . . . (J)
Brother
Toad The Wet Sprocket; *In Light Syrup* . . . . (Columbia)
Brother Jukebox
Mark Chesnutt; *Too Cold At Home* . . . . (MCA)
Brother Louie
Stories; *Billboard Top Rock 'N' Roll Hits-1973-C* . . . . (Rhino)
Brother Love's Traveling Salvation Show
Neil Diamond; *Hot August Night* . . . . (MCA)
Love At The Greek . . . . (Columbia)
Neil Diamond-Gold . . . . (MCA)
Neil Diamond-His 12 Greatest Hits . . . . (MCA)
Sweet Caroline . . . . (MCA)
Brother To The Night
Larenz Tate; *ST/Love Jones* . . . . (Columbia)
Brother Trucker
James Taylor; *Flag* . . . . (Columbia)
Brother Wolf, Sister Moon
Cult; *Love* . . . .(Sire)
Brother, Brother
Carole King; *Music* . . . . (Epic)
Brother, Can You Spare A Dime
Bing Crosby; *Bing Crosby-16 Most Requested Songs* . . . . (Legacy)
Odetta/Dr. John/John Campbell/Rufus Reid; *Strike A Deep Chord-Blues For*
The Homeless-C . . . . (Justice)
Peter, Paul & Mary; *See What Tomorrow Brings* . . . . (Warner Bros.)
Weavers; *Weavers' Greatest Hits* . . . . (Vanguard)
Brotherly Love
Keith Whitley & Earl Thomas Conley; *Kentucky Bluebird* . . . . (RCA)
Moe Bandy; *Moe Bandy's Greatest Hits* . . . . (Curb)
Brothers Ain't Shit
Roxanne Shante; *2 Nasty 4 Radio* . . . . (Cold Chillin')
Brothers Under The Bridge
Bruce Springsteen; *Tracks* . . . . (Columbia)
Brothers Under The Bridges ('83)
Bruce Springsteen; *Tracks* . . . . (Columbia)
Daniel
Elton John; *Don't Shoot Me I'm Only The Piano Player* . . . . (Polydor)
Elton John's Greatest Hits . . . . (Polydor)
Wilson Phillips; *Two Rooms-Celebrating The Songs Of Elton John & Bernie*
Taupin-C . . . . (Polydor)
Dear Brother
Hank Williams; *I Saw The Light* . . . . (Polydor)
Fire Brothers
Quicksilver Messenger Service; *Quicksilver* . . . . (Capitol)
Quicksilver Messenger Service-Anthology . . . . (Capitol)
Go Rest High On That Mountain
Vince Gill; *When Love Finds You* . . . . (MCA)
He Ain't Heavy, He's My Brother
Hollies; *Best Of The Hollies* . . . . (EMI)
Best Of The Hollies-#2 . . . . (EMI)
Chicken Soup For The Soul: I'll Be There For You-Songs Of Friendship,
Brotherhood And Sisterhood-C . . . . (Rhino)
Hollies-Epic Anthology From The Original Master Tapes . . . . (Epic)
The Hollies' Greatest Hits . . . . (Epic)
Neil Diamond; *Glory Road-1968-1972* . . . . (MCA)
Tap Root Manuscript . . . . (MCA)
He Was My Brother
Simon & Garfunkel; *Wednesday Morning 3 A.M.* . . . . (Columbia)
Highway Patrolman
Bruce Springsteen; *Nebraska* . . . . (Columbia)
I Am Your Mother Too
Keb' Mo' with Brenda Russell; *Big Wide Grin* . . . . (Sony Wonder)

I'm The Brother Of Lily Of The Valley
Henry Lewis; *Music From The New York Stage (1890-1920)-#4-1917-1920-C* . . . . (Pearl)

Little Joe The Wrangler's Sister Nell
Skip Gorman; *A Cowboy's Wild Song To His Herd* . . . . (Rounder)

Mississippi Moon
Greg Brown; *One More Goodnight Kiss* . . . . (Red House)

Night The Lights Went Out In Georgia
Lynn Anderson; *Top Of The World* . . . . (Columbia)
Reba McEntire; *For My Broken Heart* . . . . (MCA)
   Reba McEntire's Greatest Hits-#3: I'm A Survivor . . . . (MCA)
Vicki Lawrence; *Super Hits Of The '70s-Have A Nice Day-#10-C* . . . . . (Rhino)

Partners, Brothers, & Friends
Nitty Gritty Dirt Band; *Live Two Five* . . . . (Capitol)
   Twenty Years Of Dirt-Best Of The Nitty Gritty Dirt Band . . . . . . (Warner Bros.)

Peace Brother Peace
Bill Medley; *Best Of The Righteous Brothers-#2* . . . . (Curb)

Petals
Mariah Carey; *Rainbow* . . . . (Columbia)

Ricky Wants A Man Of Her Own
Bruce Springsteen; *Tracks* . . . . (Columbia)

Room With A View
Carolyn Dawn Johnson; *Room With A View* . . . . (Arista)

Straight Brother
Leon Russell & Marc Benno; *Asylum Choir II* . . . . (MCA)

Theme From "Adventures Of Pete And Pete"
Original Soundtrack; *Television's Greatest Hits-#7-Cable Ready-C* . . . . . (TVT)

Theme From "Simon And Simon"
Original Soundtrack; *Television's Greatest Hits-#3-1970s & 1980s-C* . . . . (TVT)

Theme From "The Alvin Show"
Original Soundtrack; *Television's Greatest Hits-#3-1970s & 1980s-C* . . . . (TVT)

Theme From "The Brothers Grunt"
Original Soundtrack; *Television's Greatest Hits-#7-Cable Ready-C* . . . . . (TVT)

Theme From "The Smothers Brothers Comedy Hour"
Original Soundtrack; *Television's Greatest Hits-#2-C* . . . . (TVT)

Was My Brother In The Battle
Kate & Anna McGarrigle; *Songs Of The Civil War-C* . . . . (Columbia)

What's Going On
Cyndi Lauper; *True Colors* . . . . (Portrait)
Marvin Gaye; *20/20-C* . . . . (Motown)
   Marvin Gaye Live At The London Palladium . . . . (Motown)
   Marvin Gaye-Anthology . . . . (Motown)
   Marvin Gaye's Greatest Hits/ . . . . (Motown)
   More Songs From "The Big Chill" Soundtrack-C . . . . (Motown)
   What's Going On . . . . (Motown)
Quincy Jones; *Quincy Jones-The Best* . . . . (A&M)

What's Happening, Brother
Marvin Gaye; *What's Going On* . . . . (Motown)

When It All Goes Wrong Again
Everclear; *Songs From An American Movie-#2-Good Time For A Bad Attitude* . . . . (Capitol)

FAMILY: COUSINS

See Also: **CHILDREN, FAMILY (various), MEN: GENERAL, MEN'S NAMES: A-Z, WOMEN: GENERAL, WOMEN'S NAMES: A-Z**

Cousin Dupree
Steely Dan; *Two Against Nature* . . . . (Giant)

Cousin Henry
Bobby Womack; *Back To My Roots* . . . . (Right Stuff)

Cousin Jane
Troggs; *Archeology-1967-1977* . . . . (Polydor)

Cousin Kevin
Original Cast; *Tommy* . . . . (RCA Victor)
Who; *Join Together* . . . . (MCA)
   Odds & Sods . . . . (MCA)
   ST/Tommy . . . . (Polydor)
   Tommy . . . . (MCA)

Cousin Mary
John Coltrane; *Best Of John Coltrane* . . . . (Rhino)
   Giant Steps . . . . (Rhino)

Cousin Of Mine
Bob & Marcia; *Reggae Spectacular-C* . . . . (A&M)

Cousins
Woody Herman; *Verve Jazz Masters 54* . . . . (Verve)

Kissin' Cousins
Elvis Presley; *Command Performances-Essential 60's Masters II* . . . . . . (RCA)

My Cousin In Milwaukee
Ella Fitzgerald; *George & Ira Gershwin Songbook* . . . . (Verve)

Theme From "The Patty Duke Show"
Original Soundtrack; *Just Patty: The Best Of Patty Duke* . . . . (EMI)
   Television's Greatest Hits-#1-C . . . . (TVT)

FAMILY: DAUGHTERS

See Also: **CHILDREN, CHILDREN LEAVING HOME, FAMILY (various), ORPHANS, PARENTS (various), WOMEN: GENERAL, WOMEN'S NAMES: A-Z**

Busy Man
Billy Ray Cyrus; *Shot Full Of Love* . . . . (Mercury)

Butterfly Kisses
Bob Carlisle; *Butterfly Kisses (Shades Of Grace)* . . . . (DMG/Jive)

Clementine
Bobby Darin; *Bobby Darin-At The Copa* . . . . (Bainbridge)
   The Bobby Darin Story . . . . (Atlantic)
Original Soundtrack; *Children's Favorites* . . . . (Kid Rhino/Rhino 4 Kids)

Coal Miner's Daughter
Loretta Lynn; *Coal Miner's Daughter* . . . . (MCA)
   Coal Miner's Daughter . . . . (MCA)
   Loretta Lynn-20 Greatest Hits . . . . (MCA)
   Loretta Lynn-Greatest Hits Live . . . . (K-Tel)
   Loretta Lynn's Greatest Hits-#2 . . . . (MCA)
   The Country Music Hall Of Fame-Loretta Lynn . . . . (MCA)

Crossing Muddy Waters
John Hiatt; *Crossing Muddy Waters* . . . . (Vanguard)

Daddy's Little Girl
Al Martino; *Best Of Al Martino* . . . . (Capitol)
Mills Brothers; *50th Anniversary* . . . . (Ranwood)
   All Occasions Album . . . . (Gateway)
   Best Of The Mills Brothers . . . . (MCA)
   The Mills Brothers Story . . . . (Ranwood)

Daddy's Little Girl
Nikki D; *1st Ladies Of Rap-C* . . . . (K-Tel)

Damn Right, I've Got The Blues
Buddy Guy; *Best Blues Album In The World...Ever!-C* . . . . (Virgin)
   Buddy's Baddest: The Best Of Buddy Guy . . . . (Silvertone)
   Damn Right, I've Got The Blues . . . . (Silvertone)

Daughter
Bread; *Baby I'm-A Want You* . . . . (Elektra)
   Best Of Bread-#2 . . . . (Elektra)

Daughter
Pearl Jam; *Vs.* . . . . (Epic Portrait Assoc.)

Daughters Of Texas
Band Of H.M. Royal Marines; *Hands Across The Sea-Sousa Marches* . . . (Angel)

Daughters Of The Sea
Doobie Brothers; *What Were Once Vices Are Now Habits* . . . . (Warner Bros.)

Daughters Of Time
Judy Collins; *All-Ears Review-#7-Still Amazing...-C* . . . . (Really Outstanding Music)

Delphin's Daughter
Joe Taylor; *Cool Jazz Hot Summer-#2* . . . . (Pro Jazz)
   Spellbound . . . . (RCA Victor)

Down By The Water
PJ Harvey; *ST/Basketball Diaries* . . . . (Island)
   To Bring You My Love . . . . (Island)

Down The Road
Mac McAnally; *Knots* . . . . (MCA)

Farmer's Daughter
Merle Haggard; *Amber Waves Of Grain* . . . . (Epic)
   Best Of The Best Of Merle Haggard . . . . (Liberty)
Vince Gill; *Mama's Hungry Eyes-Merle Haggard Tribute-C* . . . . (Arista)

Farmer's Daughter
Beach Boys; *Surfin' U.S.A.* . . . . (Capitol)

Farmer's Daughter
Fleetwood Mac; *Fleetwood Mac Live* . . . . (Warner Bros.)

Good Man Is Hard To Find (Pittsburgh)
Bruce Springsteen; *Tracks* . . . . (Columbia)

How Can I Help You Say Goodbye
Patty Loveless; *Only What I Feel* . . . . (Epic)
   Patty Loveless-Classics . . . . (Epic)

How Far Is Heaven
Kitty Wells; *Kitty Wells-20 Greatest Hits* . . . . (Tee Vee)

I Don't Want To Wait
Paula Cole; *Live On Letterman-From The Late Show* . . . . (Reprise)
   Songs From Dawson's Creek . . . . (Sony Music Soundtrax)
   This Fire . . . . (Imago)

I Think About You
Collin Raye; *Best Of Collin Raye-Direct Hits* . . . . (Epic)
   I Think About You . . . . (Epic)

Iceman
Bruce Springsteen; *Tracks* . . . . (Columbia)

Isn't She Lovely
Keb' Mo'; *Big Wide Grin* . . . . (Sony Wonder)
Lee Ritenour; *Best Of Lee Ritenour* . . . . (GRP)
Stevie Wonder; *Original Musiquarium* . . . . (Motown)
   Songs In The Key Of Life . . . . (Motown)

Jacob's Ladder
Mark Wills; *Mark Wills* . . . . (Mercury)

Letting Go
Suzy Bogguss; *Aces* . . . . (Liberty)

Voices In The Wind .... (Liberty)
Little Girl, The
John Michael Montgomery; *Brand New Me* .... (Atlantic)
Totally Hits-#3-C .... (Atlantic)
Little Star
Madonna; *Ray Of Light* .... (Maverick)
Mama
Spice Girls; *Diana, Princess Of Wales-Tribute-C* .... (Columbia)
Spice .... (Virgin)
Mama, He Treats Your Daughter Mean
Susan Tedeschi; *Just Won't Burn* .... (Tone Cool)
Memphis
Chuck Berry; *Chuck Berry* .... (Audio Fidelity)
Chuck Berry-Golden Hits .... (Mercury)
Chuck Berry's Greatest Hits .... (Everest)
St. Louis To Liverpool .... (Chess)
ST/Hail! Hail! Rock 'N' Roll .... (MCA)
The Chess Box-Chuck Berry .... (Chess)
Toronto Rock 'N' Roll Revival-#2-C .... (Accord)
John Cale; *IRS Greatest Hits-#2 & #3-C* .... (I.R.S.)
Johnny Rivers; *Best Of Johnny Rivers* .... (EMI)
Johnny Rivers-Anthology 1964-1977 .... (Rhino)
Lonnie Mack; *Rock Instrumental Classics-#2-'60s-C* ..... (Rhino)
Teen Beat-Instrumental Rock-1957-1965-C .... (Capitol)
Mother Mother
Tracy Bonham; *Burdens Of Being Uprigh* .... (Island)
Mrs. Brown You've Got A Lovely Daughter
Herman's Hermits; *Herman's Hermits-Their Greatest Hits* ...... (Abkco)
Something Good Again .... (Abkco)
Ms. Jackson
Outkast; *Stankonia* .... (LaFace/Arista)
My Baby Needs A Shepherd
Emmylou Harris; *Red Dirt Girl* .... (Nonesuch)
My Baby You
Marc Anthony; *Marc Anthony* .... (Columbia)
No Sir
Darryl & Don Ellis; *No Sir* .... (Epic)
Papa Can You Hear Me?
Barbra Streisand; *One Voice* .... (Columbia)
ST/Yentl .... (Columbia)
Preacher's Daughter
Lynyrd Skynyrd; *First & Last* .... (MCA)
Santa Claus' Daughter
Charlie Rich; *Charlie Rich-Complete Smash Sessions* ...... (Mercury)
Shenandoah
Bob Dylan; *Down In The Groove* .... (Columbia)
Harry Belafonte; *Harry Belafonte-Legendary Performer* ..... (RCA)
James Galway; *James Galway's Greatest Hits* .... (RCA)
Leontyne Price; *God Bless America* .... (RCA)
Van Morrison & The Chieftains; *ST/Long Journey Home: The Irish In
America* .... (RCA Victor)
Vienna Boys Choir; *International Folk Songs: Around The World With The
Vienna Boys' Choir* .... (Philips)
She's Leaving Home
Al Jarreau; *All Fly Home* .... (Warner Bros.)
Beatles; *Beatles-Box Set* .... (Capitol)
Beatles-Love Songs .... (Capitol)
Sgt. Pepper's Lonely Hearts Club Band .... (Capitol)
Somebody Killed Dewey Jones' Daughter
Lacy J. Dalton; *Takin' It Easy* .... (Columbia)
Tennessee Border
Hank Williams; *Alone With His Guitar* .... (Mercury)
I Ain't Got Nothin' But Time-1946-1947 .... (Polydor)
Red Foley; *Red Foley: The Country Music Hall
Of Fame* .... (MCA Special Prod.)
Sonny Burgess & Dave Alvin; *Tennessee Border* .... (Hightone)
Tennessee Ernie Ford; *Best Of Tennessee Ernie Ford-16 Tons Of
Boogie* .... (Rhino)
Capitol Collectors Series-Tennessee Ernie Ford ...... (Capitol)
Theme From "Blossom"
Original Soundtrack; *Television's Greatest Hits-#7-Cable Ready-C* ..... (TVT)
Theme From "Full House"
Original Soundtrack; *Television's Greatest Hits-#7-Cable Ready-C* ..... (TVT)
Theme From "My Little Margie"
Original Soundtrack; *Television's Greatest Hits-#4-Black & White
Classics-C* .... (TVT)
Theme From "My Two Dads"
Original Soundtrack; *Television's Greatest Hits-#7-Cable Ready-C* ..... (TVT)
Theme From "One Day At A Time"
Original Soundtrack; *CBS: The First 50 Years* .... (TVT)
This Little Girl Of Mine
Faron Young; *Faron Young's Greatest Hits-#3* .... (Step One)
To Be Loved
Curtis Stigers; *Songs From Dawson's Creek* .... (Sony Music Soundtrax)
Walkaway Joe
Trisha Yearwood; *Hearts In Armor* .... (MCA)
Songbook-A Collection Of Hits .... (MCA)
Who I Am
Jessica Andrews; *Who I Am* .... (DreamWorks/SKG)

Wide Open Spaces
Dixie Chicks; *Big Country Hits '99-C* .... (K-Tel)
Wide Open Spaces .... (Monument)
Wild One
Faith Hill; *Take Me As I Am* .... (Warner Bros.)
Wolverton Mountain
Claude King; *American Originals-Claude King* .... (Columbia)
Best Of Claude King .... (Gusto)
Billboard Top Country Hits-1962-C .... (Rhino)
Super Hits Of The '60s-C .... (Epic)
You Can't Lose Me
Faith Hill; *It Matters To Me* .... (Warner Bros.)

FAMILY: FATHERS, Daddy

See Also: **BABY, CHILDREN, FAMILY (various), FAMILY
PLANNING, MEN: GENERAL, MEN'S NAMES: A-Z, PARENTS
(various), TEACHING VALUES, TEENAGERS**

1941
Nilsson; *Pandemonium Shadow Show* .... (RCA)
Adam Raised A Cain
Bruce Springsteen; *Darkness On The Edge Of Town* .... (Columbia)
Alone Again (Naturally)
Gilbert O'Sullivan; *Best Of Gilbert O'Sullivan* .... (Rhino)
Billboard Top Rock 'N' Roll Hits-1972-C .... (Rhino)
Beat Me Daddy Eight To The Bar
Andrews Sisters; *Andrews Sisters-16 Great Performances* ...... (MCA)
Best Of The Andrews Sisters .... (MCA)
Boogie Woogie Bugle Girls .... (MCA)
Capitol Collectors Series-The Andrews Sisters .... (Capitol)
Commander Cody & His Lost Planet Airmen; *Lost In The Ozone* ...... (MCA)
Best Day
George Strait; *Latest Greatest Straitest Hits* .... (MCA)
Big Daddy
Heavy D; *Waterbed Hev* .... (Universal)
Big Fat Daddy
Jeannie & Jimmy Cheatham; *Midnight Mama* .... (Concord Jazz)
Box, The
Randy Travis; *This Is Me* .... (Warner Bros.)
Boy Named Sue
Johnny Cash; *Columbia Country Classics-#3-Americana-C* ...... (Columbia)
Johnny Cash's Biggest Hits .... (Columbia)
Johnny Cash's Greatest Hits-#2 .... (Columbia)
The Man In Black-His Greatest Hits .... (Legacy)
Busy Man
Billy Ray Cyrus; *Shot Full Of Love* .... (Mercury)
Butterfly Kisses
Bob Carlisle; *Butterfly Kisses (Shades Of Grace)* .... (DMG/Jive)
Cannibals
Mark Knopfler; *Golden Heart* .... (Warner Bros.)
Cat's In The Cradle
Harry Chapin; *Greatest Stories-Live* .... (Elektra)
Harry Chapin-Anthology .... (Elektra)
Verities & Balderdash .... (Elektra)
Cincinnati Daddy
Duke Ellington; *Jazz Heritage-Rockin' In Rhythm-#3-C* .. (MCA Special Prod.)
Jungle Band-Brunswick Era-#2 .... (Decca)
Coal Miner's Daughter
Loretta Lynn; *Coal Miner's Daughter* .... (MCA)
Coal Miner's Daughter .... (MCA)
Loretta Lynn-20 Greatest Hits .... (MCA)
Loretta Lynn-Greatest Hits Live .... (K-Tel)
Loretta Lynn's Greatest Hits-#2 .... (MCA)
The Country Music Hall Of Fame-Loretta Lynn .... (MCA)
Color Him Father
Linda Martell; *20 Great Hits-C* .... (Plantation)
Color Me Country .... (Plantation)
Come From The Heart
Don Williams; *Traces* .... (Capitol)
Kathy Mattea; *Willow In The Wind* .... (Mercury)
Come To Poppa
Bob Seger; *Night Moves* .... (Capitol)
Cool Daddy In A Cadillac
Elvis Hitler; *Disgraceland* .... (Restless)
Cotton Mill Man
Jim & Jesse; *Old Dominion Masters* .... (Pinecastle)
Daddy
Andrews Sisters; *Boogie Woogie Bugle Girls* .... (MCA)
Nicolette Larson; *In The Nick Of Time* .... (Warner Bros.)
Sammy Kaye & His Orchestra; *Big Band Sampler-C* .... (Columbia)
Nipper's Greatest Hits Of The '40s-#1-C .... (RCA)
*Sammy Kaye & His Orchestra Play 22 Original Big Band
Recordings* .... (Hindsight)
Daddy And Home
Jimmie Rodgers; *Best Of Jimmie Rodgers-Legendary Master Series* ..... (RCA)

Jimmie Rodgers-Early Years-1928-1929 . . . . (Rounder)
This Is Jimmie Rodgers . . . . (RCA)
Tanya Tucker; *Strong Enough To Bend* . . . . (Liberty)
Superstars Salute Jimmie Rodgers-C . . . . (Step One)
Tanya Tucker's Greatest Hits . . . . (Liberty)

Daddy Come & Get Me
Dolly Parton; *Best Of Dolly Parton* . . . . (RCA)

Daddy Cool
Boney M; *Love For Sale* . . . . (Atlantic)
Take The Heat Off Me . . . . (Atco)
Diamonds; *Best Of The Diamonds* . . . . (Rhino)

Daddy Could Swear, I Declare
Gladys Knight & The Pips; *Gladys Knight & The Pips-All The
Great Hits* . . . . (Motown)
Gladys Knight & The Pips-Anthology. . . . . (Motown)
Motown Memories-#3-C . . . . (Motown)
Neither One Of Us . . . . (Motown)

Daddy Don't Go
Jennifer Warnes; *Jennifer Warnes* . . . . (Arista)

Daddy Don't Live In That New York City No More
Steely Dan; *Katy Lied* . . . . (MCA)

Daddy Frank (The Guitar Man)
Merle Haggard; *Best Of Merle Haggard* . . . . (Capitol)
Capitol Collectors Series-Merle Haggard . . . . (Capitol)
Merle Haggard & The Strangers; *For The Record: Merle Haggard-43
Legendary Hits* . . . . (BNA)
Songs I'll Always Sing . . . . (Capitol)

Daddy Never Was The Cadillac Kind
Confederate Railroad; *Notorious* . . . . (Atlantic)

Daddy Sang Bass
Johnny Cash; *Columbia Country Classics-#5-A New Tradition-C* . . . (Columbia)
Johnny Cash's Greatest Hits-#2 . . . . (Columbia)
The Man In Black-His Greatest Hits . . . . (Legacy)

Daddy Should Have Stayed In High School
Cheap Trick; *Cheap Trick* . . . . (Epic)

Daddy Was An Old Time Preacher Man
Porter Wagoner & Dolly Parton; *Best Of Porter Wagoner & Dolly
Parton* . . . . (RCA)

Daddy What If
Bobby Bare; *Bobby Bare* . . . . (RCA)
Great Moments At The Grand Ole Opry-C . . . . (RCA)

Daddy Won't Sell The Farm
Montgomery Gentry; *Tattoos & Scars* . . . . (Columbia)

Daddy You've Been On My Mind
Joan Baez; *Farewell Angelina* . . . . (Vanguard)
Judy Collins; *Judy Collins' Fifth Album* . . . . (Elektra)
Recollections . . . . (Elektra)

Daddy, Daddy, Daddy
Janis Joplin; *ST/Janis.* . . . . (Columbia)

Daddy, What's A Train?
Utah Phillips; *Steel Rails-Classic Railroad Songs-#1-C* . . . . (Rounder)

Daddy's All Gone
James Taylor; *In The Pocket* . . . . (Warner Bros.)

Daddy's Baby
James Taylor; *Walking Man* . . . . (Warner Bros.)

Daddy's Back
Kenny Loggins; *Celebrate Me Home* . . . . (Columbia)

Daddy's Come Around
Paul Overstreet; *Heroes.* . . . . (RCA)

Daddy's Dream
Vikki Carr; *Live At The Greek Theatre* . . . . (Columbia)

Daddy's Drinking Up Our Christmas
Commander Cody; *Hillbilly Holiday-C.* . . . . (Rhino)

Daddy's Gone Grey
Lonesome Strangers; *Lonesome Strangers* . . . . (Hightone)

Daddy's Gonna Save My Soul
Golden Earring; *Switch* . . . . (MCA)

Daddy's Gonna Treat You Right
Commander Cody & His Lost Planet Airmen; *Lost In The Ozone* . . . (MCA)

Daddy's Hands
Holly Dunn; *Country Love Songs-C* . . . . (Warner Bros.)
Holly Dunn . . . . (MTM)

Daddy's Home
Shep And The Limelites; *Cruisin'-1961-C* . . . . (Increase)
Doo-Wop Ballads-#2-C . . . . (Rhino)
Oldies But Goodies-#5-C . . . . (Original Sound)
Shep And The Limelites & The Heartbeats; *Best Of The Heartbeats* . . . . (Rhino)

Daddy's Last Letter (Private First Class John H. McCormick)
Tex Ritter; *45-#1267* . . . . (Capitol)

Daddy's Little Boy
Mills Brothers; *45-#60098.* . . . . (MCA)

Daddy's Little Girl
Al Martino; *Best Of Al Martino* . . . . (Capitol)
Mills Brothers; *50th Anniversary* . . . . (Ranwood)
All Occasions Album. . . . . (Gateway)
Best Of The Mills Brothers . . . . (MCA)
The Mills Brothers Story . . . . (Ranwood)

Daddy's Little Girl
Nikki D; *1st Ladies Of Rap-C* . . . . (K-Tel)

Daddy's Money
Ricochet; *Ricochet* . . . . (Columbia)

Daddy's Song
Nilsson; *Aerial Ballet* . . . . (RCA)

Daddy's Tune
Jackson Browne; *The Pretender* . . . . (Asylum)

Dead Bodies Everywhere
Korn; *Follow The Leader* . . . . (Immortal/Epic)

Desperados Waiting For A Train
Guy Clark; *Old No. 1* . . . . (Sugar Hill)
Jerry Jeff Walker; *Best Of Jerry Jeff Walker* . . . . (MCA)
Great Gonzos . . . . (MCA)
Viva Terlingua. . . . . (MCA)
Waylon Jennings, Willie Nelson, Johnny Cash, Kris Kristofferson;
Highwayman . . . . (Columbia)
Hot Tracks-Train Super Hits-C . . . . (Epic)

Diddley Daddy
Bo Diddley; *Bo Diddley-His Best.* . . . . (Chess)
Bo Knows Bo . . . . (MCA Special Prod.)
Chris Isaak; *Heart Shaped World.* . . . . (Reprise)

Don't Cry Daddy
Elvis Presley; *Always On My Mind* . . . . (RCA)
Memphis Record . . . . (RCA)
The Top Ten Hits . . . . (RCA)
Worldwide 50 Gold Award Hits, Vol. 1, Parts 1 & 2 . . . . (RCA)

Don't Sell Daddy Any More Whiskey
Joe Val & The New England Bluegrass Boys; *Not A Word
From Home* . . . . (Rounder)

Down At Papa Joe's
Dixiebelles; *WCBS FM 101 History Of Rock-'60s-#3-C* . . . . (Collectables)

Down The Road
Mac McAnally; *Knots* . . . . (MCA)

Drop Down Mama, Let Your Papa See
John Hammond; *Best Of John Hammond* . . . . (Vanguard)
Sleepy John Estes; *Legend Of Sleepy John Estes* . . . . (Delmark)
Tom Rush; *Best Of Tom Rush: No Regrets.* . . . . (Legacy)
Tom Rush. . . . . (Columbia)

Drunken Driver
Ricky Skaggs and Kentucky Thunder; *Bluegrass Rules!* . . . . (Rounder)

Evaporated
Ben Folds Five; *Whatever And Ever Amen.* . . . . (Caroline/550)

Factory
Bruce Springsteen; *Darkness On The Edge Of Town* . . . . (Columbia)

Father
Cat Stevens; *Back To Earth* . . . . (A&M)

Father
Why Store; *The Why Store* . . . . (MCA)

Father & Son
Cat Stevens; *Cat Stevens Greatest Hits* . . . . (A&M)
Cat Stevens-Classics-#24 . . . . (A&M)
Footsteps In The Dark-Greatest Hits-#2 . . . . (A&M)
Tea For The Tillerman . . . . (A&M)

Father And A Son
Loudon Wainwright III; *Loudon Wainwright III-History* . . . . . . (Charisma)

Father Christmas
Kinks; *Billboard Rock 'N Roll Christmas-C* . . . . (Rhino)
Come Dancing With The Kinks-Best Of The Kinks 1977-1986 . . . . . . (Arista)

Father Dear Father
Doucette; *Douce Is Loose.* . . . . (Mushroom)

Father Figure
George Michael; *Faith.* . . . . (Columbia)

Father O.S.A.
Styx; *Lady* . . . . (RCA)

Father Of A Boy Named Sue
Shel Silverstein; *Songs & Stories* . . . . (Parachute)

Father Of Day, Father Of Night
Manfred Mann's Earth Band; *Solar Fire* . . . . (Polydor)

Father Of Girls
Perry Como; *Perry Como-Legendary Performer* . . . . (RCA)

Father Of Mine
Everclear; *Now That's What I Call Music!-#2-C* . . . . (Virgin)
So Much For The Afterglow . . . . (Capitol)

Father Of Night
Bob Dylan; *New Morning* . . . . (Columbia)

Father Steps In
Earl "Fatha" Hines; *Father Jumps* . . . . (RCA)
Grand Terrace Band. . . . . (Quintessence)

Father Sun
Wynonna; *Tell Me Why* . . . . (MCA)

Father To Son
Alarm; *Strength* . . . . (I.R.S.)

Father To Son
Phil Collins; *...But Seriously* . . . . (Atlantic)

Father To Son
Queen; *Queen II* . . . . (Hollywood)

Father's Table Grace
Lester Flatt; *Fifty Years Of Bluegrass Hits-#3-C* . . . . (C.M.H. Prod.)

Lester Flatt & The Nashville Grass; *The Tennessee Mountain Bluegrass Festival* . . . .(C.M.H. Prod.)

Feet Up (Pat Him On The Po-Po)
Guy Mitchell; *Definitive Guy Mitchell* . . . . (Collector's Choice)

Foggy, Foggy Dew
Burl Ives; *Best Of Burl Ives* . . . .(MCA)

Fool To Cry
Rolling Stones; *Black And Blue* . . . .(Rolling Stones)
Rewind (1971-1984) . . . .(Rolling Stones)
Sucking In The Seventies . . . .(Rolling Stones)

Forty Again
John Berry; *Faces* . . . . (Capitol)

Fox, The
Nickel Creek; *Nickel Creek* . . . . (Sugar Hill)

Fun, Fun, Fun
Beach Boys; *Beach Boys-Gift Set* . . . . (Capitol)
Best Of The Beach Boys . . . . (Capitol)
Endless Summer . . . . (Capitol)
Made In The U.S.A. . . . . (Capitol)
The Beach Boys In Concert . . . . (Brother)

Games That Daddies Play
Conway Twitty; *Conway Twitty-Number Ones-#1* . . . . (Liberty)
Conway Twitty's Greatest Hits-#2 . . . .(MCA)

God Bless The Child
Billie Holiday; *Billie Holiday's Greatest Hits* . . . . (Decca Jazz)
Billie Holiday's Greatest Hits . . . . (Legacy)
From The Original Decca Masters . . . .(MCA)
Songbook . . . . (Verve)
The Billie Holiday Story-#2 . . . . (Columbia)
Blood, Sweat & Tears; *Blood, Sweat & Tears* . . . . (Columbia)
Blood, Sweat & Tears Greatest Hits . . . . (Columbia)
Diana Ross; *ST/Lady Sings The Blues* . . . . (Motown)
Liza Minnelli; *4-Sider* . . . . (Cypress)
ST/Liza With A "Z" . . . . (Columbia)
Lou Rawls; *Best From Lou Rawls* . . . . (Capitol)

Got A Letter From My Kid Today
Asleep At The Wheel; *Tribute To The Music Of Bob Wills And The Texas Playboys-C* . . . . (Liberty)
Merle Haggard & The Strangers; *18 Rare Classics* . . . . (Curb)
Working Man Can't Get Nowhere Today . . . . (Capitol)

Greatest Man I Never Knew
Reba McEntire; *For My Broken Heart* . . . .(MCA)
Reba McEntire's Greatest Hits Volume Two . . . .(MCA)

Grown Men Don't Cry
Tim McGraw; *Set This Circus Down* . . . . (Curb)

He Didn't Have To Be
Brad Paisley; *Who Needs Pictures* . . . . (Arista)

He Walked On Water
Randy Travis; *No Holdin' Back* . . . .(Warner Bros.)

Heavenly Father
Castelles; *Home Of Grand Records* . . . . (Collectables)
Sweet Sounds Of The Castelles . . . . (Collectables)

Hello Muddah, Hello Fadduh
Allan Sherman; *Dr. Demento Presents The Greatest Novelty Records-#3-1960s-C* . . . . (Rhino)
Dr. Demento Presents The Greatest Novelty Records-C . . . . (Rhino)

Hot Rod Lincoln
Asleep At The Wheel; *Western Standard Time* . . . .(Epic)
Commander Cody & His Lost Planet Airmen; *Lost In The Ozone* . . . .(MCA)
Super Hits Of The '70s-Have A Nice Day-#8-C . . . . (Rhino)
Johnny Bond; *Best Of Johnny Bond* . . . . (Starday)

How Far Is Heaven
Kitty Wells; *Kitty Wells-20 Greatest Hits* . . . .(Tee Vee)

How'd You Like To Be My Daddy?
Farber Sisters; *Music From The New York Stage (1890-1920)-#4-1917-1920-C* . . . . (Pearl)

Hungry Eyes
Emmylou Harris; *Mama's Hungry Eyes-Merle Haggard Tribute-C* . . . . (Arista)
Merle Haggard; *For The Record: Merle Haggard-43 Legendary Hits* . . . . (BNA)

Hush Hush Hush
Paula Cole; *This Fire* . . . . (Imago)

I Am Your Mother Too
Keb' Mo' with Brenda Russell; *Big Wide Grin* . . . . (Sony Wonder)

I Don't Call Him Daddy
Doug Supernaw; *Pure Country-Best Of The '90s-C* . . . . (Priority)
Red And Rio Grande . . . . (BNA)

I Don't Call Him Daddy
Kenny Rogers; *Hearts On Fire* . . . .(Madacy)
I Prefer The Moonlight . . . . (RCA)
Kenny Rogers' Greatest Hits . . . . (RCA)

I Don't Want To Wait
Paula Cole; *Live On Letterman-From The Late Show* . . . . (Reprise)
Songs From Dawson's Creek . . . . (Sony Music Soundtrax)
This Fire . . . . (Imago)

I Think About You
Collin Raye; *Best Of Collin Raye-Direct Hits* . . . .(Epic)
I Think About You . . . .(Epic)

I Want A Girl (Just Like The Girl)
Al Jolson; *The Al Jolson Story-#1* . . . .(MCA)

Spike Jones & His City Slickers; *King Of Corn*. . . . .(Glendale)

I'm A Long Gone Daddy
George Jones; *Too WIld Too Long* . . . .(Epic)
Hank III; *Timeless: Hank Williams Tribute-C* . . . . (Lost Highway/IDJMG)
Hank Williams; *Hank Williams-24 Greatest Hits-#2* . . . .(Polydor)
Lovesick Blues . . . .(Polydor)

I'm Already There
Lonestar; *I'm Already There* . . . .(BNA)

Independence Day
Bruce Springsteen; *The River* . . . . (Columbia)
Bruce Springsteen & The E Street Band; *Bruce Springsteen & The E Street Band Live/1975-85* . . . . (Legacy)

Is Zat You, Myrtle
Carlisles; *45-#70174* . . . . (Mercury)
Louvin Brothers; *Live At New River Ranch* . . . .(Copper Creek)

It's All In Your Head
Diamond Rio; *Diamond Rio IV* . . . . (Arista)
Diamond Rio's Greatest Hits . . . . (Arista)

It's Late
Ricky Nelson; *Lonesome Town* . . . . (CEMA Special Prod.)
Ricky Nelson Volume 1 . . . . (Gold Rush)

Jacob's Ladder
Mark Wills; *Mark Wills*. . . . . (Mercury)

Just The Two Of Us
Will Smith; *Big Willie Style*. . . . . (Columbia)

Kansas City Papa
Leadbelly; *King Of The Twelve-String Guitar* . . . . (Columbia)
Leadbelly . . . . (Columbia)

Keep It Between The Lines
Ricky Van Shelton; *Backroads* . . . . (Columbia)

Key To Life, The
Vince Gill; *The Key* . . . . (MCA)

Kisses Sweeter Than Wine
Jimmie Rodgers; *Best Of Jimmie Rodgers*. . . . . (Rhino)
Cruisin'-1958-C . . . . (Increase)
Weavers; *Best Of The Weavers* . . . . (MCA)
Reunion-At Carnegie Hall-1963 . . . . (Vanguard)
Weavers At Carnegie Hall . . . . (Vanguard)
Weavers' Greatest Hits . . . . (Vanguard)

Last Game Of The Season (A Blind Man In The Bleachers)
David Geddes; *Super Hits Of The '70s-Have A Nice Day-#20-C* . . . . (Rhino)

Last Song
Elton John; *The One* . . . . (MCA)

Lawyers, Guns & Money
Warren Zevon; *Excitable Boy* . . . .(Asylum)
Quiet Normal Life-Best Of Warren Zevon . . . .(Asylum)
Stand In The Fire . . . .(Asylum)

Leader Of The Band
Dan Fogelberg; *Dan Fogelberg/Greatest Hits* . . . .(Full Moon)
Innocent Age . . . .(Full Moon)

Letter, The (That Johnny Walker Read)
Asleep At The Wheel; *Very Best Of Asleep At The Wheel Since 1970* . . . .(Relentless/Madacy)

Like Father Like Son
Lenny Kravitz; *ST/Aida*. . . . . (Island)

Living Years, The
Mike & The Mechanics; *Living Years*. . . . .(Atlantic)

Love Keep Us Together
Martin Sexton; *Black Sheep* . . . . (Eastern Front)
The American . . . .(Atlantic)

Love Without End, Amen
George Strait; *Livin' It Up* . . . . (MCA)
Ten Strait Hits . . . . (MCA)

Lullaby
Tom Rush; *Tom Rush* . . . . (Columbia)

Mama Hated Diesels
Commander Cody & His Lost Planet Airmen; *Hot Licks, Cold Steel & Trucker's Favorites* . . . . (MCA)

Man He Was, The
George Jones; *The Rock: Stone Cold Country 2001* . . . .(BNA)

Mississippi Moon
Greg Brown; *One More Goodnight Kiss* . . . . (Red House)

Momma, Where's My Daddy
Keb' Mo'; *Just Like You* . . . .(Okeh)

Mommy Where's Daddy
Red Hot Chili Peppers; *Red Hot Chili Peppers* . . . . (EMI)

Ms. Jackson
Outkast; *Stankonia* . . . .(LaFace/Arista)

My Dad
Paul Peterson; *Donna Reed's Dinner Party-C*. . . . .(Nick At Nite)

My Dad Sucks
Descendants; *Bonus Fat* . . . .(SST)
Liveage . . . .(SST)
Somery . . . .(SST)

My Daddy
Jess Pearson; *Woody Guthrie's "We Ain't Down Yet"* . . . . (Cream)

My Daddy Knows Best
Marvelettes; *Compact Command Performances-Marvelettes*. . . . . (Motown)

Marvelettes-Anthology . . . . (Motown)

My Daddy Rocks Me
Benny Goodman Sextet; *Slipped Disc-1945-1946* . . . . (Columbia)
Mae West; *Fabulous Mae West* . . . . (MCA)

My Daddy Was A Jockey
John Lee Hooker; *Detroit Blues-1950-1951* . . . . (Collectables)
Gotham Golden Classics-C . . . . (Collectables)

My Daddy Was A Milkman
Kentucky HeadHunters; *Pickin' On Nashville* . . . . (Mercury)

My Daddy Was A Travelin' Man
Brenda Kaye Perry; *45-#1021* . . . . (MRC)

My Father
Barbara Cook; *Barbara Cook-Live At Carnegie Hall* . . . . (Sony Music Classical)
Judy Collins; *Colors Of The Day-The Best Of Judy Collins* . . . . (Elektra)
So Early In The Spring, The First 15 Years . . . . (Elektra)
Who Knows Where The Time Goes . . . . (Elektra)

My Father's Eyes
Eric Clapton; *Pilgrim* . . . . (Duck/Reprise)

My Father's Fiddle
Dave Loggins; *Apprentice (In A Musical Workshop)* . . . . (Epic)

My Father's Gun
Elton John; *Tumbleweed Connection* . . . . (Polydor)

My Father's Mansions
Pete Seeger; *Essential Pete Seeger* . . . . (Vanguard)

My Father's Shoes
Level 42; *Guaranteed* . . . . (RCA)

My Father's Shoes
Leon Russell; *Will O' The Wisp* . . . . (MCA)

My Father's Song
Barbra Streisand; *Lazy Afternoon* . . . . (Columbia)

My Heart Belongs To Daddy
Ella Fitzgerald & Cole Porter; *Dream Dancing* . . . . (Pablo)
Peggy Lee; *Best Of Peggy Lee* . . . . (MCA)
Rosemary Clooney; *Rosemary Clooney Sings The Music Of Cole
Porter* . . . . (Concord Jazz)

My Hometown
Bruce Springsteen; *Born In The U.S.A.* . . . . (Columbia)
Bruce Springsteen's Greatest Hits . . . . (Columbia)

My Old Man
Jerry Jeff Walker; *Gypsy Songman* . . . . (Rykodisc)
Mr. Bojangles . . . . (Bainbridge)
Walker's Collectibles . . . . (MCA)
John Denver; *Rhymes & Reasons* . . . . (RCA)
Steve Goodman; *Say It In Private* . . . . (Asylum)

My Son Calls Another Man Daddy
Hank Williams With His Drifting Cowboys; *Hank Williams-16
Great Hits* . . . . (Everest)
Hank Williams-40 Greatest Hits . . . . (Polydor)
Rare Takes & Radio Cuts . . . . (Polydor)

Mybabydaddy
B-Rock And The Bizz; *And Then There Was Bass* . . . . (Arista)
D.J. Mix '98-#1-C . . . . (Beast)

Night I Called The Old Man Out
Garth Brooks; *In Pieces* . . . . (Liberty)

No Sir
Darryl & Don Ellis; *No Sir* . . . . (Epic)

No Son Of Mine
Genesis; *We Can't Dance* . . . . (Atlantic)

Ode To My Family
Cranberries; *No Need To Argue* . . . . (Island)

Oh! My Papa
Eddie Fisher; *Eddie Fisher's All-Time Greatest Hits-#1* . . . . (RCA)
Hebrew National Kosher Classics-C . . . . (RCA)
Nipper's Greatest Hits Of The '50s-#2-C . . . . (RCA)

Old Coyote Town
Don Williams; *Traces* . . . . (Capitol)

Only Daddy That'll Walk The Line
Hank Williams, Jr.; *Family Tradition* . . . . (WB/Curb)
Kentucky HeadHunters; *Electric Barnyard* . . . . (Mercury)
Ricky Skaggs; *My Father's Son* . . . . (Epic)
Waylon Jennings; *Best Of Waylon Jennings* . . . . (RCA)
Waylon Jennings' Greatest Hits . . . . (RCA)
Waylon Jennings-Early Years . . . . (RCA)
Willie Nelson; *Willie & Family Live* . . . . (Columbia)

Papa
Paul Anka; *Anka* . . . . (United Artists)
Times Of Your Life . . . . (United Artists)

Papa
Prince; *Come* . . . . (Warner Bros.)

Papa
Bill Anderson; *The Bill Anderson Story* . . . . (MCA)

Papa Can You Hear Me?
Barbra Streisand; *One Voice* . . . . (Columbia)
ST/Yentl . . . . (Columbia)

Papa Don't Preach
Madonna; *Immaculate Collection* . . . . (Sire)
Royal Box . . . . (Sire)
True Blue . . . . (Sire)

Papa Hobo
Paul Simon; *Paul Simon* . . . . (Columbia)

Papa Loved Mama
Garth Brooks; *Garth Brooks-Double Live* . . . . (Capitol)
Ropin' The Wind . . . . (Liberty)

Papa Loves Mambo
Perry Como; *Como's Golden Records* . . . . (RCA)
Perry Como-Pure Gold . . . . (RCA)
Perry Como's All-Time Greatest Hits-#1 . . . . (RCA)
This Is Perry Como . . . . (RCA)

Papa Rolled His Own
Tommy James And The Shondells; *Crimson & Clover/Cellophane
Symphony* . . . . (Rhino)

Papa Was A Rollin' Stone
Temptations; *20/20-C* . . . . (Motown)
25 #1 Hits From 25 Years-C . . . . (Motown)
All The Million-Sellers . . . . (Motown)
Billboard Top Rock 'N' Roll Hits-1972-C . . . . (Rhino)
Compact Command Performances-Temptations . . . . (Motown)
Temptations-Anthology-The Best Of The Temptations . . . . (Motown)

Papa's Billy Goat
Sarah Ogan Gunning; *Silver Dagger* . . . . (Rounder)

Papa's Got A Brand New Bag
James Brown; *21 Legendary Superstars-C* . . . . (Original Sound)
Everybody's Doin' The Hustle & Dead On The Double Bump . . . . . . (Polydor)
James Brown's Greatest Hits . . . . (Rhino)
Live-Hot On The One . . . . (Polydor)
Otis Redding; *The Otis Redding Story* . . . . (Atlantic)
Unlimited! . . . . (Reprise)

Parents Just Don't Understand
D.J. Jazzy Jeff & The Fresh Prince; *He's The D.J. I'm The Rapper* . . . . (Jive)

Pistol Packin' Papa
Hank Snow; *Superstars Salute Jimmie Rodgers-C* . . . . (Step One)
Jimmie Rodgers; *Riding High-1929-1930* . . . . (Rounder)
This Is Jimmie Rodgers . . . . (RCA)

Pop, Let Me Have The Car
Carl Perkins; *Restless-Columbia Recordings* . . . . (Columbia)
Whole Lotta Shakin' . . . . (Sony Music Special Prod.)

Prodigal Son
Rolling Stones; *Beggars Banquet* . . . . (Abkco)

Question Everything
8Stops7; *In Moderation* . . . . (Reprise)

Ray's Dad Cadillac
Joni Mitchell; *Night Ride Home* . . . . (Geffen)

Ricky Wants A Man Of Her Own
Bruce Springsteen; *Tracks* . . . . (Columbia)

Rockin' Daddy
Howlin' Wolf; *The Chess Box-Howlin' Wolf* . . . . (Chess)

Roots Of My Raising
Merle Haggard & The Strangers; *Capitol Collectors Series-Merle Haggard &
The Strangers* . . . . (Capitol)
For The Record: Merle Haggard-43 Legendary Hits . . . . (BNA)
Merle Haggard's Greatest Hits-#2 . . . . (Curb)

Rosalita
Bruce Springsteen; *The Wild, The Innocent & The E Street Shuffle* . . .(Columbia)
Bruce Springsteen & The E Street Band; *Bruce Springsteen & The E Street
Band Live/1975-85* . . . . (Legacy)

Saginaw, Michigan
Lefty Frizzell; *American Originals-Lefty Frizzell* . . . . (Columbia)
Billboard Top Country Hits-1964-C . . . . (Rhino)
Columbia Country Classics-#3-Americana-C . . . . (Columbia)
Lefty Frizzell's Greatest Hits . . . . (Columbia)

Salty Papa Blues
Dinah Washington; *Dinah Washington-Golden Hits* . . . . (Mercury)

Saturday's Father
4 Seasons; *25th Anniversary Collection* . . . . (Rhino)

Seein' My Father In Me
Paul Overstreet; *Sowin' Love* . . . . (RCA)

Shimmy Shakin' Daddy
Maddox Brothers & Rose; *1946-1951-#2* . . . . (Arhoolie)
America's Most Colorful Hillbilly Band . . . . (Arhoolie)

Silver Future
Monster Magnet; *ST/Heavy Metal 2000* . . . . (Restless)

Silver Haired Daddy Of Mine
Frankie Yankovic & His Yanks; *I Wish I Was 18 Again* . . . . (Smash)

So Much Like My Dad
George Strait; *Holding My Own* . . . . (MCA)
Willie Nelson; *Partners* . . . . (Columbia)

Sugar Daddy
Bellamy Brothers; *Bellamy Brothers' Greatest Hits* . . . . (MCA)
You Can Get Crazy . . . . (WB/Curb)

Sugar Daddy
Thompson Twins; *Big Trash* . . . . (Red Eye)

Sugar Daddy
Fleetwood Mac; *Fleetwood Mac* . . . . (Reprise)

Sugar Daddy
Michigan & Smiley; *Sugar Daddy* . . . . (Real Authentic Sound)

Sugar Daddy
Jackson 5; *Jackson 5-Anthology* . . . . (Motown)

Jackson 5's Greatest Hits .... (Motown)
Sweet Daddy (Your Mama's Done Gone Mad)
Little Brother Montgomery; *Chicago-Living Legends-South Side
Blues* .... (Riverside)
Sweet Little Papa
Louis Armstrong; *Hot Fives & Hot Sevens-#2* .... (Columbia)
Sweet Lovin' Daddy
Betty Wright; *Golden Classics-Betty Wright* .... (Collectables)
Fontella Bass; *Rescued-Best Of Fontella Bass* .... (Chess)
Swingin' Daddy
Buddy Knox; *Best Of Buddy Knox* .... (Rhino)
Talk To Me Daddy
Thelma Cooper/Boyfriends; *Collectables Blues Collection-#3-C* . (Collectables)
Texas Girl At The Funeral Of Her Father
Randy Newman; *Little Criminals* .... (Warner Bros.)
That Silver Haired Daddy Of Mine
Doc Watson; *My Dear Old Southern Home* .... (Sugar Hill)
Gene Autry; *The Country Music Hall Of Fame-Gene Autry-15 Of His All-
Time Greatest Hits* .... (Columbia)
That Was Your Mother
Paul Simon; *Graceland* .... (Warner Bros.)
That's My Pa
Champion Jack Dupree; *Blues For Everybody* ..... (International Mktg. Group)
The Day (That You Gave Me A Son)
Babyface; *The Day* .... (Epic)
Theme From "Augie Doggie"
Original Soundtrack; *Hanna-Barbera Classics-#1-Original Recordings Of
The World's Most Famous Cartoon Themes &
Scores* .... (Kid Rhino/Rhino 4 Kids)
*Hanna-Barbera Pic-A-Nic Basket Of Cartoon
Classics* .... (Kid Rhino/Rhino 4 Kids)
Theme From "Blossom"
Original Soundtrack; *Television's Greatest Hits-#7-Cable Ready-C* ..... (TVT)
Theme From "Davis Rules"
Original Soundtrack; *Television's Greatest Hits-#7-Cable Ready-C* ..... (TVT)
Theme From "Empty Nest"
Original Soundtrack; *Television's Greatest Hits-#7-Cable Ready-C* ..... (TVT)
Theme From "Father Knows Best"
Original Soundtrack; *Television's Greatest Hits-#4-Black & White
Classics-C* .... (TVT)
Theme From "Full House"
Original Soundtrack; *Television's Greatest Hits-#7-Cable Ready-C* ..... (TVT)
Theme From "Major Dad"
Original Soundtrack; *Television's Greatest Hits-#7-Cable Ready-C* ..... (TVT)
Theme From "My Three Sons"
Original Soundtrack; *CBS: The First 50 Years* .... (TVT)
Television's Greatest Hits-#1-C .... (TVT)
Theme From "My Two Dads"
Original Soundtrack; *Television's Greatest Hits-#7-Cable Ready-C* ..... (TVT)
Theme From "Sanford & Son"
Original Soundtrack; *Television's Greatest Hits-#3-1970s & 1980s-C* ... (TVT)
Theme From "The Courtship Of Eddie's Father" (Best Friend)
Nilsson; *Television's Greatest Hits-#2-C* .... (TVT)
Theme From "The Godfather"
Henry Mancini & Mancini Pops Orchestra; *Cinema Italiano* ...... (RCA Victor)
Roger Williams; *Greatest Movie Themes* .... (Hip-O)
There Ain't No Good Chain Gang
Johnny Cash & Waylon Jennings; *Country's Greatest Hits-#15-Outlaw
Country-C* .... (Priority)
Hot Country Rock-#1-C .... (Epic)
Johnny Cash-16 Biggest Hits-#2 .... (Legacy)
The Man In Black-His Greatest Hits .... (Legacy)
They Don't Make 'Em Like That Anymore
Boy Howdy; *She'd Give Anything* .... (Curb)
They're Moving Father's Grave To Build A Sewer
Clancy Brothers & Tommy Makem; *Luck Of The Irish* .... (Columbia)
This Child Needs Its Father
Gladys Knight & The Pips; *Neither One Of Us* .... (Motown)
To Daddy
Emmylou Harris; *Profile/Best Of Emmylou Harris* .... (Warner Bros.)
Quarter Moon In A Ten Cent Town .... (Warner Bros.)
Tombstone Blues
Bob Dylan; *Biograph* .... (Columbia)
Highway 61 Revisited .... (Columbia)
Real Live .... (Columbia)
Truckin' Dad
Dave Dudley; *Diesel Express* .... (Fifty One West)
Unconditional
Clay Davidson; *Unconditional* .... (Virgin)
Unwed Fathers
Gail Davies; *Best Of Gail Davies* .... (Capitol)
Tammy Wynette; *Best Loved Hits* .... (Epic)
Used Cars
Bruce Springsteen; *Nebraska* .... (Columbia)
Voodoo Daddy
Lonnie Brooks; *Bayou Lightning* .... (Alligator)
Walk Like A Man
Bruce Springsteen; *Tunnel Of Love* .... (Columbia)

What's Going On
Cyndi Lauper; *True Colors* .... (Portrait)
Marvin Gaye; *20/20-C* .... (Motown)
Marvin Gaye Live At The London Palladium .... (Motown)
Marvin Gaye-Anthology .... (Motown)
Marvin Gaye's Greatest Hits/ .... (Motown)
More Songs From "The Big Chill" Soundtrack-C .... (Motown)
What's Going On .... (Motown)
Quincy Jones; *Quincy Jones-The Best* .... (A&M)
When I Grow Up (To Be A Man)
Beach Boys; *Absolute Best-#1* .... (Capitol)
Beach Boys-Gift Set .... (Capitol)
Dance Dance Dance .... (Capitol)
Made In The U.S.A. .... (Capitol)
Spirit Of America .... (Capitol)
Where Corn Don't Grow
Travis Tritt; *The Restless Kind* .... (Warner Bros.)
Who I Am
Jessica Andrews; *Who I Am.* .... (DreamWorks/SKG)
With Arms Wide Open
Creed; *Human Clay* .... (Wind-up)
Now That's What I Call Music!-#6-C .... (Virgin)
You Better Sit Down Kids
Cher; *Bang, Bang The Early Years* .... (Capitol)
Your Mama Don't Dance
Loggins & Messina; *Loggins & Messina-On Stage* .... (Columbia)
Loggins And Messina .... (Columbia)
Pop Classics Of The '70s-C .... (Columbia)
The Best Of Friends .... (Columbia)
Poison; *Open Up And Say...Ahh!* .... (Capitol)
Swallow This Live .... (Capitol)
Zero And Blind Terry
Bruce Springsteen; *Tracks* .... (Columbia)

FAMILY: GENERAL, Family Life

See Also: **CHILDREN, CHILDREN LEAVING HOME, DOMESTIC
ABUSE, FAMILY (various), PARENTS (various)**

Affirmation
Savage Garden; *Affirmation* .... (Columbia)
A-sleepin' At The Foot Of The Bed
"Little" Jimmy Dickens; *Bluegrass Super Hits-C* .... (Columbia)
Black Sheep Of The Family
Blackmore's Rainbow; *Ritchie Blackmore's R-A-I-N-B-O-W* .... (Polydor)
Bulls On Parade
Rage Against The Machine; *Evil Empire* .... (Epic)
Consider Yourself
Original Broadway Cast; *Oliver!* .... (RCA Victor)
Original London Cast; *Oliver!.* .... (EMI-Angel)
Daddy Frank (The Guitar Man)
Merle Haggard; *Best Of Merle Haggard* .... (Capitol)
Capitol Collectors Series-Merle Haggard .... (Capitol)
Merle Haggard & The Strangers; *For The Record: Merle Haggard-43
Legendary Hits* .... (BNA)
Songs I'll Always Sing .... (Capitol)
Daddy Sang Bass
Johnny Cash; *Columbia Country Classics-#5-A New Tradition-C* ... (Columbia)
Johnny Cash's Greatest Hits-#2. .... (Columbia)
The Man In Black-His Greatest Hits. .... (Legacy)
Danny's Song
Anne Murray; *Anne Murray-Country* .... (Capitol)
Anne Murray's Greatest Hits .... (Capitol)
Danny's Song .... (Capitol)
Loggins & Messina; *Loggins & Messina-On Stage* .... (Columbia)
Sittin' In .... (Columbia)
The Best Of Friends .... (Columbia)
Down Home
Alabama; *Pass It On Down* .... (BMG Special Prod.)
Families
Lou Reed; *The Bells* .... (Buddha)
Family
Dar Williams; *Mortal City.* .... (Razor & Tie)
Family
Maze; *Greatest Slow Jams* .... (Right Stuff)
Joy And Pain .... (Razor & Tie)
Slow Jams-The Timeless Collection-#6-C .... (Right Stuff)
Family
Dolly Parton; *Eagle When She Flies* .... (Columbia)
Family
Original Cast; *Dreamgirls* .... (Geffen)
Family Affair
Sly & The Family Stone; *Billboard Top Rock 'N' Roll Hits-1971-C* ..... (Rhino)
Club Epic-#2-C .... (Legacy)
In Yo' Face!-History Of Funk-#2-C .... (Rhino)
Sly & The Family Stone-Anthology .... (Epic)
There's A Riot Goin' On. .... (Epic)

Steve Winwood; *Junction Seven* . . . .(Virgin)
Family And The Fishing Net, The
  Peter Gabriel; *Peter Gabriel/Plays Live* . . . . (Geffen)
    Security . . . . (Geffen)
  Primus; *Rhinoplasty* . . . . (Interscope)
Family Background
  Victor Borge; *Live!* . . . . (Sony Broadway)
Family Band
  Shakin' Apostles; *Medicine Show* . . . . (Big Tex)
Family Beat
  Bad Boys Blue; *Reggae Summer Splash-C* . . . .(Radikal)
Family Bible
  Claude Gray; *20 Great Country Recordings Of The '50s & '60s-C* . . . . (Cascade)
  Commander Cody & His Lost Planet Airmen; *Lost In The Ozone* . . . . . . (MCA)
  Ernest Tubb; *Family Bible* . . . .(Universal Special Mkts.)
  George Jones; *24 Gospel Greats* . . . .(Deluxe)
    Cup Of Loneliness-Classic Mercury Years . . . .(Mercury)
  Johnny Cash & Willie Nelson; *VH1 Storytellers* . . . .(American)
  Merle Haggard; *Land Of Many Churches* . . . .(Razor & Tie)
  Osborne Brothers; *Essential Bluegrass Album* . . . . (C.M.H. Prod.)
  Willie Nelson; *Best Of Gospel* . . . .(Universal Special Mkts.)
    Essential Willie Nelson . . . .(RCA)
    Ryman Country Homecoming 3-C . . . (Springhouse Music Grp./Chordant)
Family Bible And The Farmer's Almanac
  Randy Travis; *A Man Ain't Made Of Stone* . . . . (DreamWorks/SKG)
Family Business
  Fugees; *The Score-Edit* . . . .(Columbia)
Family Business
  Master P; *Da Last Don* . . . .(Priority)
Family Business
  Fish; *Pigpen's Birthday* . . . . (Renaissance)
Family Court
  Starlights; *Soldering-Reggae's Greatest Hits* . . . . (Heartbeat)
Family Curse
  Lonnie Brooks; *Satisfaction Guaranteed* . . . .(Alligator)
Family Dirge
  Noel Coward; *Noel Coward Sings Sail Away & Other Coward Rarities* . . .(DRG)
Family Fugue
  Original Cast; *Stop The World I Want To Get Off* . . . . (Jay)
Family Groove
  Neville Brothers; *Family Groove* . . . . (A&M)
Family Hands
  Mary Chapin Carpenter; *Hometown Girl* . . . .(Columbia)
Family In A Suitcase
  Sugar Puff Demons; *Psycho Killers-C* . . . . (Dressed To Kill)
Family Is
  Cleve Francis; *Big Country-For One And All-C* . . . . . (Music For Little People)
Family Man
  Everton Blender; *Live At The White River Reggae Bash* . . . . (Heartbeat)
Family Man
  Karyn White; *Karyn White* . . . . (Warner Bros.)
Family Man
  Pablo Cruise; *Worlds Away* . . . . (A&M)
Family Man
  Black Flag; *Family Man* . . . . (SST)
Family Man
  Daryl Hall & John Oates; *H2O* . . . .(RCA)
    Hi Octane-Hard Drivin' Hits-C . . . .(RCA)
Family Man
  James Taylor; *In The Pocket* . . . . (Warner Bros.)
Family Man
  Fleetwood Mac; *Tango In The Night* . . . . (Warner Bros.)
Family Of Man
  Three Dog Night; *Best Of Three Dog Night* . . . . (MCA)
    Joy To The World-Greatest Hits . . . . (MCA)
Family Of The Underdog
  Digital Underground; *Sons Of The P* . . . .(Tommy Boy)
Family Planning
  Depressions; *The Punk Rock Collection* . . . . (Captain Oi)
Family Reserve
  Lyle Lovett; *Joshua Judges Ruth* . . . .(Curb/MCA)
Family Reunion
  Rick Trevino; *Looking For The Light* . . . .(Columbia)
Family Reunion
  Wade Hayes; *Old Enough To Know Better* . . . . (Columbia)
Family Reunion
  David Allan Coe; *David Allan Coe-Super Hits* . . . .(Columbia)
  Oak Ridge Boys; *Best Of The Oak Ridge Boys* . . . . (Columbia)
Family Reunion
  O'Jays; *Collector's Item* . . . . (Philadelphia Int'l)
    Family Reunion . . . . (Philadelphia Int'l)
    Let Me Make Love To You . . . . (Legacy)
Family Reunion
  Carl Story; *Fifty Years Of Bluegrass Hits-4-C* . . . . (C.M.H. Prod.)
Family Reunion
  Blink-182; *Short Music For Short People-C* . . . . . . (Fat Wreck Chords)
Family Rules
  Lonnie Brooks; *Lonnie Brooks-Deluxe Edition* . . . .(Alligator)

Family Snapshot
  Peter Gabriel; *Peter Gabriel* . . . . (Geffen)
    Peter Gabriel/Plays Live . . . . (Geffen)
    Shaking The Tree-Sixteen Golden Greats . . . . (Geffen)
Family Tradition
  Hank Williams, Jr.; *20 Hits Special Collection-#1* . . . .(Curb)
    Best Of Hank & Hank . . . .(Curb)
    Family Tradition-Original Classic Hits-#3 . . . .(Curb)
    Hank Williams, Jr.-Greatest Hits-#1 . . . .(Curb)
Family Tree
  Megadeth; *Youthanasia* . . . .(Capitol)
Family Tree
  Suzy Bogguss; *Nobody Love, Nobody Gets Hurt* . . . .(Capitol)
Family Tree
  Michael Martin Murphey; *Land Of Enchantment* . . . . (Warner Bros.)
Family Tree
  Lee Roy Parnell; *Lee Roy Parnell* . . . .(Arista)
Family Troubles
  Teddy Big Boy Edwards; *Complete Recorded Works-1930-1936* . . . (Document)
Family Way, The
  Original Cast; *I Can Get It For You Wholesale* . . . . (Columbia)
Family Ways
  Soup Dragons; *This Is Our Art* . . . . (Sire)
Family Whistle
  Tony Trischka; *Alone & Together* . . . .(Alcazar)
Family Who Prays (Never Shall Part), The
  Browns; *Family Bible* . . . .(Step One)
  Jim & Jesse; *Old Dominion Masters* . . . . (Pinecastle)
  Louvin Brothers; *Live At New River Ranch* . . . . (Copper Creek)
    ST/Jesus' Son . . . . (Mammoth)
    When I Stop Dreaming: The Best Of The Louvin Brothers . . . . . .(Razor & Tie)
  Ralph Stanley; *Child Of The King* . . . . (Rebel)
Grown Men Don't Cry
  Tim McGraw; *Set This Circus Down* . . . .(Curb)
Halfway Home Cafe
  Ricky Skaggs and Kentucky Thunder; *History Of The Future* . . .(Skaggs Family)
Hands Of A Working Man
  Ty Herndon; *Big Hopes* . . . . (Epic)
Hey Little Minivan
  Austin Lounge Lizards; *Employee Of The Month* . . . . (Sugar Hill)
Holes In The Floor Of Heaven
  Steve Wariner; *Burnin' The Roadhouse Down* . . . .(Capitol)
Honeymooners
  Bruce Springsteen; *Tracks* . . . .(Columbia)
I'll Always Be Right There
  Bryan Adams; *18 Til I Die* . . . .(A&M)
    MTV Unplugged-Bryan Adams . . . .(A&M)
Is There Life Out There
  Reba McEntire; *For My Broken Heart* . . . .(MCA)
    Reba McEntire's Greatest Hits Volume Two . . . .(MCA)
Just Another Day In Paradise
  Phil Vassar; *Phil Vassar* . . . .(Arista)
Kinfolks In Carolina
  Merle Travis; *Best Of Merle Travis* . . . .(Rhino)
My Blue Heaven
  Artie Shaw; *Complete Artie Shaw-#4* . . . . (RCA)
    This Is Artie Shaw . . . .(Bluebird)
  Fats Domino; *Fats Domino-Legendary Masters* . . . . (United Artists)
    Fats Domino's Greatest Hits . . . .(Everest)
    My Blue Heaven-Best Of Fats Domino-#1 . . . . (EMI)
    Oldies But Goodies-#10-C . . . . (Original Sound)
  Frank Sinatra; *Frank Sinatra-Gift Set* . . . .(Capitol)
    Sinatra's Swingin' Session!!! . . . .(Capitol)
My Niece From Pittsburgh In 1992
  PFS; *Illustrative Problems* . . . .(Cuneiform)
Ob-La-Di, Ob-La-Da
  Beatles; *Beatles-Box Set* . . . .(Capitol)
    The Beatles (White Album) . . . .(Capitol)
    The Beatles/1967-1970 . . . . (Capitol)
Ode To My Family
  Cranberries; *No Need To Argue* . . . .(Island)
Roulette
  Bruce Springsteen; *Tracks* . . . .(Columbia)
Theme From "All In The Family"
  Original Soundtrack; *CBS: The First 50 Years* . . . .(TVT)
    Television's Greatest Hits-#3-1970s & 1980s-C . . . .(TVT)
Theme From "All My Children"
  Original Soundtrack; *Television's Greatest Hits-#5-In Living Color-C* . . . .(TVT)
Theme From "Clarissa Explains It All"
  Original Soundtrack; *Television's Greatest Hits-#7-Cable Ready-C* . . . . . .(TVT)
Theme From "Cosby"
  Original Soundtrack; *CBS: The First 50 Years* . . . .(TVT)
Theme From "Diff'rent Strokes"
  Original Soundtrack; *Television's Greatest Hits-#6-Remote Control-C* . . .(TVT)
Theme From "Eight Is Enough"
  Original Soundtrack; *Television's Greatest Hits-#6-Remote Control-C* . . .(TVT)
Theme From "Everybody Loves Raymond"
  Original Soundtrack; *CBS: The First 50 Years* . . . .(TVT)

Theme From ''Falcon Crest''
Original Soundtrack; *Television's Greatest Hits-#6-Remote Control-C* . . (TVT)
Theme From ''Family Feud''
Original Soundtrack; *Television's Greatest Hits-#6-Remote Control-C* . . (TVT)
Theme From ''Family Matters''
Original Soundtrack; *Television's Greatest Hits-#7-Cable Ready-C* . . . . . (TVT)
Theme From ''Family Ties''
Original Soundtrack; *Television's Greatest Hits-#6-Remote Control-C* . . (TVT)
Theme From ''Father Knows Best''
Original Soundtrack; *Television's Greatest Hits-#4-Black & White
Classics-C* . . . . (TVT)
Theme From ''Fresh Prince Of Bel-Air''
Original Soundtrack; *Television's Greatest Hits-#7-Cable Ready-C* . . . . . (TVT)
Theme From ''Full House''
Original Soundtrack; *Television's Greatest Hits-#7-Cable Ready-C* . . . . . (TVT)
Theme From ''Good Times''
Original Soundtrack; *CBS: The First 50 Years* . . . . (TVT)
Television's Greatest Hits-#3-1970s & 1980s-C . . . . (TVT)
Theme From ''Growing Pains''
Original Soundtrack; *Television's Greatest Hits-#6-Remote Control-C* . . (TVT)
Theme From ''Home Improvement''
Original Soundtrack; *Television's Greatest Hits-#7-Cable Ready-C* . . . . . (TVT)
Theme From ''Lost In Space''
Neil Norman; *Greatest Science Fiction Hits-#3-C* . . . .(Crescendo)
Original Soundtrack; *CBS: The First 50 Years* . . . . (TVT)
Television's Greatest Hits-#1-C . . . . (TVT)
Theme From ''Major Dad''
Original Soundtrack; *Television's Greatest Hits-#7-Cable Ready-C* . . . . . (TVT)
Theme From ''Roc''
Original Soundtrack; *Television's Greatest Hits-#7-Cable Ready-C* . . . . . (TVT)
Theme From ''Roseanne''
Original Soundtrack; *Television's Greatest Hits-#7-Cable Ready-C* . . . . . (TVT)
Theme From ''The Addams Family''
Original Soundtrack; *Television's Greatest Hits-#1-C* . . . . (TVT)
Vic Mizzy; *Elvira Presents Haunted Hits-C* . . . . (Rhino)
Haunted Hits-C . . . . (Rhino)
Original Music From ''The Addams Family'' . . . . (RCA)
Theme From ''The Adventures Of Ozzie And Harriet''
Original Soundtrack; *Television's Greatest Hits-#4-Black & White
Classics-C* . . . . (TVT)
Theme From ''The Brady Bunch''
Brady Bunch Kids; *It's A Sunshine Day-Best Of The Brady
Bunch Kids* . . . . (MCA)
Television's Greatest Hits-#2-C . . . . (TVT)
Theme From ''The Cosby Show''
Original Soundtrack; *Television's Greatest Hits-#7-Cable Ready-C* . . . . . (TVT)
Theme From ''The Donna Reed Show''
Original Soundtrack; *Donna Reed's Dinner Party-C* . . . . (Nick At Nite)
Television's Greatest Hits-#1-C . . . . (TVT)
TV Classic Themes: 25th Anniversary Edition-C . . . . (Breakable)
Theme From ''The Dukes Of Hazzard''
Waylon Jennings; *Only Daddy That'll Walk The Line-The RCA Years* . . . (RCA)
Television's Greatest Hits-#6-Remote Control-C . . . . (TVT)
Waylon Jennings' Greatest Hits-#2 . . . . (RCA)
Theme From ''The Flintstones''
Original Soundtrack; *Hanna-Barbera Classics-#1-Original Recordings Of
The World's Most Famous Cartoon Themes &
Scores* . . . . (Kid Rhino/Rhino 4 Kids)
*Hanna-Barbera Pic-A-Nic Basket Of Cartoon
Classics* . . . . (Kid Rhino/Rhino 4 Kids)
Television's Greatest Hits-#1-C . . . . (TVT)
Steve Hobbs; *Escape* . . . . (Cexton)
Theme From ''The Godfather''
Henry Mancini & Mancini Pops Orchestra; *Cinema Italiano* . . . . . .(RCA Victor)
Roger Williams; *Greatest Movie Themes* . . . . (Hip-O)
Theme From ''The Jeffersons''
Original Soundtrack; *CBS: The First 50 Years* . . . . (TVT)
Television's Greatest Hits-#3-1970s & 1980s-C . . . . (TVT)
Theme From ''The Jetsons''
Original Soundtrack; *Hanna-Barbera Pic-A-Nic Basket Of Cartoon
Classics* . . . . (Kid Rhino/Rhino 4 Kids)
Television's Greatest Hits-#1-C . . . . (TVT)
Stunners; *ST/Jetsons-The Movie* . . . . (MCA)
Theme From ''The Partridge Family''
Original Soundtrack; *Television's Greatest Hits-#2-C* . . . . (TVT)
Theme From ''The Real McCoys''
Original Soundtrack; *Television's Greatest Hits-#4-Black & White
Classics-C* . . . . (TVT)
Theme From ''The Simpsons''
Original Soundtrack; *Television's Greatest Hits-#7-Cable Ready-C* . . . . . (TVT)
Theme From ''The Smurfs''
Original Soundtrack; *Television's Greatest Hits-#3-1970s & 1980s-C* . . . (TVT)
Theme From ''The Waltons''
Original Soundtrack; *CBS: The First 50 Years* . . . . (TVT)
Television's Greatest Hits-#3-1970s & 1980s-C . . . . (TVT)
Theme From ''Thirtysomething''
Original Soundtrack; *Television's Greatest Hits-#7-Cable Ready-C* . . . . . (TVT)
They Dance Alone (Cueca Solo)
Sting; *...Nothing Like The Sun* . . . . (A&M)

Fields Of Gold-The Best Of Sting 1984-1994 . . . . (A&M)
Thicker Than Blood
Garth Brooks; *Scarecrow* . . . . (Capitol)
Time Marches On
Tracy Lawrence; *Best Of Tracy Lawrence* . . . .(Atlantic)
Time Marches On . . . .(Atlantic)
Wayward Wind
Gogi Grant; *'50s Jukebox Favorites-C* . . . . (K-Tel)
Collectables Presents The History Of Rock-#7-C . . . . (Collectables)
Lynn Anderson & Emmylou Harris; *Cowboy's Sweetheart* . . . .(Laserlight)
Patsy Cline; *The Patsy Cline Story* . . . . (MCA)
We Are Family
Sister Sledge; *Atlantic Records 50 Years-The Gold Anniversary
Collection-C* . . . .(Atlantic)
Best Of Sister Sledge-1973-1985 . . . . (Rhino)
*Chicken Soup For The Soul: I'll Be There For You-Songs Of Friendship,
Brotherhood And Sisterhood-C* . . . . (Rhino)
ST/The Full Monty . . . . (RCA Victor)
We Are Family . . . . (Rhino)
Where Were You (When The World Stopped Turning)
Alan Jackson; *Alan Jackson-Drive* . . . .(Arista)
Who's That Man
Toby Keith; *Boomtown* . . . .(Polydor Country)
Workin' Man Blues
Diamond Rio/Lee Roy Parnell/Steve Wariner; *Mama's Hungry Eyes-Merle
Haggard Tribute-C* . . . . (Arista)
Gary Morris; *These Days.* . . . . (Capitol)
Merle Haggard & The Strangers; *Best Of Country Blues* . . . . (Curb)
Capitol Collectors Series-Merle Haggard & The Strangers . . . . (Capitol)
For The Record: Merle Haggard-43 Legendary Hits . . . . (BNA)
Okie From Muskogee . . . . (Capitol)
Songs I'll Always Sing . . . . (Capitol)
Ricky Van Shelton; *Wild-Eyed Dream* . . . . (Columbia)

FAMILY: GRANDPARENTS, Grandfathers, Grandmothers
See Also: **BABY, CHILDREN, FAMILY (various), MEN: GENERAL, MEN'S NAMES: A-Z, WOMEN: GENERAL, WOMEN'S NAMES: A-Z**

Canned Goods
Greg Brown; *One More Goodnight Kiss* . . . . (Red House)
Country Boy's Tool Box
Aaron Tippin; *Tool Box.* . . . .(RCA)
Grandaddy
Judy Collins; *Times Of Our Lives* . . . . (Elektra)
Grandma Got Run Over By A Reindeer
Elmo & Patsy; *Billboard's Greatest Christmas Hits-C* . . . . (Rhino)
*Dr. Demento Presents The Greatest Novelty Records-#6-
Christmas-C* . . . . (Rhino)
Dr. Demento Presents The Greatest Novelty Records-C . . . . (Rhino)
Grandma Got Run Over By A Reindeer . . . . (Epic)
Greatest Children's Christmas Hits-C . . . . (Columbia)
Now That's What I Call Christmas!-C . . . . (UTV)
Grandma Harp
Merle Haggard; *18 Rare Classics* . . . . (Curb)
Grandma Klump
Eddie Murphy; *Eddie Murphy-Greatest Comedy Hits* . . . . (Columbia)
Grandma Told Grandpa
Lightnin' Hopkins; *Drinkin' In The Blues-Golden Classics-#1* . . . (Collectables)
Grandma's Feather Bed
John Denver; *Back Home Again* . . . . (RCA)
Grandma's Hands
Al Jarreau; *Improvisations* . . . . (Blue Moon)
Barbra Streisand; *Butterfly* . . . . (Columbia)
Bill Withers; *Bill Withers' Greatest Hits* . . . . (Columbia)
Bill Withers Live At Carnegie Hall . . . . (Columbia)
Keb' Mo'; *Big Wide Grin* . . . . (Sony Wonder)
Grandma's Killer Fruitcake
Elmo Shropshire; *Dr. Elmo's Twisted Christmas* . . . . (Laughing Stock)
Grandma's Song
Gail Davies; *Gail Davies' Greatest Hits* . . . . (Little Chickadee)
Grandma's Theme
John Cougar Mellencamp; *Scarecrow* . . . . (Riva)
Grandmother Song
Steve Martin; *Let's Get Small* . . . . (Warner Bros.)
Grandpa (Tell Me 'Bout The Good Old Days)
Judds; *Judds' Greatest Hits.* . . . . (MCA)
Rockin' With The Rhythm . . . . (MCA)
Super 10-#2-C . . . . (RCA)
Grandpa Was A Carpenter
John Prine; *John Prine-Souvenirs* . . . .(Oh Boy)
Grandpa's Gonna Sue The Pants Off Of Santa
Elmo Shropshire; *Dr. Elmo's Twisted Christmas* . . . . (Laughing Stock)
Granny
Dave Matthews Band; *Listener Supported* . . . . (RCA)
Live At Luther College . . . . (RCA)

Holes In The Floor Of Heaven
Steve Wariner; *Burnin' The Roadhouse Down* . . . . (Capitol)
I'm My Own Grandpa
Willie Nelson; *Rainbow Connection* . . . . (Island)
It's In The Book (Parts 1 & 2)
Johnny Standley; *Dr. Demento Gooses Mother-C* . . . . (Kid Rhino/Rhino 4 Kids)
Jacob's Ladder
Mark Wills; *Mark Wills* . . . . (Mercury)
Jig Saw Puzzle
Rolling Stones; *Beggars Banquet* . . . . (Abkco)
Johnny, My Love (Grandma's Diary)
Wilma Lee & Stoney Cooper; *45-#1118* . . . . (Hickory)
Kisses Sweeter Than Wine
Jimmie Rodgers; *Best Of Jimmie Rodgers* . . . . (Rhino)
Cruisin'-1958-C . . . . (Increase)
Weavers; *Best Of The Weavers* . . . . (MCA)
Reunion-At Carnegie Hall-1963 . . . . (Vanguard)
Weavers At Carnegie Hall . . . . (Vanguard)
Weavers' Greatest Hits . . . . (Vanguard)
Li'l Red Riding Hood
Sam The Sham and The Pharaohs; *Best Of Sam The Sham and The*
Pharaohs . . . . (Polydor)
Cruisin'-1966-C . . . . (Increase)
Pharaohization! (Best Of) . . . . (Rhino)
Little Old Lady (From Pasadena)
Beach Boys; *Concert/'69-Live In London* . . . . (Capitol)
Jan & Dean; *Best Of Jan & Dean* . . . . (EMI)
Billboard Top Rock 'N' Roll Hits-1964-C . . . . (Rhino)
Dead Man's Curve . . . . (EMI)
Surf City-Best Of Jan & Dean . . . . (EMI)
Love, Me
Collin Raye; *All I Can Be* . . . . (Epic)
Greatest Country Hits Of The '90s-1992-C . . . . (Columbia)
Mountain Music
Alabama; *Alabama's Greatest Hits* . . . . (RCA)
Mountain Music . . . . (RCA)
Ooh La La
Rod Stewart; *When We Were The New Boys* . . . . (Warner Bros.)
San Antonio Rose To You
Rick Trevino; *Texas Super Hits-C* . . . . (Columbia)
Strawberry Wine
Deana Carter; *Did I Shave My Legs For This?* . . . . (Capitol)
Theme From "The Real McCoys"
Original Soundtrack; *Television's Greatest Hits-#4-Black & White*
Classics-C . . . . (TVT)
When I'm Sixty-Four
Beatles; *Beatles-Box Set* . . . . (Capitol)
Sgt. Pepper's Lonely Hearts Club Band . . . . (Capitol)
Who I Am
Jessica Andrews; *Who I Am* . . . . (DreamWorks/SKG)
Who's Sucking On Grandpa's Balls Since Grandma Ain't Home
Tonight?
Frogs; *My Daughter The Broad* . . . . (Matador)
You'll Never Leave Harlan Alive
Patty Loveless; *Mountain Soul* . . . . (Epic)

FAMILY: MOTHERS, Mama, Mom

See Also: BABY, CHILDREN, FAMILY (various), FAMILY
PLANNING, PARENTS (various), TEACHING VALUES,
TEENAGERS, WOMEN: GENERAL, WOMEN'S NAMES: A-Z

26 Cents
Wilkinsons; *Nothing But Love* . . . . (Giant)
500 Miles Away From Home
Bobby Bare; *500 Miles Away From Home* . . . . (RCA)
Foy Willing; *Cowboy/The New Sound Of American Folk* . . . . (DRG)
Reba McEntire; *Starting Over* . . . . (MCA)
All The Good Ones Are Gone
Pam Tillis; *Pam Tillis' Greatest Hits* . . . . (Arista)
Alone Again (Naturally)
Gilbert O'Sullivan; *Best Of Gilbert O'Sullivan* . . . . (Rhino)
Billboard Top Rock 'N' Roll Hits-1972-C . . . . (Rhino)
And Her Mother Came Too
Bobby Short; *50 By Bobby Short* . . . . (Atlantic)
Anything
Jay-Z; *Vol. 3-Life & Times of S. Carter* . . . . (Roc-A-Fella/DJMG)
Apple Tree
Erykah Badu; *Baduizm* . . . . (Kedar Entert./Universal)
Big Bad Mamma
Foxy Brown featuring Dru Hill; *Ill Na Na* . . . . (Violator)
Big Fat Mama
Fred McDowell; *Long Way From Home* . . . . (Milestone)
Big Fat Mama
Big Joe Williams; *Legacy Of The Blues-#6* . . . . (Crescendo)
Big Girls Don't Cry
4 Seasons; *4 Seasons' Greatest Hits-#1* . . . . (Rhino)

4 Seasons-Anthology . . . . (Rhino)
Billboard Top Rock 'N' Roll Hits-1962-C . . . . (Rhino)
More Dirty Dancing-C . . . . (RCA)
Blues In The Night
Benny Goodman; *Small Groups-1941-1945* . . . . (Columbia)
Bobby Bland; *Introspective Of The Early Years* . . . . (MCA)
Dinah Shore; *Nipper's Greatest Hits Of The '40s-#1-C* . . . . (RCA)
Doc Severinsen; *Best Of Doc Severinsen* . . . . (MCA)
Frank Sinatra; *Frank Sinatra sings for Only The Lonely* . . . . (Capitol)
Jimmie Lunceford & His Orchestra; *Warner Bros.' 75 Years Entertaining*
The World-Film Music-C . . . . (Rhino)
Mel Torme; *Torme* . . . . (Verve)
Robins; *Best Of The Robins* . . . . (Crescendo)
Rosemary Clooney; *Rosemary Clooney-16 Most Requested Songs* . . . (Legacy)
Tony Bennett; *Playin' With My Friends-Bennett Sings The*
Blues-C . . . . (Columbia)
Woody Herman; *Blues On Parade* . . . . (GRP)
Woody Herman-Best Of The Decca Years . . . . (Decca)
Woody Herman & His Orchestra; *Big Bands Greatest*
Hits-#3-C . . . . (MCA Special Prod.)
Bohemian Rhapsody
Braids; *Here We Come* . . . . (Big Beat)
ST/High School High . . . . (Big Beat)
Queen; *A Night At The Opera* . . . . (Hollywood)
Classic Queen . . . . (Hollywood)
Live At Wembley '86 . . . . (Hollywood)
ST/Wayne's World . . . . (Reprise)
Bookends
Joe Walsh; *The Smoker You Drink The Player You Get* . . . . (MCA)
Burn That Candle
Bill Haley & His Comets; *Bill Haley & His Comets' Greatest Hits* . . . . . (MCA)
Bill Haley & His Comets-Golden Hits . . . . (MCA)
R-O-C-K . . . . (Sun)
Emmylou Harris; *Quarter Moon In A Ten Cent Town* . . . . (Warner Bros.)
Catfish John
Johnny Russell; *Johnny Russell's Greatest Hits* . . . . (Dominion Entert.)
Choo Choo Mama
Ten Years After; *Recorded Live* . . . . (Chrysalis)
Universal . . . . (Chrysalis)
Christmas Shoes
Newsong; *Sheltering Tree* . . . . (Benson/Jive)
Coat Of Many Colors
Dolly Parton; *Best Of Dolly Parton* . . . . (RCA)
Dolly Parton-Super Hits . . . . (Columbia)
Essential Dolly Parton-#2 . . . . (RCA)
Emmylou Harris; *Pieces Of The Sky* . . . . (Reprise)
Come To Mama
Etta James; *Seven Year Itch* . . . . (Island)
Koko Taylor; *Queen Of The Blues* . . . . (Alligator)
Come To Mama
Pete Townshend; *White City* . . . . (Atco)
Cowboy's Wild Song To His Herd
Skip Gorman; *A Cowboy's Wild Song To His Herd* . . . . (Rounder)
Crazy Mama
Rolling Stones; *Black And Blue* . . . . (Rolling Stones)
Sucking In The Seventies . . . . (Rolling Stones)
Crazy Mama
J.J. Cale; *Naturally* . . . . (MCA)
Cry Baby Cry
Beatles; *The Beatles (White Album)* . . . . (Capitol)
Daddy Frank (The Guitar Man)
Merle Haggard; *Best Of Merle Haggard* . . . . (Capitol)
Capitol Collectors Series-Merle Haggard . . . . (Capitol)
Merle Haggard & The Strangers; *For The Record: Merle Haggard-43*
Legendary Hits . . . . (BNA)
Songs I'll Always Sing . . . . (Capitol)
Daddy Sang Bass
Johnny Cash; *Columbia Country Classics-#5-A New Tradition-C* . . . (Columbia)
Johnny Cash's Greatest Hits-#2 . . . . (Columbia)
The Man In Black-His Greatest Hits . . . . (Legacy)
Daddy's Come Around
Paul Overstreet; *Heroes* . . . . (RCA)
Daddy's Little Girl
Al Martino; *Best Of Al Martino* . . . . (Capitol)
Mills Brothers; *50th Anniversary* . . . . (Ranwood)
All Occasions Album . . . . (Gateway)
Best Of The Mills Brothers . . . . (MCA)
The Mills Brothers Story . . . . (Ranwood)
Dear Brother
Hank Williams; *I Saw The Light* . . . . (Polydor)
Dear Mama
2Pac; *Death Row Greatest Hits-C* . . . . (Death Row)
Me Against The World . . . . (Interscope)
MTV Party To Go-#7-C . . . . (Tommy Boy)
Did Your Mother Come From Ireland
Bing Crosby; *Shillelaghs & Shamrocks* . . . . (MCA)
Does Your Mother Know?
Abba; *Abba Live* . . . . (Atlantic)
Abba's Greatest Hits-#2 . . . . (Atlantic)

The Singles-First 10 Years . . . .(Atlantic)
Voulez-Vous . . . .(Atlantic)

Don't Take Your Guns To Town
Johnny Cash; *Billboard Top Country Hits-1959-C* . . . . (Rhino)
Columbia Country Classics-#3-Americana-C . . . . (Columbia)
Johnny Cash-16 Biggest Hits-#2 . . . . (Legacy)
Johnny Cash's Greatest Hits . . . . (Columbia)
The Man In Black-His Greatest Hits . . . . (Legacy)

Don't Tell Your Mama
Eddie Floyd; *Eddie Floyd-Chronicle* . . . .(Stax)

Down By The Bay
Eric Heatherly; *Country Goes Raffi-C* . . . . (Rounder)

Down The Road
Mac McAnally; *Knots* . . . .(MCA)

Down With The Sickness
Disturbed; *The Sickness* . . . .(Giant)

Drop Down Mama, Let Your Papa See
John Hammond; *Best Of John Hammond* . . . . (Vanguard)
Sleepy John Estes; *Legend Of Sleepy John Estes* . . . . (Delmark)
Tom Rush; *Best Of Tom Rush: No Regrets* . . . . (Legacy)
Tom Rush . . . . (Columbia)

Earth Mother
Paul Kantner/Grace Slick; *Sunfighter* . . . .(Grunt)

Every Mother's Son
Traffic; *John Barleycorn Must Die* . . . . (Island)

Every Mother's Son
Pretenders; *Last Of The Independents* . . . .(Sire)

Fancy
Bobbi Gentry; *All-Time Country Classics-#1-C* . . . . (Capitol)
Reba McEntire; *Rumor Has It* . . . .(MCA)

Fly
Sugar Ray; *Floored* . . . . (Atlantic)

Folsom Prison Blues
Brooks & Dunn with Johnny Cash; *Red Hot + Country-C* . . . . . . (Mercury)
Johnny Cash; *Billboard Top Country Hits-1968-C* . . . . (Rhino)
Classic Cash-Hall Of Fame Series . . . . (Mercury)
Hot Tracks-Train Super Hits-C . . . .(Epic)
Jailhouse Rock (Hits From The Big House)-C . . . . .(Sony Music Special Prod.)
Johnny Cash At Folsom Prison & San Quentin . . . . (Columbia)
Johnny Cash-Original Golden Hits-#1 . . . . (Sun)
Johnny Cash's Greatest Hits-#2 . . . . (Columbia)
Superbilly . . . .(Sun)
The Man In Black-His Greatest Hits . . . . (Legacy)

For A Thousand Mothers
Jethro Tull; *Stand Up* . . . . (Chrysalis)

For Momma
Statler Brothers; *Statler Brothers Christmas Present* . . . . (Mercury)

Freaks
Live; *Secret Samadhi* . . . .(Radioactive/MCA)

Gabriel's Mother's Hiway Ballad 16 Blues
Arlo Guthrie; *Best Of Arlo Guthrie* . . . .(Warner Bros.)

Ginger Bread
Frankie Avalon; *Gold For The Road-Carburetor Classics-C* . . . .(Compose)
Venus: The Very Best Of Frankie Avalon . . . . (Collectables)

God Bless The Child
Billie Holiday; *Billie Holiday's Greatest Hits* . . . . (Decca Jazz)
Billie Holiday's Greatest Hits . . . . (Legacy)
From The Original Decca Masters . . . .(MCA)
Songbook . . . . (Verve)
The Billie Holiday Story-#2 . . . . (Columbia)
Blood, Sweat & Tears; *Blood, Sweat & Tears* . . . . (Columbia)
Blood, Sweat & Tears Greatest Hits . . . . (Columbia)
Diana Ross; *ST/Lady Sings The Blues* . . . .(Motown)
Liza Minnelli; *4-Sider* . . . . (Cypress)
ST/Liza With A "Z" . . . . (Columbia)
Lou Rawls; *Best From Lou Rawls* . . . . (Capitol)

Good Golly, Miss Molly
Creedence Clearwater Revival; *1968-1969* . . . . (Fantasy)
Bayou Country . . . . (Fantasy)
Creedence Clearwater Revival-Chronicle-#2 . . . . (Fantasy)
Little Richard; *Big Hits* . . . .(Crescendo)
Cruisin'-1958-C . . . .(Increase)
Greatest Hits Recorded Live . . . .(Epic)
Little Richard-18 Greatest Hits . . . . (Rhino)
Little Richard-His Greatest Hits . . . . (Vee-Jay)
ST/The Flamingo Kid . . . .(Motown)
Super Oldies Of The '50s-#2-C . . . .(Audio Fidelity)

Have You Seen Your Mother, Baby, Standing In The Shadow?
Rolling Stones; *Flowers* . . . . (Abkco)
got Live if you want it! . . . . (Abkco)
More Hot Rocks (big hits & fazed cookies) . . . . (Abkco)
Through The Past, Darkly (Big Hits Vol. 2) . . . . (Abkco)

He Thinks He'll Keep Her
Mary Chapin Carpenter; *Come On Come On* . . . . (Columbia)

He Would Be Sixteen
Michelle Wright; *Now & Then* . . . . (Arista)

Heirloom
Bjork; *Vespertine* . . . . (Elektra)

Hello Muddah, Hello Fadduh
Allan Sherman; *Dr. Demento Presents The Greatest Novelty Records-#3-
1960s-C* . . . . (Rhino)
Dr. Demento Presents The Greatest Novelty Records-C . . . . (Rhino)

Hobo & His Mother
Goebel Reeves; *Texas Drifter* . . . .(Glendale)

Holes In The Floor Of Heaven
Steve Wariner; *Burnin' The Roadhouse Down* . . . . (Capitol)

Hot Chili Mama
Beausoleil; *Hot Chili Mama* . . . .(Arhoolie)

How Can I Help You Say Goodbye
Patty Loveless; *Only What I Feel* . . . . (Epic)
Patty Loveless-Classics . . . . (Epic)

Hungry Eyes
Emmylou Harris; *Mama's Hungry Eyes-Merle Haggard Tribute-C* . . . . . (Arista)
Merle Haggard; *For The Record: Merle Haggard-43 Legendary Hits* . . . .(BNA)

I Am Weary (Let Me Rest)
Cox Family; *ST/O Brother, Where Art Thou?* . . . . (Mercury)

I Am Your Mother Too
Keb' Mo' with Brenda Russell; *Big Wide Grin* . . . . (Sony Wonder)

I Dreamed About Mama Last Night
Hank Williams; *Complete Hank Williams* . . . . (Mercury)
Johnny Cash; *Timeless: Hank Williams Tribute-C* . . . . . (Lost Highway/IDJMG)

I Want A Girl (Just Like The Girl)
Al Jolson; *The Al Jolson Story-#1* . . . . (MCA)
Spike Jones & His City Slickers; *King Of Corn* . . . .(Glendale)

If I Could
Barbra Streisand; *Higher Ground* . . . . (Columbia)

If Momma Was Married
Cynthia Gibb & Jennifer Beck; *ST/Gypsy* . . . .(Atlantic)
Original Cast; *Gypsy* . . . . (Columbia)

I'm A Mother
Pretenders; *Last Of The Independents* . . . .(Sire)

I'm Already Taken
Steve Wariner; *Country Cares For Kids II-C* . . . . (BNA)
Two Teardrops . . . . (Capitol)

I'm The One Mama Warned You About
Mickey Gilley; *Too Good To Stop Now* . . . . (Epic)

Is Your Mama Gonna Miss Ya?
Bryan Adams; *Waking Up The Neighbours* . . . . (A&M)

It's My Mother's Birthday Today
Arthur Tracy; *To Mother With Love-C* . . . . (ASV Living Era)

Jesus & Mama
Confederate Railroad; *Confederate Railroad* . . . .(Atlantic)

Julia
Beatles; *Beatles-Box Set* . . . . (Capitol)
ST/Imagine: John Lennon . . . . (Capitol)
The Beatles (White Album) . . . . (Capitol)

L.A. Mama
Jim Stafford; *Jim Stafford* . . . .(Polydor)

Lady Madonna
Beatles; *Beatles 1* . . . . (Capitol)
Hey Jude . . . . (Capitol)
Past Masters-Volume Two . . . . (Parlophone)
The Beatles/1967-1970. . . . . (Capitol)
Wings; *Wings Over America* . . . . (Capitol)

Letting Go
Suzy Bogguss; *Aces* . . . . (Liberty)
Voices In The Wind . . . . (Liberty)

Lightning Crashes
Live; *Throwing Copper* . . . . (Radioactive/MCA)

Little Mama
Clovers; *Down In The Alley* . . . . (Rhino)

Ma (She's) Making Eyes At Me
Eddie Cantor; *Memories* . . . . (MCA)

Mama
Roy Orbison; *Our Love Song* . . . . (Monument)
Rare Orbison II . . . . (Monument)
Roy Orbison Greatest Hits . . . . (Monument)

Mama
Spice Girls; *Diana, Princess Of Wales-Tribute-C* . . . . (Columbia)
Spice . . . .(Virgin)

Mama
Electric Light Orchestra; *Afterglow* . . . . (Epic)
Electric Light Orchestra II . . . .(Jet)

Mama
B.J. Thomas; *B.J. Thomas' Greatest Hits* . . . . (Rhino)

Mama
Genesis; *Genesis* . . . .(Atlantic)
Knebworth-The Album-C . . . .(Polydor)

Mama
Original Broadway Cast; *Sarafina! (The Music Of Liberation)* . . . .(RCA)

Mama
Jerry Vale; *Jerry Vale-17 Most Requested Songs* . . . . (Legacy)

Mama
Helen Reddy; *Live At The London Palladium* . . . . (Capitol)
Music Music . . . . (Capitol)

Mama Can't Buy You Love
Elton John; *Complete Thom Bell Sessions* . . . . (MCA)
   Elton John's Greatest Hits-1976-1986 . . . . (MCA)
Mama Chicago
Bonnie Koloc; *With You On My Side* . . . . (Flying Fish)
Mama Didn't Lie
Jan Bradley; *Best Of Chess Rhythm & Blues-#1-C* . . . . (Chess)
   ST/Hairspray . . . . (MCA Special Prod.)
Mama Done Told Me
Miracles; *Greatest Hits From The Beginning* . . . . (Motown)
Mama Don't Forget To Pray For Me
Diamond Rio; *Diamond Rio* . . . . (Arista)
   Diamond Rio's Greatest Hits . . . . (Arista)
Mama Don't Get Dressed Up For Nothing
Brooks & Dunn; *Borderline* . . . . (Arista)
Mama Don't You Tear My Clothes
Blind Snooks Eaglin; *Rural Blues* . . . . (Fantasy)
Mama From The Train
Patti Page; *Patti Page-Golden Celebration* . . . . (Mercury)
Mama Hated Diesels
Commander Cody & His Lost Planet Airmen; *Hot Licks, Cold Steel &*
   Trucker's Favorites . . . . (MCA)
Mama He's Crazy
Judds; *Judds* . . . . (RCA)
   Judds' Greatest Hits . . . . (MCA)
   Why Not Me . . . . (MCA)
Mama I'm Coming Home
Ozzy Osbourne; *The Ozzman Cometh* . . . . (Epic)
Mama Kin
Aerosmith; *Aerosmith* . . . . (Columbia)
   Aerosmith-Classics Live . . . . (Columbia)
   Gems . . . . (Columbia)
   Live! Bootleg . . . . (Columbia)
Guns N' Roses; *G N' R Lies* . . . . (Geffen)
Mama Knows The Highway
Hal Ketchum; *Sure Love* . . . . (Curb)
Mama Let Him Play
Doucette; *Mama Let Him Play* . . . . (Mushroom)
Mama Lion
David Crosby & Graham Nash; *Wind On The Water* . . . . (MCA)
Mama Said
Shirelles; *Original Rock 'N' Roll Hits Of The '60s-C* . . . . (Roulette)
   Shirelles' Greatest Hits . . . . (Everest)
   Shirelles-Anthology 1959-1964 . . . . (Rhino)
   Shirelles-Classics . . . . (Bac-Trac)
   Super Oldies Of The '60s-#3-C . . . . (Audio Fidelity)
Mama Said Knock You Out
L.L. Cool J; *Mama Said Knock You Out* . . . . (Def Jam)
Mama Sang A Song
Bill Anderson; *Bill Anderson's Greatest Hits* . . . . (Varese Sarabande)
   Country Music Classics-#17-C . . . . (K-Tel)
Mama Say
Heptones; *Night Food* . . . . (Island)
Mama Told Me Not To Come
Randy Newman; *12 Songs* . . . . (Reprise)
   Randy Newman/Live . . . . (Warner Archives)
Three Dog Night; *Best Of Three Dog Night* . . . . (MCA)
   Billboard Top Rock 'N' Roll Hits-1970-C . . . . (Rhino)
Wilson Pickett; *Wilson Pickett's Greatest Hits* . . . . (Atlantic)
Mama Tried
Grateful Dead; *Grateful Dead (Skull & Roses)* . . . . (Warner Bros.)
John Anderson & Marty Stuart; *Mama's Hungry Eyes-Merle Haggard*
   Tribute-C . . . . (Arista)
Merle Haggard; *Jailhouse Rock (Hits From The Big*
   House)-C . . . . (Sony Music Special Prod.)
Merle Haggard & The Strangers; *Best Of Merle Haggard & The*
   Strangers . . . . (Capitol)
   For The Record: Merle Haggard-43 Legendary Hits . . . . (BNA)
   Okie From Muskogee . . . . (Capitol)
   Songs I'll Always Sing . . . . (Capitol)
   Very Best Of Merle Haggard . . . . (Capitol)
Mama Used To Say
Junior; *Jr.* . . . . (Mercury)
   Sophisticated Street . . . . (London)
Mama Weer All Crazee Now
Quiet Riot; *Condition Critical* . . . . (Epic Portrait Assoc.)
Mama, He Treats Your Daughter Mean
Susan Tedeschi; *Just Won't Burn* . . . . (Tone Cool)
Mama, I'm Coming Home
Ozzy Osbourne; *No More Tears* . . . . (Epic Portrait Assoc.)
Mama's Always On Stage
Arrested Development; *3 Years 5 Months 2 Days In The Life Of* . . . . (Chrysalis)
   Arrested Development-Unplugged . . . . (Chrysalis)
Mama's Fool
Tesla; *Bust A Nut* . . . . (Geffen)
Mama's Never Seen Those Eyes
Forester Sisters; *Forester Sisters* . . . . (Warner Bros.)
Mama's Opry
Iris DeMent; *Infamous Angel* . . . . (Warner Bros.)

Mama's Pearl
Jackson 5; *3rd Album* . . . . (Motown)
   Compact Command Performances-Jackson 5 . . . . (Motown)
   Jackson 5-Anthology . . . . (Motown)
   Jackson 5's Greatest Hits . . . . (Motown)
Mammas Don't Let Your Babies Grow Up To Be Cowboys
Gibson/Miller Band; *Cowboy Super Hits-C* . . . . (Columbia)
   ST/The Cowboy Way . . . . (Epic)
Waylon Jennings & Willie Nelson; *Waylon & Willie* . . . . (RCA)
   Waylon Jennings & Willie Nelson's Greatest Hits . . . . (RCA)
Willie Nelson; *Greatest Hits (& Some That Will Be)* . . . . (Columbia)
   ST/The Electric Horseman . . . . (Columbia)
   Willie & Family Live . . . . (Columbia)
Mean Mama Blues
Bob Wills; *Stay A Little Longer-The Original Columbia*
   Recordings . . . . (Roswell/RCA)
Mer Girl
Madonna; *Ray Of Light* . . . . (Maverick)
Mindless Child Of Motherhood
Kinks; *Kink Kronikles* . . . . (Reprise)
Momma
Bob Seger; *Beautiful Loser* . . . . (Capitol)
Momma Cried
Alison Krauss & Union Station; *New Favorite* . . . . (Rounder)
Momma, Where's My Daddy
Keb' Mo'; *Just Like You* . . . . (Okeh)
Mommy Can I Come Home
Keb' Mo'; *The Door* . . . . (550/Epic/Okeh)
Mommy For A Day
Kitty Wells; *It Wasn't God Who Made Honky Tonk*
   Angels . . . . (MCA Special Prod.)
   Kitty Wells' Greatest Hits . . . . (MCA)
Mommy Where's Daddy
Red Hot Chili Peppers; *Red Hot Chili Peppers* . . . . (EMI)
Mommy, Can I Go Out & Kill Tonight
Misfits; *Walk Among Us* . . . . (Ruby)
M-O-T-H-E-R, A Word That Means The World To Me
Bobby Breen; *To Mother With Love-C* . . . . (ASV Living Era)
Mother
John Lennon; *Lennon* . . . . (Capitol)
   Live In New York City . . . . (Capitol)
   ST/Imagine: John Lennon . . . . (Capitol)
John Lennon/Plastic Ono Band; *John Lennon/Plastic Ono Band* . . . . . (Capitol)
   Shaved Fish . . . . (Capitol)
Mother
Danzig; *Thrall Demonsweatlive* . . . . (American)
Mother
Barbra Streisand; *Barbra Joan Streisand* . . . . (Columbia)
Mother
Chicago; *Chicago At Carnegie Hall* . . . . (Chicago)
   Chicago III . . . . (Chicago)
   Group Portrait . . . . (Chicago)
Mother
Roy Orbison; *Rare Orbison II* . . . . (Monument)
Mother
Police; *Synchronicity* . . . . (A&M)
Mother
Pink Floyd; *The Wall* . . . . (Columbia)
Mother (You Make Me Want To Be A)
Tammy Wynette; *Tammy Wynette's Greatest Hits-#3* . . . . (Epic)
Mother Africa
Santana; *Welcome* . . . . (Columbia)
Mother And Child Reunion
Paul Simon; *Negotiations And Love Songs, 1971-1986* . . . . (Warner Bros.)
   Paul Simon . . . . (Columbia)
   Paul Simon In Concert/Live Rhymin' . . . . (Columbia)
Mother Dear
Diana Ross & The Supremes; *Motown Legends-Diana Ross & The*
   Supremes . . . . (Motown)
Mother Dear
Styx; *Equinox* . . . . (A&M)
Mother Earth
Memphis Slim; *Memphis Slim* . . . . (Chess)
   Real Folk Blues-C . . . . (Chess)
Mother Earth
Nitty Gritty Dirt Band; *Dirt, Silver & Gold* . . . . (One Way)
Mother Earth
Merry-Go-Round; *Best Of Merry-Go-Round* . . . . (Rhino)
Mother Earth
Tom Rush; *Best Of Tom Rush: No Regrets* . . . . (Legacy)
Mother Goose
Jethro Tull; *Aqualung* . . . . (Chrysalis)
Mother I Miss You
John Tesh featuring Dalia; *Grand Passion-C* . . . . (GTS)
Mother In Law
Buddy Guy; *Left My Blues In San Francisco* . . . . (Chess)
Ernie K-Doe; *Best Of New Orleans Rhythm & Blues-#1-C* . . . . (Rhino)
   Collectables Presents The History Of Rock-#7-C . . . . (Collectables)

New Orleans Jazz & Heritage Festival-1976-C. . . . . (Rhino)
Huey Lewis and the News; *Four Chords & Several Years Ago* . . . . (Elektra)

Mother In Law Blues
Junior Parker; *Best Of Junior Parker* . . . . (MCA)

Mother In Law Song
Martin Mull; *Sex & Violins* . . . . (MCA)

Mother Machree
John McHugh; *To Mother With Love-C* . . . . (ASV Living Era)

Mother Mary
UFO; *Force It* . . . . (Chrysalis)
Strangers In The Night . . . . (Chrysalis)

Mother Mary
Julian Lennon; *Mr. Jordan* . . . . (Atlantic)

Mother Mary
Sheila E.; *Sex Cymbal* . . . . (Warner Bros.)

Mother Mother
Tracy Bonham; *Burdens Of Being Upright* . . . . (Island)

Mother, My Dear
John McCormack; *To Mother With Love-C* . . . . (ASV Living Era)

Mother Nature
Temptations; *Temptations-Anthology-The Best Of The Temptations* . . (Motown)

Mother Nature's Son
Beatles; *Beatles-Box Set* . . . . (Capitol)
The Beatles (White Album) . . . . (Capitol)
John Denver; *Evening With John Denver* . . . . (RCA)
Rocky Mountain High . . . . (RCA)

Mother Popcorn
Aerosmith; *Live! Bootleg* . . . . (Columbia)
James Brown; *Sex Machine* . . . . (Polydor)

Mother Russia
Renaissance; *Renaissance-Live At Carnegie Hall* . . . . (Sire)
Tales Of 1001 Nights-#1 . . . . (Sire)
Turn Of The Cards . . . . (Sire)

Mother Russia
Iron Maiden; *No Prayer For The Dying* . . . . (Epic)

Mother Says
Joe Walsh; *Barnstorm*. . . . . (Mobile Fidelity Sound Lab)
Best Of Joe Walsh . . . . (MCA)

Mother The Queen Of My Heart
Pete Seeger & Arlo Guthrie; *Together In Concert* . . . . (Reprise)

Mother Trucker
Shaver; *Rig Rock Deluxe: A Musical Salute To the American Truck Driver-C* . . . . (Upstart)

Motherhood
Carol Channing/Original Cast; *Hello Dolly!*. . . . . (RCA)
Original Cast; *Hello Dolly!* . . . . (RCA)

Motherless Child
Steve Miller Band; *Steve Miller Band-Anthology* . . . . (Capitol)
Your Saving Grace . . . . (Capitol)

Motherless Children
Eric Clapton; *461 Ocean Boulevard* . . . . (Polydor)
Eric Clapton-Crossroads-C . . . . (Polydor)
From The Cradle . . . . (Duck/Reprise)

Mother's Day
7 Seconds; *Soulforce Revolution* . . . . (Restless)

Mother's Day
Rick Margitza; *Hope*. . . . . (Blue Note)

Mothers Dream
Candlebox; *Candlebox* . . . . (Maverick)

Mother's Eyes
Matthews, Wright & King; *Power Of Love*. . . . . (Columbia)

Mother's Lament
Cream; *Disraeli Gears* . . . . (Polydor)

Mother's Little Helper
Rolling Stones; *Flowers* . . . . (Abkco)
Hot Rocks 1964-1971 . . . . (Abkco)
Through The Past, Darkly (Big Hits Vol. 2) . . . . (Abkco)
Tesla; *Five Man Acoustical Jam* . . . . (Geffen)

Mothers Of The Disappeared
U2; *The Joshua Tree* . . . . (Island)

Mother's Only Sleeping
Ricky Skaggs and Kentucky Thunder; *History Of The Future* . . (Skaggs Family)

Mothers Talk
Tears For Fears; *Songs From The Big Chair* . . . . (Mercury)
Tears Roll Down-The Hits-1982-1992. . . . . (Fontana)

Motorcycle Mama
Sailcat; *Back To The '70s-#2-C* . . . . (Dominion Entert.)
Super Hits Of The '70s-Have A Nice Day-#8-C . . . . (Rhino)

Motorcycle Mama
Neil Young; *Comes A Time*. . . . . (Reprise)

Movies Are A Mother To Me
Loudon Wainwright III; *Loudon Wainwright III*. . . . . (Atlantic)

Mrs. Brown You've Got A Lovely Daughter
Herman's Hermits; *Herman's Hermits-Their Greatest Hits*. . . . . (Abkco)
Something Good Again . . . . (Abkco)

Ms. Jackson
Outkast; *Stankonia* . . . . (LaFace/Arista)

Music Makin' Mama From Memphis
Hank Snow; *Best Of Hank Snow* . . . . (RCA)

My Baby Needs A Shepherd
Emmylou Harris; *Red Dirt Girl* . . . . (Nonesuch)

My Guitar Wants To Kill Your Mama
Frank Zappa; *You Can't Do That On Stage Anymore-#4*. . . . . (Rykodisc)
Mothers Of Invention; *Weasels Ripped My Flesh* . . . . (Bizarre/Straight)

My Mammy
Al Jolson; *Best Of Al Jolson* . . . . (MCA)
Let Me Sing And I'm Happy . . . . (Turner Classic Movies)
The '20s-From Broadway To Hollywood-#3-C . . . . (Flapper)
Happenings; *Happenings-Golden Hits!* . . . . (B.T. Puppy)

My Mom's A Feminist
Kristin Lems; *We Will Never Give Up* . . . . (Carolsdatter Prod.)

My Mother's Bible
Warrior River Boys; *New Beginnings* . . . . (Rounder)

My Mother's Eyes
Bette Midler; *ST/Divine Madness* . . . . (Atlantic)
Forester Sisters; *You Again* . . . . (Warner Bros.)

My Mother's Eyes
Clovers; *Love Potion No. 9* . . . . (EMI)

My Mother's Wedding Day
Original Cast; *Brigadoon* . . . . (RCA)

My Mummy's Dead
John Lennon; *Lennon* . . . . (Capitol)
John Lennon/Plastic Ono Band; *John Lennon/Plastic Ono Band* . . . . . (Capitol)

My Yiddische Momma
Sophie Tucker; *To Mother With Love-C* . . . . (ASV Living Era)

Nashville Cats
Del McCoury Band; *The Family* . . . . (Ceili Music)
Lovin' Spoonful; *Lovin' Spoonful-Anthology* . . . . (Rhino)

Never Let You Go
Third Eye Blind; *Blue* . . . . (Elektra)
Totally Hits-#2-C . . . . (Elektra)

New Mother Nature
Guess Who; *American Woman* . . . . (RCA)
Best Of The Guess Who . . . . (RCA)

Ode To My Family
Cranberries; *No Need To Argue*. . . . . (Island)

One's On The Way (Here In Topeka)
Loretta Lynn; *Loretta Lynn-20 Greatest Hits* . . . . (MCA)
Loretta Lynn-Greatest Hits Live . . . . (K-Tel)
Loretta Lynn's Greatest Hits-#2 . . . . (MCA)
The Country Music Hall Of Fame-Loretta Lynn. . . . . (MCA)

Only The Strong Survive
Elvis Presley; *From Elvis In Memphis*. . . . . (RCA)
Memphis Record. . . . . (RCA)
Jerry Butler; *Best Of Jerry Butler* . . . . (Mercury)
Best Of Jerry Butler . . . . (Rhino)

Papa Loved Mama
Garth Brooks; *Garth Brooks-Double Live*. . . . . (Capitol)
Ropin' The Wind. . . . . (Liberty)

Papa Loves Mambo
Perry Como; *Como's Golden Records* . . . . (RCA)
Perry Como-Pure Gold . . . . (RCA)
Perry Como's All-Time Greatest Hits-#1 . . . . (RCA)
This Is Perry Como. . . . . (RCA)

Parents Just Don't Understand
D.J. Jazzy Jeff & The Fresh Prince; *He's The D.J. I'm The Rapper* . . . . . . (Jive)

Peach Orchard Mamma
Big Joe Williams; *Piney Woods Blues*. . . . . (Delmark)

Pistol Packin' Mama
Al Dexter; *Columbia Country Classics-#1-Golden Age-C* . . . . (Columbia)
Great Records Of The Decade-'40s-Country-C . . . . (Curb)
Andrews Sisters; *Andrews Sisters-16 Great Performances*. . . . . (MCA)
Boogie Woogie Bugle Girls . . . . (MCA)
Bing Crosby; *Bing Crosby's Greatest Hits* . . . . (MCA)
Glenn Miller & His Army/Air Force Band; *Nipper's Greatest Hits Of The '40s-#1-C*. . . . . (RCA)

Pretty Little Dogies
Skip Gorman; *A Cowboy's Wild Song To His Herd*. . . . . (Rounder)

Pretty Penny
Stone Temple Pilots; *Purple* . . . . (Atlantic)

Pretty Wreath For Mother's Grave
Reno & Smiley; *1983 Collector's Edition-#9* . . . . . . (International Mktg. Group)

Que Sera, Sera
Doris Day; *Doris Day-16 Most Requested Songs-Encore!* . . . . (Columbia)
Doris Day's Greatest Hits . . . . (Columbia)
Radio Classics Of The '50s-C. . . . . (Columbia)
Sly & The Family Stone; *Fresh*. . . . . (Legacy)
Sly & The Family Stone-Anthology . . . . (Epic)

Rag Mama Rag
Band; *Rock Of Ages* . . . . (Capitol)
The Band . . . . (Capitol)
The Band-Gift Set . . . . (Capitol)
To Kingdom Come-The Definitive Collection. . . . . (Capitol)

RC's Mom
Dead Milkmen; *Beelzebubba* . . . . (Fever)

Remember Mother's Day
Al Jolson; *The Al Jolson Story-#5* . . . . (MCA)
Ricky Wants A Man Of Her Own
Bruce Springsteen; *Tracks* . . . . (Columbia)
Rock A Bye Your Baby With A Dixie Melody
Al Jolson; *Best Of Al Jolson* . . . . (MCA)
  Jolson Sang 'Em . . . . (Biograph)
  Music From The New York Stage (1890-1920)-#4-1917-1920-C . . . . . .(Pearl)
  The Al Jolson Story-#1 . . . . (MCA)
Jerry Lewis; *Just Sings* . . . . (Razor & Tie)
Judy Garland; *Judy Garland-At Carnegie Hall* . . . . (Capitol)
  Miss Show Business . . . . (Capitol)
  One & Only . . . . (Capitol)
Rock Me Mama
Blind Snooks Eaglin; *Country Boy In New Orleans* . . . . (Arhoolie)
Buddy Guy/Junior Mance/Junior Wells; *Buddy & The Juniors* . . . . (MCA)
Sonny Terry; *Chain Gang Blues* . . . . (Collectables)
Rock Your Mama
Ten Years After; *Alvin Lee & Company* . . . . (Deram)
  Ten Years After-London Collector . . . . (London)
Roll On Big Mama
Joe Stampley; *Encore-Joe Stampley* . . . . (Epic)
  Joe Stampley's Biggest Hits . . . . (Epic)
  Joe Stampley's Greatest Hits . . . . (Epic)
  Truckers' Jukebox-10 All-Time Radio Requests-C . . . . (Legacy)
Roots Of My Raising
Merle Haggard & The Strangers; *Capitol Collectors Series-Merle Haggard & The Strangers* . . . . (Capitol)
  For The Record: Merle Haggard-43 Legendary Hits . . . . (BNA)
  Merle Haggard's Greatest Hits-#2 . . . . (Curb)
Roses For Mama
C.W. McCall; *C.W. McCall's Greatest Hits* . . . . (Polydor)
Savannah Mama
Blind Willie McTell; *Blind Willie McTell-Early Years-1927-1932* . . . . . (Yazoo)
  Three Shades Of Blues-C . . . . (Biograph)
Blind Willie McTell & Memphis Minnie; *Love Changin' Blues* . . . . . (Biograph)
Paul Geremia; *My Kinda Place* . . . . (Flying Fish)
Save It, Pretty Mama
Lionel Hampton & His Orchestra; *Tempo & Swing* . . . . (Bluebird)
Louis Armstrong; *1940s-Small Band Sides-C* . . . . (Bluebird)
  Louis Armstrong-1928-1931 . . . . (Nimbus)
Louis Armstrong & Earl Hines; *Louis Armstrong-Vol. 4-In New York* . . . . (Columbia)
Teddy Buckner; *Salute To Louis Armstrong* . . . . (Crescendo)
Save Mother Earth
Merl Saunders; *Heavy Turbulence* . . . . (Fantasy)
Merl Saunders & Friends; *Fire Up* . . . . (Fantasy)
Merl Saunders & The Rainforest Band; *Save The Planet* . . . . . . (Sumertone)
Send A Picture Of Mother
Johnny Cash; *Johnny Cash At Folsom Prison & San Quentin* . . . . . . (Columbia)
Shake My Mother's Hand
Bill Monroe & His Blue Grass Boys; *Mule Skinner Blues* . . . . . . (RCA)
She's A Bad Mama Jama
Carl Carlton; *Carl Carlton* . . . . (20th Century Fox)
Shop Around
Captain & Tennille; *Captain & Tennille's Greatest Hits* . . . . (A&M)
Miracles; *Greatest Hits From The Beginning* . . . . (Motown)
  Hi-We're The Miracles . . . . (Motown)
Smokey Robinson & The Miracles; *16 #1 Hits From The Early '60s-C* . . . . (Motown)
  Every Great Motown Song-First 25 Years-C . . . . (Motown)
  Smokey Robinson & The Miracles' Anthology . . . . (Motown)
Shortenin' Bread
Andrews Sisters; *50th Anniversary Collection-#2* . . . . (MCA)
Original Soundtrack; *Children's Favorites* . . . . (Kid Rhino/Rhino 4 Kids)
Sam McNeil/Dent Wimmer/Others; *Old Originals-#2* . . . . (Rounder)
Sonny Terry; *Folkways Years-1944-1963* . . . . (Smithsonian Folkways)
Shut Out The Light
Bruce Springsteen; *Tracks* . . . . (Columbia)
Solitude
Edwin McCain; *Honor Among Thieves* . . . . (Lava)
Edwin McCain & Darius Rucker; *VH-1 Crossroads-C* . . . . (Atlantic)
Sometimes I Feel Like A Motherless Child
Dave Van Ronk; *Folksinger* . . . . (Prestige)
  Inside Dave Van Ronk . . . . (Fantasy)
Grant Green; *Feelin' The Spirit* . . . . (Blue Note)
  Iron City . . . . (Muse)
Jerry Butler; *Jerry Butler-Gold* . . . . (Vee-Jay)
Mormon Tabernacle Choir; *Songs Of The Civil War And Stephen Foster Favorites* . . . . (Sony Music Classical)
O.V. Wright; *O.V. Wright* . . . . (MCA)
Odetta; *Essential Odetta* . . . . (Vanguard)
Peter, Paul & Mary; *The Song Will Rise* . . . . (Warner Bros.)
Van Morrison; *Poetic Champions Compose* . . . . (Mercury)
Son Of Hickory Holler's Tramp
O.C. Smith; *Me And You* . . . . (Columbia Special Prod.)
  Story Songs-C . . . . (K-Tel)
Song For Mama
Boyz II Men; *BET-Best Of Planet Groove-C* . . . . (Virgin)

Evolution . . . . (Motown)
ST/Soul Food . . . . (LaFace)
Space Lord
Monster Magnet; *Powertrip* . . . . (A&M)
Squeezebox
Who; *By Numbers* . . . . (MCA)
  Hooligans . . . . (MCA)
  Who Greatest Hits . . . . (MCA)
Stop Your Half Steppin' Mama
Ben Vereen; *Here I Am* . . . . (Accord)
  Signed Sealed Delivered . . . . (Fifty One West)
Sugar Mama
John Lee Hooker; *Blues-#2-C* . . . . (Chess)
  House Of The Blues . . . . (Chess)
Sugar Mama
Bonnie Raitt; *Bonnie Raitt-Collection* . . . . (Warner Bros.)
  Home Plate . . . . (Warner Bros.)
Sullivan
Caroline's Spine; *Monsoon* . . . . (Hollywood)
Swanee
Al Jolson; *Al Jolson-Best Of The Decca Years* . . . . (MCA)
  Best Of Al Jolson . . . . (MCA)
  Jolson Sang 'Em . . . . (Biograph)
  Music From The New York Stage (1890-1920)-#4-1917-1920-C . . . . (Pearl)
George Gershwin; *Rhapsody In Blue* . . . . (Biograph)
Judy Garland; *Judy Garland-At Carnegie Hall* . . . . (Capitol)
  Judy Garland's All-Time Greatest Hits . . . . (Curb)
Sweet Daddy (Your Mama's Done Gone Mad)
Little Brother Montgomery; *Chicago-Living Legends-South Side Blues* . . . . (Riverside)
Sweet Mama
Allman Brothers Band; *Win, Lose Or Draw* . . . . (Polydor)
Sweet Mama Goodtimes
Mickey Gilley; *Mickey Gilley's Greatest Hits-#2* . . . . (Epic)
Sweet Mama Hurry Home Or I'll Be Gone
Leon Redbone; *On The Track* . . . . (Warner Bros.)
Sweet Mother Texas
Eddy Raven; *Eddy Raven's Greatest Hits* . . . . (Warner Bros.)
Sylvia's Mother
Dr. Hook; *Dr. Hook & The Medicine Show Revisited* . . . . . . (Columbia)
  Dr. Hook-Greatest Hits & More . . . . (Capitol)
  Super Hits Of The '70s-Have A Nice Day-#8-C . . . . (Rhino)
Take Me Home, Country Roads
John Denver; *Evening With John Denver* . . . . (RCA)
  John Denver's Greatest Hits . . . . (RCA)
  Poems, Prayers & Promises . . . . (RCA)
  Take Me Home, Country Roads & Other Hits . . . . (RCA)
Toots & The Maytals; *Brand New Second-Hand* . . . . (Rykodisc)
Teddy Boy
Beatles; *The Beatles-Anthology-#3* . . . . (Capitol)
Paul McCartney; *McCartney* . . . . (Capitol)
Teenage Immigrant Welfare Mothers On Drugs
Austin Lounge Lizards; *Live Bait* . . . . (Sugar Hill)
Tell Mama
Etta James; *Didn't It Blow Your Mind: Soul Hits Of The '70s-#1-C* . . . . . (Rhino)
  Essential Etta James . . . . (Chess)
  Tell Mama . . . . (Chess)
Janis Joplin; *Janis* . . . . (Legacy)
Savoy Brown; *Savoy Brown-London Collector* . . . . (London)
  Street Corner Talking . . . . (Deram)
Tennessee Border
Hank Williams; *Alone With His Guitar* . . . . (Mercury)
  I Ain't Got Nothin' But Time-1946-1947 . . . . (Polydor)
Red Foley; *Red Foley: The Country Music Hall Of Fame* . . . . (MCA Special Prod.)
Sonny Burgess & Dave Alvin; *Tennessee Border* . . . . (Hightone)
Tennessee Ernie Ford; *Best Of Tennessee Ernie Ford-16 Tons Of Boogie* . . . . (Rhino)
  Capitol Collectors Series-Tennessee Ernie Ford . . . . (Capitol)
That Was Your Mother
Paul Simon; *Graceland* . . . . (Warner Bros.)
That's All Right (Mama)
Arthur "Big Boy" Crudup; *Best Of The Blues* . . . . (Pair)
  That's All Right (Mama) . . . . (Bluebird)
Carl Perkins; *Restless-Columbia Recordings* . . . . (Columbia)
Elvis Presley; *For LP Fans Only* . . . . (RCA)
  Sun Story-C . . . . (Rhino)
  Sun's Greatest Hits-C . . . . (RCA)
  The Sun Sessions . . . . (RCA)
Marty Robbins; *Essential Marty Robbins-1951-1982* . . . . . . (Columbia)
Merl Saunders/Jerry Garcia/Bill Vitt/John Kahn; *Live At Keystone* . . . . (Fantasy)
Paul McCartney; *CHOBA B CCCP-The Russian Album* . . . . . . (Capitol)
Rick Nelson; *Stay Young-Epic Recordings* . . . . (Epic)
Rod Stewart; *Every Picture Tells A Story* . . . . (Mercury)
  Vintage Rod Stewart . . . . (Mercury)
Vince Gill; *ST/Honeymoon In Vegas* . . . . . (Epic/Sony Music Soundtrax)
Theme From "Alice"
Original Soundtrack; *Television's Greatest Hits-#6-Remote Control-C* . . . (TVT)

Theme From "My Mother The Car"
Original Soundtrack; *Television's Greatest Hits-#2-C* . . . . (TVT)
Theme From "One Day At A Time"
Original Soundtrack; *CBS: The First 50 Years* . . . . (TVT)
Theme From "The Donna Reed Show"
Original Soundtrack; *Donna Reed's Dinner Party-C* . . . . (Nick At Nite)
Television's Greatest Hits-#1-C . . . . (TVT)
TV Classic Themes: 25th Anniversary Edition-C . . . . (Breakable)
There Ain't No Good Chain Gang
Johnny Cash & Waylon Jennings; *Country's Greatest Hits-#15-Outlaw*
Country-C . . . . (Priority)
Hot Country Rock-#1-C . . . . (Epic)
Johnny Cash-16 Biggest Hits-#2 . . . . (Legacy)
The Man In Black-His Greatest Hits . . . . (Legacy)
Thinkin' 'Bout Your Mother
Freewheelers; *Freewheelers* . . . . (David Geffen Co.)
This Little Girl Of Mine
Faron Young; *Faron Young's Greatest Hits-#3* . . . . (Step One)
Three Times A Lady
Commodores; *All The Great Love Songs-Commodores* . . . . (Motown)
Commodores Greatest Hits . . . . (Motown)
Commodores-All The Great Hits . . . . (Motown)
Endless Love-Motown's Greatest Love Songs-C . . . . (Motown)
Natural High . . . . (Motown)
Tie Your Mother Down
Queen; *Classic Queen* . . . . (Hollywood)
Live At Wembley '86 . . . . (Hollywood)
Live Killers . . . . (Hollywood)
Tombstone Blues
Bob Dylan; *Biograph* . . . . (Columbia)
Highway 61 Revisited . . . . (Columbia)
Real Live . . . . (Columbia)
True Fine Mama
Little Richard; *Georgia Peach* . . . . (Specialty)
Little Richard-His Biggest Hits . . . . (Specialty)
TV Mama
Big Joe Turner; *Atlantic Blues-Guitar-C* . . . . (Atlantic)
Texas Style . . . . (Evidence Music)
Dizzy Gillespie & Others; *Trumpet Kings Meet Joe Turner* . . . . . . (Pablo)
Freddie King; *Freddie King* . . . . (RSO)
Johnny Winter; *Nothin' But The Blues* . . . . (Blue Sky)
TV Mama
Leon Haywood; *It's Me Again* . . . . (Casablanca)
Vision Of Mother
Ricky Skaggs; *Don't Cheat In Our Hometown* . . . . (Epic)
Stanley Brothers; *Complete Columbia Stanley Brothers* . . . . (Legacy)
Wendy
Original Cast/Mary Martin; *Peter Pan-The 1954 Broadway*
Production . . . . (RCA Victor)
What Would You Do?
City High; *City High* . . . . (Interscope)
Now That's What I Call Music!-#7-C . . . . (Virgin)
ST/Life . . . . (Rock Land/Interscope)
What's Going On
Cyndi Lauper; *True Colors* . . . . (Portrait)
Marvin Gaye; *20/20-C* . . . . (Motown)
Marvin Gaye Live At The London Palladium . . . . (Motown)
Marvin Gaye-Anthology . . . . (Motown)
Marvin Gaye's Greatest Hits/ . . . . (Motown)
More Songs From "The Big Chill" Soundtrack-C . . . . (Motown)
What's Going On . . . . (Motown)
Quincy Jones; *Quincy Jones-The Best* . . . . (A&M)
Who I Am
Jessica Andrews; *Who I Am* . . . . (DreamWorks/SKG)
Wild Week-End
Bill Anderson; *Bill Anderson-Legend* . . . . (Masters)
MCA Records 30 Years Of Hits-1958-1988-C . . . . (MCA)
Still . . . . (MCA Special Prod.)
Will The Circle Be Unbroken
Charlie Daniels Band & Friends; *Volunteer Jam 3 & 4* . . . . (Epic)
Joan Baez; *Country Music Album* . . . . (Vanguard)
The First 10 Years . . . . (Vanguard)
Nitty Gritty Dirt Band; *Will The Circle Be Unbroken* . . . . (EMI)
Roy Acuff; *Best Of Roy Acuff* . . . . (Liberty)
Willie Nelson; *Willie & Family Live* . . . . (Columbia)
Wish, The
Bruce Springsteen; *Tracks* . . . . (Columbia)
You Better Sit Down Kids
Cher; *Bang, Bang The Early Years* . . . . (Capitol)
You Can't Hurry Love
Diana Ross; *Diana Ross-The Ultimate Collection* . . . . (Motown)
Diana Ross & The Supremes; *16 #1 Hits From The Early '60s-C* . . . . (Motown)
Phil Collins; *Hello, I Must Be Going* . . . . (Atlantic)
You Can't Lose Me
Faith Hill; *It Matters To Me* . . . . (Warner Bros.)
Your Mama Don't Dance
Loggins & Messina; *Loggins & Messina-On Stage* . . . . (Columbia)
Loggins And Messina . . . . (Columbia)
Pop Classics Of The '70s-C . . . . (Columbia)

The Best Of Friends . . . . (Columbia)
Poison; *Open Up And Say...Ahh!* . . . . (Capitol)
Swallow This Live . . . . (Capitol)
Your Mom's In My Business
K-Solo; *Tell The World My Name* . . . . (Atlantic)
Your Mother Should Know
Beatles; *Beatles-Box Set* . . . . (Capitol)
Magical Mystery Tour . . . . (Capitol)
Zoomin'
Lionel Richie; *Time* . . . . (Mercury)

FAMILY: SISTERS

*See Also: **FAMILY (various), FEMINISM, WOMEN: GENERAL,**
WOMEN'S NAMES: A-Z

Angels In Waiting
Tammy Cochran; *Tammy Cochran* . . . . (Epic)
Best Friend
Brandy; *Brandy* . . . . (Atlantic)
Bonnie Jean (Little Sister)
David Lynn Jones; *Best Of Country Rock-C* . . . . (K-Tel)
Hard Times On Easy Street . . . . (Mercury)
Brother Wolf, Sister Moon
Cult; *Love* . . . . (Sire)
Capricorn Sister
Mother Love Bone; *Mother Love Bone* . . . . (Stardog)
Daddy Frank (The Guitar Man)
Merle Haggard; *Best Of Merle Haggard* . . . . (Capitol)
Capitol Collectors Series-Merle Haggard . . . . (Capitol)
Merle Haggard & The Strangers; *For The Record: Merle Haggard-43*
Legendary Hits . . . . (BNA)
Songs I'll Always Sing . . . . (Capitol)
Dance Little Sister
Rolling Stones; *It's Only Rock 'N Roll* . . . . (Rolling Stones)
Made In The Shade . . . . (Rolling Stones)
Dance Little Sister
Terence Trent D'Arby; *Introducing The Hardline According To Terence*
Trent D'Arby . . . . (Columbia)
Driving Sister
Mott The Hoople; *Mott* . . . . (Columbia)
I Am Your Mother Too
Keb' Mo' with Brenda Russell; *Big Wide Grin* . . . . (Sony Wonder)
It's A Shame (My Sister)
Monie Love & True Image; *Down To Earth* . . . . (Warner Bros.)
Lift Up Every Stone
John Hiatt; *Crossing Muddy Waters* . . . . (Vanguard)
Little Joe The Wrangler's Sister Nell
Skip Gorman; *A Cowboy's Wild Song To His Herd* . . . . (Rounder)
Little Sister
Elvis Presley; *Elvis' Golden Records, Volume 3* . . . . (RCA)
Elvis In Concert . . . . (RCA)
I Was The One . . . . (RCA)
The Top Ten Hits . . . . (RCA)
Worldwide 50 Gold Award Hits, Vol. 1, Parts 1 & 2 . . . . (RCA)
Petals
Mariah Carey; *Rainbow* . . . . (Columbia)
Pretty Penny
Stone Temple Pilots; *Purple* . . . . (Atlantic)
Ricky Wants A Man Of Her Own
Bruce Springsteen; *Tracks* . . . . (Columbia)
Sail Away Sweet Sister
Queen; *The Game* . . . . (Hollywood)
Shakespeare's Sister
Smiths; *Louder Than Bombs* . . . . (Sire)
Shimmy Like Kate
Olympics; *Meet The Marathons* . . . . (Collectables)
Official Record Album Of The Olympics . . . . (Rhino)
Sister
Nixons; *Foma* . . . . (MCA)
Sister Christian
Night Ranger; *Midnight Madness* . . . . (MCA)
Night Ranger's Greatest Hits . . . . (Camel)
Sister Don't Cry
Collective Soul; *Hints, Allegations And Things Left Unsaid* . . . . (Atlantic)
Sister Golden Hair
America; *America Live* . . . . (Warner Bros.)
Billboard Top Rock 'N' Roll Hits-1975-C . . . . (Rhino)
History-Greatest Hits . . . . (Warner Bros.)
Sister Havana
Urge Overkill; *Saturation* . . . . (Geffen)
Sister Moonshine
Supertramp; *Crisis? What Crisis?* . . . . (A&M)
Sister Morphine
Marianne Faithfull; *Blazing Away* . . . . (Island)
Marianne Faithfull's Greatest Hits . . . . (Abkco)

Rolling Stones; *Sticky Fingers*................................(Virgin)
Sister Of Pain
Vince Neil; *Exposed* .... (Warner Bros.)
Sister Rosa
Neville Brothers; *Yellow Moon* ....(A&M)
Sister Seagull
Be Bop Deluxe; *Best Of And The Rest Of Be Bop Deluxe* ....(Capitol)
Best Of Be Bop Deluxe-Raiding The Divine Archive ....(Capitol)
Futurama ....(Harvest)
Live! In The Air Age ....(Harvest)
Sisters
Rosemary Clooney & Betty Clooney; *Mothers & Daughters* .... (Concord Jazz)
Sisters Of The Moon
Fleetwood Mac; *25 Years-The Chain* ....(Warner Bros.)
Tusk ....(Warner Bros.)
Stepsisters' Lament
Barbara Ruick & Pat Carroll; *Cinderella-The CBS Television Network*
Production ....(Columbia)
Original Cast; *Cinderella-The CBS Television Production* ....(Columbia)
Theme From "Sisters"
Original Soundtrack; *Television's Greatest Hits-#7-Cable Ready-C* .....(TVT)
We Are Family
Sister Sledge; *Atlantic Records 50 Years-The Gold Anniversary*
Collection-C ....(Atlantic)
Best Of Sister Sledge-1973-1985 ....(Rhino)
Chicken Soup For The Soul: I'll Be There For You-Songs Of Friendship,
Brotherhood And Sisterhood-C ....(Rhino)
ST/The Full Monty ....(RCA Victor)
We Are Family ....(Rhino)
What's Going On
Cyndi Lauper; *True Colors* ....(Portrait)
Marvin Gaye; *20/20-C*...............................(Motown)
Marvin Gaye Live At The London Palladium ....(Motown)
Marvin Gaye-Anthology ....(Motown)
Marvin Gaye's Greatest Hits/...........................(Motown)
More Songs From "The Big Chill" Soundtrack-C ....(Motown)
What's Going On ....(Motown)
Quincy Jones; *Quincy Jones-The Best*......................(A&M)

FAMILY: SONS

**See Also: CHILDREN, CHILDREN LEAVING HOME, FAMILY
(various), MEN: GENERAL, MEN'S NAMES: A-Z, ORPHANS,
PARENTS (various)**

1941
Nilsson; *Pandemonium Shadow Show*..........................(RCA)
Adam Raised A Cain
Bruce Springsteen; *Darkness On The Edge Of Town*..............(Columbia)
Angel's Son
Strait Up featuring Lajon of Sevendust; *Strait Up-C* ....(Immortal/Virgin)
Ballad Of The Green Berets
Barry Sadler; *Cruisin'-1966-C* .... (Increase)
Hits Of The Sixties-C ....(Intercom Music)
More American Graffiti-#4-C.............................(MCA)
Nipper's Greatest Hits Of The '60s-#2-C ....(RCA)
Super Hits-#3-C ....(Gusto)
Beautiful Boy
John Lennon; *Double Fantasy*.............................(Capitol)
Best Day
George Strait; *Latest Greatest Straitest Hits* .... (MCA)
Billie Jean
Michael Jackson; *Thriller* ....(Epic)
Boy Named Sue
Johnny Cash; *Columbia Country Classics-#3-Americana-C* ....(Columbia)
Johnny Cash's Biggest Hits ....(Columbia)
Johnny Cash's Greatest Hits-#2 ....(Columbia)
The Man In Black-His Greatest Hits......................(Legacy)
Busy Man
Billy Ray Cyrus; *Shot Full Of Love* ....(Mercury)
Cannibals
Mark Knopfler; *Golden Heart* ....(Warner Bros.)
Cat's In The Cradle
Harry Chapin; *Greatest Stories-Live* ....(Elektra)
Harry Chapin-Anthology ....(Elektra)
Verities & Balderdash ....(Elektra)
City Of New Orleans
Arlo Guthrie; *Best Of Arlo Guthrie* ....(Warner Bros.)
Hobo's Lullaby ....(Reprise)
Together In Concert ....(Reprise)
HARP; *HARP* ....(Redwood)
Willie Nelson; *19 Hot Country Requests-#2-C* ....(Epic)
City Of New Orleans...................................(Columbia)
Greatest Country Hits Of The '80s-#4-C ....(Columbia)
Hot Tracks-Train Super Hits-C ....(Epic)
Train Trax-C.......................................(Sony Music Special Prod.)

Clack Clack/Oldest Living Son
John Stewart; *Last Campaign*............................ (Laserlight)
Cotton Mill Man
Jim & Jesse; *Old Dominion Masters* ....(Pinecastle)
Daddy's Little Boy
Mills Brothers; *45-#60098* ....(MCA)
Danny's Song
Anne Murray; *Anne Murray-Country* ....(Capitol)
Anne Murray's Greatest Hits ....(Capitol)
Danny's Song ....(Capitol)
Loggins & Messina; *Loggins & Messina-On Stage* ....(Columbia)
Sittin' In...(Columbia)
The Best Of Friends...................................(Columbia)
Dat Dere
Rickie Lee Jones; *Pop Pop* .... (Geffen)
Tony Bennett; *The Playground* ....(Sony Wonder)
Dead Bodies Everywhere
Korn; *Follow The Leader* ....(Immortal/Epic)
Desperados Waiting For A Train
Guy Clark; *Old No. 1* .... (Sugar Hill)
Jerry Jeff Walker; *Best Of Jerry Jeff Walker* .... (MCA)
Great Gonzos .... (MCA)
Viva Terlingua.. (MCA)
Waylon Jennings, Willie Nelson, Johnny Cash, Kris Kristofferson;
Highwayman ....(Columbia)
Hot Tracks-Train Super Hits-C ....(Epic)
D-I-V-O-R-C-E
Rosanne Cash; *Tammy Wynette...Remembered-C*............ (Asylum)
Tammy Wynette; *Super Hits Of The '60s-C*..................(Epic)
Tammy Wynette-Anniversary-20 Years Of Hits.............(Epic)
Tammy Wynette's Biggest Hits ....(Epic)
Tammy Wynette's Greatest Hits ....(Epic)
Don't Take Your Guns To Town
Johnny Cash; *Billboard Top Country Hits-1959-C* ....(Rhino)
Columbia Country Classics-#3-Americana-C ....(Columbia)
Johnny Cash-16 Biggest Hits-#2 ....(Legacy)
Johnny Cash's Greatest Hits ....(Columbia)
The Man In Black-His Greatest Hits ....(Legacy)
Drunken Driver
Ricky Skaggs and Kentucky Thunder; *Bluegrass Rules!* ....(Rounder)
Every Mother's Son
Traffic; *John Barleycorn Must Die*.........................(Island)
Every Mother's Son
Pretenders; *Last Of The Independents* .... (Sire)
Father & Son
Cat Stevens; *Cat Stevens Greatest Hits* ....(A&M)
Cat Stevens-Classics-#24 ....(A&M)
Footsteps In The Dark-Greatest Hits-#2..................(A&M)
Tea For The Tillerman ....(A&M)
Father And A Son
Loudon Wainwright III; *Loudon Wainwright III-History* ....(Charisma)
Father Of A Boy Named Sue
Shel Silverstein; *Songs & Stories*.........................(Parachute)
Father Of Mine
Everclear; *Now That's What I Call Music!-#2-C* .... (Virgin)
So Much For The Afterglow ....(Capitol)
Father To Son
Alarm; *Strength* ....(I.R.S.)
Father To Son
Phil Collins; *...But Seriously* .... (Atlantic)
Father To Son
Queen; *Queen II*.......................................(Hollywood)
Father's Table Grace
Lester Flatt; *Fifty Years Of Bluegrass Hits-#3-C* ....(C.M.H. Prod.)
Lester Flatt & The Nashville Grass; *The Tennessee Mountain Bluegrass*
Festival...(C.M.H. Prod.)
Feet Up (Pat Him On The Po-Po)
Guy Mitchell; *Definitive Guy Mitchell*..................(Collector's Choice)
Fortunate Son
Creedence Clearwater Revival; *1969*.......................(Fantasy)
Creedence Clearwater Revival-Chronicle ....(Fantasy)
Live In Europe ....(Fantasy)
More Gold ....(Fantasy)
ST/Forrest Gump..................... (Epic/Sony Music Soundtrax)
Willy & The Poor Boys ....(Fantasy)
Forty Again
John Berry; *Faces* ....(Capitol)
Give My Love To Rose
George Jones; *George Jones Sings The Hits Of His Country*
Cousins...(Razor & Tie)
Johnny Cash; *Johnny Cash-Sun Years*......................(Rhino)
He Didn't Have To Be
Brad Paisley; *Who Needs Pictures*.........................(Arista)
He Would Be Sixteen
Michelle Wright; *Now & Then* ....(Arista)
Heirloom
Bjork; *Vespertine*......................................(Elektra)
Hush Hush Hush
Paula Cole; *This Fire* ....(Imago)

I Am
Train; *Train* . . . .(Aware/C2/Columbia)
I Don't Want To Wait
Paula Cole; *Live On Letterman-From The Late Show*. . . . . (Reprise)
Songs From Dawson's Creek. . . . . (Sony Music Soundtrax)
This Fire . . . . (Imago)
I'm Already Taken
Steve Wariner; *Country Cares For Kids II-C* . . . . (BNA)
Two Teardrops . . . . (Capitol)
I'm Already There
Lonestar; *I'm Already There* . . . . (BNA)
Independence Day
Bruce Springsteen; *The River* . . . . (Columbia)
Bruce Springsteen & The E Street Band; *Bruce Springsteen & The E Street Band Live/1975-85* . . . . (Legacy)
Just The Two Of Us
Will Smith; *Big Willie Style* . . . . (Columbia)
Key To Life, The
Vince Gill; *The Key* . . . .(MCA)
Last Song
Elton John; *The One* . . . .(MCA)
Like Father Like Son
Lenny Kravitz; *ST/Aida* . . . . (Island)
Living Years, The
Mike & The Mechanics; *Living Years* . . . .(Atlantic)
Mona Lisas And Mad Hatters
Elton John; *Honky Chateau* . . . .(Rocket)
Reg Strikes Back . . . .(MCA)
The Concert For New York City-C . . . . (Columbia)
Mother Nature's Son
Beatles; *Beatles-Box Set* . . . . (Capitol)
The Beatles (White Album) . . . . (Capitol)
John Denver; *Evening With John Denver* . . . . (RCA)
Rocky Mountain High . . . . (RCA)
My Father's Eyes
Eric Clapton; *Pilgrim* . . . . (Duck/Reprise)
My Hometown
Bruce Springsteen; *Born In The U.S.A.* . . . . (Columbia)
Bruce Springsteen's Greatest Hits . . . . (Columbia)
My Son Calls Another Man Daddy
Hank Williams With His Drifting Cowboys; *Hank Williams-16 Great Hits* . . . . (Everest)
Hank Williams-40 Greatest Hits . . . . (Polydor)
Rare Takes & Radio Cuts . . . . (Polydor)
Nashville Cats
Del McCoury Band; *The Family* . . . . (Ceili Music)
Lovin' Spoonful; *Lovin' Spoonful-Anthology* . . . . (Rhino)
Native Son
Bryan Adams; *Into The Fire* . . . . (A&M)
No Son Of Mine
Genesis; *We Can't Dance* . . . .(Atlantic)
Oh! My Papa
Eddie Fisher; *Eddie Fisher's All-Time Greatest Hits-#1* . . . . . . (RCA)
Hebrew National Kosher Classics-C . . . . (RCA)
Nipper's Greatest Hits Of The '50s-#2-C . . . . (RCA)
Poor Man's Son
Rockin' Berries; *History Of British Rock-#2-C* . . . . (Rhino)
Prodigal Son
Rolling Stones; *Beggars Banquet* . . . . (Abkco)
Question Everything
8Stops7; *In Moderation* . . . . (Reprise)
Son Of A Fisherman
Tom Jones; *Memories Don't Leave Like People Do* . . . . (Parrot)
Son Of A New York Gun
Gino Vannelli; *Powerful People* . . . . (A&M)
Son Of A Poor Man
REO Speedwagon; *A Decade Of Rock And Roll 1970 To 1980* . . . .(Epic)
REO Speedwagon Live/*You Get What You Play For* . . . . (Epic)
Ridin' The Storm Out . . . .(Epic)
Son Of A Preacher Man
Dusty Springfield; *Dusty Springfield* . . . . (Rhino)
Dusty Springfield-Anthology . . . . (Mercury)
Son Of A Rotten Gambler
Anne Murray; *Anne Murray-Country* . . . . (Capitol)
Anne Murray-Country Hits . . . . (Capitol)
Love Song . . . . (Capitol)
Emmylou Harris; *Cimarron* . . . .(Warner Bros.)
Son Of A Son Of A Sailor
Jimmy Buffett; *Boats Beaches Bars & Ballads* . . . . (Margaritaville)
Son Of A Son Of A Sailor . . . .(MCA)
Songs You Know By Heart-Jimmy Buffett's Greatest Hit(s) . . . .(MCA)
You Had To Be There . . . .(MCA)
Son Of Hickory Holler's Tramp
O.C. Smith; *Me And You* . . . . (Columbia Special Prod.)
Story Songs-C . . . . (K-Tel)
Son Of Sagittarius
Eddie Kendricks; *Motown Superstar Series-#19-Eddie Kendricks* . . . (Motown)
Sullivan
Caroline's Spine; *Monsoon*. . . . . (Hollywood)

Tears In Heaven
Eric Clapton; *Diana, Princess Of Wales-Tribute-C* . . . . (Columbia)
Eric Clapton-Unplugged . . . .(Reprise)
ST/Rush . . . .(Reprise)
Teddy Boy
Beatles; *The Beatles Anthology-#3* . . . . (Capitol)
Paul McCartney; *McCartney*. . . . .(Capitol)
That Was Your Mother
Paul Simon; *Graceland* . . . . (Warner Bros.)
That's My Boy
Stan Freberg; *Capitol Collectors Series-Stan Freberg* . . . . (Capitol)
Theme From "Davis Rules"
Original Soundtrack; *Television's Greatest Hits-#7-Cable Ready-C* . . . . . (TVT)
Theme From "My Three Sons"
Original Soundtrack; *CBS: The First 50 Years* . . . . (TVT)
Television's Greatest Hits-#1-C . . . . (TVT)
Theme From "Sanford & Son"
Original Soundtrack; *Television's Greatest Hits-#3-1970s & 1980s-C* . . . (TVT)
Theme From "The Courtship Of Eddie's Father" (Best Friend)
Nilsson; *Television's Greatest Hits-#2-C* . . . . (TVT)
Used Cars
Bruce Springsteen; *Nebraska* . . . . (Columbia)
Voice Of America's Son
John Cafferty And The Beaver Brown Band; *ST/Cobra* . . . .(Scotti Bros.)
Tough All Over . . . .(Scotti Bros.)
War Baby Son Of Zorro
Daryl Hall & John Oates; *War Babies* . . . .(Atlantic)
What Would You Do?
City High; *City High* . . . .(Interscope)
Now That's What I Call Music!-#7-C . . . .(Virgin)
ST/Life . . . . (Rock Land/Interscope)
Wild Hearted Son
Cult; *Ceremony* . . . .(Sire)
Wish, The
Bruce Springsteen; *Tracks* . . . . (Columbia)
Zoomin'
Lionel Richie; *Time* . . . . (Mercury)

FAMILY: UNCLES

See Also: **FAMILY (various), MEN: GENERAL, MEN'S NAMES: A-Z**

Anything
Jay-Z; *Vol. 3-Life & Times of S. Carter* . . . .(Roc-A-Fella/DJMG)
Black Uncle Remus
Loudon Wainwright III; *Loudon Wainwright III*. . . . .(Atlantic)
Long Tall Sally
Beatles; *Past Masters-Volume One* . . . . (Parlophone)
Rock 'N' Roll Music . . . . (Capitol)
The Beatles At The Hollywood Bowl . . . . (Capitol)
The Beatles' Second Album . . . . (Capitol)
Little Richard; *Billboard Top R&B Hits-1956-C* . . . . (Rhino)
Here's Little Richard . . . .(Specialty)
Little Richard-18 Greatest Hits . . . . (Rhino)
Little Richard's Greatest Hits. (Everest)
Oldies But Goodies-#3-C . . . .(Original Sound)
ST/Heaven Help Us . . . . (EMI)
Super Oldies Of The '50s-#3-C . . . . (Audio Fidelity)
Tutti Frutti . . . .(Accord)
Me And My Uncle
Grateful Dead; *Grateful Dead (Skull & Roses)* . . . . (Warner Bros.)
Hundred Year Hall . . . .(Grateful Dead)
What A Long Strange Trip It's Been: The Best Of The Grateful Dead . . . . (Warner Bros.)
Theme From "Family Affair"
Original Soundtrack; *Television's Greatest Hits-#5-In Living Color-C* . . . (TVT)
Theme From "Fresh Prince Of Bel-Air"
Original Soundtrack; *Television's Greatest Hits-#7-Cable Ready-C* . . . . . (TVT)
Uncle Albert/Admiral Halsey
Paul And Linda McCartney; *RAM*. (Capitol)
Paul McCartney; *All The Best!* . . . . (Capitol)
Paul McCartney-Gift Set . . . . (Capitol)
Wings; *Wings Greatest* . . . . (Capitol)
Uncle Clooney Played The Banjo
Country Gazette; *Hello Operator...This Is Country Gazette*. . . . . . (Flying Fish)
Out To Lunch . . . . (Flying Fish)
Uncle Dave's Travels-Misery In Arkansas
Uncle Dave Macon; *The Country Music Hall Of Fame-Uncle Dave Macon* . . . . (MCA)
Uncle Isak Goes To Africa
Tom Wasinger; *Rock Music* . . . .(Invincible)
Uncle Jack
Spirit; *Best Of Spirit* . . . . (Epic)
Spirit. . . . . (Epic)
Spirit Of '84 . . . . (Mercury)

Time Circle .... (Epic)

Uncle John's Band
Grateful Dead; *Best Of/Skeletons From The Closet* .... (Warner Bros.)
Workingman's Dead .... (Warner Bros.)
Indigo Girls; *Deadicated-C* .... (Arista)

Uncle Pen
Bill Monroe; *Bean Blossom* .... (MCA)
Best Of Bill Monroe & His Blue Grass Boys .... (MCA)
Ricky Skaggs; *19 Hot Country Requests-#2-C* .... (Epic)
Bluegrass Super Hits-C .... (Columbia)
Columbia Country Classics-#5-A New Tradition-C .... (Columbia)
Don't Cheat In Our Hometown .... (Epic)
Live In London .... (Epic)

FARMS, Farmers

See Also: **ANIMALS: A-Z, ANIMALS: GENERAL, COUNTRY, FOOD & BEVERAGES (various), SOCIAL CLASS: RURAL, WORK**

Ain't Nobody Here But Us Chickens
Asleep At The Wheel; *Very Best Of Asleep At The Wheel Since 1970* ....(Relentless/Macady)
Louis Jordan; *Best Of Louis Jordan* .... (MCA)

Animal Farm
Kinks; *Are The Village Green Preservation Society* .... (Reprise)

Ant Farm
Young Fresh Fellows; *Men Who Loved Music* .... (Frontier)

Ant Farm
Night Soil Man; *Garden of Delights* .... (Vinyl Comm.)

Ask Any Farmer
John McCutcheon; *What It's Like* .... (Rounder)

Black Land Farmer
Sleepy LaBeef; *Bull's Night Out* .... (Sun)
Souvenirs Of Music City U.S.A.-C .... (Plantation)

Black Land Farmer
Frankie Miller; *45-#2101* .... (Gusto)

Boll Weevil Song
Brook Benton; *Brook Benton-Anthology* .... (Rhino)
It's Just A Matter Of Time-His Greatest Hits .... (Mercury)
Pick Of Brook Benton ....(Fifty One West)
Leadbelly; *Good Mornin' Blues-1936-1940* .... (Biograph)

Boy Who Wouldn't Hoe Corn
Alison Krauss & Union Station; *New Favorite* .... (Rounder)

Bushel And A Peck
Andrews Sisters; *Best Of The Andrews Sisters-#2* .... (MCA)
Original Cast; *Guys & Dolls* .... (MCA)

Cafe On The Corner
Sawyer Brown; *Cafe On The Corner* .... (Curb)

California Cotton Fields
Gram Parsons & Fallen Angels; *Live 1973* .... (Sierra)

Carry Me Back To Old Virginny
Jerry Lee Lewis; *Doin' Just Fine* .... (Accord)
Ole Tyme Country Music .... (Sun)
Sunday Down South .... (Sun)

Chug-A-Lug
Roger Miller; *Billboard Top Country Hits-1964-C* .... (Rhino)
Frat Rock!-#3-Grandson Of Frat Rock!-C .... (Rhino)

Coal Miner's Daughter
Loretta Lynn; *Coal Miner's Daughter* .... (MCA)
Coal Miner's Daughter .... (MCA)
Loretta Lynn-20 Greatest Hits .... (MCA)
Loretta Lynn-Greatest Hits Live .... (K-Tel)
Loretta Lynn's Greatest Hits-#2 .... (MCA)
The Country Music Hall Of Fame-Loretta Lynn .... (MCA)

Cotton Fields
Creedence Clearwater Revival; *1969* ....(Fantasy)
Willy & The Poor Boys ....(Fantasy)

Cotton Fields
Highwaymen; *"Michael Row The Boat Ashore"-Best Of The Highwaymen* .... (EMI)

Cotton Fields
Beach Boys; *Absolute Best-#2* .... (Capitol)
Friends-20/20 .... (Capitol)

Cotton Fields
Pogues; *Peace & Love* .... (Island)

Daddy Sang Bass
Johnny Cash; *Columbia Country Classics-#5-A New Tradition-C* ... (Columbia)
Johnny Cash's Greatest Hits-#2 .... (Columbia)
The Man In Black-His Greatest Hits .... (Legacy)

Daddy Won't Sell The Farm
Montgomery Gentry; *Tattoos & Scars* .... (Columbia)

Deportee (Plane Wreck At Los Gatos)
Arlo Guthrie & Pete Seeger; *Together In Concert* .... (Reprise)
Byrds; *The Byrds* .... (Columbia)
Cisco Houston; *Greatest Songs Of Woody Guthrie-C* .... (Vanguard)
Gene Clark & Carla Olson; *So Rebellious A Lover* .... (Rhino)

Judy Collins; *Tribute To Woody Guthrie-C* .... (Warner Bros.)
Waylon Jennings, Willie Nelson, Johnny Cash, Kris Kristofferson; *Highwayman* ....(Columbia)

Devil In The Cane Field
Mose Allison; *Down Home Piano* .... (Prestige)
Ol' Devil Mose .... (Prestige)

Diggin' My Potatoes
James Cotton; *High Compression* .... (Alligator)
Two Sides Of The Blues ....(Intermedia)

Down On The Farm
Charley Pride; *Charley Pride's Greatest Hits-#2* .... (RCA)

Down On The Farm
Little Feat; *Down On The Farm* .... (Warner Bros.)

Down On The Farm
Joe Walsh; *There Goes The Neighborhood* .... (Asylum)

Down On The Farm
Tim McGraw; *Not A Moment Too Soon* ....(Curb)
Tim McGraw's Greatest Hits ....(Curb)

Farm
Jefferson Airplane; *Volunteers* .... (RCA)

Farm, The
Aerosmith; *Nine Lives* ....(Columbia)

Farmer & The Cowman
Original Broadway Cast; *Oklahoma!* .... (RCA)

Farmer In Florida
Sally Rogers; *Love Will Guide Us* .... (Flying Fish)

Farmer John
Premiers; *Frat Rock!-#2-C* ....(Rhino)
History Of Latino Rock-#1-C ....(Rhino)

Farmer John
Neil Young & Crazy Horse; *Ragged Glory* .... (Reprise)

Farmer's Daughter
Merle Haggard; *Amber Waves Of Grain* .... (Epic)
Best Of The Best Of Merle Haggard ....(Liberty)
Vince Gill; *Mama's Hungry Eyes-Merle Haggard Tribute-C* .... (Arista)

Farmer's Daughter
Beach Boys; *Surfin' U.S.A.* ....(Capitol)

Farmer's Daughter
Fleetwood Mac; *Fleetwood Mac Live* .... (Warner Bros.)

Field Worker
David Crosby & Graham Nash; *Wind On The Water* .... (MCA)

Fields Of Gold
Sting; *Fields Of Gold-The Best Of Sting 1984-1994* .... (A&M)
Ten Summoner's Tales ....(A&M)

Fox, The
Nickel Creek; *Nickel Creek* .... (Sugar Hill)

Grow Your Own
Darlahood; *Big Fine Thing* .... (Reprise)

Harvest Moon
Neil Young; *Harvest Moon* .... (Reprise)

Heartland
George Strait; *ST/Pure Country* .... (MCA)

Heartland
Sawyer Brown; *Boys Are Back* ....(Curb)

Heartland
Steve Wariner; *Life's Highway* .... (MCA)

Heartland
U2; *Rattle And Hum* ....(Island)

High Cotton
Alabama; *Southern Star* .... (RCA)

How Do You Raise A Barn?
Original Cast; *Plain And Fancy* .... (EMI-Angel)

How Ya Gonna Keep 'Em Down On The Farm
Eddie Cantor; *Memories* .... (MCA)

I Want To Go Back To Michigan
Judy Garland; *ST/Easter Parade* ....(Rhino)

John Barleycorn
Traffic; *John Barleycorn Must Die* ....(Island)

John Deere Green
Joe Diffie; *Honky Tonk Attitude* .... (Epic)
Joe Diffie's Greatest Hits .... (Epic)

John Deere Tractor
Judds; *Judds' Greatest Hits-#2* .... (MCA)
Love Can Build A Bridge .... (MCA)

John Deere Tractor Song
Don Walser; *Uprooted: Best Of Roots Country-C* .... (Shanachie)

Junior's Farm
Paul McCartney; *All The Best!* ....(Capitol)
Wings; *Wings Greatest* ....(Capitol)

Kisses Sweeter Than Wine
Jimmie Rodgers; *Best Of Jimmie Rodgers* .... (Rhino)
Cruisin'-1958-C .... (Increase)
Weavers; *Best Of The Weavers* .... (MCA)
Reunion-At Carnegie Hall-1963 .... (Vanguard)
Weavers At Carnegie Hall .... (Vanguard)
Weavers' Greatest Hits .... (Vanguard)

Long Hard Road (Sharecropper's Dream)
Nitty Gritty Dirt Band; *Live Two Five* ....(Capitol)

Plain Dirt Fashion . . . . (Warner Bros.)
Twenty Years Of Dirt-Best Of The Nitty Gritty Dirt Band . . . . . (Warner Bros.)

Maggie's Farm
Bob Dylan; *Bob Dylan At Budokan* . . . . (Columbia)
Bob Dylan's Greatest Hits-#2 . . . . (Columbia)
Bringing It All Back Home . . . . (Columbia)
Hard Rain . . . . (Columbia)
Real Live . . . . (Columbia)

Migrant's Song, The
Luis Valdez & Augustin Lira; *Best Of Broadside 1962-1968: Anthems
Of The American Underground From The Pages Of Broadside
Magazine-C* . . . . (Smithsonian Folkways)

Most Happy Fella
Broadway Cast; *Most Happy Fella* . . . . (RCA)
Original Broadway Cast; *Most Happy Fella* . . . . (Sony Music Classical)

Naturally
Marty Stuart; *Country Goes Raffi-C* . . . . (Rounder)

Old Farm 1939
Randy Newman; *ST/The Natural* . . . . (Warner Bros.)

Old MacDonald Had A Farm
Original Soundtrack; *Toddler Favorites* . . . . (Kid Rhino/Rhino 4 Kids)

Old Man On The Farm
Randy Newman; *Little Criminals* . . . . (Warner Bros.)

Onion Field
Dandelion; *I Think I'm Gonna Be Sick* . . . . (Ruffhouse/Columbia)

Out Behind The Barn
"Little" Jimmy Dickens; *Columbia Historic Edition-"Little" Jimmy
Dickens* . . . . (Columbia)

Parchman Farm
John Mayall's Bluesbreakers; *Behind The Iron Curtain* . . . . (Crescendo)
John Mayall's Bluesbreakers-London Collector . . . . (London)
Last Of The British Blues . . . . (MCA)
John Mayall's Bluesbreakers with Eric Clapton; *John Mayall's Bluesbreakers
with Eric Clapton* . . . . (Deram)
Johnny Winter; *About Blues* . . . . (Janus)
Before The Storm . . . . (Janus)
Mose Allison; *Mose Allison* . . . . (Prestige)
Mose Allison's Greatest Hits . . . . (Prestige)

Party At The Prune Farm
Lou & Peter Berryman; *Cupid's Trash Truck* . . . . (Cornbelt)

Pastures Of Plenty
Tom Paxton; *Tribute To Woody Guthrie-C* . . . . (Warner Bros.)

Plant A Radish
Original Cast; *Fantasticks* . . . . (Polydor)

Plowed
Sponge; *Rotting Pinata* . . . . (Work)

Prairie Wedding
Mark Knopfler; *Sailing To Philadelphia* . . . . (Warner Bros.)

Rabbit In The Pea Patch
Red Clay Ramblers; *Merchant's Lunch* . . . . (Flying Fish)

Rain On The Scarecrow
John Cougar Mellencamp; *Scarecrow* . . . . (Riva)

Rainmaker
Dillards; *There Is A Time-1963-1970* . . . . (Vanguard)

Rainmaker
Traffic; *The Low Spark Of High Heeled Boys* . . . . (Island)

Reap What You Sow
Otis Rush; *Atlantic Blues-Chicago-C* . . . . (Atlantic)
Mourning In The Morning . . . . (Atlantic)

Rhythm In The Barnyard
Joe Liggins & The Honeydrippers; *Joe Liggins & The
Honeydrippers* . . . . (Specialty)

Scarecrow
Siouxsie And The Banshees; *Peepshow* . . . . (Geffen)

Sex Farm
Spinal Tap; *ST/Spinal Tap* . . . . (Polydor)

She Thinks My Tractor's Sexy
Kenny Chesney; *Everywhere We Go* . . . . (BNA)

Shoot Out On The Plantation
Leon Russell; *Best Of Leon Russell* . . . . (MCA)
Leon Russell . . . . (MCA)

Silence On The Line
Chris LeDoux; *Cowboy* . . . . (Capitol)

Sinaloa Cowboys
Bruce Springsteen; *The Ghost Of Tom Joad* . . . . (Columbia)

Somewhere Other Than The Night
Garth Brooks; *The Chase* . . . . (Liberty)

Song Of The South
Alabama; *Alabama's Greatest Hits-#2* . . . . (RCA)
Southern Star . . . . (RCA)

Sowin' Love
Paul Overstreet; *Sowin' Love* . . . . (RCA)

Strawberry Wine
Deana Carter; *Did I Shave My Legs For This?* . . . . (Capitol)

Taxes On The Farmer Feeds Us All
Ry Cooder; *Into The Purple Valley* . . . . (Reprise)

Tender Shepherd
Original Cast; *Peter Pan-The 1954 Broadway Production* . . . . . . (RCA Victor)

Tennessee Farmer
Stringbean; *Salute To Uncle Dave Macon* . . . . (Starday)

That Summer
Garth Brooks; *The Chase* . . . . (Liberty)

Theme From "Falcon Crest"
Original Soundtrack; *Television's Greatest Hits-#6-Remote Control-C* . . . (TVT)

Theme From "Green Acres"
Eddie Albert & Eva Gabor; *ST/Son In Law* . . . . (Hollywood)
Original Soundtrack; *CBS: The First 50 Years* . . . . (TVT)
Television's Greatest Hits-#1-C . . . . (TVT)

Theme From "The Magnificent Seven"
BBC Concert Orchestra; *Golden Cinema Classics-#1-The
Adventure Film* . . . . (Bainbridge)

Theme From "The Real McCoys"
Original Soundtrack; *Television's Greatest Hits-#4-Black & White
Classics-C* . . . . (TVT)

This Hard Land
Bruce Springsteen; *Bruce Springsteen's Greatest Hits* . . . . (Columbia)
Tracks . . . . (Columbia)

Three Blind Mice
Van Alexander; *Small Fry-Capitol Sings Kids Songs For
Grownups-C* . . . . (Capitol)

Trouble In The Fields
Nanci Griffith; *Lone Star State Of Mind* . . . . (MCA)
One Fair Summer Evening . . . . (MCA)

Turkey In The Straw
Stanley Brothers; *Stanley Series-Vol. 1-#3* . . . . (Copper Creek)
Vassar Clements; *Grass Routes* . . . . (Rounder)

Vermont Farmer's Song
Margaret MacArthur; *Almanac Of New England Farm Songs* . . . (Green Linnet)

When Country Comes To Town
Toby Keith; *How Do You Like Me Now?!* . . . . (DreamWorks/SKG)

Where Corn Don't Grow
Travis Tritt; *The Restless Kind* . . . . (Warner Bros.)

Where The Blacktop Ends
keith urban; *keith urban* . . . . (Capitol)

Where The Green Grass Grows
Tim McGraw; *Big Country Hits '99-C* . . . . (K-Tel)
Everywhere . . . . (Curb)
Tim McGraw's Greatest Hits . . . . (Curb)

Wolves
Garth Brooks; *No Fences* . . . . (Capitol)

You're Lookin' At Country
Loretta Lynn; *Loretta Lynn-20 Greatest Hits* . . . . (MCA)
Loretta Lynn-Greatest Hits Live . . . . (K-Tel)
Loretta Lynn's Greatest Hits-#2 . . . . (MCA)
The Country Music Hall Of Fame-Loretta Lynn . . . . (MCA)

FAST, Sudden

See Also: **BUSY, SLOW, SPORTS: CAR RACING, TIME:
GENERAL, URGENT**

5 Miles To Empty
Brownstone; *Still Climbing* . . . . (MJJ Music/Work)

All At Once You Love Her
Perry Como; *Perry Como's Greatest Hits* . . . . (RCA)

Beep Beep
Playmates; *Dr. Demento: 20th Anniversary Collection-C* . . . . (Rhino)

Casey Jones
Grateful Dead; *Best Of The Grateful Dead-Skeletons From The
Closet* . . . . (Warner Bros.)
*Bill Graham Presents The Last Days Of The
Fillmore-C* . . . . (Epic Portrait Assoc.)
Workingman's Dead . . . . (Warner Bros.)
Jerry Garcia Acoustic Band; *Almost Acoustic* . . . . (Grateful Dead)

Closer You Get, The
Alabama; *Alabama's Greatest Hits-#2* . . . . (RCA)
For The Record: 41 Number One Hits . . . . (RCA)
The Closer You Get . . . . (BMG Special Prod.)

Devil In A Fast Car
Sheena Easton; *Best Kept Secret* . . . . (EMI)

Distance, The
Cake; *Fashion Nugget* . . . . (Capricorn)

Everyday
Buddy Holly; *Buddy Holly* . . . . (MCA)
Buddy Holly-20 Golden Greats . . . . (MCA)
Buddy Holly's Greatest Hits . . . . (MCA)
From The Original Master Tapes-Buddy Holly . . . . (MCA)
Legend-From The Original Master Tapes . . . . (MCA)
The Buddy Holly Collection . . . . (MCA)

Fast As You
Dwight Yoakam; *This Time* . . . . (Reprise)

Fast Car
Tracy Chapman; *Tracy Chapman* . . . . (Elektra)

Fast Changes
Seal; *Seal 2* . . . . (Sire)

Fast Food
Stevens & Grdnic; *Dr. Demento Presents The Greatest Novelty Records-#5-
1980s-C* . . . . (Rhino)
Fast Food
Pete Townshend; *The Iron Man* . . . . (Atlantic)
Fast Moving Train
Restless Heart; *Best Of Restless Heart* . . . . (RCA)
Fast Moving Train . . . . (RCA)
Fastlove
George Michael; *Ladies & Gentlemen: The Best Of George Michael* . . . . . (Epic)
Older . . . . (DreamWorks/SKG)
Georgia On A Fast Train
Billy Joe Shaver; *Hot Tracks-Train Super Hits-C* . . . . (Epic)
Henry
New Riders Of The Purple Sage; *Best Of New Riders Of The
Purple Sage* . . . . (Columbia)
*Bill Graham Presents The Last Days Of The
Fillmore-C* . . . . (Epic Portrait Assoc.)
Home Home On The Road . . . . (Columbia)
New Riders Of The Purple Sage . . . . (Columbia)
How Fast Them Trucks Will Go
Boxcar Willie; *Truck Driving Favorites* . . . . (Madacy)
I Been To Georgia On A Fast Train
Willie Nelson; *Me & Paul* . . . . (Columbia)
I Love You
Keith Washington & Chante' Moore; *KW* . . . . (Silas)
I'm In A Hurry (And Don't Know Why)
Alabama; *American Pride* . . . . (RCA)
Johnny Needs A Fast Car
Chris Rea; *Espresso Logic* . . . . (East West)
Katie Wants A Fast One
Steve Wariner & Garth Brooks; *Faith In You* . . . . (Capitol)
Let Sally Drive
Sammy Hagar; *Ten 13* . . . . (Cabo Wabo/Beyond)
Little Honda
Beach Boys; *Absolute Best-#1* . . . . (Capitol)
All Summer Long . . . . (Capitol)
Best Of The Beach Boys . . . . (Capitol)
Spirit Of America . . . . (Capitol)
Hondells; *Beach Classics-All Original
Recordings-C* . . . . (Dunhill Compact Classics)
Cruisin'-1964-C . . . . (Increase)
Little Old Lady (From Pasadena)
Beach Boys; *Concert/'69-Live In London* . . . . (Capitol)
Jan & Dean; *Best Of Jan & Dean* . . . . (EMI)
Billboard Top Rock 'N' Roll Hits-1964-C . . . . (Rhino)
Dead Man's Curve . . . . (EMI)
Surf City-Best Of Jan & Dean . . . . (EMI)
Love Can Run Faster
Robert Palmer; *Double Fun* . . . . (Island)
MFC
Pearl Jam; *Yield* . . . . (Epic)
New York Minute
Don Henley; *End Of The Innocence* . . . . (Geffen)
One Minute Man
Missy ''Misdemeanor'' Elliot; *Miss E...So
Addictive* . . . . (Gold Mind/East West/EEG)
Quick As Rainbows
Kitchens Of Distinction; *Strange Free World* . . . . (One Little Indian)
Ray Of Light
Madonna; *GHV2* . . . . (Warner Bros.)
Ray Of Light . . . . (Maverick)
Totally Hits-#1-C . . . . (Arista)
Run
George Strait; *The Road Goes On Forever, A Collection Of Their Greatest
Recordings* . . . . (Polydor)
Rush
Big Audio Dynamite II; *Globe* . . . . (Columbia)
Rush Rush
Paula Abdul; *Spellbound* . . . . (Captive)
Should've Asked Her Faster
Ty England; *Ty England* . . . . (RCA)
Slow Down
Beatles; *Past Masters-Volume One* . . . . (Parlophone)
Speedoo
Cadillacs; *Best Of The Cadillacs* . . . . (Rhino)
Echoes Of A Rock Era-Early Years-C . . . . (Roulette)
More American Graffiti-C . . . . (MCA)
Original Rock 'N' Roll Hits Of The '50s-C . . . . (Roulette)
ST/Goodfellas . . . . (Atlantic)
Ry Cooder; *Borderline* . . . . (Warner Bros.)
Speedy Gonzales
Pat Boone; *Best Of Pat Boone* . . . . (MCA)
Speedy's Coming
Scorpions; *Best Of The Scorpions* . . . . (RCA)
Fly To The Rainbow . . . . (RCA)

Tokyo Tapes . . . . (RCA)
Suddenly
Soraya; *On Nights Like This* . . . . (Island)
Take The Short Way Home
Dionne Warwick; *Heartbreaker* . . . . (Arista)
Theme From ''Speed Racer''
Original Soundtrack; *Television's Greatest Hits-#3-1970s & 1980s-C* . . . . (TVT)
Too Fast For Love
Motley Crue; *Too Fast For Love* . . . . (Elektra)
Transfusion
Nervous Norvus; *Dr. Demento Presents The Greatest Novelty Records-#2-
1950s-C* . . . . (Rhino)
Dr. Demento: 20th Anniversary Collection-C . . . . (Rhino)
Vintage Music-#3-C . . . . (MCA)
Wacky Weirdos-C . . . . (K-Tel)
Wild Things Run Fast
Joni Mitchell; *Wild Things Run Fast* . . . . (Geffen)
Wreck Of The Old '97
Johnny Cash; *Johnny Cash At Folsom Prison & San Quentin* . . . . . . (Columbia)
Johnny Cash-Original Golden Hits-#3 . . . . (Sun)
Story Songs Of The Trains & Rivers . . . . (Sun)
Superbilly . . . . (Sun)
The Man-The World-His Music . . . . (Sun)
You Win My Love
Shania Twain; *The Woman In Me* . . . . (Mercury)

FAT, Skinny, Thin
See Also: FOOD & BEVERAGES (various)

Appointment At The Fat Clinic
Digable Planets; *Reachin'-New Refutation Of Time & Space* . . . . . . (Pendulum)
Baby Fat
Wet Willie; *Wet Willie's Greatest Hits* . . . . (Polydor)
Bacon Fat
Frank Zappa; *Broadway The Hard Way* . . . . (Rykodisc)
Our Man In Nirvana . . . . (Rhino)
Bang The Drum Slowly
Emmylou Harris; *Red Dirt Girl* . . . . (Nonesuch)
Big Fat Daddy
Jeannie & Jimmy Cheatham; *Midnight Mama* . . . . (Concord Jazz)
Big Fat Funky Booty
Spin Doctors; *Up For Grabs...Live* . . . . (Epic Portrait Assoc.)
Big Fat Ham
Jelly Roll Morton; *Immortal Jelly Roll Morton* . . . . (Milestone)
Big Fat Lady
George Benson; *Cookbook* . . . . (Columbia)
Big Fat Mama
Fred McDowell; *Long Way From Home* . . . . (Milestone)
Big Fat Mama
Big Joe Williams; *Legacy Of The Blues-#6* . . . . (Crescendo)
Big Fat Woman
Leadbelly; *Bourgeois Blues-Golden Classics-#1* . . . . (Collectables)
Tom Rush; *Blues Songs & Ballads* . . . . (Fantasy)
Bloat On
Cheech & Chong; *Let's Make A New Dope Deal* . . . . (Warner Bros.)
Brian Wilson
Barenaked Ladies; *Gordon* . . . . (Reprise)
Rock Spectacle . . . . (Reprise)
Cadillac Slim
Rick Braun; *Beat Street* . . . . (Mesa/Bluemoon)
Cellulite City
Redd Kross; *Born Innocent* . . . . (Frontier)
Creeque Alley
Mamas & The Papas; *Best Of The Mamas & The Papas* . . . . (MCA)
Mamas & The Papas' Greatest Hits . . . . (MCA)
Mamas & The Papas-16 Of Their Greatest Hits . . . . (MCA)
Davy The Fat Boy
Randy Newman; *Randy Newman* . . . . (Warner Archives)
Randy Newman/Live . . . . (Warner Archives)
Diet Song
Shel Silverstein; *Songs & Stories* . . . . (Parachute)
Fat
''Weird Al'' Yankovic; *''Weird Al'' Yankovic's Greatest Hits* . . . . (Scotti Bros.)
Dr. Demento: 20th Anniversary Collection-C . . . . (Rhino)
Even Worse . . . . (Scotti Bros.)
Paul Kantner, Grace Slick & David Freiberg; *Baron Von Tollbooth & The
Chrome Nun* . . . . (Grunt)
Fat
Violent Femmes; *3* . . . . (Slash)
Fat
Paul Kantner, Grace Slick & David Freiberg; *Baron Von Tollbooth & The
Chrome Nun* . . . . (Grunt)
Fat & Greasy
Original Cast; *Ain't Misbehavin'* . . . . (RCA)

Fat Angel
Jefferson Airplane; *2400 Fulton Street-An Anthology* . . . . (RCA)
   Bless Its Pointed Little Head . . . . (RCA)
Fat Bottomed Girls
Queen; *Jazz*. . . . . (Hollywood)
   Queen's Greatest Hits I & II . . . . (Hollywood)
Fat Boy
Billy Stewart; *Beach Music Hits-C* . . . . (Universal)
   One More Time . . . . (Chess)
   One More Time/Chess Years . . . . (Chess)
Fat Boy
Max-A-Million; *Club Hitz Of The '90s-#1-C* . . . . (Beast)
   Take Your Time . . . . (S.O.S./Zoo)
Fat Jack
Steppenwolf; *Steppenwolf 7* . . . . (MCA)
Fat Lady That Bumped Me Down
Paul Kelly; *Stand On The Positive Side* . . . . (Warner Bros.)
Fat Lip
Sum 41; *All Killer No Filler* . . . . (Island/IDJMG)
   Now That's What I Call Music!-#8-C . . . . (Virgin)
Fat Man
Fats Domino; *Best Of Fats Domino* . . . .(EMI)
   Fats Domino's Greatest Hits . . . . (MCA)
   My Blue Heaven-Best Of Fats Domino-#1 . . . .(EMI)
Fat Man
Jethro Tull; *20 Years Of Jethro Tull* . . . .(Chrysalis)
   M.U.-The Best Of Jethro Tull. . . . .(Chrysalis)
   Stand Up . . . .(Chrysalis)
Fat Man
Nazareth; *Nazareth* . . . . (A&M)
Fat Man
Radio Program Theme; *Themes From Old Times* . . . . (Viva)
Fat Man In The Bathtub
Little Feat; *Dixie Chicken* . . . .(Warner Bros.)
   Waiting For Columbus. . . . .(Warner Bros.)
Fatso
Terri Gibbs; *Take It From Me* . . . .(MCA)
Fattening Frogs For Snakes
Sonny Boy Williamson; *The Blues-#3-C* . . . . (Chess)
Fatty, Fatty
Heptones; *Night Food*. . . . . (Island)
I Like 'Em Fat Like That
Louis Jordan; *Five Guys Named Moe-Original Decca Recordings-#2*. . . .(MCA)
Me & Fat Boy
Mac Davis; *Texas In My Rear View Mirror* . . . . (Casablanca)
Pull Over
Trina; *Da Baddest B***h* . . . . (Slip 'N Slide)
Shake That Fat
Jo Jo Gunne; *Jo Jo Gunne*. . . . . (Asylum)
Short Fat Fannie
Larry Williams; *Original Rock Oldies-Golden Hits-#1-C* . . . . (Specialty)
   The Ultimate '50s Party-C . . . . (Era)
   This Is How It All Began-#2-C . . . . (Specialty)
Skin & Bone
Kinks; *Celluloid Heroes* . . . . (RCA)
   Everybody's In Show-Biz. . . . . (Rhino)
   Muswell Hillbillies . . . . (VelVel)
   The Kinks' Greatest-Celluloid Heroes. . . . . (RCA)
Skinny Boy
Chicago; *Chicago VII*. . . . .(Chicago)
   Group Portrait . . . .(Chicago)
Skinny Legs And All
Joe Tex; *I Believe I'm Gonna Make It!-Best Of Joe Tex* . . . . (Rhino)
   Joe Tex's Greatest Hits . . . . (Curb)
   Soul Years-C . . . . (Atlantic)
Skinny Minnie
Bill Haley & His Comets; *Bill Haley & His Comets' Greatest Hits* . . . . . .(MCA)
   Bill Haley & His Comets-Golden Hits . . . .(MCA)
Theme From "Fat Albert And The Cosby Kids"
Original Soundtrack; *Television's Greatest Hits-#3-1970s & 1980s-C* . . . (TVT)
Three Hundred Pounds Of Heavenly Joy
Big Twist & The Mellow Fellows; *Alligator Records 20th Anniversary
   Collection-C* . . . .(Alligator)
Howlin' Wolf; *The Chess Box-Howlin' Wolf* . . . . (Chess)
Too Fat Polka
Arthur Godfrey; *Dr. Demento Presents The Greatest Novelty Records-#1-
   1940s & Before-C* . . . . (Rhino)
Frankie Yankovic & His Yanks; *Frankie Yankovic & His Yanks'
   Greatest Hits* . . . . (Columbia)
Li'l Wally; *I Love To Polka* . . . .(Jay Jay)
Too Fat To Fuck
Blowfly; *Fresh Juice*. . . . . (Oops)
Unskinny Bop
Poison; *Flesh & Blood* . . . . (Capitol)
   Swallow This Live . . . . (Capitol)
You Can't Fool The Fat Man
Randy Newman; *Little Criminals*. . . . .(Warner Bros.)

FEAR & COURAGE, Bravery, Panic, Paranoia, Shy, Worry
See Also: CHARACTER & INTEGRITY, DANGER & DISASTER, EGO, HEROISM, HIDING, MOTIVATION, PATRIOTISM, STRONG

(Don't Fear) The Reaper
Blue Oyster Cult; *Agents Of Fortune* . . . . (Columbia)
   Extraterrestrial Live. . . . . (Columbia)
   Metalmania-C . . . . (Columbia)
   Some Enchanted Evening . . . . (Columbia)
(Man Who Shot) Liberty Valance
Gene Pitney; *Gene Pitney-Anthology 1961-1968* . . . . (Rhino)
   Gene Pitney's Greatest Hits . . . . (Evergreen Music)
   Super Oldies Of The '60s-#9-C . . . . (Audio Fidelity)
Greg Kihn; *Glass House Rock*. . . . . (Beserkley)
1984
David Bowie; *Changestwobowie* . . . . (RCA)
   David Live . . . . (Rykodisc)
   Diamond Dogs . . . . (Rykodisc)
   Fame & Fashion . . . . (RCA)
Tina Turner; *Private Dancer* . . . . (Capitol)
3am
Matchbox Twenty; *Yourself Or Someone Like You* . . . . (Lava)
Afraid
Willie Nelson; *Moonlight Becomes You* . . . .(Justice)
Afraid
Motley Crue; *Generation Swine* . . . .(Beyond)
   Motley Crue's Greatest Hits. . . . .(Beyond)
Afraid Of Love
Toto; *Toto IV* . . . . (Columbia)
Are You Hung Up
Mothers Of Invention; *We're Only In It For The Money* . . . . (Rykodisc)
Ballad Of The Green Berets
Barry Sadler; *Cruisin'-1966-C* . . . . (Increase)
   Hits Of The Sixties-C . . . . (Intercom Music)
   More American Graffiti-#4-C . . . . (MCA)
   Nipper's Greatest Hits Of The '60s-#2-C . . . . (RCA)
   Super Hits-#3-C . . . . (Gusto)
Beautiful
Mary J. Blige; *ST/How Stella Got Her Groove Back* . . . .(Flyte Tyme/MCA)
Believe
Cher; *Believe* . . . . (Warner Bros.)
   Totally Hits-#1-C . . . . (Arista)
Bent
Matchbox Twenty; *Mad Season By Matchbox Twenty* . . . . (Lava)
   Totally Hits-#3-C . . . .(Atlantic)
Better Watch Your Back
Daryl Hall & John Oates; *War Babies* . . . .(Atlantic)
Beware Of Darkness
George Harrison; *All Things Must Pass*. . . . .(Parlophone)
   Concert For Bangladesh-C . . . . (Capitol)
Bleed Together
Soundgarden; *A-Sides* . . . . (A&M)
Blister
Our Lady Peace; *Happiness...Is Not A Fish That You Can Catch* . . . . (Columbia)
Blue Train, The
Linda Ronstadt; *Feels Like Home* . . . . (Elektra)
Maura O'Connell; *Blue Is The Colour Of Hope* . . . . (Warner Bros.)
Bold As Love
Jimi Hendrix; *Axis: Bold As Love* . . . . (Reprise)
   Essential Jimi Hendrix . . . . (Reprise)
Brahma Fear
Jimmy Buffett; *Living & Dying In 3/4 Time* . . . . (MCA)
Bravado
Rush; *Roll The Bones* . . . .(Atlantic)
Brave Heart
Bill Miller; *Raven In The Snow* . . . . (Reprise)
Brave New World
Steve Miller Band; *Brave New World* . . . . (Capitol)
Brave New World
Public Image Ltd.; *9* . . . .(Virgin)
Brave New World
Choirboys; *Big Bad Noise* . . . . (WTG)
Brave Strangers
Bob Seger & Silver Bullet Band; *Stranger In Town* . . . . (Capitol)
Can't Stop Worrying
Dave Mason; *Alone Together* . . . . (MCA)
Cigarette
Ben Folds Five; *Whatever And Ever Amen* . . . .(Caroline/550)
Cold Sweat
James Brown; *Billboard Top R&B Hits-1967-C* . . . . (Rhino)
   Can Your Heart Stand It . . . .(Solid Smoke)
   James Brown's Greatest Hits . . . . (Rhino)
   Live At The Apollo-Vol. 2-Part 1 . . . . (Rhino)
Cold Sweat
Warrant; *Dirty Rotten Filthy Stinking Rich* . . . . (Columbia)
Come What May
Patti Page; *Patti Page Collection-The Mercury Years-#1* . . . . (Mercury)

Count Your Blessings (Instead Of Sheep)
Bing Crosby; *45-#29251* .... (Decca)
Eddie Fisher; *Best Of Eddie Fisher* .... (MCA)
Rosemary Clooney; *Essence Of Rosemary Clooney* .... (Legacy)
Courage
Tragically Hip; *Fully Completely* .... (MCA)
Coward Of The County
Kenny Rogers; *Kenny* .... (Liberty)
Kenny Rogers' Greatest Hits .... (EMI)
Kenny Rogers-Twenty Greatest Hits .... (EMI)
Cowards Over Pearl Harbor
Wilma Lee Cooper; *Wilma Lee Cooper* .... (Rounder)
Crawling
Linkin Park; *Hybrid Theory* .... (Warner Bros.)
Dare Me
Pointer Sisters; *Contact* .... (RCA)
Nipper's Greatest Hits Of The '80s-C .... (RCA)
Daylight Fading
Counting Crows; *Recovering The Satellites* .... (David Geffen Co.)
Dear Jean (I'm Nervous)
City Boy; *Young Men Gone West* .... (Mercury)
Don't Give Up
Peter Gabriel; *Shaking The Tree-Sixteen Golden Greats* .... (Geffen)
So .... (Geffen)
Don't Worry About Me
Doris Day; *Doris Day Sings 22 Great Songs-Original Big Band* .... (Hindsight)
Ella Fitzgerald; *Classy Pair* .... (Pablo)
Ella Fitzgerald & Joe Pass; *Easy Living* .... (Pablo)
Don't Worry, Baby
Beach Boys; *Absolute Best-#1* .... (Capitol)
Endless Summer .... (Capitol)
Fun Fun Fun .... (Capitol)
Made In The U.S.A. .... (Capitol)
Don't Worry, Be Happy
Bobby McFerrin; *Simple Pleasures* .... (EMI)
ST/Cocktail .... (Elektra)
Don'tcha Worry 'Bout A Thing
Stevie Wonder; *Innervisions* .... (Motown)
Down To My Last Broken Heart
Janie Fricke; *Greatest Country Hits Of The '80s-1980-C* .... (Columbia)
Janie Fricke-17 Greatest Hits .... (Columbia)
Janie Fricke's Greatest Hits .... (Columbia)
Down Town, The
Days Of The New; *Days Of The New* .... (Outpost/Interscope)
E-Bow The Letter
R.E.M.; *New Adventures In Hi-Fi* .... (Warner Bros.)
Fear
Sarah McLachlan; *Fumbling Towards Ecstasy* .... (Arista)
Fear Of A Black Planet
Public Enemy; *Fear Of A Black Planet* .... (Def Jam)
Fear Of Being Alone
Reba McEntire; *Reba McEntire's Greatest Hits-#3: I'm A Survivor* ..... (MCA)
What If It's You .... (MCA)
Fear Of Falling
Badlees; *River Songs* .... (Atlas)
Fear Of The Marketplace
Neil Diamond; *On The Way To The Sky* .... (Columbia)
Fear The Voices
Alice In Chains; *Music Bank* .... (Columbia)
Fearless
Pink Floyd; *Meddle* .... (Capitol)
Works .... (Capitol)
Fearless Boogie
ZZ Top; *XXX* .... (RCA)
Fly Me Courageous
Drivin' N' Cryin'; *Fly Me Courageous* .... (Island)
Fools Rush In (Where Angels Fear To Tread)
Brook Benton; *Super Oldies Of The '60s-#10-C* .... (Audio Fidelity)
Tommy Dorsey & Frank Sinatra; *Sessions-#1-February 1, 1940-July 17, 1940* .... (RCA)
For What It's Worth
Buffalo Springfield; *Buffalo Springfield* .... (Atco)
Buffalo Springfield-Retrospective .... (Atco)
Double History .... (Atco)
Hit Singles-1958-1977-C .... (Atlantic)
ST/Forrest Gump .... (Epic/Sony Music Soundtrax)
God Fearing Man
Steppenwolf; *At Your Birthday Party* .... (MCA Special Prod.)
Goodnight Moon
Shivaree; *I Oughtta Give You A Shot...* .... (Capitol)
Gotta Get Away
Offspring; *Smash* .... (Epitaph)
Gun Shy
10,000 Maniacs; *In My Tribe* .... (Elektra)
Moon Martin; *Escape From Domination* .... (Capitol)
Hero Of The Day
Metallica; *Load* .... (Elektra)

He's So Shy
Pointer Sisters; *Special Things* .... (Planet)
High Noon
Frankie Laine; *Billboard Top Movie Hits-1950-1954-C* .... (Rhino)
Tex Ritter; *Heroes Of Country Music-#4-Legends Of The West Coast-C* .... (Rhino)
The Envelope Please-Academy Award Winning Songs (1946-1957)-C .... (Rhino)
Hold Your Head Up
Argent; *Argent-Anthology-Collection Of Greatest Hits* .... (Epic)
Encore-Argent .... (Epic)
Rock Artifacts-From The Vaults-#1-C .... (Columbia)
ST/Queen's Logic .... (Epic)
Home
Staind; *Dysfunction* .... (Flip/Elektra)
Hospital Song
Ben Folds Five; *The Unauthorized Biography Of Reinhold Messner* .... (550 Music)
I Ain't Down Yet
Debbie Reynolds; *ST/The Unsinkable Molly Brown* .... (MCA)
I Alone
Live; *Throwing Copper* .... (Radioactive/MCA)
I Don't Think I Will
James Bonamy; *What I Live To Do* .... (Epic)
I Don't Worry About A Thing
Mose Allison; *Best Of Mose Allison* .... (Rhino)
I Don't Worry About A Thing .... (Rhino)
I Scare Myself
Dan Hicks & His Hot Licks; *Striking It Rich!* .... (MCA)
Thomas Dolby; *Flat Earth* .... (Capitol)
I Think I'm Paranoid
Garbage; *Now That's What I Call Music!-#2-C* .... (Virgin)
Version 2.0 .... (Almo Sounds)
I Whistle A Happy Tune
Barbara Cook; *My Little Broadway* .... (Sony Wonder)
Frank Sinatra; *Frank Sinatra Sings Rodgers & Hammerstein* ...... (Columbia)
Micky Dolenz; *Broadway Micky* .... (Kid Rhino/Rhino 4 Kids)
Original Broadway Cast; *The King And I* .... (RCA Victor)
Original Cast; *The King And I* .... (MCA)
I Will Survive
Gloria Gaynor; *Billboard Top Hits-1979-C* .... (Rhino)
I Am Woman-C .... (Nick At Nite)
Love Tracks .... (Polydor)
The Disco Years-#2-On The Beat-1978-1982-C .... (Rhino)
I Wonder What The King Is Doing Tonight
Original Cast; *Camelot* .... (Columbia)
Richard Harris; *ST/Camelot* .... (Warner Bros.)
I'm Afraid Of Me
Culture Club; *Kissing To Be Clever* .... (Virgin)
I'm Afraid To Go Home
Brian Hyland; *Brian Hyland's Greatest Hits* .... (Rhino)
Gene Pitney; *This Is Gene Pitney* .... (Out Of Print)
I'm Not Afraid
Frank Sinatra; *Frank Sinatra's Greatest Hits-#2* .... (Reprise)
I'm So Afraid
Fleetwood Mac; *25 Years-The Chain* .... (Warner Bros.)
Fleetwood Mac .... (Reprise)
Fleetwood Mac Live .... (Warner Bros.)
I'm The Bravest Individual
Original Cast; *Sweet Charity* .... (Columbia)
Impossible Dream
Andy Williams; *Andy Williams' Greatest Hits-#2* .... (Columbia)
Andy Williams-16 Most Requested Songs .... (Legacy)
Impossible Dream .... (Columbia)
Ed Ames; *Best Of Ed Ames* .... (RCA)
Ed Ames-Pure Gold .... (RCA)
Impossible Dream .... (RCA)
This Is Ed Ames .... (RCA)
Jack Jones; *Best Of Jack Jones* .... (MCA)
Kate Smith; *Best Of Kate Smith* .... (RCA)
Kate Smith-Legendary Performer .... (RCA)
Luther Vandross; *Songs* .... (Epic)
Original London Cast; *Man Of La Mancha* .... (MCA)
Robert Goulet; *Robert Goulet's Greatest Hits* .... (Columbia)
In 2 Deep
Kenny Wayne Shepherd Band; *Live On* .... (Giant)
Independence Day
Martina McBride; *The Way That I Am* .... (RCA)
It Worries Me
Frank Sinatra; *Concepts* .... (Capitol)
Where Are You? .... (Capitol)
It's Only Me
Leon Russell; *Americana* .... (Paradise)
Itsy Bitsy Teenie Weenie Yellow Polkadot Bikini
Brian Hyland; *Brian Hyland's Greatest Hits* .... (Rhino)
Dr. Demento Presents The Greatest Novelty Records-#3-1960s-C ..... (Rhino)
Vintage Music-#5-C .... (MCA)
Knock On Wood
Amii Stewart; *Double Smash Hits-C* .... (Volcano Entertainment)

Buddy Guy; *This Is Buddy Guy*. . . . . (Vanguard)
Eddie Floyd; *15 Original Big Hits-#3-C*. . . . .(Stax)
   Atlantic Rhythm & Blues 1947-1974-#6 (1966-1969)-C . . . .(Atlantic)
   Best Of Wattstax-C. . . . . (Stax)
   Super Oldies Of The '60s-#11-C . . . . (Audio Fidelity)
Eric Clapton; *Behind The Sun* . . . . (Duck/Reprise)
Ike & Tina Turner; *Ike & Tina Turner's Greatest Hits-#3* . . . . (Saja)

Learning To Live Again
Garth Brooks; *The Chase* . . . . (Liberty)

Life Line
Nilsson; *The Point* . . . . (RCA)

Living Inside Myself
Gino Vannelli; *Nightwalker* . . . . (Arista)

Look At That
Paul Simon; *You're The One*. . . . .(Warner Bros.)

Look Heart No Hands
Randy Travis; *Randy Travis' Greatest Hits-#2*. . . . .(Warner Bros.)

Murder Incorporated
Bruce Springsteen; *Bruce Springsteen's Greatest Hits*. . . . . (Columbia)

My Brave Face
Paul McCartney; *Flowers In The Dirt*. . . . . (Capitol)
   Tripping The Live Fantastic-Highlights! . . . . (Capitol)

My Heart Has A History
Paul Brandt; *Calm Before The Storm* . . . . (Reprise)

My Husband's Got No Courage In Him
Maddy Prior & June Tabor; *Silly Sisters*. . . . . (Shanachie)

Naked
Goo Goo Dolls; *A Boy Named Goo*. . . . .(Metal Blade)

Never Surrender
Triumph; *Never Surrender* . . . .(MCA)
   Stages. . . . .(MCA)

Never Surrender
Corey Hart; *Boy In The Box* . . . .(EMI)
   The Singles. . . . .(EMI)

New Worried Mind
Bob Wills; *Stay A Little Longer-The Original Columbia*
   Recordings . . . . (Roswell/RCA)

No Fear
Terri Clark; *Fearless*. . . . . (Mercury)

No, No, No
Destiny's Child; *Destiny's Child* . . . . (Grass Roots/Columbia)

On The Side Of Angels
LeAnn Rimes; *You Light Up My Life-Inspirational Songs* . . . . (Curb)

On, Brave Old Army Team
All-Star Inter-Conference Band; *College Marches At Halftime* . . . . (Alshire)
Glenn Miller; *Pennsylvania 6-5000-Sustaining*
   Remotes. . . . . (Vintage Jazz Classics)
Original Soundtrack; *Top Ten College Fight Songs* . . . . (K-Tel)

Once Bitten Twice Shy
Great White; *...Twice Shy*. . . . . (Capitol)
   Rock The First-#2-C . . . .(Sandstone Music)
Vesta Williams; *Vesta*. . . . . (A&M)

One Love At A Time
Tanya Tucker; *Tanya Tucker's Greatest Hits*. . . . . (Liberty)

Other Side Of The Game
Erykah Badu; *Baduizm* . . . . (Kedar Entert./Universal)

Panic
Smiths; *Best...I*. . . . . (Sire)
   Louder Than Bombs . . . . (Sire)
   Rank. . . . . (Sire)

Panic
Anthrax; *Armed & Dangerous* . . . .(Megaforce)
   Fistful Of Metal . . . .(Megaforce)

Panic In Detroit
David Bowie; *Aladdin Sane* . . . .(Rykodisc)
   Scary Monsters . . . .(Rykodisc)
   Sound + Vision . . . .(Rykodisc)

Panic In The World
Be Bop Deluxe; *Best Of And The Rest Of Be Bop Deluxe* . . . . (Capitol)
   Best Of Be Bop Deluxe-Raiding The Divine Archive . . . . (Capitol)
   Drastic Plastic . . . . (Capitol)

Paranoid
Black Sabbath; *Live Evil*. . . . .(Warner Bros.)
   Paranoid . . . .(Warner Bros.)
   We Sold Our Soul For Rock 'N' Roll . . . .(Warner Bros.)
Grand Funk Railroad; *Grand Funk* . . . . (Capitol)
   Live Album . . . . (Capitol)
   Mark, Don & Mel 1969-71 . . . . (Capitol)
   More Of The Best . . . . (Capitol)
Ozzy Osbourne; *Speak Of The Devil* . . . . (Jet)
   The Ozzman Cometh . . . .(Epic)
   Tribute . . . .(Epic)

Pressure
Billy Joel; *Billy Joel-Greatest Hits, Volume I & Volume II*. . . . . (Columbia)
   Nylon Curtain . . . . (Columbia)

Pressure
Neil Young; *Landing On Water* . . . . (Geffen)

Pressure
Fishbone; *Reality Of My Surroundings*. . . . . (Columbia)

Pressure
Rude Boys; *Rude Awakening* . . . .(Atlantic)

Pressure
Negative Approach; *Total Recall* . . . . (Touch & Go)

Rattlesnake
Live; *Secret Samadhi* . . . . (Radioactive/MCA)

Runaway Train
Rosanne Cash; *Greatest Country Hits Of The '80s-1988-C* . . . . (Columbia)
   Hot Tracks-Train Super Hits-C . . . . (Epic)
   King's Record Shop . . . . (Columbia)
   Rosanne Cash-Retrospective . . . . (Columbia)

Running Scared
Roy Orbison; *For The Lonely: A Roy Orbison Anthology 1959-1965*. . . . (Rhino)
   In Dreams-Greatest Hits . . . .(Orbison)
   Roy Orbison & Friends: Black & White Night-Live . . . .(Virgin)
   Roy Orbison's All-Time Greatest Hits-#1 & 2 . . . . (Monument)

Safe And Sound
Sheryl Crow; *America: A Tribute To Heroes-C* . . . .(Interscope)

San Francisco Holiday (Worry Later)
Thelonius Monk; *In Person*. . . . . (Milestone)

Scarecrow
Siouxsie And The Banshees; *Peepshow* . . . . (Geffen)

Scared
John Lennon; *Lennon* . . . . (Capitol)
   Menlove Ave. . . . . (Capitol)
   Walls And Bridges . . . . (Capitol)

Scarred & Scared
Rod Stewart; *Blondes Have More Fun* . . . . (Warner Bros.)

Scary Monsters
David Bowie; *Golden Years* . . . .(Rykodisc)
   Scary Monsters. . . . .(Rykodisc)
   The Singles-1969-1993. . . . .(Rykodisc)

Scotland The Brave
Gordon Highlanders; *Scotland: Scottish Bagpipes & Drums-C* . . . . . (Laserlight)
Original Cast; *Forever Plaid* . . . .(RCA)
Original Soundtrack; *ST/More Music From Braveheart* . . . . (Philips)

Shy
Carol Burnett/Original Cast; *Once Upon A Mattress* . . . . (MCA)

Shy Guy
Diana King; *ST/Bad Boys* . . . . (Work)
   Tougher Than Love . . . . (Work)

Silver Future
Monster Magnet; *ST/Heavy Metal 2000* . . . . (Restless)

Somebody's Watching Me
Rockwell; *Somebody's Watching Me* . . . . (Motown)

Someone To Watch Over Me
Ella Fitzgerald; *Ella Fitzgerald Sings The George & Ira Gershwin*
   Songbook. . . . . (Verve)
Elton John; *Glory Of Gershwin Featuring Larry Adler-C* . . . . (Mercury)
Frank Sinatra; *Nice 'N' Easy* . . . . (Capitol)
   The Capitol Years . . . . (Capitol)
Jack Jones; *Gershwin Album* . . . . (Columbia)
Original Broadway Cast; *Crazy For You*. . . . . (Angel)
Oscar Peterson; *My Favorite Instrument*. . . . . (Verve)
Sarah Vaughan; *Sarah Vaughan Sings George Gershwin Songbook,*
   Vol. 2 . . . .(Emarcy)
Willie Nelson; *Stardust*. . . . . (Legacy)

Sometimes
Britney Spears; *...Baby One More Time* . . . . (Jive)
   Now That's What I Call Music!-#3-C . . . . (Virgin)

Song From Moulin Rouge (Where Is Your Heart)
Percy Faith & His Orchestra; *Percy Faith & His Orchestra's All-Time*
   Greatest Hits . . . . (Columbia)

Sparrow In The Treetop
Guy Mitchell; *Guy Mitchell-16 Most Requested Songs*. . . . . (Legacy)

Stage Fright
Band; *Best Of The Band* . . . . (Capitol)
   Rock Of Ages . . . . (Capitol)
   Stage Fright . . . . (Capitol)
   The Last Waltz . . . . (Warner Bros.)
   To Kingdom Come-The Definitive Collection . . . . (Capitol)
Bob Dylan And The Band; *Before The Flood* . . . . (Columbia)

Stand And Be Counted
Crosby, Stills, Nash & Young; *Looking Forward* . . . . (Reprise)

Standing In The Shadows Of Love
Barry White; *Barry White's Greatest Hits*. . . . . (20th Century Fox)
   I've Got So Much To Give. . . . . (20th Century Fox)
Four Tops; *Four Tops' Greatest Hits* . . . . (Motown)
   Four Tops Reach Out . . . . (Motown)
   Four Tops-Anthology . . . . (Motown)
   Motown Story-First 25 Years-C . . . . (Motown)
   Motown Superstar Series-#14-Four Tops . . . . (Motown)
Rod Stewart; *Blondes Have More Fun* . . . . (Warner Bros.)

Standing Outside The Fire
Garth Brooks; *In Pieces*. . . . . (Liberty)

Staring At The Sun
U2; *Pop* . . . . (Island)

Stick It Out
Rush; *Counterparts*. . . . .(Atlantic)

Stolen Car
Bruce Springsteen; *The River* . . . . (Columbia)
   Tracks . . . . (Columbia)
Elliott Murphy; *One Step Up/Two Steps Back-The Songs Of Bruce*
   Springsteen-C . . . . (Right Stuff)

Straight Lines
Wood; *Songs From Stamford Hill* . . . . (Columbia)

Tales Of Brave Ulysses
Cream; *Disraeli Gears.* . . . . (Polydor)
   Eric Clapton-Crossroads-C . . . . (Polydor)
   Live Cream-#2 . . . . (Polydor)

Talk Back Trembling Lips
Ernest Ashworth; *Best Of Ernest Ashworth* . . . .(Curb)
Johnny Tillotson; *Cruisin'-1964-C* . . . . (Increase)

Terrified
Uncle Green; *You.* . . . . (DB)

Terrified
Pursuit Of Happiness; *Downward Road* . . . . (Mercury)

Terrified
Anacrusis; *Speed Metal-C* . . . .(Priority)

Terrified
Quiet Riot; *Terrified* . . . . (Moonstone)

Terrifying
Rolling Stones; *Steel Wheels* . . . . (Rolling Stones)

Terror On The Town
Lizzy Borden; *Menace To Society* . . . . (Metal Blade)

Terror Zone
Kreator; *Coma Of Souls* . . . . (Epic)

Terrorist Trousers
Jim Carroll Band; *Praying Mantis* . . . . (Giant)

Terrorist's Life
D.I.; *What Good Is Grief To A God* . . . . (Triple X Entert.)

Theme From "Courageous Cat & Minute Mouse"
Original Soundtrack; *Television's Greatest Hits-#2-C* . . . . (TVT)

There Are No Cats In America
Nehemiah Persoff/John Guarnieri/Warren Hays; *ST/An American Tail* . . (MCA)

Tiger
Paula Cole; *This Fire* . . . . (Imago)

Too Much Paranoias
Devo; *Live-The Mongoloid Years* . . . . (Rykodisc)
   Q: Are We Not Men? A: We Are Devo! . . . . (Warner Bros.)
   Rest Of Devo-Greatest Misses . . . . (Warner Bros.)

Too Shy
Kajagoogoo; *White Feathers* . . . . (EMI)

Too Shy To Say
Stevie Wonder; *Fulfillingness' First Finale* . . . . (Motown)

Touch Me
Doors; *Best Of The Doors* . . . . (Elektra)
   Doors 13 . . . . (Elektra)
   Doors' Greatest Hits. . . . . (Elektra)
   Soft Parade . . . . (Elektra)

Tremble For My Beloved
Collective Soul; *Dosage* . . . . (Atlantic)

Troubles
Alicia Keys; *Songs In A Minor* . . . . (J)

Under Pressure
David Bowie & Queen; *Bowie-The Singles-1969-1993* . . . . (Rykodisc)
Queen & David Bowie; *Classic Queen* . . . .(Hollywood)
   Hot Space . . . . (Hollywood)
   Queen's Greatest Hits I & II . . . . (Hollywood)

Wake Up Little Susie
Everly Brothers; *All They Had To Do Was Dream* . . . . (Rhino)
   American Graffiti-#3-C . . . . (MCA)
   Everly Brothers. . . . . (Rhino)
   Everly Brothers' All-Time Greatest Hits. . . . .(Curb)
   Oldies But Goodies-#7-C . . . .(Original Sound)
   Very Best Of The Everly Brothers . . . . (Warner Bros.)
Grateful Dead; *History Of The Grateful Dead-Vol. 1 (Bear's*
   Choice) . . . . (Warner Bros.)
Simon & Garfunkel; *The Concert In Central Park* . . . . . . (Warner Bros.)

Walk On Faith
Mike Reid; *Greatest Country Hits Of The '90s-1991-C* . . . . (Columbia)
   Turning For Home . . . . (Columbia)

Walk Unafraid
R.E.M.; *Up* . . . . (Warner Bros.)

Walkin' The Floor Over You
Asleep At The Wheel; *Western Standard Time* . . . . (Epic)
Ernest Tubb; *Legend & The Legacy.* . . . . (First Generation)
   The Ernest Tubb Story . . . . (MCA)
Ernest Tubb/Merle Haggard/Charlie Daniels; *Ernest Tubb*
   Collection-C . . . . (Step One)
Sandy Denny; *Who Knows Where The Time Goes.* . . . . (Hannibal)
Webb Pierce; *Webb Pierce-Golden Hits* . . . . (Plantation)

Whatever I Fear
Toad The Wet Sprocket; *Coil* . . . . (Columbia)

When She Cries
Restless Heart; *Big Iron Horses.* . . . . (RCA)
   Restless Heart's Greatest Hits . . . . (RCA)
   Today's Number One Country-C . . . . (K-Tel)

When You Believe
Mariah Carey & Whitney Houston; *Mariah Carey-#1's* . . . .(Columbia)
   ST/The Prince Of Egypt. . . . . (DreamWorks/SKG)
Whitney Houston & Mariah Carey; *My Love Is Your Love* . . . .(Arista)

Where Do We Go From Here
Vanessa Williams; *Vanessa Williams' Greatest Hits-The First Ten*
   Years. . . . . (Mercury)

Where You Get Love
Matthew Sweet; *Blue Sky On Mars* . . . . (Freeworld/Capitol)

White Knuckles
Elvis Costello & The Attractions; *Trust* . . . . (Rykodisc)

Whiter Shade Of Pale
Annie Lennox; *Medusa* . . . . (Arista)
Procol Harum; *Best Of Procol Harum* . . . . (A&M)
   Billboard Top Pop Hits-1967-C . . . . (Rhino)
   History Of British Rock-#8-C . . . . (Rhino)
   ST/Big Chill. . . . . (Motown)

Who Scared You
Doors; *Weird Scenes Inside The Gold Mine* . . . . (Elektra)

Who's Afraid Of The Big Bad Wolf
Barbra Streisand; *Just For The Record* . . . . (Columbia)
   The Barbra Streisand Album. . . . . (Columbia)
L.L. Cool J; *Simply Mad About The Mouse-C* . . . . (Columbia)
Mormon Tabernacle Choir & Columbia Symphony Orchestra; *When You*
   Wish Upon A Star-A Tribute To Walt Disney . . . . (CBS Masterworks)

Why Am I So Shy
Chiffons; *Chiffons-Golden Classics.* . . . .(Collectables)
   Everything You Always Wanted To Hear By . . . . (Laurie)

Wimoweh (Mbube)-The Lion Sleeps Tonight
Chet Atkins; *RCA Years* . . . . (RCA)
Kingston Trio; *Kingston Trio/From The Hungry i* . . . . (Capitol)
Nylons; *Seamless* . . . . (Open Air)
Pete Seeger; *Pete Seeger's Greatest Hits* . . . . (Columbia)
Tokens; *Billboard Top Rock 'N' Roll Hits-1961-C* . . . . (Rhino)
   Nipper's Greatest Hits Of The '60s-#1-C . . . . (RCA)
Weavers; *Weavers' Greatest Hits* . . . . (Vanguard)

Winner Of Your Heart
Johnnie & Jack & Their Tennessee Mountain Boys; *45-Out of print* . . . . . (RCA)

With A Girl Like You
Troggs; *Best Of The Troggs* . . . . (Rhino)
   History Of British Rock-#4-C . . . . (Rhino)

Wolverton Mountain
Claude King; *American Originals-Claude King* . . . . (Columbia)
   Best Of Claude King . . . . (Gusto)
   Billboard Top Country Hits-1962-C . . . . (Rhino)
   Super Hits Of The '60s-C . . . . (Epic)

Wolves
Garth Brooks; *No Fences* . . . . (Capitol)

Work It Out
Def Leppard; *Slang* . . . . (Mercury)

Work Shy
Fabulous Poodles; *Mirror Stars* . . . . (Epic)

Worried Life Blues
B.B. King; *Turn On With B.B. King* . . . . (Kent)
Eric Clapton; *24 Nights* . . . .(Duck/Reprise)
   Just One Night. . . . . (Polydor)
John Lee Hooker; *John Lee Hooker Plays & Sings The Blues* . . . . (Chess)
Lightnin' Hopkins; *Best Of Lightnin' Hopkins* . . . . (Prestige)
   How Many More Years I Got. . . . . (Fantasy)

Worried Mind
Roy Acuff; *Night Train To Memphis* . . . . (Columbia River Entert. Group)

You Can Call Me Al
Paul Simon; *Concert In The Park-August 15 1991* . . . .(Warner Bros.)
   Graceland . . . . (Warner Bros.)
   Negotiations And Love Songs, 1971-1986. . . . . (Warner Bros.)

You Don't Have To Worry
En Vogue; *Born To Sing.* . . . . (Atlantic)

You Don't Have To Worry
New Edition; *Home Again* . . . . (MCA)

You'll Never Walk Alone
Andy Williams; *Unchained Melody-Greatest Songs* . . . .(Curb)
Jim Nabors; *Jim Nabors-16 Most Requested Songs* . . . . (Legacy)
Judy Garland; *Best Of The Capitol Masters-One & Only Box* . . . . . . (Capitol)
Mormon Tabernacle Choir; *Climb Ev'ry Mountain* . . . . (Columbia)
Original Broadway Cast; *Carousel* . . . . (Angel)
Original Cast; *Carousel* . . . . (MCA)
Pink Floyd; *Meddle* . . . . (Capitol)

FEELINGS, Emotion, Lack Of Feelings, Moods, Numb, Sensitivity

See Also: **ANGER, CHARACTER & INTEGRITY, CRAZY, CRYING, DESPAIR, FEAR & COURAGE, HAPPINESS, HATE, HEART, HELP, JEALOUSY, LOVE (various), REMEMBER, SADNESS, SURPRISE**

(This Ain't) No Thinkin' Thing
Trace Adkins; *Dreamin' Out Loud.* . . . . (Capitol)

(You Make Me Feel Like) A Natural Woman
Aretha Franklin; *Aretha Franklin's Greatest Hits-1980-1994* . . . . (Arista)
Chicken Soup For The Woman's Soul-C . . . . (Rhino)
Carole King; *Tapestry* . . . .(Epic)
Celine Dion; *Tapestry Revisited: Tribute To Carole King-C* . . . . (Lava)
10,000 Horses
Candlebox; *Happy Pills* . . . .(Maverick)
All I Want
Toad The Wet Sprocket; *Fear* . . . . (Columbia)
P.S. (A Toad Retrospective) . . . . (Columbia)
Am I The Only One (Who's Ever Felt This Way)
Dixie Chicks; *Wide Open Spaces* . . . . (Monument)
And Still
Reba McEntire; *Read My Mind* . . . .(MCA)
Reba McEntire's Greatest Hits-#3: I'm A Survivor . . . .(MCA)
Anything's Better Than Feelin' The Blues
Martina McBride; *Emotion* . . . . (RCA)
Baby I'm-A Want You
Bread; *Baby I'm-A Want You* . . . . (Elektra)
Best Of Bread . . . . (Elektra)
Bread-Anthology . . . . (Elektra)
Baby You're A Rich Man
Beatles; *Beatles-Box Set* . . . . (Capitol)
Magical Mystery Tour . . . . (Capitol)
Babylon
David Gray; *White Ladder* . . . . (ATO/RCA)
Back 2 Good
Matchbox Twenty; *Yourself Or Someone Like You* . . . . (Lava)
Battle Of Who Could Care Less
Ben Folds Five; *Whatever And Ever Amen* . . . . (Caroline/550)
Be Still My Beating Heart
Sting; *...Nothing Like The Sun* . . . . (A&M)
Fields Of Gold-The Best Of Sting 1984-1994 . . . . (A&M)
Before The Blues
Colin Linden; *Raised By Wolves* . . . . (Compass)
Blue Monday
Orgy; *Candyass* . . . . (Elementree/Reprise)
Brand New Mister Me
Mel Tillis & The Statesiders; *The Ultimate Mel Tillis* . . . . (Bransounds)
Breathe
Faith Hill; *Breathe* . . . .(Warner Bros.)
But Anyway
Blues Traveler; *Blues Traveler* . . . . (A&M)
Live From The Fall . . . . (A&M)
Can't Believe
Faith Evans featuring Carl Thomas; *12'' Maxi Single* . . . . (Bad Boy/Arista)
Can't Fight This Feeling
REO Speedwagon; *REO Speedwagon-The Hits* . . . .(Epic)
T.J. Martell-Music For The Miracle-C . . . . (Epic Portrait Assoc.)
Wheels Are Turnin' . . . .(Epic)
Can't Help It
Jon B.; *Cool Relax* . . . . (Yab Yum/550)
Comfortably Numb
Pink Floyd; *Delicate Sound Of Thunder* . . . . (Columbia)
Knebworth-The Album-C . . . . (Polydor)
The Wall . . . . (Columbia)
Roger Waters; *The Wall-Live In Berlin* . . . . (Mercury)
Conviction Of The Heart
Kenny Loggins; *Leap Of Faith* . . . . (Columbia)
Outside: From The Redwoods . . . . (Columbia)
*Yesterday, Today, Tomorrow: The Greatest Hits Of Kenny
Loggins* . . . . (Columbia)
Country Comfort
Earl Scruggs & Elton John; *Earl Scruggs And Friends-C* . . . .(MCA)
Elton John; *Tumbleweed Connection* . . . . (Polydor)
Rod Stewart; *Best Of Rod Stewart-#2* . . . . (Mercury)
Gasoline Alley . . . . (Mercury)
Sing It Again, Rod . . . . (Mercury)
Cry
Crystal Gayle; *Best Of Crystal Gayle* . . . .(Warner Bros.)
Janie Fricke; *Celebration* . . . . (Columbia)
I'll Need To Hold Someone When I Cry . . . . (Columbia)
Johnnie Ray; *Best Of Johnnie Ray* . . . .(Exact)
Johnnie Ray-16 Most Requested Songs . . . . (Legacy)
Radio Classics Of The '50s-C . . . . (Columbia)
Lynn Anderson; *Lynn Anderson's Greatest Hits* . . . . (Columbia)
Ray Charles; *Ray Charles' Greatest Hits-#2* . . . . (Rhino)
Ray Charles-Anthology . . . . (Rhino)
Cuts Like A Knife
Bryan Adams; *Cuts Like A Knife* . . . . (A&M)
Live! Live! Live! . . . . (A&M)
MTV Unplugged-Bryan Adams . . . . (A&M)
So Far So Good . . . . (A&M)
Dancing On The Ceiling
Lionel Richie; *Dancing On The Ceiling* . . . . (Motown)
Didn't Cha Know
Erykah Badu; *Mama's Gun* . . . . (Motown)
Don't Fight The Feelings Of Love
Charley Pride; *Sweet Country* . . . . (RCA)

Don't Take It Personal (Just One Of Dem Days)
Monica; *Miss Thang* . . . .(Rowdy/Arista)
Don't You Care
Buckinghams; *Buckinghams' Greatest Hits* . . . . (Columbia)
Dream On
Depeche Mode; *Exciter* . . . . (Mute/Reprise)
Eclipse
Pink Floyd; *Dark Side Of The Moon* . . . . (Capitol)
Works . . . . (Capitol)
Emotion
Destiny's Child; *Survivor* . . . . (Columbia)
The Concert For New York City-C . . . . (Columbia)
Emotional
Carl Thomas; *Emotional* . . . . (Bad Boy/Arista)
Emotional Girl
Terri Clark; *Just The Same* . . . . (Mercury)
Emotions
Brenda Lee; *The Brenda Lee Story-Her Greatest Hits* . . . . (MCA)
Vintage Music-#13-C . . . . (MCA)
Emotions
Reno & Smiley; *Best Of Reno & Smiley* . . . . (Starday)
Emotions
Mariah Carey; *Emotions* . . . . (Columbia)
Fallin' In Love Never Felt So Good
Mark Chesnutt; *Confessing My Love* . . . . (MCA)
Falling For The First Time
Barenaked Ladies; *Maroon* . . . . (Reprise)
Feel Like A Number
Bob Seger & The Silver Bullet Band; *Nine Tonight* . . . . (Capitol)
Stranger In Town . . . . (Capitol)
Feel Like Makin' Love
Roberta Flack; *Atlantic Rhythm & Blues 1947-1974-#6 (1966-
1969)-C* . . . .(Atlantic)
Best Of Roberta Flack . . . .(Atlantic)
Feel Like Makin' Love . . . .(Atlantic)
Golden Age Of Black Music-1970-1975-C . . . .(Atlantic)
Golden Soul-C . . . .(Atlantic)
Feel Like Makin' Love
Bad Company; *10 From 6* . . . .(Atlantic)
Straight Shooter . . . . (Swan Song)
Feel Me Flow
Naughty By Nature; *Poverty's Paradise* . . . . (Tommy Boy)
Feel So Numb
Rob Zombie; *Sinister Urge* . . . . (Geffen)
Feelin' Good About Feelin' Bad
Patty Loveless; *When Fallen Angels Fly* . . . . (Epic)
Feelin' Love
Paula Cole; *This Fire* . . . . (Imago)
Feelin' Single, Seein' Double
Emmylou Harris; *Elite Hotel* . . . . (Reprise)
Feelings
Morris Albert; *Have A Nice Decade-The '70s Pop Culture Box-C* . . . . . . (Rhino)
Feels Like Heaven
Peter Cetera; *World Falling Down* . . . . (Warner Bros.)
Feels Like Home
LeAnn Rimes; *Sittin' On Top Of The World* . . . . (Curb)
Feels Like Home
Bonnie Raitt; *ST/Michael* . . . . (Revolution)
Chantal Kreviazuk; *Songs From Dawson's Creek* . . . . .(Sony Music Soundtrax)
Linda Ronstadt; *Feels Like Home* . . . . (Elektra)
Randy Newman; *Guilty: 30 Years Of Randy Newman* . . . . (Rhino)
Randy Newman's Faust . . . . (Reprise)
Feels Like Love
Vince Gill; *Let's Make Sure We Kiss Goodbye* . . . . (MCA)
Feels Like The First Time
Foreigner; *Classic Rock 1966-1988-C* . . . .(Atlantic)
Foreigner . . . .(Atlantic)
Records . . . .(Atlantic)
Feels So Good
Xscape; *Off The Hook* . . . . (So So Def/Columbia)
Feels So Good (Show Me Your Love)
Lina Santiago; *Best Of Dance Hits Supermix-#1 & 2-C* . . . . (Warlock)
Dance Mix USA-#5-C . . . . (Warlock)
Feels So Right
Alabama; *Alabama's Greatest Hits* . . . . (RCA)
Feels So Right . . . . (RCA)
Flashdance...What A Feeling
Irene Cara; *ST/Flashdance* . . . . (Casablanca)
Followin' A Feelin'
Sherrie Austin; *Followin' A Feelin'* . . . . (We/Madacy)
Funny Familiar Forgotten Feelings
Don Gibson; *Best Of Don Gibson-#1* . . . . (Curb)
Mandy Barnett; *I've Got A Right To Cry* . . . . (Sire)
Tom Jones; *Back To Back-Greatest Hits* . . . . (Rebound)
Country Side Of Tom Jones . . . . (London)
Tom Jones-London Collector-Greatest Hits . . . . (London)
Gettin' In The Way
Jill Scott; *Who Is Jill Scott? Words And Sounds-#1* . . . . (Hidden Beach/Epic)

Getting Sentimental Over You
Ella Fitzgerald; *Best Of Ella Fitzgerald* . . . . (Pablo)
Frank Sinatra; *I Remember Tommy* . . . . (Reprise)
Helen O'Connell; *Sentimental Journey: Capitol's Great Ladies Of Song-C* . . . . (Gold Rush)
Shirley Scott; *For Members Only/Great Scott* . . . . (MCA Special Prod.)
Tommy Dorsey & His Orchestra; *Best Of Tommy Dorsey* . . . . (Bluebird)
Best Of Tommy Dorsey & His Orchestra . . . . (Curb)

Got A Feelin'
Mamas & The Papas; *Best Of The Mamas & The Papas* . . . . (MCA)

Greed
Godsmack; *Awake* . . . . (Republic/Universal)

Gumboots
Paul Simon; *Graceland* . . . . (Warner Bros.)

Happy Girl
Beth Nielsen Chapman; *Sand And Water* . . . . (Reprise)
Martina McBride; *Evolution* . . . . (RCA)

Hearts Of Stone
Bruce Springsteen; *Tracks* . . . . (Columbia)
Southside Johnny And The Asbury Jukes; *Best Of Southside Johnny And The Asbury Jukes* . . . . (Legacy)
Cover Me (Bruce Springsteen Tribute)-C . . . . (Rhino)
Hearts Of Stone . . . . (Epic)

Hearts Of Stone
Fontane Sisters; *Hearts Of Stone-The Best Of The Fontane Sisters* . . . . (Varese Sarabande)

Heaven's What I Feel
Gloria Estefan; *Gloria!* . . . . (Epic)

High
Jimmie's Chicken Shack; *Pushing The Salmanilla Envelope* . . . . (Rocket)

Honey
Mariah Carey; *Butterfly* . . . . (Columbia)

Hooked On A Feeling
B.J. Thomas; *Best Of B.J. Thomas* . . . . (Hollywood/DNA-Rounder)
Vonda Shepard; *ST/Songs From "Ally McBeal" Featuring Vonda Shepard* . . . . (550/Epic)

How Forever Feels
Kenny Chesney; *Everywhere We Go* . . . . (BNA)
Kenny Chesney's Greatest Hits . . . . (BNA)

How Much I Feel
Ambrosia; *Ambrosia-Anthology* . . . . (Warner Bros.)
Life Beyond L.A. . . . . (Warner Bros.)
Mellow Rock Hits Of The '70s-Summer Breeze-C . . . . (Rhino)

How Your Love Makes Me Feel
Diamond Rio; *Diamond Rio's Greatest Hits* . . . . (Arista)

I Can Still Feel You
Collin Raye; *The Walls Came Down* . . . . (Epic)

I Can't Do That
Stephen Simmonds; *Spirit Tales* . . . . (Priority)

I Cry
Ja Rule; *Rule 3:36* . . . . (Murder Inc./Def Jam/IDJMG)

I Do
Lisa Loeb; *Firecracker* . . . . (Geffen)

I Do
Toya; *Totally Hits 2001-C* . . . . (Arista)
Toya . . . . (Arista)

I Feel Fine
Beatles; *Beatles 1* . . . . (Capitol)
Beatles '65 . . . . (Capitol)
Beatles-20 Greatest Hits . . . . (Capitol)
Past Masters-Volume One . . . . (Parlophone)
The Beatles/1962-1966 . . . . (Capitol)
Sweethearts Of The Rodeo; *One Time One Night* . . . . (Columbia)

I Feel Free
Belinda Carlisle; *Belinda Carlisle-Her Greatest Hits* . . . . (MCA)
Heaven On Earth . . . . (MCA)
Cream; *Eric Clapton-Crossroads-C* . . . . (Polydor)
Fresh Cream . . . . (Polydor)
Strange Brew-Very Best Of Cream . . . . (Polydor)
The Sopranos-Music From The HBO Original Series . . . . (Sony Music Soundtrax)

I Feel Pretty
Julie Andrews; *A Little Bit Of Broadway* . . . . (Columbia)
Little Richard; *The Songs Of West Side Story* . . . . (RCA Victor)
Original Cast; *ST/West Side Story* . . . . (Sony Broadway)

I Feel The Earth Move
Carole King; *Carole King's Greatest Hits* . . . . (Epic)
Tapestry . . . . (Epic)

I Got You (I Feel Good)
James Brown; *James Brown's 20 All Time Greatest Hits!* . . . . (Polydor)
Live At The Apollo . . . . (Polydor)
ST/Good Morning, Vietnam . . . . (A&M)
Very Best Of James Brown . . . . (Polydor)

I Lost It
Kenny Chesney; *Kenny Chesney's Greatest Hits* . . . . (BNA)

I Only Get This Way With You
Rick Trevino; *Learning As You Go* . . . . (Columbia)

I Second That Emotion
Smokey Robinson & The Miracles; *Smokey Robinson & The Miracles' Anthology* . . . . (Motown)
Smokey Robinson-The Ultimate Collection . . . . (Motown)
Tammy Wynette & Smokey Robinson; *Without Walls-C* . . . . (Epic)

I Think God Can Explain
Splender; *ST/Dawson's Creek-#2* . . . . (C2/Columbia)

I Understand (Just How You Feel)
Four Tunes; *45-#5132* . . . . (Jubilee)
Freddie And The Dreamers; *45-#72377* . . . . (Mercury)
G-Clefs; *45-#7500* . . . . (Terrace)
Ink Spots; *ST/Trees Lounge* . . . . (MCA)

I Wanna Fall In Love
Lila McCann; *Lila* . . . . (Asylum)

I Want To Hold Your Hand
Beatles; *Beatles 1* . . . . (Capitol)
Beatles-20 Greatest Hits . . . . (Capitol)
Meet The Beatles! . . . . (Capitol)
Past Masters-Volume One . . . . (Parlophone)
The Beatles/1962-1966 . . . . (Capitol)
Lakeside; *Galactic Grooves/Best Of Lakeside* . . . . (Right Stuff)
Your Wish Is My Command . . . . (Solar)

I Wish I Felt Nothing
Wallflowers; *Bringing Down The Horse* . . . . (Interscope)

I Wonder If You Feel The Way I Do
Asleep At The Wheel featuring Merle Haggard; *Tribute To The Music Of Bob Wills And The Texas Playboys-C* . . . . (Liberty)
Bob Wills & His Texas Playboys; *For The Last Time* . . . . (Capitol)

If You (Lovin' Me)
Silk; *Tonight* . . . . (Elektra)

If You Can't Feel It (It Ain't There)
Freddie Hart; *Best Of Freddie Hart* . . . . (CEMA Special Prod.)

I'm Feelin' You
Ginuwine; *ST/Men In Black* . . . . (Columbia)

I'm In The Mood For Love
McGuire Sisters; *Best Of The McGuire Sisters* . . . . (MCA)
Nat "King" Cole; *The Trio Recordings-#2* . . . . (Laserlight)
Ray Conniff; *Young At Heart* . . . . (Columbia)

I'm Not Feeling You
Yvette Michelle; *My Dream* . . . . (RCA)

I'm Not Supposed To Love You Anymore
Bryan White; *Between Now And Forever* . . . . (Asylum)

I'm Telling You Now
Keb' Mo'; *Slow Down* . . . . (550/Epic/Okeh)

In The Mood
Robert Plant; *Principle Of Moments* . . . . (Es Paranza)

Insensitive
Jann Arden; *Living Under June* . . . . (A&M)
Women For Women-#2-C . . . . (Mercury)

It Feels So Good
Sonique; *Hear My Cry* . . . . (Republic/Universal)
Now That's What I Call Music!-#4-C . . . . (Virgin)

It Matters To Me
Faith Hill; *It Matters To Me* . . . . (Warner Bros.)

It Must Be Love
Alan Jackson; *Under The Influence* . . . . (Arista)

It's How You Say It
Al Jarreau; *Tomorrow Today* . . . . (GRP/VMG)

I've Got A Feeling
Beatles; *Let It Be* . . . . (Capitol)
The Beatles-Anthology-#3 . . . . (Capitol)

I've Got This Feeling
Mavericks; *Trampoline* . . . . (MCA)

Leading With Your Heart
Barbra Streisand; *Higher Ground* . . . . (Columbia)

Like A Rolling Stone
Bob Dylan; *Biograph* . . . . (Columbia)
Bob Dylan At Budokan . . . . (Columbia)
Bob Dylan's Greatest Hits . . . . (Columbia)
Highway 61 Revisited . . . . (Columbia)
More American Graffiti-#4-C . . . . (MCA)
Self Portrait . . . . (Columbia)
Bob Dylan And The Band; *Before The Flood* . . . . (Columbia)
Jimi Hendrix; *ST/Jimi Plays Monterey* . . . . (Reprise)
Jimi Hendrix Experience; *Jimi Hendrix Experience* . . . . (Reprise)
Rolling Stones; *Stripped* . . . . (Virgin)

Love You Down
INOJ; *So So Def Bass All-Stars-#2-C* . . . . (So So Def/Columbia)
Total Dance Explosion-C . . . . (Columbia)

Man Ain't Supposed To Cry
Public Announcement; *Don't Hold Back* . . . . (RCA)

Man! I Feel Like A Woman
Shania Twain; *Come On Over* . . . . (Mercury)
VH-1 Divas Live-C . . . . (Epic)

Minnesota Medley
Los Lobos; *ST/Feeling Minnesota* . . . . (Atlantic)

Mood Indigo
Duke Ellington; *1954 Los Angeles Concert* . . . . (Crescendo)

    Black, Brown & Beige: 1944-1946 Band Recordings . . . . (Bluebird)
    Carnegie Hall Concert-January 23, 1943 . . . .(Prestige)
    Ellington Indigos . . . . (Columbia)
    Sophisticated Ellington . . . . (RCA)
  Ella Fitzgerald; *Ella A Nice* . . . .(Pablo)
    Ella Fitzgerald Sings-#2 . . . . (Verve)
  Four Freshmen; *Capitol Collectors Series-Four Freshman* . . . . (Capitol)
  Frank Sinatra; *In The Wee Small Hours* . . . . (Capitol)
  Jimmie Lunceford & His Orchestra; *Stomp It Off-#1-1934-1935* . . . . (GRP)
  Preservation Hall Jazz Band; *Best Of The Preservation Hall*
    Jazz Band . . . . (Columbia)
    New Orleans-#4 . . . . (Columbia)

More Than A Feeling
  Boston; *Boston* . . . .(Epic)

Much Too Young (To Feel This Damn Old)
  Garth Brooks; *Garth Brooks-Double Live* . . . . (Capitol)

My Melancholy Baby
  Barbra Streisand; *Third Album* . . . . (Columbia)
  Bing Crosby; *Hits Of 1939-C* . . . .(Living Era)
  Coleman Hawkins; *Genius Of Coleman Hawkins* . . . . (Verve)
  Dorothy Loudon; *Saloon* . . . .(DRG)
  Frank Sinatra; *Voice: The Columbia Years-1943-1952* . . . . (Columbia)
  Gene Austin; *78-#21015* . . . . (Victor)
  Jan Garber & His Orchestra; *Jan Garber & His Orchestra Play 22 Original*
    Big Band Favorites . . . . (Hindsight)
  Kate Smith; *Kate Smith-16 Most Requested Songs* . . . . (Columbia)
  Leon Redbone; *Double Time* . . . .(Warner Bros.)
  Marcels; *Best Of The Marcels* . . . . (Rhino)

N.I.B.
  Primus with Ozzy; *Nativity In Black II: Tribute To Black*
    Sabbath-C . . . . (Divine/Priority)

Narcolepsy
  Ben Folds Five; *The Unauthorized Biography Of Reinhold*
    Messner . . . . (550 Music)

Natural One
  Folk Implosion; *MTV Best Of The Buzz Bin-#2-C* . . . . (Mammoth)
  ST/Kids . . . . (London)

Needles And Pins
  Jackie DeShannon; *Very Best Of Jackie DeShannon* . . . .(EMI)
  Searchers; *History Of British Rock-#1-C* . . . . (Rhino)
    Searchers' Greatest Hits . . . . (Rhino)
  Tom Petty And The Heartbreakers; *Pack Up The Plantation-Live!* . . . . . .(MCA)

Never Felt This Way (interlude)
  Alicia Keys; *Songs In A Minor* . . . . (J)

Not That Different
  Collin Raye; *I Think About You* . . . .(Epic)

Nothing To Prove
  Caroline's Spine; *Attention Please* . . . . (Hollywood)

Obvious
  Christina Aguilera; *Christina Aguilera* . . . . (RCA)

One
  Creed; *My Own Prison* . . . . (Wind-up)

One Angry Dwarf And 200 Solemn Faces
  Ben Folds Five; *Whatever And Ever Amen* . . . . (Caroline/550)

One Emotion
  Clash; *Clash On Broadway* . . . . (Legacy)

One Emotion
  Clint Black; *One Emotion* . . . . (RCA)

One In A Million
  Aaliyah; *One In A Million* . . . . (BlackGround Enterp./Atlantic)

Only The Lonely (Know The Way I Feel)
  Roy Orbison; *For The Lonely: A Roy Orbison Anthology 1959-1965* . . . (Rhino)
    In Dreams-Greatest Hits . . . . (Orbison)
    Roy Orbison's All-Time Greatest Hits-#1 & 2 . . . . (Monument)

Operator (That's Not The Way It Feels)
  Jim Croce; *Photographs & Memories/His Greatest Hits* . . . .(Atlantic)
    Time In A Bottle/Jim Croce's Greatest Love Songs . . . .(Atlantic)
    You Don't Mess Around With Jim . . . . (Lifesong)

People That We Love, The
  Bush; *Golden State* . . . .(Atlantic)

Pretty
  Korn; *Follow The Leader* . . . .(Immortal/Epic)

Private Emotion
  Ricky Martin & Meja; *Ricky Martin* . . . . (Columbia)

Question Everything
  8Stops7; *In Moderation* . . . . (Reprise)

Ray Of Light
  Madonna; *GHV2* . . . .(Warner Bros.)
    Ray Of Light . . . . (Maverick)
    Totally Hits-#1-C . . . . (Arista)

Reunited
  Peaches & Herb; *Best Of Peaches & Herb* . . . . (Polydor)
    Chicken Soup For The Couples Soul-C . . . . (Rhino)
    Didn't It Blow Your Mind: Soul Hits Of The '70s-#20-C . . . . (Rhino)
    Only Love-1975-1979-C . . . . (JCI Assoc. Labels)

Revival
  Allman Brothers Band; *An Evening With The Allman Brothers Band-*
    First Set. . . . .(Epic)
    Beginnings . . . . (Polydor)

    Decade Of Hits-1969-1979 . . . . (Polydor)
    Dreams . . . . (Polydor)
    Idlewild South. . . . . (Polydor)

See Me, Feel Me
  Who; *ST/The Kids Are Alright.* . . . . (MCA)
    Tommy . . . . (MCA)
    Who's Last . . . . (MCA)

Selfless, Cold And Composed
  Ben Folds Five; *Whatever And Ever Amen* . . . .(Caroline/550)

Sensitivity
  Original Cast; *Once Upon A Mattress* . . . . (MCA)
  Ralph Tresvant; *New Edition Solo Hits* . . . . (MCA)
    Ralph Tresvant . . . . (MCA)

Sentimental
  Deborah Cox; *Deborah Cox* . . . . (Arista)

Sentimental Journey
  Dinah Shore; *Sentimental Journey: Capitol's Great Ladies Of*
    Song-C . . . . (Gold Rush)
  Doris Day; *Doris Day Sings 22 Great Songs-Original Big Band* . . . . (Hindsight)
  Hal McIntyre & His Orchestra; *Nipper's Greatest Hits Of The*
    '40s-#2-C. . . . . (RCA)
  Les Brown & His Orchestra; *Best Of The Big Bands-C* . . . . (Columbia)

She Said She Said
  Beatles; *Beatles-Box Set* . . . . (Capitol)
    Revolver . . . . (Capitol)

Shout
  Beatles; *The Beatles-Anthology-#1* . . . . (Capitol)
  Isley Brothers; *Nipper's Greatest Hits Of The '50s-#2-C* . . . . (RCA)
    Shout. . . . . (Collectables)
  ST/The Wanderers . . . .(Warner Bros.)
  Joey Dee & the Starliters; *Echoes Of A Rock Era-Later Years-C* . . . . (Roulette)
    Hey Let's Twist! Best Of Joey Dee & The Starliters . . . . (Rhino)
    Live At The Peppermint Lounge . . . . (Accord)
    Original Rock 'N' Roll Hits Of The '60s-C . . . . (Roulette)
    Sock Hoppin' Sixties-C . . . .(JCI Assoc. Labels)
  Otis Day & The Knights; *Shout.* . . . . (MCA)
    ST/Animal House . . . . (MCA)
  Tom Petty And The Heartbreakers; *Pack Up The Plantation-Live!* . . . . . (MCA)

Show Me The Meaning Of Being Lonely
  Backstreet Boys; *Millennium* . . . .(Jive)
    Now That's What I Call Music!-#5-C . . . .(Virgin)

Shower The People
  James Taylor; *In The Pocket* . . . . (Warner Bros.)
    James Taylor's Greatest Hits . . . . (Warner Bros.)

Slow Like Honey
  Fiona Apple; *Tidal* . . . .(Clean Slate/Work)

So Emotional
  Christina Aguilera; *Christina Aguilera* . . . . (RCA)

So Emotional
  Whitney Houston; *Whitney* . . . . (Arista)
    Whitney Houston's Greatest Hits . . . . (Arista)

Something About The Way You Look Tonight
  Elton John; *The Big Picture* . . . . (Rocket)

Sucked Out
  Superdrag; *Regretfully Yours* . . . . (Elektra)

Sure Feels Like Love
  Larry Gatlin & The Gatlin Brothers Band; *Larry Gatlin & The Gatlin*
    Brothers' Greatest Hits-#2 . . . . (Columbia)
    Larry Gatlin & The Gatlin Brothers-17 Greatest Hits . . . . (Columbia)

Sweet Emotion
  Aerosmith; *ST/Armageddon-The Album* . . . . (Columbia)

Take A Picture
  Filter; *Title Of Record* . . . . (Reprise)
    Totally Hits-#2-C . . . . (Elektra)

Talk Back Trembling Lips
  Ernest Ashworth; *Best Of Ernest Ashworth* . . . . (Curb)
  Johnny Tillotson; *Cruisin'-1964-C* . . . . (Increase)

Teenager In Love
  Dion And The Belmonts; *Classic Old & Gold-C* . . . . (Laurie)
    Collectables Presents The History Of Rock-#6-C. . . . . (Collectables)
    Dion And The Belmonts-Their Best . . . . (Laurie)
    Oldies But Goodies-#6-C . . . . (Original Sound)
    Party Time Fifties-C . . . . (JCI Assoc. Labels)

Tell Her
  Lonestar; *Lonely Grill* . . . . (BNA)

That's How You Know (When You're In Love)
  Lari White; *Best Of Lari White* . . . . (RCA)
    Wishes . . . . (RCA)

That's The Kind Of Mood I'm In
  Patty Loveless; *Strong Heart.* . . . .(Epic)

That's The Way I Feel
  Faron Young; *45-#4050* . . . . (Capitol)

There She Goes
  Sixpence None The Richer; *Sixpence None The Richer* . . . . . (Squint/Columbia)

This Can't Be Love
  Diana Krall; *Stepping Out* . . . .(Justin Time)
  Ella Fitzgerald; *Rodgers & Hart Songbook* . . . . (Verve)
  Natalie Cole; *Unforgettable With Love* . . . . (Elektra)
  Original Cast; *The Boys From Syracuse* . . . . (Angel)

Stephane Grappelli; *Compact Jazz-Stephane Grappelli* . . . . (Verve)
Various Artists; *Embraceable You-Broadway In Love* . . . . . . (Sony Broadway)
To Be Loved
Curtis Stigers; *Songs From Dawson's Creek* . . . . (Sony Music Soundtrax)
To Make You Feel My Love
Billy Joel; *Billy Joel's Greatest Hits-#3* . . . . (Columbia)
Songs From The Heart-C . . . . (Columbia)
Bob Dylan; *Time Out Of Mind* . . . . (Columbia)
Garth Brooks; *Garth Brooks-Double Live* . . . . (Capitol)
Limited Series-Box . . . . (Capitol)
ST/Hope Floats . . . . (Capitol)
Trisha Yearwood; *ST/Hope Floats* . . . . (Capitol)
To The Moon And Back
Savage Garden; *Savage Garden* . . . . (Columbia)
Tonight I Feel Like Texas
Barbara Lamb; *Tonight I Feel Like Texas* . . . . (Sugar Hill)
Torn
Natalie Imbruglia; *Left Of The Middle* . . . . (RCA)
Trainwreck Of Emotion
Lorrie Morgan; *Essential Lorrie Morgan* . . . . (RCA)
Leave The Light On . . . . (RCA)
To Get To You-Greatest Hits Collection . . . . (BNA)
Trainwreck Of Emotion
Del McCoury Band; *Steel Rails-Classic Railroad Songs-#1-C* . . . . . (Rounder)
Unforgiven II
Metallica; *Reload* . . . . (Elektra)
Unglued
Stone Temple Pilots; *Purple* . . . . (Atlantic)
Untitled (How Does It Feel)
D'Angelo; *Voodoo* . . . . (Cheeba Sound/Virgin)
Way He Makes Me Feel
Barbra Streisand; *Collection-Greatest Hits...And More* . . . . (Columbia)
ST/Yentl . . . . (Columbia)
Way You Love Me, The
Faith Hill; *Breathe* . . . . (Warner Bros.)
Totally Hits-#3-C . . . . (Atlantic)
What It Feels Like For A Girl
Madonna; *GHV2* . . . . (Warner Bros.)
Music . . . . (Maverick)
What's Love Got To Do With It
Tina Turner; *Live In Europe* . . . . (Capitol)
Private Dancer . . . . (Capitol)
Simply The Best . . . . (Capitol)
When I Dream At Night
Marc Anthony; *Marc Anthony* . . . . (Columbia)
When I Fall In Love
Celine Dion; *The Colour Of My Love* . . . . (550 Music)
Doris Day; *Doris Day-16 Most Requested Songs-Encore!* . . . . . . (Columbia)
Where Were You (When The World Stopped Turning)
Alan Jackson; *Alan Jackson-Drive* . . . . (Arista)
Where You Get Love
Matthew Sweet; *Blue Sky On Mars* . . . . (Freeworld/Capitol)
Without Expression
John Mellencamp; *Best That I Could Do-1978-1988* . . . . (Mercury)
You Can Feel Bad
Patty Loveless; *Patty Loveless-Classics* . . . . (Epic)
Super Hits Of 1996-C . . . . (Epic)
The Trouble With The Truth . . . . (Epic)
You Don't Know How It Feels
Tom Petty; *Wildflowers* . . . . (Warner Bros.)
You Make Loving Fun
Fleetwood Mac; *25 Years-The Chain* . . . . (Warner Bros.)
Fleetwood Mac's Greatest Hits . . . . (Warner Bros.)
Rumours . . . . (Warner Bros.)
Jewel; *Legacy-A Tribute To Fleetwood Mac's Rumours-C* . . . . (Lava)
You Make Me Feel (Mighty Real)
Sylvester; *ST/Young Soul Rebels* . . . . (Volcano Entertainment)
You Make Me Feel Bad
Wood; *Songs From Stamford Hill* . . . . (Columbia)
You Make Me Feel Brand New
Roberta Flack; *Set The Night To Music* . . . . (Atlantic)
You Make Me Feel Like Dancing
Leo Sayer; *Billboard Top Rock 'N' Roll Hits-1977-C* . . . . . . (Rhino)
Endless Flight . . . . (Chrysalis)
Mega Hits Dance Classics-#3-C . . . . (Priority)
You Make Me Feel So Good
Astors; *Astors Meet The Newcomers* . . . . (Stax)
You Make Me Feel So Young
Frank Sinatra; *Best Of The Capitol Years* . . . . (Capitol)
You Make My Dreams
Daryl Hall & John Oates; *Rock 'N Soul, Part 1* . . . . (RCA)
Voices . . . . (RCA)
You Never Give Me Your Money
Beatles; *Abbey Road* . . . . (Parlophone)
Beatles-Box Set . . . . (Capitol)
George Benson; *The Best* . . . . (Rebound)
You Sang To Me
Marc Anthony; *Marc Anthony* . . . . (Columbia)

Young Love
Sonny James; *Golden Jukebox Favorites* . . . . (Capitol)
Opry Legends-Sonny James . . . . (Capitol)
Stars Of The Grand Ole Opry-1926-1974-C . . . . (RCA)
Traditions In Country Music-C . . . . (Capitol)
Tab Hunter; *Fonzie's Make-Out Music-C* . . . . (Nick At Nite)
Teen Idols-C . . . . (Universal)
You're An Ocean
Fastball; *Harsh Light Of Day* . . . . (Hollywood)
You've Lost That Lovin' Feelin'
Daryl Hall & John Oates; *Voices* . . . . (RCA)
Righteous Brothers; *Best Of The Righteous Brothers* . . . . (Curb)
Billboard Top Rock 'N' Roll Hits-1965-C . . . . (Rhino)
Cruisin'-1965-C . . . . (Increase)
Unchained Melody-Very Best Of The Righteous Brothers . . . . (Polydor)

FEMINISM, Women's Independence

See Also: **FAMILY: SISTERS, GENDER CONFLICT, GENDER STEREOTYPES, PROTEST, POLITICS (various), WOMEN: GENERAL, WORK**

80's Ladies
K.T. Oslin; *80's Ladies* . . . . (RCA)
K.T. Oslin's Greatest Hits: Songs From An Aging Sex Bomb . . . . . . (RCA)
Nipper's Greatest Hits Of The '80s-C . . . . (RCA)
9 To 5
Dolly Parton; *9 To 5 And Odd Jobs* . . . . (RCA)
Best There Is . . . . (RCA)
Dolly Parton's Greatest Hits . . . . (RCA)
I Am Woman-C . . . . (Nick At Nite)
Nipper's Greatest Hits Of The '80s-C . . . . (RCA)
Awful
Hole; *Celebrity Skin* . . . . (David Geffen Co.)
Be Your Own Girl
Wallflowers; *The Wallflowers* . . . . (Virgin)
Blonde Ambition
Billy Burnette; *Soldier Of Love* . . . . (Curb)
Bread And Roses
Ani DiFranco & Utah Phillips; *Fellow Workers* . . . . (Righteous Babe)
Judy Collins; *So Early In The Spring, The First 15 Years* . . . . . . (Elektra)
Company Time
Linda Davis; *Shoot For The Moon* . . . . (Arista)
Girls Just Want To Have Fun
Cyndi Lauper; *She's So Unusual* . . . . (Portrait)
Guys Do It All The Time
Mindy McCready; *Ten Thousand Angels* . . . . (BNA)
Gym II
Meg Christian; *Turning It Over* . . . . (Olivia)
Harry's House Centerpiece
Joni Mitchell; *Hissing Of Summer Lawns* . . . . (Asylum)
He Thinks He'll Keep Her
Mary Chapin Carpenter; *Come On Come On* . . . . (Columbia)
I Am Woman
Helen Reddy; *Helen Reddy's Greatest Hits* . . . . (Capitol)
I Am Woman . . . . (Capitol)
I Am Woman-C . . . . (Nick At Nite)
I Don't Know How To Love Him . . . . (Capitol)
I Think About You
Collin Raye; *Best Of Collin Raye-Direct Hits* . . . . (Epic)
I Think About You . . . . (Epic)
I Will Survive
Gloria Gaynor; *Billboard Top Hits-1979-C* . . . . (Rhino)
I Am Woman-C . . . . (Nick At Nite)
Love Tracks . . . . (Polydor)
The Disco Years-#2-On The Beat-1978-1982-C . . . . (Rhino)
I Will...But
SHeDAISY; *The Whole Shebang* . . . . (Lyric Street)
If Women Ruled The World
Joan Armatrading; *Square The Circle* . . . . (A&M)
Independence Day
Martina McBride; *The Way That I Am* . . . . (RCA)
Independent Women Pt.1
Destiny's Child; *Now That's What I Call Music!-#6-C* . . . . (Virgin)
ST/Charlie's Angels . . . . (Columbia)
Is There Life Out There
Reba McEntire; *For My Broken Heart* . . . . (MCA)
Reba McEntire's Greatest Hits Volume Two . . . . (MCA)
Just A Girl
No Doubt; *Tragic Kingdom* . . . . (Trauma)
Lady Is A Tramp
Ella Fitzgerald; *Rodgers & Hart Songbook* . . . . (Verve)
Frank Sinatra; *Sinatra Reprise-The Very Good Years* . . . . (Reprise)
The Capitol Years . . . . (Capitol)
Frank Sinatra & Luther Vandross; *Frank Sinatra-Duets-C* . . . . . . (Capitol)
Little Bird
Sherrie Austin; *Love In The Real World* . . . . (Arista)

Little Plastic Castle
Ani DiFranco; *Little Plastic Castle* . . . . (Righteous Babe)
Man Smart, Woman Smarter
Harry Belafonte; *Harry Belafonte-Pure Gold* . . . . (RCA)
Robert Palmer; *Some People Can Do What They Like* . . . . (Island)
Rosanne Cash; *I Am Woman-C* . . . . (Nick At Nite)
   Right Or Wrong . . . . (Columbia)
Man! I Feel Like A Woman
Shania Twain; *Come On Over* . . . . (Mercury)
   VH-1 Divas Live-C . . . . (Epic)
Me & A Gun
Tori Amos; *Little Earthquakes* . . . . (Atlantic)
Modern Girl
Sheena Easton; *Best Of Sheena Easton* . . . . (EMI)
   Sheena Easton . . . . (EMI)
   Sheena Easton's Greatest Hits . . . . (EMI Special Markets)
   The World Of Sheena Easton: The Singles Collection-C . . . . (EMI)
Most Girls
Pink; *Can't Take Me Home* . . . . (LaFace)
   Totally Hits-#3-C . . . . (Atlantic)
My Mom's A Feminist
Kristin Lems; *We Will Never Give Up* . . . . (Carolsdatter Prod.)
No Man's Woman
Sinead O'Connor; *Faith & Courage* . . . . (Atlantic)
P.M.S. Blues
Dolly Parton; *Heart Songs* . . . . (Columbia)
Pill, The
Loretta Lynn; *Loretta Lynn-20 Greatest Hits* . . . . (MCA)
   The Country Music Hall Of Fame-Loretta Lynn . . . . (MCA)
Respect
Aretha Franklin; *Aretha Franklin-30 Greatest Hits* . . . . (Rhino)
   Best Of Aretha Franklin . . . . (Atlantic)
   I Am Woman-C . . . . (Nick At Nite)
   I Never Loved A Man The Way I Love You . . . . (Atlantic)
   Live At Fillmore West . . . . (Atlantic)
   Soul Years-C . . . . (Atlantic)
   ST/Forrest Gump . . . . (Epic/Sony Music Soundtrax)
Otis Redding; *History Of Otis Redding* . . . . (Atco)
   Live In Europe . . . . (Atco)
   Otis Blue-Sings Soul . . . . (Atco)
   The Otis Redding Story . . . . (Atlantic)
Reba McEntire; *Reba* . . . . (MCA)
Rose Is Still A Rose
Aretha Franklin; *A Rose Is Still A Rose* . . . . (Arista)
She's Gonna Make It
Garth Brooks; *Sevens* . . . . (Capitol)
Sisters Are Doin' It For Themselves
Ann Wilson/Nancy Wilson/Lisa Simpson; *Simpsons-The Yellow*
   Album . . . . (Geffen)
Eurythmics & Aretha Franklin; *Be Yourself Tonight* . . . . (RCA)
   Chicken Soup For The Soul: I'll Be There For You-Songs Of Friendship,
   Brotherhood And Sisterhood-C . . . . (Rhino)
   Eurythmics' Greatest Hits . . . . (Arista)
   Who's Zoomin' Who? . . . . (Arista)
Theme From "Alice"
Original Soundtrack; *Television's Greatest Hits-#6-Remote Control-C* . . (TVT)
Theme From "Cagney & Lacey"
Original Soundtrack; *CBS: The First 50 Years* . . . . (TVT)
   Television's Greatest Hits-#6-Remote Control-C . . . . (TVT)
Theme From "Maude"
Original Soundtrack; *Television's Greatest Hits-#3-1970s & 1980s-C* . . . (TVT)
Theme From "Murphy Brown"
Original Soundtrack; *CBS: The First 50 Years* . . . . (TVT)
Theme From "That Girl"
Original Soundtrack; *Television's Greatest Hits-#2-C* . . . . (TVT)
Theme From "The Mary Tyler Moore Show"
Original Soundtrack-Sonny Curtis; *CBS: The First 50 Years* . . . . (TVT)
   Television's Greatest Hits-#2-C . . . . (TVT)
Think
Aretha Franklin; *Aretha Franklin's Greatest Hits* . . . . (Atlantic)
   Aretha's Gold . . . . (Atlantic)
   Best Of Aretha Franklin . . . . (Atlantic)
   ST/The Blues Brothers . . . . (Atlantic)
Video
India.Arie; *Acoustic Soul* . . . . (Motown)
What It Feels Like For A Girl
Madonna; *GHV2* . . . . (Warner Bros.)
   Music . . . . (Maverick)
What Part Of No
Lorrie Morgan; *Lorrie Morgan's Greatest Hits* . . . . (BNA)
   Watch Me . . . . (BNA)
Woman Is The Nigger Of The World
John Lennon; *Live In New York City* . . . . (Capitol)
John Lennon/Plastic Ono Band; *Lennon* . . . . (Capitol)
   Shaved Fish . . . . (Capitol)
   Some Time In New York City . . . . (Capitol)
Woman Of Heart & Mind
Joni Mitchell; *For The Roses* . . . . (Asylum)
Joni Mitchell with Tom Scott & The L.A. Express; *Miles Of Aisles* . . . . (Asylum)

Woman Of The Year
Original Cast; *Woman Of The Year* . . . . (Bay Cities)
Woman Power
Yoko Ono; *Walking On Thin Ice Compilation* . . . . (Rykodisc)
Woman To Woman
Tammy Wynette; *Tammy Wynette-Anniversary-20 Years Of Hits* . . . . . . (Epic)
   Tammy Wynette's Greatest Hits-#3 . . . . (Epic)
   Tears Of Fire-25th Anniversary Collection . . . . (Epic)
Wynonna; *Tammy Wynette...Remembered-C* . . . . (Asylum)
Woman Walk The Line
Emmylou Harris; *Ballad Of Sally Rose* . . . . (Warner Bros.)
Highway 101; *Featuring Paulette Carlson* . . . . (Warner Bros.)
Trisha Yearwood; *Hearts In Armor* . . . . (MCA)
Woman's Got A Right To Change Her Mind
Rex Stewart & The Ellingtonians; *Rex Stewart & The*
   Ellingtonians . . . . (Riverside)
Woman's Point Of View
Shirley Murdock; *Woman's Point Of View* . . . . (Elektra)
Woman's Prerogative
Pearl Bailey; *Pearl Bailey-16 Most Requested Songs* . . . . (Legacy)
Woman's Smarter
Jolly Boys; *Sunshine 'N' Water* . . . . (Rykodisc)
Women Walk More Determined
Kristin Lems; *Oh Mama!* . . . . (Carolsdatter Prod.)
Women Will Rule The World
Ry Cooder; *Get Rhythm* . . . . (Warner Bros.)
Women's Love Rights
Laura Lee; *Laura Lee's Greatest Hits* . . . . (HDH)
XXX's And OOO's
Trisha Yearwood; *Thinkin' About You* . . . . (MCA)
You Don't Own Me
Joan Jett; *Bad Reputation* . . . . (Blackheart)
Lesley Gore; *Billboard Top Pop Hits-1964-C* . . . . (Rhino)

FIGHT, Argue, Compete, Disagree, Violence
See Also: ANGER, CRIME, DEATH, DOMESTIC ABUSE, GUNS, HATE, KILL, POLICE, PROTEST, REBELS, REVENGE, WAR

(Everything I Do) I Do It For You
Bryan Adams; *ST/Robin Hood: Prince Of Thieves* . . . . (Morgan Creek)
   Waking Up The Neighbours . . . . (A&M)
All Around The World
Oasis; *Be Here Now* . . . . (Epic)
Angel's Son
Strait Up featuring Lajon of Sevendust; *Strait Up-C* . . . . (Immortal/Virgin)
Attitude Adjustment
Hank Williams, Jr.; *Hank Williams, Jr.'s Greatest Hits-#2* . . . . . . (WB/Curb)
   Major Moves . . . . (WB/Curb)
Avenging Annie
Andy Pratt; *Andy Pratt* . . . . (Columbia)
Roger Daltrey; *Best Bits* . . . . (MCA)
   One Of The Boys . . . . (MCA)
Back In Baby's Arms
Patsy Cline; *Patsy Cline's 12 Greatest Hits* . . . . (MCA)
   The Patsy Cline Story . . . . (MCA)
Back Stabbers
O'Jays; *Billboard Top Rock 'N' Roll Hits-1972-C* . . . . (Rhino)
   Live In London . . . . (Philadelphia Int'l)
   O'Jays-Collector's Item . . . . (Philadelphia Int'l)
Bad, Bad Leroy Brown
Jim Croce; *Billboard Top Rock 'N' Roll Hits-1973-C* . . . . (Rhino)
   Down The Highway . . . . (Atlantic)
   Life & Times . . . . (Lifesong)
   Photographs & Memories/His Greatest Hits . . . . (Atlantic)
Ballad Of TV Violence
Cheap Trick; *Cheap Trick* . . . . (Epic)
Bangkok Cockfight
Martin Denny; *Exotica-Best Of Martin Denny* . . . . (Rhino)
Beat It
Michael Jackson; *Thriller* . . . . (Epic)
Beat On The Brat
Ramones; *All The Stuff & More-#1* . . . . (Sire)
   Mania . . . . (Sire)
   Ramones . . . . (Sire)
Black-Eyed Blues
Joe Cocker; *Joe Cocker* . . . . (A&M)
   Joe Cocker's Greatest Hits . . . . (A&M)
Black-Eyed Blues
Esther Phillips; *Best Of Esther Phillips* . . . . (CBS Associated)
Bodies
Drowning Pool; *Sinner* . . . . (Wind-up)
Born Fighter
Nick Lowe; *Basher: Best Of* . . . . (Columbia)
   Labour Of Lust . . . . (Columbia)
Born In The U.S.A.
Bruce Springsteen; *Born In The U.S.A.* . . . . (Columbia)

Bruce Springsteen's Greatest Hits . . . . (Columbia)
Tracks . . . . (Columbia)
Bruce Springsteen & The E Street Band; *Bruce Springsteen & The E Street Band Live/1975-85* . . . . (Legacy)

Boxer, The
Simon & Garfunkel; *Bridge Over Troubled Water* . . . . (Columbia)
Collected Works . . . . (Columbia)
Simon & Garfunkel's Greatest Hits . . . . (Columbia)
The Concert In Central Park . . . . (Warner Bros.)

Boy Is Mine
Brandy & Monica; *Never Say Never* . . . . (Atlantic)
Monica; *The Boy Is Mine* . . . . (Arista)

Boy Named Sue
Johnny Cash; *Columbia Country Classics-#3-Americana-C* . . . . . . (Columbia)
Johnny Cash's Biggest Hits . . . . (Columbia)
Johnny Cash's Greatest Hits-#2 . . . . (Columbia)
The Man In Black-His Greatest Hits . . . . (Legacy)

Boyz-N-The-Hood
Dynamite Hack; *Superfast* . . . . (Farm Club/Universal)

Break Stuff
Limp Bizkit; *Significant Other* . . . . (Flip/Interscope)

Buddy Holly
Weezer; *Weezer* . . . . (David Geffen Co.)

Can't Fight The Moonlight
LeAnn Rimes; *ST/Coyote Ugly* . . . . (London Sire/Curb)

Can't Fight This Feeling
REO Speedwagon; *REO Speedwagon-The Hits* . . . . (Epic)
T.J. Martell-Music For The Miracle-C . . . . (Epic Portrait Assoc.)
Wheels Are Turnin' . . . . (Epic)

Careful With That Mic...
Clutch; *Pure Rock Fury* . . . . (Atlantic)

Casual Affair
Tonic; *Lemon Parade* . . . . (Polydor)

Controlled By Hatred
Suicidal Tendencies; *Controlled By Hatred/Feel Like Shit...Deja Vu* . . . . . (Epic)

Coward Of The County
Kenny Rogers; *Kenny* . . . . (Liberty)
Kenny Rogers' Greatest Hits . . . . (EMI)
Kenny Rogers-Twenty Greatest Hits . . . . (EMI)

Cruel To Be Kind
Nick Lowe; *Basher: Best Of* . . . . (Columbia)
Labour Of Lust . . . . (Columbia)

Cruising For Bruising
Basia; *London Warsaw New York* . . . . (Epic)

Crush 'Em
Megadeth; *Risk* . . . . (Trauma)
ST/Universal Soldier II: The Return . . . . (Arista)

Don't Fight It
Flying Burrito Brothers; *Last Of The Red Hot Burritos* . . . . (A&M)
Kenny Loggins & Steve Perry; *High Adventure* . . . . (Columbia)
Wilson Pickett; *Best Of Wilson Pickett* . . . . (Atlantic)
Wilson Pickett's Greatest Hits . . . . (Atlantic)

El Paso
Grateful Dead; *Steal Your Face* . . . . (Grateful Dead)
Marty Robbins; *Billboard Top Country Hits-1960-C* . . . . (Rhino)
Gunfighter Ballads & Trail Songs . . . . (Legacy)
Marty Robbins' Biggest Hits . . . . (Columbia)
Radio Classics Of The '50s-C . . . . (Columbia)
Texas Super Hits-C . . . . (Columbia)

Electric Avenue
Eddy Grant; *Killer On The Rampage* . . . . (Portrait)

Every Other Time
LFO; *Life Is Good* . . . . (J)

Eye Of The Tiger
Survivor; *Eye Of The Tiger* . . . . (Scotti Bros.)
Frankenstein & Other Rock Monsters-C . . . . . . (CBS Associated)
Rocky Story-C . . . . (Scotti Bros.)
ST/Rocky III . . . . (EMI)

Face To Face
Garth Brooks; *The Chase* . . . . (Liberty)

Fight Apartheid
Peter Tosh; *No Nuclear War* . . . . (EMI)

Fight Dirty
Charlie; *Fight Dirty* . . . . (Arista)

Fight Fire With Fire
Kansas; *Best Of Kansas* . . . . (CBS Associated)
Drastic Measures . . . . (Kirshner)
Metallica; *Ride The Lightning* . . . . (Elektra)

Fight For Your Right (To Party)
Beastie Boys; *Def Jam Classics-#1-C* . . . . (Def Jam)
Heart Of Soul-C . . . . (Columbia)
Licensed To Ill . . . . (Def Jam)

Fight From The Inside
Queen; *News Of The World* . . . . (Hollywood)

Fight On
Peter Tosh; *Mystic Man* . . . . (Rolling Stones)

Fight On Christmas Fight On
John Fahey; *Essential John Fahey* . . . . (Vanguard)

John Fahey . . . . (Vanguard)

Fight Or Fall
Thin Lizzy; *Jailbreak* . . . . (Mercury)

Fight The Good Fight
Triumph; *Allied Forces* . . . . (RCA)
Stages . . . . (MCA)
Triumph-Classics . . . . (MCA)

Fight The Power
Isley Brothers; *Forever Gold* . . . . (T-Neck/Columbia)
Heat Is On . . . . (T-Neck/Columbia)
Isley Brothers' Greatest Hits . . . . (T-Neck/Columbia)
The Isley Brothers Story-#2-The T-Neck Years-1969-1985. . . . . (Rhino)

Fight The Power
Public Enemy; *Def Jam Classics-#2-C* . . . . (Def Jam)
Fear Of A Black Planet . . . . (Def Jam)
ST/Do The Right Thing . . . . (Motown)

Fight The Team Across The Field
Ohio State University Marching Band; *Across The Field* . . . . . . (Fidelity Sound)

Fightin' Side Of Me
Merle Haggard; *All American* . . . . (Capitol)
Best Of Merle Haggard . . . . (Capitol)
Capitol Collectors Series-Merle Haggard . . . . (Capitol)
The Fightin' Side Of Me . . . . (Capitol)
Merle Haggard & The Strangers; *Songs I'll Always Sing* . . . . (Capitol)

Fighting For Strangers
Steeleye Span; *Rocket Cottage; Story* . . . . (Chrysalis)

Fist City
Loretta Lynn; *Loretta Lynn-20 Greatest Hits* . . . . (MCA)
Loretta Lynn-Greatest Hits Live . . . . (K-Tel)
Loretta Lynn's Greatest Hits-#2 . . . . (MCA)
The Country Music Hall Of Fame-Loretta Lynn . . . . (MCA)

Flying Colours
Jethro Tull; *The Broadsword And The Beast* . . . . (Chrysalis)

Freak On A Leash
Korn; *Follow The Leader* . . . . (Immortal/Epic)

Freedom
Paul McCartney; *Driving Rain* . . . . (Columbia)
The Concert For New York City-C . . . . (Columbia)

Gimme Three Steps
Lynyrd Skynyrd; *Gold & Platinum* . . . . (MCA)
One More From The Road . . . . (MCA)
Pronounced Leh-nerd Skin-nerd . . . . (MCA)

Hey Man, Nice Shot
Filter; *Short Bus* . . . . (Reprise)
ST/Cable Guy . . . . (Work)

Hit The Road Jack
Ray Charles; *Ray Charles' Greatest Hits* . . . . (Rhino)
Ray Charles-Anthology . . . . (Rhino)
Ray Charles-His Greatest Hits-#2. . . . . (Dunhill Compact Classics)

Holla Holla
Ja Rule; *Venni Vetti Vecci* . . . . (Murder Inc./Def Jam/IDJMG)

How Come, How Long
Babyface & Stevie Wonder; *The Day* . . . . (Epic)

I Dare You
Black Rob; *Life Story* . . . . (Bad Boy/Arista)

I Fought The Law
Bobby Fuller Four; *Best Of The Bobby Fuller Four* . . . . (Rhino)
Heart & Soul Of Rock 'N' Roll-#1-C. . . . . (Rhino)
Jailhouse Rock (Hits From The Big House)-C . . . . (Sony Music Special Prod.)
Oldies But Goodies-#9-C . . . . (Original Sound)
Super Oldies Of The '60s-#7-C . . . . (Audio Fidelity)
Clash; *The Clash* . . . . (Epic)
The Story Of The Clash, Volume 1 . . . . (Epic)

I Made A Fist
Original Broadway Cast; *The Most Happy Fella* . . . . (Sony Music Classical)

I Saw Red
Warrant; *Cherry Pie* . . . . (Columbia)

I Wonder If Heaven Got A Ghetto
2Pac; *R U Still Down (Remember Me)* . . . . (Amaru/Jive)

If You Don't Know Me By Now
Harold Melvin And The Blue Notes; *Harold Melvin And The Blue Notes-Collector's Item* . . . . (Philadelphia Int'l)
Philly Ballads-#1-C. . . . . (Philadelphia Int'l)
Simply Red; *New Flame* . . . . (Elektra)
Simply Red's Greatest Hits . . . . (East West)

Incident On 57th Street
Bruce Springsteen; *The Wild, The Innocent & The E Street Shuffle* . . . (Columbia)

Independence Day
Martina McBride; *The Way That I Am* . . . . (RCA)

Inner London Violence
Bad Manners; *ST/Dance Craze* . . . . (Chrysalis)

It Matters To Me
Faith Hill; *It Matters To Me* . . . . (Warner Bros.)

It's All About You (Not About Me)
Tracie Spencer; *Tracie* . . . . (Capitol)

Jerry Springer
"Weird Al" Yankovic; *Running With Scissors* . . . . (Volcano Entertainment)

Jukebox Argument
Mickey Gilley; *ST/Urban Cowboy 2* . . . . (Epic)

K.S.U. Fight Song
Kent State University Marching Band; *Kent State University
Marching Band* . . . .(Fidelity Sound)
Keep On Fighting
Frankie & The Knockouts; *Below The Belt* . . . . (Millennium)
Kick A Little
Little Texas; *Kick A Little* . . . .(Warner Bros.)
King Of New Orleans
Better Than Ezra; *Friction, Baby* . . . . (Swell/Elektra)
Land Of Nightmares
Rosanne Cash; *Interiors* . . . . (Columbia)
Little Bit Me, A Little Bit You
Monkees; *Monkees' Greatest Hits* . . . . (Rhino)
Little Black Backpack
Stroke9; *Nasty Little Thoughts* . . . . (Cherry/Universal)
Little Fighter
White Lion; *Big Game* . . . . (Atlantic)
Little More Love
Vince Gill; *High Lonesome Sound* . . . .(MCA)
Living Years, The
Mike & The Mechanics; *Living Years* . . . . (Atlantic)
Love Without End, Amen
George Strait; *Livin' It Up* . . . .(MCA)
Ten Strait Hits . . . .(MCA)
Make Em Say Uhh #2
Master P; *MP Da Last Don* . . . . (No Limit/Priority)
Me & A Gun
Tori Amos; *Little Earthquakes* . . . .(Atlantic)
Mean Disposition
Rolling Stones; *Voodoo Lounge* . . . . (Virgin)
Meanest Jukebox In Town
Johnny Paycheck; *Johnny Paycheck Sings Jukebox Charlie And Other Songs
That Make The Jukebox Play* . . . .(Little Darlin')
Mending Fences
Restless Heart; *Big Iron Horses* . . . . (RCA)
Midnight Rambler
Rolling Stones; *Get Yer Ya-Ya's Out!* . . . . (Abkco)
Hot Rocks 1964-1971 . . . . (Abkco)
Let It Bleed . . . . (Abkco)
Missouri Squabble
Alex Jackson Plantation; *Territory Bands-#2-1927-1931-C* . . . . (Historical)
Mr. Shorty
Marty Robbins; *The Drifter* . . . . (Koch International)
My Way
Limp Bizkit; *Chocolate Starfish & The Hotdog Flavored
Water* . . . . (Flip/Interscope)
Nevada Fighter
Michael Nesmith; *Older Stuff* . . . .(Rhino)
Nigga Ya Love To Hate
Ice Cube; *AmeriKKKa's Most Wanted* . . . . (Priority)
Night I Called The Old Man Out
Garth Brooks; *In Pieces* . . . . (Liberty)
No Son Of Mine
Genesis; *We Can't Dance* . . . .(Atlantic)
Not On Your Love
Jeff Carson; *From Nashville With Love-C* . . . . (Curb)
Jeff Carson . . . . (Curb)
Nothing To Prove
Caroline's Spine; *Attention Please* . . . . (Hollywood)
November Rain
Guns N' Roses; *Use Your Illusion I* . . . .(Geffen)
Oh How The Years Go By
Vanessa Williams; *NBA At 50-A Musical Celebration-C* . . . . (Mercury)
One Of These Days--Pow
Jackie Gleason; *Dr. Demento Presents The Greatest Novelty Records-#2-
1950s-C* . . . . (Rhino)
One Week
Barenaked Ladies; *Stunt* . . . . (Reprise)
Totally Hits-#1-C . . . . (Arista)
Only Wanna Be With You
Hootie & The Blowfish; *Cracked Rear View* . . . .(Atlantic)
O'Reilly At The Bar
Dan Hicks & His Hot Licks; *Striking It Rich!* . . . .(MCA)
P.M.S. Blues
Dolly Parton; *Heart Songs* . . . . (Columbia)
Push Comes To Shove
Jackyl; *Push Comes To Shove* . . . . (Geffen)
Rage In The Cage
J. Geils Band; *Freeze-Frame* . . . .(EMI)
Red Roses (Won't Work Now)
Reba McEntire; *Have I Got A Deal For You* . . . .(MCA)
Red Roses For A Blue Lady
Al Martino; *Best Of Al Martino* . . . . (Capitol)
Capitol Collectors Series-Al Martino . . . . (Capitol)
Andy Williams; *Andy Williams-16 Most Requested Songs* . . . . (Legacy)
Mom & Dads; *Best Of The Mom & Dads* . . . .(Crescendo)
Roger Whittaker; *All-Time Heart-Touching Favorites* . . . . (Capitol)
Roger Whittaker-Classics Collection-#1 . . . . (Capitol)

Vaughn Monroe; *Best Of Vaughn Monroe* . . . . (RCA)
Rip Her To Shreds
Blondie; *Best Of Blondie* . . . . (Chrysalis)
Blondie . . . . (Chrysalis)
Rockaway The Days
Bruce Springsteen; *Tracks* . . . . (Columbia)
Rosie Strikes Back
Eliza Gilkyson; *Texas-A Musical Celebration-150 Years* . . . .(Tomato)
Rosanne Cash; *King's Record Shop* . . . . (Columbia)
Saturday Night's Alright For Fighting
Elton John; *Elton John's Greatest Hits* . . . .(Polydor)
Goodbye Yellow Brick Road . . . .(Polydor)
Knebworth-The Album-C . . . .(Polydor)
Rock Classics-C . . . . (K-Tel)
Who; *Two Rooms-Celebrating The Songs Of Elton John & Bernie
Taupin-C* . . . .(Polydor)
Shakin' The Blues
Screamin' Cheetah Wheelies; *Screamin' Cheetah Wheelies* . . . .(Atlantic)
Silent Treatment
Earl Thomas Conley; *Earl Thomas Conley's Greatest Hits* . . . . (RCA)
Fire & Smoke . . . . (RCA)
Small Town Saturday Night
Hal Ketchum; *Past The Point Of Rescue* . . . . (Curb)
Somebody To Shove
Soul Asylum; *Grave Dancers Union* . . . . (Columbia)
Stairs, The
Reba McEntire; *The Last One To Know* . . . . (MCA)
Stand Up & Fight Back
Jimmy Cliff; *Give Thanx* . . . . (Warner Bros.)
Stay Together For The Kids
Blink-182; *Take Off Your Pants And Jacket* . . . . (MCA)
Stop The Violence
Boogie Down Productions; *By All Means Necessary* . . . .(Jive)
Live Hardcore Worldwide-Paris-London-NYC . . . .(Jive)
Straight Tequila Night
John Anderson; *Seminole Wind* . . . .(BNA)
Today's Hot Country-C . . . . (K-Tel)
Street Fighting Man
Rod Stewart; *Best Of Rod Stewart* . . . .(Mercury)
Sing It Again, Rod . . . . (Mercury)
Storyteller/The Complete Anthology: 1964-1990 . . . . (Warner Bros.)
Rolling Stones; *Beggars Banquet* . . . .(Abkco)
Get Yer Ya-Ya's Out! . . . .(Abkco)
Hot Rocks 1964-1971 . . . .(Abkco)
Singles Collection-The London Years . . . .(Abkco)
Through The Past, Darkly (Big Hits Vol. 2) . . . . (Abkco)
Sue Me
Original Cast; *Guys & Dolls* . . . . (MCA)
Guys & Dolls . . . . (Motown)
Suicidal Rage
Death Squad; *Split You At The Seams* . . . . (Ever Rat)
T.C.U. Fight Song
Southern Methodist Mustang Band; *Southwest
Conference Jazz* . . . . (Fidelity Sound)
Take 'Em As They Come
Bruce Springsteen; *Tracks* . . . . (Columbia)
Talk Back Trembling Lips
Ernest Ashworth; *Best Of Ernest Ashworth* . . . . (Curb)
Johnny Tillotson; *Cruisin'-1964-C* . . . . (Increase)
Tears Of Rage
Band; *Best Of The Band* . . . . (Capitol)
Music From Big Pink . . . . (Capitol)
To Kingdom Come-The Definitive Collection . . . . (Capitol)
Bob Dylan And The Band; *Basement Tapes* . . . . (Columbia)
Teen Angst (What The World Needs Now)
Cracker; *Cracker* . . . .(Virgin)
Theme From ''Family Feud''
Original Soundtrack; *Television's Greatest Hits-#6-Remote Control-C* . . . (TVT)
Then You May Take Me To The Fair
Original Cast; *Camelot* . . . . (Columbia)
Vanessa Redgrave; *ST/Camelot* . . . . (Warner Bros.)
Throwing Stones
Paula Cole; *This Fire* . . . . (Imago)
Thunder Rolls, The
Garth Brooks; *Garth Brooks-Double Live* . . . . (Capitol)
No Fences . . . . (Capitol)
Time Is Running Out
Steve Winwood; *Steve Winwood* . . . . (Island)
To The Moon And Back
Savage Garden; *Savage Garden* . . . . (Columbia)
Too Weak To Fight
Clarence Carter; *Golden Age Of Black Music-1960-1970-C* . . . .(Atlantic)
Snatching It Back-The Best Of Clarence Carter . . . . (Rhino)
U.N.M. Fight Song
University Of New Mexico Lobos Pep Band; *University Of New Mexico
Lobos Pep Band* . . . . (Fidelity Sound)
Ultraviolence
New Order; *Power, Corruption & Lies* . . . . (Qwest)

Undo
Bjork; *Vespertine*. . . . . (Elektra)
Video Violence
Lou Reed; *Between Thought & Expression-Anthology* . . . .(RCA)
Vigilante Man
Bruce Springsteen; *Folkways: A Vision Shared-C*. . . . . (Columbia)
Ry Cooder; *Into The Purple Valley* . . . . (Reprise)
Woody Guthrie; *Dust Bowl Ballads* . . . . (Rounder)
Violence
Mott The Hoople; *Mott* . . . . (Columbia)
   Mott The Hoople-Live. . . . . (Columbia)
   The Ballad Of Mott: A Retrospective . . . . (Columbia)
Pet Shop Boys; *Please* . . . . (EMI)
Violence Of Truth
The The; *Mind Bomb* . . . . (Epic)
   Shades Of Blue . . . . (Epic)
Violent Crimes
Riot; *Restless Breed*. . . . . (Elektra)
Violent Times
Call; *Walls Came Down-Best Of The Mercury Years* . . . . (Mercury)
We Can Work It Out
Beatles; *"Yesterday"...And Today* . . . . (Capitol)
   Beatles 1 . . . . (Capitol)
   Beatles-20 Greatest Hits. . . . . (Capitol)
   Beatles-Box Set. . . . . (Capitol)
   Past Masters-Volume Two . . . . (Parlophone)
   The Beatles/1962-1966 . . . . (Capitol)
Paul McCartney; *Unplugged (The Official Bootleg)* . . . . (Capitol)
Stevie Wonder; *Beatles Songs By Greatest Stars* . . . . (Motown)
   Signed Sealed & Delivered . . . . (Motown)
   Stevie Wonder's Greatest Hits-#2. (Motown)
   Top 10 With A Bullet-Motown Solo Stars-C . . . . (Motown)
We Just Disagree
Billy Dean; *Fire In The Dark*. . . . . (Liberty)
Dave Mason; *Best Of Dave Mason* . . . . (Columbia)
   Let It Flow. . . . . (Columbia)
   Rock Classics Of The '70s-C. . . . . (Columbia)
We Need A Resolution
Aaliyah; *Aaliyah* . . . . (BlackGround Enterp./Atlantic)
Where's The Love
Hanson; *Middle Of Nowhere* . . . . (Mercury)

FINDING

See Also: **EYES, HIDING, LOVE (various), SEARCHING, SEEING**

(Love Will) Find A Way
Amy Grant; *Unguarded*. . . . . (A&M)
All My Life
K-Ci & JoJo; *Love Always*. . . . . (MCA)
   Now That's What I Call Music!-#1-C. . . . . (Virgin)
Apples Peaches Pumpkin Pie
Jay And The Techniques; *Cruisin'-1967-C* . . . . (Increase)
Astounded
Tantric; *Tantric* . . . . (Maverick)
Baby, Now That I've Found You
Alison Krauss & Union Station; *Best Of Austin City Limits-Country Music's*
   Finest Hour-C . . . . (Legacy)
   Now That I've Found You: A Collection. . . . . (Rounder)
Foundations; *Best Of Rock 'N Soul-C* . . . . (Priority)
   History Of British Rock-#6-C . . . . (Rhino)
Bernadette
Four Tops; *Compact Command Performances-Four Tops* . . . . (Motown)
   Four Tops' Greatest Hits . . . . (Motown)
   Four Tops Reach Out . . . . (Motown)
   Four Tops-Anthology . . . . (Motown)
   Motown Superstar Series-#14-Four Tops. . . . . (Motown)
Betcha'll Never Find
Chantay Savage; *Here We Go* . . . . (RCA)
Breathe
Nickelback; *State*. . . . . (Roadrunner)
Find A Dream
Crosby, Stills & Nash; *After The Storm* . . . . (Atlantic)
Find A Way
Amy Grant; *Amy Grant-Collection* . . . . (A&M)
   Unguarded . . . . (A&M)
Find Another Fool
Quarterflash; *Quarterflash*. . . . . (Geffen)
Find Another Love
Tams; *45-#2108*. . . . . (Gusto)
Find Me A Girl
Jacksons; *Goin' Places* . . . . (Epic)
   Philly Ballads-#2-C . . . . (Philadelphia Int'l)
Find My Way
Cameo; *ST/Thank God It's Friday*. (Casablanca)
Find Out What They Like
Original Cast; *Ain't Misbehavin'* . . . . (RCA)

Teresa Brewer; *Live At Carnegie Hall & Montreux Switzerland* . . . (Doctor Jazz)
Find The Cost Of Freedom
Crosby, Stills, Nash & Young; *4 Way Street* . . . . (Atlantic)
   So Far . . . . (Atlantic)
Find Your Way Back
Jefferson Starship; *Greatest Hits-Ten Years & Change-1979-1991*. . . . . (RCA)
   Modern Times. . . . . (Grunt)
Find Yourself A Man
Original Cast; *Funny Girl*. . . . . (Capitol)
Finder Of Lost Loves
Dionne Warwick & Glenn Jones; *The Reel Burt Bacharach-C* . . . . . . (Hip-O)
Finders Keepers, Losers Weepers
Soul Children; *Lost Soul-#1-C* . . . . (Epic)
Finders Keepers, Losers Weepers
Elvis Presley; *Elvis For Everyone!*. . . . . (RCA)
Finding My Way
Rush; *All The World's A Stage* . . . . (Mercury)
   Archives. . . . . (Mercury)
   Rush. . . . . (Mercury)
Finding You
Joe Stampley; *Backslidin'* . . . . (Epic)
For Once In My Life
Gladys Knight & The Pips; *Gladys Knight & The Pips-Anthology* . . .(Motown)
   Motown Superstar Series-#13-Gladys Knight & The Pips . . . .(Motown)
   Neither One Of Us . . . . (Motown)
Stevie Wonder; *Motown Story-First 25 Years-C* . . . . (Motown)
   Stevie Wonder-Love Songs-20 Classic Hits. . . . . (Motown)
   Stevie Wonder's Greatest Hits-#2 . . . . (Motown)
Tony Bennett; *Tony Bennett's All-Time Greatest Hits* . . . . (Columbia)
Vikki Carr; *Best Of Vikki Carr* . . . . (EMI)
For Once In Our Lives
Paul Carrack; *Blue Views*. . . . . (Ark 21)
Found A Peanut
Wonder Kids; *Really Silly Songs* . . . . (Madacy)
Found Out About You
Gin Blossoms; *New Miserable Experience* . . . . (A&M)
Give Her Thorns & She'll Find The Roses
Roger Whittaker; *Wind Beneath My Wings* . . . . (RCA)
Gonna Find Me A Bluebird
Frank Ifield; *Best Of Frank Ifield* . . . . (Curb)
Marvin Rainwater; *Greatest Hits-1957-C* . . . . (Deluxe)
   Only Country-1955-1959-C . . . . (JCI Assoc. Labels)
Royal Wade Kimes; *ST/Traveller* . . . . (Asylum)
Good Lovin's Hard To Find
Lynyrd Skynyrd; *Last Rebel*. . . . . (Atlantic)
Good Man Is Hard To Find (Pittsburgh)
Bruce Springsteen; *Tracks*. . . . . (Columbia)
Heaven Can't Be Found
Hank Williams, Jr.; *Born To Boogie* . . . . (WB/Curb)
   Hank Williams, Jr.'s Greatest Hits III. . . . . (Curb)
Heroes Are Hard To Find
Fleetwood Mac; *25 Years-The Chain* . . . . (Warner Bros.)
   Heroes Are Hard To Find . . . . (Reprise)
Hey Leonardo (She Likes Me For Me)
Blessid Union Of Souls; *Now That's What I Call Music!-#3-C* . . . . . . (Virgin)
   Walking Off The Buzz . . . . (Push/V2)
I Finally Found Someone
Barbra Streisand & Bryan Adams; *ST/The Mirror Has Two Faces* . . .(Columbia)
I Found A Dream
Bob Wills; *Bob Wills-Anthology* . . . . (Sony Music Special Prod.)
I Found A Love
Eric Clapton; *Eric Clapton-Crossroads-C* . . . . (Polydor)
Falcons; *Atlantic Rhythm & Blues 1947-1974-#4 (1958-1962)-C* . . . . (Atlantic)
Wilson Pickett; *Best Of Wilson Pickett* . . . . (Atlantic)
   Wilson Pickett's Greatest Hits. . . . . (Atlantic)
I Found A Million-Dollar Baby (In A Five-And-Ten-Cent Store)
Barbra Streisand; *ST/Funny Girl* . . . . (Columbia)
Bing Crosby; *Pennies From Heaven* . . . . (Pro-Arte)
Fred Waring's Pennsylvanians; *78-#22707* . . . . (Victor)
Nat "King" Cole; *Nat "King" Cole-Gift Set* . . . . (Capitol)
I Found Love
Quicksilver Messenger Service; *Quicksilver* . . . . (Capitol)
   Quicksilver Messenger Service-Anthology . . . . (Capitol)
   Sons Of Mercury . . . . (Rhino)
I Found Love
Lone Justice; *Shelter* . . . . (Geffen)
I Found Love
Paul Carrack; *Suburban Voodoo* . . . . (Epic)
I Found Love
Earl Scruggs & Vince Gill & Rosanne Cash; *Earl Scruggs And*
   Friends-C. . . . . (MCA)
I Found My Baby
Gap Band; *Gap Band-Ultimate Collection*. . . . . (Hip-O)
I Found Somebody
Glenn Frey; *No Fun Aloud* . . . . (Asylum)
I Found Someone
Cher; *Cher* . . . . (Geffen)
Laura Branigan; *Hold Me* . . . . (Atlantic)

I Found The Brains Of Santa Claus
Jason & The Straptones; *Demento's Mementos* . . . . (PVC)
I Have Found Me A Home
Jimmy Buffett; *White Sport Coat & A Pink Crustacean* . . . . (MCA)
I Still Haven't Found What I'm Looking For
U2; *Joshua Tree* . . . . (Island)
Rattle And Hum . . . . (Island)
If You Want To Find Love
Kenny Rogers; *Back Home Again* . . . . (Reprise)
I'll Never Find Another You
Seekers; *Best Of The Seekers* . . . . (Capitol)
History Of British Rock-#3-C . . . . (Rhino)
Sonny James; *All-Time Country Classics-#2-C* . . . . (Capitol)
Opry Legends-Sonny James . . . . (Capitol)
I've Found A New Baby
Benny Goodman; *Benny Goodman-Live At Carnegie Hall* . . . . (London)
Benny Goodman-On Stage . . . . (London)
Complete Benny Goodman-#2 . . . . (RCA)
I've Found Someone Of My Own
Free Movement; *Didn't It Blow Your Mind: Soul Hits Of The
'70s-#6-C* . . . . (Rhino)
Lost & Found
Sparks; *Profile-The Ultimate Sparks Collection* . . . . (Rhino)
Lost & Found
Brooks & Dunn; *Brand New Man* . . . . (Arista)
Lost & Found
Original Broadway Cast; *City Of Angels* . . . . (Columbia)
Lost & Found
Echo & The Bunnymen; *Echo & The Bunnymen* . . . . (Sire)
Love I Found In You
Jim Brickman; *My Romance: An Evening With Jim Brickman* . . . (Windham Hill)
Love Is Gonna Find You
Manhattans; *Forever By Your Side* . . . . (Columbia)
Love Is On The Way
Celine Dion; *Let's Talk About Love-C* . . . . (550 Music)
Dave Koz; *Dance* . . . . (Capitol)
Love She Found In Me
Gary Morris; *Gary Morris-Hits* . . . . (Warner Bros.)
Why Lady Why . . . . (Warner Bros.)
Love Will Find A Way
Sam Cooke; *The Man And His Music* . . . . (RCA)
This Is Sam Cooke . . . . (RCA)
Love Will Find A Way
Lionel Richie; *Can't Slow Down* . . . . (Motown)
Love Will Find A Way
George Howard; *Dancing In The Sun* . . . . (GRP)
Love Will Find A Way
Pablo Cruise; *Worlds Away* . . . . (A&M)
Love Will Find A Way
Yes; *Big Generator* . . . . (Atco)
Love Will Find A Way
Christina Aguilera; *Christina Aguilera* . . . . (RCA)
Love Will Find Its Way To You
Reba McEntire; *Last One To Know* . . . . (MCA)
Reba McEntire's Greatest Hits Volume Two . . . . (MCA)
Love's Found You & Me
Ed Bruce; *Ed Bruce's Greatest Hits* . . . . (MCA)
Never Find Someone Like You
Keith Martin; *ST/Bad Boys* . . . . (Work)
Now That I've Found You
Terri Clark; *How I Feel* . . . . (Mercury)
Now That We Found Love
Heavy D & The Boyz; *Peaceful Journey* . . . . (Uptown)
Third World; *Journey To Addis* . . . . (Island)
The Island Story-1962-1987-25th Anniversary-C . . . . (Island)
Oh Girl (You Know Where To Find Me)
Vince Gill; *When I Call Your Name* . . . . (MCA)
Ready For A Fall
P.J. Olsson; *Songs From Dawson's Creek* . . . . (Sony Music Soundtrax)
Reason To Believe
Rod Stewart; *Best Of Rod Stewart-#2* . . . . (Mercury)
Every Picture Tells A Story . . . . (Mercury)
Sing It Again, Rod . . . . (Mercury)
Storyteller/The Complete Anthology: 1964-1990 . . . . (Warner Bros.)
Unplugged...And Seated . . . . (Warner Bros.)
Reason To Believe
Bruce Springsteen; *Nebraska* . . . . (Columbia)
Bruce Springsteen & The E Street Band; *Bruce Springsteen & The E Street
Band Live/1975-85* . . . . (Legacy)
Rediscovery
Chicago; *Chicago VI* . . . . (Chicago)
Search Find
Bee Gees; *Spirits Having Flown* . . . . (Polydor)
Search Is Over
Survivor; *Survivor's Greatest Hits* . . . . (Scotti Bros.)
Vital Signs . . . . (Scotti Bros.)
Searchin'
Beatles; *The Beatles-Anthology-#1* . . . . (Capitol)

Someday I'll Find You
Bobby Short; *Mad About Noel Coward* . . . . (Atlantic)
Mary Martin & Noel Coward; *Together With Music* . . . . (DRG)
Somewhere They Can't Find Me
Simon & Garfunkel; *Collected Works* . . . . (Columbia)
Sounds Of Silence . . . . (Columbia)
Sure Love
Hal Ketchum; *Sure Love* . . . . (Curb)
Ten Minutes Ago
Julie Andrews & Jon Cypher; *Cinderella-The CBS Television
Production* . . . . (Columbia)
Stuart Damon & Lesley Ann Warren; *Cinderella-The CBS Television
Network Production* . . . . (Columbia)
Thank God I Found You
Mariah Carey featuring Joe & 98 Degrees; *Rainbow* . . . . (Columbia)
Thing, The
Phil Harris; *The Thing About Phil Harris* . . . . (Living Era)
This Love That I've Found
Ella Fitzgerald; *Best Of Ella Fitzgerald* . . . . (Pablo)
Till I Found You
Marty Stuart; *Tempted* . . . . (MCA)
To Find God
James Michaels; *Bouquet* . . . . (Innersong)
True Love Is Hard To Find
Bonnie Raitt; *Bonnie Raitt-Collection* . . . . (Warner Bros.)
Nine Lives . . . . (Warner Bros.)
Try To Find Another Man
Righteous Brothers; *Righteous Brothers-Anthology 1962-1974* . . . . . . (Rhino)
Until I Find You Again
Richard Marx; *Flesh And Bone* . . . . (Capitol)
Richard Marx's Greatest Hits . . . . (Capitol)
Voice Of The Heart
Diana Ross; *Take Me Higher* . . . . (Motown)
We Tell Ourselves
Clint Black; *The Hard Way* . . . . (RCA)
When I Find My Life
Marianne Faithfull; *Blazing Away* . . . . (Island)
When Love Finds You
Vince Gill; *When Love Finds You* . . . . (MCA)
While You See A Chance
Steve Winwood; *Arc Of A Diver* . . . . (Island)
Steve Winwood-Chronicles . . . . (Island)
Whispering Pines
Band; *The Band* . . . . (Capitol)
Who Found Who
Jellybean with Elisa Fiorillo; *Jellybean-Just Visiting This Planet* . . . (Chrysalis)
You Sang To Me
Marc Anthony; *Marc Anthony* . . . . (Columbia)
You'll Never Find Another Love Like Mine
Lou Rawls; *10 Years Of #1 Hits* . . . . (Philadelphia Int'l)
Lou Rawls-Classics . . . . (Philadelphia Int'l)
Lou Rawls-Live (Right Stuff) . . . . (Right Stuff)
Mega Hits Dance Classics-#2-C . . . . (Priority)
Philly Ballads-#1-C . . . . (Philadelphia Int'l)

FIRE, Ashes, Burning, Candles, Smoke
See Also: DANGER & DISASTER, DESIRE, LIGHT, HOT, SUN

(There's A) Fire In The Night
Alabama; *Roll On* . . . . (RCA)
African Flame
Herb Alpert; *Wild Romance* . . . . (A&M)
After The Fire
Pete Townshend; *Pete Townshend's Deep End Live!* . . . . (Atco)
Roger Daltrey; *Under A Raging Moon* . . . . (Atlantic)
After The Fire Is Gone
Loretta Lynn & Conway Twitty; *MCA Records 30 Years Of Hits-1958-
1988-C* . . . . (MCA)
Very Best Of Loretta Lynn & Conway Twitty . . . . (MCA)
Ain't No Smoke Without Fire
Eddie Kendricks; *Vintage '78* . . . . (Arista)
All Cried Out
Allure; *Allure* . . . . (Track Masters/Crave)
Boom! 17 Explosive Hits-C . . . . (Simitar)
Lisa Lisa; *Lisa Lisa & Cult Jam With Full Force* . . . . (Columbia)
Lisa Lisa-Super Hits . . . . (Columbia)
Past, Present & Future . . . . (TMP)
All Fired Up
Pat Benatar; *Best Shots* . . . . (Chrysalis)
Wide Awake In Dreamland . . . . (Chrysalis)
Ana's Song (Open Fire)
Silverchair; *Neon Ballroom* . . . . (Epic)
Another Bridge To Burn
Mel Tillis; *Best Of Mel Tillis* . . . . (MCA)
Ashes
Mary's Danish; *There Goes The Wondertruck* . . . . (Chameleon)

Ashes
Poco; *Cowboys & Englishmen*. . . . . (One Way)
Ashes
Martina McBride; *The Way That I Am*. . . . .(RCA)
Ashes Are Burning
Renaissance; *Tales Of 1001 Nights-#2*. . . . .(Sire)
Ashes By Now
Lee Ann Womack; *I Hope You Dance*. (MCA)
Rodney Crowell; *Rodney Crowell-Collection*. . . . . (Warner Bros.)
Ashes In The Wind
Moe Bandy; *No Regrets*. . . . .(Curb)
Ashes Of Love
Chris Hillman; *Desert Rose*. . . . .(Sugar Hill)
Desert Rose Band; *Desert Rose Band*. . . . .(Curb)
Dickey Lee; *Ashes Of Love*. . . . .(RCA)
Johnnie & Jack & Their Tennessee Mountain Boys; *Johnnie & Jack's
  Greatest Hits*. . . . . (King)
Rose Maddox; *Rose Of The West Coast Country*. . . . .(Arhoolie)
Ashes The Rain And I
James Gang; *Best Of The James Gang*. . . . . (MCA)
  James Gang Rides Again. . . . . (MCA)
  James Gang-16 Greatest Hits. . . . . (MCA)
Ashes To Ashes
David Bowie; *Changesbowie*. . . . .(Rykodisc)
  Scary Monsters. . . . . (Rykodisc)
  Sound + Vision. . . . .(Rykodisc)
  The Singles-1969-1993. . . . .(Rykodisc)
Ashes To Ashes
Wallflowers; *The Wallflowers*. . . . .(Virgin)
Ashes To Ashes
Darden Smith; *Trouble No More*. . . . . (Columbia)
Ashes To Ashes
Faith No More; *Album Of The Year*. . . . .(Reprise)
Ashes To Ashes
Gene Watson; *Honky Tonk Crazy*. . . . . (Epic)
Atlanta Burned Again Last Night
Atlanta; *Pictures*. . . . . (MCA)
Atlanta's Burning Down
Dickey Betts & Great Southern; *Dickey Betts & Great Southern*. . . . . . . (Arista)
Randy Howard; *All-American Redneck*. . . . . (Warner Bros.)
Attack Ships On Fire
Revolting Cocks; *Big Sexy Land*. . . . .(Wax Trax)
Baby I'm Burnin'
Dolly Parton; *Heartbreaker*. . . . .(RCA)
Baby's On Fire
Sammy Hagar; *Standing Hampton*. . . . . (Geffen)
Baby's On Fire
Great White; *Twice Shy*. . . . . (Capitol)
B-B-B-Burning Up With Love
Eddie Rabbitt; *The Best Year Of My Life*. . . . . (Warner Bros.)
Beautiful Disaster
311; *Live!*. . . . .(Capricorn)
  Transistor. . . . .(Capricorn)
Between Two Fires
Gary Morris; *Faded Blue*. . . . . (Warner Bros.)
  Gary Morris' Greatest Hits-#2. . . . . (Warner Bros.)
Big Black Smoke
Kinks; *Kink Kronikles*. . . . .(Reprise)
Born With A Broken Heart
Kenny Wayne Shepherd; *Ledbetter Heights*. . . . . (Giant)
Both Ends Burning
Roxy Music; *Heart Still Beating*. . . . .(Virgin)
  Siren. . . . . (Atco)
  Viva. . . . . (Reprise)
Bridge That Just Won't Burn
Conway Twitty; *Number Ones*. . . . . (MCA)
Bridges Burning
Mission U.K.; *God's Own Medicine*. (Mercury)
Brush Fire In Hoboken
Chris Stamey; *It's A Wonderful Life*. . . . . (DB)
Build A Fire
Drivin' N' Cryin'; *Fly Me Courageous*. . . . . (Island)
Burn
Bruce Cockburn; *Waiting For A Miracle-Singles 1970-1987*. . . . . (Gold Castle)
Deep Purple; *Burn*. . . . . (Warner Bros.)
  Deepest Purple/The Very Best Of Deep Purple. . . . . (Warner Bros.)
  Made In Europe. . . . . (Warner Bros.)
  When We Rock We Rock & When We Roll We Roll. . . . . (Warner Bros.)
Dream Syndicate; *Live At Raji's*. . . . . (Restless)
  Medicine Show/This Is Not The New Album. . . . . (A&M)
Burn
Jo Dee Messina; *Burn*. . . . . (Curb)
Burn Down The Bridges
Artch; *For The Sake Of Mankind*. . . . . (Metal Blade)
Burn Down The Malls
Mojo Nixon & Skid Roper; *Enigma Variations-#2-C*. . . . . . . (Enigma Capitol)
Burn Down The Mission
Elton John; *11-17-70*. . . . .(Polydor)

  Live In Australia With The Melbourne Symphony Orchestra. . . . . (MCA)
  Tumbleweed Connection. . . . . (Polydor)
  Your Songs. . . . . (Polydor)
Phil Collins & His Serious Band; *Two Rooms-Celebrating The Songs Of
  Elton John & Bernie Taupin-C*. . . . . (Polydor)
Burn Georgia Burn
Alabama; *Feels So Right*. . . . . (RCA)
Burn Hollywood Burn
Chuck D/The Roots/Zack De La Rocha; *ST/Bamboozled*. . . . .(Motown)
Public Enemy; *Fear Of A Black Planet*. . . . . (Def Jam)
Burn Me Down
Marty Stuart; *Tempted*. . . . . (MCA)
Burn Me Up
Kay Gees; *Burn Me Up*. . . . . (De-Lite)
Burn On
Randy Newman; *Sail Away*. . . . . (Reprise)
Burn One Down
Clint Black; *The Hard Way*. . . . . (RCA)
Burn Rubber On Me
Gap Band; *12'' Collection*. . . . .(Mercury)
  Gap Gold/Best Of The Gap Band. . . . .(Mercury)
  The Gap Band III. . . . .(Mercury)
Burn That Bridge
Jimmy Buffett; *Riddles In The Sand*. . . . . (MCA)
Burn That Candle
Bill Haley & His Comets; *Bill Haley & His Comets' Greatest Hits*. . . . . .(MCA)
  Bill Haley & His Comets-Golden Hits. . . . . (MCA)
  R-O-C-K. . . . . (Sun)
Emmylou Harris; *Quarter Moon In A Ten Cent Town*. . . . . . (Warner Bros.)
Burn This Disco Out
Michael Jackson; *Off The Wall*. . . . . (Epic)
Burn To Shine
Ben Harper; *Burn To Shine*. . . . . (Virgin)
Burn Your Money!
Mojo Nixon & Skid Roper; *Root Hog Or Die*. . . . .(I.R.S.)
Burned
Buffalo Springfield; *Buffalo Springfield*. . . . .(Atco)
Neil Young; *Decade*. . . . . (Reprise)
Burnin' & Lootin'
Bob Marley & The Wailers; *Bob Marley & The Wailers-Live*. . . . . . (Tuff Gong)
Wailers; *Burnin'*. . . . . (Tuff Gong)
Burnin' A Hole In My Heart
Skip Ewing; *Class Of Country-C*. . . . .(K-Tel)
  Coast Of Colorado. . . . . (MCA)
Burnin' Bush
Earth, Wind & Fire; *Spirit*. . . . .(Columbia)
Burnin' For You
Blue Oyster Cult; *Extraterrestrial Live*. . . . .(Columbia)
  Fire Of Unknown Origin. . . . .(Columbia)
Burnin' In L.A.
Lightnin' Hopkins; *Lightnin' Sam Hopkins*. . . . . (Arhoolie)
Burnin' Love
Con Funk Shun; *Burnin' Love*. . . . .(Mercury)
Burnin' Old Memories With A Brand New Flame
Kathy Mattea; *Country Hits 4: Sweet Country-C*. . . . . (Priority)
  Willow In The Wind. . . . .(Mercury)
Burnin' Sky
Bad Company; *Burnin' Sky*. . . . .(Swan Song)
Burnin' The Midnight Oil
Foghat; *Night Shift*. . . . .(Rhino)
Burnin' The Roadhouse Down
Steve Wariner & Garth Brooks; *Burnin' The Roadhouse Down*. . . . . . .(Capitol)
Burnin' Thing
Mac Davis; *Burnin' Thing*. . . . .(Columbia)
  Mac Davis' Greatest Hits. . . . .(Columbia)
Burning A Hole In My Mind
Connie Smith; *Essential Connie Smith*. . . . .(RCA)
Burning Bridges
Pink Floyd; *Pink Floyd-Gift Set*. . . . .(Capitol)
  ST/Obscured By Clouds. . . . . (Capitol)
Burning Bridges
Naked Eyes; *Best Of Naked Eyes*. . . . . (EMI)
Burning Bridges
38 Special; *Bone Against Steel*. . . . .(Charisma)
Burning Bridges
Glen Campbell; *Glen Campbell's Greatest Hits*. . . . .(Capitol)
Burning Bridges
Collective Soul; *Hints, Allegations And Things Left Unsaid*. . . . . (Atlantic)
Burning Bridges
Jack Scott; *Capitol Collectors Series-Jack Scott*. . . . .(Capitol)
  Super Oldies Of The '60s-#6-C. . . . . (Audio Fidelity)
Burning Bridges
Mike Curb Congregation; *Super Hits Of The '70s-Have A Nice
  Day-#5-C*. . . . . (Rhino)
Burning Bridges
Garth Brooks; *Ropin' The Wind*. . . . .(Liberty)
Burning Bridges
Roger Miller; *King Of The Road*. . . . . (Laserlight)

Burning Bridges
George Jones; *Jones Country* . . . .(Epic)
One Woman Man . . . .(Epic)
Burning Down
R.E.M.; *Dead Letter Office* . . . .(I.R.S.)
Suzy Bogguss; *Moment Of Truth* . . . . (Capitol)
Burning Down One Side
Robert Plant; *Pictures At Eleven* . . . . (Swan Song)
Burning Down The House
Talking Heads; *Speaking In Tongues* . . . . (Sire)
Stop Making Sense . . . . (Sire)
Burning Fingers
Shawn Phillips; *Collaboration* . . . . (A&M)
Burning Fire
Otis Spann; *Chicago/The Blues Today* . . . . (Vanguard)
Great Blues Men-C . . . . (Vanguard)
Burning For Me
Strawbs; *Burning For Me* . . . . (Oyster)
Burning Heart
Vandenberg; *Best Of Vandenberg* . . . . (Atco)
Vandenberg . . . . (Atco)
Burning Heart
Survivor; *Rocky Story-C* . . . . (Scotti Bros.)
ST/Rocky IV . . . . (Scotti Bros.)
Burning House Of Love
X; *Ain't Love Grand* . . . . (Elektra)
Best Of MTV's 120 Minutes-#2-C . . . . (Rhino)
Live At The Whisky A Go-Go . . . . (Elektra)
Burning Love
Elvis Presley; *Aloha from Hawaii via Satellite* . . . . (RCA)
Elvis Aron Presley . . . . (RCA)
Elvis-Greatest Hits, Volume One . . . . (RCA)
The Top Ten Hits . . . . (RCA)
Burning Memories
Mel Tillis; *Best Of Mel Tillis* . . . .(MCA)
Heart Healer . . . .(MCA)
Very Best Of Mel Tillis . . . .(MCA)
Ray Price; *Ray Price's Greatest Hits-#1-3* . . . . (Step One)
Burning My Rowboat
Maura O'Connell; *Real Life Story* . . . .(Warner Bros.)
Burning Of Atlanta
Claude King; *American Originals-Claude King* . . . . (Columbia)
Burning Of The Midnight Lamp
Jimi Hendrix; *Essential Jimi Hendrix* . . . . (Reprise)
Lifelines/Jimi Hendrix Story . . . . (Reprise)
Jimi Hendrix Experience; *Electric Ladyland* . . . . (Reprise)
Radio One . . . .(Rykodisc)
Living Colour; *Biscuits* . . . .(Epic)
Burning Rope
Genesis; *And Then There Were Three* . . . .(Atlantic)
Burning The Ballroom Down
Amazing Rhythm Aces; *Burning The Ballroom Down* . . . .(MCA)
Burning Up
Bad Company; *Fame & Fortune* . . . .(Atlantic)
Burning Up
Madonna; *Madonna* . . . . (Sire)
Burning Up
Judas Priest; *Hell Bent For Leather* . . . . (Columbia)
Burning Up Time
Stranglers; *No More Hereos* . . . . (A&M)
Candle In The Wind
Elton John; *Goodbye Yellow Brick Road* . . . . (Polydor)
Live In Australia With The Melbourne Symphony Orchestra . . . .(MCA)
Your Songs . . . . (Polydor)
Candle In The Wind 1997
Elton John; *Candle In The Wind 1997 (Diana, Princess Of Wales)*
(Single) . . . .(Rocket)
Candle In The Window
Alabama; *Alabama-Christmas* . . . . (RCA)
Candle Of Life
Moody Blues; *To Our Children's Children's Children* . . . . (Polydor)
Candle On The Water
Helen Reddy; *Chicken Soup For The Soul: I'll Be There For You-Songs Of
Friendship, Brotherhood And Sisterhood-C* . . . . (Rhino)
Live In London . . . . (Capitol)
ST/Pete's Dragon . . . . (Capitol)
Candlelight
Janis Ian; *Miracle Row* . . . . (Columbia)
Wishbone Ash; *New England* . . . .(Atlantic)
Candles
Pru; *Pru* . . . . (Capitol)
Candles Of Our Lives
England Dan & John Ford Coley; *Fables* . . . . (A&M)
Canned Heat
Jamiroquai; *Synkronized* . . . . (Work/Epic)
Castles Burning
Journey; *Trial By Fire* . . . . (Columbia)

Cat People (Putting Out Fire)
David Bowie; *Let's Dance* . . . . (EMI)
ST/Cat People . . . . (MCA)
The Singles-1969-1993 . . . . (Rykodisc)
Chariots Of Fire
Vangelis; *ST/Chariots Of Fire* . . . .(Polydor)
Themes . . . .(Polydor)
Cheatin' Fire
Conway Twitty; *Mr. T* . . . . (MCA)
Cigarette
Ben Folds Five; *Whatever And Ever Amen* . . . .(Caroline/550)
Cincinnati Fireball
Johnny Burnette; *Best Of Johnny Burnette-You're Sixteen* . . . . (Gold Rush)
Cities Are Burning, The
Jimmy Collier & Rev. F.D. Kirkpatrick; *Best Of Broadside 1962-1968:
Anthems Of The American Underground From The Pages Of Broadside
Magazine-C* . . . .(Smithsonian Folkways)
Cities On Flame With Rock & Roll
Blue Oyster Cult; *Blue Oyster Cult* . . . . (Columbia)
Career Of Evil . . . . (Columbia)
Extraterrestrial Live . . . . (Columbia)
On Your Feet Or On Your Knees . . . . (Columbia)
City's Burning
Heart; *Private Audition* . . . . (Epic)
Cold Blue Steel & Sweet Fire
Joni Mitchell; *For The Roses* . . . .(Asylum)
Joni Mitchell with Tom Scott & The L.A. Express; *Miles Of Aisles* . . . .(Asylum)
Cold Fire
Rush; *Counterparts* . . . .(Atlantic)
Cook With Fire
Heart; *Dog & Butterfly* . . . . (Portrait)
Crack Pipe (Burnin' My Hand)
Coolies; *Doug (A Rock Opera & Comic Book)* . . . . (DB)
Crash & Burn
April Wine; *Nature Of The Beast* . . . . (Capitol)
Crash & Burn
Pat Travers Band; *Crash & Burn* . . . . (Polydor)
Crash & Burn
Bangles; *Everything* . . . . (Columbia)
Crash & Burn
Don Dokken; *Up From The Ashes* . . . . (Geffen)
Crash & Burn
'Til Tuesday; *Everything's Different Now* . . . . (Epic)
Crash And Burn
Savage Garden; *Affirmation* . . . . (Columbia)
Crash And Burn
Sheryl Crow; *The Globe Sessions* . . . . (A&M)
Dancing In The Dark
Bruce Springsteen; *Born In The U.S.A.* . . . . (Columbia)
Bruce Springsteen's Greatest Hits . . . . (Columbia)
Desert Rose
Sting; *Brand New Day* . . . . (A&M)
Disco Inferno
Trammps; *Best Of The Trammps* . . . .(Atlantic)
Disco Inferno . . . .(Atlantic)
ST/Saturday Night Fever . . . .(Polydor)
The Disco Years-#1-Turn The Beat Around-1974-1978-C . . . . (Rhino)
Don't Let It Bring You Down
Crosby, Stills, Nash & Young; *4 Way Street* . . . .(Atlantic)
Neil Young; *After The Gold Rush* . . . . (Reprise)
Down In Flames
Semisonic; *Great Divide* . . . . (MCA)
Down In Flames
BlackHawk; *BlackHawk* . . . . (Arista)
The Hits-Love & Gravity . . . . (Arista)
Down In Flames
Dead Boys; *Young, Loud And Snotty* . . . .(Sire)
Down In Flames
Don Dokken; *Up From The Ashes* . . . . (Geffen)
Down In Flames
Little Feat; *Shake Me Up* . . . . (Morgan Creek)
Elvira
Murry Kellum; *Country Comedy-20 Country Comedy Hits* . . . .(Plantation)
Oak Ridge Boys; *Fancy Free* . . . . (MCA)
MCA Records 30 Years Of Hits-1958-1988-C . . . . (MCA)
Oak Ridge Boys' Greatest Hits 2 . . . . (MCA)
Eternal Flame
Bangles; *Bangles' Greatest Hits* . . . . (Columbia)
Everything . . . . (Columbia)
Everybody's Been Burned
Byrds; *Original Singles-#1-1965-1967* . . . . (Columbia)
The Byrds . . . . (Columbia)
Younger Than Yesterday . . . . (Columbia)
Face The Fire
Dan Fogelberg; *Phoenix* . . . .(Full Moon)
Fallen Embers
Enya; *A Day Without Rain* . . . .(Reprise)

Feed The Fire
BoDeans; *Go Slow Down* . . . . (Slash)
Feel The Fire
Claudja Berry; *Best Of Claudja Berry* . . . . (Hot Prod.)
Feel The Fire
Peabo Bryson; *The Peabo Bryson Collection* . . . . (Capitol)
Roberta Flack & Peabo Bryson; *Live & More* . . . . (Atlantic)
Feel The Fire
Stephanie Mills; *Greatest Hits In My Life* . . . . (Casablanca)
Feel The Fire
Bob James; *Obsession* . . . . (Tappan Zee)
Feel The Fire
Overkill; *Feel The Fire* . . . . (Megaforce)
Fight Fire With Fire
Kansas; *Best Of Kansas* . . . . (CBS Associated)
Drastic Measures . . . . (Kirshner)
Metallica; *Ride The Lightning* . . . . (Elektra)
Fire
Television; *Adventure* . . . . (Elektra)
Fire
Brigette McWilliams; *Too Much Woman* . . . . (Virgin)
Ohio Players; *Didn't It Blow Your Mind: Soul Hits Of The*
'70s-#14-C . . . . (Rhino)
Ohio Players-Gold . . . . (Mercury)
Fire
Bruce Springsteen & The E Street Band; *Bruce Springsteen & The E Street*
Band Live/1975-85 . . . . (Legacy)
Pointer Sisters; *Cover Me (Bruce Springsteen Tribute)-C* . . . . (Rhino)
Energy . . . . (Planet)
I Am Woman-C . . . . (Nick At Nite)
Fire
Subway; *Good Times* . . . . (Motown)
Fire
Jimi Hendrix; *Concerts* . . . . (Reprise)
Essential Jimi Hendrix, Volume 2 . . . . (Reprise)
Jimi Hendrix Experience; *Are You Experienced?* . . . . (Reprise)
Smash Hits . . . . (Reprise)
Fire
U2; *October* . . . . (Island)
Fire
Jefferson Starship; *Earth* . . . . (Grunt)
Fire
Crazy World Of Arthur Brown; *History Of British Rock-#9-C* . . . . (Rhino)
Fire
Mother's Finest; *Mother's Finest-Live* . . . . (Epic)
Fire
Red Hot Chili Peppers; *Mother's Milk* . . . . (EMI)
Fire
Robert Gordon & Link Wray; *Fresh Fish Special* . . . . (RCA)
Fire & Smoke
Earl Thomas Conley; *Earl Thomas Conley's Greatest Hits* . . . . (RCA)
Fire & Smoke . . . . (RCA)
Jukebox Saturday Night-C . . . . (RCA)
Fire And Desire
Rick James; *All The Great Motown Love Song Duets-C* . . . . (Motown)
Motown Memories-#4-C . . . . (Motown)
Reflections-Greatest Hits . . . . (Motown)
Street Songs . . . . (Motown)
Fire And Ice
Pat Benatar; *Best Shots* . . . . (Chrysalis)
Live From Earth . . . . (Chrysalis)
Precious Time . . . . (Chrysalis)
Fire And Rain
James Taylor; *James Taylor's Greatest Hits* . . . . (Warner Bros.)
Sweet Baby James . . . . (Warner Bros.)
The Concert For New York City-C . . . . (Columbia)
Sammy Kershaw; *Red Hot + Country-C* . . . . (Mercury)
Fire And Water
Free; *Best Of Free* . . . . (A&M)
Fire And Water . . . . (A&M)
Free-Live . . . . (A&M)
Fire And Water
Wilson Pickett; *Very Best Of Wilson Pickett* . . . . (Rhino)
Fire At Midnight
Jethro Tull; *Songs From The Wood* . . . . (Chrysalis)
Fire Brothers
Quicksilver Messenger Service; *Quicksilver* . . . . (Capitol)
Quicksilver Messenger Service-Anthology . . . . (Capitol)
Fire Down Below
Bob Seger; *Night Moves* . . . . (Capitol)
Bob Seger & The Silver Bullet Band; *Nine Tonight* . . . . (Capitol)
Fire Escape
Fastball; *All The Pain Money Can Buy* . . . . (Hollywood)
Fire Girl
Commodores; *Natural High* . . . . (Motown)
Fire I Can't Put Out
George Strait; *George Strait's Greatest Hits* . . . . (MCA)
Strait From The Heart . . . . (MCA)

Fire In Cairo
Cure; *Boys Don't Cry* . . . . (Elektra)
Fire In The Engine Room
Richard Thompson; *Across A Crowded Room* . . . . (Polydor)
Fire In The Hole
Steely Dan; *Can't Buy A Thrill* . . . . (MCA)
Fire In The Hole
Van Halen; *Van Halen 3* . . . . (Warner Bros.)
Fire In The Mine
Stompin' Tom Connors; *Love & Laughter* . . . . (Out Of Print)
On Tragedy Trail . . . . (Out Of Print)
Fire In The Morning
Melissa Manchester; *Melissa Manchester* . . . . (Arista)
Fire In The Sky
Nitty Gritty Dirt Band; *Twenty Years Of Dirt-Best Of The Nitty Gritty*
Dirt Band . . . . (Warner Bros.)
Fire In The Sky
Saxon; *Denim & Leather* . . . . (Capitol)
Fire In The Sky
Ozzy Osbourne; *No Rest For The Wicked* . . . . (Epic)
Fire Inside
Bob Seger & The Silver Bullet Band; *Fire Inside* . . . . (Capitol)
Fire Island
Village People; *Live & Sleazy* . . . . (Casablanca)
Village People . . . . (Casablanca)
Woody Herman; *Blowin' Up A Storm* . . . . (Pickwick)
Fire Lake
Bob Seger & The Silver Bullet Band; *Against The Wind* . . . . (Capitol)
Nine Tonight . . . . (Capitol)
Fire Of The Newly Alive
Rosanne Cash; *The Wheel* . . . . (Columbia)
Fire Of Two Old Flames
Roy Head; *In Our Room* . . . . (Elektra)
Fire Of Unknown Origin
Blue Oyster Cult; *Fire Of Unknown Origin* . . . . (Columbia)
Fire On High
Electric Light Orchestra; *Face The Music* . . . . (Jet)
Fire On The Mountain
Marshall Tucker Band; *Marshall Tucker Band's Greatest Hits* . . . . . (Capricorn)
Searchin' For A Rainbow . . . . (AJK Music)
South's Greatest Hits-C . . . . (Capricorn)
Fire On The Mountain
Bill Monroe & His Blue Grass Boys; *Kentucky Bluegrass* . . . . (MCA)
Fire On The Mountain
Grateful Dead; *Dead Set* . . . . (Arista)
Shakedown Street . . . . (Arista)
Fire Woman
Cult; *Sonic Temple* . . . . (Sire)
Fireball
Deep Purple; *Deepest Purple/The Very Best Of Deep Purple* . . . . (Warner Bros.)
Fireball . . . . (Warner Bros.)
Fireball
Fireballs; *Legends Of Rock Guitar-'50s-#2-C* . . . . (Rhino)
Fireball
Flatt & Scruggs; *Greatest Hits With The Foggy Mountain Boys* . . . . (Columbia)
Roy Acuff; *Roy Acuff's Greatest Hits* . . . . (Elektra)
Fireball Mail
John McEuen; *String Wizards* . . . . (Vanguard)
Roy Acuff; *Best Of Roy Acuff* . . . . (Liberty)
Opry Legends-Roy Acuff . . . . (Capitol)
Roy Acuff's Greatest Hits . . . . (Columbia)
Firecracker
Mass Production; *In The Purest Form* . . . . (Cotillion)
Fired Up!
Funky Green Dogs; *Get Fired Up!* . . . . (MCA)
Firehouse
Kiss; *Alive!* . . . . (Mercury)
Double Platinum . . . . (Mercury)
Kiss . . . . (Casablanca)
The Originals . . . . (Casablanca)
Fireman, The
George Strait; *Country Classics-#4-1984-1985-C* . . . . (Universal)
Does Fort Worth Ever Cross Your Mind . . . . (MCA)
George Strait's Greatest Hits-#2 . . . . (MCA)
Fires
Procol Harum; *Grand Hotel* . . . . (Chrysalis)
Fireside Song
Genesis; *Genesis-London Collector-In The Beginning* . . . . (London)
Firestarter
38 Special; *Special Forces* . . . . (A&M)
Tease; *Tease* . . . . (Epic)
Fireworks
Alabama; *Alabama-Live* . . . . (RCA)
Fireworks
Blue Oyster Cult; *Spectres* . . . . (Columbia)
Fireworks
Choirboys; *Big Bad Noise* . . . . (WTG)

Fireworks
Jose Feliciano; *Fireworks* . . . . (RCA)
Flame
Cheap Trick; *Lap Of Luxury* . . . .(Epic)
Flame Of Love
Jean Carne; *Closer Than Close* . . . .(Omni)
Flame Thrower Love
Dead Boys; *We Have Come For Your Children* . . . . (Sire)
Flame, The
Cheap Trick; *Cheap Trick's Greatest Hits* . . . .(Epic)
Lap Of Luxury . . . .(Epic)
Sex, America, Cheap Trick . . . .(Epic)
Flaming
Pink Floyd; *Nice Pair* . . . . (Capitol)
Flaming Agnes
Original Broadway Cast; *I Do! I Do!* . . . .(RCA Victor)
Flaming Telepaths
Blue Oyster Cult; *Career Of Evil* . . . . (Columbia)
Secret Treaties . . . . (Columbia)
Flaming Youth
Kiss; *Destroyer* . . . .(Casablanca)
Frances Farmer Will Have Her Revenge On Seattle
Nirvana; *In Utero* . . . . (David Geffen Co.)
From The Ashes
Martina McBride; *Emotion* . . . . (RCA)
From The Ashes
Rosanne Cash; *The Wheel* . . . . (Columbia)
Fuel
Metallica; *Reload* . . . . (Elektra)
Fuel My Fire
L7; *Hungry For Stink* . . . . (Slash)
Full Of Smoke
Christion; *Ghetto Cyrano* . . . . (Mercury)
Gonna Burn Some Bridges
Ray Price; *For The Good Times/I Won't Mention It Again* . . . . (Columbia)
Great Balls Of Fire
Jerry Lee Lewis; *Billboard Top Rock 'N' Roll Hits-1958-C* . . . . (Rhino)
Jerry Lee Lewis-Original Golden Hits-#1 . . . . (Sun)
Jerry Lee Lewis-Original Golden Hits-#1 . . . . (Sun)
Jerry Lee's Greatest! . . . . (Rhino)
Oldies But Goodies-#12-C . . . . (Original Sound)
Original Memphis Rock & Roll . . . . (Sun)
Rock & Roll Show-C . . . . (Gusto)
Twenty Classic Jerry Lee Lewis Hits . . . . (Original Sound)
Guenevere
Original Cast; *Camelot* . . . . (Columbia)
Original Soundtrack; *ST/Camelot* . . . .(Warner Bros.)
Ha!
Juvenile; *400 Degreez* . . . .(Cash Money/Universal)
Hang Fire
Rolling Stones; *Rewind (1971-1984)* . . . .(Rolling Stones)
Tattoo You . . . . (Virgin)
Hearts On Fire
Eddie Rabbitt; *Best Of Eddie Rabbitt* . . . . (Elektra)
Eddie Rabbitt's All-Time Greatest Hits . . . .(Warner Bros.)
Variations . . . . (Elektra)
Hearts On Fire
Gram Parsons; *Grievous Angel* . . . . (Reprise)
Hearts On Fire
Bryan Adams; *Into The Fire* . . . . (A&M)
Hearts On Fire
Randy Meisner; *One More Song* . . . .(Epic)
Hearts On Fire
Steve Winwood; *Roll With It* . . . . (Virgin)
Heart's On Fire
38 Special; *Strength In Numbers* . . . . (A&M)
Heaven's On Fire
Kiss; *Animalize* . . . . (Mercury)
Hear 'N Aid-C . . . . (Mercury)
Smashes, Thrashes & Hits . . . . (Mercury)
Here I Am
Patty Loveless; *Patty Loveless-Classics* . . . .(Epic)
When Fallen Angels Fly . . . .(Epic)
His Latest Flame
Residents; *The King & Eye* . . . .(Restless)
Hollywood
Wallflowers; *The Wallflowers* . . . . (Virgin)
Hong Kong Fireworks
Henry Mancini; *ST/Revenge Of The Pink Panther* . . . .(EMI)
Hot Like Fire
Aaliyah; *One In A Million* . . . . (BlackGround Enterp./Atlantic)
House Burning Down
Jimi Hendrix; *Essential Jimi Hendrix* . . . . (Reprise)
Jimi Hendrix Experience; *Electric Ladyland* . . . . (Reprise)
House On Fire
Boomtown Rats; *Boomtown Rats' Greatest Hits* . . . . (Columbia)
V Deep . . . . (Columbia)

I Can Feel The Fire
Ron Wood; *Ron Wood* . . . . (Out Of Print)
I Can't Stop The Fire
Eric Martin; *ST/Teachers* . . . . (Capitol)
I Don't Want To Set The World On Fire
Ink Spots; *Best Of The Ink Spots* . . . . (MCA)
If You Love Somebody, Set Them On Fire
Dead Milkmen; *Metaphysical Graffiti* . . . . (Enigma Capitol)
I'm On Fire
Bruce Springsteen; *Born In The U.S.A.* . . . . (Columbia)
Bruce Springsteen & The E Street Band; *Bruce Springsteen & The E Street Band Live/1975-85* . . . . (Legacy)
Dwight Twilley Band; *Super Hits Of The '70s-Have A Nice Day-#15-C* . . . . (Rhino)
Into The Fire
Dokken; *Beast From The East* . . . . (Elektra)
Tooth & Nail . . . . (Elektra)
Into The Fire
Bryan Adams; *Into The Fire* . . . . (A&M)
Into The Fire
Deep Purple; *Deep Purple In Rock* . . . . (Warner Bros.)
Jackson
Johnny Cash & June Carter; *Johnny Cash's Greatest Hits* . . . . (Columbia)
The Man In Black-His Greatest Hits . . . . (Legacy)
Nancy Sinatra & Lee Hazlewood; *Nancy Sinatra-The Hit Years* . . . . (Rhino)
Keep The Candle Burning
Kenny Rankin; *Critics Choice-#2-C* . . . .(Cypress)
Rita Coolidge; *It's Only Love* . . . . (A&M)
Keep The Fire
Kenny Loggins; *Keep The Fire* . . . . (Columbia)
Kenny Loggins Alive . . . . (Columbia)
Keep The Fire Burnin'
REO Speedwagon; *A Second Decade Of Rock And Roll 1981 To 1991* . . . . (Epic)
Good Trouble . . . .(Epic)
Jane Fonda's New & Improved Workout . . . . (Columbia)
Keep The Fire Burning
Louisiana's Le Roux; *Keep The Fire Burning* . . . . (Capitol)
Keep The Home Fire Burning
Latimore; *Get Down Tonight! Best Of T.K. Records-C* . . . . (Rhino)
Latimore III . . . . (Glades)
Millie Jackson; *Get It Out'cha System* . . . . (Spring)
Live & Uncensored . . . . (Spring)
Keeper For Every Flame
Mary Chapin Carpenter; *Stones In The Road* . . . . (Columbia)
Keeper Of The Flame
Martin Page; *In The House Of Stone And Light* . . . .(Mercury)
Keepers Of the Flame
Zamboni Brothers; *The Hockey Zone-C* . . . . (Sportsongs)
Kiss Of Fire
Georgia Gibbs; *Best Of Georgia Gibbs-The Mercury Years* . . . . . . (Chronicles)
Tony Martin; *Best Of Tony Martin On RCA* . . . . (Collector's Choice)
Lake Of Fire
Nirvana; *MTV Unplugged In New York* . . . .(David Geffen Co.)
Let Me Be The One
Blessid Union Of Souls; *Home* . . . . (EMI)
Light My Fire
Doors; *Best Of The Doors* . . . . (Elektra)
Doors . . . . (Elektra)
Doors 13 . . . . (Elektra)
Doors' Greatest Hits . . . . (Elektra)
ST/The Doors . . . . (Elektra)
Jose Feliciano; *Encore-Jose Feliciano* . . . . (RCA)
Jose Feliciano's All-Time Greatest Hits . . . . (RCA)
Light The Sky On Fire
Jefferson Starship; *Jefferson Starship-Gold* . . . . (RCA)
Lilacs & Fire
George Morgan; *Super Country Hits Of The '70s-C* . . . . (Gusto)
Little Chicago Fire
Count Basie & His Orchestra; *Live At El Morocco* . . . .(Telarc)
London's Burning
Clash; *On Broadway* . . . .(Epic)
The Clash . . . .(Epic)
The Story Of The Clash, Volume 1 . . . .(Epic)
Love That Burns
Fleetwood Mac; *25 Years-The Chain* . . . . (Warner Bros.)
Man On Fire
Wood; *Songs From Stamford Hill* . . . . (Columbia)
Matchbox
Carl Perkins; *Carl Perkins-Original Sun Greatest Hits* . . . . (Rhino)
Carl Perkins, Duane Eddy & The Mavericks; *Red Hot + Country-C* . . (Mercury)
Matchbox
Beatles; *Past Masters-Volume Two* . . . . (Parlophone)
Rock 'N' Roll Music . . . . (Capitol)
Something New . . . . (Capitol)
Midnight Fire
Steve Wariner; *Best Of Steve Wariner* . . . . (RCA)
Steve Wariner's Greatest Hits . . . .(RCA)
Molly
Sponge; *Rotting Pinata* . . . . (Work)

Motel Matches
Elvis Costello; *Girls Girls Girls* . . . . (Columbia)
Elvis Costello & The Attractions; *Get Happy!* . . . . (Rykodisc)
Moth & The Flame
Sky Saxon Blues Band; *Full Spoon Of Seedy Blues*. . . . . (Crescendo)
Moth & The Flame, Parts 1-5
Keith Jarrett; *Invocations*. . . . . (ECM)
Mustang Burn
Jack Ingram; *Hey You* . . . . (Lucky Dog)
My Ass Is On Fire
Mr. Bungle; *Mr. Bungle*. . . . . (Warner Bros.)
My Old Flame
Duke Ellington; *Nipper's Greatest Hits Of The '30s-#1-C* . . . .(RCA)
Guy Lombardo & His Royal Canadians; *Guy Lombardo-16 Most Requested*
Songs . . . . (Legacy)
J.J. Johnson; *Trombone Master*. . . . . (Columbia)
Linda Ronstadt; *Lush Life* . . . . (Asylum)
Rosemary Clooney; *Great Girl Singers Sing 22 Original*
Recordings-C. . . . . (Hindsight)
Stan Kenton & His Orchestra; *Road Show* . . . . (Capitol)
Tommy Smith; *Standards* . . . . (Blue Note)
Napalm For Breakfast
Rhythm Devils; *Apocalypse Now Sessions* . . . . (Rykodisc)
New Way (To Light Up An Old Flame)
Joe Diffie; *A Thousand Winding Roads* . . . . (Epic)
Next Thing Smokin'
Joe Diffie; *Regular Joe* . . . . (Epic)
Night The Carousel Burned Down
Todd Rundgren; *Something/Anything?* . . . . (Rhino)
No Smoke Without A Fire
Bad Company; *Dangerous Age* . . . . (Atlantic)
Nuclear Burn
Brand X; *Unorthodox Behaviour*. . . . .(Blue Plate)
Oddfellows Local 151
R.E.M.; *Document*. . . . . (EMI-Capitol Entert. Properties)
Old Flame
Alabama; *60 Years Of Country Music-C*. . . . .(RCA)
Alabama's Greatest Hits. . . . .(RCA)
Feels So Right. . . . .(RCA)
Old Flame
Church; *Priest-Aura* . . . . (Arista)
Old Flame
Juice Newton; *Old Flame* . . . .(RCA)
Old Flames Can't Hold A Candle To You
Dolly Parton; *Dolly Dolly Dolly* . . . .(RCA)
Dolly Parton's Greatest Hits . . . .(RCA)
Joe Sun; *Old Flames Can't Hold A Candle To You* . . . . (Ovation)
Merle Haggard; *Kern River* . . . . (Epic)
Old Flames Have New Names
Mark Chesnutt; *Longnecks & Short Stories*. . . . . (MCA)
Out Of The Frying Pan (& Into The Fire)
Meat Loaf; *Bat Out Of Hell II: Back Into Hell* . . . . (MCA)
Paper In Fire
John Cougar Mellencamp; *The Lonesome Jubilee*. . . . . (Mercury)
John Mellencamp; *Best That I Could Do-1978-1988* . . . . (Mercury)
Pardon Me
Incubus; *Make Yourself*. . . . . (Immortal/Epic)
Paris Is Burning
Dokken; *Breaking The Chains*. . . . . (Elektra)
Penny Lane
Beatles; *Beatles 1*. . . . . (Capitol)
Magical Mystery Tour. . . . . (Capitol)
The Beatles/1967-1970. . . . . (Capitol)
The Beatles-Anthology-#2 . . . . (Capitol)
Phoenix
Cult; *Love* . . . .(Sire)
Phoenix
Wishbone Ash; *Live Dates* . . . . (MCA)
Phoenix
Dan Fogelberg; *Phoenix* . . . . (Full Moon)
Play With Fire
Rolling Stones; *Hot Rocks 1964-1971*. (Abkco)
Out Of Our Heads. . . . . (Abkco)
Singles Collection-The London Years. (Abkco)
Playin' With Fire
Lita Ford; *Dangerous Curves* . . . .(RCA)
Lita Ford's Greatest Hits . . . .(RCA)
Playin' With Fire
Vishugruv; *Vishugruv*. . . . . (Red Light)
Playing With Fire
Lisa Lisa & Cult Jam; *Spanish Fly*. . . . . (Columbia)
Playing With Fire
David Foster; *David Foster* . . . . (Atlantic)
Playing With Fire
Sam Riney; *Playing With Fire* . . . . (Spindletop)
Playing With Fire
Richard Marx; *Rush Street*. . . . . (Capitol)

Porno For Pyros
Porno For Pyros; *Porno For Pyros*. . . . . (Warner Bros.)
Put Out The Fire
Queen; *Hot Space*. . . . .(Hollywood)
Put This Fire Out
Toni Childs; *House Of Hope* . . . .(A&M)
Quest For Fire
Iron Maiden; *Piece Of Mind*. . . . .(Capitol)
Racin' Burnin' Bridges
Ranch Romance; *Blue Blazes*. . . . . (Sugar Hill)
Ring Of Fire
Country Joe McDonald; *Best Of Country Joe McDonald-The Vanguard*
Years-1969-1975. . . . .(Vanguard)
Tonight I'm Singing Just For You . . . .(Vanguard)
Dwight Yoakam; *Guitars, Cadillacs, Etc., Etc.* . . . . (Reprise)
Earl Scruggs & Billy Bob Thornton; *Earl Scruggs And Friends-C* . . . . . (MCA)
Johnny Cash; *All Time Legends Of Country Music-C* . . . .(Legacy)
Billboard Top Country Hits-1963-C . . . .(Rhino)
Classic Cash-Hall Of Fame Series . . . .(Mercury)
Johnny Cash's Greatest Hits . . . .(Columbia)
The Man In Black-His Greatest Hits . . . .(Legacy)
Stan Ridgway & Wall Of Voodoo; *Best Of Stan Ridgway & Wall Of*
Voodoo . . . .(I.R.S.)
Wall Of Voodoo; *Ugly Americans In Australia* . . . .(I.R.S.)
Rockin' With Fire
Isley Brothers; *Showdown* . . . . (T-Neck/Columbia)
Roof Is On Fire
C & C Music Factory; *C & C Music Factory* . . . . (MCA)
Rooms On Fire
Stevie Nicks; *Other Side Of The Mirror*. . . . . (Modern)
TimeSpace-The Best Of Stevie Nicks. . . . . (Modern)
Roses In The Fire
Rosanne Cash; *The Wheel* . . . .(Columbia)
Run To The Water
Live; *The Distance To Here* . . . . (Radioactive/MCA)
Saint Agnes & The Burning Train
Sting; *Soul Cages* . . . .(A&M)
Santa Monica (Watch The World Die)
Everclear; *Sparkle And Fade* . . . .(Capitol)
Season In Hell (Fire Suite)
John Cafferty And The Beaver Brown Band; *ST/Eddie & The*
Cruisers . . . . (Scotti Bros.)
Serpentine Fire
Earth, Wind & Fire; *All 'N All* . . . .(Columbia)
Best Of Earth, Wind & Fire-#2 . . . .(Columbia)
Eternal Dance . . . .(Columbia)
Settin' The Woods On Fire
Hank Williams With His Drifting Cowboys; *24 Of Hank Williams'*
Greatest Hits . . . . (Polydor)
Hank Williams-40 Greatest Hits . . . . (Polydor)
Seventh Avenue
Rosanne Cash; *The Wheel* . . . .(Columbia)
She Keeps The Home Fires Burning
Ronnie Milsap; *Essential Ronnie Milsap* . . . . (RCA)
Shot Down In Flames
AC/DC; *Highway To Hell* . . . .(Atco)
Silence Of A Candle
Oregon; *Essential Oregon* . . . . (Vanguard)
Paul Winter Consort; *Icarus* . . . . (Epic)
Sleep Now In The Fire
Rage Against The Machine; *The Battle Of Los Angeles*. . . . . (Epic)
Sleep That Burns
Be Bop Deluxe; *Best Of And The Rest Of Be Bop Deluxe*. . . . .(Capitol)
Best Of Be Bop Deluxe-Raiding The Divine Archive. . . . .(Capitol)
Sunburst Finish . . . .(Capitol)
Slow Burn
T.G. Sheppard; *T.G. Sheppard's All-Time Greatest Hits* . . . . (Warner Bros.)
Slow Burning Memory
Vern Gosdin; *10 Years Of Greatest Hits Newly Recorded* . . . .(Columbia)
There Is A Season . . . . (Compleat)
Smoke
Ben Folds Five; *Whatever And Ever Amen*. . . . . (Caroline/550)
Smoke
Drivin' N' Cryin'; *Smoke*. . . . .(Island)
Smoke From A Distant Fire
Sanford/Townsend Band; *Smoke From A Distant Fire* . . . . (Warner Bros.)
Smoke From Your Cigarette
Belmonts; *Lost Treasures* . . . . (Relic)
Fabulons; *Harlem Holiday-New York Rhythm & Blues-#7-C* . . . . .(Collectables)
Mellows; *Yesterday's Memories* . . . . (Relic)
Smoke Gets In Your Eyes
Bryan Ferry; *Another Time Another Place*. . . . . (Reprise)
Street Life-20 Great Hits . . . . (Reprise)
Dinah Washington; *Golden Classics-Dinah Washington* . . . .(Collectables)
Lawrence Welk; *Musical Memories With Lawrence Welk*. . . . . (Ranwood)
Patti Austin; *Real Me* . . . . (Qwest)
Platters; *Encore Of Golden Hits-Platters*. . . . .(Mercury)
Oldies But Goodies-#14-C . . . . (Original Sound)

Platters Greatest Hits . . . . (Everest)
ST/Always . . . .(MCA)
ST/American Graffiti . . . .(MCA)
Super Oldies Of The '50s-#5-C . . . . (Audio Fidelity)

Smoke On The Water
Deep Purple; *Deepest Purple/The Very Best Of Deep Purple* . . . . .(Warner Bros.)
Machine Head . . . .(Warner Bros.)
Made In Japan . . . .(Warner Bros.)
Nobody's Perfect . . . . (Mercury)
When We Rock We Rock & When We Roll We Roll . . . .(Warner Bros.)

Smoke Rings In The Dark
Gary Allan; *Smoke Rings In The Dark* . . . . (MCA)

Smoke Signal
Band; *Cahoots* . . . . (Capitol)

Smokescreen
Ted Nugent; *Weekend Warriors* . . . .(Epic)

Smokestack Lightning
George Thorogood & The Destroyers; *Born To Be Bad* . . . .(Gold Rush)
Grateful Dead; *History Of The Grateful Dead-Vol. 1 (Bear's
Choice)* . . . .(Warner Bros.)
Howlin' Wolf; *Best Of Chess Blues-C* . . . . (Chess)
Between The Rails: America's Train Songs-C . . . .(Crescendo)
Blues-#1-C . . . . (Chess)
Moanin' In The Moonlight . . . . (Chess)
Lynyrd Skynyrd; *1991* . . . . (Atlantic)
Muddy Waters; *The Chess Box-Muddy Waters* . . . . (Chess)
Soundgarden; *Ultramega OK* . . . . (SST)
Yardbirds; *Five Live Yardbirds* . . . . (Rhino)
For Your Love . . . . (Accord)
Yardbirds' Greatest Hits-#1 (1964-1966) . . . . (Rhino)

Smokey Day
Zombies; *Time Of The Zombies* . . . . (Bac-Trac)

Smokey Places
Billy Walker; *Billy Walker's Greatest Hits* . . . . (Monument)
Corsairs; *Best Of Chess Rhythm & Blues-#1-C* . . . . (Chess)
Collectables Presents The History Of Rock-#5-C . . . . (Collectables)

Somebody Else's Fire
Janie Fricke; *Somebody Else's Fire* . . . . (Columbia)
Mollie O'Brien; *Every Night In The Week* . . . . (Resounding)

Something's Burning
Kenny Rogers; *Kenny Rogers-20 Great Years* . . . . (Reprise)
Kenny Rogers-Twenty Greatest Hits . . . .(EMI)
Ten Years Of Gold . . . .(EMI)
Mac Davis; *Mac Davis' Greatest Hits* . . . . (Columbia)

Spark
Tori Amos; *From The Choirgirl Hotel* . . . . (Atlantic)

Sparks Of The Tempest
Kansas; *Point Of Know Return* . . . . (Kirshner)

Spit Of Love
Bonnie Raitt; *Fundamental*. . . . . (Capitol)
Lilith Fair-A Celebration Of Women In Music-#3-C . . . . (Arista)

St. Elmo's Fire
John Parr; *Hit Singles-1980-1988-C* . . . . (Atlantic)
Romantic Hits Of The '80s-C . . . . (K-Tel)
ST/St. Elmo's Fire . . . . (Atlantic)

Standing Outside The Fire
Garth Brooks; *In Pieces* . . . . (Liberty)

Still
Macy Gray; *On How Life Is* . . . .(Epic)

Still Burnin' For You
Rob Crosby; *Solid Ground* . . . . (Arista)

Strawberries
Smooth; *Reality* . . . .(Perspective/A&M)

Streets Of Fire
Duncan Browne; *Streets Of Fire* . . . . (Sire)

Streets Of Fire
Bruce Springsteen; *Darkness On The Edge Of Town* . . . . (Columbia)

Streets On Fire
U.K. Subs; *Japan Today* . . . . (Restless)

Streets On Fire
Rhythm Corps; *Common Ground* . . . . (Epic Portrait Assoc.)

Summer's Cauldron
XTC; *Skylarking* . . . .(Geffen)

Sunny Came Home
Shawn Colvin; *1998 Grammy Nominees-C* . . . .(MCA)
A Few Small Repairs . . . . (Columbia)

Swamp Fire
Duke Ellington; *Best Of The Swing Bands-C* . . . . (Hindsight)
Black, Brown & Beige: 1944-1946 Band Recordings . . . . (Bluebird)

Sweet Fire Of Love
Robbie Robertson; *Robbie Robertson*. . . . .(Geffen)

Take Hold Of The Flame
Queensryche; *The Warning* . . . .(EMI)

Tearin' It Up (And Burnin' It Down)
Garth Brooks; *Garth Brooks-Double Live* . . . . (Capitol)

That Old Black Magic
Ella Fitzgerald; *Best Of Ella Fitzgerald* . . . .(MCA)
Big Bands Of The Swinging Years-C . . . . (Everest)

In Rome-Birthday Concert . . . . (Verve)
Frank Sinatra; *Come Swing With Me!* . . . . (Capitol)
Glenn Miller & His Orchestra; *Chattanooga Choo Choo-#1 Hits* . . . . . (Bluebird)
Judy Garland; *Best Of Judy Garland* . . . . (MCA)
Louis Prima & Keely Smith; *Memories Are Made Of This-C* . . . . (Capitol)
Marcels; *Best Of The Marcels* . . . . (Rhino)
Sammy Davis, Jr.; *Hey There-At His Dynamite Greatest* . . . . (MCA)
Spike Jones; *Best Of Spike Jones-#2* . . . . (RCA)

Theme From "Fireball XL-5"
Original Soundtrack; *Television's Greatest Hits-#1-C* . . . . (TVT)

This Wheel's On Fire
Band; *Music From Big Pink* . . . . (Capitol)
Rock Of Ages . . . . (Capitol)
The Band-Anthology-#1 . . . . (Capitol)
Bob Dylan And The Band; *Basement Tapes* . . . . (Columbia)
Byrds; *The Byrds*. . . . . (Columbia)
Ian & Sylvia; *Ian & Sylvia's Greatest Hits* . . . . (Vanguard)
Siouxsie And The Banshees; *Through The Looking Glass* . . . . (Geffen)
Twice Upon A Time-The Singles . . . . (Geffen)

Through The Fire
Chaka Khan; *I Feel For You* . . . . (Warner Bros.)

Timmy Is An Arsonist
Plow; *Shreds-#2: American Underground 1994-C* . . . . (Shredder)

To A Flame
Stephen Stills; *Stephen Stills* . . . .(Atlantic)

To The Fire
Bon Jovi; *7800 Degrees Fahrenheit* . . . . (Mercury)

Trial By Fire
Jefferson Airplane; *30 Seconds Over Winterland* . . . . (RCA)
Loves You . . . . (RCA)
Journey; *Trial By Fire* . . . . (Columbia)

Truck On Fire
White Zombie; *Soul-Crusher* . . . . (Caroline)

Tryin' To Hide A Fire In The Dark
Billy Dean; *Fire In The Dark*. . . . . (Liberty)

Unforgettable Fire
U2; *Unforgettable Fire* . . . . (Island)

Up In A Puff Of Smoke
Polly Brown; *Super Hits Of The '70s-Have A Nice Day-#14-C* . . . . (Rhino)

Vermont Is Afire In The Autumn
Lui Collins; *Made In New England* . . . . (Green Linnet)

Walk Through Fire
Bad Company; *Holy Water* . . . . (Atco)

Walking Through Fire
Mary Chapin Carpenter; *Come On Come On* . . . . (Columbia)

We Didn't Start The Fire
Billy Joel; *Storm Front* . . . . (Columbia)

Welcome To The Occupation
R.E.M.; *Document* . . . . (EMI-Capitol Entert. Properties)

We'll Burn That Bridge
Brooks & Dunn; *Hard Workin' Man* . . . . (Arista)

We've Got A Good Fire Goin'
Don Williams; *Don Williams' Greatest Country Hits* . . . . (Curb)
New Moves . . . . (Capitol)

Wheel, The
Rosanne Cash; *The Wheel* . . . . (Columbia)

Where There's Smoke There's Fire
Blues Project; *No Time Like The Right Time-Best Of The Blues
Project* . . . . (Rhino)

Where There's Smoke There's Fire
Louise Mandrell & R.C. Bannon; *Me & My R.C.* . . . . (RCA)

Which Bridge To Cross (Which Bridge To Burn)
Vince Gill; *When Love Finds You* . . . . (MCA)

Who By Fire
Leonard Cohen; *Best Of Leonard Cohen*. . . . . (Columbia)

Wildfire
Michael Martin Murphey; *'70s Greatest Rock Hits-#3-High Times-C* . .(Priority)
Best Of Michael Martin Murphey. (Liberty)
Blue Sky-Night Thunder . . . . (Epic)
Super Hits Of The '70s-Have A Nice Day-#14-C . . . . (Rhino)

Wildfire Woman
Bad Company; *Straight Shooter* . . . . (Swan Song)

You're Gonna Get Your Fingers Burned
Alan Parsons Project; *Eye In The Sky* . . . . (Arista)
Very Best Live. . . . . (RCA Victor)

FIXING, Repair
See Also: **BREAK, BUILDING & CONSTRUCTION, HOLES, TOOLS**

Back 2 Good
Matchbox Twenty; *Yourself Or Someone Like You*. . . . . (Lava)
Broken Pieces
Strato Vocalz; *Love Shouldn't Hurt-C* . . . . (Qwest)
Cupid
Sam Cooke; *Best Of Sam Cooke* . . . . (RCA)

The Man And His Music ....(RCA)
Spinners; *Love Trippin'* .... (Atlantic)
Everything Falls Apart
Dog's Eye View; *Happy Nowhere* ....(Columbia)
Fixing A Hole
Beatles; *Sgt. Pepper's Lonely Hearts Club Band*. ....(Capitol)
Handy Man
Del Shannon; *Del Shannon's Greatest Hits* ....(Curb)
Del Shannon's Greatest Hits ....(Rhino)
James Taylor; *James Taylor-Best Live* ....(Columbia)
JT ....(Columbia)
Jimmy Jones; *Billboard Top Rock 'N' Roll Hits-1960-C*. ....(Rhino)
Hard To Find 45s On CD-#1-1955-1960-C ....(Eric)
How Can You Mend A Broken Heart
Al Green; *Al Green's Greatest Hits-#1* .... (Motown)
Compact Command Performances-Al Green ....(Motown)
Let's Stay Together ....(Right Stuff)
Bee Gees; *Bee Gees-Gold* ....(Polydor)
Here At Last...Bee Gees...Live ....(Polydor)
Nobody's Child-Romanian Angel Appeal-C .... (Warner Bros.)
Hundred Pounds Of Clay
Gene McDaniels; *Best Of Gene McDaniels-A Hundred Pounds*
Of Clay. ....(Collectables)
Rock Is Dead But It Won't Lie Down-C .... (Gold Rush)
Let Me Be There
Olivia Newton-John; *Let Me Be There* ....(MCA)
Olivia Newton-John's Greatest Hits ....(MCA)
New Beginning
Tracy Chapman; *New Beginning* ....(Elektra)
Only Love Can Break A Heart
Gene Pitney; *Gene Pitney* ....(Everest)
Gene Pitney-Anthology 1961-1968. ....(Rhino)
Love Sixties-C ....(JCI Assoc. Labels)
Pick Of Gene Pitney ....(Fifty One West)
Silver Threads And Golden Needles
Honky Tonk Angels; *Honky Tonk Angels*. ....(Columbia)
Linda Ronstadt; *Don't Cry Now* ....(Asylum)
Hand Sown Home Grown ....(Capitol)
Linda Ronstadt-Retrospective ....(Capitol)
Linda Ronstadt's Greatest Hits. ....(Asylum)
Springfields; *Troubadours Of The Folk Era-#3-C*. ....(Rhino)
Sunny Came Home
Shawn Colvin; *1998 Grammy Nominees-C*. .... (MCA)
A Few Small Repairs. ....(Columbia)
There's A Hole In My Bucket
Disneyland Cast; *Children's Favorite Songs-#4* ....(Disney)
This Ole House
Rosemary Clooney; *Rosemary Clooney-16 Most Requested Songs* ....(Legacy)
Statler Brothers; *The World Of The Statler Brothers* ....(Columbia)
Stuart Hamblen; *Stuart Hamblen-A Man & His Music* .... (Lamb & Lion)
Un-Break My Heart
Toni Braxton; *Secrets* ....(LaFace)
Unglued
Stone Temple Pilots; *Purple* ....(Atlantic)
Wax Ecstatic (To Sell Angeline)
Sponge; *Wax Ecstatic* ....(Columbia)
Woman's Touch
Toby Keith; *Blue Moon* ....(Polydor Country)

FLOOD

See Also: *DANGER & DISASTER, DEATH, DROWN, OCEAN, RIVERS, WATER*

Absolutely (Story Of A Girl)
Nine Days; *Maddening Crowd* .... (550 Music)
Now That's What I Call Music!-#5-C ....(Virgin)
After The Flood
Lone Justice; *Lone Justice* ....(Geffen Goldline)
After The Flood
Talk Talk; *Laughing Stock* .... (Polydor)
Bridge Washed Out
Warner Mack; *Country's Greatest Hits-#3-C* .... (MCA)
MCA Records 30 Years Of Hits-1958-1988-C .... (MCA)
Down In The Flood
Bob Dylan; *Bob Dylan's Greatest Hits-#2* ....(Columbia)
Chris Smither; *Another Way To Find You* .... (Hightone)
Jimmy LaFave; *Trail* ....(Bohemia Beat)
Sandy Denny; *North Star Grassman And The Ravens* ....(Hannibal)
Drowning
Hootie & The Blowfish; *Cracked Rear View*. .... (Atlantic)
Five Feet High And Rising
Johnny Cash; *The Man In Black-His Greatest Hits* ....(Legacy)
Flood
Jars Of Clay; *Jars Of Clay*. ....(Silvertone)
Where Music Meets Film: Live From The Sundance Film
Festival-C ....(Beyond)

Flood
Muddy Waters; *The Chess Box-Muddy Waters* ....(Chess)
Flood
Throwing Muses; *University* .... (Sire)
Flood
Tool; *Undertow* ....(Zoo/Volcano)
Flood
Paul Oakenfold; *Global Underground 002: New York*. ...... (Boxed)
Flood And The Storm
Woody Guthrie; *Ballads Of Sacco & Vanzetti* ....(Smithsonian Collection)
Flood I
Sisters Of Mercy; *Floodland* ....(Elektra)
Flood In Houston
Savoy Brown; *Getting To The Point* .... (Rebound)
Flood Of '57
Stanley Brothers & The Clinch Mountain Boys; *Classic Bluegrass-Stanley*
Brothers & The Clinch Mountain Boys. ....(Rebel)
Flood Of '93
David Olney; *High, Wide And Lonesome*. .... (Philo)
Flood Of Sunshine
Posies; *Dear 23* .... (David Geffen Co.)
Flood Water Blues
Lonnie Johnson; *Complete Recorded Works-#1-1937-1940* ...... (Document)
Flood, The
Original Cast; *Children Of Eden* ....(RCA Victor)
Flood, The
Original Soundtrack; *ST/Noah's Ark* .... (VSI)
Flood, The (Wish I Was In Nashville)
Don Williams; *I've Got A Winner In You*. ....(Universal)
Floodin' In California
Albert King; *Crosscut Saw: Albert King In San Francisco* .... (Stax)
Floods
Pantera; *Great Southern Trendkill*. .... (Atlantic)
Floods Of South Dakota
Modern Hicks; *Out Among The Stars*. ....(Jackalope)
Galveston Flood
Tom Rush; *Best Of Tom Rush: No Regrets*. ....(Legacy)
Here Comes The Flood
Peter Gabriel; *Peter Gabriel*. ....(Atco)
Revisited ....(Atlantic)
Shaking The Tree-Sixteen Golden Greats ....(Geffen)
Last Flood
Die Krupps; *Isolation*. ....(Cleopatra)
Odyssey Of The Mind ....(Cleopatra)
Let It Rain
Mark Chesnutt; *Mark Chesnutt's Greatest Hits* ....(Decca)
Lost In The Flood
Bruce Springsteen; *Greetings From Asbury Park, N.J.* ....(Columbia)
Rain, Rain, Rain
Frankie Laine; *Frankie Laine-16 Most Requested Songs* ....(Legacy)
River, Stay 'Way From My Door
Guy Lombardo & His Royal Canadians; *Auld Lang Syne* ....(Pro-Arte)
Texas Flood
Fenton Robinson; *Somebody Loan Me A Dime* .... (Alligator)
Larry Davis; *Best Of Duke-Peacock Blues-C*. .... (MCA Special Prod.)
Stevie Ray Vaughan and Double Trouble; *Live Alive* .... (Epic)
Stevie Ray Vaughan and Double Trouble ....(Epic)
Taste Of Texas-Songs 'Bout Texas By Texans-C ....(Columbia)
Theme From "Flood"
They Might Be Giants; *Flood*. ....(Elektra)
Wasn't That A Mighty Storm
Eric Von Schmidt; *Troubadours Of The Folk Era-#1-C* ....(Rhino)

FLOORS, Ceilings

See Also: *HOUSES, HOME*

1,2,3,4 (Sumpin' New)
Coolio; *ESPN Presents Jock Jams-#2-C* .... (Tommy Boy)
MTV Party To Go-#9-C. .... (Tommy Boy)
Tommy Boy's Greatest Beats-#2-C .... (Tommy Boy)
25th Floor
Patti Smith Group; *Easter* ....(Arista)
Bodies
Drowning Pool; *Sinner*. .... (Wind-up)
Bound For The Floor
Local H; *As Good As Dead*. ....(Island)
Charlie's Shoes
Billy Walker; *Best Of Billy Walker* ....(Deluxe)
Columbia Country Classics-#4-Nashville Sound-C ....(Columbia)
Dancing On The Ceiling
Chet Baker; *Chet Baker Sings It Could Happen*
To You ....(Original Jazz Classics)
Ella Fitzgerald; *Rodgers & Hart Songbook* ....(Verve)
Frank Sinatra; *In The Wee Small Hours* ....(Capitol)
Dancing On The Ceiling
Lionel Richie; *Dancing On The Ceiling*. ....(Motown)

Floor, The
Johnny Gill; *Provocative* . . . . (Motown)
Freshmen, The
Verve Pipe; *Villains* . . . . (RCA)
Holes In The Floor Of Heaven
Steve Wariner; *Burnin' The Roadhouse Down* . . . . (Capitol)
I'm Not Supposed To Love You Anymore
Bryan White; *Between Now And Forever* . . . . (Asylum)
Jig Saw Puzzle
Rolling Stones; *Beggars Banquet* . . . . (Abkco)
Killin' Floor
Albert King; *Years Gone By* . . . . (Stax)
Howlin' Wolf; *Real Folk Blues-C.* . . . . (Chess)
Jimi Hendrix; *Kiss The Sky* . . . . (Reprise)
Live At Winterland . . . . (Rykodisc)
Jimi Hendrix Experience; *Radio One* . . . .(Rykodisc)
Set 'Em Up Joe
Vern Gosdin; *Chiseled In Stone* . . . . (Columbia)
Greatest Country Hits Of The '80s-1988-C . . . . (Columbia)
Torn
Natalie Imbruglia; *Left Of The Middle* . . . . (RCA)
Two Little Girls
Ani DiFranco; *Little Plastic Castle* . . . .(Righteous Babe)
Walkin' The Floor Over You
Asleep At The Wheel; *Western Standard Time* . . . .(Epic)
Ernest Tubb; *Legend & The Legacy* . . . . (First Generation)
The Ernest Tubb Story . . . .(MCA)
Ernest Tubb/Merle Haggard/Charlie Daniels; *Ernest Tubb Collection-C* . . . . (Step One)
Sandy Denny; *Who Knows Where The Time Goes* . . . . (Hannibal)
Webb Pierce; *Webb Pierce-Golden Hits* . . . . (Plantation)
We Danced
Brad Paisley; *Who Needs Pictures* . . . . (Arista)

FLOWERS: GENERAL, Gardens, Grass, Parks, Plants
See Also: COUNTRY, FLOWERS: ROSES, NATURE, TREES

All The King's Gardens
Joan Armatrading; *Whatever's For Us* . . . . (A&M)
Amapola (Pretty Little Poppy)
Jimmy Dorsey & His Orchestra; *Best Of Jimmy Dorsey & His Orchestra* . . . . (Curb)
April Showers
Al Jolson; *Best Of Al Jolson* . . . .(MCA)
The Al Jolson Story-#2 . . . .(MCA)
Judy Garland; *Hits Of Judy Garland* . . . . (Capitol)
Judy . . . . (Capitol)
Artificial Flowers
Bobby Darin; *The Bobby Darin Story* . . . .(Atlantic)
Azalea
Louis Armstrong & Duke Ellington; *Louis Armstrong & Duke Ellington-Complete Sessions* . . . . (Roulette)
Balboa Park
Bruce Springsteen; *The Ghost Of Tom Joad* . . . . (Columbia)
Bayou Girl
Bob Woodruff; *Dreams & Saturday Nights* . . . . (Asylum)
Berkshire Poppies
Traffic; *Mr. Fantasy* . . . . (Island)
Blossom
Candlebox; *Candlebox* . . . .(Maverick)
Blossoms In The Snow
Skyliners; *Skyliners' Greatest Hits* . . . . (Original Sound)
Blue Gardenia
Nat "King" Cole; *The Nat "King" Cole Story* . . . . (Capitol)
Central Park West
John Coltrane; *Art Of John Coltrane* . . . . (Atlantic)
Best Of John Coltrane . . . . (Atlantic)
Coltrane's Sound . . . . (Atlantic)
Cherry Blossom Time
Columbia Ballroom Orchestra; *Let's Dance-#7-Competition Dance* . . . . (Denon)
Cherry Hill Park
Billy Joe Royal; *Billy Joe Royal's Greatest Hits* . . . . (Columbia)
Super Hits Of The '70s-Have A Nice Day-#1-C . . . . (Rhino)
China Cat Sunflower
Grateful Dead; *Aoxomoxoa* . . . .(Warner Bros.)
Europe '72 . . . .(Warner Bros.)
Without A Net . . . . (Arista)
Come Back As A Flower
Stevie Wonder; *Journey Through The Secret Life Of Plants* . . . . (Motown)
Coming Up
Paul McCartney; *All The Best!* . . . . (Capitol)
Tripping The Live Fantastic-Highlights! . . . . (Capitol)
Crimson And Clover
Joan Jett & The Blackhearts; *I Love Rock 'n' Roll* . . . .(Blackheart)
Tommy James And The Shondells; *Best Of Tommy James And The Shondells* . . . . (Roulette)

Billboard Top Rock 'N' Roll Hits-1969-C . . . . (Rhino)
Jewels-#1-C . . . . (SSS International)
Tommy James And The Shondells-Anthology . . . . (Rhino)
Daisy Jane
America; *America In Concert* . . . . (Capitol)
America Live . . . . (Warner Bros.)
Hearts . . . . (Warner Bros.)
History-Greatest Hits . . . . (Warner Bros.)
Daisy Petal Pickin'
Jimmy Gilmer And The Fireballs; *Best Of Jimmy Gilmer & The Fireballs-Sugarshack* . . . .(Varese Vintage)
Daisys Up Your Butterfly
Cramps; *Stay Sick!* . . . . (Enigma Capitol)
Dandelion
Rolling Stones; *More Hot Rocks (big hits & fazed cookies)* . . . .(Abkco)
Through The Past, Darkly (Big Hits Vol. 2) . . . . (Abkco)
Dead Flowers
Rolling Stones; *Sticky Fingers* . . . .(Virgin)
Steve Earle & The Dukes; *Shut Up And Die Like An Aviator* . . . . (MCA)
Delta Dawn
Bette Midler; *Divine Miss M* . . . .(Atlantic)
Live At Last . . . . (Atlantic)
Helen Reddy; *Helen Reddy's Greatest Hits* . . . . (Capitol)
Tanya Tucker; *Tanya Tucker Live* . . . . (MCA Special Prod.)
Tanya Tucker-Greatest Hits Encore . . . . (Gold Rush)
Tanya Tucker's Greatest Hits . . . . (Columbia)
Edelweiss
Original Cast/Mary Martin; *The Sound Of Music* . . . . (Sony Broadway)
Egyptian Gardens
Kaleidoscope; *Egyptian Candy-Collection* . . . . (Epic)
Side Trips . . . . (Epic)
Elephants & Flowers
Prince; *ST/Graffiti Bridge* . . . . (Paisley Park)
Empty Garden (Hey Hey Johnny)
Elton John; *Elton John's Greatest Hits-1976-1986* . . . . (MCA)
Jump Up! . . . . (MCA)
Fading Like A Flower (Every Time You Leave)
Roxette; *Joyride* . . . . (EMI)
Flower & The Young Man
Strawbs; *Grave New World* . . . . (A&M)
Flower Is A Lovesome Thing
Ella Fitzgerald; *Jazz 'Round Midnight Again* . . . . (Verve)
Frank Morgan; *Lush Life-Billy Strayhorn Songbook* . . . . (Verve)
Vince Guaraldi; *Jazz Impressions* . . . . (Original Jazz Classics)
Flower Lady
Peter And Gordon; *Best Of Peter And Gordon* . . . . (Rhino)
Phil Ochs; *Chords Of Fame* . . . . (A&M)
Pleasures Of The Harbor . . . . (A&M)
The War Is Over-Best Of Phil Ochs . . . . (A&M)
Flowers
Emotions; *Flowers* . . . . (Columbia)
Flowers Are Red
Harry Chapin; *Legends Of The Lost & Found* . . . . (Elektra)
Living Room Suite . . . . (Elektra)
Flowers Mean Forgiveness
Frank Sinatra; *Forever Frank* . . . . (Capitol)
Flowers Never Bend With The Rainfall
Simon & Garfunkel; *Collected Works* . . . . (Columbia)
Parsley Sage Rosemary & Thyme . . . . (Columbia)
Flowers Of Guatemala
R.E.M.; *Life's Rich Pageant* . . . . (EMI-Capitol Entert. Properties)
Flowers Of The Night
Paul Kantner, Grace Slick & David Freiberg; *Baron Von Tollbooth & The Chrome Nun* . . . . (Grunt)
Flowers On The Wall
Eric Heatherly; *Swimming In Champagne* . . . . (Mercury)
Statler Brothers; *All Time Legends Of Country Music-C* . . . . (Legacy)
Best Of The Statler Brothers . . . . (Mercury)
Billboard Top Country Hits-1966-C . . . . (Rhino)
Columbia Country Classics-#3-Americana-C . . . . (Columbia)
Pop Classics Of The '60s-C . . . . (Columbia)
Forget Me Nots
Patrice Rushen; *Patrice Rushen-Anthology* . . . . (Elektra)
Straight From The Heart . . . . (Elektra)
The Disco Years-#2-On The Beat-1978-1982-C . . . . (Rhino)
Four Leaf Clover
Abra Moore; *Strangest Places* . . . . (Arista Austin)
Garden City
Orchestral Manoeuvres In The Dark; *Junk Culture* . . . . (A&M)
Garden Gate
James Gang; *James Gang Rides Again* . . . . (MCA)
Garden In The Rain
Four Aces; *Best Of The Four Aces* . . . . (MCA)
Four Aces' 20 Greatest Hits . . . . (Everest)
Precious Memories . . . . (Accord)
Garden Of Allah
Don Henley; *Actual Miles: Henley's Greatest Hits* . . . . (Geffen)
Garden Of Eden
New Riders Of The Purple Sage; *New Riders Of The Purple Sage* . . . (Columbia)

Garden Of England
Gerry Rafferty; *Right Down The Line-Best Of Gerry Rafferty* . . . . (EMI)
Garden Song
Arlo Guthrie & Pete Seeger; *Precious Friend* . . . . (Warner Bros.)
Garden, The
Magazine; *Magic Murder & The Weather* . . . . (I.R.S.)
Gardening At Night
R.E.M.; *Chronic Town* . . . . (I.R.S.)
Eponymous . . . . (I.R.S.)
Grazing In The Grass
Boney James & Rick Braun; *Shake It Up* . . . . (Warner Bros.)
Hugh Masekela; *Promise Of A Future* . . . . (Uni)
Sixties Rule! Chapter 1-C . . . . (One Way)
Green Green Grass Of Home
Burl Ives; *Best Of Burl Ives-#2* . . . . (MCA)
Elvis Presley; *Elvis Presley Today* . . . . (RCA)
Our Memories Of Elvis, Volume 2 . . . . (RCA)
George Jones; *20 Golden Pieces Of George Jones* . . . . (Bulldog)
Johnny Cash; *Johnny Cash-16 Biggest Hits-#2* . . . . (Legacy)
Tom Jones; *Country Side Of Tom Jones* . . . . (London)
Things That Matter Most To Me . . . . (Mercury)
Tom Jones-London Collector-Greatest Hits . . . . (London)
Green Grow The Lilacs
Tex Ritter; *An American Legend* . . . . (Capitol)
Best Of Tex Ritter . . . . (Capitol)
Best Of Town & Country-#3-C . . . . (Gusto)
Hillbilly Heaven . . . . (Capitol)
Green Grow The Rushes, Ho
Chieftains; *Bonaparte's Retreat* . . . . (Shanachie)
Hard To Make A Stand
Sheryl Crow; *Sheryl Crow* . . . . (A&M)
Hawaiian Lei Song
Les Jansen; *45-#1362* . . . . (Accent)
Heather On The Hill
Gene Kelly; *ST/Brigadoon* . . . . (MCA)
Original Cast; *Brigadoon* . . . . (Columbia Special Prod.)
Hissing Of Summer Lawns
Joni Mitchell; *Hissing Of Summer Lawns* . . . . (Asylum)
Hole In My Soul
Aerosmith; *Nine Lives* . . . . (Columbia)
Holland Park
John Williams; *Echoes Of London* . . . . (Columbia)
Honeysuckle Honey
Commander Cody & His Lost Planet Airmen; *Country Casanova* . . . . . . (MCA)
Hong Kong Garden
Siouxsie And The Banshees; *Once Upon A Time-The Singles* . . . . (Geffen)
House Of Flowers
Barbra Streisand; *Just For The Record* . . . . (Columbia)
Harold Arlen & Barbra Streisand; *Harold Sings Arlen (With Friend)* . . . . (Sony Music Special Prod.)
Original Cast; *House Of Flowers* . . . . (Sony Music Special Prod.)
Hyacinth House
Doors; *L.A. Woman* . . . . (Elektra)
Hyde Park ("Ah, Ooh" Song)
Jeff Kashiwa; *Another Door Opens* . . . . (Native Language)
I Can Hear The Grass Grow
Blues Magoos; *Nuggets-#11-Pop-Part 4-C* . . . . (Rhino)
Move; *Best Of The Move* . . . . (A&M)
I'd Like That
XTC; *Homespun* . . . . (Idea/TVT)
In Bloom
Nirvana; *Nevermind* . . . . (David Geffen Co.)
Inchworm
Danny Kaye; *Billboard Presents Family Lullaby Classics-C* . . . . (Kid Rhino/Rhino 4 Kids)
Victoria Jackson; *Child's Celebration Of Song-#2-C* . . (Music For Little People)
Johnny's Garden
Stephen Stills; *Manassas* . . . . (Atlantic)
Kentucky Flower
King Edward IV & The Knights; *45-#4635* . . . . (Soundwaves)
Lazy Day
Spanky & Our Gang; *Best Of Spanky & Our Gang* . . . . (Rhino)
Let It Grow
Eric Clapton; *461 Ocean Boulevard* . . . . (Polydor)
Eric Clapton-Crossroads-C . . . . (Polydor)
Lilacs & Fire
George Morgan; *Super Country Hits Of The '70s-C* . . . . (Gusto)
Lilies Of The Field
Gretchen Peters; *Gretchen Peters* . . . . (Purple Crayon Prod.)
Lily Of The Valley
Queen; *Sheer Heart Attack* . . . . (Hollywood)
Lily Of The West
Joan Baez; *Joan Baez, Vol. 2* . . . . (Vanguard)
The Joan Baez Ballad Book . . . . (Vanguard)
Lincoln Park Pirates
Steve Goodman; *No Big Surprise: The Steve Goodman Anthology* . . . . (Red Pajama)
Somebody Else's Troubles . . . . (Buddah)

Long Walk, A
Jill Scott; *Who Is Jill Scott? Words And Sounds-#1* . . . . (Hidden Beach/Epic)
Lotus
Tommy Bolin; *Teaser* . . . . (Columbia)
Lotus
R.E.M.; *Up* . . . . (Warner Bros.)
Lotus Blossom
War; *Why Can't We Be Friends* . . . . (Avenue)
Lotus Blossom
Dave Frishberg; *Getting Some Fun Out Of Life* . . . . (Concord Jazz)
Lotus Blossom
Michael Franks; *One Bad Habit* . . . . (Warner Bros.)
MacArthur Park
Andy Williams; *Andy Williams' Greatest Hits-#2* . . . . (Columbia)
Donna Summer; *Live & More* . . . . (Casablanca)
On The Radio-Greatest Hits-Volumes I & II . . . . (Casablanca)
Summer Collection . . . . (Mercury)
Walk Away-Best Of Donna Summer-1977-1980 . . . . . (Casablanca)
Richard Harris; *Love Album* . . . . (MCA)
Richard Harris-His Greatest Performances . . . . (MCA)
Tramp Shining . . . . (MCA)
Vintage Music-#13-C . . . . (MCA)
Waylon Jennings; *Are You Ready For The Country* . . . . (RCA)
Best Of Waylon Jennings . . . . (RCA)
Magnolia
Tom Petty And The Heartbreakers; *You're Gonna Get It!* . . . . (Gone Gator)
Magnolia
Screamin' Cheetah Wheelies; *Magnolia* . . . . (Mercury)
Magnolia
Poco; *Crazy Eyes* . . . . (Epic)
Magnolia
Pat Travers; *Pat Travers* . . . . (Polydor)
Magnolia Moon
Seals & Crofts; *Takin' It Easy* . . . . (Warner Bros.)
Magnolia Triangle
Kansas; *Two For The Show* . . . . (Kirshner)
March Winds And April Showers
Wingy Manone; *Wingy Manone Collection-#3-1934-1935* . . . . (Collector's Classics)
Mmm Bop
Hanson; *1998 Grammy Nominees-C* . . . . (MCA)
Middle Of Nowhere . . . . (Mercury)
Now That's What I Call Music!-#1-C . . . . (Virgin)
Three Car Garage: The Independent Recordings . . . . . . (Mercury)
Mobile Bay (Magnolia Blossoms)
Cal Smith; *Stories Of Life By Cal Smith* . . . . (Step One)
Johnny Cash; *Johnny Cash's Biggest Hits* . . . . (Columbia)
Merle Haggard & George Jones; *Taste Of Yesterday's Wine* . . . . (Epic)
Mocking Bird Hill
Patti Page; *Patti Page-16 Most Requested Songs* . . . . (Legacy)
Patti Page-Golden Hits . . . . (Mercury)
Patti Page's Greatest Hits . . . . (Columbia)
Russ Morgan; *Best Of Russ Morgan* . . . . (MCA)
Moonflower
Santana; *Moonflower* . . . . (Columbia)
Morning Glory
Oasis; *(What's The Story) Morning Glory* . . . . (Epic)
Moss Garden
David Bowie; *Heroes* . . . . (Rykodisc)
Night Blooming Jasmine
Charles Lloyd Quartet; *Night In Copenhagen* . . . . (Blue Note)
October Thorns
Flotsam & Jetsam; *When The Storm Comes Down* . . . . (MCA)
Octopus's Garden
Beatles; *Abbey Road* . . . . (Parlophone)
Beatles-Box Set . . . . (Capitol)
The Beatles/1967-1970 . . . . (Capitol)
Orange Blossom Lane
Glenn Miller & His Orchestra; *Complete Glenn Miller & His Orchestra* . . . . (Bluebird)
Complete Glenn Miller & His Orchestra-#7 . . . . (Bluebird)
Orange Blossom Mandolin
Northeast Winds; *Northeast Winds In Concert* . . . . (Folk Era)
Orange Blossom Special
Bill Monroe; *Bean Blossom* . . . . (MCA)
Bill Monroe and His Blue Grass Boys-60 Years Of Country . . . . (RCA)
Stars Of The Grand Ole Opry-1926-1974-C . . . . (RCA)
Charlie Daniels Band; *Fire On The Mountain* . . . . (Epic)
ST/Urban Cowboy 2 . . . . (Epic)
Flatt & Scruggs; *Hear The Whistles Blow* . . . . (International Mktg. Group)
Gordon Terry; *Disco Country* . . . . (Plantation)
Gordon Terry-20 Golden Souvenirs . . . . (Plantation)
Johnny Cash; *Columbia Records-1958-1986.* . . . . (Columbia)
Essential Johnny Cash . . . . (Columbia)
Johnny Cash-16 Biggest Hits-#2 . . . . (Legacy)
Johnny Cash's Greatest Hits . . . . (Columbia)
The Man In Black-His Greatest Hits . . . . (Legacy)
Train Trax-C . . . . (Sony Music Special Prod.)
Johnson Mountain Boys; *Steel Rails-Classic Railroad Songs-#1-C* . . . (Rounder)

Nitty Gritty Dirt Band; *Will The Circle Be Unbroken* . . . . (EMI)

Orange Blossom Time
Bing Crosby; *Crooner-Columbia Years-1928-1934* . . . . (Columbia)

Orchids Mean Goodbye
Carl Smith; *45-#21087* . . . . (Columbia)

Paddy's Green Shamrock Shore
Chieftains; *Another Country* . . . . (RCA)

Passion Flower
Billy Strayhorn; *Lush Life* . . . . (Red Baron)
Duke Ellington; *Big Band Hits CD Gift Set* . . . . (Capitol)
Piano Reflections . . . . (Blue Note)

Peach Blossom Spring
Yutaka; *Yutaka* . . . . (GRP)

Perfumed Garden of Gulliver Smith
Marc Bolan; *T. Rex Classics* . . . . (Cleopatra)

Playing In God's Garden
Stevie Nicks; *Street Angel* . . . . (Modern)

Please Don't Eat The Daisies
Doris Day; *Doris Day-16 Most Requested Songs-Encore!* . . . . (Columbia)

Plum Blossom
Vangelis; *China* . . . . (Polydor)
Yusef Lateef & Others; *Eastern Sounds* . . . . (Prestige)

Poison Ivy
Coasters; *Atlantic Rhythm & Blues 1947-1974-#4 (1958-1962)-C* . . . . . (Atlantic)
Billboard Top R&B Hits-1959-C . . . . (Rhino)
Coasters' Greatest Hits . . . . (Atco)
Coasters-Their Greatest Recordings-Early Years . . . . (Atco)
More American Graffiti-C . . . . (MCA)
Nylons; *Rockapella* . . . . (Windham Hill)
ST/Stealing Home . . . . (Atlantic)
Rolling Stones; *More Hot Rocks (big hits & fazed cookies)* . . . . (Abkco)

Poisoning Pigeons In The Park
Tom Lehrer; *Dr. Demento Presents The Greatest Novelty Records-C* . . . (Rhino)
Dr. Demento: 20th Anniversary Collection-C . . . . (Rhino)
Evening Wasted With Tom Lehrer . . . . (Reprise)

Poppies
Buffy Sainte-Marie; *Best Of Buffy Sainte-Marie-#2* . . . . (Vanguard)
Illuminations . . . . (Vanguard)
Native North American Child . . . . (Vanguard)

Poppies
Patti Smith; *Radio Ethiopia* . . . . (Arista)

Pretty Wreath For Mother's Grave
Reno & Smiley; *1983 Collector's Edition-#9* . . . . . . (International Mktg. Group)

Purple Heather
Van Morrison; *Hard Nose The Highway* . . . . (Polydor)

Pushing Up Daisies
Garth Brooks; *Scarecrow* . . . . (Capitol)

Pussy Willows Cat Tails
Gordon Lightfoot; *Best Of Gordon Lightfoot* . . . . (EMI)
Lightfoot . . . . (EMI)
Sunday Concert . . . . (EMI)

Rain, The Park And Other Things
Cowsills; *Cowsills* . . . . (Razor & Tie)

Roof Garden
Al Jarreau; *Al Jarreau In London* . . . . (Warner Bros.)
Breakin' Away . . . . (Warner Bros.)

Rosabella
Original Broadway Cast; *The Most Happy Fella* . . . . (Sony Music Classical)

Rose Garden
k.d. lang; *Swingin' Country Favorites-C* . . . . (Warner Bros.)
k.d. lang and The Reclines; *Angel With A Lariat* . . . . (Sire)
Lynn Anderson; *All Time Legends Of Country Music-C* . . . . (Legacy)
Country Music Classics-#4-1970-1975-C . . . . (K-Tel)
Lynn Anderson's Greatest Hits . . . . (Columbia)
Rose Garden . . . . (Columbia)
Super Hits Of The '70s-Have A Nice Day-#4-C . . . . (Rhino)
Very Special Love Song-C . . . . (Fifty One West)

Rose In The Heather
Nazareth; *Hair Of The Dog* . . . . (A&M)

Rose Is Still A Rose
Aretha Franklin; *A Rose Is Still A Rose* . . . . (Arista)

Royal Garden Blues
Bix Beiderbecke; *At The Jazz Band Ball-#2* . . . . (Columbia)
Bix Beiderbecke & His Wolverines; *History Of Classic Jazz-C* . . . . . (Riverside)
Original Broadway Cast; *Black & Blue* . . . . (DRG)
Tommy Dorsey; *Best Of Tommy Dorsey* . . . . (Bluebird)
Complete Tommy Dorsey-#2 . . . . (RCA)

Sagebrush Sports Report
Riders In The Sky; *Riders Radio Theater* . . . . (MCA)

San Francisco (Be Sure To Wear Some Flowers In Your Hair)
Scott McKenzie; *Nuggets-#10-Folk Rock-C* . . . . (Rhino)
Rock Artifacts-From The Vaults-#3-C . . . . (Columbia)
ST/Forrest Gump . . . . (Epic/Sony Music Soundtrax)
Summer Of Love-#1-C . . . . (Rhino)

Sassafras Roots
Green Day; *Dookie* . . . . (Reprise)

Saturday In The Park
Chicago; *Chicago IX-Chicago's Greatest Hits* . . . . (Chicago)

Chicago V . . . . (Chicago)
Chicken Soup For The Soul: I'll Be There For You-Songs Of Friendship,
Brotherhood And Sisterhood-C . . . . (Rhino)
Group Portrait . . . . (Chicago)
If You Leave Me Now . . . . (Chicago)
ST/My Girl . . . . (Epic)
The Heart Of Chicago-1967-1997 . . . . (Reprise)

Scarlet Begonias
Grateful Dead; *From The Mars Hotel* . . . . (Grateful Dead)

Second Hand News
Fleetwood Mac; *25 Years-The Chain* . . . . (Warner Bros.)
Rumours . . . . (Warner Bros.)
Tonic; *Legacy-A Tribute To Fleetwood Mac's Rumours-C* . . . . (Lava)

Secret Garden
Alan Parsons Project; *Eve* . . . . (Arista)

Secret Garden
Bruce Springsteen; *Bruce Springsteen's Greatest Hits* . . . . (Columbia)
ST/Jerry Maguire . . . . (Epic/Sony Music Soundtrax)

Secret Garden
Quincy Jones; *Back On The Block* . . . . (Qwest)

Secret Garden
Johnny Rivers; *Johnny Rivers-Golden Hits* . . . . (Imperial)

Secret Gardens
Judy Collins; *So Early In The Spring, The First 15 Years* . . . . (Elektra)
True Stories & Other Dreams . . . . (Elektra)

Send One Your Love
Stevie Wonder; *Journey Through The Secret Life Of Plants* . . . . (Motown)
Original Musiquarium . . . . (Motown)

Silver Dew On The Bluegrass Tonight
Johnnie Lee Wills; *Tulsa Swing* . . . . (Rounder)

Silver Stars, Purple Sage, Eyes Of Blue
Roy Rogers & Sons Of The Pioneers; *Roy Rogers & Sons Of The*
Pioneers . . . . (Varese Sarabande)

Sky Is A Poisonous Garden
Concrete Blonde; *Bloodletting* . . . . (I.R.S.)

Soldiers In The Park
Ethel Jackson; *Music From The New York Stage (1890-1920)-#1-1890-*
1908-C . . . . (Pearl)

Sugar Magnolia
Grateful Dead; *American Beauty* . . . . (Warner Bros.)
Best Of/Skeletons From The Closet . . . . (Warner Bros.)
Europe '72 . . . . (Warner Bros.)
Grateful Dead-Live-#1 . . . . (JCI Assoc. Labels)

Sunday Afternoon In The Park
Van Halen; *Fair Warning* . . . . (Warner Bros.)

Sunday In The Park With George
Original Cast; *Sunday In The Park With George* . . . . (RCA Victor)

Sunflower
Glen Campbell; *Best Of Glen Campbell* . . . . (Capitol)
Glen Campbell-Live . . . . (Capitol)
Southern Nights . . . . (Capitol)

Sunflower
Mason Williams; *Music-1968-1971* . . . . (Vanguard)

Sunflower River Blues
John Fahey; *John Fahey With Peter Lang & Leo Kottke* . . . . (Takoma)

Sunflower Slow Drag
Dick Hyman; *Scott Joplin-Greatest Hits* . . . . (RCA)
Scott Joplin; *King Of Ragtime Writers* . . . . (Biograph)

Sunshower
Chris Cornell; *ST/Great Expectations* . . . . (Atlantic)

Sweet Little Flower
Sleepy John Estes; *Electric Sleep* . . . . (Delmark)

Sweet Violets
Mitch Miller; *Sing Along With Mitch* . . . . (Columbia)

Tend My Garden
James Gang; *James Gang Rides Again* . . . . (MCA)
James Gang-16 Greatest Hits . . . . (MCA)
Live In Concert . . . . (Mobile Fidelity Sound Lab)

That's Where I Belong
Paul Simon; *You're The One* . . . . (Warner Bros.)

Thorn Tree In The Garden
Derek And The Dominos; *Layla* . . . . (Polydor)

Thorny Patch
John Gorka; *After Yesterday* . . . . (Red House)

Three Flowers
McCoy Tyner; *Soliloquy* . . . . (Blue Note)
Today & Tomorrow . . . . (Blue Note)

Three Flowers
Richard Hayward; *Ireland Of Treasures-Voices & Melodies-C* . . . . . (Capitol)

Thursday Morning Garden Club
Buddy Winfield; *45-#167* . . . . (Nationwide Sound Distrib.)

Tip-Toe Through The Tulips With Me
Tiny Tim; *Dr. Demento Presents The Greatest Novelty Records-#3-*
1960s-C . . . . (Rhino)
Silly Songs-C . . . . (K-Tel)

Touch A Four Leaf Clover
Atlantic Starr; *Atlantic Starr-Classics-#10* . . . . (A&M)
Secret Lovers: Best Of Atlantic Starr . . . . (A&M)

Yours Forever . . . . (A&M)

Tulip Or Turnip (Tell Me Dream Face)
Duke Ellington & Teresa Brewer; *It Don't Mean A Thing If It Ain't Got That Swing* . . . . (Columbia)

Tulip Time
Andrews Sisters; *Capitol Collectors Series-The Andrews Sisters* . . . . . (Capitol)
John Steel; *Music From The New York Stage (1890-1920)-#4-1917-1920-C* . . . . (Pearl)

Tumbling Tumbleweeds
Billy Vaughn; *Billy Vaughn's Greatest Hits* . . . . (Curb)
Gene Autry; *Essential Gene Autry* . . . . (Columbia)
Meat Puppets; *Meat Puppets* . . . . (SST)
Michael Martin Murphey; *Cowboy Songs* . . . . (Warner Western)
Roy Rogers/K.T. Oslin/Restless Heart; *Roy Rogers Tribute-C* . . . . . (RCA)
Sons Of The Pioneers; *The Country Music Hall Of Fame-Sons Of The Pioneers* . . . . (MCA)

Venus Flytrap & The Bug
Stevie Wonder; *Journey Through The Secret Life Of Plants* . . . . (Motown)

Violets & Silverbells
Original Cast; *Shenandoah* . . . . (RCA)

Violets For Your Furs
Frank Sinatra; *Concepts* . . . . (Capitol)
Frank Sinatra-Gift Set . . . . (Capitol)
Songs For Young Lovers & Swing Easy . . . . (Capitol)
Jesse Davis; *Horn Of Passion* . . . . (Concord Jazz)
John Coltrane; *Prestige Recordings* . . . . (Prestige)
Tommy Dorsey & Frank Sinatra; *Sessions-#1-February 1, 1940-July 17, 1940* . . . . (RCA)

Violets Of Dawn
Blues Project; *No Time Like The Right Time-Best Of The Blues Project* . . . . (Rhino)
Eric Andersen; *Best Of Eric Andersen* . . . . (Vanguard)
Troubadours Of The Folk Era-#1-C . . . . (Rhino)

Waltz Of The Flowers
Lawrence Welk; *22 All-Time Favorite Waltzes* . . . . (Ranwood)

Watch The Flowers Grow
4 Seasons; *25th Anniversary Collection* . . . . (Rhino)

When The Cactus Is In Bloom
Jimmie Rodgers; *Down The Old Road-1931-1932* . . . . (Rounder)

When The White Lilacs Bloom Again
Billy Vaughn; *Best Of Billy Vaughn* . . . . (MCA)
Billy Vaughn's Greatest Hits . . . . (Curb)

When You Wore A Tulip
Judy Garland; *Best Of Judy Garland* . . . . (MCA)

Where Have All The Flowers Gone
Johnny Rivers; *Best Of Johnny Rivers* . . . . (EMI)
Johnny Rivers-Anthology 1964-1977 . . . . (Rhino)
Kingston Trio; *Capitol Collectors Series-The Kingston Trio* . . . . (Capitol)
Songs Of Protest-C . . . . (Rhino)
Pete Seeger; *Essential Pete Seeger* . . . . (Vanguard)
Pete Seeger's Greatest Hits . . . . (Columbia)
Peter, Paul & Mary; *Peter, Paul and Mary* . . . . (Warner Bros.)
Wes Montgomery; *Wes Montgomery-Classics-#22* . . . . (A&M)

Where The Green Grass Grows
Tim McGraw; *Big Country Hits '99-C* . . . . (K-Tel)
Everywhere . . . . (Curb)
Tim McGraw's Greatest Hits . . . . (Curb)

White Sport Coat (And A Pink Carnation)
Marty Robbins; *16 Most Requested Songs Of The '50s-#2-C* . . . . (Legacy)
Lifetime Of Song-1951-1982 . . . . (Columbia)
Marty Robbins' Greatest Hits . . . . (Columbia)

Who's Gonna Mow Your Grass
Buck Owens; *Buck Owens' All-Time Greatest Hits-#1* . . . . (Curb)
Buck Owens Collection-1959-1990 . . . . (Rhino)

Wicked Garden
Stone Temple Pilots; *Core* . . . . (Atlantic)

Wild Flowers
Jimmy Smith; *Best Of Jimmy Smith* . . . . (Curb)

Wild Goose Grasses In Tarrytown
Weavers; *Weavers' Greatest Hits* . . . . (Vanguard)
Weavers-Classics . . . . (Vanguard)

Wildflower
Skylark; *Reaching For The Sky-Towering Soul From The '70s-C* . . . . . (Capitol)
Super Hits Of The '70s-Have A Nice Day-#10-C . . . . (Rhino)

Wildflower
Carter Family; *60 Years Of Country Music-C* . . . . (RCA)

Wildflower
O'Jays; *Live In London* . . . . (Philadelphia Int'l)
O'Jays-Collector's Item . . . . (Philadelphia Int'l)

Wildflowers
Dolly Parton/Emmylou Harris/Linda Ronstadt; *Trio* . . . . (Warner Bros.)

Wildflowers In A Mason Jar
John Denver; *Some Days Are Diamonds* . . . . (RCA)

Wildwood Flower
Carter Family; *Legends Of Country Guitar-#2-C* . . . . (Rhino)
Chet Atkins; *Tennessee Guitar Man* . . . . (Pair)
Hank Thompson & Merle Travis; *Great Records Of The Decade-'50s-Pop-#1-C* . . . . (Curb)
Hank Thompson's Greatest Hits-#2 . . . . (Curb)

Kentucky Colonels; *Featuring Clarence White* . . . . (Rounder)

You Are My Flower
Carter Family; *The Country Music Hall Of Fame-The Carter Family* . . . . (MCA)
Nitty Gritty Dirt Band; *Will The Circle Be Unbroken* . . . . (EMI)

You Don't Bring Me Flowers
Barbra Streisand; *Songbird* . . . . (Columbia)
Barbra Streisand & Neil Diamond; *Barbra Streisand's Greatest Hits, Volume 2* . . . . (Columbia)
Just For The Record . . . . (Columbia)
Neil Diamond; *Hot August Night II* . . . . (Columbia)
Neil Diamond & Barbra Streisand; *12 Greatest Hits-#2* . . . . (Columbia)
I'm Glad You're Here With Me Tonight . . . . (Columbia)
You Don't Bring Me Flowers . . . . (Columbia)

FLOWERS: ROSES

See Also: FLOWERS: GENERAL

American Beauty Rose
Frank Sinatra; *Come Swing With Me!* . . . . (Capitol)
Sentimental Journey . . . . (Capitol)

Are The Roses Not Blooming
Judds; *Love Can Build A Bridge* . . . . (MCA)

Arizona Rose
Waco Brothers; *Do You Think About Me* . . . . (Bloodshot)

Artificial Rose
Jimmy C. Newman; *Jimmy C. Newman's Greatest Hits* . . . . (Plantation)

Beanie G & The Rose Tattoo
Daryl Hall & John Oates; *No Goodbyes* . . . . (Atlantic)
War Babies . . . . (Atlantic)

Bed Of Roses
Oak Ridge Boys; *American Dreams* . . . . (MCA)

Bed Of Roses
Warrant; *Cherry Pie* . . . . (Columbia)

Bed Of Roses
Bon Jovi; *Keep The Faith* . . . . (Mercury)

Bed Of Roses
Judy Clay; *Stax Soul Sisters-C* . . . . (Stax)

Black Rose
Waylon Jennings; *Honky Tonk Heroes* . . . . (RCA)
Willie Nelson; *Me & Paul* . . . . (Columbia)

Black Rose
Eric Clapton; *Another Ticket* . . . . (RSO)

Black Rose
J.D. Souther; *Black Rose* . . . . (Asylum)

Black Rose
Sad Cafe; *Misplaced Ideals* . . . . (A&M)

Blue Rose Is
Pam Tillis; *Put Yourself In My Place* . . . . (Arista)

Blue Rose Of Texas
Holly Dunn; *Blue Rose Of Texas* . . . . (Warner Bros.)

Bouquet Of Roses
Eddy Arnold; *Eddy Arnold-Pure Gold* . . . . (RCA)
Eddy Arnold-Super Hits . . . . (RCA)
Eddy Arnold-The Hits . . . . (Mercury)

Bread And Roses
Ani DiFranco & Utah Phillips; *Fellow Workers* . . . . (Righteous Babe)
Judy Collins; *So Early In The Spring, The First 15 Years* . . . . (Elektra)

Buy Me A Rose
Kenny Rogers; *She Rides Wild Horses* . . . . (Dreamcatcher)

Candle In The Wind 1997
Elton John; *Candle In The Wind 1997 (Diana, Princess Of Wales) (Single)* . . . . (Rocket)

Candy And Roses
Sue Thompson; *Sue Thompson's Greatest Hits* . . . . (Curb)

Color Of Roses
Beth Nielsen Chapman; *Sand And Water* . . . . (Reprise)

Cousin Dupree
Steely Dan; *Two Against Nature* . . . . (Giant)

Days Of Wine And Roses
Andy Williams; *Andy Williams' Greatest Hits* . . . . (Columbia)
Andy Williams-16 Most Requested Songs . . . . (Legacy)
Close Enough For Love . . . . (Atco)
Days Of Wine And Roses/Moon River & Other Great Movie Themes . . . . (Columbia)
Dream Syndicate; *Days Of Wine & Roses* . . . . (Slash)
Live At Raji's . . . . (Restless)
Frank Sinatra; *Days Of Wine And Roses, Moon River, And Other Academy Award Winners* . . . . (Reprise)
Henry Mancini; *Best Of Henry Mancini* . . . . (RCA)
Henry Mancini-Pure Gold . . . . (RCA)
Peter Gunn . . . . (RCA)

Dead Flowers
Rolling Stones; *Sticky Fingers* . . . . (Virgin)
Steve Earle & The Dukes; *Shut Up And Die Like An Aviator* . . . . (MCA)

Desert Rose
Chris Hillman; *Desert Rose* . . . . (Sugar Hill)

Desert Rose Band; *Pages Of Life* . . . . (Curb)
Desert Rose
Eric Johnson; *Ah Via Musicom* . . . . (Capitol)
Desert Rose
Sting; *Brand New Day* . . . . (A&M)
Eighteen Wheels And A Dozen Roses
Kathy Mattea; *Collection Of Hits* . . . . (Mercury)
Untasted Honey . . . . (Polydor Country)
Eleven Roses
Hank Williams, Jr.; *Eleven Roses* . . . . (Polydor)
Hank Williams, Jr.-14 Greatest Hits . . . . (Polydor)
Number One Country Hits: '50s Through The '80s-C . . . . (Universal)
Standing In The Shadows . . . . (Polydor)
English Rose
Jam; *All Mad Cons* . . . . (Polydor)
Snap! . . . . (Polydor)
English Roses
Pretenders; *Pretenders II* . . . . (Sire)
Every Rose Has Its Thorn
Poison; *Open Up And Say...Ahh!* . . . . (Capitol)
Rock The First-#5-C . . . . (Sandstone Music)
Swallow This Live . . . . (Capitol)
Everything's Coming Up Roses
Ethel Merman; *Broadway Magic-The 1960s-C* . . . . (Columbia)
Original Cast; *Gypsy* . . . . (Columbia)
Original London Cast; *Gypsy* . . . . (RCA)
For The Roses
Joni Mitchell; *For The Roses* . . . . (Asylum)
Forever Like The Rose
Seals & Crofts; *Takin' It Easy* . . . . (Warner Bros.)
Give Her Thorns & She'll Find The Roses
Roger Whittaker; *Wind Beneath My Wings* . . . . (RCA)
Good Year For The Roses
George Jones & Alan Jackson; *The Bradley Barn Sessions* . . . . (MCA)
Honeysuckle Rose
Ella Fitzgerald & Count Basie; *Classy Pair* . . . . (Pablo)
Perfect Match. . . . . (Pablo)
Fats Waller; *Ain't Misbehavin'* . . . . (Everest)
Fats Waller-Legendary Performer . . . . (RCA)
Nipper's Greatest Hits Of The '30s-#1-C . . . . (RCA)
Piano Solos-1929-1941 . . . . (RCA)
The Joint Is Jumpin'. . . . . (Bluebird)
Turn On The Heat-Fats Waller Piano Solos . . . . (Bluebird)
I Don't Mind Thorns When You're The Rose
Lee Greenwood; *Country Classics-#6-1985-1986-C* . . . . (Universal)
MCA #1 Hits Of The '80s-#2-C . . . . (MCA Special Prod.)
Streamline . . . . (MCA)
I Threw Away The Rose
George Jones; *20 Golden Pieces Of George Jones* . . . . (Bulldog)
Hank Williams, Jr.; *Living Proof-MGM Recordings 1963-1975* . . . . (Mercury)
Lorrie Morgan; *Mama's Hungry Eyes-Merle Haggard Tribute-C* . . . . . (Arista)
Merle Haggard; *Merle Haggard-Best Of The Early Years* . . . . (Curb)
It Must Have Been The Roses
Grateful Dead; *Reckoning.* . . . . (Arista)
Steal Your Face . . . . (Grateful Dead)
Katie, My Southern Rose
William H. Thompson; *Music From The New York Stage (1890-1920)-#1-1890-1908-C* . . . . (Pearl)
Kiss From A Rose
Seal; *Seal 2* . . . . (Sire)
La Vie En Rose
Edith Piaf; *Voice Of The Sparrow-Very Best Of Edith Piaf.* . . . . (Capitol)
Grace Jones; *Island Life* . . . . (Island)
Louis Armstrong; *Louis Armstrong-Best Of The Decca Years-#1-The Singer-C* . . . . (Decca)
Marlene Dietrich; *The Cosmopolitan* . . . . (Columbia)
Melissa Manchester; *Tribute* . . . . (Polydor)
Last Rose Of Summer
Boston Pops Orchestra/Arthur Fiedler; *Irish Album.* . . . . (RCA)
James Galway & The Chieftains; *Over The Sea To Skye-Celtic Connection* . . . . (RCA)
Kiri Te Kanawa; *Come To The Fair* . . . . (Angel)
Phil Coulter; *Sea Of Tranquility* . . . . (Shanachie)
Last Rose Of Summer
Judas Priest; *Sin After Sin* . . . . (Columbia)
Lo, How A Rose E'er Blooming
Beane Family; *Christmas Classics From Around The World* . . . . . (Critique)
John Fahey; *Christmas Guitar-#1.* . . . . (Varrick)
New York City Gay Men's Chorus; *Christmas Comes Anew.* . . . . (Virgin)
Pete Seeger; *Traditional Christmas Carols* . . . . (Smithsonian Folkways)
Philadelphia Brass Ensemble & Eugene Ormandy; *Festival Of Carols In Brass* . . . . (Columbia)
Trapp Family Singers; *Christmas With The Trapp Family Singers* . . . . (MCA Special Prod.)
Vienna Boys Choir; *Christmas Festival-C* . . . . (RCA)
Vienna Boys Choir & Hermann Prey; *Christmas With The Vienna Boys Choir & Hermann Prey* . . . . (RCA)
Lollipops And Roses
Four Preps; *Best Of The Four Preps* . . . . (Curb)

Herb Alpert & The Tijuana Brass; *Herb Alpert & The Tijuana Brass-Classics-#1* . . . . (A&M)
Whipped Cream & Other Delights . . . . (A&M)
Jack Jones; *Jack Jones' Greatest Hits* . . . . (MCA)
Lonely Rose Of Mexico
Sons Of The Pioneers; *Tumbleweed Trails* . . . . (MCA)
Love Is A Rose
Linda Ronstadt; *Linda Ronstadt's Greatest Hits* . . . . (Asylum)
Prisoner In Disguise . . . . (Asylum)
Mexicali Rose
Bing Crosby; *Best Of Bing Crosby* . . . . (Sony Music Special Prod.)
Bob Wills; *Bob Wills-Anthology* . . . . (Sony Music Special Prod.)
Misty Roses
Johnny Mathis; *Johnny Mathis' All-Time Greatest Hits* . . . . . . (Columbia)
Sandpipers; *Four Sider* . . . . (A&M)
Sandpipers' Greatest Hits . . . . (A&M)
Tim Hardin; *Memorial Album.* . . . . (Polydor)
My Brown Eyed Texas Rose
Tex Ritter; *Arizona Days.* . . . . (MCA Special Prod.)
The Country Music Hall Of Fame-Tex Ritter . . . . (MCA)
My Little Georgia Rose
David Grisman; *Home Is Where The Heart Is* . . . . (Rounder)
Herb Pederson; *Son Of Rounder Banjo* . . . . (Rounder)
My Rose Of Old Kentucky
Bill Monroe; *Bill Monroe & Friends.* . . . . (MCA)
Bill Monroe & Flatt & Scruggs; *Bill Monroe And Flatt & Scruggs.* . . . (Rounder)
My Wild Irish Rose
Magic Organ; *22 Great Organ Favorites* . . . . (Ranwood)
Mom & Dads; *One Dozen Roses* . . . . (Crescendo)
New Mexican Rose
4 Seasons; *25th Anniversary Collection* . . . . (Rhino)
New San Antonio Rose
Bob Wills & His Texas Playboys; *Bob Wills & His Texas Playboys-Greatest Hits* . . . . (Curb)
Columbia Country Classics-#1-Golden Age-C . . . . . . (Columbia)
Essential Bob Wills & His Texas Playboys-1935-1973 . . . . (Legacy)
Dwight Yoakam & Asleep At The Wheel; *Ride With Bob-C* . . . . (DreamWorks/SKG)
Oh, The Last Rose Of Summer
Eddie Cantor; *Music From The New York Stage (1890-1920)-#4-1917-1920-C* . . . . (Pearl)
Old Rose Motel
Great White; *Psycho City* . . . . (Capitol)
One Red Rose
John Prine; *Great Days-Anthology* . . . . (Rhino)
Storm Windows. . . . . (Asylum)
One Rose (That's Left In My Heart)
Bing Crosby; *Best Of Bing Crosby* . . . . (MCA)
Leon Redbone; *Champagne Charlie* . . . . (Warner Bros.)
Orchids Mean Goodbye
Carl Smith; *45-#21087* . . . . (Columbia)
Painted, Tainted Rose
Al Martino; *Best Of Al Martino* . . . . (Capitol)
Capitol Collectors Series-Al Martino . . . . (Capitol)
Paper Roses
Kitty Wells; *Kitty Wells' Greatest Hits-#2* . . . . (Step One)
Marie Osmond; *All Time Greatest Hits Of Country-C* . . . . . . (Curb)
Marie Osmond-25 Hits-Special Collection . . . . (Curb)
Paper Rosie
Don Walser; *Here's To Country Music* . . . . (Sire)
Gene Watson; *Gene Watson's Greatest Hits* . . . . (Curb)
Osborne Brothers; *Hillbilly Fever* . . . . (C.M.H. Prod.)
Poisoned Rose
Costello Show (Featuring Elvis Costello); *King Of America* . . . . . . (Columbia)
Elvis Costello; *Girls Girls Girls* . . . . (Columbia)
Poor Man's Roses (Or A Rich Man's Gold)
Patsy Cline; *Best Of Patsy Cline* . . . . (Curb)
Forever & Always . . . . (Epic)
Stop, Look & Listen . . . . (MCA)
The Patsy Cline Story . . . . (MCA)
Reba McEntire; *Feel The Fire* . . . . (Mercury)
Prairie Rose
Roxy Music; *Country Life* . . . . (Atco)
Pretty Pink Rose
Adrian Belew; *Young Lions* . . . . (Atlantic)
Purple Rose Of Cairo
New Orleans Ragtime Orchestra; *New Orleans Jazz-C* . . . . (Arhoolie)
Ramblin' Rose
Hank Snow; *Collector's Series-Hank Snow-#2.* . . . . (RCA)
Nat "King" Cole; *Best Of Nat "King" Cole-Vol. 1.* . . . . . . (Capitol)
Memories Are Made Of This-C. . . . . (Capitol)
Ramblin' Rose
Chuck Berry; *Chuck Berry's Greatest Hits* . . . . (Everest)
Red Red Rose
Dave Mallett; *Vital Signs.* . . . . (Flying Fish)
Emmylou Harris; *Brand New Dance* . . . . (Reprise)
Red Rose
Alphaville; *Afternoons In Utopia* . . . . (Atlantic)

Alphaville-The Singles Collection . . . . (Atlantic)
Red Roses
Midnight Star; *Work It Out* . . . .(Solar)
Red Roses (Won't Work Now)
Reba McEntire; *Have I Got A Deal For You* . . . . (MCA)
Red Roses For A Blue Lady
Al Martino; *Best Of Al Martino* . . . . (Capitol)
Capitol Collectors Series-Al Martino . . . . (Capitol)
Andy Williams; *Andy Williams-16 Most Requested Songs* . . . . (Legacy)
Mom & Dads; *Best Of The Mom & Dads* . . . . (Crescendo)
Roger Whittaker; *All-Time Heart-Touching Favorites* . . . . (Capitol)
Roger Whittaker-Classics Collection-#1 . . . . (Capitol)
Vaughn Monroe; *Best Of Vaughn Monroe* . . . . (RCA)
Redneck Roses
Tracy Byrd; *No Ordinary Man* . . . . (MCA)
Room Full Of Roses
George Morgan; *Columbia Country Classics-#2-Honky Tonk*
Heroes-C . . . . (Columbia)
Mickey Gilley; *Mickey Gilley's Greatest Hits-#1* . . . . (Epic)
Ten Years Of Hits . . . . (Epic)
Rosa De San Antonio
Santiago Jimenez, Jr.; *Mero Mero De San Antonio* . . . . (Arhoolie)
Rose And A Baby Ruth, A
George Hamilton IV; *At The Hop* . . . . (MCA)
Vintage Music-#12-C . . . . (MCA)
Rose Bouquet
Phil Vassar; *Phil Vassar* . . . . (Arista)
Rose By Any Other Name
Ronnie Milsap; *Rose By Any Other Name* . . . . (Warner Bros.)
Rose Garden
k.d. lang; *Swingin' Country Favorites-C* . . . . (Warner Bros.)
k.d. lang and The Reclines; *Angel With A Lariat* . . . .(Sire)
Lynn Anderson; *All Time Legends Of Country Music-C* . . . . (Legacy)
Country Music Classics-#4-1970-1975-C . . . . (K-Tel)
Lynn Anderson's Greatest Hits . . . . (Columbia)
Rose Garden . . . . (Columbia)
Super Hits Of The '70s-Have A Nice Day-#4-C . . . . (Rhino)
Very Special Love Song-C . . . . (Fifty One West)
Rose In Paradise
Waylon Jennings; *Country Classics-#8-1986-1987-C* . . . . (Universal)
MCA #1 Hits Of The '80s-#3-C . . . . (MCA Special Prod.)
New Classic Waylon . . . . (MCA)
Rose In The Garden
Karla Bonoff; *Karla Bonoff* . . . . (Columbia)
Rose In The Heather
Nazareth; *Hair Of The Dog* . . . . (A&M)
Rose Is Still A Rose
Aretha Franklin; *A Rose Is Still A Rose* . . . . (Arista)
Rose Of Cimarron
Emmylou Harris; *Cimarron* . . . . (Warner Bros.)
Poco; *Backtracks* . . . . (MCA)
Rose Of Cimarron . . . . (MCA)
Rose Of England
Nick Lowe; *Basher: Best Of* . . . . (Columbia)
Rose Of Old Monterey
Happy Polkateers; *Happy Polkateers* . . . . (Crescendo)
Rose Of San Antone
Bashful Brother Oswald; *Don't Say Aloha* . . . . (Rounder)
Rose Of The Rio Grande
Bob Crosby & His Orchestra; *Bob Crosby & His Orchestra Play 22 Original*
Big Band Hits . . . . (Hindsight)
Duke Ellington; *Great Paris Concert* . . . . (Atlantic)
Ella Fitzgerald & Duke Ellington; *At The Cote D'Azur* . . . . (Verve)
Rose Of Tralee
Bing Crosby; *When Irish Eyes Are Smiling* . . . . (MCA)
Patrick O'Hagan; *22 Golden Shamrocks* . . . .(Rego Irish)
Rose Room
Benny Goodman; *I Like Jazz-Essence Of Benny Goodman* . . . . (Columbia)
Charlie Christian; *Genius Of The Electric Guitar* . . . . (Columbia)
Rose Tint In My World
Tim Curry & Original Roxy Cast; *Rocky Horror Show* . . . . (Rhino)
Rose, The
Bette Midler; *Hit Singles-1980-1988-C* . . . . (Atlantic)
ST/The Rose . . . . (Atlantic)
Conway Twitty; *Dream Maker* . . . . (Elektra)
Latest Greatest Hits-#1 . . . . (Warner Bros.)
Number One's: The Warner Bros. Years . . . . (Warner Bros.)
Roses
Jim Reeves; *Jim Reeves* . . . . (RCA)
Moonlight & Roses . . . . (RCA)
Roses
Janis Ian; *Aftertones* . . . . (Columbia)
Roses & Thorns
Jeannie C. Riley; *Jeannie* . . . . (Plantation)
Roses Ain't Red
Diane Pfeifer; *Diane Pfeifer* . . . . (Capitol)
Roses Are Red
Bobby Vinton; *Bobby Vinton-16 Most Requested Songs* . . . . (Legacy)

Bobby Vinton's All-Time Greatest Hits . . . . (Epic)
Spring Sensations . . . . (Epic)
Roses For Mama
C.W. McCall; *C.W. McCall's Greatest Hits* . . . . (Polydor)
Roses In The Fire
Rosanne Cash; *The Wheel* . . . . (Columbia)
Roses In The Snow
Emmylou Harris; *Roses In The Snow* . . . . (Warner Bros.)
Roses In The Winter
Merle Haggard; *Merle Haggard-His Best* . . . . (MCA)
Serving 190 Proof . . . . (MCA)
Run For The Roses
Dan Fogelberg; *Dan Fogelberg/Greatest Hits* . . . . (Full Moon)
Innocent Age . . . . (Full Moon)
Live-Greetings From The West . . . . (Full Moon)
Sally Go Round The Roses
Jaynettes; *Best Of Chess Rock 'N' Roll-#1-C* . . . . (Chess)
Cruisin'-1963-C . . . . (Increase)
Girl Groups-Story Of A Sound-C . . . . (Rhino)
Wonder Women-History Of Girl Group Sound-C . . . . (Rhino)
Yvonne Elliman; *Night Flight* . . . . (RSO)
San Antonio Rose
Asleep At The Wheel; *Western Standard Time* . . . . (Epic)
Bob Wills; *Best Of Bob Wills-#2* . . . . (MCA)
Sounds Of Texas . . . . (Capitol)
Texas State Of Mind-C . . . . (Capitol)
Floyd Cramer; *Billboard Top Country Hits-1961-C* . . . . (Rhino)
Country Love . . . . (Step One)
Patsy Cline; *The Patsy Cline Story* . . . . (MCA)
Ricky Skaggs; *Comin' Home To Stay* . . . . (Epic)
Willie Nelson; *What A Wonderful World* . . . .(Columbia)
San Antonio Rose To You
Rick Trevino; *Texas Super Hits-C* . . . .(Columbia)
Spanish Harlem
Aretha Franklin; *Aretha Franklin-30 Greatest Hits* . . . . (Rhino)
Best Of Aretha Franklin . . . . (Atlantic)
Ten Years Of Gold . . . . (Atlantic)
Ben E. King; *Ben E. King's Greatest Hits* . . . . (Atco)
Phil Spector-Back To Mono 1958-1969-C . . . . (Abkco)
Crusaders; *Crusaders-At Their Best* . . . . (Motown)
Drifters; *Drifters' Greatest Hits* . . . . (Gusto)
Spanish Rose
Santana; *Inner Secrets* . . . .(Columbia)
Spanish Rose
Van Morrison; *Bang Masters* . . . . (Epic)
Stop & Smell The Roses
Mac Davis; *Mac Davis' Greatest Hits* . . . . (Columbia)
Stop And Smell The Roses . . . . (Columbia)
Summer Of Roses
Willie Nelson; *Tougher Than Leather* . . . . (Columbia)
Sweet And Lovely
Bing Crosby; *Pennies From Heaven* . . . .(Pro-Arte)
Thelonius Monk; *Monk's Dream* . . . . (Columbia)
Woody Herman; *Essential Big Bands-C* . . . .(Verve)
Teardrop On A Rose
Hank Williams; *Alone With His Guitar* . . . . (Mercury)
Let's Turn Back The Years-1951-1953 . . . . (Polydor)
Tennessee Rose
Emmylou Harris; *Cimarron* . . . . (Warner Bros.)
Texas Rose Cafe
Little Feat; *Sailin' Shoes* . . . . (Warner Bros.)
Thank You For The Roses
Kitty Wells; *Kitty Wells' Greatest Hits* . . . . (Step One)
That's Where I Belong
Paul Simon; *You're The One* . . . . (Warner Bros.)
Throw The Roses Away
Daryl Hall & John Oates; *Marigold Sky* . . . .(Push)
Tiger Rose
Robert Hunter; *Tiger Rose* . . . . (Rykodisc)
'Til A Tear Becomes A Rose
Jann Browne; *Tell Me Why* . . . .(Curb)
'Til A Tear Becomes A Rose . . . .(Curb)
Keith Whitley; *Keith Whitley's Greatest Hits* . . . . (RCA)
Lorrie Morgan; *Lorrie Morgan's Greatest Hits* . . . . (BNA)
Till There Was You
Beatles; *Beatles-Box Set* . . . .(Capitol)
Meet The Beatles! . . . .(Capitol)
With The Beatles . . . . (Parlophone)
Original Cast; *ST/The Music Man* . . . . (Warner Bros.)
'Tis The Last Rose Of Summer
Lucy Shelton & Others; *Moore's Irish Melodies* . . . .(Nonesuch)
Two Dozen Roses
Shenandoah; *30 Years Of #1 Hits-#20-C* . . . . (Columbia)
Road Not Taken . . . . (Columbia)
Shenandoah's Greatest Hits . . . . (Columbia)
When The Roses Bloom Again
Glenn Miller & His Orchestra; *Complete Glenn Miller & His*
Orchestra . . . .(Bluebird)

Johnny Cash; *Essential Johnny Cash* . . . . (Columbia)

When The Snow Is On The Roses
Ed Ames; *Best Of Ed Ames* . . . . (RCA)
   Ed Ames-Pure Gold . . . . (RCA)
Sonny James; *American Originals-Sonny James* . . . . (Columbia)
   Sonny James' Greatest Hits . . . . (Columbia)

When You Wore A Tulip
Judy Garland; *Best Of Judy Garland* . . . .(MCA)

Winter Rose Love Awake
Wings; *Back To The Egg* . . . . (Capitol)

World Is Waiting For The Sunrise
Benny Goodman; *I Like Jazz-Essence Of Benny Goodman* . . . . (Columbia)
Benny Goodman Orchestra & Quartet; *Let's Dance* . . . . (Laserlight)
Les Paul & Mary Ford; *The World Is Waiting For The Sunrise* . . . . (Laserlight)
Roy Clark & Buck Trent; *Banjo Bandit* . . . .(MCA)

Yankee Rose
David Lee Roth; *Eat 'Em & Smile* . . . .(Warner Bros.)

Yellow Rose
Johnny Lee & Lane Brody; *'Til The Bars
   Burn Down* . . . .(Full Moon/Warner Bros.)
   You & I-Classic Country Duets-C . . . .(Warner Bros.)

Yellow Rose Of Texas
Hoyt Axton; *Songs Of The Civil War-C* . . . . (Columbia)
Michael Martin Murphey; *Cowboy Songs* . . . . (Warner Western)
Mitch Miller; *Mitch Miller-16 Most Requested Songs* . . . . (Columbia)
Roy Rogers; *Great American Singing Cowboys-C* . . . .(Republic/Universal)

Yellow Roses
Dolly Parton; *Greatest Country Hits Of The '80s-1989-C* . . . . (Columbia)
   White Limozeen . . . . (Columbia)

Yellow Roses
Ry Cooder; *Chicken Skin Music* . . . . (Reprise)

Yellow Roses On Her Gown
Johnny Mathis; *I Only Have Eyes For You* . . . . (Columbia)

FLYING, Flight

**See Also: *AIR, AIRPLANES, ANGELS, ANIMALS: BIRDS, DRUGS
(various), SKY***

(Just Like) Starting Over
John Lennon & Yoko Ono; *Double Fantasy* . . . . (Capitol)
   ST/Imagine: John Lennon . . . . (Capitol)

(Your Love Keeps Lifting Me) Higher And Higher
Bette Midler; *Bette Midler* . . . .(Atlantic)
Bonnie Bramlett; *It's Time* . . . . (Capricorn)
Jackie Wilson; *Billboard Top R&B Hits-1967-C* . . . . (Rhino)
   Jackie Wilson's Greatest Hits . . . . (Brunswick)
   Jackie Wilson's Greatest Hits-#2 . . . . (Brunswick)
   Reet Petite-Best Of Jackie Wilson . . . . (Columbia)
   The Jackie Wilson Story . . . .(Epic)
   Very Best Of Jackie Wilson . . . . (Rhino)
Rita Coolidge; *Anytime...Anywhere* . . . . (A&M)
   Havana Jam . . . . (Columbia)
   Rita Coolidge-Classics-#5 . . . . (A&M)
   Rita Coolidge's Greatest Hits . . . . (A&M)

20 Flight Rock
Eddie Cochran; *Great Hits* . . . . (Liberty)
Montrose; *Montrose* . . . .(Warner Bros.)

Above The Clouds
Electric Light Orchestra; *New World Record* . . . . (Jet)

African Night Flight
David Bowie; *Lodger* . . . .(Rykodisc)

Angel
Jimi Hendrix; *Cry Of Love* . . . . (Reprise)
   Experience Hendrix: The Best Of Jimi Hendrix . . . .(MCA)
   First Rays Of The New Rising Sun . . . . (MCA)
Rod Stewart; *Best Of Rod Stewart* . . . . (Mercury)

Angel Flying Too Close To The Ground
Willie Nelson; *Greatest Hits (& Some That Will Be)* . . . . (Columbia)
   ST/Honeysuckle Rose . . . . (Columbia)

Angel Spread Your Wings
Judy Collins; *Judith* . . . . (Elektra)

Angels In Waiting
Tammy Cochran; *Tammy Cochran* . . . .(Epic)

Army Air Corps
Fred Waring's Pennsylvanians; *Very Best Of Fred Waring & The
   Pennsylvanians* . . . . (Reader's Digest Music)
Glenn Miller; *Best Of The Lost Recordings And The Secret
   Broadcasts* . . . .(RCA Victor)
   V-Disc Recordings-Glenn Miller . . . . (Collector's Choice)

Around The World In Eighty Days
Boston Pops Orchestra/Arthur Fiedler; *Greatest Hits Of The '50s-#2* . . . . (RCA)
Frank Sinatra; *Come Fly With Me* . . . . (Capitol)
Roger Williams; *Roger Williams' Greatest Hits* . . . .(MCA)
Victor Young & His Singing Strings; *Hollywood's Greatest Hits-#2* . . . . (Telarc)

Bermuda Triangle
Fleetwood Mac; *Heroes Are Hard To Find* . . . . (Reprise)

Bermuda Triangle Blues (Flight 45)
Blondie; *Plastic Letters* . . . . (Chrysalis)

Blackbird
Beatles; *Beatles-Box Set* . . . . (Capitol)
   The Beatles (White Album) . . . . (Capitol)
Crosby, Stills & Nash; *CSN* . . . .(Atlantic)
Paul McCartney; *Unplugged (The Official Bootleg)* . . . . (Capitol)
Wings; *Wings Over America* . . . . (Capitol)

Blue Sky
Patty Griffin; *Flaming Red* . . . . (A&M)

Bomber Medley
James Gang; *Best Of The James Gang* . . . . (MCA)
   James Gang Rides Again . . . . (MCA)

Born To Fly
Sara Evans; *Born To Fly* . . . .(RCA)

Broken Wing
Martina McBride; *Evolution* . . . . (RCA)

Broken Wings
Mr. Mister; *Nipper's Greatest Hits Of The '80s-C* . . . . (RCA)
   Welcome To The Real World . . . . (RCA)

Broken Wings
Chris DeBurgh; *At The End Of A Perfect Day* . . . . (A&M)

Bumble Boogie
Freddy Martin; *Big Band In Hi Fi-#1-Let's Dance* . . . . (Capitol)

Bumble Boogie
Jo Ann Castle; *Legends Of Accordion-C* . . . . (Rhino)

Butterfly
Mariah Carey; *Butterfly* . . . . (Columbia)

Butterflyz
Alicia Keys; *Songs In A Minor* . . . . (J)

Caged Bird
Alicia Keys; *Songs In A Minor* . . . . (J)

Carried Away
George Strait; *Blue Clear Sky* . . . . (MCA)
   Latest Greatest Straitest Hits . . . . (MCA)

Come Fly With Me
Frank Sinatra; *At The Sands* . . . . (Reprise)
   Come Fly With Me . . . . (Capitol)
   Sinatra: A Man And His Music . . . . (Reprise)
   The Capitol Years . . . . (Capitol)

Comin' In On A Wing & A Prayer
Anita Ellis; *Songs That Won The War-C* . . . . . . (Columbia River Entert. Group)
Anne Shelton; *V-E Day 50th Anniversary-The Musical
   Memories-C* . . . . (Living Era)
Four Vagabonds; *The Victory Collection: The Smithsonian Remembers When
   America Went To War-C* . . . . (RCA)
Ry Cooder; *Boomer's Story* . . . . (Reprise)

Coming Into Los Angeles
Arlo Guthrie; *Best Of Arlo Guthrie* . . . . (Warner Bros.)
   Running Down The Road . . . . (Reprise)
   ST/Woodstock . . . .(Atlantic)

Cowboy Take Me Away
Dixie Chicks; *Fly* . . . . (Monument)

Cruisin'
D'Angelo; *Brown Sugar* . . . . (EMI)
Huey Lewis and Gwyneth Paltrow; *ST/Duets* . . . . (Hollywood)
Smokey Robinson; *Compact Command Performances-Smokey
   Robinson* . . . . (Motown)
   Motown Love Songs-C . . . . (Motown)
   Motown Story-First 25 Years-C . . . . (Motown)
   Where There's Smoke . . . . (Motown)

Danger Zone
Kenny Loggins; *ST/Top Gun* . . . . (Columbia)

De Bat (Fly In Me Face)
Carly Simon; *Boys In The Trees* . . . . (Elektra)

Down Here On The Ground
George Benson; *Weekend In L.A.* . . . .(Warner Bros.)

Eight Miles High
Byrds; *Fifth Dimension* . . . . (Columbia)
   Original Singles-#1-1965-1967 . . . . (Columbia)
   The Byrds . . . . (Columbia)
   The Byrds (Untitled) . . . . (Legacy)
   The Byrds' Greatest Hits . . . . (Columbia)
Leo Kottke; *Best Of Leo Kottke* . . . . (Capitol)
   Mudlark . . . . (Capitol)
Roxy Music; *Flesh + Blood* . . . . (Atco)

Elevation
U2; *All That You Can't Leave Behind* . . . . (Interscope)

Expecting To Fly
Buffalo Springfield; *Buffalo Springfield* . . . . (Atco)
   Buffalo Springfield Again . . . . (Atco)
   Buffalo Springfield-Retrospective . . . . (Atco)
Neil Young; *Decade* . . . . (Reprise)

Fear Of Falling
Badlees; *River Songs* . . . . (Atlas)

Flamingos Fly
Sammy Hagar; *Nine On A Ten Scale* . . . . (Capitol)
Van Morrison; *Period Of Transition* . . . .(Warner Bros.)

Flight (505)
Rolling Stones; *Aftermath* . . . . (Abkco)
Flight (The Higher We Fly)
John Denver; *It's About Time* . . . . (RCA)
Flight 602
Chicago; *Chicago At Carnegie Hall* . . . . (Chicago)
   Chicago III . . . . (Chicago)
   Group Portrait . . . . (Chicago)
Flight Of Icarus
Iron Maiden; *Live After Death-World Slavery Tour* . . . . (Capitol)
   Piece Of Mind . . . . (Capitol)
Flight Of The Fly
Dan Hicks & His Hot Licks; *Striking It Rich!* . . . . (MCA)
Fly
Al Jarreau; *All Fly Home* . . . . (Warner Bros.)
Chubby Checker; *Chubby Checker's Greatest Hits* . . . . (Everest)
   Echoes Of A Rock Era-Later Years-C . . . . (Roulette)
Fly
Sugar Ray; *Floored* . . . . (Atlantic)
Fly (The Angel Song)
Wilkinsons; *Nothing But Love* . . . . (Giant)
Fly Away
Peter Allen; *Best Of Peter Allen* . . . . (A&M)
   Bi-Coastal . . . . (A&M)
Fly Away
Lenny Kravitz; *5* . . . . (Virgin)
   Now That's What I Call Music!-#1-C . . . . (Virgin)
Fly Away
Patty Loveless; *If My Heart Had Windows* . . . . (MCA)
Fly Away
John Denver; *John Denver's Greatest Hits-#2* . . . . (RCA)
   Windsong . . . . (RCA)
Fly Away
Blackfoot; *Maurader* . . . . (Atco)
Fly Away Home
Ozark Mountain Daredevils; *Best Of The Ozark Mountain Daredevils* . . . (A&M)
   Men From Earth . . . . (A&M)
Fly By Night
Rush; *All The World's A Stage* . . . . (Mercury)
   Archives . . . . (Mercury)
   Fly By Night . . . . (Mercury)
Fly Fly Fly
Brewer & Shipley; *On The Road Again* . . . . (Accord)
Fly Into Night
Charly McClain; *Charly McClain's Biggest Hits* . . . . (Epic)
   Paradise . . . . (Epic)
Fly Into The Sun
Lou Reed; *New Sensations* . . . . (RCA)
Fly Into This Night
Gino Vannelli; *Best Of Gino Vannelli* . . . . (A&M)
   Gino Vannelli-Classics-#7 . . . . (A&M)
   Gist Of The Gemini . . . . (A&M)
Fly Like An Eagle
Seal; *ST/Space Jam* . . . . (Warner Sunset)
Steve Miller; *Fly Like An Eagle* . . . . (Capitol)
   ST/FM . . . . (MCA)
   Steve Miller Band-Gift Set . . . . (Capitol)
   Steve Miller Band-Live . . . . (Capitol)
   Steve Miller Band's Greatest Hits-1974-78 . . . . (Capitol)
Fly Me Courageous
Drivin' N' Cryin'; *Fly Me Courageous* . . . . (Island)
Fly Me To The Moon
Frank Sinatra; *At The Sands* . . . . (Reprise)
   It Might As Well Be Swing . . . . (Reprise)
   Sinatra: A Man And His Music . . . . (Reprise)
   The Reprise Collection . . . . (Reprise)
Fly, Robin, Fly
Silver Convention; *Best Of Silver Convention-Get Up And Boogie* . . . (Hot Prod.)
Flyer
Saga; *Heads Or Tales* . . . . (Portrait)
Flyin' High
Yularaq; *Future Tribe* . . . . (Higher Octave)
Flyin' High In The Friendly Sky
Marvin Gaye; *What's Going On* . . . . (Motown)
Flying
Beatles; *Beatles-Box Set* . . . . (Capitol)
   Magical Mystery Tour . . . . (Capitol)
Flying
Chris Isaak; *Speak Of The Devil* . . . . (Reprise)
Flying Away
Mary J. Blige; *No More Drama* . . . . (MCA)
Flying Cloud
Doobie Brothers; *What Were Once Vices Are Now Habits* . . . . . . (Warner Bros.)
Flying Colours
Jethro Tull; *The Broadsword And The Beast* . . . . (Chrysalis)
Flying High
Country Joe & The Fish; *Collected-1965-1970* . . . . (Vanguard)
   Life & Times Of Country Joe & The Fish . . . . (Vanguard)

Flying High
Karla Bonoff; *Karla Bonoff* . . . . (Columbia)
Flying High
Commodores; *Natural High* . . . . (Motown)
Flying High Again
Ozzy Osbourne; *Diary Of A Madman* . . . . (Jet)
   Tribute . . . . (Epic)
Flying Home
Benny Goodman; *Jazz Sampler-#6-C* . . . . (Columbia)
Ella Fitzgerald; *Best Of Ella Fitzgerald* . . . . (MCA)
Ella Fitzgerald & Count Basie; *Pablo Live* . . . . (Pablo)
Lionel Hampton & His Orchestra; *Flying Home* . . . . (Dunhill Compact Classics)
Flying On The Ground Is Wrong
Buffalo Springfield; *Buffalo Springfield* . . . . (Atco)
Flying Turkey Trot
REO Speedwagon; *A Decade Of Rock And Roll 1970 To 1980* . . . . (Epic)
   R.E.O. . . . . (Epic)
   REO Speedwagon Live/You Get What You Play For . . . . (Epic)
Free Fallin'
Tom Petty; *Full Moon Fever* . . . . (MCA)
Ghost Of Flight 401
Bob Welch; *Three Hearts* . . . . (Capitol)
Ginny The Flying Girl
Janis Ian; *In Harmony 2-C* . . . . (Columbia)
Give Me Wings
Michael Johnson; *Best Of Michael Johnson* . . . . (RCA)
   Hits Of '86-C . . . . (RCA)
   Wings . . . . (RCA)
Given To Fly
Pearl Jam; *Yield* . . . . (Epic)
Gonna Fly Now
Bill Conti; *ST/Rocky* . . . . (Liberty)
   ST/Rocky II . . . . (EMI)
   ST/Rocky III . . . . (EMI)
Growin' Up
Bruce Springsteen; *Greetings From Asbury Park, N.J.* . . . . . . (Columbia)
   Live 1975-1985 . . . . (Legacy)
   Tracks . . . . (Columbia)
Bruce Springsteen & The E Street Band; *Bruce Springsteen & The E Street Band Live/1975-85* . . . . (Legacy)
High Flying Bird
Elton John; *Don't Shoot Me I'm Only The Piano Player* . . . . (Polydor)
High Flying, Adored
Original Cast; *Evita* . . . . (MCA)
I Believe I Can Fly
R. Kelly; *1998 Grammy Nominees-C* . . . . (MCA)
   R. . . . . (Jive)
   ST/Space Jam . . . . (Warner Sunset)
I Get A Kick Out Of You
Ethel Merman with Johnny Green & His Orchestra; *The Ethel Merman Collection* . . . . (Razor & Tie)
   This Is Art Deco-C . . . . (Columbia)
Frank Sinatra; *My One & Only Love* . . . . (Capitol)
   Round #1 . . . . (Capitol)
   Sinatra and Swingin' Brass . . . . (Reprise)
   Sinatra-The Main Event Live . . . . (Reprise)
   The Capitol Years . . . . (Capitol)
   The Reprise Collection . . . . (Reprise)
Original Cast; *Anything Goes* . . . . (Epic)
Paul Whiteman & His Orchestra; *78-#24769* . . . . (Victor)
Icarus
Paul Winter; *Common Ground* . . . . (A&M)
Paul Winter Consort; *Earthdance* . . . . (A&M)
   Icarus . . . . (Epic)
   Pioneers Of The New Age . . . . (Columbia)
   Road . . . . (A&M)
If My Heart Had Wings
Faith Hill; *Breathe* . . . . (Warner Bros.)
I'll Fly Away
Aretha Franklin; *Diana, Princess Of Wales-Tribute-C* . . . . . . (Columbia)
I'll Fly Away
Gillian Welch & Alison Krauss; *ST/O Brother, Where Art Thou?* . . . (Mercury)
I'm Flying
Original Cast/Mary Martin; *Peter Pan-The 1954 Broadway Production* . . . . (RCA Victor)
I'm Like A Bird
Nelly Furtado; *Whoa Nelly!* . . . . (DreamWorks/SKG)
I'm Mandy Fly Me
10 CC; *10 CC's Greatest Hits-1972-1978* . . . . (Polydor)
   How Dare You! . . . . (Mercury)
   Live & Let Live . . . . (Mercury)
It Wouldn't Hurt To Have Wings
Mark Chesnutt; *Wings* . . . . (Decca)
Jet
Paul McCartney; *All The Best!* . . . . (Capitol)
Paul McCartney & Wings; *Band On The Run* . . . . (Capitol)
Wings; *Wings Greatest* . . . . (Capitol)
   Wings Over America . . . . (Capitol)

Jet Airliner
Steve Miller Band; *Book Of Dreams* . . . (Capitol)
Steve Miller Band-Gift Set . . . (Capitol)
Steve Miller Band-Live . . . (Capitol)
Steve Miller Band's Greatest Hits-1974-78 . . . (Capitol)
Jets At Dawn
Be Bop Deluxe; *Axe Victim* . . . (Capitol)
Las Vegas Turnaround
Daryl Hall & John Oates; *Abandoned Luncheonette* . . . (Atlantic)
No Goodbyes . . . (Atlantic)
Learn To Fly
Foo Fighters; *There Is Nothing Left To Lose* . . . (Roswell/RCA)
Learning To Fly
Pink Floyd; *Delicate Sound Of Thunder* . . . (Columbia)
Momentary Lapse Of Reason . . . (Columbia)
Learning To Fly
Tom Petty And The Heartbreakers; *Into The Great Wide Open* . . . (MCA)
Let Him Fly
Dixie Chicks; *Fly* . . . (Monument)
Letter, The
Box Tops; *Billboard Top Rock 'N' Roll Hits-1967-C* . . . (Rhino)
Box Tops' Greatest Hits . . . (Rhino)
Cruisin'-1967-C . . . (Increase)
Oldies But Goodies-#12-C . . . (Original Sound)
Rockin' '60s-C . . . (Priority)
Joe Cocker; *Joe Cocker Live* . . . (Capitol)
Joe Cocker-Classics-#4 . . . (A&M)
Joe Cocker's Greatest Hits . . . (A&M)
Mad Dogs & Englishmen . . . (A&M)
Vernon Green & The Medallions; *Oldies But Goodies-#1-C* . . . (Original Sound)
Vernon Green & The Medallions-Golden Classics . . . (Collectables)
Little Bird
Sherrie Austin; *Love In The Real World* . . . (Arista)
Love Light In Flight
Stevie Wonder; *ST/Woman In Red* . . . (Motown)
Lullaby Of Birdland
Ella Fitzgerald; *Best Of Ella Fitzgerald-#2* . . . (MCA)
Ella Fitzgerald With Billie Holiday . . . (MCA)
Four Freshmen; *Greatest Hits-Four Freshman* . . . (Curb)
Mel Torme; *Songs Of New York* . . . (Rhino)
Sarah Vaughan; *Sarah Vaughan-Golden Hits* . . . (Mercury)
Tito Puente & His Latin Ensemble; *Mambo Diablo* . . . (Concord Jazz)
Magic Carpet Ride
Steppenwolf; *Live Steppenwolf* . . . (MCA)
Nuggets-#9-Acid Rock-C . . . (Rhino)
Steppenwolf Gold/Their Great Hits . . . (MCA)
Steppenwolf-16 Greatest Hits . . . (MCA)
The Second . . . (MCA)
May The Bird Of Paradise Fly Up Your Nose
''Little'' Jimmy Dickens; *Columbia Country Classics-#3-Americana-C* . . . (Columbia)
Super Hits Of The '60s-C . . . (Epic)
Harlow Wilcox and the Oakies; *Cripple Cricket* . . . (Plantation)
My Baby You
Marc Anthony; *Marc Anthony* . . . (Columbia)
Natural High
Bloodstone; *Bloodstone's Greatest Hits* . . . (T-Neck/Columbia)
Didn't It Blow Your Mind: Soul Hits Of The '70s-#11-C . . . (Rhino)
Natural High
Merle Haggard & Janie Fricke; *For The Record: Merle Haggard-43 Legendary Hits* . . . (BNA)
Night Flight
Buddy Guy; *Buddy Guy-Complete Chess Studio Recordings* . . . (Chess)
Night Flight
Led Zeppelin; *Physical Graffiti* . . . (Swan Song)
Norwegian Wood (This Bird Has Flown)
Beatles; *Beatles-Box Set* . . . (Capitol)
Beatles-Love Songs . . . (Capitol)
Rubber Soul . . . (Capitol)
The Beatles/1962-1966 . . . (Capitol)
On The Wings Of Love
Jeffrey Osborne; *Jeffrey Osborne* . . . (A&M)
Over The Rainbow
Barbra Streisand; *Just For The Record* . . . (Columbia)
Dave Brubeck; *Greatest Hits From The Fantasy Years* . . . (Fantasy)
Ella Fitzgerald; *Silver Collection-Songbooks* . . . (Verve)
Judy Garland; *Best Of The Capitol Masters-One & Only Box* . . . (Capitol)
Judy Garland-At Carnegie Hall . . . (Capitol)
Judy Garland's Greatest Hits . . . (Curb)
Miss Show Business . . . (Capitol)
One & Only . . . (Capitol)
ST/The Wizard Of Oz . . . (Sony Music Special Prod.)
P.O.V. Waltz
Nilsson; *The Point* . . . (RCA)
Pegasus
Mahavishnu Orchestra; *Visions Of The Emerald Beyond* . . . (Columbia)
Pegasus
Allman Brothers Band; *Enlightened Rogues* . . . (Polydor)
Pigs On The Wing
Pink Floyd; *Animals* . . . (Columbia)
Shine On . . . (Columbia)
Pilot Error
Stephanie Mills; *Merciless* . . . (Casablanca)
Purple People Eater
Sheb Wooley; *45s On CD-#1-1956-1959-C* . . . (Mercury)
Dr. Demento: 20th Anniversary Collection-C . . . (Rhino)
Halloween Hits-C . . . (Rhino)
Horror Rock Classics-#2-C . . . (Rhino)
Super Hits-#4-C . . . (Gusto)
Ray Of Light
Madonna; *GHV2* . . . (Warner Bros.)
Ray Of Light . . . (Maverick)
Totally Hits-#1-C . . . (Arista)
Rocky Mountain High
John Denver; *Evening With John Denver* . . . (RCA)
John Denver's Greatest Hits . . . (RCA)
Rocky Mountain High . . . (RCA)
Take Me Home, Country Roads & Other Hits . . . (RCA)
Sail On Flying Dutchman
Nick Seeger; *Sail On Flying Dutchman* . . . (Biograph)
She's Gonna Fly
Collin Raye; *Tracks* . . . (Epic)
Silver Wings
Merle Haggard; *More Of The Best* . . . (Rhino)
The Seashores Of Old Mexico . . . (Epic)
Merle Haggard & Jewel; *For The Record: Merle Haggard-43 Legendary Hits* . . . (BNA)
Merle Haggard & The Strangers; *Okie From Muskogee* . . . (Capitol)
Songs I'll Always Sing . . . (Capitol)
Pam Tillis; *Mama's Hungry Eyes-Merle Haggard Tribute-C* . . . (Arista)
Slow Ride
Kenny Wayne Shepherd; *Trouble Is...* . . . (Revolution)
Space Cowboy (Yippie-Yi-Yay)
'N Sync featuring Lisa ''Left Eye'' Lopes; *No Strings Attached* . . . (Jive)
Spirits (Having Flown)
Bee Gees; *Bee Gees' Greatest* . . . (Polydor)
Spirits Having Flown . . . (Polydor)
Spread Your Wings
Queen; *Live Killers* . . . (Hollywood)
News Of The World . . . (Hollywood)
Straighten Up And Fly Right
Andrews Sisters; *Best Of The Andrews Sisters-#2* . . . (MCA)
Diana Krall; *Stepping Out* . . . (Justin Time)
Linda Ronstadt; *For Sentimental Reasons* . . . (Asylum)
Nat ''King'' Cole; *Best Of Nat ''King'' Cole-Vol. 2* . . . (Capitol)
Superman (I Wish I Could Fly Like)
Kinks; *Come Dancing With The Kinks-Best Of The Kinks 1977-1986* . . . (Arista)
Low Budget . . . (Arista)
Texas Bound And Flyin'
Jerry Reed; *ST/Smokey And The Bandit 2* . . . (MCA)
Texas Bound & Flyin' . . . (RCA)
Theme From ''Dastardly & Muttley In Their Flying Machine''
Original Soundtrack; *Hanna-Barbera Pic-A-Nic Basket Of Cartoon Classics* . . . (Kid Rhino/Rhino 4 Kids)
Television's Greatest Hits-#3-1970s & 1980s-C . . . (TVT)
Theme From ''I'll Fly Away''
Original Soundtrack; *Television's Greatest Hits-#7-Cable Ready-C* . . . (TVT)
Theme From ''Monty Python's Flying Circus''
Original Soundtrack; *Television's Greatest Hits-#2-C* . . . (TVT)
Theme From ''The Flying Nun''
Original Soundtrack; *Television's Greatest Hits-#5-In Living Color-C* . . . (TVT)
There You'll Be
Faith Hill; *ST/Pearl Harbor* . . . (Warner Bros.)
Time For Me To Fly
REO Speedwagon; *A Decade Of Rock And Roll 1970 To 1980* . . . (Epic)
REO Speedwagon-The Hits . . . (Epic)
You Can Tune A Piano But You Can't Tuna Fish . . . (Epic)
To The Moon And Back
Savage Garden; *Savage Garden* . . . (Columbia)
Travelin' Light
Eric Clapton; *Reptile* . . . (Duck/Reprise)
Up, Up & Away
5th Dimension; *5th Dimension-Anthology 1967-1973* . . . (Rhino)
Greatest Hits On Earth . . . (Arista)
Volare
Bobby Rydell; *'60s Rock 'N' Roll-#1-It's My Party-C* . . . (Dominion Entert.)
Waiting In The Wings
BBM; *Around The Next Dream* . . . (Virgin)
When I See An Elephant Fly
Barbara Cook; *Disney Album* . . . (Disney)
Cliff Edwards/Jim Carmichael/The Hall Johnson Choir; *Disney Collection-#2-C* . . . (Disney)
When The Eagle Flies
Traffic; *When The Eagle Flies* . . . (Asylum)
When The Fallen Angels Fly
Patty Loveless; *When Fallen Angels Fly* . . . (Epic)

When You Come Back Down
Nickel Creek; *Nickel Creek* . . . . (Sugar Hill)
Why Walk When You Can Fly
Mary Chapin Carpenter; *Stones In The Road*. . . . .(Columbia)
Wind Beneath My Wings
Bette Midler; *ST/Beaches* . . . . (Atlantic)
Gary Morris; *Chicken Soup For The Soul: I'll Be There For You-Songs Of
    Friendship, Brotherhood And Sisterhood-C* . . . . (Rhino)
Country Love Songs-C . . . . (Warner Bros.)
Gary Morris-Hits . . . . (Warner Bros.)
Why Lady Why . . . . (Warner Bros.)
James Galway; *Wind Beneath My Wings* . . . .(RCA)
Lee Greenwood; *Somebody's Gonna Love You* . . . . (MCA)
Lou Rawls; *When The Night Comes* . . . . (Epic)
Roger Whittaker; *Roger Whittaker Greatest Hits* . . . . (RCA)
Wind Beneath My Wings . . . . (RCA)
Willie Nelson; *City Of New Orleans* . . . . (Columbia)
Windy
Association; *Association Greatest Hits* . . . . (Warner Bros.)
Billboard Top Rock 'N' Roll Hits-1967-C . . . . (Rhino)
Summer Of Love-#1-C . . . . (Rhino)
Vintage Association . . . . (Fifty One West)
Wes Montgomery; *A Day In The Life* . . . . (A&M)
Wes Montgomery-Classics-#22 . . . . (A&M)
Wes Montgomery's Greatest Hits . . . . (A&M)
Wing And A Prayer
Laurel MacDonald; *Chroma* . . . . (Wicklow)
Wingspan . . . . (Wicklow)
Wingin' It Home To Texas
Jerry Jeff Walker; *Collectibles* . . . . (MCA)
Wings Of Your Love
Prism; *Small Change* . . . . (Capitol)
Wings Over Manhattan
Charlie Barnet; *1941* . . . . (Circle)
Wings Wetted Down
Blue Oyster Cult; *Tyranny & Mutation* . . . . (Columbia)
You Got Me Floatin'
PM Dawn; *Stone Free: A Tribute To Jimi Hendrix-C* . . . .(Reprise)

FOLLOWING

(They Long To Be) Close To You
Carpenters; *Carpenters-Classics-#2* . . . . (A&M)
Carpenters-Love Songs . . . . (A&M)
Carpenters-The Singles 1969-1973 . . . . (A&M)
From The Top . . . . (A&M)
Follow Me
Original Cast; *Camelot* . . . . (Columbia)
ST/Camelot. . . . . (Warner Bros.)
Follow Me
Uncle Kracker; *Double Wide* . . . . (Warner Bros.)
Totally Hits 2001-C . . . . (Arista)
Follow You Down
Gin Blossoms; *Congratulations I'm Sorry* . . . . (A&M)
Follow You, Follow Me
Genesis; *And Then There Were Three* . . . . (Atlantic)
Three Sides Live . . . . (Atlantic)
Follow Your Heart
Triumph; *Stages* . . . . (MCA)
Thunder Seven . . . . (MCA)
Triumph-Classics . . . . (MCA)
Follow Your Heart
John McLaughlin; *CTI Masters Of The Guitar* . . . . (CBS Associated)
My Goals Beyond . . . . (Elektra)
Follow Your Heart
Joe Farrell; *Joe Farrell Quartet*. . . . . (CBS Associated)
Followin' A Feelin'
Sherrie Austin; *Followin' A Feelin'* . . . . (We/Madacy)
Hey Pretty
Poe; *Haunted*. . . . . (FEI/Atlantic)
I Will Follow Him
Little Peggy March; *Nipper's Greatest Hits Of The '60s-#1-C* . . . .(RCA)
I'd Follow You Anywhere
Derailers; *Here Come The Derailers* . . . . (Lucky Dog)
I'll Follow The Sun
Beatles; *Beatles '65* . . . . (Capitol)
Beatles-Box Set . . . . (Capitol)
Beatles-Love Songs . . . . (Capitol)
For Sale . . . . (Capitol)
I'm Free
Who; *Join Together*. . . . . (MCA)
Tommy . . . . (MCA)
Keep Searchin' (We'll Follow The Sun)
Del Shannon; *Del Shannon's Greatest Hits*. . . . . (Rhino)
Del Shannon's Greatest Hits . . . . (Curb)
Leader Of Men
Nickelback; *State*. . . . . (Roadrunner)

Leading With Your Heart
Barbra Streisand; *Higher Ground* . . . . (Columbia)
Look What Followed Me Home
David Ball; *Thinkin' Problem* . . . . (Warner Bros.)
Love Your Way
Sophie B. Hawkins; *Songs From Dawson's Creek* . . . . (Sony Music Soundtrax)
Mr. Tambourine Man
Bob Dylan; *Biograph* . . . .(Columbia)
Bob Dylan At Budokan . . . .(Columbia)
Bob Dylan's Greatest Hits . . . .(Columbia)
Bringing It All Back Home . . . .(Columbia)
Byrds; *Billboard Top Rock 'N' Roll Hits-1965-C* . . . .(Rhino)
Original Singles-#1-1965-1967 . . . .(Columbia)
The Byrds' Greatest Hits . . . .(Columbia)
The Original Singles-1965-1967 . . . .(Columbia)
Turn! Turn! Turn! . . . .(Legacy)
My Elusive Dreams
Bobby Vinton; *Autumn Memories* . . . . (Epic)
Bobby Vinton's All-Time Greatest Hits . . . . (Epic)
Charlie Rich; *Charlie Rich-16 Biggest Hits* . . . .(Legacy)
Charlie Rich's Greatest Hits . . . . (Epic)
Charlie Rich-Super Hits . . . . (Epic)
David Houston & Tammy Wynette; *Best Of David
    Houston* . . . .(Collector's Choice)
Billboard Top Country Hits-1967-C . . . .(Rhino)
Tammy Wynette's Greatest Hits . . . . (Epic)
N.I.B.
Primus with Ozzy; *Nativity In Black II: Tribute To Black
    Sabbath-C* . . . . (Divine/Priority)
Runnin' Away With My Heart
Lonestar; *Lonestar* . . . . (BNA)
Shy Guy
Diana King; *ST/Bad Boys* . . . . (Work)
Tougher Than Love . . . . (Work)
Sour Girl
Stone Temple Pilots; *No. 4* . . . . (Atlantic)
They All Follow Me
Edna May; *Music From The New York Stage (1890-1920)-#1-1890-
    1908-C* . . . . (Pearl)
Where You Lead
Carole King; *Tapestry* . . . . (Epic)

FOOD & BEVERAGES: COFFEE, Tea

See Also: **FOOD & BEVERAGES (various), RESTAURANTS,
WAITRESSES**

Afternoon Tea
Kinks; *Something Else* . . . . (Reprise)
All The Tea In China
Buck Owens; *Kickin'* . . . .(Curb)
Another Cup Of Coffee & A Cigarette
Robbin Thompson; *Robbin Thompson* . . . . (Nemperor)
Another Cup Of Coffee (Then I'll Go)
Brook Benton; *Brook Benton-Anthology* . . . .(Rhino)
Black Coffee
k.d. lang; *Just Say Yo-#2 Of Just Say Yes-C* . . . . (Sire)
Shadowland. . . . . (Sire)
Black Coffee
Humble Pie; *Best Of Humble Pie* . . . .(A&M)
Eat It . . . .(A&M)
Black Coffee
Peggy Lee; *Best Of Peggy Lee* . . . . (MCA)
Black Coffee
Lacy J. Dalton; *Lacy J.* . . . .(Capitol)
Black Coffee
Black Flag; *Slip It In* . . . . (SST)
Black Coffee In Bed
Squeeze; *Sweets From A Stranger* . . . .(A&M)
Chock Full O'Nuts Is That Heavenly Coffee
Original Sins; *TeeVee Toons-The Commercials-#1-C* . . . .(TVT)
Cigarettes & Coffee
Otis Redding; *Best Of Otis Redding* . . . .(Atco)
Best Of Otis Redding . . . . (Atlantic)
The Otis Redding Story . . . . (Atlantic)
Coffee
Billy Falcon; *Letters From A Paper Ship* . . . .(Mercury)
Flowerhead; *Ka-Bloom* . . . . (Zoo)
Coffee & Kisses
Duke Ellington & His Orchestra; *Happy Birthday Duke-Birthday
    Sessions-#4*. . . . . (Laserlight)
Coffee At Midnite
Bluegrass Parlor Band; *Two Colors* . . . . (Pinecastle)
Coffee Beans
Moondog; *Moondog* . . . . (Columbia)
Coffee Blues
Lightnin' Hopkins; *Mojo Hand-Anthology* . . . .(Rhino)

Mississippi John Hurt; *Best Of Mississippi John Hurt* . . . . (Vanguard)
Today! . . . . (Vanguard)

Coffee Break
Will T. Massey; *Will T. Massey* . . . . (MCA)

Coffee Break
Billy McLaughlin; *Inhale Pink* . . . .(A Major Label)

Coffee Grindin' Blues
Jaybird Coleman; *Alabama Blues-1927-1931-C* . . . . (Yazoo)

Coffee Homeground
Kate Bush; *Lionheart* . . . .(EMI)

Coffee House Blues
Lightnin' Hopkins; *Best Of The Blues* . . . . (Tradition)

Coffee In A Cardboard Cup
Original Broadway Cast; *70 Girls 70* . . . . (Sony Music Classical)
Original Cast; *And The World Goes 'Round: Songs Of Kander
& Ebb* . . . . (RCA Victor)

Coffee Shoppe
Margaret Whiting; *Then & Now* . . . . (DRG)

Coffee Song (They've Got An Awful Lot Of Coffee In Brazil)
Frank Sinatra; *Frank Sinatra-16 Most Requested Songs* . . . . (Columbia)
Frank Sinatra-In The Beginning-1943-1951 . . . . (Columbia)
Frank Sinatra & Johnny Mandel; *Ring-A-Ding Ding* . . . . (Reprise)

Coffee Time
Li'l Wally; *My Polish Girlfriend & Others* . . . .(Jay Jay)

Coffee Train
David Thomas; *Monster Walks The Winter Lake* . . . . (Twin-Tone)

Coffee, Donuts & Death
Paris; *Sleeping With The Enemy* . . . . (Scarface)

Cup Of Coffee, A Sandwich And You
Enoch Light & The Charleston City All-Stars; *Music Of The 1920s-C* . . . .(MCA)

Cup Of Tea
Verve Pipe; *Villains* . . . . (RCA)

Don't Forget The Coffee Billy Joe
Tom T. Hall; *Essential Tom T. Hall-20th Anniversary Collection* . . . . (Mercury)

Espresso Logic
Chris Rea; *Espresso Logic* . . . . (East West)

Everything I Love
Alan Jackson; *Everything I Love* . . . . (Arista)

Have A Cuppa Tea
Kinks; *Muswell Hillbillies* . . . . (VelVel)

Hot Coffee
Carl Anderson; *Pieces Of A Heart* . . . . (GRP)

I Don't Sleep, I Dream
R.E.M.; *Monster* . . . .(Warner Bros.)

I'll Have Another Cup Of Coffee
Claude Gray; *Truckin' On-C* . . . . (Hollywood)

I'll Just Have A Cup Of Coffee
Claude Gray; *Super Hits-Country-1960s-C* . . . . (Gusto)

Java Jive
Ink Spots; *Best Of The Ink Spots* . . . .(MCA)
Manhattan Transfer; *Best Of The Manhattan Transfer* . . . . (Atlantic)
The Manhattan Transfer . . . . (Rhino)

Let's Have Another Cup Of Coffee
Glenn Miller; *Complete Glenn Miller & His Orchestra-#8* . . . . . . (Bluebird)
Michael Feinstein; *Remember-Michael Feinstein Sings Irving Berlin* . . (Elektra)

Morning Coffee
Joe King Carrasco & The Crowns; *Tales From The Crypt-Basement Tapes-
1979* . . . .(Roir)

One Cup Of Coffee
Bob Marley & The Wailers; *Songs Of Freedom* . . . . (Tuff Gong)

One More Cup Of Coffee
Bob Dylan; *Bob Dylan At Budokan* . . . . (Columbia)
Desire . . . . (Columbia)

Over A Cup Of Coffee
Castelles; *Sweet Sounds Of The Castelles* . . . . (Collectables)

Pennyroyal Tea
Nirvana; *In Utero* . . . . (David Geffen Co.)
MTV Unplugged In New York . . . . (David Geffen Co.)

Pot Of Coffee
Pinchers; *Reggae Jamdown-The Ras Tapes* . . . . (Rykodisc)

Smokin' Cigarettes & Drinkin' Coffee Blues
David Ball; *David Ball* . . . .(BMG Special Prod.)
Marty Robbins; *Essential Marty Robbins-1951-1982* . . . . (Columbia)

Sugar Shack
Jimmy Gilmer And The Fireballs; *Billboard Top Rock 'N' Roll Hits-
1963-C* . . . . (Rhino)
Golden Years-1963-C . . . . (Dominion Entert.)
Good Old Rock & Roll-C . . . . (International Mktg. Group)

Sunday For Tea
Peter And Gordon; *Best Of Peter And Gordon* . . . . (Rhino)

Tea For One
Led Zeppelin; *Presence* . . . . (Swan Song)

Tea For The Tillerman
Cat Stevens; *Tea For The Tillerman* . . . . (A&M)

Tea For Two
Fred Waring's Pennsylvanians; *Nipper's Greatest Hits Of The
'30s-#2-C* . . . . (RCA)
Julie Andrews; *Love Julie* . . . . (USA Music Group)

Leigh Kaplan & Lincoln Mayorga; *Dizzy Fingers* . . . . (Cambria)
Original Cast/Ruby Keeler; *No No Nanette* . . . . (Columbia)
Tommy Dorsey & His Orchestra; *Best Of Tommy Dorsey & His
Orchestra* . . . . (Curb)

Tea In The Sahara
Police; *Message In A Box-Complete Recordings* . . . . (A&M)
Synchronicity . . . . (A&M)
Sting; *Bring On The Night* . . . . (A&M)

Texas Tea Party
Benny Goodman; *Benny Goodman-Early Years* . . . .(Biograph)

That's What I Like-No Cream In My Coffee
Cooly Live; *Livewire* . . . . (RCA)

Truck Drivers Coffee Shop
Dick Reinhart & His Lone Star Boys; *Truck Driver Boogie Big Rig Hits-
1939-1969-C* . . . . (Audium)

Wake Up & Smell The Coffee
Killbilly; *Stranger In This Place* . . . . (Flying Fish)

When I Take My Sugar To Tea
Boswell Sisters; *78-#6083* . . . . (Brunswick)
Frank Sinatra; *Ring-A-Ding Ding* . . . . (Reprise)
Nat "King" Cole; *The Vocal Classics-1947-1950* . . . . (Capitol)

You're Getting To Be A Habit With Me
Betty Carter; *I Can't Help It* . . . . (GRP)
Diana Krall; *Love Scenes* . . . .(Impulse!)
Doris Day; *Golden Girl: The Columbia Recordings-1944-1966* . . . . . . (Legacy)
Frank Sinatra; *songs for Swingin' Lovers!* . . . . (Capitol)
Mel Torme; *Spotlight On Mel Torme* . . . . (Capitol)
Original Broadway Cast; *42nd Street* . . . . (RCA Victor)

You're So Vain
Carly Simon; *'70s Greatest Rock Hits-#3-High Times-C* . . . . (Priority)
Best Of Carly Simon . . . . (Elektra)
Carly Simon-Greatest Hits Live . . . . (Arista)
No Secrets . . . . (Elektra)

You're The Cream In My Coffee
Lawrence Welk; *Lawrence Welk-16 Most Requested Songs* . . . . (Columbia)
Les Brown & His Orchestra; *Best Of Les Brown & His Orchestra* . . . . . . (MCA)

FOOD & BEVERAGES: FRUIT

See Also: ***FOOD & BEVERAGES (various), RESTAURANTS***

30,000 Pounds Of Bananas
Harry Chapin; *Greatest Stories-Live* . . . . (Elektra)
Harry Chapin-Anthology . . . . (Elektra)
Verities & Balderdash . . . . (Elektra)

Apple Honey
Woody Herman; *Best Of Woody Herman & His Orchestra* . . . . (Curb)
Big Band Treasures-#2-C . . . . (Dunhill Compact Classics)
Thundering Herds-1945-1947 . . . . (Columbia)

Apple Of Your Eye
Peter Frampton; *Frampton* . . . . (A&M)

Apple Orchard
Spirit; *Spirit* . . . . (Epic)

Apple Scruffs
George Harrison; *All Things Must Pass* . . . . (Parlophone)

Apple Suckling Tree
Bob Dylan And The Band; *Basement Tapes* . . . . (Columbia)

Apple Tree
Erykah Badu; *Baduizm* . . . . (Kedar Entert./Universal)

Apples & Oranges
Pink Floyd; *Shine On* . . . . (Columbia)

Apples And Bananas
keith urban; *Country Goes Raffi-C* . . . . (Rounder)

Apples In Winter
Kim Robertson; *Angels In Disguise* . . . . (Invincible)

Apples Peaches Pumpkin Pie
Jay And The Techniques; *Cruisin'-1967-C* . . . . (Increase)

Apples, Peaches & Cherries
Peggy Lee; *Best Of Peggy Lee* . . . . (MCA)

Apples, Peaches, Bananas & Pears
Monkees; *Missing Links* . . . . (Rhino)

Apricot Love
Neil Norman; *Not Of This Earth* . . . .(Crescendo)

Attack Of The Killer Tomatoes
Lewis Lee; *Elvira Presents Haunted Hits-C* . . . . (Rhino)
Halloween Hits-C . . . . (Rhino)

Avocado Green
Johnny Winter; *About Blues* . . . .(Janus)
Before The Storm . . . .(Janus)

Baby Lemonade
Syd Barrett; *Barrett* . . . . (Capitol)

Back To The Apple
Count Basie & His Orchestra; *ST/Hannah & Her Sisters* . . . . (MCA)

Banana Boat (Day-O)
Harry Belafonte; *Belafonte '89* . . . . (EMI)
Nipper's Greatest Hits Of The '50s-#1-C . . . .(RCA)

Kinks; *Everybody's In Show-Biz* . . . . (Rhino)

Banana Man
Clifton Chenier; *Louisiana Blues & Zydeco* . . . .(Arhoolie)

Banana Republic
Boomtown Rats; *Boomtown Rats' Greatest Hits* . . . .(Columbia)
Mondo Bongo . . . . (Columbia)

Banana Republics
Jimmy Buffett; *Changes In Latitudes, Changes In Attitudes* . . . . (MCA)

Bananas
Louis Jordan & His Tympany Five; *Rock 'N Roll Call* . . . . (Bluebird)

Bananas & Cream
Kinky Friedman; *Lasso From El Paso* . . . . (Epic)

Bananas By The Bunch
Lou & Peter Berryman; *So Comfortable* . . . .(Cornbelt)

Big Apple
Tommy Dorsey & His Clambake Seven; *Nipper's Greatest Hits Of The
'30s-#2-C* . . . .(RCA)
Tommy Dorsey & His Orchestra; *Seventeen Number Ones* . . . .(RCA)

Blackberry
Black Crowes; *Three Snakes And One Charm* . . . . (American)

Blueberry Hill
Elvis Presley; *Elvis Recorded Live On Stage In Memphis* . . . .(RCA)
Loving You . . . .(RCA)
Fats Domino; *Fats Domino's Greatest Hits* . . . .(Everest)
Fats Domino's Greatest Hits . . . . (MCA)
My Blue Heaven-Best Of Fats Domino-#1 . . . . (EMI)
Little Richard; *Big Hits* . . . .(Crescendo)
Louis Armstrong; *Best Of Louis Armstrong* . . . . (MCA)
Essential Louis Armstrong . . . . (Vanguard)
I Like Jazz-Essence Of Louis Armstrong . . . . (Columbia)

Blueberry Pie
Bette Midler; *For Our Children-10th Annivesary
Edition-C* . . . . (Kid Rhino/Rhino 4 Kids)

Bruised Orange
John Prine; *Bruised Orange* . . . .(Oh Boy)

Cantaloop
US3; *Hand On The Torch* . . . .(Capitol)

Cherry
Count Basie & Mills Brothers; *Count Basie & Mills Brothers-16 Great
Performances* . . . . (MCA)
Harry James & His Orchestra; *Best Of Harry James & His Orchestra* . . . .(Curb)
Oscar Peterson & Count Basie; *Satch & Josh Again* . . . . (Pablo)
UFO; *Obsession* . . . . (Chrysalis)

Cherry
Stanley Turrentine; *Best Of Stanley Turrentine* . . . . (CBS Associated)

Cherry
UFO; *Obsession* . . . . (Chrysalis)

Cherry Blossom Time
Columbia Ballroom Orchestra; *Let's Dance-#7-Competition Dance* . . . (Denon)

Cherry Bomb
John Cougar Mellencamp; *Check It Out* . . . .(Mercury)
The Lonesome Jubilee . . . . (Mercury)

Cherry Coke
Bob's Diner; *Bob's Diner* . . . . (Digital Music Prod.)

Cherry Hill Park
Billy Joe Royal; *Billy Joe Royal's Greatest Hits* . . . .(Columbia)
Super Hits Of The '70s-Have A Nice Day-#1-C . . . .(Rhino)

Cherry Oh Baby
Rolling Stones; *Black And Blue* . . . . (Rolling Stones)
UB40; *Labour Of Love* . . . . (A&M)
Live In Moscow . . . . (A&M)

Cherry Pie
Marvin & Johnny; *Collectables Presents The History Of
Rock-#4-C* . . . . (Collectables)
Rock & Roll Festival-#1-C . . . . (Kent)

Cherry Pie
Sade; *Diamond Life* . . . . (Portrait)

Cherry Pink And Apple Blossom White
Fabulous Thunderbirds; *Butt Rockin'* . . . . (Chrysalis)
Perez Prado & His Orchestra; *This Is Perez Prado-Decade Of
The '50s* . . . .(RCA)

Cherry Red
Big Joe Turner; *Atlantic Blues-Piano-C* . . . . (Atlantic)
Boss Of The Blues . . . . (Atlantic)
Count Basie & Big Joe Turner; *Bosses* . . . . (Pablo)
Ella Fitzgerald; *These Are The Blues* . . . .(Verve)
Esther Phillips; *Confessin' The Blues-Jazzlore-#41* . . . .(Rhino)

Cherry Red
Lime Spiders; *Beethoven's Fist* . . . . (Caroline)

Cherry Red
Little Richard; *Big Hits* . . . .(Crescendo)

Cherry, Cherry
Neil Diamond; *Bang & Shout* . . . .(Bang)
Hot August Night . . . . (MCA)
Hot August Night II . . . . (Columbia)
Neil Diamond-Classics (Early Years) . . . . (Columbia)

Neil Diamond-Gold . . . . (MCA)
Neil Diamond's Greatest Hits . . . .(Bang)
Shilo . . . .(Bang)

Cherry, Cherry Coupe
Beach Boys; *Little Deuce Coupe/All Summer Long* . . . .(Capitol)

Coconut
Nilsson; *Nilsson Schmilsson* . . . .(RCA)
Nilsson's Greatest Hits . . . . (RCA)
Songwriter . . . . (RCA)

Coconut Grove
David Lee Roth; *Crazy From The Heat* . . . . (Warner Bros.)
Lovin' Spoonful; *Lovin' Spoonful-Anthology* . . . .(Rhino)

Coconut Island
Junior Brown; *12 Shades Of Brown* . . . .(Curb)

Coconut Telegraph
Jimmy Buffett; *Boats Beaches Bars & Ballads* . . . . (Margaritaville)
Coconut Telegraph . . . . (MCA)

Come On-A My House
Rosemary Clooney; *Rosemary Clooney-16 Most Requested Songs* . . . . .(Legacy)
Sentimental Journey: Pop Vocal Classics-#3-C . . . .(Rhino)

Don't Sit Under The Apple Tree
Andrews Sisters; *Andrews Sisters Greatest Hits* . . . .(Curb)
Andrews Sisters-16 Great Performances . . . . (MCA)
Capitol Collectors Series-The Andrews Sisters . . . .(Capitol)
Glenn Miller; *Memorial-1944-1969* . . . .(Bluebird)
Glenn Miller & His Orchestra; *The Unforgettable Glenn Miller & His
Orchestra* . . . . (RCA)

Don't Your Peaches Look Mellow
Luke & The Locomotives; *Luke & The Locomotives* . . . . (Audioquest)

Elderberry Wine
Elton John; *Don't Shoot Me I'm Only The Piano Player* . . . . (Polydor)

Fig Leaf Rag
Scott Joplin; *Ragtime-#2-1900-1910* . . . . (Biograph)

Fig Tree
Bunny Wailer; *Blackheart Man* . . . .(Island)

Fig Tree Bay
Peter Frampton; *Wind Of Change* . . . .(A&M)

Forbidden Fruit
Band; *Northern Lights-Southern Cross* . . . .(Capitol)

From The Vine Came The Grape
Gaylords; *X-tra Cheese-Originals By The Originals-C* . . . . (Compose)

Fruit Juicy (Hawaiian Punch)
Original Soundtrack; *TeeVee Toons-The Commercials-#1-C* . . . .(TVT)

Fruit Song
Martin Mull; *Never Perfect/Perfect* . . . . (Elektra)

Funky Avocado
Michael Hedges; *Breakfast In The Field* . . . . (Windham Hill)
Live On The Double Planet . . . . (Windham Hill)

God's Great Banana Skin
Chris Rea; *Espresso Logic* . . . .(East West)

Golden Apples Of The Sun
Judy Collins; *Golden Apples Of The Sun* . . . . (Elektra)
So Early In The Spring, The First 15 Years . . . . (Elektra)

Grapefruit Juicy Fruit
Jimmy Buffett; *Songs You Know By Heart-Jimmy Buffett's Greatest
Hit(s)* . . . . (MCA)
White Sport Coat & A Pink Crustacean . . . . (MCA)
You Had To Be There . . . . (MCA)

Grapes Of Wrath
Charlie Daniels Band; *Midnight Wind* . . . . (Epic)

Guacamole
Texas Tornados; *Hangin' On By A Thread* . . . . (Reprise)

Guava Jelly
Barbra Streisand; *Butterfly* . . . .(Columbia)
Bob Marley & The Wailers; *Songs Of Freedom* . . . . (Tuff Gong)
Owen Gray; *This Is Reggae Music-#1-C* . . . .(Island)

I Like Bananas Because They Have No Bone
Hoosier Hot Shots; *Dr. Demento Presents The Greatest Novelty Records-#1-
1940s & Before-C* . . . .(Rhino)

I Like Cherries
Audio Two; *What More Can I Say* . . . . (First Priority)

I'm A Chiquita Banana
Original Soundtrack; *TeeVee Toons-The Commercials-#1-C* . . . .(TVT)

Josephine
Wallflowers; *Bringing Down The Horse* . . . . (Interscope)

Judy In Disguise (With Glasses)
John Fred & His Playboy Band; *Billboard Top Rock 'N' Roll Hits-
1968-C* . . . .(Rhino)
Cruisin'-1967-C . . . . (Increase)
ST/Drugstore Cowboy . . . . (Novus)
Super Oldies Of The '60s-#7-C . . . . (Audio Fidelity)

Last Mango In Paris
Jimmy Buffett; *Feeding Frenzy* . . . . (MCA)
Last Mango In Paris . . . . (MCA)

Lemon Pie
Strawbs; *Best Of The Strawbs* . . . .(A&M)

Ghosts .... (A&M)

Lemon Song
Led Zeppelin; *Led Zeppelin II*.......................... (Atlantic)

Lemon Squeezing Daddy
Sultans; *Risque Rhythms: Nasty '50s R&B-C* .... (Rhino)

Lemon Tree
Kingston Trio; *Very Best Of The Kingston Trio* .... (Capitol)
Peter, Paul & Mary; *10 Years Together/The Best Of Peter, Paul
   and Mary*............................ (Warner Bros.)
   Peter, Paul and Mary .... (Warner Bros.)
Trini Lopez; *Best Of Trini Lopez* .... (Exact)

Life Is A Lemon And I Want My Money Back
Meat Loaf; *Bat Out Of Hell II: Back Into Hell* .... (MCA)

Life Is Just A Bowl Of Cherries
Ethel Merman; *The Ethel Merman Collection* .... (Razor & Tie)
Jaye P. Morgan; *The Jaye P. Morgan Story* .... (Simitar)
Original Cast; *Fosse* .... (RCA Victor)
Rudy Vallee & His Connecticut Yankees; *As Time
   Goes By* .... (Varese Sarabande)

Little Green Apples
O.C. Smith; *Pop Classics Of The '60s-C* .... (Columbia)

Naturally
Marty Stuart; *Country Goes Raffi-C* .... (Rounder)

Old Dogs, Children & Watermelon Wine
Tom T. Hall; *Essential Tom T. Hall-20th Anniversary Collection* .... (Mercury)
   Tom T. Hall's Greatest Hits-#2 .... (Mercury)

One Bad Apple
Osmonds; *Billboard Top Rock 'N' Roll Hits-1971-C* .... (Rhino)

Orange Blossom Lane
Glenn Miller & His Orchestra; *Complete Glenn Miller & His
   Orchestra* .... (Bluebird)
   Complete Glenn Miller & His Orchestra-#7 .... (Bluebird)

Orange Blossom Mandolin
Northeast Winds; *Northeast Winds In Concert*.............. (Folk Era)

Orange Blossom Special
Bill Monroe; *Bean Blossom* .... (MCA)
   Bill Monroe and His Blue Grass Boys-60 Years Of Country .... (RCA)
   Stars Of The Grand Ole Opry-1926-1974-C .... (RCA)
Charlie Daniels Band; *Fire On The Mountain* .... (Epic)
   ST/Urban Cowboy 2............................ (Epic)
Flatt & Scruggs; *Hear The Whistles Blow*........ (International Mktg. Group)
Gordon Terry; *Disco Country* .... (Plantation)
   Gordon Terry-20 Golden Souvenirs .... (Plantation)
Johnny Cash; *Columbia Records-1958-1986* .... (Columbia)
   Essential Johnny Cash......................... (Columbia)
   Johnny Cash-16 Biggest Hits-#2 .... (Legacy)
   Johnny Cash's Greatest Hits .... (Columbia)
   The Man In Black-His Greatest Hits .... (Legacy)
   Train Trax-C .... (Sony Music Special Prod.)
Johnson Mountain Boys; *Steel Rails-Classic Railroad Songs-#1-C* ... (Rounder)
Nitty Gritty Dirt Band; *Will The Circle Be Unbroken*................. (EMI)

Orange Blossom Time
Bing Crosby; *Crooner-Columbia Years-1928-1934*............ (Columbia)

Orange Juice Blues
Bob Dylan And The Band; *Basement Tapes* .... (Columbia)

Orange Sherbert
Count Basie; *Basie Big Band* ....(Pablo)

Party At The Prune Farm
Lou & Peter Berryman; *Cupid's Trash Truck*.............. (Cornbelt)

Peach
Prince; *The Hits 2* .... (Paisley Park)
   The Hits/The B-Sides .... (Paisley Park)

Peach Blossom Spring
Yutaka; *Yutaka* .... (GRP)

Peach Orchard Mamma
Big Joe Williams; *Piney Woods Blues* .... (Delmark)

Peach Picking Time Down In Georgia
Jimmie Rodgers; *My Rough & Rowdy Ways*.................. (RCA)
   This Is Jimmie Rodgers .... (RCA)
Merle Travis; *Red, White & Bluegrass-C* ....(C.M.H. Prod.)
   Superstars Salute Jimmie Rodgers-C.............. (Step One)

Peach Tree
Sonny Boy Williamson; *Real Folk Blues-C* .... (Chess)

Peach Tree Shuffle
Panama Francis; *All-Stars 1949* .... (Collectables)

Peach Window
Julianna Raye; *Something Peculiar* .... (Reprise)

Peacherine Rag
Scott Joplin; *King Of Ragtime Writers* ....(Biograph)

Peaches
Stranglers; *Stranglers' Greatest Hits-1977-1990* ....(Epic)

Peaches
Presidents Of The United States Of America; *The Presidents Of The United
   States Of America* .... (Columbia)

Peaches
Junior Parker; *Best Of Junior Parker* ....(MCA)

Peaches
Kristen Hall; *Fact & Fiction* .... (High Street)

Peaches
Captain Beefheart; *Unconditionally Guaranteed* .... (Blue Plate)

Peaches And Cream
Wayne Shorter; *Wayne Shorter*..........................(Crescendo)

Peaches And Cream
112; *Part III*...........................(Bad Boy/Arista)
   Totally Hits 2001-C .... (Arista)

Peaches And Diesel
Eric Clapton; *Slowhand*.............................(Polydor)

Peaches En Regalia
Frank Zappa; *Hot Rats*.............................. (Rykodisc)
   Swiss Cheese/Fire .... (Rhino)
Mothers Of Invention; *Fillmore East-June 1971*........... (Reprise)

Peel Me A Grape
Anita O'Day; *Time For Two* .... (Verve)
Diana Krall; *Love Scenes* .... (Impulse!)

Pineapple
Original Cast; *Cabaret* .... (Columbia)

Pineapple Princess
Annette Funicello; *Frankie Avalon/Annette Funicello* .... (K-Tel)

Pisces Apple Lady
Leon Russell; *Leon Russell* .... (MCA)

Please Don't Squeeze Da Banana
Louis Prima; *V-Disc Recordings-Louis Prima* .... (Collector's Choice)

Plum
George Benson; *Body Talk* .... (CBS Associated)
Stanley Turrentine; *Best Of Stanley Turrentine*................. (Blue Note)

Plum Blossom
Vangelis; *China*................................(Polydor)
Yusef Lateef & Others; *Eastern Sounds* ....(Prestige)

Pomegranate
Ian McCulloch; *Mysterio* ....(Sire)

Raspberries, Strawberries
Kingston Trio; *Capitol Collectors Series-The Kingston Trio* .... (Capitol)
   Sold Out/String Along .... (Capitol)

Raspberry Beret
Prince and the Revolution; *Around The World In A Day*........ (Paisley Park)

Raspberry Jam
Carole King; *Writer*............................. (Epic)

Rotten Peaches
Elton John; *Madman Across The Water* ....(Polydor)

Smith's Red Apple Rag
Skip Gorman; *A Cowboy's Wild Song To His Herd*............. (Rounder)

Stealin' Watermelons
Elvin Bishop; *Best Of Elvin Bishop* .... (Epic)
   Let It Flow ....(Capricorn)
   Live! Raisin' Hell ....(Capricorn)

Strange Fruit
Billie Holiday; *History Of The Real Billie Holiday* .... (Verve)
   Lady Sings The Blues .... (Verve)
   Songbook .... (Verve)
Nina Simone; *Compact Jazz-Nina Simone* .... (Verve)
Siouxsie And The Banshees; *Through The Looking Glass* .... (Geffen)

Strawberries
Smooth; *Reality*.................... (Perspective/A&M)

Strawberry
Everclear; *Sparkle And Fade*............................. (Capitol)

Strawberry Fields Forever
Beatles; *Beatles-Box Set* .... (Capitol)
   Magical Mystery Tour .... (Capitol)
   ST/Imagine: John Lennon .... (Capitol)
   The Beatles/1967-1970. .... (Capitol)

Strawberry Flats
Little Feat; *Hoy-Hoy!* .... (Warner Bros.)
   Little Feat. .... (Warner Bros.)

Strawberry Letter #23
Brothers Johnson; *Brothers Johnson-Classics-#11* .... (A&M)
   Right On Time .... (A&M)
Tevin Campbell; *T.E.V.I.N.*........................... (Qwest)

Strawberry Wine
Band; *Stage Fright* .... (Capitol)

Strawberry Wine
Deana Carter; *Did I Shave My Legs For This?* .... (Capitol)

Sweet Cherry Wine
Tommy James And The Shondells; *Tommy James And The Shondells-
   Anthology* .... (Rhino)
   Very Best Of Tommy James And The Shondells .... (Pair)

Sweet Guava Jelly
Lee ''Scratch'' Perry; *Soundz From The Hot Line*............. (Heartbeat)

Sweet Pear
Elvis Costello; *Mighty Like A Rose* .... (Warner Bros.)

Tangerine
Benny Goodman; *Best Of The Big Bands-C* .... (Columbia)
Dave Brubeck; *The Great Concerts...Amsterdam, Copenhagen,
   Carnegie Hall* .... (Columbia)

Frank Sinatra; *Sinatra and Swingin' Brass* . . . .(Reprise)
Harry Connick, Jr.; *25* . . . . (Columbia)
Nat ''King'' Cole; *At The Movies* . . . .(Capitol)

Tangerine
Led Zeppelin; *Led Zeppelin III* . . . . (Atlantic)
Led Zeppelin-Box Set . . . . (Atlantic)

Tempted
Squeeze; *East Side Story* . . . . (A&M)
Rock Of The '80s-#1-C . . . .(Priority)
VH-1 The Big '80s-C . . . . (Rhino)

Texas Lemon Flavor
Stefan Grossman; *Yazoo Basin Boogie* . . . .(Shanachie)

This Plum Is Too Ripe
Original Cast; *Fantasticks* . . . . (Polydor)

Tutti Frutti
Elvis Presley; *Elvis Presley* . . . .(RCA)
Rocker. . . . .(RCA)
Little Richard; *Greatest Hits Recorded Live* . . . . (Epic)
Little Richard . . . . (Specialty)
Little Richard-18 Greatest Hits . . . . (Rhino)
More American Graffiti-C . . . .(MCA)
This Is How It All Began-#2-C . . . . (Specialty)
Tribute To Black Entertainers-C . . . . (Columbia)
Queen; *Live At Wembley '86* . . . .(Hollywood)

Two Scoops Of Raisins
Common Sense; *Can I Borrow A Dollar?* . . . .(Relativity)

Underneath The Apple Tree
Michael Franks; *Tiger In The Rain* . . . . (Warner Bros.)

Watermelon
Scorpio Rising; *Pig Symphony* . . . .(Sire)
Zodiac Killers . . . .(Sire)

Watermelon
Pops Cool Love; *A Man* . . . . (Elektra)

Watermelon
John McCutcheon; *Family Garden* . . . . (Rounder)

Watermelon Crawl
Tracy Byrd; *No Ordinary Man* . . . . (MCA)

Watermelon Hangin' On The Vine
Hodges Brothers; *Watermelon Hangin' On The Vine* . . . .(Arhoolie)

Watermelon In Easter Hay
Frank Zappa; *Guitar* . . . . (Rykodisc)
Joe's Garage Acts I-III . . . . (Rykodisc)

Watermelon Man
Albert King; *Wednesday Night In San Francisco* . . . . (Stax)
Buddy Guy; *Hold That Plane* . . . .(Vanguard)
Herbie Hancock; *Best Of Herbie Hancock-The Blue Note Years.* . . . . .(Blue Note)
Head Hunters . . . . (Columbia)
Takin' Off . . . . (Blue Note)
Johnny Taylor; *Wanted One Soul Singer* . . . . (Atlantic)
Mongo Santamaria; *Mongo Santamaria's Greatest Hits* . . . .(Fantasy)
Mongo Santamaria's Greatest Hits . . . . (Columbia)
New Grass Revival; *Too Late To Turn Back Now* . . . .(Flying Fish)

Watermelon Man
Gun Club; *Miami* . . . . (I.R.S.)

Watermelon On The Vine
Stanley Brothers; *Stanley Series-Vol. 1-#2* . . . .(Copper Creek)

Watermelon Song
Hypnolovewheel; *Altered States* . . . .(Alias)

Watermelon Time In Georgia
Larry Boone; *Get In Line* . . . . (Columbia)

Watermelon Weather
Perry Como; *Yesterday And Today-A Celebration In Song* . . . .(RCA)

Watermelons
Johnny Shines; *Roots Of R&B-Tribute To Robert Johnson-C* . . . .(Columbia)

When Banana Skins Are Falling
Slim Gaillard; *Cement Mixer Putti Putti* . . . . (Folklyric)

When It's Cherry Time In Tokio
James P. Johnson; *Rare Piano Roll Solos-#2-1917* . . . . (Biograph)

When The Good Apples Fall
Seekers; *Capitol Collectors Series-The Seekers* . . . .(Capitol)

When The World Was Young
Anita O'Day; *Mello'Day* . . . .(Crescendo)
Frank Sinatra; *Point Of No Return.* . . . . (Capitol)

Why Is A Carrot More Orange Than An Orange
Amboy Dukes; *Journey To The Center Of The Mind.* . . . . (Mainstream)

Wild Cherry
Foghat; *Best Of Foghat* . . . . (Rhino)
Energized . . . . (Rhino)

Wild Cherry
Leroy Washington; *Sound Of The Swamp-Best Of Excello-#1-C* . . . .(Rhino)

Wild Strawberries
Gordon Lightfoot; *Waiting For You* . . . .(Reprise)

WPLJ (White Port Lemon Juice)
Four Deuces; *Legends Of Doo-Wop-#3-C* . . . . (Juke Box Treasures)
Mothers Of Invention; *Burnt Weeny Sandwich* . . . . (Bizarre/Straight)

Yes We Have No Bananas
Authentic Band Organ; *Catch The Brass Ring-Merry-Go-Round* . . . . . .(Klavier)
Spike Jones; *Best Of Spike Jones-#2* . . . .(RCA)

FOOD & BEVERAGES: GENERAL, Cooking, Eating, Hungry, Kitchens, Meals, Thirsty

See Also: **ALCOHOL, ANIMALS: FISH, BOTTLES, CANDY, FOOD & BEVERAGES (various), RESTAURANTS, SWEET, WAITRESSES, WATER**

3 Martini Lunch
Graham Parker; *Best Of Graham Parker 1988-1991* . . . . (RCA)

32 Flavors
Alana Davis; *Blame It On Me.* . . . .(Elektra)
Ani DiFranco; *Living In Clip* . . . . (Righteous Babe)
Not A Pretty Girl . . . . (Righteous Babe)

Abundance
Original Broadway Cast; *The Most Happy Fella* . . . . . . (Sony Music Classical)

Alan's Psychedelic Breakfast
Pink Floyd; *Atom Heart Mother* . . . .(Capitol)

Alpine Milkman
Randy Erwin; *'Til The Cows Come Home/Cowboy Rhythm* . . . .(Really Outstanding Music)

Amazing Bigfoot Diet
Mojo Nixon & Skid Roper; *Frenzy/Get Out Of My Way* . . . . (I.R.S.)

American Pie
Don McLean; *American Pie.* . . . .(EMI)
Best Of Don McLean . . . .(EMI)
Greatest Hits Then & Now . . . .(EMI)
ST/Born On The Fourth Of July. . . . .(MCA)
Madonna; *ST/The Next Big Thing* . . . . (Maverick)

Angel Food Cake
Siegel-Schwall Band; *Best Of The Siegel-Schwall Band* . . . .(Vanguard)

Animal Crackers
Melanie; *Best Of Melanie.* . . . . (Buddah)

Animal Crackers
Anne Murray; *There's A Hippo In My Tub.* . . . .(Capitol)

Another Piece Of Meat
Scorpions; *Lovedrive* . . . .(Mercury)
Worldwide Live . . . .(Mercury)

Ants In The Kitchen
Masters Of Reality; *Sunrise On The Sufferbus* . . . .(Chrysalis)

Apples Peaches Pumpkin Pie
Jay And The Techniques; *Cruisin'-1967-C* . . . .(Increase)

Astronaut Food
Sopwith Camel; *Miraculous Hump Returns.* . . . . (Reprise)

Baby Lemonade
Syd Barrett; *Barrett* . . . .(Capitol)

Back In The U.S.A.
Chuck Berry; *Chuck Berry-Golden Hits* . . . .(Mercury)
Chuck Berry's Greatest Hits . . . . (Everest)
Roll Over Beethoven . . . .(Allegiance)
The Chess Box-Chuck Berry . . . . (Chess)
Linda Ronstadt; *Linda Ronstadt's Greatest Hits, Volume Two* . . . . (Asylum)
Living In The USA . . . . (Asylum)

Bacon Fat
Frank Zappa; *Broadway The Hard Way* . . . . (Rykodisc)
Our Man In Nirvana . . . .(Rhino)

Baloney Again
Mark Knopfler; *Sailing To Philadelphia* . . . . (Warner Bros.)

Bar B Q
ZZ Top; *Rio Grande Mud.* . . . . (Warner Bros.)
Six Pack. . . . . (Warner Bros.)

Be A Pepper (Dr. Pepper)
Original Soundtrack; *TeeVee Toons-The Commercials-#1-C* . . . .(TVT)

Beef Jerky
John Lennon; *Walls And Bridges* . . . .(Capitol)

Being Boiled
Human League; *Human League's Greatest Hits* . . . .(A&M)

Big Butter And Egg Man
Louis Armstrong; *Best Of Louis Armstrong* . . . . (Audio Fidelity)
Hot Fives & Hot Sevens-#2 . . . .(Columbia)
Merle Haggard; *Kern River* . . . . (Epic)
Walking The Line . . . .(Epic)

Big Fat Ham
Jelly Roll Morton; *Immortal Jelly Roll Morton* . . . .(Milestone)

Big Mexican Dinner
Kentucky HeadHunters; *Electric Barnyard* . . . .(Mercury)

Big Mouth Blues
Gram Parsons; *G.P./Grievous Angel* . . . . (Reprise)
Gram Parsons/Fallen Angels Live-1973 . . . .(Sierra)

Binge & Purge
Clutch; *Transnational Speedway League.* . . . .(East West)

Bishop Danced
Bruce Springsteen; *Tracks* . . . .(Columbia)

Bittersweet Me
R.E.M.; *New Adventures In Hi-Fi* . . . . (Warner Bros.)

Bloat On
Cheech & Chong; *Let's Make A New Dope Deal* . . . .(Warner Bros.)

Blue Tail Fly
Burl Ives; *Best Of Burl Ives*. . . . .(MCA)
Pete Seeger; *20 Golden Pieces Of Pete Seeger* . . . . (Bulldog)
Blueberry Pie
Bette Midler; *For Our Children-10th Anniversary
Edition-C* . . . . (Kid Rhino/Rhino 4 Kids)
Blues For The Barbecue
Count Basie; *Farmers Market Barbecue* . . . .(Pablo)
Brain Stew
Green Day; *Insomniac* . . . . (Reprise)
Bread & Blood
Air Supply; *The Earth Is...* . . . . (Giant)
Bread & Water
Gary Morris; *Stones* . . . . (Liberty)
Bread And Butter
Newbeats; *Billboard Top Rock 'N' Roll Hits-1964-C*. . . . . (Rhino)
Collectables Presents The History Of Rock-#9-C . . . . . . (Collectables)
Oldies But Goodies-#2-C . . . . (Original Sound)
Bread And Butter
Waitresses; *Best Of The Waitresses* . . . . (Polydor)
Bread And Roses
Ani DiFranco & Utah Phillips; *Fellow Workers* . . . .(Righteous Babe)
Judy Collins; *So Early In The Spring, The First 15 Years* . . . . (Elektra)
Breadline Blues
New Lost City Ramblers; *Depression Songs* . . . . (Smithsonian Folkways)
Breakfast At Tiffany's
Deep Blue Something; *Home* . . . . (RainMaker/Interscope)
Breakfast At Tiffany's
Henry Mancini; *Days Of Wine And Roses* . . . . (RCA)
Breakfast For Dinosaurs
Fowler Brothers; *Breakfast For Dinosaurs*. . . . . (Fossil)
Breakfast In America
Supertramp; *Breakfast In America* . . . . (A&M)
Paris . . . . (A&M)
Supertramp-Classics-#9 . . . . (A&M)
Breakfast In Bed
Lorna Bennett; *This Is Reggae Music-#1-C* . . . . (Island)
UB40; *UB40*. . . . . (A&M)
Bring Home The Bacon
Drivin' N' Cryin'; *Scarred But Smarter* . . . . (Island)
Bring On The Rain
Jo Dee Messina with Tim McGraw; *Burn*. . . . . (Curb)
Bun & Cheese
Clement Irie & Robert French; *Dancehall Style-Best Of Reggae
Dancehall-C* . . . . (Profile)
Burgers & Fries
Charley Pride; *Burgers & Fries* . . . . (RCA)
Charley Pride's Greatest Hits . . . . (RCA)
When I Stop Leaving . . . . (RCA)
Butta Love
Next; *Rated Next*. . . . .(Divine Mill/Arista)
Buttermilk Biscuits (Keep On Square Dancin')
Sir Mix-A-Lot; *Swass*. . . . . (Nastymix)
Candy And A Currant Bun
Pink Floyd; *Saucerful Of Secrets* . . . . (Capitol)
Shine On . . . . (Columbia)
Candy And Cake
Mindy Carson; *Lost Female Hits Of The '50s-C*. . . . .(Taragon)
Candy And Cake
Evelyn Knight; *Best Of Evelyn Knight* . . . . (Collector's Choice)
Candy-Coated Popcorn, Peanuts And A Prize (Cracker Jack)
Original Soundtrack; *TeeVee Toons-The Commercials-#1-C*. . . . . (TVT)
Canned Goods
Greg Brown; *One More Goodnight Kiss*. . . . .(Red House)
Catfish Fry
Red Meat; *Alameda County Line* . . . .(Ranchero)
Catfish Sam'ich
Charles Williams; *Charles Williams*. . . . .(Mainstream)
Cheap Seats, The
Alabama; *Cheap Seats* . . . . (RCA)
Cheese & Onions
Rutles; *Rutles* . . . . (Rhino)
Cheeseburger In Paradise
Jimmy Buffett; *Son Of A Son Of A Sailor* . . . . (MCA)
Songs You Know By Heart-Jimmy Buffett's Greatest Hit(s) . . . . (MCA)
Cherry Coke
Bob's Diner; *Bob's Diner* . . . . (Digital Music Prod.)
Chewin' Gum
Ella Fitzgerald; *Ella Fitzgerald* . . . . (Laserlight)
Chewing Gum
Carter Family; *Anchored In Love-Complete Victor Recordings* . . . . . . (Rounder)
Elvis Costello; *Spike* . . . .(Warner Bros.)
Uncle Dave Macon; *Laugh Your Blues Away* . . . . (Rounder)
Chicken Cordon Blues
Steve Goodman; *Somebody Else's Troubles*. . . . . (Buddah)
Chicken Gumbo
Preston Love & Shuggie Otis; *Omaha BBQ* . . . . (Kent)

Chicken Heads
Jimmy Johnson; *Bar Room Preacher* . . . . (Alligator)
Mighty Joe Young; *Chicken Heads*. . . . .(Ovation)
Chicken Soup
Angel; *Helluva Band*. . . . . (Mercury)
Chicken Stew Part I
Geoff Muldaur & Amos Garrett; *Geoff Muldaur & Amos
Garrett*. . . . . (Flying Fish)
Chinese Kitchen
Fleshtones; *Fleshtones* . . . . (I.R.S.)
Roman Gods. . . . . (I.R.S.)
Choc'late Ice Cream Cone
Red Foley; *45-#46234*. . . . . (Decca)
Chocolate And Vanilla Pudding
Everything; *Labrador* . . . . (Capricorn)
Chocolate Buttermilk
Kool & The Gang; *Best Of Kool & The Gang-1969-
1976*. . . . . (Mercury/Funk Essentials)
Kool & The Gang . . . . (Mercury)
Live At The Sex Machine . . . . (Mercury)
Chocolate Cake
Crowded House; *Woodface* . . . . (Capitol)
Chocolate Shake
Duke Ellington; *Wicked Swing-C* . . . . (RCA Victor)
Chop Suey
Original Cast; *ST/Flower Drum Song* . . . . (Sony Music Classical)
Chop Suey Louie
Jimmy Preston; *Rock The Joint-#2-C* . . . . (Collectables)
Chopsticks
Liberace; *Liberace-16 Most Requested Songs* . . . . (Columbia)
Church
Lyle Lovett; *Joshua Judges Ruth* . . . . (Curb/MCA)
Cinnamon
Derek; *Rock Artifacts-From The Vaults-#3-C* . . . . (Columbia)
Cinnamon Girl
Neil Young & Crazy Horse; *Decade* . . . . (Reprise)
Everybody Knows This Is Nowhere . . . . (Reprise)
Live Rust . . . . (Reprise)
WELD . . . . (Reprise)
Coca Cola Cowboy
Mel Tillis; *Mel Tillis' Greatest Hits* . . . . (Curb)
Very Best Of Mel Tillis . . . . (MCA)
Cockles & Mussels
Emily Mitchell; *The Irish Album*. . . . . (RCA)
Coffee, Donuts & Death
Paris; *Sleeping With The Enemy* . . . . (Scarface)
Colorado Kool Aid
Johnny Paycheck; *Johnny Paycheck's Biggest Hits* . . . . (Epic)
Johnny Paycheck's Greatest Hits-#2 . . . . (Epic)
Take This Job And Shove It . . . . (Epic)
Come Alive (Pepsi)
Original Soundtrack; *TeeVee Toons-The Commercials-#1-C* . . . . (TVT)
Come On In My Kitchen
Delaney & Bonnie; *Delaney & Bonnie-Anthology-#2*. . . . . (Capricorn)
Duane Allman-An Anthology . . . . (Capricorn)
Robert Johnson; *King Of The Delta Blues Singers* . . . . (Columbia)
Robert Johnson-Complete Recordings. . . . . (Columbia)
Steve Miller Band; *Joker*. . . . . (Capitol)
Come On-A My House
Rosemary Clooney; *Rosemary Clooney-16 Most Requested Songs* . . . . (Legacy)
Sentimental Journey: Pop Vocal Classics-#3-C . . . . (Rhino)
Cook Of The House
Wings; *Wings At The Speed Of Sound* . . . . (Capitol)
Cook With Fire
Heart; *Dog & Butterfly* . . . . (Portrait)
Cool Water
Bob Nolan; *Sound Of A Pioneer* . . . . (Elektra)
Frankie Laine; *Frankie Laine-16 Most Requested Songs* . . . . (Legacy)
Jack Scott; *Capitol Collectors Series-Jack Scott* . . . . (Capitol)
Joni Mitchell; *Chalk Mark In A Rain Storm* . . . . (Geffen)
Marty Robbins; *Gunfighter Ballads & Trail Songs* . . . . (Legacy)
Sons Of The Pioneers; *60 Years Of Country Music-C* . . . . (RCA)
Best Of The Sons Of The Pioneers . . . . (RCA)
Cool Water . . . . (RCA)
Western Country. . . . . (Granite)
Cornflake Girl
Tori Amos; *Under The Pink* . . . . (Atlantic)
Country Ham & Red Gravy
Hotmud Family; *Live As We Know It* . . . . (Flying Fish)
Country Pie
Bob Dylan; *Nashville Skyline* . . . . (Columbia)
Cream
Prince And The New Power Generation; *Diamonds And Pearls*. . . (Paisley Park)
Cup Of Life
Ricky Martin; *Ricky Martin*. . . . . (Columbia)
Custard Pie
Led Zeppelin; *Physical Graffiti*. (Swan Song)

Days Of Pup & Taco
Lawndale; *Beyond Barbecue* . . . . (SST)
No Age-Compilation Of SST Instrumentals-C . . . . (SST)

Devil's Food
Alice Cooper; *The Alice Cooper Show* . . . . (Warner Bros.)
Welcome To My Nightmare . . . . (Atlantic)

Dill Pickle Rag I
Mark O'Connor; *Championship Years* . . . . (Country Music Foundation)

Dill Pickles Rag
Max Morath; *Ragtime Man* . . . . (Omega)

Dinner For One Please James
Nat "King" Cole; *Blossom Fell* . . . . (Capitol)
Nat "King" Cole-Gift Set . . . . (Capitol)

Dinner With Drac
Zacherle; *Rock-O-Rama-#2-C* . . . . (Abkco)

Dinner With Gershwin
Brenda Russell; *Kiss Me With The Wind* . . . . (A&M)
Donna Summer; *All Systems Go* . . . . (Geffen)

Dirty Old Egg-Sucking Dog
Johnny Cash; *Essential Johnny Cash* . . . . (Columbia)
Johnny Cash At Folsom Prison & San Quentin . . . . (Columbia)

Do You Know Exactly How (Oreo Cookies)
Original Soundtrack; *TeeVee Toons-The Commercials-#1-C* . . . . . . (TVT)

Does Your Chewing Gum Lose Its Flavor (On The Bedpost Overnight)
Lonnie Donegan; *Dr. Demento Presents The Greatest Novelty Records-#3-1960s-C* . . . . (Rhino)
Dr. Demento Presents The Greatest Novelty Records-C . . . . (Rhino)

Dogs Kids Love To Bite, The (Armour Hot Dogs)
Original Soundtrack; *TeeVee Toons-The Commercials-#1-C* . . . . . . (TVT)

Don't Eat Stuff Off The Sidewalk
Cramps; *Psychedelic Jungle/Gravest Hits* . . . . (I.R.S.)

Don't Eat The Yellow Snow
Frank Zappa; *Apostrophe/Overnite Sensation* . . . . (Rykodisc)

Donut Man
Rita Coolidge; *The Lady's Not For Sale* . . . . (A&M)

Easter Dinner
Tribe; *Abort* . . . . (Slash)

Eat A Little Something
Original Cast; *I Can Get It For You Wholesale* . . . . (Columbia)

Eat At Home
Paul And Linda McCartney; *RAM* . . . . (Capitol)

Eat It
"Weird Al" Yankovic; *"Weird Al" Yankovic's Greatest Hits* . . . . (Scotti Bros.)
Dr. Demento Presents The Greatest Novelty Records-#5-1980s-C . . . . (Rhino)
Dr. Demento: 20th Anniversary Collection-C . . . . (Rhino)
In 3-D . . . . (Scotti Bros.)

Eat The Rich
Aerosmith; *Get A Grip* . . . . (Geffen)

Eat To The Beat
Blondie; *Eat To The Beat* . . . . (Chrysalis)

Eaten Alive
Diana Ross; *Eaten Alive* . . . . (RCA)

Eggplant Pizza
Jimmy Bruno Trio; *Sleight Of Hand* . . . . (Concord Jazz)

Eggs And Sausage (In A Cadillac With Susan Michelson)
Tom Waits; *Nighthawks At The Diner* . . . . (Asylum)

Everybody Eats When They Come To My House
Cab Calloway; *Are You Hep To The Jive?-22 Sensational Tracks* . . . . . (Legacy)
Hi De Ho Man . . . . (Columbia)
Legacy's Rhythm & Soul Revue-C . . . . (Legacy)

Fast Food
Stevens & Grdnic; *Dr. Demento Presents The Greatest Novelty Records-#5-1980s-C* . . . . (Rhino)

Fast Food
Pete Townshend; *The Iron Man* . . . . (Atlantic)

Father's Table Grace
Lester Flatt; *Fifty Years Of Bluegrass Hits-#3-C* . . . . . (C.M.H. Prod.)
Lester Flatt & The Nashville Grass; *The Tennessee Mountain Bluegrass Festival* . . . . (C.M.H. Prod.)

Feed Jake
Pirates Of The Mississippi; *Pirates Of The Mississippi* . . . . (Liberty)

Feed Me
Elton John; *Rock Of The Westies* . . . . (Polydor)

Fish & Chips
Eddie & The Hot Rods; *Fish & Chips* . . . . (EMI)

Fish Heads
Barnes & Barnes; *20th Anniversary Collection* . . . . (Rhino)
Dr. Demento Presents The Greatest Novelty Records-#4-1970s-C . . . . (Rhino)

Follow The Drinking Gourd
Richie Havens; *Songs Of The Civil War-C* . . . . (Columbia)
Weavers; *Weavers' Greatest Hits* . . . . (Vanguard)

Food (Till Sunday) (No)
Click Click; *Wet Skin & Curious Eye* . . . . (Play It Again Sam)

Food Glorious Food
Original Broadway Cast; *Oliver!* . . . . (RCA Victor)
Original London Cast; *Oliver!* . . . . (EMI-Angel)

Food Phone Gas Lodging
Charlie King; *Food Phone Gas Lodging* . . . . (Flying Fish)

Fort Worth Hambone Blues
Johnny Gimble & The Texas Swing Pioneers; *Johnny Gimble's Texas Honky-Tonk Hits-C* . . . . (C.M.H. Prod.)

Found A Peanut
Wonder Kids; *Really Silly Songs* . . . . (Madacy)

Fourteen Minutes Old
Doug Stone; *Doug Stone* . . . . (Epic)

Fried Chicken
Rufus Thomas; *Hi Times-The Hi Records R&B Years* . . . . . . (Right Stuff)

Frim Fram Sauce
Diana Krall; *Stepping Out* . . . . (Justin Time)
Nat "King" Cole; *V-Disc Recordings-Nat "King" Cole* . . . (Collector's Choice)

Fruit Juicy (Hawaiian Punch)
Original Soundtrack; *TeeVee Toons-The Commercials-#1-C* . . . . . . (TVT)

Gator Tails And Monkey Ribs
Spats; *45-#10585* . . . . (ABC)

Georgy Porgy
Eric Benet featuring Faith Evans; *A Day In The Life* . . . . (Warner Bros.)
Toto; *Past To Present 1977-1990* . . . . (Columbia)
Toto . . . . (Columbia)

German Lunch
Frank Zappa; *You Can't Do That On Stage Anymore-#5* . . . . . . (Rykodisc)

Gimme A Pigfoot (And A Bottle Of Beer)
Billie Holiday; *Complete Decca Recordings* . . . . (Decca Jazz)
From The Original Decca Masters . . . . (MCA)

Gimme Some Water
Eddie Money; *Life For The Taking* . . . . (Columbia)

Ginger Bread
Frankie Avalon; *Gold For The Road-Carburetor Classics-C* . . . . (Compose)
Venus: The Very Best Of Frankie Avalon . . . . (Collectables)

Go For Soda
Kim Mitchell; *Akimbo Alogo* . . . . (Bronze)

Goodbye Earl
Dixie Chicks; *Fly* . . . . (Monument)

Grandma's Killer Fruitcake
Elmo Shropshire; *Dr. Elmo's Twisted Christmas* . . . . (Laughing Stock)

Guacamole
Texas Tornados; *Hangin' On By A Thread* . . . . (Reprise)

Hey, Good Lookin'
Hank Williams With His Drifting Cowboys; *24 Of Hank Williams' Greatest Hits* . . . . (Polydor)
Hank Williams-40 Greatest Hits . . . . (Polydor)
Hey, Good Lookin'-December 1950-July 1951 . . . . (Polydor)
Loretta Lynn & Conway Twitty; *Hey, Good Lookin'* . . . . . . (MCA Special Prod.)

Hold Tight, Hold Tight (Sea Food)
Andrews Sisters; *Andrews Sisters-16 Great Performances* . . . . (MCA)
Best Of The Andrews Sisters . . . . (MCA)
Boogie Woogie Bugle Girls . . . . (MCA)

Home Cookin'
Junior Walker & The All Stars; *Junior Walker & The All Stars' Greatest Hits* . . . . (Motown)
Junior Walker & The All Stars-Anthology . . . . (Motown)

Honey Bun
Original Cast; *South Pacific* . . . . (CBS Masterworks)

Hot Cakes
Carly Simon; *Hotcakes* . . . . (Elektra)

Hot Chili
Steve Miller Band; *Number 5* . . . . (Capitol)

Hot Chili Mama
Beausoleil; *Hot Chili Mama* . . . . (Arhoolie)

Hot Dog
Elvis Presley; *Elvis Presley* . . . . (RCA)
Essential Elvis-The First Movies . . . . (RCA)
Loving You . . . . (RCA)

Hot Dog
Led Zeppelin; *In Through The Out Door* . . . . (Swan Song)

Hot Dog
Mongo Santamaria; *Mongo Santamaria's Greatest Hits* . . . . . . (Columbia)

Hot Dogs & Cabbage
Li'l Wally; *One Man Band* . . . . (Jay Jay)

Hot Dogs & Hamburgers
John Cougar Mellencamp; *The Lonesome Jubilee* . . . . (Mercury)

Hot Pastrami
Dartells; *Frat Rock! Box Set-C* . . . . (Rhino)
Frat Rock!-#4-C . . . . (Rhino)
History Of Rock Instrumentals-#1-C . . . . (Rhino)
Son Of Frat Rock!-C . . . . (Rhino)

Hot Tamale
Jackie Mittoo; *Jackie Mittoo* . . . . (EMI)
New & Old Songs . . . . (EMI)

Hot Tamale Baby
Buckwheat Zydeco; *Best Of Louisiana Music* . . . . (Rounder)
Clifton Chenier; *Zydeco Dynamite-Anthology* . . . . (Rhino)
Zydeco Party-C . . . . (K-Tel)

How Do You Like Your Eggs In The Morning?
Jane Powell/Vic Damone/Four Freshmen; *ST/Romantic Duets From MGM Classics-C* . . . . (Turner Classic Movies)

Hunger
Waylon Jennings; *Ramblin' Man* . . . . (RCA)

Hunger Strike
Temple Of The Dog; *Temple Of The Dog* . . . . (A&M)

Hungry
Winger; *Winger* . . . . (Atlantic)

Hungry
Coasters; *It Ain't Sanitary* . . . . (Trip)

Hungry
Sammy Hagar; *Sammy Hagar* . . . . (Capitol)

Hungry (For Those Good Things)
Paul Revere And The Raiders; *Best Of Paul Revere And The
  Raiders-#1* . . . . (Bac-Trac)
Frat Rock!-C . . . . (Rhino)
Legend Of Paul Revere And The Raiders . . . . (Columbia)
Paul Revere And The Raiders' Greatest Hits . . . . (Columbia)

Hungry Eyes
Eric Carmen; *Best Of Eric Carmen* . . . . (Arista)
Dirty Dancing Live In Concert-C . . . . (RCA)
ST/Dirty Dancing . . . . (RCA)

Hungry Eyes
Emmylou Harris; *Mama's Hungry Eyes-Merle Haggard Tribute-C* . . . . (Arista)
Merle Haggard; *For The Record: Merle Haggard-43 Legendary Hits* . . . . (BNA)

Hungry For Love
Patsy Cline; *20 Golden Pieces Of Patsy Cline* . . . . (Bulldog)
Hungry For Love-Her First Recordings-#2 . . . . (Rhino)
Patsy Cline . . . . (MCA)

Hungry For Love
Todd Rundgren; *A Wizard A True Star* . . . . (Rhino)

Hungry For Your Love
Van Morrison; *ST/An Officer And A Gentleman* . . . . (Island)
Wavelength . . . . (Warner Bros.)

Hungry Heart
Bruce Springsteen; *Bruce Springsteen's Greatest Hits* . . . . (Columbia)
The River . . . . (Columbia)
Bruce Springsteen & The E Street Band; *Bruce Springsteen & The E Street
  Band/1975-85* . . . . (Legacy)

Hungry Like The Wolf
Duran Duran; *Arena* . . . . (Capitol)
Decade . . . . (Capitol)
Duran Duran (The Wedding Album) . . . . (Capitol)
Rio . . . . (Capitol)

I Ain't Gonna Eat Out My Heart Anymore
Rascals; *The Young Rascals* . . . . (Warner Special Prod.)
Time Peace/The Rascals' Greatest Hits . . . . (Atlantic)

I Ain't Gonna Give Nobody None Of My Jelly Roll
Bobby Darin/Johnny Mercer/Billy May Orchestra; *Two Of A Kind* . . . . (Atlantic)

I Am A Pizza
Peter Alsop; *Wha' D' Ya Wanna Do* . . . . (Flying Fish)

I Dream Of Ice Cream
Bananas In Pajamas; *Bumping And A-Jumping* . . . . (Capitol)

I Know An Old Lady Who Swallowed A Fly
Original Soundtrack; *More Silly Songs* . . . . (Disney)
Peter, Paul & Mary; *Peter, Paul & Mommy, Too* . . . . (Warner Bros.)

I Left My Heart At The Stage Door Canteen
Jo Stafford; *G.I. Jo* . . . . (Corinthian)

I Love Bosco
Original Soundtrack; *TeeVee Toons-The Commercials-#1-C* . . . . (TVT)

I Love Rocky Road
"Weird Al" Yankovic; *"Weird Al" Yankovic* . . . . (Volcano Entertainment)

I Need Lunch
Dead Boys; *Young, Loud And Snotty* . . . . (Sire)

I Tawt I Taw A Puddy Tat
Mel Blanc; *From The Vaults-#7-The Movies...-C* . . . . (Capitol)

I Want You (Coca-Cola)
Savage Garden; *Best Of Savage Garden* . . . . (Columbia)
Savage Garden . . . . (Columbia)

Ice Cream
Sarah McLachlan; *Fumbling Towards Ecstasy* . . . . (Arista)

Ice Cream Castles
Time; *Ice Cream Castle* . . . . (Warner Bros.)

I'd Like To Buy The World A Coke (Coca-Cola)
Original Soundtrack; *TeeVee Toons-The Commercials-#1-C* . . . . (TVT)

If I Knew You Were Comin' I'd've Baked A Cake
Bing Crosby; *The Radio Years-#4* . . . . (Crescendo)
Ethel Merman; *The Ethel Merman Collection* . . . . (Razor & Tie)

If You Like Fluff, Fluff, Fluff (Marshallow Fluff)
Original Soundtrack; *TeeVee Toons-The Commercials-#1-C* . . . . (TVT)

I'm A Woman
Maria Muldaur; *Waitress In The Donut Shop* . . . . (Warner Archives)
Peggy Lee; *I Am Woman-C* . . . . (Nick At Nite)
Peggy Lee's All-Time Greatest Hits . . . . (Curb)
Reba McEntire; *Out Of A Dream* . . . . (Mercury)

I'm Putting All My Eggs In One Basket
Carmen McRae; *Greatest Of Carmen McRae* . . . . (MCA)
Fred Astaire; *Irving Berlin Songbook* . . . . (Verve)
Irving Berlin; *American Songbook Series-Irving
  Berlin* . . . . (Smithsonian Collection)

I'm Throwing Rice
Jerry Lee Lewis; *Taste Of Country* . . . . (Sun)

In Hiding
Pearl Jam; *Yield* . . . . (Epic)

In The Cool, Cool, Cool Of The Evening
Bing Crosby; *Best Of Bing Crosby* . . . . (MCA)
Frank Sinatra; *Days Of Wine And Roses, Moon River, And Other Academy
  Award Winners* . . . . (Reprise)
Rosemary Clooney; *Rosemary Clooney-16 Most Requested Songs* . . . . (Legacy)

Incense And Peppermints
Strawberry Alarm Clock; *Billboard Top Rock 'N' Roll Hits-1967-C* . . . . (Rhino)
Cruisin'-1967-C . . . . (Increase)
Even More Nuggets-C . . . . (Rhino)
Nuggets-#8-Acid Rock-C . . . . (Rhino)

It Ain't The Meat
Swallows; *Risque Blues: It Ain't The Meat-C* . . . . (King)
Risque Rhythms: Nasty '50s R&B-C . . . . (Rhino)

It's The Real Thing (Coca-Cola)
Original Cast; *TeeVee Toons-The Commercials-#1-C* . . . . (TVT)

Jambalaya (On The Bayou)
Blue Ridge Rangers; *Blue Ridge Rangers* . . . . (Fantasy)
Fats Domino; *Fats Domino's Greatest Hits* . . . . (MCA)
Hank Williams With His Drifting Cowboys; *24 Of Hank Williams'
  Greatest Hits* . . . . (Polydor)
Hank Williams-16 Great Hits . . . . (Everest)
Hank Williams-40 Greatest Hits . . . . (Polydor)
Hank Williams, Jr.; *ST/Your Cheatin' Heart* . . . . (Sony Music Special Prod.)
Jerry Lee Lewis; *Twenty Classic Hits* . . . . (Sun)
Nitty Gritty Dirt Band; *All The Good Times* . . . . (United Artists)
Stars And Stripes Forever . . . . (Capitol)

Jelly, Jelly
Lincoln Center Jazz Orchestra; *ST/Love Jones* . . . . (Columbia)

Jesus At McDonald's
Mojo Nixon; *Get Out Of My Way* . . . . (Restless)

Jumbo Malt
Skatalites; *African Roots* . . . . (Liberty)

Junk Food Junkie
Larry Groce; *Dr. Demento Presents The Greatest Novelty Records-#4-
  1970s-C* . . . . (Rhino)

Lasagna
"Weird Al" Yankovic; *Even Worse* . . . . (Scotti Bros.)

Last Cup Of Sorrow
Faith No More; *Album Of The Year* . . . . (Reprise)

Last Meal
Asleep At The Wheel; *Very Best Of Asleep At The Wheel
  Since 1970* . . . . (Relentless/Madacy)

Leader Of Men
Nickelback; *State* . . . . (Roadrunner)

Leftovers
Millie Jackson; *Still Caught Up* . . . . (Spring)

Let's Have Another Cup Of Coffee
Glenn Miller; *Complete Glenn Miller & His Orchestra-#8* . . . . (Bluebird)
Michael Feinstein; *Remember-Michael Feinstein Sings Irving Berlin* . . (Elektra)

Life In The Foodchain
Tonio K.; *Life In The Foodchain* . . . . (Epic)

Life Is A Minestrone
10 CC; *Original Soundtrack* . . . . (Mercury)

Looking East
Jackson Browne; *Looking East* . . . . (Elektra)

Lost In The Supermarket
Clash; *London Calling* . . . . (Epic)
On Broadway . . . . (Epic)
The Story Of The Clash, Volume 1 . . . . (Epic)

Lotus
R.E.M.; *Up* . . . . (Warner Bros.)

Love Bites
Judas Priest; *Defenders Of The Faith* . . . . (Columbia)
Priest...Live! . . . . (Columbia)

Love Bites
Def Leppard; *Hysteria* . . . . (Mercury)

Love Will Keep Us Alive
Eagles; *Hell Freezes Over* . . . . (Geffen)

Lumpy Gravy
Mothers Of Invention; *Lumpy Gravy* . . . . (Rykodisc)

Lunch Hour
Rupert Holmes; *Partners In Crime* . . . . (MCA)

MacArthur Park
Andy Williams; *Andy Williams' Greatest Hits-#2* . . . . (Columbia)
Donna Summer; *Live & More* . . . . (Casablanca)
On The Radio-Greatest Hits-Volumes I & II . . . . (Casablanca)
Summer Collection . . . . (Mercury)
Walk Away-Best Of Donna Summer-1977-1980 . . . . (Casablanca)
Richard Harris; *Love Album* . . . . (MCA)
Richard Harris-His Greatest Performances . . . . (MCA)
Tramp Shining . . . . (MCA)
Vintage Music-#13-C . . . . (MCA)
Waylon Jennings; *Are You Ready For The Country* . . . . (RCA)
Best Of Waylon Jennings . . . . (RCA)

Macon Hambone Blues
Wet Willie; *Drippin' Wet/Live!* . . . . (Capricorn)
Main Course
Freddie Jackson; *Do Me Again* . . . . (Capitol)
Paul Laurence; *Underexposed* . . . . (Capitol)
Maneater
Daryl Hall & John Oates; *H2O* . . . . (RCA)
Nipper's Greatest Hits Of The '80s-C . . . . (RCA)
Rock 'N Soul, Part 1 . . . . (RCA)
Martika's Kitchen
Martika; *Martika's Kitchen* . . . . (Columbia)
Mashed Potatoes (Hot Pastrami With)
Joey Dee & the Starliters; *Hey Let's Twist! Best Of Joey Dee & The
Starliters* . . . . (Rhino)
Maximum Consumption
Kinks; *Everybody's In Show-Biz* . . . . (Rhino)
Mayonaise
Smashing Pumpkins; *Siamese Dream* . . . . (Virgin)
Mean Mr. Mustard
Beatles; *Abbey Road* . . . . (Parlophone)
Memphis Jellyroll
Stefan Grossman; *Yazoo Basin Boogie* . . . . (Shanachie)
Memphis Soul Stew
King Curtis; *Atlantic Jazz-Soul-C* . . . . (Atlantic)
Atlantic Rhythm & Blues 1947-1974-#6 (1966-1969)-C . . . . (Atlantic)
Best Of King Curtis . . . . (Atlantic)
Golden Soul-C . . . . (Atlantic)
Live At The Fillmore West . . . . (Atlantic)
Milk & Honey
Original Cast; *Milk & Honey* . . . . (RCA Victor)
Milk Cow Blues
Aerosmith; *Draw The Line* . . . . (Columbia)
Pandora's Box . . . . (Columbia)
Bob Wills & His Texas Playboys; *Best Of Bob Wills & His Texas
Playboys* . . . . (MCA)
Tiffany Transcriptions-#3 . . . . (Rhino)
Eddie Cochran; *Eddie Cochran-Legendary Masters* . . . . (EMI)
Rick Nelson; *Rick Nelson-Souvenirs* . . . . (EMI)
Ricky Nelson; *Ricky Nelson-Legendary Masters* . . . . (EMI)
Tim McGraw & Asleep At The Wheel; *Ride With Bob-C* . . (DreamWorks/SKG)
Milk It
Nirvana; *In Utero* . . . . (David Geffen Co.)
Mota
Offspring; *Ixnay On The Hombre* . . . . (Columbia)
Mother Popcorn
Aerosmith; *Live! Bootleg* . . . . (Columbia)
James Brown; *Sex Machine* . . . . (Polydor)
Mouth
Merril Bainbridge; *The Garden* . . . . (Universal)
Mr. Too Damn Good
Gerald Levert; *G* . . . . (East West)
Muffin Man
Zappa/Beefheart; *Bongo Fury* . . . . (Rykodisc)
My Big Iron Skillet
Wanda Jackson; *Rockin' In The Country-Best Of Wanda Jackson* . . . . . (Rhino)
My Bologna
"Weird Al" Yankovic; *"Weird Al" Yankovic* . . . . (Volcano Entertainment)
Dr. Demento Presents The Greatest Novelty Records-#4-1970s-C . . . . (Rhino)
Dr. Demento's Dementia Royale-C . . . . (Rhino)
My Daddy Was A Milkman
Kentucky HeadHunters; *Pickin' On Nashville* . . . . (Mercury)
Mysterious
Scorpions; *Eye II Eye* . . . . (Koch International)
Napalm For Breakfast
Rhythm Devils; *Apocalypse Now Sessions* . . . . (Rykodisc)
Need A Little Taste Of Love
Doobie Brothers; *Cycles* . . . . (Warner Bros.)
N-E-S-T-L-E-S (Nestle's Quik Chocolate Flavor)
Original Soundtrack; *TeeVee Toons-The Commercials-#1-C* . . . . (TVT)
No Milk Today
Herman's Hermits; *Herman's Hermits-Their Greatest Hits* . . . . (Abkco)
There's A Kind Of A Hush . . . . (MGM)
No Rice, No Peas, No Coconut Oil
Jolly Boys; *Beer Joint & Tailoring* . . . . (Smithsonian Folkways)
Nobody Doesn't Like Sara Lee
Original Soundtrack; *TeeVee Toons-The Commercials-#1-C* . . . . (TVT)
Now's The Time To Fall In Love
Eddie Cantor; *The Eddie Cantor Radio Show-1942-1943* . . . . . . (Original Cast)
Gene Gardos & His Orchestra; *Brother Can You Spare A Dime? Great
American Songs Of The Depression-C* . . . . (Pro-Arte)
Old Home Filler Up & Keep On A Truckin'
C.W. McCall; *C.W. McCall's Greatest Hits* . . . . (Polydor)
Wolf Creek Pass . . . . (MGM)
Old Kidney Stew Is Fine
Eddie "Cleanhead" Vinson; *Old Kidney Stew Is Fine* . . . . (Delmark)
Ole Buttermilk Sky
Hoagy Carmichael; *Ole Buttermilk Sky* . . . . (Collector's Choice)

Kay Kyser & His Orchestra; *Best Of Kay Kyser & His
Orchestra* . . . . (Collector's Choice)
Mello-Larks; *The Hoagy Carmichael Songbook-C* . . . . (Bluebird)
Willie Nelson; *What A Wonderful World* . . . . (Columbia)
On Top Of Spaghetti
Tom Glazer; *Silly Songs-C* . . . . (K-Tel)
One Meat Ball
Ry Cooder; *Ry Cooder* . . . . (Reprise)
One Meatball
Roy Bookbinder; *Hillbilly Blues Cats* . . . . (Rounder)
Onion Roll
Herb Ellis & Ray Brown Sextet; *Hot Tracks* . . . . (Concord Jazz)
Orange Sherbert
Count Basie; *Basie Big Band* . . . . (Pablo)
Oreo Cookie Blues
Lonnie Mack; *Strike Like Lightning* . . . . (Alligator)
Out Of The Frying Pan (& Into The Fire)
Meat Loaf; *Bat Out Of Hell II: Back Into Hell* . . . . (MCA)
Out To Lunch
Country Gazette; *Out To Lunch* . . . . (Flying Fish)
Eric Dolphy; *Out To Lunch* . . . . (Blue Note)
Paddy Won't You Drink Some Cider
Red Clay Ramblers; *Chuckin' The Frizz* . . . . (Flying Fish)
Pass The Pickle
Prime Minister Pete Nice & Daddy Rich; *Dust To Dust* . . . . (Def Jam/Columbia)
Peaches And Cream
112; *Part III* . . . . (Bad Boy/Arista)
Totally Hits 2001-C . . . . (Arista)
Peak Hour (Lunch Break)
Moody Blues; *Caught Live Plus Five* . . . . (Polydor)
Days Of Future Passed . . . . (Polydor)
Peanut Butter
Marathons; *Best Of Chess Vocal Groups-C* . . . . (Chess)
Cruisin'-1961-C . . . . (Increase)
Frat Rock!-#2-C . . . . (Rhino)
Son Of Frat Rock!-C . . . . (Rhino)
Peanut Butter Conspiracy
Jimmy Buffett; *White Sport Coat & A Pink Crustacean* . . . . (MCA)
Peanut Butter Time
Rolling Stones; *Made In The Shade* . . . . (Rolling Stones)
Peanut Vendor
Judy Garland; *Star Is Born* . . . . (Columbia)
Stan Kenton; *Comprehensive Stan Kenton* . . . . (Capitol)
Retrospective-Capitol Years . . . . (Blue Note)
Stan Kenton's Greatest Hits . . . . (Capitol)
The Uncollected Stan Kenton & His Orchestra-#6-1962 . . . . (Hindsight)
Peanuts
4 Seasons; *25th Anniversary Collection* . . . . (Rhino)
Police; *Outlandos D'Amour* . . . . (A&M)
Peas, Porridge Hot
Original Soundtrack; *Toddler Favorites* . . . . (Kid Rhino/Rhino 4 Kids)
Peggy's Kitchen Wall
Bruce Cockburn; *Stealing Fire* . . . . (Columbia)
Pepper
Butthole Surfers; *Electriclarryland* . . . . (Capitol)
Peppermint Man
Dick Dale And The Del-Tones; *Dick Dale And The Del-Tones'
Greatest Hits* . . . . (Crescendo)
Peppermint Stick
Elchords; *Memories Of Times Square Record Shop-#1-C* . . . . . . (Collectables)
Peppermint Twist
Joey Dee & the Starliters; *Billboard Top Rock 'N' Roll Hits-1962-C* . . . (Rhino)
Hey Let's Twist! Best Of Joey Dee & The Starliters . . . . (Rhino)
ST/American Graffiti . . . . (MCA)
Picnic
McGuire Sisters; *Songs Of Steve Allen-C* . . . . (Varese Sarabande)
Picnic In The Jungle
Snakefinger; *Chewing Hides The Sound* . . . . (Ralph)
Piece Of The Pie
Boom Crash Opera; *These Here Are Crazy Times* . . . . (Giant)
Piece Of The Pie
Kix; *Blow My Fuse* . . . . (Atlantic)
Piece Of The Pie
Jimmy Cliff; *Power & The Glory* . . . . (Columbia)
Pigmeat
Leadbelly; *King Of The Twelve-String Guitar* . . . . (Columbia)
Pigmeat Is What I Crave
Bo Carter; *Legends Of The Blues-#1-C* . . . . (Columbia)
Pizza Face
Barnes & Barnes; *Zabagabee-Best Of Barnes & Barnes* . . . . (Rhino)
Pizza In My Shorts
Da Yoopers; *Yoopy Do Wah* . . . . (You Guys)
Pizza On The Ground
Austin Lounge Lizards; *Lizard Vision* . . . . (Flying Fish)
Please Don't Eat The Daisies
Doris Day; *Doris Day-16 Most Requested Songs-Encore!* . . . . (Columbia)
Polish Sausage Polka
Li'l Wally; *Li'l Wally* . . . . (Jay Jay)

Polk Salad Annie
Elvis Presley; *Elvis As Recorded At Madison Square Garden* . . . . (RCA)
Tony Joe White; *Soul Shots-#6-Blue-Eyed Soul-C* . . . . (Rhino)
Swingin' Country Favorites-C . . . . (Warner Bros.)
Popcorn
Hot Butter; *Super Hits Of The '70s-Have A Nice Day-#9-C* . . . . (Rhino)
Popcorn Love
New Edition; *Club Classics-1982-1984-#1-C* . . . . (Warlock)
New Edition's Greatest Hits, Vol. 1 . . . . (MCA)
Popcorn Pop Pop
Jessie Hill; *Golden Classics-Ooh Poo Pah Doo* . . . . (Collectables)
Popcorn, Pretzels & Beer Waltz
Michigan Dutchmen; *Beer & Dutchmen Polkas* . . . . (Jay Jay)
Popsicle
Jan & Dean; *Jan & Dean-Legendary Masters* . . . . (EMI)
Surf City-Best Of Jan & Dean . . . . (EMI)
Popsicle
New Kids On The Block; *New Kids On The Block* . . . . (Columbia)
Popsicle
Talking Heads; *Popular Favorites-1984-1992* . . . . (Sire)
Popsicle Toes
Diana Krall; *When I Look In Your Eyes* . . . . (GRP)
Manhattan Transfer; *Coming Out* . . . . (Atlantic)
Michael Franks; *Art Of Tea* . . . . (Reprise)
Popsicles & Icicles
Murmaids; *Golden Girl Groups-C* . . . . (K-Tel)
Oldies But Goodies-#2-C . . . . (Original Sound)
Porcupine Pie
Neil Diamond; *Hot August Night* . . . . (MCA)
Moods . . . . (MCA)
Pork & Beans
Willie ''The Lion'' Smith; *Pork & Beans* . . . . (Black Lion)
Pork Chop Blues
Sam Collins; *Jailhouse Blues* . . . . (Yazoo)
Pork Chop Stomp
Grady Martin and His Winged Strings; *Legends Of Country*
Guitar-#2-C . . . . (Rhino)
Pork Chops & Gravy
Ink Spots; *If I Didn't Care* . . . . (Pro-Arte)
Potatoe Chips
King Curtis; *Scepter Records Story-C* . . . . (Capricorn)
Poundcake
Van Halen; *For Unlawful Carnal Knowledge* . . . . (Warner Bros.)
Pretty Girl Milking A Cow
Judy Garland; *Best Of Judy Garland* . . . . (MCA)
One & Only . . . . (Capitol)
Pretzel Logic
Donald Fagen & Michael McDonald; *New York Rock & Soul Revue-At The*
Beacon-C . . . . (Giant)
Steely Dan; *Pretzel Logic* . . . . (MCA)
Steely Dan's Greatest Hits . . . . (MCA)
Pretzel Man
Harry Chapin; *Legends Of The Lost & Found* . . . . (Elektra)
Punky's Dilemma
Simon & Garfunkel; *Bookends* . . . . (Columbia)
Collected Works . . . . (Columbia)
Pure Love (Captain Crunch, milk)
Ronnie Milsap; *Ronnie Milsap's Greatest Hits* . . . . (RCA)
Ronnie Milsap-Super Hits . . . . (RCA)
Purple People Eater
Sheb Wooley; *45s On CD-#1-1956-1959-C* . . . . (Mercury)
Dr. Demento: 20th Anniversary Collection-C . . . . (Rhino)
Halloween Hits-C . . . . (Rhino)
Horror Rock Classics-#2-C . . . . (Rhino)
Super Hits-#4-C . . . . (Gusto)
Quiche Lorraine
B-52's; *Tame Yourself-C* . . . . (Rhino)
Wild Planet . . . . (Warner Bros.)
Quiche Woman In A Barbecue Town
Tarwater Band; *Walking Across Egypt* . . . . (Flying Fish)
Rainbow Stew
Merle Haggard; *For The Record: Merle Haggard-43 Legendary Hits* . . . . (BNA)
Merle Haggard's Greatest Hits . . . . (MCA)
More Of The Best . . . . (Rhino)
Rainbow Stew-Live At Anaheim Stadium . . . . (MCA)
Rat In The Kitchen
UB40; *Live In Moscow* . . . . (A&M)
Rat In The Kitchen . . . . (A&M)
Rat Salad
Black Sabbath; *Paranoid* . . . . (Warner Bros.)
Rats & Roaches In My Kitchen
Silas Hogan; *Louisiana Blues* . . . . (Arhoolie)
Rats In My Kitchen
Sleepy John Estes; *Legend Of Sleepy John Estes* . . . . (Delmark)
Red Beans
Coleman Hawkins & Red Garland Trio; *Coleman Hawkins & Red*
Garland Trio . . . . (Prestige)
Kingsnakes; *19 Lucky Strikes* . . . . (Blue Wave)

Professor Longhair; *Crawfish Fiesta* . . . . (Alligator)
Red Beans And Rice
Booker T. & The M.G.s; *Back To Back: Mar-Keys & Booker T. & The*
M.G.s . . . . (Atlantic)
Best Of Booker T. & The M.G.s . . . . (Atlantic)
Legends Of Rock Guitar-'60s-#1-C . . . . (Rhino)
Red Hot Chicken
Wet Willie; *Drippin' Wet/Live!* . . . . (Capricorn)
Wet Willie's Greatest Hits . . . . (Polydor)
Redneck Eats
Frank Zappa; *200 Motels* . . . . (Rykodisc)
Refried Dreams
Tim McGraw; *Not A Moment Too Soon* . . . . (Curb)
Reno Burrito
Tom Collier; *Pacific Aire* . . . . (Nebula)
Rhapsody From Hunger
Spike Jones & His City Slickers; *Spike Jones Is Murdering The*
Classics . . . . (RCA)
Rice & Peas
Wailers Band; *I.D.* . . . . (Atlantic)
Rice Pudding
Jeff Beck Group; *Beck-Ola* . . . . (Epic)
Rock & Roll Stew
Traffic; *The Low Spark Of High Heeled Boys* . . . . (Island)
Root Beer Rag
Billy Joel; *Streetlife Serenade* . . . . (Columbia)
Rubber Biscuit
Blues Brothers; *Best Of The Blues Brothers* . . . . (Atlantic)
Briefcase Full Of Blues . . . . (Atlantic)
Rum & Coca-Cola
Andrews Sisters; *Andrews Sisters-16 Great Performances* . . . . (MCA)
Best Of The Andrews Sisters . . . . (MCA)
Boogie Woogie Bugle Girls . . . . (MCA)
Capitol Collectors Series-The Andrews Sisters . . . . (Capitol)
Professor Longhair; *Last Mardi Gras* . . . . (Atlantic)
Mardi Gras In Baton Rouge . . . . (Rhino)
Salt In My Tears, The
Dolly Parton; *Hungry Again* . . . . (Rising Tide)
Salt Of The Earth
Mick Jagger & Keith Richards; *The Concert For New York City-C* . . (Columbia)
Rolling Stones; *Beggars Banquet* . . . . (Abkco)
Salt Peanuts
Bud Powell; *Bluebird Sampler-C* . . . . (Bluebird)
Bud Powell Trio; *Time Was* . . . . (Bluebird)
Dizzy Gillespie; *Dizzy Gillespie-In The Beginning* . . . . (Prestige)
Greatest Jazz Concert Ever . . . . (Prestige)
Jazz At Massey Hall . . . . (Fantasy)
Jazz Trumpet-#2-Modern Time . . . . (Prestige)
King Of Be-Bop . . . . (Everest)
Salty Dog Blues
Flatt & Scruggs; *Earl Scruggs: His Family & Friends/Nashville*
Airplane . . . . (Collectables)
Flatt & Scruggs-20 Greatest Hits . . . . (Deluxe)
Greatest Folksingers Of The '60s-C . . . . (Vanguard)
Salty Dog Rag, A
Stefan Grossman; *Black Melodies On A Clear Afternoon* . . . . (Shanachie)
Salty Dog, A
Procol Harum; *A Salty Dog* . . . . (A&M)
Best Of Procol Harum . . . . (A&M)
Procol Harum Live In Concert with the Edmonton Symphony . . . . . . (A&M)
Procol Harum-Classics-#17 . . . . (A&M)
Sam-The Hot Dog Man
Lil Johnson; *Raunchy Business-Hot Nuts & Lollypops-C* . . . . (Legacy)
San Francisco Treat, The (Rice-A-Roni)
Original Soundtrack; *TeeVee Toons-The Commercials-#1-C* . . . . (TVT)
Sarah Cynthia Sylvia Stout
Shel Silverstein; *Dr. Demento Presents The Greatest Novelty Records-#4-*
1970s-C . . . . (Rhino)
Dr. Demento: 20th Anniversary Collection-C . . . . (Rhino)
Where The Sidewalk Ends . . . . (Columbia)
Sashimi
101 North; *101 North* . . . . (Capitol)
Sassafras Roots
Green Day; *Dookie* . . . . (Reprise)
Saturday Night Fish Fry Drag
Joe Robichaux & The New Orleans Boys; *Joe Robichaux & The New*
Orleans Boys-1933 . . . . (Folklyric)
Savoy Truffle
Beatles; *Beatles-Box Set* . . . . (Capitol)
The Beatles (White Album) . . . . (Capitol)
Scarborough Fair/Canticle (Parsley, Sage, Rosemary, Thyme)
Simon & Garfunkel; *Collected Works* . . . . (Columbia)
Parsley Sage Rosemary & Thyme . . . . (Columbia)
Simon & Garfunkel's Greatest Hits . . . . (Columbia)
ST/The Graduate . . . . (Columbia)
The Concert In Central Park . . . . (Warner Bros.)
Scottish Tea
Ted Nugent & The Amboy Dukes; *Greatest*
Collection Ever . . . . (Dunhill Compact Classics)

Scrambled Eggs
Sandy Austin; *Cajun Music-Early '50s* . . . . (Arhoolie)

Second Sitting For The Last Supper
10 CC; *Live & Let Live* . . . . (Mercury)

Shanghai Noodle Factory
Traffic; *Last Exit* . . . . (Island)

She Kept Chewing Gum
Donald Jacob; *Zydeco Blues 'N' Boogie* . . . . (Rykodisc)

She Wears Red Feathers
Guy Mitchell; *Guy Mitchell-16 Most Requested Songs* . . . . (Legacy)

Shortenin' Bread
Andrews Sisters; *50th Anniversary Collection-#2* . . . . (MCA)
Original Soundtrack; *Children's Favorites* . . . . (Kid Rhino/Rhino 4 Kids)
Sam McNeil/Dent Wimmer/Others; *Old Originals-#2* . . . . (Rounder)
Sonny Terry; *Folkways Years-1944-1963* . . . . (Smithsonian Folkways)

Sing A Song Of Sixpence
Original Soundtrack; *Children's Favorites* . . . . (Kid Rhino/Rhino 4 Kids)

Skin & Bone
Kinks; *Celluloid Heroes* . . . . (RCA)
Everybody's In Show-Biz . . . . (Rhino)
Muswell Hillbillies . . . . (VelVel)
The Kinks' Greatest-Celluloid Heroes . . . . (RCA)

Snap Crackle Pop (Kellogg's Rice Krispies)
Original Soundtrack; *TeeVee Toons-The Commercials-#1-C* . . . . (TVT)

Something Like That (barbecue, Coke)
Tim McGraw; *A Place In The Sun* . . . . (Curb)
Tim McGraw's Greatest Hits . . . . (Curb)

Song Of The South
Alabama; *Alabama's Greatest Hits-#2* . . . . (RCA)
Southern Star . . . . (RCA)

Soup For One
Chic; *Dance Dance Dance-Best Of* . . . . (Atlantic)

Soup Of The Day
Chris Rea; *Espresso Logic* . . . . (East West)

Space Lord
Monster Magnet; *Powertrip* . . . . (A&M)

Spider In My Stew
Buster Benton; *Spider In My Stew* . . . . (Ronn)

Spit Of Love
Bonnie Raitt; *Fundamental* . . . . (Capitol)
Lilith Fair-A Celebration Of Women In Music-#3-C . . . . (Arista)

St. Alphonzo's Pancake Breakfast
Frank Zappa; *Apostrophe/Overnite Sensation* . . . . (Rykodisc)

Standing Knee Deep In A River (Dying Of Thirst)
Kathy Mattea; *Lonesome Standard Time* . . . . (Mercury)

Struttin' With Some Barbecue
Louis Armstrong; *Louis Armstrong Of New Orleans* . . . . (MCA)
Louis Armstrong's Greatest Hits . . . . (Legacy)
Newport Jazz Festival All-Stars; *Newport Jazz Festival All-*
Stars . . . . (Concord Jazz)
Teddy Buckner; *Salute To Louis Armstrong* . . . . (Crescendo)

Sumthin' Sumthin'
Maxwell; *Maxwell's Urban Hang Suite* . . . . (Columbia)
ST/Love Jones . . . . (Columbia)

Sunday For Tea
Peter And Gordon; *Best Of Peter And Gordon* . . . . (Rhino)

Sunnyside Up
Teresa Brewer & The World's Greatest Jazz Band; *Good News* . . (Doctor Jazz)

Supper Time
Barbra Streisand; *People* . . . . (Columbia)
Ella Fitzgerald; *The Irving Berlin Songbook-#2* . . . . (Verve)
Johnny Cash; *Classic Cash-Hall Of Fame Series* . . . . (Mercury)
Nancy Wilson; *But Beautiful* . . . . (Blue Note)

Supper's Ready
Genesis; *Seconds Out* . . . . (Atlantic)

Suppertime
Original Cast; *Little Shop Of Horrors* . . . . (Geffen)

Suppertime
Original Cast; *You're A Good Man, Charlie Brown* . . . . (Polydor)

Sushi Girl
Tubes; *Best Of The Tubes* . . . . (Gold Rush)
Completion Backward Principle . . . . (Capitol)

Swallow The Sun
Love Exchange; *Nuggets-#10-Folk Rock-C* . . . . (Rhino)

Swamp Sauce
Albert Collins; *Albert Collins-Complete Imperial Recordings* . . . . (EMI)

Swedish Meatball
Steve Lyon; *There's No Place Like Mars* . . . . (Flying Fish)

Swedish Pastry
Bill Evans; *Time Remembered* . . . . (Milestone)
Bill Evans Trio; *At Shelly's Manne-Hole* . . . . (Riverside)
Bud Powell Trio; *Time Was* . . . . (Bluebird)

Sweet As Bear Meat
Johnny Hodges Orchestra; *Used To Be Duke* . . . . (Verve)

Sweet Gingerbread Man
Mike Curb Congregation; *Mike Curb Congregation's Greatest Hits* . . . . (Curb)

Sweet Kentucky Ham
David Frishberg; *Can't Take You Nowhere* . . . . (Fantasy)

David Frishberg-Classics . . . . (Concord Jazz)

Sweets For My Sweet
Drifters; *1959-1965-All-Time Greatest Hits And More* . . . . (Atlantic)
Very Best Of The Drifters . . . . (Rhino)

Switchin' In The Kitchen
Big Joe Turner; *Rides Again-Jazzlore-#39* . . . . (Atlantic)

Taco Grande
"Weird Al" Yankovic; *Off The Deep End* . . . . (Scotti Bros.)
The Food Album . . . . (Scotti Bros.)

Taco Stand
Normaltown Flyers; *Normaltown Flyers* . . . . (Mercury)

Taco Wagon
Dick Dale And The Del-Tones; *King Of The Surf Guitar-Best Of Dick Dale*
And The Del-Tones . . . . (Rhino)
Young Fresh Fellows; *This One's For The Ladies* . . . . (Frontier)

Tacos
Mongo Santamaria; *Skins* . . . . (Milestone)

Take Me Out To The Ball Game
Bruce Springstone; *Baseball's Greatest Hits-C* . . . . (Rhino)
Doc & Merle Watson; *Baseball's Greatest Hits-C* . . . . (Rhino)
Frank Zappa; *You Can't Do That On Stage Anymore-#4* . . . . (Rykodisc)

Tall Drink Of Water
Barbara Mandrell; *Best Of Barbara Mandrell* . . . . (Liberty)
Mel Tillis; *Best Of Branson U.S.A.-#2-C* . . . . (Curb)
Mel Tillis' Greatest Hits . . . . (Curb)

Tall Drink Of Water
Matraca Berg; *Speed Of Grace* . . . . (RCA)

Tapioca Tundra
Monkees; *Listen To The Band* . . . . (Rhino)

Taste Of Chocolate
Big Daddy Kane; *Taste Of Chocolate* . . . . (Cold Chillin')

Taste Of India
Aerosmith; *Nine Lives* . . . . (Columbia)

Tastes Just Like Chicken
Scatterbrain; *Scamboogery* . . . . (Elektra)

Teddy Bears' Picnic
Anne Murray; *There's A Hippo In My Tub* . . . . (Capitol)
Frank DeVol; *Small Fry-Capitol Sings Kids Songs For Grownups-C* . . (Capitol)

Tennessee Fish Fry
Helen O'Connell; *The Uncollected Helen O'Connell With Irv Orton's*
Orchestra . . . . (Hindsight)

Texas Cookin'
Gene Clark/Rodney Crowell/Emmylou Harris/J.J. Walker; *Texas*
Cookin' . . . . (Sugar Hill)
Guy Clark; *Guy Clark's Greatest Hits* . . . . (RCA)

Texas Stew
Louis Jordan & His Tympany Five; *Rock 'N Roll Call* . . . . (Bluebird)

Thanks For The Pepperoni
George Harrison; *All Things Must Pass* . . . . (Parlophone)

That's Amore
Dean Martin; *Best Of Dean Martin* . . . . (CEMA Special Prod.)
Dean Martin's All Time Greatest Hits . . . . (Curb)
Dean Martin's Greatest Hits . . . . (EMI)
The Capitol Years-Dean Martin . . . . (Capitol)

That's The Worst Jello
Chordiac Arrest; *1990 Top 20 Barbershop Quartets: Coney Island*
Baby-C . . . . (ISD/Intersound)

Them Belly Full
Bob Marley & The Wailers; *Bob Marley & The Wailers-Live* . . . . . (Tuff Gong)
Natty Dread . . . . (Tuff Gong)
Rebel Music . . . . (Tuff Gong)

Theme From "Picnic"
Chet Atkins; *Pickin' My Way-In Hollywood*
Alone . . . . (Mobile Fidelity Sound Lab)

They Call Me The Popcorn Man
Luther Johnson; *Lonesome In My Bedroom* . . . . (Evidence Music)

Thing That Only Eats Hippies
Dead Milkmen; *Eat Your Paisley* . . . . (Restless)
Enigma Variations-#2-C . . . . (Enigma Capitol)

Things Go Better With Coke
Original Soundtrack; *TeeVee Toons-The Commercials-#1-C* . . . . (TVT)

Those Lazy Hazy Crazy Days Of Summer
Nat "King" Cole; *Best Of Nat "King" Cole-Vol. 1* . . . . (Capitol)
Capitol Collectors Series-Nat "King" Cole . . . . (Capitol)

Tijuana Sauerkraut
Herb Alpert & The Tijuana Brass; *Lonely Bull* . . . . (A&M)

Too Much
Dave Matthews Band; *Crash* . . . . (RCA)

Too Much Barbeque
Big Twist & The Mellow Fellows; *Live From Chicago-Bigger*
Than Life . . . . (Alligator)

Too Old To Cut The Mustard
Carlisles; *45-#6348* . . . . (Mercury)
Ernest Tubb; *Ernest Tubb-Retrospective-#2* . . . . (MCA Special Prod.)

Top Hat Bar & Grille
Jim Croce; *50th Anniversary Collection* . . . . (Saja)

Tortillas & Beans
Stan Kenton; *Lighter Side* . . . . (Creative World)

Trombone Butter
Dinah Washington; *Bessie Smith Songbook* . . . . (Emarcy)
Tumble In The Rough
Stone Temple Pilots; *Tiny Music...Songs From The Vatican*
Gift Shop . . . . (Atlantic)
TV Dinners
ZZ Top; *Eliminator*. . . . .(Warner Bros.)
Two Minutes Till Lunch
Wall Of Voodoo; *Dark Continent* . . . . (A&M)
Two Triple Cheese, Side Order Of Fries
Commander Cody & His Lost Planet Airmen; *Aces High* . . . . (Relix)
Veal Chop & Pork Chop
Blind Snooks Eaglin; *Country Boy In New Orleans* . . . . (Arhoolie)
Venom Soup
Ted Nugent; *Weekend Warriors* . . . .(Epic)
Vibrant Thing (Ben & Jerry)
Q-Tip; *Amplified*. . . . . (Def Jam/IDJMG)
Waldo's Discount Donuts
Red Knuckles & The Trailblazers; *Hot Rize Presents*. . . . . (Flying Fish)
We Are Hungry Men
David Bowie; *David Bowie-London Collector-Starting Point* . . . . (London)
Starting Point. . . . .(Deram)
Wedding Cake
Jeannie C. Riley; *Things Go Better With Love* . . . . (Plantation)
Well Fed Slave/Hungry Free Man
Lucky Dube; *Taxman* . . . . (Shanachie)
When Bacon Was Scarce/Ryestraw
Red Clay Ramblers; *Twisted Laurel* . . . . (Flying Fish)
When Did We Have Sauerkraut?
Lou & Peter Berryman; *So Comfortable*. . . . . (Cornbelt)
When The Cookie Jar Is Empty
Michael Franks; *Burchfield Nines*. . . . .(Warner Bros.)
Where I Come From (cornbread, chicken)
Alan Jackson; *When Somebody Loves You* . . . . (Arista)
Whipped Cream
Herb Alpert & The Tijuana Brass; *Foursider* . . . . (A&M)
Herb Alpert & The Tijuana Brass' Greatest Hits . . . . (A&M)
Herb Alpert & The Tijuana Brass-Classics-#1 . . . . (A&M)
Whipped Cream & Other Delights . . . . (A&M)
Who Threw The Overalls In Mrs. Murphy's Chowder
Bing Crosby; *Shillelaghs & Shamrocks* . . . .(MCA)
Wild Honey
Beach Boys; *Absolute Best-#2* . . . . (Capitol)
Party!/Stack-O-Tracks. . . . . (Capitol)
Smiley Smile/Wild Honey. . . . . (Capitol)
Wild Honey Pie
Beatles; *Beatles-Box Set*. . . . . (Capitol)
The Beatles (White Album). . . . . (Capitol)
Wild Mountain Honey
Steve Miller Band; *Fly Like An Eagle*. (Capitol)
Steve Miller Band's Greatest Hits-1974-78. . . . . (Capitol)
Wild Mountain Thyme
Armstrong Family; *Wheel Of The Year-Thirty Years With The Armstrong*
Family . . . . (Flying Fish)
Byrds; *Fifth Dimension*. . . . . (Columbia)
Joan Baez; *Farewell Angelina* . . . . (Vanguard)
Wild Rice
Lee Ritenour; *Best Of Lee Ritenour* . . . .(Epic)
First Course . . . .(Epic)
Worst Pies In London
Original Cast; *Sweeney Todd* . . . . (RCA)
You Were Meant For Me
Jewel; *Pieces Of You*. . . . . (Atlantic)
Yummy Yummy Yummy
Ohio Express; *Billboard Top Rock 'N' Roll Hits-1968-C*. . . . . (Rhino)
Bubblegum Classics-#1-C. . . . . (Varese Vintage)

FOOD & BEVERAGES: VEGETABLES
See Also: FOOD & BEVERAGES (various), RESTAURANTS

Addicted To Spuds
"Weird Al" Yankovic; *"Weird Al" Yankovic's Greatest Hits* . . . . (Scotti Bros.)
The Food Album. . . . . (Scotti Bros.)
And Even The Vegetables Screamed
Legendary Pink Dots; *Golden Age* . . . . (Play It Again Sam)
Attack Of The Vegetable Men
Active Ingredient; *Extrastrength* . . . . (Bainbridge)
Boy Who Wouldn't Hoe Corn
Alison Krauss & Union Station; *New Favorite* . . . . (Rounder)
Bud The Spud
Stompin' Tom Connors; *Bud The Spud* . . . .(EMI)
Cabbage Greens
Champion Jack Dupree; *New Orleans Barrelhouse Boogie-*
Complete. . . . . (Columbia)
Call Any Vegetable
Mothers Of Invention; *Just Another Band From L.A.*. . . . . (Bizarre/Straight)

Candy Yam
Lee Dorsey; *Wheelin' And Dealin': The Definitive Collection* . . . . (Arista)
Celery Stalks At Midnight
Will Bradley; *Swing Time! Fabulous Big Band Era-1925-1955-C*. . . (Columbia)
Cheese & Onions
Rutles; *Rutles* . . . . (Rhino)
Chop Suey Louie
Jimmy Preston; *Rock The Joint-#2-C* . . . . (Collectables)
Collard Greens & Black-Eyed Peas
Bud Powell; *Best Of Bud Powell*. . . . . (Blue Note)
Country Bumpkin
Cal Smith; *16 Top Country Hits-#1-C*. (MCA)
Country's Greatest Hits-#2-C . . . . (MCA Special Prod.)
Grand Ole Opry-75 Years-#2-C. . . . . (MCA)
Don't Slay That Potato
Tom Paxton; *One Million Lawyers & Other Disasters* . . . . (Flying Fish)
Eggplant Pizza
Jimmy Bruno Trio; *Sleight Of Hand* . . . . (Concord Jazz)
Eggplant That Ate Chicago
Dr. West's Medicine Show & Junk Band; *Dr. Demento Presents The*
Greatest Novelty Records-#3-1960s-C . . . . (Rhino)
Fish & Chips
Eddie & The Hot Rods; *Fish & Chips* . . . . (EMI)
Glass Onion
Beatles; *Beatles-Box Set* . . . . (Capitol)
The Beatles (White Album) . . . . (Capitol)
Goober Peas
Burl Ives; *Burl Ives' Greatest Hits* . . . . (MCA)
Kingston Trio; *At Large/Here We Go Again!* . . . . (Capitol)
Good Old Cabbage Greens
Washboard Sam; *Rockin' My Blues Away*. . . . . (RCA)
Green Onions
Booker T. & The M.G.s; *Best Of Booker T. & The M.G.s* . . . .(Atlantic)
Billboard Top R&B Hits-1962-C . . . . (Rhino)
Green Onions . . . .(Atlantic)
ST/American Graffiti . . . . (MCA)
ST/Quadrophenia . . . . (MCA)
Hot Corn, Cold Corn
Flatt & Scruggs; *Flatt & Scruggs At Carnegie Hall!* . . . . . . (Koch International)
Hot Dogs & Cabbage
Li'l Wally; *One Man Band* . . . . (Jay Jay)
Hot Potatoes
Kinks; *Everybody's In Show-Biz* . . . . (Rhino)
Hot Potatoes
King Curtis; *Enjoy...Best Of* . . . . (Collectables)
I'm A Potato
Devo; *Hardcore-#1 (The Evolution Of Devolution)* . . . . (Rykodisc)
Lord I Love Mashed Potatoes
Mayf Nutter; *Goin' Skinny Dippin'*. . . . .(Crescendo)
Mashed Potato Time
Dee Dee Sharp; *21 Oldies But Goodies-C*. . . . . (Original Sound)
Big Bad Bossa Beat. . . . . (Original Sound)
Oldies But Goodies-#6-C. . . . . (Original Sound)
Mashed Potatoes (Hot Pastrami With)
Joey Dee & the Starliters; *Hey Let's Twist! Best Of Joey Dee & The*
Starliters . . . . (Rhino)
Motorcycle Song
Arlo Guthrie; *Alice's Restaurant*. . . . .(Reprise)
Best Of Arlo Guthrie . . . . (Warner Bros.)
Mystical Potato Head Groove Thing
Joe Satriani; *Flying In A Blue Dream* . . . . (Relativity)
Naturally
Marty Stuart; *Country Goes Raffi-C* . . . . (Rounder)
No Rice, No Peas, No Coconut Oil
Jolly Boys; *Beer Joint & Tailoring* . . . . (Smithsonian Folkways)
One Potato
Sesame Street; *The Count's Countdown* . . . . (Sony Wonder)
One Potato Two
Music Explosion; *Super K Kollection-#2-C* . . . . (Collectables)
One Potato, Two Potato
Westside Children's Singers; *Play Time: 25 Favorite Play And Party*
Songs . . . . (EMI Special Markets)
Onion Field
Dandelion; *I Think I'm Gonna Be Sick* . . . . (Ruffhouse/Columbia)
Onion In A Closet
Sergie Kuriokhin & Henry Kaiser; *Popular Science* . . . . (Rykodisc)
Onion Roll
Herb Ellis & Ray Brown Sextet; *Hot Tracks* . . . . (Concord Jazz)
Onion Skin
Boom Crash Opera; *These Here Are Crazy Times* . . . .(Giant)
Onion Song
Marvin Gaye & Tammi Terrell; *Easy* . . . . (Motown)
Marvin Gaye & Tammi Terrell's Greatest Hits . . . . (Motown)
Onion Town
John Delafose & The Eunice Playboys; *Stomp Down Zydeco-C* . . . . . (Rounder)
Pass The Peas
Maceo Parker; *Life On Planet Groove*. (Verve)

Pickin' Up The Cabbage
Cab Calloway; *Best Of The Big Bands-C*. . . . .(Columbia)
Plant A Radish
Original Cast; *Fantasticks* . . . . (Polydor)
Polk Salad Annie
Elvis Presley; *Elvis As Recorded At Madison Square Garden*. . . . .(RCA)
Tony Joe White; *Soul Shots-#6-Blue-Eyed Soul-C* . . . . (Rhino)
Swingin' Country Favorites-C . . . . (Warner Bros.)
Pope Is A Potato
Mofungo; *Bugged* . . . . (SST)
Potato Head Blues
Louis Armstrong; *Louis Armstrong-Best Of The Decca Years-#2-The
Composer-C*. . . . . (MCA)
You Rascal You . . . .(Pro-Arte)
Potato Pancake
Preston Reed; *Pointing Up* . . . .(Flying Fish)
Potato Picking
Mark Knopfler; *Screenplaying* . . . . (Warner Bros.)
ST/Cal. . . . .(Mercury)
Potato Radio
King & Moore; *Potato Radio* . . . . (Justice)
Potato Salad
Jimmy Preston; *Jimmy Preston* . . . .(Collectables)
Pumpkin
Andrew Hill; *Black Fire* . . . .(Blue Note)
Pumpkin Head
Dharma Bums; *Bliss* . . . . (Frontier)
Pumpkin Time
Darol Anger & Barbara Higbie; *Live At Montreux* . . . . (Windham Hill)
Rabbit In The Pea Patch
Red Clay Ramblers; *Merchant's Lunch* . . . . (Flying Fish)
Rat Salad
Black Sabbath; *Paranoid*. . . . . (Warner Bros.)
Rice & Peas
Wailers Band; *I.D.* . . . . (Atlantic)
Rotten Lettuce
Jeffrey Frederick & The Clamtones; *Spiders In The Moonlight* . . . . . . (Rounder)
Sauerkraut 'N' Solar Energy
Norman Blake & Others; *Norman Blake/Others* . . . .(Flying Fish)
She Cooks Me Cabbage
Champion Jack Dupree; *Blues For Everybody* . . . . .(International Mktg. Group)
Swee' Pea
Count Basie; *Best Of Count Basie & His Orchestra* . . . . (Pablo)
Sweet Pea
Tommy Roe; *Best Of Tommy Roe* . . . . (Curb)
Cruisin'-1966-C . . . . (Increase)
Tommy Roe's Greatest Hits . . . . (MCA)
Sweet Potato Pie
Al Jarreau; *We Got By* . . . .(Reprise)
Sweet Potato Pie
James Taylor; *Never Die Young* . . . .(Columbia)
Sweet Potatoe Pie
Domino; *Domino* . . . . (OutBurst)
Texas Jalapenos
Texas Rubies; *Working Girl Blues* . . . .(Monsterdisc)
Theme From "Popeye"
Original Soundtrack; *Television's Greatest Hits-#1-C* . . . . (TVT)
Tomato Paste
Flop; *Flop & The Fall Of The Mopsqueezer* . . . . (Frontier)
Tree Hugger
Rugburns; *Taking The World By Donkey*. . . . .(Priority)
Tulip Or Turnip (Tell Me Dream Face)
Duke Ellington & Teresa Brewer; *It Don't Mean A Thing If It Ain't Got That
Swing* . . . . (Columbia)
Vegetables
Beach Boys; *Smiley Smile/Wild Honey* . . . . (Capitol)
Sunshine Dream . . . . (Capitol)
Vidalia
Sammy Kershaw; *Politics Religion & Her* . . . . (Mercury)
Where Corn Don't Grow
Travis Tritt; *The Restless Kind* . . . . (Warner Bros.)
Why Is A Carrot More Orange Than An Orange
Amboy Dukes; *Journey To The Center Of The Mind*. . . . . . (Mainstream)
Wonderful Guy, A
Original Cast; *South Pacific*. . . . . (CBS Masterworks)

FOOLS, Dumb, Embarrassed, Foolish, Idiot, Stupid
See Also: INSULTS, LOVE (various), LOW SELF-ESTEEM, MISTAKES, THINKING & KNOWING

Act Naturally
Beatles; *"Yesterday"...And Today* . . . . (Capitol)
Buck Owens; *Beatles Originals* . . . . (Rhino)
Buck Owens & Ringo Starr; *Act Naturally* . . . . (Capitol)

Buck Owens & The Buckaroos; *Buck Owens & The Buckaroos-Live At
Carnegie Hall*. (Country Music Foundation)
Charley Pride; *Country Pride*. . . . . (RCA)
Johnny Russell; *20 Great Country Hits-C* . . . . (RCA)
All You Ever Do Is Bring Me Down
Mavericks; *Best Of The Mavericks-Super Colossal Smash Hits Of
The '90s* . . . .(Mercury)
Country Superstar Hits-C . . . . (Hip-O)
Honky Tonk Boogie-C . . . . (Hip-O)
Music For All Occasions . . . . (MCA)
And Fools Shine On
Brother Cane; *Best Of Rockline-C* . . . . (Priority)
Essential Southern Rock-C . . . .(House Of Blues)
Seeds . . . . (Virgin)
Another Girl
Beatles; *Beatles-Box Set*. . . . .(Capitol)
ST/Help! . . . .(Capitol)
Any Other Fool
Sadao Watanabe & Patti Austin; *Front Seat*. . . . .(Elektra)
April Fool
Pete Townshend & Ronnie Lane; *Rough Mix*. . . . . (Atlantic)
April Fool
Soul Asylum; *Grave Dancers Union* . . . .(Columbia)
April Fool
Eric Dolphy; *Here & There* . . . . (Prestige)
April Fools
Dionne Warwick; *Dionne Warwick-Anthology 1962-1971* . . . .(Rhino)
April Fools
Earl Klugh; *Living Inside Your Love* . . . . (EMI)
April Fools
Aretha Franklin; *Young, Gifted And Black* . . . . (Atlantic & Atco Remasters)
April Fool's Day Morn
Loudon Wainwright III; *Career Moves* . . . . (Virgin)
Fame & Wealth . . . .(Rounder)
April's Fool
Ray Price; *Ray Price's Greatest Hits-#4-By Request* . . . . (Step One)
April's Fool
Mark Chesnutt; *Almost Goodbye* . . . . (MCA)
April's Fool
Tracy Lawrence; *Sticks & Stones* . . . . (Atlantic)
Arms Of A Fool
Mel Tillis; *Brand New Mister Me*. . . . . (Polydor)
Mel Tillis & The Statesiders; *Best Of Mel Tillis & The Statesiders* . . . . .(MGM)
As Any Fool Can See
Tracy Lawrence; *I See It Now* . . . . (Atlantic)
Live & Unplugged. . . . . (Atlantic)
Baby Come Back
Player; *Billboard Top Hits-1978-C* . . . .(Rhino)
Mellow Rock Hits Of The '70s-Ventura Highway-C . . . .(Rhino)
Super Hits Of The '70s-Have A Nice Day-#21-C . . . .(Rhino)
Banditos
Refreshments; *Fizzy Fuzzy Big & Buzzy* . . . .(Mercury)
Barely Breathing
Duncan Sheik; *Duncan Sheik*. . . . . (Atlantic)
Be Young, Be Foolish, Be Happy
Tams; *Tam's Greatest Hits*. . . . .(Universal)
Believe Me Baby (I Lied)
Trisha Yearwood; *Everybody Knows* . . . . (MCA)
Between An Old Memory And Me
Keith Whitley; *I Wonder Do You Think Of Me*. . . . . (RCA)
Travis Tritt; *Ten Feet Tall And Bulletproof* . . . .(Warner Bros.)
Born A Fool
Freddie Hart; *Best Of Freddie Hart* . . . . (MCA)
Broadway Fools
Branford Marsalis; *Random Abstract*. . . . .(Columbia)
But Not For Me
Billie Holiday; *Silver Collection* . . . .(Verve)
Chet Baker; *Let's Get Lost-Best Of Chet Baker Sings* . . . . (Blue Note)
Ella Fitzgerald; *Ella Sings Jazz* . . . . (MCA Jazz)
Elvis Costello; *Glory Of Gershwin Featuring Larry Adler-C* . . . .(Mercury)
Harry Connick, Jr.; *ST/When Harry Met Sally* . . . .(Columbia)
Judy Garland; *Best Of Judy Garland* . . . . (MCA)
Original London Cast; *Crazy For You* . . . . (RCA)
Original Soundtrack; *Manhattan* . . . .(CBS Masterworks)
Sarah Vaughan; *Sarah Vaughan Sings George Gershwin Songbook,
Vol. 2* . . . . (Emarcy)
Bye Bye Bye
'N Sync; *No Strings Attached*. . . . . (Jive)
Now That's What I Call Music!-#6-C . . . . (Virgin)
Card Carrying Fool
Randy Travis; *No Holdin' Back* . . . .(Warner Bros.)
ST/Pink Cadillac . . . .(Warner Bros.)
Certain Kind Of Fool
Eagles; *Desperado* . . . . (Asylum)
Chain Of Fools
Aretha Franklin; *Aretha Franklin's Greatest Hits* . . . . (Atlantic)
Aretha's Gold . . . . (Atlantic)
Atlantic Rhythm & Blues 1947-1974-#6 (1966-1969)-C . . . . (Atlantic)

Best Of Aretha Franklin.................................(Atlantic)
Lady Of Soul...(Atlantic)
Clint Black & Pointer Sisters; *Rhythm Country And Blues-C*.........(MCA)

Come And Get It
Badfinger; *Best Of Badfinger*...........................(Capitol)
Beatles; *The Beatles-Anthology-#3*........................(Capitol)

Crazy
Jimmie Dale Gilmore with Willie Nelson; *Red Hot + Country-C*.....(Mercury)
Kenny Rogers; *Kenny Rogers' Greatest Hits*.....................(RCA)
What About Me?..(RCA)
Linda Ronstadt; *Hasten Down The Wind*.......................(Asylum)
Patsy Cline; *Songwriter's Tribute*...........................(MCA)
ST/Sweet Dreams......................................(MCA)
The Patsy Cline Story...................................(MCA)
Ray Price; *Ray Price's Greatest Hits-#2*.....................(Step One)
Willie Nelson; *Best Of Willie*.............................(RCA)
Healing Hands Of Time..................................(Liberty)
Nite Life-Greatest Hits & Rare Tracks.......................(Rhino)
Willie & Family Live....................................(Columbia)

Dancin' Fool
Frank Zappa; *Sheik Yerbouti*.............................(Zappa)

Dancin' Fool
Guess Who; *Greatest Of The Guess Who*......................(RCA)

Do Your Thing
7 Mile; *7 Mile*.......................................(Crave)

Does That Blue Moon Ever Shine On You
Toby Keith; *Blue Moon*...........................(Polydor Country)
Toby Keith's Greatest Hits, Volume One.....................(Mercury)

Don't Be A Fool
Loose Ends; *Look How Long*..............................(MCA)

Don't Be A Fool
Del Vikings; *Del Vikings*.............................(Collectables)

Don't Be Stupid (You Know I Love You)
Shania Twain; *Come On Over*.............................(Mercury)

Don't Say
Jon B.; *Cool Relax*.................................(Yab Yum/550)

Don't Want To Be A Fool
Luther Vandross; *Power Of Love*............................(Epic)

Dumb
Nirvana; *In Utero*..............................(David Geffen Co.)
MTV Unplugged In New York......................(David Geffen Co.)

Earth Angel
Elvis Presley; *A Golden Celebration*.........................(RCA)
New Edition; *ST/Under The Blue Moon*........................(MCA)
Penguins; *Billboard Top Rock 'N' Roll Hits-1955-C*..............(Rhino)
Golden Classics-Penguins..............................(Collectables)
Oldies But Goodies-#1-C...........................(Original Sound)
ST/American Graffiti...................................(MCA)

Emperor's New Clothes
Sinead O'Connor; *I Do Not Want What I Haven't Got*............(Ensign)

Every Time Two Fools Collide
Kenny Rogers & Dottie West; *Every Time Two Fools Collide*.........(EMI)
Kenny Rogers' Greatest Hits.............................(EMI)

Everybody Plays The Fool
Aaron Neville; *Warm Your Heart*...........................(A&M)
Main Ingredient; *Golden Classics-Main Ingredient*............(Collectables)
Nipper's Greatest Hits Of The '70s-C.......................(RCA)

Everybody's Somebody's Fool
Heartbeats; *Daddy's Home*.............................(Remember)

Everybody's Somebody's Fool
Betty Carter; *'Round Midnight*...........................(Atlantic)
Connie Francis; *Very Best Of Connie Francis*..................(Polydor)
Debby Boone; *Best Of Debby Boone*..........................(Curb)

Everything To Everyone
Everclear; *Ka-Boom!-C*.................................(Beast)
So Much For The Afterglow...............................(Capitol)

Find Another Fool
Quarterflash; *Quarterflash*.............................(Geffen)

Fool
Sanford Clark; *Billboard Top Rock 'N' Roll Hits-1956-C*..........(Rhino)
Original Classic Oldies Of The '50s & '60s-#17-C...............(MCA)

Fool #1
Brenda Lee; *The Brenda Lee Story-Her Greatest Hits*.............(MCA)
Joe Stampley/The Uniques; *Joe Stampley-Golden Hits*............(Paula)

Fool #1
Mavericks; *Trampoline*.................................(MCA)

Fool & His Money
Wang Chung; *Mosaic*..................................(Geffen)

Fool (If You Think It's Over)
Chris Rea; *New Light Through Old Windows*...................(Atlantic)
Whatever Happened To Benny Santini....................(United Artists)

Fool About A Cigarette
Tom Ball & Kenny Sultan; *Bloodshot Eyes*...................(Flying Fish)

Fool Button
Jimmy Buffett; *Son Of A Son Of A Sailor*......................(MCA)

Fool By Your Side
David Rowland & Sugar; *Pleasure*.........................(Elektra)

Fool For A Cigarette
Ry Cooder; *Paradise And Lunch*............................(Reprise)

Fool For The City
Foghat; *Best Of Foghat*.................................(Rhino)
Best Of Hard Rock-#1-C..........................(MCA Special Prod.)
Foghat-Live...(Rhino)
Fool For The City.....................................(Rhino)

Fool For You
James Taylor; *One Man Dog*............................(Warner Bros.)
Neil Diamond; *Heartlight*...............................(Columbia)
Ray Charles; *Atlantic Rhythm & Blues 1947-1974-#2 (1952-1955)-C*..(Atlantic)
Ray Charles-Live.....................................(Atlantic)
Rod Stewart; *Night On The Town*........................(Warner Bros.)
Rude Boys; *Rude Awakening*.............................(Atlantic)

Fool For Your Love
Mickey Gilley; *19 Hot Country Requests-C*.....................(Epic)
Fool For Your Love....................................(Epic)

Fool For Your Loving
Whitesnake; *Live...In The Heart Of The City*..................(Geffen)
Slip Of The Tongue...................................(Geffen)

Fool For Your Stockings
ZZ Top; *Deguello*.................................(Warner Bros.)

Fool Hearted Memory
George Strait; *George Strait's Greatest Hits*..................(MCA)
Night Game...(MCA)
Strait From The Heart..................................(MCA)

Fool In Love
Ike & Tina Turner; *Best Of Ike & Tina Turner*.................(EMI)
Best Of Sue Records-C...............................(Collectables)
Proud Mary-Best Of Ike & Tina Turner.......................(EMI)

Fool In Love
Robins; *Best Of The Robins*...........................(Crescendo)

Fool In Love
Etta James; *Sticking To My Guns*..........................(Island)

Fool In Love
Michael Smotherman; *ST/Always*..........................(MCA)

Fool In Love With You
Jim Photoglo; *45-#2487*..........................(20th Century Fox)

Fool In The Rain
Led Zeppelin; *In Through The Out Door*....................(Swan Song)
Led Zeppelin-Box Set..................................(Atlantic)

Fool On The Hill
Beatles; *Beatles-Box Set*................................(Capitol)
Magical Mystery Tour..................................(Capitol)
The Beatles/1967-1970.................................(Capitol)

Fool Such As I
Baillie & The Boys; *Lights Of Home*.........................(RCA)
Elvis Presley; *Elvis Aron Presley*...........................(RCA)
Elvis-A Legendary Performer, Volume 1......................(RCA)
Worldwide 50 Gold Award Hits, Vol. 1, Parts 1 & 2..............(RCA)

Fool To Cry
Rolling Stones; *Black And Blue*.......................(Rolling Stones)
Rewind (1971-1984).................................(Rolling Stones)
Sucking In The Seventies............................(Rolling Stones)

Fool With My Money
Special Forces; *Special Forces*..................(Empire Recording Comm.)

Fool Yourself
Bonnie Raitt; *Home Plate*.............................(Warner Bros.)
Little Feat; *Dixie Chicken*............................(Warner Bros.)

Fool, The
Lee Ann Womack; *Lee Ann Womack*..........................(Decca)

Fool, The
Quicksilver Messenger Service; *Quicksilver Messenger Service*......(Capitol)
Quicksilver Messenger Service-Anthology......................(Capitol)
Sons Of Mercury.....................................(Rhino)

Fool, The
BoDeans; *Outside Looking In*.............................(Slash)

Fool, The
38 Special; *Special Delivery*.............................(A&M)

Fool, The
Elvis Presley; *A Golden Celebration*.........................(RCA)

Fooled Again (I Don't Like It)
Tom Petty And The Heartbreakers; *Tom Petty & The
Heartbreakers*.....................................(Gone Gator)

Fooled Around & Fell In Love
Elvin Bishop; *Billboard Top Hits-1976-C*.....................(Rhino)
South's Greatest Hits-C................................(Capricorn)
Struttin' My Stuff....................................(Capricorn)

Fooled By A Feeling
Barbara Mandrell; *Just For The Record*.......................(MCA)

Foolin'
Johnny Rodriguez; *19 Hot Country Requests-#2-C*...............(Epic)

Foolin'
Def Leppard; *Pyromania*...............................(Mercury)

Foolin' Around
Patsy Cline; *Always*..................................(MCA)
ST/Sweet Dreams.....................................(MCA)
The Patsy Cline Story..................................(MCA)

Foolin' Around
Changing Faces; *Changing Faces*....................(Big Beat/Atlantic)

Fooling Yourself
Styx; *Caught In The Act*.............................(A&M)
   Grand Illusion ....(A&M)
   Styx-Classics-#15 ....(A&M)
Foolish Beat
Debbie Gibson; *Hit Singles-1980-1988-C*...........(Atlantic)
   Out Of The Blue ....(Atlantic)
Foolish Games
Jewel; *Pieces Of You* ....(Atlantic)
   ST/Batman & Robin-Music From And Inspired By The Motion Picture...(Jive)
   VH-1 Crossroads-C ....(Atlantic)
Foolish Heart
Steve Perry; *Street Talk* ....(Columbia)
Foolish Heart
Grateful Dead; *Built To Last* ....(Arista)
Foolish Heart
Sharon Bryant; *Here I Am* ....(Wing)
Foolish Little Girl
Shirelles; *Shirelles' Greatest Hits* ....(Everest)
   Shirelles-16 Greatest Hits. ....(Trip)
   Shirelles-Anthology 1959-1964 ....(Rhino)
Foolish Pride
Daryl Hall; *Three Hearts In The Happy Ending Machine* ....(RCA)
Joan Armatrading; *The Key* ....(A&M)
Foolish Pride
Travis Tritt; *Ten Feet Tall And Bulletproof* ....(Warner Bros.)
Fools
Van Halen; *Women & Children First* ....(Warner Bros.)
Fools Fall In Love
Drifters; *Atlantic Rhythm & Blues 1947-1974-#3 (1955-1958)-C*.....(Atlantic)
   Drifters-Their Greatest Recordings ....(Atco)
   ST/Book Of Love. ....(Atlantic)
Jacky Ward; *Best Of Jacky Ward*. ....(Mercury)
   Lover's Question ....(Mercury)
Fool's Gold
Stone Roses; *The Stone Roses* ....(Silvertone)
Fool's Gold
Graham Parker; *Pourin' It All Out-Mercury Years* ....(Mercury)
Graham Parker And The Rumour; *Heat Treatment* ....(Mercury)
   The Parkerilla. ....(Mercury)
Fool's Gold
Poco; *Crazy Eyes* ....(Epic)
   Ride The Country ....(Epic)
   Very Best Of Poco ....(Epic)
Fool's Gold
Thin Lizzy; *Johnny The Fox* ....(Warner Bros.)
Fool's Gold
Lee Greenwood; *Lee Greenwood's Greatest Hits* ......(MCA)
   You've Got A Good Love Comin' ....(MCA)
Fool's Hall Of Fame
Johnny Cash; *Rough Cut King Of Country Music* ....(Sun)
   The Man-The World-His Music ....(Sun)
Roy Orbison; *Roy Orbison-The Sun Years* ....(Rhino)
Fools In Love
Joe Jackson; *Live 1980/86* ....(A&M)
   Look Sharp! ....(A&M)
Fools Like Me
Jerry Lee Lewis; *Jerry Lee Lewis-Original Golden Hits-#2* ......(Sun)
   The Golden Hits Of Jerry Lee Lewis. ....(Smash)
Fool's Overture
Supertramp; *Even In The Quietest Moments* ....(A&M)
   Paris ....(A&M)
Fools Rush In (Where Angels Fear To Tread)
Brook Benton; *Super Oldies Of The '60s-#10-C* .....(Audio Fidelity)
Tommy Dorsey & Frank Sinatra; *Sessions-#1-February 1, 1940-July 17, 1940* ....(RCA)
Give This Fool Another Try
Charlie Daniels Band; *Whiskey* ....(Epic)
Heartaches Of A Fool
Willie Nelson; *Greatest Hits (& Some That Will Be)* ....(Columbia)
Heaven Help The Fool
Bob Weir; *Heaven Help The Fool* ....(Arista)
He's A Fool For You
Boz Scaggs; *My Time* ....(Columbia)
Hey There
Original Cast; *ST/Pajama Game* ....(Collectables)
Rosemary Clooney; *Essence Of Rosemary Clooney* ......(Legacy)
Honky Tonkin' Fool
Doug Supernaw; *Red And Rio Grande* ....(BNA)
   The Encore Collection ....(BMG Special Prod.)
How Do The Fools Survive
Doobie Brothers; *Minute By Minute* ....(Warner Bros.)
I Guess I'm Crazy
Jim Reeves; *Billboard Top Country Hits-1964-C* ....(Rhino)
   Essential Jim Reeves. ....(RCA)
I Know One
Charley Pride; *Charley Pride-Super Hits* ....(RCA)
Garth Brooks; *Garth Brooks* ....(Liberty)

Jim Reeves; *Essential Jim Reeves* ....(RCA)
I Make A Fool Of Myself
Frankie Valli; *25th Anniversary Collection* ....(Rhino)
I Think You've Got Your Fools Mixed Up
Brenton Wood; *Brenton Wood-18 Best* ....(Original Sound)
I Was A Fool To Care
James Taylor; *Gorilla* ....(Warner Bros.)
I Whistle A Happy Tune
Barbara Cook; *My Little Broadway* ....(Sony Wonder)
Frank Sinatra; *Frank Sinatra Sings Rodgers & Hammerstein* ....(Columbia)
Micky Dolenz; *Broadway Micky* ....(Kid Rhino/Rhino 4 Kids)
Original Broadway Cast; *The King And I* ....(RCA Victor)
Original Cast; *The King And I* ....(MCA)
If You Gotta Make A Fool Of Somebody
Aretha Franklin; *Soul '69-C* ....(Rhino)
Bonnie Raitt; *Give It Up* ....(Warner Bros.)
Eddie Floyd; *Knock On Wood* ....(Atlantic)
Huey Lewis and the News; *Four Chords & Several Years Ago* ....(Elektra)
James Ray; *Golden Classics-James Ray* ....(Collectables)
Lou Rawls; *It's Supposed To Be Fun* ....(Blue Note)
Maxine Brown; *Golden Classics-Maxine Brown* ....(Collectables)
I'm A Fool
Dino, Desi & Billy; *Even More Nuggets-C* ....(Rhino)
   Only Love-1965-1969-C ....(JCI Assoc. Labels)
I'm The Fool
Mark Knopfler; *Golden Heart* ....(Warner Bros.)
Incomplete
Sisqo; *Now That's What I Call Music!-#5-C* ....(Virgin)
   Unleash The Dragon. ....(Dragon/Def Soul/IDJMG)
Just Walking In The Rain
Johnnie Ray; *16 Most Requested Songs Of The '50s-#1-C*..........(Legacy)
   Best Of Johnnie Ray ....(Columbia)
   Johnnie Ray-16 Most Requested Songs ....(Legacy)
   Johnnie Ray's Greatest Hits ....(Sony Music Special Prod.)
Kansas You Fooler
Ozark Mountain Daredevils; *It'll Shine When It Shines* ....(A&M)
King Of The Mountain
George Strait; *Blue Clear Sky*. ....(MCA)
   Latest Greatest Straitest Hits. ....(MCA)
Kissing A Fool
George Michael; *Faith* ....(Columbia)
Little Old Wine Drinker Me
Dean Martin; *Dean Martin's Greatest Hits-#2* ....(Reprise)
   Welcome To My World ....(Reprise)
Mel Tillis; *Best Of Mel Tillis* ....(MCA)
Lovefool
Cardigans; *First Band On The Moon* ....(Mercury)
   MTV Best Of The Buzz Bin-#2-C ....(Mammoth)
Love's Made A Fool Of You
Bobby Fuller Four; *Best Of The Bobby Fuller Four* ....(Rhino)
Buddy Holly; *Rock & Roll Collection* ....(MCA)
Greg Kihn; *Greg Kihn Again* ....(Beserkley)
Lucky Me
Anne Murray; *Anne Murray-Country Hits*............(Capitol)
   Somebody's Waiting ....(Capitol)
Mama's Fool
Tesla; *Bust A Nut* ....(Geffen)
Married Man's A Fool
Blind Willie McTell; *Last Session* ....(Prestige)
Ry Cooder; *Paradise And Lunch* ....(Reprise)
Maybe He'll Notice Her Now
Mindy McCready; *Ten Thousand Angels* ....(BNA)
Maybe I'm A Fool
Aretha Franklin; *Aretha Franklin Sings The Blues* ....(Columbia)
Eddie Money; *Life For The Taking* ....(Columbia)
Mirror Mirror
Diamond Rio; *Diamond Rio*. ....(Arista)
   Diamond Rio's Greatest Hits ....(Arista)
Mr. Too Damn Good
Gerald Levert; *G* ....(East West)
My Foolish Heart
Bill Evans; *Waltz For Debby* ....(Riverside)
Carmen McRae; *Live At Bubba's* ....(Who's Who In Jazz)
John McLaughlin; *Electric Guitarist* ....(Columbia)
Liz Story; *My Foolish Heart* ....(Windham Hill)
Roberta Flack; *Set The Night To Music* ....(Atlantic)
Stephane Grappelli; *Stephanova* ....(Concord Jazz)
Tony Bennett & Bill Evans; *The Tony Bennett & Bill Evans Album*. ....(Original Jazz Classics)
My My
Seven Mary Three; *American Standard* ....(Mammoth)
Never Gonna Be Your Fool Again
Lisa Brokop; *Every Little Girl's Dream* ....(Patriot)
New Fool At An Old Game
Reba McEntire; *Country's Greatest Hits-#4-Sweet Country-C* ....(Priority)
   Reba. ....(MCA)
   Reba McEntire-Live. ....(MCA)
Nobody But A Fool (Would Love You)
Connie Smith; *Best Of Connie Smith* ....(Dominion Entert.)

Nobody Falls Like A Fool
Earl Thomas Conley; *Earl Thomas Conley's Greatest Hits* . . . . (RCA)
Nobody Falls Like A Fool . . . . (RCA)
Nobody's Fool
Kenny Loggins; *Back To Avalon* . . . . (Columbia)
ST/Caddyshack II . . . . (Columbia)
Nobody's Fool
Cinderella; *Night Songs* . . . . (Mercury)
Nobody's Fool
Poco; *Pickin' Up The Pieces* . . . .(Epic)
Norma Jean Riley
Diamond Rio; *Diamond Rio* . . . . (Arista)
Diamond Rio's Greatest Hits . . . . (Arista)
October Fool
Charlie Shoemaker & Bill Holman; *Collaboration* . . . .(Pausa)
Oh Daddy
Fleetwood Mac; *Rumours* . . . .(Warner Bros.)
Tallulah; *Legacy-A Tribute To Fleetwood Mac's Rumours-C* . . . (Lava)
Oh Me, Oh My (I'm A Fool For You Baby)
Aretha Franklin; *Aretha Franklin-30 Greatest Hits* . . . . (Rhino)
Buster Poindexter; *Buster Poindexter* . . . . (RCA)
Irma Thomas; *Simply The Best-Live!* . . . . (Rounder)
Lulu; *Super Hits Of The '70s-Have A Nice Day-#6-C* . . . . (Rhino)
One Of A Kind Pair Of Fools
Barbara Mandrell; *Barbara Mandrell-Greatest Country Hits* . . . . (Curb)
Barbara Mandrell's Greatest Hits . . . . (MCA)
Spun Gold . . . . (MCA)
Only A Fool
Black Crowes; *By Your Side* . . . . (American)
Pack Of Fools
New Grass Revival; *Commonwealth* . . . . (Flying Fish)
Poor Damned Fool
Harry Chapin; *Legends Of The Lost & Found* . . . . (Elektra)
Living Room Suite . . . . (Elektra)
Poor Fool
Ike & Tina Turner; *Ike & Tina Turner-Golden Classics* . . . . . (Collectables)
Ike & Tina Turner's Greatest Hits . . . . (Curb)
Proud Mary-Best Of Ike & Tina Turner . . . . (EMI)
Poor Little Fool
Rick Nelson; *Live In '85* . . . . (Rhino)
Ricky Nelson; *Best Of Ricky Nelson* . . . .(EMI)
EMI Legends Of Rock & Roll-24 Greatest Hits-C . . . . (EMI)
Ricky Nelson-Legendary Masters . . . . (EMI)
Pop A Top
Alan Jackson; *Under The Influence* . . . . (Arista)
Jim Ed Brown; *Essential Jim Ed Brown* . . . . (RCA)
Queen Of Hearts
Dave Edmunds; *Best Of Dave Edmunds* . . . . (Swan Song)
Repeat When Necessary . . . . (Swan Song)
Juice Newton; *All-Time Country Classics-#2-C* . . . . (Capitol)
Juice . . . . (Capitol)
Juice Newton-Greatest Hits & More . . . . (Capitol)
Juice Newton's Greatest Hits . . . . (Gold Rush)
Rodney Crowell; *Rodney Crowell-Collection* . . . .(Warner Bros.)
Reckless
Alabama; *American Pride* . . . . (RCA)
Rednecks
Randy Newman; *Good Old Boys* . . . . (Reprise)
Guilty: 30 Years Of Randy Newman . . . . (Rhino)
Rhythm Of The Rain
Cascades; *Collectables Presents The History Of Rock-#7-C* . . . . (Collectables)
Golden Years-1963-C . . . . (Dominion Entert.)
Ridiculous Thoughts
Cranberries; *No Need To Argue* . . . . (Island)
Rip It Up
Elvis Presley; *Elvis* . . . . (RCA)
Rocker . . . . (RCA)
Little Richard; *Big Hits* . . . .(Crescendo)
Grooviest 17 Original Hits . . . .(Specialty)
Little Richard-18 Greatest Hits . . . . (Rhino)
Little Richard's Greatest Hits . . . . (Everest)
Sentimental Fool
Roxy Music; *Siren* . . . . (Atco)
Sexy Sadie
Beatles; *Beatles-Box Set* . . . . (Capitol)
The Beatles (White Album) . . . . (Capitol)
Shame, Shame
Magic Lanterns; *Shame, Shame* . . . . (Collectables)
She's A Fool
Lesley Gore; *Golden Hits Of Lesley Gore* . . . . (Mercury)
Lesley Gore-Anthology . . . . (Rhino)
Ship Of Fools
Elvis Costello; *Deadicated-C* . . . . (Arista)
Grateful Dead; *From The Mars Hotel* . . . . (Grateful Dead)
Steal Your Face . . . . (Grateful Dead)
Ship Of Fools
Garland Jeffreys; *American Boy & Girl* . . . . (A&M)
Ship Of Fools
World Party; *Greenpeace/Rainbow Warriors-C* . . . .(Geffen)

Private Revolution . . . . (Ensign)
Ship Of Fools
Doors; *Morrison Hotel/Hard Rock Cafe* . . . . (Elektra)
Weird Scenes Inside The Gold Mine . . . . (Elektra)
Ship Of Fools
Bob Seger; *Night Moves* . . . . (Capitol)
Ship Of Fools
Robert Plant; *Now And Zen* . . . . (Es Paranza)
Silly Ho
TLC; *Fanmail* . . . . (LaFace)
Slippin' And Slidin'
Little Richard; *Little Richard-18 Greatest Hits* . . . . (Rhino)
Some Fools Never Learn
Steve Wariner; *One Good Night Deserves Another* . . . . (MCA)
Steve Wariner's Greatest Hits . . . . (MCA)
Statue Of A Fool
Jack Greene; *Country Hits-C* . . . . (Exact)
Jack Greene Sings His Best . . . . (Step One)
Jack Greene's Greatest Hits . . . . (International Mktg. Group)
MCA Records 30 Years Of Hits-1958-1988-C . . . . (MCA)
Ricky Van Shelton; *Ricky Van Shelton's Greatest Hits Plus* . . . . . (Columbia)
RVS III . . . . (Columbia)
Stupid Cupid
Connie Francis; *Very Best Of Connie Francis* . . . .(Polydor)
Neil Sedaka; *Neil Sedaka's All-Time Greatest Hits-#2* . . . . (RCA)
Stupid Einstein
Three O'Clock; *Sixteen Tambourines* . . . .(Frontier)
Stupid Girl
Rolling Stones; *Aftermath* . . . .(Abkco)
Singles Collection-The London Years . . . .(Abkco)
Stupid Girl
Garbage; *Garbage* . . . . (Almo Sounds)
Stupid Marriage
Specials; *Specials* . . . . (Chrysalis)
Stupid War Movies
Paleface; *Paleface* . . . .(Polydor)
Stupid, Stupid War
D.R.I.; *Dealing With It* . . . . (Metal Blade)
Stupidly Happy
XTC; *Wasp Star (Apple Venus Volume 2)* . . . . (Idea/TVT)
Sunday Morning Fool
Michael Dinner; *Great Pretenders* . . . . (Fantasy)
Tear Fell, A
Teresa Brewer; *Best Of Teresa Brewer* . . . .(MCA Jazz)
Tears Are Just For Fools
Starlites; *Harlem Holiday-New York Rhythm & Blues-#7-C* . . . . . (Collectables)
Tell The Truth
Derek And The Dominos; *Derek & The Dominos In Concert* . . . . (RSO)
Eric Clapton-Crossroads-C . . . . (Polydor)
Layla . . . . (Polydor)
Ten Feet Tall And Bulletproof
Travis Tritt; *Ten Feet Tall And Bulletproof* . . . . (Warner Bros.)
Theme From "The Three Stooges"
Original Soundtrack; *Television's Greatest Hits-#2-C* . . . . (TVT)
There Goes My Baby
Trisha Yearwood; *Where Your Road Leads* . . . . (MCA)
These Foolish Things (Remind Me Of You)
Aaron Neville; *The Grand Tour* . . . . (A&M)
Art Pepper; *Art Pepper Today* . . . . (Galaxy)
Benny Goodman; *Stompin' At The Savoy* . . . . (Bluebird)
Billie Holiday; *Billie Holiday-16 Most Requested Songs* . . . . (Legacy)
Bobby Watson; *This Little Light Of Mine* . . . .(Red)
Boston Pops Orchestra/Arthur Fiedler; *Popular Favorites By The Boston
Pops Orchestra* . . . .(Pair)
Bryan Ferry; *Street Life-20 Great Hits* . . . . (Reprise)
These Foolish Things . . . . (Reprise)
Chet Baker; *Baker's Holiday* . . . . Verve)
Somewhere Over The Rainbow . . . . (Bluebird)
Count Basie Jam; *Montreux '77-C* . . . . (Pablo)
Dave Brubeck; *Greatest Hits From The Fantasy Years* . . . . . . (Fantasy)
Dinah Washington; *In Love* . . . . (Roulette)
Frank Sinatra; *Point Of No Return* . . . . (Capitol)
Nat "King" Cole; *Just One Of Those Things (& More)* . . . . (Capitol)
Ronnie Milsap; *True Believer* . . . . (Liberty)
Ruby Braff; *Jazz Club-Mainstream-Trumpet* . . . . Verve)
Stan Getz; *Essential Stan Getz Songbook* . . . . Verve)
They'll Never Take Her Love From Me
Emmylou Harris; *Blue Kentucky Girl* . . . . (Warner Bros.)
George Jones; *George Jones Sings The Great Songs Of Leon
Payne* . . . .(Hollywood/DNA-Rounder)
Hank Williams With His Drifting Cowboys; *Hank Williams-24 Greatest
Hits-#2* . . . .(Polydor)
Hank Williams-40 Greatest Hits . . . .(Polydor)
Third Time Lucky
Foghat; *Best Of Foghat* . . . . (Rhino)
Boogie Motel . . . . (Rhino)
Thoughts Of A Fool
George Strait; *ST/Pure Country* . . . . (MCA)

Toast To The Fool
Dramatics; *Best Of The Dramatics* . . . . (Stax)
  Dramatically Yours . . . . (Stax)
  Dramatics-Live . . . . (Stax)
Today's Lonely Fool
Tracy Lawrence; *Sticks & Stones* . . . . (Atlantic)
Tonight The Heartache's On Me
Dixie Chicks; *Wide Open Spaces* . . . . (Monument)
Trying To Make A Fool Of Me
Delfonics; *Best Of The Delfonics* . . . . (Arista)
  Delfonics-Golden Classics . . . . (Collectables)
Victim Or A Fool
Rodney Crowell; *Rodney Crowell-Collection* . . . . (Warner Bros.)
Waist Deep In The Big Muddy
Pete Seeger; *Best Of Broadside 1962-1968: Anthems Of The American*
  Underground From The Pages Of Broadside
  Magazine-C . . . . (Smithsonian Folkways)
Was
Kenny Wayne Shepherd Band; *Live On* . . . . (Giant)
What A Fool Believes
Doobie Brothers; *Best Of The Doobies, Volume II* . . . . (Warner Bros.)
  Minute By Minute . . . . (Warner Bros.)
Kenny Loggins; *Kenny Loggins Alive* . . . . (Columbia)
  Nightwatch . . . . (Columbia)
What Do I Know
Ricochet; *Pure Country-Best Of The '90s-#2-C* . . . . (Priority)
  Ricochet . . . . (Columbia)
What Is This Thing Called Love
Alexander O'Neal; *All True Man* . . . . (Tabu)
  Greatest Hits Of Alexander O'Neal . . . . (Epic)
Artie Shaw; *Begin The Beguine* . . . . (Bluebird)
Charlie Parker; *Cole Porter Songbook* . . . . (Verve)
Ella Fitzgerald; *Cole Porter Songbook* . . . . (Verve)
Frank Sinatra; *Frank Sinatra Sings The Select Cole Porter* . . . . (Capitol)
Julie London; *Julie London Sings Cole Porter* . . . . (EMI)
Kay Starr; *Back To The Roots* . . . . (Crescendo)
Mel Torme; *Night & Day-Cole Porter Songbook-C* . . . . (Verve)
What Kind Of Fool
Barbra Streisand; *Collection-Greatest Hits...And More* . . . . (Columbia)
  One Voice . . . . (Columbia)
Barbra Streisand & Barry Gibb; *Guilty* . . . . (Columbia)
What Kind Of Fool
Lionel Cartwright; *Chasin' The Sun* . . . . (MCA)
What Kind Of Fool Am I
Bill Evans; *Solo Sessions-#1* . . . . (Milestone)
Marvin Gaye; *Hello Broadway* . . . . (Motown)
Original Broadway Cast; *Stop The World I Want To Get Off.* . . . . (Polydor)
Robert Goulet; *Robert Goulet-16 Most Requested Songs* . . . . (Columbia)
  Robert Goulet's Greatest Hits . . . . (Columbia)
Sammy Davis, Jr.; *Sammy Davis, Jr.'s Greatest Songs* . . . . (Curb)
What Kind Of Fool Am I
Rick Springfield; *Rick Springfield's Greatest Hits* . . . . (RCA)
  Success Hasn't Spoiled Me Yet . . . . (RCA)
What Kind Of Fool Do You Think I Am
Bill Deal & The Rhondels; *Frat Rock!-#2-C* . . . . (Rhino)
  Oldies But Goodies-#15-C . . . . (Original Sound)
What Kind Of Fool Do You Think I Am
Lee Roy Parnell; *Love Without Mercy* . . . . (Arista)
What Mattered Most
Ty Herndon; *Super Hits Of 1995-C* . . . . (Epic)
  What Mattered Most . . . . (Epic)
Who But A Fool (Thief In Paradise)
Bonnie Raitt; *Nine Lives* . . . . (Warner Bros.)
Who Will The Next Fool Be
Charlie Rich; *Charlie Rich-The Ultimate Collection* . . . . (Hip-O)
  Lonely Weekends-The Very Best Of Charlie Rich . . . . (Collectables)
Jerry Lee Lewis; *The Mercury & Smash Years Recordings* . . . . . . (Collectables)
Why Am I A Fool For You
Jarmels; *Jarmels-Golden Classics* . . . . (Collectables)
Why Do Fools Fall In Love
Beach Boys; *Spirit Of America* . . . . (Capitol)
Diamonds; *Best Of The Diamonds-The Mercury Years* . . . . (Mercury)
Diana Ross; *Why Do Fools Fall In Love* . . . . (RCA)
Frankie Lymon and The Teenagers; *Best Of Frankie Lymon and The*
  Teenagers . . . . (Rhino)
  Billboard Top Rock 'N' Roll Hits-1956-C . . . . (Rhino)
  ST/American Graffiti . . . . (MCA)
Joni Mitchell; *Shadows & Light* . . . . (Asylum)
Will Not Be Your Fool
David Bromberg; *How Late'll Ya Play 'Til?* . . . . (Fantasy)
Without You
Audrey Hepburn; *ST/My Fair Lady* . . . . (Columbia)
Julie Andrews/Original Cast; *My Fair Lady* . . . . (Columbia)
Original Cast; *My Fair Lady* . . . . (London)
Woke Up In Love
Exile; *Exile* . . . . (Epic)
  Exile's Greatest Hits . . . . (Epic)
Won't Get Fooled Again
Van Halen; *LIVE: Right here, right now.* . . . . (Warner Bros.)

Who; *ST/The Kids Are Alright* . . . . (MCA)
  The Concert For New York City-C . . . . (Columbia)
  Who Greatest Hits . . . . (MCA)
  Who's Last. . . . . (MCA)
  Who's next . . . . (MCA)
Write This Down
George Strait; *Always Never The Same* . . . . (MCA)
You Can't Fool The Fat Man
Randy Newman; *Little Criminals.* . . . . (Warner Bros.)
Young And Foolish
Eddie Fisher; *Very Best Of Eddie Fisher* . . . . (MCA)
Four Tops; *Lost & Found: Breaking Through* . . . . (Motown)
Joe Williams; *Here's To Life* . . . . (Telarc)
Nancy Kelly; *Singin' & Swingin'.* . . . . (Amherst)
Tony Bennett & Bill Evans; *The Tony Bennett & Bill Evans*
  Album . . . . (Original Jazz Classics)
You've Been In Love Too Long
Bonnie Raitt; *Takin' My Time* . . . . (Warner Bros.)
Martha & The Vandellas; *Martha Reeves & The Vandellas'*
  Greatest Hits . . . . (Motown)
  Martha Reeves & The Vandellas-Anthology . . . . (Motown)

FORGIVE, Mercy

See Also: BAD, CHARACTER & INTEGRITY, CHEATING &
LIES, FAITH, GOD, GUILT, HELP, LOVE (various), MISTAKES,
TEACHING VALUES

Affirmation
Savage Garden; *Affirmation* . . . . (Columbia)
Bridge
Queensryche; *Promised Land* . . . . (EMI)
Conviction Of The Heart
Kenny Loggins; *Leap Of Faith.* . . . . (Columbia)
  Outside: From The Redwoods . . . . (Columbia)
  Yesterday, Today, Tomorrow: The Greatest Hits Of Kenny
  Loggins . . . . (Columbia)
Criminal
Fiona Apple; *1998 Grammy Nominees-C* . . . . (MCA)
  Tidal . . . . (Clean Slate/Work)
Forgive And Forget
Blondie; *No Exit.* . . . . (Beyond)
Forgive Me
Cowboy Junkies; *Whites Off Earth Now!!* . . . . (RCA)
Forgive My Heart
Ray Price; *For The Good Times/I Won't Mention It Again* . . . . (Columbia)
Forgive Them Father
Lauryn Hill featuring Shelly Thunder; *The Miseducation Of*
  Lauryn Hill . . . . (Ruffhouse/Columbia)
Forgiveness
Macy Gray; *The Id* . . . . (Epic)
God Have Mercy On The Workin' Man
Randy Newman; *Good Old Boys* . . . . (Reprise)
God Was Drunk When He Made Me
Jim White; *No Such Place* . . . . (Luaka Bop)
Halfway Home Cafe
Ricky Skaggs and Kentucky Thunder; *History Of The Future* . . . (Skaggs Family)
Have You Ever Been Lonely (Have You Ever Been Blue)
Ernest Tubb; *Best Of Ernest Tubb* . . . . (Curb)
  The Country Music Hall Of Fame-Ernest Tubb. . . . . (MCA)
Jim Reeves & Patsy Cline; *Jim Reeves' Greatest Hits* . . . . (RCA)
Patsy Cline; *Showcase-With The Jordanaires* . . . . (MCA)
Heart Of The Matter
Don Henley; *End Of The Innocence.* . . . . (Geffen)
Husbands And Wives
Brooks & Dunn; *Big Country Hits '99-C* . . . . (K-Tel)
  If You See Her. . . . . (Arista)
Neil Diamond; *Neil Diamond-Love Songs* . . . . (MCA)
  Rainbow . . . . (MCA)
  Stones . . . . (MCA)
Roger Miller; *Best Of Roger Miller* . . . . (Mercury)
  Best Of Roger Miller-His Greatest Songs . . . . (Curb)
  Roger Miller-Super Hits . . . . (Epic)
  Roger Miller-The Hits . . . . (Mercury)
I Forgive You
Rachelle Ferrell; *Individuality (Can I Be Me?)* . . . . (Capitol)
I'm Telling You Now
Keb' Mo'; *Slow Down* . . . . (550/Epic/Okeh)
Just Between You And Me
DC Talk; *First Generation: 25 Years Of Virgin Records-C* . . . . (Virgin)
  Jesus Freak . . . . (Virgin)
Make The World Go Away
Eddy Arnold; *Best Of Eddy Arnold* . . . . (RCA)
  Billboard Top Country Hits-1965-C . . . . (Rhino)
  Eddy Arnold-Pure Gold . . . . (RCA)
  Nipper's Greatest Hits Of The '60s-#1-C . . . . (RCA)

World Of Hits . . . . (MGM)
Ray Price; *Ray Price-16 Biggest Hits* . . . . (Legacy)
Ray Price-20 Hits . . . . (Tee Vee)
My My
Seven Mary Three; *American Standard* . . . . (Mammoth)
Never An Absolution
James Horner; *ST/Titanic* . . . . (Sony Music Classical)
Please Forgive Me
Bryan Adams; *So Far So Good* . . . . (A&M)
Please Forgive Me
David Gray; *White Ladder* . . . . (ATO/RCA)
She Said
Collective Soul; *Dosage* . . . . (Atlantic)
ST/Scream 2 . . . . (Dimension/Capitol)
Shy Guy
Diana King; *ST/Bad Boys* . . . . (Work)
Tougher Than Love . . . . (Work)
Somewhere
Aretha Franklin; *Aretha's Jazz* . . . . (Rhino)
Barbra Streisand; *The Broadway Album* . . . . (Columbia)
Dave Brubeck; *Music From West Side Story* . . . . (Columbia)
Jose Carreras; *Amigos Para Siempre-Friends For Life* . . . . (Atlantic)
Original Cast; *ST/West Side Story* . . . . (Sony Broadway)
Tom Waits; *Tom Waits-Anthology* . . . . (Asylum)
Sweet Forgiveness
Bonnie Raitt; *Sweet Forgiveness* . . . . (Warner Bros.)
Sweet Forgiveness
Iris DeMent; *Infamous Angel* . . . . (Warner Bros.)
Take Me To Your World
George Jones; *Tammy Wynette...Remembered-C* . . . . (Asylum)
Tammy Wynette; *Tammy Wynette-16 Biggest Hits* . . . . (Legacy)
Tammy Wynette's Greatest Hits . . . . (Epic)
To Have You Back Again
Patty Loveless; *Long Stretch Of Lonesome* . . . . (Epic)
Unforgiven II
Metallica; *Reload* . . . . (Elektra)
When The Fallen Angels Fly
Patty Loveless; *When Fallen Angels Fly* . . . . (Epic)

FREEDOM, Independence

See Also: **CAREFREE, COUNTRIES: AMERICA, MONTHS & DATES: JULY, PATRIOTISM, POLITICS (various), PREJUDICE, PRISON, PROTEST, ROYALTY, SLAVERY**

2000 Blacks Got To Be Free
Fela Anikulapo Kuti & Roy Ayers; *Music Of Many Colours* . . . . . . (Celluloid)
50 Ways To Leave Your Lover
Paul Simon; *Greatest Hits, Etc.* . . . . (Columbia)
Negotiations And Love Songs, 1971-1986 . . . . (Warner Bros.)
Still Crazy After All These Years . . . . (Columbia)
Simon & Garfunkel; *The Concert In Central Park* . . . . (Warner Bros.)
Abolitionist Hymn
Hermes Nye; *Ballads Of The Civil War-#1 & 2* . . . . (Smithsonian Folkways)
All I Want
Offspring; *Ixnay On The Hombre* . . . . (Columbia)
Almost Independence Day
Van Morrison; *St. Dominic's Preview* . . . . (Warner Bros.)
Amarillo By Morning
George Strait; *George Strait's Greatest Hits* . . . . (MCA)
Strait From The Heart . . . . (MCA)
America
Neil Diamond; *12 Greatest Hits-#2* . . . . (Columbia)
Hot August Night II . . . . (Columbia)
ST/The Jazz Singer . . . . (Capitol)
America
Original Cast; *ST/West Side Story* . . . . (Sony Broadway)
Animal Song
Savage Garden; *Affirmation* . . . . (Columbia)
Any Bonds Today?
Andrews Sisters; *Swing Out To Victory: Songs Of World War II-C* . . . . (ISD/Intersound)
Barry Wood; *78-#27478* . . . . (Victor)
Bing Crosby; *Original Soundtrack Sessions* . . . . (Vintage Jazz Classics)
Any Which Way...Freedom
Mutabaruka; *Any Which Way...Freedom* . . . . (Shanachie)
Anything Goes
Count Basie & Tony Bennett; *Anything Goes-Capitol Sings Cole Porter-C* . . . . (Capitol)
Basie Swings Bennett Sings . . . . (Roulette)
Dionne Warwick; *Dionne Warwick Sings Cole Porter* . . . . (Arista)
Ella Fitzgerald; *Night & Day-Cole Porter Songbook-C* . . . . (Verve)
Frank Sinatra; *Frank Sinatra Sings The Select Cole Porter* . . . . . . (Capitol)
Mary Martin; *Mary Martin-16 Most Requested Songs* . . . . (Columbia)
Original Cast; *Anything Goes* . . . . (Epic)
Paul Whiteman & His Orchestra; *78-#24770* . . . . (Victor)

Yo-Yo Ma; *Anything Goes-The Music Of Cole Porter* . . . . (Columbia)
Are The Good Times Really Over (I Wish A Buck Was Still Silver)
Merle Haggard; *Big City* . . . . (Epic)
For The Record: Merle Haggard-43 Legendary Hits . . . . (BNA)
Greatest Country Hits Of The '80s-1982-C . . . . (Columbia)
His Epic Hits-First 11 To Be Continued-C . . . . (Epic)
Army Of The Free
Tennessee Ernie Ford; *Tennessee Ernie Ford Sings Songs Of The Civil War* . . . . (Capitol)
Asylum
Supertramp; *Crime Of The Century* . . . . (A&M)
Paris . . . . (A&M)
Baby, I Love Your Way/Free Bird Medley
Will To Power; *Billboard Top Hits-1988-C* . . . . (Rhino)
Will To Power . . . . (Epic)
Back In The Saddle Again
Gene Autry; *50th Anniversary* . . . . (Republic/Universal)
Columbia Country Classics-#1-Golden Age-C . . . . (Columbia)
Cowboy Hall Of Fame . . . . (Republic/Universal)
Cowboy Super Hits-C . . . . (Columbia)
Great American Singing Cowboys-C . . . . (Republic/Universal)
South Of The Border . . . . (Republic/Universal)
Ballad Of William Worthy
Phil Ochs; *Best Of Broadside 1962-1968: Anthems Of The American Underground From The Pages Of Broadside Magazine-C* . . . . (Smithsonian Folkways)
Battle Cry Of Freedom
Mormon Tabernacle Choir; *God Bless America* . . . (Sony Music Classical)
Mormon Tabernacle Choir's Greatest Hits . . . . (Columbia)
Songs Of The North & South 1861-1965 . . . . (Columbia)
The Mormon Tabernacle Choir Album . . . . (Columbia)
Be Free
Loggins & Messina; *Finale* . . . . (Columbia)
Mother Lode . . . . (Columbia)
The Best Of Friends . . . . (Columbia)
Belle, Belle, My Liberty Belle
Guy Mitchell; *Definitive Guy Mitchell* . . . . (Collector's Choice)
Guy Mitchell-16 Most Requested Songs . . . . (Legacy)
Big City
Merle Haggard; *For The Record: Merle Haggard-43 Legendary Hits* . . . (BNA)
Born Free
Andy Williams; *Andy Williams' Greatest Hits* . . . . (Columbia)
Andy Williams-16 Most Requested Songs . . . . (Legacy)
John Barry; *Film Music Of John Barry* . . . . (Columbia)
Matt Monro; *ST/Born Free* . . . . (MGM)
Roger Williams; *Best Of Roger Williams* . . . . (MCA)
Roger Williams-Golden Hits . . . . (MCA)
Born To Fly
Sara Evans; *Born To Fly* . . . . (RCA)
Break Away
Beach Boys; *Absolute Best-#2* . . . . (Capitol)
Beach Boys-Gift Set . . . . (Capitol)
Friends-20/20 . . . . (Capitol)
Spirit Of America . . . . (Capitol)
Break Away
Nick Lowe; *Basher: Best Of* . . . . (Columbia)
Break Away
Neville Brothers; *Treacherous Too!-A History Of The Neville Brothers-#2* . . . . (Rhino)
Break Away
Gail Davies; *ST/Sylvester* . . . . (RCA)
Where Is A Woman To Go . . . . (RCA)
Break Away
Art Garfunkel; *Breakaway* . . . . (Columbia)
Garfunkel . . . . (Columbia)
Break On Through (To The Other Side)
Doors; *Best Of The Doors* . . . . (Elektra)
Doors . . . . (Elektra)
Doors' Greatest Hits . . . . (Elektra)
Doors-Live . . . . (Elektra)
ST/Forrest Gump . . . . (Epic/Sony Music Soundtrax)
ST/The Doors . . . . (Elektra)
Weird Scenes Inside The Gold Mine . . . . (Elektra)
Breakaway
ZZ Top; *Antenna* . . . . (RCA)
Bumming Around
"T" Texas Tyler; *Only Country-1950-1954-C* . . . . (JCI Assoc. Labels)
Butterfly
Mariah Carey; *Butterfly* . . . . (Columbia)
Butterfly (I'll Set You Free)
Perry Como; *Perry Como Today* . . . . (RCA)
Cactus Tree
Joni Mitchell; *Joni Mitchell* . . . . (Reprise)
Joni Mitchell with Tom Scott & The L.A. Express; *Miles Of Aisles* . . . (Asylum)
Cage Of Freedom
Jon Anderson; *ST/Metropolis* . . . . (Columbia)
Chimes Of Freedom
Bob Dylan; *Another Side Of Bob Dylan* . . . . (Columbia)
Bruce Springsteen; *Chimes Of Freedom* . . . . (Columbia)

Byrds; *The Byrds* . . . . (Columbia)
  The Byrds' Greatest Hits . . . . (Columbia)
Closer To Free
BoDeans; *Chicago Bulls Greatest Hits-#3-C* . . . . . . (Atlantic)
  Go Slow Down . . . . (Slash)
  Joe Dirt Car . . . . (Reprise)
  ST/Party Of Five . . . . (Reprise)
Cowboy Take Me Away
Dixie Chicks; *Fly* . . . . (Monument)
Crazy
Alana Davis; *Blame It On Me* . . . . (Elektra)
Cry For Freedom
White Lion; *Big Game* . . . . (Atlantic)
Cry Freedom
Dave Matthews Band; *Crash* . . . . (RCA)
Cut Loose
Chrome Molly; *Angst* . . . . (I.R.S.)
Cut Loose
Paul Rodgers; *Cut Loose* . . . . (Atlantic)
Dance Into The Light
Phil Collins; *Dance Into The Light* . . . . (Atlantic)
Do Anything
Natural Selection featuring Niki Haris; *Natural Selection* . . . . (East West)
Do What You Want, Be What You Are
Daryl Hall & John Oates; *Bigger Than Both Of Us* . . . . (RCA)
  Livetime . . . . (RCA)
Don't Fence Me In
Andrews Sisters; *Andrews Sisters' All-Time Greatest Hits* . . . . (Decca)
Bing Crosby; *Best Of Bing Crosby* . . . . (MCA)
David Byrne; *Red Hot + Blue-Tribute To Cole Porter-C* . . (Chrysalis)
Ella Fitzgerald; *Cole Porter Songbook* . . . . (Verve)
Lari White/Shelby Lynne/Trisha Yearwood; *Don't Fence Me In* . . . . (RCA)
Willie Nelson & Leon Russell; *Cowboy Super Hits-C* . . (Columbia)
Don't Tread On Me
Metallica; *Metallica* . . . . (Elektra)
Don't You Get It
Mark Knopfler; *Golden Heart* . . . . (Warner Bros.)
Everybody's Free (To Wear Sunscreen)
Baz Luhrmann; *Now That's What I Call Music!-#2-C* . . . . (Virgin)
  Something For Everybody . . . . (Capitol)
Everybody's Talkin'
Nilsson; *Everybody's Talkin': The Encore Collection* . . . . (BMG Special Prod.)
  ST/Forrest Gump . . . . (Epic/Sony Music Soundtrax)
  ST/Midnight Cowboy . . . . (EMI)
Willie Nelson; *Best Of Willie* . . . . (RCA)
  Sweet Memories . . . . (RCA)
Fancy Free
Oak Ridge Boys; *Fancy Free* . . . . (MCA)
  Oak Ridge Boys' Greatest Hits 2 . . . . (MCA)
Find The Cost Of Freedom
Crosby, Stills, Nash & Young; *4 Way Street* . . . . (Atlantic)
  So Far . . . . (Atlantic)
Free
Phish; *Billy Breathes* . . . . (Elektra)
Free
Vast; *Music For People* . . . . (Elektra)
Free
Mya; *ST/Bait* . . . . (Warner Bros.)
Free As A Bird
Beatles; *The Beatles-Anthology-#1* . . . . (Capitol)
Free At Last
Dock Read & Vera Hall Ward; *Every Tone A Testimony-C* . . . . (Smithsonian Folkways)
Free Bird
Lynyrd Skynyrd; *Gold & Platinum* . . . . (MCA)
  One More From The Road . . . . (MCA)
  Pronounced Leh-nerd Skin-nerd . . . . (MCA)
  Southern By The Grace Of God-Tribute '87 . . . . . . (MCA)
Wynonna; *Skynyrd Frynds-C* . . . . (MCA)
Free Fallin'
Tom Petty; *Full Moon Fever* . . . . (MCA)
Free Girl Now
Tom Petty And The Heartbreakers; *Echo* . . . . . . (Warner Bros.)
Free Man In Paris
Joni Mitchell; *Court & Spark* . . . . (Asylum)
  Shadows & Light . . . . (Asylum)
Free Me
Roger Daltrey; *Best Bits* . . . . (MCA)
  ST/McVicar . . . . (Polydor)
Free Nelson Mandela
Special AKA; *In The Studio* . . . . (Chrysalis)
Free South Africa
Kinsey Report; *Midnight Drive* . . . . (Alligator)
Tackhead; *Friendly As A Hand Grenade* . . . . (TVT)
Free The People
Barbra Streisand; *Stoney End* . . . . (Columbia)
Delaney & Bonnie; *Best Of Delaney & Bonnie* . . . . . . (Rhino)
Free To Go
Folk Implosion; *One Part Lullaby* . . . . (Interscope)

Free Will
Rush; *Exit...Stage Left* . . . . (Mercury)
Free Your Mind
En Vogue; *Funky Divas* . . . . (East West)
Freeborn Man
Outlaws; *Bring It Back Alive* . . . . (Arista)
  Lady In Waiting . . . . (Arista)
  Legends Of Rock Guitar-'70s-C . . . . (Rhino)
Freedom
Jimi Hendrix; *Cry Of Love* . . . . (Reprise)
  Essential Jimi Hendrix . . . . (Reprise)
  Voodoo Soup . . . . (MCA)
Richie Havens; *ST/Woodstock* . . . . (Atlantic)
  The Best Of Woodstock-C . . . . (Atlantic)
Freedom
George Michael; *Listen Without Prejudice* . . . . (Columbia)
Wham! Featuring George Michael; *Make It Big* . . . . . (Columbia)
Freedom
Fleetwood Mac; *Behind The Mask* . . . . (Warner Bros.)
Freedom
Jefferson Airplane; *Jefferson Airplane* . . . . (Epic)
Freedom
Paul McCartney; *Driving Rain* . . . . (Columbia)
  The Concert For New York City-C . . . . (Columbia)
Freedom Dance (Get Free!)
Vanessa Williams; *The Comfort Zone* . . . . (Wing)
Freedom Overspill
Steve Winwood; *Back In The High Life* . . . . (Island)
Freedom Rider
Traffic; *John Barleycorn Must Die* . . . . (Island)
  On The Road . . . . (Island)
Freedom Riders
Phil Ochs; *Best Of Broadside 1962-1968: Anthems Of The American Underground From The Pages Of Broadside Magazine-C* . . . . (Smithsonian Folkways)
Freedom Song
Thin Lizzy; *Fighting* . . . . (Mercury)
Freedom Train, The
Bing Crosby; *Bing Crosby-Complete Recordings* . . . . . . (MCA)
Peggy Lee; *Peggy Lee-Complete Recordings-1941-1947* . . (Legacy)
Give Me Wings
Michael Johnson; *Best Of Michael Johnson* . . . . (RCA)
  Hits Of '86-C . . . . (RCA)
  Wings . . . . (RCA)
Give Me Your Tired, Your Poor
Mormon Tabernacle Choir; *Around The World: A Musical Journey Of Best-Loved Favorites* . . . . (Sony Music Classical)
Go Down Moses
Arlo Guthrie; *Arlo Guthrie* . . . . (Rising Son)
Fats Waller; *Ain't Misbehavin'* . . . . (Laserlight)
Paul Robeson; *Ballad For Americans* . . . . (Vanguard)
  The Power & The Glory . . . . (Columbia)
Simon Estes; *Spirituals* . . . . (Philips)
Go Where You Wanna Go
Mamas & The Papas; *Best Of The Mamas & The Papas* . . (MCA)
  Farewell To The First Golden Era . . . . (MCA)
  If You Can Believe Your Eyes & Ears . . . . (MCA)
  Mamas & The Papas-16 Of Their Greatest Hits . . . . (MCA)
God Bless The USA
Lee Greenwood; *American Patriot* . . . . (Capitol)
  God Bless America-C . . . . (Columbia)
  God Bless The USA . . . . (MCA Special Prod.)
  Inside Out/You've Got A Good Love Comin' . . . . (MCA)
  Lee Greenwood's Greatest Hits . . . . (MCA)
  Lee Greenwood's Greatest Hits-#2 . . . . (MCA)
  Today's Country Classics-C . . . . (MCA Special Prod.)
Great Day For Freedom
Pink Floyd; *The Division Bell* . . . . (Columbia)
Guinnevere
Crosby, Stills & Nash; *Crosby, Stills & Nash* . . . . . . (Atlantic)
  CSN . . . . (Atlantic)
Crosby, Stills, Nash & Young; *So Far* . . . . (Atlantic)
  Woodstock Two . . . . (Atlantic)
Here Comes The Freedom Train
Merle Haggard; *Capitol Collectors Series-Merle Haggard* . . . (Capitol)
His Eye Is On The Sparrow
Carmen McRae; *Greatest Of Carmen McRae* . . . . (MCA)
Marvin Gaye; *Musical Testament 1964-1984* . . . . (Motown)
Preservation Hall Jazz Band; *Best Of The Preservation Hall Jazz Band* . . . . (Columbia)
Soundtrack; *Streetcar Named Desire* . . . . (Allegiance)
Hungry Heart
Bruce Springsteen; *Bruce Springsteen's Greatest Hits* . . . (Columbia)
  The River . . . . (Columbia)
Bruce Springsteen & The E Street Band; *Bruce Springsteen & The E Street Band Live/1975-85* . . . . (Legacy)
I Am A Patriot
Jackson Browne; *World In Motion* . . . . (Elektra)
Little Steven; *Voice Of America* . . . . (Razor & Tie)

I Declare
Lee Roy Parnell with Keb' Mo'; *Tell The Truth* .... (Vanguard)
I Feel Free
Belinda Carlisle; *Belinda Carlisle-Her Greatest Hits* .... (MCA)
Heaven On Earth .... (MCA)
Cream; *Eric Clapton-Crossroads-C* .... (Polydor)
Fresh Cream .... (Polydor)
Strange Brew-Very Best Of Cream .... (Polydor)
The Sopranos-Music From The HBO Original Series .... (Sony Music Soundtrax)
I Need You
LeAnn Rimes; *ST/Jesus-The Epic Mini-Series* .... (Sparrow/Curb/Capitol)
I Shall Be Released
Band; *Music From Big Pink* .... (Capitol)
The Band-Anthology-#1 .... (Capitol)
The Last Waltz .... (Warner Bros.)
To Kingdom Come-The Definitive Collection .... (Capitol)
Bette Midler; *Bette Midler* .... (Atlantic)
ST/Divine Madness .... (Atlantic)
Bob Dylan; *Biograph* .... (Columbia)
Bob Dylan At Budokan .... (Columbia)
Bob Dylan's Greatest Hits-#2 .... (Columbia)
The Bootleg Series-Volumes 1-3 [Rare & Unreleased] .... (Columbia)
Bob Dylan And The Band; *Before The Flood* .... (Columbia)
Box Tops; *Box Tops' Greatest Hits* .... (Rhino)
Flying Burrito Brothers; *Farther Along-Best Of The Flying Burrito Brothers* .... (A&M)
Joan Baez; *Any Day Now: Songs Of Bob Dylan* .... (Vanguard)
Carry It On .... (Vanguard)
From Every Stage .... (A&M)
Joe Cocker; *With A Little Help From My Friends* .... (A&M)
Nina Simone; *Best Of Nina Simone* .... (Verve)
Rick Nelson; *Rick Nelson In Concert-Troubadour 1969* .... (MCA)
I Wanna Be Free
Loretta Lynn; *Loretta Lynn's Greatest Hits-#2* .... (MCA)
I Wanna Go Too Far
Trisha Yearwood; *Thinkin' About You* .... (MCA)
I Will Get There
Boyz II Men; *ST/The Prince Of Egypt-Inspirational* ...... (DreamWorks/SKG)
I.G.Y. (What A Beautiful World)
Donald Fagen; *The Nightfly* .... (Warner Bros.)
If Dogs Run Free
Bob Dylan; *New Morning* .... (Columbia)
If I Had A Hammer (The Hammer Song)
Pete Seeger; *Sing-A-Long-Live At Sanders Theatre 1980* .... (Smithsonian Folkways)
Peter, Paul & Mary; *10 Years Together/The Best Of Peter, Paul and Mary* .... (Warner Bros.)
Peter, Paul and Mary .... (Warner Bros.)
Peter, Paul and Mary In Concert .... (Warner Bros.)
Trini Lopez; *Best Of Trini Lopez* .... (Exact)
Weavers; *Weavers' Greatest Hits* .... (Vanguard)
If You Love Somebody Set Them Free
Sting; *Dream Of The Blue Turtles* .... (A&M)
I'm Free
Rolling Stones; *December's Children (and everybody's)* .... (Abkco)
More Hot Rocks (big hits & fazed cookies) .... (Abkco)
I'm Free
Who; *Join Together* .... (MCA)
Tommy .... (MCA)
I'm Free
Jon Secada; *Jon Secada* .... (SBK)
I'm Free
Soup Dragons; *Lovegod* .... (Big Life)
I'm Free (Heaven Help The Man)
Kenny Loggins; *ST/Footloose* .... (Columbia)
Independence Day
Bruce Springsteen; *The River* .... (Columbia)
Bruce Springsteen & The E Street Band; *Bruce Springsteen & The E Street Band Live/1975-85* .... (Legacy)
Independence Day
Martina McBride; *The Way That I Am* .... (RCA)
Independent Women Pt.1
Destiny's Child; *Now That's What I Call Music!-#6-C* .... (Virgin)
ST/Charlie's Angels .... (Columbia)
It's Your Thing
Isley Brothers; *Billboard Top R&B Hits-1969-C* .... (Rhino)
The Isley Brothers Story-#2-The T-Neck Years-1969-1985 .... (Rhino)
Timeless .... (T-Neck/Columbia)
Je Suis Desole
Mark Knopfler; *Golden Heart* .... (Warner Bros.)
Juneteenth
Anthony Rivers & Others; *I've Known Rivers* .... (Gramavision)
Just Between You And Me
DC Talk; *First Generation: 25 Years Of Virgin Records-C* .... (Virgin)
Jesus Freak .... (Virgin)
Justice And Independence '85
John Cougar Mellencamp; *Scarecrow* .... (Riva)
Lack Of Water
Why Store; *The Why Store* .... (MCA)
Letitgo
Prince; *Come* .... (Warner Bros.)
Letter, The
Macy Gray; *On How Life Is* .... (Epic)
Light My Fire
Doors; *Best Of The Doors* .... (Elektra)
Doors .... (Elektra)
Doors 13 .... (Elektra)
Doors' Greatest Hits .... (Elektra)
ST/The Doors .... (Elektra)
Jose Feliciano; *Encore-Jose Feliciano* .... (RCA)
Jose Feliciano's All-Time Greatest Hits .... (RCA)
Loving Arms
Dixie Chicks; *Wide Open Spaces* .... (Monument)
Many A Mile To Freedom
Traffic; *The Low Spark Of High Heeled Boys* .... (Island)
Me And Bobby McGee
Grateful Dead; *Grateful Dead (Skull & Roses)* .... (Warner Bros.)
Janis Joplin; *Janis* .... (Legacy)
Janis Joplin's Greatest Hits .... (Columbia)
Pearl .... (Legacy)
Rock Classics Of The '70s-C .... (Columbia)
Willie Nelson; *Willie Nelson Sings Kristofferson* .... (Columbia)
Money (That's What I Want)
Barrett Strong; *Motown Story-First 25 Years-C* .... (Motown)
Oldies But Goodies-#4-C .... (Original Sound)
Beatles; *Beatles-Box Set* .... (Capitol)
Rock 'N' Roll Music .... (Capitol)
The Beatles' Second Album .... (Capitol)
Buddy Guy; *Man & The Blues* .... (Vanguard)
Diana Ross & The Supremes; *Diana Ross & The Supremes Sing Motown* .... (Motown)
Jerry Lee Lewis; *Jerry Lee's Greatest!* .... (Rhino)
John Lennon; *Lennon* .... (Capitol)
Junior Walker & The All Stars; *Junior Walker & The All Stars' Greatest Hits* .... (S.O.U.L.)
Junior Walker & The All Stars-Anthology .... (Motown)
Rolling Stones; *More Hot Rocks (big hits & fazed cookies)* .... (Abkco)
Ronnie Milsap; *Lost In The Fifties Tonight* .... (RCA)
Todd Rundgren; *Something/Anything?* .... (Rhino)
Monkey Wrench
Foo Fighters; *The Colour And The Shape* .... (Roswell/RCA)
My Sacrifice
Creed; *Weathered* .... (Wind-up)
Natural One
Folk Implosion; *MTV Best Of The Buzz Bin-#2-C* .... (Mammoth)
ST/Kids .... (London)
Nigerian Marketplace
Oscar Peterson Trio; *Nigerian Marketplace* .... (Pablo)
Night
Bruce Springsteen; *Born To Run* .... (Columbia)
No More Tears (Enough Is Enough)
Barbra Streisand & Donna Summer; *Memories* .... (Columbia)
Wet .... (Columbia)
Donna Summer; *Dance Collection* .... (Casablanca)
On The Radio-Greatest Hits-Volumes I & II .... (Casablanca)
On The Loose
Saga; *Worlds Apart* .... (Portrait)
On The Loose
Europe; *Final Countdown* .... (Epic)
One Way Ticket (Because I Can)
LeAnn Rimes; *Blue* .... (MCG/Curb)
Outbound Plane
Nanci Griffith; *Little Love Affairs* .... (MCA)
Suzy Bogguss; *Aces* .... (Liberty)
People Got To Be Free
Rascals; *Atlantic's Hit Singles-1958-1977-C* .... (Atlantic)
Billboard Top Rock 'N' Roll Hits-1968-C .... (Rhino)
Hit Singles-1958-1977-C .... (Atlantic)
Rascals-Anthology 1965-1972 .... (Rhino)
Songs Of Protest-C .... (Rhino)
Very Best Of The Rascals .... (Rhino)
Philadelphia Freedom
Daryl Hall & John Oates; *Two Rooms-Celebrating The Songs Of Elton John & Bernie Taupin-C* .... (Polydor)
Elton John; *Billboard Top Rock 'N' Roll Hits-1975-C* .... (Rhino)
Elton John's Greatest Hits-#2 .... (Polydor)
Pill, The
Loretta Lynn; *Loretta Lynn-20 Greatest Hits* .... (MCA)
The Country Music Hall Of Fame-Loretta Lynn .... (MCA)
Prayer For Everybody/To Be Free
Gil Scott-Heron & Brian Jackson; *Secrets* .... (Arista)
Prisoner For Life
Skip Gorman; *A Cowboy's Wild Song To His Herd* .... (Rounder)
Redemption Song
Bob Marley & The Wailers; *Legend: The Best Of Bob Marley & The Wailers* .... (Island)

Uprising . . . . (Island)
Wyclef Jean; *America: A Tribute To Heroes-C* . . . . (Interscope)

Refugee
Tom Petty And The Heartbreakers; *Damn The Torpedoes* . . . . (MCA)
Pack Up The Plantation-Live! . . . . (MCA)

Refugee
U2; *War* . . . . (Island)

Revolution
Bob Marley & The Wailers; *Natty Dread* . . . . (Tuff Gong)

Roads To Freedom
Robin Trower; *Victims Of The Fury* . . . . (Chrysalis)

Rockin' In The Free World
Bon Jovi; *One Wild Night: Live 1985-2001* . . . . (Island)
Neil Young; *Freedom* . . . . (Reprise)
Neil Young & Crazy Horse; *WELD* . . . . (Reprise)
Pearl Jam; *8/12/00: Tampa, Florida* . . . . (Epic)

Ruby Tuesday
Rolling Stones; *Between The Buttons* . . . . (Abkco)
Flashpoint . . . . (Virgin)
Flowers . . . . (Abkco)
Hot Rocks 1964-1971 . . . . (Abkco)
Singles Collection-The London Years . . . . (Abkco)
Through The Past, Darkly (Big Hits Vol. 2) . . . . (Abkco)

Running Free
Iron Maiden; *Iron Maiden* . . . . (Capitol)
Live After Death-World Slavery Tour . . . . (Capitol)
Maiden Japan . . . . (Capitol)

Saddle Tramp
Marty Robbins; *Gunfighter Ballads & Trail Songs* . . . . (Legacy)
Marty Robbins-More Greatest Hits . . . . (Columbia)

Sailing
Christopher Cross; *Christopher Cross* . . . . (Warner Bros.)

Sailing To Philadelphia
Mark Knopfler; *Sailing To Philadelphia* . . . . (Warner Bros.)

Salvation
Cranberries; *To The Faithful Departed* . . . . (Island)

Saturday Freedom
Blue Cheer; *Good Times Are So Hard To Find-History Of Blue
Cheer* . . . . (Mercury)

Selfless, Cold And Composed
Ben Folds Five; *Whatever And Ever Amen* . . . . (Caroline/550)

Set Me Free
Utopia; *Adventures In Utopia* . . . . (Rhino)
Utopia-Anthology 1974-1985 . . . . (Rhino)

Set Me Free
Chris Rea; *Auberge* . . . . (Atco)

Set Me Free
Times Two; *Hi-Fi & Mighty* . . . . (EMI)

Set Me Free
Gene Loves Jezebel; *House Of Dolls* . . . . (Geffen)

Set Me Free
Kinks; *Kinks' Greatest Hits* . . . . (Rhino)

Set Me Free
Merle Haggard; *Ramblin' Fever* . . . . (MCA)

Set Me Free
Teddy Pendergrass; *Teddy* . . . . (Philadelphia Int'l)

Set U Free
Planet Soul; *Disco Queens-The '90s-C* . . . . (Rhino)
Energy + Harmony . . . . (Strictly Rhythm)

Set You Free This Time
Byrds; *Original Singles-#1-1965-1967* . . . . (Columbia)
Turn! Turn! Turn! . . . . (Legacy)
Gene Clark; *Echoes* . . . . (Columbia)

Simple Song Of Freedom
Tim Hardin; *Simple Songs Of Freedom: The Tim Hardin Collection* . . . (Legacy)

Sisters Are Doin' It For Themselves
Ann Wilson/Nancy Wilson/Lisa Simpson; *Simpsons-The Yellow
Album.* . . . . (Geffen)
Eurythmics & Aretha Franklin; *Be Yourself Tonight* . . . . (RCA)
*Chicken Soup For The Soul: I'll Be There For You-Songs Of Friendship,
Brotherhood And Sisterhood-C* . . . . (Rhino)
Eurythmics' Greatest Hits . . . . (Arista)
Who's Zoomin' Who? . . . . (Arista)

Sleep Come Free Me
James Taylor; *Flag* . . . . (Columbia)

Sleeping In Paris
Rosanne Cash; *The Wheel* . . . . (Columbia)

Some People Can Do What They Like
Robert Palmer; *Some People Can Do What They Like.* . . . . (Island)

Someday We'll All Be Free
Alicia Keys; *America: A Tribute To Heroes-C* . . . . (Interscope)
Donny Hathaway; *Best Of Donny Hathaway.* . . . . (Atco)
James Ingram; *It's Real* . . . . (Warner Bros.)

Song Of Freedom
Bing Crosby; *Original Soundtrack Sessions* . . . . (Vintage Jazz Classics)

Songs Of Freedom
Santana; *Freedom* . . . . (Columbia)

Stone Free
Eric Clapton; *Eric Clapton-Unplugged* . . . . (Reprise)

Jimi Hendrix; *Are You Experienced?* . . . . (Reprise)

Struggle (Free South Africa)
Rochester/Easley Band; *One Minute Of Love* . . . . (Gramavision)

Sweet Freedom
Michael McDonald; *Soundtrack Smashes-'80s & More-C* . . . . (MCA)
ST/Running Scared . . . . (MCA Special Prod.)

Take These Chains From My Heart
Hank Williams With His Drifting Cowboys; *24 Of Hank Williams'
Greatest Hits* . . . . (Polydor)
Hank Williams-40 Greatest Hits . . . . (Polydor)
Ray Charles; *Ray Charles-His Greatest Hits-#2* . . . . (Dunhill Compact Classics)

Theme From ''Greatest American Hero''
Joey Scarbury; *Television's Greatest Hits-#3-1970s & 1980s-C* . . . . (TVT)
Tube Tunes-#3-The '70s & '80s-C . . . . (Rhino)

They Dance Alone (Cueca Solo)
Sting; *...Nothing Like The Sun* . . . . (A&M)
Fields Of Gold-The Best Of Sting 1984-1994 . . . . (A&M)

Think
Aretha Franklin; *Aretha Franklin's Greatest Hits* . . . . (Atlantic)
Aretha's Gold . . . . (Atlantic)
Best Of Aretha Franklin . . . . (Atlantic)
ST/The Blues Brothers. . . . . (Atlantic)

Thrill Is Gone
B.B. King; *Best Of B.B. King* . . . . (MCA)
Live In Cook County Jail . . . . (MCA)
B.B. King & Tracy Chapman; *Deuces Wild* . . . . (MCA)

Tiger
Paula Cole; *This Fire* . . . . (Imago)

To Be Free
Chicago; *Chicago At Carnegie Hall.* . . . . (Chicago)
Chicago II . . . . (Chicago)
Group Portrait . . . . (Chicago)

Trail Of Freedom
Bill Miller; *The Red Road* . . . . (Warner Western)

Tumbling Tumbleweeds
Billy Vaughn; *Billy Vaughn's Greatest Hits* . . . . (Curb)
Gene Autry; *Essential Gene Autry* . . . . (Columbia)
Meat Puppets; *Meat Puppets* . . . . (SST)
Michael Martin Murphey; *Cowboy Songs* . . . . (Warner Western)
Roy Rogers/K.T. Oslin/Restless Heart; *Roy Rogers Tribute-C* . . . . (RCA)
Sons Of The Pioneers; *The Country Music Hall Of Fame-Sons Of The
Pioneers* . . . . (MCA)

Unbound
Robbie Robertson; *Contact From The Underworld of Redboy* . . . . (Capitol)

Voices Of Freedom
Jackson Browne/Peter Gabriel/Youssou N'Dour/Lou Reed; *Secret
Policeman's Third Ball-The Music-C.* . . . . (Virgin)
Lou Reed; *Between Thought & Expression-Anthology* . . . . (RCA)

Walkin' To Freedom
Jazzmasters; *Jazzmasters II* . . . . (JVC Musical Industries)

We Shall Be Free
Garth Brooks; *The Chase.* . . . . (Liberty)

Well Fed Slave/Hungry Free Man
Lucky Dube; *Taxman.* . . . . (Shanachie)

Where You Are
Jessica Simpson featuring Nick Lachey; *Sweet Kisses* . . . . (Columbia)

White Cliffs Of Dover
Kay Kyser & His Orchestra; *16 Most Requested Songs Of The
'40s-#1-C* . . . . (Legacy)
Lee Andrews And The Hearts; *Lee Andrews And The Hearts'
Biggest Hits* . . . . (Collectables)
Mystics; *Mystics-16 Golden Classics.* . . . . (Collectables)
Righteous Brothers; *Righteous Brothers' Greatest Hits* . . . . (Verve)
Righteous Brothers-Anthology 1962-1974 . . . . (Rhino)
Rosemary Clooney; *For The Duration.* . . . . (Concord Jazz)

Wide Open Spaces
Dixie Chicks; *Big Country Hits '99-C* . . . . (K-Tel)
Wide Open Spaces. . . . . (Monument)

Wild One
Faith Hill; *Take Me As I Am* . . . . (Warner Bros.)

Word, The
Beatles; *Beatles-Box Set.* . . . . (Capitol)
Rubber Soul. . . . . (Capitol)

You Are Free
John Charles Thomas & Lucille Rene; *Music From The New York Stage
(1890-1920)-#4-1917-1920-C* . . . . (Pearl)

You Don't Own Me
Joan Jett; *Bad Reputation.* . . . . (Blackheart)
Lesley Gore; *Billboard Top Pop Hits-1964-C* . . . . (Rhino)

You Never Give Me Your Money
Beatles; *Abbey Road.* . . . . (Parlophone)
Beatles-Box Set. . . . . (Capitol)
George Benson; *The Best.* . . . . (Rebound)

Young Hearts Run Free
Candi Staton; *The Disco Years-#3-Boogie Fever-C.* . . . . (Rhino)
Young Hearts Run Free: The Best Of Candi Staton. . . . . (Warner Bros.)

Young Turks
Rod Stewart; *Absolutely Live* . . . . (Warner Bros.)

Downtown Train-Selections From The Storyteller Anthology . . .(Warner Bros.)
Storyteller/The Complete Anthology: 1964-1990 . . . .(Warner Bros.)
Tonight I'm Yours . . . .(Warner Bros.)

Your Saving Grace
Steve Miller Band; *Best Of Steve Miller 1968-1973* . . . . (Capitol)
Steve Miller Band-Anthology . . . . (Capitol)
Your Saving Grace . . . . (Capitol)

FRIENDS, Being Dependable

See Also: CHARACTER & INTEGRITY, COUPLES, HELP, LOVE: GENERAL, TOGETHERNESS

Adios Amigo
Jim Reeves; *Best Of Jim Reeves* . . . . (RCA)
Billboard Top Country Hits-1962-C . . . . (Rhino)
Marty Robbins; *Adios Amigo* . . . . (Columbia)
American Originals-Marty Robbins . . . . (Columbia)
Marty Robbins' Greatest Hits-#4 . . . . (Columbia)

Adrian
Jewel; *Pieces Of You* . . . .(Atlantic)

African Friend
Jimmy Buffett; *Son Of A Son Of A Sailor* . . . .(MCA)

All I Really Want To Do
Bob Dylan; *Another Side Of Bob Dylan* . . . . (Columbia)
Bob Dylan At Budokan . . . . (Columbia)
Bob Dylan's Greatest Hits-#2 . . . . (Columbia)
Byrds; *Original Singles-#1-1965-1967* . . . . (Columbia)
Play Dylan . . . . (Columbia)
The Byrds . . . . (Columbia)
The Byrds' Greatest Hits . . . . (Columbia)
Cher; *Best Of Cher* . . . .(EMI)

All My Friends
Gregg Allman; *Laid Back* . . . . (Polydor)

All My Friends
Counting Crows; *This Desert Life* . . . . (David Geffen Co.)

All My Friends Were There
Kinks; *Are The Village Green Preservation Society* . . . . (Reprise)

All My Rowdy Friends (Have Settled Down)
Hank Williams, Jr.; *Hank Williams, Jr. "Live"* . . . . (WB/Curb)
Hank Williams, Jr.'s Greatest Hits . . . . (WB/Curb)
The Pressure Is On-Original Classics Collection-#7 . . . . (Curb)

All My Rowdy Friends Are Coming Over Tonight
Hank Williams, Jr.; *Great Divorce Songs For Him-C* . . . .(Warner Bros.)
Hank Williams, Jr.'s Greatest Hits-#2 . . . . (WB/Curb)
Major Moves . . . . (WB/Curb)

Angels Would Fall
Melissa Etheridge; *Breakdown* . . . . (Island)

Any Time At All
Beatles; *Rock 'N' Roll Music* . . . . (Capitol)
Something New . . . . (Capitol)

Anytime You Need A Friend
Mariah Carey; *Music Box* . . . . (Columbia)

Apple Tree
Erykah Badu; *Baduizm* . . . . (Kedar Entert./Universal)

Are Friends Electric
Gary Numan & Tubeway Army; *Replicas* . . . . (Atco)

Are We Making Love Or Making Friends
Moe Bandy; *Soft Lights And Hard Country Music* . . . . (Columbia)

Auld Lang Syne
Beach Boys; *Beach Boys Christmas Album* . . . . (Capitol)
Duke Ellington & His Orchestra; *Take The Holiday Train* . . .(Special Music Co.)
Guy Lombardo & His Royal Canadians; *All Occasions Album* . . . . . (Gateway)
Best Of Guy Lombardo . . . . (Curb)
Merry Christmas Baby-Romance & Reindeer-C . . . . (Curb)
Patti LaBelle & The Blue Belles; *A Soulful Christmas-C* . . . . . (Collectables)
Stylistics; *Stylistics-Christmas* . . . . (Amherst)

Back Door Friend
Johnny Winter; *Johnny Winter* . . . . (Columbia)
Lightnin' Hopkins; *The Jewel/Paula Records Story* . . . . (Capricorn)

Bar Room Buddies
Merle Haggard & Clint Eastwood; *ST/Bronco Billy* . . . . (Elektra)

Be Kind To Your Web-Footed Friends
Mitch Miller; *Sing Along With Mitch* . . . . (Columbia)

Be My Friend
Free; *Free-Live* . . . . (A&M)
Highway . . . . (A&M)

Be My Life's Companion
Mills Brothers; *Best Of The Mills Brothers* . . . .(MCA)
The Mills Brothers-Best Of The Decca Years . . . . (Decca)
Rosemary Clooney; *Rosemary Clooney-16 Most Requested Songs* . . . . (Legacy)

Be One Now
Little Feat; *Down On The Farm* . . . .(Warner Bros.)

Be Your Own Best Friend
Ray Stevens; *Be Your Own Best Friend* . . . .(Warner Bros.)
Feeling's Not Right Again . . . .(Warner Bros.)

Beautiful Friendship
Nat "King" Cole; *Nat "King" Cole Sings/George Shearing Plays* . . . . (Capitol)

Beautiful Friendships
Loretta Lynn & Ernest Tubb; *The Ernest Tubb/Loretta Lynn Story* . . . . . (MCA)

Beautiful Friendships
Lou Rawls; *Best From Lou Rawls* . . . . (Capitol)

Ben
Michael Jackson; *Best Of Michael Jackson* . . . . (Motown)
Jackson 5-16 Greatest Hits . . . . (Motown)
Jackson 5-Anthology . . . . (Motown)
Jacksons Live . . . . (Epic)
Michael Jackson-Anthology . . . . (Motown)
Motown Superstar Series-#7-Michael Jackson . . . . (Motown)

Best Friend
English Beat; *I Just Can't Stop It* . . . . (I.R.S.)
What Is Beat . . . . (I.R.S.)

Best Friend
Toni Braxton; *Toni Braxton* . . . . (LaFace)

Best Friend
Brandy; *Brandy* . . . .(Atlantic)

Best Friends
ET (Eddie Towns); *45-#2433* . . . . (Total Experience)

Best Friends
Basia; *London Warsaw New York* . . . . (Epic)

Best Man I Can Be
Ginuwine, R.L., Tyrese, Case; *ST/The Best Man* . . . . . .(Sony Music Soundtrax)

Best Of Friends
Peter, Paul & Mary; *Reunion* . . . . (Warner Bros.)

Best Of Friends
Dangerous Toys; *Hellacious Acres* . . . . (Columbia)

Best Old Friend
Bonnie Raitt; *The Glow* . . . .(Warner Bros.)

Blood Brothers
Bruce Springsteen; *Bruce Springsteen's Greatest Hits* . . . . (Columbia)

Bobby Jean
Bruce Springsteen; *Born In The U.S.A.* . . . . (Columbia)
Bruce Springsteen & The E Street Band; *Bruce Springsteen & The E Street Band Live/1975-85* . . . . (Legacy)

Boys & Me
Sawyer Brown; *Outskirts Of Town* . . . . (Curb)

Bridge Over Troubled Water
Aretha Franklin; *Aretha Franklin-30 Greatest Hits* . . . . (Rhino)
Aretha Franklin's Greatest Hits . . . .(Atlantic)
Live At Fillmore West . . . .(Atlantic)
Paul Simon; *America: A Tribute To Heroes-C* . . . . (Interscope)
Concert In The Park-August 15 1991 . . . .(Warner Bros.)
Paul Simon In Concert/Live Rhymin' . . . . (Columbia)
Simon & Garfunkel; *Bridge Over Troubled Water* . . . . (Columbia)
Collected Works . . . . (Columbia)
God Bless America-C . . . . (Columbia)
Simon & Garfunkel's Greatest Hits . . . . (Columbia)
The Concert In Central Park . . . .(Warner Bros.)

Buddy
De La Soul; *3 Feet High & Rising* . . . . (Tommy Boy)

Can We Still Be Friends?
Robert Palmer; *Secrets* . . . . (Island)
Rod Stewart; *Camouflage* . . . .(Warner Bros.)
Todd Rundgren; *Hermit Of Mink Hollow* . . . . (Rhino)
Todd Rundgren-Anthology 1968-1985 . . . . (Rhino)

Candle On The Water
Helen Reddy; *Chicken Soup For The Soul: I'll Be There For You-Songs Of Friendship, Brotherhood And Sisterhood-C* . . . . (Rhino)
Live In London . . . . (Capitol)
ST/Pete's Dragon . . . . (Capitol)

Can't We Be Friends
Art Tatum; *Standards* . . . . (Black Lion)
Buck Clayton & Buddy Tate; *Buck & Buddy* . . . .(Prestige)
Ella Fitzgerald & Louis Armstrong; *Ella & Louis* . . . . (Verve)
Frank Sinatra; *In The Wee Small Hours* . . . . (Capitol)
Linda Ronstadt; *Lush Life* . . . . (Asylum)

Careless Whisper
Dave Koz featuring Montell Jordan; *Dance* . . . . (Capitol)
Wham! Featuring George Michael; *Make It Big* . . . . (Columbia)
Music For The Miracle-C . . . . (Epic Portrait Assoc.)

Circle Of Friends
Ray Pillow; *20 Great Hits-C* . . . .(Plantation)
People Music . . . .(Plantation)

Cisco Kid
War; *All Day Music* . . . . (MCA)
Best Of War...And More . . . .(Avenue)
War Live! . . . .(Avenue)

Come In From The Rain
Captain & Tennille; *Captain & Tennille's Greatest Hits* . . . . (A&M)
Melissa Manchester; *Melissa Manchester's Greatest Hits* . . . . (Arista)

Company's Comin'
Porter Wagoner; *Essential Porter Wagoner* . . . . (RCA)

Consider Yourself
Original Broadway Cast; *Oliver!* . . . . (RCA Victor)

Original London Cast; *Oliver!* . . . .(EMI-Angel)
Count On Me
Whitney Houston and CeCe Winans; *ST/Waiting To Exhale* . . . . (Arista)
Cut You In
Jerry Cantrell; *Boggy Depot* . . . . (Columbia)
Dammit (Growing Up)
Blink-182; *Dude Ranch* . . . . (Cargo)
Davy The Fat Boy
Randy Newman; *Randy Newman* . . . . (Warner Archives)
Randy Newman/Live . . . . (Warner Archives)
Dawgs (Are A Man's Best Friend)
Original Cast; *Dawgs* . . . . (Glendale)
Daytime Friends
Kenny Rogers; *Daytime Friends* . . . . (EMI)
Kenny Rogers-Twenty Greatest Hits . . . . (EMI)
Ten Years Of Gold . . . . (EMI)
Dear Friends
Queen; *Sheer Heart Attack* . . . . (Hollywood)
Wings; *Wild Life* . . . . (Capitol)
Devil Ain't A Lonely Woman's Friend
Red Steagall; *45-#2824* . . . . (MCA)
Diamonds Are A Girl's Best Friend
Carol Channing; *Broadway Magic-The 1950s-C* . . . . (Columbia)
Emmylou Harris; *White Shoes* . . . . (Warner Bros.)
Marilyn Monroe; *Goodbye Primadonna* . . . . (Accord)
Pearl Bailey; *Back On Broadway* . . . . (Roulette)
Echoes Of An Era-Pearl Bailey . . . . (Roulette)
Don't Give Up
Peter Gabriel; *Shaking The Tree-Sixteen Golden Greats* . . . . (Geffen)
So . . . . (Geffen)
Don't Tell Me Your Troubles
Doc Watson; *Memories* . . . .(Sugar Hill)
Don Gibson; *45-#7566* . . . .(RCA)
Ray Charles; *Greatest Country & Western Hits* . . . . (Dunhill Compact Classics)
Ebony And Ivory
Paul McCartney & Stevie Wonder; *All The Best!* . . . . (Capitol)
Tug Of War . . . . (Gold Rush)
Emotional
Carl Thomas; *Emotional* . . . . (Bad Boy/Arista)
Everybody Hurts
R.E.M.; *Automatic For The People* . . . . (Warner Bros.)
Diana, Princess Of Wales-Tribute-C . . . . (Columbia)
Everybody's Free (To Wear Sunscreen)
Baz Luhrmann; *Now That's What I Call Music!-#2-C* . . . .(Virgin)
Something For Everybody . . . . (Capitol)
Exhale (Shoop Shoop)
Whitney Houston; *ST/Waiting To Exhale* . . . . (Arista)
Whitney Houston's Greatest Hits . . . . (Arista)
Fairweather Friend
John Cale; *Vintage Violence* . . . . (Columbia)
Fairweather Friend
Johnny Gill; *Johnny Gill* . . . . (Motown)
Faith In Me
Crosby, Stills, Nash & Young; *Looking Forward* . . . .(Reprise)
Fake Friends
Joan Jett & The Blackhearts; *Joan Jett & The Blackhearts Album* . . . . . . (MCA)
Fire And Rain
James Taylor; *James Taylor's Greatest Hits* . . . . (Warner Bros.)
Sweet Baby James . . . . (Warner Bros.)
The Concert For New York City-C . . . . (Columbia)
Sammy Kershaw; *Red Hot + Country-C* . . . . (Mercury)
Flyin' High In The Friendly Sky
Marvin Gaye; *What's Going On* . . . . (Motown)
For All Our Cowboy Friends
Red Steagall & The Coleman County Cowboys; *For All Our Cowboy
Friends* . . . . (MCA)
Freight Train Be My Friend
John Lee Hooker; *At Newport* . . . . (Vee-Jay)
Friend
Roger McGuinn; *Born To Rock & Roll* . . . . (Columbia)
Cardiff Rose . . . . (Columbia)
Friend
Winans; *Return* . . . . (Qwest)
Friend In California
Merle Haggard; *Friend In California* . . . . (Epic)
More Hot Country Requests-C . . . . (Epic)
Friend In Need
Supertramp; *Indelibly Stamped* . . . . (A&M)
Friend Is A Friend
Pete Townshend; *The Iron Man* . . . . (Atlantic)
Friend Of Mine
Kelly Price; *Soul Of A Woman* . . . . (T-Neck/Island)
Friend Of The Devil
Grateful Dead; *American Beauty* . . . . (Warner Bros.)
Best Of The Grateful Dead-Skeletons From The Closet . . . . (Warner Bros.)
Dead Set . . . . (Arista)
Lyle Lovett; *Deadicated-C* . . . . (Arista)

Friend To Friend
Diana Ross; *Diana* . . . . (Motown)
Friend, Love, Woman, Life
Mac Davis; *Baby Don't Get Hooked On Me* . . . .(Columbia)
Mac Davis' Greatest Hits . . . . (Columbia)
Friend, Lover, Wife
Johnny Paycheck; *Johnny Paycheck-16 Biggest Hits* . . . . (Epic)
Johnny Paycheck's Biggest Hits . . . . (Epic)
Friendly Beasts
Garth Brooks; *Beyond The Season* . . . .(Liberty)
Peter, Paul & Mary & The New York Choral Society; *Holiday
Celebration* . . . . (Warner Bros.)
Riders In The Sky; *Christmas The Country Way* . . . .(Rounder)
Friendly Neighborhood Narco Agent
Jef Jaisun; *Dr. Demento's Delights-C* . . . . (Warner Bros.)
Friendly Persuasion
Pat Boone; *Best Of Pat Boone* . . . . (MCA)
Pat Boone-16 Great Performances . . . . (MCA)
Friends
Razzy Bailey; *14 #1 Country Hits-C* . . . .(RCA)
Makin' Friends . . . . (RCA)
Friends
John Michael Montgomery; *John Michael Montgomery's
Greatest Hits* . . . . (Atlantic)
What I Do The Best . . . . (Atlantic)
Friends
Beach Boys; *Absolute Best-#2* . . . .(Capitol)
Friends-20/20 . . . . (Capitol)
Friends
Bette Midler; *Divine Miss M* . . . . (Atlantic)
Friends
Joe Satriani; *Extremist* . . . . (Relativity)
Friends
Led Zeppelin; *Led Zeppelin III* . . . . (Atlantic)
Friends
B.B. King; *Live & Well* . . . . (MCA)
Friends
Joan Armatrading; *Me Myself I* . . . .(A&M)
Friends
Jody Watley & Eric B. & Rakim; *You Wanna Dance With Me?* . . . . (MCA)
Friends
Elton John; *Your Songs* . . . . (Polydor)
Friends & Lovers
Bread; *Best Of Bread-#2* . . . . (Elektra)
Bread . . . . (Elektra)
Friends And Lovers
Gloria Loring & Carl Anderson; *Chicken Soup For The Couples
Soul-C* . . . . (Rhino)
*Chicken Soup For The Soul: I'll Be There For You-Songs Of Friendship,
Brotherhood And Sisterhood-C* . . . . (Rhino)
Gloria Loring . . . . (Atlantic)
Friends In Love
Dionne Warwick; *Dionne Warwick With Johnny Mathis* . . . .(Arista)
Friends In Love . . . . (Arista)
Johnny Mathis & Dionne Warwick; *Friends In Love* . . . . (Columbia)
Johnny Mathis-Love Songs . . . . (Columbia)
Friends In Low Places
Garth Brooks; *Garth Brooks-Double Live* . . . .(Capitol)
No Fences . . . .(Capitol)
Friends Of P.
Rentals; *Return Of The Rentals* . . . . (Maverick)
Friendship
Judy Garland; *Over The Rainbow* . . . .(Pro-Arte)
Original Lincoln Center Cast; *Anything Goes* . . . . (RCA Victor)
Friendship Train
Gladys Knight & The Pips; *Compact Command Performances-Gladys Knight
& The Pips* . . . . (Motown)
Gladys Knight & The Pips-All The Great Hits . . . . (Motown)
Gladys Knight & The Pips-Anthology . . . . (Motown)
Motown Superstar Series-#13-Gladys Knight & The Pips . . . . (Motown)
Funeral For A Friend
Elton John; *Goodbye Yellow Brick Road* . . . . (Polydor)
Here And There . . . . (Rocket)
Gang That Sang "Heart Of My Heart"
Four Aces; *Best Of The Four Aces* . . . . (MCA)
Girlfriend
Beautiful South; *Welcome To The Beautiful South* . . . . (Elektra)
Girlfriend
Matthew Sweet; *Girlfriend* . . . . (Zoo)
Girlfriend
Bobby Brown; *King Of Stage* . . . . (MCA)
Girlfriend
Wings; *London Town* . . . . (Capitol)
Girlfriend
Michael Jackson; *Off The Wall* . . . . (Epic)
Girlfriend
Mary Jane Girls; *Only Four You* . . . . (Motown)

Girlfriend
Pebbles; *Pebbles*..(MCA)
Girlfriend
Alicia Keys; *Songs In A Minor* ....(J)
Girlfriend Is Better
Talking Heads; *Speaking In Tongues* .... (Sire)
ST/Stop Making Sense .... (Sire)
Go On
George Strait; *George Strait*.........................(MCA)
Good Friend
Loggins & Messina; *Loggins And Messina*.......... (Columbia)
Good Friend
Violent Femmes; *Blind Leading The Naked* ....(Slash)
Good Friends
Reba McEntire; *Reba Nell McEntire* .... (Mercury)
Good Friends & A Bottle Of Wine
Ted Nugent; *Weekend Warriors* ....(Epic)
Goodbye Earl
Dixie Chicks; *Fly* .... (Monument)
Goodbye Old Buddies
Seals & Crofts; *Get Closer* ....(Warner Bros.)
Graduation (Friends Forever)
Vitamin C; *Totally Hits-#3-C* ....(Atlantic)
Vitamin C.. (Elektra)
Hello Little Friend
Joe Cocker; *Joe Cocker!* ....(A&M)
Hello Old Friend
Eric Clapton; *Eric Clapton-Crossroads-C* ....(Polydor)
No Reason To Cry .... (RSO)
Here's To Good Friends (Lowenbrau Beer)
Original Soundtrack; *TeeVee Toons-The Commercials-#1-C*.......... (TVT)
Heroes And Friends
Randy Travis; *Heroes And Friends*.............(Warner Bros.)
Randy Travis' Greatest Hits-#1 ....(Warner Bros.)
Hey Joe!
Carl Smith; *All Time Legends Of Country Music-C* .... (Legacy)
Hey, Mr. Bluebird
Ernest Tubb & Wilburn Brothers; *More Great Country
Duets-C*..............................(MCA Special Prod.)
Hold An Old Friend's Hand
Rita Coolidge; *Fall Into Spring*. ....(A&M)
Tiffany; *Hold An Old Friend's Hand* ....(MCA)
Home To You
John Michael Montgomery; *Home To You* ....(Atlantic)
How Can We Be Lovers
Michael Bolton; *Soul Provider*....................(Columbia)
How Many Friends
Who; *By Numbers*...................................(MCA)
I Ain't Going Out
Jon B.; *Cool Relax* ....(Yab Yum/550)
I Am
Train; *Train* ....(Aware/C2/Columbia)
I Think It's Gonna Rain Today
Bette Midler; *ST/Beaches*........................(Atlantic)
Judy Collins; *In My Life*.......................... (Elektra)
Neil Diamond; *Rainbow*..............................(MCA)
Stones..(MCA)
Randy Newman; *12 Songs* ....(Reprise)
Randy Newman ....(Warner Archives)
I Turn To You
Christina Aguilera; *Christina Aguilera*. .... (RCA)
I Will Always Love You
Dolly Parton; *Best Of Dolly Parton* ....(RCA)
Best There Is .... (RCA)
Chicken Soup For The Woman's Soul-C........... (Rhino)
Dolly Parton's Greatest Hits ....(RCA)
ST/Best Little Whorehouse In Texas..................(MCA)
Linda Ronstadt; *Prisoner In Disguise*..............(Asylum)
Whitney Houston; *ST/The Bodyguard* ....(Arista)
Whitney Houston's Greatest Hits. ....(Arista)
I Will Be Your Friend
Amy Grant; *Behind The Eyes* ....(A&M)
I'd Do Anything
Original Broadway Cast; *Oliver!* ....(RCA Victor)
Original London Cast; *Oliver!* .... (EMI-Angel)
If I Was Your Girlfriend
Prince; *The Hits 2* ....(Paisley Park)
The Hits/The B-Sides ....(Paisley Park)
If My Friends Could See Me Now
Original Cast/Gwen Verdon; *Sweet Charity*........ (Columbia)
If The World Had A Front Porch
Tracy Lawrence; *Best Of Tracy Lawrence*..........(Atlantic)
I See It Now ....(Atlantic)
If You Really Want To Be My Friend
Rolling Stones; *It's Only Rock 'N Roll* ....(Rolling Stones)
I'll Be
Reba McEntire; *So Good Together*..................(MCA)

I'll Be Around
Spinners; *Atlantic Rhythm & Blues 1947-1974-#6 (1966-1969)-C* ....(Atlantic)
Best Of The Spinners ....(Atlantic)
Golden Age Of Black Music-1970-1975-C..........(Atlantic)
Golden Soul-C ....(Atlantic)
Soul Years-C....................................(Atlantic)
Spinners ....(Rhino)
I'll Be By Your Side
Stevie B; *Best Of Stevie B* ....(LMR)
Love & Emotion ....(LMR)
I'll Be Good To You
Brothers Johnson; *Brothers Johnson-Classics-#11* .... (A&M)
Look Out For No. 1 ....(A&M)
Najee; *Tokyo Blue* .... (EMI)
Quincy Jones with Ray Charles & Chaka Khan; *Back On The Block* ....(Qwest)
I'll Be Missing You
Puff Daddy & Family & Faith Evans & 112; *No Way Out*......(Bad Boy/Arista)
I'll Do 4 U
Father M.C.; *Father's Day* ....(Uptown)
I'll Stand By You
Pretenders; *Last Of The Independents* ....(Sire)
I'm From The Country
Tracy Byrd; *I'm From The Country*. .... (MCA)
Inside
Patti Rothberg; *Between The 1 And The 9* .... (EMI)
It's OK
Tracy Chapman; *Telling Stories* .... (Elektra)
January Friend
Goo Goo Dolls; *Dizzy Up The Girl* ....(Warner Sunset/Reprise)
Joining You
Alanis Morissette; *Supposed Former Infatuation Junkie* .... (Maverick)
Jumper
Third Eye Blind; *Third Eye Blind* .... (Elektra)
Totally Hits-#1-C .... (Arista)
Just A Friend
Biz Markie; *Bass Waves-#3-C*.......................(Luke)
Diabolical-The Biz Never Sleeps .... (Cold Chillin')
Just Friends
Charlie Parker; *Compact Jazz-Charlie Parker* .... (Verve)
Charlie Watts Quintet; *Tribute To Charlie Parker* ....(Continuum)
Frank Sinatra; *No One Cares*. .... (Capitol)
Joe Pass; *I Remember Charlie Parker* ....(Pablo)
L.A. Four; *Just Friends* ....(Concord Jazz)
Sarah Vaughan; *Divine Sarah Vaughan-Columbia Years-1949-
1953*.. (Columbia)
Tony Bennett; *Jazz* .... (Columbia)
Wynton Marsalis Quartet; *Live At Blues Alley* .... (Columbia)
Just Friends (Sunny)
Musiq Soulchild; *Aijuswanaseing*............. (Def Soul/IDJMG)
Just Like You
Keb' Mo'; *Just Like You*...........................(Okeh)
Just Your Friends
Mink De Ville; *Return To Magenta*. .... (Capitol)
Kern River
Merle Haggard; *For The Record: Merle Haggard-43 Legendary Hits* ....(BNA)
Kern River ....(Epic)
Lean On Me
Bill Withers; *Bill Withers' Greatest Hits*. .... (Columbia)
*Chicken Soup For The Soul: I'll Be There For You-Songs Of Friendship,
Brotherhood And Sisterhood-C* .... (Rhino)
God Bless America-C .... (Columbia)
Still Bill....................................... (Columbia)
Club Nouveau; *Life Love & Pain* .... (Warner Bros.)
Grover Washington, Jr.; *Greatest Performances-Grover
Washington, Jr.*. .... (Motown)
Let Me Be The One
Mint Condition; *Definition Of A Band*. .... (Perspective/A&M)
Mint Condition-Collection (1991-1998) .... (Perspective/A&M)
Little Pal
Jimmy Roselli; *Daddy's Little Girl* .... (M&R)
Rock-A-Bye Your Baby .... (M&R)
Sold Out-Carnegie Hall Concert .... (M&R)
Little Street Where Old Friends Meet, A
Tony Bennett; *I Left My Heart In San Francisco* .... (Columbia)
Long Lost Friend
Restless Heart; *Fast Moving Train* ....(RCA)
Mama
Spice Girls; *Diana, Princess Of Wales-Tribute-C*......... (Columbia)
Spice...(Virgin)
Man Overboard
Blink-182; *The Mark, Tom & Travis Show-The Enema Strikes Back* .... (MCA)
Me And Julio Down By The Schoolyard
Paul Simon; *Greatest Hits, Etc.* .... (Columbia)
Negotiations And Love Songs, 1971-1986 .... (Warner Bros.)
Paul Simon .... (Columbia)
Paul Simon In Concert/Live Rhymin' .... (Columbia)
Simon & Garfunkel; *The Concert In Central Park* .... (Warner Bros.)
Meet On The Ledge
Fairport Convention; *Fairport Convention* .... (A&M)

Fairport Convention-*Chronicles* .... (A&M)
In Real Time-Live '87 .... (Island)
Mmm Bop
Hanson; *1998 Grammy Nominees-C* .... (MCA)
Middle Of Nowhere .... (Mercury)
Now That's What I Call Music!-#1-C .... (Virgin)
Three Car Garage: The Independent Recordings .... (Mercury)
More Than Friends
Jonathan Butler & Others; *More Than Friends* .... (Jive)
My Best Friend
Jefferson Airplane; *2400 Fulton Street-An Anthology* .... (RCA)
Surrealistic Pillow .... (RCA)
My Best Friend
Tim McGraw; *A Place In The Sun* .... (Curb)
Tim McGraw's Greatest Hits .... (Curb)
My Best Friend
Air Supply; *Lost In Love* .... (Arista)
My Best Friend
Marshall Tucker Band; *Running Like The Wind* .... (Warner Bros.)
My Best Friend Is A Buddha
Deuter; *Silence Is The Answer* .... (Kuckuck)
My Best Friend's Girl
Cars; *The Cars* .... (Elektra)
The Cars' Greatest Hits .... (Elektra)
My Buddy
Barbra Streisand; *The Way We Were* .... (Columbia)
Dr. John; *In A Sentimental Mood* .... (Warner Bros.)
Rosemary Clooney & Woody Herman; *My Buddy* ...... (Concord Jazz)
My Friend
Jimi Hendrix; *Cry Of Love* .... (Reprise)
My Friend
Take 6 (featuring Ray Charles); *Join The Band-C* .... (Reprise)
My Friends
Original Cast/Angela Lansbury/Len Cariou; *Sweeney Todd* .... (RCA)
My Friends
Red Hot Chili Peppers; *One Hot Minute* .... (Warner Bros.)
My Little Friend
Elvis Presley; *Suspicious Minds* .... (RCA)
My Old Friend
John Hiatt; *Tiki Bar Is Open* .... (Vanguard)
My One True Friend
Bette Midler; *Bathhouse Betty* .... (Warner Bros.)
My Whiskey Head Buddies
Elvin Bishop; *Don't Let The Bossman Get You Down* .... (Alligator)
Neighborhood
Vonda Shepard; *ST/Songs From "Ally McBeal" Featuring Vonda
Shepard* .... (550/Epic)
Never Ending
Wood; *Songs From Stamford Hill* .... (Columbia)
Newborn Friend
Seal; *Seal 2* .... (Sire)
No Surrender
Bruce Springsteen; *Born In The U.S.A.* .... (Columbia)
None Of Ur Friends Business
Ginuwine; *100 Percent Ginuwine* .... (550 Music)
Nothin On Me
Shawn Colvin; *A Few Small Repairs* .... (Columbia)
ST/Mr. Wrong .... (Hollywood)
Old Friends
Barry Manilow; *Showstoppers* .... (Arista)
Liza Minnelli; *Liza Minnelli-At Carnegie Hall* .... (Telarc)
Original Cast; *Merrily We Roll Along* .... (RCA)
Stephen Sondheim & Angela Lansbury & Co.; *Collector's Sondheim-C* .. (RCA)
Old Friends
Simon & Garfunkel; *Bookends* .... (Columbia)
Collected Works .... (Columbia)
The Concert In Central Park .... (Warner Bros.)
Old Friends
Willie Nelson & Roger Miller; *Old Friends* .... (Columbia)
Willie Nelson & Waylon Jennings; *Take It To The Limit* .... (Columbia)
Old Friends
Everything But The Girl; *Worldwide* .... (Atlantic)
One Sweet Day
Mariah Carey; *Daydream* .... (Columbia)
Mariah Carey & Boyz II Men; *1996 Grammy Nominees-C* .... (Columbia)
One Too Many Girlfriends
REO Speedwagon; *A Second Decade Of Rock And Roll 1981 To 1991* .... (Epic)
Life As We Know It .... (Epic)
Outside Of A Small Circle Of Friends
Phil Ochs; *The War Is Over-Best Of Phil Ochs* .... (A&M)
There & Now-Live In Vancouver-1968 .... (Rhino)
Partners, Brothers, & Friends
Nitty Gritty Dirt Band; *Live Two Five* .... (Capitol)
Twenty Years Of Dirt-Best Of The Nitty Gritty Dirt Band ...... (Warner Bros.)
Perfect
Smashing Pumpkins; *Adore* .... (Virgin)
Pride & Joy
Jon B.; *Cool Relax* .... (Yab Yum/550)

Puppy Song
Nilsson; *Harry* .... (Dunhill Compact Classics)
ST/You've Got Mail .... (Atlantic)
Pure Morning
Placebo; *Without You I'm Nothing* .... (Virgin)
Put A Little Love In Your Heart
Annie Lennox & Al Green; *ST/Scrooged* .... (A&M)
Jackie DeShannon; *Chicken Soup For The Soul: I'll Be There For You-Songs
Of Friendship, Brotherhood And Sisterhood-C* .... (Rhino)
ST/Drugstore Cowboy .... (Novus)
Very Best Of Jackie DeShannon .... (EMI)
Rachel
Buddy & Julie Miller; *Buddy & Julie Miller* .... (Hightone)
Racist Friend
Special AKA; *In The Studio* .... (Chrysalis)
Reach Out I'll Be There
Four Tops; *Compact Command Performances-Four Tops* .... (Motown)
Four Tops' Greatest Hits .... (Motown)
Four Tops Reach Out .... (Motown)
Four Tops-Anthology .... (Motown)
Motown Dance Party-#2-C .... (Motown)
Reach Out Of The Darkness
Friend And Lover; *Chicken Soup For The Soul: I'll Be There For You-Songs
Of Friendship, Brotherhood And Sisterhood-C* .... (Rhino)
Flower Power-Psychedelic Rock Classics-C .... (K-Tel)
Red Dirt Girl
Emmylou Harris; *Red Dirt Girl* .... (Nonesuch)
Red Neck Friend
Jackson Browne; *For Everyman* .... (Asylum)
Remember Me This Way
Jordan Hill; *Jordan Hill* .... (Atlantic)
ST/Casper .... (MCA)
Sally's Got A Friend In New York City
Larry McCray; *Ambition* .... (Charisma)
Saturday In The Park
Chicago; *Chicago IX-Chicago's Greatest Hits* .... (Chicago)
Chicago V .... (Chicago)
*Chicken Soup For The Soul: I'll Be There For You-Songs Of Friendship,
Brotherhood And Sisterhood-C* .... (Rhino)
Group Portrait .... (Chicago)
If You Leave Me Now .... (Chicago)
ST/My Girl .... (Epic)
The Heart Of Chicago-1967-1997 .... (Reprise)
Saying Goodbye To A Friend
Suzy Bogguss; *Give Me Some Wheels* .... (Capitol)
Secret Friend
Paul McCartney; *McCartney II* .... (Gold Rush)
Paul McCartney-Gift Set .... (Capitol)
Sending Me Angels
Kathy Mattea; *Love Travels* .... (Mercury)
Seven Days
Mary J. Blige; *Share My World* .... (MCA)
The Tour .... (MCA)
She's All I Ever Had
Ricky Martin; *Ricky Martin* .... (Columbia)
Shilo
Neil Diamond; *Glory Road-1968-1972* .... (MCA)
Hot August Night .... (MCA)
Neil Diamond-Classics (Early Years) .... (Columbia)
Neil Diamond-His 12 Greatest Hits .... (MCA)
Side By Side
Kay Starr; *Kay Starr's Greatest Hits* .... (Curb)
Mitch Miller; *Mitch Miller-16 Most Requested Songs* .... (Columbia)
Snowblind Friend
David Allan Coe; *Unchained* .... (Columbia)
Hoyt Axton; *Snowblind Friend* .... (MCA)
Steppenwolf; *Steppenwolf 7* .... (MCA)
Steppenwolf-16 Greatest Hits .... (MCA)
Solitude
Edwin McCain; *Honor Among Thieves* .... (Lava)
Edwin McCain & Darius Rucker; *VH-1 Crossroads-C* .... (Atlantic)
Some Kind Of Friend
Barry Manilow; *Barry Manilow's Greatest Hits-#1* .... (Arista)
Southside
Moby featuring Gwen Stefani; *12" Maxi Single* .... (V2)
Play .... (V2)
Stand By Me
Ben E. King; *Atlantic Soul Classics-C* .... (Warner Special Prod.)
Ben E. King's Greatest Hits .... (Atco)
Golden Age Of Black Music-1960-1970-C .... (Atlantic)
ST/Stand By Me .... (Atlantic)
Stand By Me-Best Of Ben E. King .... (Atlantic)
Drifters; *Drifters' Greatest Hits* .... (Gusto)
John Lennon; *Rock 'N' Roll* .... (Capitol)
ST/Imagine: John Lennon .... (Capitol)
The John Lennon Collection .... (Capitol)
Maurice White; *Maurice White* .... (Columbia)
Mickey Gilley; *Greatest Country Hits From The Movies-C* .... (Epic)
Mickey Gilley's Biggest Hits .... (Epic)

ST/Urban Cowboy . . . . (Asylum)
Ten Years Of Hits . . . . (Epic)
Ry Cooder; *Chicken Skin Music* . . . . (Reprise)
Steven's Last Night In Town
Ben Folds Five; *Whatever And Ever Amen* . . . . (Caroline/550)
Streets Of Philadelphia
Bruce Springsteen; *Bruce Springsteen's Greatest Hits*. . . . . (Columbia)
Diana, Princess Of Wales-Tribute-C . . . . (Columbia)
ST/Philadelphia . . . . (Epic/Sony Music Soundtrax)
Take Me There
Blackstreet & Mya featuring Mase & Blinky Blink;
Finally . . . . (Lil' Man/Interscope)
Now That's What I Call Music!-#2-C . . . . (Virgin)
ST/Rugrats . . . . (Interscope)
Thank You For Being A Friend
Andrew Gold; *All This & Heaven Too* . . . . (Asylum)
Chicken Soup For The Soul: I'll Be There For You-Songs Of Friendship,
Brotherhood And Sisterhood-C . . . . (Rhino)
Television's Greatest Hits-#6-Remote Control-C . . . . (TVT)
Thank You For Being A Friend: The Best Of Andrew Gold . . . . (Rhino)
That Old Gang Of Mine
Mitch Miller; *Sing Along With Mitch* . . . . (Columbia)
That's What Friends Are For
Dionne Warwick/Elton John/Gladys Knight/Stevie Wonder; *Dionne*
Warwick's Greatest Hits-1979-1990 . . . . (Arista)
Friends . . . . (Arista)
That's What Friends Are For
Johnny Mathis & Deniece Williams; *That's What Friends Are For* . . (Columbia)
That's What Friends Are For
Barbara Mandrell; *Best Of Barbara Mandrell* . . . . (MCA)
This Is Barbara Mandrell . . . . (MCA)
Theme From ''Anything But Love''
Original Soundtrack; *Television's Greatest Hits-#7-Cable Ready-C* . . . . . (TVT)
Theme From ''Barney And Friends''
Original Soundtrack; *Television's Greatest Hits-#7-Cable Ready-C* . . . . . (TVT)
Theme From ''Beverly Hills 90210''
John Davis; *Beverly Hills 90210: Songs From The Peach Pit* . . . . (Rhino)
ST/Beverly Hills, 90210-College Years . . . . (Giant)
Television's Greatest Hits-#7-Cable Ready-C . . . . (TVT)
Theme From ''Casper The Friendly Ghost''
Original Soundtrack; *Television's Greatest Hits-#1-C* . . . . (TVT)
Theme From ''Cheers''
Gary Portnoy; *Tube Tunes-#3-The '70s & '80s-C* . . . . (Rhino)
Original Soundtrack; *Television's Greatest Hits-#3-1970s & 1980s-C* . . . (TVT)
Theme From ''Friends'' (I'll Be There For You)
Rembrandts; *LP* . . . . (East West)
ST/Friends-Music From The TV Series . . . . (Reprise)
Theme From ''Golden Girls''
Original Soundtrack; *Television's Greatest Hits-#6-Remote Control-C* . . (TVT)
Theme From ''Laverne & Shirley''
Original Soundtrack; *Television's Greatest Hits-#3-1970s & 1980s-C* . . . (TVT)
Theme From ''The Courtship Of Eddie's Father'' (Best Friend)
Nilsson; *Television's Greatest Hits-#2-C* . . . . (TVT)
Theme From ''Three's Company''
Original Soundtrack; *Television's Greatest Hits-#3-1970s & 1980s-C* . . . (TVT)
Theme From ''What's Happening?''
Original Soundtrack; *Television's Greatest Hits-#6-Remote Control-C* . . (TVT)
There You Are
Martina McBride; *Emotion* . . . . (RCA)
There's A Place In Hell For Me And My Friends
Morrissey; *Kill Uncle* . . . . (Sire)
Thicker Than Blood
Garth Brooks; *Scarecrow* . . . . (Capitol)
Thirty-Three
Smashing Pumpkins; *Mellon Collie And The Infinite Sadness* . . . . . (Virgin)
Touch A Hand, Make A Friend
Oak Ridge Boys; *Country's Greatest Hits-#4-C* . . . . (MCA Special Prod.)
Oak Ridge Boys' Greatest Hits 3 . . . . (MCA)
Step On Out . . . . (MCA)
Staple Singers; *15 Original Big Hits-#4-C* . . . . (Stax)
Staple Singers-Chronicle . . . . (Stax)
Top Of The Stax-Twenty Greatest Hits-#2-C . . . . (Stax)
Treat You Right
Luther Vandross; *Best Of Luther Vandross...The Best Of Love* . . . . . . (Epic)
Truck Driving Buddy
Red Sovine/Willis Bros./Reno & Smiley; *Heavy Haulers* . . . . . . (Power Pak)
True Companion
Donald Fagen; *ST/Heavy Metal* . . . . (Asylum)
Steely Dan featuring Donald Fagen; *Gold-Expanded Edition* . . . . . . (MCA)
True Friends
Shannon Curfman; *Loud Guitars Big Suspicions* . . . . (Arista)
Turn Of A Friendly Card
Alan Parsons Project; *Best Of Alan Parsons Project-#2* . . . . (Arista)
Turn Of A Friendly Card . . . . (Arista)
Ugg-a-Wugg
Original Cast; *Peter Pan-The 1954 Broadway Production* . . . . . . (RCA Victor)
Uninvited
Ruth Wallis; *Laughing Gallery* . . . . (American)

User Friendly
Ian Anderson; *Walk Into Light* . . . . (Chrysalis)
Utah Carol
Harry K. McClintock; *Cowboy Songs On*
Folkways-C . . . . (Smithsonian Folkways)
Marty Robbins; *Gunfighter Ballads & Trail Songs* . . . . (Legacy)
Vacant Chair
Steve Winwood; *Steve Winwood* . . . . (Island)
Steve Winwood-Chronicles . . . . (Island)
Visiting An Old Friend
Nitty Gritty Dirt Band; *Dirt, Silver & Gold* . . . . (One Way)
Waiting On A Friend
Rolling Stones; *Rewind (1971-1984)* . . . . (Rolling Stones)
Tattoo You . . . . (Virgin)
Wannabe
Spice Girls; *First Generation: 25 Years Of Virgin Records-C* . . . . (Virgin)
MTV The Grind-#1-C . . . . (Tommy Boy)
Spice . . . . (Virgin)
We Hate It When Our Friends Become Successful
Morrissey; *Your Arsenal* . . . . (Sire)
Wedding Bells (Are Breaking Up That Old Gang Of Mine)
Four Aces; *Best Of The Four Aces* . . . . (MCA)
Weekend Friend
Con Hunley; *Con Hunley* . . . . (Warner Bros.)
West Virginia Friend
Holly Near; *Watch Out* . . . . (Redwood)
What A Friend We Have In Jesus
Nashville Superpickers; *Live From Austin City Limits* . . . . (Flying Fish)
Sweet Honey In The Rock; *We All...Every One Of Us* . . . . (Flying Fish)
What About Your Friends
TLC; *Ooooooohhh...On The TLC Tip* . . . . (LaFace)
What If I Said
Anita Cochran & Steve Wariner; *Back To You* . . . . (Warner Bros.)
Steve Wariner & Anita Cochran; *Burnin' The Roadhouse Down* . . . . . (Capitol)
What's My Age Again?
Blink-182; *Enema Of The State* . . . . (MCA)
Now That's What I Call Music!-#3-C . . . . (Virgin)
When I Take My Sugar To Tea
Boswell Sisters; *78-#6083* . . . . (Brunswick)
Frank Sinatra; *Ring-A-Ding Ding* . . . . (Reprise)
Nat ''King'' Cole; *The Vocal Classics-1947-1950* . . . . (Capitol)
Whenever I Call You ''Friend''
Kenny Loggins; *Kenny Loggins Alive* . . . . (Columbia)
Kenny Loggins & Stevie Nicks; *Nightwatch* . . . . (Columbia)
Melissa Manchester; *Melissa Manchester's Greatest Hits* . . . . (Arista)
Where The Blacktop Ends
keith urban; *keith urban* . . . . (Capitol)
Who I Am
Jessica Andrews; *Who I Am* . . . . (DreamWorks/SKG)
Why Can't We Be Friends
War; *Best Of War...And More* . . . . (Avenue)
Why Can't We Be Friends . . . . (Avenue)
Wind Beneath My Wings
Bette Midler; *ST/Beaches* . . . . (Atlantic)
Gary Morris; *Chicken Soup For The Soul: I'll Be There For You-Songs Of*
Friendship, Brotherhood And Sisterhood-C . . . . (Rhino)
Country Love Songs-C . . . . (Warner Bros.)
Gary Morris-Hits . . . . (Warner Bros.)
Why Lady Why . . . . (Warner Bros.)
James Galway; *Wind Beneath My Wings* . . . . (RCA)
Lee Greenwood; *Somebody's Gonna Love You* . . . . (MCA)
Lou Rawls; *When The Night Comes* . . . . (Epic)
Roger Whittaker; *Roger Whittaker Greatest Hits* . . . . (RCA)
Wind Beneath My Wings . . . . (RCA)
Willie Nelson; *City Of New Orleans* . . . . (Columbia)
With A Little Help From My Friends
Beatles; *Beatles-Box Set* . . . . (Capitol)
Rarities . . . . (Capitol)
Sgt. Pepper's Lonely Hearts Club Band . . . . (Capitol)
The Beatles/1967-1970 . . . . (Capitol)
Joe Cocker; *History Of British Rock-#9-C* . . . . (Rhino)
Joe Cocker-Classics-#4 . . . . (A&M)
Joe Cocker's Greatest Hits . . . . (A&M)
ST/Woodstock . . . . (Atlantic)
With A Little Help From My Friends . . . . (A&M)
Ringo Starr & His All-Star Band; *Nobody's Child-Romanian Angel*
Appeal-C . . . . (Warner Bros.)
Woman, A Lover, A Friend
Jackie Wilson; *Jackie Wilson's Greatest Hits-#2* . . . . (Brunswick)
Mr. Excitement . . . . (Rhino)
Otis Redding; *The Otis Redding Story* . . . . (Atlantic)
Yellow Submarine
Beatles; *Beatles 1* . . . . (Capitol)
Beatles-Box Set . . . . (Capitol)
Reel Music . . . . (Capitol)
Revolver . . . . (Capitol)
The Beatles/1962-1966 . . . . (Capitol)
You Can Call Me Al
Paul Simon; *Concert In The Park-August 15 1991* . . . . (Warner Bros.)

Graceland . . . . (Warner Bros.)
Negotiations And Love Songs, 1971-1986 . . . . (Warner Bros.)

You Can Depend On Me
Brenda Lee; *The Brenda Lee Story-Her Greatest Hits*. . . . . (MCA)
Count Basie; *Best Of Count Basie* . . . . (MCA)
Louis Armstrong; *Stardust* . . . . (Portrait)
Manhattan Transfer; *The Manhattan Transfer* . . . . (Rhino)

You Don't Know Me
Ray Charles; *Ray Charles-Complete Country & Western Recordings 1959-1986* . . . . (Rhino)

You Got It
Bonnie Raitt; *ST/Boys On The Side* . . . . (Arista)
Roy Orbison; *Mystery Girl* . . . . (Virgin)

Your Friend In The Cowboy Hat (The Viagra Song)
Croatan; *Violent Passion Surrogate* . . . . (Man's Ruin)

You're A Friend Of Mine
Clarence Clemons & Jackson Browne; *Hero*. . . . . (Columbia)

You're Invited But Your Friend Can't Come
Vince Neil; *ST/Encino Man* . . . . (Hollywood)

You're My Best Friend
Don Williams; *Best Of Don Williams-#2*. . . . . (MCA)
Country Comes To Carnegie Hall-C. . . . . (MCA)
Country Music Classics-#4-1970-1975-C . . . . (K-Tel)
Lovers & Best Friends . . . . (MCA)
You're My Best Friend . . . . (MCA)
Queen; *A Night At The Opera* . . . . (Hollywood)
Live Killers . . . . (Hollywood)
Queen's Greatest Hits I & II . . . . (Hollywood)

You're My Bestest Friend
Mac Davis; *Mac Davis-Very Best & More* . . . . (Casablanca)
Midnight Crazy . . . . (Casablanca)

You've Got A Friend
Barbra Streisand; *Barbra Joan Streisand* . . . . (Columbia)
Carole King; *Tapestry* . . . . (Epic)
Donny Hathaway & Roberta Flack; *Best Of Donny Hathaway* . . . . (Atco)
Jamaica Boys; *J Boys* . . . . (Reprise)
James Taylor; *James Taylor's Greatest Hits* . . . . (Warner Bros.)
Mud Slide Slim And The Blue Horizon . . . . (Warner Bros.)
Michael Jackson; *Got To Be There* . . . . (Motown)
Original Soul Of Michael Jackson . . . . (Motown)
Roberta Flack & Donny Hathaway; *Best Of Roberta Flack*. . . . . (Atlantic)
Roberta Flack & Donny Hathaway. . . . . (Atlantic)

FUN, Good Times

See Also: **CARNIVALS, DANCE, HAPPINESS, PARTY, SMILE, TOYS & GAMES, WEEKEND**

1,2,3,4 (Sumpin' New)
Coolio; *ESPN Presents Jock Jams-#2-C* . . . . (Tommy Boy)
MTV Party To Go-#9-C . . . . (Tommy Boy)
Tommy Boy's Greatest Beats-#2-C. . . . . (Tommy Boy)

59th Street Bridge Song (Feelin' Groovy)
Harper's Bizarre; *Baby Boomer Classics-More Mellow Sixties-C*. . . . . (JCI Assoc. Labels)
Better Days-C . . . . (Rhino)
Simon & Garfunkel; *Collected Works* . . . . (Columbia)
Parsley Sage Rosemary & Thyme . . . . (Columbia)
Simon & Garfunkel's Greatest Hits . . . . (Columbia)
The Concert In Central Park. . . . . (Warner Bros.)

Ain't No Fun (If The Homies Can't Have None)
Snoop Doggy Dogg; *Doggystyle* . . . . (Death Row)

Ain't No Fun (Waiting Round To Be A Millionaire)
AC/DC; *Dirty Deeds Done Dirt Cheap* . . . . (Atlantic)

Ain't No Fun To Be Alone In San Antone
Gene Watson; *Mack In The Fire* . . . . (Warner Bros.)

All I Wanna Do
Sheryl Crow; *Tuesday Night Music Club*. . . . . (A&M)

All Night Long
Faith Evans featuring Puff Daddy; *Keep The Faith* . . . . (Bad Boy/Arista)

All The Fun
Paul Overstreet; *Best Of Paul Overstreet*. . . . . (RCA)

Apples Peaches Pumpkin Pie
Jay And The Techniques; *Cruisin'-1967-C* . . . . (Increase)

Are The Good Times Really Over (I Wish A Buck Was Still Silver)
Merle Haggard; *Big City* . . . . (Epic)
For The Record: Merle Haggard-43 Legendary Hits . . . . (BNA)
Greatest Country Hits Of The '80s-1982-C . . . . (Columbia)
His Epic Hits-First 11 To Be Continued-C . . . . (Epic)

At The Zoo
Simon & Garfunkel; *Bookends* . . . . (Columbia)
Collected Works . . . . (Columbia)

Beer Barrel Polka
Andrews Sisters; *Andrews Sisters-16 Great Performances*. . . . . (MCA)
Best Of The Andrews Sisters. (MCA)
Frankie Yankovic & His Yanks; *Frankie Yankovic & His Yanks' Greatest Hits* . . . . (Columbia)

Will Glahe; *This Is Will Glahe-Decade Of The '30s*. . . . . (RCA)

Big City
Merle Haggard; *For The Record: Merle Haggard-43 Legendary Hits*. . . . (BNA)

Big Fun
Scatterbrain; *Scamboogery* . . . . (Elektra)

Big Fun
Kool & The Gang; *As One* . . . . (De-Lite)

Birthday
Beatles; *The Beatles (White Album)*. . . . .(Capitol)
Daffy Duck; *Bugs & Friends Sing The Beatles* . . . . . (Kid Rhino/Rhino 4 Kids)
Paul McCartney; *Tripping The Live Fantastic-Highlights!* . . . . (Capitol)
Texas Chainsaw Orchestra; *The Texas Chainsaw Orchestra*. . . . . (Rhino)

Blondes (Have More Fun)
Rod Stewart; *Blondes Have More Fun* . . . . (Warner Bros.)

California Sun
Ramones; *All The Stuff & More-#1* . . . . (Sire)
Leave Home. . . . . (Sire)
ST/Rock 'N' Roll High School . . . . (Sire)
Rivieras; *Beach Classics-All Original Recordings-C* . . . . (Dunhill Compact Classics)
Frat Rock!-#4-C . . . . (Rhino)
Summer & Sun-C . . . . (Rhino)

Come On (Part 1)
Jimi Hendrix Experience; *Electric Ladyland* . . . . (Reprise)

Come On Over (All I Want Is You)
Christina Aguilera; *Christina Aguilera* . . . . (RCA)

Crazy Man Crazy
Bill Haley; *Still Rockin' Around The Clock* . . . . (BMG Special Prod.)

Dance Tonight
Lucy Pearl; *Lucy Pearl*. . . . . (Overbrook/Pookie/Beyond)

Dancing Queen
Abba; *Abba Live*. . . . . (Atlantic)
Abba's Greatest Hits-#2 . . . . (Atlantic)
Arrival . . . . (Polydor)
Gold-Greatest Hits . . . . (Polydor)
The Singles-First 10 Years . . . . (Atlantic)

Dangerous Fun
Jesse Winchester; *Best Of Jesse Winchester* . . . . (Rhino)
Third Down 110 To Go . . . . (Rhino)

Dig In
Lenny Kravitz; *Lenny*. . . . . (Virgin)

Do It Again
Beach Boys; *Best Of The Beach Boys*. . . . . (Capitol)
Friends-20/20 . . . . (Capitol)
Made In The U.S.A. . . . . (Capitol)

Downtown
Neil Young; *Mirror Ball* . . . . (Reprise)

Early To Bed
Morphine; *Like Swimming* . . . . (DreamWorks/Rykodisc)

Epistle To Dippy
Donovan; *Donovan's Greatest Hits* . . . . (Epic)

Everybody Have Fun Tonight
Wang Chung; *Mosaic*. . . . . (Geffen)

Family Affair
Mary J. Blige; *No More Drama* . . . . (MCA)

Ffun
Con Funk Shun; *Secrets* . . . . (Mercury)

Finally Friday
George Jones; *Walls Can Fall* . . . . (MCA)
Working Man's Blues-C . . . . (Hip-O)

Friday On My Mind
David Bowie; *Bowie Pin Ups* . . . . (Rykodisc)
Easybeats; *Best Of The Easybeats* . . . . (Rhino)
Nuggets-Classic Collection From The Psychedelic '60s-C. . . . . . . (Rhino)

Fun
Sly & The Family Stone; *Sly & The Family Stone-Anthology* . . . . (Epic)
Sly & The Family Stone's Greatest Hits . . . . (Epic)

Fun & Games
Chuck Mangione; *Best Of Chuck Mangione* . . . . (A&M)
Chuck Mangione-Classics-#6 . . . . (A&M)
Fun & Games . . . . (A&M)

Fun & Games
Isley Brothers; *Showdown* . . . . (T-Neck/Columbia)

Fun Day
Stevie Wonder; *ST/Jungle Fever* . . . . (Motown)

Fun In Texas
Britny Fox; *Britny Fox*. . . . . (Columbia)

Fun Time
Bebe Buell; *Covers Girl* . . . . (Rhino)

Fun, Fun, Fun
Beach Boys; *Beach Boys-Gift Set* . . . . (Capitol)
Best Of The Beach Boys. . . . . (Capitol)
Endless Summer . . . . (Capitol)
Made In The U.S.A. . . . . (Capitol)
The Beach Boys In Concert . . . . (Brother)

Get 'Em Outta Here
Sprung Monkey; *Mr. Funny Face* . . . . (Surfdog/Hollywood)

Get On Up
Jodeci; *The Show, The After-Party, The Hotel* . . . . (Uptown/MCA)

Get Up & Enjoy Yourself
Head East; *Head East-Live* . . . . (A&M)
Girls Just Want To Have Fun
Cyndi Lauper; *She's So Unusual* . . . . (Portrait)
Go Deep
Janet Jackson; *Velvet Rope* . . . . (Virgin)
Gonna Have A Good Time
Easybeats; *Best Of The Easybeats* . . . . (Rhino)
Good Morning
Gene Kelly/Debbie Reynolds/Donald O'Connor; *ST/Singin' In
   The Rain* . . . .(Sony Music Special Prod.)
Good Times
Willie Nelson; *Best Of Willie* . . . . (RCA)
   Minstrel Man . . . . (RCA)
   Music From "Songwriter" . . . . (Columbia)
Good Times
Rita Coolidge; *Anytime...Anywhere* . . . . (A&M)
Good Times
Hoodoo Gurus; *Blow Your Cool* . . . . (Elektra)
Good Times
Dan Seals; *Dan Seals' Greatest Hits*. . . . . (Liberty)
   On Arrival . . . . (Capitol)
Good Times
Jimi Hendrix; *Jimi Hendrix* . . . .(Audio Fidelity)
Good Times
Rolling Stones; *Out Of Our Heads* . . . . (Abkco)
Good Times
Chic; *Plus Grands Succes De Chic* . . . . (Atlantic)
   Risque . . . . (Atlantic)
Good Times
Nat "King" Cole; *Ramblin' Rose* . . . . (Capitol)
Good Times
Persuasions; *Street Corner Symphony* . . . . (Capitol)
Good Times Bad Times
Led Zeppelin; *Led Zeppelin* . . . . (Atlantic)
Good Times Roll
Cars; *The Cars* . . . . (Elektra)
   The Cars' Greatest Hits . . . . (Elektra)
Good Times, Bad Times
Rolling Stones; *12 X 5*. . . . . (Abkco)
   Big Hits (High Tide & Green Grass) . . . . (Abkco)
   More Hot Rocks (big hits & fazed cookies) . . . . (Abkco)
   Singles Collection-The London Years . . . . (Abkco)
Grazing In The Grass
Boney James & Rick Braun; *Shake It Up* . . . .(Warner Bros.)
Hugh Masekela; *Promise Of A Future* . . . . (Uni)
   Sixties Rule! Chapter 1-C . . . . (One Way)
Have A Good Time
Paul Simon; *Greatest Hits, Etc.* . . . . (Columbia)
   Negotiations And Love Songs, 1971-1986 . . . .(Warner Bros.)
   Still Crazy After All These Years . . . . (Columbia)
Have A Good Time
Elvin Bishop; *Struttin' My Stuff* . . . . (Capricorn)
Have A Good Time
Rufus Featuring Chaka Khan; *Rufus featuring Chaka Khan*. . . .(MCA)
Having A Blast
Green Day; *Dookie* . . . . (Reprise)
Having A Party
Norma Jean; *Norma Jean* . . . . (Bearsville)
Pointer Sisters; *Having A Party* . . . . (MCA)
Rod Stewart & Ronnie Wood; *Unplugged...And Seated* . . . . . .(Warner Bros.)
Sam Cooke; *Best Of Sam Cooke* . . . . (RCA)
   Feel It . . . . (RCA)
   Live At The Harlem Square Club . . . . (RCA)
   This Is Sam Cooke . . . . (RCA)
Southside Johnny And The Asbury Jukes; *Havin' A Party With Southside
   Johnny And The Asbury Jukes.* . . . . (Epic)
Hey, Good Lookin'
Hank Williams With His Drifting Cowboys; *24 Of Hank Williams'
   Greatest Hits* . . . . (Polydor)
   Hank Williams-40 Greatest Hits . . . . (Polydor)
   Hey, Good Lookin'-December 1950-July 1951 . . . . (Polydor)
Loretta Lynn & Conway Twitty; *Hey, Good Lookin'* . . . . . .(MCA Special Prod.)
Hooch
Everything; *Super Natural* . . . .(Blackbird/Sire)
Hot Fun In The Summertime
Sly & The Family Stone; *Billboard Top R&B Hits-1969-C* . . . . (Rhino)
   Sly & The Family Stone-Anthology . . . .(Epic)
   Sly & The Family Stone's Greatest Hits. . . . .(Epic)
   Summer & Sun-C . . . . (Rhino)
House Arrest
Bryan Adams; *Waking Up The Neighbours* . . . . (A&M)
I Wanna Have Some Fun
Samantha Fox; *I Wanna Have Some Fun* . . . . (Jive)
In The Summertime
Mungo Jerry; *In The Summertime-Best Of Mungo Jerry* . . . . . (Rhino)
   Super Hits Of The '70s-Have A Nice Day-#3-C . . . . (Rhino)
Island In The Sun
Weezer; *Weezer 2001* . . . . (Geffen)

It's All Right
Impressions; *Billboard Top R&B Hits-1963-C* . . . . (Rhino)
   Cruisin'-1964-C . . . . (Increase)
   Impressions' Greatest Hits . . . . (MCA)
   ST/The Flamingo Kid . . . . (Motown)
It's In The Book (Parts 1 & 2)
Johnny Standley; *Dr. Demento Gooses Mother-C* . . . .(Kid Rhino/Rhino 4 Kids)
Jambalaya (On The Bayou)
Blue Ridge Rangers; *Blue Ridge Rangers* . . . . (Fantasy)
Fats Domino; *Fats Domino's Greatest Hits* . . . . (MCA)
Hank Williams With His Drifting Cowboys; *24 Of Hank Williams'
   Greatest Hits* . . . .(Polydor)
   Hank Williams-16 Great Hits . . . . (Everest)
   Hank Williams-40 Greatest Hits . . . . (Polydor)
Hank Williams, Jr.; *ST/Your Cheatin' Heart* . . . . (Sony Music Special Prod.)
Jerry Lee Lewis; *Twenty Classic Hits* . . . . (Sun)
Nitty Gritty Dirt Band; *All The Good Times* . . . .(United Artists)
   Stars And Stripes Forever . . . . (Capitol)
Josie
Steely Dan; *Aja* . . . . (MCA)
   Steely Dan's Greatest Hits . . . . (MCA)
Jumpin' Jack Flash
Aretha Franklin; *Aretha* . . . . (Arista)
Johnny Winter; *Live/Johnny Winter And.* . . . . (Columbia)
Peter Frampton; *Frampton Comes Alive* . . . . (A&M)
Rolling Stones; *Flashpoint* . . . . (Virgin)
   Get Yer Ya-Ya's Out! . . . .(Abkco)
   Hot Rocks 1964-1971 . . . .(Abkco)
   Love You Live . . . .(Virgin)
   ST/Jumpin' Jack Flash . . . . (Mercury)
   Through The Past, Darkly (Big Hits Vol. 2) . . . .(Abkco)
Jumpin, Jumpin
Destiny's Child; *Now That's What I Call Music!-#5-C* . . . . (Virgin)
   The Writing's On The Wall . . . . (Columbia)
Let It Whip
Dazz Band; *Dazz Band's Greatest Hits* . . . . (Motown)
   Funkology-#1-Got To Give It Up-C . . . . (Motown)
Let Me Entertain You
Original Cast; *Gypsy* . . . . (Columbia)
Original London Cast; *Gypsy* . . . . (RCA)
Pearl Bailey; *Back On Broadway* . . . . (Roulette)
   Echoes Of An Era-Pearl Bailey . . . . (Roulette)
Let Me Entertain You
Queen; *Jazz* . . . . (Hollywood)
   Live Killers . . . . (Hollywood)
Let The Good Times Roll
Barbra Streisand; *Butterfly* . . . . (Columbia)
Betty Everett & Jerry Butler; *Delicious Together* . . . . (Vee-Jay)
   Starring Betty Everett . . . . (Tradition)
Bobby Bland & B.B. King; *Together Again Live* . . . . (MCA)
Jerry Lee Lewis; *Golden Rock & Roll* . . . . (Sun)
Louis Jordan; *Best Of Louis Jordan* . . . . (MCA)
Molly Hatchet; *Flirtin' With Disaster* . . . . (Epic)
Nilsson; *Nilsson Schmilsson* . . . . (RCA)
Phoebe Snow; *Phoebe Snow* . . . . (MCA)
Ray Charles; *Genius Of Ray Charles.* . . . .(Atlantic)
Shirley & Lee; *Billboard Top R&B Hits-1956-C* . . . . (Rhino)
   History Of New Orleans R&B-#1-1950-1958-C . . . . (Rhino)
   ST/Stand By Me . . . . (Atlantic)
   Super Oldies Of The '50s-#4-C . . . . (Audio Fidelity)
Tony Bennett with B.B. King; *Playin' With My Friends-Bennett Sings The
   Blues-C* . . . . (Columbia)
Long Tall Sally
Beatles; *Past Masters-Volume One* . . . . (Parlophone)
   Rock 'N' Roll Music . . . . (Capitol)
   The Beatles At The Hollywood Bowl. . . . . (Capitol)
   The Beatles' Second Album . . . . (Capitol)
Little Richard; *Billboard Top R&B Hits-1956-C* . . . . (Rhino)
   Here's Little Richard . . . .(Specialty)
   Little Richard-18 Greatest Hits . . . . (Rhino)
   Little Richard's Greatest Hits. . . . . (Everest)
   Oldies But Goodies-#3-C . . . . (Original Sound)
   ST/Heaven Help Us . . . . (EMI)
   Super Oldies Of The '50s-#3-C . . . . (Audio Fidelity)
   Tutti Frutti . . . . (Accord)
Louisiana Hayride
Boswell Sisters; *That's How Rhythm Was Born* . . . . (Legacy)
Mama Told Me Not To Come
Randy Newman; *12 Songs.* . . . . (Reprise)
   Randy Newman/Live. . . . . (Warner Archives)
Three Dog Night; *Best Of Three Dog Night* . . . . (MCA)
   Billboard Top Rock 'N' Roll Hits-1970-C . . . . (Rhino)
Wilson Pickett; *Wilson Pickett's Greatest Hits* . . . .(Atlantic)
Man! I Feel Like A Woman
Shania Twain; *Come On Over.* . . . . (Mercury)
   VH-1 Divas Live-C . . . . (Epic)
Next Episode
Dr. Dre; *Dr. Dre 2001* . . . . (Aftermath/Interscope)
No Fun
Iggy Pop; *Elektrock-Sixties-C* . . . . (Elektra)

Stooges; *Stooges* . . . . (Elektra)
Ode To My Family
Cranberries; *No Need To Argue* . . . . (Island)
Off The Wall
Jacksons; *Jacksons Live.* . . . . (Epic)
Michael Jackson; *Off The Wall* . . . . (Epic)
Old Enough To Know Better
Wade Hayes; *Country Dance Hits-C* . . . . (Columbia)
Old Enough To Know Better . . . . (Columbia)
Steppin' Country-#2-C . . . . (Columbia)
Super Hits Of 1994-C . . . . (Columbia)
On The One For Fun
Dazz Band; *Dazz Band's Greatest Hits* . . . . (Motown)
Only The Good Die Young
Billy Joel; *Billy Joel-Greatest Hits, Volume I & Volume II* . . . . (Columbia)
KOHUEPT . . . . (Columbia)
The Stranger . . . . (Columbia)
Out With A Bang
David Lee Murphy; *Out With A Bang* . . . . (MCA)
Party Crowd
David Lee Murphy; *Out With A Bang* . . . . (MCA)
Peace Tonight
Indigo Girls; *Come On Now Social* . . . . (Epic)
Radar Gun
Bottle Rockets; *The Brooklyn Side* . . . . (East Side Digital)
Ready To Run
Dixie Chicks; *Fly* . . . . (Monument)
ST/Runaway Bride . . . . (Sony Music Soundtrax)
Real Good Time Together
Lou Reed; *Between Thought & Expression-Anthology* . . . . (RCA)
Street Hassle . . . . (Out Of Print)
Really Good Time
Roxy Music; *Country Life* . . . . (Atco)
Rip It Up
Elvis Presley; *Elvis* . . . . (RCA)
Rocker. . . . . (RCA)
Little Richard; *Big Hits* . . . . (Crescendo)
Grooviest 17 Original Hits . . . . (Specialty)
Little Richard-18 Greatest Hits . . . . (Rhino)
Little Richard's Greatest Hits . . . . (Everest)
Runaway
Janet Jackson; *Design Of A Decade-1986/1996* . . . . (A&M)
See The Funny Little Clown
Bobby Goldsboro; *10th Anniversary Album-#1* . . . . (EMI)
Bobby Goldsboro's Greatest Hits . . . . (Liberty)
Honey-Best Of Bobby Goldsboro . . . . (EMI)
Sheep Go To Heaven
Cake; *Prolonging The Magic.* . . . . (Capricorn)
Skokiaan
Four Lads; *16 Most Requested Songs Of The '50s-#2-C* . . . . (Legacy)
Some Days You Gotta Dance
Dixie Chicks; *Fly* . . . . (Monument)
Some People
Original Cast; *ST/Gypsy* . . . . (Columbia)
Stay (Wasting Time)
Dave Matthews Band; *Before These Crowded Streets.* . . . . (RCA)
Still The One
Orleans; *Dance With Me* . . . . (Rhino)
Still The One . . . . (Elektra)
Super Hits Of The '70s-Have A Nice Day-#19-C . . . . (Rhino)
Summertime, Summertime
Jamies; *Summer & Sun-C* . . . . (Rhino)
Take It Easy
Eagles; *Eagles* . . . . (Asylum)
Eagles Live . . . . (Asylum)
Eagles/Their Greatest Hits 1971-1975 . . . . (Asylum)
Hell Freezes Over . . . . (Geffen)
Jackson Browne; *For Everyman* . . . . (Asylum)
Travis Tritt; *Common Thread-Songs Of The Eagles-C* . . . . (Giant)
Take Me There
Blackstreet & Mya featuring Mase & Blinky Blink;
Finally . . . . (Lil' Man/Interscope)
Now That's What I Call Music!-#2-C . . . . (Virgin)
ST/Rugrats . . . . (Interscope)
Talk About The Good Times
Elvis Presley; *Good Times.* . . . . (RCA)
Thank The Lord For The Night Time
Neil Diamond; *Glory Road-1968-1972* . . . . (MCA)
Hot August Night II. . . . . (Columbia)
Neil Diamond-Classics (Early Years). . . . . (Columbia)
Neil Diamond-Gold . . . . (MCA)
Neil Diamond's Greatest Hits-1966-1992 . . . . (Columbia)
Thanks For All The Good Times
White Mountain Singers; *Best Of The White Mountain Singers* . . . . . . (Folk Era)
Thanks For The Memories
Benny Goodman; *Benny Goodman-More Greatest Hits* . . . . (RCA)
Bob Hope; *Thanks For The Memories.* . . . . (MCA)
Bob Hope & Shirley Ross; *The Envelope Please-Academy Award Winning
Songs-#1 (1934-1945)-C* . . . . (Rhino)

There's Going To Be A Party
Bob Wills; *Stay A Little Longer-The Original Columbia
Recordings* . . . . (Roswell/RCA)
They're Coming To Take Me Away, Ha Haaa!
Napoleon XIV; *Dr. Demento Presents The Greatest Novelty Records-#3-
1960s-C* . . . . (Rhino)
Silly Songs-C. . . . . (K-Tel)
The Second Coming. . . . . (Rhino)
Thrill Of It All
Roxy Music; *Country Life* . . . . (Atco)
Roxy Music's Greatest Hits . . . . (Atco)
Tonight We're Gonna Tear Down The Walls
Randy Travis; *Always & Forever.* . . . . (Warner Bros.)
Too Much Fun
Commander Cody & His Lost Planet Airmen; *Live From Deep In The Heart
Of Texas* . . . . (MCA)
Too Much Fun-Best Of Commander Cody & His Lost Planet Airmen. . . . (MCA)
Too Much Fun
Daryle Singletary; *Daryle Singletary.* . . . . (Giant)
Today's Country Love-C. . . . . (K-Tel)
Under The Boardwalk
Bette Midler; *ST/Beaches.* . . . . (Atlantic)
Bruce Willis; *Return Of Bruno.* . . . . (Motown)
Drifters; *Atlantic Rhythm & Blues 1947-1974-#5 (1962-1966)-C* . . . . . (Atlantic)
Drifters-16 Greatest Hits . . . . (Trip)
Drifters-Golden Hits . . . . (Atlantic)
Super Oldies Of The '60s-#5-C . . . . (Audio Fidelity)
John Mellencamp; *Rough Harvest* . . . . (Mercury)
Lynn Anderson; *What She Does Best.* . . . . (Mercury)
Rickie Lee Jones; *Girl At Her Volcano* . . . . (Warner Bros.)
Rolling Stones; *12 X 5* . . . . (Abkco)
Untouchables; *Agent Double O Soul* . . . . (Restless)
Walkin' My Baby Back Home
Johnnie Ray; *Johnnie Ray-16 Most Requested Songs* . . . . (Legacy)
Johnnie Ray's Greatest Hits . . . . (Sony Music Special Prod.)
Nat "King" Cole; *Capitol Collectors Series-Nat "King" Cole* . . . . . . (Capitol)
The Nat "King" Cole Story . . . . (Capitol)
You Ain't Much Fun
Toby Keith; *Boomtown* . . . . (Polydor Country)
You Don't Need The Wine To Have A Wonderful Time
Eddie Cantor; *Music From The New York Stage (1890-1920)-#4-1917-
1920-C* . . . . (Pearl)
You Make Loving Fun
Fleetwood Mac; *25 Years-The Chain.* . . . . (Warner Bros.)
Fleetwood Mac's Greatest Hits. . . . . (Warner Bros.)
Rumours . . . . (Warner Bros.)
Jewel; *Legacy-A Tribute To Fleetwood Mac's Rumours-C* . . . . (Lava)
You Ought To Be Havin' Fun
Tower Of Power; *Ain't Nothin' Stoppin' Us Now* . . . . (Columbia)
Young Blood
Rickie Lee Jones; *Naked Songs Live And Acoustic* . . . . (Reprise)
Rickie Lee Jones . . . . (Warner Bros.)

FURNITURE, Beds, Chairs
*See Also: **HOUSES, SLEEP***

As Long As I'm Rockin' With You
John Conlee; *Best Of John Conlee* . . . . (Curb)
In My Eyes . . . . (MCA)
John Conlee-20 Greatest Hits . . . . (MCA)
John Conlee-Legends . . . . (MCA)
A-sleepin' At The Foot Of The Bed
"Little" Jimmy Dickens; *Bluegrass Super Hits-C* . . . . . . (Columbia)
Bed Of Rose's
Screaming Trees; *Uncle Anesthesia.* . . . . (Epic)
Bed Of Rose's
Kenny Rogers; *Back Home Again* . . . . (Reprise)
Bed Of Rose's
Statler Brothers; *Bed Of Rose's* . . . . (Mercury)
Big Four Poster Bed
Brenda Lee; *Brenda Lee-Anthology-#1 & #2* . . . . (MCA)
Bus Stop Bench
Darden Smith; *Native Soil* . . . . (Watermelon)
Chair, The
George Strait; *Country Classics-#5-1985-1986-C* . . . . (Universal)
George Strait's Greatest Hits-#2. . . . . (MCA)
MCA #1 Hits Of The '80s-#1-C . . . . (MCA Special Prod.)
Something Special . . . . (MCA)
Strait Out Of The Box . . . . (MCA)
Chemicals Between Us, The
Bush; *The Science Of Things* . . . . (Trauma)
Give It To You
Jordan Knight; *Jordan Knight* . . . . (Interscope)
Good Old Desk
Nilsson; *Aerial Ballet.* . . . . (RCA)

Hour Of Gold
Emmylou Harris; *Red Dirt Girl* . . . . (Nonesuch)
I Don't Need Your Rockin' Chair
George Jones; *Platinum Country-C* . . . . (MCA)
Walls Can Fall . . . . (MCA)
I'm Gonna Change Everything
Mandy Barnett; *I've Got A Right To Cry* . . . . (Sire)
In My Bed
Dru Hill; *Dru Hill* . . . . (Island)
In My Own Little Corner
Julie Andrews; *A Little Bit Of Broadway* . . . . (Columbia)
Cinderella-The CBS Television Production . . . . (Columbia)
Lesley Ann Warren; *Cinderella-The CBS Television Network*
Production . . . . (Columbia)
Lit Up
Buckcherry; *Buckcherry* . . . . (DreamWorks/SKG)
Little Girl, The
John Michael Montgomery; *Brand New Me* . . . . (Atlantic)
Totally Hits-#3-C . . . . (Atlantic)
London Rain (Nothing Heals Like You Do)
Heather Nova; *Siren* . . . . (Big Cat)
Songs From Dawson's Creek . . . . (Sony Music Soundtrax)
Maybe We Should Just Sleep On It
Tim McGraw; *All I Want* . . . . (Curb)
Tim McGraw's Greatest Hits . . . . (Curb)
Meeting In My Bedroom
Silk; *Tonight* . . . . (Elektra)
Navajo Rug
Ian Tyson; *Cowboyography* . . . . (Sugar Hill)
Norwegian Wood (This Bird Has Flown)
Beatles; *Beatles-Box Set* . . . . (Capitol)
Beatles-Love Songs . . . . (Capitol)
Rubber Soul . . . . (Capitol)
The Beatles/1962-1966 . . . . (Capitol)
Rockin' Chair
Band; *The Band* . . . . (Capitol)
The Band-Gift Set . . . . (Capitol)
Rockin' Chair
Jerry Jeff Walker; *A Man Must Carry On* . . . . (MCA)
Rockin' Chair Money
Hank Williams; *Alone With His Guitar* . . . . (Mercury)
Rockin' Chair On The Moon
Bill Haley & His Comets; *King Of Rock & Roll* . . . . (Alshire)
Rockin' Chair Stomp
Gwen McCrae; *Didn't It Blow Your Mind: Soul Hits Of The*
'70s-#15-C . . . . (Rhino)
Get Down Tonight! Best Of T.K. Records-C . . . . (Rhino)
Hi-Lo's; *Swing-Best Of The Big Bands-C* . . . . (MCA)
Hoagy Carmichael; *Stardust Road* . . . . (MCA)
Jerry Garcia & David Grisman; *Jerry Garcia & David*
Grisman . . . . (Grateful Dead)
John Lee Hooker; *The Healer* . . . . (Chameleon)
Louis Armstrong & Jack Teagarden; *Evening With Louis Armstrong & Jack*
Teagarden-#2 . . . . (Crescendo)
Mildred Bailey; *Jazz Singers* . . . . (Prestige)
Nipper's Greatest Hits Of The '30s-#2-C . . . . (RCA)
Tom Waits; *Tom Waits-Early Years-Volume One* . . . . (Planet 3)
Rockin' With The Rhythm Of The Rain
Judds; *Judds' Greatest Hits* . . . . (MCA)
Rockin' With The Rhythm . . . . (MCA)
Rocking Chair Blues
Bessie Smith; *Bessie Smith-The Complete Recordings-#1* . . . . . . (Legacy)
Ray Charles; *20 Golden Pieces Of Ray Charles* . . . . (Bulldog)
Rocks In My Bed
Duke Ellington; *Duke Ellington & The Blanton-Webster Band* . . . (Bluebird)
Jimmy Witherspoon; *Baby Baby Baby* . . . . (Prestige)
Ray Brown All-Stars; *Don't Forget The Blues* . . . . (Concord Jazz)
Sarah Vaughan; *Duke Ellington Songbook Two* . . . . (Pablo)
Satin Sheets
Jeannie Pruett; *16 Top Country Hits-#1-C* . . . . (MCA)
Country Chart-Toppers . . . . (Dominion Entert.)
Grand Ole Opry-75 Years-#2-C . . . . (MCA)
MCA Records 30 Years Of Hits-1958-1988-C . . . . (MCA)
Shawn Colvin; *Cover Girl* . . . . (Columbia)
She Can Put Her Shoes Under My Bed (Anytime)
Johnny Duncan; *Classic Country* . . . . (Simitar)
Theme From "Designing Women" (Georgia On My Mind)
Original Soundtrack; *Television's Greatest Hits-#7-Cable Ready-C* . . . (TVT)
There Will Never Be Any Peace (Until God Is Seated At The
Conference Table)
Chi-Lites; *Chi-Lites' Greatest Hits* . . . . (Rhino)
Vacant Chair
Steve Winwood; *Steve Winwood* . . . . (Island)
Steve Winwood-Chronicles . . . . (Island)
We Just Couldn't Say Goodbye
Guy Lombardo & His Royal Canadians; *Guy Lombardo-16 Most Requested*
Songs . . . . (Legacy)
Whose Bed Have Your Boots Been Under?
Shania Twain; *The Woman In Me* . . . . (Mercury)

You Ain't Goin' Nowhere
Bob Dylan; *Bob Dylan's Greatest Hits-#2* . . . . (Columbia)
Bob Dylan And The Band; *Basement Tapes* . . . . (Columbia)
Byrds; *Best Of The Byrds-Greatest Hits-#2* . . . . (Columbia)
Byrds Play Dylan . . . . (Columbia)
Sweetheart Of The Rodeo . . . . (Columbia)
The Byrds . . . . (Columbia)
Chris Hillman & Roger McGuinn; *Will The Circle Be Unbroken-#2-C* . . . (Uni)
Joan Baez; *The First 10 Years* . . . . (Vanguard)
You Turned The Tables On Me
Anita O'Day; *Anita Sings The Most* . . . . (Verve)
Benny Goodman; *Benny Goodman's Greatest Hits* . . . . (RCA Victor)
Birth Of Swing . . . . (Bluebird)
Billie Holiday; *Solitude* . . . . (Verve)
Louis Armstrong; *Compact Jazz-Louis Armstrong* . . . . (Verve)

FUTURE, Predictions, Tomorrow

See Also: **ASTROLOGY, DANGER & DISASTER, ETERNITY,**
HISTORY, MAGIC (fortune tellers), TIME: GENERAL, TIME:
SPECIFIC, WARNINGS, YESTERDAY

(I Believe) Our Time Is Gonna Come
REO Speedwagon; *A Decade Of Rock And Roll 1970 To 1980* . . . . (Epic)
R.E.O. . . . . (Epic)
REO Speedwagon Live/You Get What You Play For . . . . (Epic)
100 Years From Now
Huey Lewis and the News; *Time Flies...Best Of Huey Lewis and*
the News . . . . (Elektra)
1999
Prince; *1999* . . . . (Warner Bros.)
21st Century Schizoid Man
King Crimson; *In The Court Of The Crimson King-An Observation By King*
Crimson . . . . (Editions E.G.)
Across The Border
Bruce Springsteen; *The Ghost Of Tom Joad* . . . . (Columbia)
All The Things You Are
Ella Fitzgerald; *Complete Jerome Kern* . . . . (Verve)
Mario Lanza; *Be My Love-Greatest Performances* . . . . (Rhino)
Willie Nelson; *Healing Hands Of Time* . . . . (Liberty)
Anthem For The Year 2000
Silverchair; *Neon Ballroom* . . . . (Epic)
Any Day Now
Ronnie Milsap; *Essential Ronnie Milsap* . . . . (RCA)
Ronnie Milsap's Greatest Hits-#2 . . . . (RCA)
Ronnie Milsap-Super Hits . . . . (RCA)
As We Lay
Kelly Price; *Mirror Mirror* . . . . (Def Soul/IDJMG)
Baby Hold On
Eddie Money; *Eddie Money* . . . . (Columbia)
Eddie Money's Greatest Hits-Sound Of Money . . . . (Columbia)
Best Is Yet To Come
Grover Washington, Jr.; *Grover Washington, Jr.-Anthology* . . . . (Elektra)
Grover Washington, Jr. & Patti LaBelle; *Best Is Yet To Come* . . . . . (Elektra)
Best Is Yet To Come
Frank Sinatra; *It Might As Well Be Swing* . . . . (Reprise)
Sinatra Reprise-The Very Good Years . . . . (Reprise)
Johnny Mathis; *I'll Buy You A Star* . . . . (Legacy)
Rosemary Clooney; *Girl Singer* . . . . (Concord Jazz)
Tony Bennett; *I Left My Heart In San Francisco* . . . . (Columbia)
The Ultimate Tony Bennett . . . . (Legacy)
Best Of Intentions
Travis Tritt; *Down The Road I Go* . . . . (Columbia)
Bring On The Rain
Jo Dee Messina with Tim McGraw; *Burn* . . . . (Curb)
Built For The Future
Fixx; *One Thing Leads To Another-Greatest Hits* . . . . (MCA)
React . . . . (MCA)
Walkabout . . . . (MCA)
Children Of The Future
Steve Miller Band; *Children Of The Future* . . . . (Capitol)
Clint Eastwood
Gorillaz; *Gorillaz* . . . . (Virgin)
Come Rain Or Come Shine
Ella Fitzgerald; *Harold Arlen Songbook-#2* . . . . (Verve)
Frank Sinatra; *Very Best Of Frank Sinatra* . . . . (Reprise)
Frank Sinatra & Gloria Estefan; *Frank Sinatra-Duets-C* . . . . . . (Capitol)
Judy Garland; *America's Treasure* . . . . (Dunhill Compact Classics)
Hits Of Judy Garland . . . . (Capitol)
Judy . . . . (Capitol)
Judy Garland-At Carnegie Hall . . . . (Capitol)
Michael Crawford; *With Love* . . . . (Atlantic)
Come Some Rainy Day
Wynonna; *The Other Side* . . . . (Curb/MCA)
Come What May
Patti Page; *Patti Page Collection-The Mercury Years-#1* . . . . (Mercury)

Coming Up
Paul McCartney; *All The Best!* .... (Capitol)
   Tripping The Live Fantastic-Highlights! .... (Capitol)
Don't Stop
Elton John; *Legacy-A Tribute To Fleetwood Mac's Rumours-C* .... (Lava)
Fleetwood Mac; *25 Years-The Chain* .... (Warner Bros.)
   Fleetwood Mac Live .... (Warner Bros.)
   Fleetwood Mac's Greatest Hits .... (Warner Bros.)
   Rumours .... (Warner Bros.)
Drive
Incubus; *Make Yourself* .... (Immortal/Epic)
   Now That's What I Call Music!-#6-C .... (Virgin)
Estimated Prophet
Burning Spear; *Deadicated-C* .... (Arista)
Grateful Dead; *Terrapin Station* .... (Arista)
Fly Like An Eagle
Seal; *ST/Space Jam* .... (Warner Sunset)
Steve Miller; *Fly Like An Eagle* .... (Capitol)
   ST/FM .... (MCA)
   Steve Miller Band-Gift Set .... (Capitol)
   Steve Miller Band-Live .... (Capitol)
   Steve Miller Band's Greatest Hits-1974-78 .... (Capitol)
Fortune Teller
Benny Spellman; *Best Of New Orleans Rhythm & Blues-#1-C* ... (Rhino)
   History Of New Orleans R&B-#2-1959-1962-C .... (Rhino)
Rolling Stones; *got Live if you Want It* .... (Abkco)
   More Hot Rocks (big hits & fazed cookies) .... (Abkco)
Friends Of P.
Rentals; *Return Of The Rentals* .... (Maverick)
From This Moment On
Shania Twain & Bryan White; *Come On Over* .... (Mercury)
From This Moment On
Anita O'Day; *Swings Cole Porter* .... (Verve)
Ella Fitzgerald; *Ella Fitzgerald Sings The Cole Porter Songbook* .... (Verve)
Frank Sinatra; *a Swingin' Affair!* .... (Capitol)
Original Soundtrack; *Kiss Me Kate* .... (Rhino)
Future
Prince; *ST/Batman* .... (Warner Bros.)
Future
Little Johnny Taylor; *45-#88* .... (Ronn)
Future Games
Fleetwood Mac; *Future Games* .... (Reprise)
Future Legend
David Bowie; *Diamond Dogs* .... (Rykodisc)
Future Shock
Hello People; *45-#15023* .... (Dunhill Compact Classics)
Future's So Bright I Gotta Wear Shades
Timbuk 3; *Greetings From Timbuk 3* .... (I.R.S.)
Goodbye Yellow Brick Road
Elton John; *Billboard Top Rock 'N' Roll Hits-1973-C* .... (Rhino)
   Elton John's Greatest Hits .... (Polydor)
   Goodbye Yellow Brick Road .... (Polydor)
Headache Tomorrow (Or A Heartache Tonight)
Mickey Gilley; *Mickey Gilley's Biggest Hits* .... (Epic)
   Ten Years Of Hits .... (Epic)
   That's All That Matters To Me .... (Epic)
Headed For The Future
Neil Diamond; *Headed For The Future* .... (Columbia)
   Hot August Night II .... (Columbia)
Here Today
Beach Boys; *Pet Sounds* .... (Capitol)
   The Pet Sounds Sessions: A 30th Anniversary Collection .... (Capitol)
Hi-Lili, Hi-Lo
Anne Murray; *There's A Hippo In My Tub* .... (Capitol)
Ray Conniff; *Encore! 16 Most Requested Songs* .... (Legacy)
How It's Going To Be
Third Eye Blind; *Third Eye Blind* .... (Elektra)
I Am Going To Like It Here
Original Cast; *ST/Flower Drum Song* .... (Sony Music Classical)
I Confess
Perry Como; *Yesterday And Today-A Celebration In Song* .... (RCA)
I Don't Live Today
Jimi Hendrix; *Concerts* .... (Reprise)
   Essential Jimi Hendrix, Volume 2 .... (Reprise)
   Kiss The Sky .... (Reprise)
Jimi Hendrix Experience; *Are You Experienced?* .... (Reprise)
I Only Know I Love You
Four Aces; *Four Aces-More Greatest Hits* .... (Varese Vintage)
I Shall Be Released
Band; *Music From Big Pink* .... (Capitol)
   The Band-Anthology-#1 .... (Capitol)
   The Last Waltz .... (Warner Bros.)
   To Kingdom Come-The Definitive Collection .... (Capitol)
Bette Midler; *Bette Midler* .... (Atlantic)
   ST/Divine Madness .... (Atlantic)
Bob Dylan; *Biograph* .... (Columbia)
   Bob Dylan At Budokan .... (Columbia)
   Bob Dylan's Greatest Hits-#2 .... (Columbia)
   The Bootleg Series-Volumes 1-3 [Rare & Unreleased] .... (Columbia)

Bob Dylan And The Band; *Before The Flood* .... (Columbia)
Box Tops; *Box Tops' Greatest Hits* .... (Rhino)
Flying Burrito Brothers; *Farther Along-Best Of The Flying Burrito*
   Brothers .... (A&M)
Joan Baez; *Any Day Now: Songs Of Bob Dylan* .... (Vanguard)
   Carry It On .... (Vanguard)
   From Every Stage .... (A&M)
Joe Cocker; *With A Little Help From My Friends* .... (A&M)
Nina Simone; *Best Of Nina Simone* .... (Verve)
Rick Nelson; *Rick Nelson In Concert-Troubadour 1969* .... (MCA)
I Still Believe
Mariah Carey; *Mariah Carey-#1's* .... (Columbia)
   MTV Unplugged-Mariah Carey .... (Columbia)
I.G.Y. (What A Beautiful World)
Donald Fagen; *The Nightfly* .... (Warner Bros.)
I'll Stick Around
Foo Fighters; *Foo Fighters* .... (Roswell/RCA)
I'm Gonna Be A Wheel Someday
Fats Domino; *Best Of Fats Domino* .... (EMI)
   Fats Domino's Greatest Hits .... (MCA)
   Fats Domino's Greatest Hits .... (Everest)
   My Blue Heaven .... (Gold Rush)
   My Blue Heaven-Best Of Fats Domino-#1 .... (EMI)
Los Lobos; *Fine Mess* .... (Motown)
I'm Gonna Leave You Tomorrow
John Schneider; *Country Classics-#6-1985-1986-C* .... (Universal)
   John Schneider's Greatest Hits .... (MCA)
   Tryin' To Outrun The Wind .... (MCA)
I'm Just An Old Chunk Of Coal (But I'm Gonna Be A Diamond
   Someday)
Billy Joe Shaver; *Restless Wind-The Legendary Billy Joe Shaver-1973-*
   1987 .... (Razor & Tie)
John Anderson; *John Anderson's Greatest Hits* .... (Warner Bros.)
In The Meantime
Spacehog; *Resident Alien* .... (Sire)
In The Year 2525 (Exordium & Terminus)
Zager & Evans; *Nipper's Greatest Hits Of The '60s-#2-C* .... (RCA)
Infinite Possibilities
Amel Larrieux; *Infinite Possibilities* .... (Epic)
It Won't Be Long Now
Barbeque Bob & Laughing Charley; *Story Of The Blues-C* .... (Columbia)
It's Going To Take Some Time
Carole King; *A Natural Woman: The Ode Collection-1968-1976* ..... (Legacy)
   Music .... (Epic)
Carpenters; *A Song For You* .... (A&M)
   Carpenters-The Singles 1969-1973 .... (A&M)
   Yesterday Once More .... (A&M)
It's Gonna Be Me
'N Sync; *No Strings Attached* .... (Jive)
   Now That's What I Call Music!-#5-C .... (Virgin)
I've Got This Feeling
Mavericks; *Trampoline* .... (MCA)
Lara's Theme
Maurice Jarre Orchestra; *Hollywood's Great*
   Composers-C .... (Columbia Special Prod.)
MGM Studio Orchestra; *ST/Dr. Zhivago* .... (MCA)
Last Kiss
J. Frank Wilson and The Cavaliers; *Billboard Top Rock 'N' Roll Hits-*
   1964-C .... (Rhino)
   Collectables Presents The History Of Rock-#2-C .... (Collectables)
   Oldies But Goodies-#9-C .... (Original Sound)
   Teenage Tragedies-C .... (Rhino)
Pearl Jam; *No Boundaries-Benefit For The Kosovar Refugees-C* .... (Epic)
Living In The Future
John Prine; *Storm Windows* .... (Asylum)
Living In The Future In A Plastic Dome
Country Joe McDonald; *Incredible Live* .... (Vanguard)
Living In The Plastic Age
Buggles; *Age Of Plastic* .... (Island)
Lookin' At Tomorrow
Beach Boys; *Surf's Up* .... (Caribou)
Love Is All You Need For The Future
Nona Gaye; *Love For The Future* .... (Third Stone)
Love Is Gonna Come At Last
Badfinger; *Airwaves* .... (Out Of Print)
   Best Of Badfinger-#2 .... (Rhino)
Love Me Tomorrow
Chicago; *Chicago 16* .... (Full Moon/Warner Bros.)
   Chicago's Greatest Hits-1982-1989 .... (Full Moon)
Love You For A Day
Ricky Martin; *Ricky Martin* .... (Columbia)
Manana
Jimmy Buffett; *Son Of A Son Of A Sailor* .... (MCA)
Maybe Someday
Cure; *Bloodflowers* .... (Fiction/Elektra)
Mmm Bop
Hanson; *1998 Grammy Nominees-C* .... (MCA)
   Middle Of Nowhere .... (Mercury)

Now That's What I Call Music!-#1-C .... (Virgin)
Three Car Garage: The Independent Recordings .... (Mercury)
More Today Than Yesterday
Spiral Staircase; *CBS Classics-Pop Classics Of The '60s-C* .... (Columbia)
Rock Artifacts-From The Vaults-#1-C .... (Columbia)
Super Hits Of The '70s-Have A Nice Day-#1-C .... (Rhino)
My Next Thirty Years
Tim McGraw; *A Place In The Sun* .... (Curb)
Tim McGraw's Greatest Hits .... (Curb)
Never Comes The Day
Moody Blues; *Caught Live Plus Five* .... (Polydor)
On The Threshold Of A Dream .... (Polydor)
This Is The Moody Blues .... (Polydor)
Next Time
Gladys Knight; *Just For You.* .... (MCA)
Next Year
Foo Fighters; *There Is Nothing Left To Lose.* .... (Roswell/RCA)
No Future In The Past
Vince Gill; *I Still Believe In You.* .... (MCA)
No More Looking Back
Kinks; *Schoolboys In Disgrace.* .... (Rhino)
Second Time Around .... (RCA)
One Day You'll Be Mine
Usher; *My Way.* .... (LaFace)
One Fine Day
Carpenters; *From The Top* .... (A&M)
Now & Then. .... (A&M)
Chiffons; *Best Of The Chiffons* .... (Laurie)
Chiffons-Golden Classics .... (Collectables)
Collectables Presents The History Of Rock-#9-C .... (Collectables)
Oldies But Goodies-#12-C. .... (Original Sound)
One Of These Days
John Lee Hooker; *That's My Story* .... (Riverside)
One Of These Days
Tim McGraw; *Everywhere* .... (Curb)
One Of These Days
Pink Floyd; *Collection Of Great Dance Songs* .... (Columbia)
Delicate Sound Of Thunder .... (Columbia)
Meddle. .... (Capitol)
Pink Floyd-Gift Set .... (Capitol)
Works. .... (Capitol)
One Of These Days
Emmylou Harris; *Elite Hotel* .... (Reprise)
Profile/Best Of Emmylou Harris .... (Warner Bros.)
One Of These Days
Neil Young; *Harvest Moon.* .... (Reprise)
One Of These Days
Nanci Griffith; *Last Of The True Believers* .... (Philo)
One Of These Days
Camper Van Beethoven; *Our Beloved Revolutionary Sweetheart* ...... (Virgin)
One Of These Days
Ten Years After; *A Space In Time.* .... (Columbia)
One Of These Days
Ronnie Hawkins and The Hawks; *Best Of Ronnie Hawkins and The Hawks.* ...... (Rhino)
One Of These Days
Matthews, Wright & King; *Dream Seekers* .... (Columbia)
One Of These Days
Tom Grant; *Just The Right Moment* .... (Verve/Forecast)
One Of These Days
Marvin Gaye; *Marvin Gaye's Greatest Hits.* .... (Motown)
One Of These Days
Velvet Underground; *V.U.* .... (Verve)
One Sweet Day
Mariah Carey; *Daydream.* .... (Columbia)
Mariah Carey & Boyz II Men; *1996 Grammy Nominees-C* ... (Columbia)
Only Time
Enya; *A Day Without Rain* .... (Reprise)
Our Day Will Come
Ruby And The Romantics; *21 Country Rock & Love Songs Of The '50s & '60s-#1-C* ...... (Laurie)
Oldies But Goodies-#12-C. .... (Original Sound)
Our Time Is Coming
Brooks & Dunn; *Hard Workin' Man* .... (Arista)
Peaceful World
John Mellencamp; *Cuttin' Heads* .... (Columbia)
God Bless America-C. .... (Columbia)
The Concert For New York City-C. .... (Columbia)
Pineapple Princess
Annette Funicello; *Frankie Avalon/Annette Funicello* ...... (K-Tel)
Premonition
John Fogerty; *Premonition* .... (Reprise)
Put Your Dreams Away (For Another Day)
Frank Sinatra; *Best Of The Columbia Years-1943-1952.* ... (Columbia)
Frank Sinatra-16 Most Requested Songs. .... (Columbia)
Sinatra: A Man And His Music .... (Reprise)
The Capitol Years .... (Capitol)
Mickey Gilley; *Put Your Dreams Away* .... (Epic)
Ten Years Of Hits. .... (Epic)

Que Sera, Sera
Doris Day; *Doris Day-16 Most Requested Songs-Encore!* ...... (Columbia)
Doris Day's Greatest Hits .... (Columbia)
Radio Classics Of The '50s-C. .... (Columbia)
Sly & The Family Stone; *Fresh.* .... (Legacy)
Sly & The Family Stone-Anthology .... (Epic)
See The Future
Front 242; *No Comment* .... (Epic)
Seven-And-A-Half Cents
John Raitt; *ST/Pajama Game* .... (Collectables)
Original Cast; *Pajama Game.* .... (Columbia)
Silver Future
Monster Magnet; *ST/Heavy Metal 2000* .... (Restless)
Sleeping In Paris
Rosanne Cash; *The Wheel.* .... (Columbia)
Some Enchanted Evening
Jay & The Americans; *Come A Little Bit Closer-Best Of Jay & The Americans* ...... (Gold Rush)
Jay & The Americans' All-Time Greatest Hits .... (Rhino)
Original Cast; *South Pacific* .... (CBS Masterworks)
Perry Como; *Perry Como's All-Time Greatest Hits-#1.* ...... (RCA)
Rosanno Brazzi; *ST/South Pacific.* .... (RCA)
Willie Nelson; *What A Wonderful World* .... (Columbia)
Some Of These Days
Cab Calloway; *Masters Of Jazz-#6-Male Vocal Classics-C* ...... (Rhino)
Leon Redbone; *On The Track* .... (Warner Bros.)
Louis Armstrong; *Louis Armstrong And The Big Bands-1928-1930.* ..... (DRG)
Mills Brothers; *Close Harmony.* .... (Ranwood)
Sophie Tucker; *Legendary Entertainers* .... (Pro-Arte)
Those Wonderful Years-Roaring '20s-C. ...... (JCI Assoc. Labels)
Somebody's Gonna Love You
Lee Greenwood; *Lee Greenwood's Greatest Hits* .... (MCA)
Somebody's Gonna Love You. .... (MCA)
Someday
Greg Kihn; *Kihnsolidation-Best Of Greg Kihn* .... (Rhino)
Someday
All-4-One; *ST/The Hunchback Of Notre Dame.* .... (Disney)
Someday
Bobby Bland; *Best Of Bobby Bland* .... (MCA)
Introspective Of The Early Years .... (MCA)
Someday
Alan Jackson; *Don't Rock The Jukebox.* .... (Arista)
Someday
Mariah Carey; *Mariah Carey* .... (Columbia)
MTV Unplugged-Mariah Carey .... (Columbia)
Someday
Shawn Colvin; *Cover Girl.* .... (Columbia)
Someday
Neil Young; *Freedom* .... (Reprise)
Someday
Steve Earle & The Dukes; *Guitar Town* .... (MCA)
Shut Up And Die Like An Aviator. .... (MCA)
Someday
BoDeans; *Outside Looking In* .... (Slash)
Someday
Flim & The BB's; *Vintage Flim & The BB's.* ...... (Digital Music Prod.)
Someday
Concrete Blonde; *Walking In London* .... (I.R.S.)
Someday (You'll Want Me To Want You)
Gene Autry; *The Country Music Hall Of Fame-Gene Autry-15 Of His All-Time Greatest Hits.* ...... (Columbia)
Mills Brothers; *Best Of The Mills Brothers* .... (MCA)
The Mills Brothers-Best Of The Decca Years. .... (Decca)
Patsy Cline; *Last Sessions* .... (MCA)
Portrait Of Patsy Cline. .... (MCA)
Vaughn Monroe; *Best Of Vaughn Monroe* .... (MCA)
Someday (You're Gonna Want Me)
Bobby Vee; *Bobby Vee-Golden Greats.* .... (Liberty)
Someday After A While
Eric Clapton; *From The Cradle.* .... (Duck/Reprise)
Someday I'll Find You
Bobby Short; *Mad About Noel Coward.* .... (Atlantic)
Mary Martin & Noel Coward; *Together With Music.* ...... (DRG)
Someday My Day Will Come
George Jones; *George Jones-Anniversary-Ten Years Of Hits.* ...... (Epic)
Still The Same Ole Me .... (Epic)
Someday My Prince Will Come
Bill Evans Trio; *Portrait In Jazz* .... (Riverside)
En Vogue; *Simply Mad About The Mouse-C.* .... (Columbia)
Lena Horne; *A New Album* .... (RCA)
Lena Horne & Phil Woods; *I Have Dreamed* .... (Novus)
Miles Davis; *I Like Jazz-Essence Of Miles Davis* .... (Columbia)
Miles Davis' Greatest Hits. .... (Columbia)
Someday My Prince Will Come .... (Columbia)
Mormon Tabernacle Choir & Columbia Symphony Orchestra; *When You Wish Upon A Star-A Tribute To Walt Disney.* ...... (CBS Masterworks)
Someday Never Comes
Creedence Clearwater Revival; *Creedence Clearwater Revival-Chronicle.* ...... (Fantasy)

Mardi Gras . . . .(Fantasy)
Someday Out Of The Blue
Elton John; *ST/The Road To El Dorado* . . . . (DreamWorks/SKG)
Someday Someday
Marvelettes; *Marvelettes-Anthology* . . . . (Motown)
Someday Soon
Chris LeDoux; *Rodeo Songs Old & New* . . . . (Liberty)
Ian & Sylvia; *Ian & Sylvia's Greatest Hits* . . . . (Vanguard)
Northern Journey . . . . (Vanguard)
Judy Collins; *Colors Of The Day-The Best Of Judy Collins* . (Elektra)
Who Knows Where The Time Goes . . . . (Elektra)
Moe Bandy; *Moe Bandy's Greatest Hits* . . . . (Columbia)
Rodeo Romeo . . . . (Columbia)
Suzy Bogguss; *Aces* . . . . (Liberty)
Suzy Bogguss' Greatest Hits . . . . (Liberty)
Someday Soon
Journey; *Departure* . . . . (Columbia)
Someday Sweetheart
Bing Crosby; *Here Lies Love* . . . . (ASV Living Era)
Peggy Lee; *You Can Depend On Me* . . . .(Glendale)
Zoot Sims; *Best Of Zoot Sims* . . . . (Pablo)
Someday We'll All Be Free
Alicia Keys; *America: A Tribute To Heroes-C* . . . . (Interscope)
Donny Hathaway; *Best Of Donny Hathaway* . . . .(Atco)
James Ingram; *It's Real* . . . . (Warner Bros.)
Someday We'll Be Together
Diana Ross & The Supremes; *20/20-C* . . . . (Motown)
Diana Ross & The Supremes' Greatest Hits-#3 . . . . . . (Motown)
Diana Ross & The Supremes-Anthology (1962-1969) . . (Motown)
Evening With Diana Ross . . . . (Motown)
Motown Story-First 25 Years-C . . . . (Motown)
Motown Superstar Series-#1-Diana Ross & The Supremes . . . . . . (Motown)
Someday We're Gonna Love Again
Barbara Lewis; *Barbara Lewis-Golden Classics* . . . .(Collectables)
Searchers; *Searchers' Greatest Hits* . . . . (Rhino)
Someday When Things Are Good
Merle Haggard; *His Epic Hits-First 11 To Be Continued-C* . (Epic)
That's The Way Love Goes . . . . (Epic)
Someday, Someway
Marshall Crenshaw; *Marshall Crenshaw* . . . . (Rhino)
ST/Nightshift . . . . (Warner Bros.)
Something's Coming
Barbra Streisand; *One Voice* . . . . (Columbia)
The Broadway Album . . . . (Columbia)
Original Cast; *ST/West Side Story* . . . . (Sony Broadway)
Somewhere
Aretha Franklin; *Aretha's Jazz* . . . . (Rhino)
Barbra Streisand; *The Broadway Album* . . . . (Columbia)
Dave Brubeck; *Music From West Side Story* . . . . (Columbia)
Jose Carreras; *Amigos Para Siempre-Friends For Life* . . . . (Atlantic)
Original Cast; *ST/West Side Story* . . . . (Sony Broadway)
Tom Waits; *Tom Waits-Anthology* . . . . (Asylum)
Somewhere Down The Line
T.G. Sheppard; *Slow Burn* . . . . (Warner Bros.)
T.G. Sheppard's All-Time Greatest Hits . . . . (Warner Bros.)
Soon
Ella Fitzgerald; *George & Ira Gershwin Songbook* . . . . (Verve)
Kiri Te Kanawa; *Kiri Sings Gershwin* . . . . (Angel)
Original Cast; *Little Night Music* . . . . (Columbia)
My One And Only . . . . (Atlantic)
Soon
Tanya Tucker; *Soon* . . . . (Liberty)
Soon
LeAnn Rimes; *I Need You* . . . . (Curb)
Sooner Or Later
Eddy Raven; *Best Of Eddy Raven* . . . . (Liberty)
Temporary Sanity . . . . (Capitol)
Sooner Or Later
Grass Roots; *Grass Roots-All-Time Greatest Hits* . . . . (MCA)
Grass Roots-Anthology (1966-1975) . . . . (Rhino)
Super Hits-#2-C . . . . (Gusto)
Sooner Or Later
Barbara Cook; *Disney Album* . . . . (Disney)
Sooner Or Later
Madonna; *I'm Breathless-Music From Dick Tracy* . . . .(Sire)
Sooner Or Later
Gary Morris; *Stones* . . . . (Liberty)
Space Cowboy (Yippie-Yi-Yay)
'N Sync featuring Lisa "Left Eye" Lopes; *No Strings Attached* . . . .(Jive)
Tell Me Tomorrow
Angela Bofill; *Angela Bofill* . . . . (Arista)
Best Of Angela Bofill . . . . (Arista)
Karyn White; *Karyn White* . . . . (Warner Bros.)
Smokey Robinson; *Blame It On Love & All The Great Hits* . . . . (Motown)
Thank You In Advance
Boyz II Men; *Nathan Michael Shawn Wanya* . . . . (Universal)
That'll Be The Day
Buddy Holly; *ST/American Graffiti* . . . . (MCA)
Buddy Holly/The Crickets; *Buddy Holly-20 Golden Greats* . . . . (MCA)

Chirping Crickets . . . . (MCA)
Crickets; *Billboard Top Rock 'N' Roll Hits-1957-C* . . . .(Rhino)
Foghat; *Best Of Foghat-#2* . . . .(Rhino)
Energized . . . .(Rhino)
Linda Ronstadt; *Hasten Down The Wind* . . . . (Asylum)
Linda Ronstadt's Greatest Hits . . . . (Asylum)
Theme From "Back To The Future"
Cincinnati Pops Orchestra/Erich Kunzel; *Star Tracks II* . . . . (Telarc)
Theme From "Lost In Space"
Neil Norman; *Greatest Science Fiction Hits-#3-C* . . . .(Crescendo)
Original Soundtrack; *CBS: The First 50 Years* . . . .(TVT)
Television's Greatest Hits-#1-C . . . .(TVT)
Theme From "Star Trek"
Cincinnati Pops Orchestra/Erich Kunzel; *Star Tracks II* . . . . (Telarc)
Theme From "Star Trek: The Next Generation"
Original Soundtrack; *Television's Greatest Hits-#7-Cable Ready-C* . . . . .(TVT)
Theme From "The Jetsons"
Original Soundtrack; *Hanna-Barbera Pic-A-Nic Basket Of Cartoon
Classics* . . . . (Kid Rhino/Rhino 4 Kids)
Television's Greatest Hits-#1-C . . . .(TVT)
Stunners; *ST/Jetsons-The Movie* . . . . (MCA)
There Ain't No Future In This
Reba McEntire; *Best Of Reba McEntire* . . . .(Mercury)
There Will Come A Day
Faith Hill; *America: A Tribute To Heroes-C* . . . . (Interscope)
Breathe . . . . (Warner Bros.)
There's No Tomorrow
Squeeze; *East Side Story* . . . .(A&M)
Tony Martin; *Nipper's Greatest Hits Of The '40s-#2-C* . . . . . . (RCA)
Things We Said Today
Beatles; *Beatles-Box Set* . . . .(Capitol)
Something New . . . .(Capitol)
The Beatles At The Hollywood Bowl . . . . (Capitol)
Paul McCartney; *Tripping The Live Fantastic-Highlights!* . . . .(Capitol)
Think Of Tomorrow
Chris Isaak; *Baja Sessions* . . . . (Reprise)
Till Then
Mills Brothers; *Best Of The Mills Brothers* . . . . (MCA)
Cab Driver . . . .(Ranwood)
Lazy River . . . . (MCA Special Prod.)
Mills Brothers . . . . (Everest)
Mills Brothers' Greatest Hits . . . . (MCA)
Time Is Running Out
Steve Winwood; *Steve Winwood* . . . .(Island)
Tomorrow
Three O'Clock; *Hoedown* . . . . (Fontana)
Sixteen Tambourines . . . . (Frontier)
Tomorrow
Silverchair; *Frogstomp* . . . . (Epic)
Tomorrow
Joe Walsh; *But Seriously Folks* . . . . (Asylum)
Tomorrow
Wall Of Voodoo; *Call Of The West* . . . . (I.R.S.)
Tomorrow
Morrissey; *Your Arsenal* . . . . (Sire)
Tomorrow
U2; *October* . . . .(Island)
Tomorrow
Poco; *Pickin' Up The Pieces* . . . . (Epic)
Tomorrow
Wings; *Wild Life* . . . .(Capitol)
Tomorrow
Information Society; *Information Society* . . . . (Tommy Boy)
Tomorrow
Jay & The Americans; *Come A Little Bit Closer-Best Of Jay & The
Americans* . . . . (Gold Rush)
Tomorrow
Jimmy Somerville & The Communards; *Jimmy Somerville-Singles Collection-
1984-1990* . . . . (London)
Tomorrow
Strawberry Alarm Clock; *Best Of The Strawberry Alarm Clock-#1* . . . (Bac-Trac)
Tomorrow
Barbra Streisand; *Songbird* . . . . (Columbia)
Original Broadway Cast; *Annie* . . . .(Columbia)
Original Cast; *ST/Annie* . . . .(Columbia)
Tomorrow & Tonight
Kiss; *Alive II* . . . . (Casablanca)
Love Gun . . . . (Casablanca)
Tomorrow (A Better You, Better Me)
Quincy Jones & Tevin Campbell; *Back On The Block* . . . . (Qwest)
Tomorrow Belongs To Me
Liza Minnelli & Joel Grey; *ST/Cabaret* . . . . (MCA)
Original Cast; *Cabaret* . . . .(Columbia)
Tomorrow Doesn't Matter Tonight
Starship; *Knee Deep In The Hoopla* . . . . (Grunt)
Tomorrow I'll Be Out Of Town
Ten Years After; *Classic Performances Of Ten Years After* . . . . (Columbia)
Universal . . . .(Chrysalis)

Tomorrow Is A Long Time
Bob Dylan; *Bob Dylan's Greatest Hits-#2* . . . . (Columbia)
Chris Hillman; *Morning Sky* . . . . (Sugar Hill)
Elvis Presley; *A Valentine Gift For You* . . . . (RCA)
Ian & Sylvia; *Four Strong Winds* . . . . (Vanguard)
  Ian & Sylvia's Greatest Hits . . . . (Vanguard)
  Troubadors Of The Folk Era-#1-C . . . . (Rhino)
Sandy Denny; *Who Knows Where The Time Goes* . . . . (Hannibal)

Tomorrow Is Such A Long Time
Rod Stewart; *Every Picture Tells A Story* . . . . (Mercury)
  Rod Stewart's Greatest Hits-#2 . . . . (Mercury)

Tomorrow Never Comes
Ernest Tubb; *The Ernest Tubb Story* . . . . (MCA)
Ernest Tubb & B.J. Thomas; *Ernest Tubb Collection-C* . . . . . . (Step One)
Slim Whitman; *Best Of Slim Whitman 1952-1972* . . . . (Rhino)

Tomorrow Never Knows
Beatles; *Beatles-Box Set* . . . . (Capitol)
  Revolver . . . . (Capitol)
Phil Collins; *Face Value* . . . . (Atlantic)

Tomorrow Night
Elvis Presley; *For Everyone* . . . . (RCA)
  Reconsider Baby . . . . (RCA)
  Sun's Greatest Hits-C . . . . (RCA)
  The Sun Sessions . . . . (RCA)
LaVern Baker; *Atlantic Rhythm & Blues 1947-1974-#2 (1952-*
  1955)-C . . . . (Atlantic)
  Soul On Fire . . . . (Atlantic)

Tomorrow Night
Barbra Streisand; *ST/Yentl* . . . . (Columbia)

Tomorrow Night
Bob Dylan; *Good As I Been To You* . . . . (Columbia)

Tomorrow Night In Baltimore
Roger Miller; *Best Of Roger Miller* . . . . (Mercury)
  More Golden Hits . . . . (Smash)

Tomorrow We'll See
Sting; *Brand New Day* . . . . (A&M)

Tomorrow's Dreams
Black Sabbath; *Black Sabbath-Vol. 4* . . . . (Warner Bros.)
  We Sold Our Soul For Rock 'N' Roll . . . . (Warner Bros.)

Tomorrow's Girls
Donald Fagen; *Kamakiriad* . . . . (Reprise)

Tomorrow's Gonna Be Another Day
Charlie Daniels Band; *Night Rider* . . . . (Epic)
  Nightrider . . . . (Epic)

Tomorrow's My Wedding Day
Country Gentlemen; *Country Songs Old & New* . . . . . . (Smithsonian Folkways)

Victims Of The Future
Gary Moore; *Gary Moore-Early Years* . . . . (WTG)
  We Want Moore . . . . (Virgin)

Vision Of The Future
Roachford; *Get Ready!* . . . . (Epic)

Wait Until Tomorrow
Jimi Hendrix; *Axis: Bold As Love* . . . . (Reprise)
Jimi Hendrix Experience; *Radio One* . . . . (Rykodisc)

Waiting For The Day
Gerry Rafferty; *City To City* . . . . (EMI)

We Shall Overcome
Bruce Springsteen; *Where Have All The Flowers Gone: The Songs Of Pete*
  Seeger . . . . (Appleseed)
James Cleveland & The Troubadors; *James Cleveland & The*
  Troubadors . . . . (Savoy)
Joan Baez; *Carry It On* . . . . (Vanguard)
  Joan Baez In Concert, Part 2 . . . . (Vanguard)
Mahalia Jackson; *God Bless America-C* . . . . (Columbia)
Pete Seeger; *Bitter & The Sweet* . . . . (Mobile Fidelity Sound Lab)
  Pete Seeger's Greatest Hits . . . . (Columbia)

We'll Meet Again
Vera Lynn; *ST/Dr. Strangelove: Music From The Films Of Stanley*
  Kubrick . . . . (Silva Classics)
  We'll Meet Again . . . . (Living Era)

When It All Goes Wrong Again
Everclear; *Songs From An American Movie-#2-Good Time For A Bad*
  Attitude . . . . (Capitol)

When My Blue Moon Turns To Gold Again
Elvis Presley; *A Golden Celebration* . . . . (RCA)
  Elvis . . . . (RCA)
  The Other Sides-Worldwide Gold Award Hits, Vol. 2 . . . . (RCA)
Merle Haggard; *Merle Haggard-His Best* . . . . (MCA)
  Ramblin' Fever . . . . (MCA)

When Tomorrow Comes
Eurythmics; *Eurythmics' Greatest Hits* . . . . (Arista)
  Greenpeace/Rainbow Warriors-C . . . . (Geffen)
  Revenge . . . . (RCA)

White Cliffs Of Dover
Kay Kyser & His Orchestra; *16 Most Requested Songs Of The*
  '40s-#1-C . . . . (Legacy)
Lee Andrews And The Hearts; *Lee Andrews And The Hearts'*
  Biggest Hits . . . . (Collectables)
Mystics; *Mystics-16 Golden Classics* . . . . (Collectables)

Righteous Brothers; *Righteous Brothers' Greatest Hits* . . . . (Verve)
  Righteous Brothers-Anthology 1962-1974 . . . . (Rhino)
Rosemary Clooney; *For The Duration* . . . . (Concord Jazz)

Who Knows What Tomorrow Will Bring
Traffic; *Traffic* . . . . (Island)

Wicker Man
Iron Maiden; *Brave New World* . . . . (Portrait)

Will 2K
Will Smith; *Willenium* . . . . (Columbia)

Will You Love Me Tomorrow
4 Seasons; *4 Seasons' Greatest Hits-#2.* . . . . (Rhino)
Carole King; *Tapestry* . . . . (Epic)
Linda Ronstadt; *Linda Ronstadt-Retrospective* . . . . (Capitol)
Lorrie Morgan; *Chicken Soup For The Woman's Soul-C* . . . . . . (Rhino)
Roberta Flack; *Best Of Roberta Flack* . . . . (Atlantic)
  Quiet Fire . . . . (Atlantic)
Shirelles; *Girl Groups-Story Of A Sound-C* . . . . (Rhino)
  More Dirty Dancing-C . . . . (RCA)
  Oldies But Goodies-#14-C . . . . (Original Sound)
  Shirelles-16 Greatest Hits . . . . (Trip)
  Shirelles-Anthology 1959-1964 . . . . (Rhino)
  Wonder Women-#2-History Of Girl Group-C . . . . (Rhino)

Wonderful
Everclear; *Now That's What I Call Music!-#5-C* . . . . (Virgin)
  Songs From An American Movie-#1-Learning How To Smile . . . . . . (Capitol)

World Tonight
Paul McCartney; *Flaming Pie* . . . . (Capitol)

Year 2003 Minus 25
Waylon Jennings & Willie Nelson; *Waylon & Willie* . . . . (RCA)

Yesterday, Today And Tomorrow
Small Faces; *From The Beginning* . . . . (Polydor)
  Small Faces-Anthology-1965-1967 . . . . (Polydor)

You'll See
Madonna; *Something To Remember* . . . . (Maverick/Sire)

Your Time Is Gonna Come
Led Zeppelin; *Led Zeppelin* . . . . (Atlantic)
  Led Zeppelin-Box Set . . . . (Atlantic)

You've Got A Good Love Comin'
Lee Greenwood; *Inside Out/You've Got A Good Love Comin'* . . . . . . (MCA)

GAMBLING, Betting, Card Games, Casino Games, Chance, Dice, Risk

See Also: CITIES: LAS VEGAS, LOSING & LOSS, LUCK, SPORTS (various), WINNING

21
Eagles; *Desperado* . . . . (Asylum)

50-50
Mothers Of Invention; *Apostrophe/Overnite Sensation* . . . . (Rykodisc)

7-11 (A Winner)
Li'l Wally; *Polish Carnival* . . . . (Jay Jay)

Ace In The Hole
George Strait; *Beyond The Blue Neon* . . . . (MCA)

Ace In The Hole
George Feyer; *Cole Porter Songbook* . . . . (Vanguard)

Aces
Suzy Bogguss; *Aces* . . . . (Liberty)

Against All Odds (Take A Look At Me Now)
Mariah Carey; *Rainbow* . . . . (Columbia)
Phil Collins; *Hit Singles-1980-1988-C* . . . . (Atlantic)
  Serious Hits...Live! . . . . (Atlantic)
  ST/Against All Odds . . . . (Atlantic)

All I Need (Is A Chance)
Take 6; *Join The Band-C* . . . . (Reprise)

American Roulette
Robbie Robertson; *Robbie Robertson* . . . . (Geffen)

Another Chance
Tammy Wynette; *Tears Of Fire-25th Anniversary Collection* . . . . . (Epic)

As Long As You Love Me
Backstreet Boys; *Backstreet Boys* . . . . (Jive)
  Now That's What I Call Music!-#1-C . . . . (Virgin)

Atlantic City Gambler
Grace Jones; *Muse* . . . . (Island)

Bad, Bad Leroy Brown
Jim Croce; *Billboard Top Rock 'N' Roll Hits-1973-C* . . . . (Rhino)
  Down The Highway . . . . (Atlantic)
  Life & Times . . . . (Lifesong)
  Photographs & Memories/His Greatest Hits . . . . (Atlantic)

Bangkok Cockfight
Martin Denny; *Exotica-Best Of Martin Denny* . . . . (Rhino)

Beatin' The Odds
Molly Hatchet; *Beatin' The Odds* . . . . (Epic)
  Double Trouble-Live . . . . (Epic)

Bet Your Heart On Me
Johnny Lee; *Johnny Lee's Greatest Hits* . . . . (Full Moon/Asylum)

Betcha Can't Cry Just One
David Frizzell & Shelly West; *In Session* . . . . (Viva)
Betcha Gonna Need My Lovin'
LaToya Jackson; *Heart Don't Lie* . . . . (Private I)
Betcha Say That
Gloria Estefan and Miami Sound Machine; *Let It Loose* . . . . (Epic)
Betcha She Don't Love You
Jessica Simpson; *Sweet Kisses* . . . . (Columbia)
Betcha The Love Bug Bitcha
Dr. Buzzard's Original ''Savannah'' Band; *Dr. Buzzard's Original
''Savannah'' Band* . . . . (RCA)
Betcha' Wouldn't Hurt Me
Quincy Jones; *Quincy Jones-Classics-#3* . . . . (A&M)
Quincy Jones-The Best . . . . (A&M)
The Dude . . . . (A&M)
Caesar's Palace Blues
UK; *Danger Money* . . . . (Editions E.G.)
Night After Night . . . . (Editions E.G.)
Call It A Loan
Jackson Browne; *Hold Out* . . . . (Asylum)
Candyman
Grateful Dead; *American Beauty* . . . . (Warner Bros.)
Dead Set . . . . (Arista)
Casino Boogie
Rolling Stones; *Exile On Main Street* . . . .(Virgin)
Chance For Heaven
Christopher Cross; *Official Music Of The XXIIIrd Olympiad* . . . . (Columbia)
Chance Of Lovin' You
Earl Thomas Conley; *Earl Thomas Conley's Greatest Hits-#2* . . . . (RCA)
Treadin' Water . . . . (RCA)
Chance, A
Kenny Chesney; *I Will Stand* . . . . (BNA)
Chances
Air Supply; *Air Supply's Greatest Hits* . . . . (Arista)
Lost In Love . . . . (Arista)
Chances Are
Bob Marley; *Chances Are* . . . . (Cotillion)
Bob Seger & Martina McBride; *ST/Hope Floats* . . . . (Capitol)
Johnny Mathis; *First 25 Years-Silver Anniversary Album*. . . . . (Columbia)
Johnny Mathis' All-Time Greatest Hits . . . . (Columbia)
Johnny Mathis' Greatest Hits . . . . (Columbia)
Johnny Mathis-Live . . . . (Columbia)
Johnny Mathis-Love Songs . . . . (Columbia)
Connection
Elastica; *Elastica* . . . . (David Geffen Co.)
Crush 'Em
Megadeth; *Risk* . . . .(Trauma)
ST/Universal Soldier II: The Return . . . . (Arista)
Curious
LSG featuring L.L. Cool J, Busta Rhymes & MC Lyte; *Levert-Sweat-
Gill* . . . . (East West)
Deal
Grateful Dead; *Dead Set* . . . . (Arista)
Jerry Garcia; *Garcia* . . . .(Grateful Dead)
Deck Of Cards
''T'' Texas Tyler; *45-#2060* . . . . (Gusto)
Bill Anderson; *American Music Greatest Hits-C* . . . . (Curb)
Best Of Bill Anderson . . . . (Curb)
Tex Ritter; *Capitol Collectors Series-Tex Ritter* . . . . (Capitol)
Tex Ritter's Greatest Hits . . . . (Curb)
Desperado
Clint Black; *Common Thread-Songs Of The Eagles-C* . . . . (Giant)
Eagles; *Desperado*. . . . . (Asylum)
Eagles Live . . . . (Asylum)
Eagles/Their Greatest Hits 1971-1975 . . . . (Asylum)
Hell Freezes Over . . . . (Geffen)
Linda Ronstadt; *Don't Cry Now* . . . . (Asylum)
Linda Ronstadt's Greatest Hits . . . . (Asylum)
Deuces Are Wild
Aerosmith; *Beavis & Butt-Head Experience* . . . . (Geffen)
Devil Went Down To Georgia
Charlie Daniels Band; *A Decade Of Hits* . . . . (Epic)
Billboard Top Hits-1979-C . . . . (Rhino)
Me & The Boys . . . . (Epic)
Million Mile Reflections . . . . (Epic)
ST/Urban Cowboy . . . . (Asylum)
Dime Queen Of Nevada
Tom Jones; *Darlin'* . . . . (Mercury)
Don't Bet Money
Whispers; *Best Of The Whispers* . . . .(Solar)
Don't Bet Money. . . . . (Solar)
Don't Stand Another Chance
Janet Jackson; *Dream Street* . . . . (A&M)
Door #1
LSG; *Levert-Sweat-Gill*. . . . . (East West)
Door Number Three
Jimmy Buffett; *A1A* . . . . (MCA)
Double Dealin' Four Flusher
Doobie Brothers; *Stampede* . . . . (Warner Bros.)

Draw Of The Cards
Kim Carnes; *Mistaken Identity*. . . . . (EMI)
Dyin' Crapshooter's Blues
Blind Willie McTell; *Atlanta Twelve-String* . . . . (Atlantic)
David Bromberg; *How Late'll Ya Play 'Til?* . . . . (Fantasy)
Dyin' Gambler
Blind James Campbell; *Blind James Campbell & His Nashville
Street Band* . . . . (Arhoolie)
Dyin' Gambler's Blues
Bessie Smith; *Bessie Smith-The Complete Recordings-#2*. . . . .(Legacy)
Every Time I Roll The Dice
Delbert McClinton; *Never Been Rocked Enough* . . . .(Curb)
Fat Chance Hotel
Public Image Ltd.; *Happy?* . . . . (Virgin)
Feels Like Love
Vince Gill; *Let's Make Sure We Kiss Goodbye* . . . . (MCA)
France Chance
Ry Cooder; *Ry Cooder* . . . . (Reprise)
From A Jack To A King
Jim Reeves; *I Love You Because* . . . . (RCA)
Jim Reeves-Pure Gold . . . . (RCA)
Ned Miller; *Billboard Top Country Hits-1963-C* . . . .(Rhino)
Ricky Van Shelton; *Loving Proof* . . . .(Columbia)
Gambler
Madonna; *ST/Vision Quest*. . . . . (Geffen)
Gambler
Whitesnake; *Slide It In* . . . . (Geffen)
Gambler
Emerson, Lake & Palmer; *Love Beach*. . . . . (Atlantic)
Gambler, The
Kenny Rogers; *Kenny Rogers' Greatest Hits* . . . . (EMI)
Kenny Rogers-Twenty Greatest Hits . . . . (EMI)
The Gambler . . . . (EMI)
Gambler's Blues
B.B. King; *Back In The Alley* . . . . (MCA)
Great Moments With B.B. King . . . . (MCA)
Otis Rush; *Atlantic Blues-Chicago-C* . . . . (Atlantic)
Gambling Man
Bonnie Raitt; *Sweet Forgiveness* . . . . (Warner Bros.)
Ghost Of A Chance
Rush; *Roll The Bones* . . . . (Atlantic)
Ghost Of A Chance With You
Billie Holiday; *Billie Holiday-Vol. 2* . . . .(Everest)
Stormy Blues . . . . (Verve)
Mel Torme; *Smooth As Velvet* . . . . (Pickwick)
Give Me One More Chance
Exile; *19 Hot Country Requests-#2-C* . . . . (Epic)
Exile's Greatest Hits . . . . (Epic)
Kentucky Hearts . . . . (Epic)
Give Me One More Shot
Alabama; *Alabama's Greatest Hits-#3* . . . . (RCA)
Go Down Gamblin'
Blood, Sweat & Tears; *Blood, Sweat & Tears Greatest Hits* . . . .(Columbia)
Good Run Of Bad Luck
Clint Black; *No Time To Kill* . . . . (RCA)
Guys & Dolls
Original Cast; *ST/Guys & Dolls*. (MCA)
Hearts Of Stone
Bruce Springsteen; *Tracks* . . . .(Columbia)
Southside Johnny And The Asbury Jukes; *Best Of Southside Johnny And The
Asbury Jukes.* . . . .(Legacy)
Cover Me (Bruce Springsteen Tribute)-C . . . .(Rhino)
Hearts Of Stone . . . . (Epic)
Hi Roller
Little Feat; *Time Loves A Hero*. . . . . (Warner Bros.)
Holdin' A Good Hand
Lee Greenwood; *Holdin' A Good Hand* . . . .(Capitol)
House Of Love
Amy Grant & Vince Gill; *House Of Love*. . . . . (A&M)
House Of The Rising Sun
Animals; *Animals Greatest Hits*. (Allegiance)
Best Of The Animals . . . . (Abkco)
Greatest Hits Live!-Rip It To Shreds . . . . (I.R.S.)
Hank Williams, Jr.; *Hank Williams, Jr. ''Live''* . . . .(WB/Curb)
Ronnie Milsap; *Ronnie Milsap-16 Greatest Hits-#2* . . . . (Trip)
I Feel Lucky
Mary Chapin Carpenter; *Come On Come On* . . . .(Columbia)
I Take My Chances
Mary Chapin Carpenter; *Come On Come On* . . . .(Columbia)
If I Lose
Ricky Skaggs and Kentucky Thunder; *Bluegrass Rules!* . . . .(Rounder)
I'll Bet You A Kangaroo
Olivia Newton-John; *Don't Stop Believin'*. . . . . (MCA)
In The Jailhouse Now
Jimmie Rodgers; *First Sessions-1927-1928-#1* . . . .(Rounder)
Short But Brilliant Life . . . . (RCA)
This Is Jimmie Rodgers . . . . (RCA)

Soggy Bottom Boys featuring Jim Blake Nelson; *ST/O Brother, Where Art Thou?* .... (Mercury)
Webb Pierce; *Best Of Webb Pierce*...................................(MCA)
   Webb Pierce-Golden Hits-#2...........................(Plantation)

I've Got The Horse Right Here
Original Cast; *Guys & Dolls* ....(MCA)

Jack O' Diamonds
Blind Snooks Eaglin; *Possum Up A Simmon Tree* ....(Arhoolie)
Odetta; *Odetta* ....(Everest)

Jack Of Hearts
Bob Dylan; *Blood On The Tracks*..........................(Columbia)

Jack Of Speed
Steely Dan; *Two Against Nature*...............................(Giant)

Jack, The
AC/DC; *High Voltage*...(Atco)
   If You Want Blood You've Got It.....................(Atlantic)

Jokers Wild
Paul Hardcastle; *Hardcastle 2* ....(JVC Musical Industries)

Jump
Van Halen; *1984*..(Warner Bros.)
   Best Of Van Halen-#1...............................(Warner Bros.)
   LIVE: Right here, right now..........................(Warner Bros.)

Kentucky Gambler
Merle Haggard & The Strangers; *Songs I'll Always Sing* ....(Capitol)

Knock On Wood
Amii Stewart; *Double Smash Hits-C* ....(Volcano Entertainment)
Buddy Guy; *This Is Buddy Guy*...........................(Vanguard)
Eddie Floyd; *15 Original Big Hits-#3-C*..........................(Stax)
   Atlantic Rhythm & Blues 1947-1974-#6 (1966-1969)-C....(Atlantic)
   Best Of Wattstax-C....................................(Stax)
   Super Oldies Of The '60s-#11-C...............(Audio Fidelity)
Eric Clapton; *Behind The Sun*......................(Duck/Reprise)
Ike & Tina Turner; *Ike & Tina Turner's Greatest Hits-#3* ....(Saja)

Las Vegas Turnaround
Daryl Hall & John Oates; *Abandoned Luncheonette* ....(Atlantic)
   No Goodbyes ....(Atlantic)

Last Chance
John Mellencamp; *Whenever We Wanted*....................(Mercury)

Last Chance
Level 42; *Pursuit Of Accidents* ....(Polydor)

Last Chance
Bryan Adams; *You Want It, You Got It* ....(A&M)

Last Chance Texaco
Rickie Lee Jones; *Naked Songs Live And Acoustic* ....(Reprise)
   Rickie Lee Jones....................................(Warner Bros.)

Let's Go To Vegas
Faith Hill; *It Matters To Me* ....(Warner Bros.)

Lido Shuffle
Boz Scaggs; *Hits!* ....(Columbia)
   Silk Degrees.......................................(Columbia)
   ST/FM..(MCA)

Lily, Rosemary And The Jack Of Hearts
Bob Dylan; *Blood On The Tracks* ....(Columbia)

Little Child
Beatles; *Meet The Beatles!* ....(Capitol)

Lottery Song
Nilsson; *Son Of Schmilsson* ....(RCA)

Louisiana Lou & Three-Card Monty John
Allman Brothers Band; *Win, Lose Or Draw* ....(Polydor)

Luck Be A Lady
Frank Sinatra; *Sinatra Reprise-The Very Good Years* ....(Reprise)
   The Reprise Collection..............................(Reprise)
Original Cast; *Guys & Dolls* ....(MCA)

Lucky Man
Bruce Springsteen; *Tracks* ....(Columbia)

Mister & Mississippi
Patti Page; *Patti Page's Greatest Hits* ....(Columbia)

Moonlight Gambler
Frankie Laine; *Frankie Laine-16 Most Requested Songs* ....(Legacy)
   Frankie Laine's Greatest Hits.......................(Columbia)

No Chance Of Losing
Jerry Garcia; *Jerry Garcia* ....(Warner Bros.)

No Cheap Thrill
Suzanne Vega; *Nine Objects Of Desire* ....(A&M)

Oldest Established (Permanent Floating Crap Game In New York)
Original Cast; *ST/Guys & Dolls* ....(MCA)

One Big Love
Emmylou Harris; *Red Dirt Girl* ....(Nonesuch)
Patty Griffin; *Flaming Red* ....(A&M)

One Of A Kind Pair Of Fools
Barbara Mandrell; *Barbara Mandrell-Greatest Country Hits* ....(Curb)
   Barbara Mandrell's Greatest Hits...................(MCA)
   Spun Gold...(MCA)

One-Eyed Jack
Garland Jeffreys; *Matador & More* ....(A&M)
   One-Eyed Jack.......................................(A&M)

Ooh Las Vegas
Emmylou Harris; *Elite Hotel* ....(Reprise)

Gram Parsons; *Grievous Angel* ....(Reprise)

Overprotected
Britney Spears; *Britney* ....(Jive)

Politics & Poker
Tom Bosley/Original Cast; *ST/Fiorello!* ....(EMI-Angel)

Queen Of Hearts
Dave Edmunds; *Best Of Dave Edmunds* ....(Swan Song)
   Repeat When Necessary..............................(Swan Song)
Juice Newton; *All-Time Country Classics-#2-C* ....(Capitol)
   Juice...(Capitol)
   Juice Newton-Greatest Hits & More..................(Capitol)
   Juice Newton's Greatest Hits ....(Gold Rush)
Rodney Crowell; *Rodney Crowell-Collection* ....(Warner Bros.)

Queen Of Spades
Styx; *Pieces Of Eight* ....(A&M)

Rambler Gambler
Joan Baez; *Very Early Joan Baez* ....(Vanguard)

Ramblin' Gamblin' Man
Bob Seger; *Live Bullet* ....(Capitol)

Rambling, Gambling Willie
Bob Dylan; *The Bootleg Series-Volumes 1-3 [Rare & Unreleased]* .. (Columbia)

Read 'Em & Weep
Barry Manilow; *Barry Manilow's Greatest Hits-#3* ....(Arista)

Ready To Take A Chance Again
Barry Manilow; *Barry Manilow's Greatest Hits-#3* ....(Arista)
   Even Now..(Arista)

Reno
Doug Supernaw; *Red And Rio Grande* ....(BNA)

Riverboat Gambler
Chris LeDoux; *Songs Of Rodeo Life* ....(Capitol)

Roll Of The Dice
Bruce Springsteen; *Human Touch*.........................(Columbia)

Roll The Bones
Rush; *Roll The Bones* ....(Atlantic)

Roll The Dice
Ian Thomas; *Riders On Dark Horses*..........................(RCA)
Ronnie Milsap; *Stranger Things Have Happened*..............(RCA)

Roulette
Bruce Springsteen; *Tracks* ....(Columbia)

Roving Gambler
Everly Brothers; *Songs Our Daddy Taught Us* ....(Rhino)
Peter Rowan; *Walls Of Time* ....(Sugar Hill)
Ramblin' Jack Elliott; *Essential Ramblin' Jack Elliott* ....(Vanguard)

Russian Roulette
Lords Of The New Church; *Killer Lords* ....(I.R.S.)
   Lords Of The New Church............................(I.R.S.)

Russian Roulette
Michelle Shocked; *Captain Swing* ....(Mercury)

Russian Roulette
Taxxi; *Expose* ....(MCA)

Russian Roulette
Hollies; *Hollies* ....(Epic)

Russian Roulette
Accept; *Russian Roulette* ....(Portrait)

Russian Roulette
Joan Armatrading; *Sleight Of Hand* ....(A&M)

Sands Of Nevada
Mark Knopfler; *Sailing To Philadelphia* ....(Warner Bros.)

Save The Last Chance
Johnny Lee; *Keep Me Hangin' On* ....(Full Moon/Warner Bros.)

Second Chance
Reivers; *Pop Beloved* ....(DB)

Second Chance
38 Special; *Rock & Roll Strategy*............................(A&M)

Seven Come Eleven
Benny Goodman; *Benny Goodman-Live At Carnegie Hall*..........(London)
Charlie Christian; *Genius Of The Electric Guitar* ....(Columbia)
Herb Ellis & Joe Pass; *Seven Come Eleven* ....(Concord Jazz)
   Two For The Road...................................(Pablo)

Smoke! Smoke! Smoke!
Commander Cody & His Lost Planet Airmen; *Country Casanova* ...... (MCA)
   Too Much Fun-Best Of Commander Cody & His Lost Planet Airmen ... (MCA)
   We've Got A Live One Here! ....(Warner Bros.)
Doc Watson; *Red Rocking Chair*.........................(Flying Fish)
Johnny Bond & His Red River Valley Boys; *All Time Legends Of Country Music-C*..(Legacy)
Merle Travis; *Johnny Gimble's Texas Honky-Tonk Hits-C*......(C.M.H. Prod.)
Tex Williams; *Birth Of A Dream-Capitol's Early Hits-C* ......(Capitol)
   Dr. Demento Presents The Greatest Novelty Records-#1-1940s & Before-C..(Rhino)

Snake Eyes
Alan Parsons Project; *Turn Of A Friendly Card* ....(Arista)

Solitaire
Elvis Presley; *Always On My Mind* ....(RCA)
   From Elvis Presley Boulevard, Memphis, Tennessee.............(RCA)

Solitaire
Laura Branigan; *Branigan 2* ....(Atlantic)

Solitaire
Stan Kenton; *Artistry In Voices & Brass* . . . .(Creative World)
Solitaire
Johnny Mathis; *Feelings* . . . . (Columbia)
Solitaire
Carpenters; *From The Top*. . . . . (A&M)
   Horizon. . . . . (A&M)
Solitaire
Neil Sedaka; *I'm A Song* . . . .(Fifty One West)
   Solitaire . . . .(Fifty One West)
Solitaire
Jerry Vale; *Jerry Vale's Greatest Hits*. . . . . (Columbia)
Solitaire
Erroll Garner; *Other Voices* . . . . (Columbia)
Solitaire
Jane Olivor; *Stay The Night* . . . . (Columbia)
Solitaire
Public Image Ltd.; *Live In Tokyo*. . . . . (Elektra)
   This Is What You Want...Is What You Get. . . . . (Elektra)
Son Of A Rotten Gambler
Anne Murray; *Anne Murray-Country* . . . . (Capitol)
   Anne Murray-Country Hits. . . . . (Capitol)
   Love Song . . . . (Capitol)
Emmylou Harris; *Cimarron*. . . . . (Warner Bros.)
Stagger Lee
Dion; *Dion-His Best* . . . . (Laurie)
Huey Lewis and the News; *Four Chords & Several Years Ago* . . . . (Elektra)
Ike & Tina Turner; *Best Of Ike & Tina Turner*. . . . . (EMI)
Lloyd Price; *Billboard Top Rock 'N' Roll Hits-1959-C*. . . . . (Rhino)
   Collectables Presents The History Of Rock-#5-C . . . . . (Collectables)
   Lloyd Price's Greatest Hits . . . . (MCA)
   Oldies But Goodies-#1-C . . . .(Original Sound)
Professor Longhair; *Rock 'N' Roll Gumbo* . . . . (Dancing Cat)
Wilson Pickett; *A Man & A Half-Best Of Wilson Pickett*. . . . . (Rhino)
Still Taking Chances
Michael Martin Murphey; *Best Of Michael Martin Murphey* . . . . (Liberty)
   Michael Martin Murphey . . . . (Liberty)
Still The Same
Bob Seger & The Silver Bullet Band; *Stranger In Town* . . . . (Capitol)
Take A Chance
Olivia Newton-John & John Travolta; *ST/Two Of A Kind* . . . . (MCA)
Take A Chance
Eric Clapton; *August* . . . .(Duck/Reprise)
Take A Chance
Divinyls; *Desperate*. . . . . (Chrysalis)
Take A Chance
Bob Seger & The Silver Bullet Band; *Fire Inside* . . . . (Capitol)
Take A Chance
Chicago; *Hot Streets* . . . . (Columbia)
Take A Chance
Kingsnakes; *Take A Chance* . . . . (Blue Wave)
Take A Chance
J; *We Are The Majority* . . . . (A&M)
Take A Chance On Me
Abba; *Abba's Greatest Hits-#2* . . . . (Atlantic)
   Billboard Top Rock 'N' Roll Hits-1978-C . . . . (Rhino)
   Gold-Greatest Hits . . . . (Polydor)
   The Album . . . . (Atlantic)
   The Singles-First 10 Years . . . . (Atlantic)
Take A Chance On Me, Baby
Capitols; *Capitols-Their Greatest Recordings* . . . . (Solid Smoke)
Taking A Chance On Love
Anita O'Day; *Anita Sings The Most*. . . . . (Verve)
Barbra Streisand; *Third Album* . . . . (Columbia)
Benny Goodman; *I Like Jazz-Essence Of Benny Goodman*. . . . . . . (Columbia)
Ella Fitzgerald; *Ella-Fitzgerald-Early Years-#2* . . . . (GRP)
Frank Sinatra; *Songs For Young Lovers & Swing Easy* . . . . (Capitol)
Johnny Mathis & Henry Mancini; *Hollywood Musicals* . . . . (Columbia)
Rosemary Clooney; *Show Tunes* . . . . (Concord Jazz)
Tony Bennett; *I Left My Heart In San Francisco* . . . . (Columbia)
That's My Story
Collin Raye; *Extremes*. . . . . (Epic)
Theme From "Let's Make A Deal"
Original Soundtrack; *Television's Greatest Hits-#5-In Living Color-C* . . . (TVT)
Theme From "Maverick"
Original Soundtrack; *Television's Greatest Hits-#2-C* . . . . (TVT)
Theme From "Mr. Lucky"
Original Soundtrack; *Television's Greatest Hits-#4-Black & White Classics-C* . . . . (TVT)
There's A Place In The World For A Gambler
Dan Fogelberg; *Dan Fogelberg-Souvenirs* . . . . (Full Moon)
   Live-Greetings From The West . . . . (Full Moon)
   ST/FM . . . . (MCA)
Tumbling Dice
Linda Ronstadt; *Linda Ronstadt's Greatest Hits, Volume Two* . . . (Asylum)
   Simple Dreams . . . . (Asylum)
   ST/FM . . . . (MCA)
Rolling Stones; *Exile On Main Street* . . . . (Virgin)

   Love You Live . . . . (Virgin)
   Made In The Shade . . . . (Rolling Stones)
   Rewind (1971-1984) . . . . (Rolling Stones)
Two Of A Kind, Workin' On A Full House
Garth Brooks; *No Fences* . . . . (Capitol)
What About Now
Lonestar; *Lonely Grill* . . . . (BNA)
Wheel Of Fortune
Cardinals; *Atlantic Rhythm & Blues 1947-1974-box-C* . . . . (Atlantic)
Kay Starr; *Capitol Collectors Series-Kay Starr* . . . .(Capitol)
Wheels Of Fortune
Doobie Brothers; *Takin' It To The Streets* . . . . (Warner Bros.)
While You See A Chance
Steve Winwood; *Arc Of A Diver* . . . .(Island)
   Steve Winwood-Chronicles . . . .(Island)
Who Played Poker With Pocahontas?
Fannie Watson; *Music From The New York Stage (1890-1920)-#4-1917-1920-C* . . . . (Pearl)
Win Or Lose
Earth, Wind & Fire; *Faces* . . . .(Columbia)
Win Or Lose
Nitty Gritty Dirt Band; *Dirt, Silver & Gold* . . . . (One Way)
Win Some, Lose Some
Scandal; *Scandal* . . . . (Columbia)
Win Some, Lose Some
Bryan Adams; *Bryan Adams* . . . . (A&M)
Ya Got Trouble
Robert Preston/Original Broadway Cast; *The Music Man* . . . . (Angel)
Robert Preston/Original Cast; *ST/The Music Man* . . . . (Warner Bros.)
   The Music Man . . . . (Gold Rush)
You Better Think Twice
Vince Gill; *When Love Finds You* . . . . (MCA)

GAS STATIONS, Car Repair, Gasoline

   See Also: **CARS (various), ENERGY, MOTORCYCLES, ROAD, TRAVELING, TRUCKS**

---

5 Miles To Empty
Brownstone; *Still Climbing* . . . .(MJJ Music/Work)
Back When Gas Was Thirty Cents A Gallon
Tom T. Hall; *Soldier Of Fortune* . . . . (RCA)
Diesel & Propane
Sandoz; *Unfamiliar Territory* . . . . (Relix)
Dollar's Worth Of Gasoline
Tom Russell; *Hurricane Season*. . . . . (Philo)
Down At The Texaco
Shams; *Quilt*. . . . . (Matador)
Ethelene (The Truckstop Queen)
Ray Stevens; *I Never Made A Record I Didn't Like* . . . . (MCA)
Fill Her Up
Earl Scruggs & Sting; *Earl Scruggs And Friends-C* . . . . (MCA)
Food Phone Gas Lodging
Charlie King; *Food Phone Gas Lodging* . . . . (Flying Fish)
Fuel
Metallica; *Reload*. . . . . (Elektra)
Gas Station Woman
Phil Ochs; *The War Is Over-Best Of Phil Ochs* . . . . (A&M)
Gasoline Alley
Rod Stewart; *Absolutely Live* . . . . (Warner Bros.)
   Best Of Rod Stewart. . . . . (Mercury)
   Gasoline Alley . . . . (Mercury)
   Sing It Again, Rod . . . . (Mercury)
   Storyteller/The Complete Anthology: 1964-1990 . . . . (Warner Bros.)
Gasoline Blues
Charley Jordan; *St. Louis Blues-1929-1935* . . . . (Yazoo)
John Mayall; *Room To Move-1969-1974-Chronicle Series* . . . . . . (Polydor)
Great Filling Station Holdup
Jimmy Buffett; *White Sport Coat & A Pink Crustacean* . . . . (MCA)
Gulf And The Shell
Clinton Gregory; *Clinton Gregory* . . . . (Polydor Country)
Heavy Fuel
Dire Straits; *On Every Street* . . . . (Warner Bros.)
How Bizarre
OMC; *How Bizarre* . . . . (Huh!/Mercury)
I Asked For Water (He Gave Me Gasoline)
Lucinda Williams; *Lucinda Williams*. . . . .(Koch International)
I Asked For Water (She Gave Me Gasoline)
Howlin' Wolf; *Howlin' Wolf-His Best* . . . . (Chess)
   The Blues-#3-C . . . . (Chess)
I Wanna Be With You
Bruce Springsteen; *Tracks* . . . .(Columbia)
Invitation To The Blues
Holly Cole; *Temptation* . . . . (Metro Blue)
Tom Waits; *Small Change* . . . . (Asylum)

It's Hard To Be A Saint In The City
Bruce Springsteen; *Greetings From Asbury Park, N.J.* . . . . (Columbia)
Live 1975-1985 . . . . (Legacy)
Tracks . . . . (Columbia)
David Bowie; *One Step Up/Two Steps Back-The Songs Of Bruce*
Springsteen-C . . . . (Right Stuff)
Jungleland
Bruce Springsteen; *Born To Run.* . . . . (Columbia)
Last Chance Texaco
Rickie Lee Jones; *Naked Songs Live And Acoustic* . . . . (Reprise)
Rickie Lee Jones. . . . .(Warner Bros.)
Little Gasoline, A
Terri Clark; *Fearless.* . . . . (Mercury)
Little Man
Alan Jackson; *High Mileage* . . . . (Arista)
Love And Texaco
Gretchen Peters; *Gretchen Peters.* . . . . (Purple Crayon Prod.)
Master Mechanic
Johnny Winter; *Serious Business* . . . . (Alligator)
Old Home Filler Up & Keep On A Truckin'
C.W. McCall; *C.W. McCall's Greatest Hits* . . . . (Polydor)
Wolf Creek Pass . . . . (MGM)
Open All Night
Bruce Springsteen; *Nebraska* . . . . (Columbia)
Peaches And Diesel
Eric Clapton; *Slowhand* . . . . (Polydor)
Pretty Little Lady From Beaumont, Texas
George Jones; *One Woman Man* . . . .(Epic)
Texas Super Hits-C . . . . (Columbia)
Promised Land
Bruce Springsteen; *Darkness On The Edge Of Town* . . . . (Columbia)
Bruce Springsteen & The E Street Band; *Bruce Springsteen & The E Street*
Band Live/1975-85 . . . . (Legacy)
Rock & Roll Gas Station
Adrenalin O.D.; *Wacky Hi-Jinks Of Adrenalin O.D.* . . . . (Buy Our Records)
Running On Empty
Jackson Browne; *Running On Empty* . . . . (Asylum)
Streak, The
Ray Stevens; *Ray Stevens' Greatest Hits* . . . . (RCA)
Ray Stevens' Greatest Hits. . . . .(MCA)
Ray Stevens-All-Time Greatest Comic Hits . . . . (Curb)
Super Hits Of The '70s-Have A Nice Day-#12-C . . . . (Rhino)
Talkin' At The Texaco
James McMurtry; *Too Long In The Wasteland* . . . . (Columbia)
Texaco Star Theme
Original Soundtrack; *TeeVee Toons-The Commercials-#1-C.* . . . . . (TVT)
Truck Stop
Mills Brothers; *Cab Driver* . . . .(Ranwood)
Truck Stop
Lenny Dee; *Best Of Lenny Dee-#2* . . . .(MCA)
Truck Stop At The End Of The World
Commander Cody; *Let's Rock* . . . .(Blind Pig)
Truck Stop Girl
Byrds; *The Byrds* . . . . (Columbia)
The Byrds (Untitled) . . . . (Legacy)
Little Feat; *Little Feat.* . . . .(Warner Bros.)
Truck Stop Rock
Commander Cody & His Lost Planet Airmen; *Hot Licks, Cold Steel &*
Trucker's Favorites. . . . .(MCA)
Two Pump Texaco
Diamond Rio; *Unbelievable* . . . . (Arista)
Under The Light Of The Texaco
Jeff Stevens & The Bullets; *Jeff Stevens & The Bullets.* . . . .(Atlantic)
Lisa Stewart; *Lisa Stewart* . . . . (BNA)
Walkaway Joe
Trisha Yearwood; *Hearts In Armor* . . . .(MCA)
Songbook-A Collection Of Hits . . . .(MCA)

GENDER CONFLICT, Gender Competition, Man-hating, Misogyny

See Also: *FEMINISM, GENDER STEREOTYPES*

Anything You Can Do (I Can Do Better)
Betty Hutton & Howard Keel; *That's Entertainment! III-C* . . . . (Angel)
Ethel Merman/Bruce Yarnell/Original Cast; *Annie Get*
Your Gun. . . . .(RCA Victor)
Ethel Merman/Ray Middleton/Original Cast; *Annie Get Your Gun* . . . . . .(MCA)
John Raitt & Bonnie Raitt; *Broadway Legend* . . . . (Angel)
Awful
Hole; *Celebrity Skin* . . . . (David Geffen Co.)
Beast Of Burden
Bette Midler; *No Frills* . . . .(Atlantic)
Rolling Stones; *Rewind (1971-1984)* . . . .(Rolling Stones)
Some Girls . . . . (Virgin)
Sucking In The Seventies . . . .(Rolling Stones)

Beep Me 911
Missy ''Misdemeanor'' Elliot; *Supa Dupa Fly* . . . . (East West)
Big Pimpin'
Jay-Z; *Vol. 3-Life & Times of S. Carter* . . . . (Roc-A-Fella/DJMG)
Children Of The Korn
Korn with Ice Cube; *Follow The Leader* . . . . (Immortal/Epic)
Female Of The Species
Space; *Spiders* . . . .(Gut/Universal)
Hymn To Him
Audrey Hepburn; *ST/My Fair Lady.* . . . . (Columbia)
Julie Andrews/Original Cast; *My Fair Lady.* . . . . (Columbia)
I Hate Men
Original Cast; *ST/Kiss Me Kate.* . . . . (Rhino)
Original Cast/Patricia Morrison; *Kiss Me Kate* . . . . (Sony Music Classical)
If You Wanna Be Happy
Jimmy Soul; *Best Of Jimmy Soul.* . . . . (Rhino)
Dick Bartley's One-Hit Wonders Of The '60s-#1-C . . . . (Rhino)
Son Of Frat Rock!-C . . . . (Rhino)
ST/Mermaids . . . . (Geffen)
ST/My Best Friend's Wedding . . . .(Work/Epic)
I'm An Ordinary Man
Rex Harrison/Original Cast; *My Fair Lady* . . . . (Columbia)
It Wasn't God Who Made Honky Tonk Angels
Kitty Wells; *Grand Ole Opry-75 Years-#1-C* . . . . (MCA)
Kitty Wells' Greatest Hits. . . . .(Step One)
The Kitty Wells Story . . . . (MCA)
Just A Girl
No Doubt; *Tragic Kingdom* . . . .(Trauma)
Kill You
Eminem; *The Marshall Mathers LP* . . . . (Aftermath/Interscope)
Livin' It Up
Ja Rule; *Pain Is Love* . . . .(Murder Inc./Def Jam/IDJMG)
Man Smart, Woman Smarter
Harry Belafonte; *Harry Belafonte-Pure Gold.* . . . .(RCA)
Robert Palmer; *Some People Can Do What They Like* . . . . (Island)
Rosanne Cash; *I Am Woman-C* . . . .(Nick At Nite)
Right Or Wrong . . . .(Columbia)
No Man's Woman
Sinead O'Connor; *Faith & Courage* . . . .(Atlantic)
One Minute Man
Missy ''Misdemeanor'' Elliot; *Miss E...So*
Addictive . . . . (Gold Mind/East West/EEG)
Ooh La La
Rod Stewart; *When We Were The New Boys* . . . . (Warner Bros.)
Pill, The
Loretta Lynn; *Loretta Lynn-20 Greatest Hits* . . . . (MCA)
The Country Music Hall Of Fame-Loretta Lynn. . . . . (MCA)
Project Chick/Project Bitch
Cash Money Millionaires; *12'' Maxi Single* . . . . (Cash Money/Universal)
Real Slim Shady
Eminem; *The Marshall Mathers LP* . . . . (Aftermath/Interscope)
Shake Ya Ass
Mystikal; *Let's Get Ready.* . . . .(Jive)
Strut
Sheena Easton; *Best Of Sheena Easton* . . . . (EMI)
Dance Mix . . . . (EMI)
Private Heaven. . . . . (EMI)
The World Of Sheena Easton: The Singles Collection-C . . . . (EMI)
What You Want
DMX; *...And Then There Was X* . . . .(Ruff Ryders/IDJMG)

GENDER STEREOTYPES, Traditional Female, Traditional Male

See Also: *FEMINISM, GENDER CONFLICT*

(You're) Having My Baby
Paul Anka; *'70s Party Killers-C* . . . . (Rhino)
Five Decades Of Hits . . . . (Curb)
Paul Anka-His Best . . . . (EMI)
Paul Anka-Live . . . . (Columbia)
Times Of Your Life . . . .(United Artists)
Anything You Can Do (I Can Do Better)
Betty Hutton & Howard Keel; *That's Entertainment! III-C* . . . . (Angel)
Ethel Merman/Bruce Yarnell/Original Cast; *Annie Get*
Your Gun . . . .(RCA Victor)
Ethel Merman/Ray Middleton/Original Cast; *Annie Get Your Gun* . . . . . (MCA)
John Raitt & Bonnie Raitt; *Broadway Legend.* . . . . (Angel)
Barbie Girl
Aqua; *Aquarium* . . . . (MCA)
Now That's What I Call Music!-#1-C . . . .(Virgin)
Born A Woman
Sandy Posey; *Best Of Sandy Posey-With Skeeter Davis* . . . . (Gusto)
Best Of Town & Country-#3-C . . . . (Gusto)
Cruisin'-1966-C . . . . (Increase)
Sandy Posey/Skeeter Davis/Wanda Jackson . . . . (Gusto)

Super Hits-#5-C . . . . (Gusto)
Boy Wanted
  Original Cast; *My One And Only* . . . . (Atlantic)
Buttons And Bows
  Dinah Shore; *16 Most Requested Songs Of The '40s-#1-C* . . . . (Legacy)
  Golden Hits Of The '40s-C . . . . (Columbia Special Prod.)
  Gene Autry; *Ridin' West-#2-C* . . . . (Crescendo)
  Songs Of The West-#3-Gene Autry & Roy Rogers-C . . . . (Rhino)
Cherchez La Femme
  Dr. Buzzard's Original ''Savannah'' Band; *Nipper's Greatest Hits Of The
    '70s-C* . . . . (RCA)
  Gloria Estefan; *Hold Me, Thrill Me, Kiss Me* . . . . (Epic)
El Macho
  Mark Knopfler; *Sailing To Philadelphia* . . . . (Warner Bros.)
Gigi
  Charles Boyer; *Romantic Songs Of Love* . . . . (Everest)
  Louis Jordan; *ST/Gigi* . . . . (Sony Music Special Prod.)
Girl That I Marry, The
  Dick Haymes; *Best Of Dick Haymes* . . . . (MCA)
  Doris Day/Original Cast; *Annie Get Your Gun* . . . . (Columbia)
  Original Broadway Cast; *Annie Get Your Gun* . . . . (Angel)
  Original Cast; *Annie Get Your Gun* . . . . (MCA)
Good Lovin' (Makes It Right)
  Tammy Wynette; *Tammy Wynette-16 Biggest Hits* . . . . (Legacy)
  Tammy Wynette-Anniversary-20 Years Of Hits . . . . (Epic)
  Tears Of Fire-25th Anniversary Collection . . . . (Epic)
Guy Is A Guy, A
  Doris Day; *Doris Day's Greatest Hits* . . . . (Columbia)
Guys & Dolls
  Original Cast; *ST/Guys & Dolls* . . . . (MCA)
Guys Do It All The Time
  Mindy McCready; *Ten Thousand Angels* . . . . (BNA)
Harry's House Centerpiece
  Joni Mitchell; *Hissing Of Summer Lawns* . . . . (Asylum)
Honey, I'm Home
  Shania Twain; *Come On Over* . . . . (Mercury)
I Can't Do That Anymore
  Faith Hill; *It Matters To Me* . . . . (Warner Bros.)
I Enjoy Being A Girl
  Original Cast; *Flower Drum Song* . . . . (Sony Music Classical)
I Feel Pretty
  Julie Andrews; *A Little Bit Of Broadway* . . . . (Columbia)
  Little Richard; *The Songs Of West Side Story* . . . . (RCA Victor)
  Original Cast; *ST/West Side Story* . . . . (Sony Broadway)
I Take It Back
  Sandy Posey; *Best Of Sandy Posey* . . . . (Collectables)
  Best Of Sandy Posey-With Skeeter Davis . . . . (Gusto)
I Want A Girl (Just Like The Girl)
  Al Jolson; *The Al Jolson Story-#1* . . . . (MCA)
  Spike Jones & His City Slickers; *King Of Corn* . . . . (Glendale)
I Will Follow Him
  Little Peggy March; *Nipper's Greatest Hits Of The '60s-#1-C* . . . . . . (RCA)
I Will Survive
  Gloria Gaynor; *Billboard Top Hits-1979-C* . . . . (Rhino)
  I Am Woman-C . . . . (Nick At Nite)
  Love Tracks . . . . (Polydor)
  The Disco Years-#2-On The Beat-1978-1982-C . . . . (Rhino)
I Will…But
  SHeDAISY; *The Whole Shebang* . . . . (Lyric Street)
I'm A Man
  Bo Diddley; *Bo Diddley-His Best* . . . . (Chess)
  Super Blues . . . . (Chess)
  *The Sopranos-Music From The HBO Original
    Series* . . . . (Sony Music Soundtrax)
  Yardbirds; *Five Live Yardbirds* . . . . (Rhino)
  History Of British Rock-#3-C . . . . (Rhino)
  Yardbirds' Greatest Hits-#1 (1964-1966) . . . . (Rhino)
I'm A Woman
  Maria Muldaur; *Waitress In The Donut Shop* . . . . (Warner Archives)
  Peggy Lee; *I Am Woman-C* . . . . (Nick At Nite)
  Peggy Lee's All-Time Greatest Hits . . . . (Curb)
  Reba McEntire; *Out Of A Dream* . . . . (Mercury)
I'm An Ordinary Man
  Rex Harrison/Original Cast; *My Fair Lady* . . . . (Columbia)
I'm That Kind Of Girl
  Patty Loveless; *On Down The Line* . . . . (MCA)
  Patty Loveless' Greatest Hits . . . . (MCA)
I've Never Been To Me
  Charlene; *Endless Love-Motown's Greatest Love Songs-C* . . . . . . (Motown)
  Hard-To-Find Motown Classics-#2-C . . . . (Motown)
  I've Never Been To Me . . . . (Motown)
  Motown Memories-#4-C . . . . (Motown)
It Works
  Alabama; *In Pictures* . . . . (RCA)
Just A Girl
  No Doubt; *Tragic Kingdom* . . . . (Trauma)
Keep Young And Beautiful
  Annie Lennox; *Diva* . . . . (Arista)

Legend Of A Cowgirl
  Imani Coppola; *Chupacapra* . . . . (Columbia)
Little Plastic Castle
  Ani DiFranco; *Little Plastic Castle* . . . . (Righteous Babe)
Lonely Women Make Good Lovers
  Bob Luman; *Bob Luman-Classic Country* . . . . (Simitar)
  Steve Wariner; *Best Of Steve Wariner* . . . . (RCA)
  Midnight Fire . . . . (RCA)
  Steve Wariner's Greatest Hits . . . . (RCA)
  Steve Wariner-Super Hits . . . . (RCA)
Man Ain't Supposed To Cry
  Public Announcement; *Don't Hold Back* . . . . (RCA)
Mannish Boy
  Muddy Waters; *Electric Mud* . . . . (Chess)
  King Of The Electric Blues . . . . (Legacy)
  The Best Blues Album In The World…Ever!-C . . . . (Virgin)
Music To Watch Girls By
  Andy Williams; *Andy Williams' Greatest Hits-#2* . . . . (Columbia)
Occasional Wife
  Faron Young; *Faron Young-Golden Hits* . . . . (Mercury)
One's On The Way (Here In Topeka)
  Loretta Lynn; *Loretta Lynn-20 Greatest Hits* . . . . (MCA)
  Loretta Lynn-Greatest Hits Live . . . . (K-Tel)
  Loretta Lynn's Greatest Hits-#2 . . . . (MCA)
  The Country Music Hall Of Fame-Loretta Lynn . . . . (MCA)
Pill, The
  Loretta Lynn; *Loretta Lynn-20 Greatest Hits* . . . . (MCA)
  The Country Music Hall Of Fame-Loretta Lynn . . . . (MCA)
Put Your Dreams Away (For Another Day)
  Frank Sinatra; *Best Of The Columbia Years-1943-1952* . . . . . . (Columbia)
  Frank Sinatra-16 Most Requested Songs . . . . (Columbia)
  Sinatra: A Man And His Music . . . . (Reprise)
  The Capitol Years . . . . (Capitol)
  Mickey Gilley; *Put Your Dreams Away* . . . . (Epic)
  Ten Years Of Hits . . . . (Epic)
Race Is On
  Dave Edmunds; *Best Of Dave Edmunds* . . . . (Swan Song)
  Twangin' . . . . (Swan Song)
  George Jones; *Best Of George Jones-1955-1967* . . . . (Rhino)
  Billboard Top Country Hits-1964-C . . . . (Rhino)
  George Jones' All-Time Greatest Hits . . . . (Epic)
  Sawyer Brown; *Boys Are Back* . . . . (Curb)
  Sawyer Brown's Greatest Hits . . . . (Curb)
Real Live Woman
  Trisha Yearwood; *Real Live Woman* . . . . (MCA)
Run For Your Life
  Beatles; *Beatles-Box Set* . . . . (Capitol)
  Rubber Soul . . . . (Capitol)
Simple Joys Of Maidenhood
  Julie Andrews; *Camelot* . . . . (Columbia)
  Various Artists; *ST/Camelot* . . . . (Warner Bros.)
Single Girl
  Sandy Posey; *Greatest Hits Of 1966-C* . . . . (Deluxe)
Sweet Old Fashioned Girl, A
  Teresa Brewer; *Music! Music! Music!-Best Of Teresa
    Brewer* . . . . (Varese Vintage)
Tammy
  Columbia Ballroom Orchestra; *Let's Dance-#7-Competition Dance* . . . (Denon)
  Debbie Reynolds; *Best Of Debbie Reynolds* . . . . (Curb)
  Tammy . . . . (MCA Special Prod.)
  Roger Williams; *Roger Williams' Greatest Hits* . . . . (MCA)
Testosterone
  Bush; *Sixteen Stone* . . . . (Trauma)
Thank Heaven For Little Girls
  Maurice Chevalier; *ST/Gigi* . . . . (Sony Music Special Prod.)
  Merle Haggard & Janie Fricke; *It's All In The Game* . . . . (Epic)
That's The Way Boys Are
  Lesley Gore; *Golden Hits Of Lesley Gore* . . . . (Mercury)
That's The Way I've Always Heard It Should Be
  Carly Simon; *Best Of Carly Simon* . . . . (Elektra)
  Carly Simon . . . . (Elektra)
Theme From ''All In The Family''
  Original Soundtrack; *CBS: The First 50 Years* . . . . (TVT)
  Television's Greatest Hits-#3-1970s & 1980s-C . . . . (TVT)
Theme From ''Who's The Boss''
  Original Soundtrack; *Television's Greatest Hits-#6-Remote Control-C* . . . (TVT)
There Is Nothin' Like A Dame
  Original Cast; *South Pacific* . . . . (CBS Masterworks)
Typical Male
  Tina Turner; *Break Every Rule* . . . . (Capitol)
  Hot Ladies Of The '80s-C . . . . (K-Tel)
  Live In Europe . . . . (Capitol)
  Simply The Best . . . . (Capitol)
Under My Thumb
  Rolling Stones; *''Still Life'' (American Concert 1981)* . . . . (Virgin)
  12 X 5 . . . . (Abkco)
  Aftermath . . . . (Abkco)
  got Live if you want it! . . . . (Abkco)
  Hot Rocks 1964-1971 . . . . (Abkco)

Who; *Odds & Sods* . . . .(MCA)
   Who's Missing . . . .(MCA)
Video
  India.Arie; *Acoustic Soul* . . . . (Motown)
Walk Like A Man
  4 Seasons; *4 Seasons' Greatest Hits-#1* . . . . (Rhino)
   4 Seasons-Anthology . . . . (Rhino)
   Billboard Top Rock 'N' Roll Hits-1963-C . . . . (Rhino)
   ST/The Wanderers . . . .(Warner Bros.)
Walk Like A Man
  Bruce Springsteen; *Tunnel Of Love* . . . . (Columbia)
What It Feels Like For A Girl
  Madonna; *GHV2* . . . .(Warner Bros.)
   Music . . . . (Maverick)
Where Have All The Cowboys Gone?
  Paula Cole; *This Fire* . . . . (Imago)
You Don't Own Me
  Joan Jett; *Bad Reputation* . . . .(Blackheart)
  Lesley Gore; *Billboard Top Pop Hits-1964-C* . . . . (Rhino)
Your Good Girl's Gonna Go Bad
  Billie Jo Spears; *Best Of Billie Jo Spears* . . . . . (CEMA Special Prod.)
   Best Of Billie Jo Spears . . . . (Razor & Tie)
  K.T. Oslin; *Tammy Wynette...Remembered-C* . . . . (Asylum)
  Tammy Wynette; *Tammy Wynette-Anniversary-20 Years Of Hits* . . . .(Epic)
   Tammy Wynette's Greatest Hits . . . .(Epic)
   Your Good Girl's Gonna Go Bad . . . . (Legacy)

GENTLE, Delicate, Soft, Tender
See Also: CHARACTER & INTEGRITY, HELP, LOVE (various)

After Tonight
  Mariah Carey; *Rainbow* . . . . (Columbia)
And I Love Her
  Beatles; *ST/A Hard Day's Night* . . . . (Capitol)
   The Beatles/1962-1966 . . . . (Capitol)
   The Beatles-Anthology-#1 . . . . (Capitol)
Blessed
  Christina Aguilera; *Christina Aguilera*. . . . . (RCA)
Burn To Shine
  Ben Harper; *Burn To Shine* . . . . (Virgin)
Come Softly To Me
  Fleetwoods; *Come Softly To Me: The Very Best Of The Fleetwoods* . . . . .(EMI)
   Only Love-1955-1959-C . . . . (Rhino)
Fair And Tender Ladies
  Whites; *A Lifetime In The Making* . . . . (Ceili Music)
Flow Gently, Sweet Afton
  Mormon Tabernacle Choir; *Old Beloved Songs* . . . . . . (Columbia)
Gentle Annie
  Kate & Anna McGarrigle; *The McGarrigle Hour* . . . . . (Hannibal)
  Linda Ronstadt; *Linda Ronstadt-Box Set* . . . . (Elektra)
  Makem & Clancy; *The Makem & Clancy Collection* . . . . (Shanachie)
Gentle On My Mind
  Elvis Presley; *From Elvis In Memphis* . . . . (RCA)
   Great Country Songs . . . . (RCA)
  Glen Campbell; *Best Of Austin City Limits-Legends Of Country Music-C* . . . . (Legacy)
   Best Of Glen Campbell . . . . (Capitol)
   Glen Campbell-Best Of The Early Years . . . . (Curb)
  John Hartford; *Me Oh My-How The Time Does Fly-Anthology* . . . . (Flying Fish)
  Patti Page; *Patti Page-16 Most Requested Songs* . . . . . . (Legacy)
Gentle Place, A
  Clannad; *Banba* . . . . (Atlantic)
  Lisa Lynne; *Daughters Of The Celtic Moon* . . . . . . (Windham Hill)
Gentle Rain
  Astrud Gilberto; *Compact Jazz-Best Of Bossa Nova Compact Jazz-C* . . . (Verve)
   The Silver Collection: The Astrud Gilberto Album . . . . (Verve)
  Tony Bennett; *The Movie Song Album* . . . . (Columbia)
Gentle Rains Of Home
  George Morgan; *45-#32886* . . . . (Decca)
Gentle To Your Senses
  Mel McDaniel; *Gentle To Your Senses* . . . . (Capitol)
Killing Me Softly With His Song
  Fugees; *Score* . . . . (Ruffhouse)
  Luther Vandross; *Songs* . . . .(Epic)
  Roberta Flack; *Atlantic Rhythm & Blues 1947-1974-#6 (1966-1969)-C* . . . .(Atlantic)
   Best Of Roberta Flack . . . . (Atlantic)
   Golden Age Of Black Music-1970-1975-C . . . . (Atlantic)
   Killing Me Softly . . . . (Atlantic)
Learning As You Go
  Rick Trevino; *Learning As You Go* . . . . (Columbia)
   Super Hits Of 1996-C . . . .(Epic)
Let's Make A Night To Remember
  Bryan Adams; *18 Til I Die* . . . . (A&M)
Love Me Tender
  Elvis Presley; *Elvis* . . . . (RCA)
   Elvis Aron Presley . . . . (RCA)

   Elvis' Golden Records . . . . (RCA)
   Elvis-A Legendary Performer, Volume 1 . . . . (RCA)
   Worldwide 50 Gold Award Hits, Vol. 1, Parts 1 & 2 . . . .(RCA)
Marie
  Tommy Dorsey & His Orchestra; *Seventeen Number Ones* . . . .(RCA)
Moon, Turn The Tides...Gently Gently Away
  Jimi Hendrix Experience; *Electric Ladyland* . . . . (Reprise)
Nice And Easy
  Walter Beasley; *For Your Pleasure*. . . . .(Shanachie)
Oh! My Papa
  Eddie Fisher; *Eddie Fisher's All-Time Greatest Hits-#1* . . . . (RCA)
   Hebrew National Kosher Classics-C . . . . (RCA)
   Nipper's Greatest Hits Of The '50s-#2-C . . . . (RCA)
Row, Row, Row Your Boat
  Bobby Darin/Johnny Mercer/Billy May Orchestra; *Two Of A Kind* . . . .(Atlantic)
  Original Soundtrack; *Children's Favorites* . . . .(Kid Rhino/Rhino 4 Kids)
  Spike Jones & His City Slickers; *King Of Corn*. . . . . . (Glendale)
San Francisco (Be Sure To Wear Some Flowers In Your Hair)
  Scott McKenzie; *Nuggets-#10-Folk Rock-C* . . . . (Rhino)
   Rock Artifacts-From The Vaults-#3-C . . . . (Columbia)
   ST/Forrest Gump . . . .(Epic/Sony Music Soundtrax)
   Summer Of Love-#1-C . . . . (Rhino)
Sentimental Lady
  Fleetwood Mac; *25 Years-The Chain* . . . . (Warner Bros.)
   Bare Trees . . . . (Reprise)
Seven Rooms Of Gloom
  Four Tops; *Four Tops' Greatest Hits* . . . . (Motown)
   Four Tops Reach Out . . . . (Motown)
   Four Tops-Anthology . . . . (Motown)
Shout
  Beatles; *The Beatles-Anthology-#1* . . . . (Capitol)
  Isley Brothers; *Nipper's Greatest Hits Of The '50s-#2-C* . . . . . .(RCA)
   Shout. . . . . (Collectables)
   ST/The Wanderers . . . . (Warner Bros.)
  Joey Dee & the Starliters; *Echoes Of A Rock Era-Later Years-C* . . . . (Roulette)
   Hey Let's Twist! Best Of Joey Dee & The Starliters . . . . (Rhino)
   Live At The Peppermint Lounge . . . . (Accord)
   Original Rock 'N' Roll Hits Of The '60s-C . . . . (Roulette)
   Sock Hoppin' Sixties-C. . . . .(JCI Assoc. Labels)
  Otis Day & The Knights; *Shout*. . . . . (MCA)
   ST/Animal House . . . . (MCA)
  Tom Petty And The Heartbreakers; *Pack Up The Plantation-Live!* . . . . . (MCA)
Soft
  Second Coming; *Second Coming* . . . . (Capitol)
Soft
  Bill Doggett; *All His Hits* . . . . (King)
   Doggett Beat For Dancing Feet . . . . (King)
Soft And Wet
  Prince; *The Hits 1* . . . . (Paisley Park)
   The Hits/The B-Sides . . . . (Paisley Park)
Soft Hearted Hana
  George Harrison; *George Harrison*. . . . .(Dark Horse)
Soft Lights And Hard Country Music
  Moe Bandy; *Honky Tonk Amnesia-The Hard Country Sound Of Moe Bandy* . . . . (Razor & Tie)
Soft Lights And Sweet Music
  John Coltrane; *John Coltrane And The Jazz Giants* . . . . . . (Fantasy)
  Victor Young & The Brunswick Orchestra with Bing Crosby; *Irving Berlin: A Hundred Years-C* . . . . (Columbia)
Soft Lips
  Hank Thompson and His Brazos Valley Boys; *45-#40211* . . . . (Capitol)
Soft Place To Fall
  Allison Moorer; *Alabama Song*. . . . . (MCA)
   ST/The Horse Whisperer . . . . (MCA)
Soft Rain
  Ray Price; *Ray Price's Greatest Hits-#1-3* . . . .(Step One)
Soft Sands
  Chordettes; *Best Of The Chordettes* . . . . (Rhino)
   Golden Classics-Chordettes. . . . . (Collectables)
Soft Shoe
  Gerry Mulligan; *Gerry Mulligan's Greatest Hits* . . . . . (RCA Victor)
Soft Summer Breeze
  Diamonds; *45-#70934*. . . . . (Mercury)
  Eddie Heywood; *Chart Toppers-Romantic Hits Of The '50s-C* . . . (Priority)
   Great Instrumental Hits Of The '50s-'80s-C . . . . . . (Rebound)
Soft, Sweet And Warm
  David Houston; *45-#10870*. (Epic)
Softest Place On Earth
  Xscape; *Traces Of My Lipstick* . . . . (So So Def/Columbia)
Softest Touch In Town
  Bobby G. Rice; *45-#031* . . . . (Republic/Universal)
Softly And Tenderly (I'll Hold You In My Arms)
  Lewis Pruitt; *45-#31095* . . . . (Decca)
Softly Whispering I Love You
  English Congregation; *Super Hits Of The '70s-Have A Nice Day-#7-C* . . (Rhino)
  Mike Curb Congregation; *Your Favorite Songs-C* . . . . . . (Curb)
  Paul Young; *From Time To Time-The Singles Collection* . . . (Columbia)
Softly, As I Leave You
  Brenda Lee; *In The Mood For Love: Classic Ballads* . . . . (Hip-O)

Elvis Presley; *Elvis Aron Presley* . . . . (RCA)
Frank Sinatra; *Frank Sinatra's Greatest Hits-#1* . . . . (Reprise)
Sinatra: A Man And His Music . . . . (Reprise)

Softly, As In A Morning Sunrise
Artie Shaw; *Artie Shaw Plays 22 Original Big Band Recordings-1938-1939* . . . . (Hindsight)
Big Bands In Hi-Fi-#1-Let's Dance-C . . . . (Capitol)
Bing Crosby; *Bing: His Legendary Years-1931-1957* . . . . (MCA)
Bobby Darin; *That's All* . . . . (Atlantic)
Dianne Reeves; *I Remember* . . . . (Blue Note)
Sonny Rollins; *Best Of Sonny Rollins-The Blue Note Years* . . . . (Blue Note)

Softly, Softly
Jaye P. Morgan; *45-#6016* . . . . (RCA Victor)

Sweet Afton
Nickel Creek; *Nickel Creek* . . . . (Sugar Hill)

Tender Hearted Sue
Rambling Rogue; *45-#6747* . . . . (Okeh)

Tender Is The Night
Andy Williams; *Moon River & Other Great Movie Themes* . . . . (Columbia)
Tony Bennett; *I Left My Heart In San Francisco* . . . . (Columbia)
Tony Bennett-16 Most Requested Songs . . . . (Legacy)

Tender Is The Night
Jackson Browne; *Lawyers In Love* . . . . (Asylum)

Tender Kisses
Tracie Spencer; *Make The Difference* . . . . (Capitol)

Tender Lie
Restless Heart; *Best Of Restless Heart* . . . . (RCA)
Big Dreams In A Small Town . . . . (RCA)
Restless Heart's Greatest Hits . . . . (RCA)

Tender Love
Force MD's; *For Lovers & Others-Greatest Hits* . . . . (Tommy Boy)
Smooth Grooves-A Sensual Collection-#2-C . . . . (Rhino)

Tender Love
Derek And The Dominos; *The Layla Sessions-20th Anniversary Edition* . . . . (Polydor)

Tender Lover
Babyface; *Tender Lover* . . . . (Solar)

Tender Moment, A
Lee Roy Parnell; *Hits And Highways Ahead* . . . . (Arista)
Love Without Mercy . . . . (Arista)
Pure Country-Best Of The '90s-C . . . . (Priority)

Tender Shepherd
Original Cast; *Peter Pan-The 1954 Broadway Production* . . . . (RCA Victor)

Tender Time
Louise Mandrell; *Best Of Louise Mandrell* . . . . (BNA)

Tender Trap (Love Is The)
Frank Sinatra; *At The Movies* . . . . (Capitol)
Best Of The Capitol Years . . . . (Capitol)
Frank Sinatra Sings The Songs Of Van Heusen & Cahn . . . . (Reprise)
Very Best Of Frank Sinatra . . . . (Reprise)
Sammy Cahn; *Evening With Sammy Cahn* . . . . (DRG)

Tender When I Want To Be
Mary Chapin Carpenter; *Stones In The Road* . . . . (Columbia)

Tender Years
George Jones; *Best Of George Jones-1955-1967* . . . . (Rhino)
Billboard Top Country Hits-1961-C . . . . (Rhino)
Essential George Jones-The Spirit Of Country . . . . (Legacy)

Tenderest Kiss
Divine Horsemen; *Devil's River* . . . . (SST)

Tenderly
Billie Holiday; *Verve Jazz Masters 47-Billie Holiday Sings Standards*. . . (Verve)
Ella Fitzgerald; *Verve Jazz Masters 24* . . . . (Verve)
Oscar Peterson; *Essential Oscar Peterson-The Swinger* . . . . (Verve)
Rosemary Clooney; *Essence Of Rosemary Clooney* . . . . (Legacy)
Rosemary Clooney-16 Most Requested Songs . . . . (Legacy)
Sarah Vaughan; *Compact Jazz-Sarah Vaughan* . . . . (Verve)
Verve Jazz Masters 42-The Jazz Sides . . . . (Verve)
Tony Bennett; *Here's To The Ladies* . . . . (Columbia)

Tenderness
Colour Club; *Sexuality* . . . . (JVC Musical Industries)

Tenderness On The Block
Warren Zevon; *Excitable Boy* . . . . (Asylum)

Theme From "Gentle Ben"
Original Soundtrack; *Television's Greatest Hits-#5-In Living Color-C* . . . (TVT)

Try A Little Tenderness
Aretha Franklin; *Sweet Bitter Love* . . . . (Columbia)
David Sanborn; *ST/The Mirror Has Two Faces* . . . . (Columbia)
Otis Redding; *Best Of Otis Redding* . . . . (Atco)
Best Of Otis Redding . . . . (Atlantic)
Live In Europe . . . . (Atco)
The Otis Redding Story . . . . (Atlantic)
Very Best Of Otis Redding . . . . (Rhino)
Three Dog Night; *Best Of Three Dog Night* . . . . (MCA)

Try A Little Tenderness
Marty Robbins; *Don't Let Me Touch You* . . . . (Columbia)
Marty Robbins' Greatest Hits-#4 . . . . (Columbia)

Walk Softly On This Heart Of Mine
Bill Monroe; *The Country Music Hall Of Fame-Bill Monroe* . . . . (MCA)
Joey Welz; *Lovin' My Country* . . . . (Capricorn)

Kentucky HeadHunters; *Best Of The Kentucky HeadHunters-Still Pickin'* . . . . (Mercury)
Pickin' On Nashville . . . . (Mercury)
Ricky Skaggs and the Dixie Chicks; *Ricky Skaggs & Friends-Big Mon: Songs Of Bill Monroe* . . . . (Skaggs Family)

While My Guitar Gently Weeps
Beatles; *Beatles-Box Set* . . . . (Capitol)
The Beatles (White Album) . . . . (Capitol)
The Beatles/1967-1970 . . . . (Capitol)
George Harrison; *Best Of George Harrison* . . . . (Capitol)
Concert For Bangladesh-C . . . . (Capitol)
Live In Japan . . . . (Dark Horse)

Woman's Touch
Toby Keith; *Blue Moon* . . . . (Polydor Country)

GOD, Church, Faiths Of The World, Jesus Christ, Prayer, Religion

See Also: **ANGELS, BAD (sin), CHARACTER & INTEGRITY, CHRISTMAS, EASTER, FAITH, FORGIVE, GRATITUDE, HEAVEN, HELL, MARRIAGE, TEACHING VALUES**

(Hey Lord) Don't Ask Me Questions
Graham Parker And The Rumour; *The Parkerilla* . . . . (Mercury)

(Love Will) Find A Way
Amy Grant; *Unguarded* . . . . (A&M)

800 Pound Jesus
Sawyer Brown; *Drive Me Wild* . . . . (Curb)

Adam Raised A Cain
Bruce Springsteen; *Darkness On The Edge Of Town* . . . . (Columbia)

Affirmation
Savage Garden; *Affirmation* . . . . (Columbia)

Ain't No God In Mexico
Waylon Jennings; *Honky Tonk Heroes* . . . . (RCA)

Alive
P.O.D.; *Satellite* . . . . (Atlantic)

All God's Chillun Got Rhythm
Judy Garland; *Judy Garland-Collector's Items-1936-1945* . . . . (MCA)

All My Life
K-Ci & JoJo; *Love Always* . . . . (MCA)
Now That's What I Call Music!-#1-C . . . . (Virgin)

Am I The Only One (Who's Ever Felt This Way)
Dixie Chicks; *Wide Open Spaces* . . . . (Monument)

Amazing Grace
Jeff Beck; *All-Star Christmas-C* . . . . (Epic)
Judy Collins; *Colors Of The Day-The Best Of Judy Collins* . . . . (Elektra)
Whales & Nightingales . . . . (Elektra)
Maverick Choir; *ST/Maverick* . . . . (Atlantic)
Nitty Gritty Dirt Band; *Will The Circle Be Unbroken-#2-C* . . . . (Uni)
Tramaine Hawkins; *God Bless America-C* . . . . (Columbia)

Amen Kind Of Love
Daryle Singletary; *All Because Of You* . . . . (Giant)
Wedding Day Music-C . . . . (Reprise)

American Pie
Don McLean; *American Pie* . . . . (EMI)
Best Of Don McLean . . . . (EMI)
Greatest Hits Then & Now . . . . (EMI)
ST/Born On The Fourth Of July . . . . (MCA)
Madonna; *ST/The Next Big Thing* . . . . (Maverick)

American Prayer
Doors; *An American Prayer-Jim Morrison* . . . . (Elektra)

Amukiriki
Les Paul; *Legend And The Legacy* . . . . (Gold Rush)

Angel
Lionel Richie; *Renaissance* . . . . (Island/IDJMG)

Angel Band
Emmylou Harris; *Angel Band* . . . . (Warner Bros.)
Stanley Brothers; *ST/O Brother, Where Art Thou?* . . . . (Mercury)
Stanley Brothers & The Clinch Mountain Boys; *Best Of Bluegrass-#1-Standards-C* . . . . (Mercury)

Angel On My Bike
Wallflowers; *Bringing Down The Horse* . . . . (Interscope)

Angel On My Shoulder
Natalie Cole; *Natalie Cole's Greatest Hits-#1* . . . . (Elektra)

Angel Without A Prayer
Deana Carter; *Love Shouldn't Hurt-C* . . . . (Qwest)

Angels Would Fall
Melissa Etheridge; *Breakdown* . . . . (Island)

Any Dream Will Do
Michael Crawford; *Michael Crawford Performs Andrew Lloyd Webber* . . . . (Atlantic)
Original Cast; *Joseph & The Amazing Technicolor Dreamcoat* . . . . (MCA)

Aqualung
Jethro Tull; *20 Years Of Jethro Tull* . . . . (Chrysalis)
Bursting Out . . . . (Chrysalis)

M.U.-The Best Of Jethro Tull . . . . (Chrysalis)
Too Old To Rock 'N' Roll: Too Young To Die! . . . . (Chrysalis)

Are You Building A Temple In Heaven
Hank Williams; *I'm So Lonesome I Could Cry-1949* . . . . (Polydor)

As I Lay Me Down
Sophie B. Hawkins; *Whaler* . . . . (Columbia)

Aurora
Bjork; *Vespertine* . . . . (Elektra)

Ave Maria
Barbra Streisand; *Barbra Streisand Christmas Album* . . . . (Columbia)
Christmas Memories . . . . (Columbia)
Carpenters; *Carpenters Christmas Portrait* . . . . (A&M)
Harry Connick, Jr.; *When My Heart Finds Christmas* . . . . (Columbia)
James Galway & The Royal Philharmonic; *James Galway's Christmas Carol* . . . . (RCA)
Luciano Pavarotti; *O Holy Night* . . . . (London)
Mario Lanza; *Christmas With Mario Lanza* . . . . (RCA)
Michael Bolton; *Diana, Princess Of Wales-Tribute-C* . . . . (Columbia)
Perry Como; *I Wish It Could Be Christmas Forever* . . . . (RCA)
Renata Tebaldi; *Christmas Stars-C* . . . . (London)
Stevie Wonder; *Motown Christmas Album-C* . . . . (Motown)
Someday At Christmas . . . . (Motown)

Avinu Malkeinu
Barbra Streisand; *Higher Ground* . . . . (Columbia)

Bad Religion
Godsmack; *Godsmack* . . . . (Republic/Universal)

Baloney Again
Mark Knopfler; *Sailing To Philadelphia* . . . . (Warner Bros.)

Battle Hymn Of The Republic, The
Charlie Sexton; *Charlie Sexton* . . . . (MCA)
Judy Collins; *Songs Of The Civil War-C* . . . . (Columbia)
Mormon Tabernacle Choir; *God Bless America* . . . . (Sony Music Classical)
Stars And Stripes Forever . . . . (Columbia)
National Philharmonic Orchestra & Chorus; *Stars And Stripes Forever-#2-C* . . . . (Volcano Entertainment)
Original Soundtrack; *School Days-Kids Classics* . . . . (Benson)
Pat Boone; *Star Spangled Banner* . . . . (Word)

Beast In Me
Johnny Cash; *American Recordings* . . . . (American)
Nick Lowe; *The Impossible Bird* . . . . (Upstart)
The Sopranos-Music From The HBO Original Series . . . . (Sony Music Soundtrax)

Beginning, The
Keb' Mo'; *The Door* . . . . (550/Epic/Okeh)

Bells Of St. Mary's, The
Bing Crosby; *My Favorite Hymns* . . . . (Universal Special Mkts.)

Bible Tells Me So
Don Cornell; *Rock 'N Roll Reunion: Class Of '55-C* . . . . (Madacy)

Big Jesus Trash Can
Birthday Party; *Best & Rarest* . . . . (Missing Link)
Birthday Party-Collection . . . . (Missing Link)

Bishop Danced
Bruce Springsteen; *Tracks* . . . . (Columbia)

Black Jesus
Everlast; *Eat At Whitey's* . . . . (Tommy Boy)

Black Messiah
Kinks; *Misfits* . . . . (Arista)

Bless The Lord
Original Cast; *Godspell* . . . . (Arista)
Soundtrack; *Godspell* . . . . (Arista)

Bless You
Martha Reeves & The Vandellas; *Compact Command Performances-Martha Reeves & The Vandellas* . . . . (Motown)
Martha Reeves & The Vandellas-Anthology . . . . (Motown)
Motown Superstar Series-#11-Martha Reeves & The Vandellas . . . . (Motown)

Bless You
John Lennon; *Lennon* . . . . (Capitol)
Menlove Ave. . . . . (Capitol)
Walls And Bridges . . . . (Capitol)

Blessed
Elton John; *Elton John-Love Songs* . . . . (MCA)
Made In England . . . . (Rocket)

Blessed
Christina Aguilera; *Christina Aguilera* . . . . (RCA)

Blessed
Al Green; *I Get Joy* . . . . (A&M)

Blessed
Simon & Garfunkel; *Collected Works* . . . . (Columbia)
Sounds Of Silence . . . . (Columbia)

Blessed Are
Joan Baez; *Blessed Are* . . . . (Vanguard)
From Every Stage . . . . (A&M)
Hits/Greatest & Others . . . . (Vanguard)

Blessed Are The Believers
Anne Murray; *Anne Murray-Country Hits* . . . . (Capitol)
Anne Murray's Greatest Hits-#2 . . . . (Capitol)

Blessed Be
Alison Krauss; *Country Goes Raffi-C* . . . . (Rounder)

Blue Eden
Neil Young & Crazy Horse; *Sleeps With Angels* . . . . (Reprise)

Bo Diddley Is Jesus
Jesus & Mary Chain; *Barbed Wire Kisses* . . . . (Warner Bros.)

Born Again
Christians; *Christians* . . . . (Island)

Broken Pieces
Strato Vocalz; *Love Shouldn't Hurt-C* . . . . (Qwest)

Brother Love's Traveling Salvation Show
Neil Diamond; *Hot August Night* . . . . (MCA)
Love At The Greek . . . . (Columbia)
Neil Diamond-Gold . . . . (MCA)
Neil Diamond-His 12 Greatest Hits . . . . (MCA)
Sweet Caroline . . . . (MCA)

Building A Mystery
Sarah McLachlan; *Lilith Fair-A Celebration Of Women In Music-C* . . . . (Arista)
Mirrorball . . . . (Arista)
Surfacing . . . . (Arista)

Burn Down The Mission
Elton John; *11-17-70* . . . . (Polydor)
Live In Australia With The Melbourne Symphony Orchestra . . . . (MCA)
Tumbleweed Connection . . . . (Polydor)
Your Songs . . . . (Polydor)
Phil Collins & His Serious Band; *Two Rooms-Celebrating The Songs Of Elton John & Bernie Taupin-C* . . . . (Polydor)

But For The Grace Of God
keith urban; *keith urban* . . . . (Capitol)

By The Book
Michael Peterson; *Michael Peterson* . . . . (Reprise)

Calling You
Hank Williams; *I Saw The Light* . . . . (Polydor)

Candyman Messiah
Army Of Lovers; *Massive Luxury Overdose* . . . . (Giant)

Can't Stand It
Wilco; *Summer Teeth* . . . . (Reprise)

Can't Take That Away (Mariah's Theme)
Mariah Carey; *Rainbow* . . . . (Columbia)

Cathedral
Crosby, Stills & Nash; *CSN* . . . . (Atlantic)
Replay . . . . (Atlantic)
Van Halen; *Diver Down* . . . . (Warner Bros.)

Cathedrals
Jump, Little Children; *Magazine* . . . . (Breaking/Atlantic)

Catholic Girls
Frank Zappa; *Joe's Garage Acts I-III* . . . . (Rykodisc)
You Can't Do That On Stage Anymore-#6 . . . . (Rykodisc)

Catholic School Girls Rule
Red Hot Chili Peppers; *Abbey Road E.P.* . . . . (EMI)
Freaky Styley . . . . (EMI)
What Hits!? . . . . (EMI)

Caught In Your Web (Swear To Your Heart)
Russell Hitchcock; *ST/Arachnophobia* . . . . (Hollywood)

Chanukah Song, The
Adam Sandler; *What The Hell Happened To Me?* . . . . (Warner Bros.)

Chapel Of Love
Dixie Cups; *Girl Groups-Story Of A Sound-C* . . . . (Rhino)
Jewels-#1-C . . . . (SSS International)
Oldies But Goodies-#11-C . . . . (Original Sound)
Original New York Rock & Roll-C . . . . (Original Sound)

Chapel On The Hill
Mello-Kings; *Mello-Kings' Greatest Hits* . . . . (Collectables)

Cheater's Prayer
Kendalls; *Stickin' Together* . . . . (Mercury)
Thank God For The Radio (& All The Hits) . . . . (Mercury)

Children Go Where I Send Thee
Michael McDonald; *In The Spirit-A Christmas Album* . . . . (MCA)
Peter, Paul & Mary & The New York Choral Society; *Holiday Celebration* . . . . (Warner Bros.)
Weavers; *Weavers At Carnegie Hall* . . . . (Vanguard)
White Mountain Singers; *Best Of The White Mountain Singers* . . . . . (Folk Era)

Chocolate Jesus
Tom Waits; *Mule Variations* . . . . (Epitaph)

Christ Child Lullaby
Judy Collins; *Golden Apples Of The Sun* . . . . (Elektra)

Christian Life
Byrds; *Sweetheart Of The Rodeo* . . . . (Columbia)
The Byrds . . . . (Columbia)

Church
Lyle Lovett; *Joshua Judges Ruth* . . . . (Curb/MCA)

Church Bells May Ring
Diamonds; *Best Of The Diamonds* . . . . (Rhino)
Willows; *Rockin' & Rollin' Wedding Songs-#1-C* . . . . (Rhino)
ST/A Rage In Harlem . . . . (MCA Special Prod.)
WCBS FM 101 History Of Rock-'50s-#2-C . . . . (Collectables)

Church Of Logic, Sin & Love
Men; *The Men* . . . . (Polydor)

Church Of The Poison Mind
Culture Club; *At Worst...The Best Of Boy George And Culture Club* . . . . . (SBK)

Colour By Numbers ....(Virgin)
Church Of Your Heart
Roxette; *Joyride* .... (EMI)
Church On Cumberland Road
Shenandoah; *Greatest Country Hits Of The '80s-1989-C* ....(Columbia)
Road Not Taken ....(Columbia)
City Of God
Rubber Rodeo; *Scenic Views*.................................. (Mercury)
Clean My Wounds
Corrosion Of Conformity; *Deliverance* ....(Columbia)
Come Back To Us Barbara Lewis Hare Krisha Beauregard
John Prine; *Common Sense* .... (Atlantic)
Great Days-Anthology ....(Rhino)
Prime Prine-The Best Of John Prine .... (Atlantic)
Comin' In On A Wing & A Prayer
Anita Ellis; *Songs That Won The War-C* ....(Columbia River Entert. Group)
Anne Shelton; *V-E Day 50th Anniversary-The Musical
Memories-C* .... (Living Era)
Four Vagabonds; *The Victory Collection: The Smithsonian Remembers When
America Went To War-C* ....(RCA)
Ry Cooder; *Boomer's Story* ....(Reprise)
Computer God
Black Sabbath; *Dehumanizer* .... (Reprise)
Convict's Prayer
Li'l Wally; *One Man Band* .... (Jay Jay)
Could I Be Your Girl
Jann Arden; *Living Under June* .... (A&M)
Count Your Blessings (Instead Of Sheep)
Bing Crosby; *45-#29251* ....(Decca)
Eddie Fisher; *Best Of Eddie Fisher* .... (MCA)
Rosemary Clooney; *Essence Of Rosemary Clooney* .... (Legacy)
Counting Blue Cars
Dishwalla; *Pet Your Friends* .... (A&M)
Cowboy's Prayer
Goebel Reeves; *Songs Of The Old West* ....(Glendale)
Texas Drifter ....(Glendale)
Creator Has A Master Plan
Pharoah Sanders; *Fire Into Music-Best Of Impulse!-#3-C* ..... (MCA/Impulse)
Karma...(MCA/Impulse)
Criminal
Fiona Apple; *1998 Grammy Nominees-C* .... (MCA)
Tidal ....(Clean Slate/Work)
Crucified
Agnostic Front; *Best Of Agnostic Front*.....................(Relativity)
Last Warning ....(Relativity)
Crucified
Fixx; *Ink* .... (Impact)
Crucified
Army Of Lovers; *Massive Luxury Overdose* .... (Giant)
Crying In The Chapel
Elvis Presley; *Elvis-A Legendary Performer, Volume 3* ....(RCA)
How Great Thou Art..(RCA)
The Top Ten Hits...(RCA)
Worldwide 50 Gold Award Hits, Vol. 1, Parts 1 & 2..........(RCA)
June Valli; *Nipper's Greatest Hits Of The '50s-#2-C* ....(RCA)
Little Richard; *Shut Up-Collection Of Rare Tracks-1951-1964* ....(Rhino)
Orioles; *Super Oldies Of The '50s-#1-C* .... (Audio Fidelity)
Rex Allen; *Only Country-1950-1954-C* ....(JCI Assoc. Labels)
Sonny Til & The Orioles; *Echoes Of A Rock Era-Early Years-C* ..... (Roulette)
Sonny Til & The Orioles' Greatest Hits ....(Collectables)
ST/American Graffiti ....(MCA)
Crystal Blue Persuasion
Tommy James And The Shondells; *Best Of Tommy James And The
Shondells* ....(Roulette)
Tommy James And The Shondells-Anthology ....(Rhino)
Daddy Sang Bass
Johnny Cash; *Columbia Country Classics-#5-A New Tradition-C* ...(Columbia)
Johnny Cash's Greatest Hits-#2............................(Columbia)
The Man In Black-His Greatest Hits........................(Legacy)
Daddy Was An Old Time Preacher Man
Porter Wagoner & Dolly Parton; *Best Of Porter Wagoner & Dolly
Parton* ....(RCA)
Daniel & The Sacred Harp
Band; *Stage Fright*..(Capitol)
The Band-Anthology-#1 ....(Capitol)
To Kingdom Come-The Definitive Collection.................(Capitol)
Daniel Prayed
Patty Loveless; *Mountain Soul* .... (Epic)
Stanley Brothers; *Stanley Brothers-On Radio* ....(Rebel)
Deacon Blues
Steely Dan; *Aja* .... (MCA)
Steely Dan-Gold ....(MCA)
Deal With The Preacher
Bad Company; *Straight Shooter* ....(Swan Song)
Dear Brother
Hank Williams; *I Saw The Light* ....(Polydor)
Dear God
Patsy Cline; *Forever & Always* .... (Epic)

Dear God
XTC; *Best Of MTV's 120 Minutes-#1-C* ....(Rhino)
Skylarking ....(Geffen)
Upsy Daisy Assortment ....(Geffen)
Dear God
Elton John; *21 At 33* .... (Polydor)
Dear Lord
Continentals; *Great Groups Of The '50s-#2-C* ....(Collectables)
Thin Lizzy; *Bad Reputation* ....(Mercury)
Deck Of Cards
''T'' Texas Tyler; *45-#2060*................................(Gusto)
Bill Anderson; *American Music Greatest Hits-C* ....(Curb)
Best Of Bill Anderson ....(Curb)
Tex Ritter; *Capitol Collectors Series-Tex Ritter* ....(Capitol)
Tex Ritter's Greatest Hits ....(Curb)
Dedicated To The One I Love
Mamas & The Papas; *Best Of The Mamas & The Papas* .... (MCA)
Farewell To The First Golden Era ....(MCA)
Original Classic Oldies Of The '50s & '60s-#13-C ....(MCA)
Shirelles; *Oldies But Goodies-#10-C* .... (Original Sound)
Shirelles' Greatest Hits ....(Everest)
Shirelles-Anthology 1959-1964.............................(Rhino)
Super Oldies Of The '50s-#4-C .... (Audio Fidelity)
Dinosaur Jesus
Barbie Bones; *Brake For Nobody* .... (Restless)
Do Right
Paul Davis; *Best Of Paul Davis* .... (Bang)
Paul Davis...(Bang)
Dominic Christ
Suicide; *Way Of Life*......................................(Wax Trax)
Don't Let Me Be Misunderstood
Animals; *Greatest Hits Live!-Rip It To Shreds*..............(I.R.S.)
Sullivan Years-British Invasion...........................(TVT)
Joe Cocker; *With A Little Help From My Friends* ....(A&M)
Don't Take The Girl
Tim McGraw; *Not A Moment Too Soon* ....(Curb)
Tim McGraw's Greatest Hits ....(Curb)
Don't Tell Me (What Love Can Do)
Van Halen; *Balance* .... (Warner Bros.)
Don't You Marry The Mormon Boys
Rosalie Sorrels; *Lonesome Roving Wolves-Songs & Ballads Of
The West* .... (Green Linnet)
Door, The
Keb' Mo'; *The Door*....................................... (550/Epic/Okeh)
Down To The River To Pray
Alison Krauss; *ST/O Brother, Where Art Thou?* ....(Mercury)
Down To The Valley
Nilsson; *Everybody's Talkin': The Encore Collection* ..... (BMG Special Prod.)
Drop Kick Me Jesus (Through The Goalposts Of Life)
Bobby Bare; *Essential Bobby Bare* .... (RCA)
D'You Know What I Mean
Oasis; *Be Here Now* .... (Epic)
Eleanor Rigby
Beatles; *Beatles 1* ....(Capitol)
Revolver ....(Capitol)
The Beatles/1962-1966 ....(Capitol)
Ray Charles; *Ray Charles' Greatest Hits-#2* ....(Rhino)
Ray Charles-Anthology.....................................(Rhino)
Everlasting Glaze
Smashing Pumpkins; *Machina: The Machines Of God* .... (Virgin)
Everything Is Everything
Lauryn Hill; *The Miseducation Of Lauryn Hill* ....(Ruffhouse/Columbia)
Everything Zen
Bush; *MTV Buzz Bin-C* .... (Mammoth)
Sixteen Stone ....(Trauma)
Failed Christian
Nick Lowe; *Dig My Mood* ....(Upstart)
Fall From Grace
Amanda Marshall; *Amanda Marshall* ....(Epic)
Family Bible
Claude Gray; *20 Great Country Recordings Ot The '50s & '60s-C* ....(Cascade)
Commander Cody & His Lost Planet Airmen; *Lost In The Ozone* ....(MCA)
Ernest Tubb; *Family Bible* .... (Universal Special Mkts.)
George Jones; *24 Gospel Greats* ....(Deluxe)
Cup Of Loneliness-Classic Mercury Years ....(Mercury)
Johnny Cash & Willie Nelson; *VH1 Storytellers* ....(American)
Merle Haggard; *Land Of Many Churches* ....(Razor & Tie)
Osborne Brothers; *Essential Bluegrass Album*...............(C.M.H. Prod.)
Willie Nelson; *Best Of Gospel* .... (Universal Special Mkts.)
Essential Willie Nelson .... (RCA)
Ryman Country Homecoming 3-C ....(Springhouse Music Grp./Chordant)
Family Who Prays (Never Shall Part), The
Browns; *Family Bible* ....(Step One)
Jim & Jesse; *Old Dominion Masters* ....(Pinecastle)
Louvin Brothers; *Live At New River Ranch* ....(Copper Creek)
ST/Jesus' Son ....(Mammoth)
When I Stop Dreaming: The Best Of The Louvin Brothers .....(Razor & Tie)
Ralph Stanley; *Child Of The King* ....(Rebel)

Far Away Eyes
Rolling Stones; *Some Girls* . . . . (Virgin)

Farther Along
Byrds; *The Byrds* . . . . (Columbia)
Elvis Presley; *Million-Dollar Quartet* . . . . (RCA)
Flying Burrito Brothers; *Farther Along-Best Of The Flying Burrito
    Brothers* . . . . (A&M)
Rose Maddox; *Rose Of The West Coast Country* . . . . (Arhoolie)

Father's Table Grace
Lester Flatt; *Fifty Years Of Bluegrass Hits-#3-C* . . . .(C.M.H. Prod.)
Lester Flatt & The Nashville Grass; *The Tennessee Mountain Bluegrass
    Festival* . . . .(C.M.H. Prod.)

Fields Have Turned Brown
Stanley Brothers & The Clinch Mountain Boys; *Bluegrass Super
    Hits-C* . . . . (Columbia)

Final Hour
Lauryn Hill; *The Miseducation Of Lauryn Hill* . . . . (Ruffhouse/Columbia)

Find A Way
Amy Grant; *Amy Grant-Collection* . . . . (A&M)
    Unguarded . . . . (A&M)

Follow The Fold
Original Cast; *ST/Guys & Dolls* . . . .(MCA)

Forever And Ever, Amen
Randy Travis; *Always & Forever* . . . .(Warner Bros.)

Forgive Them Father
Lauryn Hill featuring Shelly Thunder; *The Miseducation Of
    Lauryn Hill* . . . . (Ruffhouse/Columbia)

Forgiveness
Macy Gray; *The Id* . . . .(Epic)

Friendly Persuasion
Pat Boone; *Best Of Pat Boone* . . . .(MCA)
    Pat Boone-16 Great Performances . . . .(MCA)

From A Distance
Bette Midler; *Some People's Lives* . . . . (Atlantic)
Byrds; *20 Essential Tracks From The Box Set* . . . . (Columbia)
    The Byrds . . . . (Columbia)
Judy Collins; *Fires Of Eden* . . . . (Columbia)
Kathy Mattea; *Time Passes By* . . . . (Mercury)
Nanci Griffith; *Lone Star State Of Mind* . . . .(MCA)
    One Fair Summer Evening . . . .(MCA)

Galilee Road
Marcus Hummon; *Looking For The Child* . . . . (Velvet Armadillo)

Garden Of Allah
Don Henley; *Actual Miles: Henley's Greatest Hits* . . . .(Geffen)

Garden Of Eden
New Riders Of The Purple Sage; *New Riders Of The Purple Sage* . . . (Columbia)

German Nun
Sex Gang Children; *Ecstasy & Vendetta Over New York* . . . .(Roir)

Get Down On Your Knees And Pray
Marty Stuart; *Bluegrass Super Hits-C* . . . . (Columbia)

Get Happy
Benny Goodman; *Benny Goodman's Greatest Hits* . . . .(RCA Victor)
Ella Fitzgerald; *Harold Arlen Songbook-#2* . . . . (Verve)
Judy Garland; *Best Of Judy Garland In Hollywood* . . . . (Turner Classic Movies)
Nat Shilkret & The Victor Orchestra; *78-#22444* . . . . (Victor)

Get In Touch With Jesus
Joan Armatrading; *Back To The Night* . . . . (A&M)

Get Me To The Church On Time
Original Cast; *My Fair Lady* . . . . (Columbia)

Give More Power To The People
Chi-Lites; *Chi-Lites' Greatest Hits* . . . .(Epic)

Go Down Moses
Arlo Guthrie; *Arlo Guthrie* . . . .(Rising Son)
Fats Waller; *Ain't Misbehavin'* . . . .(Laserlight)
Paul Robeson; *Ballad For Americans* . . . . (Vanguard)
    The Power & The Glory . . . . (Columbia)
Simon Estes; *Spirituals* . . . . (Philips)

Go Rest High On That Mountain
Vince Gill; *When Love Finds You* . . . .(MCA)

Go Tell It On The Mountain
Bobby Darin; *Bobby Darin-25th Day Of December* . . . . (Atco)
Bruce Cockburn; *Christmas* . . . . (Columbia)
Dolly Parton; *Home For Christmas* . . . . (Columbia)
Don McLean; *Christmas* . . . .(Curb)
Garth Brooks; *Beyond The Season* . . . . (Liberty)
Simon & Garfunkel; *Collected Works* . . . . (Columbia)
    Wednesday Morning 3 A.M. . . . . (Columbia)
Weavers; *On Tour* . . . . (Vanguard)

Go Up Moses
Roberta Flack; *Quiet Fire* . . . . (Atlantic)

God
Tori Amos; *Under The Pink* . . . . (Atlantic)

God Ain't No Stained Glass Window
Kathy Mattea; *Kathy Mattea* . . . . (Mercury)

God Bless America
Anita Bryant; *Golden Classics-Anita Bryant* . . . . (Collectables)
Bill & Gloria Gaither; *Kennedy Center Homecoming: A Celebration Of Our
    Faith And Heritage* . . . . (Springhouse Music Grp./Chordant)

Celine Dion; *America: A Tribute To Heroes-C* . . . . (Interscope)
    God Bless America-C . . . . (Columbia)
Drew Carey; *ST/The Drew Carey Show* . . . . (Rhino)
Frank Zappa; *Uncle Meat* . . . . (Barking Pumpkin)
Kate Smith; *Best Of Kate Smith* . . . .(RCA)
    God Bless America . . . .(Pickwick)
    Kate Smith-Legendary Performer . . . . (RCA)
    Nipper's Greatest Hits Of The '30s-#1-C . . . . (RCA)
    Stars And Stripes Forever-#2-C . . . . (Volcano Entertainment)
LeAnn Rimes; *You Light Up My Life-Inspirational Songs* . . . .(Curb)
Lee Greenwood; *American Patriot* . . . . (Capitol)
Mormon Tabernacle Choir; *God Bless America* . . . .(Sony Music Classical)
Original Soundtrack; *ST/The Deer Hunter* . . . . (Capitol)
Peter Pan Kids; *I Love America Sing Along* . . . . (Compose)
Robert Shaw Chorale; *Battle Cry Of Freedom* . . . .(RCA)

God Bless America Again
Bobby Bare; *Best Of Bobby Bare* . . . . (Razor & Tie)
    Country Shots: God Bless America-C . . . . (Rhino)
Loretta Lynn & Conway Twitty; *From Seven Till Ten* . . . . (MCA Special Prod.)
    United Talent . . . . (MCA)
    Very Best Of Loretta Lynn & Conway Twitty . . . .(MCA)

God Bless The Child
Billie Holiday; *Billie Holiday's Greatest Hits* . . . . (Decca Jazz)
    Billie Holiday's Greatest Hits . . . . (Legacy)
    From The Original Decca Masters . . . . (MCA)
    Songbook . . . . (Verve)
    The Billie Holiday Story-#2 . . . . (Columbia)
Blood, Sweat & Tears; *Blood, Sweat & Tears* . . . . (Columbia)
    Blood, Sweat & Tears Greatest Hits . . . . (Columbia)
Diana Ross; *ST/Lady Sings The Blues* . . . . (Motown)
Liza Minnelli; *4-Sider* . . . . (Cypress)
    ST/Liza With A "Z" . . . . (Columbia)
Lou Rawls; *Best From Lou Rawls* . . . . (Capitol)

God Bless The Children
Loretta Lynn; *Out Of My Head And Back In My Bed* . . . .(MCA)

God Bless The Children
Motley Crue; *Shout At The Devil* . . . . (Elektra)

God Bless The Grass
Pete Seeger; *Essential Pete Seeger* . . . . (Vanguard)

God Bless The USA
Lee Greenwood; *American Patriot* . . . . (Capitol)
    God Bless America-C . . . . (Columbia)
    God Bless The USA . . . . (MCA Special Prod.)
    Inside Out/You've Got A Good Love Comin' . . . . (MCA)
    Lee Greenwood's Greatest Hits . . . . (MCA)
    Lee Greenwood's Greatest Hits-#2 . . . . (MCA)
    Today's Country Classics-C . . . . (MCA Special Prod.)

God Blessed Texas
Little Texas; *Big Time* . . . . (Warner Bros.)

God Can
Paul Kelly; *Stand On The Positive Side* . . . . (Warner Bros.)
Staples; *Unlock Your Mind* . . . . (Warner Bros.)

God Don't Live In Nashville, Tennessee
Randy Howard; *All-American Redneck* . . . . (Warner Bros.)

God Don't Make Lonely Girls
Wallflowers; *Bringing Down The Horse* . . . . (Interscope)

God Fearing Man
Steppenwolf; *At Your Birthday Party* . . . . (MCA Special Prod.)

God Gave Me Everything
Mick Jagger; *Goddess In The Doorway* . . . . (Virgin)

God Gave Noah The Rainbow Sign
Carter Family; *My Clinch Mountain Home-Their Complete Victor
    Recordings-1928-1929* . . . . (Rounder)

God Gave Rock & Roll To You
Argent; *Argent-Anthology-Collection Of Greatest Hits* . . . .(Epic)
    Encore-Argent . . . .(Epic)
Truth; *Jump* . . . . (I.R.S.)

God Have Mercy On The Workin' Man
Randy Newman; *Good Old Boys* . . . . (Reprise)

God Is Alive, Magic Is Afoot
Buffy Sainte-Marie; *Best Of Buffy Sainte-Marie* . . . . (Vanguard)
    Illuminations . . . . (Vanguard)

God Is Love
Marvin Gaye; *Marvin Gaye-Live* . . . . (Motown)
    Pops We Love You . . . . (Motown)
    What's Going On . . . . (Motown)

God Knows
Debby Boone; *Best Of Debby Boone* . . . . (Curb)
    Best Of Debby Boone . . . . (MCA)
    Midstream . . . . (Warner Bros.)

God Knows
Bob Dylan; *Under The Red Sky* . . . . (Columbia)

God Knows I'm Good
David Bowie; *Space Oddity* . . . . (Rykodisc)

God Loves A Drunk
Richard Thompson; *Rumor & Sigh* . . . . (Capitol)

God Must Be A Boogie Man
Joni Mitchell; *Mingus* . . . . (Elektra)
    Shadows & Light . . . . (Asylum)

God Must Be A Cowboy
Dan Seals; *Best Of Dan Seals* . . . . (Capitol)
   Dan Seals-Classics Collection-#1 . . . . (Capitol)
   Rebel Heart . . . . (Liberty)

God Must Have Blessed America
Glen Campbell; *Country Shots: God Bless America-C* . . . . (Rhino)

God Must Have Spent A Little More Time On You
Alabama Featuring 'N Sync; *Twentieth Century* . . . . (RCA)
   'N Sync; *'N Sync* . . . . (RCA)
   Totally Hits-#1-C . . . . (Arista)

God Of The Sun
America; *Harbor* . . . . (Warner Bros.)

God Of Thunder
Kiss; *Alive II* . . . . (Casablanca)
   Destroyer . . . . (Casablanca)
   Double Platinum . . . . (Mercury)

God Only Knows
Beach Boys; *Beach Boys' Greatest Hits* . . . . (Reprise)
   Best Of The Beach Boys-Good Vibrations . . . .(Reprise)
   Made In The U.S.A. . . . . (Capitol)
   Pet Sounds . . . . (Capitol)
   Stack 'O' Tracks . . . . (Capitol)
   The Pet Sounds Sessions: A 30th Anniversary Collection . . . . (Capitol)

God Part II
U2; *Rattle And Hum* . . . . (Island)

God Rest Ye Merry Gentlemen
Bing Crosby; *Bing Crosby Sings Christmas Songs* . . . . (MCA Special Prod.)
   Merry Christmas . . . . (MCA Special Prod.)
   Voice Of Christmas-The Complete Decca Christmas Songbook . . . . . .(Decca)
Bobby Vinton; *Christmas All-Time Greatest Records-#2-C* . . . .(Curb)
Ella Fitzgerald; *Best Of Christmas-C* . . . . (Capitol)
Garth Brooks; *Beyond The Season* . . . . (Liberty)
   Christmas For The '90s-#1-C . . . . (Liberty)
Jackie Wilson; *Merry Christmas From Jackie Wilson* . . . .(Rhino)
Kenny Rogers; *Christmas In America* . . . . (Reprise)
Leontyne Price; *Christmas Songs* . . . . (London)
Mannheim Steamroller; *Christmas Live* . . . . (American Gramaphone)
Mel Torme; *Christmas Songs* . . . . (Telarc)
Nat "King" Cole; *Cole Christmas & Kids* . . . . (Capitol)
Neil Diamond; *Neil Diamond Christmas Album* . . . . (Columbia)
Perry Como; *Season's Greetings From Perry Como* . . . . (RCA)
Randy Travis; *An Old Time Christmas* . . . . (Warner Bros.)
Roger Whittaker; *Tidings Of Comfort & Joy* . . . . (Liberty)
Smokey Robinson & The Miracles; *Season For Miracles* . . . . (Motown)
Steve Wariner; *Steve Wariner Christmas Memories* . . . . . . (MCA Special Prod.)
T Bone Burnett; *Acoustic Christmas* . . . . (Columbia)
Take 6 & The Yellowjackets; *He Is Christmas* . . . . (Reprise)

God Save The Queen
Queen; *A Night At The Opera* . . . . (Hollywood)
   Live Killers . . . . (Hollywood)

God Save The Queen
Anthrax; *Armed & Dangerous* . . . . (Megaforce)

God Save The Queen
Sex Pistols; *Never Mind The Bollocks, Here's The Sex Pistols* . . . (Warner Bros.)

God Trying To Get Your Attention
Keb' Mo'; *Slow Down* . . . . (550/Epic/Okeh)

God Was Drunk When He Made Me
Jim White; *No Such Place* . . . . (Luaka Bop)

God Will
Holly Cole Trio; *Blame It On My Youth* . . . . (Blue Note)
Lyle Lovett; *Lyle Lovett* . . . . (MCA)
   Lyle Lovett Anthology-#1-Cowboy Man . . . . (MCA)
Patty Loveless; *Up Against My Heart* . . . . (MCA)

God Won't Get You
Dolly Parton; *ST/Rhinestone* . . . . (RCA)

Godless
U.P.O.; *No Pleasantries* . . . . (Epic)

God's A Gonna Cut You Down
Odetta; *Essential Odetta* . . . . (Vanguard)

God's Children
Kinks; *Kink Kronikles* . . . . (Reprise)

God's Coloring Book
Dolly Parton; *Here You Come Again* . . . . (Dunhill Compact Classics)

God's Country
Al Jolson; *The Al Jolson Story-#4* . . . . (MCA)

God's Country
Kool & The Gang; *Forever* . . . . (Mercury)

God's Footballer
Billy Bragg; *Don't Try This At Home* . . . . (Elektra)

God's Gonna Get'cha (For That)
George Jones & Tammy Wynette; *George Jones & Tammy Wynette-16*
   Biggest Hits . . . . (Epic/Legacy)
George Jones & Tammy Wynette's Greatest Hits . . . . (Epic)

God's Great Banana Skin
Chris Rea; *Espresso Logic* . . . . (East West)

God's Own Drunk
Jimmy Buffett; *Living & Dying In 3/4 Time* . . . . (MCA)
   You Had To Be There . . . . (MCA)

God's Own Jukebox
Jesse Winchester; *Third Down 110 To Go* . . . .(Rhino)

God's Own Singer
Flying Burrito Brothers; *Burrito Deluxe* . . . .(A&M)
   Close Up The Honky Tonks . . . .(A&M)
   Farther Along-Best Of The Flying Burrito Brothers . . . .(A&M)

God's Plan
Desert Rose Band; *Pages Of Life* . . . .(Curb)

God's Song (That's Why I Love Mankind)
Randy Newman; *Sail Away* . . . . (Reprise)

Good Friday
Black Crowes; *Sho' Nuff* . . . .(American)
   Three Snakes And One Charm . . . .(American)

Good News
Staple Singers; *Swing Low Sweet Chariot* . . . .(Collectables)

Good News
Kingston Trio; *Scarlet Ribbons* . . . .(Capitol)
Mary Travers; *It's In Every One Of Us* . . . .(Chrysalis)
Sweet Honey In The Rock; *Good News* . . . . (Flying Fish)

Gospel According To Luke
Skip Ewing; *Coast Of Colorado* . . . . (MCA)

Got The Life
Korn; *Follow The Leader* . . . . (Immortal/Epic)

Gotta Serve Somebody
Bob Dylan; *Biograph* . . . .(Columbia)
   Slow Train Coming . . . .(Columbia)
   The Sopranos-Music From The HBO Original
   Series . . . . (Sony Music Soundtrax)
Bob Dylan & The Grateful Dead; *Dylan & The Dead* . . . .(Columbia)

Grandma's Hands
Al Jarreau; *Improvisations* . . . .(Blue Moon)
Barbra Streisand; *Butterfly* . . . .(Columbia)
Bill Withers; *Bill Withers' Greatest Hits* . . . .(Columbia)
   Bill Withers Live At Carnegie Hall . . . .(Columbia)
Keb' Mo'; *Big Wide Grin* . . . . (Sony Wonder)

Great Speckled Bird
Roy Acuff; *Best Of Roy Acuff* . . . .(Liberty)
   Bluegrass Super Hits-C . . . .(Columbia)
   Roy Acuff's Greatest Hits . . . .(Columbia)

Green Grow The Rushes, Ho
Chieftains; *Bonaparte's Retreat* . . . . (Shanachie)

Grow Old With Me
John Lennon; *The John Lennon Anthology* . . . .(Capitol)
   Wonsaponatime . . . .(Capitol)
Mary Chapin Carpenter; *Party Doll And Other Favorites* . . . .(Columbia)

Hail Mary
Makaveli; *The Don Killuminati: The 7 Day Theory*
   Album . . . .(Death Row/Interscope)

Hand Song, The
Nickel Creek; *Nickel Creek* . . . . (Sugar Hill)

Hands
Jewel; *Spirit* . . . . (Atlantic)

Hands To Heaven
Breathe; *All That Jazz* . . . .(A&M)

Hang On St. Christopher
Tom Waits; *Frank's Wild Years-Un Operachi Romantico* . . . .(Island)

Hannukah Rocks
Gefilte Joe & The Fish; *Tales From The Rhino-Rhino Records*
   Story-C . . . .(Rhino)

Happiness Is A Warm Gun
Beatles; *The Beatles (White Album)* . . . .(Capitol)

Happy Birthday, Jesus
Original Sins; *Bethlehem* . . . .(Bar/None)

Have A Talk With God
Stevie Wonder; *Songs In The Key Of Life* . . . .(Motown)

He Walked On Water
Randy Travis; *No Holdin' Back* . . . . (Warner Bros.)

Hear Me Lord
George Harrison; *All Things Must Pass* . . . . (Parlophone)

Heaven Is 10 Zillion Light Years Away
Stevie Wonder; *Fulfillingness' First Finale* . . . .(Motown)

Heavenly Father
Castelles; *Home Of Grand Records* . . . .(Collectables)
   Sweet Sounds Of The Castelles . . . .(Collectables)

Here I Am, Oh Lord Send Me
Mississippi John Hurt; *Best Of Mississippi John Hurt* . . . .(Vanguard)

Hero Worship
B-52's; *B-52's* . . . .(Warner Bros.)
   Wild Planet . . . . (Warner Bros.)

He's Got The Whole World In His Hands
Laurie London; *Rock 'N Roll's Greatest Hits Of All Time-#10-*
   '50s-C . . . . (Platinum Disc)
Mormon Tabernacle Choir; *Mormon Tabernacle Choir's Greatest*
   Hits-#2 . . . .(Columbia)
Odetta; *Essential Odetta* . . . . (Vanguard)

High On Jesus
Kinky Friedman; *Sold American* . . . .(Vanguard)

Higher Ground
Stevie Wonder; *Innervisions* . . . . (Motown)
Original Musiquarium . . . . (Motown)

Hill Where The Lord Hides
Chuck Mangione; *Best Of Chuck Mangione* . . . . (Mercury)
Best Of Chuck Mangione . . . . (A&M)
Chuck Mangione-Classics-#6 . . . . (A&M)
Evening Of Magic . . . . (A&M)
Friends & Love . . . . (Mercury)
Together . . . . (Mercury)

His Eye Is On The Sparrow
Carmen McRae; *Greatest Of Carmen McRae* . . . .(MCA)
Marvin Gaye; *Musical Testament 1964-1984* . . . . (Motown)
Preservation Hall Jazz Band; *Best Of The Preservation Hall
Jazz Band* . . . . (Columbia)
Soundtrack; *Streetcar Named Desire* . . . .(Allegiance)

Holy River
''AFKAP''; *Emancipation* . . . . (NPG)

Holy Thursday
Greg Brown; *Songs Of Innocence & Experience* . . . .(Red House)

Holy Water
Bad Company; *Holy Water* . . . . (Atco)

House Of The Rising Sun
Animals; *Animals Greatest Hits* . . . .(Allegiance)
Best Of The Animals . . . .(Abkco)
Greatest Hits Live!-Rip It To Shreds . . . .(I.R.S.)
Hank Williams, Jr.; *Hank Williams, Jr. ''Live''* . . . . (WB/Curb)
Ronnie Milsap; *Ronnie Milsap-16 Greatest Hits-#2* . . . . (Trip)

Houses Of The Holy
Led Zeppelin; *Led Zeppelin-Box Set* . . . . (Atlantic)
Physical Graffiti . . . . (Swan Song)

How Great Thou Art
Connie Smith; *Essential Connie Smith* . . . . (RCA)
Elvis Presley; *Elvis Recorded Live On Stage In Memphis* . . . . (RCA)
Lee Greenwood; *Lee Greenwood-Super Hits* . . . . (Epic)
Statler Brothers; *30th Anniversary Celebration* . . . . (Mercury)

Human Beings
Seal; *Human Being* . . . .(Warner Bros.)

Hundred Pounds Of Clay
Gene McDaniels; *Best Of Gene McDaniels-A Hundred Pounds
Of Clay* . . . . (Collectables)
Rock Is Dead But It Won't Lie Down-C . . . .(Gold Rush)

Hymn
James Taylor; *One Man Dog* . . . .(Warner Bros.)

Hymn
Patti Smith Group; *Wave* . . . . (Arista)

Hymn
Peter, Paul & Mary; *Late Again* . . . .(Warner Bros.)

Hymn 43
Jethro Tull; *Aqualung* . . . .(Chrysalis)
Living In The Past . . . .(Chrysalis)

Hymn For The Dudes
Mott The Hoople; *Mott* . . . . (Columbia)
Mott The Hoople's Greatest Hits . . . . (Columbia)

Hymn To Me
Brinsley Schwarz; *Brinsley Schwarz* . . . . (Capitol)

I Am The Light Of This World
Jorma Kaukonen & Tom Hobson; *Quah* . . . . (Relix)

I Believe In The Man In The Sky
Elvis Presley; *The Other Sides-Worldwide Gold Award Hits, Vol. 2* . . . . . (RCA)

I Can't Wai To Meetchu
Macy Gray; *On How Life Is* . . . .(Epic)

I Don't Want To Wait
Paula Cole; *Live On Letterman-From The Late Show* . . . . (Reprise)
Songs From Dawson's Creek . . . . (Sony Music Soundtrax)
This Fire . . . . (Imago)

I Guess The Lord Must Be In New York City
Nilsson; *Harry* . . . .(Dunhill Compact Classics)
Nilsson's Greatest Hits . . . . (RCA)

I Just Want To See His Face
Rolling Stones; *Exile On Main Street* . . . . (Virgin)

I Knew Jesus (Before He Was A Star)
Glen Campbell; *Best Of Glen Campbell* . . . . (Capitol)

I Met Her In Church
Box Tops; *Box Tops' Greatest Hits* . . . . (Rhino)

I Said A Prayer
Pam Tillis; *Every Time* . . . . (Arista)

I Saw The Light
Hank Williams; *Hank Williams-24 Greatest Hits-#2* . . . . (Polydor)
Hank Williams-40 Greatest Hits . . . . (Polydor)
I Ain't Got Nothin' But Time-1946-1947 . . . . (Polydor)
Legend In Song-With Hank Williams, Jr. . . . . (Polydor)
Rare Takes & Radio Cuts . . . . (Polydor)

I Say A Little Prayer
Aretha Franklin; *Aretha Franklin's Greatest Hits* . . . .(Atlantic)
Aretha's Gold . . . .(Atlantic)
Best Of Aretha Franklin . . . .(Atlantic)
Burt Bacharach; *Burt Bacharach-Classics-#23* . . . . (A&M)

Burt Bacharach's Greatest Hits . . . . (A&M)
Reach Out . . . . (A&M)
Diana King; *ST/My Best Friend's Wedding* . . . . (Work/Epic)
Dionne Warwick; *Dionne Warwick* . . . . (Everest)
Dionne Warwick Greatest Hits . . . . (Everest)
Dionne Warwick-Anthology 1962-1971 . . . . (Rhino)
Original Rock 'N' Roll Hits Of The '60s-C . . . . (Roulette)

I Think God Can Explain
Splender; *ST/Dawson's Creek-#2* . . . . (C2/Columbia)

I Thought Of God
Porter Wagoner; *Porter Wagoner-In Person* . . . . (Koch International)

I Used To Love Him
Lauryn Hill featuring Mary J. Blige; *The Miseducation Of
Lauryn Hill* . . . . (Ruffhouse/Columbia)

I Wish
R. Kelly; *Now That's What I Call Music!-#6-C* . . . .(Virgin)
TP-2.com . . . .(Jive)

Iceman
Bruce Springsteen; *Tracks* . . . . (Columbia)

If There's A God In Heaven
Elton John; *Blue Moves* . . . . (MCA)

If There's A God On My Side
Rosanne Cash; *The Wheel* . . . . (Columbia)

I'll Be Missing You
Puff Daddy & Family & Faith Evans & 112; *No Way Out* . . . . .(Bad Boy/Arista)

I'll Fly Away
Aretha Franklin; *Diana, Princess Of Wales-Tribute-C* . . . . (Columbia)

I'm Living With The 3-Foot Anti-Christ
Mojo Nixon; *Frenzy/Get Out Of My Way* . . . . (I.R.S.)

In God We Trust
Barefoot Jerry; *Barefoot Jerry's Grocery* . . . . (Monument)

In God's Country
U2; *Joshua Tree* . . . . (Island)

In The Chapel In The Moonlight
Kitty Kallen; *Those Wonderful Years: Music! Music!
Music!-C* . . . .(JCI Assoc. Labels)
Patti Page; *Patti Page-16 Most Requested Songs* . . . . (Legacy)
Shep Fields & His Rippling Rhythm Orchestra; *78-#6640* . . . . (Bluebird)

In The Highways
Sarah, Hannah And Leah Peasall; *ST/O Brother, Where Art Thou?* . . . (Mercury)

In The House Of Stone And Light
Martin Page; *In The House Of Stone And Light* . . . . (Mercury)

Infinite Eyes
Keb' Mo'; *Big Wide Grin* . . . . (Sony Wonder)

Inner Light
Beatles; *Past Masters-Volume Two* . . . . (Parlophone)
Rarities . . . . (Capitol)

Innocent
Fuel; *Something Like Human* . . . . (Epic)

It Ain't Necessarily So
Aretha Franklin; *The Great-First 12 Sides* . . . . (Columbia)
Cab Calloway; *Sullivan Years-Best Of Broadway* . . . . (TVT)
Cal Tjader; *Cal Tjader Plays/Mary Stallings Sings* . . . . (Fantasy)
Cher; *Glory Of Gershwin Featuring Larry Adler-C* . . . . (Mercury)
Ella Fitzgerald & Louis Armstrong; *Porgy & Bess* . . . . (Verve)
Miles Davis & His Orchestra; *Porgy & Bess* . . . . (Columbia)

It Must Be Him
Vikki Carr; *Greatest Hits* . . . .(Curb)

It Wasn't God Who Made Honky Tonk Angels
Kitty Wells; *Grand Ole Opry-75 Years-#1-C* . . . . (MCA)
Kitty Wells' Greatest Hits . . . .(Step One)
The Kitty Wells Story . . . . (MCA)

It's A Sin
George Thorogood & The Destroyers; *Bad To The Bone* . . . . (EMI)

It's A Sin
Marty Robbins; *Marty Robbins' All-Time Greatest Hits* . . . . (Columbia)

It's A Sin
Pet Shop Boys; *Actually* . . . . (EMI)

It's A Sin To Tell A Lie
Fats Waller; *20 Golden Pieces Of Fats Waller* . . . .(Bulldog)
Somethin' Smith & The Redheads; *45-#5-9093* . . . . (Epic)

It's All In Your Head
Diamond Rio; *Diamond Rio IV* . . . . (Arista)
Diamond Rio's Greatest Hits . . . . (Arista)

It's Hard To Be A Saint In The City
Bruce Springsteen; *Greetings From Asbury Park, N.J.* . . . . (Columbia)
Live 1975-1985 . . . . (Legacy)
Tracks . . . . (Columbia)
David Bowie; *One Step Up/Two Steps Back-The Songs Of Bruce
Springsteen-C* . . . . (Right Stuff)

J.A.P. Rap
2 Live Jews; *As Kosher As They Wanna Be* . . . . (Kosher)

Jesus & Mama
Confederate Railroad; *Confederate Railroad* . . . .(Atlantic)

Jesus At McDonald's
Mojo Nixon; *Get Out Of My Way* . . . . (Restless)

Jesus Boy (You Only Look Like A Man)
Billy Paul; *45-#3737* . . . . (Philadelphia Int'l)

Jesus Children Of America
Stevie Wonder; *Innervisions* . . . . (Motown)
Jesus Christ
Arlo Guthrie; *Tribute To Woody Guthrie-C* . . . . (Warner Bros.)
Cisco Houston; *Greatest Songs Of Woody Guthrie-C* . . . . (Vanguard)
U2; *Folkways: A Vision Shared-C* . . . . (Columbia)
Woody Guthrie; *Woody Guthrie* . . . . (Warner Bros.)
Jesus Gave Love Away For Free
Stephen Stills; *Manassas* . . . . (Atlantic)
Jesus Gonna Make It Alright
Sonny Terry & Brownie McGhee; *Sonny & Brownie* . . . . (A&M)
Jesus He Knows Me
Genesis; *We Can't Dance* . . . . (Atlantic)
Jesus Is Just Alright
Byrds; *Ballad Of Easy Rider* . . . . (Columbia)
Best Of The Byrds-Greatest Hits-#2 . . . . (Columbia)
The Byrds . . . . (Columbia)
Doobie Brothers; *Best Of The Doobies* . . . . (Warner Bros.)
Toulouse Street . . . . (Warner Bros.)
Jesus Is Love
Commodores; *All The Great Love Songs-Commodores* . . . . (Motown)
Heroes/Commodores . . . . (Motown)
Jesus Is My Kind Of People
Ray Price; *You're The Best Thing That Ever Happened To Me* . . . . . . (Columbia)
Jesus Is On The Mainline
Ry Cooder; *Paradise And Lunch* . . . . (Reprise)
Show Time . . . . (Warner Bros.)
Jesus Is The Answer
Paul Simon; *Paul Simon In Concert/Live Rhymin'* . . . . (Columbia)
Jesus Is The Missing Peace
Whites; *A Lifetime In The Making* . . . . (Ceili Music)
Jesus Just Left Chicago
ZZ Top; *Best Of ZZ Top* . . . . (Warner Bros.)
Six Pack . . . . (Warner Bros.)
Tres Hombres . . . . (Warner Bros.)
Jesus Met The Woman At The Well
Peter, Paul & Mary; *Peter, Paul and Mary In Concert* . . . . (Warner Bros.)
Tracy Nelson; *Deep Are The Roots* . . . . (Prestige)
Jesus On The Radio
Tom T. Hall; *Ol' T's In Town* . . . . (RCA)
Jesus Thinks You're A Jerk
Frank Zappa; *Broadway The Hard Way* . . . . (Rykodisc)
Jesus To A Child
George Michael; *Ladies & Gentlemen: The Best Of George Michael* . . . . . (Epic)
Older . . . . (DreamWorks/SKG)
Jesus Was a Capricorn
Kris Kristofferson; *Jesus was a Capricorn* . . . . (Columbia)
John 3:16
Wyclef; *Muggs Presents...The Soul Assassins-C* . . . . (Columbia)
Joseph And Mary's Boy
Alabama; *Alabama-Christmas* . . . . (RCA)
Journey From Eden
Steve Miller Band; *Recall The Beginning* . . . . (Capitol)
Steve Miller Band-Anthology . . . . (Capitol)
Judith
A Perfect Circle; *Mer De Noms* . . . . (Virgin)
Just A Closer Walk With Thee
Jim Nabors; *Jim Nabors-16 Most Requested Songs* . . . . (Legacy)
Kid Thomas; *Kid Thomas & His New Orleans Jazz Band* . . . . . (Arhoolie)
Patsy Cline; *Best Of Patsy Cline* . . . . (Curb)
Here's Patsy Cline . . . . (MCA)
Preservation Hall Jazz Band; *Best Of The Preservation Hall
Jazz Band* . . . . (Columbia)
Tom Rush; *Blues Songs & Ballads* . . . . (Fantasy)
Just A Little Talk With Jesus
Elvis Presley; *Million-Dollar Quartet* . . . . (RCA)
Just Another Day In Paradise
Phil Vassar; *Phil Vassar* . . . . (Arista)
Just Between You And Me
DC Talk; *First Generation: 25 Years Of Virgin Records-C* . . . . . (Virgin)
Jesus Freak . . . . (Virgin)
Kathleen (Catholicism Made Easier)
Randy Newman; *Little Criminals* . . . . (Warner Bros.)
Keep It Between The Lines
Ricky Van Shelton; *Backroads* . . . . (Columbia)
Keeper Of The Stars
Tracy Byrd; *No Ordinary Man* . . . . (MCA)
Kingdom Hall
Van Morrison; *Wavelength* . . . . (Warner Bros.)
Last God Of England
Pete Morton; *Frivolous Love* . . . . (Philo)
Last Kiss
J. Frank Wilson and The Cavaliers; *Billboard Top Rock 'N' Roll Hits-
1964-C* . . . . (Rhino)
Collectables Presents The History Of Rock-#2-C . . . . (Collectables)
Oldies But Goodies-#9-C . . . . (Original Sound)
Teenage Tragedies-C . . . . (Rhino)
Pearl Jam; *No Boundaries-Benefit For The Kosovar Refugees-C* . . . . . (Epic)

Lean On Me
Kirk Franklin; *The Nu Nation Project* . . . . (Gospo Centric/Interscope)
Learn To Be Still
Eagles; *Hell Freezes Over* . . . . (Geffen)
Lessons To Be Learned
Barbra Streisand; *Higher Ground* . . . . (Columbia)
Let It Be
Aretha Franklin; *Aretha Franklin's Greatest Hits* . . . . (Atlantic)
Beatles; *Beatles 1* . . . . (Capitol)
Beatles-20 Greatest Hits . . . . (Capitol)
Past Masters-Volume Two . . . . (Parlophone)
Reel Music . . . . (Capitol)
The Beatles/1967-1970 . . . . (Capitol)
Paul McCartney; *The Concert For New York City-C* . . . . (Columbia)
Tripping The Live Fantastic-Highlights! . . . . (Capitol)
Rockestra; *Kampuchea-C* . . . . (Atlantic)
Light Of The World
Original Cast; *ST/Godspell* . . . . (Arista)
Like A Prayer
Madonna; *Like A Prayer* . . . . (Sire)
Royal Box . . . . (Sire)
Listen To The Bells
Doyle Lawson & Quicksilver; *Just Over In Heaven* . . . . (Sugar Hill)
Little Girl, The
John Michael Montgomery; *Brand New Me* . . . . (Atlantic)
Totally Hits-#3-C . . . . (Atlantic)
Little Green Apples
O.C. Smith; *Pop Classics Of The '60s-C* . . . . (Columbia)
Little John Of God
Los Lobos; *The Neighborhood* . . . . (Slash)
Little Lady Preacher
Tom T. Hall; *Tom T. Hall's Greatest Hits-#2* . . . . (Mercury)
Little Old Church In England
Glenn Miller & His Orchestra; *Complete Glenn Miller & His
Orchestra* . . . . (Bluebird)
Little Priest
Original Cast; *Sweeney Todd* . . . . (RCA)
Little Tin God
Don Henley; *End Of The Innocence* . . . . (Geffen)
Livin' In The Light
Caron Wheeler; *Uk Blak* . . . . (EMI)
Livin' On A Prayer
Bon Jovi; *America: A Tribute To Heroes-C* . . . . (Interscope)
Cross Road-14 Classic Grooves . . . . (Mercury)
Slippery When Wet . . . . (Jambco)
The Concert For New York City-C . . . . (Columbia)
Lonely
Tracy Lawrence; *Lessons Learned* . . . . (Atlantic)
Looking East
Jackson Browne; *Looking East* . . . . (Elektra)
Lord Have Mercy On A Country Boy
Don Williams; *True Love* . . . . (RCA)
Lord Have Mercy On My Soul
Black Oak Arkansas; *Best Of Black Oak Arkansas* . . . . (Atco)
Black Oak Arkansas . . . . (Atco)
Live Mutha . . . . (Atco)
Lord Have Mercy On The Working Man
Travis Tritt; *T-R-O-U-B-L-E* . . . . (Warner Bros.)
Lord I Hope This Day Is Good
Don Williams; *Best Of Don Williams-#3* . . . . (MCA)
Especially For You . . . . (MCA)
Lee Ann Womack; *Grand Ole Opry-75 Years-#1-C* . . . . (MCA)
Lord I Love Mashed Potatoes
Mayf Nutter; *Goin' Skinny Dippin'* . . . . (Crescendo)
Lord I Want To Go Back To California
Jim Post; *Magic-In Concert* . . . . (Flying Fish)
Lord Loves The One
George Harrison; *Living In The Material World* . . . . (Capitol)
Lord Protect My Child
Bob Dylan; *The Bootleg Series-Volumes 1-3 [Rare & Unreleased]* . . (Columbia)
Lord Take My Hand
Maddox Brothers & Rose; *On The Air-#1 & 2* . . . . (Arhoolie)
Lord, Lord, Lord
Cyrus Chestnut; *Revelation* . . . . (Atlantic)
Lord, Lord, Lord, You Sure Been Good To Me
Preservation Hall Jazz Band; *New Orleans-#3-When The Saints Go
Marchin' In* . . . . (Columbia)
Lord's Prayer
Randy Newman; *12 Songs* . . . . (Reprise)
Lord's Prayer
Original Broadway Cast; *Sarafina! (The Music Of Liberation)* . . . . (RCA)
Lord's Prayer
Sister Janet Mead; *Super Hits Of The '70s-Have A Nice Day-#12-C* . . . . (Rhino)
Losing My Religion
R.E.M.; *Out Of Time* . . . . (Warner Bros.)
Love Keep Us Together
Martin Sexton; *Black Sheep* . . . . (Eastern Front)
The American . . . . (Atlantic)

Love Spreads
Stone Roses; *Second Coming* . . . .(Geffen)
Love That Never Fails
Jim White; *No Such Place*. . . . .(Luaka Bop)
Love Train
Keb' Mo'; *Big Wide Grin* . . . . (Sony Wonder)
O'Jays; *Billboard Top Rock 'N' Roll Hits-1973-C* . . . . (Rhino)
   O'Jays' Greatest Hits . . . . (Philadelphia Int'l)
   O'Jays-Collector's Item. . . . . (Philadelphia Int'l)
   Philadelphia Classics-C . . . . (Philadelphia Int'l)
   Train Trax-C . . . . (Sony Music Special Prod.)
Love Without End, Amen
George Strait; *Livin' It Up* . . . .(MCA)
   Ten Strait Hits . . . .(MCA)
Lover's Prayer
Randy Newman; *Randy Newman/Live* . . . .(Warner Archives)
Lullaby
Take 6; *Join The Band-C* . . . . (Reprise)
   Love Shouldn't Hurt-C. . . . . (Qwest)
Machine Messiah
Yes; *Drama* . . . .(Atlantic)
Make Me A Channel Of Your Peace
Sinead O'Connor; *Diana, Princess Of Wales-Tribute-C* . . . . (Columbia)
Maker Said Take Her
Alabama; *In Pictures* . . . . (RCA)
Mama Don't Forget To Pray For Me
Diamond Rio; *Diamond Rio* . . . . (Arista)
   Diamond Rio's Greatest Hits . . . . (Arista)
Mama Sang A Song
Bill Anderson; *Bill Anderson's Greatest Hits* . . . . (Varese Sarabande)
   Country Music Classics-#17-C . . . . (K-Tel)
Marching To Mars
Sammy Hagar; *Marching To Mars* . . . .(MCA)
Mary's Prayer
Danny Wilson; *Meet Danny Wilson* . . . . (Virgin)
Master's Call
Marty Robbins; *Gunfighter Ballads & Trail Songs* . . . . (Legacy)
Me And Jesus
Tom T. Hall; *Audiograph Alive-C* . . . .(Audiograph)
   Tom T. Hall's Greatest Hits-#1 . . . . (Mercury)
Mercedes Benz
Janis Joplin; *Pearl*. . . . . (Legacy)
   ST/Janis. . . . . (Columbia)
Michael Row The Boat Ashore
Joe & Eddie; *Best Of Joe & Eddie*. . . . .(Crescendo)
   Gospel Truth . . . .(Crescendo)
   Weavers; *Weavers' Greatest Hits*. (Vanguard)
Mighty Fortress Is Our God, A
Leontyne Price; *God Bless America* . . . . (RCA)
Miner's Prayer
Dwight Yoakam; *Guitars, Cadillacs, Etc., Etc.* . . . . (Reprise)
Miseducation Of Lauryn Hill
Lauryn Hill; *The Miseducation Of Lauryn Hill*. . . . . (Ruffhouse/Columbia)
Missionary Man
Eurythmics; *Eurythmics' Greatest Hits* . . . . (Arista)
   Revenge . . . . (RCA)
Mississippi Squirrel Revival
Ray Stevens; *Country Classics-#1-C* . . . . (Universal)
   He Thinks He's Ray Stevens . . . . (MCA)
   Ray Stevens' Greatest Hits. . . . .(MCA)
Modern Maiden's Prayer, The
Eddie Cantor; *Music From The New York Stage (1890-1920)-#4-1917-
   1920-C* . . . . (Pearl)
Most High
Jimmy Page/Robert Plant; *Walking Into Clarksdale*. . . . .(Atlantic)
Mother's Only Sleeping
Ricky Skaggs and Kentucky Thunder; *History Of The Future* . . (Skaggs Family)
Mrs. Robinson
Simon & Garfunkel; *Bookends* . . . . (Columbia)
   Collected Works . . . . (Columbia)
   Hollywood Magic-1960s-C . . . . (Columbia)
   Simon & Garfunkel's Greatest Hits . . . . (Columbia)
   ST/Forrest Gump . . . . (Epic/Sony Music Soundtrax)
   ST/The Graduate . . . . (Columbia)
   The Concert In Central Park . . . .(Warner Bros.)
Muddy Jesus
Ian Moore; *Modernday Folklore* . . . . (Capricorn)
My Best Friend Is A Buddha
Deuter; *Silence Is The Answer* . . . . (Kuckuck)
My Cup Runneth Over
Ed Ames; *My Cup Runneth Over* . . . . (RCA)
   Nipper's Greatest Hits Of The '60s-#2-C . . . . (RCA)
   George Jones; *Homecoming In Heaven* . . . . (Razor & Tie)
   Jim Nabors; *Jim Nabors-16 Most Requested Songs* . . . . (Legacy)
   Original Broadway Cast; *I Do! I Do!* . . . .(RCA Victor)
My Everything
98 Degrees; *Revelation* . . . . (Universal)
My Father's Eyes
Eric Clapton; *Pilgrim* . . . . (Duck/Reprise)

My God
Alice Cooper; *Lace And Whiskey* . . . . (Warner Bros.)
Jethro Tull; *Aqualung* . . . . (Chrysalis)
My God & I
Ray Charles; *Renaissance* . . . . (Crossover)
My God Is A Powerful God
Sister Souljah; *360 Degrees Of Power* . . . . (Epic)
My God Is Real
Al Green; *Livin' For You* . . . . (Motown)
My Head Hurts, My Feet Stink And I Don't Love Jesus
Jimmy Buffett; *Havana Daydreamin'*. . . . . (MCA)
My Lover's Prayer
Otis Redding; *The Otis Redding Story*. . . . .(Atlantic)
   Very Best Of Otis Redding . . . . (Rhino)
My Mother's Bible
Warrior River Boys; *New Beginnings* . . . . (Rounder)
My Own Prison
Creed; *My Own Prison* . . . . (Wind-up)
My Prayer
Ink Spots; *Best Of The Ink Spots* . . . . (MCA)
Platters; *Encore Of Golden Hits-Platters* . . . . (Mercury)
   Oldies But Goodies-#3-C . . . .(Original Sound)
   Platters Greatest Hits . . . . (Everest)
   Platters-Anthology . . . . (Rhino)
My Sacrifice
Creed; *Weathered* . . . . (Wind-up)
My Song
Jerry Cantrell; *Boggy Depot* . . . . (Columbia)
My Special Prayer
Percy Sledge; *Best Of Percy Sledge*. . . . .(Atlantic)
   *Percy Sledge-The Ultimate Collection-When A Man Loves A
   Woman*. . . . .(Atlantic)
My Sweet Lord
George Harrison; *All Things Must Pass*. . . . .(Parlophone)
   Best Of George Harrison . . . . (Capitol)
   Concert For Bangladesh-C . . . . (Capitol)
Nearer, My God, To Thee
Mississippi John Hurt; *Best Of Mississippi John Hurt* . . . . (Vanguard)
   Immortal Mississippi Hurt . . . . (Vanguard)
Richard Jose; *Music From The New York Stage (1890-1920)-#1-1890-
   1908-C*. . . . . (Pearl)
Never An Absolution
James Horner; *ST/Titanic* . . . .(Sony Music Classical)
New Gods
Meat Puppets; *Meat Puppets II* . . . .(SST)
   No Strings Attached . . . .(SST)
No Man's Woman
Sinead O'Connor; *Faith & Courage* . . . .(Atlantic)
Oh Happy Day
Edwin Hawkins Singers; *Didn't It Blow Your Mind: Soul Hits Of The
   '70s-#1-C*. . . . . (Rhino)
   Super Hits-#3-C . . . . (Gusto)
Five Satins; *Five Satins Sing Their Greatest Hits* . . . . (Collectables)
Oh Thank You Great Spirit
Chicago; *Chicago VIII* . . . . (Chicago)
Old
Paul Simon; *You're The One* . . . . (Warner Bros.)
Old Country Church
Hank Williams; *I Ain't Got Nothin' But Time-1946-1947*. . . . .(Polydor)
Old Master Painter
Peggy Lee; *Capitol Collectors Series-Peggy Lee-#1-Early Years* . . . . . (Capitol)
On & On
Erykah Badu; *Baduizm* . . . . (Kedar Entert./Universal)
On Holy Ground
Barbra Streisand; *Higher Ground* . . . . (Columbia)
On The Rock Where Moses Stood
Carter Family; *Worried Man Blues: Their Complete Victor Recordings-
   1930*. . . . . (Rounder)
Flatt & Scruggs; *Songs Of The Famous Carter Family* . . . . (Legacy)
One God
Barbra Streisand; *Christmas Memories*. . . . . (Columbia)
One Miner's Life-The Image Of God
Battlefield Band; *There's A Buzz*. (Flying Fish)
One Of Us
Joan Osborne; *Relish*. . . . .(Blue Gorilla/Mercury)
One Small Miracle
Bryan White; *The Right Place* . . . .(Asylum)
One Toke Over The Line
Brewer & Shipley; *'70s Greatest Rock Hits-#10-C* . . . . (Priority)
   Super Hits Of The '70s-Have A Nice Day-#4-C . . . . (Rhino)
One Voice
Billy Gilman; *One Voice* . . . . (Epic)
Only God Knows Why
Kid Rock; *Devil Without A Cause* . . . . (Top Dog/Lava/Atlantic)
Only The Good Die Young
Billy Joel; *Billy Joel-Greatest Hits, Volume I & Volume II* . . . . (Columbia)
   KOHUEPT. . . . . (Columbia)
   The Stranger. . . . . (Columbia)

Open My Heart
Yolanda Adams; *Mountain High Valley Low* . . . . (Elektra)
Outlaw's Prayer
Johnny Paycheck; *Armed & Crazy* . . . . (Epic)
   Johnny Paycheck's Biggest Hits . . . . (Epic)
Palm Sunday
Jerry Garcia; *Cats Under The Stars* . . . . (Arista)
Part Man, Part Monkey
Bruce Springsteen; *Tracks* . . . . (Columbia)
Pearl, The
Emmylou Harris; *Red Dirt Girl* . . . . (Nonesuch)
People Get Ready
Aretha Franklin; *Aretha-Lady Soul* . . . . (Atlantic)
Impressions; *Impressions' Greatest Hits* . . . . (MCA)
   Soul Shots-#5-La-La Means I Love You-C . . . . (Rhino)
   Train Trax-C . . . . (Sony Music Special Prod.)
Jeff Beck; *Flash* . . . . (Epic)
Rod Stewart; *Storyteller/The Complete Anthology: 1964-1990* . . (Warner Bros.)
Personal Jesus
Depeche Mode; *Best Of MTV's 120 Minutes-#2-C* . . . . (Rhino)
   Just Say Da-#4 Of Just Say Yes-C . . . .(Sire)
   Violator . . . .(Sire)
Phone Call From God
Ray Reeves; *Comedy For The Road-#2-C* . . . . (Hollywood/DNA-Rounder)
Pilate & Christ
Original London Cast; *Jesus Christ Superstar* . . . . (MCA)
Pilate's Dream
Original London Cast; *Jesus Christ Superstar* . . . . (MCA)
Place In This World
Michael W. Smith; *Go West Young Man* . . . . (Reunion)
Plastic Jesus
Ernie Marrs & The Marrs Family; *Best Of Broadside 1962-1968: Anthems Of The American Underground From The Pages Of Broadside Magazine-C* . . . .(Smithsonian Folkways)
Playing In God's Garden
Stevie Nicks; *Street Angel* . . . . (Modern)
Po Lazarus
James Carter & The Prisoners; *ST/O Brother, Where Art Thou?* . . . . . . (Mercury)
Poems, Prayers & Promises
John Denver; *Evening With John Denver* . . . . (RCA)
   John Denver's Greatest Hits . . . .(RCA)
   Poems, Prayers & Promises . . . .(RCA)
John Denver & The Muppets; *Rocky Mountain Holiday* . . . . (RCA)
Point Of Light
Randy Travis; *Heroes And Friends* . . . . (Warner Bros.)
   High Lonesome . . . . (Warner Bros.)
Poor Little Jesus
Weavers; *On Tour* . . . . (Vanguard)
Poor, Poor Joseph
Original Cast; *Joseph & The Amazing Technicolor Dreamcoat* . . . . . . (Polydor)
Pope Is A Potato
Mofungo; *Bugged* . . . . (SST)
Pope On A Rope (Cigarette Butt)
Squirrels; *What Gives?* . . . .(Pop Llama Prod.)
Power & The Glory
Phil Ochs; *Chords Of Fame* . . . .(A&M)
   There But For Fortune . . . . (Elektra)
Power & The Glory
Wee Papa Girls; *Be Aware* . . . .(Jive)
Power & The Glory
Limeliters; *Harmony!* . . . . (Folk Era)
   We The People-C . . . . (Folk Era)
Power & The Glory
Jimmy Cliff; *Power & The Glory* . . . . (Columbia)
Power & The Glory
Twisted Sister; *You Can't Stop Rock 'N' Roll* . . . . (Atlantic)
Power Of God
L.L. Cool J; *Mama Said Knock You Out* . . . . (Def Jam)
Praise The Lord & Pass The Ammunition
Kay Kyser & His Orchestra; *Best Of The Big Bands-C* . . . . (Columbia)
   Sentimental Favorites . . . . (Columbia)
Pray For Me
John Cougar; *John Cougar* . . . . (Riva)
Prayer
Christian Death; *Only Theatre Of Pain* . . . . (Fontana)
Joe Walsh; *The Smoker You Drink The Player You Get* . . . . (MCA)
Stevie B; *Healing* . . . . (Epic)
Prayer & A Juke Box
Little Anthony And The Imperials; *Best Of Little Anthony And The Imperials* . . . . (Rhino)
   Forever Yours . . . . (Roulette)
Prayer For Everybody/To Be Free
Gil Scott-Heron & Brian Jackson; *Secrets* . . . . (Arista)
Prayer For The Dying
Seal; *Diana, Princess Of Wales-Tribute-C* . . . . (Columbia)
   Seal 2 . . . .(Sire)
Prayin' For Daylight
Rascal Flatts; *Rascal Flatts* . . . . (Lyric Street)

Praying For Time
George Michael; *Listen Without Prejudice* . . . .(Columbia)
Praying Hands
Devo; *Live-The Mongoloid Years* . . . . (Rykodisc)
   Q: Are We Not Men? A: We Are Devo! . . . .(Warner Bros.)
Praying To The Aliens
Gary Numan & Tubeway Army; *Replicas* . . . .(Atco)
Preacher
Horace Silver; *Best Of Horace Silver-The Blue Note Years* . . . . (Blue Note)
Louis Armstrong; *Louis Armstrong's Greatest Hits* . . . .(Curb)
Preacher & The Bear
Andy Griffith; *American Originals-Andy Griffith* . . . .(Capitol)
Big Bopper; *Helloo Baby! Best Of The Big Bopper-1954-1959* . . . .(Rhino)
Rufus Thomas & Carla Thomas; *Rufus Thomas & Carla Thomas-Chronicle* . . . . (Stax)
Preacher Man
Bananarama; *Pop Life* . . . . (London)
Preacher Man
Bananarama; *Pop Life* . . . . (London)
Preacher's Daughter
Lynyrd Skynyrd; *First & Last* . . . . (MCA)
Preachin' The Blues
Bessie Smith; *Bessie Smith-The Complete Recordings-#3* . . . .(Legacy)
   Nobody's Blues But Mine . . . .(Columbia)
LaVern Baker; *LaVern Baker Sings Bessie Smith* . . . . (Atlantic)
Linda Hopkins; *Me & Bessie* . . . .(Columbia)
Preachin' The Blues
Gun Club; *Fire Of Love* . . . . (Slash)
Preaching Blues (Up Jumped The Devil)
Robert Johnson; *King Of The Delta Blues Singers-#2* . . . .(Columbia)
   Robert Johnson-Complete Recordings . . . .(Columbia)
Preaching, Praying, Singing
Bluegrass Album Band; *Bluegrass Class Of 1990* . . . .(Rounder)
Lester Flatt, Earl Scruggs & The Foggy Mountain Boys; *Lester Flatt, Earl Scruggs & The Foggy Mountain Boys-Complete Mercury Sessions* . . . .(Mercury)
Precious Little
Eleanor McEvoy; *What's Following Me?* . . . .(Columbia)
Precious Lord, Take My Hand
Linda Hopkins; *How Blue Can You Get* . . . . (Quicksilver)
Preservation Hall Jazz Band; *Best Of The Preservation Hall Jazz Band* . . . .(Columbia)
Precious Time
Van Morrison; *Back On Top* . . . . (Point Blank/Virgin)
Presence Of The Lord
Blind Faith; *Blind Faith* . . . . (Polydor)
Derek And The Dominos; *Derek & The Dominos In Concert* . . . .(RSO)
Eric Clapton; *Eric Clapton-Crossroads-C* . . . . (Polydor)
Pretty Fly For A Rabbi
"Weird Al" Yankovic; *Running With Scissors* . . . . (Volcano Entertainment)
Priests On Drugs
Paper Bag; *No Age-Compilation Of SST Instrumentals-C* . . . . (SST)
Promised Land
Band; *Moondog Matinee* . . . .(Capitol)
Chuck Berry; *Rock 'N' Roll Rarities-20 Magic Tracks* . . . .(Chess)
   The Chess Box-Chuck Berry . . . .(Chess)
Elvis Presley; *Promised Land* . . . . (RCA)
   ST/This Is Elvis . . . . (RCA)
Freddy Weller; *Country Music Classics-#11-Early '70s-C* . . . .(K-Tel)
   Freddy Weller's Greatest Hits . . . .(Columbia)
Gary Morris; *Full Moon Empty Heart* . . . .(Liberty)
Grateful Dead; *Steal Your Face* . . . . (Grateful Dead)
James Taylor; *Walking Man* . . . .(Warner Bros.)
Kingfish; *Kingfish/Alive In Eighty Five-Double Dose* . . . . (Relix)
Pure Religion
Reverend Gary Davis; *Pure Religion & Bad Company* . . . . (Smithsonian Folkways)
Put Your Hand In The Hand
Anne Murray; *Anne Murray-Country* . . . .(Capitol)
   Danny's Song . . . .(Capitol)
   Snowbird . . . .(Capitol)
Elvis Presley; *Canadian Tribute* . . . . (RCA)
   Elvis Now . . . . (RCA)
Ocean; *Super Hits Of The '70s-Have A Nice Day-#4-C* . . . .(Rhino)
Put Your Hands On The Screen
Martin Briley; *One Night With A Stranger* . . . .(Mercury)
Quicksand Jesus
Skid Row; *Slave To The Grind* . . . . (Atlantic)
Quiet
Paul Simon; *You're The One* . . . . (Warner Bros.)
Rain, Rain, Rain
Frankie Laine; *Frankie Laine-16 Most Requested Songs* . . . .(Legacy)
Redemption
Johnny Cash; *American Recordings* . . . .(American)
Redemption Day
Sheryl Crow; *Sheryl Crow* . . . .(A&M)
Resignation Superman
Big Head Todd & The Monsters; *Beautiful World* . . . .(Revolution)

Live Monsters . . . . (Revolution)
Rest My Mind On Jesus
Charles Ford Band; *Charles Ford Band* . . . . (Arhoolie)
Reverend Jack & His Roamin' Cadillac Church
Timbuk 3; *Eden Alley* . . . .(I.R.S.)
Reverend Mr. Black
Johnny Cash; *Johnny Cash's Biggest Hits* . . . . (Columbia)
Kingston Trio; *Capitol Collectors Series-The Kingston Trio* . . . . (Capitol)
Revival
Gretchen Peters; *Gretchen Peters* . . . . (Purple Crayon Prod.)
Rhythm Of The Saints
Paul Simon; *Rhythm Of The Saints* . . . .(Warner Bros.)
Rich Man's Spiritual
Gordon Lightfoot; *Lightfoot* . . . .(EMI)
Right Hand Of God
Move; *Yeah Whatever* . . . .(Atlantic)
River Of Deceit
Mad Season; *Above* . . . . (Columbia)
River Of Jordan
Ricky Skaggs; *Family & Friends* . . . . (Rounder)
Stained Glass Hour . . . . (Rounder)
Rivers Of Babylon
Boney M; *Nightflight To Venus* . . . . (Sire)
Linda Ronstadt; *Hasten Down The Wind* . . . . (Asylum)
Melodians; *Grooveyard-C* . . . . (Mango)
ST/The Harder They Come . . . . (Mango)
Road To Dead
Paula Cole; *This Fire* . . . . (Imago)
Rock Of Ages
Cristy Lane; *Amazing Grace* . . . .(EMI)
Johnny Cash; *Johnny Cash Sings Precious Memories* . . . .(Epic)
Mormon Tabernacle Choir; *Rock Of Ages-30 Favorite*
Hymns . . . . (Sony Music Classical)
Statler Brothers; *Todays' Gospel Favorites* . . . . (Mercury)
Tennessee Ernie Ford; *Country Gospel Classics-#1* . . . . (Liberty)
Rocket To God
Daryl Hall & John Oates; *ooh yeah!* . . . . (Arista)
Sabbath Prayer
Herschel Bernardi; *ST/Fiddler On The Roof* . . . . (Columbia)
Original Cast; *Fiddler On The Roof* . . . .(RCA Victor)
Sabbath, Bloody Sabbath
Anthrax; *I'm The Man* . . . . (Island)
Black Sabbath; *Sabbath Bloody Sabbath* . . . .(Warner Bros.)
We Sold Our Soul For Rock 'N' Roll . . . .(Warner Bros.)
Ozzy Osbourne; *Speak Of The Devil* . . . . (Jet)
Sacred
Depeche Mode; *101* . . . . (Sire)
Music For The Masses . . . . (Sire)
Sacred Bird
Original London Cast; *Miss Saigon* . . . .(Geffen)
Sacred Emotion
Donny Osmond; *Donny Osmond* . . . . (Capitol)
Sacred Ground
McBride & The Ride; *Sacred Ground* . . . .(MCA)
Sacred Heart
Dio; *Intermission* . . . .(Warner Bros.)
Sacred Heart . . . .(Warner Bros.)
Sacred Heart
Shakespear's Sister; *ST/Nuns On The Run* . . . . (Mercury)
Saint
Elton John; *Too Low For Zero* . . . .(MCA)
Saint
Thompson Twins; *Queer* . . . .(Warner Bros.)
Saint Agnes & The Burning Train
Sting; *Soul Cages* . . . . (A&M)
Saint Joe On The School Bus
Marcy Playground; *Marcy Playground* . . . . (Capitol)
Saint Of Me
Rolling Stones; *Bridges To Babylon* . . . . (Virgin)
No Security . . . . (Virgin)
Samson & Delilah
Blind Gary Davis; *Harlem Street Singer* . . . . (Bluesville)
Reverend Gary Davis; *From Blues To Gospel* . . . . (Biograph)
Samson & Delilah
Blasters; *Blasters-Collection* . . . . (Slash)
Samson & Delilah
Grateful Dead; *Dead Set* . . . . (Arista)
Terrapin Station . . . . (Arista)
Sanctified Lady
Marvin Gaye; *Dream Of A Lifetime* . . . . (Columbia)
Sanctify Yourself
Simple Minds; *Once Upon A Time* . . . . (A&M)
Simple Minds Live: In The City Of Light . . . . (A&M)
Save A Prayer
Duran Duran; *Arena* . . . . (Capitol)
Decade . . . . (Capitol)
Rio . . . . (Capitol)
Secret Policeman's Third Ball-The Music-C . . . . (Virgin)

Save A Prayer
Mavericks; *Trampoline* . . . . (MCA)
Say A Prayer
Breathe; *Peace Of Mind* . . . . (A&M)
Scarlet Ribbons (For Her Hair)
Harry Belafonte; *Harry Belafonte-Legendary Performer* . . . . (RCA)
Harry Belafonte's All Time Greatest Hits-#1 . . . . (RCA)
This Is Harry Belafonte . . . . (RCA)
Jim Ed Brown & Maxine Brown; *Essential Jim Ed Brown* . . . . (RCA)
Kingston Trio; *At Large/Here We Go Again!* . . . . (Capitol)
Capitol Collectors Series-The Kingston Trio . . . . (Capitol)
Lennon Sisters; *Best Of The Lennon Sisters* . . . . (Ranwood)
Les Paul; *Legend & The Legacy-#1-4* . . . . (Capitol)
NRBQ; *Diggin' Uncle Q* . . . . (Rounder)
Patti Page; *Patti Page-16 Most Requested Songs* . . . . (Legacy)
Roger Whittaker; *Roger Whittaker-Classics Collection-#2* . . . . (Liberty)
Scratchings On The Bible Belt
Rain Tree Crow; *Rain Tree Crow* . . . .(Virgin)
Second Sitting For The Last Supper
10 CC; *Live & Let Live* . . . . (Mercury)
Send Down An Angel
Allison Moorer; *The Hardest Part* . . . . (MCA)
Send It On
D'Angelo; *Voodoo* . . . .(Cheeba Sound/Virgin)
Sending Me Angels
Kathy Mattea; *Love Travels* . . . . (Mercury)
Shackles (Praise You)
Mary Mary; *Thankful* . . . . (C2/Columbia)
Shall We Gather At The River?
Chuck Wagon Gang; *16 Country-Gospel Favorites* . . . . (MCA)
Tennessee Ernie Ford; *All-Time Greatest Hymns* . . . . (Curb)
Tennessee Ernie Ford Sings 22 Favorite Hymns . . . . (Ranwood)
Shanti/Ashtangi
Madonna; *Ray Of Light* . . . . (Maverick)
She Gives Me Religion
Van Morrison; *Beautiful Vision* . . . .(Warner Bros.)
She Misses Him On Sunday The Most
Diamond Rio; *Diamond Rio IV* . . . . (Arista)
Diamond Rio's Greatest Hits . . . . (Arista)
Shine A Light
Rolling Stones; *Exile On Main Street* . . . .(Virgin)
Sin Wagon
Dixie Chicks; *Fly* . . . . (Monument)
Sinner
Neil Finn; *Try Whistling This* . . . . (Work)
Sinner's Prayer
Eric Clapton; *From The Cradle* . . . .(Duck/Reprise)
Sister Christian
Night Ranger; *Midnight Madness* . . . . (MCA)
Night Ranger's Greatest Hits . . . .(Camel)
Sit Down, You're Rockin' The Boat
Don Henley; *ST/Leap Of Faith* . . . . (MCA)
Original Cast; *Guys & Dolls* . . . . (MCA)
Skellig
Loreena McKennitt; *The Book Of Secrets* . . . . (Quinlan Rd./Warner Bros.)
Slide
Goo Goo Dolls; *Dizzy Up The Girl* . . . .(Warner Sunset/Reprise)
Slow Train
Bob Dylan; *Slow Train Coming* . . . . (Columbia)
Bob Dylan & The Grateful Dead; *Dylan & The Dead* . . . . (Columbia)
So In Love With You
U.N.V.; *Universal Nubian Voices* . . . . (Maverick/Warner Bros.)
Somebody Up There Likes Me
David Bowie; *Young Americans* . . . . (Rykodisc)
Somebody Up There Likes Me
Reba McEntire; *Sweet Sixteen* . . . . (MCA)
Sometimes Salvation
Black Crowes; *Southern Harmony & Musical Companion* . . . . . .(Def American)
Son Of A Preacher Man
Dusty Springfield; *Dusty Springfield* . . . . (Rhino)
Dusty Springfield-Anthology . . . . (Mercury)
Soul Searchin'
Leon Everette; *45-#13282* . . . . (RCA)
Soul Searchin'
Glenn Frey; *Soul Searchin'* . . . . (MCA)
Spanish Pipedream
John Prine; *John Prine* . . . .(Atlantic)
Spirit In The Sky
Kentucky HeadHunters; *Electric Barnyard* . . . . (Mercury)
Norman Greenbaum; *Billboard Top Rock 'N' Roll Hits-1970-C* . . . . (Rhino)
Super Hits Of The '70s-Have A Nice Day-#2-C . . . . (Rhino)
Spiritual Thang
Eric Benet; *True To Myself* . . . .(Jac-Mac/Warner Bros.)
St. Alphonzo's Pancake Breakfast
Frank Zappa; *Apostrophe/Overnite Sensation* . . . . (Rykodisc)
Star Of Bethlehem
Emmylou Harris & Neil Young; *Duets-C* . . . . (Reprise)
Neil Young; *Decade* . . . . (Reprise)

Neil Young, Crazy Horse & The Bullets; *American Stars 'N Bars* . . . . (Reprise)
State Trooper
Bruce Springsteen; *Nebraska* . . . . (Columbia)
The Sopranos-Music From The HBO Original
Series . . . . (Sony Music Soundtrax)
Steal Away
Jackson Southernaires; *Presenting Joy, Peace, Happiness*
& Love . . . . (MCA Special Prod.)
Reverend James Cleveland; *Reverend James Cleveland Sings With The*
World's Greatest Gospel Stars . . . . (Savoy)
Stomp
God's Property; *MTV Jams-C* . . . . (Kedar Entert./Universal)
Sun Goddess
Earth, Wind & Fire; *Eternal Dance* . . . . (Columbia)
Gratitude . . . . (Legacy)
Sun Goddess
Ramsey Lewis; *Best Of Ramsey Lewis* . . . . (Columbia)
Sun Goddess . . . . (Columbia)
Superstar
Murray Head; *Premiere Collection-Best Of Andrew Lloyd Webber-C* . . . (MCA)
Super Hits Of The '70s-Have A Nice Day-#5-C . . . . (Rhino)
Original Cast; *ST/Jesus Christ Superstar* . . . . (MCA)
Soundtrack; *Movie Greats* . . . . (MCA)
Swearin' To God
4 Seasons; *25th Anniversary Collection* . . . . (Rhino)
4 Seasons' Greatest Hits-#2 . . . . (Rhino)
Sweet Jesus
Sugar Minott; *Ghetto Child* . . . . (Heartbeat)
Sweet 'N' Sour Jesus
Supersuckers; *Smoke Of Hell* . . . . (Sub Pop)
Swing Down Chariot
Rufus; *Rags To Rufus* . . . . (MCA)
Swing Low, Sweet Chariot
Eric Clapton; *Time Pieces-#1-The Best Of Eric Clapton* . . . . (Polydor)
Glenn Miller & His Orchestra; *Moonlight Serenade* . . . . (Ranwood)
Hi-Lo's; *Suddenly It's The Hi-Lo's* . . . . (Columbia)
Jerry Garcia Acoustic Band; *Almost Acoustic* . . . . (Grateful Dead)
Joan Baez; *From Every Stage* . . . . (A&M)
Peggy Lee; *Best Of Peggy Lee* . . . . (MCA)
Take Your Burden To The Lord & Leave It There
Blind Willie Johnson; *Complete Blind Willie Johnson* . . . . (Columbia)
Talkin' Hava Negeilah Blues
Bob Dylan; *The Bootleg Series-Volumes 1-3 [Rare & Unreleased]* . . (Columbia)
Teach Them To Pray
Junior Walker & The All Stars; *Motown Superstar Series-#5-Junior Walker*
& The All Stars. . . . . (Motown)
Temple Jamaica
Peter Manning Robinson; *Phoenix Rising* . . . . (Chase Music Group)
Temple Of The Lord
Saints; *All Fools Day* . . . . (TVT)
Temple, The
20th Anniversary London Cast; *Jesus Christ Superstar* . . . . (RCA)
Ten Commandments Of Love
Bob Marley & The Wailers; *Birth Of A Legend 1963-*
1966 . . . . (Epic Portrait Assoc.)
Harvey & The Moonglows; *Best Of Chess Rock 'N' Roll-#2-C* . . . . . (Chess)
Collectables Presents The History Of Rock-#10-C . . . . (Collectables)
Cruisin'-1958-C . . . . (Increase)
Oldies But Goodies-#11-C . . . . (Original Sound)
Ten Thousand Angels
Mindy McCready; *Ten Thousand Angels* . . . . (BNA)
Tender Shepherd
Original Cast; *Peter Pan-The 1954 Broadway Production* . . . . . . (RCA Victor)
Testicle Of God (& It Was Good)
Gaye Bykers On Acid; *Stewed To The Gills* . . . . (Caroline)
Tha Crossroads
Bone Thugs-N-Harmony; *Club Mix '97* . . . . (Cold Front)
MTV Party To Go-#10-C . . . . (Tommy Boy)
Thank God
Hank Williams; *I Saw The Light* . . . . (Polydor)
Let's Turn Back The Years-1951-1953 . . . . (Polydor)
Roy Acuff; *Roy Acuff's Greatest Hits-#2* . . . . (MCA)
Thank God & Greyhound
Roy Clark; *Best Of Roy Clark* . . . . (MCA)
Great Picks And New Tricks . . . . (ISD/Intersound)
Roy Clark-Live . . . . (MCA)
Roy Clark's Greatest Hits . . . . (MCA)
Thank God For Believers
Mark Chesnutt; *Thank God For Believers* . . . . (Decca)
Thank God For Kids
Oak Ridge Boys; *Christmas For The '90s-#1-C* . . . . (Liberty)
Oak Ridge Boys' Greatest Hits 2 . . . . (MCA)
Oak Ridge Boys-Christmas . . . . (MCA Special Prod.)
Oak Ridge Boys-Collection . . . . (MCA)
Thank God For The Radio
Kendalls; *Kendalls-20 Favorites* . . . . (Epic)
Movin' Train . . . . (Mercury)
Thank God For You
Sawyer Brown; *Outskirts Of Town* . . . . (Curb)

Sawyer Brown's Greatest Hits 1990-1995 . . . . (Curb)
Thank God I Found You
Mariah Carey featuring Joe & 98 Degrees; *Rainbow* . . . . (Columbia)
Thank God I'm A Country Boy
John Denver; *Back Home Again* . . . . (RCA)
Evening With John Denver . . . . (RCA)
John Denver's Greatest Hits-#2 . . . . (RCA)
Thank God It's Monday
Dene Anton; *Texas Soul* . . . . (JRS)
Thank The Lord For The Night Time
Neil Diamond; *Glory Road-1968-1972* . . . . (MCA)
Hot August Night II . . . . (Columbia)
Neil Diamond-Classics (Early Years) . . . . (Columbia)
Neil Diamond-Gold . . . . (MCA)
Neil Diamond's Greatest Hits-1966-1992 . . . . (Columbia)
Thank U
Alanis Morissette; *Supposed Former Infatuation Junkie* . . . . (Maverick)
Thank You Lord
Bob Marley & The Wailers; *Songs Of Freedom* . . . . (Tuff Gong)
Glenn Yarbrough & The Limeliters; *Joy Across The Land* . . . . . . (Crescendo)
Heptones; *Changing Times* . . . . (Moving Target)
Thanking The Good Lord
Merle Haggard; *Chill Factor* . . . . (Epic)
That's What God Looks Like To Me
Frank Sinatra; *Trilogy: Pasts, Present, Future.* . . . . (Reprise)
That's Why God Made The Movies
Paul Simon; *ST/One-Trick Pony* . . . . (Warner Bros.)
Theme From "Exodus"
101 Strings Orchestra; *Golden Movie Themes* . . . . (Alshire)
Boston Pops Orchestra/Arthur Fiedler; *Motion Picture*
Classics-#1 . . . . (RCA Victor)
Ferrante & Teicher; *Grand Pianos* . . . . (Pair)
Theme From "Raiders Of The Lost Ark"
Neil Norman; *Greatest Science Fiction Hits-#3-C.* . . . . (Crescendo)
Theme From "The Flying Nun"
Original Soundtrack; *Television's Greatest Hits-#5-In Living Color-C.* . . . (TVT)
Then God Made Malls
Uncle Bonsai; *Myn Ynd Wymyn* . . . . (Yellow Tail)
There Goes God
Crowded House; *Woodface* . . . . (Capitol)
There Will Never Be Any Peace (Until God Is Seated At The
Conference Table)
Chi-Lites; *Chi-Lites' Greatest Hits* . . . . (Rhino)
There You Are
Martina McBride; *Emotion* . . . . (RCA)
There's A Gold Mine In The Sky
Jimmy C. Newman; *Cajun Cowboy* . . . . (Plantation)
Pat Boone; *Love Letters In The Sand* . . . . (MCA Special Prod.)
There's A Light
Doobie Brothers; *Livin' On The Fault Line* . . . . (Warner Bros.)
Thicker Than Blood
Garth Brooks; *Scarecrow* . . . . (Capitol)
Thieves In The Temple
Prince; *ST/Graffiti Bridge* . . . . (Paisley Park)
This Is My Prayer
Frank Sinatra; *The World We Knew* . . . . (Reprise)
Petula Clark; *20 Top 10 Hits Of The '50s & '60s-C* . . . . (Laurie)
Greatest Hits Of Petula Clark . . . . (Crescendo)
This Is The Way I Pray
Ella Jenkins; *African-American Folk Rhythms.* . . . . . . (Smithsonian Folkways)
This Jesus Must Die
Original London Cast; *Jesus Christ Superstar* . . . . (MCA)
This Train Is Bound For Glory
Arlo Guthrie; *Tribute To Woody Guthrie-C* . . . . (Warner Bros.)
Three Bells, The
Browns; *Billboard Top Country Hits-1959-C* . . . . (Rhino)
Nipper's Greatest Hits Of The '50s-#1-C . . . . (RCA)
Tiki Tiki Tiki Room
Original Music; *Disney Collection-#1-C* . . . . (Disney)
Time Of The Preacher Theme
Willie Nelson; *Red Headed Stranger* . . . . (Columbia)
Tin Jesus
Wire Train; *Wire Train.* . . . . (MCA)
Tippin' Home From Sunday School
Oliver Jones; *Class Act.* . . . . (Justin Time)
To Find God
James Michaels; *Bouquet.* . . . . (Innersong)
To Zion
Lauryn Hill featuring Carlos Santana; *The Miseducation Of*
Lauryn Hill. . . . . (Ruffhouse/Columbia)
Transcendance
Santana; *Moonflower* . . . . (Columbia)
Transcendental Blues
Steve Earle; *Transcendental Blues.* . . . . (Artemis)
Travelin' Prayer
Billy Joel; *Piano Man.* . . . . (Columbia)
Traveller's Prayer
George Jones & Sweethearts Of The Rodeo; *Friends In High Places-C* . . . (Epic)

Trial Before Pilate
 Original London Cast; *Jesus Christ Superstar* . . . .(MCA)
Truck Driver's Prayer
 Dave Dudley; *Diesel Express* . . . . (Fifty One West)
Truckers Prayer
 Boxcar Willie; *Truck Driving Favorites* . . . . (Madacy)
Turn! Turn! Turn! (To Everything There Is A Season)
 Byrds; *Billboard Top Rock 'N' Roll Hits-1965-C* . . . . (Rhino)
  Original Singles-#1-1965-1967 . . . . (Columbia)
  ST/Forrest Gump . . . . (Epic/Sony Music Soundtrax)
  The Byrds . . . . (Columbia)
  The Byrds' Greatest Hits . . . . (Columbia)
  Turn! Turn! Turn! . . . . (Legacy)
 Pete Seeger; *Pete Seeger's Greatest Hits* . . . . (Columbia)
  Troubadours Of The Folk Era-#2-C . . . . (Rhino)
TV Preacher Man Blues
 Glenn Sutton; *Close Encounters Of The Sutton Kind* . . . . (Mercury)
Unanswered Prayers
 Garth Brooks; *No Fences* . . . . (Capitol)
Under God
 Midge Ure; *Answers To Nothing* . . . .(Chrysalis)
Under The God
 Tin Machine; *Tin Machine* . . . .(EMI)
Vacation Bible School
 Ray Stevens; *Everything Is Beautiful* . . . .(MCA Special Prod.)
  I Have Returned . . . . (MCA)
Various Tracks
 Bob Dylan; *Saved* . . . . (Columbia)
Vaya Con Dios
 Bing Crosby; *The Radio Years-#2* . . . .(Crescendo)
 Freddy Fender; *Freddy Fender-Collection* . . . . (Reprise)
 Les Paul & Mary Ford; *Memories Are Made Of This-C* . . . . (Capitol)
 Roger Whittaker; *All-Time Heart-Touching Favorites* . . . . (Capitol)
Vicar In A Tutu
 Smiths; *Rank* . . . . (Sire)
  The Queen Is Dead . . . . (Sire)
Voice Of Harold
 R.E.M.; *Dead Letter Office* . . . .(I.R.S.)
Wages Of Sin
 Bruce Springsteen; *Tracks* . . . . (Columbia)
Watching Out For Jesus
 Rave-Ups; *Chance* . . . .(Epic)
Waterfalls
 TLC; *1996 Grammy Nominees-C* . . . . (Columbia)
  CrazySexyCool . . . . (LaFace)
We Gather Together
 Original Soundtrack; *School Days-Kids Classics* . . . . (Benson)
We Need A Lot More Of Jesus (& A Lot Less Of Rock & Roll)
 Linda Ronstadt; *Hand Sown Home Grown* . . . . (Capitol)
Well, Alright!
 CeCe Winans; *Everlasting Love* . . . .(PMG/Atlantic)
  Wow Gospel 1999-C . . . . (Verity/BMG)
Were You There (When They Crucified My Lord?)
 Johnny Cash with The Carter Family; *The Man In Black-His
  Greatest Hits* . . . . (Legacy)
What A Friend We Have In Jesus
 Nashville Superpickers; *Live From Austin City Limits* . . . . (Flying Fish)
 Sweet Honey In The Rock; *We All...Every One Of Us* . . . . (Flying Fish)
What God Wants (Part I)
 Roger Waters; *Amused To Death* . . . . (Columbia)
What If God Smoked Cannabis
 Bob Rivers; *Best Of Twisted Tunes-#2* . . . .(Atlantic)
What's This Life For
 Creed; *My Own Prison* . . . . (Wind-up)
When God Comes & Gathers His Jewels
 Hank Williams; *Health & Happiness Shows* . . . . (Mercury)
  I Saw The Light . . . .(Polydor)
 Molly O'Day & The Cumberland Mountain Folks; *Columbia Country
  Classics-#1-Golden Age-C* . . . . (Columbia)
  Hank Williams Songbook-C . . . . (Columbia)
When God Fearin' Women Get The Blues
 Martina McBride; *Martina McBride's Greatest Hits* . . . . (RCA)
When Jesus Left Birmingham
 John Mellencamp & Sounds Of Blackness; *Human Wheels* . . . . (Mercury)
When The Fallen Angels Fly
 Patty Loveless; *When Fallen Angels Fly* . . . .(Epic)
When The Saints Go Marching In
 Al Hirt; *Best Of Al Hirt* . . . . (RCA)
  Our Man-In New Orleans . . . . (Novus)
 Jerry Lee Lewis; *Jerry Lee Lewis* . . . . (Rhino)
 Louis Armstrong; *At The Crescendo* . . . .(MCA)
  Big Bands Of The Swinging Years-#1-C . . . . (Collectables)
  C'Est Si Bon . . . . (Rhino)
  Essential Louis Armstrong . . . . (Vanguard)
  Louis Armstrong Of New Orleans . . . . (MCA)
 Original Soundtrack; *Children's Favorites* . . . . (Kid Rhino/Rhino 4 Kids)
 Pete Fountain; *Best Of Pete Fountain* . . . .(MCA)
  Down On Rampart Street . . . . (Intermedia)

  Pete Fountain's New Orleans . . . . (MCA)
 Preservation Hall Jazz Band; *Best Of The Preservation Hall
  Jazz Band* . . . . (Columbia)
When You Believe
 Mariah Carey & Whitney Houston; *Mariah Carey-#1's* . . . . (Columbia)
  ST/The Prince Of Egypt . . . .(DreamWorks/SKG)
 Whitney Houston & Mariah Carey; *My Love Is Your Love* . . . . (Arista)
Where Were You (When The World Stopped Turning)
 Alan Jackson; *Alan Jackson-Drive* . . . . (Arista)
Whispering Hope
 Jo Stafford; *Capitol Collectors Series-Jo Stafford* . . . . (Capitol)
Who Am I?
 Elvis Presley; *Memphis Record* . . . .(RCA)
Who Will Save Your Soul
 Jewel; *Pieces Of You* . . . .(Atlantic)
Wholy Holy
 Aretha Franklin; *Aretha Franklin-30 Greatest Hits* . . . . (Rhino)
 Marvin Gaye; *Musical Testament 1964-1984* . . . . (Motown)
  What's Going On . . . . (Motown)
Why Me Lord
 Johnny Cash; *American Recordings* . . . . (American)
Will Jesus Wash The Bloodstains From Your Hands
 Bill Frisell; *Nashville* . . . . (Nonesuch)
 Exene Cervenka; *Running Sacred* . . . . (Rhino)
Will The Circle Be Unbroken
 Charlie Daniels Band & Friends; *Volunteer Jam 3 & 4* . . . . (Epic)
 Joan Baez; *Country Music Album* . . . . (Vanguard)
  The First 10 Years . . . . (Vanguard)
 Nitty Gritty Dirt Band; *Will The Circle Be Unbroken* . . . . (EMI)
 Roy Acuff; *Best Of Roy Acuff* . . . . (Liberty)
 Willie Nelson; *Willie & Family Live* . . . . (Columbia)
Winchester Cathedral
 New Vaudeville Band; *History Of British Rock-#7-C* . . . . (Rhino)
Wine Into Water
 T. Graham Brown; *Wine Into Water* . . . .(ISD/Intersound)
Wing And A Prayer
 Laurel MacDonald; *Chroma* . . . .(Wicklow)
  Wingspan . . . .(Wicklow)
Wings Of A Dove
 Bob Marley & The Wailers; *Birth Of A Legend 1963-
  1966* . . . . (Epic Portrait Assoc.)
 Ferlin Husky; *Billboard Top Country Hits-1960-C* . . . . (Rhino)
  Country Music Classics-#2-1960-1965-C . . . . (K-Tel)
  Ferlin Husky's Greatest Hits . . . . (Curb)
With God On Our Side
 Bob Dylan; *The Times They Are A-Changin'* . . . . (Columbia)
 Joan Baez; *The First 10 Years* . . . . (Vanguard)
 Manfred Mann; *Songs Of Protest-C* . . . . (Rhino)
 Neville Brothers; *Uptown Rulin': The Best Of The Neville Brothers* . . . . (A&M)
  Yellow Moon . . . . (A&M)
 Wire Train; *Best Of 415 Records-C* . . . . (Legacy)
Wolves
 Garth Brooks; *No Fences* . . . . (Capitol)
Wonder
 Natalie Merchant; *Tigerlily* . . . . (Elektra)
Would Jesus Wear A Rolex
 Ray Stevens; *Ray Stevens' Greatest Hits-#2* . . . . (MCA)
  Ray Stevens-All-Time Greatest Comic Hits . . . . (Curb)
  Ray Stevens-Collection . . . . (MCA)
Yah Mo B There
 James Ingram & Michael McDonald; *It's Your Night-C* . . . .(Qwest)
  The Power Of Great Music . . . . (Warner Bros.)
You Can Tell The World
 Simon & Garfunkel; *Collected Works* . . . . (Columbia)
  Wednesday Morning 3 A.M. . . . . (Columbia)
You Gotta Move
 Rolling Stones; *Love You Live* . . . .(Virgin)
  Sticky Fingers . . . .(Virgin)
Young Jews Be Proud
 2 Live Jews; *As Kosher As They Wanna Be* . . . . (Kosher)
Your Saving Grace
 Steve Miller Band; *Best Of Steve Miller 1968-1973* . . . . (Capitol)
  Steve Miller Band-Anthology . . . . (Capitol)
  Your Saving Grace . . . . (Capitol)
You're A God
 Vertical Horizon; *Everything You Want* . . . . (RCA)
You're The Reason God Made Oklahoma
 David Frizzell & Shelly West; *Carryin' On The Family
  Names* . . . . (Warner Bros.)
  Country's Greatest Hits-#9-'80s Duets-C . . . .(Priority)
  Golden Duets . . . . (Viva)

GOLD, Golden

See Also: *JEWELRY, MINING, MONEY, SILVER*

(They Long To Be) Close To You
 Carpenters; *Carpenters-Classics-#2* . . . . (A&M)

Carpenters-Love Songs .... (A&M)
Carpenters-The Singles 1969-1973 .... (A&M)
From The Top .... (A&M)
3 Chains O' Gold
Prince And The New Power Generation; *Love Symbol Album* .... (Paisley Park)
After The Goldrush
Emmylou Harris/Dolly Parton/Linda Ronstadt; *Trio II* .... (Asylum)
Neil Young; *After The Gold Rush* .... (Reprise)
Decade .... (Reprise)
Neil Young & Crazy Horse; *Live Rust* .... (Reprise)
All That Glitters Ain't Gold
Spinners; *Pick Of The Litter* .... (Atlantic)
All The Gold In California
Larry Gatlin & The Gatlin Brothers Band; *Larry Gatlin & The Gatlin*
Brothers' Greatest Hits-#2 .... (Columbia)
Larry Gatlin & The Gatlin Brothers' Greatest Hits-Encore .... (Capitol)
Larry Gatlin & The Gatlin Brothers-17 Greatest Hits .... (Columbia)
Live At 8:00 .... (Capitol)
Straight Ahead .... (Columbia)
Almost Gold
Jesus & Mary Chain; *Honey's Dead* .... (Def American)
Band Of Gold
Freda Payne; *Beachbeat Draggin'* .... (Dunhill Compact Classics)
Didn't It Blow Your Mind: Soul Hits Of The '70s-#2-C .... (Rhino)
Freda Payne's Greatest Hits .... (HDH)
Band Of Gold
Don Cherry; *Very Best Of Don Cherry* .... (Collector's Choice)
Be My Life's Companion
Mills Brothers; *Best Of The Mills Brothers* .... (MCA)
The Mills Brothers-Best Of The Decca Years .... (Decca)
Rosemary Clooney; *Rosemary Clooney-16 Most Requested Songs* .... (Legacy)
Bird In A Gilded Cage
Joan Morris & William Bolcom; *After The Ball* .... (Nonesuch)
Black Gold
Soul Asylum; *Grace Dancers Union* .... (Columbia)
Blue Moon
Billie Holiday; *Billie's Blues* .... (Blue Note)
First Verve Sessions .... (Verve)
History Of Billie Holiday .... (Verve)
Elvis Presley; *Elvis Presley* .... (RCA)
The Sun Sessions .... (RCA)
Marcels; *Best Of The Marcels* .... (Rhino)
Billboard Top Rock 'N' Roll Hits-1961-C .... (Rhino)
California Gold
Rance Allen; *Straight From The Heart* .... (Stax)
California Golden West Waltz
Golden West Singers & The Cavaliers; *45-#1378* .... (Accent)
Chains Of Gold
Sweethearts Of The Rodeo; *More Hot Country Requests-#2-C* .... (Epic)
Sweethearts Of The Rodeo .... (Columbia)
Days Of Autumn Gold
Hank Locklin; *There Never Was A Time* .... (Plantation)
Devil Comes Back To Georgia
Marc O'Connor; *Heroes* .... (Warner Bros.)
Devil Went Down To Georgia
Charlie Daniels Band; *A Decade Of Hits* .... (Epic)
Billboard Top Hits-1979-C .... (Rhino)
Me & The Boys .... (Epic)
Million Mile Reflections .... (Epic)
ST/Urban Cowboy .... (Asylum)
Down The River Of Golden Dreams
Mom & Dads; *Down The River Of Golden Dreams* .... (Crescendo)
Slim Whitman; *Home On The Range* .... (United Artists)
Everything Is Turning To Gold
Rolling Stones; *Sucking In The Seventies* .... (Rolling Stones)
Everything That Glitters (Is Not Gold)
Dan Seals; *Best Of Dan Seals* .... (Capitol)
Dan Seals' Greatest Hits .... (Liberty)
Dan Seals-Classics Collection-#2 .... (Liberty)
Won't Be Blue Anymore .... (EMI)
Fields Of Gold
Sting; *Fields Of Gold-The Best Of Sting 1984-1994* .... (A&M)
Ten Summoner's Tales .... (A&M)
Fool's Gold
Stone Roses; *The Stone Roses* .... (Silvertone)
Fool's Gold
Graham Parker; *Pourin' It All Out-Mercury Years* .... (Mercury)
Graham Parker And The Rumour; *Heat Treatment* .... (Mercury)
The Parkerilla .... (Mercury)
Fool's Gold
Poco; *Crazy Eyes* .... (Epic)
Ride The Country .... (Epic)
Very Best Of Poco .... (Epic)
Fool's Gold
Thin Lizzy; *Johnny The Fox* .... (Warner Bros.)
Fool's Gold
Lee Greenwood; *Lee Greenwood's Greatest Hits* .... (MCA)
You've Got A Good Love Comin' .... (MCA)

Fourteen Karat Mind
Gene Watson; *Gene Watson's Greatest Hits* .... (MCA)
Old Loves Never Die .... (MCA)
Gold
John Stewart; *Bombs Away Dream Babies* .... (RSO)
Spandau Ballet; *Spandau Ballet-Singles Collection* .... (Chrysalis)
True .... (Chrysalis)
Gold And Silver
Quicksilver Messenger Service; *Legends Of Rock Guitar-'60s-#1-C* .... (Rhino)
Quicksilver Messenger Service .... (Capitol)
Sons Of Mercury .... (Rhino)
Gold At The End Of My Rainbow
Be Bop Deluxe; *Modern Music* .... (Capitol)
Gold Dust Woman
Fleetwood Mac; *25 Years-The Chain* .... (Warner Bros.)
Rumours .... (Warner Bros.)
Sister Hazel; *Legacy-A Tribute To Fleetwood Mac's Rumours-C* .... (Lava)
Gold Dust Woman
Hole; *ST/City Of Angels* .... (Warner Sunset/Reprise)
Gold In Africa
Tiger; *Where Was Butler?-Calypso Documentary* .... (Folklyric)
Golden Age
Ray Stevens; *Nashville* .... (Barnaby)
Golden Age Of Leather
Blue Oyster Cult; *Spectres* .... (Columbia)
Golden Age Of Rock & Roll
Mott The Hoople; *Mott The Hoople's Greatest Hits* .... (Columbia)
The Ballad Of Mott: A Retrospective .... (Columbia)
Golden Apples Of The Sun
Judy Collins; *Golden Apples Of The Sun* .... (Elektra)
So Early In The Spring, The First 15 Years .... (Elektra)
Golden Arrow
Foghat; *Energized* .... (Rhino)
Golden Boy
Tubes; *Tubes Now* .... (A&M)
Golden Coins
Elvis Presley; *ST/Harum Scarum* .... (RCA)
Golden Country
REO Speedwagon; *A Decade Of Rock And Roll 1970 To 1980* .... (Epic)
REO Speedwagon Live/You Get What You Play For .... (Epic)
Golden Earrings
Peggy Lee; *Capitol Collectors Series-Peggy Lee-#1-Early Years* ..... (Capitol)
Peggy Lee's Greatest Hits .... (Capitol)
Golden Goose
Peter Frampton; *Somethin's Happening* .... (A&M)
Todd Rundgren; *Healing* .... (Rhino)
Golden Guitar
Bill Anderson; *Bill Anderson's Greatest Hits* .... (MCA)
The Bill Anderson Story .... (MCA)
Golden Heart
Mark Knopfler; *Golden Heart* .... (Warner Bros.)
Golden Helmet
Original London Cast; *Man Of La Mancha* .... (MCA)
Golden Lady
Stevie Wonder; *Innervisions* .... (Motown)
Golden Lark
Styx; *Man Of Miracles* .... (Wooden Nickel)
Golden Memories And Silver Tears
Jim Reeves; *Best Of Jim Reeves* .... (RCA)
Great Moments With Jim Reeves .... (RCA)
Jim Reeves' Greatest Hits .... (RCA)
Golden Mile
Babys; *Broken Heart* .... (Chrysalis)
Golden Moments
James Taylor; *In The Pocket* .... (Warner Bros.)
Golden Olden Days Of Rock & Roll
Johnny Winter; *J.D. Winter III* .... (Blue Sky)
Golden Rainbow
Looking Glass; *45-#15-2330* .... (Epic)
Seals & Crofts; *I'll Play For You* .... (Warner Bros.)
Golden Rainbow
Seals & Crofts; *I'll Play For You* .... (Warner Bros.)
Golden Ribbons
Loggins & Messina; *Loggins & Messina-On Stage* .... (Columbia)
Loggins And Messina .... (Columbia)
Golden Ring
Emmylou Harris/Linda Ronstadt/Anna & Kate McGarrigle; *Tammy*
Wynette...Remembered-C .... (Asylum)
George Jones & Tammy Wynette; *George Jones & Tammy Wynette-16*
Biggest Hits .... (Epic/Legacy)
Tammy Wynette & George Jones; *Encore-Tammy Wynette & George*
Jones .... (Epic)
Tammy Wynette & George Jones' Greatest Hits .... (Epic)
Tammy Wynette-Anniversary-20 Years Of Hits .... (Epic)
Golden Ring
Eric Clapton; *Backless* .... (Polydor)

Golden Road
Grateful Dead; *Best Of The Grateful Dead-Skeletons From The*
   Closet ....(Warner Bros.)
   Grateful Dead (Skull & Roses) ....(Warner Bros.)
Golden Rocket
Hank Snow; *All About Trains* ....(RCA)
   Best Of Hank Snow ....(RCA)
Horse Soldiers; *Between The Rails: America's Train Songs-C* .....(Crescendo)
Willie Nelson & Hank Snow; *Brand On My Heart* ....(Columbia)
Golden Slumbers
Beatles; *Abbey Road* ....(Parlophone)
   Beatles-Box Set ....(Capitol)
Golden Vanity
Pete Seeger & Arlo Guthrie; *Together In Concert* ....(Reprise)
Golden Years
David Bowie; *Changesonebowie* ....(RCA)
   Station To Station ....(Rykodisc)
   The Singles-1969-1993 ....(Rykodisc)
Goldfinger
Shirley Bassey; *13 Original James Bond Themes-C* ....(EMI)
   Best Of Shirley Bassey ....(EMI)
   Great Performances ....(EMI)
   Shirley Bassey-Live At Carnegie Hall ....(United Artists)
   Shirley Bassey's Greatest Hits ....(EMI)
   ST/Goldfinger ....(United Artists)
Gold-Tipped Boots, Black Jacket And Tie
Jethro Tull; *Catfish Rising* ....(Chrysalis)
Hanging Tree
Marty Robbins; *Gunfighter Ballads & Trail Songs* ....(Legacy)
   Hollywood Magic-1950s-C ....(Columbia)
   Lifetime Of Song-1951-1982 ....(Columbia)
   Marty Robbins' All-Time Greatest Hits ....(Columbia)
Heart Of Gold
Neil Young; *Decade* ....(Reprise)
   Harvest ....(Reprise)
Hour Of Gold
Emmylou Harris; *Red Dirt Girl* ....(Nonesuch)
House Of Gold
Hank Williams; *I'm So Lonesome I Could Cry-1949* ....(Polydor)
King Midas In Reverse
Hollies; *Best Of The Hollies-#2* ....(EMI)
   Hollies-Epic Anthology From The Original Master Tapes ......(Epic)
   The Hollies' Greatest Hits ....(Epic)
Love Is A Golden Ring
Frankie Laine; *Frankie Laine-16 Most Requested Songs* ....(Legacy)
Love Over Gold
Dire Straits; *Live-Alchemy* ....(Warner Bros.)
   Love Over Gold ....(Warner Bros.)
Man With The Golden Thumb
Jerry Reed; *Man With The Golden Thumb* ....(RCA)
Midas Touch
Original Cast; *Bells Are Ringing* ....(Columbia)
Midas Touch
Midnight Star; *Anniversary Collection* ....(Right Stuff)
Mining For Gold
Cowboy Junkies; *Trinity Session* ....(RCA)
Molten Gold
Paul Kossoff; *Koss* ....(DJM)
New Gold Dream
Simple Minds; *New Gold Dream* ....(A&M)
   Simple Minds Live: In The City Of Light ....(A&M)
New Gold Dream
Utah Saints; *Utah Saints* ....(London)
North To Alaska
Dwight Yoakam; *Under The Covers* ....(Reprise)
Johnny Horton; *American Originals-Johnny Horton* ....(Columbia)
   Billboard Top Country Hits-1961-C ....(Rhino)
   Johnny Horton's Greatest Hits ....(Columbia)
   Super Hits Of The '60s-C ....(Epic)
Ornaments Of Gold
Siouxsie And The Banshees; *Peepshow* ....(Geffen)
Pocket Full Of Gold
Vince Gill; *Pocket Full Of Gold* ....(MCA)
Poor Man's Roses (Or A Rich Man's Gold)
Patsy Cline; *Best Of Patsy Cline* ....(Curb)
   Forever & Always ....(Epic)
   Stop, Look & Listen ....(MCA)
   The Patsy Cline Story ....(MCA)
Reba McEntire; *Feel The Fire* ....(Mercury)
Power Of Gold
Dan Fogelberg; *Live-Greetings From The West* ....(Full Moon)
Dan Fogelberg & Tim Weisberg; *Dan Fogelberg/Greatest Hits* ....(Full Moon)
   Twin Sons Of Different Mothers ....(Full Moon)
Prairie Wedding
Mark Knopfler; *Sailing To Philadelphia* ....(Warner Bros.)
Rhythm In Gold
Jethro Tull; *20 Years Of Jethro Tull* ....(Chrysalis)
Ruby's Golden Wedding
Danny Wilson; *Meet Danny Wilson* ....(Virgin)

Saginaw, Michigan
Lefty Frizzell; *American Originals-Lefty Frizzell* ....(Columbia)
   Billboard Top Country Hits-1964-C ....(Rhino)
   Columbia Country Classics-#3-Americana-C ....(Columbia)
   Lefty Frizzell's Greatest Hits ....(Columbia)
Sailing Down This Golden River
Pete Seeger; *Bread & Roses Festival Of Acoustic Music-#1-C* ......(Fantasy)
   Circles & Seasons ....(Warner Bros.)
She Got The Goldmine (I Got The Shaft)
Jerry Reed; *14 #1 Country Hits-C* ....(RCA)
   Jerry Reed's Greatest Hits ....(RCA)
   Solid Country Gold-C ....(RCA)
She's A Rainbow
Rolling Stones; *Get Yer Ya-Ya's Out!* ....(Abkco)
   More Hot Rocks (big hits & fazed cookies) ....(Abkco)
   Singles Collection-The London Years ....(Abkco)
   Their Satanic Majesties Request ....(Abkco)
   Through The Past, Darkly (Big Hits Vol. 2) ....(Abkco)
Silence Is Golden
4 Seasons; *25th Anniversary Collection* ....(Rhino)
   4 Seasons-Anthology ....(Rhino)
Tremeloes; *Best Of The Tremeloes* ....(Rhino)
   History Of British Rock-#7-C ....(Rhino)
   Rock Artifacts-From The Vaults-#4-C ....(Columbia)
Silver & Gold
Dolly Parton; *Eagle When She Flies* ....(Columbia)
Silver & Gold
U2; *Rattle And Hum* ....(Island)
Silver & Gold (Our Love Is Like)
Sweethearts Of The Rodeo; *Sisters* ....(Columbia)
Silver Threads Among The Gold
Mike Auldridge; *Dobro/Blues & Bluegrass* ....(Takoma)
Silver Threads And Golden Needles
Honky Tonk Angels; *Honky Tonk Angels* ....(Columbia)
Linda Ronstadt; *Don't Cry Now* ....(Asylum)
   Hand Sown Home Grown ....(Capitol)
   Linda Ronstadt-Retrospective ....(Capitol)
   Linda Ronstadt's Greatest Hits ....(Asylum)
Springfields; *Troubadours Of The Folk Era-#3-C* ....(Rhino)
Silver Tongue & Gold Plated Lies
Hotmud Family; *Meat & Potatoes (& Stuff Like That)* ....(Flying Fish)
Silver, Blue & Gold
Bad Company; *Run With The Pack* ....(Swan Song)
Silvertown Blues
Mark Knopfler; *Sailing To Philadelphia* ....(Warner Bros.)
Sister Golden Hair
America; *America Live* ....(Warner Bros.)
   Billboard Top Rock 'N' Roll Hits-1975-C ....(Rhino)
   History-Greatest Hits ....(Warner Bros.)
Solid Gold Cadillac
Mitch Woods & The Rocket 88's; *Solid Gold Cadillac* ....(Blind Pig)
Stairway To Heaven
Led Zeppelin; *Led Zeppelin IV* ....(Atlantic)
   Led Zeppelin-Box Set ....(Atlantic)
   Remasters ....(Atlantic)
   ST/The Song Remains The Same ....(Swan Song)
Stanley Jordan; *Best Of Stanley Jordan* ....(Blue Note)
   Flying Home ....(EMI)
Streets Of Gold
Ronnie Milsap; *Pure Love* ....(RCA)
Streets Of Gold
Fabulous Thunderbirds; *Hot Number* ....(Epic Portrait Assoc.)
Sweet Summer Blue And Gold
Stone Poneys Featuring Linda Ronstadt; *The Stone Poneys Featuring Linda*
   Ronstadt ....(EMI)
Testosterone
Bush; *Sixteen Stone* ....(Trauma)
That Acapulco Gold
Rainy Daze; *Summer Of Love-#2-Turn On-Mind Expansion & Signs Of The*
   Times-C ....(Rhino)
Theme From "Golden Girls"
Original Soundtrack; *Television's Greatest Hits-#6-Remote Control-C* ... (TVT)
Theme From "Solid Gold"
Original Soundtrack; *Television's Greatest Hits-#3-1970s & 1980s-C* ... (TVT)
There's A Gold Mine In The Sky
Jimmy C. Newman; *Cajun Cowboy* ....(Plantation)
Pat Boone; *Love Letters In The Sand* ....(MCA Special Prod.)
Train Of Gold
Electric Light Orchestra; *Secret Messages* ....(Jet)
Trumpeter Blow Your Golden Horn
Michael Tilson Thomas; *Of Thee I Sing/Let 'Em Eat Cake* ....(Columbia)
When My Blue Moon Turns To Gold Again
Elvis Presley; *A Golden Celebration* ....(RCA)
   Elvis ....(RCA)
   The Other Sides-Worldwide Gold Award Hits, Vol. 2 ....(RCA)
Merle Haggard; *Merle Haggard-His Best* ....(MCA)
   Ramblin' Fever ....(MCA)
When The Golden Leaves Begin To Fall
Joe Val & The New England Bluegrass Boys; *Diamond Joe* ....(Rounder)

Joe Val & The New England Bluegrass Boys-Vol. 2 . . . . (Rounder)

When The Golden Train Comes Down
Sons Of The Pioneers; *Columbia Historic Edition-Sons Of The
Pioneers* . . . . (Columbia)
Steel Rails-Classic Railroad Songs-#1-C . . . . (Rounder)

Where The Blue Of The Night Meets The Gold Of The Day
Bing Crosby; *All-Time Best Of* . . . . (Curb)
Best Of Bing Crosby . . . . (MCA)
Where The Blue Of The Night Meets The Gold Of The Day . . . . (Biograph)

White Bird
It's A Beautiful Day; *Bill Graham Presents The Last Days Of The
Fillmore-C* . . . . (Epic Portrait Assoc.)
It's A Beautiful Day . . . . (Columbia)

Wrong Number
Cure; *Galore-The Singles-1987-1997* . . . . (Fiction/Elektra)

Your Gold Teeth
Steely Dan; *Countdown To Ecstasy* . . . . (MCA)

Your Gold Teeth II
Steely Dan; *Katy Lied* . . . . (MCA)

GOOD, Great, Wonderful

*See Also: BAD, BEST, CHARACTER & INTEGRITY,
HAPPINESS, SPECIAL*

Ac-Cent-Tchu-Ate The Positive
Andrews Sisters; *Andrews Sisters Greatest Hits* . . . . (Curb)
Bing Crosby; *Bing Crosby's Greatest Hits* . . . . (MCA)
Original Soundtrack; *ST/Bugsy* . . . . (Epic)

Ain't That Good News
David "Fathead" Newman; *Bigger & Better-Many Facets Of David
"Fathead" Newman* . . . . (Rhino)

All The Good Ones Are Gone
Pam Tillis; *Pam Tillis' Greatest Hits* . . . . (Arista)

Anything's Better Than Feelin' The Blues
Martina McBride; *Emotion* . . . . (RCA)

Au Revoir, Pleasant Dreams
Ben Bernie & His Orchestra; *78-#4943* . . . . (Brunswick)

Back For Good
Take That; *Nobody Else* . . . . (Arista)

Bad Goodbye, A
Clint Black with Wynonna; *Clint Black-The Greatest Hits* . . . . (RCA)
Grammy's Greatest Country Moments-#1-C . . . . (Atlantic)
No Time To Kill . . . . (RCA)

Badlands
Bruce Springsteen; *Bruce Springsteen's Greatest Hits* . . . . (Columbia)
Darkness On The Edge Of Town . . . . (Columbia)
Bruce Springsteen & The E Street Band; *Bruce Springsteen & The E Street
Band Live/1975-85* . . . . (Legacy)

Be Good Johnny
Men At Work; *Business As Usual* . . . . (Columbia)

Be Good To Yourself
Journey; *Journey's Greatest Hits* . . . . (Columbia)
Raised On Radio . . . . (Columbia)

Be Good To Yourself
Frankie Miller; *Full House* . . . . (Chrysalis)

Better Days
Bruce Springsteen; *Bruce Springsteen's Greatest Hits* . . . . (Columbia)
Lucky Town . . . . (Columbia)

Better In The USA
Glenn Frey; *The Allnighter* . . . . (MCA)

Better Off Dead
Elton John; *Captain Fantastic And The Brown Dirt Cowboy* . . . . . . (Polydor)

Better Off Dead
Ice Cube; *AmeriKKKa's Most Wanted* . . . . (Priority)

Better Than You
Metallica; *Reload* . . . . (Elektra)

Cannibals
Mark Knopfler; *Golden Heart* . . . . (Warner Bros.)

Can't Keep A Good Man Down
38 Special; *Special Delivery* . . . . (A&M)
Alabama; *Alabama-Live* . . . . (RCA)

Can't Take My Eyes Off You
Frankie Valli; *25th Anniversary Collection* . . . . (Rhino)
Frankie Valli-Anthology . . . . (Rhino)
Very Best Of Frankie Valli . . . . (MCA)
Lauryn Hill; *The Miseducation Of Lauryn Hill* . . . . (Ruffhouse/Columbia)

C'est Si Bon (It's So Good)
Eartha Kitt; *Lost Female Hits Of The '50s-C* . . . . (Taragon)

Change
Sheryl Crow; *Sheryl Crow* . . . . (A&M)

Cruel To Be Kind
Nick Lowe; *Basher: Best Of* . . . . (Columbia)
Labour Of Lust . . . . (Columbia)

Damn Good Cowboy
Charlie Daniels Band; *Cowboy Super Hits-C* . . . . (Columbia)
Night Rider . . . . (Epic)

Doctor Do It Good
Vernon Burch; *Get Up* . . . . (Chocolate City)

Elegantly Wasted
INXS; *Elegantly Wasted* . . . . (Mercury)

Even Better Than The Real Thing
U2; *Achtung Baby* . . . . (Island)

Even The Bad Times Are Good
Tremeloes; *Best Of The Tremeloes* . . . . (Rhino)

Feel So Good
Shirley & Lee; *Best Of New Orleans Rhythm & Blues-#1-C* . . . . . (Rhino)
Billboard Top R&B Hits-1955-C . . . . (Rhino)
History Of New Orleans R&B-#1-1950-1958-C . . . . (Rhino)

Feel So Good
Mase; *Harlem World* . . . . (Bad Boy/Arista)

Feel So Good
Jefferson Airplane; *30 Seconds Over Winterland* . . . . (RCA)
Bark . . . . (Grunt)
Flight Log (1966-1976) . . . . (Grunt)

Feel So Numb
Rob Zombie; *Sinister Urge* . . . . (Geffen)

Feelin' Good About Feelin' Bad
Patty Loveless; *When Fallen Angels Fly* . . . . (Epic)

Feels So Good
Xscape; *Off The Hook* . . . . (So So Def/Columbia)

Feels So Good (Show Me Your Love)
Lina Santiago; *Best Of Dance Hits Supermix-#1 & 2-C* . . . . (Warlock)
Dance Mix USA-#5-C . . . . (Warlock)

Few Good Things Remain
Kathy Mattea; *A Collection Of Hits* . . . . (Mercury)
Time Passes By . . . . (Mercury)

Fine & Dandy
Art Tatum; *Solo Masterpieces-#5* . . . . (Pablo)
Barbra Streisand; *People* . . . . (Columbia)
Chet Baker; *Out Of Nowhere* . . . . (Milestone)
Milt Jackson & Sonny Stitt; *Milt Jackson & Sonny Stitt-In The
Beginning* . . . . (Galaxy)

Fine Fine Day
Tony Carey; *Some Tough City* . . . . (MCA)

Fine Spring Morning
Blossom Dearie; *Blossom Dearie* . . . . (Verve)

For He's A Jolly Good Fellow
Good Time Singers; *All Occasions Album* . . . . (Gateway)

Gee Baby, Ain't I Good To You
Diana Krall; *All For You (A Dedication To The Nat "King" Cole
Trio)* . . . . (Impulse!)

Getting Better
Beatles; *Sgt. Pepper's Lonely Hearts Club Band* . . . . (Capitol)

Gimme Gimme Good Lovin'
Crazy Elephant; *Dick Bartley's One-Hit Wonders Of The '60s-#2-C* . . . (Rhino)

God Knows I'm Good
David Bowie; *Space Oddity* . . . . (Rykodisc)

Gonna Have A Good Time
Easybeats; *Best Of The Easybeats* . . . . (Rhino)

Good
Better Than Ezra; *Deluxe* . . . . (Swell/Elektra)

Good As I Was To You
Lorrie Morgan; *Greater Need* . . . . (BNA)
Lorrie Morgan-Super Hits . . . . (RCA)
To Get To You-Greatest Hits Collection . . . . (BNA)

Good Beat
Deee-Lite; *World Clique* . . . . (Elektra)

Good Day In Hell
Eagles; *On The Border* . . . . (Elektra)

Good Day Sunshine
Beatles; *Beatles-Box Set* . . . . (Capitol)
Revolver . . . . (Capitol)

Good Day To Run
Darryl Worley; *Hard Rain Don't Last* . . . . (DreamWorks/SKG)

Good Enough
Van Halen; *5150* . . . . (Warner Bros.)

Good Enough
Bobby Brown; *Bobby* . . . . (MCA)

Good Enough
Anita Baker; *Giving You The Best That I Got* . . . . (Elektra)

Good Enough
Bonnie Raitt; *Home Plate* . . . . (Warner Bros.)

Good Feelin' To Know
Poco; *Good Feelin' To Know* . . . . (Epic)
Ride The Country . . . . (Epic)
Songs Of Richie Furay . . . . (Epic)
Very Best Of Poco . . . . (Epic)

Good Friday
Cowboy Junkies; *Miles From Our Home* . . . . (Geffen)

Good Friday
Black Crowes; *Sho' Nuff* . . . . (American)
Three Snakes And One Charm . . . . (American)

Good Friday
Crust; *Crust* . . . . (Trance Syndicate)

Good Friday
Saints; *Howling* . . . .(Triple X Entert.)
Good Friend
Loggins & Messina; *Loggins And Messina*. . . . . (Columbia)
Good Friend
Violent Femmes; *Blind Leading The Naked* . . . . (Slash)
Good Friends
Reba McEntire; *Reba Nell McEntire* . . . . (Mercury)
Good Friends & A Bottle Of Wine
Ted Nugent; *Weekend Warriors* . . . .(Epic)
Good Girls
Joe; *All That I Am* . . . . (Jive)
Good Girls Don't
Knack; *Get The Knack* . . . . (Capitol)
Good Girls Go To Heaven
Charlie Floyd; *Charlie Floyd* . . . . (Liberty)
Good Hearted Woman
George Jones; *I Am What I Am* . . . .(Epic)
Waylon Jennings; *Good Hearted Woman*. . . . . (RCA)
The Outlaws . . . . (RCA)
Waylon Jennings' Greatest Hits . . . . (RCA)
Willie Nelson; *Greatest Hits (& Some That Will Be)* . . (Columbia)
Willie . . . . (RCA)
Good Intentions
Toad The Wet Sprocket; *ST/Friends-Music From The TV Series* . . . . . (Reprise)
Good Life
Betty Carter; *Atlantic Jazz-Singers-C* . . . . (Atlantic)
'Round Midnight . . . . (Atlantic)
Ernie Maresca; *22 Leaders Of The Pack-#1-C* . . . . . . (Laurie)
Frank Sinatra & Count Basie; *It Might As Well Be Swing* . . . . (Reprise)
Tony Bennett; *Tony Bennett Sings His All-Time Hall Of Fame Hits* . . . . . . (Columbia)
Tony Bennett-16 Most Requested Songs . . . . (Legacy)
Good Life
Bruce Robison; *Long Way Home From Anywhere* . . . . (Lucky Dog)
Good Love
Prince; *ST/Bright Lights Big City* . . . .(Warner Bros.)
Good Love
Anita Baker; *Giving You The Best That I Got* . . . . (Elektra)
Good Love
Klymaxx; *Maxx Is Back* . . . .(MCA)
Good Love
Poison; *Open Up And Say...Ahh!* . . . . (Capitol)
Good Lovin'
Grateful Dead; *Shakedown Street* . . . . (Arista)
Rascals; *Hit Singles-1958-1977-C* . . . . (Atlantic)
Rascals' Greatest Hits . . . . (Atlantic)
Rascals-Super Hits . . . . (Atlantic)
ST/Big Chill . . . . (Motown)
Good Lovin' (Makes It Right)
Tammy Wynette; *Tammy Wynette-16 Biggest Hits* . . . . (Legacy)
Tammy Wynette-Anniversary-20 Years Of Hits . . . .(Epic)
Tears Of Fire-25th Anniversary Collection . . . .(Epic)
Good Lovin's Hard To Find
Lynyrd Skynyrd; *Last Rebel* . . . .(Atlantic)
Good Luck Charm
Elvis Presley; *Elvis' Golden Records, Volume 3*. . . . . . . (RCA)
Number One Hits . . . . (RCA)
The Top Ten Hits . . . . (RCA)
Worldwide 50 Gold Award Hits, Vol. 1, Parts 1 & 2 . . . (RCA)
Good Man Is Hard To Find (Pittsburgh)
Bruce Springsteen; *Tracks* . . . . (Columbia)
Good Morning Girl
Journey; *Departure* . . . . (Columbia)
Good Morning Good Morning
Beatles; *Beatles-Box Set* . . . . (Capitol)
Sgt. Pepper's Lonely Hearts Club Band. . . . . (Capitol)
Good Morning Heartache
Billie Holiday; *All Or Nothing At All* . . . . (Verve)
Billie Holiday's Greatest Hits . . . . (Decca Jazz)
From The Original Decca Masters . . . .(MCA)
History Of Billie Holiday . . . . (Verve)
Diana Ross; *Diana Ross-Anthology* . . . . (Motown)
ST/Lady Sings The Blues . . . . (Motown)
Tony Bennett with Sheryl Crow; *Playin' With My Friends-Bennett Sings The Blues.* . . . . (Columbia)
Good Morning Judge
10 CC; *10 CC's Greatest Hits-1972-1978* . . . . (Polydor)
Deceptive Bends. . . . . (Mercury)
Jailhouse Rock (Hits From The Big House)-C . . . . (Sony Music Special Prod.)
Live & Let Live. . . . . (Mercury)
Good Morning Little School Girl
Grateful Dead; *Grateful Dead (Skull & Roses)* . . . . . . (Warner Bros.)
Huey Lewis and the News; *Four Chords & Several Years Ago* . . . . . (Elektra)
Johnny Winter; *Johnny Winter* . . . . (Columbia)
Live/Johnny Winter And. . . . . (Columbia)
Ten Years After; *Classic Performances Of Ten Years After* . . . . . (Columbia)
Recorded Live . . . . (Columbia)
SSSSH . . . . (Chrysalis)

Universal . . . . (Chrysalis)
Yardbirds; *Eric Clapton-Crossroads-C* . . . .(Polydor)
Five Live Yardbirds . . . . (Rhino)
Good Morning Starshine
Oliver; *'60s Rock Classics-#3-C* . . . . (Rhino)
Original Broadway Cast; *Hair.* . . . . (RCA)
Good News
Muddy Waters; *The Chess Box-Muddy Waters* . . . . (Chess)
Good News
Melissa Manchester; *Better Days & Happy Endings.* . . . . . . (Arista)
Essence Of Melissa Manchester . . . . (Arista)
Good News
Attitudes; *Good News* . . . .(Dark Horse)
Good News
Red Rider; *Don't Fight It* . . . . (Capitol)
Good News
King Curtis; *Best Of King Curtis* . . . . (Collectables)
Good News
Kingston Trio; *Scarlet Ribbons* . . . . (Capitol)
Mary Travers; *It's In Every One Of Us* . . . . (Chrysalis)
Sweet Honey In The Rock; *Good News.* . . . . (Flying Fish)
Good News
Staple Singers; *Swing Low Sweet Chariot.* . . . . . . (Collectables)
Good News Travels Fast
Jerry Lee Lewis; *When Two Worlds Collide* . . . . (Elektra)
Good News, Bad News
Eddy Raven; *Eddy Raven-Greatest Country Hits* . . . . . (Curb)
Good Old American Guest
Merle Haggard; *Big City* . . . . (Epic)
Good Old Cabbage Greens
Washboard Sam; *Rockin' My Blues Away.* . . . . (RCA)
Good Old Desk
Nilsson; *Aerial Ballet* . . . . (RCA)
Good Ole Boys From Louisiana
Jimmy C. Newman & Cajun Country; *Jimmy C. Newman & Cajun Country* . . . . (Dot)
Good Rockin' Tonight
Elvis Presley; *A Date With Elvis* . . . . (RCA)
Sun Story-C . . . . (Rhino)
The Sun Sessions . . . . (RCA)
Jerry Lee Lewis; *20 Classic Jerry Lee Lewis Hits* . . (Original Sound)
Trio Plus . . . . (Sun)
Jimmy Witherspoon; *Best Of Jimmy Witherspoon* . . . (Prestige)
'Spoon Concerts . . . . (Fantasy)
Good Run Of Bad Luck
Clint Black; *No Time To Kill* . . . . (RCA)
Good Texan
Vaughan Brothers; *Taste Of Texas-Songs 'Bout Texas By Texans-C* . . . . (Columbia)
Good Time Boy
Buffalo Springfield; *Buffalo Springfield Again* . . . . . . (Atco)
Good Time Girl
Lee Ferrell; *Hard Times* . . . . (TMS)
Good Time Man Like Me Got No Business (Singin' The Blues), A
Jim Croce; *Life & Times* . . . . (Lifesong)
Words And Music . . . . (Dunhill Compact Classics)
Good Times
Willie Nelson; *Best Of Willie* . . . . (RCA)
Minstrel Man . . . . (RCA)
Music From "Songwriter" . . . . (Columbia)
Good Times
Rita Coolidge; *Anytime...Anywhere* . . . . (A&M)
Good Times
Hoodoo Gurus; *Blow Your Cool* . . . . (Elektra)
Good Times
Dan Seals; *Dan Seals' Greatest Hits* . . . . (Liberty)
On Arrival . . . . (Capitol)
Good Times
Jimi Hendrix; *Jimi Hendrix.* . . . . (Audio Fidelity)
Good Times
Rolling Stones; *Out Of Our Heads* . . . . (Abkco)
Good Times
Chic; *Plus Grands Succes De Chic* . . . .(Atlantic)
Risque. . . . .(Atlantic)
Good Times
Nat "King" Cole; *Ramblin' Rose* . . . . (Capitol)
Good Times
Persuasions; *Street Corner Symphony.* . . . . (Capitol)
Good Times Bad Times
Led Zeppelin; *Led Zeppelin.* . . . .(Atlantic)
Good Times Roll
Cars; *The Cars.* . . . . (Elektra)
The Cars' Greatest Hits . . . . (Elektra)
Good Times, Bad Times
Rolling Stones; *12 X 5* . . . . (Abkco)
Big Hits (High Tide & Green Grass) . . . .(Abkco)
More Hot Rocks (big hits & fazed cookies) . . . . . .(Abkco)
Singles Collection-The London Years . . . .(Abkco)

Good Timin'
Jimmy Jones; *Hard To Find 45s On CD-#1-1955-1960-C* . . . . (Eric)
Good To See You
Neil Young; *Silver & Gold* . . . .(Reprise)
Good Vibrations
Beach Boys; *Beach Boys-Gift Set* . . . . (Capitol)
Billboard Top Rock 'N' Roll Hits-1966-C . . . . (Rhino)
Endless Summer . . . . (Capitol)
Good Vibrations-Thirty Years Of The Beach Boys . . . . (Capitol)
Smiley Smile/Wild Honey . . . . (Capitol)
Sunshine Dream . . . . (Capitol)
Good Vibrations
Marky Mark And The Funky Bunch; *Music For The People* . . . . . . (Interscope)
Good Woman Blues
Mel Tillis; *Mel Tillis' Greatest Hits.* . . . .(Curb)
Goodnight, Good Guy
Collective Soul; *Hints, Allegations And Things Left Unsaid* . . . . (Atlantic)
Goody Goody
Lisette Melendez; *True To Life* . . . . (Fever)
Grandpa (Tell Me 'Bout The Good Old Days)
Judds; *Judds' Greatest Hits.* . . . . (MCA)
Rockin' With The Rhythm . . . . (MCA)
Super 10-#2-C . . . . (RCA)
Have A Good Time
Paul Simon; *Greatest Hits, Etc.* . . . . (Columbia)
Negotiations And Love Songs, 1971-1986 . . . . (Warner Bros.)
Still Crazy After All These Years. . . . . (Columbia)
Have A Good Time
Elvin Bishop; *Struttin' My Stuff.* . . . .(Capricorn)
Have A Good Time
Rufus Featuring Chaka Khan; *Rufus featuring Chaka Khan* . . . . (MCA)
He Was Too Good To Me
Barbara Cook; *Barbara Cook-Live At Carnegie Hall* . . . . (Sony Music Classical)
Bette Midler; *Some People's Lives* . . . . (Atlantic)
Carmen McRae; *Carmen McRae Sings Great American
Songwriters* . . . . (Decca Jazz)
Helen Merrill; *Dream Of You* . . . . (Emarcy)
Jeri Southern; *The Very Thought Of You: The Decca Years-1951-1957* . . . (GRP)
He's A Good Ole Boy
Chely Wright; *Woman In The Moon* . . . .(Polydor Country)
Hey, Good Lookin'
Hank Williams With His Drifting Cowboys; *24 Of Hank Williams'
Greatest Hits* . . . . (Polydor)
Hank Williams-40 Greatest Hits . . . . (Polydor)
Hey, Good Lookin'-December 1950-July 1951 . . . . (Polydor)
Loretta Lynn & Conway Twitty; *Hey, Good Lookin'* . . . . . (MCA Special Prod.)
Honey
Mariah Carey; *Butterfly.* . . . . (Columbia)
Honey
Bobby Goldsboro; *Billboard Top Pop Hits-1968-C* . . . . (Rhino)
Cruisin'-1968-C . . . . (Increase)
Houston, Treat My Lady Good
Joe Stampley; *Red Wine & Blue Memories* . . . . (Epic)
How Come You Don't Call Me
Alicia Keys; *Songs In A Minor* . . . . (J)
Hungry (For Those Good Things)
Paul Revere And The Raiders; *Best Of Paul Revere And The
Raiders-#1* . . . . (Bac-Trac)
Frat Rock!-C . . . . (Rhino)
Legend Of Paul Revere And The Raiders . . . . (Columbia)
Paul Revere And The Raiders' Greatest Hits . . . . (Columbia)
Hurt Me Bad (In A Real Good Way)
Patty Loveless; *Patty Loveless' Greatest Hits* . . . . (MCA)
Up Against My Heart . . . . (MCA)
Hurts So Good
John Cougar; *American Fool.* . . . . (Riva)
I Feel Fine
Beatles; *Beatles 1.* . . . . (Capitol)
Beatles '65. . . . . (Capitol)
Beatles-20 Greatest Hits. . . . . (Capitol)
Past Masters-Volume One . . . . (Parlophone)
The Beatles/1962-1966. . . . . (Capitol)
Sweethearts Of The Rodeo; *One Time One Night* . . . . (Columbia)
I Found My Girl In The Good Old U.S.A.
Jimmie Skinner; *45-#2095.* . . . . (Gusto)
I Saved The World Today
Eurythmics; *Peace.* . . . . (Arista)
I Want You Bad (And That Ain't Good)
Collin Raye; *In This Life* . . . . (Epic)
If The Good Die Young
Tracy Lawrence; *Alibis* . . . . (Atlantic)
I'll Be Good To You
Brothers Johnson; *Brothers Johnson-Classics-#11* . . . . (A&M)
Look Out For No. 1 . . . . (A&M)
Najee; *Tokyo Blue* . . . . (EMI)
Quincy Jones with Ray Charles & Chaka Khan; *Back On The Block* . . . (Qwest)
I'm Good At Being Bad
TLC; *Fanmail.* . . . . (LaFace)

I'm Into Something Good
Herman's Hermits; *Herman's Hermits-Their Greatest Hits* . . . . (Abkco)
In The Good Old Summertime
Andrews Sisters; *45-#65016* . . . . (MCA)
Mom & Dads; *In The Good Old Summertime* . . . . (Crescendo)
It Feels So Good
Sonique; *Hear My Cry* . . . . (Republic/Universal)
Now That's What I Call Music!-#4-C . . . . (Virgin)
It Goes Like It Goes (Theme From ''Norma Rae'')
Jennifer Warnes; *Best Of Jennifer Warnes.* . . . .(Arista)
*The Envelope Please-Academy Award Winning Songs-#4 (1970-
1981)-C* . . . . (Rhino)
It Was A Very Good Year
Frank Sinatra; *Frank Sinatra-The Very Good Years* . . . . (Reprise)
September Of My Years . . . . (Reprise)
The Reprise Collection . . . . (Reprise)
*The Sopranos-Music From The HBO Original
Series* . . . . (Sony Music Soundtrax)
Frank Sinatra with Count Basie & The Orchestra; *Sinatra At The
Sands* . . . . (Reprise)
It's All Right
Impressions; *Billboard Top R&B Hits-1963-C* . . . .(Rhino)
Cruisin'-1964-C . . . . (Increase)
Impressions' Greatest Hits . . . . (MCA)
ST/The Flamingo Kid . . . . (Motown)
It's Alright
Adam Faith With The Roulettes; *History Of British Rock-#1-C* . . . . . .(Rhino)
It's Been A Great Afternoon
Merle Haggard; *For The Record: Merle Haggard-43 Legendary Hits.* . . . (BNA)
I'm Always On A Mountain When I Fall . . . . (MCA)
Merle Haggard's Greatest Hits . . . . (MCA)
More Of The Best. . . . . (Rhino)
It's Better With A Union Man
Barbra Streisand; *Pins And Needles* . . . . (Columbia)
It's Good News Week
Hedgehoppers Anonymous; *Songs Of Protest-C* . . . . (Rhino)
It's Good To Be King
Tom Petty; *Wildflowers* . . . . (Warner Bros.)
I've Seen All The Good People
Yes; *Classic Rock 1966-1988-C* . . . . (Atlantic)
The Yes Album. . . . . (Atlantic)
Yessongs . . . . (Atlantic)
Johnny B. Goode
Chuck Berry; *Chuck Berry's Greatest Hits* . . . .(Everest)
Classic Rock-#2-C . . . . (MCA)
Roll Over Beethoven . . . . (Allegiance)
ST/American Graffiti . . . . (MCA)
The Chess Box-Chuck Berry . . . . (Chess)
Elvis Presley; *Elvis In Concert.* . . . . (RCA)
From Memphis To Vegas/From Vegas To Memphis . . . . (RCA)
Grateful Dead; *Bill Graham Presents The Last Days Of The
Fillmore-C* . . . . (Epic Portrait Assoc.)
Johnny Winter; *Live/Johnny Winter And* . . . . (Columbia)
Second Winter . . . . (Columbia)
Just Good Ol' Boys
Moe Bandy & Joe Stampley; *Just Good Ol' Boys* . . . . (Columbia)
Moe Bandy & Joe Stampley's Greatest Hits . . . . (Columbia)
Trucker's Jukebox-#2-C . . . . (Legacy)
Kiss An Angel Good Mornin'
Charley Pride; *Charley Pride-24 Greatest Hits* . . . . (Tee Vee)
Pride! My 6 Latest And 6 Greatest . . . . (ISD/Intersound)
The Ultimate Charley Pride . . . . (Bransounds)
Let The Good Times Roll
Barbra Streisand; *Butterfly.* . . . . (Columbia)
Betty Everett & Jerry Butler; *Delicious Together* . . . . (Vee-Jay)
Starring Betty Everett . . . . (Tradition)
Bobby Bland & B.B. King; *Together Again Live* . . . . (MCA)
Jerry Lee Lewis; *Golden Rock & Roll* . . . . (Sun)
Louis Jordan; *Best Of Louis Jordan* . . . . (MCA)
Molly Hatchet; *Flirtin' With Disaster* . . . . (Epic)
Nilsson; *Nilsson Schmilsson* . . . . (RCA)
Phoebe Snow; *Phoebe Snow* . . . . (MCA)
Ray Charles; *Genius Of Ray Charles* . . . . (Atlantic)
Shirley & Lee; *Billboard Top R&B Hits-1956-C.* . . . . (Rhino)
History Of New Orleans R&B-#1-1950-1958-C . . . . (Rhino)
ST/Stand By Me. . . . . (Atlantic)
Super Oldies Of The '50s-#4-C . . . . (Audio Fidelity)
Tony Bennett with B.B. King; *Playin' With My Friends-Bennett Sings The
Blues-C.* . . . . (Columbia)
Life's Been Good
Eagles; *Eagles Live* . . . . (Asylum)
Joe Walsh; *But Seriously Folks* . . . . (Asylum)
ST/FM. . . . . (MCA)
Little Good News
Anne Murray; *Anne Murray's Greatest Hits-#2* . . . . (Capitol)
Little Good News. . . . . (Capitol)
Lollipop Train (You Never Had It So Good)
Grass Roots; *Grass Roots-Anthology (1966-1975)* . . . . (Rhino)
P.F. Sloan; *P.F. Sloan-Anthology.* . . . . (One Way)

Lonely Women Make Good Lovers
Bob Luman; *Bob Luman-Classic Country* . . . . (Simitar)
Steve Wariner; *Best Of Steve Wariner* . . . . (RCA)
   Midnight Fire . . . . (RCA)
   Steve Wariner's Greatest Hits . . . . (RCA)
   Steve Wariner-Super Hits . . . . (RCA)
Lookin' Good But Feelin' Bad
Original Cast; *Ain't Misbehavin'* . . . . (RCA)
Looking For A Good Sign
Daryl Hall & John Oates; *Private Eyes* . . . . (RCA)
Lord I Hope This Day Is Good
Don Williams; *Best Of Don Williams-#3* . . . . (MCA)
   Especially For You . . . . (MCA)
Lee Ann Womack; *Grand Ole Opry-75 Years-#1-C* . . . . (MCA)
Lord, Lord, Lord, You Sure Been Good To Me
Preservation Hall Jazz Band; *New Orleans-#3-When The Saints Go*
   Marchin' In . . . . (Columbia)
Love Is So Good When You're Stealing It
Z.Z. Hill; *Lost Soul-#3-C* . . . . (Epic)
Mr. Too Damn Good
Gerald Levert; *G* . . . . (East West)
Mr. Wonderful
Peggy Lee; *Best Of Peggy Lee* . . . . (MCA)
My Baby's Got Good Timing
Dan Seals; *Best Of Dan Seals* . . . . (Capitol)
   Country Gold-C . . . . (Priority)
   Dan Seals-Classics Collection-#1 . . . . (Capitol)
   Early Dan Seals . . . . (Capitol)
   San Antone . . . . (EMI)
My Radio Sure Sounds Good To Me
Larry Graham; *My Radio Sure Sounds Good To Me* . . (Warner Bros.)
My Radio Sure Sounds Good To Me
Oak Ridge Boys; *Oak Ridge Boys Have Arrived* . . . . (MCA)
Nice & Slow
Usher; *My Way* . . . . (LaFace)
No One Knows About A Good Thing
Curtis Mayfield; *New World Order* . . . . (Warner Bros.)
Norwegian Wood (This Bird Has Flown)
Beatles; *Beatles-Box Set* . . . . (Capitol)
   Beatles-Love Songs . . . . (Capitol)
   Rubber Soul . . . . (Capitol)
   The Beatles/1962-1966 . . . . (Capitol)
Nothin' But A Good Time
Poison; *Open Up And Say...Ahh!* . . . . (Capitol)
   Swallow This Live . . . . (Capitol)
Nothing Sure Looked Good On You
Gene Watson; *All-Time Country Classics-#2-C* . . . . (Capitol)
   Country's Greatest Hits-#7-C . . . . (Priority)
   Should I Come Home . . . . (Capitol)
Oh! My Papa
Eddie Fisher; *Eddie Fisher's All-Time Greatest Hits-#1* . . . . (RCA)
   Hebrew National Kosher Classics-C . . . . (RCA)
   Nipper's Greatest Hits Of The '50s-#2-C . . . . (RCA)
Oh, Lady Be Good
Benny Goodman; *Benny Goodman-Live At Carnegie Hall* . . . . . (London)
Count Basie; *Essential Count Basie-#1* . . . . (Columbia)
Count Basie Trio; *For The First Time* . . . . (Pablo)
Ella Fitzgerald; *Compact Jazz-Ella Live!* . . . . (Verve)
   Essential Ella Fitzgerald-The Great Songs . . . . (Verve)
Erroll Garner; *Original Misty* . . . . (Mercury)
Lionel Hampton & His Orchestra; *Jazz Club-Big Band* . . . . . (Verve)
Pete Fountain; *Best Of Pete Fountain* . . . . (MCA)
Supersax; *Supersax Plays Bird* . . . . (Blue Note)
On A Good Night
Wade Hayes; *On A Good Night* . . . . (Columbia)
   Super Hits Of 1996-C . . . . (Epic)
On The Good Ship Lollipop
4 Seasons; *Rarities-#1* . . . . (Rhino)
Firehouse Five Plus Two; *Goes To Sea* . . . . (Good Time Jazz)
One Fine Day
Carpenters; *From The Top* . . . . (A&M)
   Now & Then . . . . (A&M)
Chiffons; *Best Of The Chiffons* . . . . (Laurie)
   Chiffons-Golden Classics . . . . (Collectables)
   Collectables Presents The History Of Rock-#9-C . . . (Collectables)
   Oldies But Goodies-#12-C . . . . (Original Sound)
One Good Man
Michelle Wright; *The Reasons Why* . . . . (Arista)
One Good Well
Don Williams; *One Good Well* . . . . (RCA)
One Good Woman
Billy Squier; *Emotions In Motion* . . . . (Capitol)
Only The Good Die Young
Billy Joel; *Billy Joel-Greatest Hits, Volume I & Volume II* . . . . . (Columbia)
   KOHUEPT . . . . (Columbia)
   The Stranger . . . . (Columbia)
Pure Morning
Placebo; *Without You I'm Nothing* . . . . (Virgin)

Real Good Time Together
Lou Reed; *Between Thought & Expression-Anthology* . . . . (RCA)
   Street Hassle . . . . (Out Of Print)
Really Good Time
Roxy Music; *Country Life* . . . . (Atco)
Reunited
Peaches & Herb; *Best Of Peaches & Herb* . . . . (Polydor)
   Chicken Soup For The Couples Soul-C . . . . (Rhino)
   Didn't It Blow Your Mind: Soul Hits Of The '70s-#20-C . . . . . (Rhino)
   Only Love-1975-1979-C . . . . (JCI Assoc. Labels)
Right On Track
Breakfast Club; *Breakfast Club* . . . . (MCA)
   Club Disco-Dance Hits-C . . . . (MCA Special Prod.)
   Greatest Rock Hits Of The '80s-C . . . . (MCA Special Prod.)
Righteous
Eric Johnson; *Ah Via Musicom* . . . . (Capitol)
Rock Island Line
Johnny Cash; *Johnny Cash-Sun Years* . . . . (Rhino)
   Story Songs Of The Trains & Rivers . . . . (Sun)
   Vintage Years-1955-1963 . . . . (Rhino)
Sonny Terry & Brownie McGhee; *Hootin'* . . . . (Muse)
   Jazz Heritage . . . . (MCA)
Weavers; *Best Of The Weavers* . . . . (MCA)
   Weavers At Carnegie Hall . . . . (Vanguard)
   Weavers' Greatest Hits . . . . (Vanguard)
Rockin' Good Way (To Mess Around And Fall In Love)
Arthur Prysock; *Rockin' Good Way* . . . . (Milestone)
Brook Benton & Dinah Washington; *Brook Benton-Anthology* . . . . (Rhino)
Searching With My Good Eye Closed
Soundgarden; *Badmotorfinger* . . . . (A&M)
She's Been Good To Me
Marc Anthony; *Marc Anthony* . . . . (Columbia)
She's Lookin' Good
Rodger Collins; *Soul Shots-#2-The "In" Crowd-Sweet Soul-C* . . . (Rhino)
Wilson Pickett; *Very Best Of Wilson Pickett* . . . . (Rhino)
   Wilson Pickett's Greatest Hits . . . . (Atlantic)
So Good
Destiny's Child; *The Writing's On The Wall* . . . . (Columbia)
So Sad (To Watch Good Love Go Bad)
Everly Brothers; *The Reunion Concert-Live At Albert Hall 1983* . . . . . (Mercury)
   Walk Right Back: The Everly Brothers On Warner Bros.-1960-
   1969 . . . . (Warner Archives)
Frank Ifield; *Best Of Frank Ifield* . . . . (Curb)
Sweethearts Of The Rodeo; *Columbia Country Classics-#5-A New*
   Tradition-C . . . . (Columbia)
Some Change
Boz Scaggs; *My Time: A Boz Scaggs Anthology-1969-1997* . . . (Legacy)
   Some Change . . . . (Virgin)
Someday When Things Are Good
Merle Haggard; *His Epic Hits-First 11 To Be Continued-C* . . . . (Epic)
   That's The Way Love Goes . . . . (Epic)
Something Fine
Jackson Browne; *Jackson Browne* . . . . (Asylum)
Something Good
Utah Saints; *Something Good* . . . . (London)
Something Wonderful
Original Broadway Cast; *The King And I* . . . . (RCA Victor)
Original Cast; *The King And I* . . . . (MCA)
Sweet Soul Music
Arthur Conley; *Atlantic Soul Classics-C* . . . . (Warner Special Prod.)
   Golden Age Of Black Music-1960-1970-C . . . . (Atlantic)
Swinging On A Star
Bing Crosby; *All-Time Best* . . . . (Curb)
   Best Of Bing Crosby . . . . (MCA)
Dion And The Belmonts; *Dion And The Belmonts-Their Best* . . . (Laurie)
Frank Sinatra; *Frank Sinatra Sings The Songs Of Van Heusen*
   & Cahn . . . . (Reprise)
Take Good Care Of My Baby
Bobby Vee; *Best Of Bobby Vee* . . . . (EMI)
   Billboard Top Rock 'N' Roll Hits-1961-C . . . . (Rhino)
   'Til My Dreamin' Comes True-C . . . . (Capitol)
Bobby Vinton; *Bobby Vinton-16 Most Requested Songs* . . . (Legacy)
Dion; *Runaround Sue (Right Stuff)* . . . . (Right Stuff)
Tell Me I'm Not Dreamin'
Jermaine Jackson; *Jermaine Jackson* . . . . (Arista)
Tell Me Something Good
Rufus; *Rags To Rufus* . . . . (MCA)
Rufus Featuring Chaka Khan; *Classic Soul-C* . . . . (MCA)
   Live-Stompin' At The Savoy . . . . (Warner Bros.)
Testicle Of God (& It Was Good)
Gaye Bykers On Acid; *Stewed To The Gills* . . . . (Caroline)
Thanking The Good Lord
Merle Haggard; *Chill Factor* . . . . (Epic)
That Road Still Looks Real Good To Me
Lacy J. Dalton; *Lacy J.* . . . . (Capitol)
Theme From "Good Times"
Original Soundtrack; *CBS: The First 50 Years* . . . . (TVT)
   Television's Greatest Hits-#3-1970s & 1980s-C . . . . . . (TVT)

There's Nothing Too Good For My Baby
Lee Newman; *Relatively Singing: The Songs Of Jimmy McHugh, Eddie Cantor & More* . . . . (Original Cast)
They Say That Falling In Love Is Wonderful
Mark Shane & Terry Blaine; *With Thee I Swing!* . . . . (Nagel-Heyer)
Those Good Old Dreams
Carpenters; *Carpenters-Classics-#2* . . . . (A&M)
Yesterday Once More . . . . (A&M)
Those Good Old Sun Records
Sun Rhythm Section; *Old Time Rock 'N Roll* . . . .(Flying Fish)
Those Oldies But Goodies (Remind Me Of You)
John Cafferty And The Beaver Brown Band; *ST/Eddie & The Cruisers* . . . . (Scotti Bros.)
Little Caesar and The Romans; *Best Love Songs-C* . . . .(Original Sound)
Collectables Presents The History Of Rock-#2-C . . . . (Collectables)
Cruisin'-1961-C . . . . (Increase)
Oldies But Goodies-#6-C . . . . (Original Sound)
Till Good Luck Comes My Way
Original Cast; *Show Boat* . . . . (Angel)
Too Good To Be True
Michael Peterson; *Michael Peterson* . . . .(Reprise)
Too Good To Stop Now
Mickey Gilley; *Too Good To Stop Now* . . . . (Epic)
Too Little Too Late
Barenaked Ladies; *Maroon* . . . .(Reprise)
Well Respected Man
Kinks; *History Of British Rock-#4-C* . . . . (Rhino)
Kinks' Greatest Hits . . . . (Rhino)
Kinks-Size Kinkdom . . . . (Rhino)
We're Off To See The Wizard
Jewel/Jackson Browne/Ry Cooder; *The Wizard Of Oz In Concert: Dreams Come True-C* . . . . (Rhino)
Judy Garland; *A&E Biography: A Musical Anthology* . . . . (Capitol)
Original Cast; *The Wizard Of Oz* . . . . (TVT)
Original Soundtrack; *The Wizard Of Oz-Selections From The Original Motion Picture Soundtrack* . . . . (Turner Classic Movies)
We've Got A Good Fire Goin'
Don Williams; *Don Williams' Greatest Country Hits* . . . .(Curb)
New Moves . . . . (Capitol)
What A Wonderful World
Louis Armstrong; *ST/Good Morning, Vietnam* . . . . (A&M)
Vocalists-Jazz Masters-C . . . . (Bluebird)
What A Wonderful World . . . . (Decca Jazz)
Mormon Tabernacle Choir; *Songs From America's Heartland* . . . .(London)
Willie Nelson; *What A Wonderful World* . . . . (Columbia)
When It Hurts So Bad
Lauryn Hill; *The Miseducation Of Lauryn Hill* . . . . (Ruffhouse/Columbia)
When The Good Apples Fall
Seekers; *Capitol Collectors Series-The Seekers* . . . . (Capitol)
Where Have All The Good Times Gone
Kinks; *Kinks' Greatest Hits* . . . . (Rhino)
One For The Road . . . . (Arista)
Where Have All The Good Times Gone
David Bowie; *Bowie Pin Ups* . . . . (Rykodisc)
Where Have All The Good Times Gone
Van Halen; *Diver Down* . . . . (Warner Bros.)
Where Have All The Good Times Gone
Elton John; *Jump Up!* . . . . (MCA)
Whole New You
Shawn Colvin; *Whole New You* . . . . (Columbia)
Winston Tastes Good (Winston Cigarettes)
Original Soundtrack; *TeeVee Toons-The Commercials-#1-C* . . . . (TVT)
Wiser Time
Black Crowes; *Amorica* . . . . (American)
Wonderful Summer
Robin Ward; *Sixties Rule! Chapter Two-C* . . . . (One Way)
Would You Like To Take A Walk?
Ella Fitzgerald; *Ella & Friends* . . . . (Decca Jazz)
Julia Sanderson/Frank Crumit/Leonard Joy; *The Song Is...Harry Warren-C* . . . . (Living Era)
Rudy Vallee & His Connecticut Yankees; *78-#22611* . . . .(Victor)
Wouldn't It Be Nice
Beach Boys; *Absolutely Best-#2* . . . . (Capitol)
Made In The U.S.A. . . . . (Capitol)
Pet Sounds . . . . (Capitol)
Still Cruisin' . . . . (Capitol)
You Give Good Love
Whitney Houston; *Whitney Houston* . . . . (Arista)
Whitney Houston's Greatest Hits . . . . (Arista)
You'd Be So Nice To Come Home To
Dinah Shore; *Songs That Got Us Through WWII-#2-C* . . . . (Rhino)
Your Good Girl's Gonna Go Bad
Billie Jo Spears; *Best Of Billie Jo Spears* . . . . (CEMA Special Prod.)
Best Of Billie Jo Spears . . . . (Razor & Tie)
K.T. Oslin; *Tammy Wynette...Remembered-C* . . . . (Asylum)
Tammy Wynette; *Tammy Wynette-Anniversary-20 Years Of Hits* . . . . . . (Epic)
Tammy Wynette's Greatest Hits . . . . (Epic)
Your Good Girl's Gonna Go Bad . . . . (Legacy)

You're A Good Man, Charlie Brown
Original Cast; *You're A Good Man, Charlie Brown* . . . . (Polydor)
You've Got A Good Love Comin'
Lee Greenwood; *Inside Out/You've Got A Good Love Comin'* . . . . (MCA)

GOSSIP, Rumors

See Also: **CHEATING & LIES, COMMUNICATION: TALK, JEALOUSY, LOVE (various), SECRETS**

Baby It's You
Beatles; *Introducing...The Beatles* . . . . (Vee-Jay)
The Early Beatles . . . . (Capitol)
Careless Whisper
Dave Koz featuring Montell Jordan; *Dance* . . . . (Capitol)
Wham! Featuring George Michael; *Make It Big* . . . . (Columbia)
Music For The Miracle-C . . . . (Epic Portrait Assoc.)
C'mon Marianne
4 Seasons; *25th Anniversary Collection* . . . .(Rhino)
4 Seasons-Anthology . . . . (Rhino)
Freedom Overspill
Steve Winwood; *Back In The High Life* . . . . (Island)
Girls Talk
Dave Edmunds; *Best Of Dave Edmunds* . . . . (Swan Song)
Repeat When Necessary . . . . (Swan Song)
Dave Edmunds Band; *I Hear You Rockin'* . . . . (Columbia)
Elvis Costello; *Girls Girls Girls* . . . . (Columbia)
Taking Liberties . . . . (Columbia)
Linda Ronstadt; *Mad Love* . . . . (Elektra)
Grapevyne
Brownstone; *Dancin' Divas-C* . . . . (Epic Dance)
From The Bottom Up . . . . (MJJ/Epic)
I Heard
Mills Brothers; *Essential Mills Brothers: Four Boys And A Guitar* . . . . .(Legacy)
I Heard It Through The Grapevine
Creedence Clearwater Revival; *Chooglin'* . . . .(Fantasy)
Cosmo's Factory . . . . (Fantasy)
Creedence Clearwater Revival-Chronicle . . . . (Fantasy)
Creedence Clearwater Revival-Gold . . . . (Fantasy)
Movie Album . . . . (Fantasy)
Gladys Knight & The Pips; *16 #1 Hits From The Late '60s-C* . . . .(Motown)
Compact Command Performances-Gladys Knight & The Pips . . . . . . (Motown)
Every Great Motown Song-First 25 Years-C . . . . (Motown)
Motown Grammy R&B Performances Of The '60s & '70s-C . . . . . (Motown)
Motown Superstar Series-#13-Gladys Knight & The Pips . . . . (Motown)
Top 10 With A Bullet-Motown Girl Groups-C . . . . (Motown)
Marvin Gaye; *25 #1 Hits From 25 Years-C* . . . . (Motown)
Every Great Motown Hit Of Marvin Gaye . . . . (Motown)
Marvin Gaye Live At The London Palladium . . . . (Motown)
Marvin Gaye-Anthology . . . . (Motown)
Most Played Songs On America's Jukeboxes . . . . (Motown)
Motown Story-First 25 Years-C . . . . (Motown)
I Know
Luther Vandross; *I Know* . . . . (LV/Virgin)
I Wasn't With It
Jesse Powell; *'Bout It* . . . . (Silas)
I'm Still In Love With You
New Edition; *D.J. Mix '98-#1-C* . . . . (Beast)
Home Again . . . . (MCA)
Little Gossip
Original London Cast; *Man Of La Mancha* . . . . (MCA)
Loose Talk
Carl Smith; *Very Special Love Song-C* . . . . (Fifty One West)
Patsy Cline; *Live At The Opry* . . . . (MCA)
Maybe I Know
Lesley Gore; *Golden Hits Of Lesley Gore* . . . . (Mercury)
Lesley Gore-Anthology . . . . (Rhino)
Minnesota Man Claims Monkey Bowled Perfect Game
Jad Fair; *Strange But True* . . . . (Matador)
Missing You
Brooks & Dunn; *Tight Rope* . . . . (Arista)
John Waite; *'80s Greatest Rock Hits-#1-Passion & Power-C* . . . . . . (Priority)
Complete John Waite-#1-Falling Backwards . . . . (EMI)
Essential John Waite-1976-1986 . . . . (Chrysalis)
Tina Turner; *Wildest Dreams* . . . . (Virgin)
No Matter What They Say
Lil' Kim; *Notorious K.I.M.* . . . . (Queen Bee/Undeas/Atlantic)
People Will Say We're In Love
Frank Sinatra; *A Lovely Way To Spend An Evening* . . . .(ASV)
Original Broadway Cast; *Oklahoma!* . . . . (RCA)
Spaniels; *Spaniels' Golden Hits* . . . . (Juke Box Treasures)
The Acapella Collection . . . . (Juke Box Treasures)
Pick-A-Little, Talk-A-Little
Hermione Gingold & Biddys; *ST/The Music Man* . . . . (Warner Bros.)
Original Cast; *The Music Man* . . . . (Gold Rush)
Rumor Has It
Clay Walker; *Clay Walker's Greatest Hits* . . . . (Giant)

Rumor Has It . . . . (Giant)

Say It Isn't So
Dinah Washington; *Irving Berlin Always-C* . . . . (Verve)
Michael Feinstein; *Remember-Michael Feinstein Sings Irving Berlin* . . (Elektra)
Nat "King" Cole; *Spotlight On Nat "King" Cole* . . . . (Capitol)
Ray Conniff; *'S Awful Nice* . . . . (Columbia)

Take It On The Run
REO Speedwagon; *A Second Decade Of Rock And Roll 1981 To 1991* . . . .(Epic)
Hi Infidelity . . . .(Epic)
REO Speedwagon-The Hits . . . .(Epic)

Telephone Hour
Original Cast; *Bye Bye Birdie* . . . . (Columbia)
Soundtrack; *Bye Bye Birdie* . . . . (RCA)

They Don't Know
Jon B.; *Cool Relax* . . . . (Yab Yum/550)

Think Of What You've Done
Ricky Skaggs and Kentucky Thunder; *Bluegrass Rules!* . . . . (Rounder)

Til I Hear It From You
Gin Blossoms; *ST/Crossroads-VH1 Television Program* . . . . (Atlantic)
ST/Empire Records . . . . (A&M)

You Should Know Better
Kenny Wayne Shepherd Band; *Live On* . . . . (Giant)

You Talk Too Much
Joe Jones; *American Graffiti-#3-C* . . . .(MCA)
Billboard Top Rock 'N' Roll Hits-1960-C . . . . (Rhino)
Carnival Time-Best Of Ric Records-#1-C . . . . (Rounder)
Echoes Of A Rock Era-Middle Years-C . . . . (Roulette)
Original Rock 'N' Roll Hits Of The '60s-C . . . . (Roulette)

GRATITUDE, Thank You
See Also: **HAPPINESS**

(I've Had) The Time Of My Life
Bill Medley; *Best Of Bill Medley* . . . . (Curb)
Bill Medley & Jennifer Warnes; *Dirty Dancing Live In Concert-C* . . . . . . (RCA)
ST/Dirty Dancing . . . . (RCA)

(Your Love Keeps Lifting Me) Higher And Higher
Bette Midler; *Bette Midler* . . . .(Atlantic)
Bonnie Bramlett; *It's Time* . . . . (Capricorn)
Jackie Wilson; *Billboard Top R&B Hits-1967-C* . . . . (Rhino)
Jackie Wilson's Greatest Hits . . . .(Brunswick)
Jackie Wilson's Greatest Hits-#2 . . . .(Brunswick)
Reet Petite-Best Of Jackie Wilson . . . . (Columbia)
The Jackie Wilson Story . . . .(Epic)
Very Best Of Jackie Wilson . . . . (Rhino)
Rita Coolidge; *Anytime...Anywhere* . . . . (A&M)
Havana Jam . . . . (Columbia)
Rita Coolidge-Classics-#5 . . . . (A&M)
Rita Coolidge's Greatest Hits . . . . (A&M)

24/7
Kevon Edmonds; *24/7* . . . . (RCA)

All My Life
K-Ci & JoJo; *Love Always* . . . .(MCA)
Now That's What I Call Music!-#1-C . . . . (Virgin)

Angel
Shaggy; *Hotshot* . . . .(MCA)

Angel
Lionel Richie; *Renaissance* . . . . (Island/IDJMG)

Angel Of Mine
Monica; *The Boy Is Mine* . . . . (Arista)
Totally Hits-#1-C . . . . (Arista)

Angels Listened In
Crests; *Crests Greatest Hits* . . . . (Collectables)
Super Oldies Of The '50s-#3-C . . . . (Audio Fidelity)
WCBS FM 101 History Of Rock-'50s-#2-C . . . . (Collectables)

Anyone Else
Collin Raye; *The Walls Came Down* . . . .(Epic)

Anything
Jay-Z; *Vol. 3-Life & Times Of S. Carter* . . . . (Roc-A-Fella/DJMG)

Back To You
Bryan Adams; *MTV Unplugged-Bryan Adams* . . . . (A&M)

Be Thankful For What You Got
William DeVaughn; *Didn't It Blow Your Mind: Soul Hits Of The '70s-#12-C* . . . . (Rhino)
Oldies But Goodies-#11-C . . . . (Original Sound)

Because Of You
Bobby Vinton; *Bobby Vinton's Greatest Hits* . . . . (Curb)
Tony Bennett; *Tony Bennett Sings His All-Time Hall Of Fame Hits* . . . . (Columbia)
Tony Bennett-16 Most Requested Songs . . . . (Legacy)
Willie Nelson; *One For The Road* . . . . (Columbia)

Because You Love Me
Jo Dee Messina; *I'm Alright* . . . . (Curb)

Because You Loved Me
Celine Dion; *All The Way...A Decade Of Song* . . . . (550 Music)
Diana, Princess Of Wales-Tribute-C . . . . (Columbia)
Falling Into You . . . . (550 Music)

Bip Bam Thank You Ma'am
Ann Peebles; *Fill This World With Love* . . . . (Bullseye Blues)

Blessed
Christina Aguilera; *Christina Aguilera* . . . .(RCA)

But For The Grace Of God
keith urban; *keith urban.* . . . . (Capitol)

Butterfly
Crazy Town; *Gift Of Game* . . . . (Columbia)

Can't Take My Eyes Off You
Frankie Valli; *25th Anniversary Collection* . . . . (Rhino)
Frankie Valli-Anthology . . . . (Rhino)
Very Best Of Frankie Valli . . . .(MCA)
Lauryn Hill; *The Miseducation Of Lauryn Hill* . . . . . (Ruffhouse/Columbia)

Chain Of Love
Clay Walker; *Live, Laugh, Love* . . . .(Giant)

Child's Song
Tom Rush; *Best Of Tom Rush: No Regrets* . . . . (Legacy)
Tom Rush . . . . (Columbia)

Crazy Love
Brian McKnight; *Anytime* . . . . (Motown)
I Remember You . . . . (Mercury)
ST/Jason's Lyric . . . . (Mercury)
Van Morrison; *Moondance* . . . . (Warner Bros.)

Danke Schoen
Wayne Newton; *Best Of Wayne Newton-Now* . . . . (Curb)
Capitol Collectors Series-Wayne Newton . . . . (Capitol)
Jackpot! The Las Vegas Story-C . . . . (Rhino)
Wayne Newton's Greatest Hits . . . . (Curb)

Days
Kinks; *Kink Kronikles* . . . . (Reprise)

Dear Mrs. Roosevelt
Bob Dylan; *Tribute To Woody Guthrie-C* . . . . (Warner Bros.)

Drift Away
Dobie Gray; *Classic Rock-#1-C* . . . .(MCA)
Oldies But Goodies-#10-C . . . . (Original Sound)
Oldies But Goodies-#3-C . . . . (Original Sound)
Super Hits Of The '70s-Have A Nice Day-#10-C . . . . (Rhino)
Michael Bolton; *Timeless-Classics* . . . . (Columbia)
Rod Stewart; *Atlantic Crossing* . . . . (Warner Bros.)

Even If
Amel Larrieux; *Infinite Possibilities* . . . . (Epic)

Every Time I Close My Eyes
Babyface; *The Day* . . . . (Epic)

Fortunate
Maxwell; *ST/Life* . . . . (Rock Land/Interscope)

God Gave Me Everything
Mick Jagger; *Goddess In The Doorway* . . . . (Virgin)

Grown Men Don't Cry
Tim McGraw; *Set This Circus Down* . . . . (Curb)

Hats Off To Larry
Del Shannon; *Runaway Hits!* . . . . (Rhino)
Super Oldies Of The '60s-#2-C . . . . (Audio Fidelity)
WCBS FM 101 History Of Rock-'60s-#3-C . . . . (Collectables)

Help!
Beatles; *Beatles 1* . . . . (Capitol)
Beatles-20 Greatest Hits . . . . (Capitol)
Rarities . . . . (Capitol)
Reel Music . . . . (Capitol)
ST/Help! . . . . (Capitol)
The Beatles At The Hollywood Bowl. . . . . (Capitol)
The Beatles/1962-1966 . . . . (Capitol)

How Sweet It Is (To Be Loved By You)
James Taylor; *Gorilla* . . . . (Warner Bros.)
James Taylor-Best Live . . . . (Columbia)
James Taylor's Greatest Hits . . . . (Warner Bros.)
Junior Walker & The All Stars; *Junior Walker & The All Stars' Greatest Hits* . . . . (Motown)
Junior Walker & The All Stars-The Ultimate Collection . . . . (Motown)
Marvin Gaye; *20th Century Masters-The Millennium Collection-The Best Of Marvin Gaye-#1 (The '60s)* . . . . (Motown)
Marvin Gaye-Anthology . . . . (Motown)
Marvin Gaye's Greatest Hits/ . . . . (Motown)

I Can't Wait To Meetchu
Macy Gray; *On How Life Is* . . . . (Epic)

I Found Love
Earl Scruggs & Vince Gill & Rosanne Cash; *Earl Scruggs And Friends-C* . . . .(MCA)

I Thank You
Bonnie Raitt; *The Glow* . . . . (Warner Bros.)
John Cowan; *Soul'd Out* . . . . (Sugar Hill)
Sam & Dave; *Best Of Sam & Dave* . . . .(Atlantic)
Very Best Of Sam & Dave. . . . . (Rhino)
ZZ Top; *Deguello* . . . . (Warner Bros.)

I Turn To You
Christina Aguilera; *Christina Aguilera* . . . . (RCA)

In Harm's Way
Bebe Winans; *Bebe Winans* . . . .(Atlantic)

In This Life
Collin Raye; *In This Life* . . . . (Epic)

In Times Like These
Barbara Mandrell; *Barbara Mandrell's Greatest Hits* . . . . (MCA)
Spun Gold . . . . (MCA)
Jilted
Teresa Brewer; *Best Of Teresa Brewer* . . . . (MCA Jazz)
Just As I Am
Air Supply; *Air Supply* . . . . (Arista)
Keeper Of The Stars
Tracy Byrd; *No Ordinary Man* . . . . (MCA)
Kind & Generous
Natalie Merchant; *Ophelia* . . . . (Elektra)
Lady (You Bring Me Up)
Commodores; *All The Great Love Songs-Commodores* . . . . (Motown)
Commodores-All The Great Hits . . . . (Motown)
Compact Command Performances-Commodores . . . . (Motown)
Larger Than Life
Backstreet Boys; *Millennium* . . . . (Jive)
Now That's What I Call Music!-#4-C . . . . (Virgin)
Last Night
Al Jarreau; *Tomorrow Today* . . . . (GRP/VMG)
Love Of A Woman
Travis Tritt; *Down The Road I Go* . . . . (Columbia)
Lucky One
Amy Grant; *House Of Love* . . . . (A&M)
Make Me Whole
Amel Larrieux; *Infinite Possibilities* . . . . (Epic)
Mona Lisas And Mad Hatters
Elton John; *Honky Chateau* . . . . (Rocket)
Reg Strikes Back . . . . (MCA)
The Concert For New York City-C . . . . (Columbia)
My Baby You
Marc Anthony; *Marc Anthony* . . . . (Columbia)
My Darling Child
Sinead O'Connor; *Universal Mother* . . . . (Ensign)
My One True Friend
Bette Midler; *Bathhouse Betty* . . . . (Warner Bros.)
Natural High
Merle Haggard & Janie Fricke; *For The Record: Merle Haggard-43*
Legendary Hits . . . . (BNA)
Now Be Thankful
Fairport Convention; *Meet On The Ledge: The Classic Years-1967-*
1975 . . . . (A&M)
Oh Happy Day
Lawrence Welk; *Champagne Music Of Lawrence Welk* . . . . (Universal)
Oh Thank You Great Spirit
Chicago; *Chicago VIII* . . . . (Chicago)
On London Bridge
Jo Stafford; *International Hits* . . . . (Corinthian)
One In A Million
Platters; *Magic Touch-An Anthology* . . . . (Mercury)
One Voice
Billy Gilman; *One Voice* . . . . (Epic)
Other Man's Grass Is Always Greener
Petula Clark; *Petula Clark's Greatest Hits* . . . . (Crescendo)
Pride & Joy
Jon B.; *Cool Relax* . . . . (Yab Yum/550)
Room At The Top
Tom Petty And The Heartbreakers; *Echo* . . . . (Warner Bros.)
Salt Of The Earth
Mick Jagger & Keith Richards; *The Concert For New York City-C* . . (Columbia)
Rolling Stones; *Beggars Banquet* . . . . (Abkco)
Shelter From The Storm
Bob Dylan; *Blood On The Tracks* . . . . (Columbia)
Bob Dylan At Budokan . . . . (Columbia)
Hard Rain . . . . (Columbia)
Ships That Don't Come In
Joe Diffie; *Regular Joe* . . . . (Epic)
Shout
Beatles; *The Beatles-Anthology-#1* . . . . (Capitol)
Isley Brothers; *Nipper's Greatest Hits Of The '50s-#2-C* . . . . (RCA)
Shout . . . . (Collectables)
ST/The Wanderers . . . . (Warner Bros.)
Joey Dee & the Starliters; *Echoes Of A Rock Era-Later Years-C* . . . . (Roulette)
Hey Let's Twist! Best Of Joey Dee & The Starliters . . . . (Rhino)
Live At The Peppermint Lounge . . . . (Accord)
Original Rock 'N' Roll Hits Of The '60s-C . . . . (Roulette)
Sock Hoppin' Sixties-C . . . . (JCI Assoc. Labels)
Otis Day & The Knights; *Shout* . . . . (MCA)
ST/Animal House . . . . (MCA)
Tom Petty And The Heartbreakers; *Pack Up The Plantation-Live!* . . . . (MCA)
Someone To Love
Jon B.; *Bonafide* . . . . (Yab Yum/550)
Jon B. featuring Babyface; *ST/Bad Boys* . . . . (Work)
Song For Mama
Boyz II Men; *BET-Best Of Planet Groove-C* . . . . (Virgin)
Evolution . . . . (Motown)
ST/Soul Food . . . . (LaFace)

Stomp
God's Property; *MTV Jams-C* . . . . (Kedar Entert./Universal)
Stranger Than You
Joe Jackson; *Steppin' Out: The Very Best Of Joe Jackson* . . . . (A&M)
Sunshine
Coko; *Hot Coko* . . . . (RCA)
Taking You Home
Don Henley; *Inside Job* . . . . (Warner Bros.)
Thank God
Hank Williams; *I Saw The Light* . . . . (Polydor)
Let's Turn Back The Years-1951-1953 . . . . (Polydor)
Roy Acuff; *Roy Acuff's Greatest Hits-#2* . . . . (MCA)
Thank God & Greyhound
Roy Clark; *Best Of Roy Clark* . . . . (MCA)
Great Picks And New Tricks . . . . (ISD/Intersound)
Roy Clark-Live . . . . (MCA)
Roy Clark's Greatest Hits . . . . (MCA)
Thank God For Believers
Mark Chesnutt; *Thank God For Believers* . . . . (Decca)
Thank God For Kids
Oak Ridge Boys; *Christmas For The '90s-#1-C* . . . . (Liberty)
Oak Ridge Boys' Greatest Hits 2 . . . . (MCA)
Oak Ridge Boys-Christmas . . . . (MCA Special Prod.)
Oak Ridge Boys-Collection . . . . (MCA)
Thank God For The Radio
Kendalls; *Kendalls-20 Favorites* . . . . (Epic)
Movin' Train . . . . (Mercury)
Thank God For You
Sawyer Brown; *Outskirts Of Town* . . . . (Curb)
Sawyer Brown's Greatest Hits 1990-1995 . . . . (Curb)
Thank God I Found You
Mariah Carey featuring Joe & 98 Degrees; *Rainbow* . . . . (Columbia)
Thank God I'm A Country Boy
John Denver; *Back Home Again* . . . . (RCA)
Evening With John Denver . . . . (RCA)
John Denver's Greatest Hits-#2 . . . . (RCA)
Thank God It's Friday
Love And Kisses; *ST/Thank God It's Friday* . . . . (Casablanca)
Thank God It's Monday
Dene Anton; *Texas Soul* . . . . (JRS)
Thank Goodness It's Friday
Moe Bandy & Joe Stampley; *Just Good Ol' Boys* . . . . (Columbia)
Moe Bandy & Joe Stampley's Greatest Hits . . . . (Columbia)
Thank Heaven For Little Girls
Maurice Chevalier; *ST/Gigi* . . . . (Sony Music Special Prod.)
Merle Haggard & Janie Fricke; *It's All In The Game* . . . . (Epic)
Thank The Lord For The Night Time
Neil Diamond; *Glory Road-1968-1972* . . . . (MCA)
Hot August Night II . . . . (Columbia)
Neil Diamond-Classics (Early Years) . . . . (Columbia)
Neil Diamond-Gold . . . . (MCA)
Neil Diamond's Greatest Hits-1966-1992 . . . . (Columbia)
Thank U
Alanis Morissette; *Supposed Former Infatuation Junkie* . . . . (Maverick)
Thank You
Boyz II Men; *Boyz II Men II* . . . . (Motown)
Thank You
Led Zeppelin; *BBC Sessions* . . . . (Atlantic)
Led Zeppelin II . . . . (Atlantic)
Led Zeppelin-Box Set . . . . (Atlantic)
Led Zeppelin-The Complete Studio Recordings . . . . (Atlantic)
Page & Plant; *No Quarter: Jimmy Page & Robert Plant Unledded* . . . . (Atlantic)
Thank You Boys
Jane's Addiction; *Nothing's Shocking* . . . . (Warner Bros.)
Thank You Canada
Frank Jones; *45-#4595* . . . . (Soundwaves)
Thank You Falletin Me Be Mice Elf Again
Sly & The Family Stone; *In Yo' Face!-History Of Funk-#1-C* . . . . (Rhino)
Sly & The Family Stone-Anthology . . . . (Epic)
Sly & The Family Stone's Greatest Hits . . . . (Epic)
Thank You For Being A Friend
Andrew Gold; *All This & Heaven Too* . . . . (Asylum)
Chicken Soup For The Soul: I'll Be There For You-Songs Of Friendship,
Brotherhood And Sisterhood-C . . . . (Rhino)
Television's Greatest Hits-#6-Remote Control-C . . . . (TVT)
Thank You For Being A Friend: The Best Of Andrew Gold . . . . (Rhino)
Thank You For Loving Me
Bon Jovi; *Crush* . . . . (Island/IDJMG)
Thank You For Sending Me An Angel
Talking Heads; *More Songs About Buildings & Food* . . . . (Sire)
Thank You For Talking To Me, Africa
Miki Howard; *Femme Fatale* . . . . (Giant)
Sly & The Family Stone; *Sly & The Family Stone-Anthology* . . . . (Epic)
There's A Riot Goin' On . . . . (Epic)
Thank You For The Music
Abba; *Gold-Greatest Hits* . . . . (Polydor)
Thank You For The Roses
Kitty Wells; *Kitty Wells' Greatest Hits* . . . . (Step One)

Thank You Girl
Beatles; *Beatles-Box Set* . . . . (Capitol)
Past Masters-Volume One . . . . (Parlophone)
The Beatles' Second Album . . . . (Capitol)
Thank You Girl
John Hiatt; *Bring The Family* . . . . (A&M)
Thank You In Advance
Boyz II Men; *Nathan Michael Shawn Wanya* . . . . (Universal)
Thank You Lord
Bob Marley & The Wailers; *Songs Of Freedom* . . . . (Tuff Gong)
Glenn Yarbrough & The Limeliters; *Joy Across The Land* . . . . . . (Crescendo)
Heptones; *Changing Times* . . . . (Moving Target)
Thank You Pretty Baby
Brook Benton; *Brook Benton-At His Best* . . . . (Pair)
It's Just A Matter Of Time-His Greatest Hits . . . . (Mercury)
Professor Longhair; *'Fess-Anthology* . . . . (Rhino)
Thank You World
Statler Brothers; *Best Of The Statler Brothers* . . . . . (Mercury)
Thank You, Republic Airlines
Tom Paxton; *One Million Lawyers & Other Disasters* . . . . (Flying Fish)
Thanking The Good Lord
Merle Haggard; *Chill Factor* . . . . (Epic)
Thanks A Lot
Raul Malo; *Country Goes Raffi-C* . . . . (Rounder)
Thanks For All The Good Times
White Mountain Singers; *Best Of The White Mountain Singers* . . . . . (Folk Era)
Thanks For Leaving, Lucille
Sherri Jerrico; *Best Of Town & Country-#3-C* . . . . . (International Mktg. Group)
Thanks For The Beautiful Land On The Delta
Duke Ellington; *New Orleans Suite* . . . . (Atlantic)
Thanks For The Memories
Benny Goodman; *Benny Goodman-More Greatest Hits* . . . . (RCA)
Bob Hope; *Thanks For The Memories* . . . . (MCA)
Bob Hope & Shirley Ross; *The Envelope Please-Academy Award Winning Songs-#1 (1934-1945)-C* . . . . (Rhino)
Thanks For The Pepperoni
George Harrison; *All Things Must Pass* . . . . (Parlophone)
Thanks For The Ride On The MerryGoRound
Andy Badale & The Beer Garden Band; *Nashville Beer Garden* . . . . . (Ranwood)
Thanks For The Trip To Paradise
Jim & Jesse; *Music Among Friends* . . . . (Rounder)
Thanks To The Cat House
Johnny Paycheck; *Armed & Crazy* . . . . (Epic)
Thankyou
Dido; *No Angel* . . . . (Arista)
Totally Hits 2001-C . . . . (Arista)
Theme From ''The Bob Hope Show'' (Thanks For The Memories)
Original Soundtrack; *Television's Greatest Hits-#4-Black & White Classics-C* . . . . (TVT)
Then The Morning Comes
Smash Mouth; *Astro Lounge* . . . . (Interscope)
Now That's What I Call Music!-#4-C . . . . (Virgin)
There You Are
Martina McBride; *Emotion* . . . . (RCA)
There You'll Be
Faith Hill; *ST/Pearl Harbor* . . . . (Warner Bros.)
Till There Was You
Beatles; *Beatles-Box Set* . . . . (Capitol)
Meet The Beatles! . . . . (Capitol)
With The Beatles . . . . (Parlophone)
Original Cast; *ST/The Music Man* . . . . (Warner Bros.)
To Sir With Love
Lulu; *History Of British Rock-#6-C* . . . . (Rhino)
Hollywood Magic-1960s-C . . . . (Columbia)
Rock Artifacts-From The Vaults-#3-C . . . . (Columbia)
Turn The Page
Aaliyah; *ST/Music Of The Heart* . . . . . (Epic/Sony Music Soundtrax)
Unanswered Prayers
Garth Brooks; *No Fences* . . . . (Capitol)
We Gather Together
Original Soundtrack; *School Days-Kids Classics* . . . . (Benson)
What A Girl Wants
Christina Aguilera; *Christina Aguilera* . . . . (RCA)
Totally Hits-#3-C . . . . (Atlantic)
When I Close My Eyes
Shanice; *Shanice* . . . . (LaFace)
Who Put The Bomp (In The Bomp, Bomp, Bomp)
Barry Mann; *Goofy Greats-C* . . . . (K-Tel)
Sixties Rule! Chapter Two-C . . . . (One Way)
Whoever Says I Do
Geggy Tah; *Sacred Cow* . . . . (Luaka Bop)
Wifey
Next; *Totally Hits-#3-C* . . . . (Atlantic)
Welcome To Nextacy . . . . (Arista)
Wind Beneath My Wings
Bette Midler; *ST/Beaches* . . . . (Atlantic)
Gary Morris; *Chicken Soup For The Soul: I'll Be There For You-Songs Of Friendship, Brotherhood And Sisterhood-C* . . . . . . (Rhino)

Country Love Songs-C . . . . (Warner Bros.)
Gary Morris-Hits . . . . (Warner Bros.)
Why Lady Why . . . . (Warner Bros.)
James Galway; *Wind Beneath My Wings* . . . . (RCA)
Lee Greenwood; *Somebody's Gonna Love You* . . . . (MCA)
Lou Rawls; *When The Night Comes* . . . . (Epic)
Roger Whittaker; *Roger Whittaker Greatest Hits* . . . . (RCA)
Wind Beneath My Wings . . . . (RCA)
Willie Nelson; *City Of New Orleans* . . . . (Columbia)
Wish, The
Bruce Springsteen; *Tracks* . . . . (Columbia)
You Light Up My Life
Debby Boone; *Best Of Debby Boone* . . . . (Curb)
There Is Love-Wedding Songs-C . . . . (Scotti Bros.)
You Light Up My Life . . . . (MCA)
LeAnn Rimes; *You Light Up My Life-Inspirational Songs* . . . . . . (Curb)
Your Faith In Me
Jessica Simpson; *Sweet Kisses* . . . . (Columbia)
Your Precious Love
Marvin Gaye; *Last Concert Tour* . . . . (Giant)
You're My Everything
Temptations; *Temptations' Greatest Hits-#2* . . . . (Motown)
You've Made Me So Very Happy
Blood, Sweat & Tears; *Blood, Sweat & Tears* . . . . (Columbia)
Blood, Sweat & Tears Greatest Hits . . . . (Columbia)
Live & Improvised . . . . (Columbia)
Pop Classics Of The '60s-C . . . . (Columbia)

GREED

See Also: *EGO, MONEY*

(This Thing Called) Wantin' And Havin' It All
Sawyer Brown; *Greatest Hits Of Country Dance-C* . . . . (Curb)
This Thing Called Wantin' & Havin' It All . . . . (Curb)
Can I Get A...
Jay-Z featuring Amil & Ja Rule; *Vol. 2-Hard Knock Life* . . . . . . (Def Jam)
Difference, The
Wallflowers; *Bringing Down The Horse* . . . . (Interscope)
Ends
Everlast; *Whitey Ford Sings The Blues* . . . . (Tommy Boy)
Greed
Godsmack; *Awake* . . . . (Republic/Universal)
Greedy Fly
Bush; *Razorblade Suitcase* . . . . (Trauma)
Here & Now
Letters To Cleo; *Aurora Gory Alice* . . . . (Cherrydisc)
I Believe
Blessid Union Of Souls; *Home* . . . . (EMI)
I Me Mine
Beatles; *Let It Be* . . . . (Capitol)
The Beatles-Anthology-#3 . . . . (Capitol)
I'm Good At Being Bad
TLC; *Fanmail* . . . . (LaFace)
Kids Of The Baby Boom
Bellamy Brothers; *Bellamy Brothers' Greatest Hits-#3* . . . . (MCA)
Country Rap . . . . (MCA)
MCA #1 Hits Of The '80s-#3-C . . . . (MCA Special Prod.)
King Nothing
Metallica; *Load* . . . . (Elektra)
Money
Pink Floyd; *Collection Of Great Dance Songs* . . . . (Columbia)
Dark Side Of The Moon . . . . (Capitol)
Delicate Sound Of Thunder . . . . (Columbia)
Pink Floyd-Gift Set . . . . (Capitol)
Money (That's What I Want)
Barrett Strong; *Motown Story-First 25 Years-C* . . . . (Motown)
Oldies But Goodies-#4-C . . . . (Original Sound)
Beatles; *Beatles-Box Set* . . . . (Capitol)
Rock 'N' Roll Music . . . . (Capitol)
The Beatles' Second Album . . . . (Capitol)
Buddy Guy; *Man & The Blues* . . . . (Vanguard)
Diana Ross & The Supremes; *Diana Ross & The Supremes Sing Motown* . . . . (Motown)
Jerry Lee Lewis; *Jerry Lee's Greatest!* . . . . (Rhino)
John Lennon; *Lennon* . . . . (Capitol)
Junior Walker & The All Stars; *Junior Walker & The All Stars' Greatest Hits* . . . . (S.O.U.L.)
Junior Walker & The All Stars-Anthology . . . . (Motown)
Rolling Stones; *More Hot Rocks (big hits & fazed cookies)* . . . . . (Abkco)
Ronnie Milsap; *Lost In The Fifties Tonight* . . . . (RCA)
Todd Rundgren; *Something/Anything?* . . . . (Rhino)
Razor Love
Neil Young; *Silver & Gold* . . . . (Reprise)
Ruby
Ray Charles; *Love Songs* . . . . (Rhino)
Sign Of The Times
Queensryche; *Hear In The Now Frontier* . . . . (Virgin)

Somebody Else's Money
Wallflowers; *The Wallflowers* . . . .(Virgin)
Stairway To Heaven
Led Zeppelin; *Led Zeppelin IV* . . . . (Atlantic)
  Led Zeppelin-Box Set . . . . (Atlantic)
  Remasters . . . . (Atlantic)
  ST/The Song Remains The Same . . . .(Swan Song)
Stanley Jordan; *Best Of Stanley Jordan* . . . .(Blue Note)
  Flying Home . . . . (EMI)
Taking Everything
Gerald Levert; *Love & Consequences* . . . .(East West)
Too Much
Dave Matthews Band; *Crash* . . . .(RCA)

GUILT, Apology, Blame, Innocent Of Guilt, Regret, Shame, Sorry

See Also: CAPITAL PUNISHMENT, CHEATING & LIES, CRIME, FOOLS, FORGIVE, GOD, KILL, LAW & ORDER, LOVE (various), LOW SELF-ESTEEM, MISTAKES, MISTREATMENT, POLICE, PRISON, REASONS, REBELS, SADNESS, WRONG

(Eye) Hate U
"AFKAP"; *The Gold Experience* . . . . (NPG)
...Baby One More Time
Britney Spears; *...Baby One More Time* . . . .(Jive)
  Now That's What I Call Music!-#2-C . . . .(Virgin)
32 Flavors
Alana Davis; *Blame It On Me* . . . . (Elektra)
Ani DiFranco; *Living In Clip* . . . . (Righteous Babe)
  Not A Pretty Girl . . . . (Righteous Babe)
Adia
Sarah McLachlan; *Mirrorball* . . . .(Arista)
  Surfacing . . . .(Arista)
Ain't That A Shame
4 Seasons; *25th Anniversary Collection* . . . .(Rhino)
Cheap Trick; *Cheap Trick At Budokan* . . . . (Epic)
Fats Domino; *Best Of Fats Domino* . . . .(EMI)
  Fats Domino's Greatest Hits . . . .(Everest)
  Fats Domino's Greatest Hits . . . .(MCA)
  ST/American Graffiti . . . .(MCA)
Hank Williams, Jr.; *Hank Williams, Jr.-14 Greatest Hits* . . . . (Polydor)
  Standing In The Shadows . . . . (Polydor)
John Lennon; *Lennon* . . . .(Capitol)
  Rock 'N' Roll . . . .(Capitol)
All Apologies
Nirvana; *In Utero* . . . .(David Geffen Co.)
  MTV Unplugged In New York . . . .(David Geffen Co.)
All Cried Out
Allure; *Allure* . . . . (Track Masters/Crave)
  Boom! 17 Explosive Hits-C . . . . (Simitar)
Lisa Lisa; *Lisa Lisa & Cult Jam With Full Force* . . . . (Columbia)
  Lisa Lisa-Super Hits . . . . (Columbia)
  Past, Present & Future . . . .(TMP)
All I Need
Temptations; *Temptations-Anthology-The Best Of The Temptations* . . (Motown)
All Mixed Up
311; *311* . . . .(Capricorn)
All Out Of Love
Air Supply; *Air Supply's Greatest Hits* . . . .(Arista)
  Air Supply-The Definitive Collection . . . .(Arista)
  Lost In Love . . . .(Arista)
Always On My Mind
Willie Nelson; *Always On My Mind* . . . . (Columbia)
  Super Hits Of The '80s-C . . . . (Epic)
  Willie Nelson-Super Hits . . . . (Columbia)
Amanda
Don Williams; *Don Williams' Greatest Hits* . . . . (MCA)
  Volume One . . . . (MCA)
Waylon Jennings; *Waylon Jennings' Greatest Hits* . . . . (RCA)
Amigone
Goo Goo Dolls; *Dizzy Up The Girl* . . . . (Warner Sunset/Reprise)
Angels Of The Silences
Counting Crows; *Recovering The Satellites* . . . .(David Geffen Co.)
Answer Me, My Love
Nat "King" Cole; *Best Of Nat "King" Cole-Vol. 1* . . . .(Capitol)
  The Nat "King" Cole Story-#2 . . . .(Capitol)
  Unforgettable . . . .(Capitol)
Apology/Nessun Dorma
Luciano Pavarotti; *ST/The Mirror Has Two Faces* . . . . (Columbia)
As We Lay
Kelly Price; *Mirror Mirror* . . . . (Def Soul/IDJMG)
Baby Come Back
Player; *Billboard Top Hits-1978-C* . . . .(Rhino)
  Mellow Rock Hits Of The '70s-Ventura Highway-C . . . .(Rhino)
  Super Hits Of The '70s-Have A Nice Day-#21-C . . . .(Rhino)

Babylon
David Gray; *White Ladder* . . . .(ATO/RCA)
Back 2 Good
Matchbox Twenty; *Yourself Or Someone Like You* . . . .(Lava)
Back For Good
Take That; *Nobody Else* . . . .(Arista)
Back Here
BBMak; *Now That's What I Call Music!-#5-C* . . . . (Virgin)
  Sooner Or Later . . . .(Hollywood)
Back In Your Arms Again
Lorrie Morgan; *Lorrie Morgan's Greatest Hits* . . . . (BNA)
Backstreets
Bruce Springsteen; *Born To Run* . . . .(Columbia)
Bad Day
Fuel; *Now That's What I Call Music!-#8-C* . . . . (Virgin)
  Something Like Human . . . .(Epic)
Bang And Blame
R.E.M.; *Monster* . . . . (Warner Bros.)
Beast Of Burden
Bette Midler; *No Frills* . . . . (Atlantic)
Rolling Stones; *Rewind (1971-1984)* . . . .(Rolling Stones)
  Some Girls . . . . (Virgin)
  Sucking In The Seventies . . . .(Rolling Stones)
Because I Got High
Afroman; *Good Times* . . . .(Universal)
Before You Accuse Me
Bo Diddley; *Bo Diddley* . . . . (Chess)
Creedence Clearwater Revival; *1970* . . . . (Fantasy)
  Cosmo's Factory . . . . (Fantasy)
  Creedence Clearwater Revival-Chronicle-#2 . . . . (Fantasy)
  Creedence Country . . . . (Fantasy)
Eric Clapton; *Eric Clapton-Unplugged* . . . . (Reprise)
  Journeyman . . . .(Duck/Reprise)
Before You Walk Out Of My Life
Monica; *Miss Thang* . . . .(Rowdy/Arista)
Believe Me Baby (I Lied)
Trisha Yearwood; *Everybody Knows* . . . . (MCA)
Best Man I Can Be
Ginuwine, R.L., Tyrese, Case; *ST/The Best Man* . . . . . (Sony Music Soundtrax)
Best Of Intentions
Travis Tritt; *Down The Road I Go* . . . .(Columbia)
Big Girls Don't Cry
4 Seasons; *4 Seasons' Greatest Hits-#1* . . . . (Rhino)
  4 Seasons-Anthology . . . .(Rhino)
  Billboard Top Rock 'N' Roll Hits-1962-C . . . .(Rhino)
  More Dirty Dancing-C . . . . (RCA)
Big Man
Four Preps; *Best Of The Four Preps* . . . .(Curb)
  Capitol Collectors Series-Four Preps . . . .(Collectables)
Bill Bailey
Louis Armstrong; *Essential Louis Armstrong* . . . . (Vanguard)
  Louis Armstrong . . . .(Audio Fidelity)
Pearl Bailey; *Echoes Of An Era-Pearl Bailey* . . . . (Roulette)
Preservation Hall Jazz Band; *New Orleans-#1* . . . . (Columbia)
Bitch
Meredith Brooks; *Blurring The Edges* . . . . (Capitol)
Bittersweet
Fuel; *Sunburn* . . . . (550 Music)
Blame
Collective Soul; *Disciplined Breakdown* . . . . (Atlantic)
Blame
Mike & The Mechanics; *Living Years* . . . . (Atlantic)
Blame It On Cain
Elvis Costello; *My Aim Is True* . . . .(Columbia)
Blame It On Fate
Jude Cole; *Start The Car* . . . . (Reprise)
Blame It On Love
Smokey Robinson; *Blame It On Love & All The Great Hits* . . . .(Motown)
Blame It On Me
Barenaked Ladies; *Gordon* . . . . (Reprise)
Blame It On Mexico
George Strait; *Strait Country* . . . . (MCA)
  Strait Out Of The Box . . . . (MCA)
Blame It On My Youth
Nat "King" Cole; *Complete After Midnight Sessions* . . . .(Capitol)
Blame It On New York City
Dramatics; *Positive State Of Mind* . . . . (Volt)
Blame It On Texas
Mark Chesnutt; *Mark Chesnutt's Greatest Hits* . . . .(Decca)
  Too Cold At Home . . . .(MCA)
Blame It On The Boogie
Jacksons; *Destiny* . . . . (Epic)
Blame It On The Bossa Nova
Eydie Gorme; *45-#42661* . . . .(Columbia)
Blame It On The Love Of Rock & Roll
Bon Jovi; *Keep The Faith* . . . .(Mercury)
Blame It On The Rain
Milli Vanilli; *Girl You Know It's True* . . . . (Arista)

Blame It On The Stones
Kris Kristofferson; *Me & Bobby McGee*. . . . . (Columbia)
Blame It On The Sun
Stevie Wonder; *Talking Book*. . . . . (Motown)
Blame It On Your Heart
Patty Loveless; *Only What I Feel* . . . .(Epic)
Patty Loveless-Classics . . . . (Epic)
Blame The Weather
XTC; *Rag & Bone Buffet* . . . .(Geffen)
Blame The Whiskey
Paul David Wells; *Sounds Good To Me* . . . . (Capitol)
Blue On Black
Kenny Wayne Shepherd; *Trouble Is...* . . . . (Revolution)
Bohemian Rhapsody
Braids; *Here We Come* . . . . (Big Beat)
ST/High School High . . . . (Big Beat)
Queen; *A Night At The Opera* . . . . (Hollywood)
Classic Queen . . . . (Hollywood)
Live At Wembley '86 . . . . (Hollywood)
ST/Wayne's World . . . . (Reprise)
Book, The
Sheryl Crow; *Sheryl Crow* . . . . (A&M)
Boy Named Sue
Johnny Cash; *Columbia Country Classics-#3-Americana-C* . . . . (Columbia)
Johnny Cash's Biggest Hits . . . . (Columbia)
Johnny Cash's Greatest Hits-#2 . . . . (Columbia)
The Man In Black-His Greatest Hits . . . . (Legacy)
Branded Man
Merle Haggard & The Strangers; *For The Record: Merle Haggard-43*
Legendary Hits . . . . (BNA)
Breakdown
Tantric; *Tantric*. . . . .(Maverick)
Breathe
Nickelback; *State* . . . . (Roadrunner)
Bridge
Queensryche; *Promised Land*. . . . .(EMI)
Bullet Proof
Goo Goo Dolls; *Dizzy Up The Girl* . . . . (Warner Sunset/Reprise)
By The Book
Michael Peterson; *Michael Peterson* . . . . (Reprise)
Can't You Hear Me Callin'?
Ricky Skaggs; *Bluegrass Super Hits-C* . . . . (Columbia)
Favorite Country Songs . . . .(Epic)
Highway & Heartaches . . . . (Epic)
Captain Bligh
Filter; *Title Of Record*. . . . . (Reprise)
Careless Whisper
Dave Koz featuring Montell Jordan; *Dance* . . . . (Capitol)
Wham! Featuring George Michael; *Make It Big* . . . . (Columbia)
Music For The Miracle-C . . . . (Epic Portrait Assoc.)
Child Of Clay
Jimmie Rodgers; *Best Of Jimmie Rodgers* . . . . (Rhino)
C'mon Marianne
4 Seasons; *25th Anniversary Collection* . . . . (Rhino)
4 Seasons-Anthology . . . . (Rhino)
Comedown
Bush; *Sixteen Stone*. . . . . (Trauma)
Coming Back Home
Bebe Winans featuring Brian McKnight & Joe; *Love & Freedom* . . . . (Motown)
Complicated Shadows
Elvis Costello & The Attractions; *The Sopranos-Music From The HBO*
Original Series . . . . (Sony Music Soundtrax)
Confessions
Destiny's Child; *The Writing's On The Wall* . . . . (Columbia)
Couldn't Last A Moment
Collin Raye; *Tracks* . . . .(Epic)
Crazy
K-Ci & JoJo; *Now That's What I Call Music!-#6-C* . . . . (Virgin)
X. . . . .(MCA)
Criminal
Fiona Apple; *1998 Grammy Nominees-C*. . . . .(MCA)
Tidal. . . . . (Clean Slate/Work)
Cryin' Shame
Lyle Lovett and his Large Band; *Lyle Lovett and his*
Large Band . . . . (Curb/MCA)
Cryin' Shame
Faster Pussycat; *Wake Me When It's Over* . . . . (Elektra)
Crying Shame
Michael Johnson; *Best Of Michael Johnson* . . . . (RCA)
That's That. . . . . (RCA)
Crying Shame
Kate Wolf; *Evening In Austin* . . . . (Kaleidoscope)
Poet's Heart. . . . . (Kaleidoscope)
Day Job
Gin Blossoms; *Congratulations I'm Sorry* . . . . (A&M)
Outside Looking In: The Best Of The Gin Blossoms . . . . (A&M)
Dear Me
Lorrie Morgan; *Lorrie Morgan's Greatest Hits* . . . . (BNA)

Detour (Devil Took A)
Patti Page; *Patti Page-Golden Hits* . . . . (Mercury)
Devil Woman
Marty Robbins; *Billboard Top Country Hits-1962-C* . . . . (Rhino)
Columbia Country Classics-#4-Nashville Sound-C . . . . (Columbia)
Lifetime Of Song-1951-1982 . . . . (Columbia)
Marty Robbins' Greatest Hits-#4 . . . . (Columbia)
Difficult Kind, The
Sheryl Crow; *The Globe Sessions* . . . . (A&M)
Dixie Road
Lee Greenwood; *Country Classics-#3-1984-1985-C* . . . . (Universal)
Lee Greenwood's Greatest Hits . . . . (MCA)
MCA #1 Hits Of The '80s-#2-C . . . . (MCA Special Prod.)
Do For Love
2Pac featuring Eric Williams; *R U Still Down (Remember Me)* . . . .(Amaru/Jive)
Don't Be Cruel
Cheap Trick; *Cheap Trick's Greatest Hits* . . . . (Epic)
Lap Of Luxury . . . . (Epic)
Elvis Presley; *Billboard Top Rock 'N' Roll Hits-1956-C* . . . . (Rhino)
Nipper's Greatest Hits Of The '50s-#2-C . . . .(RCA)
Number One Hits . . . . (RCA)
The Great Performances . . . .(RCA)
The Top Ten Hits . . . . (RCA)
Judds; *Heartland* . . . . (MCA)
Don't Blame Me
Eric Clapton; *There's One In Every Crowd*. . . . .(Polydor)
Don't Blame Me
Dorothy Fields; *An Evening With Dorothy Fields* . . . . (DRG)
Everly Brothers; *Golden Hits Of The Everly Brothers* . . . . (Warner Bros.)
Frank Sinatra; *The Golden Days Of Radio* . . . . (K-Tel)
Nat "King" Cole; *The Trio Recordings-#1* . . . .(Laserlight)
Don't Blame Me For Colorado
Larry Gatlin & The Gatlin Brothers Band; *Partners* . . . . (Columbia)
Don't Bother Me
Beatles; *Meet The Beatles!* . . . . (Capitol)
Don't Drink The Water
Dave Matthews Band; *Before These Crowded Streets* . . . .(RCA)
Don't Let Me Be Misunderstood
Animals; *Greatest Hits Live!-Rip It To Shreds* . . . . (I.R.S.)
Sullivan Years-British Invasion . . . . (TVT)
Joe Cocker; *With A Little Help From My Friends* . . . . (A&M)
Don't Look Back In Anger
Oasis; *What's The Story Morning Glory?* . . . . (Epic)
Don't Waste Your Heart
Dixie Chicks; *Fly* . . . . (Monument)
Door, The
Keb' Mo'; *The Door* . . . .(550/Epic/Okeh)
Dream Merchant
New Birth; *Smooth Grooves-A Sensual Collection-#5-C* . . . . (Rhino)
Evaporated
Ben Folds Five; *Whatever And Ever Amen* . . . .(Caroline/550)
Everlasting Love
Carl Carlton; *Classic R&B Oldies Of The '70s-#2-C* . . . . . (MCA Special Prod.)
Gloria Estefan; *Hold Me, Thrill Me, Kiss Me* . . . . (Epic)
Robert Knight; *Everlasting Love*. . . . . (Collectables)
Every Morning
Sugar Ray; *14:59*. . . . . (Lava)
Evil On Your Mind
Jan Howard; *Grand Ladies Of The Opry-C*. . . . . (Deluxe)
Excuse Me Mr.
No Doubt; *Tragic Kingdom*. . . . .(Trauma)
Fa Fa (Never Be The Same Again)
Guster; *Lost & Gone Forever* . . . .(Hybrid/Sire)
Fiction (Dreams In Digital)
Orgy; *Vapor Transmission* . . . . (Elementree/Reprise)
Fill Her Up
Earl Scruggs & Sting; *Earl Scruggs And Friends-C* . . . . (MCA)
Follow Me
Uncle Kracker; *Double Wide* . . . . (Warner Bros.)
Totally Hits 2001-C . . . . (Arista)
Fool
Sanford Clark; *Billboard Top Rock 'N' Roll Hits-1956-C*. . . . . (Rhino)
Original Classic Oldies Of The '50s & '60s-#17-C . . . . (MCA)
Fool, The
Elvis Presley; *A Golden Celebration*. . . . .(RCA)
For Once In Our Lives
Paul Carrack; *Blue Views* . . . . (Ark 21)
For Your Love
Tevin Campbell; *Tevin Campbell* . . . .(Qwest)
Forgiveness
Macy Gray; *The Id.* . . . . (Epic)
Fred Jones Part 2
Ben Folds; *Rockin' The Suburbs* . . . . (Epic)
Freshmen, The
Verve Pipe; *Villains* . . . .(RCA)
Gave It A Name
Bruce Springsteen; *Tracks* . . . . (Columbia)

Glycerine
Bush; *Sixteen Stone* . . . .(Trauma)

Gone
Ferlin Husky; *Ferlin Husky's Greatest Hits* . . . . (Curb)
Heroes Of Country Music-#4-Legends Of The West Coast-C . . . . (Rhino)

Good Friday
Black Crowes; *Sho' Nuff* . . . . (American)
Three Snakes And One Charm . . . . (American)

Got No Shame
Brother Cane; *Brother Cane* . . . .(Virgin)

Great Pretender
Band; *Moondog Matinee* . . . . (Capitol)
Platters; *Billboard Top R&B Hits-1956-C* . . . . (Rhino)
Cruisin'-1956-C . . . . (Increase)
Encore Of Golden Hits-Platters . . . . (Mercury)
Platters-Anthology . . . . (Rhino)
ST/American Graffiti . . . . (MCA)
Super Oldies Of The '50s-#3-C . . . . (Audio Fidelity)
Roy Orbison; *Best Of Roy Orbison-Loved Standards* . . . . (Monument)
Stan Freberg; *Capitol Collectors Series-Stan Freberg* . . . . (Capitol)

Guilty
Barbra Streisand; *Collection-Greatest Hits...And More* . . . . (Columbia)
Just For The Record . . . . (Columbia)
One Voice . . . . (Columbia)
Barbra Streisand & Barry Gibb; *Guilty* . . . . (Columbia)
Bee Gees; *One Night Only* . . . . (Polydor)

Guilty
Warren Brothers; *Beautiful Day In The Cold Cruel World* . . . .(BNA)

Guilty
Bonnie Raitt; *Bonnie Raitt-Collection* . . . . (Warner Bros.)
Takin' My Time . . . . (Warner Bros.)
Randy Newman; *Good Old Boys* . . . . (Reprise)
Guilty: 30 Years Of Randy Newman . . . . (Rhino)

Guilty
Def Leppard; *Euphoria* . . . . (Mercury)

Guilty
Poorboys; *Pardon Me* . . . . (Hollywood)

Hands In The Air
Bob Seger; *It's A Mystery* . . . . (Capitol)

Hard To Say I'm Sorry
Az Yet; *Az Yet* . . . . (LaFace)
Chicago; *Chicago 16* . . . . (Full Moon/Warner Bros.)

Harmless
Mulberry Lane; *Run Your Own Race* . . . . (Refuge/MCA)

Have You Ever Been Lonely (Have You Ever Been Blue)
Ernest Tubb; *Best Of Ernest Tubb* . . . . (Curb)
The Country Music Hall Of Fame-Ernest Tubb . . . . (MCA)
Jim Reeves & Patsy Cline; *Jim Reeves' Greatest Hits* . . . .(RCA)
Patsy Cline; *Showcase-With The Jordanaires* . . . . (MCA)

He Can't Love U
Jagged Edge; *J.E. Heartbreak* . . . . (So So Def/Columbia)

He Feels Guilty
Bobbie Cryner; *Bobbie Cryner* . . . . (Epic)

Head Over Feet
Alanis Morissette; *Jagged Little Pill* . . . . (Maverick)

Heart Of The Matter
Don Henley; *End Of The Innocence* . . . . (Geffen)

Hello Darlin'
Conway Twitty; *Conway Twittty-20 Greatest Hits* . . . . (MCA)
Conway Twitty's Greatest Hits . . . . (Curb)
From The Vaults: Decca Country Classics-1934-1973-C . . . . (Decca)
Greatest Country Classics-#1-C . . . . (MCA Special Prod.)

He's Gone
Chantels; *Best Of The Chantels* . . . . (Rhino)

Hitchin' A Ride
Green Day; *Nimrod* . . . . (Reprise)

How Do I Say I'm Sorry
Tami Davis; *Only You* . . . . (Red Ant)

How Do You Sleep At Night
Wade Hayes; *When The Wrong One Loves You Right* . . . . (Columbia/DKC)

How You Remind Me
Nickelback; *Silver Side Up* . . . . (Roadrunner)

I Apologize
Anita Baker; *Rhythm Of Love* . . . . (Atlantic)

I Call Your Name
Beatles; *Past Masters-Volume One* . . . . (Parlophone)
Rock 'N' Roll Music . . . . (Capitol)
The Beatles' Second Album . . . . (Capitol)

I Cheated Me Right Out Of You
Moe Bandy; *Moe Bandy's Greatest Hits* . . . . (Columbia)

I Confess
Perry Como; *Yesterday And Today-A Celebration In Song* . . . .(RCA)

I Did It
Dave Matthews Band; *Everyday* . . . . (RCA)

I Do
Mila Mason; *That's Enough Of That* . . . . (Atlantic)

I Don't Know You Anymore
Savage Garden; *Affirmation* . . . . (Columbia)

I Don't Want To Wait
Paula Cole; *Live On Letterman-From The Late Show* . . . . (Reprise)
Songs From Dawson's Creek . . . . (Sony Music Soundtrax)
This Fire . . . . (Imago)

I Drive Myself Crazy
'N Sync; *'N Sync* . . . . (RCA)
Totally Hits-#2-C . . . . (Elektra)

I Let Her Lie
Daryle Singletary; *Daryle Singletary* . . . . (Giant)

I Meant Every Word He Said
Ricky Van Shelton; *Greatest Country Hits Of The '90s-#2-C* . . . . . .(Columbia)
RVS III . . . . (Columbia)

I Saw Her Again
Mamas & The Papas; *Best Of The Mamas & The Papas* . . . . (MCA)
Farewell To The First Golden Era . . . . (MCA)
Mamas & The Papas . . . . (MCA)

I Shot The Sheriff
Bob Marley & The Wailers; *Bob Marley & The Wailers-Live* . . . . . . (Tuff Gong)
Legend: The Best Of Bob Marley & The Wailers . . . .(Island)
This Is Reggae Music-#1-C . . . . (Island)
Eric Clapton; *461 Ocean Boulevard* . . . . (Polydor)
Eric Clapton-Crossroads-C . . . . (Polydor)
Time Pieces-#1-The Best Of Eric Clapton . . . . (Polydor)
Wailers; *Burnin'* . . . . (Tuff Gong)

I Should Know
Mavericks; *Trampoline* . . . . (MCA)

I Started A Joke
Bee Gees; *Best Of The Bee Gees-#1* . . . . (Polydor)
Here At Last...Bee Gees...Live . . . . (Polydor)
One Night Only . . . . (Polydor)
Wallflowers; *ST/Zoolander* . . . . (Hollywood)

I Take It Back
Sandy Posey; *Best Of Sandy Posey* . . . . (Collectables)
Best Of Sandy Posey-With Skeeter Davis . . . . (Gusto)

I Want My Goodbye Back
Ty Herndon; *What Mattered Most* . . . . (Epic)

I Want You Back
'N Sync; *'N Sync* . . . . (RCA)

I Was Wrong
Social Distortion; *White Light White Heat White Trash* . . . . (550 Music)

I Was Wrong
Keb' Mo'; *Slow Down* . . . . (550/Epic/Okeh)

I Won't Take The Blame
Del Amitri; *Change Everything* . . . .(A&M)

I'd Rather Have What We Had
Conway Twitty; *Two's A Party* . . . . (MCA Special Prod.)
Lee Ann Womack; *Some Things I Know* . . . .(Decca)

If I Could Turn Back The Hands Of Time
R. Kelly; *Now That's What I Call Music!-#3-C* . . . . (Virgin)
R. . . . . (Jive)

If Tomorrow Never Comes
Garth Brooks; *Garth Brooks* . . . . (Liberty)
Limited Series-Box . . . . (Capitol)
Joose; *Joose* . . . . (Flavor Unit)

If You're Ever Down In Dallas
Lee Ann Womack; *Some Things I Know* . . . .(Decca)

I'll Do Anything/I'm Sorry
Ginuwine; *The Bachelor* . . . . (550 Music)

I'm A Honky Tonk Girl
Loretta Lynn; *The Country Music Hall Of Fame-Loretta Lynn* . . . . (MCA)

I'm Sorry
Brenda Lee; *Billboard Top Pop Hits-1960-C* . . . .(Rhino)
Brenda Lee-Anthology-#1 & #2 . . . . (MCA)
The Brenda Lee Story-Her Greatest Hits . . . . (MCA)
Platters; *Enchanted-The Best Of The Platters* . . . .(Rhino)
Magic Touch-An Anthology . . . . (Mercury)

I'm The Fool
Mark Knopfler; *Golden Heart* . . . . (Warner Bros.)

I'm The Man Who Murdered Love
XTC; *Wasp Star (Apple Venus Volume 2)* . . . .(Idea/TVT)

In A Week Or Two
Diamond Rio; *Close To The Edge* . . . .(Arista)
Diamond Rio's Greatest Hits . . . .(Arista)

Indiana Wants Me
R. Dean Taylor; *Hard-To-Find Motown Classics-#2-C* . . . .(Motown)
Super Hits Of The '70s-Have A Nice Day-#3-C . . . . (Rhino)
Super Hits-#5-C . . . . (Gusto)

Innocent
Alexander O'Neal; *Alexander O'Neal* . . . . (Tabu)
All Mixed Up . . . . (Tabu)

Innocent
Garland Jeffreys; *Escape Artist* . . . . (Epic)

Innocent
Whispers; *More Of The Night* . . . .(Capitol)

Isn't It A Pity?
Mel Torme; *That's All* . . . . (Sony Music Special Prod.)
Michael Feinstein; *Pure Gershwin* . . . .(Elektra)

Isn't It A Pity?
George Harrison; *All Things Must Pass* . . . . (Parlophone)

It Ain't My Fault
Silkk The Shocker; *Charge It 2 Da Game* . . . . (No Limit/Priority)

It Wasn't God Who Made Honky Tonk Angels
Kitty Wells; *Grand Ole Opry-75 Years-#1-C* . . . . (MCA)
   Kitty Wells' Greatest Hits . . . . (Step One)
   The Kitty Wells Story . . . . (MCA)

It Wasn't Me
Shaggy; *Hotshot* . . . . (MCA)
   Now That's What I Call Music!-#6-C . . . . (Virgin)

It Worries Me
Frank Sinatra; *Concepts* . . . . (Capitol)
   Where Are You? . . . . (Capitol)

It's A Little Too Late
Mark Chesnutt; *Mark Chesnutt's Greatest Hits* . . . . (Decca)

It's A Shame (My Sister)
Monie Love & True Image; *Down To Earth* . . . . (Warner Bros.)

It's A Shame To Ship Your Wife On Sunday
Fiddlin' John Carson; *The Old Hen Cackled (& The Rooster's Going To
   Crow)* . . . . (Rounder)

It's Been Awhile
Staind; *Break The Cycle* . . . . (Flip/Elektra)

It's Not My Cross To Bear
Allman Brothers Band; *Allman Brothers Band* . . . . (Polydor)
   Beginnings . . . . (Polydor)
   Dreams . . . . (Polydor)
Gregg Allman Band; *I'm No Angel* . . . . (Epic)

It's On!
Korn; *Follow The Leader* . . . . (Immortal/Epic)

It's Over Now
112; *Part III* . . . . (Bad Boy/Arista)

I've Committed Murder
Macy Gray; *On How Life Is* . . . . (Epic)

Jaded
Aerosmith; *Just Push Play* . . . . (Columbia)
   Now That's What I Call Music!-#7-C . . . . (Virgin)

Jealous Heart
Al Morgan; *Hits Of '49-C* . . . . (ASV)
Connie Francis; *Connie Francis-Souvenirs* . . . . (Polydor)
Les Paul; *Les Paul-16 Most Requested Songs* . . . . (Columbia)
Tex Ritter; *An American Legend* . . . . (Capitol)
   Best Of Tex Ritter . . . . (Capitol)
   Hillbilly Heaven . . . . (Capitol)
   Tex Ritter's Greatest Hits . . . . (Curb)
   Tex Ritter-Vintage Collection . . . . (Capitol)

Josephine
Wallflowers; *Bringing Down The Horse* . . . . (Interscope)

Just Be A Man About It
Toni Braxton; *The Heat* . . . . (LaFace)

Just Between You And Me
DC Talk; *First Generation: 25 Years Of Virgin Records-C* . . . . (Virgin)
   Jesus Freak . . . . (Virgin)

King Nothing
Metallica; *Load* . . . . (Elektra)

Lack Of Water
Why Store; *The Why Store* . . . . (MCA)

Last Kiss
J. Frank Wilson and The Cavaliers; *Billboard Top Rock 'N' Roll Hits-
   1964-C* . . . . (Rhino)
   Collectables Presents The History Of Rock-#2-C . . . . (Collectables)
   Oldies But Goodies-#9-C . . . . (Original Sound)
   Teenage Tragedies-C . . . . (Rhino)
Pearl Jam; *No Boundaries-Benefit For The Kosovar Refugees-C* . . . . . . (Epic)

Last Train Done Gone Down
Marty Stuart; *Hot Tracks-Train Super Hits-C* . . . . (Epic)
   Let There Be Country . . . . (Columbia)

Layla
Derek And The Dominos; *Classic Rock 1966-1988-C* . . . . (Atlantic)
   Eric Clapton-Crossroads-C . . . . (Polydor)
   Layla . . . . (Polydor)
   ST/Goodfellas . . . . (Atlantic)
Eric Clapton; *Eric Clapton-Unplugged* . . . . (Reprise)

Leader Of The Pack
Bette Midler; *Divine Miss M* . . . . (Atlantic)
   ST/Divine Madness . . . . (Atlantic)
Original Cast; *Leader Of The Pack* . . . . (Elektra)
Shangri-Las; *21 Number One Hits-C* . . . . (Original Sound)
   Billboard Top Rock 'N' Roll Hits-1964-C . . . . (Rhino)
   Girl Groups-Story Of A Sound-C . . . . (Rhino)
   Golden Hits Of The Shangri-Las . . . . (Mercury)
   Oldies But Goodies-#15-C . . . . (Original Sound)
   Radio Active Hits-#2-C . . . . (Accord)
   Remember The Shangri-Las At Their Best . . . . (Collectables)

Life In Prison
Byrds; *Jailhouse Rock (Hits From The Big
   House)-C* . . . . (Sony Music Special Prod.)
   Sweetheart Of The Rodeo . . . . (Columbia)

Life Turned Her That Way
"Little" Jimmy Dickens; *I'm Little, But I'm Loud-The "Little" Jimmy
   Dickens Collection* . . . . (Razor & Tie)

Mel Tillis; *Best Of Mel Tillis* . . . . (MCA)
   Mel Tillis' Greatest Hits . . . . (Universal)
Ricky Van Shelton; *Ricky Van Shelton-16 Biggest Hits* . . . . (Legacy)
   Wild-Eyed Dream . . . . (Columbia)

Lift Up Every Stone
John Hiatt; *Crossing Muddy Waters* . . . . (Vanguard)

Little Bit Me, A Little Bit You
Monkees; *Monkees' Greatest Hits* . . . . (Rhino)

Little Darlin'
Diamonds; *Best Of The Diamonds* . . . . (Rhino)
   Billboard Top Rock 'N' Roll Hits-1957-C . . . . (Rhino)
   Cruisin'-1957-C . . . . (Increase)
   Good Time Rock 'N' Roll-C . . . . (Increase)
   Oldies But Goodies-#11-C . . . . (Original Sound)
   ST/American Graffiti . . . . (MCA)

Little Things
Bush; *Sixteen Stone* . . . . (Trauma)

Living In Shame
Supremes; *45-#442* . . . . (Motown)

Living Years, The
Mike & The Mechanics; *Living Years* . . . . (Atlantic)

Lock And Load
Bob Seger; *It's A Mystery* . . . . (Capitol)

Lonely
Tracy Lawrence; *Lessons Learned* . . . . (Atlantic)

Lonely Too Long
Patty Loveless; *Patty Loveless-Classics* . . . . (Epic)
   Super Hits Of 1996-C . . . . (Epic)
   The Trouble With The Truth . . . . (Epic)

Lonesome Town
Ricky Nelson; *Best Of Ricky Nelson* . . . . (Curb)

Long Day
Matchbox Twenty; *Yourself Or Someone Like You* . . . . (Lava)

Longneck Bottle
Garth Brooks; *Sevens* . . . . (Capitol)

Losing Lisa
Ben Folds; *Rockin' The Suburbs* . . . . (Epic)

Love Is Stronger Than Pride
Ricochet; *Ricochet* . . . . (Columbia)

Love Me
112 Featuring Mase; *Room 112* . . . . (Bad Boy/Arista)

Love Without End, Amen
George Strait; *Livin' It Up* . . . . (MCA)
   Ten Strait Hits . . . . (MCA)

Machinehead
Bush; *Sixteen Stone* . . . . (Trauma)

Make The World Go Away
Eddy Arnold; *Best Of Eddy Arnold* . . . . (RCA)
   Billboard Top Country Hits-1965-C . . . . (Rhino)
   Eddy Arnold-Pure Gold . . . . (RCA)
   Nipper's Greatest Hits Of The '60s-#1-C . . . . (RCA)
   World Of Hits . . . . (MGM)
Ray Price; *Ray Price-16 Biggest Hits* . . . . (Legacy)
   Ray Price-20 Hits . . . . (Tee Vee)

Mama Tried
Grateful Dead; *Grateful Dead (Skull & Roses)* . . . . (Warner Bros.)
John Anderson & Marty Stuart; *Mama's Hungry Eyes-Merle Haggard
   Tribute-C* . . . . (Arista)
Merle Haggard; *Jailhouse Rock (Hits From The Big
   House)-C* . . . . (Sony Music Special Prod.)
Merle Haggard & The Strangers; *Best Of Merle Haggard & The
   Strangers* . . . . (Capitol)
   For The Record: Merle Haggard-43 Legendary Hits . . . . (BNA)
   Okie From Muskogee . . . . (Capitol)
   Songs I'll Always Sing . . . . (Capitol)
   Very Best Of Merle Haggard . . . . (Capitol)

Man Overboard
Blink-182; *The Mark, Tom & Travis Show-The Enema Strikes Back* . . . . (MCA)

Mandy
Barry Manilow; *Barry Manilow II* . . . . (Arista)
   Barry Manilow's Greatest Hits-#1 . . . . (Arista)
   Live On Broadway . . . . (Arista)

Margaritaville
Jimmy Buffett; *Changes In Latitudes, Changes In Attitudes* . . . . . . (MCA)
   Songs You Know By Heart-Jimmy Buffett's Greatest Hit(s) . . . . . (MCA)
   You Had To Be There . . . . (MCA)

Master's Call
Marty Robbins; *Gunfighter Ballads & Trail Songs* . . . . (Legacy)

Maybe He'll Notice Her Now
Mindy McCready; *Ten Thousand Angels* . . . . (BNA)

Maybe I Deserve
Tank; *Force Of Nature* . . . . (BlackGround Enterp./Atlantic)

Mistakes
Mandy Barnett; *I've Got A Right To Cry* . . . . (Sire)

Mr. Dream Merchant
Jerry Butler; *Best Of Jerry Butler* . . . . (Rhino)
   Soul Shots-#2-The "In" Crowd-Sweet Soul-C . . . . (Rhino)

Ms. Jackson
Outkast; *Stankonia* . . . . (LaFace/Arista)

Murder (Or A Heart Attack)
Old 97's; *Fight Songs* . . . . (Elektra)
My Elusive Dreams
Bobby Vinton; *Autumn Memories* . . . . (Epic)
  Bobby Vinton's All-Time Greatest Hits . . . . (Epic)
Charlie Rich; *Charlie Rich-16 Biggest Hits* . . . . (Legacy)
  Charlie Rich's Greatest Hits . . . . (Epic)
  Charlie Rich-Super Hits . . . . (Epic)
David Houston & Tammy Wynette; *Best Of David
  Houston* . . . . (Collector's Choice)
  Billboard Top Country Hits-1967-C . . . . (Rhino)
  Tammy Wynette's Greatest Hits . . . . (Epic)
My Own Prison
Creed; *My Own Prison* . . . . (Wind-up)
My Own Worst Enemy
Lit; *A Place In The Sun* . . . . (RCA)
Naked
Goo Goo Dolls; *A Boy Named Goo* . . . . (Metal Blade)
Never An Absolution
James Horner; *ST/Titanic* . . . . (Sony Music Classical)
Never Blame The Rainbows For The Rain
Moody Blues; *Keys Of The Kingdom* . . . . (Polydor)
Never Ever
All Saints; *All Saints* . . . . (London)
  Now That's What I Call Music!-#1-C . . . . (Virgin)
Never Let You Go
Third Eye Blind; *Blue* . . . . (Elektra)
  Totally Hits-#2-C . . . . (Elektra)
Nights
Ed Bruce; *Night Things* . . . . (RCA)
Ninety Nine Years (Dead Or Alive)
Guy Mitchell; *Definitive Guy Mitchell* . . . . (Collector's Choice)
No Excuses
Alice In Chains; *Jar Of Flies* . . . . (Columbia)
No One Is To Blame
Howard Jones; *Best Of Howard Jones 1983-1993* . . . . (Elektra)
  Dream Into Action . . . . (Elektra)
No Regrets
Emmylou Harris; *Bluebird* . . . . (Reprise)
Tom Rush; *Best Of Tom Rush: No Regrets* . . . . (Legacy)
  The Circle Game . . . . (Elektra)
No Son Of Mine
Genesis; *We Can't Dance* . . . . (Atlantic)
Nobody Knows
Kevin Sharp; *Measure Of A Man* . . . . (143/Asylum)
Tony Rich Project; *Words* . . . . (LaFace)
Not Guilty
Bryan Adams; *Waking Up The Neighbours* . . . . (A&M)
Not Guilty
Beatles; *The Beatles-Anthology-#3* . . . . (Capitol)
Not To Blame
Joni Mitchell; *Turbulent Indigo* . . . . (Reprise)
On Bended Knee
Boyz II Men; *Boyz II Men II* . . . . (Motown)
One Sweet Day
Mariah Carey; *Daydream* . . . . (Columbia)
Mariah Carey & Boyz II Men; *1996 Grammy Nominees-C* . . . . (Columbia)
One Week
Barenaked Ladies; *Stunt* . . . . (Reprise)
  Totally Hits-#1-C . . . . (Arista)
Ooh Baby Baby
Linda Ronstadt; *Linda Ronstadt's Greatest Hits, Volume Two* . . . . (Asylum)
  Living In The USA . . . . (Asylum)
Miracles; *Best Of Smokey Robinson & The Miracles-Anthology* . . . . . . (Motown)
  Smokey Robinson's Greatest Hits-#2 . . . . (Motown)
Ooh La La
Rod Stewart; *When We Were The New Boys* . . . . (Warner Bros.)
Oops!...I Did It Again
Britney Spears; *Oops!...I Did It Again* . . . . (Jive)
Orchids Mean Goodbye
Carl Smith; *45-#21087* . . . . (Columbia)
Ordinary Life
Chad Brock; *Chad Brock* . . . . (Warner Bros.)
Out Of My Head
Fastball; *All The Pain Money Can Buy* . . . . (Hollywood)
  Now That's What I Call Music!-#3-C . . . . (Virgin)
Over Now
Alice In Chains; *Alice In Chains* . . . . (Columbia)
Pair Of Old Sneakers
George Jones; *George Jones & Tammy Wynette-16
  Biggest Hits* . . . . (Epic/Legacy)
Paper Sun
Def Leppard; *Euphoria* . . . . (Mercury)
Pardon My Heart
Neil Young & Crazy Horse; *Zuma* . . . . (Reprise)
Please Forgive Me
Bryan Adams; *So Far So Good* . . . . (A&M)

Prayin' For Daylight
Rascal Flatts; *Rascal Flatts* . . . . (Lyric Street)
Purple Rain
Prince and the Revolution; *ST/Purple Rain* . . . . (Warner Bros.)
Push It
Garbage; *Version 2.0* . . . . (Almo Sounds)
Put The Blame On Mame
Mark Murphy; *Singin' In The Rain-Capitol Sings Hollywood-C* . . . . . . (Capitol)
Put The Blame On Me
Mother Station; *Brand New Bag* . . . . (East West)
Put The Blame On Me
Eurythmics; *Savage* . . . . (RCA)
Put The Blame On Me
Elvis Presley; *Something For Everybody* . . . . (RCA)
Red Roses For A Blue Lady
Al Martino; *Best Of Al Martino* . . . . (Capitol)
  Capitol Collectors Series-Al Martino . . . . (Capitol)
Andy Williams; *Andy Williams-16 Most Requested Songs* . . . . . (Legacy)
Mom & Dads; *Best Of The Mom & Dads* . . . . (Crescendo)
Roger Whittaker; *All-Time Heart-Touching Favorites* . . . . (Capitol)
  Roger Whittaker-Classics Collection-#1 . . . . (Capitol)
Vaughn Monroe; *Best Of Vaughn Monroe* . . . . (RCA)
Regret
New Order; *Republic* . . . . (Qwest)
Regretful Blues
Nora Bayes; *Music From The New York Stage (1890-1920)-#4-1917-
  1920-C* . . . . (Pearl)
Remember Me
Marc Anthony; *Marc Anthony* . . . . (Columbia)
Repetitive Regret
Eddie Rabbitt; *Rabbit Trax* . . . . (RCA)
River
Betty Buckley; *With One Look* . . . . (Sterling)
Joni Mitchell; *Blue* . . . . (Reprise)
River Of Deceit
Mad Season; *Above* . . . . (Columbia)
Second Chance
38 Special; *Rock & Roll Strategy* . . . . (A&M)
See You Later, Alligator
Bill Haley & His Comets; *Bill Haley & His Comets* . . . . . . (Everest)
  Bill Haley & His Comets' Greatest Hits . . . . (MCA)
  Bill Haley & His Comets-Golden Hits . . . . (MCA)
  Billboard Top Rock 'N' Roll Hits-1956-C . . . . (Rhino)
  Mr. Rock 'N' Roll . . . . (Accord)
  Rock & Roll Is Here To Stay-C . . . . (Gusto)
  Rockin' & Rollin' . . . . (Accord)
Self Made Man
Montgomery Gentry; *Tattoos & Scars* . . . . (Columbia)
Shame
Stabbing Westward; *Wither Blister Burn & Peel* . . . . (Columbia)
Shame On The Moon
Bob Seger & The Silver Bullet Band; *The Distance* . . . . (Capitol)
Mac Davis; *Mac Davis-Very Best & More* . . . . (Casablanca)
Rodney Crowell; *Rodney Crowell-Collection* . . . . (Warner Bros.)
Shame On You
Indigo Girls; *Shaming Of The Sun* . . . . (Epic)
Shame Shame Shame Shame
Mark Collie; *Mark Collie* . . . . (MCA)
Shame, Shame
Magic Lanterns; *Shame, Shame* . . . . (Collectables)
Shame, Shame, Shame
Shirley & Company; *Dance Floor Divas-The '70s-C* . . . . (Rhino)
  Didn't It Blow Your Mind: Soul Hits Of The '70s-#14-C . . . . . . (Rhino)
  Shame, Shame, Shame . . . . (Collectables)
Shame, Shame, Shame
Jimmy Reed; *Best Of Jimmy Reed* . . . . (Crescendo)
Shameless
Garth Brooks; *Ropin' The Wind* . . . . (Liberty)
Shape Of My Heart
Backstreet Boys; *Black & Blue* . . . . (Jive)
  Now That's What I Call Music!-#6-C . . . . (Virgin)
She Loves You
Beatles; *Beatles 1* . . . . (Capitol)
  Beatles-20 Greatest Hits . . . . (Capitol)
  Beatles-Box Set . . . . (Capitol)
  Past Masters-Volume One . . . . (Parlophone)
  The Beatles At The Hollywood Bowl . . . . (Capitol)
  The Beatles' Second Album . . . . (Capitol)
  The Beatles/1962-1966 . . . . (Capitol)
She Said
Collective Soul; *Dosage* . . . . (Atlantic)
  ST/Scream 2 . . . . (Dimension/Capitol)
She's Not There
Santana; *Moonflower* . . . . (Columbia)
  Viva Santana! . . . . (Columbia)
Vanilla Fudge; *Vanilla Fudge* . . . . (Atco)
Zombies; *Best & The Rest Of The Zombies* . . . . (Epic)
  Billboard Top Rock 'N' Roll Hits-1964-C . . . . (Rhino)
  History Of British Rock-#1-C . . . . (Rhino)

Time Of The Zombies . . . . (Bac-Trac)
Should've Asked Her Faster
Ty England; *Ty England* . . . . (RCA)
Sin Wagon
Dixie Chicks; *Fly* . . . . (Monument)
Sleeping Single In A Double Bed
Barbara Mandrell; *Barbara Mandrell Live* . . . .(MCA)
Best Of Barbara Mandrell . . . .(MCA)
Moods . . . .(MCA)
Snap Your Fingers
Barbara Lewis; *Hello Stranger-The Best Of Barbara Lewis* . . . . (Rhino)
Dick Curless; *The Drag 'Em Off The Interstate, Sock It To 'Em Hits Of Dick Curless* . . . . (Razor & Tie)
Don Gibson; *Best Of Don Gibson-#1* . . . . (Curb)
Joe Henderson; *Discoveries Presents-Stereo Oldies-C* . . . . (Varese Vintage)
Ronnie Milsap; *Essential Ronnie Milsap* . . . . (RCA)
Heart & Soul . . . . (RCA)
Ronnie Milsap's Greatest Hits-#3 . . . . (RCA)
Some Of These Days
Cab Calloway; *Masters Of Jazz-#6-Male Vocal Classics-C* . . . . . (Rhino)
Leon Redbone; *On The Track* . . . .(Warner Bros.)
Louis Armstrong; *Louis Armstrong And The Big Bands-1928-1930* . . . . . (DRG)
Mills Brothers; *Close Harmony* . . . .(Ranwood)
Sophie Tucker; *Legendary Entertainers* . . . . (Pro-Arte)
Those Wonderful Years-Roaring '20s-C . . . . . (JCI Assoc. Labels)
Someday We'll Be Together
Diana Ross & The Supremes; *20/20-C* . . . . (Motown)
Diana Ross & The Supremes' Greatest Hits-#3 . . . . (Motown)
Diana Ross & The Supremes-Anthology (1962-1969) . . . . . . (Motown)
Evening With Diana Ross . . . . (Motown)
Motown Story-First 25 Years . . . . (Motown)
Motown Superstar Series-#1-Diana Ross & The Supremes . . . . (Motown)
Someone Else To Blame
Midnight Oil; *Place Without A Postcard* . . . . (Columbia)
Someone Should Tell Her
Mavericks; *Trampoline* . . . .(MCA)
Someone To Blame
Jesus Jones; *Liquidizer* . . . . (SBK)
Sorry I Lied
Cliff Thomas; *45-#63* . . . . (Sun)
Sorry Seems To Be The Hardest Word
Elton John; *Blue Moves* . . . .(MCA)
Elton John's Greatest Hits-#2 . . . . (Polydor)
Live In Australia With The Melbourne Symphony Orchestra . . . .(MCA)
Joe Cocker; *Two Rooms-Celebrating The Songs Of Elton John & Bernie Taupin-C* . . . . (Polydor)
Sparrow In The Treetop
Guy Mitchell; *Guy Mitchell-16 Most Requested Songs* . . . . (Legacy)
Streets Of Laredo
Buck Owens & The Buckaroos; *Buck Owens & The Buckaroos-Live At Carnegie Hall* . . . .(Country Music Foundation)
Marty Robbins; *Cowboy Super Hits-C* . . . . (Columbia)
Marty Robbins' All-Time Greatest Hits . . . . (Columbia)
Marty Robbins-More Greatest Hits . . . . (Columbia)
More Gunfighter Ballads & Trail Songs . . . . (Columbia)
Rex Allen; *Great American Singing Cowboys-C* . . . .(Republic/Universal)
Sure Gonna Miss Her
Gary Lewis And The Playboys; *Gary Lewis And The Playboys' Greatest Hits* . . . . (Curb)
Gary Lewis And The Playboys-Legendary Masters Series . . . .(EMI)
Sweet Forgiveness
Bonnie Raitt; *Sweet Forgiveness* . . . .(Warner Bros.)
Sweet Forgiveness
Iris DeMent; *Infamous Angel* . . . .(Warner Bros.)
Take It On Faith
Joshua Kadison; *Delilah Blue* . . . .(EMI)
Tequila Talkin'
Lonestar; *Lonestar* . . . . (BNA)
That's My Story
Collin Raye; *Extremes* . . . .(Epic)
There Ain't No Good Chain Gang
Johnny Cash & Waylon Jennings; *Country's Greatest Hits-#15-Outlaw Country-C* . . . . (Priority)
Hot Country Rock-#1-C . . . .(Epic)
Johnny Cash-16 Biggest Hits-#2 . . . . (Legacy)
The Man In Black-His Greatest Hits . . . . (Legacy)
There Goes My Baby
Trisha Yearwood; *Where Your Road Leads* . . . .(MCA)
They'll Never Take Her Love From Me
Emmylou Harris; *Blue Kentucky Girl* . . . .(Warner Bros.)
George Jones; *George Jones Sings The Great Songs Of Leon Payne* . . . .(Hollywood/DNA-Rounder)
Hank Williams With His Drifting Cowboys; *Hank Williams-24 Greatest Hits-#2* . . . . (Polydor)
Hank Williams-40 Greatest Hits . . . . (Polydor)
They're Hanging Me Tonight
Marty Robbins; *Gunfighter Ballads & Trail Songs* . . . . . . (Legacy)
Things I Should Have Said
Grass Roots; *Grass Roots-All-Time Greatest Hits* . . . .(MCA)

Grass Roots-Anthology (1966-1975) . . . . (Rhino)
Think Of What You've Done
Ricky Skaggs and Kentucky Thunder; *Bluegrass Rules!* . . . . (Rounder)
Tips Of My Fingers
Bill Anderson; *Bill Anderson's Greatest Hits* . . . . (MCA)
The Bill Anderson Story . . . . (MCA)
Eddy Arnold; *Best Of Eddy Arnold-#2* . . . . (Dunhill Compact Classics)
Roy Clark; *Best Of Roy Clark* . . . . (MCA)
Roy Clark's Greatest Hits . . . . (MCA)
Yesterday When I Was Young . . . . (MCA)
Steve Wariner; *I Am Ready* . . . . (Arista)
To See My Angel Cry
Conway Twitty; *Conway Twitty-Number Ones-#1* . . . . (Liberty)
Conway Twitty's Greatest Hits-#1 . . . . (MCA)
Tonight
Marc Nelson; *chocolate mood* . . . . (Columbia)
Too Sorry
Doyle Bramhall; *Bird Nest On The Ground* . . . .(Antone's)
Torn
Natalie Imbruglia; *Left Of The Middle* . . . .(RCA)
Trash
Korn; *Issues* . . . . (Immortal/Epic)
Trouble
Coldplay; *Parachutes* . . . . (Nettwerk/Capitol)
Trust
Megadeth; *Cryptic Writings* . . . . (Capitol)
Turn Back Time
Aqua; *Aquarium* . . . . (MCA)
ST/Sliding Doors . . . . (MCA)
Unsent
Alanis Morissette; *Supposed Former Infatuation Junkie* . . . . . . (Maverick)
Until It Sleeps
Metallica; *Load* . . . . (Elektra)
Victims Of Comfort
Keb' Mo'; *Keb' Mo'* . . . .(Okeh)
Wages Of Sin
Bruce Springsteen; *Tracks* . . . . (Columbia)
Walk Away
Cool For August; *Grand World* . . . . (Warner Bros.)
Walk Away Renee
Four Tops; *Compact Command Performances-Four Tops* . . . . (Motown)
Four Tops Reach Out . . . . (Motown)
Four Tops-Anthology . . . . (Motown)
Left Banke; *Cruisin'-1966-C* . . . . (Increase)
History Of The Left Banke . . . . (Rhino)
Vonda Shepard; *ST/Songs From "Ally McBeal" Featuring Vonda Shepard* . . . . (550/Epic)
Wanted
Perry Como; *Perry Como's All-Time Greatest Hits-#1* . . . . (RCA)
Perry Como's Greatest Hits . . . . (RCA)
Wash It Away
Black Lab; *Your Body Above Me* . . . .(David Geffen Co.)
Water's Edge
Seven Mary Three; *American Standard* . . . .(Mammoth)
We Need A Resolution
Aaliyah; *Aaliyah* . . . . (BlackGround Enterp./Atlantic)
Wednesday Morning, 3 AM
Simon & Garfunkel; *Collected Works* . . . . (Columbia)
Wednesday Morning 3 A.M. . . . . (Columbia)
Western Union
Elvis Presley; *From Nashville To Memphis-The Essential '60s Masters* . .(RCA)
What A Crying Shame
Mavericks; *Best Of The Mavericks-Super Colossal Smash Hits Of The '90s* . . . . (Mercury)
What A Crying Shame . . . . (MCA)
What Have I Done To Deserve This
Pet Shop Boys & Dusty Springfield; *Actually* . . . .(EMI)
Discography-Complete Singles Collection . . . .(EMI)
What I Didn't Know
Athenaeum; *Radiance* . . . .(Atlantic)
What I Meant To Say
Wade Hayes; *Old Enough To Know Better* . . . . (Columbia)
What I Really Meant To Say
Cyndi Thomson; *My World* . . . . (Capitol)
What If
Creed; *Human Clay* . . . . (Wind-up)
What Kind Of Fool Am I
Rick Springfield; *Rick Springfield's Greatest Hits* . . . . (RCA)
Success Hasn't Spoiled Me Yet . . . . (RCA)
What Mattered Most
Ty Herndon; *Super Hits Of 1995-C* . . . . (Epic)
What Mattered Most . . . . (Epic)
When A Woman's Fed Up
R. Kelly; *Now That's What I Call Music!-#2-C* . . . . (Virgin)
R. . . . . (Jive)
When She Cries
Restless Heart; *Big Iron Horses* . . . . (RCA)

Restless Heart's Greatest Hits . . . . (RCA)
Today's Number One Country-C . . . . (K-Tel)
Where Did I Go Wrong
Steve Wariner; *Country's Greatest Hits-#3-C* . . . . (Priority)
I Got Dreams . . . . (MCA)
Steve Wariner's Greatest Hits-#2 . . . . (MCA)
Where Did I Go Wrong
UB40; *UB40* . . . . (A&M)
Where Do I Go From You
Jon Secada; *Heart, Soul & A Voice* . . . . (SBK)
Who Can Blame You
Alison Krauss; *Every Time You Say Goodbye* . . . . (Rounder)
Who Needs You Baby
Clay Walker; *Hypnotize The Moon* . . . . (Giant)
Who To Blame
Posies; *Success* . . . . (Pop Llama Prod.)
Who's Sorry Now
Benny Goodman; *Stompin'* . . . . (Drive)
Big Bill Broonzy; *Black, Brown & White* . . . . (Evidence Music)
Bob Crosby; *Bob Crosby & His Orchestra* . . . . (EPM)
Connie Francis; *Dick Clark's 21 All-Time Hits-#1-C* . . . . (Original Sound)
Very Best Of Connie Francis . . . . (Polydor)
Ella Fitzgerald; *The Intimate Ella* . . . . (Verve)
Esquivel; *Space-Age Bachelor Pad Music* . . . . (Bar/None)
Glen Gray; *Moonglow: 1930-1936* . . . . (Aero Space)
Nat "King" Cole; *The Billy May Sessions* . . . . (Capitol)
Ray Anthony; *Swing Back To The '40s* . . . . (Aero Space)
Who's To Bless And Who's To Blame
Kris Kristofferson; *Who's To Bless And Who's To Blame* . . . . (One Way)
Why Pt. 2
Collective Soul; *Blender* . . . . (Atlantic)
Why Would I Say Goodbye
Brooks & Dunn; *Borderline* . . . . (Arista)
Wild Horses
Garth Brooks; *No Fences* . . . . (Capitol)
Willing To Forgive
Aretha Franklin; *Aretha Franklin's Greatest Hits-1980-1994* . . . . (Arista)
Wiser Time
Black Crowes; *Amorica* . . . . (American)
Without Blame
Ismael Lo with Marianne Faithfull; *World Music That Speaks To The
Spirit-C* . . . . (Triloka)
Working My Way Back To You
4 Seasons; *25th Anniversary Collection* . . . . (Rhino)
4 Seasons-Anthology . . . . (Rhino)
Working My Way Back To You/Forgive Me, Girl
Spinners; *Billboard Top Hits-1980-C* . . . . (Rhino)
One Of A Kind Love Affair-Anthology . . . . (Rhino)
Very Best Of The Spinners . . . . (Rhino)
You Are Everything
Dru Hill; *Enter The Dru* . . . . (Def Jam/RAL/Mercury/Island)
You Can't Deny It
Lisa Stansfield; *Affection* . . . . (Arista)
You Caused It All By Telling Lies
Hank Williams; *Alone With His Guitar* . . . . (Mercury)
Complete Hank Williams . . . . (Mercury)
You Look So Good In Love
George Strait; *George Strait's Greatest Hits* . . . . (MCA)
Right Or Wrong . . . . (MCA)
Strait Out Of The Box . . . . (MCA)
You Make Me Feel Bad
Wood; *Songs From Stamford Hill* . . . . (Columbia)
You Should've Told Me
Kelly Price; *Mirror Mirror* . . . . (Def Soul/IDJMG)
You Still Believe In Me
Beach Boys; *Pet Sounds* . . . . (Capitol)
You Still Touch Me
Sting; *Mercury Falling* . . . . (A&M)
Your Cheatin' Heart
Beck; *Timeless: Hank Williams Tribute-C* . . . . (Lost Highway/IDJMG)
Elvis Presley; *Elvis For Everyone!* . . . . (RCA)
Welcome To My World . . . . (RCA)
Frankie Laine; *Frankie Laine's 16 Greatest Hits* . . . . (Trip)
Frankie Laine's Greatest Hits . . . . (Columbia)
Hank Williams With His Drifting Cowboys; *24 Of Hank Williams'
Greatest Hits* . . . . (Polydor)
Hank Williams-16 Great Hits . . . . (Everest)
Hank Williams-40 Greatest Hits . . . . (Polydor)
Hank Williams, Jr.; *Very Best Of Hank Williams, Jr.* . . . . (Polydor)
Jerry Lee Lewis; *Live At The Star Club-Hamburg 1964* . . . . (Rhino)
The Golden Hits Of Jerry Lee Lewis . . . . (Smash)
Patsy Cline; *ST/Sweet Dreams* . . . . (MCA)
The Patsy Cline Story . . . . (MCA)
Ray Charles; *Ray Charles' Greatest Hits-#2* . . . . (Rhino)
You're The One
Paul Simon; *You're The One* . . . . (Warner Bros.)

GUNS, Arrows, Bullets, Hunting, Shooting
See Also: **CRIME, DEATH, FIGHT, KILL, LAW & ORDER, POLICE,
REBELS, WAR**

(Man Who Shot) Liberty Valance
Gene Pitney; *Gene Pitney-Anthology 1961-1968* . . . . (Rhino)
Gene Pitney's Greatest Hits . . . . (Evergreen Music)
Super Oldies Of The '60s-#9-C . . . . (Audio Fidelity)
Greg Kihn; *Glass House Rock* . . . . (Beserkley)
.357-Break It On Down
L.L. Cool J; *Bigger & Deffer* . . . . (Def Jam/Columbia)
38 Pistol Blues
Big Joe Williams; *Walkin' Blues* . . . . (Fantasy)
911
Wyclef Jean featuring Mary J. Blige; *The Ecleftic-2 Sides II
A Book* . . . . (Ruffhouse/Columbia)
Ain't Nobody Here But Us Chickens
Asleep At The Wheel; *Very Best Of Asleep At The Wheel
Since 1970* . . . . (Relentless/Madacy)
Louis Jordan; *Best Of Louis Jordan* . . . . (MCA)
American Skin (41 Shots)
Bruce Springsteen & The E Street Band; *Live In New York City* . . . . . (Columbia)
Arctic Whale Hunt
Mancini Pops Orchestra; *In Surround-Mostly Monsters Murders...* . . . . . . (RCA)
Armed
Shawn Phillips; *Collaboration* . . . . (A&M)
Armed & Crazy
Johnny Paycheck; *Armed & Crazy* . . . . (Epic)
Armed & Extremely Dangerous
Merry Clayton; *Emotion* . . . . (MCA)
Armed & Ready
Michael Schenker Group; *Essential Michael Schenker Group* . . . . . . (Chrysalis)
Michael Schenker Group . . . . (Chrysalis)
Armed With An Empty Gun
Dream Syndicate; *Medicine Show/This Is Not The New Album* . . . . (A&M)
Arrow
Cheryl Wheeler; *Cheryl Wheeler* . . . . (North Star)
Arrow
Candlebox; *Candlebox* . . . . (Maverick)
Arrow Through Me
Wings; *Back To The Egg* . . . . (Capitol)
Arrow Thru Your Heart
Lou Gramm; *Ready or Not* . . . . (Atlantic)
Arrows
Crosby, Stills & Nash; *Live It Up* . . . . (Atlantic)
At The End Of A Pointed Gun
Tannahill Weavers; *Passage* . . . . (Green Linnet)
Bad Boyz
Shyne featuring Levy, Barrington; *Shyne* . . . . (Bad Boy/Arista)
Ballad Of A Well Known Gun
Elton John; *Tumbleweed Connection* . . . . (Polydor)
Bang Bang
Cher; *Cher* . . . . (Geffen)
EMI Legends Of Rock & Roll-24 Greatest Hits-C . . . . (EMI)
Bang Bang
ZZ Top; *Rhythmeen* . . . . (RCA)
Bang Bang
Stevie Wonder; *Down To Earth* . . . . (Motown)
Bang Bang
Bar-Kays; *Too Hot To Stop* . . . . (Mercury)
Bang Bang
Vanilla Fudge; *Vanilla Fudge* . . . . (Atco)
Bang, You're Dead
Bette Midler; *Live At Last* . . . . (Atlantic)
Barrel Of A Gun
Depeche Mode; *The Singles-1986-1998* . . . . (Mute/Reprise)
Ultra . . . . (Mute/Reprise)
Barrel Of A Gun (4,3,2,1)
Guster; *Lost & Gone Forever* . . . . (Hybrid/Sire)
Battle Of New Orleans
Chet Atkins & The Boston Pops; *Best Of Chet Atkins & The
Boston Pops* . . . . (RCA)
Johnny Horton; *American Originals-Johnny Horton* . . . . (Columbia)
Johnny Horton's Greatest Hits . . . . (Columbia)
Radio Classics Of The '50s-C . . . . (Columbia)
Nitty Gritty Dirt Band; *Dirt, Silver & Gold* . . . . (One Way)
Dream . . . . (United Artists)
Stars And Stripes Forever . . . . (Capitol)
Bayonet Rap
Tom Paxton; *Compleat Tom Paxton* . . . . (Elektra)
Big Gun
AC/DC; *ST/Last Action Hero* . . . . (Columbia)
Big Guns
Skid Row; *Skid Row* . . . . (Atlantic)
Big Guns
Heatwave; *Heatwave's Greatest Hits* . . . . (Epic)

Big Iron
Marty Robbins; *Columbia Country Classics-#3-Americana-C* . . . . . (Columbia)
Gunfighter Ballads & Trail Songs . . . . (Legacy)
Marty Robbins' All-Time Greatest Hits . . . . (Columbia)
Marty Robbins-More Greatest Hits . . . . (Columbia)

Bikini Girls With Machine Guns
Cramps; *Stay Sick!* . . . .(Enigma Capitol)

Billy The Kid
Marty Robbins; *Gunfighter Ballads & Trail Songs*. . . . . (Legacy)

Blues From A Gun
Jesus & Mary Chain; *Automatic* . . . .(Warner Bros.)

Boom Bye Bye
Buju Banton; *Voice Of Jamaica* . . . . (Mercury)

Bop Gun
Ice Cube & George Clinton; *Featuring...Ice Cube* . . . . (Priority)

Born In Chicago
George Thorogood & The Destroyers; *Boogie People* . . . .(EMI)
Paul Butterfield Blues Band; *Golden Butter* . . . . (Elektra)
Paul Butterfield Blues Band . . . . (Elektra)

British Grenadiers
Cambridge Singers; *The Lark In The Clear Air* . . . . (Collegium)

Broken Arrow
Buffalo Springfield; *Buffalo Springfield Again*. . . . . (Atco)
Buffalo Springfield-Retrospective . . . . (Atco)
Neil Young; *Decade* . . . . (Reprise)

Broken Arrow
Robbie Robertson; *Robbie Robertson*. (Geffen)
Rod Stewart; *Vagabond Heart* . . . .(Warner Bros.)

Broken Arrow
Chuck Berry; *Rockin' At The Hops* . . . . (Chess)

Bubba Shot The Jukebox
Mark Chesnutt; *Longnecks & Short Stories* . . . . (MCA)

Buffalo Gun
Michael Murphey; *Swans Against The Sun* . . . .(Epic)

Bullet
Divinyls; *Divinyls* . . . . (Virgin)

Bullet From A Gun
Derek B.; *Bullet From A Gun* . . . . (Profile)

Bullet In The Chamber
Loverboy; *Lovin' Every Minute Of It* . . . . (Columbia)

Bullet In The Head
Rage Against The Machine; *Rage Against The Machine* . . (Epic Portrait Assoc.)

Bullet Proof
George Clinton; *Some Of My Best Jokes Are Friends* . . . . (Capitol)

Bullet Proof
Goo Goo Dolls; *Dizzy Up The Girl* . . . .(Warner Sunset/Reprise)

Bullet Proof
Sade; *Love Deluxe* . . . .(Epic)

Bullet The Blue Sky
U2; *Joshua Tree* . . . . (Island)
Rattle And Hum . . . . (Island)

Bullet With Butterfly Wings
Smashing Pumpkins; *Mellon Collie And The Infinite Sadness* . . . . (Virgin)

Bullet-Ridden Bodies
Accused; *Grinning Like An Undertaker* . . . . (Nastymix)

Bullets For Bafazane
Juluka; *Stand Your Ground* . . . .(Warner Bros.)

Bullets To Spare
Dokken; *Tooth & Nail* . . . . (Elektra)

Cannonball
Supertramp; *Brother Where You Bound* . . . . (A&M)
Supertramp-Classics-#9 . . . . (A&M)

Cannonball
Duane Eddy; *Compact Command Performances-Duane Eddy* . . . . . . (Motown)

Cannonball
Breeders; *Last Splash* . . . . (4AD)

Cowboys Don't Shoot Straight
Tammy Wynette; *Tammy Wynette's Biggest Hits* . . . .(Epic)
Tears Of Fire-25th Anniversary Collection . . . .(Epic)

Crossfire
Kansas; *Vinyl Confessions* . . . . (Kirshner)

Crossfire
Jethro Tull; *"A"* . . . .(Chrysalis)

Crossfire
Stevie Ray Vaughan and Double Trouble; *In Step* . . . .(Epic)

Crossfire
Scorpions; *Love At First Sting* . . . . (Mercury)

Cupid
Sam Cooke; *Best Of Sam Cooke* . . . . (RCA)
The Man And His Music . . . . (RCA)
Spinners; *Love Trippin'* . . . .(Atlantic)

Cupid's Got A Brand New Gun
Michael Penn; *March* . . . . (RCA)

Day That Curly Bill Shot Down Crazy Sam
Hollies; *Hollies* . . . .(Epic)

Deja Vu (Uptown Baby)
Lord Tariq & Peter Gunz; *Deja Vu* . . . .(Codeine/Columbia)

Dirty Weapons
Killer Dwarfs; *Dirty Weapons*. . . . . (Epic)

Don't Drop That Bomb On Me
Bryan Adams; *Waking Up The Neighbours*. . . . . (A&M)

Don't Need A Gun
Billy Idol; *Whiplash Smile*. . . . . (Chrysalis)

Don't Take Your Guns To Town
Johnny Cash; *Billboard Top Country Hits-1959-C* . . . . (Rhino)
Columbia Country Classics-#3-Americana-C . . . . (Columbia)
Johnny Cash-16 Biggest Hits-#2 . . . . (Legacy)
Johnny Cash's Greatest Hits . . . . (Columbia)
The Man In Black-His Greatest Hits. . . . . (Legacy)

Don't Tell Me (What Love Can Do)
Van Halen; *Balance* . . . . (Warner Bros.)

Down By The River
Neil Young; *Decade* . . . .(Reprise)
Neil Young & Crazy Horse; *Everybody Knows This Is Nowhere* . . . . . . (Reprise)

Easy Tonight
Five For Fighting; *America Town* . . . . (Aware/C2/Columbia)

El Paso
Grateful Dead; *Steal Your Face* . . . .(Grateful Dead)
Marty Robbins; *Billboard Top Country Hits-1960-C* . . . . (Rhino)
Gunfighter Ballads & Trail Songs . . . . (Legacy)
Marty Robbins' Biggest Hits . . . . (Columbia)
Radio Classics Of The '50s-C . . . . (Columbia)
Texas Super Hits-C . . . . (Columbia)

Elephant Gun
David Lee Roth; *Eat 'Em & Smile* . . . . (Warner Bros.)

English Boys (With Guns)
Deaf School; *English Boys/Working Girls* . . . . (Warner Bros.)

Folsom Prison Blues
Brooks & Dunn with Johnny Cash; *Red Hot + Country-C* . . . . (Mercury)
Johnny Cash; *Billboard Top Country Hits-1968-C* . . . . (Rhino)
Classic Cash-Hall Of Fame Series . . . . (Mercury)
Hot Tracks-Train Super Hits-C . . . . (Epic)
Jailhouse Rock (Hits From The Big House)-C . . . . (Sony Music Special Prod.)
Johnny Cash At Folsom Prison & San Quentin . . . . (Columbia)
Johnny Cash-Original Golden Hits-#1. . . . . (Sun)
Johnny Cash's Greatest Hits-#2 . . . . (Columbia)
Superbilly . . . . (Sun)
The Man In Black-His Greatest Hits. . . . . (Legacy)

Forty Thousand Headmen
Traffic; *Traffic* . . . . (Island)
Welcome To The Canteen . . . . (Island)

Gimme A Bullet
AC/DC; *Powerage* . . . .(Atlantic)

Go For Your Guns
Isley Brothers; *Go For Your Guns* . . . . (T-Neck/Columbia)

Gone Shootin'
AC/DC; *Powerage* . . . .(Atlantic)

Gonna Go Huntin' Tonight
Hank Williams, Jr.; *Hank Williams, Jr.'s Greatest Hits-#2* . . . . (WB/Curb)
Strong Stuff . . . . (Warner Bros.)

Gun
John Cale; *Guts* . . . . (Island)
Siouxsie And The Banshees; *Through The Looking Glass* . . . . (Geffen)

Gun Don't Mind
Winter Brothers Band; *Coast To Coast* . . . . (Atco)

Gun Love
ZZ Top; *ZZ Top's Greatest Hits* . . . . (Warner Bros.)

Gun Shy
10,000 Maniacs; *In My Tribe*. . . . . (Elektra)
Moon Martin; *Escape From Domination* . . . . (Capitol)

Guns Of Love
Pamela Rose; *Morpheus* . . . . (Grace)

Guns On The Roof
Clash; *Give 'Em Enough Rope* . . . . (Epic)

Guns, Guns, Guns
Burton Cummings; *Dream Of A Child* . . . .(Portrait)

Gunslinger
Mink De Ville; *Mink De Ville* . . . . (Capitol)

Gunsmoke
Molly Hatchet; *Flirtin' With Disaster* . . . . (Epic)
Outlaws; *Hurry Sundown* . . . . (Arista)

Happiness Is A Warm Gun
Beatles; *The Beatles (White Album)* . . . . (Capitol)

Harder Cards
Collin Raye; *Tracks*. . . . . (Epic)

Heart Is A Lonely Hunter
Reba McEntire; *Read My Mind*. . . . . (MCA)
Reba McEntire's Greatest Hits-#3: I'm A Survivor . . . . (MCA)

Hey Joe
Jimi Hendrix; *Essential Jimi Hendrix, Volume 2*. . . . . (Reprise)
Live At Winterland . . . . (Rykodisc)
Jimi Hendrix Experience; *Are You Experienced?* . . . . (Reprise)
Smash Hits . . . . (Reprise)
Love; *Best Of Love* . . . . (Rhino)

Hey Man, Nice Shot
Filter; *Short Bus* . . . .(Reprise)

ST/Cable Guy . . . . (Work)
Hit Me With Your Best Shot
Pat Benatar; *Crimes Of Passion* . . . . (Chrysalis)
Live From Earth . . . . (Chrysalis)
Homecoming Queen's Got A Gun
Julie Brown; *Dr. Demento Presents The Greatest Novelty Records-#5-
1980s-C* . . . . (Rhino)
Teenage Tragedies-C . . . . (Rhino)
Trapped In The Body Of A White Girl . . . .(Sire)
Horse & Carriage
Cam'ron featuring Mase; *Confessions Of Fire* . . . . (Untertainment/Epic)
Hunter
Free; *Best Of Free* . . . . (A&M)
Free-Live . . . . (A&M)
Hunter
Paul Rodgers; *Muddy Water Blues-Tribute To Muddy
Waters-C* . . . . (Victory Music)
Hunter
Dokken; *Under Lock & Key* . . . . (Elektra)
Hunter Gets Captured By The Game
Marvelettes; *Compact Command Performances-Marvelettes* . . . . (Motown)
Marvelettes-Anthology . . . . (Motown)
Smokey Robinson & The Miracles; *Motown Legends-Smokey Robinson &
The Miracles* . . . . (Motown)
Hunting The Wren
Steeleye Span; *Live At Last* . . . . (Chrysalis)
Hunting Tigers Out In India
Bonzo Dog Band; *Best Of The Bonzo Dog Band* . . . . (Rhino)
Tadpoles . . . . (Liberty)
I Feel Like A Bullet
Elton John; *Rock Of The Westies* . . . . (Polydor)
I Fought The Law
Bobby Fuller Four; *Best Of The Bobby Fuller Four* . . . . (Rhino)
Heart & Soul Of Rock 'N' Roll-#1-C . . . . (Rhino)
Jailhouse Rock (Hits From The Big House)-C . . . . (Sony Music Special Prod.)
Oldies But Goodies-#9-C . . . . (Original Sound)
Super Oldies Of The '60s-#7-C . . . . (Audio Fidelity)
Clash; *The Clash* . . . . (Epic)
The Story Of The Clash, Volume 1 . . . . (Epic)
I Just Shot John Lennon
Cranberries; *To The Faithful Departed* . . . . (Island)
I Shot The Sheriff
Bob Marley & The Wailers; *Bob Marley & The Wailers-Live* . . . . . . (Tuff Gong)
Legend: The Best Of Bob Marley & The Wailers . . . . (Island)
This Is Reggae Music-#1-C . . . . (Island)
Eric Clapton; *461 Ocean Boulevard* . . . . (Polydor)
Eric Clapton-Crossroads-C . . . . (Polydor)
Time Pieces-#1-The Best Of Eric Clapton . . . . (Polydor)
Wailers; *Burnin'* . . . . (Tuff Gong)
I Wanna Get Me A Gun
Bill Wyman; *Monkey Grip* . . . . (Rolling Stones)
I'll Be Your .44
Dr. Blue; *Salt City Blues-C* . . . . (Blue Wave)
Janie's Got A Gun
Aerosmith; *Pump* . . . . (Geffen)
John 3:16
Wyclef; *Muggs Presents...The Soul Assassins-C* . . . . (Columbia)
John Peel
Hermes Nye; *Anglo-American Songs* . . . . (Smithsonian Folkways)
Johnny 99
Bruce Springsteen; *Nebraska* . . . . (Columbia)
Bruce Springsteen & The E Street Band; *Bruce Springsteen & The E Street
Band Live/1975-85* . . . . (Legacy)
Johnny Cash; *Cover Me (Bruce Springsteen Tribute)-C* . . . . (Rhino)
Johnny Too Bad
Slickers; *ST/The Harder They Come* . . . . (Mango)
Taj Mahal; *Best Of Taj Mahal* . . . . (Columbia)
Mo' Roots . . . . (Legacy)
UB40; *Labour Of Love* . . . . (A&M)
Live In Moscow . . . . (A&M)
Justice In The Barrel
Jon Bon Jovi; *Blaze Of Glory-ST/Young Guns II* . . . . (Mercury)
Lawyers, Guns & Money
Warren Zevon; *Excitable Boy* . . . . (Asylum)
Quiet Normal Life-Best Of Warren Zevon . . . . (Asylum)
Stand In The Fire . . . . (Asylum)
Lay Down Your Arms
Chordettes; *Best Of The Chordettes* . . . . (Rhino)
Little Arrows
Leapy Lee; *Bubble Gum Classics-C* . . . . (MCA Special Prod.)
Country Music Classics-#3-1965-1970-C . . . . (K-Tel)
Little Girl, The
John Michael Montgomery; *Brand New Me* . . . . (Atlantic)
Totally Hits-#3-C . . . . (Atlantic)
Little Triggers
Elvis Costello; *This Year's Model* . . . . (Rykodisc)
Locked & Loaded
Jackyl; *Cut The Crap-C* . . . . (Epic)

Look Into My Eyes
Bone Thugs-N-Harmony; *Art Of War* . . . . (Ruthless/Relativity)
Love Gun
Kiss; *Alive II* . . . . (Casablanca)
Double Platinum . . . .(Mercury)
Love Gun . . . . (Casablanca)
Smashes, Thrashes & Hits . . . .(Mercury)
Love Is A Good Thing
Sheryl Crow; *Sheryl Crow* . . . .(A&M)
Love Is In Control (Finger On The Trigger)
Donna Summer; *Donna Summer* . . . . (Geffen)
Love Is Like A Bullet
Shoes; *Best Of The Shoes* . . . . (Black Vinyl)
Stolen Wishes . . . . (Black Vinyl)
Machine Gun
Jimi Hendrix; *Band Of Gypsys* . . . .(Capitol)
Essential Jimi Hendrix, Volume 2 . . . . (Reprise)
Midnight Lightning . . . . (Reprise)
ST/Jimi Hendrix . . . . (Reprise)
Machine Gun
Commodores; *Commodores Greatest Hits*. . . . .(Motown)
Commodores-All The Great Hits. . . . .(Motown)
Machine Gun. . . . .(Motown)
Machine Gun
Warrant; *Dog Eat Dog* . . . .(Columbia)
Machine Gun Kelly
James Taylor; *Mud Slide Slim And The Blue Horizon* . . . . . . (Warner Bros.)
Man Who Shot Himself
Tom T. Hall; *Places I've Done Time* . . . . (RCA)
Me & A Gun
Tori Amos; *Little Earthquakes* . . . . (Atlantic)
Murder Incorporated
Bruce Springsteen; *Bruce Springsteen's Greatest Hits* . . . .(Columbia)
My Father's Gun
Elton John; *Tumbleweed Connection* . . . . (Polydor)
Nebraska
Bruce Springsteen; *Nebraska*. . . . .(Columbia)
Bruce Springsteen & The E Street Band; *Bruce Springsteen & The E Street
Band Live/1975-85* . . . .(Legacy)
Never Bit A Bullet Like This
George Jones; *High-Tech Redneck*. (MCA)
Nigga Witta Gun
Dr. Dre; *The Chronic* . . . . (Priority)
Night The Lights Went Out In Georgia
Lynn Anderson; *Top Of The World* . . . .(Columbia)
Reba McEntire; *For My Broken Heart*. . . . . (MCA)
Reba McEntire's Greatest Hits-#3: I'm A Survivor. . . . . (MCA)
Vicki Lawrence; *Super Hits Of The '70s-Have A Nice Day-#10-C* . . . . . .(Rhino)
Nobody's Got The Gun
Mark Knopfler; *Golden Heart* . . . . (Warner Bros.)
Ohio
Crosby, Stills & Nash; *CSN* . . . . (Atlantic)
Crosby, Stills, Nash & Young; *4 Way Street* . . . . (Atlantic)
So Far . . . . (Atlantic)
Neil Young; *Decade*. . . . . (Reprise)
ST/Journey Through The Past . . . . (Warner Bros.)
Ohio/Machine Gun
Isley Brothers; *Timeless* . . . . (T-Neck/Columbia)
Our Shotgun Wedding Day
Howington Brothers & Tennessee Haymakers; *Long Gone
Daddy-C* . . . .(Collectables)
Over There
Glenn Miller; *Original Recordings-#3-Army/Air Force Band*. . . . . (Pair)
Glenn Miller & His Army/Air Force Band; *Glenn Miller-A Legendary
Performer-#3* . . . .(Bluebird)
Mormon Tabernacle Choir; *God Bless America* . . . . (Sony Music Classical)
Paradise Knife & Gun Club
Jerry Lansdowne; *Travel Light*. . . . . (Step One)
Roy Clark; *Live From Austin City Limits* . . . . (Churchill)
Pass Me The Gun
House Of Freaks; *All My Friends* . . . .(Rhino)
Pass The Ammo
C.E.B.; *Countin' Endless Bank* . . . .(Ruffhouse/Columbia)
Perfume, Powder And Lead
Lonesome River Band; *Finding The Way* . . . . (Sugar Hill)
Peter And The Wolf
Dave Van Ronk; *Peter And The Wolf*. . . . .(Alacazam)
Original Soundtrack; *Beethoven Wrote It...But It
Swings* . . . . (Sony Music Classical)
Pistol Packin' Mama
Al Dexter; *Columbia Country Classics-#1-Golden Age-C* . . . .(Columbia)
Great Records Of The Decade-'40s-Country-C . . . .(Curb)
Andrews Sisters; *Andrews Sisters-16 Great Performances* . . . . (MCA)
Boogie Woogie Bugle Girls . . . . (MCA)
Bing Crosby; *Bing Crosby's Greatest Hits* . . . . (MCA)
Glenn Miller & His Army/Air Force Band; *Nipper's Greatest Hits Of The
'40s-#1-C* . . . . (RCA)
Pistol Packin' Papa
Hank Snow; *Superstars Salute Jimmie Rodgers-C* . . . . (Step One)

Jimmie Rodgers; *Riding High-1929-1930* . . . . (Rounder)
   This Is Jimmie Rodgers . . . . (RCA)
Po Lazarus
James Carter & The Prisoners; *ST/O Brother, Where Art Thou?* . . . . . (Mercury)
Pocket Full Of Gold
Vince Gill; *Pocket Full Of Gold* . . . .(MCA)
Point Blank
Bruce Springsteen; *The River* . . . . (Columbia)
Poison Arrow
ABC; *Absolutely ABC* . . . . (Mercury)
   Lexicon Of Love . . . . (Mercury)
Poison Arrow
Flesheaters; *Prehistoric Fits-#2* . . . . (SST)
Possum Hunt
Lightnin' Hopkins; *Lost Texas Tapes-#4* . . . . (Collectables)
Praise The Lord & Pass The Ammunition
Kay Kyser & His Orchestra; *Best Of The Big Bands-C* . . . . (Columbia)
   Sentimental Favorites . . . . (Columbia)
Put Down The Gun
Poison Dart; *Dancehall Roughneck* . . . . (Heartbeat)
Put Out The Fire
Queen; *Hot Space* . . . . (Hollywood)
Radar Gun
Bottle Rockets; *The Brooklyn Side* . . . . (East Side Digital)
Ricochet
Teresa Brewer; *Best Of Teresa Brewer* . . . . (MCA Jazz)
Rifle Range
Blondie; *Blondie* . . . . (Chrysalis)
Riflemen Of Bennington
Jim Burroughs; *Songs Of Rebellion* . . . .(Audio Fidelity)
Rocky Raccoon
Beatles; *Beatles-Box Set* . . . . (Capitol)
   The Beatles (White Album) . . . . (Capitol)
Roland The Headless Thompson Gunner
Warren Zevon; *Excitable Boy* . . . . (Asylum)
   Quiet Normal Life-Best Of Warren Zevon . . . . (Asylum)
Roll Out (My Business)
Ludacris; *Word Of Mouf* . . . . (Murder Inc./Def Jam/IDJMG)
Roulette
Bruce Springsteen; *Tracks* . . . . (Columbia)
Rubber Bullets
10 CC; *10 CC's Greatest Hits-1972-1978* . . . . (Polydor)
Running Gun
Marty Robbins; *Gunfighter Ballads & Trail Songs* . . . . (Legacy)
Running Gun Blues
David Bowie; *Man Who Sold The World* . . . .(Rykodisc)
Russian Roulette
Lords Of The New Church; *Killer Lords* . . . . (I.R.S.)
   Lords Of The New Church . . . . (I.R.S.)
Russian Roulette
Michelle Shocked; *Captain Swing* . . . . (Mercury)
Russian Roulette
Taxxi; *Expose* . . . .(MCA)
Russian Roulette
Hollies; *Hollies* . . . .(Epic)
Russian Roulette
Accept; *Russian Roulette* . . . . (Portrait)
Russian Roulette
Joan Armatrading; *Sleight Of Hand* . . . . (A&M)
San Angelo
Marty Robbins; *All Around Cowboy* . . . . (Columbia)
   Essential Marty Robbins-1951-1982 . . . . (Columbia)
   More Gunfighter Ballads & Trail Songs . . . . (Columbia)
Sapphire Bullets Of Pure Love
They Might Be Giants; *Flood* . . . . (Elektra)
Saturday Night Special
Lynyrd Skynyrd; *Gold & Platinum* . . . .(MCA)
   Nuthin' Fancy . . . .(MCA)
   One More From The Road . . . .(MCA)
   Skynyrd's Innards-Their Greatest Hits . . . .(MCA)
McBride & The Ride; *Skynyrd Frynds-C* . . . .(MCA)
Sex As A Weapon
Pat Benatar; *Seven The Hard Way* . . . . (Chrysalis)
She Shot A Hole In My Soul
Clifford Curry; *Soul Shots-#2-The "In" Crowd-Sweet Soul-C* . . . . (Rhino)
Huey Lewis and the News; *Four Chords & Several Years Ago* . . . . . . (Elektra)
Shoot Down The Moon
Elton John; *Ice On Fire* . . . .(MCA)
Shoot 'Em Down
Twisted Sister; *Big Hits & Nasty Cuts* . . . . (Atlantic)
Shoot 'Em Up
Cypress Hill Crew; *ST/Juice* . . . . (S.O.U.L.)
Shoot Her If She Runs
Climax Blues Band; *Tightly Knit* . . . . (Sire)
Shoot High Aim Low
Yes; *Big Generator* . . . . (Atco)
Shoot Him
Sugarcubes; *Here Today, Tomorrow Next Week!* . . . . (Elektra)

Shoot Low Sheriff
Murry Kellum; *Country Comedy-20 Country Comedy Hits* . . . . (Plantation)
Shoot Me In The Dark
Brews Springstien; *Melting Plot* . . . . (SST)
Shoot Out At The Fantasy Factory
Traffic; *On The Road* . . . . (Island)
   Shoot Out At The Fantasy Factory . . . . (Island)
Shoot Out In Chinatown
Band; *Cahoots* . . . . (Capitol)
Shoot Out On The Plantation
Leon Russell; *Best Of Leon Russell* . . . .(MCA)
   Leon Russell . . . .(MCA)
Shoot Out The Lights
Richard & Linda Thompson; *Shoot Out The Lights* . . . .(Hannibal)
Richard Thompson; *Watching The Dark-History Of Richard*
   Thompson . . . . (Rykodisc)
Shoot Shoot
UFO; *Force It* . . . . (Chrysalis)
   Strangers In The Night . . . . (Chrysalis)
Shoot Shoot
Dio; *Sacred Heart* . . . . (Warner Bros.)
Shoot Shoot
Sons Of Freedom; *Sons Of Freedom* . . . . (Slash)
Shoot That Turkey
Holy Modal Rounders; *Alleged In Their Own Time* . . . . (Rounder)
Shoot To Thrill
AC/DC; *Back In Black* . . . . (Atco)
Shoot Your Shot
J. Geils Band; *Blow Your Face Out* . . . . (Rhino)
Junior Walker & The All Stars; *Junior Walker & The All Stars'*
   Greatest Hits . . . . (Motown)
Junior Walker & The All Stars-Anthology . . . . (Motown)
   Shotgun . . . . (Motown)
Shootin' On Narcs
Pat Gangsta; *#1 Suspect* . . . . (Atlantic)
Shot Down
Neil Diamond; *Do It* . . . . (Bang)
   Double Gold-Neil Diamond . . . . (Bang)
Shot Down
Julian Cope; *Saint Julian* . . . . (Island)
Shot Down
Icehouse; *Sidewalk* . . . . (Chrysalis)
Shot Down In Flames
AC/DC; *Highway To Hell* . . . . (Atco)
Shot Full Of Love
Chris LeDoux; *Western Underground* . . . . (Liberty)
Don Williams; *New Moves* . . . . (Capitol)
Juice Newton; *Juice* . . . . (Capitol)
   Juice Newton-Greatest Hits & More . . . . (Capitol)
Shot In The Dark
Ozzy Osbourne; *The Ozzman Cometh* . . . . (Epic)
   Ultimate Sin . . . . (CBS Associated)
Shot In The Dark
Utopia; *Adventures In Utopia* . . . . (Rhino)
Shot In The Heart
Genya Ravan; *Urban Desire* . . . . (20th Century Fox)
Shot Me Down
Nazareth; *Expect No Mercy* . . . . (A&M)
Shot Through The Heart
Jennifer Warnes; *Best Of Jennifer Warnes* . . . . (Arista)
   Shot Through The Heart . . . . (Arista)
Shotgun
Junior Walker & The All Stars; *Billboard Top R&B Hits-1965-*
   1969-C . . . . (Rhino)
   Junior Walker & The All Stars' Greatest Hits . . . . (Motown)
   Junior Walker & The All Stars-Anthology . . . . (Motown)
   Motown Superstar Series-#5-Junior Walker & The All Stars . . . . . . (Motown)
   Shotgun . . . . (Motown)
Shotgun
Los Lobos; *ST/American Me* . . . . (Virgin)
Shotgun
Tanya Tucker; *Tennessee Woman* . . . . (Capitol)
Shotgun
Vanilla Fudge; *Best Of Vanilla Fudge* . . . . (Atco)
   Vanilla Fudge-Live . . . . (Rhino)
Shotgun Blues
Blues Brothers; *Briefcase Full Of Blues* . . . . (Atlantic)
Shotgun Blues
Guns N' Roses; *Use Your Illusion II* . . . . (Geffen)
Shotgun Blues
Lightnin' Hopkins; *Best Blues Album In The World...Ever!-C* . . . . (Virgin)
   Very Best Of Lightnin' Hopkins-Blues Masters . . . . (Rhino)
Shotgun Willie
Willie Nelson; *Shotgun Willie* . . . . (Atlantic)
Shoulder Holster
Elton John; *Blue Moves* . . . .(MCA)
Sign Of The Times
Queensryche; *Hear In The Now Frontier* . . . . (Virgin)

Silver Bullet
Flo & Eddie; *History Of Flo & Eddie And The Turtles* . . . . (Rhino)
Silver Gun
Robert Palmer; *Addictions-#2* . . . . (Island)
  Pride . . . . (Island)
Sin Wagon
Dixie Chicks; *Fly* . . . . (Monument)
Smackwater Jack
Carole King; *Carole King's Greatest Hits* . . . . (Epic)
  Tapestry . . . . (Epic)
Son Of A New York Gun
Gino Vannelli; *Powerful People* . . . . (A&M)
Southside
Moby featuring Gwen Stefani; *12'' Maxi Single* . . . . (V2)
  Play . . . . (V2)
Stagger Lee
Dion; *Dion-His Best* . . . . (Laurie)
Huey Lewis and the News; *Four Chords & Several Years Ago* . . . . (Elektra)
Ike & Tina Turner; *Best Of Ike & Tina Turner* . . . . (EMI)
Lloyd Price; *Billboard Top Rock 'N' Roll Hits-1959-C* . . . . (Rhino)
  Collectables Presents The History Of Rock-#5-C . . . . (Collectables)
  Lloyd Price's Greatest Hits . . . . (MCA)
  Oldies But Goodies-#1-C . . . . (Original Sound)
Professor Longhair; *Rock 'N' Roll Gumbo* . . . . (Dancing Cat)
Wilson Pickett; *A Man & A Half-Best Of Wilson Pickett* . . . . (Rhino)
Stiff Upper Lip
AC/DC; *Stiff Upper Lip* . . . . (East West)
Sweet Little Bullet From A Pretty Blue Gun
Tom Waits; *Blue Valentine* . . . . (Asylum)
Testosterone
Bush; *Sixteen Stone* . . . . (Trauma)
That Dog Won't Hunt
Waylon Jennings; *Will The Wolf Survive* . . . . (MCA)
Theme From "Colt .45"
Original Soundtrack; *Television's Greatest Hits-#4-Black & White
  Classics-C* . . . . (TVT)
Theme From "Gunsmoke" (The Old Trail)
Billy Strange; *Great Western Themes* . . . . (Crescendo)
Original Soundtrack; *CBS: The First 50 Years* . . . . (TVT)
  Television's Greatest Hits-#4-Black & White Classics-C . . . . (TVT)
Theme From "Have Gun Will Travel" (Ballad Of Paladin)
Duane Eddy; *Duane Eddy-Pure Gold* . . . . (RCA)
Johnny Western; *Columbia Country Classics-#3-Americana-C* . . . . . (Columbia)
  Television's Greatest Hits-#7-Cable Ready-C . . . . (TVT)
Theme From "The Rifleman"
Cincinnati Pops Orchestra/Erich Kunzel; *Round-Up* . . . . (Telarc)
Original Soundtrack; *Television's Greatest Hits-#1-C* . . . . (TVT)
There Goes My Gun
Pixies; *Doolittle* . . . . (Elektra)
Tragedy
Bee Gees; *Bee Gees' Greatest* . . . . (Polydor)
  Mega Hits Dance Classics-#8-C . . . . (Priority)
  Spirits Having Flown . . . . (Polydor)
Trigga Happy Nigga
Geto Boys; *Grip It! On That Other Level* . . . . (Def American)
Trigger Happy
"Weird Al" Yankovic; *Off The Deep End* . . . . (Scotti Bros.)
Thrashpack; *Hard As Hell-#2* . . . . (Profile)
Trigger Happy Kid
Kenny Rogers And The First Edition; *Kenny Rogers And The First Edition's
  All-Time Greatest Hits-#2* . . . . (MCA Special Prod.)
Two Bullets & A Gun
Stevie Salas Colorcode; *Stevie Salas Colorcode* . . . . (Island)
Under The Gun
Aldo Nova; *Aldo Nova* . . . . (Portrait)
  Portrait Of Aldo Nova . . . . (Epic)
Under The Gun
Poco; *Backtracks* . . . . (MCA)
Under The Gun
Robin Trower; *In The Line Of Fire* . . . . (Atlantic)
Under The Gun
Suzy Bogguss; *Moment Of Truth* . . . . (Capitol)
Under The Gun
Willie Nelson & Kris Kristofferson; *Music From "Songwriter"* . . . . (Columbia)
Under The Gun
Molly Hatchet; *No Guts No Glory* . . . . (Epic)
Under The Gun
Deep Purple; *Perfect Strangers* . . . . (Mercury)
Under The Gun
Poco; *Under The Gun* . . . . (MCA)
Vote With A Bullet
Corrosion Of Conformity; *Vote With A Bullet* . . . . (Relativity)
Washington Bullets
Clash; *On Broadway* . . . . (Epic)
  Sandinista . . . . (Epic)
Watch My .38
Commander Cody & His Lost Planet Airmen; *Hot Licks, Cold Steel &
  Trucker's Favorites* . . . . (MCA)

Western Movies (My Baby Loves)
Olympics; *All-Time Greatest Hits Of Rock 'N' Roll-C* . . . . (Curb)
  American Graffiti-#3-C . . . . (MCA)
  Best Of The Olympics . . . . (Vee-Jay)
  Jumpin' Jive '50s-C . . . . (Priority)
With A Gun
Steely Dan; *Pretzel Logic* . . . . (MCA)
Woke Up This Morning
A3; *Exile On Coldharbour Lane* . . . . (C2/Columbia)
  *The Sopranos-Music From The HBO Original
  Series* . . . . (Sony Music Soundtrax)
You Can't Get A Man With A Gun
Ethel Merman/Ray Middleton/Original Cast; *Annie Get Your Gun* . . . . . (MCA)
Original Broadway Cast; *Annie Get Your Gun* . . . . (Angel)
Young Guns
Wham! Featuring George Michael; *Fantastic* . . . . (Columbia)
Youth Of The Nation
P.O.D.; *Satellite* . . . . (Atlantic)

GYPSIES

See Also: MAGIC (fortune tellers), TRAVELING

Brilliant Disguise
Bruce Springsteen; *Bruce Springsteen's Greatest Hits* . . . . (Columbia)
  Tunnel Of Love . . . . (Columbia)
Caravan
Van Morrison; *Moondance* . . . . (Warner Bros.)
Van Morrison & The Band; *The Last Waltz* . . . . (Warner Bros.)
Come What May
Patti Page; *Patti Page Collection-The Mercury Years-#1* . . . . (Mercury)
Gypsies, Tramps And Thieves
Cher; *Half-Breed* . . . . (MCA Special Prod.)
Gypsies In The Palace
Jimmy Buffett; *Feeding Frenzy* . . . . (MCA)
  Last Mango In Paris . . . . (MCA)
Gypsy Eyes
Jimi Hendrix Experience; *Electric Ladyland* . . . . (Reprise)
Gypsy Queen
Santana; *Abraxas* . . . . (Columbia)
  Lotus . . . . (Columbia)
  Moonflower . . . . (Columbia)
Gypsy Queen
Van Morrison; *His Band And The Street Choir* . . . . (Warner Bros.)
Gypsy Wind
Dan Fogelberg; *Phoenix* . . . . (Full Moon)
Gypsy Woman
Brian Hyland; *Brian Hyland's Greatest Hits* . . . . (Rhino)
  Super Hits Of The '70s-Have A Nice Day-#3-C . . . . (Rhino)
Impressions; *Billboard Top R&B Hits-1961-C* . . . . (Rhino)
  Impressions' Greatest Hits . . . . (MCA)
  Oldies But Goodies-#12-C . . . . (Original Sound)
  Vintage Music-#6-C . . . . (MCA)
Ry Cooder; *Slide Area* . . . . (Warner Bros.)
Gypsy Woman
Muddy Waters; *Real Folk Blues-C* . . . . (Chess)
  The Chess Box-Muddy Waters . . . . (Chess)
Gypsy Woman (She's Homeless)
Crystal Waters; *Red Hot + Dance-C* . . . . (Columbia)
  Surprise . . . . (Mercury)
Gypsy, The
Dinah Shore; *Dinah Shore-16 Most Requested Songs* . . . . (Legacy)
Dinah Shore with Sonny Burke & His Orchestra; *Sentimental Journey: Pop
  Vocal Classics-#1-1942-1946-C* . . . . (Rhino)
Ink Spots; *Billboard Pop Memories-1945-1949-C* . . . . (Rhino)
  Ink Spots' Greatest Hits-Original Recordings-1939-1946 . . . . (MCA)
I Almost Lost My Mind
Eddy Arnold; *World Of Hits* . . . . (MGM)
Fats Domino; *Fats Domino's Greatest Hits* . . . . (MCA)
Ivory Joe Hunter; *Since I Met You Baby* . . . . (Mercury)
Pat Boone; *Pat Boone's Greatest Hits* . . . . (Curb)
Just Like A Gypsy
Nora Bayes; *Music From The New York Stage (1890-1920)-#4-1917-
  1920-C* . . . . (Pearl)
Key West Intermezzo (I Saw You First) (Gypsy Scotty)
John Mellencamp; *Mr. Happy Go Lucky* . . . . (Mercury)
Love Potion Number 9
Clovers; *ST/American Graffiti* . . . . (MCA)
  Super Oldies Of The '50s-#7-C . . . . (Audio Fidelity)
Herb Alpert & The Tijuana Brass; *Herb Alpert & The Tijuana Brass'
  Greatest Hits* . . . . (A&M)
  Herb Alpert & The Tijuana Brass-Classics-#1 . . . . (A&M)
Searchers; *History Of British Rock-#3-C* . . . . (Rhino)
  Searchers' Greatest Hits . . . . (Rhino)

HAPPINESS, Feeling Good, High Consciousness, High On Life, Joy, Liking The Way Things Are, Natural High

See Also: BEST, CAREFREE, FUN, GOOD, GRATITUDE, LOVE (various), PAIN & HEALING, OPTIMISM, PARTY, RELAX, SMILE, THINKING & KNOWING (enlightenment)

(He's) Some Kind Of Wonderful
Carole King; *Music* ....(Epic)
(I Can't Get No) Satisfaction
Devo; *Best Of Devo-Greatest Hits* ....(Warner Bros.)
   Q: Are We Not Men? A: We Are Devo! ....(Warner Bros.)
Otis Redding; *Best Of Otis Redding* ....(Atlantic)
   History Of Otis Redding ....(Atco)
   Otis Redding ....(Atlantic)
   The Otis Redding Story ....(Atlantic)
Rolling Stones; *Big Hits (High Tide & Green Grass)* ....(Abkco)
   Flashpoint ....(Virgin)
   got Live if you want it! ....(Abkco)
   Hot Rocks 1964-1971 ....(Abkco)
   Out Of Our Heads ....(Abkco)
   Singles Collection-The London Years ....(Abkco)
(It's A) Beautiful Morning
Rascals; *Rascals' Greatest Hits* ....(Atlantic)
(I've Had) The Time Of My Life
Bill Medley; *Best Of Bill Medley* ....(Curb)
Bill Medley & Jennifer Warnes; *Dirty Dancing Live In Concert-C* ......(RCA)
   ST/Dirty Dancing ....(RCA)
(Keep Feeling) Fascination
Human League; *Fascination* ....(A&M)
(She's) Some Kind Of Wonderful
Drifters; *Drifters-16 Greatest Hits* ....(Trip)
   Drifters-Golden Hits ....(Atlantic)
   ST/More Dirty Dancing ....(RCA)
   Very Best Of The Drifters ....(Rhino)
Huey Lewis and the News; *Four Chords & Several Years Ago* ......(Elektra)
Jay & The Americans; *Sands Of Time/Wax Museum* ....(EMI)
Marvin Gaye; *I Heard It Through The Grapevine/I Want You* ......(Motown)
(You Make Me Feel Like) A Natural Woman
Aretha Franklin; *Aretha Franklin's Greatest Hits-1980-1994* ....(Arista)
   Chicken Soup For The Woman's Soul-C ....(Rhino)
Carole King; *Tapestry* ....(Epic)
Celine Dion; *Tapestry Revisited: Tribute To Carole King-C* ......(Lava)
(Your Love Keeps Lifting Me) Higher And Higher
Bette Midler; *Bette Midler* ....(Atlantic)
Bonnie Bramlett; *It's Time* ....(Capricorn)
Jackie Wilson; *Billboard Top R&B Hits-1967-C* ....(Rhino)
   Jackie Wilson's Greatest Hits ....(Brunswick)
   Jackie Wilson's Greatest Hits-#2 ....(Brunswick)
   Reet Petite-Best Of Jackie Wilson ....(Columbia)
   The Jackie Wilson Story ....(Epic)
   Very Best Of Jackie Wilson ....(Rhino)
Rita Coolidge; *Anytime...Anywhere* ....(A&M)
   Havana Jam ....(Columbia)
   Rita Coolidge-Classics-#5 ....(A&M)
   Rita Coolidge's Greatest Hits ....(A&M)
59th Street Bridge Song (Feelin' Groovy)
Harper's Bizarre; *Baby Boomer Classics-More Mellow Sixties-C* ....(JCI Assoc. Labels)
   Better Days-C ....(Rhino)
Simon & Garfunkel; *Collected Works* ....(Columbia)
   Parsley Sage Rosemary & Thyme ....(Columbia)
   Simon & Garfunkel's Greatest Hits ....(Columbia)
   The Concert In Central Park ....(Warner Bros.)
Aba Daba Honeymoon
Debbie Reynolds; *Debbie Reynolds' Greatest Hits* ....(Curb)
Aeroplane
Red Hot Chili Peppers; *One Hot Minute* ....(Warner Bros.)
Ain't It Great To Be Crazy
Wonder Kids; *Really Silly Songs* ....(Madacy)
Alive
P.O.D.; *Satellite* ....(Atlantic)
All Is Well
Chicago; *Chicago V* ....(Chicago)
All Right Now
Free; *Best Of Free* ....(A&M)
   Fire And Water ....(A&M)
   Free-Live ....(A&M)
   Rock Classics-#2-C ....(K-Tel)
   The Island Story-1962-1987-25th Anniversary-C ....(Island)
An Acceptable Level Of Ecstasy (The Wedding Song)
Lyle Lovett; *Lyle Lovett* ....(MCA)
Anticipation
Carly Simon; *Anticipation* ....(Elektra)
   Best Of Carly Simon ....(Elektra)
Apple Tree
Erykah Badu; *Baduizm* ....(Kedar Entert./Universal)

April Joy
Pat Metheny Group; *Pat Metheny Group* ....(ECM)
Are You Happy Baby?
Dottie West; *Dottie West's Greatest Hits* ....(Curb)
Aren't You Glad?
Beach Boys; *Beach Boys '69 (The Beach Boys Live In London)* ......(Capitol)
   Smiley Smile/Wild Honey ....(Capitol)
   Sunshine Dream ....(Capitol)
Aren't You Glad?
Original Broadway Cast; *The Most Happy Fella* ....(Sony Music Classical)
As Long As I'm Rockin' With You
John Conlee; *Best Of John Conlee* ....(Curb)
   In My Eyes ....(MCA)
   John Conlee-20 Greatest Hits ....(MCA)
   John Conlee-Legends ....(MCA)
At The Ballet
Original Cast; *A Chorus Line* ....(Columbia)
Baby Luv
Groove Theory; *Groove Theory* ....(Epic)
Back In Stride
Maze featuring Frankie Beverly; *Can't Stop The Love* ....(Capitol)
   Lifelines-#1 ....(Capitol)
   Live In Los Angeles ....(Capitol)
Back In The High Life Again
Steve Winwood; *Back In The High Life* ....(Island)
Back In The U.S.A.
Chuck Berry; *Chuck Berry-Golden Hits* ....(Mercury)
   Chuck Berry's Greatest Hits ....(Everest)
   Roll Over Beethoven ....(Allegiance)
   The Chess Box-Chuck Berry ....(Chess)
Linda Ronstadt; *Linda Ronstadt's Greatest Hits, Volume Two* ......(Asylum)
   Living In The USA ....(Asylum)
Back On My Feet Again
Babys; *Babys-Anthology* ....(Chrysalis)
   Union Jacks ....(Chrysalis)
Back On The Streets Again
Tower Of Power; *Bill Graham Presents The Last Days Of The Fillmore-C* ....(Epic Portrait Assoc.)
   East Bay Grease ....(Rhino)
Barbie Girl
Aqua; *Aquarium* ....(MCA)
   Now That's What I Call Music!-#1-C ....(Virgin)
Be Glad
Del Reeves; *45-#50531* ....(United Artists)
Be Happy
Mary J. Blige; *My Life* ....(Uptown/MCA)
Be My Life's Companion
Mills Brothers; *Best Of The Mills Brothers* ....(MCA)
   The Mills Brothers-Best Of The Decca Years ....(Decca)
Rosemary Clooney; *Rosemary Clooney-16 Most Requested Songs* ....(Legacy)
Be Young, Be Foolish, Be Happy
Tams; *Tam's Greatest Hits* ....(Universal)
Beautiful
Mary J. Blige; *ST/How Stella Got Her Groove Back* ....(Flyte Tyme/MCA)
Beautiful
Carole King; *Tapestry* ....(Epic)
Because Of You
Bobby Vinton; *Bobby Vinton's Greatest Hits* ....(Curb)
Tony Bennett; *Tony Bennett Sings His All-Time Hall Of Fame Hits* ....(Columbia)
   Tony Bennett-16 Most Requested Songs ....(Legacy)
Willie Nelson; *One For The Road* ....(Columbia)
Because You Love Me
Jo Dee Messina; *I'm Alright* ....(Curb)
Beer Barrel Polka
Andrews Sisters; *Andrews Sisters-16 Great Performances* ......(MCA)
   Best Of The Andrews Sisters ....(MCA)
Frankie Yankovic & His Yanks; *Frankie Yankovic & His Yanks' Greatest Hits* ....(Columbia)
Will Glahe; *This Is Will Glahe-Decade Of The '30s* ....(RCA)
Bernadette
Four Tops; *Compact Command Performances-Four Tops* ....(Motown)
   Four Tops' Greatest Hits ....(Motown)
   Four Tops Reach Out ....(Motown)
   Four Tops-Anthology ....(Motown)
   Motown Superstar Series-#14-Four Tops ....(Motown)
Best Day
George Strait; *Latest Greatest Straitest Hits* ....(MCA)
Best Days Of My Life
Johnny Mathis; *Best Days Of My Life* ....(Columbia)
   Best Of Johnny Mathis 1975-1980 ....(Columbia)
Best Days Of My Life
Rod Stewart; *Blondes Have More Fun* ....(Warner Bros.)
Better Days
Bruce Springsteen; *Bruce Springsteen's Greatest Hits* ....(Columbia)
   Lucky Town ....(Columbia)
Better Man, Better Off
Tracy Lawrence; *The Coast Is Clear* ....(Atlantic)

Beyond The Blue Horizon
Jeanette MacDonald; *Hollywood Sings-C* . . . . (Living Era)
Lou Christie; *ST/Rain Man* . . . . (Capitol)
Big Bright Green Pleasure Machine
Simon & Garfunkel; *Collected Works* . . . . (Columbia)
Parsley Sage Rosemary & Thyme . . . . (Columbia)
ST/The Graduate . . . . (Columbia)
Big Time
Neil Young & Crazy Horse; *Broken Arrow* . . . .(Reprise)
Year Of The Horse . . . .(Reprise)
Bliss
Mariah Carey; *Rainbow* . . . . (Columbia)
Blue Skies
Benny Goodman; *Benny Goodman Today* . . . .(London)
Carnegie Hall Jazz Concert . . . .(Columbia)
The Birth Of Swing (1935-1936) . . . .(Bluebird)
This Is Benny Goodman . . . .(RCA)
Bing Crosby; *Bing Crosby's Greatest Hits* . . . . (MCA)
Duke Ellington; *Carnegie Hall Concert* . . . . (Prestige)
Golden Duke . . . . (Prestige)
Willie Nelson; *Stardust* . . . . (Legacy)
Bluebird Of Happiness
Lee Andrews And The Hearts; *Gotham Recording Sessions* . . . . . .(Collectables)
Lee Andrews And The Hearts' Biggest Hits . . . . (Collectables)
Both Sides Now
Sammy Hagar; *Marching To Mars* . . . . (MCA)
Bowling Green
Everly Brothers; *Walk Right Back: The Everly Brothers On Warner Bros.-
1960-1969* . . . . (Warner Archives)
Bringing Out The Elvis
Faith Hill; *Breathe* . . . . (Warner Bros.)
Bumming Around
"T" Texas Tyler; *Only Country-1950-1954-C* . . . . . .(JCI Assoc. Labels)
But For The Grace Of God
keith urban; *keith urban* . . . . (Capitol)
Bye Bye Blues
Bert Lown; *Fabulous Thirties-C* . . . . (Pro Jazz)
Cabin On The Hill
Flatt & Scruggs; *Columbia Historic Edition-Flatt & Scruggs* . . . . (Columbia)
Lester Flatt & Earl Scruggs; *Bluegrass Super Hits-C* . . . . (Columbia)
C'est Si Bon (It's So Good)
Eartha Kitt; *Lost Female Hits Of The '50s-C* . . . . (Taragon)
Chantilly Lace
Big Bopper; *45s On CD-#1-1956-1959-C* . . . . (Mercury)
Cruisin'-1958-C . . . . (Increase)
Oldies But Goodies-#4-C . . . . (Original Sound)
ST/American Graffiti . . . . (MCA)
Jerry Lee Lewis; *"Killer" Rocks On* . . . . (Mercury)
Best Of Jerry Lee Lewis-#2 . . . . (Mercury)
Chapel Of Love
Dixie Cups; *Girl Groups-Story Of A Sound-C* . . . . (Rhino)
Jewels-#1-C . . . . (SSS International)
Oldies But Goodies-#11-C . . . .(Original Sound)
Original New York Rock & Roll-C . . . .(Original Sound)
Chattanoogie Shoe Shine Boy
Freddy Cannon; *14 Booming Hits* . . . . (Rhino)
Red Foley; *Red Foley: The Country Music Hall
Of Fame* . . . . (MCA Special Prod.)
The Nashville Sound: Owen Bradley-C . . . . (Decca)
Checkin' It Out
Van Morrison; *Wavelength* . . . . (Warner Bros.)
Cheek To Cheek
Ella Fitzgerald; *Silver Collection-Songbooks* . . . . (Verve)
Frank Sinatra; *Come Dance With Me!* . . . . (Capitol)
Fred Astaire; *Cheek To Cheek* . . . . (Pro-Arte)
Irving Berlin Songbook . . . . (Verve)
Mundell Lowe; *Mundell Lowe Quartet* . . . . (Riverside)
Pete Fountain; *Cheek To Cheek* . . . . (Ranwood)
Tommy Dorsey; *Irving Berlin 100th Anniversary Collection-C* . . . . (MCA)
Tony Bennett; *Bennett/Berlin* . . . . (Columbia)
Cheerful Little Earful
Ella Fitzgerald; *Swings Brightly With Nelson* . . . . (Verve)
Chessman's Delight
Randy Weston Trio & Cecil Payne; *Jazz A La Bohemia* . . . . (Riverside)
Cinnamon Girl
Neil Young & Crazy Horse; *Decade* . . . .(Reprise)
Everybody Knows This Is Nowhere . . . .(Reprise)
Live Rust . . . .(Reprise)
WELD . . . .(Reprise)
Clint Eastwood
Gorillaz; *Gorillaz* . . . .(Virgin)
Color My World
Petula Clark; *Petula Clark's Greatest Hits* . . . . (Crescendo)
Comfort Zone
Vanessa Williams; *The Comfort Zone* . . . . (Wing)
Comfortably Numb
Pink Floyd; *Delicate Sound Of Thunder* . . . . (Columbia)
Knebworth-The Album-C . . . . (Polydor)
The Wall . . . . (Columbia)

Roger Waters; *The Wall-Live In Berlin* . . . . (Mercury)
Comforter
Shai; *If I Ever Fall In Love* . . . .(Gasoline Alley)
Cool To Hate
Offspring; *Ixnay On The Hombre* . . . . (Columbia)
Cool, Calm, Collected
Atlantic Starr; *As The Band Turns* . . . . (A&M)
Country Comfort
Earl Scruggs & Elton John; *Earl Scruggs And Friends-C* . . . . (MCA)
Elton John; *Tumbleweed Connection* . . . . (Polydor)
Rod Stewart; *Best Of Rod Stewart-#2* . . . . (Mercury)
Gasoline Alley . . . . (Mercury)
Sing It Again, Rod . . . . (Mercury)
Country State Of Mind
Hank Williams, Jr.; *Hank Williams, Jr.'s Greatest Hits III* . . . .(Curb)
Montana Cafe . . . .(WB/Curb)
Cracklin' Rosie
Neil Diamond; *Hot August Night* . . . . (MCA)
Hot August Night II . . . .(Columbia)
Neil Diamond-His 12 Greatest Hits . . . . (MCA)
Tap Root Manuscript . . . . (MCA)
Cruisin'
D'Angelo; *Brown Sugar* . . . . (EMI)
Huey Lewis and Gwyneth Paltrow; *ST/Duets* . . . .(Hollywood)
Smokey Robinson; *Compact Command Performances-Smokey
Robinson* . . . .(Motown)
Motown Love Songs-C . . . . (Motown)
Motown Story-First 25 Years-C . . . . (Motown)
Where There's Smoke . . . . (Motown)
Crying In The Chapel
Elvis Presley; *Elvis-A Legendary Performer, Volume 3* . . . . (RCA)
How Great Thou Art . . . . (RCA)
The Top Ten Hits . . . . (RCA)
Worldwide 50 Gold Award Hits, Vol. 1, Parts 1 & 2 . . . . (RCA)
June Valli; *Nipper's Greatest Hits Of The '50s-#2-C* . . . . (RCA)
Little Richard; *Shut Up-Collection Of Rare Tracks-1951-1964* . . . . . .(Rhino)
Orioles; *Super Oldies Of The '50s-#1-C* . . . . (Audio Fidelity)
Rex Allen; *Only Country-1950-1954-C* . . . .(JCI Assoc. Labels)
Sonny Til & The Orioles; *Echoes Of A Rock Era-Early Years-C* . . . . . .(Roulette)
Sonny Til & The Orioles' Greatest Hits . . . .(Collectables)
ST/American Graffiti . . . . (MCA)
Daddy's Gonna Treat You Right
Commander Cody & His Lost Planet Airmen; *Lost In The Ozone* . . . . (MCA)
Dance The Night Away
Mavericks; *Trampoline* . . . . (MCA)
Danny's Song
Anne Murray; *Anne Murray-Country* . . . . (Capitol)
Anne Murray's Greatest Hits . . . . (Capitol)
Danny's Song . . . . (Capitol)
Loggins & Messina; *Loggins & Messina-On Stage* . . . . (Columbia)
Sittin' In . . . . (Columbia)
The Best Of Friends . . . . (Columbia)
Daydream Believer
Anne Murray; *Anne Murray's Greatest Hits* . . . . (Capitol)
I'll Always Love You . . . . (Capitol)
Monkees; *Billboard Top Rock 'N' Roll Hits-1967-C* . . . . (Rhino)
Mellow '60s-C . . . . (Priority)
Monkees' Greatest Hits . . . . (Rhino)
Days Of Wine And Roses
Andy Williams; *Andy Williams' Greatest Hits* . . . . (Columbia)
Andy Williams-16 Most Requested Songs . . . . (Legacy)
Close Enough For Love . . . . (Atco)
*Days Of Wine And Roses/Moon River & Other Great Movie
Themes* . . . . (Columbia)
Dream Syndicate; *Days Of Wine & Roses* . . . . (Slash)
Live At Raji's . . . . (Restless)
Frank Sinatra; *Days Of Wine And Roses, Moon River, And Other Academy
Award Winners* . . . . (Reprise)
Henry Mancini; *Best Of Henry Mancini* . . . . (RCA)
Henry Mancini-Pure Gold . . . . (RCA)
Peter Gunn . . . . (RCA)
Diggin' On You
TLC; *CrazySexyCool* . . . . (LaFace)
Digging Your Scene
Blow Monkeys; *Animal Magic* . . . . (RCA)
Ding Dong The Witch Is Dead
Fifth Estate; *Dick Bartley's One-Hit Wonders Of The '60s-#2-C* . . . .(Rhino)
Meco; *The Wizard Of Oz* . . . . (Millennium)
MGM Studio Orchestra; *ST/The Wizard Of Oz* . . . . . (Sony Music Special Prod.)
Dites-Moi
Original Cast; *South Pacific* . . . . (CBS Masterworks)
Do What You Do
Jermaine Jackson; *Jermaine Jackson* . . . . (Arista)
Doctor Feelgood
Aretha Franklin; *Aretha Franklin-30 Greatest Hits* . . . .(Rhino)
Aretha's Gold . . . . (Atlantic)
Best Of Aretha Franklin . . . . (Atlantic)
I Never Loved A Man The Way I Love You . . . . (Atlantic)
Live At Fillmore West . . . . (Atlantic)

Domestic Life
John Conlee; *American Faces* . . . . (Columbia)
   Greatest Country Hits Of The '80s-1987-C . . . . (Columbia)
   More Hot Country Requests-#2-C . . . .(Epic)

Don't Be So Serious
Starpoint; *It's So Delicious* . . . . (Elektra)

Don't Worry, Baby
Beach Boys; *Absolute Best-#1* . . . . (Capitol)
   Endless Summer . . . . (Capitol)
   Fun Fun Fun . . . . (Capitol)
   Made In The U.S.A. . . . . (Capitol)

Don't Worry, Be Happy
Bobby McFerrin; *Simple Pleasures* . . . .(EMI)
   ST/Cocktail . . . . (Elektra)

Dumb
Nirvana; *In Utero* . . . . (David Geffen Co.)
   MTV Unplugged In New York . . . . (David Geffen Co.)

Ease My Mind
Arrested Development; *Zingalamaduni* . . . .(Chrysalis)

Easy
Commodores; *20 Greatest Songs In Motown History-C* . . . . (Motown)
   All The Great Love Songs-Commodores . . . . (Motown)
   Commodores . . . . (Motown)
   Commodores Greatest Hits . . . . (Motown)
   Compact Command Performances-Commodores . . . . (Motown)
   Composer-Great Love Songs By Lionel Richie . . . . (Motown)
Lionel Richie; *Back To Front* . . . . (Motown)

Easy Skanking
Bob Marley & The Wailers; *Kaya* . . . . (Tuff Gong)

Encore
Cheryl Lynn; *Preppie* . . . . (Columbia)

Enjoy The Silence
Depeche Mode; *Violator* . . . . (Sire)

Enjoy Yourself
Kylie Minogue; *Enjoy Yourself* . . . .(Geffen)

Enjoy Yourself
Guy Lombardo & His Royal Canadians; *Best Of Guy Lombardo* . . . .(MCA)

Enjoy Yourself
Jacksons; *Jacksons* . . . .(Epic)

Even If
Amel Larrieux; *Infinite Possibilities* . . . .(Epic)

Everlong
Foo Fighters; *The Colour And The Shape* . . . . (Roswell/RCA)

Every Little Thing
Beatles; *Beatles VI* . . . . (Capitol)
   Beatles-Love Songs . . . . (Capitol)
   For Sale . . . . (Capitol)

Every Time I Get Around You
David Lee Murphy; *Gettin' Out The Good Stuff* . . . .(MCA)

Everybody's Free (To Wear Sunscreen)
Baz Luhrmann; *Now That's What I Call Music!-#2-C* . . . . (Virgin)
   Something For Everybody . . . . (Capitol)

Everybody's Gonna Be Happy
Kinks; *Kinks' Greatest Hits* . . . . (Rhino)
   Kinks-Size Kinkdom . . . . (Rhino)

Everybody's Got Something To Hide Except Me And My Monkey
Beatles; *The Beatles (White Album)* . . . . (Capitol)

Everyday Is A Winding Road
Sheryl Crow; *1998 Grammy Nominees-C* . . . .(MCA)
   Sheryl Crow . . . . (A&M)

Everything Is Going To Be All Right
Paul Butterfield Blues Band; *Paul Butterfield Blues Band-Live* . . . . (Elektra)

Everything Is Kinda All Right
Charlie Daniels Band; *Night Rider* . . . .(Epic)

Everything's All Right
David Bowie; *Bowie Pin Ups* . . . . (Rykodisc)

Fallin' In Love Never Felt So Good
Mark Chesnutt; *Confessing My Love* . . . .(MCA)

Feel Right
Tanya Tucker; *Changes* . . . . (Arista)

Feel So Good
Shirley & Lee; *Best Of New Orleans Rhythm & Blues-#1-C* . . . . . . (Rhino)
   Billboard Top R&B Hits-1955-C . . . . (Rhino)
   History Of New Orleans R&B-#1-1950-1958-C . . . . (Rhino)

Feel So Good
Mase; *Harlem World* . . . . (Bad Boy/Arista)

Feel So Good
Jefferson Airplane; *30 Seconds Over Winterland* . . . . (RCA)
   Bark . . . .(Grunt)
   Flight Log (1966-1976) . . . .(Grunt)

Feelin' Good About Feelin' Bad
Patty Loveless; *When Fallen Angels Fly* . . . .(Epic)

Feelin' Satisfied
Boston; *Don't Look Back* . . . .(Epic)

Feelin' Single, Seein' Double
Emmylou Harris; *Elite Hotel* . . . . (Reprise)

Feelin' So Good
Jennifer Lopez; *On The 6* . . . . (Work)

Feels Good
Tony Toni Tone; *Revival* . . . .(Wing)

Feels Like Home
LeAnn Rimes; *Sittin' On Top Of The World* . . . . (Curb)

Feels Like Home
Bonnie Raitt; *ST/Michael* . . . . (Revolution)
Chantal Kreviazuk; *Songs From Dawson's Creek* . . . . . (Sony Music Soundtrax)
Linda Ronstadt; *Feels Like Home* . . . . (Elektra)
Randy Newman; *Guilty: 30 Years Of Randy Newman* . . . . (Rhino)
   Randy Newman's Faust . . . . (Reprise)

Feels Like Love
Vince Gill; *Let's Make Sure We Kiss Goodbye* . . . . (MCA)

Feels Like The First Time
Foreigner; *Classic Rock 1966-1988-C* . . . .(Atlantic)
   Foreigner . . . .(Atlantic)
   Records . . . .(Atlantic)

Feels So Good
Chuck Mangione; *70 Miles Young* . . . . (A&M)
   Best Of Chuck Mangione . . . . (A&M)
   Chuck Mangione-Classics-#6 . . . . (A&M)
   Evening With Magic . . . . (A&M)
   Feels So Good . . . . (A&M)

Feels So Good
Xscape; *Off The Hook* . . . . (So So Def/Columbia)

Feels So Good
Van Halen; *OU812* . . . . (Warner Bros.)

Feels So Good
Surface; *Surface* . . . . (Columbia)

Feels So Good (Show Me Your Love)
Lina Santiago; *Best Of Dance Hits Supermix-#1 & 2-C* . . . . (Warlock)
   Dance Mix USA-#5-C . . . . (Warlock)

Feels So Right
Alabama; *Alabama's Greatest Hits* . . . . (RCA)
   Feels So Right . . . . (RCA)

Fine & Dandy
Art Tatum; *Solo Masterpieces-#5* . . . . (Pablo)
Barbra Streisand; *People* . . . . (Columbia)
Chet Baker; *Out Of Nowhere* . . . . (Milestone)
Milt Jackson & Sonny Stitt; *Milt Jackson & Sonny Stitt-In The Beginning* . . . . (Galaxy)

Fine & Mellow
Billie Holiday; *Essential Billie Holiday-Carnegie Hall Concert* . . . . (Verve)
   Fine & Mellow . . . . (Collectables)
   History Of The Real Billie Holiday . . . . (Verve)

Fine Fine Day
Tony Carey; *Some Tough City* . . . . (MCA)

Fit As A Fiddle (And Ready For Love)
Fred Waring's Pennsylvanians; *The Fred Waring Memorial Album* . . . . (Viper's Nest)
   Very Best Of Fred Waring & The Pennsylvanians . . . .(Reader's Digest Music)
Gene Kelly/Donald O'Connor/The MGM Studio Orchestra; *ST/Singin' In The Rain* . . . . (Turner Classic Movies)

Flashdance…What A Feeling
Irene Cara; *ST/Flashdance* . . . . (Casablanca)

For A Change
Neal McCoy; *You Gotta Love That!* . . . .(Atlantic)

For Once In My Life
Gladys Knight & The Pips; *Gladys Knight & The Pips-Anthology* . . . . (Motown)
   Motown Superstar Series-#13-Gladys Knight & The Pips . . . . (Motown)
   Neither One Of Us . . . . (Motown)
Stevie Wonder; *Motown Story-First 25 Years-C* . . . . (Motown)
   Stevie Wonder-Love Songs-20 Classic Hits . . . . (Motown)
   Stevie Wonder's Greatest Hits-#2 . . . . (Motown)
Tony Bennett; *Tony Bennett's All-Time Greatest Hits* . . . . (Columbia)
Vikki Carr; *Best Of Vikki Carr* . . . . (EMI)

Fortunate
Maxwell; *ST/Life* . . . . (Rock Land/Interscope)

From The Vine Came The Grape
Gaylords; *X-tra Cheese-Originals By The Originals-C* . . . . (Compose)

From This Moment On
Shania Twain & Bryan White; *Come On Over* . . . . (Mercury)

Fumbling Towards Ecstasy
Sarah McLachlan; *Fumbling Towards Ecstasy* . . . . (Arista)

Funiculi, Funicula
Mario Lanza; *Legendary Tenor* . . . .(RCA)

Future's So Bright I Gotta Wear Shades
Timbuk 3; *Greetings From Timbuk 3* . . . . (I.R.S.)

Gang That Sang "Heart Of My Heart"
Four Aces; *Best Of The Four Aces* . . . . (MCA)

Get Happy
Benny Goodman; *Benny Goodman's Greatest Hits* . . . . (RCA Victor)
Ella Fitzgerald; *Harold Arlen Songbook-#2* . . . . (Verve)
Judy Garland; *Best Of Judy Garland In Hollywood* . . . . (Turner Classic Movies)
Nat Shilkret & The Victor Orchestra; *78-#22444* . . . . (Victor)

Get Off (You Fascinate Me)
Patrice Rushen; *Patrice Rushen Now* . . . . (Elektra)

Gett Off
Prince And The New Power Generation; *Diamonds And Pearls* . . . (Paisley Park)

Getting Better
Beatles; *Sgt. Pepper's Lonely Hearts Club Band*................. (Capitol)
Gimme Some Lovin'
Spencer Davis Group; *Best Of The Spencer Davis Group*.......... (EMI)
Girl's Alright With Me
Temptations; *Temptations' Greatest Hits-#1* .... (Motown)
Temptations-Anthology-The Best Of The Temptations .... (Motown)
Glad
Traffic; *John Barleycorn Must Die* .... (Island)
On The Road... (Island)
Glad All Over
Dave Clark Five; *History Of The Dave Clark Five* .... (Hollywood)
Glad All Over
Jeff Beck; *Jeff Beck Group* .... (Epic)
Glad Tidings
Van Morrison; *Moondance* .... (Warner Bros.)
Glad To Be Unhappy
Mamas & The Papas; *Mamas & The Papas-16 Of Their Greatest Hits* ... (MCA)
Glory Days
Bruce Springsteen; *Born In The U.S.A.* .... (Columbia)
Bruce Springsteen's Greatest Hits .... (Columbia)
Glory Of Love
Bette Midler; *ST/Beaches* .... (Atlantic)
Peter Cetera; *Solitude/Solitaire* .... (Full Moon)
ST/The Karate Kid Part II .... (EMI)
Glory Of Love
Velvetones; *Doo-Wop Ballads-#2-C*........................ (Rhino)
Go Deep
Janet Jackson; *Velvet Rope* ....(Virgin)
Goin' Cali
Bruce Springsteen; *Tracks*............................... (Columbia)
Gold Diggers' Song (We're In The Money)
Ginger Rogers; *Lullaby Of Broadway-The Best Of Busby Berkeley At Warner
Brothers* .... (Rhino)
Good Clean Fun
Allman Brothers Band; *Seven Turns* .... (Epic)
Good Day Sunshine
Beatles; *Beatles-Box Set* .... (Capitol)
Revolver .... (Capitol)
Good Feelin' To Know
Poco; *Good Feelin' To Know* .... (Epic)
Ride The Country .... (Epic)
Songs Of Richie Furay .... (Epic)
Very Best Of Poco .... (Epic)
Good Morning
Gene Kelly/Debbie Reynolds/Donald O'Connor; *ST/Singin' In
The Rain*................................. (Sony Music Special Prod.)
Good Morning Beautiful
Steve Holy; *Blue Moon* ....(Curb)
Good Time Man Like Me Got No Business (Singin' The Blues), A
Jim Croce; *Life & Times* .... (Lifesong)
Words And Music .... (Dunhill Compact Classics)
Good To See You
Neil Young; *Silver & Gold* ....(Reprise)
Good Vibrations
Beach Boys; *Beach Boys-Gift Set* .... (Capitol)
Billboard Top Rock 'N' Roll Hits-1966-C .... (Rhino)
Endless Summer .... (Capitol)
Good Vibrations-Thirty Years Of The Beach Boys .... (Capitol)
Smiley Smile/Wild Honey .... (Capitol)
Sunshine Dream .... (Capitol)
Got The Feeling
Jeff Beck; *Rough & Ready*............................... (Epic)
Graduation Day
Beach Boys; *Beach Boys-Gift Set* .... (Capitol)
Spirit Of America .... (Capitol)
Rover Boys; *Choice Voices! Pop Vocal Group Gems Of The
'50s-C* ....(Collector's Choice)
Groovin'
Aretha Franklin; *Lady Soul* .... (Atlantic)
Booker T. & The M.G.s; *Best Of Booker T. & The M.G.s* ..... (Atlantic)
Soul Shots#3-Soul Twist-C .... (Atlantic)
Rascals; *Groovin'* .... (Warner Special Prod.)
Hit Singles-1958-1977-C .... (Atlantic)
Rascals' Greatest Hits .... (Atlantic)
ST/Platoon .... (Atlantic)
Groovy Kind Of Love
Mindbenders; *British Rock-#3-C*......................(Original Sound)
History Of British Rock-#6-C .... (Rhino)
Phil Collins; *Phil Collins-Hits* .... (Atlantic)
Serious Hits...Live! .... (Atlantic)
H.A.P.P.Y. Radio
Edwin Starr; *The Disco Years-#5-Must Be The Music-C*......... (Rhino)
Happier Than The Morning Sun
Stevie Wonder; *Music Of My Mind* .... (Motown)
Happiest Girl In The Whole U.S.A.
Donna Fargo; *Best Of Donna Fargo* .... (Curb)
Jeanne Pruett; *Stand By Your Man* .... (Allegiance)

Happiest Song On The Jukebox
Charley Pride; *Sweet Country* .... (RCA)
Happily Ever After
Case; *Now That's What I Call Music!-#3-C* .... (Virgin)
Personal Conversation .... (Def Jam/IDJMG)
Happily Married Man
Duane Allman; *Duane Allman-An Anthology-Vol. II* ....(Capricorn)
Happiness
Pointer Sisters; *Energy*.................................(Planet)
Happiness
Vanessa Williams; *Next* ....(Mercury)
Happiness
Robert Palmer; *Don't Explain* .... (EMI)
Happiness
Soul II Soul; *Keep On Movin'* .... (Virgin)
Happiness
Billy Lawrence; *One Might Say* ....(East West)
Happiness
Original Cast; *You're A Good Man, Charlie Brown*.............. (Polydor)
Happiness Is A Warm Gun
Beatles; *The Beatles (White Album)*......................(Capitol)
Happiness Lives Next Door
Willie Nelson; *Diamonds In The Rough*....................(Delmark)
Legend Begins/Wild & Willie ....(Allegiance)
Happiness Street
Georgia Gibbs; *Best Of Georgia Gibbs-The Mercury Years* ....(Chronicles)
Happy
Rolling Stones; *Exile On Main Street*.................... (Virgin)
Love You Live .... (Virgin)
Made In The Shade .... (Rolling Stones)
Happy
Bruce Springsteen; *Tracks*..............................(Columbia)
Happy
Sister Hazel; *...Somewhere More Familiar* ....(Universal)
Happy
Michael Jackson; *Best Of Michael Jackson* ....(Motown)
Music & Me...(Motown)
Happy
Boys; *Messages From The Boys*...........................(Motown)
Happy
Sunshine Company; *Nuggets-#11-Pop-Part 4-C* ....(Rhino)
Happy
Surface; *Surface*.......................................(Columbia)
Happy Anniversary
Little River Band; *Diamantina Cocktail* ....(Capitol)
Little River Band's Greatest Hits .... (Capitol)
Happy Anniversary
Slim Whitman; *Best Of Slim Whitman-Legendary Master Series* .... (EMI)
Happy 'Cause I'm Going Home
Chicago; *Chicago At Carnegie Hall*.......................(Chicago)
Chicago III ....(Chicago)
Happy Days
Pratt & McClain; *45-#0117* .... (Reprise)
Happy Days
Talking Heads; *'77*..................................... (Sire)
Happy Days Are Here Again
Barbra Streisand; *A Happening In Central Park* ....(Columbia)
Barbra Streisand's Greatest Hits ....(Columbia)
One Voice ....(Columbia)
The Barbra Streisand Album..............................(Columbia)
Leo Reisman & His Orchestra; *Nipper's Greatest Hits Of The
'30s-#1-C* .... (RCA)
Happy Endings
Liza Minnelli & Larry Kert; *ST/New York, New York* .... (EMI)
Happy Feelin's
Maze featuring Frankie Beverly; *Lifelines-#1* ....(Capitol)
Live In New Orleans ....(Capitol)
Maze featuring Frankie Beverly ....(Capitol)
Happy Girl
Beth Nielsen Chapman; *Sand And Water* .... (Reprise)
Martina McBride; *Evolution* ....(RCA)
Happy Go Lucky Local
Duke Ellington; *20 Golden Pieces Of Duke Ellington* .... (Bulldog)
All Star Road Band-#2................................... (Doctor Jazz)
Continuum .... (Fantasy)
Great Paris Concert .... (Atlantic)
Happy Heart
Andy Williams; *Andy Williams' Greatest Hits* .... (Columbia)
Petula Clark; *Petula Clark's Greatest Hits* .... (Crescendo)
Happy House
Siouxsie And The Banshees; *Kaleidoscope* .... (Geffen)
Nocturne ....(Geffen)
Once Upon A Time-The Singles............................(Geffen)
Happy Jack
Who; *Happy Jack*.. (MCA)
Meaty Beaty Big & Bouncy .... (MCA)
ST/The Kids Are Alright .... (MCA)
Who Greatest Hits .... (MCA)

Happy Loving Couples
Joe Jackson; *Look Sharp!* . . . . (A&M)
Happy Man
Chicago; *Chicago VII* . . . .(Chicago)
Chicago's Greatest Hits-#2 (1974-81) . . . .(Chicago)
Happy Man
Greg Kihn Band; *Kihnsolidation-Best Of Greg Kihn* . . . . (Rhino)
Happy Organ
Dave "Baby" Cortez; *Billboard Top Rock 'N' Roll Hits-1959-C* . . . . . . (Rhino)
History Of Rock Instrumentals-#1-C . . . . (Rhino)
Super Oldies Of The '50s-#7-C . . . .(Audio Fidelity)
Happy Song
Box Tops; *Box Tops' Greatest Hits* . . . . (Rhino)
Happy Talk
Original Cast; *South Pacific* . . . .(CBS Masterworks)
Happy To Be Just Like I Am
Taj Mahal; *Happy To Be Just Like I Am* . . . . (Columbia)
Happy Together
Flo & Eddie And The Turtles; *History Of Flo & Eddie And The
Turtles* . . . . (Rhino)
Turtles; *Billboard Top Rock 'N' Roll Hits-1967-C* . . . . (Rhino)
Cruisin'-1967-C . . . .(Increase)
Happy Together . . . . (Rhino)
Turtles-20 Greatest Hits . . . . (Rhino)
Turtlesized . . . . (Rhino)
Happy Trails
Michael Martin Murphey; *Cowboy Songs* . . . . (Warner Western)
Original Soundtrack; *Television's Greatest Hits-#1-C* . . . . (TVT)
Quicksilver Messenger Service; *Sons Of Mercury* . . . . (Rhino)
Randy Travis & Roy Rogers; *Heroes And Friends* . . . .(Warner Bros.)
Riders In The Sky; *Cowboy Way* . . . .(MCA)
Roy Rogers/Dale Evans/Dusty Rogers; *Roy Rogers Tribute-C* . . . . (RCA)
Van Halen; *Diver Down* . . . .(Warner Bros.)
Happy Wanderer
Frank Weir & His Orchestra; *Hits To Remember-C* . . . (PolyGram Special Prod.)
Joey Miskulin; *Hooked On Polkas* . . . . (K-Tel)
Original Soundtrack; *Disney Travel Songs-C* . . . .(Disney)
Hard Day's Night, A
Beatles; *Beatles 1* . . . . (Capitol)
Beatles-20 Greatest Hits . . . . (Capitol)
ST/A Hard Day's Night . . . . (Capitol)
The Beatles At The Hollywood Bowl . . . . (Capitol)
The Beatles/1962-1966 . . . . (Capitol)
Heaven On Earth
Platters; *Encore Of Golden Hits-Platters* . . . . (Mercury)
Platters-16 Greatest Hits . . . . (Trip)
Platters-Anthology . . . . (Rhino)
Red Sails In The Sunset . . . .(Allegiance)
Hi Hi Hi
Wings; *Wings Greatest* . . . . (Capitol)
High Cotton
Alabama; *Southern Star* . . . . (RCA)
High Enough
Damn Yankees; *Damn Yankees* . . . .(Warner Bros.)
High On Emotion
Chris DeBurgh; *Man On The Line* . . . . (A&M)
High On Love
Patty Loveless; *Long Stretch Of Lonesome* . . . .(Epic)
High On Love
Foghat; *Stone Blue* . . . . (Rhino)
High On Sunshine
Commodores; *Hot On The Tracks* . . . . (Motown)
High On You
Survivor; *Vital Signs* . . . . (Scotti Bros.)
High On Your Love Suite/One Mo Hit
Rick James; *Bustin' Out Of L Seven* . . . . (Gordy)
High Times
Jamiroquai; *Traveling Without Moving* . . . . (Work/Epic)
Higher
Creed; *Human Clay* . . . . (Wind-up)
Higher Ground
Stevie Wonder; *Innervisions* . . . . (Motown)
Original Musiquarium . . . . (Motown)
Higher Love
Steve Winwood; *Back In The High Life* . . . . (Island)
Steve Winwood-Chronicles . . . . (Island)
His Eye Is On The Sparrow
Carmen McRae; *Greatest Of Carmen McRae* . . . .(MCA)
Marvin Gaye; *Musical Testament 1964-1984* . . . . (Motown)
Preservation Hall Jazz Band; *Best Of The Preservation Hall
Jazz Band* . . . . (Columbia)
Soundtrack; *Streetcar Named Desire* . . . .(Allegiance)
Hold What You've Got
Joe Tex; *Atlantic Ultimate '60s Soul Smashes!-C* . . . . (Rhino)
Very Best Of Joe Tex . . . . (Rhino)
Honey
Mariah Carey; *Butterfly* . . . . (Columbia)
Honeymooners
Bruce Springsteen; *Tracks* . . . . (Columbia)

Hoop-Dee-Doo
Perry Como; *Perry Como's Greatest Hits* . . . .(RCA)
Hot Diggity (Dog Ziggity Boom)
Perry Como; *Como's Golden Records* . . . . (RCA)
Nipper's Greatest Hits Of The '50s-#2-C . . . . (RCA)
Perry Como-Pure Gold . . . . (RCA)
Perry Como's All-Time Greatest Hits-#1 . . . . (RCA)
This Is Perry Como . . . . (RCA)
Hotel Happiness
Brook Benton; *Brook Benton-Anthology* . . . . (Rhino)
It's Just A Matter Of Time-His Greatest Hits . . . . (Mercury)
Super Oldies Of The '60s-#11-C . . . . (Audio Fidelity)
How Was I To Know
John Michael Montgomery; *What I Do The Best* . . . .(Atlantic)
Hundred And Sixty Acres
Marty Robbins; *Gunfighter Ballads & Trail Songs* . . . . (Legacy)
Hungry (For Those Good Things)
Paul Revere And The Raiders; *Best Of Paul Revere And The
Raiders-#1* . . . .(Bac-Trac)
Frat Rock!-C . . . . (Rhino)
Legend Of Paul Revere And The Raiders . . . . (Columbia)
Paul Revere And The Raiders' Greatest Hits . . . . (Columbia)
Hurts So Good
John Cougar; *American Fool* . . . . (Riva)
I Am Going To Like It Here
Original Cast; *ST/Flower Drum Song* . . . .(Sony Music Classical)
I Can't Be Satisfied
Muddy Waters; *Best Of Muddy Waters* . . . . (Chess)
Hard Again . . . .(Blue Sky)
The Chess Box-Muddy Waters . . . . (Chess)
I Can't Be Satisfied
Rolling Stones; *More Hot Rocks (big hits & fazed cookies)* . . . .(Abkco)
I Can't Be Satisfied
Bee Gees; *Spirits Having Flown* . . . . (Polydor)
I Could Not Ask For More
Edwin McCain; *Messenger* . . . . (Lava)
I Enjoy Being A Girl
Original Cast; *Flower Drum Song* . . . .(Sony Music Classical)
I Feel Fine
Beatles; *Beatles 1* . . . . (Capitol)
Beatles '65 . . . . (Capitol)
Beatles-20 Greatest Hits . . . . (Capitol)
Past Masters-Volume One . . . . (Parlophone)
The Beatles/1962-1966 . . . . (Capitol)
Sweethearts Of The Rodeo; *One Time One Night* . . . . (Columbia)
I Feel For You
Chaka Khan; *I Feel For You* . . . .(Warner Bros.)
Life Is A Dance/The Remix Project . . . .(Warner Bros.)
Prince; *Prince* . . . .(Warner Bros.)
I Feel Pretty
Julie Andrews; *A Little Bit Of Broadway* . . . .(Columbia)
Little Richard; *The Songs Of West Side Story* . . . . (RCA Victor)
Original Cast; *ST/West Side Story* . . . . (Sony Broadway)
I Feel The Earth Move
Carole King; *Carole King's Greatest Hits* . . . . (Epic)
Tapestry . . . . (Epic)
I Got Rhythm
Ella Fitzgerald; *George & Ira Gershwin Songbook* . . . . (Verve)
Ethel Waters; *I Got Rhythm: The Smithsonian George Gershwin
Collection-C* . . . . (Smithsonian Collection)
Happenings; *'60s Rock Classics-#1-C* . . . . (Rhino)
Judy Garland; *Judy Garland-Collector's Items-1936-1945* . . . . (MCA)
Louis Armstrong; *Essential Louis Armstrong* . . . . (Verve)
Original Cast; *Girl Crazy* . . . . (Nonesuch)
Original London Cast; *Crazy For You* . . . . (RCA)
Robert Palmer; *Glory Of Gershwin Featuring Larry Adler-C* . . . . (Mercury)
I Got The Sun In The Morning
Ethel Merman/Bruce Yarnell/Original Cast; *Annie Get
Your Gun* . . . . (RCA Victor)
Ethel Merman/Ray Middleton/Original Cast; *Annie Get Your Gun* . . . . . (MCA)
Original Broadway Cast; *Annie Get Your Gun* . . . . (Angel)
I Got You (I Feel Good)
James Brown; *James Brown's 20 All Time Greatest Hits!* . . . .(Polydor)
Live At The Apollo . . . .(Polydor)
ST/Good Morning, Vietnam . . . . (A&M)
Very Best Of James Brown . . . .(Polydor)
I Had A Beautiful Time
Merle Haggard; *19 Hot Country Requests-#3-C* . . . . (Epic)
Friend In California . . . . (Epic)
Greatest Country Hits Of The '80s-1986-C . . . . (Columbia)
I Just Want to Satisfy You
O'Jays; *My Favorite Person/Year 2000* . . . . (Right Stuff)
I Like Ev'rybody
Original Broadway Cast; *The Most Happy Fella* . . . .(Sony Music Classical)
I Like It
Gerry And The Pacemakers; *Best Of Gerry And The Pacemakers* . . . . . . (EMI)
History Of British Rock-#2-C . . . . (Rhino)
I Like It
Blackout Allstars; *I Like It Like That-#1* . . . . (Columbia)

I Like It
Sammie; *From The Bottom To The Top* . . . . (Freeworld/Capitol)
I Like It
DeBarge; *All This Love* . . . . (Motown)
   DeBarge's Greatest Hits. . . . . (Motown)
I Like It
Brand New Heavies; *ST/Love Jones* . . . . (Columbia)
I Like It, I Love It
Tim McGraw; *All I Want* . . . . (Curb)
   Tim McGraw's Greatest Hits. . . . . (Curb)
I Said A Prayer
Pam Tillis; *Every Time* . . . . (Arista)
I Saved The World Today
Eurythmics; *Peace.* . . . . (Arista)
I Saw The Light
Hank Williams; *Hank Williams-24 Greatest Hits-#2* . . . . (Polydor)
   Hank Williams-40 Greatest Hits. . . . . (Polydor)
   I Ain't Got Nothin' But Time-1946-1947 . . . . (Polydor)
   Legend In Song-With Hank Williams, Jr. . . . . (Polydor)
   Rare Takes & Radio Cuts . . . . (Polydor)
I Want To Spread A Little Sunshine
Jack Norworth; *Music From The New York Stage (1890-1920)-#4-1917-1920-C .* . . . . (Pearl)
I Want To Take You Higher
Ike & Tina Turner; *Proud Mary-Best Of Ike & Tina Turner* . . . . (EMI)
Sly & The Family Stone; *Sly & The Family Stone-Anthology* . . . . . (Epic)
   Sly & The Family Stone's Greatest Hits. . . . . (Epic)
I Whistle A Happy Tune
Barbara Cook; *My Little Broadway* . . . . (Sony Wonder)
Frank Sinatra; *Frank Sinatra Sings Rodgers & Hammerstein* . . . . . . (Columbia)
Micky Dolenz; *Broadway Micky* . . . . (Kid Rhino/Rhino 4 Kids)
Original Broadway Cast; *The King And I* . . . . (RCA Victor)
Original Cast; *The King And I* . . . . (MCA)
I Wish I Could Have Been There
John Anderson; *Solid Ground* . . . . (BNA)
I Wouldn't Have It Any Other Way
Aaron Tippin; *Read Between The Lines.* . . . . (RCA)
Pirates Of The Mississippi; *Walk The Plank* . . . . (Liberty)
I'd Like That
XTC; *Homespun* . . . . (Idea/TVT)
If I Were A Bell
Original Cast; *Guys & Dolls* . . . . (MCA)
If I Were A Bell
Teena Marie; *Ivory* . . . . (Epic)
If It Makes You Happy
Sheryl Crow; *Sheryl Crow.* . . . . (A&M)
If You Wanna Be Happy
Jimmy Soul; *Best Of Jimmy Soul* . . . . (Rhino)
   Dick Bartley's One-Hit Wonders Of The '60s-#1-C . . . . (Rhino)
   Son Of Frat Rock!-C . . . . (Rhino)
   ST/Mermaids . . . . (Geffen)
   ST/My Best Friend's Wedding . . . . (Work/Epic)
If You're Happy & You Know It
Original Soundtrack; *Children's Favorites* . . . . (Kid Rhino/Rhino 4 Kids)
I'll Be Glad When You're Dead (You Rascal You)
Cab Calloway; *Jazz Heritage: Mr. Hi-De-Ho* . . . . (MCA)
I'll Keep You Satisfied
Billy J. Kramer With The Dakotas; *History Of British Rock-#2-C* . . . . . . (Rhino)
I'm Alright
Little Anthony And The Imperials; *Best Of Little Anthony And The Imperials.* . . . . (Rhino)
   Forever Yours. . . . . (Roulette)
   Tears On My Pillow . . . . (Accord)
I'm Alright
Rolling Stones; *got Live if you want it!* . . . . (Abkco)
   Out Of Our Heads . . . . (Abkco)
I'm Alright
Jo Dee Messina; *I'm Alright* . . . . (Curb)
I'm Alright
Kenny Loggins; *Kenny Loggins Alive* . . . . (Columbia)
   ST/Caddyshack. . . . . (Columbia)
I'm Feeling Fine
Head East; *Head East* . . . . (A&M)
   Head East-Live . . . . (A&M)
I'm Flying
Original Cast/Mary Martin; *Peter Pan-The 1954 Broadway Production* . . . . (RCA Victor)
I'm From The Country
Tracy Byrd; *I'm From The Country.* . . . . (MCA)
I'm Glad There Is You
Jimmy Dorsey & His Orchestra; *Then & Now-Fabulous New Jimmy Dorsey & His Orchestra.* . . . . (Atlantic)
Morgana King; *Stretchin' Out.* . . . . (Muse)
Peggy Lee; *Best Of Peggy Lee.* . . . . (MCA)
I'm Happy Just To Dance With You
Anne Murray; *Somebody's Waiting.* . . . . (Capitol)
Beatles; *Something New.* . . . . (Capitol)
   ST/A Hard Day's Night. . . . . (Capitol)

I'm In Love Again
George Morgan; *Room Full Of Roses-The George Morgan Collection* . . . . (Razor & Tie)
I'm Not Gonna Let It Bother Me Tonight
Atlanta Rhythm Section; *Are You Ready!* . . . . (Polydor)
   Champagne Jam . . . . (Polydor)
I'm Overjoyed
Nona Gaye; *Love For The Future* . . . . (Third Stone)
I'm Satisfied
Mississippi John Hurt; *Satisfied* . . . . (Intermedia)
   Today! . . . . (Vanguard)
I'm Satisfied
Bee Gees; *Spirits Having Flown* . . . . (Polydor)
I'm Satisfied With You
Hank Williams; *Complete Hank Williams* . . . . (Mercury)
   Lovesick Blues . . . . (ASV)
I'm Sitting On Top Of The World
Al Jolson; *Jolson Sang 'Em* . . . . (Biograph)
   The Al Jolson Story-#3 . . . . (MCA)
I'm So Excited
Pointer Sisters; *Break Out* . . . . (Planet)
I'm So Glad
Cream; *Fresh Cream* . . . . (Polydor)
   Goodbye . . . . (Polydor)
I'm So Happy I Can't Stop Crying
Sting; *Mercury Falling.* . . . . (A&M)
Toby Keith with Sting; *Dream Walkin'* . . . . (Mercury)
   Toby Keith's Greatest Hits, Volume One. . . . . (Mercury)
In The Mood
Andrews Sisters; *Andrews Sisters-16 Great Performances* . . . . (MCA)
   Boogie Woogie Bugle Girls . . . . (MCA)
   Chesterfield Broadcasts-#1 . . . . (RCA Victor)
Bette Midler; *Bette Midler* . . . . (Atlantic)
   Live At Last . . . . (Atlantic)
Glenn Miller; *Best Of Glenn Miller* . . . . (RCA)
   Glenn Miller-A Legendary Performer-#1 & 2. . . . . (Bluebird)
   The Glenn Miller Story . . . . (RCA)
Glenn Miller & His Orchestra; *Glenn Miller & His Orchestra-Pure Gold.* . . . . (Bluebird)
   The Unforgettable Glenn Miller & His Orchestra. . . . . (RCA)
Island In The Sun
Weezer; *Weezer 2001.* . . . . (Geffen)
It Feels So Good
Sonique; *Hear My Cry* . . . . (Republic/Universal)
   Now That's What I Call Music!-#4-C . . . . (Virgin)
It Was A Very Good Year
Frank Sinatra; *Frank Sinatra-The Very Good Years* . . . . (Reprise)
   September Of My Years . . . . (Reprise)
   The Reprise Collection . . . . (Reprise)
   The Sopranos-Music From The HBO Original Series . . . . (Sony Music Soundtrax)
Frank Sinatra with Count Basie & The Orchestra; *Sinatra At The Sands.* . . . . (Reprise)
Itchycoo Park
Small Faces; *Baby Boomer Classics-British Sixties-C* . . . . . . (JCI Assoc. Labels)
It's A Great Day To Be Alive
Travis Tritt; *Down The Road I Go* . . . . (Columbia)
It's A Hap-Hap-Happy Day
Dick Todd; *Dick Todd: The Canadian Crosby-His Greatest Recordings* . . . . (Living Era)
It's De-Lovely
Ella Fitzgerald; *Cole Porter Songbook.* . . . . (Verve)
Mabel Mercer; *Mabel Mercer Sings Cole Porter.* . . . . (Verve)
Sarah Vaughan; *Sarah Vaughan Sings Broadway.* . . . . (Verve)
It's Ecstasy When You Lay Down Next To Me
Barry White; *Barry White Sings For Someone You Love* . . . . . (20th Century Fox)
   Barry White's All-Time Greatest Hits. . . . . (Mercury)
It's Gonna Be Alright
Gerry And The Pacemakers; *Best Of Gerry And The Pacemakers* . . . . (EMI)
   History Of British Rock-#3-C . . . . (Rhino)
It's Gonna Be Alright
Ruby Turner; *Paradise.* . . . . (Jive)
It's Gonna Work Out Fine
Ike & Tina Turner; *Proud Mary-Best Of Ike & Tina Turner* . . . . (EMI)
   River Deep-Mountain High. . . . . (A&M)
   Super Oldies Of The '60s-#3-C . . . . (Audio Fidelity)
It's Good To Be King
Tom Petty; *Wildflowers* . . . . (Warner Bros.)
It's Wonderful
Rascals; *Nuggets-#8-Acid Rock-C* . . . . (Rhino)
   Once Upon A Time . . . . (Rhino)
   Rascals' Greatest Hits. . . . . (Atlantic)
I've Been Lonely Too Long
Rascals; *Rascals-Anthology 1965-1972.* . . . . (Rhino)
   Very Best Of The Rascals . . . . (Rhino)
I've Got The World On A String
Count Basie; *Standards.* . . . . (Verve)
Diana Krall; *Only Trust Your Heart.* . . . . (GRP)
Ella Fitzgerald; *Harold Arlen Songbook-#1.* . . . . (Verve)

Frank Sinatra; *Capitol Collectors Series-Frank Sinatra* . . . . (Capitol)
Frank Sinatra & Liza Minnelli; *Frank Sinatra-Duets-C* . . . . (Capitol)
Sarah Vaughan; *Best Of Sarah Vaughan* . . . . (Pablo)
Stephane Grappelli & Martin Taylor; *We've Got The World On A
  String* . . . . (Angel)

Jackie Wilson Said (I'm In Heaven When You Smile)
Van Morrison; *Best Of Van Morrison* . . . . (Polydor)
  St. Dominic's Preview . . . . (Warner Bros.)
  ST/Queen's Logic . . . . (Epic)

Joy
Marvin Gaye; *Midnight Love* . . . . (Columbia)
  Midnight Love & The Sexual Healing Sessions . . . . (Legacy)

Joy
Blackstreet; *Blackstreet* . . . . (Interscope)

Joy
Nilsson; *Son Of Schmilsson* . . . . (RCA)

Joy And Pain
Maze & Kurtis Blow; *Lifelines-#1* . . . . (Capitol)
Maze featuring Frankie Beverly; *Live In Los Angeles* . . . . (Capitol)
  Live In New Orleans . . . . (Capitol)

Joy And Pain
Donna Allen; *Heaven On Earth* . . . . (Oceana)

Joy And Pain
Rob Base & D.J. EZ-Rock; *It Takes Two* . . . . (Profile)

Joy Comes In The Morning
Oak Ridge Boys; *All Our Favorite Songs* . . . . (Columbia)

Joy Inside My Tears
Stevie Wonder; *Songs In The Key Of Life* . . . . (Motown)

Joy To The World
Three Dog Night; *Best Of Three Dog Night* . . . . (MCA)
  Good Feeling Music Of The Big Chill Generation-#2-C . . . . . . (Motown)
  Good Feeling Music Of The Big Chill Generation-#3-C . . . . . . (Motown)
  Joy To The World-Greatest Hits . . . . (MCA)
  ST/Big Chill . . . . (Motown)
  ST/Forrest Gump . . . . (Epic/Sony Music Soundtrax)

Joy-Pt. 1
Isaac Hayes; *Best Of Isaac Hayes-#2* . . . . (Stax)
  Enterprise-His Greatest Hits . . . . (Stax)
  Isaac Hayes' Greatest Hit Singles . . . . (Stax)
  Joy . . . . (Stax)

Jubilation
Paul Anka; *Jubilation* . . . . (Garland)
  My Way . . . . (Fifty One West)
  Very Best Of Paul Anka . . . . (Ranwood)

Just Another Day In Paradise
Phil Vassar; *Phil Vassar* . . . . (Arista)

Just To Satisfy You
Hank Williams, Jr.; *Pure Hank* . . . . (WB/Curb)
Waylon Jennings & Willie Nelson; *Best Of Waylon Jennings* . . . . (RCA)
  Collector's Series-Duets-C . . . . (RCA)
  Waylon And Company . . . . (RCA)

Keep It Gay
Original Cast; *Me & Juliet* . . . . (RCA Victor)

Keep The Customer Satisfied
Simon & Garfunkel; *Bridge Over Troubled Water* . . . . (Columbia)
  Collected Works . . . . (Columbia)

Keepin' My Lover Satisfied
Melba Moore; *Never Say Never* . . . . (Capitol)

Kicking Back In Amsterdam
Kevin Welch; *Life Down Here On Earth* . . . . (Dead Reckoning)

Kiss An Angel Good Mornin'
Charley Pride; *Charley Pride-24 Greatest Hits* . . . . (Tee Vee)
  Pride! My 6 Latest And 6 Greatest . . . . (ISD/Intersound)
  The Ultimate Charley Pride . . . . (Bransounds)

Kisses Sweeter Than Wine
Jimmie Rodgers; *Best Of Jimmie Rodgers* . . . . (Rhino)
  Cruisin'-1958-C . . . . (Increase)
Weavers; *Best Of The Weavers* . . . . (MCA)
  Reunion-At Carnegie Hall-1963 . . . . (Vanguard)
  Weavers At Carnegie Hall . . . . (Vanguard)
  Weavers' Greatest Hits . . . . (Vanguard)

Lady (You Bring Me Up)
Commodores; *All The Great Love Songs-Commodores* . . . . (Motown)
  Commodores-All The Great Hits . . . . (Motown)
  Compact Command Performances-Commodores . . . . (Motown)

Land Of The Living
Pam Tillis; *Pam Tillis' Greatest Hits* . . . . (Arista)

Last Laugh
Mark Knopfler; *Sailing To Philadelphia* . . . . (Warner Bros.)

Let Me Sing & I'm Happy
Al Jolson; *Best Of Al Jolson* . . . . (MCA)
  The Al Jolson Story-#3 . . . . (MCA)

Let The Good Times Roll
Barbra Streisand; *Butterfly* . . . . (Columbia)
Betty Everett & Jerry Butler; *Delicious Together* . . . . (Vee-Jay)
  Starring Betty Everett . . . . (Tradition)
Bobby Bland & B.B. King; *Together Again Live* . . . . (MCA)
Jerry Lee Lewis; *Golden Rock & Roll* . . . . (Sun)
Louis Jordan; *Best Of Louis Jordan* . . . . (MCA)

Molly Hatchet; *Flirtin' With Disaster* . . . . (Epic)
Nilsson; *Nilsson Schmilsson* . . . . (RCA)
Phoebe Snow; *Phoebe Snow* . . . . (MCA)
Ray Charles; *Genius Of Ray Charles* . . . . (Atlantic)
Shirley & Lee; *Billboard Top R&B Hits-1956-C* . . . . (Rhino)
  History Of New Orleans R&B-#1-1950-1958-C . . . . (Rhino)
  ST/Stand By Me . . . . (Atlantic)
  Super Oldies Of The '50s-#4-C . . . . (Audio Fidelity)
Tony Bennett with B.B. King; *Playin' With My Friends-Bennett Sings The
  Blues-C* . . . . (Columbia)

Let The Rest Of The World Go By
Mitch Miller; *Sing Along With Mitch* . . . . (Columbia)
Mom & Dads; *Down The River Of Golden Dreams* . . . . (Crescendo)

Let's Chill
Guy; *Future* . . . . (Uptown/MCA)

Let's Go All The Way
Norma Jean; *Best Of Norma Jean* . . . . (Collector's Choice)

Let's Think About Living
Bob Luman; *Bob Luman-Classic Country* . . . . (Simitar)

Life Is Beautiful
Amy Correia; *Carnival Love* . . . . (Capitol)

Life Is Happiness Indeed
Original Cast; *Candide* . . . . (Columbia)

Life's Been Good
Eagles; *Eagles Live* . . . . (Asylum)
Joe Walsh; *But Seriously Folks* . . . . (Asylum)
  ST/FM . . . . (MCA)

Lift Me Up
Yes; *Union* . . . . (Arista)

Light Up
Styx; *Equinox* . . . . (A&M)

Little Bit Of Happiness
New Christy Minstrels; *New Christy Minstrels' Greatest Hits* . . . . . (Columbia)

Little Bitty
Alan Jackson; *Everything I Love* . . . . (Arista)
Tom T. Hall; *Songs From Sopchoppy* . . . . (Mercury)
  Tom T. Hall-The Hits . . . . (Mercury)

Long Live Our Love
Shangri-Las; *Best Of The Shangri-Las* . . . . (Mercury)

Look At That
Paul Simon; *You're The One* . . . . (Warner Bros.)

Look For The Silver Lining
Alberta Hunter; *Look For The Silver Lining* . . . . (Columbia)
Chet Baker; *Let's Get Lost-Best Of Chet Baker Sings* . . . . (Blue Note)
Dave Brubeck Quartet; *Stardust* . . . . (Fantasy)
Judy Garland; *Best Of Judy Garland In Hollywood* . . . . (Turner Classic Movies)
Marion Harris; *78-#3367* . . . . (Columbia)

Lotus
R.E.M.; *Up* . . . . (Warner Bros.)

Louisiana Hayride
Boswell Sisters; *That's How Rhythm Was Born* . . . . (Legacy)

Love & Happiness
Al Green; *I'm Still In Love With You* . . . . (Right Stuff)
  Tokyo...Live . . . . (Right Stuff)

Love & Happiness
Living Colour; *Biscuits* . . . . (Epic)

Love & Happiness
John Mellencamp; *Whenever We Wanted* . . . . (Mercury)

Love (Can Make You Happy)
Mercy; *Super Oldies Of The '60s-#10-C* . . . . (Audio Fidelity)
  WCBS FM 101 History Of Rock-'60s-#2-C . . . . (Collectables)

Love Can Take Us All The Way
Jack Wagner & Valerie Carter; *Lighting Up The Night* . . . . (Qwest)

Love Is A Wonderful Thing
Michael Bolton; *Time, Love & Tenderness* . . . . (Columbia)

Love Is Alive
Judds; *Collector's Series-The Judds* . . . . (RCA)
  Judds' Greatest Hits . . . . (MCA)
  Why Not Me . . . . (MCA)

Love Is The Seventh Wave
Sting; *Dream Of The Blue Turtles* . . . . (A&M)
  Greenpeace/Rainbow Warriors-C . . . . (Geffen)

Love Walked In
Chet Baker; *Chet Baker With Strings* . . . . (Columbia)
Frank Sinatra; *Sinatra Swings* . . . . (Reprise)
  The Reprise Collection . . . . (Reprise)
Sarah Vaughan; *Complete Sarah Vaughan On Mercury-#2* . . . . . (Mercury)

Love Working On You
John Michael Montgomery; *Leave A Mark* . . . . (Atlantic)

Love You Down
INOJ; *So So Def Bass All-Stars-#2-C* . . . . (So So Def/Columbia)
  Total Dance Explosion-C . . . . (Columbia)

Lovely Night, A
Julie Andrews; *A Little Bit Of Broadway* . . . . (Columbia)
Julie Andrews/Original Cast; *Cinderella-The CBS Television
  Production* . . . . (Columbia)

Love's Gonna Live Here
Buck Owens; *Billboard Top Country Hits-1963-C* . . . . (Rhino)

Buck Owens' All-Time Greatest Hits-#2.....................(Curb)
Buck Owens & The Buckaroos; *Buck Owens & The Buckaroos-Live At
Carnegie Hall* ....(Country Music Foundation)

Lovin' What Your Lovin' Does To Me
Conway Twitty & Loretta Lynn; *Conway Twittty-20 Greatest Hits* ..... (MCA)

Luckenbach Texas (Back To The Basics Of Love)
Waylon Jennings; *Ol' Waylon* ....(RCA)
Stars Are Out In Texas-C ....(RCA)
Waylon Jennings' Greatest Hits ....(RCA)

Lucky Man
Verve; *Urban Hymns*...................................... (Hut/Virgin)

Lucky One
Alison Krauss & Union Station; *New Favorite* ....(Rounder)

Make Someone Happy
Stevie Wonder; *With A Song In My Heart* ....(Motown)

Make Someone Happy
Tower Of Power; *Ain't Nothin' Stoppin' Us Now* ....(Columbia)

Make You Happy
Celine Dion; *Falling Into You* .... (550 Music)

Make You Happy
Trey Lorenz; *ST/Men In Black*. ....(Columbia)

Makin' Happy
Crystal Waters; *Surprise* .... (Mercury)

Mellow
Elton John; *Honky Chateau* .... (Rocket)

Mellow Down Easy
Paul Butterfield Blues Band; *Golden Butter* ....(Elektra)
Greatest Folksingers Of The '60s-C ....(Vanguard)
Paul Butterfield Blues Band ....(Elektra)

Memory
Original Broadway Cast; *Cats* .... (Geffen)

Mint Car
Cure; *Wild Mood Swings* .... (Elektra)

Mocking Bird Hill
Patti Page; *Patti Page-16 Most Requested Songs* ....(Legacy)
Patti Page-Golden Hits......................................(Mercury)
Patti Page's Greatest Hits ....(Columbia)
Russ Morgan; *Best Of Russ Morgan* .... (MCA)

Most Beautiful Girl In The World
Frank Sinatra; *Strangers In The Night* ....(Reprise)
Tony Bennett; *Rodgers & Hart Songbook* ....(DRG)
Tony Bennett Sings More Great Rodgers & Hart ....(Improv)

Most Happy Fella
Broadway Cast; *Most Happy Fella* ....(RCA)
Original Broadway Cast; *Most Happy Fella* ....(Sony Music Classical)

Mota
Offspring; *Ixnay On The Hombre* ....(Columbia)

Motorcycle Cowboy
Merle Haggard; *Merle Haggard-Live At Billy Bob's*............ (Razor & Tie)

Music
Erick Sermon featuring Marvin Gaye; *Music* .... (J)
ST/What's The Worst That Can Happen? .... (Bad Boy/Arista)

My Blue Heaven
Artie Shaw; *Complete Artie Shaw-#4* ....(RCA)
This Is Artie Shaw ....(Bluebird)
Fats Domino; *Fats Domino-Legendary Masters* ....(United Artists)
Fats Domino's Greatest Hits ....(Everest)
My Blue Heaven-Best Of Fats Domino-#1 ....(EMI)
Oldies But Goodies-#10-C.............................(Original Sound)
Frank Sinatra; *Frank Sinatra-Gift Set* ....(Capitol)
Sinatra's Swingin' Session!!! ....(Capitol)

My Favorite Things
Andy Williams; *Merry Christmas* ....(Columbia)
Barbra Streisand; *Barbra Streisand Christmas Album* ....(Columbia)
Betty Carter; *Compact Jazz-Betty Carter* ....(Verve)
Diana Ross & The Supremes; *Merry Christmas* ....(Motown)
Motown Christmas Album-C ....(Motown)
Herb Alpert & The Tijuana Brass; *Herb Alpert & The Tijuana Brass
Christmas Album* .... (A&M)
John Coltrane; *Best Of John Coltrane* ....(Atlantic)
Johnny Mathis; *Give Me Your Love For Christmas*. ....(Columbia)
Julie Andrews; *ST/The Sound Of Music*. ....(RCA)
Kenny Rogers; *Kenny Rogers-Christmas* ....(EMI)
Lorrie Morgan; *Merry Christmas From London* ....(BNA)

My First Night With You
Mya; *Mya* .... (University/Interscope)

My Happiness
Andy Williams; *Unchained Melody-Greatest Songs*.................(Curb)
Connie Francis; *Very Best Of Connie Francis* ....(Polydor)
Elvis Presley; *The Great Performances*..........................(RCA)
Jim Reeves; *Jim Reeves-Pure Gold* ....(RCA)
Pied Pipers; *Capitol Collectors Series-Pied Pipers*..............(Capitol)

My Old Man
Joni Mitchell; *Blue*...(Reprise)

My Wonderful
Jessica Simpson; *Sweet Kisses*. ....(Columbia)

Natural High
Bloodstone; *Bloodstone's Greatest Hits* ....(T-Neck/Columbia)

Didn't It Blow Your Mind: Soul Hits Of The '70s-#11-C...........(Rhino)

Natural High
Merle Haggard & Janie Fricke; *For The Record: Merle Haggard-43
Legendary Hits* .... (BNA)

Neon Rainbow
Box Tops; *Box Tops' Greatest Hits* ....(Rhino)

Never Ending
Wood; *Songs From Stamford Hill* ....(Columbia)

New Attitude
Patti LaBelle; *Classic Soul-C*................................. (MCA)
I Am Woman-C .... (Nick At Nite)
Soundtrack Smashes-'80s & More-C .... (MCA)
ST/Beverly Hills Cop .... (MCA)

New Orleans Joys
Butch Thompson; *New Orleans Joys* .... (Daring)

New Soldiers Joy
Kentucky Colonels featuring Roland & Clarence White; *1965-1967* ..(Rounder)

Nice Work If You Can Get It
Billie Holiday; *Compact Jazz-Billie Holiday* ....(Verve)
Carmen McRae; *Greatest Of Carmen McRae* .... (MCA)
Ella Fitzgerald; *George & Ira Gershwin Songbook* ....(Verve)
Frank Sinatra; *My Kind Of Broadway* ....(Reprise)
Original Cast; *My One And Only* ....(Atlantic)
Sting; *Glory Of Gershwin Featuring Larry Adler-C* ....(Mercury)

O What A Thrill
Mavericks; *What A Crying Shame* .... (MCA)

Ob-La-Di, Ob-La-Da
Beatles; *Beatles-Box Set* ....(Capitol)
The Beatles (White Album) ....(Capitol)
The Beatles/1967-1970 ....(Capitol)

Oh Fab, I'm Glad (Fab Laundry Detergent)
Original Soundtrack; *TeeVee Toons-The Commercials-#1-C* ....(TVT)

Oh Happy Day
Edwin Hawkins Singers; *Didn't It Blow Your Mind: Soul Hits Of The
'70s-#1-C* ....(Rhino)
Super Hits-#3-C ....(Gusto)
Five Satins; *Five Satins Sing Their Greatest Hits*............(Collectables)

Oh Happy Day
Lawrence Welk; *Champagne Music Of Lawrence Welk* ....(Universal)

Oh How Happy
Shades Of Blue; *Oldies But Goodies-#2-C* .... (Original Sound)

Oh Marie
Sheryl Crow; *Sheryl Crow* ....(A&M)

Oh, What A Beautiful Morning
Original Broadway Cast; *Oklahoma!* ....(RCA)
Original Cast; *Oklahoma!* .... (MCA)

Old King Cole
Original Soundtrack; *Children's Favorites* .... (Kid Rhino/Rhino 4 Kids)

On The Street Where You Live
Andy Williams; *Andy Williams-16 Most Requested Songs-Encore!* ....(Legacy)
Bobby Darin; *Unreleased Capitol Sides* ....(Collector's Choice)
Eddie Fisher; *Very Best Of Eddie Fisher* ....(Taragon)
Four Tops; *Lost & Found: Breaking Through* ....(Motown)
Harry Connick, Jr.; *25* ....(Columbia)
Mel Torme; *Swings Shubert Alley* ....(Verve)
Original Cast; *My Fair Lady* ....(Columbia)
Ray Conniff; *'S Awful Nice* ....(Columbia)

On The Sunny Side Of The Street
Diana Krall; *Stepping Out* .... (Justin Time)
Frank Sinatra; *Come Swing With Me!* ....(Capitol)
One More For The Road ....(Capitol)
Sentimental Journey ....(Capitol)
The Capitol Years ....(Capitol)
Judy Garland; *Best Of Judy Garland* .... (MCA)
Louis Armstrong; *Best Of Louis Armstrong*..................... (MCA)
Chicago Concert 1956 ....(Columbia)
Jazz Club-Vocal ....(Verve)
Music Autobiography .... (MCA)
Ted Lewis & His Orchestra; *Charming Gents Of Stage & Screen-C* ....(Legacy)
Those Wonderful Years: Puttin' On The Ritz-C....(JCI Assoc. Labels)

One Fine Day
Carpenters; *From The Top* ....(A&M)
Now & Then ....(A&M)
Chiffons; *Best Of The Chiffons* ....(Laurie)
Chiffons-Golden Classics ....(Collectables)
Collectables Presents The History Of Rock-#9-C ....(Collectables)
Oldies But Goodies-#12-C ....(Original Sound)

One In A Million
Aaliyah; *One In A Million* ....(BlackGround Enterp./Atlantic)

One More Goodtime Band In Texas
Leon Rausch; *Rausch Touch* .... (Southland)

Only Happy When It Rains
Garbage; *Garbage* ....(Almo Sounds)

Optimistic
Sounds Of Blackness; *Evolution Of Gospel* .... (Perspective/A&M)

Our House
Crosby, Stills & Nash; *CSN* ....(Atlantic)
Crosby, Stills, Nash & Young; *Deja Vu* ....(Atlantic)
So Far ....(Atlantic)

ST/The Strawberry Statement . . . . (MCA)

Outrageous
Lakeside; *Outrageous*. . . . . (Solar)

Over The Rainbow
Barbra Streisand; *Just For The Record* . . . . (Columbia)
Dave Brubeck; *Greatest Hits From The Fantasy Years* . . . . (Fantasy)
Ella Fitzgerald; *Silver Collection-Songbooks* . . . . (Verve)
Judy Garland; *Best Of The Capitol Masters-One & Only Box* . . . . . . (Capitol)
  Judy Garland-At Carnegie Hall. . . . . (Capitol)
  Judy Garland's Greatest Hits . . . . (Curb)
  Miss Show Business . . . . (Capitol)
  One & Only . . . . (Capitol)
  ST/The Wizard Of Oz . . . . (Sony Music Special Prod.)

Overjoyed
Stevie Wonder; *In Square Circle* . . . . (Motown)

Paradise
Nat "King" Cole; *Nat "King" Cole-Gift Set* . . . . (Capitol)
  The Nat "King" Cole Story . . . . (Capitol)
Ray Conniff; *'S Awful Nice*. . . . . (Columbia)
Russ Colombo; *Nipper's Greatest Hits Of The '30s-#2-C* . . . . (RCA)

Passionate Kisses
Mary Chapin Carpenter; *Come On Come On* . . . . (Columbia)

Pensacola Joy
Kellis Ethridge; *Tomorrow Sky*. . . . . (Inner City)

Pink Cadillac
Bruce Springsteen; *Tracks* . . . . (Columbia)
Natalie Cole; *Everlasting* . . . . (Elektra)
  Gotta Have House-Best Of House Music-#2-C . . . . (Profile)
Southern Pacific; *Killbilly Hill* . . . .(Warner Bros.)
  Rockin' Country-C. . . . .(Warner Bros.)
  Southern Pacific's Greatest Hits . . . .(Warner Bros.)

Please Please Me
Beatles; *Beatles-Box Set* . . . . (Capitol)
  Please Please Me . . . . (Parlophone)
  The Beatles/1962-1966 . . . . (Capitol)
  The Early Beatles . . . . (Capitol)

Pleasure Seekers
System; *System*. . . . . (Mirage)

Poor Boy
Elvis Presley; *Essential Elvis-The First Movies* . . . . (RCA)
  For LP Fans Only . . . . (RCA)

Positive Vibration
Bob Marley & The Wailers; *Babylon By Bus* . . . . (Tuff Gong)
  Rastaman Vibration. . . . . (Tuff Gong)

Pride & Joy
Marvin Gaye; *Marvin Gaye Live At The London Palladium*. . . . . . . (Motown)
  Marvin Gaye-Anthology . . . . (Motown)
  Marvin Gaye's Greatest Hits . . . . (Motown)
  Marvin Gaye-Super Hits . . . . (Motown)
  That Stubborn Kinda Fellow . . . . (Motown)

Pride & Joy
Coverdale/Page; *Coverdale/Page*. . . . .(Geffen)

Pride & Joy
Lil' Ed & The Blues Imperials; *Genuine Houserockin' Music II-C* . . . (Alligator)
  Roughhousin'. . . . . (Alligator)

Purple Rain
Prince and the Revolution; *ST/Purple Rain* . . . .(Warner Bros.)

Put On A Happy Face
Dick Van Dyke; *Broadway Magic-The 1960s-C* . . . . (Columbia)
  ST/Bye Bye Birdie . . . . (RCA)
Dick Van Dyke/Original Cast; *Bye Bye Birdie* . . . . (Columbia)
Stevie Wonder; *With A Song In My Heart*. . . . . (Motown)
Tony Bennett; *Forty Years-The Artistry Of Tony Bennett*. . . . . . . (Columbia)
  Tony Bennett's All-Time Greatest Hits . . . . (Columbia)

Quarter To Three
Gary U.S. Bonds; *Best Of Gary U.S. Bonds* . . . . (Rhino)
  Best Of Gary U.S. Bonds . . . . (EMI Legends Of Rock 'N' Roll)

Rain, The Park And Other Things
Cowsills; *Cowsills*. . . . . (Razor & Tie)

Reach For The Light
Steve Winwood; *ST/Balto*. . . . . (MCA)

Reunited
Peaches & Herb; *Best Of Peaches & Herb* . . . . (Polydor)
  Chicken Soup For The Couples Soul-C . . . . (Rhino)
  Didn't It Blow Your Mind: Soul Hits Of The '70s-#20-C . . . . (Rhino)
  Only Love-1975-1979-C . . . . (JCI Assoc. Labels)

Revival
Allman Brothers Band; *An Evening With The Allman Brothers Band-*
  First Set. . . . .(Epic)
  Beginnings. . . . . (Polydor)
  Decade Of Hits-1969-1979. . . . . (Polydor)
  Dreams. . . . . (Polydor)
  Idlewild South . . . . (Polydor)

Right On Track
Breakfast Club; *Breakfast Club* . . . . (MCA)
  Club Disco-Dance Hits-C . . . . (MCA Special Prod.)
  Greatest Rock Hits Of The '80s-C . . . . (MCA Special Prod.)

Rip It Up
Elvis Presley; *Elvis* . . . . (RCA)

Rocker . . . . (RCA)
Little Richard; *Big Hits* . . . .(Crescendo)
  Grooviest 17 Original Hits. . . . .(Specialty)
  Little Richard-18 Greatest Hits . . . . (Rhino)
  Little Richard's Greatest Hits. (Everest)

Rise
Herb Alpert; *Herb Alpert-Classics-#20.* . . . . (A&M)
  Rise. . . . . (A&M)

Room At The Top
Tom Petty And The Heartbreakers; *Echo* . . . . (Warner Bros.)

Row, Row, Row Your Boat
Bobby Darin/Johnny Mercer/Billy May Orchestra; *Two Of A Kind* . . . .(Atlantic)
Original Soundtrack; *Children's Favorites*. . . . .(Kid Rhino/Rhino 4 Kids)
Spike Jones & His City Slickers; *King Of Corn*. . . . .(Glendale)

'S Wonderful
Diana Krall; *The Look Of Love* . . . .(Impulse!)
Ella Fitzgerald; *Oh, Lady Be Good! Best Of the Gershwin Songbook* . . . . (Verve)
Fred Astaire; *Steppin' Out-Astaire Sings* . . . . (Verve)
Harry Connick, Jr.; *20* . . . . (Columbia)
Ray Conniff; *Ray Conniff -16 Most Requested Songs* . . . . (Legacy)

Saddle Tramp
Marty Robbins; *Gunfighter Ballads & Trail Songs* . . . . (Legacy)
  Marty Robbins-More Greatest Hits . . . . (Columbia)

Satisfaction Guaranteed
Rare Earth; *Ecology* . . . . (Motown)

Satisfaction Guaranteed
Firm; *Firm*. . . . .(Atlantic)

Satisfaction Guaranteed
Michael Franks; *Tiger In The Rain* . . . . (Warner Bros.)

Satisfied
Martha Carson; *Stars Of The Grand Ole Opry-1926-1974-C* . . . . (RCA)

Satisfied
Rachelle Ferrell; *Individuality (Can I Be Me?)* . . . . (Capitol)

Satisfied
Van Morrison; *Common One* . . . . (Warner Bros.)

Satisfied
Richard Marx; *Repeat Offender* . . . . (EMI)

Satisfied
Ted Nugent; *State Of Shock*. . . . . (Epic)

Satisfied
Joe Cocker; *Unchain My Heart* . . . . (Capitol)

Satisfied Man
Molly Hatchet; *Double Trouble-Live* . . . . (Epic)
  The Deed Is Done . . . . (Epic)

Satisfied Mind
Bob Dylan; *Saved* . . . . (Columbia)
Byrds; *Turn! Turn! Turn!* . . . . (Legacy)
David Allan Coe; *Texas Moon* . . . . (Plantation)
Lindsey Buckingham; *Law And Order* . . . . (Asylum)
Porter Wagoner; *Porter Wagoner's Greatest* . . . . (Tudor)

Satisfied Mind
Ozark Mountain Daredevils; *It's Alive* . . . . (A&M)
  Ozark Mountain Daredevils. . . . . (A&M)

Satisfy My Soul
Bob Marley & The Wailers; *Kaya*. . . . .(Tuff Gong)
  Legend: The Best Of Bob Marley & The Wailers . . . . (Island)
Winston Jarrett; *Heartbeat Reggae Roundup* . . . . (Heartbeat)
  Solid Foundation . . . . (Heartbeat)

Satisfy Suzie
Lonnie Mack; *Attack Of The Killer V* . . . . (Alligator)
  Strike Like Lightning . . . . (Alligator)

Satisfy You
Puff Daddy Featuring R. Kelly; *Forever*. . . . .(Bad Boy/Arista)

Say You'll Be There
Spice Girls; *Now That's What I Call Music!-#1-C* . . . .(Virgin)
  Spice. . . . .(Virgin)

Sea Of Joy
Blind Faith; *Blind Faith*. . . . .(Polydor)
Eric Clapton; *History Of Eric Clapton* . . . . (Atco)

Secret
Madonna; *Bedtime Stories* . . . .(Maverick/Sire)
  GHV2 . . . . (Warner Bros.)

Set Adrift On Memory Bliss
PM Dawn; *MTV Party To Go-#2-C*. . . . . (Tommy Boy)
  Red Hot + Dance-C . . . . (Columbia)

Set U Free
Planet Soul; *Disco Queens-The '90s-C* . . . . (Rhino)
  Energy + Harmony. . . . . (Strictly Rhythm)

Sha-La-La (Make Me Happy)
Al Green; *Al Green Explores Your Mind*. . . . . (Motown)
  Al Green's Greatest Hits-#2 . . . . (Motown)
  Tokyo...Live . . . . (Right Stuff)

She Loves You
Beatles; *Beatles 1* . . . . (Capitol)
  Beatles-20 Greatest Hits . . . . (Capitol)
  Beatles-Box Set. . . . . (Capitol)
  Past Masters-Volume One . . . . (Parlophone)
  The Beatles At The Hollywood Bowl. . . . . (Capitol)

The Beatles' Second Album .... (Capitol)
The Beatles/1962-1966 .... (Capitol)
She Makes The Coming Home Worth The Being Gone
Shenandoah; *Extra Mile* .... (Columbia)
Sheila
Tommy Roe; *Billboard Top Rock 'N' Roll Hits-1962-C* .... (Rhino)
Golden Years-1962-C .... (Dominion Entert.)
Original Rock 'N' Roll Hits Of The '60s-C .... (Roulette)
Sheila .... (Accord)
Tommy Roe's Greatest Hits .... (MCA)
She's Only Happy When She's Dancin'
Bryan Adams; *Reckless* .... (A&M)
She's So High
Marc Tanner Band; *No Escape* .... (Elektra)
Shine
Ry Cooder; *Jazz* .... (Warner Bros.)
Shiny Happy People
R.E.M.; *Out Of Time* .... (Warner Bros.)
Shout
Beatles; *The Beatles-Anthology-#1* .... (Capitol)
Isley Brothers; *Nipper's Greatest Hits Of The '50s-#2-C* .... (RCA)
Shout .... (Collectables)
ST/The Wanderers .... (Warner Bros.)
Joey Dee & the Starliters; *Echoes Of A Rock Era-Later Years-C* ..... (Roulette)
Hey Let's Twist! Best Of Joey Dee & The Starliters ...... (Rhino)
Live At The Peppermint Lounge .... (Accord)
Original Rock 'N' Roll Hits Of The '60s-C .... (Roulette)
Sock Hoppin' Sixties-C .... (JCI Assoc. Labels)
Otis Day & The Knights; *Shout* .... (MCA)
ST/Animal House .... (MCA)
Tom Petty And The Heartbreakers; *Pack Up The Plantation-Live!* ...... (MCA)
Simple Joys Of Maidenhood
Julie Andrews; *Camelot* .... (Columbia)
Various Artists; *ST/Camelot* .... (Warner Bros.)
Sing A Happy Song
Taj Mahal; *Evolution* .... (Warner Bros.)
Sing A Happy Song
O'Jays; *Identify Yourself* .... (Philadelphia Int'l)
Singin' In The Rain
Gene Kelly; *ST/A Clockwork Orange* .... (Warner Bros.)
ST/Singin' In The Rain .... (Sony Music Special Prod.)
ST/Those Glorious MGM Musicals .... (MGM)
Six Days On The Road
Boxcar Willie; *Truck Driving Favorites* .... (Madacy)
Dave Dudley; *Billboard Top Country Hits-1963-C* .... (Rhino)
Country Music Classics-#2-1960-1965-C .... (K-Tel)
Legends Of Country Guitar-#2-C .... (Rhino)
Truck Driver Boogie Big Rig Hits-1939-1969-C ..... (Audium)
Flying Burrito Brothers; *Cabin Fever* .... (Relix)
Farther Along-Best Of The Flying Burrito Brothers ..... (A&M)
Last Of The Red Hot Burritos .... (A&M)
Sawyer Brown; *Six Days On The Road* .... (Curb)
Taj Mahal; *Giant Step/De Ole Folks At Home* .... (Columbia)
Legends Of Rock Guitar-'60s-#2-C .... (Rhino)
Skokiaan
Four Lads; *16 Most Requested Songs Of The '50s-#2-C* .... (Legacy)
Sleep
Little Willie John; *Best Of Little Willie John-Fever* .... (Rhino)
Soldier's Joy
Jimmy Driftwood; *Best Of Jimmy Driftwood* .... (Motown)
Marty Stuart; *Busy Bee Cafe* .... (Sugar Hill)
Nitty Gritty Dirt Band; *Dirt, Silver & Gold* .... (One Way)
Will The Circle Be Unbroken .... (EMI)
Tony Trischka; *Heartlands* .... (Rounder)
Somebody's Doin' Me Right
Glen Campbell; *Unconditional Love* .... (Liberty)
Keith Whitley; *Kentucky Bluebird* .... (RCA)
S-K-O; *S-K-O* .... (MTM)
Someday When Things Are Good
Merle Haggard; *His Epic Hits-First 11 To Be Continued-C* ..... (Epic)
That's The Way Love Goes .... (Epic)
Sometimes
Brand New Heavies; *Shelter* .... (Delicious Vinyl)
Sour Girl
Stone Temple Pilots; *No. 4* .... (Atlantic)
Standing On The Top
Temptations featuring Rick James; *Emperors Of Soul* .... (Motown)
Steppin' Out With My Baby
Fred Astaire; *Cheek To Cheek: The Irving Berlin Songbook-C* ...... (Verve)
Fred Astaire At MGM .... (Rhino)
ST/Easter Parade .... (Rhino)
Steppin' Out-Astaire Sings .... (Verve)
Tony Bennett; *MTV Unplugged-Tony Bennett* .... (Columbia)
Steppin' Out .... (Columbia)
Still Alive And Well
Edgar Winter's White Trash; *Roadwork* .... (Epic)
Johnny Winter; *Still Alive & Well* .... (Columbia)
Stomp
God's Property; *MTV Jams-C* .... (Kedar Entert./Universal)

Stuck In A Closet With Vanna White
"Weird Al" Yankovic; *Even Worse* .... (Scotti Bros.)
Stuck With You
Huey Lewis and the News; *Fore!* .... (Chrysalis)
Stupidly Happy
XTC; *Wasp Star (Apple Venus Volume 2)* .... (Idea/TVT)
Summer Of '69
Bryan Adams; *Reckless* .... (A&M)
Sunny Side To Every Situation
Original Broadway Cast; *42nd Street* .... (RCA Victor)
Sunshine On My Shoulders
John Denver; *John Denver's Greatest Hits* .... (RCA)
Take Me Home, Country Roads & Other Hits .... (RCA)
Sweet Caroline
Neil Diamond; *Glory Road-1968-1972* .... (MCA)
Hot August Night .... (MCA)
Love At The Greek .... (Columbia)
Neil Diamond-Gold .... (MCA)
Neil Diamond-His 12 Greatest Hits .... (MCA)
Sweet Little Miss Blue Eyes
Jim & Jesse/The Virginia Boys; *Appalachian Stomp: More Bluegrass
Classics-C* .... (Rhino)
Sweet Mama Goodtimes
Mickey Gilley; *Mickey Gilley's Greatest Hits-#2* .... (Epic)
T.M. Song
Beach Boys; *15 Big Ones* .... (Brother)
Take It Easy
Eagles; *Eagles* .... (Asylum)
Eagles Live .... (Asylum)
Eagles/Their Greatest Hits 1971-1975 .... (Asylum)
Hell Freezes Over .... (Geffen)
Jackson Browne; *For Everyman* .... (Asylum)
Travis Tritt; *Common Thread-Songs Of The Eagles-C* .... (Giant)
Take Me There
Blackstreet & Mya featuring Mase & Blinky Blink;
Finally .... (Lil' Man/Interscope)
Now That's What I Call Music!-#2-C .... (Virgin)
ST/Rugrats .... (Interscope)
Ten Minutes Ago
Julie Andrews & Jon Cypher; *Cinderella-The CBS Television
Production* .... (Columbia)
Stuart Damon & Lesley Ann Warren; *Cinderella-The CBS Television
Network Production* .... (Columbia)
That Don't Satisfy Me
Brother Cane; *Brother Cane* .... (Virgin)
That's The Way (I Like It)
KC And The Sunshine Band; *Best Of KC And The Sunshine Band* ...... (Rhino)
Disco Hits-#1-C .... (Rhino)
Mega Hits Dance Classics-#3-C .... (Priority)
That's The Way Of The World
Earth, Wind & Fire; *Best Of Earth, Wind & Fire-#1* .... (Legacy)
Eternal Dance .... (Columbia)
Love Shouldn't Hurt-C .... (Qwest)
Pop Classics Of The '70s-C .... (Columbia)
That's The Way Of The World .... (Legacy)
That's What I Get For Lovin' You
Diamond Rio; *Diamond Rio IV* .... (Arista)
That's Where I Belong
Paul Simon; *You're The One* .... (Warner Bros.)
That's Where The Happy People Go
Trammps; *Disco Hits-#1-C* .... (Rhino)
That's Where The Happy People Go .... (Out Of Print)
Theme From "Happy Days"
Original Soundtrack; *Television's Greatest Hits-#3-1970s & 1980s-C* ....(TVT)
Theme From "Mr. Rogers' Neighborhood"
Original Soundtrack; *Television's Greatest Hits-#2-C* .... (TVT)
They Say It's Wonderful
Frank Sinatra; *The Voice-Columbia Years-1943-1952* .... (Columbia)
Johnny Mathis; *Heavenly* .... (Columbia)
Original Cast; *Annie Get Your Gun* .... (RCA Victor)
Sarah Vaughan; *Irving Berlin Always-C* .... (Verve)
They Say That Falling In Love Is Wonderful
Mark Shane & Terry Blaine; *With Thee I Swing!* .... (Nagel-Heyer)
Things Can Only Get Better
Howard Jones; *Dream Into Action* .... (Elektra)
Things Get Better
Delaney & Bonnie; *Delaney & Bonnie & Friends On Tour With Eric
Clapton* .... (Rhino)
Thirty-Three
Smashing Pumpkins; *Mellon Collie And The Infinite Sadness* .... (Virgin)
This Can't Be Love
Diana Krall; *Stepping Out* .... (Justin Time)
Ella Fitzgerald; *Rodgers & Hart Songbook* .... (Verve)
Natalie Cole; *Unforgettable With Love* .... (Elektra)
Original Cast; *The Boys From Syracuse* .... (Angel)
Stephane Grappelli; *Compact Jazz-Stephane Grappelli* .... (Verve)
Various Artists; *Embraceable You-Broadway In Love* .... (Sony Broadway)
This Everyday Love
Rascal Flatts; *Rascal Flatts* .... (Lyric Street)

This Kiss
Faith Hill; *Faith* . . . .(Warner Bros.)
Totally Hits-#1-C . . . . (Arista)

Three Hundred Pounds Of Heavenly Joy
Big Twist & The Mellow Fellows; *Alligator Records 20th Anniversary*
Collection-C . . . . (Alligator)
Howlin' Wolf; *The Chess Box-Howlin' Wolf* . . . . (Chess)

To Zion
Lauryn Hill featuring Carlos Santana; *The Miseducation Of*
Lauryn Hill . . . . (Ruffhouse/Columbia)

Too Good To Stop Now
Mickey Gilley; *Too Good To Stop Now* . . . .(Epic)

Tree Of Joy
Jeannie C. Riley; *Country Gold-Jeannie C. Riley* . . . . (Plantation)

Trippin'
Total featuring Missy Elliott; *Kima, Keisha & Pam* . . . . (Bad Boy/Arista)

Turn Me On "Mr. Deadman"
Union Underground; *...An Education In Rebellion* . . . . (Portrait)

Twelve Thirty (Young Girls Are Coming To The Canyon)
Mamas & The Papas; *Best Of The Mamas & The Papas* . . . .(MCA)
Mamas & The Papas-16 Of Their Greatest Hits . . . .(MCA)
The Papas & The Mamas . . . .(MCA)

Two Teardrops
Steve Wariner; *Two Teardrops* . . . . (Capitol)

U Send Me
Mint Condition; *From The Mint Factory* . . . .(Perspective/A&M)

Up On The Roof
Cryan' Shames; *Scratch In The Sky* . . . . (Columbia)
Drifters; *Cruisin'-1962-C* . . . .(Increase)
Drifters' Greatest Hits . . . . (Gusto)
Drifters-16 Greatest Hits . . . . (Trip)
Drifters-Golden Hits . . . .(Atlantic)
James Taylor; *Flag* . . . . (Columbia)
The Concert For New York City-C . . . . (Columbia)
Nylons; *Four On The Floor* . . . . (Scotti Bros.)

Uptight (Everything's Alright)
Stevie Wonder; *16 #1 Hits From The Early '60s-C* . . . . (Motown)
Looking Back . . . . (Motown)
Motown Dance Party-#1-C . . . . (Motown)
Motown Legends-Stevie Wonder . . . . (Motown)
Stevie Wonder's Greatest Hits . . . . (Motown)
Uptight (Everything's Alright) . . . . (Motown)

Voice Of The Heart
Diana Ross; *Take Me Higher* . . . . (Motown)

Walkin' My Baby Back Home
Johnnie Ray; *Johnnie Ray-16 Most Requested Songs* . . . . (Legacy)
Johnnie Ray's Greatest Hits . . . . (Sony Music Special Prod.)
Nat "King" Cole; *Capitol Collectors Series-Nat "King" Cole* . . . . . (Capitol)
The Nat "King" Cole Story . . . . (Capitol)

Watermelon Weather
Perry Como; *Yesterday And Today-A Celebration In Song* . . . . (RCA)

Way He Makes Me Feel
Barbra Streisand; *Collection-Greatest Hits...And More* . . . . (Columbia)
ST/Yentl . . . . (Columbia)

Way You Make Me Feel
Michael Jackson; *Bad* . . . .(Epic)

We Believe In Happy Endings
Earl Thomas Conley & Emmylou Harris; *Duets-C* . . . . (Reprise)

We Got A Groovy Thing Goin'
Simon & Garfunkel; *Sounds Of Silence* . . . . (Columbia)

We Just Couldn't Say Goodbye
Guy Lombardo & His Royal Canadians; *Guy Lombardo-16 Most Requested*
Songs . . . . (Legacy)

When I Close My Eyes
Shanice; *Shanice* . . . . (LaFace)

When I'm Back On My Feet Again
Michael Bolton; *Soul Provider* . . . . (Columbia)

When Irish Eyes Are Smiling
Billy Shepherd Singers; *Irish Sing-Along* . . . .(MCA)
Bing Crosby; *When Irish Eyes Are Smiling* . . . .(MCA)
Dennis Day; *Irish Album* . . . . (RCA)

When Johnny Comes Marching Home
Marilyn Horne; *Beautiful Dreamer-Great American Songbook* . . . . . . (London)
Mormon Tabernacle Choir; *Songs Of The Civil War And Stephen Foster*
Favorites . . . . (Sony Music Classical)
United States Military Academy Band; *Songs Of The Civil War-C* . . (Columbia)

When My Baby Smiles At Me
Pete Fountain; *Best Of Pete Fountain* . . . .(MCA)
Ted Lewis & His Orchestra; *Music From The New York Stage (1890-1920)-*
#4-1917-C . . . . (Pearl)

When The Fallen Angels Fly
Patty Loveless; *When Fallen Angels Fly* . . . .(Epic)

When The Feeling's Right
Con Funk Shun; *Loveshine* . . . . (Out Of Print)

When You Love A Woman
Journey; *Trial By Fire* . . . . (Columbia)

Who Will Buy?
Barbra Streisand; *The Second Barbra Streisand Album* . . . . (Columbia)

Original Broadway Cast; *Oliver!* . . . . (RCA Victor)
Original London Cast; *Oliver!* . . . . (EMI-Angel)

Whole Lotta Loving
Fats Domino; *Fats Domino's All Time Greatest Hits* . . . . (Curb)
Fats Domino's Greatest Hits . . . . (CEMA Special Prod.)
My Blue Heaven . . . . (Gold Rush)
Professor Longhair; *Mardi Gras In Baton Rouge* . . . . (Rhino)

Wink
Neal McCoy; *No Doubt About It* . . . .(Atlantic)

Wish You Were Here
Incubus; *Morning View* . . . . (Epic)

Wish, The
Bruce Springsteen; *Tracks* . . . . (Columbia)

With Arms Wide Open
Creed; *Human Clay* . . . .(Wind-up)
Now That's What I Call Music!-#6-C . . . .(Virgin)

With Me
Lonestar; *I'm Already There* . . . . (BNA)

With My Eyes Wide Open I'm Dreaming
Mandy Barnett; *I've Got A Right To Cry* . . . .(Sire)
Patti Page; *Patti Page-Golden Hits* . . . . (Mercury)
Patti Page's Greatest Hits . . . . (Columbia)

Woke Up In Love
Exile; *Exile* . . . . (Epic)
Exile's Greatest Hits . . . . (Epic)

Wonderful Guy, A
Original Cast; *South Pacific* . . . . (CBS Masterworks)

Wonderful Tonight
Eric Clapton; *24 Nights* . . . . (Duck/Reprise)
Eric Clapton-Crossroads-C . . . . (Polydor)
Just One Night . . . . (Polydor)
Slowhand . . . . (Polydor)
Time Pieces-#1-The Best Of Eric Clapton . . . . (Polydor)

Wonderful World
Art Garfunkel; *Watermark* . . . . (Legacy)
Herman's Hermits; *Herman's Hermits-Their Greatest Hits* . . . . . . (Abkco)
Sam Cooke; *Best Of Sam Cooke* . . . . (RCA)
ST/Animal House . . . . (MCA)
This Is Sam Cooke . . . . (RCA)

Wonderful! Wonderful!
Johnny Mathis; *First 25 Years-Silver Anniversary Album* . . . . (Columbia)
Johnny Mathis' All-Time Greatest Hits . . . . (Columbia)
Johnny Mathis' Greatest Hits . . . . (Columbia)
Johnny Mathis-16 Most Requested Songs . . . . (Columbia)
Supremes; *I Hear A Symphony* . . . . (Motown)
Times; *Best Of Times* . . . . (Abkco)
Rock-O-Rama-#1-C . . . . (Abkco)

Words
Solomon Burke; *Best Of Solomon Burke* . . . .(Atlantic)
Home In Your Heart-Best Of Solomon Burke . . . . (Rhino)

Wouldn't It Be Loverly
Original Cast; *My Fair Lady* . . . . (Columbia)
My Fair Lady . . . . (London)

Wouldn't It Be Nice
Beach Boys; *Absolutely Best-#2* . . . . (Capitol)
Made In The U.S.A. . . . . (Capitol)
Pet Sounds . . . . (Capitol)
Still Cruisin' . . . . (Capitol)

You Are My Sunshine
Bing Crosby; *Best Of Bing Crosby* . . . . (MCA)
Bing Crosby's Greatest Hits . . . . (MCA)
Jimmie Davis; *20 Golden Souvenirs Of Music City U.S.A.-C* . . . . . (Plantation)
Best Of Jimmie Davis . . . . (MCA)
Jimmie Davis-Golden Hits . . . . (Plantation)
The Country Music Hall Of Fame-Jimmie Davis . . . . (MCA)
Mississippi John Hurt; *Best Of Mississippi John Hurt* . . . .(Vanguard)
Mitch Miller; *Mitch Miller-16 Most Requested Songs* . . . .(Columbia)
Norman Blake; *ST/O Brother, Where Art Thou?* . . . . (Mercury)
Ray Charles; *Ray Charles-Anthology* . . . . (Rhino)
Ray Charles-His Greatest Hits-#2 . . . . (Dunhill Compact Classics)
Willie Nelson & Leon Russell; *One For The Road* . . . . (Columbia)

You Are The Sunshine Of My Life
Peter Nero; *Peter Nero's Greatest Hits* . . . . (Columbia)
Stevie Wonder; *20/20-C* . . . . (Motown)
Original Musiquarium . . . . (Motown)
Talking Book . . . . (Motown)

You Bring Me Joy
Mary J. Blige; *My Life* . . . . (Uptown/MCA)

You Can Tell The World
Simon & Garfunkel; *Collected Works* . . . . (Columbia)
Wednesday Morning 3 A.M. . . . . (Columbia)

You Can't Always Get What You Want
Rolling Stones; *Flashpoint* . . . . (Virgin)
Hot Rocks 1964-1971 . . . . (Abkco)
Let It Bleed . . . . (Abkco)
Love You Live . . . . (Virgin)
Singles Collection-The London Years . . . . (Abkco)

You Give Good Love
Whitney Houston; *Whitney Houston* . . . . (Arista)

Whitney Houston's Greatest Hits .... (Arista)
You Light Up My Life
Debby Boone; *Best Of Debby Boone* .... (Curb)
There Is Love-Wedding Songs-C .... (Scotti Bros.)
You Light Up My Life .... (MCA)
LeAnn Rimes; *You Light Up My Life-Inspirational Songs* .... (Curb)
You Make Me Feel (Mighty Real)
Sylvester; *ST/Young Soul Rebels* .... (Volcano Entertainment)
You Make Me Feel Brand New
Roberta Flack; *Set The Night To Music* .... (Atlantic)
You Make Me Feel Like Dancing
Leo Sayer; *Billboard Top Rock 'N' Roll Hits-1977-C* .... (Rhino)
Endless Flight .... (Chrysalis)
Mega Hits Dance Classics-#3-C .... (Priority)
You Make Me Feel So Good
Astors; *Astors Meet The Newcomers* .... (Stax)
You Make Me Feel So Young
Frank Sinatra; *Best Of The Capitol Years* .... (Capitol)
You Make My Dreams
Daryl Hall & John Oates; *Rock 'N Soul, Part 1* .... (RCA)
Voices .... (RCA)
You Send Me
Aretha Franklin; *Aretha's Gold* .... (Atlantic)
Manhattans; *Too Hot To Stop It* .... (Columbia)
Michael Bolton; *Timeless-Classics* .... (Columbia)
Sam Cooke; *Best Of Sam Cooke* .... (RCA)
ST/American Pop .... (MCA)
The Man And His Music .... (RCA)
Young And Healthy
Bing Crosby with Guy Lombardo & His Royal Canadians; *The Song Is...Harry Warren-C* .... (Living Era)
Dick Powell & Toby Wing; *Lullaby Of Broadway-The Best Of Busby Berkeley At Warner Brothers* .... (Rhino)
Guy Lombardo & His Royal Canadians; *Guy Lombardo-16 Most Requested Songs* .... (Legacy)
Original Broadway Cast; *42nd Street* .... (RCA Victor)
Your Song
Elton John; *Elton John* .... (Polydor)
Elton John's Greatest Hits .... (Polydor)
Live In Australia With The Melbourne Symphony Orchestra .... (MCA)
Rod Stewart; *Two Rooms-Celebrating The Songs Of Elton John & Bernie Taupin-C* .... (Polydor)
You're Makin' Me High
Toni Braxton; *Secrets* .... (LaFace)
You're Not In Kansas Anymore
Jo Dee Messina; *Jo Dee Messina* .... (Curb)
You're The Inspiration
Chicago; *Chicago 17* .... (Warner Bros.)
Chicago's Greatest Hits-1982-1989 .... (Full Moon)
Peter Cetera featuring Az Yet; *You're The Inspiration-A Collection* .... (River North)
You've Got A Good Love Comin'
Lee Greenwood; *Inside Out/You've Got A Good Love Comin'* .... (MCA)
You've Made Me So Very Happy
Blood, Sweat & Tears; *Blood, Sweat & Tears* .... (Columbia)
Blood, Sweat & Tears Greatest Hits .... (Columbia)
Live & Improvised .... (Columbia)
Pop Classics Of The '60s-C .... (Columbia)
Zip A Dee Doo Dah
Barbara Cook; *Disney Album* .... (Disney)
Bing Crosby; *The Radio Years: 25 Songs* .... (Crescendo)
Jackson 5; *Motown Legends-Jackson 5* .... (Motown)
Johnny Mercer; *Capitol Collectors Series-Johnny Mercer* .... (Capitol)
Kelly Stevens & Carnival; *When You Wish Upon A Star* .....(American Variety)
Mormon Tabernacle Choir & Columbia Symphony Orchestra; *When You Wish Upon A Star-A Tribute To Walt Disney* .... (CBS Masterworks)
Ric Ocasek; *Simply Mad About The Mouse-C* .... (Columbia)
Steve Miller; *Born 2 B Blue* .... (Gold Rush)

HARD CITY LIFE, Gangsta Life
See Also: CITIES: A-Z, CITIES: GENERAL, POVERTY (ghetto)

1st Of Tha Month
Bone Thugs-N-Harmony; *E. 1999 Eternal* .... (Ruthless/Relativity)
6th Avenue Heartache
Wallflowers; *Best Of Rockline-C* .... (Priority)
Bringing It All Back Home .... (Columbia)
Backstreets
Bruce Springsteen; *Born To Run* .... (Columbia)
Bad Man
R. Kelly; *I Wish (import EP)* .... (Jive)
Black Jesus
Everlast; *Eat At Whitey's* .... (Tommy Boy)
Bling Bling
B.G.; *Chopper City In The Ghetto* .... (Cash Money/Universal)
Boyz-N-The-Hood
Dynamite Hack; *Superfast* .... (Farm Club/Universal)

Brenda's Got A Baby
Tupac; *2Pacalypse Now* .... (Priority)
Can't Deny It
Fabolous featuring Nate Dogg; *Ghetto Fabolous* ... (Desert Storm/Elektra/EEG)
Change
Keb' Mo'; *The Door* .... (550/Epic/Okeh)
Cloud Nine
Temptations; *25 Years Of Grammy Greats-C* .... (Motown)
Cloud Nine .... (Motown)
Motown Grammy R&B Performances Of The '60s & '70s-C ...... (Motown)
Motown Story-First 25 Years-C .... (Motown)
Temptations' Greatest Hits-#2 .... (Motown)
Days Of Our Livez
Bone Thugs-N-Harmony; *The Collection-#1* .... (Ruthless)
Ends
Everlast; *Whitey Ford Sings The Blues* .... (Tommy Boy)
Ghetto Supastar (That Is What You Are)
Pras Michel featuring Old Dirty Bastard & Mya; *ST/Bulworth* ..... (Interscope)
Ha!
Juvenile; *400 Degreez* .... (Cash Money/Universal)
Hail Mary
Makaveli; *The Don Killuminati: The 7 Day Theory Album* .... (Death Row/Interscope)
I Cry
Ja Rule; *Rule 3:36* .... (Murder Inc./Def Jam/IDJMG)
I Miss My Homies
Master P; *Ghetto D* .... (No Limit/Priority)
I Wish
Skee-Lo; *I Wish* .... (Sunshine/Scotti Bros.)
Stevie Wonder; *Original Musiquarium* .... (Motown)
Songs In The Key Of Life .... (Motown)
I Wish
R. Kelly; *Now That's What I Call Music!-#6-C* .... (Virgin)
TP-2.com .... (Jive)
I Wonder If Heaven Got A Ghetto
2Pac; *R U Still Down (Remember Me)* .... (Amaru/Jive)
I'll Be Around
Rappin' 4-Tay; *Don't Fight The Feelin'* .... (Rag Top/EMI)
I'm A Thug
Trick Daddy; *Thugs Are Us* .... (Slip 'N Slide/Atlantic)
Inner City Blues (Make Me Wanna Holler)
Marvin Gaye; *What's Going On* .... (Motown)
John 3:16
Wyclef; *Muggs Presents...The Soul Assassins-C* .... (Columbia)
Jungleland
Bruce Springsteen; *Born To Run* .... (Columbia)
Just In Case
Jaheim; *Ghetto Love* .... (Divine Mill/Warner Bros.)
Keep Their Heads Ringin'
Dr. Dre; *Hip Hop's Most Wanted-C* .... (Priority)
ST/Friday .... (Priority)
Look Into My Eyes
Bone Thugs-N-Harmony; *Art Of War* .... (Ruthless/Relativity)
Make Em Say Uhh #2
Master P; *MP Da Last Don* .... (No Limit/Priority)
Maria Maria
Santana; *Supernatural* .... (Arista)
Totally Hits-#2-C .... (Elektra)
More Than One Way Home
Keb' Mo'; *Just Like You* .... (Okeh)
N 2 Gether Now
Limp Bizkit; *Significant Other* .... (Flip/Interscope)
Nights In Harlem
Luther Vandross; *I Know* .... (LV/Virgin)
Project Chick/Project Bitch
Cash Money Millionaires; *12" Maxi Single* .... (Cash Money/Universal)
So Good
Destiny's Child; *The Writing's On The Wall* .... (Columbia)
Somebody Like Me
Silkk The Shocker Featuring Mya; *Made Man* .... (No Limit/Priority)
Still A G Thang
Snoop Dogg; *Da Game Is To Be Sold, Not To Be Told* ...... (No Limit/Priority)
Tenth Avenue Freeze-Out
Bruce Springsteen; *Born To Run* .... (Columbia)
Bruce Springsteen & The E Street Band; *Bruce Springsteen & The E Street Band Live/1975-85* .... (Legacy)
Theme From "Good Times"
Original Soundtrack; *CBS: The First 50 Years* .... (TVT)
Television's Greatest Hits-#3-1970s & 1980s-C .... (TVT)
Theme From "Room 222"
Original Soundtrack; *Television's Greatest Hits-#3-1970s & 1980s-C* .... (TVT)
Theme From "What's Happening?"
Original Soundtrack; *Television's Greatest Hits-#6-Remote Control-C* ...(TVT)
Trouble Man
Angie Stone; *Black Diamond* .... (Arista)
Wanna Be A Baller
Lil' Troy; *Sittin' Fat Down South* .... (Short Stop/Republic/Universal)

Westside
TQ; *They Never Saw Me Coming* . . . . (ClockWork/Epic)
What It's Like
Everlast; *Whitey Ford Sings The Blues* . . . . (Tommy Boy)
What Would You Do?
City High; *City High* . . . . (Interscope)
Now That's What I Call Music!-#7-C . . . . (Virgin)
ST/Life . . . . (Rock Land/Interscope)

HATE

See Also: **ANGER, BROTHERHOOD, DIVORCE, FEELINGS, FIGHT, GENDER CONFLICT, LOVE (various), MISTREATMENT, POLITICS (various), PREJUDICE, PROTEST, REVENGE, WAR**

(Eye) Hate U
"AFKAP"; *The Gold Experience* . . . . (NPG)
Already Home
Marc Cohn; *Burning The Daze* . . . . (Atlantic)
Avinu Malkeinu
Barbra Streisand; *Higher Ground* . . . . (Columbia)
Beautiful People
Marilyn Manson; *Antichrist Superstar* . . . . (Interscope)
Been Around The World
Puff Daddy & The Family; *No Way Out* . . . . (Bad Boy/Arista)
Bodies
Drowning Pool; *Sinner* . . . . (Wind-up)
Cool To Hate
Offspring; *Ixnay On The Hombre* . . . . (Columbia)
Corduroy
Pearl Jam; *Vitalogy* . . . .(Epic)
Dead Bodies Everywhere
Korn; *Follow The Leader* . . . .(Immortal/Epic)
Enemy
Days Of The New; *Days Of The New 2* . . . . (Outpost/Interscope)
Got The Life
Korn; *Follow The Leader* . . . .(Immortal/Epic)
Greedy Fly
Bush; *Razorblade Suitcase* . . . . (Trauma)
Hate This Place
Goo Goo Dolls; *Dizzy Up The Girl* . . . . (Warner Sunset/Reprise)
I Hate Men
Original Cast; *ST/Kiss Me Kate* . . . . (Rhino)
Original Cast/Patricia Morrison; *Kiss Me Kate* . . . . (Sony Music Classical)
I Hate My Generation
Cracker; *The Golden Age* . . . . (Virgin)
I Hate New York
Ann Jillian; *In The Middle Of Love-The Songs Of Steve Allen* . . . . . (Aero Space)
I Hate The Holidays
Venus Envy; *I'll Be Homo For Christmas* . . . .(Venus Envy)
I Hate You
D.O.A.; *War On 45/Bloodied But Unbowed* . . . .(Restless)
I Hate You
Ronnie Milsap; *Ronnie Milsap's Greatest Hits* . . . . (RCA)
I Hate You Then I Love You
Celine Dion with Luciano Pavarotti; *Let's Talk About Love-C* . . . . . . (550 Music)
I Hate You, Baby
Count Basie Big Band; *Fun Time* . . . .(Pablo)
I Hate You, Baby
Jimmy Soul; *Best Of Jimmy Soul* . . . . (Rhino)
Keep Away
Godsmack; *Godsmack* . . . .(Republic/Universal)
Kid Who Hates Summer
John McCutcheon; *John McCutcheon's Four Seasons: Summersongs* . . . . (Rounder)
Kill You
Eminem; *The Marshall Mathers LP* . . . . (Aftermath/Interscope)
Lookin' At Me
Mase Featuring Puff Daddy; *Harlem World* . . . . (Bad Boy/Arista)
Love Is Blind
Eve; *First Lady Of Ruff Ryders* . . . . (Ruff Ryders/IDJMG)
Love's In Need Of Love Today
Stevie Wonder featuring Take 6; *America: A Tribute To Heroes-C* . . . . (Interscope)
My Gift To You
Korn; *Follow The Leader* . . . .(Immortal/Epic)
Oh! How I Hate To Get Up In The Morning
Irving Berlin; *American Songbook Series-Irving Berlin* . . . .(Smithsonian Collection)
War Years-C . . . . (ISD/Intersound)
Soundtrack; *American Musical Theater-#2* . . . . (Smithsonian Collection)
Oh, How I Hate To Get Up In The Afternoon
Harry "Sweets" Edison; *Swing Trumpet Kings-C* . . . . (Verve)
Shimmer
Shawn Mullins; *Songs From Dawson's Creek* . . . . (Sony Music Soundtrax)

Soul's Core . . . . (Columbia)
Sign Of The Times
Queensryche; *Hear In The Now Frontier* . . . .(Virgin)
Take A Look Around
Limp Bizkit; *Chocolate Starfish & The Hotdog Flavored Water* . . . . (Flip/Interscope)
Throwing Stones
Paula Cole; *This Fire* . . . .(Imago)
What If
Creed; *Human Clay* . . . .(Wind-up)

HATS, Berets, Veils

See Also: **ANATOMY: HEAD, CLOTHES, FABRICS, SHOES, SHOPPING**

All Around My Hat
Steeleye Span; *All Around My Hat* . . . . (Chrysalis)
The Steeleye Span Story . . . . (Chrysalis)
Any Place I Hang My Hat Is Home
Barbra Streisand; *The Second Barbra Streisand Album* . . . . (Columbia)
Rosemary Clooney; *Rosemary Clooney Sings The Lyrics Of Johnny Mercer* . . . . (Concord Jazz)
Ballad Of The Green Berets
Barry Sadler; *Cruisin'-1966-C* . . . . (Increase)
Hits Of The Sixties-C . . . . (Intercom Music)
More American Graffiti-#4-C . . . . (MCA)
Nipper's Greatest Hits Of The '60s-#2-C . . . .(RCA)
Super Hits-#3-C . . . . (Gusto)
Bumming Around
"T" Texas Tyler; *Only Country-1950-1954-C* . . . . (JCI Assoc. Labels)
Cowboy Hat In Dallas
Charlie Daniels Band; *Homesick Heroes* . . . . (Epic)
Easter Parade
Andy Russell; *Puttin' On The Ritz-Capitol Sings Berlin-C* . . . . (Capitol)
Bing Crosby; *All Time Best Of Bing Crosby* . . . . (Curb)
Judy Garland & Fred Astaire; *ST/Easter Parade* . . . . (Rhino)
Sarah Vaughan; *Complete Sarah Vaughan On Mercury-#2* . . . . (Mercury)
Hats Off To Larry
Del Shannon; *Runaway Hits!* . . . . (Rhino)
Super Oldies Of The '60s-#2-C . . . . (Audio Fidelity)
WCBS FM 101 History Of Rock-'60s-#3-C . . . . (Collectables)
Homburg
Procol Harum; *Best Of Procol Harum* . . . . (A&M)
Procol Harum's Greatest Hits . . . . (A&M)
I Left My Hat In Haiti
Fred Astaire; *Fred Astaire At MGM* . . . . (Rhino)
ST/Royal Wedding . . . . (Sony Music Special Prod.)
I Tipped My Hat And Slowly Rode Away
Gene Autry; *Sing Cowboy Sing: The Gene Autry Collection* . . . . (Rhino)
Keeper Of The Stars
Tracy Byrd; *No Ordinary Man* . . . . (MCA)
Leopard-Skin Pill-Box Hat
Bob Dylan; *Blonde On Blonde* . . . . (Columbia)
Long Black Veil
Band; *Music From Big Pink* . . . . (Capitol)
To Kingdom Come-The Definitive Collection . . . . (Capitol)
Joan Baez; *Joan Baez In Concert, Part 2* . . . . (Vanguard)
One Day At A Time . . . . (Vanguard)
Johnny Cash; *Classic Cash-Hall Of Fame Series* . . . . (Mercury)
Johnny Cash At Folsom Prison & San Quentin . . . . (Columbia)
Lefty Frizzell; *American Originals-Lefty Frizzell* . . . . (Columbia)
Columbia Country Classics-#3-Americana-C . . . . (Columbia)
Mexican Hat Dance
Percy Faith & His Orchestra; *Percy Faith & His Orchestra's All-Time Greatest Hits* . . . . (Columbia)
New Grey Bonnet
Johnny Gimble; *Still Fiddlin' Around* . . . . (MCA)
On The Sunny Side Of The Street
Diana Krall; *Stepping Out* . . . .(Justin Time)
Frank Sinatra; *Come Swing With Me!* . . . . (Capitol)
One More For The Road . . . . (Capitol)
Sentimental Journey . . . . (Capitol)
The Capitol Years . . . . (Capitol)
Judy Garland; *Best Of Judy Garland* . . . . (MCA)
Louis Armstrong; *Best Of Louis Armstrong* . . . . (MCA)
Chicago Concert 1956 . . . . (Columbia)
Jazz Club-Vocal . . . . (Verve)
Music Autobiography . . . . (MCA)
Ted Lewis & His Orchestra; *Charming Gents Of Stage & Screen-C* . . . . (Legacy)
Those Wonderful Days: Puttin' On The Ritz-C . . . . (JCI Assoc. Labels)
Papa Was A Rollin' Stone
Temptations; *20/20-C* . . . . (Motown)
25 #1 Hits From 25 Years-C . . . . (Motown)
All The Million-Sellers . . . . (Motown)
Billboard Top Rock 'N' Roll Hits-1972-C . . . . (Rhino)

Compact Command Performances-Temptations . . . . (Motown)
Temptations-Anthology-The Best Of The Temptations . . . . (Motown)
Raspberry Beret
Prince and the Revolution; *Around The World In A Day* . . . . (Paisley Park)
Steppin' Out With My Baby
Fred Astaire; *Cheek To Cheek: The Irving Berlin Songbook-C* . . . . (Verve)
Fred Astaire At MGM . . . . (Rhino)
ST/Easter Parade . . . . (Rhino)
Steppin' Out-Astaire Sings . . . . (Verve)
Tony Bennett; *MTV Unplugged-Tony Bennett* . . . . (Columbia)
Steppin' Out . . . . (Columbia)
That's Right (You're Not From Texas)
Lyle Lovett; *Live In Texas* . . . . (MCA)
The Road To Ensenada . . . . (MCA)
Top Hat, White Tie And Tails
Fred Astaire; *Irving Berlin Songbook* . . . . (Verve)
You Can Leave Your Hat On
Joe Cocker; *Cocker* . . . . (Capitol)
Joe Cocker Live . . . . (Capitol)
ST/9 1/2 Weeks . . . . (Capitol)
Randy Newman; *Sail Away* . . . . (Reprise)
You Gotta Have A Hat
Ray Stevens; *#1 With A Bullet* . . . . (Curb)
Your Friend In The Cowboy Hat (The Viagra Song)
Croatan; *Violent Passion Surrogate* . . . . (Man's Ruin)

HEAR, Ears, Listen, Sound
See Also: **COMMUNICATION (various), SILENCE, SOUNDS**

(I Love The Sound Of) Breaking Glass
Nick Lowe; *Pure Pop For Now People* . . . . (Columbia)
Alexander's Ragtime Band
Al Jolson & Bing Crosby; *Al Jolson Story-#1* . . . . (MCA)
Immortal Al Jolson . . . . (MCA)
All Around The World
Oasis; *Be Here Now* . . . . (Epic)
Almost Hear You Sigh
Rolling Stones; *Steel Wheels* . . . . (Rolling Stones)
And A Bang On The Ear
Waterboys; *Fisherman's Blues* . . . . (Ensign)
Angels Listened In
Crests; *Crests Greatest Hits* . . . . (Collectables)
Super Oldies Of The '50s-#3-C . . . . (Audio Fidelity)
WCBS FM 101 History Of Rock-'50s-#2-C . . . . (Collectables)
Anybody Listening?
Queensryche; *Empire* . . . . (EMI)
Are You Sleeping?
Nilsson; *The Point* . . . . (RCA)
Beautiful Noise
Neil Diamond; *12 Greatest Hits-#2* . . . . (Columbia)
Beautiful Noise . . . . (Columbia)
Love At The Greek . . . . (Columbia)
Big Boss Man
B.B. King; *Six Silver Strings* . . . . (MCA)
Elvis Presley; *ST/Clambake* . . . . (RCA)
Grateful Dead; *Grateful Dead (Skull & Roses)* . . . . (Warner Bros.)
Jimmy Reed; *Best Of Jimmy Reed* . . . . (Crescendo)
Oldies But Goodies-#1-C . . . . (Original Sound)
John Hammond; *Best Of John Hammond* . . . . (Vanguard)
So Many Roads . . . . (Vanguard)
Big Noise From Winnetka
Bette Midler; *Divine Madness* . . . . (Atlantic)
Thighs And Whispers . . . . (Atlantic)
Bob Crosby & His Bob Cats; *Best Of Bob Crosby & His Bob Cats* . . . (MCA)
Bob Crosby & His Orchestra; *Bob Crosby & His Orchestra Play 22 Original
Big Band Hits* . . . . (Hindsight)
Bomb! (These Sounds Fall Into My Mind)
Bucketheads; *All In The Mind* . . . . (Big Beat/Atlantic)
Brokedown Palace
Grateful Dead; *American Beauty* . . . . (Warner Bros.)
Persuasions; *Might As Well...The Persuasions Sing
Grateful Dead* . . . . (Grateful Dead)
Bucket's Got A Hole In It, The
Preservation Hall Jazz Band; *Best Of The Preservation Hall
Jazz Band* . . . . (Columbia)
Can You Hear Me?
David Bowie; *Young Americans* . . . . (Rykodisc)
Can You Hear The Music?
Rolling Stones; *Goats Head Soup* . . . . (Rolling Stones)
Can't You Hear Me Callin'?
Ricky Skaggs; *Bluegrass Super Hits-C* . . . . (Columbia)
Favorite Country Songs . . . . (Epic)
Highway & Heartaches . . . . (Epic)
Can't You Hear Me Knockin'
Rolling Stones; *Sticky Fingers* . . . . (Virgin)

Can't You Hear My Heartbeat
Herman's Hermits; *Herman's Hermits-Their Greatest Hits* . . . . (Abkco)
Cheerful Little Earful
Ella Fitzgerald; *Swings Brightly With Nelson* . . . . (Verve)
Cryin' To Be Heard
Traffic; *Traffic* . . . . (Island)
Cum On Feel The Noise
Quiet Riot; *Metal Health* . . . . (Pasha)
Daddy Frank (The Guitar Man)
Merle Haggard; *Best Of Merle Haggard* . . . . (Capitol)
Capitol Collectors Series-Merle Haggard . . . . (Capitol)
Merle Haggard & The Strangers; *For The Record: Merle Haggard-43
Legendary Hits* . . . . (BNA)
Songs I'll Always Sing . . . . (Capitol)
Dear Doctor
Rolling Stones; *Beggars Banquet* . . . . (Abkco)
Do I Hear A Waltz?
Elizabeth Allen; *Broadway Magic-The 1960s-C* . . . . (Columbia)
Original Broadway Cast; *Do I Hear A Waltz?* . . . . . . (Sony Music Classical)
Do Nothin' Till You Hear From Me
Billie Holiday; *Compact Jazz-Billie Holiday* . . . . (Verve)
Stay With Me . . . . (Verve)
Cal Tjader & Carmen McRae; *Heat Wave* . . . . (Concord Jazz)
Diana Krall; *Stepping Out* . . . . (Justin Time)
Duke Ellington; *I Like Jazz-Essence Of Duke Ellington* . . . . (Columbia)
Duke Ellington & His Orchestra; *ST/Fabulous Baker Boys* . . . . (GRP)
Johnny Mathis; *In A Sentimental Mood-Johnny Mathis Sings
Ellington* . . . . (Columbia)
Mose Allison; *Mose Allison's Greatest Hits* . . . . (Prestige)
Do You Hear Wedding Bells
Jive Five; *Jive Five-Their Greatest Hits* . . . . (Collectables)
Do You Want To Know A Secret
Beatles; *Introducing...The Beatles* . . . . (Vee-Jay)
Please Please Me . . . . (Parlophone)
The Early Beatles . . . . (Capitol)
Don't You Hear Jerusalem Moan
Nitty Gritty Dirt Band; *Will The Circle Be Unbroken-#2-C* . . . . (Uni)
Down Under
Men At Work; *Business As Usual* . . . . (Columbia)
Earache My Eye featuring Alice Bowie
Cheech & Chong; *Dr. Demento: 20th Anniversary Collection-C* . . . . . . (Rhino)
Greatest Hit . . . . (Warner Bros.)
Wedding Album . . . . (Warner Bros.)
Enemy
Days Of The New; *Days Of The New 2* . . . . (Outpost/Interscope)
Everybody's Talkin'
Nilsson; *Everybody's Talkin': The Encore Collection* . . . . . (BMG Special Prod.)
ST/Forrest Gump . . . . (Epic/Sony Music Soundtrax)
ST/Midnight Cowboy . . . . (EMI)
Willie Nelson; *Best Of Willie* . . . . (RCA)
Sweet Memories . . . . (RCA)
Flava In Ya Ear
Craig Mack; *Funk Da World* . . . . (Arista)
Fool On The Hill
Beatles; *Beatles-Box Set* . . . . (Capitol)
Magical Mystery Tour . . . . (Capitol)
The Beatles/1967-1970 . . . . (Capitol)
For What It's Worth
Buffalo Springfield; *Buffalo Springfield* . . . . (Atco)
Buffalo Springfield-Retrospective . . . . (Atco)
Double History . . . . (Atco)
Hit Singles-1958-1977-C . . . . (Atlantic)
ST/Forrest Gump . . . . (Epic/Sony Music Soundtrax)
Go On
George Strait; *George Strait* . . . . (MCA)
Have You Heard
Duprees; *Best Of The Duprees* . . . . (Collectables)
Best Of The Duprees . . . . (Rhino)
WCBS FM 101 History Of Rock-'60s-#3-C . . . . (Collectables)
Have You Heard
Moody Blues; *Caught Live Plus Five* . . . . (Polydor)
On The Threshold Of A Dream . . . . (Polydor)
This Is The Moody Blues . . . . (Polydor)
Have You Heard The News
Ben Sidran; *Puttin' In Time On Planet Earth* . . . . (MCA)
Vikki Carr; *Live At The Greek Theatre* . . . . (Columbia)
Haven't You Heard
Patrice Rushen; *Patrice Rushen-Anthology* . . . . (Elektra)
Pizzazz . . . . (Elektra)
Haven't You Heard
George Strait; *Something Special* . . . . (MCA)
Hear Me In The Harmony
Harry Connick, Jr.; *Star Turtle* . . . . (Columbia)
Hear Me Lord
George Harrison; *All Things Must Pass* . . . . (Parlophone)
Hear My Train A'Comin'
Jimi Hendrix; *Concerts* . . . . (Reprise)
Rainbow Bridge . . . . (Reprise)

Jimi Hendrix Experience; *Radio One* . . . . (Rykodisc)
Hear Say
Soul Children; *15 Original Big Hits-#3-C* . . . . (Stax)
  Soul Children-Chronicle . . . .(Stax)
Hear The Wind Howl
Leo Kottke; *Mudlark* . . . . (Capitol)
  My Feet Are Smiling . . . . (Capitol)
Heard It All Before
Sunshine Anderson; *Your Woman* . . . . (Soullife/Atlantic)
Hey There
Original Cast; *ST/Pajama Game* . . . . (Collectables)
Rosemary Clooney; *Essence Of Rosemary Clooney* . . . . (Legacy)
High Lonesome Sound
Vince Gill; *Bluegrass Essentials-C* . . . . (Hip-O)
  High Lonesome Sound . . . .(MCA)
Vince Gill with Alison Krauss & Union Station; *Grand Ole Opry-75 Years-#1-C* . . . . (MCA)
Home On The Range
Bing Crosby; *Crooner-Columbia Years-1928-1934.* . . . . (Columbia)
Boston Pops Orchestra/Arthur Fiedler; *Yankee Doodle Dandy* . . . . (RCA)
Gene Autry; *50th Anniversary* . . . .(Republic/Universal)
  The Country Music Hall Of Fame-Gene Autry-15 Of His All-Time Greatest Hits . . . . (Columbia)
Neil Young; *ST/Where The Buffalo Roam* . . . .(Backstreet)
Homeward Bound
Paul Simon; *Paul Simon In Concert/Live Rhymin'* . . . . (Columbia)
Paul Simon & George Harrison; *Nobody's Child-Romanian Angel Appeal-C* . . . .(Warner Bros.)
Simon & Garfunkel; *Collected Works* . . . . (Columbia)
  Parsley Sage Rosemary & Thyme . . . . (Columbia)
  Simon & Garfunkel's Greatest Hits . . . . (Columbia)
  The Concert In Central Park . . . .(Warner Bros.)
Willie Nelson & Waylon Jennings; *Take It To The Limit* . . . . (Columbia)
I Can Hear Kentucky Calling Me
Chet Atkins; *Collector's Chet Atkins* . . . . (RCA)
I Can Hear Music
Beach Boys; *Friends-20/20* . . . . (Capitol)
  Sunshine Dream. . . . . (Capitol)
Beach Boys & Kathy Troccoli; *Stars And Stripes-#1* . . . .(River North)
I Can Hear The Grass Grow
Blues Magoos; *Nuggets-#11-Pop-Part 4-C* . . . . (Rhino)
Move; *Best Of The Move.* . . . . (A&M)
I Do
Lisa Loeb; *Firecracker.* . . . .(Geffen)
I Got The Hook Up
Master P featuring Sons Of Funk; *ST/I Got The Hook Up.* . . . . (No Limit/Priority)
Sons Of Funk; *The Game Of Funk* . . . . (No Limit/Priority)
I Hear A Rhapsody
John Coltrane; *Lush Life* . . . .(Prestige)
  More Lasting Than Bronze . . . .(Prestige)
  Prestige Twofer Giants-#2. . . . . (Prestige)
I Hear A Symphony
Diana Ross & The Supremes; *16 #1 Hits From The Early '60s-C* . . . . (Motown)
  Diana Ross & The Supremes' Greatest Hits . . . . (Motown)
  Diana Ross & The Supremes-25th Anniversary. . . . . (Motown)
  Diana Ross & The Supremes-Anthology (1962-1969). . . . . (Motown)
  Evening With Diana Ross . . . . (Motown)
  Every Great #1 Hit . . . . (Motown)
  Good Feeling Music Of The Big Chill Generation-#2-C . . . . (Motown)
  Motown Story-First 25 Years-C. . . . . (Motown)
Supremes; *I Hear A Symphony* . . . . (Motown)
I Hear Music
Anita O'Day; *Big Band Session* . . . . (Verve)
  Live At Mingos . . . . (Emily)
I Hear Music
Billie Holiday; *Billie Holiday-Golden Year-#2* . . . . (Columbia)
  Quintessential-#8-1939-1940 . . . . (Legacy)
  The Billie Holiday Story-#3 . . . . (Columbia)
I Hear Those Bells
Kings; *45-#1018.* . . . . (Collectables)
I Hear You Knockin'
Smiley Lewis; *Billboard Top R&B Hits-1955-C* . . . . (Rhino)
  Non-Stop Party Rock . . . .(EMI)
I Hear You Now
Jon & Vangelis; *Best Of Jon & Vangelis.* . . . . (Polydor)
  Short Stories . . . . (Polydor)
I Hear Your Voice
Lionel Richie; *Time* . . . . (Mercury)
I Heard
Mills Brothers; *Essential Mills Brothers: Four Boys And A Guitar* . . . . (Legacy)
I Heard It Through The Grapevine
Creedence Clearwater Revival; *Chooglin'.* . . . . (Fantasy)
  Cosmo's Factory. . . . . (Fantasy)
  Creedence Clearwater Revival-Chronicle. . . . . (Fantasy)
  Creedence Clearwater Revival-Gold. . . . . (Fantasy)
  Movie Album . . . . (Fantasy)
Gladys Knight & The Pips; *16 #1 Hits From The Late '60s-C* . . . . (Motown)
  Compact Command Performances-Gladys Knight & The Pips . . . . (Motown)
  Every Great Motown Song-First 25 Years-C. . . . . (Motown)

  Motown Grammy R&B Performances Of The '60s & '70s-C . . . . . (Motown)
  Motown Superstar Series-#13-Gladys Knight & The Pips . . . . . . (Motown)
  Top 10 With A Bullet-Motown Girl Groups-C . . . . (Motown)
Marvin Gaye; *25 #1 Hits From 25 Years-C.* . . . . (Motown)
  Every Great Motown Hit Of Marvin Gaye . . . . (Motown)
  Marvin Gaye Live At The London Palladium . . . . (Motown)
  Marvin Gaye-Anthology . . . . (Motown)
  Most Played Songs On America's Jukeboxes . . . . (Motown)
  Motown Story-First 25 Years-C . . . . (Motown)
I Heard The Jukebox Playing
Faron Young; *Hi Tone Poppa* . . . . (Collectables)
Kitty Wells; *The Kitty Wells Story.* . . . .(MCA)
I Talk To The Trees
Al Hirt; *Al Hirt* . . . . (Dunhill Compact Classics)
  Showtime . . . . (Allegiance)
Alan Jay Lerner; *Alan Jay Lerner Performs His Own Songs* . . . . (DRG)
Original Broadway Cast; *Paint Your Wagon.* . . . . (RCA Victor)
I Walk The Line (Revisited)
Rodney Crowell; *The Houston Kid* . . . .(Sugar Hill)
I Wanna Hear It From You
Eddy Raven; *Best Of Eddy Raven* . . . . (Curtom)
I Wanna Hear It From Your Lips
Eric Carmen; *Eric Carmen* . . . . (Geffen)
Louise Mandrell; *Dreamin'.* . . . . (RCA)
I Want To Hear A Yankee Doodle Tune
George M. Cohan; *Music From The New York Stage (1890-1920)-#1-1890-1908-C.* . . . . (Pearl)
Is That A Tear
Tracy Lawrence; *Best Of Tracy Lawrence* . . . .(Atlantic)
  Time Marches On. . . . . (Atlantic)
I've Been Working On The Railroad
Mitch Miller; *Sing Along With Mitch* . . . . (Columbia)
Original Soundtrack; *Children's Favorites* . . . .(Kid Rhino/Rhino 4 Kids)
John Doe No. 24
Mary Chapin Carpenter; *Stones In The Road* . . . . (Columbia)
Just To Hear You Say That You Love Me
Faith Hill & Tim McGraw; *Faith* . . . . (Warner Bros.)
Kind Of A Drag
Buckinghams; *Kind Of A Drag* . . . .(Sundazed Music)
  Mercy, Mercy, Mercy . . . .(Legacy Rock Artifacts Series)
Last Goodbye
Kenny Wayne Shepherd Band; *Live On* . . . .(Giant)
Last Laugh
Mark Knopfler; *Sailing To Philadelphia* . . . . (Warner Bros.)
Let's Hear It For The Boy
Deniece Williams; *Billboard Top Hits-1984-C.* . . . . (Rhino)
  ST/Footloose . . . . (Columbia)
Letting The Cables Sleep
Bush; *Science Of Things* . . . . (Trauma)
Lisa, Listen To Me
Blood, Sweat & Tears; *Blood, Sweat & Tears Greatest Hits* . . . . (Columbia)
Listen
Collective Soul; *Disciplined Breakdown.* . . . .(Atlantic)
Listen Here
Brian Auger; *Best Of Brian Auger* . . . . (Out Of Print)
Listen Like Thieves
INXS; *Listen Like Thieves.* . . . .(Atlantic)
Listen Listen
Fairport Convention; *Fairport Convention-Chronicles* . . . . (A&M)
Listen People
Herman's Hermits; *Herman's Hermits-Their Greatest Hits* . . . .(Abkco)
Listen To A Country Song
Loggins & Messina; *Loggins & Messina-On Stage.* . . . . (Columbia)
  Sittin' In . . . . (Columbia)
Lynn Anderson; *Country Chartbusters-#2* . . . . (Columbia)
  Lynn Anderson's Greatest Hits. . . . . (Columbia)
Listen To Her Heart
Tom Petty And The Heartbreakers; *You're Gonna Get It!* . . . .(Gone Gator)
Listen To Me
Buddy Holly; *Buddy Holly* . . . . (MCA)
  Buddy Holly-20 Golden Greats . . . . (MCA)
  Rock & Roll Collection. . . . . (MCA)
Listen To The Band
Monkees; *Monkees' Greatest Hits* . . . . (Rhino)
  Present . . . . (Rhino)
Listen To The Heartbeat
Billy Squier; *Emotions In Motion* . . . . (Capitol)
Listen To The Lion
Van Morrison; *It's Too Late To Stop Now* . . . . (Warner Bros.)
  St. Dominic's Preview . . . . (Warner Bros.)
Listen To The Mocking Bird
Lester Flatt; *Lester Raymond Flatt* . . . . (Flying Fish)
Listen To The Music
Doobie Brothers; *Best Of The Doobies* . . . . (Warner Bros.)
  Farewell Tour. . . . . (Warner Bros.)
  Toulouse Street. . . . . (Warner Bros.)
Listen To The Radio
Don Williams; *Best Of Don Williams-#3* . . . . (MCA)

Listen To The Radio . . . . (MCA)
Kathy Mattea; *Lonesome Standard Time* . . . . (Mercury)
Nanci Griffith; *Storms* . . . . (MCA)
Listen To What The Man Said
Wings; *Venus And Mars* . . . . (Capitol)
Wings Over America . . . . (Capitol)
Listen, The Snow Is Falling
John Lennon; *Wedding Album* . . . . (Rykodisc)
Listening To You
Who; *Tommy* . . . . (MCA)
Lonesome Whistle
Hank Williams With His Drifting Cowboys; *Between The Rails: America's*
Train Songs-C . . . . (Crescendo)
Hank Williams-24 Greatest Hits-#2 . . . . (Polydor)
Hank Williams-40 Greatest Hits . . . . (Polydor)
Johnny Cash; *Story Songs Of The Trains & Rivers* . . . . (Sun)
Little Feat; *Hoy-Hoy!* . . . . (Warner Bros.)
My Silent Love
Bing Crosby; *Where The Blue Of The Night Meets The Gold Of*
The Day . . . . (Biograph)
Peggy Lee; *Mink Jazz* . . . . (Blue Note)
Never Ending
Wood; *Songs From Stamford Hill* . . . . (Columbia)
Next Voice You Hear
Jackson Browne; *The Next Voice You Hear-Best Of Jackson Browne* . . . (Elektra)
No More "I Love You's"
Annie Lennox; *Medusa* . . . . (Arista)
Nothing To Prove
Caroline's Spine; *Attention Please* . . . . (Hollywood)
One Day In March I Go Down To The Sea And Listen
Jan Garbarek Group; *It's OK To Listen To The Gray Voice* . . . . (ECM)
One Voice
Billy Gilman; *One Voice* . . . . (Epic)
Only A Northern Song
Beatles; *The Beatles-Anthology-#2* . . . . (Capitol)
Yellow Submarine . . . . (Capitol)
Open Your Eyes
Doobie Brothers; *Minute By Minute* . . . . (Warner Bros.)
Papa Can You Hear Me?
Barbra Streisand; *One Voice* . . . . (Columbia)
ST/Yentl . . . . (Columbia)
Papa-Oom-Mow-Mow
Rivingtons; *Cruisin'-1962-C* . . . . (Increase)
EMI Legends Of Rock & Roll-24 Greatest Hits-C . . . . (EMI)
In The Still Of The Night . . . . (Capitol)
Kahuna Classics-A Collection Of Surf Music-C . . . . (K-Tel)
Monster Summer Hits-Wild Surf-C . . . . (Capitol)
Please
Chris Isaak; *Speak Of The Devil* . . . . (Reprise)
Plowed
Sponge; *Rotting Pinata* . . . . (Work)
Rhythm Of The Rain
Cascades; *Collectables Presents The History Of Rock-#7-C* . . . . . . (Collectables)
Golden Years-1963-C . . . . (Dominion Entert.)
Rumor Has It
Reba McEntire; *Reba McEntire's Greatest Hits Volume Two* . . . . (MCA)
Rumor Has It . . . . (MCA)
Rumor Has It
Clay Walker; *Clay Walker's Greatest Hits* . . . . (Giant)
Rumor Has It . . . . (Giant)
Semi-Charmed Life
Third Eye Blind; *Jock Rock 2000-C* . . . . (Tommy Boy)
Third Eye Blind . . . . (Elektra)
She
Green Day; *Dookie* . . . . (Reprise)
Shelf In The Room
Days Of The New; *Days Of The New* . . . . (Outpost/Interscope)
Shhh
Tevin Campbell; *I'm Ready* . . . . (Qwest)
Shit You Hear At Parties
Minutemen; *Ballot Result* . . . . (SST)
Singing In My Sleep
Semisonic; *Feeling Strangely Fine* . . . . (MCA)
So Far Away
Stabbing Westward; *Stabbing Westward* . . . . (Koch International)
Song For The Life
Alan Jackson; *Who I Am* . . . . (Arista)
Alison Krauss; *Too Late To Cry* . . . . (Rounder)
Jerry Jeff Walker; *A Man Must Carry On* . . . . (MCA)
John Denver; *Country Roads Collection* . . . . (RCA)
Kathy Mattea; *Walk The Way The Wind Blows* . . . . (Mercury)
Rodney Crowell; *Ain't Living Long Like This* . . . . (Warner Bros.)
Song Of A Summer Night
Original Broadway Cast; *The Most Happy Fella* . . . . (Sony Music Classical)
Sound & Vision
David Bowie; *Changestwobowie* . . . . (RCA)
Low . . . . (Rykodisc)
Sound + Vision . . . . (Rykodisc)
The Singles-1969-1993 . . . . (Rykodisc)

Sound Of Goodbye
Crystal Gayle; *Best Of Crystal Gayle* . . . . (Warner Bros.)
Cage The Songbird . . . . (Warner Bros.)
Sound Of Music
Mormon Tabernacle Choir; *Mormon Tabernacle Choir's Greatest Hits-22*
Best-Loved Favorites . . . . (Sony Masterworks)
Original Cast; *The Sound Of Music* . . . . (Sony Broadway)
Sound Of Your Voice
38 Special; *Bone Against Steel* . . . . (Charisma)
Sounds Like Love
Johnny Lee; *Johnny Lee's Greatest Hits* . . . . (Full Moon/Asylum)
Stop, Look & Listen
Patsy Cline; *Loved & Lost Again* . . . . (Fifty One West)
Rockin' Side-Her First Recordings-#3 . . . . (Rhino)
Stop, Look & Listen . . . . (MCA)
Try Again . . . . (Quicksilver)
Stop, Look & Listen
Dorsey Brothers; *1934-1935 Decca Sessions* . . . . (MCA)
Complete Tommy Dorsey-#4 . . . . (RCA)
Stop, Look & Listen
Chiffons; *Best Of The Chiffons* . . . . (Laurie)
Stop, Look & Listen
Elvis Presley; *Collector's Gold* . . . . (RCA)
Stop, Look & Listen
Donna Summer; *She Works Hard For The Money* . . . . (Mercury)
Summer Collection . . . . (Mercury)
Talking In Your Sleep
Crystal Gayle; *Classic Crystal* . . . . (EMI)
Country Gold-C . . . . (Priority)
Crystal Gayle's All-Time Greatest Hits . . . . (Curb)
When I Dream . . . . (Liberty)
Reba McEntire; *Starting Over* . . . . (MCA)
Tears Falling Down
Rosanne Cash; *The Wheel* . . . . (Columbia)
Teen Angel
Dion And The Belmonts; *Everything You Always Wanted* . . . . . . (Laurie)
Rock & Roll U.S.A.-21 Rock & Roll Favorites-#2-C . . . . (Laurie)
Mark Dinning; *Golden Years-1959-C* . . . . (Dominion Entert.)
Oldies But Goodies-#7-C . . . . (Original Sound)
ST/American Graffiti . . . . (MCA)
Teenage Tragedies-C . . . . (Rhino)
Thank U
Alanis Morissette; *Supposed Former Infatuation Junkie* . . . . (Maverick)
That's The Way I've Always Heard It Should Be
Carly Simon; *Best Of Carly Simon* . . . . (Elektra)
Carly Simon . . . . (Elektra)
There's A Kind Of Hush (All Over The World)
Carpenters; *A Kind Of Hush* . . . . (A&M)
Carpenters-Classics-#2 . . . . (A&M)
Yesterday Once More . . . . (A&M)
Herman's Hermits; *Herman's Hermits-Their Greatest Hits* . . . . (Abkco)
Til I Hear It From You
Gin Blossoms; *ST/Crossroads-VH1 Television Program* . . . . (Atlantic)
ST/Empire Records . . . . (A&M)
Till There Was You
Beatles; *Beatles-Box Set* . . . . (Capitol)
Meet The Beatles! . . . . (Capitol)
With The Beatles . . . . (Parlophone)
Original Cast; *ST/The Music Man* . . . . (Warner Bros.)
To Beat The Devil
Johnny Cash; *Johnny Cash-16 Biggest Hits-#2* . . . . (Legacy)
Tommy Can You Hear Me
Who; *Join Together* . . . . (MCA)
ST/The Kids Are Alright . . . . (MCA)
ST/Tommy . . . . (Polydor)
Tommy . . . . (MCA)
Turn On Your Radio
Nilsson; *Son Of Schmilsson* . . . . (RCA)
Turn The Beat Around
Gloria Estefan; *Hold Me, Thrill Me, Kiss Me* . . . . (Epic)
ST/The Specialist . . . . (Epic/Sony Music Soundtrax)
Vicki Sue Robinson; *Dance Floor Divas-The '70s-C* . . . . (Rhino)
Never Gonna Let You Go . . . . (RCA)
Nipper's Greatest Hits Of The '70s-C . . . . (RCA)
Uncle John's Band
Grateful Dead; *Best Of/Skeletons From The Closet* . . . . (Warner Bros.)
Workingman's Dead . . . . (Warner Bros.)
Indigo Girls; *Deadicated-C* . . . . (Arista)
Unheard Music
X; *Live At The Whisky A Go-Go* . . . . (Elektra)
Los Angeles/Wild Gift . . . . (Slash)
Van Gogh's Left Ear
Kenny Garrett; *Black Hope* . . . . (Warner Bros.)
Vincent
Don McLean; *American Pie* . . . . (EMI)
Best Of Don McLean . . . . (EMI)
Greatest Hits Then & Now . . . . (EMI)
Voice Of The Heart
Diana Ross; *Take Me Higher* . . . . (Motown)

Voices Carry
'Til Tuesday; *Voices Carry*..................................(Epic)
Wabash Cannonball
Billy Strange; *Between The Rails: America's Train Songs-C*......(Crescendo)
Nitty Gritty Dirt Band; *Will The Circle Be Unbroken*.................(EMI)
Roy Acuff; *All Time Legends Of Country Music-C* ....(Legacy)
Backstage At The Grand Ole Opry-C........................(RCA)
Best Of Roy Acuff.......................................(Liberty)
Columbia Historic Edition-Roy Acuff....................(Columbia)
Essential Roy Acuff-1936-1949 ....(Legacy)
Hot Tracks-Train Super Hits-C...............................(Epic)
Roy Acuff's Greatest Hits..............................(Columbia)
Steel Rails-Classic Railroad Songs-#1-C ....(Rounder)
Warm Machine
Bush; *Science Of Things*.................................(Trauma)
Welcome To The Occupation
R.E.M.; *Document* ....(EMI-Capitol Entert. Properties)
When Love Starts Talkin'
Wynonna; *The Other Side*............................(Curb/MCA)
Whisper My Name
Randy Travis; *This Is Me* ....(Warner Bros.)
White Noise
Jay Ferguson; *White Noise* ....(Capitol)
Yesterday, I Heard The Rain
Bill Evans; *Tokyo Concert*.............................(Fantasy)
Tony Bennett; *Essence Of Tony Bennett*....................(Columbia)
You Ain't Heard Nothing Yet
Al Jolson; *Music From The New York Stage (1890-1920)-#4-1917-
1920-C* ....(Pearl)
You Could've Heard A Heart Break
Johnny Lee; *Workin' For A Livin'* ....(Full Moon/Warner Bros.)
You Haven't Heard The Last Of Me
Moe Bandy; *You Haven't Heard The Last Of Me* ....(MCA)
Peter Allen; *Not The Boy Next Door*........................(Arista)
You Should Hear How She Talks About You
Melissa Manchester; *Hey Ricky* ....(Arista)
Melissa Manchester's Greatest Hits ....(Arista)

HEART, Valentines

See Also: BREAK, CHARACTER & INTEGRITY, FEELINGS, LOVE
(various), MARRIAGE, MOTIVATION, PAIN & HEALING, SWEET

(All Of A Sudden) My Heart Sings
Paul Anka; *Paul Anka Sings His Big 15, Vol. 2*....................(RCA)
Paul Anka-30th Anniversary Anthology ....(Rhino)
(You Sure Know Your Way) Around My Heart
Louise Mandrell & R.C. Bannon; *Me & My R.C.* ....(RCA)
5 Miles To Empty
Brownstone; *Still Climbing*....................... (MJJ Music/Work)
6th Avenue Heartache
Wallflowers; *Best Of Rockline-C* ....(Priority)
Bringing It All Back Home ....(Columbia)
Absence Of The Heart
Deana Carter; *Everything's Gonna Be Alright* ....(Capitol)
Achy Breaky Heart
Billy Ray Cyrus; *Some Gave All* ....(Mercury)
Affair Of The Heart
Rick Springfield; *Living In Oz* ....(RCA)
Rick Springfield's Greatest Hits..........................(RCA)
Affairs Of The Heart
Fleetwood Mac; *25 Years-The Chain* ....(Warner Bros.)
After All (Love Theme From Chances Are)
Cher; *Heart Of Stone*...................................(Geffen)
All Cried Out
Allure; *Allure* ....(Track Masters/Crave)
Boom! 17 Explosive Hits-C ....(Simitar)
Lisa Lisa; *Lisa Lisa & Cult Jam With Full Force* ....(Columbia)
Lisa Lisa-Super Hits ....(Columbia)
Past, Present & Future ....(TMP)
All Of Me
Billie Holiday; *Billie Holiday-Love Songs* ....(Legacy)
Count Basie; *Compact Jazz-The Standards* ....(Verve)
Diana Ross; *ST/Lady Sings The Blues*.....................(Motown)
Dinah Washington; *Compact Jazz-Dinah Washington*............(Verve)
Duke Ellington; *Jazz Party*.............................(Legacy)
Esquivel; *Music From A Sparkling Planet* ....(Bar/None)
Frank Sinatra; *Sinatra Sings His Greatest Hits* ....(Legacy)
Helen O'Connell; *Great Girl Singers Sing 22 Original
Recordings-C* ....(Hindsight)
Louis Armstrong; *Louis Armstrong's Greatest Hits*..............(Legacy)
Martha Tilton; *Sweet And Lovely: Capitol's Great Ladies Of Song-C* .. (Capitol)
Paul Whiteman & Mildred Bailey; *Those Wonderful Years: Happy Days Are
Here Again-C* .... (JCI Assoc. Labels)
Sarah Vaughan; *Essential Sarah Vaughan-The Great Songs* ....(Verve)
Willie Nelson; *Stardust*................................(Legacy)

Alone
Bee Gees; *Still Waters* ....(Polydor)
Always In My Heart
Tevin Campbell; *I'm Ready*..............................(Qwest)
Always In My Heart
Bob Seger & The Silver Bullet Band; *The Fire Inside*..............(Capitol)
American Heartbeat
Survivor; *Eye Of The Tiger*...........................(Scotti Bros.)
American Hearts
Air Supply; *Lost In Love* ....(Arista)
Among My Souvenirs
Connie Francis; *Connie Francis' Greatest Hits* ....(Polydor)
Frank Sinatra; *Columbia Years-1943-1952-Complete Recordings*.....(Legacy)
Marty Robbins; *Marty Robbins-Super Hits*.................(Columbia)
Sons Of The Pioneers; *Country & Western Memories* ....(Pair)
Anema E Core
Eddie Fisher; *Very Best Of Eddie Fisher* ....(Taragon)
Aneurysm
Nirvana; *From The Muddy Banks Of The Wishkah* ....(David Geffen Co.)
Anyone Who Had A Heart
Dionne Warwick; *Dionne Warwick Greatest Hits*................(Everest)
Dionne Warwick-Anthology 1962-1971......................(Rhino)
Sultry Soul Sisters-Wonder Women-#3-C.....................(Rhino)
April In My Heart
Billie Holiday; *Quintessential-#6-1938* ....(Columbia)
Arrow Thru Your Heart
Lou Gramm; *Ready or Not* ....(Atlantic)
Ashtray Heart
Captain Beefheart; *Doc At The Radar Station* ....(Blue Plate)
Away
Toadies; *Rubberneck*................................(Interscope)
Baby Don't Break Your Baby's Heart
Kashif; *Send Me Your Love* ....(Arista)
Baby Don't You Do It (Break My Heart)
Marvin Gaye; *Marvin Gaye-Anthology*......................(Motown)
Marvin Gaye-Super Hits ....(Motown)
Musical Testament 1964-1984 ....(Motown)
Babylon
David Gray; *White Ladder* ....(ATO/RCA)
Bad Liver & A Broken Heart
Tom Waits; *Small Change*...............................(Asylum)
Bad Of The Heart
George LaMond; *Bad Of The Heart* ....(Columbia)
Badlands
Bruce Springsteen; *Bruce Springsteen's Greatest Hits*...........(Columbia)
Darkness On The Edge Of Town..........................(Columbia)
Bruce Springsteen & The E Street Band; *Bruce Springsteen & The E Street
Band Live/1975-85* ....(Legacy)
Be Careful
Ricky Martin & Madonna; *Ricky Martin*.....................(Columbia)
Be Careful, It's My Heart
Bing Crosby & Fred Astaire; *ST/Holiday Inn* ....(MCA)
Four Freshmen; *Puttin' On The Ritz-Capitol Sings Berlin-C* ....(Capitol)
Kate Smith; *Kate Smith-16 Most Requested Songs* ....(Columbia)
Rosemary Clooney; *Rosemary Clooney Sings The Music Of Irving
Berlin*. .... (Concord Jazz)
Tommy Dorsey & Frank Sinatra; *Tommy Dorsey & Frank Sinatra's All-Time
Greatest Hits-#1* ....(Bluebird)
Be Still My Beating Heart
Sting; *...Nothing Like The Sun* ....(A&M)
Fields Of Gold-The Best Of Sting 1984-1994 ....(A&M)
Beat Of A Heart
Scandal featuring Patty Smyth; *Warrior* ....(Columbia)
Bet Your Heart On Me
Johnny Lee; *Johnny Lee's Greatest Hits* ....(Full Moon/Asylum)
Better Your Heart Than Mine
Trisha Yearwood; *The Song Remembers When* .... (MCA)
Black Hearted Woman
Allman Brothers Band; *Allman Brothers Band* ....(Polydor)
Beginnings...(Polydor)
*The Road Goes On Forever, A Collection Of Their Greatest
Recordings*. ....(Polydor)
Black Valentine
Scott Thomas Band; *California*...........................(Elektra)
Blame It On Your Heart
Patty Loveless; *Only What I Feel* ....(Epic)
Patty Loveless-Classics ....(Epic)
Blue Moon With Heartache
Rosanne Cash; *19 Hot Country Requests-#2-C* .... (Epic)
Rosanne Cash-Hits-1979-1989 ....(Columbia)
Seven Year Ache ....(Columbia)
Blue Valentine
Tom Waits; *The Heart Of Saturday Night* ....(Asylum)
Born With A Broken Heart
Kenny Wayne Shepherd; *Ledbetter Heights* ....(Giant)
Brand New Heartache
Everly Brothers; *Everly Brothers* ....(Rhino)
Everly Brothers-Cadence Classics-Their 20 Greatest Hits ....(Rhino)

Brave Heart
Bill Miller; *Raven In The Snow* ....(Reprise)
Break My Heart
Squeeze; *Cosi Fan Tutti Frutti* .... (A&M)
Break My Heart
Shakespear's Sister; *Sacred Heart*.................. (Full Frequency Range)
Break My Heart
David Ruffin; *So Soon We Changed* ....(Warner Bros.)
Broken Hearted Savior
Big Head Todd & The Monsters; *Sister Sweetly* ....(Giant)
Broken Heartland
Don Williams; *One Good Well* ....(RCA)
Broken Heartland
Holly Dunn; *Heart Full Of Love* ....(Warner Bros.)
Brokenhearted
Brandy featuring Wanya Morris; *Brandy* .... (Atlantic)
Brokenhearted Me
Anne Murray; *15 Of The Best* ....(Liberty)
Anne Murray's Greatest Hits ....(Capitol)
Broken-Hearted Melody
Sarah Vaughan; *Essential Sarah Vaughan-The Great Songs* ....(Verve)
Sarah Vaughan-Golden Hits.......................(Mercury)
Burnin' A Hole In My Heart
Skip Ewing; *Class Of Country-C* ....(K-Tel)
Coast Of Colorado ....(MCA)
Burning Heart
Vandenberg; *Best Of Vandenberg* ....(Atco)
Vandenberg ....(Atco)
Burning Heart
Survivor; *Rocky Story-C* ....(Scotti Bros.)
ST/Rocky IV ....(Scotti Bros.)
By Heart
Jim Brickman; *By Heart* .... (Windham Hill)
Call To Your Heart
Giuffria; *Giuffria* ....(Camel)
Can I Touch You...There?
Michael Bolton; *Michael Bolton's Greatest Hits-1985-1995* ....(Columbia)
Can I Trust You With My Heart
Travis Tritt; *T-R-O-U-B-L-E* ....(Warner Bros.)
Can't Break It To My Heart
Tracy Lawrence; *Alibis* .... (Atlantic)
Can't Fight The Moonlight
LeAnn Rimes; *ST/Coyote Ugly* .... (London Sire/Curb)
Can't Stop My Heart From Loving You
Aaron Neville; *The Tattooed Heart* ....(A&M)
O'Kanes; *Greatest Country Hits Of The '80s-1987-C*...........(Columbia)
More Hot Country Requests-#2-C ....(Epic)
O'Kanes ....(Columbia)
Can't You Hear My Heartbeat
Herman's Hermits; *Herman's Hermits-Their Greatest Hits* .... (Abkco)
Captain Of Her Heart
Double; *Blue* ....(A&M)
Romantic Hits Of The '80s-C ....(K-Tel)
Caught In Your Web (Swear To Your Heart)
Russell Hitchcock; *ST/Arachnophobia* ....(Hollywood)
Chains Around My Heart
Richard Marx; *Rush Street*...........................(Capitol)
Change Of Heart
Judds; *Judds* ....(RCA)
Judds' Greatest Hits ....(MCA)
Change Of Heart
Eric Carmen; *Best Of Eric Carmen* ....(Arista)
Change Of Heart................................(Arista)
Change Of Heart
Toto; *Isolation* ....(Columbia)
Change Of Heart
Tom Petty And The Heartbreakers; *Long After Dark* .... (MCA)
Change Of Heart
Stray Cats; *Rock Therapy* ....(EMI)
Change Of Heart
Cyndi Lauper; *True Colors* ....(Portrait)
Chrome Plated Heart
Melissa Etheridge; *Melissa Etheridge* ....(Island)
Church Of Your Heart
Roxette; *Joyride* .... (EMI)
Closer To The Heart
Rush; *Exit...Stage Left*..........................(Mercury)
Farewell To Kings ....(Mercury)
Rush-Chronicles................................(Mercury)
Show Of Hands.................................(Mercury)
Clouds In My Heart
Muddy Waters; *Blues Deluxe* .... (Allegiance)
Cold Cold Heart
Hank Williams; *Complete Hank Williams*..................(Mercury)
Hank Williams With His Drifting Cowboys; *24 Of Hank Williams'*
Greatest Hits ....(Polydor)
Hank Williams ....(MGM)
Hank Williams-40 Greatest Hits....................(Polydor)

Live At Opry ....(MGM)
Long Gone Lonesome Blues ....(Polydor)
Jerry Lee Lewis; *Duets*................................ (Sun)
Golden Cream Of Jerry Lee Lewis ....(Sun)
Jerry Lee Lewis & Friends-Duets ....(Sun)
Lucinda Williams; *Timeless: Hank Williams*
Tribute-C ....(Lost Highway/IDJMG)
Tony Bennett; *Tony Bennett-16 Most Requested Songs*............(Legacy)
Cold Hearted
Paula Abdul; *Forever Your Girl*........................ (Virgin)
Get Up & Dance-Dance Mixes .... (Virgin)
Come And Knock (On The Door Of My Heart)
Roy Acuff; *45-#1097* .... (Hickory)
Come From The Heart
Don Williams; *Traces* ....(Capitol)
Kathy Mattea; *Willow In The Wind* ....(Mercury)
Connection
Elastica; *Elastica* .... (David Geffen Co.)
Conviction Of The Heart
Kenny Loggins; *Leap Of Faith*.........................(Columbia)
Outside: From The Redwoods ....(Columbia)
Yesterday, Today, Tomorrow: The Greatest Hits Of Kenny
Loggins.....................................(Columbia)
Crazy From The Heart
Bellamy Brothers; *Bellamy Brothers' Greatest Hits-#3*....... (MCA)
Crazy From The Heart ....(MCA)
Crazy Heart
Forester Sisters; *Forester Sisters* ....(Warner Bros.)
Hank Williams With His Drifting Cowboys; *Hank Williams-24 Greatest*
Hits-#2 ....(Polydor)
Hank Williams-40 Greatest Hits ....(Polydor)
Hey Good Lookin' (December 1950-July 1951) ....(Polydor)
Rare Takes & Radio Cuts ....(Polydor)
Cross My Broken Heart
Jets; *Magic* ....(MCA)
Soundtrack Smashes-'80s & More-C ....(MCA)
ST/Beverly Hills Cop II ....(MCA)
Cross My Broken Heart
Suzy Bogguss; *Somewhere Between* ....(Capitol)
Cross My Heart
Johnny Lee; *Best Of Johnny Lee* ....(Curb)
New Directions ....(Curb)
Cross My Heart
Everything But The Girl; *Baby The Stars Shine Bright* .... (Sire)
Cross My Heart
Diana Ross; *Endless Love* ....(RCA)
Cross My Heart
Eighth Wonder; *Fearless* ....(WTG)
Cross My Heart
Billy Stewart; *Greatest Sides* ....(Chess)
Cross My Heart
Bruce Springsteen; *Human Touch* ....(Columbia)
Cross My Heart
Martika; *Martika* ....(Columbia)
Cross My Heart
Johnny Ace; *Memorial Album* ....(MCA)
Cross My Heart
Dolly Parton/Vince Gill/Ricky Skaggs; *Slow Dancing With*
The Moon ....(Columbia)
Cross My Heart
Tracie Spencer; *Tracie Spencer* ....(Capitol)
Cross My Heart & Hope To Die
Elvis Presley; *ST/Girl Happy* ....(RCA)
Cross My Heart I Love You
Bob Wills & His Texas Playboys; *Bob Wills & His Texas Playboys-24*
Great Hits ....(Polydor)
Cross Your Heart
Artie Shaw & The Gramercy Five; *This Is Artie Shaw* ....(Bluebird)
Brothers Figaro; *Gypsy Beat* .... (Geffen)
Crying My Heart Out For You
Diana Ross; *All The Great Love Songs-Diana Ross* ....(Motown)
Diana Ross-Anthology ....(Motown)
Crying My Heart Out For You
Doris Day; *Doris Day Sings 22 Great Songs-Original Big Band* .....(Hindsight)
The Uncollected Doris Day with The Page Cavanaugh Trio-#2 ....(Hindsight)
Crying My Heart Out Over You
Ricky Skaggs; *Greatest Country Hits Of The '80s-1981-C* ....(Columbia)
Waiting For The Sun To Shine.......................(Epic)
Cupid
Sam Cooke; *Best Of Sam Cooke* ....(RCA)
The Man And His Music ....(RCA)
Spinners; *Love Trippin'* .... (Atlantic)
Danger Heartbreak Dead Ahead
Bonnie Raitt; *Bonnie Raitt* .... (Warner Bros.)
Marvelettes; *Marvelettes' Greatest Hits* ....(Motown)
Marvelettes-Anthology ....(Motown)
ST/Good Morning, Vietnam ....(A&M)
Dear Heart
Andy Williams; *Andy Williams' Greatest Hits* ....(Columbia)

Andy Williams-16 Most Requested Songs . . . . (Legacy)

Dear Lonely Hearts
Nat ''King'' Cole; *Capitol Collectors Series-Nat ''King'' Cole* . . . . . (Capitol)
Ramblin' Rose . . . . (Capitol)

Deep In My Heart
Fleshtones; *Living Legends*. . . . .(I.R.S.)

Deep In My Heart
Club House; *Deep In My Heart (Single)* . . . . (Atlantic)

Deep In My Heart
Shells; *Golden Classics-Shells* . . . . (Collectables)

Deep In The Heart Of Texas
Bing Crosby; *Bing Crosby's Greatest Hits* . . . .(MCA)
Bob Wills; *Best Of Bob Wills & His Texas Playboys* . . . . (MCA)
Best Of Bob Wills-#2 . . . .(MCA)
Gene Autry; *Columbia Historic Edition-Gene Autry* . . . . (Columbia)
Texas Super Hits-C . . . . (Columbia)
Moe Bandy; *Taste Of Texas-Songs 'Bout Texas By Texans-C* . . . . . . (Columbia)

Deserted Cities Of The Heart
Cream; *Cream-Live-#2* . . . . (Polydor)
Wheels Of Fire . . . . (Polydor)

Devil In Her Heart
Beatles; *The Beatles' Second Album*. (Capitol)
With The Beatles . . . . (Parlophone)
Donays; *Beatles Originals* . . . . (Rhino)

Does Your Heart Beat For Me
Blue Barron; *Big Band Treasures-#2-C* . . . .(Dunhill Compact Classics)
Patsy Cline; *Always* . . . . (MCA)
Portrait Of Patsy Cline . . . . (MCA)
Russ Morgan; *Best Of Russ Morgan* . . . . (MCA)
Russ Morgan & His Orchestra; *Russ Morgan & His Orchestra Play 22*
Original Big Band Recordings . . . . (Hindsight)

Don't Be Cruel
Cheap Trick; *Cheap Trick's Greatest Hits* . . . . (Epic)
Lap Of Luxury . . . . (Epic)
Elvis Presley; *Billboard Top Rock 'N' Roll Hits-1956-C* . . . . (Rhino)
Nipper's Greatest Hits Of The '50s-#2-C . . . . (RCA)
Number One Hits . . . . (RCA)
The Great Performances . . . . (RCA)
The Top Ten Hits . . . . (RCA)
Judds; *Heartland* . . . . (MCA)

Don't Believe My Heart Can Stand Another You
Tanya Tucker; *Tanya Tucker's Greatest Hits* . . . . (MCA)
The Tanya Tucker Collection. . . . . (MCA)

Don't Go Breaking My Heart
Elton John & Kiki Dee; *Elton John's Greatest Hits-#2* . . . . (Polydor)

Don't Let The Stars Get In Your Eyes
Perry Como; *Como's Golden Records* . . . . (RCA)
Perry Como-Pure Gold . . . . (RCA)
Perry Como's All-Time Greatest Hits-#1. . . . . (RCA)
This Is Perry Como . . . . (RCA)

Doo Doo Doo Doo Doo
Rolling Stones; *Goats Head Soup*. . . . .(Rolling Stones)
Made In The Shade . . . .(Rolling Stones)
Rewind (1971-1984) . . . .(Rolling Stones)

Door Is Still Open To My Heart
Dean Martin; *Dean Martin's Greatest Hits* . . . .(EMI)
Door Is Still Open To My Heart . . . . (Reprise)

Doors Of Your Heart
English Beat; *Wha'ppen* . . . .(I.R.S.)
What Is Beat . . . .(I.R.S.)

Down To My Last Broken Heart
Janie Fricke; *Greatest Country Hits Of The '80s-1980-C* . . . . . . (Columbia)
Janie Fricke-17 Greatest Hits . . . . (Columbia)
Janie Fricke's Greatest Hits . . . . (Columbia)

Dream Is A Wish Your Heart Makes
Barbara Cook; *Disney Album* . . . .(Disney)
Linda Ronstadt; *Disney's Music From The Park-C* . . . .(Disney)
Music Of Disney's Cinderella-C . . . .(Disney)
Michael Bolton; *Simply Mad About The Mouse-C* . . . . (Columbia)
Original Soundtrack; *ST/Cinderella* . . . .(Disney)

Dreams
Corrs; *Legacy-A Tribute To Fleetwood Mac's Rumours-C* . . . . (Lava)
Fleetwood Mac; *25 Years-The Chain*. . . . .(Warner Bros.)
Fleetwood Mac Live. . . . .(Warner Bros.)
Fleetwood Mac's Greatest Hits . . . .(Warner Bros.)
Rumours. . . . .(Warner Bros.)

Drunken Hearted Man
Robert Johnson; *Robert Johnson-Complete Recordings*. . . . . (Columbia)

Dyslexic Heart
Paul Westerberg; *ST/Singles*. . . . .(Epic)

Eartheart
Kenny Rankin; *Like A Seed*. . . . .(Little David)

Elderly Woman Behind The Counter In A Small Town
Pearl Jam; *Vs.* . . . . (Epic Portrait Assoc.)

Elvira
Murry Kellum; *Country Comedy-20 Country Comedy Hits* . . . . (Plantation)
Oak Ridge Boys; *Fancy Free*. . . . .(MCA)
MCA Records 30 Years Of Hits-1958-1988-C. . . . . (MCA)
Oak Ridge Boys' Greatest Hits 2 . . . . (MCA)

E-Mail My Heart
Britney Spears; *...Baby One More Time* . . . .(Jive)

Empty Heart
Rolling Stones; *12 X 5* . . . .(Abkco)

Empty-Handed Heart
Warren Zevon; *Bad Luck Streak In Dancing School* . . . .(Asylum)

Every Beat Of My Heart
Gladys Knight & The Pips; *Gladys Knight & The Pips-Anthology* . . . . (Motown)
Hits From The Legendary Vee-Jay Records-C. . . . . (Motown)
Oldies But Goodies-#6-C . . . .(Original Sound)
Sultry Soul Sisters-Wonder Women-#3-C. . . . . (Rhino)
Rod Stewart; *Storyteller/The Complete Anthology: 1964-1990* . . (Warner Bros.)

Every Heartbeat
Amy Grant; *Heart In Motion*. . . . . (A&M)

Everything Your Heart Desires
Daryl Hall & John Oates; *ooh yeah!* . . . . (Arista)

Everywhere
Tim McGraw; *Everywhere* . . . . (Curb)

Ev'ry Heart Should Have One
Charley Pride; *Charley Pride's Greatest Hits-#2* . . . . (RCA)
Night Games. . . . . (RCA)

Excuse Me (I Think I've Got A Heartache)
Buck Owens; *Billboard Top Country Hits-1960-C* . . . . (Rhino)
Buck Owens' All-Time Greatest Hits-#1 . . . . (Curb)
Buck Owens Collection-1959-1990 . . . . (Rhino)
Mavericks; *From Hell To Paradise* . . . . (MCA)

Expressway To Your Heart
Blues Brothers; *Best Of The Blues Brothers* . . . .(Atlantic)
Soul Survivors; *Dick Bartley's One-Hit Wonders Of The '60s-#2-C* . . (Rhino)
Oldies But Goodies-#11-C . . . .(Original Sound)
Super Oldies Of The '60s-#6-C . . . . (Audio Fidelity)
When The Whistle Blows Anything Goes . . . . (Collectables)

Faith Of The Heart
Rod Stewart; *ST/Patch Adams*. . . . . (Universal)

February In My Heart
Osborne Brothers; *Some Things I Want To Sing About* . . . . (Sugar Hill)

Final Heartbreak
Jessica Simpson; *Sweet Kisses* . . . . (Columbia)

Fire Of The Newly Alive
Rosanne Cash; *The Wheel* . . . . (Columbia)

Follow Your Heart
Triumph; *Stages* . . . . (MCA)
Thunder Seven . . . . (MCA)
Triumph-Classics . . . . (MCA)

Follow Your Heart
John McLaughlin; *CTI Masters Of The Guitar* . . . . (CBS Associated)
My Goals Beyond . . . . (Elektra)

Follow Your Heart
Joe Farrell; *Joe Farrell Quartet*. . . . . (CBS Associated)

Follow Your Heart
Manhattans; *Dedicated To You-Golden Classics-#1* . . . . (Collectables)

Fool Hearted Memory
George Strait; *George Strait's Greatest Hits*. . . . . (MCA)
Night Game . . . . (MCA)
Strait From The Heart . . . . (MCA)

Foolish Heart
Steve Perry; *Street Talk*. . . . . (Columbia)

Foolish Heart
Grateful Dead; *Built To Last* . . . . (Arista)

Foolish Heart
Sharon Bryant; *Here I Am* . . . .(Wing)

Fools Rush In (Where Angels Fear To Tread)
Brook Benton; *Super Oldies Of The '60s-#10-C* . . . . (Audio Fidelity)
Tommy Dorsey & Frank Sinatra; *Sessions-#1-February 1, 1940-July 17, 1940* . . . . (RCA)

For My Broken Heart
Reba McEntire; *For My Broken Heart* . . . . (MCA)
Reba McEntire's Greatest Hits Volume Two . . . . (MCA)

Fortress Around Your Heart
Sting; *Dream Of The Blue Turtles* . . . . (A&M)
Fields Of Gold-The Best Of Sting 1984-1994 . . . . (A&M)

Frozen
Madonna; *GHV2* . . . . (Warner Bros.)
Ray Of Light . . . . (Maverick)

Gang That Sang ''Heart Of My Heart''
Four Aces; *Best Of The Four Aces*. . . . . (MCA)

Give Back My Heart
Lyle Lovett; *Pontiac* . . . . (MCA)

Give One Heart
Linda Ronstadt; *Hasten Down The Wind* . . . . (Asylum)

Golden Heart
Mark Knopfler; *Golden Heart*. . . . . (Warner Bros.)

Good Hearted Woman
George Jones; *I Am What I Am* . . . . (Epic)
Waylon Jennings; *Good Hearted Woman* . . . . (RCA)
The Outlaws . . . . (RCA)
Waylon Jennings' Greatest Hits . . . . (RCA)
Willie Nelson; *Greatest Hits (& Some That Will Be)* . . . . (Columbia)

Willie .... (RCA)

Good Morning Heartache
Billie Holiday; *All Or Nothing At All*......................... (Verve)
   Billie Holiday's Greatest Hits.......................... (Decca Jazz)
   From The Original Decca Masters............................ (MCA)
   History Of Billie Holiday .... (Verve)
Diana Ross; *Diana Ross-Anthology*........................ (Motown)
   ST/Lady Sings The Blues.............................. (Motown)
Tony Bennett with Sheryl Crow; *Playin' With My Friends-Bennett Sings The
   Blues-C* .... (Columbia)

Goodnight Sweetheart
David Kersh; *Goodnight Sweetheart*........................ (Curb)

Goodnight Sweetheart
Guy Lombardo & His Royal Canadians; *Guy Lombardo-All Time
   Favorites* .... (MCA Special Prod.)

Goodnight, Sweetheart
Flamingos; *Best Of The Flamingos* .... (Rhino)
Spaniels; *Cruisin'-1957-C*.............................. (Increase)
   Doo-Wop Ballads-#2-C .... (Rhino)
   Lovin' '50s-C .... (Priority)

Got My Heart Set On You
John Conlee; *Greatest Country Hits Of The '80s-1986-C* ..... (Columbia)
   More Hot Country Requests-C .... (Epic)

Greasy Heart
Jefferson Airplane; *Crown Of Creation*..................... (RCA)

Great Pretender
Band; *Moondog Matinee* .... (Capitol)
Platters; *Billboard Top R&B Hits-1956-C*................. (Rhino)
   Cruisin'-1956-C .... (Increase)
   Encore Of Golden Hits-Platters .... (Mercury)
   Platters-Anthology .... (Rhino)
   ST/American Graffiti .... (MCA)
   Super Oldies Of The '50s-#3-C................. (Audio Fidelity)
Roy Orbison; *Best Of Roy Orbison-Loved Standards* ...... (Monument)
Stan Freberg; *Capitol Collectors Series-Stan Freberg* .... (Capitol)

Groove Is In The Heart/What Is Love
Deee-Lite; *World Clique* .... (Elektra)

Groundzero (In Our Hearts You Remain)
Cash & Computa; *Groundzero (In Our Hearts You Remain)-CD
   Single* .... (Select)

Hang On To Your Heart
Exile; *Exile's Greatest Hits* .... (Epic)
   Hang On To Your Heart .... (Epic)

Hanging On A Heart Attack
Device; *22B3* .... (Renaissance)

Happy Birthday Broken Heart
Rex Hobart; *Forever Always Ends* .... (Bloodshot)

Happy Birthday Dear Heartache
Barbara Mandrell; *Barbara Mandrell's Greatest Hits*........ (MCA)
   Country Classics-#1-C .... (Universal)
   Today's Country Classics-C .... (MCA Special Prod.)

Happy Heart
Andy Williams; *Andy Williams' Greatest Hits* .... (Columbia)
Petula Clark; *Petula Clark's Greatest Hits* .... (Crescendo)

Hard Rock Bottom Of Your Heart
Randy Travis; *No Holdin' Back* .... (Warner Bros.)

Harden My Heart
Quarterflash; *Quarterflash*........................... (Geffen)

Haunted Heart
Sammy Kershaw; *Haunted Heart* .... (Mercury)

Have A Heart
Bonnie Raitt; *Nick Of Time* .... (Capitol)

Headache Tomorrow (Or A Heartache Tonight)
Mickey Gilley; *Mickey Gilley's Biggest Hits*.............. (Epic)
   Ten Years Of Hits .... (Epic)
   That's All That Matters To Me .... (Epic)

Headed For A Heartache
Gary Morris; *Gary Morris*..................... (Warner Bros.)
   Gary Morris-Hits .... (Warner Bros.)

Headed For A Heartbreak
Winger; *Winger*...................................... (Atlantic)

Heart
Pet Shop Boys; *Actually* .... (EMI)
   Discography-Complete Singles Collection.............. (EMI)

Heart
Nick Lowe; *Basher: Best Of* .... (Columbia)
Rockpile; *Seconds Of Pleasure* .... (Columbia)

Heart
Original Broadway Cast; *Damn Yankees*.................. (RCA)

Heart
Peggy Lee; *Peggy Lee's All-Time Greatest Hits* .... (Curb)

Heart
Neneh Cherry; *Raw Like Sushi* .... (Virgin)

Heart
Laura Branigan; *Self Control*.......................... (Atlantic)

Heart And Soul
Cleftones; *Echoes Of A Rock Era-Later Years-C* .... (Roulette)
   ST/American Graffiti .... (MCA)

Four Aces; *Four Aces' 20 Greatest Hits*...................... (Everest)
Huey Lewis and the News; *Sports* .... (Chrysalis)
Jan & Dean; *Best Of Jan & Dean* .... (EMI)
   Oldies But Goodies-#9-C .... (Original Sound)
Larry Clinton & His Orchestra; *The Hoagy Carmichael
   Songbook-C* ....(Bluebird)

Heart Attack
Olivia Newton-John; *Olivia Newton-John's Greatest Hits-#2*......... (MCA)
   Physical.. (MCA)

Heart Bowed Down, The
Henri Scott; *Music From The New York Stage (1890-1920)-#4-1917-
   1920-C* .... (Pearl)

Heart Don't Fall Now
Sawyer Brown; *Shakin'* ....(Curb)

Heart Full Of Love
Original Broadway Cast; *Les Miserables* .... (Geffen)

Heart Full Of Love
Holly Dunn; *Heart Full Of Love* .... (Warner Bros.)

Heart Full Of Soul
Chris Isaak; *Chris Isaak* .... (Warner Bros.)
Yardbirds; *History Of British Rock-#2-C*.................. (Rhino)
   Yardbirds' Greatest Hits-#1 (1964-1966) .... (Rhino)

Heart Half Empty
Ty Herndon; *What Mattered Most* .... (Epic)

Heart Hotels
Dan Fogelberg; *Dan Fogelberg/Greatest Hits* .... (Full Moon)
   Phoenix .... (Full Moon)

Heart In New York
Art Garfunkel; *Garfunkel*............................. (Columbia)
   Scissors Cut .... (Columbia)
Simon & Garfunkel; *The Concert In Central Park*......... (Warner Bros.)

Heart Is A Lonely Hunter
Reba McEntire; *Read My Mind* .... (MCA)
   Reba McEntire's Greatest Hits-#3: I'm A Survivor........ (MCA)

Heart Is In Africa
Rozalla; *Everybody's Free* .... (Epic)

Heart Like A Hurricane
Larry Stewart; *Heart Like A Hurricane* .... (Columbia)

Heart Like A Wheel
Steve Miller Band; *Circle Of Love* .... (Capitol)

Heart Like A Wheel
Linda Ronstadt; *Heart Like A Wheel* .... (Capitol)

Heart Of Glass
Blondie; *Best Of Blondie* .... (Chrysalis)
   Billboard Top Hits-1979-C ....(Rhino)
   Parallel Lines .... (Chrysalis)
   The Disco Years-#2-On The Beat-1978-1982-C ....(Rhino)

Heart Of Gold
Neil Young; *Decade*.................................. (Reprise)
   Harvest .... (Reprise)

Heart Of Innocence
Jessica Simpson; *Sweet Kisses* .... (Columbia)

Heart Of Mine
Oak Ridge Boys; *Oak Ridge Boys' Greatest Hits*............. (MCA)
   Together .... (MCA)

Heart Of Rock & Roll
Huey Lewis and the News; *Sports* .... (Chrysalis)

Heart Of Saturday Night, The (Looking For)
Shawn Colvin; *Cover Girl* .... (Columbia)
Tom Waits; *The Heart Of Saturday Night* .... (Asylum)
   Tom Waits-Anthology .... (Asylum)

Heart Of Stone
Rolling Stones; *Big Hits (High Tide & Green Grass)*............... (Abkco)
   Hot Rocks 1964-1971 .... (Abkco)
   Singles Collection-The London Years .... (Abkco)
   The Rolling Stones, Now! .... (Abkco)

Heart Of Stone
Fleetwood Mac; *25 Years-The Chain*................. (Warner Bros.)

Heart Of The Matter
Don Henley; *End Of The Innocence* .... (Geffen)

Heart Of The Night
Juice Newton; *Juice Newton-Greatest Hits & More* ....(Capitol)
   Juice Newton's Greatest Hits .... (Gold Rush)
   Quiet Lies .... (Capitol)

Heart Over Mind
Lorrie Morgan; *War Paint* .... (BNA)

Heart That You Own
Dwight Yoakam; *If There Was A Way* .... (Reprise)
   ST/White Sands .... (Morgan Creek)

Heart To Heart
Kenny Loggins; *High Adventure* .... (Columbia)
Kenny Rogers; *What About Me?* .... (RCA)

Heart To Heart Talk
Lee Ann Womack & Asleep At The Wheel; *Ride With
   Bob-C* .... (DreamWorks/SKG)

Heart Trouble
Steve Wariner; *Country Classics-#3-1984-1985-C* ....(Universal)
   One Good Night Deserves Another .... (MCA)

Steve Wariner's Greatest Hits . . . . (MCA)
Heart Trouble
Martina McBride; *The Way That I Am* . . . . (RCA)
Heart Won't Lie, The
Reba McEntire & Vince Gill; *It's Your Call* . . . . (MCA)
Reba McEntire's Greatest Hits-#3: I'm A Survivor . . . . (MCA)
Heartache Big As Texas
Ricky Van Shelton; *Texas Super Hits-C* . . . . (Columbia)
Heartache Tonight
Conway Twitty; *Latest Greatest Hits-#1* . . . . (Warner Bros.)
Lost In The Feeling . . . . (Warner Bros.)
Eagles; *Eagles Greatest Hits, Volume 2* . . . . (Asylum)
Eagles Live . . . . (Asylum)
Long Run . . . . (Asylum)
John Anderson; *Common Thread-Songs Of The Eagles-C* . . . (Giant)
Heartache, A Shadow, A Lifetime
Dave Mason; *Best Of Dave Mason* . . . . (MCA)
Dave Mason-At His Very Best . . . . (MCA)
Heartaches
Marcels; *The Doo Wop Box II* . . . . (Rhino)
Patsy Cline; *The Patsy Cline Story* . . . . (MCA)
Ted Weems & His Orchestra; *Billboard Pop Memories-1945-1949-C* . . (Rhino)
Nipper's Greatest Hits Of The '40s-#2-C . . . . (RCA)
Heartaches By The Number
Guy Mitchell; *Sentimental Journey-C* . . . . (Dominion Entert.)
Sunshine Guitar . . . . (Collectables)
Unforgettable-Love Songs-Fabulous '50s-C . . . . . . (Dominion Entert.)
Ray Price; *Columbia Country Classics-#2-Honky Tonk Heroes-C* . . (Columbia)
Ray Price's Greatest Hits . . . . (Columbia)
Ray Price's Greatest Hits-#1-3 . . . . (Step One)
Heartaches Of A Fool
Willie Nelson; *Greatest Hits (& Some That Will Be)* . . . . . (Columbia)
Heartbeat
Buddy Holly; *Legend-From The Original Master Tapes* . . . . . (MCA)
Buddy Holly/The Crickets; *Buddy Holly-20 Golden Greats* . . . (MCA)
Heartbeat
Dolly Parton; *Dolly Parton's Greatest Hits* . . . . (RCA)
Heartbeat
Don Johnson; *Heartbeat* . . . . (Epic)
Heartbeat
Dazz Band; *Jukebox* . . . . (Motown)
Heartbeat
Wham! Featuring George Michael; *Make It Big* . . . . (Columbia)
Heartbeat
Midnight Star; *Midnight Star* . . . . (Solar)
Heartbeat
Gloria Jones; *Soul Shots-#2-The ''In'' Crowd-Sweet Soul-C* . . . (Rhino)
Heartbeat In The Darkness
Don Williams; *New Moves* . . . . (Capitol)
Prime Cuts . . . . (Capitol)
Heartbeat/Free Your Body
Seduction; *Nothing Matters Without Love* . . . . (Vendettat)
Heartbeats
Yarbrough & Peoples; *Best Of Yarbrough & Peoples* . . . . . (Mercury)
Heartbreak Express
Dolly Parton; *Dolly Parton's Greatest Hits* . . . . (RCA)
Heartbreak Express . . . . (RCA)
Heartbreak Express
Delia Bell & Bill Grant; *Cheer Of The Home Fires* . . . . . . (Rounder)
Heartbreak Hotel
Albert King; *Blues For Elvis* . . . . (Stax)
Elvis Presley; *Elvis As Recorded At Madison Square Garden* . . (RCA)
Elvis' Golden Records . . . . (RCA)
Elvis-A Legendary Performer, Volume 1 . . . . (RCA)
Nipper's Greatest Hits Of The '50s-#1-C . . . . (RCA)
Worldwide 50 Gold Award Hits, Vol. 1, Parts 1 & 2 . . . . . (RCA)
Stan Freberg; *Capitol Collectors Series-Stan Freberg* . . . . (Capitol)
Willie Nelson; *Greatest Hits (& Some That Will Be)* . . . . . (Columbia)
Willie Nelson & Leon Russell: One For The Road . . . . (Columbia)
Heartbreak Hotel
Whitney Houston Featuring Faith Evans & Kelly Price; *My Love Is Your Love* . . . . (Arista)
Totally Hits-#1-C . . . . (Arista)
Whitney Houston's Greatest Hits . . . . (Arista)
Heartbreak Station
Cinderella; *Heartbreak Station* . . . . (Mercury)
Heartbreak Town
Dixie Chicks; *Fly* . . . . (Monument)
Heartbreak U.S.A.
Kitty Wells; *I Love Country-Hits Of The '60s-#1-C* . . . . . . (Priority)
Kitty Wells' Greatest Songs . . . . (Curb)
The Country Music Hall Of Fame-Kitty Wells . . . . (MCA Special Prod.)
Heartbreak, Tennessee
Johnny Paycheck; *This Is Country-C* . . . . (Pegasus/Cleopatra)
Heartbreaker
Grand Funk Railroad; *Capitol Collectors Series-Grand Funk Railroad* . . . . (Capitol)
Heartbreaker
Pat Benatar; *Best Shots* . . . . (Chrysalis)

In The Heat Of The Night . . . . (Chrysalis)
Live From Earth . . . . (Chrysalis)
Heartbreaker
Great White; *Hooked* . . . . (Capitol)
Heartbreaker
Tanya Tucker; *Love Me Like You Used To* . . . . (Liberty)
Heartbreaker
Led Zeppelin; *Led Zeppelin II* . . . . (Atlantic)
Led Zeppelin-The Complete Studio Recordings . . . . (Atlantic)
Heartbreaker
Dionne Warwick; *Heartbreaker* . . . . (Arista)
Heartbreaker
Mariah Carey; *Rainbow* . . . . (Columbia)
Heartbreaker
Bee Gees; *One Night Only* . . . . (Polydor)
Heartbroke
George Strait; *Strait From The Heart* . . . . (MCA)
Strait Out Of The Box . . . . (MCA)
Guy Clark; *Craftsman* . . . . (Philo)
Keepers . . . . (Sugar Hill)
Ricky Skaggs; *Country Gentleman: The Best Of Ricky Skaggs* . . . (Epic)
Greatest Country Hits Of The '80s-#2-C . . . . (Columbia)
Highways & Heartaches . . . . (Epic)
Live In London . . . . (Epic)
Ricky Skaggs-Super Hits . . . . (Epic)
Rodney Crowell; *Rodney Crowell-Collection* . . . . (Warner Bros.)
Heartbroke Every Day
Lonestar; *Lonestar* . . . . (BNA)
Heartland
George Strait; *ST/Pure Country* . . . . (MCA)
Heartland
Sawyer Brown; *Boys Are Back* . . . . (Curb)
Heartland
Steve Wariner; *Life's Highway* . . . . (MCA)
Heartland
U2; *Rattle And Hum* . . . . (Island)
Heartless
Heart; *Heart's Greatest Hits/Live* . . . . (Epic)
Magazine . . . . (Capitol)
Heartlight
Neil Diamond; *Heartlight* . . . . (Columbia)
Hot August Night II . . . . (Columbia)
Hearts
Marty Balin; *Balin* . . . . (EMI)
Balince-A Collection . . . . (Rhino)
Hearts
Huey Lewis and the News; *Huey Lewis and the News* . . . . (Chrysalis)
Hearts Are Gonna Roll
Hal Ketchum; *Sure Love* . . . . (Curb)
Hearts Aren't Made To Break
Lee Greenwood; *Country Classics-#5-1985-1986-C* . . . . (Universal)
Lee Greenwood's Greatest Hits-#2 . . . . (MCA)
Streamline . . . . (MCA)
Heart's Desire
Lee Roy Parnell; *We All Get Lucky Sometimes* . . . . (Career)
Hearts Don't Think (They Feel)
Natural Selection; *Natural Selection* . . . . (East West)
Hearts Of Stone
Bruce Springsteen; *Tracks* . . . . (Columbia)
Southside Johnny And The Asbury Jukes; *Best Of Southside Johnny And The Asbury Jukes* . . . . (Legacy)
Cover Me (Bruce Springsteen Tribute)-C . . . . (Rhino)
Hearts Of Stone . . . . (Epic)
Hearts Of Stone
Fontane Sisters; *Hearts Of Stone-The Best Of The Fontane Sisters* . . . . (Varese Sarabande)
Hearts On Fire
Eddie Rabbitt; *Best Of Eddie Rabbitt* . . . . (Elektra)
Eddie Rabbitt's All-Time Greatest Hits . . . . (Warner Bros.)
Variations . . . . (Elektra)
Hearts On Fire
Gram Parsons; *Grievous Angel* . . . . (Reprise)
Hearts On Fire
Bryan Adams; *Into The Fire* . . . . (A&M)
Hearts On Fire
Randy Meisner; *One More Song* . . . . (Epic)
Hearts On Fire
Steve Winwood; *Roll With It* . . . . (Virgin)
Heart's On Fire
38 Special; *Strength In Numbers* . . . . (A&M)
Heart-Shaped Box
Nirvana; *In Utero* . . . . (David Geffen Co.)
Heart-Shaped World
Chris Isaak; *Heart-Shaped World* . . . . (Reprise)
Heaven Help My Heart
Tina Arena; *Don't Ask* . . . . (Epic)
Wynonna; *Revelations* . . . . (Curb/MCA)
Wynonna-Collection . . . . (Curb)

Hello Mary Lou
Creedence Clearwater Revival; *Creedence Country* ....(Fantasy)
Rick Nelson; *Rick Nelson In Concert-Troubadour 1969* ....(MCA)
Rick Nelson-Souvenirs ....(EMI)
Ricky Nelson; *Best Of Ricky Nelson* ....(EMI)
Rick Nelson's Greatest Hits ....(Rhino)
Statler Brothers; *14 Country Favorites-C* ....(Mercury)
Pardners In Rhyme ....(Mercury)
Hello Mr. Heartache
Dixie Chicks; *Fly* ....(Monument)
Help Me Rhonda
Beach Boys; *Billboard Top Rock 'N' Roll Hits-1965-C* ....(Rhino)
California Girls ....(Capitol)
Dance Dance Dance ....(Capitol)
Endless Summer ....(Capitol)
Made In The U.S.A. ....(Capitol)
Here In My Heart
Chicago; *The Heart Of Chicago-1967-1997* ....(Reprise)
Here In My Heart
Al Martino; *Capitol Collectors Series-Al Martino* ....(Capitol)
Here In My Heart
Martina McBride; *Chicken Soup For The Woman's Soul-C* ....(Rhino)
Hero
Mariah Carey; *America: A Tribute To Heroes-C* ....(Interscope)
Diana, Princess Of Wales-Tribute-C ....(Columbia)
God Bless America-C ....(Columbia)
Mariah Carey-#1's ....(Columbia)
Music Box ....(Columbia)
He's A Heartache (Looking For A Place To Happen)
Janie Fricke; *19 Hot Country Requests-C* ....(Epic)
It Ain't Easy ....(Columbia)
Janie Fricke-17 Greatest Hits ....(Columbia)
Very Best Of Janie Fricke ....(Columbia)
Hold On My Heart
Genesis; *We Can't Dance* ....(Atlantic)
Hole Hearted
Extreme; *Pornograffitti* ....(A&M)
Home Again In My Heart
Nitty Gritty Dirt Band; *More Great Dirt-Best Of Nitty Gritty Dirt Band* ....(Warner Bros.)
Partners Brothers & Friends ....(Warner Bros.)
Home Is A Wounded Heart
Neil Diamond; *Beautiful Noise* ....(Columbia)
Home Is Where The Heart Is
Bobby Womack; *Home Is Where The Heart Is* ....(Columbia)
Gladys Knight & The Pips; *Still Together* ....(Buddah)
Kool & The Gang; *In The Heart* ....(De-Lite)
Homestead In My Heart
Amazing Rhythm Aces; *Amazing Rhythm Aces* ....(Columbia)
Honky Tonk Heart
Highway 101; *Highway 101's Greatest Hits* ....(Warner Bros.)
One-O-One ....(Warner Bros.)
Jim Owen; *45-#1164* ....(Sun)
Keith Whitley; *Don't Close Your Eyes* ....(RCA)
Hook
Blues Traveler; *Four* ....(A&M)
Hot Rod Hearts
Robbie Dupree; *Robbie Dupree* ....(Elektra)
Hotter Than Mojave In My Heart
Iris DeMent; *Infamous Angel* ....(Warner Bros.)
How Can You Mend A Broken Heart
Al Green; *Al Green's Greatest Hits-#1* ....(Motown)
Compact Command Performances-Al Green ....(Motown)
Let's Stay Together ....(Right Stuff)
Bee Gees; *Bee Gees-Gold* ....(Polydor)
Here At Last...Bee Gees...Live ....(Polydor)
Nobody's Child-Romanian Angel Appeal-C ....(Warner Bros.)
How Could An Angel Break My Heart
Kenny G with Toni Braxton; *Kenny G's Greatest Hits* ....(Arista)
Toni Braxton with Kenny G; *Diana, Princess Of Wales-Tribute-C* ...(Columbia)
Secrets ....(LaFace)
Hungry Heart
Bruce Springsteen; *Bruce Springsteen's Greatest Hits* ....(Columbia)
The River ....(Columbia)
Bruce Springsteen & The E Street Band; *Bruce Springsteen & The E Street Band Live/1975-85* ....(Legacy)
Husbands And Wives
Brooks & Dunn; *Big Country Hits '99-C* ....(K-Tel)
If You See Her ....(Arista)
Neil Diamond; *Neil Diamond-Love Songs* ....(MCA)
Rainbow ....(MCA)
Stones ....(MCA)
Roger Miller; *Best Of Roger Miller* ....(Mercury)
Best Of Roger Miller-His Greatest Songs ....(Curb)
Roger Miller-Super Hits ....(Epic)
Roger Miller-The Hits ....(Mercury)
I Ain't Gonna Eat Out My Heart Anymore
Rascals; *The Young Rascals* ....(Warner Special Prod.)
Time Peace/The Rascals' Greatest Hits ....(Atlantic)
I Ain't Gonna Let You Break My Heart Again
Bonnie Raitt; *Nick Of Time* ....(Capitol)
I Can't Stand It
Eric Clapton; *Another Ticket* ....(RSO)
Eric Clapton-Crossroads-C ....(Polydor)
I Cross My Heart
George Strait; *ST/Pure Country* ....(MCA)
I Don't Have The Heart
James Ingram; *It's Real* ....(Warner Bros.)
I Know A Heartache When I See One
Jennifer Warnes; *Best Of Jennifer Warnes* ....(Arista)
Shot Through The Heart ....(Arista)
I Left My Heart At The Stage Door Canteen
Jo Stafford; *G.I. Jo* ....(Corinthian)
I Left My Heart In Iran
Forgotten Rebels; *Surfin' On Heroin* ....(Restless)
I Left My Heart In San Francisco
Tony Bennett; *I Left My Heart In San Francisco* ....(Columbia)
Pop Classics Of The '60s-C ....(Columbia)
Tony Bennett's All-Time Greatest Hits ....(Columbia)
I Let A Song Go Out Of My Heart
Bill Jennings; *Stompin' With Bill* ....(Collectables)
Duke Ellington; *Braggin' In Brass-Immortal 1938 Year* ....(Portrait)
Joe Pass; *Portraits Of Duke Ellington* ....(Pablo)
Teresa Brewer; *Sophisticated Lady* ....(Columbia)
Tony Bennett; *Jazz* ....(Columbia)
I Love You By Heart
Sylvia & Michael Johnson; *Collector's Series-Duets-C* ....(RCA)
I Never Go Around Mirrors
Lefty Frizzell; *Grand Ole Opry-75 Years-#1-C* ....(MCA)
I Sold My Heart To The Junkman
Blue-Belles; *Super Oldies Of The '60s-#3-C* ....(Audio Fidelity)
Carmen McRae; *Sound Of Silence* ....(Atlantic)
I Think We're Alone Now
Tiffany; *Tiffany* ....(MCA)
Tiffany's Greatest Hits ....(Hip-O)
Tommy James And The Shondells; *Best Of Tommy James And The Shondells* ....(Roulette)
Billboard Top Rock 'N' Roll Hits-1967-C ....(Rhino)
Tommy James And The Shondells-Anthology ....(Rhino)
I Wanna Be A Cowboy's Sweetheart
Patsy Montana & The Prairie Ramblers; *All Time Legends Of Country Music-C* ....(Legacy)
Respect: A History Of Women In Music-C ....(Rhino)
I Will Love Again
Lara Fabian; *Lara Fabian* ....(Columbia)
I Wish You Could Have Turned My Head
Oak Ridge Boys; *Bobbie Sue* ....(MCA)
If He Should Break Your Heart
Journey; *Trial By Fire* ....(Columbia)
If I Only Had A Heart
Jack Haley; *ST/The Wizard Of Oz* ....(Sony Music Special Prod.)
Original Soundtrack; *The Wizard Of Oz-The Deluxe Edition* ....(Rhino)
The Wizard Of Oz-The Story And Songs ....(Rhino)
If My Heart Had Windows
Patty Loveless; *Country Classics-#12-1987-1988-C* ....(Universal)
If My Heart Had Windows ....(MCA)
Patty Loveless' Greatest Hits ....(MCA)
If My Heart Had Wings
Faith Hill; *Breathe* ....(Warner Bros.)
If You Leave Me Tonight I'll Cry
Jerry Wallace; *From The Vaults: Decca Country Classics-1934-1973-C* ....(Decca)
Jerry Wallace's Greatest Hits ....(Curb)
If Your Heart Ain't Busy Tonight
Tanya Tucker; *What Do I Do With Me* ....(Capitol)
If Your Heart Isn't In It
Atlantic Starr; *As The Band Turns* ....(A&M)
Atlantic Starr-Classics-#10 ....(A&M)
Secret Lovers: Best Of Atlantic Starr ....(A&M)
If You've Got Love
John Michael Montgomery; *Kickin' It Up* ....(Atlantic)
I'll Follow My Secret Heart
Mary Martin & Noel Coward; *Together With Music* ....(DRG)
I'll Hold You In My Heart (Till I Can Hold You In My Arms)
Eddy Arnold; *Best Of Eddy Arnold* ....(RCA)
Eddy Arnold-The Hits ....(Mercury)
Memories Are Made Of This ....(Mercury)
I'll Never Break Your Heart
Backstreet Boys; *Backstreet Boys* ....(Jive)
Now That's What I Call Music!-#2-C ....(Virgin)
I'll Repossess My Heart
Kitty Wells; *Kitty Wells' Greatest Hits* ....(Hollywood/DNA-Rounder)
In China Or A Woman's Heart
Kate Wolf; *Poet's Heart* ....(Kaleidoscope)
In Over My Heart
T.G. Sheppard; *Livin' On The Edge* ....(Columbia)
T.G. Sheppard's Biggest Hits ....(Columbia)

In Over My Heart
 Bobby Womack; *Someday We'll All Be Free* . . . .(Beverly Glen)
In The Heart Of A Woman
 Billy Ray Cyrus; *It Won't Be The Last* . . . . (Mercury)
In The Middle Of A Heartache
 Wanda Jackson; *Rockin' In The Country-Best Of Wanda Jackson* . . . . . . (Rhino)
 Wanda Jackson's Greatest Hits . . . . (Gusto)
In The Shape Of A Heart
 Jackson Browne; *Lives In The Balance* . . . . (Asylum)
Inside
 Ronnie Milsap; *Inside Ronnie Milsap* . . . . (RCA)
 Ronnie Milsap's Greatest Hits-#2 . . . . (RCA)
 Solid Country Gold-C . . . . (RCA)
Irish Heartbeat
 Van Morrison; *Inarticulate Speech Of The Heart* . . . .(Warner Bros.)
 Van Morrison & The Chieftains; *Irish Heartbeat* . . . . (Mercury)
It Would Be You
 Gary Allan; *It Would Be You* . . . . (Decca)
It's A Heartache
 Bonnie Tyler; *Billboard Top Hits-1978-C* . . . . (Rhino)
 It's A Heartache . . . . (RCA)
 Juice Newton; *Juice Newton-Greatest Hits & More* . . . . (Capitol)
It's A Heartache
 Ronnie Spector; *Get Down Tonight! Best Of T.K. Records-C* . . . . (Rhino)
It's For You
 Three Dog Night; *Captured Live At The Forum* . . . .(MCA)
It's Only A Heartache
 Steve Wariner; *One Good Night Deserves Another* . . . .(MCA)
I've Got A New Heartache
 Ray Price; *Ray Price's Greatest Hits* . . . . (Columbia)
 Ricky Skaggs; *Live In London* . . . .(Epic)
 More Hot Country Requests-C . . . .(Epic)
I've Got A Rock 'N' Roll Heart
 Eric Clapton; *Money And Cigarettes* . . . . (Duck/Reprise)
Janey Don't You Lose Heart
 Bruce Springsteen; *Tracks* . . . . (Columbia)
January Friend
 Goo Goo Dolls; *Dizzy Up The Girl* . . . .(Warner Sunset/Reprise)
Jealous Heart
 Al Morgan; *Hits Of '49-C* . . . . (ASV)
 Connie Francis; *Connie Francis-Souvenirs* . . . .(Polydor)
 Les Paul; *Les Paul-16 Most Requested Songs* . . . . (Columbia)
 Tex Ritter; *An American Legend* . . . . (Capitol)
 Best Of Tex Ritter . . . . (Capitol)
 Hillbilly Heaven . . . . (Capitol)
 Tex Ritter's Greatest Hits . . . . (Curb)
 Tex Ritter-Vintage Collection . . . . (Capitol)
Jealous Hearted Man
 Muddy Waters; *Hard Again* . . . . (Blue Sky)
Jealous Hearted Me
 Minnie Pearl; *Stars Of The Grand Ole Opry-1926-1974-C* . . . . (RCA)
Just Another Day In Paradise
 Phil Vassar; *Phil Vassar* . . . . (Arista)
Just Take My Heart
 Mr. Big; *Lean Into It* . . . . (Atlantic)
Ka-Ding Dong
 Diamonds; *Best Of The Diamonds-The Mercury Years* . . . . (Mercury)
Keep My Heart In Line
 Earl Thomas Conley; *Yours Truly* . . . . (RCA)
Keep This Heart In Mind
 Bonnie Raitt; *Green Light* . . . .(Warner Bros.)
Keep Tryin'
 Groove Theory; *Groove Theory* . . . .(Epic)
Kickin' My Heart Around
 Black Crowes; *By Your Side* . . . . (American)
King Of My Heart
 Melba Moore; *Read My Lips* . . . . (Capitol)
Lazarus Heart
 Sting; *...Nothing Like The Sun* . . . . (A&M)
Leading With Your Heart
 Barbra Streisand; *Higher Ground* . . . . (Columbia)
Let Me Call You Sweetheart
 Bette Midler; *ST/The Rose* . . . .(Atlantic)
 Billy Vaughn & His Orchestra; *Billy Vaughn & His Orchestra Play 22 Of
 His Greatest Hits* . . . .(Ranwood)
 Bing Crosby; *Bing Crosby-Love Songs* . . . .(Universal)
 Bob Ralston; *22 Great Organ Hits-#2* . . . . (Ranwood)
 Gene Autry; *Gene Autry-Love Songs* . . . . (Varese Sarabande)
 Lawrence Welk; *American Favorites* . . . .(Ranwood)
 Peerless Quartet; *78-#1057.* . . . . (Columbia)
Let Me Into Your Heart
 Mary Chapin Carpenter; *A Place In The World* . . . . (Columbia)
 Super Hits Of 1996-C . . . .(Epic)
Let Me Let Go
 Faith Hill; *Faith* . . . .(Warner Bros.)
Let The Heartache Ride
 Restless Heart; *Restless Heart* . . . . (RCA)
 Restless Heart's Greatest Hits . . . . (RCA)

Like We Never Had A Broken Heart
 Trisha Yearwood; *Trisha Yearwood* . . . . (MCA)
Lily, Rosemary And The Jack Of Hearts
 Bob Dylan; *Blood On The Tracks* . . . . (Columbia)
Listen To Her Heart
 Tom Petty And The Heartbreakers; *You're Gonna Get It!* . . . .(Gone Gator)
Listen To The Heartbeat
 Billy Squier; *Emotions In Motion* . . . . (Capitol)
Little Gasoline, A
 Terri Clark; *Fearless* . . . . (Mercury)
Little Left Of Center
 Randy Travis; *A Man Ain't Made Of Stone* . . . .(DreamWorks/SKG)
Long Goodbye, The
 Brooks & Dunn; *Steers & Stripes* . . . . (Arista)
Longing In Their Hearts
 Bonnie Raitt; *Longing In Their Hearts* . . . . (Capitol)
Look Heart No Hands
 Randy Travis; *Randy Travis' Greatest Hits-#2* . . . . (Warner Bros.)
Lose Your Heart
 Bob Welch; *French Kiss* . . . . (Capitol)
Love Bug Leave My Heart Alone
 Martha & The Vandellas; *Compact Command Performances-Martha Reeves
 & The Vandellas* . . . . (Motown)
 Martha Reeves & The Vandellas-Anthology . . . . (Motown)
Love Don't Care (Whose Heart It Breaks)
 Earl Thomas Conley; *Earl Thomas Conley's Greatest Hits-#2* . . . . (RCA)
 Essential Earl Thomas Conley . . . . (RCA)
 Treadin' Water . . . . (RCA)
Miseducation Of Lauryn Hill
 Lauryn Hill; *The Miseducation Of Lauryn Hill* . . . . (Ruffhouse/Columbia)
Miss You In A Heartbeat
 Def Leppard; *Retro Active* . . . . (Mercury)
Mother The Queen Of My Heart
 Pete Seeger & Arlo Guthrie; *Together In Concert* . . . .(Reprise)
Murder In My Heart For The Judge
 Lee Michaels; *Lee Michaels-Collection* . . . . (Rhino)
 Moby Grape; *Wow* . . . . (Columbia)
 Three Dog Night; *Jailhouse Rock (Hits From The Big
 House)-C* . . . . (Sony Music Special Prod.)
My Beating Heart
 Cathy Dennis; *Move To This* . . . .(Polydor)
My Bleeding Heart
 Elmore James; *Complete Fire & Enjoy Sessions-#2* . . . . (Collectables)
My Foolish Heart
 Bill Evans; *Waltz For Debby* . . . . (Riverside)
 Carmen McRae; *Live At Bubba's* . . . . (Who's Who In Jazz)
 John McLaughlin; *Electric Guitarist.* . . . . (Columbia)
 Liz Story; *My Foolish Heart* . . . .(Windham Hill)
 Roberta Flack; *Set The Night To Music* . . . .(Atlantic)
 Stephane Grappelli; *Stephanova* . . . . (Concord Jazz)
 Tony Bennett & Bill Evans; *The Tony Bennett & Bill Evans
 Album* . . . . (Original Jazz Classics)
My Funny Valentine
 Anita Baker; *Rhythm Of Love* . . . .(Atlantic)
 Anita O'Day; *Anita O'Day* . . . .(Glendale)
 Anita O'Day Sings The Winners . . . . (Verve)
 Live At The City . . . . (Emily)
 Carly Simon; *My Romance* . . . . (Arista)
 Ella Fitzgerald; *Rodgers & Hart Songbook* . . . . (Verve)
 Mel Torme; *Easy To Remember* . . . .(Glendale)
 Miles Davis; *Columbia Years-1955-1985* . . . . (Columbia)
 Cookin' With The Miles Davis Quintet . . . .(Prestige)
 Miles Davis' Greatest Hits . . . . (Columbia)
 My Funny Valentine . . . . (Columbia)
 Original Cast/Mary Martin; *Babes In Arms* . . . . (Sony Music Special Prod.)
 Stan Getz; *Artistry Of-Stan Getz-Best Of Verve Years-#1* . . . . (Verve)
My Heart
 Ronnie Milsap; *Collector's Series-Ronnie Milsap* . . . .(RCA)
 Milsap Magic . . . . (RCA)
My Heart
 Neil Young & Crazy Horse; *Sleeps With Angels* . . . .(Reprise)
My Heart Belongs To Daddy
 Ella Fitzgerald & Cole Porter; *Dream Dancing* . . . . (Pablo)
 Peggy Lee; *Best Of Peggy Lee* . . . . (MCA)
 Rosemary Clooney; *Rosemary Clooney Sings The Music Of Cole
 Porter* . . . . (Concord Jazz)
My Heart Belongs To Me
 Barbra Streisand; *Barbra Streisand's Greatest Hits, Volume 2* . . . . . . (Columbia)
 Memories . . . . (Columbia)
 Streisand Superman . . . . (Columbia)
My Heart Belongs To Only You
 Bobby Vinton; *Bobby Vinton-16 Most Requested Songs* . . . . (Legacy)
 Bobby Vinton's All-Time Greatest Hits . . . . (Epic)
 Bobby Vinton's Greatest Hits/Greatest Hits Of Love . . . . (Columbia)
My Heart Can't Tell Me No
 Rod Stewart; *Downtown Train-Selections From The Storyteller
 Anthology* . . . . (Warner Bros.)
 Out Of Order . . . . (Warner Bros.)
 Storyteller/The Complete Anthology: 1964-1990. . . . . (Warner Bros.)

My Heart Cries For You
Charlie Rich; *Charlie Rich-20 Golden Hits* . . . . (Sun)
Time For Tears-C . . . . (Sun)
Dinah Shore; *Nipper's Greatest Hits Of The '50s-#1-C* . . . . (RCA)
Guy Mitchell; *Guy Mitchell-16 Most Requested Songs* . . . . (Legacy)
My Heart Has A History
Paul Brandt; *Calm Before The Storm* . . . . (Reprise)
My Heart Has A Mind Of Its Own
Connie Francis; *Very Best Of Connie Francis* . . . . (Polydor)
Debby Boone; *Best Of Debby Boone* . . . . (Curb)
My Heart Is A Hobo
Rosemary Clooney; *Rosemary Clooney Sings The Music Of Jimmy Van
Heusen* . . . . (Concord Jazz)
My Heart Is Failing Me
Riff; *Riff* . . . . (SBK)
My Heart Is So Full Of You
Original Broadway Cast; *The Most Happy Fella* . . . . (Sony Music Classical)
My Heart Stood Still
Bud Powell; *Genius Of Bud Powell-#2* . . . . (Verve)
Frank Sinatra; *The Concert Sinatra* . . . . (Reprise)
Tony Bennett; *Rodgers & Hart Songbook* . . . . (DRG)
My Heart Tells Me
Etta Jones; *Something Nice* . . . . (Original Jazz Classics)
Nat "King" Cole; *Very Thought Of You* . . . . (Capitol)
My Heart Will Go On (Love Theme from "Titanic")
Celine Dion; *All The Way...A Decade Of Song* . . . . (550 Music)
ST/Titanic . . . . (Sony Music Classical)
Celine Dion with The Bee Gees; *Let's Talk About Love-C* . . . . (550 Music)
Kenny G; *Kenny G's Greatest Hits* . . . . (Arista)
My Heart Would Know
Hank Williams; *24 Of Hank Williams' Greatest Hits* . . . . (Polydor)
Hey Good Lookin' (December 1950-July 1951) . . . . (Polydor)
My Heart's Deep In The Heart Of Texas
Boxcar Willie; *King Of The Freight Train* . . . . (MCA Special Prod.)
My Next Broken Heart
Brooks & Dunn; *Brand New Man* . . . . (Arista)
My One And Only Heart
Perry Como; *Sing Just For You* . . . . (RCA)
My Sweetheart In Tennessee
Burnett & Rutherford; *Ramblin' Reckless Hobo* . . . . (Rounder)
My Sweetheart Lives In San Antonio
Ray Duncan; *45-#232* . . . . (Door Knob)
Never Say Die
Dixie Chicks; *Wide Open Spaces* . . . . (Monument)
Night Is Fallin' In My Heart
Diamond Rio; *Diamond Rio's Greatest Hits* . . . . (Arista)
Love A Little Stronger . . . . (Arista)
Nobody's Supposed To Be Here
Deborah Cox; *One Wish* . . . . (Arista)
Totally Hits-#1-C . . . . (Arista)
North Carolina (Home In My Heart)
Claudia Church; *Claudia Church* . . . . (Reprise)
North Carolina Tune/Child Of My Heart
Liz Carroll; *Friend Indeed* . . . . (Shanachie)
Nothin' But A Heartache
Doobie Brothers; *Livin' On The Fault Line* . . . . (Warner Bros.)
Nothing Broken But My Heart
Celine Dion; *Celine Dion* . . . . (Epic)
Nothing But Heartaches
Diana Ross & The Supremes; *Diana Ross & The Supremes'
Greatest Hits* . . . . (Motown)
Diana Ross & The Supremes-Anthology (1962-1969) . . . . (Motown)
Motown Story-First 25 Years-C . . . . (Motown)
Motown Superstar Series-#1-Diana Ross & The Supremes . . . . (Motown)
Oklahoma Heartaches & California Dreams
Kris Carpenter; *45-#203* . . . . (Door Knob)
Oklahoma Sweetheart
George Thorogood & The Destroyers; *Boogie People* . . . . (EMI)
Oklahoma Sweetheart Sally
Maddox Brothers & Rose; *America's Most Colorful Hillbilly Band* . .(Arhoolie)
Old Fashioned Love
Asleep At The Wheel featuring Suzy Bogguss; *Tribute To The Music Of Bob
Wills And The Texas Playboys-C* . . . . (Liberty)
Once You Lose Your Heart
Original Broadway Cast; *Me & My Girl* . . . . (MCA)
One Broken Heart For Sale
Elvis Presley; *Collector's Gold* . . . . (RCA)
It Happened At The World's Fair . . . . (RCA)
Worldwide 50 Gold Award Hits, Vol. 1, Parts 1 & 2 . . . . (RCA)
One Honest Heart
Reba McEntire; *If You See Him* . . . . (MCA)
Reba McEntire's Greatest Hits-#3: I'm A Survivor . . . . (MCA)
One I Gave My Heart To
Aaliyah; *One In A Million* . . . . (BlackGround Enterp./Atlantic)
One Owner Heart
T.G. Sheppard; *One Owner Heart* . . . . (WB/Curb)
T.G. Sheppard's Greatest Hits-#2 . . . . (WB/Curb)

One Rose (That's Left In My Heart)
Bing Crosby; *Best Of Bing Crosby* . . . . (MCA)
Leon Redbone; *Champagne Charlie* . . . . (Warner Bros.)
One Way Track
Ricky Skaggs and Kentucky Thunder; *History Of The Future* . . .(Skaggs Family)
Only A Lonely Heart Knows
Barbara Mandrell; *Clean Cut* . . . . (MCA)
Only A Lonely Heart Sees
Felix Cavaliere; *Castles In The Air* . . . . (Out Of Print)
Only Love Can Break A Heart
Gene Pitney; *Gene Pitney* . . . . (Everest)
Gene Pitney-Anthology 1961-1968 . . . . (Rhino)
Love Sixties-C . . . . (JCI Assoc. Labels)
Pick Of Gene Pitney . . . . (Fifty One West)
Only The Lonely (Know The Way I Feel)
Roy Orbison; *For The Lonely: A Roy Orbison Anthology 1959-1965* . . . .(Rhino)
In Dreams-Greatest Hits . . . . (Orbison)
Roy Orbison's All-Time Greatest Hits-#1 & 2 . . . . (Monument)
Only Trust Your Heart
Diana Krall; *Only Trust Your Heart* . . . . (GRP)
Open My Heart
Yolanda Adams; *Mountain High Valley Low* . . . . (Elektra)
Open The Door To Your Heart
Little Milton; *Stax Blues Masters-Blue Monday-C* . . . . (Stax)
Walking The Back Streets . . . . (Stax)
Open Up Your Heart
Buck Owens; *Buck Owens Collection-1959-1990* . . . . (Rhino)
Open Your Heart
Madonna; *Immaculate Collection* . . . . (Sire)
Royal Box . . . . (Sire)
True Blue . . . . (Sire)
Open Your Heart
Europe; *Out Of This World* . . . . (Epic)
Wings Of Tomorrow . . . . (Epic)
Open Your Heart
Human League; *Dare* . . . . (A&M)
Human League's Greatest Hits . . . . (A&M)
Out Of My Dreams
Original Broadway Cast; *Oklahoma!* . . . . (RCA)
Original Cast; *Oklahoma!* . . . . (MCA)
Owner Of A Lonely Heart
Yes; *90125* . . . . (Atco)
Pain In My Heart
Otis Redding; *Best Of Otis Redding* . . . . (Atco)
History Of Otis Redding . . . . (Atco)
In Person At The Whisky A Go Go . . . . (Rhino)
Pain In My Heart . . . . (Atco)
The Otis Redding Story . . . . (Atlantic)
Rolling Stones; *The Rolling Stones, Now!* . . . . (Abkco)
Pain In My Heart
David Johansen; *David Johansen* . . . . (Blue Sky)
Painted On My Heart
Cult; *ST/Gone In 60 Seconds* . . . . (Island)
Pardon My Heart
Neil Young & Crazy Horse; *Zuma* . . . . (Reprise)
Pass You By
Boyz II Men; *Nathan Michael Shawn Wanya* . . . . (Universal)
Peace In My Heart
Carole Bayer Sager; *Too* . . . . (Elektra)
Peg O' My Heart
Buddy Clark; *Buddy Clark-16 Most Requested Songs* . . . . (Columbia)
Three Suns; *Nipper's Greatest Hits Of The '40s-#2-C* . . . . (RCA)
Piece Of My Heart
Big Brother & The Holding Company; *Cheap Thrills* . . . . (Columbia)
Rock Classics Of The '60s-C . . . . (Columbia)
Seems Like Yesterday-#6-Late '60s-C . . . . (K-Tel)
Bryan Ferry; *These Foolish Things* . . . . (Reprise)
Delaney & Bonnie; *Best Of Delaney & Bonnie* . . . . (Rhino)
Faith Hill; *Take Me As I Am* . . . . (Warner Bros.)
Janis Joplin; *Janis Joplin In Concert* . . . . (Columbia)
Janis Joplin's Greatest Hits . . . . (Columbia)
ST/Janis . . . . (Columbia)
Sammy Hagar; *Standing Hampton* . . . . (Geffen)
Piece Of My Heart
Tara Kemp; *Tara Kemp* . . . . (Giant)
Place To Fall Apart
Merle Haggard & Janie Fricke; *For The Record: Merle Haggard-43
Legendary Hits* . . . . (BNA)
Poet's Heart
Kate Wolf; *Gold In California-Retrospective-1975-1985* . . . . (Kaleidoscope)
Poet's Heart . . . . (Kaleidoscope)
Poison Heart
Ramones; *Mondo Bizarro* . . . . (Radioactive/MCA)
Poisoned Heart & A Twisted Memory
Richard Thompson; *Hand Of Kindness* . . . . (Hannibal)
Purple Heart
David Allan Coe; *Invictus Means Unconquered* . . . . (Columbia)
Purple Heart
T Bone Burnett; *Talking Animals* . . . . (Columbia)

Put A Little Love In Your Heart
Annie Lennox & Al Green; *ST/Scrooged* . . . . (A&M)
Jackie DeShannon; *Chicken Soup For The Soul: I'll Be There For You-Songs*
Of Friendship, Brotherhood And Sisterhood-C . . . . (Rhino)
ST/Drugstore Cowboy . . . . (Novus)
Very Best Of Jackie DeShannon . . . . (EMI)
Queen Of Hearts
Dave Edmunds; *Best Of Dave Edmunds* . . . . (Swan Song)
Repeat When Necessary . . . . (Swan Song)
Juice Newton; *All-Time Country Classics-#2-C* . . . . (Capitol)
Juice . . . . (Capitol)
Juice Newton-Greatest Hits & More . . . . (Capitol)
Juice Newton's Greatest Hits . . . . (Gold Rush)
Rodney Crowell; *Rodney Crowell-Collection* . . . . (Warner Bros.)
Queen Of Hearts
Joan Baez; *Joan Baez In Concert, Part 2* . . . . (Vanguard)
The Joan Baez Ballad Book . . . . (Vanguard)
Queen Of Hearts
Whitesnake; *Snakebite* . . . . (Geffen)
Queen Of Hearts
Gregg Allman; *Laid Back* . . . . (Polydor)
Queen Of My Heart
Hank Williams, Jr.; *Hank Williams, Jr.'s Greatest Hits-#2* . . . . (WB/Curb)
Man Of Steel . . . . (WB/Curb)
Queen Of My Heart
DeBarge; *In A Special Way* . . . . (Motown)
Queen Of My Heart
Rene & Ray; *History Of Latino Rock-#1-C* . . . . (Rhino)
Queen Of The Broken Hearts
Loverboy; *Keep It Up* . . . . (Columbia)
Quit Playing Games (With My Heart)
Backstreet Boys; *Backstreet Boys* . . . . (Jive)
MTV Party To Go '98-C . . . . (Tommy Boy)
The Concert For New York City-C . . . . (Columbia)
Radio Heart
Charly McClain; *19 Hot Country Requests-#3-C* . . . . (Epic)
Charly McClain's Biggest Hits . . . . (Epic)
Greatest Country Hits Of The '80s-1985-C . . . . (Columbia)
Radio Heart . . . . (Epic)
Radio Sweetheart
Elvis Costello; *Taking Liberties* . . . . (Columbia)
Rain In My Heart
Frank Sinatra; *Cycles* . . . . (Reprise)
Raining In My Heart
Anne Murray; *New Kind Of Feeling* . . . . (Capitol)
Buddy Holly; *Buddy Holly-20 Golden Greats* . . . . (MCA)
The Buddy Holly Collection . . . . (MCA)
Vintage Music-#6-C . . . . (MCA)
Jo-el Sonnier; *Come On Joe* . . . . (RCA)
Leo Sayer; *Leo Sayer* . . . . (Warner Bros.)
Ready, Willing And Able
Lari White; *Best Of Lari White* . . . . (RCA)
Don't Fence Me In . . . . (RCA)
Rebel Heart
Rod Stewart; *Vagabond Heart* . . . . (Warner Bros.)
Rhythm Divine
Enrique Iglesias; *Enrique* . . . . (Overbrook/Interscope)
Rhythm Of My Heart
Rod Stewart; *Vagabond Heart* . . . . (Warner Bros.)
Road Of Broken Hearted Men
Bobby Bland; *Introspective Of The Early Years* . . . . (MCA)
Touch Of The Blues . . . . (MCA)
Road To Your Heart
Barbara Mandrell; *Key's In The Mailbox* . . . . (Capitol)
Road To Your Heart
Highway 101; *101 2* . . . . (Warner Bros.)
Rock And Roll Heart
Lou Reed; *Between Thought & Expression-Anthology* . . . . (RCA)
Rock And Roll Heart . . . . (Arista)
Room In Your Heart
Gladys Knight & The Pips; *Every Beat Of My Heart-*
Greatest Hits . . . . (Chameleon)
Letter Full Of Tears-Golden Classics . . . . (Collectables)
Rough & Tumble Heart
Highway 101; *Paint The Town* . . . . (Warner Bros.)
Runnin' Away With My Heart
Lonestar; *Lonestar* . . . . (BNA)
Sacred Heart
Dio; *Intermission* . . . . (Warner Bros.)
Sacred Heart . . . . (Warner Bros.)
Sacred Heart
Shakespear's Sister; *ST/Nuns On The Run* . . . . (Mercury)
Safe In My Heart
Foreigner; *Unusual Heat* . . . . (Atlantic)
Savage Earth Heart
Waterboys; *Waterboys* . . . . (Ensign)
Savage Heart
Pretty Maids; *Lethal Heroes* . . . . (Epic)

Save A Little Room In Your Heart For Me
Eddie Money; *Eddie Money* . . . . (Columbia)
Saving My Heart
Yes; *Union* . . . . (Arista)
Say What's In My Heart
Aaron Neville; *To Make You Who I Am* . . . . (A&M)
Sea Of Heartbreak
Don Gibson; *Billboard Top Country Hits-1961-C* . . . . (Rhino)
Don Gibson's All-Time Greatest Hits . . . . (RCA)
Seasons Of My Heart
George Jones; *20 Golden Pieces Of George Jones* . . . . (Bulldog)
Jerry Lee Lewis; *Golden Cream Of Jerry Lee Lewis* . . . . (Sun)
Johnny Cash; *Columbia Records-1958-1986* . . . . (Columbia)
Now, There Was A Song! Memories From The Past-C . . . . (Legacy)
Seasons Of The Heart
John Denver; *John Denver's Greatest Hits-#3* . . . . (RCA)
Seasons Of The Heart . . . . (RCA)
Second Hand Heart
Gary Morris; *Faded Blue* . . . . (Warner Bros.)
Sgt. Pepper's Lonely Hearts Club Band
Beatles; *Beatles-Box Set* . . . . (Capitol)
The Beatles/1967-1970 . . . . (Capitol)
Jimi Hendrix; *Stages-Stockholm/Paris/San Diego/Atlanta* . . . . (Reprise)
Shape Of My Heart
Sting; *Ten Summoner's Tales* . . . . (A&M)
Shape Of My Heart
Backstreet Boys; *Black & Blue* . . . . (Jive)
Now That's What I Call Music!-#6-C . . . . (Virgin)
She Drew A Broken Heart
Patty Loveless; *The Trouble With The Truth* . . . . (Epic)
She Gave Her Heart To A Soldier Boy
Roy Rogers; *The Country Music Hall Of Fame-Roy Rogers* . . . . (MCA)
She Gave Her Heart To Jethro
Tom T. Hall; *Essential Tom T. Hall-20th Anniversary Collection* . . . . (Mercury)
She Never Lets It Go To Her Heart
Tim McGraw; *All I Want* . . . . (Curb)
Tim McGraw's Greatest Hits . . . . (Curb)
She Sure Got Away With My Heart
John Anderson; *Eye Of A Hurricane* . . . . (Warner Bros.)
John Anderson's Greatest Hits-#2 . . . . (Warner Bros.)
Sheer Heart Attack
Queen; *Live Killers* . . . . (Hollywood)
News Of The World . . . . (Hollywood)
She's A Heartbreaker
Gene Pitney; *Best Of Gene Pitney* . . . . (K-Tel)
Gene Pitney-Anthology 1961-1968 . . . . (Rhino)
She's A Heartbreaker
ZZ Top; *Six Pack* . . . . (Warner Bros.)
Tejas . . . . (Warner Bros.)
She's Gonna Win Your Heart
Eddy Raven; *I Could Use Another You* . . . . (RCA)
Shot In The Heart
Genya Ravan; *Urban Desire* . . . . (20th Century Fox)
Shot Through The Heart
Jennifer Warnes; *Best Of Jennifer Warnes* . . . . (Arista)
Shot Through The Heart . . . . (Arista)
Sign Your Name
Terence Trent D'Arby; *Introducing The Hardline According To Terence*
Trent D'Arby . . . . (Columbia)
Slow Dancin'-C . . . . (K-Tel)
Silver Threads And Golden Needles
Honky Tonk Angels; *Honky Tonk Angels* . . . . (Columbia)
Linda Ronstadt; *Don't Cry Now* . . . . (Asylum)
Hand Sown Home Grown . . . . (Capitol)
Linda Ronstadt-Retrospective . . . . (Capitol)
Linda Ronstadt's Greatest Hits . . . . (Asylum)
Springfields; *Troubadours Of The Folk Era-#3-C* . . . . (Rhino)
Sing My Heart Out
O'Jays; *So Full Of Love* . . . . (Philadelphia Int'l)
Sleeping Heart
Judds; *Talk About Love* . . . . (RCA)
Why Not Me . . . . (MCA)
Soft Hearted Hana
George Harrison; *George Harrison* . . . . (Dark Horse)
Solsbury Hill
Peter Gabriel; *Peter Gabriel* . . . . (Atco)
Peter Gabriel/Plays Live . . . . (Geffen)
Shaking The Tree-Sixteen Golden Greats . . . . (Geffen)
Some Broken Hearts
Bellamy Brothers; *The Reggae Cowboys* . . . . (Bellamy Bros./Intersound)
Some Broken Hearts Never Mend
Don Williams; *Best Of Don Williams-#2* . . . . (MCA)
Don Williams-20 Greatest Hits . . . . (MCA)
Some Broken Hearts Never Mend . . . . (MCA Special Prod.)
Someday Sweetheart
Bing Crosby; *Here Lies Love* . . . . (ASV Living Era)
Peggy Lee; *You Can Depend On Me* . . . . (Glendale)
Zoot Sims; *Best Of Zoot Sims* . . . . (Pablo)

Someone Could Lose A Heart Tonight
Eddie Rabbitt; *Best Of Eddie Rabbitt/Greatest Hits-II* . . . . (Warner Bros.)
Number 1's . . . . (Warner Bros.)
Step By Step . . . . (Liberty)
Something In My Heart
Michel'le; *Michel'le* . . . . (Ruthless)
Ricky Skaggs; *Ricky Skaggs-Country Boy* . . . . (Epic)
Something Like That
Tim McGraw; *A Place In The Sun* . . . . (Curb)
Tim McGraw's Greatest Hits . . . . (Curb)
Somewhere In My Broken Heart
Billy Dean; *Billy Dean's Greatest Hits* . . . . (Liberty)
Heart Beats-Country Lovin': Songs From The Heart-C . . . . (Rhino)
Young Man . . . . (SBK)
Randy Travis; *No Holdin' Back* . . . . (Warner Bros.)
Somewhere In The Vicinity Of The Heart
Shenandoah; *In The Vicinity Of The Heart* . . . . (Capitol)
Now And Then . . . . (Capitol)
Pure Country-Best Of The '90s-#2-C . . . . (Priority)
Song From Moulin Rouge (Where Is Your Heart)
Percy Faith & His Orchestra; *Percy Faith & His Orchestra's All-Time*
Greatest Hits . . . . (Columbia)
Soul Of My Soul
Michael Bolton; *Love Shouldn't Hurt-C* . . . . (Qwest)
Speak Softly-You're Talking To My Heart
Gene Watson; *Gene Watson's Greatest Hits* . . . . (MCA)
Old Loves Never Die . . . . (MCA)
Steal Your Heart Away
Bonnie Raitt; *Longing In Their Hearts* . . . . (Capitol)
Still In My Heart
Tracie Spencer; *Tracie* . . . . (Capitol)
Still Right Here In My Heart
Pure Prairie League; *Best Of Pure Prairie League* . . . . (Mercury)
Stop Draggin' My Heart Around
Stevie Nicks with Tom Petty And The Heartbreakers; *Bella Donna* . . . (Modern)
TimeSpace-The Best Of Stevie Nicks . . . . (Modern)
Stop Steppin' On My Heart
Eddie Money; *Eddie Money's Greatest Hits-Sound Of Money* . . . . . (Columbia)
Stop, Look & Listen To Your Heart
Johnny Mathis; *I'm Coming Home* . . . . (Columbia)
Johnny Mathis-Love Songs . . . . (Columbia)
Marvin Gaye & Diana Ross; *Diana & Marvin* . . . . (Motown)
Patti Austin; *Every Home Should Have One* . . . . (Qwest)
Stylistics; *Stylistics-1st Album* . . . . (Amherst)
Storm In The Heartland
Billy Ray Cyrus; *Storm In The Heartland* . . . . (Mercury)
Story Of A Broken Heart
Johnny Cash; *Johnny Cash-Original Golden Hits-#3* . . . . (Sun)
Original Johnny Cash . . . . (Sun)
Rough Cut King Of Country Music . . . . (Sun)
The Man-The World-His Music . . . . (Sun)
Stout-Hearted Men
Barbra Streisand; *Simply Streisand* . . . . (Columbia)
Straight For The Heart
Whitesnake; *Whitesnake* . . . . (Geffen)
Straight For The Heart
Toto; *Seventh One* . . . . (Columbia)
Straight From My Heart
Sylvia; *Sylvia's Greatest Hits* . . . . (RCA)
Straight From The Heart
Peabo Bryson; *Straight From The Heart* . . . . (Elektra)
Straight From The Heart
Coyote Sisters; *Coyote Sisters* . . . . (Morocco)
Straight From The Heart
Bryan Adams; *Cuts Like A Knife* . . . . (A&M)
Straight From The Heart
Little Feat; *Down On The Farm* . . . . (Warner Bros.)
Straight From The Heart
Earth, Wind & Fire; *Powerlight* . . . . (Columbia)
Straight To My Heart
Sting; *...Nothing Like The Sun* . . . . (A&M)
Straight To The Heart
David Sanborn; *Straight To The Heart* . . . . (Warner Bros.)
Straight To The Heart
Crystal Gayle; *Best Of Crystal Gayle* . . . . (Warner Bros.)
Straight To Your Heart
Bad English; *Backlash* . . . . (Epic)
Strangers Of The Heart
Heart; *Bad Animals* . . . . (Capitol)
String Around My Heart
Cleftones; *Best Of The Cleftones* . . . . (Rhino)
Strings Of My Heart, The
Gaylords; *Best Of The Gaylords-Mercury Years* . . . . (Chronicles)
Strings On Your Heart
Meat Puppets; *Monsters* . . . . (Rykodisc)
Strong Heart
T.G. Sheppard; *Greatest Country Hits Of The '80s-1986-C* . . . . . . (Columbia)
More Hot Country Requests-C . . . . (Epic)

T.G. Sheppard's Biggest Hits . . . . (Columbia)
Subway Heart
Massacre; *Killing Time* . . . . (Celluloid)
Sweetheart
Dan Hicks & His Hot Licks; *Last Train To Hicksville* . . . . (MCA)
Maria Muldaur; *Waitress In The Donut Shop* . . . . (Warner Archives)
Sweetheart
Thin Lizzy; *Chinatown* . . . . (Warner Bros.)
Sweetheart
Frankie & The Knockouts; *Radio Daze-Pop Hits Of The '80s-#5-C* . . . . . (Rhino)
Sweetheart From Venezuela
Harry Belafonte; *Harry Belafonte-Pure Gold* . . . . (RCA)
Sweetheart Of Sigma Chi
Fred Waring's Pennsylvanians; *Very Best Of Fred Waring & The*
Pennsylvanians . . . . (Reader's Digest Music)
Gene Austin; *The Voice Of The Southland* . . . . (Living Era)
Sweetheart Of The Rodeo
Emmylou Harris; *Ballad Of Sally Rose* . . . . (Warner Bros.)
Sweetheart Of The Year
Ray Price; *Best Of Ray Price* . . . . (Columbia)
Ray Price's Greatest Hits-#3 . . . . (Step One)
Sweetheart You Done Me Wrong
Bill Monroe & His Blue Grass Boys; *Essential Bill Monroe-1945-*
1949 . . . . (Columbia)
Elvis Presley; *Million-Dollar Quartet* . . . . (RCA)
Sweethearts On Parade
Guy Lombardo & His Royal Canadians; *Best Of Guy Lombardo* . . . . (Curb)
Best Of Guy Lombardo . . . . (MCA)
Louis Armstrong; *Louis Armstrong-Vol. 7-You're Driving Me*
Crazy . . . . (Columbia)
Pete Fountain; *Pete Fountain's New Orleans* . . . . (MCA)
Roy Eldridge; *Happy Time* . . . . (Pablo)
Take A Heart
Sorrows; *History Of British Rock-#4-C* . . . . (Rhino)
Take Good Care Of My Heart
Whitney Houston & Jermaine Jackson; *Whitney Houston* . . . . (Arista)
Take It Like A Man
Michelle Wright; *Now & Then* . . . . (Arista)
Today's Top Country-C . . . . (K-Tel)
Take It To Heart
Michael McDonald; *Take It To Heart* . . . . (Reprise)
Take Me To Heart
Quarterflash; *Take Another Picture* . . . . (Geffen)
Take Me To Heart
Neville Brothers; *Family Groove* . . . . (A&M)
Take My Heart
Kool & The Gang; *Something Special* . . . . (De-Lite)
Take My Heart
Neal McCoy; *At This Moment* . . . . (Atlantic)
Take My Heart
Corey Hart; *Corey Hart-Singles* . . . . (EMI)
Take These Chains From My Heart
Hank Williams With His Drifting Cowboys; *24 Of Hank Williams'*
Greatest Hits . . . . (Polydor)
Hank Williams-40 Greatest Hits . . . . (Polydor)
Ray Charles; *Ray Charles-His Greatest Hits-#2* . . . . (Dunhill Compact Classics)
Take This Heart
Richard Marx; *Rush Street* . . . . (Capitol)
Take This Heart Of Mine
Marvin Gaye; *Marvin Gaye-Anthology* . . . . (Motown)
Motown Legends-Marvin Gaye . . . . (Motown)
Taking Everything
Gerald Levert; *Love & Consequences* . . . . (East West)
Talk To Me Lonesome Heart
James O'Gwynn; *James O'Gwynn's Greatest Hits* . . . . (Plantation)
Teardrops In My Heart
Marty Robbins; *Marty Robbins' Biggest Hits* . . . . (Columbia)
Sons Of The Pioneers; *Cool Water* . . . . (RCA)
Tearin' Up My Heart
'N Sync; *'N Sync* . . . . (RCA)
Tell It To My Heart
Taylor Dayne; *Rock The First-#6-C* . . . . (Sandstone Music)
Tell It To My Heart . . . . (Arista)
Tender Hearted Sue
Rambling Rogue; *45-#6747* . . . . (Okeh)
Texas Heartache #1
Mickey Gilley; *Put Your Dreams Away* . . . . (Epic)
Texas Size Heartache
Joe Diffie; *Joe Diffie's Greatest Hits* . . . . (Epic)
Thanks A Lot
Ernest Tubb; *The Country Music Hall Of Fame-Ernest Tubb* . . . . (MCA)
IIIrd Time Out; *IIIrd Time Out* . . . . (Rebel)
Ronnie & Rob McCoury; *Ronnie & Rob McCoury* . . . . (Rounder)
That Heart Belongs To Me
George Jones; *20 Golden Pieces Of George Jones* . . . . (Bulldog)
That's How A Heartache Begins
Patsy Cline; *Songwriter's Tribute* . . . . (MCA)

That's How Heartaches Are Made
Baby Washington; *Best Of Baby Washington* . . . . (Collectables)
That's How Heartaches Are Made . . . . (Collectables)
Marvelettes; *Deliver-Singles-1961-1971* . . . . (Motown)
Marvelettes-Anthology . . . . (Motown)

That's How You Know (When You're In Love)
Lari White; *Best Of Lari White* . . . . (RCA)
Wishes . . . . (RCA)

That's The Beat Of A Heart
Warren Brothers with Sara Evans; *King Of Nothing* . . . . (BNA)
ST/Where The Heart Is . . . . (RCA)

That's What I Get (For Losin' You)
Hal Ketchum; *Every Little Word* . . . . (Curb)

That's What My Heart Needs
Otis Redding; *Pain In My Heart* . . . . (Atco)
The Otis Redding Story . . . . (Atlantic)

That's When Your Heartaches Begin
Elvis Presley; *Elvis' Golden Records* . . . . (RCA)
Million-Dollar Quartet . . . . (RCA)
Worldwide 50 Gold Award Hits, Vol. 1, Parts 1 & 2 . . . . (RCA)

Their Hearts Were Full Of Spring
Beach Boys; *Concert/'69-Live In London* . . . . (Capitol)
Good Vibrations-Thirty Years Of The Beach Boys . . . . (Capitol)
Smiley Smile/Wild Honey . . . . (Capitol)

There Goes My Heart
Nat ''King'' Cole; *Let's Fall In Love* . . . . (Paisley Park)
Nat ''King'' Cole Sings For Two In Love-& More . . . . (Capitol)

There Goes My Heart
Mavericks; *Best Of The Mavericks-Super Colossal Smash Hits Of
The '90s* . . . . (Mercury)
What A Crying Shame . . . . (MCA)

There Goes My Heart Again
Holly Dunn; *Blue Rose Of Texas* . . . . (Warner Bros.)
Greatest Country Dance Record Ever-#1-C . . . . (Warner Bros.)
Milestones-Greatest Hits . . . . (Warner Bros.)

There Is A Tavern In The Town
Four Aces; *Four Aces-More Greatest Hits* . . . . (Varese Vintage)
Mitch Miller; *Sing Along With Mitch* . . . . (Columbia)
Stan Wolowic & The Polka Chips; *Million-Seller Polkas* . . . . . . (Capitol)

There Must Be An Angel (Playing With My Heart)
Eurythmics; *Be Yourself Tonight* . . . . (RCA)
Eurythmics' Greatest Hits . . . . (Arista)
Live-1983-1989 . . . . (Arista)

There's A Broken Heart For Every Light On Broadway
Mel Torme; *Songs Of New York* . . . . (Rhino)

There's A Hero
Billy Gilman; *God Bless America-C* . . . . (Columbia)

There's No Stopping Your Heart
Marie Osmond; *Best Of Branson U.S.A.-#1-C* . . . . (Curb)
Best Of Marie Osmond . . . . (Curb)
There's No Stopping Your Heart . . . . (Curb)

They Don't Make Hearts Like They Used To
Diamond Rio; *Diamond Rio* . . . . (Arista)

Thief Of Hearts
Melissa Manchester; *ST/Thief Of Hearts* . . . . (Casablanca)

Thief Of Hearts
Madonna; *Erotica* . . . . (Maverick/Sire)

This Broken Heart
Mavericks; *From Hell To Paradise* . . . . (MCA)

This Heart
Sweethearts Of The Rodeo; *Buffalo Zone* . . . . (Columbia)

This Heart
Aaron Tippin; *Read Between The Lines* . . . . (RCA)

This Heart Of Mine
Hi-Lo's; *Love Nest* . . . . (Sony Music Special Prod.)
Judy Garland & Victor Young & His Orchestra; *Changing My Tune-Best Of
Decca Years-#2* . . . . (Decca)

This Heart Of Mine
New Grass Revival; *Fly Through The Country* . . . . (Flying Fish)

This Heart Speaks For Itself
Bobbie Cryner; *Bobbie Cryner* . . . . (Epic)

This Heartache Never Sleeps
Mark Chesnutt; *I Don't Want To Miss A Thing* . . . . (MCA)

This Missin' You Heart Of Mine
Sawyer Brown; *Somewhere In The Night* . . . . (Liberty)

This Old Heart Of Mine
Isley Brothers; *25 Hard-To-Find Motown Classics-#3-C* . . . . . (Motown)
Good Feeling Music Of The Big Chill Generation-#1-C . . . . . . (Motown)
Greatest By Holland/Dozier/Holland-C . . . . (Motown)
Motown Story-First 25 Years-C . . . . (Motown)
Motown Superstar Series-#6-Isley Brothers . . . . (Motown)
This Old Heart Of Mine . . . . (Motown)
Rod Stewart; *Atlantic Crossing* . . . . (Warner Bros.)
Rod Stewart & Ronald Isley; *Downtown Train-Selections From The
Storyteller Anthology* . . . . (Warner Bros.)
Storyteller/The Complete Anthology: 1964-1990 . . . . . . (Warner Bros.)

This Place Hotel (Heartbreak Hotel)
Jacksons; *Jacksons Live* . . . . (Epic)

Triumph . . . . (Epic)

Three Hearts In A Tangle
Roy Drusky; *45-#31193* . . . . (Decca)

Thundering Hearts
John Cougar; *American Fool* . . . . (Riva)

Time (Clock Of The Heart)
Culture Club; *Kissing To Be Clever* . . . . (Virgin)

To The Summer In Our Hearts
Curlew; *Bee* . . . . (Cuneiform)
Live In Berlin . . . . (Cuneiform)

Tonight The Heartache's On Me
Dixie Chicks; *Wide Open Spaces* . . . . (Monument)

Too Much On My Heart
Statler Brothers; *Partners In Rhyme* . . . . (Mercury)

Too Soon To Know
Don Gibson; *Oh Lonesome Me* . . . . (Collectables)
Roy Orbison; *The Classic Roy Orbison-1965-1968* . . . . (Rhino)

Total Eclipse Of The Heart
Bonnie Tyler; *Billboard Top Hits-1983-C* . . . . (Rhino)
Faster Than The Speed Of Night . . . . (Columbia)
Seems Like Yesterday-#4-Early '80s-C . . . . (K-Tel)
Nicki French; *Dance Hits '96 Supermix-C* . . . . (Critique)
Secrets . . . . (Critique)

Touch My Heart
Ray Price; *Ray Price's Greatest Hits-#2* . . . . (Step One)

Tourette's
Nirvana; *In Utero* . . . . (David Geffen Co.)

Toy Heart
Bill Monroe; *Columbia Historic Edition-Bill Monroe* . . . . (Columbia)
Bill Monroe & Flatt & Scruggs; *Bill Monroe And Flatt & Scruggs* . . . . (Rounder)
Bill Monroe & His Blue Grass Boys; *Essential Bill Monroe-1945-
1949* . . . . (Columbia)
Ricky Skaggs; *Family & Friends* . . . . (Rounder)

Trail Of Broken Hearts
k.d. lang and The Reclines; *Absolute Torch & Twang* . . . . (Sire)

Tranquillo (Melt My Heart)
Carly Simon; *Boys In The Trees* . . . . (Elektra)

Travelin' Man
Lynyrd Skynyrd; *Live From Steel Town* . . . . (CMC Int'l)
One More From The Road . . . . (MCA)

Trippin' On A Hole In A Paper Heart
Stone Temple Pilots; *Tiny Music...Songs From The Vatican
Gift Shop* . . . . (Atlantic)

Trolley Song
Judy Garland; *Best Of Judy Garland* . . . . (MCA)
Judy Garland's All-Time Greatest Hits . . . . (Curb)
Original Broadway Cast; *Meet Me In St. Louis* . . . . (DRG)

True Heart
Oak Ridge Boys; *Country Classics-#11-1987-1988-C* . . . . . . (Universal)
Heart Beat . . . . (MCA)
Oak Ridge Boys' Greatest Hits 3 . . . . (MCA)

Tuesday Heartbreak
Stevie Wonder; *Talking Book* . . . . (Motown)

Two Hearts
Bruce Springsteen; *The River* . . . . (Columbia)
Bruce Springsteen & The E Street Band; *Bruce Springsteen & The E Street
Band Live/1975-85* . . . . (Legacy)

Two Hearts
Stephanie Mills; *Greatest Hits In My Life* . . . . (Casablanca)

Two Hearts
K.T. Oslin; *Love In A Small Town* . . . . (RCA)

Two Hearts
Pebbles; *Pebbles* . . . . (MCA)

Two Hearts
Chris Isaak; *San Francisco Days* . . . . (Reprise)

Two Hearts
Phil Collins; *Serious Hits...Live!* . . . . (Atlantic)

Two Hearts Beat As One
U2; *War* . . . . (Island)

Two Of Hearts
Stacey Q; *Better Than Heaven* . . . . (Atlantic)
Dance Traxx-#2-C . . . . (Atlantic)

Two People Fell In Love
Brad Paisley; *Brad Paisley-Part II* . . . . (Arista)

Unborn Heart
Dan Hill; *Real Love* . . . . (Columbia)

Un-Break My Heart
Toni Braxton; *Secrets* . . . . (LaFace)

Unbreakable Heart
Carlene Carter; *Little Love Letters* . . . . (Giant)
Jessica Andrews; *Heart Shaped World* . . . . (DreamWorks/SKG)

Unchain My Heart
Joe Cocker; *Joe Cocker Live* . . . . (Capitol)
Unchain My Heart . . . . (Capitol)
Ray Charles; *Ray Charles' Greatest Hits* . . . . (Rhino)
Ray Charles-Anthology . . . . (Rhino)
Ray Charles-His Greatest Hits-#1 . . . . (Dunhill Compact Classics)

Universal Heart-Beat
Juliana Hatfield; *Box Presents Big Ones Of Alternative*
  Rock-#1-C . . . . (Box Tunes)
  Only Everything . . . . (Mammoth)
Valentine
Nils Lofgren & Bruce Springsteen; *Silver Lining* . . . . (Rykodisc)
Valentine
Jim Brickman & Martina McBride; *Picture This*. . . . . (Windham Hill)
  Smooth Sounds-C . . . . (Razor & Tie)
Martina McBride & Jim Brickman; *Evolution*. . . . .(RCA)
Valentine
Willie Nelson; *Across The Borderline*. (Columbia)
Valentine
Bryan Ferry; *Boys & Girls*. . . . . (Warner Bros.)
Valentine
Replacements; *Pleased To Meet Me* . . . .(Sire)
Valentine
Belinda Carlisle; *Runaway Horses* . . . . (MCA)
Valentine
Toby Keith; *Toby Keith* . . . . (Mercury)
Valentine
Psychedelic Furs; *World Outside*. . . . . (Columbia)
Valentine Day
Paul McCartney; *McCartney* . . . . (Capitol)
  Paul McCartney-Gift Set . . . . (Capitol)
Valentine's Day
ABC; *Lexicon Of Love*. . . . . (Mercury)
Valentine's Day
James Taylor; *Never Die Young* . . . . (Columbia)
Valentine's Day
Bruce Springsteen; *Tunnel Of Love* . . . . (Columbia)
Victim Of A Broken Heart
Aldo Nova; *Portrait Of Aldo Nova* . . . . (Epic)
  Subject...Aldo Nova . . . . (Portrait)
Victim Of The Modern Heart
Earth, Wind & Fire; *Touch Of The World* . . . . (Columbia)
Voice Of The Heart
Diana Ross; *Take Me Higher* . . . . (Motown)
Walk On
U2; *America: A Tribute To Heroes-C* . . . . (Interscope)
  Now That's What I Call Music!-#8-C . . . . (Virgin)
Walk Softly
Billy "Crash" Craddock; *Billy "Crash" Craddock Live* . . . . (MCA)
  Billy "Crash" Craddock Sings His Greatest Hits . . . . (MCA)
  Easy As Pie . . . . (MCA)
Walk Softly On This Heart Of Mine
Bill Monroe; *The Country Music Hall Of Fame-Bill Monroe* . . . . (MCA)
Joey Welz; *Lovin' My Country* . . . . (Capricorn)
Kentucky HeadHunters; *Best Of The Kentucky HeadHunters-Still*
  Pickin' . . . . (Mercury)
  Pickin' On Nashville . . . . (Mercury)
Ricky Skaggs and the Dixie Chicks; *Ricky Skaggs & Friends-Big Mon: Songs*
  Of Bill Monroe . . . . (Skaggs Family)
Walkin' A Broken Heart
Don Williams; *Cafe Carolina* . . . . (MCA)
  Don Williams' Greatest Hits . . . . (MCA)
Walkin', Talkin'...Beatin' Broken Heart
Highway 101; *Country's Greatest Hits-#4-Sweet Country-C* . . . . (Priority)
  Paint The Town. . . . . (Warner Bros.)
Walls
Tom Petty And The Heartbreakers; *ST/She's The One* . . . . (Warner Bros.)
War Of The Hearts
Sade; *Promise* . . . . (Portrait)
Warm Your Heart
Aaron Neville; *Warm Your Heart* . . . . (A&M)
Drifters; *Let The Boogie Woogie Roll-Greatest Hits* . . . . (Atlantic)
Way We Make A Broken Heart
Rosanne Cash; *30 Years Of #1 Hits-#16-C* . . . . (Columbia)
  Greatest Country Hits Of The '80s-1987-C . . . . (Columbia)
  King's Record Shop . . . . (Columbia)
  Love Gets Strange-Songs Of John Hiatt-C . . . . (Rhino)
  Rosanne Cash-Hits-1979-1989 . . . . (Columbia)
Ry Cooder; *Borderline* . . . . (Warner Bros.)
We Live In Two Different Worlds
Auldridge/Bennett/Gaudreau; *This Old Town* . . . . (Rebel)
Welcome To Heartlight
Kenny Loggins; *High Adventure* . . . . (Columbia)
Whaleheart
Marnie Jones; *Grace* . . . . (Thriving Productions)
What Becomes Of The Brokenhearted
Jimmy & David Ruffin; *Motown Superstar Series-#8-Jimmy & David*
  Ruffin . . . . (Motown)
Jimmy Ruffin; *Motown Story-First 25 Years-C* . . . . (Motown)
Paul Young; *ST/Fried Green Tomatoes* . . . . (MCA)
What Can I Tell My Heart
Vanessa Williams; *The Comfort Zone* . . . . (Wing)
What Goes On
Beatles; *"Yesterday"...And Today* . . . . (Capitol)

What The Heart Wants
Collin Raye; *Best Of Collin Raye-Direct Hits* . . . . (Epic)
Whatever
En Vogue; *Bass In Your Face: Essential Drum And Bass-C* . . . . (Elektra)
What's Love Got To Do With It
Tina Turner; *Live In Europe* . . . . (Capitol)
  Private Dancer . . . . (Capitol)
  Simply The Best . . . . (Capitol)
When I Fall In Love
Celine Dion; *The Colour Of My Love* . . . . (550 Music)
Doris Day; *Doris Day-16 Most Requested Songs-Encore!*. . . . . (Columbia)
When The Heart Rules The Mind
GTR; *GTR* . . . . (Arista)
Where Do Broken Hearts Go
Whitney Houston; *Whitney* . . . . (Arista)
  Whitney Houston's Greatest Hits . . . . (Arista)
Where Do You Keep Your Heart
Tommy Dorsey & Frank Sinatra; *Dorsey/Sinatra Sessions-#1* . . . . . . (Bluebird)
  Tommy Dorsey & Frank Sinatra's All-Time Greatest Hits-#4 . . . . . . (Bluebird)
Where Does My Heart Beat Now?
Celine Dion; *Unison*. . . . . (Epic)
Whispering Heart
Empires; *Harlem Holiday-New York Rhythm & Blues-#3-C* . . . . . (Collectables)
Who Will Call You Sweetheart
Stanley Brothers & The Clinch Mountain Boys; *Best Of Bluegrass-#1-*
  Standards-C . . . . (Mercury)
Why Don't You Believe Me?
Duprees; *Best Of The Duprees* . . . . (Rhino)
  Best Of The Duprees . . . . (Collectables)
Joni James; *Platinum & Gold Hits* . . . . (Taragon)
Patti Page; *Patti Page-Golden Celebration* . . . . (Mercury)
Wild Heart
Stevie Nicks; *Wild Heart* . . . . (Modern)
Wild Heart Of The Young
Karla Bonoff; *Wild Heart Of The Young* . . . . (Columbia)
Wild Hearted Son
Cult; *Ceremony* . . . . (Sire)
Wild Hearts
Roy Orbison; *Legendary Roy Orbison* . . . . (Sony Music Special Prod.)
Wild Hearts Run Out Of Time
Roy Orbison; *King Of Hearts* . . . . (Virgin)
Winner Of Your Heart
Johnnie & Jack & Their Tennessee Mountain Boys; *45-Out of print* . . . . . (RCA)
With A Song In My Heart
Ella Fitzgerald; *Rodgers & Hart Songbook* . . . . (Verve)
Jerry Vale; *Standing Ovation!-Carnegie Hall Concert* . . . . (Columbia)
Jose Carreras; *The 3 Tenors In Concert 1994* . . . . (Teldec)
Mario Lanza; *Be My Love* . . . . (RCA)
Stevie Wonder; *Uptight (Everything's Alright)* . . . . (Motown)
With Each Beat Of My Heart
Stevie Wonder; *Characters* . . . . (Motown)
With Every Beat Of My Heart
Taylor Dayne; *Can't Fight Fate*. . . . . (Arista)
Without You
Dixie Chicks; *Fly* . . . . (Monument)
Woman Of Heart & Mind
Joni Mitchell; *For The Roses* . . . . (Asylum)
Joni Mitchell with Tom Scott & The L.A. Express; *Miles Of Aisles*. . . . (Asylum)
Woman's Touch
Toby Keith; *Blue Moon* . . . . (Polydor Country)
Wooden Heart
Elvis Presley; *For Children* . . . . (RCA)
  ST/G.I. Blues . . . . (RCA)
  Worldwide 50 Gold Award Hits, Vol. 1, Parts 1 & 2 . . . . (RCA)
Words By Heart
Billy Ray Cyrus; *It Won't Be The Last* . . . . (Mercury)
You Are Not Alone
Michael Jackson; *1996 Grammy Nominees-C* . . . . (Columbia)
  HIStory: Past, Present And Future-Book 1-C . . . . (Epic)
You Can Tell The World
Simon & Garfunkel; *Collected Works* . . . . (Columbia)
  Wednesday Morning 3 A.M. . . . . (Columbia)
You Can't Hurry Love
Diana Ross; *Diana Ross-The Ultimate Collection* . . . . (Motown)
Diana Ross & The Supremes; *16 #1 Hits From The Early '60s-C* . . . . . (Motown)
Phil Collins; *Hello, I Must Be Going* . . . . (Atlantic)
You Can't Make A Heart Love Somebody
George Strait; *Latest Greatest Straitest Hits* . . . . (MCA)
  Lead On . . . . (MCA)
You Can't Run Away From Your Heart
Lacy J. Dalton; *Dream Baby* . . . . (Columbia)
Patty Loveless; *On Down The Line* . . . . (MCA)
You Could've Heard A Heart Break
Johnny Lee; *Workin' For A Livin'* . . . . (Full Moon/Warner Bros.)
You Let Your Heart Go Too Fast
Spin Doctors; *Turn It Upside Down* . . . . (Epic)
You Put The Beat In My Heart
Eddie Rabbitt; *Best Of Eddie Rabbitt/Greatest Hits-II* . . . . (Warner Bros.)

You Win My Love
Shania Twain; *The Woman In Me* . . . . (Mercury)
You'll Be In My Heart
Phil Collins; *ST/Tarzan*. . . . . (Hollywood)
You'll Never Get To Heaven (If You Break My Heart)
Dionne Warwick; *Dionne Warwick* . . . . (Everest)
  Dionne Warwick Greatest Hits . . . . (Everest)
  Dionne Warwick-Anthology 1962-1971 . . . . (Rhino)
  Hot! Live & Otherwise. . . . . (Arista)
  Say A Little Prayer. . . . .(Dunhill Compact Classics)
Stylistics; *Best Of The Stylistics-#2.* . . . . (Amherst)
Young Hearts Run Free
Candi Staton; *The Disco Years-#3-Boogie Fever-C* . . . . (Rhino)
  Young Hearts Run Free: The Best Of Candi Staton . . . .(Warner Bros.)
Young Turks
Rod Stewart; *Absolutely Live* . . . .(Warner Bros.)
  Downtown Train-Selections From The Storyteller Anthology. . .(Warner Bros.)
  Storyteller/The Complete Anthology: 1964-1990 . . . .(Warner Bros.)
  Tonight I'm Yours . . . .(Warner Bros.)
Young-At-Heart
Bing Crosby with Guy Lombardo & His Royal Canadians; *The Radio Years:*
  20 Songs . . . . (Crescendo)
Frank Sinatra; *At The Movies* . . . . (Capitol)
  Capitol Collectors Series-Frank Sinatra . . . . (Capitol)
  Classic Sinatra . . . . (Capitol)
  Sinatra's Sinatra . . . . (Reprise)
Ray Price; *Portrait Of A Singer* . . . . (Step One)
Rosemary Clooney; *Essence Of Rosemary Clooney*. . . . . (Legacy)
Your Cheatin' Heart
Beck; *Timeless: Hank Williams Tribute-C* . . . . (Lost Highway/IDJMG)
Elvis Presley; *Elvis For Everyone!* . . . . (RCA)
  Welcome To My World. . . . . (RCA)
Frankie Laine; *Frankie Laine's 16 Greatest Hits* . . . . (Trip)
  Frankie Laine's Greatest Hits . . . . (Columbia)
Hank Williams With His Drifting Cowboys; *24 Of Hank Williams'*
  Greatest Hits . . . . (Polydor)
  Hank Williams-16 Great Hits . . . . (Everest)
  Hank Williams-40 Greatest Hits . . . . (Polydor)
Hank Williams, Jr.; *Very Best Of Hank Williams, Jr.* . . . . (Polydor)
Jerry Lee Lewis; *Live At The Star Club-Hamburg 1964* . . . . (Rhino)
  The Golden Hits of Jerry Lee Lewis . . . . (Smash)
Patsy Cline; *ST/Sweet Dreams* . . . . (MCA)
  The Patsy Cline Story . . . . (MCA)
Ray Charles; *Ray Charles' Greatest Hits-#2* . . . . (Rhino)
Your Heart's Not In It
Janie Fricke; *First Word In Memory*. (Columbia)
  Greatest Country Hits Of The '80s-1984-C . . . . (Columbia)
  Janie Fricke-17 Greatest Hits . . . . (Columbia)
  Very Best Of Janie Fricke . . . . (Columbia)
Your Selfish Heart
Stanley Brothers & The Clinch Mountain Boys; *Stanley Brothers & The*
  Clinch Mountain Boys. . . . . (King)
You're Breaking My Heart
Nilsson; *Son Of Schmilsson* . . . . (RCA)
You're Easy On The Eyes
Terri Clark; *Big Country Hits '99-C* . . . . (K-Tel)
  How I Feel . . . . (Mercury)
You're In My Heart (The Final Acclaim)
Rod Stewart; *Absolutely Live* . . . .(Warner Bros.)
  Footloose & Fancy Free . . . .(Warner Bros.)
  Rod Stewart's Greatest Hits. . . . .(Warner Bros.)
  Storyteller/The Complete Anthology: 1964-1990 . . . .(Warner Bros.)
You're The Best Break This Old Heart Ever Had
Ed Bruce; *Ed Bruce's Greatest Hits* . . . . (MCA)
  One To One . . . . (MCA)
You're The One
Paul Simon; *You're The One* . . . .(Warner Bros.)
You've Still Got A Place In My Heart
George Jones; *You've Still Got A Place In My Heart* . . . .(Epic)
Zing! Went The Strings Of My Heart
Coasters; *Coasters' Greatest Hits.* . . . . (Atco)
  Rare Soul-Beach Music Classics-#1-C . . . . (Rhino)
Frank Sinatra; *The Reprise Collection* . . . . (Reprise)
Judy Garland; *Best Of Judy Garland* . . . . (MCA)
  Best Of The Decca Years-#1-Hits!-C . . . . (Decca)
  Judy Garland-At Carnegie Hall. . . . . (Capitol)
  Judy Garland's All-Time Greatest Hits . . . . (Curb)

HEAVEN, Afterlife

See Also: **ANGELS, DEATH, DEVILS, FAITH, GOD, HAPPINESS,**
HELL, PARADISE

All That Heaven Will Allow
Bruce Springsteen; *Tunnel Of Love* . . . . (Columbia)
All This And Heaven Too
Tommy Dorsey & Frank Sinatra; *Dorsey/Sinatra Sessions-#1* . . . . . . (Bluebird)

Tommy Dorsey & Frank Sinatra's All-Time Greatest Hits-#4 . . . . . (Bluebird)
All You Want Is Heaven
Daryl Hall & John Oates; *X-Static*. . . . .(RCA)
And The Heavens Cried
Anthony Newley; *Genuis Of Anthony Newley*. . . . .(London)
Angel
Jimi Hendrix; *Cry Of Love* . . . .(Reprise)
  Experience Hendrix: The Best Of Jimi Hendrix . . . . (MCA)
  First Rays Of The New Rising Sun . . . . (MCA)
Rod Stewart; *Best Of Rod Stewart*. . . . . (Mercury)
Angel Band
Emmylou Harris; *Angel Band* . . . . (Warner Bros.)
Stanley Brothers; *ST/O Brother, Where Art Thou?* . . . . (Mercury)
Stanley Brothers & The Clinch Mountain Boys; *Best Of Bluegrass-#1-*
  Standards-C . . . . (Mercury)
Angel In My Eyes
John Michael Montgomery; *John Michael Montgomery's*
  Greatest Hits . . . . (Atlantic)
Anywhere Like Heaven
James Taylor; *Sweet Baby James* . . . . (Warner Bros.)
April 24, 1981
Rick Springfield; *Success Hasn't Spoiled Me Yet* . . . .(RCA)
Are You Building A Temple In Heaven
Hank Williams; *I'm So Lonesome I Could Cry-1949* . . . .(Polydor)
Artificial Flowers
Bobby Darin; *The Bobby Darin Story* . . . .(Atlantic)
Away
Toadies; *Rubberneck*. . . . .(Interscope)
Beginning, The
Keb' Mo'; *The Door* . . . .(550/Epic/Okeh)
Between Heaven And Hell
Zakk Wylde; *Book Of Shadows* . . . . (Spitfire)
Black Jesus
Everlast; *Eat At Whitey's.* . . . . (Tommy Boy)
Body Heavenly
Full Force; *Get Busy 1 Time* . . . . (Columbia)
Born To Fly
Sara Evans; *Born To Fly* . . . .(RCA)
Breath Away From Heaven
George Harrison; *Cloud Nine* . . . .(Dark Horse)
Buying My Way Into Heaven
Sammy Hagar; *Unboxed* . . . . (Geffen)
Can Heaven Wait
Luther Vandross; *Luther Vandross* . . . . (J)
Chance For Heaven
Christopher Cross; *Official Music Of The XXIIIrd Olympiad* . . . . . . (Columbia)
Cheek To Cheek
Ella Fitzgerald; *Silver Collection-Songbooks* . . . . (Verve)
Frank Sinatra; *Come Dance With Me!*. (Capitol)
Fred Astaire; *Cheek To Cheek* . . . . (Pro-Arte)
  Irving Berlin Songbook . . . . (Verve)
Mundell Lowe; *Mundell Lowe Quartet* . . . . (Riverside)
Pete Fountain; *Cheek To Cheek.* . . . . (Ranwood)
Tommy Dorsey; *Irving Berlin 100th Anniversary Collection-C* . . . . . . (MCA)
Tony Bennett; *Bennett/Berlin.* . . . . (Columbia)
Chock Full O'Nuts Is That Heavenly Coffee
Original Sins; *TeeVee Toons-The Commercials-#1-C* . . . . (TVT)
Circus Of Heaven
Yes; *Tormato.* . . . .(Atlantic)
Cowboy Heaven
Roy Rogers; *Peace In The Valley* . . . . (Pair)
Daddy Sang Bass
Johnny Cash; *Columbia Country Classics-#5-A New Tradition-C* . . . (Columbia)
  Johnny Cash's Greatest Hits-#2. . . . . (Columbia)
  The Man In Black-His Greatest Hits. . . . . (Legacy)
Dear Brother
Hank Williams; *I Saw The Light* . . . .(Polydor)
Dixie Road
Lee Greenwood; *Country Classics-#3-1984-1985-C* . . . . (Universal)
  Lee Greenwood's Greatest Hits. . . . . (MCA)
  MCA #1 Hits Of The '80s-#2-C . . . . (MCA Special Prod.)
Do You Wanna Go To Heaven
Original Broadway Cast; *Big River-The Adventures Of*
  Huckleberry Finn . . . . (MCA)
T.G. Sheppard; *Smooth Sailin'* . . . . (Warner Bros.)
  T.G. Sheppard's All-Time Greatest Hits. . . . . (Warner Bros.)
  T.G. Sheppard's Greatest Hits . . . .(Warner Bros./Curb)
Edge Of Heaven
Wham! Featuring George Michael; *Music From The Edge Of*
  Heaven. . . . . (Columbia)
Family Who Prays (Never Shall Part), The
Browns; *Family Bible* . . . .(Step One)
Jim & Jesse; *Old Dominion Masters* . . . .(Pinecastle)
Louvin Brothers; *Live At New River Ranch.* . . . .(Copper Creek)
  ST/Jesus' Son . . . . (Mammoth)
  When I Stop Dreaming: The Best Of The Louvin Brothers . . . . . (Razor & Tie)
Ralph Stanley; *Child Of The King* . . . . (Rebel)
Farther Along
Byrds; *The Byrds.* . . . . (Columbia)

Elvis Presley; *Million-Dollar Quartet* . . . .(RCA)
Flying Burrito Brothers; *Farther Along-Best Of The Flying Burrito Brothers* . . . . (A&M)
Rose Maddox; *Rose Of The West Coast Country* . . . .(Arhoolie)

Feels Like Heaven
Peter Cetera; *World Falling Down* . . . . (Warner Bros.)

Fifty Miles Of Elbow Room
Iris DeMent; *Infamous Angel* . . . . (Warner Bros.)
Norman & Nancy Blake; *Blind Dog* . . . . (Rounder)
Red Clay Ramblers; *Twisted Laurel* . . . . (Flying Fish)

Fish & Whistle
John Prine; *Bruised Orange* . . . . (Oh Boy)

Flip The Switch
Rolling Stones; *Bridges To Babylon* . . . .(Virgin)
No Security . . . .(Virgin)

Ghetto Heaven
Family Stand; *Chain* . . . . (Atlantic)

Go Rest High On That Mountain
Vince Gill; *When Love Finds You* . . . . (MCA)

Go To Heaven
Grateful Dead; *Go To Heaven* . . . .(Arista)

God Blessed Texas
Little Texas; *Big Time* . . . . (Warner Bros.)

God's Gonna Get'cha (For That)
George Jones & Tammy Wynette; *George Jones & Tammy Wynette-16 Biggest Hits* . . . .(Epic/Legacy)
George Jones & Tammy Wynette's Greatest Hits . . . . (Epic)

Gone Away
Offspring; *Ixnay On The Hombre* . . . .(Columbia)

Good Girls Go To Heaven
Charlie Floyd; *Charlie Floyd* . . . . (Liberty)

Good News
Kingston Trio; *Scarlet Ribbons* . . . .(Capitol)
Mary Travers; *It's In Every One Of Us* . . . .(Chrysalis)
Sweet Honey In The Rock; *Good News* . . . . (Flying Fish)

Got A Date With An Angel
Hal Kemp; *Best Of The Big Bands-C* . . . .(Columbia)
Sammy Kaye & His Orchestra; *Best Of Sammy Kaye & His Orchestra* . . (MCA)

Great Beyond, The
R.E.M.; *Man On The Moon* . . . . (Warner Bros.)
Totally Hits-#2-C . . . . (Elektra)

Great Gig In The Sky
Pink Floyd; *Dark Side Of The Moon* . . . .(Capitol)
Pink Floyd-Gift Set . . . .(Capitol)

Green Rolling Hills
Bottle Hill; *Rumor In Their Own Time-#1* . . . . (Biograph)
Emmylou Harris; *Quarter Moon In A Ten Cent Town* . . . . . (Warner Bros.)

Guitar Heaven
Neil Diamond; *On The Way To The Sky* . . . . (Columbia)

Hands To Heaven
Breathe; *All That Jazz* . . . . (A&M)

Heaven
Psychedelic Furs; *All Of This & Nothing* . . . .(Columbia)
Mirror Moves . . . .(Columbia)

Heaven
Nu Flavor; *110% Hits-C* . . . . (Simitar)
Nu Flavor . . . .(Reprise)

Heaven
Bryan Adams; *MTV Unplugged-Bryan Adams* . . . . (A&M)
Reckless . . . . (A&M)

Heaven
Solo; *Solo* . . . . (Perspective/A&M)

Heaven
Chris Rea; *Auberge* . . . . (Atco)

Heaven
Joe Cocker; *Cocker* . . . .(Capitol)

Heaven
Talking Heads; *Fear Of Music* . . . .(Sire)

Heaven
Robyn Hitchcock & The Egyptians; *Fegmania* . . . . (Slash)

Heaven
Simply Red; *Picture Book* . . . .(Elektra)

Heaven
Rolling Stones; *Tattoo You* . . . .(Virgin)

Heaven
Pere Ubu; *Terminal Tower-Archival Collection* . . . . (Twin-Tone)

Heaven
Joan Armatrading; *Track Record* . . . . (A&M)

Heaven Above Me
Peabo Bryson & Roberta Flack; *Born To Love* . . . . (Capitol)
The Peabo Bryson Collection . . . .(Capitol)

Heaven And Hell
Black Sabbath; *Heaven And Hell* . . . . (Warner Bros.)
Live Evil . . . . (Warner Bros.)

Heaven And Hell
Assembled Multitude; *Heaven And Hell-45* . . . . (Eric)

Heaven And Hell
Easybeats; *Nuggets-Classic Collection From The Psychedelic '60s-C* . . . (Rhino)

Heaven And Hell
Willie Nelson; *Phases & Stages* . . . . (Atlantic)

Heaven And Hell
Who; *Who's Missing* . . . . (MCA)

Heaven Beside You
Alice In Chains; *Alice In Chains* . . . .(Columbia)
Alice In Chains-MTV Unplugged . . . .(Columbia)

Heaven Bound Train
Carl Story; *Great American Train Songs-C* . . . .(C.M.H. Prod.)

Heaven Can Be Anywhere
Charlie Daniels Band; *Midnight Wind* . . . . (Epic)

Heaven Can Wait
Paul Young; *Other Voices* . . . .(Columbia)

Heaven Can Wait
Meat Loaf; *Bat Out Of Hell* . . . . (Epic)

Heaven Can Wait
Iron Maiden; *Somewhere In Time* . . . .(Capitol)

Heaven Can't Be Found
Hank Williams, Jr.; *Born To Boogie* . . . .(WB/Curb)
Hank Williams, Jr.'s Greatest Hits III . . . .(Curb)

Heaven Every Day
Mel Tillis & The Statesiders; *Best Of Mel Tillis & The Statesiders* . . . . .(MGM)

Heaven Help
Lenny Kravitz; *Are You Gonna Go My Way* . . . . (Virgin)

Heaven Help Me
Deon Estus; *Spell* . . . . (Mika)

Heaven Help My Heart
Tina Arena; *Don't Ask* . . . . (Epic)
Wynonna; *Revelations* . . . . (Curb/MCA)
Wynonna-Collection . . . .(Curb)

Heaven Help The Fool
Bob Weir; *Heaven Help The Fool* . . . .(Arista)

Heaven Help The Lonely
Willie Nile; *Places I Have Never Been* . . . .(Columbia)

Heaven Help Us All
Stevie Wonder; *Signed Sealed & Delivered* . . . .(Motown)
Stevie Wonder-Love Songs-20 Classic Hits . . . .(Motown)
Stevie Wonder's Greatest Hits-#2 . . . .(Motown)

Heaven In The Back Seat
Eddie Money; *Right Here* . . . .(Columbia)

Heaven In Your Arms
R.J.'s Latest Arrival; *Hold On* . . . . (Manhattan)

Heaven In Your Eyes
Loverboy; *Big Ones* . . . .(Columbia)
ST/Top Gun . . . .(Columbia)

Heaven Is 10 Zillion Light Years Away
Stevie Wonder; *Fulfillingness' First Finale* . . . .(Motown)

Heaven Is A Place On Earth
Belinda Carlisle; *Greenpeace/Rainbow Warriors-C* . . . . (Geffen)
Heaven On Earth . . . .(MCA)

Heaven Is Here
Anne Murray; *Country Collection* . . . .(Capitol)
New Kind Of Feeling . . . .(Capitol)

Heaven Is In Your Mind
Three Dog Night; *Captured Live At The Forum* . . . .(MCA)
Traffic; *Mr. Fantasy* . . . . (Island)
Winwood . . . . (United Artists)

Heaven Knows
Donna Summer; *Live & More* . . . . (Casablanca)
On The Radio-Greatest Hits-Volumes I & II . . . . (Casablanca)
Summer Collection . . . .(Mercury)

Heaven Knows
Grass Roots; *Grass Roots-All-Time Greatest Hits* . . . .(MCA)
Grass Roots-Anthology (1966-1975) . . . .(Rhino)

Heaven Knows
Commodores; *Heroes/Commodores* . . . .(Motown)

Heaven Knows
Lalah Hathaway; *Lalah Hathaway* . . . . (Virgin)

Heaven Knows
Robert Plant; *Now And Zen* . . . .(Es Paranza)

Heaven Must Be Missing An Angel
Tavares; *Best Of Tavares* . . . .(Capitol)
Sky High . . . .(Capitol)

Heaven Must Have Sent You
Bonnie Pointer; *Greatest Songs By Holland-Dozier-Holland* . . . .(Motown)
Motown Memories-#4-C . . . .(Motown)
Top 10 With A Bullet-Motown Dance Songs-C . . . .(Motown)

Heaven On Earth
Platters; *Encore Of Golden Hits-Platters* . . . .(Mercury)
Platters-16 Greatest Hits . . . . (Trip)
Platters-Anthology . . . .(Rhino)
Red Sails In The Sunset . . . .(Allegiance)

Heaven On The 7th Floor
Paul Nicholas; *Super Hits Of The '70s-Have A Nice Day-#24-C* . . . .(Rhino)

Heaven On Their Minds
Original Cast; *ST/Jesus Christ Superstar* . . . . (MCA)

Heaven Only Knows
Shangri-Las; *Best Of The Shangri-Las* . . . .(Mercury)

Golden Hits Of The Shangri-Las . . . . (Mercury)
Remember The Shangri-Las At Their Best . . . . (Collectables)

Heaven Only Knows
Emmylou Harris; *Bluebird* . . . . (Reprise)

Heaven Only Knows
Richard Marx; *Richard Marx* . . . . (Capitol)

Heaven Or Las Vegas
Cocteau Twins; *Heaven Or Las Vegas* . . . . (Capitol)

Heaven Right Here
Jeb Loy Nichols; *Just What Time It Is* . . . .(Rykodisc)

Heaven Sent
INXS; *Welcome To Wherever You Are* . . . . (Atlantic)

Heaven Sent You
Stanley Clarke; *Time Exposure* . . . .(Epic)

Heaven Tonight
Cheap Trick; *Heaven Tonight* . . . .(Epic)

Heaven, Hell Or Houston
ZZ Top; *El Loco* . . . .(Warner Bros.)
Six Pack . . . .(Warner Bros.)

Heavenly Bodies
Earl Thomas Conley; *Somewhere Between Right And Wrong* . . . . (RCA)

Heavenly Body
Chi-Lites; *Ear Candy-#2-C* . . . . (20th Century Fox)
Heavenly Body . . . . (20th Century Fox)

Heavenly Father
Castelles; *Home Of Grand Records* . . . . (Collectables)
Sweet Sounds Of The Castelles . . . . (Collectables)

Heavenly Homes
Be Bop Deluxe; *Sunburst Finish* . . . . (Capitol)

Heaven's Already Here
Collective Soul; *Hints, Allegations And Things Left Unsaid* . . . .(Atlantic)

Heaven's Just A Sin Away
Kelly Willis; *Hot Country-C* . . . .(MCA Special Prod.)
Kelly Willis . . . .(MCA)
Kendalls; *Best Of The Kendalls* . . . . (Curb)
Kendalls-20 Greatest Hits . . . . (Deluxe)

Heaven's On Fire
Kiss; *Animalize* . . . . (Mercury)
Hear 'N Aid-C . . . . (Mercury)
Smashes, Thrashes & Hits . . . . (Mercury)

Heaven's Trail
Tesla; *Five Man Acoustical Jam* . . . . (Geffen)
Great Radio Controversy . . . . (Geffen)

Heaven's What I Feel
Gloria Estefan; *Gloria!* . . . .(Epic)

Hobo Heaven
Boxcar Willie; *Boxcar Willie* . . . . (Dot)

Hold My Hand
Don Cornell; *Hold My Hand* . . . . (MCA Special Prod.)

Holdin' Heaven
Tracy Byrd; *Tracy Byrd* . . . .(MCA)

Holes In The Floor Of Heaven
Steve Wariner; *Burnin' The Roadhouse Down* . . . . (Capitol)

How Far Is Heaven
Kitty Wells; *Kitty Wells-20 Greatest Hits* . . . .(Tee Vee)

How High The Moon
Duke Ellington; *1954 Los Angeles Concert* . . . . (Crescendo)
Ella Fitzgerald; *Best Of Ella Fitzgerald* . . . .(MCA)
Les Paul & Mary Ford; *Memories Are Made Of This-C* . . . . (Capitol)
Sarah Vaughan; *Compact Jazz-Best Of The Compact Jazz Vocalists-C* . . (Verve)
Complete Sarah Vaughan On Mercury-#3 . . . . (Mercury)
Stephane Grappelli & Martin Taylor; *Just One Of Those Things* . . . . (Angel)

I Always Think I'm Up In Heaven
Watson Sisters; *Music From The New York Stage (1890-1920)-#4-1917-1920-C* . . . . (Pearl)

I Can't Wait To Meetchu
Macy Gray; *On How Life Is* . . . .(Epic)

I Dreamed Of A Hillbilly Heaven
Tex Ritter; *An American Legend* . . . . (Capitol)
Best Of Tex Ritter . . . . (Capitol)
Hillbilly Heaven . . . . (Capitol)
Opry Legends-Tex Ritter . . . . (Capitol)

I May Never Get To Heaven
Conway Twitty; *Conway Twitty-20 Greatest Hits* . . . .(MCA)
Conway Twitty Sings The Hits . . . . (MCA Special Prod.)

I Miss My Homies
Master P; *Ghetto D* . . . . (No Limit/Priority)

I Wonder If Heaven Got A Ghetto
2Pac; *R U Still Down (Remember Me)* . . . . (Amaru/Jive)

If Heaven Could Find Me
Ambrosia; *Life Beyond L.A.* . . . .(Warner Bros.)

If I Ever Lose This Heaven
Quincy Jones; *Body Heat* . . . . (A&M)
I Heard That! . . . . (A&M)
Quincy Jones-Classics-#3 . . . . (A&M)
Quincy Jones-The Best . . . . (A&M)

If There's A God In Heaven
Elton John; *Blue Moves* . . . .(MCA)

If You Wanna Get To Heaven
Hank Williams, Jr.; *High Notes* . . . . (WB/Curb)
Ozark Mountain Daredevils; *Best Of The Ozark Mountain Daredevils* . . . (A&M)
It's Alive . . . . (A&M)
Ozark Mountain Daredevils . . . . (A&M)

I'll Fly Away
Gillian Welch & Alison Krauss; *ST/O Brother, Where Art Thou?* . . . . (Mercury)

I'm Free (Heaven Help The Man)
Kenny Loggins; *ST/Footloose* . . . . (Columbia)

Immigrant Song
Led Zeppelin; *Led Zeppelin III* . . . .(Atlantic)
Led Zeppelin-Box Set . . . .(Atlantic)

Iris
Goo Goo Dolls; *Dizzy Up The Girl* . . . .(Warner Sunset/Reprise)
ST/City Of Angels . . . .(Warner Sunset/Reprise)

It's A Short Walk From Heaven To Hell
John Schneider; *Country Classics-#5-1985-1986-C* . . . . (Universal)
John Schneider's Greatest Hits . . . . (MCA)
Tryin' To Outrun The Wind . . . . (MCA)

Jackie Wilson Said (I'm In Heaven When You Smile)
Van Morrison; *Best Of Van Morrison* . . . .(Polydor)
St. Dominic's Preview . . . . (Warner Bros.)
ST/Queen's Logic . . . . (Epic)

Johnny Angel
Shelley Fabares; *Billboard Top Rock 'N' Roll Hits-1962-C* . . . . (Rhino)
ST/Mermaids . . . . (Geffen)

Knockin' On Heaven's Door
Bob Dylan; *Biograph* . . . . (Columbia)
Bob Dylan At Budokan . . . . (Columbia)
Rock Classics Of The '70s-C . . . . (Columbia)
ST/Pat Garrett & Billy The Kid . . . . (Columbia)
Bob Dylan & The Grateful Dead; *Dylan & The Dead* . . . . (Columbia)
Bob Dylan And The Band; *Before The Flood* . . . . (Columbia)
Eric Clapton; *Eric Clapton-Crossroads-C* . . . .(Polydor)
Time Pieces-#1-The Best Of Eric Clapton . . . .(Polydor)
Guns N' Roses; *ST/Days Of Thunder* . . . .(David Geffen Co.)
Use Your Illusion II . . . . (Geffen)
Jerry Garcia; *Run For The Roses* . . . . (Arista)
Randy Crawford; *Rich & Poor* . . . . (Warner Bros.)

Last Kiss
J. Frank Wilson and The Cavaliers; *Billboard Top Rock 'N' Roll Hits-1964-C* . . . . (Rhino)
Collectables Presents The History Of Rock-#2-C . . . . (Collectables)
Oldies But Goodies-9-C . . . . (Original Sound)
Teenage Tragedies-C . . . . (Rhino)
Pearl Jam; *No Boundaries-Benefit For The Kosovar Refugees-C* . . . . (Epic)

Let The Mystery Be
10,000 Maniacs; *Few & Far Between* . . . . (Elektra)
Iris DeMent; *Infamous Angel* . . . . (Warner Bros.)

Letting The Cables Sleep
Bush; *Science Of Things* . . . .(Trauma)

Life's Railway To Heaven
Merle Haggard & The Strangers; *Train Whistle Blues* . . . . (Rounder)

Little Bit Of Heaven
Natalie Cole; *Dangerous* . . . .(Modern)
Ray Charles; *Seven Spanish Angels & Other Hits* . . . . (Columbia)

Lost In You
Garth Brooks as Chris Gaines; *Garth Brooks In...The Life Of Chris Gaines* . . . . (Capitol)

Love, Me
Collin Raye; *All I Can Be* . . . . (Epic)
Greatest Country Hits Of The '90s-1992-C . . . . (Columbia)

Maid In Heaven
Be Bop Deluxe; *Best Of Be Bop Deluxe-Raiding The Divine Archive* . . . (Capitol)
Live! In The Air Age . . . .(Harvest)

Mama Sang A Song
Bill Anderson; *Bill Anderson's Greatest Hits* . . . .(Varese Sarabande)
Country Music Classics-#17-C . . . . (K-Tel)

Marriage Made In Heaven
Bob Crewe; *Motivation* . . . . (Elektra)

Michael
Highwaymen; *Billboard Top Pop Hits-1961-C* . . . . (Rhino)

Mrs. Robinson
Simon & Garfunkel; *Bookends* . . . . (Columbia)
Collected Works . . . . (Columbia)
Hollywood Magic-1960s-C . . . . (Columbia)
Simon & Garfunkel's Greatest Hits . . . . (Columbia)
ST/Forrest Gump . . . .(Epic/Sony Music Soundtrax)
ST/The Graduate . . . . (Columbia)
The Concert In Central Park . . . . (Warner Bros.)

My Blue Heaven
Artie Shaw; *Complete Artie Shaw-#4* . . . . (RCA)
This Is Artie Shaw . . . . (Bluebird)
Fats Domino; *Fats Domino-Legendary Masters* . . . .(United Artists)
Fats Domino's Greatest Hits . . . . (Everest)
My Blue Heaven-Best Of Fats Domino-#1 . . . . (EMI)
Oldies But Goodies-#10-C . . . . (Original Sound)
Frank Sinatra; *Frank Sinatra-Gift Set* . . . . (Capitol)
Sinatra's Swingin' Session!!! . . . . (Capitol)

No Depression
Johnson Mountain Boys; *Goin' Up Copper Creek-C* . . . .(Copper Creek)
Uncle Tupelo; *No Depression* . . . . (Rockville)
No Telephone In Heaven
Doc Watson; *My Dear Old Southern Home*. . . . .(Sugar Hill)
Now You're In Heaven
Julian Lennon; *Mr. Jordan* . . . . (Atlantic)
Old Man And Me
Hootie & The Blowfish; *Fairweather Johnson* . . . . (Atlantic)
One Sweet Day
Mariah Carey; *Daydream* . . . . (Columbia)
Mariah Carey & Boyz II Men; *1996 Grammy Nominees-C*. . . . . (Columbia)
Pearl, The
Emmylou Harris; *Red Dirt Girl* . . . .(Nonesuch)
Pennies From Heaven
Billie Holiday; *Billie Holiday-16 Most Requested Songs* . . . . (Legacy)
Bing Crosby; *Pennies From Heaven* . . . . (Pro-Arte)
Frank Sinatra & Nelson Riddle Orchestra; *songs for Swingin'*
Lovers!. . . . . (Capitol)
Lester Young; *Birdland All-Stars At Carnegie Hall* . . . . (Roulette)
Louis Armstrong; *RCA Victor Jazz: First Half-Century-C* . . . .(RCA)
Mandy Patinkin; *Mandy Patinkin* . . . . (Columbia)
Skyliners; *Skyliners' Greatest Hits* . . . .(Original Sound)
Stan Getz; *Essential Stan Getz Songbook* . . . . (Verve)
Stephane Grappelli; *Satin Doll-#1-Best Of Stephane Grappelli* . . . . . (Vanguard)
Poor Wayfaring Stranger
Jim Hendricks; *Appalachian Memories-Front Porch Favorites* . . . . . .(Benson)
Jo Stafford; *American Folk Songs* . . . . (Corinthian)
Ray Of Light
Madonna; *GHV2* . . . .(Warner Bros.)
Ray Of Light . . . . (Maverick)
Totally Hits-#1-C . . . . (Arista)
Redemption Day
Sheryl Crow; *Sheryl Crow* . . . . (A&M)
Redneck Heaven
Billy Ray Cyrus; *Storm In The Heartland* . . . .(Mercury)
Riding With The King
B.B. King & Eric Clapton; *Riding With The King* . . . .(Duck/Reprise)
Rock & Roll Heaven
Righteous Brothers; *Righteous Brothers-Anthology 1962-1974* . . . .(Rhino)
Rockin' Heaven Down
Heart; *Bebe Le Strange* . . . . (Epic)
Room With A View
Carolyn Dawn Johnson; *Room With A View* . . . .(Arista)
Say Hello To Heaven
Temple Of The Dog; *Temple Of The Dog* . . . . (A&M)
See You On The Other Side
Ozzy Osbourne; *Ozzmosis* . . . . (Epic)
Seven Steps To Heaven
Miles Davis; *Miles Davis' Greatest Hits* . . . .(Columbia)
Seven Steps To Heaven . . . . (Columbia)
Shall We Gather At The River?
Chuck Wagon Gang; *16 Country-Gospel Favorites* . . . . (MCA)
Tennessee Ernie Ford; *All-Time Greatest Hymns* . . . .(Curb)
Tennessee Ernie Ford Sings 22 Favorite Hymns . . . .(Ranwood)
Sh-Boom
Chords; *Atlantic Rhythm & Blues 1947-1974-#2 (1952-1955)-C* . . . . . (Atlantic)
Crew-Cuts; *Partytime '50s-C* . . . . (Priority)
Stan Freberg; *Capitol Collectors Series-Stan Freberg* . . . . (Capitol)
Sheep Go To Heaven
Cake; *Prolonging The Magic*. . . . . (Capricorn)
She's Playing Hell Trying To Get Me To Heaven
George Strait; *Strait Country*. . . . . (MCA)
Sky Fits Heaven
Madonna; *Ray Of Light* . . . . (Maverick)
Smoke! Smoke! Smoke!
Commander Cody & His Lost Planet Airmen; *Country Casanova* . . . . . (MCA)
Too Much Fun-Best Of Commander Cody & His Lost Planet Airmen . . (MCA)
We've Got A Live One Here!. . . . .(Warner Bros.)
Doc Watson; *Red Rocking Chair*. . . . .(Flying Fish)
Johnny Bond & His Red River Valley Boys; *All Time Legends Of Country*
Music-C. . . . . (Legacy)
Merle Travis; *Johnny Gimble's Texas Honky-Tonk Hits-C* . . . . . . (C.M.H. Prod.)
Tex Williams; *Birth Of A Dream-Capitol's Early Hits-C* . . . . (Capitol)
Dr. Demento Presents The Greatest Novelty Records-#1-1940s &
Before-C . . . . (Rhino)
Somebody Up There Likes Me
David Bowie; *Young Americans* . . . . (Rykodisc)
Somebody Up There Likes Me
Reba McEntire; *Sweet Sixteen* . . . . (MCA)
Somebody's Knockin'
Terri Gibbs; *Best Of Terri Gibbs* . . . . (MCA)
Country Gold-C . . . . (Priority)
Country Music Classics-#6-1980-1985-C . . . . (K-Tel)
Something Happened On The Way To Heaven
Phil Collins; *...But Seriously* . . . . (Atlantic)
Serious Hits...Live! . . . . (Atlantic)
Somewhere
Aretha Franklin; *Aretha's Jazz* . . . . (Rhino)

Barbra Streisand; *The Broadway Album* . . . .(Columbia)
Dave Brubeck; *Music From West Side Story* . . . .(Columbia)
Jose Carreras; *Amigos Para Siempre-Friends For Life* . . . . (Atlantic)
Original Cast; *ST/West Side Story* . . . . (Sony Broadway)
Tom Waits; *Tom Waits-Anthology*. . . . . (Asylum)
Stairway To Heaven
O'Jays; *Family Reunion* . . . .(Philadelphia Int'l)
O'Jays' Greatest Hits . . . .(Philadelphia Int'l)
O'Jays-Collector's Item . . . .(Philadelphia Int'l)
Stairway To Heaven
Led Zeppelin; *Led Zeppelin IV*. . . . . (Atlantic)
Led Zeppelin-Box Set . . . . (Atlantic)
Remasters . . . . (Atlantic)
ST/The Song Remains The Same . . . . (Swan Song)
Stanley Jordan; *Best Of Stanley Jordan* . . . . (Blue Note)
Flying Home . . . . (EMI)
Stairway To Heaven
Neil Sedaka; *Neil Sedaka Sings His Greatest Hits* . . . . (RCA)
Neil Sedaka's All-Time Greatest Hits . . . . (RCA)
Swing Low, Sweet Chariot
Eric Clapton; *Time Pieces-#1-The Best Of Eric Clapton* . . . . (Polydor)
Glenn Miller & His Orchestra; *Moonlight Serenade* . . . . (Ranwood)
Hi-Lo's; *Suddenly It's The Hi-Lo's* . . . .(Columbia)
Jerry Garcia Acoustic Band; *Almost Acoustic* . . . . (Grateful Dead)
Joan Baez; *From Every Stage*. . . . . (A&M)
Peggy Lee; *Best Of Peggy Lee* . . . . (MCA)
Take A Little Trip
Alabama; *American Pride* . . . . (RCA)
Taxi To Heaven
Pray For Rain; *ST/Sid & Nancy* . . . . (MCA)
Tears In Heaven
Eric Clapton; *Diana, Princess Of Wales-Tribute-C* . . . .(Columbia)
Eric Clapton-Unplugged . . . . (Reprise)
ST/Rush . . . . (Reprise)
Teenage Heaven
Eddie Cochran; *Eddie Cochran-Legendary Masters* . . . . (EMI)
Eddie Cochran's Greatest Hits . . . .(Curb)
Johnny Cymbal; *Teen Idols-C* . . . . (Universal)
Thank Heaven For Little Girls
Maurice Chevalier; *ST/Gigi* . . . . (Sony Music Special Prod.)
Merle Haggard & Janie Fricke; *It's All In The Game* . . . . (Epic)
That Lucky Old Sun
Asleep At The Wheel; *Western Standard Time* . . . . (Epic)
Bing Crosby; *The Radio Years: 25 Songs*. . . . . (Crescendo)
Frankie Laine; *Frankie Laine-16 Most Requested Songs* . . . .(Legacy)
Frankie Laine-Golden Hits . . . . (Mercury)
Frankie Laine's Greatest Hits. (Columbia)
Jerry Garcia Band; *Jerry Garcia Band*. . . . . (Arista)
Louis Armstrong; *Louis Armstrong's Greatest Hits* . . . .(Curb)
Ray Charles; *Ray Charles-Anthology*. . . . . (Rhino)
Willie Nelson; *Sound In Your Mind* . . . .(Columbia)
That's Heaven To Me
Sam Cooke; *The Man And His Music*. . . . . (RCA)
Theme From ''Highway To Heaven''
Original Soundtrack; *Television's Greatest Hits-#6-Remote Control-C* . . .(TVT)
There's A Great Camp Meeting
Fisk Jubilee Singers; *Every Tone A Testimony-C* . . . . . . (Smithsonian Folkways)
They Took The Stars Out Of Heaven
Floyd Tillman; *The Country Music Hall Of Fame-Floyd Tillman* . . . . . . (MCA)
This Is Heaven To Me
Billie Holiday; *From The Original Decca Masters* . . . . (MCA)
This Must Be Heaven
Rick Astley; *Free* . . . . (RCA)
This Nearly Was Mine
Original Cast; *South Pacific* . . . . (CBS Masterworks)
Thought I'd Died & Gone To Heaven
Bryan Adams; *Waking Up The Neighbours* . . . . (A&M)
Three Hundred Pounds Of Heavenly Joy
Big Twist & The Mellow Fellows; *Alligator Records 20th Anniversary*
Collection-C . . . . (Alligator)
Howlin' Wolf; *The Chess Box-Howlin' Wolf*. . . . . (Chess)
Three Steps To Heaven
Eddie Cochran; *Eddie Cochran-Legendary Masters* . . . . (EMI)
Eddie Cochran's Greatest Hits . . . .(Curb)
Ticket To Heaven
Dire Straits; *On Every Street* . . . . (Warner Bros.)
Together Again
Janet Jackson; *Now That's What I Call Music!-#1-C* . . . . (Virgin)
Velvet Rope . . . . (Virgin)
Too Much Heaven
Bee Gees; *Bee Gees' Greatest* . . . . (Polydor)
Transcendental Blues
Steve Earle; *Transcendental Blues* . . . . (Artemis)
Tryin' To Get To Heaven
Bob Dylan; *Time Out Of Mind* . . . .(Columbia)
Up In Heaven
Clash; *Sandinista* . . . . (Epic)
Up To Heaven (You Lift Me)
Reba McEntire; *Best Of Reba McEntire* . . . .(Mercury)

Feel The Fire . . . . (Mercury)
Walkaway Joe
   Trisha Yearwood; *Hearts In Armor* . . . . (MCA)
   Songbook-A Collection Of Hits . . . . (MCA)
Waltz Me To Heaven
   Waylon Jennings; *Waylon Jennings' Greatest Hits-#2* . . . (RCA)
We Have Heaven
   Yes; *Fragile* . . . . (Atlantic)
Wear Your Love Like Heaven
   Donovan; *Donovan's Greatest Hits* . . . . (Epic)
   Gift From A Flower To A Garden . . . . (Epic)
   Summer Of Love-#1-C . . . . (Rhino)
   Troubadour-Definitive Collection . . . . (Epic)
   Sarah McLachlan; *Solace* . . . . (Arista)
When Did You Leave Heaven?
   Bob Dylan; *Down In The Groove* . . . . (Columbia)
When Did You Leave Heaven?
   Hank Crawford; *After Hours* . . . . (Atlantic)
When I Think About Angels
   Jamie O'Neal; *Shiver* . . . . (Mercury)
When The Saints Go Marching In
   Al Hirt; *Best Of Al Hirt* . . . . (RCA)
   Our Man-In New Orleans . . . . (Novus)
   Jerry Lee Lewis; *Jerry Lee Lewis* . . . . (Rhino)
   Louis Armstrong; *At The Crescendo* . . . . (MCA)
   Big Bands Of The Swinging Years-#1-C . . . . . (Collectables)
   C'Est Si Bon . . . . (Rhino)
   Essential Louis Armstrong . . . . (Vanguard)
   Louis Armstrong Of New Orleans . . . . (MCA)
   Original Soundtrack; *Children's Favorites* . . . . . (Kid Rhino/Rhino 4 Kids)
   Pete Fountain; *Best Of Pete Fountain* . . . . (MCA)
   Down On Rampart Street . . . . (Intermedia)
   Pete Fountain's New Orleans . . . . (MCA)
   Preservation Hall Jazz Band; *Best Of The Preservation Hall
   Jazz Band* . . . . (Columbia)
When The Train Comes Along
   Uncle Dave Macon; *Grand Ole Opry-75 Years-#2-C* . . . (MCA)
Where You Get Love
   Matthew Sweet; *Blue Sky On Mars* . . . . . (Freeworld/Capitol)
Wherever You Will Go
   Calling; *Camino Palmero* . . . . (RCA)
Will The Circle Be Unbroken
   Charlie Daniels Band & Friends; *Volunteer Jam 3 & 4* . . . (Epic)
   Joan Baez; *Country Music Album* . . . . (Vanguard)
   The First 10 Years . . . . (Vanguard)
   Nitty Gritty Dirt Band; *Will The Circle Be Unbroken* . . . (EMI)
   Roy Acuff; *Best Of Roy Acuff* . . . . (Liberty)
   Willie Nelson; *Willie & Family Live* . . . . (Columbia)
Will There Be A Shopping Mall In Heaven?
   Reverend Billy C. Wirtz; *Deep Fried & Sanctified* . . . (Hightone)
Wish You Were Here
   Mark Wills; *Wish You Were Here* . . . . (Mercury)
You Are My Heaven
   Roberta Flack & Donny Hathaway; *Featuring Donny Hathaway* . . . (Atlantic)
   Roberta Flack & Peabo Bryson; *Best Of Roberta Flack* . . . (Atlantic)
   Live & More . . . . (Atlantic)
   Roberta Flack & Peabo Bryson . . . . (Atlantic)
You Make Your Own Heaven & Hell Right Here On Earth
   Temptations; *Psychedelic Shack* . . . . (Motown)
You'll Never Get To Heaven (If You Break My Heart)
   Dionne Warwick; *Dionne Warwick* . . . . (Everest)
   Dionne Warwick Greatest Hits . . . . (Everest)
   Dionne Warwick-Anthology 1962-1971 . . . . (Rhino)
   Hot! Live & Otherwise . . . . (Arista)
   Say A Little Prayer . . . . (Dunhill Compact Classics)
   Stylistics; *Best Of The Stylistics-#2* . . . . (Amherst)
Your Flag Decal Won't Get You Into Heaven Anymore
   John Prine; *John Prine* . . . . (Atlantic)

HELL

See Also: ANGELS, BAD (sin), DEATH, DEVILS, GOD, HEAVEN

(Ghost) Riders In The Sky
   Gene Autry; *50th Anniversary* . . . . (Republic/Universal)
   Cowboy Hall Of Fame . . . . (Republic/Universal)
   Johnny Cash; *The Man In Black-His Greatest Hits* . . (Legacy)
   Outlaws; *Ghost Riders* . . . . (Arista)
   Roy Clark; *Roy Clark In Concert* . . . . (MCA)
   Roy Clark's Greatest Hits . . . . (MCA)
   Superpicker . . . . (MCA)
   Vaughn Monroe; *Best Of Vaughn Monroe* . . . . . . (RCA)
   This Is Vaughn Monroe/Decade Of The '40s . . . . . (RCA)
6 Underground
   Sneaker Pimps; *Becoming X* . . . . (Virgin)
Ain't Life Hell
   Hank Cochran; *Hank Cochran* . . . . (Capitol)

And All Hell Broke Loose
   Billie Hutch; *In Tune* . . . . (Whitfield)
Angry Johnny
   Poe; *Hello* . . . . (Modern)
Aw, To Hell With Love
   Jeri Fakter & The Backporch Symphony; *Jeri Fakter & The Backporch
   Symphony* . . . . (American Variety)
Bat Out Of Hell
   Meat Loaf; *Bat Out Of Hell* . . . . (Epic)
Beer Drinkers & Hell Raisers
   ZZ Top; *Best Of ZZ Top* . . . . (Warner Bros.)
   Six Pack . . . . (Warner Bros.)
   Tres Hombres . . . . (Warner Bros.)
Between Heaven And Hell
   Zakk Wylde; *Book Of Shadows* . . . . (Spitfire)
Between The Devil And Me
   Alan Jackson; *Everything I Love* . . . . (Arista)
Black Jesus
   Everlast; *Eat At Whitey's* . . . . (Tommy Boy)
Cold Day In Hell
   Gary Moore; *After Hours* . . . . (Charisma)
Devil Made Texas
   Hermes Nye; *Cowboy Songs On Folkways-C* . . . (Smithsonian Folkways)
   Texas Folk Songs . . . . (Smithsonian Folkways)
Ding Dong The Witch Is Dead
   Fifth Estate; *Dick Bartley's One-Hit Wonders Of The '60s-#2-C* . . . (Rhino)
   Meco; *The Wizard Of Oz* . . . . (Millennium)
   MGM Studio Orchestra; *ST/The Wizard Of Oz* . . (Sony Music Special Prod.)
Downbound Train
   Chuck Berry; *Chuck Berry-The Anthology* . . . . . . (MCA)
Edge Of Heaven
   Wham! Featuring George Michael; *Music From The Edge Of
   Heaven* . . . . (Columbia)
Flip The Switch
   Rolling Stones; *Bridges To Babylon* . . . . (Virgin)
   No Security . . . . (Virgin)
From Hell To Paradise
   Mavericks; *From Hell To Paradise* . . . . (MCA)
Garden Of Allah
   Don Henley; *Actual Miles: Henley's Greatest Hits* . . . (Geffen)
Go To Hell
   Alice Cooper; *Goes To Hell* . . . . (Warner Bros.)
   The Alice Cooper Show . . . . (Warner Bros.)
Go To Hell
   Megadeth; *ST/Bill & Ted's Bogus Journey* . . . . (Interscope)
God's Gonna Get'cha (For That)
   George Jones & Tammy Wynette; *George Jones & Tammy Wynette-16
   Biggest Hits* . . . . (Epic/Legacy)
   George Jones & Tammy Wynette's Greatest Hits . . . (Epic)
Good Day In Hell
   Eagles; *On The Border* . . . . (Elektra)
Gotta Serve Somebody
   Bob Dylan; *Biograph* . . . . (Columbia)
   Slow Train Coming . . . . (Columbia)
   *The Sopranos-Music From The HBO Original
   Series* . . . . (Sony Music Soundtrax)
   Bob Dylan & The Grateful Dead; *Dylan & The Dead* . . . (Columbia)
Heaven And Hell
   Black Sabbath; *Heaven And Hell* . . . . (Warner Bros.)
   Live Evil . . . . (Warner Bros.)
Heaven And Hell
   Assembled Multitude; *Heaven And Hell-45* . . . . . . (Eric)
Heaven And Hell
   Easybeats; *Nuggets-Classic Collection From The Psychedelic '60s-C* . . . (Rhino)
Heaven And Hell
   Willie Nelson; *Phases & Stages* . . . . (Atlantic)
Heaven And Hell
   Who; *Who's Missing* . . . . (MCA)
Heaven Beside You
   Alice In Chains; *Alice In Chains* . . . . (Columbia)
   Alice In Chains-MTV Unplugged . . . . (Columbia)
Heaven, Hell Or Houston
   ZZ Top; *El Loco* . . . . (Warner Bros.)
   Six Pack . . . . (Warner Bros.)
Hell
   James Brown; *Hell* . . . . (Polydor)
Hell
   Squirrel Nut Zippers; *Hot* . . . . (Mammoth)
Hell & Half Of Georgia
   Owen Brothers; *Audiograph Alive-C* . . . . (Audiograph)
   Fool Of Fools . . . . (Audiograph)
Hell Ain't A Bad Place To Be
   AC/DC; *If You Want Blood You've Got It* . . . . . . (Atlantic)
   Let There Be Rock . . . . (Atco)
Hell Below/Stars Above
   Toadies; *Hell Below/Stars Above* . . . . (Interscope)
Hell Bent For Leather
   Judas Priest; *Hell Bent For Leather* . . . . (Columbia)

Hell Cat
Scorpions; *Best Of The Scorpions* . . . . (RCA)
 Virgin Killer . . . . (RCA)

Hell Is For Children
Pat Benatar; *Best Shots* . . . . (Chrysalis)
 Crimes Of Passion . . . . (Chrysalis)
 Live From Earth . . . . (Chrysalis)
 MTV's Rock 'N' Roll To Go-C . . . . (Elektra)
 ST/American Pop . . . . (MCA)

Hell On High Heels
Motley Crue; *New Tattoo* . . . . (Motley/Beyond)

Hell To Pay
Bonnie Raitt; *Longing In Their Hearts* . . . . (Capitol)

Hellbound Train
Savoy Brown; *Hellbound Train* . . . . (Parrot)
 Savoy Brown-London Collector . . . . (London)
 Savoy Brown's Greatest Hits-Live In Concert . . . . (Townhouse)

Helldriver
Accept; *Accept* . . . . (Portrait)
 Midnight Highway . . . . (PVC)

Hells Bells
AC/DC; *Back In Black* . . . . (Atco)
 Who Made Who . . . . (Atlantic)

Hellzapoppin'
Louis Armstrong; *What A Wonderful World* . . . . (Decca Jazz)

Highway To Hell
AC/DC; *AC/DC Live* . . . . (Atco)
 Atlantic Rock & Roll-C . . . . (Atlantic)
 Back In Black . . . . (Atco)
 Highway To Hell . . . . (Atco)

Hot Rails To Hell
Blue Oyster Cult; *Career Of Evil* . . . . (Columbia)
 Extraterrestrial Live . . . . (Columbia)
 Metal Giants-C . . . . (Columbia)
 On Your Feet Or On Your Knees . . . . (Columbia)
 Tyranny & Mutation . . . . (Columbia)

If Hell Had A Jukebox
Travis Tritt; *It's All About To Change* . . . . (Warner Bros.)

If You Wanna Get To Heaven
Hank Williams, Jr.; *High Notes* . . . . (WB/Curb)
Ozark Mountain Daredevils; *Best Of The Ozark Mountain Daredevils* . . . (A&M)
 It's Alive . . . . (A&M)
 Ozark Mountain Daredevils . . . . (A&M)

It's A Short Walk From Heaven To Hell
John Schneider; *Country Classics-#5-1985-1986-C* . . . . (Universal)
 John Schneider's Greatest Hits . . . . (MCA)
 Tryin' To Outrun The Wind . . . . (MCA)

Lake Of Fire
Nirvana; *MTV Unplugged In New York* . . . . (David Geffen Co.)

Nature Trail To Hell
''Weird Al'' Yankovic; *In 3-D* . . . . (Scotti Bros.)

One Hell Of A Woman
Mac Davis; *Mac Davis' Greatest Hits* . . . . (Columbia)

Payback Is Hell
Candy Fresh; *Just The Way I Like It* . . . . (Wrap/Ichiban)

Raisin' Hell
Elvin Bishop; *Live! Raisin' Hell* . . . . (Capricorn)

Raising Hell
Run-D.M.C.; *Raising Hell* . . . . (Profile)

Ring Of Fire
Country Joe McDonald; *Best Of Country Joe McDonald-The Vanguard Years-1969-1975* . . . . (Vanguard)
 Tonight I'm Singing Just For You . . . . (Vanguard)
Dwight Yoakam; *Guitars, Cadillacs, Etc., Etc.* . . . . (Reprise)
Earl Scruggs & Billy Bob Thornton; *Earl Scruggs And Friends-C* . . . . . . (MCA)
Johnny Cash; *All Time Legends Of Country Music-C* . . . . (Legacy)
 Billboard Top Country Hits-1963-C . . . . (Rhino)
 Classic Cash-Hall Of Fame Series . . . . (Mercury)
 Johnny Cash's Greatest Hits . . . . (Columbia)
 The Man In Black-His Greatest Hits . . . . (Legacy)
Stan Ridgway & Wall Of Voodoo; *Best Of Stan Ridgway & Wall Of Voodoo* . . . . (I.R.S.)
Wall Of Voodoo; *Ugly Americans In Australia* . . . . (I.R.S.)

Rock You To Hell
Grim Reaper; *Rock You To Hell* . . . . (RCA)

Run Like Hell
Pink Floyd; *Delicate Sound Of Thunder* . . . . (Columbia)
 Knebworth-The Album-C . . . . (Polydor)
 The Wall . . . . (Columbia)
Roger Waters; *The Wall-Live In Berlin* . . . . (Mercury)

Season In Hell (Fire Suite)
John Cafferty And The Beaver Brown Band; *ST/Eddie & The Cruisers* . . . . (Scotti Bros.)

See You In Hell
Grim Reaper; *See You In Hell* . . . . (RCA)

See You In Hell (Don't Be Late)
Yngwie Malmsteen; *Eclipse* . . . . (Polydor)

See You In Hell, Blind Boy
Ry Cooder; *ST/Crossroads* . . . . (Warner Bros.)

Sheep Go To Heaven
Cake; *Prolonging The Magic* . . . . (Capricorn)

She's Playing Hell Trying To Get Me To Heaven
George Strait; *Strait Country* . . . . (MCA)

Storming The Gates Of Hell
Riot; *Privilege Of Power* . . . . (Epic Portrait Assoc.)

Straight To Hell
Clash; *Combat Rock* . . . . (Epic)
 On Broadway . . . . (Epic)
 The Story Of The Clash, Volume 1 . . . . (Epic)

Straight To Hell
Drivin' N' Cryin'; *Mystery Road* . . . . (Island)

Summer In Hell
Fred Schneider; *Fred Schneider* . . . . (Qwest)

Sun Also Rises In Hell
XYZ; *Hungry* . . . . (Capitol)

There's A Place In Hell For Me And My Friends
Morrissey; *Kill Uncle* . . . . (Sire)

To Hell With Poverty!
Gang Of Four; *Brief History Of The Twentieth Century* . . . . (Warner Bros.)

To Hell With The Devil
Stryper; *Can't Stop The Rock: The Stryper Collection-1984-1991* . . (Hollywood)
 To Hell With The Devil . . . . (Hollywood)

War Is Hell (On The Homefront Too)
T.G. Sheppard; *Perfect Stranger* . . . . (Warner Bros.)
 T.G. Sheppard's All-Time Greatest Hits . . . . (Warner Bros.)
 T.G. Sheppard's Greatest Hits . . . . (Warner Bros./Curb)

Where You Get Love
Matthew Sweet; *Blue Sky On Mars* . . . . (Freeworld/Capitol)

Whiskey Bent & Hell Bound
Hank Williams, Jr.; *Hank Williams, Jr.'s Greatest Hits* . . . . (WB/Curb)
 Whiskey Bent & Hell Bound . . . . (WB/Curb)

You Make Your Own Heaven & Hell Right Here On Earth
Temptations; *Psychedelic Shack* . . . . (Motown)

HELLO, Getting To Know You, Greetings, Meeting, Welcome
See Also: BEGINNINGS, LEAVING, MORNING, RETURNING

Cabaret
Original Cast; *Cabaret* . . . . (Columbia)

Candy
Cameo; *12'' Collection And More* . . . . (Mercury)
 Best Of Cameo . . . . (Mercury/Funk Essentials)
 Billboard Top R&B Hits-1987-C . . . . (Rhino)
 Greatest Hits . . . . (Chronicles)
Will Smith featuring Larry Blackmon; *Big Willie Style* . . . . (Columbia)

Church Bells May Ring
Diamonds; *Best Of The Diamonds* . . . . (Rhino)
Willows; *Rockin' & Rollin' Wedding Songs-#1-C* . . . . (Rhino)
 ST/A Rage In Harlem . . . . (MCA Special Prod.)
 WCBS FM 101 History Of Rock-'50s-#2-C . . . . (Collectables)

Come In From The Rain
Captain & Tennille; *Captain & Tennille's Greatest Hits* . . . . (A&M)
Melissa Manchester; *Melissa Manchester's Greatest Hits* . . . . (Arista)

Country Bumpkin
Cal Smith; *16 Top Country Hits-#1-C* . . . . (MCA)
 Country's Greatest Hits-#2-C . . . . (MCA Special Prod.)
 Grand Ole Opry-75 Years-#2-C . . . . (MCA)

Down
Stone Temple Pilots; *No. 4* . . . . (Atlantic)

Elderly Woman Behind The Counter In A Small Town
Pearl Jam; *Vs.* . . . . (Epic Portrait Assoc.)

Getting To Know You
Original Broadway Cast; *The King And I* . . . . (RCA Victor)
Original Cast; *ST/The King And I* . . . . (Angel)
 The King And I . . . . (MCA)

Good Day Sunshine
Beatles; *Beatles-Box Set* . . . . (Capitol)
 Revolver . . . . (Capitol)

Good Girls
Joe; *All That I Am* . . . . (Jive)

Good To See You
Neil Young; *Silver & Gold* . . . . (Reprise)

Goodbye San Francisco, Hello Amsterdam
Doug Sahm; *SDQ '98* . . . . (Watermelon)

Have You Met Miss Jones
Art Tatum; *Best Of Art Tatum* . . . . (Pablo)
Coleman Hawkins; *April In Paris* . . . . (Bluebird)
Ella Fitzgerald; *Silver Collection-Songbooks* . . . . (Verve)
Frank Sinatra; *Swing Along With Me* . . . . (Reprise)
Louis Armstrong; *American Songbook* . . . . (Verve)
Tony Bennett; *Jazz* . . . . (Columbia)
 Rodgers & Hart Songbook . . . . (DRG)

Hello
Lionel Richie; *Back To Front* . . . . (Motown)

Can't Slow Down . . . . (Motown)
Truly-The Love Songs . . . . (Motown)
Luther Vandross; *Songs* . . . . (Epic)

Hello
Ginuwine; *The Bachelor* . . . . (550 Music)

Hello
Poe; *Hello* . . . . (Modern)

Hello America
Def Leppard; *On Through The Night* . . . . (Mercury)

Hello Brother
Louis Armstrong; *What A Wonderful World* . . . . (Decca Jazz)

Hello Darlin'
Conway Twitty; *Conway Twittty-20 Greatest Hits* . . . . (MCA)
Conway Twitty's Greatest Hits . . . . (Curb)
From The Vaults: Decca Country Classics-1934-1973-C . . . . . . (Decca)
Greatest Country Classics-#1-C . . . . (MCA Special Prod.)

Hello Dolly!
Carol Channing/Original Cast; *Hello Dolly!* . . . . (RCA)
Louis Armstrong; *Essential Louis Armstrong* . . . . (Vanguard)
Vintage Music-#16-C . . . . (MCA)
Original Cast; *Hello Dolly!* . . . . (RCA)

Hello From Venus
Screamin' Cheetah Wheelies; *Magnolia* . . . . (Mercury)

Hello Goodbye
Beatles; *Beatles 1* . . . . (Capitol)
Beatles-20 Greatest Hits . . . . (Capitol)
Beatles-Box Set . . . . (Capitol)
Magical Mystery Tour . . . . (Capitol)
The Beatles/1967-1970 . . . . (Capitol)

Hello Hello
Talk Show; *Talk Show* . . . . (Atlantic)

Hello In There
Bette Midler; *Live At Last* . . . . (Atlantic)
John Prine; *John Prine* . . . . (Atlantic)
John Prine-Souvenirs . . . . (Oh Boy)

Hello Little Friend
Joe Cocker; *Joe Cocker!* . . . . (A&M)

Hello Little Girl
Beatles; *The Beatles-Anthology-#1* . . . . (Capitol)

Hello Mary Lou
Creedence Clearwater Revival; *Creedence Country* . . . . (Fantasy)
Rick Nelson; *Rick Nelson In Concert-Troubadour 1969* . . . . . . (MCA)
Rick Nelson-Souvenirs . . . . (EMI)
Ricky Nelson; *Best Of Ricky Nelson* . . . . (EMI)
Rick Nelson's Greatest Hits . . . . (Rhino)
Statler Brothers; *14 Country Favorites-C* . . . . (Mercury)
Pardners In Rhyme . . . . (Mercury)

Hello Mr. Heartache
Dixie Chicks; *Fly* . . . . (Monument)

Hello Muddah, Hello Fadduh
Allan Sherman; *Dr. Demento Presents The Greatest Novelty Records-#3-
1960s-C* . . . . (Rhino)
Dr. Demento Presents The Greatest Novelty Records-C . . . . . . (Rhino)

Hello Old Friend
Eric Clapton; *Eric Clapton-Crossroads-C* . . . . (Polydor)
No Reason To Cry . . . . (RSO)

Hello Stranger
Barbara Lewis; *Atlantic Rhythm & Blues 1947-1974-#5 (1962-
1966)-C* . . . . (Atlantic)
Billboard Top R&B Hits-1963-C . . . . (Rhino)
Collectables Presents The History Of Rock-#5-C . . . . . . (Collectables)

Hello Texas
Jimmy Buffett; *ST/Urban Cowboy* . . . . (Asylum)

Hello There
Cheap Trick; *Cheap Trick At Budokan* . . . . (Epic)
In Color . . . . (Epic)
ST/Over The Edge . . . . (Warner Bros.)

Hello Trouble
Desert Rose Band; *Running* . . . . (MCA)

Hello Vietnam
Johnny Wright; *ST/Full Metal Jacket* . . . . (Warner Bros.)

Hello Walls
Faron Young; *Billboard Top Country Hits-1961-C* . . . . (Rhino)
Willie Nelson; *Essential Willie Nelson* . . . . (RCA)
Willie Nelson-Greatest Songs . . . . (Curb)

Hello, Central, Give Me No Man's Land
Al Jolson; *Music From The New York Stage (1890-1920)-#4-1917-
1920-C* . . . . (Pearl)

Hello, I Love You
Doors; *Best Of The Doors* . . . . (Elektra)
Doors' Greatest Hits . . . . (Elektra)
Doors-Box Set . . . . (Elektra)
Waiting For The Sun . . . . (Elektra)

Hello, Young Lovers
Frank Sinatra; *Frank Sinatra Sings Rodgers & Hammerstein* . . . . . . (Columbia)
Mel Torme; *Jazz 'Round Midnight-Mel Torme* . . . . (Verve)
Original Broadway Cast; *The King And I* . . . . (RCA Victor)
Original Cast; *ST/The King And I* . . . . (Angel)

Hotel California
Eagles; *Eagles Greatest Hits, Volume 2* . . . . (Asylum)
Eagles Live . . . . (Asylum)
Hell Freezes Over . . . . (Geffen)
Hotel California . . . . (Asylum)

Howdido
Jack Elliot; *Tribute To Woody Guthrie-C* . . . . (Warner Bros.)

I Knew I Loved You
Savage Garden; *Affirmation* . . . . (Columbia)
Now That's What I Call Music!-#4-C . . . . (Virgin)

I Think I Love You
Partridge Family; *Partridge Family's Greatest Hits* . . . . (Arista)

If I Knew You Were Comin' I'd've Baked A Cake
Bing Crosby; *The Radio Years-#4* . . . . (Crescendo)
Ethel Merman; *The Ethel Merman Collection* . . . . (Razor & Tie)

If You See Her, Say Hello
Bob Dylan; *Blood On The Tracks* . . . . (Columbia)

I'm Getting Used To You
Selena; *Dreaming Of You* . . . . (EMI Latin)

I've Grown Accustomed To Her Face
Rex Harrison/Original Cast; *My Fair Lady* . . . . (Columbia)
Tony Bennett; *Big Band Bash* . . . . (Intermedia)
Chicago . . . . (Dunhill Compact Classics)

Just Friends (Sunny)
Musiq Soulchild; *Aijuswanaseing* . . . . (Def Soul/IDJMG)

Just Tell Her Jim Said Hello
Elvis Presley; *Collector's Gold* . . . . (RCA)
Elvis' Gold Records, Volume 4 . . . . (RCA)
The Other Sides-Worldwide Gold Award Hits, Vol. 2 . . . . (RCA)

Kiss The Rain
Billie Myers; *A Taste Of '98-C* . . . . (Universal)
Growing Pains . . . . (Universal)

Let's Wait Awhile
Janet Jackson; *Control* . . . . (A&M)

Life Line
Nilsson; *The Point* . . . . (RCA)

Lollipop Guild
Original Cast; *The Wizard Of Oz-Selections From The Original Motion
Picture Soundtrack* . . . . (Turner Classic Movies)

Man From The South, The
Ted Weems & His Orchestra; *78-#22238* . . . . (Victor)

Meet The Swinger (Polaroid Swinger)
Original Soundtrack; *TeeVee Toons-The Commercials-#1-C* . . . . (TVT)

Meet Virginia
Train; *Now That's What I Call Music!-#4-C* . . . . (Virgin)
Train . . . . (Aware/C2/Columbia)

Most Happy Fella
Broadway Cast; *Most Happy Fella* . . . . (RCA)
Original Broadway Cast; *Most Happy Fella* . . . . (Sony Music Classical)

Psycho Circus
Kiss; *Psycho Circus* . . . . (Mercury)

Red Neck Friend
Jackson Browne; *For Everyman* . . . . (Asylum)

Saying Hello, Saying I Love You, Saying Goodbye
Jim Ed Brown & Helen Cornelius; *Jim Ed Brown & Helen Cornelius'
Greatest Hits* . . . . (RCA)

Shalom
Original Cast; *Milk & Honey* . . . . (RCA Victor)

Simple Lessons
Candlebox; *Lucy* . . . . (Maverick)

Some Enchanted Evening
Jay & The Americans; *Come A Little Bit Closer-Best Of Jay & The
Americans* . . . . (Gold Rush)
Jay & The Americans' All-Time Greatest Hits . . . . (Rhino)
Original Cast; *South Pacific* . . . . (CBS Masterworks)
Perry Como; *Perry Como's All-Time Greatest Hits-#1* . . . . . . (RCA)
Rosanno Brazzi; *ST/South Pacific* . . . . (RCA)
Willie Nelson; *What A Wonderful World* . . . . (Columbia)

Song 2
Blur; *Blur* . . . . (Virgin)

Sound Of Silence, The
Paul Simon; *Paul Simon In Concert/Live Rhymin'* . . . . (Columbia)
Simon & Garfunkel; *Collected Works* . . . . (Columbia)
More American Graffiti-#4-C . . . . (MCA)
Simon & Garfunkel's Greatest Hits . . . . (Columbia)
Sounds Of Silence . . . . (Columbia)
ST/The Graduate . . . . (Columbia)
The Concert In Central Park . . . . (Warner Bros.)

Suddenly
Soraya; *On Nights Like This* . . . . (Island)

Sympathy For The Devil
Bryan Ferry; *These Foolish Things* . . . . (Reprise)
Jane's Addiction; *Jane's Addiction* . . . . (Triple X Entert.)
Rolling Stones; *Beggars Banquet* . . . . (Abkco)
Flashpoint . . . . (Virgin)
Get Yer Ya-Ya's Out! . . . . (Abkco)
Hot Rocks 1964-1971 . . . . (Abkco)
Love You Live . . . . (Virgin)

Ten Minutes Ago
Julie Andrews & Jon Cypher; *Cinderella-The CBS Television Production* .... (Columbia)
Stuart Damon & Lesley Ann Warren; *Cinderella-The CBS Television Network Production* .... (Columbia)

Thank You In Advance
Boyz II Men; *Nathan Michael Shawn Wanya* .... (Universal)

Theme From "The Flintstones"
Original Soundtrack; *Hanna-Barbera Classics-#1-Original Recordings Of The World's Most Famous Cartoon Themes & Scores* .... (Kid Rhino/Rhino 4 Kids)
Hanna-Barbera Pic-A-Nic Basket Of Cartoon Classics .... (Kid Rhino/Rhino 4 Kids)
Television's Greatest Hits-#1-C .... (TVT)
Steve Hobbs; *Escape* .... (Cexton)

Theme From "Welcome Back, Kotter"
John Sebastian; *Best Of John Sebastian* .... (Rhino)
Original Soundtrack; *Television's Greatest Hits-#3-1970s & 1980s-C*.... (TVT)

Uninvited
Alanis Morissette; *ST/City Of Angels* .... (Warner Sunset/Reprise)

Walk Right In
Rooftop Singers; *Best Of The Rooftop Singers* .... (Vanguard)
Cruisin'-1963-C .... (Increase)
Greatest Folksingers Of The '60s-C .... (Vanguard)
ST/Forrest Gump .... (Epic/Sony Music Soundtrax)
Troubadours Of The Folk Era-#3-C .... (Rhino)

Welcome Illegal Immigrants
H.E.A.D.; *97 98* .... (Caipirinha)

Welcome To Chinatown
John Cougar; *John Cougar* .... (Riva)

Welcome To Heartlight
Kenny Loggins; *High Adventure* .... (Columbia)

Welcome To My World
Eddy Arnold; *Eddy Arnold-Pure Gold* .... (RCA)
The World Of Eddy Arnold .... (RCA)
Welcome To My World .... (RCA)
Elvis Presley; *Aloha from Hawaii via Satellite* .... (RCA)
Welcome To My World .... (RCA)
Jim Reeves; *Am I That Easy To Forget* .... (RCA)
Best Of Jim Reeves .... (RCA)
Jim Reeves .... (RCA)
Jim Reeves-Legendary Performer .... (RCA)

Welcome To Paradise
Green Day; *Dookie* .... (Reprise)

Welcome To The Boomtown
David & David; *Boomtown* .... (A&M)

Welcome To The Fold
Filter; *Title Of Record* .... (Reprise)

Welcome To The Jungle
Guns N' Roses; *Appetite For Destruction* .... (Geffen)
ST/Lean On Me .... (Warner Bros.)

Welcome To The Machine
Pink Floyd; *The Wall* .... (Columbia)

Welcome To The Occupation
R.E.M.; *Document* .... (EMI-Capitol Entert. Properties)

Welcome To The United States
Frank Zappa; *The Yellow Shark* .... (Rykodisc)

Welcome To The Working Week
Elvis Costello; *My Aim Is True* .... (Columbia)

We'll Meet Again
Vera Lynn; *ST/Dr. Strangelove: Music From The Films Of Stanley Kubrick* .... (Silva Classics)
We'll Meet Again .... (Living Era)

What If I Said
Anita Cochran & Steve Wariner; *Back To You* .... (Warner Bros.)
Steve Wariner & Anita Cochran; *Burnin' The Roadhouse Down* ...... (Capitol)

What's Happening, Brother
Marvin Gaye; *What's Going On* .... (Motown)

Where Or When
Barbra Streisand; *Color Me Barbra* .... (Columbia)
Benny Goodman; *Small Groups-1941-1945* .... (Columbia)
Bryan Ferry; *As Time Goes By* .... (Virgin)
Dion And The Belmonts; *Best Of Doo Wop Ballads-C* .... (Rhino)
Complete Dion And The Belmonts .... (Collector's Choice)
Ella Fitzgerald; *Ella Fitzgerald Sings The Rodgers & Hart Songbook* ... (Verve)
Frank Sinatra; *Sinatra At The Sands* .... (Reprise)
Johnny Mathis; *You Light Up My Life* .... (Columbia)
Peggy Lee; *Peggy Lee-Complete Recordings-1941-1947* .... (Legacy)
Wynton Marsalis; *Standard Time-#3-The Resolution Of Romance* ... (Columbia)

Why Do Hawaiians Sing Aloha?
Fats Waller; *The Middle Years-#1-1936-1938* .... (Bluebird)

With Arms Wide Open
Creed; *Human Clay* .... (Wind-up)
Now That's What I Call Music!-#6-C .... (Virgin)

Woman On The Tier (I'll See You Through)
Suzanne Vega; *ST/Dead Man Walking* .... (Columbia)

You Don't Know Me
Ray Charles; *Ray Charles-Complete Country & Western Recordings 1959-1986* ... (Rhino)

You Had Me From Hello
Kenny Chesney; *Everywhere We Go* .... (BNA)
Kenny Chesney's Greatest Hits .... (BNA)

Younger Girl
Critters; *Sixties Rule! Chapter Two-C* .... (One Way)
Lovin' Spoonful; *Lovin' Spoonful-Anthology* .... (Rhino)

HELP, Comfort, Compassion, Protect, Reassure, Rescue, Safe, Save, Shelter, Support, Sympathy

See Also: ANGELS, CHARACTER & INTEGRITY, DANGER & DISASTER, DESIRE, DESPAIR, FAITH, FEELINGS, FORGIVE, FRIENDS, GOD, GRATITUDE, HOLDING ON, HUG, LOVE (various), MOTIVATION, OPTIMISM, PAIN & HEALING, PROMISE, SADNESS, TROUBLE

(I Could Only) Whisper Your Name
Harry Connick, Jr.; *She* .... (Columbia)
ST/The Mask .... (Chaos)

(You Make Me Feel Like) A Natural Woman
Aretha Franklin; *Aretha Franklin's Greatest Hits-1980-1994* .... (Arista)
Chicken Soup For The Woman's Soul-C .... (Rhino)
Carole King; *Tapestry* .... (Epic)
Celine Dion; *Tapestry Revisited: Tribute To Carole King-C* .... (Lava)

911 Is A Joke
Public Enemy; *Fear Of A Black Planet* .... (Def Jam)
Yo! MTV Raps-C .... (Def Jam)

Acoustic #3
Goo Goo Dolls; *Dizzy Up The Girl* .... (Warner Sunset/Reprise)

Ain't No Mountain High Enough
Diana Ross; *20/20-C* .... (Motown)
25 #1 Hits From 25 Years-C .... (Motown)
Diana Ross .... (Motown)
Diana Ross-The Ultimate Collection .... (Motown)
Every Great Motown Song-First 25 Years-C .... (Motown)
Greatest Songs By Ashford & Simpson .... (Motown)
Motown Legends-Diana Ross .... (Motown)
Motown Story-First 25 Years-C .... (Motown)
Motown's Biggest Pop Hits-C .... (Motown)
TV ST/Diana-C .... (Motown)
Marvin Gaye & Tammi Terrell; *20 Greatest Songs In Motown History-C* ... (Motown)
Classic Duets-Marvin Gaye & His Women-C .... (Motown)
Marvin Gaye & Tammi Terrell's Greatest Hits .... (Motown)
Marvin Gaye Live At The London Palladium .... (Motown)
Motown Grammy R&B Performances Of The '60s & '70s-C ...... (Motown)
Performances Of The '60s & '70s-C .... (Motown)
United .... (Motown)

All The Small Things
Blink-182; *Enema Of The State* .... (MCA)
Now That's What I Call Music!-#4-C .... (Virgin)

All Through The Night
Judy Collins; *Baby's Bedtime* .... (Lightyear)

Amazing Grace
Jeff Beck; *All-Star Christmas-C* .... (Epic)
Judy Collins; *Colors Of The Day-The Best Of Judy Collins* .... (Elektra)
Whales & Nightingales .... (Elektra)
Maverick Choir; *ST/Maverick* .... (Atlantic)
Nitty Gritty Dirt Band; *Will The Circle Be Unbroken-#2-C* .... (Uni)
Tramaine Hawkins; *God Bless America-C* .... (Columbia)

Angel
Sarah McLachlan; *Mirrorball* .... (Arista)
ST/City Of Angels .... (Warner Sunset/Reprise)
Surfacing .... (Arista)
Totally Hits-#1-C .... (Arista)

Angel
Jimi Hendrix; *Cry Of Love* .... (Reprise)
Experience Hendrix: The Best Of Jimi Hendrix .... (MCA)
First Rays Of The New Rising Sun .... (MCA)
Rod Stewart; *Best Of Rod Stewart* .... (Mercury)

Angel
Aerosmith; *Permanent Vacation* .... (Geffen)

Angel
Lionel Richie; *Renaissance* .... (Island/IDJMG)

Angel On My Shoulder
Natalie Cole; *Natalie Cole's Greatest Hits-#1* .... (Elektra)

Angels
Robbie Williams; *The Egg Has Landed* .... (Capitol)

Animal Song
Savage Garden; *Affirmation* .... (Columbia)

Anything
Jay-Z; *Vol. 3-Life & Times Of S. Carter* .... (Roc-A-Fella/DJMG)

Are U Still Down?
Jon B.; *Cool Relax* .... (Yab Yum/550)

Are You There?
Oleander; *Unwind* .... (Republic/Universal)

Baby
Robert Bradley's Blackwater Surprise; *Time To Discover* .... (RCA)
Beautiful Life
Ace Of Base; *Bridge* .... (Arista)
    MTV Party To Go-#9-C .... (Tommy Boy)
Beautiful You
Oak Ridge Boys; *Together* .... (MCA)
Because You Loved Me
Celine Dion; *All The Way...A Decade Of Song* .... (550 Music)
    Diana, Princess Of Wales-Tribute-C .... (Columbia)
    Falling Into You .... (550 Music)
Bent
Matchbox Twenty; *Mad Season By Matchbox Twenty* .... (Lava)
    Totally Hits-#3-C .... (Atlantic)
Best Friend
Brandy; *Brandy* .... (Atlantic)
Best Man I Can Be
Ginuwine, R.L., Tyrese, Case; *ST/The Best Man* .... (Sony Music Soundtrax)
Between The Devil And Me
Alan Jackson; *Everything I Love* .... (Arista)
Black Balloon
Goo Goo Dolls; *Dizzy Up The Girl* .... (Warner Sunset/Reprise)
Bookends
Joe Walsh; *The Smoker You Drink The Player You Get* .... (MCA)
Both Sides Of The Story
Phil Collins; *Both Sides* .... (Atlantic)
Breathe
Nickelback; *State* .... (Roadrunner)
Bridge Over Troubled Water
Aretha Franklin; *Aretha Franklin-30 Greatest Hits* .... (Rhino)
    Aretha Franklin's Greatest Hits .... (Atlantic)
    Live At Fillmore West .... (Atlantic)
Paul Simon; *America: A Tribute To Heroes-C* .... (Interscope)
    Concert In The Park-August 15 1991 .... (Warner Bros.)
    Paul Simon In Concert/Live Rhymin' .... (Columbia)
Simon & Garfunkel; *Bridge Over Troubled Water* .... (Columbia)
    Collected Works .... (Columbia)
    God Bless America-C .... (Columbia)
    Simon & Garfunkel's Greatest Hits .... (Columbia)
    The Concert In Central Park .... (Warner Bros.)
Brother, Brother
Carole King; *Music* .... (Epic)
Bullet Proof
Goo Goo Dolls; *Dizzy Up The Girl* .... (Warner Sunset/Reprise)
By Your Side
Sade; *Lovers Rock* .... (Epic)
Can I Get A Witness
Marvin Gaye; *Marvin Gaye-Anthology* .... (Motown)
    Marvin Gaye's Greatest Hits .... (Motown)
    Marvin Gaye-Super Hits .... (Motown)
Rod Stewart; *Storyteller/The Complete Anthology: 1964-1990* ... (Warner Bros.)
Rolling Stones; *England's Newest Hit Makers/The Rolling Stones* ..... (Abkco)
Can You Help Me
Jesse Johnson's Revue; *Jesse Johnson's Revue* .... (A&M)
Can't Help Falling In Love
Elvis Presley; *Elvis* .... (RCA)
    Elvis-A Legendary Performer, Volume 1 .... (RCA)
    From Memphis To Vegas/From Vegas To Memphis .... (RCA)
    ST/Blue Hawaii .... (RCA)
Julio Iglesias; *Starry Night* .... (Columbia)
UB40; *Promises And Lies* .... (Virgin)
    ST/Sliver .... (Virgin)
Can't Help Lovin' Dat Man
Lena Horne; *20 Golden Pieces Of Lena Horne* .... (Bulldog)
    Jazz Master .... (DRG)
    Jazzy Ladies .... (Dunhill Compact Classics)
    Live On Broadway .... (Qwest)
Can't You Hear Me Knockin'
Rolling Stones; *Sticky Fingers* .... (Virgin)
Carrion
Fiona Apple; *Tidal* .... (Clean Slate/Work)
Cars
Fear Factory; *Obsolete* .... (Roadrunner)
Gary Numan; *18 Modern Rock Classics From The '80s-C* ...... (Rhino)
    Pleasure Principle .... (Atco)
Catch Me I'm Falling
Pretty Poison; *ST/Hiding Out* .... (Virgin)
Chain Of Love
Clay Walker; *Live, Laugh, Love* .... (Giant)
Change The World
Offspring; *Ixnay On The Hombre* .... (Columbia)
Changes
2Pac; *2Pac Greatest Hits* .... (Amaru/Death Row/Interscope)
Close Your Eyes
Peaches & Herb; *Love Is Strange-The Best Of Peaches & Herb* ...... (Legacy)
Clumsy
Our Lady Peace; *Clumsy* .... (Columbia)
Computer Sex And Self Help
Carl Reiner; *The 2000-Year-Old Man In The Year 2000* .... (Rhino)

Count On Me
Whitney Houston and CeCe Winans; *ST/Waiting To Exhale* .... (Arista)
Cover Me
Bruce Springsteen; *Born In The U.S.A.* .... (Columbia)
    Music For The Miracle-C .... (Epic Portrait Assoc.)
Bruce Springsteen & The E Street Band; *Bruce Springsteen & The E Street
    Band Live/1975-85* .... (Legacy)
Cover You In Kisses
John Michael Montgomery; *Leave A Mark* .... (Atlantic)
Crash And Burn
Savage Garden; *Affirmation* .... (Columbia)
Crawling In The Dark
Hoobastank; *Hoobastank* .... (Island/IDJMG)
Cry For Help
Rick Astley; *Free* .... (RCA)
Cry For Mercy
Raindogs; *Lost Souls* .... (Atco)
Cry Ophelia
Adam Cohen; *Songs From Dawson's Creek* .... (Sony Music Soundtrax)
Dammit (Growing Up)
Blink-182; *Dude Ranch* .... (Cargo)
Danny's Song
Anne Murray; *Anne Murray-Country* .... (Capitol)
    Anne Murray's Greatest Hits .... (Capitol)
    Danny's Song .... (Capitol)
Loggins & Messina; *Loggins & Messina-On Stage* .... (Columbia)
    Sittin' In .... (Columbia)
    The Best Of Friends .... (Columbia)
Dear Doctor
Rolling Stones; *Beggars Banquet* .... (Abkco)
Desperately Wanting
Better Than Ezra; *Friction, Baby* .... (Swell/Elektra)
Didn't Leave Nobody But The Baby
Emmylou Harris/Alison Krauss/Gillian Welch; *ST/O Brother, Where Art
    Thou?* .... (Mercury)
Don't Cry
Seal; *Seal 2* .... (Sire)
Don't Go Breaking My Heart
Elton John & Kiki Dee; *Elton John's Greatest Hits-#2* .... (Polydor)
Don't Laugh At Me
Mark Wills; *Wish You Were Here* .... (Mercury)
Don't Worry, Baby
Beach Boys; *Absolute Best-#1* .... (Capitol)
    Endless Summer .... (Capitol)
    Fun Fun Fun .... (Capitol)
    Made In The U.S.A. .... (Capitol)
Don'tcha Worry 'Bout A Thing
Stevie Wonder; *Innervisions* .... (Motown)
Dreamlover
Mariah Carey; *Music Box* .... (Columbia)
Drift Away
Dobie Gray; *Classic Rock-#1-C* .... (MCA)
    Oldies But Goodies-#10-C .... (Original Sound)
    Oldies But Goodies-#3-C .... (Original Sound)
    Super Hits Of The '70s-Have A Nice Day-#10-C ...... (Rhino)
Michael Bolton; *Timeless-Classics* .... (Columbia)
Rod Stewart; *Atlantic Crossing* .... (Warner Bros.)
Ease My Mind
Arrested Development; *Zingalamaduni* .... (Chrysalis)
Emotional Rescue
Rolling Stones; *Emotional Rescue* .... (Rolling Stones)
    Rewind (1971-1984) .... (Rolling Stones)
Everybody Hurts
R.E.M.; *Automatic For The People* .... (Warner Bros.)
    Diana, Princess Of Wales-Tribute-C .... (Columbia)
Everything
Mary J. Blige; *Share My World* .... (MCA)
Everything For Free
K's Choice; *Cocoon Choice* .... (550 Music)
Falling In Love Again (Can't Help It)
Billie Holiday; *Quintessential-#8-1939-1940* .... (Legacy)
Linda Ronstadt; *Lush Life* .... (Asylum)
Marlene Dietrich; *Best Of Marlene Dietrich* .... (Columbia)
    Falling In Love Again .... (MCA)
    Her Complete Decca Recordings .... (MCA)
Flood
Jars Of Clay; *Jars Of Clay* .... (Silvertone)
    *Where Music Meets Film: Live From The Sundance Film
    Festival-C* .... (Beyond)
Follow Me
Uncle Kracker; *Double Wide* .... (Warner Bros.)
    Totally Hits 2001-C .... (Arista)
For You
Bruce Springsteen; *Greetings From Asbury Park, N.J.* ...... (Columbia)
Greg Kihn; *Kihnsolidation-Best Of Greg Kihn* .... (Rhino)
    Unkihntrollable-Live .... (Rhino)
Manfred Mann's Earth Band; *Chance* .... (Warner Bros.)
For You I Will
Monica; *The Boy Is Mine* .... (Arista)

Forever More (I'll Be The One)
James Ingram; *Forever More (Love Songs, Hits & Duets)* ...... (Private Music)
John Tesh featuring James Ingram; *One World* .... (GTS)

Freak Of The Week
Marvelous 3; *Hey Album* .... (HiFi/Elektra)

From A Buick 6
Bob Dylan; *Highway 61 Revisited* .... (Columbia)

Get Born Again
Alice In Chains; *Nothing Safe* .... (Columbia)

Get Up
Amel Larrieux; *Infinite Possibilities* .... (Epic)

Gets Me Through
Ozzy Osbourne; *Down To Earth* .... (Epic)

Gimme Shelter
Goo Goo Dolls; *Jed* .... (Metal Blade)
Grand Funk Railroad; *Capitol Collectors Series-Grand Funk Railroad* .... (Capitol)
Caught In The Act .... (Capitol)
Rolling Stones; *Hot Rocks 1964-1971* .... (Abkco)
Let It Bleed .... (Abkco)
No Security .... (Virgin)

Girl Can't Help It
Journey; *Journey's Greatest Hits* .... (Columbia)
Raised On Radio .... (Columbia)

Girl Can't Help It, The
Little Richard; *Little Richard-18 Greatest Hits* .... (Rhino)
Little Richard's Greatest Hits .... (Everest)
Super Oldies Of The '50s-#3-C .... (Audio Fidelity)
Well Alright! .... (Specialty)

Golden Slumbers
Beatles; *Abbey Road* .... (Parlophone)
Beatles-Box Set .... (Capitol)

Good Old Desk
Nilsson; *Aerial Ballet* .... (RCA)

Graceland
Paul Simon; *Graceland* .... (Warner Bros.)

Greed
Godsmack; *Awake* .... (Republic/Universal)

Ground Beneath Her Feet, The
U2; *ST/The Million Dollar Hotel* .... (Interscope)

Guenevere
Original Cast; *Camelot* .... (Columbia)
Original Soundtrack; *ST/Camelot* .... (Warner Bros.)

Halfway Down
Patty Loveless; *When Fallen Angels Fly* .... (Epic)

Hands
Jewel; *Spirit* .... (Atlantic)

Hard Day's Night, A
Beatles; *Beatles 1* .... (Capitol)
Beatles-20 Greatest Hits .... (Capitol)
ST/A Hard Day's Night .... (Capitol)
The Beatles At The Hollywood Bowl .... (Capitol)
The Beatles/1962-1966 .... (Capitol)

Have A Cuppa Tea
Kinks; *Muswell Hillbillies* .... (VelVel)

Have Mercy
Judds; *Judds' Greatest Hits* .... (MCA)
Rockin' With The Rhythm .... (MCA)

Have You Seen Mary
Sponge; *Wax Ecstatic* .... (Columbia)

Hearts Of Stone
Bruce Springsteen; *Tracks* .... (Columbia)
Southside Johnny And The Asbury Jukes; *Best Of Southside Johnny And The Asbury Jukes* .... (Legacy)
Cover Me (Bruce Springsteen Tribute)-C .... (Rhino)
Hearts Of Stone .... (Epic)

Heaven
Nu Flavor; *110% Hits-C* .... (Simitar)
Nu Flavor .... (Reprise)

Heaven Help
Lenny Kravitz; *Are You Gonna Go My Way* .... (Virgin)

Heaven Help Me
Deon Estus; *Spell* .... (Mika)

Heaven Help My Heart
Tina Arena; *Don't Ask* .... (Epic)
Wynonna; *Revelations* .... (Curb/MCA)
Wynonna-Collection .... (Curb)

Heaven Help The Fool
Bob Weir; *Heaven Help The Fool* .... (Arista)

Heaven Help The Lonely
Willie Nile; *Places I Have Never Been* .... (Columbia)

Heaven Help Us All
Stevie Wonder; *Signed Sealed & Delivered* .... (Motown)
Stevie Wonder-Love Songs-20 Classic Hits .... (Motown)
Stevie Wonder's Greatest Hits-#2 .... (Motown)

Hello In There
Bette Midler; *Live At Last* .... (Atlantic)
John Prine; *John Prine* .... (Atlantic)

John Prine-Souvenirs .... (Oh Boy)

Help Is On Its Way
Little River Band; *Diamantina Cocktail* .... (Capitol)
Little River Band's Greatest Hits .... (Capitol)

Help Me
Elvis Presley; *Promised Land* .... (RCA)

Help Me
Joni Mitchell; *Court & Spark* .... (Asylum)

Help Me
Larry Gatlin; *Rain-Rainbow* .... (Columbia)

Help Me Angel
Steve Winwood; *Talking Back To The Night* .... (Island)

Help Me Hold On
Travis Tritt; *Country Club* .... (Warner Bros.)

Help Me Make It (To My Rocking Chair)
B.J. Thomas; *B.J. Thomas-More Greatest Hits* ...... (Varese Vintage)

Help Me Make It Through The Night
Bryan Ferry; *Another Time Another Place* .... (Reprise)
Gladys Knight & The Pips; *Compact Command Performances-Gladys Knight & The Pips* .... (Motown)
Gladys Knight & The Pips-Anthology .... (Motown)
Joan Baez; *Blessed Are* .... (Vanguard)
Hits/Greatest & Others .... (Vanguard)
Sammi Smith; *Super Hits Of The '70s-Have A Nice Day-#4-C* ...... (Rhino)
Willie Nelson; *Greatest Hits (& Some That Will Be)* ...... (Columbia)
Sweet Memories .... (RCA)
Willie Nelson Sings Kristofferson .... (Columbia)

Help Me Make It Through The Yard
Pinkard & Bowden; *Honky Tonk Country-C* .... (Warner Bros.)
Writers In Disguise .... (Warner Bros.)

Help Me Rhonda
Beach Boys; *Billboard Top Rock 'N' Roll Hits-1965-C* ...... (Rhino)
California Girls .... (Capitol)
Dance Dance Dance .... (Capitol)
Endless Summer .... (Capitol)
Made In The U.S.A. .... (Capitol)

Help Me Through The Day
Freddie King; *Best Of Freddie King* .... (MCA)

Help Me Up
Eric Clapton; *ST/Rush* .... (Reprise)

Help You Dream
Blasters; *Blasters-Collection* .... (Slash)
Hard Line .... (Slash)

Help Yourself
Tom Jones; *Live In Las Vegas* .... (Parrot)
Tom Jones-London Collector-Greatest Hits .... (London)

Help Yourself To My Love
Kashif; *Kashif* .... (Arista)

Help Yourselves To Each Other
Crystal Gayle; *These Days* .... (Columbia)
Don Williams; *Listen To The Radio* .... (MCA)
You're My Best Friend .... (MCA)

Help!
Beatles; *Beatles 1* .... (Capitol)
Beatles-20 Greatest Hits .... (Capitol)
Rarities .... (Capitol)
Reel Music .... (Capitol)
ST/Help! .... (Capitol)
The Beatles At The Hollywood Bowl .... (Capitol)
The Beatles/1962-1966 .... (Capitol)

Help! I'm White And I Can't Get Down
Geezinslaws; *Feelin' Good, Gittin' Up, Gittin' Down* ...... (Step One)

Helping Me Get Over You
Travis Tritt & Lari White; *The Restless Kind* ...... (Warner Bros.)

Helpless
Band & Neil Young; *The Last Waltz* .... (Warner Bros.)
Crosby, Stills, Nash & Young; *Deja Vu* .... (Atlantic)
So Far .... (Atlantic)
Neil Young; *Decade* .... (Reprise)

Helpless
Sugar; *Copper Blue* .... (Rykodisc)

Helpless
Four Tops; *Four Tops-Anthology* .... (Motown)

Helpless
Platters; *Platters-Anthology* .... (Rhino)

Helpless
Johnny Otis; *Roots Of Rock & Roll* .... (Savoy)

Helplessly Hoping
Crosby, Stills & Nash; *Crosby, Stills & Nash* .... (Atlantic)
CSN .... (Atlantic)
Crosby, Stills, Nash & Young; *So Far* .... (Atlantic)

Hey Bulldog
Beatles; *Rock 'N' Roll Music* .... (Capitol)
Yellow Submarine .... (Capitol)

Hey Jude
Beatles; *Beatles 1* .... (Capitol)
Beatles-20 Greatest Hits .... (Capitol)
Past Masters-Volume Two .... (Parlophone)

The Beatles/1967-1970 . . . . (Capitol)
Paul McCartney; *Knebworth-The Album-C* . . . . (Polydor)
Wilson Pickett; *Wilson Pickett's Greatest Hits* . . . . (Atlantic)
Hey You
Pink Floyd; *The Wall* . . . . (Columbia)
Roger Waters; *The Wall-Live In Berlin* . . . . (Mercury)
His Eye Is On The Sparrow
Carmen McRae; *Greatest Of Carmen McRae* . . . .(MCA)
Marvin Gaye; *Musical Testament 1964-1984* . . . . (Motown)
Preservation Hall Jazz Band; *Best Of The Preservation Hall*
   Jazz Band . . . . (Columbia)
Soundtrack; *Streetcar Named Desire* . . . .(Allegiance)
Hold My Hand
Hootie & The Blowfish; *Cracked Rear View* . . . . (Atlantic)
Hold On
Jamie Walters; *Jamie Walters* . . . . (Atlantic)
How Can I Help You Say Goodbye
Patty Loveless; *Only What I Feel* . . . .(Epic)
   Patty Loveless-Classics . . . .(Epic)
How Come, How Long
Babyface & Stevie Wonder; *The Day* . . . .(Epic)
How Do I Say I'm Sorry
Tami Davis; *Only You* . . . .(Red Ant)
Hushabye
Mystics; *Doo-Wop Uptempo-#2-C* . . . . (Rhino)
   Million-Dollar Memories #1-C . . . . (RCA)
   Mystics-16 Golden Classics . . . . (Collectables)
I Ain't Goin' Nowhere
Martina McBride; *Emotion* . . . . (RCA)
I Am
Train; *Train* . . . .(Aware/C2/Columbia)
I Believe
Elvis Presley; *Amazing Grace-His Greatest Sacred Performances* . . . . . . (RCA)
Frankie Laine; *Frankie Laine-16 Most Requested Songs* . . . . (Legacy)
   Frankie Laine's Greatest Hits . . . . (Columbia)
Jo Stafford; *You'll Never Walk Alone* . . . . (CEMA Special Prod.)
I Believe
Robert Plant; *Fate Of Nations* . . . .(Es Paranza)
I Can Help
Billy Swan; *Billboard Top Rock 'N' Roll Hits-1974-C* . . . . (Rhino)
   Rock This Town-Rockabilly Hits-#2-C . . . . (Rhino)
   Super Hits Of The '70s-Have A Nice Day-#13-C . . . . (Rhino)
I Can't Help Falling In Love With You
Wright Brothers; *The American Way* . . . .(KRB Music)
I Can't Help It
Michael Jackson; *Off The Wall* . . . .(Epic)
I Can't Help It
Andy Gibb & Olivia Newton-John; *A Collection Of His*
   Greatest Hits . . . . (Polydor)
   After Dark . . . . (Polydor)
I Can't Help Myself (Sugar Pie Honey Bunch)
Four Tops; *16 #1 Hits From The Early '60s-C* . . . . (Motown)
   Billboard Top R&B Hits-1965-C . . . . (Rhino)
   Four Tops' Greatest Hits . . . . (Motown)
   Four Tops-Anthology . . . . (Motown)
   Good Feeling Music Of The Big Chill Generation-#1-C . . . . (Motown)
   Motown Story-First 25 Years-C . . . . (Motown)
   Motown Superstar Series-#14-Four Tops . . . . (Motown)
   ST/Forrest Gump . . . .(Epic/Sony Music Soundtrax)
   ST/Heaven Help Us . . . .(EMI)
   ST/Into The Night . . . .(MCA)
   ST/Where The Buffalo Roam . . . . (Backstreet)
I Can't Help Remembering You
Dean Martin; *Dean Martin's Greatest Hits* . . . . (Reprise)
I Couldn't Help Myself
Sara Hickman; *Shortstop* . . . . (Elektra)
I Don't Live Today
Jimi Hendrix; *Concerts* . . . . (Reprise)
   Essential Jimi Hendrix, Volume 2 . . . . (Reprise)
   Kiss The Sky . . . . (Reprise)
Jimi Hendrix Experience; *Are You Experienced?* . . . . (Reprise)
I Need You
LeAnn Rimes; *ST/Jesus-The Epic Mini-Series* . . . . (Sparrow/Curb/Capitol)
I Saved The World Today
Eurythmics; *Peace* . . . . (Arista)
I Think God Can Explain
Splender; *ST/Dawson's Creek-#2* . . . . (C2/Columbia)
I Turn To You
Christina Aguilera; *Christina Aguilera* . . . . (RCA)
I'd Do Anything
Original Broadway Cast; *Oliver!* . . . . (RCA Victor)
Original London Cast; *Oliver!* . . . . (EMI-Angel)
If There's A God On My Side
Rosanne Cash; *The Wheel* . . . . (Columbia)
If We Fall In Love Tonight
Rod Stewart; *If We Fall In Love Tonight* . . . .(Warner Bros.)
If You Change Your Mind
Rosanne Cash; *King's Record Shop* . . . . (Columbia)

Rosanne Cash-Super Hits . . . . (Columbia)
I'll Always Be Right There
Bryan Adams; *18 Til I Die* . . . .(A&M)
   MTV Unplugged-Bryan Adams . . . . (A&M)
I'll Be
Edwin McCain; *Misguided Roses* . . . . (Lava)
I'll Be
Reba McEntire; *So Good Together* . . . . (MCA)
I'll Be Around
Spinners; *Atlantic Rhythm & Blues 1947-1974-#6 (1966-1969)-C* . . . . .(Atlantic)
   Best Of The Spinners . . . .(Atlantic)
   Golden Age Of Black Music-1970-1975-C . . . .(Atlantic)
   Golden Soul-C . . . .(Atlantic)
   Soul Years-C . . . .(Atlantic)
   Spinners . . . . (Rhino)
I'll Be Around
Rappin' 4-Tay; *Don't Fight The Feelin'* . . . . (Rag Top/EMI)
I'll Be There
Jackson 5; *Compact Command Performances-Jackson 5* . . . . (Motown)
   Jackson 5-Anthology . . . . (Motown)
   Jackson 5's Greatest Hits . . . . (Motown)
   Motown Superstar Series-#12-Jackson 5 . . . . (Motown)
   Motown's Biggest Pop Hits-C . . . . (Motown)
Mariah Carey; *MTV Unplugged-Mariah Carey* . . . . (Columbia)
I'll Be There
Gerry And The Pacemakers; *Best Of Gerry And The Pacemakers* . . . . (EMI)
   History Of British Rock-#2-C . . . . (Rhino)
I'll Be There
Escape Club; *Dollars & Sex* . . . .(Atlantic)
I'll Be There
Gail Davies; *I'll Be There* . . . . (Warner Bros.)
I'll Be There For You
Bon Jovi; *New Jersey* . . . . (Jambco)
I'll Change Your Flat Tire, Merle
Pure Prairie League; *Two Lane Highway* . . . . (RCA)
I'll Take You There
Staple Singers; *15 Original Big Hits-#1-C* . . . . (Stax)
   I Am Woman-C . . . . (Nick At Nite)
   Staple Singers' Greatest Hits . . . . (Fantasy)
   Staple Singers-Chronicle . . . . (Stax)
I'll Take You There
General Public; *ST/Threesome* . . . .(Epic/Sony Music Soundtrax)
I'm Holdin' On To Love (To Save My Life)
Shania Twain; *Come On Over* . . . . (Mercury)
I'm Your Angel
Celine Dion & R. Kelly; *All The Way...A Decade Of Song* . . . .(550 Music)
   These Are Special Times . . . .(550 Music)
R. Kelly & Celine Dion; *R.* . . . .(Jive)
In Harm's Way
Bebe Winans; *Bebe Winans* . . . .(Atlantic)
Ironic
Alanis Morissette; *Jagged Little Pill* . . . . (Maverick)
It Hurts Me Too
Keb' Mo'; *The Door* . . . .(550/Epic/Okeh)
It'll Be Me
Exile; *Back To Back: Exile* . . . . (K-Tel)
   Billboard Top Country Hits-1986-C . . . . (Rhino)
   Exile-Super Hits . . . . (Epic)
It's OK
Tracy Chapman; *Telling Stories* . . . . (Elektra)
Janey Don't You Lose Heart
Bruce Springsteen; *Tracks* . . . . (Columbia)
Jesus To A Child
George Michael; *Ladies & Gentlemen: The Best Of George Michael* . . . . . (Epic)
   Older . . . .(DreamWorks/SKG)
Jim Dandy
Black Oak Arkansas; *Best Of Black Oak Arkansas* . . . . (Atco)
   Super Hits Of The '70s-Have A Nice Day-#12-C . . . . (Rhino)
LaVern Baker; *Atlantic Rhythm & Blues 1947-1974-#3 (1955-*
   1958)-C . . . .(Atlantic)
Joining You
Alanis Morissette; *Supposed Former Infatuation Junkie* . . . . (Maverick)
Jumper
Third Eye Blind; *Third Eye Blind* . . . . (Elektra)
   Totally Hits-#1-C . . . . (Arista)
Jungle, The
Kiss; *Carnival Of Souls: The Final Sessions* . . . . (Mercury)
Just Like You
Keb' Mo'; *Just Like You* . . . .(Okeh)
Just Remember I Love You
Firefall; *Firefall's Greatest Hits* . . . . (Rhino)
   Luna Sea . . . . (Rhino)
Keep Me From The Cold
Curtis Stigers; *Time Was* . . . . (Arista)
Lack Of Water
Why Store; *The Why Store* . . . . (MCA)
Lady Lay Down
John Conlee; *Rose Colored Glasses* . . . . (Universal)

Last Night A D.J. Saved My Life
Indeep; *Last Night A D.J. Saved My Life* . . . . (Sound Of New York)
   The Disco Years-#2-On The Beat-1978-1982-C . . . . (Rhino)
Lawyers, Guns & Money
Warren Zevon; *Excitable Boy* . . . . (Asylum)
   Quiet Normal Life-Best Of Warren Zevon . . . . (Asylum)
   Stand In The Fire . . . . (Asylum)
Lean On Me
Bill Withers; *Bill Withers' Greatest Hits* . . . . (Columbia)
   Chicken Soup For The Soul: I'll Be There For You-Songs Of Friendship,
      Brotherhood And Sisterhood-C . . . . (Rhino)
   God Bless America-C . . . . (Columbia)
   Still Bill . . . . (Columbia)
Club Nouveau; *Life Love & Pain* . . . . (Warner Bros.)
Grover Washington, Jr.; *Greatest Performances-Grover*
   Washington, Jr. . . . . (Motown)
Lean On Me
Kirk Franklin; *The Nu Nation Project* . . . . (Gospo Centric/Interscope)
Learn To Fly
Foo Fighters; *There Is Nothing Left To Lose* . . . .(Roswell/RCA)
Lend A Helpin' Hand
Lynyrd Skynyrd; *Skynyrd's First & Last* . . . . (MCA)
Let Go Of The Stone
John Anderson; *Seminole Wind* . . . .(BNA)
Let It Be
Aretha Franklin; *Aretha Franklin's Greatest Hits* . . . . (Atlantic)
Beatles; *Beatles 1* . . . .(Capitol)
   Beatles-20 Greatest Hits . . . .(Capitol)
   Past Masters-Volume Two . . . . (Parlophone)
   Reel Music . . . . (Capitol)
   The Beatles/1967-1970 . . . . (Capitol)
Paul McCartney; *The Concert For New York City-C* . . . . . . (Columbia)
   Tripping The Live Fantastic-Highlights! . . . . (Capitol)
Rockestra; *Kampuchea-C* . . . . (Atlantic)
Let Your Soul Be Your Pilot
Sting; *Mercury Falling* . . . . (A&M)
Life Line
Nilsson; *The Point* . . . .(RCA)
Life Saver
Chicago; *Chicago VII* . . . . (Chicago)
Lifeline
Spandau Ballet; *True* . . . . (Chrysalis)
Lifeline
10 CC; *Bloody Tourists* . . . . (Polydor)
Lifeline
Husker Du; *Metal Circus* . . . . (SST)
Line, The
Bruce Springsteen; *The Ghost Of Tom Joad* . . . . (Columbia)
Little Wing
Derek And The Dominos; *Layla* . . . . (Polydor)
Jimi Hendrix; *Axis: Bold As Love* . . . . (Reprise)
   Concerts . . . . (Reprise)
   Essential Jimi Hendrix . . . . (Reprise)
   Lifelines/Jimi Hendrix Story . . . . (Reprise)
Sting; *...Nothing Like The Sun* . . . . (A&M)
Long Day
Matchbox Twenty; *Yourself Or Someone Like You* . . . . (Lava)
Lord I Hope This Day Is Good
Don Williams; *Best Of Don Williams-#3* . . . . (MCA)
   Especially For You . . . . (MCA)
Lee Ann Womack; *Grand Ole Opry-75 Years-#1-C* . . . . (MCA)
Love Of My Life
Sammy Kershaw; *Labor Of Love* . . . . (Mercury)
Love Rescue Me
U2; *Rattle And Hum* . . . . (Island)
Love Will Save The Day
Whitney Houston; *Whitney* . . . . (Arista)
   Whitney Houston's Greatest Hits . . . . (Arista)
Love You Save, The
Jackson 5; *14 Greatest Hits* . . . . (Motown)
   ABC . . . . (Motown)
   Goin' Back To Indiana . . . . (Motown)
   Jackson 5-Anthology . . . . (Motown)
   Jackson 5's Greatest Hits . . . . (Motown)
   Motown Superstar Series-#12-Jackson 5 . . . . (Motown)
   TV ST/Diana-C . . . . (Motown)
Love's In Need Of Love Today
Stevie Wonder featuring Take 6; *America: A Tribute To*
   Heroes-C . . . . (Interscope)
Lullaby
Shawn Mullins; *Soul's Core* . . . . (Columbia)
Lullaby
Tom Rush; *Tom Rush* . . . . (Columbia)
Malibu
Hole; *Celebrity Skin* . . . . (David Geffen Co.)
Mama Said
Shirelles; *Original Rock 'N' Roll Hits Of The '60s-C* . . . . (Roulette)
   Shirelles' Greatest Hits . . . . (Everest)

   Shirelles-Anthology 1959-1964 . . . .(Rhino)
   Shirelles-Classics . . . . (Bac-Trac)
   Super Oldies Of The '60s-#3-C . . . . (Audio Fidelity)
Man Ain't Supposed To Cry
Public Announcement; *Don't Hold Back* . . . . (RCA)
Master's Call
Marty Robbins; *Gunfighter Ballads & Trail Songs* . . . .(Legacy)
Maybe I'm Amazed
Paul McCartney; *McCartney* . . . .(Capitol)
Wings; *Wings Over America* . . . .(Capitol)
Men In Black
Will Smith; *Big Willie Style* . . . . (Columbia)
   ST/Men In Black . . . . (Columbia)
Message In A Bottle
Police; *Every Breath You Take-The Classics* . . . . (A&M)
   Regatta De Blanc . . . . (A&M)
Sting; *The Secret Policeman's Other Ball/The Music* . . . . (Rhino)
Miner's Lifeguard
Almanac Singers/Peter Seeger/Chorus; *Talking Union & Other Union*
   Songs . . . . (Smithsonian Folkways)
Mother's Little Helper
Rolling Stones; *Flowers* . . . . (Abkco)
   Hot Rocks 1964-1971 . . . . (Abkco)
   Through The Past, Darkly (Big Hits Vol. 2) . . . . (Abkco)
Tesla; *Five Man Acoustical Jam* . . . . (Geffen)
My Baby Needs A Shepherd
Emmylou Harris; *Red Dirt Girl* . . . .(Nonesuch)
My Friends
Red Hot Chili Peppers; *One Hot Minute* . . . . (Warner Bros.)
My Melancholy Baby
Barbra Streisand; *Third Album* . . . . (Columbia)
Bing Crosby; *Hits Of 1939-C* . . . . (Living Era)
Coleman Hawkins; *Genius Of Coleman Hawkins* . . . .(Verve)
Dorothy Loudon; *Saloon* . . . . (DRG)
Frank Sinatra; *Voice: The Columbia Years-1943-1952* . . . .(Columbia)
Gene Austin; *78-#21015* . . . . (Victor)
Jan Garber & His Orchestra; *Jan Garber & His Orchestra Play 22 Original*
   Big Band Favorites . . . . (Hindsight)
Kate Smith; *Kate Smith-16 Most Requested Songs* . . . . (Columbia)
Leon Redbone; *Double Time* . . . . (Warner Bros.)
Marcels; *Best Of The Marcels* . . . . (Rhino)
My Special Angel
Bobby Helms; *American Graffiti-#3-C* . . . . (MCA)
   Blue Ribbon Country-#3-C . . . .(Accord)
   Oldies But Goodies-#14-C . . . . (Original Sound)
   Pop A Billy . . . . (MCA)
   Vintage Music-#2-C . . . . (MCA)
Vogues; *Vogues' Greatest Hits* . . . . (Rhino)
   Vogues' Greatest Hits/Finest Performances . . . . (Sun)
No Help Wanted
Carlisles; *Heroes Of Country Music-#3-Legends Of Nashville-C* . . . .(Rhino)
No Refuge
Eddie Schwartz; *No Refuge* . . . . (Atco)
Nobody
Ry Cooder; *Jazz* . . . . (Warner Bros.)
Oh How The Years Go By
Vanessa Williams; *NBA At 50-A Musical Celebration-C* . . . .(Mercury)
One Voice
Billy Gilman; *One Voice* . . . . (Epic)
One, The
Backstreet Boys; *Millennium* . . . . (Jive)
Only The Strong Survive
Elvis Presley; *From Elvis In Memphis* . . . . (RCA)
   Memphis Record . . . . (RCA)
Jerry Butler; *Best Of Jerry Butler* . . . .(Mercury)
   Best Of Jerry Butler . . . . (Rhino)
Open My Heart
Yolanda Adams; *Mountain High Valley Low* . . . .(Elektra)
Paradise
Styx; *Return To Paradise* . . . . (CMC Int'l)
Past The Point Of Rescue
Hal Ketchum; *Past The Point Of Rescue* . . . .(Curb)
Place In The Sun
Pablo Cruise; *A Place In The Sun* . . . .(A&M)
Please Help
J.B. Hutto; *Chicago/The Blues Today* . . . .(Vanguard)
   Great Blues Men-C . . . .(Vanguard)
   Slideslinger . . . . (Evidence Music)
Please Help Me, I'm Falling
Hank Locklin; *Billboard Top Country Hits-1960-C* . . . .(Rhino)
   Hank Locklin-Golden Hits . . . . (Plantation)
   Nipper's Greatest Hits Of The '60s-#2-C . . . . (RCA)
   Souvenirs Of Music City U.S.A.-C . . . . (Plantation)
Janie Fricke; *Janie Fricke's Greatest Hits* . . . .(Columbia)
Pour Me
Trick Pony; *Trick Pony* . . . .(H2E/Warner Bros.)
Precious Declaration
Collective Soul; *Disciplined Breakdown* . . . .(Atlantic)

Precious Lord, Take My Hand
Linda Hopkins; *How Blue Can You Get* . . . . (Quicksilver)
Preservation Hall Jazz Band; *Best Of The Preservation Hall*
Jazz Band . . . . (Columbia)
Pretty Little Adriana
Vince Gill; *High Lonesome Sound* . . . . (MCA)
Private Emotion
Ricky Martin & Meja; *Ricky Martin* . . . . (Columbia)
Push It
Garbage; *Version 2.0* . . . . (Almo Sounds)
Queen Jane Approximately
4 Seasons; *The 4 Seasons Sing Big Hits By Bacharach/David/Dylan* . . . . (Rhino)
Bob Dylan; *Highway 61 Revisited* . . . . (Columbia)
Bob Dylan & The Grateful Dead; *Dylan & The Dead* . . . . (Columbia)
Reach Out And Touch
Diana Ross; *Diana Ross-All The Great Hits* . . . . (Motown)
Diana Ross-Anthology . . . . (Motown)
Live At Caesar's Palace . . . . (Motown)
Most Played Songs On America's Jukeboxes . . . . (Motown)
Motown Story-First 25 Years-C . . . . (Motown)
Reach Out I'll Be There
Four Tops; *Compact Command Performances-Four Tops* . . . . (Motown)
Four Tops' Greatest Hits . . . . (Motown)
Four Tops Reach Out . . . . (Motown)
Four Tops-Anthology . . . . (Motown)
Motown Dance Party-#2-C . . . . (Motown)
Reach Out Of The Darkness
Friend And Lover; *Chicken Soup For The Soul: I'll Be There For You-Songs*
Of Friendship, Brotherhood And Sisterhood-C . . . . (Rhino)
Flower Power-Psychedelic Rock Classics-C . . . . (K-Tel)
Rebecca
Pat McGhee Band; *Shine* . . . . (Giant/Warner Bros.)
Recover Your Soul
Elton John; *The Big Picture* . . . . (Rocket)
Redemption Day
Sheryl Crow; *Sheryl Crow* . . . . (A&M)
Rescue
Echo & The Bunnymen; *Crocodiles* . . . . (Sire)
Echo & The Bunnymen . . . . (Sire)
Songs To Learn & Sing-The Hits . . . . (Sire)
Rescue
Sam Harris; *Sam-I Am* . . . . (Motown)
Rescue Me
Diana Ross; *Swept Away* . . . . (RCA)
Fontella Bass; *Billboard Top R&B Hits-1965-1969-C* . . . . (Rhino)
Collectables Presents The History Of Rock-#8-C . . . . (Collectables)
Cruisin'-1965-C . . . . (Increase)
Oldies But Goodies-#12-C . . . . (Original Sound)
ST/Air America . . . . (MCA)
Red Hot & Blue Band; *Red Hot & Blue-All Time Great R&B Songs* . . . . . (Curb)
Rescue Me
Alarm; *Electric Folklore* . . . . (I.R.S.)
Eye Of The Hurricane . . . . (I.R.S.)
ST/21 Jump Street . . . . (I.R.S.)
Rescue Me
Al B. Sure!; *In Effect Mode* . . . . (Warner Bros.)
Rescue Me
Madonna; *Immaculate Collection* . . . . (Sire)
Royal Box . . . . (Sire)
Rhythm Saved The World
Bunny Berigan & His Boys; *Take It Bunny* . . . . (Sony Music Special Prod.)
Riverwide
Sheryl Crow; *The Globe Sessions* . . . . (A&M)
Rock 'N' Roll To The Rescue
Beach Boys; *Beach Boys-Gift Set* . . . . (Capitol)
Made In The U.S.A. . . . . (Capitol)
Roll To Me
Del Amitri; *ST/Crossroads-VH1 Television Program* . . . . (Atlantic)
Twisted . . . . (A&M)
Run Away
Real McCoy; *Another Night* . . . . (Arista)
Running Around Town
Billy Ray Martin; *Deadline For My Memories* . . . . (Sire)
S.O.S.
Abba; *Abba* . . . . (Atlantic)
Abba's Greatest Hits . . . . (Atlantic)
The Singles-First 10 Years . . . . (Atlantic)
S.O.S.
S.O.S. Band; *45-#5526* . . . . (Tabu)
S.O.S.
Tim Curry; *Best Of Tim Curry* . . . . (A&M)
S.O.S.
Manhattan Transfer; *Coming Out* . . . . (Atlantic)
S.O.S.
Ex-Girlfriend; *X Marks The Spot* . . . . (Reprise)
S.O.S.
Aerosmith; *Get Your Wings* . . . . (Columbia)
Live! Bootleg . . . . (Columbia)

S.O.S. Fire In The Sky
Deodato; *Motion* . . . . (Warner Bros.)
Safe And Sound
Sheryl Crow; *America: A Tribute To Heroes-C* . . . . (Interscope)
Safe In The Arms Of Love
Martina McBride; *ST/Switchback* . . . . (RCA)
Wild Angels . . . . (RCA)
Safe In The Arms Of Love
Martika; *Martika's Kitchen* . . . . (Columbia)
Turn The Tide . . . . (RCA)
Safety In Numbers
Joan Osborne; *Righteous Love* . . . . (Interscope)
Salvation
Cranberries; *To The Faithful Departed* . . . . (Island)
Save Me
Fleetwood Mac; *25 Years-The Chain* . . . . (Warner Bros.)
Behind The Mask . . . . (Warner Bros.)
Save Me
Smokey Robinson & The Miracles; *Away We A Go-Go* . . . . (Motown)
Motown Legends-Smokey Robinson & The Miracles . . . . (Motown)
Smokey Robinson & The Miracles' Anthology . . . . (Motown)
Smokey Robinson & The Miracles' Greatest Hits-#2 . . . . (Motown)
Save Me
Al Jarreau; *Jarreau* . . . . (Warner Bros.)
Save Me
Aretha Franklin; *Best Of Aretha Franklin* . . . . (Atlantic)
Save Me
Tanya Tucker; *Best Of Tanya Tucker* . . . . (MCA)
Save Me
Louise Mandrell; *Best Of The '80s...So Far-C* . . . . (RCA)
Solid Country Gold-C . . . . (RCA)
Save Me
Michael Bolton; *Time, Love & Tenderness* . . . . (Columbia)
Save Me
Public Image Ltd.; *Happy?* . . . . (Virgin)
Save Me
k.d. lang; *Ingenue* . . . . (Sire)
Save Me
Joan Armatrading; *Joan Armatrading* . . . . (A&M)
Save Me
Des'ree; *Mind Adventures* . . . . (550 Music)
Save Me
Neil Diamond; *On The Way To The Sky* . . . . (Columbia)
Save Me
Bob & Marcia; *Reggae Spectacular-C* . . . . (A&M)
Save Me
Rembrandts; *Rembrandts* . . . . (Atco)
Save Me
Crisis Party; *Rude Awakening* . . . . (Metal Blade)
Save Me
Vitamin Z; *Sharp Stone Rain* . . . . (Geffen)
Save Me
Lisa Fischer; *So Intense* . . . . (Elektra)
Save Me
Queen; *The Game* . . . . (Hollywood)
Save The Children
Diana Ross; *Diana Ross-Anthology* . . . . (Motown)
Touch Me In The Morning . . . . (Motown)
Gil Scott-Heron; *Gil Scott-Heron* . . . . (Bluebird)
Revolution Will Not Be Televised . . . . (Flying Dutchman)
Marvin Gaye; *Marvin Gaye Live At The London Palladium* . . . . (Motown)
Marvin Gaye-Anthology . . . . (Motown)
Musical Testament 1964-1984 . . . . (Motown)
What's Going On . . . . (Motown)
Save The Country
5th Dimension; *5th Dimension-Anthology 1967-1973* . . . . (Rhino)
Greatest Hits On Earth . . . . (Arista)
Bobby Darin; *Live At The Desert Inn* . . . . (Motown)
Laura Nyro; *New York Tendaberry* . . . . (Columbia)
Save The Life Of My Child
Simon & Garfunkel; *Bookends* . . . . (Columbia)
Collected Works . . . . (Columbia)
Save The People
Original Cast; *Godspell* . . . . (Arista)
Save The Whale
Nik Kershaw; *The Riddle* . . . . (MCA)
Save The Whales
Country Joe McDonald; *Bread & Roses Festival Of Acoustic*
Music-#1-C . . . . (Fantasy)
Country Joe McDonald-Classics . . . . (Fantasy)
Into The Fray . . . . (Rag Baby)
Paradise With An Ocean View . . . . (Fantasy)
Save The Whales
Danny O'Keefe; *Global Blues* . . . . (Warner Bros.)
Save The World
George Harrison; *Greenpeace-C* . . . . (A&M)
Somewhere In England . . . . (Dark Horse)

Save Tonight
 Eagle-Eye Cherry; *Desireless* . . . . (Work)
Save Yourself
 Stabbing Westward; *Darkest Days* . . . .(Columbia)
Saved
 Band; *Moondog Matinee* . . . . (Capitol)
 Commitments; *ST/The Commitments-#2* . . . . (MCA)
 Elvis Presley; *Elvis Presley Sings Leiber & Stoller* . . . . (RCA)
 LaVern Baker; *Atlantic Rhythm & Blues 1947-1974-#4 (1958-*
   1962)-C . . . . (Atlantic)
 Rock Classics Of Leiber & Stoller-C . . . . (Rhino)
 Soul On Fire . . . . (Atlantic)
 ST/Shag . . . . (Sire)
Saved
 Bob Dylan; *Saved* . . . .(Columbia)
Saved By Love
 Rik Emmett; *Absolutely* . . . . (Charisma)
Saved By Love
 Amy Grant; *Lead Me On* . . . . (A&M)
Saved By Zero
 Fixx; *One Thing Leads To Another-Greatest Hits* . . . . (MCA)
 Reach The Beach . . . . (MCA)
 React . . . . (MCA)
Saved My Life
 Fee Waybill; *Read My Lips* . . . . (Capitol)
 ST/St. Elmo's Fire . . . . (Atlantic)
Saving My Heart
 Yes; *Union* . . . . (Arista)
Say You, Say Me
 Lionel Richie; *Back To Front* . . . . (Motown)
 Dancing On The Ceiling . . . . (Motown)
Secret
 Madonna; *Bedtime Stories* . . . . (Maverick/Sire)
 GHV2 . . . . (Warner Bros.)
Secret Smile
 Semisonic; *Feeling Strangely Fine* . . . . (MCA)
Send Down An Angel
 Allison Moorer; *The Hardest Part* . . . . (MCA)
Sending Me Angels
 Kathy Mattea; *Love Travels* . . . . (Mercury)
Shackles (Praise You)
 Mary Mary; *Thankful* . . . . (C2/Columbia)
Shame
 Stabbing Westward; *Wither Blister Burn & Peel* . . . . . (Columbia)
She Said
 Collective Soul; *Dosage* . . . . (Atlantic)
 ST/Scream 2 . . . .(Dimension/Capitol)
Shelter From The Storm
 Bob Dylan; *Blood On The Tracks* . . . .(Columbia)
 Bob Dylan At Budokan . . . .(Columbia)
 Hard Rain . . . .(Columbia)
Shelter Me
 Cinderella; *Heartbreak Station* . . . . (Mercury)
 Say What U Want-Rock The Vote-C . . . . (Mercury)
 Joe Cocker; *Cocker* . . . . (Capitol)
 Joe Cocker Live . . . . (Capitol)
Shelter Of Your Eyes
 Don Williams; *Don Williams' Greatest Hits* . . . . (MCA)
Shine A Light
 Rolling Stones; *Exile On Main Street* . . . . (Virgin)
Shut Out The Light
 Bruce Springsteen; *Tracks* . . . .(Columbia)
Shy Of The Moon
 Wallflowers; *The Wallflowers* . . . .(Virgin)
Snow On The Sahara
 Anggun; *Anggun* . . . . (Epic)
So Help Me Girl
 Gary Barlow; *Open Road* . . . . (Arista)
 Joe Diffie; *Third Rock From The Sun* . . . . (Epic)
Somebody Help Me
 Spencer Davis Group; *Best Of The Spencer Davis Group* . . . . . . (EMI)
 Winwood . . . . (United Artists)
Somebody Help Me
 Iguanas; *Nuevo Boogaloo* . . . . (Margaritaville)
Somebody's Out There Watching
 Kinleys; *Kinleys II* . . . . (Epic)
Someday
 Sugar Ray; *14:59* . . . . (Lava)
 Totally Hits-#1-C . . . . (Arista)
Someone Loves You Honey
 Charley Pride; *Charley Pride's Greatest Hits* . . . . (RCA)
Someone Saved My Life Tonight
 Elton John; *Captain Fantastic And The Brown Dirt Cowboy* . . . . . . (Polydor)
 Elton John's Greatest Hits-#2 . . . . (Polydor)
Someone To Watch Over Me
 Ella Fitzgerald; *Ella Fitzgerald Sings The George & Ira Gershwin*
   Songbook . . . . (Verve)
 Elton John; *Glory Of Gershwin Featuring Larry Adler-C* . . . . . . (Mercury)

Frank Sinatra; *Nice 'N' Easy* . . . . (Capitol)
 The Capitol Years . . . . (Capitol)
 Jack Jones; *Gershwin Album* . . . .(Columbia)
 Original Broadway Cast; *Crazy For You* . . . . (Angel)
 Oscar Peterson; *My Favorite Instrument* . . . .(Verve)
 Sarah Vaughan; *Sarah Vaughan Sings George Gershwin Songbook,*
   Vol. 2 . . . . (Emarcy)
 Willie Nelson; *Stardust* . . . . (Legacy)
Sometimes Salvation
 Black Crowes; *Southern Harmony & Musical Companion* . . . . . (Def American)
Sparrow
 Simon & Garfunkel; *Wednesday Morning 3 A.M.* . . . .(Columbia)
Splackavellie
 Pressha; *Don't Get It Twisted* . . . . (Tony Mercedes/LaFace/Arista)
Stamp Out Loneliness
 Stonewall Jackson; *Stonewall Jackson-Classic Country* . . . .(Simitar)
Stand By Me
 Ben E. King; *Atlantic Soul Classics-C* . . . .(Warner Special Prod.)
 Ben E. King's Greatest Hits . . . .(Atco)
 Golden Age Of Black Music-1960-1970-C . . . . (Atlantic)
 ST/Stand By Me . . . . (Atlantic)
 Stand By Me-Best Of Ben E. King . . . . (Atlantic)
 Drifters; *Drifters' Greatest Hits* . . . . (Gusto)
 John Lennon; *Rock 'N' Roll* . . . . (Capitol)
 ST/Imagine: John Lennon . . . . (Capitol)
 The John Lennon Collection . . . . (Capitol)
 Maurice White; *Maurice White* . . . .(Columbia)
 Mickey Gilley; *Greatest Country Hits From The Movies-C* . . . . . (Epic)
 Mickey Gilley's Biggest Hits . . . . (Epic)
 ST/Urban Cowboy . . . . (Asylum)
 Ten Years Of Hits . . . . (Epic)
 Ry Cooder; *Chicken Skin Music* . . . . (Reprise)
Step Inside Love
 Beatles; *The Beatles-Anthology-#3* . . . . (Capitol)
Still On Your Side
 BBMak; *Sooner Or Later* . . . .(Hollywood)
Street To Lean On
 Crosby, Stills & Nash; *After The Storm* . . . . (Atlantic)
Sunshower
 Chris Cornell; *ST/Great Expectations* . . . . (Atlantic)
Sympathy For The Devil
 Bryan Ferry; *These Foolish Things* . . . . (Reprise)
 Jane's Addiction; *Jane's Addiction* . . . . (Triple X Entert.)
 Rolling Stones; *Beggars Banquet* . . . . (Abkco)
 Flashpoint . . . . (Virgin)
 Get Yer Ya-Ya's Out! . . . . (Abkco)
 Hot Rocks 1964-1971 . . . . (Abkco)
 Love You Live . . . . (Virgin)
Take Good Care Of My Baby
 Bobby Vee; *Best Of Bobby Vee* . . . . (EMI)
 Billboard Top Rock 'N' Roll Hits-1961-C . . . . (Rhino)
 'Til My Dreamin' Comes True-C . . . . (Capitol)
 Bobby Vinton; *Bobby Vinton-16 Most Requested Songs* . . . . . .(Legacy)
 Dion; *Runaround Sue (Right Stuff)* . . . .(Right Stuff)
Takes A Little Time
 Amy Grant; *Behind The Eyes* . . . . (A&M)
Ten Thousand Angels
 Mindy McCready; *Ten Thousand Angels* . . . . (BNA)
Tender Moment, A
 Lee Roy Parnell; *Hits And Highways Ahead* . . . . (Arista)
 Love Without Mercy . . . . (Arista)
 Pure Country-Best Of The '90s-C . . . . (Priority)
Thank You
 Boyz II Men; *Boyz II Men II* . . . .(Motown)
Thank You For Loving Me
 Bon Jovi; *Crush* . . . . (Island/IDJMG)
That's All Right (Mama)
 Arthur "Big Boy" Crudup; *Best Of The Blues* . . . . (Pair)
 That's All Right (Mama) . . . .(Bluebird)
 Carl Perkins; *Restless-Columbia Recordings* . . . . . . (Columbia)
 Elvis Presley; *For LP Fans Only* . . . . (RCA)
 Sun Story-C . . . . (Rhino)
 Sun's Greatest Hits-C . . . . (RCA)
 The Sun Sessions . . . . (RCA)
 Marty Robbins; *Essential Marty Robbins-1951-1982* . . . . . (Columbia)
 Merl Saunders/Jerry Garcia/Bill Vitt/John Kahn; *Live At Keystone* . . . . . (Fantasy)
 Paul McCartney; *CHOBA B CCCP-The Russian Album* . . . . (Capitol)
 Rick Nelson; *Stay Young-Epic Recordings* . . . . (Epic)
 Rod Stewart; *Every Picture Tells A Story* . . . .(Mercury)
 Vintage Rod Stewart . . . .(Mercury)
 Vince Gill; *ST/Honeymoon In Vegas* . . . . (Epic/Sony Music Soundtrax)
That's What Friends Are For
 Dionne Warwick/Elton John/Gladys Knight/Stevie Wonder; *Dionne*
   Warwick's Greatest Hits-1979-1990 . . . .(Arista)
 Friends . . . . (Arista)
Theme From "Friends" (I'll Be There For You)
 Rembrandts; *LP* . . . .(East West)
 ST/Friends-Music From The TV Series . . . . (Reprise)

There You Are
Martina McBride; *Emotion* . . . (RCA)
These Arms
All-4-One; *And The Music Speaks* . . . (Blitzz)
Thunder Road
Bruce Springsteen; *Born To Run* . . . (Columbia)
Bruce Springsteen's Greatest Hits . . . (Columbia)
Bruce Springsteen & The E Street Band; *Bruce Springsteen & The E Street Band Live/1975-85* . . . (Legacy)
'Til A Tear Becomes A Rose
Jann Browne; *Tell Me Why* . . . (Curb)
'Til A Tear Becomes A Rose . . . (Curb)
Keith Whitley; *Keith Whitley's Greatest Hits* . . . (RCA)
Lorrie Morgan; *Lorrie Morgan's Greatest Hits* . . . (BNA)
'Til I Can Make It On My Own
Faith Hill; *Tammy Wynette...Remembered-C* . . . (Asylum)
Kenny Rogers & Dottie West; *Kenny Rogers-Classics* . . . (EMI)
Kenny Rogers-Twenty Greatest Hits . . . (EMI)
Tammy Wynette; *Tammy Wynette's Greatest Hits-#4* . . . (Epic)
Tears Of Fire-25th Anniversary Collection . . . (Epic)
'Til I Can Make It On My Own . . . (Epic)
Time After Time
Cyndi Lauper; *Chicken Soup For The Woman's Soul-C* . . . (Rhino)
She's So Unusual . . . (Portrait)
Twelve Deadly Cyns...And Then Some . . . (Epic)
Everything But The Girl; *Acoustic* . . . (Atlantic)
INOJ & So So Def Bass All-Stars; *Time After Time (Maxi Single)* . . . (So So Def/Columbia)
Miles Davis; *Live Around The World* . . . (Warner Bros.)
You're Under Arrest . . . (Columbia)
To Be Loved
Curtis Stigers; *Songs From Dawson's Creek* . . . (Sony Music Soundtrax)
Total Eclipse Of The Heart
Bonnie Tyler; *Billboard Top Hits-1983-C* . . . (Rhino)
Faster Than The Speed Of Night . . . (Columbia)
Seems Like Yesterday-#4-Early '80s-C . . . (K-Tel)
Nicki French; *Dance Hits '96 Supermix-C* . . . (Critique)
Secrets . . . (Critique)
Troubles
Alicia Keys; *Songs In A Minor* . . . (J)
Ugg-a-Wugg
Original Cast; *Peter Pan-The 1954 Broadway Production* . . . (RCA Victor)
Up On The Roof
Cryan' Shames; *Scratch In The Sky* . . . (Columbia)
Drifters; *Cruisin'-1962-C* . . . (Increase)
Drifters' Greatest Hits . . . (Gusto)
Drifters-16 Greatest Hits . . . (Trip)
Drifters-Golden Hits . . . (Atlantic)
James Taylor; *Flag* . . . (Columbia)
The Concert For New York City-C . . . (Columbia)
Nylons; *Four On The Floor* . . . (Scotti Bros.)
Urgent
Foreigner; *Records* . . . (Atlantic)
Voice Of The Heart
Diana Ross; *Take Me Higher* . . . (Motown)
Waffle
Sevendust; *Home* . . . (TVT)
We Are The World
USA For Africa; *We Are The World-C* . . . (Columbia)
Well, Alright!
CeCe Winans; *Everlasting Love* . . . (PMG/Atlantic)
Wow Gospel 1999-C . . . (Verity/BMG)
We're All Alone
Boz Scaggs; *Boz Scaggs-Hits!* . . . (Columbia)
Slow Dancer . . . (Columbia)
Rita Coolidge; *Rita Coolidge's Greatest Hits* . . . (A&M)
When You Are Old
Gretchen Peters; *The Secret Of Life* . . . (Purple Crayon Prod.)
When You Come Back Down
Nickel Creek; *Nickel Creek* . . . (Sugar Hill)
When You Come Back To Me Again
Garth Brooks; *Scarecrow* . . . (Capitol)
When You Need Me
Bruce Springsteen; *Tracks* . . . (Columbia)
Whenever You Call
Mariah Carey; *Butterfly* . . . (Columbia)
Who Will Save Your Soul
Jewel; *Pieces Of You* . . . (Atlantic)
Wimoweh (Mbube)-The Lion Sleeps Tonight
Chet Atkins; *RCA Years* . . . (RCA)
Kingston Trio; *Kingston Trio/From The Hungry i* . . . (Capitol)
Nylons; *Seamless* . . . (Open Air)
Pete Seeger; *Pete Seeger's Greatest Hits* . . . (Columbia)
Tokens; *Billboard Top Rock 'N' Roll Hits-1961-C* . . . (Rhino)
Nipper's Greatest Hits Of The '60s-#1-C . . . (RCA)
Weavers; *Weavers' Greatest Hits* . . . (Vanguard)
Wine Into Water
T. Graham Brown; *Wine Into Water* . . . (ISD/Intersound)
Wings Of A Dove
Bob Marley & The Wailers; *Birth Of A Legend 1963-1966* . . . (Epic Portrait Assoc.)
Ferlin Husky; *Billboard Top Country Hits-1960-C* . . . (Rhino)
Country Music Classics-#2-1960-1965-C . . . (K-Tel)
Ferlin Husky's Greatest Hits . . . (Curb)
With A Little Help From My Friends
Beatles; *Beatles-Box Set* . . . (Capitol)
Rarities . . . (Capitol)
Sgt. Pepper's Lonely Hearts Club Band . . . (Capitol)
The Beatles/1967-1970 . . . (Capitol)
Joe Cocker; *History Of British Rock-#9-C* . . . (Rhino)
Joe Cocker-Classics-#4 . . . (A&M)
Joe Cocker's Greatest Hits . . . (A&M)
ST/Woodstock . . . (Atlantic)
With A Little Help From My Friends . . . (A&M)
Ringo Starr & His All-Star Band; *Nobody's Child-Romanian Angel Appeal-C* . . . (Warner Bros.)
Without You
Van Halen; *Van Halen 3* . . . (Warner Bros.)
Woman On The Tier (I'll See You Through)
Suzanne Vega; *ST/Dead Man Walking* . . . (Columbia)
Wonderwall
Oasis; *What's The Story Morning Glory?* . . . (Epic)
Work It Out
Def Leppard; *Slang* . . . (Mercury)
You Can Call Me Al
Paul Simon; *Concert In The Park-August 15 1991* . . . (Warner Bros.)
Graceland . . . (Warner Bros.)
Negotiations And Love Songs, 1971-1986 . . . (Warner Bros.)
You Cried Wolf
Todd Rundgren; *Hermit Of Mink Hollow* . . . (Rhino)
Todd Rundgren-Anthology 1968-1985 . . . (Rhino)
You Get What You Give
New Radicals; *Maybe You've Been Brainwashed Too* . . . (MCA)
Now That's What I Call Music!-#2-C . . . (Virgin)
You Won't Ever Be Lonely
Andy Griggs; *Andy Griggs* . . . (RCA)
You Wreck Me
Tom Petty; *Wildflowers* . . . (Warner Bros.)
You'll Be In My Heart
Phil Collins; *ST/Tarzan* . . . (Hollywood)
You'll Never Walk Alone
Andy Williams; *Unchained Melody-Greatest Songs* . . . (Curb)
Jim Nabors; *Jim Nabors-16 Most Requested Songs* . . . (Legacy)
Judy Garland; *Best Of The Capitol Masters-One & Only Box* . . . (Capitol)
Mormon Tabernacle Choir; *Climb Ev'ry Mountain* . . . (Columbia)
Original Broadway Cast; *Carousel* . . . (Angel)
Original Cast; *Carousel* . . . (MCA)
Pink Floyd; *Meddle* . . . (Capitol)
Your Faith In Me
Jessica Simpson; *Sweet Kisses* . . . (Columbia)
You're Not In Kansas Anymore
Jo Dee Messina; *Jo Dee Messina* . . . (Curb)
You've Got A Friend
Barbra Streisand; *Barbra Joan Streisand* . . . (Columbia)
Carole King; *Tapestry* . . . (Epic)
Donny Hathaway & Roberta Flack; *Best Of Donny Hathaway* . . . (Atco)
Jamaica Boys; *J Boys* . . . (Reprise)
James Taylor; *James Taylor's Greatest Hits* . . . (Warner Bros.)
Mud Slide Slim And The Blue Horizon . . . (Warner Bros.)
Michael Jackson; *Got To Be There* . . . (Motown)
Original Soul Of Michael Jackson . . . (Motown)
Roberta Flack & Donny Hathaway; *Best Of Roberta Flack* . . . (Atlantic)
Roberta Flack & Donny Hathaway . . . (Atlantic)
You've Got To Talk To Me
Lee Ann Womack; *Lee Ann Womack* . . . (Decca)

HEROISM

See Also: ***CHARACTER & INTEGRITY, DANGER & DISASTER, FEAR & COURAGE, HELP, PATRIOTISM, WAR, WINNING***

(Man Who Shot) Liberty Valance
Gene Pitney; *Gene Pitney-Anthology 1961-1968* . . . (Rhino)
Gene Pitney's Greatest Hits . . . (Evergreen Music)
Super Oldies Of The '60s-#9-C . . . (Audio Fidelity)
Greg Kihn; *Glass House Rock* . . . (Beserkley)
Abraham, Martin And John
Dion; *Collectables Presents The History Of Rock-#3-C* . . . (Collectables)
Dion-24 Original Classics . . . (Arista)
Songs Of Protest-C . . . (Rhino)
WCBS FM 101 History Of Rock-'60s-#2-C . . . (Collectables)
Harry Belafonte; *Harry Belafonte's All Time Greatest Hits-#1* . . . (RCA)
Smokey Robinson & The Miracles; *Smokey Robinson & The Miracles' Anthology* . . . (Motown)
Time Out For Smokey Robinson & The Miracles/Special Occasion . . . (Motown)

Are You Ready?
Creed; *Human Clay* . . . .(Wind-up)
Ballad Of Davy Crockett
Bill Hayes; *Songs Of The West-#4-Movie & Television Themes-C* . . . . . . (Rhino)
Fess Parker; *16 Most Requested Songs Of The '50s-#1-C* . . . . (Legacy)
   Columbia Country Classics-#3-Americana-C . . . .(Columbia)
   Hollywood Magic-1950s-C . . . .(Columbia)
Kentucky HeadHunters; *Electric Barnyard*. . . . .(Mercury)
Mac Wiseman; *45-#1240*. . . . .(Dot)
Original Soundtrack; *Television's Greatest Hits-#4-Black & White*
   Classics-C . . . .(TVT)
Tennessee Ernie Ford; *Capitol Collectors Series-Tennessee*
   Ernie Ford . . . .(Capitol)
Ballad Of Ira Hayes, The
Johnny Cash; *The Man In Black-His Greatest Hits* . . . . (Legacy)
Peter La Farge; *Best Of Broadside 1962-1968: Anthems Of The American*
   Underground From The Pages Of Broadside
   Magazine-C . . . .(Smithsonian Folkways)
Ballad Of Martin Luther King
Mike Millius; *Best Of Broadside 1962-1968: Anthems Of The American*
   Underground From The Pages Of Broadside
   Magazine-C . . . .(Smithsonian Folkways)
Ballad Of The Green Berets
Barry Sadler; *Cruisin'-1966-C* . . . . (Increase)
   Hits Of The Sixties-C . . . . (Intercom Music)
   More American Graffiti-#4-C . . . . (MCA)
   Nipper's Greatest Hits Of The '60s-#2-C . . . .(RCA)
   Super Hits-#3-C . . . . (Gusto)
Big Bad John
Jimmy Dean; *American Originals-Jimmy Dean* . . . . (Columbia)
   Billboard Top Country Hits-1961-C . . . .(Rhino)
   Columbia Country Classics-#3-Americana-C . . . .(Columbia)
   Jimmy Dean's Greatest Hits . . . .(Columbia)
Big Iron
Marty Robbins; *Columbia Country Classics-#3-Americana-C* . . . . . .(Columbia)
   Gunfighter Ballads & Trail Songs. . . . . (Legacy)
   Marty Robbins' All-Time Greatest Hits . . . .(Columbia)
   Marty Robbins-More Greatest Hits . . . .(Columbia)
Biko
Peter Gabriel; *Peter Gabriel* . . . . (Geffen)
   Peter Gabriel/Plays Live . . . . (Geffen)
   Shaking The Tree-Sixteen Golden Greats. . . . . (Geffen)
Billy Don't Be A Hero
Bo Donaldson & The Heywoods; *Super Hits Of The '70s-Have A Nice*
   Day-#13-C . . . .(Rhino)
Born To Run
Bruce Springsteen; *Born To Run* . . . .(Columbia)
   Chimes Of Freedom . . . .(Columbia)
Bruce Springsteen & The E Street Band; *Bruce Springsteen & The E Street*
   Band Live/1975-85 . . . . (Legacy)
Melissa Etheridge; *The Concert For New York City-C* . . . . (Columbia)
Broken Hearted Savior
Big Head Todd & The Monsters; *Sister Sweetly* . . . . (Giant)
Candle In The Wind 1997
Elton John; *Candle In The Wind 1997 (Diana, Princess Of Wales)*
   (Single) . . . .(Rocket)
Celluloid Heroes
Joan Jett; *The Hit List* . . . . (Epic)
Kinks; *Come Dancing With The Kinks-Best Of The Kinks 1977-1986* . . . (Arista)
   Everybody's In Show-Biz . . . .(Rhino)
   The Kinks' Greatest-Celluloid Heroes . . . .(RCA)
Childhood Hero
Bobby Bare; *Bare* . . . .(Columbia)
Desperados Waiting For A Train
Guy Clark; *Old No. 1* . . . .(Sugar Hill)
Jerry Jeff Walker; *Best Of Jerry Jeff Walker* . . . . (MCA)
   Great Gonzos . . . . (MCA)
   Viva Terlingua . . . . (MCA)
Waylon Jennings, Willie Nelson, Johnny Cash, Kris Kristofferson;
   Highwayman . . . .(Columbia)
   Hot Tracks-Train Super Hits-C . . . . (Epic)
Die With Your Boots On
Iron Maiden; *Live After Death-World Slavery Tour* . . . . (Capitol)
   Piece Of Mind. . . . .(Capitol)
Don Quixote
Gordon Lightfoot; *Gord's Gold*. . . . .(Reprise)
Don Quixote
Nik Kershaw; *The Riddle*. . . . . (MCA)
Eternal Idol
Black Sabbath; *Eternal Idol*. . . . . (Warner Bros.)
Everybody's Hero
Desert Rose Band; *Pages Of Life*. . . . .(Curb)
For You I Will
Monica; *The Boy Is Mine*. . . . . (Arista)
Go The Distance
Michael Bolton; *All That Matters* . . . .(Columbia)
Golden Vanity
Pete Seeger & Arlo Guthrie; *Together In Concert*. . . . .(Reprise)

Gotham City
R. Kelly; *ST/Batman & Robin-Music From And Inspired By The Motion*
   Picture . . . . (Jive)
Greatest Man I Never Knew
Reba McEntire; *For My Broken Heart*. . . . . (MCA)
   Reba McEntire's Greatest Hits Volume Two . . . . (MCA)
Hand Song, The
Nickel Creek; *Nickel Creek* . . . . (Sugar Hill)
Harriet Tubman
Holly Near & Ronnie Gilbert; *Lifeline* . . . .(Redwood)
   Redwood Collection . . . .(Redwood)
Harriet Tubman's Gonna Carry Me Home
Long Ryders; *Two-Fisted Tales* . . . .(Island)
He Walked On Water
Randy Travis; *No Holdin' Back* . . . . (Warner Bros.)
Hero
Kris Kristofferson & The Borderlords; *Third World Warrior* . . . .(Mercury)
Hero
Verve Pipe; *The Verve Pipe* . . . . (RCA)
Hero
Mariah Carey; *America: A Tribute To Heroes-C* . . . . (Interscope)
   Diana, Princess Of Wales-Tribute-C . . . .(Columbia)
   God Bless America-C . . . .(Columbia)
   Mariah Carey-#1's . . . .(Columbia)
   Music Box . . . .(Columbia)
Hero
Enrique Iglesias; *America: A Tribute To Heroes-C* . . . . (Interscope)
   Escape . . . . (Interscope)
Hero
Gladys Knight & The Pips; *Visions* . . . .(Columbia)
Hero #99
Gene Ryder; *Last Cigarette & A Blindfold*. . . . .(Mercury)
Hero Of The Day
Metallica; *Load* . . . .(Elektra)
Hero Takes A Fall
Bangles; *All Over The Place* . . . .(Columbia)
   Bangles' Greatest Hits . . . .(Columbia)
   Bangles-Super Hits . . . .(Legacy)
Hero Worship
B-52's; *B-52's* . . . .(Warner Bros.)
   Wild Planet . . . . (Warner Bros.)
Heroes
Paul Overstreet; *Heroes* . . . . (RCA)
Heroes
David Bowie; *Bridge School Concerts-#1* . . . . (Reprise)
   Changesbowie. . . . .(Rykodisc)
   The Concert For New York City-C . . . .(Columbia)
   The Singles-1969-1993 . . . .(Rykodisc)
Heroes
David & David; *Boomtown* . . . .(A&M)
Heroes
Commodores; *Heroes/Commodores* . . . .(Motown)
Heroes
Wallflowers; *ST/Godzilla-The Album* . . . . (Epic/Sony Music Soundtrax)
Heroes
Johnny Cash & Waylon Jennings; *Heroes* . . . .(Columbia)
Heroes
Waylon Jennings & Willie Nelson; *WWII* . . . . (RCA)
Heroes
Southern Pacific; *Southern Pacific*. . . . . (Warner Bros.)
Heroes & Heroines
Mary Chapin Carpenter; *Hometown Girl*. . . . .(Columbia)
Heroes & Villains
Beach Boys; *Concert/'69-Live In London* . . . .(Capitol)
   Endless Harmony . . . .(Capitol)
   Good Vibrations-Thirty Years Of The Beach Boys . . . .(Capitol)
   Made In The U.S.A. . . . .(Capitol)
   Smiley Smile/Wild Honey . . . .(Capitol)
   Sunshine Dream . . . .(Capitol)
Heroes And Friends
Randy Travis; *Heroes And Friends* . . . . (Warner Bros.)
   Randy Travis' Greatest Hits-#1 . . . . (Warner Bros.)
Heroes Are Hard To Find
Fleetwood Mac; *25 Years-The Chain* . . . . (Warner Bros.)
   Heroes Are Hard To Find . . . . (Reprise)
Heroes Die Young
Sleeze Beez; *Screwed Blued & Tattooed* . . . . (Atlantic)
Heroes Die Young
Waysted; *Save Your Prayers* . . . .(Capitol)
Heroes End
Judas Priest; *Stained Class* . . . .(Columbia)
Holding Out For A Hero
Bonnie Tyler; *ST/Footloose*. . . . .(Columbia)
Hometown Hero
Zamboni Brothers; *The Hockey Zone-C*. . . . . (Sportsongs)
Honky-Tonk Heroes
Billy Joe Shaver; *Rebels, Renegades & Ramblers-C* . . . . (Polydor)
Waylon Jennings; *Outlaws*. . . . . (RCA)

Waylon Jennings' Greatest Hits .... (RCA)

I Made A Fist
Original Broadway Cast; *The Most Happy Fella* .... (Sony Music Classical)

I Saved The World Today
Eurythmics; *Peace* .... (Arista)

I Want To Spend My Lifetime Loving You
Marc Anthony & Tina Arena; *ST/Mask Of Zorro* .... (Sony Music Classical)

I Would Die 4 U
Prince and the Revolution; *ST/Purple Rain* .... (Warner Bros.)

I'm Going To Be A Teenage Idol
Elton John; *Don't Shoot Me I'm Only The Piano Player* .... (Polydor)

Jim Dandy
Black Oak Arkansas; *Best Of Black Oak Arkansas* .... (Atco)
Super Hits Of The '70s-Have A Nice Day-#12-C .... (Rhino)
LaVern Baker; *Atlantic Rhythm & Blues 1947-1974-#3 (1955-1958)-C* .... (Atlantic)

Jukebox Hero
Foreigner; *Classic Rock 1966-1988-C* .... (Atlantic)
Records .... (Atlantic)

Let's Roll
Neil Young; *Let's Roll-CD Single* .... (Reprise)

Lion's Den
Bruce Springsteen; *Tracks* .... (Columbia)

Local Hero
Bruce Springsteen; *Lucky Town* .... (Columbia)

Longest Day
Arthur Fiedler; *Motion Picture Classics-#2* .... (RCA Victor)
Mitch Miller; *Mitch Miller-The Gang & Orchestra-Greatest Hits* ... (Columbia)
Paul Anka; *Paul Anka's 21 Golden Hits* .... (RCA)

Meadowlands
101 Strings Orchestra; *Soul Of Russia* .... (Madacy)
Jefferson Airplane; *Volunteers* .... (RCA)

My Hero
Blue Notes; *Blue Notes-Early Years* .... (Collectables)
Myron Floren; *Memory Waltzes* .... (Ranwood)

My Hero
Foo Fighters; *The Colour And The Shape* .... (Roswell/RCA)

My Heroes Have Always Been Cowboys
Willie Nelson; *All Time Legends Of Country Music-C* ..... (Legacy)
Cowboy Super Hits-C .... (Columbia)
Greatest Country Hits Of The '80s-1980-C .... (Columbia)
Greatest Hits (& Some That Will Be) .... (Columbia)
ST/My Heroes Have Always Been Cowboys .... (RCA)
ST/The Electric Horseman .... (Columbia)

Nietzche's Eyes
Paula Cole; *This Fire* .... (Imago)

Nobody's Hero
Rush; *Counterparts* .... (Atlantic)

Nolan Ryan (He's A Hero To Us All)
Jerry Jeff Walker; *Navajo Rug* .... (Rykodisc)

Real World
Matchbox Twenty; *Yourself Or Someone Like You* .... (Lava)

Remember The Heroes
Sammy Hagar; *Three Lock Box* .... (Geffen)

Resignation Superman
Big Head Todd & The Monsters; *Beautiful World* .... (Revolution)
Live Monsters .... (Revolution)

Ride Of The Valkyries
Vienna Philharmonic Orchestra; *ST/Apocalypse Now* .... (Elektra)

Riding With Private Malone
David Ball; *Amigo* .... (Razor & Tie)

Rosa Parks
Outkast; *Aquemini* .... (LaFace/Arista)

Santa Ana
Bruce Springsteen; *Tracks* .... (Columbia)

Saturday's Heroes
Business; *Business-1979-1989* .... (Blackout!)

Sister Rosa
Neville Brothers; *Yellow Moon* .... (A&M)

Some Gave All
Billy Ray Cyrus; *Some Gave All* .... (Mercury)

Splackavellie
Pressha; *Don't Get It Twisted* .... (Tony Mercedes/LaFace/Arista)

Super Heroes
Original London Cast; *Rocky Horror Show* .... (Rhino)

Superhero
Gary Barlow; *Open Road* .... (Arista)

Superman (It's Not Easy)
Five For Fighting; *America Town* .... (Aware/C2/Columbia)
The Concert For New York City-C .... (Columbia)

Theme From "Batman"
Original Soundtrack; *Television's Greatest Hits-#1-C* .... (TVT)

Theme From "Ben Hur"
BBC Concert Orchestra; *Golden Cinema Classics-#1-The Adventure Film* .... (Bainbridge)

Theme From "Daniel Boone"
Original Soundtrack; *Television's Greatest Hits-#1-C* .... (TVT)

Theme From "Flash Gordon"
Neil Norman; *Greatest Science Fiction Hits-#3-C* .... (Crescendo)

Theme From "Flipper"
Original Soundtrack; *Television's Greatest Hits-#1-C* .... (TVT)

Theme From "Greatest American Hero"
Joey Scarbury; *Television's Greatest Hits-#3-1970s & 1980s-C* .... (TVT)
Tube Tunes-#3-The '70s & '80s-C .... (Rhino)

Theme From "Hogan's Heroes"
Original Soundtrack; *CBS: The First 50 Years* .... (TVT)
Television's Greatest Hits-#2-C .... (TVT)

Theme From "Lassie"
Original Soundtrack; *Television's Greatest Hits-#4-Black & White Classics-C* .... (TVT)

Theme From "Lawrence Of Arabia"
BBC Concert Orchestra; *Golden Cinema Classics-#1-The Adventure Film* .... (Bainbridge)
Cincinnati Pops Orchestra/Erich Kunzel; *Hollywood's Greatest Hits-#1* .... (Telarc)

Theme From "Lois And Clark: The New Adventures Of Superman"
Original Soundtrack; *Television's Greatest Hits-#7-Cable Ready-C* ..... (TVT)

Theme From "Mighty Mouse"
Original Soundtrack; *Television's Greatest Hits-#2-C* .... (TVT)

Theme From "Quantum Leap"
Original Soundtrack; *Sci-Fi's Greatest Hits-#4-Defenders Of Justice* .... (TVT)
Television's Greatest Hits-#7-Cable Ready-C .... (TVT)

Theme From "Rin Tin Tin"
Original Soundtrack; *Television's Greatest Hits-#1-C* .... (TVT)

Theme From "Roger Ramjet"
Original Soundtrack; *Television's Greatest Hits-#4-Black & White Classics-C* .... (TVT)

Theme From "Shaft"
Isaac Hayes; *Isaac Hayes' Greatest Hit Singles* .... (Stax)
Pimps, Players & Private Eyes-C .... (Sire)
Top Of The Stax-Twenty Greatest Hits-C .... (Stax)

Theme From "Space Ghost Coast To Coast"
Original Soundtrack; *Television's Greatest Hits-#7-Cable Ready-C* ..... (TVT)

Theme From "Spiderman"
Original Soundtrack; *Television's Greatest Hits-#2-C* .... (TVT)

Theme From "Superman"
London Symphony Orchestra & John Williams; *ST/Superman-The Movie* .... (Warner Bros.)
Neil Norman; *Greatest Science Fiction Hits* .... (Crescendo)
Original Soundtrack; *Television's Greatest Hits-#1-C* .... (TVT)

Theme From "The Adventures Of Robin Hood"
Original Soundtrack; *Television's Greatest Hits-#2-C* .... (TVT)

Theme From "The A-Team"
Original Soundtrack; *Television's Greatest Hits-#3-1970s & 1980s-C* ... (TVT)

Theme From "The Atom Ant Show"
Original Soundtrack; *Hanna-Barbera Pic-A-Nic Basket Of Cartoon Classics* .... (Kid Rhino/Rhino 4 Kids)
Television's Greatest Hits-#5-In Living Color-C .... (TVT)

Theme From "The Green Hornet"
Original Soundtrack; *Television's Greatest Hits-#2-C* .... (TVT)

Theme From "The Lone Ranger" (William Tell Overture)
Boston Pops Orchestra; *TV Classics-C* .... (RCA)
Boston Pops Orchestra/Arthur Fiedler; *Fiedler-Greatest Hits* .... (RCA)
Original Soundtrack; *Television's Greatest Hits-#7-Cable Ready-C* ..... (TVT)
Spike Jones & His City Slickers; *Best Of Spike Jones & His City Slickers* .... (RCA)

Theme From "The Magnificent Seven"
BBC Concert Orchestra; *Golden Cinema Classics-#1-The Adventure Film* .... (Bainbridge)

Theme From "The Mighty Hercules"
Original Soundtrack; *Television's Greatest Hits-#4-Black & White Classics-C* .... (TVT)

Theme From "The Miss America Pageant" (There She Is, Miss America)
Bert Parks; *Television's Greatest Hits-#4-Black & White Classics-C* ..... (TVT)

Theme From "Underdog"
Original Soundtrack; *Television's Greatest Hits-#2-C* .... (TVT)

Theme From "Wonder Woman"
Original Soundtrack; *Television's Greatest Hits-#3-1970s & 1980s-C* ... (TVT)

Theme From "Zorro"
Original Soundtrack; *Disney Collection-#2-C* .... (Disney)

There's A Hero
Billy Gilman; *God Bless America-C* .... (Columbia)

Time Loves A Hero
Little Feat; *Time Loves A Hero* .... (Warner Bros.)
Waiting For Columbus .... (Warner Bros.)

Utah Carol
Harry K. McClintock; *Cowboy Songs On Folkways-C* .... (Smithsonian Folkways)
Marty Robbins; *Gunfighter Ballads & Trail Songs* .... (Legacy)

Utah Carroll
Skip Gorman; *A Cowboy's Wild Song To His Herd* .... (Rounder)

We Don't Need Another Hero (Thunderdome)
Tina Turner; *Live In Europe* .... (Capitol)
Simply The Best .... (Capitol)

Western Hero
Neil Young & Crazy Horse; *Sleeps With Angels* . . . . (Reprise)
When Heroes Go Down
Suzanne Vega; *99.9 F* . . . . (A&M)
Who Are Your Heroes
Bill Blue; *Givin' Good Boys A Bad Name* . . . . (Adelphi)
Wild West Hero
Electric Light Orchestra; *Out Of The Blue* . . . . (Jet)
Wind Beneath My Wings
Bette Midler; *ST/Beaches* . . . . (Atlantic)
Gary Morris; *Chicken Soup For The Soul: I'll Be There For You-Songs Of
   Friendship, Brotherhood And Sisterhood-C* . . . . (Rhino)
   Country Love Songs-C . . . . (Warner Bros.)
   Gary Morris-Hits . . . . (Warner Bros.)
   Why Lady Why . . . . (Warner Bros.)
James Galway; *Wind Beneath My Wings* . . . . (RCA)
Lee Greenwood; *Somebody's Gonna Love You* . . . . (MCA)
Lou Rawls; *When The Night Comes* . . . . (Epic)
Roger Whittaker; *Roger Whittaker Greatest Hits* . . . . (RCA)
   Wind Beneath My Wings . . . . (RCA)
Willie Nelson; *City Of New Orleans* . . . . (Columbia)
Working Class Hero
John Lennon; *Lennon* . . . . (Capitol)
John Lennon/Plastic Ono Band; *John Lennon/Plastic Ono Band* . . . . . (Capitol)
Marianne Faithfull; *Broken English* . . . . (Island)
Working Class Hero
Alan Jackson; *Don't Rock The Jukebox* . . . . (Arista)
Working Class Hero
Johnny Holm; *Work's Many Voices-#1 & 2-C* . . . . (Arhoolie)
World's Greatest, The
R. Kelly; *ST/Ali* . . . . (Interscope)
Yesterday's Hero
Bay City Rollers; *Bay City Rollers' Greatest Hits* . . . . (Arista)
Yesterday's Hero
Gene Pitney; *Gene Pitney's Greatest Hits* . . . . (Evergreen Music)
You've Got To Be A Football Hero
University Of Michigan Band; *Greatest College Football Marches* . . (Vanguard)

HIDING, Conceal, Sneak

See Also: *CHEATING & LIES, CRIME, ESCAPE, FEAR &
COURAGE, FINDING, LAW & ORDER, LOVE: FORBIDDEN LOVE,
LOW SELF-ESTEEM, PRETEND, REBELS, SEARCH, SECRETS,
TOYS & GAMES*

A World Without Love
Peter And Gordon; *Billboard Top Pop Hits-1964-C* . . . . (Rhino)
Angel's Eye
Aerosmith; *ST/Charlie's Angels* . . . . (Columbia)
Baby's Got A Brand New Baby
S-K-O; *S-K-O* . . . . (MTM)
Backstreets
Bruce Springsteen; *Born To Run* . . . . (Columbia)
Behind The Mask
Fleetwood Mac; *Behind The Mask* . . . . (Warner Bros.)
Blue Mask
Lou Reed; *Blue Mask*. . . . . (RCA)
Bookends
Joe Walsh; *The Smoker You Drink The Player You Get*. . . . . (MCA)
Can't Hide Love
Earth, Wind & Fire; *Best Of Earth, Wind & Fire-#1* . . . . (Legacy)
   Gratitude . . . . (Legacy)
Can't Hide Love
Wayman Tisdale; *Face To Face* . . . . (Atlantic)
Change The Locks
Tom Petty And The Heartbreakers; *ST/She's The One* . . . . (Warner Bros.)
Cover Me
Bruce Springsteen; *Born In The U.S.A.* . . . . (Columbia)
   Music For The Miracle-C . . . . (Epic Portrait Assoc.)
Bruce Springsteen & The E Street Band; *Bruce Springsteen & The E Street
   Band Live/1975-85* . . . . (Legacy)
Cynthia Mask
Robyn Hitchcock; *Eye*. . . . . (Rhino)
Dead Giveaway
Shalamar; *The Look*. . . . . (Solar)
Dead Giveaway
Molly Hatchet; *Take No Prisoners* . . . . (Epic)
Dead Skin Mask
Slayer; *Live-Decade Of Aggression*. . . . . (Def American)
Desperado
Clint Black; *Common Thread-Songs Of The Eagles-C* . . . . (Giant)
Eagles; *Desperado*. . . . . (Asylum)
   Eagles Live . . . . (Asylum)
   Eagles/Their Greatest Hits 1971-1975 . . . . (Asylum)
   Hell Freezes Over . . . . (Geffen)

Linda Ronstadt; *Don't Cry Now*. . . . . (Asylum)
   Linda Ronstadt's Greatest Hits . . . . (Asylum)
Duck And Run
3 Doors Down; *Better Life* . . . . (Republic/Universal)
Elegantly Wasted
INXS; *Elegantly Wasted* . . . . (Mercury)
Eli's Comin'
Laura Nyro; *Eli And The Thirteenth Confession* . . . . (Columbia)
Three Dog Night; *Best Of Three Dog Night* . . . . (MCA)
   Rockin' '60s-C . . . . (Priority)
Everybody's Got Something To Hide Except Me And My Monkey
Beatles; *The Beatles (White Album)*. (Capitol)
Footlights
Merle Haggard; *For The Record: Merle Haggard-43 Legendary Hits*. . . . (BNA)
God's Gonna Get'cha (For That)
George Jones & Tammy Wynette; *George Jones & Tammy Wynette-16
   Biggest Hits* . . . . (Epic/Legacy)
   George Jones & Tammy Wynette's Greatest Hits . . . . (Epic)
Hernando's Hideaway
Original Cast; *Pajama Game* . . . . (Columbia)
   ST/Pajama Game . . . . (Collectables)
Hidden Place
Bjork; *Vespertine*. . . . . (Elektra)
Hide
Link Wray & The Wraymen; *45-#15-2210* . . . . (Epic)
Hide & Go Seek
Big Joe Turner; *Rock This Joint* . . . . (Intermedia)
Hide & Seek
Chuck Mangione; *Evening Of Magic* . . . . (A&M)
   Feels So Good . . . . (A&M)
Hide & Seek
Howard Jones; *Action Replay*. . . . . (Elektra)
   Human's Lib . . . . (Elektra)
Hide & Seek
Bill Haley & His Comets; *Bill Haley & His Comets-Golden Hits* . . . . . . (MCA)
Hide & Seek
Spencer Davis Group; *Greatest & Latest* . . . . (Priority)
Hide In Your Shell
Supertramp; *Crime Of The Century* . . . . (A&M)
   Paris . . . . (A&M)
   Supertramp-Classics-#9 . . . . (A&M)
Hide Your Face
Spade Cooley; *Columbia Historic Edition-Spade Cooley* . . . . (Columbia)
Hide Your Love
Rolling Stones; *Goats Head Soup* . . . . (Rolling Stones)
Hideaway
Creedence Clearwater Revival; *1970*. . . . . (Fantasy)
   Creedence Clearwater Revival-Chronicle-#2. . . . . (Fantasy)
   Pendulum . . . . (Fantasy)
David Sanborn; *Casino Lights-Live At Montreux* . . . . (Warner Bros.)
   Hideaway . . . . (Warner Bros.)
   Straight To The Heart . . . . (Warner Bros.)
Freddie King; *Cruisin'-1961-C* . . . . (Increase)
John Mayall; *Down The Line* . . . . (London)
Hideaway
Beat Farmers; *Poor & Famous*. . . . . (Curb)
Hideaway
Todd Rundgren; *Ever Popular Tortured Artist Effect* . . . . (Rhino)
   Todd Rundgren-Anthology 1968-1985 . . . . (Rhino)
Hidin' From Love
Bryan Adams; *Bryan Adams* . . . . (A&M)
Hidin' Out
Patsy Cline; *Walkin' Dreams-Her First Recordings-#1*. . . . . (Rhino)
Hidin' Out
Pete Townshend; *White City* . . . . (Atco)
Hidin' Places
Shylo; *45-#811097-7* . . . . (Mercury)
Hill Where The Lord Hides
Chuck Mangione; *Best Of Chuck Mangione* . . . . (Mercury)
   Best Of Chuck Mangione . . . . (A&M)
   Chuck Mangione-Classics-#6 . . . . (A&M)
   Evening Of Magic . . . . (A&M)
   Friends & Love . . . . (Mercury)
   Together . . . . (Mercury)
House With No Curtains
Alan Jackson; *Everything I Love* . . . . (Arista)
How Did I Get By Without You
John Waite; *Complete John Waite-#1-Falling Backwards* . . . . (EMI)
   Temple Bar . . . . (Coyote/Imago)
Hypnotize The Moon
Clay Walker; *Hypnotize The Moon* . . . . (Giant)
I Am Not Hiding
Kenny Loggins; *The Unimaginable Life* . . . . (Columbia)
I Never Go Around Mirrors
Lefty Frizzell; *Grand Ole Opry-75 Years-#1-C* . . . . (MCA)
I Think We're Alone Now
Tiffany; *Tiffany* . . . . (MCA)
   Tiffany's Greatest Hits . . . . (Hip-O)

Tommy James And The Shondells; *Best Of Tommy James And The Shondells*. . . . . (Roulette)
Billboard Top Rock 'N' Roll Hits-1967-C . . . . (Rhino)
Tommy James And The Shondells-Anthology . . . . (Rhino)

I Want To Hold Your Hand
Beatles; *Beatles 1* . . . . (Capitol)
Beatles-20 Greatest Hits . . . . (Capitol)
Meet The Beatles! . . . . (Capitol)
Past Masters-Volume One . . . . (Parlophone)
The Beatles/1962-1966 . . . . (Capitol)
Lakeside; *Galactic Grooves/Best Of Lakeside* . . . . . (Right Stuff)
Your Wish Is My Command . . . . (Solar)

I'll Cry Instead
Beatles; *Beatles-Box Set* . . . . (Capitol)
Something New . . . . (Capitol)
ST/A Hard Day's Night . . . . (Capitol)

In Hiding
Pearl Jam; *Yield* . . . . (Epic)

In The Closet
Michael Jackson; *Dangerous* . . . . (Epic)

Keep Searchin' (We'll Follow The Sun)
Del Shannon; *Del Shannon's Greatest Hits* . . . . (Rhino)
Del Shannon's Greatest Hits . . . . (Curb)

Lady Picture Show
Stone Temple Pilots; *Tiny Music...Songs From The Vatican Gift Shop* . . . . (Atlantic)

Love Hides
Doors; *Absolutely Live* . . . . (Elektra)

Love Sneakin' Up On You
Bonnie Raitt; *Longing In Their Hearts* . . . . (Capitol)

Make Me A Mask
Fleetwood Mac; *25 Years-The Chain* . . . . (Warner Bros.)

Married But Not To Each Other
Barbara Mandrell; *Best Of Barbara Mandrell* . . . . (MCA)
Lovers, Friends & Strangers . . . . (MCA)
Midnight Angel . . . . (MCA)

Mask
Bauhaus; *Mask* . . . . (Beggar's Banquet)

Mask, The
Fugees; *The Score* . . . . (Ruffhouse)

My Favorite Headache
Geddy Lee; *My Favorite Headache* . . . . (Anthem/Atlantic)

Night Has A Thousand Eyes
Anita O'Day; *Night Has A Thousand Eyes* . . . . (Emily)
Bobby Vee; *Best Of Bobby Vee*. . . . . (EMI)
Bobby Vee-Legendary Masters . . . . (EMI)
Golden Years-1962-C . . . . (Dominion Entert.)

Nowhere To Run
Isley Brothers; *This Old Heart Of Mine* . . . . (Motown)
Martha & The Vandellas; *Martha Reeves & The Vandellas' Greatest Hits* . . . . (Motown)
Martha Reeves & The Vandellas-Anthology . . . . (Motown)
Motown Story-First 25 Years-C . . . . (Motown)
Motown Superstar Series-#11-Martha Reeves & The Vandellas . . . . (Motown)
ST/Sound Of "Murphy Brown" . . . . (MCA)

Nowhere To Run
Esther Phillips; *A Way To Say Goodbye* . . . . (Muse)

Nowhere To Run
J.J. Cale; *Naturally* . . . . (MCA)

Nowhere To Run
Pete Townshend & Ronnie Lane; *Rough Mix* . . . . . . (Atlantic)

Nowhere To Run
Santana; *Shango* . . . . (Columbia)

Octopus's Garden
Beatles; *Abbey Road*. . . . . (Parlophone)
Beatles-Box Set . . . . (Capitol)
The Beatles/1967-1970 . . . . (Capitol)

One Piece At A Time
Johnny Cash; *The Man In Black-His Greatest Hits*. . . . (Legacy)

Open Up Your Eyes
Tonic; *Lemon Parade* . . . . (Polydor)

Pair Of Old Sneakers
George Jones; *George Jones & Tammy Wynette-16 Biggest Hits*. . . . . (Epic/Legacy)

Peek A Boo
Cadillacs; *Best Of The Cadillacs*. . . . . (Rhino)

Peek-A-Boo
Siouxsie And The Banshees; *Peepshow* . . . . (Geffen)
Twice Upon A Time-The Singles . . . . (Geffen)

Peek-A-Boo!
Devo; *Best Of Devo-Greatest Hits*. . . . . (Warner Bros.)
EZ Listening Disc. . . . . (Rykodisc)
Oh No! It's Devo . . . . (Warner Bros.)

Prisoner In Disguise
Linda Ronstadt; *Different Drum* . . . . (Capitol)

R&B Skeletons (In The Closet)
George Clinton; *R&B Skeletons (In The Closet)* . . . . . (Capitol)

Razorblades
Chris Stills; *100 Year Thing* . . . . (Atlantic)

Reflection
Christina Aguilera; *Christina Aguilera* . . . . (RCA)
ST/Mulan . . . . (Walt Disney)

Say My Name
Destiny's Child; *The Writing's On The Wall*. . . . . (Columbia)

Secret Mountain Hideout
Michael Martin Murphey; *Blue Sky-Night Thunder* . . . . . (Epic)

Secret Place
Megadeth; *Cryptic Writings* . . . . (Capitol)

She Wore A Yellow Ribbon
Mitch Miller; *Sing Along With Mitch* . . . . (Columbia)

Shelf In The Room
Days Of The New; *Days Of The New* . . . . (Outpost/Interscope)

Sleeping With Your Devil Mask
Robyn Hitchcock; *Globe Of Frogs* . . . . (A&M)

Slip Away
Clarence Carter; *Billboard Top Pop Hits-1968-C* . . . . . . (Rhino)
Snatching It Back-The Best Of Clarence Carter. . . . . . . (Rhino)

Slippin' And Slidin'
Little Richard; *Little Richard-18 Greatest Hits* . . . . (Rhino)

Smokescreen
Ted Nugent; *Weekend Warriors* . . . . (Epic)

Smoky Places
Corsairs; *Best Of Chess Rhythm & Blues-#1-C* . . . . . . (Chess)
Hard To Find Hits Of Rock 'N Roll-#1-C . . . . (Curb)

Sneakin' Around
B.B. King; *B.B. King-16 Original Big Hits* . . . . (Fantasy)
Chet Atkins & Jerry Reed; *Sneakin' Around* . . . . . . (Columbia)
Dolly Parton & Burt Reynolds; *ST/Best Little Whorehouse In Texas* . . . . (MCA)
Little Milton; *Little Milton Sings Big Blues* . . . . (Chess)

Sneakin' Sally Through The Alley
Robert Palmer; *Addictions-#2* . . . . (Island)
Sneakin' Sally Through The Alley . . . . (Island)

Sometimes
Britney Spears; *...Baby One More Time* . . . . (Jive)
Now That's What I Call Music!-#3-C . . . . (Virgin)

Somewhere They Can't Find Me
Simon & Garfunkel; *Collected Works*. . . . . (Columbia)
Sounds Of Silence . . . . (Columbia)

Theme From "Candid Camera"
Original Soundtrack; *Television's Greatest Hits-#4-Black & White Classics-C* . . . . (TVT)

Theme From "The Lone Ranger" (William Tell Overture)
Boston Pops Orchestra; *TV Classics-C* . . . . (RCA)
Boston Pops Orchestra/Arthur Fiedler; *Fiedler-Greatest Hits* . . . (RCA)
Original Soundtrack; *Television's Greatest Hits-#7-Cable Ready-C* . . . . . (TVT)
Spike Jones & His City Slickers; *Best Of Spike Jones & His City Slickers* . . . . (RCA)

There Ain't Nobody Here But Us Chickens
Original London Cast; *Five Guys Named Moe* . . . . (Relativity)

Time To Hide
Wings; *Wings At The Speed Of Sound* . . . . (Capitol)
Wings Over America . . . . (Capitol)

Trouble's Back In Town
Wilburn Brothers; *Wilburn Brothers*. . . . . (First Generation)

Tryin' To Hide A Fire In The Dark
Billy Dean; *Fire In The Dark*. . . . . (Liberty)

Two Faces Have I
Lou Christie; *Back To The '60s-#4-C* . . . . . . (Dominion Entert.)
Enlightnin'ment-Best Of Lou Christie . . . . (Rhino)

Under The Boardwalk
Bette Midler; *ST/Beaches* . . . . (Atlantic)
Bruce Willis; *Return Of Bruno* . . . . (Motown)
Drifters; *Atlantic Rhythm & Blues 1947-1974-#5 (1962-1966)-C* . . . . . (Atlantic)
Drifters-16 Greatest Hits . . . . (Trip)
Drifters-Golden Hits . . . . (Atlantic)
Super Oldies Of The '60s-#5-C . . . . (Audio Fidelity)
John Mellencamp; *Rough Harvest* . . . . (Mercury)
Lynn Anderson; *What She Does Best* . . . . (Mercury)
Rickie Lee Jones; *Girl At Her Volcano* . . . . (Warner Bros.)
Rolling Stones; *12 X 5* . . . . (Abkco)
Untouchables; *Agent Double O Soul* . . . . (Restless)

We Hide & Seek
Jerry Douglas; *Slide Rule* . . . . (Sugar Hill)

We Kiss In A Shadow
Barbra Streisand; *The Broadway Album* . . . . (Columbia)
Original Broadway Cast; *The King And I* . . . . (RCA Victor)
Original Cast; *The King And I* . . . . (MCA)

What's Behind The Mask
Cramps; *Songs The Lord Taught Us* . . . . (I.R.S.)

When She Cries
Restless Heart; *Big Iron Horses* . . . . (RCA)
Restless Heart's Greatest Hits . . . . (RCA)
Today's Number One Country-C . . . . (K-Tel)

Who's Cheatin' Who
Alan Jackson; *Everything I Love* . . . . (Arista)

Word Games
Billy Walker; *45-#10205*. . . . . (RCA)

Lovin' and Losin' . . . . (RCA)

World Without Love, A
Peter And Gordon; *Billboard Top Pop Hits-1964-C* . . . . (Rhino)
History Of British Rock-#1-C . . . . (Rhino)
Peter & Gordon's Greatest Hits . . . . (CEMA Special Prod.)

Yesterday
Beatles; *"Yesterday"...And Today* . . . . (Capitol)
Beatles 1 . . . . (Capitol)
Beatles-20 Greatest Hits . . . . (Capitol)
Beatles-Box Set . . . . (Capitol)
Beatles-Love Songs . . . . (Capitol)
Compact Disc Singles Collection . . . . (Capitol)
The Beatles/1962-1966 . . . . (Capitol)
Elvis Presley; *On Stage-February, 1970* . . . . (RCA)
En Vogue; *Funky Divas* . . . . (East West)
Frank Sinatra; *My Way* . . . . (Reprise)
Paul McCartney; *The Concert For New York City-C* . . . . (Columbia)
Placido Domingo; *Domingo Songbook* . . . . (Sony Music Classical)
Ray Charles; *Ray Charles-His Greatest Hits-#1* . . . . (Dunhill Compact Classics)
Supremes; *I Hear A Symphony* . . . . (Motown)
Wings; *Wings Over America* . . . . (Capitol)

You Better Run
Pat Benatar; *Crimes Of Passion* . . . . (Chrysalis)
ST/Roadie . . . . (Warner Bros.)

You Can't Run Away From Your Heart
Lacy J. Dalton; *Dream Baby* . . . . (Columbia)
Patty Loveless; *On Down The Line* . . . . (MCA)

You Can't Run From Love
Eddie Rabbitt; *Best Of Eddie Rabbitt/Greatest Hits-II* . . . . (Warner Bros.)
Eddie Rabbitt-#1's . . . . (Warner Bros.)
Radio Romance . . . . (Elektra)

Your Eyes
Xscape; *Traces Of My Lipstick* . . . . (So So Def/Columbia)

You've Got To Hide Your Love Away
Beatles; *Beatles-Box Set* . . . . (Capitol)
Beatles-Love Songs . . . . (Capitol)
Reel Music . . . . (Capitol)
ST/Help! . . . . (Capitol)
The Beatles/1962-1966 . . . . (Capitol)

You've Lost That Lovin' Feelin'
Daryl Hall & John Oates; *Voices* . . . . (RCA)
Righteous Brothers; *Best Of The Righteous Brothers* . . . . (Curb)
Billboard Top Rock 'N' Roll Hits-1965-C . . . . (Rhino)
Cruisin'-1965-C . . . . (Increase)
Unchained Melody-Very Best Of The Righteous Brothers . . . . (Polydor)

HIPPIES

See Also: **BROTHERHOOD, CITIES: SAN FRANCISCO, COOL, DRAFT, DRUGS (various), PEACE, POLITICS (various), PROTEST**

Alice's Restaurant Massacree
Arlo Guthrie; *Alice's Restaurant* . . . . (Reprise)
Best Of Arlo Guthrie . . . . (Warner Bros.)

Arizona
Mark Lindsay; *Super Hits Of The '70s-Have A Nice Day-#1-C* . . . . (Rhino)

Hair
Cowsills; *Billboard Top Rock 'N' Roll Hits-1969-C* . . . . (Rhino)
Original Broadway Cast; *Hair* . . . . (RCA)

Harry The Hippie
Bobby Womack; *Bobby Womack Greatest Hits* . . . . (Liberty)
Soul Survivor . . . . (EMI)

Hippie
Blues Traveler; *Live From The Fall* . . . . (A&M)

Hippie Crash Pad
Jump With Joey; *Ska-Ba* . . . . (Rykodisc)

Hippie Dream
Neil Young; *Landing On Water* . . . . (Geffen)
Lucky Thirteen . . . . (Geffen)

Hippie Killer
Suicidal Tendencies; *Freedumb* . . . . (Side One)

Hippie With A Banjo
Those Darn Accordions!; *Clownhead* . . . . (Globe)

Hippies On A Corner
Joe Sample; *Best Of Joe Sample* . . . . (Warner Bros.)
Old Places, Old Faces . . . . (Warner Bros.)

Hippietown
Ugly Americans; *Boom Boom Baby* . . . . (Capricorn)

Hippy Fascist
Pulkas; *Earache Presents Earplugged 2-C* . . . . (Earache)
Greed . . . . (Earache)

Love Is A Good Thing
Sheryl Crow; *Sheryl Crow* . . . . (A&M)

Motorcycle Cowboy
Merle Haggard; *Merle Haggard-Live At Billy Bob's* . . . . (Razor & Tie)

Redneck In A Rock & Roll Bar
Jerry Reed; *Redneck Mothers-C* . . . . (RCA)

San Francisco (Be Sure To Wear Some Flowers In Your Hair)
Scott McKenzie; *Nuggets-#10-Folk Rock-C* . . . . (Rhino)
Rock Artifacts-From The Vaults-#3-C . . . . (Columbia)
ST/Forrest Gump . . . . (Epic/Sony Music Soundtrax)
Summer Of Love-#1-C . . . . (Rhino)

Signs
Five Man Electrical Band; *Songs Of Protest-C* . . . . (Rhino)

Uneasy Rider
Charlie Daniels Band; *A Decade Of Hits* . . . . (Epic)
Homesick Heroes . . . . (Epic)
Super Hits Of The '70s-Have A Nice Day-#11-C . . . . (Rhino)
Uneasy Rider . . . . (Epic)

Walkin' On The Sun
Smash Mouth; *Fush Yu Mang* . . . . (Interscope)

Woodstock
Crosby, Stills & Nash; *CSN* . . . . (Atlantic)
Crosby, Stills, Nash & Young; *Deja Vu* . . . . (Atlantic)
So Far . . . . (Atlantic)
Joni Mitchell; *Ladies Of The Canyon* . . . . (Reprise)
Shadows & Light . . . . (Asylum)
Joni Mitchell with Tom Scott & The L.A. Express; *Miles Of Aisles* . . . . (Asylum)

HISPANIC, Spanish

See Also: **COUNTRIES: MEXICO, COUNTRIES: SPAIN**

God Don't Make Lonely Girls
Wallflowers; *Bringing Down The Horse* . . . . (Interscope)

I Wonder Why She Kept On Saying "Si-Si-Si-Si Senor"
Al Jolson; *Music From The New York Stage (1890-1920)-#4-1917-1920-C* . . . . (Pearl)

New Spanish Two-Step
Bob Wills & His Texas Playboys; *Country Music Classics-#14-1940s-C* . . . . (K-Tel)
Essential Bob Wills & His Texas Playboys-1935-1973 . . . . (Legacy)

Shake Your Bon-Bon
Ricky Martin; *Ricky Martin* . . . . (Columbia)

Spanish Bombs
Clash; *London Calling* . . . . (Epic)
On Broadway . . . . (Epic)
The Story Of The Clash, Volume 1 . . . . (Epic)

Spanish Boots
Jeff Beck Group; *Beck-Ola* . . . . (Epic)

Spanish Caravan
Doors; *Best Of The Doors* . . . . (Elektra)
Live At The Hollywood Bowl . . . . (Elektra)
Waiting For The Sun . . . . (Elektra)
Weird Scenes Inside The Gold Mine . . . . (Elektra)

Spanish Castle Magic
Jimi Hendrix; *Axis: Bold As Love* . . . . (Reprise)
Lifelines/Jimi Hendrix Story . . . . (Reprise)
Live At Winterland . . . . (Rykodisc)
Jimi Hendrix Experience; *Radio One* . . . . (Rykodisc)

Spanish Dance
John Fahey; *Death Chants, Breakdowns & Military Waltzes* . . . . . . (Takoma)

Spanish Dancer
Steve Winwood; *Arc Of A Diver* . . . . (Island)
Steve Winwood-Chronicles . . . . (Island)

Spanish Eddie
Laura Branigan; *Hold Me* . . . . (Atlantic)

Spanish Entomologist
Leo Kottke; *Best Of Leo Kottke* . . . . (Capitol)
Greenhouse . . . . (Capitol)
Very Best Of Leo Kottke . . . . (Capitol)

Spanish Eyes
Al Martino; *Best Of Al Martino* . . . . (Capitol)
Capitol Collectors Series-Al Martino . . . . (Capitol)
Spanish Eyes . . . . (Capitol)
Buddy Merrill; *Buddy Merrill's All-Time Hits* . . . . (Accent)
Engelbert Humperdinck; *Engelbert Humperdinck-16 Most Requested Songs* . . . . (Epic)
Live In Concert/All Of Me . . . . (Epic)
Man Without Love . . . . (Mercury)

Spanish Eyes
U2; *Joshua Tree* . . . . (Island)

Spanish Fandango
Chet Atkins; *Pickin' My Way-In Hollywood Alone* . . . . (Mobile Fidelity Sound Lab)
Mississippi John Hurt; *Best Of Mississippi John Hurt* . . . . (Vanguard)

Spanish Fandango
Bob Wills & His Texas Playboys; *Bob Wills & His Texas Playboys-24 Great Hits* . . . . (Polydor)

Spanish Flea
Herb Alpert & The Tijuana Brass; *Going Places* . . . . (A&M)
Herb Alpert & The Tijuana Brass' Greatest Hits . . . . (A&M)
Herb Alpert & The Tijuana Brass-Classics-#1 . . . . (A&M)

Spanish Fly
Van Halen; *Van Halen II* . . . . (Warner Bros.)

Spanish Guitar
Squeeze; *Picadilly Collection* .... (A&M)
Spanish Guitar
Toni Braxton; *The Heat* .... (LaFace)
Spanish Harlem
Aretha Franklin; *Aretha Franklin-30 Greatest Hits* .... (Rhino)
  Best Of Aretha Franklin .... (Atlantic)
  Ten Years Of Gold .... (Atlantic)
Ben E. King; *Ben E. King's Greatest Hits* .... (Atco)
  Phil Spector-Back To Mono 1958-1969-C .... (Abkco)
Crusaders; *Crusaders-At Their Best* .... (Motown)
Drifters; *Drifters' Greatest Hits* .... (Gusto)
Spanish Harlem Incident
Bob Dylan; *Another Side Of Bob Dylan* .... (Columbia)
Byrds; *Mr. Tambourine Man* .... (Columbia)
  The Byrds .... (Columbia)
Spanish Is The Loving Tongue
Bob Dylan; *Dylan* .... (Columbia)
Emmylou Harris; *Cimarron* .... (Warner Bros.)
  Evangeline .... (Warner Bros.)
Ian & Sylvia; *Four Strong Winds* .... (Vanguard)
Ian & Sylvia's *Greatest Hits* .... (Vanguard)
Michael Martin Murphey; *Cowboy Songs* .... (Warner Western)
Spanish Jam
Grateful Dead; *Dick's Picks-#12* .... (Grateful Dead)
Spanish Key
Miles Davis; *Bitches Brew* .... (Columbia)
Spanish Lady
John Handy; *Monterey* .... (Columbia)
Spanish Moon
Little Feat; *Feats Don't Fail Me Now* .... (Warner Bros.)
  Waiting For Columbus .... (Warner Bros.)
Robert Palmer; *Some People Can Do What They Like* ... (Island)
Spanish Panic
Original Cast; *Once Upon A Mattress* .... (MCA)
Spanish Pipedream
John Prine; *John Prine* .... (Atlantic)
Spanish Rose
Santana; *Inner Secrets* .... (Columbia)
Spanish Rose
Van Morrison; *Bang Masters* .... (Epic)
Spanish Stroll
Mink De Ville; *Savoire Faire* .... (Capitol)
Spanish Town
Garland Jeffreys; *Ghost Writer* .... (A&M)
  Matador & More .... (A&M)
Spanish Two Step
Bob Wills; *Bob Wills-Anthology* .... (Sony Music Special Prod.)
Theme From "Chico And The Man"
Original Soundtrack; *Television's Greatest Hits-#5-In Living Color-C* ... (TVT)
Theme From "Zorro"
Original Soundtrack; *Disney Collection-#2-C* .... (Disney)

HISTORY, Old-fashioned, Past, Tradition

See Also: AGING, FUTURE, LOVE: LONG GONE, MONTHS & DATES (various), OLD, POLITICS (various), REMEMBER, TIME: GENERAL, TIME: SPECIFIC, WAR, YEARS: GENERAL, YEARS: SPECIFIC, YESTERDAY

(Just Like) Romeo & Juliet
Reflections; *'60s Dance Party-C* .... (Dominion Entert.)
  Sensational '60s#-1-C .... (Dominion Entert.)
1913 Massacre
Arlo Guthrie; *Hobo's Lullaby* .... (Reprise)
Jack Elliot; *Tribute To Woody Guthrie-C* .... (Warner Bros.)
Ramblin' Jack Elliott; *Greatest Songs Of Woody Guthrie-C* ...... (Vanguard)
Woody Guthrie; *Struggle* .... (Smithsonian Folkways)
Abigail Beecher
Freddy Cannon; *14 Booming Hits* .... (Rhino)
  Big Blast From Boston: The Best Of Freddy "Boom Boom" Cannon .... (Rhino)
Abolitionist Hymn
Hermes Nye; *Ballads Of The Civil War-#1 & 2* .... (Smithsonian Folkways)
All Those Yesterdays
Pearl Jam; *Yield* .... (Epic)
American Pie
Don McLean; *American Pie* .... (EMI)
  Best Of Don McLean .... (EMI)
  Greatest Hits Then & Now .... (EMI)
  ST/Born On The Fourth Of July .... (MCA)
Madonna; *ST/The Next Big Thing* .... (Maverick)
Anne Frank Story
Human Sexual Response; *Fig. 15* .... (Eat)
April The 14th, Part 1
Gillian Welch; *Time (The Revelator)* .... (Acony)

Ballad Of Davy Crockett
Bill Hayes; *Songs Of The West-#4-Movie & Television Themes-C* ..... (Rhino)
Fess Parker; *16 Most Requested Songs Of The '50s-#1-C* .... (Legacy)
  Columbia Country Classics-#3-Americana-C .... (Columbia)
  Hollywood Magic-1950s-C .... (Columbia)
Kentucky HeadHunters; *Electric Barnyard* .... (Mercury)
Mac Wiseman; *45-#1240* .... (Dot)
Original Soundtrack; *Television's Greatest Hits-#4-Black & White Classics-C* .... (TVT)
Tennessee Ernie Ford; *Capitol Collectors Series-Tennessee Ernie Ford* .... (Capitol)
Ballad Of Ira Hayes, The
Johnny Cash; *The Man In Black-His Greatest Hits* .... (Legacy)
Peter La Farge; *Best Of Broadside 1962-1968: Anthems Of The American Underground From The Pages Of Broadside Magazine-C* .... (Smithsonian Folkways)
Battle Of Bunker Hill
Jim Burroughs; *Songs Of Rebellion* .... (Audio Fidelity)
Battle Of New Orleans
Chet Atkins & The Boston Pops; *Best Of Chet Atkins & The Boston Pops* .... (RCA)
Johnny Horton; *American Originals-Johnny Horton* .... (Columbia)
  Johnny Horton's Greatest Hits .... (Columbia)
  Radio Classics Of The '50s-C .... (Columbia)
Nitty Gritty Dirt Band; *Dirt, Silver & Gold* .... (One Way)
  Dream .... (United Artists)
  Stars And Stripes Forever .... (Capitol)
Battle Of Trenton
Jim Burroughs; *Songs Of Rebellion* .... (Audio Fidelity)
Beat Goes On, The
Sonny & Cher; *Best Of Sonny & Cher* .... (Atco)
  Hit Singles-1958-1977-C .... (Atlantic)
  Sonny & Cher-Live .... (MCA)
  The Beat Goes On-Best Of Sonny & Cher .... (Rhino)
  Two Of Us .... (Atco)
Biggest Thing That Man Has Ever Done (Great Historical Bum)
Tom Paxton; *Tribute To Woody Guthrie-C* .... (Warner Bros.)
Brown Eyed Handsome Man
Buddy Holly; *Buddy Holly-20 Golden Greats* .... (MCA)
  For The First Time Anywhere .... (MCA)
  Rock & Roll Collection .... (MCA)
Chuck Berry; *Best Of The Best Of Chuck Berry* .... (International Mktg. Group)
  Roll Over Beethoven .... (Allegiance)
  The Chess Box-Chuck Berry .... (Chess)
Waylon Jennings; *Essential Waylon Jennings* .... (RCA)
  Waylon Jennings-Super Hits .... (RCA)
Carrion
Fiona Apple; *Tidal* .... (Clean Slate/Work)
Country Comfort
Earl Scruggs & Elton John; *Earl Scruggs And Friends-C* ..... (MCA)
Elton John; *Tumbleweed Connection* .... (Polydor)
Rod Stewart; *Best Of Rod Stewart-#2* .... (Mercury)
  Gasoline Alley .... (Mercury)
  Sing It Again, Rod .... (Mercury)
Cowards Over Pearl Harbor
Wilma Lee Cooper; *Wilma Lee Cooper* .... (Rounder)
Distant Melody
Original Cast/Mary Martin; *Peter Pan-The 1954 Broadway Production* .... (RCA Victor)
Done With Bonaparte
Mark Knopfler; *Golden Heart* .... (Warner Bros.)
Flood Of '57
Stanley Brothers & The Clinch Mountain Boys; *Classic Bluegrass-Stanley Brothers & The Clinch Mountain Boys* .... (Rebel)
Flood Of '93
David Olney; *High, Wide And Lonesome* .... (Philo)
Galveston Flood
Tom Rush; *Best Of Tom Rush: No Regrets* .... (Legacy)
Granada
Frankie Laine; *Frankie Laine's Greatest Hits* .... (Columbia)
Heritage
Earth, Wind & Fire; *Featuring The Boyz-Heritage* .... (Columbia)
I Don't Want To Wait
Paula Cole; *Live On Letterman-From The Late Show* .... (Reprise)
  Songs From Dawson's Creek .... (Sony Music Soundtrax)
  This Fire .... (Imago)
I Watched It All (On My Radio)
Lionel Cartwright; *I Watched It All On The Radio* .... (MCA)
If I Could Turn Back The Hands Of Time
R. Kelly; *Now That's What I Call Music!-#3-C* .... (Virgin)
  R. .... (Jive)
If I Could Turn Back Time
Cher; *Heart Of Stone* .... (Geffen)
Indian Reservation (The Lament Of The Cherokee Reservation Indian)
Don Fardon; *45-#408* .... (GNP/Crescendo)
Raiders; *Billboard Top Rock 'N' Roll Hits-1971-C* .... (Rhino)
  Legend Of Paul Revere And The Raiders .... (Columbia)
  Pop Classics Of The '70s-C .... (Columbia)
  Super Hits Of The '70s-Have A Nice Day-#5-C .... (Rhino)

It's All Been Done
Barenaked Ladies; *Stunt* . . . . (Reprise)
John Brown's Body
Pete Seeger; *American Favorite Ballads-#3* . . . . (Smithsonian Folkways)
Sonny Terry & Brownie McGhee; *Every Tone A
Testimony-C*. . . . .(Smithsonian Folkways)
Jumper
Third Eye Blind; *Third Eye Blind* . . . . (Elektra)
Totally Hits-#1-C . . . . (Arista)
Kids Of The Baby Boom
Bellamy Brothers; *Bellamy Brothers' Greatest Hits-#3* . . . . (MCA)
Country Rap . . . . (MCA)
MCA #1 Hits Of The '80s-#3-C . . . . (MCA Special Prod.)
Kiss Your Past Good-Bye
Aerosmith; *Nine Lives* . . . . (Columbia)
Lady Godiva
Peter And Gordon; *History Of British Rock-#4-C* . . . . (Rhino)
Last Cowboy Song
Ed Bruce; *16 Top Country Hits-#2-C* . . . . (MCA)
Ed Bruce's Greatest Hits . . . . (MCA)
Waylon Jennings, Willie Nelson, Johnny Cash, Kris Kristofferson; *Cowboy
Super Hits-C* . . . . (Columbia)
Highwayman . . . . (Columbia)
Leaving October
Sons Of The Desert; *Whatever Comes First* . . . . (Epic)
Legend Of A Cowgirl
Imani Coppola; *Chupacapra* . . . . (Columbia)
Little Chicago Fire
Count Basie & His Orchestra; *Live At El Morocco* . . . . (Telarc)
Little Man
Alan Jackson; *High Mileage* . . . . (Arista)
Long Ago And Far Away
Erroll Garner; *Long Ago And Far Away* . . . . (Columbia)
Glenn Miller; *Glenn Miller-A Legendary Performer-#1 & 2.* . . . . (Bluebird)
Helen Forrest & Dick Haymes; *American Songbook Series-
Jerome Kern.* . . . . (Smithsonian Collection)
Jo Stafford; *Capitol Collectors Series-Jo Stafford.* . . . . (Capitol)
International Hits . . . . (Corinthian)
Jukebox Saturday Night-Great Vocal Hits-C . . . . (Capitol)
Songs That Got Us Through WWII-C . . . . (Rhino)
ST/Bugsy . . . . (Epic)
Johnny Mathis; *Hollywood Musicals.* . . . . (Columbia)
Mantovani; *More Golden Hits.* . . . . (London)
Perry Como; *Always In My Heart-Classic Songs Of World War II-#2* . . . .(RCA)
Rosemary Clooney; *Rosemary Clooney Sings The Lyrics Of Ira
Gershwin* . . . . (Concord Jazz)
Long Time Ago
Remingtons; *Blue Frontier* . . . . (BNA)
Lost You In The Canyon
Marc Cohn; *Burning The Daze* . . . . (Atlantic)
My Heart Has A History
Paul Brandt; *Calm Before The Storm.* . . . .(Reprise)
New York Mining Disaster 1941 (Mr. Jones)
Bee Gees; *Bee Gees-Gold* . . . . (Polydor)
Here At Last...Bee Gees...Live . . . . (Polydor)
History Of British Rock-#8-C . . . . (Rhino)
Night In Summer Long Ago
Mark Knopfler; *Golden Heart* . . . . (Warner Bros.)
Night They Invented Champagne
Betty Wand/Louis Jordan/Others; *ST/Gigi* . . . . (Sony Music Special Prod.)
Original Cast; *Gigi.* . . . . (RCA Victor)
No Future In The Past
Vince Gill; *I Still Believe In You* . . . . (MCA)
Nothing As Original As You
Statler Brothers; *The Originals* . . . . (Mercury)
Old Days/Old Ways
Ronnie Laws; *Dream A Little* . . . . (HDH)
Old Fashioned Love
Asleep At The Wheel featuring Suzy Bogguss; *Tribute To The Music Of Bob
Wills And The Texas Playboys-C* . . . . (Liberty)
Old Lamplighter, The
Bing Crosby; *The Radio Years-#2* . . . . (Crescendo)
Browns; *45-#7700* . . . . (RCA)
Nipper's Greatest Hits Of The '60s-#2-C . . . . (RCA)
Kay Kyser & His Orchestra; *Best Of The Big Bands-Kay Kyser & His
Orchestra* . . . . (Legacy)
Sammy Kaye & His Orchestra; *Nipper's Greatest Hits Of The
'40s-#2-C.* . . . . (RCA)
Once Upon A Time
Frank Sinatra; *September Of My Years* . . . . (Reprise)
Tony Bennett; *I Left My Heart In San Francisco* . . . . (Columbia)
Paul Revere
Beastie Boys; *Licensed To Ill* . . . . (Def Jam)
Rap Rap Rap-C . . . . (K-Tel)
Paul Revere
Johnny Cash; *Patriot* . . . . (Columbia)
Prologue (Tradition)
Original Cast; *Fiddler On The Roof.* . . . . (RCA Victor)

Remember Pearl Harbor
Sammy Kaye & His Orchestra; *ST/Radio Days* . . . . (Novus)
Remember The Alamo
Johnny Cash; *We The People-C* . . . . (Folk Era)
Kingston Trio; *At Large/Here We Go Again!* . . . . (Capitol)
Renegades Of Funk
Rage Against The Machine; *Renegades.* . . . . (Epic)
Rime Of The Ancient Mariner
Iron Maiden; *Live After Death-World Slavery Tour* . . . . (Capitol)
Powerslave . . . . (Capitol)
Smoke
Ben Folds Five; *Whatever And Ever Amen.* . . . . (Caroline/550)
Stay You
Wood; *Songs From Dawson's Creek* . . . . (Sony Music Soundtrax)
Songs From Stamford Hill. . . . . (Columbia)
Sympathy For The Devil
Bryan Ferry; *These Foolish Things* . . . . (Reprise)
Jane's Addiction; *Jane's Addiction* . . . . (Triple X Entert.)
Rolling Stones; *Beggars Banquet.* . . . . (Abkco)
Flashpoint . . . . (Virgin)
Get Yer Ya-Ya's Out! . . . . (Abkco)
Hot Rocks 1964-1971 . . . . (Abkco)
Love You Live . . . . (Virgin)
Talking Watergate
Tom Paxton; *New Songs From The Briarpatch* . . . . (Vanguard)
Texas Flood
Fenton Robinson; *Somebody Loan Me A Dime* . . . . (Alligator)
Larry Davis; *Best Of Duke-Peacock Blues-C* . . . . (MCA Special Prod.)
Stevie Ray Vaughan and Double Trouble; *Live Alive* . . . . (Epic)
Stevie Ray Vaughan and Double Trouble . . . . (Epic)
Taste Of Texas-Songs 'Bout Texas By Texans-C . . . . (Columbia)
Theme From "All In The Family"
Original Soundtrack; *CBS: The First 50 Years.* . . . . (TVT)
Television's Greatest Hits-#3-1970s & 1980s-C. . . . . (TVT)
Theme From "Back To The Future"
Cincinnati Pops Orchestra/Erich Kunzel; *Star Tracks II* . . . . (Telarc)
Theme From "Daniel Boone"
Original Soundtrack; *Television's Greatest Hits-#1-C* . . . . (TVT)
Theme From "Little House On The Prairie"
Original Soundtrack; *Television's Greatest Hits-#3-1970s & 1980s-C* . . . .(TVT)
Theme From "Roots"
Original Soundtrack; *Television's Greatest Hits-#6-Remote Control-C* . . .(TVT)
Theme From "Summer Of '42"
George Benson; *Best Of George Benson* . . . . (CBS Associated)
White Rabbit . . . . (CBS Associated)
Peter Nero; *"Summer Of '42" Theme* . . . . (Columbia)
Peter Nero's Greatest Hits . . . . (Columbia)
Theme From "The Flintstones"
Original Soundtrack; *Hanna-Barbera Classics-#1-Original Recordings Of
The World's Most Famous Cartoon Themes &
Scores* . . . . (Kid Rhino/Rhino 4 Kids)
*Hanna-Barbera Pic-A-Nic Basket Of Cartoon
Classics* . . . . (Kid Rhino/Rhino 4 Kids)
Television's Greatest Hits-#1-C . . . . (TVT)
Steve Hobbs; *Escape* . . . . (Cexton)
Theme From "The Waltons"
Original Soundtrack; *CBS: The First 50 Years.* . . . . (TVT)
Television's Greatest Hits-#3-1970s & 1980s-C. . . . . (TVT)
They All Laughed
Carmen McRae; *Setting Standards* . . . . (Pair)
Ella Fitzgerald & Louis Armstrong & Oscar Peterson Trio; *Great American
Songwriters-#1George & Ira Gershwin-C* . . . .(Rhino)
Fred Astaire; *Starring Fred Astaire* . . . . (Columbia)
Sarah Vaughan; *Sarah Vaughan Sings George Gershwin Songbook,
Vol. 1* . . . . (Emarcy)
Tony Bennett; *Steppin' Out* . . . . (Columbia)
Three Mile Island
Pinkard & Bowden; *Writers In Disguise* . . . . (Warner Bros.)
Titanic, The
John Townley & The Press Gang; *Chesapeake Sailor's Companion* . . . (Adelphi)
Top 40 Radio (The History Of Rock)
Joey Welz; *Return Of Haley's Comet.* . . . . (Caprice Int'l)
Trashing All The Loves Of History
Snakefinger; *Greener Postures* . . . . (Ralph)
Turn Back Time
Aqua; *Aquarium* . . . . (MCA)
ST/Sliding Doors. . . . . (MCA)
Wasn't That A Mighty Storm
Eric Von Schmidt; *Troubadours Of The Folk Era-#1-C* . . . . (Rhino)
Waterloo
Abba; *Abba's Greatest Hits* . . . . (Atlantic)
Waterloo . . . . (Atlantic)
We Didn't Start The Fire
Billy Joel; *Storm Front.* . . . . (Columbia)
West Virginia Mine Disaster
Betsy Rutherford; *Betsy Rutherford.* . . . . (Biograph)
Cindy Mangsen; *Long Time Traveling.* . . . . (Hogeye)
What It Is
Mark Knopfler; *Sailing To Philadelphia* . . . . (Warner Bros.)

Who Played Poker With Pocahontas?
Fannie Watson; *Music From The New York Stage (1890-1920)-#4-1917-1920-C* . . . . (Pearl)
Wreck Of The Edmund Fitzgerald
Gordon Lightfoot; *Gord's Gold-#2* . . . .(Warner Bros.)
Summertime Dream . . . . (Reprise)
You Can Make History (Young Again)
Elton John; *Elton John-Love Songs* . . . .(MCA)
Young Jews Be Proud
2 Live Jews; *As Kosher As They Wanna Be* . . . . (Kosher)

HITCHHIKING

See Also: CARS (various), ROAD, TRAVELING, TRUCKS

500 Miles Away From Home
Bobby Bare; *500 Miles Away From Home* . . . . (RCA)
Foy Willing; *Cowboy/The New Sound Of American Folk* . . . . (DRG)
Reba McEntire; *Starting Over* . . . . (MCA)
America
David Bowie; *The Concert For New York City-C* . . . . (Columbia)
Paul Simon; *Paul Simon In Concert/Live Rhymin'* . . . . (Columbia)
Simon & Garfunkel; *Bookends* . . . . (Columbia)
Collected Works . . . . (Columbia)
Simon & Garfunkel's Greatest Hits . . . . (Columbia)
The Concert In Central Park . . . .(Warner Bros.)
Everyday Is A Winding Road
Sheryl Crow; *1998 Grammy Nominees-C* . . . .(MCA)
Sheryl Crow . . . . (A&M)
Hitchhike
Marvin Gaye; *Good Feeling Music Of The Big Chill Generation-#3-C* . . . . (Motown)
Marvin Gaye-Anthology . . . . (Motown)
Marvin Gaye's Greatest Hits . . . . (Motown)
Marvin Gaye-Super Hits . . . . (Motown)
Rolling Stones; *Out Of Our Heads* . . . . (Abkco)
Hitchin' A Ride
Vanity Fare; *Collectables Presents The History Of Rock-#1-C* . . . (Collectables)
Super Hits Of The '70s-Have A Nice Day-#2-C . . . . (Rhino)
Super Oldies Of The '60s-#11-C . . . . (Audio Fidelity)
Hitchin' A Ride
Green Day; *Nimrod* . . . . (Reprise)
Nothin' But The Taillights
Clint Black; *Nothin' But The Taillights* . . . . (RCA)
Riding My Thumb To Mexico
Johnny Rodriguez; *40 Years Of Country Music-#3-1970-1979-C* . . . . (Mercury)
All I Ever Meant To Do . . . . (Mercury)
Desperado . . . . (Mercury)
Johnny Rodriguez's Greatest Hits . . . . (Mercury)
Shy Of The Moon
Wallflowers; *The Wallflowers* . . . . (Virgin)
Sweet Hitchhiker
Creedence Clearwater Revival; *Creedence Clearwater Revival-Chronicle* . . . . (Fantasy)
Live In Europe . . . . (Fantasy)
Mardi Gras . . . . (Fantasy)
More Creedence Gold . . . . (Fantasy)
Swingin'
Tom Petty And The Heartbreakers; *Echo* . . . .(Warner Bros.)

HOLDING ON, Hanging On, Stick To

See Also: FAITH, FRIENDS, HELP, HUG, LOVE (various),
MOTIVATION, STUCK, TOGETHERNESS

Am I Wrong
Keb' Mo'; *Keb' Mo'* . . . . (Okeh)
Any Day Now
Ronnie Milsap; *Essential Ronnie Milsap* . . . . (RCA)
Ronnie Milsap's Greatest Hits-#2 . . . . (RCA)
Ronnie Milsap-Super Hits . . . . (RCA)
Austin
Blake Shelton; *Blake Shelton* . . . . (Giant)
Baby Hold On
Eddie Money; *Eddie Money* . . . . (Columbia)
Eddie Money's Greatest Hits-Sound Of Money . . . . (Columbia)
Baby's Got A Hold On Me
Nitty Gritty Dirt Band; *Hold On* . . . .(Warner Bros.)
Between An Old Memory And Me
Keith Whitley; *I Wonder Do You Think Of Me* . . . . (RCA)
Travis Tritt; *Ten Feet Tall And Bulletproof* . . . .(Warner Bros.)
Building A Mystery
Sarah McLachlan; *Lilith Fair-A Celebration Of Women In Music-C* . . . . (Arista)
Mirrorball . . . . (Arista)
Surfacing . . . . (Arista)

Can't Let Go
Mariah Carey; *Emotions* . . . . (Columbia)
MTV Unplugged-Mariah Carey . . . . (Columbia)
Can't Let Go
Laurnea; *Betta Listen* . . . . (Yab Yum)
Can't Let You Go (The Sha La Song)
Dave Koz; *Dance* . . . . (Capitol)
Day After Day
Def Leppard; *Euphoria* . . . . (Mercury)
Day In, Day Out
David Kersh; *Goodnight Sweetheart* . . . . (Curb)
Don't Keep Me Hangin' On
Sonny James; *Best Of Sonny James* . . . . (Curb)
Young Love: The Collection . . . . (Razor & Tie)
Don't Let Go
Regina Belle; *Believe In Me* . . . . (MCA)
Don't Let Go (Love)
En Vogue; *Best Of En Vogue* . . . . (Elektra)
EV3 . . . . (East West)
Don't Let Our Love Start Slippin' Away
Vince Gill; *I Still Believe In You* . . . . (MCA)
Emotional
Carl Thomas; *Emotional* . . . .(Bad Boy/Arista)
Guitars, Cadillacs
Dwight Yoakam; *Guitars, Cadillacs, Etc., Etc.* . . . . (Reprise)
Just Lookin' For A Hit . . . . (Reprise)
Hang On Sloopy
McCoys; *21 Oldies But Goodies-C* . . . . (Original Sound)
Billboard Top Rock 'N' Roll Hits-1965-C . . . . (Rhino)
Frat Rock!-C . . . . (Rhino)
Oldies But Goodies-#14-C . . . . (Original Sound)
Ramsey Lewis; *Greatest Hits Of Ramsey Lewis* . . . . (Chess)
Vintage Music-#20-C . . . . (MCA)
Hang On To This
Days Of The New; *Days Of The New* . . . .(Outpost/Interscope)
Hangin' Around
Whites; *The '80s: Country Groups' Greatest Hits-C* . . . . (K-Tel)
Whites' Greatest Hits . . . . (Curb)
Hanging By A Moment
Lifehouse; *No Name Face* . . . .(DreamWorks/SKG)
Now That's What I Call Music!-#7-C . . . . (Virgin)
Hard Times Come Easy
Richie Sambora; *Undiscovered Soul* . . . . (Mercury)
Hold Me, Thrill Me, Kiss Me
Mel Carter; *Baby Boomer Classics-Love Sixties-C* . . . .(JCI Assoc. Labels)
Hold Me, Thrill Me, Kiss Me, Kill Me
U2; *Number One Movie Hits-C* . . . . (ESX Entert.)
ST/Batman Forever . . . .(Atlantic)
Hold My Hand
Hootie & The Blowfish; *Cracked Rear View* . . . .(Atlantic)
Hold On
Triumph; *Just A Game* . . . . (RCA)
Stages . . . . (MCA)
Triumph-Classics . . . . (MCA)
Hold On
Jamie Walters; *Jamie Walters* . . . .(Atlantic)
Hold On
Xscape; *Traces Of My Lipstick* . . . . (So So Def/Columbia)
Hold On
En Vogue; *Born To Sing* . . . .(Atlantic)
Hold On
John Lennon; *Lennon* . . . . (Capitol)
John Lennon/Plastic Ono Band; *John Lennon/Plastic Ono Band* . . . . . . (Capitol)
Hold On
John Conlee; *Rose Colored Glasses* . . . . (Universal)
Hold On
Steve Winwood; *Steve Winwood* . . . . (Island)
Hold On
Wilson Phillips; *Wilson Phillips* . . . . (SBK)
Hold On (Change Is Comin')
Sounds Of Blackness; *Time For Healing* . . . . (Perspective/A&M)
Hold On To Your Dream
Stevie Wonder; *Song Review-A Greatest Hits Collection* . . . . (Motown)
ST/The Adventures Of Pinocchio . . . .(London)
Hold On! I'm A Comin'
Chuck Jackson & Maxine Brown; *Best Of Chuck Jackson* . . . . (Tomato)
Sam & Dave; *Best Of Sam & Dave* . . . .(Atlantic)
Hold What You've Got
Joe Tex; *Atlantic Ultimate '60s Soul Smashes!-C* . . . . (Rhino)
Very Best Of Joe Tex . . . . (Rhino)
Holdin'
Diamond Rio; *Diamond Rio IV* . . . . (Arista)
Diamond Rio's Greatest Hits . . . . (Arista)
Holding Back The Years
Simply Red; *Picture Book* . . . . (Elektra)
Simply Red's Greatest Hits . . . . (East West)
Holding On
Steve Winwood; *Roll With It* . . . . (Virgin)

I Can't Let Go
Linda Ronstadt; *Mad Love* . . . . (Elektra)
I Got Dreams
Steve Wariner; *I Got Dreams* . . . . (MCA)
I Only Want To Be With You
Bay City Rollers; *Bay City Rollers' Greatest Hits* . . . .(Arista)
Dusty Springfield; *Dusty Springfield-Anthology* . . . . (Mercury)
Dusty Springfield-Golden Hits . . . . (Mercury)
Vonda Shepard; *ST/Songs From ''Ally McBeal'' Featuring Vonda
Shepard* . . . .(550/Epic)
I'll Stick Around
Foo Fighters; *Foo Fighters* . . . .(Roswell/RCA)
I'm Holdin' On To Love (To Save My Life)
Shania Twain; *Come On Over* . . . . (Mercury)
Just Once In My Life
Righteous Brothers; *Best Of The Righteous Brothers* . . . . (Curb)
Phil Spector-Back To Mono 1958-1969-C . . . . (Abkco)
Righteous Brothers-Anthology 1962-1974 . . . . (Rhino)
Unchained Melody-Very Best Of The Righteous Brothers . . . . (Polydor)
Laredo
Chris Cagle; *Play It Loud* . . . . (Capitol)
Let Me Let Go
Faith Hill; *Faith* . . . . (Warner Bros.)
Let's Hang On!
4 Seasons; *Four Seasons' Greatest Hits-#2* . . . . (Rhino)
Livin' On A Prayer
Bon Jovi; *America: A Tribute To Heroes-C* . . . . (Interscope)
Cross Road-14 Classic Grooves . . . . (Mercury)
Slippery When Wet . . . . (Jambco)
The Concert For New York City-C . . . . (Columbia)
Longneck Bottle
Garth Brooks; *Sevens* . . . . (Capitol)
Lover After Me, The
Savage Garden; *Affirmation* . . . . (Columbia)
Man Holdin' On (To A Woman Lettin' Go)
Ty Herndon; *Big Hopes* . . . . (Epic)
My Guy
Mary Wells; *Mary Wells' Greatest Hits* . . . . (Motown)
My Guy . . . . (Motown)
Oldies But Goodies-#11-C . . . .(Original Sound)
Never Gonna Give You Up
Rick Astley; *Whenever You Need Somebody* . . . . (RCA)
Never Gonna Let You Go
Tina Moore; *Speed Garage Classics-C* . . . . (Logic)
Never Gonna Let You Go
Blackstreet; *Another Level* . . . . (Interscope)
No Way Out
Stone Temple Pilots; *No. 4* . . . . (Atlantic)
One Emotion
Clint Black; *One Emotion* . . . . (RCA)
Reach Out I'll Be There
Four Tops; *Compact Command Performances-Four Tops* . . . . (Motown)
Four Tops' Greatest Hits . . . . (Motown)
Four Tops Reach Out . . . . (Motown)
Four Tops-Anthology . . . . (Motown)
Motown Dance Party-#2-C . . . . (Motown)
Reflections
Diana Ross & The Supremes; *Diana Ross & The Supremes' Greatest
Hits-#3* . . . . (Motown)
Diana Ross & The Supremes-25th Anniversary . . . . (Motown)
Diana Ross & The Supremes-Anthology (1962-1969) . . . . (Motown)
Motown Story-First 25 Years-C . . . . (Motown)
Four Tops; *Four Tops-Anthology* . . . . (Motown)
Still Waters Run Deep . . . . (Motown)
Until You Love Someone: More Of The Best (1965-1970) . . . . (Rhino)
Luther Vandross; *Songs* . . . . (Epic)
Release Me
Angelina; *Angelina* . . . . (Upstairs)
Serious Hold On Me
O'Jays; *Serious* . . . . (EMI)
She Said Yes
Rhett Akins; *A Thousand Memories* . . . . (Decca)
Softly And Tenderly (I'll Hold You In My Arms)
Lewis Pruitt; *45-#31095* . . . . (Decca)
Somebody's Doin' Me Right
Glen Campbell; *Unconditional Love* . . . . (Liberty)
Keith Whitley; *Kentucky Bluebird* . . . . (RCA)
S-K-O; *S-K-O* . . . . (MTM)
Still Holding On
Clint Black & Martina McBride; *Nothin' But The Taillights* . . . . (RCA)
Martina McBride & Clint Black; *Evolution* . . . . (RCA)
Stuck In The Middle With You
Stealers Wheel; *Super Hits Of The '70s-Have A Nice Day-#10-C* . . . . . (Rhino)
Stuck On You
Elvis Presley; *Elvis' Golden Records, Volume 3* . . . . (RCA)
Number One Hits . . . . (RCA)
Return Of The Rocker . . . . (RCA)
Worldwide 50 Gold Award Hits, Vol. 1, Parts 1 & 2 . . . . (RCA)

Stuck On You
Lionel Richie; *Can't Slow Down* . . . . (Motown)
There's Your Trouble
Dixie Chicks; *Wide Open Spaces* . . . .(Monument)
Tiger Rag
Django Reinhardt; *Jazz Legacy* . . . . (Inner City)
Legendary Django Reinhardt . . . . (Crescendo)
Django Reinhardt & Stephane Grappelli; *Django Reinhardt & Stephane
Grappelli* . . . . (Crescendo)
Les Paul & Mary Ford; *Selections From ''Legend & The Legacy''* . . . (Capitol)
Louis Armstrong; *Essential Louis Armstrong* . . . . (Vanguard)
Mostly Blues . . . . (Olympic)
Stardust . . . . (Portrait)
Louis Armstrong & Friends; *20 Golden Pieces Of Louis Armstrong &
Friends* . . . . (Bulldog)
Louis Armstrong & His Orchestra; *Louis Armstrong & The Big
Bands* . . . .(Disques Swing)
Mills Brothers; *Mills Brothers-22 Great Hits* . . . . (Ranwood)
Preservation Hall Jazz Band; *Best Of The Preservation Hall
Jazz Band* . . . . (Columbia)
New Orleans-#1 . . . . (Columbia)
Touch Me Tease Me
Case Featuring Foxy Brown; *Case* . . . . (Def Jam/RAL/Mercury)
Def Jam Greatest Hits-C . . . . (Def Jam)
ST/The Nutty Professor . . . . (Def Jam)
Ultimate Hip Hop Party-1998-C . . . . (Arista)
Unconditional
Clay Davidson; *Unconditional* . . . . (Virgin)
We're Gonna Hold On
George Jones & Tammy Wynette; *George Jones & Tammy Wynette-16
Biggest Hits* . . . . (Epic/Legacy)
Why Ain't I Running
Garth Brooks; *Scarecrow* . . . . (Capitol)
You Can't Lose Me
Faith Hill; *It Matters To Me* . . . . (Warner Bros.)
You Keep Me Hangin' On
Diana Ross; *Evening With Diana Ross* . . . . (Motown)
Diana Ross & The Supremes; *Diana Ross & The Supremes-Anthology (1962-
1969)* . . . . (Motown)
Motown Story-First 25 Years-C . . . . (Motown)
Kim Wilde; *Another Step* . . . . (MCA)
Reba McEntire; *Starting Over* . . . . (MCA)
Supremes; *Billboard Top R&B Hits-1965-C* . . . . (Rhino)
Diana Ross & The Supremes' Greatest Hits-#2 . . . . (Motown)
Vanilla Fudge; *Best Of Vanilla Fudge* . . . . (Atco)
Vanilla Fudge . . . . (Atco)
Wilson Pickett; *A Man & A Half-Best Of Wilson Pickett* . . . . (Rhino)
Wilson Pickett's Greatest Hits . . . . (Atlantic)
Your Unchanging Love
Marvin Gaye; *Marvin Gaye-Anthology* . . . . (Motown)
You've Really Got A Hold On Me
Beatles; *The Beatles-Anthology-#1* . . . . (Capitol)
Smokey Robinson & The Miracles; *Best Of Smokey Robinson & The
Miracles-Anthology* . . . . (Motown)
*Great Songs & Performances That Inspired The Motown 25th Anniversary
Television Special-C.* . . . . (Motown)
Smokey Robinson-The Ultimate Collection. . . . . (Motown)

HOLES

*See Also: **BITS & PIECES, BREAK, BUILDING & CONSTRUCTION,
FIXING, OPEN & CLOSED***

Bucket's Got A Hole In It, The
Preservation Hall Jazz Band; *Best Of The Preservation Hall
Jazz Band* . . . . (Columbia)
Burning A Hole In My Mind
Connie Smith; *Essential Connie Smith* . . . . (RCA)
Darlin' Corey
Ricky Skaggs with Bruce Hornsby; *Big Mon: The Songs Of Bill
Monroe-C* . . . .(Skaggs Family)
Day In The Life, A
Beatles; *Sgt. Pepper's Lonely Hearts Club Band* . . . .(Capitol)
ST/Imagine: John Lennon . . . . (Capitol)
The Beatles/1967-1970 . . . . (Capitol)
Fire In The Hole
Van Halen; *Van Halen 3* . . . . (Warner Bros.)
Fixing A Hole
Beatles; *Sgt. Pepper's Lonely Hearts Club Band* . . . .(Capitol)
Hole In My Head
Dixie Chicks; *Fly* . . . .(Monument)
Hole In My Soul
Aerosmith; *Nine Lives* . . . . (Columbia)
Hole, The
Randy Travis; *You And You Alone* . . . . (DreamWorks/SKG)
Holes In The Floor Of Heaven
Steve Wariner; *Burnin' The Roadhouse Down* . . . .(Capitol)

Hopeless
Dionne Farris; *ST/Love Jones* . . . . (Columbia)
Matchbox
Beatles; *Past Masters-Volume Two* . . . . (Parlophone)
Rock 'N' Roll Music . . . . (Capitol)
Something New . . . . (Capitol)
Money Burns A Hole In My Pocket
Dean Martin; *Capitol Collectors Series-Dean Martin* . . . . (Capitol)
My Bucket's Got A Hole In It
Hank Williams; *Complete Hank Williams* . . *. . . . . (Mercury)
There's A Hole In My Bucket
Disneyland Cast; *Children's Favorite Songs-#4.* . . . .(Disney)
There's A Hole In The Bottom Of The Sea
Original Soundtrack; *School Days-Kids Classics* . . . . (Benson)
Trippin' On A Hole In A Paper Heart
Stone Temple Pilots; *Tiny Music...Songs From The Vatican
Gift Shop* . . . . (Atlantic)

HOLLYWOOD

See Also: **CITIES: LOS ANGELES, CITIES: NEW YORK
(Broadway), ELVIS, MOVIES, MUSIC, RADIO, RECORD
BUSINESS, SHOW BIZ, TELEVISION**

Burn Hollywood Burn
Chuck D/The Roots/Zack De La Rocha; *ST/Bamboozled.* . . . . (Motown)
Public Enemy; *Fear Of A Black Planet.* . . . .(Def Jam)
Californication
Red Hot Chili Peppers; *Californication* . . . .(Warner Bros.)
Camera One
Josh Joplin Group; *Useful Music* . . . . (Artemis)
Celebrity Skin
Hole; *Celebrity Skin* . . . . (David Geffen Co.)
Celluloid Heroes
Joan Jett; *The Hit List* . . . .(Epic)
Kinks; *Come Dancing With The Kinks-Best Of The Kinks 1977-1986* . . . (Arista)
Everybody's In Show-Biz . . . . (Rhino)
The Kinks' Greatest-Celluloid Heroes. . . . . (RCA)
Cowboys From Hollywood
Camper Van Beethoven; *Camper Van Beethoven II & III* . . . .(I.R.S.)
Down In Hollywood
Ry Cooder; *Bop Till You Drop* . . . .(Warner Bros.)
Flight 309 To Tennessee
Shelly West; *West By West* . . . . (Viva)
Gone Hollywood
Supertramp; *Breakfast In America* . . . . (A&M)
Hollywood
Connie Francis; *Rocksides-1957-1964* . . . . (Polydor)
Hollywood
Wallflowers; *The Wallflowers.* . . . . (Virgin)
Hollywood
999; *999* . . . . (Polydor)
Hollywood
America; *America Live* . . . .(Warner Bros.)
Holiday . . . .(Warner Bros.)
Hollywood
Rufus Featuring Chaka Khan; *Ask Rufus* . . . .(MCA)
Hollywood
Statler Brothers; *Atlanta Blue* . . . . (Mercury)
Hollywood
Chicago; *Chicago VI.* . . . .(Chicago)
Hollywood
Rick James; *Come Get It!* . . . . (Motown)
Hollywood
Billy Squier; *Creatures Of Habit* . . . . (Capitol)
Hollywood
Boz Scaggs; *Down Two Then Left* . . . . (Columbia)
Hollywood
Alabama; *Feels So Right.* . . . . (RCA)
Hollywood
Freddie James; *Get Up & Boogie* . . . .(Warner Bros.)
Hollywood
Shooting Star; *Hang On For Your Life* . . . . (Virgin)
Hollywood
Crystal Gayle; *Hollywood, Tennessee* . . . . (Columbia)
Hollywood
Jimmy Holiday; *How Can I Forget-Golden Classics* . . . . (Collectables)
Hollywood
Lauren Wood; *Lauren Wood* . . . .(Warner Bros.)
Hollywood (Down On Your Luck)
Thin Lizzy; *Lizzy Lives! (1976-1984)* . . . . (Gland Slamm)
Renegade . . . .(Warner Bros.)
Hollywood A Go Go
Hollywood Persuaders; *45-#58.* . . . . (Original Sound)
Hollywood Bed
Big Joe Turner; *...And The Blues'll Make You Happy Too!* . . . . (Savoy)

Have No Fear Big Joe Is Here . . . . (Savoy)
Hollywood Bed
Blasters; *Blasters-Collection.* . . . .(Slash)
Hollywood Blues
Boz Scaggs; *Moments* . . . . (Columbia)
Hollywood Dream
James Gang; *Jesse Come Home* . . . . (Atco)
Hollywood Dream
Thunderclap Newman; *Hollywood Dream* . . . . (MCA)
Hollywood Dream
Steve Miller Band; *Italian X-Rays.* . . . . (Capitol)
Hollywood Dreaming
Father's Children; *Father's Children* . . . . (Mercury)
Hollywood Heckle & Jive
England Dan & John Ford Coley; *Dr. Heckle & Mr. Jive* . . . . (Big Tree)
Hollywood Hopeful
Loudon Wainwright III; *Live One* . . . . (Rounder)
T-Shirt . . . . (Arista)
Hollywood Lady
Burt Compton & Steve Mele; *Rock 'N' Roll Genius* . . . . (Wizard)
Hollywood Movie Girls
Dusty Springfield; *It Begins Again* . . . .(United Artists)
Hollywood Nights
Bob Seger & The Silver Bullet Band; *Nine Tonight* . . . . (Capitol)
Stranger In Town . . . . (Capitol)
Hollywood Perfume
Pretenders; *Last Of The Independents* . . . .(Sire)
Hollywood Squares
Bootsy's Rubber Band; *Bootsy Player Of The Year* . . . .(Warner Bros.)
Hollywood Squares
George Strait; *Beyond The Blue Neon* . . . . (MCA)
Hollywood Swinging
Kool & The Gang; *Everything's Kool & The Gang-Greatest Hits
& More* . . . . (Mercury)
Kool & The Gang Spin Their Top Hits . . . .(De-Lite)
Hollywood Town
Manfred Mann's Earth Band; *Angel Station* . . . .(Warner Bros.)
Hollywood Waltz
Eagles; *One Of These Nights* . . . .(Asylum)
Honey Pie
Beatles; *The Beatles (White Album)* . . . . (Capitol)
The Beatles-Anthology-#3 . . . . (Capitol)
Hooray For Hollywood
Coney Island Chorus Girls; *Hot Disco Night.* . . . .(American Variety)
Ella Fitzgerald; *Harold Arlen Songbook-#1* . . . . (Verve)
Rosemary Clooney; *Rosemary Clooney Sings The Lyrics Of Johnny
Mercer* . . . .(Concord Jazz)
If Hollywood Don't Need You
Don Williams; *Best Of Don Williams-#3* . . . . (MCA)
Don Williams Sings Bob McDill. . . . . (MCA)
Listen To The Radio . . . . (MCA)
King Of Hollywood
Eagles; *The Long Run* . . . .(Asylum)
Little Hollywood Girl
Crickets; *Liberty Years* . . . . (EMI)
Long Way To Hollywood
Hank Williams, Jr.; *Hank Williams, Jr.-Early Years* . . . .(WB/Curb)
New South . . . . (Warner Bros.)
Long Way To Hollywood
Steve Young; *Seven Bridges Road* . . . . (Rounder)
Lost In Hollywood
Neil Diamond; *Headed For The Future* . . . . (Columbia)
Lost In Hollywood
Rainbow; *Down To Earth* . . . . (Polydor)
Lucky
Britney Spears; *Now That's What I Call Music!-#5-C* . . . .(Virgin)
Oops!...I Did It Again. . . . .(Jive)
Picture Show
John Prine; *The Missing Years* . . . .(Oh Boy)
Poor Little Hollywood Star
Virginia Martin; *Little Me* . . . . (RCA)
Queen Of Hollywood High
John Stewart; *Blondes.* . . . . (Allegiance)
Say Goodbye To Hollywood
Bette Midler; *Broken Blossom.* . . . .(Atlantic)
Billy Joel; *Billy Joel-Greatest Hits, Volume I & Volume II* . . . . (Columbia)
Songs In The Attic. . . . . (Columbia)
Turnstiles. . . . . (Columbia)
Sheep Go To Heaven
Cake; *Prolonging The Magic* . . . . (Capricorn)
Tulsa Time
Don Williams; *Best Of Don Williams-#2* . . . . (MCA)
Country's Greatest Hits-#6-Superstars-C . . . . (Priority)
Don Williams-Legends. . . . . (MCA)
Expressions . . . . (MCA)
Eric Clapton; *Backless* . . . .(Polydor)
Just One Night . . . .(Polydor)

We're Going To Hollywood
    Sicilian Vespers; *Sicilian Vespers* . . . . (Profile)

HOME, Homesick

    See Also: **CHILDREN, CHILDREN LEAVING HOME, DIVORCE, DOMESTIC ABUSE, FAMILY (various), HOUSES, MARRIAGE, PARENTS (various), RETURNING, SMALL TOWN LIFE, TRAVELING**

2,000 Light Years From Home
    Rolling Stones; *More Hot Rocks (big hits & fazed cookies)* . . . . . (Abkco)
    Singles Collection-The London Years . . . . (Abkco)
    Their Satanic Majesties Request . . . . (Abkco)
    Through The Past, Darkly (Big Hits Vol. 2) . . . . (Abkco)
500 Miles Away From Home
    Bobby Bare; *500 Miles Away From Home* . . . . (RCA)
    Foy Willing; *Cowboy/The New Sound Of American Folk* . . . . (DRG)
    Reba McEntire; *Starting Over* . . . . (MCA)
About To Make Me Leave Home
    Bonnie Raitt; *Bonnie Raitt-Collection* . . . . (Warner Bros.)
    Sweet Forgiveness . . . . (Warner Bros.)
Adam's Song
    Blink-182; *Enema Of The State* . . . . (MCA)
Adrian
    Jewel; *Pieces Of You* . . . . (Atlantic)
Ain't Got No Home
    Clarence "Frogman" Henry; *Best Of Chess Rock 'N' Roll-#1-C* . . . . . . (Chess)
    History Of New Orleans R&B-#1-1950-1958-C . . . . (Rhino)
    Vintage Music-#2-C . . . . (MCA)
Ain't Got No Home
    Band; *Moondog Matinee* . . . . (Capitol)
Ain't Nobody Home
    B.B. King; *Best Of B.B. King* . . . . (MCA)
    Bonnie Raitt; *Streetlights* . . . . (Warner Bros.)
Ain't Nobody Home (In California)
    John Kay; *All In Good Time* . . . . (Mercury)
All Roads Lead To You
    Chicago; *The Heart Of Chicago-1967-1988-#2* . . . . (Reprise)
All The Fun
    Paul Overstreet; *Best Of Paul Overstreet* . . . . (RCA)
All The Small Things
    Blink-182; *Enema Of The State* . . . . (MCA)
    Now That's What I Call Music!-#4-C . . . . (Virgin)
Almost Home
    Mary Chapin Carpenter; *Party Doll And Other Favorites* . . . . (Columbia)
Already Home
    Marc Cohn; *Burning The Daze* . . . . (Atlantic)
Always Comin' Home
    Whites; *A Lifetime In The Making* . . . . (Ceili Music)
Amelia
    Gretchen Peters; *Gretchen Peters* . . . . (Purple Crayon Prod.)
America
    Neil Diamond; *12 Greatest Hits-#2* . . . . (Columbia)
    Hot August Night II . . . . (Columbia)
    ST/The Jazz Singer . . . . (Capitol)
America Is My Home
    James Brown; *Best Of James Brown* . . . . (Polydor)
Angel Come Home
    Beach Boys; *L.A.-The Light Album* . . . . (Caribou)
Angeline Is Coming Home
    Badlees; *River Songs* . . . . (Atlas)
Any Place I Hang My Hat Is Home
    Barbra Streisand; *The Second Barbra Streisand Album* . . . . (Columbia)
    Rosemary Clooney; *Rosemary Clooney Sings The Lyrics Of Johnny Mercer* . . . . (Concord Jazz)
At The Stars
    Better Than Ezra; *How Does Your Garden Grow?* . . . . (Elektra)
Avalon My Home Town
    Mississippi John Hurt; *Best Of Mississippi John Hurt* . . . . (Vanguard)
Baby Come On Home
    Led Zeppelin; *Boxed Set 2* . . . . (Atlantic)
Baby Please Come Home
    Lloyd Price; *Original Rock Oldies-Golden Hits-#2-C* . . . . (Specialty)
Baby Won't You Please Come Home
    Billie Holiday; *Last Recordings* . . . . (Verve)
    Dinah Washington; *Echoes Of An Era-Dinah Washington* . . . . . . (Roulette)
    Frank Sinatra; *Night We Called It A Day* . . . . (Capitol)
    Louis Armstrong; *Most Blues* . . . . (Olympic)
    Louis Armstrong & Friends; *20 Golden Pieces Of Louis Armstrong & Friends* . . . . (Bulldog)
    Ray Charles; *20 Golden Pieces Of Ray Charles* . . . . (Bulldog)
Baby, Let Me Take You Home
    Animals; *Best Of The Animals* . . . . (Abkco)
Back Home
    Booker T. & The M.G.s; *Melting Pot* . . . . (Stax)
    Booker T. Jones; *Runaway* . . . . (MCA)

Back Home
    Beach Boys; *15 Big Ones* . . . . (Brother)
Back Home
    China Crisis; *Diary Of A Hollow Horse* . . . . (A&M)
Back Home Again
    John Denver; *Back Home Again* . . . . (RCA)
    John Denver's Greatest Hits-#2 . . . . (RCA)
Back Home Again In Indiana
    Les Paul; *Legend & The Legacy-#1-4* . . . . (Capitol)
Back Home In Derry
    Christy Moore; *Ride On* . . . . (Green Linnet)
    Spirit Of Freedom . . . . (Green Linnet)
Back Home In Huntsville Again
    Bobby Bare; *20 Great Country Hits-C* . . . . (RCA)
    20 Greatest Country Hits-C . . . . (RCA)
Back Home In Indiana
    Peggy Gilbert & The Dixie Bells; *Dixieland Jazz* . . . . (Cambria)
Back In The Day
    Blues Traveler; *Bridge* . . . . (A&M)
Back In The U.S.S.R.
    Beatles; *Beatles-Box Set* . . . . (Capitol)
    Rock 'N' Roll Music . . . . (Capitol)
    The Beatles (White Album) . . . . (Capitol)
    The Beatles/1967-1970 . . . . (Capitol)
    Billy Joel; *KOHUEPT* . . . . (Columbia)
Back In Your Own Back Yard
    Billie Holiday; *Billie Holiday* . . . . (Columbia)
    Quintessential-#5-1937-1938 . . . . (Columbia)
    The Billie Holiday Story-#1 . . . . (Columbia)
Backyard
    Pebbles with Salt-N-Pepa; *Always* . . . . (MCA)
Banana Boat (Day-O)
    Harry Belafonte; *Belafonte '89* . . . . (EMI)
    Nipper's Greatest Hits Of The '50s-#1-C . . . . (RCA)
    Kinks; *Everybody's In Show-Biz* . . . . (Rhino)
Beautiful Homes
    Chris Isaak; *San Francisco Days* . . . . (Reprise)
Bill Bailey
    Louis Armstrong; *Essential Louis Armstrong* . . . . (Vanguard)
    Louis Armstrong . . . . (Audio Fidelity)
    Pearl Bailey; *Echoes Of An Era-Pearl Bailey* . . . . (Roulette)
    Preservation Hall Jazz Band; *New Orleans-#1* . . . . (Columbia)
Blame It On Texas
    Mark Chesnutt; *Mark Chesnutt's Greatest Hits* . . . . (Decca)
    Too Cold At Home . . . . (MCA)
Blue Ridge Mountain Blues
    Blue Ridge Rangers; *Blue Ridge Rangers* . . . . (Fantasy)
    Doc Watson; *Essential Doc Watson* . . . . (Vanguard)
    Earl Scruggs & John Fogerty; *Earl Scruggs And Friends-C* . . . . . . (MCA)
    Norman Blake; *Directions* . . . . (Takoma)
Blue White Planet
    Raffi; *Country Goes Raffi-C* . . . . (Rounder)
Boll Weevil Song
    Brook Benton; *Brook Benton-Anthology* . . . . (Rhino)
    It's Just A Matter Of Time-His Greatest Hits . . . . (Mercury)
    Pick Of Brook Benton . . . . (Fifty One West)
    Leadbelly; *Good Mornin' Blues-1936-1940* . . . . (Biograph)
Boxer, The
    Simon & Garfunkel; *Bridge Over Troubled Water* . . . . (Columbia)
    Collected Works . . . . (Columbia)
    Simon & Garfunkel's Greatest Hits . . . . (Columbia)
    The Concert In Central Park . . . . (Warner Bros.)
Bring Christmas Home
    Lee Greenwood; *Lee Greenwood-Christmas To Christmas* . . . . (MCA Special Prod.)
Bring Him Home
    Original Broadway Cast; *Les Miserables* . . . . (Geffen)
Bring Home The Bacon
    Drivin' N' Cryin'; *Scarred But Smarter* . . . . (Island)
Bring It On Home
    Nighthawks; *Best Of The Blues* . . . . (Adelphi)
    Best Of The Nighthawks . . . . (Genes CD Co.)
    Side Pocket Shot . . . . (Adelphi)
Bring It On Home
    Sonny Boy Williamson; *Best Of Chess Blues-C* . . . . (Chess)
    Chess Blues Box-C . . . . (Chess)
    Real Folk Blues-C . . . . (Chess)
Bring It On Home
    Led Zeppelin; *Led Zeppelin II* . . . . (Atlantic)
Bring It On Home To Me
    Animals; *Best Of The Animals* . . . . (Abkco)
    Dave Mason; *Certified Live* . . . . (Columbia)
    Dave Mason . . . . (Columbia)
    Eddie Floyd; *Eddie Floyd-Chronicle* . . . . (Stax)
    John Lennon; *Rock 'N' Roll* . . . . (Capitol)
    Mickey Gilley; *Mickey Gilley's Greatest Hits-#2* . . . . (Playboy)
    Ten Years Of Hits . . . . (Epic)
    Paul McCartney; *CHOBA B CCCP-The Russian Album* . . . . . . (Capitol)
    Sam Cooke; *Best Of Sam Cooke* . . . . (RCA)

    The Man And His Music..................................... (RCA)
    This Is Sam Cooke .... (RCA)
    Van Morrison; *It's Too Late To Stop Now* .... (Warner Bros.)

Bring It On Home To Me
    Bill Haley & His Comets; *Rock & Roll* .... (Crescendo)

Broadway
    Goo Goo Dolls; *Dizzy Up The Girl* .... (Warner Sunset/Reprise)

Broken Home
    Papa Roach; *Infest* .... (DreamWorks/SKG)

Buffalo River Home
    John Hiatt; *Perfectly Good Guitar* .... (A&M)

Bus Fare Home
    Spaniels; *Heart & Soul-#2-C* .... (Vee-Jay)

Cabin Home On The Hill
    Ricky Skaggs; *Sweet Temptation* .... (Sugar Hill)

Cabin On The Hill
    Flatt & Scruggs; *Columbia Historic Edition-Flatt & Scruggs* ...... (Columbia)
    Lester Flatt & Earl Scruggs; *Bluegrass Super Hits-C* .... (Columbia)

California
    Joni Mitchell; *Blue* .... (Reprise)

Call Me (Come Back Home)
    Al Green; *Al Green's Greatest Hits* .... (Right Stuff)

Can't Find My Way Home
    Blind Faith; *Blind Faith* .... (Polydor)
    Eric Clapton-Crossroads-C .... (Polydor)
    ST/1969 .... (Polydor)

Celebrate Me Home
    Kenny Loggins; *Celebrate Me Home* .... (Columbia)
    Kenny Loggins Alive .... (Columbia)

Chattanooga Choo Choo
    Asleep At The Wheel; *Train Trax-C*......... (Sony Music Special Prod.)
    Billy Strange; *Railroad Man*............................ (Crescendo)
    Boston Pops Orchestra/Arthur Fiedler; *Boston Pops Orchestra/Arthur
       Fiedler* .... (RCA)
    Greatest Hits Of The '40s................................ (RCA)
    Glenn Miller; *Best Of Glenn Miller* .... (RCA)
    Decade Of The '40s-C .... (RCA)
    Glenn Miller-A Legendary Performer-#1 & 2............ (Bluebird)
    Memorial-1944-1969.................................. (Bluebird)
    Nipper's Greatest Hits Of The '40s-#1-C .... (RCA)
    Glenn Miller & His Orchestra; *Glenn Miller & His Orchestra-
       Pure Gold* .... (Bluebird)
    Tuxedo Junction; *Best Of Butterfly Records-C* .... (Hot Prod.)
    Tuxedo Junction...................................... (Butterfly)

Chicago Send Her Home
    Thelma Houston & Jerry Butler; *Two To One*........... (Motown)

Cindy, Oh Cindy
    Beach Boys; *Surfin' Safari-Surfin' Usa (Remasterd With Bonus
       Tracks)* .... (Capitol)

Closing Time
    Semisonic; *Feeling Strangely Fine* .... (MCA)
    Now That's What I Call Music!-#2-C .... (Virgin)

Come Over To My Place
    Davina; *Best Of Both Worlds* .... (Loud/RCA)

Come To My Window
    Melissa Etheridge; *The Concert For New York City-C*........ (Columbia)
    Yes I Am .... (Island)

Comin' Home
    Lynyrd Skynyrd; *First & Last*............................ (MCA)
    Gold & Platinum .... (MCA)
    Southern By The Grace Of God-Tribute '87 .... (MCA)

Comin' Home
    Delaney & Bonnie; *Best Of Delaney & Bonnie*........... (Rhino)
    Delaney & Bonnie & Friends On Tour With Eric Clapton.......... (Rhino)
    Eric Clapton-Crossroads-C .... (Polydor)

Comin' Home
    Nutmegs; *Harlem Holiday-New York Rhythm & Blues-#7-C*..... (Collectables)
    Nutmegs' Greatest Hits .... (Collectables)

Comin' Home
    Bob Seger & The Silver Bullet Band; *The Distance* .... (Capitol)

Coming Back Home
    Bebe Winans featuring Brian McKnight & Joe; *Love & Freedom* .... (Motown)

Coming Home
    Fleetwood Mac; *Heroes Are Hard To Find* .... (Reprise)
    Vintage Years .... (Sire)

Coming Home
    Cinderella; *Long Cold Winter* .... (Mercury)

Coming Home
    Holly Near; *Speed Of Light*............................ (Redwood)

Coming Home
    Scorpions; *Love At First Sting* .... (Mercury)
    World Wide Live .... (Mercury)

Coming Home Soldier
    Bobby Vinton; *Bobby Vinton's All-Time Greatest Hits* .... (Epic)

Coming Home To See You
    Supertramp; *Indelibly Stamped*.......................... (A&M)

Cottage For Sale, A
    Frank Sinatra; *No One Cares* .... (Capitol)
    Mel Torme; *Luck Be A Lady* .... (Laserlight)

Country Comfort
    Earl Scruggs & Elton John; *Earl Scruggs And Friends-C* .... (MCA)
    Elton John; *Tumbleweed Connection* ....(Polydor)
    Rod Stewart; *Best Of Rod Stewart-#2* .... (Mercury)
    Gasoline Alley .... (Mercury)
    Sing It Again, Rod..................................... (Mercury)

Cowboy Night Herd Song
    Roy Rogers & Sons Of The Pioneers; *Cowboy Super Hits-C* .... (Columbia)

Crawlin' Home Puker
    Da Yoopers; *Yoopanese* .... (You Guys)

Cry For Home
    Van Morrison; *Inarticulate Speech Of The Heart* .... (Warner Bros.)

Cut You In
    Jerry Cantrell; *Boggy Depot* .... (Columbia)

Da Doo Ron Ron (When He Walked Me Home)
    Crystals; *Best Of The Crystals*............................(Abkco)
    Good Time Rock 'N' Roll-C .... (MCA)
    Hits Of The Sixties-C .... (Intercom Music)
    Phil Spector's Greatest Hits-C .... (Spector)
    Shaun Cassidy; *Shaun Cassidy's Greatest Hits*...............(Curb)

Daddy's Home
    Shep And The Limelites; *Cruisin'-1961-C* .... (Increase)
    Doo-Wop Ballads-#2-C .... (Rhino)
    Oldies But Goodies-#5-C ....(Original Sound)
    Shep And The Limelites & The Heartbeats; *Best Of The Heartbeats* .... (Rhino)

Daddy's Home
    Jackson 5; *Jackson 5-Anthology* .... (Motown)
    Jermaine Jackson; *Motown Superstar Series-#17-Jermaine Jackson* .. (Motown)

Daddy's Home
    Cliff Richard; *Wired For Sound* .... (EMI)

Darling Are You Ever Coming Home
    Jeannie Seely; *Jeannie Seely's Greatest Hits* .... (Monument)

Darling Be Home Soon
    Joe Cocker; *Joe Cocker!* .... (A&M)
    Joe Cocker-Classics-#4 .... (A&M)
    Joe Cocker's Greatest Hits .... (A&M)
    Lovin' Spoonful; *Best Of The Lovin' Spoonful-#2* .... (Rhino)
    Lovin' '60s-C .... (Priority)
    Lovin' Spoonful-Anthology .... (Rhino)

Darling Come Back Home
    Eddie Kendricks; *Eddie Kendricks-The Ultimate Collection* .... (Motown)

Deep River Woman
    Lionel Richie; *Dancing On The Ceiling* .... (Motown)

Detroit City
    Ace Cannon; *Golden Favorites* .... (Ranwood)
    Bill Anderson; *Best Of Bill Anderson* .... (Curb)
    Bobby Bare; *Nipper's Greatest Hits Of The '60s-#2-C* .... (RCA)
    This Is Bobby Bare .... (RCA)
    Chet Atkins; *Country Gems*...............................(Pair)
    Flatt & Scruggs; *20 All-Time Great Recordings* .... (Columbia)
    Hank Williams, Jr.; *Live At Cobo Hall Detroit* ....(Polydor)
    Standing In The Shadows ....(Polydor)
    Mel Tillis; *Best Of Mel Tillis*............................ (MCA)
    Live At The Sam Houston Coliseum .... (MGM)
    Solomon Burke; *Home In Your Heart-Best Of Solomon Burke* .... (Rhino)

Devil Woman
    Marty Robbins; *Billboard Top Country Hits-1962-C* .... (Rhino)
    Columbia Country Classics-#4-Nashville Sound-C .... (Columbia)
    Lifetime Of Song-1951-1982 .... (Columbia)
    Marty Robbins' Greatest Hits-#4 .... (Columbia)

Diamonds On My Windshield
    Tom Waits; *The Heart Of Saturday Night* ....(Asylum)
    Tom Waits-Anthology...................................(Asylum)

Dirty Water
    Standells; *Best Of The Standells* .... (Rhino)
    Nuggets-Classic Collection From The Psychedelic '60s-C .... (Rhino)
    Super Oldies Of The '60s-#10-C .... (Audio Fidelity)

Do You Know The Way To San Jose
    Dionne Warwick; *Dionne Warwick Greatest Hits*.............. (Everest)
    Dionne Warwick-Anthology 1962-1971 .... (Rhino)
    Hot! Live & Otherwise .... (Arista)

Dolphins & Whales (Come Home To The Sea)
    Mannheim Steamroller; *Saving The Wildlife*........ (American Gramaphone)

Domestic Life
    John Conlee; *American Faces* .... (Columbia)
    Greatest Country Hits Of The '80s-1987-C .... (Columbia)
    More Hot Country Requests-#2-C .... (Epic)

Don't Cheat In Our Hometown
    Ricky Skaggs; *Don't Cheat In Our Hometown* .... (Epic)

Don't Come Home A'Drinkin' (With Lovin' On Your Mind)
    Loretta Lynn; *Loretta Lynn-Greatest Hits Live* .... (K-Tel)
    Loretta Lynn's Greatest Hits .... (MCA)
    MCA Records 30 Years Of Hits-1958-1988-C .... (MCA)

Don't Come Home A'Lovin' With Venison On Your Truck
    Debby McClatchy; *Someday Cafe*................... (Green Linnet)

Don't Drink The Water
    Dave Matthews Band; *Before These Crowded Streets* ....(RCA)

Don't Go Home With Your Hard On
    Leonard Cohen; *Death Of A Ladies' Man* .... (Columbia)

Don't Stay Home
311; *311* . . . . (Capricorn)
Down By The Bay
Eric Heatherly; *Country Goes Raffi-C* . . . . (Rounder)
Down Home
Original Broadway Cast; *Purlie* . . . . (RCA)
Down Home
Alabama; *Pass It On Down* . . . . (BMG Special Prod.)
Down Home
John Hiatt; *Overcoats* . . . . (Epic)
Down Home Girl
Nazareth; *Play'n' The Game* . . . . (A&M)
Down Home Girl
Rolling Stones; *The Rolling Stones, Now!* . . . . (Abkco)
Down Home In Kentucky
Frankie Jaxon; *Frankie ''Half-Pint'' Jaxon-1927-1940* . . . . . . (Sony Broadway)
Down Home In New Orleans
Magic Organ; *Traveling With The Magic Organ* . . . . . . (Ranwood)
Down Home Town
Electric Light Orchestra; *Face The Music* . . . . (Jet)
Dream Home In New Zealand
English Beat; *Wha'ppen* . . . . (I.R.S.)
Drinkin' My Way Back Home
Gene Watson; *Gene Watson's Greatest Hits* . . . . (MCA)
Little By Little . . . . (MCA)
Texas Saturday Night . . . . (MCA)
Drive
Cars; *Heartbeat City* . . . . (Elektra)
MTV's Rock 'N' Roll To Go-C . . . . (Elektra)
The Cars' Greatest Hits . . . . (Elektra)
Eat At Home
Paul And Linda McCartney; *RAM* . . . . (Capitol)
Eight More Miles
Kieran Kane/Kevin Welch; *11/12/13: Live In Melbourne,
Australia* . . . . (Dead Reckoning)
Evening Falls
Enya; *Watermark* . . . . (Reprise)
Exile
Enya; *Watermark* . . . . (Reprise)
Feels Like Home
LeAnn Rimes; *Sittin' On Top Of The World* . . . . (Curb)
Feels Like Home
Bonnie Raitt; *ST/Michael* . . . . (Revolution)
Chantal Kreviazuk; *Songs From Dawson's Creek* . . . . . . (Sony Music Soundtrax)
Linda Ronstadt; *Feels Like Home* . . . . (Elektra)
Randy Newman; *Guilty: 30 Years Of Randy Newman* . . . (Rhino)
Randy Newman's Faust . . . . (Reprise)
Ferry Cross The Mersey
Gerry And The Pacemakers; *Ferry Across The Mersey-Best Of Gerry And
The Pacemakers* . . . . (EMI)
History Of British Rock-#4-C . . . . (Rhino)
Fly Away Home
Ozark Mountain Daredevils; *Best Of The Ozark Mountain Daredevils* . . . (A&M)
Men From Earth . . . . (A&M)
Flying Home
Benny Goodman; *Jazz Sampler-#6-C* . . . . (Columbia)
Ella Fitzgerald; *Best Of Ella Fitzgerald* . . . . (MCA)
Ella Fitzgerald & Count Basie; *Pablo Live* . . . . (Pablo)
Lionel Hampton & His Orchestra; *Flying Home* . . . . (Dunhill Compact Classics)
Gary, Indiana
Original Cast; *ST/The Music Man* . . . . (Gold Rush)
Gentle Rains Of Home
George Morgan; *45-#32886* . . . . (Decca)
Get Back
Beatles; *Beatles 1* . . . . (Capitol)
Beatles-20 Greatest Hits . . . . (Capitol)
Beatles-Box Set . . . . (Capitol)
Let It Be . . . . (Capitol)
Past Masters-Volume Two . . . . (Parlophone)
Reel Music . . . . (Capitol)
Rock 'N' Roll Music . . . . (Capitol)
The Beatles/1967-1970 . . . . (Capitol)
Get Me Home
Foxy Brown; *Ill Na Na* . . . . (Violator)
Give My Love To Rose
George Jones; *George Jones Sings The Hits Of His Country
Cousins* . . . . (Razor & Tie)
Johnny Cash; *Johnny Cash-Sun Years* . . . . (Rhino)
Go Back Home
Stephen Stills; *Stephen Stills* . . . . (Atlantic)
Still Stills . . . . (Atlantic)
Go Back Home
T-Connection; *Magic* . . . . (Dash)
Go Back Home
Andrew Gold; *What's Wrong With This Picture?* . . . . . . (Asylum)
Go Home
Stevie Wonder; *In Square Circle* . . . . (Motown)

Go Home Girl
Ry Cooder; *Bop Till You Drop* . . . . (Warner Bros.)
God Bless America
Anita Bryant; *Golden Classics-Anita Bryant* . . . . (Collectables)
Bill & Gloria Gaither; *Kennedy Center Homecoming: A Celebration Of Our
Faith And Heritage* . . . . (Springhouse Music Grp./Chordant)
Celine Dion; *America: A Tribute To Heroes-C* . . . . . . (Interscope)
God Bless America-C . . . . (Columbia)
Drew Carey; *ST/The Drew Carey Show* . . . . (Rhino)
Frank Zappa; *Uncle Meat* . . . . (Barking Pumpkin)
Kate Smith; *Best Of Kate Smith* . . . . (RCA)
God Bless America . . . . (Pickwick)
Kate Smith-Legendary Performer . . . . (RCA)
Nipper's Greatest Hits Of The '30s-#1-C . . . . (RCA)
Stars And Stripes Forever-#2-C . . . . . (Volcano Entertainment)
LeAnn Rimes; *You Light Up My Life-Inspirational Songs* . . . . . . (Curb)
Lee Greenwood; *American Patriot* . . . . (Capitol)
Mormon Tabernacle Choir; *God Bless America* . . . . . . (Sony Music Classical)
Original Soundtrack; *ST/The Deer Hunter* . . . . (Capitol)
Peter Pan Kids; *I Love America Sing Along* . . . . (Compose)
Robert Shaw Chorale; *Battle Cry Of Freedom* . . . . (RCA)
Goin' Back
Byrds; *20 Essential Tracks From The Box Set* . . . . . . (Columbia)
The Byrds . . . . (Columbia)
Dusty Springfield; *Dusty Springfield-Golden Greats* . . . . . . (Philips)
Neil Young; *Comes A Time* . . . . (Reprise)
Nils Lofgren; *Best Of Nils Lofgren* . . . . (A&M)
Night After Night . . . . (A&M)
Nils Lofgren . . . . (Rykodisc)
Goin' Back
Neil Young; *Comes A Time* . . . . (Reprise)
Goin' Home
Alvin Lee/Ten Years Later; *Ride On* . . . . (RSO)
Going Home
Osmonds; *Osmonds' Greatest Hits* . . . . (Polydor)
Going Home
Rolling Stones; *Aftermath* . . . . (Abkco)
Going Home
Elvis Presley; *Collector's Gold* . . . . (RCA)
Going Home
Fats Domino; *Fats Domino-Legendary Masters* . . . . . . (United Artists)
Going Home
Kenny G; *Kenny G-Live* . . . . (Arista)
Going Home
Buddy Guy; *Left My Blues In San Francisco* . . . . (Chess)
Going Home
Little Richard; *Little Richard's Greatest Hits* . . . . (Trip)
Going Home
Dire Straits; *Live-Alchemy* . . . . (Warner Bros.)
Going Home
Santana; *Lotus* . . . . (Columbia)
Going Home To Louisiana
Chris Thomas; *The Beginning* . . . . (Arhoolie)
Golden Slumbers
Beatles; *Abbey Road* . . . . (Parlophone)
Beatles-Box Set . . . . (Capitol)
Got No More Home Than A Dog
Ian & Sylvia; *Ian & Sylvia* . . . . (Vanguard)
Ian & Sylvia's Greatest Hits . . . . (Vanguard)
Got No Reason Now For Goin' Home
Gene Watson; *Country Classics-#9-1984-1987-C* . . . . . . (Universal)
Heartaches Love & Stuff . . . . (Curb/MCA)
Texas Saturday Night . . . . (MCA)
Gotta Get You Home Tonight
Eugene Wilde; *Eugene Wilde* . . . . (Phil World)
Green Green Grass Of Home
Burl Ives; *Best Of Burl Ives-#2* . . . . (MCA)
Elvis Presley; *Elvis Presley Today* . . . . (RCA)
Our Memories Of Elvis, Volume 2 . . . . (RCA)
George Jones; *20 Golden Pieces Of George Jones* . . . . . (Bulldog)
Johnny Cash; *Johnny Cash-16 Biggest Hits-#2* . . . . . . (Legacy)
Tom Jones; *Country Side Of Tom Jones* . . . . (London)
Things That Matter Most To Me . . . . (Mercury)
Tom Jones-London Collector-Greatest Hits . . . . (London)
Gypsy Woman (She's Homeless)
Crystal Waters; *Red Hot + Dance-C* . . . . (Columbia)
Surprise . . . . (Mercury)
Halfway Home Cafe
Ricky Skaggs and Kentucky Thunder; *History Of The Future* . . . (Skaggs Family)
Happy 'Cause I'm Going Home
Chicago; *Chicago At Carnegie Hall* . . . . (Chicago)
Chicago III . . . . (Chicago)
Hard Day's Night, A
Beatles; *Beatles 1* . . . . (Capitol)
Beatles-20 Greatest Hits . . . . (Capitol)
ST/A Hard Day's Night . . . . (Capitol)
The Beatles At The Hollywood Bowl . . . . (Capitol)
The Beatles/1962-1966 . . . . (Capitol)

Harriet Tubman's Gonna Carry Me Home
Long Ryders; *Two-Fisted Tales* . . . . (Island)
He Calls Home
Candlebox; *Candlebox* . . . .(Maverick)
Heartbreak U.S.A.
Kitty Wells; *I Love Country-Hits Of The '60s-#1-C* . . . . . (Priority)
  Kitty Wells' Greatest Songs . . . . (Curb)
  The Country Music Hall Of Fame-Kitty Wells . . . . (MCA Special Prod.)
Heavenly Homes
Be Bop Deluxe; *Sunburst Finish.* . . . . (Capitol)
Home
Loretta Lynn; *Home* . . . .(MCA)
Home
Sheryl Crow; *Sheryl Crow* . . . . (A&M)
Home
Staind; *Dysfunction* . . . .(Flip/Elektra)
Home
Alan Jackson; *Alan Jackson-The Greatest Hits Collection* . . . . (Arista)
  Here In The Real World . . . . (Arista)
Home
Duncan Sheik; *Duncan Sheik* . . . .(Atlantic)
Home
Gary Puckett And The Union Gap; *Gary Puckett And The Union Gap's
  Greatest Hits* . . . . (Columbia)
Home
Jerry Lee Lewis; *Golden Cream Of Jerry Lee Lewis* . . . . (Sun)
Home
Public Image Ltd.; *Greatest Hits So Far* . . . . (Virgin)
Home
Hothouse Flowers; *Home* . . . . (London)
Home
Jamaica Boys; *Jamaica Boys* . . . .(Warner Bros.)
Home
Joe Walsh & Barnstorm; *Joe Walsh & Barnstorm* . . . .(MCA)
Home
Ian Matthews; *Some Days You Eat The Bear* . . . . (Elektra)
Home
Lene Lovich; *Stateless...Plus* . . . . (Rhino)
Home
Jethro Tull; *Stormwatch* . . . .(Chrysalis)
Home
Original Cast/Stephanie Mills; *The Wiz* . . . .(Atlantic)
Home
Joe Diffie; *Billboard Top Country Hits-1990-C* . . . . (Rhino)
  Joe Diffie's Greatest Hits . . . .(Epic)
Home & Dry
Gerry Rafferty; *City To City* . . . .(EMI)
Home Again
Al Green; *Livin' For You* . . . . (Motown)
Home Again
Barry Manilow; *Barry Manilow II* . . . . (Arista)
Home Again
Judy Collins; *Home Again* . . . . (Elektra)
Home Again
Carole King; *Tapestry.* . . . .(Epic)
Home Again
Supertramp; *Supertramp* . . . . (A&M)
Home Again
Bryan Adams; *Into The Fire* . . . . (A&M)
Home Again In My Heart
Nitty Gritty Dirt Band; *More Great Dirt-Best Of Nitty Gritty
  Dirt Band* . . . . (Warner Bros.)
  Partners Brothers & Friends . . . .(Warner Bros.)
Home Alone
R. Kelly featuring Keith Murray; *R. Kelly* . . . . (Jive)
Home At Last
Steely Dan; *Aja* . . . .(MCA)
Home Cookin'
Junior Walker & The All Stars; *Junior Walker & The All Stars'
  Greatest Hits* . . . . (Motown)
  Junior Walker & The All Stars-Anthology . . . . (Motown)
Home Grown
Neil Young, Crazy Horse & The Bullets; *American Stars 'N Bars* . . . . . (Reprise)
Home In Indiana
Magic Organ; *Traveling With The Magic Organ* . . . .(Ranwood)
Home In Louisiana
Country Gentlemen; *Home In Louisiana* . . . . (Vanguard)
  Remembrances & Forecasts . . . . (Vanguard)
Home In My Hand
Foghat; *Best Of Foghat.* . . . .(Rhino)
  Energized . . . . (Rhino)
  Foghat-Live . . . . (Rhino)
Home In San Antone
Bob Wills & His Texas Playboys; *Tiffany Transcriptions-#4-You're From
  Texas.* . . . . (Rhino)
George Strait; *The Chill Of An Early Fall.* . . . .(MCA)
Texas Playboys & Leon McAuliffe; *Greatest Hits Of Texas-C* . . . . (Rhino)
  San Antonio Rose Story . . . . (Delmark)

Home In Tennessee
Carter Family; *Longing For Old Virginia: Their Complete Victor Recordings-
  1934.* . . . . (Rounder)
Home Is A Wounded Heart
Neil Diamond; *Beautiful Noise* . . . . (Columbia)
Home Is Africa
Horace Parlan; *Afro Blue: The Roots & Rhythms Of Jazz-C* . . . . (Blue Note)
Home Is Where The Hatred Is
Esther Phillips; *Best Of Esther Phillips* . . . . (CBS Associated)
  From A Whisper To A Scream . . . . (CBS Associated)
Gil Scott-Heron; *Gil Scott-Heron* . . . . (Bluebird)
  It's Your World . . . . (Arista)
  Pieces Of A Man . . . .(Flying Dutchman)
Home Is Where The Heart Is
Bobby Womack; *Home Is Where The Heart Is* . . . . (Columbia)
Gladys Knight & The Pips; *Still Together* . . . .(Buddah)
Kool & The Gang; *In The Heart* . . . . (De-Lite)
Home Lovin' Man
Andy Williams; *Andy Williams' Greatest Hits-#2* . . . . (Columbia)
Home Of The Blues
Dwight Yoakam; *Buenas Noches From A Lonely Room* . . . . (Reprise)
Johnny Cash; *Classic Cash-Hall Of Fame Series* . . . . (Mercury)
  Johnny Cash-Legend . . . . (Sun)
  Johnny Cash-Original Golden Hits-#1. . . . . (Sun)
  Original Johnny Cash . . . . (Sun)
  Superbilly . . . . (Sun)
Home On The Range
Bing Crosby; *Crooner-Columbia Years-1928-1934* . . . . (Columbia)
Boston Pops Orchestra/Arthur Fiedler; *Yankee Doodle Dandy.* . . . .(RCA)
Gene Autry; *50th Anniversary.* . . . . (Republic/Universal)
  *The Country Music Hall Of Fame-Gene Autry-15 Of His All-Time
    Greatest Hits* . . . . (Columbia)
Neil Young; *ST/Where The Buffalo Roam.* . . . .(Backstreet)
Home Sweet Home
Carl Jackson; *Songs Of The South* . . . .(Sugar Hill)
Doc & Merle Watson; *Home Sweet Home.* . . . .(Sugar Hill)
Lawrence Welk; *200 Years Of American Music* . . . . (Ranwood)
Home Sweet Home
Motley Crue; *Theatre Of Pain.* . . . . (Elektra)
Home Sweet Home
Peter Gabriel; *Peter Gabriel* . . . .(Atlantic)
Home To Myself
Melissa Manchester; *Essence Of Melissa Manchester* . . . . (Arista)
Home To New Orleans
Queen Ida; *Caught In The Act* . . . .(Crescendo)
Home To You
John Michael Montgomery; *Home To You* . . . .(Atlantic)
Home You're Tearing Down
Loretta Lynn; *Loretta Lynn's Greatest Hits* . . . . (MCA)
Home, Sweet Oklahoma
Tom Paxton; *It Ain't Easy* . . . .(Flying Fish)
Homebound
Ted Nugent; *Cat Scratch Fever.* . . . . (Epic)
Homeboy
Michael McDonald; *Take It To Heart* . . . . (Reprise)
Homecoming
Floyd Cramer; *Forever Floyd Cramer* . . . .(Step One)
  Just Me & My Piano . . . .(Step One)
Tom T. Hall; *Essential Tom T. Hall-20th Anniversary Collection* . . . . (Mercury)
  Tom T. Hall's Greatest Hits-#1 . . . . (Mercury)
Homecomputer
Kraftwerk; *The Mix.* . . . . (Elektra)
Homegrown Western Saturday Night
Chris LeDoux; *Powder River* . . . . (Liberty)
Homeless
Paul Simon; *Graceland.* . . . . (Warner Bros.)
Homemade Love
Kenny Rogers; *Love Lifted Me* . . . . (EMI)
Homemade Lovin'
Whispers; *Whisper In Your Ear.* . . . .(Solar)
Homestead In My Heart
Amazing Rhythm Aces; *Amazing Rhythm Aces* . . . . (Columbia)
Hometown Blues
Tom Petty And The Heartbreakers; *Tom Petty & The
  Heartbreakers* . . . .(Gone Gator)
Hometown Blues
Rosanne Cash; *Seven Year Ache* . . . . (Columbia)
Hometown Honeymoon
Alabama; *American Pride.* . . . .(RCA)
Hometown New Orleans
Champion Jack Dupree; *Forever & Ever* . . . . (Bullseye Blues)
Homeward Bound
Paul Simon; *Paul Simon In Concert/Live Rhymin'* . . . . (Columbia)
Paul Simon & George Harrison; *Nobody's Child-Romanian Angel
  Appeal-C* . . . . (Warner Bros.)
Simon & Garfunkel; *Collected Works* . . . . (Columbia)
  Parsley Sage Rosemary & Thyme. . . . . (Columbia)
  Simon & Garfunkel's Greatest Hits . . . . (Columbia)
  The Concert In Central Park . . . .(Warner Bros.)

Willie Nelson & Waylon Jennings; *Take It To The Limit* . . . . (Columbia)
Homeward Bound
Fleetwood Mac; *Bare Trees*. . . . .(Reprise)
Honey, I'm Home
Shania Twain; *Come On Over* . . . . (Mercury)
House Full Of Love
Michael McDonald; *In The Spirit-A Christmas Album* . . . . (MCA)
House Is Not A Home
Burt Bacharach; *Burt Bacharach-Classics-#23*. . . . .(A&M)
Dionne Warwick; *Dionne Warwick Greatest Hits*. . . . . (Everest)
Dionne Warwick-Anthology 1962-1971 . . . . (Rhino)
Hot-Live & Otherwise. . . . . (Arista)
Say A Little Prayer . . . . (Dunhill Compact Classics)
Luther Vandross; *Best Of Luther Vandross...The Best Of Love* . . . . . (Epic)
Never Too Much . . . . (Epic)
Mavis Staples; *15 Original Big Hits-#3-C* . . . . (Stax)
Mavis Staples . . . . (Stax)
Hundred And Sixty Acres
Marty Robbins; *Gunfighter Ballads & Trail Songs* . . . . (Legacy)
Hurricane Eye
Paul Simon; *You're The One* . . . . (Warner Bros.)
I Ain't Going Out
Jon B.; *Cool Relax* . . . .(Yab Yum/550)
I Ain't Got No Home
Bob Dylan; *Tribute To Woody Guthrie-C* . . . . (Warner Bros.)
I Am Not Hiding
Kenny Loggins; *The Unimaginable Life* . . . . (Columbia)
I Have Found Me A Home
Jimmy Buffett; *White Sport Coat & A Pink Crustacean* . . . . (MCA)
I Just Came Home To Count The Memories
John Anderson; *Honky-Tonk Country-Tender Lovin' Country* . . . . .(Priority)
I Just Came Home To Count The Memories . . . . (Warner Bros.)
John Anderson's Greatest Hits . . . . (Warner Bros.)
I Left My Heart In San Francisco
Tony Bennett; *I Left My Heart In San Francisco* . . . . (Columbia)
Pop Classics Of The '60s-C . . . . (Columbia)
Tony Bennett's All-Time Greatest Hits . . . . (Columbia)
I Want To Walk You Home
Fats Domino; *Billboard Top R&B Hits-1959-C* . . . . (Rhino)
Fats Domino's Greatest Hits . . . . (MCA)
My Blue Heaven-Best Of Fats Domino-#1 . . . . (EMI)
I Wonder How The Old Folks Are At Home
Doc & Merle Watson; *Home Sweet Home* . . . . (Sugar Hill)
I Wonder If I Take You Home
Lisa Lisa & Cult Jam With Full Force; *Breakdancing* . . . . (Columbia)
Lisa Lisa & Cult Jam With Full Force . . . . (Columbia)
I Won't Be Home No More
Hank Williams With His Drifting Cowboys; *Hank Williams-24 Greatest
Hits-#2* . . . . (Polydor)
Hank Williams-40 Greatest Hits . . . . (Polydor)
I Won't Be Home Tonight
Tony Carey; *Tony Carey* . . . . (Rocket)
If You're Gone
Matchbox Twenty; *Mad Season By Matchbox Twenty* . . . . (Lava)
I'll Be Home
Barbra Streisand; *Stoney End* . . . . (Columbia)
Randy Newman; *Little Criminals* . . . . (Warner Bros.)
Randy Newman/Live . . . . (Warner Archives)
I'll Be Home
Flamingos; *Alan Freed's Memory Lane-C* . . . . (MCA)
Best Of The Flamingos . . . . (Rhino)
Super Oldies Of The '50s-#6-C . . . . (Audio Fidelity)
Platters; *Platters Greatest Hits-#2* . . . . (Curb)
I'll Be Your Shelter
Taylor Dayne; *Can't Fight Fate* . . . . (Arista)
I'll Go Home With Bonnie Jean
Original Cast; *Brigadoon.* . . . . (RCA)
I'll Take You Home Again Kathleen
Billy Shepherd Singers; *Irish Sing-Along* . . . . (MCA)
Bing Crosby; *When Irish Eyes Are Smiling* . . . . (MCA)
Slim Whitman; *Paloma Blanca-Best Of Slim Whitman-Legendary
Masters* . . . . (EMI)
I'm Afraid To Go Home
Brian Hyland; *Brian Hyland's Greatest Hits* . . . . (Rhino)
Gene Pitney; *This Is Gene Pitney*. (Out Of Print)
I'm Coming Home
Johnny Mathis; *First 25 Years-Silver Anniversary Album*. . . . . . . (Columbia)
I'm Coming Home. . . . . (Columbia)
I'm Coming Home
Left Banke; *History Of The Left Banke* . . . . (Rhino)
I'm Coming Home
Carmen McRae; *Jazzy Ladies-C* . . . . (Dunhill Compact Classics)
I'm Coming Home
Elvis Presley; *Return Of The Rocker* . . . . (RCA)
I'm Coming Home
Johnny Horton; *Truck Driver Boogie Big Rig Hits-1939-1969-C* . . . . . (Audium)
I'm Going Back To The Old Home
Doc Watson; *Legacy-A Tribute To The First Generation Of
Bluegrass-C* . . . . (Sugar Hill)

I'm Going Home
Ten Years After; *ST/Woodstock*. . . . . (Atlantic)
I'm Gonna Hire A Wino To Decorate Our Home
David Frizzell; *Family's Fine But This One's All Mine* . . . . (Warner Bros.)
I'm Like A Bird
Nelly Furtado; *Whoa Nelly!* . . . . (DreamWorks/SKG)
Immortality
Pearl Jam; *Vitalogy* . . . . (Epic)
In A Shanty In Old Shanty Town
Ink Spots; *Java Jive* . . . . (Laserlight)
In My Own Backyard
Joe Diffie; *A Thousand Winding Roads* . . . . (Epic)
Infamous Angel
Iris DeMent; *Infamous Angel* . . . . (Warner Bros.)
Ireland My Home
Anne & Francie Brolly; *Ireland My Home* . . . . (Rego Irish)
Barley Bree; *Speak Up For Old Ireland* . . . . (Shanachie)
It Won't Be Long
Beatles; *Meet The Beatles!* . . . . (Capitol)
With The Beatles . . . . (Parlophone)
It's Late
Ricky Nelson; *Lonesome Town* . . . . (CEMA Special Prod.)
Ricky Nelson Volume 1 . . . . (Gold Rush)
Josie
Steely Dan; *Aja* . . . . (MCA)
Steely Dan's Greatest Hits . . . . (MCA)
Jukebox Never Plays Home Sweet Home
Jack Greene; *45-#0016.* . . . . (EMH)
Jump Up Behind Me
James Taylor; *Hourglass* . . . . (Columbia)
Songs From The Heart-C . . . . (Columbia)
Jungle, The
Kiss; *Carnival Of Souls: The Final Sessions* . . . . (Mercury)
Keep The Home Fire Burning
Latimore; *Get Down Tonight! Best Of T.K. Records-C* . . . . (Rhino)
Latimore III . . . . (Glades)
Millie Jackson; *Get It Out'cha System* . . . . (Spring)
Live & Uncensored . . . . (Spring)
Kentucky
Everly Brothers; *All They Had To Do Was Dream* . . . . (Rhino)
Songs Our Daddy Taught Us . . . . (Rhino)
Gail Davies; *I'll Be There* . . . . (Warner Bros.)
Mac Wiseman; *Red, White & Bluegrass-C* . . . . (C.M.H. Prod.)
Osborne Brothers; *Best Of The Osborne Brothers* . . . . (MCA)
Whitstein Brothers; *Rose Of My Heart*. . . . . (Rounder)
Kiss An Angel Good Mornin'
Charley Pride; *Charley Pride-24 Greatest Hits* . . . . (Tee Vee)
Pride! My 6 Latest And 6 Greatest . . . . (ISD/Intersound)
The Ultimate Charley Pride . . . . (Bransounds)
Leaving Home Ain't Easy
Queen; *Jazz* . . . . (Hollywood)
Lend Me Your Comb
Beatles; *The Beatles-Anthology-#1* . . . . (Capitol)
Carl Perkins; *Carl Perkins-Original Sun Greatest Hits* . . . .(Rhino)
Let Me Take You Home Tonight
Boston; *Boston.* . . . . (Epic)
Let's Stay Home Together
Joe; *Better Days* . . . . (Jive)
Let's Take The Long Way Home
Cab Calloway; *Cab Calloway-1942-1947* . . . . (Classics)
Rosemary Clooney; *Rosemary Clooney Sings The Music Of Harold
Arlen* . . . . (Concord Jazz)
Letter From Home
Eddie Jefferson; *Letter From Home* . . . . (Original Jazz Classics)
Letter Home
Wendy Waldman; *Letters Home* . . . . (Cypress)
Letter Home
Memphis Slim; *All Kinds Of Blues* . . . . (Bluesville)
Letter Home
Forester Sisters; *Forester Sisters' Greatest Hits* . . . . (Warner Bros.)
Letter Home
Elvis Costello & The Brodsky Quartet; *Juliet Letters* . . . . (Warner Bros.)
Letter, The
Box Tops; *Billboard Top Rock 'N' Roll Hits-1967-C* . . . .(Rhino)
Box Tops' Greatest Hits . . . .(Rhino)
Cruisin'-1967-C . . . . (Increase)
Oldies But Goodies-#12-C . . . . (Original Sound)
Rockin' '60s-C . . . . (Priority)
Joe Cocker; *Joe Cocker Live* . . . . (Capitol)
Joe Cocker-Classics-#4. . . . . (A&M)
Joe Cocker's Greatest Hits . . . . (A&M)
Mad Dogs & Englishmen . . . . (A&M)
Vernon Green & The Medallions; *Oldies But Goodies-#1-C* . . . (Original Sound)
Vernon Green & The Medallions-Golden Classics . . . .(Collectables)
Lida Rose/Will I Ever Tell You?
Original Broadway Cast; *The Music Man* . . . . (Angel)
Original Cast; *The Music Man* . . . . (Gold Rush)
Soundtrack; *ST/The Music Man* . . . . (Warner Bros.)

Little Home In Tennessee
Bill Harrell & The Virginians; *Ballads & Bluegrass* . . . . (Adelphi)
Mac Wiseman; *Classic Bluegrass-Mac Wiseman*. . . . . (Rebel)
Little Home In West Virginia
Josh Graves; *King Of The Dobro* . . . .(C.M.H. Prod.)
Little Street Where Old Friends Meet, A
Tony Bennett; *I Left My Heart In San Francisco* . . . . (Columbia)
London Homesick Blues
David Allan Coe; *David Allan Coe's Biggest Hits* . . . . (Legacy)
Jerry Jeff Walker; *Great Gonzos*. . . . . (MCA)
Viva Terlingua . . . . (MCA)
London Rain (Nothing Heals Like You Do)
Heather Nova; *Siren* . . . . (Big Cat)
Songs From Dawson's Creek. . . . . (Sony Music Soundtrax)
Lonely Teenager
Dion; *Collectables Presents The History Of Rock-#4-C* . . . . (Collectables)
Dion-His Best . . . . (Laurie)
Everything You Always Wanted To Hear By . . . . (Laurie)
The Wanderer . . . . (Laurie)
Lonesome And A Long Way From Home
Eric Clapton; *Eric Clapton* . . . . (Polydor)
Long Long Way From Home
Foreigner; *Foreigner* . . . . (Atlantic)
Records . . . . (Atlantic)
Long Way From Home
Neil Diamond; *Double Gold-Neil Diamond* . . . . (Bang)
Just For You . . . . (Bang)
Long Way From Home
Whitesnake; *Love Hunter* . . . .(Geffen)
Look What Followed Me Home
David Ball; *Thinkin' Problem*. . . . .(Warner Bros.)
Lost Children, The
Michael Jackson; *Invincible* . . . .(Epic)
Love You For A Day
Ricky Martin; *Ricky Martin* . . . . (Columbia)
Major Tom (Coming Home)
Peter Schilling; *Different Story (World Of Lust & Crime)* . . . . (Elektra)
Error In The The System . . . . (Elektra)
Make Me The Woman That You Go Home To
Gladys Knight & The Pips; *Compact Command Performances-Gladys Knight
& The Pips* . . . . (Motown)
Gladys Knight & The Pips-All The Great Hits . . . . (Motown)
Gladys Knight & The Pips-Anthology . . . . (Motown)
Standing Ovation . . . . (S.O.U.L.)
Mama, I'm Coming Home
Ozzy Osbourne; *No More Tears* . . . .(Epic)
The Ozzman Cometh . . . .(Epic)
Martians Go Home
Shorty Rogers; *Great Moments In Jazz-C*. . . . . (Atlantic)
Meet Me Tonight By My Old Kentucky Home
Joe Val & The New England Bluegrass Boys; *Joe Val & The New England
Bluegrass Boys-Vol. 2* . . . . (Rounder)
Midnight Train To Georgia
Gladys Knight & The Pips; *Billboard Top Rock 'N' Roll Hits-1973-C*. . . (Rhino)
Gladys Knight & The Pips' Greatest Hits . . . . (Buddah)
Imagination . . . . (Right Stuff)
On & On. . . . . (Fifty One West)
Radio Active Hits-C . . . . (Accord)
Train Trax-C . . . . (Sony Music Special Prod.)
Very Best Of Gladys Knight & The Pips. . . . . (Buddah)
Miles From Our Home
Cowboy Junkies; *Miles From Our Home* . . . . (Geffen)
Mister & Mississippi
Patti Page; *Patti Page's Greatest Hits* . . . . (Columbia)
Mommy Can I Come Home
Keb' Mo'; *The Door* . . . . (550/Epic/Okeh)
More Than One Way Home
Keb' Mo'; *Just Like You* . . . . (Okeh)
My Adobe Hacienda
Bob Wills; *Best Of Bob Wills & His Texas Playboys* . . . . (MCA)
My Blue Heaven
Artie Shaw; *Complete Artie Shaw-#4* . . . . (RCA)
This Is Artie Shaw . . . . (Bluebird)
Fats Domino; *Fats Domino-Legendary Masters*. . . . . (United Artists)
Fats Domino's Greatest Hits . . . . (Everest)
My Blue Heaven-Best Of Fats Domino-#1 . . . . (EMI)
Oldies But Goodies-#10-C . . . . (Original Sound)
Frank Sinatra; *Frank Sinatra-Gift Set* . . . . (Capitol)
Sinatra's Swingin' Session!!! . . . . (Capitol)
My Dear Old Arizona Home
Rex Allen; *Back In The Saddle Again: American Cowboy
Songs-C* . . . . (New World)
My Home Ain't In The Hall Of Fame
J.D. Crowe and the New South; *My Home Ain't In The Hall
Of Fame* . . . . (Rounder)
Jonathan Edwards; *Lucky Day* . . . . (Atco)
My Home Is In The Delta
Muddy Waters; *Folk Singer* . . . . (Chess)

The Chess Box-Muddy Waters . . . . (Chess)
My Home's In Alabama
Alabama; *Alabama-Live* . . . . (RCA)
Alabama's Greatest Hits . . . . (RCA)
Gonna Have A Party...Live . . . . (RCA)
My Home's In Alabama . . . . (RCA)
My Hometown
Bruce Springsteen; *Born In The U.S.A.* . . . . (Columbia)
Bruce Springsteen's Greatest Hits . . . . (Columbia)
My Little Home Down In New Orleans
Jimmie Rodgers; *Jimmie Rodgers-Early Years-1928-1929* . . . . (Rounder)
My North Dakota Home
Lawrence Welk; *Reminiscing-#1* . . . . (Ranwood)
My Ol' Kentucky Rock & Roll Home
Original New York Cast; *Oil City Symphony* . . . .(DRG)
My Old Kentucky Home
Al Jolson; *The Al Jolson Story-#5* . . . . (MCA)
Ry Cooder; *Ry Cooder*. . . . . (Reprise)
Salli Terri; *Songs Of The American Land* . . . . (Angel)
My Second Home
Tracy Lawrence; *Alibis* . . . .(Atlantic)
My Tennessee Mountain Home
Dolly Parton; *Best Of A Great Year-#3-C* . . . . (RCA)
Best Of Dolly Parton . . . . (RCA)
My Tennessee Mountain Home. . . . . (RCA)
Rose Maddox; *Reckless Love & Bold Adventure*. . . . . (Takoma)
New Way Home
K.T. Oslin; *Greatest Hits: Songs From An Aging Sex Bomb* . . . . (RCA)
Love In A Small Town . . . . (RCA)
New York's My Home
Ray Charles; *The Genius Hits The Road* . . . . (Rhino)
Sammy Davis, Jr.; *New York Songs-C*. . . . . (Rhino)
New York's Not My Home
Jim Croce; *Photographs & Memories/His Greatest Hits* . . . .(Atlantic)
New York's Not My Home
Kid Rock; *Grits Sandwiches For Breakfast* . . . .(Jive)
Next Year
Foo Fighters; *There Is Nothing Left To Lose* . . . .(Roswell/RCA)
No Other Love
Perry Como; *Easy Listening* . . . .(Pair)
No Place But Texas
Willie Nelson; *Texas Super Hits-C* . . . . (Columbia)
The Promiseland . . . . (Columbia)
No Place Like Home
Bert Williams; *Music From The New York Stage (1890-1920)-#4-1917-
1920-C*. . . . . (Pearl)
Nobody Home
Pink Floyd; *The Wall*. . . . . (Columbia)
Roger Waters; *The Wall-Live In Berlin* . . . . (Mercury)
Nobody's Home
Clint Black; *Killin' Time* . . . . (RCA)
North Carolina (Home In My Heart)
Claudia Church; *Claudia Church* . . . . (Reprise)
North Carolina, My Home State
Andy Griffith; *American Originals-Andy Griffith* . . . . (Capitol)
Nothing As It Seems
Pearl Jam; *Binaural*. . . . . (Epic)
Oklahoma Going Home
Kate Wolf & Wildwood Flower; *Back Roads* . . . . (Rhino)
Old Folks At Home
Mormon Tabernacle Choir; *Songs Of The Civil War And Stephen Foster
Favorites* . . . .(Sony Music Classical)
Paul Robeson; *A Man & His Beliefs-Golden Classics-#2* . . . . (Collectables)
Old Home Filler Up & Keep On A Truckin'
C.W. McCall; *C.W. McCall's Greatest Hits* . . . .(Polydor)
Wolf Creek Pass . . . . (MGM)
Old Kentucky Home
Randy Newman; *12 Songs*. . . . . (Reprise)
Randy Newman/Live. (Warner Archives)
Old Man From The Mountain
Merle Haggard & The Strangers; *For The Record: Merle Haggard-43
Legendary Hits* . . . . (BNA)
On The Way Home
Buffalo Springfield; *Buffalo Springfield* . . . . (Atco)
Buffalo Springfield-Retrospective . . . . (Atco)
Last Time Around . . . . (Atco)
Crosby, Stills, Nash & Young; *4 Way Street*. . . . .(Atlantic)
One Headlight
Wallflowers; *Bringing Down The Horse* . . . .(Interscope)
One Room Country Shack
Buddy Guy; *Man & The Blues* . . . . (Vanguard)
My Time After Awhile . . . . (Vanguard)
Mercy Dee Walton; *Mercy's Troubles* . . . . (Arhoolie)
One Room Country Shack. . . . . (Specialty)
Pity & A Shame. . . . . (Prestige)
Mose Allison; *Mose Allison's Greatest Hits* . . . . (Prestige)
One Way Ticket Back Home
Don Edwards with Tom Morrell & Time-Warp Tophands; *Freight Train
Blues-Classic Railroad Songs-#4-C* . . . . (Rounder)

One Way Ticket Home
Phil Ochs; *Phil Ochs' Greatest Hits* (A&M)
The War Is Over-Best Of Phil Ochs (A&M)
Our House
Crosby, Stills & Nash; *CSN* (Atlantic)
Crosby, Stills, Nash & Young; *Deja Vu* (Atlantic)
So Far (Atlantic)
ST/The Strawberry Statement (MCA)
Our House
Madness; *Madness* (Geffen)
Over The Next Hill
Johnny Cash with The Carter Family; *Johnny Cash-16 Biggest Hits-#2* (Legacy)
Paint Me Back Home In Wyoming
Chris LeDoux; *Paint Me Back Home In Wyoming* (Liberty)
Sounds Of The Western Country (Liberty)
Papa Was A Rollin' Stone
Temptations; *20/20-C* (Motown)
25 #1 Hits From 25 Years-C (Motown)
All The Million-Sellers (Motown)
Billboard Top Rock 'N' Roll Hits-1972-C (Rhino)
Compact Command Performances-Temptations (Motown)
Temptations-Anthology-The Best Of The Temptations (Motown)
Party Till The Cows Come Home
Elvin Bishop Group; *Bill Graham Presents The Last Days Of The Fillmore-C* (Epic Portrait Assoc.)
Pictures Of Home
Deep Purple; *Machine Head* (Warner Bros.)
Please Call Home
Allman Brothers Band; *Beginnings* (Polydor)
Idlewild South (Polydor)
Gregg Allman; *Laid Back* (Polydor)
Please Come To Boston
Dave Loggins; *Apprentice (In A Musical Workshop)* (Epic)
Rock Artifacts-From The Vaults-#2-C (Legacy)
Super Hits Of The '70s-Have A Nice Day-#13-C (Rhino)
David Allan Coe; *David Allan Coe-17 Greatest Hits* (Columbia)
For The Record-The First 10 Years (Columbia)
Joan Baez; *Best Of Joan Baez* (A&M)
Joan Baez-Classics-#8 (A&M)
Reba McEntire; *Starting Over* (MCA)
Put Me On A Train Back To Texas
Waylon Jennings & Willie Nelson; *Clean Shirt* (Epic)
Hot Tracks-Train Super Hits-C (Epic)
Queen Of My Double Wide Trailer
Sammy Kershaw; *Haunted Heart* (Mercury)
Rank Stranger
Ricky Skaggs and Kentucky Thunder; *Bluegrass Rules!* (Rounder)
Ray Of Light
Madonna; *GHV2* (Warner Bros.)
Ray Of Light (Maverick)
Totally Hits-#1-C (Arista)
Roamin' Wyoming
Randy Travis; *Wind In The Wire* (Warner Bros.)
Rocky Top
Conway Twitty; *Hello Darlin'* (MCA Special Prod.)
Flying Burrito Brothers; *Close Encounters To The West Coast* (Relix)
Osborne Brothers; *Best Of The Osborne Brothers* (MCA)
Yesterday, Today & The Osborne Brothers (MCA)
Roy Clark; *Roy Clark In Concert* (MCA)
White Mountain Singers; *Best Of The White Mountain Singers* (Folk Era)
Roll On Mississippi
Charley Pride; *Charley Pride's Greatest Hits* (RCA)
Rollin' Home
Eric Andersen; *Best Of Eric Andersen* (Vanguard)
Peter, Paul & Mary; *Album 1700* (Warner Bros.)
Rollin' In My Sweet Baby's Arms
Bill Monroe; *Bean Blossom* (MCA)
Del McCoury Band; *Appalachian Stomp: Bluegrass Classics-C* (Rhino)
Dillard & Clark; *Fantastic Expedition/Through The Morning* (Mobile Fidelity Sound Lab)
Flatt & Scruggs; *Flatt & Scruggs At Carnegie Hall!* (Koch International)
Flatt & Scruggs-20 Greatest Hits (Deluxe)
Flying Burrito Brothers; *Close Encounters To The West Coast* (Relix)
Leon Russell; *Hank Wilson's Back, Vol. 1* (Right Stuff)
New Lost City Ramblers; *Greatest Folksingers Of The '60s-C* (Vanguard)
Ramblin' Jack Elliott; *Hard Travelin'* (Fantasy)
Ricky Skaggs and Kentucky Thunder; *History Of The Future* (Skaggs Family)
Tony Trischka; *Heartlands* (Rounder)
Willie Nelson; *Willie & Family Live* (Columbia)
Safe European Home
Clash; *Give 'Em Enough Rope* (Epic)
On Broadway (Epic)
The Story Of The Clash, Volume 1 (Epic)
Sailing Home For Christmas
Doug Stone; *First Christmas* (Epic)
Sailing Toward Home
Oak Ridge Boys; *All Our Favorite Songs* (Columbia)
Second Home By The Sea
Genesis; *Genesis* (Atlantic)
Sense Of Purpose
Pretenders; *Isle Of View* (Warner Bros.)
Packed (Sire)
Sentimental Journey
Dinah Shore; *Sentimental Journey: Capitol's Great Ladies Of Song-C* (Gold Rush)
Doris Day; *Doris Day Sings 22 Great Songs-Original Big Band* (Hindsight)
Hal McIntyre & His Orchestra; *Nipper's Greatest Hits Of The '40s-#2-C* (RCA)
Les Brown & His Orchestra; *Best Of The Big Bands-C* (Columbia)
Seven Rooms Of Gloom
Four Tops; *Four Tops' Greatest Hits* (Motown)
Four Tops Reach Out (Motown)
Four Tops-Anthology (Motown)
She Gonna Come Home Wit' Me
Original Broadway Cast; *Most Happy Fella* (Sony Music Classical)
She Keeps The Home Fires Burning
Ronnie Milsap; *Essential Ronnie Milsap* (RCA)
She Makes The Coming Home Worth The Being Gone
Shenandoah; *Extra Mile* (Columbia)
She's Leaving Home
Al Jarreau; *All Fly Home* (Warner Bros.)
Beatles; *Beatles-Box Set* (Capitol)
Beatles-Love Songs (Capitol)
Sgt. Pepper's Lonely Hearts Club Band (Capitol)
Show Me The Road
Bill Staines; *Going To The West* (Red House)
Show Me The Way To Go Home
Artie Shaw; *Best Of Artie Shaw* (MCA)
Randy Erwin; *Back Home* (Really Outstanding Music)
Sing Me Back Home
Alabama; *Mama's Hungry Eyes-Merle Haggard Tribute-C* (Arista)
Flying Burrito Brothers; *Farther Along-Best Of The Flying Burrito Brothers* (A&M)
Merle Haggard & The Strangers; *Best Of Merle Haggard & The Strangers* (Capitol)
Capitol Collectors Series-Merle Haggard & The Strangers (Capitol)
For The Record: Merle Haggard-43 Legendary Hits (BNA)
Okie From Muskogee (Capitol)
Songs I'll Always Sing (Capitol)
Sitting Home
Total; *Kima, Keisha & Pam* (Bad Boy/Arista)
Six Days On The Road
Boxcar Willie; *Truck Driving Favorites* (Madacy)
Dave Dudley; *Billboard Top Country Hits-1963-C* (Rhino)
Country Music Classics-#2-1960-1965-C (K-Tel)
Legends Of Country Guitar-#2-C (Rhino)
Truck Driver Boogie Big Rig Hits-1939-1969-C (Audium)
Flying Burrito Brothers; *Cabin Fever* (Relix)
Farther Along-Best Of The Flying Burrito Brothers (A&M)
Last Of The Red Hot Burritos (A&M)
Sawyer Brown; *Six Days On The Road* (Curb)
Taj Mahal; *Giant Step/De Ole Folks At Home* (Columbia)
Legends Of Rock Guitar-'60s-#2-C (Rhino)
Sloop John B
Beach Boys; *Absolute Best-#2* (Capitol)
Beach Boys '69 (The Beach Boys Live In London) (Capitol)
Beach Boys-Gift Set (Capitol)
Best Of (Good Vibrations) (Reprise)
Made In The U.S.A. (Capitol)
Pet Sounds (Capitol)
ST/Forrest Gump (Epic/Sony Music Soundtrax)
The Pet Sounds Sessions: A 30th Anniversary Collection (Capitol)
Solsbury Hill
Peter Gabriel; *Peter Gabriel* (Atco)
Peter Gabriel/Plays Live (Geffen)
Shaking The Tree-Sixteen Golden Greats (Geffen)
Sort Of Homecoming
U2; *Unforgettable Fire* (Island)
Wide Awake In America (Island)
Sparrow In The Treetop
Guy Mitchell; *Guy Mitchell-16 Most Requested Songs* (Legacy)
Subterranean Homesick Blues
Bob Dylan; *Biograph* (Columbia)
Bob Dylan's Greatest Hits (Columbia)
Bringing It All Back Home (Columbia)
The Bootleg Series-Volumes 1-3 [Rare & Unreleased] (Columbia)
Red Hot Chili Peppers; *Uplift Mofo Party Plan* (EMI)
Suburban Home
Descendants; *Liveage* (SST)
Milo Goes To College (SST)
Somery (SST)
Success Has Made A Failure Of Our Home
Sinead O'Connor; *Am I Not Your Girl?* (Ensign)
So Far...The Best Of Sinead O'Connor (EMI)
Sunny Came Home
Shawn Colvin; *1998 Grammy Nominees-C* (MCA)

A Few Small Repairs . . . . (Columbia)

Swamps Of Home
Original Cast; *Once Upon A Mattress* . . . .(MCA)

Swanee
Al Jolson; *Al Jolson-Best Of The Decca Years* . . . .(MCA)
   Best Of Al Jolson . . . .(MCA)
   Jolson Sang 'Em . . . . (Biograph)
   Music From The New York Stage (1890-1920)-#4-1917-1920-C . . . . . (Pearl)
George Gershwin; *Rhapsody In Blue* . . . . (Biograph)
Judy Garland; *Judy Garland-At Carnegie Hall* . . . . (Capitol)
   Judy Garland's All-Time Greatest Hits . . . . (Curb)

Sweet Chicago Home
David Bromberg; *How Late'll Ya Play 'Til?* . . . . (Fantasy)

Sweet Home Alabama
Alabama; *Skynyrd Frynds-C* . . . .(MCA)
Charlie Daniels Band; *Volunteer Jam VII-C* . . . .(Epic)
Hank Williams, Jr.; *Hank Williams, Jr. "Live"* . . . . (WB/Curb)
Lynyrd Skynyrd; *Billboard Top Rock 'N' Roll Hits-1974-C* . . . . (Rhino)
   Gold & Platinum . . . .(MCA)
   One More From The Road . . . .(MCA)
   Second Helping . . . .(MCA)
   South's Greatest Hits-C . . . . (Capricorn)
   ST/Forrest Gump . . . . (Epic/Sony Music Soundtrax)

Sweet Home Chicago
Blues Brothers; *ST/The Blues Brothers* . . . . (Atlantic)
Foghat; *Best Of Foghat-#2* . . . . (Rhino)
   Stone Blue . . . . (Rhino)
Junior Parker; *Best Of Junior Parker* . . . .(MCA)
Leon Russell & Marc Benno; *Asylum Choir II* . . . .(MCA)
Magic Sam; *Magic Sam-Live* . . . . (Delmark)
Robert Johnson; *King Of The Delta Blues Singers-#2* . . . . . (Columbia)
   Robert Johnson-Complete Recordings . . . . (Columbia)
Taj Mahal; *Recycling The Blues & Other Related Stuff* . . . . (Columbia)
Urban Knights; *Urban Knights 3* . . . . (Narada)

Sweet Indiana Home
Aileen Stanley; *78-#18922* . . . . (Victor)
Marion Harris; *78-#2310* . . . .(Brunswick)

Sweet Mama Hurry Home Or I'll Be Gone
Leon Redbone; *On The Track* . . . .(Warner Bros.)

Sweet Wyoming Home
Chris LeDoux; *Chris LeDoux & The Saddle Boogie Band* . . . . (Liberty)

Swing Low, Sweet Chariot
Eric Clapton; *Time Pieces-#1-The Best Of Eric Clapton* . . . . . (Polydor)
Glenn Miller & His Orchestra; *Moonlight Serenade* . . . . (Ranwood)
Hi-Lo's; *Suddenly It's The Hi-Lo's* . . . . (Columbia)
Jerry Garcia Acoustic Band; *Almost Acoustic* . . . . (Grateful Dead)
Joan Baez; *From Every Stage* . . . . (A&M)
Peggy Lee; *Best Of Peggy Lee* . . . .(MCA)

Swinging Doors
George Jones; *20 Golden Pieces Of George Jones* . . . . (Bulldog)
Merle Haggard; *Capitol Collectors Series-Merle Haggard* . . . . . (Capitol)
Merle Haggard & The Strangers; *Best Of Merle Haggard & The*
   Strangers . . . . (Capitol)
   For The Record: Merle Haggard-43 Legendary Hits . . . . (BNA)
   Okie From Muskogee . . . . (Capitol)
   Songs I'll Always Sing . . . . (Capitol)

Take Care Of Home
Dave Hollister; *Chicago '85 The Movie* . . . .(Def Squad/DreamWorks)

Take Me Back To My Old Carolina Home
Uncle Dave Macon; *Laugh Your Blues Away* . . . . (Rounder)

Take Me Back To Tulsa
Asleep At The Wheel; *Route 66* . . . . (Liberty)
   Very Best Of Asleep At The Wheel Since 1970 . . . . (Relentless/Madacy)
Bob Wills & His Texas Playboys; *All Time Legends Of Country*
   Music-C . . . . (Legacy)
   Bob Wills-Anthology . . . .(Sony Music Special Prod.)
   Columbia Country Classics-#1-Golden Age-C . . . . (Columbia)
   Tiffany Transcriptions-#2-Best Of The Tiffanys . . . . (Rhino)
Clay Walker & Asleep At The Wheel; *Ride With Bob-C* . . . (DreamWorks/SKG)

Take Me Home
Phil Collins; *Miami Vice II-C* . . . .(MCA)
   No Jacket Required . . . . (Atlantic)
   Serious Hits...Live! . . . . (Atlantic)

Take Me Home
Cher; *Night At Studio 54-C* . . . . (Casablanca)
   Take Me Home . . . . (Casablanca)

Take Me Home
Crystal Gayle; *ST/One From The Heart* . . . . (Columbia)

Take Me Home Tonight
Eddie Money; *Can't Hold Back* . . . . (Columbia)
   Eddie Money's Greatest Hits-Sound Of Money . . . . (Columbia)

Take Me Home, Country Roads
John Denver; *Evening With John Denver* . . . . (RCA)
   John Denver's Greatest Hits . . . . (RCA)
   Poems, Prayers & Promises . . . . (RCA)
   Take Me Home, Country Roads & Other Hits . . . . (RCA)
Toots & The Maytals; *Brand New Second-Hand* . . . . (Rykodisc)

Take The Long Way Home
Supertramp; *Breakfast In America* . . . . (A&M)

Paris . . . . (A&M)
Supertramp-Classics-#9 . . . . (A&M)

Take The Long Way Home
John Schneider; *Country Classics-#8-1986-1987-C* . . . . (Universal)
   John Schneider's Greatest Hits . . . .(MCA)

Take The Short Way Home
Dionne Warwick; *Heartbreaker* . . . . (Arista)

Take Your Whiskey Home
Van Halen; *Women & Children First* . . . . (Warner Bros.)

Taking You Home
Don Henley; *Inside Job* . . . . (Warner Bros.)

Teacher, The
Paul Simon; *You're The One* . . . . (Warner Bros.)

Tennessee Homesick Blues
Dolly Parton; *Best Of Dolly Parton-#3* . . . . (RCA)
   RCA Years-1967-1986 . . . . (RCA)
   ST/Rhinestone . . . . (RCA)
   Star Spangled Country-C . . . . (RCA)

That I Get Back Home
NRBQ; *Honest Dollar* . . . . (Rykodisc)

Theme From "Home Improvement"
Original Soundtrack; *Television's Greatest Hits-#7-Cable Ready-C* . . . . . (TVT)

There's No Place Like Home For The Holidays
Perry Como; *Now That's What I Call Christmas!-C* . . . . (UTV)
   Perry Como's Greatest Hits . . . . (RCA)

Thirty Days (To Come Back Home)
Chuck Berry; *Blues-#2-C* . . . . (Chess)
   Chuck Berry-Golden Hits . . . . (Mercury)
Johnny Winter; *Rock N' Roll Collection-C* . . . . (Columbia)

Thirty-Three
Smashing Pumpkins; *Mellon Collie And The Infinite Sadness* . . . . (Virgin)

This Old Man
Dana; *Dana's Best Sing & Play-Along Tunes!* . . . . (Real Music For Kidz)
Original Soundtrack; *Children's Favorites* . . . .(Kid Rhino/Rhino 4 Kids)

'Til My Baby Comes Home
Luther Vandross; *Best Of Luther Vandross...The Best Of Love* . . . . (Epic)
   Night I Fell In Love . . . . (Epic)

Tippin' Home From Sunday School
Oliver Jones; *Class Act* . . . . (Justin Time)

Tones Of Home
Blind Melon; *Blind Melon* . . . . (Capitol)

Tonight My Baby's Coming Home
Barbara Mandrell; *Best Of Barbara Mandrell* . . . . (Columbia)

Too Cold At Home
Mark Chesnutt; *Too Cold At Home* . . . .(MCA)

Train Of Love
Johnny Cash; *Johnny Cash-Legend* . . . . (Sun)
   Johnny Cash-Original Golden Hits-#1 . . . . (Sun)
   Johnny Cash-Sun Years . . . . (Rhino)
   Superbilly . . . . (Sun)
   Trucks,Trains & Airplanes-C . . . . (International Mktg. Group)

Tuck Me To Sleep In My Old Kentucky Home
Firehouse Five Plus Two; *Goes South* . . . . (Good Time Jazz)

Turning For Home
Mike Reid; *Turning For Home* . . . . (Columbia)
Oak Ridge Boys; *American Dreams* . . . .(MCA)

Two Of Us
Beatles; *Beatles-Box Set* . . . . (Capitol)
   Let It Be . . . . (Capitol)

Vahevala
Loggins & Messina; *Loggins & Messina-On Stage* . . . . (Columbia)
   Sittin' In . . . . (Columbia)
   The Best Of Friends . . . . (Columbia)

Wait
Beatles; *Beatles-Box Set* . . . . (Capitol)
   Rubber Soul . . . . (Capitol)

Walk Away Renee
Four Tops; *Compact Command Performances-Four Tops* . . . . (Motown)
   Four Tops Reach Out . . . . (Motown)
   Four Tops-Anthology . . . . (Motown)
Left Banke; *Cruisin'-1966-C* . . . . (Increase)
   History Of The Left Banke . . . . (Rhino)
Vonda Shepard; *ST/Songs From "Ally McBeal" Featuring Vonda*
   Shepard . . . . (550/Epic)

Walk On
U2; *America: A Tribute To Heroes-C* . . . . (Interscope)
   Now That's What I Call Music!-#8-C . . . . (Virgin)

Walkin' My Baby Back Home
Johnnie Ray; *Johnnie Ray-16 Most Requested Songs* . . . . (Legacy)
   Johnnie Ray's Greatest Hits . . . . (Sony Music Special Prod.)
Nat "King" Cole; *Capitol Collectors Series-Nat "King" Cole* . . . . . . (Capitol)
   The Nat "King" Cole Story . . . . (Capitol)

Walking To New Orleans
Fats Domino; *Fats Domino's All Time Greatest Hits* . . . . (Curb)
   Fats Domino's Greatest Hits . . . . (CEMA Special Prod.)
   Fats Domino's Greatest Hits . . . .(MCA)
   My Blue Heaven-Best Of Fats Domino-#1 . . . . (EMI)
   They Call Me The Fat Man . . . . (EMI)

War Is Hell (On The Homefront Too)
T.G. Sheppard; *Perfect Stranger* . . . . (Warner Bros.)
  T.G. Sheppard's All-Time Greatest Hits . . . . (Warner Bros.)
  T.G. Sheppard's Greatest Hits . . . . (Warner Bros./Curb)
West Virginia My Home
Hazel Dickens & Alice Gerrard; *Hazel Dickens & Alice Gerrard* . . . . . (Rounder)
Whatever
Ideal; *Ideal* . . . . (Noontime/Virgin)
When I Could Come Home To You
Steve Wariner; *I Got Dreams* . . . . (MCA)
  Steve Wariner's Greatest Hits-#2 . . . . (MCA)
When I Get Home
Beatles; *Beatles-Box Set* . . . . (Capitol)
  Something New . . . . (Capitol)
When Johnny Comes Marching Home
Marilyn Horne; *Beautiful Dreamer-Great American Songbook* . . . .(London)
Mormon Tabernacle Choir; *Songs Of The Civil War And Stephen Foster
  Favorites* . . . . (Sony Music Classical)
United States Military Academy Band; *Songs Of The Civil War-C* . . . (Columbia)
When My Dreamboat Comes Home
Fats Domino; *My Blue Heaven* . . . . (Gold Rush)
Kay Starr; *Capitol Collectors Series-Kay Starr* . . . . (Capitol)
Where Do We Go From Here
Vanessa Williams; *Vanessa Williams' Greatest Hits-The First Ten
  Years* . . . . (Mercury)
Why Can't You Bring Me Home
Jay & The Americans; *Come A Little Bit Closer-Best Of Jay & The
  Americans* . . . . (Gold Rush)
  Jay & The Americans' All-Time Greatest Hits . . . . (Rhino)
Why Can't You Come Home
Ex-Girlfriend; *X Marks The Spot* . . . . (Reprise)
Why Don't You Get A Job?
Offspring; *Americana* . . . . (Columbia)
Wingin' It Home To Texas
Jerry Jeff Walker; *Collectibles* . . . . (MCA)
Woman At Home
Country Joe McDonald; *Tribute To Woody Guthrie-C* . . . . (Warner Bros.)
Yellow Submarine
Beatles; *Beatles 1* . . . . (Capitol)
  Beatles-Box Set . . . . (Capitol)
  Reel Music . . . . (Capitol)
  Revolver . . . . (Capitol)
  The Beatles/1962-1966 . . . . (Capitol)
Yesterday's News Just Hit Home Today
Johnny Paycheck; *Johnny Paycheck's Biggest Hits* . . . . (Epic)
You Belong To Me
Dean Martin; *Dean Martin's All Time Greatest Hits* . . . . (Curb)
Duprees; *13 Of The Best Doo Wop Love Songs-#2-C* . . . .(Original Sound)
  Baby Boomer's Best-Mellow '60s-C . . . . (Priority)
  Best Of The Duprees . . . . (Rhino)
Jo Stafford; *Billboard Pop Memories-1950-1954-C* . . . . (Rhino)
  Jo Stafford's Greatest Hits . . . . (Curb)
Johnny Mathis; *In The Still Of The Night* . . . . (Columbia)
Patsy Cline; *Patsy Cline Sings Songs Of Love* . . . . (MCA Special Prod.)
  Sentimentally Yours . . . . (MCA)
Vonda Shepard; *ST/Songs From "Ally McBeal" Featuring Vonda
  Shepard* . . . . (550/Epic)
You Don't Have To Go Home Tonight
Triplets; *...Thicker Than Water* . . . . (Mercury)
You Wrecked My Happy Home
Various Artists; *Four Women Blues: Victor/Bluebird Recordings-C* . .(Bluebird)
You'd Be So Nice To Come Home To
Dinah Shore; *Songs That Got Us Through WWII-#2-C* . . . . (Rhino)

HOMOSEXUALS, Lesbians, Sexual Variations

See Also: SEX

Affirmation
Savage Garden; *Affirmation* . . . . (Columbia)
Ain't Nobody Straight In L.A.
Miracles; *City Of Angels* . . . . (Tamla)
All The Girls Love Alice
Elton John; *Goodbye Yellow Brick Road* . . . . (Polydor)
Ballad Of Ben Gay
Ben Gay & His Silly Savages; *Dr. Demento's Delights-C* . . . . (Warner Bros.)
Boom Bye Bye
Buju Banton; *Voice Of Jamaica* . . . . (Mercury)
Don't Pick It Up
Offspring; *Ixnay On The Hombre* . . . . (Columbia)
Dude (Looks Like A Lady)
Aerosmith; *Big Ones* . . . . (Geffen)
  Permanent Vacation . . . . (Geffen)
Eddie's First Wife
Gretchen Peters; *Gretchen Peters* . . . . (Purple Crayon Prod.)
El Macho
Mark Knopfler; *Sailing To Philadelphia* . . . . (Warner Bros.)

Flame
Metro; *Metro* . . . . (Sire)
Glad To Be Gay
Tom Robinson Band; *Power In The Darkness* . . . . (Harvest)
He's So Gay
Frank Zappa; *Thing-Fish* . . . . (Rykodisc)
Hush Hush Hush
Paula Cole; *This Fire* . . . . (Imago)
I Kissed A Girl
Jill Sobule; *Jill Sobule* . . . .(Lava)
  Lesbian Favorites-Women Like Us-C . . . .(Rhino)
I Spent My Last Ten Dollars (On Birth Control And Beer)
Two Nice Girls; *Lesbian Favorites-Women Like Us-C* . . . .(Rhino)
In Or Out
Ani DiFranco; *Lesbian Favorites-Women Like Us-C* . . . .(Rhino)
Internet Is Gay
A.C.; *I Like It When You Die* . . . . (Earache)
Killing Of Georgie
Rod Stewart; *Night On The Town* . . . . (Warner Bros.)
  Rod Stewart's Greatest Hits . . . . (Warner Bros.)
Leaping Lesbians
Meg Christian; *Face The Music* . . . .(Olivia)
Sue Fink; *Lesbian Concentrate* . . . .(Olivia)
Lola
Kinks; *Come Dancing With The Kinks-Best Of The Kinks 1977-1986* . . . .(Arista)
  Everybody's In Show-Biz . . . .(Rhino)
  Kink Kronikles . . . . (Reprise)
  Lola Versus Powerman And The Moneygoround, Part One . . . . (Reprise)
  One For The Road . . . .(Arista)
  Second Time Around . . . . (RCA)
Long Hair Queer
Vandals; *Slippery When Ill* . . . . (Restless)
Made In England
Elton John; *Made In England* . . . . (Rocket)
Masculine Women, Feminine Men
Margaret Roadknight; *Living In The Land Of Oz* . . . . (Redwood)
Out Of The Wardrobe
Kinks; *Misfits* . . . .(Arista)
Psycho Dyke
Dead Serios; *Possessed By Polka* . . . .(Long Song)
Queer
Garbage; *Garbage* . . . . (Almo Sounds)
Saint Joe On The School Bus
Marcy Playground; *Marcy Playground* . . . .(Capitol)
Straight In A Gay World
Skyhooks; *Livin' In The 70s* . . . .(Out Of Print)
Strange Night
Heart; *Bebe Le Strange* . . . . (Epic)
Sweet Transvestite
Original London Cast; *Rocky Horror Show* . . . .(Rhino)
Tim Curry; *ST/Rocky Horror Picture Show* . . . .(Rhino)
Tim Curry & Original Roxy Cast; *Rocky Horror Show* . . . .(Rhino)
Temple
Jane Siberry; *Lesbian Favorites-Women Like Us-C* . . . .(Rhino)
Theme From "Kids In The Hall"
Original Soundtrack; *Television's Greatest Hits-#7-Cable Ready-C* . . . . .(TVT)
Turned You Into A Lesbian
Mentors; *Rock Bible* . . . . (Mentor/Mind Boggler)
Two Little Girls
Ani DiFranco; *Little Plastic Castle* . . . . (Righteous Babe)
Various Tracks
Pansy Division; *Wish I'd Taken Pictures* . . . .(Lookout)
Walk On The Wild Side
Edie Brickell & New Bohemians; *ST/Flashback* . . . . (WTG)
Lou Reed; *Between Thought & Expression-Anthology* . . . . (RCA)
  Lou Reed Live . . . . (RCA)
  Transformer . . . . (RCA)
  Walk On The Wild Side-The Best Of Lou Reed . . . . (RCA)
Y.M.C.A.
Village People; *Billboard Top Dance Hits-1978-C* . . . .(Rhino)
  Billboard Top Rock 'N' Roll Hits-1979-C . . . .(Rhino)
  Cruisin' . . . . (Casablanca)
  Live & Sleazy . . . . (Casablanca)
  Night At Studio 54-C . . . . (Casablanca)
  Village People's Greatest Hits . . . .(Rhino)

HOT, Heat, Warm

*See Also: COLD, DESIRE, FIRE, HELL, SEASONS:
  SUMMER, SEX, SUN*

90 Degrees In The Shade
Heavy Shift; *Acid Jazz Test Part 2-C* . . . . (Discovery)
99 In The Shade
Bon Jovi; *New Jersey* . . . . (Jambco)
California Sun
Ramones; *All The Stuff & More-#1* . . . . (Sire)

Leave Home . . . . (Sire)
ST/Rock 'N' Roll High School . . . . (Sire)
Rivieras; *Beach Classics-All Original*
Recordings-C . . . .(Dunhill Compact Classics)
Frat Rock!-#4-C. . . . . (Rhino)
Summer & Sun-C . . . . (Rhino)

Cruel Summer
Ace Of Base; *Cruel Summer* . . . . (Arista)
Bananarama; *Bananarama* . . . . (London)

Don't Stop When You're Hot
Larry Graham; *45-#50068* . . . .(Warner Bros.)

Gonna Make You Sweat (Everybody Dance Now)
C & C Music Factory; *Gonna Make You Sweat* . . . . (Columbia)
Hot #1 Hits-C. . . . . (Foundation)

Happiness Is A Warm Gun
Beatles; *The Beatles (White Album)* . . . . (Capitol)

Heat Goes On
Asia; *Alpha* . . . .(Geffen)

Heat In Harlem
Graham Parker; *Pourin' It All Out-Mercury Years* . . . . (Mercury)
Graham Parker And The Rumour; *Stick To Me* . . . . (Mercury)
The Parkerilla . . . . (Mercury)

Heat In The Street
Pat Travers; *Go For What You Know* . . . . (Polydor)
Heat In The Street . . . . (Polydor)

Heat Is On
Glenn Frey; *Soundtrack Smashes-'80s & More-C* . . . .(MCA)
ST/Beverly Hills Cop . . . .(MCA)

Heat Is On
Isley Brothers; *Heat Is On.* . . . .(T-Neck/Columbia)

Heat Is On Is Saigon
Original London Cast; *Miss Saigon* . . . .(Geffen)

Heat Of Heat
Patti Austin; *Gettin' Away With Murder* . . . . (Qwest)

Heat Of The Moment
Asia; *Asia* . . . .(Geffen)
Then & Now . . . .(Geffen)

Heat Of The Night
Jay Ferguson; *White Noise* . . . . (Capitol)

Heat Of The Night
Bryan Adams; *Into The Fire* . . . . (A&M)

Heat Treatment
Graham Parker; *Pourin' It All Out-Mercury Years* . . . . (Mercury)
Graham Parker And The Rumour; *Heat Treatment* . . . . (Mercury)
The Parkerilla . . . . (Mercury)

Heat Wave
Linda Ronstadt; *Linda Ronstadt's Greatest Hits* . . . . (Asylum)
Prisoner In Disguise . . . . (Asylum)
Martha & The Vandellas; *Billboard Top R&B Hits-1963-C.* . . . . . (Rhino)
Martha Reeves & The Vandellas' Greatest Hits . . . . (Motown)
More American Graffiti-#4-C . . . .(MCA)
Motown Story-First 25 Years-C . . . . (Motown)
Who; *A Quick One (Happy Jack)/Sell Out* . . . .(MCA)
Two's Missing . . . .(MCA)

Heat Wave
Art Tatum; *Art Tatum Solo Masterpieces-#2* . . . .(Pablo)
Ella Fitzgerald; *The Irving Berlin Songbook-#2* . . . . (Verve)
Ernestine Anderson; *Cheek To Cheek: The Irving Berlin Songbook-C.* . . (Verve)
Ethel Waters; *Lovely Ladies Of Stage & Screen-C* . . . . (Legacy)

Hot
Roy Ayers; *You Might Be Surprised* . . . . (Columbia)

Hot
Carl Carlton; *Private Property* . . . . (Casablanca)

Hot & Nasty
Humble Pie; *Best Of Humble Pie* . . . . (A&M)
Humble Pie-Classics-#14 . . . . (A&M)
Rockin' '60s-C. . . . . (Priority)
Smokin' . . . . (A&M)

Hot & Nasty
Black Oak Arkansas; *Best Of Black Oak Arkansas.* . . . . (Atco)
Black Oak Arkansas. . . . . (Atco)
Raunch 'N' Roll . . . . (Atco)

Hot As Sun
Paul McCartney; *McCartney* . . . . (Capitol)

Hot Blooded
Foreigner; *Double Vision* . . . . (Atlantic)
Records . . . . (Atlantic)
ST/Vision Quest . . . . (Geffen)

Hot Boyz
Missy "Misdemeanor" Elliot; *Da Real World.* . . . . (East West)
Totally Hits-#2-C. . . . . (Elektra)

Hot Cakes
Carly Simon; *Hotcakes* . . . . (Elektra)

Hot Cherie
Hardline; *Double Eclipse* . . . .(MCA)

Hot Child In The City
Nick Gilder; *Billboard Top Hits-1978-C* . . . . (Rhino)
City Nights . . . . (Chrysalis)

Hot Chili
Steve Miller Band; *Number 5* . . . . (Capitol)

Hot Chili Mama
Beausoleil; *Hot Chili Mama* . . . . (Arhoolie)

Hot Coffee
Carl Anderson; *Pieces Of A Heart* . . . . (GRP)

Hot Cop
Village People; *Cruisin'* . . . . (Casablanca)
Live & Sleazy . . . . (Casablanca)
Village People's Greatest Hits . . . . (Rhino)

Hot Corn, Cold Corn
Flatt & Scruggs; *Flatt & Scruggs At Carnegie Hall!* . . . . (Koch International)

Hot Diggity (Dog Ziggity Boom)
Perry Como; *Como's Golden Records* . . . . (RCA)
Nipper's Greatest Hits Of The '50s-#2-C . . . . (RCA)
Perry Como-Pure Gold . . . . (RCA)
Perry Como's All-Time Greatest Hits-#1 . . . . (RCA)
This Is Perry Como. . . . . (RCA)

Hot Dog
Elvis Presley; *Elvis Presley* . . . . (RCA)
Essential Elvis-The First Movies . . . . (RCA)
Loving You . . . . (RCA)

Hot Dog
Led Zeppelin; *In Through The Out Door.* . . . . (Swan Song)

Hot Dog
Mongo Santamaria; *Mongo Santamaria's Greatest Hits.* . . . . (Columbia)

Hot Dusty Roads
Buffalo Springfield; *Buffalo Springfield* . . . . (Atco)

Hot For Teacher
Van Halen; *1984* . . . . (Warner Bros.)

Hot Fun In The Summertime
Sly & The Family Stone; *Billboard Top R&B Hits-1969-C* . . . . . (Rhino)
Sly & The Family Stone-Anthology . . . . (Epic)
Sly & The Family Stone's Greatest Hits . . . . (Epic)
Summer & Sun-C . . . . (Rhino)

Hot Girls In Love
Loverboy; *Big Ones* . . . . (Columbia)
Keep It Up . . . . (Columbia)

Hot 'Lanta
Allman Brothers Band; *At Fillmore East* . . . . (Capricorn)
The Road Goes On Forever, A Collection Of Their Greatest
Recordings. . . . .(Polydor)

Hot 'Lanta
38 Special; *Rock & Roll Strategy.* . . . . (A&M)

Hot Legs
Rod Stewart; *Absolutely Live* . . . . (Warner Bros.)
Footloose & Fancy Free. . . . . (Warner Bros.)
Rod Stewart's Greatest Hits . . . . (Warner Bros.)
Storyteller/The Complete Anthology: 1964-1990. . . . . (Warner Bros.)

Hot Like Fire
Aaliyah; *One In A Million* . . . . (BlackGround Enterp./Atlantic)

Hot Line
Black Sabbath; *Born Again* . . . . (Warner Bros.)

Hot Line
Sylvers; *Best Of The Sylvers* . . . . (Capitol)

Hot Lips
Django Reinhardt; *Djangologie USA-#3 & 4* . . . .(DRG)
Harry James; *Mr. Trumpet* . . . . (Hindsight)
Stephane Grappelli; *Shades Of Django.* . . . . (Verve)

Hot Love
Michael Bolton; *The Hunger.* . . . . (Columbia)

Hot Love
Cheap Trick; *Cheap Trick* . . . . (Epic)

Hot Love
Five Star; *Five Star* . . . . (Epic)

Hot Love Cold World
Bob Welch; *French Kiss* . . . . (Capitol)

Hot 'N' Ready
UFO; *Obsession* . . . . (Chrysalis)

Hot Night In New York City
Bonnie Koloc; *With You On My Side.* . . . . (Flying Fish)

Hot Nite In Dallas
Moon Martin; *Shots From A Cold Nightmare* . . . . (Capitol)

Hot Number
Foxy; *Get Down Tonight! Best Of T.K. Records-C* . . . . (Rhino)
Hot Numbers . . . . (Dash)

Hot Number
Fabulous Thunderbirds; *Hot Number* . . . . (Epic Portrait Assoc.)

Hot On A Thing Called Love
Chi-Lites; *Me And You* . . . . (20th Century Fox)

Hot Pants
James Brown; *In The Jungle Groove* . . . .(Polydor)
Revolution Of The Mind . . . .(Polydor)

Hot Pants In The Summertime
Dramatics; *Whatcha See Is Whatcha Get* . . . . (Stax)

Hot Pastrami
Dartells; *Frat Rock! Box Set-C* . . . . (Rhino)
Frat Rock!-#4-C. . . . . (Rhino)

History Of Rock Instrumentals-#1-C . . . . (Rhino)
Son Of Frat Rock!-C . . . . (Rhino)

Hot Pink
Meat Puppets; *Up On The Sun* . . . . (SST)

Hot Pink
Eddy Raven; *Right For The Flight* . . . . (Liberty)

Hot Potatoes
Kinks; *Everybody's In Show-Biz* . . . . (Rhino)

Hot Potatoes
King Curtis; *Enjoy...Best Of* . . . . (Collectables)

Hot Rails To Hell
Blue Oyster Cult; *Career Of Evil* . . . . (Columbia)
Extraterrestrial Live . . . . (Columbia)
Metal Giants-C . . . . (Columbia)
On Your Feet Or On Your Knees . . . . (Columbia)
Tyranny & Mutation . . . . (Columbia)

Hot Rockin'
Judas Priest; *Point Of Entry* . . . . (Columbia)

Hot Rod
Ray Charles; *Ray Charles-Live* . . . . (Atlantic)

Hot Rod Baby
Ronny & The Daytonas; *45-#19* . . . . (Flashback)

Hot Rod Hearts
Robbie Dupree; *Robbie Dupree* . . . . (Elektra)

Hot Rod Lincoln
Asleep At The Wheel; *Western Standard Time* . . . . (Epic)
Commander Cody & His Lost Planet Airmen; *Lost In The Ozone* . . . . . . (MCA)
Super Hits Of The '70s-Have A Nice Day-#8-C . . . . (Rhino)
Johnny Bond; *Best Of Johnny Bond* . . . . (Starday)

Hot Spot
Dazz Band; *Hot Spot* . . . . (Motown)

Hot Streets
Chicago; *Hot Streets* . . . . (Columbia)

Hot Stuff
Donna Summer; *Bad Girls* . . . . (Casablanca)
Dance Collection . . . . (Casablanca)
On The Radio-Greatest Hits-Volumes I & II . . . . (Casablanca)
Walk Away-Best Of Donna Summer-1977-1980 . . . . (Casablanca)

Hot Stuff
Whitesnake; *Come An' Get It* . . . . (Geffen)

Hot Stuff
Rolling Stones; *Black And Blue* . . . . (Rolling Stones)
Love You Live . . . . (Virgin)
Sucking In The Seventies . . . . (Rolling Stones)

Hot Summer Day
David LaFlamme; *White Bird* . . . . (Amherst)
It's A Beautiful Day; *It's A Beautiful Day* . . . . (Columbia)

Hot Summer Nights
Rick James; *Wonderful* . . . . (Reprise)

Hot Summer Nights
Walter Egan; *Not Shy* . . . . (Columbia)

Hot Summer Nights
Miami Sound Machine; *ST/Top Gun* . . . . (Columbia)

Hot Tamale
Jackie Mittoo; *Jackie Mittoo* . . . . (EMI)
New & Old Songs . . . . (EMI)

Hot Tamale Baby
Buckwheat Zydeco; *Best Of Louisiana Music* . . . . (Rounder)
Clifton Chenier; *Zydeco Dynamite-Anthology* . . . . (Rhino)
Zydeco Party-C . . . . (K-Tel)

Hot Texas Night
Mac Davis; *Texas In My Rear View Mirror* . . . . (Casablanca)

Hot To Trot
Hank Williams, Jr.; *Lone Wolf* . . . . (WB/Curb)

Hot To Trot
Wild Cherry; *Electrified Funk* . . . . (Epic)

Hot To Trot
Kings Of The Sun; *Kings Of The Sun* . . . . (RCA)

Hot Water
Level 42; *Physical Presence-#2* . . . . (Polydor)
True Colours . . . . (Polydor)
World Machine . . . . (Polydor)

Hot Water
Jefferson Starship; *Spitfire* . . . . (Grunt)

Hot Wire
Al Green; *Arista Heritage Series* . . . . (Arista)

Hot! Wild! Unrestricted! Crazy Love
Millie Jackson; *Imitation Of Love* . . . . (Jive)

Hot, Blue & Righteous
ZZ Top; *Six Pack* . . . . (Warner Bros.)
Tres Hombres . . . . (Warner Bros.)

Hot, Wet & Sticky
Galaxy; *Hot, Wet & Sticky* . . . . (Arista)

Hotter Than Mojave In My Heart
Iris DeMent; *Infamous Angel* . . . . (Warner Bros.)

I Left Something Turned On At Home
Trace Adkins; *Dreamin' Out Loud* . . . . (Capitol)

I Melt With You
Modern English; *After The Snow* . . . . (Sire)
Pillow Lips . . . . (TVT)

I Need A Hot Girl
Hot Boys; *Guerrilla Warfare* . . . . (Cash Money/Universal)

In The Heat Of The Jungle
Chris Isaak; *Heart Shaped World* . . . . (Reprise)

In The Heat Of The Night
Ray Charles; *Ray Charles-His Greatest Hits-#2* . . . . (Dunhill Compact Classics)
ST/In The Heat Of The Night . . . . (United Artists)

In The Heat Of The Night
Pat Benatar; *In The Heat Of The Night* . . . . (Chrysalis)

It's Hot Up Here
Mandy Patinkin/Bernadette Peters/Original Cast; *Sunday In The Park With George* . . . . (RCA Victor)

I've Got My Love To Keep Me Warm
Ella Fitzgerald; *The Irving Berlin Songbook-#2* . . . . (Verve)
Les Brown & His Orchestra; *16 Most Requested Songs Of The '40s-#1-C* . . . . (Legacy)
Best Of The Big Bands-C . . . . (Columbia)

Keep Each Other Warm
Barry Manilow; *Barry Manilow* . . . . (Arista)

Keep It Hot
Cameo; *Best Of Cameo-#2* . . . . (Mercury/Funk Essentials)
Feel Me . . . . (Chocolate City)

Keep It Warm
Flo & Eddie; *Best Of Flo & Eddie* . . . . (Rhino)

Long Hot Summer
Aldo Nova; *Twitch* . . . . (Portrait)

Long Hot Summer
Jimmie Rodgers; *Best Of Jimmie Rodgers* . . . . (Rhino)

Long Hot Summer
Style Council; *Introducing The Style Council* . . . . (Mercury)

Long Hot Summer Night
Jimi Hendrix Experience; *Electric Ladyland* . . . . (Reprise)

Love In The Hot Afternoon
Gene Watson; *Best Of Gene Watson* . . . . (Capitol)
Gene Watson's Greatest Hits . . . . (Curb)
Great Records Of The Decade-'70s Hits-Country-C . . . . (Curb)

Make You Sweat
Keith Sweat; *I'll Give All My Love To You* . . . . (Vintertainment)

Melt In Your Mouth
Candyman; *Ain't No Shame In My Game* . . . . (Epic)

Meltdown
AC/DC; *Stiff Upper Lip* . . . . (East West)

Memphis, Tennessee Hot Rock
Gordon Terry; *Tennessee Hot Rock* . . . . (Plantation)

Pale September
Fiona Apple; *Tidal* . . . . (Clean Slate/Work)

Peas, Porridge Hot
Original Soundtrack; *Toddler Favorites* . . . . (Kid Rhino/Rhino 4 Kids)

Pump It Hottie
Redhead Kingpin & F.B.I.; *Rap: On The Lighter Tip-C* . . . . (K-Tel)

Rainmaker
Nilsson; *Harry* . . . . (Dunhill Compact Classics)

Red Hot
Billy Lee Riley & His Little Green Men; *Red Hot: The Very Best Of Billy Lee Riley* . . . . (Collectables)
Rock This Town-Rockabilly Hits-#1-C . . . . (Rhino)
Robert Gordon; *Rock This Town-Rockabilly Hits-#2-C* . . . . (Rhino)
Robert Gordon & Link Wray; *Robert Gordon & Link Wray* . . . . (RCA)

Red Hot Chicken
Wet Willie; *Drippin' Wet/Live!* . . . . (Capricorn)
Wet Willie's Greatest Hits . . . . (Polydor)

Red Hot Poker
Rufus; *Numbers* . . . . (MCA)

Red Light Mama Red Hot
Humble Pie; *Humble Pie* . . . . (A&M)

Rhythm Of The Heat
Peter Gabriel; *Peter Gabriel/Plays Live* . . . . (Geffen)
Security . . . . (Geffen)

Rock Is Hot
Crown Heights Affair; *Dance Lady Dance* . . . . (De-Lite)

San Franciscan Nights
Eric Burdon & The Animals; *Eric Burdon & The Animals' Greatest Hits* . . . . (MGM)
History Of British Rock-#8-C . . . . (Rhino)

She Runs Hot
Little Village; *Little Village* . . . . (Reprise)

She Was Hot
Rolling Stones; *Undercover* . . . . (Rolling Stones)

She's Hot
Fabulous Thunderbirds; *Powerful Stuff* . . . . (Epic Portrait Assoc.)

Soft, Sweet And Warm
David Houston; *45-#10870* . . . . (Epic)

Some Like It Hot
Power Station; *Power Station* . . . . (Capitol)
Robert Palmer; *Addictions-#1* . . . . (Island)

Steam
Peter Gabriel; *Us* . . . . (Geffen)
Steam
Ty Herndon; *Steam* . . . . (Epic)
Steam Heat
Carol Haney; *ST/Pajama Game* . . . . (Collectables)
Janis Paige/John Raitt/Original Cast; *Pajama Game* . . . . (Columbia)
Strawberry Wine
Deana Carter; *Did I Shave My Legs For This?* . . . . (Capitol)
Summer In The City
Lovin' Spoonful; *Billboard Top Rock 'N' Roll Hits-1966-C* . . . . (Rhino)
Lovin' Spoonful-Anthology . . . . (Rhino)
Rockin' '60s-C . . . . (Priority)
Sweat (A La La La Long)
Inner Circle; *Bad Boys* . . . . (Big Beat)
Sweat (Till You Get Wet)
System; *Sweat (Till You Get Wet)* . . . . (Mirage)
Sweat (Till You Get Wet)
Oingo Boingo; *Best O' Boingo* . . . .(MCA)
Sweat (Till You Get Wet)
Brick; *Summer Heat* . . . . (Bang)
Sweat Of My Balls
CB4 & Daddy-O-Hi-C; *ST/CB4* . . . .(MCA)
Theme From ''In The Heat Of The Night''
Original Soundtrack; *Television's Greatest Hits-#7-Cable Ready-C* . . . . . (TVT)
There'll Be A Hot Time In The Old Town Tonight
Bessie Smith; *Bessie Smith-The Complete Recordings-#3* . . . . . (Legacy)
Louis Armstrong; *Best Of Louis Armstrong* . . . . (Audio Fidelity)
Turk Murphy's San Francisco Jazz Band; *Turk Murphy's San Francisco Jazz Band* . . . . (Good Time Jazz)
Woody Herman; *The Uncollected Woody Herman & His First Herd* . . . . (Hindsight)
They're Red Hot
Red Hot Chili Peppers; *Blood Sugar Sex Magik* . . . .(Warner Bros.)
Robert Johnson; *Robert Johnson-Complete Recordings* . . . . (Columbia)
This Beat Is Hot
B.G. The Prince Of Rap; *Power Of Rhythm* . . . .(Epic)
This Beat Is Hot-C . . . . (Epic)
Too Darn Hot
Ella Fitzgerald; *Cole Porter Songbook* . . . . (Verve)
Erasure; *Red Hot + Blue-Tribute To Cole Porter-C* . . . . . .(Chrysalis)
Mel Torme; *Swings Shubert Alley* . . . . (Verve)
Too Hot
Kool & The Gang; *Everything's Kool & The Gang-Greatest Hits & More* . . . . (Mercury)
Ladies Night . . . . (De-Lite)
Too Hot
Loverboy; *Big Ones* . . . . (Columbia)
Too Hot
Specials; *Specials* . . . .(Chrysalis)
Too Hot Ta Trot
Commodores; *Commodores Greatest Hits* . . . . (Motown)
Commodores-Live . . . . (Motown)
Too Hot To Handle
UFO; *Lights Out* . . . .(Chrysalis)
Strangers In The Night . . . .(Chrysalis)
Too Hot To Handle
Roosevelt Sykes; *Raining In My Heart* . . . . (Delmark)
Too Hot To Sleep
Louise Mandrell; *Too Hot To Sleep* . . . . (RCA)
Two Hot Girls (On A Hot Summer Night)
Carly Simon; *Carly Simon-Greatest Hits Live* . . . . (Arista)
Coming Around Again . . . . (Arista)
Warm & Beautiful
Wings; *Wings At The Speed Of Sound* . . . . (Capitol)
Warm & Tender
Johnny Mathis; *Johnny Mathis' Greatest Hits* . . . . (Columbia)
Warm & Tender Love
Percy Sledge; *Best Of Percy Sledge* . . . .(Atlantic)
It Tears Me Up-Best Of Percy Sledge . . . . (Rhino)
Percy Sledge-The Ultimate Collection-When A Man Loves A Woman . . . .(Atlantic)
Warm & Tender Love
Dave Mason; *Mariposa De Oro* . . . . (Columbia)
Warm All Over
Barbra Streisand; *...Just For The Record* . . . . (Columbia)
Highlights From ''Just For The Record'' . . . . (Columbia)
Original Broadway Cast; *The Most Happy Fella* . . . . . . (Sony Music Classical)
Warm It Up
Kris Kross; *Totally Krossed Out* . . . . (Ruffhouse)
Warm Love
Van Morrison; *Best Of Van Morrison* . . . . (Polydor)
Hard Nose The Highway . . . . (Polydor)
It's Too Late To Stop Now . . . .(Warner Bros.)
Warm Love
Joan Armatrading; *Show Some Emotion* . . . . (A&M)
Warm Machine
Bush; *Science Of Things* . . . . (Trauma)

Warm Summer Daze
Vybe; *Vybe* . . . . (Island)
Warm Sunday
Conrad Herwig Quintet; *The Amulet* . . . .(Ken)
Warm Valley
Duke Ellington; *Money Jungle* . . . . (Blue Note)
Paul Desmond; *Pure Desmond* . . . . (CBS Associated)
Warm Ways
Fleetwood Mac; *25 Years-The Chain* . . . . (Warner Bros.)
Fleetwood Mac . . . . (Reprise)
Warm Your Heart
Aaron Neville; *Warm Your Heart* . . . . (A&M)
Drifters; *Let The Boogie Woogie Roll-Greatest Hits* . . . .(Atlantic)
Warmth Of The Sun
Beach Boys; *Absolute Best-#1* . . . . (Capitol)
Beach Boys-Gift Set . . . . (Capitol)
Best Of The Beach Boys . . . . (Capitol)
Endless Summer . . . . (Capitol)
Fun Fun Fun . . . . (Capitol)
ST/Good Morning, Vietnam . . . . (A&M)
Warmth, The
Incubus; *Make Yourself* . . . .(Immortal/Epic)
When You're Hot, You're Hot
Jerry Reed; *60 Years Of Country Music-C* . . . .(RCA)
Best Of Jerry Reed . . . .(RCA)
Super Hits Of The '70s-Have A Nice Day-#5-C . . . . . . (Rhino)
When You're Hot, You're Hot . . . .(RCA)
White Heat, Red Hot
Judas Priest; *Stained Class* . . . . (Columbia)
White Hot
Black Flag; *In My Head* . . . .(SST)
White Hot
Red Rider; *Don't Fight It* . . . . (Capitol)
White Light/White Heat
David Bowie; *Sound + Vision* . . . . (Rykodisc)
ST/Ziggy Stardust-The Motion Picture . . . . (Rykodisc)
Lou Reed; *Rock N Roll Animal* . . . .(RCA)
Walk On The Wild Side-The Best Of Lou Reed . . . .(RCA)
Velvet Underground; *1969: Velvet Underground Live* . . . . (Mercury)
White Light/White Heat . . . . (Verve)
Wild Nights, Hot & Crazy Days
Judas Priest; *Metal Works-1973-1993* . . . . (Columbia)
Turbo . . . . (Columbia)

HOTELS, Inns, Motels
See Also: **TRAVELING**

(Margie's At) The Lincoln Park Inn
Bobby Bare; *Ryman Country Homecoming 1-C* . . . .(Springhouse Music Grp./Chordant)
Angel
Sarah McLachlan; *Mirrorball* . . . . (Arista)
ST/City Of Angels . . . .(Warner Sunset/Reprise)
Surfacing . . . . (Arista)
Totally Hits-#1-C . . . . (Arista)
Another Motel Memory
Shelly West; *David Frizzell & Shelly West-Greatest Hits-Alone & Together* . . . . (K-Tel)
At The Grand Hotel/Table With A View
Broadway Cast; *Grand Hotel* . . . .(RCA)
At The Mambo Inn
George Benson; *Tenderly* . . . . (Warner Bros.)
Back To The Hotel
N2Deep; *Back To The Hotel* . . . .(Profile)
Ballad Of John And Yoko (Hilton)
Beatles; *Beatles 1* . . . . (Capitol)
Beatles-Box Set . . . . (Capitol)
Hey Jude . . . . (Capitol)
Past Masters-Volume Two . . . . (Parlophone)
ST/Imagine: John Lennon . . . . (Capitol)
The Beatles/1967-1970 . . . . (Capitol)
Big Hotel
Big Pig; *Bonk* . . . . (A&M)
Blue Motel Room
Joni Mitchell; *Hejira* . . . .(Asylum)
Broadway Hotel
Al Stewart; *Year Of The Cat* . . . . (Arista)
Buenos Noches From A Lonely Room
Dwight Yoakam; *Buenos Noches From A Lonely Room* . . . . (Reprise)
Caesar's Palace Blues
UK; *Danger Money* . . . . (Editions E.G.)
Night After Night . . . . (Editions E.G.)
Cigarette Motel
Leaving Trains; *Kill Tunes* . . . .(SST)
Cold, Cold, Cold
Little Feat; *Feats Don't Fail Me Now* . . . . (Warner Bros.)

Sailin' Shoes . . . . (Warner Bros.)
Dinner At The Ritz
City Boy; *Dinner At The Ritz* . . . . (Mercury)
Evangeline Hotel
Katy Moffatt; *Greatest Show On Earth* . . . . (Philo)
Tom Russell; *Hurricane Season* . . . . (Philo)
Fat Chance Hotel
Public Image Ltd.; *Happy?* . . . . (Virgin)
Food Phone Gas Lodging
Charlie King; *Food Phone Gas Lodging* . . . . (Flying Fish)
Grand Hotel
Procol Harum; *Grand Hotel* . . . . (Chrysalis)
Hangdog Hotel Room
Gordon Lightfoot; *Gord's Gold-#2* . . . . (Warner Bros.)
Heart Hotels
Dan Fogelberg; *Dan Fogelberg/Greatest Hits* . . . . (Full Moon)
Phoenix . . . . (Full Moon)
Heartbreak Hotel
Albert King; *Blues For Elvis* . . . . (Stax)
Elvis Presley; *Elvis As Recorded At Madison Square Garden* . . . . . . (RCA)
Elvis' Golden Records . . . . (RCA)
Elvis-A Legendary Performer, Volume 1 . . . . (RCA)
Nipper's Greatest Hits Of The '50s-#1-C . . . . (RCA)
Worldwide 50 Gold Award Hits, Vol. 1, Parts 1 & 2 . . . . . . (RCA)
Stan Freberg; *Capitol Collectors Series-Stan Freberg* . . . . . . (Capitol)
Willie Nelson; *Greatest Hits (& Some That Will Be)* . . . . . . (Columbia)
Willie Nelson & Leon Russell: One For The Road . . . . (Columbia)
Heartbreak Hotel
Whitney Houston Featuring Faith Evans & Kelly Price; *My Love Is*
Your Love . . . . (Arista)
Totally Hits-#1-C . . . . (Arista)
Whitney Houston's Greatest Hits . . . . (Arista)
Holiday Hotel
Loggins & Messina; *Loggins & Messina-On Stage* . . . . (Columbia)
Loggins And Messina . . . . (Columbia)
Holiday Inn
Elton John; *Madman Across The Water* . . . . (Polydor)
Holiday Inn Blues
Neil Diamond; *Velvet Gloves & Spit* . . . . (MCA Special Prod.)
Honeymoon Hotel
Alice Faye; *Hooray For Hollywood* . . . . (RCA)
Dick Powell; *In Hollywood-1933-1935* . . . . (Legacy)
Ruby Keeler & Dick Powell; *ST/Lullaby Of Broadway-The Best Of Busby*
Berkeley At Warner Bros. . . . . (Rhino)
Hotel 49
Chet Baker; *In New York* . . . . (Riverside)
Hotel California
Eagles; *Eagles Greatest Hits, Volume 2* . . . . (Asylum)
Eagles Live . . . . (Asylum)
Hell Freezes Over . . . . (Geffen)
Hotel California . . . . (Asylum)
Hotel For Women
Nails; *Hotel For Women* . . . . (PVC)
Hotel Happiness
Brook Benton; *Brook Benton-Anthology* . . . . (Rhino)
It's Just A Matter Of Time-His Greatest Hits . . . . (Mercury)
Super Oldies Of The '60s-#11-C . . . . (Audio Fidelity)
Hotel Hobbies
Marillion; *Clutching At Straws* . . . . (Capitol)
Hotel Illness
Black Crowes; *Southern Harmony & Musical Companion* . . . . . (Def American)
Hotel Indiscreet
Sagittarius; *Present Tense* . . . . (Bac-Trac)
Hotel Me
Gil Evans; *Individualism Of Gil Evans* . . . . (Verve)
Hotel Rats & Photostats
Jimmy Page; *ST/Death Wish 2* . . . . (Swan Song)
Hotel Ritz
Hoyt Axton; *Rusty Old Halo* . . . . (Jeremiah)
If We're Not Back In Love By Monday
Merle Haggard; *MCA Records 30 Years Of Hits-1958-1988-C* . . . . . . (MCA)
Merle Haggard-Legends . . . . (MCA)
Merle Haggard's Greatest Hits . . . . (MCA)
More Of The Best . . . . (MCA)
Ramblin' Fever . . . . (MCA)
I'm Already There
Lonestar; *I'm Already There* . . . . (BNA)
Imperial Hotel
Stevie Nicks; *Rock A Little* . . . . (Modern)
Iron Bar Motel
Slave Raider; *What Do You Know About Rock & Roll* . . . . (Jive)
Kicking Back In Amsterdam
Kevin Welch; *Life Down Here On Earth* . . . . (Dead Reckoning)
King Of The Road
R.E.M.; *Dead Letter Office* . . . . (I.R.S.)
Roger Miller; *Billboard Top Country Hits-1965-C* . . . . (Increase)
Cruisin'-1965-C . . . . (Increase)
Roger Miller-Golden Hits . . . . (Smash)

L' Hotel
Yello; *Yello One Second* . . . . (Polydor)
Little Hotel Room
Merle Haggard; *Friendship-C* . . . . (Columbia)
It's All In The Game . . . . (Epic)
Love Or Something Like It
Kenny Rogers; *Kenny Rogers-Twenty Greatest Hits* . . . . (EMI)
Loveless Motel
Eddie Moore; *Moore Country With* . . . . (Country Int'l)
L-Ranko Motel
Bell & Shore; *El-Ranko Motel* . . . . (Really Outstanding Music)
Magic Hotel
Wild Swans; *Space Flower* . . . . (Sire)
Memory Motel
Rolling Stones; *Black And Blue* . . . . (Rolling Stones)
No Security . . . . (Virgin)
Moonlight Motel
Gun Club; *Las Vegas Story* . . . . (I.R.S.)
Motel
Connells; *Fun & Games* . . . . (TVT)
Motel
Gang Of Four; *Mall* . . . . (Polydor)
Motel Blues
Loudon Wainwright III; *Live One* . . . . (Rounder)
Motel Blues
Big Star; *Big Star Live* . . . . (Rykodisc)
Motel Eyes
Rick Springfield; *Living In Oz* . . . . (RCA)
Motel King
James Harman Band; *Do Not Disturb* . . . . (Black Top)
Motel Lover
Marvin Sease; *Real Deal* . . . . (London)
Motel Matches
Elvis Costello; *Girls Girls Girls* . . . . (Columbia)
Elvis Costello & The Attractions; *Get Happy!* . . . . (Rykodisc)
Motel Mourning
Sonny Wright; *45-#040* . . . . (Door Knob)
Motel Party Baby
Dinosaurs; *Dinosaurs* . . . . (Relix)
Motel Room In My Bed
X; *Under The Big Black Sun* . . . . (Elektra)
Motel Row
James & Michael Younger; *James & Michael Younger* . . . . (MCA)
Motel Satellite
Wellsprings Of Hope; *Phonograph* . . . . (Safety Net)
Motel Time
Larry Coryell; *Bolero* . . . . (Evidence Music)
Motels & Planes
Bill Morrissey; *Standing Eight* . . . . (Philo)
Motels And Memories
T.G. Sheppard; *Motels And Memories* . . . . (Melodyland)
Mud Shark, The
Mothers Of Invention; *Fillmore East-June 1971* . . . . (Reprise)
No Tell Motel
David Houston; *Best Of David Houston* . . . . (Gusto)
Old Rose Motel
Great White; *Psycho City* . . . . (Capitol)
One Night In The Hotel
Michel Petrucciani; *Promenade With Duke* . . . . (Blue Note)
Papa Loved Mama
Garth Brooks; *Garth Brooks-Double Live* . . . . (Capitol)
Ropin' The Wind . . . . (Liberty)
Paper Thin Hotel
Leonard Cohen; *Death Of A Ladies' Man* . . . . (Columbia)
Portmeirion
Fairport Convention; *Expletive Delighted* . . . . (Varrick)
Puttin' On The Ritz
Ella Fitzgerald; *Silver Collection-Songbooks* . . . . (Verve)
Fred Astaire; *Irving Berlin Always-C* . . . . (Verve)
Irving Berlin Songbook . . . . (Verve)
Harry Richman; *Hollywood Sings-C* . . . . (Living Era)
Those Wonderful Years: Puttin' On The Ritz-C . . . . . (JCI Assoc. Labels)
Judy Garland; *One & Only* . . . . (Capitol)
Mandy Patinkin; *Mandy Patinkin* . . . . (Columbia)
Taco; *After Eight* . . . . (RCA)
Nipper's Greatest Hits Of The '80s-C . . . . (RCA)
Rats Motel
Lord Tracy; *Deaf Gods Of Babylon* . . . . (Uni)
Roach Motel
Dead Youth; *Intense Brutality* . . . . (Grind Core Int'l)
Room 317
Original London Cast; *Miss Saigon* . . . . (Geffen)
Room 608
Horace Silver; *Best Of Horace Silver-The Blue Note Years* . . . . . . (Blue Note)
Room Service
Po', Broke & Lonely?; *No Money No Honey* . . . . (Ruthless)
Room Service
Kiss; *Dressed To Kill* . . . . (Mercury)

Room With A View
Johnny Adams; *Room With A View Of The Blues* . . . . (Rounder)
Lou Rawls; *Legendary Lou Rawls* . . . . (Blue Note)
  Lou Rawls-At Last . . . . (Blue Note)
Room With A View
Wall Of Voodoo; *Seven Days In Sammystown* . . . .(I.R.S.)
Room With A View
Noel Coward; *Live From Las Vegas & New York* . . . . (Columbia)
Room With A View
Yellowjackets; *Four Corners* . . . .(MCA)
Room With A View
Bobby Short; *Bobby Noel & Cole* . . . . (Atlantic)
Room With A View
Jeffrey Osborne; *Emotional* . . . . (A&M)
Room Without A View
Smithereens; *11* . . . . (Enigma)
Seven Doors Hotel
Europe; *Europe* . . . .(Epic)
Simple Twist Of Fate
Bob Dylan; *Blood On The Tracks* . . . . (Columbia)
  Bob Dylan At Budokan . . . . (Columbia)
Jerry Garcia Band; *Jerry Garcia Band* . . . . (Arista)
Joan Baez; *Best Of Joan Baez* . . . . (A&M)
  Diamonds & Rust . . . . (A&M)
Sitting In My Hotel
Kinks; *Everybody's In Show-Biz* . . . . (Rhino)
Standin' At The Big Hotel
Joe Ely; *Down On The Drag* . . . .(MCA)
Stompin' At The Savoy
Benny Goodman; *Benny Goodman-Pure Gold* . . . . (RCA)
  Benny Goodman's All-Time Greatest Hits . . . . (Columbia)
  Carnegie Hall Jazz Concert . . . . (Columbia)
  Stompin' At The Savoy . . . . (Bluebird)
Doc Severinsen; *Facets* . . . . (Amherst)
Ella Fitzgerald & Louis Armstrong; *Ella & Louis* . . . . (Verve)
Louis Armstrong; *Essential Louis Armstrong* . . . . (Vanguard)
There's A Small Hotel
Benny Goodman; *Birth Of Swing* . . . . (Bluebird)
  The Birth Of Swing (1935-1936) . . . . (Bluebird)
Bobby Short; *Bobby Short Celebrates Rodgers & Hart* . . . . (Atlantic)
Ella Fitzgerald; *Rodgers & Hart Songbook* . . . . (Verve)
Tony Bennett; *Rodgers & Hart Songbook* . . . . (DRG)
Third Rate Romance
Amazing Rhythm Aces; *Stacked Deck* . . . .(MCA)
Rosanne Cash; *Somewhere In The Stars* . . . . (Columbia)
Sammy Kershaw; *Cryin' Lyin' Lovin' & Leavin'-C* . . . . (Universal)
  Feelin' Good Train . . . . (Mercury)
  The Hits-Chapter 1 . . . . (Mercury)
This Hotel Room
Jimmy Buffett; *Havana Daydreamin'* . . . .(MCA)
This Place Hotel (Heartbreak Hotel)
Jacksons; *Jacksons Live* . . . .(Epic)
  Triumph . . . .(Epic)
Tropicalia
Beck; *Mutations* . . . . (David Geffen Co.)
Twenty-Four Hours From Tulsa
Burt Bacharach; *Walk On By* . . . .(MCA Special Prod.)
Gene Pitney; *Best Of Gene Pitney* . . . . (K-Tel)

HOUSES, Cabins, Roofs, Rooms

See Also: FLOORS, FURNITURE, HELP (shelter), HOME, HOTELS, WALLS

Apartment #9
Melissa Etheridge; *Tammy Wynette...Remembered-C* . . . . (Asylum)
Tammy Wynette; *Tammy Wynette-Anniversary-20 Years Of Hits* . . . .(Epic)
  Tammy Wynette's Greatest Hits . . . .(Epic)
At An Arabian House Party
Raymond Scott; *Reckless Nights & Turkish Twilights* . . . . (Columbia)
Attics Of My Life
Grateful Dead; *American Beauty* . . . .(Warner Bros.)
Baby Let's Play House
Elvis Presley; *A Date With Elvis* . . . . (RCA)
  A Golden Celebration . . . . (RCA)
  The Sun Sessions . . . . (RCA)
Baby's House
Steve Miller Band; *Steve Miller Band-Anthology* . . . . (Capitol)
  Your Saving Grace . . . . (Capitol)
Barrel House Blues
Gertrude ''Ma'' Rainey; *Queen Of The Blues-#3* . . . . (Biograph)
Barrelhouse Shakedown
Emerson, Lake & Palmer; *Works, Volume 2* . . . . (Atlantic)
Bimbombey
Jimmie Rodgers; *Best Of Jimmie Rodgers* . . . . (Rhino)
  Best Of Jimmie Rodgers . . . . (Curb)

Blow The House Down
Siouxsie And The Banshees; *Hyaena* . . . . (Geffen)
Blow The House Down
Living In A Box; *Gatecrashing* . . . . (Chrysalis)
Brick House
Commodores; *Commodores* . . . . (Motown)
  Commodores Greatest Hits . . . . (Motown)
  Commodores-All The Great Hits . . . . (Motown)
  Compact Command Performances-Commodores . . . . (Motown)
  Motown Dance Party-#2-C . . . . (Motown)
Bring It Down To My House
Asleep At The Wheel; *Tribute To The Music Of Bob Wills And The Texas Playboys-C* . . . . (Liberty)
Merle Haggard; *Country Swing Essentials-C* . . . . (Hip-O)
Burning Down The House
Talking Heads; *Speaking In Tongues* . . . .(Sire)
  Stop Making Sense . . . .(Sire)
Burning House Of Love
X; *Ain't Love Grand* . . . . (Elektra)
  Best Of MTV's 120 Minutes-#2-C . . . . (Rhino)
  Live At The Whisky A Go-Go . . . . (Elektra)
Cabin Home On The Hill
Ricky Skaggs; *Sweet Temptation* . . . . (Sugar Hill)
Cabin In The Sky
Andre Previn; *Andre Previn Plays Songs By Vernon Duke* . . . . . (Contemporary)
Mose Allison; *Creek Bank* . . . .(Prestige)
Cabin On A Mountain
Country Gazette; *Bluegrass Tonight* . . . . (Flying Fish)
Cabin On The Hill
Flatt & Scruggs; *Columbia Historic Edition-Flatt & Scruggs* . . . . . (Columbia)
Lester Flatt & Earl Scruggs; *Bluegrass Super Hits-C* . . . . (Columbia)
Candy's Room
Bruce Springsteen; *Darkness On The Edge Of Town* . . . . (Columbia)
Bruce Springsteen & The E Street Band; *Bruce Springsteen & The E Street Band Live/1975-85* . . . . (Legacy)
Coffee House Blues
Lightnin' Hopkins; *Best Of The Blues* . . . .(Tradition)
Come On-A My House
Rosemary Clooney; *Rosemary Clooney-16 Most Requested Songs* . . . . (Legacy)
  Sentimental Journey: Pop Vocal Classics-#3-C . . . . (Rhino)
Cook Of The House
Wings; *Wings At The Speed Of Sound* . . . . (Capitol)
Cottage For Sale, A
Frank Sinatra; *No One Cares* . . . . (Capitol)
Mel Torme; *Luck Be A Lady* . . . . (Laserlight)
Crack House Woman
George ''Wild Child'' Butler; *These Mean Old Blues* . . . . (Bullseye Blues)
Every Light In The House
Trace Adkins; *Dreamin' Out Loud* . . . . (Capitol)
Everybody Eats When They Come To My House
Cab Calloway; *Are You Hep To The Jive?-22 Sensational Tracks* . . . . (Legacy)
  Hi De Ho Man . . . . (Columbia)
  Legacy's Rhythm & Soul Revue-C . . . . (Legacy)
Get Out Of This House
Shawn Colvin; *A Few Small Repairs* . . . . (Columbia)
Get The Fuck Out Of My House
2 Live Crew; *As Nasty As They Wanna Be* . . . . (Luke)
Ghost In This House
Shenandoah; *Extra Mile* . . . . (Columbia)
Glass Houses
Tammy Wynette & Joe Diffie; *Without Walls-C* . . . . (Epic)
Glasshouse
Temptations; *A Song For You* . . . . (Motown)
  Temptations-25th Anniversary . . . . (Motown)
Goin' Through The Big D
Mark Chesnutt; *What A Way To Live* . . . . (Decca)
Graceland
Paul Simon; *Graceland* . . . . (Warner Bros.)
Grand Tour
Aaron Neville; *The Grand Tour* . . . . (A&M)
Guns On The Roof
Clash; *Give 'Em Enough Rope* . . . .(Epic)
Happy House
Siouxsie And The Banshees; *Kaleidoscope* . . . . (Geffen)
  Nocturne . . . . (Geffen)
  Once Upon A Time-The Singles . . . . (Geffen)
Harry's House Centerpiece
Joni Mitchell; *Hissing Of Summer Lawns* . . . . (Asylum)
Hello Walls
Faron Young; *Billboard Top Country Hits-1961-C* . . . . (Rhino)
Willie Nelson; *Essential Willie Nelson* . . . . (RCA)
  Willie Nelson-Greatest Songs . . . . (Curb)
Here In Your Bedroom
Goldfinger; *Richter* . . . . (Mojo Music/Universal)
Home
Alan Jackson; *Alan Jackson-The Greatest Hits Collection* . . . . (Arista)

Here In The Real World .... (Arista)

House
Psychedelic Furs; *Theodore: An Alternative Music Sampler*........ (Columbia)

House Arrest
Bryan Adams; *Waking Up The Neighbours*...................... (A&M)

House At Pooh Corner
Loggins & Messina; *Loggins & Messina-On Stage*.............. (Columbia)
Sittin' In .... (Columbia)
The Best Of Friends .... (Columbia)
Nitty Gritty Dirt Band; *Best Of The Nitty Gritty Dirt Band* .... (Liberty)
Best Of The Nitty Gritty Dirt Band ....(Curb)
Dirt, Silver & Gold ....(One Way)
Uncle Charlie And His Dog Teddy ....(Liberty)

House Behind A House
Bob Seger & The Silver Bullet Band; *The Distance* .... (Capitol)

House Burning Down
Jimi Hendrix; *Essential Jimi Hendrix* ....(Reprise)
Jimi Hendrix Experience; *Electric Ladyland*..................(Reprise)

House Carpenter
Bob Dylan; *The Bootleg Series-Volumes 1-3 [Rare & Unreleased]* .. (Columbia)
Joan Baez; *The Joan Baez Ballad Book*.....................(Vanguard)
Pete Seeger; *20 Golden Pieces Of Pete Seeger* .... (Bulldog)

House Cleaning
Spaniels; *Goodnight, Well It's Time To Go* ....(Vee-Jay)

House For Everyone
Traffic; *Mr. Fantasy* .... (Island)

House I Live In (That's America To Me)
Frank Sinatra; *Frank Sinatra-In The Beginning-1943-1951* .... (Columbia)
Portrait Of Sinatra-Columbia Classics ....(Legacy)
Sinatra: A Man And His Music ....(Reprise)
Sinatra-The Main Event Live ....(Reprise)

House In France
Doris Day & Andre Previn; *Duet*.........................(DRG)
Sacha Distel; *Amour Tout Court* ....(DRG)

House In The Country
Blood, Sweat & Tears; *Child Is Father To The Man* .... (Columbia)

House Is Not A Home
Burt Bacharach; *Burt Bacharach-Classics-#23*. .... (A&M)
Dionne Warwick; *Dionne Warwick Greatest Hits*................. (Everest)
Dionne Warwick-Anthology 1962-1971 ....(Rhino)
Hot-Live & Otherwise. ....(Arista)
Say A Little Prayer .... (Dunhill Compact Classics)
Luther Vandross; *Best Of Luther Vandross...The Best Of Love*. .... (Epic)
Never Too Much ....(Epic)
Mavis Staples; *15 Original Big Hits-#3-C*....................(Stax)
Mavis Staples ....(Stax)

House Is Rockin'
Stevie Ray Vaughan and Double Trouble; *In Step*.............. (Epic)

House Is Rockin'
Cheap Trick; *Dream Police*............................... (Epic)

House Of Blue Lights
Andrews Sisters; *Best Of The Andrews Sisters-#2*................ (MCA)
Asleep At The Wheel; *Asleep At The Wheel-10*................ (Epic)
Greatest Country Hits Of The '80s-1987-C .... (Columbia)
More Hot Country Requests-#2-C .... (Epic)
Trucker's Jukebox-#2-C. ....(Legacy)
Very Best Of Asleep At The Wheel Since 1970 ....(Relentless/Madacy)
Canned Heat; *Canned Heat & John Lee Hooker: Live At The Fox
Venice* ....(Rhino)
Human Conditions .... (Takoma)
Chuck Berry; *More Rock 'N' Roll Rarities-Golden Era* .... (Chess)
The Chess Box-Chuck Berry ....(Chess)
Chuck Miller; *Hard To Find 45s On CD-#1-1955-1960-C* .... (Eric)

House Of Blue Lovers
James O'Gwynn; *James O'Gwynn's Greatest Hits*.............(Plantation)
Souvenirs Of Music City U.S.A.-C ....(Plantation)

House Of Cards
Mary Chapin Carpenter; *Stones In The Road*................. (Columbia)

House Of Cards
Elton John; *Rare Masters* .... (Polydor)

House Of Flowers
Barbra Streisand; *Just For The Record* .... (Columbia)
Harold Arlen & Barbra Streisand; *Harold Sings Arlen (With
Friend)*. .... (Sony Music Special Prod.)
Original Cast; *House Of Flowers*............... (Sony Music Special Prod.)

House Of Four Doors
Moody Blues; *In Search Of The Lost Chord* .... (Polydor)

House Of Gold
Hank Williams; *I'm So Lonesome I Could Cry-1949*. .... (Polydor)

House Of Love
Amy Grant & Vince Gill; *House Of Love* .... (A&M)

House Of Marcus Lycus
George Hearn, Bob Gunton & Women; *Collector's Sondheim-C* .... (RCA)
Stephen Sondheim; *Collector's Sondheim-C* .... (RCA)

House Of Memories
Merle Haggard & The Strangers; *Best Of Merle Haggard & The
Strangers* ....(Capitol)

House Of Pain
Van Halen; *1984* .... (Warner Bros.)

House Of Pain
Faster Pussycat; *Wake Me When It's Over* ....(Elektra)

House Of Rock
James Brown; *45-#38-ZS4-06568* .... (Scotti Bros.)

House Of The Rising Sun
Animals; *Animals Greatest Hits*........................... (Allegiance)
Best Of The Animals .... (Abkco)
Greatest Hits Live!-Rip It To Shreds .... (I.R.S.)
Hank Williams, Jr.; *Hank Williams, Jr. ''Live''*...............(WB/Curb)
Ronnie Milsap; *Ronnie Milsap-16 Greatest Hits-#2* .... (Trip)

House On Fire
Boomtown Rats; *Boomtown Rats' Greatest Hits* .... (Columbia)
V Deep...(Columbia)

House On The Hill
Turtles; *Turtle Soup* ....(Rhino)
Turtle Wax-Best Of The Turtles-#2 ....(Rhino)

House On The Hill
Stevie Wonder; *For Once In My Life* ....(Motown)

House Party
J. Geils Band; *Best Of The J. Geils Band* .... (Atlantic)
Bloodshot .... (Atlantic)
Blow Your Face Out ....(Rhino)

House Song
Peter, Paul & Mary; *Album 1700* .... (Warner Bros.)

House That Jack Built
Aretha Franklin; *Aretha Franklin-30 Greatest Hits* ....(Rhino)
Aretha's Gold .... (Atlantic)

House The Dog Built
Jibri Wise One; *House The Dog Built (Single)* .... (Ear Candy)

House Upon A Hill
Paul Anka; *She's A Lady* .... (RCA)
Very Best Of Paul Anka ....(Ranwood)

House With Love In It, A
Four Lads; *Moments To Remember-Very Best Of The Four Lads* ..... (Taragon)

House With No Curtains
Alan Jackson; *Everything I Love* ....(Arista)

House Without Love
Hank Williams; *Hank Williams-24 Greatest Hits-#2*........... (Polydor)
I'm So Lonesome I Could Cry-1949 ....(Polydor)

Housecall
Shabba Ranks with Maxi Priest; *As Raw As Ever*...................(Epic)

House-Cat
Danielle Dax; *Dark Adapted Eye* .... (Sire)

Housequake
Prince; *Sign ''O'' The Times* ....(Paisley Park)

Houses
Judy Collins; *Judith* ....(Elektra)
So Early In The Spring, The First 15 Years ....(Elektra)

Houses Of The Holy
Led Zeppelin; *Led Zeppelin-Box Set* .... (Atlantic)
Physical Graffiti ....(Swan Song)

Housewife
Leon Russell; *Americana* ....(Paradise)

Husbands And Wives
Brooks & Dunn; *Big Country Hits '99-C* ....(K-Tel)
If You See Her ....(Arista)
Neil Diamond; *Neil Diamond-Love Songs*....................(MCA)
Rainbow ....(MCA)
Stones ....(MCA)
Roger Miller; *Best Of Roger Miller* ....(Mercury)
Best Of Roger Miller-His Greatest Songs ....(Curb)
Roger Miller-Super Hits ....(Epic)
Roger Miller-The Hits ....(Mercury)

Hyacinth House
Doors; *L.A. Woman* ....(Elektra)

I Don't Wanna Play House
Sara Evans; *Tammy Wynette...Remembered-C* .... (Asylum)
Tammy Wynette; *Tammy Wynette-Anniversary-20 Years Of Hits*........ (Epic)
Tammy Wynette's Greatest Hits ....(Epic)
Tammy Wynette-Super Hits. ....(Epic)

I Don't Want To Play House
Lynn Anderson; *Rose Garden* ....(Columbia)

Icehouse
Icehouse; *Icehouse* ....(Chrysalis)

If The World Had A Front Porch
Tracy Lawrence; *Best Of Tracy Lawrence*...................(Atlantic)
I See It Now ....(Atlantic)

I'm Gonna Tear Your Playhouse Down
Ann Peebles; *Ann Peebles Greatest Hits* ....(MCA)
B.B. King; *Lucille Talks Back* ....(Out Of Print)
Graham Parker; *Pourin' It All Out-Mercury Years* ....(Mercury)
Graham Parker And The Rumour; *Stick To Me* ....(Mercury)
The Parkerilla ....(Mercury)
Paul Young; *Secret Of Association* ....(Columbia)

In A Shanty In Old Shanty Town
Ink Spots; *Java Jive* . . . . (Laserlight)
In My House
Mary Jane Girls; *Motown Story-First 25 Years-C* . . . . (Motown)
Only Four You . . . . (Motown)
In My Room
Tammy Wynette & Brian Wilson; *Tammy Wynette...Remembered-C* . . (Asylum)
In The House Of Stone And Light
Martin Page; *In The House Of Stone And Light* . . . . (Mercury)
Is It Raining At Your House
Vern Gosdin; *10 Years Of Greatest Hits Newly Recorded* . . . . (Columbia)
Chiseled In Stone . . . . (Columbia)
Greatest Country Hits Of The '90s-1991-C . . . . (Columbia)
Israel In Our House
Al Jolson; *The Al Jolson Story-#5* . . . .(MCA)
It Don't Hurt
Sheryl Crow; *The Globe Sessions* . . . . (A&M)
It's My House
Diana Ross; *Composer-Greatest By Ashford & Simpson* . . . . (Motown)
Diana Ross-All The Great Hits . . . . (Motown)
Diana Ross-Anthology . . . . (Motown)
The Boss . . . . (Motown)
Jailhouse Rock
Blues Brothers; *ST/The Blues Brothers* . . . . (Atlantic)
Elvis Presley; *Billboard Top Rock 'N' Roll Hits-1957-C* . . . . (Rhino)
Elvis Recorded Live On Stage In Memphis . . . . (RCA)
Elvis-A Legendary Performer, Volume 2 . . . . (RCA)
Number One Hits . . . . (RCA)
Rocker . . . . (RCA)
Worldwide 50 Gold Award Hits, Vol. 1, Parts 1 & 2 . . . . (RCA)
Jeff Beck Group; *Beck-Ola* . . . .(Epic)
Legend In My Living Room
Annie Lennox; *Diva* . . . . (Arista)
Like Humans Do
David Byrne; *Look Into The Eyeball* . . . .(Luaka Bop)
Limehouse Blues
Anita O'Day; *Mello'Day* . . . .(Crescendo)
Benny Goodman; *Small Groups-1941-1945* . . . . (Columbia)
Dave McKenna; *Live At Maybeck Recital Hall-#2* . . . .(Concord Jazz)
Earl ''Fatha'' Hines & His Orchestra; *Monday Date* . . . . (Riverside)
Glen Gray; *Big Band Sampler-C* . . . . (Columbia)
Joe Pass; *Virtuoso-#2* . . . . (Pablo)
Kay Starr; *Back To The Roots* . . . .(Crescendo)
Little Boxes
Malvina Reynolds; *Best Of Broadside 1962-1968: Anthems Of The
American Underground From The Pages Of Broadside
Magazine-C* . . . . (Smithsonian Folkways)
Folk Classics: Roots Of American Folk Music-C . . . . (Columbia)
Pete Seeger; *Pete Seeger's Greatest Hits* . . . . (Columbia)
Little Houses
Doug Stone; *Doug Stone G.H.* . . . .(Epic)
Little Pad
Beach Boys; *Smiley Smile/Wild Honey* . . . . (Capitol)
Living In The Future In A Plastic Dome
Country Joe McDonald; *Incredible Live* . . . . (Vanguard)
Log Cabin Home In The Sky
Michael Martin Murphey; *Cowboy Christmas* . . . .(Warner Bros.)
Lonely And Gone
Montgomery Gentry; *Tattoos & Scars* . . . . (Columbia)
Love Don't Live Here Anymore
Madonna; *Like A Virgin* . . . . (Sire)
Something To Remember . . . .(Maverick/Sire)
Rose Royce; *Rose Royce III/Strikes Again!* . . . .(Whitfield)
Rose Royce's Greatest Hits . . . .(Whitfield)
Love Shack
Friends Of Distinction; *Friends Of Distinction-Golden Classics* . . (Collectables)
Love Shack
X; *Ain't Love Grand* . . . . (Elektra)
Love Shack
B-52's; *Cosmic Thing* . . . . (Reprise)
Love's The Only House
Martina McBride; *Emotion* . . . . (RCA)
Mad House
Robin Trower; *Victims Of The Fury* . . . .(Chrysalis)
Mansion In The Slums
Crowded House; *Temple Of Low Men* . . . . (Capitol)
Mansion On The Hill
Hank Williams With His Drifting Cowboys; *Hank Williams-40
Greatest Hits* . . . . (Polydor)
Lovesick Blues . . . . (Polydor)
Mansion On The Hill
Bruce Springsteen; *Nebraska* . . . . (Columbia)
Emmylou Harris & The Nash Ramblers; *At The Ryman* . . . . . . (Reprise)
Mansion On The Hill
Neil Young & Crazy Horse; *Ragged Glory* . . . . (Reprise)
WELD . . . . (Reprise)
Mi Casa, Su Casa
Perry Como; *Como's Golden Records* . . . . (RCA)

Most Beautiful Girl In The World
Frank Sinatra; *Strangers In The Night* . . . . (Reprise)
Tony Bennett; *Rodgers & Hart Songbook* . . . .(DRG)
Tony Bennett Sings More Great Rodgers & Hart . . . . (Improv)
My Baby's House
Michael Cooper; *Just What I Like* . . . . (Reprise)
My Cabin In Caroline
Lester Flatt & Earl Scruggs; *Flatt & Scruggs-20 Greatest Hits* . . . . . . (Deluxe)
Lester Flatt, Earl Scruggs & The Foggy Mountain Boys; *Lester Flatt,
Earl Scruggs & The Foggy Mountain Boys-Complete Mercury
Sessions* . . . . (Mercury)
My Father's Mansions
Pete Seeger; *Essential Pete Seeger* . . . . (Vanguard)
My Little Grass Shack In Kealakekua, Hawaii
Mom & Dads; *Blue Hawaii* . . . .(Crescendo)
Next To Nothin'
Gene Watson; *From The Heart* . . . . (Row Music Group)
On The Roofs Of Paris
Ennio Morricone; *ST/Frantic* . . . . (Elektra)
Once In A Lifetime
Talking Heads; *Remain In Light* . . . .(Sire)
ST/Stop Making Sense . . . .(Sire)
Packing House Blues
Lillian Glinn; *Lillian Glinn-1927-1929* . . . .(Document)
Pink Houses
John Cougar Mellencamp; *Rock For Amnesty-C* . . . . (Mercury)
Uh-Huh . . . . (Riva)
John Mellencamp featuring Kid Rock; *The Concert For New York
City-C* . . . . (Columbia)
Prologue (Tradition)
Original Cast; *Fiddler On The Roof* . . . . (RCA Victor)
Queen Of My Double Wide Trailer
Sammy Kershaw; *Haunted Heart* . . . . (Mercury)
Queen Of The House
Jody Miller; *20th Century Country-#1-Honky Tonk
Angels-C* . . . . (Dominion Entert.)
Queen Of The House
Diana Ross & The Supremes; *Diana Ross & The Supremes-At
The Copa* . . . . (Motown)
Rain On The Roof
Lovin' Spoonful; *Best Of The Lovin' Spoonful* . . . . (Radio Active Gold)
Lovin' Spoonful-Anthology . . . . (Rhino)
Rain On The Roof
Original Cast; *ST/Follies-In Concert* . . . . (RCA Victor)
Rainy Night House
Joni Mitchell; *Ladies Of The Canyon* . . . .(Reprise)
Joni Mitchell with Tom Scott & The L.A. Express; *Miles Of Aisles* . . . .(Asylum)
Raise The Roof
Bob James; *Joy Ride* . . . . (Warner Bros.)
Ramshackle Shack
Doc Watson; *Riding That Midnight Train* . . . .(Sugar Hill)
Ready To Go
Republica; *Republica* . . . . (RCA)
Red House
Jimi Hendrix; *Concerts* . . . . (Reprise)
Kiss The Sky . . . . (Reprise)
Lifelines/Jimi Hendrix Story . . . . (Reprise)
Live At Winterland . . . . (Rykodisc)
ST/Jimi Hendrix . . . . (Reprise)
Jimi Hendrix Experience; *Are You Experienced?* . . . .(Reprise)
Smash Hits . . . . (Reprise)
Red House
Great White; *Recovery-Live!* . . . . (Enigma Capitol)
Red House
David Byrne; *The Catherine Wheel-Complete Broadway Score* . . . .(Sire)
River, Stay 'Way From My Door
Guy Lombardo & His Royal Canadians; *Auld Lang Syne* . . . . (Pro-Arte)
Roadhouse Blues
Doors; *Best Of The Doors* . . . . (Elektra)
Doors 13 . . . . (Elektra)
Doors' Greatest Hits . . . . (Elektra)
Doors-Classics . . . . (Elektra)
Morrison Hotel/Hard Rock Cafe . . . . (Elektra)
ST/The Doors . . . . (Elektra)
Rock The House
D.J. Jazzy Jeff & The Fresh Prince; *Rock The House* . . . . (Jive)
Rockhouse
Roy Orbison; *Original Sound Of Roy Orbison* . . . . (Sun)
Roy Orbison-The Sun Years . . . . (Rhino)
Rockhouse
Ray Charles; *Best Of Ray Charles* . . . .(Atlantic)
Rollin' In My Sweet Baby's Arms
Bill Monroe; *Bean Blossom* . . . . (MCA)
Del McCoury Band; *Appalachian Stomp: Bluegrass Classics-C* . . . . . (Rhino)
Dillard & Clark; *Fantastic Expedition/Through The
Morning* . . . .(Mobile Fidelity Sound Lab)

Flatt & Scruggs; *Flatt & Scruggs At Carnegie Hall!* . . . . (Koch International)
Flatt & Scruggs-20 Greatest Hits . . . . (Deluxe)
Flying Burrito Brothers; *Close Encounters To The West Coast* . . . . (Relix)
Leon Russell; *Hank Wilson's Back, Vol. 1* . . . . (Right Stuff)
New Lost City Ramblers; *Greatest Folksingers Of The '60s-C* . . . . . (Vanguard)
Ramblin' Jack Elliott; *Hard Travelin'* . . . .(Fantasy)
Ricky Skaggs and Kentucky Thunder; *History Of The Future* . . (Skaggs Family)
Tony Trischka; *Heartlands* . . . . (Rounder)
Willie Nelson; *Willie & Family Live* . . . . (Columbia)

Roof Garden
Al Jarreau; *Al Jarreau In London* . . . . (Warner Bros.)
Breakin' Away . . . . (Warner Bros.)

Roof Is Leaking
Phil Collins; *Face Value* . . . . (Atlantic)

Roof Is On Fire
C & C Music Factory; *C & C Music Factory* . . . . (MCA)

Roof, The
Mariah Carey; *Butterfly* . . . . (Columbia)

Rooms
Mamas & The Papas; *The Papas & The Mamas* . . . . (MCA)

Rooms On Fire
Stevie Nicks; *Other Side Of The Mirror* . . . . (Modern)
TimeSpace-The Best Of Stevie Nicks. . . . . (Modern)

Seven Rooms Of Gloom
Four Tops; *Four Tops' Greatest Hits.* . . . . (Motown)
Four Tops Reach Out . . . . (Motown)
Four Tops-Anthology . . . . (Motown)

Shacks & Chalets
Critton Hollow; *Great Dreams* . . . . (Flying Fish)

Shit House Shuffle
Aerosmith; *Pandora's Box* . . . . (Columbia)

Some Enchanted Evening
Jay & The Americans; *Come A Little Bit Closer-Best Of Jay & The Americans* . . . . (Gold Rush)
Jay & The Americans' All-Time Greatest Hits . . . . (Rhino)
Original Cast; *South Pacific* . . . . (CBS Masterworks)
Perry Como; *Perry Como's All-Time Greatest Hits-#1* . . . . (RCA)
Rosanno Brazzi; *ST/South Pacific* . . . . (RCA)
Willie Nelson; *What A Wonderful World.* . . . . (Columbia)

Son Of Hickory Holler's Tramp
O.C. Smith; *Me And You* . . . . (Columbia Special Prod.)
Story Songs-C . . . . (K-Tel)

Sticks & Stones
Tracy Lawrence; *Tracy Lawrence* . . . . (Atlantic)

Stranger In My House
Ronnie Milsap; *Keyed Up* . . . . (RCA)
Ronnie Milsap's Greatest Hits-#2 . . . . (RCA)

Stranger In My House
Tamia; *Nu Day.* . . . . (Elektra)

Stranger In My Own House
Foreigner; *Agent Provocateur* . . . . (Atlantic)

Stranger In Our House Tonight
Gene Watson; *Memories To Burn* . . . . (Epic)

Stranger In The House
George Jones; *The Bradley Barn Sessions* . . . . (MCA)

Sugar Shack
Jimmy Gilmer And The Fireballs; *Billboard Top Rock 'N' Roll Hits-1963-C* . . . . (Rhino)
Golden Years-1963-C. . . . . (Dominion Entert.)
Good Old Rock & Roll-C . . . . (International Mktg. Group)

Take It To Da House
Trick Daddy; *Thugs Are Us* . . . . (Slip 'N Slide/Atlantic)

Taking Everything
Gerald Levert; *Love & Consequences* . . . . (East West)

Tear The Roof Off
Grandmaster Flash; *Ba-Dop-Boom-Bang* . . . . (Elektra)

Tear The Roof Off
Triumph; *Progressions Of Power* . . . . (MCA)

Tear The Roof Off The Sucker
Parliament; *Son Of Super Bad-C* . . . . (K-Tel)

Theme From "Full House"
Original Soundtrack; *Television's Greatest Hits-#7-Cable Ready-C* . . . . . (TVT)

Theme From "Green Acres"
Eddie Albert & Eva Gabor; *ST/Son In Law* . . . . (Hollywood)
Original Soundtrack; *CBS: The First 50 Years* . . . . (TVT)
Television's Greatest Hits-#1-C . . . . (TVT)

Theme From "Little House On The Prairie"
Original Soundtrack; *Television's Greatest Hits-#3-1970s & 1980s-C* . . . . (TVT)

There's A Cabin In The Pines
Bing Crosby; *Crooner-Columbia Years-1928-1934* . . . . (Columbia)

This House
Original Broadway Cast; *I Do! I Do!* . . . . (RCA Victor)

This House
Tracie Spencer; *Make The Difference* . . . . (Capitol)

This House Is Empty Now
Elvis Costello; *Painted From Memory* . . . . (Mercury)

This Ole House
Rosemary Clooney; *Rosemary Clooney-16 Most Requested Songs* . . . . .(Legacy)
Statler Brothers; *The World Of The Statler Brothers* . . . .(Columbia)
Stuart Hamblen; *Stuart Hamblen-A Man & His Music* . . . .(Lamb & Lion)

Tin Roof Blues
Dukes Of Dixieland; *Dixieland's Greatest Hits.* . . . . (MCA)
George Lewis; *Jazz In The Classic New Orleans Tradition* . . . . (Riverside)
Harry Connick, Jr.; *Eleven* . . . . (Columbia)
Louis Armstrong & His All-Stars; *Evening With Louis Armstrong & His All-Stars* . . . . (Crescendo)
New Orleans Rhythm Kings; *New Orleans Rhythm Kings.* . . . .(Milestone)
Pete Fountain; *High Society* . . . .(Bluebird)

Two Of A Kind, Workin' On A Full House
Garth Brooks; *No Fences* . . . .(Capitol)

Two Story House
George Jones & Tammy Wynette; *George Jones & Tammy Wynette-16 Biggest Hits* . . . . (Epic/Legacy)

Two-Story House
George Jones & Tammy Wynette; *20 Years Of Hits/First Lady Of Country.* . . . . (Epic)
George Jones' Greatest Hits-#2 . . . . (Epic)
Tears Of Fire-25th Anniversary Collection. . . . . (Epic)
Tammy Wynette & George Jones; *Encore-Tammy Wynette & George Jones.* . . . . (Epic)

Under The House
Public Image Ltd.; *Flowers Of Romance* . . . . (Warner Bros.)

Up In My Treehouse
Chet Atkins; *Sails.* . . . . (Columbia)

Up On The House Top
Jimmy Buffett; *Christmas Island* . . . . (MCA)
Michael Jackson & The Jackson 5; *Jackson 5-Christmas Album* . . . . . .(Motown)

Up On The Roof
Cryan' Shames; *Scratch In The Sky* . . . .(Columbia)
Drifters; *Cruisin'-1962-C* . . . .(Increase)
Drifters' Greatest Hits . . . . (Gusto)
Drifters-16 Greatest Hits . . . . (Trip)
Drifters-Golden Hits . . . . (Atlantic)
James Taylor; *Flag.* . . . . (Columbia)
The Concert For New York City-C . . . . (Columbia)
Nylons; *Four On The Floor* . . . . (Scotti Bros.)

Up On The Roof
Cover Girls; *We Can't Go Wrong* . . . .(Capitol)

Up The Ladder To The Roof
Bette Midler; *Live At Last* . . . . (Atlantic)
Nylons; *Best Of The Nylons* . . . . (Open Air)
One Size Fits All . . . . (Open Air)

Villa In Portugal
Pursuit Of Happiness; *Downward Road.* . . . .(Mercury)

Villa Nueva
Victor Feldman/Generation Band; *Best Of Victor Feldman/ Generation Band* . . . . (Nova)

Walk Across The Rooftops
Blue Nile; *Walk Across The Rooftops* . . . . (A&M)

We Can Have The Olympics...At Our House
Tom Paxton; *One Million Lawyers & Other Disasters* . . . . (Flying Fish)

Wendy
Original Cast/Mary Martin; *Peter Pan-The 1954 Broadway Production* . . . . (RCA Victor)

When Your House Is Not A Home
Patsy Cline; *Patsy Cline-Live-#2* . . . . (MCA)

White House Blues
Doc Watson; *Essential Doc Watson.* . . . .(Vanguard)
Doc Watson & Family; *Treasures Untold-C* . . . .(Vanguard)
Stanley Brothers; *Shadows Of The Past* . . . . (Copper Creek)

White Houses
Eric Burdon & The Animals; *Eric Burdon & The Animals' Greatest Hits* . . . .(MGM)

White Room
Cream; *Cream-Live-#2* . . . . (Polydor)
History Of British Rock-#9-C . . . .(Rhino)
Strange Brew-Very Best Of Cream . . . . (Polydor)
Wheels Of Fire . . . . (Polydor)
Eric Clapton; *24 Nights* . . . .(Duck/Reprise)
Eric Clapton-Crossroads-C . . . . (Polydor)

HUG, Cuddle, Embrace, Hold

See Also: ANATOMY: ARMS, HOLDING ON, LOVE (various)

(Let Me Be Your) Teddy Bear
Elvis Presley; *Elvis' Golden Records.* . . . . (RCA)
Elvis In Concert. . . . . (RCA)
Number One Hits. . . . . (RCA)
ST/Loving You. . . . . (RCA)

The Top Ten Hits . . . . (RCA)
After The Lights Go Down Low
 Al Hibbler; *After The Lights Go Down Low* . . . . (Atlantic)
All I Need To Know
 Kenny Chesney; *All I Need To Know* . . . . (BNA)
 Kenny Chesney's Greatest Hits . . . . (BNA)
Botcha-A-Me (Ba-Ba-Baciami Piccina)
 Rosemary Clooney; *Rosemary Clooney-16 Most Requested Songs* . . . . (Legacy)
Bushel And A Peck
 Andrews Sisters; *Best Of The Andrews Sisters-#2* . . . . (MCA)
 Original Cast; *Guys & Dolls* . . . . (MCA)
Could I Have This Kiss Forever
 Whitney Houston & Enrique Iglesias; *Whitney Houston's*
  Greatest Hits . . . . (Arista)
Cover You In Kisses
 John Michael Montgomery; *Leave A Mark* . . . . (Atlantic)
Cuddle Up A Little Closer
 Jimmy Roselli; *When Your Old Wedding Ring Was* . . . . (M&R)
Dim, Dim The Lights (I Want Some Atmosphere)
 Bill Haley; *From The Original Master Tapes-Bill Haley* . . . . (MCA)
Do It Again A Little Bit Slower
 Jon, Robin & The In Crowd; *Dick Bartley's One-Hit Wonders Of The*
  '60s-#1-C . . . . (Rhino)
Don't Let Go
 Regina Belle; *Believe In Me* . . . . (MCA)
Don't Let Go (Love)
 En Vogue; *Best Of En Vogue* . . . . (Elektra)
 EV3 . . . . (East West)
Eight Days A Week
 Beatles; *Beatles 1* . . . . (Capitol)
 Beatles VI . . . . (Capitol)
 Beatles-20 Greatest Hits . . . . (Capitol)
 The Beatles/1962-1966 . . . . (Capitol)
Embraceable You
 Billie Holiday; *Body And Soul* . . . . (Verve)
 Frank Sinatra; *The Capitol Years* . . . . (Capitol)
 MGM Studio Orchestra; *ST/American In Paris* . . . . . (Sony Music Special Prod.)
 Oleta Adams; *Glory Of Gershwin Featuring Larry Adler-C* . . . . (Mercury)
 Sarah Vaughan; *Complete Sarah Vaughan On Mercury-#1-Great Jazz Years-*
  1954-1956 . . . . (Mercury)
Falls Apart
 Sugar Ray; *14:59* . . . . (Lava)
 Totally Hits-#2-C . . . . (Elektra)
Fever
 Buddy Guy; *This Is Buddy Guy* . . . . (Vanguard)
 Elvis Presley; *A Valentine Gift For You* . . . . (RCA)
 Aloha from Hawaii via Satellite . . . . (RCA)
 Elvis Presley-Pure Gold . . . . (RCA)
 Little Willie John; *Best Of Little Willie John-Fever* . . . . (Rhino)
 Peggy Lee; *Memories Are Made Of This-C* . . . . (Capitol)
 Rita Coolidge; *Rita Coolidge-Classics-#5* . . . . (A&M)
 Rita Coolidge's Greatest Hits . . . . (A&M)
Hold Me
 Brian McKnight; *Anytime* . . . . (Motown)
Hold Me Tight
 Beatles; *Meet The Beatles!* . . . . (Capitol)
Hold Me, Thrill Me, Kiss Me
 Mel Carter; *Baby Boomer Classics-Love Sixties-C* . . . . (JCI Assoc. Labels)
Hold Me, Thrill Me, Kiss Me, Kill Me
 U2; *Number One Movie Hits-C* . . . . (ESX Entert.)
 ST/Batman Forever . . . . (Atlantic)
Hold You Tight
 Tara Kemp; *Tara Kemp* . . . . (Giant)
Holdin'
 Diamond Rio; *Diamond Rio IV* . . . . (Arista)
 Diamond Rio's Greatest Hits . . . . (Arista)
Holdin' Heaven
 Tracy Byrd; *Tracy Byrd* . . . . (MCA)
How Can I Help You Say Goodbye
 Patty Loveless; *Only What I Feel* . . . . (Epic)
 Patty Loveless-Classics . . . . (Epic)
I Can't Get Next To You
 Temptations; *All The Million-Sellers* . . . . (Motown)
 Temptations' Greatest Hits-#2 . . . . (Motown)
 Temptations-The Ultimate Collection . . . . (Motown)
I Got Id
 Pearl Jam; *Merkinball* . . . . (Epic)
I Want To Hold Your Hand
 Beatles; *Beatles 1* . . . . (Capitol)
 Beatles-20 Greatest Hits . . . . (Capitol)
 Meet The Beatles! . . . . (Capitol)
 Past Masters-Volume One . . . . (Parlophone)
 The Beatles/1962-1966 . . . . (Capitol)
 Lakeside; *Galactic Grooves/Best Of Lakeside* . . . . (Right Stuff)
 Your Wish My Command . . . . (Solar)
I Want You, I Need You, I Love You
 Elvis Presley; *Heart & Soul* . . . . (RCA)

I'll Hold You In My Heart (Till I Can Hold You In My Arms)
 Eddy Arnold; *Best Of Eddy Arnold* . . . . (RCA)
 Eddy Arnold-The Hits . . . . (Mercury)
 Memories Are Made Of This . . . . (Mercury)
I'll Make Love To You
 Boyz II Men; *Boyz II Men II* . . . . (Motown)
In The Still Of The Nite
 Dion; *Dion Sings The 15 Million Sellers* . . . . (Laurie)
 Dion's Greatest Hits . . . . (Laurie)
 Dion And The Belmonts; *Wish Upon A Star With Dion And The*
  Belmonts . . . . (Collectables)
 Five Satins; *Billboard Top R&B Hits-1956-C* . . . . (Rhino)
 Cruisin'-1956-C . . . . (Increase)
 Five Satins Sing Their Greatest Hits . . . . (Collectables)
 In The Still Of The Night . . . . (Capitol)
 ST/Dirty Dancing . . . . (RCA)
 Johnny Mathis; *In The Still Of The Night* . . . . (Columbia)
Let It Rain
 Mark Chesnutt; *Mark Chesnutt's Greatest Hits* . . . . (Decca)
Missing My Baby
 Selena; *Dreaming Of You* . . . . (EMI Latin)
My Melancholy Baby
 Barbra Streisand; *Third Album* . . . . (Columbia)
 Bing Crosby; *Hits Of 1939-C* . . . . (Living Era)
 Coleman Hawkins; *Genius Of Coleman Hawkins* . . . . (Verve)
 Dorothy Loudon; *Saloon* . . . . (DRG)
 Frank Sinatra; *Voice: The Columbia Years-1943-1952* . . . . (Columbia)
 Gene Austin; *78-#21015* . . . . (Victor)
 Jan Garber & His Orchestra; *Jan Garber & His Orchestra Play 22 Original*
  Big Band Favorites . . . . (Hindsight)
 Kate Smith; *Kate Smith-16 Most Requested Songs* . . . . (Columbia)
 Leon Redbone; *Double Time* . . . . (Warner Bros.)
 Marcels; *Best Of The Marcels* . . . . (Rhino)
Nobody Wants To Be Lonely
 Ricky Martin; *Sound Loaded* . . . . (Columbia)
Oh, What A Night
 Dells; *Billboard Top R&B Hits-1965-1969-C* . . . . (Rhino)
 Collectables Presents The History Of Rock-#9-C . . . . (Collectables)
 Cruisin'-1956-C . . . . (Increase)
 Oh, What A Night . . . . (Vee-Jay)
 Oldies But Goodies-#3-C . . . . (Original Sound)
Saturday Night At The Movies
 Drifters; *1959-1965-All-Time Greatest Hits And More* . . . . (Atlantic)
 Drifters-16 Greatest Hits . . . . (Trip)
 Drifters-Golden Hits . . . . (Atlantic)
 Save The Last Dance For Me . . . . (Fifty One West)
Seven Little Girls Sitting In The Back Seat
 Paul Evans; *Music To Remember-C* . . . . (Dominion Entert.)
Silver Future
 Monster Magnet; *ST/Heavy Metal 2000* . . . . (Restless)
Someone To Love
 Jon B.; *Bonafide* . . . . (Yab Yum/550)
 Jon B. featuring Babyface; *ST/Bad Boys* . . . . (Work)
That's How You Know (When You're In Love)
 Lari White; *Best Of Lari White* . . . . (RCA)
 Wishes . . . . (RCA)
This I Promise You
 'N Sync; *No Strings Attached* . . . . (Jive)
 Now That's What I Call Music!-#7-C . . . . (Virgin)
Trademark
 Mandy Barnett; *I've Got A Right To Cry* . . . . (Sire)
Tree Hugger
 Rugburns; *Taking The World By Donkey* . . . . (Priority)
Unison
 Bjork; *Vespertine* . . . . (Elektra)
Why Would I Say Goodbye
 Brooks & Dunn; *Borderline* . . . . (Arista)
Wild Thing
 Jimi Hendrix; *Essential Jimi Hendrix, Volume 2* . . . . (Reprise)
 Live At Winterland . . . . (Rykodisc)
 ST/Jimi Plays Monterey . . . . (Reprise)
 Tone Loc; *Loc-ed After Dark* . . . . (Delicious Vinyl)
 Rap's Biggest Hits-C . . . . (K-Tel)
 Rock The First-#6-C . . . . (Sandstone Music)
 Troggs; *Billboard Top Rock 'N' Roll Hits-1966-C* . . . . (Rhino)
 Frat Rock!-C . . . . (Rhino)
 History Of British Rock-#3-C . . . . (Rhino)
Woman In Me (Needs The Man In You)
 Shania Twain; *Woman In Me* . . . . (Mercury)
You Have The Right To Remain Silent
 Perfect Stranger; *From Nashville With Love-C* . . . . (Curb)
You've Really Got A Hold On Me
 Beatles; *The Beatles-Anthology-#1* . . . . (Capitol)
 Smokey Robinson & The Miracles; *Best Of Smokey Robinson & The*
  Miracles-Anthology . . . . (Motown)
 Great Songs & Performances That Inspired The Motown 25th Anniversary
  Television Special-C . . . . (Motown)

Smokey Robinson-*The Ultimate Collection* . . . . (Motown)

IDENTITY CRISIS, Don't Know Myself, Finding Oneself, Loss Of Identity

See Also: **AGING, CRAZY, EGO, LOW SELF-ESTEEM, SEARCH**

(Sittin' On) The Dock Of The Bay
Michael Bolton; *The Hunger* . . . . (Columbia)
Otis Redding; *(Sittin' On) The Dock Of The Bay* . . . .(Atco)
Best Of Otis Redding . . . .(Atco)
Golden Age Of Black Music-1960-1970-C . . . . (Atlantic)
Golden Soul-C . . . . (Atlantic)
Soul Years-C . . . . (Atlantic)
The Otis Redding Story . . . . (Atlantic)
10,000 Horses
Candlebox; *Happy Pills* . . . . (Maverick)
Bitter Sweet Symphony
Verve; *Urban Hymns* . . . . (Hut/Virgin)
Bittersweet Me
R.E.M.; *New Adventures In Hi-Fi* . . . . (Warner Bros.)
Change Your Mind
Sister Hazel; *Fortress* . . . . (Universal)
Child Is Gone
Fiona Apple; *Tidal* . . . .(Clean Slate/Work)
Crazy
Alana Davis; *Blame It On Me* . . . . (Elektra)
Drift Away
Dobie Gray; *Classic Rock-#1-C* . . . . (MCA)
Oldies But Goodies-#10-C . . . .(Original Sound)
Oldies But Goodies-#3-C . . . .(Original Sound)
Super Hits Of The '70s-Have A Nice Day-#10-C . . . .(Rhino)
Michael Bolton; *Timeless-Classics* . . . . (Columbia)
Rod Stewart; *Atlantic Crossing* . . . . (Warner Bros.)
Englishman In New York
Sting; *...Nothing Like The Sun* . . . . (A&M)
Fields Of Gold-The Best Of Sting 1984-1994 . . . . (A&M)
Evaporated
Ben Folds Five; *Whatever And Ever Amen* . . . . (Caroline/550)
I Am
Train; *Train* . . . . (Aware/C2/Columbia)
I Am...I Said
Neil Diamond; *Hot August Night* . . . . (MCA)
Hot August Night II . . . . (Columbia)
Neil Diamond-His 12 Greatest Hits . . . . (MCA)
Stones . . . . (MCA)
Iris
Goo Goo Dolls; *Dizzy Up The Girl* . . . . (Warner Sunset/Reprise)
ST/City Of Angels . . . . (Warner Sunset/Reprise)
James
Huffamoose; *We've Been Had Again* . . . . (Interscope)
Joining You
Alanis Morissette; *Supposed Former Infatuation Junkie* . . . . (Maverick)
Knock It On The Head
Wood; *Songs From Stamford Hill* . . . . (Columbia)
No One
Cold; *13 Ways To Bleed On Stage* . . . .(Flip/Geffen/Interscope)
One Headlight
Wallflowers; *Bringing Down The Horse* . . . . (Interscope)
Reflection
Christina Aguilera; *Christina Aguilera* . . . . (RCA)
ST/Mulan . . . . (Walt Disney)
Run Away
Real McCoy; *Another Night* . . . . (Arista)
Shame
Stabbing Westward; *Wither Blister Burn & Peel* . . . . (Columbia)
Sick Of Myself
Matthew Sweet; *100% Fun* . . . .(Zoo)
Slide
Goo Goo Dolls; *Dizzy Up The Girl* . . . . (Warner Sunset/Reprise)
So Much To Say
Dave Matthews Band; *Crash* . . . . (RCA)
Stolen Car
Bruce Springsteen; *The River* . . . . (Columbia)
Tracks . . . . (Columbia)
Elliott Murphy; *One Step Up/Two Steps Back-The Songs Of Bruce Springsteen-C* . . . . (Right Stuff)
Streets Of Philadelphia
Bruce Springsteen; *Bruce Springsteen's Greatest Hits* . . . . (Columbia)
Diana, Princess Of Wales-Tribute-C . . . . (Columbia)
ST/Philadelphia . . . . (Epic/Sony Music Soundtrax)
Tryin' To Get To Heaven
Bob Dylan; *Time Out Of Mind* . . . . (Columbia)
Where Am I Going?
Original Cast/Gwen Verdon; *Sweet Charity* . . . . (Columbia)

Wherever You Go
Clint Black; *Clint Black-The Greatest Hits* . . . . (RCA)
One Emotion . . . . (RCA)
Who Am I?
Petula Clark; *Greatest Hits Of Petula Clark* . . . . (Crescendo)
You Don't Even Know Who I Am
Patty Loveless; *Patty Loveless-Classics* . . . .(Epic)
When Fallen Angels Fly . . . . (Epic)

INSIDE/OUTSIDE

See Also: **DOORS, LEAVING, OPEN & CLOSED, OPPOSITES, WINDOWS**

Baby, It's Cold Outside
Pearl Bailey; *Pearl Bailey-16 Most Requested Songs* . . . .(Legacy)
Ray Charles; *Ray Charles-His Greatest Hits-#2* . . . .(Dunhill Compact Classics)
Birds Of A Feather
Phish; *The Story Of The Ghost* . . . . (Elektra)
Blow Up The Outside World
Soundgarden; *A-Sides* . . . . (A&M)
Down On The Upside . . . . (A&M)
Can I Touch You...There?
Michael Bolton; *Michael Bolton's Greatest Hits-1985-1995* . . . .(Columbia)
Count Me In
Gary Lewis And The Playboys; *Gary Lewis & The Playboys* . . . . . . (Gold Rush)
Gary Lewis And The Playboys' Greatest Hits . . . .(Curb)
Deep Inside
Mary J. Blige; *Mary* . . . . (MCA)
End Of Outside
Duncan Sheik; *Duncan Sheik* . . . . (Atlantic)
Everybody's Got Something To Hide Except Me And My Monkey
Beatles; *The Beatles (White Album)* . . . .(Capitol)
Fallin'
Alicia Keys; *Songs In A Minor* . . . .(J)
Totally Hits 2001-C . . . . (Arista)
Fools Rush In (Where Angels Fear To Tread)
Brook Benton; *Super Oldies Of The '60s-#10-C* . . . . (Audio Fidelity)
Tommy Dorsey & Frank Sinatra; *Sessions-#1-February 1, 1940-July 17, 1940* . . . . (RCA)
Freezing
Nick Lowe; *Dig My Mood* . . . .(Upstart)
Get 'Em Outta Here
Sprung Monkey; *Mr. Funny Face* . . . .(Surfdog/Hollywood)
Get Outta My Dreams, Get Into My Car
Billy Ocean; *Billy Ocean's Greatest Hits* . . . . (Jive)
ST/License To Drive . . . . (MCA)
Girl Inside My Head
Blues Traveler; *Bridge* . . . . (A&M)
Go Let It Out
Oasis; *Standing On The Shoulders Of Giants* . . . . (Epic)
Green Door
Jim Lowe; *Billboard Top Rock 'N' Roll Hits-1956-C* . . . .(Rhino)
Super Hits-#4-C . . . . (Gusto)
Hey Jude
Beatles; *Beatles 1* . . . .(Capitol)
Beatles-20 Greatest Hits . . . .(Capitol)
Past Masters-Volume Two . . . . (Parlophone)
The Beatles/1967-1970 . . . .(Capitol)
Paul McCartney; *Knebworth-The Album-C* . . . . (Polydor)
Wilson Pickett; *Wilson Pickett's Greatest Hits* . . . . (Atlantic)
House With No Curtains
Alan Jackson; *Everything I Love* . . . . (Arista)
Human
Pretenders; *Viva El Amor!* . . . . (Warner Bros.)
In And Out Of Love
Diana Ross; *Diana Ross-Anthology* . . . . (Motown)
In Between Dances
Pam Tillis; *Pam Tillis' Greatest Hits* . . . . (Arista)
Sweetheart's Dance . . . . (Arista)
In Or Out
Ani DiFranco; *Lesbian Favorites-Women Like Us-C* . . . . (Rhino)
Inner Light
Beatles; *Past Masters-Volume Two* . . . . (Parlophone)
Rarities . . . .(Capitol)
Inner Light
Little River Band; *Diamantina Cocktail* . . . .(Capitol)
Inside
Ronnie Milsap; *Inside Ronnie Milsap* . . . . (RCA)
Ronnie Milsap's Greatest Hits-#2 . . . . (RCA)
Solid Country Gold-C . . . . (RCA)
Inside My Love
Trina Broussard; *ST/Love Jones* . . . . (Columbia)
Inside Of Me
Little Steven & The Disciples Of Soul; *The Sopranos-Music From The HBO Original Series* . . . . (Sony Music Soundtrax)

Inside Out
Eve 6; *Eve 6* . . . . (RCA)
I've Got This Feeling
Mavericks; *Trampoline* . . . .(MCA)
Level On The Inside
Dovetail Joint; *001* . . . .(Aware/C2/Columbia)
Like Humans Do
David Byrne; *Look Into The Eyeball*. . . . .(Luaka Bop)
Livin' La Vida Loca
Ricky Martin; *Ricky Martin* . . . . (Columbia)
Out In The Cold
Judas Priest; *Priest...Live!* . . . . (Columbia)
Turbo . . . . (Columbia)
Out In The Cold
Tom Petty And The Heartbreakers; *Into The Great Wide Open* . . . .(MCA)
Out In The Cold
George Howard; *When Summer Comes* . . . . (GRP)
Out Of My Dreams
Original Broadway Cast; *Oklahoma!* . . . . (RCA)
Original Cast; *Oklahoma!* . . . .(MCA)
Out Of Sight, Out Of Mind
Five Keys; *Golden Classics-Five Keys* . . . . (Collectables)
Out Of Your Shoes
Lorrie Morgan; *Essential Lorrie Morgan* . . . . (RCA)
Leave The Light On . . . . (RCA)
Lorrie Morgan-Super Hits . . . . (RCA)
Outside
Mariah Carey; *Butterfly* . . . . (Columbia)
Outside
Staind; *Break The Cycle* . . . .(Flip/Elektra)
Outside Looking In
Mary Chapin Carpenter; *Stones In The Road* . . . . (Columbia)
Outside Of A Small Circle Of Friends
Phil Ochs; *The War Is Over-Best Of Phil Ochs* . . . . (A&M)
There & Now-Live In Vancouver-1968 . . . . (Rhino)
Outside The Law
Rundle Chowning Band; *Heart On Fire* . . . . (A&M)
Outside The Nashville City Limits
Joan Baez; *Blessed Are* . . . . (Vanguard)
Country Music Album . . . . (Vanguard)
Outskirts Of Town
Sawyer Brown; *Outskirts Of Town* . . . . (Curb)
Outta The World
Ashford & Simpson; *Solid* . . . . (Capitol)
Solid Plus Seven . . . . (Capitol)
Power Inside Of Me
Richard Marx; *ST/The Mirror Has Two Faces* . . . . (Columbia)
Reflection
Christina Aguilera; *Christina Aguilera*. . . . . (RCA)
ST/Mulan . . . . (Walt Disney)
Rollin'
Limp Bizkit; *Chocolate Starfish & The Hotdog Flavored
Water* . . . . (Flip/Interscope)
Shelf In The Room
Days Of The New; *Days Of The New* . . . . (Outpost/Interscope)
Something Inside
Boney James featuring Dave Hollister; *Ride* . . . .(Warner Bros.)
Stand Inside Your Love
Smashing Pumpkins; *Machina: The Machines Of God* . . . . (Virgin)
Standing Outside The Fire
Garth Brooks; *In Pieces* . . . . (Liberty)
Step Inside Love
Beatles; *The Beatles-Anthology-#3*. . . . . (Capitol)
Sugar Walls
Sheena Easton; *Dance Mix* . . . .(EMI)
Private Heaven . . . .(EMI)
Superman Inside
Eric Clapton; *Reptile*. . . . . (Duck/Reprise)
Surfin' U.S.A.
Beach Boys; *Absolute Best-#1* . . . . (Capitol)
Best Of The Beach Boys . . . . (Capitol)
Billboard Top Rock 'N' Roll Hits-1963-C . . . . (Rhino)
Endless Summer. . . . . (Capitol)
Made In The U.S.A. . . . . (Capitol)
Take You Out
Luther Vandross; *Luther Vandross* . . . . (J)
Testify
Rage Against The Machine; *The Battle Of Los Angeles* . . . .(Epic)
Theme From "Outer Limits"
Original Soundtrack; *Television's Greatest Hits-#2-C* . . . . (TVT)
When She Cries
Restless Heart; *Big Iron Horses* . . . . (RCA)
Restless Heart's Greatest Hits . . . . (RCA)
Today's Number One Country-C . . . . (K-Tel)
Who Walks In When I Walk Out
Bob Wills; *Stay A Little Longer-The Original Columbia
Recordings* . . . .(Roswell/RCA)

Whole Lotta Love
Led Zeppelin; *Led Zeppelin II* . . . .(Atlantic)
Led Zeppelin-Box Set . . . .(Atlantic)
Remasters . . . .(Atlantic)
ST/The Song Remains The Same. (Swan Song)
Within You Without You
Beatles; *Beatles-Box Set* . . . . (Capitol)
Sgt. Pepper's Lonely Hearts Club Band . . . . (Capitol)
You
Queensryche; *Hear In The Now Frontier* . . . .(Virgin)
You Won't Let Me In
Rosanne Cash; *The Wheel* . . . . (Columbia)

INSULTS

*See Also: **ANATOMY: REAR, ANGER, BEAUTY, COMPLAINTS,
CRAZY, FEELINGS, FOOLS, HATE, LOVE: GET LOST!, LOW
SELF-ESTEEM, SLEAZY***

Abuse Me
Silverchair; *Freak Show* . . . . (Epic)
Ain't My Bitch
Metallica; *Load* . . . . (Elektra)
All The Fuckers Live In Newport Beach
Fluf; *The Classic Years* . . . .(Headhunter)
All You Ever Do Is Bring Me Down
Mavericks; *Best Of The Mavericks-Super Colossal Smash Hits Of
The '90s*. . . . . (Mercury)
Country Superstar Hits-C. . . . .(Hip-O)
Honky Tonk Boogie-C . . . .(Hip-O)
Music For All Occasions . . . . (MCA)
American Bad Ass
Kid Rock; *History Of Rock* . . . . (Top Dog/Lava/Atlantic)
Are You Teasing Me
Carl Smith; *Carl Smith's Greatest Hits* . . . . (Gusto)
Essential Carl Smith-1950-1956 . . . . (Legacy)
Asleep At The Wheel
Wallflowers; *The Wallflowers* . . . .(Virgin)
Asshole From El Paso
Kinky Friedman; *Lasso From El Paso* . . . . (Epic)
Kinky Friedman & His Texas Jewboys; *Old Testaments & New
Revelations* . . . .(Fruit Of The Tune)
Assholes On Parade
Timbuk 3; *Best Of Timbuk 3* . . . . (I.R.S.)
Battle Of Who Could Care Less
Ben Folds Five; *Whatever And Ever Amen* . . . .(Caroline/550)
Beautiful People
Marilyn Manson; *Antichrist Superstar* . . . .(Interscope)
Better Than You
Metallica; *Reload* . . . . (Elektra)
Big Shot
Billy Joel; *52nd Street* . . . . (Columbia)
Billy Joel-Greatest Hits, Volume I & Volume II . . . . (Columbia)
KOHUEPT . . . . (Columbia)
Bills, Bills, Bills
Destiny's Child; *The Writing's On The Wall*. . . . . (Columbia)
Bird Brain Baby
Mercy Dee Walton; *Back Luck 'N' Trouble* . . . . (Arhoolie)
Bird Dog
Everly Brothers; *Best Of The Everly Brothers* . . . . (Rhino)
Billboard Top Rock 'N' Roll Hits-1958-C . . . . (Rhino)
Everly Brothers-Cadence Classics-Their 20 Greatest Hits . . . . (Rhino)
Fabulous Style Of The Everly Brothers . . . . (Rhino)
Very Best Of The Everly Brothers. . . . . (Warner Bros.)
Birdbrain
Tom Buffalo; *Birdbrain* . . . .(Beggar's Banquet)
Bird-Brain Rag
Max Morath; *The World Of Scott Joplin-#2* . . . . (Vanguard)
Birds Of A Feather
Phish; *The Story Of The Ghost* . . . . (Elektra)
Bitch
Meredith Brooks; *Blurring The Edges* . . . . (Capitol)
Bitch Betta Have My Money
AMG; *Give A Dog A Bone*. . . . . (Select)
Blame
Collective Soul; *Disciplined Breakdown*. . . . .(Atlantic)
Blame It On Your Heart
Patty Loveless; *Only What I Feel* . . . . (Epic)
Patty Loveless-Classics . . . . (Epic)
Bound For The Floor
Local H; *As Good As Dead* . . . . (Island)
Boy Named Sue
Johnny Cash; *Columbia Country Classics-#3-Americana-C* . . . . . . (Columbia)
Johnny Cash's Biggest Hits . . . . (Columbia)
Johnny Cash's Greatest Hits-#2. . . . . (Columbia)
The Man In Black-His Greatest Hits. (Legacy)

Brothers Ain't Shit
Roxanne Shante; *2 Nasty 4 Radio* .... (Cold Chillin')
Call Me Irresponsible
Frank Sinatra; *Sinatra: A Man And His Music* ....(Reprise)
Sinatra's Sinatra..(Reprise)
Jackie Gleason; *Best Of Jackie Gleason & His Orchestra* ....(Curb)
Robert Goulet; *Robert Goulet-16 Most Requested Songs* ....(Columbia)
Rosemary Clooney; *Rosemary Clooney Sings The Music Of Jimmy Van Heusen* .... (Concord Jazz)
Careful With That Mic...
Clutch; *Pure Rock Fury* .... (Atlantic)
Case Of The Ex (Whatcha Gonna Do)
Mya; *Fear Of Flying* .... (University/Interscope)
Now That's What I Call Music!-#5-C ....(Virgin)
Cathy's Clown
Everly Brothers; *Billboard Top Rock 'N' Roll Hits-1960-C* .... (Rhino)
Golden Hits Of The Everly Brothers .... (Warner Bros.)
The Reunion Concert-Live At Albert Hall 1983 ....(Mercury)
Very Best Of The Everly Brothers .... (Warner Bros.)
Reba McEntire; *Sweet Sixteen* .... (MCA)
Change
Sheryl Crow; *Sheryl Crow* .... (A&M)
Change The World
Offspring; *Ixnay On The Hombre* .... (Columbia)
Charlie Brown
Coasters; *Billboard Top Rock 'N' Roll Hits-1957-C* .... (Rhino)
Coasters' Greatest Hits ....(Atco)
Coasters-Their Greatest Recordings-Early Years ....(Atco)
Cruisin'-1959-C ....(Increase)
Super Oldies Of The '50s-#7-C .... (Audio Fidelity)
Young Blood .... (Atlantic)
Choice In The Matter
Aimee Mann; *I'm With Stupid* .... (Geffen)
Christian Life
Byrds; *Sweetheart Of The Rodeo* .... (Columbia)
The Byrds .... (Columbia)
Chump
Green Day; *Dookie* ....(Reprise)
Clumsy
Our Lady Peace; *Clumsy* .... (Columbia)
Cold Contagious
Bush; *Razorblade Suitcase* ....(Trauma)
Cold Hard Truth, The
George Jones; *Cold Hard Truth* .... (Asylum)
Jamie O'Hara; *Rise Above It* ....(RCA)
Cold Hearted
Paula Abdul; *Forever Your Girl* ....(Virgin)
Get Up & Dance-Dance Mixes ....(Virgin)
Crawlin' Home Puker
Da Yoopers; *Yoopanese*..............................(You Guys)
Crosstown Traffic
Jimi Hendrix; *Kiss The Sky* ....(Reprise)
Jimi Hendrix Experience; *Electric Ladyland* ....(Reprise)
Essential Jimi Hendrix, Volume 2 ....(Reprise)
Smash Hits ....(Reprise)
Cut You In
Jerry Cantrell; *Boggy Depot* .... (Columbia)
Daddy Could Swear, I Declare
Gladys Knight & The Pips; *Gladys Knight & The Pips-All The Great Hits* .... (Motown)
Gladys Knight & The Pips-Anthology................ (Motown)
Motown Memories-#3-C........................... (Motown)
Neither One Of Us .... (Motown)
Dammit Janet
Barry Bostwick; *ST/Rocky Horror Picture Show* .... (Rhino)
Original London Cast; *Rocky Horror Show*................ (Rhino)
Dance Of The Imbeciles
D.C. 3; *This Is The Dream* .... (SST)
Day Tripper
Beatles; *"Yesterday"...And Today*....................... (Capitol)
Beatles 1 ....(Capitol)
Beatles-Box Set .... (Capitol)
Past Masters-Volume Two .... (Parlophone)
The Beatles/1962-1966............................. (Capitol)
Jimi Hendrix Experience; *Radio One* .... (Rykodisc)
Otis Redding; *Dictionary Of Soul* ....(Atco)
The Otis Redding Story .... (Atlantic)
Sergio Mendes & Brasil '66; *Sergio Mendes & Brasil '66's Greatest Hits* .... (A&M)
December
Collective Soul; *Collective Soul* .... (Atlantic)
Dickie's Such An Asshole
Frank Zappa; *Broadway The Hard Way* .... (Rykodisc)
You Can't Do That On Stage Anymore-#3 .... (Rykodisc)
Did I Do That?
Mariah Carey; *Rainbow* .... (Columbia)
Die Nigger Die
Schoolly D; *How A Black Man Feels*..................... (Capitol)

Dirty Dawg
NKOTB; *Face The Music* ....(Columbia)
Dirty Old Egg-Sucking Dog
Johnny Cash; *Essential Johnny Cash*.....................(Columbia)
Johnny Cash At Folsom Prison & San Quentin................(Columbia)
Do The Evolution
Pearl Jam; *Yield* .... (Epic)
Dog Breath
Frank Zappa; *Uncle Meat*........................ (Barking Pumpkin)
Mothers Of Invention; *Just Another Band From L.A.* ....(Bizarre/Straight)
Donna The Prima Donna
Dion; *Bronx Blues-Columbia Recordings 1962-1965* ....(Columbia)
Dion-24 Original Classics ....(Arista)
Don't Be A Hog
Doctor Nerve; *Armed Observation*........................ (Cuneiform)
Don't Be Stupid (You Know I Love You)
Shania Twain; *Come On Over* ....(Mercury)
Don't Call Me Nigger, Whitey
Sly & The Family Stone; *Sly & The Family Stone-Anthology* ....(Epic)
Stand! ....(Epic)
Don't Come Home A'Lovin' With Venison On Your Truck
Debby McClatchy; *Someday Cafe* .... (Green Linnet)
Don't Get Mad, Get Even
Aerosmith; *Pump* .... (Geffen)
Don't Laugh At Me
Mark Wills; *Wish You Were Here* ....(Mercury)
Don't Say Nothing Bad About My Baby
Cookies; *Golden Girl Groups-C*..........................(K-Tel)
Original Rock 'N' Roll Hits Of The '60s-C ....(Roulette)
Don't Say Things You Don't Mean
Lynn Anderson; *Lynn Anderson's Greatest Hits* ....(Columbia)
Don't Tell Me What To Do
Pam Tillis; *Put Yourself In My Place* ....(Arista)
Don't Think Twice, It's All Right
Bob Dylan; *Before The Flood* ....(Columbia)
Bob Dylan's Greatest Hits-#2 ....(Columbia)
Freewheelin' ....(Columbia)
Joan Baez; *The First 10 Years* ....(Vanguard)
Wonder Who?; *Anniversary*..............................(Rhino)
Don't Think You're Smart
Memphis Slim; *Raining The Blues* .... (Fantasy)
Don't Use Your Penis (For A Brain)
Romanovsky & Phillips; *Trouble In Paradise* ....(Fresh Fruit)
Down In The Boondocks
Billy Joe Royal; *Billy Joe Royal's Greatest Hits* ....(Columbia)
Rock Classics Of The '60s-C..........................(Columbia)
Eat My Shorts
Rick Dees; *45-#89601* .... (Atlantic)
Eat Shit You Fucking Redneck
Pigface; *Eat Shit You F@$king Redneck* ....(Invisible)
Escape From The Island Of Living Puke
Zoogz Rift; *Island Of Living Puke* .... (SST)
Everything To Everyone
Everclear; *Ka-Boom!-C* .... (Beast)
So Much For The Afterglow ....(Capitol)
Extra Pale
Goo Goo Dolls; *Dizzy Up The Girl*.............. (Warner Sunset/Reprise)
Fashion Victim
Green Day; *Warning* .... (Reprise)
Fool's Hall Of Fame
Johnny Cash; *Rough Cut King Of Country Music* .... (Sun)
The Man-The World-His Music .... (Sun)
Roy Orbison; *Roy Orbison-The Sun Years*.....................(Rhino)
For All My Niggaz & Bitches
Snoop Doggy Dogg; *Doggystyle* ....(Death Row)
For Those Who Dissed Me
2 Deep; *Honey That's Show Biz* .... (Cold Chillin')
Free To Decide
Cranberries; *To The Faithful Departed* ....(Island)
Fuck Compton
Tim Dog; *Penicillin On Wax* ....(Ruffhouse)
Fuck Tha Police
N.W.A.; *Straight Outta Compton* .... (Ruthless/Priority)
Fuck You
D.O.A.; *War On 45/Bloodied But Unbowed* .... (Restless)
Fuck You, Man
Pussy Galore; *Right Now!* ....(Caroline)
Fuck Your Attitude
War Zone; *Don't Forget The Struggle...* ....(Caroline)
Geek U.S.A.
Smashing Pumpkins; *Siamese Dream* .... (Virgin)
Gentleman Is A Dope
Jo Stafford; *Jo Stafford's Greatest Hits* ....(Curb)
Morgana King; *Another Time Another Space* .... (Muse)
Get 'Em Outta Here
Sprung Monkey; *Mr. Funny Face* ....(Surfdog/Hollywood)
Get The Fuck Out
Skid Row; *Slave To The Grind*........................... (Atlantic)

Get The Fuck Out Of My House
2 Live Crew; *As Nasty As They Wanna Be* . . . . (Luke)
Go To Hell
Alice Cooper; *Goes To Hell* . . . .(Warner Bros.)
The Alice Cooper Show . . . .(Warner Bros.)
Go To Hell
Megadeth; *ST/Bill & Ted's Bogus Journey* . . . . (Interscope)
Got You (Where I Want You)
Flys; *Holiday Man* . . . .(Delicious Vinyl)
ST/Disturbing Behavior . . . . (Trauma)
Greed
Godsmack; *Awake* . . . .(Republic/Universal)
Gypsies, Tramps And Thieves
Cher; *Half-Breed* . . . . (MCA Special Prod.)
Ha!
Juvenile; *400 Degreez* . . . . (Cash Money/Universal)
He Loves U Not
Dream; *It Was All A Dream* . . . . (Bad Boy/Arista)
He Thinks He'll Keep Her
Mary Chapin Carpenter; *Come On Come On* . . . . (Columbia)
He Wasn't Man Enough
Toni Braxton; *The Heat* . . . . (LaFace)
Totally Hits-#3-C . . . . (Atlantic)
He's Misstra Know-It-All
Stevie Wonder; *Innervisions* . . . . (Motown)
Hey Stoopid
Alice Cooper; *Hey Stoopid* . . . .(Epic)
Hippy Fascist
Pulkas; *Earache Presents Earplugged 2-C* . . . .(Earache)
Greed . . . . (Earache)
Honey Chile
Martha Reeves & The Vandellas; *Compact Command Performances-Martha
Reeves & The Vandellas* . . . . (Motown)
Martha Reeves & The Vandellas-Anthology . . . . (Motown)
Motown Superstar Series-#11-Martha Reeves & The Vandellas . . . . (Motown)
Hound Dog
Elvis Presley; *Aloha from Hawaii via Satellite* . . . . (RCA)
Elvis Aron Presley . . . . (RCA)
Elvis As Recorded At Madison Square Garden . . . . (RCA)
Elvis' Golden Records . . . . (RCA)
Elvis In Concert . . . . (RCA)
Elvis Recorded Live On Stage In Memphis . . . . (RCA)
Elvis-A Legendary Performer, Volume 3 . . . . (RCA)
From Memphis To Vegas/From Vegas To Memphis . . . . (RCA)
Number One Hits . . . . (RCA)
ST/Forrest Gump . . . . (Epic/Sony Music Soundtrax)
How Insensitive
Ella Fitzgerald; *Ella Abraca Jobim* . . . .(Pablo)
Frank Sinatra & Antonio Carlos Jobim; *Francis Albert Sinatra & Antonio
Carlos Jobim* . . . . (Reprise)
Stan Getz; *Compact Jazz-Stan Getz* . . . . (Verve)
I Feel Like Homemade Shit
Fugs; *Fugs' Greatest Hits* . . . . (PVC)
I Hate You
D.O.A.; *War On 45/Bloodied But Unbowed* . . . .(Restless)
I Hate You
Ronnie Milsap; *Ronnie Milsap's Greatest Hits* . . . . (RCA)
I Hate You, Baby
Count Basie Big Band; *Fun Time* . . . . (Pablo)
I Hate You, Baby
Jimmy Soul; *Best Of Jimmy Soul* . . . . (Rhino)
I Like 'Em Big & Stupid
Julie Brown; *Trapped In The Body Of A White Girl* . . . . (Sire)
I Love You (But You're Boring)
Beautiful South; *Welcome To The Beautiful South* . . . . (Elektra)
I Never Loved A Man (The Way I Love You)
Aretha Franklin; *Aretha Franklin-30 Greatest Hits* . . . . (Rhino)
Golden Age Of Black Music-1960-1970-C . . . .(Atlantic)
ST/The Commitments . . . .(MCA)
I Really Don't Need No Light
Jeffrey Osborne; *Jeffrey Osborne* . . . . (A&M)
Idiot Wind
Bob Dylan; *Blood On The Tracks* . . . . (Columbia)
Hard Rain . . . . (Columbia)
The Bootleg Series-Volumes 1-3 [Rare & Unreleased] . . . . (Columbia)
Ignoreland
R.E.M.; *Automatic For The People* . . . .(Warner Bros.)
I'll Be Glad When You're Dead (You Rascal You)
Cab Calloway; *Jazz Heritage: Mr. Hi-De-Ho* . . . .(MCA)
I'm An Ordinary Man
Rex Harrison/Original Cast; *My Fair Lady* . . . . (Columbia)
I'm The Biggest Liar In Town
Reno & Smiley; *1983 Collector's Edition-#11* . . . . (Gusto)
I'm The Laziest Gal In Town
Julie Wilson; *Cole Porter Songbook* . . . .(DRG)
Indian Giver
1910 Fruitgum Company; *Best Of 1910 Fruitgum Company & Other
Bubblegum Smashes-#2-C* . . . . (Rhino)

Insensitive
Jann Arden; *Living Under June* . . . . (A&M)
Women For Women-#2-C . . . . (Mercury)
I've Come To Expect It From You
George Strait; *Livin' It Up* . . . . (MCA)
Ten Strait Hits . . . . (MCA)
J.A.P. Rap
2 Live Jews; *As Kosher As They Wanna Be* . . . . (Kosher)
Jack-Ass
Beck; *Odelay* . . . . (David Geffen Co.)
Jackson
Johnny Cash & June Carter; *Johnny Cash's Greatest Hits* . . . . (Columbia)
The Man In Black-His Greatest Hits . . . . (Legacy)
Nancy Sinatra & Lee Hazlewood; *Nancy Sinatra-The Hit Years* . . . . . . (Rhino)
Jesus Thinks You're A Jerk
Frank Zappa; *Broadway The Hard Way* . . . . (Rykodisc)
Judith
A Perfect Circle; *Mer De Noms* . . . .(Virgin)
Just Because
Shelton Brothers; *Classic Country Music-#1-C* . . . . . . (Smithsonian Collection)
Keep The Customer Satisfied
Simon & Garfunkel; *Bridge Over Troubled Water* . . . . (Columbia)
Collected Works . . . . (Columbia)
King Nothing
Metallica; *Load* . . . . (Elektra)
King Of Sleaze
Beat Farmers; *Loud & Plowed &...Live!* . . . . (Curb)
Poor & Famous . . . . (Curb)
Kiss This
Aaron Tippin; *People Like Us* . . . .(Lyric Street)
Lady Is A Tramp
Ella Fitzgerald; *Rodgers & Hart Songbook* . . . . (Verve)
Frank Sinatra; *Sinatra Reprise-The Very Good Years* . . . . (Reprise)
The Capitol Years . . . . (Capitol)
Frank Sinatra & Luther Vandross; *Frank Sinatra-Duets-C* . . . . (Capitol)
Laugh Laugh
Beau Brummels; *Best Of The Beau Brummels* . . . . (Rhino)
Heart & Soul Of Rock 'N' Roll-#1-C . . . . (Rhino)
Introducing The Beau Brummels . . . . (Rhino)
Nuggets-#7-Early San Francisco-C . . . . (Rhino)
Leech
Eve 6; *Eve 6* . . . . (RCA)
Level On The Inside
Dovetail Joint; *001* . . . . (Aware/C2/Columbia)
Liar
Profyle; *Nothin' But Drama* . . . . (Motown)
Liar Liar
Castaways; *Frat Rock!-#3-Grandson Of Frat Rock!-C* . . . . (Rhino)
Oldies But Goodies-#9-C . . . . (Original Sound)
ST/Good Morning, Vietnam . . . . (A&M)
Like A Rolling Stone
Bob Dylan; *Biograph* . . . . (Columbia)
Bob Dylan At Budokan . . . . (Columbia)
Bob Dylan's Greatest Hits . . . . (Columbia)
Highway 61 Revisited . . . . (Columbia)
More American Graffiti-#4-C . . . . (MCA)
Self Portrait . . . . (Columbia)
Bob Dylan And The Band; *Before The Flood* . . . . (Columbia)
Jimi Hendrix; *ST/Jimi Plays Monterey* . . . . (Reprise)
Jimi Hendrix Experience; *Jimi Hendrix Experience* . . . . (Reprise)
Rolling Stones; *Stripped* . . . .(Virgin)
Lion's Den
Bruce Springsteen; *Tracks* . . . . (Columbia)
Little Plastic Castle
Ani DiFranco; *Little Plastic Castle* . . . . (Righteous Babe)
Long Gone Geek
Procol Harum; *Best Of Procol Harum* . . . . (A&M)
Look At All Those Idiots
Simpsons; *Simpsons Sing The Blues* . . . . (Geffen)
Losing A Whole Year
Third Eye Blind; *Third Eye Blind* . . . . (Elektra)
Lump
Presidents Of The United States Of America; *Pure Frosting* . . . . . . (Columbia)
The Presidents Of The United States Of America . . . . (Columbia)
Lyin' Ass Bitch
Fishbone; *Fishbone* . . . . (Columbia)
Man Smart, Woman Smarter
Harry Belafonte; *Harry Belafonte-Pure Gold* . . . . (RCA)
Robert Palmer; *Some People Can Do What They Like* . . . . (Island)
Rosanne Cash; *I Am Woman-C* . . . . (Nick At Nite)
Right Or Wrong . . . . (Columbia)
Man With The Lightbulb Head
Robyn Hitchcock & The Egyptians; *Fegmania* . . . .(Slash)
Marry A Woman Uglier Than You
King's Singers; *10th Anniversary Concert-#2* . . . . . (Mojo Music/Universal)
May The Bird Of Paradise Fly Up Your Nose
"Little" Jimmy Dickens; *Columbia Country Classics-#3-
Americana-C* . . . . (Columbia)

Super Hits Of The '60s-C . . . . (Epic)
Harlow Wilcox and the Oakies; *Cripple Cricket* . . . .(Plantation)

More You Ignore
Morrissey; *Vauxhall And I* . . . .(Sire)

Mother In Law
Buddy Guy; *Left My Blues In San Francisco* . . . . (Chess)
Ernie K-Doe; *Best Of New Orleans Rhythm & Blues-#1-C* . . . . (Rhino)
  Collectables Presents The History Of Rock-#7-C . . . .(Collectables)
  New Orleans Jazz & Heritage Festival-1976-C . . . . (Rhino)
Huey Lewis and the News; *Four Chords & Several Years Ago* . . . . (Elektra)

Mouth
Bush; *Deconstructed* . . . .(Trauma)
  Razorblade Suitcase . . . .(Trauma)
  ST/An American Werewolf In Paris . . . .(Hollywood)

Mr. Big Stuff
Jean Knight; *'70s Hit(s) Back Again-C* . . . . (Hip-O)
  Have A Nice Decade-The '70s Pop Culture Box-C . . . . (Rhino)

Mr. Shorty
Marty Robbins; *The Drifter* . . . . (Koch International)

My Dad Sucks
Descendents; *Bonus Fat* . . . . (SST)
  Liveage . . . . (SST)
  Somery . . . . (SST)

My Little Bimbo
Clancy Hayes & The Salt Dogs; *Oh By Jingo* . . . .(Delmark)

My Way
Usher; *My Way* . . . . (LaFace)

Neanderthal Man
Hotlegs; *Rock Radio Vietnam-C* . . . . (K-Tel)
  Super Hits Of The '70s-Have A Nice Day-#3-C . . . . (Rhino)

Nigga Out The Projects
1-5ive Posse; *Lifestyles Of The Young & Crazy* . . . . (World Export)

Nigga Witta Gun
Dr. Dre; *The Chronic* . . . . (Priority)

Niggas Come In All Colors
L.A. Posse; *They Come In All Colors* . . . . (Atlantic)

Nigger Whitie
Sly Dunbar; *Sly Wicked & Slick* . . . . (Front Line)

No Scrubs
TLC; *Fanmail* . . . . (LaFace)
  Totally Hits-#1-C . . . . (Arista)

No Son Of Mine
Genesis; *We Can't Dance* . . . . (Atlantic)

No Trash In My Trailer
Gene Watson; *From The Heart* . . . . (Row Music Group)

No Way To Treat A Lady
Bonnie Raitt; *Bonnie Raitt-Collection* . . . . (Warner Bros.)
  Nine Lives . . . . (Warner Bros.)

Nobody But A Fool (Would Love You)
Connie Smith; *Best Of Connie Smith* . . . . (Dominion Entert.)

Nookie
Limp Bizkit; *Now That's What I Call Music!-#3-C* . . . .(Virgin)
  Significant Other . . . .(Flip/Interscope)

Oaf, The
Big Wreck; *In Loving Memory Of...* . . . . (Atlantic)

Oh Well - Pt. I
Fleetwood Mac; *Then Play On* . . . . (Reprise)

Osama, Yo' Mama
Ray Stevens; *Osama-Yo' Mama* . . . . (Curb)

Outside
Staind; *Break The Cycle* . . . . (Flip/Elektra)

Papa Was A Rollin' Stone
Temptations; *20/20-C* . . . . (Motown)
  25 #1 Hits From 25 Years-C . . . . (Motown)
  All The Million-Sellers . . . . (Motown)
  Billboard Top Rock 'N' Roll Hits-1972-C . . . . (Rhino)
  Compact Command Performances-Temptations . . . . (Motown)
  Temptations-Anthology-The Best Of The Temptations . . . . . . (Motown)

Paper Roses
Kitty Wells; *Kitty Wells' Greatest Hits-#2* . . . .(Step One)
Marie Osmond; *All Time Greatest Hits Of Country-C* . . . .(Curb)
  Marie Osmond-25 Hits-Special Collection . . . .(Curb)

Paper Sun
Def Leppard; *Euphoria* . . . .(Mercury)

Party Up
DMX; *...And Then There Was X* . . . . (Ruff Ryders/IDJMG)

Pencil Neck Geek
Fred Blassie; *Dr. Demento Presents The Greatest Novelty Records-#4-
  1970s-C* . . . . (Rhino)
  Dr. Demento: 20th Anniversary Collection-C . . . . (Rhino)
  Dr. Demento's Dementia Royale-C . . . . (Rhino)

Perpetual Blues Machine
Keb' Mo'; *Just Like You* . . . . (Okeh)

Piece Of Crap
Neil Young & Crazy Horse; *Sleeps With Angels* . . . .(Reprise)

Piggies
Beatles; *Beatles-Box Set* . . . . (Capitol)
  The Beatles (White Album) . . . . (Capitol)
George Harrison; *Live In Japan* . . . .(Dark Horse)

Pizza Face
Barnes & Barnes; *Zabagabee-Best Of Barnes & Barnes* . . . .(Rhino)

Plastic People
Mothers Of Invention; *Absolutely Free* . . . . (Rykodisc)

Po' White Trash
White Trash; *White Trash* . . . . (Elektra)

Popstar
Pretenders; *Viva El Amor!* . . . . (Warner Bros.)

Pore Jud Is Daid
Original Cast; *Oklahoma!* . . . . (MCA)

Potato Head Blues
Louis Armstrong; *Louis Armstrong-Best Of The Decca Years-#2-The
  Composer-C* . . . . (MCA)
  You Rascal You . . . .(Pro-Arte)

Pretty Fly (For A White Guy)
Offspring; *Americana* . . . .(Columbia)

Pretty Vacant
Joan Jett; *The Hit List* . . . .(Epic)
Sex Pistols; *Live At Chelmsford Top Security Prison* . . . . (Restless)
  Never Mind The Bollocks, Here's The Sex Pistols . . . . (Warner Bros.)

Punk & Belligerent
Warrior Soul; *Salutations From The Ghetto Nation* . . . . (David Geffen Co.)

Punk Bitch
Too $hort; *Short Dog's In The House* . . . . (Jive)

Real Niggaz
N.W.A.; *100 Miles & Runnin'* . . . . (Ruthless/Priority)
  Efil4zaggin . . . . (Ruthless/Priority)

Real Niggaz Don't Die
N.W.A.; *Efil4zaggin* . . . . (Ruthless/Priority)

Real Slim Shady
Eminem; *The Marshall Mathers LP* . . . . (Aftermath/Interscope)

Red Hot
Billy Lee Riley & His Little Green Men; *Red Hot: The Very Best Of Billy
  Lee Riley* . . . .(Collectables)
  Rock This Town-Rockabilly Hits-#1-C . . . .(Rhino)
Robert Gordon; *Rock This Town-Rockabilly Hits-#2-C* . . . .(Rhino)
Robert Gordon & Link Wray; *Robert Gordon & Link Wray* . . . . (RCA)

Rednecks
Randy Newman; *Good Old Boys* . . . . (Reprise)
  Guilty: 30 Years Of Randy Newman . . . . (Rhino)

Rich Bitch
D.O.A.; *War On 45/Bloodied But Unbowed* . . . . (Restless)

Rich Girl
Daryl Hall & John Oates; *Bigger Than Both Of Us* . . . . (RCA)
  Billboard Top Rock 'N' Roll Hits-1977-C . . . .(Rhino)
  Livetime . . . . (RCA)
  Nipper's Greatest Hits Of The '70s-C . . . . (RCA)
  Rock 'N Soul, Part 1 . . . . (RCA)
  Soulful Sounds . . . . (RCA)

Rich Little Bitch
Dash Rip Rock; *Boiled Alive!* . . . . (Mammoth)
  Not Of This World . . . . (Mammoth)

Roar Of The Masses Could Be Farts
Minutemen; *Double Nickels On The Dime* . . . . (SST)

Rock N Roll Nigger
Patti Smith Group; *Easter* . . . . (Arista)

Saint Joe On The School Bus
Marcy Playground; *Marcy Playground* . . . . (Capitol)

Sassin' The Boss
Glen Gray; *The Uncollected Glen Gray & The Casa Loma Orchestra-1939-
  1940* . . . . (Hindsight)

Say Man
Bo Diddley; *Bo Diddley-His Best* . . . . (Chess)
  Cruisin'-1959-C . . . . (Increase)

Scum Of The Earth
Kinks; *Preservation Act 2* . . . . (Rhino)

Scum Of The Earth
Rob Zombie; *ST/Mission: Impossible 2* . . . .(Hollywood)

See You In Hell (Don't Be Late)
Yngwie Malmsteen; *Eclipse* . . . . (Polydor)

See You In Hell, Blind Boy
Ry Cooder; *ST/Crossroads* . . . . (Warner Bros.)

Seen Enough
Crosby, Stills, Nash & Young; *Looking Forward* . . . . (Reprise)

Selfless, Cold And Composed
Ben Folds Five; *Whatever And Ever Amen* . . . . (Caroline/550)

Shaddap You Face
Joe Dolce; *45-#51053* . . . . (MCA)

She Ain't Ugly
Gary B.B. Coleman; *Romance Without Finance Is A Nuisance* . . .(Ichiban Int'l)

She Ain't Worth It
Glenn Medeiros; *Glenn Medeiros With Bobby Brown* . . . . (MCA)

She Loves The Jerk
John Hiatt; *Riding With The King* . . . . (Geffen)
  Y'All Caught? Ones That Got Away, 1979-85 . . . . (Geffen)
Rodney Crowell; *Street Language* . . . .(Columbia)

She's A Bitch
Missy "Misdemeanor" Elliot; *Da Real World* . . . .(East West)

She's Got Issues
Offspring; *Americana*.. (Columbia)
Short People
Randy Newman; *Dr. Demento Presents The Greatest Novelty Records-#4-1970s-C*.. (Rhino)
Little Criminals....................................(Warner Bros.)
Shut Up
Trick Daddy; *Book Of Thugs-Chapter AK Verse 47*........... (Slip 'N Slide)
Shut Up And Dance
Pointer Sisters; *Serious Slammin'*........................ (RCA)
Shut Up And Kiss Me
Mary Chapin Carpenter; *Stones In The Road*................. (Columbia)
Sick & Beautiful
Artificial Joy Club; *Melt*................................ (Interscope)
Silly Ho
TLC; *Fanmail*.. (LaFace)
Silver Tongue & Gold Plated Lies
Hotmud Family; *Meat & Potatoes (& Stuff Like That)*........ (Flying Fish)
Skinny Legs And All
Joe Tex; *I Believe I'm Gonna Make It!-Best Of Joe Tex*..... (Rhino)
Joe Tex's Greatest Hits................................... (Curb)
Soul Years-C... (Atlantic)
Sleep To Dream
Fiona Apple; *Tidal*...................................... (Clean Slate/Work)
Smashing Young Man
Collective Soul; *Collective Soul*......................... (Atlantic)
Son Of A Gun (I Betcha You Think This Song's About You)
Janet (with Carly Simon); *All For You*.................... (Virgin)
Song For The Dumped
Ben Folds Five; *Naked Baby Photos*....................... (Caroline)
ST/Mr. Wrong.. (Hollywood)
Whatever And Ever Amen................................. (Caroline/550)
Sophisticated Bitch
Public Enemy; *Yo! Bum Rush The Show*.............. (Def Jam/Columbia)
Special
Garbage; *Now That's What I Call Music!-#3-C*............. (Virgin)
Version 2.0... (Almo Sounds)
Star 69
R.E.M.; *Monster*...(Warner Bros.)
Still Water Runs The Deepest
Asleep At The Wheel featuring Willie Nelson; *Tribute To The Music Of Bob Wills And The Texas Playboys-C*......................... (Liberty)
Stop, Don't Tease Me
DeBarge; *All This Love*.................................. (Motown)
DeBarge's Greatest Hits................................. (Motown)
Sucker
Mott The Hoople; *All The Young Dudes*.................... (Columbia)
The Ballad Of Mott: A Retrospective..................... (Columbia)
Sucker In A 3-Piece Suit
Van Halen; *OU812*.......................................(Warner Bros.)
Suicide Chump
Frank Zappa; *You Are What You Is*........................(Rykodisc)
Sullen Girl
Fiona Apple; *Tidal*...................................... (Clean Slate/Work)
Surrounded By Idiots
Wrathchild America; *3-D*.................................(Atlantic)
Take Back Your Mink
Original Cast; *Guys & Dolls*.............................(MCA)
Take It Back
Cream; *Disraeli Gears*................................... (Polydor)
Take This Job And Shove It
David Allan Coe; *David Allan Coe-17 Greatest Hits*........ (Columbia)
Johnny Paycheck; *Johnny Paycheck's Biggest Hits*...........(Epic)
Johnny Paycheck's Greatest Hits-#2.......................(Epic)
Take This Job And Shove It...............................(Epic)
Truckers' Jukebox-10 All-Time Radio Requests-C.......... (Legacy)
Take This Job And Shove It Too
David Allan Coe; *I've Got Something To Say*............... (Columbia)
Testosterone
Bush; *Sixteen Stone*.................................... (Trauma)
That Girl's A Slut
Just-Ice; *Rapmasters 7-Best Of The Laughs-C*............. (Priority)
That'll Be The Day
Buddy Holly; *ST/American Graffiti*.......................(MCA)
Buddy Holly/The Crickets; *Buddy Holly-20 Golden Greats* ....(MCA)
Chirping Crickets......................................(MCA)
Crickets; *Billboard Top Rock 'N' Roll Hits-1957-C*........ (Rhino)
Foghat; *Best Of Foghat-#2*.............................. (Rhino)
Energized.. (Rhino)
Linda Ronstadt; *Hasten Down The Wind*................... (Asylum)
Linda Ronstadt's Greatest Hits.......................... (Asylum)
Then I'll Be Tired Of You
Coleman Hawkins; *Real Thing*............................(Prestige)
Jonathan Schwartz; *Alone Together*...................... (Muse)
Paul Desmond; *Late Lament*.............................. (Bluebird)
There Goes The Neighborhood
Sheryl Crow; *The Globe Sessions*........................ (A&M)

There Is A Sucker Born Ev'ry Minute
Cy Coleman; *Presents Barnum*........................... (Bainbridge)
These Boots Are Made For Walkin'
Billy Ray Cyrus; *Some Gave All*......................... (Mercury)
Nancy Sinatra; *Billboard Top Rock 'N' Roll Hits-1966-C* .... (Rhino)
Boots-Nancy Sinatra's Greatest Hits.................... (Rhino)
Think For Yourself
Beatles; *Beatles-Box Set*............................... (Capitol)
Rubber Soul.. (Capitol)
George Harrison; *Best Of George Harrison*................ (Capitol)
Throwing Stones
Paula Cole; *This Fire*.................................. (Imago)
Time Of Your Life (Good Riddance)
Green Day; *Nimrod*...................................... (Reprise)
Toilet Licking Maggot
Hell On Earth; *Biomechanical Ejaculations Of The Damned* .... (Neptune)
Too Dumb For New York City
Waylon Jennings; *Too Dumb For New York City, Too Ugly For L.A.*...... (Epic)
Too Fat Polka
Arthur Godfrey; *Dr. Demento Presents The Greatest Novelty Records-#1-1940s & Before-C*.. (Rhino)
Frankie Yankovic & His Yanks; *Frankie Yankovic & His Yanks' Greatest Hits*.. (Columbia)
Li'l Wally; *I Love To Polka*............................. (Jay Jay)
Too Good To Be True
Michael Peterson; *Michael Peterson*......................(Reprise)
Too Lazy To Work, Too Nervous To Steal
BR549; *This Is BR549*................................... (Lucky Dog)
Too Old To Cut The Mustard
Carlisles; *45-#6348*.................................... (Mercury)
Ernest Tubb; *Ernest Tubb-Retrospective-#2*........... (MCA Special Prod.)
Trapped In The Body Of A White Girl
Julie Brown; *Trapped In The Body Of A White Girl*................. (Sire)
Trashy Lady
Neon Judgement; *Horny As Hell*.......................... (Play It Again Sam)
Trashy Women
Confederate Railroad; *Confederate Railroad*.................... (Atlantic)
Treat Her Like A Prostitute
Slick Rick; *Great Adventures Of Slick Rick*............. (Def Jam/Columbia)
Turn Me On "Mr. Deadman"
Union Underground; *...An Education In Rebellion*.......... (Portrait)
Ugliest Girl In The World
Bob Dylan; *Down In The Groove*.......................... (Columbia)
Ugly
Fishbone; *Fishbone*..................................... (Columbia)
Rhythm Come Forward: Volume II-C...................... (Columbia)
Ugly
Saigon Kick; *Saigon Kick*...............................(Third Stone)
Ugly Duckling
Danny Kaye; *Hans Christian Andersen*................... (MCA)
Ugly Girl
Fleming & John; *The Way We Are*......................... (Universal)
Under My Thumb
Rolling Stones; *"Still Life" (American Concert 1981)*.............. (Virgin)
12 X 5... (Abkco)
Aftermath... (Abkco)
got Live if you want it!................................ (Abkco)
Hot Rocks 1964-1971.................................. (Abkco)
Who; *Odds & Sods*...................................... (MCA)
Who's Missing... (MCA)
Up Against The Wall Redneck Mother
Jerry Jeff Walker; *A Man Must Carry On*................. (MCA)
Best Of Jerry Jeff Walker.............................. (MCA)
Great Gonzos.. (MCA)
Venom Wearin' Denim
Junior Brown; *Semi Crazy*.............................. (Curb)
Vidiot
Ken Nordine; *Best Of Word Jazz-#1*..................... (Rhino)
Walk All Over You
AC/DC; *Highway To Hell*................................ (Atco)
Warming Up The Brain Farm
Lo Fidelity Allstars; *How To Operate With A Blown Mind*............ (Skint)
Waylon Jennings
Waylon Jennings; *Greatest Country Hits Of The '90s-1990-C*...... (Columbia)
We Will Rock You
Queen; *Live At Wembley '86*............................ (Hollywood)
Live Killers.. (Hollywood)
News Of The World..................................... (Hollywood)
Queen's Greatest Hits I & II........................... (Hollywood)
ST/FM... (MCA)
Welcome To The Fold
Filter; *Title Of Record*............................... (Reprise)
What Kind Of Love Are You On
Aerosmith; *ST/Armageddon-The Album*.................... (Columbia)
What Part Of No
Lorrie Morgan; *Lorrie Morgan's Greatest Hits*.............. (BNA)
Watch Me... (BNA)

What You Want
DMX; ...And Then There Was X .... (Ruff Ryders/IDJMG)
Whatever
Godsmack; Godsmack......................... (Republic/Universal)
What's The Ugliest Part Of Your Body
Mothers Of Invention; We're Only In It For The Money .... (Rykodisc)
What's This Shit Called Love
Meatmen; We're The Meatmen...& You Still Suck! .... (Caroline)
White Nigger
Big Boys; The Fat Elvis........................ (Touch & Go)
White Trash Wife
Exene Cervenka; Old Wives' Tales .... (Rhino)
White Trash With Cash
Southgang; Group Therapy...................... (Charisma)
Who Dat
JT Money; Pimpin' On Wax .... (Tony Mercedes/Freeworld/Priority)
Who's Your Baby Now
Mark Knopfler; Sailing To Philadelphia .... (Warner Bros.)
Why Did You Waste My Time?
Screamin' Jay Hawkins; Collectables Blues Collection-#1-C ..... (Collectables)
Why Don't You Get A Job?
Offspring; Americana .... (Columbia)
Without You
Audrey Hepburn; ST/My Fair Lady...................... (Columbia)
Julie Andrews/Original Cast; My Fair Lady .... (Columbia)
Original Cast; My Fair Lady .... (London)
Workin' It
Don Henley; Inside Job .... (Warner Bros.)
Yakety Yak
2 Live Crew; ST/Twins .... (WTG)
Coasters; Atlantic Rhythm & Blues 1947-1974-#3 (1955-1958)-C .... (Atlantic)
Billboard Top Rock 'N' Roll Hits-1958-C .... (Rhino)
Coasters' Greatest Hits .... (Atco)
Cruisin'-1958-C .... (Increase)
ST/Stand By Me. .... (Atlantic)
You Ain't Much Fun
Toby Keith; Boomtown .... (Polydor Country)
You Ain't Woman Enough
Loretta Lynn; Billboard Top Country Hits-1966-C .... (Rhino)
Legends Of Country Music-The Best Of Austin City Limits-C ..... (Columbia)
Loretta Lynn's Greatest Hits .... (MCA)
The Country Music Hall Of Fame-Loretta Lynn................. (MCA)
Shirley Brown; Diva Of Soul .... (Malaco Jazz)
You Bowed Down
Elvis Costello & The Attractions; All This Useless Beauty ...... (Warner Bros.)
You Get Ugly
Contours; Do You Love Me (Now That I Can Dance) .... (Motown)
You Give Love A Bad Name
Bon Jovi; 7800 Degrees Fahrenheit .... (Mercury)
Cross Road-14 Classic Grooves .... (Mercury)
You Make Me Feel Like A Whore
Everclear; Sparkle And Fade .... (Capitol)
You Make Me Sick
Pink; Can't Take Me Home .... (LaFace)
You Oughta Know
Alanis Morissette; 1996 Grammy Nominees-C .... (Columbia)
Jagged Little Pill. .... (Maverick)
You Smell Like Doo Doo
Get Some Crew; Booty Shake: 16 Boomin' Hits-C .... (Street Solid)
You So Dumb
Roosevelt Sykes; Roosevelt Sykes-#2-1930-1931 .... (Document)
You Stupid Jerk
Angry Samoans; Back From Samoa .... (PVC)
Gimme Samoa-31 Garbage-Pit Hits .... (PVC)
You Talk Too Much
Cheap Trick; Next Position Please .... (Epic)
You Talk Too Much
Joe Jones; American Graffiti-#3-C .... (MCA)
Billboard Top Rock 'N' Roll Hits-1960-C .... (Rhino)
Carnival Time-Best Of Ric Records-#1-C .... (Rounder)
Echoes Of A Rock Era-Middle Years-C .... (Roulette)
Original Rock 'N' Roll Hits Of The '60s-C .... (Roulette)
You Talk Too Much
George Thorogood & The Destroyers; Born To Be Bad .... (Gold Rush)
You Talk Too Much
Run-D.M.C.; King Of Rock .... (Profile)
Your Feet's Too Big
Beatles; 45-#1503 .... (Collectables)
Fats Waller; 20 Golden Pieces Of Fats Waller .... (Bulldog)
Ain't Misbehavin' .... (RCA)
Fats Waller-Legendary Performer..................... (RCA)
Joint Is Jumpin' .... (Bluebird)
Original Cast; Ain't Misbehavin'....................... (RCA)
Your Woman
White Town; MTV The Grind-#1-C .... (Tommy Boy)
Women In Technology .... (Chrysalis)
You're So Sweet, Horseflies Keep Hangin' Round Your Face
Neil Diamond; Brother Love's Traveling Salvation Show............. (MCA)

You're So Vain
Carly Simon; '70s Greatest Rock Hits-#3-High Times-C........... (Priority)
Best Of Carly Simon .... (Elektra)
Carly Simon-Greatest Hits Live .... (Arista)
No Secrets .... (Elektra)
You're The Reason Our Kids Are Ugly
Loretta Lynn & Conway Twitty; Conway Twittty-20 Greatest Hits...... (MCA)
Very Best Of Loretta Lynn & Conway Twitty .... (MCA)

INVISIBLE, Disappear

See Also: **IDENTITY CRISIS, LEAVING, MAGIC, PRETEND, SEEING**

3 Libras
A Perfect Circle; Mer De Noms .... (Virgin)
Evaporated
Ben Folds Five; Whatever And Ever Amen. .... (Caroline/550)
Hay Una Mujer Desaparecida
Holly Near; Imagine My Surprise .... (Redwood)
Holly Near & Ronnie Gilbert; Lifeline .... (Redwood)
I Can Still Feel You
Collin Raye; The Walls Came Down .... (Epic)
I Disappear
Metallica; ST/Mission: Impossible 2 ....(Hollywood)
I Don't Want To Spoil The Party
Beatles; Beatles VI ....(Capitol)
For Sale. ....(Capitol)
Rosanne Cash; Greatest Country Hits Of The '80s-1989-C........ (Columbia)
Rosanne Cash-Hits-1979-1989............... (Columbia)
I'm Looking Through You
Beatles; The Beatles-Anthology-#2 ....(Capitol)
Invisible City
Wallflowers; Bringing Down The Horse .... (Interscope)
Invisible Man
98 Degrees; 98 Degrees ....(Motown)
Invisible Touch
Genesis; Hit Singles-1980-1988-C. .... (Atlantic)
Invisible Touch .... (Atlantic)
MFC
Pearl Jam; Yield ....(Epic)
Missing
Everything But The Girl; Amplified Heart .... (Atlantic)
MTV Party To Go-#9-C. .... (Tommy Boy)
The Absolute Hits-C .... (Atlantic)
The Ultimate Dance Party-1997-C ....(Arista)
Naked
Goo Goo Dolls; A Boy Named Goo .... (Metal Blade)
No One
Cold; 13 Ways To Bleed On Stage .... (Flip/Geffen/Interscope)
Stolen Car
Bruce Springsteen; The River........................(Columbia)
Tracks ....(Columbia)
Elliott Murphy; One Step Up/Two Steps Back-The Songs Of Bruce
Springsteen-C.........................(Right Stuff)
There Is A Mountain
Donovan; Donovan's Greatest Hits .... (Epic)
Troubadour-Definitive Collection...................... (Epic)
You Won't See Me
Anne Murray; Anne Murray's Greatest Hits ....(Capitol)
Love Song ....(Capitol)
Beatles; Beatles-Box Set....................... (Capitol)
Rubber Soul......................... (Capitol)
Bryan Ferry; These Foolish Things .... (Reprise)

ISLANDS

See Also: **CITIES: A-Z, COUNTRIES: A-Z, OCEAN, PARADISE, SAILING, SHIPS, STATES: HAWAII**

26 Miles
Four Preps; True.........................(Capitol)
Avalon
Al Jolson; Best Of Al Jolson.......................... (MCA)
Jolson Sang 'Em .... (Biograph)
The Al Jolson Story-#2 .... (MCA)
Avalon
Roxy Music; Avalon........................ (Warner Bros.)
Heart Still Beating. .... (Virgin)
Street Life-20 Great Hits .... (Reprise)
Back To The Island
Leon Russell; Best Of Leon Russell .... (MCA)
Rock Of The '70s-C .... (MCA Special Prod.)
Will O' The Wisp......................... (MCA)

Bali Ha'i
Original Cast; *South Pacific* . . . .(CBS Masterworks)
Caribbean Breeze
Rippingtons; *Life In The Tropics* . . . . (Peak/Concord)
Caribbean Queen
Billy Ocean; *Billy Ocean's Greatest Hits* . . . . (Jive)
Suddenly . . . . (Jive)
Coconut Island
Junior Brown; *12 Shades Of Brown* . . . . (Curb)
Easter Island
Russ Freeman; *Nocturnal Playground* . . . . (Brainchild)
Escape From The Island Of Living Puke
Zoogz Rift; *Island Of Living Puke* . . . . (SST)
Fire Island
Village People; *Live & Sleazy* . . . . (Casablanca)
Village People . . . . (Casablanca)
Woody Herman; *Blowin' Up A Storm* . . . . (Pickwick)
Follow Me
Original Cast; *Camelot* . . . . (Columbia)
ST/Camelot . . . .(Warner Bros.)
From Hell To Paradise
Mavericks; *From Hell To Paradise* . . . .(MCA)
From The Vine Came The Grape
Gaylords; *X-tra Cheese-Originals By The Originals-C* . . . .(Compose)
I Am A Rock
Simon & Garfunkel; *Collected Works* . . . . (Columbia)
Simon & Garfunkel's Greatest Hits . . . . (Columbia)
Sounds Of Silence . . . . (Columbia)
In The Middle Of An Island
Tennessee Ernie Ford; *Capitol Collectors Series-Tennessee Ernie Ford.* . . . . (Capitol)
In Zanzibar
Emma Carus; *Music From The New York Stage (1890-1920)-#1-1890-1908-C* . . . . (Pearl)
Island
Eddy Raven; *Temporary Sanity* . . . . (Capitol)
Island
Gerry Rafferty; *City To City* . . . .(EMI)
Island
Jimmy Buffett; *Coconut Telegraph* . . . .(MCA)
Island
Sarah Vaughan; *Crazy & Mixed Up* . . . .(Pablo)
Island
Patti Austin; *Every Home Should Have One* . . . . (Qwest)
Island
Greg Kihn; *Greg Kihn Again* . . . . (Beserkley)
Island
Julie Andrews; *Julie Love* . . . . (USA Music Group)
Island
Jimmy Messina; *One More Mile* . . . .(Warner Bros.)
Island
Julia Fordham; *Porcelain* . . . . (Virgin)
Island Girl
Elton John; *Billboard Top Hits-1975-C* . . . . (Rhino)
Elton John's Greatest Hits-#2 . . . . (Polydor)
Rock Of The Westies . . . . (Polydor)
Island Girl
Beach Boys; *Still Cruisin'* . . . . (Capitol)
Island In The Sun
Weezer; *Weezer 2001* . . . .(Geffen)
Island Of Domination
Judas Priest; *Best Of Judas Priest* . . . . (RCA)
Sad Wings Of Destiny . . . . (RCA)
Island Of Love
Elvis Presley; *ST/Blue Hawaii* . . . . (RCA)
Island Of Love
Rascals; *Freedom Suite* . . . . (Rhino)
Island Of Love
Sheppards; *Sheppards-Golden Classics* . . . . (Collectables)
Island Woman
Pablo Cruise; *Pablo Cruise* . . . . (A&M)
Islands
King Crimson; *Islands* . . . .(Editions E.G.)
Islands
John Denver; *Seasons Of The Heart* . . . . (RCA)
Islands
King Crimson; *Islands* . . . .(Editions E.G.)
Islands In The Stream
Kenny Rogers & Dolly Parton; *Eyes That See In The Dark* . . . . (RCA)
Kenny Rogers' Greatest Hits . . . . (RCA)
Islands Of The Dead
Be Bop Deluxe; *Drastic Plastic* . . . . (Capitol)
Isle Of Capri
Billy Vaughn; *Billy Vaughn-22 Of His Greatest Hits* . . . .(Ranwood)
Frank Sinatra; *Come Fly With Me* . . . . (Capitol)
Isle Of You
Motels; *Little Robbers* . . . . (Capitol)

Key Largo
Bertie Higgins; *Just Another Day In Paradise* . . . . (Kat Family)
Key West Intermezzo (I Saw You First)
John Mellencamp; *Mr. Happy Go Lucky* . . . . (Mercury)
Kokomo
Beach Boys; *ST/Cocktail* . . . .(Elektra)
Still Cruisin' . . . . (Capitol)
La Isla Bonita
Madonna; *True Blue* . . . .(Sire)
Lady Of The Island
Crosby, Stills & Nash; *Crosby, Stills & Nash* . . . .(Atlantic)
CSN . . . .(Atlantic)
Manhattan Island Serenade
Leon Russell; *Carney* . . . . (Right Stuff)
Marooned
Pink Floyd; *The Division Bell* . . . . (Columbia)
Misty Isles Of Scotland
Anne & Francie Brolly; *Ireland My Home* . . . .(Rego Irish)
Monkey Island
J. Geils Band; *Best Of The J. Geils Band* . . . .(Atlantic)
Monkey Island . . . .(Atlantic)
Offshore Banking Business
Members; *At The 1980 Chelsea Night Club* . . . .(Blue Plate)
ST/Urgh! A Music War . . . . (A&M)
On A Desert Island With You
Original Cast; *Sitting Pretty* . . . . (Nightwork)
On Treasure Island
Louis Armstrong; *Louis Armstrong.* . . . . (MCA Special Prod.)
Tommy Dorsey & His Orchestra; *Seventeen Number Ones* . . . .(RCA)
One Night In Trinidad
Earl ''Fatha'' Hines; *Lionel Hampton Presents Earl ''Fatha'' Hines* . . . . (Who's Who In Jazz)
Pretty Green Island
George Tucker; *George Tucker.* . . . . (Rounder)
Rock Island Line
Johnny Cash; *Johnny Cash-Sun Years* . . . . (Rhino)
Story Songs Of The Trains & Rivers . . . .(Sun)
Vintage Years-1955-1963. . . . . (Rhino)
Sonny Terry & Brownie McGhee; *Hootin'* . . . .(Muse)
Jazz Heritage . . . . (MCA)
Weavers; *Best Of The Weavers* . . . . (MCA)
Weavers At Carnegie Hall . . . . (Vanguard)
Weavers' Greatest Hits . . . . (Vanguard)
Smiling Islands
Robbie Patton; *Orders From Headquarters* . . . .(Atlantic)
Smiling Islands
Chris Proctor; *Delicate Dance.* . . . . (Flying Fish)
Tahiti
Milt Jackson; *Milt Jackson* . . . . (Blue Note)
Tahiti Condo
Michael Nesmith; *Newer Stuff.* . . . . (Rhino)
Tahitian Moon
Michael Franks; *Objects Of Desire* . . . .(Warner Bros.)
Tahitian Moon
Porno For Pyros; *Good God's Urge* . . . .(Warner Bros.)
Tahitian Skies
Chet Atkins & Mark Knopfler; *Neck And Neck* . . . . (Columbia)
Taking Islands In Africa
Japan; *Gentlemen Take Polaroids.* . . . .(Blue Plate)
Theme From ''Fantasy Island''
Original Soundtrack; *Television's Greatest Hits-#6-Remote Control-C* . . . (TVT)
Theme From ''Gilligan's Island''
Original Soundtrack; *CBS: The First 50 Years* . . . . (TVT)
Television's Greatest Hits-#1-C . . . . (TVT)
Three Mile Island
Pinkard & Bowden; *Writers In Disguise* . . . . (Warner Bros.)
Three Mile Smile
Aerosmith; *Night In The Ruts* . . . . (Columbia)
Pandora's Box . . . . (Columbia)
Thunder Island
Jay Ferguson; *Jay Ferguson* . . . .(Asylum)
Tiki Tiki Tiki Room
Original Music; *Disney Collection-#1-C.* . . . . (Disney)
Washed Ashore (On A Lonely Island In The Sea)
Platters; *Platters-16 Greatest Hits.* . . . .(Trip)
Platters-Anthology. . . . . (Rhino)
You're An Ocean
Fastball; *Harsh Light Of Day* . . . . (Hollywood)

JEALOUSY, Envy

See Also: **ANGER, CHEATING & LIES, EGO, FEELINGS, HATE, LOVE (various), REVENGE**

(I Know) I'm Losing You
Rod Stewart; *Best Of Rod Stewart* . . . . (Mercury)

Every Picture Tells A Story........................(Mercury)
Storyteller/The Complete Anthology: 1964-1990........(Warner Bros.)
Temptations; *Temptations-Anthology-The Best Of The Temptations*..(Motown)
Temptations-The Ultimate Collection...................(Motown)

(Marie's The Name) His Latest Flame
Elvis Presley; *Elvis' Golden Records, Volume 3*...................(RCA)
ST/This Is Elvis....................................(RCA)
The Other Sides-Worldwide Gold Award Hits, Vol. 2.........(RCA)
The Top Ten Hits....................................(RCA)

32 Flavors
Alana Davis; *Blame It On Me*........................(Elektra)
Ani DiFranco; *Living In Clip*.......................(Righteous Babe)
Not A Pretty Girl..................................(Righteous Babe)

Adalida
George Strait; *Latest Greatest Straitest Hits*.............(MCA)
Lead On..(MCA)

Alright Already
Larry Stewart; *Down The Road*.........................(RCA)

Another Girl
Beatles; *Beatles-Box Set*.............................(Capitol)
ST/Help!...(Capitol)

Another Lonely Song
Tammy Wynette; *Tammy Wynette-16 Biggest Hits*............(Legacy)
Tammy Wynette-Anniversary-20 Years Of Hits..............(Epic)
Tammy Wynette-Super Hits.............................(Epic)
Tears Of Fire-25th Anniversary Collection..............(Epic)

Baby's In Black
Beatles; *Beatles '65*................................(Capitol)
Beatles-Box Set....................................(Capitol)
For Sale...(Capitol)

Back Up Buddy
Carl Smith; *Essential Carl Smith-1950-1956*............(Legacy)
Trucker's Jukebox-2-C..............................(Legacy)

Bad, Bad Leroy Brown
Jim Croce; *Billboard Top Rock 'N' Roll Hits-1973-C*.......(Rhino)
Down The Highway...................................(Atlantic)
Life & Times......................................(Lifesong)
Photographs & Memories/His Greatest Hits..............(Atlantic)

Beautiful Ones
Mariah Carey; *Butterfly*.............................(Columbia)

Bernadette
Four Tops; *Compact Command Performances-Four Tops*.....(Motown)
Four Tops' Greatest Hits............................(Motown)
Four Tops Reach Out................................(Motown)
Four Tops-Anthology................................(Motown)
Motown Superstar Series-#14-Four Tops................(Motown)

Betcha She Don't Love You
Jessica Simpson; *Sweet Kisses*........................(Columbia)

Bird Dog
Everly Brothers; *Best Of The Everly Brothers*............(Rhino)
Billboard Top Rock 'N' Roll Hits-1958-C...............(Rhino)
Everly Brothers-Cadence Classics-Their 20 Greatest Hits....(Rhino)
Fabulous Style Of The Everly Brothers.................(Rhino)
Very Best Of The Everly Brothers....................(Warner Bros.)

Boy Is Mine
Brandy & Monica; *Never Say Never*....................(Atlantic)
Monica; *The Boy Is Mine*.............................(Arista)

Brand New Mister Me
Mel Tillis & The Statesiders; *The Ultimate Mel Tillis*......(Bransounds)

Bye Bye Love
Everly Brothers; *Everly Brothers' All-Time Greatest Hits*.......(Curb)
Everly Brothers-Cadence Classics-Their 20 Greatest Hits....(Rhino)
Very Best Of The Everly Brothers....................(Warner Bros.)
Simon & Garfunkel; *Bridge Over Troubled Water*..........(Columbia)

Carol
Chuck Berry; *Berry Is On Top*.........................(Chess)
Chuck Berry-Golden Hits.............................(Mercury)
Chuck Berry's Greatest Hits.........................(Everest)
Roll Over Beethoven................................(Allegiance)
Rolling Stones; *England's Newest Hit Makers/The Rolling Stones*....(Abkco)
Get Yer Ya-Ya's Out!..............................(Abkco)

Case Of The Ex (Whatcha Gonna Do)
Mya; *Fear Of Flying*.............................(University/Interscope)
Now That's What I Call Music!-#5-C..................(Virgin)

Chain Lightning
Steely Dan; *Katy Lied*...............................(MCA)
Steely Dan-Gold....................................(MCA)

Could've Been Me
Billy Ray Cyrus; *Some Gave All*.......................(Mercury)

Curly Headed Baby
Pete Seeger; *Tribute To Woody Guthrie-C*..............(Warner Bros.)

Damn I Wish I Was Your Lover
Sophie B. Hawkins; *Tongues & Tales*....................(Columbia)

Dance Only With Me
Blossom Dearie; *Blossoms On Broadway*..................(DRG)
Maxine Sullivan & Keith Ingham Sextet; *Together (Maxine Sings Jules Styne)*......................................(Atlantic)

Difference, The
Wallflowers; *Bringing Down The Horse*.................(Interscope)

Do For Love
2Pac featuring Eric Williams; *R U Still Down (Remember Me)*....(Amaru/Jive)

Do Your Thing
7 Mile; *7 Mile*.....................................(Crave)

Does He Love You
Reba McEntire & Linda Davis; *Reba McEntire's Greatest Hits Volume Two*.......................................(MCA)

Don't Be Stupid (You Know I Love You)
Shania Twain; *Come On Over*..........................(Mercury)

Don't Mess With Bill
Marvelettes; *Compact Command Performances-Marvelettes*.......(Motown)
Marvelettes' Greatest Hits..........................(Motown)
Marvelettes-Anthology..............................(Motown)
Top 10 With A Bullet-Motown Girl Groups-C............(Motown)

Don't Mess With My Man
Irma Thomas; *We Got A Party-Best Of Ron Records-#1-C*......(Rounder)

Don't Sit Under The Apple Tree
Andrews Sisters; *Andrews Sisters Greatest Hits*.........(Curb)
Andrews Sisters-16 Great Performances...............(MCA)
Capitol Collectors Series-The Andrews Sisters..........(Capitol)
Glenn Miller; *Memorial-1944-1969*.....................(Bluebird)
Glenn Miller & His Orchestra; *The Unforgettable Glenn Miller & His Orchestra*.....................................(RCA)

Don't Take Her She's All I Got
Tracy Byrd; *Big Love*...............................(MCA)

Do-Wacka-Do
Roger Miller; *Best Of Roger Miller-His Greatest Songs*.......(Curb)
Dumb Ditties-C.....................................(K-Tel)

El Paso
Grateful Dead; *Steal Your Face*.....................(Grateful Dead)
Marty Robbins; *Billboard Top Country Hits-1960-C*..........(Rhino)
Gunfighter Ballads & Trail Songs....................(Legacy)
Marty Robbins' Biggest Hits.........................(Columbia)
Radio Classics Of The '50s-C........................(Columbia)
Texas Super Hits-C................................(Columbia)

Everybody's Key Fits My Baby's Door
Rockin' Tabby Thomas; *King Of Swamp Blues*..........(Maison De Soul)

Everything You Did
Steely Dan; *The Royal Scam*..........................(MCA)

Fist City
Loretta Lynn; *Loretta Lynn-20 Greatest Hits*............(MCA)
Loretta Lynn-Greatest Hits Live.....................(K-Tel)
Loretta Lynn's Greatest Hits-#2.....................(MCA)
The Country Music Hall Of Fame-Loretta Lynn...........(MCA)

Flavor Of The Weak
American Hi-Fi; *American Hi-Fi*.......................(Island)
Now That's What I Call Music!-#7-C..................(Virgin)

Fool, The
Lee Ann Womack; *Lee Ann Womack*.....................(Decca)

Get Off Of My Cloud
Rolling Stones; *Big Hits (High Tide & Green Grass)*........(Abkco)
December's Children (and everybody's)................(Abkco)
got Live if you want it!...........................(Abkco)
Hot Rocks 1964-1971...............................(Abkco)
Singles Collection-The London Years.................(Abkco)

Gettin' In The Way
Jill Scott; *Who Is Jill Scott? Words And Sounds-#1*.......(Hidden Beach/Epic)

Gettin' Mighty Crowded
Betty Everett; *Soul Shots-#8-C*......................(Rhino)
Very Best Of Betty Everett.........................(Vee-Jay)
Elvis Costello; *Taking Liberties*.....................(Columbia)

Girl Is Mine
Michael Jackson with Paul McCartney; *Thriller*..........(Epic)

Girlfriend
Alicia Keys; *Songs In A Minor*.......................(J)

Gotta Man
Eve; *First Lady Of Ruff Ryders*.....................(Ruff Ryders/IDJMG)

He Ain't Worth Missing
Toby Keith; *Toby Keith*.............................(Mercury)

He Don't Love You (Like I Love You)
Tony Orlando & Dawn; *'70s Greatest Rock Hits-#9-#1 Hits-C*.......(Priority)
Behind Closed Doors-'70s Swingers-C.................(Rhino)
Best Of Tony Orlando & Dawn.........................(Rhino)

He Will Break Your Heart
Jerry Butler; *Best Of Jerry Butler*...................(Rhino)

He'll Have To Go
Jim Reeves; *60 Years Of Country Music-C*..............(RCA)
Best Of Jim Reeves................................(RCA)
Billboard Top Country Hits-1960-C...................(Rhino)
Great Moments At The Grand Ole Opry-C...............(RCA)
Jim Reeves' Greatest Hits...........................(RCA)
Nipper's Greatest Hits Of The '50s-#1-C..............(RCA)
Ry Cooder; *Chicken Skin Music*.......................(Reprise)

He'll Never Love You (Like I Do)
Freddie Jackson; *Rock Me Tonight (For Old Time's Sake)*......(Capitol)

He's Got You
Brooks & Dunn; *The Greatest Hits Collection*............(Arista)

Hey Jealous Lover
Frank Sinatra; *Capitol Collectors Series-Frank Sinatra*.......(Capitol)

Hey Jealousy
Gin Blossoms; *New Miserable Experience* . . . . (A&M)
Hey Joe!
Carl Smith; *All Time Legends Of Country Music-C* . . . . (Legacy)
Him
Rupert Holmes; *Partners In Crime* . . . .(MCA)
I Ain't Gonna Eat Out My Heart Anymore
Rascals; *The Young Rascals* . . . . (Warner Special Prod.)
Time Peace/The Rascals' Greatest Hits . . . .(Atlantic)
I Can't Sleep Baby (If I)
R. Kelly; *R. Kelly* . . . . (Jive)
I Can't Stand It
Eric Clapton; *Another Ticket* . . . . (RSO)
Eric Clapton-Crossroads-C . . . . (Polydor)
I Don't Call Him Daddy
Doug Supernaw; *Pure Country-Best Of The '90s-C* . . . . (Priority)
Red And Rio Grande . . . . (BNA)
I Get The Fever
Bill Anderson; *Bill Anderson's Greatest Hits* . . . . (Varese Sarabande)
I Heard It Through The Grapevine
Creedence Clearwater Revival; *Chooglin'* . . . . (Fantasy)
Cosmo's Factory . . . . (Fantasy)
Creedence Clearwater Revival-Chronicle . . . . (Fantasy)
Creedence Clearwater Revival-Gold . . . . (Fantasy)
Movie Album . . . . (Fantasy)
Gladys Knight & The Pips; *16 #1 Hits From The Late '60s-C* . . (Motown)
Compact Command Performances-Gladys Knight & The Pips . . . . . (Motown)
Every Great Motown Song-First 25 Years-C . . . . (Motown)
Motown Grammy R&B Performances Of The '60s & '70s-C . . . (Motown)
Motown Superstar Series-#13-Gladys Knight & The Pips . . . (Motown)
Top 10 With A Bullet-Motown Girl Groups-C . . . . (Motown)
Marvin Gaye; *25 #1 Hits From 25 Years-C* . . . . (Motown)
Every Great Motown Hit Of Marvin Gaye . . . . (Motown)
Marvin Gaye Live At The London Palladium . . . . (Motown)
Marvin Gaye-Anthology . . . . (Motown)
Most Played Songs On America's Jukeboxes . . . . (Motown)
Motown Story-First 25 Years-C . . . . (Motown)
I Hope You've Learned
Ricky Skaggs and Kentucky Thunder; *Bluegrass Rules!* . . . . (Rounder)
I Hurt For You
Conway Twitty; *Final Touches* . . . .(MCA)
Deborah Allen; *45-#13776* . . . . (RCA)
I Know
Luther Vandross; *I Know* . . . .(LV/Virgin)
I Meant Every Word He Said
Ricky Van Shelton; *Greatest Country Hits Of The '90s-#2-C* . . . . . (Columbia)
RVS III . . . . (Columbia)
I Really Don't Want To Know
Charlie McCoy; *Greatest Hits Of Charlie McCoy* . . . . (Columbia)
Eddy Arnold; *Best Of Eddy Arnold* . . . . (RCA)
Essential Eddy Arnold . . . . (RCA)
Elvis Presley; *Elvis Country ("I'm 10,000 Years Old")* . . . . (RCA)
Great Country Songs . . . . (RCA)
Les Paul; *Best Of The Capitol Masters* . . . . (Gold Rush)
Les Paul & Mary Ford; *Les Paul's Greatest Hits* . . . . (Pair)
Ronnie Dove; *Ronnie Dove-His Best* . . . . (Laurie)
Tommy Edwards; *It's All In The Game-The Complete Hits Of Tommy*
Edwards . . . . (Eric)
I Want My Goodbye Back
Ty Herndon; *What Mattered Most* . . . .(Epic)
I Went To Your Wedding
Patti Page; *Patti Page-Golden Hits* . . . . (Mercury)
I Wish
Skee-Lo; *I Wish* . . . . (Sunshine/Scotti Bros.)
Stevie Wonder; *Original Musiquarium* . . . . (Motown)
Songs In The Key Of Life . . . . (Motown)
I Wish I Had A Girl
Henry Lee Summer; *Henry Lee Summer* . . . . (CBS Associated)
I Wish I Were Blind
Bruce Springsteen; *Human Touch* . . . . (Columbia)
I Wonder Who's Kissing Her Now
Bobby Darin; *Capitol Collectors Series-Bobby Darin* . . . . (Capitol)
Ted Weems & His Orchestra; *Sweetest Sounds Ever Heard-C* . . . . (Hip-O)
I'd Be Better Off (In A Pine Box)
Doug Stone; *Doug Stone* . . . .(Epic)
Greatest Country Hits Of The '90s-1990-C . . . . (Columbia)
I'd Rather Go Blind
Etta James; *Best Blues Album In The World...Ever!-C* . . . . (Virgin)
Best Blues Album In The World...Ever!-C . . . . (Virgin)
If I Fell
Beatles; *Beatles-Love Songs* . . . . (Capitol)
Something New . . . . (Capitol)
ST/A Hard Day's Night . . . . (Capitol)
If I Were You
Terri Clark; *Terri Clark* . . . . (Mercury)
If It Weren't For Him
Vince Gill & Rosanne Cash; *Collector's Series-Duets-C* . . . . (RCA)
I'll Never Be Jealous Again
Original Cast; *ST/Pajama Game* . . . . (Collectables)

I'll Think Of A Reason Later
Lee Ann Womack; *Some Things I Know* . . . . (Decca)
I'm Blue (The Gong-Gong Song)
Ikettes; *Great R&B Female Groups-Hits Of The '60s-C* . . . . (K-Tel)
I'm Not Angry
Elvis Costello; *My Aim Is True* . . . . (Columbia)
I'm Still In Love With You
New Edition; *D.J. Mix '98-#1-C* . . . .(Beast)
Home Again . . . .(MCA)
Is She Really Going Out With Him
Joe Jackson; *Live 1980/86* . . . . (A&M)
Look Sharp! . . . . (A&M)
It Could've Been Me
Billy Ray Cyrus; *Some Gave All* . . . . (Mercury)
It Hurts Me Too
Keb' Mo'; *The Door* . . . . (550/Epic/Okeh)
It's My Party
Lesley Gore; *Billboard Top Rock 'N' Roll Hits-1963-C* . . . . (Rhino)
Golden Hits Of Lesley Gore . . . . (Mercury)
Good Time Rock 'N' Roll-C . . . . (MCA)
Lesley Gore-Anthology . . . . (Rhino)
Oldies But Goodies-#3-C . . . .(Original Sound)
Jane Doe
Alicia Keys; *Songs In A Minor* . . . . (J)
Jealous
Robert Palmer; *Secrets* . . . . (Island)
Jealous
Gene Loves Jezebel; *Kiss Of Life* . . . . (Geffen)
Jealous
Rod Stewart; *Tonight I'm Yours* . . . . (Warner Bros.)
Jealous Again
Black Crowes; *Shake Your Money Maker* . . . .(Def American)
Jealous Again
Black Flag; *First Four Years* . . . .(SST)
Jealous Bone
Patty Loveless; *Patty Loveless' Greatest Hits* . . . . (MCA)
Up Against My Heart . . . . (MCA)
Jealous Dogs
Pretenders; *Pretenders II* . . . .(Sire)
Jealous Girl
New Edition; *Candy Girl* . . . .(Streetwise)
Jealous Guy
John Lennon; *Lennon* . . . . (Capitol)
ST/Imagine: John Lennon . . . . (Capitol)
John Lennon & Yoko Ono; *The John Lennon Collection* . . . . (Capitol)
John Lennon/Plastic Ono Band; *Imagine* . . . . (Capitol)
Roxy Music; *Heart Still Beating* . . . .(Virgin)
High Road . . . . (Warner Bros.)
Street Life-20 Great Hits . . . . (Reprise)
Jealous Heart
Al Morgan; *Hits Of '49-C* . . . . (ASV)
Connie Francis; *Connie Francis-Souvenirs* . . . . (Polydor)
Les Paul; *Les Paul-16 Most Requested Songs* . . . . (Columbia)
Tex Ritter; *An American Legend* . . . . (Capitol)
Best Of Tex Ritter . . . . (Capitol)
Hillbilly Heaven . . . . (Capitol)
Tex Ritter's Greatest Hits . . . . (Curb)
Tex Ritter-Vintage Collection . . . . (Capitol)
Jealous Hearted Man
Muddy Waters; *Hard Again* . . . .(Blue Sky)
Jealous Hearted Me
Minnie Pearl; *Stars Of The Grand Ole Opry-1926-1974-C* . . . .(RCA)
Jealous Kind
Joe Cocker; *Joe Cocker-Classics-#4* . . . . (A&M)
Joe Cocker's Greatest Hits . . . . (A&M)
Jealous Man
Truth; *Jump* . . . . (I.R.S.)
Jealous Man
Hoyt Axton; *Fearless* . . . . (A&M)
Jealousy
Adventures Of Stevie V; *Adventures Of Stevie V* . . . . (Mercury)
Jealousy
Natalie Merchant; *Tigerlily* . . . . (Elektra)
Jealousy
Escape Club; *Wild Wild West* . . . .(Atlantic)
Jealousy
Tommy Shaw; *What If* . . . . (A&M)
Jealousy
Frankie Miller; *Standing On The Edge* . . . . (Capitol)
Jealousy
Pet Shop Boys; *Behavior* . . . . (EMI)
Jealousy
Heart; *Passionworks* . . . .(Epic)
Jealousy
Mary Jane Girls; *Mary Jane Girls* . . . . (Motown)
Jealousy
Queen; *Jazz* . . . .(Hollywood)

Jealousy
Ronnie McDowell; *Good Time Lovin' Man* . . . . (Epic)
Jolene
Dolly Parton; *Best Of Dolly Parton* . . . . (RCA)
   Best There Is . . . . (RCA)
   Jolene . . . . (RCA)
   RCA Years-1967-1986 . . . . (RCA)
Sherrie Austin; *Followin' A Feelin'* . . . . (We/Madacy)
Judy's Turn To Cry
Lesley Gore; *'60s Dance Party-#2-C* . . . . (Dominion Entert.)
   Golden Hits Of Lesley Gore . . . . (Mercury)
   Lesley Gore-Anthology . . . . (Rhino)
Jump
Loverboy; *Get Lucky* . . . . (Columbia)
Kate
Ben Folds Five; *Whatever And Ever Amen* . . . . (Caroline/550)
Keep Your Hands Off My Baby
Trashmen; *Bird Call! The Twin City Stomp Of The
   Trashmen* . . . . (Sundazed Music)
Killer Joe
Rocky Fellers; *Scepter Records Story-C* . . . . (Capricorn)
Lady
D'Angelo; *Brown Sugar* . . . . (EMI)
Leave Him Out Of This
Steve Wariner; *I Am Ready* . . . . (Arista)
Leave My Kitten Alone
Beatles; *The Beatles-Anthology-#1* . . . . (Capitol)
Elvis Costello; *Kojak Variety* . . . . (Warner Bros.)
Little Willie John; *Best Of Little Willie John-Fever* . . . . (Rhino)
Life #9
Martina McBride; *The Way That I Am* . . . . (RCA)
Lightning's Girl
Nancy Sinatra; *How Does That Grab You?* . . . . (Sundazed Music)
Listen To Her Heart
Tom Petty And The Heartbreakers; *You're Gonna Get It!* . . . . (Gone Gator)
Living In The Footsteps Of Another Man
Chi-Lites; *Chi-Lites Greatest Hits* . . . . (Brunswick)
   Half A Love . . . . (Brunswick)
Living Proof
Ricky Van Shelton; *30 Years Of #1 Hits-#20-C* . . . . (Columbia)
   Greatest Country Hits Of The '80s-1989-C . . . . (Columbia)
   Ricky Van Shelton's Greatest Hits Plus . . . . (Columbia)
Lookin' At Me
Mase Featuring Puff Daddy; *Harlem World* . . . . (Bad Boy/Arista)
Love Blues
Keb' Mo'; *Keb' Mo'* . . . . (Okeh)
Matty Groves
Fairport Convention; *Fairport Convention-Chronicles* . . . . (A&M)
   Liege & Lief . . . . (A&M)
Muddy Water
Aretha Franklin; *Aretha Sings The Blues* . . . . (Columbia)
Sonny Terry & Brownie McGhee; *Best Of Sonny Terry & Brownie
   McGhee* . . . . (Prestige)
   Midnight Special . . . . (Fantasy)
My Best Friend's Girl
Cars; *The Cars* . . . . (Elektra)
   The Cars' Greatest Hits . . . . (Elektra)
My Name Is Not Susan
Whitney Houston; *I'm Your Baby Tonight* . . . . (Arista)
My Son Calls Another Man Daddy
Hank Williams With His Drifting Cowboys; *Hank Williams-16
   Great Hits* . . . . (Everest)
   Hank Williams-40 Greatest Hits . . . . (Polydor)
   Rare Takes & Radio Cuts . . . . (Polydor)
My Wife
Who; *ST/The Kids Are Alright* . . . . (MCA)
   Two's Missing . . . . (MCA)
   Who Greatest Hits . . . . (MCA)
   Who's next . . . . (MCA)
Na Na Hey Hey Kiss Him Goodbye
Steam; *Billboard Top Rock 'N' Roll Hits-1969-C* . . . . (Rhino)
   Super Hits Of The '70s-Have A Nice Day-#1-C . . . . (Rhino)
   Toga Rock-C . . . . (Dunhill Compact Classics)
Next Time You See Her
Eric Clapton; *Slowhand* . . . . (Polydor)
Ninety Nine Years (Dead Or Alive)
Guy Mitchell; *Definitive Guy Mitchell* . . . . (Collector's Choice)
No Reply
Beatles; *Beatles '65* . . . . (Capitol)
   Beatles-Box Set . . . . (Capitol)
   For Sale . . . . (Capitol)
Nobody Else
Tyrese; *Tyrese* . . . . (RCA)
Nobody's Darlin' But Mine
Chieftains & Emmylou Harris; *Another Country* . . . . (RCA)
Jimmie Davis; *The Country Music Hall Of Fame-Jimmie Davis* . . . . . . (MCA)
Merle Haggard; *Going Where The Lonely Go* . . . . (Epic)
None Of Ur Friends Business
Ginuwine; *100 Percent Ginuwine* . . . . (550 Music)

O.P.P.
Naughty By Nature; *MTV Party To Go-#2-C* . . . . (Tommy Boy)
Oh No
Commodores; *All The Great Love Songs-Commodores* . . . . (Motown)
   Commodores-All The Great Hits . . . . (Motown)
   In The Pocket . . . . (Motown)
   Lionel Richie-Composer Series . . . . (Motown)
   Top 10 With A Bullet-Motown Love Songs-C . . . . (Motown)
One I Love Belongs To Somebody Else, The
Count Basie & His Kansas City 3; *For The Second Time* . . . . (Pablo)
Etta Jones featuring Houston Person; *Fine & Mellow/Save Your Love
   For Me* . . . . (Muse)
Frank Sinatra; *I Remember Tommy* . . . . (Reprise)
Sheena Easton; *No Strings* . . . . (MCA)
Other Guy
Little River Band; *Little River Band's Greatest Hits* . . . . (Capitol)
Other Man's Grass Is Always Greener
Petula Clark; *Petula Clark's Greatest Hits* . . . . (Crescendo)
Out Of Your Shoes
Lorrie Morgan; *Essential Lorrie Morgan* . . . . (RCA)
   Leave The Light On . . . . (RCA)
   Lorrie Morgan-Super Hits . . . . (RCA)
Papa Loved Mama
Garth Brooks; *Garth Brooks-Double Live* . . . . (Capitol)
   Ropin' The Wind . . . . (Liberty)
Paper Doll
Bar-Kays; *Banging The Wall* . . . . (Mercury)
Mills Brothers; *Best Of The Mills Brothers* . . . . (MCA)
   Billboard Pop Memories-1940-1944-C . . . . (Rhino)
   Mills Brothers' All Time Greatest Hits . . . . (MCA)
   Mills Brothers' Greatest Hits . . . . (MCA)
   Mills Brothers-22 Great Hits . . . . (Ranwood)
   Paper Doll . . . . (MCA)
   Sentimental Journey: Pop Vocal Classics-#1-1942-1946-C . . . . (Rhino)
   The Mills Brothers-Best Of The Decca Years . . . . (Decca)
Penis Envy
Uncle Bonsai; *Lonely Grain Of Corn* . . . . (Freckle)
Please Don't Squeeze My Sharmon
Charlie Walker; *Charlie Walker-Golden Hits* . . . . (Plantation)
   Country Music Classics-#10-Late '60s-C . . . . (K-Tel)
Poor Boy
Woody Guthrie; *Legendary Woody Guthrie* . . . . (Tradition)
   Woody Guthrie . . . . (Everest)
   Worried Man Blues-Golden Classics-#1 . . . . (Collectables)
Pop Ya Collar
Usher; *All About U* . . . . (LaFace)
Potential New Boyfriend
Dolly Parton; *Best Of Dolly Parton-#3* . . . . (RCA)
Put Out The Fire
Queen; *Hot Space* . . . . (Hollywood)
Queen Of My Double Wide Trailer
Sammy Kershaw; *Haunted Heart* . . . . (Mercury)
Rocky Raccoon
Beatles; *Beatles-Box Set* . . . . (Capitol)
   The Beatles (White Album) . . . . (Capitol)
Rumor Has It
Reba McEntire; *Reba McEntire's Greatest Hits Volume Two* . . . . . . (MCA)
   Rumor Has It . . . . (MCA)
Run For Your Life
Beatles; *Beatles-Box Set* . . . . (Capitol)
   Rubber Soul . . . . (Capitol)
Sacred Ground
McBride & The Ride; *Sacred Ground* . . . . (MCA)
Santeria
Sublime; *Sublime* . . . . (Gasoline Alley)
Shame, Shame
Magic Lanterns; *Shame, Shame* . . . . (Collectables)
She Ain't The Girl For You
Kinleys; *Kinleys II* . . . . (Epic)
She Can't Love You
Destiny's Child; *The Writing's On The Wall* . . . . (Columbia)
She Used To Be Mine
Brooks & Dunn; *Hard Workin' Man* . . . . (Arista)
She Wants You
Billie; *Honey To The B* . . . . (Virgin)
She's Got The Rhythm (And I Got The Blues)
Alan Jackson; *A Lot About Livin' (And A Little 'Bout Love)* . . . . . . (Arista)
She's Got You
Patsy Cline; *12 Greatest Hits* . . . . (MCA)
   Billboard Top Country Hits-1962-C . . . . (Rhino)
   The Patsy Cline Story . . . . (MCA)
She's In Love
Mark Wills; *Wish You Were Here* . . . . (Mercury)
She's Mine Tonight
Jay Ferguson; *White Noise* . . . . (Capitol)
She's Not Cryin' Anymore
Billy Ray Cyrus; *Some Gave All* . . . . (Mercury)
She's Taken A Shine
John Berry; *Faces* . . . . (Capitol)

Silver Springs
Fleetwood Mac; *1998 Grammy Nominees-C* . . . . (MCA)
25 Years-The Chain . . . .(Warner Bros.)
The Dance . . . . (Reprise)

Sisters
Rosemary Clooney & Betty Clooney; *Mothers & Daughters*. . . . .(Concord Jazz)

Some Guys Have All The Love
Little Texas; *First Time For Everything* . . . . (Warner Bros.)

Some Guys Have All The Luck
Maxi Priest; *Best Of Me* . . . .(Charisma)
Maxi . . . . (Virgin)
Robert Palmer; *Addictions-#1*. . . . . (Island)
Rod Stewart; *Camouflage* . . . . (Warner Bros.)
Storyteller/The Complete Anthology: 1964-1990 . . . .(Warner Bros.)

Somebody Else's Guy
Jocelyn Brown; *Somebody Else's Guy* . . . . (Vinyl Dreams)

Somebody Else's Moon
Collin Raye; *In This Life* . . . .(Epic)

Somebody New
Billy Ray Cyrus; *It Won't Be The Last* . . . . (Mercury)

Somebody Stole My Gal
Benny Goodman; *B.G. In Hi-Fi* . . . . (Blue Note)
Best Of The Big Bands-C . . . . (Columbia)

Song From Moulin Rouge (Where Is Your Heart)
Percy Faith & His Orchestra; *Percy Faith & His Orchestra's All-Time
Greatest Hits*. . . . . (Columbia)

Spit Of Love
Bonnie Raitt; *Fundamental*. . . . . (Capitol)
Lilith Fair-A Celebration Of Women In Music-#3-C . . . . (Arista)

Stepsisters' Lament
Barbara Ruick & Pat Carroll; *Cinderella-The CBS Television Network
Production* . . . . (Columbia)
Original Cast; *Cinderella-The CBS Television Production* . . . . (Columbia)

Such A Night
Dr. John; *Very Best Of Dr. John* . . . . (Rhino)
Dr. John & Chris Barber; *On A Mardi Gras Day* . . . . (Great Southern)
Dr. John & The Band; *The Last Waltz*. . . . .(Warner Bros.)

Surrey With The Fringe On Top
Ellis Marsalis; *Heart Of Gold* . . . . (Columbia)
Original Broadway Cast; *Oklahoma!* . . . . (RCA)
Original Cast; *Oklahoma!*. . . . .(MCA)

Take Good Care Of Her
Adam Wade; *45-#546*. . . . . (Coed)
Sonny James; *Billboard Top Country Hits-1966-C* . . . . (Rhino)

Take Good Care Of My Baby
Bobby Vee; *Best Of Bobby Vee*. . . . .(EMI)
Billboard Top Rock 'N' Roll Hits-1961-C . . . . (Rhino)
'Til My Dreamin' Comes True-C . . . . (Capitol)
Bobby Vinton; *Bobby Vinton-16 Most Requested Songs* . . . . (Legacy)
Dion; *Runaround Sue (Right Stuff)* . . . . (Right Stuff)

Talking In Your Sleep
Crystal Gayle; *Classic Crystal* . . . .(EMI)
Country Gold-C . . . . (Priority)
Crystal Gayle's All-Time Greatest Hits . . . . (Curb)
When I Dream . . . . (Liberty)
Reba McEntire; *Starting Over* . . . .(MCA)

Tell Him No
Travis & Bob; *The History Of Dot-#2-Come Go
With Me-C* . . . . (Varese Sarabande)

Tell Laura I Love Her
Ray Peterson; *Nipper's Greatest Hits Of The '60s-#1-C* . . . . (RCA)
Teenage Tragedies-C . . . . (Rhino)

That Ain't My Truck
Rhett Akins; *A Thousand Memories* . . . . (Decca)
Cryin' Lyin' Lovin' & Leavin'-C . . . . (Universal)

Then You May Take Me To The Fair
Original Cast; *Camelot* . . . . (Columbia)
Vanessa Redgrave; *ST/Camelot* . . . .(Warner Bros.)

There Goes My Heart
Mavericks; *Best Of The Mavericks-Super Colossal Smash Hits Of
The '90s* . . . . (Mercury)
What A Crying Shame . . . .(MCA)

They Don't Know
Jon B.; *Cool Relax* . . . . (Yab Yum/550)

They Were Doin' The Mambo
Vaughn Monroe; *Very Best Of Vaughn Monroe* . . . .(Taragon)

They're Hanging Me Tonight
Marty Robbins; *Gunfighter Ballads & Trail Songs*. . . . . (Legacy)

This Boy
Beatles; *Beatles-Box Set* . . . . (Capitol)
Beatles-Love Songs . . . . (Capitol)
Meet The Beatles! . . . . (Capitol)
Past Masters-Volume One . . . . (Parlophone)
The Beatles-Anthology-#1 . . . . (Capitol)

Today's Lonely Fool
Tracy Lawrence; *Sticks & Stones* . . . . (Atlantic)

Top Of The World
Brandy featuring Mase; *Never Say Never* . . . . (Atlantic)

Two Princes
Spin Doctors; *Pocket Full Of Kryptonite*. . . . . (Epic Portrait Assoc.)

Ugly Girl
Fleming & John; *The Way We Are* . . . . (Universal)

We Hate It When Our Friends Become Successful
Morrissey; *Your Arsenal* . . . .(Sire)

Wedding Bells (Are Breaking Up That Old Gang Of Mine)
Four Aces; *Best Of The Four Aces*. . . . . (MCA)

We'll Burn That Bridge
Brooks & Dunn; *Hard Workin' Man* . . . . (Arista)

When I Take My Sugar To Tea
Boswell Sisters; *78-#6083*. . . . . (Brunswick)
Frank Sinatra; *Ring-A-Ding Ding* . . . . (Reprise)
Nat ''King'' Cole; *The Vocal Classics-1947-1950* . . . . (Capitol)

When It's Springtime In Alaska
Johnny Horton; *American Originals-Johnny Horton* . . . . (Columbia)
Johnny Horton's Greatest Hits . . . . (Columbia)

When You Need My Love
Darryl Worley; *Hard Rain Don't Last*. . . . .(DreamWorks/SKG)

Whiskey, If You Were A Woman
Highway 101; *Highway 101* . . . . (Warner Bros.)
Highway 101's Greatest Hits . . . . (Warner Bros.)

Who Walks In When I Walk Out
Bob Wills; *Stay A Little Longer-The Original Columbia
Recordings*. . . . .(Roswell/RCA)

Who's That Man
Toby Keith; *Boomtown* . . . .(Polydor Country)

Whose Bed Have Your Boots Been Under?
Shania Twain; *The Woman In Me* . . . . (Mercury)

Will You Be Loving Another Man
Bill Monroe & His Blue Grass Boys; *Essential Bill Monroe & His Blue
Grass Boys*. . . . . (Legacy)
Essential Bill Monroe-1945-1949 . . . . (Columbia)

With Me Part 1
Destiny's Child featuring JD; *Destiny's Child* . . . .(Grass Roots/Columbia)

Woman To Woman
Shirley Brown; *Didn't It Blow Your Mind: Soul Hits Of The
'70s-#15-C* . . . . (Rhino)
Top Of The Stax-Twenty Greatest Hits-C . . . . (Stax)
Woman To Woman . . . . (Stax)

X-Girlfriend
Mariah Carey; *Rainbow* . . . . (Columbia)

You Ain't Woman Enough
Loretta Lynn; *Billboard Top Country Hits-1966-C*. . . . . (Rhino)
Legends Of Country Music-The Best Of Austin City Limits-C . . . . . (Columbia)
Loretta Lynn's Greatest Hits . . . . (MCA)
The Country Music Hall Of Fame-Loretta Lynn. . . . . (MCA)
Shirley Brown; *Diva Of Soul* . . . . (Malaco Jazz)

You Belong To Me
Carly Simon; *Boys In The Trees* . . . . (Elektra)
Carly Simon-Greatest Hits . . . . (Arista)
Chicken Soup For The Woman's Soul-C . . . . (Rhino)
Doobie Brothers; *Best Of The Doobies, Volume II* . . . . (Warner Bros.)
Livin' On The Fault Line . . . . (Warner Bros.)

You Can't Do That
Beatles; *Beatles-Box Set* . . . . (Capitol)
Rock 'N' Roll Music . . . . (Capitol)
The Beatles' Second Album . . . . (Capitol)

You Oughta Know
Alanis Morissette; *1996 Grammy Nominees-C* . . . . (Columbia)
Jagged Little Pill . . . . (Maverick)

You, Me And He
Mtume; *You, Me And He* . . . . (Epic)

You're Going To Lose That Girl
Beatles; *ST/Help!* . . . . (Capitol)

You're So Vain
Carly Simon; *'70s Greatest Rock Hits-#3-High Times-C* . . . . (Priority)
Best Of Carly Simon . . . . (Elektra)
Carly Simon-Greatest Hits Live . . . . (Arista)
No Secrets . . . . (Elektra)

You've Got A Lover
Ricky Skaggs; *19 Hot Country Requests-#2-C* . . . . (Epic)
Highways & Heartaches . . . . (Epic)

JEWELRY, Diamonds, Gems, Precious Stones, Rings
See Also: GOLD, LOVE (various), MARRIAGE, MONEY, ROYALTY, SILVER

3 Chains O' Gold
Prince And The New Power Generation; *Love Symbol Album* . . . . (Paisley Park)

Angelina
Keb' Mo'; *Keb' Mo'* . . . .(Okeh)

Band Of Gold
Freda Payne; *Beachbeat Draggin'* . . . . (Dunhill Compact Classics)
Didn't It Blow Your Mind: Soul Hits Of The '70s-#2-C . . . . (Rhino)

Freda Payne's Greatest Hits .... (HDH)
Band Of Gold
Don Cherry; *Very Best Of Don Cherry* .... (Collector's Choice)
Baubles, Bangles And Beads
Frank Sinatra & Antonio Carlos Jobim; *Francis Albert Sinatra & Antonio Carlos Jobim* .... (Reprise)
Marlene Dietrich; *Marlene Dietrich-Live* .... (Columbia)
Original Cast; *Kismet* .... (Columbia)
Peggy Lee; *Best Of Peggy Lee* .... (MCA)
Percy Faith & His Orchestra; *Percy Faith & His Orchestra's All-Time Greatest Hits* .... (Columbia)
Bijou
Lambert, Hendricks & Ross; *Best Of Lambert, Hendricks & Ross* ... (Columbia)
Woody Herman; *20 Golden Pieces Of Woody Herman* .... (Bulldog)
Thundering Herds-1945-1947 .... (Columbia)
Bimbombey
Jimmie Rodgers; *Best Of Jimmie Rodgers* .... (Rhino)
Best Of Jimmie Rodgers .... (Curb)
Black Diamond
Kiss; *Alive!* .... (Mercury)
Double Platinum .... (Mercury)
Kiss .... (Casablanca)
The Originals .... (Casablanca)
Black Diamond Bay
Bob Dylan; *Desire* .... (Columbia)
Black Pearl
Sonny Charles; *Soul Shots-#2-The "In" Crowd-Sweet Soul-C* .... (Rhino)
Sonny Charles and The Checkmates, Ltd.; *Soul Shots-C* .... (Rhino)
Bling Bling
B.G.; *Chopper City In The Ghetto* .... (Cash Money/Universal)
Bo Diddley
Bo Diddley; *Good Time Rock 'N' Roll-C* .... (MCA)
History Of Rock-#5-C .... (Collectables)
Oldies But Goodies-#10-C .... (Original Sound)
ST/Rage In Harlem .... (Sire)
Buddy Holly; *Buddy Holly-20 Golden Greats* .... (MCA)
For The First Time Anywhere .... (MCA)
Breakfast At Tiffany's
Deep Blue Something; *Home* .... (RainMaker/Interscope)
Breakfast At Tiffany's
Henry Mancini; *Days Of Wine And Roses* .... (RCA)
Buried Treasure
Kenny Rogers; *Eyes That See In The Dark* .... (RCA)
Kenny Rogers' Greatest Hits .... (RCA)
Buried Treasure
Flesheaters; *Prehistoric Fits-#2* .... (SST)
Can't Buy Me Love
Beatles; *Beatles 1* .... (Capitol)
Hey Jude .... (Capitol)
Reel Music .... (Capitol)
ST/A Hard Day's Night .... (Capitol)
The Beatles At The Hollywood Bowl .... (Capitol)
The Beatles/1962-1966 .... (Capitol)
Chains Of Gold
Sweethearts Of The Rodeo; *More Hot Country Requests-#2-C* .... (Epic)
Sweethearts Of The Rodeo .... (Columbia)
Charms
Bobby Vee; *EMI Legends Of Rock & Roll-Bobby Vee* .... (Gold Rush)
Cool Pearl
Capitols; *Golden Classics-Capitols* .... (Collectables)
Crystal Blue Persuasion
Tommy James And The Shondells; *Best Of Tommy James And The Shondells* .... (Roulette)
Tommy James And The Shondells-Anthology .... (Rhino)
Crystal Chandeliers
Charley Pride; *Charley Pride-24 Greatest Hits* .... (Tee Vee)
Special Collector's Edition-#3 .... (Platinum Disc)
Cuff Link
Wings; *London Town* .... (Capitol)
Devil With A Blue Dress On & Good Golly Miss Molly
Bruce Springsteen; *ST/No Nukes-Muse Concerts* .... (Asylum)
Mitch Ryder And The Detroit Wheels; *Frat Rock!-#4-C* .... (Rhino)
Rev Up-Best Of Mitch Ryder .... (Rhino)
Son Of Frat Rock!-C .... (Rhino)
Toga Rock-C .... (Dunhill Compact Classics)
Diamond Dogs
David Bowie; *Changesbowie* .... (Rykodisc)
David Live .... (Rykodisc)
Diamond Dogs .... (Rykodisc)
The Singles-1969-1993 .... (Rykodisc)
Diamond Dust
Jeff Beck; *Blow By Blow* .... (Epic)
Diamond Girl
Seals & Crofts; *Diamond Girl* .... (Warner Bros.)
Seals & Crofts' Greatest Hits .... (Warner Bros.)
Diamond Head
Beach Boys; *Friends-20/20* .... (Capitol)
Diamond In The Dust
Mark Gray; *This Ol' Piano* .... (Columbia)

Diamond Joe
Tom Rush; *Mind Ramblin'* .... (Prestige)
Tom Rush .... (Fantasy)
Diamond Mine
Hank Williams, Jr.; *Out Of Left Field* .... (Capricorn)
Diamond Mine
Blue Rodeo; *Diamond Mine* .... (Atlantic)
Diamond Smiles
Boomtown Rats; *Fine Art Of Surfacing* .... (Columbia)
Diamonds
Chris Rea; *Deltics* .... (United Artists)
Diamonds & Rust
Joan Baez; *Best Of Joan Baez* .... (A&M)
Diamonds & Rust .... (A&M)
From Every Stage .... (A&M)
Joan Baez-Classics-#8 .... (A&M)
Diamonds & Rust
Judas Priest; *Best Of Judas Priest* .... (Columbia)
Sin After Sin .... (Columbia)
Unleashed In The East .... (Columbia)
Diamonds And Pearls
Paradons; *Back Seat Jams-C* .... (Dunhill Compact Classics)
Collectables Presents The History Of Rock-#8-C .... (Collectables)
Oldies But Goodies-#5-C .... (Original Sound)
Super Oldies Of The '60s-#3-C .... (Audio Fidelity)
Diamonds And Pearls
Prince And The New Power Generation; *Diamonds And Pearls* ... (Paisley Park)
Diamonds And Pearls
Kansas; *Vinyl Confessions* .... (Kirshner)
Diamonds Are A Girl's Best Friend
Carol Channing; *Broadway Magic-The 1950s-C* .... (Columbia)
Emmylou Harris; *White Shoes* .... (Warner Bros.)
Marilyn Monroe; *Goodbye Primadonna* .... (Accord)
Pearl Bailey; *Back On Broadway* .... (Roulette)
Echoes Of An Era-Pearl Bailey .... (Roulette)
Diamonds Are Forever
Shirley Bassey; *13 Original James Bond Themes-C* .... (EMI)
Best Of Shirley Bassey .... (EMI)
Shirley Bassey's Greatest Hits .... (EMI)
Diamonds In The Rough
John Prine; *Diamonds In The Rough* .... (Atlantic)
Diamonds In The Stars
Ray Price; *Ray Price's Greatest Hits-#3* .... (Step One)
Diamonds On My Windshield
Tom Waits; *The Heart Of Saturday Night* .... (Asylum)
Tom Waits-Anthology .... (Asylum)
Diamonds On The Soles Of Her Shoes
Paul Simon; *Concert In The Park-August 15 1991* .... (Warner Bros.)
Graceland .... (Warner Bros.)
Negotiations And Love Songs, 1971-1986 .... (Warner Bros.)
Does My Ring Hurt Your Finger
Charley Pride; *Charley Pride-24 Greatest Hits* .... (Tee Vee)
Essential Charley Pride .... (RCA)
Don't Sell This Diamond Ring
Gary Lewis And The Playboys; *Good Old Rock & Roll-C* .... (International Mktg. Group)
Dupree's Diamond Blues
Grateful Dead; *Aoxomoxoa* .... (Warner Bros.)
Emerald
Thin Lizzy; *Jailbreak* .... (Mercury)
Live And Dangerous .... (Warner Bros.)
Emerald Eyes
Eric Johnson; *Tones* .... (Reprise)
Emerald Eyes
Fleetwood Mac; *Mystery To Me* .... (Reprise)
Emerald Eyes
Jimmy Page; *Outrider* .... (Geffen)
From Here To Eternity
Michael Peterson; *Michael Peterson* .... (Reprise)
Wedding Day Music-C .... (Reprise)
Georgia Keeps Pulling On My Ring
Conway Twitty; *Classic Conway* .... (MCA)
Very Best Of Conway Twitty .... (MCA)
Give Me A Ring Sometime
Lisa Brokop; *Every Little Girl's Dream* .... (Patriot)
Golden Earrings
Peggy Lee; *Capitol Collectors Series-Peggy Lee-#1-Early Years* ...... (Capitol)
Peggy Lee's Greatest Hits .... (Capitol)
Golden Heart
Mark Knopfler; *Golden Heart* .... (Warner Bros.)
Golden Ring
Emmylou Harris/Linda Ronstadt/Anna & Kate McGarrigle; *Tammy Wynette...Remembered-C* .... (Asylum)
George Jones & Tammy Wynette; *George Jones & Tammy Wynette-16 Biggest Hits* .... (Epic/Legacy)
Tammy Wynette & George Jones; *Encore-Tammy Wynette & George Jones* .... (Epic)
Tammy Wynette & George Jones' Greatest Hits .... (Epic)

Tammy Wynette-Anniversary-20 Years Of Hits . . . .(Epic)

Golden Ring
Eric Clapton; *Backless* . . . . (Polydor)

Good Luck Charm
Elvis Presley; *Elvis' Golden Records, Volume 3.* . . . . (RCA)
Number One Hits . . . . (RCA)
The Top Ten Hits . . . . (RCA)
Worldwide 50 Gold Award Hits, Vol. 1, Parts 1 & 2 . . . . (RCA)

Green Earrings
Steely Dan; *Steely Dan-Gold* . . . . (MCA)
The Royal Scam . . . . (MCA)

Hidden Treasure
Traffic; *The Low Spark Of High Heeled Boys* . . . . (Island)

I Feel Fine
Beatles; *Beatles 1* . . . . (Capitol)
Beatles '65 . . . . (Capitol)
Beatles-20 Greatest Hits . . . . (Capitol)
Past Masters-Volume One . . . . (Parlophone)
The Beatles/1962-1966 . . . . (Capitol)
Sweethearts Of The Rodeo; *One Time One Night.* . . . . (Columbia)

I Need A Rolex
Toddy Tee; *Rhyme Syndicate Comin' Through* . . . .(Warner Bros.)

If She Don't Love You
Buffalo Club; *Buffalo Club.* . . . . (Rising Tide)

If You've Got Trouble
Beatles; *The Beatles-Anthology-#2.* . . . . (Capitol)

I'm Just An Old Chunk Of Coal (But I'm Gonna Be A Diamond Someday)
Billy Joe Shaver; *Restless Wind-The Legendary Billy Joe Shaver-1973-1987* . . . . (Razor & Tie)
John Anderson; *John Anderson's Greatest Hits* . . . .(Warner Bros.)

In A Week Or Two
Diamond Rio; *Close To The Edge.* . . . . (Arista)
Diamond Rio's Greatest Hits . . . . (Arista)

Jewel
Eddie Rabbitt; *Eddie Rabbitt* . . . . (Elektra)

Jewel
Propaganda; *Secret Wish* . . . . (Island)

Jewel Eyed Judy
Fleetwood Mac; *Kiln House* . . . . (Reprise)

Lady Came From Baltimore
Joan Baez; *Contemporary Ballad Book* . . . . (Vanguard)
Joan . . . . (Vanguard)
John Stewart; *Neon Beach* . . . . (Homecoming)
Johnny Cash; *Johnny Cash-16 Biggest Hits-#2* . . . . (Legacy)
Tim Hardin; *Hang On To A Dream-Verve Recordings* . . . . (Polydor)

Little Rock
Reba McEntire; *Whoever's In New England* . . . .(MCA)
Woman To Woman-#2-C . . . .(MCA)

Love Is A Golden Ring
Frankie Laine; *Frankie Laine-16 Most Requested Songs* . . . . (Legacy)

Lucy In The Sky With Diamonds
Beatles; *Sgt. Pepper's Lonely Hearts Club Band* . . . . (Capitol)
The Beatles/1967-1970 . . . . (Capitol)
Yellow Submarine . . . . (Capitol)
Elton John; *All This & World War 2* . . . . (20th Century Fox)
Elton John's Greatest Hits-#2 . . . . (Polydor)
John Lennon; *Lennon* . . . . (Capitol)

Magic Jewelled Limousine
Nasa; *Insha-Allah!* . . . . (Sire)
ST/Wild Orchid . . . . (Sire)

Mama's Pearl
Jackson 5; *3rd Album* . . . . (Motown)
Compact Command Performances-Jackson 5 . . . . (Motown)
Jackson 5-Anthology . . . . (Motown)
Jackson 5's Greatest Hits . . . . (Motown)

Memphis Pearl
Lucinda Williams; *Sweet Old World.* . . . . (Chameleon)

Mockingbird
Carly Simon & James Taylor; *Best Of Carly Simon & James Taylor* . . . (Elektra)
Hotcakes . . . . (Elektra)
Inez Foxx with Charlie Foxx; *Billboard Top R&B Hits-1963-C.* . . . . (Rhino)
Oldies But Goodies-#8-C. . . . . (Original Sound)
Super Oldies Of The '60s-#4-C . . . . (Audio Fidelity)
Peter, Paul & Mary; *Peter, Paul & Mommy* . . . .(Warner Bros.)

Mother Of Pearl
Roxy Music; *Roxy Music's Greatest Hits* . . . . (Atco)
Stranded. . . . . (Reprise)

On The Other Hand
Randy Travis; *Randy Travis' Greatest Hits-#1.* . . . .(Warner Bros.)
Storms Of Life . . . .(Warner Bros.)

On Treasure Island
Louis Armstrong; *Louis Armstrong* . . . .(MCA Special Prod.)
Tommy Dorsey & His Orchestra; *Seventeen Number Ones* . . . . (RCA)

Pearl From Warsaw
Klezmer Conservatory Band; *Jumpin' Night In The Garden Of Eden* . . . . (Rounder)

Pearl Necklace
ZZ Top; *El Loco* . . . .(Warner Bros.)

Six Pack . . . . (Warner Bros.)
ZZ Top's Greatest Hits . . . . (Warner Bros.)

Pearl Of The Quarter
Steely Dan; *Countdown To Ecstasy.* . . . . (MCA)

Pearls
Sade; *Love Deluxe* . . . . (Epic)

Pearls In The Snow
Michael Martin Murphey; *Cowboy Christmas* . . . . (Warner Bros.)

Pearls, The
Canadian Brass; *Red Hot Jazz-Dixieland Album* . . . . (Philips)
Jelly Roll Morton; *Jelly Roll Morton.* . . . . (Bluebird)

Pearly Queen
Dave Mason; *Certified Live.* . . . . (Columbia)
Very Best Of Dave Mason. . . . . (MCA)
Traffic; *Traffic.* . . . . (Island)

Playing Marbles With Diamonds
Steve Camp; *Doing My Best-#2* . . . . (Sparrow)

Pledge Pin
Robert Plant; *Pictures At Eleven* . . . . (Swan Song)

Pocket Full Of Gold
Vince Gill; *Pocket Full Of Gold* . . . . (MCA)

Precious Little
Eleanor McEvoy; *What's Following Me?* . . . . (Columbia)

Put That Ring On My Finger
Andrews Sisters; *50th Anniversary Collection-#2* . . . . (MCA)
Woody Herman; *Best Of The Big Bands-C* . . . . (Columbia)

Rainbow
Russ Hamilton; *45-#184* . . . .(Kapp)

Reflections In A Crystal Wind
Mimi & Richard Farina; *Best Of Mimi & Richard Farina* . . . . (Vanguard)
Reflections In A Crystal Wind. . . . . (Vanguard)

Rhinestone Cowboy
Glen Campbell; *Country's Greatest Hits-#6-Superstars-C.* . . . . (Priority)
Glen Campbell-Classics Collection . . . . (Capitol)
Glen Campbell-Live . . . . (Capitol)
Rhinestone Cowboy . . . . (Capitol)
Very Best Of Glen Campbell. . . . . (Capitol)

Ring On Her Finger, Time On Her Hands
Lee Greenwood; *Best Of Lee Greenwood-God Bless America* . . . . (Curb)
Inside Out/You've Got A Good Love Comin' . . . . (MCA)
Lee Greenwood's Greatest Hits . . . . (MCA)
Lee Greenwood-Super Hits . . . . (Epic)
Reba McEntire; *Starting Over.* . . . . (MCA)

Ruby Red
Kingston Trio; *Hidden Treasures* . . . . (Folk Era)
Treasure Chest . . . . (Folk Era)

Sapphire
Royal Philharmonic Ensemble & John Keating; *Birthstone Suite.* . . . . (USA Music Group)

Sapphire
Clash; *Sandinista.* . . . . (Epic)

Sapphire
TNT; *Tell No Tales* . . . . (Mercury)

Sapphire Bullets Of Pure Love
They Might Be Giants; *Flood* . . . . (Elektra)

Satan's Jewel Crown
Emmylou Harris; *Elite Hotel.* . . . .(Reprise)

Senorita With A Necklace Of Tears
Paul Simon; *You're The One* . . . . (Warner Bros.)

She Ain't Your Ordinary Girl
Alabama; *Alabama-Super Hits-#2* . . . .(RCA)
In Pictures . . . .(RCA)

She Is A Diamond
Original Cast; *Evita* . . . . (MCA)

She Wears My Ring
Elvis Presley; *Essential Elvis-#5-Rhythm & Country* . . . . (RCA)
Ray Price; *Ray Price-20 Hits* . . . . (Tee Vee)
Ray Price's Greatest Hits-#1-3 . . . .(Step One)

She's Taken A Shine
John Berry; *Faces* . . . . (Capitol)

Shine On Ruby Mountain
Kenny Rogers And The First Edition; *Best Of Kenny Rogers And The First Edition* . . . . (K-Tel)
Kenny Rogers And The First Edition's All-Time Greatest Hits-#2. . . . . (MCA Special Prod.)

Shine On You Crazy Diamond
Pink Floyd; *Collection Of Great Dance Songs* . . . . (Columbia)
Delicate Sound Of Thunder. . . . . (Columbia)
Wish You Were Here. . . . . (Columbia)

Some Days Are Diamonds
John Denver; *John Denver's Greatest Hits-#3* . . . .(RCA)
Some Days Are Diamonds . . . .(RCA)

Souvenirs
Gretchen Peters; *Gretchen Peters* . . . .(Purple Crayon Prod.)

Sparkling In The Sand
Tower Of Power; *East Bay Grease* . . . . (Rhino)
Live & In Living Color . . . . (Warner Bros.)

String Of Pearls
Boston Pops Orchestra/Arthur Fiedler; *Greatest Hits Of The '40s-#2.* . . . . (RCA)

Glenn Miller; *Best Of Glenn Miller* . . . . (RCA)
  Glenn Miller-A Legendary Performer-#1 & 2 . . . . (Bluebird)
  Memorial-1944-1969 . . . . (Bluebird)
  Moonlight Serenade . . . . (Bluebird)
  The Glenn Miller Story . . . . (RCA)
Glenn Miller & His Orchestra; *Glenn Miller & His Orchestra-*
  Pure Gold . . . . (Bluebird)
Lawrence Welk; *22 All-Time Big Band Favorites* . . . . (Ranwood)
Les & Larry Elgart; *Best Of The Big Bands-C* . . . . (Columbia)

Take Back Your Mink
Original Cast; *Guys & Dolls* . . . . (MCA)

Tears Of Pearls
Savage Garden; *Savage Garden* . . . . (Columbia)

This Diamond Ring
Gary Lewis And The Playboys; *Billboard Top Rock 'N' Roll Hits-*
  1965-C . . . . (Rhino)
  EMI Legends Of Rock & Roll-24 Greatest Hits-C . . . . (EMI)
  Golden Years-1965-C . . . . (Dominion Entert.)
  Spring Break-#2-Cold Kegs & Tan Legs . . . . (Capitol)

This Is For The Lover In You
Babyface; *The Day* . . . . (Epic)

Topaz
Journey; *Journey* . . . . (Columbia)
  Journey-In The Beginning . . . . (Columbia)

Topaz
B-52's; *Cosmic Thing* . . . . (Reprise)

Trouble With Diamonds
Mac McAnally; *Live & Learn* . . . . (MCA)

Turquoise Jewelry
Camper Van Beethoven; *Our Beloved Revolutionary Sweetheart* . . . . . . (Virgin)

Wear My Ring Around Your Neck
Elvis Presley; *50,000,000 Elvis Fans Can't Be Wrong-Elvis' Gold Records-*
  Volume 2 . . . . (RCA)
  Hits Like Never Before-Essential-#3 . . . . (RCA)
  The Top Ten Hits . . . . (RCA)
  Worldwide 50 Gold Award Hits, Vol. 1, Parts 1 & 2 . . . . (RCA)
Ricky Van Shelton; *Ricky Van Shelton's Greatest Hits Plus* . . . . . . (Columbia)

When God Comes & Gathers His Jewels
Hank Williams; *Health & Happiness Shows* . . . . (Mercury)
  I Saw The Light . . . . (Polydor)
Molly O'Day & The Cumberland Mountain Folks; *Columbia Country*
  Classics-#1-Golden Age-C . . . . (Columbia)
  Hank Williams Songbook-C . . . . (Columbia)

With This Ring
Platters; *Enchanted-The Best Of The Platters* . . . . (Rhino)
  Only Their Best For You . . . . (Pair)
  Rockin' & Rollin' Wedding Songs-#2-C . . . . (Rhino)
  The Musicor Years . . . . (Collectables)
T. Graham Brown; *Best Of T. Graham Brown* . . . . (Liberty)
  T. Graham Brown's All-Time Greatest Hits . . . . (Curb)

With This Ring
Sawyer Brown; *Six Days On The Road* . . . . (Curb)
  Wedding Day Music-C . . . . (Reprise)

Would Jesus Wear A Rolex
Ray Stevens; *Ray Stevens' Greatest Hits-#2* . . . . (MCA)
  Ray Stevens-All-Time Greatest Comic Hits . . . . (Curb)
  Ray Stevens-Collection . . . . (MCA)

Wrapped Around
Brad Paisley; *Brad Paisley-Part II* . . . . (Arista)

JUKEBOX

See Also: **BARS, DANCE, FUN, MUSIC, PARTY, RESTAURANTS**

A-1 On The Jukebox
Dave Edmunds; *Best Of Dave Edmunds* . . . . (Swan Song)
  Tracks On Wax 4 . . . . (Swan Song)

A-11
Buck Owens; *Buck Owens Collection-1959-1990* . . . . (Rhino)
Johnny Paycheck; *Johnny Paycheck-20 Greatest Hits* . . . . (Deluxe)

All Night Juke
Lloyd Green; *Lloyd's Of Nashville* . . . . (Boot)

Anywhere There's A Jukebox
Razzy Bailey; *Makin' Friends* . . . . (RCA)

Beer And Bones
John Michael Montgomery; *John Michael Montgomery's*
  Greatest Hits . . . . (Atlantic)
  Life's A Dance . . . . (Atlantic)

Between An Old Memory And Me
Keith Whitley; *I Wonder Do You Think Of Me* . . . . (RCA)
Travis Tritt; *Ten Feet Tall And Bulletproof* . . . . (Warner Bros.)

Brother Jukebox
Don Everly; *Best Of The Everly Brothers-Rare Solo Classics* . . . . . . (Curb)
Paul Craft; *Songwriters On Beale Street* . . . . (Syren)

Brother Jukebox
Mark Chesnutt; *Too Cold At Home* . . . . (MCA)

Bubba Shot The Jukebox
Mark Chesnutt; *Longnecks & Short Stories* . . . . (MCA)

Canned Music
Dan Hicks & His Hot Licks; *Striking It Rich!* . . . . (MCA)

Danny's All-Star Joint
Rickie Lee Jones; *Rickie Lee Jones* . . . . (Warner Bros.)

Don't Rock The Jukebox
Alan Jackson; *Alan Jackson-The Greatest Hits Collection* . . . . (Arista)
  Don't Rock The Jukebox . . . . (Arista)

Drinkin' My Baby (Off My Mind)
Eddie Rabbitt; *Best Of Eddie Rabbitt/Greatest Hits-II* . . . . . . (Warner Bros.)
  Great Divorce Songs For Him-C . . . . (Warner Bros.)
  Number 1's . . . . (Warner Bros.)
  Rocky Mountain Music . . . . (Elektra)

God's Own Jukebox
Jesse Winchester; *Third Down 110 To Go* . . . . (Rhino)

Happiest Song On The Jukebox
Charley Pride; *Sweet Country* . . . . (RCA)

Hey Mister, That's Me Up On The Jukebox
Linda Ronstadt; *Prisoner In Disguise* . . . . (Asylum)

Honky Tonk Man
Dwight Yoakam; *Guitars, Cadillacs, Etc., Etc.* . . . . (Reprise)
  Just Lookin' For A Hit . . . . (Reprise)
Johnny Horton; *All Time Legends Of Country Music-C* . . . . (Legacy)
  Columbia Country Classics-#2-Honky Tonk Heroes-C . . . . (Columbia)
Marty Robbins; *Greatest Country Hits From The Movies-C* . . . . (Epic)

Honky Tonkin' Fool
Doug Supernaw; *Red And Rio Grande* . . . . (BNA)
  The Encore Collection . . . . (BMG Special Prod.)

Human Jukebox
Scientists; *Absolute* . . . . (Sub Pop)

I Heard The Jukebox Playing
Faron Young; *Hi Tone Poppa* . . . . (Collectables)
Kitty Wells; *The Kitty Wells Story* . . . . (MCA)

I Love Rock 'N Roll
Britney Spears; *Britney* . . . . (Jive)
Joan Jett & The Blackhearts; *I Love Rock 'n' Roll* . . . . (Blackheart)
ST/*Wayne's World 2* . . . . (Reprise)

If Hell Had A Jukebox
Travis Tritt; *It's All About To Change* . . . . (Warner Bros.)

If I Didn't Have A Dime (To Play The Jukebox)
Gene Pitney; *Gene Pitney-Anthology 1961-1968* . . . . (Rhino)
  Gene Pitney's Greatest Hits . . . . (Evergreen Music)

If The Jukebox Took Teardrops
Billy Joe Royal; *Out Of The Shadows* . . . . (Atlantic)
Mike Henderson; *Country Music Made Me Do It* . . . . (RCA)

I'll Be Your Jukebox Tonight
Barbara Mandrell; *I'll Be Your Jukebox Tonight* . . . . (Capitol)

I'm A Honky Tonk Girl
Loretta Lynn; *The Country Music Hall Of Fame-Loretta Lynn* . . . . (MCA)

Jerusalem On The Jukebox
Richard Thompson; *Amnesia* . . . . (Capitol)

Jones On The Jukebox
Becky Hobbs; *All Keyed Up* . . . . (RCA)

Juke
Charlie Musselwhite; *Stone Blues* . . . . (Vanguard)
Little Walter; *Best Of Little Walter* . . . . (Chess)

Juke Box Baby
Perry Como; *Perry Como's Greatest Hits* . . . . (RCA)

Juke Box Saturday Night
Glenn Miller; *Best Of Glenn Miller* . . . . (RCA)
  Glenn Miller-A Legendary Performer-#1 & 2 . . . . (Bluebird)
  Memorial-1944-1969 . . . . (Bluebird)
  This Is Glenn Miller . . . . (RCA)
Modernaires; *Big Bands' Greatest Hits-#1-C* . . . . (Columbia)

Juke Box Saturday Night
Roy Clark; *The Ultimate Roy Clark* . . . . (Bransounds)

Juke Joint Blues
Big Joe Turner; *Best Of Joe Turner* . . . . (Pablo)
Big Joe Turner & Others; *Nobody In Mind* . . . . (Pablo)

Juke Joint Jump
Elvin Bishop; *Juke Joint Jump* . . . . (Capricorn)
  Live! Raisin' Hell . . . . (Capricorn)

Jukebox
Michael Martin Murphey; *Land Of Enchantment* . . . . (Warner Bros.)

Jukebox Argument
Mickey Gilley; *ST/Urban Cowboy 2* . . . . (Epic)

Jukebox Charlie
Johnny Paycheck; *Johnny Paycheck Sings Jukebox Charlie And Other Songs*
  That Make The Jukebox Play . . . . (Little Darlin')

Jukebox Cinderella
Johnny Duncan; *Come A Little Bit Closer* . . . . (Columbia)

Jukebox Fury
Rickie Lee Jones; *The Magazine* . . . . (Warner Bros.)

Jukebox Gypsy
Lindisfarne; *Back & Fourth* . . . . (Atco)

Jukebox Has A 45
Clinton Gregory; *Freeborn Man* . . . . (Step One)

Jukebox Help Me Find My Baby
Rhythm Rockers; *Sun Rockabillies-#1-C* . . . . (Sun)

Jukebox Hero
Foreigner; *Classic Rock 1966-1988-C* . . . . (Atlantic)
Records . . . . (Atlantic)

Jukebox In My Mind
Alabama; *Pass It On Down* . . . . (BMG Special Prod.)

Jukebox Junkie
Ken Mellons; *Ken Mellons* . . . .(Epic)

Jukebox Music
Kinks; *Come Dancing With The Kinks-Best Of The Kinks 1977-1986* . . . (Arista)
Sleepwalker . . . . (Arista)

Jukebox Never Plays Home Sweet Home
Jack Greene; *45-#0016* . . . .(EMH)

Jukebox Played Along
Gene Watson; *Back In The Fire* . . . .(Warner Bros.)
Honky Tony Country . . . .(Warner Bros.)

Jukebox With A Country Song
Doug Stone; *I Thought It Was You* . . . .(Epic)

Jump Right Out Of This Jukebox
Dale Wheeler; *Memphis Country-C* . . . . (Sun)

Kindly Keep It Country
Vince Gill; *The Key* . . . .(MCA)

Let The Jukebox Keep On Playing
Carl Perkins; *Blue Suede Shoes* . . . . (Sun)
Memphis Country-C . . . . (Sun)

Little Old Wine Drinker Me
Dean Martin; *Dean Martin's Greatest Hits-#2* . . . . (Reprise)
Welcome To My World . . . . (Reprise)
Mel Tillis; *Best Of Mel Tillis* . . . .(MCA)

Love Or Something Like It
Kenny Rogers; *Kenny Rogers-Twenty Greatest Hits* . . . . (EMI)

Lyin' Jukebox
Hank Williams, Jr.; *Maverick* . . . . (Capricorn)

Me & The Jukebox
Leon Morris & Buzz Busby; *Honky Tonk Bluegrass* . . . . (Rounder)

Meanest Jukebox In Town
Johnny Paycheck; *Johnny Paycheck Sings Jukebox Charlie And Other Songs That Make The Jukebox Play* . . . .(Little Darlin')

Music! Music! Music!
Teresa Brewer; *Best Of Teresa Brewer* . . . . (MCA Jazz)

Old Rainbow Jukebox & You
John Schneider; *Memory Like You* . . . .(MCA)

On The Verge
Collin Raye; *I Think About You* . . . . (Epic)

Out With A Bang
David Lee Murphy; *Out With A Bang* . . . .(MCA)

Over At Herbie's Juke Joint
Donald Brown; *People Music* . . . . (Muse)

Party Crowd
David Lee Murphy; *Out With A Bang* . . . .(MCA)

People Like Us
Aaron Tippin; *People Like Us* . . . . (Lyric Street)

Play The Saddest Song On The Jukebox
Carmol Taylor; *Songwriter* . . . . (Elektra)

Please Mr. Please
Olivia Newton-John; *Back To Basics-Essential Collection 1971-1992* . .(Geffen)

Please Play The Jukebox
Jimmy Martin; *One Woman Man* . . . . (International Mktg. Group)

Prayer & A Juke Box
Little Anthony And The Imperials; *Best Of Little Anthony And The Imperials* . . . . (Rhino)
Forever Yours . . . . (Roulette)

Prop Me Up Beside The Jukebox (If I Die)
Joe Diffie; *Honky Tonk Attitude* . . . .(Epic)

Put A Nickel In The Jukebox
Sharon McNight; *Another Side Of Sharon McNight* . . . . (Glendale)
Presenting Sharon McNight . . . . (Glendale)

Put A Quarter In The Jukebox
Barry Manilow; *Barry Manilow's Greatest Hits-#2* . . . . (Arista)

Put A Quarter In The Jukebox
Buck Owens; *Hot Dog!* . . . . (Capitol)

Redneck Rhythm & Blues
Brooks & Dunn; *Borderline* . . . . (Arista)

Roll Over Beethoven
Beatles; *Beatles-Box Set* . . . . (Capitol)
Rock 'N' Roll Music . . . . (Capitol)
The Beatles At The Hollywood Bowl . . . . (Capitol)
The Beatles' Second Album . . . . (Capitol)
With The Beatles . . . . (Parlophone)
Byrds; *The Byrds* . . . . (Columbia)
Chuck Berry; *Chuck Berry-Golden Hits* . . . . (Mercury)
Chuck Berry's Greatest Hits . . . . (Everest)
Cruisin'-1956-C . . . . (Increase)
Oldies But Goodies-#10-C . . . . (Original Sound)
The Chess Box-Chuck Berry . . . . (Chess)
Electric Light Orchestra; *Afterglow* . . . .(Epic)
Ole ELO . . . . (Jet)

School Days
Chuck Berry; *Best Of Chuck Berry* . . . . (Gusto)
Billboard Top Rock 'N' Roll Hits-1957-C . . . . (Rhino)
Chuck Berry-Golden Hits . . . . (Mercury)
ST/Rock 'N' Roll High School . . . . (Sire)

Set 'Em Up Joe (B24)
Vern Gosdin; *Chiseled In Stone* . . . . (Columbia)
Greatest Country Hits Of The '80s-1988-C . . . . (Columbia)

Stoned At The Jukebox
Hank Williams, Jr.; *Best Of Hank Williams, Jr.* . . . . (Curb)
Best Of Hank Williams, Jr.-#1-Roots & Branches . . . . (Mercury)
Bocephus Box-Collection-1979-1992 . . . . (Capricorn)
Lone Wolf . . . . (WB/Curb)

Straight Tequila Night
John Anderson; *Seminole Wind* . . . .(BNA)
Today's Hot Country-C . . . . (K-Tel)

That's What Makes The Jukebox Play
Moe Bandy; *Honky Tonk Amnesia-The Hard Country Sound Of Moe Bandy* . . . . (Razor & Tie)

There Ain't No Country Music On This Jukebox
Tom T. Hall; *Storyteller, Poet, Philospher* . . . . (Mercury)

There's A Song On The Jukebox
David Wills; *Columbia Country Classics-#5-A New Tradition-C* . . . . (Columbia)

Two Dollars In The Jukebox
Eddie Rabbitt; *Best Of Eddie Rabbitt/Greatest Hits-II* . . . . (Warner Bros.)
Eddie Rabbitt's All-Time Greatest Hits . . . . (Warner Bros.)
Rocky Mountain Music . . . . (Elektra)
Ten Years Of Greatest Hits . . . . (Capitol)

Two Plays For A Quarter
Kathy Hart & The Bluestars; *Tonight I Want It All* . . . .(Biograph)

Warning Labels
Doug Stone; *From The Heart* . . . . (Epic)

Who Stole The Jukebox (From Lucy's Perfume Parlor)
Johnny Bond; *Johnny Gimble's Texas Honky-Tonk Hits-C* . . . . . (C.M.H. Prod.)

Wrong Night
Reba McEntire; *If You See Him* . . . . (MCA)

Wurlitzer Prize (I Don't Want To Get Over You)
Waylon Jennings; *Waylon & Willie* . . . . (RCA)

JUNGLES

See Also: AFRICA, ANIMALS: A-Z, NATURE, TREES

Animal Song
Savage Garden; *Affirmation* . . . . (Columbia)

Animals In Jungles
China Crisis; *Working With Fire & Steel* . . . . (Warner Bros.)

Back In Judy's Jungle
Brian Eno; *Desert Island Selection* . . . . (Editions E.G.)
Taking Tiger Mountain By Strategy . . . . (Editions E.G.)

Blues From The Rainforest
Merl Saunders; *Blues From The Rainforest-A Musical Suite* . . . . . (Sumertone)

Bungle In The Jungle
Jethro Tull; *20 Years Of Jethro Tull* . . . . (Chrysalis)
M.U.-The Best Of Jethro Tull . . . . (Chrysalis)
Original Masters . . . . (Chrysalis)
War Child . . . . (Chrysalis)

Bush Doctor
Peter Tosh; *Bush Doctor* . . . . (Rolling Stones)
Captured Live . . . . (EMI)
The Toughest . . . . (Capitol)

Concrete Jungle
Bob Marley & The Wailers; *Babylon By Bus* . . . . (Tuff Gong)
Catch A Fire . . . . (Tuff Gong)
Reggae Roots-C . . . . (Garland)
This Is Reggae Music-#1-C . . . . (Island)

Concrete Jungle
Anvil; *Best Of Metal Blade-#3-C* . . . . (Metal Blade)
Strength Of Steel . . . . (Metal Blade)

Concrete Jungle
Specials; *Specials* . . . . (Chrysalis)
ST/Dance Craze . . . . (Chrysalis)

Continuing Story Of Bungalow Bill, The
Beatles; *The Beatles (White Album)* . . . . (Capitol)

Cowboy In The Jungle
Jimmy Buffett; *Son Of A Son Of A Sailor* . . . . (MCA)

Gitarzan
Ray Stevens; *Dr. Demento Presents The Greatest Novelty Records-#3-1960s-C* . . . . (Rhino)
Ray Stevens' Greatest Hits . . . . (RCA)
Ray Stevens' Greatest Hits . . . . (MCA)

Greystoke
Soundtrack; *Greystoke-Legend Of Tarzan* . . . . (Warner Bros.)

Hobo Jungle
Band; *Northern Lights-Southern Cross* . . . . (Capitol)

In The Heat Of The Jungle
Chris Isaak; *Heart Shaped World* . . . . (Reprise)

Jungle
Ashford & Simpson; *Ashford & Simpson* . . . . (Capitol)

Solid Plus Seven . . . . (Capitol)
ST/Body Rock . . . . (EMI)
Jungle
Electric Light Orchestra; *Box Of Their Best* . . . . (Jet)
Out Of The Blue . . . . (Jet)
Jungle
Dwight Twilley Band; *Jungle* . . . . (EMI)
Jungle Boogie
Kool & The Gang; *Didn't It Blow Your Mind: Soul Hits Of The*
  '70s-#12-C . . . . (Rhino)
Everything Is-Greatest Hits . . . . (Mercury)
Kool & The Gang Spin Their Top Hits . . . .(De-Lite)
Jungle Boy
Bow Wow Wow; *I Want Candy*. . . . . (RCA)
Jungle Boy
John Eddie; *John Eddie* . . . . (Columbia)
Jungle Comes Alive
Jamaica Boys; *J Boys*. . . . . (Reprise)
Jungle Drums
Artie Shaw; *Begin The Beguine*. . . . .(Pro-Arte)
This Is Artie Shaw . . . . (Bluebird)
Jungle Fever
Stevie Wonder; *ST/Jungle Fever* . . . . (Motown)
Jungle Hop
Cramps; *Psychedelic Jungle/Gravest Hits*. . . . . (I.R.S.)
Jungle Line
Joni Mitchell; *Hissing Of Summer Lawns* . . . . (Asylum)
Jungle Love
Gladys Knight & The Pips; *Glad To Be* . . . . (Allegiance)
Letter Full Of Tears-Golden Classics . . . . (Collectables)
Jungle Love
Steve Miller Band; *Book Of Dreams* . . . . (Capitol)
Steve Miller Band-Gift Set . . . . (Capitol)
Steve Miller Band-Live . . . . (Capitol)
Steve Miller Band's Greatest Hits-1974-78 . . . . (Capitol)
Jungle Strut
Gene Ammons; *Brother Jug* . . . . (Prestige)
Gene Ammons' Greatest Hits . . . . (Prestige)
Jungle Strut
Santana; *Santana*. . . . . (Columbia)
Viva Santana! . . . . (Columbia)
Jungle Time
Neil Diamond; *Beautiful Noise* . . . . (Columbia)
Jungle Work
Warren Zevon; *Bad Luck Streak In Dancing School* . . . . (Asylum)
Jungle, The
Kiss; *Carnival Of Souls: The Final Sessions* . . . . (Mercury)
Jungleland
Bruce Springsteen; *Born To Run* . . . . (Columbia)
King Of The Jungle
Lester Davenport; *When The Blues Hit You* . . . . . (Earwig Music Co.)
Life In The Jungle
John Mayall's Bluesbreakers; *Chicago Line* . . . . (Island)
Livin' In The Jungle
Flo & Eddie And The Turtles; *History Of Flo & Eddie And The*
  Turtles . . . . (Rhino)
Oakland Jungle
Wild Boyz; *It Had To Be Done* . . . . (Volt)
Oh Jungleland
Simple Minds; *Simple Minds Live: In The City Of Light* . . . . . . (A&M)
One Jungle
Fixx; *Ink* . . . . (Impact)
Picnic In The Jungle
Snakefinger; *Chewing Hides The Sound* . . . . (Ralph)
Poor Tarzan
Little Charlie & The Nightcats; *All The Way Crazy* . . . . . . (Alligator)
Queen Of The Jungle
Zarkons; *Riders In The Long Black Parade* . . . . (Enigma)
Rockin' In The Jungle
Eternals; *WCBS FM 101 History Of Rock-Doo-Wop-#2-C* . . . . (Collectables)
Run Through The Jungle
Creedence Clearwater Revival; *1970* . . . . (Fantasy)
Cosmo's Factory . . . . (Fantasy)
Creedence Clearwater Revival-Chronicle . . . . (Fantasy)
More Creedence Gold . . . . (Fantasy)
Skokiaan
Four Lads; *16 Most Requested Songs Of The '50s-#2-C* . . . . (Legacy)
Space Safari
Nazareth; *Rampant* . . . . (A&M)
Stranded In The Jungle
Cadets; *Collectables Presents The History Of Rock-#2-C* . . . (Collectables)
Cruisin'-1956-C . . . . (Increase)
Oldies But Goodies-#1-C . . . . (Original Sound)
Original Rock 'N' Roll Hits Of The '50s-C . . . . (Roulette)
New York Dolls; *In Too Much Too Soon* . . . . (Mercury)
Live In NYC-1975 . . . . (Restless)
Surfin' Safari
Beach Boys; *Absolute Best-#1* . . . . (Capitol)

Endless Summer . . . .(Capitol)
Made In The U.S.A. . . . . (Capitol)
Monster Summer Hits-Wild Surf-C . . . . (Capitol)
Swingin' Safari
Billy Vaughn; *Best Of Billy Vaughn*. . . . . (MCA)
Billy Vaughn's Greatest Hits . . . .(Curb)
Tarzan & Jane
Sparks; *Angst In My Pants* . . . . (Atlantic)
Tarzan Boy
Baltimora; *Living In The Background* . . . . (Manhattan)
Tarzan Was A Bluesman
Timbuk 3; *Eden Alley*. . . . . (I.R.S.)
Tarzan's Nuts
Madness; *One Step Beyond* . . . . (Sire)
Theme From "Daktari"
Original Soundtrack; *Television's Greatest Hits-#2-C* . . . . . . (TVT)
Theme From "George Of The Jungle"
Original Soundtrack; *Television's Greatest Hits-#2-C* . . . . . . (TVT)
Theme From "Tarzan"
Original Soundtrack; *Television's Greatest Hits-#2-C* . . . . . . (TVT)
Welcome To The Jungle
Guns N' Roses; *Appetite For Destruction* . . . . (Geffen)
ST/Lean On Me . . . . (Warner Bros.)
Why Don't You Write Me
Simon & Garfunkel; *Bridge Over Troubled Water* . . . .(Columbia)
Wimoweh (Mbube)-The Lion Sleeps Tonight
Chet Atkins; *RCA Years* . . . . (RCA)
Kingston Trio; *Kingston Trio/From The Hungry i* . . . .(Capitol)
Nylons; *Seamless* . . . . (Open Air)
Pete Seeger; *Pete Seeger's Greatest Hits* . . . . (Columbia)
Tokens; *Billboard Top Rock 'N' Roll Hits-1961-C* . . . .(Rhino)
Nipper's Greatest Hits Of The '60s-#1-C . . . . (RCA)
Weavers; *Weavers' Greatest Hits* . . . . (Vanguard)

KILL, Murder

See Also: **ANGER, BLOOD, CAPITAL PUNISHMENT, CRIME,**
DEATH, DRUGS (various), FIGHT, GUNS, HATE, LAW & ORDER,
PRISON, REBELS, SUICIDE, WAR

"Murder", He Says
Roy Eldridge/Gene Krupa Orchestra/Anita O'Day; *Uptown* . . . .(Columbia)
(Man Who Shot) Liberty Valance
Gene Pitney; *Gene Pitney-Anthology 1961-1968*. . . . .(Rhino)
Gene Pitney's Greatest Hits . . . . (Evergreen Music)
Super Oldies Of The '60s-#9-C . . . . (Audio Fidelity)
Greg Kihn; *Glass House Rock* . . . .(Beserkley)
1913 Massacre
Arlo Guthrie; *Hobo's Lullaby* . . . . (Reprise)
Jack Elliot; *Tribute To Woody Guthrie-C*. . . . . (Warner Bros.)
Ramblin' Jack Elliott; *Greatest Songs Of Woody Guthrie-C* . . . .(Vanguard)
Woody Guthrie; *Struggle* . . . . (Smithsonian Folkways)
Adam Raised A Cain
Bruce Springsteen; *Darkness On The Edge Of Town* . . . .(Columbia)
American Skin (41 Shots)
Bruce Springsteen & The E Street Band; *Live In New York City* . . . . .(Columbia)
Angry Johnny
Poe; *Hello*. . . . . (Modern)
Annihilate This Week
Black Flag; *Loose Nut* . . . . (SST)
Another One In The Dark
Wallflowers; *The Wallflowers* . . . . (Virgin)
Bad Boyz
Shyne featuring Levy, Barrington; *Shyne* . . . . (Bad Boy/Arista)
Ballad Of Danny Bailey
Elton John; *Goodbye Yellow Brick Road* . . . . (Polydor)
Before You Kill Us All
Randy Travis; *This Is Me* . . . . (Warner Bros.)
Big Iron
Marty Robbins; *Columbia Country Classics-#3-Americana-C* . . . . . .(Columbia)
Gunfighter Ballads & Trail Songs . . . . (Legacy)
Marty Robbins' All-Time Greatest Hits . . . . (Columbia)
Marty Robbins-More Greatest Hits. . . . . (Columbia)
Billy The Kid
Marty Robbins; *Gunfighter Ballads & Trail Songs* . . . . (Legacy)
Blood On The Dance Floor
Michael Jackson; *Blood On The Dance Floor-HIStory...* . . . .(MJJ Music/Work)
Bohemian Rhapsody
Braids; *Here We Come* . . . .(Big Beat)
ST/High School High. . . . .(Big Beat)
Queen; *A Night At The Opera*. . . . .(Hollywood)
Classic Queen . . . .(Hollywood)
Live At Wembley '86 . . . .(Hollywood)
ST/Wayne's World. . . . . (Reprise)
Boom Bye Bye
Buju Banton; *Voice Of Jamaica* . . . .(Mercury)

Born In Chicago
George Thorogood & The Destroyers; *Boogie People* . . . .(EMI)
Paul Butterfield Blues Band; *Golden Butter* . . . . (Elektra)
Paul Butterfield Blues Band . . . . (Elektra)

Born To Kill
Damned; *Damned Damned Damned* . . . . (Frontier)
Final Damnation . . . .(Restless)

Born To Kill
Gillan; *Double Trouble* . . . .(Metal Blade)

Breakfast In Mayfair
Fairport Convention; *Babbacombe Lee* . . . . (A&M)
Fairport Convention-Chronicles . . . . (A&M)

Brenda's Got A Baby
Tupac; *2Pacalypse Now* . . . . (Priority)

Bullet In The Head
Rage Against The Machine; *Rage Against The Machine* . . (Epic Portrait Assoc.)

Bullet-Ridden Bodies
Accused; *Grinning Like An Undertaker* . . . . (Nastymix)

Careful With That Axe Eugene
Pink Floyd; *Relics* . . . . (Capitol)
Ummagumma . . . . (Capitol)

Cocaine Done Killed My Baby
Mance Lipscomb; *Texas Songwriter-#2* . . . . (Arhoolie)

Cold Hard Facts Of Life, The
Porter Wagoner; *Essential Porter Wagoner* . . . . (RCA)
Porter Wagoner's Greatest Hits . . . . (Pair)

Complicated Shadows
Elvis Costello & The Attractions; *The Sopranos-Music From The HBO
Original Series* . . . . (Sony Music Soundtrax)

Continuing Story Of Bungalow Bill, The
Beatles; *The Beatles (White Album)* . . . . (Capitol)

Cop Killer
Ice-T; *Body Count* . . . .(Warner Bros.)

Cortez The Killer
Neil Young & Crazy Horse; *Decade* . . . . (Reprise)
Live Rust . . . . (Reprise)
Zuma . . . . (Reprise)

Crush, Kill, Destroy
Elvis Hitler; *Hellbilly* . . . .(Restless)

Cure Me...Or Kill Me
Gilby Clarke; *Pawnshop Guitars* . . . . (Virgin)

Curiosity Killed The Cat
Curiosity Killed The Cat; *Keep Your Distance* . . . . (Mercury)

Cuts You Up
Peter Murphy; *Deep* . . . . (Beggar's Banquet)

Cuttin' Heads
John Mellencamp; *Cuttin' Heads* . . . . (Columbia)

Day That Curly Bill Shot Down Crazy Sam
Hollies; *Hollies* . . . .(Epic)

Delia's Gone
Johnny Cash; *American Recordings* . . . . (American)

Dial A Hitman
Big Audio Dynamite; *No. 10 Upping St.* . . . . (Columbia)

Dire Wolf
Grateful Dead; *Reckoning* . . . .(Arista)
Workingman's Dead . . . .(Warner Bros.)

Dirty Deeds Done Dirt Cheap
AC/DC; *Dirty Deeds Done Dirt Cheap* . . . . (Atlantic)

Disarm
Smashing Pumpkins; *Siamese Dream* . . . . (Virgin)

Disco Strangler
Eagles; *Long Run* . . . . (Asylum)

Disco's Out, Murder's In
Suicidal Tendencies; *Lights...Camera...Revolution* . . . .(Epic)

Divide & Conquer
Husker Du; *Flip Your Wig* . . . . (SST)

Don't Kill It Carol
Manfred Mann's Earth Band; *Angel Station* . . . .(Warner Bros.)

Don't Kill The Animals
Lene Lovich; *Animal Liberation-C* . . . . (Wax Trax)
Lene Lovich & Nina Hagen; *Tame Yourself-C* . . . . (Rhino)

Don't Kill The Whale
Yes; *Tormato* . . . . (Atlantic)
Yesshows . . . . (Atlantic)

Don't Slay That Potato
Tom Paxton; *One Million Lawyers & Other Disasters* . . . . . (Flying Fish)

Down By The River
Neil Young; *Decade* . . . . (Reprise)
Neil Young & Crazy Horse; *Everybody Knows This Is Nowhere* . . . . . . (Reprise)

Down By The Water
PJ Harvey; *ST/Basketball Diaries* . . . . (Island)
To Bring You My Love . . . . (Island)

Dressed To Kill
Nazareth; *Fool Circle* . . . . (A&M)
Nazareth-Classics-#16 . . . . (A&M)
'Snaz . . . . (A&M)

Dressed To Kill
Lita Ford; *Dancin' On The Edge* . . . . (Mercury)

El Paso
Grateful Dead; *Steal Your Face* . . . .(Grateful Dead)
Marty Robbins; *Billboard Top Country Hits-1960-C* . . . . (Rhino)
Gunfighter Ballads & Trail Songs . . . . (Legacy)
Marty Robbins' Biggest Hits . . . . (Columbia)
Radio Classics Of The '50s-C . . . . (Columbia)
Texas Super Hits-C . . . . (Columbia)

Ends
Everlast; *Whitey Ford Sings The Blues* . . . . (Tommy Boy)

Euthanasia Waltz
Brand X; *Livestock* . . . .(Blue Plate)
Unorthodox Behaviour . . . .(Blue Plate)

Everything I Love
Alan Jackson; *Everything I Love* . . . . (Arista)

Excitable Boy
Warren Zevon; *Excitable Boy* . . . .(Asylum)
Quiet Normal Life-Best Of Warren Zevon . . . .(Asylum)
Stand In The Fire . . . .(Asylum)

Folsom Prison Blues
Brooks & Dunn with Johnny Cash; *Red Hot + Country-C* . . . . (Mercury)
Johnny Cash; *Billboard Top Country Hits-1968-C* . . . . (Rhino)
Classic Cash-Hall Of Fame Series . . . . (Mercury)
Hot Tracks-Train Super Hits-C . . . . (Epic)
Jailhouse Rock (Hits From The Big House)-C . . . . (Sony Music Special Prod.)
Johnny Cash At Folsom Prison & San Quentin . . . . (Columbia)
Johnny Cash-Original Golden Hits-#1 . . . .(Sun)
Johnny Cash's Greatest Hits-#2 . . . . (Columbia)
Superbilly . . . .(Sun)
The Man In Black-His Greatest Hits . . . . (Legacy)

Frankie & Johnny
Brook Benton; *Endlessly-The Best Of Brook Benton* . . . . (Rhino)
Doc Watson; *Favorites-Doc Watson* . . . . (Liberty)
Jerry Lee Lewis; *Jerry Lee's Greatest!* . . . . (Rhino)

Genocide
Judas Priest; *Hero Hero* . . . . (RCA)
Sad Wings Of Destiny . . . . (RCA)
Unleashed In The East . . . . (Columbia)

Gettin' Away With Murder
Slaughterhouse; *Face Reality* . . . . (Metal Blade)

Ghostbusters
Ray Parker Jr.; *Chartbusters* . . . . (Arista)
Elvira Presents Haunted Hits-C . . . . (Rhino)
Greatest Movie Rock Hits-C . . . . (Rhino)
ST/Ghostbusters . . . . (Arista)

Gimme All Your Lovin' Or I Will Kill You
Macy Gray; *The Id.* . . . . (Epic)

Given To Fly
Pearl Jam; *Yield* . . . . (Epic)

Goodbye Earl
Dixie Chicks; *Fly* . . . . (Monument)

Harder Cards
Collin Raye; *Tracks* . . . . (Epic)

He Was My Brother
Simon & Garfunkel; *Wednesday Morning 3 A.M.* . . . . (Columbia)

Here Comes President Kill Again
XTC; *Oranges & Lemons* . . . . (Geffen)

Here Comes The Hotstepper
Ini Kamoze; *Here Comes The Hotstepper* . . . . (Columbia)
MTV Party To Go-#7-C . . . .(Tommy Boy)

Hey Joe
Jimi Hendrix; *Essential Jimi Hendrix, Volume 2* . . . .(Reprise)
Live At Winterland . . . . (Rykodisc)
Jimi Hendrix Experience; *Are You Experienced?* . . . . (Reprise)
Smash Hits . . . . (Reprise)
Love; *Best Of Love* . . . . (Rhino)

Hippie Killer
Suicidal Tendencies; *Freedumb* . . . .(Side One)

Hold Me, Thrill Me, Kiss Me, Kill Me
U2; *Number One Movie Hits-C* . . . . (ESX Entert.)
ST/Batman Forever . . . .(Atlantic)

Hook's Tango
Original Cast/Cyril Ritchard; *Peter Pan-The 1954 Broadway
Production* . . . . (RCA Victor)

How Come, How Long
Babyface & Stevie Wonder; *The Day* . . . . (Epic)

How To Kill A Radio Consultant
Public Enemy; *Apocalypse 91...The Enemy Strikes Black* . .(Def Jam/Columbia)
Greatest Misses . . . . (Chaos)

Hurricane
Bob Dylan; *Desire* . . . . (Columbia)

I Am A Predator
Ted Nugent; *Intensities In 10 Cities* . . . . (Epic)

I Don't Like Mondays
Bob Geldof & Johnny Fingers; *The Secret Policeman's Other Ball/The
Music* . . . . (Rhino)
Boomtown Rats; *Fine Art Of Surfacing* . . . . (Columbia)

I Hope You've Learned
Ricky Skaggs and Kentucky Thunder; *Bluegrass Rules!* . . . . (Rounder)

I Just Shot John Lennon
Cranberries; *To The Faithful Departed* . . . . (Island)
I Love A Murder Mystery
Jerry Lewis; *Capitol Collectors Series-Jerry Lewis* . . . . (Capitol)
I Shot The Sheriff
Bob Marley & The Wailers; *Bob Marley & The Wailers-Live* . . . . . (Tuff Gong)
   Legend: The Best Of Bob Marley & The Wailers . . . . (Island)
   This Is Reggae Music-#1-C . . . . (Island)
Eric Clapton; *461 Ocean Boulevard* . . . . (Polydor)
   Eric Clapton-Crossroads-C . . . . (Polydor)
   Time Pieces-#1-The Best Of Eric Clapton . . . . (Polydor)
Wailers; *Burnin'* . . . . (Tuff Gong)
If Drinkin' Don't Kill Me (Her Memory Will)
George Jones; *10 Years Of Hits* . . . . (Epic)
   I Am What I Am . . . . (Epic)
If I Had A Rocket Launcher (Central America)
Bruce Cockburn; *Stealing Fire* . . . . (Columbia)
   Waiting For A Miracle-Singles 1970-1987 . . . . (Gold Castle)
I'll Be Missing You
Puff Daddy & Family & Faith Evans & 112; *No Way Out* . . . . . (Bad Boy/Arista)
I'm The Man Who Murdered Love
XTC; *Wasp Star (Apple Venus Volume 2)* . . . . (Idea/TVT)
Indiana Wants Me
R. Dean Taylor; *Hard-To-Find Motown Classics-#2-C* . . . . (Motown)
   Super Hits Of The '70s-Have A Nice Day-#3-C . . . . (Rhino)
   Super Hits-#5-C . . . . (Gusto)
It's Gonna Kill Me
Filter; *Title Of Record* . . . . (Reprise)
I've Committed Murder
Macy Gray; *On How Life Is* . . . . (Epic)
Jeannie Needs A Shooter
Warren Zevon; *Bad Luck Streak In Dancing School* . . . . (Asylum)
   Stand In The Fire . . . . (Asylum)
Johnny 99
Bruce Springsteen; *Nebraska* . . . . (Columbia)
Bruce Springsteen & The E Street Band; *Bruce Springsteen & The E Street*
   Band Live/1975-85 . . . . (Legacy)
Johnny Cash; *Cover Me (Bruce Springsteen Tribute)-C* . . . . (Rhino)
Jungle, The
Kiss; *Carnival Of Souls: The Final Sessions* . . . . (Mercury)
Kill City
Iggy Pop & James Williamson; *Kill City* . . . . (Bomp)
Kill For Peace
Fugs; *Best Of Broadside 1962-1968: Anthems Of The American Underground*
   From The Pages Of Broadside Magazine-C . . . . (Smithsonian Folkways)
   Fugs . . . . (ESP Disk)
   Fugs 4 Rounders Score . . . . (ESP Disk)
Kill Surf City
Jesus & Mary Chain; *Barbed Wire Kisses* . . . . (Warner Bros.)
Kill The King
Rainbow; *Long Live Rock 'n' Roll* . . . . (Polydor)
   Rainbow-On Stage . . . . (Oyster)
Kill You
Eminem; *The Marshall Mathers LP* . . . . (Aftermath/Interscope)
Killed A Cat
Kenny Rankin; *Silver Morning* . . . . (Little David)
Killer
Alice Cooper; *Killer* . . . . (Warner Bros.)
Killer
Pat Travers; *Boom Boom...The Best Of* . . . . (Polydor)
Killer
Kiss; *Creatures Of The Night* . . . . (Casablanca)
Killer
Adamski; *Liveandirect* . . . . (MCA)
Killer
Seal; *Seal* . . . . (Sire)
Killer Cut
Charlie; *Fight Dirty* . . . . (Arista)
Killer Joe
Quincy Jones; *I Heard That!* . . . . (A&M)
   Quincy Jones-Classics-#3 . . . . (A&M)
   Quincy Jones-The Best . . . . (A&M)
   ST/Listen Up-The Lives Of Quincy Jones . . . . (Qwest)
   Walking In Space . . . . (A&M)
Killer Queen
Queen; *Live Killers* . . . . (Hollywood)
   Queen's Greatest Hits I & II . . . . (Hollywood)
   Sheer Heart Attack . . . . (Hollywood)
Killer Without A Cause
Thin Lizzy; *Bad Reputation* . . . . (Mercury)
Killer's Eyes
Kinks; *Give The People What They Want* . . . . (Arista)
Killer's Instinct
Pat Travers; *Heat In The Street* . . . . (Polydor)
Killin' Floor
Albert King; *Years Gone By* . . . . (Stax)
Howlin' Wolf; *Real Folk Blues-C* . . . . (Chess)
Jimi Hendrix; *Kiss The Sky* . . . . (Reprise)
   Live At Winterland . . . . (Rykodisc)

Jimi Hendrix Experience; *Radio One* . . . . (Rykodisc)
Killin' Time
Clint Black; *Killin' Time* . . . . (RCA)
   RCA Award Winners-C . . . . (RCA)
Killing An Arab
Cure; *Boys Don't Cry* . . . . (Elektra)
   Standing On A Beach-The Singles . . . . (Elektra)
Killing Machine
Judas Priest; *Hell Bent For Leather* . . . . (Columbia)
Killing Me Softly With His Song
Fugees; *Score* . . . . (Ruffhouse)
Luther Vandross; *Songs* . . . . (Epic)
Roberta Flack; *Atlantic Rhythm & Blues 1947-1974-#6 (1966-*
   1969)-C . . . . (Atlantic)
   Best Of Roberta Flack . . . . (Atlantic)
   Golden Age Of Black Music-1970-1975-C . . . . (Atlantic)
   Killing Me Softly . . . . (Atlantic)
Killing Moon
Echo & The Bunnymen; *Ocean Rain* . . . . (Sire)
   Songs To Learn & Sing-The Hits . . . . (Sire)
Killing Of Georgie
Rod Stewart; *Night On The Town* . . . . (Warner Bros.)
   Rod Stewart's Greatest Hits . . . . (Warner Bros.)
Killing The Blues
John Prine; *Pink Cadillac* . . . . (Asylum)
Shawn Colvin; *Cover Girl* . . . . (Columbia)
Killing The Fly
Union Underground; *...An Education In Rebellion* . . . . (Portrait)
Learning To Live Again
Garth Brooks; *The Chase* . . . . (Liberty)
Life In Prison
Byrds; *Jailhouse Rock (Hits From The Big*
   House)-C . . . . (Sony Music Special Prod.)
   Sweetheart Of The Rodeo . . . . (Columbia)
Life Takes A Life
Jon Butcher Axis; *Jon Butcher Axis* . . . . (Polydor)
Lily, Rosemary And The Jack Of Hearts
Bob Dylan; *Blood On The Tracks* . . . . (Columbia)
Little Girl, The
John Michael Montgomery; *Brand New Me* . . . . (Atlantic)
   Totally Hits-#3-C . . . . (Atlantic)
Little Things
Bush; *Sixteen Stone* . . . . (Trauma)
Loose Ends
Bruce Springsteen; *Tracks* . . . . (Columbia)
Loser
Beck; *Mellow Gold-C* . . . . (David Geffen Co.)
Love Is Blind
Eve; *First Lady Of Ruff Ryders* . . . . (Ruff Ryders/IDJMG)
Lovin' You Is Killing Me
Alabama; *Mountain Music* . . . . (RCA)
Mack The Knife
Bobby Darin; *Bobby Darin-At The Copa* . . . . (Bainbridge)
   Hit Singles-1958-1977-C . . . . (Atlantic)
   The Bobby Darin Story . . . . (Atlantic)
Frank Sinatra; *The Reprise Collection* . . . . (Reprise)
Louis Armstrong; *Best Of Louis Armstrong* . . . . (Vanguard)
Manslaughter
EPMD; *Business As Usual* . . . . (Def Jam)
Massacre
Thin Lizzy; *Johnny The Fox* . . . . (Warner Bros.)
   Live And Dangerous . . . . (Warner Bros.)
Matty Groves
Fairport Convention; *Fairport Convention-Chronicles* . . . . (A&M)
   Liege & Lief . . . . (A&M)
Maxwell's Silver Hammer
Beatles; *Abbey Road* . . . . (Parlophone)
Mommy, Can I Go Out & Kill Tonight
Misfits; *Walk Among Us* . . . . (Ruby)
Mr. Shorty
Marty Robbins; *The Drifter* . . . . (Koch International)
Murder
Selecter; *Selected Selections* . . . . (Chrysalis)
   Too Much Pressure . . . . (Chrysalis)
Murder
David Gilmour; *About Face* . . . . (Columbia)
Murder
General Public; *Hand To Mouth* . . . . (I.R.S.)
Murder
Cavedogs; *Soul Martini* . . . . (Capitol)
Murder
New Order; *Substance* . . . . (Qwest)
Murder (Or A Heart Attack)
Old 97's; *Fight Songs* . . . . (Elektra)
Murder By Numbers
Police; *Synchronicity* . . . . (A&M)
Murder By Suicide
Gary Richrath; *Only The Strong Survive* . . . . (Crescendo)

Murder Gonna Be My Crime
Sippie Wallace; *Women Be Wise* . . . . (Alligator)
Murder In High Heels
Kiss; *Animalize* . . . . (Mercury)
Murder In My Heart For The Judge
Lee Michaels; *Lee Michaels-Collection* . . . . (Rhino)
Moby Grape; *Wow* . . . . (Columbia)
Three Dog Night; *Jailhouse Rock (Hits From The Big
House)-C* . . . . (Sony Music Special Prod.)
Murder In The First Degree
Elvin Bishop; *Don't Let The Bossman Get You Down* . . . . (Alligator)
Murder In The Skies
Gary Moore; *Gary Moore-Early Years* . . . .(WTG)
We Want Moore . . . . (Virgin)
Murder Inc.
Murder Inc.; *Murder Inc.* . . . . (RCA)
Murder Incorporated
Bruce Springsteen; *Bruce Springsteen's Greatest Hits* . . . . (Columbia)
Murder Mystery
Velvet Underground; *The Velvet Underground* . . . . (Verve)
Murder Of Love
Propaganda; *Secret Wish* . . . . (Island)
Murder Of One
Counting Crows; *August And Everything After* . . . . (David Geffen Co.)
Murder On Music Row
George Strait & Alan Jackson; *Latest Greatest Straitest Hits* . . . .(MCA)
Murder One
Awesome Dre & The Hardcore Committee; *You Can't Hold
Me Back* . . . . (Priority)
Murder Rap
Above The Law; *Livin' Like Hustlers* . . . . (Ruthless)
Murder Story
Simple Minds; *Life In A Day* . . . . (Virgin)
Murder Style
Lords Of The New Church; *Method To Our Madness* . . . .(I.R.S.)
Murder Was The Case
Snoop Doggy Dogg; *Doggystyle* . . . . (Death Row)
Murder, Tonight, In The Trailer Park
Cowboy Junkies; *Black-Eyed Man* . . . . (RCA)
Murdered By Love
Gary Stewart; *Brand New* . . . . (Hightone)
Murderer's Confession
Original Broadway Cast; *Mystery Of Edwin Drood* . . . . (Polydor)
My Gift To You
Korn; *Follow The Leader* . . . .(Immortal/Epic)
My Guitar Wants To Kill Your Mama
Frank Zappa; *You Can't Do That On Stage Anymore-#4* . . . .(Rykodisc)
Mothers Of Invention; *Weasels Ripped My Flesh* . . . . (Bizarre/Straight)
Nebraska
Bruce Springsteen; *Nebraska* . . . . (Columbia)
Bruce Springsteen & The E Street Band; *Bruce Springsteen & The E Street
Band Live/1975-85* . . . . (Legacy)
Never Kill Another Man
Steve Miller Band; *Steve Miller Band-Anthology* . . . . (Capitol)
Steve Miller Band-Number 5 . . . . (Capitol)
New Timer
Bruce Springsteen; *The Ghost Of Tom Joad* . . . . (Columbia)
Night The Lights Went Out In Georgia
Lynn Anderson; *Top Of The World* . . . . (Columbia)
Reba McEntire; *For My Broken Heart* . . . .(MCA)
Reba McEntire's Greatest Hits-#3: I'm A Survivor . . . .(MCA)
Vicki Lawrence; *Super Hits Of The '70s-Have A Nice Day-#10-C* . . . . . . (Rhino)
Ninety Nine Years (Dead Or Alive)
Guy Mitchell; *Definitive Guy Mitchell* . . . . (Collector's Choice)
Nobody Knows But Me
Jimmie Rodgers; *Riding High-1929-1930* . . . . (Rounder)
Merle Haggard & The Strangers; *Same Train Different Time* . . . . (Capitol)
November 22, 1963
Original Cast; *Assassins* . . . . (RCA)
Oh! How I Hate To Get Up In The Morning
Irving Berlin; *American Songbook Series-Irving
Berlin* . . . .(Smithsonian Collection)
War Years-C . . . . (ISD/Intersound)
Soundtrack; *American Musical Theater-#2* . . . .(Smithsonian Collection)
One Of These Days
Pink Floyd; *Collection Of Great Dance Songs* . . . . (Columbia)
Delicate Sound Of Thunder . . . . (Columbia)
Meddle . . . . (Capitol)
Pink Floyd-Gift Set . . . . (Capitol)
Works . . . . (Capitol)
Overkill
Motorhead; *No Sleep At All* . . . . (Roadracer)
No Sleep 'Til Hammersmith . . . .(Castle Music America)
Overkill . . . .(Castle Music America)
Overkill
Men At Work; *Cargo* . . . . (Columbia)
Papa Loved Mama
Garth Brooks; *Garth Brooks-Double Live* . . . . (Capitol)

Ropin' The Wind . . . . (Liberty)
Pigs, Sheep & Wolves
Paul Simon; *You're The One* . . . . (Warner Bros.)
Pinkville Helicopter
Thom Parrott; *Best Of Broadside 1962-1968: Anthems Of The American
Underground From The Pages Of Broadside
Magazine-C* . . . .(Smithsonian Folkways)
Please
Chris Isaak; *Speak Of The Devil* . . . . (Reprise)
Po Lazarus
James Carter & The Prisoners; *ST/O Brother, Where Art Thou?* . . . . . . (Mercury)
Pocket Full Of Gold
Vince Gill; *Pocket Full Of Gold* . . . . (MCA)
Point Blank
Bruce Springsteen; *The River* . . . . (Columbia)
Poisoning Pigeons In The Park
Tom Lehrer; *Dr. Demento Presents The Greatest Novelty Records-C* . . . (Rhino)
Dr. Demento: 20th Anniversary Collection-C . . . . (Rhino)
Evening Wasted With Tom Lehrer . . . . (Reprise)
Pretty Polly
Judy Collins; *Who Knows Where The Time Goes* . . . . (Elektra)
Stanley Brothers; *Complete Columbia Stanley Brothers* . . . . (Legacy)
Folk Classics: Roots Of American Folk Music-C . . . . (Columbia)
Long Journey Home . . . . (Rebel)
Psycho Killer
Talking Heads; *'77* . . . . (Sire)
Name Of This Band Is Talking Heads . . . . (Sire)
ST/Stop Making Sense . . . . (Sire)
Psycho Man
Black Sabbath; *Reunion* . . . . (Epic)
Put Out The Fire
Queen; *Hot Space* . . . .(Hollywood)
Rock 'N' Roll Murder
Leaving Trains; *Loser Illusion-Pt. 0* . . . .(SST)
Rocky Raccoon
Beatles; *Beatles-Box Set* . . . . (Capitol)
The Beatles (White Album) . . . . (Capitol)
Salt On A Slug
Black Flag; *Family Man* . . . .(SST)
Salting Of The Slug
Riders In The Sky; *Cowboy Way* . . . . (MCA)
Search & Destroy
Dictators; *10 Roir Years-Anthology-C* . . . . (Roir)
Live-F..k 'Em If They Can't Take A Joke . . . . (Roir)
Manifest Destiny . . . . (Asylum)
Search & Destroy
Deadly Blessing; *Ascend From The Cauldron* . . . . (New Renaissance)
Search & Destroy
Overlords; *Organic?* . . . . (Antler Subway)
Search & Destroy
Iggy & The Stooges; *Raw Power* . . . . (Columbia)
Serial Killa
Snoop Doggy Dogg; *Doggystyle* . . . . (Death Row)
She's Just Killing Me
ZZ Top; *Rhythmeen* . . . .(RCA)
ST/From Dusk Till Dawn . . . .(Epic/Sony Music Soundtrax)
Shoot Her If She Runs
Climax Blues Band; *Tightly Knit* . . . . (Sire)
Sky Is A Poisonous Garden
Concrete Blonde; *Bloodletting* . . . . (I.R.S.)
Somebody Got Murdered
Clash; *On Broadway* . . . . (Epic)
Sandinista . . . . (Epic)
The Story Of The Clash, Volume 1 . . . . (Epic)
Somebody Killed Dewey Jones' Daughter
Lacy J. Dalton; *Takin' It Easy* . . . . (Columbia)
Speed Kills
Steve Gibbons Band; *Caught In The Act* . . . . (MCA)
St. George & The Dragonet
Stan Freberg; *Greatest Hits-Stan Freberg* . . . . (Curb)
Tip Of The Freberg: The Stan Freberg Collection-1951-1998 . . . . (Rhino)
Stagger Lee
Dion; *Dion-His Best* . . . . (Laurie)
Huey Lewis and the News; *Four Chords & Several Years Ago* . . . . (Elektra)
Ike & Tina Turner; *Best Of Ike & Tina Turner* . . . . (EMI)
Lloyd Price; *Billboard Top Rock 'N' Roll Hits-1959-C* . . . . (Rhino)
Collectables Presents The History Of Rock-#5-C . . . . (Collectables)
Lloyd Price's Greatest Hits . . . . (MCA)
Oldies But Goodies-#1-C . . . .(Original Sound)
Professor Longhair; *Rock 'N' Roll Gumbo* . . . . (Dancing Cat)
Wilson Pickett; *A Man & A Half-Best Of Wilson Pickett* . . . . (Rhino)
Strange Fruit
Billie Holiday; *History Of The Real Billie Holiday* . . . . (Verve)
Lady Sings The Blues . . . . (Verve)
Songbook . . . . (Verve)
Nina Simone; *Compact Jazz-Nina Simone* . . . . (Verve)
Siouxsie And The Banshees; *Through The Looking Glass* . . . . (Geffen)
Stranglehold
Ted Nugent; *Double Live Gonzo* . . . . (Epic)

Heavy Metal Memories-C. . . . . (Rhino)
Ted Nugent . . . . (Epic)
Stranglehold
Paul McCartney; *Press To Play*. . . . . (Capitol)
Style Kills
Robert Palmer; *Addictions-#1* . . . . (Island)
Theme From ''Murder, She Wrote''
Original Soundtrack; *CBS: The First 50 Years* . . . . (TVT)
Theme From ''Twin Peaks''
Original Soundtrack; *Television's Greatest Hits-#7-Cable Ready-C* . . . . . (TVT)
They're Hanging Me Tonight
Marty Robbins; *Gunfighter Ballads & Trail Songs* . . . . (Legacy)
This Drinkin' Will Kill Me
Dwight Yoakam; *Hillbilly Deluxe* . . . . (Reprise)
Thunder Rolls, The
Garth Brooks; *Garth Brooks-Double Live* . . . . (Capitol)
No Fences . . . . (Capitol)
Time To Kill
UK; *Night After Night* . . . . (Editions E.G.)
UK . . . . (Editions E.G.)
Time To Kill
Band; *Stage Fright*. . . . . (Capitol)
Time To Kill
Alice Cooper; *Raise Your Fist And Yell* . . . . (MCA)
To Kill A Hooker
N.W.A.; *Efil4zaggin* . . . . (Ruthless/Priority)
Tom Dooley
Doc Watson; *Doc Watson* . . . . (Vanguard)
Essential Doc Watson . . . . (Vanguard)
Out In The Country . . . . (Intermedia)
Kingston Trio; *Capitol Collectors Series-The Kingston Trio* . . . . (Capitol)
From The Hungry i . . . . (Capitol)
Kingston Trio's Greatest Hits . . . . (Curb)
Tom Dooley . . . . (Capitol)
Troubadours Of The Folk Era-#3-C . . . . (Rhino)
Tomb Of The Unknown Love
Cassell Webb; *Songs Of A Stranger*. . . . . (Venture)
Kenny Rogers; *The Heart Of The Matter*. . . . . (RCA)
Video Killed The Radio Star
Bruce Woolley & The Camera Club; *Bruce Woolley & The
Camera Club* . . . . (Columbia)
Buggles; *Age Of Plastic*. . . . . (Island)
Rock Of The '80s-#2-C . . . . (Priority)
The Island Story-1962-1987-25th Anniversary-C . . . . (Island)
View To A Kill
Duran Duran; *Decade* . . . . (Capitol)
ST/A View To A Kill . . . . (Capitol)
Virgin Killer
Scorpions; *Best Of The Scorpions* . . . . (RCA)
Virgin Killer . . . . (RCA)
Waitress, The
Tori Amos; *Under The Pink* . . . . (Atlantic)
Watch The Girl Destroy Me
Possum Dixon; *Possum Dixon*. (Interscope)
Whiskey In The Jar
Metallica; *Garage Inc.*. . . . . (Elektra)
Wolves
Garth Brooks; *No Fences*. . . . . (Capitol)
You Can't Kill Rock & Roll
Ozzy Osbourne; *Diary Of A Madman* . . . . (Jet)
Your Disease
Saliva; *Every Six Seconds* . . . . (Island/IDJMG)
Zoomin'
Lionel Richie; *Time* . . . . (Mercury)

KINGS, Kingdom, Princes

See Also: **BOSSES, CELEBRITIES: SPECIFIC, COUNTRIES: A-
Z, MEN'S NAMES: A-Z, POLITICS (various), POWER &
CONTROL, PRESIDENTS, PROTEST, QUEENS, ROYALTY,
SOCIAL CLASS: GENERAL**

All The King's Castles
Shawn Phillips; *Bright White*. . . . . (A&M)
All The King's Gardens
Joan Armatrading; *Whatever's For Us* . . . . (A&M)
All The King's Horses
Triumph; *Surveillance*. . . . . (MCA)
All The King's Horses
Nazareth; *Expect No Mercy*. . . . . (A&M)
All The King's Horses
Lynn Anderson; *Lynn Anderson's Greatest Hits-#2* . . . . (Columbia)
All The King's Horses
Firm; *Mean Business* . . . . (Atlantic)
All The King's Horses
Aretha Franklin; *Young, Gifted And Black* . . . . (Atlantic & Atco Remasters)

All The King's Weight
Andy Pratt; *Andy Pratt*. . . . . (Columbia)
Bob Wills Is Still The King
Clint Black & Asleep At The Wheel; *Ride With Bob-C* . . . . (DreamWorks/SKG)
Camelot
Original 1982 London Cast; *Camelot*. . . . . (Varese Sarabande)
Original Cast; *Camelot*. . . . . (Columbia)
Richard Burton; *Broadway Magic-The 1960s-C* . . . . (Columbia)
Richard Harris; *ST/Camelot* . . . . (Warner Bros.)
Cannibal King
Shivaree; *I Oughtta Give You A Shot...* . . . . (Capitol)
Capricorn Kings
Lee Wright; *45-#7628* . . . . (Prairie Dog)
Connecticut Yankee In The Court Of King Arthur
Robert Fripp & The League Of Crafty Guitarists; *Show Of
Hands* . . . . (Editions E.G.)
Court Of The Crimson King-Part 1
King Crimson; *In The Court Of The Crimson King-An Observation By King
Crimson* . . . . (Editions E.G.)
Crawling King Snake
Doors; *L.A. Woman* . . . . (Elektra)
John Lee Hooker; *Best Of John Lee Hooker*. . . . . (Crescendo)
World's Greatest Blues Singer . . . . (Vee-Jay)
Muddy Waters; *They Call Me Muddy Waters* . . . . (Chess)
Cry Baby Cry
Beatles; *The Beatles (White Album)* . . . . (Capitol)
Davy Crockett
Hermes Nye; *Ballads Of The Civil War-#1 & 2* . . . . (Smithsonian Folkways)
Electric Kingdom
Twilight 22; *Twilight 22*. . . . . (Vanguard)
Emperor Of Wyoming
Neil Young; *Neil Young*. . . . . (Reprise)
Emperor's New Clothes
Sinead O'Connor; *I Do Not Want What I Haven't Got*. . . . . (Ensign)
Every Man A King
Randy Newman; *Good Old Boys* . . . . (Reprise)
Everybody Wants To Rule The World
Tears For Fears; *Knebworth-The Album-C* . . . . (Polydor)
Music For The Miracle-C . . . . (Epic Portrait Assoc.)
Songs From The Big Chair . . . . (Mercury)
Farewell To Kings
Rush; *Farewell To Kings* . . . . (Mercury)
From A Jack To A King
Jim Reeves; *I Love You Because* . . . . (RCA)
Jim Reeves-Pure Gold . . . . (RCA)
Ned Miller; *Billboard Top Country Hits-1963-C* . . . . (Rhino)
Ricky Van Shelton; *Loving Proof* . . . . (Columbia)
Go Let It Out
Oasis; *Standing On The Shoulders Of Giants* . . . . (Epic)
Heroes
Wallflowers; *ST/Godzilla-The Album* . . . . (Epic/Sony Music Soundtrax)
I Just Can't Wait To Be King
Elton John; *ST/The Lion King* . . . . (Walt Disney)
I Used To Be A King
Graham Nash; *Songs For Beginners* . . . . (Atlantic)
I Wonder What The King Is Doing Tonight
Original Cast; *Camelot*. . . . . (Columbia)
Richard Harris; *ST/Camelot* . . . . (Warner Bros.)
If I Were King Of The Forest
Bert Lahr; *ST/The Wizard Of Oz* . . . . (Sony Music Special Prod.)
I'm A King Bee
Muddy Waters; *King Bee* . . . . (Blue Sky)
Rolling Stones; *England's Newest Hit Makers/The Rolling Stones* . . . . . (Abkco)
Slim Harpo; *Best Of Slim Harpo* . . . . (Rhino)
Blues Classics-C . . . . (K-Tel)
I'm Henry The VIII, I Am
Herman's Hermits; *Herman's Hermits-Their Greatest Hits* . . . . (Abkco)
Something Good Again . . . . (Abkco)
In The Hall Of The Mountain King
Duke Ellington; *Three Suites* . . . . (Columbia)
Electric Light Orchestra; *On The Third Day* . . . . (Jet)
Sounds Incorporated; *History Of British Rock-#3-C* . . . . (Rhino)
It's Good To Be King
Tom Petty; *Wildflowers* . . . . (Warner Bros.)
Jeremy
Pearl Jam; *Ten* . . . . (Epic Portrait Assoc.)
Kill The King
Rainbow; *Long Live Rock 'n' Roll* . . . . (Polydor)
Rainbow-On Stage . . . . (Oyster)
King
Count Basie; *Basie's Best*. . . . . (Pausa)
UB40; *1980-1983*. . . . . (A&M)
King & Queen
Moody Blues; *Caught Live Plus Five*. . . . . (Polydor)
King & Queen Of America
Eurythmics; *Eurythmics' Greatest Hits* . . . . (Arista)
We Too Are One . . . . (Arista)

King & Queen Of England
Sandy Denny; *Circle Dance-Hokey Pokey Charity-C* . . . . (Green Linnet)
King Cobra
King Cobra; *Powerhouse Music* . . . . (AJK Music)
King Cobra
Herbie Hancock; *Best Of Herbie Hancock-The Blue Note Years* . . . . (Blue Note)
King Cobra
Tom Scott & The L.A. Express; *Tom Scott & The L.A. Express* . . . . (Epic)
King Cockroach
Chick Corea Elektric Band; *Chick Corea Elektric Band* . . . . (GRP)
King Cool
Donnie Iris; *King Cool* . . . . (MCA)
King Cotton
Mormon Tabernacle Choir; *Stars And Stripes Forever* . . . . (Columbia)
King Creole
Elvis Presley; *Hits Like Never Before-Essential-#3* . . . . (RCA)
ST/King Creole . . . . (RCA)
The Great Performances . . . . (RCA)
The Other Sides-Worldwide Gold Award Hits, Vol. 2 . . . . (RCA)
King David
Judy Collins; *Bread & Roses* . . . . (Elektra)
King For A Day
Thompson Twins; *Here's To Future Days* . . . . (Arista)
King For A Day
XTC; *Oranges & Lemons* . . . . (Geffen)
King Has Lost His Crown
Abba; *Voulez-Vous* . . . . (Atlantic)
King Herod's Song
Original London Cast; *Jesus Christ Superstar* . . . . (MCA)
King Heroin
James Chance & The Contortions; *Live In New York* . . . . (Roir)
New York Rockers-C . . . . (Roir)
Soul Exorcism . . . . (Roir)
King Heroin
Jazzy Jeff; *On Fire* . . . . (Jive)
King Heroin
James Brown; *There It Is* . . . . (Polydor)
King Holiday
King Dream Chorus & The Holiday Crew; *45-#884442-7* . . . . (Mercury)
King Is Half-Undressed
Jellyfish; *Bellybutton* . . . . (Charisma)
King Kong
Frank Zappa; *Uncle Meat* . . . . (Barking Pumpkin)
You Can't Do That On Stage Anymore-#3 . . . . (Rykodisc)
King Kong
Kinks; *Kink Kronikles* . . . . (Reprise)
King Kong's Monkey
Gary U.S. Bonds; *45-#1031* . . . . (LeGrand)
King Midas In Reverse
Hollies; *Best Of The Hollies-#2* . . . . (EMI)
Hollies-Epic Anthology From The Original Master Tapes . . . . (Epic)
The Hollies' Greatest Hits . . . . (Epic)
King Must Die
Elton John; *Elton John* . . . . (Polydor)
Live In Australia With The Melbourne Symphony Orchestra . . . . (MCA)
King Nothing
Metallica; *Load* . . . . (Elektra)
King Of All
Al Green; *Truth N' Time* . . . . (Motown)
King Of All The World
Old 97's; *Satellite Rides* . . . . (Elektra)
King Of Hollywood
Eagles; *The Long Run* . . . . (Asylum)
King Of Kansas
Skywalk; *Fall Into Winter Jazz Sampler '88* . . . . (MCA)
King Of My Heart
Melba Moore; *Read My Lips* . . . . (Capitol)
King Of New Orleans
Better Than Ezra; *Friction, Baby* . . . . (Swell/Elektra)
King Of New York
Schoolly D; *How A Black Man Feels* . . . . (Capitol)
King Of Nothing
Seals & Crofts; *Seals & Crofts' Greatest Hits* . . . . (Warner Bros.)
King Of Oak Street
Kenny Rogers; *The Gambler* . . . . (EMI)
Kenny Rogers And The First Edition; *Country Songs* . . . . . (MCA Special Prod.)
King Of Oklahoma
Michael Franks; *Previously Unavailable* . . . . (DRG)
King Of Pain
Police; *Every Breath You Take-The Classics* . . . . (A&M)
MTV's Rock 'N' Roll To Go-C . . . . (Elektra)
Synchronicity . . . . (A&M)
King Of Paris
Jo Stafford; *By Request* . . . . (Corinthian)
King Of Rats
Neighborhoods; *Neighborhoods* . . . . (Third Stone)
King Of Rock
Run-D.M.C.; *King Of Rock* . . . . (Profile)

Mr. Magic's Rap Attack-C . . . . (Profile)
King Of Sleaze
Beat Farmers; *Loud & Plowed &...Live!* . . . . (Curb)
Poor & Famous . . . . (Curb)
King Of Sorrow
Sade; *Lovers Rock* . . . . (Epic)
King Of Soul
James Brown; *ST/Doctor Detroit* . . . . (Backstreet)
King Of The Castle
Soup Dragons; *This Is Our Art* . . . . (Sire)
King Of The Cowboys
Amazing Rhythm Aces; *Stacked Deck* . . . . (MCA)
Roy Rogers & Dusty Rogers; *Roy Rogers Tribute-C* . . . . (RCA)
King Of The Dogs
Spread Eagle; *Open To The Public* . . . . (MCA)
King Of The Dollar
School Of Fish; *School Of Fish* . . . . (Capitol)
King Of The Hill
Minutemen; *Ballot Result* . . . . (SST)
Project: Mersh . . . . (SST)
King Of The Hill
Roger McGuinn; *Back From Rio* . . . . (Arista)
King Of The Hill
Quiet Riot; *Quiet Riot* . . . . (Pasha)
King Of The Jungle
Lester Davenport; *When The Blues Hit You* . . . . (Earwig Music Co.)
King Of The Mountain
Bon Jovi; *7800 Degrees Fahrenheit* . . . . (Mercury)
King Of The Mountain
George Strait; *Blue Clear Sky* . . . . (MCA)
Latest Greatest Straitest Hits . . . . (MCA)
King Of The New York Streets
Dion; *Yo Frankie* . . . . (Arista)
King Of The Night Time World
Kiss; *Alive II* . . . . (Casablanca)
Destroyer . . . . (Casablanca)
King Of The Road
R.E.M.; *Dead Letter Office* . . . . (I.R.S.)
Roger Miller; *Billboard Top Country Hits-1965-C* . . . . (Rhino)
Cruisin'-1965-C . . . . (Increase)
Roger Miller-Golden Hits . . . . (Smash)
King Of The Silver Screen
Alice Cooper; *Lace And Whiskey* . . . . (Warner Bros.)
King Of The Surf Guitar
Dick Dale And The Del-Tones; *Beach Classics-All Original
Recordings-C* . . . . (Dunhill Compact Classics)
Dick Dale And The Del-Tones' Greatest Hits . . . . (Crescendo)
Tigers Loose . . . . (Rhino)
King Of The Wheels
Bobby Fuller Four; *Best Of The Bobby Fuller Four* . . . . (Rhino)
King Of The World
Steely Dan; *Countdown To Ecstasy* . . . . (MCA)
Steely Dan-Gold . . . . (MCA)
King Of Wishful Thinking
Go West; *ST/Pretty Woman* . . . . (EMI)
King Porter's Stomp
Benny Goodman; *Benny Goodman-Live At Carnegie Hall* . . . . (London)
Birth Of Swing . . . . (Bluebird)
The Birth Of Swing (1935-1936) . . . . (Bluebird)
This Is Benny Goodman . . . . (RCA)
King Tut
Steve Martin & Toot Uncommons; *Dr. Demento Presents The Greatest
Novelty Records-#4-1970s-C* . . . . (Rhino)
Dr. Demento Presents The Greatest Novelty Records-C . . . . (Rhino)
King Without A Queen
Lefty Frizzell; *Columbia Historic Edition-Lefty Frizzell* . . . . (Columbia)
Kingdom Come
David Bowie; *Scary Monsters* . . . . (Rykodisc)
Sound + Vision . . . . (Rykodisc)
Kingdom Hall
Van Morrison; *Wavelength* . . . . (Warner Bros.)
Kingdom Of Swing
Benny Goodman; *Complete Benny Goodman-#7* . . . . (RCA)
Complete Benny Goodman-#8 . . . . (RCA)
Kingfish
Randy Newman; *Good Old Boys* . . . . (Reprise)
Kings
Steely Dan; *Can't Buy A Thrill* . . . . (MCA)
Kings & Queens
Aerosmith; *Aerosmith-Classics Live* . . . . (Columbia)
Aerosmith's Greatest Hits . . . . (Columbia)
Draw The Line . . . . (Columbia)
King's Chorale
Mountain; *Best Of Mountain* . . . . (Columbia)
King's Highway
Tom Petty And The Heartbreakers; *Into The Great Wide Open* . . . . (MCA)
Kings Road
Tom Petty And The Heartbreakers; *Hard Promises* . . . . (MCA)

King's Song, The
Edward M. Favor; *Music From The New York Stage (1890-1920)-#1-1890-1908-C* . . . .(Pearl)
Kiss That Frog
Peter Gabriel; *Us* . . . . (Geffen)
Lord Of The Highway
Joe Ely; *Lord Of The Highway*. . . . . (Hightone)
Lord Of The Thighs
Aerosmith; *Aerosmith-Classics Live* . . . .(Columbia)
Gems . . . .(Columbia)
Get Your Wings . . . .(Columbia)
Live! Bootleg . . . .(Columbia)
Pandora's Box . . . .(Columbia)
Love Spreads
Stone Roses; *Second Coming* . . . . (Geffen)
Lovely Night, A
Julie Andrews; *A Little Bit Of Broadway*. . . . .(Columbia)
Julie Andrews/Original Cast; *Cinderella-The CBS Television Production* . . . .(Columbia)
Midas Touch
Original Cast; *Bells Are Ringing* . . . .(Columbia)
Midas Touch
Midnight Star; *Anniversary Collection* . . . .(Right Stuff)
Most High
Jimmy Page/Robert Plant; *Walking Into Clarksdale* . . . . (Atlantic)
Motel King
James Harman Band; *Do Not Disturb* . . . .(Black Top)
My Kingdom
Echo & The Bunnymen; *Ocean Rain*. . . . .(Sire)
My Kingdom Come
Lords Of The New Church; *Method To Our Madness* . . . . (I.R.S.)
My Kingdom For A Car
Gene Parsons; *Melodies*. . . . . (Sierra)
My Kingdom For A Car
Jason & The Scorchers; *Thunder & Fire* . . . . (A&M)
My Kingdom For A Car
Phil Ochs; *Phil Ochs' Greatest Hits* . . . . (A&M)
My Lord & Master
Barbra Streisand; *People* . . . .(Columbia)
Original Broadway Cast; *The King And I* . . . . (RCA Victor)
Original Cast; *The King And I* . . . . (MCA)
Nasty Dogs & Funky Kings
ZZ Top; *Fandango* . . . . (Warner Bros.)
Six Pack . . . . (Warner Bros.)
Oh King Richard
Rodney Crowell; *Hot Country Rock-#2-C*. . . . . (Epic)
Street Language . . . .(Columbia)
Old King Cole
Original Soundtrack; *Children's Favorites* . . . . (Kid Rhino/Rhino 4 Kids)
Orange King
Cafe Noir; *Window To The Sea* . . . . (Carpe Diem)
Out To Bomb Fresh Kings
Doctor Nerve; *Armed Observation* . . . . (Cuneiform)
Palace Of The King
Freddie King; *Best Of Freddie King* . . . . (MCA)
Pharaoh's Host Got Lost
Lawrence McKiver; *Every Tone A Testimony-C* . . . . . .(Smithsonian Folkways)
Pinball Wizard
Elton John; *Elton John's Greatest Hits-#2* . . . . (Polydor)
Pete Townshend; *Another Scoop*. . . . . (Atco)
Pete Townshend's Deep End Live! . . . . (Atco)
Rod Stewart; *Best Of Rod Stewart* . . . .(Mercury)
Sing It Again, Rod. . . . .(Mercury)
Storyteller/The Complete Anthology: 1964-1990 . . . . (Warner Bros.)
Who; *Meaty Beaty Big & Bouncy* . . . . (MCA)
ST/The Kids Are Alright . . . . (MCA)
ST/Tommy . . . . (Polydor)
Tommy . . . . (MCA)
Who Greatest Hits. . . . . (MCA)
Who's Last . . . . (MCA)
Possum Kingdom
Toadies; *ESPN Presents X Games-#1-C* . . . .(Tommy Boy)
Rubberneck. . . . . (Interscope)
Precious Time
Van Morrison; *Back On Top* . . . .(Point Blank/Virgin)
Prince Charming
Adam Ant; *Antics In The Forbidden Zone* . . . . (Epic)
Prince Charming . . . . (Epic)
Prince Is Giving A Ball
Television Cast; *Cinderella-The CBS Television Network Production* . . . .(Columbia)
Prince Of Darkness
Nylons; *Best Of The Nylons*. (Open Air)
One Size Fits All . . . . (Open Air)
Prince Of Darkness
Indigo Girls; *Back On The Bus Y'All* . . . . (Epic)
Indigo Girls . . . . (Epic)
Prince Of Darkness
Big Daddy Kane; *Prince Of Darkness*. . . . .(Cold Chillin')

Prince Of Darkness
Alice Cooper; *Raise Your Fist And Yell* . . . . (MCA)
Prince Of Darkness
Miles Davis; *Sorcerer* . . . .(Columbia)
Prince Of The Punks
Kinks; *One For The Road* . . . .(Arista)
Prince Of Tides
Jimmy Buffett; *Hot Water* . . . . (MCA)
Prince Of Whales
Joachim Kuhn; *Dynamics* . . . .(Creative Music Prod.)
Prince Of Whales
Amy & Leslie; *Amy & Leslie* . . . . (Alcazar)
Princes Of The Universe
Queen; *A Kind Of Magic* . . . .(Hollywood)
Radio Kingdom
Beach Boys; *Holland* . . . . (Brother)
Rain King
Counting Crows; *August And Everything After* . . . . (David Geffen Co.)
Rascal King
Mighty Mighty Bosstones; *Let's Face It* . . . . (Big Rig/Mercury)
Live From The Middle East . . . . (Big Rig/Mercury)
Riding With The King
John Hiatt; *Riding With The King*. . . . . (Geffen)
Y'All Caught? Ones That Got Away, 1979-85 . . . . (Geffen)
Riding With The King
B.B. King & Eric Clapton; *Riding With The King*. . . . .(Duck/Reprise)
Rock 'N' Roll Is King
Electric Light Orchestra; *Afterglow* . . . . (Epic)
Secret Messages . . . . (Jet)
Satan's Kingdom
Jimmy Cliff; *I Am The Living* . . . . (MCA)
Seven-And-A-Half Cents
John Raitt; *ST/Pajama Game* . . . .(Collectables)
Original Cast; *Pajama Game* . . . .(Columbia)
Sing A Song Of Sixpence
Original Soundtrack; *Children's Favorites* . . . . (Kid Rhino/Rhino 4 Kids)
Someday My Prince Will Come
Bill Evans Trio; *Portrait In Jazz* . . . .(Riverside)
En Vogue; *Simply Mad About The Mouse-C* . . . .(Columbia)
Lena Horne; *A New Album* . . . . (RCA)
Lena Horne & Phil Woods; *I Have Dreamed* . . . .(Novus)
Miles Davis; *I Like Jazz-Essence Of Miles Davis*. . . . .(Columbia)
Miles Davis' Greatest Hits . . . .(Columbia)
Someday My Prince Will Come . . . .(Columbia)
Mormon Tabernacle Choir & Columbia Symphony Orchestra; *When You Wish Upon A Star-A Tribute To Walt Disney* . . . . (CBS Masterworks)
Speed King
Deep Purple; *Deepest Purple/The Very Best Of Deep Purple* . . . .(Warner Bros.)
In Rock . . . . (Warner Bros.)
Suburban King
Pat Benatar; *Tropico* . . . .(Chrysalis)
Sun King
Beatles; *Abbey Road* . . . . (Parlophone)
Beatles-Box Set . . . .(Capitol)
Sun King
Cult; *Sonic Temple* . . . . (Sire)
Temple Of The King
Blackmore's Rainbow; *Ritchie Blackmore's R-A-I-N-B-O-W* . . . . (Polydor)
Theme From ''Fresh Prince Of Bel-Air''
Original Soundtrack; *Television's Greatest Hits-#7-Cable Ready-C* . . . . .(TVT)
Trash Can King
Nick Seeger; *Sail On Flying Dutchman* . . . . (Biograph)
TV Is King
Tubes; *Remote Control* . . . .(A&M)
Two Princes
Spin Doctors; *Pocket Full Of Kryptonite* . . . .(Epic Portrait Assoc.)
Your Love Is King
Sade; *Diamond Life* . . . .(Portrait)

KISSING, Making Out

See Also: **ANATOMY (various), DESIRE, LOVE (various), PARENTS: CONCERNED ABOUT TEEN LOVE, SEX, SEX: RESISTING TEMPTATION**

('Til) I Kissed You
Everly Brothers; *Everly Brothers-Cadence Classics-Their 20 Greatest Hits* . . . .(Rhino)
Fabulous Style Of The Everly Brothers . . . .(Rhino)
Very Best Of The Everly Brothers . . . . (Warner Bros.)
All At Once You Love Her
Perry Como; *Perry Como's Greatest Hits* . . . . (RCA)
All I've Got To Do
Beatles; *Meet The Beatles!* . . . .(Capitol)
All My Loving
Beatles; *Meet The Beatles!* . . . .(Capitol)

The Beatles At The Hollywood Bowl . . . . (Capitol)
The Beatles/1962-1966 . . . . (Capitol)
With The Beatles . . . . (Parlophone)

All The Places (I Will Kiss You)
Aaron Hall; *Inside Of You* . . . .(MCA)

Always Late (With Your Kisses)
Dwight Yoakam; *Hillbilly Deluxe* . . . . (Reprise)
Jo-el Sonnier; *Jo-el Sonnier-Complete Mercury Sessions* . . . . (Mercury)
Lefty Frizzell; *American Originals-Lefty Frizzell* . . . . (Columbia)
Best Of Lefty Frizzell . . . . (Rhino)
Lefty Frizzell's Greatest Hits . . . . (Columbia)
Willie Nelson; *To Lefty From Willie* . . . . (Columbia)

As We Kiss Goodnight
Iguanas; *Nuevo Boogaloo* . . . .(Margaritaville)

Ask Of You
Raphael Saadiq; *ST/Higher Learning* . . . .(550 Music)

Baby's Smile Woman's Kiss
Johnny Duncan; *Best Of Johnny Duncan* . . . . (Columbia)

Before I Let You Go
Blackstreet; *Blackstreet* . . . . (Interscope)

Besame Mucho
Beatles; *The Beatles-Anthology-#1* . . . . (Capitol)

Blowing Kisses In The Wind
Paula Abdul; *Spellbound* . . . . (Captive)

Blue Kiss
Jane Wiedlin; *Jane Wiedlin* . . . .(I.R.S.)

Blue Kiss
Chuck Loeb; *Listen.* . . . . (Shanachie)

Botcha-A-Me (Ba-Ba-Baciami Piccina)
Rosemary Clooney; *Rosemary Clooney-16 Most Requested Songs* . . . . (Legacy)

Boys
Beatles; *Beatles-Box Set* . . . . (Capitol)
Please Please Me . . . . (Parlophone)
Rock 'N' Roll Music . . . . (Capitol)
The Beatles At The Hollywood Bowl . . . . (Capitol)
The Early Beatles . . . . (Capitol)
Shirelles; *Shirelles-Anthology 1959-1964* . . . . (Rhino)

Breathless
Corrs; *In Blue* . . . .(143/Lava/Atlantic)
Totally Hits-#3-C . . . . (Atlantic)

But I Do Love You
LeAnn Rimes; *I Need You.* . . . . (Curb)

Butterflies
Michael Jackson; *Invincible.* . . . .(Epic)

Butterfly Kisses
Bob Carlisle; *Butterfly Kisses (Shades Of Grace)* . . . .(DMG/Jive)

Candy Kisses
Tony Bennett; *I Left My Heart In San Francisco* . . . . (Columbia)

Candy Kisses
Elton Britt; *The RCA Years* . . . . (Collector's Choice)
George Morgan; *Room Full Of Roses-The George Morgan
Collection* . . . . (Razor & Tie)
Lorrie Morgan; *Essential Lorrie Morgan* . . . . (RCA)
Roy Rogers; *Best Of Roy Rogers* . . . . (Curb)

Candy Man
Fred Neil; *Little Bit Of Rain* . . . . (Elektra)
Mickey Gilley & Charly McClain; *It Takes Believers* . . . .(Epic)
Roy Orbison; *In Dreams-Greatest Hits* . . . . (Orbison)
Roy Orbison Greatest Hits . . . . (Monument)
Roy Orbison's All-Time Greatest Hits-#1 & 2 . . . . (Monument)
Very Best Of Roy Orbison . . . . (Monument)

Coffee & Kisses
Duke Ellington & His Orchestra; *Happy Birthday Duke-Birthday
Sessions-#4* . . . . (Laserlight)

Could I Have This Kiss Forever
Whitney Houston & Enrique Iglesias; *Whitney Houston's
Greatest Hits* . . . . (Arista)

Cousin Dupree
Steely Dan; *Two Against Nature.* . . . .(Giant)

Cover You In Kisses
John Michael Montgomery; *Leave A Mark.* . . . . (Atlantic)

Do It Again A Little Bit Slower
Jon, Robin & The In Crowd; *Dick Bartley's One-Hit Wonders Of The
'60s-#1-C* . . . . (Rhino)

Don't Get Me Started
Rhett Akins; *Somebody New.* . . . . (Decca)

Every Little Kiss
Bruce Hornsby & The Range; *The Way It Is* . . . . (RCA)

Fire
Bruce Springsteen & The E Street Band; *Bruce Springsteen & The E Street
Band Live/1975-85* . . . . (Legacy)
Pointer Sisters; *Cover Me (Bruce Springsteen Tribute)-C* . . . . (Rhino)
Energy . . . . (Planet)
I Am Woman-C. . . . . (Nick At Nite)

For Your Love
Ed Townsend; *The Glory Of Love-'50s Sweet & Soulful Love
Songs-C.* . . . . (Hip-O)
Peaches & Herb; *The Glory Of Love-'60s Sweet & Soulful Love
Songs-C.* . . . . (Hip-O)

French Kiss
Lil Louis & His World; *This Beat Is Hot-C* . . . . (Epic)

Georgy Porgy
Eric Benet featuring Faith Evans; *A Day In The Life* . . . . . (Warner Bros.)
Toto; *Past To Present 1977-1990* . . . . (Columbia)
Toto . . . .(Columbia)

Give Him A Great Big Kiss
Shangri-Las; *Best Of The Girl Groups-#1-C* . . . . (Rhino)
Remember The Shangri-Las At Their Best . . . . (Collectables)

Give The Girl A Kiss
Bruce Springsteen; *Tracks* . . . . (Columbia)

Heart And Soul
Cleftones; *Echoes Of A Rock Era-Later Years-C* . . . . (Roulette)
ST/American Graffiti . . . . (MCA)
Four Aces; *Four Aces' 20 Greatest Hits* . . . . (Everest)
Huey Lewis and the News; *Sports.* . . . . (Chrysalis)
Jan & Dean; *Best Of Jan & Dean* . . . . (EMI)
Oldies But Goodies-#9-C . . . .(Original Sound)
Larry Clinton & His Orchestra; *The Hoagy Carmichael
Songbook-C.* . . . . (Bluebird)

Hold Me, Thrill Me, Kiss Me
Mel Carter; *Baby Boomer Classics-Love Sixties-C* . . . .(JCI Assoc. Labels)

Hold Me, Thrill Me, Kiss Me, Kill Me
U2; *Number One Movie Hits-C* . . . . (ESX Entert.)
ST/Batman Forever . . . .(Atlantic)

Honey To The Bee
Billie; *Honey To The B* . . . .(Virgin)

I Kissed A Girl
Jill Sobule; *Jill Sobule* . . . . Lava)
Lesbian Favorites-Women Like Us-C. . . . . (Rhino)

I Kissed The Bus
Geezinslaw Brothers; *Feelin' Good, Gittin' Up, Gittin' Down* . . . .(Step One)

I Should Have Known Better
Beatles; *A Hard Day's Night.* . . . . (Parlophone)

I Wanna Be Loved By You
Helen Kane; *Nipper's Greatest Hits Of The '20s-#1-C* . . . . (RCA)

I Was Born When You Kissed Me
Whispers; *Excellence* . . . . (Allegiance)
Shhhh . . . . (Dore)

I Wonder Who's Kissing Her Now
Bobby Darin; *Capitol Collectors Series-Bobby Darin* . . . . (Capitol)
Ted Weems & His Orchestra; *Sweetest Sounds Ever Heard-C* . . . . (Hip-O)

In France They Kiss On Main Street
Joni Mitchell; *Hissing Of Summer Lawns* . . . .(Asylum)
Shadows & Light . . . .(Asylum)

Innamorata
Dean Martin; *Capitol Collectors Series-Dean Martin.* . . . . (Capitol)
Dean Martin's All Time Greatest Hits . . . . (Curb)
Jerry Vale; *Essence Of Jerry Vale* . . . . (Legacy)
Jerry Vale-17 Most Requested Songs . . . . (Legacy)
Jerry Vale's Greatest Hits . . . . (Columbia)

Is Zat You, Myrtle
Carlisles; *45-#70174* . . . . (Mercury)
Louvin Brothers; *Live At New River Ranch.* . . . . (Copper Creek)

It's Been A Long, Long Time
Bing Crosby; *Best Of Bing Crosby* . . . . (MCA)
Harry James & His Orchestra; *Words & Music Of World
War II-C* . . . . (Columbia)
Harry James & Kitty Kallen; *Best Of The Big Bands-C.* . . . . (Columbia)
Jan Garber & His Orchestra; *Best Of Jan Garber* . . . . (MCA)
Louis Armstrong; *Hello Dolly! & Other Hits* . . . . (MCA)

It's In His Kiss (Shoop Shoop Song)
Betty Everett; *Billboard Top R&B Hits-1964-C* . . . . (Rhino)
Hits Of The Sixties-C . . . . (Intercom Music)
More American Graffiti-C . . . . (MCA)
Oldies But Goodies-#3-C . . . .(Original Sound)
Very Best Of Betty Everett . . . . (Vee-Jay)
Wonder Women-History Of Girl Group Sound-C. . . . . (Rhino)
Cher; *ST/Mermaids* . . . . (Geffen)
Vonda Shepard; *ST/Songs From ''Ally McBeal'' Featuring Vonda
Shepard* . . . .(550/Epic)

Keep The Ball Rollin'
Jay And The Techniques; *Bubblegum Classics-#4-C* . . . .(Varese Vintage)

Kiss
Prince and the Revolution; *Around The World In A Day* . . . . (Paisley Park)
Parade-Music From ''Under The Cherry Moon'' . . . . (Paisley Park)

Kiss
Cure; *Kiss Me Kiss Me Kiss Me.* . . . . (Elektra)

Kiss
Tom Jones; *Move Closer.* . . . .(Jive)

Kiss An Angel Good Mornin'
Charley Pride; *Charley Pride-24 Greatest Hits* . . . . (Tee Vee)
Pride! My 6 Latest And 6 Greatest . . . .(ISD/Intersound)
The Ultimate Charley Pride . . . .(Bransounds)

Kiss And Say Goodbye
Manhattans; *Best Of The Manhattans-Kiss And Say Goodbye* . . . . (Legacy)
Manhattans Greatest Hits . . . . (Columbia)

Kiss Away The Pain
Patti LaBelle; *Winner In You.* . . . . (MCA)

Kiss For Cinderella
Michael Tilson Thomas; *Of Thee I Sing/Let 'Em Eat Cake* . . . . (Columbia)
Kiss From A Rose
Seal; *Seal 2* . . . .(Sire)
Kiss Him Goodbye
Nylons; *Happy Together* . . . . (Open Air)
Kiss Me
Original Cast; *Sweeney Todd* . . . .(RCA)
Kiss Me
Sixpence None The Richer; *Sixpence None The Richer* . . . . . . (Squint/Columbia)
Songs From Dawson's Creek . . . .(Sony Music Soundtrax)
Kiss Me
Gutterboy; *Gutterboy* . . . . (Mercury)
Kiss Me
Indecent Obsession; *Indio* . . . . (MCA)
Kiss Me
Whycliffe; *Rough Side* . . . . (MCA)
Kiss Me
El Cincos; *Taste Of Doo Wop-#1-C* . . . . (Vee-Jay)
Kiss Me Again
101 Strings Orchestra; *World's Greatest Standards* . . . . (Alshire)
Victor Herbert; *Victor Herbert* . . . . (Alshire)
Wayne King & His Orchestra; *Best Of Wayne King* . . . . (MCA)
Kiss Me Baby
Beach Boys; *Best Of The Beach Boys* . . . . (Capitol)
Dance Dance Dance . . . . (Capitol)
Today/Summer Days (& Summer Nights!) . . . . (Capitol)
Kiss Me Deadly
Lita Ford; *Best Of Lita Ford* . . . . (Dreamland)
Lita . . . . (Dreamland)
Kiss Me In The Car
John Berry; *John Berry* . . . . (Liberty)
Kiss Me In The Rain
Barbra Streisand; *Wet* . . . . (Columbia)
Kiss Me On The Bus
Replacements; *Tim* . . . .(Sire)
Kiss Me, I'm Gone
Marty Stuart; *Love And Luck* . . . . (MCA)
Kiss Of Fire
Georgia Gibbs; *Best Of Georgia Gibbs-The Mercury Years* . . . . (Chronicles)
Tony Martin; *Best Of Tony Martin On RCA* . . . . (Collector's Choice)
Kiss On My List
Daryl Hall & John Oates; *Rock 'N Soul, Part 1* . . . . (RCA)
Voices . . . . (RCA)
Kiss That Frog
Peter Gabriel; *Us* . . . . (Geffen)
Kiss The Bride
Elton John; *Elton John's Greatest Hits-1976-1986* . . . . (MCA)
Too Low For Zero . . . . (MCA)
Kiss The Rain
Billie Myers; *A Taste Of '98-C* . . . . (Universal)
Growing Pains . . . . (Universal)
Kiss The World Goodbye
Kris Kristofferson; *Border Lord* . . . . (Columbia)
Kiss Them For Me
Siouxsie And The Banshees; *Superstition* . . . . (Geffen)
Kiss This
Aaron Tippin; *People Like Us* . . . . (Lyric Street)
Kiss To Build A Dream On
Louis Armstrong; *Best Of Louis Armstrong* . . . . (MCA)
Essential Louis Armstrong . . . . (Vanguard)
Hello Dolly! & Other Hits . . . . (MCA)
Kiss You All Over
Exile; *Best Of Exile* . . . . (MCA)
Exile's Greatest Hits . . . . (MCA)
Mixed Emotions . . . . (MCA)
Kiss Your Past Good-Bye
Aerosmith; *Nine Lives* . . . . (Columbia)
Kisses In The Rain
Rick Braun; *Kisses In The Rain* . . . . (Warner Bros.)
Kisses Sweeter Than Wine
Jimmie Rodgers; *Best Of Jimmie Rodgers* . . . . (Rhino)
Cruisin'-1958-C . . . . (Increase)
Weavers; *Best Of The Weavers* . . . . (MCA)
Reunion-At Carnegie Hall-1963 . . . . (Vanguard)
Weavers At Carnegie Hall . . . . (Vanguard)
Weavers' Greatest Hits . . . . (Vanguard)
Kissin' Cousins
Elvis Presley; *Command Performances-Essential 60's Masters II* . . . .(RCA)
Kissin' You
Total; *Total* . . . . (Bad Boy/Arista)
Kissing A Fool
George Michael; *Faith* . . . . (Columbia)
Kissing You
Keith Washington; *Make Time For Love* . . . .(Qwest)
Knock Me A Kiss
Gene Krupa Orchestra & Roy Eldridge; *1940s-The Singers-C* . . . . . . (Columbia)
Louis Jordan; *Best Of Louis Jordan* . . . . (MCA)

No Moe! Louis Jordan's Greatest Hits . . . .(Verve)
Language Of The Kiss
Indigo Girls; *Swamp Ophelia* . . . .(Epic)
Last Kiss
J. Frank Wilson and The Cavaliers; *Billboard Top Rock 'N' Roll Hits-*
1964-C . . . . (Rhino)
Collectables Presents The History Of Rock-#2-C . . . .(Collectables)
Oldies But Goodies-#9-C . . . . (Original Sound)
Teenage Tragedies-C . . . . (Rhino)
Pearl Jam; *No Boundaries-Benefit For The Kosovar Refugees-C* . . . .(Epic)
Let's Make Sure We Kiss Goodbye
Vince Gill; *Let's Make Sure We Kiss Goodbye* . . . . (MCA)
Love Potion Number 9
Clovers; *ST/American Graffiti* . . . . (MCA)
Super Oldies Of The '50s-#7-C . . . . (Audio Fidelity)
Herb Alpert & The Tijuana Brass; *Herb Alpert & The Tijuana Brass'*
Greatest Hits . . . . (A&M)
Herb Alpert & The Tijuana Brass-Classics-#1 . . . . (A&M)
Searchers; *History Of British Rock-#3-C* . . . . (Rhino)
Searchers' Greatest Hits . . . . (Rhino)
Lullaby Of Birdland
Ella Fitzgerald; *Best Of Ella Fitzgerald-#2* . . . . (MCA)
Ella Fitzgerald With Billie Holiday . . . . (MCA)
Four Freshmen; *Greatest Hits-Four Freshman* . . . .(Curb)
Mel Torme; *Songs Of New York* . . . . (Rhino)
Sarah Vaughan; *Sarah Vaughan-Golden Hits* . . . .(Mercury)
Tito Puente & His Latin Ensemble; *Mambo Diablo* . . . . (Concord Jazz)
Mama From The Train
Patti Page; *Patti Page-Golden Celebration* . . . .(Mercury)
Marie
Tommy Dorsey & His Orchestra; *Seventeen Number Ones* . . . . (RCA)
Memories Are Made Of This
Dean Martin; *Billboard Pop Memories-1955-1959-C* . . . .(Rhino)
Dean Martin-Love Songs . . . . (Ranwood)
Dean Martin's All Time Greatest Hits . . . .(Curb)
Mouth
Merril Bainbridge; *The Garden* . . . . (Universal)
My Lips Remember Your Kisses
Nat ''King'' Cole; *1941-1943* . . . . (Classics)
Na Na Hey Hey Kiss Him Goodbye
Steam; *Billboard Top Rock 'N' Roll Hits-1969-C* . . . . (Rhino)
Super Hits Of The '70s-Have A Nice Day-#1-C . . . . (Rhino)
Toga Rock-C . . . . (Dunhill Compact Classics)
Never Been Kissed
Sherrie Austin; *Love In The Real World* . . . .(Arista)
One More Kiss
Original Broadway Cast; *Follies* . . . . (Capitol)
Follies . . . . (Capitol)
One More Kiss
Paul McCartney; *Paul McCartney-Gift Set* . . . . (Capitol)
Passionate Kisses
Mary Chapin Carpenter; *Come On Come On* . . . . (Columbia)
Perfect Kiss
New Order; *Best Of MTV's 120 Minutes-#2-C* . . . . (Rhino)
Low-Life . . . . (Qwest)
Substance . . . . (Qwest)
Possession
Sarah McLachlan; *Fumbling Towards Ecstasy* . . . .(Arista)
Prelude To A Kiss
Bing Crosby & Others; *Tribute To Duke* . . . .(Concord Jazz)
Carmen McRae; *Any Old Time* . . . . (Denon)
Diane Schuur; *Diane Schuur-Love Songs* . . . .(GRP)
Duke Ellington; *Ellington Indigos* . . . . (Columbia)
Duke Ellington & His Orchestra; *Digital Duke* . . . . (GRP)
Nancy Wilson; *But Beautiful* . . . . (Blue Note)
Renee Fleming; *Salute To American Music* . . . . (RCA)
Sarah Vaughan; *Jazz 'Round Midnight-Sarah Vaughan* . . . .(Verve)
Pucker Up Buttercup
Junior Walker & The All Stars; *Junior Walker & The All Stars'*
Greatest Hits . . . . (Motown)
Purple Haze
Cure; *Stone Free: A Tribute To Jimi Hendrix-C* . . . . (Reprise)
Jimi Hendrix; *Kiss The Sky* . . . . (Reprise)
ST/Jimi Hendrix . . . . (Reprise)
Jimi Hendrix Experience; *Are You Experienced?* . . . . (Reprise)
Essential Jimi Hendrix . . . . (Reprise)
Radio One . . . . (Rykodisc)
Smash Hits . . . . (Reprise)
Winger; *Winger* . . . . (Atlantic)
Put That Kiss Back Where You Found It
Benny Goodman; *All The Cats Join In* . . . . (Columbia)
Reunited
Peaches & Herb; *Best Of Peaches & Herb* . . . . (Polydor)
Chicken Soup For The Couples Soul-C . . . . (Rhino)
Didn't It Blow Your Mind: Soul Hits Of The '70s-#20-C . . . . . . (Rhino)
Only Love-1975-1979-C . . . . (JCI Assoc. Labels)
Say It With A Kiss
Billie Holiday; *Quintessential-#6-1938* . . . . (Columbia)
The Billie Holiday Story-#3 . . . . (Columbia)

Scary Kisses
Voice Of The Beehive; *Sex And Misery* . . . . (Discovery)
Sealed With A Kiss
Bobby Vinton; *Bobby Vinton's Greatest Hits* . . . . (Curb)
Brian Hyland; *Cruisin'-1962-C* . . . .(Increase)
Oldies But Goodies-#2-C . . . . (Original Sound)
Original Rock 'N' Roll Hits Of The '50s-C . . . . (Roulette)
Lettermen; *Best Of The Lettermen-#2* . . . . (Capitol)
Capitol Collectors Series-The Lettermen. . . . . (Capitol)
Seven Little Girls Sitting In The Back Seat
Paul Evans; *Music To Remember-C* . . . . (Dominion Entert.)
Shut Up And Kiss Me
Mary Chapin Carpenter; *Stones In The Road* . . . . (Columbia)
Steal My Kisses
Ben Harper; *Burn To Shine* . . . . (Virgin)
Now That's What I Call Music!-#4-C . . . . (Virgin)
Such A Night
Elvis Presley; *From Nashville To Memphis-The Essential '60s Masters* . . (RCA)
Suck My Kiss
Red Hot Chili Peppers; *Blood Sugar Sex Magik* . . . .(Warner Bros.)
Summer Kisses, Winter Tears
Elvis Presley; *Collector's Gold* . . . . (RCA)
Sweet Kisses
Jessica Simpson; *Sweet Kisses* . . . . (Columbia)
Sweet Kisses
Van & Schenck; *Music From The New York Stage (1890-1920)-#4-1917-1920-C* . . . . (Pearl)
Taste Of Honey
Barbra Streisand; *The Barbra Streisand Album* . . . . (Columbia)
Beatles; *Beatles-Box Set* . . . . (Capitol)
Please Please Me . . . . (Parlophone)
The Early Beatles . . . . (Capitol)
Herb Alpert; *Midnight Sun* . . . . (A&M)
Herb Alpert & The Tijuana Brass; *Herb Alpert & The Tijuana Brass' Greatest Hits* . . . . (A&M)
Herb Alpert & The Tijuana Brass-Classics-#1 . . . . (A&M)
Tony Bennett; *Forty Years-The Artistry Of Tony Bennett.* . . . . . . (Columbia)
Television Kiss
Lave Love; *Aphrodisia* . . . . (Sky)
Tender Kisses
Tracie Spencer; *Make The Difference* . . . . (Capitol)
Tenderest Kiss
Divine Horsemen; *Devil's River* . . . . (SST)
Then He Kissed Me
Crystals; *Best Of The Crystals* . . . . (Abkco)
Phil Spector-Back To Mono 1958-1969-C . . . . (Abkco)
Then I Kissed Her
Beach Boys; *California Girls* . . . . (Capitol)
Sunshine Dream . . . . (Capitol)
Today/Summer Days (& Summer Nights!) . . . . (Capitol)
This Kiss
Faith Hill; *Faith* . . . .(Warner Bros.)
Totally Hits-#1-C . . . . (Arista)
This Magic Moment
Drifters; *Drifters' Greatest Hits* . . . . (Gusto)
Drifters-Golden Hits . . . . (Atlantic)
Jay & The Americans; *Come A Little Bit Closer-Best Of Jay & The Americans* . . . .(Gold Rush)
Jay & The Americans' All-Time Greatest Hits. . . . . (Rhino)
Marvin Gaye; *M.P.G.* . . . . (Motown)
This Year's Kisses
Billie Holiday; *Quintessential-#3-1936-1937* . . . . (Columbia)
June Christy; *Misty June Christy* . . . . (Blue Note)
Lester Young & Roy Eldridge; *Jazz Giants* . . . . (Verve)
Trademark
Mandy Barnett; *I've Got A Right To Cry.* . . . . (Sire)
Veni-Vidi-Vici (I Came, I Saw, I Conquered)
Gaylords; *Best Of The Gaylords* . . . .(Chronicles)
Vision Of A Kiss
B-52's; *Good Stuff* . . . . (Reprise)
Voodoo Kiss
Mr. Big; *Lean Into It* . . . . (Atlantic)
We Kiss In A Shadow
Barbra Streisand; *The Broadway Album* . . . . (Columbia)
Original Broadway Cast; *The King And I* . . . .(RCA Victor)
Original Cast; *The King And I.* . . . . (MCA)
We've Only Just Begun
Barbra Streisand; *Just For The Record* . . . . (Columbia)
Carpenters; *Carpenters-Classics-#2.* . . . . (A&M)
Carpenters-The Singles 1969-1973 . . . . (A&M)
Close To You . . . . (A&M)
From The Top . . . . (A&M)
Yesterday Once More. . . . . (A&M)
What Would Happen
Meredith Brooks; *Blurring The Edges* . . . . (Capitol)
While You Loved Me
Rascal Flatts; *Rascal Flatts.* . . . . (Lyric Street)
Whole Lotta Loving
Fats Domino; *Fats Domino's All Time Greatest Hits* . . . . (Curb)

Fats Domino's Greatest Hits . . . . (CEMA Special Prod.)
My Blue Heaven . . . . (Gold Rush)
Professor Longhair; *Mardi Gras In Baton Rouge* . . . . (Rhino)
Wishful Thinking
Wynn Stewart; *Heroes Of Country Music-#4-Legends Of The West Coast-C* . . . . (Rhino)
XXX's And OOO's
Trisha Yearwood; *Thinkin' About You* . . . . (MCA)
You Shouldn't Kiss Me Like This
Toby Keith; *How Do You Like Me Now?!* . . . .(DreamWorks/SKG)
You'd Be Surprised
Eddie Cantor; *Music From The New York Stage (1890-1920)-#4-1917-1920-C* . . . . (Pearl)
Johnnie Ray; *45-#40154* . . . . (Columbia)
Marilyn Monroe; *Never Before & Never Again-1953-1954* . . . . (DRG)
Orrin Tucker & His Orchestra; *Best Of Orrin Tucker & His Orchestra* . . .(DRG)
You're Gonna Miss Me When I'm Gone
Brooks & Dunn; *Brooks & Dunn-The Greatest Hits Collection* . . . . (Arista)
Waitin' On Sundown . . . . (Arista)

LATE

See Also: **BUSY, NIGHT, TIME: GENERAL, TIME: SPECIFIC, URGENT**

10 Days Late
Third Eye Blind; *Blue* . . . . (Elektra)
Always Late (With Your Kisses)
Dwight Yoakam; *Hillbilly Deluxe* . . . .(Reprise)
Jo-el Sonnier; *Jo-el Sonnier-Complete Mercury Sessions* . . . . (Mercury)
Lefty Frizzell; *American Originals-Lefty Frizzell* . . . . (Columbia)
Best Of Lefty Frizzell . . . . (Rhino)
Lefty Frizzell's Greatest Hits . . . . (Columbia)
Willie Nelson; *To Lefty From Willie* . . . . (Columbia)
Another Nine Minutes
Yankee Grey; *Untamed* . . . . (Monument)
Born Too Late
Poni-Tails; *Original Classic Oldies Of The '50s-#4-C* . . . . (MCA)
Expressway To Your Heart
Blues Brothers; *Best Of The Blues Brothers* . . . .(Atlantic)
Soul Survivors; *Dick Bartley's One-Hit Wonders Of The '60s-#2-C* . . . . (Rhino)
Oldies But Goodies-#11-C . . . .(Original Sound)
Super Oldies Of The '60s-#6-C . . . . (Audio Fidelity)
When The Whistle Blows Anything Goes . . . . (Collectables)
I'm Already Taken
Steve Wariner; *Country Cares For Kids II-C* . . . .(BNA)
Two Teardrops . . . . (Capitol)
In A Week Or Two
Diamond Rio; *Close To The Edge* . . . . (Arista)
Diamond Rio's Greatest Hits . . . . (Arista)
It's A Little Too Late
Tanya Tucker; *Can't Run From Yourself* . . . . (Liberty)
It's A Little Too Late
Mark Chesnutt; *Mark Chesnutt's Greatest Hits* . . . . (Decca)
It's Late
Ricky Nelson; *Lonesome Town* . . . . (CEMA Special Prod.)
Ricky Nelson Volume 1 . . . . (Gold Rush)
It's Too Late
Amy Grant; *Tapestry Revisited: Tribute To Carole King-C* . . . . (Lava)
Carole King; *Her Greatest Hits* . . . . (Epic)
Tapestry . . . . (Epic)
Gloria Estefan; *Hold Me, Thrill Me, Kiss Me* . . . . (Epic)
It's Too Late
Derek And The Dominos; *Layla* . . . . (Polydor)
Late Great Johnny Ace, The
Paul Simon; *Hearts & Bones.* . . . . (Warner Bros.)
Late Show, The
Jackson Browne; *Late For The Sky* . . . .(Asylum)
Later On
Jefferson Starship; *Windows Of Heaven* . . . .(CMC Int'l)
Later Tonight
Pet Shop Boys; *Please.* . . . . (EMI)
One Promise Too Late
Reba McEntire; *Country Classics-#10-1987-C.* . . . . (Universal)
Reba McEntire's Greatest Hits. . . . . (MCA)
What Am I Gonna Do About You . . . . (MCA)
See You In Hell (Don't Be Late)
Yngwie Malmsteen; *Eclipse* . . . .(Polydor)
She's Not There
Santana; *Moonflower.* . . . . (Columbia)
Viva Santana! . . . . (Columbia)
Vanilla Fudge; *Vanilla Fudge* . . . . (Atco)
Zombies; *Best & The Rest Of The Zombies* . . . . (Epic)
Billboard Top Rock 'N' Roll Hits-1964-C . . . . (Rhino)
History Of British Rock-#1-C . . . . (Rhino)
Time Of The Zombies . . . .(Bac-Trac)

Slow Poke
Ray Conniff; *Speak To Me Of Love* . . . . (Columbia)
So Help Me Girl
Gary Barlow; *Open Road* . . . . (Arista)
Joe Diffie; *Third Rock From The Sun* . . . . (Epic)
Sparrow In The Treetop
Guy Mitchell; *Guy Mitchell-16 Most Requested Songs* . . . . (Legacy)
Spring Will Be A Little Late This Year
Sarah Vaughan; *Divine Sarah Vaughan-Columbia Years-1949-*
1953 . . . . (Columbia)
In Hi-Fi . . . . (Sony Music Special Prod.)
Theme From "The Late Late Show"
Original Soundtrack; *Television's Greatest Hits-#1-C* . . . . (TVT)
Theme From "The Late Show With David Letterman"
Original Soundtrack; *CBS: The First 50 Years* . . . . (TVT)
Television's Greatest Hits-#7-Cable Ready-C . . . . (TVT)
There Goes My Baby
Trisha Yearwood; *Where Your Road Leads* . . . . (MCA)
Too Late, Too Soon
Jon Secada; *Secada* . . . . (Capitol)
Too Little Too Late
Barenaked Ladies; *Maroon* . . . . (Reprise)
Torn
Natalie Imbruglia; *Left Of The Middle* . . . . (RCA)
Traffic Jam
Artie Shaw; *Begin The Beguine* . . . . (Bluebird)
Ella Fitzgerald & Chick Webb; *Ella Sings/Chick Swings* . . . . (Olympic)
Traffic Jam
James Taylor; *JT* . . . . (Columbia)
Undun
Guess Who; *American Woman, These Eyes & Other Hits* . . . . (RCA)
Best Of The Guess Who . . . . (RCA)
Wheel, The
Rosanne Cash; *The Wheel* . . . . (Columbia)

LAW & ORDER, Court System, Justice, Lawyers

See Also: CAPITAL PUNISHMENT, CRIME, FIGHT, FREEDOM,
GUILT, GUNS, POLICE, POLITICS (various), POWER & CONTROL,
PRISON, REBELS

(Eye) Hate U
"AFKAP"; *The Gold Experience* . . . . (NPG)
(Man Who Shot) Liberty Valance
Gene Pitney; *Gene Pitney-Anthology 1961-1968* . . . . (Rhino)
Gene Pitney's Greatest Hits . . . . (Evergreen Music)
Super Oldies Of The '60s-#9-C . . . . (Audio Fidelity)
Greg Kihn; *Glass House Rock* . . . . (Beserkley)
Against The Law
Warrant; *Dirty Rotten Filthy Stinking Rich* . . . . (Columbia)
All Is Fair In Love And War
Ronnie Milsap; *Club* . . . . (RCA)
All Of The Law
Psychedelic Furs; *Midnight To Midnight* . . . . (Columbia)
Auntie's Municipal Court
Monkees; *Birds Bees & The Monkees* . . . . (Rhino)
Authority Song
John Cougar Mellencamp; *Uh-Huh* . . . . (Riva)
Bad Boys Get Spanked
Pretenders; *Pretenders II* . . . . (Sire)
Bangkok Attorney
Doves; *Affinity* . . . . (Elektra)
Book Of Rules
Heptones; *Night Food* . . . . (Island)
This Is Reggae Music-#1-C . . . . (Island)
Breaking All The Rules
Peter Frampton; *Breaking All The Rules* . . . . (A&M)
Shine On-Collection . . . . (A&M)
Breaking All The Rules
Ozzy Osbourne; *No Rest For The Wicked* . . . . (Epic)
Brown Eyed Handsome Man
Buddy Holly; *Buddy Holly-20 Golden Greats* . . . . (MCA)
For The First Time Anywhere . . . . (MCA)
Rock & Roll Collection . . . . (MCA)
Chuck Berry; *Best Of The Best Of Chuck Berry* . . . . . (International Mktg. Group)
Roll Over Beethoven . . . . (Allegiance)
The Chess Box-Chuck Berry . . . . (Chess)
Waylon Jennings; *Essential Waylon Jennings* . . . . (RCA)
Waylon Jennings-Super Hits . . . . (RCA)
Coming Into Los Angeles
Arlo Guthrie; *Best Of Arlo Guthrie* . . . . (Warner Bros.)
Running Down The Road . . . . (Reprise)
ST/Woodstock . . . . (Atlantic)
Complicated Shadows
Elvis Costello & The Attractions; *The Sopranos-Music From The HBO*
Original Series . . . . (Sony Music Soundtrax)

Crime & Punishment
Agony Column; *Brave Words & Bloody Knuckles* . . . . (Big Chief)
Criminal
Fiona Apple; *1998 Grammy Nominees-C* . . . . (MCA)
Tidal . . . . (Clean Slate/Work)
Evidence
Steve Lacy & Don Cherry; *Evidence* . . . . (New Jazz)
Thelonius Monk; *Atlantic Jazz-Bebop-C* . . . . (Atlantic)
Best Of Thelonius Monk . . . . (Blue Note)
Evidence . . . . (Milestone)
Exhibit "A"
Shok Paris; *Steel & Starlight* . . . . (I.R.S.)
Exhibit A
Art Blakey; *Ritual* . . . . (Blue Note)
Art Taylor; *Taylor's Wailers* . . . . (Prestige)
F. Lee Bailey Blues
Sugar Ray & The Bluetones; *Don't Stand In My Way* . . . . (Bullseye Blues)
Fair
Ben Folds Five; *Whatever And Ever Amen* . . . . (Caroline/550)
Goin' By The Book
Johnny Cash; *Mystery Of Life* . . . . (Mercury)
Good Morning Judge
10 CC; *10 CC's Greatest Hits-1972-1978* . . . . (Polydor)
Deceptive Bends . . . . (Mercury)
Jailhouse Rock (Hits From The Big House)-C . . . . (Sony Music Special Prod.)
Live & Let Live . . . . (Mercury)
I Can't Drive 55
Sammy Hagar; *VOA* . . . . (Geffen)
I Did It
Dave Matthews Band; *Everyday* . . . . (RCA)
I Fought The Law
Bobby Fuller Four; *Best Of The Bobby Fuller Four* . . . . (Rhino)
Heart & Soul Of Rock 'N' Roll-#1-C . . . . (Rhino)
Jailhouse Rock (Hits From The Big House)-C . . . . (Sony Music Special Prod.)
Oldies But Goodies-#9-C . . . . (Original Sound)
Super Oldies Of The '60s-#7-C . . . . (Audio Fidelity)
Clash; *The Clash* . . . . (Epic)
The Story Of The Clash, Volume 1 . . . . (Epic)
I Won't Let You Do That To Me
Luther Vandross; *One Night With You-The Best Of Love-#2* . . . . (LV/Epic)
If I Had A Hammer (The Hammer Song)
Pete Seeger; *Sing-A-Long-Live At Sanders*
Theatre 1980 . . . . (Smithsonian Folkways)
Peter, Paul & Mary; *10 Years Together/The Best Of Peter, Paul*
and Mary . . . . (Warner Bros.)
Peter, Paul and Mary . . . . (Warner Bros.)
Peter, Paul and Mary In Concert . . . . (Warner Bros.)
Trini Lopez; *Best Of Trini Lopez* . . . . (Exact)
Weavers; *Weavers' Greatest Hits* . . . . (Vanguard)
If There's Any Justice
Lee Greenwood; *Country Classics-#11-1987-1988-C* . . . . (Universal)
If There's Any Justice . . . . (Panorama)
Lee Greenwood's Greatest Hits-#2 . . . . (MCA)
I'm A Lonesome Fugitive
Merle Haggard; *Merle Haggard-16 Biggest Hits* . . . . (Legacy)
Merle Haggard & The Strangers; *Best Of Merle Haggard & The*
Strangers . . . . (Capitol)
Capitol Collectors Series-Merle Haggard & The Strangers . . . . (Capitol)
Songs I'll Always Sing . . . . (Capitol)
Roy Buchanan; *Roy Buchanan* . . . . (Polydor)
Innocent
Alexander O'Neal; *Alexander O'Neal* . . . . (Tabu)
All Mixed Up . . . . (Tabu)
Innocent
Garland Jeffreys; *Escape Artist* . . . . (Epic)
Innocent
Whispers; *More Of The Night* . . . . (Capitol)
Judge Baby I'm Back
Cliff Nobles & Co.; *The Horse* . . . . (Phil. L.A.)
Justice
Art Blakey & His Jazz Messengers; *History Of Art Blakey/Jazz*
Messengers . . . . (Blue Note)
Justice
Bruce Cockburn; *Inner City Front* . . . . (Columbia)
Justice
Ziggy Marley & The Melody Makers; *One Bright Day* . . . . (Virgin)
Justice
Little Steven; *Voice Of America* . . . . (Razor & Tie)
Justice And Independence '85
John Cougar Mellencamp; *Scarecrow* . . . . (Riva)
Justice In Ontario
Steve Earle & The Dukes; *The Hard Way* . . . . (MCA)
Justice In The Barrel
Jon Bon Jovi; *Blaze Of Glory-ST/Young Guns II* . . . . (Mercury)
Justice In Truth
Brenda Russell; *Brenda Russell's Greatest Hits* . . . . (A&M)
Justice Tonight/Rock It Over
Clash; *Black Market Clash* . . . . (Epic)

Keepin' Out Of Mischief Now
Barbra Streisand; *Just For The Record* . . . . (Columbia)
   The Barbra Streisand Album . . . . (Columbia)
Bobby Henderson; *Handful Of Keys* . . . . (Vanguard)
Fats Waller; *Turn On The Heat-Fats Waller Piano Solos* . . . . (Bluebird)
Louis Armstrong; *Satch Plays Fats* . . . . (Columbia)

Knife Feels Like Justice
Brian Setzer; *Knife Feels Like Justice* . . . . (EMI)

Knoxville Courthouse Blues
Hank Williams, Jr.; *Major Moves* . . . . (WB/Curb)

Lady Came From Baltimore
Joan Baez; *Contemporary Ballad Book* . . . . (Vanguard)
   Joan . . . . (Vanguard)
John Stewart; *Neon Beach* . . . . (Homecoming)
Johnny Cash; *Johnny Cash-16 Biggest Hits-#2* . . . . (Legacy)
Tim Hardin; *Hang On To A Dream-Verve Recordings* . . . . (Polydor)

Law Is For The Protection Of The People
Kris Kristofferson; *Me & Bobby McGee* . . . . (Columbia)

Laws Must Change
John Mayall; *Best Of John Mayall* . . . . (Polydor)
   The Turning Point . . . . (Polydor)
John Mayall's Bluesbreakers; *Behind The Iron Curtain* . . . . . (Crescendo)

Lawyers
Billy Walker; *45-#2056* . . . . (Caprice)

Lawyers In Love
Jackson Browne; *Lawyers In Love* . . . . (Asylum)

Lawyers, Guns & Money
Warren Zevon; *Excitable Boy* . . . . (Asylum)
   Quiet Normal Life-Best Of Warren Zevon . . . . (Asylum)
   Stand In The Fire . . . . (Asylum)

Laying Down The Law
INXS & Jimmy Barnes; *ST/The Lost Boys* . . . . (Atlantic)

Laying Down The Law
Law; *Law* . . . . (Atlantic)

Legal Matter
Who; *Meaty Beaty Big & Bouncy* . . . . (MCA)
   The Who Sings "My Generation" . . . . (MCA)

Lily, Rosemary And The Jack Of Hearts
Bob Dylan; *Blood On The Tracks* . . . . (Columbia)

Living Proof
Ricky Van Shelton; *30 Years Of #1 Hits-#20-C* . . . . (Columbia)
   Greatest Country Hits Of The '80s-1989-C . . . . (Columbia)
   Ricky Van Shelton's Greatest Hits Plus . . . . (Columbia)

Long Arm Of The Law
Kenny Rogers; *Kenny Rogers' Greatest Hits* . . . . (EMI)

Love In The First Degree
Alabama; *Alabama-Live* . . . . (RCA)
   Alabama's Greatest Hits . . . . (RCA)
   Feels So Right . . . . (RCA)
   Nipper's Greatest Hits Of The '80s-C . . . . (RCA)

Love Is Stronger Than Justice
Sting; *Ten Summoner's Tales* . . . . (A&M)

Love Is The Only Law
Ziggy Marley & The Melody Makers; *One Bright Day* . . . . . (Virgin)

Mammas Don't Let Your Babies Grow Up To Be Cowboys
Gibson/Miller Band; *Cowboy Super Hits-C* . . . . (Columbia)
   ST/The Cowboy Way . . . . (Epic)
Waylon Jennings & Willie Nelson; *Waylon & Willie* . . . . (RCA)
   Waylon Jennings & Willie Nelson's Greatest Hits . . . . (RCA)
Willie Nelson; *Greatest Hits (& Some That Will Be)* . . . . . (Columbia)
   ST/The Electric Horseman . . . . (Columbia)
   Willie & Family Live . . . . (Columbia)

Maxwell's Silver Hammer
Beatles; *Abbey Road* . . . . (Parlophone)

Murder In My Heart For The Judge
Lee Michaels; *Lee Michaels-Collection* . . . . (Rhino)
Moby Grape; *Wow* . . . . (Columbia)
Three Dog Night; *Jailhouse Rock (Hits From The Big House)-C* . . . . (Sony Music Special Prod.)

Murphy's Law
Murphy's Law; *Murphy's Law* . . . . (Rock Hotel)

Murphy's Law
Cheri; *Best Disco In Town-#1-C* . . . . (Hip-O)

Murphy's Law
Al Jarreau; *High Crime* . . . . (Warner Bros.)

My Attorney Bernie
David Frishberg; *Can't Take You Nowhere* . . . . (Fantasy)
   David Frishberg-Classics . . . . (Concord Jazz)

Night The Lights Went Out In Georgia
Lynn Anderson; *Top Of The World* . . . . (Columbia)
Reba McEntire; *For My Broken Heart* . . . . (MCA)
   Reba McEntire's Greatest Hits-#3: I'm A Survivor . . . . (MCA)
Vicki Lawrence; *Super Hits Of The '70s-Have A Nice Day-#10-C* . . . . . . (Rhino)

Ninety Nine Years (Dead Or Alive)
Guy Mitchell; *Definitive Guy Mitchell* . . . . (Collector's Choice)

No Alibis
Eric Clapton; *Journeyman* . . . . (Duck/Reprise)

No Law Or Order
Hanoi Rocks; *Oriental Beat* . . . . (Geffen)

Old Judge Jones
Les Dudek; *Say No More* . . . . (Columbia)

One Million Lawyers
Tom Paxton; *One Million Lawyers & Other Disasters* . . . . . . (Flying Fish)

Other Side Of The Game
Erykah Badu; *Baduizm* . . . . (Kedar Entert./Universal)

Oughta Be A Law
Lamont Cranston Band; *Up From The Alley* . . . . (Waterhouse)
   Upper Mississippi Shakedown-Best Of . . . . (Era)
Lee Roy Parnell; *Country's Greatest Hits-#8-Lonely Hearts-C* . . . . . (Priority)
   Lee Roy Parnell . . . . (Arista)

Perry Mason
Ozzy Osbourne; *Ozzmosis* . . . . (Epic)

Philadelphia Lawyer
Rose Maddox; *Rose Of The West Coast Country* . . . . (Arhoolie)
   Super Country Hits Of The '40s-C . . . . (Gusto)
Willie Nelson; *Tribute To Woody Guthrie And Leadbelly-C* . . . . . . (Columbia)
Woody Guthrie; *Cowboy Songs On Folkways-C* . . . . . (Smithsonian Folkways)

Policy Of Truth
Depeche Mode; *Violator* . . . . (Sire)

Prohibition Blues
Nora Bayes; *Music From The New York Stage (1890-1920)-#4-1917-1920-C* . . . . (Pearl)

Punishment Fits The Crime
Ramones; *Brain Drain* . . . . (Sire)

Read Me My Rights
Ann Peebles; *Fulltime Love* . . . . (Bullseye Blues)
Dalton Reed; *Louisiana Soul Man* . . . . (Bullseye Blues)

Regulate
Warren G. & Nate Dogg; *ST/Above The Rim* . . . . (Death Row)

Right And Wrong
Joe Jackson; *Big World* . . . . (A&M)

Right To Remain Silent
Doug Stone; *I Thought It Was You* . . . . (Epic)

Rock & Roll Lawyer
Austin Lounge Lizards; *Lizard Vision* . . . . (Flying Fish)

Rules & Regulations
Public Image Ltd.; *Greatest Hits So Far* . . . . (Virgin)
   Happy? . . . . (Virgin)

Straight Time
Bruce Springsteen; *The Ghost Of Tom Joad* . . . . (Columbia)

Sue Me
Doctor Ice; *Mic Stalker* . . . . (Jive)
   Rap Wit' Cha 2-C . . . . (K-Tel)

Sue Me
Original Cast; *Guys & Dolls* . . . . (MCA)
   Guys & Dolls . . . . (Motown)

Sue Me, Sue You Blues
George Harrison; *Living In The Material World* . . . . (Capitol)

Supreme Court Judges
Michael Tilson Thomas; *Of Thee I Sing/Let 'Em Eat Cake* . . . . . . (Columbia)

Sweetest Taboo
Sade; *Promise* . . . . (Portrait)

Talk To The Lawyer
David Lindley & El Rayo-X; *Win This Record* . . . . (Elektra)

Tell It To The Judge
Monotones; *Best Of Chess Vocal Groups-C* . . . . (Chess)

Tell It To The Judge On Sunday
Long Ryders; *Native Sons* . . . . (Frontier)

Ten Commandments Of Love
Bob Marley & The Wailers; *Birth Of A Legend 1963-1966* . . . . (Epic Portrait Assoc.)
Harvey & The Moonglows; *Best Of Chess Rock 'N' Roll-#2-C* . . . . (Chess)
   Collectables Presents The History Of Rock-#10-C . . . . (Collectables)
   Cruisin'-1958-C . . . . (Increase)
   Oldies But Goodies-#11-C . . . . (Original Sound)

Testify
Greg Kihn; *Kihnsolidation-Best Of Greg Kihn* . . . . (Rhino)

Testify
Melissa Etheridge; *Brave & Crazy* . . . . (Island)

Testify
Peter Tosh; *No Nuclear War* . . . . (EMI)

Testify
David Bromberg; *Sideman Serenade* . . . . (Rounder)

Testify (I Wanna)
Johnnie Taylor; *15 Original Big Hits-#4-C* . . . . (Stax)
   Top Of The Stax-Twenty Greatest Hits-#2-C . . . . (Stax)
Parliament; *Soul Shots-#9-More Dance Party-C* . . . . (Rhino)
Stevie Ray Vaughan and Double Trouble; *Texas Flood* . . . . . . (Epic)

Testimony
Sweet Honey In The Rock; *We All...Every One Of Us* . . . . . . (Flying Fish)

Testimony
Robbie Robertson; *Robbie Robertson* . . . . (Geffen)

Texas Lawman
Regulators; *Regulators* . . . . (Polydor)

That's The Law
Point Blank; *Point Blank* . . . . (Arista)

Theme From "Hardcastle And McCormick"
Original Soundtrack; *Television's Greatest Hits-#6-Remote Control-C* . . . (TVT)
Theme From "Ironside"
Original Soundtrack; *Television's Greatest Hits-#1-C* . . . . (TVT)
Theme From "Judd For The Defense"
Original Soundtrack; *Television's Greatest Hits-#5-In Living Color-C* . . . (TVT)
Theme From "L.A. Law"
Original Soundtrack; *Television's Greatest Hits-#3-1970s & 1980s-C*. . . . (TVT)
Theme From "Law And Order"
Original Soundtrack; *Television's Greatest Hits-#7-Cable Ready-C* . . . . . (TVT)
Theme From "Night Court"
Original Soundtrack; *Television's Greatest Hits-#6-Remote Control-C* . . . (TVT)
Theme From "Paper Chase"
Original Soundtrack; *Television's Greatest Hits-#6-Remote Control-C* . . . (TVT)
Theme From "Perry Mason"
Blues Brothers; *Made In America* . . . . (Atlantic)
Jerry Goodman; *It's Alive* . . . . (Private Music)
Original Soundtrack; *CBS: The First 50 Years* . . . . (TVT)
Television's Greatest Hits-#1-C . . . . (TVT)
TV Theme Sing-Along Album . . . . (Rhino)
Theme From "The People's Court"
Original Soundtrack; *Television's Greatest Hits-#6-Remote Control-C* . . . (TVT)
There Ought To Be A Law
Five Keys; *Aladdin Years* . . . . (EMI)
There's No Justice
George Jones; *George Jones Sings The Great Songs Of Leon
    Payne* . . . . (Hollywood/DNA-Rounder)
Trial
Pink Floyd; *Shine On* . . . . (Columbia)
The Wall . . . . (Columbia)
Roger Waters; *The Wall-Live In Berlin* . . . . (Mercury)
Trial Before Pilate
Original London Cast; *Jesus Christ Superstar.* . . . . (MCA)
Verdict
Professor Griff & His Last Asiatic Disciples; *Pawns In The Game* . . . . . .(Luke)
Week In A County Jail, A
Tom T. Hall; *Storyteller, Poet, Philospher* . . . . (Mercury)
Tom T. Hall's Greatest Hits-#1. . . . . (Mercury)
You Have The Right To Remain Silent
Perfect Stranger; *From Nashville With Love-C* . . . . (Curb)
You Made A Wanted Man Of Me
Ronnie McDowell; *19 Hot Country Requests-#2-C* . . . . (Epic)
Country Boy's Heart. . . . . (Epic)
Older Women & Other Greatest Hits . . . . (Epic)

LEAVING, Farewell, Goodbye

See Also: **AIRPLANES, BUS, CARS (various), CHILDREN
LEAVING HOME, DEATH, DIVORCE, ENDINGS, ESCAPE, HELLO,
HITCHHIKING, HOME, LOSING & LOSS, LOVE (various),
MOTORCYCLES, REBELS, RETURNING, SADNESS, SAILING,
SEPARATION, SHIPS, TAXI, TRAINS, TRAVELING, TRUCKS**

(Now You See Me) Now You Don't
Lee Ann Womack; *Some Things I Know* . . . . (Decca)
(Pack Your) Suitcase Blues
Karrin Allyson; *I Didn't Know About You* . . . . (Concord Jazz)
49 Bye-Byes
Crosby, Stills & Nash; *Crosby, Stills & Nash* . . . . (Atlantic)
4th Of July, Asbury Park (Sandy)
Bruce Springsteen; *The Wild, The Innocent & The E Street Shuffle* . . . (Columbia)
Bruce Springsteen & The E Street Band; *Bruce Springsteen & The E Street
    Band Live/1975-85* . . . . (Legacy)
50 Ways To Leave Your Lover
Paul Simon; *Greatest Hits, Etc.* . . . . (Columbia)
Negotiations And Love Songs, 1971-1986 . . . . (Warner Bros.)
Still Crazy After All These Years . . . . (Columbia)
Simon & Garfunkel; *The Concert In Central Park* . . . . (Warner Bros.)
Across The Border
Bruce Springsteen; *The Ghost Of Tom Joad* . . . . (Columbia)
Adios
Jimmy Webb; *Suspending Disbelief* . . . . (Elektra)
Linda Ronstadt; *Cry Like A Rainstorm-Howl Like The Wind* . . . . . . (Elektra)
Adios Amigo
Jim Reeves; *Best Of Jim Reeves.* . . . . (RCA)
Billboard Top Country Hits-1962-C. . . . . (Rhino)
Marty Robbins; *Adios Amigo.* . . . . (Columbia)
American Originals-Marty Robbins . . . . (Columbia)
Marty Robbins' Greatest Hits-#4 . . . . (Columbia)
Ain't That A Shame
4 Seasons; *25th Anniversary Collection* . . . . (Rhino)
Cheap Trick; *Cheap Trick At Budokan* . . . . (Epic)
Fats Domino; *Best Of Fats Domino* . . . . (EMI)
Fats Domino's Greatest Hits . . . . (Everest)
Fats Domino's Greatest Hits . . . . (MCA)
ST/American Graffiti . . . . (MCA)
Hank Williams, Jr.; *Hank Williams, Jr.-14 Greatest Hits* . . . . (Polydor)

Standing In The Shadows . . . . (Polydor)
John Lennon; *Lennon* . . . . (Capitol)
Rock 'N' Roll . . . . (Capitol)
All My Loving
Beatles; *Meet The Beatles!* . . . . (Capitol)
The Beatles At The Hollywood Bowl . . . . (Capitol)
The Beatles/1962-1966 . . . . (Capitol)
With The Beatles . . . . (Parlophone)
Almost Goodbye
Mark Chesnutt; *Almost Goodbye* . . . . (MCA)
Aloha (Also Means Goodbye)
Screamin' Scott Simon; *Transmissions From Space* . . . .(Rhino)
Always Be My Baby
Mariah Carey; *Daydream.* . . . . (Columbia)
Am I The Only One
Marc Anthony; *Marc Anthony* . . . .(Columbia)
American Pie
Don McLean; *American Pie* . . . . (EMI)
Best Of Don McLean . . . . (EMI)
Greatest Hits Then & Now . . . . (EMI)
ST/Born On The Fourth Of July. . . . . (MCA)
Madonna; *ST/The Next Big Thing* . . . . (Maverick)
American Woman
Guess Who; *American Woman.* . . . . (RCA)
Best Of The Guess Who . . . . (RCA)
Greatest Of The Guess Who . . . . (RCA)
Nipper's Greatest Hits Of The '70s-C . . . . (RCA)
Rock Classics-C . . . . (K-Tel)
Lenny Kravitz; *5* . . . . (Virgin)
Now That's What I Call Music!-#3-C . . . . (Virgin)
ST/Austin Powers-The Spy Who Shagged Me . . . . (Maverick)
Angel Of The Morning
Juice Newton; *All-Time Country Classics-#2-C* . . . .(Capitol)
Juice . . . . (Capitol)
Juice Newton-Greatest Hits & More . . . . (Capitol)
Juice Newton's Greatest Hits . . . . (Gold Rush)
Merrilee Rush; *Dick Bartley's One-Hit Wonders Of The '60s-#2-C* . . . . (Rhino)
Mellow '60s-C. . . . . (Priority)
Angel's Eye
Aerosmith; *ST/Charlie's Angels* . . . .(Columbia)
Angry All The Time
Bruce Robison with Kelly Willis; *Wrapped* . . . .(Lucky Dog)
Tim McGraw with Faith Hill; *Set This Circus Down* . . . .(Curb)
Any Old Wind That Blows
Johnny Cash; *Johnny Cash-16 Biggest Hits-#2* . . . .(Legacy)
Arms Of The One Who Loves You
Xscape; *Traces Of My Lipstick.* . . . . (So So Def/Columbia)
Arrivederci Roma
Jerry Vale; *Jerry Vale Sings The Great Italian Hits* . . . .(Columbia)
Jerry Vale-17 Most Requested Songs . . . .(Legacy)
Mario Lanza; *Best Of Mario Lanza* . . . . (RCA)
Legendary Tenor . . . . (RCA)
Mario Lanza-Legendary Performer . . . . (RCA)
As We Lay
Kelly Price; *Mirror Mirror.* . . . . (Def Soul/IDJMG)
Au Revoir, Paris
Andy Williams; *Under Paris Skies* . . . . (Varese Vintage)
Au Revoir, Pleasant Dreams
Ben Bernie & His Orchestra; *78-#4943* . . . . (Brunswick)
Auf Wiedersehen
Cheap Trick; *Heaven Tonight* . . . . (Epic)
Auf Wiederseh'n, My Dear
Greta Keller; *These Foolish Things* . . . . (ASV)
Auf Wiedersehn-Sweetheart
Vera Lynn; *Those Wonderful Years: Tenderly-C* . . . . (JCI Assoc. Labels)
Austin
Blake Shelton; *Blake Shelton* . . . . (Giant)
Away Out On The Mountain
Jimmie Rodgers; *Best Of Jimmie Rodgers-Legendary Master Series* . . . . (RCA)
Essential Jimmie Rodgers . . . . (RCA)
First Sessions-1927-1928-#1 . . . . (Rounder)
My Rough & Rowdy Ways . . . . (RCA)
This Is Jimmie Rodgers . . . . (RCA)
Skip Gorman; *A Cowboy's Wild Song To His Herd* . . . . (Rounder)
Tim & Mollie O'Brien; *Away Out On The Mountain* . . . . (Sugar Hill)
Babe I'm Gonna Leave You
Led Zeppelin; *Led Zeppelin* . . . . (Atlantic)
Led Zeppelin-Box Set . . . . (Atlantic)
Baby Don't Go
Sonny & Cher; *The Beat Goes On-Best Of Sonny & Cher* . . . . (Rhino)
The Two Of Us. . . . . (Atco)
Bad Goodbye, A
Clint Black with Wynonna; *Clint Black-The Greatest Hits* . . . . (RCA)
Grammy's Greatest Country Moments-#1-C . . . . (Atlantic)
No Time To Kill . . . . (RCA)
Before You Walk Out Of My Life
Monica; *Miss Thang* . . . . (Rowdy/Arista)
Better Man, Better Off
Tracy Lawrence; *The Coast Is Clear* . . . . (Atlantic)

Big Goodbye
Great White; *Psycho City* .... (Capitol)
Bizounce
Olivia; *Olivia* .... (J)
Bohemian Rhapsody
Braids; *Here We Come* .... (Big Beat)
ST/High School High .... (Big Beat)
Queen; *A Night At The Opera* .... (Hollywood)
Classic Queen .... (Hollywood)
Live At Wembley '86 .... (Hollywood)
ST/Wayne's World .... (Reprise)
Bon Voyage
Original Cast; *Candide* ....(RCA Victor)
Boom Bye Bye
Buju Banton; *Voice Of Jamaica* .... (Mercury)
Brokedown Palace
Grateful Dead; *American Beauty* ....(Warner Bros.)
Persuasions; *Might As Well...The Persuasions Sing
Grateful Dead* .... (Grateful Dead)
Butterfly
Mariah Carey; *Butterfly* .... (Columbia)
By Heart
Jim Brickman; *By Heart* ....(Windham Hill)
By The Time I Get To Phoenix
Glen Campbell; *All-Time Country Classics-#1-C* .... (Capitol)
Glen Campbell-Classics Collection .... (Capitol)
Glen Campbell-Live .... (Capitol)
Glen Campbell's Greatest Hits .... (Capitol)
Very Best Of Glen Campbell .... (Capitol)
Reba McEntire; *Starting Over* ....(MCA)
Bye Bye Blackbird
Dean Martin; *Swingin' Down Yonder* .... (Capitol)
Joe Cocker; *With A Little Help From My Friends* ..... (A&M)
Liza Minnelli; *ST/Liza With A "Z"* .... (Columbia)
Miles Davis; *Ballads* .... (Columbia)
Miles Davis Quintet/Jazz Sampler #2 .... (Columbia)
Miles Davis Quintet; *Round About Midnight* ...... (Columbia)
Bye Bye Bye
'N Sync; *No Strings Attached* .... (Jive)
Now That's What I Call Music!-#6-C .... (Virgin)
Bye Bye Love
Everly Brothers; *Everly Brothers' All-Time Greatest Hits* ..... (Curb)
Everly Brothers-Cadence Classics-Their 20 Greatest Hits ..... (Rhino)
Very Best Of The Everly Brothers ....(Warner Bros.)
Simon & Garfunkel; *Bridge Over Troubled Water* .... (Columbia)
Bye, Bye
Jo Dee Messina; *I'm Alright* .... (Curb)
Call Me Gone
Patti LaBelle; *When A Woman Loves* ....(MCA)
Candle In The Wind
Elton John; *Goodbye Yellow Brick Road* ....(Polydor)
Live In Australia With The Melbourne Symphony Orchestra ....(MCA)
Your Songs .... (Polydor)
Candle In The Wind 1997
Elton John; *Candle In The Wind 1997 (Diana, Princess Of Wales)
(Single)* ....(Rocket)
Can't Really Be Gone
Tim McGraw; *All I Want* .... (Curb)
Can't Stay
Dave Hollister; *Ghetto Hymns* ....(Def Squad/DreamWorks)
Can't You See
Alabama; *Alabama-Live* .... (RCA)
Charlie Daniels Band; *Volunteer Jam VII-C* ....(Epic)
Hank Williams, Jr.; *Hank Williams, Jr. & Friends* ... (Polydor)
Rebels, Renegades & Ramblers-C .... (Polydor)
Standing In The Shadows .... (Polydor)
Marshall Tucker Band; *Marshall Tucker Band* .... (AJK Music)
Searchin' For A Rainbow .... (AJK Music)
Cara Mia
Jay & The Americans; *I Got Rhythm-C* .... (K-Tel)
Jay & The Americans' Greatest Hits ..... (CEMA Special Prod.)
Jay & The Americans' Greatest Hits .... (Curb)
Carey
Joni Mitchell; *Blue* .... (Reprise)
Joni Mitchell with Tom Scott & The L.A. Express; *Miles Of Aisles* .... (Asylum)
Carrion
Fiona Apple; *Tidal* .... (Clean Slate/Work)
Carrying Your Love With Me
George Strait; *Carrying Your Love With Me* ....(MCA)
Latest Greatest Straitest Hits ....(MCA)
Change
Sheryl Crow; *Sheryl Crow* .... (A&M)
Change My Mind
John Berry; *Faces* .... (Capitol)
Child Is Gone
Fiona Apple; *Tidal* .... (Clean Slate/Work)
Child's Song
Tom Rush; *Best Of Tom Rush: No Regrets* .... (Legacy)
Tom Rush .... (Columbia)

Cold Day In July
Dixie Chicks; *Fly* .... (Monument)
Joy White; *Between Midnight & Hindsight* .... (Columbia)
Ray Price; *For The Good Times/I Won't Mention It Again* .... (Columbia)
Suzy Bogguss; *Voices In The Wind* .... (Liberty)
Come With Me
Shai; *Blackface* .... (Gasoline Alley)
Cowboy Love Song
Skip Gorman; *A Cowboy's Wild Song To His Herd* .... (Rounder)
Crossing Muddy Waters
John Hiatt; *Crossing Muddy Waters* .... (Vanguard)
Cruel Summer
Ace Of Base; *Cruel Summer* .... (Arista)
Bananarama; *Bananarama* .... (London)
Cry On
Little Texas; *First Time For Everything* .... (Warner Bros.)
Great Divorce Songs For Him-C .... (Warner Bros.)
Crying Time
Buck Owens & Emmylou Harris; *Act Naturally* ..... (Capitol)
Ray Charles; *Ray Charles' Greatest Hits* .... (Rhino)
Ray Charles-Anthology .... (Rhino)
Ray Charles-His Greatest Hits-#1 ..... (Dunhill Compact Classics)
Daniel
Elton John; *Don't Shoot Me I'm Only The Piano Player* .... (Polydor)
Elton John's Greatest Hits .... (Polydor)
Wilson Phillips; *Two Rooms-Celebrating The Songs Of Elton John & Bernie
Taupin-C* .... (Polydor)
Day That She Left Tulsa (In A Chevy)
Wade Hayes; *When The Wrong One Loves You Right* .... (Columbia/DKC)
Daylight Fading
Counting Crows; *Recovering The Satellites* .... (David Geffen Co.)
Delta Dawn
Bette Midler; *Divine Miss M* .... (Atlantic)
Live At Last .... (Atlantic)
Helen Reddy; *Helen Reddy's Greatest Hits* .... (Capitol)
Tanya Tucker; *Tanya Tucker Live* .... (MCA Special Prod.)
Tanya Tucker-Greatest Hits Encore .... (Gold Rush)
Tanya Tucker's Greatest Hits .... (Columbia)
Deportee (Plane Wreck At Los Gatos)
Arlo Guthrie & Pete Seeger; *Together In Concert* ..... (Reprise)
Byrds; *The Byrds* .... (Columbia)
Cisco Houston; *Greatest Songs Of Woody Guthrie-C* ..... (Vanguard)
Gene Clark & Carla Olson; *So Rebellious A Lover* ..... (Rhino)
Judy Collins; *Tribute To Woody Guthrie-C* ..... (Warner Bros.)
Waylon Jennings, Willie Nelson, Johnny Cash, Kris Kristofferson;
Highwayman .... (Columbia)
Different Drum
Linda Ronstadt; *Different Drum* .... (Capitol)
Linda Ronstadt-Retrospective .... (Capitol)
Linda Ronstadt's Greatest Hits .... (Asylum)
Stone Poneys Featuring Linda Ronstadt; *Baby Boomer Classics-Mellow
'60s-C* .... (JCI Assoc. Labels)
On The Road Again-Rock's New Frontiers-C .... (Capitol)
The Stone Poneys Featuring Linda Ronstadt .... (EMI)
Victoria Shaw; *Victoria Shaw* .... (Reprise)
Don't Ever Leave Me
Patsy Cline; *Legendary Patsy Cline* .... (Pair)
Peggy Lee; *Moments Like This* .... (Chesky)
Don't Forget To Cry
Mandy Barnett; *I've Got A Right To Cry* .... (Sire)
Don't Leave Me
Blackstreet; *Another Level* .... (Interscope)
Don't Leave Me This Way
Thelma Houston; *Billboard Top Rock 'N' Roll Hits-1977-C* .... (Rhino)
Disco Nights-#6-C .... (Rebound)
Motown's Leading Ladies-C .... (Motown)
Don't Let Me Leave
Marc Anthony; *Marc Anthony* .... (Columbia)
Don't Sleep In The Subway
Frank Sinatra; *Frank Sinatra* .... (Reprise)
Petula Clark; *Petula Clark's Greatest Hits* ....(Crescendo)
Summer Of Love-#1-C .... (Rhino)
Don't Think Twice, It's All Right
Bob Dylan; *Before The Flood* .... (Columbia)
Bob Dylan's Greatest Hits-#2 .... (Columbia)
Freewheelin' .... (Columbia)
Joan Baez; *The First 10 Years* .... (Vanguard)
Wonder Who?; *Anniversary* .... (Rhino)
Drinkin' My Baby Goodbye
Charlie Daniels Band; *Me & The Boys* .... (Epic)
El Paso
Grateful Dead; *Steal Your Face* ....(Grateful Dead)
Marty Robbins; *Billboard Top Country Hits-1960-C* ..... (Rhino)
Gunfighter Ballads & Trail Songs .... (Legacy)
Marty Robbins' Biggest Hits .... (Columbia)
Radio Classics Of The '50s-C .... (Columbia)
Texas Super Hits-C .... (Columbia)
End Of The World
Skeeter Davis; *Best Of Skeeter Davis* .... (Gusto)

Billboard Top Country Hits-1963-C. . . . . (Rhino)
Nipper's Greatest Hits Of The '60s-#1-C. . . . . (RCA)
Stars Of The Grand Ole Opry-1926-1974-C. . . . . (RCA)
Super Country Hits Of The '60s-C. (Gusto)

Evaporated
Ben Folds Five; *Whatever And Ever Amen* . . . . (Caroline/550)

Everybody's Talkin'
Nilsson; *Everybody's Talkin': The Encore Collection* . . . . (BMG Special Prod.)
ST/Forrest Gump . . . . (Epic/Sony Music Soundtrax)
ST/Midnight Cowboy . . . . (EMI)
Willie Nelson; *Best Of Willie*. . . . . (RCA)
Sweet Memories . . . . (RCA)

Everyone's Gone To The Moon
Jonathan King; *British Rock-#3-C* . . . . (Original Sound)
History Of British Rock-#7-C . . . . (Rhino)

Everytime You Go Away
Daryl Hall & John Oates; *Best Of Daryl Hall & John Oates* . . . . . (RCA)
Voices . . . . (RCA)
Paul Young; *From Time To Time-The Singles Collection* . . . . (Columbia)
Secret Of Association . . . . (Columbia)
T.J. Martell-Music For The Miracle-C. . . . . (Epic Portrait Assoc.)

Fading Like A Flower (Every Time You Leave)
Roxette; *Joyride* . . . . (EMI)

Falls Apart
Sugar Ray; *14:59* . . . . (Lava)
Totally Hits-#2-C . . . . (Elektra)

Fancy Free
Oak Ridge Boys; *Fancy Free* . . . . (MCA)
Oak Ridge Boys' Greatest Hits 2 . . . . (MCA)

Fare Thee Well Love
Rankin Family; *North Country* . . . . (Guardian/Angel)
The Rankins-Collection . . . . (Rounder)

Farewell To Ireland
Phil Cunningham; *Airs & Graces* . . . . (Green Linnet)

Farewell To Kings
Rush; *Farewell To Kings* . . . . (Mercury)

Farewell To Maine
Paul Sullivan; *Sketches Of Maine* . . . . (River Music)

Farewell To Tarwathie
Judy Collins; *Colors Of The Day-The Best Of Judy Collins* . . . . (Elektra)
So Early In The Spring, The First 15 Years. . . . . (Elektra)
Whales & Nightingales . . . . (Elektra)

Father Of Mine
Everclear; *Now That's What I Call Music!-#2-C*. . . . .(Virgin)
So Much For The Afterglow . . . . (Capitol)

Flight 309 To Tennessee
Shelly West; *West By West* . . . . (Viva)

For Your Love
Tevin Campbell; *Tevin Campbell* . . . . (Qwest)

Free Bird
Lynyrd Skynyrd; *Gold & Platinum* . . . . (MCA)
One More From The Road . . . . (MCA)
Pronounced Leh-nerd Skin-nerd. (MCA)
Southern By The Grace Of God-Tribute '87 . . . . (MCA)
Wynonna; *Skynyrd Frynds-C* . . . . (MCA)

Free To Go
Folk Implosion; *One Part Lullaby*. . . . . (Interscope)

Georgia On A Fast Train
Billy Joe Shaver; *Hot Tracks-Train Super Hits-C* . . . . (Epic)

Get Gone
Ideal; *Ideal*. . . . . (Noontime/Virgin)
Now That's What I Call Music!-#3-C . . . .(Virgin)

Getting Out Of Town
Original Broadway Cast; *42nd Street* . . . . (RCA Victor)

Give Me One Reason
Tracy Chapman; *New Beginning* . . . . (Elektra)

Go Now!
Moody Blues; *History Of British Rock-#5-C*. . . . . (Rhino)
Moody Blues-Anthology . . . . (Polydor)
Wings; *Wings Over America* . . . . (Capitol)

Goin' Cali
Bruce Springsteen; *Tracks*. . . . . (Columbia)

Going Away Party
Manhattan Transfer & Willie Nelson & Asleep At The Wheel; *Ride With Bob-C*. . . . . (DreamWorks/SKG)

Gone
'N Sync; *Celebrity*. . . . . (Jive)

Gonna Get Along Without Ya Now
Patience & Prudence; *Lost Hits Of The 50's-C* . . . . (EMI Special Markets)

Gonna Get Along Without You Now
Maureen McGovern; *Baby I'm Yours* . . . . (RCA Victor)
Skeeter Davis; *Essential Skeeter Davis* . . . . (RCA)

Good Bye
Martina McBride; *Emotion*. . . . . (RCA)

Good Girls
Joe; *All That I Am* . . . . (Jive)

Goodbye
Jagged Edge; *Jagged Little Thrill* . . . . (So So Def/Columbia)

Goodbye
Alicia Keys; *Songs In A Minor*. . . . .(J)

Goodbye Angel
Fleetwood Mac; *25 Years-The Chain* . . . . (Warner Bros.)

Goodbye Baby
Jack Scott; *Classic Hits: Hard To Find Original Recordings-C*. . . . .(Curb)
Jack Scott's Greatest Hits . . . .(Curb)

Goodbye Blue Monday
City Boy; *Dinner At The Ritz* . . . .(Mercury)

Goodbye Blue Sky
Pink Floyd; *The Wall* . . . .(Columbia)
Roger Waters; *The Wall-Live In Berlin* . . . .(Mercury)

Goodbye Blue Sky
Daryl Braithwaite; *Higher Than Hope* . . . .(Epic Portrait Assoc.)
Rise . . . .(Epic Portrait Assoc.)

Goodbye Comes Hard For Me
Mark Chesnutt; *Red Hot + Country-C* . . . .(Mercury)

Goodbye Cruel World
James Darren; *Best Of James Darren*. . . . .(Rhino)
Billboard Top Rock 'N' Roll Hits-1961-C . . . .(Rhino)

Goodbye Earl
Dixie Chicks; *Fly* . . . .(Monument)

Goodbye England's Rose (Princess Diana)
Elton John; *Countdown Singers-England's Rose-C* . . . . (Madacy)

Goodbye Girl
David Gates; *Bread-Retrospective* . . . .(Rhino)
Super Hits Of The '70s-Have A Nice Day-#21-C . . . .(Rhino)

Goodbye Jimmy Goodbye
Kathy Linden; *Rock 'N Roll Relix: 1954-1959-C* . . . .(Eclipse)

Goodbye Lament
Iommi; *Iommi*. . . . . (Divine/Priority)

Goodbye Monday Blues
Si Kahn; *Home* . . . . (Flying Fish)

Goodbye Montana
George Winston; *Summer* . . . . (Windham Hill)

Goodbye Ohio
Too Much Joy; *Cereal Killers* . . . . (Giant)

Goodbye Old Buddies
Seals & Crofts; *Get Closer* . . . . (Warner Bros.)

Goodbye San Francisco, Hello Amsterdam
Doug Sahm; *SDQ '98* . . . .(Watermelon)

Goodbye Says It All
BlackHawk; *BlackHawk* . . . .(Arista)

Goodbye Sunday
Everything But The Girl; *Idlewild* . . . . (Sire)

Goodbye To Love
Carpenters; *Carpenters-Classics-#2* . . . .(A&M)
Carpenters-Love Songs . . . .(A&M)

Goodbye To Love
Wayne Smith; *Wicked Inna Dance Hall* . . . . (Rohit)

Goodbye To Romance
Ozzy Osbourne; *The Ozzman Cometh* . . . . (Epic)

Goodbye To Tennessee
Reilly & Maloney; *Reilly & Maloney-Alive* . . . .(Freckle)

Goodbye To You
Scandal; *I Am Woman-C* . . . . (Nick At Nite)
Patty Smyth's Greatest Hits Featuring Scandal . . . .(Legacy)

Goodbye Yellow Brick Road
Elton John; *Billboard Top Rock 'N' Roll Hits-1973-C* . . . .(Rhino)
Elton John's Greatest Hits . . . . (Polydor)
Goodbye Yellow Brick Road . . . . (Polydor)

Goodnight, Sweetheart, Goodnight
McGuire Sisters; *McGuire Sisters-Anthology* . . . . (MCA)

Gotta Travel On
Bill Monroe & His Blue Grass Boys; *20th Century Masters-The Millennium Collection-The Best Of Bill Monroe* . . . . (MCA)
Country's Greatest Hits-#1-C . . . . (MCA Special Prod.)

Happy Trails
Michael Martin Murphey; *Cowboy Songs* . . . . (Warner Western)
Original Soundtrack; *Television's Greatest Hits-#1-C* . . . .(TVT)
Quicksilver Messenger Service; *Sons Of Mercury* . . . .(Rhino)
Randy Travis & Roy Rogers; *Heroes And Friends* . . . . (Warner Bros.)
Riders In The Sky; *Cowboy Way* . . . . (MCA)
Roy Rogers/Dale Evans/Dusty Rogers; *Roy Rogers Tribute-C* . . . . (RCA)
Van Halen; *Diver Down* . . . . (Warner Bros.)

Harbor Lights
Boz Scaggs; *Silk Degrees*. . . . .(Columbia)
Dinah Washington; *Complete Dinah Washington On Mercury-#2-1950-1952* . . . .(Mercury)
Dinah Washington-Golden Hits . . . .(Mercury)
For Lonely Lovers . . . .(Mercury)
This Is My Story. . . . .(Mercury)
Platters; *Super Oldies Of The '60s-#9-C* . . . . (Audio Fidelity)

Hard To Say Goodbye, My Love
Original Cast; *Dreamgirls* . . . . (Geffen)

Have A Nice Rest Of Your Life
Randy Travis; *Great Divorce Songs For Him-C* . . . . (Warner Bros.)
No Holdin' Back . . . . (Warner Bros.)

He Left A Lot To Be Desired
Ricochet; *Blink Of An Eye*. . . . . (Columbia)
Heartache Big As Texas
Ricky Van Shelton; *Texas Super Hits-C* . . . . (Columbia)
He'll Have To Go
Jim Reeves; *60 Years Of Country Music-C* . . . . (RCA)
   Best Of Jim Reeves . . . . (RCA)
   Billboard Top Country Hits-1960-C . . . . (Rhino)
   Great Moments At The Grand Ole Opry-C . . . . (RCA)
   Jim Reeves' Greatest Hits . . . . (RCA)
   Nipper's Greatest Hits Of The '50s-#1-C . . . . (RCA)
Ry Cooder; *Chicken Skin Music* . . . . (Reprise)
Hello Goodbye
Beatles; *Beatles 1* . . . . (Capitol)
   Beatles-20 Greatest Hits . . . . (Capitol)
   Beatles-Box Set . . . . (Capitol)
   Magical Mystery Tour . . . . (Capitol)
   The Beatles/1967-1970 . . . . (Capitol)
Hello Mary Lou
Creedence Clearwater Revival; *Creedence Country*. . . . . (Fantasy)
Rick Nelson; *Rick Nelson In Concert-Troubadour 1969* . . . . (MCA)
   Rick Nelson-Souvenirs . . . . (EMI)
Ricky Nelson; *Best Of Ricky Nelson* . . . . (EMI)
   Rick Nelson's Greatest Hits . . . . (Rhino)
Statler Brothers; *14 Country Favorites-C* . . . . (Mercury)
   Pardners In Rhyme . . . . (Mercury)
Hello Walls
Faron Young; *Billboard Top Country Hits-1961-C* . . . . (Rhino)
Willie Nelson; *Essential Willie Nelson* . . . . (RCA)
   Willie Nelson-Greatest Songs . . . . (Curb)
Helplessly Hoping
Crosby, Stills & Nash; *Crosby, Stills & Nash* . . . . (Atlantic)
   CSN . . . . (Atlantic)
Crosby, Stills, Nash & Young; *So Far* . . . . (Atlantic)
Here We Go Again
Aretha Franklin; *A Rose Is Still A Rose* . . . . (Arista)
Here's To The Night
Eve 6; *Horrorscope* . . . . (RCA)
   Totally Hits 2001-C . . . . (Arista)
Heroes & Villains
Beach Boys; *Concert/'69-Live In London* . . . . (Capitol)
   Endless Harmony . . . . (Capitol)
   Good Vibrations-Thirty Years Of The Beach Boys . . . . (Capitol)
   Made In The U.S.A. . . . . (Capitol)
   Smiley Smile/Wild Honey. . . . . (Capitol)
   Sunshine Dream. . . . . (Capitol)
He's Gone
Chantels; *Best Of The Chantels*. . . . . (Rhino)
Hey Girl
Billy Joel; *Billy Joel's Greatest Hits-#3* . . . . (Columbia)
Freddie Scott; *Freddie Scott Sings And Sings And Sings* . . . . (Collectables)
Michael McDonald; *Best Of Smooth Jazz-#2-Under The*
   Covers-C. . . . . (Warner Bros.)
   Blink Of An Eye . . . . (Reprise)
Righteous Brothers; *Best Of The Righteous Brothers-#2* . . . . (Curb)
High Noon
Frankie Laine; *Billboard Top Movie Hits-1950-1954-C*. . . . . (Rhino)
Tex Ritter; *Heroes Of Country Music-#4-Legends Of The West*
   Coast-C. . . . . (Rhino)
   The Envelope Please-Academy Award Winning Songs (1946-
   1957)-C . . . . (Rhino)
Hit The Road Jack
Ray Charles; *Ray Charles' Greatest Hits* . . . . (Rhino)
   Ray Charles-Anthology . . . . (Rhino)
   Ray Charles-His Greatest Hits-#2 . . . . (Dunhill Compact Classics)
Hopeless
Dionne Farris; *ST/Love Jones* . . . . (Columbia)
How A Cowgirl Says Goodbye
Tracy Lawrence; *The Coast Is Clear* . . . . (Atlantic)
How Can I Help You Say Goodbye
Patty Loveless; *Only What I Feel* . . . . (Epic)
   Patty Loveless-Classics . . . . (Epic)
How Could I
Marc Anthony; *Marc Anthony* . . . . (Columbia)
How Do I Live
LeAnn Rimes; *Absolute Dance Hits-C*. . . . . (Curb)
   You Light Up My Life-Inspirational Songs . . . . (Curb)
Trisha Yearwood; *Songbook-A Collection Of Hits* . . . . (MCA)
How Do You Say Auf Wiedersehen
George Shearing & Mel Torme; *Top Drawer* . . . . (Concord Jazz)
How Do You Tell The One
After 7; *Reflections* . . . . (Virgin)
How Long Gone
Brooks & Dunn; *If You See Her* . . . . (Arista)
I Ain't Goin' Down
Nashville Bluegrass Band; *Waitin' For The Hard Times To Go* . . . . . (Sugar Hill)
I Couldn't See You Leavin'
Conway Twitty; *Crazy In Love* . . . . (MCA)

I Don't Believe In Goodbye
Sawyer Brown; *Sawyer Brown's Greatest Hits 1990-1995*. . . . . (Curb)
I Don't Wanna Play House
Sara Evans; *Tammy Wynette...Remembered-C* . . . . (Asylum)
Tammy Wynette; *Tammy Wynette-Anniversary-20 Years Of Hits* . . . . (Epic)
   Tammy Wynette's Greatest Hits . . . . (Epic)
   Tammy Wynette-Super Hits . . . . (Epic)
I Don't Want To Spoil The Party
Beatles; *Beatles VI* . . . . (Capitol)
   For Sale . . . . (Capitol)
Rosanne Cash; *Greatest Country Hits Of The '80s-1989-C* . . . . (Columbia)
   Rosanne Cash-Hits-1979-1989 . . . . (Columbia)
I Get The Fever
Bill Anderson; *Bill Anderson's Greatest Hits* . . . . (Varese Sarabande)
I Go To Pieces
Del Shannon; *Rock On!* . . . . (Gone Gator)
Peter And Gordon; *Best Of Peter And Gordon* . . . . (Rhino)
   History Of British Rock-#3-C . . . . (Rhino)
Southern Pacific; *County Line*. . . . . (Warner Bros.)
   Southern Pacific's Greatest Hits . . . . (Warner Bros.)
I Guess The Lord Must Be In New York City
Nilsson; *Harry*. . . . . (Dunhill Compact Classics)
   Nilsson's Greatest Hits . . . . (RCA)
I Left My Heart In San Francisco
Tony Bennett; *I Left My Heart In San Francisco*. . . . . (Columbia)
   Pop Classics Of The '60s-C . . . . (Columbia)
   Tony Bennett's All-Time Greatest Hits . . . . (Columbia)
I Take It Back
Sandy Posey; *Best Of Sandy Posey* . . . . (Collectables)
   Best Of Sandy Posey-With Skeeter Davis . . . . (Gusto)
I Tipped My Hat And Slowly Rode Away
Gene Autry; *Sing Cowboy Sing: The Gene Autry Collection*. . . . . (Rhino)
I Want My Goodbye Back
Ty Herndon; *What Mattered Most*. . . . . (Epic)
I Was Wrong
Keb' Mo'; *Slow Down*. (550/Epic/Okeh)
I Went To Your Wedding
Patti Page; *Patti Page-Golden Hits* . . . . (Mercury)
I Won't Be Home No More
Hank Williams With His Drifting Cowboys; *Hank Williams-24 Greatest*
   Hits-#2. . . . . (Polydor)
   Hank Williams-40 Greatest Hits. . . . . (Polydor)
I Won't Mention It Again
Ray Price; *Ray Price's Greatest Hits-#1-3* . . . . (Step One)
   Ray Price-Super Hits . . . . (Columbia)
Reba McEntire; *Starting Over*. (MCA)
If Ever I Would Leave You
Richard Harris; *ST/Camelot* . . . . (Warner Bros.)
Robert Goulet; *Robert Goulet's Greatest Hits*. . . . . (Columbia)
Robert Goulet/Original Cast; *Camelot* . . . . (Columbia)
If Leaving Me Is Easy
Phil Collins; *Face Value* . . . . (Atlantic)
If You Go Away
Neil Diamond; *Neil Diamond-Love Songs* . . . . (MCA)
   Rainbow . . . . (MCA)
   Stones . . . . (MCA)
If You Leave
Destiny's Child; *The Writing's On The Wall*. . . . . (Columbia)
If You Leave Me Now
Chicago; *Chicago's Greatest Hits-#2 (1974-81)*. . . . . (Chicago)
   If You Leave Me Now . . . . (Chicago)
If You Leave Me Tonight I'll Cry
Jerry Wallace; *From The Vaults: Decca Country Classics-1934-*
   1973-C. . . . . (Decca)
   Jerry Wallace's Greatest Hits . . . . (Curb)
If You're Gone
Matchbox Twenty; *Mad Season By Matchbox Twenty* . . . . (Lava)
I'll Be On My Way
Beatles; *Live At The BBC* . . . . (Apple)
I'll Fly Away
Aretha Franklin; *Diana, Princess Of Wales-Tribute-C* . . . . (Columbia)
I'll Follow The Sun
Beatles; *Beatles '65*. . . . . (Capitol)
   Beatles-Box Set. . . . . (Capitol)
   Beatles-Love Songs . . . . (Capitol)
   For Sale . . . . (Capitol)
I'll Kiss The World Goodbye
J.J. Cale; *Really* . . . . (Mercury)
I'll Let You Know Before I Leave
Jorma Kaukonen & Tom Hobson; *Quah* . . . . (Relix)
I'll See You Again
Frank Sinatra; *Point Of No Return* . . . . (Capitol)
I'm Leaving
Aaron Tippin; *What This Country Needs* . . . . (Lyric Street)
I'm Not Running Anymore
John Mellencamp; *John Mellencamp* . . . . (Columbia)
Immortality
Celine Dion with The Bee Gees; *Let's Talk About Love-C* . . . . (550 Music)

Independence Day
Bruce Springsteen; *The River* .... (Columbia)
Bruce Springsteen & The E Street Band; *Bruce Springsteen & The E Street
    Band Live/1975-85* .... (Legacy)
Indescribably Blue
Elvis Presley; *Elvis' Gold Records, Volume 4* .... (RCA)
    From Nashville To Memphis-The Essential '60s Masters .... (RCA)
Interstate Love Song
Stone Temple Pilots; *Purple* .... (Atlantic)
It's A Little Too Late
Mark Chesnutt; *Mark Chesnutt's Greatest Hits* .... (Decca)
It's So Hard To Say Goodbye To Yesterday
Boyz II Men; *Cooleyhighharmony* .... (Motown)
G.C. Cameron; *Motown Memories-#3-C* .... (Motown)
It's Time For Love
Chi-Lites; *Chi-Lites' Greatest Hits-#2* .... (Rhino)
It's Too Late
Derek And The Dominos; *Layla* .... (Polydor)
Jamaica Farewell
Harry Belafonte; *Calypso* .... (RCA)
    Harry Belafonte-Legendary Performer .... (RCA)
    Harry Belafonte-Pure Gold .... (RCA)
    Harry Belafonte's All Time Greatest Hits-#1 .... (RCA)
    This Is Harry Belafonte .... (RCA)
Je Suis Desole
Mark Knopfler; *Golden Heart* .... (Warner Bros.)
Johnny Bye-Bye
Bruce Springsteen; *Tracks* .... (Columbia)
Kansas City
Beatles; *Beatles VI* .... (Capitol)
    Beatles-Box Set .... (Capitol)
    Rock 'N' Roll Music .... (Capitol)
    Super Oldies Of The '60s-#10-C .... (Audio Fidelity)
Bill Haley & His Comets; *Bill Haley & His Comets' Greatest Hits* ..... (Everest)
Fats Domino; *Fats Domino's Greatest Hits* .... (Everest)
Wilbert Harrison; *American Graffiti-#3-C* .... (MCA)
    Billboard Top Rock 'N' Roll Hits-1959-C .... (Rhino)
    Cruisin'-1959-C .... (Increase)
    Echoes Of A Rock Era-Middle Years-C .... (Roulette)
    Super Oldies Of The '50s-#2-C .... (Audio Fidelity)
Key To The Highway
David Bromberg; *You Should See The Rest Of The Band* .... (Fantasy)
Derek And The Dominos; *Eric Clapton-Crossroads-C* .... (Polydor)
    Layla .... (Polydor)
John Hammond; *Best Of John Hammond* .... (Vanguard)
Little Walter; *Best Of Little Walter-#2* .... (Chess)
    Blues-#2-C .... (Chess)
Sonny Terry & Brownie McGhee; *Great Blues Men-C* ...... (Vanguard)
Kiss And Say Goodbye
Manhattans; *Best Of The Manhattans-Kiss And Say Goodbye* ..... (Legacy)
    Manhattans Greatest Hits .... (Columbia)
Kiss Him Goodbye
Nylons; *Happy Together* .... (Open Air)
Kiss The World Goodbye
Kris Kristofferson; *Border Lord* .... (Columbia)
Kiss This
Aaron Tippin; *People Like Us* .... (Lyric Street)
Kiss Your Past Good-Bye
Aerosmith; *Nine Lives* .... (Columbia)
Land Of Hope And Dreams
Bruce Springsteen & The E Street Band; *God Bless America-C* ..... (Columbia)
    Live In New York City .... (Columbia)
Laredo
Chris Cagle; *Play It Loud* .... (Capitol)
Last Chance To Turn Around
Gene Pitney; *Best Of Gene Pitney* .... (K-Tel)
    Gene Pitney-Anthology 1961-1968. .... (Rhino)
Last Goodbye
Jeff Buckley; *Grace* .... (Columbia)
Last Goodbye
Kenny Wayne Shepherd Band; *Live On* .... (Giant)
Last Thing On My Mind
Porter Wagoner & Dolly Parton; *Essential Porter Wagoner & Dolly
    Parton* .... (RCA)
Last Train Done Gone Down
Marty Stuart; *Hot Tracks-Train Super Hits-C* .... (Epic)
    Let There Be Country .... (Columbia)
Last Train To Clarksville
Monkees; *Monkees* .... (Arista)
    Monkees' Greatest Hits .... (Rhino)
    Monkees-Live-1967 .... (Rhino)
    Then & Now...The Best Of The Monkees .... (Arista)
Learning As You Go
Rick Trevino; *Learning As You Go* .... (Columbia)
    Super Hits Of 1996-C .... (Epic)
Leavin' And Sayin' Goodbye
Faron Young; *Faron Young-Golden Hits* .... (Mercury)
    Faron Young's Greatest Hits-#1-3 .... (Step One)

Leavin' Memphis, Frisco Bound
Jesse Fuller; *Frisco Bound* .... (Arhoolie)
    Lone Cat .... (Good Time Jazz)
Leavin' Texas
Jerry Jeff Walker; *A Man Must Carry On* .... (MCA)
    Best Of Jerry Jeff Walker .... (MCA)
Leavin' Train
Bruce Springsteen; *Tracks* .... (Columbia)
Leaving Home Ain't Easy
Queen; *Jazz* .... (Hollywood)
Leaving Kansas City
George Jackson; *Sweet Down Home Delta Blues* .... (Amblin')
Leaving Las Vegas
Sheryl Crow; *Tuesday Night Music Club* .... (A&M)
Leaving Lexington
Fiction Brothers; *Things Are Coming My Way* .... (Flying Fish)
Leaving London
Tom Paxton; *Compleat Tom Paxton* .... (Elektra)
    Outward Bound .... (Elektra)
Leaving Louisiana In The Broad Daylight
Emmylou Harris; *Quarter Moon In A Ten Cent Town* .... (Warner Bros.)
Oak Ridge Boys; *Have Arrived* .... (MCA)
    Oak Ridge Boys' Greatest Hits .... (MCA)
Rodney Crowell; *Ain't Living Long Like This* ...... (Warner Bros.)
    Rodney Crowell-Collection .... (Warner Bros.)
Leaving October
Sons Of The Desert; *Whatever Comes First* .... (Epic)
Leaving Of Liverpool
Clancy Brothers; *Clancy Brothers Greatest Hits* .... (Vanguard)
Leaving On A Jet Plane
Chantal Kreviazuk; *ST/Armageddon-The Album* .... (Columbia)
John Denver; *John Denver's Greatest Hits* .... (RCA)
    Rhymes & Reasons .... (RCA)
Kendalls; *Super Country Hits Of The '70s-C* .... (Gusto)
Peter, Paul & Mary; *10 Years Together/The Best Of Peter, Paul
    and Mary* .... (Warner Bros.)
    Album 1700 .... (Warner Bros.)
Leaving Port
James Horner; *ST/Titanic* .... (Sony Music Classical)
Leaving Sedona
Don Harriss; *Elevations* .... (Sonic Atmospheres)
Leaving This Town
Beach Boys; *Holland* .... (Brother)
    The Beach Boys In Concert .... (Brother)
Leaving Town
Dexter Freebish; *Life Of Saturdays* .... (Capitol)
Leaving West Virginia
Kathy Mattea; *Walk The Way The Wind Blows* .... (Mercury)
Let's Make Sure We Kiss Goodbye
Vince Gill; *Let's Make Sure We Kiss Goodbye* .... (MCA)
Let's Take All Night (To Say Goodbye)
Barry Manilow; *If I Should Love Again* .... (Arista)
Letter, The
Macy Gray; *On How Life Is* .... (Epic)
Light Years
Pearl Jam; *Binaural* .... (Epic)
Linger
Jonatha Brooke; *Steady Pull* .... (Bad Dog)
Little Gasoline, A
Terri Clark; *Fearless* .... (Mercury)
Little Girls, Goodbye
John Charles Thomas; *Music From The New York Stage (1890-1920)-#4-
    1917-1920-C* .... (Pearl)
Little Good-byes
SHeDAISY; *The Whole Shebang* .... (Lyric Street)
Long Goodbye
Bruce Springsteen; *Human Touch* .... (Columbia)
Long Road, The
Eddie Vedder; *America: A Tribute To Heroes-C* .... (Interscope)
Loose Talk
Carl Smith; *Very Special Love Song-C* .... (Fifty One West)
Patsy Cline; *Live At The Opry* .... (MCA)
Lovefool
Cardigans; *First Band On The Moon* .... (Mercury)
    MTV Best Of The Buzz Bin-#2-C .... (Mammoth)
Lovesick Blues
Gary Morris; *Plain Brown Wrapper* .... (Warner Bros.)
Hank Williams With His Drifting Cowboys; *24 Of Hank Williams'
    Greatest Hits* .... (Polydor)
    Lovesick Blues .... (Polydor)
Linda Ronstadt; *Linda Ronstadt-Retrospective* .... (Capitol)
    Silk Purse .... (Capitol)
Patsy Cline; *Live At The Opry* .... (MCA)
Ryan Adams; *Timeless: Hank Williams Tribute-C* .... (Lost Highway/IDJMG)
Luxury: Cococure
Maxwell; *Embrya* .... (Columbia)
Magical Mystery Tour
Beatles; *Magical Mystery Tour* .... (Capitol)

Reel Music . . . . (Capitol)
The Beatles/1967-1970 . . . . (Capitol)
Mama From The Train
Patti Page; *Patti Page-Golden Celebration* . . . . (Mercury)
Maybe He'll Notice Her Now
Mindy McCready; *Ten Thousand Angels* . . . . (BNA)
Maybe Someday
Cure; *Bloodflowers* . . . . (Fiction/Elektra)
Maybe We Should Just Sleep On It
Tim McGraw; *All I Want* . . . . (Curb)
Tim McGraw's Greatest Hits . . . . (Curb)
Me And Julio Down By The Schoolyard
Paul Simon; *Greatest Hits, Etc.* . . . . (Columbia)
Negotiations And Love Songs, 1971-1986 . . . . (Warner Bros.)
Paul Simon . . . . (Columbia)
Paul Simon In Concert/Live Rhymin' . . . . (Columbia)
Simon & Garfunkel; *The Concert In Central Park* . . . . . . (Warner Bros.)
Mean Mama Blues
Bob Wills; *Stay A Little Longer-The Original Columbia*
Recordings . . . . (Roswell/RCA)
MFC
Pearl Jam; *Yield* . . . . (Epic)
Midnight Train To Georgia
Gladys Knight & The Pips; *Billboard Top Rock 'N' Roll Hits-1973-C* . . (Rhino)
Gladys Knight & The Pips' Greatest Hits . . . . (Buddah)
Imagination . . . . (Right Stuff)
On & On . . . . (Fifty One West)
Radio Active Hits-C . . . . (Accord)
Train Trax-C . . . . (Sony Music Special Prod.)
Very Best Of Gladys Knight & The Pips . . . . (Buddah)
Miss Blue
Filter; *Title Of Record* . . . . (Reprise)
Mistakes
Mandy Barnett; *I've Got A Right To Cry* . . . . (Sire)
Modern Age, The
Strokes; *Is This It* . . . . (RCA)
Monkey Wrench
Foo Fighters; *The Colour And The Shape* . . . . (Roswell/RCA)
Moscow Farewell
Ennio Morricone; *Film Music-#1* . . . . (Virgin Movie Music)
Movin' On
Mya featuring Silkk The Shocker; *Mya* . . . . . . (University/Interscope)
Movin' Out
Aerosmith; *Aerosmith* . . . . (Columbia)
Aerosmith-Classics Live 2 . . . . (Columbia)
Pandora's Box . . . . (Columbia)
Movin' Out
Billy Joel; *Billy Joel-Greatest Hits, Volume I & Volume II* . . . . . . (Columbia)
Stranger . . . . (Columbia)
Movin' Out
Sonny Rollins; *Movin' Out* . . . . (Prestige)
My Antonia
Emmylou Harris; *Red Dirt Girl* . . . . (Nonesuch)
My Baby Left Me
Arthur ''Big Boy'' Crudup; *That's All Right (Mama)* . . . . (Bluebird)
Creedence Clearwater Revival; *Cosmo's Factory* . . . . (Fantasy)
Creedence Country . . . . (Fantasy)
Elvis Presley; *Elvis Recorded Live On Stage In Memphis* . . . . (RCA)
My Hero
Foo Fighters; *The Colour And The Shape* . . . . (Roswell/RCA)
My Hometown
Bruce Springsteen; *Born In The U.S.A.* . . . . (Columbia)
Bruce Springsteen's Greatest Hits . . . . (Columbia)
My Song
Jerry Cantrell; *Boggy Depot* . . . . (Columbia)
My Whole World Ended (The Moment You Left Me)
David Ruffin; *David Ruffin-At His Best* . . . . (Motown)
Motown Year By Year-The Sound Of Young America-1969-C . . . . . (Motown)
Spinners; *Best Of The Spinners* . . . . (Motown)
Na Na Hey Hey Kiss Him Goodbye
Steam; *Billboard Top Rock 'N' Roll Hits-1969-C* . . . . (Rhino)
Super Hits Of The '70s-Have A Nice Day-#1-C . . . . (Rhino)
Toga Rock-C . . . . (Dunhill Compact Classics)
Neither One Of Us (Wants To Be First To Say Goodbye)
Gladys Knight & The Pips; *Gladys Knight & The Pips-All The*
Great Hits . . . . (Motown)
Gladys Knight & The Pips-Anthology . . . . (Motown)
Gladys Knight & The Pips-Superstars Series-#13 . . . . (Motown)
Motown Grammy R&B Performances Of The '60s & '70s-C . . . . . (Motown)
Neither One Of Us . . . . (Motown)
Never Can Say Goodbye
Jackson 5; *Jackson 5's Greatest Hits* . . . . (Motown)
Jackson 5-The Ultimate Collection . . . . (Motown)
Never Did Say Goodbye
Lisa Brokop; *Every Little Girl's Dream* . . . . (Patriot)
New York's Not My Home
Jim Croce; *Photographs & Memories/His Greatest Hits* . . . . (Atlantic)
Next Plane To London
Rose Garden; *Only Love-1965-1969-C* . . . . (JCI Assoc. Labels)

Next Year
Foo Fighters; *There Is Nothing Left To Lose* . . . . (Roswell/RCA)
Night Before
Beatles; *Beatles-Box Set* . . . . (Capitol)
Rock 'N' Roll Music . . . . (Capitol)
ST/Help! . . . . (Capitol)
No Easy Goodbye
South Sixty Five; *South Sixty Five* . . . . (Atlantic)
No Expectations
Rolling Stones; *Beggars Banquet* . . . . (Abkco)
More Hot Rocks (big hits & fazed cookies) . . . . (Abkco)
Singles Collection-The London Years . . . . (Abkco)
No One
Cold; *13 Ways To Bleed On Stage* . . . . (Flip/Geffen/Interscope)
No Regrets
Emmylou Harris; *Bluebird* . . . . (Reprise)
Tom Rush; *Best Of Tom Rush: No Regrets* . . . . (Legacy)
The Circle Game . . . . (Elektra)
Nothin' But The Taillights
Clint Black; *Nothin' But The Taillights* . . . . (RCA)
Nothin On Me
Shawn Colvin; *A Few Small Repairs* . . . . (Columbia)
ST/Mr. Wrong . . . . (Hollywood)
Oh Me, Oh My, Sweet Baby
Diamond Rio; *Close To The Edge* . . . . (Arista)
George Strait; *Beyond The Blue Neon* . . . . (MCA)
Oh, Pretty Woman
2 Live Crew; *As Clean As They Wanna Be* . . . . (Luke)
Al Green; *Al Green's Greatest Hits-#2* . . . . (Motown)
I'm Still In Love With You . . . . (Right Stuff)
Ricky Van Shelton; *RVS III* . . . . (Columbia)
Roy Orbison; *In Dreams-Greatest Hits* . . . . (Orbison)
Roy Orbison's All-Time Greatest Hits-#1 & 2 . . . . (Monument)
ST/Pretty Woman . . . . (EMI)
Van Halen; *Diver Down* . . . . (Warner Bros.)
One Less Bell To Answer
5th Dimension; *5th Dimension-Anthology 1967-1973* . . . . (Rhino)
Greatest Hits On Earth . . . . (Arista)
Barbra Streisand; *Barbra Joan Streisand* . . . . (Columbia)
Gladys Knight & The Pips; *Gladys Knight & The Pips-Anthology* . . . (Motown)
If I Were Your Woman . . . . (Motown)
Only Living Boy In New York
Simon & Garfunkel; *Bridge Over Troubled Water* . . . . (Columbia)
Collected Works . . . . (Columbia)
Ophelia
Band; *Best Of The Band* . . . . (Capitol)
Northern Lights-Southern Cross . . . . (Capitol)
The Last Waltz . . . . (Warner Bros.)
To Kingdom Come-The Definitive Collection . . . . (Capitol)
Orchids Mean Goodbye
Carl Smith; *45-#21087* . . . . (Columbia)
Over The Rise
Bruce Springsteen; *Tracks* . . . . (Columbia)
Pack Up Her Trunk Blues
Tommy Bradley; *Complete Recorded Works-1928-1932* . . . . . . (Document)
Pack Your Lies And Go
Celinda Pink; *Victimized* . . . . (Step One)
Pack'd My Bags
Rufus; *Rufusized* . . . . (MCA)
Stompin' At The Savoy . . . . (Warner Bros.)
Packed Up And Left
Mac McAnally; *Mac McAnally* . . . . (DreamWorks/SKG)
Porcelain
Moby; *Play* . . . . (V2)
ST/Playing By Heart . . . . (Capitol)
ST/The Beach . . . . (Sire)
Power Of Good-Bye
Madonna; *GHV2* . . . . (Warner Bros.)
Ray Of Light . . . . (Maverick)
Pre-Road Downs
Crosby, Stills & Nash; *Crosby, Stills & Nash* . . . . (Atlantic)
Prisoner For Life
Skip Gorman; *A Cowboy's Wild Song To His Herd* . . . . (Rounder)
Ramble On
Led Zeppelin; *Led Zeppelin II* . . . . (Atlantic)
Led Zeppelin-Box Set . . . . (Atlantic)
Remasters . . . . (Atlantic)
Ramblin' Man
Allman Brothers Band; *Best Of The Allman Brothers Band* . . . . . . (Polydor)
Billboard Top Rock 'N' Roll Hits-1973-C . . . . (Rhino)
Brothers & Sisters . . . . (Polydor)
Decade Of Hits-1969-1979 . . . . (Polydor)
Dreams . . . . (Polydor)
Rock Classics-C . . . . (K-Tel)
South's Greatest Hits-C . . . . (Capricorn)
The Road Goes On Forever, A Collection Of Their Greatest
Recordings . . . . (Polydor)
Wipe The Windows-Check The Oil-Dollar Gas . . . . (Capricorn)

Ramblin' Man
Hank Williams; *24 Of Hank Williams' Greatest Hits* . . . . (Polydor)
   Hank Williams-16 Great Hits . . . . (Everest)
   Hank Williams-40 Greatest Hits . . . . (Polydor)
Hank Williams, Jr.; *Rowdy* . . . . (WB/Curb)
   ST/Your Cheatin' Heart . . . . (Sony Music Special Prod.)
Kieran Kane; *Steel Rails-Classic Railroad Songs-#1-C* . . . . (Rounder)

Remember Me
Journey; *ST/Armageddon-The Album* . . . . (Columbia)

Restless
Carl Perkins; *Jive After Five-Best Of Carl Perkins-1959-1978* . . . . (Rhino)
Mark O'Connor; *Great Divorce Songs For Him-C* . . . . (Warner Bros.)
   The New Nashville Cats . . . . (Warner Bros.)

Rhythm Of The Rain
Cascades; *Collectables Presents The History Of Rock-#7-C* . . . . . (Collectables)
   Golden Years-1963-C . . . . (Dominion Entert.)

River And The Highway
Pam Tillis; *All Of This Love* . . . . (Arista)
   Pam Tillis' Greatest Hits . . . . (Arista)

Ruby Tuesday
Rolling Stones; *Between The Buttons* . . . . (Abkco)
   Flashpoint . . . . (Virgin)
   Flowers . . . . (Abkco)
   Hot Rocks 1964-1971 . . . . (Abkco)
   Singles Collection-The London Years . . . . (Abkco)
   Through The Past, Darkly (Big Hits Vol. 2) . . . . (Abkco)

Saint Joe On The School Bus
Marcy Playground; *Marcy Playground* . . . . (Capitol)

Save Tonight
Eagle-Eye Cherry; *Desireless* . . . . (Work)

Say Goodbye To Hollywood
Bette Midler; *Broken Blossom* . . . . (Atlantic)
Billy Joel; *Billy Joel-Greatest Hits, Volume I & Volume II* . . . . (Columbia)
   Songs In The Attic . . . . (Columbia)
   Turnstiles . . . . (Columbia)

Say You Love Me Or Say Goodbye
REO Speedwagon; *A Decade Of Rock And Roll 1970 To 1980* . . . . (Epic)
   You Can Tune A Piano But You Can't Tuna Fish . . . . (Epic)

Saying Goodbye To A Friend
Suzy Bogguss; *Give Me Some Wheels* . . . . (Capitol)

Saying Hello, Saying I Love You, Saying Goodbye
Jim Ed Brown & Helen Cornelius; *Jim Ed Brown & Helen Cornelius'*
   Greatest Hits . . . . (RCA)

Sealed With A Kiss
Bobby Vinton; *Bobby Vinton's Greatest Hits* . . . . (Curb)
Brian Hyland; *Cruisin'-1962-C* . . . . (Increase)
   Oldies But Goodies-#2-C . . . . (Original Sound)
   Original Rock 'N' Roll Hits Of The '50s-C . . . . (Roulette)
Lettermen; *Best Of The Lettermen-#2* . . . . (Capitol)
   Capitol Collectors Series-The Lettermen . . . . (Capitol)

See You Later, Alligator
Bill Haley & His Comets; *Bill Haley & His Comets* . . . . (Everest)
   Bill Haley & His Comets' Greatest Hits . . . . (MCA)
   Bill Haley & His Comets-Golden Hits . . . . (MCA)
   Billboard Top Rock 'N' Roll Hits-1956-C . . . . (Rhino)
   Mr. Rock 'N' Roll . . . . (Accord)
   Rock & Roll Is Here To Stay-C . . . . (Gusto)
   Rockin' & Rollin' . . . . (Accord)

Semi-Charmed Life
Third Eye Blind; *Jock Rock 2000-C* . . . . (Tommy Boy)
   Third Eye Blind . . . . (Elektra)

She Cried
Jay & The Americans; *Come A Little Bit Closer-Best Of Jay & The*
   Americans . . . . (Gold Rush)
   Jay & The Americans' All-Time Greatest Hits . . . . (Rhino)
   Jay & The Americans' Greatest Hits . . . . (Curb)

She Even Woke Me Up To Say Goodbye
Jerry Lee Lewis; *Best Of Jerry Lee Lewis* . . . . (Smash)
   Heartbreak . . . . (Tomato)
Kenny Rogers And The First Edition; *Kenny Rogers And The First Edition-*
   Love Songs . . . . (MCA Special Prod.)

She's Leaving Home
Al Jarreau; *All Fly Home* . . . . (Warner Bros.)
Beatles; *Beatles-Box Set* . . . . (Capitol)
   Beatles-Love Songs . . . . (Capitol)
   Sgt. Pepper's Lonely Hearts Club Band . . . . (Capitol)

She's Sure Taking It Well
Kevin Sharp; *Measure Of A Man* . . . . (143/Asylum)

Shiver Me Timbers
Bette Midler; *Live At Last* . . . . (Atlantic)
   Songs For The New Depression . . . . (Atlantic)
   ST/Divine Madness . . . . (Atlantic)
Tom Waits; *The Heart Of Saturday Night* . . . . (Asylum)

Shut Up And Drive
Chely Wright; *Woman In The Moon* . . . . (Polydor Country)

Silver Wings
Merle Haggard; *More Of The Best* . . . . (Rhino)
   The Seashores Of Old Mexico . . . . (Epic)

Merle Haggard & Jewel; *For The Record: Merle Haggard-43*
   Legendary Hits . . . . (BNA)
Merle Haggard & The Strangers; *Okie From Muskogee* . . . . (Capitol)
   Songs I'll Always Sing . . . . (Capitol)
Pam Tillis; *Mama's Hungry Eyes-Merle Haggard Tribute-C* . . . . (Arista)

Smile
Lonestar; *Lonely Grill* . . . . (BNA)

Smoke Rings In The Dark
Gary Allan; *Smoke Rings In The Dark* . . . . (MCA)

So Long, Frank Lloyd Wright
Simon & Garfunkel; *Bridge Over Troubled Water* . . . . (Columbia)

Softly, As I Leave You
Brenda Lee; *In The Mood For Love: Classic Ballads* . . . . (Hip-O)
Elvis Presley; *Elvis Aron Presley* . . . . (RCA)
Frank Sinatra; *Frank Sinatra's Greatest Hits-#1* . . . . (Reprise)
   Sinatra: A Man And His Music . . . . (Reprise)

Somebody Should Leave
Reba McEntire; *Grand Ole Opry-75 Years-#2-C* . . . . (MCA)
   MCA #1 Hits Of The '80s-#2-C . . . . (MCA Special Prod.)
   My Kind Of Country . . . . (MCA)
   Reba McEntire's Greatest Hits . . . . (MCA)

Somebody's Always Saying Goodbye
Anne Murray; *Anne Murray-Country Hits* . . . . (Capitol)
   Hottest Night Of The Year . . . . (Capitol)

Someone's Gotta Cry
Jean Shepard; *45-#5392* . . . . (Capitol)

Sound Of Goodbye
Crystal Gayle; *Best Of Crystal Gayle* . . . . (Warner Bros.)
   Cage The Songbird . . . . (Warner Bros.)

Sour Girl
Stone Temple Pilots; *No. 4* . . . . (Atlantic)

Southbound Train
Julie Gold; *When October Goes: Autumn Love Songs-C* . . . . (Philo)
Nanci Griffith; *Flyer* . . . . (Elektra)

Southern California
George Jones & Tammy Wynette; *George Jones & Tammy Wynette-16*
   Biggest Hits . . . . (Epic/Legacy)
Tammy Wynette & George Jones; *Encore-Tammy Wynette & George*
   Jones . . . . (Epic)
   Tammy Wynette & George Jones' Greatest Hits . . . . (Epic)

Standing In The Doorway
Bob Dylan; *Time Out Of Mind* . . . . (Columbia)

Standing On The Edge Of Goodbye
John Berry; *Standing On The Edge* . . . . (Capitol)

Standing Tall
Lorrie Morgan; *Lorrie Morgan's Greatest Hits* . . . . (BNA)

Steven's Last Night In Town
Ben Folds Five; *Whatever And Ever Amen* . . . . (Caroline/550)

Sticks & Stones
Tracy Lawrence; *Tracy Lawrence* . . . . (Atlantic)

Sullivan
Caroline's Spine; *Monsoon* . . . . (Hollywood)

Summer Song
Chad & Jeremy; *Best Of Chad & Jeremy* . . . . (K-Tel)
   Capitol Gold-Best Of Chad & Jeremy . . . . (Capitol)
   History Of British Rock-#2-C . . . . (Rhino)

Take Your Memory With You
Vince Gill; *Platinum Country-C* . . . . (JCI Assoc. Labels)
   Pocket Full Of Gold . . . . (MCA)
   Vince Gill-Souvenirs . . . . (MCA)

Tell Me I Was Dreaming
Travis Tritt; *Ten Feet Tall And Bulletproof* . . . . (Warner Bros.)
   Travis Tritt's Greatest Hits-From The Beginning . . . . (Warner Bros.)

Tell Me Why
Wynonna; *Tell Me Why* . . . . (MCA)

Terence's Farewell To Kathleen
John McCormack; *Ireland Of Treasures-Voices & Melodies-C* . . . . . . (Capitol)

That Ain't No Way To Go
Brooks & Dunn; *Hard Workin' Man* . . . . (Arista)

That'll Be The Day
Buddy Holly; *ST/American Graffiti* . . . . (MCA)
Buddy Holly/The Crickets; *Buddy Holly-20 Golden Greats* . . . . (MCA)
   Chirping Crickets . . . . (MCA)
Crickets; *Billboard Top Rock 'N' Roll Hits-1957-C* . . . . (Rhino)
Foghat; *Best Of Foghat-#2* . . . . (Rhino)
   Energized . . . . (Rhino)
Linda Ronstadt; *Hasten Down The Wind* . . . . (Asylum)
   Linda Ronstadt's Greatest Hits . . . . (Asylum)

That's Okay
Marc Anthony; *Marc Anthony* . . . . (Columbia)

Then You Can Tell Me Goodbye
Casinos; *Then You Can Tell Me Goodbye* . . . . (Varese Vintage)
Neal McCoy; *Neal McCoy's Greatest Hits* . . . . (Atlantic)

There Goes
Alan Jackson; *Everything I Love* . . . . (Arista)

There Goes My Baby
Trisha Yearwood; *Where Your Road Leads* . . . . (MCA)

There Goes My Everything
Elvis Presley; *Elvis Country ("I'm 10,000 Years Old")* . . . . (RCA)

Engelbert Humperdinck; *Engelbert Humperdinck-16 Most Requested Songs*. . . . .(Epic)
Floyd Cramer; *Special Songs Of Love* . . . . (Step One)
Jack Greene; *Billboard Top Country Hits-1966-C* . . . . (Rhino)

There Is A Tavern In The Town
Four Aces; *Four Aces-More Greatest Hits* . . . . (Varese Vintage)
Mitch Miller; *Sing Along With Mitch* . . . . (Columbia)
Stan Wolowic & The Polka Chips; *Million-Seller Polkas* . . . . (Capitol)

There You Go
Johnny Cash; *The Man In Black-His Greatest Hits*. . . . . (Legacy)

These Lips Don't Know How To Say Goodbye
Doug Stone; *Doug Stone*. . . . .(Epic)
Greatest Country Hits Of The '90s-1991-C . . . . (Columbia)
Forester Sisters; *Sincerely*. . . . .(Warner Bros.)

Thinking About Leaving
Dwight Yoakam; *Last Chance For A Thousand Years-Greatest Hits From The '90s*. . . . . (Reprise)

Ticket To Ride
Beatles; *Beatles 1* . . . . (Capitol)
Beatles-20 Greatest Hits . . . . (Capitol)
Beatles-Box Set . . . . (Capitol)
Reel Music . . . . (Capitol)
ST/Help!. . . . . (Capitol)
The Beatles At The Hollywood Bowl . . . . (Capitol)
The Beatles/1962-1966 . . . . (Capitol)
Carpenters; *Carpenters-Classics-#2*. . . . . (A&M)
Carpenters-The Singles 1969-1973 . . . . (A&M)
From The Top . . . . (A&M)
Ticket To Ride . . . . (A&M)
Yesterday Once More. . . . . (A&M)
Vanilla Fudge; *Best Of Vanilla Fudge* . . . . (Atco)
Vanilla Fudge . . . . (Atco)

Till The Next Goodbye
Rolling Stones; *It's Only Rock 'N Roll* . . . .(Rolling Stones)

Till We Meet Again
Mills Brothers; *Best Of The Mills Brothers*. . . . .(MCA)
Mitch Miller; *Sing Along With Mitch* . . . . (Columbia)

Time (Keeps Flowing Like A River)
Alan Parsons Project; *Best Of The Alan Parsons Project* . . . . (Arista)
Turn Of A Friendly Card . . . . (Arista)

Time Of Your Life (Good Riddance)
Green Day; *Nimrod*. . . . . (Reprise)

To Sir With Love
Lulu; *History Of British Rock-#6-C* . . . . (Rhino)
Hollywood Magic-1960s-C . . . . (Columbia)
Rock Artifacts-From The Vaults-#3-C . . . . (Columbia)

Too Much
Elvis Presley; *Elvis' Golden Records* . . . . (RCA)
The Top Ten Hits . . . . (RCA)
Worldwide 50 Gold Award Hits, Vol. 1, Parts 1 & 2 . . . . (RCA)

Toot Toot Tootsie (Goo'Bye)
Al Jolson; *Al Jolson-Best Of The Decca Years* . . . . (MCA)
Best Of Al Jolson . . . .(MCA)
Liza Minnelli; *Liza Minnelli-At Carnegie Hall*. . . . . (Telarc)

Train Leaves Here This Morning
Eagles; *Eagles* . . . . (Asylum)

Tucker's Town
Hootie & The Blowfish; *Fairweather Johnson*. . . . . (Atlantic)

Turn On Your Radio
Nilsson; *Son Of Schmilsson* . . . . (RCA)

Unable To Stay, Unwilling To Leave
James Horner; *ST/Titanic* . . . . (Sony Music Classical)

Un-Break My Heart
Toni Braxton; *Secrets* . . . . (LaFace)

Understand Your Man
Johnny Cash; *Billboard Top Country Hits-1964-C*. . . . . (Rhino)
Johnny Cash's Greatest Hits . . . . (Columbia)
The Man In Black-His Greatest Hits . . . . (Legacy)

Up And Gone
McCarters; *Better Be Home Soon* . . . .(Warner Bros.)

Vaya Con Dios
Bing Crosby; *The Radio Years-#2* . . . . (Crescendo)
Freddy Fender; *Freddy Fender-Collection*. . . . . (Reprise)
Les Paul & Mary Ford; *Memories Are Made Of This-C* . . . . (Capitol)
Roger Whittaker; *All-Time Heart-Touching Favorites*. . . . . (Capitol)

Volcano Girls
Veruca Salt; *Eight Arms To Hold You*. . . . .(Geffen)

Wake Me Up Before You Go Go
Wham! Featuring George Michael; *Billboard Top Hits-1984-C* . . . . (Rhino)
Make It Big. . . . . (Columbia)
ST/Zoolander. . . . . (Hollywood)

Walk Away
James Gang; *Best Of The James Gang* . . . .(MCA)
James Gang-16 Greatest Hits . . . .(MCA)
Thirds. . . . .(One Way)
Joe Walsh; *Best Of Joe Walsh*. . . . .(MCA)
You Can't Argue With A Sick Mind . . . .(MCA)

Walk Away
Cool For August; *Grand World* . . . .(Warner Bros.)

Walk Away
Cheap Trick; *Busted* . . . . (Epic)

Walk Away
Dionne Warwick; *Dionne Warwick's Greatest Hits-1979-1990* . . . . (Arista)

Walk Away
Indigo Girls; *Strange Fire* . . . . (Epic)

Walk Away
Michael Bolton; *The Hunger*. (Columbia)

Walk Away
Sisters Of Mercy; *First & Last & Always* . . . .(Elektra)

Walk Away
Tom Kell; *One Sad Night* . . . . (Warner Bros.)

Walk Away
Donna Summer; *Bad Girls* . . . .(Casablanca)
Dance Collection . . . .(Casablanca)
Walk Away-Best Of Donna Summer-1977-1980 . . . .(Casablanca)

Walk Away From Love
David Ruffin; *David Ruffin-At His Best*. . . . . (Motown)
Jimmy & David Ruffin; *Motown Superstar Series-#8-Jimmy & David Ruffin* . . . . (Motown)

Walk Away Renee
Four Tops; *Compact Command Performances-Four Tops* . . . . (Motown)
Four Tops Reach Out . . . . (Motown)
Four Tops-Anthology . . . . (Motown)
Left Banke; *Cruisin'-1966-C* . . . . (Increase)
History Of The Left Banke . . . . (Rhino)
Vonda Shepard; *ST/Songs From "Ally McBeal" Featuring Vonda Shepard* . . . .(550/Epic)

Walk On
Sonny Terry & Brownie McGhee; *Coffeehouse Blues* . . . . (Vee-Jay)
Real Blues Brothers-C . . . . (Dunhill Compact Classics)

Walk On
U2; *America: A Tribute To Heroes-C* . . . .(Interscope)
Now That's What I Call Music!-#8-C . . . .(Virgin)

Walk On
Neil Young; *Decade* . . . . (Reprise)
On The Beach . . . . (Reprise)

Walk On
Reba McEntire; *Reba McEntire's Greatest Hits Volume Two* . . . . (MCA)
Sweet Sixteen . . . . (MCA)

Walk On By
Dionne Warwick; *Dionne Warwick-Anthology 1962-1971* . . . . (Rhino)
Hot! Live & Otherwise . . . . (Arista)
I Am Woman-C . . . .(Nick At Nite)
Oldies But Goodies-#15-C . . . .(Original Sound)
Scepter Records Story-C . . . . (Capricorn)
Isaac Hayes; *Isaac Hayes' Greatest Hit Singles* . . . . (Stax)
Melissa Manchester; *Romantic Hits Of The '80s-C* . . . . (K-Tel)
Tribute . . . . (Polydor)
Sybil; *Sybil* . . . .(Next Plateau/London/Island)

Walking On Broken Glass
Annie Lennox; *Diva* . . . . (Arista)

Watch Me
Lorrie Morgan; *Lorrie Morgan's Greatest Hits* . . . .(BNA)
Watch Me . . . .(BNA)

We Don't Have To Do It
Tanya Tucker; *Soon* . . . . (Liberty)

Wednesday Morning, 3 AM
Simon & Garfunkel; *Collected Works*. . . . . (Columbia)
Wednesday Morning 3 A.M. . . . . (Columbia)

We'll Sing In The Sunshine
Gale Garnett; *21 Country Rock & Love Songs Of The '50s & '60s-#1-C*. . . . .(Laurie)
Nipper's Greatest Hits Of The '60s-#1-C . . . .(RCA)

What About Us
Total; *Kima, Keisha & Pam*. . . . .(Bad Boy/Arista)
LaFace Records Presents The Platinum Collection-C . . . . (LaFace)
ST/Soul Food . . . . (LaFace)

What Is And What Should Never Be
Jimmy Page & Black Crowes; *Live At The Greek* . . . . (TVT)
Led Zeppelin; *BBC Sessions* . . . .(Atlantic)
Led Zeppelin II . . . .(Atlantic)
Led Zeppelin-Box Set . . . .(Atlantic)
Led Zeppelin-The Complete Studio Recordings . . . .(Atlantic)

When The Midnight Choo Choo Leaves For Alabam'
Andrews Sisters; *Best Of The Andrews Sisters-#2*. . . . . (MCA)
Judy Garland & Fred Astaire; *ST/Easter Parade* . . . . (Rhino)

When The Rainbow Comes
World Party; *Goodbye Jumbo* . . . . (Ensign)

When You're Gone
Cranberries; *To The Faithful Departed* . . . . (Island)

Where Did You Go?
Full Devil Jacket; *Full Devil Jacket*. . . . . (Island/IDJMG)

Where I Wanna Be
Donell Jones; *Where I Wanna Be* . . . . (LaFace)

Who Needs You Baby
Clay Walker; *Hypnotize The Moon* . . . .(Giant)

Why Would I Say Goodbye
Brooks & Dunn; *Borderline* . . . . (Arista)

Wide Open Spaces
Dixie Chicks; *Big Country Hits '99-C* . . . . (K-Tel)
Wide Open Spaces . . . . (Monument)
Wild World
Cat Stevens; *Cat Stevens Greatest Hits* . . . . (A&M)
Tea For The Tillerman . . . . (A&M)
Jimmy Cliff; *In Concert-Best Of Jimmy Cliff* . . . . (Reprise)
Reggae Spectacular-C . . . . (A&M)
Maxi Priest; *Best Of Me* . . . . (Charisma)
Maxi . . . . (Virgin)
Will You Be Staying After Sunday
Peppermint Rainbow; *Bubble Gum Classics-C* . . . . (MCA Special Prod.)
Wishing I Was There
Natalie Imbruglia; *Left Of The Middle* . . . . (RCA)
Wooden Ships
Crosby, Stills & Nash; *Crosby, Stills & Nash* . . . . (Atlantic)
CSN . . . . (Atlantic)
Crosby, Stills, Nash & Young; *So Far* . . . . (Atlantic)
ST/Woodstock . . . . (Atlantic)
Jefferson Airplane; *2400 Fulton Street-An Anthology* . . . . (RCA)
Flight Log (1966-1976) . . . . (Grunt)
Loves You . . . . (RCA)
Volunteers . . . . (RCA)
Would I Lie To You
Eurythmics; *Be Yourself Tonight* . . . . (RCA)
Eurythmics' Greatest Hits . . . . (Arista)
Write This Down
George Strait; *Always Never The Same* . . . . (MCA)
Wrong Side Of Memphis
Matraca Berg; *Bittersweet Surrender* . . . . (RCA)
Trisha Yearwood; *Grand Ole Opry-75 Years-#1-C* . . . . (MCA)
Hearts In Armor . . . . (MCA)
Yesterday
Shanice; *Shanice* . . . . (LaFace)
You Better Sit Down Kids
Cher; *Bang, Bang The Early Years* . . . . (Capitol)
You Don't Know Me
Ray Charles; *Ray Charles-Complete Country & Western Recordings 1959-1986* . . . . (Rhino)
You Keep Running Away
Four Tops; *Four Tops-Anthology* . . . . (Motown)
You Lie
Reba McEntire; *Reba McEntire's Greatest Hits Volume Two* . . . . . . (MCA)
Rumor Has It . . . . (MCA)
You're Gone
Diamond Rio; *Unbelievable* . . . . (Arista)
You're Gonna Change (Or I'm Gonna Leave)
Hank Williams With His Drifting Cowboys; *Hank Williams-24 Greatest Hits-#2* . . . . (Polydor)
Hank Williams-40 Greatest Hits . . . . (Polydor)
Health & Happiness Shows . . . . (Mercury)
Hank Williams, Jr.; *A Tribute To My Father* . . . . (Curb)
Tom Petty; *Timeless: Hank Williams Tribute-C* . . . (Lost Highway/IDJMG)
You're Gonna Make Me Lonesome When You Go
Bob Dylan; *Blood On The Tracks* . . . . (Columbia)
You're Gonna Miss Me When I'm Gone
Brooks & Dunn; *Brooks & Dunn-The Greatest Hits Collection* . . . . . . (Arista)
Waitin' On Sundown . . . . (Arista)

LIFE, Alive, Destiny, Fate, Living, Philosophy, Reality, Survive

See Also: **ADVICE, AGING, BABY, BACK ON MY FEET, BIRTHDAY, CAPITAL PUNISHMENT, CIRCLES, DEATH, GOD, HARD CITY LIFE, KILL, LOVE (various), QUESTION & ANSWERS, SMALL TOWN LIFE, TRUTH, WORK**

(Can't Live Without...) Love & Affection
Nelson; *After The Rain* . . . . (David Geffen Co.)
(I've Had) The Time Of My Life
Bill Medley; *Best Of Bill Medley* . . . . (Curb)
Bill Medley & Jennifer Warnes; *Dirty Dancing Live In Concert-C* . . . . . (RCA)
ST/Dirty Dancing . . . . (RCA)
10 Miles To Go On A 9 Mile Road
Jim White; *No Such Place* . . . . (Luaka Bop)
10,000 Horses
Candlebox; *Happy Pills* . . . . (Maverick)
3am
Matchbox Twenty; *Yourself Or Someone Like You* . . . . (Lava)
59th Street Bridge Song (Feelin' Groovy)
Harper's Bizarre; *Baby Boomer Classics-More Mellow Sixties-C* . . . . (JCI Assoc. Labels)
Better Days-C . . . . (Rhino)
Simon & Garfunkel; *Collected Works* . . . . (Columbia)
Parsley Sage Rosemary & Thyme . . . . (Columbia)
Simon & Garfunkel's Greatest Hits . . . . (Columbia)

The Concert In Central Park . . . . (Warner Bros.)
Ace In The Hole
George Strait; *Beyond The Blue Neon* . . . . (MCA)
Adam Raised A Cain
Bruce Springsteen; *Darkness On The Edge Of Town* . . . . (Columbia)
Adrian
Jewel; *Pieces Of You* . . . . (Atlantic)
Affirmation
Savage Garden; *Affirmation* . . . . (Columbia)
Afraid
Motley Crue; *Generation Swine* . . . . (Beyond)
Motley Crue's Greatest Hits . . . . (Beyond)
Again
Lenny Kravitz; *Lenny Kravitz's Greatest Hits* . . . . (Virgin)
Now That's What I Call Music!-#6-C . . . . (Virgin)
Ah! Sweet Mystery Of Life
Bing Crosby; *Little Bit Of Irish* . . . . (Atlantic)
Nelson Eddy; *Through The Years* . . . . (Living Era)
Ain't Got No (I Got Life)
Original Cast; *ST/Hair* . . . . (RCA)
Ain't It The Life
Foo Fighters; *There Is Nothing Left To Lose* . . . . (Roswell/RCA)
Ain't Life Hell
Hank Cochran; *Hank Cochran* . . . . (Capitol)
Ain't No Good Life
Lynyrd Skynyrd; *Street Survivors* . . . . (MCA)
Alfie
Barbra Streisand; *What About Today* . . . . (Columbia)
Dionne Warwick; *Dionne Warwick Greatest Hits* . . . . (Everest)
Dionne Warwick-Anthology 1962-1971 . . . . (Rhino)
Alive
Pearl Jam; *Ten* . . . . (Epic Portrait Assoc.)
Alive
Beastie Boys; *Sounds Of Silence* . . . . (Grand Royal)
Alive
P.O.D.; *Satellite* . . . . (Atlantic)
Alive & Kicking
Simple Minds; *Once Upon A Time* . . . . (A&M)
Simple Minds Live: In The City Of Light . . . . (A&M)
Alive Again
Chicago; *Chicago's Greatest Hits-#2 (1974-81)* . . . . (Chicago)
Hot Streets . . . . (Columbia)
All Around The World Or The Myth Of Fingerprints
Paul Simon; *Graceland* . . . . (Warner Bros.)
All I Want
Offspring; *Ixnay On The Hombre* . . . . (Columbia)
All I Want Is A Life
Tim McGraw; *All I Want* . . . . (Curb)
All In Love Is Fair
Stevie Wonder; *Innervisions* . . . . (Motown)
All My Friends
Counting Crows; *This Desert Life* . . . . (David Geffen Co.)
All My Life
Kenny Rogers; *We've Got Tonight* . . . . (Razor & Tie)
All My Life
Linda Ronstadt; *Cry Like A Rainstorm-Howl Like The Wind* . . . . . . (Elektra)
All Of My Life
Barbra Streisand; *ST/The Mirror Has Two Faces* . . . . (Columbia)
All The Fuckers Live In Newport Beach
Fluf; *The Classic Years* . . . . (Headhunter)
All The Way
Celine Dion; *All The Way...A Decade Of Song* . . . . (550 Music)
All Things Must Pass
George Harrison; *All Things Must Pass* . . . . (Parlophone)
All You Need Is Love
Beatles; *Beatles 1* . . . . (Capitol)
Compact Disc Singles Collection . . . . (Capitol)
Magical Mystery Tour . . . . (Capitol)
The Beatles/1967-1970 . . . . (Capitol)
Yellow Submarine . . . . (Capitol)
Along The Road
Dan Fogelberg; *Phoenix* . . . . (Full Moon)
Amanda
Don Williams; *Don Williams' Greatest Hits* . . . . (MCA)
Volume One . . . . (MCA)
Waylon Jennings; *Waylon Jennings' Greatest Hits* . . . . (RCA)
Amigone
Goo Goo Dolls; *Dizzy Up The Girl* . . . . (Warner Sunset/Reprise)
Amukiriki
Les Paul; *Legend And The Legacy* . . . . (Gold Rush)
Analyse
Cranberries; *Wake Up And Smell The Coffee* . . . . (MCA)
And I Love You So
Perry Como; *Perry Como's Greatest Hits* . . . . (RCA)
And So It Goes
Billy Joel; *Storm Front* . . . . (Columbia)
And The Beat Goes On
Whispers; *Club Epic-#1-C* . . . . (Legacy)

And When I Die
Blood, Sweat & Tears; *Blood, Sweat & Tears* . . . . (Columbia)
Blood, Sweat & Tears Greatest Hits . . . . (Columbia)
Blood, Sweat & Tears In Concert. . . . . (Columbia)
Laura Nyro; *First Songs* . . . . (Columbia)
Live At The Bottom Line . . . .(Cypress)

Angel From Montgomery
Bonnie Raitt; *Streetlights* . . . .(Warner Bros.)
Bonnie Raitt & John Prine; *Bonnie Raitt-Collection* . . . .(Warner Bros.)
John Prine; *John Prine* . . . . (Atlantic)
John Prine-Souvenirs. . . . . (Oh Boy)

Angel's Eye
Aerosmith; *ST/Charlie's Angels* . . . . (Columbia)

Angels Working Overtime
Deana Carter; *Everything's Gonna Be Alright* . . . . (Capitol)

Angry All The Time
Bruce Robison with Kelly Willis; *Wrapped* . . . . (Lucky Dog)
Tim McGraw with Faith Hill; *Set This Circus Down* . . . . (Curb)

Animal Song
Savage Garden; *Affirmation* . . . . (Columbia)

Ants Marching
Dave Matthews Band; *Under The Table And Dreaming.* . . . . (RCA)

Apple Tree
Erykah Badu; *Baduizm* . . . . (Kedar Entert./Universal)

Army Life
Leadbelly; *Easy Rider.* . . . . (Smithsonian Folkways)

As Long As I Live
Count Basie; *Standards* . . . . (Verve)
Count Basie Trio; *For The First Time.* . . . .(Pablo)
Ella Fitzgerald; *Harold Arlen Songbook-#2* . . . . (Verve)

At The Beginning
Richard Marx & Donna Lewis; *ST/Anastasia-Music From The Motion
Picture* . . . .(Atlantic)

Attics Of My Life
Grateful Dead; *American Beauty* . . . .(Warner Bros.)

Autumn Of My Life
Bobby Goldsboro; *10th Anniversary Album-#1* . . . .(EMI)
Bobby Goldsboro's Greatest Hits . . . . (Liberty)

Avinu Malkeinu
Barbra Streisand; *Higher Ground.* . . . . (Columbia)

Awake
Godsmack; *Awake* . . . .(Republic/Universal)

Back In The Day
Blues Traveler; *Bridge* . . . . (A&M)

Back In The High Life Again
Steve Winwood; *Back In The High Life* . . . . (Island)

Back In The U.S.A.
Chuck Berry; *Chuck Berry-Golden Hits* . . . . (Mercury)
Chuck Berry's Greatest Hits . . . . (Everest)
Roll Over Beethoven . . . . (Allegiance)
The Chess Box-Chuck Berry . . . . (Chess)
Linda Ronstadt; *Linda Ronstadt's Greatest Hits, Volume Two.* . . . . . . (Asylum)
Living In The USA . . . . (Asylum)

Back Into My Life
UFO; *Best Of The Rest Of UFO* . . . .(Chrysalis)
Mechanix. . . . .(Chrysalis)

Back Into My Life Again
Spencer Davis Group; *Best Of The Spencer Davis Group* . . . .(EMI)

Back On The Chain Gang
Pretenders; *Learning To Crawl.* . . . . (Sire)
Pretenders-The Singles . . . . (Sire)
ST/King Of Comedy . . . .(Warner Bros.)

Back On Top
Van Morrison; *Back On Top* . . . . (Point Blank/Virgin)

Back To Life
Soul II Soul; *Keep On Movin'.* . . . . (Virgin)

Badge
Cream; *Goodbye* . . . . (Polydor)
Strange Brew-Very Best Of Cream . . . . (Polydor)

Badlands
Bruce Springsteen; *Bruce Springsteen's Greatest Hits.* . . . . (Columbia)
Darkness On The Edge Of Town . . . . (Columbia)
Bruce Springsteen & The E Street Band; *Bruce Springsteen & The E Street
Band Live/1975-85* . . . . (Legacy)

Barbie Girl
Aqua; *Aquarium* . . . . (MCA)
Now That's What I Call Music!-#1-C . . . . (Virgin)

Be My Life's Companion
Mills Brothers; *Best Of The Mills Brothers.* . . . .(MCA)
The Mills Brothers-Best Of The Decca Years. . . . .(Decca)
Rosemary Clooney; *Rosemary Clooney-16 Most Requested Songs* . . . . (Legacy)

Beat Goes On, The
Sonny & Cher; *Best Of Sonny & Cher* . . . . (Atco)
Hit Singles-1958-1977-C. . . . . (Atlantic)
Sonny & Cher-Live . . . . (MCA)
The Beat Goes On-Best Of Sonny & Cher . . . . (Rhino)
Two Of Us . . . . (Atco)

Beautiful Day
U2; *All That You Can't Leave Behind* . . . . (Interscope)

Now That's What I Call Music!-#6-C . . . . (Virgin)

Beautiful Life
Ace Of Base; *Bridge* . . . . (Arista)
MTV Party To Go-#9-C . . . . (Tommy Boy)

Beautiful Noise
Neil Diamond; *12 Greatest Hits-#2.* . . . . (Columbia)
Beautiful Noise . . . . (Columbia)
Love At The Greek . . . . (Columbia)

Beauty Is Only Skin Deep
Temptations; *Good Feeling Music Of The Big Chill
Generation-#1-C* . . . . (Motown)
Motown Story-First 25 Years-C . . . . (Motown)
Motown's Mustang-A Motown Video-C . . . . (Motown)
Temptations-Anthology-The Best Of The Temptations . . . . (Motown)

Been There
Clint Black with Steve Wariner; *D'lectrified.* . . . .(RCA)

Before I Go
John Hiatt; *Crossing Muddy Waters* . . . . (Vanguard)

Beginning, The
Keb' Mo'; *The Door* . . . .(550/Epic/Okeh)

Being Alive
Barbra Streisand; *The Broadway Album* . . . . (Columbia)
Mandy Patinkin; *Dress Casual* . . . . (Columbia)
Original Cast; *Company* . . . . (Columbia)

Believe
Cher; *Believe* . . . . (Warner Bros.)
Totally Hits-#1-C . . . . (Arista)

Bend It Until It Breaks
John Anderson; *John Anderson's Greatest Hits* . . . .(BNA)

Bent
Matchbox Twenty; *Mad Season By Matchbox Twenty* . . . . (Lava)
Totally Hits-#3-C . . . .(Atlantic)

Best Days Of My Life
Johnny Mathis; *Best Days Of My Life* . . . . (Columbia)
Best Of Johnny Mathis 1975-1980 . . . . (Columbia)

Best Days Of My Life
Rod Stewart; *Blondes Have More Fun* . . . . (Warner Bros.)

Best Things
Filter; *Title Of Record* . . . .(Reprise)

Best Things In Life Are Free
June Allyson; *ST/Good News* . . . . (Sony Music Special Prod.)
Luther Vandross & Janet Jackson; *ST/Mo' Money* . . . .(Bluebird)
Mel Torme; *Easy To Remember* . . . . (Glendale)
Sam Cooke; *Sam Cooke-At The Copa* . . . . (RCA)

Best Year Of My Life
Eddie Rabbitt; *Number 1's* . . . . (Warner Bros.)
The Best Year Of My Life . . . . (Warner Bros.)

Big Bang Baby
Stone Temple Pilots; *Tiny Music...Songs From The Vatican
Gift Shop* . . . .(Atlantic)

Big Yellow Taxi
Amy Grant; *House Of Love* . . . . (A&M)
Joni Mitchell; *Ladies Of The Canyon* . . . . (Reprise)
Joni Mitchell with Tom Scott & The L.A. Express; *Miles Of Aisles* . . . .(Asylum)

Bitter Sweet Symphony
Verve; *Urban Hymns* . . . . (Hut/Virgin)

Black Chick, White Guy
Kid Rock; *Devil Without A Cause* . . . . (Top Dog/Lava/Atlantic)

Blackbird
Beatles; *Beatles-Box Set* . . . . (Capitol)
The Beatles (White Album) . . . . (Capitol)
Crosby, Stills & Nash; *CSN.* . . . .(Atlantic)
Paul McCartney; *Unplugged (The Official Bootleg)* . . . . (Capitol)
Wings; *Wings Over America* . . . . (Capitol)

Blood Brothers
Bruce Springsteen; *Bruce Springsteen's Greatest Hits* . . . . (Columbia)

Born To Be Alive
Patrick Hernandez; *Let's Dance-DJ's Collection* . . . . (Columbia)

Born To Be With You
Chordettes; *Best Of The Chordettes* . . . . (Rhino)
Chordettes Greatest Hits . . . . (Everest)
Lil' Bit Of Gold 3'' CD Series-C . . . . (Rhino)

Born To Fly
Sara Evans; *Born To Fly* . . . .(RCA)

Both Sides Now
Joni Mitchell; *Clouds* . . . .(Reprise)
Judy Collins; *Colors Of The Day-The Best Of Judy Collins* . . . . (Elektra)
So Early In The Spring, The First 15 Years . . . . (Elektra)
Wildflowers . . . . (Elektra)
Neil Diamond; *Neil Diamond-Gold* . . . . (MCA)
Neil Diamond-Love Songs . . . . (MCA)
Rainbow . . . . (MCA)
Touching You Touching Me . . . . (MCA)

Both Sides Now
Sammy Hagar; *Marching To Mars* . . . . (MCA)

Bound For The Floor
Local H; *As Good As Dead* . . . . (Island)

Bowling Green
Everly Brothers; *Walk Right Back: The Everly Brothers On Warner Bros.-1960-1969* . . . . (Warner Archives)

Breakdown
Tantric; *Tantric* . . . . (Maverick)

Breath Of Life
Brian Setzer; *Knife Feels Like Justice* . . . . (EMI)

Breath Of Life
Erasure; *Chorus* . . . .(Sire)

Breathe In The Air
Pink Floyd; *Dark Side Of The Moon* . . . . (Capitol)
Pink Floyd-Gift Set . . . . (Capitol)

Broadway
Goo Goo Dolls; *Dizzy Up The Girl* . . . . (Warner Sunset/Reprise)

Bug, The
Dire Straits; *On Every Street* . . . . (Warner Bros.)
Mary Chapin Carpenter; *Come On Come On* . . . . (Columbia)

But Anyway
Blues Traveler; *Blues Traveler* . . . . (A&M)
Live From The Fall . . . . (A&M)

Ca Plane Por Moi (This Life's For Me)
Plastic Bertrand; *Ca Plane Por Moi (This Life's For Me)* . . . .(Sire)

Camera One
Josh Joplin Group; *Useful Music* . . . . (Artemis)

Cancer
Filter; *Title Of Record* . . . .(Reprise)

Candle In The Wind
Elton John; *Goodbye Yellow Brick Road* . . . . (Polydor)
Live In Australia With The Melbourne Symphony Orchestra . . . . (MCA)
Your Songs . . . . (Polydor)

Candle In The Wind 1997
Elton John; *Candle In The Wind 1997 (Diana, Princess Of Wales) (Single)* . . . . (Rocket)

Candle Of Life
Moody Blues; *To Our Children's Children's Children* . . . . (Polydor)

Can't Get Enough
Patty Loveless; *Patty Loveless-Classics* . . . . (Epic)

Cast Your Fate To The Wind
Sandpipers; *Guantanamera* . . . . (A&M)
Vince Guaraldi; *Original Jazz Classics-#1* . . . . (Fantasy)
Vince Guaraldi's Greatest Hits . . . . (Fantasy)

C'est La Vie
Robbie Nevil; *Heart Of Rock-C* . . . . (Columbia)
Robbie Nevil . . . . (EMI)

C'est La Vie
Emmylou Harris; *Luxury Liner* . . . . (Warner Bros.)
Profile/Best Of Emmylou Harris . . . . (Warner Bros.)

C'est La Vie
Emerson, Lake & Palmer; *Emerson, Lake & Palmer In Concert* . . . . . . (Atlantic)
Works, Volume 1 . . . . (Rhino)

C'est La Vie
Patti LaBelle; *Golden "Philly" Classics* . . . . (Collectables)

C'est La Vie
Queen Ida & Her Bon Temps Zydeco Band; *Queen Ida On Tour* . . . (Crescendo)
Zydeco A La Mode . . . . (Crescendo)

Chain Of Love
Clay Walker; *Live, Laugh, Love* . . . . (Giant)

Change Partners
Rosanne Cash; *The Wheel* . . . . (Columbia)

Change Your Mind
Sister Hazel; *Fortress* . . . . (Universal)

Changes
2Pac; *2Pac Greatest Hits* . . . . (Amaru/Death Row/Interscope)

Chattahoochee
Alan Jackson; *A Lot About Livin' (And A Little 'Bout Love)* . . . . . . (Arista)

Chop Suey
Original Cast; *ST/Flower Drum Song* . . . . (Sony Music Classical)

Circle Game, The
Buffy Sainte-Marie; *Best Of Buffy Sainte-Marie* . . . . (Vanguard)
Fire & Fleet & Candlelight . . . . (Vanguard)
Ian & Sylvia; *Ian & Sylvia's Greatest Hits* . . . . (Vanguard)
Joni Mitchell; *Ladies Of The Canyon* . . . . (Reprise)
Joni Mitchell with Tom Scott & The L.A. Express; *Miles Of Aisles* . . . (Asylum)
Tom Rush; *Classic Rush* . . . . (Elektra)
The Circle Game . . . . (Elektra)

Circle Of Life
Elton John; *Elton John-Love Songs* . . . . (MCA)
ST/The Lion King . . . . (Walt Disney)
Original Cast; *The Lion King* . . . . (Disney)

Clean My Wounds
Corrosion Of Conformity; *Deliverance* . . . . (Columbia)

Cold Hard Facts Of Life, The
Porter Wagoner; *Essential Porter Wagoner* . . . . (RCA)
Porter Wagoner's Greatest Hits . . . .(Pair)

Color Of Roses
Beth Nielsen Chapman; *Sand And Water* . . . . (Reprise)

Come Alive (Pepsi)
Original Soundtrack; *TeeVee Toons-The Commercials-#1-C* . . . . . (TVT)

Comin' In And Out Of Your Life
Barbra Streisand; *Collection-Greatest Hits...And More* . . . .(Columbia)
Memories . . . .(Columbia)

Coming Back To Life
Pink Floyd; *The Division Bell* . . . .(Columbia)

Country Boy Can Survive
Hank Williams, Jr.; *America (The Way I See It)* . . . .(WB/Curb)
Hank Williams, Jr. "Live" . . . .(WB/Curb)
Hank Williams, Jr.'s Greatest Hits . . . .(WB/Curb)
ST/Pressure Is On . . . .(WB/Curb)

Country Bumpkin
Cal Smith; *16 Top Country Hits-#1-C* . . . . (MCA)
Country's Greatest Hits-#2-C . . . . (MCA Special Prod.)
Grand Ole Opry-75 Years-#2-C . . . . (MCA)

Crazy
Alana Davis; *Blame It On Me* . . . .(Elektra)

Cup Of Life
Ricky Martin; *Ricky Martin* . . . .(Columbia)

Dancing In The Key Of Life
Steve Arrington; *Dance Traxx-C* . . . . (Atlantic)
Dancing In The Key Of Life . . . . (Atlantic)

Darkness On The Edge Of Town
Bruce Springsteen; *Darkness On The Edge Of Town* . . . .(Columbia)
Bruce Springsteen & The E Street Band; *Bruce Springsteen & The E Street Band Live/1975-85* . . . .(Legacy)

Day By Day
Carmen McRae; *Great American Songbook* . . . . (Atlantic)
Frank Sinatra; *Come Swing With Me!* . . . .(Capitol)
Frank Sinatra-16 Most Requested Songs . . . . (Columbia)
Sarah Vaughan; *Complete Sarah Vaughan On Mercury-#3.* . . . . . .(Mercury)
Misty . . . .(Mercury)

Day By Day
Generation X; *Generation X.* . . . .(Chrysalis)

Day By Day
Hooters; *Nervous Night* . . . . (Columbia)

Day By Day
Original Cast; *Godspell* . . . .(Arista)

Day In The Life, A
Beatles; *Sgt. Pepper's Lonely Hearts Club Band* . . . .(Capitol)
ST/Imagine: John Lennon . . . .(Capitol)
The Beatles/1967-1970 . . . .(Capitol)

Days Of Our Livez
Bone Thugs-N-Harmony; *The Collection-#1.* . . . .(Ruthless)

Dead & Alive
Dead Boys; *We Have Come For Your Children* . . . . (Sire)

Dead Or Alive
Oingo Boingo; *Boingo Alive* . . . . (MCA)
Good For Your Soul . . . . (A&M)

Dead Or Alive
Journey; *Escape* . . . .(Columbia)

Dead Or Alive
Deep Purple; *Nobody's Perfect* . . . .(Mercury)

Dead Or Alive
Too $hort; *Short Dog's In The House* . . . . (Jive)

Dear God
XTC; *Best Of MTV's 120 Minutes-#1-C* . . . .(Rhino)
Skylarking . . . . (Geffen)
Upsy Daisy Assortment . . . . (Geffen)

Didn't Cha Know
Erykah Badu; *Mama's Gun* . . . .(Motown)

Dig In
Lenny Kravitz; *Lenny.* . . . . (Virgin)

Dim Lights Thick Smoke & Loud Loud Music
Flatt & Scruggs; *Golden Era* . . . .(Rounder)
Flying Burrito Brothers; *Close Encounters To The West Coast* . . . . (Relix)
Farther Along-Best Of The Flying Burrito Brothers . . . . (A&M)
Ricky Skaggs and Kentucky Thunder; *History Of The Future* . . .(Skaggs Family)

Dirt Road, The
Sawyer Brown; *Dirt Road* . . . .(Curb)

Dites-Moi
Original Cast; *South Pacific* . . . . (CBS Masterworks)

Do Something
Macy Gray; *On How Life Is* . . . . (Epic)
ST/Music Of The Heart . . . . (Epic/Sony Music Soundtrax)

Does This Bus Stop At 82nd Street?
Bruce Springsteen; *Greetings From Asbury Park, N.J.* . . . .(Columbia)
Tracks . . . .(Columbia)

Dog's Life
Gentle Giant; *Octopus* . . . .(Columbia)

Domestic Life
John Conlee; *American Faces* . . . . (Columbia)
Greatest Country Hits Of The '80s-1987-C . . . . (Columbia)
More Hot Country Requests-#2-C . . . . (Epic)

Don't Pick It Up
Offspring; *Ixnay On The Hombre.* . . . . (Columbia)

Don't Seem Right
Steve James; *Two Track Mind* . . . .(Antone's)

Don't Throw Your Life Away
Vickie Winans; *The Lady* . . . .(MCA)
Don't Wanna Live Without It
Pablo Cruise; *Worlds Away* . . . . (A&M)
Down The Road
Mac McAnally; *Knots* . . . .(MCA)
Dream Is Still Alive
Wilson Phillips; *Wilson Phillips* . . . . (SBK)
Dream Of Life
Billie Holiday; *Billie Holiday* . . . . (Columbia)
The Billie Holiday Story-#1 . . . . (Columbia)
Carmen McRae; *Greatest Of Carmen McRae* . . . .(MCA)
Dream Of Life
Patti Smith; *Dream Of Life* . . . . (Arista)
Dream On
Depeche Mode; *Exciter* . . . . (Mute/Reprise)
Dream On
Aerosmith; *Aerosmith* . . . . (Columbia)
Aerosmith-Classics Live . . . . (Columbia)
Aerosmith's Greatest Hits . . . . (Columbia)
Live! Bootleg . . . . (Columbia)
Drivin' My Life Away
Eddie Rabbitt; *Eddie Rabbitt's All-Time Greatest Hits* . . . .(Warner Bros.)
Eddie Rabbitt's Greatest Hits-#2 . . . .(Warner Bros.)
Horizon . . . . (Elektra)
Number 1's . . . .(Warner Bros.)
Ten Years Of Greatest Hits . . . . (Capitol)
Drop Kick Me Jesus (Through The Goalposts Of Life)
Bobby Bare; *Essential Bobby Bare* . . . . (RCA)
Drunk Is Better Than Dead
Push Stars; *ST/Malcolm In The Middle* . . . .(Restless)
Dust In The Wind
Kansas; *Best Of Kansas* . . . . (CBS Associated)
Point Of Know Return . . . . (Kirshner)
Two For The Show . . . . (Kirshner)
Early To Bed
Morphine; *Like Swimming* . . . . (DreamWorks/Rykodisc)
Easy As Life
Tina Turner; *ST/Aida* . . . . (Island)
Easy Living
Billie Holiday; *Quintessential-#4-1937* . . . . (Columbia)
Ella Fitzgerald & Joe Pass; *Easy Living* . . . .(Pablo)
Paul Desmond; *Easy Living* . . . . (Bluebird)
Eclipse
Pink Floyd; *Dark Side Of The Moon* . . . . (Capitol)
Works . . . . (Capitol)
Empty Lives
Graham Parker; *Passion Is No Ordinary Word-Graham Parker Anthology-1976-1991* . . . . (Rhino)
Up Escalator . . . . (Razor & Tie)
End Of The World
Skeeter Davis; *Best Of Skeeter Davis* . . . . (Gusto)
Billboard Top Country Hits-1963-C . . . . (Rhino)
Nipper's Greatest Hits Of The '60s-#1-C . . . . (RCA)
Stars Of The Grand Ole Opry-1926-1974-C . . . . (RCA)
Super Country Hits Of The '60s-C . . . . (Gusto)
End, The
Beatles; *Abbey Road* . . . . (Parlophone)
Every Day Of My Life
Open Skyz; *Open Skyz* . . . . (Zito)
Every Day Of My Life
McGuire Sisters; *McGuire Sisters' Greatest Hits* . . . .(MCA)
McGuire Sisters-Anthology . . . .(MCA)
Everybody's Free (To Wear Sunscreen)
Baz Luhrmann; *Now That's What I Call Music!-#2-C* . . . (Virgin)
Something For Everybody . . . . (Capitol)
Everybody's Had The Blues
Merle Haggard & The Strangers; *For The Record: Merle Haggard-43 Legendary Hits* . . . . (BNA)
Everyday
Phil Collins; *Both Sides* . . . . (Atlantic)
Everyday Is A Winding Road
Sheryl Crow; *1998 Grammy Nominees-C* . . . .(MCA)
Sheryl Crow . . . . (A&M)
Everyday People
Sly & The Family Stone; *Sly & The Family Stone-Anthology* . . . . . .(Epic)
Sly & The Family Stone's Greatest Hits . . . .(Epic)
Stand! . . . .(Epic)
Everything Is Beautiful
Ray Stevens; *Everything Is Beautiful* . . . . (MCA Special Prod.)
Everything Must Change
Barbra Streisand; *Higher Ground* . . . . (Columbia)
Ev'ry Day Of My Life
McGuire Sisters; *McGuire Sisters-Anthology* . . . .(MCA)
Exhale (Shoop Shoop)
Whitney Houston; *ST/Waiting To Exhale* . . . . (Arista)
Whitney Houston's Greatest Hits . . . . (Arista)
Factory
Bruce Springsteen; *Darkness On The Edge Of Town* . . . . (Columbia)

Fair
Ben Folds Five; *Whatever And Ever Amen* . . . .(Caroline/550)
Family Affair
Sly & The Family Stone; *Billboard Top Rock 'N' Roll Hits-1971-C* . . . . . (Rhino)
Club Epic-#2-C . . . . (Legacy)
In Yo' Face!-History Of Funk-#2-C . . . . (Rhino)
Sly & The Family Stone-Anthology . . . . (Epic)
There's A Riot Goin' On . . . . (Epic)
Steve Winwood; *Junction Seven* . . . . (Virgin)
Fast Car
Tracy Chapman; *Tracy Chapman* . . . . (Elektra)
Fearless Boogie
ZZ Top; *XXX* . . . . (RCA)
Ferry Cross The Mersey
Gerry And The Pacemakers; *Ferry Across The Mersey-Best Of Gerry And The Pacemakers* . . . . (EMI)
History Of British Rock-#4-C . . . . (Rhino)
Finer Things, The
Steve Winwood; *Back In The High Life* . . . . (Island)
For Once In My Life
Gladys Knight & The Pips; *Gladys Knight & The Pips-Anthology* . . . . (Motown)
Motown Superstar Series-#13-Gladys Knight & The Pips . . . . (Motown)
Neither One Of Us . . . . (Motown)
Stevie Wonder; *Motown Story-First 25 Years-C* . . . . (Motown)
Stevie Wonder-Love Songs-20 Classic Hits . . . . (Motown)
Stevie Wonder's Greatest Hits-#2 . . . . (Motown)
Tony Bennett; *Tony Bennett's All-Time Greatest Hits* . . . . . (Columbia)
Vikki Carr; *Best Of Vikki Carr* . . . . (EMI)
For Once In Our Lives
Paul Carrack; *Blue Views* . . . . (Ark 21)
For Your Life
Led Zeppelin; *Presence* . . . . (Swan Song)
Forty Six & 2
Tool; *Aenima* . . . . (Freeworld/Capitol)
Freedom
Paul McCartney; *Driving Rain* . . . . (Columbia)
The Concert For New York City-C . . . . (Columbia)
Friend, Love, Woman, Life
Mac Davis; *Baby Don't Get Hooked On Me* . . . . (Columbia)
Mac Davis' Greatest Hits . . . . (Columbia)
Gambler, The
Kenny Rogers; *Kenny Rogers' Greatest Hits* . . . . (EMI)
Kenny Rogers-Twenty Greatest Hits . . . . (EMI)
The Gambler . . . . (EMI)
Game Of Life
Billy Paul; *First Class* . . . . (Philadelphia Int'l)
Get A Life
Julian Lennon; *Help Yourself* . . . .(Atlantic)
Get A Life/Fairplay
Soul II Soul; *Keep On Movin'* . . . .(Virgin)
Get Out Of My Life, Woman
Lee Dorsey; *History Of New Orleans R&B-#3-1962-1970-C* . . . . (Rhino)
Paul Butterfield Blues Band; *East-West* . . . . (Elektra)
Golden Butter . . . . (Elektra)
Get Out The Map
Indigo Girls; *Shaming Of The Sun* . . . . (Epic)
Give Me Love (Give Me Peace On Earth)
George Harrison; *Best Of George Harrison* . . . . (Capitol)
Living In The Material World . . . . (Capitol)
Give To Live
Sammy Hagar; *I Never Said Goodbye* . . . . (Geffen)
Glamorous Life
Sheila E.; *The Glamorous Life* . . . . (Warner Bros.)
Glamorous Life
Original London Cast; *A Little Night Music* . . . . (RCA)
Glory Days
Bruce Springsteen; *Born In The U.S.A.* . . . . (Columbia)
Bruce Springsteen's Greatest Hits . . . . (Columbia)
Go Let It Out
Oasis; *Standing On The Shoulders Of Giants* . . . . (Epic)
Go On
George Strait; *George Strait* . . . . (MCA)
God Bless The Child
Billie Holiday; *Billie Holiday's Greatest Hits* . . . .(Decca Jazz)
Billie Holiday's Greatest Hits . . . . (Legacy)
From The Original Decca Masters . . . .(MCA)
Songbook . . . . (Verve)
The Billie Holiday Story-#2 . . . . (Columbia)
Blood, Sweat & Tears; *Blood, Sweat & Tears* . . . . (Columbia)
Blood, Sweat & Tears Greatest Hits . . . . (Columbia)
Diana Ross; *ST/Lady Sings The Blues* . . . . (Motown)
Liza Minnelli; *4-Sider* . . . . (Cypress)
ST/Liza With A "Z" . . . . (Columbia)
Lou Rawls; *Best From Lou Rawls* . . . . (Capitol)
God Is Alive, Magic Is Afoot
Buffy Sainte-Marie; *Best Of Buffy Sainte-Marie* . . . . (Vanguard)
Illuminations . . . . (Vanguard)
Goin' Back
Byrds; *20 Essential Tracks From The Box Set* . . . . . . (Columbia)

The Byrds . . . . (Columbia)
Dusty Springfield; *Dusty Springfield-Golden Greats* . . . . (Philips)
Neil Young; *Comes A Time* . . . . (Reprise)
Nils Lofgren; *Best Of Nils Lofgren* . . . . (A&M)
   Night After Night . . . . (A&M)
   Nils Lofgren . . . . (Rykodisc)
Going To Live In L.A.
Roger Waters; *45-#38-07180* . . . . (Columbia)
Gonna Get A Life
Mark Chesnutt; *Mark Chesnutt's Greatest Hits* . . . . (Decca)
   What A Way To Live . . . . (Decca)
Good Life
Betty Carter; *Atlantic Jazz-Singers-C* . . . . (Atlantic)
   'Round Midnight . . . . (Atlantic)
Ernie Maresca; *22 Leaders Of The Pack-#1-C* . . . . (Laurie)
Frank Sinatra & Count Basie; *It Might As Well Be Swing* . . . . (Reprise)
Tony Bennett; *Tony Bennett Sings His All-Time Hall Of
   Fame Hits* . . . . (Columbia)
   Tony Bennett-16 Most Requested Songs . . . . (Legacy)
Good Life
Bruce Robison; *Long Way Home From Anywhere* . . . . (Lucky Dog)
Good Morning Good Morning
Beatles; *Beatles-Box Set* . . . . (Capitol)
   Sgt. Pepper's Lonely Hearts Club Band . . . . (Capitol)
Good Timin'
Jimmy Jones; *Hard To Find 45s On CD-#1-1955-1960-C* . . . . (Eric)
Got A Lot O' Livin' To Do!
Elvis Presley; *Loving You* . . . . (RCA)
   The Great Performances . . . . (RCA)
   The Other Sides-Worldwide Gold Award Hits, Vol. 2 . . . . (RCA)
Got The Life
Korn; *Follow The Leader* . . . . (Immortal/Epic)
Got To Get You Into My Life
Beatles; *Beatles-Box Set* . . . . (Capitol)
   Revolver . . . . (Capitol)
   Rock 'N' Roll Music . . . . (Capitol)
   The Beatles-Anthology-#2 . . . . (Capitol)
Earth, Wind & Fire; *Best Of Earth, Wind & Fire-#1* . . . . (Legacy)
   ST/Sgt. Pepper's Lonely Hearts Club Band . . . . (RSO)
Paul McCartney & Wings; *Kampuchea-C* . . . . (Atlantic)
Gotta Serve Somebody
Bob Dylan; *Biograph* . . . . (Columbia)
   Slow Train Coming . . . . (Columbia)
   *The Sopranos-Music From The HBO Original
    Series* . . . . (Sony Music Soundtrax)
Bob Dylan & The Grateful Dead; *Dylan & The Dead* . . . . (Columbia)
Graduation (Friends Forever)
Vitamin C; *Totally Hits-#3-C* . . . . (Atlantic)
   Vitamin C . . . . (Elektra)
Green, Green
New Christy Minstrels; *New Christy Minstrels' Greatest Hits* . . . . . (Columbia)
Grow Old With Me
John Lennon; *The John Lennon Anthology* . . . . (Capitol)
   Wonsaponatime . . . . (Capitol)
Mary Chapin Carpenter; *Party Doll And Other Favorites* . . . . (Columbia)
Guess Things Happen That Way
Johnny Cash; *The Man In Black-His Greatest Hits* . . . . (Legacy)
Hakuna Matata
Jimmy Cliff; *Disney's Greatest Pop Hits-C* . . . . (Disney)
Nathan Lane/Ernie Sabella/Jason Weaver/Joseph Williams; *ST/The
   Lion King* . . . . (Walt Disney)
Original Cast; *The Lion King* . . . . (Disney)
Rembrandts; *Disney's Music From The Park-C* . . . . (Disney)
Hand Of Fate
Rolling Stones; *Black And Blue* . . . . (Rolling Stones)
Handcuffed To A Fence In Mississippi
Jim White; *No Such Place* . . . . (Luaka Bop)
Hangin' In
Tanya Tucker; *Soon* . . . . (Liberty)
Hanging Tree
Marty Robbins; *Gunfighter Ballads & Trail Songs* . . . . (Legacy)
   Hollywood Magic-1950s-C . . . . (Columbia)
   Lifetime Of Song-1951-1982 . . . . (Columbia)
   Marty Robbins' All-Time Greatest Hits . . . . (Columbia)
Happening, The
Diana Ross; *Diana Ross-Anthology* . . . . (Motown)
Diana Ross & The Supremes; *Diana Ross & The Supremes-Superstar
   Series-#1* . . . . (Motown)
Happy
Bruce Springsteen; *Tracks* . . . . (Columbia)
Happy
Sister Hazel; *...Somewhere More Familiar* . . . . (Universal)
Hard Knock Life
Original Broadway Cast; *Annie* . . . . (Columbia)
Hard Knock Life (Ghetto Anthem)
Jay-Z; *Now That's What I Call Music!-#2-C* . . . . (Virgin)
   Vol. 2-Hard Knock Life . . . . (Def Jam)
Hard Life
Little River Band; *Backstage Pass* . . . . (Capitol)

First Under The Wire . . . . (Capitol)
Hard Life
Roger Daltrey; *Daltrey* . . . . (MCA)
Hard Times Come Easy
Richie Sambora; *Undiscovered Soul* . . . . (Mercury)
Hardest Thing
98 Degrees; *98 Degrees And Rising* . . . . (Universal)
   Now That's What I Call Music!-#3-C . . . . (Virgin)
Heartache, A Shadow, A Lifetime
Dave Mason; *Best Of Dave Mason* . . . . (MCA)
   Dave Mason-At His Very Best . . . . (MCA)
Hello Brother
Louis Armstrong; *What A Wonderful World* . . . . (Decca Jazz)
Here And Now
Luther Vandross; *Best Of Luther Vandross...The Best Of Love* . . . . . (Epic)
Here We Are
Alabama; *Pass It On Down* . . . . (BMG Special Prod.)
Here We Are
Gloria Estefan; *Cuts Both Ways* . . . . (Epic)
Heroes & Villains
Beach Boys; *Concert/'69-Live In London* . . . . (Capitol)
   Endless Harmony . . . . (Capitol)
   Good Vibrations-Thirty Years Of The Beach Boys . . . . (Capitol)
   Made In The U.S.A. . . . . (Capitol)
   Smiley Smile/Wild Honey . . . . (Capitol)
   Sunshine Dream . . . . (Capitol)
Hey, Cinderella
Suzy Bogguss; *Something Up My Sleeve* . . . . (Liberty)
High Head Blues
Black Crowes; *Amorica* . . . . (American)
High Hopes And Empty Pockets
McBride & The Ride; *McBride & The Ride* . . . . (MCA)
High Noon
Frankie Laine; *Billboard Top Movie Hits-1950-1954-C* . . . . (Rhino)
Tex Ritter; *Heroes Of Country Music-#4-Legends Of The West
   Coast-C* . . . . (Rhino)
   *The Envelope Please-Academy Award Winning Songs (1946-
   1957)-C* . . . . (Rhino)
Hour Of Gold
Emmylou Harris; *Red Dirt Girl* . . . . (Nonesuch)
House I Live In (That's America To Me)
Frank Sinatra; *Frank Sinatra-In The Beginning-1943-1951* . . . . . . (Columbia)
   Portrait Of Sinatra-Columbia Classics . . . . (Legacy)
   Sinatra: A Man And His Music . . . . (Reprise)
   Sinatra-The Main Event Live . . . . (Reprise)
How Am I Supposed To Live Without You
Laura Branigan; *Branigan 2* . . . . (Atlantic)
Michael Bolton; *Soul Provider* . . . . (Columbia)
How Beautiful The Days
Original Broadway Cast; *The Most Happy Fella* . . . . (Sony Music Classical)
How Can I Help You Say Goodbye
Patty Loveless; *Only What I Feel* . . . . (Epic)
   Patty Loveless-Classics . . . . (Epic)
How Did I Get By Without You
John Waite; *Complete John Waite-#1-Falling Backwards* . . . . (EMI)
   Temple Bar . . . . (Coyote/Imago)
How Do I Live
LeAnn Rimes; *Absolute Dance Hits-C* . . . . (Curb)
   You Light Up My Life-Inspirational Songs . . . . (Curb)
Trisha Yearwood; *Songbook-A Collection Of Hits* . . . . (MCA)
How Do The Fools Survive
Doobie Brothers; *Minute By Minute* . . . . (Warner Bros.)
How Much Is It Worth To Live In L.A.
Waylon Jennings; *New Classic Waylon* . . . . (MCA)
Human Beings
Seal; *Human Being* . . . . (Warner Bros.)
Human Nature
Michael Jackson; *Thriller* . . . . (Epic)
Miles Davis; *You're Under Arrest* . . . . (Columbia)
Hundred Million Miracles
Original Cast; *Flower Drum Song* . . . . (Sony Music Classical)
Hurricane Eye
Paul Simon; *You're The One* . . . . (Warner Bros.)
I Ain't Livin' Long Like This
Emmylou Harris; *Quarter Moon In A Ten Cent Town* . . . . (Warner Bros.)
Rodney Crowell; *I Ain't Livin' Long Like This* . . . . (Warner Bros.)
   Rodney Crowell-Collection . . . . (Warner Bros.)
Waylon Jennings; *Waylon Jennings' Greatest Hits-#2* . . . . (RCA)
   What Goes Around Comes Around . . . . (RCA)
I Alone
Live; *Throwing Copper* . . . . (Radioactive/MCA)
I Can't Live Without Your Love
Teddy Pendergrass; *45-#02462* . . . . (Philadelphia Int'l)
I Choose
Offspring; *Ixnay On The Hombre* . . . . (Columbia)
I Come Alive
Jay Ferguson; *White Noise* . . . . (Capitol)

I Disappear
Metallica; *ST/Mission: Impossible 2* . . . . (Hollywood)
I Don't Live Today
Jimi Hendrix; *Concerts* . . . . (Reprise)
  Essential Jimi Hendrix, Volume 2 . . . . (Reprise)
  Kiss The Sky . . . . (Reprise)
Jimi Hendrix Experience; *Are You Experienced?* . . . . (Reprise)
I Don't Need Your Rockin' Chair
George Jones; *Platinum Country-C* . . . . (MCA)
  Walls Can Fall . . . . (MCA)
I Don't Wanna Live Without Your Love
Chicago; *Chicago 19* . . . . (Reprise)
  Chicago's Greatest Hits-1982-1989 . . . . (Full Moon)
I Don't Want To Live Without You
Foreigner; *Inside Information* . . . . (Atlantic)
I Don't Want To Wait
Paula Cole; *Live On Letterman-From The Late Show* . . . . (Reprise)
  Songs From Dawson's Creek . . . . (Sony Music Soundtrax)
  This Fire . . . . (Imago)
I Get Up I Get Down
Yes; *Close To The Edge* . . . . (Atlantic)
I Got A Mind To Give Up Living
Paul Butterfield Blues Band; *East-West* . . . . (Elektra)
I Hope You Dance
Lee Ann Womack; *I Hope You Dance* . . . . (MCA)
I Know There's An Answer
Beach Boys; *Pet Sounds* . . . . (Capitol)
  The Pet Sounds Sessions: A 30th Anniversary Collection . . . . . . (Capitol)
I Know What I Know
Paul Simon; *Graceland* . . . . (Warner Bros.)
I Like Ev'rybody
Original Broadway Cast; *The Most Happy Fella* . . . . . . (Sony Music Classical)
I Live For Your Love
Natalie Cole; *Everlasting* . . . . (Elektra)
I Live My Life For You
Firehouse; *3* . . . . (Epic)
  Good Acoustics . . . . (Epic)
I Love
Tom T. Hall; *Tom T. Hall's Greatest Hits-#2* . . . . (Mercury)
  Tom T. Hall-The Hits . . . . (Mercury)
I Love The Life I Live
Mose Allison; *Best Of Mose Allison* . . . . (Rhino)
  Mose Allison-Alive . . . . (Atlantic)
Muddy Waters; *The Chess Box-Muddy Waters* . . . . (Chess)
I Love You
Keith Washington & Chante' Moore; *KW* . . . . (Silas)
I Never Thought I'd Live To Be A Hundred
Moody Blues; *To Our Children's Children's Children* . . . . (Polydor)
I Never Thought I'd Live To Be A Million
Moody Blues; *To Our Children's Children's Children* . . . . (Polydor)
I Try
Macy Gray; *Now That's What I Call Music!-#4-C* . . . . (Virgin)
  On How Life Is . . . . (Epic)
I Wanna Be A Cowboy's Sweetheart
Patsy Montana & The Prairie Ramblers; *All Time Legends Of Country
  Music-C* . . . . (Legacy)
  Respect: A History Of Women In Music-C . . . . (Rhino)
I Want To Live In A Wigwam
Cat Stevens; *Footsteps In The Dark-Greatest Hits-#2* . . . . (A&M)
I Want To Spend My Lifetime Loving You
Marc Anthony & Tina Arena; *ST/Mask Of Zorro* . . . . (Sony Music Classical)
I Was Wrong
Social Distortion; *White Light White Heat White Trash* . . . . (550 Music)
I Will Buy You A New Life
Everclear; *Now That's What I Call Music!-#1-C* . . . . (Virgin)
  So Much For The Afterglow . . . . (Capitol)
I Will Remember You
Sarah McLachlan; *Mirrorball* . . . . (Arista)
  ST/Brothers McMullen . . . . (Arista)
  Surfacing . . . . (Arista)
  Totally Hits-#2-C . . . . (Elektra)
I Will Survive
Gloria Gaynor; *Billboard Top Hits-1979-C* . . . . (Rhino)
  I Am Woman-C . . . . (Nick At Nite)
  Love Tracks . . . . (Polydor)
  The Disco Years-#2-On The Beat-1978-1982-C . . . . (Rhino)
I'd Rather Be Dead
Nilsson; *Son Of Schmilsson* . . . . (RCA)
If He Walked Into My Life
Original Cast; *Mame* . . . . (Columbia)
If I Could
Barbra Streisand; *Higher Ground* . . . . (Columbia)
If It Makes You Happy
Sheryl Crow; *Sheryl Crow* . . . . (A&M)
I'll Stick Around
Foo Fighters; *Foo Fighters* . . . . (Roswell/RCA)
I'm A Survivor
Reba McEntire; *Reba McEntire's Greatest Hits-#3: I'm A Survivor* . . . . . (MCA)

I'm Alive
Hollies; *Best Of The Hollies* . . . . (EMI)
  History Of British Rock-#2-C . . . . (Rhino)
I'm Alive
Kiss; *Asylum* . . . . (Mercury)
I'm Alive
Tommy James And The Shondells; *Crimson & Clover/Cellophane
  Symphony* . . . . (Rhino)
I'm Alive
Mose Allison; *Ever Since The World Ended* . . . . (Blue Note)
I'm Alive
April Wine; *First Glance* . . . . (Capitol)
I'm Alive
Gamma; *Gamma* . . . . (Elektra)
I'm Alive
Neil Diamond; *Heartlight* . . . . (Columbia)
I'm Alive
Spooky Tooth; *Hell Or High Water* . . . . (Accord)
  Mirror . . . . (Island)
I'm Alive
Jackson Browne; *I'm Alive* . . . . (Elektra)
I'm Alive
Tarney/Spencer Band; *Run For Your Life* . . . . (A&M)
I'm Alive
Seal; *Seal 2* . . . . (Sire)
I'm Alive
Electric Light Orchestra; *ST/Xanadu* . . . . (MCA)
I'm An Ordinary Man
Rex Harrison/Original Cast; *My Fair Lady* . . . . (Columbia)
I'm Gonna Wash That Man Right Outta My Hair
Mitzi Gaynor; *ST/South Pacific* . . . . (RCA)
Original Cast; *South Pacific* . . . . (CBS Masterworks)
Weather Girls; *Success* . . . . (Columbia)
I'm Holdin' On To Love (To Save My Life)
Shania Twain; *Come On Over* . . . . (Mercury)
I'm In A Hurry (And Don't Know Why)
Alabama; *American Pride* . . . . (RCA)
I'm Still Alive
Trisha Yearwood; *Real Live Woman* . . . . (MCA)
I'm Tired Of Living This Lie
Bob Wills & His Texas Playboys; *Bob Wills & His Texas Playboys-24
  Great Hits* . . . . (Polydor)
Imitation Of Life
R.E.M.; *Reveal* . . . . (Warner Bros.)
In My Life
Beatles; *Beatles-Love Songs* . . . . (Capitol)
  Rubber Soul . . . . (Capitol)
  ST/Imagine: John Lennon . . . . (Capitol)
  The Beatles/1962-1966 . . . . (Capitol)
Crosby, Stills & Nash; *After The Storm* . . . . (Atlantic)
Judy Collins; *Colors Of The Day-The Best Of Judy Collins* . . . . (Elektra)
  In My Life . . . . (Elektra)
In My Life
Original Broadway Cast; *Les Miserables* . . . . (Geffen)
In My Life
Patti Austin; *Love Is Gonna Getcha* . . . . (GRP)
In My Life
Glen Campbell; *Still Within The Sound Of My Voice* . . . . (MCA)
In Pictures
Alabama; *Alabama-Super Hits* . . . . (RCA)
  In Pictures . . . . (RCA)
In The Summertime
Mungo Jerry; *In The Summertime-Best Of Mungo Jerry* . . . . (Rhino)
  Super Hits Of The '70s-Have A Nice Day-#3-C . . . . (Rhino)
In This Life
Collin Raye; *In This Life* . . . . (Epic)
Inner Light
Beatles; *Past Masters-Volume Two* . . . . (Parlophone)
  Rarities . . . . (Capitol)
Inside Of Me
Little Steven & The Disciples Of Soul; *The Sopranos-Music From The HBO
  Original Series* . . . . (Sony Music Soundtrax)
Into Each Life Some Rain Must Fall
Ella Fitzgerald; *Ella & Friends* . . . . (Decca Jazz)
Ink Spots; *Encore Of Golden Hits-Ink Spots* . . . . (Juke Box Treasures)
Invisible City
Wallflowers; *Bringing Down The Horse* . . . . (Interscope)
Iris
Goo Goo Dolls; *Dizzy Up The Girl* . . . . (Warner Sunset/Reprise)
  ST/City Of Angels . . . . (Warner Sunset/Reprise)
Ironic
Alanis Morissette; *Jagged Little Pill* . . . . (Maverick)
Is There Life Out There
Reba McEntire; *For My Broken Heart* . . . . (MCA)
  Reba McEntire's Greatest Hits Volume Two . . . . (MCA)
Isn't Life Strange
Moody Blues; *A Night At Red Rocks With The Colorado Symphony
  Orchestra* . . . . (Polydor)

Seventh Sojourn . . . . (Polydor)
This Is The Moody Blues . . . . (Polydor)
Voices In The Sky-The Best Of The Moody Blues . . . . (Threshold)

It Goes Like It Goes (Theme From "Norma Rae")
Jennifer Warnes; *Best Of Jennifer Warnes* . . . . (Arista)
*The Envelope Please-Academy Award Winning Songs-#4 (1970-
1981)-C* . . . . (Rhino)

It Was A Very Good Year
Frank Sinatra; *Frank Sinatra-The Very Good Years* . . . . (Reprise)
September Of My Years . . . . (Reprise)
The Reprise Collection . . . . (Reprise)
*The Sopranos-Music From The HBO Original
Series* . . . . (Sony Music Soundtrax)
Frank Sinatra with Count Basie & The Orchestra; *Sinatra At The
Sands* . . . . (Reprise)

It's A Great Day To Be Alive
Travis Tritt; *Down The Road I Go* . . . . (Columbia)

It's All About The Benjamins
Puff Daddy & The Family; *No Way Out* . . . . (Bad Boy/Arista)

It's All Coming Back
Keb' Mo'; *The Door* . . . . (550/Epic/Okeh)

It's My Life
Talk Talk; *It's My Life* . . . . (EMI)
Very Best Of Talk Talk-Natural History . . . . (EMI)

It's My Life
Charlie Daniels Band; *Saddle Tramp* . . . . (Epic)

It's My Life
Animals; *Animals Greatest Hits* . . . . (Allegiance)
Best Of The Animals . . . . (Abkco)

It's My Life
Bon Jovi; *Crush* . . . . (Island/IDJMG)
Now That's What I Call Music!-#5-C . . . . (Virgin)
The Concert For New York City-C . . . . (Columbia)

It's My Life Baby
Bobby Bland; *Barefoot Rock & You Got Me* . . . . (MCA)
Best Of Bobby Bland-#2 . . . . (MCA)
Johnny Winter; *Guitar Slinger* . . . . (Alligator)
Junior Wells; *It's My Life Baby* . . . . (Vanguard)

It's My Time
Martina McBride; *Emotion* . . . . (RCA)

It's No Good
Depeche Mode; *Ultra* . . . . (Mute/Reprise)

It's Not Up To You
Bjork; *Vespertine* . . . . (Elektra)

It's The Hard-Knock Life
Original Broadway Cast; *Annie* . . . . (Columbia)
Original Cast; *ST/Annie* . . . . (Columbia)

I've Got Life
Take 6; *Join The Band-C* . . . . (Reprise)

I've Got The World On A String
Count Basie; *Standards* . . . . (Verve)
Diana Krall; *Only Trust Your Heart* . . . . (GRP)
Ella Fitzgerald; *Harold Arlen Songbook-#1* . . . . (Verve)
Frank Sinatra; *Capitol Collectors Series-Frank Sinatra* . . . . . . (Capitol)
Frank Sinatra & Liza Minnelli; *Frank Sinatra-Duets-C* . . . . . . (Capitol)
Sarah Vaughan; *Best Of Sarah Vaughan* . . . . (Pablo)
Stephane Grappelli & Martin Taylor; *We've Got The World On A
String* . . . . (Angel)

J.A.R. (Jason Andrew Relva)
Green Day; *ST/Angus* . . . . (Reprise)

James
Huffamoose; *We've Been Had Again* . . . . (Interscope)

Je Suis Desole
Mark Knopfler; *Golden Heart* . . . . (Warner Bros.)

Joe Knows How To Live
Eddy Raven; *Best Of Eddy Raven* . . . . (RCA)
Nitty Gritty Dirt Band; *Hold On* . . . . (Warner Bros.)

Jump Up Behind Me
James Taylor; *Hourglass* . . . . (Columbia)
Songs From The Heart-C . . . . (Columbia)

Jungle, The
Kiss; *Carnival Of Souls: The Final Sessions* . . . . (Mercury)

Jungleland
Bruce Springsteen; *Born To Run* . . . . (Columbia)

Just Another Day
John Mellencamp; *Mr. Happy Go Lucky* . . . . (Mercury)

Just Another Day In Paradise
Phil Vassar; *Phil Vassar* . . . . (Arista)

Just One Of Those Things
Bobby Short; *Loves Cole Porter* . . . . (Atlantic)
Ella Fitzgerald; *Best Of The Song Books: Love Songs* . . . . . . (Verve)
Frank Sinatra; *Timeless* . . . . (Pair)
Lena Horne; *American Songbook Series-Cole Porter* . . (Smithsonian Collection)
Lester Lanin; *Best Of The Big Bands-C* . . . . (Columbia)
Louis Armstrong; *Jazz Masters-#1-Louis Armstrong* . . . . (Verve)
Peggy Lee; *Peggy Lee Sings For You* . . . . (Avid)
Sarah Vaughan; *Essential Sarah Vaughan-The Great Songs* . . . (Verve)

Just Seven Numbers
Four Tops; *Compact Command Performances-Four Tops* . . . . . (Motown)

Four Tops-Anthology . . . . (Motown)

Just The Two Of Us
Will Smith; *Big Willie Style* . . . . (Columbia)

Just The Way It Is, Baby
Rembrandts; *Rembrandts* . . . . (Atco)

Keep It Between The Lines
Ricky Van Shelton; *Backroads* . . . . (Columbia)

Keep On The Sunny Side
Randy Scruggs with Earl Scruggs & Doc Watson; *Red Hot +
Country-C* . . . . (Mercury)
Whites; *ST/O Brother, Where Art Thou?* . . . . (Mercury)

Keep Yourself Alive
Queen; *Live Killers* . . . . (Hollywood)
Queen . . . . (Hollywood)
Queen's Greatest Hits I & II . . . . (Hollywood)

Key To Life, The
Vince Gill; *The Key* . . . . (MCA)

Kids Aren't Alright
Offspring; *Americana* . . . . (Columbia)

Killing Yourself To Live
Black Sabbath; *Sabbath Bloody Sabbath* . . . . (Warner Bros.)

Kisses Sweeter Than Wine
Jimmie Rodgers; *Best Of Jimmie Rodgers* . . . . (Rhino)
Cruisin'-1958-C . . . . (Increase)
Weavers; *Best Of The Weavers* . . . . (MCA)
Reunion-At Carnegie Hall-1963 . . . . (Vanguard)
Weavers At Carnegie Hall . . . . (Vanguard)
Weavers' Greatest Hits . . . . (Vanguard)

Kodachrome
Paul Simon; *Greatest Hits, Etc.* . . . . (Columbia)
Negotiations And Love Songs, 1971-1986. . . . . (Warner Bros.)
There Goes Rhymin' Simon . . . . (Columbia)
Simon & Garfunkel; *The Concert In Central Park.* . . . . . (Warner Bros.)

La Vie En Rose
Edith Piaf; *Voice Of The Sparrow-Very Best Of Edith Piaf* . . . . (Capitol)
Grace Jones; *Island Life* . . . . (Island)
Louis Armstrong; *Louis Armstrong-Best Of The Decca Years-#1-The
Singer-C* . . . . (Decca)
Marlene Dietrich; *The Cosmopolitan* . . . . (Columbia)
Melissa Manchester; *Tribute* . . . . (Polydor)

Lady Picture Show
Stone Temple Pilots; *Tiny Music...Songs From The Vatican
Gift Shop.* . . . . (Atlantic)

Land Of The Living
Pam Tillis; *Pam Tillis' Greatest Hits* . . . . (Arista)

Last Cup Of Sorrow
Faith No More; *Album Of The Year* . . . . (Reprise)

Last Day, The
Marilyn Scott; *Avenues Of Love* . . . . (Warner Bros.)

Last Night A D.J. Saved My Life
Indeep; *Last Night A D.J. Saved My Life* . . . . . . (Sound Of New York)
The Disco Years-#2-On The Beat-1978-1982-C . . . . (Rhino)

Last Night On Earth
U2; *Pop* . . . . (Island)

Laughing At Life
Billie Holiday; *Billie Holiday.* . . . . (Columbia)
Quintessential-#8-1939-1940 . . . . (Legacy)
The Billie Holiday Story-#2. . . . . (Columbia)

Learn How To Live
Billy Squier; *Emotions In Motion.* . . . . (Capitol)

Learn To Be Still
Eagles; *Hell Freezes Over* . . . . (Geffen)

Learning As You Go
Rick Trevino; *Learning As You Go* . . . . (Columbia)
Super Hits Of 1996-C . . . . (Epic)

Learning To Live Again
Garth Brooks; *The Chase* . . . . (Liberty)

Leaving Town
Dexter Freebish; *Life Of Saturdays* . . . . (Capitol)

Lesson In Survival
Joni Mitchell; *For The Roses* . . . . (Asylum)

Lessons To Be Learned
Barbra Streisand; *Higher Ground* . . . . (Columbia)

Let It Flow
Toni Braxton; *Secrets.* . . . . (LaFace)
ST/Waiting To Exhale . . . . (Arista)

Let Me Live Another Day
Lisa Brokop; *Every Little Girl's Dream.* . . . . (Patriot)

Let Me Make Something In Your Life
Steve Winwood; *Steve Winwood* . . . . (Island)

Let The Mystery Be
10,000 Maniacs; *Few & Far Between* . . . . (Elektra)
Iris DeMent; *Infamous Angel* . . . . (Warner Bros.)

Let's Live For Today
Grass Roots; *At The Hop* . . . . (MCA)
Grass Roots-All-Time Greatest Hits . . . . (MCA)
Let's Live For Today . . . . (MCA Special Prod.)
Summer Of Love-#1-C. . . . . (Rhino)
Vintage Music-#10-C . . . . (MCA)

Let's Make Sure We Kiss Goodbye
Vince Gill; *Let's Make Sure We Kiss Goodbye* . . . . (MCA)
Let's Talk About Love
Celine Dion with The Bee Gees; *Let's Talk About Love-C* . . . . (550 Music)
Let's Think About Living
Bob Luman; *Bob Luman-Classic Country* . . . . (Simitar)
Life
Sly & The Family Stone; *Sly & The Family Stone-Anthology* . . . . (Epic)
Sly & The Family Stone's Greatest Hits . . . . (Epic)
Life
K-Ci & JoJo; *It's Real* . . . . (Rock Land/Interscope)
Life
Elvis Presley; *Love Letters From Elvis* . . . . (RCA)
Life #9
Martina McBride; *The Way That I Am* . . . . (RCA)
Life (Everybody Needs Somebody)
Haddaway; *Haddaway* . . . . (Arista)
Life After Death
Ian Hunter; *You're Never Alone With A Schizophrenic* . . . . (Razor & Tie)
Life Ain't Easy
Dr. Hook & The Medicine Show; *Dr. Hook At His Best* . . . . (Queen)
Life And How To Live It
R.E.M.; *Fables Of The Reconstruction* . . . . (I.R.S.)
Life As We Knew It
Kathy Mattea; *Class Of Country-C* . . . . (K-Tel)
Collection Of Hits . . . . (Mercury)
Untasted Honey . . . . (Polydor Country)
Life Beyond L.A.
Ambrosia; *Life Beyond L.A.* . . . . (Warner Bros.)
Life During Wartime
Talking Heads; *Fear Of Music* . . . . (Sire)
Name Of This Band Is Talking Heads . . . . (Sire)
ST/Stop Making Sense . . . . (Sire)
Life For The Taking
Eddie Money; *Life For The Taking* . . . . (Columbia)
Life Gets Away
Clint Black; *Clint Black-The Greatest Hits* . . . . (RCA)
One Emotion . . . . (RCA)
Life Goes On
Johnny Cash; *Story Songs Of The Trains & Rivers* . . . . (Sun)
The Man-The World-His Music . . . . (Sun)
Life Goes On
Little Texas; *Little Texas' Greatest Hits* . . . . (Warner Bros.)
Life Goes On
Peabo Bryson; *All My Love* . . . . (Capitol)
Life Goes On
Big Mama Thornton; *Big Mama Thornton With Muddy Waters*
Blues Band . . . . (Arhoolie)
Life Goes On
Utopia; *Deface The Music* . . . . (Rhino)
Life Goes On
Leon Haywood; *Double My Pleasure* . . . . (MCA)
Life Goes On
Poison; *Flesh & Blood* . . . . (Capitol)
Life Goes On
Jones Girls; *Jones Girls* . . . . (MCA)
Life Goes On
Kinks; *Sleepwalker* . . . . (Arista)
Life Goes On
Charlie Rich; *Fool Strikes Again* . . . . (United Artists)
Nobody But You . . . . (United Artists)
Life Has Its Little Ups & Downs
Charlie Rich; *Best Of Charlie Rich* . . . . (Epic)
Charlie Rich's Greatest Hits . . . . (Epic)
Life Has Just Begun
Spirit; *12 Dreams Of Dr. Sardonicus* . . . . (Epic)
Life In A Northern Town
Dream Academy; *Dream Academy* . . . . (Warner Bros.)
Life In A Song
Marshall Tucker Band; *Carolina Dreams* . . . . (Capricorn)
Life In London
Pat Travers; *Boom Boom...The Best Of* . . . . (Polydor)
Putting It Straight . . . . (Polydor)
Life In One Day
Howard Jones; *Dream Into Action* . . . . (Elektra)
Life In Prison
Byrds; *Jailhouse Rock (Hits From The Big*
House)-C . . . . (Sony Music Special Prod.)
Sweetheart Of The Rodeo . . . . (Columbia)
Life In The Air Age
Be Bop Deluxe; *Live! In The Air Age* . . . . (Harvest)
Sunburst Finish . . . . (Capitol)
Life In The Bloodstream
Guess Who; *Best Of The Guess Who-#2* . . . . (RCA)
Life In The Fast Lane
Eagles; *Eagles Live* . . . . (Asylum)
Hotel California . . . . (Asylum)
ST/FM . . . . (MCA)

Life In The Foodchain
Tonio K.; *Life In The Foodchain* . . . . (Epic)
Life In The Jungle
John Mayall's Bluesbreakers; *Chicago Line* . . . . (Island)
Life Is A Carnival
Band; *Best Of The Band* . . . . (Capitol)
Cahoots . . . . (Capitol)
Rock Of Ages . . . . (Capitol)
The Band-Anthology-#2 . . . . (Capitol)
The Last Waltz . . . . (Warner Bros.)
Life Is A Highway
Tom Cochrane; *Mad Mad World* . . . . (Capitol)
Life Is A Lady
Santana; *Inner Secrets* . . . . (Columbia)
Life Is A Lemon And I Want My Money Back
Meat Loaf; *Bat Out Of Hell II: Back Into Hell* . . . . (MCA)
Life Is A Long Song
Jethro Tull; *Living In The Past* . . . . (Chrysalis)
Life Is A Minestrone
10 CC; *Original Soundtrack* . . . . (Mercury)
Life Is A Rock (But The Radio Rolled Me)
Reunion; *Super Hits Of The '70s-Have A Nice Day-#13-C* . . . . (Rhino)
Life Is A Song Worth Singing
Johnny Mathis; *I'm Coming Home* . . . . (Columbia)
Teddy Pendergrass; *Life Is A Song Worth Singing* . . . . (Philadelphia Int'l)
Life Is A Woman
Original Cast/Sammy Davis, Jr.; *Stop The World I Want To*
Get Off . . . . (Warner Bros.)
Life Is Beautiful
Amy Correia; *Carnival Love* . . . . (Capitol)
Life Is But A Dream
Harptones; *Echoes Of A Rock Era-The Harptones* . . . . (Roulette)
ST/Goodfellas . . . . (Atlantic)
Super Oldies Of The '50s-#4-C . . . . (Audio Fidelity)
Life Is Happiness Indeed
Original Cast; *Candide* . . . . (Columbia)
Life Is Just A Bowl Of Cherries
Ethel Merman; *The Ethel Merman Collection* . . . . (Razor & Tie)
Jaye P. Morgan; *The Jaye P. Morgan Story* . . . . (Simitar)
Original Cast; *Fosse* . . . . (RCA Victor)
Rudy Vallee & His Connecticut Yankees; *As Time*
Goes By . . . . (Varese Sarabande)
Life Is Just A Tire Swing
Jimmy Buffett; *A1A* . . . . (MCA)
Life Is Sweet
Natalie Merchant; *Ophelia* . . . . (Elektra)
Life Line
Nilsson; *The Point* . . . . (RCA)
Life Of Illusion
Joe Walsh; *There Goes The Neighborhood* . . . . (Asylum)
Life On A Chain
Pete Yorn; *Musicforthemorningafter* . . . . (Columbia)
Life On Mars?
David Bowie; *Hunky Dory* . . . . (Rykodisc)
The Singles-1969-1993 . . . . (Rykodisc)
Life On The Road
Kinks; *Sleepwalker* . . . . (Arista)
Life Saver
Chicago; *Chicago VII* . . . . (Chicago)
Life So Changed, A
James Horner; *ST/Titanic* . . . . (Sony Music Classical)
Life So Cruel
Charlie; *Lines* . . . . (Janus)
Life Takes A Life
Jon Butcher Axis; *Jon Butcher Axis* . . . . (Polydor)
Life To Win
Motorhead; *Ace Of Spades* . . . . (Mercury)
Life Turned Her That Way
"Little" Jimmy Dickens; *I'm Little, But I'm Loud-The "Little" Jimmy*
Dickens Collection . . . . (Razor & Tie)
Mel Tillis; *Best Of Mel Tillis* . . . . (MCA)
Mel Tillis' Greatest Hits . . . . (Universal)
Ricky Van Shelton; *Ricky Van Shelton-16 Biggest Hits* . . . . (Legacy)
Wild-Eyed Dream . . . . (Columbia)
Life, The
Alicia Keys; *Songs In A Minor* . . . . (J)
Lifeline
Spandau Ballet; *True* . . . . (Chrysalis)
Lifeline
10 CC; *Bloody Tourists* . . . . (Polydor)
Lifeline
Husker Du; *Metal Circus* . . . . (SST)
Life's A Bitch
Shooter; *Songs From Dawson's Creek* . . . . (Sony Music Soundtrax)
Life's A Dance
John Michael Montgomery; *Life's A Dance* . . . . (Atlantic)
Life's A Song
Kool & The Gang; *Force* . . . . (De-Lite)

Life's Been Good
Eagles; *Eagles Live* . . . . (Asylum)
Joe Walsh; *But Seriously Folks* . . . . (Asylum)
ST/FM . . . . (MCA)

Life's Highway
Steve Wariner; *Country Classics-#2-Today's Country Classics-C* . . . (Universal)
Grand Ole Opry-75 Years-#2-C . . . . (MCA)
Life's Highway . . . . (MCA)

Life's In One Day
Howard Jones; *Dream Into Action* . . . . (Elektra)

Life's Just A Ballgame
Womack & Womack; *Conscience* . . . . (Island)

Life's Like Poetry
Lefty Frizzell; *Legendary Lefty Frizzell* . . . . (MCA)

Life's Little Ups And Downs
Ricky Van Shelton; *RVS III* . . . . (Columbia)

Life's Railway To Heaven
Merle Haggard & The Strangers; *Train Whistle Blues* . . . . (Rounder)

Life's What You Make It
Talk Talk; *Colour Of Spring* . . . . (EMI)

Lifestyles Of The Not-So-Rich & Famous
Tracy Byrd; *No Ordinary Man* . . . . (MCA)

Lifetime
Maxwell; *Now* . . . . (Columbia)

Lightning Does The Work
Chad Brock; *Chad Brock* . . . . (Warner Bros.)

Like A Prayer
Madonna; *Like A Prayer* . . . . (Sire)
Royal Box . . . . (Sire)

Like Humans Do
David Byrne; *Look Into The Eyeball* . . . . (Luaka Bop)

Little Bitty
Alan Jackson; *Everything I Love* . . . . (Arista)
Tom T. Hall; *Songs From Sopchoppy* . . . . (Mercury)
Tom T. Hall-The Hits . . . . (Mercury)

Little Plastic Castle
Ani DiFranco; *Little Plastic Castle* . . . . (Righteous Babe)

Little Things Mean A Lot
Kitty Kallen; *Hard To Find 45s On CD-#3-The Mid '50s-C* . . . . (Eric)
McGuire Sisters; *Best Of The McGuire Sisters* . . . . (MCA)

Live & Learn
Joe Public; *Joe Public* . . . . (Columbia)

Live Again
Tarney/Spencer Band; *Run For Your Life* . . . . (A&M)

Live And Let Die
Paul McCartney; *13 Original James Bond Themes-C* . . . . (EMI)
All The Best! . . . . (Capitol)
Wings; *ST/Live And Let Die* . . . . (EMI)
Wings Greatest . . . . (Capitol)
Wings Over America . . . . (Capitol)

Live For Loving You
Gloria Estefan; *Into The Light* . . . . (Epic)

Live For The Music
Bad Company; *10 From 6* . . . . (Atlantic)
Run With The Pack . . . . (Swan Song)

Live For Today
Lords Of The New Church; *Is Nothing Sacred* . . . . (I.R.S.)
Killer Lords . . . . (I.R.S.)

Live For Today
Jeffrey Osborne; *Don't Stop* . . . . (A&M)

Live For Today
Sweet; *Off The Record* . . . . (Capitol)

Live For Today
Toto; *Turn Back* . . . . (Columbia)

Live Forever
Oasis; *Definitely Maybe* . . . . (Epic)

Live In Vain
Frankie Miller; *Full House* . . . . (Chrysalis)

Live It Up
Isley Brothers; *Forever Gold* . . . . (T-Neck/Columbia)
Isley Brothers' Greatest Hits . . . . (T-Neck/Columbia)
Live It Up . . . . (T-Neck/Columbia)

Live It Up
Ted Nugent; *Cat Scratch Fever* . . . . (Epic)

Live It Up
Crosby, Stills & Nash; *Live It Up* . . . . (Atlantic)

Live Life
Kinks; *Misfits* . . . . (Arista)

Live Now Pay Later
Foghat; *Girls To Chat & Boys To Bounce* . . . . (Rhino)

Live Through This (Fifteen Stories)
Mighty Joe Plum; *Happiest Dogs* . . . . (Atlantic)

Live To Tell
Madonna; *Immaculate Collection* . . . . (Sire)
Royal Box . . . . (Sire)
Something To Remember . . . . (Maverick/Sire)
True Blue . . . . (Sire)

Live Until I Die
Clay Walker; *Clay Walker* . . . . (Giant)

Live Wire
AC/DC; *High Voltage* . . . . (Atco)
Martha & The Vandellas; *Compact Command Performances-Martha Reeves & The Vandellas* . . . . (Motown)
Martha Reeves & The Vandellas' Greatest Hits . . . . (Motown)
Martha Reeves & The Vandellas-Anthology . . . . (Motown)

Live With Me
Rolling Stones; *Get Yer Ya-Ya's Out!* . . . . (Abkco)
Let It Bleed . . . . (Abkco)

Live, Laugh, Love
Clay Walker; *Live, Laugh, Love* . . . . (Giant)

Lively Up Yourself
Bob Marley & The Wailers; *Babylon By Bus* . . . . (Tuff Gong)
Bob Marley & The Wailers-Live . . . . (Tuff Gong)
Natty Dread . . . . (Tuff Gong)

Livin' Ain't Livin'
Firefall; *Firefall* . . . . (Rhino)

Livin' Alone
Beck, Bogert & Appice; *Beck, Bogert & Appice* . . . . (Epic)

Livin' At The End Of The Rainbow
Dave & Sugar; *That's The Way Love Should Be* . . . . (RCA)

Livin' For Me
Garland Jeffreys; *American Boy & Girl* . . . . (A&M)

Livin' For The Weekend
O'Jays; *Family Reunion* . . . . (Philadelphia Int'l)
O'Jays-Collector's Item . . . . (Philadelphia Int'l)

Livin' For You
Al Green; *Al Green's Greatest Hits-#2* . . . . (Hi)
Compact Command Performances-Al Green . . . . (Motown)
Livin' For You . . . . (Motown)

Livin' For Your Love
Melba Moore; *Never Say Never* . . . . (Capitol)

Livin' In South Central L.A.
South Central Posse; *We're All In The Same Gang-C* . . . . (Warner Bros.)

Livin' In The Jungle
Flo & Eddie And The Turtles; *History Of Flo & Eddie And The Turtles* . . . . (Rhino)

Livin' In The Life
Isley Brothers; *Go For Your Guns* . . . . (T-Neck/Columbia)

Livin' In These Troubled Times
Crystal Gayle; *Crystal Gayle Greatest Hits* . . . . (Columbia)
Hollywood, Tennessee . . . . (Columbia)

Livin' La Vida Loca
Ricky Martin; *Ricky Martin* . . . . (Columbia)

Livin' On A Prayer
Bon Jovi; *America: A Tribute To Heroes-C* . . . . (Interscope)
Cross Road-14 Classic Grooves . . . . (Mercury)
Slippery When Wet . . . . (Jambco)
The Concert For New York City-C . . . . (Columbia)

Livin' On Borrowed Time
Travis Tritt; *Down The Road I Go* . . . . (Columbia)

Livin' On Love
Alan Jackson; *Who I Am* . . . . (Arista)

Livin' On The Edge
Aerosmith; *Get A Grip* . . . . (Geffen)

Livin' On The Fault Line
Doobie Brothers; *Livin' On The Fault Line* . . . . (Warner Bros.)

Livin' Thing
Electric Light Orchestra; *Electric Light Orchestra's Greatest Hits* . . . . (Jet)
Exposition . . . . (Epic)
New World Record . . . . (Jet)

Livin' Without You
Nitty Gritty Dirt Band; *Best Of The Nitty Gritty Dirt Band* . . . . (Curb)
Dirt, Silver & Gold . . . . (One Way)
Uncle Charlie And His Dog Teddy . . . . (Liberty)
Workin' Band . . . . (Warner Bros.)

Living & Learning
Mel Tillis & The Statesiders; *Mel Tillis & The Statesiders-24 Great Hits* . . . . (MGM)

Living A Little, Laughing A Little
John Hiatt; *Warming Up To The Ice Age* . . . . (Geffen)
Spinners; *New & Improved* . . . . (Atlantic)
Spinners-Live . . . . (Atlantic)

Living Dead Girl
Rob Zombie; *Hellbilly Deluxe* . . . . (Geffen)

Living For The City
Stevie Wonder; *Innervisions* . . . . (Motown)
Original Musiquarium . . . . (Motown)

Living For You
Sonny & Cher; *Best Of Sonny & Cher* . . . . (Atco)
Two Of Us . . . . (Atco)

Living Forever
Genesis; *We Can't Dance* . . . . (Atlantic)

Living In A Dream
Band; *Islands* . . . . (Capitol)
The Band-Anthology-#2 . . . . (Capitol)

Living In A Dream
Arc Angels; *Arc Angels* . . . . (David Geffen Co.)
Living In A Dream
Sea Level; *On The Edge* . . . . (Capricorn)
Living In A Fantasy
Leo Sayer; *All The Best* . . . .(Chrysalis)
Living In A Moment
Ty Herndon; *Living In A Moment* . . . .(Epic)
Super Hits Of 1996-C . . . .(Epic)
Living In America
Aztec Two-Step; *See It Was Like This...Acoustic Retrospective* . . . (Flying Fish)
Living In America
James Brown; *Gravity* . . . . (Scotti Bros.)
Rocky Story-C . . . . (Scotti Bros.)
ST/Rocky IV . . . . (Scotti Bros.)
Living In America
Donna Summer; *Donna Summer* . . . .(Geffen)
Living In America
Hiroshima; *East* . . . .(Epic)
Living In China
Men Without Hats; *Rhythm Of Youth* . . . .(MCA)
Living In Danger
Ace Of Base; *The Sign* . . . . (Arista)
Living In Europe
Thompson Twins; *In The Name Of Love* . . . . (Arista)
Living In Paradise
Elvis Costello; *This Year's Model* . . . . (Rykodisc)
Living In Shame
Supremes; *45-#442* . . . . (Motown)
Living In Sin
Bon Jovi; *New Jersey* . . . . (Jambco)
Living In The Blues
Johnny Winter; *About Blues* . . . .(Janus)
Before The Storm . . . .(Janus)
Living In The Footsteps Of Another Man
Chi-Lites; *Chi-Lites Greatest Hits* . . . .(Brunswick)
Half A Love . . . .(Brunswick)
Living In The Future
John Prine; *Storm Windows* . . . . (Asylum)
Living In The Future In A Plastic Dome
Country Joe McDonald; *Incredible Live* . . . . (Vanguard)
Living In The Ghetto
Toots & The Maytals; *Reggae Got Soul* . . . . (Island)
Living In The Material World
George Harrison; *Living In The Material World* . . . . (Capitol)
Living In The Past
Jethro Tull; *''M.U.''-Best Of* . . . .(Chrysalis)
20 Years Of Jethro Tull . . . .(Chrysalis)
Original Masters . . . .(Chrysalis)
Too Old To Rock 'N' Roll: Too Young To Die! . . . .(Chrysalis)
Living In The Plastic Age
Buggles; *Age Of Plastic* . . . . (Island)
Living In The Promiseland
Willie Nelson; *30 Years Of #1 Hits-#18-C* . . . . (Columbia)
Greatest Country Hits Of The '80s-1986-C . . . . (Columbia)
More Hot Country Requests-C . . . .(Epic)
The Promiseland . . . . (Columbia)
Living In The U.S.A.
Steve Miller Band; *Best Of Steve Miller 1968-1973* . . . . (Capitol)
On The Road Again-Rock's New Frontiers-C . . . . (Capitol)
Sailor . . . . (Capitol)
Steve Miller Band-Anthology . . . . (Capitol)
Steve Miller Band-Live . . . . (Capitol)
Living Inside Your Love
Earl Klugh; *Best Of Earl Klugh* . . . . (Blue Note)
Living Inside Your Love . . . .(EMI)
George Benson; *George Benson-Collection* . . . . (Warner Bros.)
Living Inside Your Love . . . .(Warner Bros.)
Living Is Easy
Cleo Laine; *Born On A Friday* . . . . (RCA)
Living It Down
Freddy Fender; *Best Of Freddy Fender* . . . .(MCA)
Living Legend
Kris Kristofferson; *Easter Land* . . . . (Columbia)
Havana Jam . . . . (Columbia)
Waylon Jennings, Willie Nelson, Johnny Cash, Kris Kristofferson;
Highwayman 2 . . . . (Columbia)
Living Lovin' Wreck
Jerry Lee Lewis; *Golden Rock & Roll* . . . . (Sun)
Original Jerry Lee Lewis . . . . (Sun)
Living Loving Maid
Led Zeppelin; *Led Zeppelin II* . . . .(Atlantic)
Living Loving Voices
Jerry Lee Lewis; *45-#48* . . . . (Sun)
Living My Life Just For You
Jerry Butler; *It All Comes Out In My Song* . . . . (Motown)
Living Next Door To Alice
Johnny Carver; *Best Of Johnny Carver* . . . .(MCA)

Living On My Own
Freddie Mercury; *The Great Pretender* . . . . (Hollywood)
Living On The Edge Of The World
Bruce Springsteen; *Tracks* . . . . (Columbia)
Living On The Highway
Freddie King; *Best Of Freddie King* . . . . (MCA)
Living On The Open Road
Delaney & Bonnie; *Duane Allman-An Anthology* . . . . (Capricorn)
Living Proof
Ricky Van Shelton; *30 Years Of #1 Hits-#20-C* . . . . (Columbia)
Greatest Country Hits Of The '80s-1989-C . . . . (Columbia)
Ricky Van Shelton's Greatest Hits Plus . . . . (Columbia)
Living The Blues
Bob Dylan; *Self Portrait* . . . . (Columbia)
Living Together
Bee Gees; *Spirits Having Flown* . . . .(Polydor)
Living Together
Jacksons; *Jacksons* . . . . (Epic)
Living Together
Whispers; *One For The Money* . . . .(Soul Train)
Living Together, Growing Together
Burt Bacharach; *Burt Bacharach-Classics-#23* . . . . (A&M)
Burt Bacharach's Greatest Hits . . . . (A&M)
Living Together . . . . (A&M)
Living With A Hernia
''Weird Al'' Yankovic; *''Weird Al'' Yankovic's Greatest Hits* . . . .(Scotti Bros.)
Polka Party . . . .(Scotti Bros.)
Living With AIDS
Romanovsky & Phillips; *Brave Boys-Best & More Of Romanovsky &*
Phillips . . . . (Fresh Fruit)
Emotional Rollercoaster . . . . (Fresh Fruit)
Living Without You
Randy Newman; *Randy Newman* . . . . (Warner Archives)
Randy Newman/Live . . . . (Warner Archives)
Living Without Your Love
Dusty Springfield; *Living Without Your Love* . . . . (EMI)
Never Trust A Man In A Rented Tuxedo . . . . (EMI)
Joe Cocker; *Cocker* . . . . (Capitol)
Living Years, The
Mike & The Mechanics; *Living Years* . . . .(Atlantic)
London Life
Ian & Sylvia; *Ian & Sylvia's Greatest Hits* . . . . (Vanguard)
Nashville . . . . (Vanguard)
Long And Winding Road, The
Beatles; *Beatles 1* . . . . (Capitol)
Beatles-20 Greatest Hits . . . . (Capitol)
Beatles-Love Songs . . . . (Capitol)
Let It Be . . . . (Capitol)
Reel Music . . . . (Capitol)
The Beatles/1967-1970 . . . . (Capitol)
Paul McCartney; *Tripping The Live Fantastic-Highlights!* . . . . (Capitol)
Wings; *Wings Over America* . . . . (Capitol)
Long As I Live
John Michael Montgomery; *John Michael Montgomery* . . . .(Atlantic)
Long Live Rock
Who; *Odds & Sods* . . . . (MCA)
ST/The Kids Are Alright . . . . (MCA)
Who's Last . . . . (MCA)
Long Live Rock 'N' Roll
Rainbow; *Finyl Vinyl* . . . . (Mercury)
Long Live Rock 'n' Roll . . . .(Polydor)
Long Live Rock 'N' Roll
Elvis Presley; *Elvis Aron Presley* . . . . (RCA)
Long Promised Road
Beach Boys; *10 Years Of Harmony* . . . .(Caribou)
Surf's Up . . . .(Caribou)
Look At That
Paul Simon; *You're The One* . . . . (Warner Bros.)
Look Through Any Window
Hollies; *History Of British Rock-#6-C* . . . . (Rhino)
The Hollies' Greatest Hits . . . . (Epic)
Lot Of Living To Do
Original Broadway Cast; *Bye Bye Birdie* . . . . (Columbia)
Original Cast; *ST/Bye Bye Birdie* . . . . (RCA)
Lottery Song
Nilsson; *Son Of Schmilsson* . . . . (RCA)
Love Ain't For Keeping
Who; *Who's next* . . . . (MCA)
Love Alive
Heart; *California Jam 2* . . . . (Columbia)
Little Queen . . . . (Portrait)
Love Don't Live Here Anymore
Madonna; *Like A Virgin* . . . . (Sire)
Something To Remember . . . .(Maverick/Sire)
Rose Royce; *Rose Royce III/Strikes Again!* . . . . (Whitfield)
Rose Royce's Greatest Hits . . . . (Whitfield)
Love Is Alive
Judds; *Collector's Series-The Judds* . . . . (RCA)
Judds' Greatest Hits . . . . (MCA)

Why Not Me . . . . (MCA)

Love Is Alive
Joe Cocker; *Night Calls* . . . . (Capitol)

Love Is Alive
Gary Wright; *Dream Weaver* . . . . (Warner Bros.)

Love Is All
Marc Anthony; *Marc Anthony* . . . . (Columbia)

Love Of A Lifetime
Larry Gatlin & The Gatlin Brothers Band; *Alive & Well...Living In The Land*
Of... . . . . (Columbia)
Country Love-C . . . . (K-Tel)
Live At 8:00. . . . . (Capitol)
The Gatlin Brothers' Biggest Hits. . . . . (Columbia)

Love Of A Lifetime
Firehouse; *Firehouse* . . . . (Epic)

Love Of My Life
Sammy Kershaw; *Labor Of Love* . . . . (Mercury)

Love Of My Life
Brian McKnight; *Superhero* . . . . (Motown)

Love Of Your Own, A
Average White Band; *Pickin' Up The Pieces-Best Of The Average White*
Band (1974-1980) . . . . (Rhino)
Smooth Grooves-A Sensual Collection-#1-C . . . . (Rhino)
Soul Searching . . . . (Rhino)

Love Remains
Collin Raye; *I Think About You* . . . . (Epic)

Love Will Keep Us Alive
Eagles; *Hell Freezes Over* . . . . (Geffen)

Love's The Only House
Martina McBride; *Emotion* . . . .(RCA)

Love's Train
Con Funk Shun; *Love's Train-C* . . . . (Mercury)
Smooth Grooves-A Sensual Collection-#1-C . . . . (Rhino)
To The Max . . . . (Mercury)

Lucky Man
Verve; *Urban Hymns* . . . . (Hut/Virgin)

Mach 5
Presidents Of The United States Of America; *Presidents Of The United States*
Of America II . . . . (Columbia)

Made To Love Ya
Gerald Levert; *Gerald's World* . . . . (East West)

Mahogany (Do You Know Where You're Going To), Theme From "Mahogany"
Diana Ross; *20/20-C* . . . . (Motown)
Diana Ross . . . . (Motown)
Diana Ross-Anthology . . . . (Motown)
Diana Ross-The Ultimate Collection . . . . (Motown)
Evening With Diana Ross . . . . (Motown)

Make My Life With You
Oak Ridge Boys; *Country Classics-#1-C* . . . . (Universal)
MCA #1 Hits Of The '80s-#1-C . . . . (MCA Special Prod.)
Oak Ridge Boys' Greatest Hits 2 . . . . (MCA)

Man In The Mirror
Michael Jackson; *Bad* . . . . (Epic)

Man In The Mirror
Jim Glaser; *Man In The Mirror* . . . . (Noble Vision)

Man Of La Mancha
Original Cast; *Lost In The Stars* . . . . (MCA)
Original London Cast; *Man Of La Mancha* . . . . (MCA)

Many A Long & Lonesome Highway
Rodney Crowell; *Keys To The Highway* . . . . (Columbia)
Taste Of Texas-Songs 'Bout Texas By Texans-C . . . . (Columbia)

Many Rivers To Cross
Jimmy Cliff; *In Concert-Best Of Jimmy Cliff* . . . . . . (Reprise)
Reggae Spectacular-C . . . . (A&M)
ST/The Harder They Come . . . . (Mango)
Wonderful World, Beautiful People . . . . (A&M)
Linda Ronstadt; *Prisoner In Disguise* . . . . (Asylum)
UB40; *Labour Of Love* . . . . (A&M)

Marching To Mars
Sammy Hagar; *Marching To Mars* . . . . (MCA)

Maria Maria
Santana; *Supernatural* . . . . (Arista)
Totally Hits-#2-C . . . . (Elektra)

Meaning Of Life
Offspring; *Ixnay On The Hombre* . . . . (Columbia)

Meant To Be
Sammy Kershaw; *Politics Religion & Her* . . . . (Mercury)

Meet Virginia
Train; *Now That's What I Call Music!-#4-C* . . . . (Virgin)
Train . . . . (Aware/C2/Columbia)

Memories Are Made Of This
Dean Martin; *Billboard Pop Memories-1955-1959-C* . . . . (Rhino)
Dean Martin-Love Songs . . . . (Ranwood)
Dean Martin's All Time Greatest Hits . . . . (Curb)

Mi Vida Loca
Pam Tillis; *Sweetheart's Dance* . . . . (Arista)

Miner's Life
Tom Juravich; *Out Of Darkness (Mine Workers' Story)* . . . . . . (Flying Fish)

Weavers; *Reunion-At Carnegie Hall-1963-#2* . . . . (Vanguard)

Mississippi
Bob Dylan; *"Love And Theft"* . . . . (Columbia)
Sheryl Crow; *The Globe Sessions* . . . . (A&M)

Money (That's What I Want)
Barrett Strong; *Motown Story-First 25 Years-C* . . . . . . (Motown)
Oldies But Goodies-#4-C . . . . (Original Sound)
Beatles; *Beatles-Box Set.* . . . . (Capitol)
Rock 'N' Roll Music . . . . (Capitol)
The Beatles' Second Album . . . . (Capitol)
Buddy Guy; *Man & The Blues* . . . . (Vanguard)
Diana Ross & The Supremes; *Diana Ross & The Supremes Sing*
Motown . . . . (Motown)
Jerry Lee Lewis; *Jerry Lee's Greatest!* . . . . (Rhino)
John Lennon; *Lennon* . . . . (Capitol)
Junior Walker & The All Stars; *Junior Walker & The All Stars'*
Greatest Hits . . . . (S.O.U.L.)
Junior Walker & The All Stars-Anthology . . . . (Motown)
Rolling Stones; *More Hot Rocks (big hits & fazed cookies)* . . . (Abkco)
Ronnie Milsap; *Lost In The Fifties Tonight* . . . . (RCA)
Todd Rundgren; *Something/Anything?* . . . . (Rhino)

More Than One Way Home
Keb' Mo'; *Just Like You* . . . . (Okeh)

More You Live, The More You Love
A Flock Of Seagulls; *Best Of A Flock Of Seagulls* . . . . . (Jive)
Story Of A Young Heart . . . . (Columbia)

Mournin' Glory Story
Nilsson; *Harry* . . . . (Dunhill Compact Classics)

Muzzle
Smashing Pumpkins; *Mellon Collie And The Infinite Sadness* . . . . (Virgin)

My Baby You
Marc Anthony; *Marc Anthony* . . . . (Columbia)

My Back Pages
Bob Dylan; *Another Side Of Bob Dylan* . . . . (Columbia)
Bob Dylan's Greatest Hits-#2 . . . . (Columbia)
Byrds; *20 Essential Tracks From The Box Set* . . . . . . (Columbia)
Byrds Play Dylan . . . . (Columbia)
The Byrds' Greatest Hits . . . . (Columbia)
Younger Than Yesterday . . . . (Columbia)

My Fate Is In Your Hands
Fats Waller; *Piano Solos-1929-1941* . . . . (RCA)
Rare Piano Roll Solos-#3 . . . . (Biograph)
Turn On The Heat-Fats Waller Piano Solos . . . . (Bluebird)

My Father's Eyes
Eric Clapton; *Pilgrim* . . . . (Duck/Reprise)

My Heart Will Go On (Love Theme from "Titanic")
Celine Dion; *All The Way...A Decade Of Song* . . . . . . (550 Music)
ST/Titanic . . . . (Sony Music Classical)
Celine Dion with The Bee Gees; *Let's Talk About Love-C* . . (550 Music)
Kenny G; *Kenny G's Greatest Hits* . . . . (Arista)

My Life
Billy Joel; *52nd Street* . . . . (Columbia)
Billy Joel-Greatest Hits, Volume I & Volume II . . . . . (Columbia)

My Life (Throw It Away If I Want To)
Bill Anderson; *Best Of Bill Anderson* . . . . (Curb)

My Life As A Dog
Active Ingredient; *Extrastrength* . . . . (Bainbridge)

My Life In The Suicide Ranks
Tears For Fears; *Saturnine Martial & Lunatic* . . . . . . (Fontana)

My Life Is A Mediocre Piece Of Shit
Alice Donut; *Bucketfuls Of Sickness And Horror In An Otherwise*
Meaningless Life . . . . (Alternative Tentacles)

My Next Thirty Years
Tim McGraw; *A Place In The Sun* . . . . (Curb)
Tim McGraw's Greatest Hits . . . . (Curb)

My Sexual Life
Everclear; *Sparkle And Fade* . . . . (Capitol)

My Way
Elvis Presley; *Aloha from Hawaii via Satellite* . . . . (RCA)
Canadian Tribute . . . . (RCA)
Elvis In Concert . . . . (RCA)
Frank Sinatra; *Frank Sinatra's Greatest Hits-#2* . . . . . (Reprise)
My Way . . . . (Reprise)
Sinatra Reprise-The Very Good Years . . . . (Reprise)
Sinatra-The Main Event Live . . . . (Reprise)
The Reprise Collection . . . . (Reprise)
Paul Anka; *Very Best Of Paul Anka* . . . . (Ranwood)

Neon Rainbow
Box Tops; *Box Tops' Greatest Hits* . . . . (Rhino)

Never Been So Loved (In All My Life)
Charley Pride; *14 #1 Country Hits-C* . . . . (RCA)
Charley Pride's Greatest Hits . . . . (RCA)

Never In My Life
Mountain; *Best Of Mountain* . . . . (Columbia)
Mountain Climbing! . . . . (Columbia)
Twin Peaks . . . . (Columbia)

New Attitude
Patti LaBelle; *Classic Soul-C* . . . . (MCA)
I Am Woman-C . . . . (Nick At Nite)

Soundtrack Smashes-'80s & More-C . . . .(MCA)
ST/Beverly Hills Cop . . . .(MCA)

Nietzche's Eyes
Paula Cole; This Fire . . . . (Imago)

Night Life
Willie Nelson; Country Willie . . . . (United Artists)
Healing Hands Of Time . . . . (Liberty)
Souvenirs Of Music City U.S.A.-C . . . . (Plantation)
Willie . . . . (RCA)
Willie & Family Live . . . . (Columbia)

Night Life
Miracles; Miracles' Greatest Hits . . . . (Motown)

Night Life
Thin Lizzy; Night Life . . . . (Mercury)

Night Life
Ray Price; Ray Price's Greatest Hits-#2 . . . . (Step One)

Night Life
Charlie Daniels Band & Friends; Volunteer Jam 3 & 4 . . . .(Epic)

Nine Lives
Aerosmith; Nine Lives . . . . (Columbia)

No Expectations
Rolling Stones; Beggars Banquet . . . . (Abkco)
More Hot Rocks (big hits & fazed cookies) . . . . (Abkco)
Singles Collection-The London Years . . . . (Abkco)

No Man's Land
John Michael Montgomery; John Michael Montgomery . . . .(Atlantic)

No Tears Left
Crosby, Stills, Nash & Young; Looking Forward . . . . (Reprise)

No Time To Live
Traffic; Traffic . . . . (Island)

Nothing Left Behind Us
Richard Marx; Paid Vacation . . . . (Capitol)

Now I Know
Lari White; Wishes . . . . (RCA)

O.D'd On Life Itself
Blue Oyster Cult; Tyranny & Mutation . . . . (Columbia)

Ob-La-Di, Ob-La-Da
Beatles; Beatles-Box Set . . . . (Capitol)
The Beatles (White Album) . . . . (Capitol)
The Beatles/1967-1970 . . . . (Capitol)

Ocean Of Life
Gene Cotton; No Strings Attached . . . . (Ariola America)

Ode To My Family
Cranberries; No Need To Argue . . . . (Island)

Off The Wall
Jacksons; Jacksons Live . . . .(Epic)
Michael Jackson; Off The Wall . . . .(Epic)

Oh How The Years Go By
Vanessa Williams; NBA At 50-A Musical Celebration-C . . . . (Mercury)

Ol' Man River
Al Jolson; Best Of Al Jolson . . . .(MCA)
The Al Jolson Story-#6 . . . .(MCA)
Frank Sinatra; The Concert Sinatra . . . . (Reprise)
Voice: The Columbia Years-1943-1952 . . . . (Columbia)
Paul Robeson; A Lonesome Road . . . .(Living Era)
American Balladeer-Golden Classics-#1-C . . . . (Collectables)
William Warfield; ST/All Those Glorious MGM Musicals . . . . (MGM)
William Warfield/Original Cast; Show Boat . . . . (Columbia)

Old
Paul Simon; You're The One . . . .(Warner Bros.)

On & On
Erykah Badu; Baduizm . . . . (Kedar Entert./Universal)

On The Street Where You Live
Andy Williams; Andy Williams-16 Most Requested Songs-Encore! . . . (Legacy)
Bobby Darin; Unreleased Capitol Sides . . . . (Collector's Choice)
Eddie Fisher; Very Best Of Eddie Fisher . . . .(Taragon)
Four Tops; Lost & Found: Breaking Through . . . . (Motown)
Harry Connick, Jr.; 25 . . . . (Columbia)
Mel Torme; Swings Shubert Alley . . . . (Verve)
Original Cast; My Fair Lady . . . . (Columbia)
Ray Conniff; 'S Awful Nice . . . . (Columbia)

Once In A Lifetime
Original Broadway Cast; Stop The World I Want To Get Off . . . . (Polydor)
Original Cast/Sammy Davis, Jr.; Stop The World I Want To
Get Off. . . . .(Warner Bros.)
Sammy Davis, Jr.; Sammy Davis, Jr.'s Greatest Hits . . . . . (Reprise)

Once In A Lifetime
Michael Bolton; ST/Only You . . . . (Columbia)

Once In A Lifetime
Talking Heads; Remain In Light . . . . (Sire)
ST/Stop Making Sense . . . . (Sire)

Once In A Lifetime
Aretha Franklin; After Hours . . . . (Columbia)

Once In A Lifetime
Chicago; Chicago 17 . . . .(Warner Bros.)

Once Upon A Lifetime
Alabama; American Pride . . . . (RCA)

One Day At A Time
John Lennon; Lennon . . . . (Capitol)

One Day At A Time
Cristy Lane; Cristy Lane-At Her Best . . . . (EMI)

One Day At A Time
Willie Nelson; Me & Paul . . . . (Columbia)
Willie . . . . (RCA)
Willie & Family Live . . . . (Columbia)

One Love In My Lifetime
Diana Ross; Diana Ross . . . . (Motown)
Diana Ross-Anthology . . . . (Motown)

One Miner's Life-The Image Of God
Battlefield Band; There's A Buzz . . . .(Flying Fish)

One Night A Day
Garth Brooks; In Pieces . . . . (Liberty)

One Of The Living
Tina Turner; ST/Beyond Thunderdome . . . . (Capitol)

One Of The Survivors
Kinks; Preservation Act 1 . . . . (Rhino)
The Kinks' Greatest-Celluloid Heroes . . . . (RCA)

One Thing Leads To Another
Fixx; One Thing Leads To Another-Greatest Hits . . . . (MCA)
Reach The Beach . . . . (MCA)

One's On The Way (Here In Topeka)
Loretta Lynn; Loretta Lynn-20 Greatest Hits . . . . (MCA)
Loretta Lynn-Greatest Hits Live . . . . (K-Tel)
Loretta Lynn's Greatest Hits-#2 . . . . (MCA)
The Country Music Hall Of Fame-Loretta Lynn . . . . (MCA)

Only God Knows Why
Kid Rock; Devil Without A Cause . . . . (Top Dog/Lava/Atlantic)

Only Living Boy In New York
Simon & Garfunkel; Bridge Over Troubled Water . . . . (Columbia)
Collected Works . . . . (Columbia)

Only One You
T.G. Sheppard; Best Of T.G. Sheppard . . . .(Curb)
T.G. Sheppard's All-Time Greatest Hits . . . . (Warner Bros.)

Only The Strong Survive
REO Speedwagon; A Decade Of Rock And Roll 1970 To 1980 . . . . (Epic)
Nine Lives . . . . (Epic)

Only You (And You Alone)
Platters; Cruisin'-1955-C . . . . (Increase)
Encore Of Golden Hits-Platters . . . . (Mercury)
Millennium Collection-20th Century Masters . . . . (Mercury)

Open My Heart
Yolanda Adams; Mountain High Valley Low . . . . (Elektra)

Open Your Eyes
Yes; Open Your Eyes . . . .(Beyond)

Opposites
Eric Clapton; There's One In Every Crowd . . . .(Polydor)

Optimistic
Radiohead; Kid A . . . . (Capitol)

Ordinary Life
Chad Brock; Chad Brock . . . . (Warner Bros.)

Other Man's Grass Is Always Greener
Petula Clark; Petula Clark's Greatest Hits . . . .(Crescendo)

Other Side Of Life
Moody Blues; Other Side Of Life . . . .(Polydor)

Other Side Of This Life
Fred Neil; Little Bit Of Rain . . . . (Elektra)
Troubadours Of The Folk Era-#2-C . . . . (Rhino)
Jefferson Airplane; Bless Its Pointed Little Head . . . .(RCA)
Loves You . . . . (RCA)
Peter, Paul & Mary; Peter, Paul and Mary Album . . . . (Warner Bros.)

Out With A Bang
David Lee Murphy; Out With A Bang . . . . (MCA)

Outtasite (Outta Mind)
Wilco; Being There . . . . (Reprise)

Overprotected
Britney Spears; Britney . . . . (Jive)

P.O.V. Waltz
Nilsson; The Point . . . . (RCA)

Painted Perfect
One Way Ride; Strait Up! . . . . (Refuge/MCA)

Papa Can You Hear Me?
Barbra Streisand; One Voice . . . . (Columbia)
ST/Yentl . . . . (Columbia)

Paper In Fire
John Cougar Mellencamp; The Lonesome Jubilee . . . . (Mercury)
John Mellencamp; Best That I Could Do-1978-1988 . . . . (Mercury)

Paper Sun
Def Leppard; Euphoria . . . . (Mercury)

Passin' Thru
Earl Scruggs & Don Henley & Johnny Cash; Earl Scruggs And
Friends-C . . . . (MCA)
Randy Scruggs; Crown Of Jewels . . . . (Reprise)
Randy Scruggs & Joan Osborne; ST/Happy Texas . . . . (Arista)

Patience
Guns N' Roses; G N' R Lies . . . . (Geffen)

Peace Tonight
Indigo Girls; *Come On Now Social* . . . . (Epic)
Pearl, The
Emmylou Harris; *Red Dirt Girl* . . . .(Nonesuch)
Pennies From Heaven
Billie Holiday; *Billie Holiday-16 Most Requested Songs* . . . . (Legacy)
Bing Crosby; *Pennies From Heaven* . . . .(Pro-Arte)
Frank Sinatra & Nelson Riddle Orchestra; *songs for Swingin'*
    Lovers! . . . . (Capitol)
Lester Young; *Birdland All-Stars At Carnegie Hall* . . . . (Roulette)
Louis Armstrong; *RCA Victor Jazz: First Half-Century-C* . . . .(RCA)
Mandy Patinkin; *Mandy Patinkin* . . . .(Columbia)
Skyliners; *Skyliners' Greatest Hits* . . . .(Original Sound)
Stan Getz; *Essential Stan Getz Songbook* . . . . (Verve)
Stephane Grappelli; *Satin Doll-#1-Best Of Stephane Grappelli* . . . . . (Vanguard)
Penny Lane
Beatles; *Beatles 1* . . . . (Capitol)
    Magical Mystery Tour . . . . (Capitol)
    The Beatles/1967-1970 . . . . (Capitol)
    The Beatles-Anthology-#2 . . . . (Capitol)
Picture From Life's Other Side
George Jones; *Hallelujah Weekend* . . . . (Epic)
Goebel Reeves; *Texas Drifter* . . . . (Glendale)
Hank Williams; *Beyond The Sunset* . . . . (Polydor)
    Hey Good Lookin' (December 1950-July 1951) . . . . (Polydor)
Pictured Life
Scorpions; *Best Of The Scorpions* . . . .(RCA)
    Tokyo Tapes . . . .(RCA)
    Virgin Killer . . . .(RCA)
Planets Of Life
Whispers; *I Can Remember* . . . . (Accord)
    Vintage Whispers . . . . (Solar)
Pop Life
Prince and the Revolution; *Around The World In A Day* . . . . (Paisley Park)
Prayer For The Dying
Seal; *Diana, Princess Of Wales-Tribute-C* . . . . (Columbia)
    Seal 2 . . . .(Sire)
Precious Time
Van Morrison; *Back On Top* . . . .(Point Blank/Virgin)
Prime Of Life
Neil Young & Crazy Horse; *Sleeps With Angels* . . . .(Reprise)
Prisoner For Life
Skip Gorman; *A Cowboy's Wild Song To His Herd* . . . . (Rounder)
Private Life
Grace Jones; *Island Life* . . . . (Island)
    Warm Leatherette . . . . (Island)
Private Life
Pretenders; *Pretenders* . . . .(Sire)
Prologue (Tradition)
Original Cast; *Fiddler On The Roof* . . . . (RCA Victor)
Prove It All Night
Bruce Springsteen; *Darkness On The Edge Of Town* . . . . (Columbia)
Pushing Up Daisies
Garth Brooks; *Scarecrow* . . . . (Capitol)
Que Sera, Sera
Doris Day; *Doris Day-16 Most Requested Songs-Encore!* . . . . (Columbia)
    Doris Day's Greatest Hits . . . . (Columbia)
    Radio Classics Of The '50s-C . . . . (Columbia)
Sly & The Family Stone; *Fresh* . . . . (Legacy)
    Sly & The Family Stone-Anthology . . . . (Epic)
Raise Your Hand
Bruce Springsteen & The E Street Band; *Bruce Springsteen & The E Street*
    Band Live/1975-85 . . . . (Legacy)
Eddie Floyd; *Knock On Wood* . . . . (Atlantic)
    Stax/Volt Revue-#2-Live In Paris-C . . . . (Atlantic)
J. Geils Band; *Blow Your Face Out* . . . . (Rhino)
Rat Race
Bob Marley & The Wailers; *Babylon By Bus* . . . . (Tuff Gong)
    Rastaman Vibration . . . . (Tuff Gong)
    Rebel Music . . . . (Tuff Gong)
Razorblades
Chris Stills; *100 Year Thing* . . . . (Atlantic)
Reach Out Of The Darkness
Friend And Lover; *Chicken Soup For The Soul: I'll Be There For You-Songs*
    Of Friendship, Brotherhood And Sisterhood-C . . . . (Rhino)
    Flower Power-Psychedelic Rock Classics-C . . . . (K-Tel)
Real Life
Simple Minds; *Real Life* . . . .(A&M)
Real Life
Phil Woods & His Little Big Band; *Real Life* . . . . (Chesky)
Real Life
John Cougar Mellencamp; *The Lonesome Jubilee* . . . . (Mercury)
Real Life (I Never Was The Same Again)
Jeff Carson; *Real Life* . . . .(Curb)
Real Life Love
Larry Stewart; *Heart Like A Hurricane* . . . . (Columbia)
Real Live Woman
Trisha Yearwood; *Real Live Woman* . . . . (MCA)

Reap What You Sow
Otis Rush; *Atlantic Blues-Chicago-C* . . . . (Atlantic)
    Mourning In The Morning . . . . (Atlantic)
Reasons For Living
Duncan Sheik; *Duncan Sheik* . . . . (Atlantic)
    ST/E.R.-Original Television Theme Music And Score . . . . (Atlantic)
Rebecca
Pat McGhee Band; *Shine* . . . . (Giant/Warner Bros.)
Reflections Of My Life
Marmalade; *History Of British Rock-#1-C* . . . . (Rhino)
    London Collector-Rock Invasion-C . . . . (London)
    Super Hits Of The '70s-Have A Nice Day-#2-C . . . . (Rhino)
Remember (Christmas)
Nilsson; *Son Of Schmilsson* . . . . (RCA)
Rest Of Mine, The
Trace Adkins; *Big Time* . . . . (Capitol)
Rhythm Of Life
Original Cast; *Sweet Charity* . . . . (Columbia)
Rhythm Of Life
Oleta Adams; *Circle Of One* . . . . (Fontana)
Rhythm Of Life
Richard Marx; *Richard Marx* . . . . (Capitol)
Right Here/Human Nature
SWV; *It's About Time* . . . .(RCA)
Right On
Marvin Gaye; *What's Going On* . . . . (Motown)
Ripple
Grateful Dead; *American Beauty* . . . . (Warner Bros.)
    Reckoning . . . . (Arista)
    What A Long Strange Trip It's Been: The Best Of The
        Grateful Dead . . . . (Warner Bros.)
Jane's Addiction; *Deadicated-C* . . . . (Arista)
River Of Dreams
Billy Joel; *River Of Dreams* . . . . (Columbia)
River Of Life
REO Speedwagon; *This Time We Mean It* . . . . (Epic)
River Of Life
Neville Brothers; *Brother's Keeper* . . . . (A&M)
River, The
Garth Brooks; *Ropin' The Wind* . . . . (Liberty)
    The Limited Series . . . . (Capitol)
River, The
Bruce Springsteen; *Bruce Springsteen's Greatest Hits* . . . . (Columbia)
    The River . . . . (Columbia)
Bruce Springsteen & The E Street Band; *Bruce Springsteen & The E Street*
    Band Live/1975-85 . . . . (Legacy)
Road You Leave Behind
David Lee Murphy; *Gettin' Out The Good Stuff* . . . . (MCA)
Roads Of Life
Bobby Womack; *Roads Of Life* . . . . (Arista)
Rock Is My Life And This Is My Song
Bachman-Turner Overdrive; *Not Fragile* . . . . (Mercury)
Rockin' My Life Away
Jerry Lee Lewis; *Rockin' My Life Away* . . . . (Tomato)
    Survivors . . . . (Columbia)
    Swingin' Country Favorites-C . . . . (Warner Bros.)
Roll With It
Steve Winwood; *Rock The First-#2-C* . . . . (Sandstone Music)
    Roll With It . . . . (Virgin)
    ST/Nuns On The Run . . . . (Mercury)
Rose Garden
k.d. lang; *Swingin' Country Favorites-C* . . . . (Warner Bros.)
k.d. lang and The Reclines; *Angel With A Lariat* . . . . (Sire)
Lynn Anderson; *All Time Legends Of Country Music-C* . . . . (Legacy)
    Country Music Classics-#4-1970-1975-C . . . . (K-Tel)
    Lynn Anderson's Greatest Hits . . . . (Columbia)
    Rose Garden . . . . (Columbia)
    Super Hits Of The '70s-Have A Nice Day-#4-C . . . . (Rhino)
    Very Special Love Song-C . . . . (Fifty One West)
Row, Row, Row Your Boat
Bobby Darin/Johnny Mercer/Billy May Orchestra; *Two Of A Kind* . . . . (Atlantic)
Original Soundtrack; *Children's Favorites* . . . . (Kid Rhino/Rhino 4 Kids)
Spike Jones & His City Slickers; *King Of Corn* . . . . (Glendale)
Ruby Tuesday
Rolling Stones; *Between The Buttons* . . . . (Abkco)
    Flashpoint . . . . (Virgin)
    Flowers . . . . (Abkco)
    Hot Rocks 1964-1971 . . . . (Abkco)
    Singles Collection-The London Years . . . . (Abkco)
    Through The Past, Darkly (Big Hits Vol. 2) . . . . (Abkco)
Run Away
Real McCoy; *Another Night* . . . . (Arista)
Run For Your Life
Beatles; *Beatles-Box Set* . . . . (Capitol)
    Rubber Soul . . . . (Capitol)
Run To The Water
Live; *The Distance To Here* . . . .(Radioactive/MCA)
Sailor's Life
Fairport Convention; *Fairport Convention-Chronicles* . . . . (A&M)

Unhalfbricking. . . . . (A&M)
Judy Collins; *Maid Of Constant Sorrow* . . . . (Elektra)
Saturday Nite Live
Masta Ace Incorporated; *SlaughtaHouse* . . . .(Delicious Vinyl)
Save The Life Of My Child
Simon & Garfunkel; *Bookends* . . . . (Columbia)
Collected Works . . . . (Columbia)
Saved My Life
Fee Waybill; *Read My Lips* . . . . (Capitol)
ST/St. Elmo's Fire . . . . (Atlantic)
Say You, Say Me
Lionel Richie; *Back To Front* . . . . (Motown)
Dancing On The Ceiling . . . . (Motown)
Secret
Madonna; *Bedtime Stories* . . . .(Maverick/Sire)
GHV2 . . . .(Warner Bros.)
Secret Life Of Arabia
David Bowie; *Heroes* . . . . 'Rykodisc)
Secret O' Life
James Taylor; *JT* . . . . (Columbia)
Secret Of Life
Faith Hill; *Faith* . . . .(Warner Bros.)
Gretchen Peters; *The Secret Of Life* . . . . (Purple Crayon Prod.)
Secret To A Long Life
Michelle Shocked; *Arkansas Traveler* . . . . (Mercury)
Texas Campfire Tapes . . . . (Mercury)
Semi-Charmed Life
Third Eye Blind; *Jock Rock 2000-C* . . . . (Tommy Boy)
Third Eye Blind . . . . (Elektra)
Senorita With A Necklace Of Tears
Paul Simon; *You're The One* . . . .(Warner Bros.)
Separate Lives
Phil Collins; *Serious Hits…Live!* . . . . (Atlantic)
Phil Collins & Marilyn Martin; *ST/White Nights* . . . . (Atlantic)
Sh-Boom
Chords; *Atlantic Rhythm & Blues 1947-1974-#2 (1952-1955)-C* . . . . . . (Atlantic)
Crew-Cuts; *Partytime '50s-C* . . . . (Priority)
Stan Freberg; *Capitol Collectors Series-Stan Freberg* . . . . (Capitol)
She Said
Collective Soul; *Dosage* . . . .(Atlantic)
ST/Scream 2 . . . . (Dimension/Capitol)
Sheep Go To Heaven
Cake; *Prolonging The Magic* . . . . (Capricorn)
She's Out Of My Life
Jacksons; *Jacksons Live* . . . .(Epic)
Michael Jackson; *Off The Wall* . . . .(Epic)
Shimmer
Shawn Mullins; *Songs From Dawson's Creek* . . . . (Sony Music Soundtrax)
Soul's Core . . . . (Columbia)
Shining Star
Earth, Wind & Fire; *Best Of Earth, Wind & Fire-#1* . . . . (Legacy)
Eternal Dance . . . . (Columbia)
Gratitude . . . . (Legacy)
That's The Way Of The World . . . . (Legacy)
Shoes You're Wearing
Clint Black; *Nothin' But The Taillights* . . . . (RCA)
Show Me Love
Robyn; *Robyn Is Here* . . . . (RCA)
Showman's Life
Jesse Winchester; *Best Of Jesse Winchester* . . . . (Rhino)
Touch On The Rainy Side . . . . (Rhino)
Sign, The
Ace Of Base; *The Sign* . . . . (Arista)
Signs Of Life
Steven Curtis Chapman; *Signs Of Life* . . . . (Sparrow)
Simple Life
Elton John; *The One* . . . .(MCA)
Simple Life
Andy Childs; *Andy Childs* . . . . (RCA)
Simple Life
Ricky Skaggs; *My Father's Son* . . . .(Epic)
Simple Twist Of Fate
Bob Dylan; *Blood On The Tracks* . . . . (Columbia)
Bob Dylan At Budokan . . . . (Columbia)
Jerry Garcia Band; *Jerry Garcia Band* . . . . (Arista)
Joan Baez; *Best Of Joan Baez* . . . . (A&M)
Diamonds & Rust . . . . (A&M)
Simple Twist Of Fate
Tim Curry; *Best Of Tim Curry* . . . . (A&M)
Sing A Song
Earth, Wind & Fire; *Best Of Earth, Wind & Fire-#1* . . . . (Legacy)
Eternal Dance . . . . (Columbia)
Gratitude . . . . (Legacy)
Sing C'Est La Vie
Sonny & Cher; *Beat Goes On* . . . . (Atco)
Best Of Sonny & Cher . . . . (Atco)
Two Of Us . . . . (Atco)
Single Life
Cameo; *Single Life* . . . . (Casablanca)

Skellig
Loreena McKennitt; *The Book Of Secrets* . . . . (Quinlan Rd./Warner Bros.)
Sky Fits Heaven
Madonna; *Ray Of Light* . . . . (Maverick)
So Alive
Love And Rockets; *Love And Rockets* . . . .(Beggar's Banquet)
So It Goes
Nick Lowe; *Basher: Best Of* . . . . (Columbia)
Pure Pop For Now People . . . . (Columbia)
ST/Rock 'N' Roll High School . . . .(Sire)
So It Goes
Wes Cunningham; *12 Ways To Win People To Your Way Of
Thinking* . . . .(Warner Bros.)
Sole Survivor
Asia; *Asia* . . . . (Geffen)
Live In Moscow . . . . (Rhino)
Some Change
Boz Scaggs; *My Time: A Boz Scaggs Anthology-1969-1997* . . . . (Legacy)
Some Change . . . . (Virgin)
Some Days You Gotta Dance
Dixie Chicks; *Fly* . . . . (Monument)
Some Folks Lives Roll Easy
Paul Simon; *Still Crazy After All These Years* . . . . (Columbia)
Some People
Original Cast; *ST/Gypsy* . . . . (Columbia)
Some Things Are Meant To Be
Linda Davis; *Some Things Are Meant To Be* . . . . (Arista)
Someone Saved My Life Tonight
Elton John; *Captain Fantastic And The Brown Dirt Cowboy* . . . .(Polydor)
Elton John's Greatest Hits-#2 . . . .(Polydor)
Something Beautiful Remains
Tina Turner; *Wildest Dreams* . . . .(Virgin)
Something Kinda Funny
Spice Girls; *Spice* . . . .(Virgin)
Something That We Do
Clint Black; *Country Cares For Kids II-C* . . . .(BNA)
Nothin' But The Taillights . . . .(RCA)
Song For The Life
Alan Jackson; *Who I Am* . . . . (Arista)
Alison Krauss; *Too Late To Cry* . . . . (Rounder)
Jerry Jeff Walker; *A Man Must Carry On* . . . . (MCA)
John Denver; *Country Roads Collection* . . . . (RCA)
Kathy Mattea; *Walk The Way The Wind Blows* . . . . (Mercury)
Rodney Crowell; *Ain't Living Long Like This* . . . . (Warner Bros.)
Soul Survivor
Rolling Stones; *Exile On Main Street* . . . .(Virgin)
Southern California
George Jones & Tammy Wynette; *George Jones & Tammy Wynette-16
Biggest Hits* . . . .(Epic/Legacy)
Tammy Wynette & George Jones; *Encore-Tammy Wynette & George
Jones* . . . . (Epic)
Tammy Wynette & George Jones' Greatest Hits . . . . (Epic)
Southside
Moby featuring Gwen Stefani; *12'' Maxi Single* . . . .(V2)
Play . . . .(V2)
Spaniard That Blighted My Life
Al Jolson; *Music From The New York Stage (1890-1920)-#3-1913-
1917-C* . . . . (Pearl)
Spend A Lifetime
Jamiroquai; *Traveling Without Moving* . . . . (Work/Epic)
Spice Of Life
Manhattan Transfer; *Bodies & Souls* . . . .(Atlantic)
Stairway To Heaven
Led Zeppelin; *Led Zeppelin IV* . . . .(Atlantic)
Led Zeppelin-Box Set . . . .(Atlantic)
Remasters . . . .(Atlantic)
ST/The Song Remains The Same . . . . (Swan Song)
Stanley Jordan; *Best Of Stanley Jordan* . . . . (Blue Note)
Flying Home . . . . (EMI)
Standing Together
George Benson; *Standing Together* . . . . (GRP)
Start A New Life
REO Speedwagon; *Ridin' The Storm Out* . . . . (Epic)
Starting A New Life
Van Morrison; *Tupelo Honey* . . . .(Polydor)
Steamboat
Beach Boys; *Carl & The Passions/Holland* . . . . (Capitol)
Holland . . . .(Brother)
Step By Step
Whitney Houston; *ST/The Preacher's Wife* . . . . (Arista)
Still Alive And Well
Edgar Winter's White Trash; *Roadwork* . . . . (Epic)
Johnny Winter; *Still Alive & Well* . . . . (Columbia)
Stinkfist
Tool; *Aenima* . . . . (Freeworld/Capitol)
Stones In The Road
Mary Chapin Carpenter; *Stones In The Road* . . . . (Columbia)

Storms Of Life
Randy Travis; *Storms Of Life* . . . . (Warner Bros.)
Story Of My Life
Don Williams; *Lovers & Best Friends* . . . . (MCA)
   Yellow Moon . . . . (MCA)
Marty Robbins; *Essential Marty Robbins-1951-1982* . . . . (Columbia)
   Lifetime Of Song-1951-1982 . . . . (Columbia)
   Marty Robbins' Greatest Hits . . . . (Columbia)
Story Of My Life
Neil Diamond; *Headed For The Future* . . . . (Columbia)
Story Of My Life
Unrelated Segments; *Nuggets-#11-Pop-Part 4-C* . . . . (Rhino)
Straight Lines
Wood; *Songs From Stamford Hill* . . . . (Columbia)
Street Life
Crusaders; *Mega Hits Dance Classics-#7-C* . . . . (Priority)
   Street Life . . . . (MCA)
Street Life
Neil Diamond; *Beautiful Noise* . . . . (Columbia)
   Love At The Greek . . . . (Columbia)
Street Life
Herb Alpert; *Herb Alpert-Classics-#20* . . . . (A&M)
   Rise . . . . (A&M)
Street Life
Roxy Music; *Stranded* . . . . (Reprise)
   Street Life-20 Great Hits . . . . (Reprise)
Strenuous Life
Dick Hyman; *Scott Joplin-Greatest Hits* . . . . (RCA)
Scott Joplin; *King Of Ragtime Writers* . . . . (Biograph)
Strong Enough To Bend
Tanya Tucker; *Strong Enough To Bend* . . . . (Liberty)
   Tanya Tucker's Greatest Hits . . . . (Liberty)
Summer Side Of Life
Gordon Lightfoot; *Gord's Gold* . . . . (Reprise)
   Summer Side Of Life . . . . (Reprise)
Sun Don't Shine On The Same Folks All The Time
Sawyer Brown; *Sawyer Brown* . . . . (Curb)
Survival
O'Jays; *O'Jays-Collector's Item* . . . . (Philadelphia Int'l)
   Survival . . . . (Philadelphia Int'l)
Survival
Roachford; *Get Ready!* . . . . (Epic)
Survival
Moody Blues; *Octave* . . . . (Polydor)
Survival
Leonard Dillon The Ethiopian; *On The Road Again* . . . . (Heartbeat)
Survival
Bob Marley & The Wailers; *Survival* . . . . (Island)
Survival
Yes; *Yes* . . . . (Atlantic)
   Yesterdays . . . . (Atlantic)
Survival Handbook Vs. Global Extinction
Sister Souljah; *360 Degrees Of Power* . . . . (Epic)
Survive
Jimmy Buffett; *Boats Beaches Bars & Ballads* . . . . (Margaritaville)
   Volcano . . . . (MCA)
Surviving The Life
Neil Diamond; *Beautiful Noise* . . . . (Columbia)
   Love At The Greek . . . . (Columbia)
Survivor
Destiny's Child; *Now That's What I Call Music!-#7-C* . . . . (Virgin)
   Survivor . . . . (Columbia)
Susannah's Still Alive
Kinks; *Kink Kronikles* . . . . (Reprise)
Sway
Rolling Stones; *Sticky Fingers* . . . . (Virgin)
Sweet Life
Marie Osmond & Paul Davis; *All In Love* . . . . (Curb)
Paul Davis; *Best Of Paul Davis* . . . . (Bang)
   Singer Of Songs-Teller Of Tales . . . . (Bang)
Take A Look Around
Limp Bizkit; *Chocolate Starfish & The Hotdog Flavored*
   Water . . . . (Flip/Interscope)
Take It To The Limit
Eagles; *Eagles Live* . . . . (Asylum)
   Eagles/Their Greatest Hits 1971-1975 . . . . (Asylum)
   One Of These Nights . . . . (Asylum)
Taking My Life In Your Hands
Elvis Costello & The Brodsky Quartet; *Juliet Letters* . . . . (Warner Bros.)
Tapestry
Carole King; *Tapestry* . . . . (Epic)
Tattoos & Scars
Montgomery Gentry; *Tattoos & Scars* . . . . (Columbia)
Terrorist's Life
D.I.; *What Good Is Grief To A God* . . . . (Triple X Entert.)
Thankyou
Dido; *No Angel* . . . . (Arista)
   Totally Hits 2001-C . . . . (Arista)

That's All There Is To That
Dinah Washington; *Complete Dinah Washington On Mercury-#6-1958-*
   1960 . . . . (Mercury)
Etta Jones; *Something Nice* . . . . (Original Jazz Classics)
Nat "King" Cole & The Four Knights; *From The Vaults-#6-Best*
   Of '56 . . . . (Capitol/EMI)
That's Just About Right
BlackHawk; *BlackHawk* . . . . (Arista)
   The Hits-Love & Gravity . . . . (Arista)
That's Just The Way It Is
Phil Collins; *...But Seriously* . . . . (Atlantic)
That's Life
David Lee Roth; *Eat 'Em & Smile* . . . . (Warner Bros.)
Frank Sinatra; *Frank Sinatra's Greatest Hits!* . . . . (Reprise)
   Frank Sinatra-The Reprise Collection . . . . (Reprise)
   Sinatra Reprise-The Very Good Years . . . . (Reprise)
   That's Life . . . . (Reprise)
That's The Way
Jo Dee Messina; *Burn* . . . . (Curb)
That's The Way It Goes
Benny Goodman & Peggy Lee; *Best Of The Big Bands-#2* . . . . (Columbia)
   Featuring Peggy Lee . . . . (Columbia)
Harptones; *WCBS FM 101 History Of Rock-Groups-#2-C* . . . . . . (Collectables)
That's The Way It Goes
George Harrison; *Best Of Dark Horse 1976-1989* . . . . (Dark Horse)
   Gone Troppo . . . . (Dark Horse)
That's The Way It Goes
Harptones; *WCBS FM 101 History Of Rock-Groups-#2-C* . . . . . . (Collectables)
That's The Way It Is
Celine Dion; *All The Way...A Decade Of Song* . . . . (550 Music)
   Collector's Series-Celine Dion-#1 . . . . (550 Music)
That's The Way Of The World
Earth, Wind & Fire; *Best Of Earth, Wind & Fire-#1* . . . . (Legacy)
   Eternal Dance . . . . (Columbia)
   Love Shouldn't Hurt-C . . . . (Qwest)
   Pop Classics Of The '70s-C . . . . (Columbia)
   That's The Way Of The World . . . . (Legacy)
That's The Way That The World Goes Round
John Prine; *Bruised Orange* . . . . (Oh Boy)
   Great Days-Anthology . . . . (Rhino)
   John Prine-Live . . . . (Oh Boy)
Theme From "As The World Turns"
Rosemary Joyce & Bill Bartholomew; *Soap Opera Themes* . . . . . . (Crescendo)
Theme From "Clarissa Explains It All"
Original Soundtrack; *Television's Greatest Hits-#7-Cable Ready-C* . . . . . . (TVT)
Theme From "Facts Of Life"
Original Soundtrack; *Television's Greatest Hits-#3-1970s & 1980s-C* . . . . (TVT)
Theme From "Lifestyles Of The Rich And Famous"
Original Soundtrack; *Television's Greatest Hits-#6-Remote Control-C* . . . (TVT)
Theme From "One Day At A Time"
Original Soundtrack; *CBS: The First 50 Years* . . . . (TVT)
Theme From "One Life To Live"
Rosemary Joyce & Bill Bartholomew; *Soap Opera Themes* . . . . . . (Crescendo)
Then The Morning Comes
Smash Mouth; *Astro Lounge* . . . . (Interscope)
   Now That's What I Call Music!-#4-C . . . . (Virgin)
Then You Look At Me
Celine Dion; *All The Way...A Decade Of Song* . . . . (550 Music)
There Are Many Stops Along The Way
Joe Sample; *Joe Sample-Collection* . . . . (GRP)
   Rainbow Seeker . . . . (MCA)
There But For Fortune
Joan Baez; *Hits/Greatest & Others* . . . . (Vanguard)
   The First 10 Years . . . . (Vanguard)
Phil Ochs; *Original New Folks* . . . . (Vanguard)
   There But For Fortune . . . . (Elektra)
There's A Light
Doobie Brothers; *Livin' On The Fault Line* . . . . (Warner Bros.)
There's A Lull In My Life
Ella Fitzgerald; *Essential Ella Fitzgerald-The Great Songs* . . . . (Verve)
   Like Someone In Love . . . . (Verve)
These Are The Days Of Our Lives
George Michael & Lisa Stansfield; *Five Live-C* . . . . (Hollywood)
Queen; *Classic Queen* . . . . (Hollywood)
   Innuendo . . . . (Hollywood)
Third Rock From The Sun
Joe Diffie; *A Thousand Winding Roads* . . . . (Epic)
Thirty-Three
Smashing Pumpkins; *Mellon Collie And The Infinite Sadness* . . . . . . (Virgin)
This Black Cat Has 9 Lives
Louis Armstrong; *What A Wonderful World* . . . . (Bluebird)
This Door Swings Both Ways
Herman's Hermits; *Herman's Hermits-Their Greatest Hits* . . . . (Abkco)
This Hard Land
Bruce Springsteen; *Bruce Springsteen's Greatest Hits* . . . . (Columbia)
   Tracks . . . . (Columbia)
This Part Of Town
Widespread Panic; *Don't Tell The Band* . . . . (Widespread/SRG)

This Time
Curtis Stigers; *Time Was*. . . . . (Arista)
Three Bells, The
Browns; *Billboard Top Country Hits-1959-C*. . . . . (Rhino)
Nipper's Greatest Hits Of The '50s-#1-C . . . . (RCA)
Through Your Hands
Don Henley; *ST/Michael* . . . . (Revolution)
Thunder Road
Bruce Springsteen; *Born To Run*. . . . . (Columbia)
Bruce Springsteen's Greatest Hits. (Columbia)
Bruce Springsteen & The E Street Band; *Bruce Springsteen & The E Street Band Live/1975-85* . . . . (Legacy)
Time
Pink Floyd; *Dark Side Of The Moon*. (Capitol)
Delicate Sound Of Thunder . . . . (Columbia)
Pink Floyd-Gift Set . . . . (Capitol)
Time In A Bottle
Jim Croce; *50th Anniversary Collection*. . . . . (Saja)
Photographs & Memories/His Greatest Hits. . . . . (Atlantic)
Time In A Bottle/Jim Croce's Greatest Love Songs . . . . (Atlantic)
Time Of Your Life (Good Riddance)
Green Day; *Nimrod*. . . . . (Reprise)
Time Waits For No One
Hilltoppers; *P.S. I Love You (The Best Of The Hilltoppers)* . . . . (Varese Vintage)
Times Of Your Life
Paul Anka; *Paul Anka-30th Anniversary Anthology*. . . . . (Rhino)
Paul Anka-His Best . . . .(EMI)
Times They Are A-Changin'
Billy Joel; *KOHUEPT* . . . . (Columbia)
Bob Dylan; *Biograph* . . . . (Columbia)
Bob Dylan At Budokan . . . . (Columbia)
Bob Dylan's Greatest Hits . . . . (Columbia)
The Bootleg Series-Volumes 1-3 [Rare & Unreleased] . . . . (Columbia)
The Times They Are A-Changin' . . . . (Columbia)
Byrds; *The Byrds* . . . . (Columbia)
Turn! Turn! Turn! . . . . (Legacy)
Peter, Paul & Mary; *Peter, Paul and Mary In Concert* . . . .(Warner Bros.)
Simon & Garfunkel; *Collected Works* . . . . (Columbia)
Wednesday Morning 3 A.M. . . . . (Columbia)
To Ev'ry Girl-To Ev'ry Boy (The Meaning Of Love)
Johnnie Ray; *45-#40252* . . . . (Columbia)
To Give (The Reason I Live)
4 Seasons; *25th Anniversary Collection* . . . . (Rhino)
Very Best Of The 4 Seasons . . . .(MCA)
To Keep My Love Alive
Ella Fitzgerald; *Rodgers & Hart Songbook* . . . . (Verve)
Mary Martin & Richard Rodgers; *Mary Martin Sings, Richard Rodgers Plays* . . . . (RCA)
To Life
Original Cast; *Fiddler On The Roof* . . . .(RCA Victor)
To Live And Die In L.A.
Wang Chung; *ST/To Live And Die In L.A.* . . . .(Geffen)
To Live Is To Die
Metallica; *...And Justice For All* . . . . (Elektra)
Tomorrow Never Knows
Beatles; *Beatles-Box Set* . . . . (Capitol)
Revolver. . . . . (Capitol)
Phil Collins; *Face Value* . . . . (Atlantic)
Top Of The World
Brandy featuring Mase; *Never Say Never* . . . . (Atlantic)
Touch Of Grey
Grateful Dead; *Heart Of Rock-C* . . . . (Columbia)
In The Dark . . . . (Arista)
Tragedy
Emmylou Harris; *Red Dirt Girl* . . . . (Nonesuch)
Transcendental Blues
Steve Earle; *Transcendental Blues* . . . . (Artemis)
Treat 'Em Right
Chubb Rock; *Freddy's Dead-Final Nightmare* . . . .(Metal Blade)
Nasty Wax-C . . . . (K-Tel)
Treat Them Like They Want To Be Treated
Father M.C.; *Father's Day* . . . . (Uptown)
Tree Of Life
Les Baxter & His Orchestra; *Brazil Now-African Blue*. . . . .(Crescendo)
Trip Free Life
Hazies; *Vinnie Smokin' In The Big Room* . . . .(EMI)
Tripping Billies
Dave Matthews Band; *Crash* . . . . (RCA)
Trying To Live My Life Without You
Bob Seger & The Silver Bullet Band; *Nine Tonight* . . . . (Capitol)
Turn The Page
Metallica; *Garage Inc.* . . . . (Elektra)
Turn! Turn! Turn! (To Everything There Is A Season)
Byrds; *Billboard Top Rock 'N' Roll Hits-1965-C* . . . . (Rhino)
Original Singles-#1-1965-1967 . . . . (Columbia)
ST/Forrest Gump . . . .(Epic/Sony Music Soundtrax)
The Byrds . . . . (Columbia)
The Byrds' Greatest Hits . . . . (Columbia)

Turn! Turn! Turn!. . . . . (Legacy)
Pete Seeger; *Pete Seeger's Greatest Hits* . . . . (Columbia)
Troubadours Of The Folk Era-#2-C . . . . (Rhino)
Twice In A Lifetime
Michael Lington; *Vivid* . . . .(Samson)
Twist Of Fate
Olivia Newton-John; *Back To Basics-Essential Collection 1971-1992* . (Geffen)
Chicken Soup For The Woman's Soul-C . . . . (Rhino)
ST/Two Of A Kind . . . . (MCA)
Two Little Girls
Ani DiFranco; *Little Plastic Castle* . . . . (Righteous Babe)
Two Lives
Bonnie Raitt; *Sweet Forgiveness*. . . . . (Warner Bros.)
Carpenters; *Voice Of The Heart* . . . .(A&M)
Randy Crawford; *Secret Combination* . . . . (Warner Bros.)
Two Step
Dave Matthews Band; *Crash*. . . . .(RCA)
Two Teardrops
Steve Wariner; *Two Teardrops* . . . . (Capitol)
Understanding
Candlebox; *Lucy* . . . . (Maverick)
Undo
Bjork; *Vespertine* . . . . (Elektra)
Universal Heart-Beat
Juliana Hatfield; *Box Presents Big Ones Of Alternative Rock-#1-C* . . . . (Box Tunes)
Only Everything . . . .(Mammoth)
Up Where We Belong
Joe Cocker; *Joe Cocker Live* . . . . (Capitol)
Joe Cocker & Jennifer Warnes; *ST/An Officer And A Gentleman* . . . . (Island)
The Island Story-1962-1987-25th Anniversary-C . . . . (Island)
Victim Of Life's Circumstances
Vince Gill; *Best Of Vince Gill* . . . . (RCA)
Vienna Life
Lawrence Welk; *22 All-Time Favorite Waltzes* . . . . (Ranwood)
Vietnam Veteran Still Alive
Country Joe McDonald; *Into The Fray* . . . . (Rag Baby)
Voices
Disturbed; *The Sickness* . . . .(Giant)
Waiting For The Light To Change
Tonic; *Sugar* . . . . (Universal)
Wake Up & Live
Bob Marley & The Wailers; *Survival* . . . .(Tuff Gong)
Wake Up & Live
Cab Calloway; *Best Of The Big Bands-C* . . . . (Columbia)
Walk Hand In Hand
Andy Williams; *I Like Your Kind Of Love-The Best Of The Cadence Years* . . . .(Varese Vintage)
Walk Of Life
Dire Straits; *Brothers In Arms*. (Warner Bros.)
Money For Nothing. . . . . (Warner Bros.)
Walls
Tom Petty And The Heartbreakers; *ST/She's The One* . . . . (Warner Bros.)
Wanted Dead Or Alive
Bon Jovi; *Slippery When Wet* . . . .(Jambco)
The Concert For New York City-C . . . . (Columbia)
Warm Machine
Bush; *Science Of Things* . . . . (Trauma)
Warning
Green Day; *Warning* . . . . (Reprise)
Way Down The Line
Offspring; *Ixnay On The Hombre* . . . . (Columbia)
Way It Is
Bruce Hornsby & The Range; *Heart Of Rock-C* . . . . (Columbia)
Nipper's Greatest Hits Of The '80s-C . . . . (RCA)
The Way It Is. . . . . (RCA)
We Can Work It Out
Beatles; *"Yesterday"...And Today* . . . . (Capitol)
Beatles 1 . . . . (Capitol)
Beatles-20 Greatest Hits . . . . (Capitol)
Beatles-Box Set. . . . . (Capitol)
Past Masters-Volume Two . . . . (Parlophone)
The Beatles/1962-1966. . . . . (Capitol)
Paul McCartney; *Unplugged (The Official Bootleg)* . . . . (Capitol)
Stevie Wonder; *Beatles Songs By Greatest Stars* . . . . (Motown)
Signed Sealed & Delivered . . . . (Motown)
Stevie Wonder's Greatest Hits-#2 . . . . (Motown)
Top 10 With A Bullet-Motown Solo Stars-C . . . . (Motown)
We Gotta Live Together
Jimi Hendrix; *Band Of Gypsys* . . . . (Capitol)
We Loved It Away
George Jones & Tammy Wynette; *George Jones & Tammy Wynette-16 Biggest Hits* . . . . (Epic/Legacy)
What Are You Doing In My Life
Tom Petty And The Heartbreakers; *Damn The Torpedoes* . . . . (MCA)
What Are You Doing The Rest Of Your Life?
Barbra Streisand; *Just For The Record* . . . . (Columbia)
The Way We Were. . . . . (Columbia)

Carmen McRae; *Great American Songbook* . . . . (Atlantic)
Joe Pass; *Best Of Joe Pass* . . . . (Pablo)

What Do You Want From Life
Tubes; *T.R.A.S.H. (Tubes Rarities And Smash Hits)* . . . . (A&M)
  Tubes . . . . (A&M)
  What Do You Want From Live . . . . (A&M)

What I Got
Sublime; *Now That's What I Call Music!-#2-C* . . . .(Virgin)
  Sublime . . . . (Gasoline Alley)

What Is Life
George Harrison; *All Things Must Pass* . . . .(Parlophone)
  Best Of George Harrison . . . . (Capitol)
  Live In Japan . . . .(Dark Horse)

What It Is
Mark Knopfler; *Sailing To Philadelphia* . . . . (Warner Bros.)

What It's Like
Everlast; *Whitey Ford Sings The Blues* . . . .(Tommy Boy)

What Would You Do?
City High; *City High* . . . . (Interscope)
  Now That's What I Call Music!-#7-C . . . .(Virgin)
  ST/Life . . . . (Rock Land/Interscope)

What Would You Say
Dave Matthews Band; *MTV Buzz Bin-C* . . . . (Mammoth)
  Under The Table And Dreaming . . . .(RCA)

What's This Life For
Creed; *My Own Prison* . . . . (Wind-up)

What's Up With That
ZZ Top; *Rhythmeen* . . . .(RCA)

Wheel Of Fortune
Cardinals; *Atlantic Rhythm & Blues 1947-1974-box-C* . . . . (Atlantic)
Kay Starr; *Capitol Collectors Series-Kay Starr* . . . . (Capitol)

Wheel Of Life
Rance Allen; *Straight From The Heart* . . . . (Stax)

Wheels Of Life
Gino Vannelli; *Best Of Gino Vannelli* . . . . (A&M)
  Brother To Brother . . . . (A&M)
  Gino Vannelli-Classics-#7 . . . . (A&M)

When I Dream At Night
Marc Anthony; *Marc Anthony* . . . . (Columbia)

When I Find My Life
Marianne Faithfull; *Blazing Away* . . . . (Island)

When It All Goes Wrong Again
Everclear; *Songs From An American Movie-#2-Good Time For A Bad
  Attitude* . . . . (Capitol)

When The Going Gets Tough, The Tough Get Going
Billy Ocean; *Billy Ocean's Greatest Hits* . . . .(Jive)
  Love Zone . . . .(Jive)

Whenever Wherever
Shakira; *Laundry Service* . . . . (Epic)

Where Corn Don't Grow
Travis Tritt; *The Restless Kind* . . . . (Warner Bros.)

Where Love Lives
Alison Limerick; *Club Cutz 2-C* . . . .(RCA)

Where Were You (When The World Stopped Turning)
Alan Jackson; *Alan Jackson-Drive* . . . . (Arista)

Where Your Road Leads
Trisha Yearwood & Garth Brooks; *Where Your Road Leads* . . . . (MCA)

Where'm I Gonna Live?
Billy Ray Cyrus; *Some Gave All* . . . . (Mercury)

Wherever You Go
Clint Black; *Clint Black-The Greatest Hits* . . . .(RCA)
  One Emotion . . . .(RCA)

While You Loved Me
Rascal Flatts; *Rascal Flatts* . . . . (Lyric Street)

While You See A Chance
Steve Winwood; *Arc Of A Diver* . . . . (Island)
  Steve Winwood-Chronicles . . . . (Island)

Who Wants To Live Forever
Queen; *A Kind Of Magic* . . . . (Hollywood)
  Classic Queen . . . . (Hollywood)
  Diana, Princess Of Wales-Tribute-C . . . . (Columbia)

Wicker Man
Iron Maiden; *Brave New World* . . . . (Portrait)

Wild Life
Wings; *Wild Life* . . . . (Capitol)

Wild Life
INXS; *Kick* . . . . (Atlantic)

Wild Side Of Life
Freddy Fender; *Before The Next Teardrop Falls* . . . . (Universal)
  Best Of Freddy Fender . . . . (MCA)
Hank Thompson; *Best Of Hank Thompson* . . . . (Gusto)
  Capitol Collectors Series-Hank Thompson . . . . (Capitol)
  Hank Thompson's All-Time Greatest Hits . . . . (Curb)
  Traditions In Country Music-C . . . . (Capitol)
Rod Stewart; *Night On The Town* . . . . (Warner Bros.)

Wild Wild Life
Talking Heads; *Popular Favorites-1984-1992* . . . . (Sire)
  True Stories . . . . (Sire)

Will The Wolf Survive
Los Lobos; *How Will The Wolf Survive* . . . . (Slash)
Waylon Jennings; *Country Classics-#6-1985-1986-C* . . . .(Universal)
  New Classic Waylon . . . . (MCA)
  Will The Wolf Survive . . . . (MCA)

Winter Of My Life
Freddy Fender; *Are You Ready For Freddy* . . . . (MCA)

Within You Without You
Beatles; *Beatles-Box Set* . . . .(Capitol)
  Sgt. Pepper's Lonely Hearts Club Band . . . . (Capitol)

Without A Song
Duke Ellington; *Great Ellington Units* . . . . (Bluebird)
Frank Sinatra; *My Kind Of Broadway* . . . . (Reprise)
James Ray; *Golden Classics-James Ray* . . . .(Collectables)
Supremes; *I Hear A Symphony* . . . . (Motown)
Tommy Dorsey & Frank Sinatra; *Tommy Dorsey & Frank Sinatra's All-Time
  Greatest Hits-#1* . . . . (Bluebird)
Willie Nelson; *What A Wonderful World* . . . . (Columbia)

Woman On The Tier (I'll See You Through)
Suzanne Vega; *ST/Dead Man Walking* . . . . (Columbia)

Wonder
Natalie Merchant; *Tigerlily* . . . . (Elektra)

World Leader Pretend
R.E.M.; *Green* . . . . (Warner Bros.)

Worried Life Blues
B.B. King; *Turn On With B.B. King* . . . . (Kent)
Eric Clapton; *24 Nights* . . . .(Duck/Reprise)
  Just One Night . . . . (Polydor)
John Lee Hooker; *John Lee Hooker Plays & Sings The Blues* . . . .(Chess)
Lightnin' Hopkins; *Best Of Lightnin' Hopkins* . . . . (Prestige)
  How Many More Years I Got . . . . (Fantasy)

Written In The Stars
Elton John & LeAnn Rimes; *ST/Aida* . . . .(Island)

Yellow Submarine
Beatles; *Beatles 1* . . . .(Capitol)
  Beatles-Box Set . . . . (Capitol)
  Reel Music . . . . (Capitol)
  Revolver . . . . (Capitol)
  The Beatles/1962-1966 . . . . (Capitol)

You Are The Sunshine Of My Life
Peter Nero; *Peter Nero's Greatest Hits* . . . . (Columbia)
Stevie Wonder; *20/20-C* . . . . (Motown)
  Original Musiquarium . . . . (Motown)
  Talking Book . . . . (Motown)

You Can't Always Get What You Want
Rolling Stones; *Flashpoint* . . . . (Virgin)
  Hot Rocks 1964-1971 . . . . (Abkco)
  Let It Bleed . . . . (Abkco)
  Love You Live . . . . (Virgin)
  Singles Collection-The London Years . . . . (Abkco)

You Can't Make A Heart Love Somebody
George Strait; *Latest Greatest Straitest Hits* . . . . (MCA)
  Lead On . . . . (MCA)

You Can't Resist It
Lyle Lovett; *Live In Texas* . . . . (MCA)
Patricia Conroy; *You Can't Resist* . . . .(Intersound)

You Decorated My Life
Kenny Rogers; *Kenny Rogers' Greatest Hits* . . . . (EMI)
  Kenny Rogers-20 Great Years . . . . (Reprise)
  Kenny Rogers-Twenty Greatest Hits . . . . (EMI)

You Gotta Be
Des'ree; *Diana, Princess Of Wales-Tribute-C* . . . . (Columbia)
  I Ain't Movin' . . . . (550 Music)

You Learn
Alanis Morissette; *Jagged Little Pill* . . . . (Maverick)

You Light Up My Life
Debby Boone; *Best Of Debby Boone* . . . .(Curb)
  There Is Love-Wedding Songs-C . . . . (Scotti Bros.)
  You Light Up My Life . . . . (MCA)
LeAnn Rimes; *You Light Up My Life-Inspirational Songs* . . . .(Curb)

You Stepped Into My Life
Bee Gees; *Bee Gees' Greatest* . . . . (Polydor)
  Children Of The World . . . .(RSO)

You Were Meant For Me
Jewel; *Pieces Of You* . . . . (Atlantic)

You Were Meant For Me
Gene Kelly; *ST/Singin' In The Rain* . . . .(Turner Classic Movies)
Sting; *ST/The Object Of My Affection* . . . . (Ark 21)

You'll See
Madonna; *Something To Remember* . . . .(Maverick/Sire)

Young-At-Heart
Bing Crosby with Guy Lombardo & His Royal Canadians; *The Radio Years:
  20 Songs* . . . . (Crescendo)
Frank Sinatra; *At The Movies* . . . . (Capitol)
  Capitol Collectors Series-Frank Sinatra . . . . (Capitol)
  Classic Sinatra . . . . (Capitol)
  Sinatra's Sinatra . . . . (Reprise)
Ray Price; *Portrait Of A Singer* . . . . (Step One)
Rosemary Clooney; *Essence Of Rosemary Clooney* . . . . (Legacy)

Your Life Is Now
John Mellencamp; *John Mellencamp* . . . . (Columbia)
You're Never Fully Dressed Without A Smile
Original Broadway Cast; *Annie* . . . . (Columbia)
Yours (Quierme Mucho)
Benny Goodman & His Orchestra featuring Helen Forrest; *Best Of The Big Bands Featuring Helen Forrest* . . . . (Columbia)
Jimmy Dorsey & His Orchestra featuring Bob Eberly & Helen O'Connell; *Best Of Jimmy Dorsey & His Orchestra* . . . . (Curb)
Vera Lynn; *We'll Meet Again* . . . . (Living Era)

LIGHT, Bright, Lamps, Lights, Shine

See Also: ENERGY, FAITH, FIRE, GOD, LIGHTHOUSES, MOON, MORNING, NIGHT, REFLECTIONS, SHADOWS, STARS, SUN

(Turn Out The Light And) Love Me Tonight
Don Williams; *Best Of Don Williams-#2* . . . . (MCA)
Don Williams-20 Greatest Hits . . . . (MCA)
16 Candles
Crests; *Alan Freed's Memory Lane-C* . . . . (MCA)
Billboard Top Rock 'N' Roll Hits-1959-C . . . . (Rhino)
Crests Greatest Hits . . . . (Collectables)
Cruisin'-1959-C . . . . (Increase)
Oldies But Goodies-#14-C . . . . (Original Sound)
Rock & Roll U.S.A.-21 Rock & Roll Favorites-#2-C . . . . (Laurie)
ST/American Graffiti . . . . (MCA)
After The Lights Go Down Low
Al Hibbler; *After The Lights Go Down Low* . . . . (Atlantic)
Alabama Shine
Ken Pollard; *45-#1183* . . . . (Eagle Int'l)
All At Once You Love Her
Perry Como; *Perry Como's Greatest Hits* . . . . (RCA)
All The Small Things
Blink-182; *Enema Of The State* . . . . (MCA)
Now That's What I Call Music!-#4-C . . . . (Virgin)
And Fools Shine On
Brother Cane; *Best Of Rockline-C* . . . . (Priority)
Essential Southern Rock-C . . . . (House Of Blues)
Seeds . . . . (Virgin)
Angel
Jon Secada; *Jon Secada* . . . . (SBK)
Aurora
Bjork; *Vespertine* . . . . (Elektra)
Aurora Borealis
Meat Puppets; *Meat Puppets II* . . . . (SST)
Aurora Borealis
C.W. McCall; *C.W. McCall's Greatest Hits* . . . . (Polydor)
Behind Closed Doors
Charlie Rich; *American Originals-Charlie Rich* . . . . (Columbia)
Behind Closed Doors . . . . (Epic)
Charlie Rich's Greatest Hits . . . . (Epic)
Columbia Country Classics-#4-Nashville Sound-C . . . . (Columbia)
Bend Me, Shape Me
American Breed; *The Ultimate History Of Rock 'N' Roll-#7-C* . . . . (K-Tel)
Blackbird
Beatles; *Beatles-Box Set* . . . . (Capitol)
The Beatles (White Album) . . . . (Capitol)
Crosby, Stills & Nash; *CSN* . . . . (Atlantic)
Paul McCartney; *Unplugged (The Official Bootleg)* . . . . (Capitol)
Wings; *Wings Over America* . . . . (Capitol)
Blinded By The Light
Bruce Springsteen; *Greetings From Asbury Park, N.J.* . . . . (Columbia)
Manfred Mann's Earth Band; *Roaring Silence* . . . .(Warner Bros.)
Blue Moon Of Kentucky
Bill Monroe; *American Originals-Bill Monroe* . . . . (Columbia)
Bean Blossom . . . . (MCA)
Best Of Bill Monroe & His Blue Grass Boys . . . . (MCA)
Bill Monroe & His Blue Grass Boys; *Bluegrass Super Hits-C* . . . . (Columbia)
Elvis Presley; *A Date With Elvis* . . . . (RCA)
A Golden Celebration . . . . (RCA)
The Sun Sessions . . . . (RCA)
Bright Lights And Country Music
Bill Anderson; *Bill Anderson's Greatest Hits* . . . . (MCA)
Burn To Shine
Ben Harper; *Burn To Shine* . . . . (Virgin)
Burning Of The Midnight Lamp
Jimi Hendrix; *Essential Jimi Hendrix* . . . . (Reprise)
Lifelines/Jimi Hendrix Story . . . . (Reprise)
Jimi Hendrix Experience; *Electric Ladyland* . . . . (Reprise)
Radio One . . . . (Rykodisc)
Living Colour; *Biscuits* . . . . (Epic)
By The Light Of The Silvery Moon
Al Jolson; *The Al Jolson Story-#1* . . . . (MCA)
Doris Day; *Day At The Movies* . . . . (Columbia)
Julie Andrews; *A Little Bit Of Broadway* . . . . (Columbia)
Mitch Miller; *34 All-Time Great Sing-Along Selections-C* . . . . (Columbia)

Sing Along With Mitch . . . . (Columbia)
Can't Take That Away (Mariah's Theme)
Mariah Carey; *Rainbow* . . . . (Columbia)
Chasin' That Neon Rainbow
Alan Jackson; *Here In The Real World* . . . . (Arista)
Come Cryin' To Me
Lonestar; *Crazy Nights* . . . .(BNA)
Coming Out Of The Dark
Gloria Estefan; *Gloria Estefan's Greatest Hits* . . . . (Epic)
God Bless America-C . . . . (Columbia)
Hot #1 Hits-C . . . . (Foundation)
Into The Light . . . . (Epic)
Crystal Chandeliers
Charley Pride; *Charley Pride-24 Greatest Hits* . . . . (Tee Vee)
Special Collector's Edition-#3 . . . .(Platinum Disc)
Dance By The Light Of The Moon
Olympics; *Meet The Marathons* . . . . (Collectables)
Dance Into The Light
Phil Collins; *Dance Into The Light* . . . .(Atlantic)
Dancing In The Dark
Barbara Cook; *Barbara Cook-Live At Carnegie Hall* . . . . (Sony Music Classical)
Diana Krall; *The Look Of Love* . . . . (Impulse!)
Fred Waring's Pennsylvanians; *78-#22708* . . . . (Victor)
Tony Bennett; *Forty Years-The Artistry Of Tony Bennett* . . . . (Columbia)
Jazz . . . . (Columbia)
Day After Day
Def Leppard; *Euphoria* . . . . (Mercury)
Dim Lights Thick Smoke & Loud Loud Music
Flatt & Scruggs; *Golden Era* . . . . (Rounder)
Flying Burrito Brothers; *Close Encounters To The West Coast* . . . .(Relix)
Farther Along-Best Of The Flying Burrito Brothers . . . . (A&M)
Ricky Skaggs and Kentucky Thunder; *History Of The Future* . . (Skaggs Family)
Dim, Dim The Lights (I Want Some Atmosphere)
Bill Haley; *From The Original Master Tapes-Bill Haley* . . . . (MCA)
Downtown
B-52's; *B-52's* . . . . (Warner Bros.)
Frank Sinatra; *Strangers In The Night* . . . . (Reprise)
Petula Clark; *Dick Clark's 21 All-Time Hits-#2-C* . . . . (Original Sound)
Petula Clark's Greatest Hits . . . .(Crescendo)
Electrolite
Michael Stipe/Mike Mills; *Tibetan Freedom Concert* . . . . (Capitol)
R.E.M.; *New Adventures In Hi-Fi* . . . . (Warner Bros.)
End Is The Beginning Is The End
Smashing Pumpkins; *ST/Batman & Robin-Music From And Inspired By The Motion Picture* . . . .(Jive)
Every Light In The House
Trace Adkins; *Dreamin' Out Loud* . . . . (Capitol)
Eye
Smashing Pumpkins; *ST/Lost Highway* . . . .(Interscope)
Finer Things, The
Steve Winwood; *Back In The High Life* . . . . (Island)
Footlights
Merle Haggard; *For The Record: Merle Haggard-43 Legendary Hits* . . . .(BNA)
Freak On A Leash
Korn; *Follow The Leader* . . . . (Immortal/Epic)
From A Window
Billy J. Kramer With The Dakotas; *History Of British Rock-#3-C* . . . . . . (Rhino)
Chad & Jeremy; *Best Of Chad & Jeremy* . . . . (One Way)
Glow Worm
Mills Brothers; *Best Of The Mills Brothers* . . . . (MCA)
Cab Driver . . . . (Ranwood)
Mills Brothers' Greatest Hits . . . . (MCA)
Mills Brothers-16 Great Performances . . . . (MCA)
God Bless America
Anita Bryant; *Golden Classics-Anita Bryant* . . . . (Collectables)
Bill & Gloria Gaither; *Kennedy Center Homecoming: A Celebration Of Our Faith And Heritage* . . . .(Springhouse Music Grp./Chordant)
Celine Dion; *America: A Tribute To Heroes-C* . . . .(Interscope)
God Bless America-C . . . . (Columbia)
Drew Carey; *ST/The Drew Carey Show* . . . . (Rhino)
Frank Zappa; *Uncle Meat* . . . . (Barking Pumpkin)
Kate Smith; *Best Of Kate Smith* . . . . (RCA)
God Bless America . . . .(Pickwick)
Kate Smith-Legendary Performer . . . . (RCA)
Nipper's Greatest Hits Of The '30s-#1-C . . . .(RCA)
Stars And Stripes Forever-#2-C . . . . (Volcano Entertainment)
LeAnn Rimes; *You Light Up My Life-Inspirational Songs* . . . . (Curb)
Lee Greenwood; *American Patriot* . . . . (Capitol)
Mormon Tabernacle Choir; *God Bless America* . . . . (Sony Music Classical)
Original Soundtrack; *ST/The Deer Hunter* . . . . (Capitol)
Peter Pan Kids; *I Love America Sing Along* . . . . (Compose)
Robert Shaw Chorale; *Battle Cry Of Freedom* . . . .(RCA)
Goodnight Moon
Shivaree; *I Oughtta Give You A Shot* . . . . (Capitol)
Harbor Lights
Boz Scaggs; *Silk Degrees* . . . . (Columbia)
Dinah Washington; *Complete Dinah Washington On Mercury-#2-1950-1952* . . . . (Mercury)
Dinah Washington-Golden Hits . . . . (Mercury)

For Lonely Lovers . . . . (Mercury)
This Is My Story . . . . (Mercury)
Platters; *Super Oldies Of The '60s-#9-C* . . . . (Audio Fidelity)

Healing Hands
Elton John; *Sleeping With The Past* . . . . (MCA)

Heirloom
Bjork; *Vespertine* . . . . (Elektra)

Holding On
Steve Winwood; *Roll With It* . . . . (Virgin)

House Of Love
Amy Grant & Vince Gill; *House Of Love* . . . . (A&M)

How Was I To Know
John Michael Montgomery; *What I Do The Best* . . . . (Atlantic)

Humans Being
Van Halen; *Best Of Van Halen-#1* . . . . (Warner Bros.)

I Am The Light Of This World
Jorma Kaukonen & Tom Hobson; *Quah* . . . . (Relix)

I Got To Find My Baby
Animals; *In The Beginning* . . . . (Sundazed Music)

I Know A Place
Petula Clark; *History Of British Rock-#7-C* . . . . (Rhino)
Petula Clark's Greatest Hits . . . . (Crescendo)

I Really Don't Need No Light
Jeffrey Osborne; *Jeffrey Osborne* . . . . (A&M)

I Saw The Light
Hank Williams; *Hank Williams-24 Greatest Hits-#2* . . . . (Polydor)
Hank Williams-40 Greatest Hits . . . . (Polydor)
I Ain't Got Nothin' But Time-1946-1947 . . . . (Polydor)
Legend In Song-With Hank Williams, Jr. . . . . (Polydor)
Rare Takes & Radio Cuts . . . . (Polydor)

I Shall Be Released
Band; *Music From Big Pink* . . . . (Capitol)
The Band-Anthology-#1 . . . . (Capitol)
The Last Waltz . . . . (Warner Bros.)
To Kingdom Come-The Definitive Collection . . . . (Capitol)
Bette Midler; *Bette Midler* . . . . (Atlantic)
ST/Divine Madness . . . . (Atlantic)
Bob Dylan; *Biograph* . . . . (Columbia)
Bob Dylan At Budokan . . . . (Columbia)
Bob Dylan's Greatest Hits-#2 . . . . (Columbia)
The Bootleg Series-Volumes 1-3 [Rare & Unreleased] . . . . (Columbia)
Bob Dylan And The Band; *Before The Flood* . . . . (Columbia)
Box Tops; *Box Tops' Greatest Hits* . . . . (Rhino)
Flying Burrito Brothers; *Farther Along-Best Of The Flying Burrito Brothers* . . . . (A&M)
Joan Baez; *Any Day Now: Songs Of Bob Dylan* . . . . (Vanguard)
Carry It On . . . . (Vanguard)
From Every Stage . . . . (A&M)
Joe Cocker; *With A Little Help From My Friends* . . . . (A&M)
Nina Simone; *Best Of Nina Simone* . . . . (Verve)
Rick Nelson; *Rick Nelson In Concert-Troubadour 1969* . . . . . . (MCA)

In The House Of Stone And Light
Martin Page; *In The House Of Stone And Light* . . . . (Mercury)

Inner Light
Beatles; *Past Masters-Volume Two* . . . . (Parlophone)
Rarities . . . . (Capitol)

Inner Light
Little River Band; *Diamantina Cocktail* . . . . (Capitol)

It's Your Song
Garth Brooks; *Big Country Hits '99-C* . . . . (K-Tel)
Garth Brooks-Double Live . . . . (Capitol)

Kiss From A Rose
Seal; *Seal 2* . . . . (Sire)

Let's Put Out The Lights And Go To Sleep
Rudy Vallee; *American Legend Series-Vagabond Lover* . . . . (Pro-Arte)

Light Don't Shine
Southside Johnny And The Asbury Jukes; *Hearts Of Stone* . . . . (Epic)

Light In Your Eyes
Blessid Union Of Souls; *Blessid Union Of Souls* . . . . (Capitol)

Light In Your Eyes
LeAnn Rimes; *Blue* . . . . (MCG/Curb)

Light Years
Pearl Jam; *Binaural* . . . . (Epic)

Lights
Journey; *Infinity* . . . . (Columbia)
Journey-Captured . . . . (Columbia)

Lili Marlene
Marlene Dietrich; *Best Of Marlene Dietrich* . . . . (Columbia)
Essential Marlene Dietrich . . . . (Capitol)
Live At The Cafe De Paris . . . . (Columbia)
This Is Art Deco-C . . . . (Columbia)

Lit Up
Buckcherry; *Buckcherry* . . . . (DreamWorks/SKG)

Lost In The Neon World
Be Bop Deluxe; *Modern Music* . . . . (Capitol)

Lover After Me, The
Savage Garden; *Affirmation* . . . . (Columbia)

Low Light
Pearl Jam; *Yield* . . . . (Epic)

Massachusetts
Bee Gees; *Bee Gees-Gold* . . . . (Polydor)
Here At Last...Bee Gees...Live . . . . (Polydor)

Miami 2017
Billy Joel; *Songs In The Attic* . . . . (Columbia)
The Concert For New York City-C . . . . (Columbia)
Turnstiles . . . . (Columbia)

Mona Lisas And Mad Hatters
Elton John; *Honky Chateau* . . . . (Rocket)
Reg Strikes Back . . . . (MCA)
The Concert For New York City-C . . . . (Columbia)

Moonlight Serenade
Frank Sinatra; *Moonlight Sinatra* . . . . (Reprise)
The Reprise Collection . . . . (Reprise)
Glenn Miller; *Best Of Glenn Miller-#2* . . . . (RCA)
Glenn Miller-A Legendary Performer-#1 & 2 . . . . (Bluebird)
Memorial-1944-1969 . . . . (Bluebird)
Nipper's Greatest Hits Of The '30s-#1-C . . . . (RCA)
The Glenn Miller Story . . . . (RCA)
Glenn Miller & His Orchestra; *Glenn Miller & His Orchestra-Pure Gold* . . . . (Bluebird)

Most High
Jimmy Page/Robert Plant; *Walking Into Clarksdale* . . . . (Atlantic)

Neon Moon
Brooks & Dunn; *Brand New Man* . . . . (Arista)

Neon Moonlight
Rosco Martinez; *Neon Moonlight (Single)* . . . . (Zoo)

Neon Rainbow
Box Tops; *Box Tops' Greatest Hits* . . . . (Rhino)

Night Is Fallin' In My Heart
Diamond Rio; *Diamond Rio's Greatest Hits* . . . . (Arista)
Love A Little Stronger . . . . (Arista)

Night Lights
Nat "King" Cole; *Night Lights* . . . . (Capitol/EMI)

Night The Lights Went Out In Georgia
Lynn Anderson; *Top Of The World* . . . . (Columbia)
Reba McEntire; *For My Broken Heart* . . . . (MCA)
Reba McEntire's Greatest Hits-#3: I'm A Survivor . . . . (MCA)
Vicki Lawrence; *Super Hits Of The '70s-Have A Nice Day-#10-C* . . . . . (Rhino)

No Leaf Clover
Metallica; *S&M* . . . . (Elektra)

No Reply
Beatles; *Beatles '65* . . . . (Capitol)
Beatles-Box Set . . . . (Capitol)
For Sale . . . . (Capitol)

Northern Lights
Val Gardena; *On The Bridge* . . . . (Mercury)

Northern Lights
Bruce Cockburn; *Dancing In The Dragon's Jaws* . . . . (Columbia)

Northern Lights
Duke Ellington; *The Ellington Suites* . . . . (Original Jazz Classics)

Northern Lights
Rippingtons; *Kilimanjaro* . . . . (GRP)

Nothin' But The Taillights
Clint Black; *Nothin' But The Taillights* . . . . (RCA)

Old Flames Can't Hold A Candle To You
Dolly Parton; *Dolly Dolly Dolly* . . . . (RCA)
Dolly Parton's Greatest Hits . . . . (RCA)
Joe Sun; *Old Flames Can't Hold A Candle To You* . . . . (Ovation)
Merle Haggard; *Kern River* . . . . (Epic)

Old Lamplighter, The
Bing Crosby; *The Radio Years-#2* . . . . (Crescendo)
Browns; *45-#7700* . . . . (RCA)
Nipper's Greatest Hits Of The '60s-#2-C . . . . (RCA)
Kay Kyser & His Orchestra; *Best Of The Big Bands-Kay Kyser & His Orchestra* . . . . (Legacy)
Sammy Kaye & His Orchestra; *Nipper's Greatest Hits Of The '40s-#2-C* . . . . (RCA)

On Broadway
Drifters; *Drifters-16 Greatest Hits* . . . . (Trip)
Drifters-Golden Hits . . . . (Atlantic)
George Benson; *George Benson-Collection* . . . . (Warner Bros.)
ST/All That Jazz . . . . (Casablanca)
Weekend In L.A. . . . . (Warner Bros.)

One Headlight
Wallflowers; *Bringing Down The Horse* . . . . (Interscope)

One, The
Backstreet Boys; *Millennium* . . . . (Jive)

Party Lights
Claudine Clark; *Collectables Presents The History Of Rock-#4-C* . . . . (Collectables)
Wonder Women-History Of Girl Group Sound-C . . . . (Rhino)

Party Lights
Natalie Cole; *Natalie Cole-Collection* . . . . (Capitol)
Natalie Cole-Live . . . . (Capitol)
Unpredictable . . . . (Capitol)

Party Lights
Gap Band; *The Gap Band II* . . . . (Mercury)

Philadelphia Freedom
Daryl Hall & John Oates; *Two Rooms-Celebrating The Songs Of Elton John & Bernie Taupin-C* . . . . (Polydor)
Elton John; *Billboard Top Rock 'N' Roll Hits-1975-C* . . . . (Rhino)
Elton John's Greatest Hits-#2 . . . . (Polydor)

Private Emotion
Ricky Martin & Meja; *Ricky Martin* . . . . (Columbia)

Ray Of Light
Madonna; *GHV2* . . . .(Warner Bros.)
Ray Of Light . . . . (Maverick)
Totally Hits-#1-C . . . . (Arista)

Reach For The Light
Steve Winwood; *ST/Balto.* . . . .(MCA)

Reach Out Of The Darkness
Friend And Lover; *Chicken Soup For The Soul: I'll Be There For You-Songs Of Friendship, Brotherhood And Sisterhood-C* . . . . (Rhino)
Flower Power-Psychedelic Rock Classics-C . . . . (K-Tel)

Red Light Special
TLC; *CrazySexyCool* . . . . (LaFace)

Searchin' My Soul
Vonda Shepard; *ST/Songs From ''Ally McBeal'' Featuring Vonda Shepard* . . . . (550/Epic)
The Radical Light . . . .(Vesperally)

See The Light
Aldo Nova; *Aldo Nova* . . . . (Portrait)
Portrait Of Aldo Nova . . . .(Epic)

See The Light
Marty Balin; *Better Generation* . . . .(GWE)

See The Light
Five Americans; *Nuggets-Classic Collection From The Psychedelic '60s-C* . . . . (Rhino)

See The Light
Jeff Healey Band; *See The Light* . . . . (Arista)

See The Light
Earth, Wind & Fire; *That's The Way Of The World* . . . . (Legacy)

Seventh Avenue
Rosanne Cash; *The Wheel* . . . . (Columbia)

She's Taken A Shine
John Berry; *Faces* . . . . (Capitol)

Shimmer
Fuel; *Sunburn* . . . . (550 Music)

Shimmer
Shawn Mullins; *Songs From Dawson's Creek* . . . . (Sony Music Soundtrax)
Soul's Core . . . . (Columbia)

Shine
Collective Soul; *Hints, Allegations And Things Left Unsaid* . . . .(Atlantic)

Shine
Jon B.; *Cool Relax* . . . . (Yab Yum/550)

Shine
Amel Larrieux; *Infinite Possibilities* . . . .(Epic)

Shine A Light
Rolling Stones; *Exile On Main Street* . . . . (Virgin)

Shine On Me
Andy Griggs & Waylon Jennings; *You Won't Ever Be Lonely* . . . . . . (RCA)

Shine Silently
Nils Lofgren; *Nils* . . . . (A&M)
Nils Lofgren-Classics-#13 . . . . (A&M)

Shining In The Light
Jimmy Page/Robert Plant; *Walking Into Clarksdale.* . . . . (Atlantic)

Shining Star
Earth, Wind & Fire; *Best Of Earth, Wind & Fire-#1* . . . . (Legacy)
Eternal Dance . . . . (Columbia)
Gratitude . . . . (Legacy)
That's The Way Of The World . . . . (Legacy)

Shut Out The Light
Bruce Springsteen; *Tracks* . . . . (Columbia)

Soft Lights And Hard Country Music
Moe Bandy; *Honky Tonk Amnesia-The Hard Country Sound Of Moe Bandy* . . . . (Razor & Tie)

Soft Lights And Sweet Music
John Coltrane; *John Coltrane And The Jazz Giants* . . . . (Fantasy)
Victor Young & The Brunswick Orchestra with Bing Crosby; *Irving Berlin: A Hundred Years-C* . . . . (Columbia)

Southside
Moby featuring Gwen Stefani; *12'' Maxi Single* . . . . (V2)
Play . . . . (V2)

Step Into The Light
Dust For Life; *Dust For Life* . . . . (Wind-up)

Sweetheart
Jermaine Dupri & Mariah Carey; *Presents Life In 1472-Original Soundtrack* . . . . (So So Def/Columbia)
Mariah Carey featuring Jermaine Dupri; *Mariah Carey-#1's* . . . . . . (Columbia)

That's What Friends Are For
Dionne Warwick/Elton John/Gladys Knight/Stevie Wonder; *Dionne Warwick's Greatest Hits-1979-1990* . . . . (Arista)
Friends . . . . (Arista)

Theme From ''Dr. Kildare'' (Three Stars Will Shine Tonight)
Betty Carter; *'Round Midnight* . . . . (Atlantic)

Original Soundtrack; *Television's Greatest Hits-#4-Black & White Classics-C* . . . . (TVT)

Theme From ''The Guiding Light''
Rosemary Joyce & Bill Bartholomew; *Soap Opera Themes* . . . .(Crescendo)

This Little Light
Elizabeth Cook; *Country Goes Raffi-C* . . . . (Rounder)
Odetta; *Freedom Is A Constant Struggle-C* . . . . (Folk Era)
Paul Robeson; *American Balladeer-Golden Classics-#1-C* . . . . . . (Collectables)
Raffi; *Rise And Shine* . . . . (Rounder)
Steeles; *ST/Corrina, Corrina* . . . . (RCA)

To Love Somebody
Bee Gees; *Bee Gees-Gold* . . . .(Polydor)
History Of British Rock-#7-C . . . . (Rhino)
Jimmy Somerville; *Jimmy Somerville-Singles Collection-1984-1990* . .(London)
Michael Bolton; *Timeless-Classics* . . . . (Columbia)

Turn Off The Light
Nelly Furtado; *Whoa Nelly!* . . . .(DreamWorks/SKG)

Turn On Your Love Light
Bobby Bland; *Bobby Bland's Greatest Hits-#1* . . . . (MCA)
Psychedelic '60s-#6-C . . . . (Collectables)
Turn On Your Love Light-The Duke Recordings-#2 . . . . (MCA)
Grateful Dead; *Best Of The Grateful Dead-Skeletons From The Closet.* . . . . (Warner Bros.)
Fillmore East-2/11/69 . . . . (Arista)
Live/Dead . . . . (Warner Bros.)
Two From The Vault . . . . (Grateful Dead)

Turn On Your Radio
Nilsson; *Son Of Schmilsson* . . . . (RCA)

Upstairs By A Chinese Lamp
Laura Nyro; *Christmas & The Beads Of Sweat* . . . . (Columbia)

Waffle
Sevendust; *Home.* . . . . (TVT)

Waiting For The Light To Change
Tonic; *Sugar* . . . . (Universal)

Welcome To Heartlight
Kenny Loggins; *High Adventure* . . . . (Columbia)

We're All Alone
Boz Scaggs; *Boz Scaggs-Hits!* . . . . (Columbia)
Slow Dancer . . . . (Columbia)
Rita Coolidge; *Rita Coolidge's Greatest Hits* . . . . (A&M)

When He Shines
Sheena Easton; *Sheena Easton's Greatest Hits* . . . . . (EMI Special Markets)
The World Of Sheena Easton: The Singles Collection-C . . . . (EMI)

When The Lights Go Out
Bruce Springsteen; *Tracks* . . . . (Columbia)

When The Lights Go Out
Five; *5* . . . . (Arista)
Totally Hits-#1-C . . . . (Arista)

When The Lovelight Starts Shining Through His Eyes
Diana Ross & The Supremes; *Diana Ross & The Supremes' Greatest Hits* . . . . (Motown)
Diana Ross & The Supremes-Anthology (1962-1969) . . . . (Motown)
Motown Superstar Series-#1-Diana Ross & The Supremes . . . . (Motown)
Supremes; *Where Did Our Love Go* . . . . (Motown)

When The Moon Shines On The Moonshine
Bert Williams; *Music From The New York Stage (1890-1920)-#4-1917-1920-C* . . . . (Pearl)

White Light/White Heat
David Bowie; *Sound + Vision* . . . . (Rykodisc)
ST/Ziggy Stardust-The Motion Picture . . . . (Rykodisc)
Lou Reed; *Rock N Roll Animal* . . . . (RCA)
Walk On The Wild Side-The Best Of Lou Reed . . . . (RCA)
Velvet Underground; *1969: Velvet Underground Live* . . . . (Mercury)
White Light/White Heat . . . . (Verve)

Whole New You
Shawn Colvin; *Whole New You.* . . . . (Columbia)

Yellow
Coldplay; *Now That's What I Call Music!-#6-C* . . . .(Virgin)
Parachutes . . . . (Nettwerk/Capitol)

You Can't Be A Beacon (If Your Light Don't Shine)
Donna Fargo; *Country Gospel-#4-C* . . . . (Platinum Disc)
The Happiest Girl In The Whole U.S.A. . . . . (Universal)

You Light Up My Life
Debby Boone; *Best Of Debby Boone.* . . . . (Curb)
There Is Love-Wedding Songs-C . . . . (Scotti Bros.)
You Light Up My Life . . . . (MCA)
LeAnn Rimes; *You Light Up My Life-Inspirational Songs* . . . . (Curb)

You're Not In Kansas Anymore
Jo Dee Messina; *Jo Dee Messina.* . . . . (Curb)

LIGHTHOUSES

See Also: **DANGER & DISASTER, HELP, HOUSES, LIGHT, OCEAN, SAILING, SHIPS**

I Wanna Marry A Lighthouse Keeper
Erika Eigen; *ST/A Clockwork Orange* . . . . (Warner Bros.)

Lighthouse
James Taylor; *Gorilla* . . . . (Warner Bros.)
Northern Lights; *Can't Buy Your Way* . . . . (Flying Fish)

Lighthouse
Rusty Draper; *Rusty Draper's Greatest Hits* . . . . (Collector's Choice)

Lighthouse
David West; *Titanic: Epic Songs Of The Sea-C* . . . . (C.M.H. Prod.)

Lighthouse
Cache Valley Drifters; *White Room* . . . . (C.M.H. Prod.)

Lighthouse
Flock; *Dinosaur Swamps* . . . . (One Way)

Lighthouse
Julie Simon; *The Vineyard Sound-#2-C* . . . . (Critique)

Lighthouse Act 1911
Steinbecks; *From The Wrestling Chair To The Sea* . . . . (Summershine)

Lighthouse On The Shore
Norman Blake; *Lighthouse On The Shore* . . . . (Rounder)

Lighthouse, The
Laurie Lewis; *The Oak And The Laurel* . . . . (Rounder)

Lighthouse, The
Hector Zazou; *Songs From The Cold Seas* . . . . (Columbia)

Lighthouse, The
J.D. Sumner; *Elvis' Gospel Favorites* . . . . (Arrival)

Lighthouse's Tale
Nickel Creek; *Nickel Creek* . . . . (Sugar Hill)

My Lighthouse
Pulp; *Countdown (1992-1983)* . . . . (VelVel)
It . . . . (VelVel)

Seventh Avenue
Rosanne Cash; *The Wheel* . . . . (Columbia)

When You Come Back To Me Again
Garth Brooks; *Scarecrow* . . . . (Capitol)

You Can't Be A Beacon (If Your Light Don't Shine)
Donna Fargo; *Country Gospel-#4-C* . . . . (Platinum Disc)
The Happiest Girl In The Whole U.S.A. . . . . (Universal)

LITTLE, Little In Amount

See Also: BIG, BITS & PIECES, SMALL (things of small size)

A Little Night Music
Original Cast; *Little Night Music* . . . . (Columbia)

Bring A Little Lovin'
Easybeats; *Best Of The Easybeats* . . . . (Rhino)

Cheerful Little Earful
Ella Fitzgerald; *Swings Brightly With Nelson* . . . . (Verve)

Come A Little Bit Closer
Jay & The Americans; *Good Vibrations (Sounds Of Top 40 Radio: 1964-1967)-C* . . . . (Capitol)
Jay & The Americans' All-Time Greatest Hits . . . . (Rhino)
Jay & The Americans' Greatest Hits . . . . (CEMA Special Prod.)

Come A Little Bit Closer
Fleetwood Mac; *25 Years-The Chain* . . . . (Warner Bros.)

Come A Little Bit Closer
Johnny Duncan & Janie Fricke; *Johnny Duncan & Janie Fricke's Greatest Hits* . . . . (Columbia)
Nice 'N' Easy . . . . (Columbia)

Crazy
Alana Davis; *Blame It On Me* . . . . (Elektra)

Cry Just A Little
Marie Osmond; *I Only Wanted You* . . . . (Capitol)

Cry Just A Little Bit
Sylvia; *Sylvia's Greatest Hits* . . . . (RCA)

Downtime
Jo Dee Messina; *Burn* . . . . (Warner Bros.)

Eat A Little Something
Original Cast; *I Can Get It For You Wholesale* . . . . (Columbia)

Every Day A Little Death
Original Cast; *Little Night Music* . . . . (Columbia)
Original London Cast; *Little Night Music* . . . . (RCA)

Every Little Bit Hurts
Brenda Holloway; *Motown Love Songs-C* . . . . (Motown)
Motown Memories-#2-C . . . . (Motown)
Motown Story-First 25 Years-C . . . . (Motown)
Gladys Knight & The Pips; *Gladys Knight & The Pips-Anthology* . . . . (Motown)
Motown Legends-Gladys Knight & The Pips . . . . (Motown)
Spencer Davis Group; *Best Of The Spencer Davis Group* . . . . (EMI)
Best Of The Spencer Davis Group . . . . (Rhino)

For A Little While
Tim McGraw; *Everywhere* . . . . (Curb)
Tim McGraw's Greatest Hits . . . . (Curb)

Give A Little
Nicolette Larson; *Nicolette* . . . . (Warner Bros.)

Give A Little Bit
Supertramp; *Even In The Quietest Moments* . . . . (A&M)
Supertramp-Classics-#9 . . . . (A&M)

Give A Little Love
Ziggy Marley & The Melody Makers; *Hey World!* . . . . (EMI)
ST/Men At Work . . . . (Mesa)
ST/Tequila Sunrise . . . . (Capitol)
Time Has Come...Best Of Ziggy Marley & The Melody Makers . . . . (EMI)

Give A Little Love
Judds; *Judds' Greatest Hits* . . . . (MCA)

Give A Little Love
Marvin Gaye & Tammi Terrell; *United* . . . . (Motown)

Give A Little Love
Stylistics; *45-#1136* . . . . (Streetwise)

God Must Have Spent A Little More Time On You
Alabama Featuring 'N Sync; *Twentieth Century* . . . . (RCA)
'N Sync; *'N Sync* . . . . (RCA)
Totally Hits-#1-C . . . . (Arista)

Gotta Give A Little Love
Timmy Thomas; *Gotta Give A Little Love* . . . . (Gold Mountain)

Growin' A Little Each Day
Doobie Brothers; *Doobie Brothers* . . . . (Warner Bros.)

How Little We Know
Frank Sinatra; *Best Of The Capitol Years* . . . . (Capitol)
Capitol Collectors Series-Frank Sinatra . . . . (Capitol)

I Cry Just A Little Bit
Shakin' Stevens; *Greatest Hits Of The '80s-Get Into The Greed-C* . . . . (Risky Business)

I Just Want You
Ozzy Osbourne; *Ozzmosis* . . . . (Epic)
The Ozzman Cometh . . . . (Epic)

I Miss You A Little
John Michael Montgomery; *John Michael Montgomery's Greatest Hits* . . . . (Atlantic)

I Want To Spread A Little Sunshine
Jack Norworth; *Music From The New York Stage (1890-1920)-#4-1917-1920-C* . . . . (Pearl)

I'm Gonna Love You Just A Little More Baby
Barry White; *Barry White's Greatest Hits* . . . . (20th Century Fox)

It Only Hurts For A Little While
Ames Brothers; *Best Of The Ames Brothers* . . . . (Pair)
Anne Murray; *Croonin'* . . . . (SBK)
Margo Smith; *Best Of Margo Smith* . . . . (MCA Special Prod.)

It's A Little Too Late
Tanya Tucker; *Can't Run From Yourself* . . . . (Liberty)

It's A Little Too Late
Mark Chesnutt; *Mark Chesnutt's Greatest Hits* . . . . (Decca)

Junkie Doll
Mark Knopfler; *Sailing To Philadelphia* . . . . (Warner Bros.)

Just A Little
Beau Brummels; *Best Of The Beau Brummels* . . . . (Rhino)
Introducing The Beau Brummels . . . . (Rhino)
Nuggets-#7-Early San Francisco-C . . . . (Rhino)
Super Oldies Of The '60s-#8-C . . . . (Audio Fidelity)

Just A Little Bit
Etta James; *Tell Mama* . . . . (Chess)
Jerry Butler; *Unavailable 16/Original Nitty Gritty* . . . . (Vee-Jay)
Mitch Ryder And The Detroit Wheels; *Rev Up-Best Of Mitch Ryder* . . . . (Rhino)
Steve Miller; *Born 2 B Blue* . . . . (Gold Rush)

Just A Little Bit Better
Herman's Hermits; *Herman's Hermits-Their Greatest Hits* . . . . (Abkco)

Just A Little Bit Of Love
Celine Dion; *Let's Talk About Love-C* . . . . (550 Music)

Just A Little Bit Of Rain
Fred Neil; *Just A Little Bit Of Rain* . . . . (Elektra)
Linda Ronstadt; *Linda Ronstadt-Retrospective* . . . . (Capitol)

Just A Little Bit Of You
Jackson 5; *Jackson 5-Anthology* . . . . (Motown)
Michael Jackson; *Forever Michael* . . . . (Motown)
Michael Jackson-Anthology . . . . (Motown)
Motown Superstar Series-#7-Michael Jackson . . . . (Motown)

Just A Little Bit South Of North Carolina
Chuck Foster & Jimmy Castle; *The Uncollected Chuck Foster & His Orchestra-1940* . . . . (Hindsight)
Dean Martin; *Swingin' Down Yonder* . . . . (Capitol)

Just A Little Closer
Pointer Sisters; *We Are The World-C* . . . . (Columbia)

Just A Little Closer
Robbie Nevil; *Robbie Nevil* . . . . (EMI)

Just A Little Love
B.B. King; *Live & Well* . . . . (MCA)

Just A Little Love
Reba McEntire; *Just A Little Love* . . . . (MCA)
Reba McEntire's Greatest Hits . . . . (MCA)

Just A Little Love
38 Special; *Strength In Numbers* . . . . (A&M)

Just A Little Lovin' (Will Go A Long, Long Way)
Eddy Arnold; *Best Of Eddy Arnold*. . . . . (RCA)
Eddy Arnold-Pure Gold. . . . . (RCA)

Just A Little Too Much
Rick Nelson; *All My Best* . . . . (MCA)
Rick Nelson-Souvenirs. . . . . (EMI)

Kick A Little
Little Texas; *Kick A Little*. . . . . (Warner Bros.)

Lil' Ain't Enough
David Lee Roth; *Little Ain't Enough* . . . . (Warner Bros.)

Little Bit Better
Herman's Hermits; *45-#4042* . . . . (Abkco)

Little Bit Crazy
Eddy Raven; *Eddy Raven's Greatest Hits*. . . . . (Warner Bros.)

Little Bit In Love
Patty Loveless; *16 Top Country Hits-#4-C*. . . . . (MCA)
If My Heart Had Windows . . . . (MCA)

Little Bit In Love
Julie Andrews; *A Little Bit Of Broadway* . . . . (Columbia)
Original Broadway Cast; *Wonderful Town*. . . . . (MCA)

Little Bit Independent
Fats Waller; *Complete Fats Waller-#3-1935-1936*. . . . . (RCA)

Little Bit Me, A Little Bit You
Monkees; *Monkees' Greatest Hits* . . . . (Rhino)

Little Bit More
Dr. Hook; *Dr. Hook-Greatest Hits & More* . . . . (Capitol)
Rock Me Gently-Mellow Rock's Greatest-C . . . . (EMI)

Little Bit Of Emotion
Kinks; *Low Budget* . . . . (Arista)

Little Bit Of Green
Elvis Presley; *Back In Memphis* . . . . (RCA)
From Memphis To Vegas/From Vegas To Memphis . . . . (RCA)

Little Bit Of Happiness
New Christy Minstrels; *New Christy Minstrels' Greatest Hits* . . . . . (Columbia)

Little Bit Of Heaven
Natalie Cole; *Dangerous* . . . . (Modern)
Ray Charles; *Seven Spanish Angels & Other Hits*. . . . . (Columbia)

Little Bit Of Love
Free; *Best Of Free*. . . . . (A&M)

Little Bit Of Love (Is All It Takes)
New Edition; *All For Love* . . . . (MCA)

Little Bit Of Snow
Howard Jones; *One To One* . . . . (Elektra)

Little Bit Of Soap
Jarmels; *Collectables Presents The History Of Rock-#7-C*. . . . . . (Collectables)
Jarmels-Golden Classics . . . . (Collectables)
Laurie Golden Oldies. . . . . (Laurie)
Million-Dollar Memories #1-C. . . . . (RCA)
Pick Hits Of The Radio Good Guys-C . . . . (Laurie)
Paul Davis; *Best Of Paul Davis*. . . . . (Bang)
Little Bit Of Paul Davis . . . . (Bang)

Little Bit Of Soul
Music Explosion; *Best Of Ohio Express & Other Bubblegum*
Smashes-#1-C. . . . . (Rhino)
Cruisin'-1967-C . . . . (Increase)
Million-Dollar Memories #1-C. . . . . (RCA)

Little Bit Of Sympathy
Robin Trower; *Bridge Of Sighs*. . . . . (Chrysalis)
Robin Trower-Live. . . . . (Chrysalis)

Little Bit Of You
Lee Roy Parnell; *We All Get Lucky Sometimes* . . . . (Career)

Little Bit South Of Saskatoon
Sonny James; *American Originals-Sonny James* . . . . (Columbia)

Little Brains, A Little Talent
Original Broadway Cast; *Damn Yankees* . . . . (RCA)

Little By Little
Rolling Stones; *England's Newest Hit Makers/The Rolling Stones* . . . . . (Abkco)

Little By Little
James House; *Days Gone By*. . . . . (Epic)

Little By Little
Dusty Springfield; *Dusty Springfield-Golden Hits* . . . . (Mercury)

Little By Little
Robert Plant; *Little By Little-Collector's Edition* . . . . (Es Paranza)
Shaken 'N' Stirred . . . . (Es Paranza)

Little By Little
Nighthawks; *Open All Nite* . . . . (Adelphi)

Little Cocaine
Lee Clayton; *Naked City* . . . . (Capitol)

Little Crazy
Fight; *War Of Words*. . . . . (Epic)

Little Dab'll Do Ya (Brylcreem)
Original Soundtrack; *TeeVee Toons-The Commercials-#1-C*. . . . . . (TVT)

Little Gasoline, A
Terri Clark; *Fearless*. . . . . (Mercury)

Little Good News
Anne Murray; *Anne Murray's Greatest Hits-#2* . . . . (Capitol)

Little Good News . . . . (Capitol)

Little Gossip
Original London Cast; *Man Of La Mancha*. . . . . (MCA)

Little Less Talk And A Lot More Action
Toby Keith; *Toby Keith*. . . . . (Mercury)

Little Love
Juice Newton; *Can't Wait All Night* . . . . (RCA)
New Breed . . . . (RCA)

Little More Love
Olivia Newton-John; *Olivia Newton-John's Greatest Hits-#2* . . . . (MCA)
Totally Hot . . . . (MCA)

Little More Love
Vince Gill; *High Lonesome Sound* . . . . (MCA)

Little More Love
Janie Fricke; *It Ain't Easy* . . . . (Columbia)

Little Night Dancin'
John Cougar; *John Cougar*. . . . . (Riva)

Little Old Fashioned Karma
Willie Nelson; *Tougher Than Leather*. . . . . (Columbia)

Little Past Little Rock
Lee Ann Womack; *Some Things I Know*. . . . . (Decca)

Little Rootie Tootie
Thelonius Monk; *High Priest* . . . . (Prestige)
In Person . . . . (Milestone)
Memorial Album. . . . . (Milestone)
Piano Giants. . . . . (Prestige)
Reflections #1 . . . . (Prestige)
Thelonius Monk . . . . (Milestone)
Thelonius Monk Trio . . . . (Prestige)

Little Star
Madonna; *Ray Of Light* . . . . (Maverick)

Little T & A
Rolling Stones; *Tattoo You* . . . . (Virgin)

Little Things
Tanya Tucker; *Complicated* . . . . (Capitol)

Little White Cloud That Cried
Johnnie Ray; *Best Of Johnnie Ray*. . . . . (Columbia)
Best Of Johnnie Ray. . . . . (Exact)
Johnnie Ray's Greatest Hits . . . . (Sony Music Special Prod.)

Living A Little, Laughing A Little
John Hiatt; *Warming Up To The Ice Age* . . . . (Geffen)
Spinners; *New & Improved*. . . . . (Atlantic)
Spinners-Live . . . . (Atlantic)

Love A Little Stronger
Diamond Rio; *'90s Hot Country-C*. . . . . (K-Tel)
Diamond Rio's Greatest Hits . . . . (Arista)
Diamond Rio-Super Hits . . . . (Arista)
Hit Country '96-C . . . . (K-Tel)
Love A Little Stronger. . . . . (Arista)

Love's Been A Little Bit Hard On Me
Juice Newton; *Juice Newton-Greatest Hits & More* . . . . (Capitol)
Juice Newton's Greatest Hits . . . . (Gold Rush)
Quiet Lies . . . . (Capitol)

Mambo No. 5 (A Little Bit Of...)
Lou Bega; *A Little Bit Of Mambo* . . . . (RCA)
Totally Hits-#2-C . . . . (Elektra)

Minimum Love
Mac McAnally; *Nothin' But The Truth* . . . . (Geffen)

Need A Little Taste Of Love
Doobie Brothers; *Cycles* . . . . (Warner Bros.)

Not Enough
Van Halen; *Balance* . . . . (Warner Bros.)

Nothing As It Seems
Pearl Jam; *Binaural*. . . . . (Epic)

Only Here For A Little While
Billy Dean; *Young Man* . . . . (SBK)

Peking Theme (So Little Time)
Andy Williams; *ST/55 Days At Peking* . . . . (Varese Sarabande)

Precious Little
Eleanor McEvoy; *What's Following Me?*. . . . . (Columbia)

Put A Little Love Away
Emotions; *Sunshine* . . . . (Stax)
The Emotions-Chronicle . . . . (Stax)

Put A Little Love In Your Heart
Annie Lennox & Al Green; *ST/Scrooged* . . . . (A&M)
Jackie DeShannon; *Chicken Soup For The Soul: I'll Be There For You-Songs*
Of Friendship, Brotherhood And Sisterhood-C . . . . (Rhino)
ST/Drugstore Cowboy . . . . (Novus)
Very Best Of Jackie DeShannon . . . . (EMI)

Run For Your Life
Beatles; *Beatles-Box Set* . . . . (Capitol)
Rubber Soul . . . . (Capitol)

Save A Little Room In Your Heart For Me
Eddie Money; *Eddie Money* . . . . (Columbia)

Shine A Little Love
Electric Light Orchestra; *Afterglow*. . . . . (Epic)
Box Of Their Best . . . . (Jet)
Discovery . . . . (Jet)

Spare Me A Little Of Your Love
Fleetwood Mac; *Bare Trees*. . . . .(Reprise)
Spend A Little Time
Joan Armatrading; *Whatever's For Us* . . . . (A&M)
Stand A Little Rain
Nitty Gritty Dirt Band; *Live Two Five* . . . . (Capitol)
Twenty Years Of Dirt-Best Of The Nitty Gritty Dirt Band. . . . . (Warner Bros.)
Stay
4 Seasons; *4 Seasons' Greatest Hits-#1*. . . . . (Rhino)
Jackson Browne; *Running On Empty* . . . . (Asylum)
Maurice Williams & The Zodiacs; *Best Of Maurice Williams & The
Zodiacs*. . . . . (Collectables)
Billboard Top Rock 'N' Roll Hits-1960-C . . . . (Rhino)
Cruisin'-1960-C . . . . (Increase)
Rock & Roll Is Here To Stay-C . . . . (Gusto)
ST/Dirty Dancing . . . . (RCA)
Stay A Little Longer
Bob Wills; *Sounds Of Texas* . . . . (Capitol)
Bob Wills & His Texas Playboys; *Bob Wills & His Texas Playboys-
Anthology 1935-1973* . . . . (Rhino)
Tiffany Transcriptions-#2-Best Of The Tiffanys . . . . (Rhino)
Willie Nelson; *Greatest Hits (& Some That Will Be)* . . . . . . (Columbia)
Willie & Family Live. . . . . (Columbia)
Take A Little Rhythm
Ali Thompson; *Take A Little Rhythm*. . . . . (A&M)
Take Me For A Little While
Coverdale/Page; *Coverdale/Page* . . . . (Geffen)
Takes A Little Time
Amy Grant; *Behind The Eyes* . . . . (A&M)
This Lil' Game We Play
Subway; *Good Times*. . . . . (Biv 10/Motown)
Too Little Too Late
Barenaked Ladies; *Maroon* . . . .(Reprise)
Try A Little Harder
Rolling Stones; *Singles Collection-The London Years* . . . . (Abkco)
Try A Little Kindness
Glen Campbell; *Best Of Glen Campbell* . . . . (Capitol)
Glen Campbell-Best Of The Early Years . . . .(Curb)
Glen Campbell's Greatest Hits . . . . (Capitol)
Try A Little Tenderness
Aretha Franklin; *Sweet Bitter Love* . . . . (Columbia)
David Sanborn; *ST/The Mirror Has Two Faces* . . . . (Columbia)
Otis Redding; *Best Of Otis Redding*. (Atco)
Best Of Otis Redding. . . . . (Atlantic)
Live In Europe . . . . (Atco)
The Otis Redding Story. . . . . (Atlantic)
Very Best Of Otis Redding . . . . (Rhino)
Three Dog Night; *Best Of Three Dog Night*. . . . . (MCA)
Try A Little Tenderness
Rod Stewart; *Out Of Order* . . . . (Warner Bros.)
Try A Little Tenderness
Marty Robbins; *Don't Let Me Touch You* . . . . (Columbia)
Marty Robbins' Greatest Hits-#4 . . . . (Columbia)
Unwashed & Somewhat Slightly Dazed
David Bowie; *Space Oddity* . . . . (Rykodisc)
What A Little Moonlight Can Do
Billie Holiday; *Billie Holiday's Greatest Hits*. . . . . (Legacy)
Billie's Best . . . . (Verve)
First Verve Sessions . . . . (Verve)
History Of The Real Billie Holiday. . . . . (Verve)
Songbook . . . . (Verve)
Diana Ross; *ST/Lady Sings The Blues* . . . . (Motown)
Will He Wait A Little Longer
Stanley Brothers; *Stanley Series-Vol. 1-#3* . . . . (Copper Creek)
With A Little Bit Of Luck
Julie Andrews/Original Cast; *My Fair Lady* . . . . (Columbia)
Kiri Te Kanawa & Jeremy Irons/Original Cast; *My Fair Lady* . . . .(London)
Stanley Holloway; *ST/My Fair Lady*. . . . . (Columbia)
With A Little Help From My Friends
Beatles; *Beatles-Box Set* . . . . (Capitol)
Rarities . . . . (Capitol)
Sgt. Pepper's Lonely Hearts Club Band . . . . (Capitol)
The Beatles/1967-1970. . . . . (Capitol)
Joe Cocker; *History Of British Rock-#9-C*. . . . . (Rhino)
Joe Cocker-Classics-#4 . . . . (A&M)
Joe Cocker's Greatest Hits . . . . (A&M)
ST/Woodstock . . . . (Atlantic)
With A Little Help From My Friends . . . . (A&M)
Ringo Starr & His All-Star Band; *Nobody's Child-Romanian Angel
Appeal-C* . . . . (Warner Bros.)
With A Little Luck
Paul McCartney; *All The Best!* . . . . (Capitol)
Wings; *London Town*. . . . . (Capitol)
Wings Greatest . . . . (Capitol)
World Is A Little Bit Under The Weather
Meters; *Trick Bag* . . . . (Reprise)
Your Little Secret
Melissa Etheridge; *Your Little Secret* . . . . (Island)

LONELY, Missing You

See Also: **DESPAIR, EMPTY, LOSING & LOSS, LOVE (various),
SADNESS, SEPARATION, SOLITUDE**

(I Don't Know Why) But I Do
Clarence "Frogman" Henry; *ST/Forrest Gump* . . (Epic/Sony Music Soundtrax)
(Lost His Love) On Our Last Date
Emmylou Harris; *Profile II-The Best Of Emmylou Harris* . . . .(Warner Bros.)
(Sittin' On) The Dock Of The Bay
Michael Bolton; *The Hunger* . . . .(Columbia)
Otis Redding; *(Sittin' On) The Dock Of The Bay* . . . .(Atco)
Best Of Otis Redding . . . .(Atco)
Golden Age Of Black Music-1960-1970-C . . . .(Atlantic)
Golden Soul-C. . . . . (Atlantic)
Soul Years-C . . . . (Atlantic)
The Otis Redding Story . . . . (Atlantic)
(Who Says) You Can't Have It All
Alan Jackson; *A Lot About Livin' (And A Little 'Bout Love)* . . . .(Arista)
(Without You) What Do I Do With Me
Tanya Tucker; *What Do I Do With Me* . . . .(Capitol)
...Baby One More Time
Britney Spears; *...Baby One More Time* . . . . (Jive)
Now That's What I Call Music!-#2-C . . . .(Virgin)
100% Chance Of Rain
Gary Morris; *Anything Goes* . . . .(Warner Bros.)
Gary Morris-Hits . . . .(Warner Bros.)
1-900-2LONELY
David Grey; *Signature* . . . . (JRS)
2,000 Light Years From Home
Rolling Stones; *More Hot Rocks (big hits & fazed cookies)*. . . . . (Abkco)
Singles Collection-The London Years . . . . (Abkco)
Their Satanic Majesties Request . . . . (Abkco)
Through The Past, Darkly (Big Hits Vol. 2) . . . . (Abkco)
26 Cents
Wilkinsons; *Nothing But Love* . . . . (Giant)
4 Seasons Of Loneliness
Boyz II Men; *Evolution* . . . . (Motown)
500 Miles Away From Home
Bobby Bare; *500 Miles Away From Home* . . . . (RCA)
Foy Willing; *Cowboy/The New Sound Of American Folk* . . . . (DRG)
Reba McEntire; *Starting Over* . . . . (MCA)
6, 8, 12
Brian McKnight; *Back At One* . . . .(Motown)
A World Without Love
Peter And Gordon; *Billboard Top Pop Hits-1964-C* . . . .(Rhino)
Abilene
George Hamilton IV; *Billboard Top Country Hits-1963-C* . . . . (Rhino)
Nipper's Greatest Hits Of The '60s-C . . . . (RCA)
Sonny James; *American Originals-Sonny James*. . . . .(Columbia)
Texas Super Hits-C . . . .(Columbia)
Waylon Jennings; *Outlaw Reunion-#1*. . . . .(Aura)
Absence Of The Heart
Deana Carter; *Everything's Gonna Be Alright* . . . .(Capitol)
Absolutely Sweet Marie
Bob Dylan; *Blonde On Blonde* . . . .(Columbia)
Act Naturally
Beatles; *"Yesterday"...And Today* . . . . (Capitol)
Buck Owens; *Beatles Originals* . . . . (Rhino)
Buck Owens & Ringo Starr; *Act Naturally*. . . . . (Capitol)
Buck Owens & The Buckaroos; *Buck Owens & The Buckaroos-Live At
Carnegie Hall*. . . . . (Country Music Foundation)
Charley Pride; *Country Pride*. . . . . (RCA)
Johnny Russell; *20 Great Country Hits-C* . . . . (RCA)
Adam's Song
Blink-182; *Enema Of The State* . . . . (MCA)
Ain't No Fun To Be Alone In San Antone
Gene Watson; *Mack In The Fire* . . . .(Warner Bros.)
Ain't No Sunshine When She's Gone
Bill Withers; *Bill Withers' Greatest Hits* . . . .(Columbia)
Bill Withers Live At Carnegie Hall . . . .(Columbia)
Michael Jackson; *Original Soul Of Michael Jackson*. . . . .(Motown)
Ain't That Lonely Yet
Dwight Yoakam; *Last Chance For A Thousand Years-Greatest Hits From
The '90s* . . . . (Reprise)
This Time . . . . (Reprise)
All Alone
Joe Satriani; *Time Machine* . . . .(Relativity)
All Alone
Frank Sinatra; *Frank Sinatra-Complete Reprise Studio Recordings* . . . (Reprise)
Rosemary Clooney; *Some Of The Best-Rosemary Clooney* . . . . (Laserlight)
All Alone In Austin
Marty Mitchell; *You Are The Sunshine Of My Life*. . . . . (MC)
All Alone In California
Dan Hill; *Hold On* . . . .(20th Century Fox)
All Along
Blessid Union Of Souls; *Home*. . . . .(EMI)

All By Myself
Celine Dion; *Falling Into You* . . . . (550 Music)
Eric Carmen; *Best Of Eric Carmen* . . . . (Arista)
Billboard Top Rock 'N' Roll Hits-1976-C . . . . (Rhino)
All By Myself
Bobby Darin; *Puttin' On The Ritz-Capitol Sings Berlin-C* . . . . (Capitol)
Ella Fitzgerald; *Blue Skies: The Irving Berlin Songbook-C* . . . . (Verve)
Nat ''King'' Cole; *Ramblin' Rose* . . . . (Capitol)
All Dressed Up & Lonely
Jim Reeves; *Touch Of Velvet* . . . . (RCA)
All Lonesome Cowboys
Pure Prairie League; *Takin' The Stage* . . . . (RCA)
All My Loving
Beatles; *Meet The Beatles!* . . . . (Capitol)
The Beatles At The Hollywood Bowl . . . . (Capitol)
The Beatles/1962-1966 . . . . (Capitol)
With The Beatles . . . . (Parlophone)
All Roads Lead To You
Chicago; *The Heart Of Chicago-1967-1988-#2* . . . . (Reprise)
All The Good Ones Are Gone
Pam Tillis; *Pam Tillis' Greatest Hits* . . . . (Arista)
Almost Honest
Megadeth; *Cryptic Writings* . . . . (Capitol)
ST/Mortal Kombat 3: Annihilation . . . . (TVT)
Alone
Bee Gees; *Still Waters* . . . . (Polydor)
Alone Again (Naturally)
Gilbert O'Sullivan; *Best Of Gilbert O'Sullivan* . . . . (Rhino)
Billboard Top Rock 'N' Roll Hits-1972-C . . . . (Rhino)
Alone And Forsaken
Emmylou Harris & Mark Knopfler; *Timeless: Hank Williams*
Tribute-C . . . . (Lost Highway/IDJMG)
Hank Williams; *Alone And Forsaken* . . . . (Mercury)
Alone With His Guitar . . . . (Mercury)
Hank Williams-The Original Singles Collection . . . . (Polydor)
Alone At A Drive In Movie
Olivia Newton-John & John Travolta; *ST/Grease* . . . . (Polydor)
Original Broadway Cast; *Grease* . . . . (Polydor)
Alone In Manitoba
Humphrey & The Dumptrucks; *Six Days Of Paper Ladies* . . . . (Boot)
Alone In Paris
Alphonse Mouzon; *Best Of Alphonse Mouzon* . . . . (Black Sun)
Early Spring . . . . (Tenacious)
Along Comes Mary
Association; *Association Greatest Hits* . . . . (Warner Bros.)
Vintage Association . . . . (Fifty One West)
Already Missing You
Gerald Levert & Eddie Levert, Sr.; *Father And Son* . . . . (East West)
Am I The Only One (Who's Ever Felt This Way)
Dixie Chicks; *Wide Open Spaces* . . . . (Monument)
Amy's Back In Austin
Little Texas; *Kick A Little* . . . . (Warner Bros.)
Little Texas' Greatest Hits . . . . (Warner Bros.)
An Ant Alone
Bob Telson & Little Village; *An Ant Alone-Songs From The*
Warrior Ant . . . . (Gramavision)
An Innocent Man
Billy Joel; *An Innocent Man* . . . . (Columbia)
And I Love You So
Perry Como; *Perry Como's Greatest Hits* . . . . (RCA)
Angels Get Lonesome Sometimes
Hank Williams, Jr.; *Hank Williams, Jr.-Early Years* . . . . (WB/Curb)
One Night Stands . . . . (Warner Bros.)
Another Lonely Saturday Night
Greg Kihn Band; *With The Naked Eye* . . . . (Beserkley)
Another Lonely Song
Tammy Wynette; *Tammy Wynette-16 Biggest Hits* . . . . (Legacy)
Tammy Wynette-Anniversary-20 Years Of Hits . . . .(Epic)
Tammy Wynette-Super Hits . . . .(Epic)
Tears Of Fire-25th Anniversary Collection . . . .(Epic)
Another Night
Ricky Skaggs and Kentucky Thunder; *Bluegrass Rules!* . . . . (Rounder)
Another Saturday Night
Cat Stevens; *Cat Stevens Greatest Hits* . . . . (A&M)
Jimmy Buffett; *Margaritaville Cafe Late Night Menu* . . . .(Margaritaville)
Sam Cooke; *The Man And His Music* . . . . (RCA)
This Is Sam Cooke . . . . (RCA)
Anytime
Brian McKnight; *Anytime* . . . . (Motown)
Now That's What I Call Music!-#1-C . . . . (Virgin)
Apartment #9
Melissa Etheridge; *Tammy Wynette...Remembered-C* . . . . (Asylum)
Tammy Wynette; *Tammy Wynette-Anniversary-20 Years Of Hits* . . . .(Epic)
Tammy Wynette's Greatest Hits . . . .(Epic)
Are You Lonely For Me
Rude Boys; *Rude Awakening* . . . . (Atlantic)
Are You Lonesome To-night?
Elvis Presley; *A Valentine Gift For You* . . . . (RCA)
Elvis' Golden Records, Volume 3 . . . . (RCA)

From Memphis To Vegas/From Vegas To Memphis . . . .(RCA)
Worldwide 50 Gold Award Hits, Vol. 1, Parts 1 & 2 . . . .(RCA)
As I Lay Me Down
Sophie B. Hawkins; *Whaler* . . . . (Columbia)
Ask The Lonely
Vonda Shepard; *ST/Songs From ''Ally McBeal'' Featuring Vonda*
Shepard . . . .(550/Epic)
At Seventeen
Janis Ian; *Between The Lines* . . . . (Columbia)
Super Hits Of The '70s-Have A Nice Day-#15-C . . . . (Rhino)
Autumn Leaves
Barbra Streisand; *Je m'appelle Barbra* . . . . (Columbia)
Frank Sinatra; *Night We Called It A Day* . . . . (Capitol)
Nat ''King'' Cole; *Blossom Fell* . . . . (Capitol)
Roger Miller; *Music Of The 1950s-C* . . . . (MCA)
Roger Williams; *Best Of Roger Williams* . . . . (MCA)
Roger Williams-Golden Hits-#2 . . . . (MCA)
Baby I Need Your Loving
Four Tops; *Four Tops' Greatest Hits* . . . . (Motown)
Four Tops-Anthology . . . . (Motown)
The Ultimate Collection-Four Tops . . . . (Motown)
Johnny Rivers; *Johnny Rivers' Greatest Hits* . . . . (Capitol)
Johnny Rivers-Anthology 1964-1977 . . . . (Rhino)
Back 2 Good
Matchbox Twenty; *Yourself Or Someone Like You* . . . . (Lava)
Back Here
BBMak; *Now That's What I Call Music!-#5-C* . . . .(Virgin)
Sooner Or Later . . . . (Hollywood)
Back On The Street Again
Sunshine Company; *Even More Nuggets-C* . . . . (Rhino)
Back To The World
Tevin Campbell; *Back To The World* . . . . (Qwest)
Band Of Gold
Freda Payne; *Beachbeat Draggin'* . . . . (Dunhill Compact Classics)
Didn't It Blow Your Mind: Soul Hits Of The '70s-#2-C . . . . . . (Rhino)
Freda Payne's Greatest Hits . . . .(HDH)
Be My Life's Companion
Mills Brothers; *Best Of The Mills Brothers* . . . . (MCA)
The Mills Brothers-Best Of The Decca Years . . . . (Decca)
Rosemary Clooney; *Rosemary Clooney-16 Most Requested Songs* . . . . (Legacy)
Be With You
Enrique Iglesias; *Enrique* . . . . (Overbrook/Interscope)
Because Of You
98 Degrees; *98 Degrees And Rising* . . . . (Universal)
Now That's What I Call Music!-#2-C . . . .(Virgin)
Before You Kill Us All
Randy Travis; *This Is Me* . . . . (Warner Bros.)
Behind Blue Eyes
Who; *Hooligans* . . . . (MCA)
Join Together . . . . (MCA)
Who's Last . . . . (MCA)
Who's next . . . . (MCA)
Bits And Pieces
Dave Clark Five; *History Of The Dave Clark Five* . . . . (Hollywood)
Bleeders
Wallflowers; *Bringing Down The Horse* . . . . (Interscope)
Blue
LeAnn Rimes; *Blue* . . . . (MCG/Curb)
Blue Bayou
Linda Ronstadt; *Linda Ronstadt's Greatest Hits, Volume Two* . . . . . . (Asylum)
Simple Dreams . . . . (Asylum)
Roy Orbison; *For The Lonely: A Roy Orbison Anthology 1959-1965* . . . (Rhino)
In Dreams-Greatest Hits . . . . (Orbison)
Roy Orbison-More Greatest Hits . . . . (Monument)
Roy Orbison's All-Time Greatest Hits-#1 & 2 . . . . (Monument)
Roy Orbison & Friends; *Black & White Night-Live* . . . . (Virgin)
Blue Kentucky Girl
Emmylou Harris; *Blue Kentucky Girl* . . . . (Warner Bros.)
Profile II-The Best Of Emmylou Harris . . . . (Warner Bros.)
Loretta Lynn; *Loretta Lynn's Greatest Hits* . . . . (MCA)
Blue Moon
Billie Holiday; *Billie's Blues* . . . . (Blue Note)
First Verve Sessions . . . . (Verve)
History Of Billie Holiday . . . . (Verve)
Elvis Presley; *Elvis Presley* . . . . (RCA)
The Sun Sessions . . . . (RCA)
Marcels; *Best Of The Marcels* . . . . (Rhino)
Billboard Top Rock 'N' Roll Hits-1961-C . . . . (Rhino)
Blue Side Of Lonesome
George Jones; *George Jones Sings The Great Songs Of Leon*
Payne . . . .(Hollywood/DNA-Rounder)
Jim Reeves; *Best Of Jim Reeves-#4* . . . . (RCA)
Blues Leave Me Alone
Eric Clapton; *From The Cradle* . . . . (Duck/Reprise)
Boxcars
Butch Hancock; *Eats Away The Night* . . . . (Sugar Hill)
Joe Ely; *Best Of Joe Ely* . . . . (MCA)
Freight Train Blues-Classic Railroad Songs-#4-C . . . . (Rounder)
Honky Tonk Masquerade . . . . (MCA)

Rosie Flores; *Rockabilly Filly* . . . . . (Hightone)
Brick
Ben Folds Five; *Whatever And Ever Amen* . . . . . (Caroline/550)
Broken Home
Papa Roach; *Infest* . . . . . (DreamWorks/SKG)
Brokenhearted
Brandy featuring Wanya Morris; *Brandy* . . . . . (Atlantic)
Buenos Noches From A Lonely Room
Dwight Yoakam; *Buenas Noches From A Lonely Room* . . . . . (Reprise)
Burning Of The Midnight Lamp
Jimi Hendrix; *Essential Jimi Hendrix* . . . . . (Reprise)
Lifelines/Jimi Hendrix Story . . . . . (Reprise)
Jimi Hendrix Experience; *Electric Ladyland* . . . . . (Reprise)
Radio One . . . . . (Rykodisc)
Living Colour; *Biscuits* . . . . . (Epic)
Bury Me Not On The Lone Prairie
Jimmy C. Newman; *Cajun Cowboy* . . . . . (Plantation)
But Not For Me
Billie Holiday; *Silver Collection* . . . . . (Verve)
Chet Baker; *Let's Get Lost-Best Of Chet Baker Sings* . . . . . (Blue Note)
Ella Fitzgerald; *Ella Sings Jazz* . . . . . (MCA Jazz)
Elvis Costello; *Glory Of Gershwin Featuring Larry Adler-C* . . . . . (Mercury)
Harry Connick, Jr.; *ST/When Harry Met Sally* . . . . . (Columbia)
Judy Garland; *Best Of Judy Garland* . . . . . (MCA)
Original London Cast; *Crazy For You* . . . . . (RCA)
Original Soundtrack; *Manhattan* . . . . . (CBS Masterworks)
Sarah Vaughan; *Sarah Vaughan Sings George Gershwin Songbook, Vol. 2* . . . . . (Emarcy)
Bye Bye Love
Everly Brothers; *Everly Brothers' All-Time Greatest Hits* . . . . . (Curb)
Everly Brothers-Cadence Classics-Their 20 Greatest Hits . . . . . (Rhino)
Very Best Of The Everly Brothers . . . . . (Warner Bros.)
Simon & Garfunkel; *Bridge Over Troubled Water* . . . . . (Columbia)
California
Joni Mitchell; *Blue* . . . . . (Reprise)
Can't Find My Way Home
Blind Faith; *Blind Faith* . . . . . (Polydor)
Eric Clapton-Crossroads-C . . . . . (Polydor)
ST/1969 . . . . . (Polydor)
Can't You Hear Me Callin'?
Ricky Skaggs; *Bluegrass Super Hits-C* . . . . . (Columbia)
Favorite Country Songs . . . . . (Epic)
Highway & Heartaches . . . . . (Epic)
Cat's In The Cradle
Harry Chapin; *Greatest Stories-Live* . . . . . (Elektra)
Harry Chapin-Anthology . . . . . (Elektra)
Verities & Balderdash . . . . . (Elektra)
Changing Partners
Bing Crosby; *Bing Crosby* . . . . . (MCA Special Prod.)
Kay Starr; *Capitol Collectors Series-Kay Starr* . . . . . (Capitol)
Patti Page; *Patti Page-Golden Hits* . . . . . (Mercury)
Charlie Brown's Parents
Dishwalla; *Pet Your Friends* . . . . . (A&M)
Chemicals Between Us, The
Bush; *The Science Of Things* . . . . . (Trauma)
Cindy, Oh Cindy
Beach Boys; *Surfin' Safari-Surfin' Usa (Remasterd With Bonus Tracks)* . . . . . (Capitol)
Circus Girl
Gretchen Peters; *The Secret Of Life* . . . . . (Purple Crayon Prod.)
Clementine
Bobby Darin; *Bobby Darin-At The Copa* . . . . . (Bainbridge)
The Bobby Darin Story . . . . . (Atlantic)
Original Soundtrack; *Children's Favorites* . . . . . (Kid Rhino/Rhino 4 Kids)
Come Back To Me
Janet Jackson; *Janet Jackson's Rhythm Nation 1814* . . . . . (A&M)
Come On Back
Carlene Carter; *I Fell In Love* . . . . . (Reprise)
Come See About Me
Diana Ross & The Supremes; *16 #1 Hits From The Early '60s-C* . . . . . (Motown)
Diana Ross & The Supremes' Greatest Hits . . . . . (Motown)
Diana Ross & The Supremes-Anthology (1962-1969) . . . . . (Motown)
Diana Ross & The Supremes-At The Copa . . . . . (Motown)
Every Great #1 Hit . . . . . (Motown)
Girl Groups-Story Of A Sound-C . . . . . (Rhino)
Motown Story-First 25 Years-C . . . . . (Motown)
Motown Superstar Series-#1-Diana Ross & The Supremes . . . . . (Motown)
Corrina, Corrina
Asleep At The Wheel featuring Brooks & Dunn; *Tribute To The Music Of Bob Wills And The Texas Playboys-C* . . . . . (Liberty)
Big Joe Turner; *Best Of Big Joe Turner* . . . . . (Pablo)
Big Joe Turner's Greatest Hits . . . . . (Atlantic)
Bob Dylan; *Freewheelin'* . . . . . (Columbia)
Ray Peterson; *Good Old Rock & Roll-C* . . . . . (International Mktg. Group)
Super Hits-#1-C . . . . . (Gusto)
Steppenwolf; *Live Steppenwolf* . . . . . (MCA)
Could've Been
Tiffany; *Tiffany* . . . . . (MCA)
Tiffany's Greatest Hits . . . . . (Hip-O)
Cowboy's Wild Song To His Herd
Skip Gorman; *A Cowboy's Wild Song To His Herd* . . . . . (Rounder)
Creep
TLC; *CrazySexyCool* . . . . . (LaFace)
Cry Softly Lonely One
Roy Orbison; *Classic (1965-1968)* . . . . . (Rhino)
Crying
Don McLean; *Best Of Don McLean* . . . . . (EMI)
Greatest Hits Then & Now . . . . . (EMI)
Roy Orbison; *For The Lonely: 18 Greatest Hits* . . . . . (Rhino)
For The Lonely: A Roy Orbison Anthology 1959-1965 . . . . . (Rhino)
In Dreams-Greatest Hits . . . . . (Orbison)
Roy Orbison's All-Time Greatest Hits-#1 & 2 . . . . . (Monument)
Crying, Waiting, Hoping
Buddy Holly; *Buddy Holly Collection* . . . . . (MCA)
Marshall Crenshaw; *ST/La Bamba* . . . . . (Slash)
Dangerously Lonely
Johnny Lee; *Best Of Johnny Lee* . . . . . (Curb)
Daniel
Elton John; *Don't Shoot Me I'm Only The Piano Player* . . . . . (Polydor)
Elton John's Greatest Hits . . . . . (Polydor)
Wilson Phillips; *Two Rooms-Celebrating The Songs Of Elton John & Bernie Taupin-C* . . . . . (Polydor)
Darling Be Home Soon
Joe Cocker; *Joe Cocker!* . . . . . (A&M)
Joe Cocker-Classics-#4 . . . . . (A&M)
Joe Cocker's Greatest Hits . . . . . (A&M)
Lovin' Spoonful; *Best Of The Lovin' Spoonful-#2* . . . . . (Rhino)
Lovin' '60s-C . . . . . (Priority)
Lovin' Spoonful-Anthology . . . . . (Rhino)
Dear Heart
Andy Williams; *Andy Williams' Greatest Hits* . . . . . (Columbia)
Andy Williams-16 Most Requested Songs . . . . . (Legacy)
Dear Lonely Hearts
Nat "King" Cole; *Capitol Collectors Series-Nat "King" Cole* . . . . . (Capitol)
Ramblin' Rose . . . . . (Capitol)
Dear Uncle Sam
Loretta Lynn; *Honky Tonk Girl: The Loretta Lynn Collection* . . . . . (MCA)
Loretta Lynn's Greatest Hits . . . . . (MCA)
Dedicated To The One I Love
Mamas & The Papas; *Best Of The Mamas & The Papas* . . . . . (MCA)
Farewell To The First Golden Era . . . . . (MCA)
Original Classic Oldies Of The '50s & '60s-#13-C . . . . . (MCA)
Shirelles; *Oldies But Goodies-#10-C* . . . . . (Original Sound)
Shirelles' Greatest Hits . . . . . (Everest)
Shirelles-Anthology 1959-1964 . . . . . (Rhino)
Super Oldies Of The '50s-#4-C . . . . . (Audio Fidelity)
Detroit City
Ace Cannon; *Golden Favorites* . . . . . (Ranwood)
Bill Anderson; *Best Of Bill Anderson* . . . . . (Curb)
Bobby Bare; *Nipper's Greatest Hits Of The '60s-#2-C* . . . . . (RCA)
This Is Bobby Bare . . . . . (RCA)
Chet Atkins; *Country Gems* . . . . . (Pair)
Flatt & Scruggs; *20 All-Time Great Recordings* . . . . . (Columbia)
Hank Williams, Jr.; *Live At Cobo Hall Detroit* . . . . . (Polydor)
Standing In The Shadows . . . . . (Polydor)
Mel Tillis; *Best Of Mel Tillis* . . . . . (MCA)
Live At The Sam Houston Coliseum . . . . . (MGM)
Solomon Burke; *Home In Your Heart-Best Of Solomon Burke* . . . . . (Rhino)
Devil Ain't A Lonely Woman's Friend
Red Steagall; *45-#2824* . . . . . (MCA)
Dinner For One Please James
Nat "King" Cole; *Blossom Fell* . . . . . (Capitol)
Nat "King" Cole-Gift Set . . . . . (Capitol)
Dirt Road Blues
Bob Dylan; *Time Out Of Mind* . . . . . (Columbia)
Distance, The
Cake; *Fashion Nugget* . . . . . (Capricorn)
Does That Blue Moon Ever Shine On You
Toby Keith; *Blue Moon* . . . . . (Polydor Country)
Toby Keith's Greatest Hits, Volume One . . . . . (Mercury)
Doggie In The Window
Patti Page; *Patti Page-16 Most Requested Songs* . . . . . (Legacy)
Patti Page-Golden Hits . . . . . (Mercury)
Patti Page's Greatest Hits . . . . . (Columbia)
Donna
Los Lobos; *ST/La Bamba* . . . . . (Slash)
Ritchie Valens; *American Graffiti-#3-C* . . . . . (MCA)
Best Of Ritchie Valens . . . . . (Rhino)
Heart & Soul Of Rock 'N' Roll-#1-C . . . . . (Rhino)
History Of Latino Rock-#1-C . . . . . (Rhino)
History Of Ritchie Valens . . . . . (Rhino)
Don't Be Cruel
Cheap Trick; *Cheap Trick's Greatest Hits* . . . . . (Epic)
Lap Of Luxury . . . . . (Epic)
Elvis Presley; *Billboard Top Rock 'N' Roll Hits-1956-C* . . . . . (Rhino)
Nipper's Greatest Hits Of The '50s-#2-C . . . . . (RCA)
Number One Hits . . . . . (RCA)
The Great Performances . . . . . (RCA)

The Top Ten Hits . . . . (RCA)
Judds; *Heartland* . . . . (MCA)

Don't Let Me Be Lonely Tonight
James Taylor; *James Taylor's Greatest Hits* . . . . (Warner Bros.)
One Man Dog . . . . (Warner Bros.)

Don't The Girls All Get Prettier At Closing Time
Mickey Gilley; *Make It Like The First Time* . . . . (ISD/Intersound)

Downtown
B-52's; *B-52's* . . . . (Warner Bros.)
Frank Sinatra; *Strangers In The Night* . . . . (Reprise)
Petula Clark; *Dick Clark's 21 All-Time Hits-#2-C* . . . . (Original Sound)
Petula Clark's Greatest Hits . . . . (Crescendo)

Dream A Little Dream Of Me
Ella Fitzgerald; *All That Jazz* . . . . (Pablo)
Mama Cass; *Mama's Big Ones-Her Greatest Hits* . . . . (MCA)
Mama Cass With The Mamas & The Papas; *Best Of The Mamas & The Papas* . . . . (MCA)
Mamas & The Papas-20 Golden Hits . . . . (MCA)
Wayne King & His Orchestra; *78-#22643* . . . . (Victor)

Dreams
Corrs; *Legacy-A Tribute To Fleetwood Mac's Rumours-C* . . . . . . (Lava)
Fleetwood Mac; *25 Years-The Chain* . . . . (Warner Bros.)
Fleetwood Mac Live . . . . (Warner Bros.)
Fleetwood Mac's Greatest Hits . . . . (Warner Bros.)
Rumours . . . . (Warner Bros.)

Eighteen Wheels And A Dozen Roses
Kathy Mattea; *Collection Of Hits* . . . . (Mercury)
Untasted Honey . . . . (Polydor Country)

Eleanor Rigby
Beatles; *Beatles 1* . . . . (Capitol)
Revolver . . . . (Capitol)
The Beatles/1962-1966 . . . . (Capitol)
Ray Charles; *Ray Charles' Greatest Hits-#2* . . . . (Rhino)
Ray Charles-Anthology . . . . (Rhino)

Empty Bed Blues
Bessie Smith; *Bessie Smith-The Collection* . . . . (Legacy)
Empty Bed Blues . . . . (Columbia)
Bette Midler; *Broken Blossom* . . . . (Atlantic)
LaVern Baker; *Atlantic Jazz-Singers-C* . . . . (Atlantic)
LaVern Baker Sings Bessie Smith . . . . (Atlantic)

Estranged
Guns N' Roses; *Use Your Illusion II* . . . . (Geffen)

Every Light In The House
Trace Adkins; *Dreamin' Out Loud* . . . . (Capitol)

Everytime You Go Away
Daryl Hall & John Oates; *Best Of Daryl Hall & John Oates* . . . . . . (RCA)
Voices . . . . (RCA)
Paul Young; *From Time To Time-The Singles Collection* . . . . (Columbia)
Secret Of Association . . . . (Columbia)
T.J. Martell-Music For The Miracle-C . . . . (Epic Portrait Assoc.)

Faded Love
Bob Wills & His Texas Playboys; *Bob Wills & His Texas Playboys-24 Great Hits* . . . . (Polydor)
For The Last Time . . . . (Capitol)
Tiffany Transcriptions-#2-Best Of The Tiffanys . . . . (Rhino)
Mickey Gilley; *Mickey Gilley's Greatest Hits-#1* . . . . (Epic)
Patsy Cline; *12 Greatest Hits* . . . . (MCA)
Shawn Colvin & Lyle Lovett & Asleep At The Wheel; *Ride With Bob-C* . . . . (DreamWorks/SKG)
Willie Nelson; *Greatest Hits (& Some That Will Be)* . . . . (Columbia)

Fading Like A Flower (Every Time You Leave)
Roxette; *Joyride* . . . . (EMI)

Fare Thee Well Love
Rankin Family; *North Country* . . . . (Guardian/Angel)
The Rankins-Collection . . . . (Rounder)

Father
Why Store; *The Why Store* . . . . (MCA)

Fear Of Being Alone
Reba McEntire; *Reba McEntire's Greatest Hits-#3: I'm A Survivor* . . . . (MCA)
What If It's You . . . . (MCA)

Finder Of Lost Loves
Dionne Warwick & Glenn Jones; *The Reel Burt Bacharach-C* . . . . . . (Hip-O)

Fire And Rain
James Taylor; *James Taylor's Greatest Hits* . . . . (Warner Bros.)
Sweet Baby James . . . . (Warner Bros.)
The Concert For New York City-C . . . . (Columbia)
Sammy Kershaw; *Red Hot + Country-C* . . . . (Mercury)

Full Moon And Empty Arms
Frank Sinatra; *A Lovely Way To Spend An Evening* . . . . (ASV)
Sarah Vaughan; *Slightly Classical* . . . . (Roulette)

Funny Familiar Forgotten Feelings
Don Gibson; *Best Of Don Gibson-#1* . . . . (Curb)
Mandy Barnett; *I've Got A Right To Cry* . . . . (Sire)
Tom Jones; *Back To Back-Greatest Hits* . . . . (Rebound)
Country Side Of Tom Jones . . . . (London)
Tom Jones-London Collector-Greatest Hits . . . . (London)

Gal That Got Away
Four Freshmen; *Voices In Love-Love Lost* . . . . (Collector's Choice)
Frank Sinatra; *Complete Capitol Singles Collection* . . . . (Capitol)

Ghost Town
Don Cherry; *Columbia & Monument Sides* . . . . (Collector's Choice)

Glamorous Life
Sheila E.; *The Glamorous Life* . . . . (Warner Bros.)

Go Your Own Way
Cranberries; *Legacy-A Tribute To Fleetwood Mac's Rumours-C* . . . . . . (Lava)
Fleetwood Mac; *25 Years-The Chain* . . . . (Warner Bros.)
Fleetwood Mac Live . . . . (Warner Bros.)
Fleetwood Mac's Greatest Hits . . . . (Warner Bros.)
Rumours . . . . (Warner Bros.)

God Don't Make Lonely Girls
Wallflowers; *Bringing Down The Horse* . . . . (Interscope)

Going Where The Lonely Go
Merle Haggard; *For The Record: Merle Haggard-43 Legendary Hits* . . . (BNA)

Gone Crazy
Alan Jackson; *High Mileage* . . . . (Arista)

Good
Better Than Ezra; *Deluxe* . . . . (Swell/Elektra)

Goodnight Sweetheart
David Kersh; *Goodnight Sweetheart* . . . . (Curb)

Got A Letter From My Kid Today
Asleep At The Wheel; *Tribute To The Music Of Bob Wills And The Texas Playboys-C* . . . . (Liberty)
Merle Haggard & The Strangers; *18 Rare Classics* . . . . (Curb)
Working Man Can't Get Nowhere Today . . . . (Capitol)

Got To Get You Into My Life
Beatles; *Beatles-Box Set* . . . . (Capitol)
Revolver . . . . (Capitol)
Rock 'N' Roll Music . . . . (Capitol)
The Beatles-Anthology-#2 . . . . (Capitol)
Earth, Wind & Fire; *Best Of Earth, Wind & Fire-#1* . . . . (Legacy)
ST/Sgt. Pepper's Lonely Hearts Club Band . . . . (RSO)
Paul McCartney & Wings; *Kampuchea-C* . . . . (Atlantic)

Grand Tour
Aaron Neville; *The Grand Tour* . . . . (A&M)

Great Pretender
Band; *Moondog Matinee* . . . . (Capitol)
Platters; *Billboard Top R&B Hits-1956-C* . . . . (Rhino)
Cruisin'-1956-C . . . . (Increase)
Encore Of Golden Hits-Platters . . . . (Mercury)
Platters-Anthology . . . . (Rhino)
ST/American Graffiti . . . . (MCA)
Super Oldies Of The '50s-#3-C . . . . (Audio Fidelity)
Roy Orbison; *Best Of Roy Orbison-Loved Standards* . . . . (Monument)
Stan Freberg; *Capitol Collectors Series-Stan Freberg* . . . . . . (Capitol)

Green Grow The Lilacs
Tex Ritter; *An American Legend* . . . . (Capitol)
Best Of Tex Ritter . . . . (Capitol)
Best Of Town & Country-#3-C . . . . (Gusto)
Hillbilly Heaven . . . . (Capitol)

Ground Beneath Her Feet, The
U2; *ST/The Million Dollar Hotel* . . . . (Interscope)

Guitars, Cadillacs
Dwight Yoakam; *Guitars, Cadillacs, Etc., Etc.* . . . . (Reprise)
Just Lookin' For A Hit . . . . (Reprise)

Harbor Lights
Boz Scaggs; *Silk Degrees* . . . . (Columbia)
Dinah Washington; *Complete Dinah Washington On Mercury-#2-1950-1952* . . . . (Mercury)
Dinah Washington-Golden Hits . . . . (Mercury)
For Lonely Lovers . . . . (Mercury)
This Is My Story . . . . (Mercury)
Platters; *Super Oldies Of The '60s-#9-C* . . . . (Audio Fidelity)

Have You Ever Been Lonely (Have You Ever Been Blue)
Ernest Tubb; *Best Of Ernest Tubb* . . . . (Curb)
The Country Music Hall Of Fame-Ernest Tubb . . . . (MCA)
Jim Reeves & Patsy Cline; *Jim Reeves' Greatest Hits* . . . . (RCA)
Patsy Cline; *Showcase-With The Jordanaires* . . . . (MCA)

Have You Seen Mary
Sponge; *Wax Ecstatic* . . . . (Columbia)

Heart Is A Lonely Hunter
Reba McEntire; *Read My Mind* . . . . (MCA)
Reba McEntire's Greatest Hits-#3: I'm A Survivor . . . . (MCA)

Heartache Big As Texas
Ricky Van Shelton; *Texas Super Hits-C* . . . . (Columbia)

Heartaches By The Number
Guy Mitchell; *Sentimental Journey-C* . . . . (Dominion Entert.)
Sunshine Guitar . . . . (Collectables)
Unforgettable-Love Songs-Fabulous '50s-C . . . . (Dominion Entert.)
Ray Price; *Columbia Country Classics-#2-Honky Tonk Heroes-C* . . . (Columbia)
Ray Price's Greatest Hits . . . . (Columbia)
Ray Price's Greatest Hits-#1-3 . . . . (Step One)

Heartbreak Hotel
Albert King; *Blues For Elvis* . . . . (Stax)
Elvis Presley; *Elvis As Recorded At Madison Square Garden* . . . . . . (RCA)
Elvis' Golden Records . . . . (RCA)
Elvis-A Legendary Performer, Volume 1 . . . . (RCA)
Nipper's Greatest Hits Of The '50s-#1-C . . . . (RCA)
Worldwide 50 Gold Award Hits, Vol. 1, Parts 1 & 2 . . . . . . (RCA)

Stan Freberg; *Capitol Collectors Series-Stan Freberg* . . . . (Capitol)
Willie Nelson; *Greatest Hits (& Some That Will Be)* . . . . (Columbia)
Willie Nelson & Leon Russell: One For The Road . . . . (Columbia)

Heartbreak U.S.A.
Kitty Wells; *I Love Country-Hits Of The '60s-#1-C* . . . . (Priority)
Kitty Wells' Greatest Songs . . . . (Curb)
The Country Music Hall Of Fame-Kitty Wells . . . . (MCA Special Prod.)

Heaven Help The Lonely
Willie Nile; *Places I Have Never Been* . . . . (Columbia)

He'll Have To Go
Jim Reeves; *60 Years Of Country Music-C* . . . . (RCA)
Best Of Jim Reeves . . . . (RCA)
Billboard Top Country Hits-1960-C . . . . (Rhino)
Great Moments At The Grand Ole Opry-C . . . . (RCA)
Jim Reeves' Greatest Hits . . . . (RCA)
Nipper's Greatest Hits Of The '50s-#1-C . . . . (RCA)
Ry Cooder; *Chicken Skin Music* . . . . (Reprise)

Hello In There
Bette Midler; *Live At Last* . . . . (Atlantic)
John Prine; *John Prine* . . . . (Atlantic)
John Prine-Souvenirs . . . . (Oh Boy)

Hello Walls
Faron Young; *Billboard Top Country Hits-1961-C* . . . . (Rhino)
Willie Nelson; *Essential Willie Nelson* . . . . (RCA)
Willie Nelson-Greatest Songs . . . . (Curb)

Here In My Heart
Al Martino; *Capitol Collectors Series-Al Martino* . . . . (Capitol)

Hey Bulldog
Beatles; *Rock 'N' Roll Music* . . . . (Capitol)
Yellow Submarine . . . . (Capitol)

High Country Snows
Dan Fogelberg; *High Country Snows* . . . . (Full Moon)

High Lonesome Sound
Vince Gill; *Bluegrass Essentials-C* . . . . (Hip-O)
High Lonesome Sound . . . . (MCA)
Vince Gill with Alison Krauss & Union Station; *Grand Ole Opry-75*
Years-#1-C . . . . (MCA)

Hold On
Jamie Walters; *Jamie Walters* . . . . (Atlantic)

Home
Staind; *Dysfunction* . . . . (Flip/Elektra)

Home Again
Carole King; *Tapestry* . . . . (Epic)

Homeward Bound
Paul Simon; *Paul Simon In Concert/Live Rhymin'* . . . . (Columbia)
Paul Simon & George Harrison; *Nobody's Child-Romanian Angel*
Appeal-C . . . . (Warner Bros.)
Simon & Garfunkel; *Collected Works* . . . . (Columbia)
Parsley Sage Rosemary & Thyme . . . . (Columbia)
Simon & Garfunkel's Greatest Hits . . . . (Columbia)
The Concert In Central Park . . . . (Warner Bros.)
Willie Nelson & Waylon Jennings; *Take It To The Limit* . . . . . . (Columbia)

Honey
Bobby Goldsboro; *Billboard Top Pop Hits-1968-C* . . . . (Rhino)
Cruisin'-1968-C . . . . (Increase)

Honey To The Bee
Billie; *Honey To The B* . . . . (Virgin)

How Am I Supposed To Live Without You
Laura Branigan; *Branigan 2* . . . . (Atlantic)
Michael Bolton; *Soul Provider* . . . . (Columbia)

How Do I Live
LeAnn Rimes; *Absolute Dance Hits-C* . . . . (Curb)
You Light Up My Life-Inspirational Songs . . . . (Curb)
Trisha Yearwood; *Songbook-A Collection Of Hits* . . . . (MCA)

How Long Gone
Brooks & Dunn; *If You See Her* . . . . (Arista)

Hubbin' It
Asleep At The Wheel featuring Huey Lewis; *Tribute To The Music Of Bob*
Wills And The Texas Playboys-C . . . . (Liberty)

Human Touch
Bruce Springsteen; *Bruce Springsteen's Greatest Hits* . . . . (Columbia)
Human Touch . . . . (Columbia)

Husbands And Wives
Brooks & Dunn; *Big Country Hits '99-C* . . . . (K-Tel)
If You See Her . . . . (Arista)
Neil Diamond; *Neil Diamond-Love Songs* . . . . (MCA)
Rainbow . . . . (MCA)
Stones . . . . (MCA)
Roger Miller; *Best Of Roger Miller* . . . . (Mercury)
Best Of Roger Miller-His Greatest Songs . . . . (Curb)
Roger Miller-Super Hits . . . . (Epic)
Roger Miller-The Hits . . . . (Mercury)

I Ain't Got Nobody
Bob Wills; *Stay A Little Longer-The Original Columbia*
Recordings . . . . (Roswell/RCA)
Preservation Hall Jazz Band; *Best Of The Preservation Hall*
Jazz Band . . . . (Columbia)

I Am A Rock
Simon & Garfunkel; *Collected Works* . . . . (Columbia)

Simon & Garfunkel's Greatest Hits . . . . (Columbia)
Sounds Of Silence . . . . (Columbia)

I Can Still Feel You
Collin Raye; *The Walls Came Down* . . . . (Epic)

I Can't Reach Her Anymore
Sammy Kershaw; *Haunted Heart* . . . . (Mercury)

I Can't Stop Loving You
Don Gibson; *60 Years Of Country Music-C* . . . . (RCA)
Collector's Series-Don Gibson . . . . (RCA)
Stars Of The Grand Ole Opry-1926-1974-C . . . . (RCA)
Elvis Presley; *Aloha from Hawaii via Satellite* . . . . (RCA)
Elvis As Recorded At Madison Square Garden . . . . (RCA)
Elvis Recorded Live On Stage In Memphis . . . . (RCA)
From Memphis To Vegas/From Vegas To Memphis . . . . (RCA)
Ray Charles; *Ray Charles' Greatest Hits-#2* . . . . (Rhino)
Ray Charles-Anthology . . . . (Rhino)
Roy Orbison; *Best Of Roy Orbison-Loved Standards* . . . . (Monument)
Legendary Roy Orbison . . . . (Sony Music Special Prod.)

I Count The Minutes
Ricky Martin; *Ricky Martin* . . . . (Columbia)

I Don't Wanna
Aaliyah; *Next Friday* . . . . (Priority)

I Don't Wanna Live Without Your Love
Chicago; *Chicago 19* . . . . (Reprise)
Chicago's Greatest Hits-1982-1989 . . . . (Full Moon)

I Don't Want To Miss A Thing
Aerosmith; *ST/Armageddon-The Album* . . . . (Columbia)
Mark Chesnutt; *I Don't Want To Miss A Thing* . . . . (MCA)

I Drive Myself Crazy
'N Sync; *'N Sync* . . . . (RCA)
Totally Hits-#2-C . . . . (Elektra)

I Get Lonely
Janet; *Velvet Rope* . . . . (Virgin)

I Go To Pieces
Del Shannon; *Rock On!* . . . . (Gone Gator)
Peter And Gordon; *Best Of Peter And Gordon* . . . . (Rhino)
History Of British Rock-#3-C . . . . (Rhino)
Southern Pacific; *County Line* . . . . (Warner Bros.)
Southern Pacific's Greatest Hits . . . . (Warner Bros.)

I Got The Hook Up
Master P featuring Sons Of Funk; *ST/I Got The Hook Up* . . . (No Limit/Priority)
Sons Of Funk; *The Game Of Funk* . . . . (No Limit/Priority)

I Guess That's Why They Call It The Blues
Elton John; *Elton John's Greatest Hits-1976-1986* . . . . (MCA)
Too Low For Zero . . . . (MCA)

I Knew You When
Billy Joe Royal; *Billy Joe Royal's Greatest Hits* . . . . (Columbia)

I Looked Away
Derek And The Dominos; *Layla* . . . . (Polydor)

I Love You Drops
Bill Anderson; *Bill Anderson's Greatest Hits* . . . . (Varese Sarabande)

I Miss My Homies
Master P; *Ghetto D* . . . . (No Limit/Priority)

I Miss You
Aaron Hall; *The Truth* . . . . (Silas)

I Miss You A Little
John Michael Montgomery; *John Michael Montgomery's*
Greatest Hits . . . . (Atlantic)

I Need You
Beatles; *ST/Help!* . . . . (Capitol)

I Still Miss Someone
Johnny Cash; *The Man In Black-His Greatest Hits* . . . . (Legacy)

I Think It's Gonna Rain Today
Bette Midler; *ST/Beaches* . . . . (Atlantic)
Judy Collins; *In My Life* . . . . (Elektra)
Neil Diamond; *Rainbow* . . . . (MCA)
Stones . . . . (MCA)
Randy Newman; *12 Songs* . . . . (Reprise)
Randy Newman . . . . (Warner Archives)

I Walk Alone
Marty Robbins; *Lifetime Of Song-1951-1982* . . . . (Columbia)
Marty Robbins' All-Time Greatest Hits . . . . (Columbia)
Marty Robbins' Greatest Hits-#3 . . . . (Columbia)

I Walk Alone
Los Lobos; *The Neighborhood* . . . . (Slash)

I Will Wait
Hootie & The Blowfish; *Musical Chairs* . . . . (Atlantic)

I Wish
R. Kelly; *Now That's What I Call Music!-#6-C* . . . . (Virgin)
TP-2.com . . . . (Jive)

I'd Die Without You
PM Dawn; *Bliss Album...?* . . . . (Gee Street)

I'd Rather Miss You
Little Texas; *First Time For Everything* . . . . (Warner Bros.)

If He Should Break Your Heart
Journey; *Trial By Fire* . . . . (Columbia)

If Heaven Could Find Me
Ambrosia; *Life Beyond L.A.* . . . . (Warner Bros.)

If I Didn't Have You
Randy Travis; *Randy Travis' Greatest Hits-#1* . . . . (Warner Bros.)
If My Heart Had Wings
Faith Hill; *Breathe* . . . . (Warner Bros.)
If You Needed Somebody
Bad Company; *Holy Water* . . . . (Atco)
If You Think You're Lonely Now
Bobby Womack; *The Poet* . . . . (Razor & Tie)
K-Ci Hailey; *ST/Jason's Lyric* . . . . (Mercury)
I'll Be Missing You
Puff Daddy & Family & Faith Evans & 112; *No Way Out* . . . . (Bad Boy/Arista)
I'll Be Seeing You
Billie Holiday; *Billie Holiday At Carnegie Hall-Billie Holiday Story-#6* . . . . (Verve)
Essential Billie Holiday-Carnegie Hall Concert . . . . (Verve)
Jackie Gleason; *Best Of Jackie Gleason & His Orchestra* . . . . (Curb)
Judy Collins; *Judith* . . . . (Elektra)
Skyliners; *Skyliners' Greatest Hits* . . . . (Original Sound)
Tommy Dorsey & Frank Sinatra; *Those Wonderful Years (WWII Love Songs)-C* . . . . (JCI Assoc. Labels)
Tommy Dorsey & His Orchestra; *Kiss The Boys Goodbye-Classic Songs Of WWII-#1* . . . . (RCA)
I'll Sail My Ship Alone
George Jones; *20 Golden Pieces Of George Jones* . . . . (Bulldog)
Mickey Gilley; *Mickey Gilley's Greatest Hits-#1* . . . . (Epic)
Patsy Cline; *Always* . . . . (MCA)
Portrait Of Patsy Cline . . . . (MCA)
Ray Price; *Ray Price's Greatest Hits-#1-3* . . . . (Step One)
I'll Walk Alone
Dinah Shore; *Dinah Shore's Greatest Hits* . . . . (Curtom)
I'm A Lonesome Fugitive
Merle Haggard; *Merle Haggard-16 Biggest Hits* . . . . (Legacy)
Merle Haggard & The Strangers; *Best Of Merle Haggard & The Strangers* . . . . (Capitol)
Capitol Collectors Series-Merle Haggard & The Strangers . . . . (Capitol)
Songs I'll Always Sing . . . . (Capitol)
Roy Buchanan; *Roy Buchanan* . . . . (Polydor)
I'm Blue (The Gong-Gong Song)
Ikettes; *Great R&B Female Groups-Hits Of The '60s-C* . . . . (K-Tel)
I'm Gonna Miss You In The Morning
Quincy Jones; *Quincy Jones-Classics-#3* . . . . (A&M)
Quincy Jones-The Best . . . . (A&M)
Sounds... And Stuff Like That!! . . . . (A&M)
I'm Gonna Sit Right Down And Write Myself A Letter
Billy Williams; *Stardust: The Classic Decca Hits & Standards Collection-C* . . . . (Decca)
Fats Waller; *Fats Waller* . . . . (RCA Special Prod.)
Frank Sinatra; *Sinatra-Basie* . . . . (Reprise)
Songs For Young Lovers & Swing Easy . . . . (Capitol)
Nat "King" Cole; *Just One Of Those Things (& More)* . . . . (Capitol)
Nat "King" Cole-Gift Set . . . . (Capitol)
Original Cast; *Ain't Misbehavin'* . . . . (RCA)
I'm Just Talkin' About Tonight
Toby Keith; *Pull My Chain* . . . . (DreamWorks/SKG)
I'm Lonesome Without You
Country Gentlemen; *Sugar Hill Collection* . . . . (Sugar Hill)
Lonesome Standard Time; *Legacy-A Tribute To The First Generation Of Bluegrass-C* . . . . (Sugar Hill)
Stanley Brothers & The Clinch Mountain Boys; *Classic Bluegrass-Stanley Brothers & The Clinch Mountain Boys* . . . . (Rebel)
I'm So Lonesome I Could Cry
B.J. Thomas; *B.J. Thomas' Greatest Hits* . . . . (Rhino)
Cowboy Junkies; *Trinity Session* . . . . (RCA)
Hank Williams; *24 Of Hank Williams' Greatest Hits* . . . . (Polydor)
Hank Williams-40 Greatest Hits . . . . (Polydor)
I'm So Lonesome I Could Cry-1949 . . . . (Polydor)
Hank Williams, Jr.; *Very Best Of Hank Williams, Jr.* . . . . (Polydor)
Jim Rooney; *One Day At A Time* . . . . (Rounder)
Johnny Cash; *Hank Williams Songbook-C* . . . . (Columbia)
Keb' Mo'; *Timeless: Hank Williams Tribute-C* . . . . (Lost Highway/IDJMG)
I'm Thinking Tonight Of My Blue Eyes
Gene Autry; *All Time Legends Of Country Music-C* . . . . (Legacy)
In Pictures
Alabama; *Alabama-Super Hits* . . . . (RCA)
In Pictures . . . . (RCA)
In The Valley
Marty Robbins; *Gunfighter Ballads & Trail Songs* . . . . (Legacy)
Incomplete
Sisqo; *Now That's What I Call Music!-#5-C* . . . . (Virgin)
Unleash The Dragon . . . . (Dragon/Def Soul/IDJMG)
Inside
Patti Rothberg; *Between The 1 And The 9* . . . . (EMI)
Invitation To The Blues
Holly Cole; *Temptation* . . . . (Metro Blue)
Tom Waits; *Small Change* . . . . (Asylum)
Is Your Mama Gonna Miss Ya?
Bryan Adams; *Waking Up The Neighbours* . . . . (A&M)
It Gets Lonely In A Small Town
Greg Brown; *One More Goodnight Kiss* . . . . (Red House)
It Might As Well Rain Until September
Carole King; *More American Graffiti-C* . . . . (MCA)
It Won't Be Long
Beatles; *Meet The Beatles!* . . . . (Capitol)
With The Beatles . . . . (Parlophone)
It's A Lonesome Old Town (When You're Not Around)
Ben Bernie & His Orchestra featuring Donald Saxon; *78-#4943* . . . . (Brunswick)
Frank Sinatra; *Sings For Only The Lonely* . . . . (EMI-Capitol Entert. Properties)
Lena Horne; *Love Is The Thing* . . . . (RCA)
Les Paul; *Les Paul's Greatest Hits* . . . . (Pair)
Sting; *ST/Leaving Las Vegas* . . . . (Pangaea)
It's Lonely Out There
Pam Tillis; *All Of This Love* . . . . (Arista)
It's Over
Roy Orbison; *Roy Orbison's All-Time Greatest Hits-#1 & 2* . . . . (Monument)
Roy Orbison-Super Hits . . . . (Columbia)
Very Best Of Roy Orbison . . . . (Virgin)
I've Been Lonely Too Long
Rascals; *Rascals-Anthology 1965-1972* . . . . (Rhino)
Very Best Of The Rascals . . . . (Rhino)
Jimmy Mack
Martha & The Vandellas; *Billboard Top R&B Hits-1967-C* . . . . (Rhino)
Compact Command Performances-Martha Reeves & The Vandellas . . . . (Motown)
Martha Reeves & The Vandellas-Anthology . . . . (Motown)
Motown Story-First 25 Years-C . . . . (Motown)
Motown Superstar Series-#11-Martha Reeves & The Vandellas . . . . (Motown)
Top 10 With A Bullet-Motown Girl Groups-C . . . . (Motown)
John Doe No. 24
Mary Chapin Carpenter; *Stones In The Road* . . . . (Columbia)
Johnny Has Gone For A Soldier
Jo Stafford; *American Folk Songs* . . . . (Corinthian)
Just A Little Lovin' (Will Go A Long, Long Way)
Eddy Arnold; *Best Of Eddy Arnold* . . . . (RCA)
Eddy Arnold-Pure Gold . . . . (RCA)
Just Call Me Lonesome
Radney Foster; *Del Rio, TX 1959* . . . . (Arista)
Just Walking In The Rain
Johnnie Ray; *16 Most Requested Songs Of The '50s-#1-C* . . . . (Legacy)
Best Of Johnnie Ray . . . . (Columbia)
Johnnie Ray-16 Most Requested Songs . . . . (Legacy)
Johnnie Ray's Greatest Hits . . . . (Sony Music Special Prod.)
Kindly Keep It Country
Vince Gill; *The Key* . . . . (MCA)
King Of The Mountain
George Strait; *Blue Clear Sky* . . . . (MCA)
Latest Greatest Straitest Hits . . . . (MCA)
Kiss The Rain
Billie Myers; *A Taste Of '98-C* . . . . (Universal)
Growing Pains . . . . (Universal)
Last Lonely Eagle
New Riders Of The Purple Sage; *Best Of New Riders Of The Purple Sage* . . . . (Columbia)
New Riders Of The Purple Sage . . . . (Columbia)
Last Waltz, The
Engelbert Humperdinck; *Engelbert Humperdinck-16 Most Requested Songs* . . . . (Epic)
Last Worthless Evening
Don Henley; *End Of The Innocence* . . . . (Geffen)
Lately
Divine; *Fairy Tales* . . . . (Pendulum)
Laugh Laugh
Beau Brummels; *Best Of The Beau Brummels* . . . . (Rhino)
Heart & Soul Of Rock 'N' Roll-#1-C . . . . (Rhino)
Introducing The Beau Brummels . . . . (Rhino)
Nuggets-#7-Early San Francisco-C . . . . (Rhino)
Layla
Derek And The Dominos; *Classic Rock 1966-1988-C* . . . . (Atlantic)
Eric Clapton-Crossroads-C . . . . (Polydor)
Layla . . . . (Polydor)
ST/Goodfellas . . . . (Atlantic)
Eric Clapton; *Eric Clapton-Unplugged* . . . . (Reprise)
Leave It Alone
Living Colour; *Stain* . . . . (Epic)
Leave It Alone
Forester Sisters; *Forester Sisters' Greatest Hits* . . . . (Warner Bros.)
Leaving October
Sons Of The Desert; *Whatever Comes First* . . . . (Epic)
Leaving On A Jet Plane
Chantal Kreviazuk; *ST/Armageddon-The Album* . . . . (Columbia)
John Denver; *John Denver's Greatest Hits* . . . . (RCA)
Rhymes & Reasons . . . . (RCA)
Kendalls; *Super Country Hits Of The '70s-C* . . . . (Gusto)
Peter, Paul & Mary; *10 Years Together/The Best Of Peter, Paul and Mary* . . . . (Warner Bros.)
Album 1700 . . . . (Warner Bros.)
Letter, The
Box Tops; *Billboard Top Rock 'N' Roll Hits-1967-C* . . . . (Rhino)
Box Tops' Greatest Hits . . . . (Rhino)

Cruisin'-1967-C . . . . (Increase)
Oldies But Goodies-#12-C . . . . (Original Sound)
Rockin' '60s-C . . . . (Priority)
Joe Cocker; *Joe Cocker Live* . . . . (Capitol)
Joe Cocker-Classics-#4 . . . . (A&M)
Joe Cocker's Greatest Hits . . . . (A&M)
Mad Dogs & Englishmen . . . . (A&M)
Vernon Green & The Medallions; *Oldies But Goodies-#1-C* . . . (Original Sound)
Vernon Green & The Medallions-Golden Classics . . . . (Collectables)

Life Goes On
Little Texas; *Little Texas' Greatest Hits* . . . . (Warner Bros.)

Life Line
Nilsson; *The Point* . . . . (RCA)

Like A Rolling Stone
Bob Dylan; *Biograph*. . . . . (Columbia)
Bob Dylan At Budokan . . . . (Columbia)
Bob Dylan's Greatest Hits . . . . (Columbia)
Highway 61 Revisited . . . . (Columbia)
More American Graffiti-#4-C . . . . (MCA)
Self Portrait . . . . (Columbia)
Bob Dylan And The Band; *Before The Flood* . . . . (Columbia)
Jimi Hendrix; *ST/Jimi Plays Monterey* . . . . (Reprise)
Jimi Hendrix Experience; *Jimi Hendrix Experience* . . . . (Reprise)
Rolling Stones; *Stripped* . . . . (Virgin)

Little Child
Beatles; *Meet The Beatles!* . . . . (Capitol)

Little White Cloud That Cried
Johnnie Ray; *Best Of Johnnie Ray* . . . . (Columbia)
Best Of Johnnie Ray . . . . (Exact)
Johnnie Ray's Greatest Hits . . . . (Sony Music Special Prod.)

Livin' Alone
Beck, Bogert & Appice; *Beck, Bogert & Appice* . . . . (Epic)

Livin' Without You
Nitty Gritty Dirt Band; *Best Of The Nitty Gritty Dirt Band* . . . (Curb)
Dirt, Silver & Gold . . . . (One Way)
Uncle Charlie And His Dog Teddy . . . . (Liberty)
Workin' Band . . . . (Warner Bros.)

Living Without You
Randy Newman; *Randy Newman* . . . . (Warner Archives)
Randy Newman/Live . . . . (Warner Archives)

Living Without Your Love
Dusty Springfield; *Living Without Your Love* . . . . (EMI)
Never Trust A Man In A Rented Tuxedo . . . . (EMI)
Joe Cocker; *Cocker* . . . . (Capitol)

Loneliness Of Evening
Stuart Damon; *Cinderella-The CBS Television Network
Production* . . . . (Columbia)

Lonely
Tracy Lawrence; *Lessons Learned* . . . . (Atlantic)

Lonely
Britney Spears; *Britney* . . . . (Jive)

Lonely And Gone
Montgomery Gentry; *Tattoos & Scars* . . . . (Columbia)

Lonely At The Top
Randy Newman; *Randy Newman/Live* . . . . (Warner Archives)
Sail Away . . . . (Reprise)

Lonely Avenue
Crickets; *Liberty Years* . . . . (EMI)
Ramsey Lewis Trio; *Greatest Hits Of Ramsey Lewis* . . . . . (Chess)
Ray Charles; *Birth Of Soul-Complete Atlantic R&B 1952-1959-C* . . . (Atlantic)

Lonely Blue Boy
Conway Twitty; *Conway Twitty's Greatest Hits* . . . . (Curb)
Very Best Of Conway Twitty . . . . (MCA)

Lonely Boy
Andrew Gold; *Listen To The Music-'70s California-C* . . . . . (Rhino)
Super Hits Of The '70s-Have A Nice Day-#19-C . . . . (Rhino)
What's Wrong With This Picture? . . . . (Asylum)

Lonely Bull (El Solo Torro)
Herb Alpert & The Tijuana Brass; *Four Sider* . . . . (A&M)
Herb Alpert & The Tijuana Brass' Greatest Hits . . . . . . (A&M)
Herb Alpert & The Tijuana Brass-Classics-#1 . . . . (A&M)
The Lonely Bull . . . . (A&M)

Lonely Child
Styx; *Equinox* . . . . (A&M)

Lonely Children
Foreigner; *Double Vision*. . . . . (Atlantic)

Lonely Days
Bee Gees; *Bee Gees-Gold* . . . . (Polydor)
Here At Last...Bee Gees...Live . . . . (Polydor)
One Night Only . . . . (Polydor)

Lonely Daze
Ginuwine; *The Bachelor* . . . . (550 Music)

Lonely Girls
Lucinda Williams; *Essence* . . . . (Lost Highway/IDJMG)

Lonely Goatherd
Julie Andrews; *ST/The Sound Of Music*. . . . . (RCA)
Original Cast/Mary Martin; *The Sound Of Music* . . . . (Sony Broadway)

Lonely Is The Night
Billy Squier; *Don't Say No* . . . . (Capitol)

Lonely Looking Sky
Neil Diamond; *Love At The Greek* . . . . (Columbia)
ST/Jonathan Livingston Seagull . . . . (Columbia)

Lonely Nights
Mickey Gilley; *Greatest Country Hits Of The '80s-1982-C*. . . . . (Columbia)
Mickey Gilley's Biggest Hits . . . . (Epic)
Ten Years Of Hits . . . . (Epic)
You Don't Know Me . . . . (Epic)

Lonely Nights
White Lion; *Pride* . . . . (Atlantic)

Lonely Nights
Bryan Adams; *You Want It, You Got It* . . . . (A&M)

Lonely Ol' Night
John Cougar Mellencamp; *Scarecrow* . . . . (Riva)

Lonely Rose Of Mexico
Sons Of The Pioneers; *Tumbleweed Trails* . . . . (MCA)

Lonely Side Of Love
Patty Loveless; *Country's Greatest Hits-#8-Lonely Hearts-C* . . . . (Priority)
Honky Tonk Angel . . . . (MCA)
Patty Loveless' Greatest Hits . . . . (MCA)

Lonely Stranger
Eric Clapton; *Eric Clapton-Unplugged* . . . . (Reprise)

Lonely Street
Andy Williams; *Andy Williams' Greatest Hits-#2* . . . . . . (Columbia)
Best Of Andy Williams. . . . . (Curb)
Emmylou Harris; *Bluebird* . . . . (Reprise)
George Jones; *20 Golden Pieces Of George Jones* . . . . . . (Bulldog)
Kitty Wells; *Kitty Wells' Greatest Hits* . . . . (Step One)
Mel Tillis; *American Originals-Mel Tillis* . . . . (Columbia)
Patsy Cline; *Sentimentally Yours* . . . . (MCA)

Lonely Surfer
Jack Nitzsche; *Surfin' Hits-C* . . . . (Rhino)
Surfin' Sixties-C . . . . (JCI Assoc. Labels)

Lonely Teardrops
Jackie Wilson; *Billboard Top R&B Hits-1958-C* . . . . (Rhino)
Reet Petite-Best Of Jackie Wilson . . . . (Columbia)
The Jackie Wilson Story . . . . (Epic)
The Jackie Wilson Story-#2 . . . . (Epic)

Lonely Teenager
Dion; *Collectables Presents The History Of Rock-#4-C* . . . . . . (Collectables)
Dion-His Best . . . . (Laurie)
Everything You Always Wanted To Hear By . . . . (Laurie)
The Wanderer . . . . (Laurie)

Lonely Too Long
Rascals; *Collections* . . . . (Warner Special Prod.)
The Ultimate Rascals . . . . (Warner Special Prod.)

Lonely Too Long
Shenandoah; *Now And Then* . . . . (Capitol)

Lonely Too Long
Patty Loveless; *Patty Loveless-Classics* . . . . (Epic)
Super Hits Of 1996-C . . . . (Epic)
The Trouble With The Truth . . . . (Epic)

Lonely Weekend
Yellowjackets; *Samurai Samba* . . . . (Warner Bros.)

Lonely Weekends
Charlie Rich; *Charlie Rich-Complete Smash Sessions*. . . . . . (Mercury)
Lonely Weekends . . . . (Sun)
Sun's Greatest Hits-C . . . . (RCA)
Shelby Lynne; *Tough All Over* . . . . (Epic)

Lonely Wind
Kansas; *Kansas* . . . . (Kirshner)
Two For The Show. . . . . (Kirshner)

Lonely Woman
Branford Marsalis; *Random Abstract*. . . . . (Columbia)
Chris Connors; *Atlantic Jazz-Singers-C*. . . . . (Atlantic)
Modern Jazz Quartet; *Lonely Woman* . . . . (Atlantic)
Sarah Vaughan; *Complete Sarah Vaughan On Mercury-#1-Great Jazz Years-
1954-1956* . . . . (Mercury)
Sylvia Sims; *Atlantic Jazz-Singers-C.* . . . . (Atlantic)

Lonely Women Make Good Lovers
Bob Luman; *Bob Luman-Classic Country* . . . . (Simitar)
Steve Wariner; *Best Of Steve Wariner* . . . . (RCA)
Midnight Fire . . . . (RCA)
Steve Wariner's Greatest Hits . . . . (RCA)
Steve Wariner-Super Hits . . . . (RCA)

Lonely Won't Leave Me Alone
Trace Adkins; *Big Time* . . . . (Capitol)

Lonesome And A Long Way From Home
Eric Clapton; *Eric Clapton*. . . . . (Polydor)

Lonesome Cowboy
Elvis Presley; *Essential Elvis-The First Movies* . . . . (RCA)
Loving You . . . . (RCA)

Lonesome Day Blues
Bob Dylan; *"Love And Theft"* . . . . (Columbia)

Lonesome Indian
Country Gazette; *American & Clean* . . . . (Flying Fish)

Lonesome Jailhouse Blues
Aunt Molly Jackson; *Library Of Congress Recordings* . . . . . . (Rounder)

Lonesome L.A. Cowboy
New Riders Of The Purple Sage; *Adventures Of Panama Red* . . . . . . (Columbia)
Midnight Moonlight . . . . (Relix)
Lonesome Road
4 Seasons; *25th Anniversary Collection* . . . . (Rhino)
Anita O'Day; *Rules Of The Road* . . . .(Pablo)
Frank Sinatra; *The Capitol Years* . . . . (Capitol)
Preservation Hall Jazz Band; *New Orleans-#4* . . . . (Columbia)
Tommy Dorsey; *Sentimental Memories* . . . . (Pair)
Lonesome Road
Van Morrison; *Too Long In Exile* . . . . (Polydor)
Lonesome Road Blues
Big Bill Broonzy; *Feelin' Low Down* . . . .(Crescendo)
Lonesome Road Blues . . . .(Crescendo)
Kentucky Colonels/Clarence White/Doc Watson; *Long Journey Home-
Newport Folk Festival-1964* . . . . (Vanguard)
Muddy Waters; *Muddy Waters Sings Big Bill Broonzy*. . . . . (Chess)
Lonesome Roads
Dwight Yoakam; *This Time* . . . . (Reprise)
Lonesome Rodeo Cowboy
George Strait; *Livin' It Up* . . . .(MCA)
Lonesome Roving Wolves
Rosalie Sorrels; *Lonesome Roving Wolves-Songs & Ballads Of
The West* . . . .(Green Linnet)
Lonesome Standard Time
Kathy Mattea; *Lonesome Standard Time* . . . . (Mercury)
Lonesome Town
Ricky Nelson; *Best Of Ricky Nelson* . . . . (Curb)
Lonesome Valley
Fairfield Four; *ST/O Brother, Where Art Thou?* . . . . (Mercury)
Lonesome Whistle
Hank Williams With His Drifting Cowboys; *Between The Rails: America's
Train Songs-C*. . . . .(Crescendo)
Hank Williams-24 Greatest Hits-#2. (Polydor)
Hank Williams-40 Greatest Hits. . . . . (Polydor)
Johnny Cash; *Story Songs Of The Trains & Rivers* . . . . (Sun)
Little Feat; *Hoy-Hoy!* . . . .(Warner Bros.)
Lonesome, I Know You Too Well
Shawn Mullins; *Beneath The Velvet Sun* . . . . (Columbia)
Long Gone Lonesome Blues
Hank Williams With His Drifting Cowboys; *Hank Williams-24 Greatest
Hits-#2* . . . . (Polydor)
Hank Williams-40 Greatest Hits. . . . . (Polydor)
Sheryl Crow; *Timeless: Hank Williams Tribute-C* . . . . . (Lost Highway/IDJMG)
Long Lonely Highway
Elvis Presley; *ST/Kissin' Cousins*. . . . . (RCA)
Longfellow Serenade
Neil Diamond; *12 Greatest Hits-#2* . . . . (Columbia)
Love At The Greek . . . . (Columbia)
On The Way To The Sky . . . . (Columbia)
Serenade . . . . (Columbia)
Louie Louie
Kingsmen; *Best Of The Kingsmen* . . . . (Rhino)
Billboard Top Rock 'N' Roll Hits-1963-C . . . . (Rhino)
Cruisin'-1963-C . . . .(Increase)
Frat Rock!-C . . . . (Rhino)
Oldies But Goodies-#11-C . . . . (Original Sound)
Rock & Roll Is Here To Stay-C. . . . . (Gusto)
ST/Quadrophenia . . . .(MCA)
WCBS FM 101 History Of Rock-'60s-#1-C . . . . (Collectables)
Louisiana Lonely
Narvel Felts; *45-#114* . . . .(GMC)
Love Don't Live Here Anymore
Madonna; *Like A Virgin* . . . . (Sire)
Something To Remember. . . . .(Maverick/Sire)
Rose Royce; *Rose Royce III/Strikes Again!* . . . .(Whitfield)
Rose Royce's Greatest Hits . . . .(Whitfield)
Love Is Here And Now You're Gone
Diana Ross; *Diana Ross-Anthology* . . . . (Motown)
Love Letters
Diana Krall; *The Look Of Love* . . . . (Impulse!)
Elvis Presley; *A Valentine Gift For You* . . . . (RCA)
Elvis' Gold Records, Volume 4 . . . . (RCA)
Love Letters From Elvis . . . . (RCA)
Ketty Lester; *Sultry Soul Sisters-Wonder Women-#3-C* . . . . (Rhino)
Peggy Lee; *Best Of Peggy Lee* . . . . (MCA)
Ronnie Milsap; *Lost In The Fifties Tonight* . . . . (RCA)
Love Me
Elvis Presley; *24 Karat Hits!* . . . .(Dunhill Compact Classics)
Love Will Never Do (Without You)
Janet Jackson; *Janet Jackson's Rhythm Nation 1814* . . . . (A&M)
Lucky
Britney Spears; *Now That's What I Call Music!-#5-C* . . . . (Virgin)
Oops!...I Did It Again . . . . (Jive)
Man This Lonely, A
Brooks & Dunn; *Borderline* . . . . (Arista)
Many A Long & Lonesome Highway
Rodney Crowell; *Keys To The Highway* . . . . (Columbia)
Taste Of Texas-Songs 'Bout Texas By Texans-C . . . . (Columbia)

Maybe It Was Memphis
Pam Tillis; *Pam Tillis' Greatest Hits* . . . . (Arista)
Pam Tillis-Collection . . . . (Warner Bros.)
Put Yourself In My Place . . . . (Arista)
Melancholy Blue
Trisha Yearwood; *Inside Out* . . . . (MCA)
Message To Michael
Dionne Warwick; *Dionne Warwick*. . . . .(Everest)
Dionne Warwick Greatest Hits . . . . (Everest)
Dionne Warwick-Anthology 1962-1971 . . . . (Rhino)
Hot! Live & Otherwise . . . . (Arista)
Original Rock 'N' Roll Hits Of The '60s-C . . . . (Roulette)
Mirror Mirror
Diamond Rio; *Diamond Rio* . . . . (Arista)
Diamond Rio's Greatest Hits . . . . (Arista)
Miss Me Blind
Culture Club; *Colour By Numbers* . . . .(Virgin)
Miss You
Mick Jagger & Keith Richards; *The Concert For New York City-C* . . (Columbia)
Rolling Stones; *Rewind (1971-1984)* . . . . (Rolling Stones)
Some Girls . . . .(Virgin)
Flashpoint . . . .(Virgin)
Miss You In A Heartbeat
Def Leppard; *Retro Active* . . . . (Mercury)
Miss You Like Crazy
Natalie Cole; *Good To Be Back* . . . . (Elektra)
Missin' You
Little Feat; *Time Loves A Hero* . . . . (Warner Bros.)
Missing
Everything But The Girl; *Amplified Heart*. . . . .(Atlantic)
MTV Party To Go-#9-C . . . .(Tommy Boy)
The Absolute Hits-C . . . .(Atlantic)
The Ultimate Dance Party-1997-C . . . . (Arista)
Missing My Baby
Selena; *Dreaming Of You* . . . .(EMI Latin)
Missing You
Brooks & Dunn; *Tight Rope* . . . . (Arista)
John Waite; *'80s Greatest Rock Hits-#1-Passion & Power-C* . . . . . . (Priority)
Complete John Waite-#1-Falling Backwards. . . . . (EMI)
Essential John Waite-1976-1986 . . . . (Chrysalis)
Tina Turner; *Wildest Dreams* . . . . (Virgin)
Missing You
Brandy/Tamia/Gladys Knight/Chaka Khan; *ST/Set It Off*. . . . . (East West)
Missing You
Mary J. Blige; *Share My World* . . . . (MCA)
The Tour . . . . (MCA)
Missing You
Steve Perry; *Greatest Hits + Five Unreleased* . . . . (Columbia)
Missing You
Case; *Open Letter* . . . . (Def Soul/IDJMG)
Missing You Now
Michael Bolton; *Time, Love & Tenderness* . . . . (Columbia)
Mister Sandman
Chordettes; *Best Of The Chordettes* . . . . (Rhino)
Emmylou Harris; *Evangeline* . . . . (Warner Bros.)
Profile II-The Best Of Emmylou Harris . . . . (Warner Bros.)
Mommy Can I Come Home
Keb' Mo'; *The Door* . . . . (550/Epic/Okeh)
Mood Indigo
Duke Ellington; *1954 Los Angeles Concert* . . . .(Crescendo)
Black, Brown & Beige: 1944-1946 Band Recordings. . . . . (Bluebird)
Carnegie Hall Concert-January 23, 1943 . . . .(Prestige)
Ellington Indigos . . . . (Columbia)
Sophisticated Ellington . . . . (RCA)
Ella Fitzgerald; *Ella A Nice* . . . . (Pablo)
Ella Fitzgerald Sings-#2. . . . . (Verve)
Four Freshmen; *Capitol Collectors Series-Four Freshman* . . . . (Capitol)
Frank Sinatra; *In The Wee Small Hours*. . . . . (Capitol)
Jimmie Lunceford & His Orchestra; *Stomp It Off-#1-1934-1935* . . . . . . (GRP)
Preservation Hall Jazz Band; *Best Of The Preservation Hall
Jazz Band*. . . . . (Columbia)
New Orleans-#4 . . . . (Columbia)
Moonlight On The Colorado
Sons Of The Pioneers; *Songs Of The Trail* . . . .(Pair)
More Than That
Backstreet Boys; *Black & Blue* . . . .(Jive)
Now That's What I Call Music!-#8-C . . . . (Virgin)
Mother I Miss You
John Tesh featuring Dalia; *Grand Passion-C* . . . . (GTS)
Motherless Child
Steve Miller Band; *Steve Miller Band-Anthology* . . . . (Capitol)
Your Saving Grace . . . . (Capitol)
Motherless Children
Eric Clapton; *461 Ocean Boulevard* . . . .(Polydor)
Eric Clapton-Crossroads-C . . . .(Polydor)
From The Cradle . . . . (Duck/Reprise)
Mr. Jones
Counting Crows; *August And Everything After*. . . . . (David Geffen Co.)

Mr. Lonely
Bobby Vinton; *Bobby Vinton-16 Most Requested Songs* . . . . (Legacy)
Bobby Vinton's All-Time Greatest Hits . . . . (Epic)

My All
Mariah Carey; *Butterfly* . . . . (Columbia)
Mariah Carey-#1's . . . . (Columbia)
VH-1 Divas Live-C . . . . (Epic)

My Arms Stay Open All Night
Tanya Tucker; *Tanya Tucker's Greatest Hits* . . . . (Liberty)

My Baby Needs A Shepherd
Emmylou Harris; *Red Dirt Girl* . . . . (Nonesuch)

My Clone Sleeps Alone
Pat Benatar; *In The Heat Of The Night* . . . . (Chrysalis)

My First Night Alone Without You
Bonnie Raitt; *Bonnie Raitt-Collection* . . . . (Warner Bros.)
Home Plate . . . . (Warner Bros.)
Jane Olivor; *First Night* . . . . (Columbia)

My First Night Without You
Cyndi Lauper; *Night To Remember* . . . . (Epic)

My Heart Cries For You
Charlie Rich; *Charlie Rich-20 Golden Hits* . . . . (Sun)
Time For Tears-C . . . . (Sun)
Dinah Shore; *Nipper's Greatest Hits Of The '50s-#1-C* . . . . (RCA)
Guy Mitchell; *Guy Mitchell-16 Most Requested Songs* . . . . (Legacy)

My Heroes Have Always Been Cowboys
Willie Nelson; *All Time Legends Of Country Music-C* . . . . (Legacy)
Cowboy Super Hits-C . . . . (Columbia)
Greatest Country Hits Of The '80s-1980-C . . . . (Columbia)
Greatest Hits (& Some That Will Be) . . . . (Columbia)
ST/My Heroes Have Always Been Cowboys . . . . (RCA)
ST/The Electric Horseman . . . . (Columbia)

My World Is Empty Without You
Diana Ross; *Diana Ross-Anthology* . . . . (Motown)
Evening With Diana Ross . . . . (Motown)
Stevie Wonder; *Down To Earth* . . . . (Motown)

Neon Moon
Brooks & Dunn; *Brand New Man* . . . . (Arista)

Never Ending
Wood; *Songs From Stamford Hill* . . . . (Columbia)

Never Knew Lonely
Vince Gill; *When I Call Your Name* . . . . (MCA)

New York's A Lonely Town
Tradewinds; *Beach Classics-All Original
Recordings-C* . . . . (Dunhill Compact Classics)
Original Golden Hits Of The Great Groups-#1-C . . . . (SSS International)
Surfin' Hits-C . . . . (Rhino)

Next Plane To London
Rose Garden; *Only Love-1965-1969-C* . . . . (JCI Assoc. Labels)

Next To Nothin'
Gene Watson; *From The Heart* . . . . (Row Music Group)

Nights
Ed Bruce; *Night Things* . . . . (RCA)

Nights Are Forever Without You
England Dan & John Ford Coley; *Best Of England Dan & John Ford
Coley* . . . . (Big Tree)
Nights Are Forever Without You . . . . (Big Tree)

No Love
Kevon Edmonds; *24/7* . . . . (RCA)

No More Lonely Nights
Paul McCartney; *All The Best!* . . . . (Capitol)
ST/Give my regards to Broad Street . . . . (Columbia)

No One
Cold; *13 Ways To Bleed On Stage* . . . . (Flip/Geffen/Interscope)

No One To Run With
Allman Brothers Band; *Where It All Begins* . . . . (Epic)

No Other Love
Perry Como; *Easy Listening* . . . . (Pair)

No Woman, No Cry
Bob Marley; *Bob Marley & The Wailers-Live* . . . . (Tuff Gong)
Bob Marley & The Wailers; *Legend: The Best Of Bob Marley & The
Wailers* . . . . (Island)
Natty Dread . . . . (Tuff Gong)
Songs Of Freedom . . . . (Tuff Gong)
Londonbeat; *In The Blood* . . . . (Radioactive/MCA)

Nobody Knows
Kevin Sharp; *Measure Of A Man* . . . . (143/Asylum)
Tony Rich Project; *Words* . . . . (LaFace)

Nobody Wants To Be Lonely
Ricky Martin; *Sound Loaded* . . . . (Columbia)

Nobody's Home
Clint Black; *Killin' Time* . . . . (RCA)

North To Alaska
Dwight Yoakam; *Under The Covers* . . . . (Reprise)
Johnny Horton; *American Originals-Johnny Horton* . . . . (Columbia)
Billboard Top Country Hits-1961-C . . . . (Rhino)
Johnny Horton's Greatest Hits . . . . (Columbia)
Super Hits Of The '60s-C . . . . (Epic)

Nothin' But The Taillights
Clint Black; *Nothin' But The Taillights* . . . . (RCA)

Now I Know
Lari White; *Wishes* . . . . (RCA)

Obviously Five Believers
Bob Dylan; *Blonde On Blonde* . . . . (Columbia)

Oh Lonesome Me
Don Gibson; *20 Top 10 Hits Of The '50s & '60s-C* . . . . (Laurie)
Collector's Series-Don Gibson . . . . (RCA)
Don Gibson's All-Time Greatest Hits . . . . (RCA)
Nipper's Greatest Hits Of The '50s-#1-C . . . . (RCA)
Johnny Cash; *Get Rhythm* . . . . (Sun)
Johnny Cash-Original Golden Hits-#3 . . . . (Sun)
Kentucky HeadHunters; *Pickin' On Nashville* . . . . (Mercury)
Neil Young; *After The Gold Rush* . . . . (Reprise)

Oh Marie
Sheryl Crow; *Sheryl Crow* . . . . (A&M)

Oh! My Papa
Eddie Fisher; *Eddie Fisher's All-Time Greatest Hits-#1* . . . . (RCA)
Hebrew National Kosher Classics-C . . . . (RCA)
Nipper's Greatest Hits Of The '50s-#2-C . . . . (RCA)

Oh, Baby Mine (I Get So Lonely)
Chet Atkins; *Tennessee Guitar Man* . . . . (Pair)
Four Knights; *Those Wonderful Years: Mr. Sandman-C* . . . . (JCI Assoc. Labels)

Oh, Pretty Woman
2 Live Crew; *As Clean As They Wanna Be* . . . . (Luke)
Al Green; *Al Green's Greatest Hits-#2* . . . . (Motown)
I'm Still In Love With You . . . . (Right Stuff)
Ricky Van Shelton; *RVS III* . . . . (Columbia)
Roy Orbison; *In Dreams-Greatest Hits* . . . . (Orbison)
Roy Orbison's All-Time Greatest Hits-#1 & 2 . . . . (Monument)
ST/Pretty Woman . . . . (EMI)
Van Halen; *Diver Down* . . . . (Warner Bros.)

Old Folks At Home
Mormon Tabernacle Choir; *Songs Of The Civil War And Stephen Foster
Favorites* . . . . (Sony Music Classical)
Paul Robeson; *A Man & His Beliefs-Golden Classics-#2* . . . . . (Collectables)

On A Bus To St. Cloud
Gretchen Peters; *The Secret Of Life* . . . . (Purple Crayon Prod.)
Trisha Yearwood; *Thinkin' About You* . . . . (MCA)

On My Own
Patti LaBelle & Michael McDonald; *Chicken Soup For The Couples
Soul-C* . . . . (Rhino)
Patti LaBelle's Greatest Hits . . . . (MCA)
Winner In You . . . . (MCA)

On The Banks Of The Old Pontchartrain
Hank Williams; *American Legends-#18* . . . . (Laserlight)
Complete Hank Williams . . . . (Mercury)

One
Nilsson; *Aerial Ballet* . . . . (RCA)
Everybody's Talkin': The Encore Collection . . . . (BMG Special Prod.)
Nilsson-All-Time Greatest Hits . . . . (RCA)
Three Dog Night; *Best Of Three Dog Night* . . . . (MCA)
Captured Live At The Forum . . . . (MCA)
Joy To The World-Greatest Hits . . . . (MCA)

One Headlight
Wallflowers; *Bringing Down The Horse* . . . . (Interscope)

One Is A Lonely Number
George Jones; *Truckin' On-C* . . . . (Hollywood)

One Less Bell To Answer
5th Dimension; *5th Dimension-Anthology 1967-1973* . . . . (Rhino)
Greatest Hits On Earth . . . . (Arista)
Barbra Streisand; *Barbra Joan Streisand* . . . . (Columbia)
Gladys Knight & The Pips; *Gladys Knight & The Pips-Anthology* . . . (Motown)
If I Were Your Woman . . . . (Motown)

One Lonely Night
REO Speedwagon; *REO Speedwagon-The Hits* . . . . (Epic)
Wheels Are Turnin' . . . . (Epic)

One More Astronaut
I Mother Earth; *Scenery And Fish* . . . . (Capitol)

Only A Lonely Heart Knows
Barbara Mandrell; *Clean Cut* . . . . (MCA)

Only A Lonely Heart Sees
Felix Cavaliere; *Castles In The Air* . . . . (Out Of Print)

Only On Days That End In "Y"
Clay Walker; *Hypnotize The Moon* . . . . (Giant)

Only The Lonely
Frank Sinatra; *Frank Sinatra sings for Only The Lonely* . . . . . . (Capitol)
The Capitol Years . . . . (Capitol)

Only The Lonely
Motels; *All Four One* . . . . (Capitol)
Best Of The Motels-No Vacancy . . . . (Capitol)

Only The Lonely
Aretha Franklin; *Aretha Franklin Sings The Blues* . . . . (Columbia)

Only The Lonely (Know The Way I Feel)
Roy Orbison; *For The Lonely: A Roy Orbison Anthology 1959-1965* . . . (Rhino)
In Dreams-Greatest Hits . . . . (Orbison)
Roy Orbison's All-Time Greatest Hits-#1 & 2 . . . . (Monument)

Only When Ur Lonely
Ginuwine; *The Bachelor* . . . . (550 Music)

Open Up My Window
　Christopher Cross; *Window* . . . .(Rhythm Safari)
Ophelia
　Band; *Best Of The Band* . . . . (Capitol)
　　Northern Lights-Southern Cross . . . . (Capitol)
　　The Last Waltz . . . .(Warner Bros.)
　　To Kingdom Come-The Definitive Collection . . . . (Capitol)
Orphan Girl
　Emmylou Harris; *Wrecking Ball* . . . . (Asylum)
　Gillian Welch; *Revival* . . . . (Almo Sounds)
　Tim O'Brien; *Away Out On The Mountain* . . . . (Sugar Hill)
Outside
　Staind; *Break The Cycle* . . . . (Flip/Elektra)
Owner Of A Lonely Heart
　Yes; *90125* . . . . (Atco)
Papa Was A Rollin' Stone
　Temptations; *20/20-C* . . . . (Motown)
　　25 #1 Hits From 25 Years-C . . . . (Motown)
　　All The Million-Sellers . . . . (Motown)
　　Billboard Top Rock 'N' Roll Hits-1972-C . . . . (Rhino)
　　Compact Command Performances-Temptations . . . . (Motown)
　　Temptations-Anthology-The Best Of The Temptations . . . . . . (Motown)
Paper Cup
　5th Dimension; *Up-Up And Away-The Definitive Collection* . . . . . (Arista)
Pay You Back With Interest
　Hollies; *Best Of The Hollies* . . . .(EMI)
　　History Of British Rock-#4-C . . . . (Rhino)
　　The Hollies' Greatest Hits . . . .(Epic)
Peggy Sue
　Buddy Holly; *Billboard Top Rock 'N' Roll Hits-1957-C* . . . . . . (Rhino)
　　Buddy Holly . . . .(MCA)
　　Buddy Holly-20 Golden Greats . . . . (MCA)
　　Buddy Holly's Greatest Hits . . . . (MCA)
　　More American Graffiti-C . . . .(MCA)
　　Oldies But Goodies-#4-C . . . . (Original Sound)
　　Rock & Roll Collection . . . .(MCA)
People Are Strange
　Doors; *Best Of The Doors* . . . . (Elektra)
Petals
　Mariah Carey; *Rainbow* . . . . (Columbia)
Piano Man
　Billy Joel; *Billy Joel-Greatest Hits, Volume I & Volume II* . . . . (Columbia)
　　Piano Man . . . . (Columbia)
　　Rock Classics Of The '70s-C . . . . (Columbia)
Picture Of Me (Without You)
　George Jones; *Best Of George Jones* . . . .(Epic)
　　Columbia Country Classics-#4-Nashville Sound-C . . . . (Columbia)
　　George Jones-Anniversary-Ten Years Of Hits . . . .(Epic)
　　George Jones-Super Hits . . . .(Epic)
　Lorrie Morgan; *Lorrie Morgan's Greatest Hits* . . . . (BNA)
　　Something In Red . . . . (RCA)
Please Mister Postman
　Beatles; *Beatles-Box Set* . . . . (Capitol)
　　The Beatles' Second Album . . . . (Capitol)
　　With The Beatles . . . . (Parlophone)
　Carpenters; *Carpenters-Classics-#2* . . . . (A&M)
　　Horizon . . . . (A&M)
　　Yesterday Once More . . . . (A&M)
　Marvelettes; *Billboard Top Rock 'N' Roll Hits-1961-C* . . . . . . (Rhino)
　　Marvelettes' Greatest Hits . . . . (Motown)
　　Marvelettes-Anthology . . . . (Motown)
　　Motown Story-First 25 Years-C . . . . (Motown)
Please Remember Me
　Tim McGraw; *A Place In The Sun* . . . . (Curb)
　　Tim McGraw's Greatest Hits . . . . (Curb)
Prayin' For Daylight
　Rascal Flatts; *Rascal Flatts* . . . . (Lyric Street)
Pretty Little Adriana
　Vince Gill; *High Lonesome Sound* . . . . (MCA)
Private Conversation
　Lyle Lovett; *The Road To Ensenada* . . . . (MCA)
Put It On Me
　Ja Rule featuring Li'l Mo And Vita; *Rule 3:36* . . . (Murder Inc./Def Jam/IDJMG)
Rainy Day Women #12 & 35
　Bob Dylan; *Blonde On Blonde* . . . . (Columbia)
　　Bob Dylan's Greatest Hits . . . . (Columbia)
　　Rock Classics Of The '60s-C . . . . (Columbia)
　　ST/Forrest Gump . . . . (Epic/Sony Music Soundtrax)
　　Bob Dylan And The Band; Before The Flood . . . . (Columbia)
Ramblin' Jack (A Lonesome Hobo)
　Skip Gorman; *A Cowboy's Wild Song To His Herd* . . . . (Rounder)
Refried Dreams
　Tim McGraw; *Not A Moment Too Soon* . . . . (Curb)
Ring On Her Finger, Time On Her Hands
　Lee Greenwood; *Best Of Lee Greenwood-God Bless America* . . . . (Curb)
　　Inside Out/You've Got A Good Love Comin' . . . .(MCA)
　　Lee Greenwood's Greatest Hits . . . .(MCA)
　　Lee Greenwood-Super Hits . . . .(Epic)
　Reba McEntire; *Starting Over* . . . .(MCA)

Rockabilly Blues (Texas 1955)
　Johnny Cash; *Texas Super Hits-C* . . . . (Columbia)
Rocky Road Blues
　Bill Monroe & His Blue Grass Boys; *All Time Legends Of Country*
　　Music-C . . . . (Legacy)
Room At The Top Of The Stairs
　David Grisman; *Retrograss* . . . .(Acoustic Disc)
　Leo Kottke; *Leo Kottke-Live* . . . . (Private Music)
　　Peculiaroso . . . . (Private Music)
　Stanley Brothers & The Clinch Mountain Boys; *Ralph Stanley-50th*
　　Anniversary . . . . (Rebel)
　Stella Parton; *Stella Parton-Anthology* . . . . (Renaissance)
Round About Way
　George Strait; *Carrying Your Love With Me* . . . . (MCA)
　　Latest Greatest Straitest Hits . . . . (MCA)
Runaway
　Lovemongers featuring Ann & Nancy Wilson; *Love Shouldn't Hurt-C* . . (Qwest)
San Francisco Is A Lonely Town
　Orion; *Sunrise* . . . . (Sun)
Santa Monica
　Savage Garden; *Savage Garden* . . . . (Columbia)
Saturday Night (Is The Loneliest Night In The Week)
　Frank Sinatra; *Come Dance With Me!* . . . . (Capitol)
　　Frank Sinatra-16 Most Requested Songs . . . . (Columbia)
　　Frank Sinatra-In The Beginning-1943-1951 . . . . (Columbia)
　　Portrait Of Sinatra-Columbia Classics . . . . (Legacy)
　　The Capitol Years . . . . (Capitol)
Scar Tissue
　Red Hot Chili Peppers; *Californication* . . . . (Warner Bros.)
Sealed With A Kiss
　Bobby Vinton; *Bobby Vinton's Greatest Hits* . . . . (Curb)
　Brian Hyland; *Cruisin'-1962-C* . . . . (Increase)
　　Oldies But Goodies-#2-C . . . . (Original Sound)
　　Original Rock 'N' Roll Hits Of The '50s-C . . . . (Roulette)
　Lettermen; *Best Of The Lettermen-#2* . . . . (Capitol)
　　Capitol Collectors Series-The Lettermen . . . . (Capitol)
Sentimental
　Deborah Cox; *Deborah Cox* . . . . (Arista)
Senza Una Donna (Without A Woman)
　Paul Young; *From Time To Time-The Singles Collection* . . . . (Columbia)
　Zucchero & Paul Young; *Zucchero & Paul Young* . . . . (London)
Seven Rooms Of Gloom
　Four Tops; *Four Tops' Greatest Hits* . . . . (Motown)
　　Four Tops Reach Out . . . . (Motown)
　　Four Tops-Anthology . . . . (Motown)
Sgt. Pepper's Lonely Hearts Club Band
　Beatles; *Beatles-Box Set* . . . . (Capitol)
　　The Beatles/1967-1970 . . . . (Capitol)
　Jimi Hendrix; *Stages-Stockholm/Paris/San Diego/Atlanta* . . . . (Reprise)
Shadow Of A Lonely Man
　Alan Parsons Project; *Pyramid* . . . . (Arista)
She Makes The Coming Home Worth The Being Gone
　Shenandoah; *Extra Mile* . . . . (Columbia)
She Misses Him
　Tim Rushlow; *Tim Rushlow* . . . .(Atlantic)
She Misses Him On Sunday The Most
　Diamond Rio; *Diamond Rio IV* . . . . (Arista)
　　Diamond Rio's Greatest Hits . . . . (Arista)
She Won't Be Lonely Long
　Lee Roy Parnell; *Hits And Highways Ahead* . . . . (Arista)
Show Me The Meaning Of Being Lonely
　Backstreet Boys; *Millennium* . . . . (Jive)
　　Now That's What I Call Music!-#5-C . . . . (Virgin)
Since I Don't Have You
　Rick Nelson; *Best Of Rick Nelson 1963-1975* . . . . (MCA)
　Ronnie McDowell; *Best Of Ronnie McDowell* . . . . (Curb)
　Ronnie Milsap; *Back To The Grindstone* . . . . (RCA)
　Skyliners; *Doo-Wop Ballads-#2-C* . . . . (Rhino)
　　La Bamba & Other Original Hits-C . . . . (Laurie)
　　Oldies But Goodies-#5-C . . . . (Original Sound)
　　Skyliners' Greatest Hits . . . . (Original Sound)
Since I Don't Have You
　Marty Stuart; *Hillbilly Rock* . . . . (MCA)
Since You've Been Gone
　Luther Vandross; *Songs* . . . . (Epic)
Single Girl
　Sandy Posey; *Greatest Hits Of 1966-C* . . . . (Deluxe)
Sister
　Nixons; *Foma* . . . . (MCA)
Sitting Home
　Total; *Kima, Keisha & Pam.* . . . .(Bad Boy/Arista)
Six O'Clock
　Lovin' Spoonful; *Lovin' Spoonful-Anthology* . . . . (Rhino)
Sleeping In Paris
　Rosanne Cash; *The Wheel* . . . . (Columbia)
Sleeping Single In A Double Bed
　Barbara Mandrell; *Barbara Mandrell Live* . . . . (MCA)
　　Best Of Barbara Mandrell . . . . (MCA)
　　Moods . . . . (MCA)

Sloop John B
Beach Boys; *Absolute Best-#2*.................................(Capitol)
  Beach Boys '69 (The Beach Boys Live In London)........(Capitol)
  Beach Boys-Gift Set....................................(Capitol)
  Best Of (Good Vibrations)...............................(Reprise)
  Made In The U.S.A......................................(Capitol)
  Pet Sounds..(Capitol)
  ST/Forrest Gump.................(Epic/Sony Music Soundtrax)
  The Pet Sounds Sessions: A 30th Anniversary Collection......(Capitol)

So Far Away
Carole King; *A Natural Woman: The Ode Collection-1968-1976*.....(Legacy)
  Tapestry...(Epic)
Rod Stewart; *If We Fall In Love Tonight*...............(Warner Bros.)
  Tapestry Revisited: Tribute To Carole King-C...........(Lava)

So How Come (No One Loves Me)
Everly Brothers; *Heartaches 'N' Harmonies*...................(Rhino)

Soldier Boy
Shirelles; *Billboard Top Rock 'N' Roll Hits-1962-C*.........(Rhino)
  Oldies But Goodies-#4-C........................(Original Sound)
  Shirelles-Anthology 1959-1964..........................(Rhino)
  ST/The Wanderers..............................(Warner Bros.)

Solitaire
Elvis Presley; *Always On My Mind*...........................(RCA)
  From Elvis Presley Boulevard, Memphis, Tennessee.........(RCA)

Solitaire
Laura Branigan; *Branigan 2*...............................(Atlantic)

Solitaire
Stan Kenton; *Artistry In Voices & Brass*..............(Creative World)

Solitaire
Johnny Mathis; *Feelings*.................................(Columbia)

Solitaire
Carpenters; *From The Top*...................................(A&M)
  Horizon..(A&M)

Solitaire
Neil Sedaka; *I'm A Song*............................(Fifty One West)
  Solitaire......................................(Fifty One West)

Solitaire
Jerry Vale; *Jerry Vale's Greatest Hits*....................(Columbia)

Solitaire
Erroll Garner; *Other Voices*...............................(Columbia)

Solitaire
Jane Olivor; *Stay The Night*..............................(Columbia)

Solitaire
Public Image Ltd.; *Live In Tokyo*.........................(Elektra)
  This Is What You Want...Is What You Get...............(Elektra)

Solitary Man
Chris Isaak; *San Francisco Days*...........................(Reprise)
Neil Diamond; *Glory Road-1968-1972*.........................(MCA)
  Hot August Night.......................................(MCA)
  Neil Diamond-Classics (Early Years)..................(Columbia)
  Neil Diamond-Gold......................................(MCA)
  Neil Diamond's Greatest Hits-1966-1992...............(Columbia)

Some Broken Hearts Never Mend
Don Williams; *Best Of Don Williams-#2*......................(MCA)
  Don Williams-20 Greatest Hits..........................(MCA)
  Some Broken Hearts Never Mend.............(MCA Special Prod.)

Some Enchanted Evening
Jay & The Americans; *Come A Little Bit Closer-Best Of Jay & The
  Americans*..(Gold Rush)
Jay & The Americans' All-Time Greatest Hits...................(Rhino)
Original Cast; *South Pacific*........................(CBS Masterworks)
Perry Como; *Perry Como's All-Time Greatest Hits-#1*..........(RCA)
Rosanno Brazzi; *ST/South Pacific*...........................(RCA)
Willie Nelson; *What A Wonderful World*.....................(Columbia)

Some Of These Days
Cab Calloway; *Masters Of Jazz-#6-Male Vocal Classics-C*.......(Rhino)
Leon Redbone; *On The Track*........................(Warner Bros.)
Louis Armstrong; *Louis Armstrong And The Big Bands-1928-1930*......(DRG)
Mills Brothers; *Close Harmony*...........................(Ranwood)
Sophie Tucker; *Legendary Entertainers*....................(Pro-Arte)
  Those Wonderful Years-Roaring '20s-C..........(JCI Assoc. Labels)

Somebody's Somebody
''AFKAP''; *Emancipation*....................................(NPG)

Someday We'll Be Together
Diana Ross & The Supremes; *20/20-C*.......................(Motown)
  Diana Ross & The Supremes' Greatest Hits-#3..........(Motown)
  Diana Ross & The Supremes-Anthology (1962-1969)......(Motown)
  Evening With Diana Ross...............................(Motown)
  Motown Story-First 25 Years-C.........................(Motown)
  Motown Superstar Series-#1-Diana Ross & The Supremes.......(Motown)

Somehow Tonight
Ricky Skaggs and Kentucky Thunder; *Bluegrass Rules!*........(Rounder)

Someone To Watch Over Me
Ella Fitzgerald; *Ella Fitzgerald Sings The George & Ira Gershwin
  Songbook*..(Verve)
Elton John; *Glory Of Gershwin Featuring Larry Adler-C*......(Mercury)
Frank Sinatra; *Nice 'N' Easy*.............................(Capitol)
  The Capitol Years....................................(Capitol)
Jack Jones; *Gershwin Album*...............................(Columbia)

Original Broadway Cast; *Crazy For You*......................(Angel)
Oscar Peterson; *My Favorite Instrument*.....................(Verve)
Sarah Vaughan; *Sarah Vaughan Sings George Gershwin Songbook,
  Vol. 2*...(Emarcy)
Willie Nelson; *Stardust*..................................(Legacy)

Sometimes I Feel Like A Motherless Child
Dave Van Ronk; *Folksinger*...............................(Prestige)
  Inside Dave Van Ronk................................(Fantasy)
Grant Green; *Feelin' The Spirit*........................(Blue Note)
  Iron City..(Muse)
Jerry Butler; *Jerry Butler-Gold*..........................(Vee-Jay)
Mormon Tabernacle Choir; *Songs Of The Civil War And Stephen Foster
  Favorites*......................................(Sony Music Classical)
O.V. Wright; *O.V. Wright*...................................(MCA)
Odetta; *Essential Odetta*................................(Vanguard)
Peter, Paul & Mary; *The Song Will Rise*...............(Warner Bros.)
Van Morrison; *Poetic Champions Compose*...................(Mercury)

Spanish Eyes
Ricky Martin; *Ricky Martin*..............................(Columbia)

Stamp Out Loneliness
Stonewall Jackson; *Stonewall Jackson-Classic Country*........(Simitar)

Standing In The Doorway
Bob Dylan; *Time Out Of Mind*.............................(Columbia)

Stay (I Missed You)
Lisa Loeb; *ST/Reality Bites*...............................(RCA)

Still
Commodores; *Best Of The Commodores-Anthology*..............(Motown)
  Commodores-All The Great Hits........................(Motown)
  Commodores-The Ultimate Collection...................(Motown)
Lionel Richie; *Back To Front*............................(Motown)
  Truly-The Love Songs.................................(Motown)

Still Dancin' With You
Wade Hayes; *Old Enough To Know Better*...................(Columbia)

Still In My Heart
Tracie Spencer; *Tracie*..................................(Capitol)

Stronger
Britney Spears; *Now That's What I Call Music!-#6-C*.........(Virgin)
  Oops!...I Did It Again................................(Jive)

Sukiyaki
4 P.M.; *Now's The Time*................(Next Plateau/London/Island)
Kyu Sakamoto; *When AM Was King-C*........................(Capitol)
Taste Of Honey; *Golden Honey*............................(Capitol)
  Twice As Sweet.......................................(Capitol)

Summer Days Alone
Brothers Four; *Brothers Four-Greatest Hits*...............(Columbia)

Summer Rain
Carl Thomas; *Emotional*............................(Bad Boy/Arista)

Sun Ain't Gonna Shine Anymore
Walker Brothers; *History Of British Rock-#7-C*.............(Rhino)
  Love Sixties-C................................(JCI Assoc. Labels)

Sunday Morning Coming Down
Johnny Cash; *Classic Cash-Hall Of Fame Series*............(Mercury)
  Johnny Cash's Greatest Hits-#2......................(Columbia)
  The Man In Black-His Greatest Hits...................(Legacy)
Kris Kristofferson; *Me & Bobby McGee*....................(Columbia)
  Songs Of Kris Kristofferson.........................(Columbia)
Vikki Carr; *Best Of Vikki Carr*............................(EMI)
Willie Nelson; *Willie*.....................................(RCA)
  Willie Nelson Sings Kristofferson...................(Columbia)

Swallowed
Bush; *Razorblade Suitcase*................................(Trauma)

Sweet Sixteen
Destiny's Child; *The Writing's On The Wall*...............(Columbia)

Take Your Memory With You
Vince Gill; *Platinum Country-C*...................(JCI Assoc. Labels)
  Pocket Full Of Gold..................................(MCA)
  Vince Gill-Souvenirs.................................(MCA)

Talk To Me Lonesome Heart
James O'Gwynn; *James O'Gwynn's Greatest Hits*.............(Plantation)

Tears Of The Lonely
Mickey Gilley; *Mickey Gilley's Biggest Hits*...............(Epic)
  Ten Years Of Love....................................(Epic)

Teenage Dirtbag
Wheatus; *Wheatus*..(Columbia)

Tell Me Why
Beatles; *Beatles-Box Set*.................................(Capitol)
  Something New..(Capitol)
  ST/A Hard Day's Night................................(Capitol)

Tennessee Lonesome Blues
Jim & Jesse; *In The Tradition*............................(Rounder)

Tenth Avenue Freeze-Out
Bruce Springsteen; *Born To Run*..........................(Columbia)
Bruce Springsteen & The E Street Band; *Bruce Springsteen & The E Street
  Band Live/1975-85*....................................(Legacy)

Texas
Merle Haggard; *Friend In California*........................(Epic)
Merle Haggard & Freddy Powers; *Texas Super Hits-C*........(Columbia)

Texas Women (Don't Stay Lonely Long)
Brooks & Dunn; *Hard Workin' Man*...........................(Arista)

That's Not Me
Beach Boys; *Pet Sounds* . . . . (Capitol)
  The Pet Sounds Sessions: A 30th Anniversary Collection . . . . (Capitol)
That's Okay
Marc Anthony; *Marc Anthony* . . . . (Columbia)
There's A Tear In My Beer
Hank Williams, Jr. & Hank Williams, Sr.; *Complete Hank Williams* . . (Mercury)
  Hank Williams, Jr.'s Greatest Hits III . . . . (Curb)
Think Of Me
Buck Owens & The Buckaroos; *Buck Owens Collection-1959-1990* . . . . (Rhino)
  Very Best Of Buck Owens-#2 . . . . (Rhino)
This Is Me Missing You
James House; *Days Gone By* . . . .(Epic)
  Super Hits Of 1995-C . . . .(Epic)
This Lonely Place
Goldfinger; *Hang-Ups* . . . . (Mojo Music/Universal)
This Masquerade
Carpenters; *Carpenters-Classics-#2* . . . . (A&M)
  Now & Then . . . . (A&M)
  Yesterday Once More . . . . (A&M)
David Sanborn; *Pearls* . . . . (Elektra)
George Benson; *Breezin'* . . . .(Warner Bros.)
  George Benson-Collection . . . .(Warner Bros.)
Leon Russell; *Best Of Leon Russell* . . . . (MCA)
  Carney . . . . (Right Stuff)
  Gimme Shelter! The Best Of Leon Russell . . . . (Capitol)
This Missin' You Heart Of Mine
Sawyer Brown; *Somewhere In The Night* . . . . (Liberty)
This Nearly Was Mine
Original Cast; *South Pacific* . . . . (CBS Masterworks)
Thorn Tree In The Garden
Derek And The Dominos; *Layla* . . . . (Polydor)
Tired Of Being Alone
Al Green; *Al Green's Greatest Hits* . . . . (Right Stuff)
  Tokyo...Live . . . . (Right Stuff)
Today My World Slipped Away
George Strait; *Carrying Your Love With Me* . . . .(MCA)
  Latest Greatest Straitest Hits . . . .(MCA)
Vern Gosdin; *10 Years Of Greatest Hits Newly Recorded* . . . . (Columbia)
  Legends Of The Silver Eagle-C . . . . (King Biscuit Entert.)
  Today My World Slipped Away . . . . (AMI)
Today's Lonely Fool
Tracy Lawrence; *Sticks & Stones* . . . . (Atlantic)
Travelin' All Alone
Billie Holiday; *Billie Holiday* . . . . (Columbia)
  Legacy Box-1933-1958 . . . . (Columbia)
  Quintessential-#5-1937-1938 . . . . (Columbia)
  The Billie Holiday Story-#1 . . . . (Columbia)
Tryin' To Get Over You
Vince Gill; *I Still Believe In You* . . . .(MCA)
Trying To Live My Life Without You
Bob Seger & The Silver Bullet Band; *Nine Tonight* . . . . (Capitol)
Tumble In The Rough
Stone Temple Pilots; *Tiny Music...Songs From The Vatican
  Gift Shop* . . . . (Atlantic)
Tumbling Tumbleweeds
Billy Vaughn; *Billy Vaughn's Greatest Hits* . . . . (Curb)
Gene Autry; *Essential Gene Autry* . . . . (Columbia)
Meat Puppets; *Meat Puppets* . . . . (SST)
Michael Martin Murphey; *Cowboy Songs* . . . . (Warner Western)
Roy Rogers/K.T. Oslin/Restless Heart; *Roy Rogers Tribute-C* . . . . (RCA)
Sons Of The Pioneers; *The Country Music Hall Of Fame-Sons Of The
  Pioneers* . . . .(MCA)
Turn The Page
Metallica; *Garage Inc.* . . . . (Elektra)
Twinkle, Twinkle Lucky Star
Merle Haggard; *Chill Factor* . . . .(Epic)
  Greatest Country Hits Of The '80s-1988-C . . . . (Columbia)
Two Less Lonely People In The World
Air Supply; *Now & Forever* . . . . (Arista)
Unchained Melody
Elvis Presley; *Always On My Mind* . . . . (RCA)
  Moody Blue . . . . (RCA)
  The Great Performances . . . . (RCA)
George Benson; *Livin' Inside Your Love* . . . .(Warner Bros.)
LeAnn Rimes; *LeAnn Rimes-Early Years-Unchained Melody* . . . . . (MCG/Curb)
Platters; *Platters Greatest Hits* . . . . (Everest)
  Red Sails In The Sunset . . . . (Allegiance)
Richard Clayderman; *Richard Clayderman Plays Love Songs Of The
  World* . . . . (Columbia)
Righteous Brothers; *Righteous Brothers' Greatest Hits* . . . . (Verve)
  ST/Ghost . . . . (Varese Sarabande)
Willie Nelson; *Stardust* . . . . (Legacy)
Uninvited
Ruth Wallis; *Laughing Gallery* . . . . (American)
Until My Dreams Come True
Jack Greene; *Until My Dreams Come True* . . . . (Decca)
Until The End Of Time
Foreigner; *Mr. Moonlight* . . . . (Generama/Rhythm Safari)

Waiting For Tonight
Tom Petty; *Playback* . . . . (MCA)
Walkin' After Midnight
Garth Brooks; *The Chase* . . . . (Liberty)
Loretta Lynn; *I Remember Patsy* . . . . (MCA)
Oak Ridge Boys; *Unstoppable* . . . . (RCA)
Patsy Cline; *20 Golden Pieces Of Patsy Cline* . . . .(Bulldog)
  Let The Teardrops Fall . . . . (Accord)
  Live At The Opry . . . . (MCA)
  Patsy Cline . . . . (MCA)
  Patsy Cline's Greatest Hits . . . . (MCA)
  The Patsy Cline Story . . . . (MCA)
Walkin' By Myself
Jimmy Rogers; *Best Of Chess Blues-C* . . . . (Chess)
Johnny Winter; *Hot & Blue* . . . . (Blue Sky)
  Scorchin' Blues . . . . (Epic Portrait Assoc.)
  Walkin' By Myself . . . . (Relix)
  White . . . . (Blue Sky)
Wander This World
Jonny Lang; *Wander This World* . . . . (A&M)
Wandering Stranger
Lionel Richie; *Lionel Richie* . . . . (Motown)
War Is Hell (On The Homefront Too)
T.G. Sheppard; *Perfect Stranger* . . . . (Warner Bros.)
  T.G. Sheppard's All-Time Greatest Hits . . . . (Warner Bros.)
  T.G. Sheppard's Greatest Hits . . . .(Warner Bros./Curb)
Washed Ashore (On A Lonely Island In The Sea)
Platters; *Platters-16 Greatest Hits* . . . .(Trip)
  Platters-Anthology . . . . (Rhino)
Wasted Days And Wasted Nights
Freddy Fender; *Before The Next Teardrop Falls* . . . . (Universal)
  Best Of Freddy Fender . . . . (MCA)
  Country Comes To Carnegie Hall-C . . . . (MCA)
  Happy Trails . . . . (United Artists)
  Texas Country . . . . (United Artists)
  The Freddy Fender Collection . . . . (MCA)
We All Sleep Alone
Cher; *Cher* . . . . (Geffen)
Wedding Bells (Are Breaking Up That Old Gang Of Mine)
Four Aces; *Best Of The Four Aces* . . . . (MCA)
We've Got Tonight
Bob Seger & The Silver Bullet Band; *Nine Tonight* . . . . (Capitol)
  Stranger In Town . . . . (Capitol)
Kenny Rogers & Sheena Easton; *Kenny Rogers/Kim Carnes/Sheena Easton/
  Dottie West* . . . . (EMI)
  Kenny Rogers-25 Greatest Hits . . . . (EMI)
  Kenny Rogers-Greatest Country Hits . . . . (Curb)
  Kenny Rogers-Twenty Greatest Hits . . . . (EMI)
  We've Got Tonight . . . . (Razor & Tie)
What A Dream
Conway Twitty; *Conway Twitty's Greatest Hits* . . . . (Curb)
Patti Page; *45-#70416* . . . . (Mercury)
Slim Harpo; *Raining In My Heart* . . . . (Hip-O)
What Are We Doin' Lonesome
Larry Gatlin & The Gatlin Brothers Band; *Best Of The Gatlins-All The Gold
  In California* . . . . (Legacy)
  Larry Gatlin & The Gatlin Brothers' Greatest Hits-#2 . . . . (Columbia)
  Larry Gatlin & The Gatlin Brothers-17 Greatest Hits . . . . (Columbia)
What Becomes Of The Brokenhearted
Jimmy & David Ruffin; *Motown Superstar Series-#8-Jimmy & David
  Ruffin* . . . . (Motown)
Jimmy Ruffin; *Motown Story-First 25 Years-C* . . . . (Motown)
Paul Young; *ST/Fried Green Tomatoes* . . . . (MCA)
What Do I Know
Ricochet; *Pure Country-Best Of The '90s-#2-C* . . . .(Priority)
  Ricochet . . . . (Columbia)
What I Didn't Know
Athenaeum; *Radiance* . . . .(Atlantic)
What Is Truth
Johnny Cash; *The Man In Black-His Greatest Hits* . . . . (Legacy)
What'll I Do
Nat "King" Cole; *The Vocal Classics-1947-1950* . . . . (Capitol)
Rosemary Clooney; *Rosemary Clooney Sings The Music Of Irving
  Berlin* . . . . (Concord Jazz)
When Can I See You Again
Babyface; *For The Cool In You* . . . . (Epic)
When I Call Your Name
Vince Gill; *When I Call Your Name* . . . . (MCA)
When I Need You
Celine Dion; *Let's Talk About Love-C* . . . .(550 Music)
Leo Sayer; *'70s Greatest Rock Hits-#5-Kickin' Back-C* . . . .(Priority)
  Show Must Go On-Anthology . . . . (Rhino)
When My Blue Moon Turns To Gold Again
Elvis Presley; *A Golden Celebration* . . . . (RCA)
  Elvis . . . . (RCA)
  The Other Sides-Worldwide Gold Award Hits, Vol. 2 . . . . (RCA)
Merle Haggard; *Merle Haggard-His Best* . . . . (MCA)
  Ramblin' Fever . . . . (MCA)

When Your House Is Not A Home
Patsy Cline; *Patsy Cline-Live-#2* . . . . (MCA)
Where Do I Go From You
Jon Secada; *Heart, Soul & A Voice*
. . . . (SBK)
Where Does My Heart Beat Now?
Celine Dion; *Unison* . . . . (Epic)
Where've You Been
Kathy Mattea; *Collection Of Hits* . . . . (Mercury)
Willow In The Wind . . . . (Mercury)
White Sport Coat (And A Pink Carnation)
Marty Robbins; *16 Most Requested Songs Of The '50s-#2-C* . . . . (Legacy)
Lifetime Of Song-1951-1982. . . . . (Columbia)
Marty Robbins' Greatest Hits . . . . (Columbia)
Who Can I Run To
Xscape; *Off The Hook* . . . . (So So Def/Columbia)
Smooth Love: Ultimate R&B Love Songs-C . . . . (EMI)
Who Can I Turn To (When Nobody Needs Me)
Tony Bennett; *Tony Bennett Sings His All-Time Hall Of Fame Hits*
Fame Hits . . . . (Columbia)
Whole New You
Shawn Colvin; *Whole New You* . . . . (Columbia)
Who's Lonely Now
Highway 101; *Country's Greatest Hits-#8-Lonely Hearts-C* . . . . (Priority)
Highway 101's Greatest Hits . . . . (Warner Bros.)
Paint The Town . . . . (Warner Bros.)
Why Don't You Believe Me?
Duprees; *Best Of The Duprees* . . . . (Rhino)
Best Of The Duprees . . . . (Collectables)
Joni James; *Platinum & Gold Hits* . . . . (Taragon)
Patti Page; *Patti Page-Golden Celebration* . . . . (Mercury)
Wildest Times Of The World
Vonda Shepard; *ST/Songs From ''Ally McBeal'' Featuring Vonda Shepard*
Shepard . . . . (550/Epic)
Wish You Were Here
Limp Bizkit & John Rzeznik; *America: A Tribute To Heroes-C* . . . . (Interscope)
Pink Floyd; *Collection Of Great Dance Songs* . . . . (Columbia)
Delicate Sound Of Thunder . . . . (Columbia)
Wish You Were Here . . . . (Columbia)
Wish You Were Here
Mark Wills; *Wish You Were Here* . . . . (Mercury)
Wish You Were Here
Bing Crosby; *The Radio Years: 20 Songs* . . . . (Crescendo)
Eddie Fisher; *Best Of Eddie Fisher* . . . . (MCA)
Wish You Were Here
Incubus; *Morning View* . . . . (Epic)
Without Her
Nilsson; *Pandemonium Shadow Show.* . . . . (RCA)
Without You
Doobie Brothers; *Best Of The Doobies* . . . . (Warner Bros.)
Captain & Me . . . . (Warner Bros.)
Without You
Dixie Chicks; *Fly.* . . . . (Monument)
Without You
Nilsson; *Nilsson Schmilsson* . . . . (RCA)
Nilsson's Greatest Hits . . . . (RCA)
Nipper's Greatest Hits Of The '70s-C. . . . . (RCA)
Without You
Van Halen; *Van Halen 3* . . . . (Warner Bros.)
Without You
Charlie Wilson; *Bridging The Gap* . . . . (Major Hits)
Without You
Asia; *Asia* . . . . (Geffen)
Without You
Motley Crue; *Dr. Feelgood* . . . . (Elektra)
Without You
David Bowie; *Let's Dance.* . . . . (EMI)
Without You
Mariah Carey; *Music Box* . . . . (Columbia)
Without You
Alison Moyet; *Raindancing.* . . . . (Columbia)
Without You
Beat Rodeo; *Staying Out Late With Beat Rodeo* . . . . (I.R.S.)
Without You (Not Another Lonely Night)
Frankie & The Knockouts; *Below The Belt* . . . . (Millennium)
Woman's Touch
Toby Keith; *Blue Moon* . . . . (Polydor Country)
World I Know, The
Collective Soul; *Collective Soul* . . . . (Atlantic)
World Without Love, A
Peter And Gordon; *Billboard Top Pop Hits-1964-C* . . . . (Rhino)
History Of British Rock-#1-C . . . . (Rhino)
Peter & Gordon's Greatest Hits . . . . (CEMA Special Prod.)
Yearning (Just For You)
Asleep At The Wheel featuring Vince Gill; *Tribute To The Music Of Bob Wills And The Texas Playboys-C* . . . . (Liberty)
Wills And The Texas Playboys-C . . . . (Liberty)
Bob Wills & His Texas Playboys; *For The Last Time* . . . . (Capitol)
Yer Blues
Beatles; *The Beatles (White Album)* . . . . (Capitol)

You Are Not Alone
Michael Jackson; *1996 Grammy Nominees-C* . . . .(Columbia)
HIStory: Past, Present And Future-Book 1-C . . . .(Epic)
You Belong To Me
Dean Martin; *Dean Martin's All Time Greatest Hits* . . . .(Curb)
Duprees; *13 Of The Best Doo Wop Love Songs-#2-C* . . . . (Original Sound)
Baby Boomer's Best-Mellow '60s-C . . . . (Priority)
Best Of The Duprees . . . .(Rhino)
Jo Stafford; *Billboard Pop Memories-1950-1954-C* . . . .(Rhino)
Jo Stafford's Greatest Hits . . . .(Curb)
Johnny Mathis; *In The Still Of The Night* . . . .(Columbia)
Patsy Cline; *Patsy Cline Sings Songs Of Love* . . . . (MCA Special Prod.)
Sentimentally Yours. . . . .(MCA)
Vonda Shepard; *ST/Songs From ''Ally McBeal'' Featuring Vonda Shepard*
Shepard . . . . (550/Epic)
You Can't Hurry Love
Diana Ross; *Diana Ross-The Ultimate Collection* . . . .(Motown)
Diana Ross & The Supremes; *16 #1 Hits From The Early '60s-C* . . . . .(Motown)
Phil Collins; *Hello, I Must Be Going* . . . . (Atlantic)
You Could Have Been With Me
Sheena Easton; *Sheena Easton's Greatest Hits* . . . . . .(EMI Special Markets)
The World Of Sheena Easton: The Singles Collection-C. . . . .(EMI)
You Don't Have To Say You Love Me
Dusty Springfield; *Dusty Springfield-Golden Hits* . . . .(Mercury)
History Of British Rock-#7-C . . . .(Rhino)
Elvis Presley; *Elvis As Recorded At Madison Square Garden* . . . . . (RCA)
That's The Way It Is. . . . . (RCA)
The Other Sides-Worldwide Gold Award Hits, Vol. 2 . . . . . (RCA)
Vikki Carr; *Best Of Vikki Carr* . . . .(EMI)
You Don't Know How It Feels
Tom Petty; *Wildflowers* . . . . (Warner Bros.)
You Don't Seem To Miss Me
Patty Loveless; *Long Stretch Of Lonesome* . . . . (Epic)
Patty Loveless-Classics. . . . . (Epic)
You Still Touch Me
Sting; *Mercury Falling.* . . . . (A&M)
You Were Meant For Me
Jewel; *Pieces Of You* . . . . (Atlantic)
You Won't Be Lonely Now
Billy Ray Cyrus; *Southern Rain* . . . .(Monument)
You Won't Ever Be Lonely
Andy Griggs; *Andy Griggs.* . . . . (RCA)
You'll Never Know
Dick Haymes; *Best Of Dick Haymes* . . . .(Curb)
You'll Never Know . . . . (MCA Special Prod.)
Dick Haymes & His Song Spinners; *Billboard Pop Memories-1940-1944-C*
1944-C . . . .(Rhino)
Billboard Top Movie Hits-1940s-C. . . . .(Rhino)
You'll Never Walk Alone
Andy Williams; *Unchained Melody-Greatest Songs* . . . .(Curb)
Jim Nabors; *Jim Nabors-16 Most Requested Songs* . . . . (Legacy)
Judy Garland; *Best Of The Capitol Masters-One & Only Box* . . . .(Capitol)
Mormon Tabernacle Choir; *Climb Ev'ry Mountain* . . . .(Columbia)
Original Broadway Cast; *Carousel* . . . .(Angel)
Original Cast; *Carousel* . . . .(MCA)
Pink Floyd; *Meddle* . . . .(Capitol)
You're Gonna Make Me Lonesome When You Go
Bob Dylan; *Blood On The Tracks* . . . .(Columbia)
You're Gonna Miss Me When I'm Gone
Flatt & Scruggs; *20 All-Time Great Recordings.* . . . .(Columbia)
Muddy Waters; *Muddy Waters-Complete Plantation Recordings-1941-1942*
1942. . . . .(Chess)
You're Gonna Miss Me When I'm Gone
Brooks & Dunn; *Brooks & Dunn-The Greatest Hits Collection.* . . . . . .(Arista)
Waitin' On Sundown . . . .(Arista)
You're Not Alone
Chicago; *Chicago 19* . . . . (Reprise)
You're Only Lonely
J.D. Souther; *Radio Daze-Pop Hits Of The '80s-#1-C* . . . .(Rhino)
You're Only Lonely . . . .(Legacy)
You're Still On My Mind
Byrds; *Sweetheart Of The Rodeo* . . . .(Columbia)
Zero
Smashing Pumpkins; *Mellon Collie And The Infinite Sadness* . . . . (Virgin)

LOSING & LOSS, Defeat, Failure, Lose Someone, Suffer A Loss

See Also: *DEATH, DESPAIR, DIVORCE, LONELY, LOVE (various), LOST & MISPLACED, SADNESS, SEPARATION, WINNING*

(I Know) I'm Losing You
Rod Stewart; *Best Of Rod Stewart* . . . .(Mercury)
Every Picture Tells A Story . . . .(Mercury)
Storyteller/The Complete Anthology: 1964-1990 . . . . . . (Warner Bros.)
Temptations; *Temptations-Anthology-Best Of The Temptations* . . .(Motown)

Temptations-The Ultimate Collection . . . . (Motown)
(Lost His Love) On Our Last Date
Emmylou Harris; *Profile II-The Best Of Emmylou Harris* . . . .(Warner Bros.)
50,000 Names
George Jones; *The Rock: Stone Cold Country 2001* . . . . (BNA)
After The Love Is Gone
Earth, Wind & Fire; *Best Of Earth, Wind & Fire-#2* . . . . (Columbia)
Earth, Wind & Fire-Greatest Hits-#1 . . . . (Legacy)
All Eyes On Me
Goo Goo Dolls; *Dizzy Up The Girl* . . . . (Warner Sunset/Reprise)
Alone Again (Naturally)
Gilbert O'Sullivan; *Best Of Gilbert O'Sullivan* . . . . (Rhino)
Billboard Top Rock 'N' Roll Hits-1972-C . . . . (Rhino)
Am I Losing You
Jim Reeves; *Best Of Jim Reeves* . . . . (RCA)
Essential Jim Reeves . . . . (RCA)
Jim Reeves' Greatest Hits . . . . (RCA)
Ronnie Milsap; *Ronnie Milsap's Greatest Hits-#2* . . . . (RCA)
American Tune
Paul Simon; *Paul Simon In Concert/Live Rhymin'* . . . . (Columbia)
There Goes Rhymin' Simon . . . . (Columbia)
Simon & Garfunkel; *The Concert In Central Park* . . . .(Warner Bros.)
Anybody Seen My Baby?
Rolling Stones; *1998 Grammy Nominees-C* . . . .(MCA)
Bridges To Babylon . . . . (Virgin)
Ask The Lonely
Vonda Shepard; *ST/Songs From "Ally McBeal" Featuring Vonda
Shepard* . . . . (550/Epic)
Back On The Chain Gang
Pretenders; *Learning To Crawl* . . . . (Sire)
Pretenders-The Singles . . . . (Sire)
ST/King Of Comedy . . . .(Warner Bros.)
Back On The Street Again
Sunshine Company; *Even More Nuggets-C* . . . . (Rhino)
Bad Loser
Joy Lynn White; *Wild Love* . . . . (Columbia)
Bang The Drum Slowly
Emmylou Harris; *Red Dirt Girl* . . . . (Nonesuch)
Better Class Of Losers
Randy Travis; *High Lonesome* . . . .(Warner Bros.)
Better Days (And The Bottom Drops Out)
Citizen King; *Mobile Estates* . . . .(Warner Bros.)
Big Yellow Taxi
Amy Grant; *House Of Love* . . . . (A&M)
Joni Mitchell; *Ladies Of The Canyon* . . . . (Reprise)
Joni Mitchell with Tom Scott & The L.A. Express; *Miles Of Aisles* . . . . (Asylum)
Billy Don't Be A Hero
Bo Donaldson & The Heywoods; *Super Hits Of The '70s-Have A Nice
Day-#13-C* . . . . (Rhino)
Black Balloon
Goo Goo Dolls; *Dizzy Up The Girl* . . . .(Warner Sunset/Reprise)
Blue Autumn
Bobby Goldsboro; *10th Anniversary Album-#1* . . . .(EMI)
Bobby Goldsboro's Greatest Hits . . . . (Liberty)
Honey-Best Of Bobby Goldsboro . . . .(EMI)
Can't Get Used To Losing You
Andy Williams; *Andy Williams' Greatest Hits* . . . . (Columbia)
Andy Williams-16 Most Requested Songs . . . . (Legacy)
*Days Of Wine And Roses/Moon River & Other Great Movie
Themes* . . . . (Columbia)
Damn Right, I've Got The Blues
Buddy Guy; *Best Blues Album In The World...Ever!-C* . . . . (Virgin)
Buddy's Baddest: The Best Of Buddy Guy . . . . (Silvertone)
Damn Right, I've Got The Blues . . . . (Silvertone)
Darkness On The Edge Of Town
Bruce Springsteen; *Darkness On The Edge Of Town* . . . . (Columbia)
Bruce Springsteen & The E Street Band; *Bruce Springsteen & The E Street
Band Live/1975-85* . . . . (Legacy)
Darling Lorraine
Paul Simon; *You're The One* . . . .(Warner Bros.)
Day I Tried To Live, The
Soundgarden; *A-Sides* . . . . (A&M)
Superunknown . . . . (A&M)
Distance, The
Cake; *Fashion Nugget* . . . . (Capricorn)
Don't Drink The Water
Dave Matthews Band; *Before These Crowded Streets* . . . . (RCA)
Don't Let The Sun Go Down On Me
Elton John; *Caribou* . . . .(Rocket)
Elton John's Greatest Hits . . . .(Polydor)
Live In Australia With The Melbourne Symphony Orchestra . . . .(MCA)
Elton John & George Michael; *Duets-C* . . . .(MCA)
George Michael & Elton John; *Two Rooms-Celebrating The Songs Of Elton
John & Bernie Taupin-C* . . . .(Polydor)
Don't Take Your Love From Me
Etta James; *These Foolish Things-The Classic Balladry Of Etta James* . . .(MCA)
King Sisters; *Spotlight On The King Sisters* . . . . (Capitol)
Three Suns; *Very Best Of The Three Suns* . . . . (Taragon)

Don't Wanna Lose You
Gloria Estefan; *Billboard Top Hits-1989-C* . . . . (Rhino)
Cuts Both Ways . . . . (Epic)
Diana, Princess Of Wales-Tribute-C . . . . (Columbia)
Gloria Estefan's Greatest Hits . . . . (Epic)
Dreams
Corrs; *Legacy-A Tribute To Fleetwood Mac's Rumours-C* . . . . (Lava)
Fleetwood Mac; *25 Years-The Chain* . . . . (Warner Bros.)
Fleetwood Mac Live . . . . (Warner Bros.)
Fleetwood Mac's Greatest Hits . . . . (Warner Bros.)
Rumours . . . . (Warner Bros.)
Elderly Woman Behind The Counter In A Small Town
Pearl Jam; *Vs.* . . . . (Epic Portrait Assoc.)
Everyone's Gone To The Moon
Jonathan King; *British Rock-#3-C* . . . .(Original Sound)
History Of British Rock-#7-C . . . . (Rhino)
Everything I Love
Alan Jackson; *Everything I Love* . . . . (Arista)
Everything To Everyone
Everclear; *Ka-Boom!-C* . . . .(Beast)
So Much For The Afterglow . . . . (Capitol)
Failed Christian
Nick Lowe; *Dig My Mood* . . . . (Upstart)
Falling Away From Me
Korn; *Issues* . . . .(Immortal/Epic)
Father Of Mine
Everclear; *Now That's What I Call Music!-#2-C* . . . .(Virgin)
So Much For The Afterglow . . . . (Capitol)
Fear Of Falling
Badlees; *River Songs* . . . .(Atlas)
Fire And Rain
James Taylor; *James Taylor's Greatest Hits* . . . . (Warner Bros.)
Sweet Baby James . . . . (Warner Bros.)
The Concert For New York City-C . . . . (Columbia)
Sammy Kershaw; *Red Hot + Country-C* . . . . (Mercury)
Foolish Little Girl
Shirelles; *Shirelles' Greatest Hits* . . . . (Everest)
Shirelles-16 Greatest Hits . . . .(Trip)
Shirelles-Anthology 1959-1964 . . . . (Rhino)
Free To Go
Folk Implosion; *One Part Lullaby* . . . .(Interscope)
Friends
John Michael Montgomery; *John Michael Montgomery's
Greatest Hits* . . . .(Atlantic)
What I Do The Best . . . .(Atlantic)
From Hell To Paradise
Mavericks; *From Hell To Paradise* . . . . (MCA)
Full Forever
Goo Goo Dolls; *Dizzy Up The Girl* . . . .(Warner Sunset/Reprise)
Go Walking Down There
Chris Isaak; *Forever Blue* . . . . (Reprise)
Good Run Of Bad Luck
Clint Black; *No Time To Kill* . . . . (RCA)
Got 'Til It's Gone
Janet featuring Q-Tip & Joni Mitchell; *Velvet Rope* . . . . (Virgin)
Graceland
Paul Simon; *Graceland* . . . . (Warner Bros.)
Halloween Parade
Lou Reed; *New York* . . . .(Sire)
He's Got You
Brooks & Dunn; *The Greatest Hits Collection* . . . . (Arista)
Homeless
Paul Simon; *Graceland* . . . . (Warner Bros.)
Honey
Bobby Goldsboro; *Billboard Top Pop Hits-1968-C* . . . . (Rhino)
Cruisin'-1968-C . . . . (Increase)
I Ain't Got No Home
Bob Dylan; *Tribute To Woody Guthrie-C* . . . . (Warner Bros.)
I Almost Lost My Mind
Eddy Arnold; *World Of Hits* . . . . (MGM)
Fats Domino; *Fats Domino's Greatest Hits* . . . . (MCA)
Ivory Joe Hunter; *Since I Met You Baby* . . . . (Mercury)
Pat Boone; *Pat Boone's Greatest Hits* . . . . (Curb)
I Don't Want To Lose Your Love
Bobby Caldwell; *Cat In The Hat* . . . . (Sin-Drome)
I Don't Want To Lose Your Love
B Angie B; *B Angie B* . . . .(Bust It)
I Fought The Law
Bobby Fuller Four; *Best Of The Bobby Fuller Four* . . . . (Rhino)
Heart & Soul Of Rock 'N' Roll-#1-C . . . . (Rhino)
Jailhouse Rock (Hits From The Big House)-C . . . . (Sony Music Special Prod.)
Oldies But Goodies-#9-C . . . .(Original Sound)
Super Oldies Of The '60s-#7-C . . . . (Audio Fidelity)
Clash; *The Clash* . . . . (Epic)
The Story Of The Clash, Volume 1 . . . . (Epic)
I Had Too Much To Dream (Last Night)
Electric Prunes; *Even More Nuggets-C* . . . . (Rhino)
Nuggets-#1-The Hits-C . . . . (Rhino)

Summer Of Love-#1-C . . . . (Rhino)

I Lost It
Kenny Chesney; *Kenny Chesney's Greatest Hits* . . . .(BNA)

I Lost On Jeopardy
"Weird Al" Yankovic; *"Weird Al" Yankovic's Greatest Hits*. . . . (Scotti Bros.)
In 3-D . . . . (Scotti Bros.)

I Surrender Dear
Bing Crosby; *Pennies From Heaven* . . . .(Pro-Arte)
Where The Blue Of The Night Meets The Gold Of The Day . . . . (Biograph)
Count Basie; *Basie & Zoot* . . . . (Pablo)
Jam-#3 . . . . (Pablo)
Loose Walk . . . . (Pablo)
Count Basie & His Kansas City 3; *For The Second Time* . . . . (Pablo)
Gus Arnheim & His Orchestra featuring Bing Crosby; *78-#22618* . . . . .(Victor)
Mel Torme; *Smooth As Velvet* . . . .(Pickwick)
Rosemary Clooney; *Rosemary Clooney Sings Bing* . . . .(Concord Jazz)

I Went To Your Wedding
Patti Page; *Patti Page-Golden Hits* . . . .(Mercury)

If I Ever Lose My Faith In You
Sting; *Fields Of Gold-The Best Of Sting 1984-1994* . . . . (A&M)
Ten Summoner's Tales . . . . (A&M)

If I Lose
Ricky Skaggs and Kentucky Thunder; *Bluegrass Rules!*. . . . .(Rounder)

If There's A God On My Side
Rosanne Cash; *The Wheel* . . . .(Columbia)

I'm A Honky Tonk Girl
Loretta Lynn; *The Country Music Hall Of Fame-Loretta Lynn* . . . . (MCA)

I'm A Loser
Beatles; *Beatles '65* . . . .(Capitol)

I'm Always On A Mountain When I Fall
Merle Haggard; *For The Record: Merle Haggard-43 Legendary Hits* . . . .(BNA)

I'm Losing You
John Lennon; *Double Fantasy* . . . .(Capitol)
The John Lennon Anthology . . . .(Capitol)
The John Lennon Collection . . . .(Capitol)
Wonsaponatime . . . .(Capitol)

In The End
Linkin Park; *Hybrid Theory*. . . . . (Warner Bros.)

I've Tried Everything
Eurythmics; *The Sopranos-Music From The HBO Original
Series* . . . .(Sony Music Soundtrax)

Janey Don't You Lose Heart
Bruce Springsteen; *Tracks*. . . . .(Columbia)

Jesus To A Child
George Michael; *Ladies & Gentlemen: The Best Of George Michael* . . . . . (Epic)
Older. . . . . (DreamWorks/SKG)

Kern River
Merle Haggard; *For The Record: Merle Haggard-43 Legendary Hits* . . . .(BNA)
Kern River . . . . (Epic)

Kids Aren't Alright
Offspring; *Americana* . . . .(Columbia)

King Nothing
Metallica; *Load* . . . .(Elektra)

Last Cowboy Song
Ed Bruce; *16 Top Country Hits-#2-C* . . . . (MCA)
Ed Bruce's Greatest Hits . . . . (MCA)
Waylon Jennings, Willie Nelson, Johnny Cash, Kris Kristofferson; *Cowboy
Super Hits-C* . . . .(Columbia)
Highwayman. . . . .(Columbia)

Last Kiss
J. Frank Wilson and The Cavaliers; *Billboard Top Rock 'N' Roll Hits-
1964-C* . . . .(Rhino)
Collectables Presents The History Of Rock-#2-C . . . .(Collectables)
Oldies But Goodies-#9-C . . . .(Original Sound)
Teenage Tragedies-C . . . .(Rhino)
Pearl Jam; *No Boundaries-Benefit For The Kosovar Refugees-C* . . . . . . (Epic)

Last Resort
Papa Roach; *Infest* . . . . (DreamWorks/SKG)

Last Song
Elton John; *The One* . . . . (MCA)

Leaving October
Sons Of The Desert; *Whatever Comes First* . . . . (Epic)

Light Years
Pearl Jam; *Binaural* . . . . (Epic)

Like A Rolling Stone
Bob Dylan; *Biograph*. . . . .(Columbia)
Bob Dylan At Budokan . . . .(Columbia)
Bob Dylan's Greatest Hits . . . .(Columbia)
Highway 61 Revisited . . . .(Columbia)
More American Graffiti-#4-C . . . . (MCA)
Self Portrait . . . .(Columbia)
Bob Dylan And The Band; *Before The Flood* . . . .(Columbia)
Jimi Hendrix; *ST/Jimi Plays Monterey* . . . .(Reprise)
Jimi Hendrix Experience; *Jimi Hendrix Experience* . . . .(Reprise)
Rolling Stones; *Stripped* . . . . (Virgin)

Listen People
Herman's Hermits; *Herman's Hermits-Their Greatest Hits* . . . . (Abkco)

Lose This Skin
Clash; *Sandinista* . . . . (Epic)

Loser
Beck; *Mellow Gold-C* . . . . (David Geffen Co.)

Loser
3 Doors Down; *Better Life* . . . . (Republic/Universal)

Losing A Whole Year
Third Eye Blind; *Third Eye Blind*. . . . .(Elektra)

Losing Lisa
Ben Folds; *Rockin' The Suburbs* . . . . (Epic)

Losing My Religion
R.E.M.; *Out Of Time* . . . .(Warner Bros.)

Lost Ones
Lauryn Hill; *The Miseducation Of Lauryn Hill* . . . .(Ruffhouse/Columbia)

Lost You In The Canyon
Marc Cohn; *Burning The Daze*. . . . .(Atlantic)

Lucky Me
Anne Murray; *Anne Murray-Country Hits*. . . . .(Capitol)
Somebody's Waiting . . . .(Capitol)

Mercy Mercy Me (The Ecology)
Marvin Gaye; *Every Great Motown Hit Of Marvin Gaye*. . . . .(Motown)
Marvin Gaye-Anthology . . . .(Motown)
Marvin Gaye's Greatest Hits . . . .(Motown)
What's Going On. . . . .(Motown)
Robert Palmer; *Don't Explain* . . . . (EMI)

Message Of Love
Journey; *Trial By Fire* . . . .(Columbia)

Moonlight Gambler
Frankie Laine; *Frankie Laine-16 Most Requested Songs* . . . .(Legacy)
Frankie Laine's Greatest Hits . . . .(Columbia)

My Antonia
Emmylou Harris; *Red Dirt Girl* . . . .(Nonesuch)

My Baby Needs A Shepherd
Emmylou Harris; *Red Dirt Girl* . . . .(Nonesuch)

My City Of Ruin
Bruce Springsteen; *America: A Tribute To Heroes-C* . . . .(Interscope)

My Oklahoma Home (It Blowed Away)
Sis Cunningham; *Best Of Broadside 1962-1968: Anthems Of The American
Underground From The Pages Of Broadside
Magazine-C* . . . .(Smithsonian Folkways)

Nearly Lost You
Screaming Trees; *Sweet Oblivion*. . . . . (Epic)

Nevertheless
Frank Sinatra; *Best Of The Columbia Years-1943-1952* . . . .(Columbia)
McGuire Sisters; *McGuire Sisters-Anthology* . . . . (MCA)

Nobody Wins
Brenda Lee; *Brenda Lee-Greatest Country Hits* . . . . (MCA)

Nobody Wins
Radney Foster; *Del Rio, TX 1959* . . . .(Arista)

Nobody Wins
Elton John; *The Fox* . . . . (Geffen)

Not Counting You
Garth Brooks; *Garth Brooks* . . . .(Liberty)

Oaf, The
Big Wreck; *In Loving Memory Of...* . . . . (Atlantic)

Only Losers Take The Bus (Dump The Dead)
Fatima Mansions; *Viva Dead Ponies* . . . .(Radioactive/MCA)

Reno
Doug Supernaw; *Red And Rio Grande* . . . . (BNA)

Resignation Superman
Big Head Todd & The Monsters; *Beautiful World* . . . .(Revolution)
Live Monsters . . . .(Revolution)

Rock Bottom
Wynonna; *Tell Me Why* . . . . (MCA)

Sands Of Nevada
Mark Knopfler; *Sailing To Philadelphia* . . . .(Warner Bros.)

Schism
Tool; *Lateralus*. . . . . (Volcano Entertainment)

Second Fiddle
Kay Starr; *Essential RCA Singles Collection* . . . .(Taragon)

Secret Place
Megadeth; *Cryptic Writings*. . . . .(Capitol)

Shame Shame Shame Shame
Mark Collie; *Mark Collie* . . . . (MCA)

Silver Medals & Sweet Memories
Statler Brothers; *Best Of The Statler Brothers-Rides Again-#2* . . . . . .(Mercury)
Short Stories . . . .(Mercury)

Silvertown Blues
Mark Knopfler; *Sailing To Philadelphia* . . . .(Warner Bros.)

Simple Joys Of Maidenhood
Julie Andrews; *Camelot*. . . . .(Columbia)
Various Artists; *ST/Camelot* . . . .(Warner Bros.)

Since I Lost My Baby
Temptations; *Temptations' Greatest Hits-#1*. . . . .(Motown)
Temptations-Anthology-The Best Of The Temptations . . . .(Motown)
Temptations-The Ultimate Collection . . . .(Motown)

Something Beautiful Remains
Tina Turner; *Wildest Dreams*. . . . . (Virgin)

Something In The Night
Bruce Springsteen; *Darkness On The Edge Of Town* . . . .(Columbia)

Sometimes It Hurts
Stabbing Westward; *Darkest Days* . . . . (Columbia)
Speedway At Nazareth
Mark Knopfler; *Sailing To Philadelphia*. . . . .(Warner Bros.)
Success Has Made A Failure Of Our Home
Sinead O'Connor; *Am I Not Your Girl?* . . . .(Ensign)
So Far...The Best Of Sinead O'Connor . . . .(EMI)
Sucked Out
Superdrag; *Regretfully Yours* . . . . (Elektra)
Sullivan
Caroline's Spine; *Monsoon*. . . . . (Hollywood)
Sweetest Thing
U2; *Best Of 1980-1990* . . . . (Island)
Now That's What I Call Music!-#2-C . . . . (Virgin)
Teenage Failure
Chad & Jeremy; *History Of British Rock-#7-C* . . . . (Rhino)
Painted Dayglow Smile-Collection . . . . (Columbia)
Tennessee Waltz
Cowboy Copas; *45-#696* . . . . (King)
Emmylou Harris; *Cimarron* . . . .(Warner Bros.)
Country's Greatest Hits-#5-C . . . .(Warner Bros.)
New Tradition Sings The Old Tradition-C . . . .(Warner Bros.)
Guy Lombardo & His Royal Canadians; *Best Of Guy Lombardo* . . . . (Curb)
Hank Williams, Jr.; *Living Proof-MGM Recordings 1963-1975* . . . . . (Mercury)
Lacy J. Dalton; *Lacy J. Dalton's Greatest Hits* . . . . (Columbia)
Les Paul & Mary Ford; *Les Paul-Selections From Legend & Legacy*. . . (Capitol)
Patti Page; *Patti Page-Golden Hits* . . . . (Mercury)
Patti Page's Greatest Hits . . . . (Columbia)
Roy Acuff; *Essential Roy Acuff-1936-1949* . . . . (Legacy)
Roy Acuff's Greatest Hits . . . . (Columbia)
Roy Rogers; *Best Of Roy Rogers* . . . . (Curb)
Sammy Kaye & His Orchestra; *Best Of The Big Bands-C* . . . . (Columbia)
Spike Jones & His City Slickers; *Best Of Spike Jones & His City Slickers* . . . . (RCA)
That's The Way Love Goes
Merle Haggard; *30 Years Of #1 Hits-#16-C* . . . . (Columbia)
His Epic Hits-First 11 To Be Continued-C . . . . (Epic)
Merle Haggard-Super Hits . . . . (Epic)
That's The Way Love Goes. . . . . (Epic)
Merle Haggard & Jewel; *For The Record: Merle Haggard-43 Legendary Hits* . . . . (BNA)
This Uncivil War
Martina McBride; *Emotion*. . . . . (RCA)
Today My World Slipped Away
George Strait; *Carrying Your Love With Me* . . . . (MCA)
Latest Greatest Straitest Hits . . . . (MCA)
Vern Gosdin; *10 Years Of Greatest Hits Newly Recorded* . . . . (Columbia)
Legends Of The Silver Eagle-C . . . . (King Biscuit Entert.)
Today My World Slipped Away . . . . (AMI)
Too Legit To Quit
Hammer; *Too Legit To Quit* . . . . (Capitol)
Too Many Ways To Fall
Arc Angels; *Arc Angels* . . . . (David Geffen Co.)
Tryin' To Get To Heaven
Bob Dylan; *Time Out Of Mind* . . . . (Columbia)
Tulsa Time
Don Williams; *Best Of Don Williams-#2* . . . .(MCA)
Country's Greatest Hits-#6-Superstars-C . . . . (Priority)
Don Williams-Legends . . . .(MCA)
Expressions . . . .(MCA)
Eric Clapton; *Backless* . . . . (Polydor)
Just One Night . . . . (Polydor)
Two Out Of Three Ain't Bad
Meat Loaf; *Bat Out Of Hell*. . . . .(Epic)
Hits Out Of Hell . . . .(Epic)
We Are The Champions
Big Blue Wrecking Crew; *Baseball's Greatest Hits-C* . . . . (Rhino)
Queen; *Billboard Top Rock 'N' Roll Hits-1978-C* . . . . (Rhino)
Live At Wembley '86 . . . . (Hollywood)
Live Killers . . . . (Hollywood)
News Of The World . . . . (Hollywood)
Queen's Greatest Hits I & II . . . . (Hollywood)
What Mattered Most
Ty Herndon; *Super Hits Of 1995-C* . . . .(Epic)
What Mattered Most . . . .(Epic)
What's Made Milwaukee Famous (Has Made A Loser Out Of Me)
Jerry Lee Lewis; *Heartbreak* . . . . (Tomato)
Milestones . . . . (Rhino)
Rod Stewart; *Best Of Rod Stewart* . . . . (Mercury)
Storyteller/The Complete Anthology: 1964-1990 . . . .(Warner Bros.)
When Heroes Go Down
Suzanne Vega; *99.9 F* . . . . (A&M)
Why Do I Feel So Sad
Alicia Keys; *Songs In A Minor* . . . . (J)
Woke Up This Morning
A3; *Exile On Coldharbour Lane* . . . . (C2/Columbia)
The Sopranos-Music From The HBO Original Series . . . . (Sony Music Soundtrax)

Yesterday's Winner Is A Loser Today
Ernest Tubb; *Ernest Tubb Collection-C* . . . .(Step One)
You Can't Lose Me
Faith Hill; *It Matters To Me*. . . . . (Warner Bros.)
You Don't Know What You've Got (Until You Lose It)
Ral Donner; *You Don't Know What You've Got (Until You Lose It)*. . . . . (Collectables)
Youngstown
Bruce Springsteen; *The Ghost Of Tom Joad* . . . . (Columbia)
You're Going To Lose That Girl
Beatles; *ST/Help!* . . . . (Capitol)
You've Lost That Lovin' Feelin'
Daryl Hall & John Oates; *Voices* . . . . (RCA)
Righteous Brothers; *Best Of The Righteous Brothers* . . . . (Curb)
Billboard Top Rock 'N' Roll Hits-1965-C . . . . (Rhino)
Cruisin'-1965-C . . . . (Increase)
Unchained Melody-Very Best Of The Righteous Brothers . . . .(Polydor)

LOST & MISPLACED, Adrift, Gone Astray, Lose One's Way, Missing

See Also: FINDING, LOVE: SEARCHING FOR LOVE, LOSING & LOSS, SEARCH, SOCIAL OUTCASTS, TRAVELING

A Tisket, A Tasket
Ella Fitzgerald; *Best Of Ella Fitzgerald* . . . . (MCA)
Ella Fitzgerald . . . . (Laserlight)
Glenn Miller & His Army/Air Force Band; *Glenn Miller & His Army/Air Force Band* . . . .(Laserlight)
Tommy Dorsey; *Complete Tommy Dorsey-#7* . . . .(RCA)
All Out Of Love
Air Supply; *Air Supply's Greatest Hits* . . . . (Arista)
Air Supply-The Definitive Collection . . . . (Arista)
Lost In Love . . . . (Arista)
Amazing Grace
Jeff Beck; *All-Star Christmas-C* . . . . (Epic)
Judy Collins; *Colors Of The Day-The Best Of Judy Collins* . . . . (Elektra)
Whales & Nightingales . . . . (Elektra)
Maverick Choir; *ST/Maverick* . . . .(Atlantic)
Nitty Gritty Dirt Band; *Will The Circle Be Unbroken-#2-C* . . . . (Uni)
Tramaine Hawkins; *God Bless America-C* . . . . (Columbia)
America
David Bowie; *The Concert For New York City-C* . . . . (Columbia)
Paul Simon; *Paul Simon In Concert/Live Rhymin'* . . . . (Columbia)
Simon & Garfunkel; *Bookends* . . . . (Columbia)
Collected Works . . . . (Columbia)
Simon & Garfunkel's Greatest Hits . . . . (Columbia)
The Concert In Central Park . . . . (Warner Bros.)
American Tune
Paul Simon; *Paul Simon In Concert/Live Rhymin'* . . . . (Columbia)
There Goes Rhymin' Simon . . . . (Columbia)
Simon & Garfunkel; *The Concert In Central Park* . . . . (Warner Bros.)
Between Heaven And Hell
Zakk Wylde; *Book Of Shadows*. (Spitfire)
Bittersweet Me
R.E.M.; *New Adventures In Hi-Fi* . . . . (Warner Bros.)
Blue Jay Way
Beatles; *Beatles-Box Set* . . . . (Capitol)
Magical Mystery Tour . . . . (Capitol)
Born In The U.S.A.
Bruce Springsteen; *Born In The U.S.A.* . . . . (Columbia)
Bruce Springsteen's Greatest Hits . . . . (Columbia)
Tracks . . . . (Columbia)
Bruce Springsteen & The E Street Band; *Bruce Springsteen & The E Street Band/1975-85* . . . . (Legacy)
Born To Lose
Johnny Cash; *Johnny Cash* . . . . (Everest)
Original Johnny Cash . . . . (Sun)
Rough Cut King Of Country Music. . . . . (Sun)
The Man-The World-His Music . . . . (Sun)
Ray Charles; *Ray Charles-His Greatest Hits-#1* . . . . (Dunhill Compact Classics)
But For The Grace Of God
keith urban; *keith urban*. . . . . (Capitol)
Carnival
Natalie Merchant; *Tigerlily* . . . . (Elektra)
Child Is Gone
Fiona Apple; *Tidal* . . . .(Clean Slate/Work)
Didn't Cha Know
Erykah Badu; *Mama's Gun* . . . . (Motown)
Drift Away
Dobie Gray; *Classic Rock-#1-C* . . . . (MCA)
Oldies But Goodies-#10-C . . . .(Original Sound)
Oldies But Goodies-#3-C . . . .(Original Sound)
Super Hits Of The '70s-Have A Nice Day-#10-C . . . . (Rhino)
Michael Bolton; *Timeless-Classics*. . . . . (Columbia)
Rod Stewart; *Atlantic Crossing*. . . . . (Warner Bros.)

Evening Falls
Enya; *Watermark*. . . . .(Reprise)
Fall From Grace
Amanda Marshall; *Amanda Marshall* . . . . (Epic)
Finders Keepers, Losers Weepers
Soul Children; *Lost Soul-#1-C*. . . . . (Epic)
Finders Keepers, Losers Weepers
Elvis Presley; *Elvis For Everyone!* . . . . (RCA)
Fort Worth Blues
Guy Clark; *Cold Dog Soup* . . . .(Sugar Hill)
Free To Decide
Cranberries; *To The Faithful Departed* . . . . (Island)
Ghost-Town Of My Brain
Jim White; *No Such Place* . . . . (Luaka Bop)
Glory Days
Bruce Springsteen; *Born In The U.S.A.* . . . .(Columbia)
Bruce Springsteen's Greatest Hits . . . .(Columbia)
Godless
U.P.O.; *No Pleasantries* . . . . (Epic)
Goodbye Earl
Dixie Chicks; *Fly* . . . . (Monument)
I Ain't Down Yet
Debbie Reynolds; *ST/The Unsinkable Molly Brown* . . . . (MCA)
I Got Lost In His Arms
Original Broadway Cast; *Annie Get Your Gun* . . . . (Angel)
I Lost My Gal From Memphis
New Sunshine Jazz Band; *Too Much Mustard* . . . . (Biograph)
Tex Williams; *Tex Williams-Vintage Collections* . . . .(Capitol)
I Lost My Sugar In Salt Lake City
Johnny Mercer; *Capitol Collectors Series-Johnny Mercer* . . . .(Capitol)
I Will Get There
Boyz II Men; *ST/The Prince Of Egypt-Inspirational* . . . . . . (DreamWorks/SKG)
I'd Surrender All
Randy Travis; *High Lonesome* . . . .(Warner Bros.)
If I Ever Lose This Heaven
Quincy Jones; *Body Heat*. . . . . (A&M)
I Heard That! . . . . (A&M)
Quincy Jones-Classics-#3 . . . . (A&M)
Quincy Jones-The Best . . . . (A&M)
If She Knew What She Wants
Bangles; *Bangles' Greatest Hits* . . . .(Columbia)
Different Light . . . .(Columbia)
I'm Like A Bird
Nelly Furtado; *Whoa Nelly!* . . . . (DreamWorks/SKG)
It's Alright
Candlebox; *Happy Pills* . . . . (Maverick)
It's In The Book (Parts 1 & 2)
Johnny Standley; *Dr. Demento Gooses Mother-C*. . . . (Kid Rhino/Rhino 4 Kids)
Janey Don't You Lose Heart
Bruce Springsteen; *Tracks* . . . .(Columbia)
Jesus Is The Missing Peace
Whites; *A Lifetime In The Making* . . . .(Ceili Music)
John Doe No. 24
Mary Chapin Carpenter; *Stones In The Road* . . . .(Columbia)
Let Your Soul Be Your Pilot
Sting; *Mercury Falling* . . . . (A&M)
Like A Rolling Stone
Bob Dylan; *Biograph*. . . . .(Columbia)
Bob Dylan At Budokan . . . .(Columbia)
Bob Dylan's Greatest Hits . . . .(Columbia)
Highway 61 Revisited . . . .(Columbia)
More American Graffiti-#4-C . . . . (MCA)
Self Portrait . . . .(Columbia)
Bob Dylan And The Band; *Before The Flood* . . . .(Columbia)
Jimi Hendrix; *ST/Jimi Plays Monterey* . . . .(Reprise)
Jimi Hendrix Experience; *Jimi Hendrix Experience* . . . .(Reprise)
Rolling Stones; *Stripped* . . . .(Virgin)
Long Lost Friend
Restless Heart; *Fast Moving Train* . . . . (RCA)
Lose That Long Face
Judy Garland; *A Star Is Born* . . . .(Columbia)
Lose Your Heart
Bob Welch; *French Kiss* . . . .(Capitol)
Losing My Mind
Bobby Short; *50 By Bobby Short*. . . . . (Atlantic)
Cleo Laine; *Cleo Laine Sings Sondheim* . . . . (RCA)
Liza Minnelli; *Results* . . . . (Epic)
Original Broadway Cast; *Follies* . . . .(Capitol)
Original Cast; *ST/Follies-In Concert* . . . .(RCA Victor)
Lost & Found
Sparks; *Profile-The Ultimate Sparks Collection* . . . . (Rhino)
Lost & Found
Brooks & Dunn; *Brand New Man* . . . . (Arista)
Lost & Found
Original Broadway Cast; *City Of Angels* . . . .(Columbia)
Lost & Found
Echo & The Bunnymen; *Echo & The Bunnymen*. . . . .(Sire)

Lost April
Nat ''King'' Cole; *Nat ''King'' Cole (Box Set)* . . . .(Capitol)
Unforgettable . . . .(Capitol)
Lost Children, The
Michael Jackson; *Invincible* . . . . (Epic)
Lost Highway
Hank Williams With His Drifting Cowboys; *Hank Williams-24 Greatest
    Hits-#2* . . . . (Polydor)
Hank Williams-40 Greatest Hits . . . . (Polydor)
Nitty Gritty Dirt Band; *Will The Circle Be Unbroken* . . . . (EMI)
Lost In A Dream
REO Speedwagon; *A Decade Of Rock And Roll 1970 To 1980* . . . . (Epic)
Lost In A Dream . . . . (Epic)
Lost In A Dream
Buster Brown; *New King Of The Blues* . . . .(Collectables)
Lost In A Dream
Johnny Otis; *Roots Of Rock & Roll* . . . .(Savoy)
Lost In A Lost World
Moody Blues; *Seventh Sojourn* . . . . (Polydor)
Lost In America
Crack The Sky; *From The Greenhouse* . . . .(Grudge)
Lost In Hollywood
Neil Diamond; *Headed For The Future* . . . .(Columbia)
Lost In Hollywood
Rainbow; *Down To Earth*. . . . . (Polydor)
Lost In Love
Air Supply; *Air Supply's Greatest Hits* . . . .(Arista)
Air Supply-The Definitive Collection. . . . .(Arista)
Lost In Love. . . . .(Arista)
Lost In Love: Dream 2-C . . . . (Madacy)
Rock On 1980-C . . . . (Madacy)
Lost In Mexico
Billy Joe Walker, Jr.; *Treehouse* . . . . (MCA)
Lost In The Fifties Tonight
Ronnie Milsap; *Lost In The Fifties Tonight* . . . . (RCA)
Ronnie Milsap's Greatest Hits-#2 . . . . (RCA)
Lost In The Flood
Bruce Springsteen; *Greetings From Asbury Park, N.J.* . . . .(Columbia)
Lost In The Lights Of Broadway
Bernie Shanahan; *Bernie Shanahan* . . . . (Atlantic)
Lost In The Neon World
Be Bop Deluxe; *Modern Music* . . . .(Capitol)
Lost In The Ozone
Commander Cody; *We've Got A Live One Here!* . . . . (Warner Bros.)
Lost In The Stars
Frank Sinatra; *My Kind Of Broadway* . . . . (Reprise)
Mormon Tabernacle Choir; *Climb Ev'ry Mountain* . . . .(Columbia)
Original Cast; *Lost In The Stars* . . . . (MCA)
Sarah Vaughan; *Complete Sarah Vaughan On Mercury-#2*. . . . .(Mercury)
Sheila Jordan; *Lost & Found* . . . . (Muse)
Tony Bennett; *Forty Years-The Artistry Of Tony Bennett* . . . .(Columbia)
Lost In The Supermarket
Clash; *London Calling* . . . . (Epic)
On Broadway . . . . (Epic)
The Story Of The Clash, Volume 1 . . . . (Epic)
Lost In You
Garth Brooks as Chris Gaines; *Garth Brooks In...The Life Of Chris
    Gaines* . . . .(Capitol)
Lost In Your Eyes
Jeff Healey Band; *Feel This* . . . .(Arista)
Lost In Your Eyes
Debbie Gibson; *Electric Youth*. (Atlantic)
Lost John
Doc Watson; *On Stage (Featuring Merle Watson)*. . . . .(Vanguard)
Reverend Gary Davis; *Legendary Rev. Gary Davis-#1* . . . .(Biograph)
Woody Guthrie; *Woody Guthrie-Early Years* . . . . (Tradition)
Lost John Boogied His Way Into Mexico
Maddox Brothers & Rose; *On The Air-#1 & 2* . . . . (Arhoolie)
Lost My Drivin' Wheel
Tom Rush; *Best Of Tom Rush: No Regrets*. . . . .(Legacy)
Tom Rush. . . . .(Columbia)
Lost Paraguayos
Rod Stewart; *Best Of Rod Stewart-#2* . . . .(Mercury)
Sing It Again, Rod . . . .(Mercury)
Lost Queen
Shok Paris; *Steel & Starlight* . . . .(I.R.S.)
Lost Soul
Bruce Hornsby & Shawn Colvin; *A Night On The Town* . . . . (RCA)
Lost Weekend
Sarah Vaughan/Lol Creme/Kevin Godley; *Consequences*. . . . .(Mercury)
Lost Weekend
Wall Of Voodoo; *Call Of The West* . . . .(I.R.S.)
Lost Weekend
Woody Herman & The Woodchoppers; *1940s-Small Groups-C* . . . . .(Columbia)
Lost Weekend
Lloyd Cole & The Commotions; *Easy Pieces* . . . .(Capitol)
Lost Weekend
Roy Lanham; *Legends Of Country Guitar-#1-C* . . . .(Rhino)

Lost Weekend
Del Fuegos; *Smoking In The Fields* . . . . (RCA)
Lost Weekend
Beat Farmers; *Tales Of The New West* . . . . (Rhino)
Lost Without Your Love
Bread; *Bread-Anthology* . . . . (Elektra)
Bread-Retrospective . . . . (Rhino)
Love Your Way
Sophie B. Hawkins; *Songs From Dawson's Creek* . . . . . (Sony Music Soundtrax)
M.T.A.
Kingston Trio; *25 Years Non-Stop* . . . .(Xeres)
Best Of The Kingston Trio . . . . (Capitol)
Capitol Collectors Series-The Kingston Trio. . . . . (Capitol)
Scarlet Ribbons . . . . (Capitol)
Very Best Of The Kingston Trio . . . . (Capitol)
Marooned
Pink Floyd; *The Division Bell* . . . . (Columbia)
Mona Lisa's Lost Her Smile
David Allan Coe; *19 Hot Country Requests-#2-C* . . . .(Epic)
David Allan Coe-17 Greatest Hits . . . . (Columbia)
For The Record-The First 10 Years . . . . (Columbia)
Greatest Country Hits Of The '80s-1984-C . . . . (Columbia)
Just Divorced . . . . (Columbia)
Mota
Offspring; *Ixnay On The Hombre* . . . . (Columbia)
My Baby Needs A Shepherd
Emmylou Harris; *Red Dirt Girl* . . . . (Nonesuch)
Never Surrender
Triumph; *Never Surrender* . . . . (MCA)
Stages . . . . (MCA)
Never Surrender
Corey Hart; *Boy In The Box* . . . . (EMI)
The Singles . . . .(EMI)
No Chance Of Losing
Jerry Garcia; *Jerry Garcia* . . . .(Warner Bros.)
No One
Cold; *13 Ways To Bleed On Stage* . . . . (Flip/Geffen/Interscope)
No Time To Lose
Tarney/Spencer Band; *Run For Your Life* . . . . (A&M)
On Top Of Old Smokey
Bing Crosby; *The Radio Years-#3* . . . . (Crescendo)
Weavers; *Best Of The Weavers* . . . .(MCA)
Reunion-At Carnegie Hall-1963-#2 . . . . (Vanguard)
Weavers' Greatest Hits . . . . (Vanguard)
Once You Lose Your Heart
Original Broadway Cast; *Me & My Girl* . . . . (MCA)
Peggy Suicide Is Missing
Julian Cope; *Jehovahkill*. . . . . (Island)
Rhythm Divine
Enrique Iglesias; *Enrique* . . . .(Overbrook/Interscope)
Rikki Don't Lose That Number
Steely Dan; *Classic Rock-#2-C* . . . .(MCA)
Decade Of Steely Dan . . . . (MCA)
Pretzel Logic . . . . (MCA)
Steely Dan's Greatest Hits . . . . (MCA)
Since I Lost You
Genesis; *We Can't Dance* . . . .(Atlantic)
Snow On The Sahara
Anggun; *Anggun* . . . .(Epic)
Someone Could Lose A Heart Tonight
Eddie Rabbitt; *Best Of Eddie Rabbitt/Greatest Hits-II* . . . .(Warner Bros.)
Number 1's . . . .(Warner Bros.)
Step By Step . . . . (Liberty)
Someone To Watch Over Me
Ella Fitzgerald; *Ella Fitzgerald Sings The George & Ira Gershwin*
Songbook . . . . (Verve)
Elton John; *Glory Of Gershwin Featuring Larry Adler-C* . . . . (Mercury)
Frank Sinatra; *Nice 'N' Easy*. . . . . (Capitol)
The Capitol Years . . . . (Capitol)
Jack Jones; *Gershwin Album* . . . . (Columbia)
Original Broadway Cast; *Crazy For You* . . . . (Angel)
Oscar Peterson; *My Favorite Instrument* . . . . (Verve)
Sarah Vaughan; *Sarah Vaughan Sings George Gershwin Songbook,*
Vol. 2 . . . . (Emarcy)
Willie Nelson; *Stardust*. . . . . (Legacy)
Stranded In The Jungle
Cadets; *Collectables Presents The History Of Rock-#2-C* . . . . (Collectables)
Cruisin'-1956-C . . . . (Increase)
Oldies But Goodies-#1-C . . . . (Original Sound)
Original Rock 'N' Roll Hits Of The '50s-C . . . . (Roulette)
New York Dolls; *In Too Much Too Soon* . . . . (Mercury)
Live In NYC-1975 . . . . (Restless)
Theme From "Lost In Space"
Neil Norman; *Greatest Science Fiction Hits-#3-C* . . . .(Crescendo)
Original Soundtrack; *CBS: The First 50 Years* . . . . (TVT)
Television's Greatest Hits-#1-C . . . . (TVT)
Theme From "Raiders Of The Lost Ark"
Neil Norman; *Greatest Science Fiction Hits-#3-C* . . . .(Crescendo)

Theme From "The Brothers Grunt"
Original Soundtrack; *Television's Greatest Hits-#7-Cable Ready-C* . . . . . (TVT)
Then You Look At Me
Celine Dion; *All The Way...A Decade Of Song* . . . .(550 Music)
There You Are
Martina McBride; *Emotion* . . . . (RCA)
Undun
Guess Who; *American Woman, These Eyes & Other Hits*. . . . .(RCA)
Best Of The Guess Who . . . . (RCA)
Wander This World
Jonny Lang; *Wander This World* . . . . (A&M)
Wandering Stranger
Lionel Richie; *Lionel Richie* . . . . (Motown)
Way, The
Fastball; *All The Pain Money Can Buy* . . . . (Hollywood)
Now That's What I Call Music!-#1-C . . . . (Virgin)
We Don't Need Another Hero (Thunderdome)
Tina Turner; *Live In Europe* . . . . (Capitol)
Simply The Best . . . . (Capitol)
Where Has My Little Dog Gone
Horace Heidt & His Musical Knights; *The Uncollected Horace Heidt & His*
Musical Knights-1939 . . . .(Hindsight)
Whiffenpoof Song
Bing Crosby & Fred Waring & His Glee Club; *Bing Crosby's*
Greatest Hits . . . . (MCA)
Count Basie & Mills Brothers; *Count Basie & Mills Brothers-16 Great*
Performances . . . . (MCA)
Louis Armstrong; *Best Of Louis Armstrong* . . . . (MCA)
Mitch Miller; *34 All-Time Great Sing-Along Selections-C* . . . . (Columbia)
Statler Brothers; *The World Of The Statler Brothers*. . . . . (Columbia)
Whispering Pines
Band; *The Band*. . . . . (Capitol)
Win Or Lose
Earth, Wind & Fire; *Faces*. . . . . (Columbia)
Win Or Lose
Nitty Gritty Dirt Band; *Dirt, Silver & Gold*. . . . . (One Way)
Win Some, Lose Some
Scandal; *Scandal* . . . . (Columbia)
Win Some, Lose Some
Bryan Adams; *Bryan Adams* . . . . (A&M)
Win, Lose Or Draw
Allman Brothers Band; *Best Of The Allman Brothers Band* . . . .(Polydor)
Win, Lose Or Draw . . . . (Polydor)
Winner/Loser
Stomu Yamashta & Go; *Live From Paris* . . . . (Island)
Stomu Yamashta & Go . . . . (Island)
Winners & Losers
Rossington-Collins Band; *Anytime, Anyplace, Anywhere* . . . . (MCA)
Without You
Dixie Chicks; *Fly* . . . . (Monument)
Work It Out
Def Leppard; *Slang* . . . . (Mercury)
You Nearly Lose Your Mind
Ernest Tubb/Willie Nelson/Waylon Jennings; *Ernest Tubb*
Collection-C . . . .(Step One)
Merle Haggard & Janie Fricke; *It's All In The Game* . . . . (Epic)
You Shouldn't Kiss Me Like This
Toby Keith; *How Do You Like Me Now?!*. . . . .(DreamWorks/SKG)
You're Lost, Little Girl
Doors; *Doors 13* . . . . (Elektra)
Strange Days . . . . (Elektra)

LOVE: BACK TOGETHER

See Also: COUPLES, DESIRE, KISSING, LOVE (various),
RETURNING, SEPARATION, TOGETHERNESS

(Best Part Of) Breakin' Up
Ronettes; *Best Of The Ronettes* . . . .(Abkco)
Phil Spector-Back To Mono 1958-1969-C . . . .(Abkco)
98.6
Keith; *'60s Pop-#1-Those Were The Days-C* . . . . (Dominion Entert.)
Austin
Blake Shelton; *Blake Shelton* . . . .(Giant)
Back In Baby's Arms
Patsy Cline; *Patsy Cline's 12 Greatest Hits* . . . . (MCA)
The Patsy Cline Story. . . . . (MCA)
Back In My Arms Again
Diana Ross & The Supremes; *Diana Ross & The Supremes'*
Greatest Hits . . . . (Motown)
Diana Ross & The Supremes-25th Anniversary . . . . (Motown)
Diana Ross & The Supremes-Anthology (1962-1969) . . . . (Motown)
Every Great #1 Hit . . . . (Motown)
Motown Story-First 25 Years-C . . . . (Motown)
Blue Bayou
Linda Ronstadt; *Linda Ronstadt's Greatest Hits, Volume Two* . . . .(Asylum)

Simple Dreams . . . . (Asylum)
Roy Orbison; *For The Lonely: A Roy Orbison Anthology 1959-1965* . . . . (Rhino)
In Dreams-Greatest Hits . . . . (Orbison)
Roy Orbison-More Greatest Hits . . . . (Monument)
Roy Orbison's All-Time Greatest Hits-#1 & 2 . . . . (Monument)
Roy Orbison & Friends; *Black & White Night-Live* . . . . (Virgin)
Homeward Bound
Paul Simon; *Paul Simon In Concert/Live Rhymin'* . . . . (Columbia)
Paul Simon & George Harrison; *Nobody's Child-Romanian Angel Appeal-C* . . . . (Warner Bros.)
Simon & Garfunkel; *Collected Works* . . . . (Columbia)
Parsley Sage Rosemary & Thyme . . . . (Columbia)
Simon & Garfunkel's Greatest Hits . . . . (Columbia)
The Concert In Central Park . . . . (Warner Bros.)
Willie Nelson & Waylon Jennings; *Take It To The Limit* . . . . (Columbia)
I Said A Prayer
Pam Tillis; *Every Time* . . . . (Arista)
It's All Coming Back To Me Now
Celine Dion; *All The Way...A Decade Of Song* . . . . (550 Music)
Falling Into You . . . . (550 Music)
It's Been A Long, Long Time
Bing Crosby; *Best Of Bing Crosby* . . . . (MCA)
Harry James & His Orchestra; *Words & Music Of World War II-C* . . . . (Columbia)
Harry James & Kitty Kallen; *Best Of The Big Bands-C* . . . . (Columbia)
Jan Garber & His Orchestra; *Best Of Jan Garber* . . . . (MCA)
Louis Armstrong; *Hello Dolly! & Other Hits* . . . . (MCA)
Jimmy Mack
Martha & The Vandellas; *Billboard Top R&B Hits-1967-C* . . . . (Rhino)
Compact Command Performances-Martha Reeves & The Vandellas . . . . (Motown)
Martha Reeves & The Vandellas-Anthology . . . . (Motown)
Motown Story-First 25 Years-C . . . . (Motown)
Motown Superstar Series-#11-Martha Reeves & The Vandellas . . . . (Motown)
Top 10 With A Bullet-Motown Girl Groups-C . . . . (Motown)
Judy's Turn To Cry
Lesley Gore; *'60s Dance Party-#2-C* . . . . (Dominion Entert.)
Golden Hits Of Lesley Gore . . . . (Mercury)
Lesley Gore-Anthology . . . . (Rhino)
Letter, The
Box Tops; *Billboard Top Rock 'N' Roll Hits-1967-C* . . . . (Rhino)
Box Tops' Greatest Hits . . . . (Rhino)
Cruisin'-1967-C . . . . (Increase)
Oldies But Goodies-#12-C . . . . (Original Sound)
Rockin' '60s-C . . . . (Priority)
Joe Cocker; *Joe Cocker Live* . . . . (Capitol)
Joe Cocker-Classics-#4 . . . . (A&M)
Joe Cocker's Greatest Hits . . . . (A&M)
Mad Dogs & Englishmen . . . . (A&M)
Vernon Green & The Medallions; *Oldies But Goodies-#1-C* . . (Original Sound)
Vernon Green & The Medallions-Golden Classics . . . . (Collectables)
Lida Rose/Will I Ever Tell You?
Original Broadway Cast; *The Music Man* . . . . (Angel)
Original Cast; *The Music Man* . . . . (Gold Rush)
Soundtrack; *ST/The Music Man* . . . . (Warner Bros.)
Maybe He'll Notice Her Now
Mindy McCready; *Ten Thousand Angels* . . . . (BNA)
My Boyfriend's Back
Angels; *Billboard Top Rock 'N' Roll Hits-1963-C* . . . . (Rhino)
Girl Groups-Story Of A Sound-C . . . . (Rhino)
My Boyfriend's Back . . . . (Collectables)
Oldies But Goodies-#11-C . . . . (Original Sound)
ST/The Wanderers . . . . (Warner Bros.)
Wonder Women-#2-History Of Girl Group-C . . . . (Rhino)
Reunited
Peaches & Herb; *Best Of Peaches & Herb* . . . . (Polydor)
Chicken Soup For The Couples Soul-C . . . . (Rhino)
Didn't A Blow Your Mind: Soul Hits Of The '70s-#20-C . . . . . . (Rhino)
Only Love-1975-1979-C . . . . (JCI Assoc. Labels)
Right Back Where We Started From
Maxine Nightingale; *Mega Hits Dance Classics-#10-C* . . . . (Priority)
She Couldn't Change Me
Montgomery Gentry; *Carrying On* . . . . (Columbia)
Someday We'll Be Together
Diana Ross & The Supremes; *20/20-C* . . . . (Motown)
Diana Ross & The Supremes' Greatest Hits-#3 . . . . (Motown)
Diana Ross & The Supremes-Anthology (1962-1969) . . . . (Motown)
Evening With Diana Ross . . . . (Motown)
Motown Story-First 25 Years-C . . . . (Motown)
Motown Superstar Series-#1-Diana Ross & The Supremes . . . . . (Motown)
Starting Over Again
Natalie Cole; *Good To Be Back* . . . . (Elektra)
Together Again
Buck Owens; *Buck Owens' All-Time Greatest Hits-#1* . . . . (Curb)
Very Best Of Buck Owens-#1 . . . . (Curb)
Emmylou Harris; *Elite Hotel* . . . . (Reprise)
Profile/Best Of Emmylou Harris . . . . (Warner Bros.)
Together Again
Janet Jackson; *Now That's What I Call Music!-#1-C* . . . . (Virgin)

Velvet Rope . . . . (Virgin)
We Just Couldn't Say Goodbye
Guy Lombardo & His Royal Canadians; *Guy Lombardo-16 Most Requested Songs* . . . . (Legacy)
We'll Be Together Again
Barbara Cook; *All I Ask Of You* . . . . (DRG)
Billie Holiday; *Verve Jazz Masters 47-Billie Holiday Sings Standards* . . . (Verve)
Frankie Laine; *The Frankie Laine Collection* . . . . (Mercury)
Lena Horne; *We'll Be Together Again* . . . . (Blue Note)
Louis Armstrong; *Essential Louis Armstrong* . . . . (Verve)
McCoy Tyner; *Priceless Jazz Collection* . . . . (GRP)
Rosemary Clooney; *Do You Miss New York?* . . . . (Concord Jazz)
Sammy Davis, Jr.; *Sammy Davis, Jr.'s Greatest Hits-#2* . . . . (Dunhill Compact Classics)

LOVE: CAN'T GET OVER YOU

See Also: *DESIRE, DIVORCE, ENDINGS, HOLDING ON, KISSING, LEAVING, LONELY, LOSING & LOSS, LOVE (various), SADNESS*

(Marie's The Name) His Latest Flame
Elvis Presley; *Elvis' Golden Records, Volume 3* . . . . (RCA)
ST/This Is Elvis . . . . (RCA)
The Other Sides-Worldwide Gold Award Hits, Vol. 2 . . . . (RCA)
The Top Ten Hits . . . . (RCA)
100% Chance Of Rain
Gary Morris; *Anything Goes* . . . . (Warner Bros.)
Gary Morris-Hits . . . . (Warner Bros.)
4 Seasons Of Loneliness
Boyz II Men; *Evolution* . . . . (Motown)
5 Steps
Dru Hill; *Dru Hill* . . . . (Island)
6, 8, 12
Brian McKnight; *Back At One* . . . . (Motown)
Ain't No Mountain High Enough
Diana Ross; *20/20-C* . . . . (Motown)
25 #1 Hits From 25 Years-C . . . . (Motown)
Diana Ross . . . . (Motown)
Diana Ross-The Ultimate Collection . . . . (Motown)
Every Great Motown Song-First 25 Years-C . . . . (Motown)
Greatest Songs By Ashford & Simpson . . . . (Motown)
Motown Legends-Diana Ross . . . . (Motown)
Motown Story-First 25 Years-C . . . . (Motown)
Motown's Biggest Pop Hits-C . . . . (Motown)
TV ST/Diana-C . . . . (Motown)
Marvin Gaye & Tammi Terrell; *20 Greatest Songs In Motown History-C* . . . . (Motown)
Classic Duets-Marvin Gaye & His Women-C . . . . (Motown)
Marvin Gaye & Tammi Terrell's Greatest Hits . . . . (Motown)
Marvin Gaye Live At The London Palladium . . . . (Motown)
Motown Grammy R&B Performances Of The '60s & '70s-C . . . (Motown)
Performances Of The '60s & '70s-C . . . . (Motown)
United . . . . (Motown)
Ain't No Sunshine When She's Gone
Bill Withers; *Bill Withers' Greatest Hits* . . . . (Columbia)
Bill Withers Live At Carnegie Hall . . . . (Columbia)
Michael Jackson; *Original Soul Of Michael Jackson* . . . . (Motown)
Ain't That Peculiar
Marvin Gaye; *Marvin Gaye-Anthology* . . . . (Motown)
All You Ever Do Is Bring Me Down
Mavericks; *Best Of The Mavericks-Super Colossal Smash Hits Of The '90s* . . . . (Mercury)
Country Superstar Hits-C . . . . (Hip-O)
Honky Tonk Boogie-C . . . . (Hip-O)
Music For All Occasions . . . . (MCA)
Almost A Memory Now
BlackHawk; *Strong Enough* . . . . (Arista)
The Hits-Love & Gravity . . . . (Arista)
Almost Honest
Megadeth; *Cryptic Writings* . . . . (Capitol)
ST/Mortal Kombat 3: Annihilation . . . . (TVT)
Always
Bon Jovi; *Cross Road-14 Classic Grooves* . . . . (Mercury)
Always Be My Baby
Mariah Carey; *Daydream* . . . . (Columbia)
Always On My Mind
Willie Nelson; *Always On My Mind* . . . . (Columbia)
Super Hits Of The '80s-C . . . . (Epic)
Willie Nelson-Super Hits . . . . (Columbia)
Always Something There To Remind Me
Naked Eyes; *Best Of Naked Eyes* . . . . (Gold Rush)
Sandie Shaw; *Burt Bacharach Songbook-C* . . . . (Varese Sarabande)
Amy's Back In Austin
Little Texas; *Kick A Little* . . . . (Warner Bros.)
Little Texas' Greatest Hits . . . . (Warner Bros.)
And Still
Reba McEntire; *Read My Mind* . . . . (MCA)

Reba McEntire's Greatest Hits-#3: I'm A Survivor . . . .(MCA)
Angel
Jon Secada; *Jon Secada* . . . . (SBK)
Angels Of The Silences
Counting Crows; *Recovering The Satellites* . . . . (David Geffen Co.)
Another Lonely Song
Tammy Wynette; *Tammy Wynette-16 Biggest Hits* . . . . (Legacy)
Tammy Wynette-Anniversary-20 Years Of Hits . . . .(Epic)
Tammy Wynette-Super Hits . . . .(Epic)
Tears Of Fire-25th Anniversary Collection . . . .(Epic)
Another Night
Ricky Skaggs and Kentucky Thunder; *Bluegrass Rules!* . . . . (Rounder)
Another You
David Kersh; *Goodnight Sweetheart* . . . . (Curb)
Anything
SWV; *It's About Time* . . . . (RCA)
ST/Above The Rim . . . . (Death Row)
Anything But Down
Sheryl Crow; *The Globe Sessions* . . . . (A&M)
Anything's Better Than Feelin' The Blues
Martina McBride; *Emotion* . . . . (RCA)
Anytime
Eddie Fisher; *Best Of Eddie Fisher* . . . .(MCA)
Eddy Arnold, the Tennessee Plowboy and his Guitar; *Nipper's Greatest Hits*
Of The '40s-#2-C . . . . (RCA)
Patsy Cline; *Best Of Patsy Cline* . . . .(MCA Special Prod.)
Anytime
Brian McKnight; *Anytime* . . . . (Motown)
Now That's What I Call Music!-#1-C . . . . (Virgin)
Apartment #9
Melissa Etheridge; *Tammy Wynette...Remembered-C* . . . . (Asylum)
Tammy Wynette; *Tammy Wynette-Anniversary-20 Years Of Hits* . . . .(Epic)
Tammy Wynette's Greatest Hits . . . .(Epic)
April In Portugal
Eartha Kitt; *Best Of Eartha Kitt* . . . .(MCA)
Are You Lonesome To-night?
Elvis Presley; *A Valentine Gift For You* . . . . (RCA)
Elvis' Golden Records, Volume 3 . . . . (RCA)
From Memphis To Vegas/From Vegas To Memphis . . . . (RCA)
Worldwide 50 Gold Award Hits, Vol. 1, Parts 1 & 2 . . . . (RCA)
Arms Of The One Who Loves You
Xscape; *Traces Of My Lipstick* . . . .(So So Def/Columbia)
Ashes Of Love
Chris Hillman; *Desert Rose* . . . . (Sugar Hill)
Desert Rose Band; *Desert Rose Band* . . . . (Curb)
Dickey Lee; *Ashes Of Love* . . . . (RCA)
Johnnie & Jack & Their Tennessee Mountain Boys; *Johnnie & Jack's*
Greatest Hits . . . . (King)
Rose Maddox; *Rose Of The West Coast Country* . . . . (Arhoolie)
Austin
Blake Shelton; *Blake Shelton* . . . . (Giant)
Autumn Leaves
Barbra Streisand; *Je m'appelle Barbra* . . . . (Columbia)
Frank Sinatra; *Night We Called It A Day* . . . . (Capitol)
Nat "King" Cole; *Blossom Fell* . . . . (Capitol)
Roger Miller; *Music Of The 1950s-C* . . . .(MCA)
Roger Williams; *Best Of Roger Williams* . . . .(MCA)
Roger Williams-Golden Hits-#2 . . . .(MCA)
Baby Come Back To Me (The Morse Code Of Love)
Manhattan Transfer; *Bop doo-wopp* . . . . (Atlantic)
Baby's In Black
Beatles; *Beatles '65* . . . . (Capitol)
Beatles-Box Set . . . . (Capitol)
For Sale . . . . (Capitol)
Back Here
BBMak; *Now That's What I Call Music!-#5-C* . . . . (Virgin)
Sooner Or Later . . . . (Hollywood)
Back To The World
Tevin Campbell; *Back To The World* . . . . (Qwest)
Band Of Gold
Freda Payne; *Beachbeat Draggin'* . . . .(Dunhill Compact Classics)
Didn't It Blow Your Mind: Soul Hits Of The '70s-#2-C . . . . (Rhino)
Freda Payne's Greatest Hits . . . . (HDH)
Bang Bang
Cher; *Cher* . . . . (Geffen)
EMI Legends Of Rock & Roll-24 Greatest Hits-C . . . .(EMI)
Bar Exam
Derailers; *Here Come The Derailers* . . . . (Lucky Dog)
Beer And Bones
John Michael Montgomery; *John Michael Montgomery's*
Greatest Hits . . . . (Atlantic)
Life's A Dance . . . . (Atlantic)
Begging To You
Marty Robbins; *Essential Marty Robbins-1951-1982* . . . . (Columbia)
Marty Robbins-16 Biggest Hits . . . . (Legacy)
Begin The Beguine
Art Tatum; *Solos-1940* . . . .(MCA)
Ella Fitzgerald; *Cole Porter Songbook* . . . . (Verve)

Johnny Mathis; *Best Days Of My Life* . . . . (Columbia)
First 25 Years-Silver Anniversary Album . . . . (Columbia)
Johnny Mathis-Live . . . . (Columbia)
Tony Bennett; *Forty Years-The Artistry Of Tony Bennett* . . . . (Columbia)
Betcha She Don't Love You
Jessica Simpson; *Sweet Kisses* . . . . (Columbia)
Better Things To Do
Terri Clark; *Terri Clark* . . . . (Mercury)
Big River
Grateful Dead; *One From The Vault* . . . .(Grateful Dead)
Steal Your Face . . . .(Grateful Dead)
Johnny Cash; *Johnny Cash-Legend* . . . . (Sun)
Johnny Cash's Greatest Hits-#2 . . . . (Columbia)
Johnny Cash-Sun Years . . . . (Rhino)
Superbilly . . . . (Sun)
The Man In Black-His Greatest Hits . . . . (Legacy)
Rosanne Cash; *Right Or Wrong* . . . . (Columbia)
Billy Dale
Asleep At The Wheel featuring Dolly Parton; *Tribute To The Music Of Bob*
Wills And The Texas Playboys-C . . . . (Liberty)
Bits And Pieces
Dave Clark Five; *History Of The Dave Clark Five* . . . . (Hollywood)
Black Is Black
Los Bravos; *History Of British Rock-#7-C* . . . . (Rhino)
London Collector-Rock Invasion-C . . . . (London)
Blue On Black
Kenny Wayne Shepherd; *Trouble Is...* . . . . (Revolution)
Blue Train, The
Linda Ronstadt; *Feels Like Home* . . . . (Elektra)
Maura O'Connell; *Blue Is The Colour Of Hope* . . . . (Warner Bros.)
Bluer Than Blue
Michael Johnson; *The Michael Johnson Album* . . . . (EMI)
Then & Now . . . .(ISD/Intersound)
Blurry
Puddle Of Mudd; *Come Clean* . . . .(Flawless/Geffen/Interscope)
Bouquet Of Roses
Eddy Arnold; *Eddy Arnold-Pure Gold* . . . . (RCA)
Eddy Arnold-Super Hits . . . . (RCA)
Eddy Arnold-The Hits . . . . (Mercury)
Boys Of Summer
Don Henley; *Building The Perfect Beast* . . . . (Geffen)
Brand New Mister Me
Mel Tillis & The Statesiders; *The Ultimate Mel Tillis* . . . .(Bransounds)
Brandy
Looking Glass; *Billboard Top Rock 'N' Roll Hits-1972-C* . . . . (Rhino)
Rock Artifacts-From The Vaults-#2-C . . . . (Legacy)
Breakin' Me
Jonny Lang; *Wander This World* . . . . (A&M)
Bridge That Just Won't Burn
Conway Twitty; *Number Ones* . . . . (MCA)
Broken Down In Tiny Pieces
Billy "Crash" Craddock; *Crash's Smashes: The Hits Of Billy "Crash"*
Craddock . . . . (Razor & Tie)
Burning A Hole In My Mind
Connie Smith; *Essential Connie Smith* . . . . (RCA)
Burning Of The Midnight Lamp
Jimi Hendrix; *Essential Jimi Hendrix* . . . . (Reprise)
Lifelines/Jimi Hendrix Story . . . . (Reprise)
Jimi Hendrix Experience; *Electric Ladyland* . . . . (Reprise)
Radio One . . . . (Rykodisc)
Living Colour; *Biscuits* . . . . (Epic)
Bury Me Beneath The Willow
Jimmie Davis; *Best Of Jimmie Davis* . . . . (MCA)
Ricky Skaggs; *Skaggs & Rice-The Essential Old-Time Country Duet*
Recordings . . . .(Sugar Hill)
Wilma Lee Cooper; *Wilma Lee Cooper* . . . . (Rounder)
Woody Guthrie; *Woody Guthrie-#1 & 2* . . . . (Collectables)
But Not For Me
Billie Holiday; *Silver Collection* . . . . (Verve)
Chet Baker; *Let's Get Lost-Best Of Chet Baker Sings* . . . . (Blue Note)
Ella Fitzgerald; *Ella Sings Jazz* . . . .(MCA Jazz)
Elvis Costello; *Glory Of Gershwin Featuring Larry Adler-C* . . . . (Mercury)
Harry Connick, Jr.; *ST/When Harry Met Sally* . . . . (Columbia)
Judy Garland; *Best Of Judy Garland* . . . . (MCA)
Original London Cast; *Crazy For You* . . . . (RCA)
Original Soundtrack; *Manhattan* . . . . (CBS Masterworks)
Sarah Vaughan; *Sarah Vaughan Sings George Gershwin Songbook,*
Vol. 2 . . . . (Emarcy)
By The Time I Get To Phoenix
Glen Campbell; *All-Time Country Classics-#1-C* . . . . (Capitol)
Glen Campbell-Classics Collection . . . . (Capitol)
Glen Campbell-Live . . . . (Capitol)
Glen Campbell's Greatest Hits . . . . (Capitol)
Very Best Of Glen Campbell . . . . (Capitol)
Reba McEntire; *Starting Over* . . . . (MCA)
Bye Bye Love
Everly Brothers; *Everly Brothers' All-Time Greatest Hits* . . . . (Curb)
Everly Brothers-Cadence Classics-Their 20 Greatest Hits . . . . (Rhino)
Very Best Of The Everly Brothers . . . . (Warner Bros.)

Simon & Garfunkel; *Bridge Over Troubled Water* . . . . (Columbia)
Can't Get Used To Losing You
Andy Williams; *Andy Williams' Greatest Hits* . . . . (Columbia)
Andy Williams-16 Most Requested Songs . . . . (Legacy)
*Days Of Wine And Roses/Moon River & Other Great Movie
Themes* . . . . (Columbia)
Can't Let Go
Mariah Carey; *Emotions* . . . . (Columbia)
MTV Unplugged-Mariah Carey . . . . (Columbia)
Can't Stand Losing You
Police; *Every Breath You Take-The Classics* . . . . (A&M)
Can't Wait
Bob Dylan; *Time Out Of Mind* . . . . (Columbia)
Can't You See
Alabama; *Alabama-Live* . . . . (RCA)
Charlie Daniels Band; *Volunteer Jam VII-C* . . . . (Epic)
Hank Williams, Jr.; *Hank Williams, Jr. & Friends* . . . . (Polydor)
Rebels, Renegades & Ramblers-C . . . . (Polydor)
Standing In The Shadows . . . . (Polydor)
Marshall Tucker Band; *Marshall Tucker Band* . . . . (AJK Music)
Searchin' For A Rainbow . . . . (AJK Music)
Charmaine
Frank Sinatra; *Frank Sinatra-Complete Reprise Studio Recordings* . . . . (Reprise)
Mantovani; *Mantovani-Golden Hits* . . . . (London)
Mom & Dads; *Good Night Sweetheart* . . . . (Crescendo)
Tommy Dorsey; *Best Of Tommy Dorsey* . . . . (MCA)
Cold Cold Heart
Hank Williams; *Complete Hank Williams* . . . . (Mercury)
Hank Williams With His Drifting Cowboys; *24 Of Hank Williams'
Greatest Hits* . . . . (Polydor)
Hank Williams . . . . (MGM)
Hank Williams-40 Greatest Hits . . . . (Polydor)
Live At Opry . . . . (MGM)
Long Gone Lonesome Blues . . . . (Polydor)
Jerry Lee Lewis; *Duets* . . . . (Sun)
Golden Cream Of Jerry Lee Lewis . . . . (Sun)
Jerry Lee Lewis & Friends-Duets . . . . (Sun)
Lucinda Williams; *Timeless: Hank Williams
Tribute-C* . . . . (Lost Highway/IDJMG)
Tony Bennett; *Tony Bennett-16 Most Requested Songs* . . . . (Legacy)
Could've Been
Tiffany; *Tiffany* . . . . (MCA)
Tiffany's Greatest Hits . . . . (Hip-O)
Crash And Burn
Sheryl Crow; *The Globe Sessions* . . . . (A&M)
Crybaby
Mariah Carey featuring Snoop Dogg; *Rainbow* . . . . (Columbia)
Crying
Don McLean; *Best Of Don McLean* . . . . (EMI)
Greatest Hits Then & Now . . . . (EMI)
Roy Orbison; *For The Lonely: 18 Greatest Hits* . . . . (Rhino)
For The Lonely: A Roy Orbison Anthology 1959-1965 . . . . (Rhino)
In Dreams-Greatest Hits . . . . (Orbison)
Roy Orbison's All-Time Greatest Hits-#1 & 2 . . . . (Monument)
Crying, Waiting, Hoping
Buddy Holly; *Buddy Holly Collection* . . . . (MCA)
Marshall Crenshaw; *ST/La Bamba* . . . . (Slash)
Dance On Little Girl
Paul Anka; *Best Of Paul Anka* . . . . (Rhino)
Paul Anka Sings His Big 15, Vol. 2 . . . . (RCA)
Paul Anka-30th Anniversary Anthology . . . . (Rhino)
Paul Anka's 21 Golden Hits . . . . (RCA)
She's A Lady . . . . (RCA)
Dancing With Tears In My Eyes
Ray Conniff; *Young At Heart* . . . . (Columbia)
Deep Down
Pam Tillis; *All Of This Love* . . . . (Arista)
Pam Tillis-Super Hits . . . . (Arista)
Deep Purple
Art Tatum; *Group Masterpieces-#2* . . . . (Pablo)
Masterpieces . . . . (MCA)
Solo Masterpieces-#3 . . . . (Pablo)
Johnny Mathis; *First 25 Years-Silver Anniversary Album* . . . . (Columbia)
Nino Tempo & April Stevens; *Hit Singles-1958-1977-C* . . . . . . (Atlantic)
Sarah Vaughan; *After Hours* . . . . (Sony Music Special Prod.)
Divine Sarah Vaughan-Columbia Years-1949-1953 . . . . (Columbia)
Deja Voodoo
Kenny Wayne Shepherd; *Ledbetter Heights* . . . . (Giant)
Difficult Kind, The
Sheryl Crow; *The Globe Sessions* . . . . (A&M)
Dirt Road Blues
Bob Dylan; *Time Out Of Mind* . . . . (Columbia)
Does That Blue Moon Ever Shine On You
Toby Keith; *Blue Moon* . . . . (Polydor Country)
Toby Keith's Greatest Hits, Volume One . . . . (Mercury)
Dream About You
Stevie B; *Funky Melody* . . . . (Emporia West/Thump)
Dry Lightning
Bruce Springsteen; *The Ghost Of Tom Joad* . . . . (Columbia)

Easy On The Pain
Michael Martin Murphey; *Cowboy Songs Four* . . . . (Valley Entert.)
Echoes Of Love
Doobie Brothers; *Best Of The Doobies, Volume II* . . . . (Warner Bros.)
Livin' On The Fault Line . . . . (Warner Bros.)
Pointer Sisters; *Energy* . . . . (Planet)
Echoes Of Love
Elvis Presley; *ST/Kissin' Cousins* . . . . (RCA)
Echoes Of Love
Kim Richey; *Kim Richey* . . . . (Mercury)
Everybody Knows
Trisha Yearwood; *Everybody Knows* . . . . (MCA)
Everything's Changed
Lonestar; *Country Cares For Kids II-C* . . . . (BNA)
Crazy Nights . . . . (BNA)
Lonely Grill . . . . (BNA)
Everywhere
Tim McGraw; *Everywhere* . . . . (Curb)
Except For Monday
Lorrie Morgan; *Lorrie Morgan's Greatest Hits* . . . . (BNA)
Something In Red . . . . (RCA)
Faded Love
Bob Wills & His Texas Playboys; *Bob Wills & His Texas Playboys-24
Great Hits* . . . . (Polydor)
For The Last Time . . . . (Capitol)
Tiffany Transcriptions-#2-Best Of The Tiffanys . . . . (Rhino)
Mickey Gilley; *Mickey Gilley's Greatest Hits-#1* . . . . (Epic)
Patsy Cline; *12 Greatest Hits* . . . . (MCA)
Shawn Colvin & Lyle Lovett & Asleep At The Wheel; *Ride With
Bob-C* . . . . (DreamWorks/SKG)
Willie Nelson; *Greatest Hits (& Some That Will Be)* . . . . (Columbia)
Fair
Ben Folds Five; *Whatever And Ever Amen* . . . . (Caroline/550)
Few More Memories
Dolly Parton; *The Grass Is Blue* . . . . (Sugar Hill)
Fire I Can't Put Out
George Strait; *George Strait's Greatest Hits* . . . . (MCA)
Strait From The Heart . . . . (MCA)
Flowers On The Wall
Eric Heatherly; *Swimming In Champagne* . . . . (Mercury)
Statler Brothers; *All Time Legends Of Country Music-C* . . . . . . (Legacy)
Best Of The Statler Brothers . . . . (Mercury)
Billboard Top Country Hits-1966-C . . . . (Rhino)
Columbia Country Classics-#3-Americana-C . . . . (Columbia)
Pop Classics Of The '60s-C . . . . (Columbia)
Flying
Chris Isaak; *Speak Of The Devil* . . . . (Reprise)
Fool
Sanford Clark; *Billboard Top Rock 'N' Roll Hits-1956-C* . . . . . . (Rhino)
Original Classic Oldies Of The '50s & '60s-#17-C . . . . (MCA)
Fool, The
Lee Ann Womack; *Lee Ann Womack* . . . . (Decca)
Foolish Little Girl
Shirelles; *Shirelles' Greatest Hits* . . . . (Everest)
Shirelles-16 Greatest Hits . . . . (Trip)
Shirelles-Anthology 1959-1964 . . . . (Rhino)
Forever
Mariah Carey; *Daydream* . . . . (Columbia)
Fourth Of July
Mariah Carey; *Butterfly* . . . . (Columbia)
From The Bottom Of My Heart
Britney Spears; *...Baby One More Time* . . . . (Jive)
Funny Familiar Forgotten Feelings
Don Gibson; *Best Of Don Gibson-#1* . . . . (Curb)
Mandy Barnett; *I've Got A Right To Cry* . . . . (Sire)
Tom Jones; *Back To Back-Greatest Hits* . . . . (Rebound)
Country Side Of Tom Jones . . . . (London)
Tom Jones-London Collector-Greatest Hits . . . . (London)
Georgia On My Mind
Billie Holiday; *God Bless The Child* . . . . (Columbia)
The Billie Holiday Story-#2 . . . . (Columbia)
Hoagy Carmichael; *Hoagy Carmichael-Legendary Performer* . . . . . . (RCA)
Hoagy Sings Carmichael . . . . (EMI)
Mildred Bailey; *Harlem Lullaby* . . . . (ASV)
Preservation Hall Jazz Band; *Best Of The Preservation Hall
Jazz Band* . . . . (Columbia)
Ray Charles; *Ray Charles' Greatest Hits-#2* . . . . (Rhino)
Ray Charles-Anthology . . . . (Rhino)
Willie Nelson; *Greatest Hits (& Some That Will Be)* . . . . (Columbia)
Stardust . . . . (Legacy)
Willie & Family Live . . . . (Columbia)
Ghost Of You And Me
BBMak; *Sooner Or Later* . . . . (Hollywood)
Ghost Town
Don Cherry; *Columbia & Monument Sides* . . . . (Collector's Choice)
Give Myself A Party
Mandy Barnett; *I've Got A Right To Cry* . . . . (Sire)
Gloria: The Enchantment Medley
Jesse Powell; *Jesse Powell* . . . . (Silas)

Go Walking Down There
Chris Isaak; *Forever Blue* . . . (Reprise)
Go Where You Wanna Go
Mamas & The Papas; *Best Of The Mamas & The Papas* . . . (MCA)
Farewell To The First Golden Era . . . (MCA)
If You Can Believe Your Eyes & Ears . . . (MCA)
Mamas & The Papas-16 Of Their Greatest Hits . . . (MCA)
Going For A Drive
Tammy Rogers; *The Speed Of Love* . . . (Dead Reckoning)
Going Where The Lonely Go
Merle Haggard; *For The Record: Merle Haggard-43 Legendary Hits* . . . (BNA)
Gone
Ferlin Husky; *Ferlin Husky's Greatest Hits* . . . (Curb)
Heroes Of Country Music-#4-Legends Of The West Coast-C . . . (Rhino)
Gone
'N Sync; *Celebrity* . . . (Jive)
Gone Crazy
Alan Jackson; *High Mileage* . . . (Arista)
Good
Better Than Ezra; *Deluxe* . . . (Swell/Elektra)
Good Bye
Martina McBride; *Emotion* . . . (RCA)
Good Morning Heartache
Billie Holiday; *All Or Nothing At All* . . . (Verve)
Billie Holiday's Greatest Hits . . . (Decca Jazz)
From The Original Decca Masters . . . (MCA)
History Of Billie Holiday . . . (Verve)
Diana Ross; *Diana Ross-Anthology* . . . (Motown)
ST/Lady Sings The Blues . . . (Motown)
Tony Bennett with Sheryl Crow; *Playin' With My Friends-Bennett Sings The Blues-C* . . . (Columbia)
Got 'Til It's Gone
Janet featuring Q-Tip & Joni Mitchell; *Velvet Rope* . . . (Virgin)
Great Pretender
Band; *Moondog Matinee* . . . (Capitol)
Platters; *Billboard Top R&B Hits-1956-C* . . . (Rhino)
Cruisin'-1956-C . . . (Increase)
Encore Of Golden Hits-Platters . . . (Mercury)
Platters-Anthology . . . (Rhino)
ST/American Graffiti . . . (MCA)
Super Oldies Of The '50s-#3-C . . . (Audio Fidelity)
Roy Orbison; *Best Of Roy Orbison-Loved Standards* . . . (Monument)
Stan Freberg; *Capitol Collectors Series-Stan Freberg* . . . (Capitol)
Guitars, Cadillacs
Dwight Yoakam; *Guitars, Cadillacs, Etc., Etc.* . . . (Reprise)
Just Lookin' For A Hit . . . (Reprise)
Hangin' Around
Whites; *The '80s: Country Groups' Greatest Hits-C* . . . (K-Tel)
Whites' Greatest Hits . . . (Curb)
Happy Birthday Dear Heartache
Barbara Mandrell; *Barbara Mandrell's Greatest Hits* . . . (MCA)
Country Classics-#1-C . . . (Universal)
Today's Country Classics-C . . . (MCA Special Prod.)
He Stopped Loving Her Today
George Jones; *All Time Legends Of Country Music-C* . . . (Legacy)
First Time Live! . . . (Epic)
George Jones-Anniversary-Ten Years Of Hits . . . (Epic)
Greatest Country Hits Of The '80s-1980-C . . . (Columbia)
Greatest Hits From The Jukebox-C . . . (Epic)
I Am What I Am . . . (Epic)
Heart Won't Lie, The
Reba McEntire & Vince Gill; *It's Your Call* . . . (MCA)
Reba McEntire's Greatest Hits-#3: I'm A Survivor . . . (MCA)
Heartaches
Marcels; *The Doo Wop Box II* . . . (Rhino)
Patsy Cline; *The Patsy Cline Story* . . . (MCA)
Ted Weems & His Orchestra; *Billboard Pop Memories-1945-1949-C* . . (Rhino)
Nipper's Greatest Hits Of The '40s-#2-C . . . (RCA)
Heartaches By The Number
Guy Mitchell; *Sentimental Journey-C* . . . (Dominion Entert.)
Sunshine Guitar . . . (Collectables)
Unforgettable-Love Songs-Fabulous '50s-C . . . (Dominion Entert.)
Ray Price; *Columbia Country Classics-#2-Honky Tonk Heroes-C* . . (Columbia)
Ray Price's Greatest Hits . . . (Columbia)
Ray Price's Greatest Hits-#1-3 . . . (Step One)
Heartbreak Hotel
Albert King; *Blues For Elvis* . . . (Stax)
Elvis Presley; *Elvis As Recorded At Madison Square Garden* . . . (RCA)
Elvis' Golden Records . . . (RCA)
Elvis-A Legendary Performer, Volume 1 . . . (RCA)
Nipper's Greatest Hits Of The '50s-#1-C . . . (RCA)
Worldwide 50 Gold Award Hits, Vol. 1, Parts 1 & 2 . . . (RCA)
Stan Freberg; *Capitol Collectors Series-Stan Freberg* . . . (Capitol)
Willie Nelson; *Greatest Hits (& Some That Will Be)* . . . (Columbia)
Willie Nelson & Leon Russell: One For The Road . . . (Columbia)
Heartbreaker
Mariah Carey; *Rainbow* . . . (Columbia)
Hello Darlin'
Conway Twitty; *Conway Twittty-20 Greatest Hits* . . . (MCA)
Conway Twitty's Greatest Hits . . . (Curb)
From The Vaults: Decca Country Classics-1934-1973-C . . . (Decca)
Greatest Country Classics-#1-C . . . (MCA Special Prod.)
Hello Walls
Faron Young; *Billboard Top Country Hits-1961-C* . . . (Rhino)
Willie Nelson; *Essential Willie Nelson* . . . (RCA)
Willie Nelson-Greatest Songs . . . (Curb)
Helping Me Get Over You
Travis Tritt & Lari White; *The Restless Kind* . . . (Warner Bros.)
Here Comes The Rain
Mavericks; *Music For All Occasions* . . . (MCA)
Here I Am (Just When I Thought I Was Over You)
Air Supply; *Air Supply-The Definitive Collection* . . . (Arista)
He's Gone
Chantels; *Best Of The Chantels* . . . (Rhino)
He's Got You
Brooks & Dunn; *The Greatest Hits Collection* . . . (Arista)
Hit Or Miss (Waited Too Long)
New Found Glory; *New Found Glory* . . . (Drive-Thru)
Honky Tonk Truth
Brooks & Dunn; *Brooks & Dunn-The Greatest Hits Collection* . . . (Arista)
Hopelessly Devoted To You
Olivia Newton-John; *Grammy's Greatest Moments-#3-C* . . . (Atlantic)
Olivia Newton-John's Greatest Hits-#2 . . . (MCA)
ST/Grease . . . (Polydor)
How Can You Mend A Broken Heart
Al Green; *Al Green's Greatest Hits-#1* . . . (Motown)
Compact Command Performances-Al Green . . . (Motown)
Let's Stay Together . . . (Right Stuff)
Bee Gees; *Bee Gees-Gold* . . . (Polydor)
Here At Last...Bee Gees...Live . . . (Polydor)
Nobody's Child-Romanian Angel Appeal-C . . . (Warner Bros.)
How Come You Don't Call Me
Alicia Keys; *Songs In A Minor* . . . (J)
How's It Goin' Down
DMX; *It's Dark And Hell Is Hot* . . . (Def Jam)
I Call Your Name
Beatles; *Past Masters-Volume One* . . . (Parlophone)
Rock 'N' Roll Music . . . (Capitol)
The Beatles' Second Album . . . (Capitol)
I Can Still Feel You
Collin Raye; *The Walls Came Down* . . . (Epic)
I Can't Get Over You
Brooks & Dunn; *If You See Her* . . . (Arista)
I Can't Get You Off My Mind
Bob Dylan; *Timeless: Hank Williams Tribute-C* . . . (Lost Highway/IDJMG)
Hank Williams; *Complete Hank Williams* . . . (Mercury)
Health & Happiness Shows . . . (Mercury)
Patty Loveless; *If My Heart Had Windows* . . . (MCA)
I Can't Help It (If I'm Still In Love With You)
Hank Williams With His Drifting Cowboys; *24 Of Hank Williams' Greatest Hits* . . . (Polydor)
Hank Williams-40 Greatest Hits . . . (Polydor)
Hank Williams, Jr.; *ST/Your Cheatin' Heart* . . . (Sony Music Special Prod.)
Johnny Cash; *First Years* . . . (Allegiance)
Johnny Cash & Jerry Lee Lewis; *Singing Story Teller* . . . (Sun)
Johnny Tillotson; *Poetry In Motion: The Best Of Johnny Tillotson* . . . (Varese Vintage)
Linda Ronstadt; *Heart Like A Wheel* . . . (Capitol)
Linda Ronstadt-Retrospective . . . (Capitol)
Ricky Nelson; *Ricky Nelson Sings Again* . . . (Liberty)
Ricky Nelson-Legendary Masters . . . (EMI)
I Can't Help Myself (Sugar Pie Honey Bunch)
Four Tops; *16 #1 Hits From The Early '60s-C* . . . (Motown)
Billboard Top R&B Hits-1965-C . . . (Rhino)
Four Tops' Greatest Hits . . . (Motown)
Four Tops-Anthology . . . (Motown)
Good Feeling Music Of The Big Chill Generation-#1-C . . . (Motown)
Motown Story-First 25 Years-C . . . (Motown)
Motown Superstar Series-#14-Four Tops . . . (Motown)
ST/Forrest Gump . . . (Epic/Sony Music Soundtrax)
ST/Heaven Help Us . . . (EMI)
ST/Into The Night . . . (MCA)
ST/Where The Buffalo Roam . . . (Backstreet)
I Can't Quit You Baby
Led Zeppelin; *Coda* . . . (Atlantic)
Led Zeppelin . . . (Atlantic)
Led Zeppelin-Box Set . . . (Atlantic)
I Can't Stop Loving You
Don Gibson; *60 Years Of Country Music-C* . . . (RCA)
Collector's Series-Don Gibson . . . (RCA)
Stars Of The Grand Ole Opry-1926-1974-C . . . (RCA)
Elvis Presley; *Aloha from Hawaii via Satellite* . . . (RCA)
Elvis As Recorded At Madison Square Garden . . . (RCA)
Elvis Recorded Live On Stage In Memphis . . . (RCA)
From Memphis To Vegas/From Vegas To Memphis . . . (RCA)
Ray Charles; *Ray Charles' Greatest Hits-#2* . . . (Rhino)
Ray Charles-Anthology . . . (Rhino)
Roy Orbison; *Best Of Roy Orbison-Loved Standards* . . . (Monument)

Legendary Roy Orbison . . . . (Sony Music Special Prod.)

I Could Never Take The Place Of Your Man
Jordan Knight; *Jordan Knight* . . . . (Interscope)

I Could Use Another You
Eddy Raven; *Best Of Eddy Raven* . . . .(Curtom)

I Cried
Patti Page; *Patti Page's Greatest Hits-Finest Performances* . . . . (Sun)

I Don't Have The Heart
James Ingram; *It's Real* . . . . (Warner Bros.)

I Don't Know You Anymore
Savage Garden; *Affirmation* . . . . (Columbia)

I Don't Wanna Talk About It Now
Emmylou Harris; *Red Dirt Girl* . . . . (Nonesuch)

I Don't Want To
Toni Braxton; *Secrets* . . . . (LaFace)

I Drive Myself Crazy
'N Sync; *'N Sync* . . . .(RCA)
Totally Hits-#2-C . . . . (Elektra)

I Fall To Pieces
Aaron Neville & Trisha Yearwood; *Rhythm Country And Blues-C* . . . . . . (MCA)
Patsy Cline; *12 Greatest Hits* . . . . (MCA)
Always . . . . (MCA)
ST/Sweet Dreams . . . . (MCA)
The Patsy Cline Story . . . . (MCA)

I Forgot To Remember To Forget
Elvis Presley; *A Date With Elvis* . . . .(RCA)
Johnny Cash; *Survivors, The* . . . . (Razor & Tie)

I Get The Fever
Bill Anderson; *Bill Anderson's Greatest Hits* . . . .(Varese Sarabande)

I Go To Pieces
Del Shannon; *Rock On!* . . . .(Gone Gator)
Peter And Gordon; *Best Of Peter And Gordon* . . . . (Rhino)
History Of British Rock-#3-C . . . . (Rhino)
Southern Pacific; *County Line* . . . . (Warner Bros.)
Southern Pacific's Greatest Hits . . . . (Warner Bros.)

I Got Id
Pearl Jam; *Merkinball* . . . . (Epic)

I Got The Blues
Rolling Stones; *Sticky Fingers* . . . .(Virgin)

I Had A Dream
Paul Revere And The Raiders; *Legend Of Paul Revere* . . . . (Legacy)

I Had Too Much To Dream (Last Night)
Electric Prunes; *Even More Nuggets-C* . . . . (Rhino)
Nuggets-#1-The Hits-C . . . . (Rhino)
Summer Of Love-#1-C . . . . (Rhino)

I Know
Kim Richey; *Bitter Sweet* . . . . (Mercury)

I Let A Song Go Out Of My Heart
Bill Jennings; *Stompin' With Bill* . . . . (Collectables)
Duke Ellington; *Braggin' In Brass-Immortal 1938 Year* . . . . (Portrait)
Joe Pass; *Portraits Of Duke Ellington* . . . . (Pablo)
Teresa Brewer; *Sophisticated Lady* . . . . (Columbia)
Tony Bennett; *Jazz* . . . . (Columbia)

I Looked Away
Derek And The Dominos; *Layla* . . . . (Polydor)

I Meant Every Word He Said
Ricky Van Shelton; *Greatest Country Hits Of The '90s-#2-C* . . . . . . (Columbia)
RVS III . . . . (Columbia)

I Miss You A Little
John Michael Montgomery; *John Michael Montgomery's
Greatest Hits* . . . . (Atlantic)

I Never Go Around Mirrors
Lefty Frizzell; *Grand Ole Opry-75 Years-#1-C* . . . . (MCA)

I Still Believe
Mariah Carey; *Mariah Carey-#1's* . . . . (Columbia)
MTV Unplugged-Mariah Carey . . . . (Columbia)

I Still Miss Someone
Johnny Cash; *The Man In Black-His Greatest Hits* . . . . (Legacy)

I Thought About You
Billie Holiday; *Lady Sings The Blues* . . . . (Verve)
Dinah Washington; *What A Diff'rence A Day Makes* . . . . (Mercury)
Frank Sinatra & Nelson Riddle Orchestra; *songs for Swingin'
Lovers!* . . . . (Capitol)
Rosemary Clooney; *Rosemary Clooney Sings The Music Of Jimmy Van
Heusen* . . . . (Concord Jazz)
Tony Bennett; *Perfectly Frank* . . . . (Columbia)

I Try
Macy Gray; *Now That's What I Call Music!-#4-C* . . . .(Virgin)
On How Life Is . . . . (Epic)

I Will Buy You A New Life
Everclear; *Now That's What I Call Music!-#1-C* . . . .(Virgin)
So Much For The Afterglow . . . . (Capitol)

I Will Love Again
Lara Fabian; *Lara Fabian* . . . . (Columbia)

I Wonder Do You Think Of Me
Keith Whitley; *I Wonder Do You Think Of Me* . . . .(RCA)

I'd Rather Go Blind
Etta James; *Best Blues Album In The World...Ever!-C* . . . . (Virgin)

Best Blues Album In The World...Ever!-C . . . . (Virgin)

If Drinkin' Don't Kill Me (Her Memory Will)
George Jones; *10 Years Of Hits* . . . . (Epic)
I Am What I Am . . . . (Epic)

If He Should Break Your Heart
Journey; *Trial By Fire* . . . . (Columbia)

If I Could Turn Back The Hands Of Time
R. Kelly; *Now That's What I Call Music!-#3-C* . . . . (Virgin)
R. . . . . (Jive)

If You See Her, Say Hello
Bob Dylan; *Blood On The Tracks* . . . .(Columbia)

If You See Him/If You See Her
Brooks & Dunn & Reba McEntire; *If You See Her* . . . .(Arista)
Reba McEntire & Brooks & Dunn; *If You See Him* . . . . (MCA)
Reba McEntire's Greatest Hits-#3: I'm A Survivor . . . . (MCA)

If You're Ever Down In Dallas
Lee Ann Womack; *Some Things I Know* . . . .(Decca)

I'll Go On Loving You
Alan Jackson; *High Mileage* . . . .(Arista)

I'll Think Of Something
Mark Chesnutt; *Longnecks & Short Stories* . . . . (MCA)
Mark Chesnutt's Greatest Hits . . . .(Decca)

I'm A Honky Tonk Girl
Loretta Lynn; *The Country Music Hall Of Fame-Loretta Lynn* . . . . (MCA)

I'm Blue (The Gong-Gong Song)
Ikettes; *Great R&B Female Groups-Hits Of The '60s-C* . . . . . .(K-Tel)

I'm Goin' Down
Mary J. Blige; *My Life* . . . . (Uptown/MCA)

I'm Gonna Sit Right Down And Write Myself A Letter
Billy Williams; *Stardust: The Classic Decca Hits & Standards
Collection-C* . . . .(Decca)
Fats Waller; *Fats Waller* . . . . (RCA Special Prod.)
Frank Sinatra; *Sinatra-Basie* . . . . (Reprise)
Songs For Young Lovers & Swing Easy . . . . (Capitol)
Nat "King" Cole; *Just One Of Those Things (& More)* . . . . . . (Capitol)
Nat "King" Cole-Gift Set . . . .(Capitol)
Original Cast; *Ain't Misbehavin'* . . . . (RCA)

I'm Lonesome Without You
Country Gentlemen; *Sugar Hill Collection* . . . . (Sugar Hill)
Lonesome Standard Time; *Legacy-A Tribute To The First Generation Of
Bluegrass-C* . . . . (Sugar Hill)
Stanley Brothers & The Clinch Mountain Boys; *Classic Bluegrass-Stanley
Brothers & The Clinch Mountain Boys* . . . . (Rebel)

I'm Not In Love
10 CC; *10 CC's Greatest Hits-1972-1978* . . . . (Polydor)
Super Hits Of The '70s-Have A Nice Day-#14-C . . . .(Rhino)
Will To Power; *Journey Home* . . . . (Epic)

I'm Not Supposed To Love You Anymore
Bryan White; *Between Now And Forever* . . . . (Asylum)

I'm Over You
Keith Whitley; *I Wonder Do You Think Of Me* . . . . (RCA)
Keith Whitley's Greatest Hits . . . . (RCA)

I'm So Happy I Can't Stop Crying
Sting; *Mercury Falling* . . . . (A&M)
Toby Keith with Sting; *Dream Walkin'* . . . .(Mercury)
Toby Keith's Greatest Hits, Volume One . . . . (Mercury)

I'm Sorry
Brenda Lee; *Billboard Top Pop Hits-1960-C* . . . .(Rhino)
Brenda Lee-Anthology-#1 & #2 . . . . (MCA)
The Brenda Lee Story-Her Greatest Hits . . . .(MCA)
Platters; *Enchanted-The Best Of The Platters* . . . . (Rhino)
Magic Touch-An Anthology . . . . (Mercury)

I'm Walking Behind You
Eddie Fisher; *Very Best Of Eddie Fisher* . . . . (MCA)
Frank Sinatra; *Capitol Collectors Series-Frank Sinatra* . . . .(Capitol)
Concepts . . . . (Capitol)
Point Of No Return . . . . (Capitol)

In Another World
Joe Diffie; *In Another World* . . . . (Monument)

In Dreams
Roy Orbison; *For The Lonely: A Roy Orbison Anthology 1959-1965* . . . . (Rhino)
In Dreams-Greatest Hits . . . . (Orbison)

In The Valley
Marty Robbins; *Gunfighter Ballads & Trail Songs* . . . .(Legacy)

Incomplete
Sisqo; *Now That's What I Call Music!-#5-C* . . . . (Virgin)
Unleash The Dragon . . . . (Dragon/Def Soul/IDJMG)

It Don't Hurt
Sheryl Crow; *The Globe Sessions* . . . . (A&M)

It Happened In Monterey
Frank Sinatra & Nelson Riddle Orchestra; *songs for Swingin'
Lovers!* . . . .(Capitol)
Mel Torme & The Mel-Tones; *Back In Town* . . . . (Verve)

It Happens To Be Me
Earl "Fatha" Hines; *At Home* . . . . (Delmark)

It Only Hurts For A Little While
Ames Brothers; *Best Of The Ames Brothers* . . . . (Pair)
Anne Murray; *Croonin'* . . . .(SBK)
Margo Smith; *Best Of Margo Smith* . . . . (MCA Special Prod.)

It Should Have Been Easy
Whites; *45-#52953* .... (Curb/MCA)
It Wouldn't Hurt To Have Wings
Mark Chesnutt; *Wings* .... (Decca)
It's All Coming Back To Me Now
Celine Dion; *All The Way...A Decade Of Song*................ (550 Music)
   Falling Into You...................................... (550 Music)
It's The Same Old Song
Four Tops; *Billboard Top R&B Hits-1965-C* .... (Rhino)
   Compact Command Performances-Four Tops .... (Motown)
   Four Tops' Greatest Hits .... (Motown)
   Four Tops-Anthology............................... (Motown)
Jealousy
Natalie Merchant; *Tigerlily*.............................. (Elektra)
Just A Little Lovin' (Will Go A Long, Long Way)
Eddy Arnold; *Best Of Eddy Arnold*........................... (RCA)
   Eddy Arnold-Pure Gold.............................. (RCA)
Just As Much As Ever
Bobby Vinton; *Bobby Vinton-16 Most Requested Songs* .... (Legacy)
Just Walking In The Rain
Johnnie Ray; *16 Most Requested Songs Of The '50s-#1-C* .... (Legacy)
   Best Of Johnnie Ray............................... (Columbia)
   Johnnie Ray-16 Most Requested Songs .... (Legacy)
   Johnnie Ray's Greatest Hits .... (Sony Music Special Prod.)
King Of Sorrow
Sade; *Lovers Rock*..(Epic)
King Of The Mountain
George Strait; *Blue Clear Sky*.............................(MCA)
   Latest Greatest Straitest Hits.....................(MCA)
Last Kiss
J. Frank Wilson and The Cavaliers; *Billboard Top Rock 'N' Roll Hits-*
   1964-C..(Rhino)
   Collectables Presents The History Of Rock-#2-C ....(Collectables)
   Oldies But Goodies-#9-C..................... (Original Sound)
   Teenage Tragedies-C................................(Rhino)
Pearl Jam; *No Boundaries-Benefit For The Kosovar Refugees-C*........(Epic)
Last Night I Didn't Get To Sleep At All
5th Dimension; *Greatest Hits On Earth* .... (Arista)
Lately
Divine; *Fairy Tales*.................................. (Pendulum)
Leaving October
Sons Of The Desert; *Whatever Comes First* ....(Epic)
Let Me Let Go
Faith Hill; *Faith* ....(Warner Bros.)
Lilly Dale
Bob Wills & His Texas Playboys; *The Country Music Hall Of Fame-Bob*
   Wills .... (Universal)
Little Bit Of Soap
Jarmels; *Collectables Presents The History Of Rock-#7-C* ...... (Collectables)
   Jarmels-Golden Classics .... (Collectables)
   Laurie Golden Oldies .... (Laurie)
   Million-Dollar Memories #1-C .... (RCA)
   Pick Hits Of The Radio Good Guys-C .... (Laurie)
Paul Davis; *Best Of Paul Davis*............................. (Bang)
   Little Bit Of Paul Davis .... (Bang)
Little Old Wine Drinker Me
Dean Martin; *Dean Martin's Greatest Hits-#2*................ (Reprise)
   Welcome To My World............................... (Reprise)
Mel Tillis; *Best Of Mel Tillis*............................(MCA)
Little Past Little Rock
Lee Ann Womack; *Some Things I Know* .... (Decca)
Little White Lies
Dick Haymes with Gordon Jenkins & His Orchestra; *Sentimental Journey:*
   Pop Vocal Classics-#2-1947-1950-C .... (Rhino)
Dinah Shore; *Dinah Shore-16 Most Requested Songs-Encore!* .... (Legacy)
Fred Waring's Pennsylvanians featuring Clare Hanlon; *Very Best Of Fred*
   Waring & The Pennsylvanians .... (Reader's Digest Music)
Tommy Dorsey; *Best Of Tommy Dorsey* .... (Bluebird)
   Complete Tommy Dorsey-#6 .... (RCA)
Livin' Without You
Nitty Gritty Dirt Band; *Best Of The Nitty Gritty Dirt Band*........... (Curb)
   Dirt, Silver & Gold............................... (One Way)
   Uncle Charlie And His Dog Teddy................... (Liberty)
   Workin' Band.................................(Warner Bros.)
Living Lovin' Wreck
Jerry Lee Lewis; *Golden Rock & Roll*......................... (Sun)
   Original Jerry Lee Lewis .... (Sun)
Living Without You
Randy Newman; *Randy Newman* ....(Warner Archives)
   Randy Newman/Live..........................(Warner Archives)
Lonely
Tracy Lawrence; *Lessons Learned* ....(Atlantic)
Lonely Teardrops
Jackie Wilson; *Billboard Top R&B Hits-1958-C* .... (Rhino)
   Reet Petite-Best Of Jackie Wilson .... (Columbia)
   The Jackie Wilson Story...........................(Epic)
   The Jackie Wilson Story-#2 ....(Epic)
Lonely Won't Leave Me Alone
Trace Adkins; *Big Time* .... (Capitol)

Long December
Counting Crows; *Recovering The Satellites* .... (David Geffen Co.)
Long Hot Summer Night
Jimi Hendrix Experience; *Electric Ladyland* .... (Reprise)
Long Long Time
Linda Ronstadt; *Different Drum* .... (Capitol)
   Linda Ronstadt-Retrospective .... (Capitol)
   Linda Ronstadt's Greatest Hits .... (Asylum)
   Silk Purse .... (Capitol)
Longneck Bottle
Garth Brooks; *Sevens* .... (Capitol)
Look What Followed Me Home
David Ball; *Thinkin' Problem* .... (Warner Bros.)
Love Hangover
Diana Ross; *20 Greatest Songs In Motown History-C*........... (Motown)
   20/20-C.. (Motown)
   Diana Ross-All The Great Hits .... (Motown)
   Diana Ross-Anthology.............................. (Motown)
   Diana Ross-The Ultimate Collection .... (Motown)
Love Is Blue
Andre Kostelanetz; *Andre Kostelanetz-16 Most Requested Songs* ... (Columbia)
Paul Mauriat; *Love Is Blue*...............................(Mercury)
Sandpipers; *Softly* .... (A&M)
Love Letters From Old Mexico
Leslie Satcher; *Love Letters* .... (Warner Bros.)
Love Letters In The Sand
Mac Wiseman; *24 Greatest Bluegrass Hits-C*........... (C.M.H. Prod.)
Pat Boone; *Best Of Pat Boone*.............................. (MCA)
   Pat Boone-16 Great Performances .... (MCA)
   Vintage Music-#2-C............................... (MCA)
Ted Black & His Orchestra; *78-#22799* .... (Victor)
Love Sick
Bob Dylan; *Time Out Of Mind* .... (Columbia)
Lover After Me, The
Savage Garden; *Affirmation* .... (Columbia)
Magnolia
J.J. Cale; *Naturally* .... (MCA)
Man Holdin' On (To A Woman Lettin' Go)
Ty Herndon; *Big Hopes*................................. (Epic)
Mandy
Barry Manilow; *Barry Manilow II* .... (Arista)
   Barry Manilow's Greatest Hits-#1 .... (Arista)
   Live On Broadway .... (Arista)
Meanwhile
George Strait; *Always Never The Same* .... (MCA)
Melancholy Blue
Trisha Yearwood; *Inside Out* .... (MCA)
Memories To Burn
Gene Watson; *Country Heartbreakers-C* .... (K-Tel)
Million Miles
Bob Dylan; *Time Out Of Mind* .... (Columbia)
Mirage
Tommy James And The Shondells; *Tommy James And The Shondells-*
   Anthology .... (Rhino)
Mirror Mirror
Diamond Rio; *Diamond Rio* .... (Arista)
   Diamond Rio's Greatest Hits .... (Arista)
Misery And Gin
Merle Haggard; *Back To The Barrooms* .... (MCA)
   Merle Haggard's Greatest Hits .... (MCA)
   Rainbow Stew-Live At Anaheim Stadium .... (MCA)
Missing You
Brooks & Dunn; *Tight Rope* .... (Arista)
John Waite; *'80s Greatest Rock Hits-#1-Passion & Power-C* .... (Priority)
   Complete John Waite-#1-Falling Backwards .... (EMI)
   Essential John Waite-1976-1986 .... (Chrysalis)
Tina Turner; *Wildest Dreams* .... (Virgin)
Missing You
Case; *Open Letter* .... (Def Soul/IDJMG)
Mistakes
Mandy Barnett; *I've Got A Right To Cry* ....(Sire)
Misty Blue
Dorothy Moore; *Blues Is Alright* .... (Malaco)
   Misty Blue....................................... (Malaco)
   Sexy Soul-C .... (K-Tel)
Eddy Arnold; *Best Of Eddy Arnold-#2* .... (Dunhill Compact Classics)
   Country Gold-Eddy Arnold .... (RCA)
   This Is Eddy Arnold .... (RCA)
Wilma Burgess; *From The Vaults: Decca Country Classics-1934-*
   1973-C... (Decca)
Mood Indigo
Duke Ellington; *1954 Los Angeles Concert* ....(Crescendo)
   Black, Brown & Beige: 1944-1946 Band Recordings............ (Bluebird)
   Carnegie Hall Concert-January 23, 1943 ....(Prestige)
   Ellington Indigos .... (Columbia)
   Sophisticated Ellington...........................(RCA)
Ella Fitzgerald; *Ella A Nice* .... (Pablo)
   Ella Fitzgerald Sings-#5 .... (Verve)
Four Freshmen; *Capitol Collectors Series-Four Freshman* .... (Capitol)

Frank Sinatra; *In The Wee Small Hours* . . . . (Capitol)
Jimmie Lunceford & His Orchestra; *Stomp It Off-#1-1934-1935* . . . . (GRP)
Preservation Hall Jazz Band; *Best Of The Preservation Hall
    Jazz Band* . . . . (Columbia)
    New Orleans-#4 . . . . (Columbia)

Most Beautiful Girl
Charlie Rich; *Behind Closed Doors* . . . . (Epic)
    Charlie Rich's Greatest Hits . . . . (Epic)
    Columbia Country Classics-#4-Nashville Sound-C . . . . (Columbia)

My All
Mariah Carey; *Butterfly* . . . . (Columbia)
    Mariah Carey-#1's . . . . (Columbia)
    VH-1 Divas Live-C . . . . (Epic)

My Name Is Not Susan
Whitney Houston; *I'm Your Baby Tonight* . . . . (Arista)

My Old Flame
Duke Ellington; *Nipper's Greatest Hits Of The '30s-#1-C* . . . . (RCA)
Guy Lombardo & His Royal Canadians; *Guy Lombardo-16 Most Requested
    Songs* . . . . (Legacy)
J.J. Johnson; *Trombone Master* . . . . (Columbia)
Linda Ronstadt; *Lush Life* . . . . (Asylum)
Rosemary Clooney; *Great Girl Singers Sing 22 Original
    Recordings-C* . . . . (Hindsight)
Stan Kenton & His Orchestra; *Road Show* . . . . (Capitol)
Tommy Smith; *Standards* . . . . (Blue Note)

My Shoes Keep Walking Back To You
Ray Price; *All Time Legends Of Country Music-C* . . . . (Legacy)
    Essential Ray Price-1951-1962 . . . . (Columbia)
    Ray Price's Greatest Hits . . . . (Columbia)

My World Is Empty Without You
Diana Ross; *Diana Ross-Anthology* . . . . (Motown)
    Evening With Diana Ross . . . . (Motown)
Stevie Wonder; *Down To Earth* . . . . (Motown)

Needles And Pins
Jackie DeShannon; *Very Best Of Jackie DeShannon* . . . . (EMI)
Searchers; *History Of British Rock-#1-C* . . . . (Rhino)
    Searchers' Greatest Hits . . . . (Rhino)
Tom Petty And The Heartbreakers; *Pack Up The Plantation-Live!* . . . . . (MCA)

Neon Moon
Brooks & Dunn; *Brand New Man* . . . . (Arista)

Never Again, Again
Lee Ann Womack; *Lee Ann Womack* . . . . (Decca)

Never Had A Dream Come True
S Club 7; *Now That's What I Call Music!-#7-C* . . . . (Virgin)
    S Club 7 . . . . (A&M)

New San Antonio Rose
Bob Wills & His Texas Playboys; *Bob Wills & His Texas Playboys-
    Greatest Hits* . . . . (Curb)
    Columbia Country Classics-#1-Golden Age-C . . . . (Columbia)
    Essential Bob Wills & His Texas Playboys-1935-1973 . . . . (Legacy)
Dwight Yoakam & Asleep At The Wheel; *Ride With
    Bob-C* . . . . (DreamWorks/SKG)

Next To Nothin'
Gene Watson; *From The Heart* . . . . (Row Music Group)

Night Lights
Nat "King" Cole; *Night Lights* . . . . (Capitol/EMI)

Night To Remember
Joe Diffie; *A Night To Remember* . . . . (Epic)

No Getting Over You
Kilauea; *Diamond Collection* . . . . (Brainchild)

Nobody Knows
Kevin Sharp; *Measure Of A Man* . . . . (143/Asylum)
Tony Rich Project; *Words* . . . . (LaFace)

Nookie
Limp Bizkit; *Now That's What I Call Music!-#3-C* . . . . (Virgin)
    Significant Other . . . . (Flip/Interscope)

Nothin' But The Wheel
Patty Loveless; *Only What I Feel* . . . . (Epic)
    Patty Loveless-Classics . . . . (Epic)

Oh Lonesome Me
Don Gibson; *20 Top 10 Hits Of The '50s & '60s-C* . . . . (Laurie)
    Collector's Series-Don Gibson . . . . (RCA)
    Don Gibson's All-Time Greatest Hits . . . . (RCA)
    Nipper's Greatest Hits Of The '50s-#1-C . . . . (RCA)
Johnny Cash; *Get Rhythm* . . . . (Sun)
    Johnny Cash-Original Golden Hits-#3 . . . . (Sun)
Kentucky HeadHunters; *Pickin' On Nashville* . . . . (Mercury)
Neil Young; *After The Gold Rush* . . . . (Reprise)

On A Bus To St. Cloud
Gretchen Peters; *The Secret Of Life* . . . . (Purple Crayon Prod.)
Trisha Yearwood; *Thinkin' About You* . . . . (MCA)

Once A Day
Connie Smith; *Billboard Top Country Hits-1964-C* . . . . (Rhino)
    Connie Smith-Super Hits . . . . (RCA)
    Essential Connie Smith . . . . (RCA)

Once You've Loved Somebody
Dixie Chicks; *Wide Open Spaces* . . . . (Monument)

One Less Bell To Answer
5th Dimension; *5th Dimension-Anthology 1967-1973* . . . . (Rhino)

Greatest Hits On Earth . . . . (Arista)
Barbra Streisand; *Barbra Joan Streisand* . . . . (Columbia)
Gladys Knight & The Pips; *Gladys Knight & The Pips-Anthology* . . . . (Motown)
    If I Were Your Woman . . . . (Motown)

One More Day
Diamond Rio; *One More Day* . . . . (Arista)

Only On Days That End In "Y"
Clay Walker; *Hypnotize The Moon* . . . . (Giant)

Ophelia
Band; *Best Of The Band* . . . . (Capitol)
    Northern Lights-Southern Cross . . . . (Capitol)
    The Last Waltz . . . . (Warner Bros.)
    To Kingdom Come-The Definitive Collection . . . . (Capitol)

Orchids Mean Goodbye
Carl Smith; *45-#21087* . . . . (Columbia)

Otherside
Red Hot Chili Peppers; *Californication* . . . . (Warner Bros.)

Out Of My Bones
Randy Travis; *You And You Alone* . . . . (DreamWorks/SKG)

Out Of Sight, Out Of Mind
Five Keys; *Golden Classics-Five Keys* . . . . (Collectables)

Over You
Gary Puckett And The Union Gap; *Best Of Gary
    Puckett* . . . . (Hollywood/DNA-Rounder)
    Gary Puckett-Super Hits . . . . (Legacy)

Painted On My Heart
Cult; *ST/Gone In 60 Seconds* . . . . (Island)

Please
Kinleys; *Just Between You And Me* . . . . (Epic)

Please Remember Me
Tim McGraw; *A Place In The Sun* . . . . (Curb)
    Tim McGraw's Greatest Hits . . . . (Curb)

Poor Boy
Woody Guthrie; *Legendary Woody Guthrie* . . . . (Tradition)
    Woody Guthrie . . . . (Everest)
    Worried Man Blues-Golden Classics-#1 . . . . (Collectables)

Pop A Top
Alan Jackson; *Under The Influence* . . . . (Arista)
Jim Ed Brown; *Essential Jim Ed Brown* . . . . (RCA)

Prisoner Of Love
Art Tatum; *Solo Masterpieces-#3* . . . . (Pablo)
Frank Sinatra; *Sinatra & Strings* . . . . (Reprise)
Perry Como; *Como's Golden Records* . . . . (RCA)
    Nipper's Greatest Hits Of The '40s-#2-C . . . . (RCA)
    Perry Como-Pure Gold . . . . (RCA)
    This Is Perry Como . . . . (RCA)

Reflections
Diana Ross & The Supremes; *Diana Ross & The Supremes' Greatest
    Hits-#3* . . . . (Motown)
    Diana Ross & The Supremes-25th Anniversary . . . . (Motown)
    Diana Ross & The Supremes-Anthology (1962-1969) . . . . (Motown)
    Motown Story-First 25 Years-C . . . . (Motown)
Four Tops; *Four Tops-Anthology* . . . . (Motown)
    Still Waters Run Deep . . . . (Motown)
    Until You Love Someone: More Of The Best (1965-1970) . . . . (Rhino)
Luther Vandross; *Songs* . . . . (Epic)

Refried Dreams
Tim McGraw; *Not A Moment Too Soon* . . . . (Curb)

Release Me
Angelina; *Angelina* . . . . (Upstairs)

Remember Me
Marc Anthony; *Marc Anthony* . . . . (Columbia)

Rhapsody In The Rain
Lou Christie; *Enlighten'ment-Best Of Lou Christie* . . . . (Rhino)

Rhythm Of The Rain
Cascades; *Collectables Presents The History Of Rock-#7-C* . . . . . (Collectables)
    Golden Years-1963-C . . . . (Dominion Entert.)

Ridin' That Midnight Train
Ricky Skaggs and Kentucky Thunder; *Bluegrass Rules!* . . . . (Rounder)

Right In Time
Lucinda Williams; *Car Wheels On A Gravel Road* . . . . (Mercury)

Right Or Wrong
George Strait; *George Strait's Greatest Hits* . . . . (MCA)
    Right Or Wrong . . . . (MCA)
    Strait Out Of The Box . . . . (MCA)
Reba McEntire & Asleep At The Wheel; *Ride With
    Bob-C* . . . . (DreamWorks/SKG)

Roamin' Wyoming
Randy Travis; *Wind In The Wire* . . . . (Warner Bros.)

Roof, The
Mariah Carey; *Butterfly* . . . . (Columbia)

Round About Way
George Strait; *Carrying Your Love With Me* . . . . (MCA)
    Latest Greatest Straitest Hits . . . . (MCA)

San Francisco Days
Chris Isaak; *San Francisco Days* . . . . (Reprise)

Send Me The Pillow You Dream On
Browns; *45-#7804* . . . . (RCA)
Dwight Yoakam; *Buenas Noches From A Lonely Room* . . . . (Reprise)

Hank Locklin; *Hank Locklin-20 Golden Souvenirs* (RCA)
Nipper's Greatest Hits Of The '50s-#1-C (RCA)
Please Help Me I'm Falling (Collectables)
Stars Of The Grand Ole Opry-1926-1974-C (RCA)
Johnny Tillotson; *Golden Classics-Johnny Tillotson* (Collectables)
Willie Nelson & Hank Snow; *Brand On My Heart* (Columbia)

Sentimental
Deborah Cox; *Deborah Cox* (Arista)

Set 'Em Up Joe
Vern Gosdin; *Chiseled In Stone* (Columbia)
Greatest Country Hits Of The '80s-1988-C (Columbia)

She's Gone
Eric Clapton; *Pilgrim* (Duck/Reprise)

She's Got You
Patsy Cline; *12 Greatest Hits* (MCA)
Billboard Top Country Hits-1962-C (Rhino)
The Patsy Cline Story (MCA)

She's In Love
Mark Wills; *Wish You Were Here* (Mercury)

Signed, Sealed, Delivered I'm Yours
Stevie Wonder; *20/20-C* (Motown)
Motown Grammy R&B Performances Of The '60s & '70s-C (Motown)
Stevie Wonder's Greatest Hits-#2 (Motown)
Uptight (Everything's Alright) (Motown)

Silver Springs
Fleetwood Mac; *1998 Grammy Nominees-C* (MCA)
25 Years-The Chain (Warner Bros.)
The Dance (Reprise)

Since I Don't Have You
Rick Nelson; *Best Of Rick Nelson 1963-1975* (MCA)
Ronnie McDowell; *Best Of Ronnie McDowell* (Curb)
Ronnie Milsap; *Back To The Grindstone* (RCA)
Skyliners; *Doo-Wop Ballads-#2-C* (Rhino)
La Bamba & Other Original Hits-C (Laurie)
Oldies But Goodies-#5-C (Original Sound)
Skyliners' Greatest Hits (Original Sound)

Since I Don't Have You
Marty Stuart; *Hillbilly Rock* (MCA)

Since I Lost My Baby
Temptations; *Temptations' Greatest Hits-#1* (Motown)
Temptations-Anthology-The Best Of The Temptations (Motown)
Temptations-The Ultimate Collection (Motown)

Sing A Sad Song
Merle Haggard; *Epic Collection-Recorded Live* (Epic)
For The Record: Merle Haggard-43 Legendary Hits (BNA)
More Of The Best (Rhino)
Sing A Sad Song (Capitol)
Merle Haggard & The Strangers; *Songs I'll Always Sing* (Capitol)

Sing Me A Love Song To Baby
Billy Walker; *45-#14422* (MGM)

Sitting Home
Total; *Kima, Keisha & Pam* (Bad Boy/Arista)

Sleeping Single In A Double Bed
Barbara Mandrell; *Barbara Mandrell Live* (MCA)
Best Of Barbara Mandrell (MCA)
Moods (MCA)

Smiling Up The Frown
Agents Of Good Roots; *One By One* (RCA)
Where'd You Get That Vibe? (RCA)

Some Broken Hearts
Bellamy Brothers; *The Reggae Cowboys* (Bellamy Bros./Intersound)

Some Broken Hearts Never Mend
Don Williams; *Best Of Don Williams-#2* (MCA)
Don Williams-20 Greatest Hits (MCA)
Some Broken Hearts Never Mend (MCA Special Prod.)

Some Things Never Change
Tim McGraw; *A Place In The Sun* (Curb)

Somebody's Crying
Chris Isaak; *Forever Blue* (Reprise)
VH-1 Crossroads-C (Atlantic)

Someday Out Of The Blue
Elton John; *ST/The Road To El Dorado* (DreamWorks/SKG)

Someday We'll Know
New Radicals; *Maybe You've Been Brainwashed Too* (MCA)

Sometimes It Hurts
Stabbing Westward; *Darkest Days* (Columbia)

Southern California
George Jones & Tammy Wynette; *George Jones & Tammy Wynette-16 Biggest Hits* (Epic/Legacy)
Tammy Wynette & George Jones; *Encore-Tammy Wynette & George Jones* (Epic)
Tammy Wynette & George Jones' Greatest Hits (Epic)

Spanish Eyes
Ricky Martin; *Ricky Martin* (Columbia)

Spanish Is The Loving Tongue
Bob Dylan; *Dylan* (Columbia)
Emmylou Harris; *Cimarron* (Warner Bros.)
Evangeline (Warner Bros.)
Ian & Sylvia; *Four Strong Winds* (Vanguard)
Ian & Sylvia's Greatest Hits (Vanguard)
Michael Martin Murphey; *Cowboy Songs* (Warner Western)

Spring Will Be A Little Late This Year
Sarah Vaughan; *Divine Sarah Vaughan-Columbia Years-1949-1953* (Columbia)
In Hi-Fi (Sony Music Special Prod.)

Standing In The Doorway
Bob Dylan; *Time Out Of Mind* (Columbia)

Stardust
Artie Shaw; *Begin The Beguine* (Bluebird)
Artie Shaw & His Orchestra; *22 Original Big Band Recordings-C* (Hindsight)
Nipper's Greatest Hits Of The '40s-#1-C (RCA)
Benny Goodman; *Benny Goodman Sextet featuring Charlie Christian-1939-1941* (Columbia)
Benny Goodman-Live At Carnegie Hall (London)
Carly Simon; *Come Upstairs* (Warner Bros.)
Coleman Hawkins; *Hollywood Stampede* (Capitol)
Dave Brubeck; *Art Of Dave Brubeck* (Atlantic)
Greatest Hits From The Fantasy Years (Fantasy)
Dave Brubeck Quartet; *Jazz At Oberlin* (Fantasy)
Stardust (Fantasy)
Frank Sinatra; *Sinatra & Strings* (Reprise)
Harry Connick, Jr.; *25* (Columbia)
Hoagy Carmichael; *Nipper's Greatest Hits Of The '30s-#1-C* (RCA)
Stardust Road (MCA)
Johnny Mathis; *Feelings* (Columbia)
First 25 Years-Silver Anniversary Album (Columbia)
Nat "King" Cole; *The Nat "King" Cole Story* (Capitol)
Rob Wasserman & Aaron Neville; *Duets-C* (MCA)
Roger Williams; *Best Of Roger Williams* (MCA)
Tommy Dorsey; *Best Of Tommy Dorsey* (Bluebird)
This Is Tommy Dorsey (RCA)
Tommy Dorsey & Frank Sinatra; *Stardust* (Bluebird)
Wayne King & His Orchestra; *78-#22656* (Victor)

Still
Commodores; *Best Of The Commodores-Anthology* (Motown)
Commodores-All The Great Hits (Motown)
Commodores-The Ultimate Collection (Motown)
Lionel Richie; *Back To Front* (Motown)
Truly-The Love Songs (Motown)

Still
Macy Gray; *On How Life Is* (Epic)

Still
Bill Anderson; *Best Of Bill Anderson* (Curb)
Bill Anderson's Greatest Hits (Varese Sarabande)
Billboard Top Country Hits-1963-C (Rhino)
From The Vaults: Decca Country Classics-1934-1973-C (Decca)
Grand Ole Opry-75 Years-#2-C (MCA)

Still Dancin' With You
Wade Hayes; *Old Enough To Know Better* (Columbia)

Still Got The Blues
Gary Moore; *Ballads & Blues-1982-1994* (Charisma)
Out In The Fields-The Very Best Of Gary Moore (Virgin)
Still Got The Blues (Charisma)
Stanley Jordan; *Best Of Stanley Jordan* (Blue Note)

Still In My Heart
Tracie Spencer; *Tracie* (Capitol)

Stop Draggin' My Heart Around
Stevie Nicks with Tom Petty And The Heartbreakers; *Bella Donna* (Modern)
TimeSpace-The Best Of Stevie Nicks (Modern)

Stormy
Classics IV; *Back To The '60s-#4-C* (Dominion Entert.)
Spring Break-#2-Cold Kegs & Tan Legs (Capitol)
Very Best Of The Classics IV (EMI)
Santana; *Inner Secrets* (Columbia)

Straight Tequila Night
John Anderson; *Seminole Wind* (BNA)
Today's Hot Country-C (K-Tel)

Sukiyaki
4 P.M.; *Now's The Time* (Next Plateau/London/Island)
Kyu Sakamoto; *When AM Was King-C* (Capitol)
Taste Of Honey; *Golden Honey* (Capitol)
Twice As Sweet (Capitol)

Summer Song
Chad & Jeremy; *Best Of Chad & Jeremy* (K-Tel)
Capitol Gold-Best Of Chad & Jeremy (Capitol)
History Of British Rock-#2-C (Rhino)

Sun Ain't Gonna Shine Anymore
Walker Brothers; *History Of British Rock-#7-C* (Rhino)
Love Sixties-C (JCI Assoc. Labels)

Sure Gonna Miss Her
Gary Lewis And The Playboys; *Gary Lewis And The Playboys' Greatest Hits* (Curb)
Gary Lewis And The Playboys-Legendary Masters Series (EMI)

Sweet Dreams (Of You)
Chet Atkins & Mark Knopfler; *Neck And Neck* (Columbia)
Don Gibson; *Don Gibson-18 Greatest Hits* (Curb)
Don Gibson's All-Time Greatest Hits (RCA)
Emmylou Harris; *Brand New Dance* (Reprise)
Elite Hotel (Reprise)

Profile/Best Of Emmylou Harris (Warner Bros.)
Jim Reeves; *Jim Reeves' Greatest Hits* (RCA)
Patsy Cline; *Patsy Cline's Greatest Hits* (MCA)
ST/Sweet Dreams (MCA)
The Patsy Cline Story (MCA)
Reba McEntire; *Out Of A Dream* (Mercury)

Take Good Care Of Her
Adam Wade; *45-#546* (Coed)
Sonny James; *Billboard Top Country Hits-1966-C* (Rhino)

Take Good Care Of My Baby
Bobby Vee; *Best Of Bobby Vee* (EMI)
Billboard Top Rock 'N' Roll Hits-1961-C (Rhino)
'Til My Dreamin' Comes True-C (Capitol)
Bobby Vinton; *Bobby Vinton-16 Most Requested Songs* (Legacy)
Dion; *Runaround Sue (Right Stuff)* (Right Stuff)

Take Your Memory With You
Vince Gill; *Platinum Country-C* (JCI Assoc. Labels)
Pocket Full Of Gold (MCA)
Vince Gill-Souvenirs (MCA)

Tear Fell, A
Teresa Brewer; *Best Of Teresa Brewer* (MCA Jazz)

Tears Of A Clown
English Beat; *I Just Can't Stop It* (I.R.S.)
What Is Beat (I.R.S.)
Smokey Robinson & The Miracles; *25 #1 Hits From 25 Years-C* (Motown)
Billboard Top Rock 'N' Roll Hits-1970-C (Rhino)
Compact Command Performances-Smokey Robinson & The Miracles (Motown)
Endless Love-Motown's Greatest Love Songs-C (Motown)
Smokey Robinson & The Miracles' Anthology (Motown)
Tears Of A Clown (Motown)

Tears On My Pillow
Chimes; *Golden Groups-C* (Specialty)
Original Rock Oldies-Golden Hits-#2-C (Specialty)
Kylie Minogue; *Enjoy Yourself* (Geffen)
Little Anthony And The Imperials; *Best Of Little Anthony And The Imperials* (EMI)
Best Of Little Anthony And The Imperials (Rhino)
Billboard Top R&B Hits-1958-C (Rhino)
Good Time Rock 'N' Roll-C (MCA)
Lorrie Morgan; *Something In Red* (RCA)
New Edition & Little Anthony; *Under The Blue Moon* (MCA)
Reba McEntire; *Feel The Fire* (Mercury)
Sha Na Na; *ST/Grease* (Polydor)

Tell Me Why
Wynonna; *Tell Me Why* (MCA)

Tempted
Squeeze; *East Side Story* (A&M)
Rock Of The '80s-#1-C (Priority)
VH-1 The Big '80s-C (Rhino)

Tennessee Waltz
Cowboy Copas; *45-#696* (King)
Emmylou Harris; *Cimarron* (Warner Bros.)
Country's Greatest Hits-#5-C (Warner Bros.)
New Tradition Sings The Old Tradition-C (Warner Bros.)
Guy Lombardo & His Royal Canadians; *Best Of Guy Lombardo* (Curb)
Hank Williams, Jr.; *Living Proof-MGM Recordings 1963-1975* (Mercury)
Lacy J. Dalton; *Lacy J. Dalton's Greatest Hits* (Columbia)
Les Paul & Mary Ford; *Les Paul-Selections From Legend & Legacy* (Capitol)
Patti Page; *Patti Page-Golden Hits* (Mercury)
Patti Page's Greatest Hits (Columbia)
Roy Acuff; *Essential Roy Acuff-1936-1949* (Legacy)
Roy Acuff's Greatest Hits (Columbia)
Roy Rogers; *Best Of Roy Rogers* (Curb)
Sammy Kaye & His Orchestra; *Best Of The Big Bands-C* (Columbia)
Spike Jones & His City Slickers; *Best Of Spike Jones & His City Slickers* (RCA)

That Girl Who Waits On Tables
Ronnie Milsap; *Collector's Series-Ronnie Milsap* (RCA)
Where My Heart Is (RCA)

That Thing You Do!
Wonders; *ST/That Thing You Do!* (Epic)

There's A Tear In My Beer
Hank Williams, Jr. & Hank Williams, Sr.; *Complete Hank Williams* (Mercury)
Hank Williams, Jr.'s Greatest Hits III (Curb)

These Eyes
Guess Who; *Best Of The Guess Who* (RCA)
Greatest Of The Guess Who (RCA)
Nipper's Greatest Hits Of The '60s-#1-C (RCA)
Track Record-Collection (RCA)

They'll Never Take Her Love From Me
Emmylou Harris; *Blue Kentucky Girl* (Warner Bros.)
George Jones; *George Jones Sings The Great Songs Of Leon Payne* (Hollywood/DNA-Rounder)
Hank Williams With His Drifting Cowboys; *Hank Williams-24 Greatest Hits-#2* (Polydor)
Hank Williams-40 Greatest Hits (Polydor)

They're Coming To Take Me Away, Ha Haaa!
Napoleon XIV; *Dr. Demento Presents The Greatest Novelty Records-#3-1960s-C* (Rhino)

Silly Songs-C (K-Tel)
The Second Coming (Rhino)

Think Of Me
Buck Owens & The Buckaroos; *Buck Owens Collection-1959-1990* (Rhino)
Very Best Of Buck Owens-#2 (Rhino)

This Heartache Never Sleeps
Mark Chesnutt; *I Don't Want To Miss A Thing* (MCA)

Thorn Tree In The Garden
Derek And The Dominos; *Layla* (Polydor)

Thrill Is Gone
B.B. King; *Best Of B.B. King* (MCA)
Live In Cook County Jail (MCA)
B.B. King & Tracy Chapman; *Deuces Wild* (MCA)

'Til I Fell In Love With You
Bob Dylan; *Time Out Of Mind* (Columbia)

'Til I Gain Control Again
Crystal Gayle; *Best Of Crystal Gayle* (Warner Bros.)
True Love (Elektra)
Emmylou Harris; *Elite Hotel* (Reprise)
Rodney Crowell; *Rodney Crowell* (Warner Bros.)
Rodney Crowell-Collection (Warner Bros.)
Willie Nelson; *Greatest Hits (& Some That Will Be)* (Columbia)
Willie Nelson & Waylon Jennings; *Take It To The Limit* (Columbia)
Willie & Family Live (Columbia)
Willie Nelson & Waylon Jennings' Greatest Hits (Columbia)

Tips Of My Fingers
Bill Anderson; *Bill Anderson's Greatest Hits* (MCA)
The Bill Anderson Story (MCA)
Eddy Arnold; *Best Of Eddy Arnold-#2* (Dunhill Compact Classics)
Roy Clark; *Best Of Roy Clark* (MCA)
Roy Clark's Greatest Hits (MCA)
Yesterday When I Was Young (MCA)
Steve Wariner; *I Am Ready* (Arista)

To See My Angel Cry
Conway Twitty; *Conway Twitty-Number Ones-#1* (Liberty)
Conway Twitty's Greatest Hits-#1 (MCA)

Today I Started Loving You Again
Blue Ridge Rangers; *Blue Ridge Rangers* (Fantasy)
Merle Haggard; *Best Of The Best Of Merle Haggard* (Liberty)
Merle Haggard-Super Hits-#2 (Epic)

Too Much
Elvis Presley; *Elvis' Golden Records* (RCA)
The Top Ten Hits (RCA)
Worldwide 50 Gold Award Hits, Vol. 1, Parts 1 & 2 (RCA)

Too Soon To Know
Don Gibson; *Oh Lonesome Me* (Collectables)
Roy Orbison; *The Classic Roy Orbison-1965-1968* (Rhino)

Touch Me
Willie Nelson; *Best Of Willie Nelson* (Capitol)

Traces
Classics IV; *Very Best Of The Classics IV* (EMI)
Classics IV Featuring Dennis Yost; *Oldies But Goodies-#11-C* (Original Sound)
Ronnie Milsap; *Ronnie Milsap-16 Greatest Hits-#2* (Trip)

Tracks Of My Tears, The
Bryan Ferry; *These Foolish Things* (Reprise)
Gladys Knight & The Pips; *Gladys Knight & The Pips-Anthology* (Motown)
Johnny Rivers; *Best Of Johnny Rivers* (EMI)
Linda Ronstadt; *Linda Ronstadt's Greatest Hits* (Asylum)
Prisoner In Disguise (Asylum)
Smokey Robinson & The Miracles; *Billboard Top R&B Hits-1965-1969-C* (Rhino)
Smokey Robinson & The Miracles' Anthology (Motown)
Smokey Robinson & The Miracles' Greatest Hits-#2 (Motown)
ST/Big Chill (Motown)
ST/Sound Of "Murphy Brown" (MCA)

Trouble's Back In Town
Wilburn Brothers; *Wilburn Brothers* (First Generation)

True Love Never Dies
Earl Scruggs & Gary Scruggs & Travis Tritt; *Earl Scruggs And Friends-C* (MCA)
Kevin Welch; *Kevin Welch* (Reprise)

Tryin' To Get Over You
Vince Gill; *I Still Believe In You* (MCA)

Turn My Head
Live; *Secret Samadhi* (Radioactive/MCA)

Un-Break My Heart
Toni Braxton; *Secrets* (LaFace)

Until I Find You Again
Richard Marx; *Flesh And Bone* (Capitol)
Richard Marx's Greatest Hits (Capitol)

Until My Dreams Come True
Jack Greene; *Until My Dreams Come True* (Decca)

Until The End Of Time
Foreigner; *Mr. Moonlight* (Generama/Rhythm Safari)

Until You Come Back To Me
Aretha Franklin; *Aretha Franklin-30 Greatest Hits* (Rhino)
Best Of Aretha Franklin (Atlantic)
Golden Age Of Black Music-1970-1975-C (Atlantic)

Basia; *Brave New Hope* . . . .(Epic)
   London Warsaw New York. . . . .(Epic)
Hil St. Soul; *Soul Organic* . . . . (Dome/Select-O-Hits)
Miki Howard; *Miki Howard* . . . . (Atlantic)
Stevie Wonder; *Stevie Wonder-Love Songs-20 Classic Hits* . . . . (Motown)

Valerie
Steve Winwood; *Steve Winwood-Chronicles* . . . . (Island)
   Talking Back To The Night. . . . . (Island)

Visions Of Johanna
Bob Dylan; *Biograph* . . . . (Columbia)
   Blonde On Blonde . . . . (Columbia)

Walk On By
Dionne Warwick; *Dionne Warwick-Anthology 1962-1971* . . . . (Rhino)
   Hot! Live & Otherwise. . . . . (Arista)
   I Am Woman-C. . . . . (Nick At Nite)
   Oldies But Goodies-#15-C. . . . . (Original Sound)
   Scepter Records Story-C . . . . (Capricorn)
Isaac Hayes; *Isaac Hayes' Greatest Hit Singles* . . . .(Stax)
Melissa Manchester; *Romantic Hits Of The '80s-C* . . . . (K-Tel)
   Tribute . . . . (Polydor)
Sybil; *Sybil* . . . . (Next Plateau/London/Island)

Walk Softly
Billy "Crash" Craddock; *Billy "Crash" Craddock Live* . . . .(MCA)
   Billy "Crash" Craddock Sings His Greatest Hits . . . .(MCA)
   Easy As Pie . . . . (MCA)

Walking In A Hurricane
John Fogerty; *Blue Moon Swamp* . . . .(Warner Bros.)

Wasted Days And Wasted Nights
Freddy Fender; *Before The Next Teardrop Falls* . . . . (Universal)
   Best Of Freddy Fender. . . . . (MCA)
   Country Comes To Carnegie Hall-C . . . . (MCA)
   Happy Trails . . . . (United Artists)
   Texas Country . . . . (United Artists)
   The Freddy Fender Collection. . . . . (MCA)

What I Really Meant To Say
Cyndi Thomson; *My World* . . . . (Capitol)

What If
Babyface; *Face 2 Face* . . . . (Arista)

What She's Doing Now
Garth Brooks; *Ropin' The Wind* . . . . (Liberty)

Whatever Comes First
Sons Of The Desert; *Whatever Comes First* . . . .(Epic)

When I Close My Eyes
Kenny Chesney; *Kenny Chesney's Greatest Hits* . . . . (BNA)
   Me And You . . . . (BNA)

When I Stop Dreaming
Jim & Jesse; *All Time Legends Of Country Music-C* . . . . (Legacy)
   Bluegrass Super Hits-C . . . . (Columbia)

When You Love Someone
Sammy Kershaw; *Maybe Not Tonight* . . . . (Mercury)

When You Need My Love
Darryl Worley; *Hard Rain Don't Last* . . . .(DreamWorks/SKG)

When Your House Is Not A Home
Patsy Cline; *Patsy Cline-Live-#2* . . . .(MCA)

Where Are You Now
Trisha Yearwood; *Real Live Woman* . . . .(MCA)

Whipping Post
Allman Brothers Band; *Allman Brothers Band.* . . . . (Polydor)
   At Fillmore East. . . . . (Capricorn)
   Beginnings. . . . . (Polydor)
   Decade Of Hits-1969-1979 . . . . (Polydor)
   Dreams . . . . (Polydor)
   The Road Goes On Forever, A Collection Of Their Greatest
     Recordings. . . . . (Polydor)

Why Does It Hurt So Bad
Whitney Houston; *ST/Waiting To Exhale.* . . . . (Arista)

Why Does Love Got To Be So Sad?
Derek And The Dominos; *Layla.* . . . . (Polydor)

Wichita Lineman
Dwight Yoakam; *Under The Covers.* . . . . (Reprise)
Glen Campbell; *Best Of Glen Campbell* . . . . (Capitol)
   Country Music Classics-#3-1965-1970-C . . . . (K-Tel)
   Glen Campbell-Classics Collection. . . . . (Capitol)
   Glen Campbell-Live . . . . (Capitol)
   Glen Campbell's Greatest Hits . . . . (Capitol)
   Jimmy Webb Collection . . . . (Columbia)

Wind Cries Mary
Jimi Hendrix; *Essential Jimi Hendrix, Volume 2* . . . . (Reprise)
Jimi Hendrix Experience; *Are You Experienced?.* . . . . (Reprise)
   Smash Hits. . . . . (Reprise)

Wine Me Up
Faron Young; *Faron Young-Golden Hits* . . . . (Mercury)
   Faron Young-The Hits. . . . . (Mercury)

Without Her
Nilsson; *Pandemonium Shadow Show* . . . . (RCA)

Without You
Dixie Chicks; *Fly* . . . . (Monument)

Without You
Nilsson; *Nilsson Schmilsson* . . . . (RCA)

   Nilsson's Greatest Hits. . . . . (RCA)
   Nipper's Greatest Hits Of The '70s-C . . . . (RCA)

Woman (Sensuous Woman)
Don Gibson; *Don Gibson-18 Greatest Hits.* . . . . (Curb)
Mark Chesnutt; *Almost Goodbye.* . . . . (MCA)

Wurlitzer Prize (I Don't Want To Get Over You)
Waylon Jennings; *Waylon & Willie.* . . . . (RCA)

www.Memory
Alan Jackson; *Under The Influence* . . . . (Arista)

Yes It Is
Beatles; *Beatles VI* . . . . (Capitol)
   Beatles-Box Set. . . . . (Capitol)
   Beatles-Love Songs . . . . (Capitol)
   Past Masters-Volume One . . . . (Parlophone)

You Are My Sunshine
Bing Crosby; *Best Of Bing Crosby* . . . . (MCA)
   Bing Crosby's Greatest Hits. . . . . (MCA)
Jimmie Davis; *20 Golden Souvenirs Of Music City U.S.A.-C* . . . . . .(Plantation)
   Best Of Jimmie Davis . . . . (MCA)
   Jimmie Davis-Golden Hits . . . . (Plantation)
   The Country Music Hall Of Fame-Jimmie Davis . . . . (MCA)
Mississippi John Hurt; *Best Of Mississippi John Hurt* . . . . (Vanguard)
Mitch Miller; *Mitch Miller-16 Most Requested Songs* . . . . (Columbia)
Norman Blake; *ST/O Brother, Where Art Thou?.* . . . . (Mercury)
Ray Charles; *Ray Charles-Anthology* . . . . (Rhino)
   Ray Charles-His Greatest Hits-#2 . . . . (Dunhill Compact Classics)
Willie Nelson & Leon Russell; *One For The Road* . . . . (Columbia)

You Don't Have To Say You Love Me
Dusty Springfield; *Dusty Springfield-Golden Hits* . . . . (Mercury)
   History Of British Rock-#7-C . . . . (Rhino)
Elvis Presley; *Elvis As Recorded At Madison Square Garden.* . . . . (RCA)
   That's The Way It Is . . . . (RCA)
   The Other Sides-Worldwide Gold Award Hits, Vol. 2 . . . . (RCA)
Vikki Carr; *Best Of Vikki Carr* . . . . (EMI)

You Look So Good In Love
George Strait; *George Strait's Greatest Hits.* . . . . (MCA)
   Right Or Wrong . . . . (MCA)
   Strait Out Of The Box . . . . (MCA)

You Should Have Been Gone By Now
Eddy Raven; *Best Of Eddy Raven* . . . . (RCA)

You Stay With Me
Ricky Martin; *Ricky Martin.* . . . . (Columbia)

You Still Touch Me
Sting; *Mercury Falling* . . . . (A&M)

You Were Mine
Dixie Chicks; *Big Country Hits '99-C* . . . . (K-Tel)
   Wide Open Spaces . . . . (Monument)

Young Blood
Bad Company; *Run With The Pack* . . . . (Swan Song)
Coasters; *Coasters' Greatest Hits* . . . . (Atco)
   Coasters-Their Greatest Recordings-Early Years . . . . (Atco)
   The Ultimate Coasters . . . . (Warner Special Prod.)

Younger Girl
Critters; *Sixties Rule! Chapter Two-C* . . . . (One Way)
Lovin' Spoonful; *Lovin' Spoonful-Anthology.* . . . . (Rhino)

You're A Big Girl Now
Bob Dylan; *Blood On The Tracks* . . . . (Columbia)

You're Breaking My Heart
Nilsson; *Son Of Schmilsson* . . . . (RCA)

You're Only Lonely
J.D. Souther; *Radio Daze-Pop Hits Of The '80s-#1-C* . . . . (Rhino)
   You're Only Lonely . . . . (Legacy)

You're Out Doing What I'm Here Doing Without
Gene Watson; *Gene Watson's Greatest Hits* . . . . (MCA)
   Sometimes I Get Lucky . . . . (MCA)

You're Still On My Mind
Byrds; *Sweetheart Of The Rodeo* . . . . (Columbia)

**LOVE: CHOOSE ME, Be Mine, I'm Better For You, Let Me
Be The One, We Should Be Together, Wish You
Were Mine**

   *See Also: **DECISIONS, DESIRE, JEALOUSY, KISSING, LOVE
(various), MARRIAGE, PRETEND***

"In" Crowd, The
Dobie Gray; *Beg, Scream & Shout! The Big Ol' Box Of '60s Soul-C* . . . . (Rhino)
   Dobie Gray Sings For In Crowders That Go "Go Go" . . . . (Collectables)
Ramsey Lewis; *Greatest Hits Of Ramsey Lewis* . . . . (Chess)
   Party Super Hits-C . . . . (Columbia)
   Ramsey Lewis' Greatest Hits . . . . (Columbia)

#1 Crush
Garbage; *ST/William Shakespeare's Romeo & Juliet* . . . . (Capitol)

(They Long To Be) Close To You
Carpenters; *Carpenters-Classics-#2* . . . . (A&M)

Carpenters-*Love Songs* .... (A&M)
Carpenters-*The Singles 1969-1973* .... (A&M)
From The Top .... (A&M)
(You Drive Me) Crazy
Britney Spears; *...Baby One More Time* ....(Jive)
Now That's What I Call Music!-#4-C ....(Virgin)
16 Candles
Crests; *Alan Freed's Memory Lane-C* .... (MCA)
Billboard Top Rock 'N' Roll Hits-1959-C .... (Rhino)
Crests Greatest Hits .... (Collectables)
Cruisin'-1959-C .... (Increase)
Oldies But Goodies-#14-C .... (Original Sound)
Rock & Roll U.S.A.-21 Rock & Roll Favorites-#2-C ......(Laurie)
ST/American Graffiti .... (MCA)
2 Become 1
Spice Girls; *Spice* ....(Virgin)
21st Century Sha La La La Girl
Def Leppard; *Euphoria* .... (Mercury)
24-7 Man
Robert Cray Band; *Take Your Shoes Off* .... (Rykodisc)
49 Bye-Byes
Crosby, Stills & Nash; *Crosby, Stills & Nash* .... (Atlantic)
4th Of July, Asbury Park (Sandy)
Bruce Springsteen; *The Wild, The Innocent & The E Street Shuffle* . . . (Columbia)
Bruce Springsteen & The E Street Band; *Bruce Springsteen & The E Street Band Live/1975-85* .... (Legacy)
634-5789
Ry Cooder; *Borderline* .... (Warner Bros.)
Wilson Pickett; *Wilson Pickett's Greatest Hits* .... (Atlantic)
808
Blaque; *Blaque* .... (Track Masters/Columbia)
Adalida
George Strait; *Latest Greatest Straitest Hits* .... (MCA)
Lead On .... (MCA)
After The Lights Go Down Low
Al Hibbler; *After The Lights Go Down Low* .... (Atlantic)
Alice In Wonderland
Neil Sedaka; *Neil Sedaka's All-Time Greatest Hits* ....(RCA)
All Alone
Frank Sinatra; *Frank Sinatra-Complete Reprise Studio Recordings* . . .(Reprise)
Rosemary Clooney; *Some Of The Best-Rosemary Clooney* ....(Laserlight)
All Day And All Of The Night
Kinks; *British Rock-#1-C* ....(Original Sound)
God Save The Kinks! .... (Castle Music America)
History Of British Rock-#2-C .... (Rhino)
All For You
Janet; *All For You* ....(Virgin)
Now That's What I Call Music!-#7-C ....(Virgin)
All I Have To Do Is Dream
Everly Brothers; *All They Had To Do Was Dream* .... (Rhino)
Best Of The Everly Brothers .... (Rhino)
Fabulous Style Of The Everly Brothers .... (Rhino)
Heartaches 'N' Harmonies .... (Rhino)
Oldies But Goodies-#12-C .... (Original Sound)
ST/Stealing Home .... (Atlantic)
Very Best Of The Everly Brothers .... (Warner Bros.)
Nitty Gritty Dirt Band; *Best Of The Nitty Gritty Dirt Band* .... (Liberty)
Heartbreak Hotel-C .... (EMI)
All I Have To Give
Backstreet Boys; *Backstreet Boys* ....(Jive)
Now That's What I Call Music!-#3-C ....(Virgin)
All Or Nothing
O-Town; *O-Town* .... (J)
Totally Hits 2001-C .... (Arista)
All The Things (Your Man Won't Do)
Joe; *ST/Don't Be A Menace To South Central* .... (Island)
All The Things You Are
Ella Fitzgerald; *Complete Jerome Kern* .... (Verve)
Mario Lanza; *Be My Love-Greatest Performances* .... (Rhino)
Willie Nelson; *Healing Hands Of Time* .... (Liberty)
All The Way
Celine Dion; *All The Way...A Decade Of Song* .... (550 Music)
All Through The Night
Original Broadway Cast; *Anything Goes* .... (RCA Victor)
Alone
Bee Gees; *Still Waters* .... (Polydor)
Alone With You
Faron Young; *'50s Hits-Country-#1-C* .... (Curb)
Faron Young's All-Time Greatest Hits .... (Curb)
Faron Young's Greatest Hits-#2 ....(Step One)
Always
Bon Jovi; *Cross Road-14 Classic Grooves* .... (Mercury)
Always On Time
Ja Rule; *Pain Is Love* ....(Murder Inc./Def Jam/IDJMG)
Am I Dreamin'
Xscape; *Traces Of My Lipstick* .... (So So Def/Columbia)
Am I Wrong
Keb' Mo'; *Keb' Mo'* .... (Okeh)

Amapola (Pretty Little Poppy)
Jimmy Dorsey & His Orchestra; *Best Of Jimmy Dorsey & His Orchestra* ....(Curb)
Anema E Core
Eddie Fisher; *Very Best Of Eddie Fisher* .... (Taragon)
Angels
Earl Scruggs & Melissa Etheridge; *Earl Scruggs And Friends-C* .... (MCA)
Angels Would Fall
Melissa Etheridge; *Breakdown* ....(Island)
Annie Waits
Ben Folds; *Rockin' The Suburbs* .... (Epic)
Another Night
Real McCoy; *Another Night* ....(Arista)
Anticipating
Britney Spears; *Britney* ....(Jive)
Any Time At All
Beatles; *Rock 'N' Roll Music* ....(Capitol)
Something New ....(Capitol)
Anyday
Derek And The Dominos; *Layla* .... (Polydor)
Anything
3T; *Brotherhood* ....(Columbia)
Anything Goes
Count Basie & Tony Bennett; *Anything Goes-Capitol Sings Cole Porter-C* ....(Capitol)
Basie Swings Bennett Sings .... (Roulette)
Dionne Warwick; *Dionne Warwick Sings Cole Porter* ....(Arista)
Ella Fitzgerald; *Night & Day-Cole Porter Songbook-C* ....(Verve)
Frank Sinatra; *Frank Sinatra Sings The Select Cole Porter* .... (Capitol)
Mary Martin; *Mary Martin-16 Most Requested Songs* .... (Columbia)
Original Cast; *Anything Goes* .... (Epic)
Paul Whiteman & His Orchestra; *78-#24770* .... (Victor)
Yo-Yo Ma; *Anything Goes-The Music Of Cole Porter* ....(Columbia)
Apples Peaches Pumpkin Pie
Jay And The Techniques; *Cruisin'-1967-C* .... (Increase)
Are U Still Down?
Jon B.; *Cool Relax* .... (Yab Yum/550)
Are You Happy Baby?
Dottie West; *Dottie West's Greatest Hits* ....(Curb)
Are You Lonesome To-night?
Elvis Presley; *A Valentine Gift For You* .... (RCA)
Elvis' Golden Records, Volume 3 .... (RCA)
From Memphis To Vegas/From Vegas To Memphis .... (RCA)
Worldwide 50 Gold Award Hits, Vol. 1, Parts 1 & 2 .... (RCA)
Are You Satisfied?
Rusty Draper; *Rusty Draper's Greatest Hits* ....(Collector's Choice)
Are You There?
Oleander; *Unwind* .... (Republic/Universal)
Arizona
Mark Lindsay; *Super Hits Of The '70s-Have A Nice Day-#1-C* .... (Rhino)
As Long As You Love Me
Backstreet Boys; *Backstreet Boys* ....(Jive)
Now That's What I Call Music!-#1-C .... (Virgin)
Ascension (Don't Ever Wonder)
Maxwell; *Maxwell's Urban Hang Suite* ....(Columbia)
Baby
Brandy; *1996 Grammy Nominees-C* ....(Columbia)
Brandy .... (Atlantic)
Baby
Robert Bradley's Blackwater Surprise; *Time To Discover* .... (RCA)
Baby Hold On
Eddie Money; *Eddie Money* ....(Columbia)
Eddie Money's Greatest Hits-Sound Of Money ....(Columbia)
Baby I Need Your Loving
Four Tops; *Four Tops' Greatest Hits* ....(Motown)
Four Tops-Anthology ....(Motown)
The Ultimate Collection-Four Tops ....(Motown)
Johnny Rivers; *Johnny Rivers' Greatest Hits* ....(Capitol)
Johnny Rivers-Anthology 1964-1977 .... (Rhino)
Baby I'm-A Want You
Bread; *Baby I'm-A Want You* ....(Elektra)
Best Of Bread ....(Elektra)
Bread-Anthology ....(Elektra)
Baby It's You
Beatles; *Introducing...The Beatles* ....(Vee-Jay)
The Early Beatles ....(Capitol)
Baby, Come Over (This Is Our Night)
Samantha Mumba; *Gotta Tell You* ...... (Wildcard/Polydor/Interscope)
Baby, Come To Me
Patti Austin (with James Ingram); *'80s Greatest Rock Hits-#13-Soft Sounds-C* ....(Priority)
Chicken Soup For The Couples Soul-C .... (Rhino)
Every Home Should Have One .... (Qwest)
Quiet Storms 2-C .... (MCA)
Baby, I Love You
Aretha Franklin; *Aretha Franklin-30 Greatest Hits* ....(Rhino)
Babydoll
Mariah Carey; *Butterfly* ....(Columbia)

Back At One
Brian McKnight; *Back At One* . . . . (Motown)
Mark Wills; *Permanently* . . . . (Mercury)
Bad Girl
Jon B.; *Cool Relax* . . . . (Yab Yum/550)
Band Of Gold
Don Cherry; *Very Best Of Don Cherry* . . . . (Collector's Choice)
Bargain
Who; *Who's next.* . . . .(MCA)
Barrel Of A Gun (4,3,2,1)
Guster; *Lost & Gone Forever* . . . . (Hybrid/Sire)
Be My Baby
Linda Ronstadt; *Dedicated To The One I Love* . . . . (Elektra)
Melissa Etheridge; *Concert For The Rock & Roll Hall Of Fame-C* . . (Columbia)
Ronettes; *Best Of The Ronettes* . . . . (Abkco)
Phil Spector-Back To Mono 1958-1969-C . . . . (Abkco)
ST/Dirty Dancing . . . . (RCA)
Be My Baby Tonight
John Michael Montgomery; *John Michael Montgomery's*
Greatest Hits . . . . (Atlantic)
Kickin' It Up . . . . (Atlantic)
Be My Life's Companion
Mills Brothers; *Best Of The Mills Brothers* . . . . (MCA)
The Mills Brothers-Best Of The Decca Years . . . . (Decca)
Rosemary Clooney; *Rosemary Clooney-16 Most Requested Songs* . . . . (Legacy)
Be My Little Bumble Bee
Jonathan & Darlene Edwards; *Jonathan & Darlene Edwards'*
Greatest Hits . . . .(Corinthian)
Be My Love
Mario Lanza; *Be My Love-Greatest Performances* . . . . (Rhino)
Nipper's Greatest Hits Of The '50s-#1-C . . . . (RCA)
Be My Lover
La Bouche; *All Mixed Up* . . . . (RCA)
ST/A Night At The Roxbury . . . . (DreamWorks/SKG)
Sweet Dreams . . . . (RCA)
Beast Of Burden
Bette Midler; *No Frills* . . . . (Atlantic)
Rolling Stones; *Rewind (1971-1984)* . . . .(Rolling Stones)
Some Girls . . . . (Virgin)
Sucking In The Seventies . . . .(Rolling Stones)
Beautiful Ones
Mariah Carey; *Butterfly* . . . . (Columbia)
Beautiful You
Oak Ridge Boys; *Together* . . . .(MCA)
Because
Dave Clark Five; *History Of The Dave Clark Five* . . . . (Hollywood)
Because Of You
98 Degrees; *98 Degrees And Rising* . . . . (Universal)
Now That's What I Call Music!-#2-C . . . . (Virgin)
Begging To You
Marty Robbins; *Essential Marty Robbins-1951-1982* . . . . (Columbia)
Marty Robbins-16 Biggest Hits . . . . (Legacy)
Believe Me Baby (I Lied)
Trisha Yearwood; *Everybody Knows* . . . .(MCA)
Bend Me, Shape Me
American Breed; *The Ultimate History Of Rock 'N' Roll-#7-C* . . (K-Tel)
Bent
Matchbox Twenty; *Mad Season By Matchbox Twenty* . . . . (Lava)
Totally Hits-#3-C . . . . (Atlantic)
Bernadette
Four Tops; *Compact Command Performances-Four Tops* . . . . (Motown)
Four Tops' Greatest Hits . . . . (Motown)
Four Tops Reach Out . . . . (Motown)
Four Tops-Anthology . . . . (Motown)
Motown Superstar Series-#14-Four Tops . . . . (Motown)
Besame Mucho
Beatles; *The Beatles-Anthology-#1* . . . . (Capitol)
Best Is Yet To Come
Frank Sinatra; *It Might As Well Be Swing* . . . . (Reprise)
Sinatra Reprise-The Very Good Years . . . . (Reprise)
Johnny Mathis; *I'll Buy You A Star* . . . . (Legacy)
Rosemary Clooney; *Girl Singer* . . . .(Concord Jazz)
Tony Bennett; *I Left My Heart In San Francisco* . . . . (Columbia)
The Ultimate Tony Bennett . . . . (Legacy)
Betcha She Don't Love You
Jessica Simpson; *Sweet Kisses* . . . . (Columbia)
Bicycle Built For Two
Kidsongs; *Cars, Boats, Trains, Planes* . . . . (Sony Wonder)
Original Soundtrack; *School Days-Kids Classics* . . . . (Benson)
Big Daddy
Heavy D; *Waterbed Hev* . . . . (Universal)
Big Love
Tracy Byrd; *Big Love* . . . .(MCA)
Big Poppa
Notorious B.I.G.; *MTV Party To Go-#8-C* . . . . (Tommy Boy)
Ready To Die . . . . (Bad Boy/Arista)
Blackberry
Black Crowes; *Three Snakes And One Charm* . . . . (American)

Blue Angel
Roy Orbison; *For The Lonely: 18 Greatest Hits* . . . . (Rhino)
In Dreams-Greatest Hits . . . .(Orbison)
Roy Orbison Greatest Hits . . . . (Monument)
Roy Orbison's All-Time Greatest Hits-#1 & 2 . . . . (Monument)
Very Best Of Roy Orbison . . . . (Monument)
Bobby's Girl
Marcie Blaine; *Collectables Presents The History Of Rock-#5-C* . . (Collectables)
Million-Dollar Memories-#2-C . . . .(RCA)
WCBS FM 101 History Of Rock-'60s-#5-C . . . . (Collectables)
Body And Soul
Benny Goodman & His Orchestra; *Benny Goodman's*
Greatest Hits . . . . (RCA Victor)
Benny Goodman Trio; *Ken Burns Jazz Collection-The Benny*
Goodman Trio . . . . (Legacy)
Billie Holiday; *Billie Holiday-16 Most Requested Songs* . . . . (Legacy)
Body And Soul . . . . (Verve)
The Billie Holiday Story-#2 . . . . (Columbia)
This Is Jazz #32: Billie Holiday Sings Standards . . . . (Columbia)
Verve Jazz Masters 47-Billie Holiday Sings Standards . . . . . . (Legacy)
Carly Simon; *Torch* . . . . (Warner Bros.)
Coleman Hawkins; *Coleman Hawkins' Greatest Hits.* . . . . (RCA Victor)
Verve Jazz Masters 34 . . . . (Verve)
Diana Krall; *Stepping Out* . . . .(Justin Time)
Eddie Jefferson; *Body And Soul* . . . . (Original Jazz Classics)
Letter From Home . . . . (Original Jazz Classics)
Main Man . . . . (Inner City)
The Jazz Singer . . . .(Evidence Music)
Louis Armstrong; *Essential Louis Armstrong* . . . . (Verve)
Louis Armstrong-Love Songs . . . . (Legacy)
Musical Autobiography-#2 . . . . (MCA)
Satchmo At Symphony Hall . . . . (Decca Jazz)
Verve Jazz Masters 1 . . . . (Verve)
Manhattan Transfer; *Best Of The Manhattan Transfer* . . . .(Atlantic)
Extensions . . . . (Rhino)
Manhattan Transfer-Anthology-Down In Birdland . . . . (Rhino)
Paul Whiteman & His Orchestra; *78-#2297* . . . . (Columbia)
Sarah Vaughan; *How Long Has This Been Going On?* . . . . (Pablo)
One Night Stand-The Town Hall Concert-1947 . . . . (Blue Note)
Sarah Vaughan. . . . . (Everest)
Bohemian Like You
Dandy Warhols; *Thirteen Tales From Urban Bohemia* . . . . (Capitol)
Borderline
Madonna; *Immaculate Collection* . . . . (Sire)
Madonna . . . . (Sire)
Royal Box . . . . (Sire)
Born To Run
Bruce Springsteen; *Born To Run* . . . . (Columbia)
Chimes Of Freedom . . . . (Columbia)
Bruce Springsteen & The E Street Band; *Bruce Springsteen & The E Street*
Band Live/1975-85 . . . . (Legacy)
Melissa Etheridge; *The Concert For New York City-C* . . . . (Columbia)
Botcha-A-Me (Ba-Ba-Baciami Piccina)
Rosemary Clooney; *Rosemary Clooney-16 Most Requested Songs* . . . . (Legacy)
Bounce With Me
Lil Bow Wow; *Beware Of Dog* . . . . (So So Def/Columbia)
ST/Big Momma's House . . . . (So So Def/Columbia)
Boy Is Mine
Brandy & Monica; *Never Say Never* . . . .(Atlantic)
Monica; *The Boy Is Mine.* . . . . (Arista)
Boys
Britney Spears; *Britney* . . . .(Jive)
Brand New Day
Sting; *Brand New Day.* . . . . (A&M)
Brass In Pocket (I'm Special)
Pretenders; *Pretenders* . . . . (Sire)
Pretenders-The Singles . . . . (Sire)
Breaking All The Rules
She Moves; *Boom! 17 Explosive Hits-C* . . . . (Simitar)
Breaking All The Rules . . . . (Geffen)
Breathless
Corrs; *In Blue* . . . . (143/Lava/Atlantic)
Totally Hits-#3-C . . . .(Atlantic)
Bring It All To Me
Blaque; *Blaque* . . . . (Track Masters/Columbia)
Buckets Of Rain
Bob Dylan; *Blood On The Tracks* . . . . (Columbia)
Build Me Up Buttercup
Foundations; *Billboard Top Rock 'N' Roll Hits-1969-C* . . . . (Rhino)
History Of British Rock-#9-C . . . . (Rhino)
ST/There's Something About Mary. . . . . (Capitol)
Burn
Jo Dee Messina; *Burn* . . . . (Curb)
Burn Me Down
Marty Stuart; *Tempted.* . . . . (MCA)
Burn To Shine
Ben Harper; *Burn To Shine* . . . . (Virgin)
Bus Stop Song, The (Paper Of Pins)
Four Lads; *Moments To Remember-Very Best Of The Four Lads* . . . . . (Taragon)

Can I Count On You
McBride & The Ride; *Burnin' Up The Road* (MCA)
Can I Touch You...There?
Michael Bolton; *Michael Bolton's Greatest Hits-1985-1995* (Columbia)
Can We
SWV; *Release Some Tension* (RCA)
Candy
Cameo; *12'' Collection And More* (Mercury)
Best Of Cameo (Mercury/Funk Essentials)
Billboard Top R&B Hits-1987-C (Rhino)
Greatest Hits (Chronicles)
Will Smith featuring Larry Blackmon; *Big Willie Style* (Columbia)
Candy Man
Fred Neil; *Little Bit Of Rain* (Elektra)
Mickey Gilley & Charly McClain; *It Takes Believers* (Epic)
Roy Orbison; *In Dreams-Greatest Hits* (Orbison)
Roy Orbison Greatest Hits (Monument)
Roy Orbison's All-Time Greatest Hits-#1 & 2 (Monument)
Very Best Of Roy Orbison (Monument)
Can't Buy Me Love
Beatles; *Beatles 1* (Capitol)
Hey Jude (Capitol)
Reel Music (Capitol)
ST/A Hard Day's Night (Capitol)
The Beatles At The Hollywood Bowl (Capitol)
The Beatles/1962-1966 (Capitol)
Can't Fight The Moonlight
LeAnn Rimes; *ST/Coyote Ugly* (London Sire/Curb)
Can't Take My Eyes Off You
Frankie Valli; *25th Anniversary Collection* (Rhino)
Frankie Valli-Anthology (Rhino)
Very Best Of Frankie Valli (MCA)
Lauryn Hill; *The Miseducation Of Lauryn Hill* (Ruffhouse/Columbia)
Can't You Hear My Heartbeat
Herman's Hermits; *Herman's Hermits-Their Greatest Hits* (Abkco)
Can't You See
Total; *Total* (Bad Boy/Arista)
Total featuring Notorious B.I.G.; *Bad Boy Greatest Hits-#1-C* (Bad Boy/Arista)
ST/New Jersey Drive-#1-C (Tommy Boy)
Caramel
City High; *City High* (Interscope)
Carol
Chuck Berry; *Berry Is On Top* (Chess)
Chuck Berry-Golden Hits (Mercury)
Chuck Berry's Greatest Hits (Everest)
Roll Over Beethoven (Allegiance)
Rolling Stones; *England's Newest Hit Makers/The Rolling Stones* (Abkco)
Get Yer Ya-Ya's Out! (Abkco)
Carrie-Anne
Hollies; *Best Of The Hollies* (EMI)
Evolution (Epic)
Hollies-Epic Anthology From The Original Master Tapes (Epic)
The Hollies' Greatest Hits (Epic)
Case Of The Ex (Whatcha Gonna Do)
Mya; *Fear Of Flying* (University/Interscope)
Now That's What I Call Music!-#5-C (Virgin)
Catch The Wind
Donovan; *Donovan-Hits* (Epic)
Donovan's Greatest Hits (Epic)
History Of British Rock-#2-C (Rhino)
The Secret Policeman's Other Ball/The Music (Rhino)
Cecilia
Simon & Garfunkel; *Bridge Over Troubled Water* (Columbia)
Collected Works (Columbia)
Simon & Garfunkel's Greatest Hits (Columbia)
C'est Si Bon (It's So Good)
Eartha Kitt; *Lost Female Hits Of The '50s-C* (Taragon)
Chair, The
George Strait; *Country Classics-#5-1985-1986-C* (Universal)
George Strait's Greatest Hits-#2 (MCA)
MCA #1 Hits Of The '80s-#1-C (MCA Special Prod.)
Something Special (MCA)
Strait Out Of The Box (MCA)
Chance, A
Kenny Chesney; *I Will Stand* (BNA)
Chances Are
Bob Marley; *Chances Are* (Cotillion)
Bob Seger & Martina McBride; *ST/Hope Floats* (Capitol)
Johnny Mathis; *First 25 Years-Silver Anniversary Album* (Columbia)
Johnny Mathis' All-Time Greatest Hits (Columbia)
Johnny Mathis' Greatest Hits (Columbia)
Johnny Mathis-Live (Columbia)
Johnny Mathis-Love Songs (Columbia)
Cheers 2 U
Playa; *Cheers 2 U* (Def Soul/Def Jam/RAL/Mercury)
Cherish
Association; *Association Greatest Hits* (Warner Bros.)
Billboard Top Pop Hits-1966-C (Rhino)
Church Bells May Ring
Diamonds; *Best Of The Diamonds* (Rhino)
Willows; *Rockin' & Rollin' Wedding Songs-#1-C* (Rhino)
ST/A Rage In Harlem (MCA Special Prod.)
WCBS FM 101 History Of Rock-'50s-#2-C (Collectables)
Cindy, Oh Cindy
Beach Boys; *Surfin' Safari-Surfin' Usa (Remasterd With Bonus Tracks)* (Capitol)
Cold Cold Heart
Hank Williams; *Complete Hank Williams* (Mercury)
Hank Williams With His Drifting Cowboys; *24 Of Hank Williams' Greatest Hits* (Polydor)
Hank Williams (MGM)
Hank Williams-40 Greatest Hits (Polydor)
Live At Opry (MGM)
Long Gone Lonesome Blues (Polydor)
Jerry Lee Lewis; *Duets* (Sun)
Golden Cream Of Jerry Lee Lewis (Sun)
Jerry Lee Lewis & Friends-Duets (Sun)
Lucinda Williams; *Timeless: Hank Williams Tribute-C* (Lost Highway/IDJMG)
Tony Bennett; *Tony Bennett-16 Most Requested Songs* (Legacy)
Come A Little Bit Closer
Fleetwood Mac; *25 Years-The Chain* (Warner Bros.)
Heroes Are Hard To Find (Reprise)
Come And Get Your Love
Real McCoy; *Another Night* (Arista)
Redbone; *Rock Artifacts-From The Vaults-#2-C* (Legacy)
Rockin' '70s-C (Columbia Special Prod.)
Wovoka (Columbia)
Come And Knock (On The Door Of My Heart)
Roy Acuff; *45-#1097* (Hickory)
Come Cryin' To Me
Lonestar; *Crazy Nights* (BNA)
Come Fly With Me
Frank Sinatra; *At The Sands* (Reprise)
Come Fly With Me (Capitol)
Sinatra: A Man And His Music (Reprise)
The Capitol Years (Capitol)
Come Go With Me
Del Vikings; *1956 Audition Tapes* (Collectables)
Billboard Top R&B Hits-1957-C (Rhino)
Oldies But Goodies-#3-C (Original Sound)
ST/American Graffiti (MCA)
ST/Stand By Me (Atlantic)
Come On
Billy Lawrence; *12'' Maxi Single* (East West)
Come On (Part 1)
Jimi Hendrix Experience; *Electric Ladyland* (Reprise)
Come On Back
Keb' Mo'; *The Door* (550/Epic/Okeh)
Come On Down To My Boat
Every Mother's Son; *Battle Of The Bands-#3-C* (K-Tel)
Come On Over (All I Want Is You)
Christina Aguilera; *Christina Aguilera* (RCA)
Come Over To My Place
Davina; *Best Of Both Worlds* (Loud/RCA)
Come See About Me
Diana Ross & The Supremes; *16 #1 Hits From The Early '60s-C* (Motown)
Diana Ross & The Supremes' Greatest Hits (Motown)
Diana Ross & The Supremes-Anthology (1962-1969) (Motown)
Diana Ross & The Supremes-At The Copa (Motown)
Every Great #1 Hit (Motown)
Girl Groups-Story Of A Sound-C (Rhino)
Motown Story-First 25 Years-C (Motown)
Motown Superstar Series-#1-Diana Ross & The Supremes (Motown)
Come See Me
112; *112* (Bad Boy/Arista)
Come Softly To Me
Fleetwoods; *Come Softly To Me: The Very Best Of The Fleetwoods* (EMI)
Only Love-1955-1959-C (Rhino)
Come To My Window
Melissa Etheridge; *The Concert For New York City-C* (Columbia)
Yes I Am (Island)
Come With Me
Shai; *Blackface* (Gasoline Alley)
Come With Me
Keith Sweat featuring Ronald Isley; *Keith Sweat* (Elektra)
Coming Back Home
Bebe Winans featuring Brian McKnight & Joe; *Love & Freedom* (Motown)
Common Disaster
Cowboy Junkies; *Lay It Down* (Geffen)
Communication Breakdown
Led Zeppelin; *Led Zeppelin* (Atlantic)
Led Zeppelin-Box Set (Atlantic)
Cool Relax
Jon B.; *Cool Relax* (Yab Yum/550)
Could I Be
Wood; *Songs From Stamford Hill* (Columbia)

Could I Have This Kiss Forever
Whitney Houston & Enrique Iglesias; *Whitney Houston's Greatest Hits* . . . . (Arista)
Cousin Dupree
Steely Dan; *Two Against Nature* . . . . (Giant)
Cowboy Love
John Michael Montgomery; *John Michael Montgomery* . . . . (Atlantic)
John Michael Montgomery's Greatest Hits . . . . (Atlantic)
Crash Into Me
Dave Matthews Band; *Crash* . . . . (RCA)
Crazy
K-Ci & JoJo; *Now That's What I Call Music!-#6-C* . . . . (Virgin)
X. . . . . (MCA)
Crazy For This Girl
Evan And Jaron; *Evan And Jaron* . . . . (Columbia)
Now That's What I Call Music!-#6-C . . . . (Virgin)
Cruisin'
D'Angelo; *Brown Sugar* . . . .(EMI)
Huey Lewis and Gwyneth Paltrow; *ST/Duets* . . . . (Hollywood)
Smokey Robinson; *Compact Command Performances-Smokey Robinson* . . . . (Motown)
Motown Love Songs-C . . . . (Motown)
Motown Story-First 25 Years-C . . . . (Motown)
Where There's Smoke . . . . (Motown)
Crush With Eyeliner
R.E.M.; *Monster* . . . .(Warner Bros.)
Cry Baby
Enchanters; *Billboard Top R&B Hits-1963-C* . . . . (Rhino)
Soul Shots-#5-La-La Means I Love You-C . . . . (Rhino)
Garnet Mimms; *18 Soulful Ballads-C* . . . . (Rhino)
Beg, Scream & Shout! The Big Ol' Box Of '60s Soul-C . . . . (Rhino)
Janis Joplin; *Janis Joplin's Greatest Hits* . . . . (Columbia)
Pearl . . . . (Legacy)
ST/Janis . . . . (Columbia)
Cupid
Sam Cooke; *Best Of Sam Cooke* . . . . (RCA)
The Man And His Music . . . . (RCA)
Spinners; *Love Trippin'* . . . . (Atlantic)
Cupid
112; *112* . . . . (Bad Boy/Arista)
Curious
LSG featuring L.L. Cool J, Busta Rhymes & MC Lyte; *Levert-Sweat-Gill* . . . . (East West)
Damn I Wish I Was Your Lover
Sophie B. Hawkins; *Tongues & Tales* . . . . (Columbia)
Dance With Me
Drifters; *Drifters-16 Greatest Hits* . . . . (Deluxe)
Dance With Me
112; *Part III* . . . . (Bad Boy/Arista)
David Duchovny
Bree Sharp; *Cheap & Evil Girl* . . . . (Trauma)
Diary
Bread; *Baby I'm-A Want You* . . . . (Elektra)
Best Of Bread . . . . (Elektra)
Bread-Anthology . . . . (Elektra)
Did You Ever Love Somebody
Jessica Simpson; *Songs From Dawson's Creek* . . . . (Sony Music Soundtrax)
Did You Ever See A Dream Walking
Bing Crosby; *Crosby Classics* . . . . (Columbia)
Hal Kemp & Skinnay Ennis; *The Uncollected Hal Kemp-#2 & #3* . . . (Hindsight)
Dinah
Bing Crosby; *Bing Crosby-16 Most Requested Songs* . . . . (Legacy)
Cab Calloway; *Best Of The Big Bands-C* . . . . (Columbia)
Cliff Edwards; *Singin' In The Rain* . . . . (ASV)
Count Basie & Ethel Waters; *Tribute To Black Entertainers-C* . . . . . (Columbia)
Duke Ellington; *Jubilee Stomp* . . . . (Bluebird)
Ethel Waters; *Am I Blue?* . . . . (ASV)
Fats Waller; *Ain't Misbehavin': 25 Greatest Hits* . . . .(Living Era)
Lionel Hampton & His Orchestra; *Tempo & Swing* . . . . (Bluebird)
Louis Armstrong; *Louis Armstrong-Vol. 6-St. Louis Blues* . . . . (Columbia)
Mills Brothers; *50th Anniversary* . . . . (Ranwood)
Distant Drums
Jim Reeves; *Best Of The Best Of Jim Reeves* . . . . (King)
Billboard Top Country Hits-1966-C . . . . (Rhino)
Essential Jim Reeves . . . . (RCA)
Dizzy Miss Lizzy
Beatles; *Beatles VI* . . . . (Capitol)
Rock 'N' Roll Music . . . . (Capitol)
The Beatles At The Hollywood Bowl . . . . (Capitol)
Ronnie Hawkins and The Hawks; *Best Of Ronnie Hawkins and The Hawks* . . . . (Rhino)
Do Ya Think I'm Sexy?
Rod Stewart; *Absolutely Live* . . . . (Warner Bros.)
Blondes Have More Fun . . . . (Warner Bros.)
Rod Stewart's Greatest Hits . . . . (Warner Bros.)
Do You Love Me (Now That I Can Dance?)
Contours; *Frat Rock!-C* . . . . (Rhino)
Greatest Movie Rock Hits-C . . . . (Rhino)
Oldies But Goodies-#12-C . . . . (Original Sound)

ST/More Dirty Dancing . . . . (RCA)
ST/The Wanderers . . . . (Warner Bros.)
Dave Clark Five; *History Of The Dave Clark Five* . . . . (Hollywood)
Do Your Thing
7 Mile; *7 Mile* . . . . (Crave)
Don't Close Your Eyes
Keith Whitley; *Don't Close Your Eyes* . . . . (RCA)
Keith Whitley's Greatest Hits . . . . (RCA)
Don't Get Above Your Raising
Lester Flatt, Earl Scruggs & The Foggy Mountain Boys; *Bluegrass Super Hits-C* . . . . (Columbia)
Don't Go To Strangers
T. Graham Brown; *Best Of T. Graham Brown* . . . . (Curb)
Don't Let Go (Love)
En Vogue; *Best Of En Vogue* . . . . (Elektra)
EV3 . . . . (East West)
Don't Let Me Down
Beatles; *Past Masters-Volume Two* . . . . (Parlophone)
Don't Let The Stars Get In Your Eyes
Perry Como; *Como's Golden Records* . . . . (RCA)
Perry Como-Pure Gold . . . . (RCA)
Perry Como's All-Time Greatest Hits-#1 . . . . (RCA)
This Is Perry Como . . . . (RCA)
Don't Make It Easy For Me
Earl Thomas Conley; *Very Best Of Earl Thomas Conley* . . . . (RCA)
Don't You Know
Keb' Mo'; *The Door* . . . . (550/Epic/Okeh)
Don't You Know I Care
Cleo Laine; *Solitude* . . . . (RCA Victor)
Duke Ellington; *Black, Brown & Beige: 1944-1946 Band Recordings* . . . . (Bluebird)
Joe Williams; *Every Day: The Best Of The Verve Years* . . . . (Verve)
Door #1
LSG; *Levert-Sweat-Gill* . . . . (East West)
Down In Flames
BlackHawk; *BlackHawk* . . . . (Arista)
The Hits-Love & Gravity . . . . (Arista)
Dream A Little Dream Of Me
Ella Fitzgerald; *All That Jazz* . . . . (Pablo)
Mama Cass; *Mama's Big Ones-Her Greatest Hits* . . . . (MCA)
Mama Cass With The Mamas & The Papas; *Best Of The Mamas & The Papas* . . . . (MCA)
Mamas & The Papas-20 Golden Hits . . . . (MCA)
Wayne King & His Orchestra; *78-#22643* . . . . (Victor)
Dream Baby (How Long Must I Dream)
Lacy J. Dalton; *Dream Baby* . . . . (Columbia)
Greatest Country Hits Of The '80s-1983-C . . . . (Columbia)
Lacy J. Dalton's Greatest Hits . . . . (Columbia)
Roy Orbison; *For The Lonely: 18 Greatest Hits* . . . . (Rhino)
For The Lonely: A Roy Orbison Anthology 1959-1965 . . . . (Rhino)
In Dreams-Greatest Hits . . . . (Orbison)
Roy Orbison's All-Time Greatest Hits-#1 & 2 . . . . (Monument)
Dream River
Mavericks; *Trampoline* . . . . (MCA)
Dreaming Of You
Selena; *Dreaming Of You* . . . . (EMI Latin)
Drops Of Jupiter (Tell Me)
Train; *Drops Of Jupiter* . . . . (Aware/C2/Columbia)
Dum Dum
Brenda Lee; *Brenda Lee-Anthology-#1 & #2* . . . . (MCA)
Earth Angel
Elvis Presley; *A Golden Celebration* . . . . (RCA)
New Edition; *ST/Under The Blue Moon* . . . . (MCA)
Penguins; *Billboard Top Rock 'N' Roll Hits-1955-C* . . . . (Rhino)
Golden Classics-Penguins . . . . (Collectables)
Oldies But Goodies-#1-C . . . . (Original Sound)
ST/American Graffiti . . . . (MCA)
Easier Said Than Done
Essex; *Best Of The Girl Groups-#2-C* . . . . (Rhino)
Billboard Top Rock 'N' Roll Hits-1963-C . . . . (Rhino)
Original Rock 'N' Roll Hits Of The '60s-C . . . . (Roulette)
Eddie My Love
Fontane Sisters; *History Of Dot-#1-Young Love-C* . . . . (Varese Sarabande)
Eight Days A Week
Beatles; *Beatles 1* . . . . (Capitol)
Beatles VI . . . . (Capitol)
Beatles-20 Greatest Hits . . . . (Capitol)
The Beatles/1962-1966 . . . . (Capitol)
Elevation
U2; *All That You Can't Leave Behind* . . . . (Interscope)
Eloise
Damned; *Light At The End Of The Tunnel* . . . . (MCA)
Essence
Lucinda Williams; *Essence* . . . . (Lost Highway/IDJMG)
Every Breath You Take
Police; *Every Breath You Take-The Classics* . . . . (A&M)
Synchronicity . . . . (A&M)
Tammy Wynette & Sting; *Without Walls-C* . . . . (Epic)

Every Day
Stevie Nicks; *Trouble In Shangri-La* . . . .(Reprise)
Everything You Want
Vertical Horizon; *Everything You Want* . . . .(RCA)
Totally Hits-#3-C . . . . (Atlantic)
Expressway To Your Heart
Blues Brothers; *Best Of The Blues Brothers* . . . . (Atlantic)
Soul Survivors; *Dick Bartley's One-Hit Wonders Of The '60s-#2-C* . . . . . (Rhino)
Oldies But Goodies-#11-C . . . .(Original Sound)
Super Oldies Of The '60s-#6-C . . . . (Audio Fidelity)
When The Whistle Blows Anything Goes . . . . (Collectables)
Extra Ordinary
Better Than Ezra; *Closer* . . . .(Beyond)
Faded
soulDecision; *No One Does It Better* . . . . (MCA)
Now That's What I Call Music!-#5-C . . . .(Virgin)
Faith In Me
Crosby, Stills, Nash & Young; *Looking Forward* . . . .(Reprise)
Fantasy
Mariah Carey; *Daydream* . . . .(Columbia)
Feels So Good (Show Me Your Love)
Lina Santiago; *Best Of Dance Hits Supermix-#1 & 2-C* . . . .(Warlock)
Dance Mix USA-#5-C . . . . (Warlock)
Final Heartbreak
Jessica Simpson; *Sweet Kisses* . . . . (Columbia)
Finer Things, The
Steve Winwood; *Back In The High Life* . . . . (Island)
Fire
Subway; *Good Times* . . . . (Motown)
First Taste
Fiona Apple; *Tidal* . . . .(Clean Slate/Work)
Fix
Blackstreet; *Another Level* . . . . (Interscope)
Flavor Of The Weak
American Hi-Fi; *American Hi-Fi* . . . . (Island)
Now That's What I Call Music!-#7-C . . . .(Virgin)
Flying Away
Mary J. Blige; *No More Drama* . . . . (MCA)
Follow Me
Uncle Kracker; *Double Wide* . . . . (Warner Bros.)
Totally Hits 2001-C . . . . (Arista)
Fool For Your Love
Mickey Gilley; *19 Hot Country Requests-C* . . . . (Epic)
Fool For Your Love . . . . (Epic)
Fool In Love
Robins; *Best Of The Robins* . . . . (Crescendo)
Fool In Love
Etta James; *Sticking To My Guns* . . . . (Island)
Fools Rush In (Where Angels Fear To Tread)
Brook Benton; *Super Oldies Of The '60s-#10-C* . . . . (Audio Fidelity)
Tommy Dorsey & Frank Sinatra; *Sessions-#1-February 1, 1940-July 17, 1940* . . . .(RCA)
For Your Love
Yardbirds; *Best Of The Yardbirds* . . . . (Rhino)
Dick Clark's 21 All-Time Hits-#3-C . . . .(Original Sound)
History Of British Rock-#1-C . . . . (Rhino)
Yardbirds' Greatest Hits-#1 (1964-1966) . . . . (Rhino)
For Your Love
Ed Townsend; *The Glory Of Love-'50s Sweet & Soulful Love Songs-C* . . . . (Hip-O)
Peaches & Herb; *The Glory Of Love-'60s Sweet & Soulful Love Songs-C* . . . . (Hip-O)
For Your Precious Love
Jerry Butler; *Best Of Jerry Butler* . . . . (Rhino)
Freak Like Me
Macy Gray; *The Id* . . . . (Epic)
Freek'n You
Jodeci; *MTV Party To Go-#7-C* . . . .(Tommy Boy)
The Show, The After-Party, The Hotel . . . .(Uptown/MCA)
Friends
John Michael Montgomery; *John Michael Montgomery's Greatest Hits* . . . . (Atlantic)
What I Do The Best . . . . (Atlantic)
From A Window
Billy J. Kramer With The Dakotas; *History Of British Rock-#3-C* . . . . . . (Rhino)
Chad & Jeremy; *Best Of Chad & Jeremy* . . . . (One Way)
From Me To You
Beatles; *Beatles 1* . . . . (Capitol)
Past Masters-Volume One . . . .(Parlophone)
The Beatles/1962-1966 . . . . (Capitol)
The Beatles-Anthology-#1 . . . . (Capitol)
Generous Palmstroke
Bjork; *Vespertine* . . . . (Elektra)
Get Involved
Raphael Saadiq featuring Q-Tip; *ST/PJ's* . . . . (Hollywood)
Get It On Tonite
Montell Jordan; *Get It On...Tonite* . . . . (Def Soul/IDJMG)
Now That's What I Call Music!-#4-C . . . .(Virgin)

Get Ready
Rare Earth; *Earth Tones-Essential* . . . . (Motown)
Very Best Of Rare Earth . . . .(Motown)
Temptations; *Temptations-Anthology-The Best Of The Temptations* . . .(Motown)
Temptations-The Ultimate Collection . . . .(Motown)
Gimme All Your Lovin' Or I Will Kill You
Macy Gray; *The Id* . . . . (Epic)
Gimme Little Sign
Brenton Wood; *18 Best-Brenton Wood* . . . . (Original Sound)
Collectables Presents The History Of Rock-#7-C . . . .(Collectables)
Cruisin'-1957-C . . . . (Increase)
Soul Shots-#3-Soul Twist-C . . . . (Rhino)
Gimme What You Got
Keb' Mo'; *The Door* . . . . (550/Epic/Okeh)
Girl Inside My Head
Blues Traveler; *Bridge* . . . . (A&M)
Girl Like You
Smithereens; *11* . . . . (Enigma)
Girl, You'll Be A Woman Soon
Neil Diamond; *Double Gold-Neil Diamond* . . . . (Bang)
Hot August Night . . . . (MCA)
Neil Diamond-Classics (Early Years) . . . .(Columbia)
Neil Diamond's Greatest Hits . . . . (Bang)
Girls Dem Sugar
Beenie Man; *Art And Life* . . . . (Virgin)
Give It To You
Jordan Knight; *Jordan Knight* . . . . (Interscope)
Give Me Just One Night (Una Noche)
98 Degrees; *Now That's What I Call Music!-#5-C* . . . . (Virgin)
Revelation . . . .(Universal)
Go Your Own Way
Cranberries; *Legacy-A Tribute To Fleetwood Mac's Rumours-C* . . . .(Lava)
Fleetwood Mac; *25 Years-The Chain* . . . . (Warner Bros.)
Fleetwood Mac Live . . . . (Warner Bros.)
Fleetwood Mac's Greatest Hits . . . . (Warner Bros.)
Rumours . . . . (Warner Bros.)
Golden Lady
Stevie Wonder; *Innervisions* . . . .(Motown)
Good Lovin'
Grateful Dead; *Shakedown Street* . . . .(Arista)
Rascals; *Hit Singles-1958-1977-C* . . . . (Atlantic)
Rascals' Greatest Hits . . . . (Atlantic)
Rascals-Super Hits . . . . (Atlantic)
ST/Big Chill . . . . (Motown)
Good Luck Charm
Elvis Presley; *Elvis' Golden Records, Volume 3* . . . . (RCA)
Number One Hits . . . . (RCA)
The Top Ten Hits . . . . (RCA)
Worldwide 50 Gold Award Hits, Vol. 1, Parts 1 & 2 . . . . (RCA)
Goodnight My Love (Pleasant Dreams)
Fleetwoods; *Best Of The Fleetwoods* . . . . (Rhino)
Fleetwoods' Greatest Hits . . . . (CEMA Special Prod.)
Jesse Belvin; *Collectables Presents The History Of Rock-#9-C* . . . .(Collectables)
Oldies But Goodies-#2-C . . . . (Original Sound)
Got To Get You Into My Life
Beatles; *Beatles-Box Set* . . . .(Capitol)
Revolver . . . .(Capitol)
Rock 'N' Roll Music . . . . (Capitol)
The Beatles-Anthology-#2 . . . . (Capitol)
Earth, Wind & Fire; *Best Of Earth, Wind & Fire-#1* . . . . (Legacy)
ST/Sgt. Pepper's Lonely Hearts Club Band . . . . (RSO)
Paul McCartney & Wings; *Kampuchea-C* . . . . (Atlantic)
Got You (Where I Want You)
Flys; *Holiday Man* . . . . (Delicious Vinyl)
ST/Disturbing Behavior . . . . (Trauma)
Gotta Be
Jagged Edge; *A Jagged Era* . . . . (So So Def/Columbia)
Grease Megamix
Grease Megamix; *Pure Disco* . . . . (A&M)
Great Balls Of Fire
Jerry Lee Lewis; *Billboard Top Rock 'N' Roll Hits-1958-C* . . . .(Rhino)
Jerry Lee Lewis-Original Golden Hits-#1 . . . . (Sun)
Jerry Lee Lewis-Original Golden Hits-#1 . . . . (Sun)
Jerry Lee's Greatest! . . . . (Rhino)
Oldies But Goodies-#12-C . . . . (Original Sound)
Original Memphis Rock & Roll . . . . (Sun)
Rock & Roll Show-C . . . . (Gusto)
Twenty Classic Jerry Lee Lewis Hits . . . . (Original Sound)
Guava Jelly
Barbra Streisand; *Butterfly* . . . .(Columbia)
Bob Marley & The Wailers; *Songs Of Freedom* . . . . (Tuff Gong)
Owen Gray; *This Is Reggae Music-#1-C* . . . .(Island)
Gumboots
Paul Simon; *Graceland* . . . . (Warner Bros.)
Gypsy Eyes
Jimi Hendrix Experience; *Electric Ladyland* . . . . (Reprise)
Handy Man
Del Shannon; *Del Shannon's Greatest Hits* . . . .(Curb)
Del Shannon's Greatest Hits . . . .(Rhino)

James Taylor; *James Taylor-Best Live* . . . . (Columbia)
   JT . . . . (Columbia)
Jimmy Jones; *Billboard Top Rock 'N' Roll Hits-1960-C* . . . . (Rhino)
   Hard To Find 45s On CD-#1-1955-1960-C . . . . (Eric)

Hangin' Around
Whites; *The '80s: Country Groups' Greatest Hits-C* . . . . (K-Tel)
   Whites' Greatest Hits . . . . (Curb)

Happy Birthday, Sweet Sixteen
Neil Sedaka; *Neil Sedaka Sings His Greatest Hits* . . . . (RCA)
   Neil Sedaka Sings The Hits . . . . (RCA)
   Neil Sedaka's All-Time Greatest Hits . . . . (RCA)

Have I The Right?
Honeycombs; *Watch Your Step: The Beat Era-#1-C* . . . . (Collectables)

Have You Ever?
Brandy; *Never Say Never* . . . . (Atlantic)

He Can't Love U
Jagged Edge; *J.E. Heartbreak* . . . . (So So Def/Columbia)

He Don't Love You (Like I Love You)
Tony Orlando & Dawn; *'70s Greatest Rock Hits-#9-#1 Hits-C* . . . . . . (Priority)
   Behind Closed Doors-'70s Swingers-C . . . . (Rhino)
   Best Of Tony Orlando & Dawn . . . . (Rhino)

He Left A Lot To Be Desired
Ricochet; *Blink Of An Eye* . . . . (Columbia)

He Will Break Your Heart
Jerry Butler; *Best Of Jerry Butler* . . . . (Rhino)

Heartbroke Every Day
Lonestar; *Lonestar* . . . . (BNA)

Heaven
Nu Flavor; *110% Hits-C* . . . . (Simitar)
   Nu Flavor . . . . (Reprise)

He'll Have To Go
Jim Reeves; *60 Years Of Country Music-C* . . . . (RCA)
   Best Of Jim Reeves . . . . (RCA)
   Billboard Top Country Hits-1960-C . . . . (Rhino)
   Great Moments At The Grand Ole Opry-C . . . . (RCA)
   Jim Reeves' Greatest Hits . . . . (RCA)
   Nipper's Greatest Hits Of The '50s-#1-C . . . . (RCA)
Ry Cooder; *Chicken Skin Music* . . . . (Reprise)

Hello
Lionel Richie; *Back To Front* . . . . (Motown)
   Can't Slow Down . . . . (Motown)
   Truly-The Love Songs . . . . (Motown)
Luther Vandross; *Songs* . . . . (Epic)

Hello Little Girl
Beatles; *The Beatles-Anthology-#1* . . . . (Capitol)

Help Me Rhonda
Beach Boys; *Billboard Top Rock 'N' Roll Hits-1965-C* . . . . (Rhino)
   California Girls . . . . (Capitol)
   Dance Dance Dance . . . . (Capitol)
   Endless Summer . . . . (Capitol)
   Made In The U.S.A. . . . . (Capitol)

Here I Am (Come And Take Me)
Al Green; *Al Green-Anthology* . . . . (Right Stuff)
   Al Green's Greatest Hits . . . . (Right Stuff)
   Call Me . . . . (Right Stuff)

Here In My Heart
Al Martino; *Capitol Collectors Series-Al Martino* . . . . (Capitol)

Hero
Enrique Iglesias; *America: A Tribute To Heroes-C* . . . . (Interscope)
   Escape . . . . (Interscope)

Heroes Are Hard To Find
Fleetwood Mac; *25 Years-The Chain* . . . . (Warner Bros.)
   Heroes Are Hard To Find . . . . (Reprise)

He's So Fine
Chiffons; *Best Of The Girl Groups-#1-C* . . . . (Rhino)
   Billboard Top Rock 'N' Roll Hits-1963-C . . . . (Rhino)
   Chiffons Greatest Hits . . . . (Right Stuff)
Jody Miller; *Jody Miller's Greatest Hits* . . . . (Epic)

Hey Joe!
Carl Smith; *All Time Legends Of Country Music-C* . . . . (Legacy)

Hey Lover
L.L. Cool J; *All World* . . . . (Def Jam)
   Mr. Smith . . . . (Def Jam)
   MTV Party To Go-#9-C . . . . (Tommy Boy)

Hey Pretty
Poe; *Haunted* . . . . (FEI/Atlantic)

Hey, Good Lookin'
Hank Williams With His Drifting Cowboys; *24 Of Hank Williams'*
   Greatest Hits . . . . (Polydor)
   Hank Williams-40 Greatest Hits . . . . (Polydor)
   Hey, Good Lookin'-December 1950-July 1951 . . . . (Polydor)
Loretta Lynn & Conway Twitty; *Hey, Good Lookin'* . . . . . . (MCA Special Prod.)

Hold Me Tight
Beatles; *Meet The Beatles!* . . . . (Capitol)

Hold Me, Thrill Me, Kiss Me
Mel Carter; *Baby Boomer Classics-Love Sixties-C* . . . . (JCI Assoc. Labels)

Hold My Hand
Hootie & The Blowfish; *Cracked Rear View* . . . . (Atlantic)

Hold My Hand
Don Cornell; *Hold My Hand* . . . . (MCA Special Prod.)

Hold On! I'm A Comin'
Chuck Jackson & Maxine Brown; *Best Of Chuck Jackson* . . . . (Tomato)
Sam & Dave; *Best Of Sam & Dave* . . . . (Atlantic)

Honey Pie
Beatles; *The Beatles (White Album)* . . . . (Capitol)
   The Beatles-Anthology-#3 . . . . (Capitol)

Honey, Do You Love Me, Huh
Hank Williams; *Complete Hank Williams* . . . . (Mercury)

Honeycomb
Jimmie Rodgers; *Best Of Jimmie Rodgers* . . . . (Rhino)
   Best Of Jimmie Rodgers . . . . (Curb)

Hoochie Coochie Man
Eric Clapton; *From The Cradle* . . . . (Duck/Reprise)
Eric Clapton featuring Buddy Guy; *The Concert For New York*
   City-C . . . . (Columbia)

Hot Blooded
Foreigner; *Double Vision* . . . . (Atlantic)
   Records . . . . (Atlantic)
   ST/Vision Quest . . . . (Geffen)

Hot Boyz
Missy "Misdemeanor" Elliot; *Da Real World* . . . . (East West)
   Totally Hits-#2-C . . . . (Elektra)

Hot Diggity (Dog Ziggity Boom)
Perry Como; *Como's Golden Records* . . . . (RCA)
   Nipper's Greatest Hits Of The '50s-#2-C . . . . (RCA)
   Perry Como-Pure Gold . . . . (RCA)
   Perry Como's All-Time Greatest Hits-#1 . . . . (RCA)
   This Is Perry Como . . . . (RCA)

How Deep Is Your Love
Dru Hill featuring Redman; *Enter The Dru* . . . . . (Def Jam/RAL/Mercury/Island)
   ST/Rush Hour . . . . (Def Jam)

How Do I Make You
Linda Ronstadt; *Linda Ronstadt's Greatest Hits, Volume Two* . . . . (Asylum)
   Mad Love . . . . (Elektra)

How Do You Do It
Beatles; *The Beatles-Anthology-#1* . . . . (Capitol)

How High The Moon
Duke Ellington; *1954 Los Angeles Concert* . . . . (Crescendo)
Ella Fitzgerald; *Best Of Ella Fitzgerald* . . . . (MCA)
Les Paul & Mary Ford; *Memories Are Made Of This-C* . . . . (Capitol)
Sarah Vaughan; *Compact Jazz-Best Of The Compact Jazz Vocalists-C* . . (Verve)
   Complete Sarah Vaughan On Mercury-#3 . . . . (Mercury)
Stephane Grappelli & Martin Taylor; *Just One Of Those Things* . . . . . . (Angel)

How Many More Times
Led Zeppelin; *Led Zeppelin* . . . . (Atlantic)

How Was I To Know
John Michael Montgomery; *What I Do The Best* . . . . (Atlantic)

I Ain't Got Nobody
Bob Wills; *Stay A Little Longer-The Original Columbia*
   Recordings . . . . (Roswell/RCA)
Preservation Hall Jazz Band; *Best Of The Preservation Hall*
   Jazz Band . . . . (Columbia)

I Am That Man
Brooks & Dunn; *Borderline* . . . . (Arista)

I Beg Of You
Elvis Presley; *50,000,000 Elvis Fans Can't Be Wrong-Elvis' Gold Records-*
   Volume 2 . . . . (RCA)
   The King Of Rock 'N' Roll-The Complete 50's Masters . . . . (RCA)
   The Top Ten Hits . . . . (RCA)
   Worldwide 50 Gold Award Hits, Vol. 1, Parts 1 & 2 . . . . (RCA)

I Belong To You (Every Time I See Your Face)
Rome; *Rome* . . . . (RCA)

I Can Do That
Montell Jordan; *Let's Ride* . . . . (Def Jam/RAL/Mercury)

I Can Dream, Can't I?
Andrews Sisters; *Best Of The Andrews Sisters* . . . . (MCA)

I Can Love You Better
Dixie Chicks; *Wide Open Spaces* . . . . (Monument)

I Can Love You Like That
All-4-One; *1996 Grammy Nominees-C* . . . . (Columbia)
   And The Music Speaks . . . . (Blitzz)
John Michael Montgomery; *John Michael Montgomery* . . . . (Atlantic)

I Can Make It Better
Luther Vandross; *Your Secret Love* . . . . (LV/Epic)

I Can't Get Next To You
Temptations; *All The Million-Sellers* . . . . (Motown)
   Temptations' Greatest Hits-#2 . . . . (Motown)
   Temptations-The Ultimate Collection . . . . (Motown)

I Can't Get Started
Anita O'Day; *Jazz 'Round Midnight-Anita O'Day* . . . . (Verve)
Bunny Berigan & His Orchestra; *An Evening At Rao's: Songs From An*
   Italian Restaurant-C . . . . (Legacy)
   Idiot's Guide To Jazz-C . . . . (RCA Victor)
   The Pied Piper . . . . (Bluebird)
   The Swingingest Sounds Ever Heard-C . . . . (Hip-O)
Ella Fitzgerald; *Compact Jazz-Ella Fitzgerald* . . . . (Verve)
Lester Young; *Best Of Lester Young* . . . . (Pablo)

I Confess
Perry Como; *Yesterday And Today-A Celebration In Song* .... (RCA)
I Do
Toya; *Totally Hits 2001-C* .... (Arista)
Toya .... (Arista)
I Do (Whatcha Say Boo)
Jon B.; *Cool Relax* .... (Yab Yum/550)
I Don't Even Know Your Name
Mavericks; *Trampoline* .... (MCA)
I Don't Know Why You Don't Want Me
Rosanne Cash; *Rosanne Cash-Hits-1979-1989* .... (Columbia)
Rosanne Cash-Super Hits .... (Columbia)
I Don't Want To Set The World On Fire
Ink Spots; *Best Of The Ink Spots* .... (MCA)
I Go Blind
Hootie & The Blowfish; *ST/Friends-Music From The TV Series* .... (Reprise)
I Hope You Want Me Too
Mavericks; *Trampoline* .... (MCA)
I Hurt For You
Conway Twitty; *Final Touches* .... (MCA)
Deborah Allen; *45-#13776* .... (RCA)
I Just Want To Be Your Everything
Andy Gibb; *Andy Gibb-A Collection Of His Greatest Hits* .... (Polydor)
I Know One
Charley Pride; *Charley Pride-Super Hits* .... (RCA)
Garth Brooks; *Garth Brooks* .... (Liberty)
Jim Reeves; *Essential Jim Reeves* .... (RCA)
I Love Me Some Him
Toni Braxton; *Secrets* .... (LaFace)
I Make A Fool Of Myself
Frankie Valli; *25th Anniversary Collection* .... (Rhino)
I Need To Know
Marc Anthony; *Marc Anthony* .... (Columbia)
Now That's What I Call Music!-#4-C .... (Virgin)
I Need You Now
Eddie Fisher; *Very Best Of Eddie Fisher* .... (MCA)
I Need Your Love Tonight
Elvis Presley; *50,000,000 Elvis Fans Can't Be Wrong-Elvis' Gold Records-Volume 2* .... (RCA)
The Top Ten Hits .... (RCA)
I Only Came For You
Wood; *Songs From Stamford Hill* .... (Columbia)
I Saw You Dancing
Yaki-Da; *Pride* .... (London)
I Say A Little Prayer
Aretha Franklin; *Aretha Franklin's Greatest Hits* .... (Atlantic)
Aretha's Gold .... (Atlantic)
Best Of Aretha Franklin .... (Atlantic)
Burt Bacharach; *Burt Bacharach-Classics-#23* .... (A&M)
Burt Bacharach's Greatest Hits .... (A&M)
Reach Out .... (A&M)
Diana King; *ST/My Best Friend's Wedding* .... (Work/Epic)
Dionne Warwick; *Dionne Warwick* .... (Everest)
Dionne Warwick Greatest Hits .... (Everest)
Dionne Warwick-Anthology 1962-1971 .... (Rhino)
Original Rock 'N' Roll Hits Of The '60s-C .... (Roulette)
I Second That Emotion
Smokey Robinson & The Miracles; *Smokey Robinson & The Miracles' Anthology* .... (Motown)
Smokey Robinson-The Ultimate Collection .... (Motown)
Tammy Wynette & Smokey Robinson; *Without Walls-C* .... (Epic)
I Should Have Known Better
Beatles; *A Hard Day's Night* .... (Parlophone)
I Still Believe
Mariah Carey; *Mariah Carey-#1's* .... (Columbia)
MTV Unplugged-Mariah Carey .... (Columbia)
I Surrender Dear
Bing Crosby; *Pennies From Heaven* .... (Pro-Arte)
Where The Blue Of The Night Meets The Gold Of The Day .... (Biograph)
Count Basie; *Basie & Zoot* .... (Pablo)
Jam-#3 .... (Pablo)
Loose Walk .... (Pablo)
Count Basie & His Kansas City 3; *For The Second Time* .... (Pablo)
Gus Arnheim & His Orchestra featuring Bing Crosby; *78-#22618* .... (Victor)
Mel Torme; *Smooth As Velvet* .... (Pickwick)
Rosemary Clooney; *Rosemary Clooney Sings Bing* .... (Concord Jazz)
I Think I'm Paranoid
Garbage; *Now That's What I Call Music!-#2-C* .... (Virgin)
Version 2.0 .... (Almo Sounds)
I Try
Macy Gray; *Now That's What I Call Music!-#4-C* .... (Virgin)
On How Life Is .... (Epic)
I Wanna B With U
Fun Factory; *Close To You* .... (Curb)
Fun-Tastic .... (Curb)
I Wanna Be Down
Brandy; *Brandy* .... (Atlantic)
MTV Party To Go-#7-C .... (Tommy Boy)
I Wanna Be Loved By You
Helen Kane; *Nipper's Greatest Hits Of The '20s-#1-C* .... (RCA)
I Wanna Be With You
Bruce Springsteen; *Tracks* .... (Columbia)
I Wanna Be With You
Mandy Moore; *I Wanna Be With You* .... (550 Music)
Now That's What I Call Music!-#5-C .... (Virgin)
I Wanna Be Your Lover
Prince; *Prince* .... (Warner Bros.)
I Wanna Be Your Lover
Bob Dylan; *Biograph* .... (Columbia)
I Wanna Be Your Man
Beatles; *Meet The Beatles!* .... (Capitol)
Rock 'N' Roll Music .... (Capitol)
I Wanna Get Next To You
Rose Royce; *Mellow Classics-C* .... (MCA Special Prod.)
Rose Royce's Greatest Hits .... (Whitfield)
ST/Car Wash .... (MCA)
I Wanna Know
Joe; *My Name Is Joe* .... (Jive)
Now That's What I Call Music!-#4-C .... (Virgin)
I Wanna Love Him So Bad
Jelly Beans; *Best Of The Girl Groups-#1-C* .... (Rhino)
I Wanna Love You Forever
Jessica Simpson; *Sweet Kisses* .... (Columbia)
I Want Candy
Bow Wow Wow; *Best Of Bow Wow Wow* .... (RCA)
I Want Candy .... (RCA)
Strangeloves; *Frat Rock!-#3-Grandson Of Frat Rock!-C* .... (Rhino)
I Want To Be The One
Lonestar; *I'm Already There* .... (BNA)
I Want To Be Your Man
Roger; *Unlimited!* .... (Reprise)
I Want To Hold Your Hand
Beatles; *Beatles 1* .... (Capitol)
Beatles-20 Greatest Hits .... (Capitol)
Meet The Beatles! .... (Capitol)
Past Masters-Volume One .... (Parlophone)
The Beatles/1962-1966 .... (Capitol)
Lakeside; *Galactic Grooves/Best Of Lakeside* .... (Right Stuff)
Your Wish Is My Command .... (Solar)
I Want You To Want Me
Cheap Trick; *Cheap Trick At Budokan* .... (Epic)
Cheap Trick's Greatest Hits .... (Epic)
In Color .... (Epic)
ST/Private Parts .... (Warner Bros.)
I Want You, I Need You, I Love You
Elvis Presley; *Heart & Soul* .... (RCA)
I Will...But
SHeDAISY; *The Whole Shebang* .... (Lyric Street)
I'd Follow You Anywhere
Derailers; *Here Come The Derailers* .... (Lucky Dog)
I'd Lie For You (And That's The Truth)
Meat Loaf; *Welcome To The Neighborhood* .... (MCA)
If I Could Only Win Your Love
Emmylou Harris; *Pieces Of The Sky* .... (Reprise)
Profile/Best Of Emmylou Harris .... (Warner Bros.)
If I Fell
Beatles; *Beatles-Love Songs* .... (Capitol)
Something New .... (Capitol)
ST/A Hard Day's Night .... (Capitol)
If I Never Stop Loving You
David Kersh; *If I Never Stop Loving You* .... (Curb)
If We Fall In Love Tonight
Rod Stewart; *If We Fall In Love Tonight* .... (Warner Bros.)
If You Asked Me To
Celine Dion; *All The Way...A Decade Of Song* .... (550 Music)
Celine Dion .... (Epic)
Patti LaBelle; *Be Yourself* .... (MCA)
Soundtrack Smashes-'80s & More-C .... (MCA)
ST/License To Kill .... (MCA)
If You Change Your Mind
Rosanne Cash; *King's Record Shop* .... (Columbia)
Rosanne Cash-Super Hits .... (Columbia)
If You Ever Have Forever In Mind
Vince Gill; *The Key* .... (MCA)
If You Go Away
Neil Diamond; *Neil Diamond-Love Songs* .... (MCA)
Rainbow .... (MCA)
Stones .... (MCA)
If You Leave Me Tonight I'll Cry
Jerry Wallace; *From The Vaults: Decca Country Classics-1934-1973-C* .... (Decca)
Jerry Wallace's Greatest Hits .... (Curb)
If You Love Me
Mint Condition; *Life's Aquarium* .... (Elektra)
If You Love Me Really Love Me
Kay Starr; *Kay Starr's Greatest Hits* .... (Curb)

If You Loved Me
Tracy Lawrence; *Time Marches On* . . . . (Atlantic)
If Your Heart Ain't Busy Tonight
Tanya Tucker; *What Do I Do With Me* . . . . (Capitol)
If You're Ever Down In Dallas
Lee Ann Womack; *Some Things I Know* . . . . (Decca)
I'll Be
Edwin McCain; *Misguided Roses* . . . . (Lava)
I'll Be Home
Barbra Streisand; *Stoney End* . . . . (Columbia)
Randy Newman; *Little Criminals* . . . .(Warner Bros.)
Randy Newman/Live . . . .(Warner Archives)
I'll Get You
Beatles; *Past Masters-Volume One* . . . . (Parlophone)
The Beatles' Second Album . . . . (Capitol)
I'll Keep You Satisfied
Billy J. Kramer With The Dakotas; *History Of British Rock-#2-C* . . . . . (Rhino)
I'll Never Break Your Heart
Backstreet Boys; *Backstreet Boys* . . . . (Jive)
Now That's What I Call Music!-#2-C . . . . (Virgin)
I'm A One- Woman Man
George Jones; *Essential George Jones-The Spirit Of Country* . . . . (Legacy)
George Jones-Super Hits . . . .(Epic)
One Woman Man . . . .(Epic)
Who's Gonna Fill Their Shoes . . . .(Epic)
Glen Campbell; *Still Within The Sound Of My Voice* . . . .(MCA)
Johnny Horton; *American Originals-Johnny Horton* . . . . (Columbia)
Honky Tonk Man-The Essential Johnny Horton-1956-1960 . . . . . (Legacy)
I'm Already Taken
Steve Wariner; *Country Cares For Kids II-C* . . . . (BNA)
Two Teardrops . . . . (Capitol)
I'm Every Woman
Chaka Khan; *Chicken Soup For The Soul: I'll Be There For You-Songs Of Friendship, Brotherhood And Sisterhood-C* . . . . (Rhino)
Epiphany: The Best Of Chaka Khan-#1 . . . . (Reprise)
I Am Woman-C . . . . (Nick At Nite)
Whitney Houston; *ST/The Bodyguard* . . . . (Arista)
Whitney Houston's Greatest Hits . . . . (Arista)
I'm Gonna Get You
Eddy Raven; *Best Of Eddy Raven* . . . . (Curtom)
Eddy Raven-Greatest Country Hits . . . . (Curb)
I'm Gonna Knock On Your Door
Eddie Hodges; *History Of Cadence Records-#1-C* . . . . (Varese Vintage)
I'm Gonna Make You Love Me
Diana Ross; *Diana Ross-Anthology* . . . . (Motown)
Diana Ross-The Ultimate Collection . . . . (Motown)
Temptations; *Temptations-Anthology-The Best Of The Temptations* . . (Motown)
I'm Gonna Make You Love Me
Jayhawks; *Smile* . . . . (American/Columbia)
I'm Gonna Make You Mine
Lou Christie; *Enlightnin'ment-Best Of Lou Christie* . . . . (Rhino)
I'm Here
Temptations; *Earresistable* . . . . (Motown)
I'm In Love Again
Fats Domino; *My Blue Heaven* . . . .(Gold Rush)
I'm Not The Only One
Filter; *Title Of Record* . . . . (Reprise)
I'm Telling You Now
Freddie And The Dreamers; *History Of British Rock-#1-C* . . . . (Rhino)
I'm The Fool
Mark Knopfler; *Golden Heart* . . . .(Warner Bros.)
I'm Waiting For The Day
Beach Boys; *Pet Sounds* . . . . (Capitol)
The Pet Sounds Sessions: A 30th Anniversary Collection . . . . (Capitol)
I'm Wondering
Stevie Wonder; *Stevie Wonder's Greatest Hits-#1* . . . . (Motown)
Imagination
Tamia; *Tamia* . . . . (Qwest)
In The Chapel In The Moonlight
Kitty Kallen; *Those Wonderful Years: Music! Music! Music!-C* . . . . (JCI Assoc. Labels)
Patti Page; *Patti Page-16 Most Requested Songs* . . . . (Legacy)
Shep Fields & His Rippling Rhythm Orchestra; *78-#6640* . . . . (Bluebird)
In The Still Of The Nite
Dion; *Dion Sings The 15 Million Sellers* . . . . (Laurie)
Dion's Greatest Hits . . . . (Laurie)
Dion And The Belmonts; *Wish Upon A Star With Dion And The Belmonts* . . . . (Collectables)
Five Satins; *Billboard Top R&B Hits-1956-C* . . . . (Rhino)
Cruisin'-1956-C . . . .(Increase)
Five Satins Sing Their Greatest Hits . . . . (Collectables)
In The Still Of The Night . . . . (Capitol)
ST/Dirty Dancing . . . . (RCA)
Johnny Mathis; *In The Still Of The Night* . . . . (Columbia)
Innamorata
Dean Martin; *Capitol Collectors Series-Dean Martin* . . . . (Capitol)
Dean Martin's All Time Greatest Hits . . . . (Curb)
Jerry Vale; *Essence Of Jerry Vale* . . . . (Legacy)
Jerry Vale-17 Most Requested Songs . . . . (Legacy)

Jerry Vale's Greatest Hits . . . . (Columbia)
Inside My Love
Trina Broussard; *ST/Love Jones* . . . . (Columbia)
Invisible Man
98 Degrees; *98 Degrees* . . . . (Motown)
Islands In The Stream
Kenny Rogers & Dolly Parton; *Eyes That See In The Dark* . . . .(RCA)
Kenny Rogers' Greatest Hits . . . .(RCA)
It Hurts Me Too
Bob Dylan; *Self Portrait* . . . . (Columbia)
Elmore James; *Golden Classics-Elmore James* . . . . (Collectables)
Eric Clapton; *From The Cradle* . . . . (Duck/Reprise)
It Hurts Me Too
Keb' Mo'; *The Door* . . . . (550/Epic/Okeh)
It's A Lonesome Old Town (When You're Not Around)
Ben Bernie & His Orchestra featuring Donald Saxon; *78-#4943* . . . (Brunswick)
Frank Sinatra; *Sings For Only The Lonely* . . . . . (EMI-Capitol Entert. Properties)
Lena Horne; *Love Is The Thing* . . . .(RCA)
Les Paul; *Les Paul's Greatest Hits* . . . .(Pair)
Sting; *ST/Leaving Las Vegas* . . . . (Pangaea)
It's About Time
Public Announcement; *All Work, No Play* . . . . (A&M)
It's Alright
Adam Faith With The Roulettes; *History Of British Rock-#1-C* . . . . (Rhino)
It's Gonna Be Me
'N Sync; *No Strings Attached* . . . .(Jive)
Now That's What I Call Music!-#5-C . . . . (Virgin)
It's Midnight Cinderella
Garth Brooks; *Fresh Horses* . . . . (Capitol)
Limited Series Box . . . . (Capitol)
It's No Good
Depeche Mode; *Ultra* . . . . (Mute/Reprise)
It's On Tonight
Sam Salter; *It's On Tonight* . . . . (LaFace)
It's Only A Paper Moon
Art Blakey & His Jazz Messengers; *Big Beat* . . . . (Blue Note)
Bing Crosby; *The Radio Years-#2* . . . .(Crescendo)
David Rose & His Orchestra; *Music Of The 1930s-C* . . . . (MCA)
Ella Fitzgerald; *Harold Arlen Songbook-#2* . . . . (Verve)
Frank Sinatra; *Round #1* . . . . (Capitol)
Mystics; *Mystics-16 Golden Classics* . . . . (Collectables)
Nat "King" Cole; *Capitol Sings Harold Arlen: Over The Rainbow-C* . . . . (Gold Rush)
The Nat "King" Cole Story . . . . (Capitol)
Sammy Kaye & His Orchestra; *Sammy Kaye & His Orchestra Play 22 Original Big Band Recordings* . . . . (Hindsight)
It's Only Make Believe
Conway Twitty; *Conway Twitty-Number Ones-#1* . . . . (Liberty)
Conway Twitty's Greatest Hits-#2 . . . . (MCA)
Conway's #1 Classics-#2 . . . . (Warner Bros.)
Very Best Of Conway Twitty . . . . (MCA)
Glen Campbell; *Very Best Of Glen Campbell* . . . . (Capitol)
I've Got My Eyes On You
Jessica Simpson; *Sweet Kisses* . . . . (Columbia)
I've Got This Feeling
Mavericks; *Trampoline* . . . . (MCA)
Ivory Tower
Cathy Carr; *Jukebox Classics-#2-C* . . . . (Rhino)
J'ai Fait Tout
Emmylou Harris; *Red Dirt Girl* . . . . (Nonesuch)
Johnny Angel
Shelley Fabares; *Billboard Top Rock 'N' Roll Hits-1962-C* . . . . (Rhino)
ST/Mermaids . . . . (Geffen)
Josephine
Wallflowers; *Bringing Down The Horse* . . . .(Interscope)
Jump
Van Halen; *1984* . . . . (Warner Bros.)
Best Of Van Halen-#1 . . . . (Warner Bros.)
LIVE: Right here, right now. . . . . (Warner Bros.)
Just Friends (Sunny)
Musiq Soulchild; *Aijuswanaseing* . . . . (Def Soul/IDJMG)
Just My Imagination (Running Away With Me)
Rolling Stones; *"Still Life" (American Concert 1981)* . . . .(Virgin)
Some Girls . . . . (Virgin)
Temptations; *12 #1 Hits From The '70s-C* . . . . (Motown)
20 Greatest Songs In Motown History-C . . . . (Motown)
25 #1 Hits From 25 Years-C . . . . (Motown)
All The Million-Sellers . . . . (Motown)
Compact Command Performances-Temptations . . . . (Motown)
Temptations-25th Anniversary . . . . (Motown)
Temptations-Anthology-The Best Of The Temptations . . . . (Motown)
Just To Hear You Say That You Love Me
Faith Hill & Tim McGraw; *Faith* . . . . (Warner Bros.)
Ka-Ding Dong
Diamonds; *Best Of The Diamonds-The Mercury Years* . . . . (Mercury)
Key West Intermezzo (I Saw You First)
John Mellencamp; *Mr. Happy Go Lucky* . . . . (Mercury)
Kiddio
Brook Benton; *Best Of Brook Benton* . . . . (Mercury)

Brook Benton-Golden Hits . . . . (Mercury)
Endlessly-The Best Of Brook Benton . . . . (Rhino)
Knock Down Walls
Tonic; *Sugar* . . . . (Universal)
Knock Three Times
Tony Orlando & Dawn; *Best Of Tony Orlando & Dawn* . . . . (Rhino)
Ladder
Joan Osborne; *Lilith Fair-A Celebration Of Women In Music-C* . . . . . . (Arista)
Relish . . . .(Blue Gorilla/Mercury)
Lady
Jack Jones; *Best Of Jack Jones* . . . . (MCA)
The Impossible Dream . . . . (Universal)
Lady In My Life
Marc Nelson; *chocolate mood* . . . . (Columbia)
Layla
Derek And The Dominos; *Classic Rock 1966-1988-C* . . . . (Atlantic)
Eric Clapton-Crossroads-C . . . . (Polydor)
Layla . . . . (Polydor)
ST/Goodfellas . . . . (Atlantic)
Eric Clapton; *Eric Clapton-Unplugged* . . . .(Reprise)
Let Me Be The One
Blessid Union Of Souls; *Home* . . . . (EMI)
Let Me Call You Sweetheart
Bette Midler; *ST/The Rose* . . . . (Atlantic)
Billy Vaughn & His Orchestra; *Billy Vaughn & His Orchestra Play 22 Of
His Greatest Hits* . . . . (Ranwood)
Bing Crosby; *Bing Crosby-Love Songs* . . . . (Universal)
Bob Ralston; *22 Great Organ Hits-#2* . . . . (Ranwood)
Gene Autry; *Gene Autry-Love Songs* . . . .(Varese Sarabande)
Lawrence Welk; *American Favorites* . . . . (Ranwood)
Peerless Quartet; *78-#1057* . . . . (Columbia)
Let Me Into Your Heart
Mary Chapin Carpenter; *A Place In The World* . . . . (Columbia)
Super Hits Of 1996-C . . . . (Epic)
Let Me Touch You For Awhile
Alison Krauss & Union Station; *New Favorite* . . . . (Rounder)
Let Old Mother Nature Have Her Way
Carl Smith; *Columbia Country Classics-#2-Honky Tonk Heroes-C* . .(Columbia)
Essential Carl Smith-1950-1956. . . . . (Legacy)
Seldom Scene; *After Midnight* . . . .(Sugar Hill)
Let's Fall To Pieces Together
George Strait; *George Strait's Greatest Hits* . . . . (MCA)
Right Or Wrong . . . . (MCA)
Strait Out Of The Box . . . . (MCA)
Let's Get Married
Jagged Edge; *J.E. Heartbreak* . . . . (So So Def/Columbia)
Let's Get Together
Hayley Mills; *Classic Disney-#1-60 Years Of Musical Magic-C* . . . . . .(Disney)
*Family Friendship Classics-The Most Memorable Songs From Film &
Television-C.* . . . . (Rhino)
Let's Go All The Way
Norma Jean; *Best Of Norma Jean* . . . . (Collector's Choice)
Let's Live For Today
Grass Roots; *At The Hop* . . . . (MCA)
Grass Roots-All-Time Greatest Hits . . . . (MCA)
Let's Live For Today. . . . . (MCA Special Prod.)
Summer Of Love-#1-C . . . . (Rhino)
Vintage Music-#10-C . . . . (MCA)
Let's Lock The Door (And Throw Away The Key)
Jay & The Americans; *Jay & The Americans' All-Time Greatest Hits* . . .(Rhino)
Let's Stay Together
Al Green; *Al Green's Greatest Hits* . . . .(Right Stuff)
Let's Stay Together . . . .(Right Stuff)
Tokyo...Live . . . .(Right Stuff)
Life Is But A Dream
Harptones; *Echoes Of A Rock Era-The Harptones* . . . . (Roulette)
ST/Goodfellas . . . . (Atlantic)
Super Oldies Of The '50s-#4-C. . . . . (Audio Fidelity)
Lifetime
Maxwell; *Now* . . . . (Columbia)
Li'l Red Riding Hood
Sam The Sham and The Pharaohs; *Best Of Sam The Sham and The
Pharaohs* . . . . (Polydor)
Cruisin'-1966-C. . . . . (Increase)
Pharaohization! (Best Of). . . . . (Rhino)
Linda Let Me Be The One
Bruce Springsteen; *Tracks.* . . . . (Columbia)
Linger
Cranberries; *Everybody Else Is Doing It, So Why Can't We?* . . . .(Island)
Little Child
Beatles; *Meet The Beatles!* . . . . (Capitol)
Little Shoe Maker
Eddie Fisher; *Very Best Of Eddie Fisher* . . . . (Taragon)
Gaylords; *Choice Voices! Pop Vocal Group Gems Of The
'50s-C* . . . . (Collector's Choice)
Lonely Too Long
Patty Loveless; *Patty Loveless-Classics* . . . . (Epic)
Super Hits Of 1996-C . . . . (Epic)
The Trouble With The Truth . . . . (Epic)

Long Long Time
Linda Ronstadt; *Different Drum.* . . . . (Capitol)
Linda Ronstadt-Retrospective. . . . . (Capitol)
Linda Ronstadt's Greatest Hits . . . . (Asylum)
Silk Purse . . . . (Capitol)
Looking Back To See
Goldie Hill & Justin Tubb; *Justin Tubb-Star Of The Grand
Ole Opry* . . . . (Starday)
Jim Ed Brown & Maxine Brown; *Essential Jim Ed Brown* . . . . (RCA)
Losing My Religion
R.E.M.; *Out Of Time* . . . .(Warner Bros.)
Louie Louie
Kingsmen; *Best Of The Kingsmen* . . . . (Rhino)
Billboard Top Rock 'N' Roll Hits-1963-C. . . . . (Rhino)
Cruisin'-1963-C . . . . (Increase)
Frat Rock!-C . . . . (Rhino)
Oldies But Goodies-#11-C . . . . (Original Sound)
Rock & Roll Is Here To Stay-C . . . . (Gusto)
ST/Quadrophenia . . . . (MCA)
WCBS FM 101 History Of Rock-'60s-#1-C. . . . .(Collectables)
Love
Musiq Soulchild; *Aijuswanaseing* . . . . (Def Soul/IDJMG)
Love Is All Around
Troggs; *Best Of The Troggs* . . . . (Rhino)
History Of British Rock-#8-C . . . . (Rhino)
Love Is All We Need
Mary J. Blige; *Share My World* . . . . (MCA)
Love Lessons
Tracy Byrd; *Love Lessons* . . . . (MCA)
Love Me Do
Beatles; *Beatles 1* . . . .(Capitol)
Past Masters-Volume One. . . . . (Parlophone)
Please Please Me . . . . (Parlophone)
The Beatles/1962-1966 . . . . (Capitol)
The Beatles-Anthology-#1. . . . . (Capitol)
Love Me Tender
Elvis Presley; *Elvis.* . . . . (RCA)
Elvis Aron Presley. . . . . (RCA)
Elvis' Golden Records. . . . . (RCA)
Elvis-A Legendary Performer, Volume 1. . . . . (RCA)
Worldwide 50 Gold Award Hits, Vol. 1, Parts 1 & 2. . . . . (RCA)
Love Will Be Waiting
Kevon Edmonds; *24/7* . . . . (RCA)
Love You Down
INOJ; *So So Def Bass All-Stars-#2-C.* . . . . (So So Def/Columbia)
Total Dance Explosion-C . . . . (Columbia)
Love You Save, The
Jackson 5; *14 Greatest Hits* . . . .(Motown)
ABC. . . . .(Motown)
Goin' Back To Indiana . . . . (Motown)
Jackson 5-Anthology. . . . . (Motown)
Jackson 5's Greatest Hits . . . . (Motown)
Motown Superstar Series-#12-Jackson 5 . . . . (Motown)
TV ST/Diana-C. . . . . (Motown)
Love Your Way
Sophie B. Hawkins; *Songs From Dawson's Creek* . . . . (Sony Music Soundtrax)
Lover In Me, The
Sheena Easton; *The Lover In Me* . . . . (MCA)
Love's Train
Con Funk Shun; *Love's Train-C* . . . .(Mercury)
Smooth Grooves-A Sensual Collection-#1-C . . . . (Rhino)
To The Max . . . . (Mercury)
Loving Cup
Rolling Stones; *Exile On Main Street.* . . . . (Virgin)
Make Me Believe
Martina McBride; *Emotion* . . . . (RCA)
Make Me Yours
Bettye Swann; *Make Me Yours-Golden Classics* . . . .(Collectables)
Man Loves His Money
Angie Stone; *Black Diamond.* . . . .(Arista)
Man This Lonely, A
Brooks & Dunn; *Borderline.* . . . .(Arista)
Mandy
Eddie Cantor; *Irving Berlin: A Hundred Years-C* . . . .(Columbia)
Fats Waller; *Breakin' The Ice: The Early Years, Part 1 (1934-
1935)* . . . . (Bluebird)
Van & Schenck; *Music From The New York Stage (1890-1920)-#4-1917-
1920-C.* . . . . (Pearl)
Margie
Cab Calloway; *More Big Band Greatest Hits-C.* . . . . (RCA Victor)
Eddie Cantor; *Eddie Cantor-The Columbia Years: 1922-1940* . . . . . .(Legacy)
Jimmy Lunceford; *Big Bands Of The Swinging Years-#2-C* . . . . .(Collectables)
Maria
Blondie; *No Exit.* . . . . (Beyond)
Marie
Tommy Dorsey & His Orchestra; *Seventeen Number Ones* . . . . (RCA)
Martha My Dear
Beatles; *Beatles-Box Set.* . . . . (Capitol)
The Beatles (White Album) . . . . (Capitol)

Meet Me In The Morning
Bob Dylan; *Blood On The Tracks* . . . . (Columbia)
Michelle
Beatles; *Beatles-Love Songs* . . . . (Capitol)
Rubber Soul . . . . (Capitol)
The Beatles/1962-1966 . . . . (Capitol)
Midnight Confessions
Grass Roots; *Grass Roots-Anthology (1966-1975)* . . . . (Rhino)
Original Rock 'N' Roll Hits Of The '60s-C . . . . (Roulette)
Vintage Music-#9-C . . . . (MCA)
Mimi
Maurice Chevalier; *Early Movie Hits* . . . . (DRG)
Nipper's Greatest Hits Of The '30s-#1-C . . . . (RCA)
ST/Pepe . . . . (DRG)
Molly
Sponge; *Rotting Pinata* . . . . (Work)
Moon Love
Frank Sinatra; *Moonlight Sinatra* . . . . (Reprise)
Glenn Miller; *Essential Glenn Miller* . . . . (Bluebird)
Glenn Miller's Greatest Hits . . . . (RCA Victor)
Moonlight Bay
Beatles; *The Beatles-Anthology-#1* . . . . (Capitol)
Bing Crosby; *The Radio Years-#4* . . . . (Crescendo)
The Radio Years: 20 Songs . . . . (Crescendo)
Drifters; *Clyde McPhatter & The Drifters-Rockin' & Driftin'* . . . . (Collectables)
Glenn Miller; *Big Bands-#1-C* . . . . (Universal)
More Than That
Backstreet Boys; *Black & Blue* . . . . (Jive)
Now That's What I Call Music!-#8-C . . . . (Virgin)
Movin' On
Mya featuring Silkk The Shocker; *Mya* . . . . (University/Interscope)
Mrs. Steven Rudy
Mark McGuinn; *Mark McGuinn* . . . . (VFR)
My Arms Stay Open All Night
Tanya Tucker; *Tanya Tucker's Greatest Hits* . . . . (Liberty)
My Boo
Ghost Town DJ's; *So So Def Bass All-Stars-#2-C* . . . . . . (So So Def/Columbia)
So So Def Bass All-Stars-C . . . . (So So Def/Columbia)
Total Dance Explosion-C . . . . (Columbia)
My Cherie Amour
Stevie Wonder; *My Cherie Amour* . . . . (Motown)
Natural Wonder . . . . (Motown)
Song Review-A Greatest Hits Collection . . . . (Motown)
Stevie Wonder's Greatest Hits-#2 . . . . (Motown)
My Everything
98 Degrees; *Revelation* . . . . (Universal)
My Future Just Passed
Shirley Horn; *Loads Of Love-Horn With Horns* . . . . (Verve)
My Love And Devotion
Perry Como; *Long-Lost Hits* . . . . (Collector's Choice)
My Love Is The Shhh!
Somethin' For The People; *This Time It's Personal* . . . . (Warner Bros.)
My Prayer
Ink Spots; *Best Of The Ink Spots* . . . . (MCA)
Platters; *Encore Of Golden Hits-Platters* . . . . (Mercury)
Oldies But Goodies-#3-C . . . . (Original Sound)
Platters Greatest Hits . . . . (Everest)
Platters-Anthology . . . . (Rhino)
My Reverie
Ella Fitzgerald; *Clap Hands, Here Comes Charlie* . . . . (Verve)
Ray Conniff; *Concert In Rhythm-#1* . . . . (Columbia)
Sarah Vaughan; *Sarah Slightly Classical* . . . . (Rounder)
My Sharona
Knack; *Billboard Top Hits-1979-C* . . . . (Rhino)
Get The Knack . . . . (Capitol)
Rock Of The '80s-C . . . . (Priority)
My Silent Love
Bing Crosby; *Where The Blue Of The Night Meets The Gold Of The Day* . . . . (Biograph)
Peggy Lee; *Mink Jazz* . . . . (Blue Note)
My Way
Usher; *My Way* . . . . (LaFace)
Mysterious
Scorpions; *Eye II Eye* . . . . (Koch International)
N.I.B.
Primus with Ozzy; *Nativity In Black II: Tribute To Black Sabbath-C* . . . . (Divine/Priority)
Na Na Hey Hey Kiss Him Goodbye
Steam; *Billboard Top Rock 'N' Roll Hits-1969-C* . . . . (Rhino)
Super Hits Of The '70s-Have A Nice Day-#1-C . . . . . . (Rhino)
Toga Rock-C . . . . (Dunhill Compact Classics)
Natural One
Folk Implosion; *MTV Best Of The Buzz Bin-#2-C* . . . . . . (Mammoth)
ST/Kids . . . . (London)
Never Gonna Let You Go
Faith Evans; *Keep The Faith* . . . . (Bad Boy/Arista)
Next Door To An Angel
Neil Sedaka; *Neil Sedaka Sings His Greatest Hits* . . . . (RCA)

Neil Sedaka's All-Time Greatest Hits . . . . (RCA)
Night And Day
Bette Midler; *Some People's Lives* . . . . (Atlantic)
Billie Holiday; *Legacy Box-1933-1958.* . . . . (Columbia)
Ella Fitzgerald; *Cole Porter Songbook* . . . . (Verve)
Frank Sinatra; *Nipper's Greatest Hits Of The '40s-#1-C* . . . . . (RCA)
Sinatra & Strings . . . . (Reprise)
Sinatra Reprise-The Very Good Years . . . . (Reprise)
Sinatra: A Man And His Music . . . . (Reprise)
The Capitol Years . . . . (Capitol)
The Reprise Collection . . . . (Reprise)
Fred Astaire; *Cheek To Cheek* . . . . (Pro-Arte)
Steppin' Out-Astaire Sings . . . . (Verve)
Tony Bennett; *Perfectly Frank* . . . . (Columbia)
U2; *Red Hot + Blue-Tribute To Cole Porter-C* . . . . (Chrysalis)
No Diggity
Blackstreet; *Another Level* . . . . (Interscope)
No One
Marc Anthony; *Marc Anthony.* . . . . (Columbia)
No Strings Attached
'N Sync; *No Strings Attached* . . . . (Jive)
No, No, No
Destiny's Child; *Destiny's Child* . . . . (Grass Roots/Columbia)
Nobody Else
Tyrese; *Tyrese* . . . . (RCA)
Nobody Wants To Be Lonely
Ricky Martin; *Sound Loaded* . . . . (Columbia)
Norma Jean Riley
Diamond Rio; *Diamond Rio* . . . . (Arista)
Diamond Rio's Greatest Hits . . . . (Arista)
Not That Different
Collin Raye; *I Think About You* . . . . (Epic)
Nothing But A Heartache
Flirtations; *Soul Shots-#2-The "In" Crowd-Sweet Soul-C* . . . . . (Rhino)
Oh Julie
Crescendos; *In The Still Of The Night* . . . . (Capitol)
Southern Rhythm 'N' Rock-Best Of Excello-#2-C . . . . . (Rhino)
Oh You Beautiful Doll
Guy Lombardo & His Royal Canadians; *Dance To Songs Everybody Knows* . . . . (MCA)
Oh, Baby Mine (I Get So Lonely)
Chet Atkins; *Tennessee Guitar Man* . . . . (Pair)
Four Knights; *Those Wonderful Years: Mr. Sandman-C* . . . . (JCI Assoc. Labels)
Oh, Pretty Woman
2 Live Crew; *As Clean As They Wanna Be* . . . . (Luke)
Al Green; *Al Green's Greatest Hits-#2* . . . . (Motown)
I'm Still In Love With You. . . . . (Right Stuff)
Ricky Van Shelton; *RVS III* . . . . (Columbia)
Roy Orbison; *In Dreams-Greatest Hits* . . . . (Orbison)
Roy Orbison's All-Time Greatest Hits-#1 & 2 . . . . . . (Monument)
ST/Pretty Woman . . . . (EMI)
Van Halen; *Diver Down* . . . . (Warner Bros.)
Oh, Pretty Woman (Can't Make You Love Me)
Albert King; *The Ultimate Collection-Albert King* . . . . (Rhino)
On A Carousel
Hollies; *Best Of The Hollies* . . . . (EMI)
History Of British Rock-#6-C . . . . (Rhino)
The Hollies' Greatest Hits . . . . (Epic)
One
George Jones & Tammy Wynette; *George Jones Collection* . . . . (MCA)
Grand Ole Opry-75 Years-#2-C . . . . (MCA)
One . . . . (MCA)
One And Only Man
Steve Winwood; *Refugees Of The Heart* . . . . (Virgin)
One Bad Apple
Osmonds; *Billboard Top Rock 'N' Roll Hits-1971-C* . . . . . . (Rhino)
One Belief Away
Bonnie Raitt; *Fundamental* . . . . (Capitol)
One Big Love
Emmylou Harris; *Red Dirt Girl* . . . . (Nonesuch)
Patty Griffin; *Flaming Red* . . . . (A&M)
One Day You'll Be Mine
Usher; *My Way* . . . . (LaFace)
One Fine Day
Carpenters; *From The Top* . . . . (A&M)
Now & Then . . . . (A&M)
Chiffons; *Best Of The Chiffons* . . . . (Laurie)
Chiffons-Golden Classics . . . . (Collectables)
Collectables Presents The History Of Rock-#9-C . . . . . (Collectables)
Oldies But Goodies-#12-C . . . . (Original Sound)
One I Love Belongs To Somebody Else, The
Count Basie & His Kansas City 3; *For The Second Time* . . . . (Pablo)
Etta Jones featuring Houston Person; *Fine & Mellow/Save Your Love For Me* . . . . (Muse)
Frank Sinatra; *I Remember Tommy* . . . . (Reprise)
Sheena Easton; *No Strings* . . . . (MCA)
One Step Closer
Doobie Brothers; *Best Of The Doobies, Volume II* . . . . . (Warner Bros.)
One Step Closer . . . . (Warner Bros.)

One, The
Backstreet Boys; *Millennium*. . . . .(Jive)
Only One For Me, The
Brian McKnight; *Anytime* . . . . (Motown)
Only Wanna Be With You
Hootie & The Blowfish; *Cracked Rear View*. . . . . (Atlantic)
Only You
112; *112*. . . . . (Bad Boy/Arista)
Bad Boy Greatest Hits-#1-C. . . . . (Bad Boy/Arista)
Ultimate Hip Hop Party-1998-C . . . . (Arista)
Ooh Aah…Just A Little Bit
Gina G; *Fresh!*. . . . . (Eternal/Warner Bros.)
Party Doll
Buddy Knox; *Best Of Buddy Knox*. . . . . (Rhino)
Billboard Top Rock 'N' Roll Hits-1957-C . . . . (Rhino)
ST/American Graffiti . . . . (MCA)
Pay You Back With Interest
Hollies; *Best Of The Hollies* . . . . (EMI)
History Of British Rock-#4-C . . . . (Rhino)
The Hollies' Greatest Hits . . . . (Epic)
Perfect Drug
Nine Inch Nails; *ST/Lost Highway* . . . . (Interscope)
Pick Me Up On Your Way Down
Charlie Walker; *Columbia Country Classics-#2-Honky Tonk
Heroes-C* . . . . (Columbia)
Heroes Of Country Music-#2-Legends Of Honky Tonk-C . . . . (Rhino)
Harlan Howard; *All-Time Favorite Country Songwriter* . . . . (Koch International)
Please
Bing Crosby; *Bing Crosby-16 Most Requested Songs* . . . . (Legacy)
Please Come To Boston
Dave Loggins; *Apprentice (In A Musical Workshop)* . . . . (Epic)
Rock Artifacts-From The Vaults-#2-C . . . . (Legacy)
Super Hits Of The '70s-Have A Nice Day-#13-C . . . . (Rhino)
David Allan Coe; *David Allan Coe-17 Greatest Hits* . . . . . . (Columbia)
For The Record-The First 10 Years . . . . (Columbia)
Joan Baez; *Best Of Joan Baez* . . . . (A&M)
Joan Baez-Classics-#8 . . . . (A&M)
Reba McEntire; *Starting Over* . . . . (MCA)
Please Don't Tell Her
Big Head Todd & The Monsters; *Beautiful World*. . . . . (Revolution)
Live Monsters . . . . (Revolution)
Please Love Me Forever
Bobby Vinton; *Bobby Vinton-16 Most Requested Songs* . . . . (Legacy)
Bobby Vinton's All-Time Greatest Hits. . . . . (Epic)
Please Love Me Forever . . . . (Epic)
Pledging My Time
Bob Dylan; *Blonde On Blonde* . . . . (Columbia)
Luther "Guitar Jr." Johnson; *Tangled Up In Blues-Songs Of Bob Dylan-This
Ain't No Tribute-C* . . . . (House Of Blues)
Possession
Sarah McLachlan; *Fumbling Towards Ecstasy* . . . . (Arista)
Prairie Wedding
Mark Knopfler; *Sailing To Philadelphia* . . . . (Warner Bros.)
Pre-Road Downs
Crosby, Stills & Nash; *Crosby, Stills & Nash* . . . . (Atlantic)
Pretty Ballerina
Left Banke; *History Of The Left Banke* . . . . (Rhino)
Nuggets-#11-Pop-Part 4-C . . . . (Rhino)
Pretty Blue Eyes
Steve Lawrence; *Best Of Steve Lawrence* . . . . (Taragon)
Pretty Girl
Jon B.; *Bonafide*. . . . . (Yab Yum/550)
Private Emotion
Ricky Martin & Meja; *Ricky Martin* . . . . (Columbia)
Problems
Everly Brothers; *Everly Brothers' All-Time Greatest Hits*. . . . . . . (Curb)
Everly Brothers-Cadence Classics-Their 20 Greatest Hits . . . . (Rhino)
Fabulous Style Of The Everly Brothers. . . . . (Rhino)
Promise
Jagged Edge; *J.E. Heartbreak* . . . . (So So Def/Columbia)
Promises
Def Leppard; *Euphoria* . . . . (Mercury)
Put It On Me
Ja Rule featuring Li'l Mo And Vita; *Rule 3:36* . . . (Murder Inc./Def Jam/IDJMG)
Put Your Dreams Away (For Another Day)
Frank Sinatra; *Best Of The Columbia Years-1943-1952* . . . . (Columbia)
Frank Sinatra-16 Most Requested Songs . . . . (Columbia)
Sinatra: A Man And His Music . . . . (Reprise)
The Capitol Years . . . . (Capitol)
Mickey Gilley; *Put Your Dreams Away*. . . . . (Epic)
Ten Years Of Hits . . . . (Epic)
R U Still Down
2Pac; *R U Still Down (Remember Me)*. . . . . (Amaru/Jive)
Rags To Riches
Tony Bennett; *Tony Bennett-16 Most Requested Songs* . . . . (Legacy)
Tony Bennett's All-Time Greatest Hits . . . . (Columbia)
Tony Bennett & Percy Faith & His Orchestra; *Radio Classics Of The
'50s-C* . . . . (Columbia)

Ragtop Cadillac
Lonestar; *Lonestar* . . . . (BNA)
Ready, Willing And Able
Lari White; *Best Of Lari White* . . . . (RCA)
Don't Fence Me In. . . . . (RCA)
Relating To A Psychopath
Macy Gray; *The Id* . . . . (Epic)
Reminiscing
Little River Band; *'70's Super Groups-C*. . . . .(Rhino)
Reminiscing: The Twentieth Anniversary Collection . . . . (Rhino)
Rendezvous
Bruce Springsteen; *Tracks* . . . .(Columbia)
Gary U.S. Bonds; *Best Of Gary U.S. Bonds* . . . .(EMI Legends Of Rock 'N' Roll)
Greg Kihn; *Kihnsolidation-Best Of Greg Kihn* . . . . (Rhino)
Greg Kihn Band; *Cover Me (Bruce Springsteen Tribute)-C* . . . .(Rhino)
Rhythm Divine
Enrique Iglesias; *Enrique*. . . . . (Overbrook/Interscope)
Right Here Right Now
Charlie Major & Joy Lynn White; *444* . . . . (Dead Reckoning)
Right Man For The Job
Charlie Robison; *Step Right Up* . . . .(Lucky Dog)
Room At The Top Of The Stairs
David Grisman; *Retrograss* . . . . (Acoustic Disc)
Leo Kottke; *Leo Kottke-Live* . . . . (Private Music)
Peculiaroso . . . . (Private Music)
Stanley Brothers & The Clinch Mountain Boys; *Ralph Stanley-50th
Anniversary* . . . .(Rebel)
Stella Parton; *Stella Parton-Anthology* . . . .(Renaissance)
Ruby Baby
Beatles; *The Beatles featuring Tony Sheridan-In The Beginning (Circa
1960)* . . . . (Polydor)
Dion; *Bronx Blues-Columbia Recordings 1962-1965* . . . .(Columbia)
Dion-24 Original Classics . . . .(Arista)
Donald Fagen; *The Nightfly* . . . . (Warner Bros.)
Drifters; *Atlantic Rhythm & Blues 1947-1974-#3 (1955-1958)-C* . . . . . (Atlantic)
Drifters-Their Greatest Recordings . . . .(Atco)
Let The Boogie Woogie Roll-Greatest Hits . . . . (Atlantic)
Rush Rush
Paula Abdul; *Spellbound* . . . . (Captive)
Sad Eyes
Bruce Springsteen; *Tracks* . . . .(Columbia)
Trisha Yearwood; *Real Live Woman* . . . . (MCA)
Sail Away
David Gray; *White Ladder* . . . .(ATO/RCA)
Salty Dog Blues
Flatt & Scruggs; *Earl Scruggs: His Family & Friends/Nashville
Airplane* . . . .(Collectables)
Flatt & Scruggs-20 Greatest Hits . . . .(Deluxe)
Greatest Folksingers Of The '60s-C . . . .(Vanguard)
San Antonio Girl
Steve Earle & The Dukes; *Exit 0* . . . . (MCA)
Sara Smile
After 7; *Very Best Of After 7*. . . . . (Virgin)
Daryl Hall & John Oates; *Best Of Daryl Hall & John Oates* . . . . (RCA)
Daryl Hall & John Oates. . . . . (RCA)
Livetime. . . . . (RCA)
Rock 'N Soul, Part 1 . . . . (RCA)
Soulful Sounds. . . . . (RCA)
Satisfy You
Puff Daddy Featuring R. Kelly; *Forever* . . . . (Bad Boy/Arista)
Save Your Heart For Me
Gary Lewis And The Playboys; *Gary Lewis & The Playboys* . . . . . . (Gold Rush)
Gary Lewis And The Playboys' Greatest Hits . . . .(Curb)
Say It
Voices Of Theory; *Voices Of Theory* . . . .(H.O.L.A./Red Ant)
Say Say Say
Paul McCartney & Michael Jackson; *All The Best!* . . . .(Capitol)
Pipes Of Peace . . . .(Capitol)
Say When
Lonestar; *Crazy Nights*. . . . . (BNA)
Say You'll Be There
Spice Girls; *Now That's What I Call Music!-#1-C* . . . . (Virgin)
Spice . . . . (Virgin)
Sea Cruise
Billy "Crash" Craddock; *Billy "Crash" Craddock's Greatest Hits* . . . .(Capitol)
Changes. . . . .(Capitol)
Frankie Ford; *American Hot Wax*. . . . . (A&M)
Best Of New Orleans Rhythm & Blues-#2-C . . . . (Rhino)
Oldies But Goodies-#3-C . . . . (Original Sound)
Rock & Roll Show-C . . . .(Gusto)
Glenn Frey; *No Fun Aloud* . . . .(Asylum)
Johnny Rivers; *Johnny Rivers-Anthology 1964-1977* . . . . (Capitol)
Nighthawks; *Best Of The Nighthawks* . . . . (Genes CD Co.)
Robert Gordon & Link Wray; *Fresh Fish Special* . . . . (RCA)
Secret Love
Doris Day; *Doris Day's Greatest Hits* . . . .(Columbia)
Hollywood Magic-1950s-C . . . .(Columbia)
Frank Sinatra; *Days Of Wine And Roses, Moon River, And Other Academy
Award Winners* . . . .(Reprise)

Freddy Fender; *Freddy Fender-Collection* . . . . (Reprise)
Guy Lombardo & His Royal Canadians; *Golden Medleys* . . . .(MCA)
Moonglows; *Doo-Wop's Greatest Hits-C* . . . .(Vee-Jay)
Nancy Wilson; *Capitol Sings The Best Movie Songs-C* . . . . (Capitol)
Slim Whitman; *Best Of Slim Whitman 1952-1972* . . . . (Rhino)
   Slim Whitman's Greatest Hits . . . . (Curb)

Sentimental Me
Ames Brothers; *Best Of The Ames Brothers* . . . . (Pair)

Set U Free
Planet Soul; *Disco Queens-The '90s-C* . . . . (Rhino)
   Energy + Harmony . . . .(Strictly Rhythm)

Shadow Dancing
Andy Gibb; *Andy Gibb's Greatest Hits* . . . . (RSO)
   Collection Of His Greatest Hits . . . . (Polydor)
   Shadow Dancing . . . . (RSO)

Shake Your Bon-Bon
Ricky Martin; *Ricky Martin* . . . . (Columbia)

Shame, Shame
Magic Lanterns; *Shame, Shame* . . . . (Collectables)

Shape Of My Heart
Backstreet Boys; *Black & Blue* . . . . (Jive)
   Now That's What I Call Music!-#6-C . . . . (Virgin)

Sh-Boom
Chords; *Atlantic Rhythm & Blues 1947-1974-#2 (1952-1955)-C* . . . . . .(Atlantic)
Crew-Cuts; *Partytime '50s-C* . . . . (Priority)
Stan Freberg; *Capitol Collectors Series-Stan Freberg* . . . . (Capitol)

She Ain't The Girl For You
Kinleys; *Kinleys II* . . . .(Epic)

She Bangs
Ricky Martin; *Sound Loaded* . . . . (Columbia)

She Can Put Her Shoes Under My Bed (Anytime)
Johnny Duncan; *Classic Country* . . . . (Simitar)

She Can't Love You
Destiny's Child; *The Writing's On The Wall* . . . . (Columbia)

She Wants You
Billie; *Honey To The B* . . . . (Virgin)

Sherry
4 Seasons; *4 Seasons' Greatest Hits-#1* . . . . (Rhino)
   4 Seasons-Anthology . . . . (Rhino)
   ST/The Wanderers . . . .(Warner Bros.)

She's A Fool
Lesley Gore; *Golden Hits Of Lesley Gore* . . . . (Mercury)
   Lesley Gore-Anthology . . . . (Rhino)

She's So High
Tal Bachman; *Tal Bachman* . . . . (Columbia)

Shine
Jon B.; *Cool Relax* . . . . (Yab Yum/550)

Shipoopi
Original Broadway Cast; *The Music Man* . . . . (Angel)
Original Cast; *The Music Man* . . . .(Gold Rush)

Shiver
Coldplay; *Parachutes* . . . . (Nettwerk/Capitol)

Should've Asked Her Faster
Ty England; *Ty England* . . . . (RCA)

Show Me The Meaning Of Being Lonely
Backstreet Boys; *Millennium* . . . . (Jive)
   Now That's What I Call Music!-#5-C . . . . (Virgin)

Silence Is Golden
4 Seasons; *25th Anniversary Collection* . . . . (Rhino)
   4 Seasons-Anthology . . . . (Rhino)
Tremeloes; *Best Of The Tremeloes* . . . . (Rhino)
   History Of British Rock-#7-C . . . . (Rhino)
   Rock Artifacts-From The Vaults-#4-C . . . . (Columbia)

Sincerely
McGuire Sisters; *Billboard Pop Memories-1955-1959-C* . . . . (Rhino)
   McGuire Sisters' Greatest Hits . . . .(MCA)
Moonglows; *13 Of The Best Doo Wop Love Songs-C* . . . . (Original Sound)
   Billboard Top Rock 'N' Roll Hits-1955-C . . . . (Rhino)
   Moonglows-Their Greatest Hits . . . . (Chess)

Sit Down I Think I Love You
Buffalo Springfield; *Buffalo Springfield-Retrospective* . . . . (Atco)

Sittin' On Go
Bryan White; *Between Now And Forever* . . . . (Asylum)

Sixty Minute Man
Billy Ward & His Dominoes; *Rock & Roll Show-C* . . . . (Gusto)
Dominos; *Oldies But Goodies-#5-C* . . . . (Original Sound)
Rufus Thomas & Carla Thomas; *Rufus Thomas & Carla Thomas-Chronicle* . . . .(Stax)

Slide
Goo Goo Dolls; *Dizzy Up The Girl* . . . . (Warner Sunset/Reprise)

Slip Away
Clarence Carter; *Billboard Top Pop Hits-1968-C* . . . . (Rhino)
   Snatching It Back-The Best Of Clarence Carter . . . . (Rhino)

Slow Like Honey
Fiona Apple; *Tidal* . . . . (Clean Slate/Work)

Small Talk
Doris Day & John Raitt; *ST/Pajama Game* . . . . (Collectables)
Original Cast; *Pajama Game* . . . . (Columbia)

Smoke! Smoke! Smoke!
Commander Cody & His Lost Planet Airmen; *Country Casanova* . . . . . (MCA)
   Too Much Fun-Best Of Commander Cody & His Lost Planet Airmen . . (MCA)
   We've Got A Live One Here! . . . . (Warner Bros.)
Doc Watson; *Red Rocking Chair* . . . .(Flying Fish)
Johnny Bond & His Red River Valley Boys; *All Time Legends Of Country Music-C* . . . . (Legacy)
Merle Travis; *Johnny Gimble's Texas Honky-Tonk Hits-C* . . . . . (C.M.H. Prod.)
Tex Williams; *Birth Of A Dream-Capitol's Early Hits-C* . . . . (Capitol)
   Dr. Demento Presents The Greatest Novelty Records-#1-1940s & Before-C . . . . (Rhino)

Smooth
Santana featuring Rob Thomas; *Supernatural* . . . . (Arista)
   Totally Hits-#1-C . . . . (Arista)

So Help Me Girl
Gary Barlow; *Open Road* . . . . (Arista)
Joe Diffie; *Third Rock From The Sun* . . . . (Epic)

So Many Ways
Braxtons; *So Many Ways* . . . .(Atlantic)

Softest Place On Earth
Xscape; *Traces Of My Lipstick* . . . . (So So Def/Columbia)

Soldier Boy
Shirelles; *Billboard Top Rock 'N' Roll Hits-1962-C* . . . . (Rhino)
   Oldies But Goodies-#4-C . . . . (Original Sound)
   Shirelles-Anthology 1959-1964 . . . . (Rhino)
   ST/The Wanderers . . . .(Warner Bros.)

Somebody
Bryan Adams; *Greenpeace/Rainbow Warriors-C* . . . . (Geffen)
   Reckless . . . . (A&M)
   So Far So Good . . . . (A&M)

Somebody Like Me
Eddy Arnold; *Best Of Eddy Arnold-#2* . . . . (Dunhill Compact Classics)

Somebody To Love
Jefferson Airplane; *2400 Fulton Street-An Anthology* . . . . (RCA)
   Loves You . . . . (RCA)
   Nipper's Greatest Hits Of The '60s-#1-C . . . . (RCA)
   Surrealistic Pillow . . . . (RCA)
   The Worst Of Jefferson Airplane . . . . (RCA)

Someday Soon
Chris LeDoux; *Rodeo Songs Old & New* . . . . (Liberty)
Ian & Sylvia; *Ian & Sylvia's Greatest Hits* . . . . (Vanguard)
   Northern Journey . . . . (Vanguard)
Judy Collins; *Colors Of The Day-The Best Of Judy Collins* . . . . . . (Elektra)
   Who Knows Where The Time Goes . . . . (Elektra)
Moe Bandy; *Moe Bandy's Greatest Hits* . . . . (Columbia)
   Rodeo Romeo . . . . (Columbia)
Suzy Bogguss; *Aces* . . . . (Liberty)
   Suzy Bogguss' Greatest Hits . . . . (Liberty)

Somehow, Somewhere, Someway
Kenny Wayne Shepherd; *Trouble Is...* . . . . (Revolution)

Someone Loves You Honey
Charley Pride; *Charley Pride's Greatest Hits* . . . .(RCA)

Someone Should Tell Her
Mavericks; *Trampoline* . . . . (MCA)

Somethin' Stupid
Frank & Nancy Sinatra; *Frank Sinatra's Greatest Hits!* . . . . (Reprise)
   The World We Knew . . . . (Reprise)
Nancy Sinatra & Frank Sinatra; *Boots-Nancy Sinatra's Greatest Hits* . . . (Rhino)

Sometimes
Strokes; *Is This It* . . . .(RCA)

Somewhere In My Broken Heart
Billy Dean; *Billy Dean's Greatest Hits* . . . . (Liberty)
   Heart Beats-Country Lovin': Songs From The Heart-C . . . . (Rhino)
   Young Man . . . . (SBK)
Randy Travis; *No Holdin' Back* . . . . (Warner Bros.)

Soul Man
Blues Brothers; *Best Of The Blues Brothers* . . . .(Atlantic)
   Blues Brothers-The Definitive Collection . . . .(Atlantic)
   Briefcase Full Of Blues . . . .(Atlantic)
Sam & Dave; *Best Of Sam & Dave* . . . .(Atlantic)
   Golden Age Of Black Music-1960-1970-C . . . .(Atlantic)
   Soul Men . . . . (Rhino)

Spanish Eyes
Ricky Martin; *Ricky Martin* . . . . (Columbia)

Spanish Guitar
Toni Braxton; *The Heat* . . . .(LaFace)

Spend The Night
Rahsaan Patterson; *Rahsaan Patterson* . . . . (MCA)

Squeeze Me In
Garth Brooks; *Scarecrow* . . . . (Capitol)

Standing Still
Jewel; *This Way* . . . .(Atlantic)

Starlight, Starbright
Linda Scott; *45-#133* . . . .(Eric)

Stay
Temptations; *Phoenix Rising* . . . . (Motown)

Stay As Sweet As You Are
Art Tatum; *Art Tatum Solo Masterpieces-#1* . . . . (Pablo)
Betty Carter; *It's Not About The Melody* . . . . (Verve)

Jimmie Grier & His Orchestra; 78-#7307 .... (Brunswick)
Nat ''King'' Cole; *Love Is The Thing* .... (Capitol)

Stay Forever
Hal Ketchum; *Every Little Word* .... (Curb)
From Nashville With Love-C .... (Curb)
Hal Ketchum-The Hits .... (MCG/Curb)

Stay The Night
IMx; *IMx* .... (MCA)

Steal My Kisses
Ben Harper; *Burn To Shine* .... (Virgin)
Now That's What I Call Music!-#4-C .... (Virgin)

Steal Your Love
Lucinda Williams; *Essence* .... (Lost Highway/IDJMG)

Steam Heat
Carol Haney; *ST/Pajama Game* .... (Collectables)
Janis Paige/John Raitt/Original Cast; *Pajama Game* .... (Columbia)

Stellar
Incubus; *Make Yourself* .... (Immortal/Epic)

Step Inside Love
Beatles; *The Beatles-Anthology-#3* .... (Capitol)

Still...You Turn Me On
Emerson, Lake & Palmer; *Best Of Emerson, Lake & Palmer* .... (Rhino)
Brain Salad Surgery .... (Rhino)
From The Beginning-The Greg Lake Retrospective .... (Rhino)

Stop By
Rahsaan Patterson; *Rahsaan Patterson* .... (MCA)

Stop! In The Name Of Love
Diana Ross & The Supremes; *16 #1 Hits From The Early '60s-C* ..... (Motown)
Diana Ross & The Supremes' Greatest Hits .... (Motown)
Diana Ross & The Supremes-Anthology (1962-1969) .... (Motown)
Evening With Diana Ross .... (Motown)
Girl Groups-Story Of A Sound-C .... (Rhino)
Motown Superstar Series-#1-Diana Ross & The Supremes .... (Motown)
Hollies; *45-#89819* .... (Atlantic)
Supremes; *Billboard Top Pop Hits-1965-C* .... (Rhino)

Straight Up
Chante Moore; *Exposed* .... (Silas)

Stranded In The Jungle
Cadets; *Collectables Presents The History Of Rock-#2-C* ...... (Collectables)
Cruisin'-1956-C .... (Increase)
Oldies But Goodies-#1-C .... (Original Sound)
Original Rock 'N' Roll Hits Of The '50s-C .... (Roulette)
New York Dolls; *In Too Much Too Soon* .... (Mercury)
Live In NYC-1975 .... (Restless)

Stranger
Johnny Duncan; *Country Music Classics-#12-C* .... (K-Tel)
Johnny Duncan-Classic Country .... (Simitar)

Stranger In Paradise
Arthur Lyman; *Pearly Shells* .... (Crescendo)
Bing Crosby; *The Radio Years: 20 Songs* .... (Crescendo)
Original Cast; *Kismet* .... (Columbia)
Tony Bennett; *Tony Bennett-16 Most Requested Songs* .... (Legacy)
Tony Bennett's All-Time Greatest Hits .... (Columbia)

Such A Night
Dr. John; *Very Best Of Dr. John* .... (Rhino)
Dr. John & Chris Barber; *On A Mardi Gras Day* .... (Great Southern)
Dr. John & The Band; *The Last Waltz* .... (Warner Bros.)

Sugar Walls
Sheena Easton; *Dance Mix* .... (EMI)
Private Heaven .... (EMI)

Sugar, Sugar
Archies; *Billboard Top Rock 'N' Roll Hits-1969-C* .... (Rhino)

Suite: Judy Blue Eyes
Crosby, Stills & Nash; *Crosby, Stills & Nash* .... (Atlantic)
CSN .... (Atlantic)
ST/Woodstock .... (Atlantic)
Crosby, Stills, Nash & Young; *So Far* .... (Atlantic)

Sunshine Girl
Parade; *More Nuggets-C* .... (Rhino)

Superman
R.E.M.; *Life's Rich Pageant* .... (EMI-Capitol Entert. Properties)

Superwoman
Lil' Mo; *Based On A True Story* .... (Gold Mind/East West/EEG)

Sure To Fall (In Love With You)
Carl Perkins; *Boppin' The Blues* .... (Columbia)

Susie Q
Creedence Clearwater Revival; *1968-1969* .... (Fantasy)
Chooglin' .... (Fantasy)
Creedence Clearwater Revival .... (Fantasy)
Creedence Clearwater Revival-Chronicle .... (Fantasy)
Creedence Clearwater Revival-Gold .... (Fantasy)
Live In Europe .... (Fantasy)
Dale Dawkins; *Collectables Presents The History Of Rock-#3-C* .. (Collectables)
Legends Of Rock Guitar-'50s-#1-C .... (Rhino)
Rockin' Rebels-C .... (K-Tel)
Jose Feliciano; *Jose Feliciano's All-Time Greatest Hits* .... (RCA)

Sweet Lady
Tyrese; *Tyrese* .... (RCA)

Sweet Pea
Tommy Roe; *Best Of Tommy Roe* .... (Curb)
Cruisin'-1966-C .... (Increase)
Tommy Roe's Greatest Hits .... (MCA)

Sweetheart
Jermaine Dupri & Mariah Carey; *Presents Life In 1472-Original
Soundtrack* .... (So So Def/Columbia)
Mariah Carey featuring Jermaine Dupri; *Mariah Carey-#1's* .... (Columbia)

Sweetheart
Dan Hicks & His Hot Licks; *Last Train To Hicksville* .... (MCA)
Maria Muldaur; *Waitress In The Donut Shop* .... (Warner Archives)

Swing My Way
K.P. & Envyi; *ST/Can't Hardly Wait* .... (Elektra)

Take Me
George Jones; *George Jones' Greatest Hits* .... (Epic)
George Jones & Tammy Wynette; *George Jones & Tammy Wynette-16
Biggest Hits* .... (Epic/Legacy)

Take Me To Your World
George Jones; *Tammy Wynette...Remembered-C* .... (Asylum)
Tammy Wynette; *Tammy Wynette-16 Biggest Hits* .... (Legacy)
Tammy Wynette's Greatest Hits .... (Epic)

Taker, The
Kris Kristofferson; *The Silver Tongued Devil And I* .... (Columbia)
Waylon Jennings; *Essential Waylon Jennings* .... (RCA)
Only Daddy That'll Walk The Line-The RCA Years .... (RCA)

Tearin' Up My Heart
'N Sync; *'N Sync* .... (RCA)

Teenage Dirtbag
Wheatus; *Wheatus* .... (Columbia)

Tell It Like It Is
Aaron Neville; *Classic Aaron Neville* .... (Rounder)
Soul Shots-#5-La-La Means I Love You-C .... (Rhino)
Super Oldies Of The '60s-#7-C .... (Audio Fidelity)
Tell It Like It Is .... (Curb)
Tell it Like It Is-Golden Classics .... (Collectables)
Treacherous: A History Of The Neville Brothers .... (Rhino)
Billy Joe Royal; *Billy Joe Royal's Greatest Hits* .... (Atlantic)
Tell It Like It Is .... (Atlantic)
George Benson; *Best Of George Benson* .... (A&M)
UB40; *Live In Moscow* .... (A&M)
Rat In The Kitchen .... (A&M)

Tell Me
Groove Theory; *Groove Theory* .... (Epic)
MTV Party To Go-#9-C .... (Tommy Boy)

Tell Me What You See
Beatles; *Beatles VI* .... (Capitol)
Beatles-Box Set .... (Capitol)
Beatles-Love Songs .... (Capitol)

Tell Me When
Human League; *Octopus* .... (East West)

Temporary Like Achilles
Bob Dylan; *Blonde On Blonde* .... (Columbia)

That's All
Tennessee Ernie Ford; *The Ultimate Tennessee Ernie Ford* ..... (Razor & Tie)

That's All I Want From You
Jaye P. Morgan; *The Jaye P. Morgan Story* .... (Simitar)

That's As Close As I'll Get To Loving You
Aaron Tippin; *Aaron Tippin-Super Hits* .... (RCA)
Essential Aaron Tippin .... (RCA)
Greatest Hits And Then Some .... (RCA)
Tool Box .... (RCA)

That's The Way Love Goes
Janet Jackson; *janet.* .... (Virgin)

The Action
Keb' Mo'; *Just Like You* .... (Okeh)

Then You Can Tell Me Goodbye
Casinos; *Then You Can Tell Me Goodbye* .... (Varese Vintage)
Neal McCoy; *Neal McCoy's Greatest Hits* .... (Atlantic)

There Is
Dells; *Dells* .... (Chess)
On Their Corner-Best Of The Dells .... (MCA)
There Is .... (Chess)

There She Goes
Babyface; *Face 2 Face* .... (Arista)

There You Have It
BlackHawk; *Big Country Hits '99-C* .... (K-Tel)
The Sky's The Limit .... (Arista)

There's Your Trouble
Dixie Chicks; *Wide Open Spaces* .... (Monument)

They Can't Take That Away From Me
Billie Holiday; *God Bless The Child* .... (Pro-Arte)
I Like Jazz-Essence Of Billie Holiday .... (Columbia)
Diana Krall; *Love Scenes* .... (Impulse!)
Ella Fitzgerald; *Ella & Louis Again* .... (Verve)
Frank Sinatra; *My Kind Of Broadway* .... (Reprise)
Frank Sinatra & Natalie Cole; *Duets* .... (Capitol)
Fred Astaire; *Starring Fred Astaire* .... (Columbia)
Kate Smith; *Best Of Kate Smith* .... (Curb)
Lisa Stansfield; *Glory Of Gershwin Featuring Larry Adler-C* ...... (Mercury)

Mary Lou Williams; *Mary Lou Williams In London* . . . . (Crescendo)
Original Broadway Cast; *Crazy For You* . . . . (Angel)
Original London Cast; *Crazy For You* . . . . (RCA)
Patti Austin; *The Real Me* . . . . (Qwest)
Sarah Vaughan; *Sarah Vaughan Sings George Gershwin Songbook,*
  Vol. 1. . . . . (Emarcy)
Stanley Turrentine; *Blue Gershwin.* . . . . (Blue Note)

Things We Said Today
Beatles; *Beatles-Box Set* . . . . (Capitol)
  Something New . . . . (Capitol)
  The Beatles At The Hollywood Bowl . . . . (Capitol)
Paul McCartney; *Tripping The Live Fantastic-Highlights!* . . . . (Capitol)

Think About Love
Dolly Parton; *Best There Is* . . . . (RCA)

Thinkin' 'Bout It
Gerald Levert; *Love & Consequences.* . . . . (East West)

This Boy
Beatles; *Beatles-Box Set* . . . . (Capitol)
  Beatles-Love Songs . . . . (Capitol)
  Meet The Beatles! . . . . (Capitol)
  Past Masters-Volume One . . . . (Parlophone)
  The Beatles-Anthology-#1 . . . . (Capitol)

This Is For The Lover In You
Babyface; *The Day* . . . . (Epic)

This Is Your Night
Amber; *ESPN Presents Jock Jams-#2-C* . . . . (Tommy Boy)
  This Is Your Night . . . . (Tommy Boy)

This Lil' Game We Play
Subway; *Good Times* . . . . (Biv 10/Motown)

Three Little Words
Carmen McRae; *Great American Songbook* . . . . (Atlantic)
Duke Ellington & His Orchestra; *Nipper's Greatest Hits Of The*
  '30s-#2-C . . . . (RCA)
Nat ''King'' Cole; *L-O-V-E* . . . . (Capitol)

Thunder Road
Bruce Springsteen; *Born To Run.* . . . . (Columbia)
  Bruce Springsteen's Greatest Hits . . . . (Columbia)
Bruce Springsteen & The E Street Band; *Bruce Springsteen & The E Street*
  Band Live/1975-85 . . . . (Legacy)

Tie A Yellow Ribbon Round The Ole Oak Tree
Dawn Featuring Tony Orlando; *'70s Party Killers-C* . . . . (Rhino)
  Fantastic-#1-C. . . . . (K-Tel)
Frank Sinatra; *Some Nice Things I've Missed* . . . . (Reprise)
Lawrence Welk; *Best Of Lawrence Welk-20 Great Hits* . . . . . .(Ranwood)
Sonny James & Karla Taylor; *Classic Country Duets-C* . . . . (Curb)

Till Then
Mills Brothers; *Best Of The Mills Brothers.* . . . .(MCA)
  Cab Driver. . . . . (Ranwood)
  Lazy River . . . . (MCA Special Prod.)
  Mills Brothers . . . . (Everest)
  Mills Brothers' Greatest Hits. . . . . (MCA)

Till We Two Are One
Eddy Howard; *Best Of Eddy Howard-The Mercury Years* . . . . (Mercury)
Georgie Shaw; *45-#28937* . . . . (Decca)
Louis Jordan; *One Guy Named Louis* . . . . (Blue Note)

Till You Love Me
Reba McEntire; *Read My Mind.* . . . . (MCA)

Time After Time (Annelise)
R.E.M.; *Reckoning* . . . . (I.R.S.)

To Be Loved By You
Wynonna; *Revelations* . . . . (Curb/MCA)
  Wynonna-Collection . . . . (Curb)

To Know Him, Is To Love Him
Dolly Parton/Emmylou Harris/Linda Ronstadt; *Trio* . . . .(Warner Bros.)
Teddy Bears; *At The Hop-'50s Rock 'N' Roll* . . . . (K-Tel)
  Phil Spector-Back To Mono 1958-1969-C . . . . (Abkco)

To Love Somebody
Bee Gees; *Bee Gees-Gold.* . . . . (Polydor)
  History Of British Rock-#7-C . . . . (Rhino)
Jimmy Somerville; *Jimmy Somerville-Singles Collection-1984-1990* . . (London)
Michael Bolton; *Timeless-Classics.* . . . . (Columbia)

To Love You More
Celine Dion with The Bee Gees; *All The Way...A Decade*
  Of Song . . . . (550 Music)
  Let's Talk About Love-C . . . . (550 Music)

To Make You Feel My Love
Billy Joel; *Billy Joel's Greatest Hits-#3* . . . . (Columbia)
  Songs From The Heart-C . . . . (Columbia)
Bob Dylan; *Time Out Of Mind* . . . . (Columbia)
Garth Brooks; *Garth Brooks-Double Live* . . . . (Capitol)
  Limited Series-Box. . . . . (Capitol)
  ST/Hope Floats . . . . (Capitol)
Trisha Yearwood; *ST/Hope Floats* . . . . (Capitol)

To The Moon And Back
Savage Garden; *Savage Garden* . . . . (Columbia)

Too Close
Next; *Rated Next.* . . . .(Divine Mill/Arista)

Too Much Heaven
Bee Gees; *Bee Gees' Greatest* . . . . (Polydor)

Touch Me
Solo; *4 Bruthas & A Bass* . . . . (Perspective/A&M)

Touch Me Tease Me
Case Featuring Foxy Brown; *Case* . . . . (Def Jam/RAL/Mercury)
  Def Jam Greatest Hits-C . . . . (Def Jam)
  ST/The Nutty Professor . . . . (Def Jam)
  Ultimate Hip Hop Party-1998-C . . . . (Arista)

Tracy
Cuff Links; *Super Hits Of The '70s-Have A Nice Day-#1-C* . . . . (Rhino)

Travelin' Light
Eric Clapton; *Reptile* . . . . (Duck/Reprise)

Truly
Lionel Richie; *Back To Front* . . . . (Motown)
  Lionel Richie . . . . (Motown)

Turn Off The Light
Nelly Furtado; *Whoa Nelly!.* . . . .(DreamWorks/SKG)

Turn On Your Love Light
Bobby Bland; *Bobby Bland's Greatest Hits-#1* . . . . (MCA)
  Psychedelic '60s-#6-C . . . . (Collectables)
  Turn On Your Love Light-The Duke Recordings-#2 . . . . (MCA)
Grateful Dead; *Best Of The Grateful Dead-Skeletons From The*
  Closet. . . . . (Warner Bros.)
  Fillmore East-2/11/69 . . . . (Arista)
  Live/Dead. . . . . (Warner Bros.)
  Two From The Vault. . . . .(Grateful Dead)

Twist And Shout
Beatles; *Beatles-Box Set* . . . . (Capitol)
  Please Please Me . . . . (Parlophone)
  Rock 'N' Roll Music . . . . (Capitol)
  ST/Imagine: John Lennon . . . . (Capitol)
  The Beatles At The Hollywood Bowl. . . . . (Capitol)
  The Early Beatles . . . . (Capitol)
Buck Owens & The Buckaroos; *Buck Owens & The Buckaroos-Live At*
  Carnegie Hall. . . . . (Country Music Foundation)
Isley Brothers; *Best Of The Isley Brothers.* . . . . (Curb)
  Cruisin'-1963-C. . . . . (Increase)
  Frat Rock!-C . . . . (Rhino)
  Oldies But Goodies-#10-C . . . . (Original Sound)
  Solid Gold Music-WCBS FM 101-'60s-#1-C . . . . (Collectables)
  Toga Rock-C. . . . . (Dunhill Compact Classics)
Mamas & The Papas; *Best Of The Mamas & The Papas* . . . . (MCA)
Who; *Who's Last.* . . . . (MCA)

Two Princes
Spin Doctors; *Pocket Full Of Kryptonite* . . . . . . (Epic Portrait Assoc.)

Two Tickets To Paradise
Eddie Money; *Eddie Money* . . . . (Columbia)
  Eddie Money's Greatest Hits-Sound Of Money . . . . (Columbia)
  Unplug It In . . . . (Columbia)

U Know What's Up
Donell Jones; *Totally Hits-#2-C* . . . . (Elektra)
  Where I Wanna Be . . . . (LaFace)

Unless
Guy Mitchell; *Definitive Guy Mitchell* . . . . (Collector's Choice)

Until You Come Back To Me
Aretha Franklin; *Aretha Franklin-30 Greatest Hits* . . . . (Rhino)
  Best Of Aretha Franklin . . . .(Atlantic)
  Golden Age Of Black Music-1970-1975-C . . . .(Atlantic)
Basia; *Brave New Hope.* . . . . (Epic)
  London Warsaw New York . . . . (Epic)
Hil St. Soul; *Soul Organic* . . . .(Dome/Select-O-Hits)
Miki Howard; *Miki Howard* . . . .(Atlantic)
Stevie Wonder; *Stevie Wonder-Love Songs-20 Classic Hits* . . . . (Motown)

Untitled (How Does It Feel)
D'Angelo; *Voodoo* . . . .(Cheeba Sound/Virgin)

Up, Up & Away
5th Dimension; *5th Dimension-Anthology 1967-1973* . . . . (Rhino)
  Greatest Hits On Earth. . . . . (Arista)

Waiting For A Star To Fall
Boy Meets Girl; *Nipper's Greatest Hits Of The '80s-C* . . . . (RCA)
  Reel Life . . . . (RCA)

Waiting For Love
3T; *ST/Men In Black* . . . . (Columbia)

Walk On By
Leroy Van Dyke; *Billboard Top Country Hits-1961-C* . . . . (Rhino)
  Country Classics-C . . . . (Sun)
  Country Music Classics-#2-1960-1965-C . . . . (K-Tel)
  Souvenirs Of Music City U.S.A.-C . . . . (Plantation)

Walking In A Hurricane
John Fogerty; *Blue Moon Swamp* . . . . (Warner Bros.)

Want You Bad
Offspring; *Conspiracy Of One* . . . . (Columbia)

Watch The Flowers Grow
4 Seasons; *25th Anniversary Collection* . . . . (Rhino)

Watch This
Clay Walker; *Rumor Has It* . . . .(Giant)

We Belong Together
Rickie Lee Jones; *Naked Songs Live And Acoustic* . . . . (Reprise)
  Pirates . . . . (Warner Bros.)

We Belong Together
Spinners; *Spinners* .... (Rhino)
We Belong Together
Robert & Johnny; *Doo Wop's Greatest Hits-C* .... (K-Tel)
We Belong Together
Peaches & Herb; *Love Is Strange-The Best Of Peaches & Herb* .... (Legacy)
We Belong Together
Los Lobos; *ST/La Bamba* .... (Slash)
Ritchie Valens; *Brown Eyed Soul...East L.A.-#2-C* .... (Rhino)
We Must Be In Love
Pure Soul; *Pure Soul* .... (Stepsun/Interscope)
Welcome To My World
Eddy Arnold; *Eddy Arnold-Pure Gold* .... (RCA)
The World Of Eddy Arnold .... (RCA)
Welcome To My World .... (RCA)
Elvis Presley; *Aloha from Hawaii via Satellite* .... (RCA)
Welcome To My World .... (RCA)
Jim Reeves; *Am I That Easy To Forget* .... (RCA)
Best Of Jim Reeves .... (RCA)
Jim Reeves .... (RCA)
Jim Reeves-Legendary Performer .... (RCA)
What A Dream
Conway Twitty; *Conway Twitty's Greatest Hits* .... (Curb)
Patti Page; *45-#70416* .... (Mercury)
Slim Harpo; *Raining In My Heart* .... (Hip-O)
What Are We Doin' Lonesome
Larry Gatlin & The Gatlin Brothers Band; *Best Of The Gatlins-All The Gold In California* .... (Legacy)
Larry Gatlin & The Gatlin Brothers' Greatest Hits-#2 .... (Columbia)
Larry Gatlin & The Gatlin Brothers-17 Greatest Hits .... (Columbia)
What Do I Know
Ricochet; *Pure Country-Best Of The '90s-#2-C* .... (Priority)
Ricochet .... (Columbia)
What Does It Take (To Win Your Love)
Junior Walker & The All Stars; *Billboard Top R&B Hits-1965-1969-C* .... (Rhino)
Junior Walker & The All Stars' Greatest Hits .... (Motown)
Junior Walker & The All Stars-Anthology .... (Motown)
Oldies But Goodies-#13-C .... (Original Sound)
What If It's You
Reba McEntire; *What If It's You* .... (MCA)
What Is And What Should Never Be
Jimmy Page & Black Crowes; *Live At The Greek* .... (TVT)
Led Zeppelin; *BBC Sessions* .... (Atlantic)
Led Zeppelin II .... (Atlantic)
Led Zeppelin-Box Set .... (Atlantic)
Led Zeppelin-The Complete Studio Recordings .... (Atlantic)
What You Want
Mase Featuring Total; *Harlem World* .... (Bad Boy/Arista)
What You Won't Do For Love
Bobby Caldwell; *Love Shouldn't Hurt-C* .... (Qwest)
Go West; *Chicken Soup For The Woman's Soul-C* .... (Rhino)
Whatever
En Vogue; *Bass In Your Face: Essential Drum And Bass-C* .... (Elektra)
What's It Gonna Be
Dusty Springfield; *Dusty Springfield-Anthology* .... (Mercury)
What's Stopping You
O'Jays; *Love You To Tears* .... (Volcano Entertainment)
What's Your Name
Don & Juan; *WCBS FM 101 History Of Rock-For Lovers-#2-C* ... (Collectables)
When I'm Sixty-Four
Beatles; *Beatles-Box Set* .... (Capitol)
Sgt. Pepper's Lonely Hearts Club Band .... (Capitol)
When The Lights Go Out
Five; *5* .... (Arista)
Totally Hits-#1-C .... (Arista)
When We Dance
Sting; *All This Time* .... (Starwave)
Fields Of Gold-The Best Of Sting 1984-1994 .... (A&M)
When Will I See You Again
Three Degrees; *Didn't It Blow Your Mind: Soul Hits Of The '70s-#14-C* .... (Rhino)
Mega Hits Dance Classics-#2-C .... (Priority)
When You Talk About Love
Patti LaBelle; *Flame* .... (MCA)
Live! One Night Only .... (MCA)
Whenever Wherever Whatever
Maxwell; *Maxwell's Urban Hang Suite* .... (Columbia)
Whenever You Come Around
Vince Gill; *When Love Finds You* .... (MCA)
Why Didn't You Call Me
Macy Gray; *On How Life Is* .... (Epic)
Why Does Love Got To Be So Sad?
Derek And The Dominos; *Layla* .... (Polydor)
Why Don't You Believe Me?
Duprees; *Best Of The Duprees* .... (Rhino)
Best Of The Duprees .... (Collectables)
Joni James; *Platinum & Gold Hits* .... (Taragon)
Patti Page; *Patti Page-Golden Celebration* .... (Mercury)
Why Don't You Fall In Love With Me?
Les Elgart; *Best Of The Big Bands: Sophisticated Swing* .... (Columbia)
Will You Be Staying After Sunday
Peppermint Rainbow; *Bubble Gum Classics-C* .... (MCA Special Prod.)
Winner Of Your Heart
Johnnie & Jack & Their Tennessee Mountain Boys; *45-Out of print* ..... (RCA)
Wishful Thinking
Wynn Stewart; *Heroes Of Country Music-#4-Legends Of The West Coast-C* .... (Rhino)
Wishin' & Hopin'
Ani DiFranco; *ST/My Best Friend's Wedding* .... (Work/Epic)
Dusty Springfield; *Dusty Springfield-Golden Hits* .... (Mercury)
History Of British Rock-#6-C .... (Rhino)
Wishing Well
Terence Trent D'Arby; *Introducing The Hardline According To Terence Trent D'Arby* .... (Columbia)
Wishlist
Pearl Jam; *Yield* .... (Epic)
With A Girl Like You
Troggs; *Best Of The Troggs* .... (Rhino)
History Of British Rock-#4-C .... (Rhino)
With Me Part 1
Destiny's Child featuring JD; *Destiny's Child* .... (Grass Roots/Columbia)
With My Eyes Wide Open I'm Dreaming
Mandy Barnett; *I've Got A Right To Cry* .... (Sire)
Patti Page; *Patti Page-Golden Hits* .... (Mercury)
Patti Page's Greatest Hits .... (Columbia)
Wolverton Mountain
Claude King; *American Originals-Claude King* .... (Columbia)
Best Of Claude King .... (Gusto)
Billboard Top Country Hits-1962-C .... (Rhino)
Super Hits Of The '60s-C .... (Epic)
Woman
Peter And Gordon; *Best Of Peter And Gordon* .... (Rhino)
History Of British Rock-#4-C .... (Rhino)
Wonderful World
Art Garfunkel; *Watermark* .... (Legacy)
Herman's Hermits; *Herman's Hermits-Their Greatest Hits* .... (Abkco)
Sam Cooke; *Best Of Sam Cooke* .... (RCA)
ST/Animal House .... (MCA)
This Is Sam Cooke .... (RCA)
Words Of Love
Beatles; *Beatles VI* .... (Capitol)
Beatles-Box Set .... (Capitol)
Beatles-Love Songs .... (Capitol)
For Sale .... (Capitol)
Buddy Holly; *Buddy Holly* .... (MCA)
Legend-From The Original Master Tapes .... (MCA)
Rock & Roll Collection .... (MCA)
Buddy Holly/The Crickets; *Buddy Holly-20 Golden Greats* .... (MCA)
Would You Like To Take A Walk?
Ella Fitzgerald; *Ella & Friends* .... (Decca Jazz)
Julia Sanderson/Frank Crumit/Leonard Joy; *The Song Is...Harry Warren-C* .... (Living Era)
Rudy Vallee & His Connecticut Yankees; *78-#22611* .... (Victor)
Wrapped Around
Brad Paisley; *Brad Paisley-Part II* .... (Arista)
You
Jesse Powell; *'Bout It* .... (Silas)
You Are My Sunshine
Bing Crosby; *Best Of Bing Crosby* .... (MCA)
Bing Crosby's Greatest Hits .... (MCA)
Jimmie Davis; *20 Golden Souvenirs Of Music City U.S.A.-C* .... (Plantation)
Best Of Jimmie Davis .... (MCA)
Jimmie Davis-Golden Hits .... (Plantation)
The Country Music Hall Of Fame-Jimmie Davis .... (MCA)
Mississippi John Hurt; *Best Of Mississippi John Hurt* .... (Vanguard)
Mitch Miller; *Mitch Miller-16 Most Requested Songs* .... (Columbia)
Norman Blake; *ST/O Brother, Where Art Thou?* .... (Mercury)
Ray Charles; *Ray Charles-Anthology* .... (Rhino)
Ray Charles-His Greatest Hits-#2 .... (Dunhill Compact Classics)
Willie Nelson & Leon Russell; *One For The Road* .... (Columbia)
You Are Not Alone
Michael Jackson; *1996 Grammy Nominees-C* .... (Columbia)
HIStory: Past, Present And Future-Book 1-C .... (Epic)
You Belong To Me
Dean Martin; *Dean Martin's All Time Greatest Hits* .... (Curb)
Duprees; *13 Of The Best Doo Wop Love Songs-#2-C* .... (Original Sound)
Baby Boomer's Best-Mellow '60s-C .... (Priority)
Best Of The Duprees .... (Rhino)
Jo Stafford; *Billboard Pop Memories-1950-1954-C* .... (Rhino)
Jo Stafford's Greatest Hits .... (Curb)
Johnny Mathis; *In The Still Of The Night* .... (Columbia)
Patsy Cline; *Patsy Cline Sings Songs Of Love* .... (MCA Special Prod.)
Sentimentally Yours .... (MCA)
Vonda Shepard; *ST/Songs From "Ally McBeal" Featuring Vonda Shepard* .... (550/Epic)
You Cheated
Shields; *Oldies But Goodies-#3-C* .... (Original Sound)

You Don't Have To Be A Star
Marilyn McCoo & Billy Davis, Jr.; *Soft Rockin' '70s #2* . . . . (Madacy)

You Don't Have To Hurt No More
Mint Condition; *Definition Of A Band* . . . . (Perspective/A&M)
Mint Condition-Collection (1991-1998) . . . . (Perspective/A&M)

You Don't Know Me
Ray Charles; *Ray Charles-Complete Country & Western Recordings 1959-1986* . . . . (Rhino)

You Got To Me
Neil Diamond; *Neil Diamond's Greatest Hits-1966-1992* . . . . (Columbia)

You Have The Right To Remain Silent
Perfect Stranger; *From Nashville With Love-C* . . . . (Curb)

You Know What I Mean
Turtles; *Turtles-20 Greatest Hits* . . . . (Rhino)

You Know What To Do
Beatles; *The Beatles-Anthology-#1* . . . . (Capitol)

You Made Me Love You
Judy Garland; *Best Of Judy Garland* . . . . (MCA)
Judy Garland's All-Time Greatest Hits . . . . (Curb)
Patsy Cline; *Sentimentally Yours* . . . . (MCA)

You May Be Right
Billy Joel; *Billy Joel-Greatest Hits, Volume I & Volume II* . . . . (Columbia)
Glass Houses . . . . (Columbia)

You Need To Be With Me
Susan Tedeschi; *Just Won't Burn* . . . . (Tone Cool)

You Rock My World
Michael Jackson; *Invincible* . . . .(Epic)

You Should Be Mine (Don't Waste Your Time)
Brian McKnight; *Anytime* . . . . (Motown)

You Should Be Mine (The Woo Woo Song)
Jeffrey Osborne; *Emotional* . . . . (A&M)

You Shouldn't Kiss Me Like This
Toby Keith; *How Do You Like Me Now?!* . . . . (DreamWorks/SKG)

You Stay With Me
Ricky Martin; *Ricky Martin* . . . . (Columbia)

You You You
Ames Brothers; *Very Best Of The Ames Brothers* . . . . (Taragon)

You'll Accomp'ny Me
Bob Seger & The Silver Bullet Band; *Against The Wind* . . . . (Capitol)
Nine Tonight . . . . (Capitol)

You'll Never Know
Dick Haymes; *Best Of Dick Haymes* . . . . (Curb)
You'll Never Know . . . . (MCA Special Prod.)
Dick Haymes & His Song Spinners; *Billboard Pop Memories-1940-1944-C* . . . . (Rhino)
Billboard Top Movie Hits-1940s-C . . . . (Rhino)

You'll Never Never Know
Platters; *Magic Touch-An Anthology* . . . . (Mercury)
Very Best Of The Platters . . . . (Mercury)

Young World
Rick Nelson; *Rick Nelson's Greatest Hits* . . . . (Rhino)
Ricky Nelson; *All My Best* . . . . (MCA)
Best Of Rick Nelson-#2 . . . . (EMI)
Teenage Idol . . . . (Liberty)

Your Eyes
Xscape; *Traces Of My Lipstick* . . . . (So So Def/Columbia)

You're An Ocean
Fastball; *Harsh Light Of Day* . . . . (Hollywood)

You're Going To Lose That Girl
Beatles; *ST/Help!* . . . . (Capitol)

You're Still A Young Man
Tower Of Power; *Bump City* . . . .(Warner Bros.)
Live & In Living Color . . . .(Warner Bros.)

You're The One
Vogues; *Back To The '60s-#2-C* . . . . (Dominion Entert.)
Vogues' Greatest Hits . . . . (Rhino)

You're The One
SWV; *MTV Party To Go-#10-C* . . . . (Tommy Boy)
New Beginning . . . . (RCA)
SWV's Greatest Hits . . . . (Beast)

Yum, Ticky, Ticky, Tum, Tum
Original Broadway Cast; *Carnival* . . . . (Polydor)

LOVE: COMMITTED OR NOT?, Free Love, Not Committed, One-night Stands, Playing The Field

See Also: CHEATING & LIES, DECISIONS, DESIRE, KISSING, LEAVING, LOVE (various), SEX

(If You're Not In It...) I'm Outta Here!
Shania Twain; *The Woman In Me* . . . . (Mercury)

51st Anniversary
Jimi Hendrix Experience; *Are You Experienced?* . . . . (Reprise)

After The Thrill Is Gone
Eagles; *Eagles Greatest Hits, Volume 2* . . . . (Asylum)
One Of These Nights . . . . (Asylum)

After Tonight
Mariah Carey; *Rainbow* . . . . (Columbia)

All Er Nothin'
Original Broadway Cast; *Oklahoma!* . . . . (RCA)
Original Cast; *Oklahoma!* . . . . (MCA)

All Or Nothing
O-Town; *O-Town* . . . . (J)
Totally Hits 2001-C . . . . (Arista)

Almost Doesn't Count
Brandy; *Never Say Never* . . . . (Atlantic)
Totally Hits-#1-C . . . . (Arista)

Almost Doesn't Count
Mark Wills; *Permanently* . . . . (Mercury)

Along Comes Mary
Association; *Association Greatest Hits* . . . . (Warner Bros.)
Vintage Association . . . . (Fifty One West)

Always On Time
Ja Rule; *Pain Is Love* . . . . (Murder Inc./Def Jam/IDJMG)

Angel Of The Morning
Juice Newton; *All-Time Country Classics-#2-C* . . . . (Capitol)
Juice . . . . (Capitol)
Juice Newton-Greatest Hits & More . . . . (Capitol)
Juice Newton's Greatest Hits . . . . (Gold Rush)
Merrilee Rush; *Dick Bartley's One-Hit Wonders Of The '60s-#2-C* . . . . . (Rhino)
Mellow '60s-C . . . . (Priority)

Another Way
Tevin Campbell; *Tevin Campbell* . . . . (Qwest)

Any Man Of Mine
Shania Twain; *1996 Grammy Nominees-C* . . . . (Columbia)
The Woman In Me . . . . (Mercury)
Snoopy; *Snoopy's Country Classiks On Toys* . . . . (Lightyear)

Any Old Wind That Blows
Johnny Cash; *Johnny Cash-16 Biggest Hits-#2* . . . . (Legacy)

Are You On The Road To Lovin' Me Again
Debby Boone; *Best Of Debby Boone* . . . . (Curb)

Ashes By Now
Lee Ann Womack; *I Hope You Dance* . . . . (MCA)
Rodney Crowell; *Rodney Crowell-Collection* . . . . (Warner Bros.)

Babe I'm Gonna Leave You
Led Zeppelin; *Led Zeppelin* . . . .(Atlantic)
Led Zeppelin-Box Set . . . .(Atlantic)

Baby
Robert Bradley's Blackwater Surprise; *Time To Discover* . . . . (RCA)

Baby Don't Get Hooked On Me
Mac Davis; *Mac Davis' Greatest Hits* . . . . (Columbia)
Super Hits Of The '70s-Have A Nice Day-#20-C . . . . (Rhino)

Back 2 Good
Matchbox Twenty; *Yourself Or Someone Like You* . . . . (Lava)

Barrel Of A Gun
Depeche Mode; *The Singles-1986-1998* . . . . (Mute/Reprise)
Ultra . . . . (Mute/Reprise)

Be Happy
Mary J. Blige; *My Life* . . . . (Uptown/MCA)

Between Me And You
Ja Rule featuring Christina Milian; *Rule 3:36* . . . . (Murder Inc./Def Jam/IDJMG)

Blood On The Dance Floor
Michael Jackson; *Blood On The Dance Floor-HIStory* . . . . (MJJ Music/Work)

Born In The Dark
Doug Stone; *Faith In Me Faith In You* . . . . (Columbia)
Steppin' Country-#2-C . . . . (Columbia)

Build Me Up Buttercup
Foundations; *Billboard Top Rock 'N' Roll Hits-1969-C* . . . . (Rhino)
History Of British Rock-#9-C . . . . (Rhino)
ST/There's Something About Mary . . . . (Capitol)

Can I Count On You
McBride & The Ride; *Burnin' Up The Road* . . . . (MCA)

Case Of The Ex (Whatcha Gonna Do)
Mya; *Fear Of Flying* . . . . (University/Interscope)
Now That's What I Call Music!-#5-C . . . . (Virgin)

Casual Affair
Tonic; *Lemon Parade* . . . .(Polydor)

Chains
Patty Loveless; *Honky Tonk Angel* . . . . (MCA)
Patty Loveless' Greatest Hits . . . . (MCA)

Come What May
Patti Page; *Patti Page Collection-The Mercury Years-#1* . . . . (Mercury)

Commitment
LeAnn Rimes; *Big Country Hits '99-C* . . . . (K-Tel)
Sittin' On Top Of The World . . . . (Curb)

Count Me In
Deana Carter; *Did I Shave My Legs For This?* . . . . (Capitol)

Cross Over The Bridge
Patti Page; *Patti Page-Golden Hits* . . . . (Mercury)
Patti Page's Greatest Hits . . . . (Columbia)

Crush
Jennifer Paige; *Jennifer Paige* . . . . (Hollywood)

Crush
Lila McCann; *Something In The Air* . . . .(Asylum)

Cry Of The Wild Goose
Frankie Laine; *Frankie Laine-Golden Hits* . . . . (Mercury)

Cuddly Toy
Nilsson; *Pandemonium Shadow Show*. . . . . (RCA)

Darned If I Don't (Danged If I Do)
Shenandoah; *In The Vicinity Of The Heart* . . . . (Capitol)

Day Tripper
Beatles; *"Yesterday"...And Today* . . . . (Capitol)
Beatles 1 . . . . (Capitol)
Beatles-Box Set. . . . . (Capitol)
Past Masters-Volume Two . . . . (Parlophone)
The Beatles/1962-1966. . . . . (Capitol)
Jimi Hendrix Experience; *Radio One* . . . . (Rykodisc)
Otis Redding; *Dictionary Of Soul* . . . . (Atco)
The Otis Redding Story. . . . . (Atlantic)
Sergio Mendes & Brasil '66; *Sergio Mendes & Brasil '66's
    Greatest Hits* . . . . (A&M)

Days Of The Week
Stone Temple Pilots; *Shangri-La-Dee-Da.* . . . . (Atlantic)

Deep Water
Asleep At The Wheel; *Asleep At The Wheel* . . . . (MCA Special Prod.)
Asleep At The Wheel featuring Garth Brooks; *Tribute To The Music Of Bob
    Wills And The Texas Playboys-C* . . . . (Liberty)
Bob Wills & His Texas Playboys; *Bob Wills & His Texas Playboys-
    Anthology 1935-1973* . . . . (Rhino)
Essential Bob Wills & His Texas Playboys-1935-1973 . . . . (Legacy)
George Strait; *George Strait-Number 7.* . . . . (MCA)
Willie Nelson; *San Antonio Rose.* . . . . (Columbia)

Did You Ever Have To Make Up Your Mind?
Lovin' Spoonful; *Best Of The Lovin' Spoonful* . . . . (Rhino)
Lovin' Spoonful-Anthology. . . . . (Rhino)

Different Drum
Linda Ronstadt; *Different Drum* . . . . (Capitol)
Linda Ronstadt-Retrospective . . . . (Capitol)
Linda Ronstadt's Greatest Hits. . . . . (Asylum)
Stone Poneys Featuring Linda Ronstadt; *Baby Boomer Classics-Mellow
    '60s-C* . . . . (JCI Assoc. Labels)
On The Road Again-Rock's New Frontiers-C. . . . . (Capitol)
The Stone Poneys Featuring Linda Ronstadt. . . . . (EMI)
Victoria Shaw; *Victoria Shaw* . . . . (Reprise)

Do You Know (What It Takes)
Robyn; *Robyn Is Here* . . . . (RCA)

Does He Love You
Reba McEntire & Linda Davis; *Reba McEntire's Greatest Hits
    Volume Two* . . . . (MCA)

Don't Close Your Eyes
Keith Whitley; *Don't Close Your Eyes* . . . . (RCA)
Keith Whitley's Greatest Hits . . . . (RCA)

Don't Keep Me Hangin' On
Sonny James; *Best Of Sonny James.* . . . . (Curb)
Young Love: The Collection . . . . (Razor & Tie)

Don't Think Twice, It's All Right
Bob Dylan; *Before The Flood* . . . . (Columbia)
Bob Dylan's Greatest Hits-#2 . . . . (Columbia)
Freewheelin'. . . . . (Columbia)
Joan Baez; *The First 10 Years* . . . . (Vanguard)
Wonder Who?; *Anniversary* . . . . (Rhino)

Don't Waste Your Heart
Dixie Chicks; *Fly.* . . . . (Monument)

Dream Walkin'
Toby Keith; *Dream Walkin'* . . . . (Mercury)
Toby Keith's Greatest Hits, Volume One . . . . (Mercury)

Drive My Car
Beatles; *"Yesterday"...And Today* . . . . (Capitol)
Rock 'N' Roll Music . . . . (Capitol)
The Beatles/1962-1966 . . . . (Capitol)

Fastlove
George Michael; *Ladies & Gentlemen: The Best Of George Michael* . . . . . (Epic)
Older. . . . . (DreamWorks/SKG)

Fire Escape
Fastball; *All The Pain Money Can Buy* . . . . (Hollywood)

Fireman, The
George Strait; *Country Classics-#4-1984-1985-C* . . . . (Universal)
Does Fort Worth Ever Cross Your Mind. . . . . (MCA)
George Strait's Greatest Hits-#2 . . . . (MCA)

Five Minutes
Lorrie Morgan; *Lorrie Morgan's Greatest Hits.* . . . . (BNA)
Lorrie Morgan-Super Hits . . . . (RCA)
Pam Tillis; *Pam Tillis-Collection* . . . . (Warner Bros.)

Flavor Of The Weak
American Hi-Fi; *American Hi-Fi* . . . . (Island)
Now That's What I Call Music!-#7-C . . . . (Virgin)

Fool In Love
Robins; *Best Of The Robins* . . . . (Crescendo)

Free
Mya; *ST/Bait* . . . . (Warner Bros.)

Free Bird
Lynyrd Skynyrd; *Gold & Platinum* . . . . (MCA)
One More From The Road . . . . (MCA)

Pronounced Leh-nerd Skin-nerd . . . . (MCA)
Southern By The Grace Of God-Tribute '87 . . . . (MCA)
Wynonna; *Skynyrd Frynds-C* . . . . (MCA)

Georgy Porgy
Eric Benet featuring Faith Evans; *A Day In The Life* . . . . (Warner Bros.)
Toto; *Past To Present 1977-1990.* . . . . (Columbia)
Toto . . . . (Columbia)

Get It Together
702; *No Doubt* . . . . (Biv 10/Motown)

Gimme Little Sign
Brenton Wood; *18 Best-Brenton Wood* . . . . (Original Sound)
Collectables Presents The History Of Rock-#7-C . . . . . . (Collectables)
Cruisin'-1957-C . . . . (Increase)
Soul Shots-#3-Soul Twist-C. . . . . (Rhino)

Girls, Girls, Girls
Jay-Z; *Girls, Girls, Girls* . . . . (Roc-A-Fella/DJMG)

Go Away
Lorrie Morgan; *Lorrie Morgan-Super Hits* . . . . (RCA)
Shakin' Things Up . . . . (BNA)
To Get To You-Greatest Hits Collection . . . . (BNA)

Go Your Own Way
Cranberries; *Legacy-A Tribute To Fleetwood Mac's Rumours-C* . . . . . (Lava)
Fleetwood Mac; *25 Years-The Chain* . . . . (Warner Bros.)
Fleetwood Mac Live . . . . (Warner Bros.)
Fleetwood Mac's Greatest Hits . . . . (Warner Bros.)
Rumours . . . . (Warner Bros.)

Good Girls
Joe; *All That I Am* . . . . (Jive)

Good Woman Blues
Mel Tillis; *Mel Tillis' Greatest Hits* . . . . (Curb)

Gotta Tell You
Samantha Mumba; *Gotta Tell You* . . . . (Wildcard/Polydor/Interscope)
Now That's What I Call Music!-#6-C . . . . (Virgin)

Half As Much
Rosemary Clooney; *Rosemary Clooney-16 Most Requested Songs* . . . . . (Legacy)

Harry
Macy Gray; *The Id* . . . . (Epic)

Helping Me Get Over You
Travis Tritt & Lari White; *The Restless Kind* . . . . (Warner Bros.)

Here's To The Night
Eve 6; *Horrorscope* . . . . (RCA)
Totally Hits 2001-C . . . . (Arista)

High Enough
Damn Yankees; *Damn Yankees* . . . . (Warner Bros.)

Honey, Do You Love Me, Huh
Hank Williams; *Complete Hank Williams* . . . . (Mercury)

Honky Tonk Man
Dwight Yoakam; *Guitars, Cadillacs, Etc., Etc.* . . . . (Reprise)
Just Lookin' For A Hit. . . . . (Reprise)
Johnny Horton; *All Time Legends Of Country Music-C* . . . . (Legacy)
Columbia Country Classics-#2-Honky Tonk Heroes-C . . . . . (Columbia)
Marty Robbins; *Greatest Country Hits From The Movies-C* . . . . . (Epic)

How Can I Be Sure
Rascals; *Groovin'.* . . . . (Warner Special Prod.)
Rascals-Anthology 1965-1972 . . . . (Rhino)
The Ultimate Rascals . . . . (Warner Special Prod.)
Very Best Of The Rascals . . . . (Rhino)

How Deep Is Your Love
Bee Gees; *Bee Gees' Greatest* . . . . (Polydor)
ST/Saturday Night Fever. . . . . (Polydor)

How Deep Is Your Love
Dru Hill featuring Redman; *Enter The Dru* . . . . (Def Jam/RAL/Mercury/Island)
ST/Rush Hour. . . . . (Def Jam)

I Can't Help Myself (Sugar Pie Honey Bunch)
Four Tops; *16 #1 Hits From The Early '60s-C* . . . . (Motown)
Billboard Top R&B Hits-1965-C. . . . . (Rhino)
Four Tops' Greatest Hits. . . . . (Motown)
Four Tops-Anthology . . . . (Motown)
Good Feeling Music Of The Big Chill Generation-#1-C. . . . . (Motown)
Motown Story-First 25 Years-C . . . . (Motown)
Motown Superstar Series-#14-Four Tops . . . . (Motown)
ST/Forrest Gump. . . . . (Epic/Sony Music Soundtrax)
ST/Heaven Help Us . . . . (EMI)
ST/Into The Night . . . . (MCA)
ST/Where The Buffalo Roam . . . . (Backstreet)

I Confess
Perry Como; *Yesterday And Today-A Celebration In Song* . . . . . . (RCA)

I Could Fall In Love
Selena; *Dreaming Of You* . . . . (EMI Latin)

I Could Never Take The Place Of Your Man
Jordan Knight; *Jordan Knight* . . . . (Interscope)

I Just Wanna Love U (Give It 2 Me)
Jay-Z; *Dynasty-Roc La Familia 2000* . . . . (Roc-A-Fella/DJMG)

I Second That Emotion
Smokey Robinson & The Miracles; *Smokey Robinson & The Miracles'
    Anthology* . . . . (Motown)
Smokey Robinson-The Ultimate Collection. . . . . (Motown)
Tammy Wynette & Smokey Robinson; *Without Walls-C* . . . . (Epic)

I Will...But
SHeDAISY; *The Whole Shebang* . . . . (Lyric Street)
I Wish
Carl Thomas; *Emotional* . . . . (Bad Boy/Arista)
I Wonder Why
Dion And The Belmonts; *Doo-Wop Uptempo-#2-C* . . . . (Rhino)
   Everything You Always Wanted . . . . (Laurie)
   Million-Dollar Memories #1-C . . . . (RCA)
   Oldies But Goodies-#12-C . . . . (Original Sound)
   Super Oldies Of The '50s-#7-C . . . . (Audio Fidelity)
   You Found The Vocal Group Sound-#1-C . . . . (Solid Smoke)
I'd Really Love To See You Tonight
England Dan & John Ford Coley; *Best Of England Dan & John Ford
   Coley* . . . . (Big Tree)
   Hit Singles-1958-1977-C . . . . (Atlantic)
   Nights Are Forever Without You . . . . (Big Tree)
If I Give My Heart To You
Nat "King" Cole; *Nat "King" Cole (Box Set)* . . . . (Capitol)
If This Is It
Huey Lewis and the News; *Sports* . . . .(Chrysalis)
   *The Heart Of Rock & Roll-The Best Of Huey Lewis and
   the News* . . . . (Chrysalis)
   Time Flies...Best Of Huey Lewis and the News . . . . . (Elektra)
If You Leave
Destiny's Child; *The Writing's On The Wall* . . . . (Columbia)
If You Really Love Me
Stevie Wonder; *Stevie Wonder's Greatest Hits-#2* . . . . . (Motown)
   Where I'm Coming From . . . . (Motown)
I'll Try
Alan Jackson; *Alan Jackson-The Greatest Hits Collection* . . . . (Arista)
I'm Just Talkin' About Tonight
Toby Keith; *Pull My Chain* . . . . (DreamWorks/SKG)
I'm Like A Bird
Nelly Furtado; *Whoa Nelly!* . . . . (DreamWorks/SKG)
I'm Real
Jennifer Lopez; *J. Lo* . . . . (Epic)
   Now That's What I Call Music!-#8-C . . . . (Virgin)
In Between Dances
Pam Tillis; *Pam Tillis' Greatest Hits* . . . . (Arista)
   Sweetheart's Dance . . . . (Arista)
Insensitive
Jann Arden; *Living Under June* . . . . (A&M)
   Women For Women-#2-C . . . . (Mercury)
Inside Out
Eve 6; *Eve 6* . . . . (RCA)
Is That A Tear
Tracy Lawrence; *Best Of Tracy Lawrence* . . . . (Atlantic)
   Time Marches On . . . . (Atlantic)
Is You Is Or Is You Ain't My Baby
Diana Krall; *Only Trust Your Heart* . . . . (GRP)
Louis Jordan; *Five Guys Named Moe-Original Decca Recordings-#2* . . . .(MCA)
   Rock 'N Roll . . . . (Mercury)
I've Been Wrong Before
Deborah Allen; *Cheat The Night* . . . . (RCA)
Just Ain't
Lester Flatt, Earl Scruggs & The Foggy Mountain Boys; *Essential Flatt &
   Scruggs-'Tis Sweet To Be Remembered* . . . . (Legacy)
Just Another Girl
Monica; *ST/Down To Earth* . . . .(Epic)
Kryptonite
3 Doors Down; *Better Life* . . . . (Republic/Universal)
   Now That's What I Call Music!-#5-C . . . . (Virgin)
Ladder
Joan Osborne; *Lilith Fair-A Celebration Of Women In Music-C* . . . . . (Arista)
   Relish . . . . (Blue Gorilla/Mercury)
Lady Bird
Nancy Sinatra & Lee Hazlewood; *Fairy Tales & Fantasies-Best Of* . . . (Rhino)
Let's Get Down
Tony Toni Tone; *House Of Music* . . . . (Mercury)
   Tony Toni Tone-Hits . . . . (Mercury)
   Ultimate Hip Hop Party-1998-C . . . . (Arista)
Little Sister
Elvis Presley; *Elvis' Golden Records, Volume 3* . . . . (RCA)
   Elvis In Concert . . . . (RCA)
   I Was The One . . . . (RCA)
   The Top Ten Hits . . . . (RCA)
   Worldwide 50 Gold Award Hits, Vol. 1, Parts 1 & 2 . . . (RCA)
Little Woman
Bobby Sherman; *Bobby Sherman's Greatest Hits* . . . . (K-Tel)
   Bubblegum Classics-#3-C . . . . (Varese Vintage)
Lonely Women Make Good Lovers
Bob Luman; *Bob Luman-Classic Country* . . . . (Simitar)
Steve Wariner; *Best Of Steve Wariner* . . . . (RCA)
   Midnight Fire . . . . (RCA)
   Steve Wariner's Greatest Hits . . . . (RCA)
   Steve Wariner-Super Hits . . . . (RCA)
Love And Marriage
Dinah Shore; *45-#6266* . . . . (RCA)

Frank Sinatra; *Capitol Collectors Series-Frank Sinatra* . . . . (Capitol)
   Sinatra: A Man And His Music . . . . (Reprise)
   The Capitol Years . . . . (Capitol)
   The Reprise Collection . . . . (Reprise)
Love Don't Love Me
Eric Benet; *ST/The Brothers* . . . . (Warner Bros.)
Love Or Something Like It
Kenny Rogers; *Kenny Rogers-Twenty Greatest Hits* . . . . . . (EMI)
Love The One You're With
Crosby, Stills & Nash; *Replay* . . . .(Atlantic)
Crosby, Stills, Nash & Young; *4 Way Street* . . . .(Atlantic)
Luther Vandross; *Songs* . . . . (Epic)
Stephen Stills; *Hit Singles-1958-1977-C* . . . .(Atlantic)
   Stephen Stills . . . .(Atlantic)
   Still . . . .(Atlantic)
Love Thing
Spice Girls; *Spice* . . . . (Virgin)
Loved Too Much
Ty Herndon; *Living In A Moment* . . . . (Epic)
Lucky One
Alison Krauss & Union Station; *New Favorite* . . . . (Rounder)
Make Me Believe
Martina McBride; *Emotion* . . . .(RCA)
Matchbox
Beatles; *Past Masters-Volume Two* . . . . (Parlophone)
   Rock 'N' Roll Music . . . . (Capitol)
   Something New . . . . (Capitol)
Matrimony: Maybe You
Maxwell; *Embrya* . . . . (Columbia)
Mimi
Maurice Chevalier; *Early Movie Hits* . . . .(DRG)
   Nipper's Greatest Hits Of The '30s-#1-C . . . . (RCA)
   ST/Pepe . . . .(DRG)
Mister & Mississippi
Patti Page; *Patti Page's Greatest Hits* . . . . (Columbia)
Modern Girl
Sheena Easton; *Best Of Sheena Easton* . . . . (EMI)
   Sheena Easton . . . . (EMI)
   Sheena Easton's Greatest Hits . . . . (EMI Special Markets)
   The World Of Sheena Easton: The Singles Collection-C . . (EMI)
Mustang Sally
Rascals; *Rascals' Greatest Hits* . . . .(Atlantic)
Wilson Pickett; *A Man & A Half-Best Of Wilson Pickett* . . . . (Rhino)
   Atlantic Rhythm & Blues 1947-1974-#6 (1966-1969)-C . . .(Atlantic)
   Best Of Wilson Pickett . . . .(Atlantic)
   Wilson Pickett's Greatest Hits . . . .(Atlantic)
   Wilson Pickett-Super Hits . . . .(Atlantic)
Young Rascals; *The Young Rascals* . . . . (Warner Special Prod.)
My Name Is Not Susan
Whitney Houston; *I'm Your Baby Tonight* . . . . (Arista)
New Beginning
Stir; *Holy Dogs* . . . . (Capitol)
Night Before
Beatles; *Beatles-Box Set* . . . . (Capitol)
   Rock 'N' Roll Music . . . . (Capitol)
   ST/Help! . . . . (Capitol)
No More (Baby I'ma Do Right)
3LW; *3LW* . . . . (Epic)
   Now That's What I Call Music!-#6-C . . . .(Virgin)
Nobody's Got The Gun
Mark Knopfler; *Golden Heart* . . . . (Warner Bros.)
Norwegian Wood (This Bird Has Flown)
Beatles; *Beatles-Box Set* . . . . (Capitol)
   Beatles-Love Songs . . . . (Capitol)
   Rubber Soul . . . . (Capitol)
   The Beatles/1962-1966 . . . . (Capitol)
Occasional Wife
Faron Young; *Faron Young-Golden Hits* . . . . (Mercury)
One Love At A Time
Tanya Tucker; *Tanya Tucker's Greatest Hits* . . . . (Liberty)
One Minute Man
Missy "Misdemeanor" Elliot; *Miss E...So
   Addictive* . . . . (Gold Mind/East West/EEG)
One Night Love Affair
Bryan Adams; *Reckless* . . . . (A&M)
One Night Stand
J-Shin featuring La Tocha Scott; *My Soul, My Life* . . . .(Atlantic)
One Night Stand
Janis Joplin; *Farewell Song* . . . . (Columbia)
   Janis Joplin-Super Hits . . . . (Epic)
One Step Closer
Doobie Brothers; *Best Of The Doobies, Volume II* . . . . . . (Warner Bros.)
   One Step Closer . . . . (Warner Bros.)
One Woman Man
Dave Hollister; *Chicago '85 The Movie* . . . . (Def Squad/DreamWorks)
Oops!...I Did It Again
Britney Spears; *Oops!...I Did It Again* . . . .(Jive)
Part-Time Lover
Stevie Wonder; *In Square Circle* . . . . (Motown)

Please Come To Boston
Dave Loggins; *Apprentice (In A Musical Workshop)* . . . . (Epic)
  Rock Artifacts-From The Vaults-#2-C . . . . (Legacy)
  Super Hits Of The '70s-Have A Nice Day-#13-C . . . . (Rhino)
David Allan Coe; *David Allan Coe-17 Greatest Hits* . . . . (Columbia)
  For The Record-The First 10 Years . . . . (Columbia)
Joan Baez; *Best Of Joan Baez* . . . . (A&M)
  Joan Baez-Classics-#8 . . . . (A&M)
Reba McEntire; *Starting Over* . . . . (MCA)

Poor Little Fool
Rick Nelson; *Live In '85* . . . . (Rhino)
Ricky Nelson; *Best Of Ricky Nelson* . . . . (EMI)
  EMI Legends Of Rock & Roll-24 Greatest Hits-C . . . . (EMI)
  Ricky Nelson-Legendary Masters . . . . (EMI)

Poor Side Of Town
Johnny Rivers; *Best Of Johnny Rivers* . . . . (EMI)
  Changes/Rewind . . . . (EMI)
  Johnny Rivers-Anthology 1964-1977 . . . . (Rhino)
  Very Best Of Johnny Rivers . . . . (EMI)

Puppy Love
Lil Bow Wow Featuring Jagged Edge; *Beware Of Dog* . . (So So Def/Columbia)

Queen Of My Double Wide Trailer
Sammy Kershaw; *Haunted Heart* . . . . (Mercury)

Ready To Run
Dixie Chicks; *Fly* . . . . (Monument)
  ST/Runaway Bride . . . . (Sony Music Soundtrax)

Roving Kind, The
Guy Mitchell; *Guy Mitchell-16 Most Requested Songs* . . . . (Legacy)

Runaround
Fleetwoods; *Best Of The Fleetwoods* . . . . (Rhino)

Sad Eyed Lady Of The Lowlands
Bob Dylan; *Blonde On Blonde* . . . . (Columbia)
Joan Baez; *Any Day Now: Songs Of Bob Dylan* . . . . (Vanguard)
  Lovesong Album . . . . (Vanguard)

Say You Love Me Or Say Goodbye
REO Speedwagon; *A Decade Of Rock And Roll 1970 To 1980* . . . . (Epic)
  You Can Tune A Piano But You Can't Tuna Fish . . . . (Epic)

See Saw
Moonglows; *Moonglows-Their Greatest Hits* . . . . (Chess)

See You In September
Chiffons; *Best Of The Chiffons* . . . . (Laurie)
Happenings; *ST/Purple People Eater* . . . . (AJK Music)
Tempos; *Cruisin'-1960-C* . . . . (Increase)
  ST/American Graffiti . . . . (MCA)

Shimmer
Fuel; *Sunburn* . . . . (550 Music)

Silly Ho
TLC; *Fanmail* . . . . (LaFace)

Simple Twist Of Fate
Bob Dylan; *Blood On The Tracks* . . . . (Columbia)
  Bob Dylan At Budokan . . . . (Columbia)
Jerry Garcia Band; *Jerry Garcia Band* . . . . (Arista)
Joan Baez; *Best Of Joan Baez* . . . . (A&M)
  Diamonds & Rust . . . . (A&M)

Sin Wagon
Dixie Chicks; *Fly* . . . . (Monument)

Sixty Minute Man
Billy Ward & His Dominoes; *Rock & Roll Show-C* . . . . (Gusto)
Dominos; *Oldies But Goodies-#5-C* . . . . (Original Sound)
Rufus Thomas & Carla Thomas; *Rufus Thomas & Carla Thomas-Chronicle* . . . . (Stax)

Slow Down
Beatles; *Past Masters-Volume One* . . . . (Parlophone)

Smoke From A Distant Fire
Sanford/Townsend Band; *Smoke From A Distant Fire* . . . . (Warner Bros.)

Smooth
Santana featuring Rob Thomas; *Supernatural* . . . . (Arista)
  Totally Hits-#1-C . . . . (Arista)

Some Days You Gotta Dance
Dixie Chicks; *Fly* . . . . (Monument)

Song From Moulin Rouge (Where Is Your Heart)
Percy Faith & His Orchestra; *Percy Faith & His Orchestra's All-Time Greatest Hits* . . . . (Columbia)

South Of The Border (Down Mexico Way)
Bob Wills & His Texas Playboys; *Best Of Bob Wills & His Texas Playboys* . . . . (MCA)
  Bob Wills & His Texas Playboys-Greatest Hits . . . . (Curb)
Frank Sinatra; *Capitol Collectors Series-Frank Sinatra* . . . . (Capitol)
  Come Fly With Me . . . . (Capitol)
Gene Autry; *The Country Music Hall Of Fame-Gene Autry-15 Of His All-Time Greatest Hits* . . . . (Columbia)
Patsy Cline; *Always* . . . . (MCA)
  The Patsy Cline Story . . . . (MCA)
Willie Nelson; *What A Wonderful World* . . . . (Columbia)

Souvenirs
Gretchen Peters; *Gretchen Peters* . . . . (Purple Crayon Prod.)

Speedoo
Cadillacs; *Best Of The Cadillacs* . . . . (Rhino)
  Echoes Of A Rock Era-Early Years-C . . . . (Roulette)

  More American Graffiti-C . . . . (MCA)
  Original Rock 'N' Roll Hits Of The '50s-C . . . . (Roulette)
  ST/Goodfellas . . . . (Atlantic)
Ry Cooder; *Borderline* . . . . (Warner Bros.)

Splackavellie
Pressha; *Don't Get It Twisted* . . . . (Tony Mercedes/LaFace/Arista)

Stay Or Let It Go
Brian McKnight; *Back At One* . . . . (Motown)

Straight Up
Paula Abdul; *Disco Queens-The '80s-C* . . . . (Rhino)
  First Generation: 25 Years Of Virgin Records-C . . . . (Virgin)
  Forever Your Girl . . . . (Virgin)
  Shut Up And Dance . . . . (Virgin)
  Shut Up And Dance (The Dance Mixes) . . . . (Virgin)

Sweet Talkin' Guy
Chiffons; *Best Of The Chiffons* . . . . (Laurie)
  Chiffons-Golden Classics . . . . (Collectables)
  Collectables Presents The History Of Rock-#1-C . . . . (Collectables)
  Everything You Always Wanted . . . . (Laurie)

Tattler
Ry Cooder; *Paradise And Lunch* . . . . (Reprise)

Tell It Like It Is
Aaron Neville; *Classic Aaron Neville* . . . . (Rounder)
  Soul Shots-#5-La-La Means I Love You-C . . . . (Rhino)
  Super Oldies Of The '60s-#7-C . . . . (Audio Fidelity)
  Tell It Like It Is . . . . (Curb)
  Tell it Like It Is-Golden Classics . . . . (Collectables)
  Treacherous: A History Of The Neville Brothers . . . . (Rhino)
Billy Joe Royal; *Billy Joe Royal's Greatest Hits* . . . . (Atlantic)
  Tell It Like It Is . . . . (Atlantic)
George Benson; *Best Of George Benson* . . . . (A&M)
UB40; *Live In Moscow* . . . . (A&M)
  Rat In The Kitchen . . . . (A&M)

Tell Me It's Real
K-Ci & JoJo; *It's Real* . . . . (Rock Land/Interscope)
  Now That's What I Call Music!-#3-C . . . . (Virgin)

Temptation
Destiny's Child; *The Writing's On The Wall* . . . . (Columbia)

Tequila Sunrise
Alan Jackson; *Common Thread-Songs Of The Eagles-C* . . . . (Giant)
Eagles; *Desperado* . . . . (Asylum)
  Eagles/Their Greatest Hits 1971-1975 . . . . (Asylum)
  Hell Freezes Over . . . . (Geffen)

That Ain't My Truck
Rhett Akins; *A Thousand Memories* . . . . (Decca)
  Cryin' Lyin' Lovin' & Leavin'-C . . . . (Universal)

That Other Woman
Changing Faces; *Visit Me* . . . . (Atlantic)

Third Rate Romance
Amazing Rhythm Aces; *Stacked Deck* . . . . (MCA)
Rosanne Cash; *Somewhere In The Stars* . . . . (Columbia)
Sammy Kershaw; *Cryin' Lyin' Lovin' & Leavin'-C* . . . . (Universal)
  Feelin' Good Train . . . . (Mercury)
  The Hits-Chapter 1 . . . . (Mercury)

Tomorrow Night
Elvis Presley; *For Everyone* . . . . (RCA)
  Reconsider Baby . . . . (RCA)
  Sun's Greatest Hits-C . . . . (RCA)
  The Sun Sessions . . . . (RCA)
LaVern Baker; *Atlantic Rhythm & Blues 1947-1974-#2 (1952-1955)-C* . . . . (Atlantic)
  Soul On Fire . . . . (Atlantic)

Travelin' Man
Lynyrd Skynyrd; *Live From Steel Town* . . . . (CMC Int'l)
  One More From The Road . . . . (MCA)

Travelin' Man
Ricky Nelson; *Best Of Ricky Nelson* . . . . (EMI)
  Rick Nelson's Greatest Hits . . . . (Rhino)

Trying To Love Two Women
Oak Ridge Boys; *Oak Ridge Boys' Greatest Hits* . . . . (MCA)
  Oak Ridge Boys-Collection . . . . (MCA)
  Together . . . . (MCA)

Tumbling Dice
Linda Ronstadt; *Linda Ronstadt's Greatest Hits, Volume Two* . . . . . (Asylum)
  Simple Dreams . . . . (Asylum)
  ST/FM . . . . (MCA)
Rolling Stones; *Exile On Main Street* . . . . (Virgin)
  Love You Live . . . . (Virgin)
  Made In The Shade . . . . (Rolling Stones)
  Rewind (1971-1984) . . . . (Rolling Stones)

Up And Gone
McCarters; *Better Be Home Soon* . . . . (Warner Bros.)

We'll Sing In The Sunshine
Gale Garnett; *21 Country Rock & Love Songs Of The '50s & '60s-#1-C* . . . . (Laurie)
  Nipper's Greatest Hits Of The '60s-#1-C . . . . (RCA)

We've Got Tonight
Bob Seger & The Silver Bullet Band; *Nine Tonight* . . . . (Capitol)
  Stranger In Town . . . . (Capitol)

Kenny Rogers & Sheena Easton; *Kenny Rogers/Kim Carnes/Sheena Easton/
   Dottie West* . . . .(EMI)
Kenny Rogers-25 Greatest Hits . . . . (EMI)
Kenny Rogers-Greatest Country Hits . . . . (Curb)
Kenny Rogers-Twenty Greatest Hits . . . . (EMI)
We've Got Tonight . . . . (Razor & Tie)

What You Want
   Mase Featuring Total; *Harlem World* . . . .(Bad Boy/Arista)

What You Want
   DMX; *...And Then There Was X* . . . .(Ruff Ryders/IDJMG)

When Will I See You Again
   Three Degrees; *Didn't It Blow Your Mind: Soul Hits Of The
      '70s-#14-C* . . . . (Rhino)
   Mega Hits Dance Classics-#2-C . . . . (Priority)

When You Ask About Love
   Crickets; *45-#9-55153* . . . .(Brunswick)

Where Do You Go
   No Mercy; *No Mercy* . . . . (Arista)

Where I Wanna Be
   Donell Jones; *Where I Wanna Be* . . . . (LaFace)

Who Is He And What Is He To You
   Me'Shell Ndegeocello; *Peace Beyond Passion* . . . .(Maverick)

Why Ain't I Running
   Garth Brooks; *Scarecrow* . . . . (Capitol)

Wild Horses
   Garth Brooks; *No Fences* . . . . (Capitol)

Will You Be Loving Another Man
   Bill Monroe & His Blue Grass Boys; *Essential Bill Monroe & His Blue
      Grass Boys* . . . . (Legacy)
   Essential Bill Monroe-1945-1949 . . . . (Columbia)

Will You Be Staying After Sunday
   Peppermint Rainbow; *Bubble Gum Classics-C* . . . . (MCA Special Prod.)

Will You Love Me Tomorrow
   4 Seasons; *4 Seasons' Greatest Hits-#2* . . . . (Rhino)
   Carole King; *Tapestry.* . . . .(Epic)
   Linda Ronstadt; *Linda Ronstadt-Retrospective* . . . . (Capitol)
   Lorrie Morgan; *Chicken Soup For The Woman's Soul-C* . . . . (Rhino)
   Roberta Flack; *Best Of Roberta Flack* . . . .(Atlantic)
   Quiet Fire . . . .(Atlantic)
   Shirelles; *Girl Groups-Story Of A Sound-C* . . . . (Rhino)
   More Dirty Dancing-C. . . . .(RCA)
   Oldies But Goodies-#14-C. . . . . (Original Sound)
   Shirelles-16 Greatest Hits . . . .(Trip)
   Shirelles-Anthology 1959-1964 . . . .(RCA)
   Wonder Women-#2-History Of Girl Group-C . . . . (Rhino)

Wishing I Was There
   Natalie Imbruglia; *Left Of The Middle* . . . . (RCA)

You Keep Running Away
   Four Tops; *Four Tops-Anthology* . . . . (Motown)

You Lie
   Reba McEntire; *Reba McEntire's Greatest Hits Volume Two* . . . .(MCA)
   Rumor Has It . . . .(MCA)

You Make Me Sick
   Pink; *Can't Take Me Home.* . . . . (LaFace)

You Shouldn't Kiss Me Like This
   Toby Keith; *How Do You Like Me Now?!.* . . . . (DreamWorks/SKG)

You Stay With Me
   Ricky Martin; *Ricky Martin* . . . . (Columbia)

LOVE: CRUSHES, Infatuation

See Also: **AGING, DESIRE, FEELINGS, KISSING, LOVE (various),
TEENAGERS, YOUNG**

#1 Crush
   Garbage; *ST/William Shakespeare's Romeo & Juliet* . . . . (Capitol)

21st Century Sha La La La Girl
   Def Leppard; *Euphoria.* . . . . (Mercury)

Abigail Beecher
   Freddy Cannon; *14 Booming Hits.* . . . . (Rhino)
   *Big Blast From Boston: The Best Of Freddy "Boom Boom"
      Cannon.* . . . . (Rhino)

Baby Don't Get Hooked On Me
   Mac Davis; *Mac Davis' Greatest Hits* . . . . (Columbia)
   Super Hits Of The '70s-Have A Nice Day-#20-C. . . . . (Rhino)

Bobbie Ann Mason
   Rick Trevino; *Looking For The Light* . . . . (Columbia)

Boy From New York City
   Ad-Libs; *Jewels-#1-C.* . . . . (SSS International)
   Oldies But Goodies-#6-C. . . . . (Original Sound)
   Original Golden Hits Of The Great Groups-#1-C. . . . . . . (SSS International)
   Original New York Rock & Roll-#1-C. . . . . (SSS International)
   Manhattan Transfer; *Best Of The Manhattan Transfer* . . . .(Atlantic)
   Mecca For Moderns. . . . .(Atlantic)

California Girls
   Beach Boys; *Beach Boys '69 (The Beach Boys Live In London).* . . . . . . (Capitol)
   Best Of The Beach Boys-#2 . . . . (Capitol)

Endless Summer . . . . (Capitol)
Good Vibrations-Thirty Years Of The Beach Boys . . . . (Capitol)
The Beach Boys In Concert . . . . (Brother)
David Lee Roth; *Crazy From The Heat* . . . . (Warner Bros.)
ST/Down & Out In Beverly Hills . . . . (Warner Bros.)

Carlene
   Phil Vassar; *Phil Vassar* . . . . (Arista)

Chantilly Lace
   Big Bopper; *45s On CD-#1-1956-1959-C.* . . . . (Mercury)
   Cruisin'-1958-C. . . . . (Increase)
   Oldies But Goodies-#4-C . . . .(Original Sound)
   ST/American Graffiti . . . . (MCA)
   Jerry Lee Lewis; *"Killer" Rocks On.* . . . . (Mercury)
   Best Of Jerry Lee Lewis-#2. . . . . (Mercury)

Chewy Chewy
   Ohio Express; *Best Of Ohio Express & Other Bubblegum
      Smashes-#1-C* . . . . (Rhino)
   Best Of Ohio Express & Other Bubblegum Smashes-#1-C. . . . . . . (Rhino)
   Bubblegum's Greatest Hits-#2-C. . . . . (Accord)
   Fabulous Bubblegum Years-C . . . . (Fifty One West)

Could This Be Magic
   Dubs; *Doo Wop Memories-#1-C.* . . . . (Rhino)

Crush
   Jennifer Paige; *Jennifer Paige.* . . . . (Hollywood)

Crush
   Lila McCann; *Something In The Air* . . . .(Asylum)

Crush
   Zhane'; *Saturday Night.* . . . . (Motown)

Crush
   Dave Matthews Band; *Before These Crowded Streets* . . . .(RCA)

Crush On U
   Lil' Kim; *Hard Core* . . . .(Atlantic)

Crush On You
   Jets; *Best Of The Jets* . . . . (MCA)
   Heartthrob Hits-C . . . . (Rhino)

Crush On You
   Bruce Springsteen; *The River* . . . . (Columbia)

Crush With Eyeliner
   R.E.M.; *Monster.* . . . . (Warner Bros.)

Cynthia
   Bruce Springsteen; *Tracks* . . . . (Columbia)

Daddy's Money
   Ricochet; *Ricochet* . . . . (Columbia)

David Duchovny
   Bree Sharp; *Cheap & Evil Girl* . . . . (Trauma)

Denis
   Blondie; *Blonde And Beyond-Rarities & Oddities* . . . . (Gold Rush)
   Once More Into The Bleach . . . . (Gold Rush)
   Plastic Letters . . . . (Chrysalis)
   The Platinum Collection. . . . . (Chrysalis)

Denise
   Randy & The Rainbows; *Doo-Wop Uptempo-#2-C* . . . . (Rhino)
   Super Oldies Of The '60s-#4-C . . . . (Audio Fidelity)
   WCBS FM 101 History Of Rock-'60s-#1-C . . . . (Collectables)

Do You Know You Are My Sunshine
   Statler Brothers; *Statler Brothers-30th Anniversary Celebration* . . . . . (Mercury)

Edge Of Seventeen
   Stevie Nicks; *Bella Donna* . . . .(Modern)

El Paso
   Grateful Dead; *Steal Your Face.* . . . .(Grateful Dead)
   Marty Robbins; *Billboard Top Country Hits-1960-C* . . . . (Rhino)
   Gunfighter Ballads & Trail Songs . . . . (Legacy)
   Marty Robbins' Biggest Hits . . . . (Columbia)
   Radio Classics Of The '50s-C. . . . . (Columbia)
   Texas Super Hits-C. . . . . (Columbia)

Fool For Your Love
   Mickey Gilley; *19 Hot Country Requests-C* . . . . (Epic)
   Fool For Your Love . . . . (Epic)

Give Him A Great Big Kiss
   Shangri-Las; *Best Of The Girl Groups-#1-C.* . . . . (Rhino)
   Remember The Shangri-Las At Their Best . . . . (Collectables)

God Don't Make Lonely Girls
   Wallflowers; *Bringing Down The Horse* . . . . (Interscope)

Hello, I Love You
   Doors; *Best Of The Doors* . . . . (Elektra)
   Doors' Greatest Hits . . . . (Elektra)
   Doors-Box Set . . . . (Elektra)
   Waiting For The Sun. . . . . (Elektra)

He's So Fine
   Chiffons; *Best Of The Girl Groups-#1-C.* . . . . (Rhino)
   Billboard Top Rock 'N' Roll Hits-1963-C. . . . . (Rhino)
   Chiffons Greatest Hits . . . . (Right Stuff)
   Jody Miller; *Jody Miller's Greatest Hits.* . . . . (Epic)

Hey Lover
   L.L. Cool J; *All World* . . . . (Def Jam)
   Mr. Smith. . . . . (Def Jam)
   MTV Party To Go-#9-C . . . . (Tommy Boy)

I'm Already Taken
   Steve Wariner; *Country Cares For Kids II-C* . . . . (BNA)

Two Teardrops . . . . (Capitol)
I've Got A Crush On You
Carly Simon; *Glory Of Gershwin Featuring Larry Adler-C* . . . . (Mercury)
Ella Fitzgerald; *Compact Jazz-Ella Fitzgerald* . . . . (Verve)
Frank Sinatra; *I've Got A Crush On You* . . . . (Legacy)
  Nice 'N' Easy . . . . (Capitol)
Frank Sinatra & Barbra Streisand; *Frank Sinatra-Duets-C* . . . . (Capitol)
Linda Ronstadt; *What's New* . . . . (Asylum)
Life's A Dance
John Michael Montgomery; *Life's A Dance* . . . . (Atlantic)
New Girl In School
Jan & Dean; *Jan & Dean-Legendary Masters* . . . . (EMI)
  Surf City-Best Of Jan & Dean . . . . (EMI)
Norma Jean Riley
Diamond Rio; *Diamond Rio* . . . . (Arista)
  Diamond Rio's Greatest Hits . . . . (Arista)
One In A Million
Aaliyah; *One In A Million* . . . . (BlackGround Enterp./Atlantic)
Popsicles & Icicles
Murmaids; *Golden Girl Groups-C* . . . . (K-Tel)
  Oldies But Goodies-#2-C . . . . (Original Sound)
Sick Of Myself
Matthew Sweet; *100% Fun* . . . . (Zoo)
Sittin' Up In My Room
Brandy; *ST/Waiting To Exhale* . . . . (Arista)
Something Like That
Tim McGraw; *A Place In The Sun* . . . . (Curb)
  Tim McGraw's Greatest Hits . . . . (Curb)
Tall Paul
Annette with the Afterbeats; *Best Of Annette Funicello* . . . . (Rhino)
  Sherman Brothers . . . . (Disney)
  Too Cute-C . . . . (Dunhill Compact Classics)
Teenage Crush
Tommy Sands; *Steady Date With Tommy Sands* . . . . (Collectables)
Tell Me Why
Belmonts; *Classic Old & Gold-C* . . . . (Laurie)
  I Got Rhythm-C . . . . (K-Tel)
That Girl
Maxi Priest featuring Shaggy; *Man With The Fun* . . . . (Virgin)
  Reggae Party 1999-C . . . . (Island)
Thee Cool Cats
Beatles; *The Beatles-Anthology-#1* . . . . (Capitol)
Theme From "The Many Loves Of Dobie Gillis"
Original Soundtrack; *CBS: The First 50 Years* . . . . (TVT)
  Television's Greatest Hits-#1-C . . . . (TVT)
  TV Classic Themes: 25th Anniversary Edition-C . . . . (Breakable)
There She Goes
Babyface; *Face 2 Face* . . . . (Arista)
When You Ask About Love
Crickets; *45-#9-55153* . . . . (Brunswick)
When You Walk In The Room
Jackie DeShannon; *Best Of Jackie DeShannon* . . . . (Rhino)
  Very Best Of Jackie DeShannon . . . . (Collectables)
Pam Tillis; *Pam Tillis' Greatest Hits* . . . . (Arista)
  Pam Tillis-Super Hits . . . . (Arista)
  Sweetheart's Dance . . . . (Arista)
You Walked In
Lonestar; *Crazy Nights* . . . . (BNA)
Young Blood
Bad Company; *Run With The Pack* . . . . (Swan Song)
Coasters; *Coasters' Greatest Hits* . . . . (Atco)
  Coasters-Their Greatest Recordings-Early Years . . . . (Atco)
  The Ultimate Coasters . . . . (Warner Special Prod.)
You're Still A Young Man
Tower Of Power; *Bump City* . . . . (Warner Bros.)
  Live & In Living Color . . . . (Warner Bros.)

LOVE: DANGERS OF LOVE, Futility Of Love,

Love Can Hurt

*See Also: **ADVICE, BREAK, CHEATING & LIES, DESIRE, FOOLS, HEART, KISSING, LEAVING, LOSING & LOSS, LOVE (various), PAIN & HEALING, PARENTS: CONCERNED ABOUT TEEN LOVE, SADNESS, SEX: RESISTING TEMPTATION, WARNINGS***

(I'd Be) A Legend In My Time
Don Gibson; *Best Of Don Gibson-#1* . . . . (Curb)
Leon Russell; *Legend In My Time: Hank Wilson-#3* . . . . (Ark 21)
Ronnie Milsap; *Ronnie Milsap's Greatest Hits* . . . . (RCA)
(You're The) Devil In Disguise
Elvis Presley; *Elvis' Gold Records, Volume 4* . . . . (RCA)
  The Top Ten Hits . . . . (RCA)
911
Wyclef Jean featuring Mary J. Blige; *The Ecleftic-2 Sides II*
  A Book . . . . (Ruffhouse/Columbia)
Aberdeen
Kenny Wayne Shepherd; *Ledbetter Heights* . . . . (Giant)

Act Naturally
Beatles; *"Yesterday"...And Today* . . . . (Capitol)
Buck Owens; *Beatles Originals* . . . . (Rhino)
Buck Owens & Ringo Starr; *Act Naturally* . . . . (Capitol)
Buck Owens & The Buckaroos; *Buck Owens & The Buckaroos-Live At
  Carnegie Hall* . . . . (Country Music Foundation)
Charley Pride; *Country Pride* . . . . (RCA)
Johnny Russell; *20 Great Country Hits-C* . . . . (RCA)
After The Blackbird Sings
Wallflowers; *The Wallflowers* . . . . (Virgin)
All In Love Is Fair
Stevie Wonder; *Innervisions* . . . . (Motown)
All The Good Ones Are Gone
Pam Tillis; *Pam Tillis' Greatest Hits* . . . . (Arista)
Almost Honest
Megadeth; *Cryptic Writings* . . . . (Capitol)
  ST/Mortal Kombat 3: Annihilation . . . . (TVT)
Always Wanting You
Merle Haggard & The Strangers; *For The Record: Merle Haggard-43
  Legendary Hits* . . . . (BNA)
Am I The Only One (Who's Ever Felt This Way)
Dixie Chicks; *Wide Open Spaces* . . . . (Monument)
And The Beat Goes On
Whispers; *Club Epic-#1-C* . . . . (Legacy)
April In Portugal
Eartha Kitt; *Best Of Eartha Kitt* . . . . (MCA)
Ashes By Now
Lee Ann Womack; *I Hope You Dance* . . . . (MCA)
Rodney Crowell; *Rodney Crowell-Collection* . . . . (Warner Bros.)
At My Front Door
Nilsson; *Son Of Schmilsson* . . . . (RCA)
At Seventeen
Janis Ian; *Between The Lines* . . . . (Columbia)
  Super Hits Of The '70s-Have A Nice Day-#15-C . . . . (Rhino)
Baby Did A Bad Thing
Chris Isaak; *Forever Blue* . . . . (Reprise)
  ST/Eyes Wide Shut . . . . (Reprise)
Barracuda
Heart; *Heart's Greatest Hits/Live* . . . . (Epic)
  Little Queen . . . . (Portrait)
Be Careful
Ricky Martin & Madonna; *Ricky Martin* . . . . (Columbia)
Beautiful Ones
Mariah Carey; *Butterfly* . . . . (Columbia)
Beautiful Stranger
Madonna; *GHV2* . . . . (Warner Bros.)
  ST/Austin Powers-The Spy Who Shagged Me . . . . (Maverick)
  Totally Hits-#2-C . . . . (Elektra)
Bitch
Rolling Stones; *Made In The Shade* . . . . (Rolling Stones)
  Sticky Fingers . . . . (Virgin)
Bitter Pill
Motley Crue; *Motley Crue's Greatest Hits* . . . . (Beyond)
Blistered
Johnny Cash; *Johnny Cash-16 Biggest Hits-#2* . . . . (Legacy)
Blues In The Night
Benny Goodman; *Small Groups-1941-1945* . . . . (Columbia)
Bobby Bland; *Introspective Of The Early Years* . . . . (MCA)
Dinah Shore; *Nipper's Greatest Hits Of The '40s-#1-C* . . . . (RCA)
Doc Severinsen; *Best Of Doc Severinsen* . . . . (MCA)
Frank Sinatra; *Frank Sinatra sings for Only The Lonely* . . . . (Capitol)
Jimmie Lunceford & His Orchestra; *Warner Bros.' 75 Years Entertaining
  The World-Film Music-C* . . . . (Rhino)
Mel Torme; *Torme* . . . . (Verve)
Robins; *Best Of The Robins* . . . . (Crescendo)
Rosemary Clooney; *Rosemary Clooney-16 Most Requested Songs* . . . . (Legacy)
Tony Bennett; *Playin' With My Friends-Bennett Sings The
  Blues-C* . . . . (Columbia)
Woody Herman; *Blues On Parade* . . . . (GRP)
  Woody Herman-Best Of The Decca Years . . . . (Decca)
Woody Herman & His Orchestra; *Big Bands Greatest
  Hits-#3-C* . . . . (MCA Special Prod.)
Borrowed Love
Earl Scruggs & Dwight Yoakam; *Earl Scruggs And Friends-C* . . . . . . (MCA)
Brand New Day
Sting; *Brand New Day* . . . . (A&M)
Brick
Ben Folds Five; *Whatever And Ever Amen* . . . . (Caroline/550)
But Not For Me
Billie Holiday; *Silver Collection* . . . . (Verve)
Chet Baker; *Let's Get Lost-Best Of Chet Baker Sings* . . . . (Blue Note)
Ella Fitzgerald; *Ella Sings Jazz* . . . . (MCA Jazz)
Elvis Costello; *Glory Of Gershwin Featuring Larry Adler-C* . . . . . (Mercury)
Harry Connick, Jr.; *ST/When Harry Met Sally* . . . . (Columbia)
Judy Garland; *Best Of Judy Garland* . . . . (MCA)
Original London Cast; *Crazy For You* . . . . (RCA)
Original Soundtrack; *Manhattan* . . . . (CBS Masterworks)
Sarah Vaughan; *Sarah Vaughan Sings George Gershwin Songbook,
  Vol. 2* . . . . (Emarcy)

Can I Get A Witness
Marvin Gaye; *Marvin Gaye-Anthology* (Motown)
Marvin Gaye's Greatest Hits (Motown)
Marvin Gaye-Super Hits (Motown)
Rod Stewart; *Storyteller/The Complete Anthology: 1964-1990* (Warner Bros.)
Rolling Stones; *England's Newest Hit Makers/The Rolling Stones* (Abkco)
Can't Change Me
Chris Cornell; *Euphoria Morning* (A&M)
Chains
Beatles; *Please Please Me* (Parlophone)
The Early Beatles (Capitol)
Carole King; *Pearls* (Capitol)
Cookies; *Introducing...The Beatles* (Vee-Jay)
Chains
Patty Loveless; *Honky Tonk Angel* (MCA)
Patty Loveless' Greatest Hits (MCA)
Chains
Tina Arena; *Don't Ask* (Epic)
Chance, A
Kenny Chesney; *I Will Stand* (BNA)
Charlie's Shoes
Billy Walker; *Best Of Billy Walker* (Deluxe)
Columbia Country Classics-#4-Nashville Sound-C (Columbia)
Cheers 2 U
Playa; *Cheers 2 U* (Def Soul/Def Jam/RAL/Mercury)
Chemistry
Semisonic; *All About Chemistry* (MCA)
Cherchez La Femme
Dr. Buzzard's Original "Savannah" Band; *Nipper's Greatest Hits Of The '70s-C* (RCA)
Gloria Estefan; *Hold Me, Thrill Me, Kiss Me* (Epic)
Climb That Hill
Tom Petty And The Heartbreakers; *ST/She's The One* (Warner Bros.)
Cold Cold Heart
Hank Williams; *Complete Hank Williams* (Mercury)
Hank Williams With His Drifting Cowboys; *24 Of Hank Williams' Greatest Hits* (Polydor)
Hank Williams (MGM)
Hank Williams-40 Greatest Hits (Polydor)
Live At Opry (MGM)
Long Gone Lonesome Blues (Polydor)
Jerry Lee Lewis; *Duets* (Sun)
Golden Cream Of Jerry Lee Lewis (Sun)
Jerry Lee Lewis & Friends-Duets (Sun)
Lucinda Williams; *Timeless: Hank Williams Tribute-C* (Lost Highway/IDJMG)
Tony Bennett; *Tony Bennett-16 Most Requested Songs* (Legacy)
Come Back When You Grow Up
Bobby Vee; *Best Of Bobby Vee* (EMI)
Bobby Vee-Legendary Masters (EMI)
Good Vibrations (Sounds Of Top 40 Radio: 1964-1967)-C (Capitol)
Come What May
Patti Page; *Patti Page Collection-The Mercury Years-#1* (Mercury)
Cool It Now
New Edition; *New Edition* (MCA)
New Edition's Greatest Hits, Vol. 1 (MCA)
Crash And Burn
Sheryl Crow; *The Globe Sessions* (A&M)
Crazy
Jimmie Dale Gilmore with Willie Nelson; *Red Hot + Country-C* (Mercury)
Kenny Rogers; *Kenny Rogers' Greatest Hits* (RCA)
What About Me? (RCA)
Linda Ronstadt; *Hasten Down The Wind* (Asylum)
Patsy Cline; *Songwriter's Tribute* (MCA)
ST/Sweet Dreams (MCA)
The Patsy Cline Story (MCA)
Ray Price; *Ray Price's Greatest Hits-#2* (Step One)
Willie Nelson; *Best Of Willie* (RCA)
Healing Hands Of Time (Liberty)
Nite Life-Greatest Hits & Rare Tracks (Rhino)
Willie & Family Live (Columbia)
Criminal
Fiona Apple; *1998 Grammy Nominees-C* (MCA)
Tidal (Clean Slate/Work)
Curly Headed Baby
Pete Seeger; *Tribute To Woody Guthrie-C* (Warner Bros.)
Cuts Like A Knife
Bryan Adams; *Cuts Like A Knife* (A&M)
Live! Live! Live! (A&M)
MTV Unplugged-Bryan Adams (A&M)
So Far So Good (A&M)
Damn Thing Called Love
After 7; *Reflections* (Virgin)
Dance, The
Garth Brooks; *Garth Brooks* (Liberty)
Garth Brooks-Double Live (Capitol)
Day Tripper
Beatles; *"Yesterday"...And Today* (Capitol)
Beatles 1 (Capitol)
Beatles-Box Set (Capitol)
Past Masters-Volume Two (Parlophone)
The Beatles/1962-1966 (Capitol)
Jimi Hendrix Experience; *Radio One* (Rykodisc)
Otis Redding; *Dictionary Of Soul* (Atco)
The Otis Redding Story (Atlantic)
Sergio Mendes & Brasil '66; *Sergio Mendes & Brasil '66's Greatest Hits* (A&M)
Desert Rose
Sting; *Brand New Day* (A&M)
Devil In Her Heart
Beatles; *The Beatles' Second Album* (Capitol)
With The Beatles (Parlophone)
Donays; *Beatles Originals* (Rhino)
Did You Ever Love Somebody
Jessica Simpson; *Songs From Dawson's Creek* (Sony Music Soundtrax)
Diving To Be Deeper
Sinead Lohan; *No Mermaid* (Grapevine)
Do For Love
2Pac featuring Eric Williams; *R U Still Down (Remember Me)* (Amaru/Jive)
Do You Love Me That Much?
Peter Cetera; *You're The Inspiration-A Collection* (River North)
Don't Believe My Heart Can Stand Another You
Tanya Tucker; *Tanya Tucker's Greatest Hits* (MCA)
The Tanya Tucker Collection (MCA)
Don't Feel Like Cryin'
Abra Moore; *Strangest Places* (Arista Austin)
Don't Let The Stars Get In Your Eyes
Perry Como; *Como's Golden Records* (RCA)
Perry Como-Pure Gold (RCA)
Perry Como's All-Time Greatest Hits-#1 (RCA)
This Is Perry Como (RCA)
Down In Flames
BlackHawk; *BlackHawk* (Arista)
The Hits-Love & Gravity (Arista)
Down To My Last Broken Heart
Janie Fricke; *Greatest Country Hits Of The '80s-1980-C* (Columbia)
Janie Fricke-17 Greatest Hits (Columbia)
Janie Fricke's Greatest Hits (Columbia)
Eddie's First Wife
Gretchen Peters; *Gretchen Peters* (Purple Crayon Prod.)
El Paso
Grateful Dead; *Steal Your Face* (Grateful Dead)
Marty Robbins; *Billboard Top Country Hits-1960-C* (Rhino)
Gunfighter Ballads & Trail Songs (Legacy)
Marty Robbins' Biggest Hits (Columbia)
Radio Classics Of The '50s-C (Columbia)
Texas Super Hits-C (Columbia)
Emotional Girl
Terri Clark; *Just The Same* (Mercury)
Every Morning
Sugar Ray; *14:59* (Lava)
Every Which Way But Loose
Eddie Rabbitt; *Billboard Top Movie Hits-1970s-C* (Rhino)
I Love Country-Hits Of The '90s-#4-C (Priority)
Warner Bros.' 75 Years Entertaining The World-Film Music-C (Rhino)
Everything You Want
Vertical Horizon; *Everything You Want* (RCA)
Totally Hits-#3-C (Atlantic)
Fair
Ben Folds Five; *Whatever And Ever Amen* (Caroline/550)
Fair And Tender Ladies
Whites; *A Lifetime In The Making* (Ceili Music)
Fallin'
Alicia Keys; *Songs In A Minor* (J)
Totally Hits 2001-C (Arista)
Falling In Love (Is Hard On The Knees)
Aerosmith; *A Little South Of Sanity* (Geffen)
Nine Lives (Columbia)
Fear Of Being Alone
Reba McEntire; *Reba McEntire's Greatest Hits-#3: I'm A Survivor* (MCA)
What If It's You (MCA)
Female Of The Species
Space; *Spiders* (Gut/Universal)
Fool #1
Brenda Lee; *The Brenda Lee Story-Her Greatest Hits* (MCA)
Joe Stampley/The Uniques; *Joe Stampley-Golden Hits* (Paula)
Fool, The
Lee Ann Womack; *Lee Ann Womack* (Decca)
Gal That Got Away
Four Freshmen; *Voices In Love-Love Lost* (Collector's Choice)
Frank Sinatra; *Complete Capitol Singles Collection* (Capitol)
Georgy Porgy
Eric Benet featuring Faith Evans; *A Day In The Life* (Warner Bros.)
Toto; *Past To Present 1977-1990* (Columbia)
Toto (Columbia)
Girl I Knew Somewhere, The
Monkees; *Monkees' Greatest Hits* (Rhino)

Girl Inside My Head
Blues Traveler; *Bridge*. . . . . (A&M)
Glad To Be Unhappy
Mamas & The Papas; *Mamas & The Papas-16 Of Their Greatest Hits* . . . (MCA)
Gold Dust Woman
Fleetwood Mac; *25 Years-The Chain* . . . . (Warner Bros.)
   Rumours . . . . (Warner Bros.)
Sister Hazel; *Legacy-A Tribute To Fleetwood Mac's Rumours-C* . . . . (Lava)
Good Girls
Joe; *All That I Am* . . . .(Jive)
Good Lovin' (Makes It Right)
Tammy Wynette; *Tammy Wynette-16 Biggest Hits* . . . . (Legacy)
   Tammy Wynette-Anniversary-20 Years Of Hits . . . . (Epic)
   Tears Of Fire-25th Anniversary Collection . . . . (Epic)
Goodbye Cruel World
James Darren; *Best Of James Darren* . . . . (Rhino)
   Billboard Top Rock 'N' Roll Hits-1961-C . . . . (Rhino)
Goodbye To Love
Carpenters; *Carpenters-Classics-#2* . . . . (A&M)
   Carpenters-Love Songs . . . . (A&M)
Graceland
Paul Simon; *Graceland* . . . . (Warner Bros.)
Half As Much
Rosemary Clooney; *Rosemary Clooney-16 Most Requested Songs* . . . . (Legacy)
Heart Of Glass
Blondie; *Best Of Blondie* . . . . (Chrysalis)
   Billboard Top Hits-1979-C . . . . (Rhino)
   Parallel Lines . . . . (Chrysalis)
   The Disco Years-#2-On The Beat-1978-1982-C . . . . (Rhino)
Heartbreak Hotel
Albert King; *Blues For Elvis* . . . . (Stax)
Elvis Presley; *Elvis As Recorded At Madison Square Garden* . . . . (RCA)
   Elvis' Golden Records . . . . (RCA)
   Elvis-A Legendary Performer, Volume 1 . . . . (RCA)
   Nipper's Greatest Hits Of The '50s-#1-C . . . . (RCA)
   Worldwide 50 Gold Award Hits, Vol. 1, Parts 1 & 2 . . . . (RCA)
Stan Freberg; *Capitol Collectors Series-Stan Freberg* . . . . (Capitol)
Willie Nelson; *Greatest Hits (& Some That Will Be)* . . . . . . (Columbia)
   Willie Nelson & Leon Russell: One For The Road . . . . (Columbia)
Heartbreaker
Pat Benatar; *Best Shots* . . . . (Chrysalis)
   In The Heat Of The Night . . . . (Chrysalis)
   Live From Earth . . . . (Chrysalis)
Heartbroke Every Day
Lonestar; *Lonestar*. . . . . (BNA)
Hearts Of Stone
Fontane Sisters; *Hearts Of Stone-The Best Of The Fontane*
   Sisters . . . . (Varese Sarabande)
Heat Wave
Linda Ronstadt; *Linda Ronstadt's Greatest Hits* . . . . (Asylum)
   Prisoner In Disguise . . . . (Asylum)
Martha & The Vandellas; *Billboard Top R&B Hits-1963-C* . . . . . (Rhino)
   Martha Reeves & The Vandellas' Greatest Hits . . . . (Motown)
   More American Graffiti-#4-C . . . . (MCA)
   Motown Story-First 25 Years-C . . . . (Motown)
Who; *A Quick One (Happy Jack)/Sell Out* . . . . (MCA)
   Two's Missing . . . . (MCA)
Hello Trouble
Desert Rose Band; *Running* . . . . (MCA)
Here Comes My Baby
Tremeloes; *Best Of The Tremeloes* . . . . (Rhino)
Here Today
Beach Boys; *Pet Sounds* . . . . (Capitol)
   The Pet Sounds Sessions: A 30th Anniversary Collection . . . . (Capitol)
Here We Go Again
Ray Charles; *Ray Charles-Anthology* . . . . (Rhino)
Here's That Rainy Day
Frank Sinatra; *The Capitol Years* . . . . (Capitol)
Gene Ammons; *The Boss Is Back* . . . . (Prestige)
Kenny Rankin; *Kenny Rankin Album* . . . . (Little David)
Rosemary Clooney; *Rosemary Clooney Sings Ballads* . . . . (Concord Jazz)
Tony Bennett; *Perfectly Frank* . . . . (Columbia)
He's A Heartache (Looking For A Place To Happen)
Janie Fricke; *19 Hot Country Requests-C* . . . . (Epic)
   It Ain't Easy . . . . (Columbia)
   Janie Fricke-17 Greatest Hits . . . . (Columbia)
   Very Best Of Janie Fricke . . . . (Columbia)
Hey There
Original Cast; *ST/Pajama Game* . . . . (Collectables)
Rosemary Clooney; *Essence Of Rosemary Clooney* . . . . (Legacy)
Highway 29
Bruce Springsteen; *The Ghost Of Tom Joad* . . . . (Columbia)
Hi-Lili, Hi-Lo
Anne Murray; *There's A Hippo In My Tub* . . . . (Capitol)
Ray Conniff; *Encore! 16 Most Requested Songs* . . . . (Legacy)
Hole, The
Randy Travis; *You And You Alone* . . . . (DreamWorks/SKG)
Honky Tonk Women
Elton John; *11-17-70* . . . . (Polydor)

Humble Pie; *Best Of Humble Pie* . . . . (A&M)
   Eat It . . . . (A&M)
   Humble Pie-Classics-#14 . . . . (A&M)
Ike & Tina Turner; *Best Of Ike & Tina Turner* . . . . (EMI)
   Get Back . . . . (Liberty)
Joe Cocker; *Mad Dogs & Englishmen* . . . . (A&M)
Rolling Stones; *Get Yer Ya-Ya's Out!* . . . . (Abkco)
   Hot Rocks 1964-1971 . . . . (Abkco)
   Love You Live . . . . (Virgin)
   Through The Past, Darkly (Big Hits Vol. 2) . . . . (Abkco)
Willie Nelson & Leon Russell; *Half Nelson-C* . . . . (Columbia)
How Can I Be Sure
Rascals; *Groovin'*. . . . . (Warner Special Prod.)
   Rascals-Anthology 1965-1972 . . . . (Rhino)
   The Ultimate Rascals . . . . (Warner Special Prod.)
   Very Best Of The Rascals . . . . (Rhino)
How Can You Mend A Broken Heart
Al Green; *Al Green's Greatest Hits-#1* . . . . (Motown)
   Compact Command Performances-Al Green . . . . (Motown)
   Let's Stay Together . . . . (Right Stuff)
Bee Gees; *Bee Gees-Gold* . . . . (Polydor)
   Here At Last...Bee Gees...Live . . . . (Polydor)
   Nobody's Child-Romanian Angel Appeal-C . . . . (Warner Bros.)
Hurt By Love
BoDeans; *Blend* . . . . (Reprise)
Hurts So Good
John Cougar; *American Fool* . . . . (Riva)
Hurts To Be In Love
Gino Vannelli; *Black Cars* . . . . (CBS Associated)
I Don't Even Know Your Name
Alan Jackson; *Alan Jackson-The Greatest Hits Collection* . . . . (Arista)
   Who I Am . . . . (Arista)
I Don't Make Promises (I Can't Break)
Shannon Curfman; *Loud Guitars Big Suspicions* . . . . (Arista)
I Don't Wanna Talk About It Now
Emmylou Harris; *Red Dirt Girl* . . . . (Nonesuch)
I Lost It
Kenny Chesney; *Kenny Chesney's Greatest Hits* . . . . (BNA)
I Make A Fool Of Myself
Frankie Valli; *25th Anniversary Collection* . . . . (Rhino)
I Never Loved A Man (The Way I Love You)
Aretha Franklin; *Aretha Franklin-30 Greatest Hits* . . . . (Rhino)
   Golden Age Of Black Music-1960-1970-C . . . . (Atlantic)
   ST/The Commitments . . . . (MCA)
I Never Will Marry
Bailey Brothers; *Early Days Of Bluegrass-#6* . . . . (Rounder)
Carter Family; *Wildwood Flower*. . . . . (ASV Living Era)
Linda Ronstadt; *Simple Dreams* . . . . (Asylum)
I Think I'll Just Stay Here And Drink
Merle Haggard; *For The Record: Merle Haggard-43 Legendary Hits*. . . . (BNA)
I Used To Love Him
Lauryn Hill featuring Mary J. Blige; *The Miseducation Of*
   Lauryn Hill . . . . (Ruffhouse/Columbia)
If I Fell
Beatles; *Beatles-Love Songs* . . . . (Capitol)
   Something New . . . . (Capitol)
   ST/A Hard Day's Night . . . . (Capitol)
If I Give My Heart To You
Nat "King" Cole; *Nat "King" Cole (Box Set)* . . . . (Capitol)
If I Wanted To
Melissa Etheridge; *Yes I Am*. . . . . (Island)
If It Ain't Love (Let's Leave It Alone)
Connie Smith; *Essential Connie Smith*. . . . . (RCA)
Whites; *Whites' Greatest Hits* . . . . (Curb)
If She Don't Love You
Buffalo Club; *Buffalo Club* . . . . (Rising Tide)
If We Fall In Love Tonight
Rod Stewart; *If We Fall In Love Tonight* . . . . (Warner Bros.)
If You Can Do Anything Else
George Strait; *George Strait*. . . . . (MCA)
If You Leave
Destiny's Child; *The Writing's On The Wall* . . . . (Columbia)
I'll Be On My Way
Beatles; *Live At The BBC* . . . . (Apple)
I'll Never Fall In Love Again
Dionne Warwick; *Billboard Top Soft Rock Hits-1970-C* . . . . (Rhino)
   Her Classic Songs-#1 . . . . (Curb)
Elvis Presley; *From Elvis Presley Boulevard, Memphis, Tennessee* . . . . (RCA)
Mary Chapin Carpenter; *ST/My Best Friend's Wedding* . . . . (Work/Epic)
I'll Never Love This Way Again
Dionne Warwick; *Dionne Warwick's Greatest Hits-1979-1990* . . . . (Arista)
   Grammy's Greatest Moments-#4-C . . . . (Atlantic)
I'm A Believer
Monkees; *Billboard Top Rock 'N' Roll Hits-1966-C* . . . . (Rhino)
   Monkees' Greatest Hits . . . . (Rhino)
   More Of The Monkees . . . . (Rhino)
   Oldies But Goodies-#3-C . . . . (Original Sound)
Neil Diamond; *Live In America* . . . . (Columbia)

Neil Diamond's Greatest Hits-1966-1992 . . . . (Columbia)
September Morn. . . . . (Columbia)
Smash Mouth; *Now That's What I Call Music!-#8-C* . . . . (Virgin)
ST/Shrek . . . . (Interscope)
I'm Not Strong Enough To Say No
BlackHawk; *Strong Enough* . . . . (Arista)
I'm Still Alive
Trisha Yearwood; *Real Live Woman* . . . . (MCA)
I'm The Man Who Murdered Love
XTC; *Wasp Star (Apple Venus Volume 2)* . . . . (Idea/TVT)
Imagine That
Diamond Rio; *Diamond Rio's Greatest Hits* . . . . (Arista)
Into Each Life Some Rain Must Fall
Ella Fitzgerald; *Ella & Friends* . . . . (Decca Jazz)
Ink Spots; *Encore Of Golden Hits-Ink Spots* . . . . (Juke Box Treasures)
Invisible Touch
Genesis; *Hit Singles-1980-1988-C* . . . . (Atlantic)
Invisible Touch . . . . (Atlantic)
Invitation To The Blues
Holly Cole; *Temptation* . . . . (Metro Blue)
Tom Waits; *Small Change* . . . . (Asylum)
It Hurts To Be In Love
Betty Everett; *Very Best Of Betty Everett* . . . . (Vee-Jay)
Gene Pitney; *Gene Pitney-Anthology 1961-1968* . . . . (Rhino)
Gene Pitney's Greatest Hits . . . . (Evergreen Music)
It Must Be Love
Alan Jackson; *Under The Influence* . . . . (Arista)
It's Four In The Morning
Faron Young; *Faron Young-Golden Hits* . . . . (Mercury)
Faron Young-The Hits . . . . (Mercury)
It's Gonna Be Me
'N Sync; *No Strings Attached* . . . . (Jive)
Now That's What I Call Music!-#5-C . . . . (Virgin)
It's Lonely Out There
Pam Tillis; *All Of This Love* . . . . (Arista)
I've Been Wrong Before
Deborah Allen; *Cheat The Night* . . . . (RCA)
I've Got You Under My Skin
4 Seasons; *25th Anniversary Collection* . . . . (Rhino)
Diana Krall; *When I Look In Your Eyes* . . . . (GRP)
Frank Sinatra; *At The Sands* . . . . (Reprise)
Round #1 . . . . (Capitol)
Sinatra: A Man And His Music . . . . (Reprise)
Sinatra's Sinatra . . . . (Reprise)
The Reprise Collection. . . . . (Reprise)
Frank Sinatra & Bono; *Frank Sinatra-Duets-C* . . . . (Capitol)
Frank Sinatra & Nelson Riddle Orchestra; *songs for Swingin'*
Lovers! . . . . (Capitol)
Just My Luck
Kim Richey; *Kim Richey* . . . . (Mercury)
Just To See You Smile
Tim McGraw; *Everywhere* . . . . (Curb)
Tim McGraw's Greatest Hits . . . . (Curb)
Kaw-Liga
Hank Williams; *Alone With His Guitar* . . . . (Mercury)
Hank Williams-40 Greatest Hits . . . . (Polydor)
Hank Williams-The Hits-#2 . . . . (Mercury)
Kiss Of Fire
Georgia Gibbs; *Best Of Georgia Gibbs-The Mercury Years* . . . . . (Chronicles)
Tony Martin; *Best Of Tony Martin On RCA* . . . . (Collector's Choice)
Knock Down Walls
Tonic; *Sugar* . . . . (Universal)
Last Time I Saw Richard
Joni Mitchell; *Blue* . . . . (Reprise)
Learning The Game
Buddy Holly; *Complete Buddy Holly* . . . . (MCA)
The Buddy Holly Collection. . . . . (MCA)
Let It Loose
Rolling Stones; *Exile On Main Street* . . . . (Virgin)
Let's Make Sure We Kiss Goodbye
Vince Gill; *Let's Make Sure We Kiss Goodbye* . . . . (MCA)
Letters From The Wasteland
Wallflowers; *Breach* . . . . (Interscope)
Life In Prison
Byrds; *Jailhouse Rock (Hits From The Big*
House)-C . . . . (Sony Music Special Prod.)
Sweetheart Of The Rodeo. . . . . (Columbia)
Life Turned Her That Way
''Little'' Jimmy Dickens; *I'm Little, But I'm Loud-The ''Little'' Jimmy*
Dickens Collection . . . . (Razor & Tie)
Mel Tillis; *Best Of Mel Tillis.* . . . . (MCA)
Mel Tillis' Greatest Hits . . . . (Universal)
Ricky Van Shelton; *Ricky Van Shelton-16 Biggest Hits* . . . . . . (Legacy)
Wild-Eyed Dream . . . . (Columbia)
Like A Hurricane
Neil Young; *Decade* . . . . (Reprise)
Neil Young & Crazy Horse; *Live Rust* . . . . (Reprise)
Neil Young, Crazy Horse & The Bullets; *American Stars 'N Bars* . . . . . (Reprise)

Lilies Of The Field
Gretchen Peters; *Gretchen Peters* . . . . (Purple Crayon Prod.)
Little Town Flirt
Del Shannon; *Del Shannon's Greatest Hits.* . . . . (Rhino)
Del Shannon's Greatest Hits . . . . (Curb)
Livin' La Vida Loca
Ricky Martin; *Ricky Martin.* . . . . (Columbia)
Long Long Time
Linda Ronstadt; *Different Drum* . . . . (Capitol)
Linda Ronstadt-Retrospective . . . . (Capitol)
Linda Ronstadt's Greatest Hits . . . . (Asylum)
Silk Purse . . . . (Capitol)
Look What Love Has Done
Patty Smyth; *ST/Junior* . . . . (MCA)
Love
Musiq Soulchild; *Aijuswanaseing* . . . . (Def Soul/IDJMG)
Love Ain't Easy
Big House; *Big House* . . . . (MCA)
Love Bites
Judas Priest; *Defenders Of The Faith* . . . . (Columbia)
Priest...Live! . . . . (Columbia)
Love Bites
Def Leppard; *Hysteria.* . . . . (Mercury)
Love Blues
Keb' Mo'; *Keb' Mo'* . . . . (Okeh)
Love Bug Leave My Heart Alone
Martha & The Vandellas; *Compact Command Performances-Martha Reeves*
& The Vandellas . . . . (Motown)
Martha Reeves & The Vandellas-Anthology . . . . (Motown)
Love Don't Love Me
Eric Benet; *ST/The Brothers* . . . . (Warner Bros.)
Love Hurts
Cher; *Love Hurts* . . . . (Geffen)
Emmylou Harris & Gram Parsons; *Duets-C* . . . . (Reprise)
Gram Parsons; *Grievous Angel* . . . . (Reprise)
Jim Capaldi; *The Island Story-1962-1987-25th Anniversary-C* . . . . . . (Island)
Judy Collins; *Bread & Roses* . . . . (Elektra)
Nazareth; *Hair Of The Dog* . . . . (A&M)
Hot Tracks . . . . (A&M)
Nazareth-Classics-#16 . . . . (A&M)
'Snaz. . . . . (A&M)
Roy Orbison; *Legendary Roy Orbison* . . . . (Sony Music Special Prod.)
Roy Orbison's All-Time Greatest Hits-#1 & 2 . . . . (Monument)
Love Hurts
Ralph Tresvant; *Ralph Tresvant* . . . . (MCA)
Love Hurts
Jon B.; *Cool Relax.* . . . . (Yab Yum/550)
Love Is A Battlefield
Pat Benatar; *Best Shots* . . . . (Chrysalis)
I Am Woman-C . . . . (Nick At Nite)
Live From Earth . . . . (Chrysalis)
Love Is A Stranger
Eurythmics; *Eurythmics' Greatest Hits.* . . . . (Arista)
Sweet Dreams (Are Made Of This) . . . . (RCA)
Love Is Blind
Eve; *First Lady Of Ruff Ryders* . . . . (Ruff Ryders/IDJMG)
Love Is Here And Now You're Gone
Diana Ross; *Diana Ross-Anthology* . . . . (Motown)
Love Is Like An Itching In My Heart
Diana Ross & The Supremes; *Beg, Scream & Shout! The Big Ol' Box Of*
'60s Soul-C . . . . (Rhino)
Love Is Strange
Mickey and Sylvia; *Legends Of Guitar-Rock The 50's-#2-C* . . . . . . (Rhino)
Nipper's Greatest Hits Of The '50s-#2-C . . . . (RCA)
Oldies But Goodies-#4-C . . . . (Original Sound)
ST/Dirty Dancing . . . . (RCA)
Love Or Confusion
Jimi Hendrix Experience; *Are You Experienced?* . . . . (Reprise)
Love Stinks
J. Geils Band; *Flashback-Best Of The J. Geils Band* . . . . (EMI)
J. Geils Band-Anthology-Houseparty. . . . . (Rhino)
Love Stinks . . . . (EMI)
ST/More Music From The Motion Picture-The Wedding Singer . . . (Maverick)
Love T.K.O.
Bette Midler; *Bette* . . . . (Warner Bros.)
Love Thing
Spice Girls; *Spice* . . . . (Virgin)
Love You Save, The
Jackson 5; *14 Greatest Hits* . . . . (Motown)
ABC . . . . (Motown)
Goin' Back To Indiana . . . . (Motown)
Jackson 5-Anthology . . . . (Motown)
Jackson 5's Greatest Hits . . . . (Motown)
Motown Superstar Series-#12-Jackson 5 . . . . (Motown)
TV ST/Diana-C . . . . (Motown)
Love's Been A Little Bit Hard On Me
Juice Newton; *Juice Newton-Greatest Hits & More* . . . . (Capitol)
Juice Newton's Greatest Hits . . . . (Gold Rush)

Quiet Lies . . . . (Capitol)
Lucky Man
Bruce Springsteen; *Tracks* . . . . (Columbia)
Maggie May
Rod Stewart; *Absolutely Live* . . . . (Warner Bros.)
Best Of Rod Stewart . . . . (Mercury)
Billboard Top Rock 'N' Roll Hits-1971-C . . . . (Rhino)
Every Picture Tells A Story . . . . (Mercury)
Rod Stewart's Greatest Hits . . . . (Warner Bros.)
Sing It Again, Rod . . . . (Mercury)
Storyteller/The Complete Anthology: 1964-1990 . . . . . . (Warner Bros.)
Malibu
Hole; *Celebrity Skin*. . . . . (David Geffen Co.)
Mama Said
Shirelles; *Original Rock 'N' Roll Hits Of The '60s-C* . . . . (Roulette)
Shirelles' Greatest Hits. . . . . (Everest)
Shirelles-Anthology 1959-1964 . . . . (Rhino)
Shirelles-Classics . . . . (Bac-Trac)
Super Oldies Of The '60s-#3-C . . . . (Audio Fidelity)
Marie
Tommy Dorsey & His Orchestra; *Seventeen Number Ones*. . . . . (RCA)
Miserable
Lit; *Place In The Sun* . . . . (RCA)
Missing You
Mary J. Blige; *Share My World* . . . . (MCA)
The Tour . . . . (MCA)
Mona Lisa
Carl Mann; *Original Memphis Rock & Roll* . . . . (Sun)
Sun Story-C . . . . (Rhino)
Elvis Presley; *Elvis-A Legendary Performer, Volume 4* . . . . (RCA)
Jim Reeves; *Jim Reeves-Pure Gold* . . . . (RCA)
Nat "King" Cole; *Best Of Nat "King" Cole-Vol. 1* . . . . (Capitol)
Capitol Collectors Series-Nat "King" Cole. . . . . (Capitol)
The Nat "King" Cole Story . . . . (Capitol)
Unforgettable . . . . (Capitol)
Neville Brothers; *Fiyo On The Bayou* . . . . (A&M)
Moonlight Gambler
Frankie Laine; *Frankie Laine-16 Most Requested Songs* . . . . (Legacy)
Frankie Laine's Greatest Hits . . . . (Columbia)
Must To Avoid, A
Herman's Hermits; *Herman's Hermits-Their Greatest Hits* . . . . (Abkco)
My Heart Has A History
Paul Brandt; *Calm Before The Storm* . . . . (Reprise)
My Lover Man
Bruce Springsteen; *Tracks* . . . . (Columbia)
My Next Broken Heart
Brooks & Dunn; *Brand New Man* . . . . (Arista)
My True Story
Jive Five; *Back Seat Jams-C* . . . . (Dunhill Compact Classics)
Billboard Top R&B Hits-1961-C . . . . (Rhino)
Cruisin'-1961-C . . . . (Increase)
Jive Five-Their Greatest Hits . . . . (Collectables)
Oldies But Goodies-#4-C . . . . (Original Sound)
Never Let You Go
Third Eye Blind; *Blue* . . . . (Elektra)
Totally Hits-#2-C . . . . (Elektra)
Nevertheless
Frank Sinatra; *Best Of The Columbia Years-1943-1952* . . . . . . (Columbia)
McGuire Sisters; *McGuire Sisters-Anthology* . . . . (MCA)
No Man's Woman
Sinead O'Connor; *Faith & Courage* . . . . (Atlantic)
No More "I Love You's"
Annie Lennox; *Medusa* . . . . (Arista)
No One Said It Would Be Easy
Sheryl Crow; *Tuesday Night Music Club*. . . . . (A&M)
No Strings Attached
'N Sync; *No Strings Attached* . . . . (Jive)
Nobody's Supposed To Be Here
Deborah Cox; *One Wish* . . . . (Arista)
Totally Hits-#1-C . . . . (Arista)
Not Enough
Van Halen; *Balance* . . . . (Warner Bros.)
Nothing But A Heartache
Flirtations; *Soul Shots-#2-The "In" Crowd-Sweet Soul-C* . . . . (Rhino)
Ol' Red
Blake Shelton; *Blake Shelton*. . . . . (Giant)
On A Night Like This
Trick Pony; *Trick Pony* . . . . (H2E/Warner Bros.)
On And On
Stephen Bishop; *Best Of Bish* . . . . (Rhino)
One Bad Apple
Osmonds; *Billboard Top Rock 'N' Roll Hits-1971-C* . . . . . (Rhino)
One More Try
Divine; *Fairy Tales* . . . . (Pendulum)
Only Love (The Ballad Of Sleeping Beauty)
Sophie B. Hawkins; *Whaler*. . . . . (Columbia)
Only Love Can Break A Heart
Gene Pitney; *Gene Pitney* . . . . (Everest)
Gene Pitney-Anthology 1961-1968. . . . . (Rhino)

Love Sixties-C . . . . (JCI Assoc. Labels)
Pick Of Gene Pitney . . . . (Fifty One West)
Only One For Me, The
Brian McKnight; *Anytime* . . . . (Motown)
Only Sixteen
Dr. Hook; *Bankrupt* . . . . (Capitol)
Dr. Hook-Greatest Hits & More . . . . (Capitol)
Great Records Of The Decade-'70s Hits-#2-C . . . . (Curb)
Little Bit More . . . . (Capitol)
Sam Cooke; *Best Of Sam Cooke*. . . . . (RCA)
The Man And His Music . . . . (RCA)
This Is Sam Cooke . . . . (RCA)
Ooh La La
Rod Stewart; *When We Were The New Boys* . . . . (Warner Bros.)
Oops!...I Did It Again
Britney Spears; *Oops!...I Did It Again* . . . . (Jive)
Paper Doll
Bar-Kays; *Banging The Wall* . . . . (Mercury)
Mills Brothers; *Best Of The Mills Brothers* . . . . (MCA)
Billboard Pop Memories-1940-1944-C . . . . (Rhino)
Mills Brothers' All Time Greatest Hits . . . . (MCA)
Mills Brothers' Greatest Hits . . . . (MCA)
Mills Brothers-22 Great Hits. . . . . (Ranwood)
Paper Doll . . . . (MCA)
Sentimental Journey: Pop Vocal Classics-#1-1942-1946-C . . . . . . (Rhino)
The Mills Brothers-Best Of The Decca Years . . . . (Decca)
People That We Love, The
Bush; *Golden State*. . . . . (Atlantic)
Piece Of My Heart
Big Brother & The Holding Company; *Cheap Thrills* . . . . . (Columbia)
Rock Classics Of The '60s-C . . . . (Columbia)
Seems Like Yesterday-#6-Late '60s-C . . . . (K-Tel)
Bryan Ferry; *These Foolish Things* . . . . (Reprise)
Delaney & Bonnie; *Best Of Delaney & Bonnie* . . . . (Rhino)
Faith Hill; *Take Me As I Am* . . . . (Warner Bros.)
Janis Joplin; *Janis Joplin In Concert* . . . . (Columbia)
Janis Joplin's Greatest Hits . . . . (Columbia)
ST/Janis . . . . (Columbia)
Sammy Hagar; *Standing Hampton*. . . . . (Geffen)
Poison Ivy
Coasters; *Atlantic Rhythm & Blues 1947-1974-#4 (1958-1962)-C* . . . . (Atlantic)
Billboard Top R&B Hits-1959-C . . . . (Rhino)
Coasters' Greatest Hits. . . . . (Atco)
Coasters-Their Greatest Recordings-Early Years. . . . . (Atco)
More American Graffiti-C . . . . (MCA)
Nylons; *Rockapella* . . . . (Windham Hill)
ST/Stealing Home . . . . (Atlantic)
Rolling Stones; *More Hot Rocks (big hits & fazed cookies)* . . . . (Abkco)
Poor Butterfly
Sarah Vaughan; *Compact Jazz-Sarah Vaughan*. . . . . (Verve)
Live In Japan . . . . (Mainstream)
Sarah Vaughan-Golden Hits . . . . (Mercury)
Sonny Rollins; *Best Of Sonny Rollins-The Blue Note Years* . . . . . . (Blue Note)
Sonny Rollins-Vol. 2 . . . . (Blue Note)
Price Of Love
Bryan Ferry; *Let's Stick Together* . . . . (Virgin)
Cactus Brothers; *Cactus Brothers* . . . . (Liberty)
Everly Brothers; *The Reunion Concert-Live At Albert Hall 1983* . . . . . (Mercury)
*Walk Right Back: The Everly Brothers On Warner Bros.-1960-
1969* . . . . (Warner Archives)
Poco; *Crazy Loving-Best Of Poco-1975-1982* . . . . (MCA)
Problems
Everly Brothers; *Everly Brothers' All-Time Greatest Hits*. . . . . (Curb)
Everly Brothers-Cadence Classics-Their 20 Greatest Hits . . . . (Rhino)
Fabulous Style Of The Everly Brothers . . . . (Rhino)
Queen Of Hearts
Dave Edmunds; *Best Of Dave Edmunds* . . . . (Swan Song)
Repeat When Necessary . . . . (Swan Song)
Juice Newton; *All-Time Country Classics-#2-C* . . . . (Capitol)
Juice . . . . (Capitol)
Juice Newton-Greatest Hits & More . . . . (Capitol)
Juice Newton's Greatest Hits . . . . (Gold Rush)
Rodney Crowell; *Rodney Crowell-Collection* . . . . (Warner Bros.)
Razor Love
Neil Young; *Silver & Gold*. (Reprise)
Ready For A Fall
P.J. Olsson; *Songs From Dawson's Creek* . . . . (Sony Music Soundtrax)
Refugee
Tom Petty And The Heartbreakers; *Damn The Torpedoes* . . . . (MCA)
Pack Up The Plantation-Live! . . . . (MCA)
Ring Of Fire
Country Joe McDonald; *Best Of Country Joe McDonald-The Vanguard
Years-1969-1975* . . . . (Vanguard)
Tonight I'm Singing Just For You . . . . (Vanguard)
Dwight Yoakam; *Guitars, Cadillacs, Etc., Etc.* . . . . (Reprise)
Earl Scruggs & Billy Bob Thornton; *Earl Scruggs And Friends-C* . . . . . (MCA)
Johnny Cash; *All Time Legends Of Country Music-C* . . . . . (Legacy)
Billboard Top Country Hits-1963-C . . . . (Rhino)
Classic Cash-Hall Of Fame Series . . . . (Mercury)
Johnny Cash's Greatest Hits. . . . . (Columbia)

The Man In Black-His Greatest Hits . . . . (Legacy)
Stan Ridgway & Wall Of Voodoo; *Best Of Stan Ridgway & Wall Of
   Voodoo* . . . .(I.R.S.)
Wall Of Voodoo; *Ugly Americans In Australia* . . . . (I.R.S.)

River And The Highway
Pam Tillis; *All Of This Love* . . . . (Arista)
   Pam Tillis' Greatest Hits . . . . (Arista)

Rocky Raccoon
Beatles; *Beatles-Box Set* . . . . (Capitol)
   The Beatles (White Album) . . . . (Capitol)

Rose Garden
k.d. lang; *Swingin' Country Favorites-C* . . . .(Warner Bros.)
k.d. lang and The Reclines; *Angel With A Lariat* . . . . (Sire)
Lynn Anderson; *All Time Legends Of Country Music-C* . . . . (Legacy)
   Country Music Classics-#4-1970-1975-C . . . . (K-Tel)
   Lynn Anderson's Greatest Hits . . . . (Columbia)
   Rose Garden . . . . (Columbia)
   Super Hits Of The '70s-Have A Nice Day-#4-C . . . . (Rhino)
   Very Special Love Song-C . . . . (Fifty One West)

Rose Is Still A Rose
Aretha Franklin; *A Rose Is Still A Rose* . . . . (Arista)

Roving Kind, The
Guy Mitchell; *Guy Mitchell-16 Most Requested Songs* . . . . (Legacy)

Saddle Tramp
Marty Robbins; *Gunfighter Ballads & Trail Songs* . . . . (Legacy)
   Marty Robbins-More Greatest Hits . . . . (Columbia)

Safe In The Arms Of Love
Martina McBride; *ST/Switchback* . . . . (RCA)
   Wild Angels . . . . (RCA)

Safety In Numbers
Joan Osborne; *Righteous Love* . . . . (Interscope)

Say When
Lonestar; *Crazy Nights* . . . . (BNA)

Send In The Clowns
Barbra Streisand; *The Broadway Album* . . . . (Columbia)
Carmen McRae; *Sarah-Dedicated To You* . . . . (Novus)
Frank Sinatra; *The Reprise Collection* . . . . (Reprise)
Judy Collins; *Judith* . . . . (Elektra)
   So Early In The Spring, The First 15 Years . . . . (Elektra)
Original Cast; *Little Night Music* . . . . (Columbia)

Seven Days
Mary J. Blige; *Share My World* . . . .(MCA)
   The Tour . . . .(MCA)

Shadowboxer
Fiona Apple; *Tidal* . . . . (Clean Slate/Work)

She Ain't Worth It
Glenn Medeiros; *Glenn Medeiros With Bobby Brown* . . . .(MCA)

She Bangs
Ricky Martin; *Sound Loaded* . . . . (Columbia)

She's A Heartbreaker
Gene Pitney; *Best Of Gene Pitney* . . . . (K-Tel)
   Gene Pitney-Anthology 1961-1968 . . . . (Rhino)

She's A River
Simple Minds; *Good News From The Next World* . . . . (Virgin)

She's Not There
Santana; *Moonflower* . . . . (Columbia)
   Viva Santana! . . . . (Columbia)
Vanilla Fudge; *Vanilla Fudge* . . . . (Atco)
Zombies; *Best & The Rest Of The Zombies* . . . .(Epic)
   Billboard Top Rock 'N' Roll Hits-1964-C . . . . (Rhino)
   History Of British Rock-#1-C . . . . (Rhino)
   Time Of The Zombies . . . . (Bac-Trac)

She's The One
Bruce Springsteen; *Born To Run* . . . . (Columbia)

Shimmer
Fuel; *Sunburn* . . . . (550 Music)

Shut Up And Drive
Chely Wright; *Woman In The Moon* . . . . (Polydor Country)

Sick Of Myself
Matthew Sweet; *100% Fun* . . . . (Zoo)

Sleepwalker
Wallflowers; *Breach* . . . . (Interscope)

Smoke Gets In Your Eyes
Bryan Ferry; *Another Time Another Place* . . . . (Reprise)
   Street Life-20 Great Hits . . . . (Reprise)
Dinah Washington; *Golden Classics-Dinah Washington* . . . . (Collectables)
Lawrence Welk; *Musical Memories With Lawrence Welk* . . . .(Ranwood)
Patti Austin; *Real Me* . . . . (Qwest)
Platters; *Encore Of Golden Hits-Platters* . . . . (Mercury)
   Oldies But Goodies-#14-C . . . . (Original Sound)
   Platters Greatest Hits . . . . (Everest)
   ST/Always . . . .(MCA)
   ST/American Graffiti . . . .(MCA)
   Super Oldies Of The '50s-#5-C . . . . (Audio Fidelity)

So It Goes
Wes Cunningham; *12 Ways To Win People To Your Way Of
   Thinking* . . . .(Warner Bros.)

Social Disease
Bon Jovi; *Slippery When Wet* . . . . (Jambco)

Somebody's Knockin'
Terri Gibbs; *Best Of Terri Gibbs* . . . . (MCA)
   Country Gold-C . . . . (Priority)
   Country Music Classics-#6-1980-1985-C . . . . (K-Tel)

Someone To Call My Lover
Janet; *All For You* . . . . (Virgin)
   Now That's What I Call Music!-#8-C . . . . (Virgin)

Sometimes
Strokes; *Is This It* . . . . (RCA)

Sometimes Love Just Ain't Enough
Patty Smyth with Don Henley; *Patty Smyth* . . . . (MCA)

Spit Of Love
Bonnie Raitt; *Fundamental* . . . . (Capitol)
   Lilith Fair-A Celebration Of Women In Music-#3-C . . . . (Arista)

Stars
Hum; *You'd Prefer An Astronaut* . . . . (RCA)

Start Me Up
Rolling Stones; *"Still Life" (American Concert 1981)* . . . .(Virgin)
   Flashpoint . . . . (Virgin)
   Tattoo You . . . . (Virgin)

Starting Over Again
Steve Wariner; *Best Of Steve Wariner* . . . . (MCA Special Prod.)
   Country Classics-#7-1986-1987-C . . . . (Universal)
   Life's Highway . . . .(MCA)
   Steve Wariner's Greatest Hits . . . . (MCA)

Statue Of A Fool
Jack Greene; *Country Hits-C* . . . . (Exact)
   Jack Greene Sings His Best . . . . (Step One)
   Jack Greene's Greatest Hits . . . . (International Mktg. Group)
   MCA Records 30 Years Of Hits-1958-1988-C . . . .(MCA)
Ricky Van Shelton; *Ricky Van Shelton's Greatest Hits Plus* . . . . . . (Columbia)
   RVS III . . . . (Columbia)

Stranger In Paradise
Arthur Lyman; *Pearly Shells* . . . . (Crescendo)
Bing Crosby; *The Radio Years: 20 Songs* . . . .(Crescendo)
Original Cast; *Kismet* . . . . (Columbia)
Tony Bennett; *Tony Bennett-16 Most Requested Songs* . . . . (Legacy)
   Tony Bennett's All-Time Greatest Hits . . . . (Columbia)

Sullen Girl
Fiona Apple; *Tidal* . . . . (Clean Slate/Work)

Summertime
Sundays; *Static & Silence* . . . . (David Geffen Co.)

Sweet Misery
Amel Larrieux; *Infinite Possibilities* . . . . (Epic)

Sweet Talkin' Guy
Chiffons; *Best Of The Chiffons* . . . . (Laurie)
   Chiffons-Golden Classics . . . . (Collectables)
   Collectables Presents The History Of Rock-#1-C . . . . (Collectables)
   Everything You Always Wanted . . . . (Laurie)

Sweetest Thing
U2; *Best Of 1980-1990* . . . . (Island)
   Now That's What I Call Music!-#2-C . . . . (Virgin)

Take Time To Know Her
Percy Sledge; *Best Of Percy Sledge* . . . . (Atlantic)
   It Tears Me Up-Best Of Percy Sledge . . . . (Rhino)

Taker, The
Kris Kristofferson; *The Silver Tongued Devil And I* . . . . (Columbia)
Waylon Jennings; *Essential Waylon Jennings* . . . .(RCA)
   Only Daddy That'll Walk The Line-The RCA Years . . . .(RCA)

Tears Falling Down
Rosanne Cash; *The Wheel* . . . . (Columbia)

Tempted
Marty Stuart; *Tempted* . . . . (MCA)

Tender Trap (Love Is The)
Frank Sinatra; *At The Movies* . . . . (Capitol)
   Best Of The Capitol Years . . . . (Capitol)
   Frank Sinatra Sings The Songs Of Van Heusen & Cahn . . . . (Reprise)
   Very Best Of Frank Sinatra . . . . (Reprise)
Sammy Cahn; *Evening With Sammy Cahn* . . . . (DRG)

Texas Tornado
Tracy Lawrence; *Best Of Tracy Lawrence* . . . . (Atlantic)
   I See It Now . . . .(Atlantic)

That's As Close As I'll Get To Loving You
Aaron Tippin; *Aaron Tippin-Super Hits* . . . . (RCA)
   Essential Aaron Tippin . . . . (RCA)
   Greatest Hits And Then Some . . . . (RCA)
   Tool Box . . . . (RCA)

That's The Way It Is
Celine Dion; *All The Way...A Decade Of Song* . . . .(550 Music)
   Collector's Series-Celine Dion-#1 . . . .(550 Music)

There You Go
Johnny Cash; *The Man In Black-His Greatest Hits* . . . . (Legacy)

Things We Do For Love
10 CC; *Deceptive Bends* . . . . (Mercury)
   Super Hits Of The '70s-Have A Nice Day-#19-C . . . . (Rhino)
Amy Grant; *ST/Mr. Wrong* . . . . (Hollywood)

'Til I Get It Right
Tammy Wynette; *Tammy Wynette's Biggest Hits* . . . . (Epic)
   Tammy Wynette's Greatest Hits-#3 . . . . (Epic)

Tears Of Fire-25th Anniversary Collection . . . . (Epic)
Trisha Yearwood; *Tammy Wynette...Remembered-C* . . . . (Asylum)

'Til You Do Me Right
After 7; *Rock On 1995-C* . . . . (Madacy)
Very Best Of After 7 . . . . (Virgin)

To Have And Not To Hold
Madonna; *Ray Of Light* . . . . (Maverick)

Tomb Of The Unknown Love
Cassell Webb; *Songs Of A Stranger* . . . . (Venture)
Kenny Rogers; *The Heart Of The Matter* . . . . (RCA)

Tonight
Marc Nelson; *chocolate mood* . . . . (Columbia)

Total Eclipse Of The Heart
Bonnie Tyler; *Billboard Top Hits-1983-C* . . . . (Rhino)
Faster Than The Speed Of Night . . . . (Columbia)
Seems Like Yesterday-#4-Early '80s-C . . . . (K-Tel)
Nicki French; *Dance Hits '96 Supermix-C* . . . . (Critique)
Secrets . . . . (Critique)

Tragedy
Emmylou Harris; *Red Dirt Girl* . . . . (Nonesuch)

Tryin' To Love Two
William Bell; *Coming Back For More* . . . . (Razor & Tie)

Trying To Love Two Women
Oak Ridge Boys; *Oak Ridge Boys' Greatest Hits* . . . . (MCA)
Oak Ridge Boys-Collection . . . . (MCA)
Together . . . . (MCA)

Two Little Girls
Ani DiFranco; *Little Plastic Castle* . . . . (Righteous Babe)

Unpretty
TLC; *Fanmail* . . . . (LaFace)

Walking In A Hurricane
John Fogerty; *Blue Moon Swamp* . . . . (Warner Bros.)

Wayward Wind
Gogi Grant; *'50s Jukebox Favorites-C* . . . . (K-Tel)
Collectables Presents The History Of Rock-#7-C . . . . (Collectables)
Lynn Anderson & Emmylou Harris; *Cowboy's Sweetheart* . . . . (Laserlight)
Patsy Cline; *The Patsy Cline Story* . . . . (MCA)

We Loved It Away
George Jones & Tammy Wynette; *George Jones & Tammy Wynette-16 Biggest Hits* . . . . (Epic/Legacy)

We Tell Ourselves
Clint Black; *The Hard Way* . . . . (RCA)

What If I Said
Anita Cochran & Steve Wariner; *Back To You* . . . . (Warner Bros.)
Steve Wariner & Anita Cochran; *Burnin' The Roadhouse Down* . . . (Capitol)

What Is This Thing Called Love
Alexander O'Neal; *All True Man* . . . . (Tabu)
Greatest Hits Of Alexander O'Neal . . . . (Epic)
Artie Shaw; *Begin The Beguine* . . . . (Bluebird)
Charlie Parker; *Cole Porter Songbook* . . . . (Verve)
Ella Fitzgerald; *Cole Porter Songbook* . . . . (Verve)
Frank Sinatra; *Frank Sinatra Sings The Select Cole Porter* . . . . (Capitol)
Julie London; *Julie London Sings Cole Porter* . . . . (EMI)
Kay Starr; *Back To The Roots* . . . . (Crescendo)
Mel Torme; *Night & Day-Cole Porter Songbook-C* . . . . (Verve)

What You Won't Do For Love
Bobby Caldwell; *Love Shouldn't Hurt-C* . . . . (Qwest)
Go West; *Chicken Soup For The Woman's Soul-C* . . . . (Rhino)

Whatever
En Vogue; *Bass In Your Face: Essential Drum And Bass-C* . . . . (Elektra)

What'll I Do
Nat ''King'' Cole; *The Vocal Classics-1947-1950* . . . . (Capitol)
Rosemary Clooney; *Rosemary Clooney Sings The Music Of Irving Berlin* . . . . (Concord Jazz)

What's Forever For
Michael Martin Murphey; *Best Of Michael Martin Murphey* . . . . (Liberty)
What's Forever For . . . . (EMI Special Markets)

What's Love Got To Do With It
Tina Turner; *Live In Europe* . . . . (Capitol)
Private Dancer . . . . (Capitol)
Simply The Best . . . . (Capitol)

When I Fall In Love
Celine Dion; *The Colour Of My Love* . . . . (550 Music)
Doris Day; *Doris Day-16 Most Requested Songs-Encore!* . . . . . (Columbia)

When It Hurts So Bad
Lauryn Hill; *The Miseducation Of Lauryn Hill* . . . . (Ruffhouse/Columbia)

When Will I Be Loved
Everly Brothers; *Everly Brothers' All-Time Greatest Hits* . . . . (Curb)
Fabulous Style Of The Everly Brothers . . . . (Rhino)
Oldies But Goodies-#11-C . . . . (Original Sound)
Linda Ronstadt; *Heart Like A Wheel* . . . . (Capitol)
Linda Ronstadt's Greatest Hits . . . . (Asylum)

Where Do We Go From Here
Vanessa Williams; *Vanessa Williams' Greatest Hits-The First Ten Years* . . . . (Mercury)

Where Have All The Cowboys Gone?
Paula Cole; *This Fire* . . . . (Imago)

Where You Get Love
Matthew Sweet; *Blue Sky On Mars* . . . . (Freeworld/Capitol)

Who Needs You Baby
Clay Walker; *Hypnotize The Moon* . . . . (Giant)

Who's Cheatin' Who
Alan Jackson; *Everything I Love* . . . . (Arista)

Why Do Fools Fall In Love
Beach Boys; *Spirit Of America* . . . . (Capitol)
Diamonds; *Best Of The Diamonds-The Mercury Years* . . . . (Mercury)
Diana Ross; *Why Do Fools Fall In Love* . . . . (RCA)
Frankie Lymon and The Teenagers; *Best Of Frankie Lymon and The Teenagers* . . . . (Rhino)
Billboard Top Rock 'N' Roll Hits-1956-C . . . . (Rhino)
ST/American Graffiti . . . . (MCA)
Joni Mitchell; *Shadows & Light* . . . . (Asylum)

Why Does Love Got To Be So Sad?
Derek And The Dominos; *Layla* . . . . (Polydor)

Why They Call It Falling
Lee Ann Womack; *I Hope You Dance* . . . . (MCA)

Why Was I Born
Billie Holiday; *Quintessential-#3-1936-1937* . . . . (Columbia)
Elisabeth Welch; *Elisabeth Welch Sings Jerome Kern* . . . . (RCA)
Frank Sinatra; *Voice: The Columbia Years-1943-1952* . . . . . (Columbia)
Lena Horne; *20 Golden Pieces Of Lena Horne* . . . . (Bulldog)
The Lady . . . . (Dunhill Compact Classics)

Wicked Game
Chris Isaak; *Heart Shaped World* . . . . (Reprise)
ST/Wild At Heart . . . . (Polydor)

Woman To Woman
Tammy Wynette; *Tammy Wynette-Anniversary-20 Years Of Hits* . . . . . . (Epic)
Tammy Wynette's Greatest Hits-#3 . . . . (Epic)
Tears Of Fire-25th Anniversary Collection . . . . (Epic)
Wynonna; *Tammy Wynette...Remembered-C* . . . . (Asylum)

Wrong Again
Martina McBride; *Big Country Hits '99-C* . . . . (K-Tel)
Country Cares For Kids II-C . . . . (BNA)
Evolution . . . . (RCA)

Wrong Number
Cure; *Galore-The Singles-1987-1997* . . . . (Fiction/Elektra)

You Always Hurt The One You Love
Brenda Lee; *The Brenda Lee Story-Her Greatest Hits* . . . . (MCA)
Clarence Henry; *Rich Roots* . . . . (Allegiance)
Mills Brothers; *Best Of The Mills Brothers* . . . . (MCA)
Mills Brothers' Greatest Hits . . . . (MCA)
Mills Brothers-16 Great Performances . . . . (MCA)
Spike Jones & His City Slickers; *Best Of Spike Jones & His City Slickers* . . . . (RCA)

You Better Think Twice
Vince Gill; *When Love Finds You* . . . . (MCA)

You Can Love Yourself
Keb' Mo'; *Just Like You* . . . . (Okeh)

You Can't Make A Heart Love Somebody
George Strait; *Latest Greatest Straitest Hits* . . . . (MCA)
Lead On . . . . (MCA)

You Got Me
Roots featuring Erykah Badu; *Things Fall Apart* . . . . (MCA)

You Have The Right To Remain Silent
Perfect Stranger; *From Nashville With Love-C* . . . . (Curb)

You're Easy On The Eyes
Terri Clark; *Big Country Hits '99-C* . . . . (K-Tel)
How I Feel . . . . (Mercury)

You're Gonna Make Me Lonesome When You Go
Bob Dylan; *Blood On The Tracks* . . . . (Columbia)

You're The One
Paul Simon; *You're The One* . . . . (Warner Bros.)

You've Really Got A Hold On Me
Beatles; *The Beatles-Anthology-#1* . . . . (Capitol)
Smokey Robinson & The Miracles; *Best Of Smokey Robinson & The Miracles-Anthology* . . . . (Motown)
Great Songs & Performances That Inspired The Motown 25th Anniversary Television Special-C . . . . (Motown)
Smokey Robinson-The Ultimate Collection . . . . (Motown)

LOVE: DEVOTION, Being Faithful, Commitment, Loyalty In Love, Our Love Will Last

See Also: **CHARACTER & INTEGRITY, ETERNITY, FAITH, FRIENDS, KISSING, LOVE (various), MARRIAGE, PROMISE, TRUTH**

''Star Is Born'' (Evergreen), Love Theme From ''A Star Is Born''
Barbra Streisand; *Barbra Streisand's Greatest Hits* . . . . (Columbia)
Barbra Streisand's Greatest Hits, Volume 2 . . . . (Columbia)
Diana, Princess Of Wales-Tribute-C . . . . (Columbia)
Memories . . . . (Columbia)
ST/A Star Is Born . . . . (Columbia)
Luther Vandross; *Songs* . . . . (Epic)
Paul Williams; *Paul Williams-Classics* . . . . (A&M)

#1 Crush
Garbage; *ST/William Shakespeare's Romeo & Juliet* . . . . (Capitol)
(Everything I Do) I Do It For You
Bryan Adams; *ST/Robin Hood: Prince Of Thieves* . . . .(Morgan Creek)
Waking Up The Neighbours . . . . (A&M)
(Just Like) Romeo & Juliet
Reflections; *'60s Dance Party-C* . . . . (Dominion Entert.)
Sensational '60s-#1-C . . . . (Dominion Entert.)
24/7
Kevon Edmonds; *24/7* . . . . (RCA)
After All These Years
Jim Brickman & Anne Cochran; *Visions Of Love* . . . . (Windham Hill)
Ain't Misbehavin'
Fats Waller; *20 Golden Pieces Of Fats Waller* . . . .(Bulldog)
Ain't Misbehavin' . . . . (RCA)
Fats Waller-Legendary Performer . . . . (RCA)
Fats Waller-Live-#2 . . . . (Giants Of Jazz)
Piano Solos-1929-1941 . . . . (RCA)
Hank Williams, Jr.; *Five-O* . . . . (WB/Curb)
Hank Williams, Jr.'s Greatest Hits III . . . . (Curb)
Ain't No Mountain High Enough
Diana Ross; *20/20-C* . . . . (Motown)
25 #1 Hits From 25 Years-C . . . . (Motown)
Diana Ross . . . . (Motown)
Diana Ross-The Ultimate Collection . . . . (Motown)
Every Great Motown Song-First 25 Years-C . . . . (Motown)
Greatest Songs By Ashford & Simpson . . . . (Motown)
Motown Legends-Diana Ross . . . . (Motown)
Motown Story-First 25 Years-C . . . . (Motown)
Motown's Biggest Pop Hits-C . . . . (Motown)
TV ST/Diana-C . . . . (Motown)
Marvin Gaye & Tammi Terrell; *20 Greatest Songs In Motown
History-C* . . . . (Motown)
Classic Duets-Marvin Gaye & His Women-C . . . . (Motown)
Marvin Gaye & Tammi Terrell's Greatest Hits . . . . (Motown)
Marvin Gaye Live At The London Palladium . . . . (Motown)
Motown Grammy R&B Performances Of The '60s & '70s-C . . . . . (Motown)
Performances Of The '60s & '70s-C . . . . (Motown)
United . . . . (Motown)
All Er Nothin'
Original Broadway Cast; *Oklahoma!* . . . . (RCA)
Original Cast; *Oklahoma!* . . . .(MCA)
All I Do Is Dream Of You
Debbie Reynolds/The MGM Studio Chorus; *ST/Singin' In
The Rain* . . . . (Turner Classic Movies)
Jan Garber & His Orchestra; *78-#24629* . . . . (Victor)
All I Have To Give
Backstreet Boys; *Backstreet Boys* . . . . (Jive)
Now That's What I Call Music!-#3-C . . . . (Virgin)
All I Have To Offer You Is Me
Aaron Tippin; *Essential Aaron Tippin* . . . . (RCA)
Charley Pride; *Charley Pride-Super Hits* . . . . (RCA)
Essential Charley Pride . . . . (RCA)
Ricky Van Shelton; *Fried Green Tomatoes* . . . . (Audium)
All I Need
Xscape; *Traces Of My Lipstick* . . . . (So So Def/Columbia)
All My Life
K-Ci & JoJo; *Love Always* . . . .(MCA)
Now That's What I Call Music!-#1-C . . . . (Virgin)
All My Love
Patti Page; *Patti Page Collection-The Mercury Years-#1* . . . . (Mercury)
All My Loving
Beatles; *Meet The Beatles!* . . . . (Capitol)
The Beatles At The Hollywood Bowl . . . . (Capitol)
The Beatles/1962-1966 . . . . (Capitol)
With The Beatles . . . . (Parlophone)
All The Way
Celine Dion; *All The Way...A Decade Of Song* . . . . (550 Music)
Almost Grown
Chuck Berry; *Berry Is On Top* . . . . (Chess)
Cruisin'-1959-C . . . .(Increase)
Roll Over Beethoven . . . . (Allegiance)
ST/American Graffiti . . . . (MCA)
The Chess Box-Chuck Berry . . . . (Chess)
Almost Persuaded
David Houston; *Super Hits Of The '60s-C* . . . .(Epic)
Alone Together
Judy Garland; *Judy Garland-At Carnegie Hall* . . . . (Capitol)
Always
Bon Jovi; *Cross Road-14 Classic Grooves* . . . . (Mercury)
Always
Frank Sinatra; *I've Got A Crush On You* . . . . (Legacy)
Willie Nelson; *One For The Road* . . . . (Columbia)
Always And Forever
Heatwave; *Heatwave's Greatest Hits* . . . .(Epic)
Too Hot To Handle . . . .(Epic)
Luther Vandross; *Songs* . . . .(Epic)
Whistle; *Always And Forever* . . . . (Select)

Always Be My Baby
Mariah Carey; *Daydream* . . . . (Columbia)
Always True To You In My Fashion
Blossom Dearie; *Night & Day-Cole Porter Songbook-C* . . . . (Verve)
Original Cast; *Kiss Me Kate* . . . .(EMI-Angel)
Peggy Lee & George Shearing; *Anything Goes-Capitol Sings Cole
Porter-C* . . . . (Capitol)
Amazed
Lonestar; *Lonely Grill* . . . .(BNA)
Totally Hits-#2-C . . . . (Elektra)
Amen Kind Of Love
Daryle Singletary; *All Because Of You* . . . .(Giant)
Wedding Day Music-C . . . . (Reprise)
Anema E Core
Eddie Fisher; *Very Best Of Eddie Fisher* . . . . (Taragon)
Angel
Shaggy; *Hotshot* . . . . (MCA)
Angels
Earl Scruggs & Melissa Etheridge; *Earl Scruggs And Friends-C* . . . . . (MCA)
Anniversary Song
Al Jolson; *Al Jolson-Best Of The Decca Years* . . . . (MCA)
Cocktail Hour . . . . (Columbia River Entert. Group)
Dinah Shore; *Buttons & Bows* . . . . (ASV)
Dinah Shore-16 Most Requested Songs-Encore! . . . . (Legacy)
Django Reinhardt; *Verve Jazz Masters 38* . . . . (Verve)
Eva Cassidy; *Time After Time* . . . . (Blix Street)
Guy Lombardo & His Royal Canadians; *Enjoy Yourself, The Hits Of Guy
Lombardo* . . . . (MCA)
Another You, Another Me
Brady Seals; *The Truth* . . . . (Reprise)
Wedding Day Music-C . . . . (Reprise)
Anything
Third Eye Blind; *Blue* . . . . (Elektra)
Anything
3T; *Brotherhood* . . . . (Columbia)
Anything And Everything
Martina McBride; *Emotion* . . . . (RCA)
Anything For You
Gloria Estefan; *Gloria Estefan's Greatest Hits* . . . . (Epic)
Gloria Estefan and Miami Sound Machine; *Billboard Top Hits-
1988-C* . . . . (Rhino)
Let It Loose . . . .(Epic)
Arms Of The One Who Loves You
Xscape; *Traces Of My Lipstick* . . . . (So So Def/Columbia)
As Long As He Needs Me
Original Broadway Cast; *Oliver!* . . . . (RCA Victor)
Original London Cast; *Oliver!* . . . .(EMI-Angel)
As Long As You Love Me
Backstreet Boys; *Backstreet Boys* . . . .(Jive)
Now That's What I Call Music!-#1-C . . . . (Virgin)
At The Beginning
Richard Marx & Donna Lewis; *ST/Anastasia-Music From The Motion
Picture* . . . .(Atlantic)
Atlantic City
Bruce Springsteen; *Bruce Springsteen's Greatest Hits* . . . . (Columbia)
Nebraska . . . . (Columbia)
Auf Wiedersehn-Sweetheart
Vera Lynn; *Those Wonderful Years: Tenderly-C* . . . .(JCI Assoc. Labels)
Austin
Blake Shelton; *Blake Shelton* . . . .(Giant)
Baby It's You
Beatles; *Introducing...The Beatles* . . . . (Vee-Jay)
The Early Beatles . . . . (Capitol)
Baby Luv
Groove Theory; *Groove Theory* . . . . (Epic)
Baby, I'm For Real
Originals; *Hitsville USA-The Motown Singles Collection-1959-
1971-C* . . . . (Motown)
Motown Love Songs-C . . . . (Motown)
Baby, I'm Yours
Barbara Lewis; *Hello Stranger-The Best Of Barbara Lewis* . . . . (Rhino)
Babylon
David Gray; *White Ladder* . . . . (ATO/RCA)
Back At One
Brian McKnight; *Back At One* . . . . (Motown)
Mark Wills; *Permanently* . . . . (Mercury)
Ballerina Girl
Lionel Richie; *Dancing On The Ceiling* . . . . (Motown)
Band Of Gold
Don Cherry; *Very Best Of Don Cherry* . . . . (Collector's Choice)
Bargain
Who; *Who's next* . . . . (MCA)
Be My Baby
Linda Ronstadt; *Dedicated To The One I Love* . . . . (Elektra)
Melissa Etheridge; *Concert For The Rock & Roll Hall Of Fame-C* . . . (Columbia)
Ronettes; *Best Of The Ronettes* . . . . (Abkco)
Phil Spector-Back To Mono 1958-1969-C . . . . (Abkco)
ST/Dirty Dancing . . . . (RCA)

Be My Life's Companion
Mills Brothers; *Best Of The Mills Brothers* . . . . (MCA)
The Mills Brothers-Best Of The Decca Years . . . . (Decca)
Rosemary Clooney; *Rosemary Clooney-16 Most Requested Songs* . . . . (Legacy)
Because You Loved Me
Celine Dion; *All The Way...A Decade Of Song* . . . . (550 Music)
Diana, Princess Of Wales-Tribute-C . . . . (Columbia)
Falling Into You . . . . (550 Music)
Before The Next Teardrop Falls
Freddy Fender; *Before The Next Teardrop Falls* . . . . (Universal)
Best Of Freddy Fender . . . . (MCA)
Oldies But Goodies-#2-C . . . . (Original Sound)
Super Hits Of The '70s-Have A Nice Day-#17-C . . . . (Rhino)
Ray Anthony; *Great Golden Hits* . . . . (Ranwood)
Believe Me If All Those Endearing Young Charms
Bronn Journey; *Celtic Journey* . . . . (Phileo)
Mitch Miller; *Favorite Irish Sing-Alongs* . . . . (Legacy)
Roger Whittaker; *Danny Boy & Other Irish Favorites* . . . . (RCA Victor)
Belle, Belle, My Liberty Belle
Guy Mitchell; *Definitive Guy Mitchell* . . . . (Collector's Choice)
Guy Mitchell-16 Most Requested Songs . . . . (Legacy)
Bernadette
Four Tops; *Compact Command Performances-Four Tops* . . . . (Motown)
Four Tops' Greatest Hits . . . . (Motown)
Four Tops Reach Out . . . . (Motown)
Four Tops-Anthology . . . . (Motown)
Motown Superstar Series-#14-Four Tops . . . . (Motown)
Bess You Is My Woman Now
Miles Davis & His Orchestra; *Porgy & Bess* . . . . (Columbia)
Original Cast; *Porgy & Bess* . . . . (MCA)
Best Of Intentions
Travis Tritt; *Down The Road I Go* . . . . (Columbia)
Best Of My Love
Emotions; *Club Columbia-C* . . . . (Columbia)
Rejoice . . . . (Columbia)
ST/Queen's Logic . . . . (Epic)
Best Of My Love
Brooks & Dunn; *Common Thread-Songs Of The Eagles-C* . . . . (Giant)
Eagles; *Eagles/Their Greatest Hits 1971-1975* . . . . (Asylum)
On The Border . . . . (Elektra)
Betcha By Golly, Wow
"AFKAP"; *Emancipation* . . . . (NPG)
Johnny Mathis; *First Time Ever I Saw Your Face* . . . . (Columbia)
Stylistics; *Best Of The Stylistics* . . . . (Amherst)
Between Now And Forever
Bryan White; *Between Now And Forever* . . . . (Asylum)
Wedding Day Music-C . . . . (Reprise)
Blessed
Christina Aguilera; *Christina Aguilera* . . . . (RCA)
Bottles And Cans
Angie Stone; *Mahogany Soul* . . . . (J)
Boys Of Summer
Don Henley; *Building The Perfect Beast* . . . . (Geffen)
Buicks To The Moon
Alan Jackson; *Everything I Love* . . . . (Arista)
By Heart
Jim Brickman; *By Heart* . . . . (Windham Hill)
By Your Side
Sade; *Lovers Rock* . . . . (Epic)
Calendar Girl
Neil Sedaka; *Neil Sedaka Sings His Greatest Hits* . . . . (RCA)
Neil Sedaka-Greatest Hits Live . . . . (K-Tel)
Neil Sedaka's All-Time Greatest Hits . . . . (RCA)
Can I Count On You
McBride & The Ride; *Burnin' Up The Road* . . . . (MCA)
Can't Help Lovin' Dat Man
Lena Horne; *20 Golden Pieces Of Lena Horne* . . . . (Bulldog)
Jazz Master . . . . (DRG)
Jazzy Ladies-C . . . . (Dunhill Compact Classics)
Live On Broadway . . . . (Qwest)
Can't Stop My Heart From Loving You
Aaron Neville; *The Tattooed Heart* . . . . (A&M)
O'Kanes; *Greatest Country Hits Of The '80s-1987-C* . . . . (Columbia)
More Hot Country Requests-#2-C . . . . (Epic)
O'Kanes . . . . (Columbia)
Cara Mia
Jay & The Americans; *I Got Rhythm-C* . . . . (K-Tel)
Jay & The Americans' Greatest Hits . . . . (CEMA Special Prod.)
Jay & The Americans' Greatest Hits . . . . (Curb)
Carrying Your Love With Me
George Strait; *Carrying Your Love With Me* . . . . (MCA)
Latest Greatest Straitest Hits . . . . (MCA)
Ceremony, The
George Jones & Tammy Wynette; *George Jones & Tammy Wynette-16 Biggest Hits* . . . . (Epic/Legacy)
George Jones & Tammy Wynette's Greatest Hits . . . . (Epic)
Chapel Of Love
Dixie Cups; *Girl Groups-Story Of A Sound-C* . . . . (Rhino)
Jewels-#1-C . . . . (SSS International)
Oldies But Goodies-#11-C . . . . (Original Sound)
Original New York Rock & Roll-C . . . . (Original Sound)
Chasing Forever
Will Smith; *Big Willie Style* . . . . (Columbia)
Cheers 2 U
Playa; *Cheers 2 U* . . . . (Def Soul/Def Jam/RAL/Mercury)
Cherish
Kool & The Gang; *Celebration-1979-1987* . . . . (Mercury)
Emergency . . . . (Mercury)
Kool & The Gang's All-Time Greatest Hits . . . . (Curb)
Cherish
Association; *Association Greatest Hits* . . . . (Warner Bros.)
Billboard Top Pop Hits-1966-C . . . . (Rhino)
Come On Back
Keb' Mo'; *The Door* . . . . (550/Epic/Okeh)
Come Rain Or Come Shine
Ella Fitzgerald; *Harold Arlen Songbook-#2* . . . . (Verve)
Frank Sinatra; *Very Best Of Frank Sinatra* . . . . (Reprise)
Frank Sinatra & Gloria Estefan; *Frank Sinatra-Duets-C* . . . . (Capitol)
Judy Garland; *America's Treasure* . . . . (Dunhill Compact Classics)
Hits Of Judy Garland . . . . (Capitol)
Judy . . . . (Capitol)
Judy Garland-At Carnegie Hall . . . . (Capitol)
Michael Crawford; *With Love* . . . . (Atlantic)
Commitment
LeAnn Rimes; *Big Country Hits '99-C* . . . . (K-Tel)
Sittin' On Top Of The World . . . . (Curb)
Could It Be I'm Falling In Love
Spinners; *One Of A Kind Love Affair-Anthology* . . . . (Rhino)
Spinners . . . . (Rhino)
Very Best Of The Spinners . . . . (Rhino)
Count Me In
Gary Lewis And The Playboys; *Gary Lewis & The Playboys* . . . . . . (Gold Rush)
Gary Lewis And The Playboys' Greatest Hits . . . . (Curb)
Crazy Love
Brian McKnight; *Anytime* . . . . (Motown)
I Remember You . . . . (Mercury)
ST/Jason's Lyric . . . . (Mercury)
Van Morrison; *Moondance* . . . . (Warner Bros.)
Crazy Things I Do
Sammie; *From The Bottom To The Top* . . . . (Freeworld/Capitol)
Cupid
Sam Cooke; *Best Of Sam Cooke* . . . . (RCA)
The Man And His Music . . . . (RCA)
Spinners; *Love Trippin'* . . . . (Atlantic)
Dedicated To The One I Love
Mamas & The Papas; *Best Of The Mamas & The Papas* . . . . (MCA)
Farewell To The First Golden Era . . . . (MCA)
Original Classic Oldies Of The '50s & '60s-#13-C . . . . (MCA)
Shirelles; *Oldies But Goodies-#10-C* . . . . (Original Sound)
Shirelles' Greatest Hits . . . . (Everest)
Shirelles-Anthology 1959-1964 . . . . (Rhino)
Super Oldies Of The '50s-#4-C . . . . (Audio Fidelity)
Deeper Than The Holler
Randy Travis; *Randy Travis' Greatest #1 Hits* . . . . (Warner Bros.)
Randy Travis' Greatest Hits-#1 . . . . (Warner Bros.)
Devoted To You
Carly Simon; *Boys In The Trees* . . . . (Elektra)
Everly Brothers; *All-Time Original Hits* . . . . (Rhino)
Everly Brothers' Greatest Hits . . . . (Delta)
Very Best Of The Everly Brothers . . . . (Warner Bros.)
Wake Up, Little Suzie . . . . (Delta)
Linda Ronstadt; *Dedicated To The One I Love* . . . . (Elektra)
Devotion
Earth, Wind & Fire; *Best Of Earth, Wind & Fire-#2* . . . . (Columbia)
Elements Of Love: The Ballads . . . . (Legacy)
Gratitude . . . . (Legacy)
Open Our Eyes . . . . (Columbia)
Do You Love Me?
Original Cast; *Fiddler On The Roof* . . . . (RCA Victor)
Doesn't Really Matter
Janet Jackson; *Now That's What I Call Music!-#5-C* . . . . (Virgin)
ST/Nutty Professor 2: The Klumps . . . . (Def Soul/IDJMG)
Don't Be Cruel
Cheap Trick; *Cheap Trick's Greatest Hits* . . . . (Epic)
Lap Of Luxury . . . . (Epic)
Elvis Presley; *Billboard Top Rock 'N' Roll Hits-1956-C* . . . . (Rhino)
Nipper's Greatest Hits Of The '50s-#2-C . . . . (RCA)
Number One Hits . . . . (RCA)
The Great Performances . . . . (RCA)
The Top Ten Hits . . . . (RCA)
Judds; *Heartland* . . . . (MCA)
Don't Go Breaking My Heart
Elton John & Kiki Dee; *Elton John's Greatest Hits-#2* . . . . (Polydor)
Don't Let Me Leave
Marc Anthony; *Marc Anthony* . . . . (Columbia)
Don't Let The Stars Get In Your Eyes
Perry Como; *Como's Golden Records* . . . . (RCA)
Perry Como-Pure Gold . . . . (RCA)

Perry Como's All-Time Greatest Hits-#1 . . . . (RCA)
This Is Perry Como . . . . (RCA)
Don't Tell Me
Madonna; *GHV2* . . . . (Warner Bros.)
Music . . . .(Maverick)
Don't You Know What The Night Can Do?
Steve Winwood; *Roll With It* . . . . (Virgin)
Down On My Knees
Beth Nielsen Chapman; *Beth Nielsen Chapman* . . . . (Reprise)
Trisha Yearwood; *Hearts In Armor* . . . .(MCA)
Drink, Swear, Steal & Lie
Michael Peterson; *Michael Peterson* . . . . (Reprise)
Drive All Night
Bruce Springsteen; *The River* . . . . (Columbia)
Endless Love
Diana Ross & Lionel Richie; *25 Years Of Grammy Greats-C* . . . . . . (Motown)
All The Great Motown Love Song Duets-C . . . . (Motown)
Motown Story-First 25 Years-C . . . . (Motown)
ST/Endless Love . . . . (Mercury)
Luther Vandross & Mariah Carey; *Songs* . . . .(Epic)
Enough Of Me
Melissa Etheridge; *Breakdown* . . . . (Island)
Ever True Evermore
Mandy Barnett; *I've Got A Right To Cry* . . . . (Sire)
Everlasting Love
Carl Carlton; *Classic R&B Oldies Of The '70s-#2-C* . . . . .(MCA Special Prod.)
Gloria Estefan; *Hold Me, Thrill Me, Kiss Me* . . . .(Epic)
Robert Knight; *Everlasting Love* . . . . (Collectables)
Every Day Of My Life
McGuire Sisters; *McGuire Sisters' Greatest Hits* . . . .(MCA)
McGuire Sisters-Anthology . . . .(MCA)
Every Heartbeat
Amy Grant; *Heart In Motion* . . . . (A&M)
Every Morning
Keb' Mo'; *Keb' Mo'* . . . .(Okeh)
Every River
Kim Richey; *Bitter Sweet* . . . . (Mercury)
Every Woman In The World
Air Supply; *Air Supply's Greatest Hits* . . . .(Arista)
Air Supply-The Definitive Collection . . . . (Arista)
Lost In Love . . . . (Arista)
Everything
Mary J. Blige; *Share My World* . . . .(MCA)
Ev'ry Day Of My Life
McGuire Sisters; *McGuire Sisters-Anthology* . . . .(MCA)
Faith In You
Steve Wariner; *Faith In You* . . . . (Capitol)
Feels Like Love
Vince Gill; *Let's Make Sure We Kiss Goodbye* . . . .(MCA)
For You
Kenny Lattimore; *Kenny Lattimore* . . . . (Columbia)
Modern Bride Presents The Wedding Album-C . . . . (Columbia)
Songs From The Heart-C . . . . (Columbia)
For You I Will
Monica; *The Boy Is Mine* . . . . (Arista)
For Your Love
Yardbirds; *Best Of The Yardbirds* . . . . (Rhino)
Dick Clark's 21 All-Time Hits-#3-C . . . . (Original Sound)
History Of British Rock-#1-C . . . . (Rhino)
Yardbirds' Greatest Hits-#1 (1964-1966) . . . . (Rhino)
For Your Love
Stevie Wonder; *Conversation Peace* . . . . (Motown)
Natural Wonder . . . . (Motown)
Song Review-A Greatest Hits Collection . . . . (Motown)
For Your Love
Tevin Campbell; *Tevin Campbell* . . . . (Qwest)
Forever
Mariah Carey; *Daydream* . . . . (Columbia)
Forever And Ever, Amen
Randy Travis; *Always & Forever* . . . .(Warner Bros.)
Forever Love
Reba McEntire; *If You See Him* . . . .(MCA)
Reba McEntire's Greatest Hits-#3: I'm A Survivor . . . . (MCA)
Forever More
Puff Johnson; *Miracle* . . . .(Work)
Forever More (I'll Be The One)
James Ingram; *Forever More (Love Songs, Hits & Duets)* . . . . . . (Private Music)
John Tesh featuring James Ingram; *One World* . . . . (GTS)
Forever's As Far As I'll Go
Alabama; *Alabama's Greatest Hits-#3* . . . . (RCA)
Alabama-Super Hits . . . . (RCA)
For The Record: 41 Number One Hits . . . . (RCA)
Pass It On Down . . . .(BMG Special Prod.)
From Here To Eternity
Michael Peterson; *Michael Peterson* . . . . (Reprise)
Wedding Day Music-C . . . . (Reprise)
From Me To You
Beatles; *Beatles 1* . . . . (Capitol)

Past Masters-Volume One . . . .(Parlophone)
The Beatles/1962-1966 . . . . (Capitol)
The Beatles-Anthology-#1 . . . . (Capitol)
From This Moment On
Shania Twain & Bryan White; *Come On Over* . . . . (Mercury)
Give Me Forever (I Do)
John Tesh featuring James Ingram; *Grand Passion-C* . . . . (GTS)
Giving You The Best That I Got
Anita Baker; *Giving You The Best That I Got* . . . . (Elektra)
God Only Knows
Beach Boys; *Beach Boys' Greatest Hits* . . . . (Reprise)
Best Of The Beach Boys-Good Vibrations . . . . (Reprise)
Made In The U.S.A. . . . . (Capitol)
Pet Sounds . . . . (Capitol)
Stack 'O' Tracks . . . . (Capitol)
The Pet Sounds Sessions: A 30th Anniversary Collection . . . . (Capitol)
Golden Heart
Mark Knopfler; *Golden Heart* . . . . (Warner Bros.)
Got To Be There
Michael Jackson; *Best Of Michael Jackson* . . . . (Motown)
Michael Jackson-Anthology . . . . (Motown)
Gotta Be
Jagged Edge; *A Jagged Era* . . . . (So So Def/Columbia)
Gotta Man
Eve; *First Lady Of Ruff Ryders* . . . .(Ruff Ryders/IDJMG)
Ground Beneath Her Feet, The
U2; *ST/The Million Dollar Hotel* . . . .(Interscope)
Grow Old With Me
John Lennon; *The John Lennon Anthology* . . . . (Capitol)
Wonsaponatime . . . . (Capitol)
Mary Chapin Carpenter; *Party Doll And Other Favorites* . . . . (Columbia)
Hand Song, The
Nickel Creek; *Nickel Creek* . . . .(Sugar Hill)
Happily Ever After
Case; *Now That's What I Call Music!-#3-C* . . . . (Virgin)
Personal Conversation . . . .(Def Jam/IDJMG)
Happy Together
Flo & Eddie And The Turtles; *History Of Flo & Eddie And The Turtles* . . . . (Rhino)
Turtles; *Billboard Top Rock 'N' Roll Hits-1967-C* . . . . (Rhino)
Cruisin'-1967-C . . . . (Increase)
Happy Together . . . . (Rhino)
Turtles-20 Greatest Hits . . . . (Rhino)
Turtlesized . . . . (Rhino)
Hardest Thing
98 Degrees; *98 Degrees And Rising* . . . . (Universal)
Now That's What I Call Music!-#3-C . . . .(Virgin)
Have You Ever Really Loved A Woman?
Bryan Adams; *18 Til I Die* . . . .(A&M)
Number One Movie Hits-C . . . . (ESX Entert.)
ST/Don Juan De Marco . . . . (A&M)
He Loves U Not
Dream; *It Was All A Dream* . . . .(Bad Boy/Arista)
He Stopped Loving Her Today
George Jones; *All Time Legends Of Country Music-C* . . . . (Legacy)
First Time Live! . . . . (Epic)
George Jones-Anniversary-Ten Years Of Hits . . . . (Epic)
Greatest Country Hits Of The '80s-1980-C . . . . (Columbia)
Greatest Hits From The Jukebox-C . . . . (Epic)
I Am What I Am . . . . (Epic)
Heartbreaker
Bee Gees; *One Night Only* . . . .(Polydor)
Heaven
Nu Flavor; *110% Hits-C* . . . . (Simitar)
Nu Flavor . . . .(Reprise)
Her Man
Gary Allan; *Cryin' Lyin' Lovin' & Leavin'-C* . . . . (Universal)
Used Heart For Sale . . . .(Decca)
Waylon Jennings; *The Eagle* . . . . (Epic)
Here In My Heart
Chicago; *The Heart Of Chicago-1967-1997* . . . .(Reprise)
Hey Jealous Lover
Frank Sinatra; *Capitol Collectors Series-Frank Sinatra* . . . . (Capitol)
High Noon
Frankie Laine; *Billboard Top Movie Hits-1950-1954-C* . . . . (Rhino)
Tex Ritter; *Heroes Of Country Music-#4-Legends Of The West Coast-C* . . . . (Rhino)
The Envelope Please-Academy Award Winning Songs (1946-1957)-C . . . . (Rhino)
Hold On
Jamie Walters; *Jamie Walters* . . . .(Atlantic)
Holdin'
Diamond Rio; *Diamond Rio IV* . . . . (Arista)
Diamond Rio's Greatest Hits . . . . (Arista)
Hopelessly Devoted To You
Olivia Newton-John; *Grammy's Greatest Moments-#3-C* . . . .(Atlantic)
Olivia Newton-John's Greatest Hits-#2 . . . . (MCA)
ST/Grease . . . .(Polydor)

Hour Of Gold
Emmylou Harris; *Red Dirt Girl* . . . . (Nonesuch)
House At Pooh Corner
Loggins & Messina; *Loggins & Messina-On Stage* . . . . (Columbia)
  Sittin' In . . . . (Columbia)
  The Best Of Friends . . . . (Columbia)
Nitty Gritty Dirt Band; *Best Of The Nitty Gritty Dirt Band* . . . . (Liberty)
  Best Of The Nitty Gritty Dirt Band . . . . (Curb)
  Dirt, Silver & Gold . . . . (One Way)
  Uncle Charlie And His Dog Teddy . . . . (Liberty)
How Deep Is The Ocean? (How High Is The Sky?)
Diana Krall; *Love Scenes* . . . . (Impulse!)
Frank Sinatra; *Nice 'N' Easy* . . . . (Capitol)
Liza Minnelli; *Liza Minnelli-At Carnegie Hall* . . . . (Telarc)
How Did I Get By Without You
John Waite; *Complete John Waite-#1-Falling Backwards* . . . . (EMI)
  Temple Bar . . . . (Coyote/Imago)
How Do I Live
LeAnn Rimes; *Absolute Dance Hits-C* . . . . (Curb)
  You Light Up My Life-Inspirational Songs . . . . (Curb)
Trisha Yearwood; *Songbook-A Collection Of Hits* . . . . (MCA)
I Ain't Goin' Nowhere
Martina McBride; *Emotion* . . . . (RCA)
I Am Yours
Derek And The Dominos; *Layla* . . . . (Polydor)
I Believe In You And Me
Whitney Houston; *ST/The Preacher's Wife* . . . . (Arista)
I Believe In You And Me
Four Tops; *Smooth Grooves-Weddings Songs-C* . . . . (Rhino)
  When She Was My Girl . . . . (Casablanca)
I Belong To You
Toni Braxton; *Toni Braxton* . . . . (LaFace)
I Can't Help Myself (Sugar Pie Honey Bunch)
Four Tops; *16 #1 Hits From The Early '60s-C* . . . . (Motown)
  Billboard Top R&B Hits-1965-C . . . . (Rhino)
  Four Tops' Greatest Hits . . . . (Motown)
  Four Tops-Anthology . . . . (Motown)
  Good Feeling Music Of The Big Chill Generation-#1-C . . . . (Motown)
  Motown Story-First 25 Years-C . . . . (Motown)
  Motown Superstar Series-#14-Four Tops . . . . (Motown)
  ST/Forrest Gump . . . . (Epic/Sony Music Soundtrax)
  ST/Heaven Help Us . . . . (EMI)
  ST/Into The Night . . . . (MCA)
  ST/Where The Buffalo Roam . . . . (Backstreet)
I Cross My Heart
George Strait; *ST/Pure Country* . . . . (MCA)
I Do
Paul Brandt; *Calm Before The Storm* . . . . (Reprise)
I Do (Cherish You)
98 Degrees; *98 Degrees And Rising* . . . . (Universal)
Mark Wills; *Wish You Were Here* . . . . (Mercury)
I Don't Want To Miss A Thing
Aerosmith; *ST/Armageddon-The Album* . . . . (Columbia)
Mark Chesnutt; *I Don't Want To Miss A Thing* . . . . (MCA)
I Got A Woman
Ray Charles; *Ray Charles' Greatest Hits* . . . . (Rhino)
  Ray Charles-Anthology . . . . (Rhino)
I Have To Surrender
Ty Herndon; *Living In A Moment* . . . . (Epic)
I Live My Life For You
Firehouse; *3* . . . . (Epic)
  Good Acoustics . . . . (Epic)
I Love You Always Forever
Donna Lewis; *Now In A Minute* . . . . (Atlantic)
  The Absolute Hits-C . . . . (Atlantic)
I Never Loved A Man (The Way I Love You)
Aretha Franklin; *Aretha Franklin-30 Greatest Hits* . . . . (Rhino)
  Golden Age Of Black Music-1960-1970-C . . . . (Atlantic)
  ST/The Commitments . . . . (MCA)
I Only Know I Love You
Four Aces; *Four Aces-More Greatest Hits* . . . . (Varese Vintage)
I Only Want To Be With You
Bay City Rollers; *Bay City Rollers' Greatest Hits* . . . . (Arista)
Dusty Springfield; *Dusty Springfield-Anthology* . . . . (Mercury)
  Dusty Springfield-Golden Hits . . . . (Mercury)
Vonda Shepard; *ST/Songs From "Ally McBeal" Featuring Vonda*
  Shepard . . . . (550/Epic)
I Say A Little Prayer
Aretha Franklin; *Aretha Franklin's Greatest Hits* . . . . (Atlantic)
  Aretha's Gold . . . . (Atlantic)
  Best Of Aretha Franklin . . . . (Atlantic)
Burt Bacharach; *Burt Bacharach-Classics-#23* . . . . (A&M)
  Burt Bacharach's Greatest Hits . . . . (A&M)
  Reach Out . . . . (A&M)
Diana King; *ST/My Best Friend's Wedding* . . . . (Work/Epic)
Dionne Warwick; *Dionne Warwick* . . . . (Everest)
  Dionne Warwick Greatest Hits . . . . (Everest)
  Dionne Warwick-Anthology 1962-1971 . . . . (Rhino)
  Original Rock 'N' Roll Hits Of The '60s-C . . . . (Roulette)

I Second That Emotion
Smokey Robinson & The Miracles; *Smokey Robinson & The Miracles'*
  Anthology . . . . (Motown)
  Smokey Robinson-The Ultimate Collection . . . . (Motown)
Tammy Wynette & Smokey Robinson; *Without Walls-C* . . . . (Epic)
I Still Love You
Next; *Rated Next* . . . . (Divine Mill/Arista)
I Surrender Dear
Bing Crosby; *Pennies From Heaven* . . . . (Pro-Arte)
  Where The Blue Of The Night Meets The Gold Of The Day . . . . (Biograph)
Count Basie; *Basie & Zoot* . . . . (Pablo)
  Jam-#3 . . . . (Pablo)
  Loose Walk . . . . (Pablo)
Count Basie & His Kansas City 3; *For The Second Time* . . . . (Pablo)
Gus Arnheim & His Orchestra featuring Bing Crosby; *78-#22618* . . . . . (Victor)
Mel Torme; *Smooth As Velvet* . . . . (Pickwick)
Rosemary Clooney; *Rosemary Clooney Sings Bing* . . . . (Concord Jazz)
I Swear
All-4-One; *All-4-One* . . . . (Blitzz)
John Michael Montgomery; *John Michael Montgomery's*
  Greatest Hits . . . . (Atlantic)
  Kickin' It Up . . . . (Atlantic)
I Used To Love Him
Lauryn Hill featuring Mary J. Blige; *The Miseducation Of*
  Lauryn Hill . . . . (Ruffhouse/Columbia)
I Walk The Line
Johnny Cash; *Johnny Cash At Folsom Prison & San Quentin* . . . . . . (Columbia)
  Johnny Cash-Legends . . . . (Dunhill Compact Classics)
  Johnny Cash-Original Golden Hits-#1 . . . . (Sun)
  Johnny Cash's Greatest Hits . . . . (Columbia)
  Johnny Cash-Sun Years . . . . (Rhino)
  Memphis Country-C . . . . (Sun)
  Show Time . . . . (Sun)
  Souvenirs Of Music City U.S.A.-C . . . . (Plantation)
  Sun Story-C . . . . (Rhino)
  Superbilly . . . . (Sun)
  The Man In Black-His Greatest Hits . . . . (Legacy)
I Want To Spend My Lifetime Loving You
Marc Anthony & Tina Arena; *ST/Mask Of Zorro* . . . . (Sony Music Classical)
I Was Made To Love Her
Stevie Wonder; *16 #1 Hits From The Late '60s-C* . . . . (Motown)
  Stevie Wonder's Greatest Hits . . . . (Motown)
I Wasn't With It
Jesse Powell; *'Bout It* . . . . (Silas)
I Will
Beatles; *The Beatles (White Album)* . . . . (Capitol)
  The Beatles-Anthology-#3 . . . . (Capitol)
Ben Taylor; *ST/Bye Bye, Love* . . . . (Giant)
Dean Martin; *Dean Martin's Greatest Hits* . . . . (EMI)
I Will Follow Him
Little Peggy March; *Nipper's Greatest Hits Of The '60s-#1-C* . . . . . . (RCA)
I Will, If You Will
John Berry; *Faces* . . . . (Capitol)
I Will...But
SHeDAISY; *The Whole Shebang* . . . . (Lyric Street)
I'd Do Anything For Love
Meat Loaf; *Bat Out Of Hell II: Back Into Hell* . . . . (MCA)
I'd Follow You Anywhere
Derailers; *Here Come The Derailers* . . . . (Lucky Dog)
I'd Lie For You (And That's The Truth)
Meat Loaf; *Welcome To The Neighborhood* . . . . (MCA)
If
Bread; *Best Of Bread* . . . . (Elektra)
  Bread-Anthology . . . . (Elektra)
  Bread-Retrospective . . . . (Rhino)
  Manna . . . . (Rhino)
If
Perry Como; *Perry Como's All-Time Greatest Hits-#1* . . . . (RCA)
If I Could
Barbra Streisand; *Higher Ground* . . . . (Columbia)
If I Could Build My Whole World Around You
Marvin Gaye & Tammi Terrell; *Every Great Motown Hit Of*
  Marvin Gaye . . . . (Motown)
  Marvin Gaye & Tammi Terrell's Greatest Hits . . . . (Motown)
  Marvin Gaye-Anthology . . . . (Motown)
  Motown Superstar Series-#2-Marvin Gaye . . . . (Motown)
  United . . . . (Motown)
If I Could Turn Back The Hands Of Time
R. Kelly; *Now That's What I Call Music!-#3-C* . . . . (Virgin)
  R. . . . . (Jive)
If I Never Stop Loving You
David Kersh; *If I Never Stop Loving You* . . . . (Curb)
If I Should Fall Behind
Bruce Springsteen; *In Concert/MTV Plugged* . . . . (Columbia)
  Lucky Town . . . . (Columbia)
Faith Hill; *Breathe* . . . . (Warner Bros.)
Linda Ronstadt; *We Ran* . . . . (Elektra)
If My Heart Had Wings
Faith Hill; *Breathe* . . . . (Warner Bros.)

If Tomorrow Never Comes
Garth Brooks; *Garth Brooks* . . . . (Liberty)
  Limited Series-Box . . . . (Capitol)
Joose; *Joose* . . . . (Flavor Unit)

If You Can Do Anything Else
George Strait; *George Strait* . . . . (MCA)

If You Can't Feel It (It Ain't There)
Freddie Hart; *Best Of Freddie Hart* . . . . (CEMA Special Prod.)

If You Ever Have Forever In Mind
Vince Gill; *The Key* . . . . (MCA)

If You Had My Love
Jennifer Lopez; *On The 6* . . . . (Work)

If You Love Me Really Love Me
Kay Starr; *Kay Starr's Greatest Hits* . . . . (Curb)

If You Loved Me
Tracy Lawrence; *Time Marches On* . . . . (Atlantic)

If You Want Me To Stay
Red Hot Chili Peppers; *Freaky Styley* . . . . (EMI)
  Out In L.A. . . . . (EMI)
  What Hits!? . . . . (EMI)
Sly & The Family Stone; *Fresh* . . . . (Legacy)
  Sly & The Family Stone-Anthology . . . . (Epic)

I'll Always Be Right There
Bryan Adams; *18 Til I Die* . . . . (A&M)
  MTV Unplugged-Bryan Adams . . . . (A&M)

I'll Be
Edwin McCain; *Misguided Roses* . . . . (Lava)

I'll Be There
Jackson 5; *Compact Command Performances-Jackson 5* . . . . (Motown)
  Jackson 5-Anthology . . . . (Motown)
  Jackson 5's Greatest Hits . . . . (Motown)
  Motown Superstar Series-#12-Jackson 5 . . . . (Motown)
  Motown's Biggest Pop Hits-C . . . . (Motown)
Mariah Carey; *MTV Unplugged-Mariah Carey* . . . . (Columbia)

I'll Be There For You
Bon Jovi; *New Jersey* . . . . (Jambco)

I'll Go On Loving You
Alan Jackson; *High Mileage* . . . . (Arista)

I'll Still Be Loving You
Restless Heart; *Wheels* . . . . (RCA)

I'll Still Love You More
Trisha Yearwood; *Where Your Road Leads* . . . . (MCA)

I'll Take Care Of You
Dixie Chicks; *Wide Open Spaces* . . . . (Monument)

I'll Try
Alan Jackson; *Alan Jackson-The Greatest Hits Collection* . . . . (Arista)

I'll Walk Alone
Dinah Shore; *Dinah Shore's Greatest Hits* . . . . (Curtom)

I'm A One- Woman Man
George Jones; *Essential George Jones-The Spirit Of Country* . . . (Legacy)
  George Jones-Super Hits . . . . (Epic)
  One Woman Man . . . . (Epic)
  Who's Gonna Fill Their Shoes . . . . (Epic)
Glen Campbell; *Still Within The Sound Of My Voice* . . . . (MCA)
Johnny Horton; *American Originals-Johnny Horton* . . . . (Columbia)
  Honky Tonk Man-The Essential Johnny Horton-1956-1960 . . . . . . (Legacy)

I'm Gonna Make You Love Me
Jayhawks; *Smile* . . . . (American/Columbia)

I'm Holdin' On To Love (To Save My Life)
Shania Twain; *Come On Over* . . . . (Mercury)

I'm Still In Love With You
New Edition; *D.J. Mix '98-#1-C* . . . . (Beast)
  Home Again . . . . (MCA)

I'm Walking Behind You
Eddie Fisher; *Very Best Of Eddie Fisher* . . . . (MCA)
Frank Sinatra; *Capitol Collectors Series-Frank Sinatra* . . . . . . (Capitol)
  Concepts . . . . (Capitol)
  Point Of No Return . . . . (Capitol)

Imagine That
Diamond Rio; *Diamond Rio's Greatest Hits* . . . . (Arista)

Immortality
Celine Dion with The Bee Gees; *Let's Talk About Love-C* . . . . . (550 Music)

In Another's Eyes
Trisha Yearwood & Garth Brooks; *Songbook-A Collection Of Hits* . . . . . (MCA)

In Harm's Way
Bebe Winans; *Bebe Winans* . . . . (Atlantic)

In My Life
Beatles; *Beatles-Love Songs* . . . . (Capitol)
  Rubber Soul . . . . (Capitol)
  ST/Imagine: John Lennon . . . . (Capitol)
  The Beatles/1962-1966 . . . . (Capitol)
Crosby, Stills & Nash; *After The Storm* . . . . (Atlantic)
Judy Collins; *Colors Of The Day-The Best Of Judy Collins* . . . (Elektra)
  In My Life . . . . (Elektra)

In The Chapel In The Moonlight
Kitty Kallen; *Those Wonderful Years: Music! Music!*
  Music!-C . . . . (JCI Assoc. Labels)
Patti Page; *Patti Page-16 Most Requested Songs* . . . . (Legacy)

Shep Fields & His Rippling Rhythm Orchestra; *78-#6640* . . . . (Bluebird)

Inside Of Me
Little Steven & The Disciples Of Soul; *The Sopranos-Music From The HBO*
  Original Series . . . . (Sony Music Soundtrax)

Islands In The Stream
Kenny Rogers & Dolly Parton; *Eyes That See In The Dark* . . . . (RCA)
  Kenny Rogers' Greatest Hits . . . . (RCA)

It All Depends On Linda
Johnny Burnette; *Best Of Johnny Burnette-You're Sixteen* . . . . . (Gold Rush)

It Won't Be Long
Beatles; *Meet The Beatles!* . . . . (Capitol)
  With The Beatles . . . . (Parlophone)

It'll Be Me
Exile; *Back To Back: Exile* . . . . (K-Tel)
  Billboard Top Country Hits-1986-C . . . . (Rhino)
  Exile-Super Hits . . . . (Epic)

It's A Woman's World
Four Aces; *Best Of The Four Aces* . . . . (MCA)

It's All About You
Luther Vandross; *One Night With You-The Best Of Love-#2* . . . (LV/Epic)

It's In Your Eyes (Any Time At All)
Phil Collins; *Dance Into The Light* . . . . (Atlantic)

It's What I Do
Billy Dean; *It's What I Do* . . . . (Capitol)
  Luv Collection-Real Luv . . . . (EMI)

It's Your Love
Tim McGraw with Faith Hill; *Everywhere* . . . . (Curb)
  Tim McGraw's Greatest Hits . . . . (Curb)

J'ai Fait Tout
Emmylou Harris; *Red Dirt Girl* . . . . (Nonesuch)

Jimmy Mack
Martha & The Vandellas; *Billboard Top R&B Hits-1967-C* . . . . . (Rhino)
  Compact Command Performances-Martha Reeves & The
  Vandellas . . . . (Motown)
  Martha Reeves & The Vandellas-Anthology . . . . (Motown)
  Motown Story-First 25 Years-C . . . . (Motown)
  Motown Superstar Series-#11-Martha Reeves & The Vandellas . . . (Motown)
  Top 10 With A Bullet-Motown Girl Groups-C . . . . (Motown)

Just In Case
Jaheim; *Ghetto Love* . . . . (Divine Mill/Warner Bros.)

Just To Hear You Say That You Love Me
Faith Hill & Tim McGraw; *Faith* . . . . (Warner Bros.)

Keep On Loving You
REO Speedwagon; *A Second Decade Of Rock And Roll 1981 To 1991* . . . (Epic)
  Hi Infidelity . . . . (Epic)
  REO Speedwagon-The Hits . . . . (Epic)

Keeper Of The Flame
Martin Page; *In The House Of Stone And Light* . . . . (Mercury)

Lady
Kenny Rogers; *Kenny Rogers' Greatest Hits* . . . . (EMI)
  Kenny Rogers-20 Great Years . . . . (Reprise)
  Kenny Rogers-Love Songs . . . . (Capitol)
  Kenny Rogers-Twenty Greatest Hits . . . . (EMI)
Lionel Richie; *Time* . . . . (Mercury)
Roger Williams; *Roger Williams' Greatest Hits* . . . . (Curb)

Lara's Theme
Maurice Jarre Orchestra; *Hollywood's Great*
  Composers-C . . . . (Columbia Special Prod.)
MGM Studio Orchestra; *ST/Dr. Zhivago* . . . . (MCA)

Last Night's Letter
K-Ci & JoJo; *Love Always* . . . . (MCA)

Leaving Town
Dexter Freebish; *Life Of Saturdays* . . . . (Capitol)

Let's Build A World Together
George Jones & Tammy Wynette; *George Jones & Tammy Wynette-16*
  Biggest Hits . . . . (Epic/Legacy)

Let's Hang On!
4 Seasons; *Four Seasons' Greatest Hits-#2* . . . . (Rhino)

Let's Stay Together
Al Green; *Al Green's Greatest Hits* . . . . (Right Stuff)
  Let's Stay Together . . . . (Right Stuff)
  Tokyo...Live . . . . (Right Stuff)

Let's Stay Together
Eric Benet; *True To Myself* . . . . (Jac-Mac/Warner Bros.)

Lida Rose/Will I Ever Tell You?
Original Broadway Cast; *The Music Man* . . . . (Angel)
Original Cast; *The Music Man* . . . . (Gold Rush)
Soundtrack; *ST/The Music Man* . . . . (Warner Bros.)

Lighthouse's Tale
Nickel Creek; *Nickel Creek* . . . . (Sugar Hill)

Little Green Apples
O.C. Smith; *Pop Classics Of The '60s-C* . . . . (Columbia)

Little Things Mean A Lot
Kitty Kallen; *Hard To Find 45s On CD-#3-The Mid '50s-C* . . . . (Eric)
McGuire Sisters; *Best Of The McGuire Sisters* . . . . (MCA)

Livin' On A Prayer
Bon Jovi; *America: A Tribute To Heroes-C* . . . . (Interscope)
  Cross Road-14 Classic Grooves . . . . (Mercury)

Slippery When Wet . . . .(Jambco)
The Concert For New York City-C . . . . (Columbia)

Living In A Moment
Ty Herndon; *Living In A Moment* . . . . (Epic)
Super Hits Of 1996-C . . . . (Epic)

Long As I Live
John Michael Montgomery; *John Michael Montgomery* . . . . (Atlantic)

Long Live Our Love
Shangri-Las; *Best Of The Shangri-Las* . . . . (Mercury)

Longer
Dan Fogelberg; *Dan Fogelberg/Greatest Hits* . . . . (Full Moon)
Phoenix . . . . (Full Moon)

Love (Can Make You Happy)
Mercy; *Super Oldies Of The '60s-#10-C* . . . . (Audio Fidelity)
WCBS FM 101 History Of Rock-'60s-#2-C . . . .(Collectables)

Love A Little Stronger
Diamond Rio; *'90s Hot Country-C* . . . . (K-Tel)
Diamond Rio's Greatest Hits . . . .(Arista)
Diamond Rio-Super Hits . . . .(Arista)
Hit Country '96-C . . . . (K-Tel)
Love A Little Stronger . . . .(Arista)

Love Can Move Mountains
Celine Dion; *All The Way...A Decade Of Song* . . . . (550 Music)
Celine Dion . . . . (Epic)

Love For All Seasons
Christina Aguilera; *Christina Aguilera* . . . .(RCA)

Love I Found In You
Jim Brickman; *My Romance: An Evening With Jim Brickman* . . (Windham Hill)

Love Is All
Marc Anthony; *Marc Anthony* . . . . (Columbia)

Love Is All Around
Troggs; *Best Of The Troggs* . . . . (Rhino)
History Of British Rock-#8-C . . . . (Rhino)

Love Me Tender
Elvis Presley; *Elvis* . . . .(RCA)
Elvis Aron Presley . . . .(RCA)
Elvis' Golden Records . . . .(RCA)
Elvis-A Legendary Performer, Volume 1 . . . .(RCA)
Worldwide 50 Gold Award Hits, Vol. 1, Parts 1 & 2 . . . .(RCA)

Love Of My Life
Sammy Kershaw; *Labor Of Love* . . . . (Mercury)

Love Will Be Waiting
Kevon Edmonds; *24/7* . . . .(RCA)

Love Will Keep Us Alive
Eagles; *Hell Freezes Over* . . . . (Geffen)

Love Will Keep Us Together
Captain & Tennille; *Billboard Top Hits-1975-C* . . . . (Rhino)
Captain & Tennille's Greatest Hits . . . . (A&M)

Love Your Way
Sophie B. Hawkins; *Songs From Dawson's Creek* . . . . .(Sony Music Soundtrax)

Love, Me
Collin Raye; *All I Can Be* . . . . (Epic)
Greatest Country Hits Of The '90s-1992-C . . . . (Columbia)

Made To Love Ya
Gerald Levert; *Gerald's World* . . . . (East West)

Man Ain't Supposed To Cry
Public Announcement; *Don't Hold Back* . . . .(RCA)

Maybe I'm Amazed
Paul McCartney; *McCartney* . . . . (Capitol)
Wings; *Wings Over America* . . . . (Capitol)

Midnight Train To Georgia
Gladys Knight & The Pips; *Billboard Top Rock 'N' Roll Hits-1973-C* . . (Rhino)
Gladys Knight & The Pips' Greatest Hits . . . .(Buddah)
Imagination . . . . (Right Stuff)
On & On . . . . (Fifty One West)
Radio Active Hits-C . . . . (Accord)
Train Trax-C . . . . (Sony Music Special Prod.)
Very Best Of Gladys Knight & The Pips . . . .(Buddah)

Miles To Go (Before I Sleep)
Celine Dion; *Let's Talk About Love-C* . . . . (550 Music)

More (Than)
Perry Como; *Perry Como's Greatest Hits* . . . .(RCA)

More Love
Kim Carnes; *Gypsy Honeymoon-The Best Of Kim Carnes* . . . . (Gold Rush)
Smokey Robinson & The Miracles; *Smokey Robinson & The Miracles'*
Anthology . . . .(Motown)
Smokey Robinson-The Ultimate Collection . . . . (Motown)

More Than That
Backstreet Boys; *Black & Blue* . . . .(Jive)
Now That's What I Call Music!-#8-C . . . .(Virgin)

More Than You'll Ever Know
Travis Tritt; *The Restless Kind* . . . . (Warner Bros.)

More Today Than Yesterday
Spiral Staircase; *CBS Classics-Pop Classics Of The '60s-C* . . . . . (Columbia)
Rock Artifacts-From The Vaults-#1-C . . . . (Columbia)
Super Hits Of The '70s-Have A Nice Day-#1-C . . . . (Rhino)

Mr. Too Damn Good
Gerald Levert; *G* . . . . (East West)

My Antonia
Emmylou Harris; *Red Dirt Girl* . . . .(Nonesuch)

My Baby Loves Me
Martina McBride; *The Way That I Am* . . . . (RCA)

My Baby You
Marc Anthony; *Marc Anthony* . . . .(Columbia)

My Cup Runneth Over
Ed Ames; *My Cup Runneth Over* . . . . (RCA)
Nipper's Greatest Hits Of The '60s-#2-C . . . . (RCA)
George Jones; *Homecoming In Heaven* . . . .(Razor & Tie)
Jim Nabors; *Jim Nabors-16 Most Requested Songs* . . . .(Legacy)
Original Broadway Cast; *I Do! I Do!* . . . . (RCA Victor)

My Everything
98 Degrees; *Revelation* . . . .(Universal)

My Favorite Girl
Dave Hollister; *Ghetto Hymns* . . . .(Def Squad/DreamWorks)

My First Love
Avant; *My Thoughts* . . . . (MCA)

My Girl
Mamas & The Papas; *Best Of The Mamas & The Papas* . . . . (MCA)
Otis Redding; *Best Of Otis Redding* . . . . (Atco)
Rolling Stones; *Flowers* . . . .(Abkco)
Temptations; *All The Million-Sellers* . . . .(Motown)
ST/Big Chill . . . .(Motown)
Temptations' Greatest Hits-#1 . . . .(Motown)
Temptations-25th Anniversary . . . .(Motown)
Temptations-Anthology-The Best Of The Temptations . . . . . .(Motown)

My Guy
Mary Wells; *Mary Wells' Greatest Hits* . . . . (Motown)
My Guy . . . .(Motown)
Oldies But Goodies-#11-C . . . . (Original Sound)

My Heart Cries For You
Charlie Rich; *Charlie Rich-20 Golden Hits* . . . . (Sun)
Time For Tears-C . . . . (Sun)
Dinah Shore; *Nipper's Greatest Hits Of The '50s-#1-C* . . . . (RCA)
Guy Mitchell; *Guy Mitchell-16 Most Requested Songs* . . . .(Legacy)

My Heart Will Go On (Love Theme from "Titanic")
Celine Dion; *All The Way...A Decade Of Song* . . . . (550 Music)
ST/Titanic . . . . (Sony Music Classical)
Celine Dion with The Bee Gees; *Let's Talk About Love-C* . . . . (550 Music)
Kenny G; *Kenny G's Greatest Hits* . . . .(Arista)

My Kind Of Woman, My Kind Of Man
Patty Loveless; *Patty Loveless-Classics* . . . . (Epic)
Vince Gill with Patty Loveless; *The Key* . . . . (MCA)

My Love
Little Texas; *Big Time* . . . . (Warner Bros.)

My Love
Petula Clark; *History Of British Rock-#7-C* . . . .(Rhino)
Petula Clark's Greatest Hits . . . .(Crescendo)

My Love And Devotion
Perry Como; *Long-Lost Hits* . . . .(Collector's Choice)

My Love Goes On And On
Chris Cagle; *Play It Loud* . . . .(Capitol)

My Love Is Your Love
Whitney Houston; *My Love Is Your Love* . . . .(Arista)
Totally Hits-#2-C . . . .(Elektra)

My Love Will Not Let You Down
Bruce Springsteen; *Tracks* . . . .(Columbia)

My Mammy
Al Jolson; *Best Of Al Jolson* . . . . (MCA)
Let Me Sing And I'm Happy . . . .(Turner Classic Movies)
The '20s-From Broadway To Hollywood-#3-C . . . . (Flapper)
Happenings; *Happenings-Golden Hits!* . . . . (B.T. Puppy)

My Man
Barbra Streisand; *Barbra Streisand's Greatest Hits* . . . .(Columbia)
Live Concert At The Forum . . . .(Columbia)
My Name Is Barbra . . . .(Columbia)
ST/Funny Girl . . . .(Columbia)
Billie Holiday; *Billie Holiday-Live* . . . .(Verve)
Essential Billie Holiday-Carnegie Hall Concert . . . . (Verve)
Diana Ross; *Evening With Diana Ross* . . . .(Motown)
ST/Lady Sings The Blues . . . . (Motown)
Ella Fitzgerald & Tommy Flanagan Trio; *Montreux '77-C* . . . . (Pablo)
Peggy Lee; *Peggy Lee's All-Time Greatest Hits* . . . . (Curb)
Sarah Vaughan; *Jazz 'Round Midnight-Sarah Vaughan* . . . . (Verve)

My Melancholy Baby
Barbra Streisand; *Third Album* . . . .(Columbia)
Bing Crosby; *Hits Of 1939-C* . . . .(Living Era)
Coleman Hawkins; *Genius Of Coleman Hawkins* . . . . (Verve)
Dorothy Loudon; *Saloon* . . . . (DRG)
Frank Sinatra; *Voice: The Columbia Years-1943-1952* . . . .(Columbia)
Gene Austin; *78-#21015* . . . . (Victor)
Jan Garber & His Orchestra; *Jan Garber & His Orchestra Play 22 Original*
Big Band Favorites . . . . (Hindsight)
Kate Smith; *Kate Smith-16 Most Requested Songs* . . . .(Columbia)
Leon Redbone; *Double Time* . . . . (Warner Bros.)
Marcels; *Best Of The Marcels* . . . .(Rhino)

My Truly, Truly Fair
Guy Mitchell; *Guy Mitchell-16 Most Requested Songs* . . . .(Legacy)

My Woman, My Woman, My Wife
Marty Robbins; *Lifetime Of Song-1951-1982* . . . . (Columbia)
Marty Robbins' All-Time Greatest Hits . . . . (Columbia)
Natural High
Merle Haggard & Janie Fricke; *For The Record: Merle Haggard-43
Legendary Hits* . . . . (BNA)
Near You
Francis Craig & His Orchestra; *Cigar Classics-#1-The Standards-C* . . . . (Hip-O)
George Jones & Tammy Wynette; *George Jones & Tammy Wynette-16
Biggest Hits* . . . . (Epic/Legacy)
Never Be Anyone Else But You
Ricky Nelson; *Best Of Ricky Nelson* . . . .(EMI)
Never Ending Song Of Love
Conway Twitty & Loretta Lynn; *Lead Me On* . . . .(MCA)
Delaney & Bonnie; *Best Of Delaney & Bonnie* . . . . (Rhino)
Super Hits Of The '70s-Have A Nice Day-#16-C . . . . (Rhino)
Never Gonna Let You Go
Faith Evans; *Keep The Faith* . . . . (Bad Boy/Arista)
Never Make A Promise
Dru Hill; *Dru Hill* . . . . (Island)
Never My Love
Association; *Association Greatest Hits* . . . .(Warner Bros.)
Songs That Made Them Famous . . . . (Pair)
There Is Still Love-Anniversary Songs-C . . . . (Scotti Bros.)
Never Say Die
Dixie Chicks; *Wide Open Spaces* . . . . (Monument)
No Guarantee
Chico DeBarge; *Long Time No See* . . . . (Kedar Entert./Universal)
MTV Jams-C . . . . (Kedar Entert./Universal)
ST/Hoodlum . . . . (Interscope)
No One
Marc Anthony; *Marc Anthony* . . . . (Columbia)
No Other Love
Perry Como; *Easy Listening* . . . . (Pair)
No Place That Far
Sara Evans; *No Place That Far* . . . . (RCA)
Nobody I Know
Peter And Gordon; *History Of British Rock-#1-C* . . . . (Rhino)
Not Fade Away
Buddy Holly/The Crickets; *Buddy Holly-20 Golden Greats* . . . .(MCA)
Buddy Holly's Greatest Hits . . . . (MCA)
From The Original Master Tapes-Buddy Holly . . . .(MCA)
Legend-From The Original Master Tapes . . . . (MCA)
The Buddy Holly Collection . . . . (MCA)
Grateful Dead; *Dick's Picks-#2* . . . . (Arista)
Dozin' At The Knick . . . . (Arista)
Rolling Stones; *Big Hits (High Tide & Green Grass)* . . . .(Abkco)
England's Newest Hit Makers/The Rolling Stones . . . . (Abkco)
got Live if you want it! . . . . (Abkco)
More Hot Rocks (big hits & fazed cookies) . . . . (Abkco)
Singles Collection-The London Years . . . . (Abkco)
Stripped . . . . (Virgin)
Not On Your Love
Jeff Carson; *From Nashville With Love-C* . . . . (Curb)
Jeff Carson . . . . (Curb)
Nothin' To Somethin'
Gerald Levert; *G* . . . . (East West)
Nothing Even Matters
Lauryn Hill featuring D'Angelo; *The Miseducation Of
Lauryn Hill* . . . . (Ruffhouse/Columbia)
Oh How Happy
Shades Of Blue; *Oldies But Goodies-#2-C* . . . . (Original Sound)
Oh Promise Me
Liberace; *Piano Magic* . . . .(Sony Music Special Prod.)
Tommy Dorsey; *Tommy Dorsey-1937-1938* . . . .(Classics)
Old Fashioned Love
Asleep At The Wheel featuring Suzy Bogguss; *Tribute To The Music Of Bob
Wills And The Texas Playboys-C* . . . . (Liberty)
Old Man And Me
Hootie & The Blowfish; *Fairweather Johnson* . . . .(Atlantic)
On My Word Of Honor
Platters; *Enchanted-The Best Of The Platters* . . . . (Rhino)
One Love In My Lifetime
Diana Ross; *Diana Ross* . . . . (Motown)
Diana Ross-Anthology . . . . (Motown)
One Woman Man
Dave Hollister; *Chicago '85 The Movie* . . . .(Def Squad/DreamWorks)
One, The
Backstreet Boys; *Millennium* . . . . (Jive)
Only Daddy That'll Walk The Line
Hank Williams, Jr.; *Family Tradition* . . . .(WB/Curb)
Kentucky HeadHunters; *Electric Barnyard* . . . . (Mercury)
Ricky Skaggs; *My Father's Son* . . . .(Epic)
Waylon Jennings; *Best Of Waylon Jennings* . . . . (RCA)
Waylon Jennings' Greatest Hits . . . . (RCA)
Waylon Jennings-Early Years . . . . (RCA)
Willie Nelson; *Willie & Family Live* . . . . (Columbia)
Only One For Me, The
Brian McKnight; *Anytime* . . . . (Motown)

Only You (And You Alone)
Platters; *Cruisin'-1955-C* . . . . (Increase)
Encore Of Golden Hits-Platters . . . . (Mercury)
Millennium Collection-20th Century Masters . . . . (Mercury)
Our Love Is Here To Stay
Elton John; *Glory Of Gershwin Featuring Larry Adler-C* . . . . (Mercury)
Tony Bennett; *Tony Bennett At Carnegie Hall* . . . . . (Sony Music Special Prod.)
Penny
Joe Stampley; *Best Of Joe Stampley* . . . .(Varese Sarabande)
Perfect Day
Collective Soul; *Blender* . . . .(Atlantic)
Please Love Me Forever
Bobby Vinton; *Bobby Vinton-16 Most Requested Songs* . . . . (Legacy)
Bobby Vinton's All-Time Greatest Hits . . . . (Epic)
Please Love Me Forever . . . . (Epic)
Poor Butterfly
Sarah Vaughan; *Compact Jazz-Sarah Vaughan* . . . . (Verve)
Live In Japan . . . . (Mainstream)
Sarah Vaughan-Golden Hits . . . . (Mercury)
Sonny Rollins; *Best Of Sonny Rollins-The Blue Note Years* . . . . (Blue Note)
Sonny Rollins-Vol. 2 . . . . (Blue Note)
Power Of Love
Celine Dion; *All The Way...A Decade Of Song* . . . .(550 Music)
The Colour Of My Love . . . .(550 Music)
Pride & Joy
Jon B.; *Cool Relax* . . . .(Yab Yum/550)
Promise
Jagged Edge; *J.E. Heartbreak* . . . . (So So Def/Columbia)
Promise Ain't Enough
Daryl Hall & John Oates; *Marigold Sky* . . . . (Push)
Modern Bride Presents The Wedding Album-C . . . . (Columbia)
Promise I Make
Dakota Moon; *Dakota Moon* . . . . (Elektra)
Prove It All Night
Bruce Springsteen; *Darkness On The Edge Of Town* . . . . (Columbia)
Put It On Me
Ja Rule featuring Li'l Mo And Vita; *Rule 3:36* . . .(Murder Inc./Def Jam/IDJMG)
Reach Out I'll Be There
Four Tops; *Compact Command Performances-Four Tops* . . . . (Motown)
Four Tops' Greatest Hits . . . . (Motown)
Four Tops Reach Out . . . . (Motown)
Four Tops-Anthology . . . . (Motown)
Motown Dance Party-#2-C . . . . (Motown)
Real Love
Beatles; *The Beatles-Anthology-#2* . . . . (Capitol)
John Lennon; *ST/Imagine: John Lennon* . . . . (Capitol)
Remember Me
Journey; *ST/Armageddon-The Album* . . . . (Columbia)
Rest Of Mine, The
Trace Adkins; *Big Time* . . . . (Capitol)
Right Here Waiting
Richard Marx; *Chicken Soup For The Woman's Soul-C* . . . . (Rhino)
Repeat Offender . . . . (EMI)
Rock Wit U
Alicia Keys; *Songs In A Minor* . . . . (J)
Run To The Water
Live; *The Distance To Here* . . . . (Radioactive/MCA)
Runaround
Fleetwoods; *Best Of The Fleetwoods* . . . . (Rhino)
Sara Smile
After 7; *Very Best Of After 7* . . . .(Virgin)
Daryl Hall & John Oates; *Best Of Daryl Hall & John Oates* . . . .(RCA)
Daryl Hall & John Oates . . . . (RCA)
Livetime . . . . (RCA)
Rock 'N Soul, Part 1 . . . . (RCA)
Soulful Sounds . . . . (RCA)
Satisfy You
Puff Daddy Featuring R. Kelly; *Forever* . . . .(Bad Boy/Arista)
Save The Last Dance For Me
Buck Owens; *Buck Owens Collection-1959-1990* . . . . (Rhino)
Dolly Parton; *Best Of Dolly Parton-#3* . . . . (RCA)
Great Pretender . . . . (RCA)
Drifters; *20 Top 10 Hits Of The '50s & '60s-C* . . . .(Laurie)
Atlantic Rhythm & Blues 1947-1974-#4 (1958-1962)-C . . . . .(Atlantic)
Billboard Top Rock 'N' Roll Hits-1960-C . . . . (Rhino)
Cruisin'-1960-C . . . . (Increase)
Drifters-Golden Hits . . . . (Atlantic)
Emmylou Harris; *Blue Kentucky Girl* . . . . (Warner Bros.)
Profile II-The Best Of Emmylou Harris . . . . (Warner Bros.)
Jerry Lee Lewis; *20 Classic Jerry Lee Lewis Hits* . . . .(Original Sound)
Duets . . . . (Sun)
Jerry Lee Lewis-Original Golden Hits-#2 . . . . (Sun)
Monsters . . . . (Sun)
Say When
Lonestar; *Crazy Nights* . . . . (BNA)
See You In September
Chiffons; *Best Of The Chiffons* . . . .(Laurie)
Happenings; *ST/Purple People Eater* . . . . (AJK Music)
Tempos; *Cruisin'-1960-C* . . . . (Increase)

ST/*American Graffiti* .... (MCA)

She Believes In Me
Kenny Rogers; *Kenny Rogers-20 Great Years* .... (Reprise)

She Is His Only Need
Wynonna; *Wynonna* .... (MCA)
Wynonna-Collection .... (Curb)

She Misses Him
Tim Rushlow; *Tim Rushlow* .... (Atlantic)

She Never Lets It Go To Her Heart
Tim McGraw; *All I Want* .... (Curb)
Tim McGraw's Greatest Hits .... (Curb)

She Wears My Ring
Elvis Presley; *Essential Elvis-#5-Rhythm & Country* .... (RCA)
Ray Price; *Ray Price-20 Hits* .... (Tee Vee)
Ray Price's Greatest Hits-#1-3 .... (Step One)

She's A Woman
Beatles; *Beatles '65* .... (Capitol)
Beatles-Box Set .... (Capitol)
Compact Disc Singles Collection .... (Capitol)
Past Masters-Volume One .... (Parlophone)
The Beatles At The Hollywood Bowl .... (Capitol)
Jeff Beck; *Blow By Blow* .... (Epic)

She's All I Ever Had
Ricky Martin; *Ricky Martin* .... (Columbia)

She's All I Got
Jimmy Cozier; *Jimmy Cozier* .... (J)

She's Got It All
Kenny Chesney; *I Will Stand* .... (BNA)

Slide
Goo Goo Dolls; *Dizzy Up The Girl* .... (Warner Sunset/Reprise)

Smooth
Santana featuring Rob Thomas; *Supernatural* .... (Arista)
Totally Hits-#1-C .... (Arista)

So In Love
Alfred Drake & Patricia Morrison; *Those Wonderful Years: On Broadway-C* .... (JCI Assoc. Labels)
Original Cast; *Kiss Me Kate* .... (EMI-Angel)
Original Cast/Patricia Morrison; *Kiss Me Kate* .... (Sony Music Classical)

So In Love With You
U.N.V.; *Universal Nubian Voices* .... (Maverick/Warner Bros.)

So Much In Love
Tymes; *20th Century Rocks-#9-'60's Vocal Groups-I Got Rhythm-C* .... (Dominion Entert.)

Soldier Boy
Shirelles; *Billboard Top Rock 'N' Roll Hits-1962-C* .... (Rhino)
Oldies But Goodies-#4-C .... (Original Sound)
Shirelles-Anthology 1959-1964 .... (Rhino)
ST/*The Wanderers* .... (Warner Bros.)

Someday
Sugar Ray; *14:59* .... (Lava)
Totally Hits-#1-C .... (Arista)

Something That We Do
Clint Black; *Country Cares For Kids II-C* .... (BNA)
Nothin' But The Taillights .... (RCA)

Song For Mama
Boyz II Men; *BET-Best Of Planet Groove-C* .... (Virgin)
Evolution .... (Motown)
ST/*Soul Food* .... (LaFace)

Spend My Life With You
Eric Benet; *A Day In The Life* .... (Warner Bros.)

Spirit Of A Boy, Wisdom Of A Man
Randy Travis; *Big Country Hits '99-C* .... (K-Tel)
You And You Alone .... (DreamWorks/SKG)

Stand By Me
Ben E. King; *Atlantic Soul Classics-C* .... (Warner Special Prod.)
Ben E. King's Greatest Hits .... (Atco)
Golden Age Of Black Music-1960-1970-C .... (Atlantic)
ST/*Stand By Me* .... (Atlantic)
Stand By Me-Best Of Ben E. King .... (Atlantic)
Drifters; *Drifters' Greatest Hits* .... (Gusto)
John Lennon; *Rock 'N' Roll* .... (Capitol)
ST/*Imagine: John Lennon* .... (Capitol)
The John Lennon Collection .... (Capitol)
Maurice White; *Maurice White* .... (Columbia)
Mickey Gilley; *Greatest Country Hits From The Movies-C* ..... (Epic)
Mickey Gilley's Biggest Hits .... (Epic)
ST/*Urban Cowboy* .... (Asylum)
Ten Years Of Hits .... (Epic)
Ry Cooder; *Chicken Skin Music* .... (Reprise)

Stand By Your Man
Elton John; *Tammy Wynette...Remembered-C* .... (Asylum)
Lyle Lovett and his Large Band; *Lyle Lovett and his Large Band* .... (Curb/MCA)
Tammy Wynette; *Columbia Country Classics-#4-Nashville Sound-C* .... (Columbia)
ST/*Sleepless In Seattle* .... (Epic/Sony Music Soundtrax)
Tammy Wynette's Biggest Hits .... (Epic)
Tears Of Fire-25th Anniversary Collection .... (Epic)

Stand Inside Your Love
Smashing Pumpkins; *Machina: The Machines Of God* .... (Virgin)

Standing Together
George Benson; *Standing Together* .... (GRP)

Stars Over Texas
Tracy Lawrence; *Best Of Tracy Lawrence* .... (Atlantic)
Time Marches On .... (Atlantic)

Still In Love
Brian McKnight; *I Remember You* .... (Mercury)

Still On Your Side
BBMak; *Sooner Or Later* .... (Hollywood)

Stranded In The Jungle
Cadets; *Collectables Presents The History Of Rock-#2-C* .... (Collectables)
Cruisin'-1956-C .... (Increase)
Oldies But Goodies-#1-C .... (Original Sound)
Original Rock 'N' Roll Hits Of The '50s-C .... (Roulette)
New York Dolls; *In Too Much Too Soon* .... (Mercury)
Live In NYC-1975 .... (Restless)

Strong Enough To Bend
Tanya Tucker; *Strong Enough To Bend* .... (Liberty)
Tanya Tucker's Greatest Hits .... (Liberty)

Sweet Baby
Macy Gray; *The Id* .... (Epic)

Tall, Tall Trees
Alan Jackson; *Alan Jackson-The Greatest Hits Collection* ...... (Arista)
George Jones; *Cup Of Loneliness-Classic Mercury Years* .... (Mercury)
George Jones-The Hits .... (Mercury)
Roger Miller; *King Of The Road-Genius Of Roger Miller* .... (Mercury)
Roger Miller-The Hits .... (Mercury)

Thank God For Believers
Mark Chesnutt; *Thank God For Believers* .... (Decca)

Thank God I Found You
Mariah Carey featuring Joe & 98 Degrees; *Rainbow* .... (Columbia)

Thank You
Led Zeppelin; *BBC Sessions* .... (Atlantic)
Led Zeppelin II .... (Atlantic)
Led Zeppelin-Box Set .... (Atlantic)
Led Zeppelin-The Complete Studio Recordings .... (Atlantic)
Page & Plant; *No Quarter: Jimmy Page & Robert Plant Unledded* .... (Atlantic)

Thank You In Advance
Boyz II Men; *Nathan Michael Shawn Wanya* .... (Universal)

That's All
Tennessee Ernie Ford; *The Ultimate Tennessee Ernie Ford* ...... (Razor & Tie)

That's All I Want From You
Jaye P. Morgan; *The Jaye P. Morgan Story* .... (Simitar)

Then You Can Tell Me Goodbye
Casinos; *Then You Can Tell Me Goodbye* .... (Varese Vintage)
Neal McCoy; *Neal McCoy's Greatest Hits* .... (Atlantic)

There Once Was A Man
Original Cast; *Pajama Game* .... (Columbia)
ST/*Pajama Game* .... (Collectables)

There You Are
Martina McBride; *Emotion* .... (RCA)

They Don't Know
Jon B.; *Cool Relax* .... (Yab Yum/550)

Think Of Tomorrow
Chris Isaak; *Baja Sessions* .... (Reprise)

This I Promise You
'N Sync; *No Strings Attached* .... (Jive)
Now That's What I Call Music!-#7-C .... (Virgin)

This Is For The Lover In You
Babyface; *The Day* .... (Epic)

This Is Me
Dream; *It Was All A Dream* .... (Bad Boy/Arista)
Totally Hits 2001-C .... (Arista)

This Time
Curtis Stigers; *Time Was* .... (Arista)

'Til A Tear Becomes A Rose
Jann Browne; *Tell Me Why* .... (Curb)
'Til A Tear Becomes A Rose .... (Curb)
Keith Whitley; *Keith Whitley's Greatest Hits* .... (RCA)
Lorrie Morgan; *Lorrie Morgan's Greatest Hits* .... (BNA)

Till I Waltz Again With You
Teresa Brewer; *Best Of Teresa Brewer* .... (MCA Jazz)

Till We Two Are One
Eddy Howard; *Best Of Eddy Howard-The Mercury Years* ...... (Mercury)
Georgie Shaw; *45-#28937* .... (Decca)
Louis Jordan; *One Guy Named Louis* .... (Blue Note)

Time After Time
Cyndi Lauper; *Chicken Soup For The Woman's Soul-C* .... (Rhino)
She's So Unusual .... (Portrait)
Twelve Deadly Cyns...And Then Some .... (Epic)
Everything But The Girl; *Acoustic* .... (Atlantic)
INOJ & So So Def Bass All-Stars; *Time After Time (Maxi Single)* .... (So So Def/Columbia)
Miles Davis; *Live Around The World* .... (Warner Bros.)
You're Under Arrest .... (Columbia)

Time In A Bottle
Jim Croce; *50th Anniversary Collection* .... (Saja)

Photographs & Memories/His Greatest Hits . . . (Atlantic)
Time In A Bottle/Jim Croce's Greatest Love Songs . . . (Atlantic)

To Be Loved By You
Wynonna; *Revelations* . . . (Curb/MCA)
Wynonna-Collection . . . (Curb)

To Know Him, Is To Love Him
Dolly Parton/Emmylou Harris/Linda Ronstadt; *Trio* . . . (Warner Bros.)
Teddy Bears; *At The Hop-'50s Rock 'N' Roll* . . . (K-Tel)
Phil Spector-Back To Mono 1958-1969-C . . . (Abkco)

To Love You More
Celine Dion with The Bee Gees; *All The Way...A Decade Of Song* . . . (550 Music)
Let's Talk About Love-C . . . (550 Music)

To Make You Feel My Love
Billy Joel; *Billy Joel's Greatest Hits-#3* . . . (Columbia)
Songs From The Heart-C . . . (Columbia)
Bob Dylan; *Time Out Of Mind* . . . (Columbia)
Garth Brooks; *Garth Brooks-Double Live* . . . (Capitol)
Limited Series-Box . . . (Capitol)
ST/Hope Floats . . . (Capitol)
Trisha Yearwood; *ST/Hope Floats* . . . (Capitol)

Touch Me
Doors; *Best Of The Doors* . . . (Elektra)
Doors 13 . . . (Elektra)
Doors' Greatest Hits . . . (Elektra)
Soft Parade . . . (Elektra)

Travelin' Soldier
Bruce Robison; *Bruce Robison* . . . (Vireo)

True
George Strait; *Latest Greatest Straitest Hits* . . . (MCA)
One Step At A Time . . . (MCA)

True Friends
Shannon Curfman; *Loud Guitars Big Suspicions* . . . (Arista)

True Love
Elton John & Kiki Dee; *Duets-C* . . . (MCA)
Four Aces; *Best Of The Four Aces* . . . (MCA)
Johnny Mathis & Henry Mancini; *Hollywood Musicals* . . . (Columbia)
Patsy Cline; *Always* . . . (MCA)
The Patsy Cline Story . . . (MCA)
Roger Whittaker; *Best Loved Ballads-#2* . . . (Liberty)

Truly
Lionel Richie; *Back To Front* . . . (Motown)
Lionel Richie . . . (Motown)

Truly Madly Deeply
Savage Garden; *Savage Garden* . . . (Columbia)

Tu Amor
Jon B.; *Cool Relax* . . . (Yab Yum/550)

Unconditional
Clay Davidson; *Unconditional* . . . (Virgin)

Until The End Of Time
Guy & Ralna; *22 Golden Country Classics* . . . (Ranwood)

Until The Real Thing Comes Along
Andy Kirk; *Sweetest Sounds Ever Heard-C* . . . (Hip-O)
Billie Holiday; *God Bless The Child* . . . (Columbia)
Quintessential-#9-1940-1942 . . . (Columbia)
Dean Martin; *The Capitol Years-Dean Martin* . . . (Capitol)
Frank Sinatra & The Quincy Jones Orchestra; *Frank Sinatra-Complete Reprise Studio Recordings* . . . (Reprise)

Uptight (Everything's Alright)
Stevie Wonder; *16 #1 Hits From The Early '60s-C* . . . (Motown)
Looking Back . . . (Motown)
Motown Dance Party-#1-C . . . (Motown)
Motown Legends-Stevie Wonder . . . (Motown)
Stevie Wonder's Greatest Hits . . . (Motown)
Uptight (Everything's Alright) . . . (Motown)

Valentine
Jim Brickman & Martina McBride; *Picture This* . . . (Windham Hill)
Smooth Sounds-C . . . (Razor & Tie)
Martina McBride & Jim Brickman; *Evolution* . . . (RCA)

Vaya Con Dios
Bing Crosby; *The Radio Years-#2* . . . (Crescendo)
Freddy Fender; *Freddy Fender-Collection* . . . (Reprise)
Les Paul & Mary Ford; *Memories Are Made Of This-C* . . . (Capitol)
Roger Whittaker; *All-Time Heart-Touching Favorites* . . . (Capitol)

Wait
Beatles; *Beatles-Box Set* . . . (Capitol)
Rubber Soul . . . (Capitol)

Walk Hand In Hand
Andy Williams; *I Like Your Kind Of Love-The Best Of The Cadence Years* . . . (Varese Vintage)

We Loved It Away
George Jones & Tammy Wynette; *George Jones & Tammy Wynette-16 Biggest Hits* . . . (Epic/Legacy)

We'll Be Together Again
Barbara Cook; *All I Ask Of You* . . . (DRG)
Billie Holiday; *Verve Jazz Masters 47-Billie Holiday Sings Standards* . . (Verve)
Frankie Laine; *The Frankie Laine Collection* . . . (Mercury)
Lena Horne; *We'll Be Together Again* . . . (Blue Note)
Louis Armstrong; *Essential Louis Armstrong* . . . (Verve)
McCoy Tyner; *Priceless Jazz Collection* . . . (GRP)
Rosemary Clooney; *Do You Miss New York?* . . . (Concord Jazz)
Sammy Davis, Jr.; *Sammy Davis, Jr.'s Greatest Hits-#2* . . . (Dunhill Compact Classics)

We're Gonna Hold On
George Jones & Tammy Wynette; *George Jones & Tammy Wynette-16 Biggest Hits* . . . (Epic/Legacy)

We've Only Just Begun
Barbra Streisand; *Just For The Record* . . . (Columbia)
Carpenters; *Carpenters-Classics-#2* . . . (A&M)
Carpenters-The Singles 1969-1973 . . . (A&M)
Close To You . . . (A&M)
From The Top . . . (A&M)
Yesterday Once More . . . (A&M)

What A Girl Wants
Christina Aguilera; *Christina Aguilera* . . . (RCA)
Totally Hits-#3-C . . . (Atlantic)

Whatever Way The Wind Blows
Kelly Willis; *One More Time-MCA Recordings* . . . (MCA)

When A Woman Loves A Man
Lee Roy Parnell; *We All Get Lucky Sometimes* . . . (Career)

When I Need You
Celine Dion; *Let's Talk About Love-C* . . . (550 Music)
Leo Sayer; *'70s Greatest Rock Hits-#5-Kickin' Back-C* . . . (Priority)
Show Must Go On-Anthology . . . (Rhino)

When I Said I Do
Clint Black & Lisa Hartman Black; *D'lectrified* . . . (RCA)

When You Are Old
Gretchen Peters; *The Secret Of Life* . . . (Purple Crayon Prod.)

When You Come Back Down
Nickel Creek; *Nickel Creek* . . . (Sugar Hill)

When You Love Someone
Sammy Kershaw; *Maybe Not Tonight* . . . (Mercury)

When You Need Me
Bruce Springsteen; *Tracks* . . . (Columbia)

Whenever Wherever
Shakira; *Laundry Service* . . . (Epic)

Whenever You Call
Mariah Carey; *Butterfly* . . . (Columbia)

Where You Lead
Carole King; *Tapestry* . . . (Epic)

Where Your Road Leads
Trisha Yearwood & Garth Brooks; *Where Your Road Leads* . . . (MCA)

Wherever You Will Go
Calling; *Camino Palmero* . . . (RCA)

Whither Thou Goest
Les Paul & Mary Ford; *Best Of The Capitol Masters* . . . (Gold Rush)
Les Paul's All-Time Greatest Hits . . . (EMI Special Markets)

Why Don't You Believe Me?
Duprees; *Best Of The Duprees* . . . (Rhino)
Best Of The Duprees . . . (Collectables)
Joni James; *Platinum & Gold Hits* . . . (Taragon)
Patti Page; *Patti Page-Golden Celebration* . . . (Mercury)

Wifey
Next; *Totally Hits-#3-C* . . . (Atlantic)
Welcome To Nextacy . . . (Arista)

Wind Beneath My Wings
Bette Midler; *ST/Beaches* . . . (Atlantic)
Gary Morris; *Chicken Soup For The Soul: I'll Be There For You-Songs Of Friendship, Brotherhood And Sisterhood-C* . . . (Rhino)
Country Love Songs-C . . . (Warner Bros.)
Gary Morris-Hits . . . (Warner Bros.)
Why Lady Why . . . (Warner Bros.)
James Galway; *Wind Beneath My Wings* . . . (RCA)
Lee Greenwood; *Somebody's Gonna Love You* . . . (MCA)
Lou Rawls; *When The Night Comes* . . . (Epic)
Roger Whittaker; *Roger Whittaker Greatest Hits* . . . (RCA)
Wind Beneath My Wings . . . (RCA)
Willie Nelson; *City Of New Orleans* . . . (Columbia)

With Just One Look In Your Eyes
Charly McClain & Wayne Massey; *19 Hot Country Requests-#3-C* . . . (Epic)
Charly McClain's Biggest Hits . . . (Epic)
Radio Heart . . . (Epic)
Ten Year Anniversary . . . (Epic)

With This Ring
Platters; *Enchanted-The Best Of The Platters* . . . (Rhino)
Only Their Best For You . . . (Pair)
Rockin' & Rollin' Wedding Songs-#2-C . . . (Rhino)
The Musicor Years . . . (Collectables)
T. Graham Brown; *Best Of T. Graham Brown* . . . (Liberty)
T. Graham Brown's All-Time Greatest Hits . . . (Curb)

With This Ring
Sawyer Brown; *Six Days On The Road* . . . (Curb)
Wedding Day Music-C . . . (Reprise)

Wolverton Mountain
Claude King; *American Originals-Claude King* . . . (Columbia)
Best Of Claude King . . . (Gusto)
Billboard Top Country Hits-1962-C . . . (Rhino)
Super Hits Of The '60s-C . . . (Epic)

Wrapped Around Your Finger
Police; *Every Breath You Take-The Classics* . . . . (A&M)
   Message In A Box-Complete Recordings . . . . (A&M)
   Police-Live . . . . (A&M)
   Synchronicity . . . . (A&M)
Written In The Stars
Elton John & LeAnn Rimes; *ST/Aida* . . . . (Island)
Yellow
Coldplay; *Now That's What I Call Music!-#6-C* . . . .(Virgin)
   Parachutes . . . . (Nettwerk/Capitol)
You
Jesse Powell; *'Bout It.* . . . . (Silas)
You And You Alone
Vince Gill; *High Lonesome Sound* . . . . (MCA)
You Are Everything
Dru Hill; *Enter The Dru.* . . . .(Def Jam/RAL/Mercury/Island)
You Are The Sunshine Of My Life
Peter Nero; *Peter Nero's Greatest Hits* . . . . (Columbia)
Stevie Wonder; *20/20-C* . . . . (Motown)
   Original Musiquarium . . . . (Motown)
   Talking Book. . . . . (Motown)
You Belong To Me
Carly Simon; *Boys In The Trees* . . . . (Elektra)
   Carly Simon-Greatest Hits Live . . . . (Arista)
   Chicken Soup For The Woman's Soul-C. . . . . (Rhino)
Doobie Brothers; *Best Of The Doobies, Volume II* . . . . (Warner Bros.)
   Livin' On The Fault Line. . . . . (Warner Bros.)
You Brought A New Kind Of Love To Me
Ella Fitzgerald; *Ella Swings Lightly* . . . . (Verve)
You Have No Idea
Pamela Rose; *Morpheus* . . . . (Grace)
You Keep Running Away
Four Tops; *Four Tops-Anthology* . . . . (Motown)
You Still Believe In Me
Beach Boys; *Pet Sounds* . . . . (Capitol)
You Won't Be Lonely Now
Billy Ray Cyrus; *Southern Rain* . . . . (Monument)
You Won't Ever Be Lonely
Andy Griggs; *Andy Griggs* . . . . (RCA)
You'll Always Be Loved By Me
Brooks & Dunn; *Tight Rope* . . . . (Arista)
You'll Never Know
Dick Haymes; *Best Of Dick Haymes* . . . . (Curb)
   You'll Never Know . . . . (MCA Special Prod.)
Dick Haymes & His Song Spinners; *Billboard Pop Memories-1940-*
   1944-C . . . . (Rhino)
   Billboard Top Movie Hits-1940s-C . . . . (Rhino)
Young Love
Sonny James; *Golden Jukebox Favorites* . . . . (Capitol)
   Opry Legends-Sonny James . . . . (Capitol)
   Stars Of The Grand Ole Opry-1926-1974-C. . . . . (RCA)
   Traditions In Country Music-C. . . . . (Capitol)
Tab Hunter; *Fonzie's Make-Out Music-C* . . . . (Nick At Nite)
   Teen Idols-C . . . . (Universal)
Your Everything
keith urban; *keith urban* . . . . (Capitol)
Your Unchanging Love
Marvin Gaye; *Marvin Gaye-Anthology* . . . . (Motown)
You're All I Need To Get By
Aretha Franklin; *Aretha Franklin-30 Greatest Hits.* . . . . (Rhino)
Marvin Gaye; *Marvin Gaye's Greatest Hits* . . . . (Motown)
Marvin Gaye & Tammi Terrell; *Chicken Soup For The Couples*
   Soul-C . . . . (Rhino)
   Every Great Motown Hit Of Marvin Gaye . . . . (Motown)
   The Glory Of Love-'60s Sweet & Soulful Love Songs-C . . . . (Hip-O)
You're My Everything
Temptations; *Temptations' Greatest Hits-#2* . . . . (Motown)
You're Still The One
Shania Twain; *Come On Over.* . . . . (Mercury)
You're The Cream In My Coffee
Lawrence Welk; *Lawrence Welk-16 Most Requested Songs* . . . . . . (Columbia)
Les Brown & His Orchestra; *Best Of Les Brown & His Orchestra* . . . . . . (MCA)
You're The One
Paul Simon; *You're The One* . . . . (Warner Bros.)
Yours (Quierme Mucho)
Benny Goodman & His Orchestra featuring Helen Forrest; *Best Of The Big*
   Bands Featuring Helen Forrest . . . . (Columbia)
Jimmy Dorsey & His Orchestra featuring Bob Eberly & Helen O'Connell;
   Best Of Jimmy Dorsey & His Orchestra. . . . . (Curb)
Vera Lynn; *We'll Meet Again* . . . . (Living Era)
You've Got To Talk To Me
Lee Ann Womack; *Lee Ann Womack* . . . . (Decca)
You've Made Me So Very Happy
Blood, Sweat & Tears; *Blood, Sweat & Tears* . . . . (Columbia)
   Blood, Sweat & Tears Greatest Hits . . . . (Columbia)
   Live & Improvised . . . . (Columbia)
   Pop Classics Of The '60s-C . . . . (Columbia)

LOVE: DON'T WANT TO BREAK UP, Come Back, Don't Go, I'm Coming Back, Take Me Back

See Also: **DESIRE, FORGIVE, GUILT, HOLDING ON, KISSING, LEAVING, LOSING & LOSS, LOVE (various), PAIN & HEALING, RETURNING, SADNESS**

(Eye) Hate U
''AFKAP''; *The Gold Experience* . . . .(NPG)
...Baby One More Time
Britney Spears; *...Baby One More Time* . . . . (Jive)
   Now That's What I Call Music!-#2-C . . . . (Virgin)
49 Bye-Byes
Crosby, Stills & Nash; *Crosby, Stills & Nash.* . . . . (Atlantic)
Absence Of The Heart
Deana Carter; *Everything's Gonna Be Alright* . . . .(Capitol)
Against All Odds (Take A Look At Me Now)
Mariah Carey; *Rainbow* . . . .(Columbia)
Phil Collins; *Hit Singles-1980-1988-C.* . . . . (Atlantic)
   Serious Hits...Live! . . . . (Atlantic)
   ST/Against All Odds . . . . (Atlantic)
Ain't Too Proud To Beg
Rolling Stones; *It's Only Rock 'N Roll* . . . .(Rolling Stones)
Temptations; *Motown Story-First 25 Years-C* . . . . (Motown)
   ST/Big Chill. . . . . (Motown)
   Temptations' Greatest Hits-#1 . . . . (Motown)
   Temptations-25th Anniversary . . . . (Motown)
   Temptations-Anthology-The Best Of The Temptations . . . . (Motown)
All Of Me
Billie Holiday; *Billie Holiday-Love Songs* . . . .(Legacy)
Count Basie; *Compact Jazz-The Standards* . . . .(Verve)
Diana Ross; *ST/Lady Sings The Blues* . . . . (Motown)
Dinah Washington; *Compact Jazz-Dinah Washington* . . . .(Verve)
Duke Ellington; *Jazz Party.* . . . .(Legacy)
Esquivel; *Music From A Sparkling Planet* . . . .(Bar/None)
Frank Sinatra; *Sinatra Sings His Greatest Hits* . . . .(Legacy)
Helen O'Connell; *Great Girl Singers Sing 22 Original*
   Recordings-C . . . .(Hindsight)
Louis Armstrong; *Louis Armstrong's Greatest Hits* . . . .(Legacy)
Martha Tilton; *Sweet And Lovely: Capitol's Great Ladies Of Song-C.* . .(Capitol)
Paul Whiteman & Mildred Bailey; *Those Wonderful Years: Happy Days Are*
   Here Again-C . . . .(JCI Assoc. Labels)
Sarah Vaughan; *Essential Sarah Vaughan-The Great Songs* . . . .(Verve)
Willie Nelson; *Stardust* . . . .(Legacy)
All Out Of Love
Air Supply; *Air Supply's Greatest Hits* . . . . (Arista)
   Air Supply-The Definitive Collection. . . . . (Arista)
   Lost In Love. . . . . (Arista)
Alone
Bee Gees; *Still Waters* . . . . (Polydor)
Always Be My Baby
Mariah Carey; *Daydream.* . . . . (Columbia)
Always On My Mind
Willie Nelson; *Always On My Mind* . . . .(Columbia)
   Super Hits Of The '80s-C . . . .(Epic)
   Willie Nelson-Super Hits . . . .(Columbia)
Am I That Easy To Forget
Carl Belew; *24 Hits: Best Of Country Stars On LP-C* . . . . (Tee Vee)
Debbie Reynolds; *Debbie Reynolds' Greatest Hits* . . . .(Curb)
Engelbert Humperdinck; *Engelbert Humperdinck-16 Most Requested*
   Songs . . . .(Epic)
Angel
Aerosmith; *Permanent Vacation* . . . . (Geffen)
Angelina
Keb' Mo'; *Keb' Mo'.* . . . . (Okeh)
Angels Of The Silences
Counting Crows; *Recovering The Satellites.* . . . . (David Geffen Co.)
Answer Me, My Love
Nat ''King'' Cole; *Best Of Nat ''King'' Cole-Vol. 1* . . . .(Capitol)
   The Nat ''King'' Cole Story-#2 . . . .(Capitol)
   Unforgettable . . . .(Capitol)
Anybody Seen My Baby?
Rolling Stones; *1998 Grammy Nominees-C.* . . . . (MCA)
   Bridges To Babylon . . . . (Virgin)
Anymore
Travis Tritt; *It's All About To Change* . . . . (Warner Bros.)
   Travis Tritt's Greatest Hits-From The Beginning . . . . (Warner Bros.)
Anything
SWV; *It's About Time* . . . . (RCA)
   ST/Above The Rim . . . . (Death Row)
Anything
3T; *Brotherhood.* . . . . (Columbia)
Anything For You
Gloria Estefan; *Gloria Estefan's Greatest Hits* . . . . (Epic)
Gloria Estefan and Miami Sound Machine; *Billboard Top Hits-*
   1988-C . . . . (Rhino)
   Let It Loose . . . . (Epic)

Anytime
Brian McKnight; *Anytime*. . . . . (Motown)
Now That's What I Call Music!-#1-C . . . . (Virgin)
Apartment #9
Melissa Etheridge; *Tammy Wynette...Remembered-C* . . . . (Asylum)
Tammy Wynette; *Tammy Wynette-Anniversary-20 Years Of Hits* . . . .(Epic)
Tammy Wynette's Greatest Hits. . . . .(Epic)
Are You Lonesome To-night?
Elvis Presley; *A Valentine Gift For You* . . . . (RCA)
Elvis' Golden Records, Volume 3 . . . . (RCA)
From Memphis To Vegas/From Vegas To Memphis . . . . (RCA)
Worldwide 50 Gold Award Hits, Vol. 1, Parts 1 & 2 . . . . (RCA)
Are You Satisfied?
Rusty Draper; *Rusty Draper's Greatest Hits* . . . . (Collector's Choice)
Arms Of The One Who Loves You
Xscape; *Traces Of My Lipstick* . . . .(So So Def/Columbia)
At This Moment
Billy Vera & The Beaters; *Billboard Top Hits-1987-C*. . . . . (Rhino)
By Request: Best Of Billy Vera & The Beaters. . . . . (Rhino)
Awake
Godsmack; *Awake* . . . .(Republic/Universal)
Baby Come Back
Player; *Billboard Top Hits-1978-C*. . . . . (Rhino)
Mellow Rock Hits Of The '70s-Ventura Highway-C . . . . (Rhino)
Super Hits Of The '70s-Have A Nice Day-#21-C . . . . (Rhino)
Baby Don't Go
Sonny & Cher; *The Beat Goes On-Best Of Sonny & Cher* . . . . (Rhino)
The Two Of Us . . . . (Atco)
Baby I Need Your Loving
Four Tops; *Four Tops' Greatest Hits* . . . . (Motown)
Four Tops-Anthology. . . . . (Motown)
The Ultimate Collection-Four Tops. (Motown)
Johnny Rivers; *Johnny Rivers' Greatest Hits* . . . . (Capitol)
Johnny Rivers-Anthology 1964-1977. (Rhino)
Baby It's You
Beatles; *Introducing...The Beatles* . . . .(Vee-Jay)
The Early Beatles. . . . . (Capitol)
Baby Love
Diana Ross; *Diana Ross-The Ultimate Collection* . . . . (Motown)
Supremes; *Motown Classic Hits-#5-C* . . . . (Motown)
Temptations; *ST/My Girl 2* . . . .(Epic)
Baby, Now That I've Found You
Alison Krauss & Union Station; *Best Of Austin City Limits-Country Music's
Finest Hour-C* . . . . (Legacy)
Now That I've Found You: A Collection . . . . (Rounder)
Foundations; *Best Of Rock 'N Soul-C*. . . . . (Priority)
History Of British Rock-#6-C . . . . (Rhino)
Babylon
David Gray; *White Ladder* . . . . (ATO/RCA)
Back For Good
Take That; *Nobody Else* . . . . (Arista)
Back Here
BBMak; *Now That's What I Call Music!-#5-C*. . . . . (Virgin)
Sooner Or Later. . . . . (Hollywood)
Back In Your Arms
Bruce Springsteen; *Tracks* . . . . (Columbia)
Back In Your Arms Again
Lorrie Morgan; *Lorrie Morgan's Greatest Hits* . . . . (BNA)
Back To The World
Tevin Campbell; *Back To The World* . . . . (Qwest)
Be With You
Enrique Iglesias; *Enrique* . . . .(Overbrook/Interscope)
Before I Let You Go
Blackstreet; *Blackstreet* . . . . (Interscope)
Before The Next Teardrop Falls
Freddy Fender; *Before The Next Teardrop Falls* . . . . (Universal)
Best Of Freddy Fender. . . . . (MCA)
Oldies But Goodies-#2-C . . . . (Original Sound)
Super Hits Of The '70s-Have A Nice Day-#17-C . . . . (Rhino)
Ray Anthony; *Great Golden Hits* . . . .(Ranwood)
Before You Walk Out Of My Life
Monica; *Miss Thang* . . . . (Rowdy/Arista)
Bell Bottom Blues
Derek And The Dominos; *Layla*. . . . . (Polydor)
Eric Clapton; *24 Nights* . . . . (Duck/Reprise)
Betcha She Don't Love You
Jessica Simpson; *Sweet Kisses* . . . . (Columbia)
Bill Bailey
Louis Armstrong; *Essential Louis Armstrong*. . . . . (Vanguard)
Louis Armstrong . . . . (Audio Fidelity)
Pearl Bailey; *Echoes Of An Era-Pearl Bailey*. . . . . (Roulette)
Preservation Hall Jazz Band; *New Orleans-#1* . . . . (Columbia)
Billy Dale
Asleep At The Wheel featuring Dolly Parton; *Tribute To The Music Of Bob
Wills And The Texas Playboys-C* . . . . (Liberty)
Black Is Black
Los Bravos; *History Of British Rock-#7-C* . . . . (Rhino)
London Collector-Rock Invasion-C . . . . (London)

Blue Kentucky Girl
Emmylou Harris; *Blue Kentucky Girl* . . . . (Warner Bros.)
Profile II-The Best Of Emmylou Harris . . . . (Warner Bros.)
Loretta Lynn; *Loretta Lynn's Greatest Hits* . . . . (MCA)
Blurry
Puddle Of Mudd; *Come Clean* . . . . (Flawless/Geffen/Interscope)
Body And Soul
Benny Goodman & His Orchestra; *Benny Goodman's
Greatest Hits* . . . . (RCA Victor)
Benny Goodman Trio; *Ken Burns Jazz Collection-The Benny
Goodman Trio* . . . . (Legacy)
Billie Holiday; *Billie Holiday-16 Most Requested Songs* . . . . (Legacy)
Body And Soul . . . . (Verve)
The Billie Holiday Story-#2 . . . . (Columbia)
This Is Jazz #32: Billie Holiday Sings Standards . . . . (Columbia)
Verve Jazz Masters 47-Billie Holiday Sings Standards . . . . (Verve)
Carly Simon; *Torch*. . . . . (Warner Bros.)
Coleman Hawkins; *Coleman Hawkins' Greatest Hits* . . . . (RCA Victor)
Verve Jazz Masters 34 . . . . (Verve)
Diana Krall; *Stepping Out* . . . . (Justin Time)
Eddie Jefferson; *Body And Soul* . . . . (Original Jazz Classics)
Letter From Home . . . . (Original Jazz Classics)
Main Man . . . . (Inner City)
The Jazz Singer. . . . . (Evidence Music)
Louis Armstrong; *Essential Louis Armstrong* . . . . (Verve)
Louis Armstrong-Love Songs . . . . (Legacy)
Musical Autobiography-#2. . . . . (MCA)
Satchmo At Symphony Hall . . . . (Decca Jazz)
Verve Jazz Masters 1 . . . . (Verve)
Manhattan Transfer; *Best Of The Manhattan Transfer* . . . .(Atlantic)
Extensions . . . . (Rhino)
Manhattan Transfer-Anthology-Down In Birdland . . . . (Rhino)
Paul Whiteman & His Orchestra; *78-#2297* . . . . (Columbia)
Sarah Vaughan; *How Long Has This Been Going On?* . . . . (Pablo)
One Night Stand-The Town Hall Concert-1947 . . . . (Blue Note)
Sarah Vaughan. . . . . (Everest)
Brand New Day
Sting; *Brand New Day*. . . . . (A&M)
Breakin' Me
Jonny Lang; *Wander This World*. . . . . (A&M)
Breaking Up Is Hard To Do
Gloria Estefan; *Hold Me, Thrill Me, Kiss Me* . . . . (Epic)
Neil Sedaka; *Billboard Top Rock 'N' Roll Hits-1962-C* . . . . (Rhino)
Neil Sedaka's All-Time Greatest Hits . . . . (RCA)
Shelley Fabares; *Things We Did Last Summer* . . . . (Collectables)
Bring It On Home
Led Zeppelin; *Led Zeppelin II* . . . .(Atlantic)
Broken Down In Tiny Pieces
Billy "Crash" Craddock; *Crash's Smashes: The Hits Of Billy "Crash"
Craddock* . . . . (Razor & Tie)
Can I Change My Mind
Tyrone Davis; *Soul Shots-#2-The "In" Crowd-Sweet Soul-C* . . . . (Rhino)
Tyrone Davis' Greatest Hits . . . . (Rhino)
Can You See Me
Jimi Hendrix; *ST/Jimi Plays Monterey* . . . . (Reprise)
Jimi Hendrix Experience; *Are You Experienced?* . . . . (Reprise)
Smash Hits . . . . (Reprise)
Can't Hang Up The Phone
Stonewall Jackson; *45-#42628* . . . . (Columbia)
Can't You Hear Me Callin'?
Ricky Skaggs; *Bluegrass Super Hits-C* . . . . (Columbia)
Favorite Country Songs . . . . (Epic)
Highway & Heartaches . . . . (Epic)
Chains Of Love
Erasure; *Innocents* . . . .(Sire)
Just Say Yo-#2 Of Just Say Yes-C . . . .(Sire)
Change My Mind
John Berry; *Faces* . . . . (Capitol)
Click-Clack
Dicky Doo And The Don'ts; *Greatest Hit Singles Collection-C* . . . . (Laserlight)
Clown, The
Conway Twitty; *Latest Greatest Hits-#1* . . . . (Warner Bros.)
Number One's: The Warner Bros. Years . . . . (Warner Bros.)
Southern Comfort. . . . . (Warner Bros.)
C'mon Marianne
4 Seasons; *25th Anniversary Collection* . . . . (Rhino)
4 Seasons-Anthology . . . . (Rhino)
Come On Back
Keb' Mo'; *The Door* . . . . (550/Epic/Okeh)
Come See About Me
Diana Ross & The Supremes; *16 #1 Hits From The Early '60s-C* . . . . (Motown)
Diana Ross & The Supremes' Greatest Hits. . . . . (Motown)
Diana Ross & The Supremes-Anthology (1962-1969) . . . . (Motown)
Diana Ross & The Supremes-At The Copa . . . . (Motown)
Every Great #1 Hit . . . . (Motown)
Girl Groups-Story Of A Sound-C . . . . (Rhino)
Motown Story-First 25 Years-C . . . . (Motown)
Motown Superstar Series-#1-Diana Ross & The Supremes . . . . (Motown)

Congo
Genesis; *Calling All Stations* . . . . (Atlantic)
Couldn't Last A Moment
Collin Raye; *Tracks* . . . . (Epic)
Cowboy Love Song
Skip Gorman; *A Cowboy's Wild Song To His Herd* . . . . (Rounder)
Crazy
K-Ci & JoJo; *Now That's What I Call Music!-#6-C* . . . . (Virgin)
X . . . . (MCA)
Creep
TLC; *CrazySexyCool* . . . . (LaFace)
Crying Shame
Michael Johnson; *Best Of Michael Johnson* . . . . (RCA)
That's That . . . . (RCA)
Crying Time
Buck Owens & Emmylou Harris; *Act Naturally* . . . . (Capitol)
Ray Charles; *Ray Charles' Greatest Hits* . . . . (Rhino)
Ray Charles-Anthology . . . . (Rhino)
Ray Charles-His Greatest Hits-#1 . . . . (Dunhill Compact Classics)
Darling Come Back Home
Eddie Kendricks; *Eddie Kendricks-The Ultimate Collection* . . . . (Motown)
Do Your Thing
7 Mile; *7 Mile* . . . . (Crave)
Don't Be Cruel
Cheap Trick; *Cheap Trick's Greatest Hits* . . . . (Epic)
Lap Of Luxury . . . . (Epic)
Elvis Presley; *Billboard Top Rock 'N' Roll Hits-1956-C* . . . . (Rhino)
Nipper's Greatest Hits Of The '50s-#2-C . . . . (RCA)
Number One Hits . . . . (RCA)
The Great Performances . . . . (RCA)
The Top Ten Hits . . . . (RCA)
Judds; *Heartland* . . . . (MCA)
Don't Bother Me
Beatles; *Meet The Beatles!* . . . . (Capitol)
Don't Ever Leave Me
Patsy Cline; *Legendary Patsy Cline* . . . . (Pair)
Peggy Lee; *Moments Like This* . . . . (Chesky)
Don't Go Away
Oasis; *Be Here Now* . . . . (Epic)
Don't Leave Me
Blackstreet; *Another Level*. . . . . (Interscope)
Don't Leave Me This Way
Thelma Houston; *Billboard Top Rock 'N' Roll Hits-1977-C* . . . . . . (Rhino)
Disco Nights-#6-C . . . . (Rebound)
Motown's Leading Ladies-C . . . . (Motown)
Don't Let Me Leave
Marc Anthony; *Marc Anthony* . . . . (Columbia)
Don't Pass Me By
Beatles; *The Beatles (White Album)* . . . . (Capitol)
The Beatles-Anthology-#3 . . . . (Capitol)
Don't Pull Your Love
Hamilton, Joe Frank & Reynolds; *'70s Biggest Hits-C* . . . . (MCA Special Prod.)
Hamilton, Joe Frank & Reynolds' Greatest Hits . . . . (MCA Special Prod.)
Rock Around The Oldies-#4-C . . . . (MCA Special Prod.)
Don't Sleep In The Subway
Frank Sinatra; *Frank Sinatra* . . . . (Reprise)
Petula Clark; *Petula Clark's Greatest Hits* . . . . (Crescendo)
Summer Of Love-#1-C . . . . (Rhino)
Don't Take Your Love From Me
Etta James; *These Foolish Things-The Classic Balladry Of Etta James* . . (MCA)
King Sisters; *Spotlight On The King Sisters* . . . . (Capitol)
Three Suns; *Very Best Of The Three Suns* . . . . (Taragon)
Don't Toss Us Away
Lone Justice; *Lone Justice* . . . . (Geffen Goldline)
This World Is Not My Home . . . . (Geffen)
Patty Loveless; *Honky Tonk Angel* . . . . (MCA)
Patty Loveless' Greatest Hits . . . . (MCA)
Don't You Care
Buckinghams; *Buckinghams' Greatest Hits* . . . . (Columbia)
Down On My Knees
Beth Nielsen Chapman; *Beth Nielsen Chapman* . . . . (Reprise)
Trisha Yearwood; *Hearts In Armor* . . . . (MCA)
Dream Merchant
New Birth; *Smooth Grooves-A Sensual Collection-#5-C* . . . . (Rhino)
Emotion
Destiny's Child; *Survivor* . . . . (Columbia)
The Concert For New York City-C . . . . (Columbia)
Everlasting Love
Carl Carlton; *Classic R&B Oldies Of The '70s-#2-C* . . . . . . (MCA Special Prod.)
Gloria Estefan; *Hold Me, Thrill Me, Kiss Me* . . . . (Epic)
Robert Knight; *Everlasting Love* . . . . (Collectables)
Every Breath You Take
Police; *Every Breath You Take-The Classics* . . . . (A&M)
Synchronicity . . . . (A&M)
Tammy Wynette & Sting; *Without Walls-C* . . . . (Epic)
Falling, Falling, Falling
Mandy Barnett; *I've Got A Right To Cry* . . . . (Sire)
For No One
Beatles; *Beatles-Box Set* . . . . (Capitol)

Beatles-Love Songs . . . . (Capitol)
Revolver . . . . (Capitol)
Emmylou Harris; *Pieces Of The Sky* . . . . (Reprise)
For Your Love
Tevin Campbell; *Tevin Campbell*. . . . . (Qwest)
Forget Me Nots
Patrice Rushen; *Patrice Rushen-Anthology* . . . . (Elektra)
Straight From The Heart . . . . (Elektra)
The Disco Years-#2-On The Beat-1978-1982-C . . . . (Rhino)
Gal That Got Away
Four Freshmen; *Voices In Love-Love Lost* . . . . (Collector's Choice)
Frank Sinatra; *Complete Capitol Singles Collection* . . . . (Capitol)
Ghost Town
Don Cherry; *Columbia & Monument Sides* . . . . (Collector's Choice)
Girlfriend
Alicia Keys; *Songs In A Minor* . . . . (J)
Give Me One More Shot
Alabama; *Alabama's Greatest Hits-#3* . . . . (RCA)
Gloria: The Enchantment Medley
Jesse Powell; *Jesse Powell* . . . . (Silas)
Gone
Ferlin Husky; *Ferlin Husky's Greatest Hits* . . . . (Curb)
Heroes Of Country Music-#4-Legends Of The West Coast-C . . . . . . (Rhino)
Gone
'N Sync; *Celebrity* . . . . (Jive)
Harbor Lights
Boz Scaggs; *Silk Degrees* . . . . (Columbia)
Dinah Washington; *Complete Dinah Washington On Mercury-#2-1950-1952* . . . . (Mercury)
Dinah Washington-Golden Hits . . . . (Mercury)
For Lonely Lovers . . . . (Mercury)
This Is My Story. . . . . (Mercury)
Platters; *Super Oldies Of The '60s-#9-C* . . . . (Audio Fidelity)
Harmless
Mulberry Lane; *Run Your Own Race* . . . . (Refuge/MCA)
Hate This Place
Goo Goo Dolls; *Dizzy Up The Girl* . . . . (Warner Sunset/Reprise)
Hats Off To Larry
Del Shannon; *Runaway Hits!* . . . . (Rhino)
Super Oldies Of The '60s-#2-C . . . . (Audio Fidelity)
WCBS FM 101 History Of Rock-'60s-#3-C . . . . (Collectables)
Have You Ever Been Lonely (Have You Ever Been Blue)
Ernest Tubb; *Best Of Ernest Tubb* . . . . (Curb)
The Country Music Hall Of Fame-Ernest Tubb. . . . . (MCA)
Jim Reeves & Patsy Cline; *Jim Reeves' Greatest Hits* . . . . (RCA)
Patsy Cline; *Showcase-With The Jordanaires* . . . . (MCA)
He Can't Love U
Jagged Edge; *J.E. Heartbreak* . . . . (So So Def/Columbia)
He'll Have To Go
Jim Reeves; *60 Years Of Country Music-C* . . . . (RCA)
Best Of Jim Reeves . . . . (RCA)
Billboard Top Country Hits-1960-C . . . . (Rhino)
Great Moments At The Grand Ole Opry-C . . . . (RCA)
Jim Reeves' Greatest Hits . . . . (RCA)
Nipper's Greatest Hits Of The '50s-#1-C . . . . (RCA)
Ry Cooder; *Chicken Skin Music* . . . . (Reprise)
Hello Darlin'
Conway Twitty; *Conway Twittty-20 Greatest Hits* . . . . (MCA)
Conway Twitty's Greatest Hits . . . . (Curb)
From The Vaults: Decca Country Classics-1934-1973-C . . . . (Decca)
Greatest Country Classics-#1-C . . . . (MCA Special Prod.)
Hemorrhage (In My Hands)
Fuel; *Now That's What I Call Music!-#6-C* . . . . (Virgin)
Something Like Human . . . . (Epic)
Here In My Heart
Chicago; *The Heart Of Chicago-1967-1997* . . . . (Reprise)
Here In Your Bedroom
Goldfinger; *Richter* . . . . (Mojo Music/Universal)
Hey Baby (They're Playing Our Song)
Buckinghams; *Mercy, Mercy, Mercy* . . . . (Legacy Rock Artifacts Series)
Hey Girl
Billy Joel; *Billy Joel's Greatest Hits-#3* . . . . (Columbia)
Freddie Scott; *Freddie Scott Sings And Sings And Sings* . . . . (Collectables)
Michael McDonald; *Best Of Smooth Jazz-#2-Under The Covers-C* . . . . (Warner Bros.)
Blink Of An Eye . . . . (Reprise)
Righteous Brothers; *Best Of The Righteous Brothers-#2* . . . . (Curb)
High Noon
Frankie Laine; *Billboard Top Movie Hits-1950-1954-C* . . . . (Rhino)
Tex Ritter; *Heroes Of Country Music-#4-Legends Of The West Coast-C* . . . . (Rhino)
The Envelope Please-Academy Award Winning Songs (1946-1957)-C . . . . (Rhino)
Hit The Road Jack
Ray Charles; *Ray Charles' Greatest Hits* . . . . (Rhino)
Ray Charles-Anthology. . . . . (Rhino)
Ray Charles-His Greatest Hits-#2. . . . . (Dunhill Compact Classics)
Home
Staind; *Dysfunction* . . . . (Flip/Elektra)

House Of Love
Amy Grant & Vince Gill; *House Of Love* . . . . (A&M)

How Come You Don't Call Me
Alicia Keys; *Songs In A Minor* . . . . (J)

How Do I Say I'm Sorry
Tami Davis; *Only You* . . . .(Red Ant)

How Long Gone
Brooks & Dunn; *If You See Her* . . . . (Arista)

Hurt So Bad
Lettermen; *The Lettermen's All-Time Greatest Hits* . . . . (Capitol)
Linda Ronstadt; *Linda Ronstadt's Greatest Hits, Volume Two* . . . . (Asylum)
    Mad Love . . . . (Elektra)
Little Anthony And The Imperials; *Best Of Little Anthony And The
    Imperials* . . . . (Rhino)
    Best Of Little Anthony And The Imperials . . . .(EMI)

I Am Your Woman
Syleena Johnson; *Chapter One: Love, Pain & Forgiveness* . . . . (Jive)

I Apologize
Anita Baker; *Rhythm Of Love* . . . . (Atlantic)

I Call Your Name
Beatles; *Past Masters-Volume One* . . . . (Parlophone)
    Rock 'N' Roll Music . . . . (Capitol)
    The Beatles' Second Album . . . . (Capitol)

I Can't Do That
Stephen Simmonds; *Spirit Tales* . . . . (Priority)

I Can't Live Without Your Love
Teddy Pendergrass; *45-#02462* . . . . (Philadelphia Int'l)

I Can't Sleep Baby (If I)
R. Kelly; *R. Kelly* . . . . (Jive)

I Can't Stay Mad At You
Skeeter Davis; *Nipper's Greatest Hits Of The '60s-#2-C* . . . . (RCA)

I Care 'Bout You
Milestone; *ST/Soul Food* . . . . (LaFace)

I Do Love You
Billy Stewart; *Best Of Chess Rhythm & Blues-#2-C* . . . . (Chess)
    I Do Love You . . . . (MCA Special Prod.)
    One More Time . . . . (Chess)
    Smooth Grooves-The '60s-#2-C . . . . (Rhino)
GQ; *Didn't It Blow Your Mind: Soul Hits Of The '70s-#20-C* . . . (Rhino)
    Smooth Grooves-A Sensual Collection-#5-C . . . . (Rhino)

I Don't Wanna
Aaliyah; *Next Friday* . . . . (Priority)

I Don't Want To Know
Fleetwood Mac; *Rumours* . . . .(Warner Bros.)
Goo Goo Dolls; *Legacy-A Tribute To Fleetwood Mac's Rumours-C* . . . . . (Lava)

I Don't Want To Spoil The Party
Beatles; *Beatles VI* . . . . (Capitol)
    For Sale . . . . (Capitol)
Rosanne Cash; *Greatest Country Hits Of The '80s-1989-C* . . . . . . (Columbia)
    Rosanne Cash-Hits-1979-1989 . . . . (Columbia)

I Drive Myself Crazy
'N Sync; *'N Sync* . . . . (RCA)
    Totally Hits-#2-C . . . . (Elektra)

I Got Dreams
Steve Wariner; *I Got Dreams* . . . . (MCA)

I Got The Hook Up
Master P featuring Sons Of Funk; *ST/I Got The Hook Up* . . . . (No Limit/Priority)
Sons Of Funk; *The Game Of Funk* . . . . (No Limit/Priority)

I Got To Find My Baby
Animals; *In The Beginning* . . . . (Sundazed Music)

I Guess I'm Crazy
Jim Reeves; *Billboard Top Country Hits-1964-C* . . . . (Rhino)
    Essential Jim Reeves . . . . (RCA)

I Heard It Through The Grapevine
Creedence Clearwater Revival; *Chooglin'* . . . . (Fantasy)
    Cosmo's Factory . . . . (Fantasy)
    Creedence Clearwater Revival-Chronicle . . . . (Fantasy)
    Creedence Clearwater Revival-Gold . . . . (Fantasy)
    Movie Album . . . . (Fantasy)
Gladys Knight & The Pips; *16 #1 Hits From The Late '60s-C* . . . (Motown)
    Compact Command Performances-Gladys Knight & The Pips . . . . . (Motown)
    Every Great Motown Song-First 25 Years-C . . . . (Motown)
    Motown Grammy R&B Performances Of The '60s & '70s-C . . . (Motown)
    Motown Superstar Series-#13-Gladys Knight & The Pips . . . (Motown)
    Top 10 With A Bullet-Motown Girl Groups-C . . . . (Motown)
Marvin Gaye; *25 #1 Hits From 25 Years-C* . . . . (Motown)
    Every Great Motown Hit Of Marvin Gaye . . . . (Motown)
    Marvin Gaye Live At The London Palladium . . . . (Motown)
    Marvin Gaye-Anthology . . . . (Motown)
    Most Played Songs On America's Jukeboxes . . . . (Motown)
    Motown Story-First 25 Years-C . . . . (Motown)

I Let A Song Go Out Of My Heart
Bill Jennings; *Stompin' With Bill* . . . . (Collectables)
Duke Ellington; *Braggin' In Brass-Immortal 1938 Year* . . . . (Portrait)
Joe Pass; *Portraits Of Duke Ellington* . . . .(Pablo)
Teresa Brewer; *Sophisticated Lady* . . . . (Columbia)
Tony Bennett; *Jazz* . . . . (Columbia)

I Need You
Beatles; *ST/Help!* . . . . (Capitol)

I Still Love You
Next; *Rated Next* . . . . (Divine Mill/Arista)

I Understand (Just How You Feel)
Four Tunes; *45-#5132* . . . . (Jubilee)
Freddie And The Dreamers; *45-#72377* . . . . (Mercury)
G-Clefs; *45-#7500* . . . . (Terrace)
Ink Spots; *ST/Trees Lounge* . . . . (MCA)

I Wanna Feel That Way Again
Tracy Byrd; *I'm From The Country* . . . . (MCA)

I Want It That Way
Backstreet Boys; *Millennium* . . . . (Jive)

I Want My Goodbye Back
Ty Herndon; *What Mattered Most* . . . . (Epic)

I Want You Back
Jackson 5; *Billboard Top Rock 'N' Roll Hits-1970-C* . . . . (Rhino)
    Jackson 5's Greatest Hits . . . . (Motown)
    Jackson 5-The Ultimate Collection . . . . (Motown)

I Want You Back
'N Sync; *'N Sync* . . . . (RCA)

I Was Wrong
Keb' Mo'; *Slow Down* . . . . (550/Epic/Okeh)

I Wonder If You Feel The Way I Do
Asleep At The Wheel featuring Merle Haggard; *Tribute To The Music Of
    Bob Wills And The Texas Playboys-C* . . . . (Liberty)
Bob Wills & His Texas Playboys; *For The Last Time* . . . . . . (Capitol)

I Won't Let You Do That To Me
Luther Vandross; *One Night With You-The Best Of Love-#2* . . . . (LV/Epic)

If Ever You're In My Arms Again
Peabo Bryson; *Straight From The Heart* . . . . (Elektra)

If He Should Break Your Heart
Journey; *Trial By Fire* . . . . (Columbia)

If I Lose
Ricky Skaggs and Kentucky Thunder; *Bluegrass Rules!* . . . . (Rounder)

If I Was A Drinkin' Man
Neal McCoy; *Neal McCoy's Greatest Hits* . . . .(Atlantic)
    Neal McCoy-Super Hits . . . .(Atlantic)
    You Gotta Love That! . . . .(Atlantic)

If You Go
Jon Secada; *Heart, Soul & A Voice* . . . . (SBK)

If You Leave Me Now
Chicago; *Chicago's Greatest Hits-#2 (1974-81)* . . . . (Chicago)
    If You Leave Me Now . . . . (Chicago)

If You Love Me, Baby
Beatles; *In The Beginning-The Early Tapes* . . . . (Polydor)

If You Loved Me
Tracy Lawrence; *Time Marches On* . . . .(Atlantic)

If You're Gone
Matchbox Twenty; *Mad Season By Matchbox Twenty* . . . . (Lava)

I'll Be Back
Beatles; *Beatles '65* . . . . (Capitol)
    Beatles-Love Songs . . . . (Capitol)

I'll Be There For You
Bon Jovi; *New Jersey* . . . . (Jambco)

I'll Come Runnin'
Connie Smith; *Essential Connie Smith* . . . . (RCA)

I'll Go Crazy
Andy Griggs; *You Won't Ever Be Lonely* . . . . (RCA)

I'm Going To Sit Right Down And Cry Over You
Elvis Presley; *Elvis Presley* . . . . (RCA)

I'm Losing You
John Lennon; *Double Fantasy* . . . . (Capitol)
    The John Lennon Anthology . . . . (Capitol)
    The John Lennon Collection . . . . (Capitol)
    Wonsaponatime . . . . (Capitol)

I'm Not Giving You Up
Gloria Estefan; *Destiny* . . . . (Epic)

Incomplete
Sisqo; *Now That's What I Call Music!-#5-C* . . . . (Virgin)
    Unleash The Dragon . . . . (Dragon/Def Soul/IDJMG)

It Happens To Be Me
Earl "Fatha" Hines; *At Home* . . . . (Delmark)

It's All About You (Not About Me)
Tracie Spencer; *Tracie* . . . . (Capitol)

It's In Your Eyes (Any Time At All)
Phil Collins; *Dance Into The Light* . . . .(Atlantic)

It's Only Love
Beatles; *The Beatles-Anthology-#2* . . . . (Capitol)

It's Time For Love
Chi-Lites; *Chi-Lites' Greatest Hits-#2* . . . . (Rhino)

It's Too Late
Derek And The Dominos; *Layla* . . . .(Polydor)

I've Got A Right To Cry
Mandy Barnett; *I've Got A Right To Cry* . . . .(Sire)

Just As Much As Ever
Bobby Vinton; *Bobby Vinton-16 Most Requested Songs* . . . . . (Legacy)

Just Once In My Life
Righteous Brothers; *Best Of The Righteous Brothers* . . . . (Curb)
    Phil Spector-Back To Mono 1958-1969-C . . . .(Abkco)

Righteous Brothers-Anthology 1962-1974 . . . . (Rhino)
Unchained Melody-Very Best Of The Righteous Brothers . . . . (Polydor)

Keep The Fire Burnin'
REO Speedwagon; *A Second Decade Of Rock And Roll 1981 To 1991* . . . . (Epic)
Good Trouble . . . . (Epic)
Jane Fonda's New & Improved Workout . . . . (Columbia)

Kentucky Rain
Elvis Presley; *Elvis Presley-Pure Gold* . . . . (RCA)
Memphis Record . . . . (RCA)
Worldwide 50 Gold Award Hits, Vol. 1, Parts 1 & 2 . . . . (RCA)

Laredo
Chris Cagle; *Play It Loud* . . . . (Capitol)

Last Goodbye
Jeff Buckley; *Grace* . . . . (Columbia)

Last Night I Didn't Get To Sleep At All
5th Dimension; *Greatest Hits On Earth* . . . . (Arista)

Last Thing On My Mind
Porter Wagoner & Dolly Parton; *Essential Porter Wagoner & Dolly Parton* . . . . (RCA)

Lately
Divine; *Fairy Tales* . . . . (Pendulum)

Leavin' And Sayin' Goodbye
Faron Young; *Faron Young-Golden Hits* . . . . (Mercury)
Faron Young's Greatest Hits-#1-3 . . . . (Step One)

Leavin' Train
Bruce Springsteen; *Tracks* . . . . (Columbia)

Let Love Come Between Us
James & Bobby Purify; *Bubblegum Classics-#4-C* . . . . (Varese Vintage)

Let's Hang On!
4 Seasons; *Four Seasons' Greatest Hits-#2* . . . . (Rhino)

Let's Stay Together
Eric Benet; *True To Myself* . . . . (Jac-Mac/Warner Bros.)

Lie To Me
Jonny Lang; *Lie To Me* . . . . (A&M)

Light In Your Eyes
Blessid Union Of Souls; *Blessid Union Of Souls* . . . . (Capitol)

Like Strangers
Everly Brothers; *All They Had To Do Was Dream* . . . . (Rhino)
Everly Brothers' Greatest Hits . . . . (Delta)
Everly Brothers-Cadence Classics-Their 20 Greatest Hits . . . . (Rhino)

Lilly Dale
Bob Wills & His Texas Playboys; *The Country Music Hall Of Fame-Bob Wills* . . . . (Universal)

Little Darlin'
Diamonds; *Best Of The Diamonds* . . . . (Rhino)
Billboard Top Rock 'N' Roll Hits-1957-C . . . . (Rhino)
Cruisin'-1957-C . . . . (Increase)
Good Time Rock 'N' Roll-C . . . . (MCA)
Oldies But Goodies-#11-C . . . . (Original Sound)
ST/American Graffiti . . . . (MCA)

Little More Love
Vince Gill; *High Lonesome Sound* . . . . (MCA)

Little Red Rodeo
Collin Raye; *Best Of Collin Raye-Direct Hits* . . . . (Epic)

Lonely Teardrops
Jackie Wilson; *Billboard Top R&B Hits-1958-C* . . . . (Rhino)
Reet Petite-Best Of Jackie Wilson . . . . (Columbia)
The Jackie Wilson Story . . . . (Epic)
The Jackie Wilson Story-#2 . . . . (Epic)

Long Hot Summer Night
Jimi Hendrix Experience; *Electric Ladyland* . . . . (Reprise)

Look What Love Has Done
Patty Smyth; *ST/Junior* . . . . (MCA)

Loola Loo
Keb' Mo'; *The Door* . . . . (550/Epic/Okeh)

Love Me
Elvis Presley; *24 Karat Hits!* . . . . (Dunhill Compact Classics)

Love Me
112 Featuring Mase; *Room 112* . . . . (Bad Boy/Arista)

Love Will Be Waiting
Kevon Edmonds; *24/7* . . . . (RCA)

Love Will Find A Way
Christina Aguilera; *Christina Aguilera* . . . . (RCA)

Lovefool
Cardigans; *First Band On The Moon* . . . . (Mercury)
MTV Best Of The Buzz Bin-#2-C . . . . (Mammoth)

Lucille
Everly Brothers; *Golden Hits Of The Everly Brothers* . . . . (Warner Bros.)
The Reunion Concert-Live At Albert Hall 1983 . . . . (Mercury)
Very Best Of The Everly Brothers . . . . (Warner Bros.)
Little Richard; *American Graffiti-#3-C* . . . . (MCA)
Big Hits . . . . (Crescendo)
Little Richard's Greatest Hits . . . . (Everest)
Oldies But Goodies-#12-C . . . . (Original Sound)

Mad Season
Matchbox Twenty; *Mad Season By Matchbox Twenty* . . . . (Lava)

Make The World Go Away
Eddy Arnold; *Best Of Eddy Arnold* . . . . (RCA)

Billboard Top Country Hits-1965-C . . . . (Rhino)
Eddy Arnold-Pure Gold . . . . (RCA)
Nipper's Greatest Hits Of The '60s-#1-C . . . . (RCA)
World Of Hits . . . . (MGM)
Ray Price; *Ray Price-16 Biggest Hits* . . . . (Legacy)
Ray Price-20 Hits . . . . (Tee Vee)

Massachusetts
Bee Gees; *Bee Gees-Gold* . . . . (Polydor)
Here At Last...Bee Gees...Live . . . . (Polydor)

Maybe
Nilsson; *Harry* . . . . (Dunhill Compact Classics)

Maybe We Should Just Sleep On It
Tim McGraw; *All I Want* . . . . (Curb)
Tim McGraw's Greatest Hits . . . . (Curb)

Message Of Love
Journey; *Trial By Fire* . . . . (Columbia)

Misery
Beatles; *Introducing...The Beatles* . . . . (Vee-Jay)
Rarities . . . . (Capitol)

Miss Blue
Filter; *Title Of Record* . . . . (Reprise)

Most Precarious
Blues Traveler; *Straight On Till Morning* . . . . (A&M)

Mr. Dream Merchant
Jerry Butler; *Best Of Jerry Butler* . . . . (Rhino)
Soul Shots-#2-The "In" Crowd-Sweet Soul-C . . . . (Rhino)

Muddy Water
Aretha Franklin; *Aretha Sings The Blues* . . . . (Columbia)
Sonny Terry & Brownie McGhee; *Best Of Sonny Terry & Brownie McGhee* . . . . (Prestige)
Midnight Special . . . . (Fantasy)

My Heart Cries For You
Charlie Rich; *Charlie Rich-20 Golden Hits* . . . . (Sun)
Time For Tears-C . . . . (Sun)
Dinah Shore; *Nipper's Greatest Hits Of The '50s-#1-C* . . . . (RCA)
Guy Mitchell; *Guy Mitchell-16 Most Requested Songs* . . . . (Legacy)

My Love Is For Real
Paula Abdul; *Head Over Heels* . . . . (Captive/Virgin)

My Lover Man
Bruce Springsteen; *Tracks* . . . . (Columbia)

My My
Seven Mary Three; *American Standard* . . . . (Mammoth)

My Own Worst Enemy
Lit; *A Place In The Sun* . . . . (RCA)

My Shoes Keep Walking Back To You
Ray Price; *All Time Legends Of Country Music-C* . . . . (Legacy)
Essential Ray Price-1951-1962 . . . . (Columbia)
Ray Price's Greatest Hits . . . . (Columbia)

Never Find Someone Like You
Keith Martin; *ST/Bad Boys* . . . . (Work)

Never Gonna Let You Go
Blackstreet; *Another Level* . . . . (Interscope)

Never Let You Go
Third Eye Blind; *Blue* . . . . (Elektra)
Totally Hits-#2-C . . . . (Elektra)

Night Before
Beatles; *Beatles-Box Set* . . . . (Capitol)
Rock 'N' Roll Music . . . . (Capitol)
ST/Help! . . . . (Capitol)

No Love
Kevon Edmonds; *24/7* . . . . (RCA)

Nothing Compares 2 U
Sinead O'Connor; *I Do Not Want What I Haven't Got* . . . . (Ensign)

Obviously Five Believers
Bob Dylan; *Blonde On Blonde* . . . . (Columbia)

Oh Baby Doll
Chuck Berry; *The Chess Box-Chuck Berry* . . . . (Chess)

Oh Darling
Beatles; *Abbey Road* . . . . (Parlophone)
The Beatles-Anthology-#3 . . . . (Capitol)

Oh! Carol
Neil Sedaka; *Neil Sedaka Sings His Greatest Hits* . . . . (RCA)
Neil Sedaka's All-Time Greatest Hits . . . . (RCA)
Nipper's Greatest Hits Of The '50s-#1-C . . . . (RCA)

On Bended Knee
Boyz II Men; *Boyz II Men II* . . . . (Motown)

One After 909
Beatles; *Let It Be* . . . . (Capitol)
The Beatles-Anthology-#1 . . . . (Capitol)

One Way Track
Ricky Skaggs and Kentucky Thunder; *History Of The Future* . . . (Skaggs Family)

Only One Road
Celine Dion; *The Colour Of My Love* . . . . (550 Music)

Over My Shoulder
Mike & The Mechanics; *Beggar On A Beach Of Gold* . . . . (Atlantic)

Past The Point Of Rescue
Hal Ketchum; *Past The Point Of Rescue* . . . . (Curb)

Photograph
Ringo Starr; *Blast From Your Past* . . . . (Gold Rush)
Ringo . . . . (Capitol)
Please Don't Go Girl
New Kids On The Block; *Hangin' Tough* . . . . (Columbia)
No More Games/Remix Album . . . . (Columbia)
Please Mr. Sun
Johnnie Ray; *Back To The Early '50s* . . . . (Dominion Entert.)
Johnnie Ray-16 Most Requested Songs . . . . (Legacy)
Vogues; *Vogues' Greatest Hits* . . . . (Rhino)
Prayin' For Daylight
Rascal Flatts; *Rascal Flatts* . . . . (Lyric Street)
Promise
Jagged Edge; *J.E. Heartbreak* . . . . (So So Def/Columbia)
Quitter Never Wins, A
Jonny Lang; *Lie To Me* . . . . (A&M)
Real World
Matchbox Twenty; *Yourself Or Someone Like You* . . . . (Lava)
Reason For Breathing
Babyface; *Collection Of His Greatest Hits* . . . . (Arista/Epic)
Remember
Jimi Hendrix Experience; *Are You Experienced?* . . . . (Reprise)
Revival
Gretchen Peters; *Gretchen Peters* . . . . (Purple Crayon Prod.)
Rhythm Of The Night
Corona; *Hot Luv-Ultimate Dance Songs Collection-C* . . . . (EMI)
Rhythm Of The Night . . . . (East West)
DeBarge; *DeBarge's Greatest Hits* . . . . (Motown)
Motown Story-First 25 Years-C . . . . (Motown)
Rhythm Of The Night . . . . (Motown)
Road To Dead
Paula Cole; *This Fire* . . . . (Imago)
Rose And A Baby Ruth, A
George Hamilton IV; *At The Hop* . . . . (MCA)
Vintage Music-#12-C . . . . (MCA)
Rose Colored Glasses
John Conlee; *Backstage At The Grand Ole Opry-C* . . . . (RCA)
Grand Ole Opry-75 Years-#1-C . . . . (MCA)
John Conlee-Legends . . . . (MCA)
John Conlee's Greatest Hits . . . . (MCA)
MCA Records 30 Years Of Hits-1958-1988-C . . . . (MCA)
Rose Colored Glasses . . . . (Universal)
Run Baby Run (Back Into My Arms)
Newbeats; *Collectables Presents The History Of Rock-#10-C* . . . . (Collectables)
Newbeats-Golden Classics Edition . . . . (Collectables)
Tremeloes; *Best Of The Tremeloes* . . . . (Rhino)
Running Scared
Roy Orbison; *For The Lonely: A Roy Orbison Anthology 1959-1965* . . . (Rhino)
In Dreams-Greatest Hits . . . . (Orbison)
Roy Orbison & Friends: Black & White Night-Live . . . . (Virgin)
Roy Orbison's All-Time Greatest Hits-#1 & 2 . . . . (Monument)
San Francisco Days
Chris Isaak; *San Francisco Days* . . . . (Reprise)
Save Your Heart For Me
Gary Lewis And The Playboys; *Gary Lewis & The Playboys* . . . . (Gold Rush)
Gary Lewis And The Playboys' Greatest Hits . . . . (Curb)
Second Chance
38 Special; *Rock & Roll Strategy* . . . . (A&M)
Sentimental
Deborah Cox; *Deborah Cox* . . . . (Arista)
Seven Rooms Of Gloom
Four Tops; *Four Tops' Greatest Hits* . . . . (Motown)
Four Tops Reach Out . . . . (Motown)
Four Tops-Anthology . . . . (Motown)
Shame
Stabbing Westward; *Wither Blister Burn & Peel* . . . . (Columbia)
She Loves You
Beatles; *Beatles 1* . . . . (Capitol)
Beatles-20 Greatest Hits . . . . (Capitol)
Beatles-Box Set . . . . (Capitol)
Past Masters-Volume One . . . . (Parlophone)
The Beatles At The Hollywood Bowl . . . . (Capitol)
The Beatles' Second Album . . . . (Capitol)
The Beatles/1962-1966 . . . . (Capitol)
Shout
Beatles; *The Beatles-Anthology-#1* . . . . (Capitol)
Isley Brothers; *Nipper's Greatest Hits Of The '50s-#2-C* . . . . (RCA)
Shout . . . . (Collectables)
ST/The Wanderers . . . . (Warner Bros.)
Joey Dee & the Starliters; *Echoes Of A Rock Era-Later Years-C* . . . . (Roulette)
Hey Let's Twist! Best Of Joey Dee & The Starliters . . . . (Rhino)
Live At The Peppermint Lounge . . . . (Accord)
Original Rock 'N' Roll Hits Of The '60s-C . . . . (Roulette)
Sock Hoppin' Sixties-C . . . . (JCI Assoc. Labels)
Otis Day & The Knights; *Shout* . . . . (MCA)
ST/Animal House . . . . (MCA)
Tom Petty And The Heartbreakers; *Pack Up The Plantation-Live!* . . . . (MCA)
Sincerely
McGuire Sisters; *Billboard Pop Memories-1955-1959-C* . . . . (Rhino)
McGuire Sisters' Greatest Hits . . . . (MCA)
Moonglows; *13 Of The Best Doo Wop Love Songs-C* . . . . (Original Sound)
Billboard Top Rock 'N' Roll Hits-1955-C . . . . (Rhino)
Moonglows-Their Greatest Hits . . . . (Chess)
Sitting Home
Total; *Kima, Keisha & Pam* . . . . (Bad Boy/Arista)
Snap Your Fingers
Barbara Lewis; *Hello Stranger-The Best Of Barbara Lewis* . . . . (Rhino)
Dick Curless; *The Drag 'Em Off The Interstate, Sock It To 'Em Hits Of Dick Curless* . . . . (Razor & Tie)
Don Gibson; *Best Of Don Gibson-#1* . . . . (Curb)
Joe Henderson; *Discoveries Presents-Stereo Oldies-C* . . . . (Varese Vintage)
Ronnie Milsap; *Essential Ronnie Milsap* . . . . (RCA)
Heart & Soul . . . . (RCA)
Ronnie Milsap's Greatest Hits-#3 . . . . (RCA)
So Sad (To Watch Good Love Go Bad)
Everly Brothers; *The Reunion Concert-Live At Albert Hall 1983* . . . . (Mercury)
Walk Right Back: The Everly Brothers On Warner Bros.-1960-1969 . . . . (Warner Archives)
Frank Ifield; *Best Of Frank Ifield* . . . . (Curb)
Sweethearts Of The Rodeo; *Columbia Country Classics-#5-A New Tradition-C* . . . . (Columbia)
Someday I'll Find You
Bobby Short; *Mad About Noel Coward* . . . . (Atlantic)
Mary Martin & Noel Coward; *Together With Music* . . . . (DRG)
Someday We'll Be Together
Diana Ross & The Supremes; *20/20-C* . . . . (Motown)
Diana Ross & The Supremes' Greatest Hits-#3 . . . . (Motown)
Diana Ross & The Supremes-Anthology (1962-1969) . . . . (Motown)
Evening With Diana Ross . . . . (Motown)
Motown Story-First 25 Years-C . . . . (Motown)
Motown Superstar Series-#1-Diana Ross & The Supremes . . . . (Motown)
Somehow Tonight
Ricky Skaggs and Kentucky Thunder; *Bluegrass Rules!* . . . . (Rounder)
Southern California
George Jones & Tammy Wynette; *George Jones & Tammy Wynette-16 Biggest Hits* . . . . (Epic/Legacy)
Tammy Wynette & George Jones; *Encore-Tammy Wynette & George Jones* . . . . (Epic)
Tammy Wynette & George Jones' Greatest Hits . . . . (Epic)
Space Between, The
Dave Matthews Band; *Everyday* . . . . (RCA)
Standing In The Shadows Of Love
Barry White; *Barry White's Greatest Hits* . . . . (20th Century Fox)
I've Got So Much To Give . . . . (20th Century Fox)
Four Tops; *Four Tops' Greatest Hits* . . . . (Motown)
Four Tops Reach Out . . . . (Motown)
Four Tops-Anthology . . . . (Motown)
Motown Story-First 25 Years-C . . . . (Motown)
Motown Superstar Series-#14-Four Tops . . . . (Motown)
Rod Stewart; *Blondes Have More Fun* . . . . (Warner Bros.)
Stay (I Missed You)
Lisa Loeb; *ST/Reality Bites* . . . . (RCA)
Still
Bill Anderson; *Best Of Bill Anderson* . . . . (Curb)
Bill Anderson's Greatest Hits . . . . (Varese Sarabande)
Billboard Top Country Hits-1963-C . . . . (Rhino)
From The Vaults: Decca Country Classics-1934-1973-C . . . . (Decca)
Grand Ole Opry-75 Years-#2-C . . . . (MCA)
Still Holding On
Clint Black & Martina McBride; *Nothin' But The Taillights* . . . . (RCA)
Martina McBride & Clint Black; *Evolution* . . . . (RCA)
Stop! In The Name Of Love
Diana Ross & The Supremes; *16 #1 Hits From The Early '60s-C* . . . . (Motown)
Diana Ross & The Supremes' Greatest Hits . . . . (Motown)
Diana Ross & The Supremes-Anthology (1962-1969) . . . . (Motown)
Evening With Diana Ross . . . . (Motown)
Girl Groups-Story Of A Sound-C . . . . (Rhino)
Motown Superstar Series-#1-Diana Ross & The Supremes . . . . (Motown)
Hollies; *45-#89819* . . . . (Atlantic)
Supremes; *Billboard Top Pop Hits-1965-C* . . . . (Rhino)
Sukiyaki
4 P.M.; *Now's The Time* . . . . (Next Plateau/London/Island)
Kyu Sakamoto; *When AM Was King-C* . . . . (Capitol)
Taste Of Honey; *Golden Honey* . . . . (Capitol)
Twice As Sweet . . . . (Capitol)
Take 54
Nilsson; *Son Of Schmilsson* . . . . (RCA)
Take It On Faith
Joshua Kadison; *Delilah Blue* . . . . (EMI)
Take Me To Your World
George Jones; *Tammy Wynette...Remembered-C* . . . . (Asylum)
Tammy Wynette; *Tammy Wynette-16 Biggest Hits* . . . . (Legacy)
Tammy Wynette's Greatest Hits . . . . (Epic)
Teenager In Love
Dion And The Belmonts; *Classic Old & Gold-C* . . . . (Laurie)
Collectables Presents The History Of Rock-#6-C . . . . (Collectables)
Dion And The Belmonts-Their Best . . . . (Laurie)
Oldies But Goodies-#6-C . . . . (Original Sound)
Party Time Fifties-C . . . . (JCI Assoc. Labels)

Tell Me (You're Coming Back)
Rolling Stones; *Big Hits (High Tide & Green Grass)* . . . . (Abkco)
England's Newest Hit Makers/The Rolling Stones . . . . (Abkco)
More Hot Rocks (big hits & fazed cookies) . . . . (Abkco)
Singles Collection-The London Years . . . . (Abkco)

Tell Me Why
Beatles; *Beatles-Box Set* . . . . (Capitol)
Something New . . . . (Capitol)
ST/A Hard Day's Night . . . . (Capitol)

Tequila Talkin'
Lonestar; *Lonestar* . . . . (BNA)

Then You Can Tell Me Goodbye
Casinos; *Then You Can Tell Me Goodbye* . . . . (Varese Vintage)
Neal McCoy; *Neal McCoy's Greatest Hits* . . . . (Atlantic)

There Goes My Heart
Mavericks; *Best Of The Mavericks-Super Colossal Smash Hits Of
The '90s* . . . . (Mercury)
What A Crying Shame . . . . (MCA)

Things Aren't Funny Anymore
Merle Haggard; *Capitol Collectors Series-Merle Haggard* . . . . (Capitol)
Epic Collection-Recorded Live . . . . (Epic)
Merle Haggard-Country Boy . . . . (Pair)

Thinkin' 'Bout It
Gerald Levert; *Love & Consequences* . . . . (East West)

This Boy
Beatles; *Beatles-Box Set* . . . . (Capitol)
Beatles-Love Songs . . . . (Capitol)
Meet The Beatles! . . . . (Capitol)
Past Masters-Volume One . . . . (Parlophone)
The Beatles-Anthology-#1 . . . . (Capitol)

This Woman And This Man
Clay Walker; *If I Could Make A Living* . . . . (Giant)

Ticket To Ride
Beatles; *Beatles 1* . . . . (Capitol)
Beatles-20 Greatest Hits . . . . (Capitol)
Beatles-Box Set . . . . (Capitol)
Reel Music . . . . (Capitol)
ST/Help! . . . . (Capitol)
The Beatles At The Hollywood Bowl . . . . (Capitol)
The Beatles/1962-1966 . . . . (Capitol)
Carpenters; *Carpenters-Classics-#2* . . . . (A&M)
Carpenters-The Singles 1969-1973 . . . . (A&M)
From The Top . . . . (A&M)
Ticket To Ride . . . . (A&M)
Yesterday Once More . . . . (A&M)
Vanilla Fudge; *Best Of Vanilla Fudge* . . . . (Atco)
Vanilla Fudge . . . . (Atco)

To Have You Back Again
Patty Loveless; *Long Stretch Of Lonesome* . . . . (Epic)

To Love You More
Celine Dion with The Bee Gees; *All The Way...A Decade
Of Song* . . . . (550 Music)
Let's Talk About Love-C . . . . (550 Music)

Tonight You Belong To Me
Patience & Prudence; *Great Jukebox Hits Of The
'50s-#2-C* . . . . (CEMA Special Prod.)

Too Little Too Late
Barenaked Ladies; *Maroon* . . . . (Reprise)

Twinkle, Twinkle Lucky Star
Merle Haggard; *Chill Factor* . . . . (Epic)
Greatest Country Hits Of The '80s-1988-C . . . . (Columbia)

Twisted
Keith Sweat; *Keith Sweat* . . . . (Elektra)

Two Dozen Roses
Shenandoah; *30 Years Of #1 Hits-#20-C* . . . . (Columbia)
Road Not Taken . . . . (Columbia)
Shenandoah's Greatest Hits . . . . (Columbia)

Un-Break My Heart
Toni Braxton; *Secrets* . . . . (LaFace)

Unchained Melody
Elvis Presley; *Always On My Mind* . . . . (RCA)
Moody Blue . . . . (RCA)
The Great Performances . . . . (RCA)
George Benson; *Livin' Inside Your Love* . . . . (Warner Bros.)
LeAnn Rimes; *LeAnn Rimes-Early Years-Unchained Melody* . . . . . (MCG/Curb)
Platters; *Platters Greatest Hits* . . . . (Everest)
Red Sails In The Sunset . . . . (Allegiance)
Richard Clayderman; *Richard Clayderman Plays Love Songs Of The
World* . . . . (Columbia)
Righteous Brothers; *Righteous Brothers' Greatest Hits* . . . . (Verve)
ST/Ghost . . . . (Varese Sarabande)
Willie Nelson; *Stardust* . . . . (Legacy)

Us
Celine Dion; *Let's Talk About Love-C* . . . . (550 Music)

Walkin' Away
Diamond Rio; *Diamond Rio IV* . . . . (Arista)
Diamond Rio's Greatest Hits . . . . (Arista)

Walkin' The Floor Over You
Asleep At The Wheel; *Western Standard Time* . . . . (Epic)

Ernest Tubb; *Legend & The Legacy* . . . . (First Generation)
The Ernest Tubb Story . . . . (MCA)
Ernest Tubb/Merle Haggard/Charlie Daniels; *Ernest Tubb
Collection-C* . . . . (Step One)
Sandy Denny; *Who Knows Where The Time Goes* . . . . (Hannibal)
Webb Pierce; *Webb Pierce-Golden Hits* . . . . (Plantation)

Walking After You
Foo Fighters; *The Colour And The Shape* . . . . (Roswell/RCA)

Walking On Broken Glass
Annie Lennox; *Diva* . . . . (Arista)

Walls
Tom Petty And The Heartbreakers; *ST/She's The One* . . . . (Warner Bros.)

Wanted
Perry Como; *Perry Como's All-Time Greatest Hits-#1* . . . . (RCA)
Perry Como's Greatest Hits . . . . (RCA)

We Can Work It Out
Beatles; *"Yesterday"...And Today* . . . . (Capitol)
Beatles 1 . . . . (Capitol)
Beatles-20 Greatest Hits . . . . (Capitol)
Beatles-Box Set . . . . (Capitol)
Past Masters-Volume Two . . . . (Parlophone)
The Beatles/1962-1966 . . . . (Capitol)
Paul McCartney; *Unplugged (The Official Bootleg)* . . . . (Capitol)
Stevie Wonder; *Beatles Songs By Greatest Stars* . . . . (Motown)
Signed Sealed & Delivered . . . . (Motown)
Stevie Wonder's Greatest Hits-#2 . . . . (Motown)
Top 10 With A Bullet-Motown Solo Stars-C . . . . (Motown)

We Just Couldn't Say Goodbye
Guy Lombardo & His Royal Canadians; *Guy Lombardo-16 Most Requested
Songs* . . . . (Legacy)

We're Not Making Love No More
Dru Hill; *ST/Soul Food* . . . . (LaFace)

Western Union
Elvis Presley; *From Nashville To Memphis-The Essential '60s Masters* . . (RCA)

What About Us
Total; *Kima, Keisha & Pam* . . . . (Bad Boy/Arista)
LaFace Records Presents The Platinum Collection-C . . . . (LaFace)
ST/Soul Food . . . . (LaFace)

What Do I Have To Do?
Stabbing Westward; *Wither Blister Burn & Peel* . . . . (Columbia)

What I Didn't Know
Athenaeum; *Radiance* . . . . (Atlantic)

What I Meant To Say
Wade Hayes; *Old Enough To Know Better* . . . . (Columbia)

What You Won't Do For Love
Bobby Caldwell; *Love Shouldn't Hurt-C* . . . . (Qwest)
Go West; *Chicken Soup For The Woman's Soul-C* . . . . (Rhino)

Wheel, The
Rosanne Cash; *The Wheel* . . . . (Columbia)

When It's Over
Sugar Ray; *Sugar Ray* . . . . (Lava)
Totally Hits 2001-C . . . . (Arista)

When She Cries
Restless Heart; *Big Iron Horses* . . . . (RCA)
Restless Heart's Greatest Hits . . . . (RCA)
Today's Number One Country-C . . . . (K-Tel)

When Somebody Loves You
Alan Jackson; *When Somebody Loves You* . . . . (Arista)

Where Did Our Love Go
Diana Ross; *Diana Ross-The Ultimate Collection* . . . . (Motown)
Diana Ross & The Supremes; *Every Great Motown Song-First 25
Years-C* . . . . (Motown)

Where Do I Go From You
Jon Secada; *Heart, Soul & A Voice* . . . . (SBK)

Whispering Wind
Mandy Barnett; *I've Got A Right To Cry* . . . . (Sire)

Who Can I Turn To (When Nobody Needs Me)
Tony Bennett; *Tony Bennett Sings His All-Time Hall Of
Fame Hits* . . . . (Columbia)

Why
Beatles; *The Beatles featuring Tony Sheridan-In The Beginning (Circa
1960)* . . . . (Polydor)

Why Didn't You Call Me
Macy Gray; *On How Life Is* . . . . (Epic)

Wild Horses
Rolling Stones; *Hot Rocks 1964-1971* . . . . (Abkco)
Made In The Shade . . . . (Rolling Stones)
Singles Collection-The London Years . . . . (Abkco)
Sticky Fingers . . . . (Virgin)

Wildest Times Of The World
Vonda Shepard; *ST/Songs From "Ally McBeal" Featuring Vonda
Shepard* . . . . (550/Epic)

Woman, Woman
Union Gap Featuring Gary Puckett; *Best Of Gary
Puckett* . . . . (Hollywood/DNA-Rounder)
Gary Puckett And The Union Gap's Greatest Hits . . . . (Columbia)

Word Games
Billy Walker; *45-#10205* . . . . (RCA)
Lovin' and Losin' . . . . (RCA)

Words
- Bee Gees; *Bee Gees-Gold*. . . . . (Polydor)
  - *Here At Last...Bee Gees...Live* . . . . (Polydor)
  - *History Of British Rock-#9-C* . . . . (Rhino)
- Elvis Presley; *From Memphis To Vegas/From Vegas To Memphis* . . . . . . (RCA)
  - *That's The Way It Is* . . . . (RCA)
- Joan Armatrading; *Shouting Stage* . . . . (A&M)
- Rita Coolidge; *Anytime...Anywhere* . . . . (A&M)
  - *Rita Coolidge-Classics-#5* . . . . (A&M)
  - *Rita Coolidge's Greatest Hits* . . . . (A&M)

Working My Way Back To You
- 4 Seasons; *25th Anniversary Collection* . . . . (Rhino)
  - *4 Seasons-Anthology* . . . . (Rhino)

Working My Way Back To You/Forgive Me, Girl
- Spinners; *Billboard Top Hits-1980-C* . . . . (Rhino)
  - *One Of A Kind Love Affair-Anthology* . . . . (Rhino)
  - *Very Best Of The Spinners* . . . . (Rhino)

Write This Down
- George Strait; *Always Never The Same* . . . .(MCA)

www.Memory
- Alan Jackson; *Under The Influence* . . . . (Arista)

Yes!
- Chad Brock; *Yes!* . . . .(Warner Bros.)

You Are Everything
- Dru Hill; *Enter The Dru* . . . . (Def Jam/RAL/Mercury/Island)

You Are Not Alone
- Michael Jackson; *1996 Grammy Nominees-C* . . . . (Columbia)
  - *HIStory: Past, Present And Future-Book 1-C* . . . .(Epic)

You Belong To Me
- Dean Martin; *Dean Martin's All Time Greatest Hits* . . . . (Curb)
- Duprees; *13 Of The Best Doo Wop Love Songs-#2-C* . . . . . (Original Sound)
  - *Baby Boomer's Best-Mellow '60s-C* . . . . (Priority)
  - *Best Of The Duprees* . . . . (Rhino)
- Jo Stafford; *Billboard Pop Memories-1950-1954-C.* . . . . . . (Rhino)
  - *Jo Stafford's Greatest Hits.* . . . . (Curb)
- Johnny Mathis; *In The Still Of The Night* . . . . (Columbia)
- Patsy Cline; *Patsy Cline Sings Songs Of Love* . . . .(MCA Special Prod.)
  - *Sentimentally Yours* . . . .(MCA)
- Vonda Shepard; *ST/Songs From ''Ally McBeal'' Featuring Vonda Shepard* . . . . (550/Epic)

You Belong To Me
- Carly Simon; *Boys In The Trees* . . . . (Elektra)
  - *Carly Simon-Greatest Hits Live* . . . . (Arista)
  - *Chicken Soup For The Woman's Soul-C* . . . . (Rhino)
- Doobie Brothers; *Best Of The Doobies, Volume II* . . . .(Warner Bros.)
  - *Livin' On The Fault Line* . . . .(Warner Bros.)

You Like Me Too Much
- Beatles; *ST/Help!* . . . . (Capitol)

You Must Love Me
- Madonna; *ST/Evita-Music From The Motion Picture* . . . . .(Warner Bros.)

You Still Touch Me
- Sting; *Mercury Falling* . . . . (A&M)

You Were Meant For Me
- Jewel; *Pieces Of You* . . . . (Atlantic)

You Won't See Me
- Anne Murray; *Anne Murray's Greatest Hits* . . . . (Capitol)
  - *Love Song* . . . . (Capitol)
- Beatles; *Beatles-Box Set* . . . . (Capitol)
  - *Rubber Soul* . . . . (Capitol)
- Bryan Ferry; *These Foolish Things* . . . . (Reprise)

You're Gonna Make Me Lonesome When You Go
- Bob Dylan; *Blood On The Tracks* . . . . (Columbia)

You've Lost That Lovin' Feelin'
- Daryl Hall & John Oates; *Voices* . . . . (RCA)
- Righteous Brothers; *Best Of The Righteous Brothers* . . . . (Curb)
  - *Billboard Top Rock 'N' Roll Hits-1965-C* . . . . (Rhino)
  - *Cruisin'-1965-C* . . . .(Increase)
  - *Unchained Melody-Very Best Of The Righteous Brothers* . . . . . (Polydor)

Zip-Lock
- Lit; *A Place In The Sun* . . . . (RCA)

LOVE: FALLING IN LOVE, Courting, Dating,
Discovery Of Love

See Also: CRAZY, DESIRE, FALLING, FEELINGS, FINDING, HAPPINESS, KISSING, LOVE (various)

(Just Like) Starting Over
- John Lennon & Yoko Ono; *Double Fantasy* . . . . (Capitol)
  - *ST/Imagine: John Lennon* . . . . (Capitol)

('Til) I Kissed You
- Everly Brothers; *Everly Brothers-Cadence Classics-Their 20 Greatest Hits* . . . . (Rhino)
  - *Fabulous Style Of The Everly Brothers* . . . . (Rhino)
  - *Very Best Of The Everly Brothers* . . . .(Warner Bros.)

(When You Fall In Love) Everything's A Waltz
- Ed Bruce; *One To One* . . . .(MCA)

(You Drive Me) Crazy
- Britney Spears; *...Baby One More Time* . . . .(Jive)
  - *Now That's What I Call Music!-#4-C* . . . .(Virgin)

(You Make Me Feel Like) A Natural Woman
- Aretha Franklin; *Aretha Franklin's Greatest Hits-1980-1994* . . . . (Arista)
  - *Chicken Soup For The Woman's Soul-C* . . . . (Rhino)
- Carole King; *Tapestry* . . . . (Epic)
- Celine Dion; *Tapestry Revisited: Tribute To Carole King-C* . . . .(Lava)

1-2-3
- Len Barry; *24 Of The Grooviest Hits Of All Time! The '60s Ultimate Collection-#1-C.* . . . .(Sundazed Music)

24/7
- Kevon Edmonds; *24/7*. . . . .(RCA)

911
- Wyclef Jean featuring Mary J. Blige; *The Ecleftic-2 Sides II A Book* . . . .(Ruffhouse/Columbia)

After Party
- Koffee Brown; *Mars/Venus* . . . . (Arista)

Ah! Sweet Mystery Of Life
- Bing Crosby; *Little Bit Of Irish* . . . .(Atlantic)
- Nelson Eddy; *Through The Years* . . . . (Living Era)

All At Once You Love Her
- Perry Como; *Perry Como's Greatest Hits* . . . . (RCA)

All My Life
- K-Ci & JoJo; *Love Always.* . . . . (MCA)
  - *Now That's What I Call Music!-#1-C.* . . . .(Virgin)

All Roads Lead To You
- Chicago; *The Heart Of Chicago-1967-1988-#2* . . . . (Reprise)

All Shook Up
- Elvis Presley; *Elvis Aron Presley* . . . . (RCA)
  - *Elvis As Recorded At Madison Square Garden* . . . . (RCA)
  - *Elvis' Golden Records* . . . . (RCA)
  - *Elvis Presley-Pure Gold.* . . . . (RCA)
  - *From Memphis To Vegas/From Vegas To Memphis.* . . . .(RCA)

Am I Dreaming
- Ol Skool featuring Keith Sweat & Xscape; *Ol Skool* . . . . (Keia/Universal)

Angel Of Mine
- Monica; *The Boy Is Mine.* . . . . (Arista)
  - *Totally Hits-#1-C* . . . . (Arista)

Angels Listened In
- Crests; *Crests Greatest Hits* . . . . (Collectables)
  - *Super Oldies Of The '50s-#3-C* . . . . (Audio Fidelity)
  - *WCBS FM 101 History Of Rock-'50s-#2-C* . . . . (Collectables)

April In Paris
- Charlie Parker; *Charlie Parker With Strings* . . . . (Verve)
  - *Verve Years-1950-1951* . . . . (Verve)
- Ella Fitzgerald & Oscar Peterson; *Ella & Oscar* . . . . (Pablo)
- Frank Sinatra; *Come Fly With Me* . . . . (Capitol)
- Mel Torme; *Mel Torme* . . . .(Glendale)
- Sarah Vaughan; *Complete Sarah Vaughan On Mercury-#1-Great Jazz Years-1954-1956* . . . . (Mercury)
  - *Sarah Vaughan* . . . . (Emarcy)
- Wynton Marsalis; *Marsalis Standard Time-#1* . . . . (Columbia)
  - *Perspectives: Columbia Jazz Sampler* . . . . (Columbia)

April In Portugal
- Eartha Kitt; *Best Of Eartha Kitt.* . . . . (MCA)

Are We In Trouble Now
- Mark Knopfler; *Golden Heart* . . . . (Warner Bros.)

Around The World
- Bing Crosby; *Heart Beats-Closer Than A Kiss-Crooner Classics-C* . . . . (Rhino)
- Frank Sinatra; *Come Fly With Me* . . . . (Capitol)
- McGuire Sisters; *McGuire Sisters-Anthology* . . . . (MCA)

Arthur's Theme (Best That You Can Do)
- Christopher Cross; *ST/Arthur* . . . . (Warner Bros.)

As Time Goes By
- Andy Williams; *Moon River & Other Great Movie Themes* . . . . (Columbia)
- Barbra Streisand; *Third Album* . . . . (Columbia)
- Frank Sinatra; *Point Of No Return* . . . . (Capitol)
- Johnny Mathis; *Best Days Of My Life* . . . . (Columbia)
  - *First 25 Years-Silver Anniversary Album.* . . . . (Columbia)
- Natalie Cole; *Take A Look.* . . . . (Elektra)
- Nilsson; *A Little Touch Of Schmilsson In The Night* . . . . (RCA)
  - *Nilsson's Greatest Hits* . . . . (RCA)
- Willie Nelson; *Without A Song* . . . . (Columbia)

At The Beginning
- Richard Marx & Donna Lewis; *ST/Anastasia-Music From The Motion Picture* . . . .(Atlantic)

Baby Face
- Al Jolson; *The Al Jolson Story-#3* . . . . (MCA)
  - *World's Greatest* . . . . (MCA)
- Kinks; *Everybody's In Show-Biz.* . . . . (Rhino)

Back At One
- Brian McKnight; *Back At One.* . . . . (Motown)
- Mark Wills; *Permanently* . . . . (Mercury)

Beautiful
- Mary J. Blige; *ST/How Stella Got Her Groove Back* . . . . . .(Flyte Tyme/MCA)

Beautiful Stranger
- Madonna; *GHV2* . . . . (Warner Bros.)
  - *ST/Austin Powers-The Spy Who Shagged Me.* . . . . (Maverick)

Totally Hits-#2-C . . . . (Elektra)

Beechwood 4-5789
Carpenters; *Made In America* . . . . (A&M)
Marvelettes; *Compact Command Performances-Marvelettes* . . . . (Motown)
  Marvelettes' Greatest Hits . . . . (Motown)
  Marvelettes-Anthology . . . . (Motown)
  More American Graffiti-#4-C . . . . (MCA)

Believe What You Say
Rick Nelson; *Rick Nelson In Concert-Troubadour 1969* . . . . (MCA)
Ricky Nelson; *Ricky Nelson Volume 1* . . . . (Gold Rush)
  Ricky Nelson's All Time Greatest Hits . . . . (Curb)
  Rock This Town-Rockabilly Hits-#1-C . . . . (Rhino)

Best Is Yet To Come
Frank Sinatra; *It Might As Well Be Swing* . . . . (Reprise)
  Sinatra Reprise-The Very Good Years . . . . (Reprise)
Johnny Mathis; *I'll Buy You A Star* . . . . (Legacy)
Rosemary Clooney; *Girl Singer* . . . . (Concord Jazz)
Tony Bennett; *I Left My Heart In San Francisco* . . . . (Columbia)
  The Ultimate Tony Bennett . . . . (Legacy)

Best Thing
Savage Garden; *Affirmation* . . . . (Columbia)

Betcha By Golly, Wow
''AFKAP''; *Emancipation* . . . . (NPG)
Johnny Mathis; *First Time Ever I Saw Your Face* . . . . (Columbia)
Stylistics; *Best Of The Stylistics* . . . . (Amherst)

Bewitched
Anita O'Day; *Anita Sings The Most* . . . . (Verve)
Barbra Streisand; *Third Album* . . . . (Columbia)
Doris Day; *Doris Day's Greatest Hits* . . . . (Columbia)
Original Cast; *Pal Joey* . . . . (Columbia)

Blue Clear Sky
George Strait; *Blue Clear Sky* . . . . (MCA)
  Latest Greatest Straitest Hits . . . . (MCA)

Blue Moon
Billie Holiday; *Billie's Blues* . . . . (Blue Note)
  First Verve Sessions . . . . (Verve)
  History Of Billie Holiday . . . . (Verve)
Elvis Presley; *Elvis Presley* . . . . (RCA)
  The Sun Sessions . . . . (RCA)
Marcels; *Best Of The Marcels* . . . . (Rhino)
  Billboard Top Rock 'N' Roll Hits-1961-C . . . . (Rhino)

Blueberry Hill
Elvis Presley; *Elvis Recorded Live On Stage In Memphis* . . . . (RCA)
  Loving You . . . . (RCA)
Fats Domino; *Fats Domino's Greatest Hits* . . . . (Everest)
  Fats Domino's Greatest Hits . . . . (MCA)
  My Blue Heaven-Best Of Fats Domino-#1 . . . . (EMI)
Little Richard; *Big Hits* . . . . (Crescendo)
Louis Armstrong; *Best Of Louis Armstrong* . . . . (MCA)
  Essential Louis Armstrong . . . . (Vanguard)
  I Like Jazz-Essence Of Louis Armstrong . . . . (Columbia)

Bombastic Love
Britney Spears; *Britney* . . . . (Jive)

Brand New Man
Brooks & Dunn; *Brand New Man* . . . . (Arista)

Brand New Me
Dusty Springfield; *Brand New Me* . . . . (Rhino)

Burnin' Old Memories With A Brand New Flame
Kathy Mattea; *Country Hits 4: Sweet Country-C* . . . . (Priority)
  Willow In The Wind . . . . (Mercury)

Bus Stop
Hollies; *Best Of The Hollies* . . . . (EMI)
  History Of British Rock-#3-C . . . . (Rhino)
  The Hollies' Greatest Hits . . . . (Epic)

Butterfly
Crazy Town; *Gift Of Game* . . . . (Columbia)

California Nights
Lesley Gore; *Summer & Sun-C* . . . . (Rhino)

Canadian Sunset
Andy Williams; *Andy Williams-16 Most Requested Songs* . . . . (Legacy)
Etta Jones; *Etta Jones' Greatest Hits* . . . . (Prestige)
  Something Nice . . . . (Original Jazz Classics)

Candy Girl
4 Seasons; *25th Anniversary Collection* . . . . (Rhino)
  4 Seasons-Anthology . . . . (Rhino)
  Lil' Bit Of Gold 3'' CD Series-C . . . . (Rhino)

Can't Help Falling In Love
Elvis Presley; *Elvis* . . . . (RCA)
  Elvis-A Legendary Performer, Volume 1 . . . . (RCA)
  From Elvis In Vegas/From Vegas To Memphis . . . . (RCA)
  ST/Blue Hawaii . . . . (RCA)
Julio Iglesias; *Starry Night* . . . . (Columbia)
UB40; *Promises And Lies* . . . . (Virgin)
  ST/Sliver . . . . (Virgin)

Caravan
Duke Ellington; *Best Of Duke Ellington* . . . . (Capitol)
  Money Jungle . . . . (Blue Note)
Ella Fitzgerald; *Montreux '75* . . . . (Pablo)

Johnny Mathis; *In A Sentimental Mood-Johnny Mathis Sings*
  Ellington . . . . (Columbia)
Wynton Marsalis; *Marsalis Standard Time-#1* . . . . (Columbia)

Carrie-Anne
Hollies; *Best Of The Hollies* . . . . (EMI)
  Evolution . . . . (Epic)
  Hollies-Epic Anthology From The Original Master Tapes . . . . (Epic)
  The Hollies' Greatest Hits . . . . (Epic)

Changing Partners
Bing Crosby; *Bing Crosby* . . . . (MCA Special Prod.)
Kay Starr; *Capitol Collectors Series-Kay Starr* . . . . (Capitol)
Patti Page; *Patti Page-Golden Hits* . . . . (Mercury)

Cherry Pink And Apple Blossom White
Fabulous Thunderbirds; *Butt Rockin'.* . . . . (Chrysalis)
Perez Prado & His Orchestra; *This Is Perez Prado-Decade Of*
  The '50s . . . . (RCA)

Claudette
Dwight Yoakam; *Under The Covers* . . . . (Reprise)
Everly Brothers; *Everly Brothers' Greatest Hits* . . . . (Delta)
  Everly Brothers-Cadence Classics-Their 20 Greatest Hits . . . . (Rhino)
Roy Orbison; *Roy Orbison-The Sun Years* . . . . (Rhino)
  Very Best Of Roy Orbison . . . . (Virgin)

Closer You Get, The
Alabama; *Alabama's Greatest Hits-#2* . . . . (RCA)
  For The Record: 41 Number One Hits . . . . (RCA)
  The Closer You Get . . . . (BMG Special Prod.)

Cocktails For Two
Duke Ellington & His Orchestra; *No. 1 Hits Greatest Hits-C* . . . . . (RCA Victor)
Spike Jones; *Dinner Music...For People Who Aren't Very Hungry!* . . . . (Rhino)
  Dr. Demento Presents The Greatest Novelty Records-#1-1940s &
  Before-C . . . . (Rhino)
  Dr. Demento: 20th Anniversary Collection-C . . . . (Rhino)
  Nipper's Greatest Hits Of The '40s-#1-C . . . . (RCA)
Spike Jones & His City Slickers; *Best Of Spike Jones & His City*
  Slickers . . . . (RCA)

Color My World
Petula Clark; *Petula Clark's Greatest Hits* . . . . (Crescendo)

Colour My World
Chicago; *Chicago At Carnegie Hall.* . . . . (Chicago)
  Chicago II . . . . (Chicago)
  Chicago IX-Chicago's Greatest Hits. . . . . (Chicago)

Come See Me
112; *112* . . . . (Bad Boy/Arista)

Complicated
Carolyn Dawn Johnson; *Room With A View.* . . . . (Arista)

Could It Be I'm Falling In Love
Spinners; *One Of A Kind Love Affair-Anthology* . . . . (Rhino)
  Spinners. . . . . (Rhino)
  Very Best Of The Spinners . . . . (Rhino)

Could This Be Magic
Dubs; *Doo Wop Memories-#1-C* . . . . (Rhino)

Country Bumpkin
Cal Smith; *16 Top Country Hits-#1-C* . . . . (MCA)
  Country's Greatest Hits-#2-C. . . . . (MCA Special Prod.)
  Grand Ole Opry-75 Years-#2-C . . . . (MCA)

Crazy For This Girl
Evan And Jaron; *Evan And Jaron* . . . . (Columbia)
  Now That's What I Call Music!-#6-C . . . . (Virgin)

Crazy Little Thing Called Love
Dwight Yoakam; *Last Chance For A Thousand Years-Greatest Hits From*
  The '90s . . . . (Reprise)
Queen; *Queen's Greatest Hits I & II* . . . . (Hollywood)
  The Game . . . . (Hollywood)

Crimson And Clover
Joan Jett & The Blackhearts; *I Love Rock 'n' Roll* . . . . (Blackheart)
Tommy James And The Shondells; *Best Of Tommy James And The*
  Shondells . . . . (Roulette)
  Billboard Top Rock 'N' Roll Hits-1969-C. . . . . (Rhino)
  Jewels-#1-C. . . . . (SSS International)
  Tommy James And The Shondells-Anthology . . . . (Rhino)

Da Doo Ron Ron (When He Walked Me Home)
Crystals; *Good Time Rock 'N' Roll-C* . . . . (Abkco)
  Good Time Rock 'N' Roll-C . . . . (MCA)
  Hits Of The Sixties-C . . . . (Intercom Music)
  Phil Spector's Greatest Hits-C . . . . (Spector)
Shaun Cassidy; *Shaun Cassidy's Greatest Hits* . . . . (Curb)

Dancing In The Dark
Barbara Cook; *Barbara Cook-Live At Carnegie Hall* . . . (Sony Music Classical)
Diana Krall; *The Look Of Love.* . . . . (Impulse!)
Fred Waring's Pennsylvanians; *78-#22708* . . . . (Victor)
Tony Bennett; *Forty Years-The Artistry Of Tony Bennett* . . . . . (Columbia)
  Jazz . . . . (Columbia)

Darling Be Home Soon
Joe Cocker; *Joe Cocker!.* . . . . (A&M)
  Joe Cocker-Classics-#4. . . . . (A&M)
  Joe Cocker's Greatest Hits . . . . (A&M)
Lovin' Spoonful; *Best Of The Lovin' Spoonful-#2* . . . . (Rhino)
  Lovin' '60s-C . . . . (Priority)
  Lovin' Spoonful-Anthology . . . . (Rhino)

Darling Lorraine
Paul Simon; *You're The One*............................(Warner Bros.)
Deep Water
Asleep At The Wheel; *Asleep At The Wheel*............(MCA Special Prod.)
Asleep At The Wheel featuring Garth Brooks; *Tribute To The Music Of Bob Wills And The Texas Playboys-C*..............................(Liberty)
Bob Wills & His Texas Playboys; *Bob Wills & His Texas Playboys-Anthology 1935-1973*.................................. (Rhino)
Essential Bob Wills & His Texas Playboys-1935-1973............ (Legacy)
George Strait; *George Strait-Number 7*.........................(MCA)
Willie Nelson; *San Antonio Rose*.............................(Columbia)
Diggin' On You
TLC; *CrazySexyCool*.......................................(LaFace)
Dizzy
Tommy Roe; *Original Classic Oldies Of The '60s-#10-C*......(MCA)
Super Hits-#1-C..(Gusto)
Tommy Roe's Greatest Hits...................................(MCA)
Do Wah Diddy Diddy
Manfred Mann; *Best Of Manfred Mann*............. (EMI Special Markets)
Billboard Top Rock 'N' Roll Hits-1964-C....................(Rhino)
History Of British Rock-#2-C...............................(Rhino)
Do You Know
Xscape; *Traces Of My Lipstick*.....................(So So Def/Columbia)
Do You Love Me That Much?
Peter Cetera; *You're The Inspiration-A Collection*..............(River North)
Do You Want To
Xscape; *Off The Hook*..............................(So So Def/Columbia)
Do You Want To Know A Secret
Beatles; *Introducing...The Beatles*...........................(Vee-Jay)
Please Please Me..(Parlophone)
The Early Beatles...(Capitol)
Don't Get Me Started
Rhett Akins; *Somebody New*.................................(Decca)
Don't Happen Twice
Kenny Chesney; *Kenny Chesney's Greatest Hits*................. (BNA)
Don't Let Go
Regina Belle; *Believe In Me*................................(MCA)
Don't Stop
Wade Hayes; *Old Enough To Know Better*.................. (Columbia)
Steppin' Country-#2-C.....................................(Columbia)
Super Hits Of 1995-C......................................(Epic)
Down In Flames
BlackHawk; *BlackHawk*.....................................(Arista)
The Hits-Love & Gravity....................................(Arista)
Earth Angel
Elvis Presley; *A Golden Celebration*.........................(RCA)
New Edition; *ST/Under The Blue Moon*.......................(MCA)
Penguins; *Billboard Top Rock 'N' Roll Hits-1955-C*..............(Rhino)
Golden Classics-Penguins..............................(Collectables)
Oldies But Goodies-#1-C..............................(Original Sound)
ST/American Graffiti......................................(MCA)
Eternal Flame
Bangles; *Bangles' Greatest Hits*............................(Columbia)
Everything...(Columbia)
Ever True Evermore
Mandy Barnett; *I've Got A Right To Cry*.....................(Sire)
Everlong
Foo Fighters; *The Colour And The Shape*................(Roswell/RCA)
Every Little Thing I Do
Soul For Real; *100% Party-Hits Of The '90s-#2-C*.............(Priority)
Candy Rain..(Uptown/MCA)
Fall In Love
Kenny Chesney; *All I Need To Know*.........................(BNA)
Kenny Chesney's Greatest Hits..............................(BNA)
Fallin'
Connie Francis; *Very Best Of Connie Francis*..................(Polydor)
Fallin'
Alicia Keys; *Songs In A Minor*............................. (J)
Totally Hits 2001-C.......................................(Arista)
Fallin' In Love Never Felt So Good
Mark Chesnutt; *Confessing My Love*.........................(MCA)
Falling In Love (Is Hard On The Knees)
Aerosmith; *A Little South Of Sanity*........................(Geffen)
Nine Lives...(Columbia)
Falling In Love Again (Can''t Help It)
Billie Holiday; *Quintessential-#8-1939-1940*...................(Legacy)
Linda Ronstadt; *Lush Life*.................................(Asylum)
Marlene Dietrich; *Best Of Marlene Dietrich*...................(Columbia)
Falling In Love Again......................................(MCA)
Her Complete Decca Recordings.............................(MCA)
Falling In Love With Love
Frank Sinatra; *The V-Discs: The Columbia Years-1943-1952*........ (Legacy)
Gene Ammons; *Jug & Dodo*................................(Prestige)
Helen Merrill; *Helen Merrill*.........................(Giants Of Jazz)
Marian McPartland; *Reprise*..........................(Concord Jazz)
Tony Bennett; *If I Ruled The World: Song For The Jet Set*......... (Columbia)
Falling Into You
Celine Dion; *Falling Into You*.............................(550 Music)

Feels Like Home
LeAnn Rimes; *Sittin' On Top Of The World*.....................(Curb)
Feels Like Home
Bonnie Raitt; *ST/Michael*................................(Revolution)
Chantal Kreviazuk; *Songs From Dawson's Creek*.....(Sony Music Soundtrax)
Linda Ronstadt; *Feels Like Home*...........................(Elektra)
Randy Newman; *Guilty: 30 Years Of Randy Newman*...............(Rhino)
Randy Newman's Faust.....................................(Reprise)
Feels Like Love
Vince Gill; *Let's Make Sure We Kiss Goodbye*.................. (MCA)
Feels So Good
Xscape; *Off The Hook*.............................(So So Def/Columbia)
Fire Of The Newly Alive
Rosanne Cash; *The Wheel*.................................(Columbia)
First Time Ever I Saw Your Face
Celine Dion; *All The Way...A Decade Of Song*..................(550 Music)
Roberta Flack; *Atlantic Rhythm & Blues 1947-1974-#6 (1966-1969)-C*...(Atlantic)
Best Of Roberta Flack....................................(Atlantic)
First Take...(Atlantic)
Fishin' In The Dark
Nitty Gritty Dirt Band; *Billboard Top Country Hits-1987-C*.......... (Rhino)
Hold On..(Warner Bros.)
More Great Dirt-Best Of Nitty Gritty Dirt Band................ (Warner Bros.)
Fit As A Fiddle (and Ready For Love)
Fred Waring's Pennsylvanians; *The Fred Waring Memorial Album*..(Viper's Nest)
Very Best Of Fred Waring & The Pennsylvanians....(Reader's Digest Music)
Gene Kelly/Donald O'Connor/The MGM Studio Orchestra; *ST/Singin' In The Rain*...........................(Turner Classic Movies)
Flying
Chris Isaak; *Speak Of The Devil*...........................(Reprise)
Fools Rush In (Where Angels Fear To Tread)
Brook Benton; *Super Oldies Of The '60s-#10-C*............. (Audio Fidelity)
Tommy Dorsey & Frank Sinatra; *Sessions-#1-February 1, 1940-July 17, 1940*...(RCA)
For A Change
Neal McCoy; *You Gotta Love That!*..........................(Atlantic)
For Once In Our Lives
Paul Carrack; *Blue Views*................................. (Ark 21)
For The First Time
Kenny Loggins; *ST/One Fine Day*...........................(Columbia)
For You I Will
Aaron Tippin; *What This Country Needs*.....................(Lyric Street)
Froggie Went A Courtin'
Doc Watson; *Essential Doc Watson*.........................(Vanguard)
Home Again...(Vanguard)
Gee Whiz
Kathy Young with The Innocents; *45-#6019*................... (Virgo)
Get Me To The World On Time
Electric Prunes; *Nuggets-Original Artyfacts From The First Psychedelic Era-1965-1968-C*..(Rhino)
Gettin' Together
Tommy James And The Shondells; *Tommy James And The Shondells-Anthology*..(Rhino)
Getting Sentimental Over You
Ella Fitzgerald; *Best Of Ella Fitzgerald*......................(Pablo)
Frank Sinatra; *I Remember Tommy*..........................(Reprise)
Helen O'Connell; *Sentimental Journey: Capitol's Great Ladies Of Song-C*...(Gold Rush)
Shirley Scott; *For Members Only/Great Scott*.......... (MCA Special Prod.)
Tommy Dorsey & His Orchestra; *Best Of Tommy Dorsey*......... (Bluebird)
Best Of Tommy Dorsey & His Orchestra......................(Curb)
Girl Like You
Rascals; *Groovin'*..................................(Warner Special Prod.)
Rascals' Greatest Hits.....................................(Atlantic)
Girl Next Door
Musiq Soulchild; *Aijuswanaseing*.................... (Def Soul/IDJMG)
God Must Have Spent A Little More Time On You
Alabama Featuring 'N Sync; *Twentieth Century*...................(RCA)
'N Sync; *'N Sync*..(RCA)
Totally Hits-#1-C...(Arista)
Goin' Gone
Kathy Mattea; *Collection Of Hits*...........................(Mercury)
Untasted Honey....................................(Polydor Country)
Good Timin'
Jimmy Jones; *Hard To Find 45s On CD-#1-1955-1960-C*............(Eric)
Good Vibrations
Beach Boys; *Beach Boys-Gift Set*...........................(Capitol)
Billboard Top Rock 'N' Roll Hits-1966-C....................(Rhino)
Endless Summer..(Capitol)
Good Vibrations-Thirty Years Of The Beach Boys.............(Capitol)
Smiley Smile/Wild Honey..................................(Capitol)
Sunshine Dream..(Capitol)
Got A Date With An Angel
Hal Kemp; *Best Of The Big Bands-C*........................(Columbia)
Sammy Kaye & His Orchestra; *Best Of Sammy Kaye & His Orchestra* .. (MCA)
Got To Get You Into My Life
Beatles; *Beatles-Box Set*..................................(Capitol)

Revolver . . . . (Capitol)
Rock 'N' Roll Music . . . . (Capitol)
The Beatles-Anthology-#2 . . . . (Capitol)
Earth, Wind & Fire; Best Of Earth, Wind & Fire-#1 . . . . (Legacy)
ST/Sgt. Pepper's Lonely Hearts Club Band . . . . (RSO)
Paul McCartney & Wings; Kampuchea-C . . . . (Atlantic)

Gotta Be
Jagged Edge; A Jagged Era . . . . (So So Def/Columbia)

Grease Megamix
Grease Megamix; Pure Disco . . . . (A&M)

Guilty
Def Leppard; Euphoria . . . . (Mercury)

Gypsy Woman
Brian Hyland; Brian Hyland's Greatest Hits . . . . (Rhino)
Super Hits Of The '70s-Have A Nice Day-#3-C . . . . (Rhino)
Impressions; Billboard Top R&B Hits-1961-C . . . . (Rhino)
Impressions' Greatest Hits . . . . (MCA)
Oldies But Goodies-#12-C . . . . (Original Sound)
Vintage Music-#6-C . . . . (MCA)
Ry Cooder; Slide Area . . . . (Warner Bros.)

Hanging By A Moment
Lifehouse; No Name Face . . . . (DreamWorks/SKG)
Now That's What I Call Music!-#7-C . . . . (Virgin)

Hanging Tree
Marty Robbins; Gunfighter Ballads & Trail Songs . . . . (Legacy)
Hollywood Magic-1950s-C . . . . (Columbia)
Lifetime Of Song-1951-1982 . . . . (Columbia)
Marty Robbins' All-Time Greatest Hits . . . . (Columbia)

Happening, The
Diana Ross; Diana Ross-Anthology . . . . (Motown)
Diana Ross & The Supremes; Diana Ross & The Supremes-Superstar
Series-#1 . . . . (Motown)

Head Over Feet
Alanis Morissette; Jagged Little Pill . . . . (Maverick)

Head Over Heels
Allure; The Greatest Dance Album In The World-C . . . . (Epic)
Allure featuring NAS; Allure . . . . (Track Masters/Crave)

Heart And Soul
Cleftones; Echoes Of A Rock Era-Later Years-C . . . . (Roulette)
ST/American Graffiti . . . . (MCA)
Four Aces; Four Aces' 20 Greatest Hits . . . . (Everest)
Huey Lewis and the News; Sports . . . . (Chrysalis)
Jan & Dean; Best Of Jan & Dean . . . . (EMI)
Oldies But Goodies-#9-C . . . . (Original Sound)
Larry Clinton & His Orchestra; The Hoagy Carmichael
Songbook-C . . . . (Bluebird)

Heart's Desire
Lee Roy Parnell; We All Get Lucky Sometimes . . . . (Career)

Heat Wave
Linda Ronstadt; Linda Ronstadt's Greatest Hits . . . . (Asylum)
Prisoner In Disguise . . . . (Asylum)
Martha & The Vandellas; Billboard Top R&B Hits-1963-C . . . . . . (Rhino)
Martha Reeves & The Vandellas' Greatest Hits . . . . (Motown)
More American Graffiti-#4-C . . . . (MCA)
Motown Story-First 25 Years-C . . . . (Motown)
Who; A Quick One (Happy Jack)/Sell Out . . . . (MCA)
Two's Missing . . . . (MCA)

Help Me
Joni Mitchell; Court & Spark . . . . (Asylum)

Here Comes The Rain Again
Eurythmics; Eurythmics' Greatest Hits . . . . (Arista)
Eurythmics' Greatest Hits . . . . (Arista)

Hey There
Original Cast; ST/Pajama Game . . . . (Collectables)
Rosemary Clooney; Essence Of Rosemary Clooney . . . . . . (Legacy)

Hidden Place
Bjork; Vespertine . . . . (Elektra)

High And The Mighty
Les Baxter & His Orchestra; Instrumental Gems Of The
'50s-C . . . . (Collector's Choice)
Roger Williams; Roger Williams' Greatest Hits . . . . (Curb)
Victor Young & His Orchestra; Hard To Find Orchestral
Instrumentals-C . . . . (Eric)
Victor Young & His Singing Strings; Billboard Top Movie Hits-1950-
1954-C . . . . (Rhino)

Hold Me, Thrill Me, Kiss Me
Mel Carter; Baby Boomer Classics-Love Sixties-C . . . . (JCI Assoc. Labels)

Hold My Hand
Don Cornell; Hold My Hand . . . . (MCA Special Prod.)

Holdin' Heaven
Tracy Byrd; Tracy Byrd . . . . (MCA)

Holding On
Steve Winwood; Roll With It . . . . (Virgin)

Hooked On A Feeling
B.J. Thomas; Best Of B.J. Thomas . . . . (Hollywood/DNA-Rounder)
Vonda Shepard; ST/Songs From "Ally McBeal" Featuring Vonda
Shepard . . . . (550/Epic)

Hot Diggity (Dog Ziggity Boom)
Perry Como; Como's Golden Records . . . . (RCA)

Nipper's Greatest Hits Of The '50s-#2-C . . . . (RCA)
Perry Como-Pure Gold . . . . (RCA)
Perry Como's All-Time Greatest Hits-#1 . . . . (RCA)
This Is Perry Como . . . . (RCA)

How Come, How Long
Babyface & Stevie Wonder; The Day . . . . (Epic)

How Do I Get There
Deana Carter; Did I Shave My Legs For This? . . . . (Capitol)

How Do You Fall In Love
Alabama; For The Record: 41 Number One Hits . . . . (RCA)

How Will I Know
Whitney Houston; Soul Train 25th Anniv. Hall Of Fame-Box . . . . . . (MCA)
Whitney Houston . . . . (Arista)
Whitney Houston's Greatest Hits . . . . (Arista)

Hypnotize The Moon
Clay Walker; Hypnotize The Moon . . . . (Giant)

Hypnotized
Linda Jones; 20 Golden Classics . . . . (Collectables)
Soul Classics-#1-C . . . . (Collectables)

I Am Going To Like It Here
Original Cast; ST/Flower Drum Song . . . . (Sony Music Classical)

I Am Not Hiding
Kenny Loggins; The Unimaginable Life . . . . (Columbia)

I Can't Help Falling In Love With You
Wright Brothers; The American Way . . . . (KRB Music)

I Could Fall In Love
Selena; Dreaming Of You . . . . (EMI Latin)

I Do
Toya; Totally Hits 2001-C . . . . (Arista)
Toya . . . . (Arista)

I Don't Even Know Your Name
Mavericks; Trampoline . . . . (MCA)

I Don't Think I Will
James Bonamy; What I Live To Do . . . . (Epic)

I Feel Pretty
Julie Andrews; A Little Bit Of Broadway . . . . (Columbia)
Little Richard; The Songs Of West Side Story . . . . (RCA Victor)
Original Cast; ST/West Side Story . . . . (Sony Broadway)

I Fell In Love With A Prostitute
James Peterson; The Kingsnake Collection: Bag O' Blues-C . . . . . . (Kingsnake)

I Finally Found Someone
Barbra Streisand & Bryan Adams; ST/The Mirror Has Two Faces . . . (Columbia)

I Found A Million-Dollar Baby (In A Five-And-Ten-Cent Store)
Barbra Streisand; ST/Funny Girl . . . . (Columbia)
Bing Crosby; Pennies From Heaven . . . . (Pro-Arte)
Fred Waring's Pennsylvanians; 78-#22707 . . . . (Victor)
Nat "King" Cole; Nat "King" Cole-Gift Set . . . . (Capitol)

I Found Love
Earl Scruggs & Vince Gill & Rosanne Cash; Earl Scruggs And
Friends-C . . . . (MCA)

I Get A Kick Out Of You
Ethel Merman with Johnny Green & His Orchestra; The Ethel Merman
Collection . . . . (Razor & Tie)
This Is Art Deco-C . . . . (Columbia)
Frank Sinatra; My One & Only Love . . . . (Capitol)
Round #1 . . . . (Capitol)
Sinatra and Swingin' Brass . . . . (Reprise)
Sinatra-The Main Event Live . . . . (Reprise)
The Capitol Years . . . . (Capitol)
The Reprise Collection . . . . (Reprise)
Original Cast; Anything Goes . . . . (Epic)
Paul Whiteman & His Orchestra; 78-#24769 . . . . (Victor)

I Got A Love Jones For You
Refugee Camp All-Stars; ST/Love Jones . . . . (Columbia)

I Have To Surrender
Ty Herndon; Living In A Moment . . . . (Epic)

I Hope You Want Me Too
Mavericks; Trampoline . . . . (MCA)

I Knew I Loved You
Savage Garden; Affirmation . . . . (Columbia)
Now That's What I Call Music!-#4-C . . . . (Virgin)

I Like It, I Love It
Tim McGraw; All I Want . . . . (Curb)
Tim McGraw's Greatest Hits . . . . (Curb)

I Love Me Some Him
Toni Braxton; Secrets . . . . (LaFace)

I Love Rock 'N Roll
Britney Spears; Britney . . . . (Jive)
Joan Jett & The Blackhearts; I Love Rock 'n' Roll . . . . . . (Blackheart)
ST/Wayne's World 2 . . . . (Reprise)

I Love You
Martina McBride; Emotion . . . . (RCA)
ST/Runaway Bride . . . . (Sony Music Soundtrax)

I Love You
Keith Washington & Chante' Moore; KW . . . . (Silas)

I Loved You Once In Silence
Original Cast; Camelot . . . . (Columbia)
Original Soundtrack; ST/Camelot . . . . (Warner Bros.)

I Only Get This Way With You
Rick Trevino; *Learning As You Go* . . . . (Columbia)
I Only Have Eyes For You
Art Garfunkel; *Breakaway* . . . . (Columbia)
   Garfunkel . . . . (Columbia)
Flamingos; *Doo-Wop Ballads-#2-C* . . . . (Rhino)
   Echoes Of A Rock Era-Middle Years-C . . . . (Roulette)
   ST/American Graffiti . . . . (MCA)
I Only Want To Be With You
Bay City Rollers; *Bay City Rollers' Greatest Hits* . . . . . (Arista)
Dusty Springfield; *Dusty Springfield-Anthology* . . . . . . (Mercury)
   Dusty Springfield-Golden Hits . . . . (Mercury)
Vonda Shepard; *ST/Songs From "Ally McBeal" Featuring Vonda
   Shepard* . . . . (550/Epic)
I Remember It Well
Original Cast; *Gigi* . . . . (RCA Victor)
I Saw Her Standing There
Beatles; *Introducing...The Beatles* . . . . (Vee-Jay)
   Meet The Beatles! . . . . (Capitol)
   Please Please Me . . . . (Parlophone)
   Rock 'N' Roll Music . . . . (Capitol)
   The Beatles-Anthology-#1 . . . . (Capitol)
Paul McCartney; *Tripping The Live Fantastic-Highlights!* . . . . . (Capitol)
I Saw Him Standing There
Tiffany; *Tiffany* . . . . (MCA)
   Tiffany's Greatest Hits . . . . (Hip-O)
I Should Have Known Better
Beatles; *A Hard Day's Night* . . . . (Parlophone)
I Talk To The Trees
Al Hirt; *Al Hirt* . . . . (Dunhill Compact Classics)
   Showtime . . . . (Allegiance)
Alan Jay Lerner; *Alan Jay Lerner Performs His Own Songs* . . . . . (DRG)
Original Broadway Cast; *Paint Your Wagon* . . . . . . (RCA Victor)
I Think About It All The Time
John Berry; *Standing On The Edge* . . . . (Capitol)
I Think I'm In Love With You
Jessica Simpson; *Now That's What I Call Music!-#5-C* . . . . (Virgin)
   Sweet Kisses . . . . (Columbia)
I Wanna Fall In Love
Lila McCann; *Lila*. . . . . (Asylum)
I Want To Hold Your Hand
Beatles; *Beatles 1* . . . . (Capitol)
   Beatles-20 Greatest Hits . . . . (Capitol)
   Meet The Beatles! . . . . (Capitol)
   Past Masters-Volume One . . . . (Parlophone)
   The Beatles/1962-1966 . . . . (Capitol)
Lakeside; *Galactic Grooves/Best Of Lakeside* . . . . (Right Stuff)
   Your Wish Is My Command . . . . (Solar)
I Wish
Carl Thomas; *Emotional*. . . . . (Bad Boy/Arista)
I'd Really Love To See You Tonight
England Dan & John Ford Coley; *Best Of England Dan & John Ford
   Coley* . . . . (Big Tree)
   Hit Singles-1958-1977-C . . . . (Atlantic)
   Nights Are Forever Without You . . . . (Big Tree)
If I Fall You're Going Down With Me
Dixie Chicks; *Fly* . . . . (Monument)
If I Fell
Beatles; *Beatles-Love Songs*. . . . . (Capitol)
   Something New . . . . (Capitol)
   ST/A Hard Day's Night . . . . (Capitol)
If I Had My Way
Nancy Wilson; *If I Had My Way* . . . . (Columbia)
If We Fall In Love Tonight
Rod Stewart; *If We Fall In Love Tonight*. . . . . . . (Warner Bros.)
If You Could Only See
Tonic; *Lemon Parade* . . . . (Polydor)
   Now That's What I Call Music!-#1-C . . . . (Virgin)
If You Had My Love
Jennifer Lopez; *On The 6* . . . . (Work)
I'll Never Fall In Love Again
Dionne Warwick; *Billboard Top Soft Rock Hits-1970-C* . . . (Rhino)
   Her Classic Songs-#1. . . . . (Curb)
Elvis Presley; *From Elvis Presley Boulevard, Memphis, Tennessee.* . . . (RCA)
Mary Chapin Carpenter; *ST/My Best Friend's Wedding* . . . . . (Work/Epic)
I'm A Believer
Monkees; *Billboard Top Rock 'N' Roll Hits-1966-C* . . . . (Rhino)
   Monkees' Greatest Hits . . . . (Rhino)
   More Of The Monkees . . . . (Rhino)
   Oldies But Goodies-#3-C . . . . (Original Sound)
Neil Diamond; *Live In America* . . . . (Columbia)
   Neil Diamond's Greatest Hits-1966-1992 . . . . (Columbia)
   September Morn. . . . . (Columbia)
Smash Mouth; *Now That's What I Call Music!-#8-C* . . . . (Virgin)
   ST/Shrek . . . . (Interscope)
I'm Getting Used To You
Selena; *Dreaming Of You* . . . . (EMI Latin)
I'm Happy Just To Dance With You
Anne Murray; *Somebody's Waiting* . . . . (Capitol)

Beatles; *Something New* . . . . (Capitol)
   ST/A Hard Day's Night. (Capitol)
I'm In Love Again
Fats Domino; *My Blue Heaven* . . . . (Gold Rush)
I'm Into Something Good
Herman's Hermits; *Herman's Hermits-Their Greatest Hits* . . . . (Abkco)
I'm Not At All In Love
Original Cast/Doris Day; *ST/Pajama Game* . . . . (Collectables)
I'm Not Strong Enough To Say No
BlackHawk; *Strong Enough* . . . . (Arista)
I'm Only In It For The Love
John Conlee; *Best Of John Conlee.* . . . . (Curb)
   John Conlee-20 Greatest Hits . . . . (MCA)
In And Out Of Love
Diana Ross; *Diana Ross-Anthology* . . . . (Motown)
In The Mood
Andrews Sisters; *Andrews Sisters-16 Great Performances*. . . . (MCA)
   Boogie Woogie Bugle Girls . . . . (MCA)
   Chesterfield Broadcasts-#1 . . . . (RCA Victor)
Bette Midler; *Bette Midler.* . . . . (Atlantic)
   Live At Last. . . . . (Atlantic)
Glenn Miller; *Best Of Glenn Miller.* . . . . (RCA)
   Glenn Miller-A Legendary Performer-#1 & 2 . . . . (Bluebird)
   The Glenn Miller Story . . . . (RCA)
Glenn Miller & His Orchestra; *Glenn Miller & His Orchestra-
   Pure Gold* . . . . (Bluebird)
   The Unforgettable Glenn Miller & His Orchestra . . . . . . (RCA)
In The Still Of The Nite
Dion; *Dion Sings The 15 Million Sellers* . . . . (Laurie)
   Dion's Greatest Hits. . . . . (Laurie)
Dion And The Belmonts; *Wish Upon A Star With Dion And The
   Belmonts* . . . . (Collectables)
Five Satins; *Billboard Top R&B Hits-1956-C* . . . . (Rhino)
   Cruisin'-1956-C . . . . (Increase)
   Five Satins Sing Their Greatest Hits. . . . . (Collectables)
   In The Still Of The Night . . . . (Capitol)
   ST/Dirty Dancing . . . . (RCA)
Johnny Mathis; *In The Still Of The Night* . . . . (Columbia)
Invisible Touch
Genesis; *Hit Singles-1980-1988-C* . . . . (Atlantic)
   Invisible Touch . . . . (Atlantic)
It Could Happen To You
Chet Baker; *Chet Baker Sings It Could Happen
   To You* . . . . (Original Jazz Classics)
Doris Day; *Best Of The Big Bands-Doris Day* . . . . (Legacy)
Eydie Gorme; *Best Of Eydie Gorme* . . . . (Curb)
Jo Stafford; *Songs That Got Us Through WWII-#2-C* . . . . (Rhino)
Rosemary Clooney; *Rosemary Clooney Sings The Music Of Jimmy Van
   Heusen.* . . . . (Concord Jazz)
Shirley Horn; *Close Enough For Love* . . . . (Verve)
Sonny Rollins; *The Sound Of Sonny* . . . . . . (Original Jazz Classics)
It Happened In Sun Valley
Glenn Miller & His Orchestra; *Complete Glenn Miller & His
   Orchestra.* . . . . (Bluebird)
It Must Be Love
Ty Herndon; *Big Hopes.* . . . . (Epic)
It Must Be Love
Alan Jackson; *Under The Influence*. . . . . (Arista)
It Was
Chely Wright; *Single White Female* . . . . (MCA)
It's In His Kiss (Shoop Shoop Song)
Betty Everett; *Billboard Top R&B Hits-1964-C* . . . . . . (Rhino)
   Hits Of The Sixties-C . . . . (Intercom Music)
   More American Graffiti-C . . . . (MCA)
   Oldies But Goodies-#3-C . . . . (Original Sound)
   Very Best Of Betty Everett . . . . (Vee-Jay)
   Wonder Women-History Of Girl Group Sound-C . . . . (Rhino)
Cher; *ST/Mermaids* . . . . (Geffen)
Vonda Shepard; *ST/Songs From "Ally McBeal" Featuring Vonda
   Shepard* . . . . (550/Epic)
It's Late
Ricky Nelson; *Lonesome Town*. . . . . (CEMA Special Prod.)
   Ricky Nelson Volume 1 . . . . (Gold Rush)
It's Only Love
Beatles; *The Beatles-Anthology-#2* . . . . (Capitol)
It's So Easy
Buddy Holly; *Buddy Holly's Greatest Hits* . . . . (MCA)
   From The Original Master Tapes-Buddy Holly . . . . . . (MCA)
Linda Ronstadt; *Linda Ronstadt's Greatest Hits, Volume Two* . . . (Asylum)
   Simple Dreams . . . . (Asylum)
It's Such A Small World
Rodney Crowell & Rosanne Cash; *Dynamic Duets-Super Hits-C* . . . (Columbia)
   Rodney Crowell-Super Hits . . . . (Columbia)
I've Been Lonely Too Long
Rascals; *Rascals-Anthology 1965-1972* . . . . (Rhino)
   Very Best Of The Rascals . . . . (Rhino)
I've Got The World On A String
Count Basie; *Standards* . . . . (Verve)
Diana Krall; *Only Trust Your Heart* . . . . (GRP)

Ella Fitzgerald; *Harold Arlen Songbook-#1* . . . . (Verve)
Frank Sinatra; *Capitol Collectors Series-Frank Sinatra* . . . . (Capitol)
Frank Sinatra & Liza Minnelli; *Frank Sinatra-Duets-C* . . . . (Capitol)
Sarah Vaughan; *Best Of Sarah Vaughan* . . . . (Pablo)
Stephane Grappelli & Martin Taylor; *We've Got The World On A*
String . . . . (Angel)

I've Got You Under My Skin
4 Seasons; *25th Anniversary Collection* . . . . (Rhino)
Diana Krall; *When I Look In Your Eyes* . . . . (GRP)
Frank Sinatra; *At The Sands* . . . . (Reprise)
Round #1 . . . . (Capitol)
Sinatra: A Man And His Music . . . . (Reprise)
Sinatra's Sinatra . . . . (Reprise)
The Reprise Collection . . . . (Reprise)
Frank Sinatra & Bono; *Frank Sinatra-Duets-C* . . . . (Capitol)
Frank Sinatra & Nelson Riddle Orchestra; *songs for Swingin'*
Lovers! . . . . (Capitol)

I've Just Seen A Face
Beatles; *Rubber Soul* . . . . (Capitol)
Paul McCartney; *Unplugged (The Official Bootleg)* . . . . (Capitol)
Wings; *Wings Over America* . . . . (Capitol)

Just Between You And Me
Kinleys; *Just Between You And Me* . . . . (Epic)

Just My Luck
Kim Richey; *Kim Richey* . . . . (Mercury)

Kiss To Build A Dream On
Louis Armstrong; *Best Of Louis Armstrong* . . . . (MCA)
Essential Louis Armstrong . . . . (Vanguard)
Hello Dolly! & Other Hits. . . . . (MCA)

Lady Came From Baltimore
Joan Baez; *Contemporary Ballad Book* . . . . (Vanguard)
Joan . . . . (Vanguard)
John Stewart; *Neon Beach* . . . . (Homecoming)
Johnny Cash; *Johnny Cash-16 Biggest Hits-#2* . . . . (Legacy)
Tim Hardin; *Hang On To A Dream-Verve Recordings* . . . . (Polydor)

Last Waltz, The
Engelbert Humperdinck; *Engelbert Humperdinck-16 Most Requested*
Songs . . . . (Epic)

Lead On
George Strait; *Latest Greatest Straitest Hits* . . . . (MCA)
Lead On . . . . (MCA)

Let's Fall In Love
Diana Krall; *When I Look In Your Eyes* . . . . (GRP)
Frank Sinatra; *The Reprise Collection* . . . . (Reprise)
Louis Armstrong & Oscar Peterson; *Verve Elite Edition Collector's*
Disc-C . . . . (Verve)
Tony Bennett; *Tony Bennett Sings A String Of Harold*
Arlen . . . . (Columbia Special Prod.)

Let's Lock The Door (And Throw Away The Key)
Jay & The Americans; *Jay & The Americans' All-Time Greatest Hits* . . . (Rhino)

Like Dreamers Do
Beatles; *The Beatles-Anthology-#1* . . . . (Capitol)

Like The Rain
Clint Black; *Clint Black-The Greatest Hits* . . . . (RCA)

Little Arrows
Leapy Lee; *Bubble Gum Classics-C* . . . . (MCA Special Prod.)
Country Music Classics-#3-1965-1970-C . . . . (K-Tel)

Long Walk, A
Jill Scott; *Who Is Jill Scott? Words And Sounds-#1* . . . . . . (Hidden Beach/Epic)

Look Of Love, The
Andy Williams; *Born Free-Love Andy* . . . . (Collectables)
Legend At His Best . . . . (Collectables)
Anita Baker; *Rhythm Of Love* . . . . (Atlantic)
Diana Krall; *The Look Of Love* . . . . (Impulse!)
Dionne Warwick; *Hidden Gems-Best Of Dionne Warwick-#2* . . . . . . (Rhino)
Neil Diamond; *As Time Goes By-The Movie Album* . . . . (Columbia)
Sergio Mendes & Brasil '66; *Sergio Mendes-Classics-#18.* . . . . (A&M)

Looking Back To See
Goldie Hill & Justin Tubb; *Justin Tubb-Star Of The Grand*
Ole Opry . . . . (Starday)
Jim Ed Brown & Maxine Brown; *Essential Jim Ed Brown* . . . . (RCA)

Looking Through Your Eyes
LeAnn Rimes; *Sittin' On Top Of The World* . . . . (Curb)
ST/Quest For Camelot . . . . (Curb/Atlantic)

Lost In You
Garth Brooks as Chris Gaines; *Garth Brooks In...The Life Of Chris*
Gaines . . . . (Capitol)

Love
Musiq Soulchild; *Aijuswanaseing* . . . . (Def Soul/IDJMG)

Love Gets Me Every Time
Shania Twain; *Come On Over* . . . . (Mercury)

Love I Found In You
Jim Brickman; *My Romance: An Evening With Jim Brickman* . . (Windham Hill)

Love Is A Many-Splendored Thing
Andy Williams; *Moon River & Other Great Movie Themes* . . . . (Columbia)
Four Aces; *Billboard Pop Memories-1955-1959-C* . . . . (Rhino)
Four Aces' Greatest Hits . . . . (MCA)

Love Like This
Faith Evans; *Keep The Faith* . . . . (Bad Boy/Arista)

Love Or Confusion
Jimi Hendrix Experience; *Are You Experienced?* . . . . (Reprise)

Love Walked In
Chet Baker; *Chet Baker With Strings* . . . . (Columbia)
Frank Sinatra; *Sinatra Swings* . . . . (Reprise)
The Reprise Collection . . . . (Reprise)
Sarah Vaughan; *Complete Sarah Vaughan On Mercury-#2.* . . . . . (Mercury)

Love Working On You
John Michael Montgomery; *Leave A Mark* . . . . (Atlantic)

Lovely Night, A
Julie Andrews; *A Little Bit Of Broadway* . . . . (Columbia)
Julie Andrews/Original Cast; *Cinderella-The CBS Television*
Production . . . . (Columbia)

Lovely Rita
Beatles; *Sgt. Pepper's Lonely Hearts Club Band* . . . . (Capitol)

Lucky One
Amy Grant; *House Of Love* . . . . (A&M)

Magic Touch, (You've Got) The
Platters; *Enchanted-The Best Of The Platters* . . . . (Rhino)

Magnet And Steel
Walter Egan; *Rock Artifacts-From The Vaults-#2-C* . . . . (Legacy)

Make It Happen
Mariah Carey; *Emotions* . . . . (Columbia)
MTV Unplugged-Mariah Carey . . . . (Columbia)

Mama He's Crazy
Judds; *Judds* . . . . (RCA)
Judds' Greatest Hits . . . . (MCA)
Why Not Me . . . . (MCA)

Mambo No. 5 (A Little Bit Of...)
Lou Bega; *A Little Bit Of Mambo* . . . . (RCA)
Totally Hits-#2-C . . . . (Elektra)

Maria Maria
Santana; *Supernatural* . . . . (Arista)
Totally Hits-#2-C . . . . (Elektra)

Marian The Librarian
Original Broadway Cast; *The Music Man* . . . . (Angel)
Robert Preston; *ST/The Music Man* . . . . (Warner Bros.)

Mint Car
Cure; *Wild Mood Swings* . . . . (Elektra)

Miracle Of Love
Eileen Rodgers; *Hard To Find 45s On CD-#3-The Mid '50s-C* . . . . . . (Eric)

Missing You
Mary J. Blige; *Share My World* . . . . (MCA)
The Tour . . . . (MCA)

Misty
Erroll Garner; *Other Voices* . . . . (Columbia)
Johnny Mathis; *First 25 Years-Silver Anniversary Album* . . . . (Columbia)
Heavenly . . . . (Columbia)
Johnny Mathis' All-Time Greatest Hits . . . . (Columbia)
Johnny Mathis-Live . . . . (Columbia)
Sarah Vaughan; *Sarah Vaughan-Golden Hits* . . . . (Mercury)

Moonglow
Art Tatum; *Solo Masterpieces-#1* . . . . (Pablo)
Billie Holiday; *First Verve Sessions.* . . . . (Verve)
Count Basie; *The Standards* . . . . (Verve)

More
Trace Adkins; *More...* . . . . (Capitol)

Mr. Moonlight
Beatles; *Beatles '65* . . . . (Capitol)
Beatles-Box Set. . . . . (Capitol)
For Sale. . . . . (Capitol)

Mr. Wonderful
Peggy Lee; *Best Of Peggy Lee* . . . . (MCA)

My Best Friend
Tim McGraw; *A Place In The Sun* . . . . (Curb)
Tim McGraw's Greatest Hits . . . . (Curb)

My Everything
98 Degrees; *Revelation* . . . . (Universal)

My First Night With You
Mya; *Mya* . . . . (University/Interscope)

My Heart Stood Still
Bud Powell; *Genius Of Bud Powell-#2* . . . . (Verve)
Frank Sinatra; *The Concert Sinatra* . . . . (Reprise)
Tony Bennett; *Rodgers & Hart Songbook* . . . . (DRG)

My Kind Of Girl
Collin Raye; *Best Of Collin Raye-Direct Hits* . . . . (Epic)
Extremes . . . . (Epic)

My One And Only Heart
Perry Como; *Sing Just For You* . . . . (RCA)

Never Been Kissed
Sherrie Austin; *Love In The Real World.* . . . . (Arista)

New
No Doubt; *Return Of Saturn.* . . . . (Interscope)
ST/Go . . . . (Work/Epic)

Night In Summer Long Ago
Mark Knopfler; *Golden Heart* . . . . (Warner Bros.)

Nightingale Sang In Berkeley Square
Harry Connick, Jr.; *We Are In Love* . . . . (Columbia)

Manhattan Transfer; *Best Of The Manhattan Transfer* . . . .(Atlantic)
   Mecca For Moderns. . . . .(Atlantic)
Tony Bennett; *Perfectly Frank* . . . . (Columbia)
No Moon At All
Anita O'Day; *In A Mellow Tone* . . . . (DRG)
Billy Stritch; *Billy Stritch* . . . . (DRG)
Not That Different
Collin Raye; *I Think About You* . . . . (Epic)
Nothin' New Under The Moon
LeAnn Rimes; *Sittin' On Top Of The World* . . . . (Curb)
Now That I've Found You
Terri Clark; *How I Feel* . . . . (Mercury)
Now's The Time To Fall In Love
Eddie Cantor; *The Eddie Cantor Radio Show-1942-1943* . . . .(Original Cast)
Gene Gardos & His Orchestra; *Brother Can You Spare A Dime? Great
   American Songs Of The Depression-C* . . . . (Pro-Arte)
Ob-La-Di, Ob-La-Da
Beatles; *Beatles-Box Set* . . . . (Capitol)
   The Beatles (White Album) . . . . (Capitol)
   The Beatles/1967-1970 . . . . (Capitol)
Oh Happy Day
Lawrence Welk; *Champagne Music Of Lawrence Welk*. . . . . (Universal)
On A Carousel
Hollies; *Best Of The Hollies* . . . . (EMI)
   History Of British Rock-#6-C . . . . (Rhino)
   The Hollies' Greatest Hits . . . .(Epic)
On A Good Night
Wade Hayes; *On A Good Night* . . . . (Columbia)
   Super Hits Of 1996-C. . . . .(Epic)
On A Night Like This
Trick Pony; *Trick Pony*. . . . . (H2E/Warner Bros.)
On London Bridge
Jo Stafford; *International Hits* . . . .(Corinthian)
On The Banks Of The Old Pontchartrain
Hank Williams; *American Legends-#18* . . . .(Laserlight)
   Complete Hank Williams . . . . (Mercury)
On The Street Where You Live
Andy Williams; *Andy Williams-16 Most Requested Songs-Encore!* . . . (Legacy)
Bobby Darin; *Unreleased Capitol Sides* . . . . (Collector's Choice)
Eddie Fisher; *Very Best Of Eddie Fisher* . . . .(Taragon)
Four Tops; *Lost & Found: Breaking Through* . . . . (Motown)
Harry Connick, Jr.; *25*. . . . . (Columbia)
Mel Torme; *Swings Shubert Alley*. . . . . (Verve)
Original Cast; *My Fair Lady* . . . . (Columbia)
Ray Conniff; *'S Awful Nice* . . . . (Columbia)
On The Verge
Collin Raye; *I Think About You* . . . .(Epic)
One Boy, One Girl
Collin Raye; *Best Of Collin Raye-Direct Hits* . . . .(Epic)
   I Think About You . . . .(Epic)
One Hour With You
Nelson Eddy; *When I'm Calling You* . . . .(Living Era)
One In A Million
Platters; *Magic Touch-An Anthology* . . . . (Mercury)
One Night At A Time
George Strait; *Carrying Your Love With Me* . . . . (MCA)
   Latest Greatest Straitest Hits . . . . (MCA)
Out Of My Dreams
Original Broadway Cast; *Oklahoma!* . . . . (RCA)
Original Cast; *Oklahoma!* . . . . (MCA)
Pagan Poetry
Bjork; *Vespertine* . . . . (Elektra)
Paradise
Styx; *Return To Paradise* . . . . (CMC Int'l)
Patricia
Perez Prado & His Orchestra; *Nipper's Greatest Hits Of The
   '50s-#2-C* . . . . (RCA)
Perry Como; *Perry Como's Greatest Hits* . . . . (RCA)
People Will Say We're In Love
Frank Sinatra; *A Lovely Way To Spend An Evening* . . . . (ASV)
Original Broadway Cast; *Oklahoma!* . . . . (RCA)
Spaniels; *Spaniels' Golden Hits* . . . . (Juke Box Treasures)
   The Acapella Collection . . . . (Juke Box Treasures)
Picnic
McGuire Sisters; *Songs Of Steve Allen-C* . . . . (Varese Sarabande)
Pineapple Princess
Annette Funicello; *Frankie Avalon/Annette Funicello* . . . . (K-Tel)
Pink
Aerosmith; *Nine Lives* . . . . (Columbia)
Pittsburgh, Pennsylvania
101 Strings Orchestra; *Million-Seller Hits From Mexico* . . . . (Alshire)
Guy Mitchell; *Guy Mitchell-16 Most Requested Songs* . . . . (Legacy)
Please Forgive Me
David Gray; *White Ladder* . . . . (ATO/RCA)
Please Help Me, I'm Falling
Hank Locklin; *Billboard Top Country Hits-1960-C* . . . . (Rhino)
   Hank Locklin-Golden Hits . . . . (Plantation)
   Nipper's Greatest Hits Of The '60s-#2-C . . . . (RCA)
   Souvenirs Of Music City U.S.A.-C . . . . (Plantation)

Janie Fricke; *Janie Fricke's Greatest Hits*. . . . . (Columbia)
Powerful Thing
Trisha Yearwood; *Where Your Road Leads* . . . . (MCA)
Pretty Ballerina
Left Banke; *History Of The Left Banke* . . . . (Rhino)
   Nuggets-#11-Pop-Part 4-C . . . . (Rhino)
Purple Haze
Cure; *Stone Free: A Tribute To Jimi Hendrix-C* . . . . (Reprise)
Jimi Hendrix; *Kiss The Sky* . . . . (Reprise)
   ST/Jimi Hendrix . . . . (Reprise)
Jimi Hendrix Experience; *Are You Experienced?* . . . . (Reprise)
   Essential Jimi Hendrix . . . . (Reprise)
   Radio One . . . . (Rykodisc)
   Smash Hits . . . . (Reprise)
Winger; *Winger*. . . . .(Atlantic)
Rain, The Park And Other Things
Cowsills; *Cowsills* . . . . (Razor & Tie)
Real Love
Beatles; *The Beatles-Anthology-#2* . . . . (Capitol)
John Lennon; *ST/Imagine: John Lennon* . . . . (Capitol)
Rebecca Lynn
Bryan White; *Bryan White* . . . .(Asylum)
Reminiscing
Little River Band; *'70's Super Groups-C* . . . . (Rhino)
   Reminiscing: The Twentieth Anniversary Collection . . . . (Rhino)
Ricky Wants A Man Of Her Own
Bruce Springsteen; *Tracks* . . . . (Columbia)
Rock Show, The
Blink-182; *Now That's What I Call Music!-#8-C* . . . . (Virgin)
   Take Off Your Pants And Jacket . . . . (MCA)
Rockin' Good Way (To Mess Around And Fall In Love)
Arthur Prysock; *Rockin' Good Way* . . . . (Milestone)
Brook Benton & Dinah Washington; *Brook Benton-Anthology* . . . . (Rhino)
Rodeo Or Mexico
Garth Brooks; *Scarecrow* . . . . (Capitol)
Runaway
Corrs; *Forgiven, Not Forgotten*. . . . . (143/Asylum)
Runnin' Away With My Heart
Lonestar; *Lonestar*. . . . .(BNA)
Running Around Town
Billy Ray Martin; *Deadline For My Memories* . . . .(Sire)
Running Out Of Reasons To Run
Rick Trevino; *Learning As You Go* . . . . (Columbia)
Sawyer Brown; *Wide Open* . . . . (Curb)
Save The Best For Last
Vanessa Williams; *Grammy's Greatest Moments-#2-C* . . . .(Atlantic)
   The Comfort Zone. . . . .(Wing)
   Women For Women-C . . . . (Mercury)
Second Fiddle
Kay Starr; *Essential RCA Singles Collection* . . . . (Taragon)
September
Earth, Wind & Fire; *Best Of Earth, Wind & Fire-#1* . . . . (Legacy)
   Eternal Dance . . . . (Columbia)
   Mega Hits Dance Classics-#7-C . . . . (Priority)
Seven Angels
Bruce Springsteen; *Tracks* . . . . (Columbia)
Seven Days
Mary J. Blige; *Share My World* . . . . (MCA)
   The Tour. . . . . (MCA)
Shall We Dance
Ella Fitzgerald; *George & Ira Gershwin Songbook*. . . . . (Verve)
She Walks This Earth
Sting; *Love Affair-Music Of Ivan Lins-C* . . . . (Telarc)
She Wears Red Feathers
Guy Mitchell; *Guy Mitchell-16 Most Requested Songs* . . . . (Legacy)
She's More
Andy Griggs; *You Won't Ever Be Lonely* . . . . (RCA)
She's Taken A Shine
John Berry; *Faces* . . . . (Capitol)
Simple Joys Of Maidenhood
Julie Andrews; *Camelot* . . . . (Columbia)
Various Artists; *ST/Camelot* . . . . (Warner Bros.)
Singing In My Sleep
Semisonic; *Feeling Strangely Fine* . . . . (MCA)
Sleepwalker
Wallflowers; *Breach* . . . . (Interscope)
Smile Like Yours
Natalie Cole; *ST/A Smile Like Yours* . . . . (Elektra)
So Emotional
Christina Aguilera; *Christina Aguilera* . . . . (RCA)
So Emotional
Whitney Houston; *Whitney* . . . . (Arista)
   Whitney Houston's Greatest Hits . . . . (Arista)
So Help Me Girl
Gary Barlow; *Open Road* . . . . (Arista)
Joe Diffie; *Third Rock From The Sun* . . . .(Epic)
So Into You
Tamia; *Tamia* . . . . (Qwest)

Soft Summer Breeze
Diamonds; *45-#70934* . . . . . (Mercury)
Eddie Heywood; *Chart Toppers-Romantic Hits Of The '50s-C* . . . . . (Priority)
Great Instrumental Hits Of The '50s-'80s-C . . . . . (Rebound)
Sold (The Grundy County Auction Incident)
John Michael Montgomery; *Drew's Famous Country Party Music-C* . . . . . (Turn Up The Music)
John Michael Montgomery . . . . . (Atlantic)
John Michael Montgomery's Greatest Hits . . . . . (Atlantic)
Some Enchanted Evening
Jay & The Americans; *Come A Little Bit Closer-Best Of Jay & The Americans* . . . . . (Gold Rush)
Jay & The Americans' All-Time Greatest Hits . . . . . (Rhino)
Original Cast; *South Pacific* . . . . . (CBS Masterworks)
Perry Como; *Perry Como's All-Time Greatest Hits-#1* . . . . . (RCA)
Rosanno Brazzi; *ST/South Pacific* . . . . . (RCA)
Willie Nelson; *What A Wonderful World* . . . . . (Columbia)
Somebody Like Me
Silkk The Shocker Featuring Mya; *Made Man* . . . . . (No Limit/Priority)
Someone To Love
Jon B.; *Bonafide* . . . . . (Yab Yum/550)
Jon B. featuring Babyface; *ST/Bad Boys* . . . . . (Work)
Something
Beatles; *Abbey Road* . . . . . (Parlophone)
Beatles 1 . . . . . (Capitol)
The Beatles/1967-1970 . . . . . (Capitol)
The Beatles-Anthology-#3 . . . . . (Capitol)
Something To Talk About
Bonnie Raitt; *Luck Of The Draw* . . . . . (Capitol)
Sometimes
Britney Spears; *...Baby One More Time* . . . . . (Jive)
Now That's What I Call Music!-#3-C . . . . . (Virgin)
Somewhere In The Vicinity Of The Heart
Shenandoah; *In The Vicinity Of The Heart* . . . . . (Capitol)
Now And Then . . . . . (Capitol)
Pure Country-Best Of The '90s-#2-C . . . . . (Priority)
Son Of A Preacher Man
Dusty Springfield; *Dusty Springfield* . . . . . (Rhino)
Dusty Springfield-Anthology . . . . . (Mercury)
Soul Singing
Black Crowes; *Lions* . . . . . (V2)
South Of The Border (Down Mexico Way)
Bob Wills & His Texas Playboys; *Best Of Bob Wills & His Texas Playboys* . . . . . (MCA)
Bob Wills & His Texas Playboys-Greatest Hits . . . . . (Curb)
Frank Sinatra; *Capitol Collectors Series-Frank Sinatra* . . . . . (Capitol)
Come Fly With Me . . . . . (Capitol)
Gene Autry; *The Country Music Hall Of Fame-Gene Autry-15 Of His All-Time Greatest Hits* . . . . . (Columbia)
Patsy Cline; *Always* . . . . . (MCA)
The Patsy Cline Story . . . . . (MCA)
Willie Nelson; *What A Wonderful World* . . . . . (Columbia)
Step By Step
Eddie Rabbitt; *Best Of Eddie Rabbitt/Greatest Hits-II* . . . . . (Warner Bros.)
Number 1's . . . . . (Warner Bros.)
Such A Night
Elvis Presley; *From Nashville To Memphis-The Essential '60s Masters* . . . (RCA)
Suddenly
Soraya; *On Nights Like This* . . . . . (Island)
Summer Means New Love
Beach Boys; *Today/Summer Days (& Summer Nights!)* . . . . . (Capitol)
Summertime
Sundays; *Static & Silence* . . . . . (David Geffen Co.)
Sunday For Tea
Peter And Gordon; *Best Of Peter And Gordon* . . . . . (Rhino)
Sunshine
Coko; *Hot Coko* . . . . . (RCA)
Sure Feels Like Love
Larry Gatlin & The Gatlin Brothers Band; *Larry Gatlin & The Gatlin Brothers' Greatest Hits-#2* . . . . . (Columbia)
Larry Gatlin & The Gatlin Brothers-17 Greatest Hits . . . . . (Columbia)
Sure To Fall (In Love With You)
Carl Perkins; *Boppin' The Blues* . . . . . (Columbia)
Sway
Bobby Rydell; *Born With A Smile* . . . . . (Plum)
Dean Martin; *Best Of Dean Martin* . . . . . (CEMA Special Prod.)
Dean Martin's All Time Greatest Hits . . . . . (Curb)
That's Amore: The Best Of Dean Martin . . . . . (Capitol)
Sweetheart
Jermaine Dupri & Mariah Carey; *Presents Life In 1472-Original Soundtrack* . . . . . (So So Def/Columbia)
Mariah Carey featuring Jermaine Dupri; *Mariah Carey-#1's* . . . . . (Columbia)
Take You Out
Luther Vandross; *Luther Vandross* . . . . . (J)
Taking You Home
Don Henley; *Inside Job* . . . . . (Warner Bros.)
Tell Him
Barbra Streisand & Celine Dion; *Higher Ground* . . . . . (Columbia)
Celine Dion & Barbra Streisand; *Let's Talk About Love-C* . . . . . (550 Music)
Tell Me When
Human League; *Octopus* . . . . . (East West)
Ten Minutes Ago
Julie Andrews & Jon Cypher; *Cinderella-The CBS Television Production* . . . . . (Columbia)
Stuart Damon & Lesley Ann Warren; *Cinderella-The CBS Television Network Production* . . . . . (Columbia)
Ten Pound Hammer
Aaron Tippin; *Tool Box* . . . . . (RCA)
Tenderly
Billie Holiday; *Verve Jazz Masters 47-Billie Holiday Sings Standards* . . . (Verve)
Ella Fitzgerald; *Verve Jazz Masters 24* . . . . . (Verve)
Oscar Peterson; *Essential Oscar Peterson-The Swinger* . . . . . (Verve)
Rosemary Clooney; *Essence Of Rosemary Clooney* . . . . . (Legacy)
Rosemary Clooney-16 Most Requested Songs . . . . . (Legacy)
Sarah Vaughan; *Compact Jazz-Sarah Vaughan* . . . . . (Verve)
Verve Jazz Masters 42-The Jazz Sides . . . . . (Verve)
Tony Bennett; *Here's To The Ladies* . . . . . (Columbia)
Texas Tornado
Tracy Lawrence; *Best Of Tracy Lawrence* . . . . . (Atlantic)
I See It Now . . . . . (Atlantic)
Thank You In Advance
Boyz II Men; *Nathan Michael Shawn Wanya* . . . . . (Universal)
That Was Your Mother
Paul Simon; *Graceland* . . . . . (Warner Bros.)
That's Amore
Dean Martin; *Best Of Dean Martin* . . . . . (CEMA Special Prod.)
Dean Martin's All Time Greatest Hits . . . . . (Curb)
Dean Martin's Greatest Hits . . . . . (EMI)
The Capitol Years-Dean Martin . . . . . (Capitol)
That's How You Know (When You're In Love)
Lari White; *Best Of Lari White* . . . . . (RCA)
Wishes . . . . . (RCA)
That's The Beat Of A Heart
Warren Brothers with Sara Evans; *King Of Nothing* . . . . . (BNA)
ST/Where The Heart Is . . . . . (RCA)
That's The Kind Of Mood I'm In
Patty Loveless; *Strong Heart* . . . . . (Epic)
Theme From "The Dating Game"
Original Soundtrack; *Television's Greatest Hits-#5-In Living Color-C* . . . (TVT)
There's A Moon Out Tonight
Capris; *20 Top 10 Hits Of The '50s & '60s-C* . . . . . (Laurie)
22 Leaders Of The Pack-#2-C . . . . . (Laurie)
Collectables Presents The History Of Rock-#3-C . . . . . (Collectables)
There's A Moon Out Tonight . . . . . (Collectables)
There's No Stopping Your Heart
Marie Osmond; *Best Of Branson U.S.A.-#1-C* . . . . . (Curb)
Best Of Marie Osmond . . . . . (Curb)
There's No Stopping Your Heart . . . . . (Curb)
These Are The Times
Dru Hill; *Enter The Dru* . . . . . (Def Jam/RAL/Mercury/Island)
They Say That Falling In Love Is Wonderful
Mark Shane & Terry Blaine; *With Thee I Swing!* . . . . . (Nagel-Heyer)
Thinkin' About You
Trisha Yearwood; *Thinkin' About You* . . . . . (MCA)
This Can't Be Love
Diana Krall; *Stepping Out* . . . . . (Justin Time)
Ella Fitzgerald; *Rodgers & Hart Songbook* . . . . . (Verve)
Natalie Cole; *Unforgettable With Love* . . . . . (Elektra)
Original Cast; *The Boys From Syracuse* . . . . . (Angel)
Stephane Grappelli; *Compact Jazz-Stephane Grappelli* . . . . . (Verve)
Various Artists; *Embraceable You-Broadway In Love* . . . . . (Sony Broadway)
This Is Your Night
Amber; *ESPN Presents Jock Jams-#2-C* . . . . . (Tommy Boy)
This Is Your Night . . . . . (Tommy Boy)
This Kiss
Faith Hill; *Faith* . . . . . (Warner Bros.)
Totally Hits-#1-C . . . . . (Arista)
This Magic Moment
Drifters; *Drifters' Greatest Hits* . . . . . (Gusto)
Drifters-Golden Hits . . . . . (Atlantic)
Jay & The Americans; *Come A Little Bit Closer-Best Of Jay & The Americans* . . . . . (Gold Rush)
Jay & The Americans' All-Time Greatest Hits . . . . . (Rhino)
Marvin Gaye; *M.P.G.* . . . . . (Motown)
'Til I Get It Right
Tammy Wynette; *Tammy Wynette's Biggest Hits* . . . . . (Epic)
Tammy Wynette's Greatest Hits-#3 . . . . . (Epic)
Tears Of Fire-25th Anniversary Collection . . . . . (Epic)
Trisha Yearwood; *Tammy Wynette...Remembered-C* . . . . . (Asylum)
Till There Was You
Beatles; *Beatles-Box Set* . . . . . (Capitol)
Meet The Beatles! . . . . . (Capitol)
With The Beatles . . . . . (Parlophone)
Original Cast; *ST/The Music Man* . . . . . (Warner Bros.)
Timber I'm Falling In Love
Patty Loveless; *Country's Greatest Hits-#4-Sweet Country-C* . . . . . (Priority)
Honky Tonk Angel . . . . . (MCA)
Patty Loveless' Greatest Hits . . . . . (MCA)

Too Late To Turn Back Now
Cornelius Brothers & Sister Rose; *Radio Days: '70s Pop-C* . . . . (EMI Special Markets)

Total Eclipse Of The Heart
Bonnie Tyler; *Billboard Top Hits-1983-C* . . . . (Rhino)
Faster Than The Speed Of Night . . . . (Columbia)
Seems Like Yesterday-#4-Early '80s-C . . . . (K-Tel)
Nicki French; *Dance Hits '96 Supermix-C* . . . .(Critique)
Secrets . . . . (Critique)

Trippin'
Total featuring Missy Elliott; *Kima, Keisha & Pam* . . . . (Bad Boy/Arista)

Twenty-Four Hours From Tulsa
Burt Bacharach; *Walk On By* . . . .(MCA Special Prod.)
Gene Pitney; *Best Of Gene Pitney* . . . . (K-Tel)

Twilight Time
Platters; *Pick Of The Platters* . . . . (Fifty One West)
Platters . . . . (Everest)
Platters-16 Greatest Hits . . . . (Trip)
Platters-Anthology . . . . (Rhino)
Sold Out . . . . (Fifty One West)
Willie Nelson; *What A Wonderful World* . . . . (Columbia)

Two Less Lonely People In The World
Air Supply; *Now & Forever* . . . . (Arista)

Two People Fell In Love
Brad Paisley; *Brad Paisley-Part II* . . . . (Arista)

U Got It Bad
Usher; *8701* . . . . (LaFace)

Unbelievable
Diamond Rio; *Unbelievable* . . . . (Arista)

Under The Boardwalk
Bette Midler; *ST/Beaches* . . . .(Atlantic)
Bruce Willis; *Return Of Bruno* . . . . (Motown)
Drifters; *Atlantic Rhythm & Blues 1947-1974-#5 (1962-1966)-C* . . . . . (Atlantic)
Drifters-16 Greatest Hits . . . . (Trip)
Drifters-Golden Hits . . . .(Atlantic)
Super Oldies Of The '60s-#5-C . . . .(Audio Fidelity)
John Mellencamp; *Rough Harvest* . . . . (Mercury)
Lynn Anderson; *What She Does Best* . . . . (Mercury)
Rickie Lee Jones; *Girl At Her Volcano* . . . .(Warner Bros.)
Rolling Stones; *12 X 5.* . . . . (Abkco)
Untouchables; *Agent Double O Soul* . . . .(Restless)

Unforgettable
Nat ''King'' Cole; *Capitol Collectors Series-Nat ''King'' Cole* . . . . . . (Capitol)
The Nat ''King'' Cole Story . . . . (Capitol)
Unforgettable . . . . (Capitol)
Natalie Cole with Nat ''King'' Cole; *Unforgettable With Love* . . . . . . (Elektra)

Uptown Girl
Billy Joel; *An Innocent Man* . . . . (Columbia)
Billy Joel-Greatest Hits, Volume I & Volume II . . . . . . (Columbia)
KOHUEPT. . . . . (Columbia)

Veni-Vidi-Vici (I Came, I Saw, I Conquered)
Gaylords; *Best Of The Gaylords* . . . .(Chronicles)

Waiting For Tonight
Jennifer Lopez; *Now That's What I Call Music!-#4-C* . . . . (Virgin)
On The 6. . . . . (Work)

Walkin' My Baby Back Home
Johnnie Ray; *Johnnie Ray-16 Most Requested Songs* . . . . (Legacy)
Johnnie Ray's Greatest Hits . . . . (Sony Music Special Prod.)
Nat ''King'' Cole; *Capitol Collectors Series-Nat ''King'' Cole* . . . (Capitol)
The Nat ''King'' Cole Story . . . . (Capitol)

Watch This
Clay Walker; *Rumor Has It.* . . . .(Giant)

Waterloo
Abba; *Abba's Greatest Hits* . . . .(Atlantic)
Waterloo . . . .(Atlantic)

We Danced
Brad Paisley; *Who Needs Pictures* . . . . (Arista)

Wear My Ring Around Your Neck
Elvis Presley; *50,000,000 Elvis Fans Can't Be Wrong-Elvis' Gold Records-Volume 2* . . . . (RCA)
Hits Like Never Before-Essential-#3 . . . . (RCA)
The Top Ten Hits . . . . (RCA)
Worldwide 50 Gold Award Hits, Vol. 1, Parts 1 & 2 . . . . . (RCA)
Ricky Van Shelton; *Ricky Van Shelton's Greatest Hits Plus* . . . (Columbia)

What A Diff'rence A Day Makes
Dinah Washington; *What A Diff'rence A Day Makes* . . . . (Mercury)

What Are We Doin' Lonesome
Larry Gatlin & The Gatlin Brothers Band; *Best Of The Gatlins-All The Gold In California* . . . . (Legacy)
Larry Gatlin & The Gatlin Brothers' Greatest Hits-#2 . . . . (Columbia)
Larry Gatlin & The Gatlin Brothers-17 Greatest Hits . . . . . . (Columbia)

What Do You Say To That
George Strait; *Always Never The Same.* . . . .(MCA)

What If I Said
Anita Cochran & Steve Wariner; *Back To You* . . . .(Warner Bros.)
Steve Wariner & Anita Cochran; *Burnin' The Roadhouse Down* . . . . . (Capitol)

What The Heart Wants
Collin Raye; *Best Of Collin Raye-Direct Hits.* . . . .(Epic)

When Boy Meets Girl
Terri Clark; *Terri Clark.* . . . . (Mercury)

When I Dream At Night
Marc Anthony; *Marc Anthony.* . . . . (Columbia)

When I Fall In Love
Celine Dion; *The Colour Of My Love* . . . .(550 Music)
Doris Day; *Doris Day-16 Most Requested Songs-Encore!* . . . . (Columbia)

When Love Starts Talkin'
Wynonna; *The Other Side* . . . .(Curb/MCA)

When The Fallen Angels Fly
Patty Loveless; *When Fallen Angels Fly* . . . . (Epic)

When You Put Your Hands On Me
Christina Aguilera; *Christina Aguilera* . . . .(RCA)

Where Do We Go From Here
Vanessa Williams; *Vanessa Williams' Greatest Hits-The First Ten Years* . . . . (Mercury)

Which Bridge To Cross (Which Bridge To Burn)
Vince Gill; *When Love Finds You* . . . . (MCA)

Who Put The Bomp (In The Bomp, Bomp, Bomp)
Barry Mann; *Goofy Greats-C* . . . . (K-Tel)
Sixties Rule! Chapter Two-C . . . . (One Way)

Why Ain't I Running
Garth Brooks; *Scarecrow* . . . . (Capitol)

Why Do Fools Fall In Love
Beach Boys; *Spirit Of America* . . . . (Capitol)
Diamonds; *Best Of The Diamonds-The Mercury Years.* . . . . (Mercury)
Diana Ross; *Why Do Fools Fall In Love* . . . .(RCA)
Frankie Lymon and The Teenagers; *Best Of Frankie Lymon and The Teenagers* . . . . (Rhino)
Billboard Top Rock 'N' Roll Hits-1956-C . . . . (Rhino)
ST/American Graffiti . . . . (MCA)
Joni Mitchell; *Shadows & Light* . . . .(Asylum)

Why Don't You Fall In Love With Me?
Les Elgart; *Best Of The Big Bands: Sophisticated Swing* . . . . (Columbia)

Why They Call It Falling
Lee Ann Womack; *I Hope You Dance* . . . . (MCA)

Winter Wonderland
Air Supply; *Air Supply Christmas Album* . . . . (Arista)
White Christmas . . . . (Word)
Alexander O'Neal; *My Gift To You* . . . . (Tabu)
Amy Grant; *Home For Christmas* . . . . (A&M)
Andrews Sisters; *Andrews Sisters-Christmas* . . . . . . (MCA Special Prod.)
Anne Murray; *Best Of The Season* . . . .(EMI America)
Aretha Franklin; *Rock 'N' Roll Christmas Classics-C* . . . . (Music For Little People)
Barbara Mandrell; *Christmas At Our House* . . . . (MCA Special Prod.)
Tennessee Christmas-C . . . . (MCA)
Bing Crosby; *Bing Crosby Christmas Classics* . . . . (Capitol)
Blue Notes; *Rhythm & Blues Christmas-#1-C* . . . .(Collectables)
Brenda Lee; *Jingle Bell Rock* . . . . (MCA Special Prod.)
Carnie & Wendy Wilson; *Hey Santa!* . . . . (SBK)
Darlene Love; *Christmas Gift For You From Phil Spector-C* . . . . (Rhino)
Phil Spector-Back To Mono 1969-C . . . . (Abkco)
Phil Spector's Christmas Album-C. . . . . (Passport)
Eddy Arnold; *Christmas With Eddy Arnold* . . . . (RCA)
Elvis Presley; *If Every Day Was Like Christmas* . . . . (RCA)
Eurythmics; *Very Special Christmas-C.* . . . . (A&M)
Faron Young; *Country Christmas* . . . .(Step One)
Frank Sinatra; *Christmas Songs By Sinatra* . . . .(Legacy)
George Strait; *Merry Christmas Strait To You* . . . . (MCA Special Prod.)
Hank Crawford; *We Got A Good Thing Going* . . . .(Kudo)
Johnny Mercer & The Pied Pipers; *Merry Christmas Baby-Romance & Reindeer-C* . . . . (Capitol)
Kathie Lee Gifford; *It's Christmas Time* . . . . (Warner Bros.)
Kenny Rogers; *Christmas In America.* . . . . (Reprise)
London Symphony Orchestra; *Christmas Traditions* . . . . . . (Special Music Co.)
Merle Haggard; *Merle Haggard-Christmas Gift.* . . . . (Curb)
Patti LaBelle & The Blue Belles; *A Soulful Christmas-C* . . . . . . (Collectables)
Randy Travis; *An Old Time Christmas* . . . . (Warner Bros.)
Robert Goulet; *Essence Of Christmas* . . . . (A&M)
Rosie O'Donnell & Macy Gray; *Another Rosie Christmas-C* . . . . . . (Columbia)
Tanya Tucker; *Christmas For The '90s-#1-C* . . . . (Liberty)
Tony Bennett; *Now That's What I Call Christmas!-C.* . . . .(UTV)
Travis Tritt; *Christmas-Loving Time Of The Year.* . . . . . (Warner Bros.)

Wishing Well
Terence Trent D'Arby; *Introducing The Hardline According To Terence Trent D'Arby.* . . . . (Columbia)

With My Eyes Wide Open I'm Dreaming
Mandy Barnett; *I've Got A Right To Cry.* . . . .(Sire)
Patti Page; *Patti Page-Golden Hits* . . . . (Mercury)
Patti Page's Greatest Hits . . . . (Columbia)

With You
Lila McCann; *Something In The Air* . . . .(Asylum)

Without You
Charlie Wilson; *Bridging The Gap* . . . . (Major Hits)

Woke Up In Love
Exile; *Exile* . . . . (Epic)
Exile's Greatest Hits . . . . (Epic)

Words Of Love
Beatles; *Beatles VI*..(Capitol)
Beatles-Box Set.................................(Capitol)
Beatles-Love Songs................................(Capitol)
For Sale....................................(Capitol)
Buddy Holly; *Buddy Holly*............................(MCA)
Legend-From The Original Master Tapes........(MCA)
Rock & Roll Collection........................(MCA)
Buddy Holly/The Crickets; *Buddy Holly-20 Golden Greats*..........(MCA)

Workin' On A Groovy Thing
Patti Drew; *Soul Shots-#2-The ''In'' Crowd-Sweet Soul-C*.......(Rhino)
Tell Him-Golden Classics...................(Collectables)

Wrong Again
Martina McBride; *Big Country Hits '99-C*.....................(K-Tel)
Country Cares For Kids II-C....................(BNA)
Evolution............................(RCA)

Wrong Night
Reba McEntire; *If You See Him*.......................(MCA)

Yellow
Coldplay; *Now That's What I Call Music!-#6-C*...............(Virgin)
Parachutes..........................(Nettwerk/Capitol)

Yes!
Chad Brock; *Yes!*....................................(Warner Bros.)

Yes, I'm Ready
Barbara Mason; *Cruisin'-1965-C*.....................(Increase)
Teri DeSario; *Casablanca Records Greatest Hits-C*............(Casablanca)

You Alone
Perry Como; *Perry Como's Greatest Hits*....................(RCA)

You Beat Me To The Punch
Mary Wells; *Hitsville USA-The Motown Singles Collection-1959-1971-C*........(Motown)
Mary Wells' Greatest Hits..................(Motown)

You Can't Hurry Love
Diana Ross; *Diana Ross-The Ultimate Collection*............(Motown)
Diana Ross & The Supremes; *16 #1 Hits From The Early '60s-C*.....(Motown)
Phil Collins; *Hello, I Must Be Going*..................(Atlantic)

You Go To My Head
Billie Holiday; *At Storyville*.....................(Black Lion)
First Verve Sessions........................(Verve)
Bing Crosby; *The Radio Years: 20 Songs*...........(Crescendo)
Frank Sinatra; *Nice 'N' Easy*....................(Capitol)
Round #1.....................................(Capitol)
Voice: The Columbia Years-1943-1952..........(Columbia)
Linda Ronstadt; *For Sentimental Reasons*.................(Asylum)

You Got Me
Roots featuring Erykah Badu; *Things Fall Apart*...........(MCA)

You Had Me From Hello
Kenny Chesney; *Everywhere We Go*.......................(BNA)
Kenny Chesney's Greatest Hits..................(BNA)

You Light Up My Life
Debby Boone; *Best Of Debby Boone*....................(Curb)
There Is Love-Wedding Songs-C............(Scotti Bros.)
You Light Up My Life.........................(MCA)
LeAnn Rimes; *You Light Up My Life-Inspirational Songs*.......(Curb)

You Made Me Love You
Judy Garland; *Best Of Judy Garland*....................(MCA)
Judy Garland's All-Time Greatest Hits........(Curb)
Patsy Cline; *Sentimentally Yours*....................(MCA)

You Make Loving Fun
Fleetwood Mac; *25 Years-The Chain*............(Warner Bros.)
Fleetwood Mac's Greatest Hits.........(Warner Bros.)
Rumours..............................(Warner Bros.)
Jewel; *Legacy-A Tribute To Fleetwood Mac's Rumours-C*......(Lava)

You Make Me Wanna...
Usher; *My Way*................................(LaFace)
Totally Hits-#1-C............................(Arista)

You Sang To Me
Marc Anthony; *Marc Anthony*...................(Columbia)

You Shouldn't Kiss Me Like This
Toby Keith; *How Do You Like Me Now?!*.....(DreamWorks/SKG)

You Showed Me
Turtles; *Turtles-20 Greatest Hits*....................(Rhino)

You Turned The Tables On Me
Anita O'Day; *Anita Sings The Most*...................(Verve)
Benny Goodman; *Benny Goodman's Greatest Hits*......(RCA Victor)
Birth Of Swing.............................(Bluebird)
Billie Holiday; *Solitude*............................(Verve)
Louis Armstrong; *Compact Jazz-Louis Armstrong*...........(Verve)

Younger Than Springtime
Original Cast; *South Pacific*...............(CBS Masterworks)

You're Beginning To Get To Me
Clay Walker; *Clay Walker's Greatest Hits*.................(Giant)

You're Getting To Be A Habit With Me
Betty Carter; *I Can't Help It*......................(GRP)
Diana Krall; *Love Scenes*.........................(Impulse!)
Doris Day; *Golden Girl: The Columbia Recordings-1944-1966*.......(Legacy)
Frank Sinatra; *songs for Swingin' Lovers!*..............(Capitol)
Mel Torme; *Spotlight On Mel Torme*..................(Capitol)
Original Broadway Cast; *42nd Street*..............(RCA Victor)

You're Sixteen
Johnny Burnette; *ST/American Graffiti*....................(MCA)
Ringo Starr; *Blast From Your Past*..............(Gold Rush)
Ringo.....................................(Capitol)

You're The Reason Why
Ebonys; *The Philly Sound-Kenny Gamble, Leon Huff & The Story Of Brotherly Love 1966-1976-C*.................(Legacy)

Zing! Went The Strings Of My Heart
Coasters; *Coasters' Greatest Hits*....................(Atco)
Rare Soul-Beach Music Classics-#1-C...........(Rhino)
Frank Sinatra; *The Reprise Collection*..............(Reprise)
Judy Garland; *Best Of Judy Garland*....................(MCA)
Best Of The Decca Years-#1-Hits!-C.........(Decca)
Judy Garland-At Carnegie Hall..............(Capitol)
Judy Garland's All-Time Greatest Hits.........(Curb)

LOVE: FORBIDDEN LOVE

See Also: **CHEATING & LIES, DESIRE, HIDING, KISSING, LOVE (various), PARENTS: CONCERNED ABOUT TEEN LOVE, POVERTY, PREJUDICE, SECRETS, SEX: RESISTING TEMPTATION, SOCIAL CLASS: GENERAL, TEENAGERS, YOUNG**

After The Fire Is Gone
Loretta Lynn & Conway Twitty; *MCA Records 30 Years Of Hits-1958-1988-C*.......(MCA)
Very Best Of Loretta Lynn & Conway Twitty.........(MCA)

Always Wanting You
Merle Haggard & The Strangers; *For The Record: Merle Haggard-43 Legendary Hits*.................(BNA)

Anyway
Keb' Mo'; *The Door*.....................(550/Epic/Okeh)

As We Lay
Kelly Price; *Mirror Mirror*...............(Def Soul/IDJMG)

Bed Of Rose's
Statler Brothers; *Bed Of Rose's*....................(Mercury)

Between Me And You
Ja Rule featuring Christina Milian; *Rule 3:36* ... (Murder Inc./Def Jam/IDJMG)

Body Bumpin'
Mytown; *Mytown*....................(Cherry/Universal)

Born Too Late
Poni-Tails; *Original Classic Oldies Of The '50s-#4-C*.............(MCA)

Borrowed Love
Earl Scruggs & Dwight Yoakam; *Earl Scruggs And Friends-C*........(MCA)

Breaking All The Rules
She Moves; *Boom! 17 Explosive Hits-C*.................(Simitar)
Breaking All The Rules......................(Geffen)

Can't You See That She's Mine
Dave Clark Five; *History Of The Dave Clark Five*...........(Hollywood)

Come On Down To My Boat
Every Mother's Son; *Battle Of The Bands-#3-C*...........(K-Tel)

Cuttin' Heads
John Mellencamp; *Cuttin' Heads*...................(Columbia)

Dawn (Go Away)
4 Seasons; *25th Anniversary Collection*...............(Rhino)
4 Seasons-Anthology........................(Rhino)

Diana
Paul Anka; *21 Legendary Superstars-C*............(Original Sound)
Billboard Top Rock 'N' Roll Hits-1957-C.........(Rhino)
Paul Anka's 21 Golden Hits...................(RCA)

Don't Make It Easy For Me
Earl Thomas Conley; *Very Best Of Earl Thomas Conley*.....(RCA)

Down In The Boondocks
Billy Joe Royal; *Billy Joe Royal's Greatest Hits*.........(Columbia)
Rock Classics Of The '60s-C..................(Columbia)

El Paso
Grateful Dead; *Steal Your Face*...............(Grateful Dead)
Marty Robbins; *Billboard Top Country Hits-1960-C*...............(Rhino)
Gunfighter Ballads & Trail Songs.............(Legacy)
Marty Robbins' Biggest Hits.................(Columbia)
Radio Classics Of The '50s-C................(Columbia)
Texas Super Hits-C.........................(Columbia)

Forbidden Love
Madonna; *Bedtime Stories*.............(Maverick/Sire)
Something To Remember...............(Maverick/Sire)

Ginger Bread
Frankie Avalon; *Gold For The Road-Carburetor Classics-C*.......(Compose)
Venus: The Very Best Of Frankie Avalon.........(Collectables)

Girl, You'll Be A Woman Soon
Neil Diamond; *Double Gold-Neil Diamond*..................(Bang)
Hot August Night...........................(MCA)
Neil Diamond-Classics (Early Years)............(Columbia)
Neil Diamond's Greatest Hits.................(Bang)

Go Away Little Girl
Happenings; *The Ultimate History Of Rock 'N' Roll-#6-C*............(K-Tel)
Steve Lawrence; *Steve Lawrence's Greatest Hits*...............(Columbia)

Hang On Sloopy
McCoys; *21 Oldies But Goodies-C* . . . . (Original Sound)
Billboard Top Rock 'N' Roll Hits-1965-C . . . . (Rhino)
Frat Rock!-C . . . . (Rhino)
Oldies But Goodies-#14-C . . . . (Original Sound)
Ramsey Lewis; *Greatest Hits Of Ramsey Lewis* . . . . (Chess)
Vintage Music-#20-C . . . . (MCA)

Have You Ever Loved A Woman
Derek And The Dominos; *Layla* . . . . (Polydor)

Heartspark Dollarsign
Everclear; *Sparkle And Fade* . . . . (Capitol)

Heaven's What I Feel
Gloria Estefan; *Gloria!* . . . . (Epic)

I Believe
Blessid Union Of Souls; *Home* . . . . (EMI)

I Think We're Alone Now
Tiffany; *Tiffany* . . . . (MCA)
Tiffany's Greatest Hits . . . . (Hip-O)
Tommy James And The Shondells; *Best Of Tommy James And The
Shondells* . . . . (Roulette)
Billboard Top Rock 'N' Roll Hits-1967-C . . . . (Rhino)
Tommy James And The Shondells-Anthology . . . . (Rhino)

I'd Rather Have What We Had
Conway Twitty; *Two's A Party* . . . . (MCA Special Prod.)
Lee Ann Womack; *Some Things I Know* . . . . (Decca)

If I Were A Carpenter
Bobby Darin; *Live At The Desert Inn* . . . . (Motown)
Four Tops; *Compact Command Performances-Four Tops* . . . . (Motown)
Four Tops Reach Out . . . . (Motown)
Four Tops-Anthology . . . . (Motown)
Johnny Cash & June Carter; *The Man In Black-His Greatest Hits* . . . . . (Legacy)
Tim Hardin; *Memorial Album* . . . . (Polydor)

I'm Not Strong Enough To Say No
BlackHawk; *Strong Enough* . . . . (Arista)

Is Zat You, Myrtle
Carlisles; *45-#70174* . . . . (Mercury)
Louvin Brothers; *Live At New River Ranch* . . . . (Copper Creek)

Isle Of Capri
Billy Vaughn; *Billy Vaughn-22 Of His Greatest Hits* . . . . (Ranwood)
Frank Sinatra; *Come Fly With Me* . . . . (Capitol)

Jacob's Ladder
Mark Wills; *Mark Wills* . . . . (Mercury)

Keep Searchin' (We'll Follow The Sun)
Del Shannon; *Del Shannon's Greatest Hits* . . . . (Rhino)
Del Shannon's Greatest Hits . . . . (Curb)

Leader Of The Pack
Bette Midler; *Divine Miss M* . . . . (Atlantic)
ST/Divine Madness . . . . (Atlantic)
Original Cast; *Leader Of The Pack* . . . . (Elektra)
Shangri-Las; *21 Number One Hits-C* . . . . (Original Sound)
Billboard Top Rock 'N' Roll Hits-1964-C . . . . (Rhino)
Girl Groups-Story Of A Sound-C . . . . (Rhino)
Golden Hits Of The Shangri-Las . . . . (Mercury)
Oldies But Goodies-#15-C . . . . (Original Sound)
Radio Active Hits-#2-C . . . . (Accord)
Remember The Shangri-Las At Their Best . . . . (Collectables)

Line, The
Bruce Springsteen; *The Ghost Of Tom Joad* . . . . (Columbia)

Love You Down
INOJ; *So So Def Bass All-Stars-#2-C* . . . . (So So Def/Columbia)
Total Dance Explosion-C . . . . (Columbia)

Midnight Confessions
Grass Roots; *Grass Roots-Anthology (1966-1975)* . . . . (Rhino)
Original Rock 'N' Roll Hits Of The '60s-C . . . . (Roulette)
Vintage Music-#9-C . . . . (MCA)

Midnight Mary
Joey Powers; *Dick Bartley's One-Hit Wonders Of The '60s-#1-C* . . . (Rhino)

My Sharona
Knack; *Billboard Top Hits-1979-C* . . . . (Rhino)
Get The Knack . . . . (Capitol)
Rock Of The '80s-C . . . . (Priority)

Next Lifetime
Erykah Badu; *Baduizm* . . . . (Kedar Entert./Universal)

Not Too Young To Get Married
Bob B. Soxx/Blue Jeans; *Phil Spector-Back To Mono 1958-1969-C* . . . . (Abkco)
Darlene Love; *Best Of Darlene Love* . . . . (Abkco)

One Day You'll Be Mine
Usher; *My Way* . . . . (LaFace)

Rag Doll
4 Seasons; *25th Anniversary Collection* . . . . (Rhino)
4 Seasons' Greatest Hits-#2 . . . . (Rhino)
4 Seasons-Anthology . . . . (Rhino)
Billboard Top Rock 'N' Roll Hits-1964-C . . . . (Rhino)

Saginaw, Michigan
Lefty Frizzell; *American Originals-Lefty Frizzell* . . . . (Columbia)
Billboard Top Country Hits-1964-C . . . . (Columbia)
Columbia Country Classics-#3-Americana-C . . . . (Columbia)
Lefty Frizzell's Greatest Hits . . . . (Columbia)

Slipping Around
Ernest Tubb; *45-#46173* . . . . (Decca)
Margaret Whiting & Jimmy Wakely; *45-#40224* . . . . (Capitol)

Society's Child (Baby I've Been Thinking)
Janis Ian; *Songs Of Protest-C* . . . . (Rhino)
The Bottom Line Encore Collection . . . . (Bottom Line)
Lou Gramm; *A Foreigner In His Own Land: Best Of Early
Years* . . . . (Collectables)
Past Times Behind Rock & Roll-C . . . . (Intermedia)

Someday Soon
Chris LeDoux; *Rodeo Songs Old & New* . . . . (Liberty)
Ian & Sylvia; *Ian & Sylvia's Greatest Hits* . . . . (Vanguard)
Northern Journey . . . . (Vanguard)
Judy Collins; *Colors Of The Day-The Best Of Judy Collins* . . . (Elektra)
Who Knows Where The Time Goes . . . . (Elektra)
Moe Bandy; *Moe Bandy's Greatest Hits* . . . . (Columbia)
Rodeo Romeo . . . . (Columbia)
Suzy Bogguss; *Aces* . . . . (Liberty)
Suzy Bogguss' Greatest Hits . . . . (Liberty)

Somewhere
Aretha Franklin; *Aretha's Jazz* . . . . (Rhino)
Barbra Streisand; *The Broadway Album* . . . . (Columbia)
Dave Brubeck; *Music From West Side Story* . . . . (Columbia)
Jose Carreras; *Amigos Para Siempre-Friends For Life* . . . . (Atlantic)
Original Cast; *ST/West Side Story* . . . . (Sony Broadway)
Tom Waits; *Tom Waits-Anthology* . . . . (Asylum)

Spanish Is The Loving Tongue
Bob Dylan; *Dylan* . . . . (Columbia)
Emmylou Harris; *Cimarron* . . . . (Warner Bros.)
Evangeline . . . . (Warner Bros.)
Ian & Sylvia; *Four Strong Winds* . . . . (Vanguard)
Ian & Sylvia's Greatest Hits . . . . (Vanguard)
Michael Martin Murphey; *Cowboy Songs* . . . . (Warner Western)

Sweet Misery
Amel Larrieux; *Infinite Possibilities* . . . . (Epic)

Tennessee Border
Hank Williams; *Alone With His Guitar* . . . . (Mercury)
I Ain't Got Nothin' But Time-1946-1947 . . . . (Polydor)
Red Foley; *Red Foley: The Country Music Hall
Of Fame* . . . . (MCA Special Prod.)
Sonny Burgess & Dave Alvin; *Tennessee Border* . . . . (Hightone)
Tennessee Ernie Ford; *Best Of Tennessee Ernie Ford-16 Tons Of
Boogie* . . . . (Rhino)
Capitol Collectors Series-Tennessee Ernie Ford . . . . (Capitol)

Two Different Worlds
Robert Goulet; *My Love Forgive Me-Sincerely Yours Robert
Goulet* . . . . (Collector's Choice)

Two Princes
Spin Doctors; *Pocket Full Of Kryptonite* . . . . (Epic Portrait Assoc.)

Uninvited
Alanis Morissette; *ST/City Of Angels* . . . . (Warner Sunset/Reprise)

War Is Hell (On The Homefront Too)
T.G. Sheppard; *Perfect Stranger* . . . . (Warner Bros.)
T.G. Sheppard's All-Time Greatest Hits . . . . (Warner Bros.)
T.G. Sheppard's Greatest Hits . . . . (Warner Bros./Curb)

We Really Shouldn't Be Doing This
George Strait; *Latest Greatest Straitest Hits* . . . . (MCA)
One Step At A Time . . . . (MCA)

What If It's You
Reba McEntire; *What If It's You* . . . . (MCA)

What Would Happen
Meredith Brooks; *Blurring The Edges* . . . . (Capitol)

When Country Comes To Town
Toby Keith; *How Do You Like Me Now?!* . . . . (DreamWorks/SKG)

With One Exception
David Houston; *American Originals-David Houston* . . . . (Columbia)
Best Of David Houston . . . . (Curb)

Wolverton Mountain
Claude King; *American Originals-Claude King* . . . . (Columbia)
Best Of Claude King . . . . (Gusto)
Billboard Top Country Hits-1962-C . . . . (Rhino)
Super Hits Of The '60s-C . . . . (Epic)

You
Queensryche; *Hear In The Now Frontier* . . . . (Virgin)

You Make Me Wanna…
Usher; *My Way* . . . . (LaFace)
Totally Hits-#1-C . . . . (Arista)

Young Blood
Bad Company; *Run With The Pack* . . . . (Swan Song)
Coasters; *Coasters' Greatest Hits* . . . . (Atco)
Coasters-Their Greatest Recordings-Early Years . . . . (Atco)
The Ultimate Coasters . . . . (Warner Special Prod.)

Young Girl
Union Gap Featuring Gary Puckett; *Billboard Top Pop Hits-1968-C* . . . (Rhino)

Younger Girl
Critters; *Sixties Rule! Chapter Two-C* . . . . (One Way)
Lovin' Spoonful; *Lovin' Spoonful-Anthology* . . . . (Rhino)

Your Love's On The Line
Earl Thomas Conley; *Very Best Of Earl Thomas Conley* . . . . (RCA)

LOVE: GENERAL, Being In Love, I'm Yours, Romance, What Love Is

See Also: BROTHERHOOD, CHARACTER & INTEGRITY, DESIRE, FAITH, FAMILY (various), FEELINGS, FRIENDS, GOD, HAPPINESS, HELP, KISSING, LOVE (various), PEACE, SEX

(All Of A Sudden) My Heart Sings
Paul Anka; *Paul Anka Sings His Big 15, Vol. 2* . . . . (RCA)
Paul Anka-30th Anniversary Anthology . . . . (Rhino)
(Can't Live Without...) Love & Affection
Nelson; *After The Rain* . . . . (David Geffen Co.)
(He's) Some Kind Of Wonderful
Carole King; *Music* . . . . (Epic)
(I Could Only) Whisper Your Name
Harry Connick, Jr.; *She* . . . . (Columbia)
ST/The Mask . . . . (Chaos)
(I Don't Know Why) But I Do
Clarence "Frogman" Henry; *ST/Forrest Gump* . . (Epic/Sony Music Soundtrax)
(It's Just) The Way That You Love Me
Paula Abdul; *Forever Your Girl* . . . . (Virgin)
Shut Up And Dance (The Dance Mixes) . . . . (Virgin)
(I've Had) The Time Of My Life
Bill Medley; *Best Of Bill Medley* . . . . (Curb)
Bill Medley & Jennifer Warnes; *Dirty Dancing Live In Concert-C* . . . . . . (RCA)
ST/Dirty Dancing . . . . (RCA)
(Just Like) Starting Over
John Lennon & Yoko Ono; *Double Fantasy* . . . . (Capitol)
ST/Imagine: John Lennon . . . . (Capitol)
(Love Will) Find A Way
Amy Grant; *Unguarded* . . . . (A&M)
(Only A) Summer Love
REO Speedwagon; *R.E.O.* . . . . (Epic)
REO Speedwagon Live/You Get What You Play For . . . . (Epic)
(Our Love) Don't Throw It All Away
Bee Gees; *Bee Gees' Greatest* . . . . (Polydor)
(She's) Some Kind Of Wonderful
Drifters; *Drifters-16 Greatest Hits* . . . . (Trip)
Drifters-Golden Hits . . . . (Atlantic)
ST/More Dirty Dancing . . . . (RCA)
Very Best Of The Drifters . . . . (Rhino)
Huey Lewis and the News; *Four Chords & Several Years Ago* . . . . (Elektra)
Jay & The Americans; *Sands Of Time/Wax Museum* . . . . (EMI)
Marvin Gaye; *I Heard It Through The Grapevine/I Want You* . . . . . . (Motown)
(This Ain't) No Thinkin' Thing
Trace Adkins; *Dreamin' Out Loud* . . . . (Capitol)
(You Make Me Feel Like) A Natural Woman
Aretha Franklin; *Aretha Franklin's Greatest Hits-1980-1994* . . . . (Arista)
Chicken Soup For The Woman's Soul-C . . . . (Rhino)
Carole King; *Tapestry* . . . . (Epic)
Celine Dion; *Tapestry Revisited: Tribute To Carole King-C* . . . . (Lava)
(Your Love Keeps Lifting Me) Higher And Higher
Bette Midler; *Bette Midler* . . . . (Atlantic)
Bonnie Bramlett; *It's Time* . . . . (Capricorn)
Jackie Wilson; *Billboard Top R&B Hits-1967-C* . . . . (Rhino)
Jackie Wilson's Greatest Hits . . . . (Brunswick)
Jackie Wilson's Greatest Hits-#2 . . . . (Brunswick)
Reet Petite-Best Of Jackie Wilson . . . . (Columbia)
The Jackie Wilson Story . . . . (Epic)
Very Best Of Jackie Wilson . . . . (Rhino)
Rita Coolidge; *Anytime...Anywhere* . . . . (A&M)
Havana Jam . . . . (Columbia)
Rita Coolidge-Classics-#5 . . . . (A&M)
Rita Coolidge's Greatest Hits . . . . (A&M)
(You're) Having My Baby
Paul Anka; *'70s Party Killers-C* . . . . (Rhino)
Five Decades Of Hits . . . . (Curb)
Paul Anka-His Best . . . . (EMI)
Paul Anka-Live . . . . (Columbia)
Times Of Your Life . . . . (United Artists)
10 Miles To Go On A 9 Mile Road
Jim White; *No Such Place* . . . . (Luaka Bop)
100% Pure Love
Crystal Waters; *Storyteller* . . . . (Mercury)
1952 Vincent Black Lightning
Richard Thompson; *Richard Thompson-Best Of Capitol Years* . . . . . . (Capitol)
26 Cents
Wilkinsons; *Nothing But Love* . . . . (Giant)
50 Ways To Leave Your Lover
Paul Simon; *Greatest Hits, Etc.* . . . . (Columbia)
Negotiations And Love Songs, 1971-1986 . . . . (Warner Bros.)
Still Crazy After All These Years . . . . (Warner Bros.)
Simon & Garfunkel; *The Concert In Central Park* . . . . (Warner Bros.)
98.6
Keith; *'60s Pop-#1-Those Were The Days-C* . . . . (Dominion Entert.)
A Mi Esposa Con Amor
Sonny James; *A Mi Esposa Con Amor* . . . . (Columbia)

American Originals-Sonny James . . . . (Columbia)
Aba Daba Honeymoon
Debbie Reynolds; *Debbie Reynolds' Greatest Hits* . . . . (Curb)
ABC
Jackson 5; *ABC* . . . . (Motown)
Jackson 5-Anthology . . . . (Motown)
Jackson 5's Greatest Hits . . . . (Motown)
Abilene
George Hamilton IV; *Billboard Top Country Hits-1963-C* . . . . (Rhino)
Nipper's Greatest Hits Of The '60s-#2-C . . . . (RCA)
Sonny James; *American Originals-Sonny James* . . . . (Columbia)
Texas Super Hits-C . . . . (Columbia)
Waylon Jennings; *Outlaw Reunion-#1* . . . . (Aura)
About A Quarter To Nine
Original Broadway Cast; *42nd Street* . . . . (RCA Victor)
Absolutely (Story Of A Girl)
Nine Days; *Maddening Crowd* . . . . (550 Music)
Now That's What I Call Music!-#5-C . . . . (Virgin)
Across The Border
Bruce Springsteen; *The Ghost Of Tom Joad* . . . . (Columbia)
Addicted To Love
Robert Palmer; *Addictions-#1* . . . . (Island)
Riptide . . . . (Island)
The Island Story-1962-1987-25th Anniversary-C . . . . (Island)
Tina Turner; *Live In Europe* . . . . (Capitol)
Addictive Love
BeBe & CeCe Winans; *Different Lifestyles* . . . . (Capitol)
Affection
Jody Watley; *Affection* . . . . (Bellmark)
Affirmation
Savage Garden; *Affirmation* . . . . (Columbia)
Afraid
Willie Nelson; *Moonlight Becomes You* . . . . (Justice)
Afraid Of Love
Toto; *Toto IV* . . . . (Columbia)
After All
Patty Loveless; *Country Classics-#10-1987-C* . . . . (Universal)
Patty Loveless . . . . (MCA)
Woman To Woman-#2-C . . . . (MCA)
After Party
Koffee Brown; *Mars/Venus* . . . . (Arista)
After The Lovin'
Engelbert Humperdinck; *All Of Me-In Concert* . . . . (Epic)
Engelbert Humperdinck-16 Most Requested Songs . . . . (Epic)
Engelbert Humperdinck-Super Hits . . . . (Epic)
After The Rain Has Fallen
Sting; *Brand New Day* . . . . (A&M)
Again
Janet Jackson; *janet.* . . . . (Virgin)
Ain't Got Nothin' On Us
John Michael Montgomery; *What I Do The Best* . . . . (Atlantic)
Ain't No Woman (Like The One I Got)
Four Tops; *Ain't No Woman (Like The One I Got)* . . . . (MCA Special Prod.)
Four Tops' Greatest Hits (1972-1976) . . . . (MCA)
Ain't Nothing Like The Real Thing
Marvin Gaye & Tammi Terrell; *Every Great Motown Hit Of Marvin Gaye* . . . . (Motown)
Marvin Gaye's Greatest Hits . . . . (Motown)
Motown 40 Forever-C . . . . (Motown)
Vince Gill & Gladys Knight; *Rhythm Country And Blues-C* . . . . (MCA)
Ain't Seen Love Like That
Mr. Big; *Bump Ahead* . . . . (Atlantic)
Ain't She Sweet?
Beatles; *History Of British Rock-#5-C* . . . . (Rhino)
The Beatles-Anthology-#3 . . . . (Capitol)
Erroll Garner; *Body And Soul* . . . . (Legacy)
Frank Sinatra; *Sinatra and Swingin' Brass* . . . . (Reprise)
Pearl Bailey; *Pearl Bailey-16 Most Requested Songs* . . . . (Legacy)
Air That I Breathe
Hollies; *Best Of The Hollies-#2* . . . . (EMI)
Hollies . . . . (Epic)
Hollies-Epic Anthology From The Original Master Tapes . . . . (Epic)
Alfie
Barbra Streisand; *What About Today* . . . . (Columbia)
Dionne Warwick; *Dionne Warwick Greatest Hits* . . . . (Everest)
Dionne Warwick-Anthology 1962-1971 . . . . (Rhino)
All 4 Love
Color Me Badd; *C.M.B.* . . . . (Giant)
MTV Party To Go-#2-C . . . . (Tommy Boy)
All About Me Intro
Xscape; *Traces Of My Lipstick* . . . . (So So Def/Columbia)
All For Love
Bryan Adams/Rod Stewart/Sting; *ST/The Three Musketeers* . . . . (A&M/Hollywood)
All For You
Sister Hazel; *...Somewhere More Familiar* . . . . (Universal)
Sister Hazel . . . . (Universal)
All I Am To You
Tammy Wynette & Aaron Neville; *Without Walls-C* . . . . (Epic)

All I Do Is Think Of You
Jackson 5; *Baddest Love Jams-Volume 3-After The Dance-C* . . . . (Motown)
Jackson 5-Anthology . . . . (Motown)
Troop; *Attitude* . . . . (Atlantic)
All I Know
Art Garfunkel; *Angel Clare* . . . . (Columbia)
Garfunkel . . . . (Columbia)
All I Need To Know
Kenny Chesney; *All I Need To Know* . . . . (BNA)
Kenny Chesney's Greatest Hits . . . . (BNA)
All I Want Is You
U2; *ST/Reality Bites* . . . . (RCA)
All Is Fair In Love And War
Ronnie Milsap; *Club* . . . . (RCA)
All I've Got To Do
Beatles; *Meet The Beatles!* . . . . (Capitol)
All Of My Love
Gap Band; *Round Trip* . . . . (Capitol)
All Over You
Live; *Throwing Copper* . . . . (Radioactive/MCA)
All Roads Lead To You
Steve Wariner; *14 #1 Country Hits-C* . . . . (RCA)
Best Of The '80s...So Far-C . . . . (RCA)
Steve Wariner . . . . (RCA)
Steve Wariner's Greatest Hits . . . . (RCA)
All Tangled Up In Love
Gus Hardin & Earl Thomas Conley; *Collector's Series-Duets-C* . . . . (RCA)
Wall Of Tears . . . . (RCA)
All That I Can Say
Mary J. Blige; *Mary* . . . . (MCA)
All The Fun
Paul Overstreet; *Best Of Paul Overstreet* . . . . (RCA)
All The Love In The World
Dionne Warwick; *Heartbreaker* . . . . (Arista)
All The Love In The World
Outfield; *Play Deep* . . . . (Columbia)
All The Love Is On The Radio
Tom Jones; *45-#880173* . . . . (Mercury)
All The Love Of The Universe
Santana; *Caravanserai* . . . . (Columbia)
All The Small Things
Blink-182; *Enema Of The State* . . . . (MCA)
Now That's What I Call Music!-#4-C . . . . (Virgin)
All These Things
Joe Stampley; *Best Of Joe Stampley* . . . . (Varese Sarabande)
All Through The Night
Cyndi Lauper; *She's So Unusual* . . . . (Portrait)
Twelve Deadly Cyns...And Then Some . . . . (Epic)
Jules Shear; *Horse Of A Different Color: The Jules Shear Collection-1976-
1989* . . . . (Razor & Tie)
All You Need Is Love
Beatles; *Beatles 1* . . . . (Capitol)
Compact Disc Singles Collection . . . . (Capitol)
Magical Mystery Tour . . . . (Capitol)
The Beatles/1967-1970 . . . . (Capitol)
Yellow Submarine . . . . (Capitol)
Always Makin' Love
Kentucky HeadHunters; *Electric Barnyard* . . . . (Mercury)
Am I Ever Gonna Fall In Love In New York
Grace Jones; *Fame* . . . . (Island)
Amanda
Don Williams; *Don Williams' Greatest Hits* . . . . (MCA)
Volume One . . . . (MCA)
Waylon Jennings; *Waylon Jennings' Greatest Hits* . . . . (RCA)
Amazed
Lonestar; *Lonely Grill* . . . . (BNA)
Totally Hits-#2-C . . . . (Elektra)
American Made
Oak Ridge Boys; *American Made* . . . . (MCA)
Oak Ridge Boys' Greatest Hits 2 . . . . (MCA)
Amukiriki
Les Paul; *Legend And The Legacy* . . . . (Gold Rush)
An Affair To Remember
Original Soundtrack; *ST/An Affair To Remember* . . . . (Epic)
And I Love Her
Beatles; *ST/A Hard Day's Night* . . . . (Capitol)
The Beatles/1962-1966 . . . . (Capitol)
The Beatles-Anthology-#1 . . . . (Capitol)
And I Love You So
Perry Como; *Perry Como's Greatest Hits* . . . . (RCA)
And Our Feelings
Babyface; *For The Cool In You* . . . . (Epic)
And The Angels Sing
Ella Fitzgerald; *Lady Time* . . . . (Pablo)
And You And I
Yes; *Close To The Edge* . . . . (Atlantic)
Yessongs . . . . (Atlantic)

Angel
Madonna; *Like A Virgin* . . . . (Sire)
Angel
Lionel Richie; *Renaissance* . . . . (Island/IDJMG)
Angel Baby
John Lennon; *Lennon* . . . . (Capitol)
Menlove Ave. . . . . (Capitol)
Rosie And The Originals; *Cruisin'-1960-C* . . . . (Increase)
Rock Gems-Classics From Small Label Era-C . . . . (Motown)
Super Oldies Of The '60s-#1-C . . . . (Audio Fidelity)
WCBS FM 101 History Of Rock-'60s-#1-C . . . . (Collectables)
Angel In My Eyes
John Michael Montgomery; *John Michael Montgomery's
Greatest Hits* . . . . (Atlantic)
Angels
Robbie Williams; *The Egg Has Landed* . . . . (Capitol)
Angels Don't Fall In Love
Bangles; *Different Light* . . . . (Columbia)
Annie's Song
John Denver; *Back Home Again* . . . . (RCA)
Evening With John Denver . . . . (RCA)
John Denver's Greatest Hits-#2 . . . . (RCA)
Another Nine Minutes
Yankee Grey; *Untamed* . . . . (Monument)
Another Sad Love Song
Toni Braxton; *Toni Braxton* . . . . (LaFace)
Another You
David Kersh; *Goodnight Sweetheart* . . . . (Curb)
Any Lucky Penny
Nikki Hassman; *Songs From Dawson's Creek* . . . . (Sony Music Soundtrax)
Any Time, Any Place
Janet Jackson; *janet.* . . . . (Virgin)
Anyone Else
Collin Raye; *The Walls Came Down* . . . . (Epic)
Anyway You Want Me
Elvis Presley; *Elvis' Golden Records* . . . . (RCA)
Apricot Love
Neil Norman; *Not Of This Earth* . . . . (Crescendo)
April Love
L.T.D.; *L.T.D.-Classics-#27 (Featuring Jeffrey Osborne)* . . . . (A&M)
Arabian Love Call
Art Neville; *That Old Time Rock 'N' Roll* . . . . (Specialty)
Arabian Lover
Duke Ellington; *Jungle Nights In Harlem* . . . . (Bluebird)
Are You Lovin' Me Like I'm Lovin' You
Ronnie Milsap; *Back To The Grindstone* . . . . (RCA)
Arms Of The One Who Loves You
Xscape; *Traces Of My Lipstick* . . . . (So So Def/Columbia)
As I Lay Me Down
Sophie B. Hawkins; *Whaler* . . . . (Columbia)
As Long As I'm Rockin' With You
John Conlee; *Best Of John Conlee* . . . . (Curb)
In My Eyes . . . . (MCA)
John Conlee-20 Greatest Hits . . . . (MCA)
John Conlee-Legends . . . . (MCA)
Ask Me Why
Beatles; *Please Please Me* . . . . (Parlophone)
At Midnight (My Love Will Lift You Up)
Rufus Featuring Chaka Khan; *Ask Rufus* . . . . (MCA)
Live-Stompin' At The Savoy . . . . (Warner Bros.)
At The Same Time
Barbra Streisand; *Higher Ground* . . . . (Columbia)
Au Clair De La Lune
Maurice Andre; *Children's Songs* . . . . (CBS Masterworks)
Auf Wiederseh'n, My Dear
Greta Keller; *These Foolish Things* . . . . (ASV)
Autumn Of My Life
Bobby Goldsboro; *10th Anniversary Album-#1* . . . . (EMI)
Bobby Goldsboro's Greatest Hits . . . . (Liberty)
Ava Adore
Smashing Pumpkins; *Adore* . . . . (Virgin)
Baby (You've Got What It Takes)
Brook Benton & Dinah Washington; *Cruisin'-1960-C* . . . . (Increase)
Endlessly-The Best Of Brook Benton . . . . (Rhino)
Baby Baby
Miracles; *Two Classics: Time Out/Special Occasion* . . . . (Motown)
Smokey Robinson & The Miracles; *Away We A Go-Go* . . . . . . (Motown)
Baby Baby
Frankie Lymon and The Teenagers; *Best Of Frankie Lymon and The
Teenagers* . . . . (Rhino)
Baby Baby
Amy Grant; *Heart In Motion* . . . . (A&M)
Baby Come Back To Me (The Morse Code Of Love)
Manhattan Transfer; *Bop doo-wopp* . . . . (Atlantic)
Baby I Love Your Way
Big Mountain; *ST/Reality Bites* . . . . (RCA)
Baby I'm Ready
Ricky Van Shelton; *Wild-Eyed Dream* . . . . (Columbia)

Baby I'm Ready
Levert; *Rope A Dope Style* . . . . (Atlantic)
Baby That's When I Come Runnin'
Luther Vandross; *One Night With You-The Best Of Love-#2* . . . . (LV/Epic)
Baby, I Love You
Andy Kim; *Andy Kim Greatest Hits* . . . . (Dunhill Compact Classics)
Ronettes; *Best Of The Ronettes* . . . . (Abkco)
Phil Spector-Back To Mono 1958-1969-C . . . . (Abkco)
Baby, I Love Your Way
Big Mountain; *Chicken Soup For The Woman's Soul-C* . . . . (Rhino)
Peter Frampton; *Frampton Comes Alive* . . . . (A&M)
Peter Frampton's Greatest Hits . . . . (A&M)
Shine On-Collection . . . . (A&M)
Baby, I Love Your Way/Free Bird Medley
Will To Power; *Billboard Top Hits-1988-C* . . . . (Rhino)
Will To Power . . . . (Epic)
Baby's Got A Hold On Me
Nitty Gritty Dirt Band; *Hold On* . . . . (Warner Bros.)
Back To You
Bryan Adams; *MTV Unplugged-Bryan Adams* . . . . (A&M)
Back Up Buddy
Carl Smith; *Essential Carl Smith-1950-1956* . . . . (Legacy)
Trucker's Jukebox-#2-C . . . . (Legacy)
Backdoor Love Affair
ZZ Top; *Best Of ZZ Top* . . . . (Warner Bros.)
Six Pack . . . . (Warner Bros.)
ZZ Top . . . . (Warner Bros.)
Bad Case Of Love
B.B. King; *Blues On The Bayou* . . . . (MCA)
Bad Love
Eric Clapton; *24 Nights* . . . . (Duck/Reprise)
Journeyman . . . . (Duck/Reprise)
Bad To Me
Billy J. Kramer With The Dakotas; *History Of British Rock-#1-C* . . . . . . (Rhino)
Rock Is Dead But It Won't Lie Down-C . . . . (Gold Rush)
Badlands
Bruce Springsteen; *Bruce Springsteen's Greatest Hits* . . . . (Columbia)
Darkness On The Edge Of Town . . . . (Columbia)
Bruce Springsteen & The E Street Band; *Bruce Springsteen & The E Street
Band/1975-85* . . . . (Legacy)
Bag Lady
Erykah Badu; *Mama's Gun* . . . . (Motown)
Ballad Of A Teenage Queen
Johnny Cash; *Johnny Cash* . . . . (Sun)
Johnny Cash-Original Golden Hits-#2 . . . . (Sun)
Johnny Cash-Sun Years . . . . (Rhino)
ST/Harper Valley PTA . . . . (Sun)
The Legend . . . . (Plantation)
The Man In Black-His Greatest Hits . . . . (Legacy)
Band Played On, The
Guy Lombardo & His Royal Canadians; *Guy Lombardo-All Time
Favorites* . . . . (MCA Special Prod.)
Barbara Ann
Beach Boys; *Beach Boys '69 (The Beach Boys Live In London)* . . . . . . (Capitol)
Beach Boys-Gift Set . . . . (Capitol)
Best Of The Beach Boys-#2 . . . . (Capitol)
Frat Rock!-C . . . . (Rhino)
Spirit Of America . . . . (Capitol)
Regents; *Cruisin'-1961-C* . . . . (Increase)
Original Rock 'N' Roll Hits Of The '60s-C . . . . (Roulette)
ST/American Graffiti . . . . (MCA)
Who; *Who's Missing* . . . . (MCA)
Be Near Me
ABC; *How To Be A Zillionaire* . . . . (Mercury)
Be True
Bruce Springsteen; *Tracks* . . . . (Columbia)
Beat Goes On, The
Sonny & Cher; *Best Of Sonny & Cher* . . . . (Atco)
Hit Singles-1958-1977-C . . . . (Atlantic)
Sonny & Cher-Live . . . . (MCA)
The Beat Goes On-Best Of Sonny & Cher . . . . (Rhino)
Two Of Us . . . . (Atco)
Beautiful
Carole King; *Tapestry* . . . . (Epic)
Beautiful People
Bobby Vee; *Very Best Of Bobby Vee* . . . . (Collectables)
Beauty And The Beast
Celine Dion & Peabo Bryson; *All The Way...A Decade Of Song* . . . . (550 Music)
Celine Dion . . . . (Epic)
ST/Beauty And The Beast . . . . (Disney)
Be-Bop-A-Lula
Everly Brothers; *Everly Brothers* . . . . (Rhino)
Gene Vincent and His Blue Caps; *Billboard Top Rock 'N' Roll Hits-
1956-C* . . . . (Rhino)
ST/Wild At Heart . . . . (Polydor)
Jerry Lee Lewis; *Monsters* . . . . (Sun)
Trio Plus . . . . (Sun)
John Lennon; *Rock 'N' Roll* . . . . (Capitol)

Because
Beatles; *Abbey Road* . . . . (Parlophone)
Beatles-Box Set . . . . (Capitol)
Because I Love You (The Postman Song)
Stevie B; *Because I Love You (The Postman Song)* . . . . (LMR)
Best Of Stevie B . . . . (LMR)
Love & Emotion . . . . (LMR)
Because Of Love
Janet Jackson; *janet.* . . . . (Virgin)
Because Of You
Bobby Vinton; *Bobby Vinton's Greatest Hits* . . . . (Curb)
Tony Bennett; *Tony Bennett Sings His All-Time Hall Of
Fame Hits* . . . . (Columbia)
Tony Bennett-16 Most Requested Songs . . . . (Legacy)
Willie Nelson; *One For The Road* . . . . (Columbia)
Because The Night
10,000 Maniacs; *MTV's Unplugged* . . . . (Elektra)
Bruce Springsteen & The E Street Band; *Bruce Springsteen & The E Street
Band Live/1975-85* . . . . (Legacy)
Patti Smith Group; *Cover Me (Bruce Springsteen Tribute)-C* . . . . (Rhino)
Easter . . . . (Arista)
Because You Love Me
Jo Dee Messina; *I'm Alright* . . . . (Curb)
Before I Go
John Hiatt; *Crossing Muddy Waters* . . . . (Vanguard)
Behind Closed Doors
Charlie Rich; *American Originals-Charlie Rich* . . . . (Columbia)
Behind Closed Doors . . . . (Epic)
Charlie Rich's Greatest Hits . . . . (Epic)
Columbia Country Classics-#4-Nashville Sound-C . . . . (Columbia)
Behind These Prison Walls Of Love
Blue Sky Boys; *Blue Sky Boys In Concert-1964* . . . . (Rounder)
Country Gentlemen; *Folk Songs & Bluegrass* . . . . . (Smithsonian Folkways)
Peter Rowan; *All On A Rising Day* . . . . (Sugar Hill)
Being In Love
Original Cast; *ST/The Music Man* . . . . (Warner Bros.)
Being With You
Smokey Robinson; *Billboard Top Hits-1981-C* . . . . (Rhino)
Blame It On Love & All The Great Hits . . . . (Motown)
Smokey Robinson-The Ultimate Collection . . . . (Motown)
Believe
Elton John; *Elton John-Love Songs* . . . . (MCA)
Made In England . . . . (Rocket)
Believe In Me
Eric Clapton; *Reptile* . . . . (Duck/Reprise)
Believe In You
Jude Cole; *I Don't Know Why I Act This Way* . . . . (Island)
Bells Are Ringing
Original Cast; *Bells Are Ringing* . . . . (Columbia)
Best Of Love, The
Michael Bolton; *All That Matters* . . . . (Columbia)
Best Things In Life Are Free
June Allyson; *ST/Good News* . . . . (Sony Music Special Prod.)
Luther Vandross & Janet Jackson; *ST/Mo' Money* . . . . (Bluebird)
Mel Torme; *Easy To Remember* . . . . (Glendale)
Sam Cooke; *Sam Cooke-At The Copa* . . . . (RCA)
Betcha Gonna Need My Lovin'
LaToya Jackson; *Heart Don't Lie* . . . . (Private I)
Better Days
Bruce Springsteen; *Bruce Springsteen's Greatest Hits* . . . . (Columbia)
Lucky Town . . . . (Columbia)
Better Love
Londonbeat; *In The Blood* . . . . (Radioactive/MCA)
Better Man
Warren Brothers; *Beautiful Day In The Cold Cruel World* . . . . (BNA)
Between The Devil And Me
Alan Jackson; *Everything I Love* . . . . (Arista)
Big Deal
LeAnn Rimes; *LeAnn Rimes* . . . . (Curb)
Big Love
Fleetwood Mac; *25 Years-The Chain* . . . . (Warner Bros.)
Fleetwood Mac's Greatest Hits . . . . (Warner Bros.)
Tango In The Night . . . . (Warner Bros.)
Big Love
Delevantes; *Long About That Time* . . . . (Rounder)
Big Love
Bellamy Brothers; *Bellamy Brothers' Greatest Hits-#3* . . . . (MCA)
Rebels Without A Clue . . . . (MCA)
Bigger Than The Beatles
Joe Diffie; *Life's So Funny* . . . . (Epic)
Bimbombey
Jimmie Rodgers; *Best Of Jimmie Rodgers* . . . . (Rhino)
Best Of Jimmie Rodgers . . . . (Curb)
Black Is The Color Of My True Love's Hair
Joan Baez; *Best Of Joan Baez* . . . . (A&M)
Joan Baez In Concert . . . . (Vanguard)
The Joan Baez Ballad Book . . . . (Vanguard)
Blame It On Love
Smokey Robinson; *Blame It On Love & All The Great Hits* . . . . (Motown)

Blame It On The Bossa Nova
Eydie Gorme; *45-#42661* . . . . (Columbia)
Blessed Be
Alison Krauss; *Country Goes Raffi-C* . . . . (Rounder)
Blind Love & Whiskey
Little Mike & The Tornadoes; *Heart Attack* . . . . (Blind Pig)
Bliss
Mariah Carey; *Rainbow* . . . . (Columbia)
Blue
Joni Mitchell; *Blue* . . . . (Reprise)
Joni Mitchell with Tom Scott & The L.A. Express; *Miles Of Aisles* . . . . (Asylum)
Blue Bayou
Linda Ronstadt; *Linda Ronstadt's Greatest Hits, Volume Two* . . (Asylum)
   Simple Dreams . . . . (Asylum)
Roy Orbison; *For The Lonely: A Roy Orbison Anthology 1959-1965* . . . (Rhino)
   In Dreams-Greatest Hits . . . . (Orbison)
   Roy Orbison-More Greatest Hits . . . . (Monument)
   Roy Orbison's All-Time Greatest Hits-#1 & 2 . . . . . (Monument)
Roy Orbison & Friends; *Black & White Night-Live* . . . . (Virgin)
Blue Skies
Benny Goodman; *Benny Goodman Today* . . . . (London)
   Carnegie Hall Jazz Concert . . . . (Columbia)
   The Birth Of Swing (1935-1936) . . . . (Bluebird)
   This Is Benny Goodman . . . . (RCA)
Bing Crosby; *Bing Crosby's Greatest Hits* . . . . (MCA)
Duke Ellington; *Carnegie Hall Concert* . . . . (Prestige)
   Golden Duke . . . . (Prestige)
Willie Nelson; *Stardust* . . . . (Legacy)
Bold As Love
Jimi Hendrix; *Axis: Bold As Love* . . . . (Reprise)
   Essential Jimi Hendrix . . . . (Reprise)
Book Of Love
Monotones; *Bedrock-Late '50s/'60s Rock 'N' Roll* . . . . . . (Allegiance)
   Best Of Chess Rock 'N' Roll-#1-C . . . . (Chess)
   Original Golden Rock Oldies-#1-C . . . . (Specialty)
   ST/American Graffiti . . . . (MCA)
   Super Oldies Of The '50s-#2-C . . . . (Audio Fidelity)
Book Of Love
Fleetwood Mac; *Mirage* . . . . (Warner Bros.)
Book Of Love
Book Of Love; *Book Of Love* . . . . (Sire)
Boom! It Was Over
Robert Ellis Orrall; *Flying Colors.* . . . . (RCA)
Born To Be With You
Chordettes; *Best Of The Chordettes* . . . . (Rhino)
   Chordettes Greatest Hits . . . . (Everest)
   Lil' Bit Of Gold 3'' CD Series-C . . . . (Rhino)
Born To Love You
Fabulous Thunderbirds; *Walk That Walk Talk That Talk* . . (Epic Portrait Assoc.)
Born To Love You
Karen Brooks; *Hearts On Fire* . . . . (Warner Bros.)
Born To Love You
Mark Collie; *Mark Collie* . . . . (MCA)
Born To Love You
Temptations; *Temptin'* . . . . (Motown)
Born To Love You
Michael Nesmith; *Best Of (1970-1973)* . . . . (Rhino)
Both Sides Now
Joni Mitchell; *Clouds* . . . . (Reprise)
Judy Collins; *Colors Of The Day-The Best Of Judy Collins* . . . . (Elektra)
   So Early In The Spring, The First 15 Years . . . . (Elektra)
   Wildflowers . . . . (Elektra)
Neil Diamond; *Neil Diamond-Gold* . . . . (MCA)
   Neil Diamond-Love Songs . . . . (MCA)
   Rainbow . . . . (MCA)
   Touching You Touching Me . . . . (MCA)
Boys
Beatles; *Beatles-Box Set* . . . . (Capitol)
   Please Please Me . . . . (Parlophone)
   Rock 'N' Roll Music . . . . (Capitol)
   The Beatles At The Hollywood Bowl . . . . (Capitol)
   The Early Beatles . . . . (Capitol)
Shirelles; *Shirelles-Anthology 1959-1964* . . . . (Rhino)
Breathe
Faith Hill; *Breathe* . . . . (Warner Bros.)
Bridge Washed Out
Warner Mack; *Country's Greatest Hits-#3-C* . . . . (MCA)
   MCA Records 30 Years Of Hits-1958-1988-C . . . . . . (MCA)
Bring A Little Lovin'
Easybeats; *Best Of The Easybeats* . . . . (Rhino)
Bring It Down To My House
Asleep At The Wheel; *Tribute To The Music Of Bob Wills And The Texas Playboys-C* . . . . (Liberty)
Merle Haggard; *Country Swing Essentials-C* . . . . (Hip-O)
Brother, Brother
Carole King; *Music.* . . . . (Epic)
Brotherly Love
Keith Whitley & Earl Thomas Conley; *Kentucky Bluebird* . . . . (RCA)
Moe Bandy; *Moe Bandy's Greatest Hits* . . . . (Curb)

Brownsville Blues
Hammie Nixon; *Tappin' That Thing* . . . . (High Water)
Burnin' Love
Con Funk Shun; *Burnin' Love* . . . . (Mercury)
Burning House Of Love
X; *Ain't Love Grand* . . . . (Elektra)
   Best Of MTV's 120 Minutes-#2-C . . . . (Rhino)
   Live At The Whisky A Go-Go . . . . (Elektra)
Burning Love
Elvis Presley; *Aloha from Hawaii via Satellite* . . . . (RCA)
   Elvis Aron Presley . . . . (RCA)
   Elvis-Greatest Hits, Volume One . . . . (RCA)
   The Top Ten Hits . . . . (RCA)
Bushel And A Peck
Andrews Sisters; *Best Of The Andrews Sisters-#2.* . . . . (MCA)
Original Cast; *Guys & Dolls* . . . . (MCA)
Business Of Love
Charlie Daniels; *The Door.* . . . . (Sparrow)
But For The Grace Of God
keith urban; *keith urban.* . . . . (Capitol)
But I Do Love You
LeAnn Rimes; *I Need You* . . . . (Curb)
Butta Love
Next; *Rated Next* . . . . (Divine Mill/Arista)
Butterfly
Mariah Carey; *Butterfly.* . . . . (Columbia)
Butterfly Kisses
Bob Carlisle; *Butterfly Kisses (Shades Of Grace)* . . . . (DMG/Jive)
Butterflyz
Alicia Keys; *Songs In A Minor* . . . . (J)
Button Up Your Overcoat
Rose Murphy; *Rose Murphy Sings Again* . . . . (MCA)
Sarah Vaughan; *Sarah Vaughan* . . . . (Everest)
Buttons And Bows
Dinah Shore; *16 Most Requested Songs Of The '40s-#1-C* . . . . (Legacy)
   Golden Hits Of The '40s-C . . . . (Columbia Special Prod.)
Gene Autry; *Ridin' West-#2-C* . . . . (Crescendo)
   Songs Of The West-#3-Gene Autry & Roy Rogers-C . . . . . . (Rhino)
Buy Me A Rose
Kenny Rogers; *She Rides Wild Horses* . . . . (Dreamcatcher)
By A Waterfall
Ruby Keeler & Dick Powell; *Lullaby Of Broadway-The Best Of Busby Berkeley At Warner Brothers.* . . . . (Rhino)
Sammy Fain; *Sammy Sings Fain* . . . . (Living Era)
By The Light Of The Silvery Moon
Al Jolson; *The Al Jolson Story-#1* . . . . (MCA)
Doris Day; *Day At The Movies* . . . . (Columbia)
Julie Andrews; *A Little Bit Of Broadway* . . . . (Columbia)
Mitch Miller; *34 All-Time Great Sing-Along Selections-C* . . . . . (Columbia)
   Sing Along With Mitch . . . . (Columbia)
Cadillac Style
Sammy Kershaw; *Don't Go Near The Water* . . . . (Mercury)
California Nights
Lesley Gore; *Summer & Sun-C* . . . . (Rhino)
Call Me Irresponsible
Frank Sinatra; *Sinatra: A Man And His Music* . . . . (Reprise)
   Sinatra's Sinatra . . . . (Reprise)
Jackie Gleason; *Best Of Jackie Gleason & His Orchestra.* . . . . . . (Curb)
Robert Goulet; *Robert Goulet-16 Most Requested Songs* . . . . . (Columbia)
Rosemary Clooney; *Rosemary Clooney Sings The Music Of Jimmy Van Heusen.* . . . . (Concord Jazz)
Callin' Baton Rouge
Garth Brooks; *In Pieces.* . . . . (Liberty)
New Grass Revival; *New Grass Revival-Anthology* . . . . (Liberty)
Oak Ridge Boys; *Room Service.* . . . . (MCA Special Prod.)
Calling To You
Robert Plant; *Fate Of Nations* . . . . (Es Paranza)
Can I Get A Witness
Marvin Gaye; *Marvin Gaye-Anthology.* . . . . (Motown)
   Marvin Gaye's Greatest Hits . . . . (Motown)
   Marvin Gaye-Super Hits . . . . (Motown)
Rod Stewart; *Storyteller/The Complete Anthology: 1964-1990* . . (Warner Bros.)
Rolling Stones; *England's Newest Hit Makers/The Rolling Stones.* . . . (Abkco)
Can You Feel The Love Tonight
Elton John; *ST/The Lion King* . . . . (Walt Disney)
John Tesh; *Sax On The Beach* . . . . (GTS)
Candy Rain
Soul For Real; *Candy Rain* . . . . (Uptown/MCA)
Candy Store Love
Valchords; *Legends Of Doo-Wop-#1-C* . . . . (Juke Box Treasures)
Can't Buy Me Love
Beatles; *Beatles 1* . . . . (Capitol)
   Hey Jude. . . . . (Capitol)
   Reel Music . . . . (Capitol)
   ST/A Hard Day's Night. . . . . (Capitol)
   The Beatles At The Hollywood Bowl. . . . . (Capitol)
   The Beatles/1962-1966. . . . . (Capitol)
Can't Get Enough Of You Baby
Smash Mouth; *Astro Lounge.* . . . . (Interscope)

ST/Can't Hardly Wait .... (Elektra)

Can't Get Enough Of Your Love
Taylor Dayne; *Soul Dancing* .... (Arista)

Can't Get Enough Of Your Love
Bad Company; *Bad Company* .... (Swan Song)

Can't Get Enuff
Winger; *In The Heart Of The Young* .... (Atlantic)

Can't Hide Love
Earth, Wind & Fire; *Best Of Earth, Wind & Fire-#1* ... (Legacy)
Gratitude .... (Legacy)

Can't Hide Love
Wayman Tisdale; *Face To Face* .... (Atlantic)

Can't Let Her Go
Boyz II Men; *Evolution* .... (Motown)

Can't We Try
Dan Hill; *Dan Hill* .... (Columbia)
Greatest Hits And More...Let Me Show You ...... (Spontaneous)
Dan Hill & Vonda Shepherd; *Chicken Soup For The Couples Soul-C* .... (Rhino)

Caravan Of Love
Isley, Jasper, Isley; *Caravan Of Love* .... (CBS Associated)

Careless Love
Dinah Washington; *Bessie Smith Songbook* .... (Emarcy)
Pete Fountain; *Mr. New Orleans* .... (MCA)
Preservation Hall Jazz Band; *Best Of The Preservation Hall Jazz Band* ..... (Columbia)
New Orleans-#3-When The Saints Go Marchin' In ..... (Columbia)

Carmen
Paula Cole; *This Fire* .... (Imago)

Carried Away
George Strait; *Blue Clear Sky* .... (MCA)
Latest Greatest Straitest Hits .... (MCA)

Case Of You
Joni Mitchell; *Blue* .... (Reprise)
Joni Mitchell with Tom Scott & The L.A. Express; *Miles Of Aisles* ... (Asylum)

Chain Of Love
Clay Walker; *Live, Laugh, Love* .... (Giant)

Chances Are
Bob Marley; *Chances Are* .... (Cotillion)
Bob Seger & Martina McBride; *ST/Hope Floats* ..... (Capitol)
Johnny Mathis; *First 25 Years-Silver Anniversary Album* ..... (Columbia)
Johnny Mathis' All-Time Greatest Hits .... (Columbia)
Johnny Mathis' Greatest Hits .... (Columbia)
Johnny Mathis-Live .... (Columbia)
Johnny Mathis-Love Songs .... (Columbia)

Change The World
Eric Clapton; *ST/Phenomenon* .... (Reprise)

Charms
Bobby Vee; *EMI Legends Of Rock & Roll-Bobby Vee* ..... (Gold Rush)

Chasing Forever
Will Smith; *Big Willie Style* .... (Columbia)

Check Yes Or No
George Strait; *Strait Out Of The Box* .... (MCA)

Cheek To Cheek
Ella Fitzgerald; *Silver Collection-Songbooks* ...... (Verve)
Frank Sinatra; *Come Dance With Me!* .... (Capitol)
Fred Astaire; *Cheek To Cheek* .... (Pro-Arte)
Irving Berlin Songbook .... (Verve)
Mundell Lowe; *Mundell Lowe Quartet* .... (Riverside)
Pete Fountain; *Cheek To Cheek* .... (Ranwood)
Tommy Dorsey; *Irving Berlin 100th Anniversary Collection-C* ..... (MCA)
Tony Bennett; *Bennett/Berlin* .... (Columbia)

Cherish
Kool & The Gang; *Celebration-1979-1987* .... (Mercury)
Emergency .... (Mercury)
Kool & The Gang's All-Time Greatest Hits .... (Curb)

Cherish
Madonna; *Immaculate Collection* .... (Sire)
Like A Prayer .... (Sire)
Royal Box .... (Sire)

Cherokee Maiden
Asleep At The Wheel; *Ride With Bob-C* ...... (DreamWorks/SKG)
Merle Haggard; *All Time Greatest Hits Of Country-C* ..... (Curb)
Capitol Collectors Series-Merle Haggard .... (Capitol)

Cherry, Cherry
Neil Diamond; *Bang & Shout* .... (Bang)
Hot August Night .... (MCA)
Hot August Night II .... (Columbia)
Neil Diamond-Classics (Early Years) .... (Columbia)
Neil Diamond-Gold .... (MCA)
Neil Diamond's Greatest Hits .... (Bang)
Shilo .... (Bang)

Chime Bells
Elton Britt; *The RCA Years* .... (Collector's Choice)
Jody King; *Photographs & Memories* .... (Capricorn)

Chuck E.'s In Love
Rickie Lee Jones; *Rickie Lee Jones* .... (Warner Bros.)

Church Of Logic, Sin & Love
Men; *The Men* .... (Polydor)

Cinnamon Girl
Neil Young & Crazy Horse; *Decade* .... (Reprise)
Everybody Knows This Is Nowhere .... (Reprise)
Live Rust .... (Reprise)
WELD .... (Reprise)

Close Enough To Perfect
Alabama; *Alabama-Super Hits-#2* .... (RCA)
Essential Alabama .... (RCA)
Mountain Music .... (RCA)

Close Your Eyes
Peaches & Herb; *Love Is Strange-The Best Of Peaches & Herb* ..... (Legacy)

C'mon And Get My Love
Cathy Dennis; *Move To This* .... (Polydor)
D-Mob; *Gold On Black* .... (Full Frequency Range)
Little Bit Of This Little Bit Of That .... (London)

Coal Miner's Daughter
Loretta Lynn; *Coal Miner's Daughter* .... (MCA)
Coal Miner's Daughter .... (MCA)
Loretta Lynn-20 Greatest Hits .... (MCA)
Loretta Lynn-Greatest Hits Live .... (K-Tel)
Loretta Lynn's Greatest Hits-#2 .... (MCA)
The Country Music Hall Of Fame-Loretta Lynn .... (MCA)

Cocoon
Bjork; *Vespertine* .... (Elektra)

Cold Love
Donna Summer; *The Wanderer* .... (Geffen)

Color Him Father
Linda Martell; *20 Great Hits-C* .... (Plantation)
Color Me Country .... (Plantation)

Color My World
Petula Clark; *Petula Clark's Greatest Hits* .... (Crescendo)

Colour Of Love
Billy Ocean; *Billy Ocean's Greatest Hits* .... (Jive)
Tear Down These Walls .... (Jive)

Come A Little Bit Closer
Johnny Duncan & Janie Fricke; *Johnny Duncan & Janie Fricke's Greatest Hits* ..... (Columbia)
Nice 'N' Easy .... (Columbia)

Come From The Heart
Don Williams; *Traces* .... (Capitol)
Kathy Mattea; *Willow In The Wind* .... (Mercury)

Come On Let's Go
Los Lobos; *And A Time To Dance* .... (Slash)
Just Another Band From East L.A. .... (Slash)
ST/La Bamba .... (Slash)
Ritchie Valens; *Best Of Ritchie Valens* .... (Rhino)
Oldies But Goodies-#4-C .... (Original Sound)
The Ritchie Valens Story .... (Del Fi)

Come On-A My House
Rosemary Clooney; *Rosemary Clooney-16 Most Requested Songs* ..... (Legacy)
Sentimental Journey: Pop Vocal Classics-#3-C ..... (Rhino)

Comin' On Strong
Sudden Change; *Comin' On Strong (Single)* ..... (East West)

Coming Out Of The Dark
Gloria Estefan; *Gloria Estefan's Greatest Hits* .... (Epic)
God Bless America-C .... (Columbia)
Hot #1 Hits-C .... (Foundation)
Into The Light .... (Epic)

Coming Up
Paul McCartney; *All The Best!* .... (Capitol)
Tripping The Live Fantastic-Highlights! .... (Capitol)

Completely
Michael Bolton; *The One Thing* .... (Columbia)

Computer In Love
Perrey & Kingsley; *Essential Perrey & Kingsley* ... (Vanguard)
The In Sound From Way Out! .... (Vanguard)

Computer Love
Kraftwerk; *Computer World* .... (Elektra)
The Mix .... (Elektra)

Computer Love
Zapp; *Smooth Grooves-A Sensual Collection-#9-C* .... (Rhino)
Zapp & Roger; *All The Greatest Hits* .... (Reprise)

Computer Love
Techmaster P.E.B.; *Bass Computer* .... (Newtown)

Computer Love
NKRU; *Freaky To You* .... (RCA)

Confidential
Fleetwoods; *Best Of The Fleetwoods* .... (Rhino)
Radiators; *Zig-Zaggin' Through Ghostland* .... (Epic)
Sonny Knight; *Oldies But Goodies-#1-C* ..... (Original Sound)

Cool Love
Wanda Jackson; *Rockin' In The Country-Best Of Wanda Jackson* ..... (Rhino)

Cool Love
Sheena Easton; *The Lover In Me* .... (MCA)

Cool Love
Pablo Cruise; *Reflector* .... (A&M)

Could This Be Love
Jennifer Lopez; *On The 6* .... (Work)

Cover You In Kisses
John Michael Montgomery; *Leave A Mark* . . . . (Atlantic)
Cowboy Take Me Away
Dixie Chicks; *Fly* . . . . (Monument)
Cracklin' Rosie
Neil Diamond; *Hot August Night* . . . .(MCA)
Hot August Night II . . . . (Columbia)
Neil Diamond-His 12 Greatest Hits . . . .(MCA)
Tap Root Manuscript . . . .(MCA)
Cradle Of Love
Billy Idol; *Charmed Life* . . . .(Chrysalis)
ST/Adventures Of Ford Fairlane . . . . (Elektra)
Cradle Of Love
Johnny Preston; *Running Bear* . . . . (Collectables)
Crazy For You
Madonna; *Immaculate Collection* . . . . (Sire)
Royal Box . . . . (Sire)
Something To Remember . . . . (Maverick/Sire)
ST/Vision Quest . . . . (Geffen)
Crazy For You
Eboni Foster; *Just What You Want* . . . . (Nightbird/MCA)
Crazy For You
Heartbeats; *Best Of The Heartbeats* . . . . (Rhino)
Crazy For Your Love
Exile; *Exile's Greatest Hits* . . . .(Epic)
Greatest Country Hits Of The '80s-1985-C . . . . (Columbia)
Kentucky Hearts . . . .(Epic)
Crazy For Your Love
Bee Gees; *E-S-P* . . . .(Warner Bros.)
Crazy In Love
Kenny Rogers; *Love Is Strange* . . . . (Reprise)
Crazy In Love
Joe Cocker; *Civilized Man* . . . . (Capitol)
Crazy Love
Paul Anka; *Best Of Paul Anka* . . . . (Rhino)
Paul Anka's 21 Golden Hits . . . . (RCA)
Vintage Years '57-'61 . . . . (Sire)
Crazy Love
Brian McKnight; *Anytime* . . . . (Motown)
I Remember You . . . . (Mercury)
ST/Jason's Lyric . . . . (Mercury)
Van Morrison; *Moondance* . . . .(Warner Bros.)
Crazy Love
Poco; *Backtracks* . . . .(MCA)
Poco-Legend . . . . (MCA)
Crazy Love
Allman Brothers Band; *Decade Of Hits-1969-1979* . . . .(Polydor)
Crazy Love
Joey Dee & the Starliters; *Hey Let's Twist! Best Of Joey Dee & The
Starliters* . . . . (Rhino)
Crazy Love
Buddy Guy; *Left My Blues In San Francisco* . . . . (Chess)
Crazy Love
Rita Coolidge; *Rita Coolidge-Classics-#5* . . . . (A&M)
Crazy Love
Aaron Neville Featuring Robbie Robertson; *ST/Phenomenon* . . . . (Reprise)
Crazy Love
Bryan Ferry; *ST/She's Having A Baby* . . . .(I.R.S.)
Crime Of Passion
Ricky Van Shelton; *More Hot Country Requests-#2-C* . . . .(Epic)
Wild-Eyed Dream . . . . (Columbia)
Crime Of Passion
Diana Ross; *Eaten Alive* . . . . (RCA)
Crime Of Passion
Bonnie Raitt; *Nine Lives* . . . .(Warner Bros.)
Crime Of Passion
Rita Coolidge; *Satisfied* . . . . (A&M)
Crime Of Passion
Loudon Wainwright III; *Unrequited* . . . . (Columbia)
Cross My Heart I Love You
Bob Wills & His Texas Playboys; *Bob Wills & His Texas Playboys-24
Great Hits* . . . . (Polydor)
Cry For Love
Iggy Pop; *Blah Blah Blah* . . . . (A&M)
Cuban Love Song
George Shearing; *Best Of George Shearing* . . . . (Capitol)
Cuddle Up A Little Closer
Jimmy Roselli; *When Your Old Wedding Ring Was* . . . .(M&R)
Cupid's Got A Brand New Gun
Michael Penn; *March* . . . . (RCA)
Cupid's Trash Truck
Lou & Peter Berryman; *Cupid's Trash Truck* . . . . (Cornbelt)
Damn Thing Called Love
After 7; *Reflections* . . . . (Virgin)
Dancing Days
Led Zeppelin; *Houses Of The Holy* . . . . (Atlantic)
Stone Temple Pilots; *Encomium: Tribute To Led Zeppelin-C* . . . . . . (Atlantic)

Dancing On The Ceiling
Chet Baker; *Chet Baker Sings It Could Happen
To You* . . . . (Original Jazz Classics)
Ella Fitzgerald; *Rodgers & Hart Songbook* . . . . (Verve)
Frank Sinatra; *In The Wee Small Hours.* . . . . (Capitol)
Danny's Song
Anne Murray; *Anne Murray-Country* . . . . (Capitol)
Anne Murray's Greatest Hits . . . . (Capitol)
Danny's Song . . . . (Capitol)
Loggins & Messina; *Loggins & Messina-On Stage* . . . . (Columbia)
Sittin' In . . . . (Columbia)
The Best Of Friends . . . . (Columbia)
Darlin'
Beach Boys; *Absolute Best-#2.* . . . . (Capitol)
Concert/'69-Live In London . . . . (Capitol)
Smiley Smile/Wild Honey . . . . (Capitol)
Sunshine Dream . . . . (Capitol)
Darling Be Home Soon
Joe Cocker; *Joe Cocker!* . . . . (A&M)
Joe Cocker-Classics-#4 . . . . (A&M)
Joe Cocker's Greatest Hits . . . . (A&M)
Lovin' Spoonful; *Best Of The Lovin' Spoonful-#2* . . . . (Rhino)
Lovin' '60s-C . . . . (Priority)
Lovin' Spoonful-Anthology . . . . (Rhino)
Darling Lorraine
Paul Simon; *You're The One* . . . . (Warner Bros.)
Darling Pretty
Mark Knopfler; *Golden Heart* . . . . (Warner Bros.)
Day In, Day Out
David Kersh; *Goodnight Sweetheart.* . . . . (Curb)
Daydream Believer
Anne Murray; *Anne Murray's Greatest Hits* . . . . (Capitol)
I'll Always Love You . . . . (Capitol)
Monkees; *Billboard Top Rock 'N' Roll Hits-1967-C* . . . . (Rhino)
Mellow '60s-C . . . . (Priority)
Monkees' Greatest Hits . . . . (Rhino)
Daydreamin'
Tatyana Ali; *Kiss The Sky* . . . . (MJJ Music/Work)
Days Like This
Kenny Lattimore; *From The Soul Of Man.* . . . . (Columbia)
Dear John & Marsha Letter
Stan Freberg; *Capitol Collectors Series-Stan Freberg* . . . . (Capitol)
Declaration Of Love
Celine Dion; *Falling Into You* . . . .(550 Music)
Deeper And Deeper
Madonna; *Erotica* . . . .(Maverick/Sire)
GHV2 . . . . (Warner Bros.)
Deeper The Love
Whitesnake; *Slip Of The Tongue* . . . . (Geffen)
Denis
Blondie; *Blonde And Beyond-Rarities & Oddities* . . . . (Gold Rush)
Once More Into The Bleach . . . . (Gold Rush)
Plastic Letters . . . . (Chrysalis)
The Platinum Collection. . . . . (Chrysalis)
Denise
Randy & The Rainbows; *Doo-Wop Uptempo-#2-C* . . . . (Rhino)
Super Oldies Of The '60s-#4-C . . . . (Audio Fidelity)
WCBS FM 101 History Of Rock-'60s-#1-C . . . . (Collectables)
Devil Or Angel
Bobby Vee; *Best Of Bobby Vee* . . . . (EMI)
Bobby Vee-Golden Greats . . . . (Liberty)
Bobby Vee-Legendary Masters. . . . . (EMI)
Clovers; *Atlantic Rhythm & Blues 1947-1974-#3 (1955-1958)-C.* . . . . . (Atlantic)
Oldies But Goodies-#2-C . . . . (Original Sound)
Very Best Of The Clovers . . . . (Rhino)
Discotheque
U2; *Pop* . . . . (Island)
Dites-Moi
Original Cast; *South Pacific* . . . . (CBS Masterworks)
Do I Love You Because You're Beautiful
Julie Andrews & Jon Cypher; *Cinderella-The CBS Television
Production* . . . . (Columbia)
Rodgers & Hammerstein Songbook . . . . (Sony Music Classical)
Mel Torme; *Mel Torme-16 Most Requested Songs* . . . . (Columbia)
Stuart Damon & Lesley Ann Warren; *Cinderella-The CBS Television
Network Production* . . . . (Columbia)
Do It Again A Little Bit Slower
Jon, Robin & The In Crowd; *Dick Bartley's One-Hit Wonders Of The
'60s-#1-C.* . . . . (Rhino)
Do Me Right
Pebbles; *Pebbles* . . . . (MCA)
Do Me Right
Guy; *Future.* . . . . (Uptown/MCA)
Do Right Woman, Do Right Man
Aretha Franklin; *Aretha Franklin-30 Greatest Hits* . . . . (Rhino)
ST/Dead Presidents . . . . (Capitol)
Commitments; *ST/The Commitments* . . . . (MCA)
Do You Love Me?
Jonathan Butler; *Do You Love Me?* . . . . (N2K)

Do You Really Love Me
Brian Culbertson; *Somethin' 'Bout Love* . . . . (Atlantic)
Does He Love You
Reba McEntire & Linda Davis; *Reba McEntire's Greatest Hits
Volume Two* . . . . (MCA)
Does She Love That Man?
Breathe; *Peace Of Mind* . . . . (A&M)
Doggie In The Window
Patti Page; *Patti Page-16 Most Requested Songs* . . . . (Legacy)
Patti Page-Golden Hits . . . . (Mercury)
Patti Page's Greatest Hits . . . . (Columbia)
Dolphin's Cry
Live; *The Distance To Here* . . . . (Radioactive/MCA)
Don't Be Stupid (You Know I Love You)
Shania Twain; *Come On Over* . . . . (Mercury)
Don't Cry My Lady Love
Quicksilver Messenger Service; *Quicksilver Messenger Service-
Anthology* . . . . (Capitol)
Don't Fight The Feelings Of Love
Charley Pride; *Sweet Country* . . . .(RCA)
Don't Hold Back Your Love
Daryl Braithwaite; *Higher Than Hope* . . . . (Epic Portrait Assoc.)
Rise . . . . (Epic Portrait Assoc.)
Daryl Hall & John Oates; *Change Of Season.* . . . . (Arista)
Don't Know Much
Linda Ronstadt & Aaron Neville; *Chicken Soup For The Couples
Soul-C* . . . . (Rhino)
Cry Like A Rainstorm-Howl Like The Wind . . . . (Elektra)
Don't Make Love To Mary
Merle Travis; *Johnny Gimble's Texas Honky-Tonk Hits-C* . . . . . . (C.M.H. Prod.)
Don't Make Me Over
Dionne Warwick; *Beg, Scream & Shout! The Big Ol' Box Of '60s
Soul-C* . . . . (Rhino)
Dionne Warwick Collection-Her All-Time Greatest Hits . . . . (Rhino)
Jennifer Warnes; *Shot Through The Heart* . . . . (Arista)
Don't Sit Under The Apple Tree
Andrews Sisters; *Andrews Sisters Greatest Hits* . . . . (Curb)
Andrews Sisters-16 Great Performances . . . . (MCA)
Capitol Collectors Series-The Andrews Sisters . . . . (Capitol)
Glenn Miller; *Memorial-1944-1969* . . . . (Bluebird)
Glenn Miller & His Orchestra; *The Unforgettable Glenn Miller & His
Orchestra.* . . . . (RCA)
Don't Take Her She's All I Got
Tracy Byrd; *Big Love.* . . . . (MCA)
Don't Take It Personal (Just One Of Dem Days)
Monica; *Miss Thang* . . . .(Rowdy/Arista)
Don't Take The Girl
Tim McGraw; *Not A Moment Too Soon* . . . . (Curb)
Tim McGraw's Greatest Hits . . . . (Curb)
Don't Talk (Put Your Head On My Shoulder)
Beach Boys; *Pet Sounds* . . . . (Capitol)
The Pet Sounds Sessions: A 30th Anniversary Collection. . . . . (Capitol)
Linda Ronstadt; *Winter Light* . . . . (Elektra)
Don't Tell Me
Madonna; *GHV2* . . . . (Warner Bros.)
Music . . . . (Maverick)
Don't Tell Me You Love Me
Night Ranger; *Dawn Patrol.* . . . .(Camel)
Night Ranger's Greatest Hits . . . . (Camel)
Don't Throw Your Love Away
Searchers; *History Of British Rock-#2-C.* . . . . (Rhino)
Searchers' Greatest Hits. . . . . (Rhino)
Don't Wanna Fall In Love
Jane Child; *Jane Child.* . . . . (Warner Bros.)
Don't Worry 'bout Me
Frank Sinatra; *Capitol Collectors Series-Frank Sinatra* . . . . (Capitol)
Don't Worry, Baby
Beach Boys; *Absolute Best-#1.* . . . . (Capitol)
Endless Summer . . . . (Capitol)
Fun Fun Fun . . . . (Capitol)
Made In The U.S.A. . . . . (Capitol)
Down In The Valley
Elvis Presley; *Reconsider Baby.* . . . .(RCA)
Leadbelly; *Defense Blues-Golden Classics-#2* . . . . (Collectables)
Pete Seeger; *American Favorite Ballads-#1* . . . . (Smithsonian Folkways)
Down The Aisle Of Love
Quin-Tones; *Rockin' & Rollin' Wedding Songs-#2-C.* . . . . (Rhino)
Dr. Love
Whispers; *Excellence* . . . . (Allegiance)
Shhhh . . . . (Dore)
Dr. Love
Bananarama; *Deep Sea Skiving.* . . . . (London)
Dream On
Depeche Mode; *Exciter* . . . . (Mute/Reprise)
Dream With No Love
Gerald Levert; *ST/Bamboozled* . . . . (Motown)
Drink To Me Only With Thine Eyes
Paul Robeson; *Essential Paul Robeson* . . . . (Vanguard)

Roger Whittaker; *Folk Songs Of Our Time* . . . .(RCA)
Drive
Cars; *Heartbeat City* . . . .(Elektra)
MTV's Rock 'N' Roll To Go-C. . . . . (Elektra)
The Cars' Greatest Hits. . . . . (Elektra)
Drive South
John Hiatt; *Slow Turning* . . . .(A&M)
Suzy Bogguss; *Voices In The Wind* . . . .(Liberty)
Drive-In Movies & Dashboard Lights
Nanci Griffith; *Storms* . . . . (MCA)
Drowned World (My Substitute For Love)
Madonna; *GHV2* . . . . (Warner Bros.)
Ray Of Light . . . . (Maverick)
Drowning
Backstreet Boys; *The Hits-Chapter 1.* . . . . (Jive)
Drowning In The Sea Of Love
Boz Scaggs; *Live At The Beacon-C* . . . . (Giant)
Joe Simon; *Didn't It Blow Your Mind: Soul Hits Of The '70s-#7-C.* . . .(Rhino)
Music In My Bones: The Best Of Joe Simon . . . . (Rhino)
Ringo Starr; *Ringo The 4th.* . . . . (Atlantic)
Duke Of Earl
Gene Chandler; *21 Oldies But Goodies-C* . . . . (Original Sound)
Billboard Top Rock 'N' Roll Hits-1962-C. . . . . (Rhino)
Cruisin'-1962-C . . . .(Increase)
Oldies But Goodies-#6-C . . . . (Original Sound)
New Edition; *Under The Blue Moon* . . . . (MCA)
Dulcinea
Original Cast; *ST/Man Of La Mancha* . . . . (MCA)
Dum Dum
Brenda Lee; *Brenda Lee-Anthology-#1 & #2.* . . . . (MCA)
Dust On The Bottle
David Lee Murphy; *Out With A Bang* . . . . (MCA)
Earth, The Sun, The Rain
Color Me Badd; *Now & Forever* . . . . (Giant)
East Of The Sun & West Of The Moon
Al Cohn & Zoot Sims; *RCA Victor Jazz: First Half-Century-C* . . . .(RCA)
Billie Holiday; *Billie's Best* . . . . (Verve)
Diana Krall; *When I Look In Your Eyes* . . . .(GRP)
Tommy Dorsey & Frank Sinatra; *Stardust.* . . . .(Bluebird)
Easter Parade
Andy Russell; *Puttin' On The Ritz-Capitol Sings Berlin-C* . . . .(Capitol)
Bing Crosby; *All Time Best Of Bing Crosby.* . . . . (Curb)
Judy Garland & Fred Astaire; *ST/Easter Parade* . . . . (Rhino)
Sarah Vaughan; *Complete Sarah Vaughan On Mercury-#2.* . . . . . . (Mercury)
Easy Come Easy Go
George Strait; *Easy Come Easy Go* . . . . (MCA)
Easy Loving
Freddie Hart; *Best Of Freddie Hart* . . . . (CEMA Special Prod.)
Elephants In Love
Jean-Luc Ponty; *Fables* . . . . (Atlantic)
Elusive Butterfly (Of Love)
Bob Lind; *Good Vibrations (Sounds Of Top 40 Radio: 1964-1967)-C* . .(Capitol)
Elvira
Murry Kellum; *Country Comedy-20 Country Comedy Hits* . . . . (Plantation)
Oak Ridge Boys; *Fancy Free* . . . . (MCA)
MCA Records 30 Years Of Hits-1958-1988-C. . . . . (MCA)
Oak Ridge Boys' Greatest Hits 2. . . . . (MCA)
Embraceable You
Billie Holiday; *Body And Soul* . . . . (Verve)
Frank Sinatra; *The Capitol Years* . . . .(Capitol)
MGM Studio Orchestra; *ST/American In Paris* . . . . . (Sony Music Special Prod.)
Oleta Adams; *Glory Of Gershwin Featuring Larry Adler-C* . . . . . . (Mercury)
Sarah Vaughan; *Complete Sarah Vaughan On Mercury-#1-Great Jazz Years-
1954-1956* . . . . (Mercury)
Emotionally Yours
Bob Dylan; *Empire Burlesque* . . . .(Columbia)
O'Jays; *Emotionally Yours.* . . . . (EMI)
Emotions
Brenda Lee; *The Brenda Lee Story-Her Greatest Hits* . . . . (MCA)
Vintage Music-#13-C . . . . (MCA)
Emotions
Reno & Smiley; *Best Of Reno & Smiley* . . . . (Starday)
Emotions
Mariah Carey; *Emotions* . . . .(Columbia)
End Of The Road
Boyz II Men; *Cooleyhighharmony.* . . . .(Motown)
End, The
Beatles; *Abbey Road* . . . .(Parlophone)
Endless Love
Diana Ross & Lionel Richie; *25 Years Of Grammy Greats-C* . . . . . .(Motown)
All The Great Motown Love Song Duets-C . . . .(Motown)
Motown Story-First 25 Years-C . . . .(Motown)
ST/Endless Love . . . . (Mercury)
Luther Vandross & Mariah Carey; *Songs* . . . .(Epic)
Eva Braun (I Never Loved)
Boomtown Rats; *Tonic For The Troops* . . . .(Columbia)
Even If
Amel Larrieux; *Infinite Possibilities* . . . .(Epic)

Even The Bad Times Are Good
Tremeloes; *Best Of The Tremeloes* (Rhino)
Even The Nights Are Better
Air Supply; *Air Supply's Greatest Hits* (Arista)
Now & Forever (Arista)
Everlasting Love
Carl Carlton; *Classic R&B Oldies Of The '70s-#2-C* (MCA Special Prod.)
Gloria Estefan; *Hold Me, Thrill Me, Kiss Me* (Epic)
Robert Knight; *Everlasting Love* (Collectables)
Every Little Girl's Dream
Lisa Brokop; *Every Little Girl's Dream* (Patriot)
Every Little Thing
Beatles; *Beatles VI* (Capitol)
Beatles-Love Songs (Capitol)
For Sale (Capitol)
Every Morning
Sugar Ray; *14:59* (Lava)
Every Other Time
LFO; *Life Is Good* (J)
Every Time I Close My Eyes
Babyface; *The Day* (Epic)
Every Time I Get Around You
David Lee Murphy; *Gettin' Out The Good Stuff* (MCA)
Everybody Loves Somebody
Dean Martin; *Dean Martin's Greatest Hits* (EMI)
Everybody's Trying To Be My Baby
Beatles; *Beatles '65* (Capitol)
For Sale (Capitol)
The Beatles-Anthology-#2 (Capitol)
Carl Perkins; *Blue Suede Shoes: The Very Best Of Carl Perkins* (Collectables)
Carl Perkins' Greatest Hits/Finest Performances (Sun)
Carl Perkins-Original Sun Greatest Hits (Rhino)
Everyday
Dave Matthews Band; *America: A Tribute To Heroes-C* (Interscope)
Everyday (RCA)
Everything
Jody Watley; *Jody Watley's Greatest Hits* (MCA)
Quiet Storms-'80s Jams-#1-C (MCA)
Thinking About You-Modern Love Songs-C (Hip-O)
Everywhere
Fleetwood Mac; *25 Years-The Chain* (Warner Bros.)
Fleetwood Mac's Greatest Hits (Warner Bros.)
Tango In The Night (Warner Bros.)
Everywhere I Go
Shawn Mullins; *Beneath The Velvet Sun* (Columbia)
Fabulous Character
Sarah Vaughan; *Complete Sarah Vaughan On Mercury-#1-Great Jazz Years-1954-1956* (Mercury)
Face Of Love
Rosie O'Donnell & Jewel; *Another Rosie Christmas-C* (Columbia)
Factory Girl
Rolling Stones; *Beggars Banquet* (Abkco)
Faded Pictures
Case Featuring Joe; *Personal Conversation* (Def Jam/IDJMG)
Faking Love
T.G. Sheppard & Karen Brooks; *Perfect Stranger* (Warner Bros.)
T.G. Sheppard's All-Time Greatest Hits (Warner Bros.)
T.G. Sheppard's Greatest Hits-#2 (WB/Curb)
You & I-Classic Country Duets-C (Warner Bros.)
Fall From Grace
Amanda Marshall; *Amanda Marshall* (Epic)
Fallin' Out Of Love
Reba McEntire; *Reba McEntire's Greatest Hits-#3: I'm A Survivor* (MCA)
Rumor Has It (MCA)
Falling For The First Time
Barenaked Ladies; *Maroon* (Reprise)
Falling In Love (Uh-Oh)
Miami Sound Machine; *Primitive Love* (Epic)
Falling In Love With Love
Frank Sinatra; *The V-Discs: The Columbia Years-1943-1952* (Legacy)
Gene Ammons; *Jug & Dodo* (Prestige)
Helen Merrill; *Helen Merrill* (Giants Of Jazz)
Marian McPartland; *Reprise* (Concord Jazz)
Tony Bennett; *If I Ruled The World: Song For The Jet Set* (Columbia)
Falling Out Of Love
John & Audrey Wiggins; *John & Audrey* (Mercury)
Fanny
Bee Gees; *Bee Gees' Greatest* (Polydor)
Main Course (RSO)
Fat Boy
Billy Stewart; *Beach Music Hits-C* (Universal)
One More Time (Chess)
One More Time/Chess Years (Chess)
Feelin' Love
Paula Cole; *This Fire* (Imago)
Feelin' Single, Seein' Double
Emmylou Harris; *Elite Hotel* (Reprise)
Feels Like Love
Vince Gill; *Let's Make Sure We Kiss Goodbye* (MCA)
Feels Like The First Time
Foreigner; *Classic Rock 1966-1988-C* (Atlantic)
Foreigner (Atlantic)
Records (Atlantic)
Feels So Good
Xscape; *Off The Hook* (So So Def/Columbia)
Feels So Right
Alabama; *Alabama's Greatest Hits* (RCA)
Feels So Right (RCA)
Femininity
Eric Benet; *True To Myself* (Jac-Mac/Warner Bros.)
Fever
Buddy Guy; *This Is Buddy Guy* (Vanguard)
Elvis Presley; *A Valentine Gift For You* (RCA)
Aloha from Hawaii via Satellite (RCA)
Elvis Presley-Pure Gold (RCA)
Little Willie John; *Best Of Little Willie John-Fever* (Rhino)
Peggy Lee; *Memories Are Made Of This-C* (Capitol)
Rita Coolidge; *Rita Coolidge-Classics-#5* (A&M)
Rita Coolidge's Greatest Hits (A&M)
Fever
Bruce Springsteen; *18 Tracks* (Columbia)
Southside Johnny And The Asbury Jukes; *Cover Me (Bruce Springsteen Tribute)-C* (Rhino)
Havin' A Party With Southside Johnny And The Asbury Jukes (Epic)
I Don't Want To Go Home (Epic)
Fields Of Gold
Sting; *Fields Of Gold-The Best Of Sting 1984-1994* (A&M)
Ten Summoner's Tales (A&M)
Fifty-Fifty Love
Lee Roy Parnell; *Lee Roy Parnell* (Arista)
Two Steppin' Country-#1-C (Priority)
Fill Her Up
Earl Scruggs & Sting; *Earl Scruggs And Friends-C* (MCA)
Find Another Love
Tams; *45-#2108* (Gusto)
Five O'Clock World
Hal Ketchum; *Past The Point Of Rescue* (Curb)
Vogues; *ST/Good Morning, Vietnam* (A&M)
Vogues' Greatest Hits (SSS International)
Vogues' Greatest Hits (Rhino)
Flesh And Blood
Johnny Cash; *Johnny Cash's Biggest Hits* (Columbia)
The Man In Black-His Greatest Hits (Legacy)
Fly
Sugar Ray; *Floored* (Atlantic)
Fly (The Angel Song)
Wilkinsons; *Nothing But Love* (Giant)
Fool For Your Loving
Whitesnake; *Live...In The Heart Of The City* (Geffen)
Slip Of The Tongue (Geffen)
Fool In Love
Ike & Tina Turner; *Best Of Ike & Tina Turner* (EMI)
Best Of Sue Records-C (Collectables)
Proud Mary-Best Of Ike & Tina Turner (EMI)
Fool In Love
Michael Smotherman; *ST/Always* (MCA)
Fooled Around & Fell In Love
Elvin Bishop; *Billboard Top Hits-1976-C* (Rhino)
South's Greatest Hits-C (Capricorn)
Struttin' My Stuff (Capricorn)
Fools Fall In Love
Drifters; *Atlantic Rhythm & Blues 1947-1974-#3 (1955-1958)-C* (Atlantic)
Drifters-Their Greatest Recordings (Atco)
ST/Book Of Love (Atlantic)
Jacky Ward; *Best Of Jacky Ward* (Mercury)
Lover's Question (Mercury)
Fools In Love
Joe Jackson; *Live 1980/86* (A&M)
Look Sharp! (A&M)
For Emily, Wherever I May Find Her
Simon & Garfunkel; *Collected Works* (Columbia)
Parsley Sage Rosemary & Thyme (Columbia)
Simon & Garfunkel's Greatest Hits (Columbia)
For Once In My Life
Gladys Knight & The Pips; *Gladys Knight & The Pips-Anthology* (Motown)
Motown Superstar Series-#13-Gladys Knight & The Pips (Motown)
Neither One Of Us (Motown)
Stevie Wonder; *Motown Story-First 25 Years-C* (Motown)
Stevie Wonder-Love Songs-20 Classic Hits (Motown)
Stevie Wonder's Greatest Hits-#2 (Motown)
Tony Bennett; *Tony Bennett's All-Time Greatest Hits* (Columbia)
Vikki Carr; *Best Of Vikki Carr* (EMI)
For You Blue
Beatles; *Beatles-Box Set* (Capitol)
Let It Be (Capitol)
George Harrison; *Best Of George Harrison* (Capitol)
For Your Eyes Only
Sheena Easton; *13 Original James Bond Themes-C* (EMI)

ST/For Your Eyes Only . . . . (Liberty)

For Your Love
Fleetwood Mac; *Mystery To Me* . . . . (Reprise)

For Your Love
Ed Townsend; *The Glory Of Love-'50s Sweet & Soulful Love
Songs-C* . . . . (Hip-O)
Peaches & Herb; *The Glory Of Love-'60s Sweet & Soulful Love
Songs-C* . . . . (Hip-O)

Forever In Love
Kenny G; *Breathless* . . . . (Arista)

Fortress Around Your Heart
Sting; *Dream Of The Blue Turtles* . . . . (A&M)
Fields Of Gold-The Best Of Sting 1984-1994 . . . . (A&M)

Fortunate
Maxwell; *ST/Life* . . . . (Rock Land/Interscope)

Frankie
Bruce Springsteen; *Tracks* . . . . (Columbia)

Frankie & Johnny
Brook Benton; *Endlessly-The Best Of Brook Benton* . . . . (Rhino)
Doc Watson; *Favorites-Doc Watson* . . . . (Liberty)
Jerry Lee Lewis; *Jerry Lee's Greatest!* . . . . (Rhino)

Freeway Of Love
Aretha Franklin; *Who's Zoomin' Who?* . . . . (Arista)

Friday I'm In Love
Cure; *Wish* . . . . (Elektra)

Friday On My Mind
David Bowie; *Bowie Pin Ups* . . . . (Rykodisc)
Easybeats; *Best Of The Easybeats* . . . . (Rhino)
Nuggets-Classic Collection From The Psychedelic '60s-C . . . . . (Rhino)

Friendly Persuasion
Pat Boone; *Best Of Pat Boone* . . . . (MCA)
Pat Boone-16 Great Performances . . . . (MCA)

Friends & Lovers
Bread; *Best Of Bread-#2* . . . . (Elektra)
Bread . . . . (Elektra)

Friends And Lovers
Gloria Loring & Carl Anderson; *Chicken Soup For The Couples
Soul-C* . . . . (Rhino)
*Chicken Soup For The Soul: I'll Be There For You-Songs Of Friendship,
Brotherhood And Sisterhood-C* . . . . (Rhino)
Gloria Loring . . . . (Atlantic)

Friends In Love
Dionne Warwick; *Dionne Warwick With Johnny Mathis* . . . . (Arista)
Friends In Love . . . . (Arista)
Johnny Mathis & Dionne Warwick; *Friends In Love* . . . . (Columbia)
Johnny Mathis-Love Songs . . . . (Columbia)

From A Distance
Bette Midler; *Some People's Lives* . . . . (Atlantic)
Byrds; *20 Essential Tracks From The Box Set* . . . . (Columbia)
The Byrds . . . . (Columbia)
Judy Collins; *Fires Of Eden* . . . . (Columbia)
Kathy Mattea; *Time Passes By* . . . . (Mercury)
Nanci Griffith; *Lone Star State Of Mind* . . . . (MCA)
One Fair Summer Evening . . . . (MCA)

From The Vine Came The Grape
Gaylords; *X-tra Cheese-Originals By The Originals-C* . . . . (Compose)

From This Moment On
Anita O'Day; *Swings Cole Porter* . . . . (Verve)
Ella Fitzgerald; *Ella Fitzgerald Sings The Cole Porter Songbook* . . . . . (Verve)
Frank Sinatra; *a Swingin' Affair!* . . . . (Capitol)
Original Soundtrack; *Kiss Me Kate* . . . . (Rhino)

Game Of Love
Wayne Fontana & The Mindbenders; *45s On CD-#2-1960-1966-C* . . . (Mercury)
ST/Good Morning, Vietnam . . . . (A&M)
Super Oldies Of The '60s-#10-C . . . . (Audio Fidelity)

Gee
Crows; *WCBS FM 101 History Of Rock-Group Sounds-#3-C* . . . . . (Collectables)

Gee Baby, Ain't I Good To You
Diana Krall; *All For You (A Dedication To The Nat "King" Cole
Trio)* . . . . (Impulse!)

Generous Palmstroke
Bjork; *Vespertine* . . . . (Elektra)

Get It On (Bang A Gong)
Power Station; *Power Station* . . . . (Capitol)
T. Rex; *Electric Warrior* . . . . (Reprise)

Get Out The Map
Indigo Girls; *Shaming Of The Sun* . . . . (Epic)

Get Together
Big Mountain; *Resistance* . . . . (Giant)
Youngbloods; *Best Of The Youngbloods* . . . . (RCA)
Billboard Top Rock 'N' Roll Hits-1969-C . . . . (Rhino)
*Chicken Soup For The Soul: I'll Be There For You-Songs Of Friendship,
Brotherhood And Sisterhood-C* . . . . (Rhino)
ST/Forrest Gump . . . . (Epic/Sony Music Soundtrax)
Summer Of Love-#1-C . . . . (Rhino)

Gettin' In The Way
Jill Scott; *Who Is Jill Scott? Words And Sounds-#1* . . . . . . (Hidden Beach/Epic)

Getting Back Into Love
Gerald Alston; *Getting Back Into Love (Single)* . . . . (Taj)

Getting Better
Beatles; *Sgt. Pepper's Lonely Hearts Club Band* . . . . (Capitol)

Ghost Of You
Richard Thompson; *Richard Thompson-Best Of Capitol Years* . . . . . . (Capitol)

Gift Of Love
Jerry Butler; *Best Of Jerry Butler* . . . . (Vee-Jay)
Jerry Butler and The Impressions; *For Your Precious Love* . . . . . (Vee-Jay)

Gift Of Love
David Ball; *Steppin' Out* . . . . (RCA)

Gift Of Love
Sweet Honey In The Rock; *Other Side* . . . . (Flying Fish)

Gift Of Love
Bette Midler; *Some People's Lives* . . . . (Atlantic)

Gimme Gimme Good Lovin'
Crazy Elephant; *Dick Bartley's One-Hit Wonders Of The '60s-#2-C* . . . . (Rhino)

Gimme Some Lovin'
Spencer Davis Group; *Best Of The Spencer Davis Group* . . . . (EMI)

Girl I Love
Led Zeppelin; *BBC Sessions* . . . . (Atlantic)

Girl's Alright With Me
Temptations; *Temptations' Greatest Hits-#1* . . . . (Motown)
Temptations-Anthology-The Best Of The Temptations . . . . (Motown)

Give A Little Love
Ziggy Marley & The Melody Makers; *Hey World!* . . . . (EMI)
ST/Men At Work . . . . (Mesa)
ST/Tequila Sunrise . . . . (Capitol)
Time Has Come...Best Of Ziggy Marley & The Melody Makers . . . . . (EMI)

Give A Little Love
Judds; *Judds' Greatest Hits* . . . . (MCA)

Give A Little Love
Marvin Gaye & Tammi Terrell; *United* . . . . (Motown)

Give A Little Love
Stylistics; *45-#1136* . . . . (Streetwise)

Give It Up
ZZ Top; *Recycler* . . . . (Warner Bros.)

Give Me Just A Little More Time
Chairmen Of The Board; *Chairmen Of The Board's Greatest Hits* . . . . . (HDH)

Give Me Love (Give Me Peace On Earth)
George Harrison; *Best Of George Harrison* . . . . (Capitol)
Living In The Material World . . . . (Capitol)

Give Me You
Mary J. Blige; *Mary* . . . . (MCA)

Give Me Your Love For Christmas
Johnny Mathis; *Give Me Your Love For Christmas* . . . . (Columbia)

Give The Girl A Kiss
Bruce Springsteen; *Tracks* . . . . (Columbia)

Given To Fly
Pearl Jam; *Yield* . . . . (Epic)

Givin' Water To A Drowning Man
Lee Roy Parnell; *We All Get Lucky Sometimes* . . . . (Career)

Glad All Over
Dave Clark Five; *History Of The Dave Clark Five* . . . . (Hollywood)

Glory Of Love
Bette Midler; *ST/Beaches* . . . . (Atlantic)
Peter Cetera; *Solitude/Solitaire* . . . . (Full Moon)
ST/The Karate Kid Part II . . . . (EMI)

Glory Of Love
Velvetones; *Doo-Wop Ballads-#2-C* . . . . (Rhino)

Glow Worm
Mills Brothers; *Best Of The Mills Brothers* . . . . (MCA)
Cab Driver . . . . (Ranwood)
Mills Brothers' Greatest Hits . . . . (MCA)
Mills Brothers-16 Great Performances . . . . (MCA)

Go On With The Wedding
Patti Page; *Patti Page-Golden Celebration* . . . . (Mercury)

God Is Love
Marvin Gaye; *Marvin Gaye-Live* . . . . (Motown)
Pops We Love You . . . . (Motown)
What's Going On . . . . (Motown)

God Loves A Drunk
Richard Thompson; *Rumor & Sigh* . . . . (Capitol)

Goin' Out Of My Head
Lettermen; *Best Of The Lettermen-#2* . . . . (Capitol)
The Lettermen's All-Time Greatest Hits . . . . (Capitol)
Little Anthony And The Imperials; *Best Of Little Anthony And The
Imperials* . . . . (Rhino)
EMI Legends Of Rock & Roll-24 Greatest Hits-C . . . . (EMI)

Golden Ring
Emmylou Harris/Linda Ronstadt/Anna & Kate McGarrigle; *Tammy
Wynette...Remembered-C* . . . . (Asylum)
George Jones & Tammy Wynette; *George Jones & Tammy Wynette-16
Biggest Hits* . . . . (Epic/Legacy)
Tammy Wynette & George Jones; *Encore-Tammy Wynette & George
Jones* . . . . (Epic)
Tammy Wynette & George Jones' Greatest Hits . . . . (Epic)
Tammy Wynette-Anniversary-20 Years Of Hits . . . . (Epic)

Good Day Sunshine
Beatles; *Beatles-Box Set* . . . . (Capitol)

Revolver . . . . (Capitol)

Good Love
Prince; *ST/Bright Lights Big City* . . . . (Warner Bros.)

Good Love
Anita Baker; *Giving You The Best That I Got* . . . . (Elektra)

Good Love
Klymaxx; *Maxx Is Back* . . . . (MCA)

Good Love
Poison; *Open Up And Say...Ahh!* . . . . (Capitol)

Good Lovin' (Makes It Right)
Tammy Wynette; *Tammy Wynette-16 Biggest Hits* . . . . (Legacy)
Tammy Wynette-Anniversary-20 Years Of Hits . . . . (Epic)
Tears Of Fire-25th Anniversary Collection . . . . (Epic)

Good Lovin's Hard To Find
Lynyrd Skynyrd; *Last Rebel* . . . . (Atlantic)

Good Morning Beautiful
Steve Holy; *Blue Moon* . . . . (Curb)

Good Run Of Bad Luck
Clint Black; *No Time To Kill* . . . . (RCA)

Goodbye To Love
Wayne Smith; *Wicked Inna Dance Hall* . . . . (Rohit)

Goodbye To Romance
Ozzy Osbourne; *The Ozzman Cometh* . . . . (Epic)

Goodnight Irene
Jim Reeves; *Jim Reeves-Pure Gold* . . . . (RCA)
Johnny Cash; *Rough Cut King Of Country Music* . . . . (Sun)
The Man-The World-His Music . . . . (Sun)
Ry Cooder; *Chicken Skin Music* . . . . (Reprise)
Weavers; *Best Of The Weavers* . . . . (MCA)
Weavers At Carnegie Hall . . . . (Vanguard)
Weavers' Greatest Hits . . . . (Vanguard)

Goodnight My Love
Benny Goodman; *Benny Goodman-Pure Gold* . . . . (RCA)
Best Of Benny Goodman . . . . (RCA)
Complete Benny Goodman-#4 . . . . (RCA)
This Is Benny Goodman . . . . (RCA)
Sarah Vaughan; *Divine Sarah Vaughan-Columbia Years-1949-
1953* . . . . (Columbia)

Goodnight Sweetheart
David Kersh; *Goodnight Sweetheart* . . . . (Curb)

Goodnight Sweetheart
Guy Lombardo & His Royal Canadians; *Guy Lombardo-All Time
Favorites* . . . . (MCA Special Prod.)

Goodnight, Well It's Time To Go
Chuck Berry; *Chuck Berry's Greatest Hits* . . . . (Everest)
Spaniels; *Goodnight, Well It's Time To Go* . . . . (Vee-Jay)
Hits From The Legendary Vee-Jay Records-C . . . . (Motown)
ST/American Graffiti . . . . (MCA)

Got A Love For You
Jomanda; *Someone To Love Me* . . . . (Big Beat)

Got To Be Love
Paul Hardcastle; *Hardcastle 2* . . . . (JVC Musical Industries)

Gotta Have You
Stevie Wonder; *ST/Jungle Fever* . . . . (Motown)

Greatest Love Of All
George Benson; *George Benson-Collection* . . . . (Warner Bros.)
ST/The Greatest . . . . (Arista)
Weekend In L.A. . . . . (Warner Bros.)
Whitney Houston; *Whitney Houston* . . . . (Arista)
Whitney Houston's Greatest Hits . . . . (Arista)

Greatest Love On Earth
Chicago; *Hot Streets* . . . . (Columbia)

Greatest Romance Ever Sold
Prince; *Rave Un2 The Joy Fantastic* . . . . (NPG)

Green Grass
Gary Lewis And The Playboys; *Gary Lewis & The Playboys* . . . . . . (Gold Rush)
Gary Lewis And The Playboys' Greatest Hits . . . . (Curb)

Groove Is In The Heart/What Is Love
Deee-Lite; *World Clique* . . . . (Elektra)

Groovin'
Aretha Franklin; *Lady Soul* . . . . (Atlantic)
Booker T. & The M.G.s; *Best Of Booker T. & The M.G.s* . . . . . . (Atlantic)
Soul Shots-#3-Soul Twist-C . . . . (Rhino)
Rascals; *Groovin'* . . . . (Warner Special Prod.)
Hit Singles-1958-1977-C . . . . (Atlantic)
Rascals' Greatest Hits . . . . (Atlantic)
ST/Platoon . . . . (Atlantic)

Groovy Kind Of Love
Mindbenders; *British Rock-#3-C* . . . . (Original Sound)
History Of British Rock-#6-C . . . . (Rhino)
Phil Collins; *Phil Collins-Hits* . . . . (Atlantic)
Serious Hits...Live! . . . . (Atlantic)

Guilty
Warren Brothers; *Beautiful Day In The Cold Cruel World* . . . . (BNA)

Gun Love
ZZ Top; *ZZ Top's Greatest Hits* . . . . (Warner Bros.)

Guns Of Love
Pamela Rose; *Morpheus* . . . . (Grace)

Guys & Dolls
Original Cast; *ST/Guys & Dolls* . . . . (MCA)

Halfway Home Cafe
Ricky Skaggs and Kentucky Thunder; *History Of The Future* . . (Skaggs Family)

Hammer Of Love
Bad Company; *The Original Bad Company Anthology* . . . . (Elektra)

Handful Of Dust
Patty Loveless; *When Fallen Angels Fly* . . . . (Epic)

Happiness Street
Georgia Gibbs; *Best Of Georgia Gibbs-The Mercury Years* . . . . . . (Chronicles)

Happy
Bruce Springsteen; *Tracks* . . . . (Columbia)

Happy Together
Flo & Eddie And The Turtles; *History Of Flo & Eddie And The
Turtles* . . . . (Rhino)
Turtles; *Billboard Top Rock 'N' Roll Hits-1967-C* . . . . (Rhino)
Cruisin'-1967-C . . . . (Increase)
Happy Together . . . . (Rhino)
Turtles-20 Greatest Hits . . . . (Rhino)
Turtlesized . . . . (Rhino)

Hard Day's Night, A
Beatles; *Beatles 1* . . . . (Capitol)
Beatles-20 Greatest Hits . . . . (Capitol)
ST/A Hard Day's Night . . . . (Capitol)
The Beatles At The Hollywood Bowl . . . . (Capitol)
The Beatles/1962-1966 . . . . (Capitol)

Hard Lovin' Woman
Mark Collie; *Unleashed* . . . . (MCA)

Hard Times Come Easy
Richie Sambora; *Undiscovered Soul* . . . . (Mercury)

Hard To Be A Husband, Hard To Be A Wife
Chely Wright & Brad Paisley; *Grand Ole Opry-75 Years-#2-C* . . . . (MCA)

Have I Told You Lately?
Rod Stewart; *Unplugged...And Seated* . . . . (Warner Bros.)
Vagabond Heart . . . . (Warner Bros.)
Van Morrison; *Best Of Van Morrison* . . . . (Polydor)

Have You Ever Been (To Electric Ladyland)
Jimi Hendrix Experience; *Electric Ladyland* . . . . (Reprise)

He Talks To Me
Lorrie Morgan; *Leave The Light On* . . . . (RCA)
Lorrie Morgan's Greatest Hits . . . . (BNA)
Lorrie Morgan-Super Hits . . . . (RCA)
To Get To You-Greatest Hits Collection . . . . (BNA)

Head Over Heels
Go-Go's; *Go-Go's Greatest* . . . . (I.R.S.)
Talk Show . . . . (I.R.S.)

Head Over Heels
Tears For Fears; *Songs From The Big Chair* . . . . (Mercury)

Head Over Heels
Tony Terry; *Tony Terry* . . . . (Epic)

Heart Full Of Love
Original Broadway Cast; *Les Miserables* . . . . (Geffen)

Heart Full Of Love
Holly Dunn; *Heart Full Of Love* . . . . (Warner Bros.)

Heart To Heart Talk
Lee Ann Womack & Asleep At The Wheel; *Ride With
Bob-C* . . . . (DreamWorks/SKG)

Hearts Of Stone
Bruce Springsteen; *Tracks* . . . . (Columbia)
Southside Johnny And The Asbury Jukes; *Best Of Southside Johnny And The
Asbury Jukes* . . . . (Legacy)
Cover Me (Bruce Springsteen Tribute)-C . . . . (Rhino)
Hearts Of Stone . . . . (Epic)

Heaven On Earth
Platters; *Encore Of Golden Hits-Platters* . . . . (Mercury)
Platters-16 Greatest Hits . . . . (Trip)
Platters-Anthology . . . . (Rhino)
Red Sails In The Sunset . . . . (Allegiance)

Hell Below/Stars Above
Toadies; *Hell Below/Stars Above* . . . . (Interscope)

Hello Mary Lou
Creedence Clearwater Revival; *Creedence Country* . . . . (Fantasy)
Rick Nelson; *Rick Nelson In Concert-Troubadour 1969* . . . . (MCA)
Rick Nelson-Souvenirs . . . . (EMI)
Ricky Nelson; *Best Of Ricky Nelson* . . . . (EMI)
Rick Nelson's Greatest Hits . . . . (Rhino)
Statler Brothers; *14 Country Favorites-C* . . . . (Mercury)
Pardners In Rhyme . . . . (Mercury)

Hello, Young Lovers
Frank Sinatra; *Frank Sinatra Sings Rodgers & Hammerstein* . . . . . (Columbia)
Mel Torme; *Jazz 'Round Midnight-Mel Torme* . . . . (Verve)
Original Broadway Cast; *The King And I* . . . . (RCA Victor)
Original Cast; *ST/The King And I* . . . . (Angel)

Helplessly Hoping
Crosby, Stills & Nash; *Crosby, Stills & Nash* . . . . (Atlantic)
CSN . . . . (Atlantic)
Crosby, Stills, Nash & Young; *So Far* . . . . (Atlantic)

Helter Skelter
Aerosmith; *Pandora's Box* . . . . (Columbia)

Beatles; *Beatles-Box Set* . . . . (Capitol)
 Rarities . . . . (Capitol)
 Rock 'N' Roll Music . . . . (Capitol)
 The Beatles (White Album) . . . . (Capitol)
Motley Crue; *Shout At The Devil* . . . . (Elektra)
Pat Benatar; *Precious Time* . . . . (Chrysalis)
Siouxsie And The Banshees; *Nocturne* . . . . (Geffen)
 The Scream . . . . (Geffen)
U2; *Rattle And Hum* . . . . (Island)
Here
Tony Martin; *Best Of Tony Martin On RCA* . . . . (Collector's Choice)
Here, There & Everywhere
Beatles; *Beatles-Box Set* . . . . (Capitol)
 Beatles-Love Songs . . . . (Capitol)
 Revolver . . . . (Capitol)
Kenny Loggins; *Kenny Loggins Alive* . . . . (Columbia)
Heroes & Villains
Beach Boys; *Concert/'69-Live In London* . . . . (Capitol)
 Endless Harmony . . . . (Capitol)
 Good Vibrations-Thirty Years Of The Beach Boys . . . . (Capitol)
 Made In The U.S.A. . . . . (Capitol)
 Smiley Smile/Wild Honey . . . . (Capitol)
 Sunshine Dream . . . . (Capitol)
He's A Rebel
Crystals; *Good Time Rock 'N' Roll-C* . . . . (MCA)
 Phil Spector's Greatest Hits-C . . . . (Spector)
Hey Leonardo (She Likes Me For Me)
Blessid Union Of Souls; *Now That's What I Call Music!-#3-C* . . . (Virgin)
 Walking Off The Buzz . . . . (Push/V2)
Hey, Sweet Darling
Iguanas; *Nuevo Boogaloo* . . . . (Margaritaville)
High And The Mighty
Les Baxter & His Orchestra; *Instrumental Gems Of The '50s-C* . . . . (Collector's Choice)
Roger Williams; *Roger Williams' Greatest Hits* . . . . (Curb)
Victor Young & His Orchestra; *Hard To Find Orchestral Instrumentals-C* . . . . (Eric)
Victor Young & His Singing Strings; *Billboard Top Movie Hits-1950-1954-C* . . . . (Rhino)
High Country Snows
Dan Fogelberg; *High Country Snows* . . . . (Full Moon)
High On Love
Patty Loveless; *Long Stretch Of Lonesome* . . . . (Epic)
High On Love
Foghat; *Stone Blue* . . . . (Rhino)
High On You
Survivor; *Vital Signs* . . . . (Scotti Bros.)
High On Your Love Suite/One Mo Hit
Rick James; *Bustin' Out Of L Seven* . . . . (Gordy)
High Powered Love
Emmylou Harris; *Cowgirl's Prayer* . . . . (Asylum)
Hold Me Tight
Beatles; *Meet The Beatles!* . . . . (Capitol)
Hold You Tight
Tara Kemp; *Tara Kemp* . . . . (Giant)
Holes In The Floor Of Heaven
Steve Wariner; *Burnin' The Roadhouse Down* . . . . (Capitol)
Home To You
John Michael Montgomery; *Home To You* . . . . (Atlantic)
Honey
Mariah Carey; *Butterfly* . . . . (Columbia)
Honey
Bobby Goldsboro; *Billboard Top Pop Hits-1968-C* . . . . . (Rhino)
 Cruisin'-1968-C . . . . (Increase)
Honey Bun
Original Cast; *South Pacific* . . . . (CBS Masterworks)
Honey Love
R. Kelly & Public Announcement; *Born Into The '90s* . . . . . (Jive)
Honey To The Bee
Billie; *Honey To The B* . . . . (Virgin)
Honky Tonk Women Love Redneck Men
Ronnie McDowell; *American Music* . . . . (Curb)
Hot Girls In Love
Loverboy; *Big Ones* . . . . (Columbia)
 Keep It Up . . . . (Columbia)
Hot Love
Michael Bolton; *The Hunger* . . . . (Columbia)
Hot Love
Cheap Trick; *Cheap Trick* . . . . (Epic)
Hot Love
Five Star; *Five Star* . . . . (Epic)
Hot On A Thing Called Love
Chi-Lites; *Me And You* . . . . (20th Century Fox)
House Full Of Love
Michael McDonald; *In The Spirit-A Christmas Album* . . . . . . (MCA)
House Of Love
Amy Grant & Vince Gill; *House Of Love* . . . . (A&M)
House With Love In It, A
Four Lads; *Moments To Remember-Very Best Of The Four Lads* . . . . (Taragon)

Houston (Means I'm One Day Closer To You)
Larry Gatlin & The Gatlin Brothers Band; *19 Hot Country Requests-C* . . . (Epic)
 Greatest Country Hits Of The '80s-1983-C . . . . (Columbia)
 Larry Gatlin & The Gatlin Brothers' Greatest Hits-Encore . . . . (Columbia)
 Larry Gatlin & The Gatlin Brothers-17 Greatest Hits . . . (Columbia)
How Deep Is The Ocean? (How High Is The Sky?)
Diana Krall; *Love Scenes* . . . . (Impulse!)
Frank Sinatra; *Nice 'N' Easy* . . . . (Capitol)
Liza Minnelli; *Liza Minnelli-At Carnegie Hall* . . . . (Telarc)
How Do You Like Your Eggs In The Morning?
Jane Powell/Vic Damone/Four Freshmen; *ST/Romantic Duets From MGM Classics-C* . . . . (Turner Classic Movies)
How Forever Feels
Kenny Chesney; *Everywhere We Go* . . . . (BNA)
 Kenny Chesney's Greatest Hits . . . . (BNA)
How Little We Know
Frank Sinatra; *Best Of The Capitol Years* . . . . (Capitol)
 Capitol Collectors Series-Frank Sinatra . . . . (Capitol)
How Many More Times
Led Zeppelin; *Led Zeppelin* . . . . (Atlantic)
How Much
Mariah Carey; *Rainbow* . . . . (Columbia)
How Much I Feel
Ambrosia; *Ambrosia-Anthology* . . . . (Warner Bros.)
 Life Beyond L.A. . . . . (Warner Bros.)
 Mellow Rock Hits Of The '70s-Summer Breeze-C . . . . (Rhino)
How Sweet It Is (To Be Loved By You)
James Taylor; *Gorilla* . . . . (Warner Bros.)
 James Taylor-Best Live . . . . (Columbia)
 James Taylor's Greatest Hits . . . . (Warner Bros.)
Junior Walker & The All Stars; *Junior Walker & The All Stars' Greatest Hits* . . . . (Motown)
 Junior Walker & The All Stars-The Ultimate Collection . . . (Motown)
Marvin Gaye; *20th Century Masters-The Millennium Collection-The Best Of Marvin Gaye-#1 (The '60s)* . . . . (Motown)
 Marvin Gaye-Anthology . . . . (Motown)
 Marvin Gaye's Greatest Hits/ . . . . (Motown)
How To Handle A Woman
Original Cast; *Camelot* . . . . (Columbia)
Richard Harris; *ST/Camelot* . . . . (Warner Bros.)
How Your Love Makes Me Feel
Diamond Rio; *Diamond Rio's Greatest Hits* . . . . (Arista)
Human Touch
Rick Springfield; *Living In Oz* . . . . (RCA)
 Rick Springfield's Greatest Hits . . . . (RCA)
Human Touch
Elvis Costello & The Attractions; *Get Happy!* . . . . (Rykodisc)
Human Touch
Joe Jackson; *Blaze Of Glory* . . . . (A&M)
Hungry For Love
Patsy Cline; *20 Golden Pieces Of Patsy Cline* . . . . (Bulldog)
 Hungry For Love-Her First Recordings-#2 . . . . (Rhino)
 Patsy Cline . . . . (MCA)
Hungry For Love
Todd Rundgren; *A Wizard A True Star* . . . . (Rhino)
Hurdy Gurdy Man
Butthole Surfers; *ST/Dumb And Dumber* . . . . (RCA)
Donovan; *Donovan's Greatest Hits* . . . . (Epic)
 Hurdy Gurdy Man . . . . (Epic)
I Adore Mi Amor
Color Me Badd; *C.M.B.* . . . . (Giant)
I Ain't Never
Webb Pierce; *Billboard Top Country Hits-1959-C* . . . . (Rhino)
 Grand Ole Opry-75 Years-#2-C . . . . (MCA)
 Webb Pierce-Greatest Hits/Finest Performances . . . . . . (Sun)
I Alone
Live; *Throwing Copper* . . . . (Radioactive/MCA)
I Believe In Love
Paula Cole Band; *Amen* . . . . (Warner Bros.)
I Believe In Love
Dixie Chicks; *America: A Tribute To Heroes-C* . . . . . . (Interscope)
I Can Hear Music
Beach Boys; *Friends-20/20* . . . . (Capitol)
 Sunshine Dream . . . . (Capitol)
Beach Boys & Kathy Troccoli; *Stars And Stripes-#1* . . . . (River North)
I Can Love You
Mary J. Blige; *Share My World* . . . . (MCA)
I Can't Make You Love Me
Bonnie Raitt; *Luck Of The Draw* . . . . (Capitol)
I Could Not Ask For More
Edwin McCain; *Messenger* . . . . (Lava)
I Count The Minutes
Ricky Martin; *Ricky Martin* . . . . (Columbia)
I Did It
Dave Matthews Band; *Everyday* . . . . (RCA)
I Do (Whatcha Say Boo)
Jon B.; *Cool Relax* . . . . (Yab Yum/550)
I Do It For Your Love
Paul Simon; *Greatest Hits, Etc.* . . . . (Columbia)

I Don't Know Why
Frank Sinatra; *The Golden Days Of Radio* . . . . (K-Tel)
I Don't Know Why I Love You
House Of Love; *House Of Love* . . . . (Fontana)
I Don't Want To Lose Your Love
Bobby Caldwell; *Cat In The Hat* . . . . (Sin-Drome)
I Don't Want To Lose Your Love
B Angie B; *B Angie B* . . . . (Bust It)
I Don't Want To Miss A Thing
Aerosmith; *ST/Armageddon-The Album* . . . . (Columbia)
Mark Chesnutt; *I Don't Want To Miss A Thing* . . . . (MCA)
I Feel Fine
Beatles; *Beatles 1* . . . . (Capitol)
  Beatles '65 . . . . (Capitol)
  Beatles-20 Greatest Hits . . . . (Capitol)
  Past Masters-Volume One . . . . (Parlophone)
  The Beatles/1962-1966 . . . . (Capitol)
Sweethearts Of The Rodeo; *One Time One Night* . . . . (Columbia)
I Feel The Earth Move
Carole King; *Carole King's Greatest Hits* . . . . (Epic)
  Tapestry . . . . (Epic)
I Fell In Love
Carlene Carter; *I Fell In Love* . . . . (Reprise)
I Fell In Love Again Last Night
Forester Sisters; *Country Love Songs-C* . . . . (Warner Bros.)
  Forester Sisters . . . . (Warner Bros.)
  Forester Sisters' Greatest Hits . . . . (Warner Bros.)
I Found Love
Quicksilver Messenger Service; *Quicksilver* . . . . (Capitol)
  Quicksilver Messenger Service-Anthology . . . . (Capitol)
  Sons Of Mercury . . . . (Rhino)
I Found Love
Lone Justice; *Shelter* . . . . (Geffen)
I Found Love
Paul Carrack; *Suburban Voodoo* . . . . (Epic)
I Go Crazy
Paul Davis; *Best Of Paul Davis* . . . . (Bang)
  Billboard Top Hits-1978-C . . . . (Rhino)
  Paul Davis' Greatest Hits . . . . (Epic)
  Singer Of Songs-Teller Of Tales . . . . (Bang)
I Go Wild
Rolling Stones; *Voodoo Lounge* . . . . (Virgin)
I Got Lost In His Arms
Original Broadway Cast; *Annie Get Your Gun* . . . . (Angel)
I Got Rhythm
Ella Fitzgerald; *George & Ira Gershwin Songbook* . . . . (Verve)
Ethel Waters; *I Got Rhythm: The Smithsonian George Gershwin
  Collection-C* . . . . (Smithsonian Collection)
Happenings; *'60s Rock Classics-#1-C* . . . . (Rhino)
Judy Garland; *Judy Garland-Collector's Items-1936-1945* . . . . (MCA)
Louis Armstrong; *Essential Louis Armstrong* . . . . (Verve)
Original Cast; *Girl Crazy* . . . . (Nonesuch)
Original London Cast; *Crazy For You* . . . . (RCA)
Robert Palmer; *Glory Of Gershwin Featuring Larry Adler-C* . . . . . . (Mercury)
I Got You
Split Enz; *History Never Repeats-Best Of Split Enz* . . . . (A&M)
  True Colours . . . . (A&M)
I Got You
Dwight Yoakam; *Buenas Noches From A Lonely Room* . . . . . . (Reprise)
  Just Lookin' For A Hit . . . . (Reprise)
I Got You
Shenandoah; *Extra Mile* . . . . (Columbia)
I Got You (I Feel Good)
James Brown; *James Brown's 20 All Time Greatest Hits!* . . . . . (Polydor)
  Live At The Apollo . . . . (Polydor)
  ST/Good Morning, Vietnam . . . . (A&M)
  Very Best Of James Brown . . . . (Polydor)
I Guess That's Why They Call It The Blues
Elton John; *Elton John's Greatest Hits-1976-1986* . . . . (MCA)
  Too Low For Zero . . . . (MCA)
I Hate You Then I Love You
Celine Dion with Luciano Pavarotti; *Let's Talk About Love-C* . . . . . (550 Music)
I Have Dreamed
Barbra Streisand; *The Broadway Album* . . . . (Columbia)
Original Broadway Cast; *The King And I* . . . . (RCA Victor)
Original Cast; *The King And I* . . . . (MCA)
I Have Learned To Respect The Power Of Love
Angela Winbush; *Real Thing* . . . . (Mercury)
Stephanie Mills; *Stephanie Mills* . . . . (MCA)
I Hear A Symphony
Diana Ross & The Supremes; *16 #1 Hits From The Early '60s-C* . . . . (Motown)
  Diana Ross & The Supremes' Greatest Hits . . . . (Motown)
  Diana Ross & The Supremes-25th Anniversary . . . . (Motown)
  Diana Ross & The Supremes-Anthology (1962-1969) . . . . . (Motown)
  Evening With Diana Ross . . . . (Motown)
  Every Great #1 Hit . . . . (Motown)
  Good Feeling Music Of The Big Chill Generation-#2-C . . . . (Motown)
  Motown Story-First 25 Years-C . . . . (Motown)

Supremes; *I Hear A Symphony* . . . . (Motown)
I Honestly Love You
Olivia Newton-John; *Back To The Basics-Essential Collection* . . . . . . (Geffen)
  Back With A Heart . . . . (MCA)
  If You Love Me Let Me Know . . . . (MCA)
  Olivia Newton-John's Greatest Hits . . . . (MCA)
I Just Can't Stop Loving You
Michael Jackson & Siedah Garrett; *Bad* . . . . (Epic)
  HIStory: Past, Present And Future-Book 1-C . . . . (Epic)
I Just Wanna Be Loved By You
Patty Loveless; *Patty Loveless-Classics* . . . . (Epic)
I Just Wanna Stop
Gino Vannelli; *Best Of Gino Vannelli* . . . . (A&M)
  Brother To Brother . . . . (A&M)
  Gino Vannelli-Classics-#7 . . . . (A&M)
I Just Want To Make Love To You
Bill Medley; *Best Of Bill Medley* . . . . (MCA)
Cold Blood; *Bill Graham Presents The Last Days Of The
  Fillmore-C* . . . . (Epic Portrait Assoc.)
Etta James; *Etta James-At Last* . . . . (Chess)
Foghat; *Best Of Foghat* . . . . (Rhino)
  Foghat . . . . (Rhino)
Muddy Waters; *Best Of Muddy Waters* . . . . (Chess)
  The Chess Box-Muddy Waters . . . . (Chess)
Righteous Brothers; *Righteous Brothers-Anthology 1962-1974* . . . . (Rhino)
Rolling Stones; *England's Newest Hit Makers/The Rolling Stones* . . . . (Abkco)
  Singles Collection-The London Years . . . . (Abkco)
Van Morrison; *It's Too Late To Stop Now* . . . . (Warner Bros.)
I Knew You Were Waiting (For Me)
Aretha Franklin & George Michael; *Aretha Franklin's Greatest Hits-1980-
  1994* . . . . (Arista)
  Billboard Top Hits-1987-C . . . . (Rhino)
  Chicken Soup For The Couples Soul-C . . . . (Rhino)
I Know What I Know
Paul Simon; *Graceland* . . . . (Warner Bros.)
I Know Where Love Lives
Hal Ketchum; *Past The Point Of Rescue* . . . . (Curb)
I Like It
Sammie; *From The Bottom To The Top* . . . . (Freeworld/Capitol)
I Like The Way
Tommy James And The Shondells; *Tommy James And The Shondells-
  Anthology* . . . . (Rhino)
I Like You
Culture Beat; *Horizon* . . . . (Epic)
I Love
Tom T. Hall; *Tom T. Hall's Greatest Hits-#2* . . . . (Mercury)
  Tom T. Hall-The Hits . . . . (Mercury)
I Love How You Love Me
Bobby Vinton; *Bobby Vinton-16 Most Requested Songs* . . . . . . (Legacy)
  Bobby Vinton's All-Time Greatest Hits . . . . (Epic)
I Love L.A.
Randy Newman; *Trouble In Paradise* . . . . (Warner Bros.)
I Love London
Tommy Page; *Tommy Page* . . . . (Sire)
I Love Me Some Him
Toni Braxton; *Secrets* . . . . (LaFace)
I Love Mickey
Mickey Mantle & Teresa Brewer; *Baseball's Greatest Hits-C* . . . . . (Rhino)
I Love Paris
Frank Sinatra; *Frank Sinatra Sings The Select Cole Porter* . . . . (Capitol)
  Sinatra Sings...of love and things . . . . (Capitol)
I Love Rocky Road
''Weird Al'' Yankovic; *''Weird Al'' Yankovic* . . . . . (Volcano Entertainment)
I Love The Life I Live
Mose Allison; *Best Of Mose Allison* . . . . (Rhino)
  Mose Allison-Alive . . . . (Atlantic)
Muddy Waters; *The Chess Box-Muddy Waters* . . . . (Chess)
I Love The Night
Blue Oyster Cult; *Spectres* . . . . (Columbia)
I Love The Night
Joe Cocker; *Civilized Man* . . . . (Capitol)
I Love The Night Life
Alicia Bridges; *Alicia Bridges* . . . . (Polydor)
  Night At Studio 54-C . . . . (Casablanca)
  Oldies But Goodies-#14-C . . . . (Original Sound)
  Polydor Dance Classics-C . . . . (Polydor)
I Love The Radio
Joey Welz; *Return Of Haley's Comet* . . . . (Caprice Int'l)
I Love The Way You Love Me
John Michael Montgomery; *Life's A Dance* . . . . (Atlantic)
I Love You
Celine Dion; *Falling Into You* . . . . (550 Music)
I Love You
Volumes; *Best Of Doo Wop Uptempo-#2-C* . . . . (Rhino)
  I Love You-Golden Classics . . . . (Collectables)
I Love You
Climax Blues Band; *Flying The Flag* . . . . (Warner Bros.)
I Love You (But You're Boring)
Beautiful South; *Welcome To The Beautiful South* . . . . (Elektra)

I Love You Drops
Bill Anderson; *Bill Anderson's Greatest Hits* . . . . (Varese Sarabande)
I Love You Period
Dan Baird; *Love Songs For The Hearing Impaired* . . . . (Def American)
I Love Your Guts
Elvis Hitler; *Disgraceland* . . . . (Restless)
I Love Your Smile
Shanice; *Inner Child* . . . . (Motown)
I Loved You
Will Smith; *Big Willie Style* . . . . (Columbia)
I Loves You Porgy/Porgy, I's Your Woman
Barbra Streisand; *The Broadway Album* . . . . (Columbia)
I May Be Wrong
Frankie Laine; *The Uncollected Frankie Laine* . . . . (Hindsight)
I May Be Wrong (But I Think You're Wonderful)
Doris Day; *Doris Day-16 Most Requested Songs-Encore!* . . . . (Columbia)
Harry James; *Harry James-22 Original Big Band Recordings* . . . . . . (Hindsight)
I Need A Lover
John Cougar; *John Cougar* . . . . (Riva)
Pat Benatar; *In The Heat Of The Night* . . . . (Chrysalis)
I Need You
LeAnn Rimes; *ST/Jesus-The Epic Mini-Series* . . . . (Sparrow/Curb/Capitol)
I Need Your Love
Boston; *Walk On* . . . . (MCA)
I Need Your Lovin'
Don Gardner & Dee Dee Ford; *Cruisin'-1962-
1963-C* . . . . (Dunhill Compact Classics)
Super Oldies Of The '60s-#4-C . . . . (Audio Fidelity)
I Need Your Lovin'
Temptations; *Cloud Nine* . . . . (Motown)
I Need Your Lovin'
Alyson Williams; *Raw* . . . . (Def Jam)
I Never Knew Love
Doug Stone; *More Love* . . . . (Epic)
I Really Don't Want To Know
Charlie McCoy; *Greatest Hits Of Charlie McCoy* . . . . (Columbia)
Eddy Arnold; *Best Of Eddy Arnold* . . . . (RCA)
Essential Eddy Arnold . . . . (RCA)
Elvis Presley; *Elvis Country ("I'm 10,000 Years Old")* . . . . (RCA)
Great Country Songs . . . . (RCA)
Les Paul; *Best Of The Capitol Masters* . . . . (Gold Rush)
Les Paul & Mary Ford; *Les Paul's Greatest Hits* . . . . (Pair)
Ronnie Dove; *Ronnie Dove-His Best* . . . . (Laurie)
Tommy Edwards; *It's All In The Game-The Complete Hits Of Tommy
Edwards* . . . . (Eric)
I Really Love You
Channels; *Harlem Holiday-New York Rhythm & Blues-#3-C* . . . . . (Collectables)
Stereos; *Best Of Doo Wop Uptempo-#1-C* . . . . (Rhino)
I Said I Love You
Babyface; *The Day* . . . . (Epic)
I See It Now
Tracy Lawrence; *I See It Now* . . . . (Atlantic)
I See The Lovelight In Your Eyes
Conway Twitty; *Number Ones* . . . . (MCA)
I Still Believe In You
Vince Gill; *I Still Believe In You* . . . . (MCA)
I Thank You
Bonnie Raitt; *The Glow* . . . . (Warner Bros.)
John Cowan; *Soul'd Out* . . . . (Sugar Hill)
Sam & Dave; *Best Of Sam & Dave* . . . . (Atlantic)
Very Best Of Sam & Dave . . . . (Rhino)
ZZ Top; *Deguello* . . . . (Warner Bros.)
I Think I Love You Too Much
Jeff Healey Band; *Hell To Pay* . . . . (Arista)
I Try To Think About Elvis
Patty Loveless; *Patty Loveless-Classics* . . . . (Epic)
When Fallen Angels Fly . . . . (Epic)
I Turn To You
Christina Aguilera; *Christina Aguilera* . . . . (RCA)
I Wanna Be Loved By You
Helen Kane; *Nipper's Greatest Hits Of The '20s-#1-C* . . . . (RCA)
I Wanna Love Like That
Tony Thompson; *Sexsational* . . . . (Giant/Warner Bros.)
I Want To Be Loved Like That
Shenandoah; *Best Of Shenandoah* . . . . (RCA)
I Want You
Juliet Roberts; *Natural Thing* . . . . (Reprise)
I Want You
Savage Garden; *Best Of Savage Garden* . . . . (Columbia)
Savage Garden . . . . (Columbia)
I Want Your Love
Chris Isaak; *San Francisco Days* . . . . (Reprise)
I Will Wait
Hootie & The Blowfish; *Musical Chairs* . . . . (Atlantic)
Ice Cream
Sarah McLachlan; *Fumbling Towards Ecstasy* . . . . (Arista)
Iceman
Bruce Springsteen; *Tracks* . . . . (Columbia)

I'd Give Anything
Gerald Levert; *Groove On* . . . . (East West)
I'd Like That
XTC; *Homespun* . . . . (Idea/TVT)
I'd Love You All Over Again
Alan Jackson; *Here In The Real World* . . . . (Arista)
I'd Rather Ride Around With You
Reba McEntire; *What If It's You* . . . . (MCA)
Ida Red
Asleep At The Wheel featuring Jody Nix, Huey Lewis & Willie Nelson;
Tribute To The Music Of Bob Wills And The Texas Playboys-C . . . . (Liberty)
Bob Wills & His Texas Playboys; *Bob Wills & His Texas Playboys-
Greatest Hits* . . . . (Curb)
Tiffany Transcriptions-#2-Best Of The Tiffanys . . . . (Rhino)
If
Bread; *Best Of Bread* . . . . (Elektra)
Bread-Anthology . . . . (Elektra)
Bread-Retrospective . . . . (Rhino)
Manna . . . . (Rhino)
If I Could Make A Living
Clay Walker; *Clay Walker's Greatest Hits* . . . . (Giant)
If I Could Make A Living . . . . (Giant)
If I Didn't Care
Connie Francis; *Very Best Of Connie Francis* . . . . (Polydor)
Hilltoppers; *45-#15220* . . . . (Dot)
Ink Spots; *Best Of The Ink Spots* . . . . (MCA)
If I Didn't Care . . . . (Pro-Arte)
Ink Spots' Greatest Hits-Original Recordings-1939-1946 . . . . . . (MCA)
ST/The Shawshank Redemption . . . . (Epic)
Moments; *Best Of The Moments: Love On A Two-Way Street* . . . . . (Rhino)
Platters; *Magic Touch-An Anthology* . . . . (Mercury)
Very Best Of The Platters . . . . (Mercury)
If I Ever Fall In Love
Shai; *If I Ever Fall In Love* . . . . (Gasoline Alley)
If I Had A Hammer (The Hammer Song)
Pete Seeger; *Sing-A-Long-Live At Sanders
Theatre 1980* . . . . (Smithsonian Folkways)
Peter, Paul & Mary; *10 Years Together/The Best Of Peter, Paul
and Mary* . . . . (Warner Bros.)
Peter, Paul and Mary . . . . (Warner Bros.)
Peter, Paul and Mary In Concert . . . . (Warner Bros.)
Trini Lopez; *Best Of Trini Lopez* . . . . (Exact)
Weavers; *Weavers' Greatest Hits* . . . . (Vanguard)
If I Had You
Frank Sinatra; *Round #1* . . . . (Capitol)
Voice: The Columbia Years-1943-1952 . . . . (Columbia)
Judy Garland; *Judy Garland-Collector's Items-1936-1945* . . . . (MCA)
Platters; *Platters Greatest Hits* . . . . (Everest)
If I Had You
Alabama; *Southern Star* . . . . (RCA)
If I Only Had A Heart
Jack Haley; *ST/The Wizard Of Oz* . . . . (Sony Music Special Prod.)
Original Soundtrack; *The Wizard Of Oz-The Deluxe Edition* . . . . . . (Rhino)
The Wizard Of Oz-The Story And Songs . . . . (Rhino)
If I Were A Carpenter
Bobby Darin; *Live At The Desert Inn* . . . . (Motown)
Four Tops; *Compact Command Performances-Four Tops* . . . . (Motown)
Four Tops Reach Out . . . . (Motown)
Four Tops-Anthology . . . . (Motown)
Johnny Cash & June Carter; *The Man In Black-His Greatest Hits* . . . . (Legacy)
Tim Hardin; *Memorial Album* . . . . (Polydor)
If I Were You
Collin Raye; *All I Can Be* . . . . (Epic)
Best Of Collin Raye-Direct Hits . . . . (Epic)
If It Isn't Love
New Edition; *Heart Break* . . . . (MCA)
New Edition's Greatest Hits, Vol. 1 . . . . (MCA)
If The Love Fits Wear It
Leslie Pearl; *Words & Music* . . . . (RCA)
If There Hadn't Been You
Billy Dean; *Billy Dean* . . . . (Liberty)
If Walls Could Talk
Celine Dion; *All The Way...A Decade Of Song* . . . . (550 Music)
If You Ain't Lovin' (You Ain't Livin')
Faron Young; *Heroes Of Country Music-#3-Legends Of Nashville-C* . . . (Rhino)
*Live Fast, Love Hard: Original Capitol Recordings-1952-
1962-C* . . . . (Country Music Foundation)
George Strait; *If You Ain't Lovin' You Ain't Livin'* . . . . (MCA)
Ten Strait Hits . . . . (MCA)
If You Go Away
Neil Diamond; *Neil Diamond-Love Songs* . . . . (MCA)
Rainbow . . . . (MCA)
Stones . . . . (MCA)
If You Love Me (Let Me Know)
Olivia Newton-John; *Back To Basics-Essential Collection 1971-1992* . . (Geffen)
If You Love Me Let Me Know . . . . (MCA)
Olivia Newton-John's Greatest Hits . . . . (MCA)
If You Love Somebody
Kevin Sharp; *Measure Of A Man* . . . . (143/Asylum)

If You Love Somebody Set Them Free
Sting; *Dream Of The Blue Turtles*. . . . . (A&M)
If You Love Somebody, Set Them On Fire
Dead Milkmen; *Metaphysical Graffiti* . . . . (Enigma Capitol)
If You Loved Me
Laura Branigan; *Branigan* . . . . (Atlantic)
If You Wanna Touch Her, Ask!
Shania Twain; *Come On Over* . . . . (Mercury)
If You Want Me To
Joe Diffie; *A Thousand Winding Roads* . . . . (Epic)
If You Want To Find Love
Kenny Rogers; *Back Home Again*. (Reprise)
I'll Be Home
Flamingos; *Alan Freed's Memory Lane-C* . . . . (MCA)
 Best Of The Flamingos. . . . . (Rhino)
 Super Oldies Of The '50s-#6-C . . . . (Audio Fidelity)
 Platters; *Platters Greatest Hits-#2* . . . . (Curb)
I'll Be Loving You
Collage; *Chapter One* . . . . (Metropolitan)
I'll Be Seeing You
Billie Holiday; *Billie Holiday At Carnegie Hall-Billie Holiday
 Story-#6* . . . . (Verve)
 Essential Billie Holiday-Carnegie Hall Concert . . . . (Verve)
 Jackie Gleason; *Best Of Jackie Gleason & His Orchestra* . . . . (Curb)
 Judy Collins; *Judith* . . . . (Elektra)
 Skyliners; *Skyliners' Greatest Hits*. . . . . (Original Sound)
 Tommy Dorsey & Frank Sinatra; *Those Wonderful Years (WWII Love
 Songs)-C* . . . . (JCI Assoc. Labels)
 Tommy Dorsey & His Orchestra; *Kiss The Boys Goodbye-Classic Songs Of
 WWII-#1* . . . . (RCA)
I'll Be There For You/You're All I Need
Method Man & Mary J. Blige; *Def Jam Music Group 10th
 Anniversary-C* . . . . (Def Jam)
I'll Give All My Love To You
Keith Sweat; *I'll Give All My Love To You* . . . . (Vintertainment)
I'll Go Down Loving You
Shenandoah; *Under The Kudzu* . . . . (RCA)
I'll Have To Say I Love You In A Song
Jim Croce; *Baby Boomer Classics-Love Seventies-C* . . . . . . (JCI Assoc. Labels)
 Billboard Top Soft Rock Hits-1974-C . . . . (Rhino)
 Dim The Lights-C. . . . . (K-Tel)
I'll Hold You In My Heart (Till I Can Hold You In My Arms)
Eddy Arnold; *Best Of Eddy Arnold*. . . . . (RCA)
 Eddy Arnold-The Hits . . . . (Mercury)
 Memories Are Made Of This . . . . (Mercury)
I'll Never Stop Loving You
Gary Morris; *Anything Goes* . . . .(Warner Bros.)
 Gary Morris-Hits. . . . .(Warner Bros.)
I'll Never Stop Loving You
Doris Day & James Cagney; *Love Me Or Leave Me* . . . (Columbia Special Prod.)
I'm A Hundred Percent For You
Fats Waller; *Breakin' The Ice: The Early Years, Part 1 (1934-
 1935)*. . . . . (Bluebird)
I'm A Man
Spencer Davis Group; *Baby Boomer Classics-Rockin'
 Sixties-C* . . . . (JCI Assoc. Labels)
 Best Of The Spencer Davis Group . . . .(EMI)
I'm Already There
Lonestar; *I'm Already There*. . . . . (BNA)
I'm Glad There Is You
Jimmy Dorsey & His Orchestra; *Then & Now-Fabulous New Jimmy Dorsey
 & His Orchestra* . . . .(Atlantic)
 Morgana King; *Stretchin' Out* . . . . (Muse)
 Peggy Lee; *Best Of Peggy Lee* . . . .(MCA)
I'm Gonna Love You Just A Little More Baby
Barry White; *Barry White's Greatest Hits* . . . . (20th Century Fox)
I'm In Love
Lisa Keith; *Walkin' In The Sun* . . . .(Perspective/A&M)
I'm In Love Again
George Morgan; *Room Full Of Roses-The George Morgan
 Collection* . . . . (Razor & Tie)
I'm In Love With My Car
Queen; *A Night At The Opera* . . . . (Hollywood)
 Live Killers . . . . (Hollywood)
I'm In Love With My Little Red Tricycle
Napoleon XIV; *The Second Coming*. . . . . (Rhino)
I'm In The Mood
Cece Peniston; *Thought Ya Knew* . . . . (A&M)
I'm In The Mood For Love
McGuire Sisters; *Best Of The McGuire Sisters* . . . .(MCA)
 Nat "King" Cole; *The Trio Recordings-#2* . . . . (Laserlight)
 Ray Conniff; *Young At Heart* . . . . (Columbia)
I'm Only In It For The Love
John Conlee; *Best Of John Conlee* . . . . (Curb)
 John Conlee-20 Greatest Hits . . . .(MCA)
I'm Ready
Tevin Campbell; *I'm Ready* . . . . (Qwest)
I'm So Into You
Peabo Bryson; *The Peabo Bryson Collection* . . . . (Capitol)

SWV; *It's About Time* . . . .(RCA)
I'm Still In Love With You
Al Green; *Al Green's Greatest Hits*. . . . . (Right Stuff)
 Billboard Hot Soul Hits-1972-C . . . . (Rhino)
 I'm Still In Love With You. (Right Stuff)
 Slow Jams-'70s-#2-C . . . . (Right Stuff)
I'm Telling You Now
Freddie And The Dreamers; *History Of British Rock-#1-C* . . . . (Rhino)
I'm Thinking Tonight Of My Blue Eyes
Gene Autry; *All Time Legends Of Country Music-C* . . . . (Legacy)
I'm Your Puppet
James & Bobby Purify; *Oldies But Goodies-#12-C* . . . .(Original Sound)
 Soul Shots-#5-La-La Means I Love You-C . . . . (Rhino)
 Sweet & Soulful '60s-C. . . . . (K-Tel)
Imaginary Lover
Atlanta Rhythm Section; *Champagne Jam* . . . .(Polydor)
Imagine
Diana Ross; *Best Of The Beatles Songs-C* . . . . (Motown)
 Diana Ross-Anthology . . . . (Motown)
 Touch Me In The Morning . . . . (Motown)
 Joan Baez; *Best Of Joan Baez* . . . . (A&M)
 Come From The Shadows . . . . (A&M)
 John Lennon; *Lennon* . . . . (Capitol)
 Live In New York City . . . . (Capitol)
 ST/Imagine: John Lennon . . . . (Capitol)
 John Lennon & Yoko Ono; *The John Lennon Collection* . . . . (Capitol)
 John Lennon/Plastic Ono Band; *Imagine* . . . . (Capitol)
 Shaved Fish . . . . (Capitol)
 Neil Young; *America: A Tribute To Heroes-C* . . . .(Interscope)
In The Midnight Hour
Rascals; *Classic Rock 1966-1988-C* . . . .(Atlantic)
 ST/More Songs From ''The Big Chill'' . . . . (Motown)
 Time Peace/The Rascals' Greatest Hits . . . .(Atlantic)
 Roxy Music; *Flesh + Blood* . . . . (Atco)
 Street Life-20 Great Hits . . . . (Reprise)
 Wilson Pickett; *Atlantic Rhythm & Blues 1947-1974-#5 (1962-
 1966)-C* . . . .(Atlantic)
 Best Of Wilson Pickett . . . .(Atlantic)
 Frat Rock!-#4-C . . . . (Rhino)
 Golden Soul-C . . . .(Atlantic)
 Soul Years-C . . . .(Atlantic)
 Wilson Pickett's Greatest Hits . . . .(Atlantic)
In The Summertime (You Don't Want My Love)
Roger Miller; *Roger Miller's Greatest Hits*. . . . .(Smash)
In This Life
Collin Raye; *In This Life* . . . . Epic)
In Times Like These
Barbara Mandrell; *Barbara Mandrell's Greatest Hits* . . . . (MCA)
 Spun Gold. . . . . (MCA)
Indian Love Call
Jeanette MacDonald & Nelson Eddy; *Jeanette MacDonald & Nelson Eddy-
 Legendary Performer* . . . .(RCA)
 Ray Stevens; *Misty* . . . . (Barnaby)
 Very Best Of Ray Stevens . . . . (Barnaby)
 Slim Whitman; *Best Of Slim Whitman 1952-1972* . . . . (Rhino)
 Paloma Blanca-Best Of Slim Whitman-Legendary Masters. . . . . (EMI)
Indian Summer Love
Con Funk Shun; *Secrets* . . . . (Mercury)
Indiana Wants Me
R. Dean Taylor; *Hard-To-Find Motown Classics-#2-C* . . . . (Motown)
 Super Hits Of The '70s-Have A Nice Day-#3-C . . . . (Rhino)
 Super Hits-#5-C . . . . (Gusto)
Inside My Love
Trina Broussard; *ST/Love Jones* . . . . (Columbia)
Iris
Goo Goo Dolls; *Dizzy Up The Girl* . . . .(Warner Sunset/Reprise)
 ST/City Of Angels . . . .(Warner Sunset/Reprise)
Irish Love Song
Mormon Tabernacle Choir; *Old Beloved Songs* . . . . (Columbia)
Island Of Love
Elvis Presley; *ST/Blue Hawaii*. . . . .(RCA)
Island Of Love
Rascals; *Freedom Suite* . . . . (Rhino)
Island Of Love
Sheppards; *Sheppards-Golden Classics* . . . . (Collectables)
Isn't It Romantic
Michael Feinstein; *Isn't It Romantic* . . . . (Elektra)
 Tony Bennett; *Rodgers & Hart Songbook*. . . . .(DRG)
It Had To Be You
Harry Connick, Jr.; *ST/When Harry Met Sally* . . . . (Columbia)
It Must Be Love
Alan Jackson; *Under The Influence*. . . . . (Arista)
It Must Have Been Love
Roxette; *ST/Pretty Woman*. . . . . (EMI)
It Takes A Lot To Laugh, It Takes A Train To Cry
Bob Dylan; *Highway 61 Revisited*. . . . . (Columbia)
 The Bootleg Series-Volumes 1-3 [Rare & Unreleased] . . . . (Columbia)
 Mike Bloomfield/Al Kooper/Stephen Stills; *Super Session* . . . . (Columbia)

It Takes Two
Marvin Gaye & Kim Weston; *Hitsville USA-The Motown Singles Collection-1959-1971-C* . . . . (Motown)
It Won't Be Over You
Steve Wariner; *Steve Wariner-Drive* . . . . (Arista)
It Works
Alabama; *In Pictures* . . . . (RCA)
It's A Woman's World
Four Aces; *Best Of The Four Aces* . . . . (MCA)
It's All About You
Luther Vandross; *One Night With You-The Best Of Love-#2* . . . . (LV/Epic)
It's All In The Game
Four Tops; *Compact Command Performances-Four Tops* . . . . (Motown)
Four Tops-Anthology . . . . (Motown)
George Benson; *Weekend In L.A.* . . . . (Warner Bros.)
Nat ''King'' Cole; *Nat ''King'' Cole-Gift Set* . . . . (Capitol)
Tommy Edwards; *Oldies But Goodies-#7-C* . . . . (Original Sound)
It's All In The Movies
Merle Haggard & The Strangers; *Country's Greatest Hits-#6-Superstars-C* . . . . (Priority)
For The Record: Merle Haggard-43 Legendary Hits . . . . (BNA)
It's All The Same To Me
Billy Ray Cyrus; *Best Of Billy Ray Cyrus-Cover To Cover* . . . . . (Mercury)
It's All Too Much
Beatles; *Yellow Submarine* . . . . (Capitol)
It's Alright
Candlebox; *Happy Pills* . . . . (Maverick)
It's Been Awhile
Staind; *Break The Cycle* . . . . (Flip/Elektra)
It's For You
Three Dog Night; *Captured Live At The Forum* . . . . (MCA)
It's How You Say It
Al Jarreau; *Tomorrow Today* . . . . (GRP/VMG)
It's Love
King's X; *Faith Hope Love* . . . . (Megaforce)
It's Time For Love
Don Williams; *Best Of Don Williams-#4* . . . . (MCA)
Cafe Carolina . . . . (MCA)
Don Williams Sings Bob McDill . . . . (MCA)
Till The Rivers All Run Dry . . . . (MCA Special Prod.)
It's Time For Love
James Brown; *Love Overdue* . . . . (Scotti Bros.)
It's Time For Love
Chi-Lites; *Chi-Lites' Greatest Hits-#2* . . . . (Rhino)
It's Your Body
Johnny Gill; *Let's Get The Mood Right* . . . . (Motown)
It's Your Love
Tim McGraw with Faith Hill; *Everywhere* . . . . (Curb)
Tim McGraw's Greatest Hits . . . . (Curb)
I've Always Got You
Robin Zander; *Robin Zander* . . . . (Interscope)
I've Found Someone Of My Own
Free Movement; *Didn't It Blow Your Mind: Soul Hits Of The '70s-#6-C* . . . . (Rhino)
I've Got A Crush On You
Carly Simon; *Glory Of Gershwin Featuring Larry Adler-C* . . . . . . (Mercury)
Ella Fitzgerald; *Compact Jazz-Ella Fitzgerald* . . . . (Verve)
Frank Sinatra; *I've Got A Crush On You* . . . . (Legacy)
Nice 'N' Easy . . . . (Capitol)
Frank Sinatra & Barbra Streisand; *Frank Sinatra-Duets-C* . . . . (Capitol)
Linda Ronstadt; *What's New* . . . . (Asylum)
I've Got A Lot To Learn About Love
Storm; *Storm* . . . . (Interscope)
I've Got A Tiger By The Tail
Buck Owens; *Billboard Top Country Hits-1965-C* . . . . (Rhino)
Buck Owens & The Buckaroos; *Buck Owens & The Buckaroos-Live At Carnegie Hall* . . . . (Country Music Foundation)
Harlan Howard; *All-Time Favorite Country Songwriter* . . . . (Koch International)
Rick Springfield; *Living In Oz* . . . . (RCA)
I've Got My Love To Keep Me Warm
Ella Fitzgerald; *The Irving Berlin Songbook-#2* . . . . (Verve)
Les Brown & His Orchestra; *16 Most Requested Songs Of The '40s-#1-C* . . . . (Legacy)
Best Of The Big Bands-C . . . . (Columbia)
I've Got Sand In My Shoes
Drifters; *1959-1965-All-Time Greatest Hits And More* . . . . (Atlantic)
Very Best Of The Drifters . . . . (Rhino)
Jambalaya (On The Bayou)
Blue Ridge Rangers; *Blue Ridge Rangers* . . . . (Fantasy)
Fats Domino; *Fats Domino's Greatest Hits* . . . . (MCA)
Hank Williams With His Drifting Cowboys; *24 Of Hank Williams' Greatest Hits* . . . . (Polydor)
Hank Williams-16 Great Hits . . . . (Everest)
Hank Williams-40 Greatest Hits . . . . (Polydor)
Hank Williams, Jr.; *ST/Your Cheatin' Heart* . . . . . . (Sony Music Special Prod.)
Jerry Lee Lewis; *Twenty Classic Hits* . . . . (Sun)
Nitty Gritty Dirt Band; *All The Good Times* . . . . (United Artists)
Stars And Stripes Forever . . . . (Capitol)

Jane Doe
Alicia Keys; *Songs In A Minor* . . . . (J)
Jesus & Mama
Confederate Railroad; *Confederate Railroad* . . . . (Atlantic)
Jesus To A Child
George Michael; *Ladies & Gentlemen: The Best Of George Michael* . . . . . (Epic)
Older . . . . (DreamWorks/SKG)
Joanna
Kool & The Gang; *Everything Is-Greatest Hits* . . . . (Mercury)
In The Heart . . . . (De-Lite)
John Deere Green
Joe Diffie; *Honky Tonk Attitude* . . . . (Epic)
Joe Diffie's Greatest Hits . . . . (Epic)
Johnny I Love You
Booker T. & The M.G.s; *Booker T. & The M.G.s' Greatest Hits* . . . . (Stax)
Johnny, My Love (Grandma's Diary)
Wilma Lee & Stoney Cooper; *45-#1118* . . . . (Hickory)
Julia
Beatles; *Beatles-Box Set* . . . . (Capitol)
ST/Imagine: John Lennon . . . . (Capitol)
The Beatles (White Album) . . . . (Capitol)
Julie, Do Ya Love Me
Bobby Sherman; *Rock & Roll Is Here To Stay-C* . . . . (Gusto)
Super Hits Of The '70s-Have A Nice Day-#3-C . . . . (Rhino)
Jump Up Behind Me
James Taylor; *Hourglass* . . . . (Columbia)
Songs From The Heart-C . . . . (Columbia)
Jungle Love
Gladys Knight & The Pips; *Glad To Be* . . . . (Allegiance)
Letter Full Of Tears-Golden Classics . . . . (Collectables)
Jungle Love
Steve Miller Band; *Book Of Dreams* . . . . (Capitol)
Steve Miller Band-Gift Set . . . . (Capitol)
Steve Miller Band-Live . . . . (Capitol)
Steve Miller Band's Greatest Hits-1974-78 . . . . (Capitol)
Jungleland
Bruce Springsteen; *Born To Run* . . . . (Columbia)
Just A Little Bit Of Love
Celine Dion; *Let's Talk About Love-C* . . . . (550 Music)
Just A Little Love
Reba McEntire; *Just A Little Love* . . . . (MCA)
Reba McEntire's Greatest Hits . . . . (MCA)
Just A Little Love
B.B. King; *Live & Well* . . . . (MCA)
Just A Little Love
38 Special; *Strength In Numbers* . . . . (A&M)
Just A Little Lovin' (Early In The Mornin')
Barbra Streisand; *Stoney End* . . . . (Columbia)
Dusty Springfield; *Dusty In Memphis* . . . . (Rhino)
Just A Touch Of Love
Slave; *Everybody Dance! Best Of Remixed Dance Classics-C* . . . . (Rhino)
Slide And Other Hits . . . . (Flashback)
Just Another Day In Paradise
Phil Vassar; *Phil Vassar* . . . . (Arista)
Just As I Am
Air Supply; *Air Supply* . . . . (Arista)
Just Between You And Me
Kinleys; *Just Between You And Me* . . . . (Epic)
Just Crazy Love
Fleetwood Mac; *Mystery To Me* . . . . (Reprise)
Just Let Me Be In Love
Tracy Byrd; *Ten Rounds* . . . . (RCA)
Just Like A Woman
Bob Dylan; *Before The Flood* . . . . (Columbia)
Biograph . . . . (Columbia)
Blonde On Blonde . . . . (Columbia)
Bob Dylan At Budokan . . . . (Columbia)
Bob Dylan's Greatest Hits . . . . (Columbia)
Byrds; *The Byrds* . . . . (Columbia)
Just Remember I Love You
Firefall; *Firefall's Greatest Hits* . . . . (Rhino)
Luna Sea . . . . (Rhino)
Just The Way You Are
Billy Joel; *Billy Joel-Greatest Hits, Volume I & Volume II* . . . . (Columbia)
Pop Classics Of The '70s-C . . . . (Columbia)
The Stranger . . . . (Columbia)
Just To Be Close To You
Commodores; *20th Century Masters-The Millennium Collection-The Best Of The Commodores* . . . . (Motown)
All The Great Love Songs-Commodores . . . . (Motown)
Lionel Richie; *Truly-The Love Songs* . . . . (Motown)
Just To Be Loved
Al Jarreau; *Tomorrow Today* . . . . (GRP/VMG)
Just You And I And The Moon
Jose Collins; *Music From The New York Stage (1890-1920)-#3-1913-1917-C* . . . . (Pearl)
Justify My Love
Madonna; *Immaculate Collection* . . . . (Sire)

Royal Box. . . . . (Sire)

Kansas City Song
Buck Owens; *Buck Owens Collection-1959-1990* . . . . (Rhino)

Kathy's Song
Simon & Garfunkel; *Collected Works* . . . . (Columbia)
Simon & Garfunkel's Greatest Hits . . . . (Columbia)
Sounds Of Silence . . . . (Columbia)

Keep It Gay
Original Cast; *Me & Juliet* . . . .(RCA Victor)

Keep On Growing
Derek And The Dominos; *Layla.* . . . . (Polydor)
Sheryl Crow; *ST/Boys On The Side.* . . . . (Arista)

Keep On Keepin' On
MC Lyte Featuring Xscape; *Bad As I Wanna B* . . . . (East West)
ST/Sunset Park. . . . . (East West)

Keep On Loving Me
O'Jays; *Emotionally Yours* . . . .(EMI)

Keep Young And Beautiful
Annie Lennox; *Diva* . . . . (Arista)

Keeper Of The Stars
Tracy Byrd; *No Ordinary Man* . . . .(MCA)

Kentucky Woman
Deep Purple; *Purple Passages* . . . .(Warner Bros.)
When We Rock We Rock & When We Roll We Roll . . . .(Warner Bros.)
Gary Puckett And The Union Gap; *Gary Puckett And The Union Gap's*
Greatest Hits . . . .(Bac-Trac)
Neil Diamond; *Love At The Greek* . . . . (Columbia)
Neil Diamond-Classics (Early Years) . . . . (Columbia)
Neil Diamond-Gold . . . .(MCA)

Kiss An Angel Good Mornin'
Charley Pride; *Charley Pride-24 Greatest Hits* . . . .(Tee Vee)
Pride! My 6 Latest And 6 Greatest . . . . (ISD/Intersound)
The Ultimate Charley Pride. . . . . (Bransounds)

Kiss From A Rose
Seal; *Seal 2* . . . . (Sire)

Kiss Me
Sixpence None The Richer; *Sixpence None The Richer* . . . . .(Squint/Columbia)
Songs From Dawson's Creek. . . . . (Sony Music Soundtrax)

Kiss You All Over
Exile; *Best Of Exile.* . . . .(MCA)
Exile's Greatest Hits . . . .(MCA)
Mixed Emotions . . . .(MCA)

Kisses Sweeter Than Wine
Jimmie Rodgers; *Best Of Jimmie Rodgers* . . . . (Rhino)
Cruisin'-1958-C . . . .(Increase)
Weavers; *Best Of The Weavers* . . . .(MCA)
Reunion-At Carnegie Hall-1963 . . . . (Vanguard)
Weavers At Carnegie Hall . . . . (Vanguard)
Weavers' Greatest Hits . . . . (Vanguard)

Knock On Wood
Amii Stewart; *Double Smash Hits-C* . . . .(Volcano Entertainment)
Buddy Guy; *This Is Buddy Guy.* . . . . (Vanguard)
Eddie Floyd; *15 Original Big Hits-#3-C.* . . . .(Stax)
Atlantic Rhythm & Blues 1947-1974-#6 (1966-1969)-C . . . . (Atlantic)
Best Of Wattstax-C. . . . .(Stax)
Super Oldies Of The '60s-#11-C . . . .(Audio Fidelity)
Eric Clapton; *Behind The Sun.* . . . . (Duck/Reprise)
Ike & Tina Turner; *Ike & Tina Turner's Greatest Hits-#3* . . . . (Saja)

La La Means I Love You
Delfonics; *Billboard Top R&B Hits-1968-C.* . . . . (Rhino)
Lovin' '60s-C . . . . (Priority)
Oldies But Goodies-#12-C. . . . . (Original Sound)
Soul Shots-#5-La-La Means I Love You-C . . . . (Rhino)
Todd Rundgren; *A Wizard A True Star* . . . . (Rhino)
Back To The Bars. . . . . (Rhino)

Labor Of Love
Radney Foster; *Labor Of Love* . . . . (Arista)

Ladder
Joan Osborne; *Lilith Fair-A Celebration Of Women In Music-C* . . . . . . (Arista)
Relish. . . . . (Blue Gorilla/Mercury)

Lady
D'Angelo; *Brown Sugar.* . . . .(EMI)

Lady (You Bring Me Up)
Commodores; *All The Great Love Songs-Commodores* . . . . (Motown)
Commodores-All The Great Hits . . . . (Motown)
Compact Command Performances-Commodores . . . . (Motown)

Lady Down On Love
Alabama; *Alabama-Live.* . . . . (RCA)
Alabama's Greatest Hits-#2 . . . . (RCA)
Closer You Get. . . . . (RCA)

Lady Takes The Cowboy Every Time
Larry Gatlin & The Gatlin Brothers Band; *Houston To Denver* . . . . . (Columbia)
The Gatlin Brothers' Biggest Hits . . . . (Columbia)

Lady's In Love With You
Annie Ross & Gerry Mulligan; *Annie Ross Sings A Song With Gerry*
Mulligan . . . .(EMI)
Shirley Ross; *Thanks For The Memories* . . . . (Decca)

Landslide
Fleetwood Mac; *25 Years-The Chain* . . . .(Warner Bros.)

Fleetwood Mac. . . . . (Reprise)
Fleetwood Mac Live . . . . (Warner Bros.)
The Dance . . . . (Reprise)
Smashing Pumpkins; *Pisces Iscariot.* . . . .(Virgin)

Language Of Love
Dan Fogelberg; *Windows & Walls* . . . .(Full Moon)

Language Of Love
John D. Loudermilk; *45-#47-7938* . . . .(RCA)

Language Of Love
Steve Wariner; *I Got Dreams* . . . . (MCA)

Language Of Love
Orleans; *Grown-Up Children* . . . . (MCA)

Language Of Love
Intrigues; *Intrigues-Golden Classics.* . . . .(Collectables)

Language Of Love
Heart; *Passionworks* . . . . (Epic)

Las Palabras De Amor
Queen; *Hot Space* . . . . (Hollywood)

Last Chance Texaco
Rickie Lee Jones; *Naked Songs Live And Acoustic* . . . . (Reprise)
Rickie Lee Jones . . . . (Warner Bros.)

Last Date
Floyd Cramer; *Last Date/On The Rebound* . . . . (Collectables)

Last Love Letter
Alison Krauss & Union Station; *Every Time You Say Goodbye* . . . . . . (Rounder)

Last Love Song
Hank Williams, Jr.; *Hank Williams, Jr.-14 Greatest Hits* . . . .(Polydor)
Standing In The Shadows . . . .(Polydor)

Last Love Song
Cat Stevens; *Back To Earth.* . . . . (A&M)

Last Night
Az Yet; *Az Yet* . . . . (LaFace)

Last Night
Al Jarreau; *Tomorrow Today* . . . .(GRP/VMG)

Last Night's Letter
K-Ci & JoJo; *Love Always.* . . . . (MCA)

Last Train To Clarksville
Monkees; *Monkees* . . . . (Arista)
Monkees' Greatest Hits . . . . (Rhino)
Monkees-Live-1967 . . . . (Rhino)
Then & Now...The Best Of The Monkees . . . . (Arista)

Lately
Tyrese; *Tyrese.* . . . . (RCA)

Laurie (Strange Things Happen)
Dickey Lee; *Collector's Essentials-#1-1960s-C.* . . . .(Varese Sarabande)

Lay Down Your Arms
Chordettes; *Best Of The Chordettes* . . . . (Rhino)

Lazy Day
Spanky & Our Gang; *Best Of Spanky & Our Gang* . . . . (Rhino)

Leading With Your Heart
Barbra Streisand; *Higher Ground* . . . . (Columbia)

Learning How To Love You
John Hiatt; *Bring The Family* . . . . (A&M)

Learning How To Love You
George Harrison; *33 1/3* . . . . (Dark Horse)

Leopards In Love
Zummos; *Modern Marriage* . . . . (A&M)

Lessons To Be Learned
Barbra Streisand; *Higher Ground* . . . . (Columbia)

Let It Rain
Mark Chesnutt; *Mark Chesnutt's Greatest Hits* . . . . (Decca)

Let Love Come Between Us
James & Bobby Purify; *Bubblegum Classics-#4-C.* . . . .(Varese Vintage)

Let Me Love You Tonight
Pure Prairie League; *Firin' Up* . . . .(Casablanca)
Let Me Love You Tonight & Other Hits . . . .(RCA)

Let Me Make Love To You
O'Jays; *O'Jays-Collector's Item.* . . . .(Philadelphia Int'l)
Survival . . . . (Philadelphia Int'l)

Let Me Make Love To You
Charlie Gonzales; *Charlie Gonzales* . . . .(Collectables)

Let My Love Open The Door
Pete Townshend; *Empty Glass* . . . . (Atco)

Let The Good Times Roll
Barbra Streisand; *Butterfly* . . . . (Columbia)
Betty Everett & Jerry Butler; *Delicious Together* . . . . (Vee-Jay)
Starring Betty Everett . . . .(Tradition)
Bobby Bland & B.B. King; *Together Again Live* . . . . (MCA)
Jerry Lee Lewis; *Golden Rock & Roll* . . . . (Sun)
Louis Jordan; *Best Of Louis Jordan* . . . . (MCA)
Molly Hatchet; *Flirtin' With Disaster* . . . . (Epic)
Nilsson; *Nilsson Schmilsson* . . . . (RCA)
Phoebe Snow; *Phoebe Snow.* . . . . (MCA)
Ray Charles; *Genius Of Ray Charles.* . . . .(Atlantic)
Shirley & Lee; *Billboard Top R&B Hits-1956-C.* . . . . (Rhino)
History Of New Orleans R&B-#1-1950-1958-C . . . . (Rhino)
ST/Stand By Me . . . .(Atlantic)
Super Oldies Of The '50s-#4-C . . . . (Audio Fidelity)

Tony Bennett with B.B. King; *Playin' With My Friends-Bennett Sings The Blues-C* . . . . (Columbia)
Let Your Love Flow
Bellamy Brothers; *Bellamy Brothers' Greatest Hits* . . . . (MCA)
Best Of The Bellamy Brothers . . . . (Curb)
Let's Fall In Love
Diana Krall; *When I Look In Your Eyes* . . . . (GRP)
Frank Sinatra; *The Reprise Collection* . . . . (Reprise)
Louis Armstrong & Oscar Peterson; *Verve Elite Edition Collector's Disc-C* . . . . (Verve)
Tony Bennett; *Tony Bennett Sings A String Of Harold Arlen* . . . . (Columbia Special Prod.)
Let's Go To Vegas
Faith Hill; *It Matters To Me* . . . . (Warner Bros.)
Let's Hear It For The Boy
Deniece Williams; *Billboard Top Hits-1984-C* . . . . (Rhino)
ST/Footloose . . . . (Columbia)
Let's Live For Today
Grass Roots; *At The Hop* . . . . (MCA)
Grass Roots-All-Time Greatest Hits . . . . (MCA)
Let's Live For Today . . . . (MCA Special Prod.)
Summer Of Love-#1-C . . . . (Rhino)
Vintage Music-#10-C . . . . (MCA)
Let's Take The Long Way Home
Cab Calloway; *Cab Calloway-1942-1947* . . . . (Classics)
Rosemary Clooney; *Rosemary Clooney Sings The Music Of Harold Arlen* . . . . (Concord Jazz)
Let's Talk About Love
Celine Dion with The Bee Gees; *Let's Talk About Love-C* . . . . (550 Music)
Let's Think About Living
Bob Luman; *Bob Luman-Classic Country* . . . . (Simitar)
Letter, The
Box Tops; *Billboard Top Rock 'N' Roll Hits-1967-C* . . . . (Rhino)
Box Tops' Greatest Hits . . . . (Rhino)
Cruisin'-1967-C . . . . (Increase)
Oldies But Goodies-#12-C . . . . (Original Sound)
Rockin' '60s-C . . . . (Priority)
Joe Cocker; *Joe Cocker Live* . . . . (Capitol)
Joe Cocker-Classics-#4 . . . . (A&M)
Joe Cocker's Greatest Hits . . . . (A&M)
Mad Dogs & Englishmen . . . . (A&M)
Vernon Green & The Medallions; *Oldies But Goodies-#1-C* . . . (Original Sound)
Vernon Green & The Medallions-Golden Classics . . . . (Collectables)
Lick Summer Love
Hanoi Rocks; *Back To Mystery City* . . . . (Geffen)
Lida Rose/Will I Ever Tell You?
Original Broadway Cast; *The Music Man* . . . . (Angel)
Original Cast; *The Music Man* . . . . (Gold Rush)
Soundtrack; *ST/The Music Man* . . . . (Warner Bros.)
Lie To You For Your Love
Bellamy Brothers; *Howard & David* . . . . (MCA)
Life (Everybody Needs Somebody)
Haddaway; *Haddaway* . . . . (Arista)
Like A River To The Sea
Steve Wariner; *I Am Ready* . . . . (Arista)
Like I Love You
Amy Grant; *Behind The Eyes* . . . . (A&M)
Lili Marlene
Marlene Dietrich; *Best Of Marlene Dietrich* . . . . (Columbia)
Essential Marlene Dietrich . . . . (Capitol)
Live At The Cafe De Paris . . . . (Columbia)
This Is Art Deco-C . . . . (Columbia)
Listen People
Herman's Hermits; *Herman's Hermits-Their Greatest Hits* . . . . (Abkco)
Little Bit In Love
Patty Loveless; *16 Top Country Hits-#4-C* . . . . (MCA)
If My Heart Had Windows . . . . (MCA)
Little Bit In Love
Julie Andrews; *A Little Bit Of Broadway* . . . . (Columbia)
Original Broadway Cast; *Wonderful Town* . . . . (MCA)
Little Bit Of You
Lee Roy Parnell; *We All Get Lucky Sometimes* . . . . (Career)
Little Bitty Pretty One
Huey Lewis and the News; *Four Chords & Several Years Ago* . . . . (Elektra)
Jackson 5; *Jackson 5-16 Greatest Hits* . . . . (Motown)
Jackson 5-Anthology . . . . (Motown)
Lookin' Through The Windows . . . . (Motown)
Motown Legends-Jackson 5 . . . . (Motown)
Top 10 With A Bullet-Motown Male Groups-C . . . . (Motown)
Thurston Harris; *Billboard Top R&B Hits-1957-C* . . . . (Rhino)
Collectables Presents The History Of Rock-#2-C . . . . (Collectables)
Little Blue Man
Betty Johnson; *45-#13146* . . . . (Atlantic)
Little Green Valley
Marty Robbins; *Gunfighter Ballads & Trail Songs* . . . . (Legacy)
Little Left Of Center
Randy Travis; *A Man Ain't Made Of Stone* . . . . (DreamWorks/SKG)
Little Less Talk And A Lot More Action
Toby Keith; *Toby Keith* . . . . (Mercury)
Little More Love
Olivia Newton-John; *Olivia Newton-John's Greatest Hits-#2* . . . . (MCA)
Totally Hot . . . . (MCA)
Little More Love
Janie Fricke; *It Ain't Easy* . . . . (Columbia)
Little Things
Tanya Tucker; *Complicated* . . . . (Capitol)
Little Wing
Derek And The Dominos; *Layla* . . . . (Polydor)
Jimi Hendrix; *Axis: Bold As Love* . . . . (Reprise)
Concerts . . . . (Reprise)
Essential Jimi Hendrix . . . . (Reprise)
Lifelines/Jimi Hendrix Story . . . . (Reprise)
Sting; *...Nothing Like The Sun* . . . . (A&M)
Live For Loving You
Gloria Estefan; *Into The Light* . . . . (Epic)
Live, Laugh, Love
Clay Walker; *Live, Laugh, Love* . . . . (Giant)
Livin' On Love
Alan Jackson; *Who I Am* . . . . (Arista)
Living Inside Your Love
Earl Klugh; *Best Of Earl Klugh* . . . . (Blue Note)
Living Inside Your Love . . . . (EMI)
George Benson; *George Benson-Collection* . . . . (Warner Bros.)
Living Inside Your Love . . . . (Warner Bros.)
Living Loving Maid
Led Zeppelin; *Led Zeppelin II* . . . . (Atlantic)
Living Without Your Love
Dusty Springfield; *Living Without Your Love* . . . . (EMI)
Never Trust A Man In A Rented Tuxedo . . . . (EMI)
Joe Cocker; *Cocker* . . . . (Capitol)
Loddy Lo
Chubby Checker; *Chubby Checker's Dance Party* . . . . (K-Tel)
Chubby Checker's Greatest Hits . . . . (Everest)
London Luck & Love
Daryl Hall & John Oates; *Bigger Than Both Of Us* . . . . (RCA)
London Rain (Nothing Heals Like You Do)
Heather Nova; *Siren* . . . . (Big Cat)
Songs From Dawson's Creek . . . . (Sony Music Soundtrax)
Lonely Days
Bee Gees; *Bee Gees-Gold* . . . . (Polydor)
Here At Last...Bee Gees...Live . . . . (Polydor)
One Night Only . . . . (Polydor)
Lonely Side Of Love
Patty Loveless; *Country's Greatest Hits-#8-Lonely Hearts-C* . . . . (Priority)
Honky Tonk Angel . . . . (MCA)
Patty Loveless' Greatest Hits . . . . (MCA)
Lonely Too Long
Patty Loveless; *Patty Loveless-Classics* . . . . (Epic)
Super Hits Of 1996-C . . . . (Epic)
The Trouble With The Truth . . . . (Epic)
Long Ago And Far Away
Erroll Garner; *Long Ago And Far Away* . . . . (Columbia)
Glenn Miller; *Glenn Miller-A Legendary Performer-#1 & 2* . . . . (Bluebird)
Helen Forrest & Dick Haymes; *American Songbook Series-Jerome Kern* . . . . (Smithsonian Collection)
Jo Stafford; *Capitol Collectors Series-Jo Stafford* . . . . (Capitol)
International Hits . . . . (Corinthian)
Jukebox Saturday Night-Great Vocal Hits-C . . . . (Capitol)
Songs That Got Us Through WWII-C . . . . (Rhino)
ST/Bugsy . . . . (Epic)
Johnny Mathis; *Hollywood Musicals* . . . . (Columbia)
Mantovani; *More Golden Hits* . . . . (London)
Perry Como; *Always In My Heart-Classic Songs Of World War II-#2* . . . . (RCA)
Rosemary Clooney; *Rosemary Clooney Sings The Lyrics Of Ira Gershwin* . . . . (Concord Jazz)
Long Long Long
Beatles; *The Beatles (White Album)* . . . . (Capitol)
Look At That
Paul Simon; *You're The One* . . . . (Warner Bros.)
Look Of Love (Part One)
ABC; *Lexicon Of Love* . . . . (Mercury)
Look What Followed Me Home
David Ball; *Thinkin' Problem* . . . . (Warner Bros.)
Looking For Another Pure Love
Stevie Wonder; *Talking Book* . . . . (Motown)
Lord I Love Mashed Potatoes
Mayf Nutter; *Goin' Skinny Dippin'* . . . . (Crescendo)
Lost In Love
Air Supply; *Air Supply's Greatest Hits* . . . . (Arista)
Air Supply-The Definitive Collection . . . . (Arista)
Lost In Love . . . . (Arista)
Lost In Love: Dream 2-C . . . . (Madacy)
Rock On 1980-C . . . . (Madacy)
Love
Musiq Soulchild; *Aijuswanaseing* . . . . (Def Soul/IDJMG)
Love
Kenny Loggins; *Love Shouldn't Hurt-C* . . . . (Qwest)

Love
Paul Simon; *You're The One*. . . . .(Warner Bros.)
Love & Happiness
Al Green; *I'm Still In Love With You*. . . . . (Right Stuff)
   Tokyo...Live. . . . . (Right Stuff)
Love & Happiness
Living Colour; *Biscuits*. . . . .(Epic)
Love & Happiness
John Mellencamp; *Whenever We Wanted*. . . . . (Mercury)
Love Ain't For Keeping
Who; *Who's next*. . . . .(MCA)
Love Ain't Like That
Faith Hill; *Faith*. . . . .(Warner Bros.)
Love And Luck
Marty Stuart; *Love And Luck*. . . . . (MCA)
Love And Marriage
Dinah Shore; *45-#6266*. . . . . (RCA)
Frank Sinatra; *Capitol Collectors Series-Frank Sinatra*. . . . . (Capitol)
   Sinatra: A Man And His Music. . . . . (Reprise)
   The Capitol Years. . . . . (Capitol)
   The Reprise Collection. (Reprise)
Love And Understanding
Cher; *Love Hurts*. . . . .(Geffen)
Love And Understanding
Blue Rodeo; *Diamond Mine*. . . . . (Atlantic)
Love And Understanding
Kool & The Gang; *Kool & The Gang Spin Their Top Hits*. . . . . (De-Lite)
Love At First Sight
Outlaws; *Playin' To Win*. . . . . (Arista)
Love At First Sight
Styx; *End Of The Century*. . . . . (A&M)
Love At First Sight
Kylie Minogue; *Kylie*. . . . .(Geffen)
Love At First Sight
Mello-Kings; *Mello-Kings' Greatest Hits*. . . . . (Collectables)
Love At The Five & Dime
Kathy Mattea; *Collection Of Hits*. . . . . (Mercury)
   Fourteen Country Favorites-C. . . . . (Mercury)
   Walk The Way The Wind Blows. . . . . (Mercury)
Nanci Griffith; *Last Of The True Believers*. . . . . (Philo)
   One Fair Summer Evening. . . . .(MCA)
Love Bizarre
Sheila E.; *Romance 1600*. . . . . (Paisley Park)
Love Bug Leave My Heart Alone
Martha & The Vandellas; *Compact Command Performances-Martha Reeves
   & The Vandellas*. . . . . (Motown)
   Martha Reeves & The Vandellas-Anthology. . . . . (Motown)
Love (Can Make You Happy)
Mercy; *Super Oldies Of The '60s-#10-C*. . . . .(Audio Fidelity)
   WCBS FM 101 History Of Rock-'60s-#2-C. . . . . (Collectables)
Love Can Build A Bridge
Judds; *Love Can Build A Bridge*. . . . .(MCA)
Love Can Run Faster
Robert Palmer; *Double Fun*. . . . . (Island)
Love Changes Everything
Michael Crawford; *Michael Crawford Performs Andrew Lloyd
   Webber*. . . . .(Atlantic)
Love Colours
Pretenders; *Last Of The Independents*. . . . . (Sire)
Love Come Down
Evelyn "Champagne" King; *Best Of Evelyn "Champagne" King-Love
   Come Down*. . . . . (RCA)
James Ingram; *It's Real*. . . . .(Warner Bros.)
Love Comes To Everyone
George Harrison; *Best Of Dark Horse 1976-1989*. . . . . (Dark Horse)
   George Harrison. . . . . (Dark Horse)
Love Didn't Do It
Linda Davis; *Shoot For The Moon*. . . . . (Arista)
Love Disease
Butterfield Blues Band; *The Butterfield Blues Band/Live*. . . . . (Elektra)
Love Don't Care (Whose Heart It Breaks)
Earl Thomas Conley; *Earl Thomas Conley's Greatest Hits-#2*. . . . . (RCA)
   Essential Earl Thomas Conley. . . . . (RCA)
   Treadin' Water. . . . . (RCA)
Love Don't Live Here Anymore
Madonna; *Like A Virgin*. . . . . (Sire)
   Something To Remember. . . . . (Maverick/Sire)
Rose Royce; *Rose Royce III/Strikes Again!*. . . . .(Whitfield)
   Rose Royce's Greatest Hits. . . . .(Whitfield)
Love Don't Love You
En Vogue; *Funky Divas*. . . . . (East West)
Love Don't Love You Anymore
Luther Vandross; *Your Secret Love*. . . . . (LV/Epic)
Love Eyes
Nancy Sinatra; *Sugar*. . . . . (Sundazed Music)
   The Hit Years. . . . . (Rhino)
Love For Sale
Charlie Parker; *Cole Porter Songbook*. . . . . (Verve)

Dexter Gordon; *Blue Porter*. . . . . (Blue Note)
Dr. John; *In A Sentimental Mood*. . . . . (Warner Bros.)
Ella Fitzgerald; *Cole Porter Songbook*. . . . . (Verve)
Fine Young Cannibals; *Red Hot + Blue-Tribute To Cole Porter-C*. . . (Chrysalis)
Tony Bennett; *I Left My Heart In San Francisco*. . . . . . (Columbia)
Love From Tokyo
Rita Coolidge; *Rita Coolidge-Classics-#5*. . . . . (A&M)
Love Gun
Kiss; *Alive II*. . . . . (Casablanca)
   Double Platinum. . . . . (Mercury)
   Love Gun. . . . . (Casablanca)
   Smashes, Thrashes & Hits. . . . . (Mercury)
Love Has A Mind Of Its Own
Donna Summer; *She Works Hard For The Money*. . . . . (Mercury)
Love Has A Mind Of Its Own
Oak Ridge Boys; *Where The Fast Lane Ends*. . . . . (MCA)
Love Her Madly
Doors; *Best Of The Doors*. (Elektra)
   Doors-Classics. . . . . (Elektra)
   L.A. Woman. . . . . (Elektra)
   Weird Scenes Inside The Gold Mine. . . . . (Elektra)
Love Hurts Love Heals
Daryl Hall & John Oates; *Beauty On A Back Street*. . . . . (RCA)
Love In An Elevator
Aerosmith; *Pump*. . . . . (Geffen)
Love In The First Degree
Alabama; *Alabama-Live*. . . . . (RCA)
   Alabama's Greatest Hits. (RCA)
   Feels So Right. . . . . (RCA)
   Nipper's Greatest Hits Of The '80s-C. . . . . (RCA)
Love In The Hot Afternoon
Gene Watson; *Best Of Gene Watson*. . . . . (Capitol)
   Gene Watson's Greatest Hits. . . . . (Curb)
   Great Records Of The Decade-'70s Hits-Country-C. . . . . . (Curb)
Love In The Ice Age
Pat Benatar; *Tropico*. . . . . (Chrysalis)
Love In The Midnight
Styx; *Cornerstone*. . . . . (A&M)
Love In Vain
Rolling Stones; *Get Yer Ya-Ya's Out!*. . . . .(Abkco)
   Let It Bleed. . . . .(Abkco)
Love In Your Eyes
Eddie Money; *Nothing To Lose*. . . . . (Columbia)
Love Is
Vanessa Williams & Brian McKnight; *ST/Beverly Hills, 90210-College
   Years*. . . . .(Giant)
Love Is A Beautiful Thing
Tina Turner; *Diana, Princess Of Wales-Tribute-C*. . . . . (Columbia)
Love Is A Contact Sport
Whitney Houston; *Whitney*. (Arista)
Love Is A Dangerous Game
Millie Jackson; *Back To The Shit*. . . . . (Jive)
Thelma Houston; *Qualifying Heat*. . . . . (MCA)
Love Is A Drug
Gretchen Peters; *Gretchen Peters*. . . . . (Purple Crayon Prod.)
Love Is A Golden Ring
Frankie Laine; *Frankie Laine-16 Most Requested Songs*. . . . . (Legacy)
Love Is A Good Thing
Sheryl Crow; *Sheryl Crow*. (A&M)
Love Is A Hurtin' Thing
Lou Rawls; *Best Of Lou Rawls*. . . . . (Capitol)
   Lou Rawls-Live (Right Stuff). . . . . (Right Stuff)
   Soul Shots-#5-La-La Means I Love You-C. . . . . . . (Rhino)
Love Is A Many-Splendored Thing
Andy Williams; *Moon River & Other Great Movie Themes*. . . . . . (Columbia)
Four Aces; *Billboard Pop Memories-1955-1959-C*. . . . . . . (Rhino)
   Four Aces' Greatest Hits. . . . . (MCA)
Love Is A Rose
Linda Ronstadt; *Linda Ronstadt's Greatest Hits*. . . . . (Asylum)
   Prisoner In Disguise. . . . . (Asylum)
Love Is A Wonderful Thing
Michael Bolton; *Time, Love & Tenderness*. . . . . (Columbia)
Love Is Alive
Judds; *Collector's Series-The Judds*. . . . . (RCA)
   Judds' Greatest Hits. . . . . (MCA)
   Why Not Me. . . . . (MCA)
Love Is Alive
Joe Cocker; *Night Calls*. . . . . (Capitol)
Love Is Alive
Gary Wright; *Dream Weaver*. . . . . (Warner Bros.)
Love Is All We Need
Mary J. Blige; *Share My World*. . . . . (MCA)
Love Is All You Need For The Future
Nona Gaye; *Love For The Future*. . . . .(Third Stone)
Love Is Alright Tonight
Rick Springfield; *Rick Springfield's Greatest Hits*. . . . . (RCA)
   Working Class Dog. . . . . (RCA)
Love Is Blue
Andre Kostelanetz; *Andre Kostelanetz-16 Most Requested Songs*. . . (Columbia)

Paul Mauriat; *Love Is Blue* .... (Mercury)
Sandpipers; *Softly* .... (A&M)

Love Is Dangerous
Fleetwood Mac; *25 Years-The Chain* .... (Warner Bros.)

Love Is Gonna Come At Last
Badfinger; *Airwaves* .... (Out Of Print)
Best Of Badfinger-#2 .... (Rhino)

Love Is Gonna Find You
Manhattans; *Forever By Your Side* .... (Columbia)

Love Is In Control (Finger On The Trigger)
Donna Summer; *Donna Summer* .... (Geffen)

Love Is Just A Game
Larry Gatlin & The Gatlin Brothers Band; *Larry Gatlin & The Gatlin Brothers' Greatest Hits* .... (Columbia)
Larry Gatlin & The Gatlin Brothers-17 Greatest Hits .... (Columbia)
Live At 8:00. .... (Capitol)

Love Is Like A Baseball Game
Intruders; *Intruders-Super Hits* .... (Philadelphia Int'l)

Love Is Like A Bullet
Shoes; *Best Of The Shoes* .... (Black Vinyl)
Stolen Wishes .... (Black Vinyl)

Love Is Like A Butterfly
Dolly Parton; *Best Of Dolly Parton* .... (RCA)
Collector's Series-Dolly Parton .... (RCA)

Love Is Like A Rock
Donnie Iris; *King Cool.* .... (MCA)

Love Is On The Way
Celine Dion; *Let's Talk About Love-C* .... (550 Music)
Dave Koz; *Dance.* .... (Capitol)

Love Is On The Way
Saigon Kick; *The Lizard* .... (Third Stone)

Love Is So Good When You're Stealing It
Z.Z. Hill; *Lost Soul-#3-C* .... (Epic)

Love Is Strange
Mickey and Sylvia; *Legends Of Guitar-Rock The 50's-#2-C* .... (Rhino)
Nipper's Greatest Hits Of The '50s-#2-C .... (RCA)
Oldies But Goodies-#4-C .... (Original Sound)
ST/Dirty Dancing .... (RCA)

Love Is Strong
Rolling Stones; *Voodoo Lounge* .... (Virgin)

Love Is Stronger Than Justice
Sting; *Ten Summoner's Tales* .... (A&M)

Love Is Stronger Than Pride
Ricochet; *Ricochet.* .... (Columbia)

Love Is The Drug
Grace Jones; *Island Life.* .... (Island)
Warm Leatherette .... (Island)
Roxy Music; *Heart Still Beating* .... (Virgin)
Roxy Music-Atlantic Years 1973-1980 .... (Atco)
Roxy Music's Greatest Hits .... (Atco)
Siren. .... (Atco)
Street Life-20 Great Hits. .... (Reprise)

Love Is The Healing
Roberta Flack & Donny Hathaway; *Blue Lights In The Basement* .... (Atlantic)

Love Is The Message
MFSB; *Philadelphia Classics-C* .... (Philadelphia Int'l)

Love Is The Only Law
Ziggy Marley & The Melody Makers; *One Bright Day* .... (Virgin)

Love Is The Power
Michael Bolton; *This Is The Time-The Christmas Album* .... (Columbia)

Love Is The Right Place
Bryan White; *The Right Place* .... (Asylum)

Love Is The Seventh Wave
Sting; *Dream Of The Blue Turtles* .... (A&M)
Greenpeace/Rainbow Warriors-C .... (Geffen)

Love Letters
Diana Krall; *The Look Of Love* .... (Impulse!)
Elvis Presley; *A Valentine Gift For You.* .... (RCA)
Elvis' Gold Records, Volume 4. .... (RCA)
Love Letters From Elvis .... (RCA)
Ketty Lester; *Sultry Soul Sisters-Wonder Women-#3-C* .... (Rhino)
Peggy Lee; *Best Of Peggy Lee.* .... (MCA)
Ronnie Milsap; *Lost In The Fifties Tonight* .... (RCA)

Love Letters
Smokey Robinson; *Quiet Storm* .... (Motown)

Love Letters
Joe Walsh; *You Bought It-You Name It* .... (Warner Bros.)

Love Lifted Me
Collective Soul; *Hints, Allegations And Things Left Unsaid* ...... (Atlantic)

Love Light In Flight
Stevie Wonder; *ST/Woman In Red* .... (Motown)

Love Machine
Miracles; *12 #1 Hits From The '70s-C* .... (Motown)
20/20-C. .... (Motown)
Billboard Top Hits-1976-C. .... (Rhino)
Motown Story-First 25 Years-C .... (Motown)
Top 10 With A Bullet-Motown Dance Songs-C. .... (Motown)

Love Machine
Country Joe & The Fish; *C.J. Fish.* .... (Vanguard)

Life & Times Of Country Joe & The Fish .... (Vanguard)

Love Machine
Wham! Featuring George Michael; *Fantastic* .... (Columbia)

Love Machine
Paul Butterfield Blues Band; *Keep On Movin'.* .... (Elektra)

Love Machine
Uriah Heep; *Look At Yourself.* .... (Mercury)
Uriah Heep-Live .... (Mercury)

Love Machine
W.A.S.P.; *W.A.S.P.* .... (Capitol)

Love Makes A Woman
Barbara Acklin; *Soul Shots-#2-The ''In'' Crowd-Sweet Soul-C* ...... (Rhino)

Love Makes The World Go Round
Deon Jackson; *Deon Jackson-Golden Classics* .... (Collectables)
Oldies But Goodies-#15-C .... (Original Sound)
Soul Shots-#2-The ''In'' Crowd-Sweet Soul-C .... (Rhino)
Super Oldies Of The '60s-#7-C .... (Audio Fidelity)

Love Makes The World Go Round
Madonna; *True Blue.* .... (Sire)

Love Makes The World Go Round
Jo Basile; *Hit Broadway Musicals* .... (Audio Fidelity)
Original Broadway Cast; *Me & My Girl* .... (MCA)
Original Cast; *Me & My Girl* .... (EMI)

Love Makes Things Happen
Pebbles; *Always* .... (MCA)

Love Me Down
Atlantic Starr; *Atlantic Starr-Classics-#10* .... (A&M)
Secret Lovers: Best Of Atlantic Starr. .... (A&M)
Freddie Jackson; *Do Me Again.* .... (Capitol)

Love Me Just For Me
Special Generation; *Take It To The Floor* .... (Bust It)

Love Me Over Again
Don Williams; *Best Of Don Williams-#3* .... (MCA)
Don Williams' Greatest Hits .... (MCA)
Lovers & Best Friends .... (MCA)

Love Me Tender
Elvis Presley; *Elvis.* .... (RCA)
Elvis Aron Presley. .... (RCA)
Elvis' Golden Records. .... (RCA)
Elvis-A Legendary Performer, Volume 1. .... (RCA)
Worldwide 50 Gold Award Hits, Vol. 1, Parts 1 & 2 ...... (RCA)

Love Me Tomorrow
Chicago; *Chicago 16* .... (Full Moon/Warner Bros.)
Chicago's Greatest Hits-1982-1989 .... (Full Moon)

Love Moves In Mysterious Ways
Michael English; *Hope.* .... (Curb)

Love Of A Lifetime
Larry Gatlin & The Gatlin Brothers Band; *Alive & Well...Living In The Land Of...* .... (Columbia)
Country Love-C. .... (K-Tel)
Live At 8:00. .... (Capitol)
The Gatlin Brothers' Biggest Hits .... (Columbia)

Love Of A Lifetime
Firehouse; *Firehouse.* .... (Epic)

Love Of A Woman
Travis Tritt; *Down The Road I Go* .... (Columbia)

Love Of Your Own, A
Average White Band; *Pickin' Up The Pieces-Best Of The Average White Band (1974-1980)* .... (Rhino)
Smooth Grooves-A Sensual Collection-#1-C .... (Rhino)
Soul Searching .... (Rhino)

Love On Arrival
Dan Seals; *Dan Seals' Greatest Hits* .... (Liberty)
On Arrival. .... (Capitol)

Love On My Mind
Xscape; *Hummin' Comin' At 'Cha.* .... (So So Def/Columbia)

Love On My Mind Tonight
Temptations; *45-#1666* .... (Gordy)

Love On The Telephone
Foreigner; *Head Games* .... (Atlantic)

Love On Top Of Love-Killer Kiss
Grace Jones; *Bulletproof Heart* .... (Capitol)

Love Out Loud
Earl Thomas Conley; *Earl Thomas Conley's Greatest Hits-#2* ...... (RCA)
Heart Of It All .... (RCA)

Love Over Gold
Dire Straits; *Live-Alchemy* .... (Warner Bros.)
Love Over Gold. .... (Warner Bros.)

Love Overboard
Gladys Knight & The Pips; *All Our Love* .... (MCA)
Soul Survivors-Best Of Gladys Knight & The Pips-1973-1988 ...... (Rhino)

Love Parade
Dream Academy; *Dream Academy* .... (Warner Bros.)

Love Potion Number 9
Clovers; *ST/American Graffiti* .... (MCA)
Super Oldies Of The '50s-#7-C .... (Audio Fidelity)
Herb Alpert & The Tijuana Brass; *Herb Alpert & The Tijuana Brass' Greatest Hits* .... (A&M)
Herb Alpert & The Tijuana Brass-Classics-#1 .... (A&M)

Searchers; *History Of British Rock-#3-C* . . . . (Rhino)
Searchers' Greatest Hits . . . . (Rhino)
Love Power
Dionne Warwick & Jeffrey Osborne; *Chicken Soup For The Couples Soul-C* . . . . (Rhino)
Reservations For Two . . . . (Arista)
Love Remains
Collin Raye; *I Think About You* . . . .(Epic)
Love Rescue Me
U2; *Rattle And Hum* . . . . (Island)
Love Rollercoaster
Ohio Players; *Honey* . . . . (Mercury)
Ohio Players-Gold . . . . (Mercury)
The Jam . . . . (Mercury)
Red Hot Chili Peppers; *ST/Beavis & Butt-Head Do America* . . . . (Geffen)
Love Saw It
Karyn White; *Karyn White* . . . .(Warner Bros.)
Love Scene
Joe; *All That I Am* . . . . (Jive)
Love School
Divinyls; *Divinyls* . . . . (Virgin)
Love Shack
Friends Of Distinction; *Friends Of Distinction-Golden Classics* . . (Collectables)
Love Shack
X; *Ain't Love Grand* . . . . (Elektra)
Love Shack
B-52's; *Cosmic Thing* . . . . (Reprise)
Love She Found In Me
Gary Morris; *Gary Morris-Hits* . . . .(Warner Bros.)
Why Lady Why . . . .(Warner Bros.)
Love Shouldn't Hurt
All Star Group; *Love Shouldn't Hurt-C* . . . . (Qwest)
Love Sneakin' Up On You
Bonnie Raitt; *Longing In Their Hearts* . . . . (Capitol)
Love So Beautiful, A
Michael Bolton; *Michael Bolton's Greatest Hits-1985-1995* . . . . (Columbia)
Roy Orbison; *Mystery Girl* . . . . (Virgin)
ST/Indecent Proposal . . . .(MCA)
Love Song
Kenny Rogers; *Kenny Rogers-Twenty Greatest Hits* . . . .(EMI)
Love Will Turn You Around . . . .(EMI)
Love Song
Oak Ridge Boys; *American Made* . . . .(MCA)
Oak Ridge Boys' Greatest Hits 2 . . . .(MCA)
Love Song
Anne Murray; *Anne Murray's Greatest Hits* . . . . (Capitol)
Love Song . . . . (Capitol)
Loggins & Messina; *Full Sail* . . . . (Columbia)
Love Song
Original Cast; *Pippin* . . . . (Motown)
Threepenny Opera . . . . (Polydor)
Love Song
Cure; *Disintegration* . . . . (Elektra)
Mixed Up . . . . (Elektra)
Love Song
Madonna; *Like A Prayer* . . . . (Sire)
Love Song
Damned; *Final Damnation* . . . .(Restless)
Light At The End Of The Tunnel . . . .(MCA)
Love Song
Elton John; *Here And There* . . . .(Rocket)
Tumbleweed Connection . . . . (Polydor)
Love Song
Tesla; *Five Man Acoustical Jam* . . . .(Geffen)
Great Radio Controversy . . . . (Geffen)
Love Song
Lee Greenwood; *Inside Out/You've Got A Good Love Comin'* . . . .(MCA)
Love Song For Iowa
Bonnie Koloc; *With You On My Side* . . . . (Flying Fish)
Love Spreads
Stone Roses; *Second Coming* . . . .(Geffen)
Love Story
Randy Newman; *Randy Newman* . . . .(Warner Archives)
Love Story
Jethro Tull; *20 Years Of Jethro Tull* . . . . (Chrysalis)
Living In The Past . . . .(Chrysalis)
Love Story
Stephen Stills; *Stills* . . . . (Columbia)
Love Story
Tanita Tikaram; *Sweet Keeper* . . . . (Reprise)
Love Takes Time
Ralph Tresvant; *Ralph Tresvant* . . . .(MCA)
Love Takes Time
Orleans; *Forever* . . . . (Infinity)
Love Takes Time
Mariah Carey; *Mariah Carey* . . . . (Columbia)
Love Talks
Ronnie McDowell; *In A New York Minute* . . . .(Epic)

Older Women & Other Greatest Hits . . . . (Epic)
Love That Burns
Fleetwood Mac; *25 Years-The Chain* . . . . (Warner Bros.)
Love That Never Fails
Jim White; *No Such Place* . . . . (Luaka Bop)
Love The World Away
Kenny Rogers; *Kenny Rogers' Greatest Hits* . . . . (EMI)
Kenny Rogers-Twenty Greatest Hits . . . . (EMI)
ST/Urban Cowboy . . . .(Asylum)
Love TKO
Teddy Pendergrass; *TP* . . . . (Philadelphia Int'l)
Love To Love You Baby
Donna Summer; *Donna Summer's Greatest Hits* . . . . (Casablanca)
Live & More . . . . (Casablanca)
Love To Love You Baby . . . . (Casablanca)
On The Radio-Greatest Hits-Volumes I & II . . . . (Casablanca)
No Doubt; *ST/Zoolander* . . . . (Hollywood)
Love Train
Keb' Mo'; *Big Wide Grin* . . . . (Sony Wonder)
O'Jays; *Billboard Top Rock 'N' Roll Hits-1973-C* . . . . (Rhino)
O'Jays' Greatest Hits . . . . (Philadelphia Int'l)
O'Jays-Collector's Item . . . . (Philadelphia Int'l)
Philadelphia Classics-C . . . . (Philadelphia Int'l)
Train Trax-C . . . . (Sony Music Special Prod.)
Love Travels
Kathy Mattea; *Love Travels* . . . . (Mercury)
Love U More
Sunscreem; *O3* . . . . (Columbia)
Love Under New Management
Miki Howard; *Miki Howard* . . . .(Atlantic)
Love Untold
Paul Westerberg; *Eventually* . . . .(Reprise)
Love Walks In
Van Halen; *5150* . . . . (Warner Bros.)
Love Will Bring Her Around
Rob Crosby; *Solid Ground* . . . . (Arista)
Love Will Find A Way
Sam Cooke; *The Man And His Music* . . . . (RCA)
This Is Sam Cooke . . . . (RCA)
Love Will Find A Way
George Howard; *Dancing In The Sun* . . . . (GRP)
Love Will Find A Way
Lionel Richie; *Can't Slow Down* . . . . (Motown)
Love Will Find A Way
Yes; *Big Generator* . . . . (Atco)
Love Will Find A Way
Christina Aguilera; *Christina Aguilera* . . . . (RCA)
Love Will Find A Way
Pablo Cruise; *Worlds Away* . . . . (A&M)
Love Will Lead You Back
Taylor Dayne; *Can't Fight Fate* . . . . (Arista)
Chicken Soup For The Woman's Soul-C . . . . (Rhino)
Love Will Never Do (Without You)
Janet Jackson; *Janet Jackson's Rhythm Nation 1814* . . . . (A&M)
Love Will Save The Day
Whitney Houston; *Whitney* . . . . (Arista)
Whitney Houston's Greatest Hits . . . . (Arista)
Love Will Turn You Around
Kenny Rogers; *Kenny Rogers-Twenty Greatest Hits* . . . . (EMI)
Love Will Turn You Around . . . . (EMI)
Love Without End, Amen
George Strait; *Livin' It Up* . . . . (MCA)
Ten Strait Hits . . . . (MCA)
Love Without Mercy
Lee Roy Parnell; *Love Without Mercy* . . . . (Arista)
Mike Reid; *Twilight Town* . . . . (Columbia)
Love Won't Let Me Wait
Luther Vandross; *Any Love* . . . . (Epic)
Best Of Luther Vandross...The Best Of Love . . . . (Epic)
Major Harris; *Atlantic Rhythm & Blues 1947-1974-#6 (1966-1969)-C* . . . .(Atlantic)
Major Harris-Live . . . .(WMOT)
My Way . . . .(Atlantic)
Love You Down
INOJ; *So So Def Bass All-Stars-#2-C* . . . . (So So Def/Columbia)
Total Dance Explosion-C . . . . (Columbia)
Love You Period
Dan Baird; *Love Songs For The Hearing Impaired* . . . .(Def American)
Love You Til Tuesday
David Bowie; *David Bowie-London Collector-Starting Point* . . . .(London)
Love You Till Tuesday . . . .(London)
Love You To
Beatles; *Revolver* . . . . (Capitol)
Love, Love, Love
Clovers; *Clovers-Dance Party* . . . . (Collectables)
Love...Thy Will Be Done
Martika; *Martika's Kitchen* . . . . (Columbia)

Love-itis
J. Geils Band; *Blow Your Face Out* . . . . (Rhino)
Hotline . . . . (Atlantic)
Loveless Motel
Eddie Moore; *Moore Country With* . . . . (Country Int'l)
Lover
Ella Fitzgerald; *Rodgers & Hart Songbook* . . . . (Verve)
John Coltrane; *Last Trane* . . . . (Prestige)
Tony Bennett; *Rodgers & Hart Songbook* . . . .(DRG)
Lover Boy
Billy Ocean; *Billy Ocean's Greatest Hits* . . . .(Jive)
Suddenly . . . .(Jive)
Lover Boy
Supertramp; *Even In The Quietest Moments* . . . . (A&M)
Lover Man (Oh, Where Can You Be?)
Barbra Streisand; *Simply Streisand* . . . .(Columbia)
Billie Holiday; *Fine & Mellow* . . . .(Collectables)
History Of The Real Billie Holiday . . . . (Verve)
Blossom Dearie; *Blossom Dearie* . . . .(Verve)
Lena Horne; *Goes Latin & Sings Your Requests* . . . .(DRG)
Sarah Vaughan; *Compact Jazz-Sarah Vaughan* . . . . (Verve)
Jazz 'Round Midnight-Sarah Vaughan . . . . (Verve)
Sonny Stitt; *Soul Classics* . . . . (Prestige)
Lover Please
Billy Swan; *Best Of Billy Swan* . . . . (Legacy)
Clyde McPhatter; *Baby Boomer Classics-Heart & Soul*
Fifties-C . . . .(JCI Assoc. Labels)
Lovergirl
Teena Marie; *Club Epic-#1-C* . . . . (Legacy)
Starchild . . . . (Epic)
Lovers After All
Melissa Manchester & Peabo Bryson; *Chicken Soup For The Couples
Soul-C* . . . . (Rhino)
Lovers In The Night
Toto; *Toto IV* . . . . (Columbia)
Lover's Prayer
Randy Newman; *Randy Newman/Live* . . . . (Warner Archives)
Love's Been A Little Bit Hard On Me
Juice Newton; *Juice Newton-Greatest Hits & More* . . . . (Capitol)
Juice Newton's Greatest Hits . . . . (Gold Rush)
Quiet Lies . . . . (Capitol)
Love's Found You & Me
Ed Bruce; *Ed Bruce's Greatest Hits* . . . . (MCA)
Love's Gonna Fall Here Tonight
Razzy Bailey; *Anthology* . . . . (Renaissance)
Love's Gonna Get'cha
Boogie Down Productions; *Edutainment (Education + Entertainment)* . . . .(Jive)
Yo! MTV Raps-#2-C . . . . (Def Jam)
Love's Gonna Live Here
Buck Owens; *Billboard Top Country Hits-1963-C* . . . . (Rhino)
Buck Owens' All-Time Greatest Hits-#2 . . . .(Curb)
Buck Owens & The Buckaroos; *Buck Owens & The Buckaroos-Live At
Carnegie Hall* . . . . (Country Music Foundation)
Love's Got A Hold On You
Alan Jackson; *Don't Rock The Jukebox* . . . . (Arista)
Love's In Need Of Love Today
Stevie Wonder featuring Take 6; *America: A Tribute To
Heroes-C* . . . . (Interscope)
Love's Made A Fool Of You
Bobby Fuller Four; *Best Of The Bobby Fuller Four* . . . . (Rhino)
Buddy Holly; *Rock & Roll Collection* . . . . (MCA)
Greg Kihn; *Greg Kihn Again* . . . . (Beserkley)
Loves Me Like A Rock
Oak Ridge Boys; *Best Of The Oak Ridge Boys* . . . .(Columbia)
Paul Simon; *Greatest Hits, Etc.* . . . .(Columbia)
Negotiations And Love Songs, 1971-1986 . . . . (Warner Bros.)
Paul Simon In Concert/Live Rhymin' . . . .(Columbia)
There Goes Rhymin' Simon . . . . (Columbia)
Love's The Only House
Martina McBride; *Emotion* . . . .(RCA)
Lovetown
Peter Gabriel; *ST/Philadelphia* . . . . (Epic/Sony Music Soundtrax)
Lovin' All Night
Rodney Crowell; *Greatest Country Hits Of The '90s-#2-C* . . . .(Columbia)
Life Is Messy . . . .(Columbia)
Lovin' What Your Lovin' Does To Me
Conway Twitty & Loretta Lynn; *Conway Twittty-20 Greatest Hits* . . . . . (MCA)
Lovin' You
Minnie Riperton; *Capitol Gold-Best Of Minnie Riperton* . . . .(Capitol)
Deep Soul-#1-C . . . . (Priority)
Perfect Angel . . . . (Epic)
Lovin' You
Dolly Parton; *Here You Come Again* . . . . (Dunhill Compact Classics)
Lovin' Spoonful; *Lovin' Spoonful-Anthology* . . . . (Rhino)
Lovin' You Is Killing Me
Alabama; *Mountain Music* . . . .(RCA)
Lovin', Touchin', Squeezin'
Journey; *Evolution* . . . .(Columbia)

Journey-Captured . . . .(Columbia)
Journey's Greatest Hits . . . .(Columbia)
Loving Arms
Dixie Chicks; *Wide Open Spaces* . . . .(Monument)
Loving Blind
Clint Black; *Put Yourself In My Shoes* . . . . (RCA)
Loving The Alien
David Bowie; *The Singles-1969-1993* . . . . (Rykodisc)
Loving You
Elvis Presley; *Elvis' Golden Records* . . . . (RCA)
Elvis Presley Sings Leiber & Stoller . . . . (RCA)
Elvis Presley-Pure Gold . . . . (RCA)
Essential Elvis-The First Movies . . . . (RCA)
ST/Loving You . . . . (RCA)
Loving You
Bobby Darin; *Splish Splash-Best Of Bobby Darin-#1* . . . . (Atlantic)
Loving You
Kenny G; *Kenny G's Greatest Hits* . . . . (Arista)
Loving You
Jonathan Butler; *Jonathan Butler* . . . . (Jive)
Loving You
Mavericks; *Music For All Occasions* . . . . (MCA)
Loving You
Alicia Keys; *Songs In A Minor* . . . .(J)
Loving You Sunday Morning
Scorpions; *Lovedrive* . . . .(Mercury)
World Wide Live . . . .(Mercury)
Loving You With My Eyes
Starland Vocal Band; *4 x 4* . . . . (Windsong)
Luckenbach Texas (Back To The Basics Of Love)
Waylon Jennings; *Ol' Waylon* . . . . (RCA)
Stars Are Out In Texas-C . . . . (RCA)
Waylon Jennings' Greatest Hits . . . . (RCA)
Lucky In Love
Sarah Vaughan; *Complete Sarah Vaughan On Mercury-#2* . . . .(Mercury)
Complete Sarah Vaughan On Mercury-#3 . . . .(Mercury)
Lucky In Love
Mick Jagger; *She's The Boss* . . . .(Columbia)
Lucky Love
Ace Of Base; *Bridge.* . . . .(Arista)
Lullaby Of Birdland
Ella Fitzgerald; *Best Of Ella Fitzgerald-#2* . . . . (MCA)
Ella Fitzgerald With Billie Holiday. . . . . (MCA)
Four Freshmen; *Greatest Hits-Four Freshman* . . . .(Curb)
Mel Torme; *Songs Of New York.* . . . . (Rhino)
Sarah Vaughan; *Sarah Vaughan-Golden Hits* . . . .(Mercury)
Tito Puente & His Latin Ensemble; *Mambo Diablo* . . . .(Concord Jazz)
Mad Love
Linda Ronstadt; *Different Drum.* . . . . (Capitol)
Made For Lovin' You
Doug Stone; *From The Heart.* . . . . (Epic)
Made For Loving You
Doug Stone; *From The Heart.* . . . . (Epic)
Magazine Lover
Pieces; *Pieces.* . . . . (United Artists)
Make Love Like A Man
Def Leppard; *Adrenalize* . . . .(Mercury)
Make Love To Me
Anne Murray; *Croonin'.* . . . .(SBK)
Make Love To The Music
Maria Muldaur; *Southern Winds* . . . . (Warner Bros.)
Make Me Lose Control
Eric Carmen; *Best Of Eric Carmen* . . . .(Arista)
Dirty Dancing Live In Concert-C . . . . (RCA)
Maker Said Take Her
Alabama; *In Pictures* . . . . (RCA)
Makin' Love
Kiss; *Alive II.* . . . . (Casablanca)
Double Platinum . . . .(Mercury)
Rock & Roll Over . . . . (Casablanca)
Makin' Love
Floyd Robinson; *Nipper's Greatest Hits Of The '50s-#1-C* . . . . (RCA)
Makin' Love
Climax Blues Band; *Shine On* . . . . (Sire)
Making Love
Roberta Flack; *I'm The One* . . . . (Atlantic)
Making Love In A Subaru
Damaskas; *Dr. Demento's Dementia Royale-C* . . . .(Rhino)
Making Love Out Of Nothing At All
Air Supply; *Air Supply's Greatest Hits* . . . .(Arista)
Making Memories
Frankie Laine; *Very Best Of The ABC Years* . . . . (Taragon)
Mama
Spice Girls; *Diana, Princess Of Wales-Tribute-C* . . . .(Columbia)
Spice . . . . (Virgin)
Mama Can't Buy You Love
Elton John; *Complete Thom Bell Sessions* . . . . (MCA)
Elton John's Greatest Hits-1976-1986 . . . . (MCA)

Man Of Me
Gary Allan; *Alright Guy* . . . . (MCA)
Man Of My Word
Collin Raye; *Extremes* . . . . (Epic)
Many A New Day
Original Cast; *Oklahoma!* . . . . (MCA)
March Winds And April Showers
Wingy Manone; *Wingy Manone Collection-#3-1934-1935* . . . . (Collector's Classics)
Maria
Original Cast; *ST/West Side Story* . . . . (Sony Broadway)
Maria
Johnny Mathis; *Johnny Mathis' All-Time Greatest Hits* . . . . (Columbia)
Maria
Marvin Gaye; *Romantically Yours* . . . . (Columbia)
Marrying For Love
Original Cast/Dinah Shore; *Call Me Madam* . . . . (RCA)
Martian Love Song
Hypnolovewheel; *Angel Food* . . . . (Alias)
Marvin I Love You
Marvin The Paranoid Android; *Dr. Demento Presents The Greatest Novelty Records-#5-1980s-C* . . . . (Rhino)
Mary In The Morning
Al Martino; *Al Martino's Greatest Hits* . . . . (EMI Special Markets)
May This Be Love
Emmylou Harris; *Wrecking Ball* . . . . (Asylum)
Jimi Hendrix; *Are You Experienced?* . . . . (Reprise)
Me & My Old Lady
Offspring; *Ixnay On The Hombre* . . . . (Columbia)
Me And You
Kenny Chesney; *All I Need To Know* . . . . (BNA)
Me And You . . . . (BNA)
Me Too
Toby Keith; *Blue Moon* . . . . (Polydor Country)
Toby Keith's Greatest Hits, Volume One . . . . (Mercury)
Meaning Of Love, The
Michael McDonald; *Blue Obsession* . . . . (Ramp)
Meet In The Middle
Diamond Rio; *Diamond Rio* . . . . (Arista)
Diamond Rio's Greatest Hits . . . . (Arista)
Meet Me In Montana
Dan Seals & Marie Osmond; *Best Of Dan Seals* . . . . (Capitol)
Won't Be Blue Anymore . . . .(EMI)
Marie Osmond & Dan Seals; *Country Duets Two By Two-C* . . . . (Capitol)
There's No Stopping Your Heart . . . . (Curb)
Mellow Yellow
Donovan; *Donovan's Greatest Hits* . . . . (Epic)
Seems Like Yesterday-#5-Mid '60s-C . . . . (K-Tel)
Memories Are Made Of This
Dean Martin; *Billboard Pop Memories-1955-1959-C* . . . . (Rhino)
Dean Martin-Love Songs . . . .(Ranwood)
Dean Martin's All Time Greatest Hits . . . . (Curb)
Mending Fences
Restless Heart; *Big Iron Horses* . . . . (RCA)
Message Of Love
Pretenders; *Extended Play* . . . . (Sire)
Pretenders II . . . . (Sire)
Pretenders-The Singles . . . . (Sire)
Message Of Love
Jimi Hendrix; *Band Of Gypsys* . . . . (Capitol)
Midnight Lover
Leon Russell; *Americana* . . . . (Paradise)
Mind Games
John Lennon; *Mind Games* . . . . (Capitol)
John Lennon/Plastic Ono Band; *Shaved Fish* . . . . (Capitol)
Minimum Love
Mac McAnally; *Nothin' But The Truth* . . . .(Geffen)
Miss You
Mick Jagger & Keith Richards; *The Concert For New York City-C* . . (Columbia)
Rolling Stones; *Rewind (1971-1984)* . . . .(Rolling Stones)
Some Girls . . . . (Virgin)
Flashpoint . . . . (Virgin)
Missing My Baby
Selena; *Dreaming Of You* . . . . (EMI Latin)
Modern Love
David Bowie; *Let's Dance* . . . .(EMI)
The Singles-1969-1993 . . . .(Rykodisc)
Monday Love
Tara Kemp; *Tara Kemp* . . . .(Giant)
Money Burns A Hole In My Pocket
Dean Martin; *Capitol Collectors Series-Dean Martin* . . . . (Capitol)
Money In The Bank
John Anderson; *On Solid Ground* . . . . (BNA)
Moon Over Georgia
Shenandoah; *Extra Mile* . . . . (Columbia)
Shenandoah's Greatest Hits . . . . (Columbia)
Moonlight Bay
Beatles; *The Beatles-Anthology-#1* . . . . (Capitol)

Bing Crosby; *The Radio Years-#4* . . . .(Crescendo)
The Radio Years: 20 Songs . . . .(Crescendo)
Drifters; *Clyde McPhatter & The Drifters-Rockin' & Driftin'* . . . . (Collectables)
Glenn Miller; *Big Bands-#1-C* . . . . (Universal)
Moonlight Mile
Rolling Stones; *Sticky Fingers* . . . . (Virgin)
More I See You
Boston Pops Orchestra/Arthur Fiedler; *Music For Every Mood-Yesterday* . . . . (RCA)
Chet Baker; *Chet Baker Sings It Could Happen To You* . . . . (Original Jazz Classics)
Chris Montez; *Bachelor Pad Pleasures-C* . . . . (Chronicles)
Dick Haymes; *Best Of Dick Haymes* . . . . (Curb)
Nat ''King'' Cole; *Very Thought Of You* . . . . (Capitol)
More Love
Doug Stone; *More Love* . . . . (Epic)
More Than You Know
Barbra Streisand; *ST/Funny Lady* . . . . (Arista)
More Than You'll Ever Know
Barbra Streisand; *Simply Streisand* . . . . (Columbia)
Billie Holiday; *Quintessential-#7-1938-1939* . . . . (Legacy)
Dinah Washington; *Jazz 'Round Midnight-Dinah Washington* . . . . (Verve)
Frank Sinatra; *Everything Happens To Me* . . . . (Reprise)
Johnny Mathis; *Heavenly* . . . . (Columbia)
Morning Train (Nine To Five)
Sheena Easton; *Sheena Easton* . . . . (EMI)
Most Beautiful Girl In The World
Frank Sinatra; *Strangers In The Night* . . . . (Reprise)
Tony Bennett; *Rodgers & Hart Songbook* . . . . (DRG)
Tony Bennett Sings More Great Rodgers & Hart . . . . (Improv)
Motel Lover
Marvin Sease; *Real Deal* . . . .(London)
Mr. Lee
Bobbettes; *Billboard Top R&B Hits-1957-C* . . . . (Rhino)
ST/Stand By Me . . . . (Atlantic)
Pointer Sisters; *Rock Rhythm & Blues-C* . . . . (Warner Bros.)
Murder Of Love
Propaganda; *Secret Wish* . . . . (Island)
Murdered By Love
Gary Stewart; *Brand New* . . . .(Hightone)
Muscle Of Love
Alice Cooper; *Alice Cooper's Greatest Hits* . . . . (Warner Bros.)
Muscle Of Love . . . . (Warner Bros.)
Music To Watch Girls By
Andy Williams; *Andy Williams' Greatest Hits-#2* . . . . (Columbia)
Music! Music! Music!
Teresa Brewer; *Best Of Teresa Brewer* . . . .(MCA Jazz)
Muskrat Love
America; *America Live* . . . . (Warner Bros.)
Hat Trick . . . . (Warner Bros.)
History-Greatest Hits . . . . (Warner Bros.)
Captain & Tennille; *Captain & Tennille's Greatest Hits* . . . . (A&M)
My Autumn Love
Frank Chacksfield; *Unmistakable* . . . .(Rim)
My Baby Just Cares For Me
Frank Sinatra; *Strangers In The Night* . . . . (Reprise)
My Baby Must Be A Magician
Marvelettes; *Marvelettes-The Ultimate Collection* . . . . (Motown)
My Baby You
Marc Anthony; *Marc Anthony* . . . . (Columbia)
My Beloved
Pamela Rose; *Morpheus* . . . . (Grace)
My Best Friend
Tim McGraw; *A Place In The Sun* . . . . (Curb)
Tim McGraw's Greatest Hits . . . . (Curb)
My Bonnie Lies Over The Ocean
Beatles With Tony Sheridan; *History Of British Rock-#5-C* . . . . (Rhino)
The Beatles featuring Tony Sheridan-In The Beginning (Circa 1960) . . . .(Polydor)
Ed McCurdy; *Best Of Ed McCurdy* . . . . (Tradition)
Mitch Miller; *Favorite Irish Sing-Alongs* . . . . (Legacy)
My Boyfriend's Back
Angels; *Billboard Top Rock 'N' Roll Hits-1963-C* . . . . (Rhino)
Girl Groups-Story Of A Sound-C . . . . (Rhino)
My Boyfriend's Back . . . . (Collectables)
Oldies But Goodies-#11-C . . . . (Original Sound)
ST/The Wanderers . . . . (Warner Bros.)
Wonder Women-#2-History Of Girl Group-C . . . . (Rhino)
My Cup Runneth Over
Ed Ames; *My Cup Runneth Over* . . . . (RCA)
Nipper's Greatest Hits Of The '60s-#2-C . . . . (RCA)
George Jones; *Homecoming In Heaven* . . . . (Razor & Tie)
Jim Nabors; *Jim Nabors-16 Most Requested Songs* . . . . (Legacy)
Original Broadway Cast; *I Do! I Do!* . . . . (RCA Victor)
My Darling Child
Sinead O'Connor; *Universal Mother* . . . . (Ensign)
My Defenses Are Down
Ethel Merman/Bruce Yarnell/Original Cast; *Annie Get Your Gun* . . . . (RCA Victor)

Original Broadway Cast; *Annie Get Your Gun* .... (Angel)
My Funny Valentine
Anita Baker; *Rhythm Of Love* .... (Atlantic)
Anita O'Day; *Anita O'Day* .... (Glendale)
Anita O'Day Sings The Winners .... (Verve)
Live At The City .... (Emily)
Carly Simon; *My Romance* .... (Arista)
Ella Fitzgerald; *Rodgers & Hart Songbook* .... (Verve)
Mel Torme; *Easy To Remember* .... (Glendale)
Miles Davis; *Columbia Years-1955-1985* .... (Columbia)
Cookin' With The Miles Davis Quintet .... (Prestige)
Miles Davis' Greatest Hits .... (Columbia)
My Funny Valentine .... (Columbia)
Original Cast/Mary Martin; *Babes In Arms* .... (Sony Music Special Prod.)
Stan Getz; *Artistry Of-Stan Getz-Best Of Verve Years-#1* .... (Verve)
My Girl
Mamas & The Papas; *Best Of The Mamas & The Papas* .... (MCA)
Otis Redding; *Best Of Otis Redding* .... (Atco)
Rolling Stones; *Flowers* .... (Abkco)
Temptations; *All The Million-Sellers* .... (Motown)
ST/Big Chill .... (Motown)
Temptations' Greatest Hits-#1 .... (Motown)
Temptations-25th Anniversary .... (Motown)
Temptations-Anthology-The Best Of The Temptations .... (Motown)
My Girl
Aerosmith; *Pump* .... (Geffen)
My Heart Is So Full Of You
Original Broadway Cast; *The Most Happy Fella* .... (Sony Music Classical)
My Lips Remember Your Kisses
Nat "King" Cole; *1941-1943* .... (Classics)
My Louisiana Love
Bill Monroe & Mel Tillis; *Bill Monroe & Friends* .... (MCA)
My Love Is In America
Chieftains; *10--Cotton-Eyed Joe* .... (Shanachie)
My Lover's Prayer
Otis Redding; *The Otis Redding Story* .... (Atlantic)
Very Best Of Otis Redding .... (Rhino)
My Man
Regina Belle; *Passion* .... (Columbia)
My Man
Jeannie C. Riley; *Jeannie C. Riley's Greatest Hits* .... (Plantation)
My Maria
B.W. Stevenson; *Nipper's Greatest Hits Of The '70s-C* .... (RCA)
Super Hits Of The '70s-Have A Nice Day-#11-C .... (Rhino)
Brooks & Dunn; *Borderline* .... (Arista)
My Melody Of Love
Frank Sinatra & Ray Anthony; *Capitol Collectors Series-Frank Sinatra* .... (Capitol)
My Old Man
Joni Mitchell; *Blue* .... (Reprise)
My Only Love
Statler Brothers; *Atlanta Blue* .... (Mercury)
Statler Brothers' Greatest Hits .... (Mercury)
My Silent Love
Bing Crosby; *Where The Blue Of The Night Meets The Gold Of The Day* .... (Biograph)
Peggy Lee; *Mink Jazz* .... (Blue Note)
My Song
Jerry Cantrell; *Boggy Depot* .... (Columbia)
My Special Angel
Bobby Helms; *American Graffiti-#3-C* .... (MCA)
Blue Ribbon Country-#3-C .... (Accord)
Oldies But Goodies-#14-C .... (Original Sound)
Pop A Billy .... (MCA)
Vintage Music-#2-C .... (MCA)
Vogues; *Vogues' Greatest Hits* .... (Rhino)
Vogues' Greatest Hits/Finest Performances .... (Sun)
My Strongest Weakness
Wynonna; *Wynonna* .... (MCA)
My Summer Love
Malta; *High Pressure* .... (JVC Musical Industries)
Naughty Girls Need Love Too
Samantha Fox; *Samantha Fox* .... (Jive)
Near You
Francis Craig & His Orchestra; *Cigar Classics-#1-The Standards-C* .... (Hip-O)
George Jones & Tammy Wynette; *George Jones & Tammy Wynette-16 Biggest Hits* .... (Epic/Legacy)
Need A Little Taste Of Love
Doobie Brothers; *Cycles* .... (Warner Bros.)
Need Your Love
Cheap Trick; *Cheap Trick At Budokan* .... (Epic)
Dream Police .... (Epic)
Need Your Loving Tonight
Queen; *The Game* .... (Hollywood)
Neon Rainbow
Box Tops; *Box Tops' Greatest Hits* .... (Rhino)
Never Been In Love Before
Chicago; *Chicago VIII* .... (Chicago)
Never Been In Love Before
Marva Hicks; *Marva Hicks* .... (Polydor)
Never Been So Loved (In All My Life)
Charley Pride; *14 #1 Country Hits-C* .... (RCA)
Charley Pride's Greatest Hits .... (RCA)
Never Ending Song Of Love
Conway Twitty & Loretta Lynn; *Lead Me On* .... (MCA)
Delaney & Bonnie; *Best Of Delaney & Bonnie* .... (Rhino)
Super Hits Of The '70s-Have A Nice Day-#16-C .... (Rhino)
Never Felt This Way (interlude)
Alicia Keys; *Songs In A Minor* .... (J)
Never On Sunday
Andy Williams; *Moon River & Other Great Movie Themes* .... (Columbia)
Boston Pops Orchestra/Arthur Fiedler; *Greatest Hits Of The '60s* .... (RCA)
Motion Picture Classics-#1 .... (RCA Victor)
Boston Pops Orchestra/John Williams; *Digital Jukebox* .... (Philips)
Chordettes; *Chordettes Greatest Hits* .... (Everest)
Never Too Busy
Kenny Lattimore; *Kenny Lattimore* .... (Columbia)
Nevertheless
Frank Sinatra; *Best Of The Columbia Years-1943-1952* .... (Columbia)
McGuire Sisters; *McGuire Sisters-Anthology* .... (MCA)
New York, New York
Ryan Adams; *Gold* .... (Lost Highway/IDJMG)
Next Plane To London
Rose Garden; *Only Love-1965-1969-C* .... (JCI Assoc. Labels)
Nice Work If You Can Get It
Billie Holiday; *Compact Jazz-Billie Holiday* .... (Verve)
Carmen McRae; *Greatest Of Carmen McRae* .... (MCA)
Ella Fitzgerald; *George & Ira Gershwin Songbook* .... (Verve)
Frank Sinatra; *My Kind Of Broadway* .... (Reprise)
Original Cast; *My One And Only* .... (Atlantic)
Sting; *Glory Of Gershwin Featuring Larry Adler-C* .... (Mercury)
Nickels & Dimes & Love
John Michael Montgomery; *Life's A Dance* .... (Atlantic)
Vern Gosdin; *Nickels & Dimes & Love* .... (Columbia)
Night And Day
Bette Midler; *Some People's Lives* .... (Atlantic)
Billie Holiday; *Legacy Box-1933-1958* .... (Columbia)
Ella Fitzgerald; *Cole Porter Songbook* .... (Verve)
Frank Sinatra; *Nipper's Greatest Hits Of The '40s-#1-C* .... (RCA)
Sinatra & Strings .... (Reprise)
Sinatra Reprise-The Very Good Years .... (Reprise)
Sinatra: A Man And His Music .... (Reprise)
The Capitol Years .... (Capitol)
The Reprise Collection .... (Reprise)
Fred Astaire; *Cheek To Cheek* .... (Pro-Arte)
Steppin' Out-Astaire Sings .... (Verve)
Tony Bennett; *Perfectly Frank* .... (Columbia)
U2; *Red Hot + Blue-Tribute To Cole Porter-C* .... (Chrysalis)
Night Fever
Bee Gees; *Bee Gees' Greatest* .... (Polydor)
ST/Saturday Night Fever .... (Polydor)
Nine Lives
Aerosmith; *Nine Lives* .... (Columbia)
No Doubt About It
Neal McCoy; *Wink* .... (Atlantic)
No Future In The Past
Vince Gill; *I Still Believe In You* .... (MCA)
No Help Wanted
Carlisles; *Heroes Of Country Music-#3-Legends Of Nashville-C* .... (Rhino)
No Not Much
Four Lads; *Four Lads-16 Most Requested Songs* .... (Legacy)
No One Needs To Know
Shania Twain; *The Woman In Me* .... (Mercury)
No Tell Lover
Chicago; *Chicago's Greatest Hits-#2 (1974-81)* .... (Chicago)
Group Portrait .... (Chicago)
Hot Streets .... (Columbia)
If You Leave Me Now .... (Chicago)
No, Not Much
Four Lads; *Four Lads-16 Most Requested Songs* .... (Legacy)
Vogues; *Vogues' Greatest Hits* .... (Rhino)
Nobody Does It Better
Carly Simon; *13 Original James Bond Themes-C* .... (EMI)
Carly Simon-Greatest Hits Live .... (Arista)
ST/The Spy Who Loved Me .... (EMI)
Nobody Else
Tyrese; *Tyrese* .... (RCA)
North To Alaska
Dwight Yoakam; *Under The Covers* .... (Reprise)
Johnny Horton; *American Originals-Johnny Horton* .... (Columbia)
Billboard Top Country Hits-1961-C .... (Rhino)
Johnny Horton's Greatest Hits .... (Columbia)
Super Hits Of The '60s-C .... (Epic)
Norwegian Wood (This Bird Has Flown)
Beatles; *Beatles-Box Set* .... (Capitol)
Beatles-Love Songs .... (Capitol)
Rubber Soul .... (Capitol)

The Beatles/1962-1966 . . . . (Capitol)

Not Enough Hours In The Night
Doug Supernaw; *You Still Got Me* . . . . (Giant)

Not Enough Love In The World
Don Henley; *Building The Perfect Beast* . . . .(Geffen)

Nothin' My Love Can't Fix
Joey Lawrence; *Joey Lawrence* . . . . (Impact)

Nothing In Common But Love
Twister Alley; *Twister Alley* . . . . (Mercury)

Nothing Left Behind Us
Richard Marx; *Paid Vacation* . . . . (Capitol)

Nothing Really Matters
Madonna; *Ray Of Light* . . . .(Maverick)

Now And Forever
Richard Marx; *Paid Vacation* . . . . (Capitol)

Now That I Know Love
Kenny Loggins; *The Unimaginable Life* . . . . (Columbia)

Now That We Found Love
Heavy D & The Boyz; *Peaceful Journey* . . . .(Uptown)
Third World; *Journey To Addis* . . . . (Island)
The Island Story-1962-1987-25th Anniversary-C . . . . (Island)

Nuttin' But Love
Heavy D & The Boyz; *Nuttin' But Love* . . . . (Uptown)

O What A Thrill
Mavericks; *What A Crying Shame* . . . .(MCA)

Object Of My Affection
Boswell Sisters; *That's How Rhythm Was Born* . . . . (Legacy)
Jimmie Grier & His Orchestra; *More #1 Hits From The
1930s-C* . . . .(Sony Music Special Prod.)
Pinky Tomlin; *Pop Music: The Early Years-1890-1950-C* . . . . (Sony)

October-Love Song
Chris & Cosey; *Funky Alternatives-18 Techno Remixes-C* . . . .(Roir)

Of Thee I Sing
Sarah Vaughan; *Sarah Vaughan Sings George Gershwin* . . . . (Verve)

Off The Hook
Jody Watley; *12'' Maxi Single* . . . . (Atlantic)

Oh Daddy
Fleetwood Mac; *Rumours*. . . . .(Warner Bros.)
Tallulah; *Legacy-A Tribute To Fleetwood Mac's Rumours-C* . . . . (Lava)

Oh How The Years Go By
Vanessa Williams; *NBA At 50-A Musical Celebration-C* . . . . (Mercury)

Oh Johnny, Oh Johnny, Oh!
Andrews Sisters; *Andrews Sisters' All-Time Greatest Hits* . . . . (Decca)
Boogie Woogie Bugle Boy . . . . (Pro-Arte)

Oh! My Papa
Eddie Fisher; *Eddie Fisher's All-Time Greatest Hits-#1* . . . . (RCA)
Hebrew National Kosher Classics-C . . . . (RCA)
Nipper's Greatest Hits Of The '50s-#2-C . . . . (RCA)

Oh, Boy!
Buddy Holly; *Buddy Holly's Greatest Hits*. . . . .(MCA)
Legend-From The Original Master Tapes . . . . (MCA)

Oh, What A Night
Dells; *Billboard Top R&B Hits-1965-1969-C* . . . . (Rhino)
Collectables Presents The History Of Rock-#9-C . . . . (Collectables)
Cruisin'-1956-C . . . .(Increase)
Oh, What A Night . . . .(Vee-Jay)
Oldies But Goodies-#3-C . . . . (Original Sound)

Old Brown Shoe
Beatles; *Beatles-Box Set* . . . . (Capitol)
Hey Jude . . . . (Capitol)
Past Masters-Volume Two . . . . (Parlophone)

Old Fashioned Love
Asleep At The Wheel featuring Suzy Bogguss; *Tribute To The Music Of Bob
Wills And The Texas Playboys-C* . . . . (Liberty)

Old Flames Can't Hold A Candle To You
Dolly Parton; *Dolly Dolly Dolly* . . . . (RCA)
Dolly Parton's Greatest Hits . . . . (RCA)
Joe Sun; *Old Flames Can't Hold A Candle To You*. . . . . (Ovation)
Merle Haggard; *Kern River* . . . .(Epic)

Old Love
Eric Clapton; *Eric Clapton-Unplugged* . . . . (Reprise)

On Again Off Again
Nashville Bluegrass Band; *Waitin' For The Hard Times To Go* . . . . . (Sugar Hill)

On My Own
Original Broadway Cast; *Les Miserables* . . . .(Geffen)

On The Side Of Angels
LeAnn Rimes; *You Light Up My Life-Inspirational Songs* . . . . (Curb)

Once In Love With Amy
Barry Manilow; *Showstoppers* . . . . (Arista)
Lawrence Welk; *My Personal Favorites* . . . .(Ranwood)
Mel Torme; *Swings Shubert Alley* . . . . (Verve)

Once Upon A Lifetime
Alabama; *American Pride* . . . . (RCA)

One
U2; *Achtung Baby*. . . . . (Island)

One After 909
Beatles; *Let It Be* . . . . (Capitol)
The Beatles-Anthology-#1 . . . . (Capitol)

One Emotion
Clint Black; *One Emotion* . . . .(RCA)

One I Loved Back Then (Corvette Song)
George Jones; *19 Hot Country Requests-#3-C* . . . . (Epic)
George Jones-Super Hits . . . . (Epic)
Greatest Country Hits Of The '80s-1986-C . . . . (Columbia)
Who's Gonna Fill Their Shoes . . . . (Epic)

One Of These Days
Tim McGraw; *Everywhere* . . . . (Curb)

One Of Those Love Songs
Xscape; *Traces Of My Lipstick* . . . . (So So Def/Columbia)

One On One
Daryl Hall & John Oates; *H2O* . . . .(RCA)
Live At The Apollo . . . . (RCA)
Rock 'N Soul, Part 1 . . . . (RCA)
Soulful Sounds . . . . (RCA)

One, The
Elton John; *Elton John-Love Songs*. . . . . (MCA)
The One . . . . (MCA)

Only A Fool
Black Crowes; *By Your Side* . . . . (American)

Only In America
Jay & The Americans; *Come A Little Bit Closer-Best Of Jay & The
Americans* . . . . (Gold Rush)
Jay & The Americans' All-Time Greatest Hits . . . . (Rhino)

Only Love
Wynonna; *Tell Me Why*. . . . . (MCA)

Only Love (The Ballad Of Sleeping Beauty)
Sophie B. Hawkins; *Whaler* . . . . (Columbia)

Only Love Is Worth This Pain
Country Joe McDonald; *Hold On It's Coming* . . . . (Vanguard)

Only Time
Enya; *A Day Without Rain*. . . . .(Reprise)

Oogum Boogum Song
Brenton Wood; *Collectables Presents The History Of
Rock-#9-C* . . . . (Collectables)
Oldies But Goodies-#7-C . . . .(Original Sound)
Soul Shots-#2-The ''In'' Crowd-Sweet Soul-C. . . . . (Rhino)

Ooh Baby Baby
Linda Ronstadt; *Linda Ronstadt's Greatest Hits, Volume Two* . . . .(Asylum)
Living In The USA . . . .(Asylum)
Miracles; *Best Of Smokey Robinson & The Miracles-Anthology* . . . . . (Motown)
Smokey Robinson's Greatest Hits-#2 . . . . (Motown)

Open Up My Window
Christopher Cross; *Window*. . . . . (Rhythm Safari)

Opposites Attract
Paula Abdul; *Forever Your Girl* . . . .(Virgin)
Rock The First-#3-C . . . .(Priority)
Shut Up And Dance (The Dance Mixes) . . . .(Virgin)

Opposites Attract
Natalie Cole; *Dangerous* . . . .(Modern)

Our Love Is Here To Stay
Elton John; *Glory Of Gershwin Featuring Larry Adler-C* . . . .(Mercury)
Tony Bennett; *Tony Bennett At Carnegie Hall* . . . . . (Sony Music Special Prod.)

Our Love Is Like A Holiday
Michael Bolton; *Now That's What I Call Christmas!-C* . . . .(UTV)

Our Love Is On The Faultline
Crystal Gayle; *Best Of Crystal Gayle* . . . . (Warner Bros.)
True Love . . . . (Elektra)

Our Summer Love
Joey Welz; *Best Of Joey Welz-Decades*. . . . . (Caprice Int'l)
Blue Memories . . . .(Caprice Int'l)

Our Teenage Love
Torquays; *45-#66* . . . .(Original Sound)

Our Time Has Come
Wood; *Songs From Stamford Hill*. . . . . (Columbia)

Our Winter Love
Lettermen; *Capitol Collectors Series-The Lettermen* . . . . (Capitol)

Over My Head
Fleetwood Mac; *25 Years-The Chain* . . . . (Warner Bros.)
Fleetwood Mac. . . . .(Reprise)
Fleetwood Mac Live . . . . (Warner Bros.)
Fleetwood Mac's Greatest Hits . . . . (Warner Bros.)

P.S. I Love You
Bette Midler; *ST/For The Boys* . . . .(Atlantic)
Billie Holiday; *Lady Sings The Blues* . . . . (Verve)
Bing Crosby; *Thanks For The Memories Mr. Crosby* . . . . (J-Bird)
Dion; *Dion-His Best* . . . .(Laurie)
Kay Starr; *Too Marvelous For Words-Capitol Sings Jonny Mercer-C* . . (Capitol)
Mel Torme; *That's All* . . . . (Sony Music Special Prod.)
Rosemary Clooney; *Rosemary Clooney Sings The Lyrics Of Johnny
Mercer*. . . . . (Concord Jazz)
Tom T. Hall; *Natural Dreams* . . . . (Mercury)
Woody Herman; *Best Of The Big Bands-C* . . . . (Columbia)

P.S. I Love You
Beatles; *Beatles-Box Set* . . . . (Capitol)
Beatles-Love Songs . . . . (Capitol)
Introducing...The Beatles . . . .(Vee-Jay)

Please Please Me . . . . (Parlophone)
   The Early Beatles . . . . (Capitol)
Pale September
   Fiona Apple; *Tidal* . . . .(Clean Slate/Work)
Papa Loved Mama
   Garth Brooks; *Garth Brooks-Double Live* . . . .(Capitol)
   Ropin' The Wind . . . . (Liberty)
Papa Loves Mambo
   Perry Como; *Como's Golden Records* . . . .(RCA)
   Perry Como-Pure Gold . . . .(RCA)
   Perry Como's All-Time Greatest Hits-#1 . . . .(RCA)
   This Is Perry Como . . . .(RCA)
Pardon My Heart
   Neil Young & Crazy Horse; *Zuma* . . . .(Reprise)
Paris Loves Lovers
   Don Ameche & Hildelgard Neff; *Cole Porter-A Centennial*
    Celebration-C . . . .(RCA)
Peace, Love & Understanding (What's So Funny About)
   Curtis Stigers; *ST/The Bodyguard* . . . .(Arista)
   Elvis Costello & The Attractions; *Armed Forces* . . . .(Rykodisc)
   Best Of Elvis Costello & The Attractions . . . . (Columbia)
Peggy Sue
   Buddy Holly; *Billboard Top Rock 'N' Roll Hits-1957-C* . . . .(Rhino)
   Buddy Holly . . . .(MCA)
   Buddy Holly-20 Golden Greats . . . . (MCA)
   Buddy Holly's Greatest Hits . . . .(MCA)
   More American Graffiti-C . . . . (MCA)
   Oldies But Goodies-#4-C . . . .(Original Sound)
   Rock & Roll Collection . . . . (MCA)
Penny Lover
   Lionel Richie; *Back To Front* . . . . (Motown)
   Can't Slow Down . . . . (Motown)
Personality
   Lloyd Price; *Lloyd Price's Greatest Hits* . . . . (MCA)
   Lloyd Price's Greatest Hits . . . . (Curb)
Personally
   Karla Bonoff; *Wild Heart Of The Young* . . . . (Columbia)
Picture Of Love
   Continentals; *Doo-Wop Era-Harlem, New York-40 Hits-C* . . . . (Collectables)
Picture Of Our Love
   Mickey Gilley; *Gilley* . . . . (Epic)
Places I've Never Been
   Mark Wills; *Mark Wills* . . . . (Mercury)
Play Me
   Neil Diamond; *Moods* . . . . (MCA)
   Neil Diamond-His 12 Greatest Hits . . . . (MCA)
   Neil Diamond-Love Songs . . . . (MCA)
Please Love Me Forever
   Bobby Vinton; *Bobby Vinton-16 Most Requested Songs* . . . . .(Legacy)
   Bobby Vinton's All-Time Greatest Hits . . . . (Epic)
   Please Love Me Forever . . . .(Epic)
Please Mister Postman
   Beatles; *Beatles-Box Set* . . . . (Capitol)
   The Beatles' Second Album . . . . (Capitol)
   With The Beatles . . . . (Parlophone)
   Carpenters; *Carpenters-Classics-#2* . . . .(A&M)
   Horizon . . . . (A&M)
   Yesterday Once More . . . . (A&M)
   Marvelettes; *Billboard Top Rock 'N' Roll Hits-1961-C* . . . . (Rhino)
   Marvelettes' Greatest Hits . . . . (Motown)
   Marvelettes-Anthology . . . .(Motown)
   Motown Story-First 25 Years-C . . . .(Motown)
Pledging My Love
   David Allan Coe; *David Allan Coe-17 Greatest Hits* . . . . . .(Columbia)
   David Allan Coe's Biggest Hits . . . .(Legacy)
   Elvis Presley; *A Touch Of Platinum-#2* . . . .(RCA)
   Moody Blue . . . . (RCA)
   Emmylou Harris; *Great Wedding Songs-C* . . . .(Warner Bros.)
   Profile II-The Best Of Emmylou Harris . . . .(Warner Bros.)
   Freddy Fender; *Freddy Fender-Collection* . . . . (Increase)
   Johnny Ace; *Cruisin'-1955-C* . . . . (Increase)
   Duke-Peacock Greatest Hits . . . . (MCA)
   Memorial Album . . . . (MCA)
   Oldies But Goodies-#10-C . . . .(Original Sound)
   ST/A Rage In Harlem . . . . (MCA Special Prod.)
   Marvin Gaye & Diana Ross; *Diana & Marvin* . . . .(Motown)
   Teresa Brewer; *Best Of Teresa Brewer* . . . . (MCA Jazz)
Poison Love
   Blood On The Saddle; *Poison Love* . . . . (Charisma)
Poison Love
   T Bone Burnett; *T Bone Burnett* . . . .(Dot)
Poor Boy
   Elvis Presley; *Essential Elvis-The First Movies* . . . . (RCA)
   For LP Fans Only . . . . (RCA)
Poor People Of Paris
   Les Baxter & His Orchestra; *Memories Are Made Of This-C* . . .(Capitol)
Popcorn Love
   New Edition; *Club Classics-1982-1984-#1-C* . . . . (Warlock)
   New Edition's Greatest Hits, Vol. 1 . . . . (MCA)

Portrait Of My Love
   Dee Clark; *Best Of Dee Clark* . . . .(Vee-Jay)
   Lettermen; *Best Of The Lettermen* . . . .(Capitol)
Portuguese Love
   Teena Marie; *It Must Be Magic* . . . . (Motown)
   Teena Marie's Greatest Hits . . . . (Motown)
Power Of Love
   Charley Pride; *Charley Pride's Greatest Hits-#2* . . . . (RCA)
   Power Of Love . . . .(RCA)
Power Of Love
   Air Supply; *Air Supply* . . . .(Arista)
Power Of Love
   T. Graham Brown; *Brilliant Conversationalist* . . . .(Capitol)
Power Of Love
   Trixter; *Hear!* . . . . (MCA)
Power Of Love
   Jennifer Rush; *Jennifer Rush* . . . . (Epic)
Power Of Love
   Nana Mouskouri; *Nana* . . . . (Philips)
   Only Love-Very Best Of Nana Mouskouri . . . . (Rhino)
Power Of Love
   Lee Roy Parnell; *On The Road* . . . .(Arista)
Power Of Love
   Luther Vandross; *Power Of Love* . . . . (Epic)
Power Of Love
   Huey Lewis and the News; *ST/Back To The Future* . . . . (MCA)
Power Of Love
   Laura Branigan; *Touch* . . . .(Atlantic)
Power Of Love
   T Bone Burnett; *Truth Decay* . . . .(Takoma)
Power Of Love
   Deee-Lite; *World Clique* . . . .(Elektra)
Power Of My Love
   Elvis Presley; *From Elvis In Memphis* . . . . (RCA)
   Memphis Record . . . . (RCA)
Powerful Thing
   Trisha Yearwood; *Where Your Road Leads* . . . . (MCA)
Pretending Love
   Little Johnny & Ted Taylor; *Super Taylors* . . . .(Ronn)
Price Of Love
   Bon Jovi; *7800 Degrees Fahrenheit* . . . .(Mercury)
Price Of Love
   Roger Daltrey; *ST/Secret Of My Success* . . . . (MCA)
Price Of Love
   Bad English; *Bad English* . . . .(Epic)
   Legends Of Pop In The '90s-C . . . . (Madacy)
Pride (In The Name Of Love)
   Clivilles & Cole; *Greatest Remixes-#1* . . . .(Columbia)
   ST/Gladiator . . . .(Columbia)
   U2; *Greenpeace/Rainbow Warriors-C* . . . . (Geffen)
   Rattle And Hum . . . .(Island)
   Unforgettable Fire . . . .(Island)
Prisoner Of Love
   Foreigner; *Very Best Of Foreigner...And Beyond* . . . .(Atlantic)
Prisoner Of Love
   Bloodstone; *Bloodstone's Greatest Hits* . . . . (T-Neck/Columbia)
Prisoner Of Love
   Pat Benatar; *Crimes Of Passion* . . . .(Chrysalis)
Prisoner Of Love
   Miami Sound Machine; *Eyes Of Innocence* . . . . (Epic)
Prisoner Of Love
   Kiss; *Hot In The Shade* . . . .(Mercury)
Prisoner Of Love
   Truth; *Jump* . . . .(I.R.S.)
Prisoner Of Love
   James Brown; *Live At The Apollo-Vol. 2-Part 2* . . . . (Rhino)
Prisoner Of Your Love
   Player; *Danger Zone* . . . . (RSO)
Promise Kept, A
   James Horner; *ST/Titanic* . . . . (Sony Music Classical)
Pure Love
   Ronnie Milsap; *Ronnie Milsap's Greatest Hits* . . . . (RCA)
   Ronnie Milsap-Super Hits . . . . (RCA)
Push Push
   Paula Abdul; *Spellbound* . . . .(Captive)
Pushing Up Daisies
   Garth Brooks; *Scarecrow* . . . .(Capitol)
Put A Little Love Away
   Emotions; *Sunshine* . . . .(Stax)
   The Emotions-Chronicle . . . . (Stax)
Put A Little Love In Your Heart
   Annie Lennox & Al Green; *ST/Scrooged* . . . .(A&M)
   Jackie DeShannon; *Chicken Soup For The Soul: I'll Be There For You-Songs*
    Of Friendship, Brotherhood And Sisterhood-C . . . . (Rhino)
   ST/Drugstore Cowboy . . . . (Novus)
   Very Best Of Jackie DeShannon . . . .(EMI)
Put Your Arms Around Me, Honey
   Fats Domino; *They Call Me The Fat Man* . . . .(EMI)

Judy Garland; *Best Of Judy Garland-From MGM Classic Films* . . . . (MCA)
Sammy Kaye & His Orchestra; *Best Of Sammy Kaye & His Orchestra* . . . (MCA)
Queen Of My Double Wide Trailer
Sammy Kershaw; *Haunted Heart* . . . . (Mercury)
Race Is On
Dave Edmunds; *Best Of Dave Edmunds* . . . . (Swan Song)
Twangin' . . . . (Swan Song)
George Jones; *Best Of George Jones-1955-1967* . . . . (Rhino)
Billboard Top Country Hits-1964-C . . . . (Rhino)
George Jones' All-Time Greatest Hits . . . . (Epic)
Sawyer Brown; *Boys Are Back* . . . . (Curb)
Sawyer Brown's Greatest Hits . . . . (Curb)
Rachel
Buddy & Julie Miller; *Buddy & Julie Miller* . . . . (Hightone)
Racing In The Street
Bruce Springsteen; *Darkness On The Edge Of Town* . . . . (Columbia)
Bruce Springsteen & The E Street Band; *Bruce Springsteen & The E Street
Band/1975-85* . . . . (Legacy)
Radar For Love
Kiss; *Asylum* . . . . (Mercury)
Radar Love
Golden Earring; *'70s Greatest Rock Hits-#1-Hard N' Heavy-C* . . . . . . (Priority)
Classic Rock-#1-C . . . . (MCA)
Golden Earring-Live . . . . (MCA)
Moontan . . . . (MCA)
Super Hits Of The '70s-Have A Nice Day-#13-C . . . . (Rhino)
Radio Lover
George Jones; *By Request* . . . . (Epic)
Jones Country . . . . (Epic)
One Woman Man . . . . (Epic)
Rainbow
Russ Hamilton; *45-#184* . . . . (Kapp)
Real Life Love
Larry Stewart; *Heart Like A Hurricane* . . . . (Columbia)
Real Live Woman
Trisha Yearwood; *Real Live Woman* . . . . (MCA)
Real Love
Jody Watley; *Larger Than Life* . . . . (MCA)
You Wanna Dance With Me? . . . . (MCA)
Real Love
Beatles; *The Beatles-Anthology-#2* . . . . (Capitol)
John Lennon; *ST/Imagine: John Lennon* . . . . (Capitol)
Real Love
Dolly Parton & Kenny Rogers; *Best Of Dolly Parton-#3* . . . . (RCA)
Real Love
Bob Seger & The Silver Bullet Band; *Fire Inside* . . . . (Capitol)
Real Love
El DeBarge; *Gemini* . . . . (Motown)
Real Love
Doobie Brothers; *One Step Closer* . . . . (Warner Bros.)
Real Love
Ashford & Simpson; *Real Love* . . . . (Capitol)
Real Love
Skyy; *Start Of A Romance* . . . . (Atlantic)
Real Love
Slaughter; *The Wild Life* . . . . (Chrysalis)
Real Love
Mary J. Blige; *What's The 411?* . . . . (Uptown)
Reason, The
Celine Dion with Carole King; *Let's Talk About Love-C* . . . . (550 Music)
Redneck Romance
Nine Pound Hammer; *Live At The Vera* . . . . (Scooch Pooch)
Redneck Romeo
Confederate Railroad; *Notorious* . . . . (Atlantic)
Regular Thang
Ovis; *Schadenfreude* . . . . (Restless)
Rendezvous
Bruce Springsteen; *Tracks* . . . . (Columbia)
Gary U.S. Bonds; *Best Of Gary U.S. Bonds* . . . (EMI Legends Of Rock 'N' Roll)
Greg Kihn; *Kihnsolidation-Best Of Greg Kihn* . . . . (Rhino)
Greg Kihn Band; *Cover Me (Bruce Springsteen Tribute)-C* . . . . (Rhino)
Rescue Me
Diana Ross; *Swept Away* . . . . (RCA)
Fontella Bass; *Billboard Top R&B Hits-1965-1969-C* . . . . (Rhino)
Collectables Presents The History Of Rock-#8-C . . . . (Collectables)
Cruisin'-1965-C . . . . (Increase)
Oldies But Goodies-#12-C . . . . (Original Sound)
ST/Air America . . . . (MCA)
Red Hot & Blue Band; *Red Hot & Blue-All Time Great R&B Songs* . . . . (Curb)
Respect
Aretha Franklin; *Aretha Franklin-30 Greatest Hits* . . . . (Rhino)
Best Of Aretha Franklin . . . . (Atlantic)
I Am Woman-C . . . . (Nick At Nite)
I Never Loved A Man The Way I Love You . . . . (Atlantic)
Live At Fillmore West . . . . (Atlantic)
Soul Years-C . . . . (Atlantic)
ST/Forrest Gump . . . . (Epic/Sony Music Soundtrax)
Otis Redding; *History Of Otis Redding* . . . . (Atco)

Live In Europe . . . . (Atco)
Otis Blue-Sings Soul . . . . (Atco)
The Otis Redding Story . . . . (Atlantic)
Reba McEntire; *Reba* . . . . (MCA)
Revival
Allman Brothers Band; *An Evening With The Allman Brothers Band-
First Set* . . . . (Epic)
Beginnings . . . . (Polydor)
Decade Of Hits-1969-1979 . . . . (Polydor)
Dreams . . . . (Polydor)
Idlewild South . . . . (Polydor)
Rhythm Of Love
Scorpions; *Best Of Rockers 'N' Ballads* . . . . (Mercury)
Savage Amusement . . . . (Mercury)
Rhythm Of Love
Yes; *Big Generator* . . . . (Atco)
Yesyears . . . . (Atco)
Rhythm Of Love
Screaming Iguanas Of Love; *Screaming Iguanas Of Love* . . . . (Long Song)
Richest Man On Earth
Paul Overstreet; *Sowin' Love* . . . . (RCA)
Right In Time
Lucinda Williams; *Car Wheels On A Gravel Road* . . . . (Mercury)
Right Kind Of Love
Jeremy Jordan; *Try My Love* . . . . (Giant)
Right On
Marvin Gaye; *What's Going On* . . . . (Motown)
Right On The Money
Alan Jackson; *Big Country Hits '99-C* . . . . (K-Tel)
High Mileage . . . . (Arista)
Right Where I Need To Be
Gary Allan; *Smoke Rings In The Dark* . . . . (MCA)
River And The Highway
Pam Tillis; *All Of This Love* . . . . (Arista)
Pam Tillis' Greatest Hits . . . . (Arista)
River Deep, Mountain High
Celine Dion; *Falling Into You* . . . . (550 Music)
Erasure; *Innocents* . . . . (Sire)
Four Tops; *Four Tops-Anthology* . . . . (Motown)
Ike & Tina Turner; *Best Of Ike & Tina Turner* . . . . (EMI)
Phil Spector's Greatest Hits-C . . . . (Spector)
Proud Mary-Best Of Ike & Tina Turner . . . . (EMI)
Tina Turner; *Simply The Best* . . . . (Capitol)
River Of Endless Love
Moody Blues; *Sur La Mer* . . . . (Polydor)
River Of Love
Lynch Mob; *Wicked Sensation* . . . . (Elektra)
River Of Love
John Denver; *Farewell Andromeda* . . . . (RCA)
River Of Love
Angels; *My Boyfriend's Back* . . . . (Collectables)
River Of Love
David Foster; *River Of Love* . . . . (Atlantic)
River Of Love
Richie Sambora; *Stranger In This Town* . . . . (Mercury)
River Of Love
T Bone Burnett; *T Bone Burnett* . . . . (Dot)
Road Goes On Forever, The
Joe Ely; *Love & Danger* . . . . (MCA)
Rock & Roll Love Letter
Bay City Rollers; *Bay City Rollers' Greatest Hits* . . . . (Arista)
Rock & Roll Love Letters . . . . (Arista)
Rock Love
Steve Miller Band; *Rock Love* . . . . (Capitol)
Utopia; *Adventures In Utopia* . . . . (Rhino)
Rock Me In The Rhythm Of Your Love
Eddy Raven; *Best Of Eddy Raven* . . . . (Liberty)
Right For The Flight . . . . (Liberty)
Rocket O' Love
Knack; *Serious Fun* . . . . (Charisma)
Rockin' The Boat Of Love
Jerry Lee Lewis; *Golden Rock & Roll* . . . . (Sun)
Rockin' With The Rhythm Of The Rain
Judds; *Judds' Greatest Hits* . . . . (MCA)
Rockin' With The Rhythm . . . . (MCA)
Romance In Durango
Bob Dylan; *Biograph* . . . . (Columbia)
Desire . . . . (Columbia)
Romantic
Karyn White; *Ritual Of Love* . . . . (Warner Bros.)
Romeo & Juliet
Chambers Brothers; *The Time Has Come* . . . . (Columbia)
Roni
Bobby Brown; *Dance!...Ya Know It!* . . . . (MCA)
Don't Be Cruel . . . . (MCA)
Room At The Top
Tom Petty And The Heartbreakers; *Echo* . . . . (Warner Bros.)

Room With A View
Carolyn Dawn Johnson; *Room With A View* . . . . (Arista)
Rosabella
Original Broadway Cast; *The Most Happy Fella* . . . . (Sony Music Classical)
Rose Of San Antone
Bashful Brother Oswald; *Don't Say Aloha* . . . . (Rounder)
Rose, Rose I Love You
Frankie Laine; *Frankie Laine's Greatest Hits* . . . . (Columbia)
Roses Are Red
Bobby Vinton; *Bobby Vinton-16 Most Requested Songs* . . . . (Legacy)
   Bobby Vinton's All-Time Greatest Hits . . . . (Epic)
   Spring Sensations . . . . (Epic)
'Round The Clock Lovin'
Gail Davies; *Best Of Gail Davies* . . . . (Capitol)
K.T. Oslin; *This Woman* . . . . (RCA)
Rub You The Right Way
Johnny Gill; *Johnny Gill* . . . . (Motown)
Rumor Has It
Clay Walker; *Clay Walker's Greatest Hits* . . . . (Giant)
   Rumor Has It . . . . (Giant)
Run
George Strait; *The Road Goes On Forever, A Collection Of Their Greatest*
   Recordings . . . . (Polydor)
Run To My Lovin' Arms
Jay & The Americans; *Jay & The Americans'*
   Greatest Hits . . . . (CEMA Special Prod.)
Runaway Love
En Vogue & Mob; *Runaway Love* . . . . (East West)
Runaway Love
Mass Order; *Maybe One Day* . . . . (Columbia)
Runaway Love
BoDeans; *Outside Looking In* . . . . (Slash)
'S Wonderful
Diana Krall; *The Look Of Love* . . . . (Impulse!)
Ella Fitzgerald; *Oh, Lady Be Good! Best Of the Gershwin Songbook* . . . . (Verve)
Fred Astaire; *Steppin' Out-Astaire Sings* . . . . (Verve)
Harry Connick, Jr.; *20* . . . . (Columbia)
Ray Conniff; *Ray Conniff -16 Most Requested Songs* . . . . (Legacy)
Safe In The Arms Of Love
Martika; *Martika's Kitchen* . . . . (Columbia)
   Turn The Tide . . . . (RCA)
Said I Loved You...But I Lied
Michael Bolton; *The One Thing* . . . . (Columbia)
Same Ol' Love
Ricky Skaggs; *My Father's Son* . . . . (Epic)
Same Ole Love
Billy Cobham; *Billy's Best Hits* . . . . (GRP)
Same Ole Love
Anita Baker; *Rapture* . . . . (Elektra)
San Antonio Girl
Lyle Lovett; *Lyle Lovett Anthology-#1-Cowboy Man* . . . . (MCA)
San Diego Serenade
Nanci Griffith; *Late Night Grande Hotel* . . . . (MCA)
Tom Waits; *The Heart Of Saturday Night* . . . . (Asylum)
   Tom Waits-Anthology . . . . (Asylum)
Sapphire Bullets Of Pure Love
They Might Be Giants; *Flood* . . . . (Elektra)
Sara
Fleetwood Mac; *25 Years-The Chain* . . . . (Warner Bros.)
   Fleetwood Mac Live . . . . (Warner Bros.)
   Fleetwood Mac's Greatest Hits . . . . (Warner Bros.)
   Tusk . . . . (Warner Bros.)
Sara
Bob Dylan; *Desire* . . . . (Columbia)
Satellite Of Love
Lou Reed; *Between Thought & Expression-Anthology* . . . . (RCA)
   City Lights . . . . (Arista)
   Lou Reed Live . . . . (RCA)
   Transformer . . . . (RCA)
   Walk On The Wild Side-The Best Of Lou Reed . . . . (RCA)
Saturday Love
Cherrelle & Alexander O'Neal; *Club Epic-#1-C* . . . . (Legacy)
   High Priority . . . . (Tabu)
Saturday Night (I Get All My Lovin')
Billy Strange; *Best Of Billy Strange* . . . . (Crescendo)
Saturday Night At The Movies
Drifters; *1959-1965-All-Time Greatest Hits And More* . . . . (Atlantic)
   Drifters-16 Greatest Hits . . . . (Trip)
   Drifters-Golden Hits . . . . (Atlantic)
   Save The Last Dance For Me . . . . (Fifty One West)
Save Some Love
Keedy; *Chase The Clouds* . . . . (Arista)
Save Tonight
Eagle-Eye Cherry; *Desireless* . . . . (Work)
Saved By Love
Rik Emmett; *Absolutely* . . . . (Charisma)
Saved By Love
Amy Grant; *Lead Me On* . . . . (A&M)

Saving All My Love For You
Whitney Houston; *Whitney Houston* . . . . (Arista)
   Whitney Houston's Greatest Hits . . . . (Arista)
Saving All My Love For You
Tom Waits; *Heartattack & Vine* . . . . (Asylum)
Saving Forever For You
Shanice; *ST/Beverly Hills, 90210-College Years* . . . . (Giant)
Say You Love Me
Fleetwood Mac; *25 Years-The Chain* . . . . (Warner Bros.)
   Fleetwood Mac . . . . (Reprise)
   Fleetwood Mac Live . . . . (Warner Bros.)
   Fleetwood Mac's Greatest Hits . . . . (Warner Bros.)
Say You Love Me
Jo-el Sonnier; *Come On Joe* . . . . (RCA)
Say You Love Me
Ce Ce Rogers; *Never Give Up* . . . . (Atlantic)
Saying Hello, Saying I Love You, Saying Goodbye
Jim Ed Brown & Helen Cornelius; *Jim Ed Brown & Helen Cornelius'*
   Greatest Hits . . . . (RCA)
School Boy Romance
Danny & The Juniors; *Rockin' With Danny & The*
   Juniors . . . . (MCA Special Prod.)
Sea Of Love
Honeydrippers; *Volume One* . . . . (Es Paranza)
Phil Phillips With The Twilights; *Cruisin'-1959-C* . . . . (Increase)
   Remember When-C . . . . (Garland)
Sealed With A Kiss
Bobby Vinton; *Bobby Vinton's Greatest Hits* . . . . (Curb)
Brian Hyland; *Cruisin'-1962-C* . . . . (Increase)
   Oldies But Goodies-#2-C . . . . (Original Sound)
   Original Rock 'N' Roll Hits Of The '50s-C . . . . (Roulette)
Lettermen; *Best Of The Lettermen-#2* . . . . (Capitol)
   Capitol Collectors Series-The Lettermen . . . . (Capitol)
Searching For My Love
Bobby Moore & The Rhythm Aces; *Best Of Chess Rhythm &*
   Blues-#1-C . . . . (Chess)
   Soul Shots-#10-More Sweet Soul-C . . . . (Rhino)
   Soul Shots-#2-The "In" Crowd-Sweet Soul-C . . . . (Rhino)
Huey Lewis and the News; *Four Chords & Several Years Ago* . . . . . . (Elektra)
Secret
Madonna; *Bedtime Stories* . . . . (Maverick/Sire)
   GHV2 . . . . (Warner Bros.)
Secret Love
Doris Day; *Doris Day's Greatest Hits* . . . . (Columbia)
   Hollywood Magic-1950s-C . . . . (Columbia)
Frank Sinatra; *Days Of Wine And Roses, Moon River, And Other Academy*
   Award Winners . . . . (Reprise)
Freddy Fender; *Freddy Fender-Collection* . . . . (Reprise)
Guy Lombardo & His Royal Canadians; *Golden Medleys* . . . . (MCA)
Moonglows; *Doo-Wop's Greatest Hits-C* . . . . (Vee-Jay)
Nancy Wilson; *Capitol Sings The Best Movie Songs-C* . . . . (Capitol)
Slim Whitman; *Best Of Slim Whitman 1952-1972* . . . . (Rhino)
   Slim Whitman's Greatest Hits . . . . (Curb)
Secret Lovers
Atlantic Starr; *As The Band Turns* . . . . (A&M)
   Atlantic Starr-Classics-#10 . . . . (A&M)
   Secret Lovers: Best Of Atlantic Starr . . . . (A&M)
Secret Of The Sea
Billy Bragg & Wilco; *Mermaid Avenue-#2* . . . . (Elektra)
Send Her My Love
Journey; *Frontiers* . . . . (Columbia)
   Journey's Greatest Hits . . . . (Columbia)
Send One Your Love
Stevie Wonder; *Journey Through The Secret Life Of Plants* . . . . (Motown)
   Original Musiquarium . . . . (Motown)
Sendin' All My Love
Jets; *Best Of The Jets* . . . . (MCA)
   Magic . . . . (MCA)
Sending All My Love
Linear; *Linear* . . . . (Atlantic)
September In The Rain
Chad & Jeremy; *Capitol Gold-Best Of Chad & Jeremy* . . . . (Capitol)
   The Soft Sound Of Chad & Jeremy . . . . (K-Tel)
Dinah Washington; *Dinah Washington-Golden Hits* . . . . (Mercury)
   This Is My Story . . . . (Mercury)
Doris Day; *Doris Day Sings 22 Great Songs-Original Big Band* . . . (Hindsight)
Duprees; *Best Of The Duprees* . . . . (Rhino)
Frank Sinatra; *Round #1* . . . . (Capitol)
   Sinatra's Swingin' Session!!! . . . . (Capitol)
Joe Williams; *Swingin'...At Birdland* . . . . (Roulette)
Marty Robbins; *Essential Marty Robbins-1951-1982* . . . . (Columbia)
Peggy Lee; *You Can Depend On Me* . . . . (Glendale)
September Love
Kool & The Gang; *In The Heart* . . . . (De-Lite)
Serpentine Fire
Earth, Wind & Fire; *All 'N All* . . . . (Columbia)
   Best Of Earth, Wind & Fire-#2 . . . . (Columbia)
   Eternal Dance . . . . (Columbia)

Sha La La Means I Love You
Barry White; *The Man* . . . . (Mercury)
Shadow Of Love
Damned; *Light At The End Of The Tunnel* . . . . (MCA)
Phantasmagoria . . . . (MCA)
Shadow Of Love
Laura Branigan; *Touch* . . . . (Atlantic)
Shadow Of Your Love
Temptations; *Power* . . . . (Motown)
Shadows Of Love
Bing Crosby; *Crooner-Columbia Years-1928-1934* . . . . . . (Columbia)
Glen Gray; *Best Of The Big Bands-C* . . . . (Columbia)
Rayburn Anthony; *45-#55053* . . . . (Mercury)
Shake The Sugar Tree
Pam Tillis; *Homeward Looking Angel* . . . . (Arista)
Shake You Down
Gregory Abbott; *Heart Of Soul-C* . . . . (Columbia)
Shake You Down . . . . (Columbia)
Slow Dancin'-C . . . . (K-Tel)
Shake Your Love
Debbie Gibson; *Out Of The Blue* . . . . (Atlantic)
Shake Your Love
Climax Blues Band; *FM/Live* . . . . (Sire)
She Don't Love Nobody
Desert Rose Band; *Running* . . . . (MCA)
She Don't Love Nobody
Nick Lowe; *Basher: Best Of* . . . . (Columbia)
She Gave Her Heart To A Soldier Boy
Roy Rogers; *The Country Music Hall Of Fame-Roy Rogers* . . . (MCA)
She Loves The Jerk
John Hiatt; *Riding With The King* . . . . (Geffen)
Y'All Caught? Ones That Got Away, 1979-85 . . . . (Geffen)
Rodney Crowell; *Street Language* . . . . (Columbia)
She Said Yes
Rhett Akins; *A Thousand Memories* . . . . (Decca)
She Thinks I Still Care
Elvis Presley; *Moody Blue* . . . . (RCA)
George Jones; *Best Of George Jones-1955-1967* . . . . (Rhino)
Billboard Top Country Hits-1962-C . . . . (Rhino)
George Jones' All-Time Greatest Hits . . . . (Epic)
George Jones-Super Hits-#2 . . . . (Epic)
She Was Only Seventeen (He Was One Year More)
Marty Robbins; *American Originals-Marty Robbins* . . . . . . (Columbia)
Marty Robbins' Greatest Hits . . . . (Columbia)
She'd Give Anything
Boy Howdy; *She'd Give Anything* . . . . (Curb)
Sheik Of Araby
Beatles; *The Beatles-Anthology-#1* . . . . (Capitol)
Benny Goodman; *Benny Goodman Sextet featuring Charlie Christian-1939-1941* . . . . (Columbia)
Django Reinhardt; *Djangologie USA-#1* . . . . (Disques Swing)
Fred Astaire; *Three Evenings With Fred Astaire* . . . . (DRG)
Leon Redbone; *Double Time* . . . . (Warner Bros.)
Sheila
Tommy Roe; *Billboard Top Rock 'N' Roll Hits-1962-C* . . . . . (Rhino)
Golden Years-1962-C . . . . (Dominion Entert.)
Original Rock 'N' Roll Hits Of The '60s-C . . . . (Roulette)
Sheila . . . . (Accord)
Tommy Roe's Greatest Hits . . . . (MCA)
Shelter From The Storm
Bob Dylan; *Blood On The Tracks* . . . . (Columbia)
Bob Dylan At Budokan . . . . (Columbia)
Hard Rain . . . . (Columbia)
Shenandoah
Bob Dylan; *Down In The Groove* . . . . (Columbia)
Harry Belafonte; *Harry Belafonte-Legendary Performer* . . . . . . (RCA)
James Galway; *James Galway's Greatest Hits* . . . . (RCA)
Leontyne Price; *God Bless America* . . . . (RCA)
Van Morrison & The Chieftains; *ST/Long Journey Home: The Irish In America* . . . . (RCA Victor)
Vienna Boys Choir; *International Folk Songs: Around The World With The Vienna Boys' Choir* . . . . (Philips)
She's About A Mover
Sir Douglas Quintet; *Best Of The Sir Douglas Quintet* . . . . . (Takoma)
Texas Music-#3-Garage Bands & Psychedelia-C . . . . (Rhino)
She's All I Got
Johnny Paycheck; *Johnny Paycheck-16 Biggest Hits* . . . . (Epic)
Johnny Paycheck's Biggest Hits . . . . (Epic)
She's Always A Woman
Billy Joel; *Billy Joel-Greatest Hits, Volume I & Volume II* . . . . . . (Columbia)
The Stranger . . . . (Columbia)
She's Every Woman
Garth Brooks; *Fresh Horses* . . . . (Capitol)
She's Funny That Way (I Got A Woman Crazy For Me)
Art Tatum; *Solo Masterpieces-#8* . . . . (Pablo)
Count Basie Jam; *Montreux '77-C* . . . . (Pablo)
Frank Sinatra; *At The Movies* . . . . (Capitol)
Nice 'N' Easy . . . . (Capitol)
Jackie Gleason; *Lush Moods* . . . . (Pair)

Nat "King" Cole; *Big Band Cole* . . . . (Blue Note)
She's Got A Way
Billy Joel; *Billy Joel-Greatest Hits, Volume I & Volume II* . . . . (Columbia)
Cold Spring Harbor . . . . (Columbia)
Songs In The Attic . . . . (Columbia)
She's Got That Look In Her Eyes
Alabama; *Dancin' On The Boulevard* . . . . (RCA)
She's In Love
Mark Wills; *Wish You Were Here* . . . . (Mercury)
She's In Love With A Rodeo Man
Chris LeDoux; *Songs Of Rodeo & Country* . . . . (Liberty)
Don Williams; *Don Williams' Greatest Hits* . . . . (MCA)
She's In Love With The Boy
Trisha Yearwood; *Trisha Yearwood* . . . . (MCA)
She's My Girl
Turtles; *'60s Sound Explosion-C* . . . . (K-Tel)
Nuggets-#9-Acid Rock-C . . . . (Rhino)
Turtles-20 Greatest Hits . . . . (Rhino)
She's Ready For Someone To Love Her
Kenny Rogers; *I Prefer The Moonlight* . . . . (RCA)
Kenny Rogers' Greatest Hits . . . . (RCA)
She's Taken A Shine
John Berry; *Faces* . . . . (Capitol)
She's The One
Bruce Springsteen; *Born To Run* . . . . (Columbia)
Shimmer
Shawn Mullins; *Songs From Dawson's Creek* . . . . . . (Sony Music Soundtrax)
Soul's Core . . . . (Columbia)
Shine A Little Love
Electric Light Orchestra; *Afterglow* . . . . (Epic)
Box Of Their Best . . . . (Jet)
Discovery . . . . (Jet)
Shine On Me
Andy Griggs & Waylon Jennings; *You Won't Ever Be Lonely* . . . . . . (RCA)
Shining In The Light
Jimmy Page/Robert Plant; *Walking Into Clarksdale* . . . . (Atlantic)
Shining Star
Manhattans; *After Midnight* . . . . (Columbia)
Manhattans Greatest Hits . . . . (Columbia)
Seems Like Yesterday-#4-Early '80s-C . . . . (K-Tel)
Ship Of Love
Nutmegs; *Echoes Down The Hall-16 Original Doo-Wop Hits-C* . . . . . . (Arista)
Nutmegs' Greatest Hits . . . . (Collectables)
Shorty Falls In Love
Dan Hicks & His Hot Licks; *Where's The Money?* . . . . (MCA)
Shot Full Of Love
Chris LeDoux; *Western Underground* . . . . (Liberty)
Don Williams; *New Moves* . . . . (Capitol)
Juice Newton; *Juice* . . . . (Capitol)
Juice Newton-Greatest Hits & More . . . . (Capitol)
Shout
Beatles; *The Beatles-Anthology-#1* . . . . (Capitol)
Isley Brothers; *Nipper's Greatest Hits Of The '50s-#2-C* . . . . (RCA)
Shout . . . . (Collectables)
ST/The Wanderers . . . . (Warner Bros.)
Joey Dee & the Starliters; *Echoes Of A Rock Era-Later Years-C* . . . . . (Roulette)
Hey Let's Twist! Best Of Joey Dee & The Starliters . . . . (Rhino)
Live At The Peppermint Lounge . . . . (Accord)
Original Rock 'N' Roll Hits Of The '60s-C . . . . (Roulette)
Sock Hoppin' Sixties-C . . . . (JCI Assoc. Labels)
Otis Day & The Knights; *Shout* . . . . (MCA)
ST/Animal House . . . . (MCA)
Tom Petty And The Heartbreakers; *Pack Up The Plantation-Live!* . . . . (MCA)
Shouting Out Love
Emotions; *15 Original Big Hits-#2-C* . . . . (Stax)
Sunshine . . . . (Stax)
The Emotions-Chronicle . . . . (Stax)
Show Me
Julie Andrews/Original Cast; *My Fair Lady* . . . . (Columbia)
Show Me Love
Robyn; *Robyn Is Here* . . . . (RCA)
Show Me Love
Robin S; *Show Me Love* . . . . (Big Beat)
Shower Me With Your Love
Surface; *2nd Wave* . . . . (Columbia)
Best Of Surface...A Nice Time 4 Lovin' . . . . (Columbia)
Power Jams-Today's Hottest Hits-C . . . . (K-Tel)
Shower The People
James Taylor; *In The Pocket* . . . . (Warner Bros.)
James Taylor's Greatest Hits . . . . (Warner Bros.)
Silly Love Songs
Paul McCartney; *All The Best!* . . . . (Capitol)
ST/Give my regards to Broad Street . . . . (Columbia)
Wings; *Wings At The Speed Of Sound* . . . . (Capitol)
Wings Greatest . . . . (Capitol)
Wings Over America . . . . (Capitol)
Silver & Gold (Our Love Is Like)
Sweethearts Of The Rodeo; *Sisters* . . . . (Columbia)

Silver Future
Monster Magnet; *ST/Heavy Metal 2000* . . . . (Restless)
Since I Fell For You
Charlie Rich; *Charlie Rich's Greatest Hits* . . . . (Epic)
Lenny Welch; *20 Million-Dollar Memories-#1-C* . . . .(Laurie)
  Golden Years-1963-C . . . . (Dominion Entert.)
  Oldies But Goodies-#12-C . . . .(Original Sound)
Michael Bolton; *Timeless-Classics* . . . . (Columbia)
Natalie Cole & Reba McEntire; *Rhythm Country And Blues-C* . . . . (MCA)
Ramsey Lewis Trio; *Greatest Hits Of Ramsey Lewis* . . . . (Chess)
Skyliners; *Doo-Wop Ballads-#2-C* . . . . (Rhino)
  La Bamba & Other Original Hits-C . . . .(Laurie)
  Oldies But Goodies-#5-C . . . .(Original Sound)
Sing
Travis; *Invisible Band* . . . . (Independiente/Epic)
Sing About Love
Lynn Anderson; *Lynn Anderson's Greatest Hits-#2* . . . . (Columbia)
  Top Of The World . . . . (Columbia)
Six O'Clock
Lovin' Spoonful; *Lovin' Spoonful-Anthology* . . . . (Rhino)
Sixteen Reasons
Connie Stevens; *Only Rock 'N Roll-1960-1964-#1 Radio Hits-C* . . . . (Rhino)
Slave To Love
Bryan Ferry; *Boys And Girls* . . . . (Reprise)
Roxy Music; *Street Life-20 Great Hits* . . . . (Reprise)
Sleeping In Paris
Rosanne Cash; *The Wheel* . . . . (Columbia)
Smoky Places
Corsairs; *Best Of Chess Rhythm & Blues-#1-C* . . . . (Chess)
  Hard To Find Hits Of Rock 'N Roll-#1-C . . . . (Curb)
So Fine
Fiestas; *Baby Boomer Classics-Party Time Fifties-C* . . . .(JCI Assoc. Labels)
  Baby Boomer's Best-Jumpin' Jive 50's-C . . . . (Priority)
So Many Ways
Brook Benton; *Brook Benton-Golden Hits* . . . . (Mercury)
So Much In Love
All-4-One; *All-4-One* . . . . (Blitzz)
So Much Love
Blood, Sweat & Tears; *Child Is Father To The Man* . . . . (Columbia)
So Much Love
B Angie B; *B Angie B* . . . .(Bust It)
So You Think You're In Love
Robyn Hitchcock & The Egyptians; *Perspex Island* . . . . (A&M)
Softly And Tenderly (I'll Hold You In My Arms)
Lewis Pruitt; *45-#31095* . . . . (Decca)
Softly Whispering I Love You
English Congregation; *Super Hits Of The '70s-Have A Nice Day-#7-C* . . (Rhino)
Mike Curb Congregation; *Your Favorite Songs-C* . . . . (Curb)
Paul Young; *From Time To Time-The Singles Collection* . . . . (Columbia)
Softly, As I Leave You
Brenda Lee; *In The Mood For Love: Classic Ballads* . . . .(Hip-O)
Elvis Presley; *Elvis Aron Presley* . . . . (RCA)
Frank Sinatra; *Frank Sinatra's Greatest Hits-#1* . . . . (Reprise)
  Sinatra: A Man And His Music . . . . (Reprise)
Soldier Of Love
Marshall Crenshaw; *Marshall Crenshaw* . . . . (Rhino)
Soldier Of Love
Donny Osmond; *Donny Osmond* . . . . (Capitol)
Soldier Of Love
Lee Greenwood; *Love's On The Way* . . . . (Liberty)
Soldier Of Love
Kenny Rogers; *Love Is Strange* . . . . (Reprise)
Soldier Of Love
Nitty Gritty Dirt Band; *Workin' Band* . . . . (Warner Bros.)
Solid
Ashford & Simpson; *Chicken Soup For The Couples Soul-C* . . . . (Rhino)
  Solid . . . . (Capitol)
  Solid Plus Seven . . . . (Capitol)
Some Bridges
Jackson Browne; *Looking East* . . . . (Elektra)
Some Girls Do
Sawyer Brown; *Dirt Road* . . . . (Curb)
Some Guys Have All The Love
Little Texas; *First Time For Everything* . . . . (Warner Bros.)
Some Things Are Meant To Be
Linda Davis; *Some Things Are Meant To Be* . . . . (Arista)
Somebody Loves Me
Meat Loaf; *Glory Of Gershwin Featuring Larry Adler-C* . . . . (Mercury)
Somebody To Love
George Michael & Queen; *Five Live-C* . . . . (Hollywood)
Queen; *Day At The Races* . . . . (Hollywood)
  Queen's Greatest Hits I & II . . . . (Hollywood)
Somebody's Doin' Me Right
Glen Campbell; *Unconditional Love* . . . . (Liberty)
Keith Whitley; *Kentucky Bluebird* . . . . (RCA)
S-K-O; *S-K-O* . . . . (MTM)
Somebody's Gonna Love You
Lee Greenwood; *Lee Greenwood's Greatest Hits* . . . . (MCA)

Somebody's Gonna Love You . . . . (MCA)
Someday (You'll Want Me To Want You)
Gene Autry; *The Country Music Hall Of Fame-Gene Autry-15 Of His All-*
  Time Greatest Hits . . . . (Columbia)
Mills Brothers; *Best Of The Mills Brothers* . . . . (MCA)
  The Mills Brothers-Best Of The Decca Years . . . . (Decca)
Patsy Cline; *Last Sessions* . . . . (MCA)
  Portrait Of Patsy Cline . . . . (MCA)
Vaughn Monroe; *Best Of Vaughn Monroe* . . . . (MCA)
Someday (You're Gonna Want Me)
Bobby Vee; *Bobby Vee-Golden Greats* . . . . (Liberty)
Someday We're Gonna Love Again
Barbara Lewis; *Barbara Lewis-Golden Classics* . . . . (Collectables)
Searchers; *Searchers' Greatest Hits* . . . . (Rhino)
Something In Red
Lorrie Morgan; *Lorrie Morgan's Greatest Hits* . . . . (BNA)
  Something In Red . . . . (RCA)
  To Get To You-Greatest Hits Collection . . . . (BNA)
Something So Right
Annie Lennox; *Medusa* . . . . (Arista)
Barbra Streisand; *The Way We Were* . . . . (Columbia)
Paul Simon; *1964-1993-Box Set.* . . . . (Warner Bros.)
  There Goes Rhymin' Simon . . . . (Columbia)
Something To Remember You By
Dinah Shore; *Blues In The Night* . . . . (ASV)
Judy Garland & Bing Crosby; *Mail Call! Armed Forces Radio*
  Broadcasts . . . . (Laserlight)
Libby Holman; *78-#4910* . . . . (Brunswick)
Something Wonderful
Original Broadway Cast; *The King And I* . . . . (RCA Victor)
Original Cast; *The King And I* . . . . (MCA)
Sometimes Love Just Ain't Enough
Patty Smyth with Don Henley; *Patty Smyth* . . . . (MCA)
Somewhere Other Than The Night
Garth Brooks; *The Chase* . . . . (Liberty)
Song For The Asking
Simon & Garfunkel; *Bridge Over Troubled Water* . . . . (Columbia)
Songbird
Duncan Sheik; *Legacy-A Tribute To Fleetwood Mac's Rumours-C* . . . . . .(Lava)
Fleetwood Mac; *25 Years-The Chain.* . . . . (Warner Bros.)
  Rumours . . . . (Warner Bros.)
Soul Of Love
Paul Rodgers; *Now & Live* . . . . (VelVel)
Sounds Like Love
Johnny Lee; *Johnny Lee's Greatest Hits* . . . . (Full Moon/Asylum)
Sour Times (Nobody Loves Me)
Portishead; *Dummy* . . . .(Go! Discs)
Southern Loving
Jim Ed Brown; *Essential Jim Ed Brown* . . . . (RCA)
Sowin' Love
Paul Overstreet; *Sowin' Love* . . . . (RCA)
Spare Me A Little Of Your Love
Fleetwood Mac; *Bare Trees* . . . . (Reprise)
Sparkling Brown Eyes
Webb Pierce with the Wilburn Brothers; *King Of The Honky-Tonk: From The*
  Original Decca Masters-1952-1959 . . . . (Country Music Foundation)
  Webb Pierce-Greatest Hits/Finest Performances . . . . (Sun)
Spilled Perfume
Pam Tillis; *Sweetheart's Dance* . . . . (Arista)
Spooky
Atlanta Rhythm Section; *Underdog* . . . . (Polydor)
Classics IV; *Ghastly Grooves-C.* . . . . (K-Tel)
  Good Vibrations (Sounds Of Top 40 Radio: 1964-1967)-C . . . .(Capitol)
  Spooky . . . . (Liberty)
  Very Best Of The Classics IV . . . . (EMI)
Spring Affair
Donna Summer; *Billboard Top Dance Hits-1976-C* . . . .(Rhino)
  Four Seasons Of Love . . . . (Casablanca)
  Live & More . . . . (Casablanca)
Stairway To Heaven
Neil Sedaka; *Neil Sedaka Sings His Greatest Hits* . . . . (RCA)
  Neil Sedaka's All-Time Greatest Hits . . . . (RCA)
Stand Up (Kick Love Into Motion)
Def Leppard; *Adrenalize* . . . . (Mercury)
Starry Eyes
Motley Crue; *Too Fast For Love* . . . . (Elektra)
Stay (Wasting Time)
Dave Matthews Band; *Before These Crowded Streets* . . . . (RCA)
Stay The Night
Chicago; *Chicago 17* . . . . (Warner Bros.)
  Chicago's Greatest Hits-1982-1989 . . . . (Full Moon)
Stay The Night
Jane Olivor; *Jane Olivor In Concert* . . . . (Columbia)
  Stay The Night . . . . (Columbia)
Stealing Love
Emotions; *The Emotions-Chronicle* . . . . (Stax)
Steam
Ty Herndon; *Steam* . . . . (Epic)

Still In Love
Lionel Richie; *Louder Than Words*. . . . . (Mercury)
Still The One
Orleans; *Dance With Me* . . . . (Rhino)
  Still The One . . . . (Elektra)
  Super Hits Of The '70s-Have A Nice Day-#19-C . . . . (Rhino)
Stolen Car
Bruce Springsteen; *The River* . . . . (Columbia)
  Tracks . . . . (Columbia)
Elliott Murphy; *One Step Up/Two Steps Back-The Songs Of Bruce*
  Springsteen-C . . . . (Right Stuff)
Stoned Love
Diana Ross & The Supremes; *ST/Forrest Gump* . . (Epic/Sony Music Soundtrax)
Stop To Love
Luther Vandross; *Best Of Luther Vandross...The Best Of Love* . . . . (Epic)
  Give Me The Reason . . . .(Epic)
Story Book Of Love
Whispers; *Excellence* . . . .(Allegiance)
  Shhhh . . . . (Dore)
Story Of Love
Desert Rose Band; *Pages Of Life* . . . . (Curb)
Storybook Love
Mark Knopfler & Willy DeVille; *ST/The Princess Bride* . . . .(Warner Bros.)
Storybook Lovers
4 Seasons; *Who Loves You* . . . .(Warner Bros.)
Storybook Of Love
Rozalla; *Everybody's Free* . . . .(Epic)
Straight A's In Love
Johnny Cash; *Johnny Cash-Original Golden Hits-#3*. . . . . (Sun)
  King Of Country Music . . . . (Sun)
  Sun Story-C . . . . (Rhino)
Strings Of Love
Edie Brickell; *Ghost Of A Dog* . . . .(Geffen)
Stuck On You
Elvis Presley; *Elvis' Golden Records, Volume 3*. . . . . (RCA)
  Number One Hits . . . . (RCA)
  Return Of The Rocker . . . . (RCA)
  Worldwide 50 Gold Award Hits, Vol. 1, Parts 1 & 2 . . . . (RCA)
Stuck On You
Lionel Richie; *Can't Slow Down* . . . . (Motown)
Stuck With You
Huey Lewis and the News; *Fore!* . . . .(Chrysalis)
Stupid Cupid
Connie Francis; *Very Best Of Connie Francis* . . . . (Polydor)
Neil Sedaka; *Neil Sedaka's All-Time Greatest Hits-#2*. . . . . (RCA)
Stupidly Happy
XTC; *Wasp Star (Apple Venus Volume 2)* . . . . (Idea/TVT)
Subway Love
Gary Windo; *Deep Water* . . . . (Antilles)
Suddenly
Billy Ocean; *Best Love Songs-C* . . . . (Original Sound)
  Billy Ocean's Greatest Hits . . . . (Jive)
  Suddenly . . . . (Jive)
Sugar Shack
Jimmy Gilmer And The Fireballs; *Billboard Top Rock 'N' Roll Hits-*
  1963-C . . . . (Rhino)
  Golden Years-1963-C . . . . (Dominion Entert.)
  Good Old Rock & Roll-C . . . . . . (International Mktg. Group)
Suitelady
Maxwell; *Maxwell's Urban Hang Suite* . . . . (Columbia)
Summer (The First Time)
Bobby Goldsboro; *Honey-Best Of Bobby Goldsboro* . . . .(EMI)
Summer Love
Chris Rea; *Espresso Logic* . . . . (East West)
Summer Of Love
Jefferson Airplane; *Jefferson Airplane* . . . .(Epic)
Summer Of Love
B-52's; *Bouncing Off The Satellites* . . . .(Warner Bros.)
Summer Rain
Carl Thomas; *Emotional*. . . . . (Bad Boy/Arista)
Summer Romance
Rolling Stones; *Emotional Rescue* . . . .(Rolling Stones)
Summerlove
Neil Diamond; *ST/The Jazz Singer* . . . . (Capitol)
Summertime Love
Ta Mara & The Seen; *Ta Mara & The Seen* . . . . (A&M)
Sumthin' Sumthin'
Maxwell; *Maxwell's Urban Hang Suite* . . . . (Columbia)
  ST/Love Jones . . . . (Columbia)
Sunday Kind Of Love
Ben Sidran; *That's Life I Guess* . . . . (Bluebird)
Ella Fitzgerald; *Best Of Ella Fitzgerald-#2*. . . . .(MCA)
Harptones; *Collectables Presents The History Of Rock-#6-C* . . . . (Collectables)
Kenny Rankin; *Inside Kenny Rankin* . . . .(Little David)
Reba McEntire; *Reba* . . . .(MCA)
Sunshine Of Your Love
Cream; *Cream-Live-#2* . . . . (Polydor)
  Disraeli Gears . . . . (Polydor)

History Of British Rock-#8-C . . . . (Rhino)
  Strange Brew-Very Best Of Cream . . . .(Polydor)
Eric Clapton; *24 Nights* . . . . (Duck/Reprise)
  Eric Clapton-Crossroads-C . . . . (Polydor)
  Knebworth-The Album-C . . . . (Polydor)
Sure Love
Hal Ketchum; *Sure Love* . . . . (Curb)
Surely I Love You
Huey Lewis and the News; *Four Chords & Several Years Ago* . . . . (Elektra)
Sway
Bobby Rydell; *Born With A Smile* . . . .(Plum)
Dean Martin; *Best Of Dean Martin* . . . . (CEMA Special Prod.)
  Dean Martin's All Time Greatest Hits . . . . (Curb)
  That's Amore: The Best Of Dean Martin . . . . (Capitol)
Sweet And Lovely
Bing Crosby; *Pennies From Heaven* . . . .(Pro-Arte)
Thelonius Monk; *Monk's Dream* . . . . (Columbia)
Woody Herman; *Essential Big Bands-C* . . . . (Verve)
Sweet Caroline
Neil Diamond; *Glory Road-1968-1972*. . . . . (MCA)
  Hot August Night . . . . (MCA)
  Love At The Greek . . . . (Columbia)
  Neil Diamond-Gold . . . . (MCA)
  Neil Diamond-His 12 Greatest Hits . . . . (MCA)
Sweet Dreams
Air Supply; *Air Supply's Greatest Hits* . . . . (Arista)
  The One That You Love . . . . (Arista)
Sweet Fire Of Love
Robbie Robertson; *Robbie Robertson* . . . . (Geffen)
Sweet Life
Marie Osmond & Paul Davis; *All In Love* . . . . (Curb)
Paul Davis; *Best Of Paul Davis* . . . .(Bang)
  Singer Of Songs-Teller Of Tales . . . .(Bang)
Sweet Little Miss Blue Eyes
Jim & Jesse/The Virginia Boys; *Appalachian Stomp: More Bluegrass*
  Classics-C . . . . (Rhino)
Sweet Love
Commodores; *All The Great Love Songs-Commodores* . . . . (Motown)
  Commodores Greatest Hits . . . . (Motown)
  Lionel Richie-Composer Series . . . . (Motown)
Sweet Love
Anita Baker; *Rapture* . . . . (Elektra)
Sweet Lover Hangover
Love And Rockets; *Sweet F.A.* . . . . (American)
Sweet Lover Man
Pointer Sisters; *Best Of The Pointer Sisters 1978-1981*. . . . . (RCA)
  Sweet & Soulful . . . . (RCA)
Sweet Lovin'
Poco; *Good Feelin' To Know* . . . . (Epic)
  Very Best Of Poco. . . . . (Epic)
Sweet Lovin' Daddy
Betty Wright; *Golden Classics-Betty Wright* . . . . (Collectables)
Fontella Bass; *Rescued-Best Of Fontella Bass* . . . .(Chess)
Sweet Rosalyn
Sheryl Crow; *Sheryl Crow*. . . . .(A&M)
Sweet Summer Lovin'
Dolly Parton; *Essential Dolly Parton* . . . . (RCA)
Sweetest Days
Vanessa Williams; *The Sweetest Days* . . . . (Uptown/MCA)
Sweetest Thing
Refugee Camp All-Stars featuring Lauryn Hill; *ST/Love Jones* . . . . . (Columbia)
Sweetest Thing (I've Ever Known)
Juice Newton; *Country Love-C* . . . . (K-Tel)
  Juice Newton-Greatest Hits & More . . . . (Capitol)
  Juice Newton's Greatest Country Hits . . . .(Curb)
Sweethearts Together
Rolling Stones; *Voodoo Lounge* . . . .(Virgin)
Swing Wide Your Gate Of Love
Hank Thompson; *Hank Thompson's Greatest Hits*. . . . .(Step One)
  The Country Music Hall Of Fame-Hank Thompson . . . . (MCA)
Take A Bow
Madonna; *Bedtime Stories* . . . .(Maverick/Sire)
  GHV2 . . . . (Warner Bros.)
  Something To Remember . . . .(Maverick/Sire)
Take Care Of Home
Dave Hollister; *Chicago '85 The Movie* . . . . (Def Squad/DreamWorks)
Take It Like A Man
Michelle Wright; *Now & Then* . . . .(Arista)
  Today's Top Country-C . . . . (K-Tel)
Take Me Back To My Love In China
Durell Coleman; *Durell Coleman* . . . . (Island)
Take Me For A Little While
Coverdale/Page; *Coverdale/Page* . . . . (Geffen)
Take Me In Your Arms & Love Me
Gladys Knight & The Pips; *Everybody Needs Love/If I Were Your*
  Woman. . . . . (Motown)
  Gladys Knight & The Pips-Anthology . . . . (Motown)
Takin' Love Into My Own Hands
Sylvester; *12 By 12-Collection* . . . . (Megatone)

Taking A Chance On Love
Anita O'Day; *Anita Sings The Most*. (Verve)
Barbra Streisand; *Third Album* . . . . (Columbia)
Benny Goodman; *I Like Jazz-Essence Of Benny Goodman*. . . . . . . (Columbia)
Ella Fitzgerald; *Ella-Fitzgerald-Early Years-#2* . . . . (GRP)
Frank Sinatra; *Songs For Young Lovers & Swing Easy* . . . . (Capitol)
Johnny Mathis & Henry Mancini; *Hollywood Musicals* . . . . (Columbia)
Rosemary Clooney; *Show Tunes* . . . . (Concord Jazz)
Tony Bennett; *I Left My Heart In San Francisco* . . . . (Columbia)

Tangled Up In Blue
Bob Dylan; *Biograph*. . . . . (Columbia)
Blood On The Tracks . . . . (Columbia)
Real Live . . . . (Columbia)
The Bootleg Series-Volumes 1-3 [Rare & Unreleased] . . . . (Columbia)

Taste Of Bitter Love
Gladys Knight & The Pips; *Best Of Gladys Knight & The Pips-The Columbia Years* . . . . (Columbia)

Taste Of Honey
Barbra Streisand; *The Barbra Streisand Album* . . . . (Columbia)
Beatles; *Beatles-Box Set* . . . . (Capitol)
Please Please Me . . . . (Parlophone)
The Early Beatles . . . . (Capitol)
Herb Alpert; *Midnight Sun* . . . . (A&M)
Herb Alpert & The Tijuana Brass; *Herb Alpert & The Tijuana Brass' Greatest Hits* . . . . (A&M)
Herb Alpert & The Tijuana Brass-Classics-#1 . . . . (A&M)
Tony Bennett; *Forty Years-The Artistry Of Tony Bennett* . . . . . . (Columbia)

Teacher, The
Paul Simon; *You're The One* . . . . (Warner Bros.)

Teen Angel
Dion And The Belmonts; *Everything You Always Wanted* . . . . (Laurie)
Rock & Roll U.S.A.-21 Rock & Roll Favorites-#2-C . . . . (Laurie)
Mark Dinning; *Golden Years-1959-C* . . . . (Dominion Entert.)
Oldies But Goodies-#7-C . . . . (Original Sound)
ST/American Graffiti . . . . (MCA)
Teenage Tragedies-C . . . . (Rhino)

Teenage Love
Frankie Lymon and The Teenagers; *Best Of Frankie Lymon and The Teenagers* . . . . (Rhino)

Teenage Vows Of Love
Dreamer; *Spotlite Series-Goldisc Records-#1-C* . . . . (Collectables)

Tell Laura I Love Her
Ray Peterson; *Nipper's Greatest Hits Of The '60s-#1-C* . . . . (RCA)
Teenage Tragedies-C . . . . (Rhino)

Tell Me That You Love Me
Eric Clapton; *Backless* . . . . (Polydor)

Tell Me Why
Elvis Presley; *A Valentine Gift For You*. . . . . (RCA)
The King Of Rock 'N' Roll-The Complete 50's Masters . . . . (RCA)
The Other Sides-Worldwide Gold Award Hits, Vol. 2 . . . . (RCA)

Tell Me Why
Bobby Vinton; *Bobby Vinton-16 Most Requested Songs* . . . . . . (Legacy)
Bobby Vinton's Greatest Hits/Greatest Hits Of Love . . . . (Columbia)
Four Aces; *Four Aces' Greatest Hits* . . . . (MCA)

Tell The Truth
Derek And The Dominos; *Derek & The Dominos In Concert* . . . . . . (RSO)
Eric Clapton-Crossroads-C . . . . (Polydor)
Layla . . . . (Polydor)

Ten Commandments Of Love
Bob Marley & The Wailers; *Birth Of A Legend 1963-1966* . . . . (Epic Portrait Assoc.)
Harvey & The Moonglows; *Best Of Chess Rock 'N' Roll-#2-C* . . . . (Chess)
Collectables Presents The History Of Rock-#10-C. . . . . (Collectables)
Cruisin'-1958-C . . . . (Increase)
Oldies But Goodies-#11-C . . . . (Original Sound)

Tender Love
Force MD's; *For Lovers & Others-Greatest Hits* . . . . (Tommy Boy)
Smooth Grooves-A Sensual Collection-#2-C . . . . (Rhino)

Tender Love
Derek And The Dominos; *The Layla Sessions-20th Anniversary Edition* . . . . (Polydor)

Tender Moment, A
Lee Roy Parnell; *Hits And Highways Ahead* . . . . (Arista)
Love Without Mercy . . . . (Arista)
Pure Country-Best Of The '90s-C . . . . (Priority)

Tender When I Want To Be
Mary Chapin Carpenter; *Stones In The Road* . . . . (Columbia)

Tenderly
Billie Holiday; *Verve Jazz Masters 47-Billie Holiday Sings Standards*. . . (Verve)
Ella Fitzgerald; *Verve Jazz Masters 24* . . . . (Verve)
Oscar Peterson; *Essential Oscar Peterson-The Swinger* . . . . (Verve)
Rosemary Clooney; *Essence Of Rosemary Clooney* . . . . (Legacy)
Rosemary Clooney-16 Most Requested Songs . . . . (Legacy)
Sarah Vaughan; *Compact Jazz-Sarah Vaughan* . . . . (Verve)
Verve Jazz Masters 42-The Jazz Sides . . . . (Verve)
Tony Bennett; *Here's To The Ladies* . . . . (Columbia)

Texas
Merle Haggard; *Friend In California* . . . . (Epic)
Merle Haggard & Freddy Powers; *Texas Super Hits-C* . . . . (Columbia)

Texas I Love You
Marty Robbins; *Lost & Found* . . . . (Columbia)

Texas Love Song
Elton John; *Don't Shoot Me I'm Only The Piano Player* . . . . (Polydor)

Thank God For You
Sawyer Brown; *Outskirts Of Town*. . . . . (Curb)
Sawyer Brown's Greatest Hits 1990-1995 . . . . (Curb)

Thank The Lord For The Night Time
Neil Diamond; *Glory Road-1968-1972* . . . . (MCA)
Hot August Night II . . . . (Columbia)
Neil Diamond-Classics (Early Years) . . . . (Columbia)
Neil Diamond-Gold. . . . . (MCA)
Neil Diamond's Greatest Hits-1966-1992 . . . . (Columbia)

Thank You
Boyz II Men; *Boyz II Men II* . . . . (Motown)

Thank You For Loving Me
Bon Jovi; *Crush* . . . . (Island/IDJMG)

Thank You Girl
Beatles; *Beatles-Box Set*. . . . . (Capitol)
Past Masters-Volume One. . . . . (Parlophone)
The Beatles' Second Album . . . . (Capitol)

Thankyou
Dido; *No Angel*. . . . . (Arista)
Totally Hits 2001-C . . . . (Arista)

That Means A Lot
Beatles; *The Beatles-Anthology-#2* . . . . (Capitol)

That Old Devil Called Love
Chet Baker; *Baker's Holiday* . . . . (Verve)
Compact Jazz-Chet Baker . . . . (Verve)
Ella Fitzgerald; *All That Jazz* . . . . (Pablo)

That's All Right (Mama)
Arthur "Big Boy" Crudup; *Best Of The Blues* . . . . (Pair)
That's All Right (Mama) . . . . (Bluebird)
Carl Perkins; *Restless-Columbia Recordings*. . . . . (Columbia)
Elvis Presley; *For LP Fans Only* . . . . (RCA)
Sun Story-C . . . . (Rhino)
Sun's Greatest Hits-C . . . . (RCA)
The Sun Sessions . . . . (RCA)
Marty Robbins; *Essential Marty Robbins-1951-1982* . . . . (Columbia)
Merl Saunders/Jerry Garcia/Bill Vitt/John Kahn; *Live At Keystone*. . . . (Fantasy)
Paul McCartney; *CHOBA B CCCP-The Russian Album* . . . . (Capitol)
Rick Nelson; *Stay Young-Epic Recordings* . . . . (Epic)
Rod Stewart; *Every Picture Tells A Story*. . . . . (Mercury)
Vintage Rod Stewart . . . . (Mercury)
Vince Gill; *ST/Honeymoon In Vegas* . . . . . (Epic/Sony Music Soundtrax)

That's Amore
Dean Martin; *Best Of Dean Martin* . . . . (CEMA Special Prod.)
Dean Martin's All Time Greatest Hits. . . . . (Curb)
Dean Martin's Greatest Hits . . . . (EMI)
The Capitol Years-Dean Martin . . . . (Capitol)

That's How You Know It's Love
Deana Carter; *Did I Shave My Legs For This?* . . . . (Capitol)

That's Not Love
Keb' Mo'; *Just Like You*. . . . . (Okeh)

That's The Way It Is
Celine Dion; *All The Way...A Decade Of Song* . . . . (550 Music)
Collector's Series-Celine Dion-#1 . . . . (550 Music)

That's The Way Love Goes
Merle Haggard; *30 Years Of #1 Hits-#16-C*. . . . . (Columbia)
His Epic Hits-First 11 To Be Continued-C . . . . (Epic)
Merle Haggard-Super Hits . . . . (Epic)
That's The Way Love Goes . . . . (Epic)
Merle Haggard & Jewel; *For The Record: Merle Haggard-43 Legendary Hits* . . . . (BNA)

That's The Way Love Goes
Kirk Whalum; *For You*. . . . . (Warner Bros.)

That's The Way Love Goes
Janet Jackson; *janet*. . . . . (Virgin)

That's The Way Of The World
Earth, Wind & Fire; *Best Of Earth, Wind & Fire-#1* . . . . (Legacy)
Eternal Dance . . . . (Columbia)
Love Shouldn't Hurt-C . . . . (Qwest)
Pop Classics Of The '70s-C . . . . (Columbia)
That's The Way Of The World . . . . (Legacy)

That's What I Get For Lovin' You
Diamond Rio; *Diamond Rio IV* . . . . (Arista)

That's What I Get For Lovin' You
Chet Atkins; *Country Gems* . . . . (Pair)

That's What Love Is For
Amy Grant; *Heart In Motion* . . . . (A&M)

That's Where You Take Me
Britney Spears; *Britney* . . . . (Jive)

Theme From "Anything But Love"
Original Soundtrack; *Television's Greatest Hits-#7-Cable Ready-C* . . . . (TVT)

Theme From "I Love Lucy"
Original Soundtrack; *CBS: The First 50 Years*. . . . . (TVT)
Television's Greatest Hits-#1-C . . . . (TVT)
TV Theme Sing-Along Album . . . . (Rhino)

Theme From "Love Story"
Andy Williams; *Andy Williams' Greatest Hits-#2* . . . . (Columbia)
 Love Story . . . . (Columbia)
Cincinnati Pops Orchestra/Erich Kunzel; *Hollywood's Greatest
 Hits-#1* . . . . (Telarc)
Francis Lai; *ST/Love Story* . . . .(MCA)
Johnny Mathis; *Johnny Mathis' All-Time Greatest Hits* . . . . . . (Columbia)
 Johnny Mathis-16 Most Requested Songs . . . . (Columbia)
Peter Nero; *Peter Nero's Greatest Hits* . . . . (Columbia)

Theme From "Love, American Style"
Original Soundtrack; *Television's Greatest Hits-#2-C* . . . . (TVT)
 TV Classic Themes: 25th Anniversary Edition-C . . . . (Breakable)

Theme From "Mad About You"
Original Soundtrack; *Television's Greatest Hits-#7-Cable Ready-C* . . . . (TVT)

Theme From "Rawhide"
Blues Brothers; *Original Soundtrack* . . . .(Atlantic)
Frankie Laine; *CBS: The First 50 Years* . . . . (TVT)
 Cowboy Super Hits-C . . . . (Columbia)
 Television's Greatest Hits-#2-C . . . . (TVT)
Riders In The Sky; *Cowboy Songs* . . . . (Rounder)

Theme From "The Love Boat"
Original Soundtrack; *Television's Greatest Hits-#3-1970s & 1980s-C* . . (TVT)

Theme From "The Many Loves Of Dobie Gillis"
Original Soundtrack; *CBS: The First 50 Years* . . . . (TVT)
 Television's Greatest Hits-#1-C . . . . (TVT)
 TV Classic Themes: 25th Anniversary Edition-C . . . . (Breakable)

Then Again
Alabama; *Pass It On Down* . . . .(BMG Special Prod.)

Then Came You
Dionne Warwick & Spinners; *Chicken Soup For The Couples Soul-C* . . (Rhino)
 Very Best Of Dionne Warwick . . . . (Rhino)
Spinners & Dionne Warwick; *Best Of The Spinners* . . . . (Atlantic)

Then You Look At Me
Celine Dion; *All The Way...A Decade Of Song* . . . . (550 Music)

There Goes Another Love Song
Outlaws; *Bring It Back Alive* . . . . (Arista)
 Greatest Hits Of The Outlaws-High Tides Forever . . . . (Arista)
 Southern Fried Rock . . . . (K-Tel)

There She Goes
Sixpence None The Richer; *Sixpence None The Richer* . . . . . .(Squint/Columbia)

There You'll Be
Faith Hill; *ST/Pearl Harbor* . . . .(Warner Bros.)

There's A Kind Of Hush (All Over The World)
Carpenters; *A Kind Of Hush* . . . . (A&M)
 Carpenters-Classics-#2 . . . . (A&M)
 Yesterday Once More . . . . (A&M)
Herman's Hermits; *Herman's Hermits-Their Greatest Hits* . . . . . (Abkco)

There's No Love In Tennessee
Barbara Mandrell; *Barbara Mandrell's Greatest Hits* . . . .(MCA)
 Country Classics-#3-1984-1985-C . . . . (Universal)

These Arms
All-4-One; *And The Music Speaks* . . . . (Blitzz)

They Call It Making Love
Tammy Wynette; *Tears Of Fire-25th Anniversary Collection* . . . .(Epic)
Tammy Wynette & George Jones; *Encore-Tammy Wynette & George
 Jones* . . . .(Epic)

They Were Doin' The Mambo
Vaughn Monroe; *Very Best Of Vaughn Monroe* . . . .(Taragon)

They're Playin' Our Song
Neal McCoy; *Neal McCoy's Greatest Hits* . . . . (Atlantic)
 You Gotta Love That! . . . . (Atlantic)

Thicker Than Blood
Garth Brooks; *Scarecrow* . . . . (Capitol)

Thing Called Love
Johnny Cash; *Johnny Cash-16 Biggest Hits-#2* . . . . (Legacy)
 The Man In Black-His Greatest Hits . . . . (Legacy)

Thing Called Love
Bonnie Raitt; *Nick Of Time* . . . . (Capitol)

Things We Said Today
Beatles; *Beatles-Box Set* . . . . (Capitol)
 Something New . . . . (Capitol)
 The Beatles At The Hollywood Bowl . . . . (Capitol)
Paul McCartney; *Tripping The Live Fantastic-Highlights!* . . . . . . (Capitol)

Thirty-Three
Smashing Pumpkins; *Mellon Collie And The Infinite Sadness* . . . . . . (Virgin)

This Ain't The Summer Of Love
Blue Oyster Cult; *Agents Of Fortune* . . . . (Columbia)

This Broken Heart
Mavericks; *From Hell To Paradise* . . . .(MCA)

This Crazy Love
Oak Ridge Boys; *Country Classics-#10-1987-C* . . . . (Universal)
 Oak Ridge Boys' Greatest Hits 3 . . . .(MCA)
 This Crazy Love . . . .(MCA Special Prod.)
 Where The Fast Lane Ends . . . .(MCA)

This Everyday Love
Rascal Flatts; *Rascal Flatts* . . . . (Lyric Street)

This Girl's In Love With You
Dionne Warwick; *Dionne Warwick-At Her Very Best* . . . . (Pair)

Petula Clark; *Greatest Hits Of Petula Clark* . . . .(Crescendo)

This Guy's In Love With You
Burt Bacharach; *Burt Bacharach-Classics-#23* . . . . (A&M)
 Burt Bacharach's Greatest Hits . . . . (A&M)
Herb Alpert & The Tijuana Brass; *Herb Alpert & The Tijuana Brass-Greatest
 Hits-#2* . . . . (A&M)

This Is Love
Regina Belle; *Quiet Storm* . . . . (Columbia)
 Stay With Me . . . . (Columbia)

This Is Love
Gladys Knight; *Good Woman* . . . .(MCA)

This Is Love
Mary Chapin Carpenter; *Stones In The Road* . . . . (Columbia)

This Is Me Missing You
James House; *Days Gone By* . . . . (Epic)
 Super Hits Of 1995-C . . . . (Epic)

This Is My Song
Petula Clark; *Greatest Hits Of Petula Clark* . . . .(Crescendo)

This Love
Tammy Wynette & Cliff Richard; *Without Walls-C* . . . . (Epic)

This Love
Commodores; *All The Great Love Songs-Commodores* . . . . (Motown)

This Love
Daniel Ash; *Coming Down* . . . .(Beggar's Banquet)

This Love
Bad Company; *Fame & Fortune* . . . .(Atlantic)

This Love That I've Found
Ella Fitzgerald; *Best Of Ella Fitzgerald* . . . . (Pablo)

This Night Won't Last Forever
Bill LaBounty; *The Right Direction* . . . . (Noteworthy)
 This Night Won't Last Forever . . . . (Warner Bros.)
Michael Johnson; *Dialogue* . . . . (EMI)
 Have A Nice Night-Romantic Hits Of The '70s-C . . . . (Rhino)
 Radio Daze-Pop Hits Of The '80s-#1-C . . . . (Rhino)
 Then & Now . . . .(ISD/Intersound)
Moe Bandy; *Many Mansions* . . . . (Curb)
Sawyer Brown; *Six Days On The Road* . . . . (Curb)

This Romeo Ain't Got Julie Yet
Diamond Rio; *Close To The Edge* . . . . (Arista)

This Time
Curtis Stigers; *Time Was* . . . . (Arista)

This Woman Needs
SHeDAISY; *The Whole Shebang* . . . .(Lyric Street)

Three Times A Lady
Commodores; *All The Great Love Songs-Commodores* . . . . (Motown)
 Commodores Greatest Hits . . . . (Motown)
 Commodores-All The Great Hits . . . . (Motown)
 Endless Love-Motown's Greatest Love Songs-C . . . . (Motown)
 Natural High . . . . (Motown)

Through The Eyes Of Love
Melissa Manchester; *Melissa Manchester's Greatest Hits* . . . . . . (Arista)
 ST/Ice Castles . . . . (Arista)

Thundercrack
Bruce Springsteen; *Tracks* . . . . (Columbia)

Tie You Up (The Pain Of Love)
Rolling Stones; *Undercover* . . . . (Rolling Stones)

'Til I Fell In Love With You
Bob Dylan; *Time Out Of Mind* . . . . (Columbia)

Time & Love
Sawyer Brown; *Dirt Road* . . . . (Curb)

Time & Love
Barbra Streisand; *Stoney End* . . . . (Columbia)
Laura Nyro; *New York Tendaberry* . . . . (Columbia)

Time For Love
Shirley Horn; *Here's To Life* . . . . (Verve)
Tony Bennett; *Forty Years-The Artistry Of Tony Bennett* . . . . . . (Columbia)
 Tony Bennett's All-Time Greatest Hits . . . . (Columbia)

Time For Love
Kenny Rogers; *They Don't Make 'Em Like They Used To* . . . . (RCA)

Time Waits For No One
Hilltoppers; *P.S. I Love You (The Best Of The Hilltoppers)* . . . . .(Varese Vintage)

Time, Love & Tenderness
Michael Bolton; *Time, Love & Tenderness* . . . . (Columbia)

Timeless & True Love
McCarters; *Country Love Songs-C* . . . . (Warner Bros.)
 The Gift . . . . (Warner Bros.)

To All The Girls I've Loved Before
Julio Iglesias & Willie Nelson; *1100 Bel Air Place* . . . . (Columbia)
Merle Haggard & Janie Fricke; *It's All In The Game* . . . . (Epic)
Willie Nelson & Julio Iglesias; *Greatest Country Hits Of The '80s-
 1984-C* . . . . (Columbia)
 Half Nelson-C . . . . (Columbia)

To Be A Lover
Billy Idol; *Vital Idol* . . . . (Chrysalis)
 Whiplash Smile . . . . (Chrysalis)

To Be Loved
Curtis Stigers; *Songs From Dawson's Creek* . . . . (Sony Music Soundtrax)

To Be With You
Mr. Big; *Lean Into It* . . . .(Atlantic)

To Be With You
Mavericks; *Trampoline* . . . (MCA)
To Each His Own
Eddy Howard & His Orchestra; *Big Band Treasures-#2-C* . . . (Dunhill Compact Classics)
The Uncollected Eddy Howard & His Orchestra-1946-1951 . . . (Hindsight)
Ink Spots; *Best Of The Ink Spots* . . . (MCA)
Ink Spots' Greatest Hits-Original Recordings-1939-1946 . . . (MCA)
Platters; *More Encore Of Golden Hits* . . . (Mercury)
Willie Nelson; *What A Wonderful World* . . . (Columbia)
Without A Song . . . (Columbia)
To Germany With Love
Alphaville; *Forever Young* . . . (Atlantic)
To Keep My Love Alive
Ella Fitzgerald; *Rodgers & Hart Songbook* . . . (Verve)
Mary Martin & Richard Rodgers; *Mary Martin Sings, Richard Rodgers Plays* . . . (RCA)
To Know Him, Is To Love Him
Dolly Parton/Emmylou Harris/Linda Ronstadt; *Trio* . . . (Warner Bros.)
Teddy Bears; *At The Hop-'50s Rock 'N' Roll* . . . (K-Tel)
Phil Spector-Back To Mono 1958-1969-C . . . (Abkco)
To Love Somebody
Bee Gees; *Bee Gees-Gold* . . . (Polydor)
History Of British Rock-#7-C . . . (Rhino)
Jimmy Somerville; *Jimmy Somerville-Singles Collection-1984-1990* . . (London)
Michael Bolton; *Timeless-Classics* . . . (Columbia)
To Make You Love Me (What Can I Say)
Alexander O'Neal; *All Mixed Up* . . . (Tabu)
Hearsay . . . (Tabu)
To Me
South Sixty Five; *South Sixty Five* . . . (Atlantic)
To Sir With Love
Lulu; *History Of British Rock-#6-C* . . . (Rhino)
Hollywood Magic-1960s-C . . . (Columbia)
Rock Artifacts-From The Vaults-#3-C . . . (Columbia)
Together Again
Janet Jackson; *Now That's What I Call Music!-#1-C* . . . (Virgin)
Velvet Rope . . . (Virgin)
Tomorrow
Strawberry Alarm Clock; *Best Of The Strawberry Alarm Clock-#1* . . (Bac-Trac)
Tonight Is So Right For Love
Elvis Presley; *ST/G.I. Blues* . . . (RCA)
Tonight My Love Tonight
Paul Anka; *Paul Anka-30th Anniversary Anthology* . . . (Rhino)
Paul Anka's 21 Golden Hits . . . (RCA)
Tonight Someone's Falling In Love
Johnny Carver; *Afternoon Delight* . . . (MCA Special Prod.)
Best Of Johnny Carver . . . (MCA)
Tonight We Just Might Fall In Love Again
Hal Ketchum; *Every Little Word* . . . (Curb)
Tonight You Belong To Me
Patience & Prudence; *Great Jukebox Hits Of The '50s-#2-C* . . . (CEMA Special Prod.)
Tonight, I Celebrate My Love
Peabo Bryson; *Tonight I Celebrate My Love* . . . (Capitol)
Peabo Bryson & Roberta Flack; *Born To Love* . . . (Capitol)
Quiet Storms 2-C . . . (MCA)
The Peabo Bryson Collection . . . (Capitol)
Roberta Flack; *Softly With These Songs-The Best Of Roberta Flack* . . . (Atlantic)
Tonight's All Right For Love
Elvis Presley; *Elvis-A Legendary Performer, Volume 1* . . . (RCA)
Too Busy Being In Love
Doug Stone; *From The Heart* . . . (Epic)
Too Busy Thinking About My Baby
Manhattan Transfer; *Tonin'* . . . (Atlantic)
Marvin Gaye; *Every Great Motown Hit Of Marvin Gaye* . . . (Motown)
Superhits . . . (Motown)
Too Fast For Love
Motley Crue; *Too Fast For Love* . . . (Elektra)
Too Late For Love
Def Leppard; *Pyromania* . . . (Mercury)
Too Many Lovers
Crystal Gayle; *Crystal Gayle Greatest Hits* . . . (Capitol)
Greatest Country Hits Of The '80s-1981-C . . . (Columbia)
These Days . . . (Columbia)
Too Much Fun
Daryle Singletary; *Daryle Singletary* . . . (Giant)
Today's Country Love-C . . . (K-Tel)
Too Much Love
Bread; *Best Of Bread* . . . (Elektra)
Manna . . . (Rhino)
Toot Toot Tootsie (Goo'Bye)
Al Jolson; *Al Jolson-Best Of The Decca Years* . . . (MCA)
Best Of Al Jolson . . . (MCA)
Liza Minnelli; *Liza Minnelli-At Carnegie Hall* . . . (Telarc)
Torn Between Two Lovers
Mary McGregor; *'70s Greatest Rock Hits-#9-#1 Hits-C* . . . (Priority)
Touch Me In The Morning
Diana Ross; *12 #1 Hits From The '70s-C* . . . (Motown)
20 Greatest Songs In Motown History-C . . . (Motown)
Diana Ross-All The Great Hits . . . (Motown)
Diana Ross-Anthology . . . (Motown)
Diana Ross-The Ultimate Collection . . . (Motown)
Evening With Diana Ross . . . (Motown)
Touch Me In The Morning . . . (Motown)
Train Of Love
Johnny Cash; *Johnny Cash-Legend* . . . (Sun)
Johnny Cash-Original Golden Hits-#1 . . . (Sun)
Johnny Cash-Sun Years . . . (Rhino)
Superbilly . . . (Sun)
Trucks,Trains & Airplanes-C . . . (International Mktg. Group)
Train Of Love
Neil Young; *Sleeps With Angels* . . . (Reprise)
Tranquillo (Melt My Heart)
Carly Simon; *Boys In The Trees* . . . (Elektra)
Trashing All The Loves Of History
Snakefinger; *Greener Postures* . . . (Ralph)
Treasure Of Love, The
Clyde McPhatter; *Greatest Hits-Clyde McPhatter* . . . (Curb)
Treat Her Like A Lady
Celine Dion; *Let's Talk About Love-C* . . . (550 Music)
Tremble For My Beloved
Collective Soul; *Dosage* . . . (Atlantic)
Trials
Jackopierce; *Finest Hour* . . . (A&M)
Truck Driver's Sweetheart
Karl & Harty; *Truck Driver Boogie Big Rig Hits-1939-1969-C* . . . (Audium)
Marcie Dickerson; *Country Gold-Marcie Dickerson* . . . (Plantation)
Truck Of Love
Blitzspeer; *Saves* . . . (Epic)
Truckload Of Lovin'
Albert King; *I'm In A Phone Booth Baby* . . . (Stax)
Masterworks . . . (Atlantic)
The Tomato Years . . . (Tomato)
Truckload Of Lovin' . . . (Tomato)
True Companion
Marc Cohn; *Marc Cohn* . . . (Atlantic)
True Fine Love
Steve Miller Band; *Book Of Dreams* . . . (Capitol)
Steve Miller Band-Gift Set . . . (Capitol)
Steve Miller Band's Greatest Hits-1974-78 . . . (Capitol)
True Love
Glenn Frey; *Soul Searchin'* . . . (MCA)
True Love
Vince Gill; *Essential Vince Gill* . . . (RCA)
I Never Knew Lonely . . . (RCA)
True Love
Pat Alger & Trisha Yearwood; *True Love & Other Short Stories-C* . . . (Sugar Hill)
True Love
Elton John & Kiki Dee; *Duets-C* . . . (MCA)
Four Aces; *Best Of The Four Aces* . . . (MCA)
Johnny Mathis & Henry Mancini; *Hollywood Musicals* . . . (Columbia)
Patsy Cline; *Always* . . . (MCA)
The Patsy Cline Story . . . (MCA)
Roger Whittaker; *Best Loved Ballads-#2* . . . (Liberty)
True Love
Neville Brothers; *Family Groove* . . . (A&M)
True Love
Joan Armatrading; *Square The Circle* . . . (A&M)
True Love
Jefferson Airplane; *Jefferson Airplane* . . . (Epic)
True Love Is Hard To Find
Bonnie Raitt; *Bonnie Raitt-Collection* . . . (Warner Bros.)
Nine Lives . . . (Warner Bros.)
True Love Never Dies
Earl Scruggs & Gary Scruggs & Travis Tritt; *Earl Scruggs And Friends-C* . . . (MCA)
Kevin Welch; *Kevin Welch* . . . (Reprise)
True Love Travels On A Gravel Road
Elvis Presley; *From Elvis In Memphis* . . . (RCA)
Memphis Record . . . (RCA)
Percy Sledge; *It Tears Me Up-Best Of Percy Sledge* . . . (Rhino)
True Love, True Love (If You Can Cry)
Drifters; *1959-1965-All-Time Greatest Hits And More* . . . (Atlantic)
Drifters-Golden Hits . . . (Atlantic)
Truth About You, The
Rosanne Cash; *The Wheel* . . . (Columbia)
Try A Little Kindness
Glen Campbell; *Best Of Glen Campbell* . . . (Capitol)
Glen Campbell-Best Of The Early Years . . . (Curb)
Glen Campbell's Greatest Hits . . . (Capitol)
Try A Little Tenderness
Aretha Franklin; *Sweet Bitter Love* . . . (Columbia)
David Sanborn; *ST/The Mirror Has Two Faces* . . . (Columbia)
Otis Redding; *Best Of Otis Redding* . . . (Atco)
Best Of Otis Redding . . . (Atlantic)

Live In Europe .... (Atco)
The Otis Redding Story .... (Atlantic)
Very Best Of Otis Redding .... (Rhino)
Three Dog Night; *Best Of Three Dog Night* ....(MCA)

Try Too Hard
Dave Clark Five; *History Of The Dave Clark Five* .... (Hollywood)

Tunnel Of Love
Dire Straits; *Live-Alchemy* ....(Warner Bros.)
Making Movies ....(Warner Bros.)
Money For Nothing ....(Warner Bros.)
ST/*An Officer And A Gentleman* .... (Island)

Tunnel Of Love
Byrds; *Byrdmaniax* .... (Columbia)

Tunnel Of Love
Bruce Springsteen; *Tunnel Of Love* .... (Columbia)

Turn The Page
Aaliyah; ST/*Music Of The Heart* ......(Epic/Sony Music Soundtrax)

Turtle Dovin'
Coasters; *50 Coastin' Classics-C* .... (Rhino)
Coasters-Their Greatest Recordings-Early Years .... (Atco)
Young Blood .... (Atlantic)

Tutti Frutti
Elvis Presley; *Elvis Presley* .... (RCA)
Rocker .... (RCA)
Little Richard; *Greatest Hits Recorded Live* .... (Epic)
Little Richard .... (Specialty)
Little Richard-18 Greatest Hits .... (Rhino)
More American Graffiti-C .... (MCA)
This Is How It All Began-#2-C .... (Specialty)
Tribute To Black Entertainers-C .... (Columbia)
Queen; *Live At Wembley '86* .... (Hollywood)

Tweedlee Dee
Ike & Tina Turner; *Ike & Tina Turner's Greatest Hits-#3* ..... (Saja)
LaVern Baker; *20 Million-Dollar Memories-#1-C* .... (Laurie)
Billboard Top Rock 'N' Roll Hits-1955-C .... (Rhino)

Two For The Road
Bruce Springsteen; *Tracks* .... (Columbia)

Two Lovers
Mary Wells; *Hitsville USA-The Motown Singles Collection-1959-1971-C* .... (Motown)
Mary Wells' Greatest Hits .... (Motown)

Two Out Of Three Ain't Bad
Meat Loaf; *Bat Out Of Hell* ....(Epic)
Hits Out Of Hell ....(Epic)

Two Sleepy People
Art Garfunkel; *Up 'Til Now* .... (Columbia)
Fats Waller; *Fats Waller-Masterpieces-#3* .... (EPM)
Jo Sullivan Loesser & Others; *Loesser By Loesser* .... (DRG)
Kay Kyser & His Orchestra; *Best Of The Big Bands-C* .... (Columbia)

Two Step
Dave Matthews Band; *Crash* .... (RCA)

Under African Skies
Paul Simon; *Graceland* ....(Warner Bros.)

Under The Moon Of Love
Curtis Lee; *Phil Spector-Back To Mono 1958-1969-C* .... (Abkco)

Undercover Lover
38 Special; *Tour De Force* .... (A&M)

Undercover Lover
Dazz Band; *Jukebox* .... (Motown)

Unequal Love
Crosby, Stills & Nash; *After The Storm* .... (Atlantic)

Unfaithfully Yours (One Love)
Stephen Bishop; *Best Of Bish* .... (Rhino)

Unison
Bjork; *Vespertine* .... (Elektra)

Unselfish Lover
Full Force; *Full Force* .... (Columbia)

Until The Real Thing Comes Along
Andy Kirk; *Sweetest Sounds Ever Heard-C* .... (Hip-O)
Billie Holiday; *God Bless The Child* .... (Columbia)
Quintessential-#9-1940-1942 .... (Columbia)
Dean Martin; *The Capitol Years-Dean Martin* .... (Capitol)
Frank Sinatra & The Quincy Jones Orchestra; *Frank Sinatra-Complete Reprise Studio Recordings* .... (Reprise)

Until Your Love Comes Back Around
RTZ; *Return To Zero* .... (Giant)

Up Where We Belong
Joe Cocker; *Joe Cocker Live* .... (Capitol)
Joe Cocker & Jennifer Warnes; *ST/An Officer And A Gentleman* .... (Island)
The Island Story-1962-1987-25th Anniversary-C .... (Island)

Upside Down
Diana Ross; *Billboard Top Dance Hits-1980-C* .... (Rhino)
Billboard Top Hits-1980-C .... (Rhino)
Diana .... (Motown)
Diana Ross-All The Great Hits .... (Motown)
Diana Ross-Anthology .... (Motown)

Valerie Loves Me
Material Issue; *International Pop Overthrow* .... (Mercury)

Valleri
Monkees; *Birds Bees & The Monkees* .... (Rhino)
Missing Links .... (Rhino)
More Greatest Hits Of The Monkees .... (Arista)
Nuggets-Classic Collection From The Psychedelic '60s-C .... (Rhino)

Very Thought Of You, The
Diane Schuur; *A Time For Love: Priceless Jazz-C* ....(GRP)
Ray Noble & His Orchestra; *The Sweetest Sounds Ever Heard-C* ...... (Hip-O)
Those Wonderful Years: Puttin' On The Ritz-C ......(JCI Assoc. Labels)
Wynton Marsalis; *The Very Thought Of You: Jazz For Lovers-C* .... (Legacy)

Violets Of Dawn
Blues Project; *No Time Like The Right Time-Best Of The Blues Project* .... (Rhino)
Eric Andersen; *Best Of Eric Andersen* .... (Vanguard)
Troubadours Of The Folk Era-#1-C .... (Rhino)

Vision Of Love
Mariah Carey; *Mariah Carey* .... (Columbia)
MTV Unplugged-Mariah Carey .... (Columbia)

Vivrant Thing
Q-Tip; *Amplified* ....(Def Jam/IDJMG)

Volare
Bobby Rydell; *'60s Rock 'N' Roll-#1-It's My Party-C* ...... (Dominion Entert.)

Vows Of Love
Paragons; *Best Of The Paragons* .... (Collectables)

Waiting For Love
Alias; *Alias* .... (EMI)

Walk Away From Love
David Ruffin; *David Ruffin-At His Best* .... (Motown)
Jimmy & David Ruffin; *Motown Superstar Series-#8-Jimmy & David Ruffin* .... (Motown)

Walk On Faith
Mike Reid; *Greatest Country Hits Of The '90s-1991-C* ..... (Columbia)
Turning For Home .... (Columbia)

Walkin' In The Rain With The One I Love
Love Unlimited; *Didn't It Blow Your Mind: Soul Hits Of The '70s-#11-C* .... (Rhino)

Walkin' My Baby Back Home
Johnnie Ray; *Johnnie Ray-16 Most Requested Songs* .... (Legacy)
Johnnie Ray's Greatest Hits .... (Sony Music Special Prod.)
Nat "King" Cole; *Capitol Collectors Series-Nat "King" Cole* .... (Capitol)
The Nat "King" Cole Story .... (Capitol)

Walls
Pamela Rose; *Morpheus* .... (Grace)

Waltz Across Texas
Ernest Tubb; *Ernest Tubb's Greatest Hits* .... (MCA)
The Country Music Hall Of Fame-Ernest Tubb .... (MCA)
Ernest Tubb & Willie Nelson; *Ernest Tubb Collection-C* .....(Step One)

Waltz You Saved For Me
Bob Wills; *Bob Wills-Anthology* .... (Sony Music Special Prod.)
Lawrence Welk; *22 All-Time Big Band Favorites* .... (Ranwood)
Mom & Dads; *Mom & Dads-20 Favorite Waltzes* ....(Crescendo)
Wayne King & His Orchestra; *Best Of Wayne King* .... (MCA)

Wanna Be Startin' Somethin'
Michael Jackson; *HIStory: Past, Present And Future-Book 1-C* .... (Epic)
Thriller .... (Epic)

Wannabe
Spice Girls; *First Generation: 25 Years Of Virgin Records-C* ....(Virgin)
MTV The Grind-#1-C .... (Tommy Boy)
Spice ....(Virgin)

Warm & Tender Love
Percy Sledge; *Best Of Percy Sledge* ....(Atlantic)
It Tears Me Up-Best Of Percy Sledge .... (Rhino)
Percy Sledge-The Ultimate Collection-When A Man Loves A Woman ....(Atlantic)

Warm & Tender Love
Dave Mason; *Mariposa De Oro* .... (Columbia)

Warm Love
Van Morrison; *Best Of Van Morrison* ....(Polydor)
Hard Nose The Highway ....(Polydor)
It's Too Late To Stop Now .... (Warner Bros.)

Warm Love
Joan Armatrading; *Show Some Emotion* .... (A&M)

Water Of Love
Dire Straits; *Dire Straits* .... (Warner Bros.)
Judds; *Collection-1983-1990* .... (RCA)
River Of Time .... (RCA)

Watermelon Weather
Perry Como; *Yesterday And Today-A Celebration In Song* .... (RCA)

Way He Makes Me Feel
Barbra Streisand; *Collection-Greatest Hits...And More* .... (Columbia)
ST/*Yentl* .... (Columbia)

Way She Loves Me
Richard Marx; *Paid Vacation* .... (Capitol)

Way That You Love, The
Vanessa Williams; *The Sweetest Days* .... (Uptown/MCA)

Way We Were, The
Barbra Streisand; *Just For The Record* .... (Columbia)
ST/*The Way We Were* .... (Columbia)

Way You Do The Things You Do
Rita Coolidge; *Rita Coolidge's Greatest Hits* . . . .(A&M)
Temptations; *Temptations' Greatest Hits-#1* . . . . (Motown)
 Temptations-Anthology-The Best Of The Temptations . . . .(Motown)
 Temptations-The Ultimate Collection. . . . .(Motown)
UB40; *Labour Of Love II.* . . . .(Virgin)

Way You Look Tonight, The
Billie Holiday; *Quintessential-#2-1936.* . . . . (Columbia)
Erroll Garner; *Body And Soul* . . . .(Legacy)
Frank Sinatra; *Days Of Wine And Roses, Moon River, And Other Academy*
 Award Winners . . . .(Reprise)
 Sinatra Reprise-The Very Good Years . . . .(Reprise)
 The Reprise Collection . . . .(Reprise)
Fred Astaire; *Steppin' Out-Astaire Sings.* . . . .(Verve)
Lettermen; *Best Of The Lettermen-All Original Recordings* . . . .(Curb)
 Capitol Collectors Series-The Lettermen . . . . (Capitol)
 The Lettermen's All-Time Greatest Hits. . . . . (Capitol)
Tony Bennett; *ST/My Best Friend's Wedding* . . . . (Work/Epic)

Way You Love Me, The
Faith Hill; *Breathe* . . . . (Warner Bros.)
 Totally Hits-#3-C . . . . (Atlantic)

Way, The
Jill Scott; *Who Is Jill Scott? Words And Sounds-#1* . . . . . . (Hidden Beach/Epic)

Ways Of A Woman In Love
Johnny Cash; *Best Of Johnny Cash* . . . .(Curb)
 Essential Johnny Cash . . . . (Columbia)
 Johnny Cash-Sun Years . . . . (Rhino)

We Can Love
Larry Stewart; *Down The Road* . . . . (RCA)

We Danced Anyway
Deana Carter; *Did I Shave My Legs For This?.* . . . . (Capitol)

We Don't Have To Talk (About Love)
Peabo Bryson; *Don't Play With Fire* . . . . (Capitol)
 The Peabo Bryson Collection . . . . (Capitol)

We Don't Make Love Anymore
Anne Murray; *Country Collection.* . . . . (Capitol)
 Let's Keep It That Way . . . . (Liberty)

We Got The Love
Restless Heart; *Big Iron Horses.* . . . . (RCA)

We Love U.S.A.
Li'l Wally; *Happy Birthday, America* . . . . (Jay Jay)

We Must Be In Love
Pure Soul; *Pure Soul* . . . .(Stepsun/Interscope)

We Should Be Making Love
Huey Lewis and the News; *Hard At Play.* . . . . (EMI)

We Were In Love
Toby Keith; *Dream Walkin'* . . . . (Mercury)
 Toby Keith's Greatest Hits, Volume One . . . . (Mercury)

Wear Your Love Like Heaven
Donovan; *Donovan's Greatest Hits.* . . . . (Epic)
 Gift From A Flower To A Garden. . . . . (Epic)
 Summer Of Love-#1-C . . . . (Rhino)
 Troubadour-Definitive Collection . . . . (Epic)
Sarah McLachlan; *Solace* . . . .(Arista)

Wednesday Morning, 3 AM
Simon & Garfunkel; *Collected Works* . . . . (Columbia)
 Wednesday Morning 3 A.M. . . . . (Columbia)

Weekend Love
Golden Earring; *No Promises-No Debts* . . . . (Polydor)

Weekend Love
Queen Latifah; *Black Reign.* . . . . (Motown)

We're All Alone
Boz Scaggs; *Boz Scaggs-Hits!.* . . . . (Columbia)
 Slow Dancer . . . . (Columbia)
Rita Coolidge; *Rita Coolidge's Greatest Hits* . . . .(A&M)

Western Movies (My Baby Loves)
Olympics; *All-Time Greatest Hits Of Rock 'N' Roll-C* . . . . (Curb)
 American Graffiti-#3-C . . . . (MCA)
 Best Of The Olympics . . . . (Vee-Jay)
 Jumpin' Jive '50s-C . . . . (Priority)

We've Got Tonight
Bob Seger & The Silver Bullet Band; *Nine Tonight* . . . . (Capitol)
 Stranger In Town . . . . (Capitol)
Kenny Rogers & Sheena Easton; *Kenny Rogers/Kim Carnes/Sheena Easton/*
 Dottie West . . . . (EMI)
 Kenny Rogers-25 Greatest Hits . . . . (EMI)
 Kenny Rogers-Greatest Country Hits . . . . (Curb)
 Kenny Rogers-Twenty Greatest Hits. . . . . (EMI)
 We've Got Tonight . . . . (Razor & Tie)

What A Diff'rence A Day Makes
Dinah Washington; *What A Diff'rence A Day Makes* . . . . (Mercury)

What Are You Doing The Rest Of Your Life?
Barbra Streisand; *Just For The Record* . . . . (Columbia)
 The Way We Were . . . . (Columbia)
Carmen McRae; *Great American Songbook* . . . . (Atlantic)
Joe Pass; *Best Of Joe Pass* . . . . (Pablo)

What Is Love
Deee-Lite; *World Clique* . . . . (Elektra)

What Is Love
Howard Jones; *Best Of Howard Jones 1983-1993* . . . .(Elektra)
 Human's Lib . . . . (Elektra)

What Is Love
En Vogue; *Funky Divas* . . . .(East West)

What Is Love
Haddaway; *House Of Groove.* . . . . (Arista)

What Is Love
Shangri-Las; *Remember The Shangri-Las At Their Best* . . . .(Collectables)

What Is Love
Shirelles; *Shirelles-16 Greatest Hits* . . . . (Trip)

What Is Love
Marc Almond; *Tenement Symphony* . . . . (Sire)

What Is This Thing Called Love
Alexander O'Neal; *All True Man* . . . . (Tabu)
 Greatest Hits Of Alexander O'Neal. . . . . (Epic)
Artie Shaw; *Begin The Beguine* . . . . (Bluebird)
Charlie Parker; *Cole Porter Songbook* . . . . (Verve)
Ella Fitzgerald; *Cole Porter Songbook.* . . . .(Verve)
Frank Sinatra; *Frank Sinatra Sings The Select Cole Porter* . . . . (Capitol)
Julie London; *Julie London Sings Cole Porter.* . . . . (EMI)
Kay Starr; *Back To The Roots* . . . . (Crescendo)
Mel Torme; *Night & Day-Cole Porter Songbook-C* . . . .(Verve)

What Kind Of Love
Rodney Crowell; *Life Is Messy.* . . . . (Columbia)

What Kind Of Love Are You On
Aerosmith; *ST/Armageddon-The Album* . . . . (Columbia)

What Love Is
"C" Company & Terry Nelson; *Mark Wills* . . . .(Mercury)

What Might Have Been
Little Texas; *Big Time* . . . . (Warner Bros.)

What She Is (Is A Woman In Love)
Earl Thomas Conley; *Heart Of It All* . . . . (RCA)

What The Cowgirls Do
Vince Gill; *When Love Finds You* . . . . (MCA)

What The World Needs Now Is Love
Burt Bacharach; *Burt Bacharach's Greatest Hits* . . . .(A&M)
Jackie DeShannon; *Flower Power-Psychedelic Rock Classics-C* . . . .(K-Tel)
 Good Vibrations (Sounds Of Top 40 Radio: 1964-1967)-C . . . .(Capitol)
 Oldies But Goodies-#14-C . . . . (Original Sound)
 ST/Forrest Gump. . . . . (Epic/Sony Music Soundtrax)
 ST/My Best Friend's Wedding. . . . . (Work/Epic)
 Very Best Of Jackie DeShannon . . . . (EMI)
Luther Vandross; *Songs* . . . . (Epic)
Tom Clay; *20 Hard-To-Find Motown Classics-#2-C* . . . .(Motown)

What We Really Want
Rosanne Cash; *Interiors* . . . . (Columbia)

Whatever
Ideal; *Ideal* . . . .(Noontime/Virgin)

What's In It For Me
John Berry; *John Berry* . . . .(Liberty)

What's It To You
Clay Walker; *Clay Walker* . . . . (Giant)

What's This Shit Called Love
Meatmen; *We're The Meatmen...& You Still Suck!* . . . . (Caroline)

When A Man Loves A Woman
Bette Midler; *ST/The Rose* . . . . (Atlantic)
Michael Bolton; *Time, Love & Tenderness* . . . .(Columbia)
Percy Sledge; *Atlantic Rhythm & Blues 1947-1974-#5 (1962-*
 1966)-C . . . . (Atlantic)
 Atlantic Soul Classics-C . . . .(Warner Special Prod.)
 Best Of Percy Sledge . . . . (Atlantic)
 Golden Age Of Black Music-1960-1970-C . . . . (Atlantic)
 ST/Platoon . . . . (Atlantic)

When A Man Loves A Woman
Barbara Mandrell; *Best Of Barbara Mandrell* . . . .(Liberty)
 Key's In The Mailbox . . . . (Capitol)

When Did You Stop Loving Me
George Strait; *ST/Pure Country* . . . . (MCA)

When He Shines
Sheena Easton; *Sheena Easton's Greatest Hits* . . . . (EMI Special Markets)
 The World Of Sheena Easton: The Singles Collection-C. . . . . (EMI)

When I Close My Eyes
Shanice; *Shanice* . . . .(LaFace)

When I Fall In Love
Celine Dion; *The Colour Of My Love* . . . . (550 Music)
Doris Day; *Doris Day-16 Most Requested Songs-Encore!.* . . . .(Columbia)

When I Look In Your Eyes
Diana Krall; *When I Look In Your Eyes* . . . . (GRP)

When I Take My Sugar To Tea
Boswell Sisters; *78-#6083* . . . . (Brunswick)
Frank Sinatra; *Ring-A-Ding Ding* . . . . (Reprise)
Nat "King" Cole; *The Vocal Classics-1947-1950* . . . . (Capitol)

When I Think About Angels
Jamie O'Neal; *Shiver* . . . . (Mercury)

When Love Finds You
Vince Gill; *When Love Finds You* . . . . (MCA)

When My Baby Smiles At Me
Pete Fountain; *Best Of Pete Fountain* . . . . (MCA)

Ted Lewis & His Orchestra; *Music From The New York Stage (1890-1920)-#4-1917-1920-C* . . . . (Pearl)

When My Blue Moon Turns To Gold Again
Elvis Presley; *A Golden Celebration* . . . . (RCA)
  Elvis . . . . (RCA)
  The Other Sides-Worldwide Gold Award Hits, Vol. 2 . . . . . (RCA)
Merle Haggard; *Merle Haggard-His Best.* . . . . (MCA)
  Ramblin' Fever . . . . (MCA)

When Somebody Loves You
Alan Jackson; *When Somebody Loves You* . . . . (Arista)

When The Lovelight Starts Shining Through His Eyes
Diana Ross & The Supremes; *Diana Ross & The Supremes' Greatest Hits* . . . . (Motown)
  Diana Ross & The Supremes-Anthology (1962-1969) . . . . . (Motown)
  Motown Superstar Series-#1-Diana Ross & The Supremes . . . . (Motown)
Supremes; *Where Did Our Love Go* . . . . (Motown)

When We Make Love
Alabama; *Roll On* . . . . (RCA)

When You Call On Me/Baby That's When I Come Runnin'
Luther Vandross; *One Night With You-The Best Of Love-#2* . . . . (LV/Epic)

When You Come Back To Me Again
Garth Brooks; *Scarecrow* . . . . (Capitol)

When You Dance I Can Really Love
Neil Young; *After The Gold Rush* . . . . (Reprise)
Neil Young & Crazy Horse; *Live Rust* . . . . (Reprise)

When You Love A Woman
Journey; *Trial By Fire.* . . . . (Columbia)

When You Love Someone
Bryan Adams; *MTV Unplugged-Bryan Adams* . . . . (A&M)

When You Love Someone
Anita Baker & James Ingram; *ST/Forget Paris* . . . . (Elektra)

When You Say Nothing At All
Alison Krauss & Union Station; *Kieth Whitley-A Tribute Album* . . . . (BNA)
  Now That I've Found You: A Collection . . . . (Rounder)
  ST/Switchback . . . . (RCA)
Keith Whitley; *Billboard Top Country Hits-1988-C* . . . . . . (Rhino)
  Country Wedding Album-C . . . . (Scotti Bros.)
  Don't Close Your Eyes . . . . (RCA)
  Essential Keith Whitley . . . . (RCA)
  Keith Whitley's Greatest Hits . . . . (RCA)

When You Wore A Tulip
Judy Garland; *Best Of Judy Garland* . . . . (MCA)

Where Is My Love?
El DeBarge; *Heart Mind & Soul* . . . . (Reprise)

Where Love Lives
Alison Limerick; *Club Cutz 2-C* . . . . (RCA)

Where The Bands Are
Bruce Springsteen; *Tracks* . . . . (Columbia)

Where The Blue Of The Night Meets The Gold Of The Day
Bing Crosby; *All-Time Best Of* . . . . (Curb)
  Best Of Bing Crosby. . . . . (MCA)
  Where The Blue Of The Night Meets The Gold Of The Day . . . . . (Biograph)

Where Were You (When The World Stopped Turning)
Alan Jackson; *Alan Jackson-Drive* . . . . (Arista)

Where Were You When I Was Falling In Love
Lobo; *Lobo's Greatest Hits* . . . . (Curb)
  Your Favorite Songs-C . . . . (Curb)

Where You Are
Jessica Simpson featuring Nick Lachey; *Sweet Kisses* . . . . (Columbia)

While My Guitar Gently Weeps
Beatles; *Beatles-Box Set* . . . . (Capitol)
  The Beatles (White Album) . . . . (Capitol)
  The Beatles/1967-1970 . . . . (Capitol)
George Harrison; *Best Of George Harrison* . . . . (Capitol)
  Concert For Bangladesh-C . . . . (Capitol)
  Live In Japan . . . . (Dark Horse)

Whispering Hope
Jo Stafford; *Capitol Collectors Series-Jo Stafford* . . . . . (Capitol)

Who Do You Love, I Hope
Original Broadway Cast; *Annie Get Your Gun* . . . . (Angel)

Whoever Finds This I Love You
Oak Ridge Boys; *All Our Favorite Songs* . . . . (Columbia)

Whole Lotta Love
Led Zeppelin; *Led Zeppelin II.* . . . . (Atlantic)
  Led Zeppelin-Box Set . . . . (Atlantic)
  Remasters . . . . (Atlantic)
  ST/The Song Remains The Same . . . . (Swan Song)

Whole Lotta Love On The Line
Aaron Tippin; *Call Of The Wild* . . . . (RCA)
  Greatest Hits And Then Some . . . . (RCA)
Charley Pride; *Best Of Charley Pride.* . . . . (Curb)

Whole Lotta Loving
Fats Domino; *Fats Domino's All Time Greatest Hits* . . . . (Curb)
  Fats Domino's Greatest Hits . . . . (CEMA Special Prod.)
  My Blue Heaven . . . . (Gold Rush)
Professor Longhair; *Mardi Gras In Baton Rouge* . . . . (Rhino)

Whole New World (Aladdin's Theme)
Peabo Bryson & Regina Belle; *ST/Aladdin.* . . . . (Disney)
Regina Belle & Peabo Bryson; *Passion* . . . . (Columbia)

Who's Makin' Love
Blues Brothers; *Blues Brothers-The Definitive Collection* . . . . (Atlantic)
  Made In America . . . . (Atlantic)
Johnnie Taylor; *Billboard Top R&B Hits-1965-1969-C* . . . . (Rhino)
  Johnnie Taylor-Super Hits . . . . (Stax)
  Oldies But Goodies-#5-C . . . . (Original Sound)
  Top Of The Stax-Twenty Greatest Hits-C . . . . (Stax)

Why
Frankie Avalon; *Frankie Avalon's Greatest Hits* . . . . . . (Curb)

Why Do Fools Fall In Love
Beach Boys; *Spirit Of America* . . . . (Capitol)
Diamonds; *Best Of The Diamonds-The Mercury Years.* . . . . (Mercury)
Diana Ross; *Why Do Fools Fall In Love* . . . . (RCA)
Frankie Lymon and The Teenagers; *Best Of Frankie Lymon and The Teenagers* . . . . (Rhino)
  Billboard Top Rock 'N' Roll Hits-1956-C . . . . (Rhino)
  ST/American Graffiti . . . . (MCA)
Joni Mitchell; *Shadows & Light* . . . . (Asylum)

Why Do I Feel So Sad
Alicia Keys; *Songs In A Minor* . . . . (J)

Why Do I LoveYou?
Barbara Cook; *Oscar Winners: The Lyrics Of Oscar Hammerstein II* . . . . (DRG)
Charlie Parker; *Yesterdays: The Jerome Kern Songbook-C* . . . . (Verve)
Margaret Whiting; *The Jerome Kern Songbook: A Fine Romance-C* . . . . (Verve)
Original Cast; *Show Boat* . . . . (RCA Victor)
  ST/Show Boat . . . . (Rhino)
Stephane Grappelli; *Stephane Grappelli Plays Berlin, Kern, Porter And Rodgers & Hart* . . . . (EMI-Angel)

Why I Love You So Much
Monica; *Miss Thang* . . . . (Rowdy/Arista)

Wild & Crazy Love
Mary Jane Girls; *Only Four You* . . . . (Motown)

Wild About My Lovin'
Stone Poneys Featuring Linda Ronstadt; *The Stone Poneys Featuring Linda Ronstadt.* . . . . (EMI)

Wild Honey
Beach Boys; *Absolute Best-#2.* . . . . (Capitol)
  Party!/Stack-O-Tracks . . . . (Capitol)
  Smiley Smile/Wild Honey . . . . (Capitol)

Wild Honey Pie
Beatles; *Beatles-Box Set* . . . . (Capitol)
  The Beatles (White Album) . . . . (Capitol)

Wild Is Love
Nat "King" Cole; *Nat "King" Cole (Box Set)* . . . . (Capitol)
  The Nat "King" Cole Story . . . . (Capitol)

Wild Love
Chris Isaak; *Chris Isaak* . . . . (Warner Bros.)

Wild Thing
Jimi Hendrix; *Essential Jimi Hendrix, Volume 2.* . . . . . . (Reprise)
  Live At Winterland . . . . (Rykodisc)
  ST/Jimi Plays Monterey . . . . (Reprise)
Tone Loc; *Loc-ed After Dark* . . . . (Delicious Vinyl)
  Rap's Biggest Hits-C . . . . (K-Tel)
  Rock The First-#6-C . . . . (Sandstone Music)
Troggs; *Billboard Top Rock 'N' Roll Hits-1966-C* . . . . . . (Rhino)
  Frat Rock!-C . . . . (Rhino)
  History Of British Rock-#3-C . . . . (Rhino)

Will It Be Love By Morning
Michael Martin Murphey; *Best Of Michael Martin Murphey* . . . . (Liberty)
  Heart Never Lies . . . . (Liberty)

Will You Love Me Tomorrow
4 Seasons; *4 Seasons' Greatest Hits-#2.* . . . . (Rhino)
Carole King; *Tapestry* . . . . (Epic)
Linda Ronstadt; *Linda Ronstadt-Retrospective.* . . . . (Capitol)
Lorrie Morgan; *Chicken Soup For The Woman's Soul-C* . . . . (Rhino)
Roberta Flack; *Best Of Roberta Flack.* . . . . (Atlantic)
  Quiet Fire . . . . (Atlantic)
Shirelles; *Girl Groups-Story Of A Sound-C* . . . . (Rhino)
  More Dirty Dancing-C . . . . (RCA)
  Oldies But Goodies-#14-C . . . . (Original Sound)
  Shirelles-16 Greatest Hits . . . . (Trip)
  Shirelles-Anthology 1959-1964 . . . . (Rhino)
  Wonder Women-#2-History Of Girl Group-C . . . . (Rhino)

Wings Of A Dove
Bob Marley & The Wailers; *Birth Of A Legend 1963-1966.* . . . . (Epic Portrait Assoc.)
Ferlin Husky; *Billboard Top Country Hits-1960-C* . . . . . . (Rhino)
  Country Music Classics-#2-1960-1965-C . . . . (K-Tel)
  Ferlin Husky's Greatest Hits . . . . (Curb)

Wings Of Your Love
Prism; *Small Change.* . . . . (Capitol)

Wink
Neal McCoy; *No Doubt About It* . . . . (Atlantic)

Winter Rose Love Awake
Wings; *Back To The Egg* . . . . (Capitol)

Wintertime Love
Doors; *Waiting For The Sun* . . . . (Elektra)

Wish You Were Here
Mark Wills; *Wish You Were Here* . . . . (Mercury)

With A Little Help From My Friends
Beatles; *Beatles-Box Set* ....(Capitol)
  Rarities ....(Capitol)
  Sgt. Pepper's Lonely Hearts Club Band ....(Capitol)
  The Beatles/1967-1970 ....(Capitol)
Joe Cocker; *History Of British Rock-#9-C* ....(Rhino)
  Joe Cocker-Classics-#4 ....(A&M)
  Joe Cocker's Greatest Hits ....(A&M)
  ST/Woodstock ....(Atlantic)
  With A Little Help From My Friends ....(A&M)
Ringo Starr & His All-Star Band; *Nobody's Child-Romanian Angel*
  Appeal-C ....(Warner Bros.)

With Love From Alberta
Jim Post; *Shipshape* ....(Flying Fish)

With Me
Lonestar; *I'm Already There* ....(BNA)

With You I'm Born Again
Billy Preston & Syreeta; *15 Of Motown's Greatest Love Songs* ......(Motown)
  Endless Love-Motown's Greatest Love Songs-C ....(Motown)
  Hard-To-Find Motown Classics-#2-C ....(Motown)
  Motown Story-First 25 Years-#3-C ....(Motown)

Within You Without You
Beatles; *Beatles-Box Set* ....(Capitol)
  Sgt. Pepper's Lonely Hearts Club Band ....(Capitol)

Woke Up In Love
Exile; *Exile* ....(Epic)
  Exile's Greatest Hits ....(Epic)

Woman At Home
Country Joe McDonald; *Tribute To Woody Guthrie-C* ....(Warner Bros.)

Woman In Love
Barbra Streisand; *A Collection: Greatest Hits...And More* ......(Columbia)
  Guilty ....(Columbia)

Woman In Love
Frankie Laine; *Frankie's Gold-Greatest Hits-#2* ....(Playback)

Woman In Love
Ronnie Milsap; *Ronnie Milsap's Greatest Hits-#3* ....(RCA)
  Stranger Things Have Happened ....(RCA)

Woman In Me (Needs The Man In You)
Shania Twain; *Woman In Me* ....(Mercury)

Woman Loves
Steve Wariner; *I Am Ready* ....(Arista)

Woman's Worth, A
Alicia Keys; *Songs In A Minor* ....(J)

Women's Love Rights
Laura Lee; *Laura Lee's Greatest Hits* ....(HDH)

Wonderful Guy, A
Original Cast; *South Pacific* ....(CBS Masterworks)

Wonderful Tonight
Eric Clapton; *24 Nights* ....(Duck/Reprise)
  Eric Clapton-Crossroads-C ....(Polydor)
  Just One Night ....(Polydor)
  Slowhand ....(Polydor)
  Time Pieces-#1-The Best Of Eric Clapton ....(Polydor)

Word, The
Beatles; *Beatles-Box Set* ....(Capitol)
  Rubber Soul ....(Capitol)

Words
Solomon Burke; *Best Of Solomon Burke* ....(Atlantic)
  Home In Your Heart-Best Of Solomon Burke ....(Rhino)

Words Of Love
Mamas & The Papas; *Best Of The Mamas & The Papas* ....(MCA)
  Farewell To The First Golden Era ....(MCA)
  Mamas & The Papas-16 Of Their Greatest Hits ....(MCA)
  Mama's Big Ones-Her Greatest Hits ....(MCA)

World Is Waiting For The Sunrise
Benny Goodman; *I Like Jazz-Essence Of Benny Goodman* ....(Columbia)
Benny Goodman Orchestra & Quartet; *Let's Dance* ....(Laserlight)
Les Paul & Mary Ford; *The World Is Waiting For The Sunrise* ....(Laserlight)
Roy Clark & Buck Trent; *Banjo Bandit* ....(MCA)

Would They Love Him Down In Shreveport
George Jones; *Hallelujah Weekend* ....(Epic)
Oak Ridge Boys; *Bobbie Sue* ....(MCA)

Wrapped Up In You
Garth Brooks; *Scarecrow* ....(Capitol)

Yearning (Just For You)
Asleep At The Wheel featuring Vince Gill; *Tribute To The Music Of Bob*
  Wills And The Texas Playboys-C ....(Liberty)
Bob Wills & His Texas Playboys; *For The Last Time* ....(Capitol)

You Always Hurt The One You Love
Brenda Lee; *The Brenda Lee Story-Her Greatest Hits.* ....(MCA)
Clarence Henry; *Rich Roots* ....(Allegiance)
Mills Brothers; *Best Of The Mills Brothers* ....(MCA)
  Mills Brothers' Greatest Hits ....(MCA)
  Mills Brothers-16 Great Performances ....(MCA)
Spike Jones & His City Slickers; *Best Of Spike Jones & His City*
  Slickers ....(RCA)

You And I
Eddie Rabbitt & Crystal Gayle; *Best Of Eddie Rabbitt/Greatest*
  Hits-II ....(Warner Bros.)

  Chicken Soup For The Couples Soul-C ....(Rhino)

You And The Mona Lisa
Shawn Colvin; *A Few Small Repairs* ....(Columbia)

You Are
Lionel Richie; *Lionel Richie.* ....(Motown)

You Are My Lady
Freddie Jackson; *Greatest Hits Of Freddie Jackson.* ....(Capitol)

You Are My Love
Jamiroquai; *Traveling Without Moving* ....(Work/Epic)

You Are So Beautiful
Joe Cocker; *Chicken Soup For The Soul: Love And Inspiration-C* ......(Rhino)
  Joe Cocker-Super Hits ....(Legacy)
  Organic ....(550 Music)
Kenny Rogers; *Timepiece* ....(Atlantic)

You Are The Sunshine Of My Life
Peter Nero; *Peter Nero's Greatest Hits* ....(Columbia)
Stevie Wonder; *20/20-C.* ....(Motown)
  Original Musiquarium ....(Motown)
  Talking Book ....(Motown)

You Are The Woman
Firefall; *Firefall* ....(Rhino)
  Firefall's Greatest Hits ....(Rhino)

You Belong To Me
Bob Dylan; *ST/Natural Born Killers* ....(Nothing)

You Bring Me Joy
Mary J. Blige; *My Life* ....(Uptown/MCA)

You Can Depend On Me
Brenda Lee; *The Brenda Lee Story-Her Greatest Hits* ......(MCA)
Count Basie; *Best Of Count Basie* ....(MCA)
Louis Armstrong; *Stardust* ....(Portrait)
Manhattan Transfer; *The Manhattan Transfer* ....(Rhino)

You Can Love Yourself
Keb' Mo'; *Just Like You.* ....(Okeh)

You Can Make History (Young Again)
Elton John; *Elton John-Love Songs* ....(MCA)

You Can Never Ask Too Much (Of Love)
Take 6; *Join The Band-C* ....(Reprise)

You Can't Hurry Love
Diana Ross; *Diana Ross-The Ultimate Collection* ....(Motown)
Diana Ross & The Supremes; *16 #1 Hits From The Early '60s-C* .....(Motown)
Phil Collins; *Hello, I Must Be Going* ....(Atlantic)

You Can't Lose Me
Faith Hill; *It Matters To Me* ....(Warner Bros.)

You Can't Run From Love
Eddie Rabbitt; *Best Of Eddie Rabbitt/Greatest Hits-II* ....(Warner Bros.)
  Eddie Rabbitt-#1's ....(Warner Bros.)
  Radio Romance ....(Elektra)

You Can't Stop Love
Schulyer, Knobloch & Overstreet; *S.K.O.* ....(MTM)

You Come To My Senses
Chicago; *Twenty 1* ....(Full Moon)

You Do Something To Me
Frank Sinatra; *Concepts* ....(Capitol)
Ray Conniff; *Ray Conniff -16 Most Requested Songs* ....(Legacy)

You Gets No Love
Faith Evans; *Faithfully.* ....(Bad Boy/Arista)

You Give Good Love
Whitney Houston; *Whitney Houston* ....(Arista)
  Whitney Houston's Greatest Hits ....(Arista)

You Give Love A Bad Name
Bon Jovi; *7800 Degrees Fahrenheit.* ....(Mercury)
  Cross Road-14 Classic Grooves ....(Mercury)

You Got It All
Jets; *Best Of The Jets* ....(MCA)
  Smooth Moves-New Jack Ballads-#1-C ....(Rhino)

You Got What It Takes
Dave Clark Five; *History Of The Dave Clark Five* ....(Hollywood)
Marv Johnson; *All-Time Greatest Hits Of Rock 'N' Roll-C* ....(Curb)

You Gotta Be
Des'ree; *Diana, Princess Of Wales-Tribute-C* ....(Columbia)
  I Ain't Movin' ....(550 Music)

You Gotta Be My Baby
Dolly Parton; *Red Hot + Country-C.* ....(Mercury)

You Gotta Love Someone
Elton John; *ST/Days Of Thunder* ....(David Geffen Co.)

You Have Been Loved
George Michael; *Diana, Princess Of Wales-Tribute-C* ....(Columbia)
  Older ....(DreamWorks/SKG)

You Like Me Too Much
Beatles; *ST/Help!* ....(Capitol)

You Make Me Feel (Mighty Real)
Sylvester; *ST/Young Soul Rebels* ....(Volcano Entertainment)

You Make Me Feel Brand New
Roberta Flack; *Set The Night To Music* ....(Atlantic)

You Make Me Feel Like Dancing
Leo Sayer; *Billboard Top Rock 'N' Roll Hits-1977-C* .....(Rhino)
  Endless Flight ....(Chrysalis)
  Mega Hits Dance Classics-#3-C ....(Priority)

You Make Me Feel So Good
Astors; *Astors Meet The Newcomers* . . . . (Stax)
You Make Me Feel So Young
Frank Sinatra; *Best Of The Capitol Years* . . . . (Capitol)
You Make My Dreams
Daryl Hall & John Oates; *Rock 'N Soul, Part 1* . . . . (RCA)
Voices . . . . (RCA)
You Move Me
Cassandra Wilson; *ST/Love Jones* . . . . (Columbia)
You Move Me
Garth Brooks; *Sevens* . . . . (Capitol)
You Oughta Be In Pictures
Doris Day; *Sentimental Journey* . . . . (Hindsight)
Jackie Gleason; *The Romantic Moods Of Jackie Gleason* . . . . (Capitol)
Rudy Vallee & His Connecticut Yankees; *78-#24580* . . . . (Victor)
You Send Me
Aretha Franklin; *Aretha's Gold* . . . . (Atlantic)
Manhattans; *Too Hot To Stop It* . . . . (Columbia)
Michael Bolton; *Timeless-Classics* . . . . (Columbia)
Sam Cooke; *Best Of Sam Cooke* . . . . (RCA)
ST/American Pop . . . . (MCA)
The Man And His Music . . . . (RCA)
You Used To Love Me
Faith Evans; *Faith Evans* . . . . (Bad Boy/Arista)
ST/All That . . . . (Loud/RCA)
The Ultimate Hip Hop Party-1998-C . . . . (Arista)
You Want This
Janet Jackson; *janet.* . . . . (Virgin)
You Were Meant For Me
Gene Kelly; *ST/Singin' In The Rain* . . . . (Turner Classic Movies)
Sting; *ST/The Object Of My Affection* . . . . (Ark 21)
You'll Be Back (Every Night In My Dreams)
Statler Brothers; *Years Ago* . . . . (Mercury)
You'll Never Find Another Love Like Mine
Lou Rawls; *10 Years Of #1 Hits* . . . . (Philadelphia Int'l)
Lou Rawls-Classics . . . . (Philadelphia Int'l)
Lou Rawls-Live (Right Stuff) . . . . (Right Stuff)
Mega Hits Dance Classics-#2-C . . . . (Priority)
Philly Ballads-#1-C . . . . (Philadelphia Int'l)
Young Man, Older Woman
Millie Jackson; *Very Best Of Millie Jackson* . . . . (Jive)
Your Faith In Me
Jessica Simpson; *Sweet Kisses* . . . . (Columbia)
Your Love
Tammy Wynette; *Higher Ground* . . . . (Epic)
More Hot Country Requests-#2-C . . . . (Epic)
Tears Of Fire-25th Anniversary Collection . . . . (Epic)
Your Love
Boyz II Men; *Cooleyhighharmony* . . . . (Motown)
Your Love
Outfield; *Play Deep* . . . . (Columbia)
Your Love
Dan Seals; *Won't Be Blue Anymore* . . . . (EMI)
Your Love Amazes Me
John Berry; *John Berry* . . . . (Liberty)
Your Love Is A Miracle
Mark Chesnutt; *Too Cold At Home* . . . . (MCA)
Your Love Is King
Sade; *Diamond Life* . . . . (Portrait)
Your Love-Part 2
Keith Sweat; *I'll Give All My Love To You* . . . . (Vintertainment)
Your Old Love Letters
Ricky Skaggs; *Favorite Country Songs* . . . . (Epic)
Waitin' For The Sun To Shine . . . . (Epic)
Your Precious Love
Marvin Gaye; *Last Concert Tour* . . . . (Giant)
Your Secret Love
Luther Vandross; *Your Secret Love* . . . . (LV/Epic)
You're Always On My Mind
SWV; *It's About Time* . . . . (RCA)
You're In Love
Wilson Phillips; *Chicken Soup For The Woman's Soul-C* . . . . (Rhino)
Wilson Phillips . . . . (SBK)
You're My Driving Wheel
Diana Ross & The Supremes; *Diana Ross & The Supremes' Greatest Hits & Rare Classics* . . . . (Motown)
You're My Man
Lynn Anderson; *Country Music Classics-#11-Early '70s-C* . . . . (K-Tel)
Lynn Anderson Anthology: The Columbia Years . . . . (Renaissance)
You're My World
Cilla Black; *History Of British Rock-#2-C* . . . . (Rhino)
You're The Best Break This Old Heart Ever Had
Ed Bruce; *Ed Bruce's Greatest Hits* . . . . (MCA)
One To One . . . . (MCA)
You're The Inspiration
Chicago; *Chicago 17* . . . . (Warner Bros.)
Chicago's Greatest Hits-1982-1989 . . . . (Full Moon)

Peter Cetera featuring Az Yet; *You're The Inspiration-A Collection* . . . . (River North)
You're The One
Vogues; *Back To The '60s-#2-C* . . . . (Dominion Entert.)
Vogues' Greatest Hits . . . . (Rhino)
Yours
Shai; *If I Ever Fall In Love* . . . . (Gasoline Alley)
You've Been In Love Too Long
Bonnie Raitt; *Takin' My Time* . . . . (Warner Bros.)
Martha & The Vandellas; *Martha Reeves & The Vandellas' Greatest Hits* . . . . (Motown)
Martha Reeves & The Vandellas-Anthology . . . . (Motown)
You've Got A Lover
Ricky Skaggs; *19 Hot Country Requests-#2-C* . . . . (Epic)
Highways & Heartaches . . . . (Epic)
You've Got A Way
Shania Twain; *Come On Over* . . . . (Mercury)
ST/Notting Hill . . . . (Mercury)
You've Made Me So Very Happy
Blood, Sweat & Tears; *Blood, Sweat & Tears* . . . . (Columbia)
Blood, Sweat & Tears Greatest Hits . . . . (Columbia)
Live & Improvised . . . . (Columbia)
Pop Classics Of The '60s-C . . . . (Columbia)
Yummy Yummy Yummy
Ohio Express; *Billboard Top Rock 'N' Roll Hits-1968-C* . . . . (Rhino)
Bubblegum Classics-#1-C . . . . (Varese Vintage)

LOVE: GET LOST!, I'm Over You, You're Not My Type

See Also: **BACK ON MY FEET, CHEATING & LIES, DIVORCE, ENDINGS, LEAVING, LOVE (various)**

(If You're Not In It...) I'm Outta Here!
Shania Twain; *The Woman In Me* . . . . (Mercury)
(I'm Not Your) Steppin' Stone
Monkees; *Monkees' Greatest Hits* . . . . (Rhino)
(Now You See Me) Now You Don't
Lee Ann Womack; *Some Things I Know* . . . . (Decca)
50 Ways To Leave Your Lover
Paul Simon; *Greatest Hits, Etc.* . . . . (Columbia)
Negotiations And Love Songs, 1971-1986 . . . . (Warner Bros.)
Still Crazy After All These Years . . . . (Columbia)
Simon & Garfunkel; *The Concert In Central Park* . . . . (Warner Bros.)
Ain't My Bitch
Metallica; *Load* . . . . (Elektra)
Ain't That Lonely Yet
Dwight Yoakam; *Last Chance For A Thousand Years-Greatest Hits From The '90s* . . . . (Reprise)
This Time . . . . (Reprise)
American Woman
Guess Who; *American Woman* . . . . (RCA)
Best Of The Guess Who . . . . (RCA)
Greatest Of The Guess Who . . . . (RCA)
Nipper's Greatest Hits Of The '70s-C . . . . (RCA)
Rock Classics-C . . . . (K-Tel)
Lenny Kravitz; *5* . . . . (Virgin)
Now That's What I Call Music!-#3-C . . . . (Virgin)
ST/Austin Powers-The Spy Who Shagged Me . . . . (Maverick)
Another Girl
Beatles; *Beatles-Box Set* . . . . (Capitol)
ST/Help! . . . . (Capitol)
Backfield In Motion
Mel & Tim; *Collectables Presents The History Of Rock-#4-C* . . . . (Collectables)
Oldies But Goodies-#2-C . . . . (Original Sound)
Soul Shots-#2-The "In" Crowd-Sweet Soul-C . . . . (Rhino)
Super Oldies Of The '60s-#10-C . . . . (Audio Fidelity)
Billie Jean
Michael Jackson; *Thriller* . . . . (Epic)
Bills, Bills, Bills
Destiny's Child; *The Writing's On The Wall* . . . . (Columbia)
Bizounce
Olivia; *Olivia* . . . . (J)
Blame It On Your Heart
Patty Loveless; *Only What I Feel* . . . . (Epic)
Patty Loveless-Classics . . . . (Epic)
Bumble Bee
LaVern Baker; *Live In Hollywood '91* . . . . (Rhino)
Searchers; *Searchers' Greatest Hits* . . . . (Rhino)
Burnin' Old Memories With A Brand New Flame
Kathy Mattea; *Country Hits 4: Sweet Country-C* . . . . (Priority)
Willow In The Wind . . . . (Mercury)
Bye Bye
'N Sync; *No Strings Attached* . . . . (Jive)
Now That's What I Call Music!-#6-C . . . . (Virgin)
Bye, Bye
Jo Dee Messina; *I'm Alright* . . . . (Curb)

Cathy's Clown
Everly Brothers; *Billboard Top Rock 'N' Roll Hits-1960-C* . . . . (Rhino)
   Golden Hits Of The Everly Brothers . . . . (Warner Bros.)
   The Reunion Concert-Live At Albert Hall 1983 . . . . (Mercury)
   Very Best Of The Everly Brothers . . . . (Warner Bros.)
Reba McEntire; *Sweet Sixteen* . . . . (MCA)

Change The Locks
Tom Petty And The Heartbreakers; *ST/She's The One* . . . . (Warner Bros.)

Coca Cola Cowboy
Mel Tillis; *Mel Tillis' Greatest Hits* . . . . (Curb)
   Very Best Of Mel Tillis . . . . (MCA)

Cousin Dupree
Steely Dan; *Two Against Nature* . . . . (Giant)

Crazy Love, Vol. II
Paul Simon; *Graceland* . . . . (Warner Bros.)

Crosstown Traffic
Jimi Hendrix; *Kiss The Sky* . . . . (Reprise)
Jimi Hendrix Experience; *Electric Ladyland* . . . . (Reprise)
   Essential Jimi Hendrix, Volume 2 . . . . (Reprise)
   Smash Hits . . . . (Reprise)

Cry On
Little Texas; *First Time For Everything* . . . . (Warner Bros.)
   Great Divorce Songs For Him-C . . . . (Warner Bros.)

Devil Woman
Marty Robbins; *Billboard Top Country Hits-1962-C* . . . . (Rhino)
   Columbia Country Classics-#4-Nashville Sound-C . . . . (Columbia)
   Lifetime Of Song-1951-1982. . . . . (Columbia)
   Marty Robbins' Greatest Hits-#4 . . . . (Columbia)

Did I Do That?
Mariah Carey; *Rainbow.* . . . . (Columbia)

Don't Come Home A'Drinkin' (With Lovin' On Your Mind)
Loretta Lynn; *Loretta Lynn-Greatest Hits Live* . . . . (K-Tel)
   Loretta Lynn's Greatest Hits . . . . (MCA)
   MCA Records 30 Years Of Hits-1958-1988-C . . . . (MCA)

Don't Come Home A'Lovin' With Venison On Your Truck
Debby McClatchy; *Someday Cafe* . . . . (Green Linnet)

Don't Waste Your Heart
Dixie Chicks; *Fly* . . . . (Monument)

Down To My Last Teardrop
Tanya Tucker; *Tanya Tucker's Greatest Hits-1990-1992* . . . . (Capitol)
   What Do I Do With Me . . . . (Capitol)

End Of The Line
Bob Wills & His Texas Playboys; *Bob Wills & His Texas Playboys-24*
   Great Hits . . . . (Polydor)
Buddy Emmons; *Buddy Emmons Sings Bob Wills.* . . . . (Flying Fish)
Jason Roberts & Asleep At The Wheel; *Ride With Bob-C* . . (DreamWorks/SKG)

Friends In Low Places
Garth Brooks; *Garth Brooks-Double Live* . . . . (Capitol)
   No Fences . . . . (Capitol)

G.H.E.T.T.O.U.T.
Changing Faces; *All Day, All Night* . . . . (Big Beat/Atlantic)

Georgia On A Fast Train
Billy Joe Shaver; *Hot Tracks-Train Super Hits-C* . . . . (Epic)

Get Gone
Ideal; *Ideal.* . . . . (Noontime/Virgin)
   Now That's What I Call Music!-#3-C . . . . (Virgin)

Get It On Tonite
Montell Jordan; *Get It On...Tonite* . . . . (Def Soul/IDJMG)
   Now That's What I Call Music!-#4-C . . . . (Virgin)

Get Out Of This House
Shawn Colvin; *A Few Small Repairs* . . . . (Columbia)

Girlfriend/Boyfriend
Blackstreet featuring Janet; *Finally.* . . . . (Lil' Man/Interscope)

Girl's Gotta Do (What A Girl's Gotta Do)
Mindy McCready; *Ten Thousand Angels* . . . . (BNA)

God Will
Holly Cole Trio; *Blame It On My Youth.* . . . . (Blue Note)
Lyle Lovett; *Lyle Lovett.* . . . . (MCA)
   Lyle Lovett Anthology-#1-Cowboy Man . . . . (MCA)
Patty Loveless; *Up Against My Heart* . . . . (MCA)

Gonna Get Along Without Ya Now
Patience & Prudence; *Lost Hits Of The 50's-C* . . . . . . (EMI Special Markets)

Good As I Was To You
Lorrie Morgan; *Greater Need* . . . . (BNA)
   Lorrie Morgan-Super Hits . . . . (RCA)
   To Get To You-Greatest Hits Collection . . . . (BNA)

Goodbye To You
Scandal; *I Am Woman-C* . . . . (Nick At Nite)
   Patty Smyth's Greatest Hits Featuring Scandal . . . . (Legacy)

Happy Birthday
Loretta Lynn; *Loretta Lynn's Greatest Hits.* . . . . (MCA)

Have A Nice Rest Of Your Life
Randy Travis; *Great Divorce Songs For Him-C* . . . . (Warner Bros.)
   No Holdin' Back . . . . (Warner Bros.)

Heard It All Before
Sunshine Anderson; *Your Woman* . . . . (Soullife/Atlantic)

Heartbreaker
Led Zeppelin; *Led Zeppelin II* . . . . (Atlantic)
   Led Zeppelin-The Complete Studio Recordings . . . . (Atlantic)

Here's A Quarter (Call Someone Who Cares)
Travis Tritt; *It's All About To Change* . . . . (Warner Bros.)

Hey Honey- I'm Packin' You In!
Bryan Adams; *Waking Up The Neighbours* . . . .(A&M)

Hit The Road Jack
Ray Charles; *Ray Charles' Greatest Hits* . . . .(Rhino)
   Ray Charles-Anthology . . . .(Rhino)
   Ray Charles-His Greatest Hits-#2. . . . . (Dunhill Compact Classics)

Hole In My Head
Dixie Chicks; *Fly* . . . . (Monument)

Hound Dog
Elvis Presley; *Aloha from Hawaii via Satellite.* . . . . (RCA)
   Elvis Aron Presley. . . . . (RCA)
   Elvis As Recorded At Madison Square Garden . . . . (RCA)
   Elvis' Golden Records. . . . . (RCA)
   Elvis In Concert. . . . . (RCA)
   Elvis Recorded Live On Stage In Memphis . . . . (RCA)
   Elvis-A Legendary Performer, Volume 3. . . . . (RCA)
   From Memphis To Vegas/From Vegas To Memphis . . . . (RCA)
   Number One Hits. . . . . (RCA)
   ST/Forrest Gump. . . . . (Epic/Sony Music Soundtrax)

I Ain't Gonna Let You Break My Heart Again
Bonnie Raitt; *Nick Of Time* . . . .(Capitol)

I Got Mexico
Eddy Raven; *14 #1 Country Hits-C* . . . . (RCA)
   Best Of Eddy Raven. . . . . (RCA)
   I Could Use Another You. . . . . (RCA)

I Learned From The Best
Whitney Houston; *My Love Is Your Love* . . . .(Arista)

I Really Don't Need No Light
Jeffrey Osborne; *Jeffrey Osborne.* . . . .(A&M)

I Will Survive
Gloria Gaynor; *Billboard Top Hits-1979-C* . . . .(Rhino)
   I Am Woman-C . . . . (Nick At Nite)
   Love Tracks . . . . (Polydor)
   The Disco Years-#2-On The Beat-1978-1982-C . . . . (Rhino)

Idiot Wind
Bob Dylan; *Blood On The Tracks* . . . . (Columbia)
   Hard Rain . . . . (Columbia)
   The Bootleg Series-Volumes 1-3 [Rare & Unreleased]. . . . . (Columbia)

If U Can't Dance
Spice Girls; *Spice* . . . . (Virgin)

If Your Girl Only Knew
Aaliyah; *MTV Party To Go '98-C* . . . . (Tommy Boy)
   One In A Million . . . .(BlackGround Enterp./Atlantic)

I'm Gonna Wash That Man Right Outta My Hair
Mitzi Gaynor; *ST/South Pacific* . . . . (RCA)
   Original Cast; *South Pacific* . . . . (CBS Masterworks)
Weather Girls; *Success.* . . . . (Columbia)

I'm Looking Through You
Beatles; *The Beatles-Anthology-#2* . . . .(Capitol)

It's My Time
Martina McBride; *Emotion* . . . . (RCA)

It's Not Right But It's Okay
Whitney Houston; *My Love Is Your Love* . . . .(Arista)

I've Had It
Danielle Brisebois; *Portable Life* . . . . (RCA)

Jilted
Teresa Brewer; *Best Of Teresa Brewer* . . . . (MCA Jazz)

Just Be A Man About It
Toni Braxton; *The Heat* . . . .(LaFace)

Just Because
Shelton Brothers; *Classic Country Music-#1-C* . . . .(Smithsonian Collection)

Keep Away
Godsmack; *Godsmack.* . . . . (Republic/Universal)

Kickin' My Heart Around
Black Crowes; *By Your Side* . . . .(American)

Kiss Off
Violent Femmes; *Violent Femmes* . . . . (Slash)

Kiss This
Aaron Tippin; *People Like Us* . . . . (Lyric Street)

Last Goodbye
Kenny Wayne Shepherd Band; *Live On* . . . . (Giant)

Let's Call The Whole Thing Off
Fred Astaire; *Steppin' Out-Astaire Sings* . . . .(Verve)

Letting Go
Sozzi; *Songs From Dawson's Creek* . . . . (Sony Music Soundtrax)

Liar
Profyle; *Nothin' But Drama* . . . .(Motown)

Life Goes On
Little Texas; *Little Texas' Greatest Hits* . . . . (Warner Bros.)

Little Gasoline, A
Terri Clark; *Fearless* . . . .(Mercury)

Little Good-byes
SHeDAISY; *The Whole Shebang.* . . . . (Lyric Street)

Little Maggie
Kingston Trio; *Tom Dooley* . . . . (Capitol)
Ricky Skaggs and Kentucky Thunder; *Bluegrass Rules!* . . . .(Rounder)

Lonely
Britney Spears; *Britney* . . . . (Jive)
Mr. Big Stuff
Jean Knight; *'70s Hit(s) Back Again-C* . . . . (Hip-O)
Have A Nice Decade-The '70s Pop Culture Box-C . . . . (Rhino)
Mustang Burn
Jack Ingram; *Hey You* . . . . (Lucky Dog)
My Boyfriend's Back
Angels; *Billboard Top Rock 'N' Roll Hits-1963-C* . . . . (Rhino)
Girl Groups-Story Of A Sound-C . . . . (Rhino)
My Boyfriend's Back . . . . (Collectables)
Oldies But Goodies-#11-C . . . . (Original Sound)
ST/The Wanderers . . . .(Warner Bros.)
Wonder Women-#2-History Of Girl Group-C . . . . (Rhino)
My Favorite Girl
Dave Hollister; *Ghetto Hymns* . . . .(Def Squad/DreamWorks)
No Man's Woman
Sinead O'Connor; *Faith & Courage* . . . .(Atlantic)
No More
Ruff Endz; *Love Crimes* . . . .(Epic)
No Scrubs
TLC; *Fanmail* . . . . (LaFace)
Totally Hits-#1-C . . . . (Arista)
No Trash In My Trailer
Gene Watson; *From The Heart* . . . .(Row Music Group)
Not A Second Time
Beatles; *With The Beatles* . . . . (Parlophone)
Not Gon' Cry
Mary J. Blige; *Share My World* . . . . (MCA)
Nothin' But The Taillights
Clint Black; *Nothin' But The Taillights* . . . . (RCA)
Nothin On Me
Shawn Colvin; *A Few Small Repairs* . . . . (Columbia)
ST/Mr. Wrong . . . . (Hollywood)
Now That She's Gone
Destiny's Child; *The Writing's On The Wall* . . . . (Columbia)
Oaf, The
Big Wreck; *In Loving Memory Of* . . . .(Atlantic)
Pack Your Lies And Go
Celinda Pink; *Victimized* . . . . (Step One)
Paper Roses
Kitty Wells; *Kitty Wells' Greatest Hits-#2* . . . . (Step One)
Marie Osmond; *All Time Greatest Hits Of Country-C* . . . . . (Curb)
Marie Osmond-25 Hits-Special Collection . . . . (Curb)
Perpetual Blues Machine
Keb' Mo'; *Just Like You* . . . . (Okeh)
Pet Names
Smash Mouth; *Fush Yu Mang* . . . . (Interscope)
Red Rubber Ball
Cyrkle; *Even More Nuggets-C* . . . . (Rhino)
Pop Classics Of The '60s-C . . . . (Columbia)
Red Rubber Ball (A Collection) . . . . (Columbia)
Release Me
Dolly Parton; *Country & Western* . . . .(Intercom Music)
Dolly Parton & Donna Fargo; *Queens Of Country* . . . .(Intermedia)
Elvis Presley; *On Stage-February, 1970* . . . . (RCA)
Welcome To My World . . . . (RCA)
Engelbert Humperdinck; *Engelbert Humperdinck-His Greatest Hits* . . . (Parrot)
Live In Concert/All Of Me . . . .(Epic)
Release Me . . . . (Mercury)
Esther Phillips; *Atlantic Rhythm & Blues 1947-1974-#5 (1962-1966)-C* . . . . (Atlantic)
Billboard Top R&B Hits-1962-C . . . . (Rhino)
Oldies But Goodies-#9-C . . . . (Original Sound)
Kitty Wells; *Kitty Wells' Greatest Hits* . . . .(MCA)
The Kitty Wells Story . . . .(MCA)
Lefty Frizzell; *Lefty Frizzell's Greatest Hits* . . . . (Columbia)
Meli'sa Morgan; *Still In Love With You* . . . . (Pendulum)
Ray Price; *Ray Price's Greatest Hits* . . . . (Columbia)
Ray Price's Greatest Hits-#1-3 . . . . (Step One)
Wilson Phillips; *Wilson Phillips* . . . . (SBK)
Return To Sender
Elvis Presley; *Girls Girls Girls* . . . . (RCA)
The Great Performances . . . . (RCA)
The Top Ten Hits . . . . (RCA)
Worldwide 50 Gold Award Hits, Vol. 1, Parts 1 & 2 . . . (RCA)
Ricochet
Teresa Brewer; *Best Of Teresa Brewer* . . . . (MCA Jazz)
Sail On
Commodores; *All The Great Love Songs-Commodores* . . . . (Motown)
Commodores-All The Great Hits . . . . (Motown)
Lionel Richie-Composer Series . . . . (Motown)
Midnight Magic . . . . (Motown)
See You Later, Alligator
Bill Haley & His Comets; *Bill Haley & His Comets* . . . . (Everest)
Bill Haley & His Comets' Greatest Hits . . . .(MCA)
Bill Haley & His Comets-Golden Hits . . . .(MCA)
Billboard Top Rock 'N' Roll Hits-1956-C . . . . (Rhino)
Mr. Rock 'N' Roll . . . . (Accord)

Rock & Roll Is Here To Stay-C . . . . (Gusto)
Rockin' & Rollin' . . . . (Accord)
Separated
Avant; *My Thoughts* . . . . (MCA)
Seven Little Girls Sitting In The Back Seat
Paul Evans; *Music To Remember-C* . . . . (Dominion Entert.)
She Drew A Broken Heart
Patty Loveless; *The Trouble With The Truth* . . . . (Epic)
Sign, The
Ace Of Base; *The Sign* . . . . (Arista)
Silence On The Line
Chris LeDoux; *Cowboy* . . . . (Capitol)
Silly Ho
TLC; *Fanmail* . . . . (LaFace)
Silver Threads And Golden Needles
Honky Tonk Angels; *Honky Tonk Angels* . . . . (Columbia)
Linda Ronstadt; *Don't Cry Now* . . . . (Asylum)
Hand Sown Home Grown . . . . (Capitol)
Linda Ronstadt-Retrospective . . . . (Capitol)
Linda Ronstadt's Greatest Hits . . . . (Asylum)
Springfields; *Troubadours Of The Folk Era-#3-C* . . . . . (Rhino)
Skinny Legs And All
Joe Tex; *I Believe I'm Gonna Make It!-Best Of Joe Tex* . . . . . (Rhino)
Joe Tex's Greatest Hits . . . . (Curb)
Soul Years-C . . . . (Atlantic)
Sleep To Dream
Fiona Apple; *Tidal* . . . .(Clean Slate/Work)
Slippin' And Slidin'
Little Richard; *Little Richard-18 Greatest Hits* . . . . (Rhino)
So Fine
Mint Condition; *From The Mint Factory* . . . . . (Perspective/A&M)
So Good
Destiny's Child; *The Writing's On The Wall* . . . . (Columbia)
Son Of A Gun (I Betcha You Think This Song's About You)
Janet (with Carly Simon); *All For You* . . . . (Virgin)
Song For The Dumped
Ben Folds Five; *Naked Baby Photos* . . . . (Caroline)
ST/Mr. Wrong . . . . (Hollywood)
Whatever And Ever Amen . . . .(Caroline/550)
Special
Garbage; *Now That's What I Call Music!-#3-C* . . . .(Virgin)
Version 2.0 . . . .(Almo Sounds)
Still Water Runs The Deepest
Asleep At The Wheel featuring Willie Nelson; *Tribute To The Music Of Bob Wills And The Texas Playboys-C* . . . . (Liberty)
Stronger
Britney Spears; *Now That's What I Call Music!-#6-C* . . . . .(Virgin)
Oops!...I Did It Again . . . . (Jive)
Strut
Sheena Easton; *Best Of Sheena Easton* . . . . (EMI)
Dance Mix . . . . (EMI)
Private Heaven . . . . (EMI)
The World Of Sheena Easton: The Singles Collection-C . . . . (EMI)
Survivor
Destiny's Child; *Now That's What I Call Music!-#7-C* . . . . (Virgin)
Survivor . . . . (Columbia)
Sweet Emotion
Aerosmith; *ST/Armageddon-The Album* . . . . (Columbia)
Sweet Music Man
Dolly Parton; *Here You Come Again* . . . . (Dunhill Compact Classics)
Kenny Rogers; *Daytime Friends* . . . . (EMI)
Reba McEntire; *Reba McEntire's Greatest Hits-#3: I'm A Survivor* . . . (MCA)
Take A Bow
Madonna; *Bedtime Stories* . . . .(Maverick/Sire)
GHV2 . . . . (Warner Bros.)
Something To Remember . . . .(Maverick/Sire)
Take It Back
Reba McEntire; *It's Your Call* . . . . (MCA)
Reba McEntire's Greatest Hits-#3: I'm A Survivor . . . . . (MCA)
Tell It To The Rain
4 Seasons; *4 Seasons' Greatest Hits-#2* . . . . (Rhino)
4 Seasons-Anthology . . . . (Rhino)
That Don't Impress Me Much
Shania Twain; *Come On Over* . . . . (Mercury)
There You Go
Pink; *Can't Take Me Home* . . . . (LaFace)
Think For Yourself
Beatles; *Beatles-Box Set* . . . . (Capitol)
Rubber Soul . . . . (Capitol)
George Harrison; *Best Of George Harrison* . . . . (Capitol)
Too Gone Too Long
Randy Travis; *Always & Forever* . . . . (Warner Bros.)
Great Divorce Songs For Him-C . . . . (Warner Bros.)
Randy Travis' Greatest Hits-#1 . . . . (Warner Bros.)
Too Gone, Too Long
En Vogue; *Best Of En Vogue* . . . . (Elektra)
EV3 . . . . (East West)
Too Lazy To Work, Too Nervous To Steal
BR549; *This Is BR549* . . . . (Lucky Dog)

Tyrone
Erykah Badu; *Erykah Badu-Live* . . . . (Kedar Entert./Universal)
Untouchable Face
Ani DiFranco; *Dilate* . . . . (Righteous Babe)
Living In Clip . . . . (Righteous Babe)
Ups & Downs
Paul Revere And The Raiders; *Legend Of Paul Revere And The Raiders* . . . . (Columbia)
Paul Revere And The Raiders' Greatest Hits . . . . (Columbia)
Walk Softly On This Heart Of Mine
Bill Monroe; *The Country Music Hall Of Fame-Bill Monroe* . . . . (MCA)
Joey Welz; *Lovin' My Country* . . . . (Capricorn)
Kentucky HeadHunters; *Best Of The Kentucky HeadHunters-Still Pickin'* . . . . (Mercury)
Pickin' On Nashville . . . . (Mercury)
Ricky Skaggs and the Dixie Chicks; *Ricky Skaggs & Friends-Big Mon: Songs Of Bill Monroe* . . . . (Skaggs Family)
Watch Me
Lorrie Morgan; *Lorrie Morgan's Greatest Hits* . . . . (BNA)
Watch Me . . . . (BNA)
What Part Of No
Lorrie Morgan; *Lorrie Morgan's Greatest Hits* . . . . (BNA)
Watch Me . . . . (BNA)
Whatever
Godsmack; *Godsmack* . . . . (Republic/Universal)
When God Fearin' Women Get The Blues
Martina McBride; *Martina McBride's Greatest Hits* . . . . (RCA)
When You Think Of Me
Eric Benet; *A Day In The Life* . . . . (Warner Bros.)
Where Were You When I Needed You
Bangles; *Bangles' Greatest Hits* . . . . (Columbia)
Grass Roots; *Grass Roots-All-Time Greatest Hits* . . . . (MCA)
Grass Roots-Anthology (1966-1975) . . . . (Rhino)
Whose Bed Have Your Boots Been Under?
Shania Twain; *The Woman In Me* . . . . (Mercury)
Why Don't You Get A Job?
Offspring; *Americana* . . . . (Columbia)
Without You
Audrey Hepburn; *ST/My Fair Lady* . . . . (Columbia)
Julie Andrews/Original Cast; *My Fair Lady* . . . . (Columbia)
Original Cast; *My Fair Lady* . . . . (London)
Would I Lie To You
Eurythmics; *Be Yourself Tonight* . . . . (RCA)
Eurythmics' Greatest Hits . . . . (Arista)
Yeah, Whatever
Splender; *Halfway Down The Sky* . . . . (Columbia)
You Can Feel Bad
Patty Loveless; *Patty Loveless-Classics* . . . . (Epic)
Super Hits Of 1996-C . . . . (Epic)
The Trouble With The Truth . . . . (Epic)
You Keep Me Hangin' On
Diana Ross; *Evening With Diana Ross* . . . . (Motown)
Diana Ross & The Supremes; *Diana Ross & The Supremes-Anthology (1962-1969)* . . . . (Motown)
Motown Story-First 25 Years-C . . . . (Motown)
Kim Wilde; *Another Step* . . . . (MCA)
Reba McEntire; *Starting Over* . . . . (MCA)
Supremes; *Billboard Top R&B Hits-1965-C* . . . . (Rhino)
Diana Ross & The Supremes' Greatest Hits-#2 . . . . (Motown)
Vanilla Fudge; *Best Of Vanilla Fudge* . . . . (Atco)
Vanilla Fudge . . . . (Atco)
Wilson Pickett; *A Man & A Half-Best Of Wilson Pickett* . . . . (Rhino)
Wilson Pickett's Greatest Hits . . . . (Atlantic)
You Should've Told Me
Kelly Price; *Mirror Mirror* . . . . (Def Soul/IDJMG)
Your Feet's Too Big
Beatles; *45-#1503* . . . . (Collectables)
Fats Waller; *20 Golden Pieces Of Fats Waller* . . . . (Bulldog)
Ain't Misbehavin' . . . . (RCA)
Fats Waller-Legendary Performer . . . . (RCA)
Joint Is Jumpin' . . . . (Bluebird)
Original Cast; *Ain't Misbehavin'* . . . . (RCA)
Your Woman
White Town; *MTV The Grind-#1-C* . . . . (Tommy Boy)
Women In Technology . . . . (Chrysalis)
You're Breaking My Heart
Nilsson; *Son Of Schmilsson* . . . . (RCA)
You're Still A Young Man
Tower Of Power; *Bump City* . . . . (Warner Bros.)
Live & In Living Color . . . . (Warner Bros.)

LOVE: LONG GONE, Love Lost, Memories Of Love
See Also: GUILT, LOSING & LOSS, LOVE (various), REMEMBER

1959
John Anderson; *Country Love Songs-#3-C* . . . . (Warner Bros.)
John Anderson's Greatest Hits . . . . (Warner Bros.)

Absolutely Sweet Marie
Bob Dylan; *Blonde On Blonde* . . . . (Columbia)
All Along
Blessid Union Of Souls; *Home* . . . . (EMI)
Always On My Mind
Willie Nelson; *Always On My Mind* . . . . (Columbia)
Super Hits Of The '80s-C . . . . (Epic)
Willie Nelson-Super Hits . . . . (Columbia)
Among My Souvenirs
Connie Francis; *Connie Francis' Greatest Hits* . . . . (Polydor)
Frank Sinatra; *Columbia Years-1943-1952-Complete Recordings* . . . . (Legacy)
Marty Robbins; *Marty Robbins-Super Hits* . . . . (Columbia)
Sons Of The Pioneers; *Country & Western Memories* . . . . (Pair)
And Still
Reba McEntire; *Read My Mind* . . . . (MCA)
Reba McEntire's Greatest Hits-#3: I'm A Survivor . . . . (MCA)
Ask The Lonely
Vonda Shepard; *ST/Songs From "Ally McBeal" Featuring Vonda Shepard* . . . . (550/Epic)
Autumn Serenade
Harry James & His Orchestra; *70 Ounces Of Big Band-Instrumentals-C* . . . . (Compose)
John Coltrane & Johnny Hartman; *John Coltrane & Johnny Hartman* . . . . (GRP)
Mel Torme; *Velvet & Brass* . . . . (Concord Jazz)
Back On The Chain Gang
Pretenders; *Learning To Crawl* . . . . (Sire)
Pretenders-The Singles . . . . (Sire)
ST/King Of Comedy . . . . (Warner Bros.)
Backstreets
Bruce Springsteen; *Born To Run* . . . . (Columbia)
Begin The Beguine
Art Tatum; *Solos-1940* . . . . (MCA)
Ella Fitzgerald; *Cole Porter Songbook* . . . . (Verve)
Johnny Mathis; *Best Days Of My Life* . . . . (Columbia)
First 25 Years-Silver Anniversary Album . . . . (Columbia)
Johnny Mathis-Live . . . . (Columbia)
Tony Bennett; *Forty Years-The Artistry Of Tony Bennett* . . . . (Columbia)
Better Things To Do
Terri Clark; *Terri Clark* . . . . (Mercury)
Between An Old Memory And Me
Keith Whitley; *I Wonder Do You Think Of Me* . . . . (RCA)
Travis Tritt; *Ten Feet Tall And Bulletproof* . . . . (Warner Bros.)
Blue Velvet
Bobby Vinton; *Bobby Vinton-16 Most Requested Songs* . . . . (Legacy)
Bobby Vinton's All-Time Greatest Hits . . . . (Epic)
Bobby Vinton's Greatest Hits/Greatest Hits Of Love . . . . (Columbia)
Blueberry Hill
Elvis Presley; *Elvis Recorded Live On Stage In Memphis* . . . . (RCA)
Loving You . . . . (RCA)
Fats Domino; *Fats Domino's Greatest Hits* . . . . (Everest)
Fats Domino's Greatest Hits . . . . (MCA)
My Blue Heaven-Best Of Fats Domino-#1 . . . . (EMI)
Little Richard; *Big Hits* . . . . (Crescendo)
Louis Armstrong; *Best Of Louis Armstrong* . . . . (MCA)
Essential Louis Armstrong . . . . (Vanguard)
I Like Jazz-Essence Of Louis Armstrong . . . . (Columbia)
Breakfast At Tiffany's
Henry Mancini; *Days Of Wine And Roses* . . . . (RCA)
Bright Lights And Country Music
Bill Anderson; *Bill Anderson's Greatest Hits* . . . . (MCA)
Bring On The Night
Bruce Springsteen; *Tracks* . . . . (Columbia)
Brown Eyed Girl
Isley Brothers; *Live It Up* . . . . (T-Neck/Columbia)
Jimmy Buffett; *One Particular Harbour* . . . . (MCA)
Van Morrison; *Bang Masters* . . . . (Epic)
Best Of Van Morrison . . . . (Polydor)
ST/Born On The Fourth Of July . . . . (MCA)
ST/Sleeping With The Enemy . . . . (Columbia)
Wonder Years-Music From Emmy Shows/Era-C . . . . (Atlantic)
Burning A Hole In My Mind
Connie Smith; *Essential Connie Smith* . . . . (RCA)
By The Book
Michael Peterson; *Michael Peterson* . . . . (Reprise)
Caroline, No
Beach Boys; *Pet Sounds* . . . . (Capitol)
The Pet Sounds Sessions: A 30th Anniversary Collection . . . . (Capitol)
Chemicals Between Us, The
Bush; *The Science Of Things* . . . . (Trauma)
Come Some Rainy Day
Wynonna; *The Other Side* . . . . (Curb/MCA)
Cry Like A Baby
Box Tops; *Billboard Top Rock 'N' Roll Hits-1968-C* . . . . (Rhino)
Box Tops' Greatest Hits . . . . (Rhino)
Super Hits-#5-C . . . . (Gusto)
WCBS FM 101 History Of Rock-'60s-#4-C . . . . (Collectables)
Dance Hall Days
Wang Chung; *Points On The Curve* . . . . (Geffen)

Danke Schoen
Wayne Newton; *Best Of Wayne Newton-Now* . . . . . (Curb)
Capitol Collectors Series-Wayne Newton . . . . . (Capitol)
Jackpot! The Las Vegas Story-C . . . . . (Rhino)
Wayne Newton's Greatest Hits . . . . . (Curb)
Deep Purple
Art Tatum; *Group Masterpieces-#2* . . . . . (Pablo)
Masterpieces . . . . . (MCA)
Solo Masterpieces-#3 . . . . . (Pablo)
Johnny Mathis; *First 25 Years-Silver Anniversary Album* . . . . . (Columbia)
Nino Tempo & April Stevens; *Hit Singles-1958-1977-C* . . . . . (Atlantic)
Sarah Vaughan; *After Hours* . . . . . (Sony Music Special Prod.)
Divine Sarah Vaughan-Columbia Years-1949-1953 . . . . . (Columbia)
Difficult Kind, The
Sheryl Crow; *The Globe Sessions* . . . . . (A&M)
Diggin' Up Bones
Randy Travis; *Storms Of Life* . . . . . (Warner Bros.)
Do You Sleep?
Lisa Loeb & Nine Stories; *Tails* . . . . . (Geffen)
Don't Feel Like Cryin'
Abra Moore; *Strangest Places* . . . . . (Arista Austin)
Don't Happen Twice
Kenny Chesney; *Kenny Chesney's Greatest Hits* . . . . . (BNA)
Everything I Own
Bread; *Baby I'm-A Want You* . . . . . (Elektra)
Best Of Bread . . . . . (Elektra)
Bread-Anthology . . . . . (Elektra)
Faded Love
Bob Wills & His Texas Playboys; *Bob Wills & His Texas Playboys-24 Great Hits* . . . . . (Polydor)
For The Last Time . . . . . (Capitol)
Tiffany Transcriptions-#2-Best Of The Tiffanys . . . . . (Rhino)
Mickey Gilley; *Mickey Gilley's Greatest Hits-#1* . . . . . (Epic)
Patsy Cline; *12 Greatest Hits* . . . . . (MCA)
Shawn Colvin & Lyle Lovett & Asleep At The Wheel; *Ride With Bob-C* . . . . . (DreamWorks/SKG)
Willie Nelson; *Greatest Hits (& Some That Will Be)* . . . . . (Columbia)
Fool
Sanford Clark; *Billboard Top Rock 'N' Roll Hits-1956-C* . . . . . (Rhino)
Original Classic Oldies Of The '50s & '60s-#17-C . . . . . (MCA)
Foolish Pride
Travis Tritt; *Ten Feet Tall And Bulletproof* . . . . . (Warner Bros.)
For A Little While
Tim McGraw; *Everywhere* . . . . . (Curb)
Tim McGraw's Greatest Hits . . . . . (Curb)
For You
Bruce Springsteen; *Greetings From Asbury Park, N.J.* . . . . . (Columbia)
Greg Kihn; *Kihnsolidation-Best Of Greg Kihn* . . . . . (Rhino)
Unkihntrollable-Live . . . . . (Rhino)
Manfred Mann's Earth Band; *Chance* . . . . . (Warner Bros.)
Forever
Mariah Carey; *Daydream* . . . . . (Columbia)
Free As A Bird
Beatles; *The Beatles-Anthology-#1* . . . . . (Capitol)
Funny Familiar Forgotten Feelings
Don Gibson; *Best Of Don Gibson-#1* . . . . . (Curb)
Mandy Barnett; *I've Got A Right To Cry* . . . . . (Sire)
Tom Jones; *Back To Back-Greatest Hits* . . . . . (Rebound)
Country Side Of Tom Jones . . . . . (London)
Tom Jones-London Collector-Greatest Hits . . . . . (London)
Funny How Time Slips Away
Al Green & Lyle Lovett; *Rhythm Country And Blues-C* . . . . . (MCA)
Jimmy Elledge; *Nipper's Greatest Hits Of The '60s-#2-C* . . . . . (RCA)
RCA's Greatest One-Hit Wonders-C . . . . . (RCA)
Willie Nelson; *Best Of Willie Nelson* . . . . . (Capitol)
Collector's Series-Willie Nelson . . . . . (RCA)
Healing Hands Of Time . . . . . (Liberty)
My Own Way . . . . . (RCA)
San Antonio Rose . . . . . (Columbia)
Willie & Family Live . . . . . (Columbia)
Willie Nelson & Faron Young; *Funny How Time Slips Away* . . . . . (Columbia)
Gentle On My Mind
Elvis Presley; *From Elvis In Memphis* . . . . . (RCA)
Great Country Songs . . . . . (RCA)
Glen Campbell; *Best Of Austin City Limits-Legends Of Country Music-C* . . . . . (Legacy)
Best Of Glen Campbell . . . . . (Capitol)
Glen Campbell-Best Of The Early Years . . . . . (Curb)
John Hartford; *Me Oh My-How The Time Does Fly-Anthology* . . . . (Flying Fish)
Patti Page; *Patti Page-16 Most Requested Songs* . . . . . (Legacy)
Girl From The North Country
Bob Dylan; *Freewheelin'* . . . . . (Columbia)
Nashville Skyline . . . . . (Columbia)
Real Live . . . . . (Columbia)
Joe Cocker; *Mad Dogs & Englishmen* . . . . . (A&M)
Johnny Cash with Bob Dylan; *The Man In Black-His Greatest Hits* . . . . (Legacy)
Good Life
Bruce Robison; *Long Way Home From Anywhere* . . . . . (Lucky Dog)

Great Pretender
Band; *Moondog Matinee* . . . . . (Capitol)
Platters; *Billboard Top R&B Hits-1956-C* . . . . . (Rhino)
Cruisin'-1956-C . . . . . (Increase)
Encore Of Golden Hits-Platters . . . . . (Mercury)
Platters-Anthology . . . . . (Rhino)
ST/American Graffiti . . . . . (MCA)
Super Oldies Of The '50s-#3-C . . . . . (Audio Fidelity)
Roy Orbison; *Best Of Roy Orbison-Loved Standards* . . . . . (Monument)
Stan Freberg; *Capitol Collectors Series-Stan Freberg* . . . . . (Capitol)
Guess Things Happen That Way
Johnny Cash; *The Man In Black-His Greatest Hits* . . . . . (Legacy)
Hanging Tree
Marty Robbins; *Gunfighter Ballads & Trail Songs* . . . . . (Legacy)
Hollywood Magic-1950s-C . . . . . (Columbia)
Lifetime Of Song-1951-1982 . . . . . (Columbia)
Marty Robbins' All-Time Greatest Hits . . . . . (Columbia)
Harbor Lights
Boz Scaggs; *Silk Degrees* . . . . . (Columbia)
Dinah Washington; *Complete Dinah Washington On Mercury-#2-1950-1952* . . . . . (Mercury)
Dinah Washington-Golden Hits . . . . . (Mercury)
For Lonely Lovers . . . . . (Mercury)
This Is My Story . . . . . (Mercury)
Platters; *Super Oldies Of The '60s-#9-C* . . . . . (Audio Fidelity)
He Wasn't Man Enough
Toni Braxton; *The Heat* . . . . . (LaFace)
Totally Hits-#3-C . . . . . (Atlantic)
Heart Won't Lie, The
Reba McEntire & Vince Gill; *It's Your Call* . . . . . (MCA)
Reba McEntire's Greatest Hits-#3: I'm A Survivor . . . . . (MCA)
Hearts Of Stone
Bruce Springsteen; *Tracks* . . . . . (Columbia)
Southside Johnny And The Asbury Jukes; *Best Of Southside Johnny And The Asbury Jukes* . . . . . (Legacy)
Cover Me (Bruce Springsteen Tribute)-C . . . . . (Rhino)
Hearts Of Stone . . . . . (Epic)
Hello Darlin'
Conway Twitty; *Conway Twittty-20 Greatest Hits* . . . . . (MCA)
Conway Twitty's Greatest Hits . . . . . (Curb)
From The Vaults: Decca Country Classics-1934-1973-C . . . . . (Decca)
Greatest Country Classics-#1-C . . . . . (MCA Special Prod.)
I Can Still Make Cheyenne
George Strait; *Blue Clear Sky* . . . . . (MCA)
Latest Greatest Straitest Hits . . . . . (MCA)
I Got Mexico
Eddy Raven; *14 #1 Country Hits-C* . . . . . (RCA)
Best Of Eddy Raven . . . . . (RCA)
I Could Use Another You . . . . . (RCA)
I Knew You When
Billy Joe Royal; *Billy Joe Royal's Greatest Hits* . . . . . (Columbia)
I Knew You When
Pamela Rose; *Morpheus* . . . . . (Grace)
I Remember Holding You
Boys Club; *'80s Greatest Rock Hits-Teen Idols-C* . . . . . (Priority)
Boys Club . . . . . (MCA)
Retro Lunchbox-Gooey Love Songs-C . . . . . (ISD/Intersound)
I Still Miss Someone
Johnny Cash; *The Man In Black-His Greatest Hits* . . . . . (Legacy)
I Used To Love Him
Lauryn Hill featuring Mary J. Blige; *The Miseducation Of Lauryn Hill* . . . . . (Ruffhouse/Columbia)
I Went To Your Wedding
Patti Page; *Patti Page-Golden Hits* . . . . . (Mercury)
I'll Remember April
Cal Tjader; *Mambo With Cal Tjader* . . . . . (Fantasy)
Charlie Parker; *Charlie Parker With Strings* . . . . . (Verve)
Chet Baker; *Chet Baker* . . . . . (Emarcy)
Cleo Laine; *Cleo's Choice* . . . . . (Crescendo)
Doris Day & The Frank DeVol Orchestra; *Hooray For Hollywood-#1-C* . . . . . (Columbia)
Erroll Garner; *Erroll Garner-Concert By The Sea* . . . . . (Columbia)
Frank Sinatra; *Point Of No Return* . . . . . (Capitol)
June Christy; *June Christy-#2-1957* . . . . . (Hindsight)
Modern Jazz Quartet; *Concorde* . . . . . (Prestige)
Modern Jazz Quartet . . . . . (Prestige)
Stephane Grappelli & Martin Taylor; *Just One Of Those Things* . . . . . (Angel)
Wynton Marsalis; *Standard Time-#2-Intimacy Calling* . . . . . (Columbia)
I'm So Lonesome I Could Cry
B.J. Thomas; *B.J. Thomas' Greatest Hits* . . . . . (Rhino)
Cowboy Junkies; *Trinity Session* . . . . . (RCA)
Hank Williams; *24 Of Hank Williams' Greatest Hits* . . . . . (Polydor)
Hank Williams-40 Greatest Hits . . . . . (Polydor)
I'm So Lonesome I Could Cry-1949 . . . . . (Polydor)
Hank Williams, Jr.; *Very Best Of Hank Williams, Jr.* . . . . . (Polydor)
Jim Rooney; *One Day At A Time* . . . . . (Rounder)
Johnny Cash; *Hank Williams Songbook-C* . . . . . (Columbia)
Keb' Mo'; *Timeless: Hank Williams Tribute-C* . . . . . (Lost Highway/IDJMG)

Isle Of Capri
Billy Vaughn; *Billy Vaughn-22 Of His Greatest Hits* . . . . . (Ranwood)
Frank Sinatra; *Come Fly With Me* . . . . . (Capitol)
It Was A Very Good Year
Frank Sinatra; *Frank Sinatra-The Very Good Years* . . . . . (Reprise)
September Of My Years . . . . . (Reprise)
The Reprise Collection . . . . . (Reprise)
The Sopranos-Music From The HBO Original Series . . . . . (Sony Music Soundtrax)
Frank Sinatra with Count Basie & The Orchestra; *Sinatra At The Sands* . . . . . (Reprise)
It's All Coming Back To Me Now
Celine Dion; *All The Way...A Decade Of Song* . . . . . (550 Music)
Falling Into You . . . . . (550 Music)
Just Friends
Charlie Parker; *Compact Jazz-Charlie Parker* . . . . . (Verve)
Charlie Watts Quintet; *Tribute To Charlie Parker* . . . . . (Continuum)
Frank Sinatra; *No One Cares* . . . . . (Capitol)
Joe Pass; *I Remember Charlie Parker* . . . . . (Pablo)
L.A. Four; *Just Friends* . . . . . (Concord Jazz)
Sarah Vaughan; *Divine Sarah Vaughan-Columbia Years-1949-1953* . . . . . (Columbia)
Tony Bennett; *Jazz* . . . . . (Columbia)
Wynton Marsalis Quartet; *Live At Blues Alley* . . . . . (Columbia)
Just One Of Those Things
Bobby Short; *Loves Cole Porter* . . . . . (Atlantic)
Ella Fitzgerald; *Best Of The Song Books: Love Songs* . . . . . (Verve)
Frank Sinatra; *Timeless* . . . . . (Pair)
Lena Horne; *American Songbook Series-Cole Porter* . . (Smithsonian Collection)
Lester Lanin; *Best Of The Big Bands-C* . . . . . (Columbia)
Louis Armstrong; *Jazz Masters-#1-Louis Armstrong* . . . . . (Verve)
Peggy Lee; *Peggy Lee Sings For You* . . . . . (Avid)
Sarah Vaughan; *Essential Sarah Vaughan-The Great Songs* . . . . . (Verve)
Kern River
Merle Haggard; *For The Record: Merle Haggard-43 Legendary Hits* . . . . (BNA)
Kern River . . . . . (Epic)
Kohoutek
R.E.M.; *Fables Of The Reconstruction* . . . . . (I.R.S.)
Lonely And Gone
Montgomery Gentry; *Tattoos & Scars* . . . . . (Columbia)
Long Gone Lonesome Blues
Hank Williams With His Drifting Cowboys; *Hank Williams-24 Greatest Hits-#2* . . . . . (Polydor)
Hank Williams-40 Greatest Hits . . . . . (Polydor)
Sheryl Crow; *Timeless: Hank Williams Tribute-C* . . . . . (Lost Highway/IDJMG)
Love Letters From Old Mexico
Leslie Satcher; *Love Letters* . . . . . (Warner Bros.)
Love So Beautiful, A
Michael Bolton; *Michael Bolton's Greatest Hits-1985-1995* . . . . . (Columbia)
Roy Orbison; *Mystery Girl* . . . . . (Virgin)
ST/Indecent Proposal . . . . . (MCA)
Loving Arms
Dixie Chicks; *Wide Open Spaces* . . . . . (Monument)
Maybe It Was Memphis
Pam Tillis; *Pam Tillis' Greatest Hits* . . . . . (Arista)
Pam Tillis-Collection . . . . . (Warner Bros.)
Put Yourself In My Place . . . . . (Arista)
Missing You
Mary J. Blige; *Share My World* . . . . . (MCA)
The Tour . . . . . (MCA)
Missing You
Steve Perry; *Greatest Hits + Five Unreleased* . . . . . (Columbia)
More Than A Feeling
Boston; *Boston* . . . . . (Epic)
Most Beautiful Girl In The World
Frank Sinatra; *Strangers In The Night* . . . . . (Reprise)
Tony Bennett; *Rodgers & Hart Songbook* . . . . . (DRG)
Tony Bennett Sings More Great Rodgers & Hart . . . . . (Improv)
Muzzle
Smashing Pumpkins; *Mellon Collie And The Infinite Sadness* . . . . . (Virgin)
My Girl Josephine
Fats Domino; *Fats Domino's Greatest Hits* . . . . . (MCA)
They Call Me The Fat Man . . . . . (EMI)
My Old Flame
Duke Ellington; *Nipper's Greatest Hits Of The '30s-#1-C* . . . . . (RCA)
Guy Lombardo & His Royal Canadians; *Guy Lombardo-16 Most Requested Songs* . . . . . (Legacy)
J.J. Johnson; *Trombone Master* . . . . . (Columbia)
Linda Ronstadt; *Lush Life* . . . . . (Asylum)
Rosemary Clooney; *Great Girl Singers Sing 22 Original Recordings-C* . . . . . (Hindsight)
Stan Kenton & His Orchestra; *Road Show* . . . . . (Capitol)
Tommy Smith; *Standards* . . . . . (Blue Note)
My Song
Jerry Cantrell; *Boggy Depot* . . . . . (Columbia)
Neighborhood
Vonda Shepard; *ST/Songs From "Ally McBeal" Featuring Vonda Shepard* . . . . . (550/Epic)
Never Too Far
Mariah Carey; *Glitter* . . . . . (Virgin)
Nights
Ed Bruce; *Night Things* . . . . . (RCA)
Nineteen
Old 97's; *Fight Songs* . . . . . (Elektra)
Not Dark Yet
Bob Dylan; *Time Out Of Mind* . . . . . (Columbia)
Old Flames Can't Hold A Candle To You
Dolly Parton; *Dolly Dolly Dolly* . . . . . (RCA)
Dolly Parton's Greatest Hits . . . . . (RCA)
Joe Sun; *Old Flames Can't Hold A Candle To You* . . . . . (Ovation)
Merle Haggard; *Kern River* . . . . . (Epic)
Once In A While
Tommy Dorsey; *Boogie Woogie* . . . . . (Pro-Arte)
Once Upon A Time
Frank Sinatra; *September Of My Years* . . . . . (Reprise)
Tony Bennett; *I Left My Heart In San Francisco* . . . . . (Columbia)
Out Of My Bones
Randy Travis; *You And You Alone* . . . . . (DreamWorks/SKG)
Please Remember Me
Tim McGraw; *A Place In The Sun* . . . . . (Curb)
Tim McGraw's Greatest Hits . . . . . (Curb)
Reflections
Diana Ross & The Supremes; *Diana Ross & The Supremes' Greatest Hits-#3* . . . . . (Motown)
Diana Ross & The Supremes-25th Anniversary . . . . . (Motown)
Diana Ross & The Supremes-Anthology (1962-1969) . . . . . (Motown)
Motown Story-First 25 Years-C . . . . . (Motown)
Four Tops; *Four Tops-Anthology* . . . . . (Motown)
Still Waters Run Deep . . . . . (Motown)
Until You Love Someone: More Of The Best (1965-1970) . . . . . (Rhino)
Luther Vandross; *Songs* . . . . . (Epic)
Refried Dreams
Tim McGraw; *Not A Moment Too Soon* . . . . . (Curb)
Remember Me
Marc Anthony; *Marc Anthony* . . . . . (Columbia)
River Of No Return
Marilyn Monroe; *I Wanna Be Loved By You* . . . . . (Eclipse)
Riverwide
Sheryl Crow; *The Globe Sessions* . . . . . (A&M)
Sail On
Commodores; *All The Great Love Songs-Commodores* . . . . . (Motown)
Commodores-All The Great Hits . . . . . (Motown)
Lionel Richie-Composer Series . . . . . (Motown)
Midnight Magic . . . . . (Motown)
Scarborough Fair/Canticle
Simon & Garfunkel; *Collected Works* . . . . . (Columbia)
Parsley Sage Rosemary & Thyme . . . . . (Columbia)
Simon & Garfunkel's Greatest Hits . . . . . (Columbia)
ST/The Graduate . . . . . (Columbia)
The Concert In Central Park . . . . . (Warner Bros.)
Seventh Avenue
Rosanne Cash; *The Wheel* . . . . . (Columbia)
She Doesn't Need Me Anymore
Peter Cetera; *You're The Inspiration-A Collection* . . . . . (River North)
She Used To Be Somebody's Baby
Larry Gatlin & The Gatlin Brothers Band; *Greatest Country Hits Of The '80s-1986-C* . . . . . (Columbia)
The Gatlin Brothers' Biggest Hits . . . . . (Columbia)
She's Gone
Eric Clapton; *Pilgrim* . . . . . (Duck/Reprise)
Silver Springs
Fleetwood Mac; *1998 Grammy Nominees-C* . . . . . (MCA)
25 Years-The Chain . . . . . (Warner Bros.)
The Dance . . . . . (Reprise)
Someday
Sugar Ray; *14:59* . . . . . (Lava)
Totally Hits-#1-C . . . . . (Arista)
Someone You Used To Know
Collin Raye; *Big Country Hits '99-C* . . . . . (K-Tel)
The Walls Came Down . . . . . (Epic)
Something Beautiful Remains
Tina Turner; *Wildest Dreams* . . . . . (Virgin)
Something Like That
Tim McGraw; *A Place In The Sun* . . . . . (Curb)
Tim McGraw's Greatest Hits . . . . . (Curb)
South Of Santa Fe
Brooks & Dunn; *If You See Her* . . . . . (Arista)
Stardust
Artie Shaw; *Begin The Beguine* . . . . . (Bluebird)
Artie Shaw & His Orchestra; *22 Original Big Band Recordings-C* . . . (Hindsight)
Nipper's Greatest Hits Of The '40s-#1-C . . . . . (RCA)
Benny Goodman; *Benny Goodman Sextet featuring Charlie Christian-1939-1941* . . . . . (Columbia)
Benny Goodman-Live At Carnegie Hall . . . . . (London)
Carly Simon; *Come Upstairs* . . . . . (Warner Bros.)
Coleman Hawkins; *Hollywood Stampede* . . . . . (Capitol)

Dave Brubeck; *Art Of Dave Brubeck* . . . . (Atlantic)
  Greatest Hits From The Fantasy Years . . . . (Fantasy)
Dave Brubeck Quartet; *Jazz At Oberlin* . . . . (Fantasy)
  Stardust . . . . (Fantasy)
Frank Sinatra; *Sinatra & Strings* . . . . (Reprise)
Harry Connick, Jr.; *25* . . . . (Columbia)
Hoagy Carmichael; *Nipper's Greatest Hits Of The '30s-#1-C* . . . . . . (RCA)
  Stardust Road . . . . (MCA)
Johnny Mathis; *Feelings* . . . . (Columbia)
  First 25 Years-Silver Anniversary Album . . . . (Columbia)
Nat ''King'' Cole; *The Nat ''King'' Cole Story* . . . . (Capitol)
Rob Wasserman & Aaron Neville; *Duets-C* . . . . (MCA)
Roger Williams; *Best Of Roger Williams* . . . . (MCA)
Tommy Dorsey; *Best Of Tommy Dorsey* . . . . (Bluebird)
  This Is Tommy Dorsey . . . . (RCA)
Tommy Dorsey & Frank Sinatra; *Stardust* . . . . (Bluebird)
Wayne King & His Orchestra; *78-#22656* . . . . (Victor)

Staring At The Sun
U2; *Pop* . . . . (Island)

Still
Commodores; *Best Of The Commodores-Anthology* . . . . (Motown)
  Commodores-All The Great Hits . . . . (Motown)
  Commodores-The Ultimate Collection . . . . (Motown)
Lionel Richie; *Back To Front* . . . . (Motown)
  Truly-The Love Songs . . . . (Motown)

Still Dancin' With You
Wade Hayes; *Old Enough To Know Better* . . . . (Columbia)

Still Got The Blues
Gary Moore; *Ballads & Blues-1982-1994* . . . . (Charisma)
  Out In The Fields-The Very Best Of Gary Moore . . . . (Virgin)
  Still Got The Blues . . . . (Charisma)
Stanley Jordan; *Best Of Stanley Jordan* . . . . (Blue Note)

Such A Night
Elvis Presley; *From Nashville To Memphis-The Essential '60s Masters* . . (RCA)

Take Good Care Of My Baby
Bobby Vee; *Best Of Bobby Vee* . . . . (EMI)
  Billboard Top Rock 'N' Roll Hits-1961-C . . . . (Rhino)
  'Til My Dreamin' Comes True-C . . . . (Capitol)
Bobby Vinton; *Bobby Vinton-16 Most Requested Songs* . . . . (Legacy)
Dion; *Runaround Sue (Right Stuff)* . . . . (Right Stuff)

Tennessee Waltz
Cowboy Copas; *45-#696* . . . . (King)
Emmylou Harris; *Cimarron* . . . . (Warner Bros.)
  Country's Greatest Hits-#5-C . . . . (Warner Bros.)
  New Tradition Sings The Old Tradition-C . . . . (Warner Bros.)
Guy Lombardo & His Royal Canadians; *Best Of Guy Lombardo* . . . . . (Curb)
Hank Williams, Jr.; *Living Proof-MGM Recordings 1963-1975* . . . (Mercury)
Lacy J. Dalton; *Lacy J. Dalton's Greatest Hits* . . . . (Columbia)
Les Paul & Mary Ford; *Les Paul-Selections From Legend & Legacy* . . (Capitol)
Patti Page; *Patti Page-Golden Hits* . . . . (Mercury)
  Patti Page's Greatest Hits . . . . (Columbia)
Roy Acuff; *Essential Roy Acuff-1936-1949* . . . . (Legacy)
  Roy Acuff's Greatest Hits . . . . (Columbia)
Roy Rogers; *Best Of Roy Rogers* . . . . (Curb)
Sammy Kaye & His Orchestra; *Best Of The Big Bands-C* . . . . . (Columbia)
Spike Jones & His City Slickers; *Best Of Spike Jones & His City
  Slickers* . . . . (RCA)

That's Another Song
Bryan White; *Between Now And Forever* . . . . (Asylum)

Theme From ''The Sandpiper'' (Shadow Of Your Smile)
Astrud Gilberto; *ST/Sandpiper* . . . . (Verve)
  *The Envelope Please-Academy Award Winning Songs-#3 (1958-
  1969)-C* . . . . (Rhino)
Barbra Streisand; *My Name Is Barbra, Two* . . . . (Columbia)
Boston Pops Orchestra/Arthur Fiedler; *Greatest Hits Of The '60s-#2* . . . (RCA)
  Motion Picture Classics-#1 . . . . (RCA Victor)
  Music For Every Mood-Yesterday . . . . (RCA)
Carmen McRae; *Carmen McRae-Alive* . . . . (Mainstream)
  I Want You . . . . (Mainstream)
Frank Sinatra; *At The Sands* . . . . (Reprise)
  The Reprise Collection . . . . (Reprise)
Henry Mancini; *Days Of Wine And Roses* . . . . (RCA)
James Morrison; *Snappy Doo* . . . . (Atlantic)
Jose Carreras; *Hollywood Golden Classics* . . . . (Atlantic)
Marvin Gaye; *Romantically Yours* . . . . (Columbia)
Tony Bennett; *Academy Award Winners: 16 Most Requested* . . . . . . (LeGrand)
  The Movie Song Album . . . . (Columbia)
  Tony Bennett-16 Most Requested Songs . . . . (Legacy)
  Tony Bennett's All-Time Greatest Hits . . . . (Columbia)

Third Man Theme (Harry Lime Theme)
Band; *Moondog Matinee* . . . . (Capitol)
Dukes Of Dixieland; *Dukes Of Dixieland's Greatest Hits* . . . . . . (MCA)
Guy Lombardo & His Royal Canadians; *Best Of Guy Lombardo* . . . . . (Curb)

This Diamond Ring
Gary Lewis And The Playboys; *Billboard Top Rock 'N' Roll Hits-
  1965-C* . . . . (Rhino)
  EMI Legends Of Rock & Roll-24 Greatest Hits-C . . . . (EMI)
  Golden Years-1965-C . . . . (Dominion Entert.)
  Spring Break-#2-Cold Kegs & Tan Legs . . . . (Capitol)

Those Oldies But Goodies (Remind Me Of You)
John Cafferty And The Beaver Brown Band; *ST/Eddie & The
  Cruisers* . . . . (Scotti Bros.)
Little Caesar and The Romans; *Best Love Songs-C* . . . . . . (Original Sound)
  Collectables Presents The History Of Rock-#2-C . . . . (Collectables)
  Cruisin'-1961-C . . . . (Increase)
  Oldies But Goodies-#6-C . . . . (Original Sound)

Thousand Times A Day
Patty Loveless; *The Trouble With The Truth* . . . . (Epic)

Time After Time
Cyndi Lauper; *Chicken Soup For The Woman's Soul-C* . . . . (Rhino)
  She's So Unusual . . . . (Portrait)
  Twelve Deadly Cyns...And Then Some . . . . (Epic)
Everything But The Girl; *Acoustic* . . . . (Atlantic)
INOJ & So So Def Bass All-Stars; *Time After Time (Maxi
  Single)* . . . . (So So Def/Columbia)
Miles Davis; *Live Around The World* . . . . (Warner Bros.)
  You're Under Arrest . . . . (Columbia)

Tonight The Heartache's On Me
Dixie Chicks; *Wide Open Spaces* . . . . (Monument)

Too Gone Too Long
Randy Travis; *Always & Forever* . . . . (Warner Bros.)
  Great Divorce Songs For Him-C . . . . (Warner Bros.)
  Randy Travis' Greatest Hits-#1 . . . . (Warner Bros.)

Too Gone, Too Long
En Vogue; *Best Of En Vogue* . . . . (Elektra)
  EV3 . . . . (East West)

Traces
Classics IV; *Very Best Of The Classics IV* . . . . (EMI)
Classics IV Featuring Dennis Yost; *Oldies But
  Goodies-#11-C* . . . . (Original Sound)
Ronnie Milsap; *Ronnie Milsap-16 Greatest Hits-#2* . . . . (Trip)

U Remind Me
Usher; *8701* . . . . (LaFace)
  Totally Hits 2001-C . . . . (Arista)

Unsent
Alanis Morissette; *Supposed Former Infatuation Junkie* . . . . (Maverick)

Way We Were, The
Barbra Streisand; *Just For The Record* . . . . (Columbia)
  ST/The Way We Were . . . . (Columbia)

What Becomes Of The Brokenhearted
Jimmy & David Ruffin; *Motown Superstar Series-#8-Jimmy & David
  Ruffin* . . . . (Motown)
Jimmy Ruffin; *Motown Story-First 25 Years-C* . . . . (Motown)
Paul Young; *ST/Fried Green Tomatoes* . . . . (MCA)

What She's Doing Now
Garth Brooks; *Ropin' The Wind* . . . . (Liberty)

When I Call Your Name
Vince Gill; *When I Call Your Name* . . . . (MCA)

When She Was My Girl
Four Tops; *When She Was My Girl* . . . . (Casablanca)

Where Do I Go From You
Jon Secada; *Heart, Soul & A Voice* . . . . (SBK)

Who Needs Pictures
Brad Paisley; *Who Needs Pictures* . . . . (Arista)

Why I'm Walkin'
Stonewall Jackson; *Columbia Country Classics-#2-Honky Tonk
  Heroes-C* . . . . (Columbia)
  Waterloo . . . . (Laserlight)

Wildest Times Of The World
Vonda Shepard; *ST/Songs From ''Ally McBeal'' Featuring Vonda
  Shepard* . . . . (550/Epic)

Wonderful
Adam Ant; *Wonderful* . . . . (Capitol)

World We Knew (Over And Over)
Frank Sinatra; *Frank Sinatra's Greatest Hits!* . . . . (Reprise)
  The World We Knew . . . . (Reprise)

You Can Feel Bad
Patty Loveless; *Patty Loveless-Classics* . . . . (Epic)
  Super Hits Of 1996-C . . . . (Epic)
  The Trouble With The Truth . . . . (Epic)

LOVE: LOOKING FOR THE WORDS, Can't Find The Words, Things We Should Have Said

See Also: COMMUNICATION: WORDS, DESIRE, KISSING, LOVE (various)

(I Don't Know Why) But I Do
Clarence ''Frogman'' Henry; *ST/Forrest Gump* . . . (Epic/Sony Music Soundtrax)

All For You
Sister Hazel; *...Somewhere More Familiar* . . . . (Universal)
  Sister Hazel . . . . (Universal)

All That I Can Say
Mary J. Blige; *Mary* . . . . (MCA)

Because Of You
98 Degrees; *98 Degrees And Rising* . . . . (Universal)

Now That's What I Call Music!-#2-C . . . .(Virgin)

Betcha By Golly, Wow
''AFKAP''; *Emancipation* . . . . (NPG)
Johnny Mathis; *First Time Ever I Saw Your Face* . . . . (Columbia)
Stylistics; *Best Of The Stylistics* . . . .(Amherst)

Cherish
Association; *Association Greatest Hits* . . . . (Warner Bros.)
Billboard Top Pop Hits-1966-C . . . . (Rhino)

Communication Breakdown
Led Zeppelin; *Led Zeppelin* . . . . (Atlantic)
Led Zeppelin-Box Set . . . . (Atlantic)

Do I Have To Come Right Out & Say It
Buffalo Springfield; *Buffalo Springfield* . . . . (Atco)

Easier Said Than Done
Essex; *Best Of The Girl Groups-#2-C* . . . . (Rhino)
Billboard Top Rock 'N' Roll Hits-1963-C . . . . (Rhino)
Original Rock 'N' Roll Hits Of The '60s-C . . . . (Roulette)

Goodbye
Alicia Keys; *Songs In A Minor* . . . . (J)

Hard To Say
Dan Fogelberg; *Dan Fogelberg/Greatest Hits* . . . . (Full Moon)
Innocent Age . . . . (Full Moon)

Hard To Say I'm Sorry
Az Yet; *Az Yet* . . . . (LaFace)
Chicago; *Chicago 16* . . . . (Full Moon/Warner Bros.)

Have You Ever?
Brandy; *Never Say Never* . . . . (Atlantic)

Heart Won't Lie, The
Reba McEntire & Vince Gill; *It's Your Call* . . . . (MCA)
Reba McEntire's Greatest Hits-#3: I'm A Survivor . . . . (MCA)

Honey
Mariah Carey; *Butterfly* . . . .(Columbia)

How Did I Get By Without You
John Waite; *Complete John Waite-#1-Falling Backwards* . . . . (EMI)
Temple Bar . . . . (Coyote/Imago)

How Do I Get There
Deana Carter; *Did I Shave My Legs For This?*. . . . .(Capitol)

How Do I Say I'm Sorry
Tami Davis; *Only You* . . . . (Red Ant)

How Do You Tell The One
After 7; *Reflections* . . . .(Virgin)

How Your Love Makes Me Feel
Diamond Rio; *Diamond Rio's Greatest Hits* . . . .(Arista)

I Can't Tell You Why
Brownstone; *From The Bottom Up* . . . . (MJJ/Epic)
Eagles; *Eagles Greatest Hits, Volume 2* . . . . (Asylum)
Eagles Live . . . . (Asylum)
The Long Run . . . . (Asylum)
Vince Gill; *Common Thread-Songs Of The Eagles-C* . . . . (Giant)

I Want To Tell You
Beatles; *Revolver* . . . . (Capitol)

If I Loved You
Barbra Streisand; *The Broadway Album* . . . .(Columbia)
Original Cast; *Carousel* . . . . (MCA)

If Tomorrow Never Comes
Garth Brooks; *Garth Brooks* . . . . (Liberty)
Limited Series-Box . . . . (Capitol)
Joose; *Joose* . . . .(Flavor Unit)

I'll Have To Say I Love You In A Song
Jim Croce; *Baby Boomer Classics-Love Seventies-C* . . . . . .(JCI Assoc. Labels)
Billboard Top Soft Rock Hits-1974-C . . . . (Rhino)
Dim The Lights-C . . . . (K-Tel)

In A Week Or Two
Diamond Rio; *Close To The Edge* . . . .(Arista)
Diamond Rio's Greatest Hits . . . . (Arista)

In Harm's Way
Bebe Winans; *Bebe Winans* . . . . (Atlantic)

It Matters To Me
Faith Hill; *It Matters To Me* . . . . (Warner Bros.)

It Would Be You
Gary Allan; *It Would Be You* . . . .(Decca)

It's Too Late
Derek And The Dominos; *Layla* . . . . (Polydor)

Julia
Beatles; *Beatles-Box Set* . . . . (Capitol)
ST/Imagine: John Lennon . . . . (Capitol)
The Beatles (White Album) . . . . (Capitol)

Let 'Er Rip
Dixie Chicks; *Wide Open Spaces* . . . . (Monument)

Let's Lock The Door (And Throw Away The Key)
Jay & The Americans; *Jay & The Americans' All-Time Greatest Hits* . . . (Rhino)

Lonely
Tracy Lawrence; *Lessons Learned* . . . . (Atlantic)

Losing My Religion
R.E.M.; *Out Of Time* . . . . (Warner Bros.)

Lullaby Of Birdland
Ella Fitzgerald; *Best Of Ella Fitzgerald-#2* . . . . (MCA)
Ella Fitzgerald With Billie Holiday . . . . (MCA)

Four Freshmen; *Greatest Hits-Four Freshman* . . . .(Curb)
Mel Torme; *Songs Of New York* . . . . (Rhino)
Sarah Vaughan; *Sarah Vaughan-Golden Hits* . . . . (Mercury)
Tito Puente & His Latin Ensemble; *Mambo Diablo* . . . . (Concord Jazz)

Me Too
Toby Keith; *Blue Moon* . . . . (Polydor Country)
Toby Keith's Greatest Hits, Volume One. . . . . (Mercury)

Mourning
Tantric; *Tantric* . . . . (Maverick)

Never Had A Dream Come True
S Club 7; *Now That's What I Call Music!-#7-C* . . . . (Virgin)
S Club 7 . . . . (A&M)

No, No, No
Destiny's Child; *Destiny's Child* . . . . (Grass Roots/Columbia)

Radiation Vibe
Fountains Of Wayne; *Fountains Of Wayne* . . . . (Tag/Atlantic)

Redundant
Green Day; *Nimrod* . . . . (Reprise)

She Walks This Earth
Sting; *Love Affair-Music Of Ivan Lins-C* . . . . (Telarc)

Single White Female
Chely Wright; *Single White Female* . . . . (MCA)

Somebody To Love
Jefferson Airplane; *2400 Fulton Street-An Anthology* . . . . (RCA)
Loves You . . . . (RCA)
Nipper's Greatest Hits Of The '60s-#1-C . . . . (RCA)
Surrealistic Pillow . . . . (RCA)
The Worst Of Jefferson Airplane . . . . (RCA)

Something About The Way You Look Tonight
Elton John; *The Big Picture* . . . . (Rocket)

Tell Her
Lonestar; *Lonely Grill* . . . . (BNA)

Things I Should Have Said
Grass Roots; *Grass Roots-All-Time Greatest Hits* . . . . (MCA)
Grass Roots-Anthology (1966-1975) . . . . (Rhino)

Tip Of My Tongue
Tommy Quickly; *History Of British Rock-#1-C* . . . . (Rhino)

Tropicalia
Beck; *Mutations* . . . . (David Geffen Co.)

Tu Amor
Jon B.; *Cool Relax* . . . . (Yab Yum/550)

What Do You Say
Reba McEntire; *So Good Together* . . . . (MCA)

What I Really Meant To Say
Cyndi Thomson; *My World* . . . .(Capitol)

When You Walk In The Room
Jackie DeShannon; *Best Of Jackie DeShannon* . . . . (Rhino)
Very Best Of Jackie DeShannon . . . . (Collectables)
Pam Tillis; *Pam Tillis' Greatest Hits* . . . . (Arista)
Pam Tillis-Super Hits . . . . (Arista)
Sweetheart's Dance . . . . (Arista)

Without You
Charlie Wilson; *Bridging The Gap* . . . .(Major Hits)

You Have No Idea
Pamela Rose; *Morpheus* . . . . (Grace)

You Know What I Mean
Turtles; *Turtles-20 Greatest Hits* . . . . (Rhino)

You Should've Told Me
Kelly Price; *Mirror Mirror* . . . . (Def Soul/IDJMG)

Your Song
Elton John; *Elton John* . . . . (Polydor)
Elton John's Greatest Hits . . . . (Polydor)
Live In Australia With The Melbourne Symphony Orchestra . . . . (MCA)
Rod Stewart; *Two Rooms-Celebrating The Songs Of Elton John & Bernie Taupin-C* . . . . (Polydor)

LOVE: LOVE & MONEY

*See Also: **CHARACTER & INTEGRITY, DESIRE, GOLD, GREED, JEWELRY, KISSING, LOVE (various), MONEY, POVERTY, PROSTITUTES, SLEAZY, SOCIAL CLASS: GENERAL***

(I'm Not Your) Steppin' Stone
Monkees; *Monkees' Greatest Hits* . . . . (Rhino)

(Just Like) Romeo & Juliet
Reflections; *'60s Dance Party-C* . . . . (Dominion Entert.)
Sensational '60s-#1-C . . . . (Dominion Entert.)

Always True To You In My Fashion
Blossom Dearie; *Night & Day-Cole Porter Songbook-C* . . . . (Verve)
Original Cast; *Kiss Me Kate* . . . . (EMI-Angel)
Peggy Lee & George Shearing; *Anything Goes-Capitol Sings Cole Porter-C* . . . . (Capitol)

And Your Bird Can Sing
Beatles; *''Yesterday''...And Today* . . . . (Capitol)
Revolver . . . . (Capitol)

Angelina
Keb' Mo'; *Keb' Mo'.* . . . . (Okeh)

Anyway
Keb' Mo'; *The Door* . . . . (550/Epic/Okeh)
Best Of Me
Mya featuring Jadakiss; *Fear Of Flying* . . . .(University/Interscope)
Bird In A Gilded Cage
Joan Morris & William Bolcom; *After The Ball* . . . . (Nonesuch)
Buy Me A Rose
Kenny Rogers; *She Rides Wild Horses* . . . . (Dreamcatcher)
Candy's Room
Bruce Springsteen; *Darkness On The Edge Of Town* . . . . (Columbia)
Bruce Springsteen & The E Street Band; *Bruce Springsteen & The E Street Band/1975-85* . . . . (Legacy)
Can't Buy Me Love
Beatles; *Beatles 1* . . . . (Capitol)
Hey Jude . . . . (Capitol)
Reel Music . . . . (Capitol)
ST/A Hard Day's Night . . . . (Capitol)
The Beatles At The Hollywood Bowl . . . . (Capitol)
The Beatles/1962-1966 . . . . (Capitol)
Could It Be
Jaheim; *Ghetto Love* . . . .(Divine Mill/Warner Bros.)
Crazy Things I Do
Sammie; *From The Bottom To The Top* . . . .(Freeworld/Capitol)
Diamonds Are A Girl's Best Friend
Carol Channing; *Broadway Magic-The 1950s-C* . . . . (Columbia)
Emmylou Harris; *White Shoes* . . . .(Warner Bros.)
Marilyn Monroe; *Goodbye Primadonna* . . . . (Accord)
Pearl Bailey; *Back On Broadway* . . . . (Roulette)
Echoes Of An Era-Pearl Bailey . . . . (Roulette)
For Your Love
Stevie Wonder; *Conversation Peace* . . . . (Motown)
Natural Wonder . . . . (Motown)
Song Review-A Greatest Hits Collection . . . . (Motown)
Gimme What You Got
Keb' Mo'; *The Door* . . . . (550/Epic/Okeh)
Give Me You
Mary J. Blige; *Mary* . . . .(MCA)
He Talks To Me
Lorrie Morgan; *Leave The Light On* . . . . (RCA)
Lorrie Morgan's Greatest Hits . . . . (BNA)
Lorrie Morgan-Super Hits . . . . (RCA)
To Get To You-Greatest Hits Collection . . . . (BNA)
Hit 'Em Up Style (Oops!)
Blu Cantrell; *So Blu* . . . . (Arista)
Totally Hits 2001-C . . . . (Arista)
Hot Boyz
Missy "Misdemeanor" Elliot; *Da Real World* . . . . (East West)
Totally Hits-#2-C . . . . (Elektra)
House With Love In It, A
Four Lads; *Moments To Remember-Very Best Of The Four Lads* . . . . .(Taragon)
How Do You Like Me Now?!
Toby Keith; *How Do You Like Me Now?!* . . . .(DreamWorks/SKG)
I Can't Give You Anything But Love
Diana Krall; *When I Look In Your Eyes* . . . .(GRP)
Ella Fitzgerald; *Fine And Mellow* . . . . (Pablo)
The Intimate Ella . . . . (Verve)
Judy Garland; *Judy Garland's All-Time Greatest Hits* . . . . . . (Curb)
Louis Armstrong; *Complete Town Hall Concert* . . . . (RCA)
I Feel Fine
Beatles; *Beatles 1* . . . . (Capitol)
Beatles '65 . . . . (Capitol)
Beatles-20 Greatest Hits . . . . (Capitol)
Past Masters-Volume One . . . . (Parlophone)
The Beatles/1962-1966 . . . . (Capitol)
Sweethearts Of The Rodeo; *One Time One Night* . . . . . . (Columbia)
I Just Wanna Love U (Give It 2 Me)
Jay-Z; *Dynasty-Roc La Familia 2000* . . . . (Roc-A-Fella/DJMG)
If She Don't Love You
Buffalo Club; *Buffalo Club* . . . . (Rising Tide)
If You Ain't Lovin' (You Ain't Livin')
Faron Young; *Heroes Of Country Music-#3-Legends Of Nashville-C* . . . (Rhino)
Live Fast, Love Hard: Original Capitol Recordings-1952-1962-C . . . .(Country Music Foundation)
George Strait; *If You Ain't Lovin' You Ain't Livin'* . . . .(MCA)
Ten Strait Hits . . . .(MCA)
If You've Got The Money I've Got The Time
Lefty Frizzell; *American Originals-Lefty Frizzell* . . . . (Columbia)
Columbia Country Classics-#2-Honky Tonk Heroes-C . . . . (Columbia)
Lefty Frizzell's Greatest Hits . . . . (Columbia)
Willie Nelson; *Greatest Hits (& Some That Will Be)* . . . . . . (Columbia)
Sound In Your Mind . . . . (Columbia)
Willie & Family Live . . . . (Columbia)
I'll Trade (A Million Bucks)
Keith Sweat featuring Lil' Mo; *Didn't See Me Coming* . . . . (Elektra)
Incomplete
Sisqo; *Now That's What I Call Music!-#5-C* . . . . (Virgin)
Unleash The Dragon . . . . (Dragon/Def Soul/IDJMG)
Independent Women Pt.1
Destiny's Child; *Now That's What I Call Music!-#6-C* . . . . (Virgin)

ST/Charlie's Angels . . . . (Columbia)
Just Because
Shelton Brothers; *Classic Country Music-#1-C* . . . . . (Smithsonian Collection)
King Of The Mountain
George Strait; *Blue Clear Sky* . . . . (MCA)
Latest Greatest Straitest Hits . . . . (MCA)
Knock Down Walls
Tonic; *Sugar* . . . . (Universal)
Little Things
Tanya Tucker; *Complicated* . . . . (Capitol)
Livin' On A Prayer
Bon Jovi; *America: A Tribute To Heroes-C* . . . .(Interscope)
Cross Road-14 Classic Grooves . . . .(Mercury)
Slippery When Wet . . . .(Jambco)
The Concert For New York City-C . . . . (Columbia)
Love Don't Cost A Thing
Jennifer Lopez; *J. Lo* . . . . (Epic)
Now That's What I Call Music!-#6-C . . . . (Virgin)
Material Girl
Madonna; *Immaculate Collection* . . . .(Sire)
Like A Virgin . . . .(Sire)
Royal Box . . . .(Sire)
Money (That's What I Want)
Barrett Strong; *Motown Story-First 25 Years-C* . . . . (Motown)
Oldies But Goodies-#4-C . . . .(Original Sound)
Beatles; *Beatles-Box Set* . . . . (Capitol)
Rock 'N' Roll Music . . . . (Capitol)
The Beatles' Second Album . . . . (Capitol)
Buddy Guy; *Man & The Blues* . . . . (Vanguard)
Diana Ross & The Supremes; *Diana Ross & The Supremes Sing Motown* . . . . (Motown)
Jerry Lee Lewis; *Jerry Lee's Greatest!* . . . . (Rhino)
John Lennon; *Lennon* . . . . (Capitol)
Junior Walker & The All Stars; *Junior Walker & The All Stars' Greatest Hits* . . . .(S.O.U.L.)
Junior Walker & The All Stars-Anthology . . . . (Motown)
Rolling Stones; *More Hot Rocks (big hits & fazed cookies)* . . . .(Abkco)
Ronnie Milsap; *Lost In The Fifties Tonight* . . . . (RCA)
Todd Rundgren; *Something/Anything?* . . . . (Rhino)
Most Girls
Pink; *Can't Take Me Home* . . . . (LaFace)
Totally Hits-#3-C . . . .(Atlantic)
New Worried Mind
Bob Wills; *Stay A Little Longer-The Original Columbia Recordings* . . . .(Roswell/RCA)
No Guarantee
Chico DeBarge; *Long Time No See* . . . . (Kedar Entert./Universal)
MTV Jams-C . . . .(Kedar Entert./Universal)
ST/Hoodlum . . . .(Interscope)
No More
Ruff Endz; *Love Crimes* . . . . (Epic)
Now's The Time To Fall In Love
Eddie Cantor; *The Eddie Cantor Radio Show-1942-1943* . . . . . . (Original Cast)
Gene Gardos & His Orchestra; *Brother Can You Spare A Dime? Great American Songs Of The Depression-C* . . . . (Pro-Arte)
Pittsburgh, Pennsylvania
101 Strings Orchestra; *Million-Seller Hits From Mexico* . . . . (Alshire)
Guy Mitchell; *Guy Mitchell-16 Most Requested Songs* . . . . (Legacy)
Poor Boy
Elvis Presley; *Essential Elvis-The First Movies* . . . . (RCA)
For LP Fans Only . . . . (RCA)
Poor Boy
Woody Guthrie; *Legendary Woody Guthrie* . . . .(Tradition)
Woody Guthrie . . . . (Everest)
Worried Man Blues-Golden Classics-#1 . . . . (Collectables)
Pretty Litle Lady From Beaumont, Texas
George Jones; *One Woman Man* . . . . (Epic)
Texas Super Hits-C . . . . (Columbia)
Ride Wit Me
Nelly; *Country Grammar* . . . .(Fo' Reel/Universal)
Now That's What I Call Music!-#7-C . . . . (Virgin)
Satin Sheets
Jeannie Pruett; *16 Top Country Hits-#1-C* . . . . (MCA)
Country Chart-Toppers . . . . (Dominion Entert.)
Grand Ole Opry-75 Years-#2-C . . . . (MCA)
MCA Records 30 Years Of Hits-1958-1988-C . . . . . (MCA)
Shawn Colvin; *Cover Girl* . . . . (Columbia)
She Ain't Your Ordinary Girl
Alabama; *Alabama-Super Hits-#2* . . . . (RCA)
In Pictures . . . . (RCA)
She's A Woman
Beatles; *Beatles '65* . . . . (Capitol)
Beatles-Box Set . . . . (Capitol)
Compact Disc Singles Collection . . . . (Capitol)
Past Masters-Volume One . . . . (Parlophone)
The Beatles At The Hollywood Bowl . . . . (Capitol)
Jeff Beck; *Blow By Blow* . . . . (Epic)
Sticks & Stones
Tracy Lawrence; *Tracy Lawrence* . . . .(Atlantic)

Sweet Kisses
Jessica Simpson; *Sweet Kisses*. . . . . (Columbia)
Take Back Your Mink
Original Cast; *Guys & Dolls* . . . . (MCA)
Tell Me (I'll Be Around)
Shades; *110% Love Jams-C*. . . . . (Simitar)
Shades. . . . . (Motown)
Tender Moment, A
Lee Roy Parnell; *Hits And Highways Ahead* . . . . (Arista)
Love Without Mercy . . . . (Arista)
Pure Country-Best Of The '90s-C. . . . . (Priority)
That's All
Tennessee Ernie Ford; *The Ultimate Tennessee Ernie Ford* . . . . . (Razor & Tie)
There It Is
Ginuwine; *Life* . . . . (Epic)
There's Nothing Too Good For My Baby
Lee Newman; *Relatively Singing: The Songs Of Jimmy McHugh, Eddie
Cantor & More* . . . . (Original Cast)
Too Busy Thinking About My Baby
Manhattan Transfer; *Tonin'*. . . . . (Atlantic)
Marvin Gaye; *Every Great Motown Hit Of Marvin Gaye* . . . . (Motown)
Superhits. . . . . (Motown)
Treasure Of Love, The
Clyde McPhatter; *Greatest Hits-Clyde McPhatter* . . . . (Curb)
Two Story House
George Jones & Tammy Wynette; *George Jones & Tammy Wynette-16
Biggest Hits* . . . . (Epic/Legacy)
Walking To New Orleans
Fats Domino; *Fats Domino's All Time Greatest Hits* . . . . (Curb)
Fats Domino's Greatest Hits . . . . (CEMA Special Prod.)
Fats Domino's Greatest Hits . . . . (MCA)
My Blue Heaven-Best Of Fats Domino-#1 . . . . (EMI)
They Call Me The Fat Man . . . . (EMI)
When You Think Of Me
Eric Benet; *A Day In The Life* . . . . (Warner Bros.)
Why Baby Why
Charley Pride; *Charley Pride's Greatest Hits-#2* . . . . (RCA)
George Jones; *George Jones' All-Time Greatest Hits* . . . . (Epic)
George Jones-Super Hits . . . . (Epic)
Red Sovine & Webb Pierce; *Greatest Country Duets Of All
Time-C*. . . . . (MCA Special Prod.)
Webb Pierce; *Webb Pierce-Golden Hits-#2* . . . . (Plantation)
Willie Nelson & Waylon Jennings; *Take It To The Limit* . . . . (Columbia)
Worried Mind
Roy Acuff; *Night Train To Memphis*. . . . . (Columbia River Entert. Group)

LOVE: MAKING LOVE

See Also: **DESIRE, FAMILY PLANNING, KISSING, LOVE (various),
PARENTS: CONCERNED ABOUT TEEN LOVE, SEX, SEX:
RESISTING TEMPTATION**

(Turn Out The Light And) Love Me Tonight
Don Williams; *Best Of Don Williams-#2*. . . . . (MCA)
Don Williams-20 Greatest Hits. . . . . (MCA)
1959
John Anderson; *Country Love Songs-#3-C* . . . . (Warner Bros.)
John Anderson's Greatest Hits . . . . (Warner Bros.)
2 Become 1
Spice Girls; *Spice*. . . . . (Virgin)
4:37 AM (Arabs With Knives & West German Skies)
Roger Waters; *Pros & Cons Of Hitchhiking* . . . . (Columbia)
808
Blaque; *Blaque* . . . . (Track Masters/Columbia)
All The Places (I Will Kiss You)
Aaron Hall; *Inside Of You* . . . . (MCA)
Anywhere
112; *Room 112*. . . . . (Bad Boy/Arista)
Are U Still Down?
Jon B.; *Cool Relax* . . . . (Yab Yum/550)
As We Lay
Kelly Price; *Mirror Mirror* . . . . (Def Soul/IDJMG)
Ask Of You
Raphael Saadiq; *ST/Higher Learning* . . . . (550 Music)
Bad Girl
Jon B.; *Cool Relax* . . . . (Yab Yum/550)
Be My Lover
La Bouche; *All Mixed Up* . . . . (RCA)
ST/A Night At The Roxbury. . . . . (DreamWorks/SKG)
Sweet Dreams . . . . (RCA)
Beast Of Burden
Bette Midler; *No Frills* . . . . (Atlantic)
Rolling Stones; *Rewind (1971-1984)*. . . . . (Rolling Stones)
Some Girls . . . . (Virgin)
Sucking In The Seventies. . . . . (Rolling Stones)
Behind Closed Doors
Charlie Rich; *American Originals-Charlie Rich* . . . . (Columbia)

Behind Closed Doors . . . . (Epic)
Charlie Rich's Greatest Hits . . . . (Epic)
Columbia Country Classics-#4-Nashville Sound-C . . . .(Columbia)
Between Me And You
Ja Rule featuring Christina Milian; *Rule 3:36* . . . (Murder Inc./Def Jam/IDJMG)
Birds And The Bees
Jewel Akens; *American Graffiti-#3-C* . . . . (MCA)
Collectables Presents The History Of Rock-#4-C . . . .(Collectables)
Cruisin'-1965-C . . . . (Increase)
Oldies But Goodies-#9-C . . . . (Original Sound)
Super Hits-#3-C . . . . (Gusto)
Breathe
Faith Hill; *Breathe* . . . . (Warner Bros.)
Bring Down The Moon
Pamela Rose; *Morpheus*. . . . . (Grace)
Bring It On
Keith Washington; *KW* . . . . (Silas)
Brown Eyed Girl
Isley Brothers; *Live It Up* . . . . (T-Neck/Columbia)
Jimmy Buffett; *One Particular Harbour* . . . . (MCA)
Van Morrison; *Bang Masters* . . . . (Epic)
Best Of Van Morrison . . . . (Polydor)
ST/Born On The Fourth Of July. . . . . (MCA)
ST/Sleeping With The Enemy. . . . . (Columbia)
Wonder Years-Music From Emmy Shows/Era-C . . . . (Atlantic)
Brown Skin
India.Arie; *Acoustic Soul* . . . . (Motown)
Caligula
Macy Gray; *On How Life Is* . . . . (Epic)
Can I Touch You...There?
Michael Bolton; *Michael Bolton's Greatest Hits-1985-1995* . . . .(Columbia)
Cocoon
Bjork; *Vespertine* . . . . (Elektra)
Cool Relax
Jon B.; *Cool Relax* . . . . (Yab Yum/550)
Dance With Me
Debelah Morgan; *Dance With Me* . . . . (Atlantic)
Totally Hits-#3-C . . . . (Atlantic)
Dancin'
Guy; *Guy-III*. . . . . (MCA)
Don't Rush (Take Love Slowly)
K-Ci & JoJo; *Love Always* . . . . (MCA)
Don't Worry, Baby
Beach Boys; *Absolute Best-#1* . . . . (Capitol)
Endless Summer . . . . (Capitol)
Fun Fun Fun . . . . (Capitol)
Made In The U.S.A. . . . . (Capitol)
Every Morning
Sugar Ray; *14:59* . . . . (Lava)
Faded
soulDecision; *No One Does It Better* . . . . (MCA)
Now That's What I Call Music!-#5-C . . . . (Virgin)
Feel Like Makin' Love
Roberta Flack; *Atlantic Rhythm & Blues 1947-1974-#6 (1966-
1969)-C* . . . . (Atlantic)
Best Of Roberta Flack . . . . (Atlantic)
Feel Like Makin' Love. . . . . (Atlantic)
Golden Age Of Black Music-1970-1975-C . . . . (Atlantic)
Golden Soul-C. . . . . (Atlantic)
Feel Like Makin' Love
Bad Company; *10 From 6* . . . . (Atlantic)
Straight Shooter . . . . (Swan Song)
Feelin' Love
Paula Cole; *This Fire* . . . . (Imago)
Feels So Good
Xscape; *Off The Hook* . . . . (So So Def/Columbia)
First Night
Monica; *The Boy Is Mine* . . . . (Arista)
First Time Ever I Saw Your Face
Celine Dion; *All The Way...A Decade Of Song* . . . . (550 Music)
Roberta Flack; *Atlantic Rhythm & Blues 1947-1974-#6 (1966-
1969)-C* . . . . (Atlantic)
Best Of Roberta Flack . . . . (Atlantic)
First Take . . . . (Atlantic)
Fourth Of July
Mariah Carey; *Butterfly* . . . .(Columbia)
Friend, Lover, Wife
Johnny Paycheck; *Johnny Paycheck-16 Biggest Hits* . . . . (Epic)
Johnny Paycheck's Biggest Hits . . . . (Epic)
Give It To You
Jordan Knight; *Jordan Knight* . . . . (Interscope)
Give You What You Want
Chico DeBarge; *Game* . . . . (Motown)
Hold Me
Brian McKnight; *Anytime* . . . . (Motown)
Hold On
Xscape; *Traces Of My Lipstick* . . . . (So So Def/Columbia)
I Ain't Going Out
Jon B.; *Cool Relax* . . . . (Yab Yum/550)

I Can Do That
Montell Jordan; *Let's Ride* . . . .(Def Jam/RAL/Mercury)

I Never Made Love (Till I Made Love With You)
Mac Davis; *Country Classics-#5-1985-1986-C* . . . . (Universal)
Till I Made It With You . . . . (MCA)

I Wanna Be Loved
Andrews Sisters; *Best Of The Andrews Sisters* . . . . (MCA)

I Wanna Be Loved By You
Helen Kane; *Nipper's Greatest Hits Of The '20s-#1-C* . . . . (RCA)

I'd Do Anything For Love
Meat Loaf; *Bat Out Of Hell II: Back Into Hell* . . . . (MCA)

If We're Not Back In Love By Monday
Merle Haggard; *MCA Records 30 Years Of Hits-1958-1988-C* . . . .(MCA)
Merle Haggard-Legends . . . .(MCA)
Merle Haggard's Greatest Hits . . . . (MCA)
More Of The Best . . . .(MCA)
Ramblin' Fever . . . . (MCA)

If You (Lovin' Me)
Silk; *Tonight* . . . . (Elektra)

I'll Make Love To You
Boyz II Men; *Boyz II Men II* . . . . (Motown)

I'm A Man
Bo Diddley; *Bo Diddley-His Best* . . . . (Chess)
Super Blues . . . . (Chess)
*The Sopranos-Music From The HBO Original
  Series* . . . . (Sony Music Soundtrax)
Yardbirds; *Five Live Yardbirds* . . . . (Rhino)
History Of British Rock-#3-C . . . . (Rhino)
Yardbirds' Greatest Hits-#1 (1964-1966) . . . . (Rhino)

It's All About Me
Mya featuring Sisqo of Dru Hill; *Mya* . . . . (University/Interscope)

It's Now Or Never
Elvis Presley; *Elvis Presley-Love Songs* . . . . (RCA)
Heart & Soul . . . . (RCA)
Worldwide 50 Gold Award Hits, Vol. 1, Parts 1 & 2 . . . . . . (RCA)

Just In Case
Jaheim; *Ghetto Love* . . . .(Divine Mill/Warner Bros.)

Just Like A Woman
Bob Dylan; *Before The Flood* . . . . (Columbia)
Biograph . . . . (Columbia)
Blonde On Blonde . . . . (Columbia)
Bob Dylan At Budokan . . . . (Columbia)
Bob Dylan's Greatest Hits . . . . (Columbia)
Byrds; *The Byrds* . . . . (Columbia)

Keep The Ball Rollin'
Jay And The Techniques; *Bubblegum Classics-#4-C* . . . . (Varese Vintage)

Lady In My Life
Marc Nelson; *chocolate mood* . . . . (Columbia)

Lady Lay Down
John Conlee; *Rose Colored Glasses* . . . . (Universal)

Lady Of The Island
Crosby, Stills & Nash; *Crosby, Stills & Nash* . . . .(Atlantic)
CSN . . . .(Atlantic)

Last Night
Az Yet; *Az Yet* . . . . (LaFace)

Last Time Lover
Spice Girls; *Spice* . . . . (Virgin)

Let The Good Times Roll
Barbra Streisand; *Butterfly* . . . . (Columbia)
Betty Everett & Jerry Butler; *Delicious Together* . . . . (Vee-Jay)
Starring Betty Everett . . . . (Tradition)
Bobby Bland & B.B. King; *Together Again Live* . . . .(MCA)
Jerry Lee Lewis; *Golden Rock & Roll* . . . . (Sun)
Louis Jordan; *Best Of Louis Jordan* . . . . (MCA)
Molly Hatchet; *Flirtin' With Disaster* . . . .(Epic)
Nilsson; *Nilsson Schmilsson* . . . . (RCA)
Phoebe Snow; *Phoebe Snow* . . . . (MCA)
Ray Charles; *Genius Of Ray Charles* . . . .(Atlantic)
Shirley & Lee; *Billboard Top R&B Hits-1956-C* . . . . (Rhino)
History Of New Orleans R&B-#1-1950-1958-C . . . . (Rhino)
ST/Stand By Me . . . . (Rhino)
Super Oldies Of The '50s-#4-C . . . .(Audio Fidelity)
Tony Bennett with B.B. King; *Playin' With My Friends-Bennett Sings The
  Blues-C* . . . . (Columbia)

Let's Chase Each Other Around The Room
Merle Haggard; *19 Hot Country Requests-#2-C* . . . .(Epic)
For The Record: Merle Haggard-43 Legendary Hits . . . .(BNA)
It's All In The Game . . . .(Epic)

Let's Go All The Way
Norma Jean; *Best Of Norma Jean* . . . . (Collector's Choice)

Let's Make A Night To Remember
Bryan Adams; *18 Til I Die* . . . . (A&M)

Let's Make Love
Faith Hill & Tim McGraw; *Breathe* . . . .(Warner Bros.)
Tim McGraw & Faith Hill; *Tim McGraw's Greatest Hits* . . . . (Curb)

Like A Virgin
Madonna; *Immaculate Collection* . . . . (Sire)
Like A Virgin . . . . (Sire)
Royal Box . . . . (Sire)

Lonely Women Make Good Lovers
Bob Luman; *Bob Luman-Classic Country* . . . . (Simitar)
Steve Wariner; *Best Of Steve Wariner* . . . . (RCA)
Midnight Fire . . . . (RCA)
Steve Wariner's Greatest Hits . . . . (RCA)
Steve Wariner-Super Hits . . . . (RCA)

Longfellow Serenade
Neil Diamond; *12 Greatest Hits-#2* . . . . (Columbia)
Love At The Greek . . . . (Columbia)
On The Way To The Sky . . . . (Columbia)
Serenade . . . . (Columbia)

Losing A Whole Year
Third Eye Blind; *Third Eye Blind* . . . . (Elektra)

Love Child
Diana Ross & The Supremes; *Billboard Top Rock 'N' Roll Hits-
  1968-C* . . . . (Rhino)
Diana Ross & The Supremes' Greatest Hits-#3 . . . . (Motown)
Diana Ross & The Supremes-Anthology (1962-1969) . . . . . . (Motown)
Every Great #1 Hit . . . . (Motown)
Motown Story-First 25 Years-C . . . . (Motown)
Motown's Biggest Pop Hits-C . . . . (Motown)
Sweet Sensation; *Love Child* . . . . (Atco)

Love Scene
Joe; *All That I Am* . . . .(Jive)

Love Thing
Spice Girls; *Spice* . . . . (Virgin)

Love You For A Day
Ricky Martin; *Ricky Martin* . . . . (Columbia)

Love You To
Beatles; *Revolver* . . . . (Capitol)

Luv 2 Luv You
Timbaland & Magoo; *Welcome To Our World* . . (BlackGround Enterp./Atlantic)

Make Love To Me
Jo Stafford; *America's Most Versatile Singing Star* . . . . (Corinthian)

Make Yourself Comfortable
Sarah Vaughan; *Essential Sarah Vaughan-The Great Songs* . . . . . (Verve)

Making Love
Roberta Flack; *I'm The One* . . . .(Atlantic)

Mannish Boy
Muddy Waters; *Electric Mud* . . . . (Chess)
King Of The Electric Blues . . . . (Legacy)
The Best Blues Album In The World...Ever!-C . . . . (Virgin)

Never Gonna Let You Go
Blackstreet; *Another Level* . . . .(Interscope)

Nobody
Keith Sweat; *Keith Sweat* . . . . (Elektra)

Nobody Does It Better
Carly Simon; *13 Original James Bond Themes-C* . . . . (EMI)
Carly Simon-Greatest Hits Live . . . . (Arista)
ST/The Spy Who Loved Me . . . . (EMI)

Ooh Aah...Just A Little Bit
Gina G; *Fresh!* . . . . (Eternal/Warner Bros.)

Paradise
Nat "King" Cole; *Nat "King" Cole-Gift Set* . . . . (Capitol)
The Nat "King" Cole Story . . . . (Capitol)
Ray Conniff; *'S Awful Nice* . . . . (Columbia)
Russ Colombo; *Nipper's Greatest Hits Of The '30s-#2-C* . . . . (RCA)

Party Doll
Buddy Knox; *Best Of Buddy Knox* . . . . (Rhino)
Billboard Top Rock 'N' Roll Hits-1957-C . . . . (Rhino)
ST/American Graffiti . . . . (MCA)

Practice What You Preach
Barry White; *The Icon Is Love* . . . . (A&M)

Pretty Girl
Jon B.; *Bonafide* . . . .(Yab Yum/550)

Prove It All Night
Bruce Springsteen; *Darkness On The Edge Of Town* . . . . (Columbia)

R U Still Down
2Pac; *R U Still Down (Remember Me)* . . . .(Amaru/Jive)

Right Time Of The Night
Jennifer Warnes; *Best Of Jennifer Warnes* . . . . (Arista)
Jennifer Warnes . . . . (Arista)

Rock The Boat
Aaliyah; *Aaliyah* . . . . (BlackGround Enterp./Atlantic)

Rollin' In My Sweet Baby's Arms
Bill Monroe; *Bean Blossom* . . . . (MCA)
Del McCoury Band; *Appalachian Stomp: Bluegrass Classics-C* . . . . . . (Rhino)
Dillard & Clark; *Fantastic Expedition/Through The
  Morning* . . . .(Mobile Fidelity Sound Lab)
Flatt & Scruggs; *Flatt & Scruggs At Carnegie Hall!* . . . .(Koch International)
Flatt & Scruggs-20 Greatest Hits . . . . (Deluxe)
Flying Burrito Brothers; *Close Encounters To The West Coast* . . . . (Relix)
Leon Russell; *Hank Wilson's Back, Vol. 1* . . . .(Right Stuff)
New Country Ramblers; *Greatest Folksingers Of The '60s-C* . . . . . (Vanguard)
Ramblin' Jack Elliott; *Hard Travelin'* . . . . (Fantasy)
Ricky Skaggs and Kentucky Thunder; *History Of The Future* . . (Skaggs Family)

Tony Trischka; *Heartlands* . . . . (Rounder)
Willie Nelson; *Willie & Family Live* . . . . (Columbia)
Roof, The
Mariah Carey; *Butterfly* . . . . (Columbia)
Set U Free
Planet Soul; *Disco Queens-The '90s-C* . . . . (Rhino)
Energy + Harmony . . . . (Strictly Rhythm)
Sexual Healing
Marvin Gaye; *Last Concert Tour* . . . . (Giant)
Midnight Love . . . . (Columbia)
Seems Like Yesterday-#4-Early '80s-C . . . . (K-Tel)
Tribute To Black Entertainers-C . . . . (Columbia)
Max-A-Million; *Take Your Time* . . . . (S.O.S./Zoo)
Sixty Minute Man
Billy Ward & His Dominoes; *Rock & Roll Show-C* . . . . (Gusto)
Dominos; *Oldies But Goodies-#5-C* . . . . (Original Sound)
Rufus Thomas & Carla Thomas; *Rufus Thomas & Carla Thomas-*
Chronicle . . . . (Stax)
Slow Ride
Kenny Wayne Shepherd; *Trouble Is...* . . . . (Revolution)
Softest Place On Earth
Xscape; *Traces Of My Lipstick* . . . . (So So Def/Columbia)
Spend The Night
Rahsaan Patterson; *Rahsaan Patterson* . . . . (MCA)
Stay The Night
IMx; *IMx* . . . . (MCA)
Strawberries
Smooth; *Reality* . . . . (Perspective/A&M)
Sweet Sexy Thing
Nu Flavor; *Nu Flavor* . . . . (Reprise)
Teach Me Tonight
Al Jarreau; *Al Jarreau In London* . . . . (Warner Bros.)
Breakin' Away . . . . (Warner Bros.)
Diane Schuur; *Diane Schuur-Collection* . . . . (GRP)
Ella Fitzgerald; *Montreux '75* . . . . (Pablo)
Phoebe Snow; *Best Of Phoebe Snow* . . . . (Columbia)
It Looks Like Snow . . . . (Columbia)
Sarah Vaughan; *How Long Has This Been Going On?* . . . . . . (Pablo)
Tender Lover
Babyface; *Tender Lover* . . . . (Solar)
That's The Way (I Like It)
KC And The Sunshine Band; *Best Of KC And The Sunshine Band* . . . . . (Rhino)
Disco Hits-#1-C . . . . (Rhino)
Mega Hits Dance Classics-#3-C . . . . (Priority)
That's The Way Love Goes
Janet Jackson; *janet.* . . . . (Virgin)
These Are The Times
Dru Hill; *Enter The Dru* . . . . (Def Jam/RAL/Mercury/Island)
This Is For The Lover In You
Babyface; *The Day* . . . . (Epic)
This Is Your Night
Amber; *ESPN Presents Jock Jams-#2-C* . . . . (Tommy Boy)
This Is Your Night . . . . (Tommy Boy)
Treat Her Right
Commitments; *ST/The Commitments* . . . . (MCA)
George Thorogood & The Destroyers; *Born To Be Bad* . . . . (Gold Rush)
Roy Head And The Traits; *Billboard Top Rock 'N' Roll Hits-1965-C* . . . . (Rhino)
Under The Boardwalk
Bette Midler; *ST/Beaches* . . . . (Atlantic)
Bruce Willis; *Return Of Bruno* . . . . (Motown)
Drifters; *Atlantic Rhythm & Blues 1947-1974-#5 (1962-1966)-C* . . . . . (Atlantic)
Drifters-16 Greatest Hits . . . . (Trip)
Drifters-Golden Hits . . . . (Atlantic)
Super Oldies Of The '60s-#5-C . . . . (Audio Fidelity)
John Mellencamp; *Rough Harvest* . . . . (Mercury)
Lynn Anderson; *What She Does Best* . . . . (Mercury)
Rickie Lee Jones; *Girl At Her Volcano* . . . . (Warner Bros.)
Rolling Stones; *12 X 5* . . . . (Abkco)
Untouchables; *Agent Double O Soul* . . . . (Restless)
Untitled (How Does It Feel)
D'Angelo; *Voodoo* . . . . (Cheeba Sound/Virgin)
Wait
Huffamoose; *We've Been Had Again* . . . . (Interscope)
What I've Got In Mind
Billie Jo Spears; *Best Of Billie Jo Spears* . . . . (Razor & Tie)
What's On Tonight
Montell Jordan; *More...* . . . . (Mercury)
When The Lights Go Out
Five; *5* . . . . (Arista)
Totally Hits-#1-C . . . . (Arista)
Wild Week-End
Bill Anderson; *Bill Anderson-Legend* . . . . (Masters)
MCA Records 30 Years Of Hits-1958-1988-C . . . . (MCA)
Still . . . . (MCA Special Prod.)
You've Got A Way
Shania Twain; *Come On Over* . . . . (Mercury)

ST/*Notting Hill* . . . . (Mercury)

LOVE: MEN TALKING TO MEN

See Also: *ADVICE, DESIRE, GOSSIP, INSULTS, JEALOUSY,*
LOVE (various), WARNINGS

Baby Doll
Andy Williams; *Andy Williams* . . . . (Madacy)
Back Up Buddy
Carl Smith; *Essential Carl Smith-1950-1956* . . . . (Legacy)
Trucker's Jukebox-#2-C . . . . (Legacy)
Be Glad
Del Reeves; *45-#50531* . . . . (United Artists)
Bird Dog
Everly Brothers; *Best Of The Everly Brothers* . . . . (Rhino)
Billboard Top Rock 'N' Roll Hits-1958-C . . . . (Rhino)
Everly Brothers-Cadence Classics-Their 20 Greatest Hits . . . . (Rhino)
Fabulous Style Of The Everly Brothers . . . . (Rhino)
Very Best Of The Everly Brothers . . . . (Warner Bros.)
Brand New Mister Me
Mel Tillis & The Statesiders; *The Ultimate Mel Tillis* . . . . (Bransounds)
Cold Hard Truth, The
George Jones; *Cold Hard Truth* . . . . (Asylum)
Jamie O'Hara; *Rise Above It* . . . . (RCA)
Don't Take Her She's All I Got
Tracy Byrd; *Big Love* . . . . (MCA)
Girl Is Mine
Michael Jackson with Paul McCartney; *Thriller* . . . . (Epic)
Hey Joe!
Carl Smith; *All Time Legends Of Country Music-C* . . . . (Legacy)
Hurt Her Once For Me
Wilburn Brothers; *Only Country-1965-1969-C* . . . . . (JCI Assoc. Labels)
I Could Have Told You
Frank Sinatra; *No One Cares* . . . . (Capitol)
I Was The One
Elvis Presley; *Elvis' Golden Records* . . . . (RCA)
If She Don't Love You
Buffalo Club; *Buffalo Club* . . . . (Rising Tide)
Keep Your Hands Off My Baby
Trashmen; *Bird Call! The Twin City Stomp Of The*
Trashmen . . . . (Sundazed Music)
Leave My Kitten Alone
Beatles; *The Beatles-Anthology-#1* . . . . (Capitol)
Elvis Costello; *Kojak Variety* . . . . (Warner Bros.)
Little Willie John; *Best Of Little Willie John-Fever* . . . . (Rhino)
Little Town Flirt
Del Shannon; *Del Shannon's Greatest Hits* . . . . (Rhino)
Del Shannon's Greatest Hits . . . . (Curb)
Maneater
Daryl Hall & John Oates; *H2O* . . . . (RCA)
Nipper's Greatest Hits Of The '80s-C . . . . (RCA)
Rock 'N Soul, Part 1 . . . . (RCA)
Please Don't Squeeze My Sharmon
Charlie Walker; *Charlie Walker-Golden Hits* . . . . (Plantation)
Country Music Classics-#10-Late '60s-C . . . . (K-Tel)
She Can Put Her Shoes Under My Bed (Anytime)
Johnny Duncan; *Classic Country* . . . . (Simitar)
She Loves You
Beatles; *Beatles 1* . . . . (Capitol)
Beatles-20 Greatest Hits . . . . (Capitol)
Beatles-Box Set . . . . (Capitol)
Past Masters-Volume One . . . . (Parlophone)
The Beatles At The Hollywood Bowl . . . . (Capitol)
The Beatles' Second Album . . . . (Capitol)
The Beatles/1962-1966 . . . . (Capitol)
Straight Tequila Night
John Anderson; *Seminole Wind* . . . . (BNA)
Today's Hot Country-C . . . . (K-Tel)
Take Care Of Home
Dave Hollister; *Chicago '85 The Movie* . . . . (Def Squad/DreamWorks)
Take Good Care Of Her
Adam Wade; *45-#546* . . . . (Coed)
Sonny James; *Billboard Top Country Hits-1966-C* . . . . (Rhino)
Take Good Care Of My Baby
Bobby Vee; *Best Of Bobby Vee* . . . . (EMI)
Billboard Top Rock 'N' Roll Hits-1961-C . . . . (Rhino)
'Til My Dreamin' Comes True-C . . . . (Capitol)
Bobby Vinton; *Bobby Vinton-16 Most Requested Songs* . . . . . (Legacy)
Dion; *Runaround Sue (Right Stuff)* . . . . (Right Stuff)
Tell Laura I Love Her
Ray Peterson; *Nipper's Greatest Hits Of The '60s-#1-C* . . . . . (RCA)
Teenage Tragedies-C . . . . (Rhino)
Too Good To Be True
Michael Peterson; *Michael Peterson* . . . . (Reprise)
Treat Her Like A Lady
Joe; *My Name Is Joe* . . . . (Jive)

Treat Her Right
Sawyer Brown; *This Thing Called Wantin' & Havin' It All* . . . . (Curb)
You're Going To Lose That Girl
Beatles; *ST/Help!* . . . . (Capitol)

LOVE: MY IDEAL

See Also: BEST, BRAGGING, COMPLIMENTS, DREAMS,
HAPPINESS, KISSING, LOVE (various), PRETEND, SPECIAL

Ain't No Woman (Like The One I Got)
Four Tops; *Ain't No Woman (Like The One I Got)* . . . . (MCA Special Prod.)
Four Tops' Greatest Hits (1972-1976) . . . . (MCA)
Ain't Nothing 'Bout You
Brooks & Dunn; *Steers & Stripes* . . . . (Arista)
Ain't She Sweet?
Beatles; *History Of British Rock-#5-C* . . . . (Rhino)
The Beatles-Anthology-#3 . . . . (Capitol)
Erroll Garner; *Body And Soul* . . . . (Legacy)
Frank Sinatra; *Sinatra and Swingin' Brass* . . . . (Reprise)
Pearl Bailey; *Pearl Bailey-16 Most Requested Songs* . . . . (Legacy)
All That Heaven Will Allow
Bruce Springsteen; *Tunnel Of Love* . . . . (Columbia)
All The Things You Are
Ella Fitzgerald; *Complete Jerome Kern* . . . . (Verve)
Mario Lanza; *Be My Love-Greatest Performances* . . . . (Rhino)
Willie Nelson; *Healing Hands Of Time* . . . . (Liberty)
Any Man Of Mine
Shania Twain; *1996 Grammy Nominees-C* . . . . (Columbia)
The Woman In Me . . . . (Mercury)
Snoopy; *Snoopy's Country Classiks On Toys* . . . . (Lightyear)
Baby You Got It
Brenton Wood; *18 Best-Brenton Wood* . . . . (Original Sound)
Back At One
Brian McKnight; *Back At One* . . . . (Motown)
Mark Wills; *Permanently* . . . . (Mercury)
Bernadette
Four Tops; *Compact Command Performances-Four Tops* . . . . (Motown)
Four Tops' Greatest Hits . . . . (Motown)
Four Tops Reach Out . . . . (Motown)
Four Tops-Anthology . . . . (Motown)
Motown Superstar Series-#14-Four Tops . . . . (Motown)
Betcha By Golly, Wow
''AFKAP''; *Emancipation* . . . . (NPG)
Johnny Mathis; *First Time Ever I Saw Your Face* . . . . (Columbia)
Stylistics; *Best Of The Stylistics* . . . . (Amherst)
Bitch
Meredith Brooks; *Blurring The Edges* . . . . (Capitol)
Boy From New York City
Ad-Libs; *Jewels-#1-C* . . . . (SSS International)
Oldies But Goodies-#6-C . . . . (Original Sound)
Original Golden Hits Of The Great Groups-#1-C . . . . (SSS International)
Original New York Rock & Roll-#1-C . . . . (SSS International)
Manhattan Transfer; *Best Of The Manhattan Transfer* . . . . (Atlantic)
Mecca For Moderns . . . . (Atlantic)
Boy Wanted
Original Cast; *My One And Only* . . . . (Atlantic)
Brand New Day
Sting; *Brand New Day* . . . . (A&M)
Buckaroo
Lee Ann Womack; *Lee Ann Womack* . . . . (Decca)
Caligula
Macy Gray; *On How Life Is* . . . . (Epic)
Can't Take My Eyes Off You
Frankie Valli; *25th Anniversary Collection* . . . . (Rhino)
Frankie Valli-Anthology . . . . (Rhino)
Very Best Of Frankie Valli . . . . (MCA)
Lauryn Hill; *The Miseducation Of Lauryn Hill* . . . . (Ruffhouse/Columbia)
Chances Are
Bob Marley; *Chances Are* . . . . (Cotillion)
Bob Seger & Martina McBride; *ST/Hope Floats* . . . . (Capitol)
Johnny Mathis; *First 25 Years-Silver Anniversary Album* . . . . (Columbia)
Johnny Mathis' All-Time Greatest Hits . . . . (Columbia)
Johnny Mathis' Greatest Hits . . . . (Columbia)
Johnny Mathis-Live . . . . (Columbia)
Johnny Mathis-Love Songs . . . . (Columbia)
Darling Be Home Soon
Joe Cocker; *Joe Cocker!* . . . . (A&M)
Joe Cocker-Classics-#4 . . . . (A&M)
Joe Cocker's Greatest Hits . . . . (A&M)
Lovin' Spoonful; *Best Of The Lovin' Spoonful-#2* . . . . (Rhino)
Lovin' '60s-C . . . . (Priority)
Lovin' Spoonful-Anthology . . . . (Rhino)
Every Woman In The World
Air Supply; *Air Supply's Greatest Hits* . . . . (Arista)
Air Supply-The Definitive Collection . . . . (Arista)
Lost In Love . . . . (Arista)

Everything You Want
Vertical Horizon; *Everything You Want* . . . . (RCA)
Totally Hits-#3-C . . . . (Atlantic)
Exactly Like You
Andy Williams; *Moon River-Days Of Wine And Roses* . . . . (Columbia)
Sarah Vaughan; *Complete Sarah Vaughan On Mercury-#1-Great Jazz Years-*
1954-1956 . . . . (Mercury)
Willie Nelson; *Somewhere Over The Rainbow* . . . . (Columbia)
Girl That I Marry, The
Dick Haymes; *Best Of Dick Haymes* . . . . (MCA)
Doris Day/Original Cast; *Annie Get Your Gun* . . . . (Columbia)
Original Broadway Cast; *Annie Get Your Gun* . . . . (Angel)
Original Cast; *Annie Get Your Gun* . . . . (MCA)
God Must Have Spent A Little More Time On You
Alabama Featuring 'N Sync; *Twentieth Century* . . . . (RCA)
'N Sync; *'N Sync* . . . . (RCA)
Totally Hits-#1-C . . . . (Arista)
Holdin' Heaven
Tracy Byrd; *Tracy Byrd* . . . . (MCA)
Holding Out For A Hero
Bonnie Tyler; *ST/Footloose* . . . . (Columbia)
Hundred Pounds Of Clay
Gene McDaniels; *Best Of Gene McDaniels-A Hundred Pounds*
Of Clay . . . . (Collectables)
Rock Is Dead But It Won't Lie Down-C . . . . (Gold Rush)
I Am Made Of You
Ricky Martin; *Ricky Martin* . . . . (Columbia)
I Knew I Loved You
Savage Garden; *Affirmation* . . . . (Columbia)
Now That's What I Call Music!-#4-C . . . . (Virgin)
If You Love Me
Brownstone; *From The Bottom Up* . . . . (MJJ/Epic)
MTV Party To Go-#8-C . . . . (Tommy Boy)
I'm Holdin' On To Love (To Save My Life)
Shania Twain; *Come On Over* . . . . (Mercury)
I'm Satisfied With You
Hank Williams; *Complete Hank Williams* . . . . (Mercury)
Lovesick Blues . . . . (ASV)
Image Of A Girl
Safaris; *Brown Eyed Soul...East L.A.-#3-C* . . . . (Rhino)
In A Perfect World
Gretchen Peters; *Gretchen Peters* . . . . (Purple Crayon Prod.)
It Had To Be You
Harry Connick, Jr.; *ST/When Harry Met Sally* . . . . (Columbia)
Just The Way You Are
Billy Joel; *Billy Joel-Greatest Hits, Volume I & Volume II* . . . . (Columbia)
Pop Classics Of The '70s-C . . . . (Columbia)
The Stranger . . . . (Columbia)
Kissin' You
Total; *Total* . . . . (Bad Boy/Arista)
Long Ago And Far Away
Erroll Garner; *Long Ago And Far Away* . . . . (Columbia)
Glenn Miller; *Glenn Miller-A Legendary Performer-#1 & 2* . . . . (Bluebird)
Helen Forrest & Dick Haymes; *American Songbook Series-*
Jerome Kern . . . . (Smithsonian Collection)
Jo Stafford; *Capitol Collectors Series-Jo Stafford* . . . . (Capitol)
International Hits . . . . (Corinthian)
Jukebox Saturday Night-Great Vocal Hits-C . . . . (Capitol)
Songs That Got Us Through WWII-C . . . . (Rhino)
ST/Bugsy . . . . (Epic)
Johnny Mathis; *Hollywood Musicals* . . . . (Columbia)
Mantovani; *More Golden Hits* . . . . (London)
Perry Como; *Always In My Heart-Classic Songs Of World War II-#2* . . . . (RCA)
Rosemary Clooney; *Rosemary Clooney Sings The Lyrics Of Ira*
Gershwin . . . . (Concord Jazz)
Love I Found In You
Jim Brickman; *My Romance: An Evening With Jim Brickman* . . . (Windham Hill)
Love Of My Life
Jim Brickman featuring Michael W. Smith; *Destiny* . . . . (Windham Hill)
Love Of My Life
Brian McKnight; *Superhero* . . . . (Motown)
Make Me Whole
Amel Larrieux; *Infinite Possibilities* . . . . (Epic)
Maria
Blondie; *No Exit* . . . . (Beyond)
Mint Car
Cure; *Wild Mood Swings* . . . . (Elektra)
My Favorite Memory
Merle Haggard; *For The Record: Merle Haggard-43 Legendary Hits* . . . . (BNA)
My Guy
Mary Wells; *Mary Wells' Greatest Hits* . . . . (Motown)
My Guy . . . . (Motown)
Oldies But Goodies-#11-C . . . . (Original Sound)
My Kind Of Girl
Collin Raye; *Best Of Collin Raye-Direct Hits* . . . . (Epic)
Extremes . . . . (Epic)
My Kind Of Woman, My Kind Of Man
Patty Loveless; *Patty Loveless-Classics* . . . . (Epic)

Vince Gill with Patty Loveless; *The Key* . . . . (MCA)
My Wild Irish Rose
Magic Organ; *22 Great Organ Favorites* . . . . (Ranwood)
Mom & Dads; *One Dozen Roses* . . . . (Crescendo)
My Wonderful
Jessica Simpson; *Sweet Kisses* . . . . (Columbia)
Of Thee I Sing
Sarah Vaughan; *Sarah Vaughan Sings George Gershwin* . . . . (Verve)
Old Master Painter
Peggy Lee; *Capitol Collectors Series-Peggy Lee-#1-Early Years* . . . . . (Capitol)
Only You (And You Alone)
Platters; *Cruisin'-1955-C* . . . . (Increase)
Encore Of Golden Hits-Platters . . . . (Mercury)
Millennium Collection-20th Century Masters . . . . (Mercury)
Perfect Drug
Nine Inch Nails; *ST/Lost Highway* . . . . (Interscope)
Perfect Love
Trisha Yearwood; *Songbook-A Collection Of Hits* . . . . (MCA)
Poetry In Motion
Johnny Tillotson; *10 Top Ten Hits-#1* . . . . (Laurie)
American Graffiti-#3-C . . . . (MCA)
Jukebox Classics-#1-C . . . . (Rhino)
Mellow '60s-C . . . . (Priority)
Million-Dollar Memories-#2-C . . . . (RCA)
She's All I Ever Had
Ricky Martin; *Ricky Martin* . . . . (Columbia)
She's Always Right
Clay Walker; *Live, Laugh, Love* . . . . (Giant)
She's More
Andy Griggs; *You Won't Ever Be Lonely* . . . . (RCA)
She's So High
Tal Bachman; *Tal Bachman* . . . . (Columbia)
Short Skirt/Long Jacket
Cake; *Comfort Eagle* . . . . (Columbia)
Shy Guy
Diana King; *ST/Bad Boys* . . . . (Work)
Tougher Than Love . . . . (Work)
Smooth
Santana featuring Rob Thomas; *Supernatural* . . . . (Arista)
Totally Hits-#1-C . . . . (Arista)
So Into You
Tamia; *Tamia* . . . . (Qwest)
Sold (The Grundy County Auction Incident)
John Michael Montgomery; *Drew's Famous Country Party
Music-C* . . . . (Turn Up The Music)
John Michael Montgomery . . . . (Atlantic)
John Michael Montgomery's Greatest Hits . . . . (Atlantic)
Stand Inside Your Love
Smashing Pumpkins; *Machina: The Machines Of God* . . . . (Virgin)
Sweetheart Of Sigma Chi
Fred Waring's Pennsylvanians; *Very Best Of Fred Waring & The
Pennsylvanians* . . . . (Reader's Digest Music)
Gene Austin; *The Voice Of The Southland* . . . . (Living Era)
That Girl's Been Spyin' On Me
Billy Dean; *It's What I Do* . . . . (Capitol)
There She Goes
Babyface; *Face 2 Face* . . . . (Arista)
This Everyday Love
Rascal Flatts; *Rascal Flatts* . . . . (Lyric Street)
Unbelievable
Diamond Rio; *Unbelievable* . . . . (Arista)
Unusually Unusual
Lonestar; *I'm Already There* . . . . (BNA)
Venus
Frankie Avalon; *21 Oldies But Goodies-C* . . . . (Original Sound)
'50s Sock Hop-C . . . . (K-Tel)
Billboard Top Rock 'N' Roll Hits-1959-C . . . . (Rhino)
Oldies But Goodies-#10-C . . . . (Original Sound)
Venus
Shocking Blue; *'70s Smash Hits-#1-C* . . . . (Rhino)
Billboard Top Rock 'N' Roll Hits-1970-C . . . . (Rhino)
Oldies But Goodies-#15-C . . . . (Original Sound)
Super Hits Of The '70s-Have A Nice Day-#1-C . . . . (Rhino)
Venus In Blue Jeans
Jimmy Clanton; *All-Star Chartbusters* . . . . (Intermedia)
Golden Years-1962-C . . . . (Dominion Entert.)
Walking In The Rain
Jay & The Americans; *Come A Little Bit Closer-Best Of Jay & The
Americans* . . . . (Gold Rush)
Jay & The Americans' All-Time Greatest Hits . . . . (Rhino)
Jay & The Americans' Greatest Hits . . . . (Curb)
Rhythm Of The Rain-C . . . . (Varese Vintage)
Ronettes; *Best Of The Ronettes* . . . . (Abkco)
Phil Spector-Back To Mono 1958-1969-C . . . . (Abkco)
We Must Be In Love
Pure Soul; *Pure Soul* . . . . (Stepsun/Interscope)
What If It's You
Reba McEntire; *What If It's You* . . . . (MCA)

When My Dreamboat Comes Home
Fats Domino; *My Blue Heaven* . . . . (Gold Rush)
Kay Starr; *Capitol Collectors Series-Kay Starr* . . . . (Capitol)
Wishin' & Hopin'
Ani DiFranco; *ST/My Best Friend's Wedding* . . . . (Work/Epic)
Dusty Springfield; *Dusty Springfield-Golden Hits* . . . . (Mercury)
History Of British Rock-#6-C . . . . (Rhino)
Yellow Rose Of Texas
Hoyt Axton; *Songs Of The Civil War-C* . . . . (Columbia)
Michael Martin Murphey; *Cowboy Songs* . . . . (Warner Western)
Mitch Miller; *Mitch Miller-16 Most Requested Songs* . . . . (Columbia)
Roy Rogers; *Great American Singing Cowboys-C* . . . . . . (Republic/Universal)
You Are So Beautiful
Joe Cocker; *Chicken Soup For The Soul: Love And Inspiration-C* . . . . . (Rhino)
Joe Cocker-Super Hits . . . . (Legacy)
Organic . . . . (550 Music)
Kenny Rogers; *Timepiece* . . . . (Atlantic)
You Got What It Takes
Dave Clark Five; *History Of The Dave Clark Five* . . . . (Hollywood)
Marv Johnson; *All-Time Greatest Hits Of Rock 'N' Roll-C* . . . . (Curb)
You Walked In
Lonestar; *Crazy Nights* . . . . (BNA)
You Want This
Janet Jackson; *janet.* . . . . (Virgin)
You'd Be So Nice To Come Home To
Dinah Shore; *Songs That Got Us Through WWII-#2-C* . . . . (Rhino)
Young Blood
Bad Company; *Run With The Pack* . . . . (Swan Song)
Coasters; *Coasters' Greatest Hits* . . . . (Atco)
Coasters-Their Greatest Recordings-Early Years . . . . (Atco)
The Ultimate Coasters . . . . (Warner Special Prod.)

LOVE: ON THE ROPES, Fear Of Losing You, Love In Trouble, Not Really Love Anymore

See Also: COLD, DECISIONS, DIVORCE, ENDINGS, FIGHT, GOSSIP, HOLDING ON, LEAVING, LOSING & LOSS, LOVE (various), SADNESS

(Eye) Hate U
"AFKAP"; *The Gold Experience* . . . . (NPG)
(I Know) I'm Losing You
Rod Stewart; *Best Of Rod Stewart* . . . . (Mercury)
Every Picture Tells A Story . . . . (Mercury)
Storyteller/The Complete Anthology: 1964-1990 . . . . (Warner Bros.)
Temptations; *Temptations-Anthology-The Best Of The Temptations*. . . (Motown)
Temptations-The Ultimate Collection . . . . (Motown)
(Just Like) Romeo & Juliet
Reflections; *'60s Dance Party-C* . . . . (Dominion Entert.)
Sensational '60s-#1-C . . . . (Dominion Entert.)
10 Days Late
Third Eye Blind; *Blue* . . . . (Elektra)
Absence Of The Heart
Deana Carter; *Everything's Gonna Be Alright* . . . . (Capitol)
Achy Breaky Heart
Billy Ray Cyrus; *Some Gave All* . . . . (Mercury)
After The Love Is Gone
Earth, Wind & Fire; *Best Of Earth, Wind & Fire-#2* . . . . (Columbia)
Earth, Wind & Fire-Greatest Hits-#1 . . . . (Legacy)
All I Want
Joni Mitchell; *Blue* . . . . (Reprise)
Joni Mitchell with Tom Scott & The L.A. Express; *Miles Of Aisles*. . . . (Asylum)
All Or Nothing
O-Town; *O-Town* . . . . (J)
Totally Hits 2001-C . . . . (Arista)
All Out Of Love
Air Supply; *Air Supply's Greatest Hits* . . . . (Arista)
Air Supply-The Definitive Collection . . . . (Arista)
Lost In Love . . . . (Arista)
All These Years
Sawyer Brown; *Cafe On The Corner* . . . . (Curb)
Almost Goodbye
Mark Chesnutt; *Almost Goodbye* . . . . (MCA)
Always On My Mind
Willie Nelson; *Always On My Mind* . . . . (Columbia)
Super Hits Of The '80s-C . . . . (Epic)
Willie Nelson-Super Hits . . . . (Columbia)
Am I Getting Through (Part I & II)
Sheryl Crow; *The Globe Sessions* . . . . (A&M)
Am I Losing You
Jim Reeves; *Best Of Jim Reeves* . . . . (RCA)
Essential Jim Reeves . . . . (RCA)
Jim Reeves' Greatest Hits . . . . (RCA)
Ronnie Milsap; *Ronnie Milsap's Greatest Hits-#2* . . . . (RCA)
Am I The Only One
Marc Anthony; *Marc Anthony* . . . . (Columbia)

Angry All The Time
Bruce Robison with Kelly Willis; *Wrapped* . . . . (Lucky Dog)
Tim McGraw with Faith Hill; *Set This Circus Down* . . . . (Curb)
Ants Marching
Dave Matthews Band; *Under The Table And Dreaming* . . . . (RCA)
Any Day Now
Ronnie Milsap; *Essential Ronnie Milsap* . . . . (RCA)
Ronnie Milsap's Greatest Hits-#2 . . . . (RCA)
Ronnie Milsap-Super Hits . . . . (RCA)
Anymore
Roy Drusky; *Anymore* . . . . (Decca)
Anymore
Travis Tritt; *It's All About To Change* . . . . (Warner Bros.)
Travis Tritt's Greatest Hits-From The Beginning . . . . (Warner Bros.)
Anything But Down
Sheryl Crow; *The Globe Sessions* . . . . (A&M)
As Any Fool Can See
Tracy Lawrence; *I See It Now* . . . . (Atlantic)
Live & Unplugged . . . . (Atlantic)
Baby I Need Your Loving
Four Tops; *Four Tops' Greatest Hits* . . . . (Motown)
Four Tops-Anthology . . . . (Motown)
The Ultimate Collection-Four Tops . . . . (Motown)
Johnny Rivers; *Johnny Rivers' Greatest Hits* . . . . (Capitol)
Johnny Rivers-Anthology 1964-1977 . . . . (Rhino)
Baby's Got A Brand New Baby
S-K-O; *S-K-O* . . . . (MTM)
Beast Of Burden
Bette Midler; *No Frills* . . . . (Atlantic)
Rolling Stones; *Rewind (1971-1984)* . . . . (Rolling Stones)
Some Girls . . . . (Virgin)
Sucking In The Seventies . . . . (Rolling Stones)
Before The Blues
Colin Linden; *Raised By Wolves* . . . . (Compass)
Best Of My Love
Brooks & Dunn; *Common Thread-Songs Of The Eagles-C* . . . . (Giant)
Eagles; *Eagles/Their Greatest Hits 1971-1975* . . . . (Asylum)
On The Border . . . . (Elektra)
Better Man
Pearl Jam; *Vitalogy* . . . . (Epic)
Blue Moon With Heartache
Rosanne Cash; *19 Hot Country Requests-#2-C* . . . .(Epic)
Rosanne Cash-Hits-1979-1989 . . . . (Columbia)
Seven Year Ache . . . . (Columbia)
Boo
Macy Gray; *The Id* . . . .(Epic)
Breakfast At Tiffany's
Deep Blue Something; *Home* . . . . (RainMaker/Interscope)
Breathe
Nickelback; *State* . . . . (Roadrunner)
Brilliant Disguise
Bruce Springsteen; *Bruce Springsteen's Greatest Hits* . . . . (Columbia)
Tunnel Of Love . . . . (Columbia)
Buy Me A Rose
Kenny Rogers; *She Rides Wild Horses* . . . . (Dreamcatcher)
Can I Change My Mind
Tyrone Davis; *Soul Shots-#2-The "In" Crowd-Sweet Soul-C* . . . . (Rhino)
Tyrone Davis' Greatest Hits . . . . (Rhino)
Can't Really Be Gone
Tim McGraw; *All I Want* . . . . (Curb)
Can't Stop Lovin' You
Van Halen; *Balance* . . . . (Warner Bros.)
Carolina Blues
Blues Traveler; *Straight On Till Morning* . . . . (A&M)
Carolyn
Merle Haggard & The Strangers; *For The Record: Merle Haggard-43
Legendary Hits* . . . . (BNA)
Carrion
Fiona Apple; *Tidal* . . . . (Clean Slate/Work)
Chain, The
Fleetwood Mac; *25 Years-The Chain* . . . .(Warner Bros.)
Rumours . . . . (Warner Bros.)
Shawn Colvin; *Legacy-A Tribute To Fleetwood Mac's Rumours-C* . . . . . (Lava)
Chains Of Love
Erasure; *Innocents* . . . . (Sire)
Just Say Yo-#2 Of Just Say Yes-C . . . . (Sire)
Chains Of Love
Big Joe Turner; *Big Joe Turner's Greatest Hits* . . . . (Atlantic)
In The Evening . . . . (Pablo)
Turns On The Blues . . . . (Kent)
Bobby Bland; *Introspective Of The Early Years* . . . . (MCA)
Spotlighting The Man . . . . (MCA)
Mickey Gilley; *First Class* . . . . (Playboy)
Mickey Gilley's Biggest Hits . . . .(Epic)
Change My Mind
John Berry; *Faces* . . . . (Capitol)
Charlie's Shoes
Billy Walker; *Best Of Billy Walker* . . . . (Deluxe)

Columbia Country Classics-#4-Nashville Sound-C . . . . (Columbia)
Choppy Water (Rocky Marriage Breakdown)
Connie Kaldor; *Small Cafe* . . . . (Philo)
Cold As Ice
Foreigner; *Foreigner* . . . .(Atlantic)
Records . . . . (Atlantic)
ST/FM . . . . (MCA)
Cold Cold Heart
Hank Williams; *Complete Hank Williams* . . . . (Mercury)
Hank Williams With His Drifting Cowboys; *24 Of Hank Williams'
Greatest Hits* . . . . (Polydor)
Hank Williams . . . . (MGM)
Hank Williams-40 Greatest Hits . . . . (Polydor)
Live At Opry . . . . (MGM)
Long Gone Lonesome Blues . . . . (Polydor)
Jerry Lee Lewis; *Duets* . . . . (Sun)
Golden Cream Of Jerry Lee Lewis . . . . (Sun)
Jerry Lee Lewis & Friends-Duets . . . . (Sun)
Lucinda Williams; *Timeless: Hank Williams
Tribute-C* . . . . (Lost Highway/IDJMG)
Tony Bennett; *Tony Bennett-16 Most Requested Songs* . . . . (Legacy)
Confessions
Destiny's Child; *The Writing's On The Wall* . . . . (Columbia)
Congo
Genesis; *Calling All Stations* . . . .(Atlantic)
Corrina, Corrina
Asleep At The Wheel featuring Brooks & Dunn; *Tribute To The Music Of
Bob Wills And The Texas Playboys-C* . . . . (Liberty)
Big Joe Turner; *Best Of Big Joe Turner* . . . . (Pablo)
Big Joe Turner's Greatest Hits . . . . (Atlantic)
Bob Dylan; *Freewheelin'* . . . . (Columbia)
Ray Peterson; *Good Old Rock & Roll-C* . . . . (International Mktg. Group)
Super Hits-#1-C . . . . (Gusto)
Steppenwolf; *Live Steppenwolf* . . . . (MCA)
Creep
TLC; *CrazySexyCool* . . . . (LaFace)
Damn Thing Called Love
After 7; *Reflections* . . . . (Virgin)
Dangling Conversation
Simon & Garfunkel; *Parsley Sage Rosemary & Thyme* . . . . (Columbia)
Days Of The Week
Stone Temple Pilots; *Shangri-La-Dee-Da* . . . .(Atlantic)
Dear Me
Lorrie Morgan; *Lorrie Morgan's Greatest Hits* . . . .(BNA)
Dis-Satisfied
Bill Anderson & Jan Howard; *More Great Country
Duets-C* . . . . (MCA Special Prod.)
Do For Love
2Pac featuring Eric Williams; *R U Still Down (Remember Me)* . . . .(Amaru/Jive)
Do Right
Jimmie's Chicken Shack; *Bring Your Own Stereo* . . . . (Rocket)
Does My Ring Hurt Your Finger
Charley Pride; *Charley Pride-24 Greatest Hits* . . . . (Tee Vee)
Essential Charley Pride . . . . (RCA)
Dollhouse
Bruce Springsteen; *Tracks* . . . . (Columbia)
Don't Leave Me
Blackstreet; *Another Level* . . . .(Interscope)
Don't Let Our Love Start Slippin' Away
Vince Gill; *I Still Believe In You* . . . . (MCA)
Don't Say
Jon B.; *Cool Relax* . . . .(Yab Yum/550)
Don't Sleep In The Subway
Frank Sinatra; *Frank Sinatra* . . . .(Reprise)
Petula Clark; *Petula Clark's Greatest Hits* . . . . (Crescendo)
Summer Of Love-#1-C . . . . (Rhino)
Don't Think I'm Not
Kandi; *Hey Kandi* . . . . (So So Def/Columbia)
Now That's What I Call Music!-#5-C . . . . (Virgin)
Don't Wanna Lose You
Gloria Estefan; *Billboard Top Hits-1989-C* . . . . (Rhino)
Cuts Both Ways . . . . (Epic)
Diana, Princess Of Wales-Tribute-C . . . . (Columbia)
Gloria Estefan's Greatest Hits . . . . (Epic)
Don't Worry 'bout Me
Frank Sinatra; *Capitol Collectors Series-Frank Sinatra* . . . . (Capitol)
Don't You Care
Buckinghams; *Buckinghams' Greatest Hits* . . . . (Columbia)
Dreams
Corrs; *Legacy-A Tribute To Fleetwood Mac's Rumours-C* . . . . (Lava)
Fleetwood Mac; *25 Years-The Chain* . . . . (Warner Bros.)
Fleetwood Mac Live . . . . (Warner Bros.)
Fleetwood Mac's Greatest Hits . . . . (Warner Bros.)
Rumours . . . . (Warner Bros.)
Drown
Son Volt; *Trace* . . . . (Warner Bros.)
Engine Engine #9
Roger Miller; *Best Of Roger Miller-#2-King Of The Road* . . . . (Mercury)

Best Of Roger Miller-His Greatest Songs . . . . (Curb)
King Of The Road-Genius Of Roger Miller . . . . (Mercury)
Roger Miller-Golden Hits . . . . (Smash)
Roger Miller-The Hits . . . . (Mercury)
Train Trax-C . . . . (Sony Music Special Prod.)

Evil Ways
Santana; *Best Of Santana* . . . . (Legacy)
Santana . . . . (Columbia)
Santana's Greatest Hits . . . . (Columbia)
Viva Santana! . . . . (Columbia)

Ex-Factor
Lauryn Hill; *The Miseducation Of Lauryn Hill* . . . . (Ruffhouse/Columbia)

Fool #1
Mavericks; *Trampoline* . . . . (MCA)

For No One
Beatles; *Beatles-Box Set* . . . . (Capitol)
Beatles-Love Songs . . . . (Capitol)
Revolver . . . . (Capitol)
Emmylou Harris; *Pieces Of The Sky* . . . . (Reprise)

Forget Me Nots
Patrice Rushen; *Patrice Rushen-Anthology* . . . . (Elektra)
Straight From The Heart . . . . (Elektra)
The Disco Years-#2-On The Beat-1978-1982-C . . . . (Rhino)

Frozen
Madonna; *GHV2* . . . . (Warner Bros.)
Ray Of Light . . . . (Maverick)

Get It Together
702; *No Doubt* . . . . (Biv 10/Motown)

Girl
Beatles; *Beatles-Box Set* . . . . (Capitol)
Beatles-Love Songs . . . . (Capitol)
Rubber Soul . . . . (Capitol)
The Beatles/1962-1966 . . . . (Capitol)

Girlfriend
Alicia Keys; *Songs In A Minor* . . . . (J)

Give Me One Reason
Tracy Chapman; *New Beginning* . . . . (Elektra)

Glycerine
Bush; *Sixteen Stone* . . . . (Trauma)

Goodnight My Love (Pleasant Dreams)
Fleetwoods; *Best Of The Fleetwoods* . . . . (Rhino)
Fleetwoods' Greatest Hits . . . . (CEMA Special Prod.)
Jesse Belvin; *Collectables Presents The History Of Rock-#9-C* . . . (Collectables)
Oldies But Goodies-#2-C . . . . (Original Sound)

Got A Feelin'
Mamas & The Papas; *Best Of The Mamas & The Papas* . . . . (MCA)

Gotta Tell You
Samantha Mumba; *Gotta Tell You* . . . . (Wildcard/Polydor/Interscope)
Now That's What I Call Music!-#6-C . . . . (Virgin)

Hail, Hail
Pearl Jam; *No Code* . . . . (Epic)

Harmless
Mulberry Lane; *Run Your Own Race* . . . . (Refuge/MCA)

Hate This Place
Goo Goo Dolls; *Dizzy Up The Girl* . . . . (Warner Sunset/Reprise)

Heartbreaker
Bee Gees; *One Night Only* . . . . (Polydor)

Here I Am
Patty Loveless; *Patty Loveless-Classics* . . . . (Epic)
When Fallen Angels Fly . . . . (Epic)

Here We Go Again
Aretha Franklin; *A Rose Is Still A Rose* . . . . (Arista)

Here's That Rainy Day
Frank Sinatra; *The Capitol Years* . . . . (Capitol)
Gene Ammons; *The Boss Is Back* . . . . (Prestige)
Kenny Rankin; *Kenny Rankin Album* . . . . (Little David)
Rosemary Clooney; *Rosemary Clooney Sings Ballads* . . . . (Concord Jazz)
Tony Bennett; *Perfectly Frank* . . . . (Columbia)

Him Or Me, What's It Going To Be
Paul Revere And The Raiders; *Essential Ride-'63-'67* . . . . (Legacy)

Hole In My Pocket
Ricky Van Shelton; *Loving Proof* . . . . (Columbia)
Ricky Van Shelton-16 Biggest Hits . . . . (Legacy)
Ricky Van Shelton-Super Hits-#2 . . . . (Columbia)

Home
Sheryl Crow; *Sheryl Crow* . . . . (A&M)

House Of Love
Amy Grant & Vince Gill; *House Of Love* . . . . (A&M)

House With No Curtains
Alan Jackson; *Everything I Love* . . . . (Arista)

How Do You Tell The One
After 7; *Reflections* . . . . (Virgin)

How It's Going To Be
Third Eye Blind; *Third Eye Blind* . . . . (Elektra)

How Long
Ace; *Lava Love-C* . . . . (K-Tel)
Super Hits Of The '70s-Have A Nice Day-#14-C . . . . (Rhino)

I Am Your Woman
Syleena Johnson; *Chapter One: Love, Pain & Forgiveness* . . . . (Jive)

I Can't Do That
Stephen Simmonds; *Spirit Tales* . . . . (Priority)

I Can't Do That Anymore
Faith Hill; *It Matters To Me* . . . . (Warner Bros.)

I Can't Stand Still
Don Henley; *I Can't Stand Still* . . . . (Asylum)

I Can't Tell You Why
Brownstone; *From The Bottom Up* . . . . (MJJ/Epic)
Eagles; *Eagles Greatest Hits, Volume 2* . . . . (Asylum)
Eagles Live . . . . (Asylum)
The Long Run . . . . (Asylum)
Vince Gill; *Common Thread-Songs Of The Eagles-C* . . . . (Giant)

I Care 'Bout You
Milestone; *ST/Soul Food* . . . . (LaFace)

I Do
Lisa Loeb; *Firecracker* . . . . (Geffen)

I Don't Wanna
Aaliyah; *Next Friday* . . . . (Priority)

I Don't Wanna Go On With You Like That
Elton John; *Reg Strikes Back* . . . . (MCA)

I Don't Want To Know
Fleetwood Mac; *Rumours* . . . . (Warner Bros.)
Goo Goo Dolls; *Legacy-A Tribute To Fleetwood Mac's Rumours-C* . . . . (Lava)

I Don't Want To Spoil The Party
Beatles; *Beatles VI* . . . . (Capitol)
For Sale . . . . (Capitol)
Rosanne Cash; *Greatest Country Hits Of The '80s-1989-C* . . . . . . (Columbia)
Rosanne Cash-Hits-1979-1989 . . . . (Columbia)

I Got The Hook Up
Master P featuring Sons Of Funk; *ST/I Got The Hook Up* . . . (No Limit/Priority)
Sons Of Funk; *The Game Of Funk* . . . . (No Limit/Priority)

I Guess I'm Crazy
Jim Reeves; *Billboard Top Country Hits-1964-C* . . . . (Rhino)
Essential Jim Reeves . . . . (RCA)

I Guess You Had To Be There
Lorrie Morgan; *To Get To You-Greatest Hits Collection* . . . . (BNA)
Watch Me . . . . (BNA)

I Heard It Through The Grapevine
Creedence Clearwater Revival; *Chooglin'* . . . . (Fantasy)
Cosmo's Factory . . . . (Fantasy)
Creedence Clearwater Revival-Chronicle . . . . (Fantasy)
Creedence Clearwater Revival-Gold . . . . (Fantasy)
Movie Album . . . . (Fantasy)
Gladys Knight & The Pips; *16 #1 Hits From The Late '60s-C* . . . . . (Motown)
Compact Command Performances-Gladys Knight & The Pips . . . . (Motown)
Every Great Motown Song-First 25 Years-C . . . . (Motown)
Motown Grammy R&B Performances Of The '60s & '70s-C . . . (Motown)
Motown Superstar Series-#13-Gladys Knight & The Pips . . . . (Motown)
Top 10 With A Bullet-Motown Girl Groups-C . . . . (Motown)
Marvin Gaye; *25 #1 Hits From 25 Years-C* . . . . (Motown)
Every Great Motown Hit Of Marvin Gaye . . . . (Motown)
Marvin Gaye Live At The London Palladium . . . . (Motown)
Marvin Gaye-Anthology . . . . (Motown)
Most Played Songs On America's Jukeboxes . . . . (Motown)
Motown Story-First 25 Years-C . . . . (Motown)

I Hope You've Learned
Ricky Skaggs and Kentucky Thunder; *Bluegrass Rules!* . . . . . . (Rounder)

I Know She Still Loves Me
George Strait; *Platinum Country-C* . . . . (MCA)
Strait Out Of The Box . . . . (MCA)

I Let Her Lie
Daryle Singletary; *Daryle Singletary* . . . . (Giant)

I Lost It
Kenny Chesney; *Kenny Chesney's Greatest Hits* . . . . (BNA)

I Saw Her Again
Mamas & The Papas; *Best Of The Mamas & The Papas* . . . . (MCA)
Farewell To The First Golden Era . . . . (MCA)
Mamas & The Papas . . . . (MCA)

I Take It Back
Sandy Posey; *Best Of Sandy Posey* . . . . (Collectables)
Best Of Sandy Posey-With Skeeter Davis . . . . (Gusto)

I Won't Let You Do That To Me
Luther Vandross; *One Night With You-The Best Of Love-#2* . . . . . (LV/Epic)

If I Were You
Terri Clark; *Terri Clark* . . . . (Mercury)

If This Is It
Huey Lewis and the News; *Sports* . . . . (Chrysalis)
*The Heart Of Rock & Roll-The Best Of Huey Lewis and
    the News* . . . . (Chrysalis)
Time Flies...Best Of Huey Lewis and the News . . . . (Elektra)

If We're Not Back In Love By Monday
Merle Haggard; *MCA Records 30 Years Of Hits-1958-1988-C* . . . . . (MCA)
Merle Haggard-Legends . . . . (MCA)
Merle Haggard's Greatest Hits . . . . (MCA)
More Of The Best . . . . (MCA)
Ramblin' Fever . . . . (MCA)

If You Don't Know Me By Now
Harold Melvin And The Blue Notes; *Harold Melvin And The Blue Notes-
    Collector's Item* . . . . (Philadelphia Int'l)

Philly Ballads-#1-C . . . . (Philadelphia Int'l)
Simply Red; *New Flame* . . . . (Elektra)
Simply Red's Greatest Hits . . . . (East West)

If You Think You're Lonely Now
Bobby Womack; *The Poet* . . . . (Razor & Tie)
K-Ci Hailey; *ST/Jason's Lyric* . . . . (Mercury)

If You're Gone
Matchbox Twenty; *Mad Season By Matchbox Twenty* . . . . (Lava)

I'll Go Crazy
Andy Griggs; *You Won't Ever Be Lonely* . . . . (RCA)

I'll Never Be Jealous Again
Original Cast; *ST/Pajama Game* . . . . (Collectables)

I'm Down
Beatles; *The Beatles-Anthology-#2* . . . . (Capitol)
Paul McCartney; *The Concert For New York City-C* . . . . (Columbia)

I'm Losing You
John Lennon; *Double Fantasy* . . . . (Capitol)
The John Lennon Anthology . . . . (Capitol)
The John Lennon Collection . . . . (Capitol)
Wonsaponatime . . . . (Capitol)

I'm Not Giving You Up
Gloria Estefan; *Destiny* . . . .(Epic)

I'm Still In Love With You
New Edition; *D.J. Mix '98-#1-C* . . . .(Beast)
Home Again . . . .(MCA)

In A Perfect World
Gretchen Peters; *Gretchen Peters* . . . . (Purple Crayon Prod.)

In My Bed
Dru Hill; *Dru Hill* . . . . (Island)

In Too Deep
Sum 41; *All Killer No Filler* . . . . (Island/IDJMG)

It Matters To Me
Faith Hill; *It Matters To Me* . . . .(Warner Bros.)

It Worries Me
Frank Sinatra; *Concepts* . . . . (Capitol)
Where Are You? . . . . (Capitol)

It's All About You (Not About Me)
Tracie Spencer; *Tracie* . . . . (Capitol)

It's In Your Eyes (Any Time At All)
Phil Collins; *Dance Into The Light* . . . . (Atlantic)

It's Not Love (But It's Not Bad)
Merle Haggard & The Strangers; *For The Record: Merle Haggard-43*
Legendary Hits . . . . (BNA)

It's Only Love
Beatles; *The Beatles-Anthology-#2* . . . . (Capitol)

It's Too Late
Amy Grant; *Tapestry Revisited: Tribute To Carole King-C* . . . . . . (Lava)
Carole King; *Her Greatest Hits* . . . .(Epic)
Tapestry . . . .(Epic)
Gloria Estefan; *Hold Me, Thrill Me, Kiss Me* . . . .(Epic)

Jackson
Johnny Cash & June Carter; *Johnny Cash's Greatest Hits* . . . . . (Columbia)
The Man In Black-His Greatest Hits . . . . (Legacy)
Nancy Sinatra & Lee Hazlewood; *Nancy Sinatra-The Hit Years* . . . . (Rhino)

Jimmy Mack
Martha & The Vandellas; *Billboard Top R&B Hits-1967-C* . . . . (Rhino)
Compact Command Performances-Martha Reeves & The
Vandellas . . . . (Motown)
Martha Reeves & The Vandellas-Anthology . . . . (Motown)
Motown Story-First 25 Years . . . . (Motown)
Motown Superstar Series-#11-Martha Reeves & The Vandellas . . . . (Motown)
Top 10 With A Bullet-Motown Girl Groups-C . . . . (Motown)

Jolene
Dolly Parton; *Best Of Dolly Parton* . . . . (RCA)
Best There Is . . . . (RCA)
Jolene . . . . (RCA)
RCA Years-1967-1986 . . . . (RCA)
Sherrie Austin; *Followin' A Feelin'* . . . . (We/Madacy)

Kansas City
Beatles; *Beatles VI* . . . . (Capitol)
Beatles-Box Set . . . . (Capitol)
Rock 'N' Roll Music . . . . (Capitol)
Super Oldies Of The '60s-#10-C . . . .(Audio Fidelity)
Bill Haley & His Comets; *Bill Haley & His Comets' Greatest Hits* . . . . (Everest)
Fats Domino; *Fats Domino's Greatest Hits* . . . . (Everest)
Wilbert Harrison; *American Graffiti-#3-C* . . . .(MCA)
Billboard Top Rock 'N' Roll Hits-1959-C . . . . (Rhino)
Cruisin'-1959-C . . . . (Increase)
Echoes Of A Rock Era-Middle Years-C . . . . (Roulette)
Super Oldies Of The '50s-#2-C . . . .(Audio Fidelity)

Keep The Fire Burnin'
REO Speedwagon; *A Second Decade Of Rock And Roll 1981 To 1991* . . . .(Epic)
Good Trouble . . . .(Epic)
Jane Fonda's New & Improved Workout . . . . (Columbia)

Kiss And Say Goodbye
Manhattans; *Best Of The Manhattans-Kiss And Say Goodbye* . . . . . (Legacy)
Manhattans Greatest Hits . . . . (Columbia)

Kiss The Rain
Billie Myers; *A Taste Of '98-C* . . . . (Universal)

Growing Pains . . . . (Universal)

Laredo
Chris Cagle; *Play It Loud* . . . . (Capitol)

Laughing Out Loud
Wallflowers; *Bringing Down The Horse* . . . .(Interscope)

Let 'Er Rip
Dixie Chicks; *Wide Open Spaces* . . . . (Monument)

Let Her Cry
Hootie & The Blowfish; *1996 Grammy Nominees-C* . . . . (Columbia)
Cracked Rear View . . . .(Atlantic)

Let Love Come Between Us
James & Bobby Purify; *Bubblegum Classics-#4-C* . . . .(Varese Vintage)

Letter, The (That Johnny Walker Read)
Asleep At The Wheel; *Very Best Of Asleep At The Wheel*
Since 1970 . . . .(Relentless/Madacy)

Life #9
Martina McBride; *The Way That I Am* . . . .(RCA)

Linger
Jonatha Brooke; *Steady Pull* . . . . (Bad Dog)

Little Bit Me, A Little Bit You
Monkees; *Monkees' Greatest Hits* . . . . (Rhino)

Long Goodbye, The
Brooks & Dunn; *Steers & Stripes* . . . . (Arista)

Look What Love Has Done
Patty Smyth; *ST/Junior* . . . . (MCA)

Loola Loo
Keb' Mo'; *The Door* . . . .(550/Epic/Okeh)

Loose Ends
Bruce Springsteen; *Tracks* . . . . (Columbia)

Loose Talk
Carl Smith; *Very Special Love Song-C* . . . . (Fifty One West)
Patsy Cline; *Live At The Opry* . . . . (MCA)

Losing Lisa
Ben Folds; *Rockin' The Suburbs* . . . . (Epic)

Love Don't Live Here Anymore
Madonna; *Like A Virgin* . . . .(Sire)
Something To Remember . . . .(Maverick/Sire)
Rose Royce; *Rose Royce III/Strikes Again!* . . . . (Whitfield)
Rose Royce's Greatest Hits . . . . (Whitfield)

Love Is A Battlefield
Pat Benatar; *Best Shots* . . . . (Chrysalis)
I Am Woman-C . . . .(Nick At Nite)
Live From Earth . . . . (Chrysalis)

Love Is The Power
Michael Bolton; *This Is The Time-The Christmas Album* . . . . (Columbia)

Love Me Like You Used To
Tanya Tucker; *Love Me Like You Used To* . . . . (Liberty)
Tanya Tucker-Love Songs . . . . (Capitol)
Tanya Tucker's Greatest Hits . . . . (Liberty)

Loving This Way
Collin Raye with Bobbie Eakes; *Tracks* . . . . (Epic)

Make It Hot
Nicole; *Make It Hot* . . . . (Gold Mind/East West/EEG)

Mama, He Treats Your Daughter Mean
Susan Tedeschi; *Just Won't Burn* . . . .(Tone Cool)

Man On Fire
Wood; *Songs From Stamford Hill* . . . . (Columbia)

Mary Queen Of Arkansas
Bruce Springsteen; *Greetings From Asbury Park, N.J.* . . . . (Columbia)
Tracks . . . . (Columbia)

Maybe
Nilsson; *Harry* . . . . (Dunhill Compact Classics)

Maybe He'll Notice Her Now
Mindy McCready; *Ten Thousand Angels* . . . .(BNA)

Maybe Not Tonight
Lorrie Morgan & Sammy Kershaw; *To Get To You-Greatest Hits*
Collection . . . .(BNA)

Maybe That's Something
Sheryl Crow; *The Globe Sessions* . . . . (A&M)

Maybe We Should Just Sleep On It
Tim McGraw; *All I Want* . . . . (Curb)
Tim McGraw's Greatest Hits . . . . (Curb)

Maybelline
Chuck Berry; *Chuck Berry-Golden Hits* . . . . (Mercury)
Chuck Berry's Greatest Hits . . . . (Everest)
Cruisin'-1955-C . . . . (Increase)
Oldies But Goodies-#11-C . . . . (Original Sound)
Super Oldies Of The '50s-#5-C . . . . (Audio Fidelity)
Johnny Rivers; *Johnny Rivers-Anthology 1964-1977* . . . . (Rhino)
Very Best Of Johnny Rivers . . . . (EMI)

Meeting Across The River
Bruce Springsteen; *Born To Run* . . . . (Columbia)

Midnight Blue
Melissa Manchester; *Melissa* . . . . (Arista)
Melissa Manchester's Greatest Hits . . . . (Arista)

Missing The War
Ben Folds Five; *Whatever And Ever Amen* . . . .(Caroline/550)

Move It On Over
George Thorogood & The Destroyers; *Move It On Over* . . . . (Rounder)
Hank Williams; *Complete Hank Williams* . . . . (Mercury)
Much Too Young (To Feel This Damn Old)
Garth Brooks; *Garth Brooks-Double Live* . . . . (Capitol)
My Elusive Dreams
Bobby Vinton; *Autumn Memories* . . . . (Epic)
Bobby Vinton's All-Time Greatest Hits . . . . (Epic)
Charlie Rich; *Charlie Rich-16 Biggest Hits* . . . . (Legacy)
Charlie Rich's Greatest Hits . . . . (Epic)
Charlie Rich-Super Hits . . . . (Epic)
David Houston & Tammy Wynette; *Best Of David
Houston* . . . . (Collector's Choice)
Billboard Top Country Hits-1967-C . . . . (Rhino)
Tammy Wynette's Greatest Hits . . . . (Epic)
My Favorite Mistake
Sheryl Crow; *Now That's What I Call Music!-#2-C* . . . . (Virgin)
The Globe Sessions . . . . (A&M)
My Way
Limp Bizkit; *Chocolate Starfish & The Hotdog Flavored
Water* . . . . (Flip/Interscope)
Neither One Of Us (Wants To Be First To Say Goodbye)
Gladys Knight & The Pips; *Gladys Knight & The Pips-All The
Great Hits* . . . . (Motown)
Gladys Knight & The Pips-Anthology . . . . (Motown)
Gladys Knight & The Pips-Superstars Series-#13 . . . . (Motown)
Motown Grammy R&B Performances Of The '60s & '70s-C . . . . . (Motown)
Neither One Of Us . . . . (Motown)
Never Can Say Goodbye
Jackson 5; *Jackson 5's Greatest Hits* . . . . (Motown)
Jackson 5-The Ultimate Collection . . . . (Motown)
Never Gonna Let You Go
Blackstreet; *Another Level* . . . . (Interscope)
Never There
Cake; *Now That's What I Call Music!-#2-C* . . . . (Virgin)
Prolonging The Magic . . . . (Capricorn)
New Beginning
Stir; *Holy Dogs* . . . . (Capitol)
New Favorite
Alison Krauss & Union Station; *New Favorite* . . . . (Rounder)
Nietzche's Eyes
Paula Cole; *This Fire* . . . . (Imago)
Night Is Fallin' In My Heart
Diamond Rio; *Diamond Rio's Greatest Hits* . . . . (Arista)
Love A Little Stronger . . . . (Arista)
No More (Baby I'ma Do Right)
3LW; *3LW* . . . . (Epic)
Now That's What I Call Music!-#6-C . . . . (Virgin)
No News
Lonestar; *Lonestar* . . . . (BNA)
No Reply
Beatles; *Beatles '65* . . . . (Capitol)
Beatles-Box Set . . . . (Capitol)
For Sale . . . . (Capitol)
Occasional Wife
Faron Young; *Faron Young-Golden Hits* . . . . (Mercury)
On The Down Low
Brian McKnight; *I Remember You* . . . . (Mercury)
One More Last Chance
Vince Gill; *I Still Believe In You* . . . . (MCA)
The Ultimate Country Party-C . . . . (Arista)
Vince Gill-Souvenirs . . . . (MCA)
One Small Miracle
Bryan White; *The Right Place* . . . . (Asylum)
One That You Love, The
Air Supply; *Air Supply-The Definitive Collection* . . . . (Arista)
Outside
Staind; *Break The Cycle* . . . . (Flip/Elektra)
Overs
Simon & Garfunkel; *Bookends* . . . . (Columbia)
Collected Works . . . . (Columbia)
Paper Tiger
Sue Thompson; *Collectables Presents The History Of
Rock-#4-C* . . . . (Collectables)
Golden Classics-Sue Thompson . . . . (Collectables)
Sue Thompson's Greatest Hits . . . . (Curb)
Pass You By
Boyz II Men; *Nathan Michael Shawn Wanya* . . . . (Universal)
Past The Point Of Rescue
Hal Ketchum; *Past The Point Of Rescue* . . . . (Curb)
Please
Kinleys; *Just Between You And Me* . . . . (Epic)
Please Please Me
Beatles; *Beatles-Box Set* . . . . (Capitol)
Please Please Me . . . . (Parlophone)
The Beatles/1962-1966 . . . . (Capitol)
The Early Beatles . . . . (Capitol)
Promise
Jagged Edge; *J.E. Heartbreak* . . . . (So So Def/Columbia)

Push
Matchbox Twenty; *Yourself Or Someone Like You* . . . . (Lava)
Quit Playing Games (With My Heart)
Backstreet Boys; *Backstreet Boys* . . . . (Jive)
MTV Party To Go '98-C . . . . (Tommy Boy)
The Concert For New York City-C . . . . (Columbia)
Quitter Never Wins, A
Jonny Lang; *Lie To Me* . . . . (A&M)
Quittin' Time
Mary Chapin Carpenter; *Greatest Country Hits Of The '90s-
1990-C* . . . . (Columbia)
State Of The Heart . . . . (Columbia)
Razor Love
Neil Young; *Silver & Gold* . . . . (Reprise)
Reasons Why
Nickel Creek; *Nickel Creek* . . . . (Sugar Hill)
Red Roses For A Blue Lady
Al Martino; *Best Of Al Martino* . . . . (Capitol)
Capitol Collectors Series-Al Martino . . . . (Capitol)
Andy Williams; *Andy Williams-16 Most Requested Songs* . . . . (Legacy)
Mom & Dads; *Best Of The Mom & Dads* . . . . (Crescendo)
Roger Whittaker; *All-Time Heart-Touching Favorites* . . . . (Capitol)
Roger Whittaker-Classics Collection-#1 . . . . (Capitol)
Vaughn Monroe; *Best Of Vaughn Monroe* . . . . (RCA)
Redundant
Green Day; *Nimrod* . . . . (Reprise)
Right Now
SR-71; *Now You See Inside* . . . . (RCA)
Road To Dead
Paula Cole; *This Fire* . . . . (Imago)
Rose And A Baby Ruth, A
George Hamilton IV; *At The Hop* . . . . (MCA)
Vintage Music-#12-C . . . . (MCA)
Rose Colored Glasses
John Conlee; *Backstage At The Grand Ole Opry-C* . . . . (RCA)
Grand Ole Opry-75 Years-#1-C . . . . (MCA)
John Conlee-Legends . . . . (MCA)
John Conlee's Greatest Hits . . . . (MCA)
MCA Records 30 Years Of Hits-1958-1988-C . . . . (MCA)
Rose Colored Glasses . . . . (Universal)
Run For Your Life
Beatles; *Beatles-Box Set* . . . . (Capitol)
Rubber Soul . . . . (Capitol)
Runaway Train
Rosanne Cash; *Greatest Country Hits Of The '80s-1988-C* . . . . (Columbia)
Hot Tracks-Train Super Hits-C . . . . (Epic)
King's Record Shop . . . . (Columbia)
Rosanne Cash-Retrospective . . . . (Columbia)
San Francisco Days
Chris Isaak; *San Francisco Days* . . . . (Reprise)
Satin Sheets
Jeannie Pruett; *16 Top Country Hits-#1-C* . . . . (MCA)
Country Chart-Toppers . . . . (Dominion Entert.)
Grand Ole Opry-75 Years-#2-C . . . . (MCA)
MCA Records 30 Years Of Hits-1958-1988-C . . . . (MCA)
Shawn Colvin; *Cover Girl* . . . . (Columbia)
Say It Isn't So
Dinah Washington; *Irving Berlin Always-C* . . . . (Verve)
Michael Feinstein; *Remember-Michael Feinstein Sings Irving Berlin* . . . (Elektra)
Nat "King" Cole; *Spotlight On Nat "King" Cole* . . . . (Capitol)
Ray Conniff; *'S Awful Nice* . . . . (Columbia)
Say My Name
Destiny's Child; *The Writing's On The Wall* . . . . (Columbia)
Schism
Tool; *Lateralus* . . . . (Volcano Entertainment)
Send Down An Angel
Allison Moorer; *The Hardest Part* . . . . (MCA)
Shake, Rattle And Roll
Big Joe Turner; *Big Joe Turner's Greatest Hits* . . . . (Atlantic)
Every Day I Have The Blues . . . . (Pablo)
Oldies But Goodies-#2-C . . . . (Original Sound)
Soul Years-C . . . . (Atlantic)
Bill Haley & His Comets; *Bill Haley & His Comets' Greatest Hits* . . . . . (MCA)
Bill Haley & His Comets-Golden Hits . . . . (MCA)
Elvis Presley; *For LP Fans Only* . . . . (RCA)
Rocker . . . . (RCA)
ST/This Is Elvis . . . . (RCA)
Fats Domino; *Fats Domino's Greatest Hits* . . . . (MCA)
Huey Lewis and the News; *Four Chords & Several Years Ago* . . . . (Elektra)
NRBQ; *At Yankee Stadium* . . . . (Mercury)
Vern Gosdin; *Best Of Vern Gosdin* . . . . (Warner Bros.)
Shoe Was On The Other Foot
Patti LaBelle; *Flame* . . . . (MCA)
Shotgun Blues
Lightnin' Hopkins; *Best Blues Album In The World...Ever!-C* . . . . . (Virgin)
Very Best Of Lightnin' Hopkins-Blues Masters . . . . (Rhino)
Sky Is Crying
Albert King; *I'm In A Phone Booth Baby* . . . . (Stax)
Years Gone By . . . . (Stax)

Elmore James; *Elmore James-Complete Fire & Enjoy*
 Sessions-#1 . . . . (Collectables)
 Red Hot Blues . . . . (Intermedia)
Eric Clapton; *Eric Clapton-Crossroads-C* . . . . (Polydor)
George Thorogood & The Destroyers; *George Thorogood & The Destroyers-
 Live* . . . . (EMI)
 Move It On Over . . . . (Rounder)
Stevie Ray Vaughan and Double Trouble; *The Sky Is Crying* . . . . (Epic)

Slow Down
 Beatles; *Past Masters-Volume One* . . . . (Parlophone)

Smoke From A Distant Fire
 Sanford/Townsend Band; *Smoke From A Distant Fire* . . . . (Warner Bros.)

So Far Away
 Stabbing Westward; *Stabbing Westward* . . . . (Koch International)

So It Goes
 Wes Cunningham; *12 Ways To Win People To Your Way Of
 Thinking* . . . . (Warner Bros.)

So Sad (To Watch Good Love Go Bad)
 Everly Brothers; *The Reunion Concert-Live At Albert Hall 1983* . . . . . (Mercury)
 *Walk Right Back: The Everly Brothers On Warner Bros.-1960-
 1969* . . . . (Warner Archives)
 Frank Ifield; *Best Of Frank Ifield* . . . . (Curb)
 Sweethearts Of The Rodeo; *Columbia Country Classics-#5-A New
 Tradition-C* . . . . (Columbia)

Somebody Should Leave
 Reba McEntire; *Grand Ole Opry-75 Years-#2-C* . . . . (MCA)
 MCA #1 Hits Of The '80s-#2-C . . . . (MCA Special Prod.)
 My Kind Of Country . . . . (MCA)
 Reba McEntire's Greatest Hits . . . . (MCA)

Someone Should Tell Her
 Mavericks; *Trampoline* . . . . (MCA)

Something In Red
 Lorrie Morgan; *Lorrie Morgan's Greatest Hits* . . . . (BNA)
 Something In Red . . . . (RCA)
 To Get To You-Greatest Hits Collection . . . . (BNA)

Space Between, The
 Dave Matthews Band; *Everyday* . . . . (RCA)

Spark
 Tori Amos; *From The Choirgirl Hotel* . . . . (Atlantic)

Splackavellie
 Pressha; *Don't Get It Twisted* . . . . (Tony Mercedes/LaFace/Arista)

Standing In The Shadows Of Love
 Barry White; *Barry White's Greatest Hits* . . . . (20th Century Fox)
 I've Got So Much To Give . . . . (20th Century Fox)
 Four Tops; *Four Tops' Greatest Hits* . . . . (Motown)
 Four Tops Reach Out . . . . (Motown)
 Four Tops-Anthology . . . . (Motown)
 Motown Story-First 25 Years-C . . . . (Motown)
 Motown Superstar Series-#14-Four Tops . . . . (Motown)
 Rod Stewart; *Blondes Have More Fun* . . . . (Warner Bros.)

Standing On The Edge Of Goodbye
 John Berry; *Standing On The Edge* . . . . (Capitol)

Still Holding On
 Clint Black & Martina McBride; *Nothin' But The Taillights* . . . . (RCA)
 Martina McBride & Clint Black; *Evolution* . . . . (RCA)

Stolen Car
 Bruce Springsteen; *The River* . . . . (Columbia)
 Tracks . . . . (Columbia)
 Elliott Murphy; *One Step Up/Two Steps Back-The Songs Of Bruce
 Springsteen-C* . . . . (Right Stuff)

Stop! In The Name Of Love
 Diana Ross & The Supremes; *16 #1 Hits From The Early '60s-C* . . . . (Motown)
 Diana Ross & The Supremes' Greatest Hits . . . . (Motown)
 Diana Ross & The Supremes-Anthology (1962-1969) . . . . (Motown)
 Evening With Diana Ross . . . . (Motown)
 Girl Groups-Story Of A Sound-C . . . . (Rhino)
 Motown Superstar Series-#1-Diana Ross & The Supremes . . . . . . (Motown)
 Hollies; *45-#89819* . . . . (Atlantic)
 Supremes; *Billboard Top Pop Hits-1965-C* . . . . (Rhino)

Storm Of Love
 Buck Owens; *Together Again/My Heart Skips A Beat* . . . . . . (Sundazed Music)

Stranger In My House
 Tamia; *Nu Day* . . . . (Elektra)

Suite: Judy Blue Eyes
 Crosby, Stills & Nash; *Crosby, Stills & Nash* . . . . (Atlantic)
 CSN . . . . (Atlantic)
 ST/Woodstock . . . . (Atlantic)
 Crosby, Stills, Nash & Young; *So Far* . . . . (Atlantic)

Suspicion
 Elvis Presley; *ST/Pot Luck* . . . . (RCA)
 Terry Stafford; *Billboard Top Rock 'N' Roll Hits-1964-C* . . . . (Rhino)
 Cruisin'-1964-C . . . . (Increase)
 Oldies But Goodies-#8-C . . . . (Original Sound)

Suspicious Minds
 Elvis Presley; *Aloha from Hawaii via Satellite* . . . . (RCA)
 From Memphis To Vegas/From Vegas To Memphis . . . . (RCA)
 Memphis Record . . . . (RCA)
 Nipper's Greatest Hits Of The '60s-#2-C . . . . (RCA)
 ST/This Is Elvis . . . . (RCA)

Sweetest Thing
 U2; *Best Of 1980-1990* . . . . (Island)
 Now That's What I Call Music!-#2-C . . . . (Virgin)

Tainted Love
 Soft Cell; *Memorabilia-The Singles* . . . . (Polydor)
 Non-Stop Erotic Cabaret . . . . (Sire)
 The Ultimate New Wave Dance Party-1998-C . . . . (Arista)

Take It On The Run
 REO Speedwagon; *A Second Decade Of Rock And Roll 1981 To 1991* . . . . (Epic)
 Hi Infidelity . . . . (Epic)
 REO Speedwagon-The Hits . . . . (Epic)

Take The Highway
 Marshall Tucker Band; *Best Of The Marshall Tucker Band-The Capricorn
 Years* . . . . (Era)
 Marshall Tucker Band . . . . (AJK Music)
 Where We All Belong . . . . (AJK Music)

Take These Chains From My Heart
 Hank Williams With His Drifting Cowboys; *24 Of Hank Williams'
 Greatest Hits* . . . . (Polydor)
 Hank Williams-40 Greatest Hits . . . . (Polydor)
 Ray Charles; *Ray Charles-His Greatest Hits-#2* . . . . (Dunhill Compact Classics)

Talk Back Trembling Lips
 Ernest Ashworth; *Best Of Ernest Ashworth* . . . . (Curb)
 Johnny Tillotson; *Cruisin'-1964-C* . . . . (Increase)

Talk Show Shhh!
 Shae Jones; *Talk Show* . . . . (Universal)

Talkin' To Myself
 Lonesome River Band; *Talkin' To Myself* . . . . (Sugar Hill)

Talking In Your Sleep
 Crystal Gayle; *Classic Crystal* . . . . (EMI)
 Country Gold-C . . . . (Priority)
 Crystal Gayle's All-Time Greatest Hits . . . . (Curb)
 When I Dream . . . . (Liberty)
 Reba McEntire; *Starting Over* . . . . (MCA)

Telefone (Long Distance Love Affair)
 Sheena Easton; *Best Kept Secret* . . . . (EMI)
 Sheena Easton's Greatest Hits . . . . (EMI Special Markets)
 The World Of Sheena Easton: The Singles Collection-C . . . . . . (EMI)

Tell Her
 Lonestar; *Lonely Grill* . . . . (BNA)

Tell Me I Was Dreaming
 Travis Tritt; *Ten Feet Tall And Bulletproof* . . . . (Warner Bros.)
 Travis Tritt's Greatest Hits-From The Beginning . . . . (Warner Bros.)

There It Is
 Ginuwine; *Life* . . . . (Epic)

Think
 Aretha Franklin; *Aretha Franklin's Greatest Hits* . . . . (Atlantic)
 Aretha's Gold . . . . (Atlantic)
 Best Of Aretha Franklin . . . . (Atlantic)
 ST/The Blues Brothers . . . . (Atlantic)

This Flight Tonight
 Joni Mitchell; *Blue* . . . . (Reprise)

This Woman And This Man
 Clay Walker; *If I Could Make A Living* . . . . (Giant)

Thorny Patch
 John Gorka; *After Yesterday* . . . . (Red House)

Thrill Is Gone
 B.B. King; *Best Of B.B. King* . . . . (MCA)
 Live In Cook County Jail . . . . (MCA)
 B.B. King & Tracy Chapman; *Deuces Wild* . . . . (MCA)

Throwing Stones
 Paula Cole; *This Fire* . . . . (Imago)

Til I Hear It From You
 Gin Blossoms; *ST/Crossroads-VH1 Television Program* . . . . (Atlantic)
 ST/Empire Records . . . . (A&M)

Too Cold At Home
 Mark Chesnutt; *Too Cold At Home* . . . . (MCA)

Too Little Too Late
 Barenaked Ladies; *Maroon* . . . . (Reprise)

Total Eclipse Of The Heart
 Bonnie Tyler; *Billboard Top Hits-1983-C* . . . . (Rhino)
 Faster Than The Speed Of Night . . . . (Columbia)
 Seems Like Yesterday-#4-Early '80s-C . . . . (K-Tel)
 Nicki French; *Dance Hits '96 Supermix-C* . . . . (Critique)
 Secrets . . . . (Critique)

Treat Her Like A Lady
 Joe; *My Name Is Joe* . . . . (Jive)

Treat Me Right
 Pat Benatar; *Crimes Of Passion* . . . . (Chrysalis)
 ST/An Officer And A Gentleman . . . . (Island)

Tyrone
 Erykah Badu; *Erykah Badu-Live* . . . . (Kedar Entert./Universal)

Us
 Celine Dion; *Let's Talk About Love-C* . . . . (550 Music)

Voices Carry
 'Til Tuesday; *Voices Carry* . . . . (Epic)

Wages Of Sin
 Bruce Springsteen; *Tracks* . . . . (Columbia)

Walk Like I Do
William Topley; *Spanish Wells* . . . . (Mercury)
Walkin' Away
Diamond Rio; *Diamond Rio IV* . . . . (Arista)
   Diamond Rio's Greatest Hits . . . . (Arista)
Walkin' The Floor Over You
Asleep At The Wheel; *Western Standard Time* . . . . (Epic)
Ernest Tubb; *Legend & The Legacy* . . . . (First Generation)
   The Ernest Tubb Story . . . . (MCA)
Ernest Tubb/Merle Haggard/Charlie Daniels; *Ernest Tubb
   Collection-C* . . . . (Step One)
Sandy Denny; *Who Knows Where The Time Goes.* . . . . (Hannibal)
Webb Pierce; *Webb Pierce-Golden Hits* . . . . (Plantation)
Water Runs Dry
Boyz II Men; *Boyz II Men II* . . . . (Motown)
We Can Work It Out
Beatles; *''Yesterday''...And Today* . . . . (Capitol)
   Beatles 1 . . . . (Capitol)
   Beatles-20 Greatest Hits . . . . (Capitol)
   Beatles-Box Set. . . . . (Capitol)
   Past Masters-Volume Two . . . . (Parlophone)
   The Beatles/1962-1966 . . . . (Capitol)
Paul McCartney; *Unplugged (The Official Bootleg)* . . . . . . (Capitol)
Stevie Wonder; *Beatles Songs By Greatest Stars* . . . . (Motown)
   Signed Sealed & Delivered . . . . (Motown)
   Stevie Wonder's Greatest Hits-#2. . . . . (Motown)
   Top 10 With A Bullet-Motown Solo Stars-C . . . . (Motown)
We Just Disagree
Billy Dean; *Fire In The Dark.* . . . . (Liberty)
Dave Mason; *Best Of Dave Mason* . . . . (Columbia)
   Let It Flow. . . . . (Columbia)
   Rock Classics Of The '70s-C. . . . . (Columbia)
We Live In Two Different Worlds
Auldridge/Bennett/Gaudreau; *This Old Town* . . . . (Rebel)
We Need A Resolution
Aaliyah; *Aaliyah* . . . . (BlackGround Enterp./Atlantic)
We're Not Making Love No More
Dru Hill; *ST/Soul Food* . . . . (LaFace)
Western Movies (My Baby Loves)
Olympics; *All-Time Greatest Hits Of Rock 'N' Roll-C* . . . . . . (Curb)
   American Graffiti-#3-C . . . . (MCA)
   Best Of The Olympics . . . . (Vee-Jay)
   Jumpin' Jive '50s-C . . . . (Priority)
What Goes On
Beatles; *''Yesterday''...And Today* . . . . (Capitol)
What It's Like To Be Me
Britney Spears; *Britney* . . . . (Jive)
What You're Doing
Beatles; *For Sale* . . . . (Capitol)
Whatever Happens
Michael Jackson; *Invincible* . . . . (Epic)
Whatever You Say
Martina McBride; *Evolution* . . . . (RCA)
What's Forever For
Michael Martin Murphey; *Best Of Michael Martin Murphey* . . . . (Liberty)
   What's Forever For . . . . (EMI Special Markets)
Wheel, The
Rosanne Cash; *The Wheel* . . . . (Columbia)
When Doves Cry
Ginuwine; *The Bachelor* . . . . (550 Music)
Prince and the Revolution; *ST/Purple Rain* . . . . (Warner Bros.)
When I Come Around
Green Day; *Dookie* . . . . (Reprise)
When You Need My Love
Darryl Worley; *Hard Rain Don't Last* . . . . (DreamWorks/SKG)
Where Did Our Love Go
Diana Ross; *Diana Ross-The Ultimate Collection.* . . . . (Motown)
Diana Ross & The Supremes; *Every Great Motown Song-First 25
   Years-C* . . . . (Motown)
Where Have All The Cowboys Gone?
Paula Cole; *This Fire* . . . . (Imago)
Where's The Love
Hanson; *Middle Of Nowhere* . . . . (Mercury)
Which Bridge To Cross (Which Bridge To Burn)
Vince Gill; *When Love Finds You* . . . . (MCA)
Whispering Pines
Johnny Horton; *Johnny Horton's Greatest Hits* . . . . (Columbia)
Who Walks In When I Walk Out
Bob Wills; *Stay A Little Longer-The Original Columbia
   Recordings.* . . . . (Roswell/RCA)
Why
Annie Lennox; *Diva* . . . . (Arista)
Why Baby Why
Charley Pride; *Charley Pride's Greatest Hits-#2* . . . . (RCA)
George Jones; *George Jones' All-Time Greatest Hits* . . . . (Epic)
   George Jones-Super Hits . . . . (Epic)
Red Sovine & Webb Pierce; *Greatest Country Duets Of All
   Time-C* . . . . (MCA Special Prod.)
Webb Pierce; *Webb Pierce-Golden Hits-#2* . . . . (Plantation)

Willie Nelson & Waylon Jennings; *Take It To The Limit* . . . . (Columbia)
Why Don't You Write Me
Simon & Garfunkel; *Bridge Over Troubled Water* . . . . (Columbia)
Why I'm Here
Oleander; *February Son.* . . . . (Republic/Universal)
   Now That's What I Call Music!-#3-C . . . . (Virgin)
   Oleander Live At The Fillmore . . . . (Republic/Universal)
Why Pt. 2
Collective Soul; *Blender* . . . . (Atlantic)
With Me Part 1
Destiny's Child featuring JD; *Destiny's Child* . . . . (Grass Roots/Columbia)
Woman, Woman
Union Gap Featuring Gary Puckett; *Best Of Gary
   Puckett* . . . . (Hollywood/DNA-Rounder)
   Gary Puckett And The Union Gap's Greatest Hits . . . . (Columbia)
Woman's Threat
R. Kelly; *TP-2.com* . . . . (Jive)
Words
Monkees; *Missing Links-#2* . . . . (Rhino)
   Monkees' Greatest Hits. . . . . (Rhino)
   More Greatest Hits Of The Monkees. . . . . (Arista)
Worlds Apart
Vince Gill; *High Lonesome Sound* . . . . (MCA)
Wrapped Around Your Finger
Dan Hill; *I'm Doing Fine* . . . . (Spontaneous)
Write This Down
George Strait; *Always Never The Same* . . . . (MCA)
You Can't Do That
Beatles; *Beatles-Box Set.* . . . . (Capitol)
   Rock 'N' Roll Music . . . . (Capitol)
   The Beatles' Second Album. . . . . (Capitol)
You Don't Even Know Who I Am
Patty Loveless; *Patty Loveless-Classics.* . . . . (Epic)
   When Fallen Angels Fly . . . . (Epic)
You Don't Seem To Miss Me
Patty Loveless; *Long Stretch Of Lonesome* . . . . (Epic)
   Patty Loveless-Classics. . . . . (Epic)
You Must Love Me
Madonna; *ST/Evita-Music From The Motion Picture* . . . . (Warner Bros.)
You Won't Let Me In
Rosanne Cash; *The Wheel* . . . . (Columbia)
You're Gonna Change (Or I'm Gonna Leave)
Hank Williams With His Drifting Cowboys; *Hank Williams-24 Greatest
   Hits-#2* . . . . (Polydor)
   Hank Williams-40 Greatest Hits . . . . (Polydor)
   Health & Happiness Shows . . . . (Mercury)
Hank Williams, Jr.; *A Tribute To My Father* . . . . (Curb)
Tom Petty; *Timeless: Hank Williams Tribute-C* . . . . (Lost Highway/IDJMG)
You're Gonna Miss Me When I'm Gone
Brooks & Dunn; *Brooks & Dunn-The Greatest Hits Collection.* . . . . (Arista)
   Waitin' On Sundown . . . . (Arista)
You've Lost That Lovin' Feelin'
Daryl Hall & John Oates; *Voices* . . . . (RCA)
Righteous Brothers; *Best Of The Righteous Brothers.* . . . . . . (Curb)
   Billboard Top Rock 'N' Roll Hits-1965-C. . . . . (Rhino)
   Cruisin'-1965-C . . . . (Increase)
   Unchained Melody-Very Best Of The Righteous Brothers . . . . . . (Polydor)
You've Really Got A Hold On Me
Beatles; *The Beatles-Anthology-#1* . . . . (Capitol)
Smokey Robinson & The Miracles; *Best Of Smokey Robinson &
   Miracles-Anthology* . . . . (Motown)
   *Great Songs & Performances That Inspired The Motown 25th Anniversary
   Television Special-C.* . . . . (Motown)
   Smokey Robinson-The Ultimate Collection. . . . . (Motown)
Zip-Lock
Lit; *A Place In The Sun.* . . . . (RCA)

LOVE: PAINFUL BREAK-UP, Bitter Break-up, It's Over

See Also: **DESPAIR, DIVORCE, ENDINGS, FIGHT, LEAVING,
LOSING & LOSS, LOVE (various), PAIN & HEALING, SADNESS**

(Best Part Of) Breakin' Up
Ronettes; *Best Of The Ronettes* . . . . (Abkco)
   Phil Spector-Back To Mono 1958-1969-C . . . . (Abkco)
(Lost His Love) On Our Last Date
Emmylou Harris; *Profile II-The Best Of Emmylou Harris* . . . . (Warner Bros.)
96 Tears
? & The Mysterians; *? & The Mysterians.* . . . . (Collectables)
   Ten Roir Years. . . . . (Roir)
Act Naturally
Beatles; *''Yesterday''...And Today* . . . . (Capitol)
Buck Owens; *Beatles Originals* . . . . (Rhino)
Buck Owens & Ringo Starr; *Act Naturally.* . . . . (Capitol)
Buck Owens & The Buckaroos; *Buck Owens & The Buckaroos-Live At
   Carnegie Hall.* . . . . (Country Music Foundation)
Charley Pride; *Country Pride.* . . . . (RCA)

Johnny Russell; *20 Great Country Hits-C* . . . . (RCA)

Adios
Jimmy Webb; *Suspending Disbelief* . . . . (Elektra)
Linda Ronstadt; *Cry Like A Rainstorm-Howl Like The Wind* . . . . (Elektra)

After The Ball
Barbara Cook/Original Cast; *Show Boat* . . . . (Columbia)

Against All Odds (Take A Look At Me Now)
Mariah Carey; *Rainbow* . . . . (Columbia)
Phil Collins; *Hit Singles-1980-1988-C* . . . . (Atlantic)
Serious Hits...Live! . . . . (Atlantic)
ST/Against All Odds . . . . (Atlantic)

Ain't That A Shame
4 Seasons; *25th Anniversary Collection* . . . . (Rhino)
Cheap Trick; *Cheap Trick At Budokan* . . . .(Epic)
Fats Domino; *Best Of Fats Domino* . . . .(EMI)
Fats Domino's Greatest Hits . . . . (Everest)
Fats Domino's Greatest Hits . . . . (MCA)
ST/American Graffiti . . . .(MCA)
Hank Williams, Jr.; *Hank Williams, Jr.-14 Greatest Hits* . . . . . (Polydor)
Standing In The Shadows . . . . (Polydor)
John Lennon; *Lennon* . . . . (Capitol)
Rock 'N' Roll . . . . (Capitol)

All Cried Out
Allure; *Allure* . . . .(Track Masters/Crave)
Boom! 17 Explosive Hits-C . . . . (Simitar)
Lisa Lisa; *Lisa Lisa & Cult Jam With Full Force* . . . . (Columbia)
Lisa Lisa-Super Hits . . . . (Columbia)
Past, Present & Future . . . . (TMP)

All In Love Is Fair
Stevie Wonder; *Innervisions* . . . . (Motown)

All Of Me
Billie Holiday; *Billie Holiday-Love Songs* . . . . (Legacy)
Count Basie; *Compact Jazz-The Standards* . . . . (Verve)
Diana Ross; *ST/Lady Sings The Blues* . . . . (Motown)
Dinah Washington; *Compact Jazz-Dinah Washington* . . . . . (Verve)
Duke Ellington; *Jazz Party* . . . . (Legacy)
Esquivel; *Music From A Sparkling Planet* . . . . (Bar/None)
Frank Sinatra; *Sinatra Sings His Greatest Hits* . . . . (Legacy)
Helen O'Connell; *Great Girl Singers Sing 22 Original
Recordings-C* . . . . (Hindsight)
Louis Armstrong; *Louis Armstrong's Greatest Hits* . . . . . . (Legacy)
Martha Tilton; *Sweet And Lovely: Capitol's Great Ladies Of Song-C* . . (Capitol)
Paul Whiteman & Mildred Bailey; *Those Wonderful Years: Happy Days Are
Here Again-C* . . . . (JCI Assoc. Labels)
Sarah Vaughan; *Essential Sarah Vaughan-The Great Songs* . . . . (Verve)
Willie Nelson; *Stardust* . . . . (Legacy)

All That You Are (x3)
Econoline Crush; *Devil You Know* . . . .(Restless)

All Things Considered
Yankee Grey; *Untamed* . . . . (Monument)

All Things Must Pass
George Harrison; *All Things Must Pass* . . . . (Parlophone)

Almost
George Morgan; *Room Full Of Roses-The George Morgan
Collection* . . . . (Razor & Tie)
The Late, Great George Morgan: 14 Greatest Hits . . . . (Power Play)

Almost Doesn't Count
Brandy; *Never Say Never* . . . . (Atlantic)
Totally Hits-#1-C . . . . (Arista)

Almost Over You
Sheena Easton; *Best Of Sheena Easton* . . . . (EMI)
Sheena Easton's Greatest Hits . . . . (EMI Special Markets)
The World Of Sheena Easton: The Singles Collection-C . . . . (EMI)

Alone Again (Naturally)
Gilbert O'Sullivan; *Best Of Gilbert O'Sullivan* . . . . (Rhino)
Billboard Top Rock 'N' Roll Hits-1972-C . . . . (Rhino)

Always Be My Baby
Mariah Carey; *Daydream* . . . . (Columbia)

Always On My Mind
Willie Nelson; *Always On My Mind* . . . . (Columbia)
Super Hits Of The '80s-C . . . .(Epic)
Willie Nelson-Super Hits . . . . (Columbia)

Am I Blue
George Strait; *Country Classics-#11-1987-1988-C* . . . . (Universal)
George Strait's Greatest Hits-#2 . . . .(MCA)
MCA #1 Hits Of The '80s-#3-C . . . . . . (MCA Special Prod.)
Ocean Front Property . . . . (MCA)

Am I Blue
Barbra Streisand; *ST/Funny Lady* . . . . (Arista)
Billie Holiday; *God Bless The Child* . . . . (Columbia)
Ray Charles; *Genius Of Ray Charles* . . . . (Atlantic)

Angelina
Keb' Mo'; *Keb' Mo'* . . . .(Okeh)

Angie
Rolling Stones; *Goats Head Soup* . . . .(Rolling Stones)
Made In The Shade . . . .(Rolling Stones)
Rewind (1971-1984) . . . .(Rolling Stones)

Anna
Beatles; *Beatles-Box Set* . . . . (Capitol)

Please Please Me . . . .(Parlophone)
The Early Beatles . . . . (Capitol)

Another One In The Dark
Wallflowers; *The Wallflowers* . . . .(Virgin)

Another Story
Ernest Tubb; *Ernest Tubb's Greatest Hits* . . . . (MCA)

April In Portugal
Eartha Kitt; *Best Of Eartha Kitt* . . . . (MCA)

Are You Happy Baby?
Dottie West; *Dottie West's Greatest Hits* . . . . (Curb)

Ashes Of Love
Chris Hillman; *Desert Rose* . . . .(Sugar Hill)
Desert Rose Band; *Desert Rose Band* . . . .(Curb)
Dickey Lee; *Ashes Of Love* . . . . (RCA)
Johnnie & Jack & Their Tennessee Mountain Boys; *Johnnie & Jack's
Greatest Hits* . . . . (King)
Rose Maddox; *Rose Of The West Coast Country* . . . . (Arhoolie)

At This Moment
Billy Vera & The Beaters; *Billboard Top Hits-1987-C* . . . . . . (Rhino)
By Request: Best Of Billy Vera & The Beaters . . . . (Rhino)

Baby Doll
Andy Williams; *Andy Williams* . . . .(Madacy)

Backstreets
Bruce Springsteen; *Born To Run* . . . . (Columbia)

Bad Goodbye, A
Clint Black with Wynonna; *Clint Black-The Greatest Hits* . . . . (RCA)
Grammy's Greatest Country Moments-#1-C . . . .(Atlantic)
No Time To Kill . . . . (RCA)

Band Of Gold
Freda Payne; *Beachbeat Draggin'* . . . .(Dunhill Compact Classics)
Didn't It Blow Your Mind: Soul Hits Of The '70s-#2-C . . . . (Rhino)
Freda Payne's Greatest Hits . . . .(HDH)

Barely Breathing
Duncan Sheik; *Duncan Sheik* . . . .(Atlantic)

Be With You
Enrique Iglesias; *Enrique* . . . . (Overbrook/Interscope)

Be Your Own Girl
Wallflowers; *The Wallflowers* . . . .(Virgin)

Beaches Of Cheyenne
Garth Brooks; *Fresh Horses* . . . . (Capitol)
Limited Series Box . . . . (Capitol)

Beautiful Brown Eyes
Rosemary Clooney; *Songs From The Girl Singer-A Musical
Autobiography* . . . . (Concord Jazz)

Beep Me 911
Missy ''Misdemeanor'' Elliot; *Supa Dupa Fly* . . . . (East West)

Believe
Cher; *Believe* . . . . (Warner Bros.)
Totally Hits-#1-C . . . . (Arista)

Best I Ever Had (Grey Sky Morning)
Vertical Horizon; *Everything You Want* . . . .(RCA)

Better Man, Better Off
Tracy Lawrence; *The Coast Is Clear* . . . .(Atlantic)

Big Girls Don't Cry
4 Seasons; *4 Seasons' Greatest Hits-#1* . . . . (Rhino)
4 Seasons-Anthology . . . . (Rhino)
Billboard Top Rock 'N' Roll Hits-1962-C . . . . (Rhino)
More Dirty Dancing . . . . (RCA)

Big Man
Four Preps; *Best Of The Four Preps* . . . . (Curb)
Capitol Collectors Series-Four Preps . . . . (Collectables)

Big Yellow Taxi
Amy Grant; *House Of Love* . . . .(A&M)
Joni Mitchell; *Ladies Of The Canyon* . . . . (Reprise)
Joni Mitchell with Tom Scott & The L.A. Express; *Miles Of Aisles* . . . .(Asylum)

Bits And Pieces
Dave Clark Five; *History Of The Dave Clark Five* . . . . (Hollywood)

Blue
LeAnn Rimes; *Blue* . . . .(MCG/Curb)

Blue Autumn
Bobby Goldsboro; *10th Anniversary Album-#1* . . . . (EMI)
Bobby Goldsboro's Greatest Hits . . . . (Liberty)
Honey-Best Of Bobby Goldsboro . . . . (EMI)

Blue Eyes Blue
Eric Clapton; *Clapton Chronicles-The Best Of Eric Clapton 1981-
1999* . . . . (Reprise)
ST/Runaway Bride . . . .(Sony Music Soundtrax)

Blue Monday
Orgy; *Candyass* . . . . (Elementree/Reprise)

Blue Moon Of Kentucky
Bill Monroe; *American Originals-Bill Monroe* . . . . (Columbia)
Bean Blossom . . . . (MCA)
Best Of Bill Monroe & His Blue Grass Boys . . . . (MCA)
Bill Monroe & His Blue Grass Boys; *Bluegrass Super Hits-C* . . . . . (Columbia)
Elvis Presley; *A Date With Elvis* . . . . (RCA)
A Golden Celebration . . . . (RCA)
The Sun Sessions . . . . (RCA)

Boy From Tupelo
Emmylou Harris; *Red Dirt Girl* . . . . (Nonesuch)

Break It To Me Gently
Brenda Lee; *Brenda Lee-Anthology-#1 & #2* . . . (MCA)
The Brenda Lee Story-Her Greatest Hits . . . (MCA)
Juice Newton; *Juice Newton's Greatest Country Hits* . . . (Curb)
Juice Newton's Greatest Hits . . . (Gold Rush)
Breakdown
Mariah Carey featuring Bone Thugs-N-Harmony; *Butterfly* . . . (Columbia)
Breakfast At Tiffany's
Deep Blue Something; *Home* . . . (RainMaker/Interscope)
Breaking Up Is Hard To Do
Gloria Estefan; *Hold Me, Thrill Me, Kiss Me* . . . (Epic)
Neil Sedaka; *Billboard Top Rock 'N' Roll Hits-1962-C* . . . (Rhino)
Neil Sedaka's All-Time Greatest Hits . . . (RCA)
Shelley Fabares; *Things We Did Last Summer* . . . (Collectables)
Brokenhearted
Brandy featuring Wanya Morris; *Brandy* . . . (Atlantic)
Broken-Hearted Melody
Sarah Vaughan; *Essential Sarah Vaughan-The Great Songs* . . . (Verve)
Sarah Vaughan-Golden Hits . . . (Mercury)
Burning A Hole In My Mind
Connie Smith; *Essential Connie Smith* . . . (RCA)
By The Time I Get To Phoenix
Glen Campbell; *All-Time Country Classics-#1-C* . . . (Capitol)
Glen Campbell-Classics Collection . . . (Capitol)
Glen Campbell-Live . . . (Capitol)
Glen Campbell's Greatest Hits . . . (Capitol)
Very Best Of Glen Campbell . . . (Capitol)
Reba McEntire; *Starting Over* . . . (MCA)
Bye Bye Bye
'N Sync; *No Strings Attached* . . . (Jive)
Now That's What I Call Music!-#6-C . . . (Virgin)
Bye Bye Love
Everly Brothers; *Everly Brothers' All-Time Greatest Hits* . . . (Curb)
Everly Brothers-Cadence Classics-Their 20 Greatest Hits . . . (Rhino)
Very Best Of The Everly Brothers . . . (Warner Bros.)
Simon & Garfunkel; *Bridge Over Troubled Water* . . . (Columbia)
Call The Police
Hot Chocolate; *Hot Chocolate* . . . (Big Tree)
Nat "King" Cole; *From The Very Beginning* . . . (MCA)
Can't Believe
Faith Evans featuring Carl Thomas; *12" Maxi Single* . . . (Bad Boy/Arista)
Can't Let Go
Laurnea; *Betta Listen* . . . (Yab Yum)
Can't Really Be Gone
Tim McGraw; *All I Want* . . . (Curb)
Can't Stand It
Wilco; *Summer Teeth* . . . (Reprise)
Can't Stand Losing You
Police; *Every Breath You Take-The Classics* . . . (A&M)
Can't Stay
Dave Hollister; *Ghetto Hymns* . . . (Def Squad/DreamWorks)
Can't Wait
Bob Dylan; *Time Out Of Mind* . . . (Columbia)
Careless Whisper
Dave Koz featuring Montell Jordan; *Dance* . . . (Capitol)
Wham! Featuring George Michael; *Make It Big* . . . (Columbia)
Music For The Miracle-C . . . (Epic Portrait Assoc.)
Cinderella
Britney Spears; *Britney* . . . (Jive)
Cold Day In July
Dixie Chicks; *Fly* . . . (Monument)
Joy White; *Between Midnight & Hindsight* . . . (Columbia)
Ray Price; *For The Good Times/I Won't Mention It Again* . . . (Columbia)
Suzy Bogguss; *Voices In The Wind* . . . (Liberty)
Cold Irons Bound
Bob Dylan; *Time Out Of Mind* . . . (Columbia)
Comedown
Bush; *Sixteen Stone* . . . (Trauma)
Contagious
Isley Brothers featuring Ronald Isley; *Eternal* . . . (DreamWorks/SKG)
Cottage For Sale, A
Frank Sinatra; *No One Cares* . . . (Capitol)
Mel Torme; *Luck Be A Lady* . . . (Laserlight)
Couldn't Last A Moment
Collin Raye; *Tracks* . . . (Epic)
Crazy
Jimmie Dale Gilmore with Willie Nelson; *Red Hot + Country-C* . . . (Mercury)
Kenny Rogers; *Kenny Rogers' Greatest Hits* . . . (RCA)
What About Me? . . . (RCA)
Linda Ronstadt; *Hasten Down The Wind* . . . (Asylum)
Patsy Cline; *Songwriter's Tribute* . . . (MCA)
ST/Sweet Dreams . . . (MCA)
The Patsy Cline Story . . . (MCA)
Ray Price; *Ray Price's Greatest Hits-#2* . . . (Step One)
Willie Nelson; *Best Of Willie* . . . (RCA)
Healing Hands Of Time . . . (Liberty)
Nite Life-Greatest Hits & Rare Tracks . . . (Rhino)
Willie & Family Live . . . (Columbia)
Cry
Roxette; *Look Sharp!* . . . (EMI)
Cry Baby
Enchanters; *Billboard Top R&B Hits-1963-C* . . . (Rhino)
Soul Shots-#5-La-La Means I Love You-C . . . (Rhino)
Garnet Mimms; *18 Soulful Ballads-C* . . . (Rhino)
Beg, Scream & Shout! The Big Ol' Box Of '60s Soul-C . . . (Rhino)
Janis Joplin; *Janis Joplin's Greatest Hits* . . . (Columbia)
Pearl . . . (Legacy)
ST/Janis . . . (Columbia)
Cry Love
John Hiatt; *Walk On* . . . (Capitol)
Cry, Cry Darling
Ricky Skaggs with Dolly Parton; *Big Mon: The Songs Of Bill Monroe-C* . . . (Skaggs Family)
Crying
Don McLean; *Best Of Don McLean* . . . (EMI)
Greatest Hits Then & Now . . . (EMI)
Roy Orbison; *For The Lonely: 18 Greatest Hits* . . . (Rhino)
For The Lonely: A Roy Orbison Anthology 1959-1965 . . . (Rhino)
In Dreams-Greatest Hits . . . (Orbison)
Roy Orbison's All-Time Greatest Hits-#1 & 2 . . . (Monument)
Dallas
Alan Jackson; *Don't Rock The Jukebox* . . . (Arista)
Dammit (Growing Up)
Blink-182; *Dude Ranch* . . . (Cargo)
Dance, The
Garth Brooks; *Garth Brooks* . . . (Liberty)
Garth Brooks-Double Live . . . (Capitol)
Dawn (Go Away)
4 Seasons; *25th Anniversary Collection* . . . (Rhino)
4 Seasons-Anthology . . . (Rhino)
Days
Kinks; *Kink Kronikles* . . . (Reprise)
Dear John Letter
Jean Shepard; *Heroes Of Country Music-#4-Legends Of The West Coast-C* . . . (Rhino)
Jean Shepard & Ferlin Husky; *Classic Duets-C* . . . (Liberty)
Denial
Sevendust; *Home* . . . (TVT)
Different Drum
Linda Ronstadt; *Different Drum* . . . (Capitol)
Linda Ronstadt-Retrospective . . . (Capitol)
Linda Ronstadt's Greatest Hits . . . (Asylum)
Stone Poneys Featuring Linda Ronstadt; *Baby Boomer Classics-Mellow '60s-C* . . . (JCI Assoc. Labels)
On The Road Again-Rock's New Frontiers-C . . . (Capitol)
The Stone Poneys Featuring Linda Ronstadt . . . (EMI)
Victoria Shaw; *Victoria Shaw* . . . (Reprise)
Distance, The
Cake; *Fashion Nugget* . . . (Capricorn)
D-I-V-O-R-C-E
Rosanne Cash; *Tammy Wynette...Remembered-C* . . . (Asylum)
Tammy Wynette; *Super Hits Of The '60s-C* . . . (Epic)
Tammy Wynette-Anniversary-20 Years Of Hits . . . (Epic)
Tammy Wynette's Biggest Hits . . . (Epic)
Tammy Wynette's Greatest Hits . . . (Epic)
Donna
Los Lobos; *ST/La Bamba* . . . (Slash)
Ritchie Valens; *American Graffiti-#3-C* . . . (MCA)
Best Of Ritchie Valens . . . (Rhino)
Heart & Soul Of Rock 'N' Roll-#1-C . . . (Rhino)
History Of Latino Rock-#1-C . . . (Rhino)
History Of Ritchie Valens . . . (Rhino)
Don't Bother Me
Beatles; *Meet The Beatles!* . . . (Capitol)
Don't Come Around
Macy Gray featuring Sunshine Anderson; *The Id* . . . (Epic)
Don't Forget To Cry
Mandy Barnett; *I've Got A Right To Cry* . . . (Sire)
Don't It Make My Brown Eyes Blue
Crystal Gayle; *Classic Crystal* . . . (EMI)
Heartbreak Hotel-C . . . (EMI)
ST/Convoy . . . (Polydor)
We Must Believe In Magic . . . (United Artists)
Don't Speak
No Doubt; *Tragic Kingdom* . . . (Trauma)
Don't Tell Me Your Troubles
Doc Watson; *Memories* . . . (Sugar Hill)
Don Gibson; *45-#7566* . . . (RCA)
Ray Charles; *Greatest Country & Western Hits* . . . (Dunhill Compact Classics)
Don't Think Twice, It's All Right
Bob Dylan; *Before The Flood* . . . (Columbia)
Bob Dylan's Greatest Hits-#2 . . . (Columbia)
Freewheelin' . . . (Columbia)
Joan Baez; *The First 10 Years* . . . (Vanguard)
Wonder Who?; *Anniversary* . . . (Rhino)
Down
Amel Larrieux; *Infinite Possibilities* . . . (Epic)

Downtime
Jo Dee Messina; *Burn*. . . . .(Warner Bros.)
Dreams
Corrs; *Legacy-A Tribute To Fleetwood Mac's Rumours-C* . . . . . . (Lava)
Fleetwood Mac; *25 Years-The Chain* . . . .(Warner Bros.)
   Fleetwood Mac Live. . . . .(Warner Bros.)
   Fleetwood Mac's Greatest Hits . . . .(Warner Bros.)
   Rumours. . . . .(Warner Bros.)
Drinkin' My Baby (Off My Mind)
Eddie Rabbitt; *Best Of Eddie Rabbitt/Greatest Hits-II* . . . .(Warner Bros.)
   Great Divorce Songs For Him-C . . . .(Warner Bros.)
   Number 1's . . . .(Warner Bros.)
   Rocky Mountain Music . . . . (Elektra)
Drinkin' My Baby Goodbye
Charlie Daniels Band; *Me & The Boys* . . . .(Epic)
Easy Tonight
Five For Fighting; *America Town* . . . .(Aware/C2/Columbia)
Emotional
Carl Thomas; *Emotional*. . . . . (Bad Boy/Arista)
End Of The Road
Boyz II Men; *Cooleyhighharmony* . . . . (Motown)
End Of The World
Skeeter Davis; *Best Of Skeeter Davis* . . . . (Gusto)
   Billboard Top Country Hits-1963-C . . . . (Rhino)
   Nipper's Greatest Hits Of The '60s-#1-C . . . . (RCA)
   Stars Of The Grand Ole Opry-1926-1974-C . . . . (RCA)
   Super Country Hits Of The '60s-C . . . . (Gusto)
Enough Of Me
Melissa Etheridge; *Breakdown*. . . . . (Island)
Everybody Knows
Trisha Yearwood; *Everybody Knows* . . . . (MCA)
Everything I Love
Alan Jackson; *Everything I Love*. . . . . (Arista)
Ex-Girlfriend
No Doubt; *Return Of Saturn* . . . . (Interscope)
Fair
Ben Folds Five; *Whatever And Ever Amen* . . . .(Caroline/550)
Falling, Falling, Falling
Mandy Barnett; *I've Got A Right To Cry*. . . . . (Sire)
Fancy Free
Oak Ridge Boys; *Fancy Free* . . . .(MCA)
   Oak Ridge Boys' Greatest Hits 2 . . . . (MCA)
Fare Thee Well Love
Rankin Family; *North Country* . . . . (Guardian/Angel)
   The Rankins-Collection . . . . (Rounder)
Fast As You
Dwight Yoakam; *This Time* . . . . (Reprise)
Feelin' Good About Feelin' Bad
Patty Loveless; *When Fallen Angels Fly*. . . . .(Epic)
Final Heartbreak
Jessica Simpson; *Sweet Kisses* . . . . (Columbia)
Flight 309 To Tennessee
Shelly West; *West By West* . . . . (Viva)
Fool #1
Brenda Lee; *The Brenda Lee Story-Her Greatest Hits* . . . . (MCA)
Joe Stampley/The Uniques; *Joe Stampley-Golden Hits* . . . . (Paula)
Fool, The
Elvis Presley; *A Golden Celebration* . . . . (RCA)
Foolish Games
Jewel; *Pieces Of You*. . . . .(Atlantic)
   ST/Batman & Robin-Music From And Inspired By The Motion Picture . . (Jive)
   VH-1 Crossroads-C . . . .(Atlantic)
Foolish Pride
Travis Tritt; *Ten Feet Tall And Bulletproof* . . . .(Warner Bros.)
For Crying Out Loud
Anita Cochran; *Anita* . . . .(Warner Bros.)
Forever Has Come To An End
Buddy & Julie Miller; *Buddy & Julie Miller*. . . . .(Hightone)
Free Bird
Lynyrd Skynyrd; *Gold & Platinum*. . . . .(MCA)
   One More From The Road. . . . . (MCA)
   Pronounced Leh-nerd Skin-nerd . . . . (MCA)
   Southern By The Grace Of God-Tribute '87 . . . . (MCA)
Wynonna; *Skynyrd Frynds-C* . . . . (MCA)
Friends
John Michael Montgomery; *John Michael Montgomery's*
   Greatest Hits. . . . .(Atlantic)
   What I Do The Best . . . .(Atlantic)
From The Bottom Of My Heart
Britney Spears; *...Baby One More Time* . . . . (Jive)
Gal That Got Away
Four Freshmen; *Voices In Love-Love Lost* . . . . (Collector's Choice)
Frank Sinatra; *Complete Capitol Singles Collection*. . . . . (Capitol)
Get Gone
Ideal; *Ideal* . . . .(Noontime/Virgin)
   Now That's What I Call Music!-#3-C . . . . (Virgin)
Getting Over You
Janis Ian; *Hunger* . . . .(Windham Hill)

Jim Brickman; *Visions Of Love* . . . .(Windham Hill)
Give It Up Or Let Me Go
Dixie Chicks; *Wide Open Spaces* . . . . (Monument)
Go Now!
Moody Blues; *History Of British Rock-#5-C* . . . . (Rhino)
   Moody Blues-Anthology. . . . . (Polydor)
Wings; *Wings Over America* . . . . (Capitol)
Go Your Own Way
Cranberries; *Legacy-A Tribute To Fleetwood Mac's Rumours-C* . . . . . . (Lava)
Fleetwood Mac; *25 Years-The Chain* . . . . (Warner Bros.)
   Fleetwood Mac Live . . . . (Warner Bros.)
   Fleetwood Mac's Greatest Hits . . . . (Warner Bros.)
   Rumours. . . . . (Warner Bros.)
Going Away Party
Manhattan Transfer & Willie Nelson & Asleep At The Wheel; *Ride With*
   Bob-C . . . .(DreamWorks/SKG)
Gold Dust Woman
Fleetwood Mac; *25 Years-The Chain* . . . . (Warner Bros.)
   Rumours. . . . . (Warner Bros.)
Sister Hazel; *Legacy-A Tribute To Fleetwood Mac's Rumours-C* . . . . . . (Lava)
Golden Ring
Emmylou Harris/Linda Ronstadt/Anna & Kate McGarrigle; *Tammy*
   Wynette...Remembered-C . . . .(Asylum)
George Jones & Tammy Wynette; *George Jones & Tammy Wynette-16*
   Biggest Hits . . . .(Epic/Legacy)
Tammy Wynette & George Jones; *Encore-Tammy Wynette & George*
   Jones . . . . (Epic)
   Tammy Wynette & George Jones' Greatest Hits . . . . (Epic)
   Tammy Wynette-Anniversary-20 Years Of Hits . . . . (Epic)
Gonna Find Me A Bluebird
Frank Ifield; *Best Of Frank Ifield*. . . . . (Curb)
Marvin Rainwater; *Greatest Hits-1957-C* . . . . (Deluxe)
   Only Country-1955-1959-C . . . .(JCI Assoc. Labels)
Royal Wade Kimes; *ST/Traveller* . . . .(Asylum)
Good
Better Than Ezra; *Deluxe* . . . . (Swell/Elektra)
Good As I Was To You
Lorrie Morgan; *Greater Need* . . . . (BNA)
   Lorrie Morgan-Super Hits . . . . (RCA)
   To Get To You-Greatest Hits Collection. . . . . (BNA)
Good Bye
Martina McBride; *Emotion* . . . . (RCA)
Good Friday
Black Crowes; *Sho' Nuff* . . . . (American)
   Three Snakes And One Charm . . . . (American)
Good Times Bad Times
Led Zeppelin; *Led Zeppelin*. . . . .(Atlantic)
Goodbye
Jagged Edge; *Jagged Little Thrill* . . . . (So So Def/Columbia)
Goodbye
Alicia Keys; *Songs In A Minor* . . . . (J)
Goodbye Lament
Iommi; *Iommi* . . . .(Divine/Priority)
Goodbye To You
Scandal; *I Am Woman-C* . . . .(Nick At Nite)
   Patty Smyth's Greatest Hits Featuring Scandal . . . . (Legacy)
Graceland
Paul Simon; *Graceland* . . . . (Warner Bros.)
Great Pretender
Band; *Moondog Matinee*. . . . . (Capitol)
Platters; *Billboard Top R&B Hits-1956-C*. . . . . (Rhino)
   Cruisin'-1956-C . . . . (Increase)
   Encore Of Golden Hits-Platters . . . . (Mercury)
   Platters-Anthology . . . . (Rhino)
   ST/American Graffiti . . . . (MCA)
   Super Oldies Of The '50s-#3-C . . . . (Audio Fidelity)
Roy Orbison; *Best Of Roy Orbison-Loved Standards* . . . . (Monument)
Stan Freberg; *Capitol Collectors Series-Stan Freberg* . . . . (Capitol)
Happening, The
Diana Ross; *Diana Ross-Anthology* . . . . (Motown)
Diana Ross & The Supremes; *Diana Ross & The Supremes-Superstar*
   Series-#1 . . . . (Motown)
Hats Off To Larry
Del Shannon; *Runaway Hits!* . . . . (Rhino)
   Super Oldies Of The '60s-#2-C . . . . (Audio Fidelity)
   WCBS FM 101 History Of Rock-'60s-#3-C . . . . (Collectables)
He Was Too Good To Me
Barbara Cook; *Barbara Cook-Live At Carnegie Hall* . . . .(Sony Music Classical)
Bette Midler; *Some People's Lives* . . . .(Atlantic)
Carmen McRae; *Carmen McRae Sings Great American*
   Songwriters . . . . (Decca Jazz)
Helen Merrill; *Dream Of You* . . . .(Emarcy)
Jeri Southern; *The Very Thought Of You: The Decca Years-1951-1957* . . . (GRP)
Healing Hands
Elton John; *Sleeping With The Past*. (MCA)
Heart Of The Matter
Don Henley; *End Of The Innocence* . . . . (Geffen)
Heartache Big As Texas
Ricky Van Shelton; *Texas Super Hits-C* . . . . (Columbia)

Heartaches
Marcels; *The Doo Wop Box II* . . . . (Rhino)
Patsy Cline; *The Patsy Cline Story* . . . . (MCA)
Ted Weems & His Orchestra; *Billboard Pop Memories-1945-1949-C* . . . (Rhino)
Nipper's Greatest Hits Of The '40s-#2-C . . . . (RCA)
Heartbreak Hotel
Albert King; *Blues For Elvis* . . . . (Stax)
Elvis Presley; *Elvis As Recorded At Madison Square Garden* . . . . (RCA)
Elvis' Golden Records . . . . (RCA)
Elvis-A Legendary Performer, Volume 1 . . . . (RCA)
Nipper's Greatest Hits Of The '50s-#1-C . . . . (RCA)
Worldwide 50 Gold Award Hits, Vol. 1, Parts 1 & 2 . . . . (RCA)
Stan Freberg; *Capitol Collectors Series-Stan Freberg* . . . . (Capitol)
Willie Nelson; *Greatest Hits (& Some That Will Be)* . . . . (Columbia)
Willie Nelson & Leon Russell: One For The Road . . . . (Columbia)
Heartbreak Hotel
Whitney Houston Featuring Faith Evans & Kelly Price; *My Love Is Your Love* . . . . (Arista)
Totally Hits-#1-C . . . . (Arista)
Whitney Houston's Greatest Hits . . . . (Arista)
Heartbreak, Tennessee
Johnny Paycheck; *This Is Country-C* . . . . (Pegasus/Cleopatra)
Heartbreaker
Grand Funk Railroad; *Capitol Collectors Series-Grand Funk Railroad* . . . . (Capitol)
Heartbreaker
Great White; *Hooked* . . . . (Capitol)
Heartbreaker
Tanya Tucker; *Love Me Like You Used To* . . . . (Liberty)
Heartbreaker
Dionne Warwick; *Heartbreaker* . . . . (Arista)
Heartbroke
George Strait; *Strait From The Heart* . . . . (MCA)
Strait Out Of The Box . . . . (MCA)
Guy Clark; *Craftsman* . . . . (Philo)
Keepers . . . . (Sugar Hill)
Ricky Skaggs; *Country Gentleman: The Best Of Ricky Skaggs* . . . . (Legacy)
Greatest Country Hits Of The '80s-#2-C . . . . (Columbia)
Highways & Heartaches . . . . (Epic)
Live In London . . . . (Epic)
Ricky Skaggs-Super Hits . . . . (Epic)
Rodney Crowell; *Rodney Crowell-Collection* . . . . (Warner Bros.)
Hello Mr. Heartache
Dixie Chicks; *Fly* . . . . (Monument)
Hello Walls
Faron Young; *Billboard Top Country Hits-1961-C* . . . . (Rhino)
Willie Nelson; *Essential Willie Nelson* . . . . (RCA)
Willie Nelson-Greatest Songs . . . . (Curb)
Help Me Rhonda
Beach Boys; *Billboard Top Rock 'N' Roll Hits-1965-C* . . . . (Rhino)
California Girls . . . . (Capitol)
Dance Dance Dance . . . . (Capitol)
Endless Summer . . . . (Capitol)
Made In The U.S.A. . . . . (Capitol)
Hemorrhage (In My Hands)
Fuel; *Now That's What I Call Music!-#6-C* . . . . (Virgin)
Something Like Human . . . . (Epic)
Here Comes The Rain
Mavericks; *Music For All Occasions* . . . . (MCA)
Here's A Quarter (Call Someone Who Cares)
Travis Tritt; *It's All About To Change* . . . . (Warner Bros.)
He's Got You
Brooks & Dunn; *The Greatest Hits Collection* . . . . (Arista)
Hey, Mr. Bluebird
Ernest Tubb & Wilburn Brothers; *More Great Country Duets-C* . . . . (MCA Special Prod.)
High And Dry
Marty Brown; *High And Dry* . . . . (MCA)
High Lonesome Sound
Vince Gill; *Bluegrass Essentials-C* . . . . (Hip-O)
High Lonesome Sound . . . . (MCA)
Vince Gill with Alison Krauss & Union Station; *Grand Ole Opry-75 Years-#1-C* . . . . (MCA)
Hit 'Em Up Style (Oops!)
Blu Cantrell; *So Blu* . . . . (Arista)
Totally Hits 2001-C . . . . (Arista)
Hole In My Soul
Aerosmith; *Nine Lives* . . . . (Columbia)
How A Cowgirl Says Goodbye
Tracy Lawrence; *The Coast Is Clear* . . . . (Atlantic)
How Could An Angel Break My Heart
Kenny G with Toni Braxton; *Kenny G's Greatest Hits* . . . . (Arista)
Toni Braxton with Kenny G; *Diana, Princess Of Wales-Tribute-C* . . . (Columbia)
Secrets . . . . (LaFace)
How Could I
Marc Anthony; *Marc Anthony* . . . . (Columbia)
How Could You
K-Ci & JoJo; *Love Always* . . . . (MCA)
How I Got To Memphis
Bobby Bare; *This Is Bare Country* . . . . (Mercury)
Otis Williams & The Midnight Cowboys; *From Where I Stand: The Black Experience In Country Music-C* . . . . (Warner Bros.)
How It's Going To Be
Third Eye Blind; *Third Eye Blind* . . . . (Elektra)
How Many Tears
Bobby Vee; *Bobby Vee-Legendary Masters* . . . . (EMI)
How Was I To Know
Reba McEntire; *Forever Reba* . . . . (Universal)
What If It's You . . . . (MCA)
Human
Pretenders; *Viva El Amor!* . . . . (Warner Bros.)
Hungry Heart
Bruce Springsteen; *Bruce Springsteen's Greatest Hits* . . . . (Columbia)
The River . . . . (Columbia)
Bruce Springsteen & The E Street Band; *Bruce Springsteen & The E Street Band Live/1975-85* . . . . (Legacy)
I Ain't Ever Satisfied
Gretchen Peters; *The Secret Of Life* . . . . (Purple Crayon Prod.)
Steve Earle & The Dukes; *Ain't Ever Satisfied: The Steve Earle Collection* . . . . (Hip-O)
Exit 0 . . . . (MCA)
Shut Up And Die Like An Aviator . . . . (MCA)
I Almost Lost My Mind
Eddy Arnold; *World Of Hits* . . . . (MGM)
Fats Domino; *Fats Domino's Greatest Hits* . . . . (MCA)
Ivory Joe Hunter; *Since I Met You Baby* . . . . (Mercury)
Pat Boone; *Pat Boone's Greatest Hits* . . . . (Curb)
I Call Your Name
Beatles; *Past Masters-Volume One* . . . . (Parlophone)
Rock 'N' Roll Music . . . . (Capitol)
The Beatles' Second Album . . . . (Capitol)
I Cheated Me Right Out Of You
Moe Bandy; *Moe Bandy's Greatest Hits* . . . . (Columbia)
I Could Have Told You
Frank Sinatra; *No One Cares* . . . . (Capitol)
I Could Use Another You
Eddy Raven; *Best Of Eddy Raven* . . . . (Curtom)
I Cried
Patti Page; *Patti Page's Greatest Hits-Finest Performances* . . . . (Sun)
I Didn't Know My Own Strength
Lorrie Morgan; *Lorrie Morgan's Greatest Hits* . . . . (BNA)
Reflections-Limited Edition Greatest Hits . . . . (BNA)
I Do
Mila Mason; *That's Enough Of That* . . . . (Atlantic)
I Don't Ever Want To See You Again
Uncle Sam; *Uncle Sam* . . . . (Stone Creek/Epic)
I Don't Have The Heart
James Ingram; *It's Real* . . . . (Warner Bros.)
I Don't Know
Gretchen Peters; *Gretchen Peters* . . . . (Purple Crayon Prod.)
I Don't Make Promises (I Can't Break)
Shannon Curfman; *Loud Guitars Big Suspicions* . . . . (Arista)
I Don't Want To
Toni Braxton; *Secrets* . . . . (LaFace)
I Don't Want To See You Again
Peter And Gordon; *Peter & Gordon's Greatest Hits* . . . . (CEMA Special Prod.)
I Go To Pieces
Del Shannon; *Rock On!* . . . . (Gone Gator)
Peter And Gordon; *Best Of Peter And Gordon* . . . . (Rhino)
History Of British Rock-#3-C . . . . (Rhino)
Southern Pacific; *County Line* . . . . (Warner Bros.)
Southern Pacific's Greatest Hits . . . . (Warner Bros.)
I Got Id
Pearl Jam; *Merkinball* . . . . (Epic)
I Got To Find My Baby
Animals; *In The Beginning* . . . . (Sundazed Music)
I Heard It Through The Grapevine
Creedence Clearwater Revival; *Chooglin'* . . . . (Fantasy)
Cosmo's Factory . . . . (Fantasy)
Creedence Clearwater Revival-Chronicle . . . . (Fantasy)
Creedence Clearwater Revival-Gold . . . . (Fantasy)
Movie Album . . . . (Fantasy)
Gladys Knight & The Pips; *16 #1 Hits From The Late '60s-C* . . . . (Motown)
Compact Command Performances-Gladys Knight & The Pips . . . . (Motown)
Every Great Motown Song-First 25 Years-C . . . . (Motown)
Motown Grammy R&B Performances Of The '60s & '70s-C . . . . (Motown)
Motown Superstar Series-#13-Gladys Knight & The Pips . . . . (Motown)
Top 10 With A Bullet-Motown Girl Groups-C . . . . (Motown)
Marvin Gaye; *25 #1 Hits From 25 Years-C* . . . . (Motown)
Every Great Motown Hit Of Marvin Gaye . . . . (Motown)
Marvin Gaye Live At The London Palladium . . . . (Motown)
Marvin Gaye-Anthology . . . . (Motown)
Most Played Songs On America's Jukeboxes . . . . (Motown)
Motown Story-First 25 Years-C . . . . (Motown)
I Know
Dionne Farris; *Wild Seed - Wild Flower* . . . . (Columbia)

I Let Her Lie
Daryle Singletary; *Daryle Singletary* . . . . (Giant)
I Looked Away
Derek And The Dominos; *Layla* . . . . (Polydor)
I Lost It
Kenny Chesney; *Kenny Chesney's Greatest Hits* . . . . (BNA)
I Lost My Gal From Memphis
New Sunshine Jazz Band; *Too Much Mustard* . . . . (Biograph)
Tex Williams; *Tex Williams-Vintage Collections* . . . . (Capitol)
I May Never Get To Heaven
Conway Twitty; *Conway Twittty-20 Greatest Hits* . . . .(MCA)
Conway Twitty Sings The Hits . . . . (MCA Special Prod.)
I Might Even Quit Lovin' You
Mark Chesnutt; *Thank God For Believers* . . . . (Decca)
I Need You
Beatles; *ST/Help!* . . . . (Capitol)
I Saw The Light
Wynonna; *Wynonna* . . . .(MCA)
I Should Know
Mavericks; *Trampoline* . . . .(MCA)
I Take It Back
Sandy Posey; *Best Of Sandy Posey* . . . . (Collectables)
Best Of Sandy Posey-With Skeeter Davis . . . . (Gusto)
I Think I'll Just Stay Here And Drink
Merle Haggard; *For The Record: Merle Haggard-43 Legendary Hits* . . . . (BNA)
I Was The One
Elvis Presley; *Elvis' Golden Records* . . . . (RCA)
I Will Always Love You
Dolly Parton; *Best Of Dolly Parton* . . . . (RCA)
Best There Is . . . . (RCA)
Chicken Soup For The Woman's Soul-C . . . . (Rhino)
Dolly Parton's Greatest Hits . . . . (RCA)
ST/Best Little Whorehouse In Texas. . . . .(MCA)
Linda Ronstadt; *Prisoner In Disguise* . . . . (Asylum)
Whitney Houston; *ST/The Bodyguard* . . . . (Arista)
Whitney Houston's Greatest Hits. . . . . (Arista)
I Will Love Again
Lara Fabian; *Lara Fabian* . . . . (Columbia)
I Will Remember You
Sarah McLachlan; *Mirrorball*. . . . . (Arista)
ST/Brothers McMullen . . . . (Arista)
Surfacing . . . . (Arista)
Totally Hits-#2-C . . . . (Elektra)
I Will Survive
Gloria Gaynor; *Billboard Top Hits-1979-C* . . . . (Rhino)
I Am Woman-C. . . . . (Nick At Nite)
Love Tracks . . . . (Polydor)
The Disco Years-#2-On The Beat-1978-1982-C . . . . (Rhino)
I Wish
Carl Thomas; *Emotional*. . . . . (Bad Boy/Arista)
I Wonder If You Feel The Way I Do
Asleep At The Wheel featuring Merle Haggard; *Tribute To The Music Of*
Bob Wills And The Texas Playboys-C. (Liberty)
Bob Wills & His Texas Playboys; *For The Last Time*. . . . . (Capitol)
I Won't Cry Anymore
Etta James; *These Foolish Things-The Classic Balladry Of Etta James* . . .(MCA)
Marvin Gaye; *Romantically Yours* . . . . (Columbia)
I Won't Mention It Again
Ray Price; *Ray Price's Greatest Hits-#1-3* . . . . (Step One)
Ray Price-Super Hits . . . . (Columbia)
Reba McEntire; *Starting Over* . . . .(MCA)
I Would've Loved You Anyway
Trisha Yearwood; *Inside Out* . . . .(MCA)
Idiot Wind
Bob Dylan; *Blood On The Tracks* . . . . (Columbia)
Hard Rain . . . . (Columbia)
The Bootleg Series-Volumes 1-3 [Rare & Unreleased] . . . . (Columbia)
If I Was A Drinkin' Man
Neal McCoy; *Neal McCoy's Greatest Hits* . . . . (Atlantic)
Neal McCoy-Super Hits . . . . (Atlantic)
You Gotta Love That! . . . . (Atlantic)
If You Could Only See
Tonic; *Lemon Parade* . . . . (Polydor)
Now That's What I Call Music!-#1-C . . . . (Virgin)
If You See Her, Say Hello
Bob Dylan; *Blood On The Tracks* . . . . (Columbia)
I'll Be On My Way
Beatles; *Live At The BBC* . . . . (Apple)
I'll Cry Instead
Beatles; *Beatles-Box Set* . . . . (Capitol)
Something New . . . . (Capitol)
ST/A Hard Day's Night . . . . (Capitol)
I'll Follow The Sun
Beatles; *Beatles '65* . . . . (Capitol)
Beatles-Box Set . . . . (Capitol)
Beatles-Love Songs . . . . (Capitol)
For Sale . . . . (Capitol)
I'll Repossess My Heart
Kitty Wells; *Kitty Wells' Greatest Hits* . . . . (Hollywood/DNA-Rounder)

I'm A Loser
Beatles; *Beatles '65*. . . . . (Capitol)
I'm Alright
Kim Richey; *Bitter Sweet* . . . . (Mercury)
I'm Always On A Mountain When I Fall
Merle Haggard; *For The Record: Merle Haggard-43 Legendary Hits* . . . .(BNA)
I'm Gonna Change Everything
Mandy Barnett; *I've Got A Right To Cry* . . . . (Sire)
I'm Leaving
Aaron Tippin; *What This Country Needs* . . . . (Lyric Street)
I'm Not Supposed To Love You Anymore
Bryan White; *Between Now And Forever* . . . .(Asylum)
I'm Waiting For The Day
Beach Boys; *Pet Sounds* . . . . (Capitol)
The Pet Sounds Sessions: A 30th Anniversary Collection . . . . (Capitol)
In A Perfect World
Lorrie Morgan; *Shakin' Things Up* . . . . (BNA)
In The End
Linkin Park; *Hybrid Theory* . . . . (Warner Bros.)
Indescribably Blue
Elvis Presley; *Elvis' Gold Records, Volume 4* . . . . (RCA)
From Nashville To Memphis-The Essential '60s Masters . . . .(RCA)
Interstate Love Song
Stone Temple Pilots; *Purple* . . . .(Atlantic)
Is It Over Yet
Wynonna; *Tell Me Why* . . . . (MCA)
Is It Really Over?
Jim Reeves; *Essential Jim Reeves* . . . . (RCA)
It Isn't Right
Platters; *Enchanted-The Best Of The Platters* . . . . (Rhino)
Magic Touch-An Anthology . . . . (Mercury)
It Must Be Him
Vikki Carr; *Greatest Hits* . . . . (Curb)
It Only Hurts For A Little While
Ames Brothers; *Best Of The Ames Brothers* . . . . (Pair)
Anne Murray; *Croonin'* . . . . (SBK)
Margo Smith; *Best Of Margo Smith* . . . . (MCA Special Prod.)
It Wasn't God Who Made Honky Tonk Angels
Kitty Wells; *Grand Ole Opry-75 Years-#1-C* . . . . (MCA)
Kitty Wells' Greatest Hits . . . . (Step One)
The Kitty Wells Story . . . . (MCA)
It Would Be You
Gary Allan; *It Would Be You* . . . . (Decca)
It's A Heartache
Bonnie Tyler; *Billboard Top Hits-1978-C* . . . . (Rhino)
It's A Heartache . . . . (RCA)
Juice Newton; *Juice Newton-Greatest Hits & More* . . . . (Capitol)
It's A Heartache
Ronnie Spector; *Get Down Tonight! Best Of T.K. Records-C* . . . . (Rhino)
It's A Little Too Late
Mark Chesnutt; *Mark Chesnutt's Greatest Hits* . . . . (Decca)
It's All Over Now
Bobby Womack; *Lookin' For A Love-Best Of Bobby Womack-1968-*
1975 . . . . (Razor & Tie)
John Anderson; *Great Divorce Songs For Him-C* . . . . (Warner Bros.)
John Anderson's Greatest Hits-#2 . . . . (Warner Bros.)
Rod Stewart; *Best Of Rod Stewart* . . . . (Mercury)
Gasoline Alley . . . . (Mercury)
Vintage Rod Stewart . . . . (Mercury)
Rolling Stones; *12 X 5* . . . .(Abkco)
Big Hits (High Tide & Green Grass) . . . .(Abkco)
More Hot Rocks (big hits & fazed cookies). . . . . (Abkco)
Singles Collection-The London Years . . . . (Abkco)
Ry Cooder; *Paradise And Lunch* . . . . (Reprise)
It's All Right
Impressions; *Billboard Top R&B Hits-1963-C* . . . . (Rhino)
Cruisin'-1964-C . . . . (Increase)
Impressions' Greatest Hits . . . . (MCA)
ST/The Flamingo Kid . . . . (Motown)
It's Almost Tomorrow
Dream Weavers; *Hard To Find 45s On CD-#3-The Mid '50s-C* . . . .(Eric)
It's Four In The Morning
Faron Young; *Faron Young-Golden Hits* . . . . (Mercury)
Faron Young-The Hits . . . . (Mercury)
It's My Party
Lesley Gore; *Billboard Top Rock 'N' Roll Hits-1963-C* . . . . (Rhino)
Golden Hits Of Lesley Gore . . . . (Mercury)
Good Time Rock 'N' Roll-C . . . . (MCA)
Lesley Gore-Anthology . . . . (Rhino)
Oldies But Goodies-#3-C . . . . (Original Sound)
It's Not Right But It's Okay
Whitney Houston; *My Love Is Your Love* . . . . (Arista)
It's Over
Roy Orbison; *Roy Orbison's All-Time Greatest Hits-#1 & 2* . . . . . . (Monument)
Roy Orbison-Super Hits . . . . (Columbia)
Very Best Of Roy Orbison. . . . . (Virgin)
It's Over Now
Deborah Cox; *One Wish* . . . . (Arista)

It's Over Now
112; *Part III* . . . . (Bad Boy/Arista)
It's Too Late
Amy Grant; *Tapestry Revisited: Tribute To Carole King-C* . . . . (Lava)
Carole King; *Her Greatest Hits* . . . . (Epic)
Tapestry . . . . (Epic)
Gloria Estefan; *Hold Me, Thrill Me, Kiss Me* . . . . (Epic)
It's Too Late
Derek And The Dominos; *Layla* . . . . (Polydor)
I've Had Enough
Regina Belle; *Believe In Me* . . . . (MCA)
Jamaica Farewell
Harry Belafonte; *Calypso* . . . . (RCA)
Harry Belafonte-Legendary Performer . . . . (RCA)
Harry Belafonte-Pure Gold . . . . (RCA)
Harry Belafonte's All Time Greatest Hits-#1 . . . . (RCA)
This Is Harry Belafonte . . . . (RCA)
Je Suis Desole
Mark Knopfler; *Golden Heart* . . . . (Warner Bros.)
Jealous Heart
Al Morgan; *Hits Of '49-C* . . . . (ASV)
Connie Francis; *Connie Francis-Souvenirs* . . . . (Polydor)
Les Paul; *Les Paul-16 Most Requested Songs* . . . . (Columbia)
Tex Ritter; *An American Legend* . . . . (Capitol)
Best Of Tex Ritter . . . . (Capitol)
Hillbilly Heaven . . . . (Capitol)
Tex Ritter's Greatest Hits . . . . (Curb)
Tex Ritter-Vintage Collection . . . . (Capitol)
Joy
Nilsson; *Son Of Schmilsson* . . . . (RCA)
Just Be A Man About It
Toni Braxton; *The Heat* . . . . (LaFace)
Just Like A Woman
Bob Dylan; *Before The Flood* . . . . (Columbia)
Biograph . . . . (Columbia)
Blonde On Blonde . . . . (Columbia)
Bob Dylan At Budokan . . . . (Columbia)
Bob Dylan's Greatest Hits . . . . (Columbia)
Byrds; *The Byrds* . . . . (Columbia)
Just One Of Those Things
Bobby Short; *Loves Cole Porter* . . . . (Atlantic)
Ella Fitzgerald; *Best Of The Song Books: Love Songs* . . . . (Verve)
Frank Sinatra; *Timeless* . . . . (Pair)
Lena Horne; *American Songbook Series-Cole Porter* . . (Smithsonian Collection)
Lester Lanin; *Best Of The Big Bands-C* . . . . (Columbia)
Louis Armstrong; *Jazz Masters-#1-Louis Armstrong* . . . . (Verve)
Peggy Lee; *Peggy Lee Sings For You* . . . . (Avid)
Sarah Vaughan; *Essential Sarah Vaughan-The Great Songs* . . . . (Verve)
Just To See You Smile
Tim McGraw; *Everywhere* . . . . (Curb)
Tim McGraw's Greatest Hits . . . . (Curb)
Kentucky Rain
Elvis Presley; *Elvis Presley-Pure Gold* . . . . (RCA)
Memphis Record . . . . (RCA)
Worldwide 50 Gold Award Hits, Vol. 1, Parts 1 & 2 . . . . (RCA)
Kind Of A Drag
Buckinghams; *Kind Of A Drag* . . . . (Sundazed Music)
Mercy, Mercy, Mercy . . . . (Legacy Rock Artifacts Series)
Kindly Keep It Country
Vince Gill; *The Key* . . . . (MCA)
Kiss And Say Goodbye
Manhattans; *Best Of The Manhattans-Kiss And Say Goodbye* . . . . (Legacy)
Manhattans Greatest Hits . . . . (Columbia)
Kiss Off
Violent Femmes; *Violent Femmes* . . . . (Slash)
Land Of The Living
Pam Tillis; *Pam Tillis' Greatest Hits* . . . . (Arista)
Last Day Of Our Acquaintance
Sinead O'Connor; *I Do Not Want What I Haven't Got* . . . . (Ensign)
Last Goodbye
Jeff Buckley; *Grace* . . . . (Columbia)
Last Goodbye
Kenny Wayne Shepherd Band; *Live On* . . . . (Giant)
Last Train Done Gone Down
Marty Stuart; *Hot Tracks-Train Super Hits-C* . . . . (Epic)
Let There Be Country . . . . (Columbia)
Last Waltz, The
Engelbert Humperdinck; *Engelbert Humperdinck-16 Most Requested
Songs* . . . . (Epic)
Learning As You Go
Rick Trevino; *Learning As You Go* . . . . (Columbia)
Super Hits Of 1996-C . . . . (Epic)
Learning The Game
Buddy Holly; *Complete Buddy Holly* . . . . (MCA)
The Buddy Holly Collection . . . . (MCA)
Leavin' And Sayin' Goodbye
Faron Young; *Faron Young-Golden Hits* . . . . (Mercury)
Faron Young's Greatest Hits-#1-3 . . . . (Step One)

Let Him Fly
Dixie Chicks; *Fly* . . . . (Monument)
Let It Flow
Toni Braxton; *Secrets* . . . . (LaFace)
ST/Waiting To Exhale . . . . (Arista)
Let Me Fall
Wood; *Songs From Stamford Hill* . . . . (Columbia)
Letters From The Wasteland
Wallflowers; *Breach* . . . . (Interscope)
Letting Go
Sozzi; *Songs From Dawson's Creek* . . . . (Sony Music Soundtrax)
Lie To Me
Jonny Lang; *Lie To Me* . . . . (A&M)
Like Strangers
Everly Brothers; *All They Had To Do Was Dream* . . . . (Rhino)
Everly Brothers' Greatest Hits . . . . (Delta)
Everly Brothers-Cadence Classics-Their 20 Greatest Hits . . . . (Rhino)
Like There Ain't No Yesterday
BlackHawk; *Strong Enough* . . . . (Arista)
The Hits-Love & Gravity . . . . (Arista)
Lion's Den
Bruce Springsteen; *Tracks* . . . . (Columbia)
Lipstick Promises
George Ducas; *George Ducas* . . . . (Capitol)
I Love Country-Hits Of The '90s-#4-C . . . . (Priority)
Little Bird
Sherrie Austin; *Love In The Real World* . . . . (Arista)
Little Bitty Tear
Burl Ives; *Best Of Burl Ives-#2* . . . . (MCA)
Burl Ives Live . . . . (MCA)
MCA Records 30 Years Of Hits-1958-1988-C . . . . (MCA)
Hank Cochran; *45-#47062* . . . . (Elektra)
Lonely
Tracy Lawrence; *Lessons Learned* . . . . (Atlantic)
Lonely Weekends
Charlie Rich; *Charlie Rich-Complete Smash Sessions* . . . . (Mercury)
Lonely Weekends . . . . (Sun)
Sun's Greatest Hits-C . . . . (RCA)
Shelby Lynne; *Tough All Over* . . . . (Epic)
Lonesome Town
Ricky Nelson; *Best Of Ricky Nelson* . . . . (Curb)
Losing A Whole Year
Third Eye Blind; *Third Eye Blind* . . . . (Elektra)
Lost Without Your Love
Bread; *Bread-Anthology* . . . . (Elektra)
Bread-Retrospective . . . . (Rhino)
Love Is Like A Cigarette
Duke Ellington; *Rockin' In Rhythm* . . . . (ASV)
Love T.K.O.
Bette Midler; *Bette* . . . . (Warner Bros.)
Lovesick Blues
Gary Morris; *Plain Brown Wrapper* . . . . (Warner Bros.)
Hank Williams With His Drifting Cowboys; *24 Of Hank Williams'
Greatest Hits* . . . . (Polydor)
Lovesick Blues . . . . (Polydor)
Linda Ronstadt; *Linda Ronstadt-Retrospective* . . . . (Capitol)
Silk Purse . . . . (Capitol)
Patsy Cline; *Live At The Opry* . . . . (MCA)
Ryan Adams; *Timeless: Hank Williams Tribute-C* . . . . . (Lost Highway/IDJMG)
Loving This Way
Collin Raye with Bobbie Eakes; *Tracks* . . . . (Epic)
Lucky 4 You (Tonight I'm Just Me)
SHeDAISY; *The Whole Shebang* . . . . (Lyric Street)
Mailman, Bring Me No More Blues
Beatles; *The Beatles-Anthology-#3* . . . . (Capitol)
Buddy Holly; *Buddy Holly* . . . . (MCA)
Maybe
Chantels; *Back To The '50s-C* . . . . (Dominion Entert.)
Fabulous '50s-#3-C . . . . (Dominion Entert.)
Ink Spots; *Ink Spots' Greatest Hits-Original Recordings-1939-1946* . . . . (MCA)
Ink Spots-The Anthology . . . . (MCA)
Maybe Someday
Cure; *Bloodflowers* . . . . (Fiction/Elektra)
Midnight Blue
Melissa Manchester; *Melissa* . . . . (Arista)
Melissa Manchester's Greatest Hits . . . . (Arista)
Misery
Asleep At The Wheel featuring Marty Stuart; *Tribute To The Music Of Bob
Wills And The Texas Playboys-C* . . . . (Liberty)
Modern Age, The
Strokes; *Is This It* . . . . (RCA)
Most Beautiful Girl
Charlie Rich; *Behind Closed Doors* . . . . (Epic)
Charlie Rich's Greatest Hits . . . . (Epic)
Columbia Country Classics-#4-Nashville Sound-C . . . . (Columbia)
Most Likely You'll Go Your Way & I'll Go Mine
Bob Dylan; *Biograph* . . . . (Columbia)
Blonde On Blonde . . . . (Columbia)

Bob Dylan And The Band; *Before The Flood* . . . . (Columbia)
Mourning
Tantric; *Tantric* . . . .(Maverick)
Movin' On
Mya featuring Silkk The Shocker; *Mya* . . . . (University/Interscope)
Mrs. Brown You've Got A Lovely Daughter
Herman's Hermits; *Herman's Hermits-Their Greatest Hits* . . . . (Abkco)
Something Good Again . . . . (Abkco)
Ms. Jackson
Outkast; *Stankonia* . . . . (LaFace/Arista)
Must You Throw Dirt In My Face
Elvis Costello; *Kojak Variety* . . . .(Warner Bros.)
Louvin Brothers; *45-#4822* . . . . (Capitol)
My Baby Left Me
Arthur "Big Boy" Crudup; *That's All Right (Mama)* . . . . (Bluebird)
Creedence Clearwater Revival; *Cosmo's Factory* . . . . (Fantasy)
Creedence Country . . . . (Fantasy)
Elvis Presley; *Elvis Recorded Live On Stage In Memphis* . . . . (RCA)
My My
Seven Mary Three; *American Standard* . . . . (Mammoth)
My Whole World Ended (The Moment You Left Me)
David Ruffin; *David Ruffin-At His Best* . . . . (Motown)
Motown Year By Year-The Sound Of Young America-1969-C . . . . . . (Motown)
Spinners; *Best Of The Spinners* . . . . (Motown)
Myself Without You
Reba McEntire; *Reba McEntire's Greatest Hits-#3: I'm A Survivor* . . . . .(MCA)
Mystery Train
Band; *Moondog Matinee* . . . . (Capitol)
The Band-Anthology-#2 . . . . (Capitol)
The Last Waltz . . . .(Warner Bros.)
To Kingdom Come-The Definitive Collection . . . . (Capitol)
Elvis Presley; *For LP Fans Only* . . . . (RCA)
The Sun Sessions . . . . (RCA)
Junior Parker; *Between The Rails: America's Train Songs-C* . . . . . . (Crescendo)
Neil Young; *Neil & The Shocking Pinks* . . . . (Geffen)
Neville Brothers; *Brother's Keeper* . . . . (A&M)
Paul Butterfield Blues Band; *Golden Butter* . . . . (Elektra)
Paul Butterfield Blues Band . . . . (Elektra)
Sam The Sham and The Pharaohs; *Best Of Sam The Sham and The*
Pharaohs . . . . (Polydor)
Naima
John Coltrane; *Afro Blue Impressions* . . . .(Pablo)
Never Ever
All Saints; *All Saints* . . . . (London)
Now That's What I Call Music!-#1-C . . . . (Virgin)
Never Let You Go
Third Eye Blind; *Blue* . . . . (Elektra)
Totally Hits-#2-C . . . . (Elektra)
New Worried Mind
Bob Wills; *Stay A Little Longer-The Original Columbia*
Recordings . . . . (Roswell/RCA)
New York, New York
Ryan Adams; *Gold* . . . . (Lost Highway/IDJMG)
No Easy Goodbye
South Sixty Five; *South Sixty Five* . . . . (Atlantic)
No Expectations
Rolling Stones; *Beggars Banquet* . . . . (Abkco)
More Hot Rocks (big hits & fazed cookies) . . . . (Abkco)
Singles Collection-The London Years . . . . (Abkco)
No Milk Today
Herman's Hermits; *Herman's Hermits-Their Greatest Hits* . . . . (Abkco)
There's A Kind Of A Hush . . . . (MGM)
No More
Ruff Endz; *Love Crimes* . . . .(Epic)
No Regrets
Emmylou Harris; *Bluebird* . . . . (Reprise)
Tom Rush; *Best Of Tom Rush: No Regrets* . . . . (Legacy)
The Circle Game . . . . (Elektra)
Nobody Knows
Kevin Sharp; *Measure Of A Man* . . . . (143/Asylum)
Tony Rich Project; *Words* . . . . (LaFace)
Not Gon' Cry
Mary J. Blige; *Share My World* . . . . (MCA)
Nothin' But The Taillights
Clint Black; *Nothin' But The Taillights* . . . . (RCA)
Nothin' But The Wheel
Patty Loveless; *Only What I Feel* . . . .(Epic)
Patty Loveless-Classics . . . .(Epic)
Nothing Compares 2 U
Sinead O'Connor; *I Do Not Want What I Haven't Got* . . . . (Ensign)
Now That She's Gone
Destiny's Child; *The Writing's On The Wall* . . . . (Columbia)
Oh Darling
Beatles; *Abbey Road* . . . . (Parlophone)
The Beatles-Anthology-#3 . . . . (Capitol)
Oh Me, Oh My, Sweet Baby
Diamond Rio; *Close To The Edge* . . . . (Arista)
George Strait; *Beyond The Blue Neon* . . . .(MCA)

On My Own
Peach Union; *Audiopeach* . . . . (Epic)
ST/Sliding Doors . . . . (MCA)
On My Own
Patti LaBelle & Michael McDonald; *Chicken Soup For The Couples*
Soul-C . . . . (Rhino)
Patti LaBelle's Greatest Hits . . . . (MCA)
Winner In You . . . . (MCA)
On My Own
Reba McEntire; *Starting Over* . . . . (MCA)
One
Metallica; *...And Justice For All* . . . . (Elektra)
One
Nilsson; *Aerial Ballet* . . . . (RCA)
Everybody's Talkin': The Encore Collection . . . . (BMG Special Prod.)
Nilsson-All-Time Greatest Hits . . . . (RCA)
Three Dog Night; *Best Of Three Dog Night* . . . . (MCA)
Captured Live At The Forum . . . . (MCA)
Joy To The World-Greatest Hits . . . . (MCA)
One I Gave My Heart To
Aaliyah; *One In A Million* . . . . (BlackGround Enterp./Atlantic)
One Of Us Must Know (Sooner Or Later)
Bob Dylan; *Blonde On Blonde* . . . . (Columbia)
One Way Track
Ricky Skaggs and Kentucky Thunder; *History Of The Future* . . (Skaggs Family)
Only On Days That End In "Y"
Clay Walker; *Hypnotize The Moon* . . . .(Giant)
Only The Lonely (Know The Way I Feel)
Roy Orbison; *For The Lonely: A Roy Orbison Anthology 1959-1965* . . . . (Rhino)
In Dreams-Greatest Hits . . . .(Orbison)
Roy Orbison's All-Time Greatest Hits-#1 & 2 . . . . (Monument)
Only The Strong Survive
Elvis Presley; *From Elvis In Memphis* . . . . (RCA)
Memphis Record . . . . (RCA)
Jerry Butler; *Best Of Jerry Butler* . . . . (Mercury)
Best Of Jerry Butler . . . . (Rhino)
Over My Shoulder
Patty Loveless; *When Fallen Angels Fly* . . . .(Epic)
Over The Rise
Bruce Springsteen; *Tracks* . . . . (Columbia)
Party Crowd
David Lee Murphy; *Out With A Bang* . . . . (MCA)
Party Time
T.G. Sheppard; *Great Divorce Songs For Him-C* . . . . (Warner Bros.)
T.G. Sheppard's All-Time Greatest Hits . . . . (Warner Bros.)
T.G. Sheppard's Greatest Hits . . . .(Warner Bros./Curb)
Perfect
Smashing Pumpkins; *Adore* . . . .(Virgin)
Pet Names
Smash Mouth; *Fush Yu Mang* . . . .(Interscope)
Petals
Mariah Carey; *Rainbow* . . . . (Columbia)
Place To Fall Apart
Merle Haggard & Janie Fricke; *For The Record: Merle Haggard-43*
Legendary Hits . . . .(BNA)
Planets Of The Universe
Stevie Nicks; *Trouble In Shangri-La* . . . . (Reprise)
Please Don't Talk About Me When I'm Gone
Ann-Margret; *Let Me Entertain You* . . . . (RCA)
Arlo Guthrie & Pete Seeger; *Precious Friend* . . . . (Warner Bros.)
Billie Holiday; *Compact Jazz-Billie Holiday* . . . . (Verve)
Music For Torching: Billie Holiday Story-#5 . . . . (Verve)
The Ultimate Billie Holiday . . . . (Verve)
Ella Fitzgerald & Count Basie; *Perfect Match* . . . . (Pablo)
Frank Sinatra; *Swing Along With Me* . . . . (Reprise)
Gene Austin; *The Voice Of The Southland* . . . . (Living Era)
Harry Connick, Jr.; *20* . . . . (Columbia)
Leon Redbone; *Champagne Charlie* . . . . (Warner Bros.)
Ray Price; *Portrait Of A Singer* . . . . (Step One)
Please Mr. Sun
Johnnie Ray; *Back To The Early '50s* . . . . (Dominion Entert.)
Johnnie Ray-16 Most Requested Songs . . . . (Legacy)
Vogues; *Vogues' Greatest Hits* . . . . (Rhino)
Porcelain
Moby; *Play* . . . .(V2)
ST/Playing By Heart . . . . (Capitol)
ST/The Beach . . . . (Sire)
Pour Me
Trick Pony; *Trick Pony* . . . . (H2E/Warner Bros.)
Power Of Good-Bye
Madonna; *GHV2* . . . . (Warner Bros.)
Ray Of Light . . . . (Maverick)
Prayin' For Daylight
Rascal Flatts; *Rascal Flatts* . . . .(Lyric Street)
Promises
Cranberries; *Bury The Hatchet* . . . . (Island/IDJMG)
Purple Rain
Prince and the Revolution; *ST/Purple Rain* . . . . (Warner Bros.)

Re-Arranged
Limp Bizkit; *Significant Other* . . . .(Flip/Interscope)
Reason For Breathing
Babyface; *Collection Of His Greatest Hits* . . . .(Arista/Epic)
Red House
Jimi Hendrix; *Concerts* . . . .(Reprise)
Kiss The Sky . . . .(Reprise)
Lifelines/Jimi Hendrix Story . . . .(Reprise)
Live At Winterland . . . .(Rykodisc)
ST/Jimi Hendrix . . . .(Reprise)
Jimi Hendrix Experience; *Are You Experienced?* . . . .(Reprise)
Smash Hits . . . .(Reprise)
Red Rubber Ball
Cyrkle; *Even More Nuggets-C.* . . . . (Rhino)
Pop Classics Of The '60s-C . . . .(Columbia)
Red Rubber Ball (A Collection) . . . .(Columbia)
Reflections
Diana Ross & The Supremes; *Diana Ross & The Supremes' Greatest
Hits-#3* . . . .(Motown)
Diana Ross & The Supremes-25th Anniversary . . . .(Motown)
Diana Ross & The Supremes-Anthology (1962-1969) . . . . .(Motown)
Motown Story-First 25 Years-C . . . .(Motown)
Four Tops; *Four Tops-Anthology* . . . .(Motown)
Still Waters Run Deep . . . .(Motown)
Until You Love Someone: More Of The Best (1965-1970) . . .(Rhino)
Luther Vandross; *Songs*. . . . .(Epic)
Remember
Jimi Hendrix Experience; *Are You Experienced?* . . . .(Reprise)
Remember (Walkin' In The Sand)
Aerosmith; *Aerosmith's Greatest Hits*. . . . .(Columbia)
Night In The Ruts . . . .(Columbia)
Go-Go's; *Return To The Valley Of The Go-Go's* . . . . (I.R.S.)
Shangri-Las; *Girl Groups-Story Of A Sound-C* . . . .(Rhino)
Oldies But Goodies-#6-C . . . .(Original Sound)
Original Golden Hits Of The Great Groups-#1-C . . . . .(SSS International)
ST/Goodfellas. . . . .(Atlantic)
Revival
Gretchen Peters; *Gretchen Peters* . . . .(Purple Crayon Prod.)
Rexall
Dave Navarro; *Trust No One* . . . .(Capitol)
Rhapsody In The Rain
Lou Christie; *Enlightnin'ment-Best Of Lou Christie* . . . .(Rhino)
River
Betty Buckley; *With One Look* . . . .(Sterling)
Joni Mitchell; *Blue*. . . . .(Reprise)
Rock, The
George Jones; *The Rock: Stone Cold Country 2001* . . . .(BNA)
Rocky Road Blues
Bill Monroe & His Blue Grass Boys; *All Time Legends Of Country
Music-C* . . . .(Legacy)
Rose Bouquet
Phil Vassar; *Phil Vassar* . . . .(Arista)
Roses In The Fire
Rosanne Cash; *The Wheel* . . . .(Columbia)
Runaround Sue
Dion; *Billboard Top Rock 'N' Roll Hits-1961-C* . . . .(Rhino)
Everything You Always Wanted To Hear . . . .(Laurie)
Million-Dollar Memories #1-C. . . . .(RCA)
Oldies But Goodies-#7-C . . . .(Original Sound)
ST/The Flamingo Kid . . . .(Motown)
ST/The Wanderers . . . .(Warner Bros.)
Runaway
Bonnie Raitt; *Bonnie Raitt-Collection* . . . .(Warner Bros.)
Sweet Forgiveness . . . .(Warner Bros.)
Del Shannon; *Billboard Top Rock 'N' Roll Hits-1961-C* . . . .(Rhino)
Cruisin'-1961-C . . . .(Increase)
Del Shannon's Greatest Hits . . . .(Rhino)
Heart & Soul Of Rock 'N' Roll-#1-C . . . .(Rhino)
Little Town Flirt . . . .(Rhino)
ST/American Graffiti . . . .(MCA)
Elvis Presley; *Collector's Gold* . . . .(RCA)
Runnin' Away With My Heart
Lonestar; *Lonestar*. . . . .(BNA)
Sad Lookin' Moon
Alabama; *Dancin' On The Boulevard* . . . .(RCA)
For The Record: 41 Number One Hits . . . .(RCA)
Santa Monica (Watch The World Die)
Everclear; *Sparkle And Fade* . . . .(Capitol)
Saying Hello, Saying I Love You, Saying Goodbye
Jim Ed Brown & Helen Cornelius; *Jim Ed Brown & Helen Cornelius'
Greatest Hits* . . . .(RCA)
Second Hand News
Fleetwood Mac; *25 Years-The Chain* . . . .(Warner Bros.)
Rumours . . . .(Warner Bros.)
Tonic; *Legacy-A Tribute To Fleetwood Mac's Rumours-C* . . . .(Lava)
Second Wind
Darryl Worley; *Hard Rain Don't Last* . . . .(DreamWorks/SKG)
See You Later, Alligator
Bill Haley & His Comets; *Bill Haley & His Comets* . . . .(Everest)

Bill Haley & His Comets' Greatest Hits . . . .(MCA)
Bill Haley & His Comets-Golden Hits. . . . .(MCA)
Billboard Top Rock 'N' Roll Hits-1956-C. . . . .(Rhino)
Mr. Rock 'N' Roll . . . .(Accord)
Rock & Roll Is Here To Stay-C . . . .(Gusto)
Rockin' & Rollin' . . . .(Accord)
Self Made Man
Montgomery Gentry; *Tattoos & Scars*. . . . .(Columbia)
Selfless, Cold And Composed
Ben Folds Five; *Whatever And Ever Amen*. . . . .(Caroline/550)
Semi-Charmed Life
Third Eye Blind; *Jock Rock 2000-C* . . . .(Tommy Boy)
Third Eye Blind . . . .(Elektra)
Shame
Stabbing Westward; *Wither Blister Burn & Peel* . . . .(Columbia)
She Cried
Jay & The Americans; *Come A Little Bit Closer-Best Of Jay & The
Americans*. . . . .(Gold Rush)
Jay & The Americans' All-Time Greatest Hits . . . .(Rhino)
Jay & The Americans' Greatest Hits . . . .(Curb)
She Even Woke Me Up To Say Goodbye
Jerry Lee Lewis; *Best Of Jerry Lee Lewis* . . . . (Smash)
Heartbreak . . . .(Tomato)
Kenny Rogers And The First Edition; *Kenny Rogers And The First Edition-
Love Songs* . . . .(MCA Special Prod.)
She's Got The Rhythm (And I Got The Blues)
Alan Jackson; *A Lot About Livin' (And A Little 'Bout Love)* . . . .(Arista)
She's Not There
Santana; *Moonflower*. . . . .(Columbia)
Viva Santana! . . . .(Columbia)
Vanilla Fudge; *Vanilla Fudge* . . . .(Atco)
Zombies; *Best & The Rest Of The Zombies* . . . .(Epic)
Billboard Top Rock 'N' Roll Hits-1964-C . . . .(Rhino)
History Of British Rock-#1-C . . . .(Rhino)
Time Of The Zombies . . . .(Bac-Trac)
She's Out Of My Life
Jacksons; *Jacksons Live* . . . .(Epic)
Michael Jackson; *Off The Wall* . . . .(Epic)
She's Sure Taking It Well
Kevin Sharp; *Measure Of A Man* . . . .(143/Asylum)
Shut Up And Drive
Chely Wright; *Woman In The Moon* . . . .(Polydor Country)
Silver Springs
Fleetwood Mac; *1998 Grammy Nominees-C* . . . .(MCA)
25 Years-The Chain. . . . .(Warner Bros.)
The Dance . . . .(Reprise)
Silver Wings
Merle Haggard; *More Of The Best* . . . .(Rhino)
The Seashores Of Old Mexico . . . .(Epic)
Merle Haggard & Jewel; *For The Record: Merle Haggard-43
Legendary Hits* . . . .(BNA)
Merle Haggard & The Strangers; *Okie From Muskogee* . . . .(Capitol)
Songs I'll Always Sing . . . .(Capitol)
Pam Tillis; *Mama's Hungry Eyes-Merle Haggard Tribute-C* . . . .(Arista)
Singing The Blues
Guy Mitchell; *CBS Classics-Radio Classics Of The '50s-C* . . . . . .(Columbia)
Guy Mitchell-16 Most Requested Songs . . . .(Legacy)
Sittin' On Top Of The World
Bob Dylan; *Good As I Been To You* . . . .(Columbia)
Bob Wills & His Texas Playboys; *Bob Wills & His Texas Playboys-24
Great Hits* . . . .(Polydor)
Bob Wills-Anthology . . . . (Sony Music Special Prod.)
Tiffany Transcriptions-#8-More Of The Best . . . .(Rhino)
Cream; *Wheels Of Fire*. . . . .(Polydor)
Doc Watson; *Doc Watson* . . . .(Vanguard)
Greatest Folksingers Of The '60s-C . . . .(Vanguard)
Old Timey Concert . . . .(Vanguard)
Grateful Dead; *Grateful Dead (Skull & Roses)* . . . .(Warner Bros.)
Jerry Jeff Walker; *Will The Circle Be Unbroken-#2-C*. . . . .(Uni)
Ray Charles; *20 Golden Pieces Of Ray Charles* . . . .(Bulldog)
Sweet Honey In The Rock; *Believe I'll Run On, See What The End's
Gonna Be* . . . .(Redwood)
Sleep To Dream
Fiona Apple; *Tidal* . . . .(Clean Slate/Work)
Slow Surprise
Emmylou Harris; *Grand Ole Opry-75 Years-#1-C* . . . .(MCA)
Smile
Lonestar; *Lonely Grill* . . . .(BNA)
Smoke
Ben Folds Five; *Whatever And Ever Amen*. . . . .(Caroline/550)
Smoke Gets In Your Eyes
Bryan Ferry; *Another Time Another Place* . . . .(Reprise)
Street Life-20 Great Hits . . . .(Reprise)
Dinah Washington; *Golden Classics-Dinah Washington* . . . .(Collectables)
Lawrence Welk; *Musical Memories With Lawrence Welk*. . . . . . .(Ranwood)
Patti Austin; *Real Me* . . . .(Qwest)
Platters; *Encore Of Golden Hits-Platters* . . . .(Mercury)
Oldies But Goodies-#14-C . . . .(Original Sound)
Platters Greatest Hits . . . .(Everest)

ST/Always . . . . (MCA)
ST/American Graffiti . . . . (MCA)
Super Oldies Of The '50s-#5-C . . . . (Audio Fidelity)
Smoke Rings In The Dark
Gary Allan; Smoke Rings In The Dark . . . . (MCA)
So Much For Pretending
Bryan White; Between Now And Forever . . . . (Asylum)
So Sad To Say
Mighty Mighty Bosstones; Pay Attention . . . . (Big Rig/DJMG)
So Very Hard To Go
Tower Of Power; Didn't It Blow Your Mind: Soul Hits Of The
'70s-#17-C . . . . (Rhino)
Tower Of Power . . . . (Warner Bros.)
Some Of These Days
Cab Calloway; Masters Of Jazz-#6-Male Vocal Classics-C . . . . (Rhino)
Leon Redbone; On The Track . . . . (Warner Bros.)
Louis Armstrong; Louis Armstrong And The Big Bands-1928-1930 . . . . (DRG)
Mills Brothers; Close Harmony . . . . (Ranwood)
Sophie Tucker; Legendary Entertainers . . . . (Pro-Arte)
Those Wonderful Years-Roaring '20s-C . . . . (JCI Assoc. Labels)
Someone's Gotta Cry
Jean Shepard; 45-#5392 . . . . (Capitol)
Somewhere In My Broken Heart
Billy Dean; Billy Dean's Greatest Hits . . . . (Liberty)
Heart Beats-Country Lovin': Songs From The Heart-C . . . . (Rhino)
Young Man . . . . (SBK)
Randy Travis; No Holdin' Back . . . . (Warner Bros.)
Song For The Dumped
Ben Folds Five; Naked Baby Photos . . . . (Caroline)
ST/Mr. Wrong . . . . (Hollywood)
Whatever And Ever Amen . . . . (Caroline/550)
Soon
LeAnn Rimes; I Need You . . . . (Curb)
Sound Of Goodbye
Crystal Gayle; Best Of Crystal Gayle . . . . (Warner Bros.)
Cage The Songbird . . . . (Warner Bros.)
Sour Girl
Stone Temple Pilots; No. 4 . . . . (Atlantic)
Special
Garbage; Now That's What I Call Music!-#3-C . . . . (Virgin)
Version 2.0 . . . . (Almo Sounds)
Standin' At The Station
Keb' Mo'; Just Like You . . . . (Okeh)
Standing Tall
Lorrie Morgan; Lorrie Morgan's Greatest Hits . . . . (BNA)
Sticks & Stones
Tracy Lawrence; Tracy Lawrence . . . . (Atlantic)
Still Holding On
Clint Black & Martina McBride; Nothin' But The Taillights . . . . . (RCA)
Martina McBride & Clint Black; Evolution . . . . (RCA)
Still Rainin'
Jonny Lang; Wander This World . . . . (A&M)
Storm, The
Garth Brooks; Scarecrow . . . . (Capitol)
Stormy Weather
Billie Holiday; Fine & Mellow . . . . (Collectables)
Jazz Club-Vocal . . . . (Verve)
Ethel Waters; Fabulous Thirties-C . . . . (Pro Jazz)
Frank Sinatra; No One Cares . . . . (Capitol)
Jackie Wilson; Mr. Excitement . . . . (Rhino)
Judy Garland; Judy Garland-At Carnegie Hall . . . . (Capitol)
Lena Horne; 20 Golden Pieces Of Lena Horne . . . . (Bulldog)
Goes Latin & Sings Your Requests . . . . (DRG)
Live On Broadway . . . . (Qwest)
Nipper's Greatest Hits Of The '40s-#1-C . . . . (RCA)
Pixies; Bossanova . . . . (Elektra)
Tony Bennett with Natalie Cole; Playin' With My Friends-Bennett Sings The
Blues-C . . . . (Columbia)
Willie Nelson & Leon Russell; One For The Road . . . . (Columbia)
Sunday Will Never Be The Same
Spanky & Our Gang; Flower Power-Psychedelic Rock Classics-C . . . . . (K-Tel)
Surefire (Never Enough)
Econoline Crush; Devil You Know . . . . (Restless)
Sweet Dreams (Of You)
Chet Atkins & Mark Knopfler; Neck And Neck . . . . (Columbia)
Don Gibson; Don Gibson-18 Greatest Hits . . . . (Curb)
Don Gibson's All-Time Greatest Hits . . . . (RCA)
Emmylou Harris; Brand New Dance . . . . (Reprise)
Elite Hotel . . . . (Reprise)
Profile/Best Of Emmylou Harris . . . . (Warner Bros.)
Jim Reeves; Jim Reeves' Greatest Hits . . . . (RCA)
Patsy Cline; Patsy Cline's Greatest Hits . . . . (MCA)
ST/Sweet Dreams . . . . (MCA)
The Patsy Cline Story . . . . (MCA)
Reba McEntire; Out Of A Dream . . . . (Mercury)
Swinging Doors
George Jones; 20 Golden Pieces Of George Jones . . . . (Bulldog)
Merle Haggard; Capitol Collectors Series-Merle Haggard . . . . . . (Capitol)

Merle Haggard & The Strangers; Best Of Merle Haggard & The
Strangers . . . . (Capitol)
For The Record: Merle Haggard-43 Legendary Hits . . . . (BNA)
Okie From Muskogee . . . . (Capitol)
Songs I'll Always Sing . . . . (Capitol)
Take A Bow
Madonna; Bedtime Stories . . . . (Maverick/Sire)
GHV2 . . . . (Warner Bros.)
Something To Remember . . . . (Maverick/Sire)
Take A Message To Mary
Bob Dylan; Self Portrait . . . . (Columbia)
Everly Brothers; Everly Brothers-All-Time Original Hits . . . . (Rhino)
Everly Brothers-Cadence Classics-Their 20 Greatest Hits . . . . . (Rhino)
Rockpile; Seconds Of Pleasure . . . . (Columbia)
Take These Chains From My Heart
Hank Williams With His Drifting Cowboys; 24 Of Hank Williams'
Greatest Hits . . . . (Polydor)
Hank Williams-40 Greatest Hits . . . . (Polydor)
Ray Charles; Ray Charles-His Greatest Hits-#2 . . . . (Dunhill Compact Classics)
Take Time To Know Her
Percy Sledge; Best Of Percy Sledge . . . . (Atlantic)
It Tears Me Up-Best Of Percy Sledge . . . . (Rhino)
Take Your Memory With You
Vince Gill; Platinum Country-C . . . . (JCI Assoc. Labels)
Pocket Full Of Gold . . . . (MCA)
Vince Gill-Souvenirs . . . . (MCA)
Taking Everything
Gerald Levert; Love & Consequences . . . . (East West)
Tear Fell, A
Teresa Brewer; Best Of Teresa Brewer . . . . (MCA Jazz)
Tell Me I Was Dreaming
Travis Tritt; Ten Feet Tall And Bulletproof . . . . (Warner Bros.)
Travis Tritt's Greatest Hits-From The Beginning . . . . . . (Warner Bros.)
Tell Me Why
Mavericks; Trampoline . . . . (MCA)
Tequila Sunrise
Alan Jackson; Common Thread-Songs Of The Eagles-C . . . . (Giant)
Eagles; Desperado . . . . (Asylum)
Eagles/Their Greatest Hits 1971-1975 . . . . (Asylum)
Hell Freezes Over . . . . (Geffen)
Thanks A Lot
Ernest Tubb; The Country Music Hall Of Fame-Ernest Tubb . . . . . . (MCA)
IIIrd Time Out; IIIrd Time Out . . . . (Rebel)
Ronnie & Rob McCoury; Ronnie & Rob McCoury . . . . (Rounder)
That Ain't My Truck
Rhett Akins; A Thousand Memories . . . . (Decca)
Cryin' Lyin' Lovin' & Leavin'-C . . . . (Universal)
That Ain't No Way To Go
Brooks & Dunn; Hard Workin' Man . . . . (Arista)
That Other Woman
Changing Faces; Visit Me . . . . (Atlantic)
That's All There Is To That
Dinah Washington; Complete Dinah Washington On Mercury-#6-1958-
1960 . . . . (Mercury)
Etta Jones; Something Nice . . . . (Original Jazz Classics)
Nat "King" Cole & The Four Knights; From The Vaults-#6-Best
Of '56 . . . . (Capitol/EMI)
That's Enough Of That
Mila Mason; That's Enough Of That . . . . (Atlantic)
That's Okay
Marc Anthony; Marc Anthony . . . . (Columbia)
That's The Way I Feel
Faron Young; 45-#4050 . . . . (Capitol)
That's The Way Love Is
Marvin Gaye; M.P.G. . . . . (Motown)
Marvin Gaye-Anthology . . . . (Motown)
Marvin Gaye-Super Hits . . . . (Motown)
There Goes
Alan Jackson; Everything I Love . . . . (Arista)
There Goes My Baby
Trisha Yearwood; Where Your Road Leads . . . . (MCA)
There Goes My Everything
Elvis Presley; Elvis Country ("I'm 10,000 Years Old") . . . . (RCA)
Engelbert Humperdinck; Engelbert Humperdinck-16 Most Requested
Songs . . . . (Epic)
Floyd Cramer; Special Songs Of Love . . . . (Step One)
Jack Greene; Billboard Top Country Hits-1966-C . . . . (Rhino)
There Goes My Heart
Mavericks; Best Of The Mavericks-Super Colossal Smash Hits Of
The '90s . . . . (Mercury)
What A Crying Shame . . . . (MCA)
There Is A Tavern In The Town
Four Aces; Four Aces-More Greatest Hits . . . . (Varese Vintage)
Mitch Miller; Sing Along With Mitch . . . . (Columbia)
Stan Wolowic & The Polka Chips; Million-Seller Polkas . . . . . . (Capitol)
There Is No Arizona
Jamie O'Neal; Shiver . . . . (Mercury)
There's A Whole Lot About A Woman (A Man Don't Know)
Jack Greene; 45-#32823 . . . . (Decca)

There's Your Trouble
Dixie Chicks; *Wide Open Spaces* . . . (Monument)
These Eyes
Guess Who; *Best Of The Guess Who* . . . (RCA)
Greatest Of The Guess Who . . . (RCA)
Nipper's Greatest Hits Of The '60s-#1-C . . . (RCA)
Track Record-Collection . . . (RCA)
They're Coming To Take Me Away, Ha Haaa!
Napoleon XIV; *Dr. Demento Presents The Greatest Novelty Records-#3-1960s-C* . . . (Rhino)
Silly Songs-C . . . (K-Tel)
The Second Coming . . . (Rhino)
They're Hanging Me Tonight
Marty Robbins; *Gunfighter Ballads & Trail Songs* . . . (Legacy)
Things Aren't Funny Anymore
Merle Haggard; *Capitol Collectors Series-Merle Haggard* . . . (Capitol)
Epic Collection-Recorded Live . . . (Epic)
Merle Haggard-Country Boy . . . (Pair)
Things I Should Have Said
Grass Roots; *Grass Roots-All-Time Greatest Hits* . . . (MCA)
Grass Roots-Anthology (1966-1975) . . . (Rhino)
Things That I Used To Do
Guitar Slim; *Blues Classics-C* . . . (K-Tel)
Think Of You
Usher; *Usher* . . . (LaFace)
This Ain't A Love Song
Bon Jovi; *These Days* . . . (Mercury)
This Nearly Was Mine
Original Cast; *South Pacific* . . . (CBS Masterworks)
Three Cigarettes In An Ashtray
k.d. lang; *New Tradition Sings The Old Tradition-C* . . . (Warner Bros.)
k.d. lang and The Reclines; *Angel With A Lariat* . . . (Sire)
Patsy Cline; *20 Golden Pieces Of Patsy Cline* . . . (Bulldog)
Patsy Cline . . . (MCA)
Stop Look & Listen . . . (MCA)
Walkin' Dreams-Her First Recordings-#1 . . . (Rhino)
Three Hearts In A Tangle
Roy Drusky; *45-#31193* . . . (Decca)
Thrill Is Gone
B.B. King; *Best Of B.B. King* . . . (MCA)
Live In Cook County Jail . . . (MCA)
B.B. King & Tracy Chapman; *Deuces Wild* . . . (MCA)
Ticket To Ride
Beatles; *Beatles 1* . . . (Capitol)
Beatles-20 Greatest Hits . . . (Capitol)
Beatles-Box Set . . . (Capitol)
Reel Music . . . (Capitol)
ST/Help! . . . (Capitol)
The Beatles At The Hollywood Bowl . . . (Capitol)
The Beatles/1962-1966 . . . (Capitol)
Carpenters; *Carpenters-Classics-#2* . . . (A&M)
Carpenters-The Singles 1969-1973 . . . (A&M)
From The Top . . . (A&M)
Ticket To Ride . . . (A&M)
Yesterday Once More . . . (A&M)
Vanilla Fudge; *Best Of Vanilla Fudge* . . . (Atco)
Vanilla Fudge . . . (Atco)
'Til I Can Make It On My Own
Faith Hill; *Tammy Wynette...Remembered-C* . . . (Asylum)
Kenny Rogers & Dottie West; *Kenny Rogers-Classics* . . . (EMI)
Kenny Rogers-Twenty Greatest Hits . . . (EMI)
Tammy Wynette; *Tammy Wynette's Greatest Hits-#4* . . . (Epic)
Tears Of Fire-25th Anniversary Collection . . . (Epic)
'Til I Can Make It On My Own . . . (Epic)
'Til I Fell In Love With You
Bob Dylan; *Time Out Of Mind* . . . (Columbia)
Time Changes Everything
Bob Wills & His Texas Playboys; *Bob Wills & His Texas Playboys-Anthology 1935-1973* . . . (Rhino)
Columbia Country Classics-#1-Golden Age-C . . . (Columbia)
Essential Bob Wills & His Texas Playboys-1935-1973 . . . (Legacy)
Roy Rogers; *The Country Music Hall Of Fame-Roy Rogers* . . . (MCA)
Time Of Your Life (Good Riddance)
Green Day; *Nimrod* . . . (Reprise)
Together
Nilsson; *Aerial Ballet* . . . (RCA)
Tonight You Belong To Me
Patience & Prudence; *Great Jukebox Hits Of The '50s-#2-C* . . . (CEMA Special Prod.)
Too Good To Be True
Michael Peterson; *Michael Peterson* . . . (Reprise)
Too Late, Too Soon
Jon Secada; *Secada* . . . (Capitol)
Too Soon To Know
Don Gibson; *Oh Lonesome Me* . . . (Collectables)
Roy Orbison; *The Classic Roy Orbison-1965-1968* . . . (Rhino)
Torn
Natalie Imbruglia; *Left Of The Middle* . . . (RCA)
Tragedy
Fleetwoods; *Best Of The Fleetwoods* . . . (Rhino)
Thomas Wayne With the DeLons; *Greatest Hit Singles Collection-C* . . . (Laserlight)
Tragedy
Emmylou Harris; *Red Dirt Girl* . . . (Nonesuch)
Trainwreck Of Emotion
Lorrie Morgan; *Essential Lorrie Morgan* . . . (RCA)
Leave The Light On . . . (RCA)
To Get To You-Greatest Hits Collection . . . (BNA)
Trouble In Mind
Bob Wills; *Stay A Little Longer-The Original Columbia Recordings* . . . (Roswell/RCA)
Trouble In Paradise
Bruce Springsteen; *Tracks* . . . (Columbia)
Trust
Megadeth; *Cryptic Writings* . . . (Capitol)
Twisted
Keith Sweat; *Keith Sweat* . . . (Elektra)
Two Faces Have I
Lou Christie; *Back To The '60s-#4-C* . . . (Dominion Entert.)
Enlightnin'ment-Best Of Lou Christie . . . (Rhino)
Two Pina Coladas
Garth Brooks; *Sevens* . . . (Capitol)
Two Story House
George Jones & Tammy Wynette; *George Jones & Tammy Wynette-16 Biggest Hits* . . . (Epic/Legacy)
Tyrone
Erykah Badu; *Erykah Badu-Live* . . . (Kedar Entert./Universal)
U Don't Love Me
Kumbia Kings; *Amor Familia Respeto* . . . (EMI Latin)
Ugly Girl
Fleming & John; *The Way We Are* . . . (Universal)
Un-Break My Heart
Toni Braxton; *Secrets* . . . (LaFace)
Understand Your Man
Johnny Cash; *Billboard Top Country Hits-1964-C* . . . (Rhino)
Johnny Cash's Greatest Hits . . . (Columbia)
The Man In Black-His Greatest Hits . . . (Legacy)
Until You Come Back To Me
Aretha Franklin; *Aretha Franklin-30 Greatest Hits* . . . (Rhino)
Best Of Aretha Franklin . . . (Atlantic)
Golden Age Of Black Music-1970-1975-C . . . (Atlantic)
Basia; *Brave New Hope* . . . (Epic)
London Warsaw New York . . . (Epic)
Hil St. Soul; *Soul Organic* . . . (Dome/Select-O-Hits)
Miki Howard; *Miki Howard* . . . (Atlantic)
Stevie Wonder; *Stevie Wonder-Love Songs-20 Classic Hits* . . . (Motown)
Untouchable Face
Ani DiFranco; *Dilate* . . . (Righteous Babe)
Living In Clip . . . (Righteous Babe)
Victim Of A Broken Heart
Aldo Nova; *Portrait Of Aldo Nova* . . . (Epic)
Subject...Aldo Nova . . . (Portrait)
Wailing Of The Willow
Nilsson; *Aerial Ballet* . . . (RCA)
Walk Away Renee
Four Tops; *Compact Command Performances-Four Tops* . . . (Motown)
Four Tops Reach Out . . . (Motown)
Four Tops-Anthology . . . (Motown)
Left Banke; *Cruisin'-1966-C* . . . (Increase)
History Of The Left Banke . . . (Rhino)
Vonda Shepard; *ST/Songs From "Ally McBeal" Featuring Vonda Shepard* . . . (550/Epic)
Walk Like A Man
4 Seasons; *4 Seasons' Greatest Hits-#1* . . . (Rhino)
4 Seasons-Anthology . . . (Rhino)
Billboard Top Rock 'N' Roll Hits-1963-C . . . (Rhino)
ST/The Wanderers . . . (Warner Bros.)
Walk On By
Dionne Warwick; *Dionne Warwick-Anthology 1962-1971* . . . (Rhino)
Hot! Live & Otherwise . . . (Arista)
I Am Woman-C . . . (Nick At Nite)
Oldies But Goodies-#15-C . . . (Original Sound)
Scepter Records Story-C . . . (Capricorn)
Isaac Hayes; *Isaac Hayes' Greatest Hit Singles* . . . (Stax)
Melissa Manchester; *Romantic Hits Of The '80s-C* . . . (K-Tel)
Tribute . . . (Polydor)
Sybil; *Sybil* . . . (Next Plateau/London/Island)
Walking To New Orleans
Fats Domino; *Fats Domino's All Time Greatest Hits* . . . (Curb)
Fats Domino's Greatest Hits . . . (CEMA Special Prod.)
Fats Domino's Greatest Hits . . . (MCA)
My Blue Heaven-Best Of Fats Domino-#1 . . . (EMI)
They Call Me The Fat Man . . . (EMI)
Wasting My Time
Default; *Fallout* . . . (TVT)
Way We Make A Broken Heart
Rosanne Cash; *30 Years Of #1 Hits-#16-C* . . . (Columbia)

Greatest Country Hits Of The '80s-1987-C (Columbia)
King's Record Shop (Columbia)
Love Gets Strange-Songs Of John Hiatt-C (Rhino)
Rosanne Cash-Hits-1979-1989 (Columbia)
Ry Cooder; *Borderline* (Warner Bros.)
Western Union
Five Americans; *Back To The '60s-Rock 'N' Roll-C* (Dominion Entert.)
Nuggets-#1-The Hits-C (Rhino)
What A Crying Shame
Mavericks; *Best Of The Mavericks-Super Colossal Smash Hits Of The '90s* (Mercury)
What A Crying Shame (MCA)
What I Didn't Know
Athenaeum; *Radiance* (Atlantic)
What I Need To Do
Kenny Chesney; *Everywhere We Go* (BNA)
Kenny Chesney's Greatest Hits (BNA)
What Kind Of Fool Am I
Rick Springfield; *Rick Springfield's Greatest Hits* (RCA)
Success Hasn't Spoiled Me Yet (RCA)
What Mattered Most
Ty Herndon; *Super Hits Of 1995-C* (Epic)
What Mattered Most (Epic)
What Now My Love
Barbra Streisand; *Je m'appelle Barbra* (Columbia)
Elvis Presley; *Alternate Aloha* (RCA)
Frank Sinatra; *That's Life* (Reprise)
Frank Sinatra & Aretha Franklin; *Frank Sinatra-Duets-C* (Capitol)
Herb Alpert & The Tijuana Brass; *Herb Alpert & The Tijuana Brass-Classics-#1* (A&M)
Herb Alpert & The Tijuana Brass-Greatest Hits-#2 (A&M)
Robert Goulet; *Robert Goulet-16 Most Requested Songs* (Columbia)
Temptations; *In A Mellow Mood* (Motown)
Whatever Comes First
Sons Of The Desert; *Whatever Comes First* (Epic)
What's Made Milwaukee Famous (Has Made A Loser Out Of Me)
Jerry Lee Lewis; *Heartbreak* (Tomato)
Milestones (Rhino)
Rod Stewart; *Best Of Rod Stewart* (Mercury)
Storyteller/The Complete Anthology: 1964-1990 (Warner Bros.)
When A Woman's Fed Up
R. Kelly; *Now That's What I Call Music!-#2-C* (Virgin)
R. (Jive)
When I Call Your Name
Vince Gill; *When I Call Your Name* (MCA)
When I Stop Dreaming
Jim & Jesse; *All Time Legends Of Country Music-C* (Legacy)
Bluegrass Super Hits-C (Columbia)
When Two Worlds Collide
Rex Allen, Jr.; *20 Golden Souvenirs Of Music City U.S.A.-C* (Plantation)
Roger Miller; *Best Of Roger Miller-His Greatest Songs* (Curb)
When You Ask About Love
Crickets; *45-#9-55153* (Brunswick)
When You Think Of Me
Eric Benet; *A Day In The Life* (Warner Bros.)
Where Did You Go?
Full Devil Jacket; *Full Devil Jacket* (Island/IDJMG)
Where I Wanna Be
Donell Jones; *Where I Wanna Be* (LaFace)
Where Is The Love
Celine Dion; *Let's Talk About Love-C* (550 Music)
Jesse & Trina; *ST/Dead Presidents* (Capitol)
Roberta Flack; *Softly With These Songs-The Best Of Roberta Flack* (Atlantic)
Roberta Flack & Donny Hathaway; *Roberta Flack & Donny Hathaway* (Atlantic)
Which Side Of The Glass
George Strait; *George Strait* (MCA)
While You Loved Me
Rascal Flatts; *Rascal Flatts* (Lyric Street)
White Sport Coat (And A Pink Carnation)
Marty Robbins; *16 Most Requested Songs Of The '50s-#2-C* (Legacy)
Lifetime Of Song-1951-1982 (Columbia)
Marty Robbins' Greatest Hits (Columbia)
Who Do U Love
Deborah Cox; *Deborah Cox* (Arista)
Ultimate Dance Party-1997-C (Arista)
Who Will Call You Sweetheart
Stanley Brothers & The Clinch Mountain Boys; *Best Of Bluegrass-#1-Standards-C* (Mercury)
Who Will The Next Fool Be
Charlie Rich; *Charlie Rich-The Ultimate Collection* (Hip-O)
Lonely Weekends-The Very Best Of Charlie Rich (Collectables)
Jerry Lee Lewis; *The Mercury & Smash Years Recordings* (Collectables)
Who's Your Baby Now
Mark Knopfler; *Sailing To Philadelphia* (Warner Bros.)
Widow's Walk
Suzanne Vega; *Songs In Red & Gray* (A&M)
Wild Side Of Life
Freddy Fender; *Before The Next Teardrop Falls* (Universal)
Best Of Freddy Fender (MCA)
Hank Thompson; *Best Of The Best Of Hank Thompson* (Gusto)
Capitol Collectors Series-Hank Thompson (Capitol)
Hank Thompson's All-Time Greatest Hits (Curb)
Traditions In Country Music-C (Capitol)
Rod Stewart; *Night On The Town* (Warner Bros.)
Wild World
Cat Stevens; *Cat Stevens Greatest Hits* (A&M)
Tea For The Tillerman (A&M)
Jimmy Cliff; *In Concert-Best Of Jimmy Cliff* (Reprise)
Reggae Spectacular-C (A&M)
Maxi Priest; *Best Of Me* (Charisma)
Maxi (Virgin)
Willow Weep For Me
Art Tatum; *Best Of Art Tatum* (Pablo)
Solo Masterpieces-#1 (Pablo)
Billie Holiday; *Billie Holiday-Live* (Verve)
Billie's Blues (Blue Note)
Lady Sings The Blues (Verve)
Stormy Blues (Verve)
Chad & Jeremy; *Best Of Chad & Jeremy* (Capitol)
History Of British Rock-#3-C (Rhino)
Super Oldies Of The '60s-#11-C (Audio Fidelity)
Dinah Shore; *Dinah Shore-16 Most Requested Songs* (Legacy)
Lou Rawls; *Legendary Lou Rawls* (Blue Note)
Roy Eldridge; *Best Of Roy Eldridge* (Pablo)
Steve Miller; *Born 2 B Blue* (Gold Rush)
Without Her
Nilsson; *Pandemonium Shadow Show* (RCA)
Without You
Dixie Chicks; *Fly* (Monument)
Worried Mind
Roy Acuff; *Night Train To Memphis* (Columbia River Entert. Group)
Worst That Could Happen
Brooklyn Bridge; *Billboard Top Pop Hits-1969-C* (Rhino)
Brooklyn Bridge-Greatest Hits (Collectables)
Yeah, Whatever
Splender; *Halfway Down The Sky* (Columbia)
Yester Love
Smokey Robinson & The Miracles; *Best Of Smokey Robinson & The Miracles-Anthology* (Motown)
Smokey Robinson-The Ultimate Collection (Motown)
Yesterday
Beatles; *"Yesterday"...And Today* (Capitol)
Beatles 1 (Capitol)
Beatles-20 Greatest Hits (Capitol)
Beatles-Box Set (Capitol)
Beatles-Love Songs (Capitol)
Compact Disc Singles Collection (Capitol)
The Beatles/1962-1966 (Capitol)
Elvis Presley; *On Stage-February, 1970* (RCA)
En Vogue; *Funky Divas* (East West)
Frank Sinatra; *My Way* (Reprise)
Paul McCartney; *The Concert For New York City-C* (Columbia)
Placido Domingo; *Domingo Songbook* (Sony Music Classical)
Ray Charles; *Ray Charles-His Greatest Hits-#1* (Dunhill Compact Classics)
Supremes; *I Hear A Symphony* (Motown)
Wings; *Wings Over America* (Capitol)
Yesterday
Shanice; *Shanice* (LaFace)
Yester-Me, Yester-You, Yesterday
Stevie Wonder; *My Cherie Amour* (Motown)
Stevie Wonder's Greatest Hits-#2 (Motown)
You Are My Sunshine
Bing Crosby; *Best Of Bing Crosby* (MCA)
Bing Crosby's Greatest Hits (MCA)
Jimmie Davis; *20 Golden Souvenirs Of Music City U.S.A.-C* (Plantation)
Best Of Jimmie Davis (MCA)
Jimmie Davis-Golden Hits (Plantation)
The Country Music Hall Of Fame-Jimmie Davis (MCA)
Mississippi John Hurt; *Best Of Mississippi John Hurt* (Vanguard)
Mitch Miller; *Mitch Miller-16 Most Requested Songs* (Columbia)
Norman Blake; *ST/O Brother, Where Art Thou?* (Mercury)
Ray Charles; *Ray Charles-Anthology* (Rhino)
Ray Charles-His Greatest Hits-#2 (Dunhill Compact Classics)
Willie Nelson & Leon Russell; *One For The Road* (Columbia)
You Are Not Alone
Michael Jackson; *1996 Grammy Nominees-C* (Columbia)
HIStory: Past, Present And Future-Book 1-C (Epic)
You Bring Me Up
K-Ci & JoJo; *Love Always* (MCA)
You Can Feel Bad
Patty Loveless; *Patty Loveless-Classics* (Epic)
Super Hits Of 1996-C (Epic)
The Trouble With The Truth (Epic)
You Caused It All By Telling Lies
Hank Williams; *Alone With His Guitar* (Mercury)
Complete Hank Williams (Mercury)
You Could Have Been With Me
Sheena Easton; *Sheena Easton's Greatest Hits* (EMI Special Markets)

The World Of Sheena Easton: The Singles Collection-C . . . . (EMI)

You Keep Me Hangin' On
Diana Ross; *Evening With Diana Ross* . . . . (Motown)
Diana Ross & The Supremes; *Diana Ross & The Supremes-Anthology (1962-1969)* . . . . (Motown)
Motown Story-First 25 Years-C . . . . (Motown)
Kim Wilde; *Another Step*. . . . . (MCA)
Reba McEntire; *Starting Over* . . . . (MCA)
Supremes; *Billboard Top R&B Hits-1965-C* . . . . (Rhino)
Diana Ross & The Supremes' Greatest Hits-#2 . . . . (Motown)
Vanilla Fudge; *Best Of Vanilla Fudge*. (Atco)
Vanilla Fudge . . . . (Atco)
Wilson Pickett; *A Man & A Half-Best Of Wilson Pickett*. . . . . . (Rhino)
Wilson Pickett's Greatest Hits . . . . (Atlantic)

You Make Me Feel Bad
Wood; *Songs From Stamford Hill* . . . . (Columbia)

You Make Me Wanna…
Usher; *My Way* . . . . (LaFace)
Totally Hits-#1-C . . . . (Arista)

You Oughta Know
Alanis Morissette; *1996 Grammy Nominees-C* . . . . (Columbia)
Jagged Little Pill. . . . . (Maverick)

You Said The Words
Wood; *Songs From Stamford Hill* . . . . (Columbia)

You Should've Told Me
Kelly Price; *Mirror Mirror* . . . . (Def Soul/IDJMG)

You Turned The Tables On Me
Anita O'Day; *Anita Sings The Most*. (Verve)
Benny Goodman; *Benny Goodman's Greatest Hits* . . . . (RCA Victor)
Birth Of Swing . . . . (Bluebird)
Billie Holiday; *Solitude* . . . . (Verve)
Louis Armstrong; *Compact Jazz-Louis Armstrong* . . . . (Verve)

You Wanted More
Tonic; *ST/American Pie*. . . . . (Universal)
Sugar . . . . (Universal)

You Were Meant For Me
Jewel; *Pieces Of You* . . . . (Atlantic)

You Were Mine
Dixie Chicks; *Big Country Hits '99-C* . . . . (K-Tel)
Wide Open Spaces . . . . (Monument)

You Were Mine
Fireflies; *Oldies But Goodies-#6-C* . . . . (Original Sound)

You Were On My Mind
We Five; *Baby Boomer Classics-Folk Sixties-C* . . . . . .(JCI Assoc. Labels)
Billboard Top Pop Hits-1965-C . . . . (Rhino)

You Win Again
Hank Williams With His Drifting Cowboys; *24 Of Hank Williams' Greatest Hits* . . . . (Polydor)
Hank Williams-40 Greatest Hits. . . . . (Polydor)
Jerry Lee Lewis; *Heartbreak* . . . . (Tomato)
Memphis Country-C . . . . (Sun)
Rockin' My Life Away . . . . (Tomato)
Taste Of Country. . . . . (Sun)
The Golden Hits Of Jerry Lee Lewis . . . . (Smash)
Johnny Cash; *Johnny Cash-Original Golden Hits-#3* . . . . (Sun)
Keith Richards; *Timeless: Hank Williams Tribute-C*. . . . (Lost Highway/IDJMG)
Keith Whitley; *Kentucky Bluebird*. . . . .(RCA)
Mary Chapin Carpenter; *Greatest Country Hits Of The '90s-#2-C* . . . (Columbia)
Tommy Edwards; *It's All In The Game-The Complete Hits Of Tommy Edwards*. . . . . (Eric)

You Won't See Me
Anne Murray; *Anne Murray's Greatest Hits* . . . . (Capitol)
Love Song . . . . (Capitol)
Beatles; *Beatles-Box Set*. . . . . (Capitol)
Rubber Soul . . . . (Capitol)
Bryan Ferry; *These Foolish Things* . . . . (Reprise)

You Wouldn't Believe
311; *From Chaos*. . . . . (Volcano Entertainment)

Your Cheatin' Heart
Beck; *Timeless: Hank Williams Tribute-C* . . . . . . (Lost Highway/IDJMG)
Elvis Presley; *Elvis For Everyone!* . . . .(RCA)
Welcome To My World . . . .(RCA)
Frankie Laine; *Frankie Laine's 16 Greatest Hits* . . . . (Trip)
Frankie Laine's Greatest Hits . . . . (Columbia)
Hank Williams With His Drifting Cowboys; *24 Of Hank Williams' Greatest Hits* . . . . (Polydor)
Hank Williams-16 Great Hits . . . . (Everest)
Hank Williams-40 Greatest Hits. . . . . (Polydor)
Hank Williams, Jr.; *Very Best Of Hank Williams, Jr.* . . . . (Polydor)
Jerry Lee Lewis; *Live At The Star Club-Hamburg 1964* . . . . . . (Rhino)
The Golden Hits Of Jerry Lee Lewis . . . . (Smash)
Patsy Cline; *ST/Sweet Dreams*. . . . . (MCA)
The Patsy Cline Story . . . . (MCA)
Ray Charles; *Ray Charles' Greatest Hits-#2* . . . . (Rhino)

Your Selfish Heart
Stanley Brothers & The Clinch Mountain Boys; *Stanley Brothers & The Clinch Mountain Boys* . . . . (King)

You're A Big Girl Now
Bob Dylan; *Blood On The Tracks* . . . . (Columbia)

You're Gone
Diamond Rio; *Unbelievable*. . . . . (Arista)

You've Got To Hide Your Love Away
Beatles; *Beatles-Box Set*. . . . . (Capitol)
Beatles-Love Songs . . . . (Capitol)
Reel Music. . . . . (Capitol)
ST/Help! . . . . (Capitol)
The Beatles/1962-1966 . . . . (Capitol)

LOVE: SEARCHING FOR LOVE, Needing Love

See Also: **DESIRE, FINDING, LONELY, LOVE (various), SEARCH**

5 Miles To Empty
Brownstone; *Still Climbing* . . . . (MJJ Music/Work)

A World Without Love
Peter And Gordon; *Billboard Top Pop Hits-1964-C* . . . .(Rhino)

Aberdeen
Kenny Wayne Shepherd; *Ledbetter Heights* . . . . (Giant)

Again
Lenny Kravitz; *Lenny Kravitz's Greatest Hits* . . . . (Virgin)
Now That's What I Call Music!-#6-C . . . . (Virgin)

All At Once You Love Her
Perry Como; *Perry Como's Greatest Hits* . . . . (RCA)

All By Myself
Celine Dion; *Falling Into You* . . . . (550 Music)
Eric Carmen; *Best Of Eric Carmen* . . . . (Arista)
Billboard Top Rock 'N' Roll Hits-1976-C . . . . (Rhino)

All I Really Want
Alanis Morissette; *Jagged Little Pill* . . . . (Maverick)

All My Friends
Counting Crows; *This Desert Life* . . . . (David Geffen Co.)

All My Love
Patti Page; *Patti Page Collection-The Mercury Years-#1* . . . .(Mercury)

All That She Wants
Ace Of Base; *All That She Wants* . . . . (Arista)

All The Good Ones Are Gone
Pam Tillis; *Pam Tillis' Greatest Hits* . . . . (Arista)

Alone
Bee Gees; *Still Waters* . . . . (Polydor)

Angels Listened In
Crests; *Crests Greatest Hits* . . . . (Collectables)
Super Oldies Of The '50s-#3-C . . . . (Audio Fidelity)
WCBS FM 101 History Of Rock-'50s-#2-C. . . . . (Collectables)

Annie Waits
Ben Folds; *Rockin' The Suburbs* . . . . (Epic)

Another Saturday Night
Cat Stevens; *Cat Stevens Greatest Hits* . . . . (A&M)
Jimmy Buffett; *Margaritaville Cafe Late Night Menu* . . (Margaritaville)
Sam Cooke; *The Man And His Music* . . . . (RCA)
This Is Sam Cooke . . . . (RCA)

Another Way
Tevin Campbell; *Tevin Campbell*. . . . . (Qwest)

Are We In Trouble Now
Mark Knopfler; *Golden Heart* . . . . (Warner Bros.)

Around The World
Bing Crosby; *Heart Beats-Closer Than A Kiss-Crooner Classics-C* . . . . .(Rhino)
Frank Sinatra; *Come Fly With Me* . . . . (Capitol)
McGuire Sisters; *McGuire Sisters-Anthology* . . . . (MCA)

Around The World In Eighty Days
Boston Pops Orchestra/Arthur Fiedler; *Greatest Hits Of The '50s-#2* . . . . (RCA)
Frank Sinatra; *Come Fly With Me* . . . . (Capitol)
Roger Williams; *Roger Williams' Greatest Hits* . . . . (MCA)
Victor Young & His Singing Strings; *Hollywood's Greatest Hits-#2* . . . (Telarc)

At Seventeen
Janis Ian; *Between The Lines* . . . . (Columbia)
Super Hits Of The '70s-Have A Nice Day-#15-C . . . . (Rhino)

Baubles, Bangles And Beads
Frank Sinatra & Antonio Carlos Jobim; *Francis Albert Sinatra & Antonio Carlos Jobim* . . . . (Reprise)
Marlene Dietrich; *Marlene Dietrich-Live* . . . . (Columbia)
Original Cast; *Kismet* . . . . (Columbia)
Peggy Lee; *Best Of Peggy Lee* . . . . (MCA)
Percy Faith & His Orchestra; *Percy Faith & His Orchestra's All-Time Greatest Hits* . . . . (Columbia)

Be Happy
Mary J. Blige; *My Life* . . . . (Uptown/MCA)

Bernadette
Four Tops; *Compact Command Performances-Four Tops* . . . . . . (Motown)
Four Tops' Greatest Hits . . . . (Motown)
Four Tops Reach Out . . . . (Motown)
Four Tops-Anthology . . . . (Motown)
Motown Superstar Series-#14-Four Tops . . . . (Motown)

Betcha By Golly, Wow
"AFKAP"; *Emancipation*. . . . .(NPG)
Johnny Mathis; *First Time Ever I Saw Your Face* . . . . (Columbia)

Stylistics; *Best Of The Stylistics* . . . . (Amherst)
Blue Moon
  Billie Holiday; *Billie's Blues* . . . . (Blue Note)
    First Verve Sessions . . . . (Verve)
    History Of Billie Holiday . . . . (Verve)
  Elvis Presley; *Elvis Presley* . . . . (RCA)
    The Sun Sessions . . . . (RCA)
  Marcels; *Best Of The Marcels* . . . . (Rhino)
    Billboard Top Rock 'N' Roll Hits-1961-C . . . . (Rhino)
Born To Fly
  Sara Evans; *Born To Fly* . . . . (RCA)
Boy Wanted
  Original Cast; *My One And Only* . . . . (Atlantic)
Brand New Key
  Deana Carter; *Everything's Gonna Be Alright* . . . . (Capitol)
  Melanie; *Best Of Melanie* . . . . (Rhino)
    Super Hits Of The '70s-Have A Nice Day-#7-C . . . . (Rhino)
Bring On The Night
  Bruce Springsteen; *Tracks* . . . . (Columbia)
Brown Eyed Handsome Man
  Buddy Holly; *Buddy Holly-20 Golden Greats* . . . . (MCA)
    For The First Time Anywhere . . . . (MCA)
    Rock & Roll Collection . . . . (MCA)
  Chuck Berry; *Best Of The Best Of Chuck Berry* . . . . (International Mktg. Group)
    Roll Over Beethoven . . . . (Allegiance)
    The Chess Box-Chuck Berry . . . . (Chess)
  Waylon Jennings; *Essential Waylon Jennings* . . . . (RCA)
    Waylon Jennings-Super Hits . . . . (RCA)
But Not For Me
  Billie Holiday; *Silver Collection* . . . . (Verve)
  Chet Baker; *Let's Get Lost-Best Of Chet Baker Sings* . . . . . . (Blue Note)
  Ella Fitzgerald; *Ella Sings Jazz* . . . . (MCA Jazz)
  Elvis Costello; *Glory Of Gershwin Featuring Larry Adler-C* . . . (Mercury)
  Harry Connick, Jr.; *ST/When Harry Met Sally* . . . . (Columbia)
  Judy Garland; *Best Of Judy Garland* . . . . (MCA)
  Original London Cast; *Crazy For You* . . . . (RCA)
  Original Soundtrack; *Manhattan* . . . . (CBS Masterworks)
  Sarah Vaughan; *Sarah Vaughan Sings George Gershwin Songbook,*
    Vol. 2 . . . . (Emarcy)
Changing Partners
  Bing Crosby; *Bing Crosby* . . . . (MCA Special Prod.)
  Kay Starr; *Capitol Collectors Series-Kay Starr* . . . . (Capitol)
  Patti Page; *Patti Page-Golden Hits* . . . . (Mercury)
Chante's Got A Man
  Chante Moore; *Now That's What I Call Music!-#3-C* . . . . . . (Virgin)
    This Moment Is Mine . . . . (Silas)
Cheerful Little Earful
  Ella Fitzgerald; *Swings Brightly With Nelson* . . . . (Verve)
Chemistry
  Semisonic; *All About Chemistry* . . . . (MCA)
Cherchez La Femme
  Dr. Buzzard's Original "Savannah" Band; *Nipper's Greatest Hits Of The*
    '70s-C . . . . (RCA)
  Gloria Estefan; *Hold Me, Thrill Me, Kiss Me* . . . . (Epic)
Climb That Hill
  Tom Petty And The Heartbreakers; *ST/She's The One* . . . . (Warner Bros.)
Closing Time
  Semisonic; *Feeling Strangely Fine* . . . . (MCA)
    Now That's What I Call Music!-#2-C . . . . (Virgin)
Commitment
  LeAnn Rimes; *Big Country Hits '99-C* . . . . (K-Tel)
    Sittin' On Top Of The World . . . . (Curb)
Cover Me
  Bruce Springsteen; *Born In The U.S.A.* . . . . (Columbia)
    Music For The Miracle-C . . . . (Epic Portrait Assoc.)
  Bruce Springsteen & The E Street Band; *Bruce Springsteen & The E Street*
    Band Live/1975-85 . . . . (Legacy)
Deep Inside
  Mary J. Blige; *Mary* . . . . (MCA)
Dixie Road
  Lee Greenwood; *Country Classics-#3-1984-1985-C* . . . . . . (Universal)
    Lee Greenwood's Greatest Hits . . . . (MCA)
    MCA #1 Hits Of The '80s-#2-C . . . . (MCA Special Prod.)
Do Ya Think I'm Sexy?
  Rod Stewart; *Absolutely Live* . . . . (Warner Bros.)
    Blondes Have More Fun . . . . (Warner Bros.)
    Rod Stewart's Greatest Hits . . . . (Warner Bros.)
Down
  Stone Temple Pilots; *No. 4* . . . . (Atlantic)
Dreamin'
  Johnny Burnette; *Best Of Johnny Burnette-You're Sixteen* . . (Gold Rush)
    Rock Is Dead But It Won't Lie Down-C . . . . (Gold Rush)
Dreamlover
  Mariah Carey; *Music Box* . . . . (Columbia)
Everybody Needs Somebody To Love
  Blues Brothers; *Best Of The Blues Brothers* . . . . (Atlantic)
Everyday
  Buddy Holly; *Buddy Holly* . . . . (MCA)
    Buddy Holly-20 Golden Greats . . . . (MCA)

    Buddy Holly's Greatest Hits . . . . (MCA)
    From The Original Master Tapes-Buddy Holly . . . . (MCA)
    Legend-From The Original Master Tapes . . . . (MCA)
    The Buddy Holly Collection . . . . (MCA)
Fall From Grace
  Amanda Marshall; *Amanda Marshall* . . . . (Epic)
Feels Like Home
  Bonnie Raitt; *ST/Michael* . . . . (Revolution)
  Chantal Kreviazuk; *Songs From Dawson's Creek* . . . . . (Sony Music Soundtrax)
  Linda Ronstadt; *Feels Like Home* . . . . (Elektra)
  Randy Newman; *Guilty: 30 Years Of Randy Newman* . . . . . . (Rhino)
    Randy Newman's Faust . . . . (Reprise)
For A Change
  Neal McCoy; *You Gotta Love That!* . . . . (Atlantic)
For Emily, Wherever I May Find Her
  Simon & Garfunkel; *Collected Works* . . . . (Columbia)
    Parsley Sage Rosemary & Thyme . . . . (Columbia)
    Simon & Garfunkel's Greatest Hits . . . . (Columbia)
Girls In Love
  Gary Lewis And The Playboys; *Gary Lewis And The Playboys-Legendary*
    Masters Series . . . . (EMI)
Good Girls
  Joe; *All That I Am* . . . . (Jive)
Good Luck Charm
  Elvis Presley; *Elvis' Golden Records, Volume 3* . . . . (RCA)
    Number One Hits . . . . (RCA)
    The Top Ten Hits . . . . (RCA)
    Worldwide 50 Gold Award Hits, Vol. 1, Parts 1 & 2 . . . . . (RCA)
Good Man Is Hard To Find (Pittsburgh)
  Bruce Springsteen; *Tracks* . . . . (Columbia)
Goodbye To Love
  Carpenters; *Carpenters-Classics-#2* . . . . (A&M)
    Carpenters-Love Songs . . . . (A&M)
Goodnight My Someone
  Shirley Jones; *ST/The Music Man* . . . . (Warner Bros.)
Got Me Wrong
  Alice In Chains; *Alice In Chains-MTV Unplugged* . . . . (Columbia)
    ST/Clerks . . . . (Chaos)
Happy
  Rolling Stones; *Exile On Main Street* . . . . (Virgin)
    Love You Live . . . . (Virgin)
    Made In The Shade . . . . (Rolling Stones)
Heart Is A Lonely Hunter
  Reba McEntire; *Read My Mind* . . . . (MCA)
    Reba McEntire's Greatest Hits-#3: I'm A Survivor . . . . (MCA)
Heart Of Gold
  Neil Young; *Decade* . . . . (Reprise)
    Harvest . . . . (Reprise)
Heart Of Innocence
  Jessica Simpson; *Sweet Kisses* . . . . (Columbia)
Heaven Help My Heart
  Tina Arena; *Don't Ask* . . . . (Epic)
  Wynonna; *Revelations* . . . . (Curb/MCA)
    Wynonna-Collection . . . . (Curb)
Help!
  Beatles; *Beatles 1* . . . . (Capitol)
    Beatles-20 Greatest Hits . . . . (Capitol)
    Rarities . . . . (Capitol)
    Reel Music . . . . (Capitol)
    ST/Help! . . . . (Capitol)
    The Beatles At The Hollywood Bowl . . . . (Capitol)
    The Beatles/1962-1966 . . . . (Capitol)
He's A Heartache (Looking For A Place To Happen)
  Janie Fricke; *19 Hot Country Requests-C* . . . . (Epic)
    It Ain't Easy . . . . (Columbia)
    Janie Fricke-17 Greatest Hits . . . . (Columbia)
    Very Best Of Janie Fricke . . . . (Columbia)
Higher Love
  Steve Winwood; *Back In The High Life* . . . . (Island)
    Steve Winwood-Chronicles . . . . (Island)
Hi-Lili, Hi-Lo
  Anne Murray; *There's A Hippo In My Tub* . . . . (Capitol)
  Ray Conniff; *Encore! 16 Most Requested Songs* . . . . (Legacy)
Holding On
  Steve Winwood; *Roll With It* . . . . (Virgin)
Holding Out For A Hero
  Bonnie Tyler; *ST/Footloose* . . . . (Columbia)
How I Got To Memphis
  Bobby Bare; *This Is Bare Country* . . . . (Mercury)
  Otis Williams & The Midnight Cowboys; *From Where I Stand: The Black*
    Experience In Country Music-C . . . . (Warner Bros.)
Human Touch
  Bruce Springsteen; *Bruce Springsteen's Greatest Hits* . . . . (Columbia)
    Human Touch . . . . (Columbia)
I Am Not Hiding
  Kenny Loggins; *The Unimaginable Life* . . . . (Columbia)
I Am That Man
  Brooks & Dunn; *Borderline* . . . . (Arista)

I Finally Found Someone
Barbra Streisand & Bryan Adams; *ST/The Mirror Has Two Faces* . . . (Columbia)
I Knew I Loved You
Savage Garden; *Affirmation*. . . . . (Columbia)
   Now That's What I Call Music!-#4-C . . . .(Virgin)
I Need A Man To Love
Big Brother & The Holding Company; *Cheap Thrills* . . . . (Columbia)
I Wanna Be A Cowboy's Sweetheart
Patsy Montana & The Prairie Ramblers; *All Time Legends Of Country
   Music-C* . . . . (Legacy)
   Respect: A History Of Women In Music-C . . . . (Rhino)
I Wanna Dance With Somebody (Who Loves Me)
Whitney Houston; *Whitney* . . . . (Arista)
   Whitney Houston's Greatest Hits . . . . (Arista)
I Wanna Fall In Love
Lila McCann; *Lila* . . . . (Asylum)
I Want A Girl (Just Like The Girl)
Al Jolson; *The Al Jolson Story-#1* . . . . (MCA)
Spike Jones & His City Slickers; *King Of Corn* . . . . (Glendale)
I Want To Be In Love
Melissa Etheridge; *Skin* . . . . (Island/IDJMG)
I Will
Beatles; *The Beatles (White Album)* . . . . (Capitol)
   The Beatles-Anthology-#3 . . . . (Capitol)
Ben Taylor; *ST/Bye Bye, Love* . . . . (Giant)
Dean Martin; *Dean Martin's Greatest Hits* . . . . (EMI)
I Wish
Skee-Lo; *I Wish* . . . . (Sunshine/Scotti Bros.)
Stevie Wonder; *Original Musiquarium* . . . . (Motown)
   Songs In The Key Of Life . . . . (Motown)
If I Only Had A Heart
Jack Haley; *ST/The Wizard Of Oz* . . . . (Sony Music Special Prod.)
Original Soundtrack; *The Wizard Of Oz-The Deluxe Edition* . . . . (Rhino)
   The Wizard Of Oz-The Story And Songs . . . . (Rhino)
I'll Know
Original Cast; *ST/Guys & Dolls* . . . . (MCA)
I'll Never Find Another You
Seekers; *Best Of The Seekers* . . . . (Capitol)
   History Of British Rock-#3-C . . . . (Rhino)
Sonny James; *All-Time Country Classics-#2-C* . . . . (Capitol)
   Opry Legends-Sonny James . . . . (Capitol)
I'll Trade (A Million Bucks)
Keith Sweat featuring Lil' Mo; *Didn't See Me Coming* . . . . (Elektra)
I'm That Kind Of Girl
Patty Loveless; *On Down The Line* . . . . (MCA)
   Patty Loveless' Greatest Hits . . . . (MCA)
In And Out Of Love
Diana Ross; *Diana Ross-Anthology*. . . . . (Motown)
In Between Dances
Pam Tillis; *Pam Tillis' Greatest Hits* . . . . (Arista)
   Sweetheart's Dance . . . . (Arista)
In My Life
Patti Austin; *Love Is Gonna Getcha* . . . . (GRP)
I've Been Lonely Too Long
Rascals; *Rascals-Anthology 1965-1972* . . . . (Rhino)
   Very Best Of The Rascals . . . . (Rhino)
I've Got A Feeling
Beatles; *Let It Be* . . . . (Capitol)
   The Beatles-Anthology-#3 . . . . (Capitol)
Jesus To A Child
George Michael; *Ladies & Gentlemen: The Best Of George Michael* . . . . . (Epic)
   Older . . . . (DreamWorks/SKG)
Kansas City
Beatles; *Beatles VI*. . . . . (Capitol)
   Beatles-Box Set. . . . . (Capitol)
   Rock 'N' Roll Music . . . . (Capitol)
   Super Oldies Of The '60s-#10-C . . . . (Audio Fidelity)
Bill Haley & His Comets; *Bill Haley & His Comets' Greatest Hits*. . . . . (Everest)
Fats Domino; *Fats Domino's Greatest Hits*. . . . . (Everest)
Wilbert Harrison; *American Graffiti-#3-C* . . . . (MCA)
   Billboard Top Rock 'N' Roll Hits-1959-C . . . . (Rhino)
   Cruisin'-1959-C . . . . (Increase)
   Echoes Of A Rock Era-Middle Years-C . . . . (Roulette)
   Super Oldies Of The '50s-#2-C. . . . . (Audio Fidelity)
Keep Me From The Cold
Curtis Stigers; *Time Was* . . . . (Arista)
Last Chance Texaco
Rickie Lee Jones; *Naked Songs Live And Acoustic* . . . . (Reprise)
   Rickie Lee Jones . . . . (Warner Bros.)
Last Kiss
J. Frank Wilson and The Cavaliers; *Billboard Top Rock 'N' Roll Hits-
   1964-C* . . . . (Rhino)
   Collectables Presents The History Of Rock-#2-C . . . . (Collectables)
   Oldies But Goodies-#9-C . . . . (Original Sound)
   Teenage Tragedies-C . . . . (Rhino)
Pearl Jam; *No Boundaries-Benefit For The Kosovar Refugees-C* . . . . . . (Epic)
Lead On
George Strait; *Latest Greatest Straitest Hits* . . . . (MCA)
   Lead On . . . . (MCA)

Life On A Chain
Pete Yorn; *Musicforthemorningafter* . . . . (Columbia)
Like There Ain't No Yesterday
BlackHawk; *Strong Enough*. . . . . (Arista)
   The Hits-Love & Gravity . . . . (Arista)
Little Star
Elegants; *Billboard Top Rock 'N' Roll Hits-1958-C* . . . . (Rhino)
   Oldies But Goodies-#5-C . . . . (Original Sound)
   Super Oldies Of The '50s-#7-C . . . . (Audio Fidelity)
Loneliness Of Evening
Stuart Damon; *Cinderella-The CBS Television Network
   Production* . . . . (Columbia)
Long Ago And Far Away
Erroll Garner; *Long Ago And Far Away* . . . . (Columbia)
Glenn Miller; *Glenn Miller-A Legendary Performer-#1 & 2* . . . .(Bluebird)
Helen Forrest & Dick Haymes; *American Songbook Series-
   Jerome Kern* . . . . (Smithsonian Collection)
Jo Stafford; *Capitol Collectors Series-Jo Stafford* . . . . (Capitol)
   International Hits . . . . (Corinthian)
   Jukebox Saturday Night-Great Vocal Hits-C . . . . (Capitol)
   Songs That Got Us Through WWII-C . . . . (Rhino)
   ST/Bugsy . . . . (Epic)
Johnny Mathis; *Hollywood Musicals* . . . . (Columbia)
Mantovani; *More Golden Hits* . . . . (London)
Perry Como; *Always In My Heart-Classic Songs Of World War II-#2* . . . . (RCA)
Rosemary Clooney; *Rosemary Clooney Sings The Lyrics Of Ira
   Gershwin* . . . . (Concord Jazz)
Lookin' For Love
Babys; *Babys* . . . . (Chrysalis)
Johnny Lee; *Country Love Songs-C* . . . . (Warner Bros.)
   Johnny Lee's Greatest Hits . . . . (Full Moon/Asylum)
   ST/Urban Cowboy . . . . (Asylum)
Looking For A New Love
Jody Watley; *Do You Wanna Dance With Me?* . . . . (MCA)
   Jody Watley . . . . (MCA)
Love (Can Make You Happy)
Mercy; *Super Oldies Of The '60s-#10-C* . . . . (Audio Fidelity)
   WCBS FM 101 History Of Rock-'60s-#2-C . . . . (Collectables)
Love Don't Love Me
Eric Benet; *ST/The Brothers* . . . . (Warner Bros.)
Love I Found In You
Jim Brickman; *My Romance: An Evening With Jim Brickman* . . . (Windham Hill)
Love Is On The Way
Celine Dion; *Let's Talk About Love-C* . . . . (550 Music)
Dave Koz; *Dance* . . . . (Capitol)
Love Will Find Its Way To You
Reba McEntire; *Last One To Know* . . . . (MCA)
   Reba McEntire's Greatest Hits Volume Two. . . . . (MCA)
Lucky Me
Anne Murray; *Anne Murray-Country Hits*. . . . . (Capitol)
   Somebody's Waiting . . . . (Capitol)
Mama Said
Shirelles; *Original Rock 'N' Roll Hits Of The '60s-C*. . . . . (Roulette)
   Shirelles' Greatest Hits . . . . (Everest)
   Shirelles-Anthology 1959-1964. . . . . (Rhino)
   Shirelles-Classics . . . . (Bac-Trac)
   Super Oldies Of The '60s-#3-C . . . . (Audio Fidelity)
Man I Love
Benny Goodman; *Carnegie Hall Jazz Concert* . . . . (Columbia)
Betty Carter; *'S Wonderful-Gershwin Songbook* . . . . (Verve)
Billie Holiday; *I Like Jazz-Essence Of Billie Holiday* . . . . (Columbia)
Carmen McRae; *Blue Series-Female Vocals-C* . . . . (Blue Note)
Diana Ross; *ST/Lady Sings The Blues* . . . . (Motown)
Ella Fitzgerald; *Mack The Knife-Ella Fitzgerald In Berlin* . . . . (Verve)
Harry James; *Hollywood Magic-1950s-C* . . . . (Columbia)
Kate Bush; *Glory Of Gershwin Featuring Larry Adler-C* . . . . (Mercury)
Mary Lou Williams; *Best Of Mary Lou Williams* . . . . (Pablo)
Matrimony: Maybe You
Maxwell; *Embrya*. . . . . (Columbia)
Mister Sandman
Chordettes; *Best Of The Chordettes* . . . . (Rhino)
Emmylou Harris; *Evangeline* . . . . (Warner Bros.)
   Profile II-The Best Of Emmylou Harris . . . . (Warner Bros.)
Moonlight Gambler
Frankie Laine; *Frankie Laine-16 Most Requested Songs* . . . . (Legacy)
   Frankie Laine's Greatest Hits . . . . (Columbia)
Morning Side Of The Mountain, The
Tommy Edwards; *It's All In The Game-The Complete Hits Of Tommy
   Edwards* . . . . (Eric)
Most Girls
Pink; *Can't Take Me Home* . . . . (LaFace)
   Totally Hits-#3-C . . . . (Atlantic)
Mr. Jones
Counting Crows; *August And Everything After* . . . . (David Geffen Co.)
My Beloved
Pamela Rose; *Morpheus*. . . . . (Grace)
My Love Will Not Let You Down
Bruce Springsteen; *Tracks* . . . . (Columbia)

Night
Bruce Springsteen; *Born To Run*. . . . . (Columbia)
Nobody Wants To Be Lonely
Ricky Martin; *Sound Loaded* . . . . (Columbia)
Nobody's Supposed To Be Here
Deborah Cox; *One Wish* . . . . (Arista)
Totally Hits-#1-C. . . . . (Arista)
Oh Marie
Sheryl Crow; *Sheryl Crow* . . . . (A&M)
One Belief Away
Bonnie Raitt; *Fundamental*. . . . . (Capitol)
One Big Love
Emmylou Harris; *Red Dirt Girl* . . . . (Nonesuch)
Patty Griffin; *Flaming Red* . . . . (A&M)
One Honest Heart
Reba McEntire; *If You See Him* . . . .(MCA)
Reba McEntire's Greatest Hits-#3: I'm A Survivor. . . . . (MCA)
Orchids Mean Goodbye
Carl Smith; *45-#21087* . . . . (Columbia)
Pass You By
Boyz II Men; *Nathan Michael Shawn Wanya*. . . . . (Universal)
Please Remember Me
Tim McGraw; *A Place In The Sun* . . . . (Curb)
Tim McGraw's Greatest Hits. . . . . (Curb)
Pretend
Nat "King" Cole; *Capitol Collectors Series-Nat "King" Cole* . . . . . (Capitol)
The Nat "King" Cole Story. . . . . (Capitol)
Unforgettable. . . . . (Capitol)
Private Conversation
Lyle Lovett; *The Road To Ensenada*. . . . .(MCA)
Question
Moody Blues; *A Night At Red Rocks With The Colorado Symphony Orchestra* . . . . (Polydor)
A Question Of Balance. . . . . (Polydor)
This Is The Moody Blues. . . . . (Polydor)
Ready For A Fall
P.J. Olsson; *Songs From Dawson's Creek* . . . . (Sony Music Soundtrax)
Real Love
Beatles; *The Beatles-Anthology-#2*. (Capitol)
John Lennon; *ST/Imagine: John Lennon* . . . . (Capitol)
Ricky Wants A Man Of Her Own
Bruce Springsteen; *Tracks*. . . . . (Columbia)
Running Out Of Reasons To Run
Rick Trevino; *Learning As You Go* . . . . (Columbia)
Sawyer Brown; *Wide Open*. . . . . (Curb)
Safe In The Arms Of Love
Martina McBride; *ST/Switchback*. (RCA)
Wild Angels . . . . (RCA)
Searchin'
Coasters; *50 Coastin' Classics-C* . . . . (Rhino)
All-Star Chartbusters. . . . . (Intermedia)
Coasters' Greatest Hits. . . . . (Atco)
Golden Years-1957-C . . . . (Dominion Entert.)
Oldies But Goodies-#8-C. (Original Sound)
The Ultimate Coasters. . . . . (Warner Special Prod.)
Very Best Of The Coasters . . . . (Rhino)
Spencer Davis Group; *Best Of The Spencer Davis Group* . . . .(EMI)
Best Of The Spencer Davis Group . . . . (Rhino)
Searchin'
Beatles; *The Beatles-Anthology-#1*. . . . . (Capitol)
Searchin' My Soul
Vonda Shepard; *ST/Songs From "Ally McBeal" Featuring Vonda Shepard*. . . . . (550/Epic)
The Radical Light. . . . . (Vesperally)
Searching For Love
Bobby Porter; *Capricorn Records Presents-Fire/Fury Story-C* . . . . (Capricorn)
She's More
Andy Griggs; *You Won't Ever Be Lonely* . . . . (RCA)
Shop Around
Captain & Tennille; *Captain & Tennille's Greatest Hits* . . . . (A&M)
Miracles; *Greatest Hits From The Beginning* . . . . (Motown)
Hi-We're The Miracles . . . . (Motown)
Smokey Robinson & The Miracles; *16 #1 Hits From The Early '60s-C* . . . . (Motown)
Every Great Motown Song-First 25 Years-C. . . . . (Motown)
Smokey Robinson & The Miracles' Anthology. . . . . (Motown)
Short Skirt/Long Jacket
Cake; *Comfort Eagle* . . . . (Columbia)
Shy Guy
Diana King; *ST/Bad Boys* . . . .(Work)
Tougher Than Love . . . .(Work)
Simple Twist Of Fate
Bob Dylan; *Blood On The Tracks* . . . . (Columbia)
Bob Dylan At Budokan. . . . . (Columbia)
Jerry Garcia Band; *Jerry Garcia Band* . . . . (Arista)
Joan Baez; *Best Of Joan Baez* . . . . (A&M)
Diamonds & Rust. . . . . (A&M)
Single Girl
Sandy Posey; *Greatest Hits Of 1966-C*. . . . . (Deluxe)

Single White Female
Chely Wright; *Single White Female* . . . . (MCA)
So How Come (No One Loves Me)
Everly Brothers; *Heartaches 'N' Harmonies*. . . . . (Rhino)
Soft Place To Fall
Allison Moorer; *Alabama Song*. . . . . (MCA)
ST/The Horse Whisperer . . . . (MCA)
Some Enchanted Evening
Jay & The Americans; *Come A Little Bit Closer-Best Of Jay & The Americans* . . . . (Gold Rush)
Jay & The Americans' All-Time Greatest Hits . . . . (Rhino)
Original Cast; *South Pacific* . . . . (CBS Masterworks)
Perry Como; *Perry Como's All-Time Greatest Hits-#1*. . . . . (RCA)
Rosanno Brazzi; *ST/South Pacific*. (RCA)
Willie Nelson; *What A Wonderful World* . . . . (Columbia)
Somebody Somewhere
Original Broadway Cast; *The Most Happy Fella*. . . . . . (Sony Music Classical)
Somebody To Love
Jefferson Airplane; *2400 Fulton Street-An Anthology*. . . . . (RCA)
Loves You . . . . (RCA)
Nipper's Greatest Hits Of The '60s-#1-C. . . . . (RCA)
Surrealistic Pillow . . . . (RCA)
The Worst Of Jefferson Airplane . . . . (RCA)
Somebody's Somebody
"AFKAP"; *Emancipation* . . . . (NPG)
Somebody's Somebody
Christina Aguilera; *Christina Aguilera*. . . . . (RCA)
Someday My Prince Will Come
Bill Evans Trio; *Portrait In Jazz* . . . . (Riverside)
En Vogue; *Simply Mad About The Mouse-C*. . . . . (Columbia)
Lena Horne; *A New Album* . . . . (RCA)
Lena Horne & Phil Woods; *I Have Dreamed* . . . . (Novus)
Miles Davis; *I Like Jazz-Essence Of Miles Davis* . . . . (Columbia)
Miles Davis' Greatest Hits . . . . (Columbia)
Someday My Prince Will Come . . . . (Columbia)
Mormon Tabernacle Choir & Columbia Symphony Orchestra; *When You Wish Upon A Star-A Tribute To Walt Disney*. . . . . (CBS Masterworks)
Someone Else's Star
Bryan White; *Bryan White* . . . .(Asylum)
Real Luv: Ultimate Country Love Songs-C. . . . . (EMI)
Someone Is Looking For Someone Like You
Gail Davies; *Best Of Gail Davies* . . . . (Lifesong)
Someone To Call My Lover
Janet; *All For You* . . . .(Virgin)
Now That's What I Call Music!-#8-C. . . . .(Virgin)
Someone To Watch Over Me
Ella Fitzgerald; *Ella Fitzgerald Sings The George & Ira Gershwin Songbook*. . . . . (Verve)
Elton John; *Glory Of Gershwin Featuring Larry Adler-C*. . . . . . . (Mercury)
Frank Sinatra; *Nice 'N' Easy* . . . . (Capitol)
The Capitol Years. . . . . (Capitol)
Jack Jones; *Gershwin Album*. . . . . (Columbia)
Original Broadway Cast; *Crazy For You*. . . . . (Angel)
Oscar Peterson; *My Favorite Instrument* . . . . (Verve)
Sarah Vaughan; *Sarah Vaughan Sings George Gershwin Songbook, Vol. 2* . . . . (Emarcy)
Willie Nelson; *Stardust*. . . . . (Legacy)
Somewhere In My Broken Heart
Billy Dean; *Billy Dean's Greatest Hits* . . . . (Liberty)
Heart Beats-Country Lovin': Songs From The Heart-C. . . . . (Rhino)
Young Man . . . . (SBK)
Randy Travis; *No Holdin' Back* . . . . (Warner Bros.)
Soon
Tanya Tucker; *Soon* . . . . (Liberty)
Souvenirs
Gretchen Peters; *Gretchen Peters* . . . .(Purple Crayon Prod.)
Stand Beside Me
Jo Dee Messina; *Big Country Hits '99-C*. . . . . (K-Tel)
I'm Alright . . . . (Curb)
Standing Knee Deep In A River (Dying Of Thirst)
Kathy Mattea; *Lonesome Standard Time* . . . . (Mercury)
Summertime
Sundays; *Static & Silence* . . . . (David Geffen Co.)
Sunshine
Coko; *Hot Coko*. . . . . (RCA)
Take You Out
Luther Vandross; *Luther Vandross* . . . . (J)
Taking You Home
Don Henley; *Inside Job*. (Warner Bros.)
That's The Way It Is
Celine Dion; *All The Way...A Decade Of Song* . . . .(550 Music)
Collector's Series-Celine Dion-#1 . . . .(550 Music)
Theme From "The Single Guy"
Original Soundtrack; *Television's Greatest Hits-#7-Cable Ready-C* . . . . (TVT)
This
Rod Stewart; *A Spanner In The Works* . . . . (Warner Bros.)
Three Coins In The Fountain
Andy Williams; *Moon River & Other Great Movie Themes* . . . . . . (Columbia)

Doris Day & Frank De Vol Orchestra; *Hooray For
    Hollywood-#2-C* .... (Columbia)
Four Aces; *Billboard Top Movie Hits-1950-1954-C* .... (Rhino)
    Four Aces' Greatest Hits .... (MCA)
Frank Sinatra; *At The Movies* .... (Capitol)
    Capitol Collectors Series-Frank Sinatra .... (Capitol)
Harry James; *Harry James Plays The Songs That Sold A Million* .... (Columbia)
Julius LaRosa; *The Envelope Please-Academy Award Winning Songs-#2
    (1946-1957)-C* .... (Rhino)
'Til I Get It Right
Tammy Wynette; *Tammy Wynette's Biggest Hits* .... (Epic)
    Tammy Wynette's Greatest Hits-#3 .... (Epic)
    Tears Of Fire-25th Anniversary Collection .... (Epic)
Trisha Yearwood; *Tammy Wynette...Remembered-C* .... (Asylum)
To Ev'ry Girl-To Ev'ry Boy (The Meaning Of Love)
Johnnie Ray; *45-#40252* .... (Columbia)
To The Moon And Back
Savage Garden; *Savage Garden* .... (Columbia)
Too Much Heaven
Bee Gees; *Bee Gees' Greatest* .... (Polydor)
Treasure Of Love, The
Clyde McPhatter; *Greatest Hits-Clyde McPhatter* .... (Curb)
Venus
Frankie Avalon; *21 Oldies But Goodies-C* .... (Original Sound)
    '50s Sock Hop-C .... (K-Tel)
    Billboard Top Rock 'N' Roll Hits-1959-C .... (Rhino)
    Oldies But Goodies-#10-C .... (Original Sound)
Waiting
Nilsson; *Harry* .... (Dunhill Compact Classics)
Waiting For The Light To Change
Tonic; *Sugar* .... (Universal)
Waiting For Tonight
Tom Petty; *Playback* .... (MCA)
Waiting For Tonight
Jennifer Lopez; *Now That's What I Call Music!-#4-C* .... (Virgin)
    On The 6 .... (Work)
Walk In The Sun
Bruce Hornsby; *Hot House* .... (RCA)
Walkin' After Midnight
Garth Brooks; *The Chase* .... (Liberty)
Loretta Lynn; *I Remember Patsy* .... (MCA)
Oak Ridge Boys; *Unstoppable* .... (RCA)
Patsy Cline; *20 Golden Pieces Of Patsy Cline* .... (Bulldog)
    Let The Teardrops Fall .... (Accord)
    Live At The Opry .... (MCA)
    Patsy Cline .... (MCA)
    Patsy Cline's Greatest Hits .... (MCA)
    The Patsy Cline Story .... (MCA)
Walking In A Hurricane
John Fogerty; *Blue Moon Swamp* .... (Warner Bros.)
Western Union
Five Americans; *Back To The '60s-Rock 'N' Roll-C* .... (Dominion Entert.)
    Nuggets-#1-The Hits-C .... (Rhino)
What Becomes Of The Brokenhearted
Jimmy & David Ruffin; *Motown Superstar Series-#8-Jimmy & David
    Ruffin* .... (Motown)
Jimmy Ruffin; *Motown Story-First 25 Years-C* .... (Motown)
Paul Young; *ST/Fried Green Tomatoes* .... (MCA)
What Kind Of Fool Am I
Bill Evans; *Solo Sessions-#1* .... (Milestone)
Marvin Gaye; *Hello Broadway* .... (Motown)
Original Broadway Cast; *Stop The World I Want To Get Off* .. (Polydor)
Robert Goulet; *Robert Goulet-16 Most Requested Songs* .... (Columbia)
    Robert Goulet's Greatest Hits .... (Columbia)
Sammy Davis, Jr.; *Sammy Davis, Jr.'s Greatest Songs* .... (Curb)
What's Your Name
Don & Juan; *WCBS FM 101 History Of Rock-For Lovers-#2-C* ... (Collectables)
Wheel Of Fortune
Cardinals; *Atlantic Rhythm & Blues 1947-1974-box-C* .... (Atlantic)
Kay Starr; *Capitol Collectors Series-Kay Starr* .... (Capitol)
When I Come Around
Green Day; *Dookie* .... (Reprise)
When I Dream At Night
Marc Anthony; *Marc Anthony* .... (Columbia)
When Will I Be Loved
Everly Brothers; *Everly Brothers' All-Time Greatest Hits* ..... (Curb)
    Fabulous Style Of The Everly Brothers .... (Rhino)
    Oldies But Goodies-#11-C .... (Original Sound)
Linda Ronstadt; *Heart Like A Wheel* .... (Capitol)
    Linda Ronstadt's Greatest Hits .... (Asylum)
When You Love A Woman
Journey; *Trial By Fire* .... (Columbia)
Where Have All The Cowboys Gone?
Paula Cole; *This Fire* .... (Imago)
Where's The Love
Hanson; *Middle Of Nowhere* .... (Mercury)
While You See A Chance
Steve Winwood; *Arc Of A Diver* .... (Island)
    Steve Winwood-Chronicles .... (Island)

Who
Mandy Barnett; *I've Got A Right To Cry* .... (Sire)
Who Can I Run To
Xscape; *Off The Hook* .... (So So Def/Columbia)
    Smooth Love: Ultimate R&B Love Songs-C .... (EMI)
With A Little Help From My Friends
Beatles; *Beatles-Box Set* .... (Capitol)
    Rarities .... (Capitol)
    Sgt. Pepper's Lonely Hearts Club Band .... (Capitol)
    The Beatles/1967-1970 .... (Capitol)
Joe Cocker; *History Of British Rock-#9-C* .... (Rhino)
    Joe Cocker-Classics-#4. .... (A&M)
    Joe Cocker's Greatest Hits .... (A&M)
    ST/Woodstock .... (Atlantic)
    With A Little Help From My Friends .... (A&M)
Ringo Starr & His All-Star Band; *Nobody's Child-Romanian Angel
    Appeal-C* .... (Warner Bros.)
Woman's Touch
Toby Keith; *Blue Moon* .... (Polydor Country)
World Without Love, A
Peter And Gordon; *Billboard Top Pop Hits-1964-C* .... (Rhino)
    History Of British Rock-#1-C .... (Rhino)
    Peter & Gordon's Greatest Hits .... (CEMA Special Prod.)
Wouldn't It Be Loverly
Original Cast; *My Fair Lady* .... (Columbia)
    My Fair Lady .... (London)
You Light Up My Life
Debby Boone; *Best Of Debby Boone* .... (Curb)
    There Is Love-Wedding Songs-C .... (Scotti Bros.)
    You Light Up My Life .... (MCA)
LeAnn Rimes; *You Light Up My Life-Inspirational Songs* ... (Curb)
You May Be Right
Billy Joel; *Billy Joel-Greatest Hits, Volume I & Volume II* ... (Columbia)
    Glass Houses .... (Columbia)
You Win My Love
Shania Twain; *The Woman In Me* .... (Mercury)
Young Lust
Pink Floyd; *1980-1981 Wall Live-Is There Anybody Out There.* .... (Columbia)
    The Wall .... (Columbia)
Roger Waters & Bryan Adams; *The Wall-Live In Berlin* ..... (Mercury)

LOVE: SOMEBODY DONE SOMEBODY WRONG

*See Also: **ANGER, CHEATING & LIES, COMPLAINTS, DIVORCE,
ENDINGS, GUILT, INSULTS, LOVE (various), MISTREATMENT,
PAIN & HEALING, REVENGE, SADNESS, WRONG***

(Eye) Hate U
"AFKAP"; *The Gold Experience* .... (NPG)
(Hey Won't You Play) Another Somebody Done Somebody Wrong Song
B.J. Thomas; *Class Of Country-1975-1979-C* .... (Hip-O)
5 Miles To Empty
Brownstone; *Still Climbing* .... (MJJ Music/Work)
Adelaide's Lament
Original Cast; *Guys & Dolls* .... (MCA)
    Guys & Dolls .... (Motown)
After The Fire Is Gone
Loretta Lynn & Conway Twitty; *MCA Records 30 Years Of Hits-1958-
    1988-C* .... (MCA)
    Very Best Of Loretta Lynn & Conway Twitty .... (MCA)
Ain't That A Shame
4 Seasons; *25th Anniversary Collection* .... (Rhino)
Cheap Trick; *Cheap Trick At Budokan* .... (Epic)
Fats Domino; *Best Of Fats Domino* .... (EMI)
    Fats Domino's Greatest Hits .... (Everest)
    Fats Domino's Greatest Hits .... (MCA)
    ST/American Graffiti .... (MCA)
Hank Williams, Jr.; *Hank Williams, Jr.-14 Greatest Hits* .... (Polydor)
    Standing In The Shadows .... (Polydor)
John Lennon; *Lennon* .... (Capitol)
    Rock 'N' Roll .... (Capitol)
Ain't That Peculiar
Marvin Gaye; *Marvin Gaye-Anthology* .... (Motown)
All Cried Out
Allure; *Allure* .... (Track Masters/Crave)
    Boom! 17 Explosive Hits-C .... (Simitar)
Lisa Lisa; *Lisa Lisa & Cult Jam With Full Force* .... (Columbia)
    Lisa Lisa-Super Hits .... (Columbia)
    Past, Present & Future .... (TMP)
All I Need
Temptations; *Temptations-Anthology-The Best Of The Temptations* .. (Motown)
All N My Grill
Missy "Misdemeanor" Elliot; *Da Real World* .... (East West)
All These Years
Sawyer Brown; *Cafe On The Corner* .... (Curb)

Almost
George Morgan; *Room Full Of Roses-The George Morgan Collection* .... (Razor & Tie)
The Late, Great George Morgan: 14 Greatest Hits .... (Power Play)
Alone And Forsaken
Emmylou Harris & Mark Knopfler; *Timeless: Hank Williams Tribute-C* .... (Lost Highway/IDJMG)
Hank Williams; *Alone And Forsaken* .... (Mercury)
Alone With His Guitar .... (Mercury)
Hank Williams-The Original Singles Collection .... (Polydor)
Am I Wrong
Keb' Mo'; *Keb' Mo'* .... (Okeh)
Anything But Down
Sheryl Crow; *The Globe Sessions* .... (A&M)
Ashes By Now
Lee Ann Womack; *I Hope You Dance* .... (MCA)
Rodney Crowell; *Rodney Crowell-Collection* .... (Warner Bros.)
Baby Did A Bad Thing
Chris Isaak; *Forever Blue* .... (Reprise)
ST/Eyes Wide Shut .... (Reprise)
Baby Doll
Andy Williams; *Andy Williams* .... (Madacy)
Baby Love
Diana Ross; *Diana Ross-The Ultimate Collection* .... (Motown)
Supremes; *Motown Classic Hits-#5-C* .... (Motown)
Temptations; *ST/My Girl 2* ....(Epic)
Backfield In Motion
Mel & Tim; *Collectables Presents The History Of Rock-#4-C* .... (Collectables)
Oldies But Goodies-#2-C .... (Original Sound)
Soul Shots-#2-The ''In'' Crowd-Sweet Soul-C .... (Rhino)
Super Oldies Of The '60s-#10-C .... (Audio Fidelity)
Band Of Gold
Freda Payne; *Beachbeat Draggin'* .... (Dunhill Compact Classics)
Didn't It Blow Your Mind: Soul Hits Of The '70s-#2-C .... (Rhino)
Freda Payne's Greatest Hits .... (HDH)
Beep Me 911
Missy ''Misdemeanor'' Elliot; *Supa Dupa Fly* .... (East West)
Bill Bailey
Louis Armstrong; *Essential Louis Armstrong* .... (Vanguard)
Louis Armstrong .... (Audio Fidelity)
Pearl Bailey; *Echoes Of An Era-Pearl Bailey* .... (Roulette)
Preservation Hall Jazz Band; *New Orleans-#1* .... (Columbia)
Black Chick, White Guy
Kid Rock; *Devil Without A Cause* .... (Top Dog/Lava/Atlantic)
Blue
LeAnn Rimes; *Blue* .... (MCG/Curb)
Blue Eyes Blue
Eric Clapton; *Clapton Chronicles-The Best Of Eric Clapton 1981-1999* .... (Reprise)
ST/Runaway Bride .... (Sony Music Soundtrax)
Blue Moon With Heartache
Rosanne Cash; *19 Hot Country Requests-#2-C* ....(Epic)
Rosanne Cash-Hits-1979-1989 .... (Columbia)
Seven Year Ache .... (Columbia)
Blue On Black
Kenny Wayne Shepherd; *Trouble Is...* .... (Revolution)
Book, The
Sheryl Crow; *Sheryl Crow* .... (A&M)
Broken Wing
Martina McBride; *Evolution* .... (RCA)
Burning A Hole In My Mind
Connie Smith; *Essential Connie Smith* .... (RCA)
But It's Alright
J.J. Jackson; *Didn't It Blow Your Mind: Soul Hits Of The '70s-#3-C* .... (Rhino)
Soul Shots-C .... (Rhino)
Bye Bye Bye
'N Sync; *No Strings Attached* .... (Jive)
Now That's What I Call Music!-#6-C .... (Virgin)
Can't You Hear Me Callin'?
Ricky Skaggs; *Bluegrass Super Hits-C* .... (Columbia)
Favorite Country Songs ....(Epic)
Highway & Heartaches ....(Epic)
Carolyn
Merle Haggard & The Strangers; *For The Record: Merle Haggard-43 Legendary Hits* .... (BNA)
Cathy's Clown
Everly Brothers; *Billboard Top Rock 'N' Roll Hits-1960-C* .... (Rhino)
Golden Hits Of The Everly Brothers .... (Warner Bros.)
The Reunion Concert-Live At Albert Hall 1983 .... (Mercury)
Very Best Of The Everly Brothers .... (Warner Bros.)
Reba McEntire; *Sweet Sixteen* .... (MCA)
Chain Of Fools
Aretha Franklin; *Aretha Franklin's Greatest Hits* .... (Atlantic)
Aretha's Gold .... (Atlantic)
Atlantic Rhythm & Blues 1947-1974-#6 (1966-1969)-C .... (Atlantic)
Best Of Aretha Franklin .... (Atlantic)
Lady Of Soul .... (Atlantic)
Clint Black & Pointer Sisters; *Rhythm Country And Blues-C* .... (MCA)

Chains
Patty Loveless; *Honky Tonk Angel* .... (MCA)
Patty Loveless' Greatest Hits .... (MCA)
Chante's Got A Man
Chante Moore; *Now That's What I Call Music!-#3-C* ....(Virgin)
This Moment Is Mine .... (Silas)
Cold Cold Heart
Hank Williams; *Complete Hank Williams* .... (Mercury)
Hank Williams With His Drifting Cowboys; *24 Of Hank Williams' Greatest Hits* .... (Polydor)
Hank Williams .... (MGM)
Hank Williams-40 Greatest Hits .... (Polydor)
Live At Opry .... (MGM)
Long Gone Lonesome Blues .... (Polydor)
Jerry Lee Lewis; *Duets* .... (Sun)
Golden Cream Of Jerry Lee Lewis .... (Sun)
Jerry Lee Lewis & Friends-Duets .... (Sun)
Lucinda Williams; *Timeless: Hank Williams Tribute-C* .... (Lost Highway/IDJMG)
Tony Bennett; *Tony Bennett-16 Most Requested Songs* .... (Legacy)
Cold Hard Facts Of Life, The
Porter Wagoner; *Essential Porter Wagoner* .... (RCA)
Porter Wagoner's Greatest Hits .... (Pair)
Dazed And Confused
Led Zeppelin; *Classic Rock 1966-1988-C* .... (Atlantic)
Led Zeppelin .... (Atlantic)
Led Zeppelin-Box Set .... (Atlantic)
ST/The Song Remains The Same .... (Swan Song)
Don't Be Cruel
Bobby Brown; *Chart Toppers-R&B Hits Of The '80s-C* .... (Priority)
Don't Say
Jon B.; *Cool Relax* .... (Yab Yum/550)
Don't You Care
Buckinghams; *Buckinghams' Greatest Hits* .... (Columbia)
Down
Amel Larrieux; *Infinite Possibilities* .... (Epic)
Fine
Whitney Houston; *Totally Hits-#3-C* .... (Atlantic)
Whitney Houston's Greatest Hits .... (Arista)
Flavor Of The Weak
American Hi-Fi; *American Hi-Fi* .... (Island)
Now That's What I Call Music!-#7-C .... (Virgin)
Frankie & Johnny
Brook Benton; *Endlessly-The Best Of Brook Benton* .... (Rhino)
Doc Watson; *Favorites-Doc Watson* .... (Liberty)
Jerry Lee Lewis; *Jerry Lee's Greatest!* .... (Rhino)
Free Girl Now
Tom Petty And The Heartbreakers; *Echo* .... (Warner Bros.)
Friend Of Mine
Kelly Price; *Soul Of A Woman* .... (T-Neck/Island)
Ghost Of You And Me
BBMak; *Sooner Or Later* .... (Hollywood)
Girl I Knew Somewhere, The
Monkees; *Monkees' Greatest Hits* .... (Rhino)
Go On
George Strait; *George Strait* .... (MCA)
Gonna Get Along Without Ya Now
Patience & Prudence; *Lost Hits Of The 50's-C* .... (EMI Special Markets)
Goodbye Baby
Jack Scott; *Classic Hits: Hard To Find Original Recordings-C* .... (Curb)
Jack Scott's Greatest Hits .... (Curb)
Grapevyne
Brownstone; *Dancin' Divas-C* .... (Epic Dance)
From The Bottom Up .... (MJJ/Epic)
Guitars, Cadillacs
Dwight Yoakam; *Guitars, Cadillacs, Etc., Etc.* .... (Reprise)
Just Lookin' For A Hit .... (Reprise)
Heard It All Before
Sunshine Anderson; *Your Woman* .... (Soullife/Atlantic)
Heartbreak Hotel
Whitney Houston Featuring Faith Evans & Kelly Price; *My Love Is Your Love* .... (Arista)
Totally Hits-#1-C .... (Arista)
Whitney Houston's Greatest Hits .... (Arista)
Heartbreaker
Mariah Carey; *Rainbow* .... (Columbia)
Heartbreaker
Led Zeppelin; *Led Zeppelin II* .... (Atlantic)
Led Zeppelin-The Complete Studio Recordings .... (Atlantic)
Heartbreaker
Bee Gees; *One Night Only* .... (Polydor)
Hello Darlin'
Conway Twitty; *Conway Twittty-20 Greatest Hits* .... (MCA)
Conway Twitty's Greatest Hits .... (Curb)
From The Vaults: Decca Country Classics-1934-1973-C .... (Decca)
Greatest Country Classics-#1-C .... (MCA Special Prod.)
Hemorrhage (In My Hands)
Fuel; *Now That's What I Call Music!-#6-C* .... (Virgin)

Something Like Human. . . . . (Epic)
Here We Go Again
Aretha Franklin; *A Rose Is Still A Rose* . . . . (Arista)
Hero Takes A Fall
Bangles; *All Over The Place* . . . . (Columbia)
Bangles' Greatest Hits . . . .(Columbia)
Bangles-Super Hits . . . . (Legacy)
Hey Joe
Jimi Hendrix; *Essential Jimi Hendrix, Volume 2* . . . .(Reprise)
Live At Winterland . . . .(Rykodisc)
Jimi Hendrix Experience; *Are You Experienced?* . . . .(Reprise)
Smash Hits . . . .(Reprise)
Love; *Best Of Love* . . . . (Rhino)
Highway Chile
Jimi Hendrix Experience; *Are You Experienced?* . . . .(Reprise)
How Could You
K-Ci & JoJo; *Love Always* . . . . (MCA)
How You Remind Me
Nickelback; *Silver Side Up* . . . .(Roadrunner)
I Can See For Miles
Who; *Hooligans* . . . . (MCA)
Join Together . . . . (MCA)
Meaty Beaty Big & Bouncy . . . . (MCA)
ST/The Kids Are Alright . . . . (MCA)
The Who Sell Out . . . . (MCA)
I Cry
Ja Rule; *Rule 3:36* . . . .(Murder Inc./Def Jam/IDJMG)
I Do
Lisa Loeb; *Firecracker* . . . . (Geffen)
I Heard It Through The Grapevine
Creedence Clearwater Revival; *Chooglin'* . . . .(Fantasy)
Cosmo's Factory . . . .(Fantasy)
Creedence Clearwater Revival-Chronicle . . . .(Fantasy)
Creedence Clearwater Revival-Gold . . . .(Fantasy)
Movie Album . . . .(Fantasy)
Gladys Knight & The Pips; *16 #1 Hits From The Late '60s-C* . . . . (Motown)
Compact Command Performances-Gladys Knight & The Pips . . . . . (Motown)
Every Great Motown Song-First 25 Years-C . . . . (Motown)
Motown Grammy R&B Performances Of The '60s & '70s-C . . . . . . (Motown)
Motown Superstar Series-#13-Gladys Knight & The Pips . . . . (Motown)
Top 10 With A Bullet-Motown Girl Groups-C . . . . (Motown)
Marvin Gaye; *25 #1 Hits From 25 Years-C* . . . . (Motown)
Every Great Motown Hit Of Marvin Gaye . . . . (Motown)
Marvin Gaye Live At The London Palladium . . . . (Motown)
Marvin Gaye-Anthology . . . . (Motown)
Most Played Songs On America's Jukeboxes . . . . (Motown)
Motown Story-First 25 Years-C . . . . (Motown)
I Hurt For You
Conway Twitty; *Final Touches* . . . . (MCA)
Deborah Allen; *45-#13776* . . . . (RCA)
I Just Don't Understand
Ann Margret; *Nipper's Greatest Hits Of The '60s-#1-C* . . . . (RCA)
I Learned From The Best
Whitney Houston; *My Love Is Your Love* . . . . (Arista)
I Never Loved A Man (The Way I Love You)
Aretha Franklin; *Aretha Franklin-30 Greatest Hits* . . . . (Rhino)
Golden Age Of Black Music-1960-1970-C . . . . (Atlantic)
ST/The Commitments . . . . (MCA)
I Wish You Didn't Love Me So Much
''Little'' Jimmy Dickens; *All Time Legends Of Country Music-C* . . . . . (Legacy)
I'm A Fool
Dino, Desi & Billy; *Even More Nuggets-C* . . . . (Rhino)
Only Love-1965-1969-C. . . . .(JCI Assoc. Labels)
I'm Looking Through You
Beatles; *The Beatles-Anthology-#2* . . . . (Capitol)
Indian Giver
1910 Fruitgum Company; *Best Of 1910 Fruitgum Company & Other
Bubblegum Smashes-#2-C* . . . . (Rhino)
Insensitive
Jann Arden; *Living Under June* . . . . (A&M)
Women For Women-#2-C . . . .(Mercury)
It Hurts Me Too
Bob Dylan; *Self Portrait* . . . . (Columbia)
Elmore James; *Golden Classics-Elmore James*. . . . .(Collectables)
Eric Clapton; *From The Cradle* . . . .(Duck/Reprise)
It Hurts Me Too
Keb' Mo'; *The Door* . . . .(550/Epic/Okeh)
It Wasn't God Who Made Honky Tonk Angels
Kitty Wells; *Grand Ole Opry-75 Years-#1-C* . . . . (MCA)
Kitty Wells' Greatest Hits . . . .(Step One)
The Kitty Wells Story . . . . (MCA)
It Wasn't Me
Shaggy; *Hotshot* . . . . (MCA)
Now That's What I Call Music!-#6-C . . . .(Virgin)
It's About Time
Public Announcement; *All Work, No Play*. . . . . (A&M)
It's All Over Now
Bobby Womack; *Lookin' For A Love-Best Of Bobby Womack-1968-
1975* . . . .(Razor & Tie)

John Anderson; *Great Divorce Songs For Him-C* . . . . (Warner Bros.)
John Anderson's Greatest Hits-#2* . . . . (Warner Bros.)
Rod Stewart; *Best Of Rod Stewart* . . . .(Mercury)
Gasoline Alley . . . .(Mercury)
Vintage Rod Stewart . . . .(Mercury)
Rolling Stones; *12 X 5* . . . . (Abkco)
Big Hits (High Tide & Green Grass) . . . . (Abkco)
More Hot Rocks (big hits & fazed cookies) . . . . (Abkco)
Singles Collection-The London Years . . . . (Abkco)
Ry Cooder; *Paradise And Lunch* . . . .(Reprise)
It's Not Right But It's Okay
Whitney Houston; *My Love Is Your Love* . . . .(Arista)
It's Over Now
Deborah Cox; *One Wish* . . . .(Arista)
I've Been Hurt
Bill Deal & The Rhondels; *Best Of Bill Deal & The Rhondels* . . . .(Rhino)
Oldies But Goodies-#7-C . . . . (Original Sound)
Soul Shots-#2-The ''In'' Crowd-Sweet Soul-C . . . .(Rhino)
Soul Shots-#6-Blue-Eyed Soul-C. . . . .(Rhino)
I've Got A Right To Cry
Mandy Barnett; *I've Got A Right To Cry* . . . . (Sire)
Just Another Girl
Monica; *ST/Down To Earth* . . . .(Epic)
Kickin' My Heart Around
Black Crowes; *By Your Side*. . . . .(American)
Kiss This
Aaron Tippin; *People Like Us* . . . . (Lyric Street)
Last Chance To Turn Around
Gene Pitney; *Best Of Gene Pitney* . . . .(K-Tel)
Gene Pitney-Anthology 1961-1968 . . . .(Rhino)
Laugh Laugh
Beau Brummels; *Best Of The Beau Brummels* . . . .(Rhino)
Heart & Soul Of Rock 'N' Roll-#1-C . . . .(Rhino)
Introducing The Beau Brummels . . . .(Rhino)
Nuggets-#7-Early San Francisco-C . . . .(Rhino)
Laughing Out Loud
Wallflowers; *Bringing Down The Horse* . . . .(Interscope)
Lemon Song
Led Zeppelin; *Led Zeppelin II* . . . . (Atlantic)
Lesson In Leavin'
Dottie West; *Special Delivery* . . . . (EMI)
Jo Dee Messina; *I'm Alright*. . . . .(Curb)
Let's See How Far You Get
BR549; *This Is BR549* . . . .(Lucky Dog)
Liar
Profyle; *Nothin' But Drama* . . . .(Motown)
Life Turned Her That Way
''Little'' Jimmy Dickens; *I'm Little, But I'm Loud-The ''Little'' Jimmy
Dickens Collection* . . . .(Razor & Tie)
Mel Tillis; *Best Of Mel Tillis* . . . . (MCA)
Mel Tillis' Greatest Hits . . . . (Universal)
Ricky Van Shelton; *Ricky Van Shelton-16 Biggest Hits*. . . . .(Legacy)
Wild-Eyed Dream . . . . (Columbia)
Lion's Den
Bruce Springsteen; *Tracks* . . . .(Columbia)
Lipstick On Your Collar
Connie Francis; *Very Best Of Connie Francis* . . . . (Polydor)
Little Sister
Elvis Presley; *Elvis' Golden Records, Volume 3* . . . . (RCA)
Elvis In Concert. . . . . (RCA)
I Was The One . . . . (RCA)
The Top Ten Hits . . . . (RCA)
Worldwide 50 Gold Award Hits, Vol. 1, Parts 1 & 2 . . . . (RCA)
Little White Lies
Dick Haymes with Gordon Jenkins & His Orchestra; *Sentimental Journey:
Pop Vocal Classics-#2-1947-1950-C.* . . . .(Rhino)
Dinah Shore; *Dinah Shore-16 Most Requested Songs-Encore!* . . . . (Legacy)
Fred Waring's Pennsylvanians featuring Clare Hanlon; *Very Best Of Fred
Waring & The Pennsylvanians* . . . . (Reader's Digest Music)
Tommy Dorsey; *Best Of Tommy Dorsey* . . . . (Bluebird)
Complete Tommy Dorsey-#6. . . . . (RCA)
Lost Ones
Lauryn Hill; *The Miseducation Of Lauryn Hill* . . . .(Ruffhouse/Columbia)
Love Bug Leave My Heart Alone
Martha & The Vandellas; *Compact Command Performances-Martha Reeves
& The Vandellas* . . . .(Motown)
Martha Reeves & The Vandellas-Anthology . . . . (Motown)
Love Is Blind
Eve; *First Lady Of Ruff Ryders* . . . . (Ruff Ryders/IDJMG)
Love Is Here And Now You're Gone
Diana Ross; *Diana Ross-Anthology* . . . .(Motown)
Maggie May
Rod Stewart; *Absolutely Live* . . . .(Warner Bros.)
Best Of Rod Stewart. . . . .(Mercury)
Billboard Top Rock 'N' Roll Hits-1971-C. . . . .(Rhino)
Every Picture Tells A Story . . . .(Mercury)
Rod Stewart's Greatest Hits . . . .(Warner Bros.)
Sing It Again, Rod . . . .(Mercury)
Storyteller/The Complete Anthology: 1964-1990 . . . .(Warner Bros.)

Mama, He Treats Your Daughter Mean
Susan Tedeschi; *Just Won't Burn* (Tone Cool)
Maybe I Deserve
Tank; *Force Of Nature* (BlackGround Enterp./Atlantic)
Maybe I Know
Lesley Gore; *Golden Hits Of Lesley Gore* (Mercury)
Lesley Gore-Anthology (Rhino)
Mountain Of Love
Charley Pride; *Charley Pride's Greatest Hits-#2* (RCA)
Solid Country Gold-C (RCA)
David Houston; *American Originals-David Houston* (Columbia)
Harold Dorman; *Collectables Presents The History Of Rock-#10-C* (Collectables)
Johnny Rivers; *Best Of Johnny Rivers* (EMI)
Johnny Rivers-Anthology 1964-1977 (Rhino)
Mrs. Steven Rudy
Mark McGuinn; *Mark McGuinn* (VFR)
Must You Throw Dirt In My Face
Elvis Costello; *Kojak Variety* (Warner Bros.)
Louvin Brothers; *45-#4822* (Capitol)
Never Ever
All Saints; *All Saints* (London)
Now That's What I Call Music!-#1-C (Virgin)
Never Let You Go
Third Eye Blind; *Blue* (Elektra)
Totally Hits-#2-C (Elektra)
New Beginning
Stir; *Holy Dogs* (Capitol)
Ninety Nine Years (Dead Or Alive)
Guy Mitchell; *Definitive Guy Mitchell* (Collector's Choice)
Nobody But A Fool (Would Love You)
Connie Smith; *Best Of Connie Smith* (Dominion Entert.)
Nookie
Limp Bizkit; *Now That's What I Call Music!-#3-C* (Virgin)
Significant Other (Flip/Interscope)
Nothing But Heartaches
Diana Ross & The Supremes; *Diana Ross & The Supremes' Greatest Hits* (Motown)
Diana Ross & The Supremes-Anthology (1962-1969) (Motown)
Motown Story-First 25 Years-C (Motown)
Motown Superstar Series-#1-Diana Ross & The Supremes (Motown)
Oh! Carol
Neil Sedaka; *Neil Sedaka Sings His Greatest Hits* (RCA)
Neil Sedaka's All-Time Greatest Hits (RCA)
Nipper's Greatest Hits Of The '50s-#1-C (RCA)
Party Time
T.G. Sheppard; *Great Divorce Songs For Him-C* (Warner Bros.)
T.G. Sheppard's All-Time Greatest Hits (Warner Bros.)
T.G. Sheppard's Greatest Hits (Warner Bros./Curb)
Piece Of My Heart
Big Brother & The Holding Company; *Cheap Thrills* (Columbia)
Rock Classics Of The '60s-C (Columbia)
Seems Like Yesterday-#6-Late '60s-C (K-Tel)
Bryan Ferry; *These Foolish Things* (Reprise)
Delaney & Bonnie; *Best Of Delaney & Bonnie* (Rhino)
Faith Hill; *Take Me As I Am* (Warner Bros.)
Janis Joplin; *Janis Joplin In Concert* (Columbia)
Janis Joplin's Greatest Hits (Columbia)
ST/Janis (Columbia)
Sammy Hagar; *Standing Hampton* (Geffen)
Poor Little Fool
Rick Nelson; *Live In '85* (Rhino)
Ricky Nelson; *Best Of Ricky Nelson* (EMI)
EMI Legends Of Rock & Roll-24 Greatest Hits-C (EMI)
Ricky Nelson-Legendary Masters (EMI)
Poor Poor Pitiful Me
Linda Ronstadt; *Linda Ronstadt's Greatest Hits, Volume Two* (Asylum)
Simple Dreams (Asylum)
Terri Clark; *Just The Same* (Mercury)
Warren Zevon; *A Quiet Normal Life-Best Of* (Asylum)
Stand In The Fire (Asylum)
Popstar
Pretenders; *Viva El Amor!* (Warner Bros.)
Pretty Polly
Judy Collins; *Who Knows Where The Time Goes* (Elektra)
Stanley Brothers; *Complete Columbia Stanley Brothers* (Legacy)
Folk Classics: Roots Of American Folk Music-C (Columbia)
Long Journey Home (Rebel)
Quit Playing Games (With My Heart)
Backstreet Boys; *Backstreet Boys* (Jive)
MTV Party To Go '98-C (Tommy Boy)
The Concert For New York City-C (Columbia)
Reflections
Diana Ross & The Supremes; *Diana Ross & The Supremes' Greatest Hits-#3* (Motown)
Diana Ross & The Supremes-25th Anniversary (Motown)
Diana Ross & The Supremes-Anthology (1962-1969) (Motown)
Motown Story-First 25 Years-C (Motown)
Four Tops; *Four Tops-Anthology* (Motown)
Still Waters Run Deep (Motown)
Until You Love Someone: More Of The Best (1965-1970) (Rhino)
Luther Vandross; *Songs* (Epic)
Refugee
Tom Petty And The Heartbreakers; *Damn The Torpedoes* (MCA)
Pack Up The Plantation-Live! (MCA)
Return Of The Mack
Mark Morrison; *Return Of The Mack* (Atlantic)
Ricochet
Teresa Brewer; *Best Of Teresa Brewer* (MCA Jazz)
Right Or Wrong
George Strait; *George Strait's Greatest Hits* (MCA)
Right Or Wrong (MCA)
Strait Out Of The Box (MCA)
Reba McEntire & Asleep At The Wheel; *Ride With Bob-C* (DreamWorks/SKG)
Ring On Her Finger, Time On Her Hands
Lee Greenwood; *Best Of Lee Greenwood-God Bless America* (Curb)
Inside Out/You've Got A Good Love Comin' (MCA)
Lee Greenwood's Greatest Hits (MCA)
Lee Greenwood-Super Hits (Epic)
Reba McEntire; *Starting Over* (MCA)
Room At The Top Of The Stairs
David Grisman; *Retrograss* (Acoustic Disc)
Leo Kottke; *Leo Kottke-Live* (Private Music)
Peculiaroso (Private Music)
Stanley Brothers & The Clinch Mountain Boys; *Ralph Stanley-50th Anniversary* (Rebel)
Stella Parton; *Stella Parton-Anthology* (Renaissance)
Rose Is Still A Rose
Aretha Franklin; *A Rose Is Still A Rose* (Arista)
Runaround, The
Xscape; *Traces Of My Lipstick* (So So Def/Columbia)
Same Script, Different Cast
Whitney Houston & Deborah Cox; *Whitney Houston's Greatest Hits* (Arista)
See You Later, Alligator
Bill Haley & His Comets; *Bill Haley & His Comets* (Everest)
Bill Haley & His Comets' Greatest Hits (MCA)
Bill Haley & His Comets-Golden Hits (MCA)
Billboard Top Rock 'N' Roll Hits-1956-C (Rhino)
Mr. Rock 'N' Roll (Accord)
Rock & Roll Is Here To Stay-C (Gusto)
Rockin' & Rollin' (Accord)
Selfless, Cold And Composed
Ben Folds Five; *Whatever And Ever Amen* (Caroline/550)
Separated
Avant; *My Thoughts* (MCA)
Shake, Rattle And Roll
Big Joe Turner; *Big Joe Turner's Greatest Hits* (Atlantic)
Every Day I Have The Blues (Pablo)
Oldies But Goodies-#2-C (Original Sound)
Soul Years-C (Atlantic)
Bill Haley & His Comets; *Bill Haley & His Comets' Greatest Hits* (MCA)
Bill Haley & His Comets-Golden Hits (MCA)
Elvis Presley; *For LP Fans Only* (RCA)
Rocker (RCA)
ST/This Is Elvis (RCA)
Fats Domino; *Fats Domino's Greatest Hits* (MCA)
Huey Lewis and the News; *Four Chords & Several Years Ago* (Elektra)
NRBQ; *At Yankee Stadium* (Mercury)
Vern Gosdin; *Best Of Vern Gosdin* (Warner Bros.)
Shame Shame Shame Shame
Mark Collie; *Mark Collie* (MCA)
Shame, Shame
Magic Lanterns; *Shame, Shame* (Collectables)
She Drew A Broken Heart
Patty Loveless; *The Trouble With The Truth* (Epic)
She's A Fool
Lesley Gore; *Golden Hits Of Lesley Gore* (Mercury)
Lesley Gore-Anthology (Rhino)
She's Got Issues
Offspring; *Americana* (Columbia)
She's Not There
Santana; *Moonflower* (Columbia)
Viva Santana! (Columbia)
Vanilla Fudge; *Vanilla Fudge* (Atco)
Zombies; *Best & The Rest Of The Zombies* (Epic)
Billboard Top Rock 'N' Roll Hits-1964-C (Rhino)
History Of British Rock-#1-C (Rhino)
Time Of The Zombies (Bac-Trac)
Shoe Was On The Other Foot
Patti LaBelle; *Flame* (MCA)
Sick & Beautiful
Artificial Joy Club; *Melt* (Interscope)
Singing The Blues
Guy Mitchell; *CBS Classics-Radio Classics Of The '50s-C* (Columbia)
Guy Mitchell-16 Most Requested Songs (Legacy)
Sky Is Crying
Albert King; *I'm In A Phone Booth Baby* (Stax)

Years Gone By . . . . (Stax)
Elmore James; *Elmore James-Complete Fire & Enjoy*
   Sessions-#1 . . . . (Collectables)
   Red Hot Blues . . . . (Intermedia)
Eric Clapton; *Eric Clapton-Crossroads-C* . . . . (Polydor)
George Thorogood & The Destroyers; *George Thorogood & The Destroyers-*
   Live . . . . (EMI)
   Move It On Over . . . . (Rounder)
Stevie Ray Vaughan and Double Trouble; *The Sky Is Crying* . . . . (Epic)

So Fine
Mint Condition; *From The Mint Factory* . . . . (Perspective/A&M)

Someone You Use
Vonda Shepard; *ST/Songs From "Ally McBeal" Featuring Vonda*
   Shepard . . . . (550/Epic)

Son Of A Gun (I Betcha You Think This Song's About You)
Janet (with Carly Simon); *All For You.* . . . . (Virgin)

Standing In The Doorway
Bob Dylan; *Time Out Of Mind* . . . . (Columbia)

Standing In The Shadows Of Love
Barry White; *Barry White's Greatest Hits* . . . . (20th Century Fox)
   I've Got So Much To Give . . . . (20th Century Fox)
Four Tops; *Four Tops' Greatest Hits.* . . . . (Motown)
   Four Tops Reach Out . . . . (Motown)
   Four Tops-Anthology . . . . (Motown)
   Motown Story-First 25 Years-C . . . . (Motown)
   Motown Superstar Series-#14-Four Tops. . . . . (Motown)
Rod Stewart; *Blondes Have More Fun* . . . . (Warner Bros.)

Still
Macy Gray; *On How Life Is* . . . . (Epic)

Still Water Runs The Deepest
Asleep At The Wheel featuring Willie Nelson; *Tribute To The Music Of Bob*
   Wills And The Texas Playboys-C . . . . (Liberty)

Stutter
Joe featuring Mystikal; *My Name Is Joe* . . . . (Jive)
   Now That's What I Call Music!-#8-C . . . . (Virgin)

Sue Me
Original Cast; *Guys & Dolls* . . . . (MCA)
   Guys & Dolls . . . . (Motown)

Take Time To Know Her
Percy Sledge; *Best Of Percy Sledge.* . . . . (Atlantic)
   It Tears Me Up-Best Of Percy Sledge . . . . (Rhino)

Taker, The
Kris Kristofferson; *The Silver Tongued Devil And I* . . . . (Columbia)
Waylon Jennings; *Essential Waylon Jennings.* . . . . (RCA)
   Only Daddy That'll Walk The Line-The RCA Years . . . . . . (RCA)

Tell Mama
Etta James; *Didn't It Blow Your Mind: Soul Hits Of The '70s-#1-C* . . . . . (Rhino)
   Essential Etta James . . . . (Chess)
   Tell Mama . . . . (Chess)
Janis Joplin; *Janis* . . . . (Legacy)
Savoy Brown; *Savoy Brown-London Collector.* . . . . (London)
   Street Corner Talking . . . . (Deram)

Tell Me Why
Beatles; *Beatles-Box Set* . . . . (Capitol)
   Something New . . . . (Capitol)
   ST/A Hard Day's Night . . . . (Capitol)

That Other Woman
Changing Faces; *Visit Me* . . . . (Atlantic)

That's Not Love
Keb' Mo'; *Just Like You* . . . . (Okeh)

That's The Way I Feel
Faron Young; *45-#4050.* . . . . (Capitol)

Things That I Used To Do
Guitar Slim; *Blues Classics-C* . . . . (K-Tel)

Think Of What You've Done
Ricky Skaggs and Kentucky Thunder; *Bluegrass Rules!* . . . . (Rounder)

Think Of You
Usher; *Usher* . . . . (LaFace)

Thinkin' 'Bout It
Gerald Levert; *Love & Consequences* . . . . (East West)

This Diamond Ring
Gary Lewis And The Playboys; *Billboard Top Rock 'N' Roll Hits-*
   1965-C . . . . (Rhino)
   EMI Legends Of Rock & Roll-24 Greatest Hits-C . . . . (EMI)
   Golden Years-1965-C . . . . (Dominion Entert.)
   Spring Break-#2-Cold Kegs & Tan Legs . . . . (Capitol)

This Is Me
Dream; *It Was All A Dream* . . . . (Bad Boy/Arista)
   Totally Hits 2001-C . . . . (Arista)

This Lonely Place
Goldfinger; *Hang-Ups.* . . . . (Mojo Music/Universal)

Thrill Is Gone
B.B. King; *Best Of B.B. King* . . . . (MCA)
   Live In Cook County Jail. . . . . (MCA)
B.B. King & Tracy Chapman; *Deuces Wild* . . . . (MCA)

Thunder Rolls, The
Garth Brooks; *Garth Brooks-Double Live* . . . . (Capitol)
   No Fences . . . . (Capitol)

'Til You Do Me Right
After 7; *Rock On 1995-C* . . . . (Madacy)
   Very Best Of After 7. . . . . (Virgin)

Too Much
Elvis Presley; *Elvis' Golden Records* . . . . (RCA)
   The Top Ten Hits . . . . (RCA)
   Worldwide 50 Gold Award Hits, Vol. 1, Parts 1 & 2 . . . . . . (RCA)

Treat Her Like A Lady
Celine Dion; *Let's Talk About Love-C* . . . . (550 Music)

Trouble
Coldplay; *Parachutes.* . . . . (Nettwerk/Capitol)

Tryin' To Get To Heaven
Bob Dylan; *Time Out Of Mind* . . . . (Columbia)

U Don't Love Me
Kumbia Kings; *Amor Familia Respeto* . . . . (EMI Latin)

U Remind Me
Usher; *8701* . . . . (LaFace)
   Totally Hits 2001-C . . . . (Arista)

Up And Gone
McCarters; *Better Be Home Soon.* . . . . (Warner Bros.)

Wanted
Perry Como; *Perry Como's All-Time Greatest Hits-#1* . . . . (RCA)
   Perry Como's Greatest Hits . . . . (RCA)

What About Us
Total; *Kima, Keisha & Pam* . . . . (Bad Boy/Arista)
   LaFace Records Presents The Platinum Collection-C . . . . (LaFace)
   ST/Soul Food . . . . (LaFace)

What Goes On
Beatles; *"Yesterday"...And Today* . . . . (Capitol)

What I Didn't Know
Athenaeum; *Radiance* . . . . (Atlantic)

When You Think Of Me
Eric Benet; *A Day In The Life.* . . . . (Warner Bros.)

Whiskey In The Jar
Metallica; *Garage Inc.* . . . . (Elektra)

Whiskey Under The Bridge
Brooks & Dunn; *Brooks & Dunn-The Greatest Hits Collection.* . . . . . . (Arista)
   Waitin' On Sundown . . . . (Arista)

White Sport Coat (And A Pink Carnation)
Marty Robbins; *16 Most Requested Songs Of The '50s-#2-C.* . . . . (Legacy)
   Lifetime Of Song-1951-1982 . . . . (Columbia)
   Marty Robbins' Greatest Hits . . . . (Columbia)

Who Do U Love
Deborah Cox; *Deborah Cox.* . . . . (Arista)
   Ultimate Dance Party-1997-C . . . . (Arista)

Who Will The Next Fool Be
Charlie Rich; *Charlie Rich-The Ultimate Collection* . . . . (Hip-O)
   Lonely Weekends-The Very Best Of Charlie Rich . . . . . (Collectables)
Jerry Lee Lewis; *The Mercury & Smash Years Recordings* . . . . . . (Collectables)

Who's Sorry Now
Benny Goodman; *Stompin'* . . . . (Drive)
Big Bill Broonzy; *Black, Brown & White.* . . . . (Evidence Music)
Bob Crosby; *Bob Crosby & His Orchestra* . . . . (EPM)
Connie Francis; *Dick Clark's 21 All-Time Hits-#1-C.* . . . . . . (Original Sound)
   Very Best Of Connie Francis. . . . . (Polydor)
Ella Fitzgerald; *The Intimate Ella* . . . . (Verve)
Esquivel; *Space-Age Bachelor Pad Music* . . . . (Bar/None)
Glen Gray; *Moonglow: 1930-1936* . . . . (Aero Space)
Nat "King" Cole; *The Billy May Sessions* . . . . (Capitol)
Ray Anthony; *Swing Back To The '40s* . . . . (Aero Space)

Why Baby Why
Charley Pride; *Charley Pride's Greatest Hits-#2.* . . . . (RCA)
George Jones; *George Jones' All-Time Greatest Hits* . . . . (Epic)
   George Jones-Super Hits . . . . (Epic)
Red Sovine & Webb Pierce; *Greatest Country Duets Of All*
   Time-C . . . . (MCA Special Prod.)
Webb Pierce; *Webb Pierce-Golden Hits-#2.* . . . . (Plantation)
Willie Nelson & Waylon Jennings; *Take It To The Limit* . . . . . . (Columbia)

Why Don't You Get A Job?
Offspring; *Americana* . . . . (Columbia)

Why Oh Why
Celine Dion; *Let's Talk About Love-C* . . . . (550 Music)

Wicked Game
Chris Isaak; *Heart Shaped World.* . . . . (Reprise)
   ST/Wild At Heart. . . . . (Polydor)

Words
Bee Gees; *Bee Gees-Gold* . . . . (Polydor)
   Here At Last...Bee Gees...Live . . . . (Polydor)
   History Of British Rock-#9-C . . . . (Rhino)
Elvis Presley; *From Memphis To Vegas/From Vegas To Memphis* . . . . . (RCA)
   That's The Way It Is. . . . . (RCA)
Joan Armatrading; *Shouting Stage* . . . . (A&M)
Rita Coolidge; *Anytime...Anywhere.* . . . . (A&M)
   Rita Coolidge-Classics-#5 . . . . (A&M)
   Rita Coolidge's Greatest Hits . . . . (A&M)

You Bring Me Up
K-Ci & JoJo; *Love Always* . . . . (MCA)

You Cheated
Shields; *Oldies But Goodies-#3-C* . . . . (Original Sound)

You Don't Have To Hurt No More
Mint Condition; *Definition Of A Band* . . . . (Perspective/A&M)
Mint Condition-Collection (1991-1998) . . . . (Perspective/A&M)

You Oughta Know
Alanis Morissette; *1996 Grammy Nominees-C.* . . . . (Columbia)
Jagged Little Pill . . . .(Maverick)

You Should Be Mine (Don't Waste Your Time)
Brian McKnight; *Anytime.* . . . . (Motown)

You Should Know Better
Kenny Wayne Shepherd Band; *Live On* . . . . (Giant)

You Should've Told Me
Kelly Price; *Mirror Mirror* . . . .(Def Soul/IDJMG)

You Will Have To Pay
Tex Ritter; *Tex Ritter's Greatest Hits* . . . . (Curb)

You Win Again
Hank Williams With His Drifting Cowboys; *24 Of Hank Williams'*
Greatest Hits. . . . .(Polydor)
Hank Williams-40 Greatest Hits . . . . (Polydor)
Jerry Lee Lewis; *Heartbreak* . . . . (Tomato)
Memphis Country-C . . . . (Sun)
Rockin' My Life Away . . . . (Tomato)
Taste Of Country . . . . (Sun)
The Golden Hits Of Jerry Lee Lewis . . . . (Smash)
Johnny Cash; *Johnny Cash-Original Golden Hits-#3.* . . . . (Sun)
Keith Richards; *Timeless: Hank Williams Tribute-C* . . . (Lost Highway/IDJMG)
Keith Whitley; *Kentucky Bluebird* . . . . (RCA)
Mary Chapin Carpenter; *Greatest Country Hits Of The '90s-#2-C.* . . (Columbia)
Tommy Edwards; *It's All In The Game-The Complete Hits Of Tommy*
Edwards . . . . (Eric)

You'll Never Get To Heaven (If You Break My Heart)
Dionne Warwick; *Dionne Warwick* . . . . (Everest)
Dionne Warwick Greatest Hits . . . . (Everest)
Dionne Warwick-Anthology 1962-1971 . . . . (Rhino)
Hot! Live & Otherwise . . . . (Arista)
Say A Little Prayer . . . .(Dunhill Compact Classics)
Stylistics; *Best Of The Stylistics-#2.* . . . . (Amherst)

Your Cheatin' Heart
Beck; *Timeless: Hank Williams Tribute-C* . . . . (Lost Highway/IDJMG)
Elvis Presley; *Elvis For Everyone!* . . . . (RCA)
Welcome To My World. . . . . (RCA)
Frankie Laine; *Frankie Laine's 16 Greatest Hits* . . . . (Trip)
Frankie Laine's Greatest Hits . . . . (Columbia)
Hank Williams With His Drifting Cowboys; *24 Of Hank Williams'*
Greatest Hits. . . . .(Polydor)
Hank Williams-16 Great Hits . . . . (Everest)
Hank Williams-40 Greatest Hits . . . . (Polydor)
Hank Williams, Jr.; *Very Best Of Hank Williams, Jr.* . . . . (Polydor)
Jerry Lee Lewis; *Live At The Star Club-Hamburg 1964* . . . . (Rhino)
The Golden Hits Of Jerry Lee Lewis . . . . (Smash)
Patsy Cline; *ST/Sweet Dreams* . . . .(MCA)
The Patsy Cline Story. . . . . (MCA)
Ray Charles; *Ray Charles' Greatest Hits-#2* . . . . (Rhino)

Your Selfish Heart
Stanley Brothers & The Clinch Mountain Boys; *Stanley Brothers & The*
Clinch Mountain Boys. . . . . (King)

Your Woman
White Town; *MTV The Grind-#1-C* . . . . (Tommy Boy)
Women In Technology . . . .(Chrysalis)

You're Driving Me Crazy
Art Pepper; *Return Of Art Pepper-Complete Aladdin*
Recordings-#1. . . . . (Blue Note)
Big Joe Turner; *Boss Of The Blues* . . . .(Atlantic)
Dinah Shore; *Love & Kisses Dinah.* . . . . (RCA)
Frank Sinatra; *Strangers In The Night* . . . . (Reprise)
Louis Armstrong; *Louis Armstrong-Vol. 7-You're Driving Me*
Crazy. . . . . (Columbia)

You're Going To Lose That Girl
Beatles; *ST/Help!* . . . . (Capitol)

You're Still On My Mind
Byrds; *Sweetheart Of The Rodeo* . . . . (Columbia)

You've Really Got A Hold On Me
Beatles; *The Beatles-Anthology-#1.* . . . . (Capitol)
Smokey Robinson & The Miracles; *Best Of Smokey Robinson & The*
Miracles-Anthology . . . . (Motown)
Great Songs & Performances That Inspired The Motown 25th Anniversary
Television Special-C . . . . (Motown)
Smokey Robinson-The Ultimate Collection . . . . (Motown)

LOVE: TEMPTATION, Can't Resist, Flirting

*See Also: **BEAUTY, DESIRE, HOLDING ON, KISSING, LOVE**
(various), PARENTS: CONCERNED ABOUT TEEN LOVE, SEX,
SEX: RESISTING TEMPTATION*

Adalida
George Strait; *Latest Greatest Straitest Hits.* . . . .(MCA)
Lead On . . . .(MCA)

After Party
Koffee Brown; *Mars/Venus* . . . . (Arista)

After The Lights Go Down Low
Al Hibbler; *After The Lights Go Down Low* . . . .(Atlantic)

Almost Persuaded
David Houston; *Super Hits Of The '60s-C* . . . . (Epic)

Ana's Song (Open Fire)
Silverchair; *Neon Ballroom.* . . . . (Epic)

Baby Don't Get Hooked On Me
Mac Davis; *Mac Davis' Greatest Hits.* . . . . (Columbia)
Super Hits Of The '70s-Have A Nice Day-#20-C . . . . (Rhino)

Be Still My Beating Heart
Sting; *...Nothing Like The Sun* . . . . (A&M)
Fields Of Gold-The Best Of Sting 1984-1994 . . . . (A&M)

Bette Davis Eyes
Kim Carnes; *Best Of Kim Carnes* . . . . (EMI Special Markets)
Billboard Top Hits-1981-C . . . . (Rhino)
Mistaken Identity . . . . (EMI)

Blood On The Dance Floor
Michael Jackson; *Blood On The Dance Floor-HIStory...* . . . . . (MJJ Music/Work)

Bootylicious
Destiny's Child; *Now That's What I Call Music!-#8-C* . . . .(Virgin)
Survivor . . . . (Columbia)

Breathless
Corrs; *In Blue* . . . . (143/Lava/Atlantic)
Totally Hits-#3-C . . . .(Atlantic)

Brown Eyed Handsome Man
Buddy Holly; *Buddy Holly-20 Golden Greats.* . . . . (MCA)
For The First Time Anywhere. . . . . (MCA)
Rock & Roll Collection. . . . . (MCA)
Chuck Berry; *Best Of The Best Of Chuck Berry* . . . . (International Mktg. Group)
Roll Over Beethoven . . . . (Allegiance)
The Chess Box-Chuck Berry . . . . (Chess)
Waylon Jennings; *Essential Waylon Jennings* . . . . (RCA)
Waylon Jennings-Super Hits . . . . (RCA)

Caligula
Macy Gray; *On How Life Is.* . . . . (Epic)

Can't Fight This Feeling
REO Speedwagon; *REO Speedwagon-The Hits* . . . . (Epic)
T.J. Martell-Music For The Miracle-C . . . . (Epic Portrait Assoc.)
Wheels Are Turnin' . . . . (Epic)

Can't Help Falling In Love
Elvis Presley; *Elvis* . . . . (RCA)
Elvis-A Legendary Performer, Volume 1 . . . . (RCA)
From Memphis To Vegas/From Vegas To Memphis . . . . (RCA)
ST/Blue Hawaii . . . . (RCA)
Julio Iglesias; *Starry Night* . . . . (Columbia)
UB40; *Promises And Lies* . . . . (Virgin)
ST/Sliver . . . . (Virgin)

Can't Help It
Jon B.; *Cool Relax.* . . . .(Yab Yum/550)

Come A Little Bit Closer
Jay & The Americans; *Good Vibrations (Sounds Of Top 40 Radio: 1964-*
1967)-C . . . . (Capitol)
Jay & The Americans' All-Time Greatest Hits . . . . (Rhino)
Jay & The Americans' Greatest Hits . . . . (CEMA Special Prod.)

Cousin Dupree
Steely Dan; *Two Against Nature* . . . .(Giant)

Cross Over The Bridge
Patti Page; *Patti Page-Golden Hits* . . . . (Mercury)
Patti Page's Greatest Hits . . . . (Columbia)

Desert Rose
Sting; *Brand New Day.* . . . . (A&M)

Devil With A Blue Dress On & Good Golly Miss Molly
Bruce Springsteen; *ST/No Nukes-Muse Concerts* . . . .(Asylum)
Mitch Ryder And The Detroit Wheels; *Frat Rock!-#4-C* . . . . (Rhino)
Rev Up-Best Of Mitch Ryder . . . . (Rhino)
Son Of Frat Rock!-C. . . . . (Rhino)
Toga Rock-C. . . . . (Dunhill Compact Classics)

Devil Woman
Marty Robbins; *Billboard Top Country Hits-1962-C* . . . . (Rhino)
Columbia Country Classics-#4-Nashville Sound-C . . . . (Columbia)
Lifetime Of Song-1951-1982 . . . . (Columbia)
Marty Robbins' Greatest Hits-#4 . . . . (Columbia)

Diggin' On You
TLC; *CrazySexyCool* . . . . (LaFace)

Don't Fight The Feelings Of Love
Charley Pride; *Sweet Country* . . . . (RCA)

Don't Go To Strangers
T. Graham Brown; *Best Of T. Graham Brown* . . . . (Curb)

Don't Let Go (Love)
En Vogue; *Best Of En Vogue.* . . . . (Elektra)
EV3. . . . . (East West)

Don't Make Me Come Over There And Love You
George Strait; *George Strait* . . . . (MCA)

Don't Stop
Wade Hayes; *Old Enough To Know Better* . . . . (Columbia)
Steppin' Country-#2-C. . . . . (Columbia)

Super Hits Of 1995-C . . . . (Epic)
Evil On Your Mind
Jan Howard; *Grand Ladies Of The Opry-C* . . . . (Deluxe)
Feelin' Love
Paula Cole; *This Fire* . . . . (Imago)
Fire
Bruce Springsteen & The E Street Band; *Bruce Springsteen & The E Street
Band Live/1975-85* . . . . (Legacy)
Pointer Sisters; *Cover Me (Bruce Springsteen Tribute)-C* . . . . (Rhino)
Energy . . . . (Planet)
I Am Woman-C . . . . (Nick At Nite)
First Night
Monica; *The Boy Is Mine* . . . . (Arista)
Follow Me
Original Cast; *Camelot* . . . . (Columbia)
ST/Camelot . . . . (Warner Bros.)
Follow Me
Uncle Kracker; *Double Wide* . . . . (Warner Bros.)
Totally Hits 2001-C . . . . (Arista)
Girl Inside My Head
Blues Traveler; *Bridge* . . . . (A&M)
Go Away Little Girl
Happenings; *The Ultimate History Of Rock 'N' Roll-#6-C* . . . . (K-Tel)
Steve Lawrence; *Steve Lawrence's Greatest Hits* . . . . (Columbia)
Goodnight, Sweetheart, Goodnight
McGuire Sisters; *McGuire Sisters-Anthology* . . . . (MCA)
Heartbreaker
Mariah Carey; *Rainbow* . . . . (Columbia)
Heaven's Just A Sin Away
Kelly Willis; *Hot Country-C* . . . . (MCA Special Prod.)
Kelly Willis . . . . (MCA)
Kendalls; *Best Of The Kendalls* . . . . (Curb)
Kendalls-20 Greatest Hits . . . . (Deluxe)
Heaven's What I Feel
Gloria Estefan; *Gloria!* . . . . (Epic)
Honky Tonk Man
Dwight Yoakam; *Guitars, Cadillacs, Etc., Etc.* . . . . (Reprise)
Just Lookin' For A Hit . . . . (Reprise)
Johnny Horton; *All Time Legends Of Country Music-C* . . . . (Legacy)
Columbia Country Classics-#2-Honky Tonk Heroes-C . . . . (Columbia)
Marty Robbins; *Greatest Country Hits From The Movies-C* . . . . (Epic)
Hypnotize The Moon
Clay Walker; *Hypnotize The Moon* . . . . (Giant)
I Can't Help Falling In Love With You
Wright Brothers; *The American Way* . . . . (KRB Music)
I Can't Help Myself (Sugar Pie Honey Bunch)
Four Tops; *16 #1 Hits From The Early '60s-C* . . . . (Motown)
Billboard Top R&B Hits-1965-C . . . . (Rhino)
Four Tops' Greatest Hits . . . . (Motown)
Four Tops-Anthology . . . . (Motown)
Good Feeling Music Of The Big Chill Generation-#1-C . . . . . . (Motown)
Motown Story-First 25 Years-C . . . . (Motown)
Motown Superstar Series-#14-Four Tops . . . . (Motown)
ST/Forrest Gump . . . . (Epic/Sony Music Soundtrax)
ST/Heaven Help Us. . . . . (EMI)
ST/Into The Night . . . . (MCA)
ST/Where The Buffalo Roam. . . . . (Backstreet)
I Could Fall In Love
Selena; *Dreaming Of You* . . . . (EMI Latin)
I Don't Want To Have To Marry You
Jim Ed Brown & Helen Cornelius; *Jim Ed Brown & Helen Cornelius'
Greatest Hits* . . . . (RCA)
I Know What Boys Like
Waitresses; *Best Of The Waitresses* . . . . (Polydor)
Just Can't Get Enough: New Wave Hits Of The '80s-#5-C. . . . . . . (Rhino)
I Like It, I Love It
Tim McGraw; *All I Want* . . . . (Curb)
Tim McGraw's Greatest Hits . . . . (Curb)
I Try
Macy Gray; *Now That's What I Call Music!-#4-C* . . . . (Virgin)
On How Life Is . . . . (Epic)
I Wanna Be Loved
Andrews Sisters; *Best Of The Andrews Sisters* . . . . (MCA)
I Want You
Savage Garden; *Best Of Savage Garden* . . . . (Columbia)
Savage Garden . . . . (Columbia)
If Ever I Would Leave You
Richard Harris; *ST/Camelot.* . . . . (Warner Bros.)
Robert Goulet; *Robert Goulet's Greatest Hits* . . . . (Columbia)
Robert Goulet/Original Cast; *Camelot* . . . . (Columbia)
If You (Lovin' Me)
Silk; *Tonight* . . . . (Elektra)
I'm A Bad, Bad Man
Ethel Merman/Bruce Yarnell/Original Cast; *Annie Get
Your Gun* . . . . (RCA Victor)
I'm Not Strong Enough To Say No
BlackHawk; *Strong Enough* . . . . (Arista)
Invitation To The Blues
Holly Cole; *Temptation* . . . . (Metro Blue)

Tom Waits; *Small Change* . . . . (Asylum)
Irresistible
Jessica Simpson; *Irresistible* . . . . (Columbia)
I've Got You Under My Skin
4 Seasons; *25th Anniversary Collection* . . . . (Rhino)
Diana Krall; *When I Look In Your Eyes* . . . . (GRP)
Frank Sinatra; *At The Sands* . . . . (Reprise)
Round #1 . . . . (Capitol)
Sinatra: A Man And His Music . . . . (Reprise)
Sinatra's Sinatra . . . . (Reprise)
The Reprise Collection . . . . (Reprise)
Frank Sinatra & Bono; *Frank Sinatra-Duets-C* . . . . (Capitol)
Frank Sinatra & Nelson Riddle Orchestra; *songs for swingin'
Lovers!* . . . . (Capitol)
Jimmy Mack
Martha & The Vandellas; *Billboard Top R&B Hits-1967-C* . . . . (Rhino)
*Compact Command Performances-Martha Reeves & The
Vandellas* . . . . (Motown)
Martha Reeves & The Vandellas-Anthology . . . . (Motown)
Motown Story-First 25 Years-C . . . . (Motown)
Motown Superstar Series-#11-Martha Reeves & The Vandellas . . . (Motown)
Top 10 With A Bullet-Motown Girl Groups-C . . . . (Motown)
Jump Right In
Urge; *Master Of Styles* . . . . (Immortal/Epic)
Keep Your Distance
Buddy & Julie Miller; *Buddy & Julie Miller* . . . . (Hightone)
Richard Thompson; *Rumor & Sigh* . . . . (Capitol)
Kiss Of Fire
Georgia Gibbs; *Best Of Georgia Gibbs-The Mercury Years* . . . . . . (Chronicles)
Tony Martin; *Best Of Tony Martin On RCA* . . . . (Collector's Choice)
Lickin'
Black Crowes; *Lions* . . . . (V2)
Lightnin' Strikes
Lou Christie; *Oldies But Goodies-#14-C* . . . . (Original Sound)
Li'l Red Riding Hood
Sam The Sham and The Pharaohs; *Best Of Sam The Sham and The
Pharaohs* . . . . (Polydor)
Cruisin'-1966-C . . . . (Increase)
Pharaohization! (Best Of) . . . . (Rhino)
Little Town Flirt
Del Shannon; *Del Shannon's Greatest Hits* . . . . (Rhino)
Del Shannon's Greatest Hits . . . . (Curb)
Livin' La Vida Loca
Ricky Martin; *Ricky Martin* . . . . (Columbia)
Loose Change
Bruce Springsteen; *Tracks* . . . . (Columbia)
Love Will Keep Us Together
Captain & Tennille; *Billboard Top Hits-1975-C* . . . . (Rhino)
Captain & Tennille's Greatest Hits . . . . (A&M)
Ma (She's) Making Eyes At Me
Eddie Cantor; *Memories* . . . . (MCA)
Macarena
Los Del Rio; *Club Cutz* . . . . (RCA)
Macarena Mix . . . . (Ariola America)
Mama He's Crazy
Judds; *Judds* . . . . (RCA)
Judds' Greatest Hits . . . . (MCA)
Why Not Me . . . . (MCA)
Mercy, Mercy, Mercy
Buckinghams; *Mercy, Mercy, Mercy* . . . . . . (Legacy Rock Artifacts Series)
Time & Charges-Portraits . . . . (Sundazed Music)
Mouth
Merril Bainbridge; *The Garden* . . . . (Universal)
Mr. Man
Alicia Keys with Jimmy Cozier; *Songs In A Minor* . . . . (J)
Mysterious
Scorpions; *Eye II Eye* . . . . (Koch International)
N.I.B.
Primus with Ozzy; *Nativity In Black II: Tribute To Black
Sabbath-C.* . . . . (Divine/Priority)
New
No Doubt; *Return Of Saturn.* . . . . (Interscope)
ST/Go . . . . (Work/Epic)
Next Lifetime
Erykah Badu; *Baduizm.* . . . . (Kedar Entert./Universal)
No One Else On Earth
Wynonna; *Wynonna* . . . . (MCA)
On The Verge
Collin Raye; *I Think About You* . . . . (Epic)
One Promise Too Late
Reba McEntire; *Country Classics-#10-1987-C* . . . . (Universal)
Reba McEntire's Greatest Hits . . . . (MCA)
What Am I Gonna Do About You . . . . (MCA)
Only The Good Die Young
Billy Joel; *Billy Joel-Greatest Hits, Volume I & Volume II* . . . . (Columbia)
KOHUEPT . . . . (Columbia)
The Stranger . . . . (Columbia)
Pink Cadillac
Bruce Springsteen; *Tracks* . . . . (Columbia)

Natalie Cole; *Everlasting* . . . . (Elektra)
  Gotta Have House-Best Of House Music-#2-C . . . . (Profile)
Southern Pacific; *Killbilly Hill* . . . .(Warner Bros.)
  Rockin' Country-C . . . .(Warner Bros.)
  Southern Pacific's Greatest Hits . . . . (Warner Bros.)

Pure Morning
Placebo; *Without You I'm Nothing* . . . . (Virgin)

Save Your Heart For Me
Gary Lewis And The Playboys; *Gary Lewis & The Playboys* . . . .(Gold Rush)
  Gary Lewis And The Playboys' Greatest Hits . . . . (Curb)

Secret Garden
Bruce Springsteen; *Bruce Springsteen's Greatest Hits* . . . . (Columbia)
  ST/Jerry Maguire . . . . (Epic/Sony Music Soundtrax)

Seduces Me
Celine Dion; *Falling Into You* . . . . (550 Music)

Sex And Candy
Marcy Playground; *Marcy Playground* . . . . (Capitol)
  Now That's What I Call Music!-#1-C . . . . (Virgin)

Shame Shame Shame Shame
Mark Collie; *Mark Collie* . . . .(MCA)

She's A Heartbreaker
Gene Pitney; *Best Of Gene Pitney* . . . .(K-Tel)
  Gene Pitney-Anthology 1961-1968 . . . . (Rhino)

She's Every Woman
Garth Brooks; *Fresh Horses* . . . . (Capitol)

Shine
Jon B.; *Cool Relax* . . . . (Yab Yum/550)

Simply Irresistible
Robert Palmer; *Super Nova* . . . . (Island)

So Help Me Girl
Gary Barlow; *Open Road* . . . . (Arista)
Joe Diffie; *Third Rock From The Sun* . . . .(Epic)

Taste Of India
Aerosmith; *Nine Lives* . . . . (Columbia)

Teach Me Tonight
Al Jarreau; *Al Jarreau In London* . . . .(Warner Bros.)
  Breakin' Away . . . .(Warner Bros.)
Diane Schuur; *Diane Schuur-Collection* . . . . (GRP)
Ella Fitzgerald; *Montreux '75* . . . . (Pablo)
Phoebe Snow; *Best Of Phoebe Snow* . . . . (Columbia)
  It Looks Like Snow . . . . (Columbia)
Sarah Vaughan; *How Long Has This Been Going On?* . . . .(Pablo)

Temptation
Destiny's Child; *The Writing's On The Wall* . . . . (Columbia)

Temptation
Bing Crosby; *Bing Crosby-16 Most Requested Songs* . . . . (Legacy)
  Bing Crosby-Love Songs . . . . (Universal)
Perry Como; *Perry Como-Pure Gold* . . . .(RCA)
  Perry Como's All-Time Greatest Hits-#1 . . . .(RCA)
  Perry Como's Greatest Hits . . . . (RCA)

Temptation Eyes
Grass Roots; *Grass Roots-All-Time Greatest Hits* . . . . (MCA)
  Grass Roots-Anthology (1966-1975) . . . . (Rhino)

Tempted
Squeeze; *East Side Story* . . . .(A&M)
  Rock Of The '80s-#1-C . . . . (Priority)
  VH-1 The Big '80s-C . . . . (Rhino)

Tempted
Marty Stuart; *Tempted* . . . .(MCA)

Ten Thousand Angels
Mindy McCready; *Ten Thousand Angels* . . . . (BNA)

That Old Black Magic
Ella Fitzgerald; *Best Of Ella Fitzgerald* . . . .(MCA)
  Big Bands Of The Swinging Years-C . . . .(Everest)
  In Rome-Birthday Concert . . . .(Verve)
Frank Sinatra; *Come Swing With Me!* . . . .(Capitol)
Glenn Miller & His Orchestra; *Chattanooga Choo Choo-#1 Hits* . . . . (Bluebird)
Judy Garland; *Best Of Judy Garland* . . . .(MCA)
Louis Prima & Keely Smith; *Memories Are Made Of This-C* . . . .(Capitol)
Marcels; *Best Of The Marcels* . . . . (Rhino)
Sammy Davis, Jr.; *Hey There-At His Dynamite Greatest* . . . . (MCA)
Spike Jones; *Best Of Spike Jones-#2* . . . . (RCA)

The 13th
Cure; *Wild Mood Swings* . . . . (Elektra)

Too Close
Next; *Rated Next* . . . .(Divine Mill/Arista)

Too Close For Comfort
Eydie Gorme; *Eydie Gorme* . . . .(Taragon)

Touch Me Tease Me
Case Featuring Foxy Brown; *Case* . . . .(Def Jam/RAL/Mercury)
  Def Jam Greatest Hits-C . . . .(Def Jam)
  ST/The Nutty Professor . . . .(Def Jam)
  Ultimate Hip Hop Party-1998-C . . . . (Arista)

T-R-O-U-B-L-E
Elvis Presley; *A Touch Of Platinum-#2* . . . .(RCA)
Travis Tritt; *Travis Tritt's Greatest Hits-From The Beginning* . . . .(Warner Bros.)
  T-R-O-U-B-L-E . . . .(Warner Bros.)

Trouble's Back In Town
Wilburn Brothers; *Wilburn Brothers* . . . . (First Generation)

Trust
Megadeth; *Cryptic Writings* . . . . (Capitol)

Twenty-Four Hours From Tulsa
Burt Bacharach; *Walk On By* . . . . (MCA Special Prod.)
Gene Pitney; *Best Of Gene Pitney* . . . .(K-Tel)

Unforgettable
Nat "King" Cole; *Capitol Collectors Series-Nat "King" Cole* . . . .(Capitol)
  The Nat "King" Cole Story . . . . (Capitol)
  Unforgettable . . . . (Capitol)
Natalie Cole with Nat "King" Cole; *Unforgettable With Love* . . . . . . (Elektra)

Waiting For Love
3T; *ST/Men In Black* . . . . (Columbia)

What If I Said
Anita Cochran & Steve Wariner; *Back To You* . . . . (Warner Bros.)
Steve Wariner & Anita Cochran; *Burnin' The Roadhouse Down* . . . . . . (Capitol)

What Would Happen
Meredith Brooks; *Blurring The Edges* . . . . (Capitol)

When You Put Your Hands On Me
Christina Aguilera; *Christina Aguilera* . . . .(RCA)

Wicked Game
Chris Isaak; *Heart Shaped World* . . . . (Reprise)
  ST/Wild At Heart . . . .(Polydor)

Will You Be Loving Another Man
Bill Monroe & His Blue Grass Boys; *Essential Bill Monroe & His Blue*
  Grass Boys . . . . (Legacy)
  Essential Bill Monroe-1945-1949 . . . . (Columbia)

With One Exception
David Houston; *American Originals-David Houston* . . . . (Columbia)
  Best Of David Houston . . . . (Curb)

Woman To Woman
Tammy Wynette; *Tammy Wynette-Anniversary-20 Years Of Hits* . . . . . . (Epic)
  Tammy Wynette's Greatest Hits-#3 . . . . (Epic)
  Tears Of Fire-25th Anniversary Collection . . . . (Epic)
Wynonna; *Tammy Wynette...Remembered-C* . . . .(Asylum)

You Blew Me Off
Bare Jr.; *Boo-Tay* . . . . (Immortal/Epic)
  ST/Cruel Intentions . . . . (Virgin)

You Can't Resist It
Lyle Lovett; *Live In Texas* . . . . (MCA)
Patricia Conroy; *You Can't Resist* . . . . (Intersound)

You Can't Run Away From It
Four Aces; *Four Aces-More Greatest Hits* . . . .(Varese Vintage)

You Made Me Love You
Judy Garland; *Best Of Judy Garland* . . . . (MCA)
  Judy Garland's All-Time Greatest Hits . . . . (Curb)
Patsy Cline; *Sentimentally Yours* . . . . (MCA)

You Make Me Wanna...
Usher; *My Way* . . . . (LaFace)
  Totally Hits-#1-C . . . . (Arista)

Young Girl
Union Gap Featuring Gary Puckett; *Billboard Top Pop Hits-1968-C* . . . . (Rhino)

Younger Girl
Critters; *Sixties Rule! Chapter Two-C* . . . . (One Way)
Lovin' Spoonful; *Lovin' Spoonful-Anthology* . . . . (Rhino)

Your Love's On The Line
Earl Thomas Conley; *Very Best Of Earl Thomas Conley* . . . .(RCA)

LOVE: US AGAINST THE WORLD

See Also: **FAITH, FIGHT, FREEDOM, KISSING, LOVE (various),
MOTIVATION, REBELS, TOGETHERNESS**

Against All Odds (Take A Look At Me Now)
Mariah Carey; *Rainbow* . . . . (Columbia)
Phil Collins; *Hit Singles-1980-1988-C* . . . .(Atlantic)
  Serious Hits...Live! . . . .(Atlantic)
  ST/Against All Odds . . . .(Atlantic)

Against The Wind
Bob Seger & The Silver Bullet Band; *Against The Wind* . . . . (Capitol)
  Nine Tonight . . . . (Capitol)
  ST/Forrest Gump . . . .(Epic/Sony Music Soundtrax)

Ain't No Stoppin' Us Now
Luther Vandross; *Songs* . . . . (Epic)

Alone Together
Judy Garland; *Judy Garland-At Carnegie Hall* . . . . (Capitol)

At The Stars
Better Than Ezra; *How Does Your Garden Grow?* . . . . (Elektra)

Born To Run
Bruce Springsteen; *Born To Run* . . . . (Columbia)
  Chimes Of Freedom . . . .(Columbia)
Bruce Springsteen & The E Street Band; *Bruce Springsteen & The E Street*
  Band Live/1975-85 . . . . (Legacy)
Melissa Etheridge; *The Concert For New York City-C* . . . . (Columbia)

Breaking All The Rules
She Moves; *Boom! 17 Explosive Hits-C* . . . . (Simitar)
  Breaking All The Rules . . . . (Geffen)

Doesn't Really Matter
Janet Jackson; *Now That's What I Call Music!-#5-C*. . . . .(Virgin)
ST/Nutty Professor 2: The Klumps . . . . (Def Soul/IDJMG)

Don't Look Back
Bruce Springsteen; *Tracks*. . . . .(Columbia)
Knack; *One Step Up/Two Steps Back-The Songs Of Bruce
Springsteen-C* . . . .(Right Stuff)
Retrospective-Best Of The Knack . . . .(Gold Rush)

How Deep Is Your Love
Bee Gees; *Bee Gees' Greatest* . . . . (Polydor)
ST/Saturday Night Fever . . . . (Polydor)

I Know
Luther Vandross; *I Know*. . . . . (LV/Virgin)

Me & My Old Lady
Offspring; *Ixnay On The Hombre* . . . .(Columbia)

No Matter What
Boyzone; *Where We Belong* . . . .(Ravenous/Mercury/IDJMG)

One Headlight
Wallflowers; *Bringing Down The Horse* . . . . (Interscope)

Run To The Water
Live; *The Distance To Here*. . . . . (Radioactive/MCA)

They All Laughed
Carmen McRae; *Setting Standards* . . . .(Pair)
Ella Fitzgerald & Louis Armstrong & Oscar Peterson Trio; *Great American
Songwriters-#1George & Ira Gershwin-C* . . . . (Rhino)
Fred Astaire; *Starring Fred Astaire*. . . . . (Columbia)
Sarah Vaughan; *Sarah Vaughan Sings George Gershwin Songbook,
Vol. 1* . . . .(Emarcy)
Tony Bennett; *Steppin' Out*. . . . . (Columbia)

They Don't Know
Tracey Ullman; *Best Of Tracey Ullman*. . . . . (Rhino)
You Broke My Heart In 17 Places . . . . (MCA)

Tonight's The Night (Gonna Be All Right)
Rod Stewart; *Absolutely Live* . . . . (Warner Bros.)
Downtown Train-Selections From The Storyteller Anthology . . (Warner Bros.)
Night On The Town . . . . (Warner Bros.)
Rod Stewart's Greatest Hits . . . . (Warner Bros.)

Two Sparrows In A Hurricane
Tanya Tucker; *Can't Run From Yourself*. . . . . (Liberty)
Tanya Tucker's Greatest Hits-1990-1992 . . . . (Capitol)

We Gotta Get Out Of This Place
Animals; *Best Of The Animals* . . . . (Abkco)
Greatest Hits Live!-Rip It To Shreds . . . . (I.R.S.)
Sullivan Years-British Invasion . . . .(TVT)
Fear; *The Record* . . . . (Slash)

We're In This Together
Nine Inch Nails; *The Fragile* . . . . (Nothing)

Whole New World (Aladdin's Theme)
Peabo Bryson & Regina Belle; *ST/Aladdin* . . . . (Disney)
Regina Belle & Peabo Bryson; *Passion*. . . . . (Columbia)

You And Me Against The World
Helen Reddy; *Helen Reddy's Greatest Hits*. . . . . (Capitol)

You And Me Against The World
Roy Rogers; *Best Of Roy Rogers* . . . . (Curb)

You'll Be In My Heart
Phil Collins; *ST/Tarzan* . . . . (Hollywood)

LOVE: WOMEN TALKING TO WOMEN

*See Also: **ADVICE, DESIRE, GOSSIP, INSULTS, JEALOUSY,
LOVE (various), WARNINGS***

Cold Hearted
Paula Abdul; *Forever Your Girl* . . . .(Virgin)
Get Up & Dance-Dance Mixes . . . .(Virgin)

Does He Love You
Reba McEntire & Linda Davis; *Reba McEntire's Greatest Hits
Volume Two* . . . . (MCA)

Don't Mess With Bill
Marvelettes; *Compact Command Performances-Marvelettes*. . . . . . (Motown)
Marvelettes' Greatest Hits . . . . (Motown)
Marvelettes-Anthology . . . . (Motown)
Top 10 With A Bullet-Motown Girl Groups-C . . . . (Motown)

Don't Mess With My Man
Irma Thomas; *We Got A Party-Best Of Ron Records-#1-C* . . . . (Rounder)

Fist City
Loretta Lynn; *Loretta Lynn-20 Greatest Hits* . . . . (MCA)
Loretta Lynn-Greatest Hits Live . . . . (K-Tel)
Loretta Lynn's Greatest Hits-#2 . . . . (MCA)
The Country Music Hall Of Fame-Loretta Lynn . . . . (MCA)

Fool, The
Lee Ann Womack; *Lee Ann Womack* . . . . (Decca)

Gettin' In The Way
Jill Scott; *Who Is Jill Scott? Words And Sounds-#1* . . . . . . (Hidden Beach/Epic)

Good Lovin' (Makes It Right)
Tammy Wynette; *Tammy Wynette-16 Biggest Hits*. . . . . (Legacy)
Tammy Wynette-Anniversary-20 Years Of Hits . . . . (Epic)

Tears Of Fire-25th Anniversary Collection. . . . . (Epic)

He Loves U Not
Dream; *It Was All A Dream* . . . . (Bad Boy/Arista)

He Wasn't Man Enough
Toni Braxton; *The Heat* . . . .(LaFace)
Totally Hits-#3-C . . . . (Atlantic)

He's A Heartache (Looking For A Place To Happen)
Janie Fricke; *19 Hot Country Requests-C* . . . . (Epic)
It Ain't Easy. . . . .(Columbia)
Janie Fricke-17 Greatest Hits . . . .(Columbia)
Very Best Of Janie Fricke . . . .(Columbia)

If He Moves His Lips
Shemekia Copeland; *Wicked* . . . . (Alligator)

I've Never Been To Me
Charlene; *Endless Love-Motown's Greatest Love Songs-C* . . . . (Motown)
Hard-To-Find Motown Classics-#2-C . . . .(Motown)
I've Never Been To Me . . . .(Motown)
Motown Memories-#4-C . . . .(Motown)

Jolene
Dolly Parton; *Best Of Dolly Parton* . . . . (RCA)
Best There Is . . . . (RCA)
Jolene . . . . (RCA)
RCA Years-1967-1986 . . . . (RCA)
Sherrie Austin; *Followin' A Feelin'* . . . .(We/Madacy)

On My Own
Reba McEntire; *Starting Over* . . . . (MCA)

Potential New Boyfriend
Dolly Parton; *Best Of Dolly Parton-#3* . . . . (RCA)

Same Script, Different Cast
Whitney Houston & Deborah Cox; *Whitney Houston's Greatest Hits*. . . .(Arista)

She's Single Again
Janie Fricke; *19 Hot Country Requests-#3-C* . . . . (Epic)
Greatest Country Hits Of The '80s-1985-C . . . .(Columbia)
Janie Fricke-17 Greatest Hits . . . .(Columbia)
Very Best Of Janie Fricke . . . .(Columbia)
Reba McEntire; *Have I Got A Deal For You* . . . . (MCA)

Something Wonderful
Original Broadway Cast; *The King And I* . . . . (RCA Victor)
Original Cast; *The King And I* . . . . (MCA)

Stepsisters' Lament
Barbara Ruick & Pat Carroll; *Cinderella-The CBS Television Network
Production* . . . . (Columbia)
Original Cast; *Cinderella-The CBS Television Production* . . . . (Columbia)

Sweet Talkin' Guy
Chiffons; *Best Of The Chiffons*. . . . . (Laurie)
Chiffons-Golden Classics . . . .(Collectables)
Collectables Presents The History Of Rock-#1-C . . . .(Collectables)
Everything You Always Wanted. . . . . (Laurie)

With Me Part 1
Destiny's Child featuring JD; *Destiny's Child* . . . . . (Grass Roots/Columbia)

Woman To Woman
Tammy Wynette; *Tammy Wynette-Anniversary-20 Years Of Hits* . . . . (Epic)
Tammy Wynette's Greatest Hits-#3 . . . . (Epic)
Tears Of Fire-25th Anniversary Collection . . . . (Epic)
Wynonna; *Tammy Wynette...Remembered-C* . . . . (Asylum)

Woman To Woman
Shirley Brown; *Didn't It Blow Your Mind: Soul Hits Of The
'70s-#15-C* . . . . (Rhino)
Top Of The Stax-Twenty Greatest Hits-C . . . . (Stax)
Woman To Woman . . . . (Stax)

Women Be Wise
Bonnie Raitt; *Bonnie Raitt* . . . . (Warner Bros.)

X-Girlfriend
Mariah Carey; *Rainbow* . . . .(Columbia)

You Ain't Woman Enough
Loretta Lynn; *Billboard Top Country Hits-1966-C* . . . . (Rhino)
Legends Of Country Music-The Best Of Austin City Limits-C. . . . . .(Columbia)
Loretta Lynn's Greatest Hits. . . . . (MCA)
The Country Music Hall Of Fame-Loretta Lynn . . . . (MCA)
Shirley Brown; *Diva Of Soul* . . . . (Malaco Jazz)

LOVE: YOUNG LOVE, Puppy Love, Teen Love

*See Also: **AGING, DESIRE, FAMILY PLANNING, KISSING,
LOVE (various), PARENTS: CONCERNED ABOUT TEEN LOVE,
TEENAGERS, YOUNG***

16 Candles
Crests; *Alan Freed's Memory Lane-C* . . . . (MCA)
Billboard Top Rock 'N' Roll Hits-1959-C . . . . (Rhino)
Crests Greatest Hits . . . .(Collectables)
Cruisin'-1959-C . . . . (Increase)
Oldies But Goodies-#14-C . . . . (Original Sound)
Rock & Roll U.S.A.-21 Rock & Roll Favorites-#2-C. . . . . (Laurie)
ST/American Graffiti . . . . (MCA)

Angels Working Overtime
Deana Carter; *Everything's Gonna Be Alright* . . . .(Capitol)

April Love
Pat Boone; *Best Of Pat Boone*. . . . .(MCA)
   Pat Boone's Greatest Hits . . . . (Curb)
At Seventeen
Janis Ian; *Between The Lines* . . . . (Columbia)
   Super Hits Of The '70s-Have A Nice Day-#15-C. . . . . (Rhino)
Be-Bop-A-Lula
Everly Brothers; *Everly Brothers* . . . . (Rhino)
Gene Vincent and His Blue Caps; *Billboard Top Rock 'N' Roll Hits-*
   1956-C . . . . (Rhino)
   ST/Wild At Heart . . . . (Polydor)
Jerry Lee Lewis; *Monsters* . . . . (Sun)
   Trio Plus . . . . (Sun)
John Lennon; *Rock 'N' Roll* . . . . (Capitol)
Bed Of Rose's
Statler Brothers; *Bed Of Rose's*. (Mercury)
Born Too Late
Poni-Tails; *Original Classic Oldies Of The '50s-#4-C* . . . .(MCA)
Brown Eyed Girl
Isley Brothers; *Live It Up* . . . .(T-Neck/Columbia)
Jimmy Buffett; *One Particular Harbour* . . . .(MCA)
Van Morrison; *Bang Masters* . . . .(Epic)
   Best Of Van Morrison . . . . (Polydor)
   ST/Born On The Fourth Of July . . . .(MCA)
   ST/Sleeping With The Enemy . . . . (Columbia)
   Wonder Years-Music From Emmy Shows/Era-C . . . . (Atlantic)
Chattahoochee
Alan Jackson; *A Lot About Livin' (And A Little 'Bout Love)*. . . . . . . (Arista)
Come Back When You Grow Up
Bobby Vee; *Best Of Bobby Vee*. . . . .(EMI)
   Bobby Vee-Legendary Masters . . . . (EMI)
   Good Vibrations (Sounds Of Top 40 Radio: 1964-1967)-C . . . . (Capitol)
Dawn (Go Away)
4 Seasons; *25th Anniversary Collection* . . . . (Rhino)
   4 Seasons-Anthology . . . . (Rhino)
Fill Me In
Craig David; *Born To Do It*. . . . .(Wildside/Atlantic)
   Totally Hits 2001-C . . . . (Arista)
Ginger Bread
Frankie Avalon; *Gold For The Road-Carburetor Classics-C*. . . . . . .(Compose)
   Venus: The Very Best Of Frankie Avalon. . . . . (Collectables)
Grease Megamix
Grease Megamix; *Pure Disco*. . . . . (A&M)
Happy Birthday, Sweet Sixteen
Neil Sedaka; *Neil Sedaka Sings His Greatest Hits* . . . . (RCA)
   Neil Sedaka Sings The Hits . . . . (RCA)
   Neil Sedaka's All-Time Greatest Hits . . . . (RCA)
Hello, Young Lovers
Frank Sinatra; *Frank Sinatra Sings Rodgers & Hammerstein* . . . . . . (Columbia)
Mel Torme; *Jazz 'Round Midnight-Mel Torme* . . . . (Verve)
Original Broadway Cast; *The King And I* . . . .(RCA Victor)
Original Cast; *ST/The King And I* . . . . (Angel)
I Got You Babe
Cher with Beavis & Butt-head; *The Beavis & Butt-head*
   Experience-C . . . . (Geffen)
Sonny & Cher; *I Got You Babe* . . . . (Rhino)
   The Beat Goes On-Best Of Sonny & Cher . . . . (Rhino)
UB40 & Chrissie Hynde; *Chicken Soup For The Couples Soul-C* . . . . . (Rhino)
I Think We're Alone Now
Tiffany; *Tiffany*. . . . .(MCA)
   Tiffany's Greatest Hits . . . . (Hip-O)
Tommy James And The Shondells; *Best Of Tommy James And The*
   Shondells. . . . . (Roulette)
   Billboard Top Rock 'N' Roll Hits-1967-C . . . . (Rhino)
   Tommy James And The Shondells-Anthology . . . . (Rhino)
I Was Made To Love Her
Stevie Wonder; *16 #1 Hits From The Late '60s-C* . . . . (Motown)
   Stevie Wonder's Greatest Hits . . . . (Motown)
Leader Of The Pack
Bette Midler; *Divine Miss M* . . . . (Atlantic)
   ST/Divine Madness . . . . (Atlantic)
Original Cast; *Leader Of The Pack* . . . . (Elektra)
Shangri-Las; *21 Number One Hits-C* . . . .(Original Sound)
   Billboard Top Rock 'N' Roll Hits-1964-C . . . . (Rhino)
   Girl Groups-Story Of A Sound-C . . . . (Rhino)
   Golden Hits Of The Shangri-Las . . . . (Mercury)
   Oldies But Goodies-#15-C . . . .(Original Sound)
   Radio Active Hits-#2-C . . . . (Accord)
   Remember The Shangri-Las At Their Best . . . . (Collectables)
Lend Me Your Comb
Beatles; *The Beatles-Anthology-#1*. . . . . (Capitol)
Carl Perkins; *Carl Perkins-Original Sun Greatest Hits* . . . . (Rhino)
Life's A Dance
John Michael Montgomery; *Life's A Dance* . . . . (Atlantic)
Love And Texaco
Gretchen Peters; *Gretchen Peters* . . . . (Purple Crayon Prod.)
Love Keep Us Together
Martin Sexton; *Black Sheep* . . . .(Eastern Front)
   The American. . . . . (Atlantic)

My Baby
Lil' Romeo; *My Baby* . . . . (Soulja/Priority)
My Sharona
Knack; *Billboard Top Hits-1979-C*. . . . . (Rhino)
   Get The Knack . . . . (Capitol)
   Rock Of The '80s-C . . . . (Priority)
Not Too Young To Get Married
Bob B. Soxx/Blue Jeans; *Phil Spector-Back To Mono 1958-1969-C* . . . .(Abkco)
Darlene Love; *Best Of Darlene Love*. . . . .(Abkco)
Popular
Nada Surf; *High/Low* . . . . (Elektra)
Pretty Little Miss
Patty Loveless; *Mountain Soul* . . . . (Epic)
Puppy Love
Donny Osmond; *Donny Osmond's Greatest Hits* . . . . (Curb)
Ike & Tina Turner; *Ike & Tina Turner-Golden Classics* . . . . . . (Collectables)
Little Jimmy Rivers & The Tops; *Memories Of Times Square Record*
   Shop-#10-C . . . . (Collectables)
Paul Anka; *Paul Anka-30th Anniversary Anthology* . . . . (Rhino)
   Paul Anka's 21 Golden Hits . . . . (RCA)
Puppy Love
Lil Bow Wow Featuring Jagged Edge; *Beware Of Dog* . . (So So Def/Columbia)
Rag Doll
4 Seasons; *25th Anniversary Collection* . . . . (Rhino)
   4 Seasons' Greatest Hits-#2 . . . . (Rhino)
   4 Seasons-Anthology . . . . (Rhino)
   Billboard Top Rock 'N' Roll Hits-1964-C . . . . (Rhino)
Rebecca Lynn
Bryan White; *Bryan White* . . . .(Asylum)
Ricky Wants A Man Of Her Own
Bruce Springsteen; *Tracks* . . . . (Columbia)
She's In Love With The Boy
Trisha Yearwood; *Trisha Yearwood* . . . . (MCA)
Sixteen Going On Seventeen
Original Cast; *The Sound Of Music* . . . .(Sony Broadway)
Slow Down
Beatles; *Past Masters-Volume One*. . . . .(Parlophone)
So Young And In Love
Bruce Springsteen; *Tracks* . . . . (Columbia)
Someday Soon
Chris LeDoux; *Rodeo Songs Old & New* . . . . (Liberty)
Ian & Sylvia; *Ian & Sylvia's Greatest Hits* . . . . (Vanguard)
   Northern Journey . . . . (Vanguard)
Judy Collins; *Colors Of The Day-The Best Of Judy Collins* . . . . . . (Elektra)
   Who Knows Where The Time Goes. . . . . (Elektra)
Moe Bandy; *Moe Bandy's Greatest Hits* . . . . (Columbia)
   Rodeo Romeo . . . . (Columbia)
Suzy Bogguss; *Aces* . . . . (Liberty)
   Suzy Bogguss' Greatest Hits. (Liberty)
Something Like That
Tim McGraw; *A Place In The Sun*. . . . . (Curb)
   Tim McGraw's Greatest Hits . . . . (Curb)
Son Of A Preacher Man
Dusty Springfield; *Dusty Springfield* . . . . (Rhino)
   Dusty Springfield-Anthology . . . . (Mercury)
Strawberry Wine
Deana Carter; *Did I Shave My Legs For This?* . . . . (Capitol)
Summer Of '69
Bryan Adams; *Reckless*. . . . . (A&M)
Summer Song
Chad & Jeremy; *Best Of Chad & Jeremy* . . . . (K-Tel)
   Capitol Gold-Best Of Chad & Jeremy . . . . (Capitol)
   History Of British Rock-#2-C . . . . (Rhino)
Sweet Little Sixteen
Beatles; *45-#1502* . . . . (Collectables)
Chuck Berry; *Best Of The Best Of Chuck Berry* . . . . (International Mktg. Group)
   Chuck Berry-Golden Hits. (Mercury)
   Chuck Berry-Greatest Hits Live . . . . (Quicksilver)
   Cruisin'-1965-C . . . . (Increase)
   Oldies But Goodies-#12-C . . . .(Original Sound)
Jerry Lee Lewis; *Jerry Lee Lewis-Original Golden Hits-#3* . . . . (Sun)
Jerry Lee Lewis & Friends; *Jerry Lee Lewis & Friends-Duets* . . . . . . (Sun)
John Lennon; *Lennon* . . . . (Capitol)
   Rock 'N' Roll . . . . (Capitol)
Tammy
Columbia Ballroom Orchestra; *Let's Dance-#7-Competition Dance* . . . .(Denon)
Debbie Reynolds; *Best Of Debbie Reynolds* . . . . (Curb)
   Tammy . . . .(MCA Special Prod.)
Roger Williams; *Roger Williams' Greatest Hits* . . . . (MCA)
Teenager In Love
Dion And The Belmonts; *Classic Old & Gold-C* . . . . (Laurie)
   Collectables Presents The History Of Rock-#6-C . . . . (Collectables)
   Dion And The Belmonts-Their Best . . . .(Laurie)
   Oldies But Goodies-#6-C . . . .(Original Sound)
   Party Time Fifties-C. . . . .(JCI Assoc. Labels)
Telephone Hour
Original Cast; *Bye Bye Birdie* . . . . (Columbia)
Soundtrack; *Bye Bye Birdie*. . . . . (RCA)

That Summer
Garth Brooks; *The Chase*. . . . . (Liberty)
Theme From "A Summer Place"
Andy Williams; *Moon River & Other Great Movie Themes* . . . . (Columbia)
Percy Faith & His Orchestra; *Best Love Songs-C* . . . . (Original Sound)
 Billboard Top Pop Hits-1960-C . . . . (Rhino)
 Percy Faith & His Orchestra-16 Most Requested Songs . . . . (Columbia)
 Percy Faith & His Orchestra's All-Time Greatest Hits . . . . (Columbia)
 Percy Faith & His Orchestra's Greatest Hits. . . . . (Columbia)
Too Young
Donny Osmond; *Donny Osmond's Greatest Hits* . . . .(Curb)
Nat "King" Cole; *Nat "King" Cole-Greatest Hits* . . . . (Capitol)
Wake Up Little Susie
Everly Brothers; *All They Had To Do Was Dream* . . . . (Rhino)
 American Graffiti-#3-C . . . . (MCA)
 Everly Brothers. . . . . (Rhino)
 Everly Brothers' All-Time Greatest Hits. . . . . (Curb)
 Oldies But Goodies-#7-C . . . . (Original Sound)
 Very Best Of The Everly Brothers . . . . (Warner Bros.)
Grateful Dead; *History Of The Grateful Dead-Vol. 1 (Bear's Choice)* . . . . (Warner Bros.)
Simon & Garfunkel; *The Concert In Central Park* . . . . (Warner Bros.)
Wear My Ring Around Your Neck
Elvis Presley; *50,000,000 Elvis Fans Can't Be Wrong-Elvis' Gold Records-Volume 2* . . . .(RCA)
 Hits Like Never Before-Essential-#3 . . . .(RCA)
 The Top Ten Hits . . . .(RCA)
 Worldwide 50 Gold Award Hits, Vol. 1, Parts 1 & 2. . . . .(RCA)
Ricky Van Shelton; *Ricky Van Shelton's Greatest Hits Plus* . . . . (Columbia)
When Boy Meets Girl
Terri Clark; *Terri Clark*. . . . . (Mercury)
When Country Comes To Town
Toby Keith; *How Do You Like Me Now?!* . . . . (DreamWorks/SKG)
When You Ask About Love
Crickets; *45-#9-55153*. . . . . (Brunswick)
When You're Young And In Love
Marvelettes; *Marvelettes-The Ultimate Collection* . . . . (Motown)
Where I Wanna Be
Donell Jones; *Where I Wanna Be*. . . . .(LaFace)
White Sport Coat (And A Pink Carnation)
Marty Robbins; *16 Most Requested Songs Of The '50s-#2-C* . . . . (Legacy)
 Lifetime Of Song-1951-1982. . . . . (Columbia)
 Marty Robbins' Greatest Hits. . . . . (Columbia)
Wouldn't It Be Nice
Beach Boys; *Absolutely Best-#2* . . . . (Capitol)
 Made In The U.S.A. . . . . (Capitol)
 Pet Sounds . . . . (Capitol)
 Still Cruisin' . . . . (Capitol)
Young Love
Sonny James; *Golden Jukebox Favorites* . . . . (Capitol)
 Opry Legends-Sonny James . . . . (Capitol)
 Stars Of The Grand Ole Opry-1926-1974-C. . . . . (RCA)
 Traditions In Country Music-C. . . . . (Capitol)
Tab Hunter; *Fonzie's Make-Out Music-C* . . . . (Nick At Nite)
 Teen Idols-C . . . . (Universal)
Young Love
Janet Jackson; *Janet Jackson*. . . . . (A&M)
Young Love
Teena Marie; *Baddest Love Jams-Volume 1-Quite Storm-C* . . . . (Motown)
 Best Of Teena Marie . . . . (Motown)
Young World
Rick Nelson; *Rick Nelson's Greatest Hits* . . . . (Rhino)
Ricky Nelson; *All My Best* . . . . (MCA)
 Best Of Rick Nelson-#2 . . . . (EMI)
 Teenage Idol . . . . (Liberty)
Younger Girl
Critters; *Sixties Rule! Chapter Two-C* . . . . (One Way)
Lovin' Spoonful; *Lovin' Spoonful-Anthology* . . . . (Rhino)
You're Still A Young Man
Tower Of Power; *Bump City* . . . . (Warner Bros.)
 Live & In Living Color . . . . (Warner Bros.)
Zero And Blind Terry
Bruce Springsteen; *Tracks* . . . . (Columbia)

LOW SELF-ESTEEM, Feel Unlovable, Insecurity, Self-criticism, Self-doubt, Self-hatred

See Also: ANGER, DESPAIR, EGO, FOOLS, GUILT, MISTAKES, SADNESS, SLEAZY, SOCIAL OUTCASTS, SUICIDE

(Sittin' On) The Dock Of The Bay
Michael Bolton; *The Hunger* . . . . (Columbia)
Otis Redding; *(Sittin' On) The Dock Of The Bay*. . . . . (Atco)
 Best Of Otis Redding. . . . . (Atco)
 Golden Age Of Black Music-1960-1970-C. . . . . (Atlantic)
 Golden Soul-C . . . . (Atlantic)

 Soul Years-C . . . . (Atlantic)
 The Otis Redding Story . . . . (Atlantic)
All My Friends
Counting Crows; *This Desert Life* . . . . (David Geffen Co.)
Am I Getting Through (Part I & II)
Sheryl Crow; *The Globe Sessions* . . . .(A&M)
Army
Ben Folds Five; *The Unauthorized Biography Of Reinhold Messner* . . . . (550 Music)
At Seventeen
Janis Ian; *Between The Lines* . . . .(Columbia)
 Super Hits Of The '70s-Have A Nice Day-#15-C . . . .(Rhino)
Barrel Of A Gun
Depeche Mode; *The Singles-1986-1998* . . . .(Mute/Reprise)
 Ultra . . . .(Mute/Reprise)
Beast In Me
Johnny Cash; *American Recordings* . . . .(American)
Nick Lowe; *The Impossible Bird* . . . .(Upstart)
 The Sopranos-Music From The HBO Original Series . . . . (Sony Music Soundtrax)
Because I Got High
Afroman; *Good Times* . . . . (Universal)
Bent
Matchbox Twenty; *Mad Season By Matchbox Twenty*. . . . .(Lava)
 Totally Hits-#3-C . . . . (Atlantic)
Best Of Intentions
Travis Tritt; *Down The Road I Go* . . . .(Columbia)
Better Days (And The Bottom Drops Out)
Citizen King; *Mobile Estates* . . . . (Warner Bros.)
Big Man
Four Preps; *Best Of The Four Preps*. . . . .(Curb)
 Capitol Collectors Series-Four Preps . . . .(Collectables)
Bitch
Meredith Brooks; *Blurring The Edges* . . . .(Capitol)
Bittersweet
Fuel; *Sunburn*. . . . . (550 Music)
Bleeding Me
Metallica; *Load* . . . . (Elektra)
Bound For The Floor
Local H; *As Good As Dead* . . . .(Island)
Cancer
Filter; *Title Of Record* . . . . (Reprise)
Come Down
Toad The Wet Sprocket; *Coil*. . . . .(Columbia)
Crawling
Linkin Park; *Hybrid Theory* . . . . (Warner Bros.)
Day I Tried To Live, The
Soundgarden; *A-Sides* . . . .(A&M)
 Superunknown. . . . . (A&M)
Distance, The
Cake; *Fashion Nugget* . . . .(Capricorn)
Don't Let Me Be Misunderstood
Animals; *Greatest Hits Live!-Rip It To Shreds* . . . . (I.R.S.)
 Sullivan Years-British Invasion . . . .(TVT)
Joe Cocker; *With A Little Help From My Friends* . . . .(A&M)
Down With The Sickness
Disturbed; *The Sickness* . . . . (Giant)
Everything Falls Apart
Dog's Eye View; *Happy Nowhere* . . . .(Columbia)
Fa Fa (Never Be The Same Again)
Guster; *Lost & Gone Forever* . . . . (Hybrid/Sire)
Fakin' It
Simon & Garfunkel; *Bookends*. . . . .(Columbia)
 Collected Works . . . .(Columbia)
Flagpole Sitta
Harvey Danger; *Now That's What I Call Music!-#1-C* . . . . (Virgin)
 Where Have All The Merrymakers Gone . . . . (Slash)
Freak Of The Week
Marvelous 3; *Hey Album* . . . .(HiFi/Elektra)
Galaxie
Blind Melon; *Soup* . . . .(Capitol)
Gave It A Name
Bruce Springsteen; *Tracks* . . . . (Columbia)
Geek Stink Breath
Green Day; *Insomniac* . . . . (Reprise)
Gonna Get A Life
Mark Chesnutt; *Mark Chesnutt's Greatest Hits* . . . .(Decca)
 What A Way To Live . . . .(Decca)
Hanginaround
Counting Crows; *This Desert Life* . . . . (David Geffen Co.)
Help! I'm White And I Can't Get Down
Geezinslaws; *Feelin' Good, Gittin' Up, Gittin' Down* . . . . (Step One)
Hero
Verve Pipe; *The Verve Pipe* . . . . (RCA)
Hurt
Nine Inch Nails; *The Downward Spiral* . . . . (Interscope)
I Got Id
Pearl Jam; *Merkinball* . . . . (Epic)

I Think I'm Paranoid
Garbage; *Now That's What I Call Music!-#2-C* . . . . (Virgin)
Version 2.0. . . . . (Almo Sounds)
I Wish
Skee-Lo; *I Wish* . . . . (Sunshine/Scotti Bros.)
Stevie Wonder; *Original Musiquarium* . . . . (Motown)
Songs In The Key Of Life . . . . (Motown)
It's Been Awhile
Staind; *Break The Cycle* . . . .(Flip/Elektra)
It's On!
Korn; *Follow The Leader* . . . .(Immortal/Epic)
I've Been Down That Road Before
Hank Williams; *Alone And Forsaken* . . . . (Mercury)
Beyond The Sunset . . . . (Polydor)
Joining You
Alanis Morissette; *Supposed Former Infatuation Junkie* . . . .(Maverick)
Just Let Me Be In Love
Tracy Byrd; *Ten Rounds* . . . . (RCA)
Just Like Anyone
Soul Asylum; *Let Your Dim Light Shine* . . . . (Columbia)
Kathy's Song
Simon & Garfunkel; *Collected Works* . . . . (Columbia)
Simon & Garfunkel's Greatest Hits . . . . (Columbia)
Sounds Of Silence . . . . (Columbia)
Keep Tryin'
Groove Theory; *Groove Theory* . . . .(Epic)
Last Resort
Papa Roach; *Infest* . . . .(DreamWorks/SKG)
Lock And Load
Bob Seger; *It's A Mystery* . . . . (Capitol)
Long Day
Matchbox Twenty; *Yourself Or Someone Like You* . . . . (Lava)
Long Way Down
Goo Goo Dolls; *A Boy Named Goo*. . . . .(Metal Blade)
Loser
3 Doors Down; *Better Life* . . . .(Republic/Universal)
Love Don't Love Me
Eric Benet; *ST/The Brothers*. . . . .(Warner Bros.)
Man That I've Become
Nick Lowe; *Dig My Mood* . . . . (Upstart)
Me
Paula Cole; *This Fire* . . . . (Imago)
Me
Staind; *Dysfunction* . . . .(Flip/Elektra)
More Human Than Human
White Zombie; *Astro-Creep: 2000 Songs Of Love* . . . .(Geffen)
My Life Is A Mediocre Piece Of Shit
Alice Donut; *Bucketfuls Of Sickness And Horror In An Otherwise
Meaningless Life*. (Alternative Tentacles)
My Own Prison
Creed; *My Own Prison* . . . . (Wind-up)
My Own Worst Enemy
Lit; *A Place In The Sun* . . . . (RCA)
One Of These Days
Tim McGraw; *Everywhere* . . . . (Curb)
Outside
Mariah Carey; *Butterfly* . . . . (Columbia)
Pennyroyal Tea
Nirvana; *In Utero* . . . . (David Geffen Co.)
MTV Unplugged In New York . . . . (David Geffen Co.)
Poor Poor Pitiful Me
Linda Ronstadt; *Linda Ronstadt's Greatest Hits, Volume Two*. . . . . . .(Asylum)
Simple Dreams. . . . . (Asylum)
Terri Clark; *Just The Same* . . . . (Mercury)
Warren Zevon; *A Quiet Normal Life-Best Of* . . . . (Asylum)
Stand In The Fire . . . . (Asylum)
River
Betty Buckley; *With One Look* . . . . (Sterling)
Joni Mitchell; *Blue* . . . . (Reprise)
River Of Deceit
Mad Season; *Above*. . . . . (Columbia)
Self Made Man
Montgomery Gentry; *Tattoos & Scars* . . . . (Columbia)
Shallow End Of The Gene Pool
Austin Lounge Lizards; *Small Minds* . . . . (Sugar Hill)
She Said
Collective Soul; *Dosage* . . . .(Atlantic)
ST/Scream 2 . . . . (Dimension/Capitol)
Sick Of Myself
Matthew Sweet; *100% Fun* . . . . (Zoo)
Someday
Sugar Ray; *14:59* . . . . (Lava)
Totally Hits-#1-C . . . . (Arista)
Staring At The Sun
U2; *Pop*. . . . . (Island)
Surefire (Never Enough)
Econoline Crush; *Devil You Know* . . . .(Restless)

Swallowed
Bush; *Razorblade Suitcase* . . . .(Trauma)
Teenage Dirtbag
Wheatus; *Wheatus*. . . . . (Columbia)
Thank God For Believers
Mark Chesnutt; *Thank God For Believers*. . . . . (Decca)
Too Much
Dave Matthews Band; *Crash*. . . . .(RCA)
Torn
Creed; *My Own Prison* . . . .(Wind-up)
Trash
Korn; *Issues*. . . . . (Immortal/Epic)
Uninvited
Ruth Wallis; *Laughing Gallery*. . . . . (American)
Unpretty
TLC; *Fanmail*. . . . . (LaFace)
Warped
Red Hot Chili Peppers; *One Hot Minute* . . . . (Warner Bros.)
Whatever I Fear
Toad The Wet Sprocket; *Coil* . . . . (Columbia)
Why Pt. 2
Collective Soul; *Blender* . . . .(Atlantic)
You Bowed Down
Elvis Costello & The Attractions; *All This Useless Beauty* . . . . . . (Warner Bros.)
You Know Me Better Than That
George Strait; *Strait Out Of The Box*. . . . . (MCA)
The Chill Of An Early Fall . . . . (MCA)
You're A God
Vertical Horizon; *Everything You Want* . . . . (RCA)
Youth Of The Nation
P.O.D.; *Satellite* . . . .(Atlantic)

LUCK, Fortunate
See Also: CITIES: LAS VEGAS, GAMBLING, LIFE (fate), LOSING & LOSS, WINNING

Any Lucky Penny
Nikki Hassman; *Songs From Dawson's Creek* . . . .(Sony Music Soundtrax)
Back In The U.S.S.R.
Beatles; *Beatles-Box Set* . . . . (Capitol)
Rock 'N' Roll Music . . . . (Capitol)
The Beatles (White Album) . . . . (Capitol)
The Beatles/1967-1970. . . . . (Capitol)
Billy Joel; *KOHUEPT*. . . . . (Columbia)
Bad Luck
Harold Melvin And The Blue Notes; *Harold Melvin And The Blue Notes-
Collector's Item*. . . . . (Philadelphia Int'l)
Harold Melvin And The Blue Notes-Vol. 12 . . . . (Philadelphia Int'l)
Philadelphia Classics-C. . . . . (Philadelphia Int'l)
Bad Luck
B.B. King; *B.B. King-16 Original Big Hits*. . . . .(Fantasy)
Bad Luck Streak In Dancing School
Warren Zevon; *Bad Luck Streak In Dancing School* . . . .(Asylum)
Best Day
George Strait; *Latest Greatest Straitest Hits* . . . . (MCA)
Better Luck Next Time
Judy Garland & Clinton Sundberg; *ST/Easter Parade* . . . . (Rhino)
Bowling Green
Everly Brothers; *Walk Right Back: The Everly Brothers On Warner Bros.-
1960-1969* . . . . (Warner Archives)
Circle Of Life
Elton John; *Elton John-Love Songs*. . . . . (MCA)
ST/The Lion King . . . . (Walt Disney)
Original Cast; *The Lion King*. . . . . (Disney)
Cowboys Don't Get Lucky All The Time
Gene Watson; *Beautiful Country*. . . . . (Capitol)
ST/Convoy. . . . .(Polydor)
Dear Mrs. Roosevelt
Bob Dylan; *Tribute To Woody Guthrie-C* . . . . (Warner Bros.)
Every Little Thing
Beatles; *Beatles VI* . . . . (Capitol)
Beatles-Love Songs . . . . (Capitol)
For Sale . . . . (Capitol)
Fortunate Son
Creedence Clearwater Revival; *1969* . . . .(Fantasy)
Creedence Clearwater Revival-Chronicle . . . .(Fantasy)
Live In Europe . . . .(Fantasy)
More Gold . . . .(Fantasy)
ST/Forrest Gump . . . .(Epic/Sony Music Soundtrax)
Willy & The Poor Boys. . . . .(Fantasy)
Four Leaf Clover
Abra Moore; *Strangest Places*. . . . . (Arista Austin)
Friday The 13th
Alvin Lee; *Rocket Fuel* . . . . (RSO)
Friday The 13th Child
David Clayton-Thomas; *Clayton* . . . . (MCA)

Gone At Last
Paul Simon; *Still Crazy After All These Years* . . . . (Columbia)
Good Luck Charm
Elvis Presley; *Elvis' Golden Records, Volume 3* . . . . (RCA)
   Number One Hits . . . . (RCA)
   The Top Ten Hits . . . . (RCA)
   Worldwide 50 Gold Award Hits, Vol. 1, Parts 1 & 2 . . . . (RCA)
Good Run Of Bad Luck
Clint Black; *No Time To Kill* . . . . (RCA)
Hard Luck Stories
Richard & Linda Thompson; *Pour Down Like Silver* . . . . (Hannibal)
Hard Luck Stories
Neil Young; *Landing On Water* . . . . (Geffen)
Hard Luck Story
Elton John; *Rock Of The Westies* . . . . (Polydor)
Hard Luck Woman
Garth Brooks; *Kiss My Ass-C* . . . . (Mercury)
Kiss; *Alive II* . . . . (Casablanca)
   Double Platinum . . . . (Mercury)
   Rock & Roll Over . . . . (Casablanca)
Hollywood (Down On Your Luck)
Thin Lizzy; *Lizzy Lives! (1976-1984)* . . . . (Gland Slamm)
   Renegade . . . . (Warner Bros.)
How The West Was Won And Where It Got Us
R.E.M.; *New Adventures In Hi-Fi* . . . . (Warner Bros.)
I Always Get Lucky With You
George Jones; *19 Hot Country Requests-C* . . . . (Epic)
   By Request . . . . (Epic)
   Shine On . . . . (Epic)
Merle Haggard; *Big City* . . . . (Epic)
I Feel Lucky
Mary Chapin Carpenter; *Come On Come On* . . . . (Columbia)
I'm Just A Lucky So And So
Diana Krall; *Stepping Out* . . . . (Justin Time)
Duke Ellington; *Sophisticated Ellington* . . . . (RCA)
Ella Fitzgerald; *Fine And Mellow* . . . . (Pablo)
I'm Looking Over A Four Leaf Clover
Al Jolson; *Best Of Al Jolson* . . . . (MCA)
   Rainbow 'Round My Shoulder . . . . (MCA Special Prod.)
Jerry Lee Lewis; *I Am What I Am* . . . . (MCA)
I'm Lucky
Joan Armatrading; *Joan Armatrading-Classics-#21* . . . . (A&M)
   Track Record . . . . (A&M)
   Walk Under Ladders . . . . (A&M)
It's Such A Small World
Rodney Crowell & Rosanne Cash; *Dynamic Duets-Super Hits-C* . . . (Columbia)
Rodney Crowell-*Super Hits* . . . . (Columbia)
I've Got Beginner's Luck
Fred Astaire; *Top Hat, White Tie And Tails* . . . . (ASV)
Gregory Hines & Patti Austin; *Hollywood Bowl Orchestra's Greatest Hits-C* . . . . (Philips)
Just Lucky I Guess
Steve Goodman; *High & Outside* . . . . (Asylum)
Just My Luck
Deele; *Street Beat* . . . . (Solar)
Just My Luck
Kim Richey; *Kim Richey* . . . . (Mercury)
Knock On Wood
Amii Stewart; *Double Smash Hits-C* . . . . (Volcano Entertainment)
Buddy Guy; *This Is Buddy Guy* . . . . (Vanguard)
Eddie Floyd; *15 Original Big Hits-#3-C* . . . . (Stax)
   Atlantic Rhythm & Blues 1947-1974-#6 (1966-1969)-C . . . . . . (Atlantic)
   Best Of Wattstax-C . . . . (Stax)
   Super Oldies Of The '60s-#11-C . . . . (Audio Fidelity)
Eric Clapton; *Behind The Sun* . . . . (Duck/Reprise)
Ike & Tina Turner; *Ike & Tina Turner's Greatest Hits-#3* . . . . . . (Saja)
Lady Luck
Journey; *Evolution* . . . . (Columbia)
   Journey-Captured . . . . (Columbia)
Lady Luck
Kenny Loggins; *Celebrate Me Home* . . . . (Columbia)
Lady Luck
Restless Heart; *Fast Moving Train* . . . . (RCA)
Lady Luck
David Lee Roth; *Little Ain't Enough* . . . . (Warner Bros.)
London Luck & Love
Daryl Hall & John Oates; *Bigger Than Both Of Us* . . . . (RCA)
Love And Luck
Marty Stuart; *Love And Luck* . . . . (MCA)
Luck Be A Lady
Frank Sinatra; *Sinatra Reprise-The Very Good Years* . . . . (Reprise)
   The Reprise Collection . . . . (Reprise)
   Original Cast; Guys & Dolls . . . . (MCA)
Luck Of The Irish
John Lennon/Plastic Ono Band; *Sometime In New York City* . . . . (Capitol)
Luck's In
Steve Winwood; *Steve Winwood* . . . . (Island)
Lucky
Britney Spears; *Now That's What I Call Music!-#5-C* . . . . (Virgin)

   Oops!...I Did It Again . . . . (Jive)
Lucky Charm
Boys; *Messages From The Boys* . . . . (Motown)
Lucky For You
REO Speedwagon; *You Can Tune A Piano But You Can't Tuna Fish* . . . . (Epic)
Lucky Guy
Rickie Lee Jones; *Pirates* . . . . (Warner Bros.)
Lucky Guy
Todd Rundgren; *Hermit Of Mink Hollow* . . . . (Rhino)
Lucky In Love
Sarah Vaughan; *Complete Sarah Vaughan On Mercury-#2* . . . . . . (Mercury)
   Complete Sarah Vaughan On Mercury-#3 . . . . (Mercury)
Lucky In Love
Mick Jagger; *She's The Boss* . . . . (Columbia)
Lucky Love
Ace Of Base; *Bridge* . . . . (Arista)
Lucky Man
Emerson, Lake & Palmer; *Best Of Emerson, Lake & Palmer* . . . . . (Rhino)
   Emerson, Lake & Palmer . . . . (Atlantic)
Lucky Man
Bruce Springsteen; *Tracks* . . . . (Columbia)
Lucky Man
Verve; *Urban Hymns* . . . . (Hut/Virgin)
Lucky Me
Anne Murray; *Anne Murray-Country Hits* . . . . (Capitol)
   Somebody's Waiting . . . . (Capitol)
Lucky Moon
Oak Ridge Boys; *Unstoppable* . . . . (RCA)
Lucky Number
Artie Shaw; *Complete Artie Shaw-#6* . . . . (RCA)
Lucky Number
Lene Lovich; *Stateless...Plus* . . . . (Rhino)
Lucky One
Laura Branigan; *Best Of Branigan* . . . . (Atlantic)
   Self Control . . . . (Atlantic)
Lucky One
Amy Grant; *House Of Love* . . . . (A&M)
Lucky One
Alison Krauss & Union Station; *New Favorite* . . . . (Rounder)
Lucky Ones
Loverboy; *Big Ones* . . . . (Columbia)
   Get Lucky . . . . (Columbia)
Lucky Star
Madonna; *Immaculate Collection* . . . . (Sire)
   Madonna . . . . (Sire)
   MTV's Rock 'N' Roll To Go-C . . . . (Elektra)
   Royal Box . . . . (Sire)
Lucky Town
Bruce Springsteen; *Lucky Town* . . . . (Columbia)
Moonlight Gambler
Frankie Laine; *Frankie Laine-16 Most Requested Songs* . . . . (Legacy)
   Frankie Laine's Greatest Hits . . . . (Columbia)
Mr. Lucky
John Lee Hooker; *Mr. Lucky* . . . . (Point Blank/Virgin)
   Urban Blues . . . . (MCA)
Mr. Lucky
Henry Mancini; *Henry Mancini-Pure Gold* . . . . (RCA)
   Peter Gunn . . . . (RCA)
No Leaf Clover
Metallica; *S&M* . . . . (Elektra)
O Lucky Man
Alan Price; *ST/O Lucky Man* . . . . (Warner Bros.)
Animals; *Greatest Hits Live!-Rip It To Shreds* . . . . (I.R.S.)
Oaf, The
Big Wreck; *In Loving Memory Of...* . . . . (Atlantic)
Oh Happy Day
Lawrence Welk; *Champagne Music Of Lawrence Welk* . . . . (Universal)
Only The Lucky
Walter Egan; *Fundamental Roll* . . . . (Columbia)
Other Man's Grass Is Always Greener
Petula Clark; *Petula Clark's Greatest Hits* . . . . (Crescendo)
Penny
Joe Stampley; *Best Of Joe Stampley* . . . . (Varese Sarabande)
Running Out Of Luck
Mick Jagger; *She's The Boss* . . . . (Columbia)
Semi-Charmed Life
Third Eye Blind; *Jock Rock 2000-C* . . . . (Tommy Boy)
   Third Eye Blind . . . . (Elektra)
She'd Rather Be With Me
Turtles; *Best Of The Turtles-Golden Archive Series* . . . . (Rhino)
   Oldies But Goodies-#3-C . . . . (Original Sound)
   Turtles-20 Greatest Hits . . . . (Rhino)
Some Guys Have All The Luck
Maxi Priest; *Best Of Me* . . . . (Charisma)
   Maxi . . . . (Virgin)
Robert Palmer; *Addictions-#1* . . . . (Island)
Rod Stewart; *Camouflage* . . . . (Warner Bros.)
   Storyteller/The Complete Anthology: 1964-1990 . . . . (Warner Bros.)

Sometimes I Get Lucky And Forget
Gene Watson; *Gene Watson's Greatest Hits* . . . . (MCA)
   Sometimes I Get Lucky . . . . (MCA)
Superstition
Stevie Wonder; *20/20-C* . . . . (Motown)
   Original Musiquarium . . . . (Motown)
   Talking Book . . . . (Motown)
That Lucky Old Sun
Asleep At The Wheel; *Western Standard Time* . . . .(Epic)
Bing Crosby; *The Radio Years: 25 Songs* . . . . (Crescendo)
Frankie Laine; *Frankie Laine-16 Most Requested Songs* . . . . (Legacy)
   Frankie Laine-Golden Hits . . . . (Mercury)
   Frankie Laine's Greatest Hits . . . . (Columbia)
Jerry Garcia Band; *Jerry Garcia Band* . . . . (Arista)
Louis Armstrong; *Louis Armstrong's Greatest Hits* . . . . (Curb)
Ray Charles; *Ray Charles-Anthology* . . . . (Rhino)
Willie Nelson; *Sound In Your Mind* . . . . (Columbia)
That's The Way Love Goes
Merle Haggard; *30 Years Of #1 Hits-#16-C* . . . . (Columbia)
   His Epic Hits-First 11 To Be Continued-C . . . .(Epic)
   Merle Haggard-Super Hits . . . .(Epic)
   That's The Way Love Goes . . . .(Epic)
Merle Haggard & Jewel; *For The Record: Merle Haggard-43*
   Legendary Hits . . . . (BNA)
Third Time Lucky
Foghat; *Best Of Foghat* . . . . (Rhino)
   Boogie Motel . . . . (Rhino)
Three Coins In The Fountain
Andy Williams; *Moon River & Other Great Movie Themes* . . . . . . (Columbia)
Doris Day & Frank De Vol Orchestra; *Hooray For*
   Hollywood-#2-C . . . . (Columbia)
Four Aces; *Billboard Top Movie Hits-1950-1954-C* . . . . (Rhino)
   Four Aces' Greatest Hits . . . . (MCA)
Frank Sinatra; *At The Movies* . . . . (Capitol)
   Capitol Collectors Series-Frank Sinatra . . . . (Capitol)
Harry James; *Harry James Plays The Songs That Sold A Million* . . . (Columbia)
Julius LaRosa; *The Envelope Please-Academy Award Winning Songs-#2*
   (1946-1957)-C . . . . (Rhino)
Till Good Luck Comes My Way
Original Cast; *Show Boat* . . . . (Angel)
Touch A Four Leaf Clover
Atlantic Starr; *Atlantic Starr-Classics-#10* . . . . (A&M)
   Secret Lovers: Best Of Atlantic Starr . . . . (A&M)
   Yours Forever . . . . (A&M)
Try Your Luck
Four Coins; *20 Great Love Songs Of The '50s & '60s-#2-C* . . . . (Laurie)
   22 Leaders Of The Pack-#1-C . . . . (Laurie)
Twinkle, Twinkle Lucky Star
Merle Haggard; *Chill Factor* . . . .(Epic)
   Greatest Country Hits Of The '80s-1988-C . . . . (Columbia)
Unlucky Girl
Big Mama Thornton; *Ball N' Chain* . . . . (Arhoolie)
We've Only Just Begun
Barbra Streisand; *Just For The Record* . . . . (Columbia)
Carpenters; *Carpenters-Classics-#2* . . . . (A&M)
   Carpenters-The Singles 1969-1973 . . . . (A&M)
   Close To You . . . . (A&M)
   From The Top . . . . (A&M)
   Yesterday Once More . . . . (A&M)
Wheel Of Fortune
Cardinals; *Atlantic Rhythm & Blues 1947-1974-box-C* . . . . (Atlantic)
Kay Starr; *Capitol Collectors Series-Kay Starr* . . . . (Capitol)
With A Little Bit Of Luck
Julie Andrews/Original Cast; *My Fair Lady* . . . . (Columbia)
Kiri Te Kanawa & Jeremy Irons/Original Cast; *My Fair Lady* . . . . . . (London)
Stanley Holloway; *ST/My Fair Lady* . . . . (Columbia)
With A Little Luck
Paul McCartney; *All The Best!* . . . . (Capitol)
Wings; *London Town* . . . . (Capitol)
   Wings Greatest . . . . (Capitol)
You Got Lucky
Tom Petty And The Heartbreakers; *Long After Dark* . . . . (MCA)
   Pack Up The Plantation-Live! . . . .(MCA)

MACHINES, Mind Control, Radar, Robots

See Also: BUSINESS & INDUSTRY, COMPUTERS, POWER & CONTROL, RADIO, TELEPHONE, TELEVISION

1983... (A Merman I Should Turn To Be)
Jimi Hendrix Experience; *Electric Ladyland* . . . . (Reprise)
Another Brick In The Wall, Part 2
Class Of '99; *ST/The Faculty* . . . . (Columbia)
Pink Floyd; *Collection Of Great Dance Songs* . . . . (Columbia)
   Delicate Sound Of Thunder . . . . (Columbia)
   The Wall . . . . (Columbia)
Roger Waters; *The Wall-Live In Berlin* . . . . (Mercury)

Answering Machine
Rupert Holmes; *Partners In Crime* . . . . (MCA)
Answering Machine
Kinsey Report; *Edge Of The City* . . . .(Alligator)
Answering Machine
Replacements; *Let It Be* . . . . (Twin-Tone)
Austin
Blake Shelton; *Blake Shelton* . . . .(Giant)
Automatic
Jennifer Rush; *Jennifer Rush* . . . . (Epic)
Automatic
Prince; *1999* . . . . (Warner Bros.)
Automatic
Go-Go's; *Beauty & The Beat* . . . . (I.R.S.)
Automatic
Pointer Sisters; *Break Out* . . . . (Planet)
Automatic Man
Michael Sembello; *Bossa Nova Hotel* . . . . (Warner Bros.)
Automation
Howard Jones; *Dream Into Action* . . . . (Elektra)
Big Bright Green Pleasure Machine
Simon & Garfunkel; *Collected Works* . . . . (Columbia)
   Parsley Sage Rosemary & Thyme . . . . (Columbia)
   ST/The Graduate . . . . (Columbia)
Brainwash
Rick Danko; *Rick Danko* . . . . (Arista)
Brainwash
Telex; *Sex* . . . . (PVC)
Brainwashed
Kinks; *Arthur Or The Decline And Fall Of The British Empire* . . . . . . (Reprise)
   Everybody's In Show-Biz . . . . (Rhino)
Brainwashed
Nuclear Assault; *Survive* . . . . (I.R.S.)
Check My Machine
Paul McCartney; *McCartney II* . . . . (Gold Rush)
   Paul McCartney-Gift Set . . . . (Capitol)
Cool The Engines
Boston; *Third Stage* . . . . (MCA)
Custom Machine
Beach Boys; *Beach Boys-Gift Set* . . . . (Capitol)
   Little Deuce Coupe/All Summer Long . . . . (Capitol)
   Spirit Of America . . . . (Capitol)
Dancing Machine
Jackson 5; *14 Greatest Hits* . . . . (Motown)
   Billboard Top Rock 'N' Roll Hits-1974-C . . . . (Rhino)
   Get It Together . . . . (Motown)
   Jackson 5-Anthology . . . . (Motown)
   Motown Dance Party-#2-C . . . . (Motown)
   Motown Story-First 25 Years-C . . . . (Motown)
   Motown Superstar Series-#12-Jackson 5 . . . . (Motown)
   Top 10 With A Bullet-Motown Dance Songs-C . . . . (Motown)
Download (I Will)
Expanding Man; *Head To The Ground* . . . . (Columbia)
   ST/The Cable Guy . . . . (Work)
Feel Like A Number
Bob Seger & The Silver Bullet Band; *Nine Tonight* . . . . (Capitol)
   Stranger In Town . . . . (Capitol)
Fire In The Engine Room
Richard Thompson; *Across A Crowded Room* . . . .(Polydor)
Flip The Switch
Rolling Stones; *Bridges To Babylon* . . . .(Virgin)
   No Security . . . .(Virgin)
Freak A Zoid
Midnight Star; *Midnight Star's Greatest Hits* . . . .(Solar)
   No Parking On The Dance Floor . . . .(Solar)
Helpless Automation
Men At Work; *Business As Usual* . . . . (Columbia)
I Am A Machine
Guess Who; *No Strings Attached* . . . .(SST)
Meat Puppets; *Mirage* . . . .(SST)
I Am Not Mechanical
Judy Mowatt; *Only A Woman* . . . . (Shanachie)
I Am Your Robot
Elton John; *Jump Up!* . . . . (MCA)
I Love You (Miss Robot)
Buggles; *Age Of Plastic* . . . . (Island)
I Robot
Alan Parsons Project; *Best Of Alan Parsons Project-#2* . . . . (Arista)
   I Robot . . . . (Arista)
   Instrumental Voyages . . . . (Arista)
I'm Not A Robot
Newcleus; *Jam On Revenge* . . . . (Sunnyview)
Jocko Homo
Devo; *Best Of Devo-Greatest Hits* . . . . (Warner Bros.)
   Q: Are We Not Men? A: We Are Devo! . . . . (Warner Bros.)
   Rest Of Devo-Greatest Misses . . . . (Warner Bros.)

John Henry
  ''Little'' Jimmy Dickens; *Columbia Historic Edition-''Little'' Jimmy Dickens* . . . . (Columbia)
  Harry Belafonte; *Harry Belafonte-At Carnegie Hall* . . . . (RCA)
  Harry Belafonte-Legendary Performer . . . . (RCA)
  Harry Belafonte's All Time Greatest Hits-#1 . . . . (RCA)
  Merle Travis; *Great American Train Songs-C* . . . . (C.M.H. Prod.)
  Odetta; *Essential Odetta* . . . . (Vanguard)
  Greatest Folksingers Of The '60s-C . . . . (Vanguard)
  Woody Guthrie; *Immortal Woody Guthrie-Golden Classics-#2* . . . (Collectables)
  Legendary Woody Guthrie . . . . (Tradition)
Killing Machine
  Judas Priest; *Hell Bent For Leather* . . . . (Columbia)
Lean, Mean, Lovin' Machine
  Lee Greenwood; *You've Got A Good Love Comin'* . . . . (MCA)
Living In The Plastic Age
  Buggles; *Age Of Plastic* . . . . (Island)
Logical Song
  Supertramp; *Breakfast In America* . . . . (A&M)
  Paris . . . . (A&M)
  Supertramp-Classics-#9 . . . . (A&M)
Lost My Drivin' Wheel
  Tom Rush; *Best Of Tom Rush: No Regrets* . . . . (Legacy)
  Tom Rush . . . . (Columbia)
Love In An Elevator
  Aerosmith; *Pump* . . . . (Geffen)
Love Machine
  Miracles; *12 #1 Hits From The '70s-C* . . . . (Motown)
  20/20-C . . . . (Motown)
  Billboard Top Hits-1976-C . . . . (Rhino)
  Motown Story-First 25 Years-C . . . . (Motown)
  Top 10 With A Bullet-Motown Dance Songs-C . . . . (Motown)
Love Machine
  Country Joe & The Fish; *C.J. Fish* . . . . (Vanguard)
  Life & Times Of Country Joe & The Fish . . . . (Vanguard)
Love Machine
  Wham! Featuring George Michael; *Fantastic* . . . . (Columbia)
Love Machine
  Paul Butterfield Blues Band; *Keep On Movin'* . . . . (Elektra)
Love Machine
  Uriah Heep; *Look At Yourself* . . . . (Mercury)
  Uriah Heep-Live . . . . (Mercury)
Love Machine
  W.A.S.P.; *W.A.S.P.* . . . . (Capitol)
M.A.C.H.I.N.E.
  Stimulators; *Loud Fast Rules!* . . . . (Roir)
Machine Messiah
  Yes; *Drama* . . . . (Atlantic)
Machine Stops
  Level 42; *Standing In The Light* . . . . (Polydor)
Machinehead
  Bush; *Sixteen Stone* . . . . (Trauma)
Machinery
  Sheena Easton; *Madness* . . . . (EMI)
  Money & Music . . . . (EMI)
Machinery
  Savage Republic; *Tragic Figures* . . . . (Independent Project)
Machines
  Giorgio Moroder; *ST/Metropolis* . . . . (Columbia)
Machines
  Queen; *Queen-The Works* . . . . (Hollywood)
Machines
  Modern English; *Ricochet Days* . . . . (Sire)
Master Mechanic
  Johnny Winter; *Serious Business* . . . . (Alligator)
Money Machine
  James Taylor; *In The Pocket* . . . . (Warner Bros.)
Mr. Roboto
  Styx; *Caught In The Act* . . . . (A&M)
  Kilroy Was Here . . . . (A&M)
  Styx-Classics-#15 . . . . (A&M)
Muswell Hillbilly
  Kinks; *Everybody's In Show-Biz* . . . . (Rhino)
  Muswell Hillbillies . . . . (VelVel)
My Clone Sleeps Alone
  Pat Benatar; *In The Heat Of The Night* . . . . (Chrysalis)
New Machine Pt. 1
  Pink Floyd; *Momentary Lapse Of Reason* . . . . (Columbia)
  Shine On . . . . (Columbia)
New Machine Pt. 2
  Pink Floyd; *Momentary Lapse Of Reason* . . . . (Columbia)
  Shine On . . . . (Columbia)
One Hit Wonder
  Everclear; *So Much For The Afterglow* . . . . (Capitol)
One Piece At A Time
  Johnny Cash; *The Man In Black-His Greatest Hits* . . . . (Legacy)
Perpetual Blues Machine
  Keb' Mo'; *Just Like You* . . . . (Okeh)

Propaganda Machine
  1927; *...Ish* . . . . (Atlantic)
Radar Blues
  Dave Dudley & Charlie Doublas; *Diesel Duets* . . . . (Sun)
Radar For Love
  Kiss; *Asylum* . . . . (Mercury)
Radar Gun
  Bottle Rockets; *The Brooklyn Side* . . . . (East Side Digital)
Radar Love
  Golden Earring; *'70s Greatest Rock Hits-#1-Hard N' Heavy-C* . . . . . . (Priority)
  Classic Rock-#1-C . . . . (MCA)
  Golden Earring-Live . . . . (MCA)
  Moontan . . . . (MCA)
  Super Hits Of The '70s-Have A Nice Day-#13-C . . . . (Rhino)
Radar Rider
  Riggs; *ST/Heavy Metal* . . . . (Asylum)
Rhythm Machine
  Bad Company; *Desolation Angels* . . . . (Swan Song)
Robot
  Robin Gibb; *Secret Agent* . . . . (Mirage)
Robot Girl
  Was (Not Was); *What Up Dog?* . . . . (Chrysalis)
Robot Man
  Scorpions; *Best Of The Scorpions* . . . . (RCA)
  In Trance . . . . (RCA)
  Tokyo Tapes . . . . (RCA)
Robot Man
  Connie Francis; *Rocksides-1957-1964* . . . . (Polydor)
Robot Police
  Baby Buddha; *Music For Teenage Sex* . . . . (Posh Boy)
Robot Portrait
  Quincy Jones & His Orchestra; *Quintessence* . . . . (MCA/Impulse)
Robots
  Kraftwerk; *Man Machine* . . . . (Capitol)
  The Mix . . . . (Elektra)
Rock & Roll Machine
  Triumph; *Rock & Roll Machine* . . . . (MCA)
  Stages . . . . (MCA)
  Triumph-Classics . . . . (MCA)
Sex Machine
  James Brown; *Revolution Of The Mind* . . . . (Polydor)
  John Wagner Coalition; *Shades Of Brown-James Brown's Greatest* . . . . . (Koala)
She Makes Me Shake Like A Soul Machine
  Unrest; *Kustom Karnal Blackxploitation* . . . . (Caroline)
She's My Machine
  David Lee Roth; *Your Filthy Little Mouth* . . . . (Reprise)
Situation
  Heart; *Private Audition* . . . . (Epic)
Sixty Minute Man
  Billy Ward & His Dominoes; *Rock & Roll Show-C* . . . . (Gusto)
  Dominos; *Oldies But Goodies-#5-C* . . . . (Original Sound)
  Rufus Thomas & Carla Thomas; *Rufus Thomas & Carla Thomas-Chronicle* . . . . (Stax)
Steel Monkey
  Jethro Tull; *Crest Of A Knave* . . . . (Chrysalis)
Street Machine
  Super Stocks; *Monster Summer Hits-Drag City-C* . . . . (Capitol)
Suicide Machine
  Death; *Best Of Death* . . . . (Relativity)
Suicide Machine
  Swell; *...Well?* . . . . (Def American)
Surfin' Sex Machine
  Pajama Slave Dancers; *Blood Sweat & Beers* . . . . (Restless)
Theme From ''Dastardly & Muttley In Their Flying Machine''
  Original Soundtrack; *Hanna-Barbera Pic-A-Nic Basket Of Cartoon Classics* . . . . (Kid Rhino/Rhino 4 Kids)
  Television's Greatest Hits-#3-1970s & 1980s-C . . . . (TVT)
Theme From ''The Bionic Woman''
  Original Soundtrack; *Television's Greatest Hits-#5-In Living Color-C* . . . (TVT)
Theme From ''The Six Million Dollar Man''
  Original Soundtrack; *Television's Greatest Hits-#5-In Living Color-C* . . . (TVT)
Third Stone From The Sun
  Jimi Hendrix; *Essential Jimi Hendrix* . . . . (Reprise)
  Kiss The Sky . . . . (Reprise)
  Jimi Hendrix Experience; *Are You Experienced?* . . . . (Reprise)
Time Machine
  Grand Funk Railroad; *Capitol Collectors Series-Grand Funk Railroad* . . . . (Capitol)
  Legends Of Rock Guitar-'70s-C . . . . (Rhino)
  Mark, Don & Mel 1969-71 . . . . (Capitol)
  On Time . . . . (Capitol)
Time Machine
  T. Graham Brown; *Come As You Were* . . . . (Capitol)
Time Machine
  Barbra Streisand; *Emotions* . . . . (Columbia)
Time Machine
  Black Sabbath; *Dehumanizer* . . . . (Reprise)
  ST/Wayne's World . . . . (Reprise)

Tin Man, The
Kenny Chesney; *In My Wildest Dreams* . . . . (Capricorn)
Turn On Your Radar
Prism; *Small Change* . . . . (Capitol)
TVC 15
David Bowie; *Fame & Fashion* . . . . (RCA)
Sound + Vision. . . . .(Rykodisc)
ST/Chrisiane F. . . . . (RCA)
Stage . . . . (Rykodisc)
Station To Station. . . . . (Rykodisc)
The Singles-1969-1993 . . . . (Rykodisc)
War Machine
Kiss; *Creatures Of The Night* . . . . (Casablanca)
Way Back Machine
Heart; *Rock The House ''Live''* . . . . (Capitol)
Welcome To The Machine
Pink Floyd; *The Wall* . . . . (Columbia)
When The Machines Rock
Gary Numan & Tubeway Army; *Replicas* . . . . (Atco)
You're My Driving Wheel
Diana Ross & The Supremes; *Diana Ross & The Supremes' Greatest Hits & Rare Classics* . . . . (Motown)
Zamboni
Martin Zellar; *The Hockey Zone-C* . . . . (Sportsongs)

MAGIC, Fortune Tellers, Magicians, Miracles, Supernatural, Voodoo, Wizardry

See Also: ASTROLOGY, FUTURE, GYPSIES, INVISIBLE, MONSTERS, SPIRITS, UFO'S

(Now You See Me) Now You Don't
Lee Ann Womack; *Some Things I Know* . . . . (Decca)
(You've Got) The Magic Touch
Platters; *Encore Of Golden Hits-Platters* . . . . (Mercury)
Abracadabra
Steve Miller Band; *Abracadabra* . . . . (Capitol)
Steve Miller Band-Live . . . . (Capitol)
Abra-Ca-Dabra
De Franco Family; *The DeFranco Family* . . . .(DeFranco Entert.)
Ain't No Trick (It Takes Magic)
Lee Greenwood; *Inside Out/You've Got A Good Love Comin'* . . . .(MCA)
Lee Greenwood's Greatest Hits . . . .(MCA)
All I Need Is A Miracle
Mike & The Mechanics; *Classic Rock 1966-1988-C* . . . . (Atlantic)
Mike & The Mechanics . . . . (Atlantic)
Amazed
Lonestar; *Lonely Grill*. . . . . (BNA)
Totally Hits-#2-C. . . . . (Elektra)
Amazing
Aerosmith; *Get A Grip* . . . .(Geffen)
Angel
Lionel Richie; *Renaissance* . . . .(Island/IDJMG)
Animal Magic
Belouis Some; *Animal Magic* . . . . (Capitol)
Animal Magic
Blow Monkeys; *Animal Magic* . . . . (RCA)
Animal Magic
Peter Gabriel; *Peter Gabriel* . . . . (Atlantic)
Any Lucky Penny
Nikki Hassman; *Songs From Dawson's Creek* . . . . (Sony Music Soundtrax)
As If You Read My Mind
Stevie Wonder; *Hotter Than July* . . . . (Motown)
Astral Traveller
Yes; *Time And A Word* . . . . (Atlantic)
Yesterdays . . . . (Atlantic)
Astral Weeks
Van Morrison; *Astral Weeks*. . . . .(Warner Bros.)
Bad Magik
Godsmack; *Awake* . . . .(Republic/Universal)
Belgian Tom's Hat Trick
Whitesnake; *Trouble* . . . .(Geffen)
Bermuda Triangle
Fleetwood Mac; *Heroes Are Hard To Find* . . . . (Reprise)
Bermuda Triangle Blues (Flight 45)
Blondie; *Plastic Letters* . . . .(Chrysalis)
Bibbidi-Bobbidi-Boo
Mormon Tabernacle Choir & Columbia Symphony Orchestra; *When You Wish Upon A Star-A Tribute To Walt Disney* . . . .(CBS Masterworks)
Original Soundtrack; *Cinderella* . . . .(Disney)
Verna Felton/Ilene Woods/Disney Chorus; *Disney Collection-#1-C* . . . .(Disney)
Black Magic Woman
Fleetwood Mac; *25 Years-The Chain* . . . .(Warner Bros.)
Vintage Years. . . . . (Sire)
Santana; *Abraxas* . . . . (Columbia)

Moonflower . . . . (Columbia)
Rock Classics Of The '70s-C . . . . (Columbia)
Santana's Greatest Hits . . . . (Columbia)
Viva Santana! . . . . (Columbia)
Book Of Miracles
Fleetwood Mac; *45-#7-28317* . . . . (Warner Bros.)
Box Of Miracles
Barefoot Servants; *Barefoot Servants* . . . . (Epic)
Boy In The Bubble
Paul Simon; *Graceland* . . . . (Warner Bros.)
Can You Read My Mind
Maureen McGovern; *Maureen McGovern* . . . . (Warner Bros.)
Cool Magic
Steve Miller Band; *Abracadabra* . . . . (Capitol)
Could It Be Magic
Barry Manilow; *Barry Manilow/Live* . . . . (Arista)
Barry Manilow's Greatest Hits-#2 . . . . (Arista)
The Manilow Collection-Twenty Classic Hits . . . . (Arista)
Donna Summer; *Love Trilogy* . . . .(Casablanca)
Could This Be Magic
Dubs; *Doo Wop Memories-#1-C* . . . . (Rhino)
December Will Be Magic Again
Kate Bush; *December Will Be Magic Again-12''* . . . . (EMI)
Deja Voodoo
Kenny Wayne Shepherd; *Ledbetter Heights* . . . .(Giant)
Deja Vu
Teena Marie; *Compact Command Performances-Teena Marie* . . . . . . (Motown)
Teena Marie's Greatest Hits . . . . (Motown)
Wild & Peaceful . . . . (Motown)
Deja Vu
Crosby, Stills, Nash & Young; *Deja Vu* . . . .(Atlantic)
So Far . . . .(Atlantic)
Deja Vu
Dionne Warwick; *Dionne* . . . . (Arista)
Perfect 10 III . . . . (Arista)
Deja Vu
Statler Brothers; *Maple Street Memories* . . . . (Mercury)
Deja Vu
Iron Maiden; *Somewhere In Time* . . . . (Capitol)
Disappear
Church; *Seance* . . . . (Arista)
INXS; *X*. . . . .(Atlantic)
Do You Believe In Magic
Lovin' Spoonful; *Lovin' Spoonful-Anthology* . . . . (Rhino)
E.S.P.
Duke Ellington; *Duke Ellington-Vol. 3-Studio Sessions-New York-1962* . . .(Saja)
In The Uncommon Market . . . . (Pablo)
E.S.P.
Miles Davis; *E.S.P.* . . . . (Columbia)
Miles Davis' Greatest Hits . . . . (Columbia)
E.S.P.
Deee-Lite; *World Clique* . . . . (Elektra)
Enchanted
Platters; *Encore Of Golden Hits-Platters* . . . . (Mercury)
E-S-P
Bee Gees; *E-S-P* . . . . (Warner Bros.)
Even Better Than The Real Thing
U2; *Achtung Baby* . . . . (Island)
Every Day Is Halloween
Ministry; *Twelve-Inch Singles-1981-1984* . . . . (Wax Trax)
Every Little Thing He Does Is Magic
Shawn Colvin; *Cover Girl* . . . . (Columbia)
Every Little Thing She Does Is Magic
Police; *Every Breath You Take-The Classics*. . . . . (A&M)
Ghost In The Machine . . . . (A&M)
Eye In The Sky
Alan Parsons Project; *Eye In The Sky* . . . . (Arista)
Turn Of A Friendly Card . . . . (Arista)
Fascinating Rhythm
Fred Astaire; *Crazy Feet!* . . . . (ASV Living Era)
Follow Me
Original Cast; *Camelot* . . . . (Columbia)
ST/Camelot . . . . (Warner Bros.)
Fortune Teller
Benny Spellman; *Best Of New Orleans Rhythm & Blues-#1-C* . . . . (Rhino)
History Of New Orleans R&B-#2-1959-1962-C . . . . (Rhino)
Rolling Stones; *got Live if you want it!* . . . .(Abkco)
More Hot Rocks (big hits & fazed cookies). . . . .(Abkco)
Friday The 13th
Alvin Lee; *Rocket Fuel* . . . . (RSO)
Friday The 13th Child
David Clayton-Thomas; *Clayton* . . . . (MCA)
Friends Of P.
Rentals; *Return Of The Rentals* . . . . (Maverick)
Funky Cold Medina
Tone Loc; *Loc-ed After Dark* . . . . (Delicious Vinyl)
Genie In A Bottle
Christina Aguilera; *Christina Aguilera* . . . .(RCA)

Totally Hits-#2-C . . . . (Elektra)

God Is Alive, Magic Is Afoot
Buffy Sainte-Marie; *Best Of Buffy Sainte-Marie* . . . . (Vanguard)
Illuminations . . . . (Vanguard)

Granada
Frankie Laine; *Frankie Laine's Greatest Hits* . . . . (Columbia)

Grand Illusion
Styx; *Grand Illusion* . . . . (A&M)
Styx-Classics-#15 . . . . (A&M)

Grand Illusion
Eric Clapton; *August* . . . . (Duck/Reprise)

Great Beyond, The
R.E.M.; *Man On The Moon* . . . . (Warner Bros.)
Totally Hits-#2-C . . . . (Elektra)

Haunted Heart
Sammy Kershaw; *Haunted Heart* . . . . (Mercury)

He Walked On Water
Randy Travis; *No Holdin' Back* . . . . (Warner Bros.)

Hocus Pocus
Focus; *Best Of Focus* . . . . (I.R.S.)
Dutch Masters-Selection Of Their Finest . . . . (Sire)
Moving Waves . . . . (I.R.S.)

Hocus Pocus
Gary Hoey; *Animal Instinct* . . . . (Reprise)

Hundred Million Miracles
Original Cast; *Flower Drum Song* . . . . (Sony Music Classical)

Hypnotized
Fleetwood Mac; *25 Years-The Chain* . . . . (Warner Bros.)

I Can See For Miles
Who; *Hooligans* . . . . (MCA)
Join Together . . . . (MCA)
Meaty Beaty Big & Bouncy . . . . (MCA)
ST/The Kids Are Alright . . . . (MCA)
The Who Sell Out . . . . (MCA)

I Need A Miracle
Grateful Dead; *Shakedown Street* . . . . (Arista)

I Put A Spell On You
Creedence Clearwater Revival; *1968-1969* . . . . (Fantasy)
Creedence Clearwater Revival . . . . (Fantasy)
Creedence Clearwater Revival-Chronicle . . . . (Fantasy)
More Creedence Gold . . . . (Fantasy)
Screamin' Jay Hawkins; *At Home With Screamin' Jay Hawkins* . . . . . (Columbia)
Elvira Presents Haunted Hits-C . . . . (Rhino)
Rock & Roll Show-C . . . . (Gusto)

If It's Magic
Stevie Wonder; *Songs In The Key Of Life* . . . . (Motown)
Tuck & Patti; *Love Warriors* . . . . (Windham Hill)

If You Could Read My Mind
Gordon Lightfoot; *Gord's Gold* . . . . (Reprise)
If You Could Read My Mind . . . . (Reprise)
Sit Down Young Stranger . . . . (Reprise)

Impossible
Jack Jones; *Hooray For Love: Gentlemen Of Song-#1-C* . . . . . . (Capitol)

Impossible!; It's Possible!
Celeste Holm & Lesley Ann Warren; *Cinderella-The CBS Television Network Production* . . . . (Columbia)

Into The Mystic
Van Morrison; *Moondance* . . . . (Warner Bros.)
Too Late To Stop Now . . . . (Warner Bros.)

Invisible Man
98 Degrees; *98 Degrees* . . . . (Motown)

It Was
Chely Wright; *Single White Female* . . . . (MCA)

It's A Miracle
Barry Manilow; *Barry Manilow II* . . . . (Arista)
Barry Manilow/Live . . . . (Arista)
Barry Manilow's Greatest Hits-#1 . . . . (Arista)

It's A Miracle
Culture Club; *Colour By Numbers* . . . . (Virgin)

It's Gonna Take A Miracle
Deniece Williams; *Niecy* . . . . (Columbia)
Laura Nyro & LaBelle; *It's Gonna Take A Miracle* . . . . (Columbia)

It's Magic
Dinah Washington; *What A Diff'rence A Day Makes* . . . . (Mercury)
Doris Day; *Doris Day's Greatest Hits* . . . . (Columbia)
Michael Feinstein; *Michael Feinstein Sings The Jule Styne Songbook* . . . . (Nonesuch)
Sarah Vaughan; *Complete Sarah Vaughan On Mercury-#1-Great Jazz Years-1954-1956* . . . . (Mercury)

Little Miss Magic
Jimmy Buffett; *Boats Beaches Bars & Ballads* . . . . (Margaritaville)
Coconut Telegraph . . . . (MCA)

Little Shoe Maker
Eddie Fisher; *Very Best Of Eddie Fisher* . . . . (Taragon)
Gaylords; *Choice Voices! Pop Vocal Group Gems Of The '50s-C* . . . . (Collector's Choice)

Livin' La Vida Loca
Ricky Martin; *Ricky Martin* . . . . (Columbia)

Love Potion Number 9
Clovers; *ST/American Graffiti* . . . . (MCA)
Super Oldies Of The '50s-#7-C . . . . (Audio Fidelity)
Herb Alpert & The Tijuana Brass; *Herb Alpert & The Tijuana Brass' Greatest Hits* . . . . (A&M)
Herb Alpert & The Tijuana Brass-Classics-#1 . . . . (A&M)
Searchers; *History Of British Rock-#3-C* . . . . (Rhino)
Searchers' Greatest Hits . . . . (Rhino)

Magic
Pilot; *Super Hits Of The '70s-Have A Nice Day-#14-C* . . . . (Rhino)

Magic
Cars; *Heartbeat City* . . . . (Elektra)
The Cars' Greatest Hits . . . . (Elektra)

Magic
Moody Blues; *Keys Of The Kingdom* . . . . (Polydor)

Magic
Michael Nesmith; *Newer Stuff* . . . . (Rhino)

Magic
Eddie Money; *Nothing To Lose* . . . . (Columbia)

Magic
Olivia Newton-John; *Olivia Newton-John's Greatest Hits-#2* . . . . . (MCA)

Magic
Electric Light Orchestra; *ST/Xanadu* . . . . (MCA)

Magic
Status Quo; *Status Quo* . . . . (Mercury)

Magic Bus
Who; *Live At Leeds* . . . . (MCA)
Magic Bus-The Who On Tour . . . . (MCA)
Meaty Beaty Big & Bouncy . . . . (MCA)
ST/The Kids Are Alright . . . . (MCA)
Who Greatest Hits . . . . (MCA)
Who's Last . . . . (MCA)

Magic Carpet Ride
Steppenwolf; *Live Steppenwolf* . . . . (MCA)
Nuggets-#9-Acid Rock-C . . . . (Rhino)
Steppenwolf Gold/Their Great Hits . . . . (MCA)
Steppenwolf-16 Greatest Hits . . . . (MCA)
The Second . . . . (MCA)

Magic Fingers (25 Cents)
Birdsongs Of The Mesozoic; *Faultline* . . . . (Cuneiform)

Magic Hotel
Wild Swans; *Space Flower* . . . . (Sire)

Magic In December
Tom Barabas; *Incredible Invincible Sampler* . . . . (Invincible)

Magic Jewelled Limousine
Nasa; *Insha-Allah!* . . . . (Sire)
ST/Wild Orchid . . . . (Sire)

Magic Man
Heart; *Dreamboat Annie* . . . . (Capitol)
Heart's Greatest Hits/Live . . . . (Epic)

Magic Mirror
Whirlers; *Harlem Holiday-New York Rhythm & Blues-#1-C* . . . . (Collectables)

Magic Mirror
Leon Russell; *Carney* . . . . (Right Stuff)

Magic Moon
Peter Frampton; *Something's Happening* . . . . (A&M)

Magic Power
Triumph; *Allied Forces* . . . . (RCA)
Stages . . . . (MCA)
Triumph-Classics . . . . (MCA)

Magic Touch, (You've Got) The
Platters; *Enchanted-The Best Of The Platters* . . . . (Rhino)

Magic, Magic
Original Broadway Cast; *Carnival* . . . . (Polydor)

Magical Mystery Tour
Beatles; *Magical Mystery Tour* . . . . (Capitol)
Reel Music . . . . (Capitol)
The Beatles/1967-1970 . . . . (Capitol)

Make The Music Magic
Be Bop Deluxe; *Modern Music* . . . . (Capitol)

Master's Call
Marty Robbins; *Gunfighter Ballads & Trail Songs* . . . . (Legacy)

Me Wise Magic
Van Halen; *Best Of Van Halen-#1* . . . . (Warner Bros.)

Midnight Magic
38 Special; *Rock & Roll Strategy* . . . . (A&M)

Midnight Magic
Commodores; *Midnight Magic* . . . . (Motown)

Miracle
Queen; *Classic Queen* . . . . (Hollywood)
Miracle . . . . (Hollywood)

Miracle
Moody Blues; *Sur La Mer* . . . . (Polydor)

Miracle
Whitney Houston; *I'm Your Baby Tonight* . . . . (Arista)

Miracle
Stylistics; *Best Of The Stylistics-#2* . . . . (Amherst)

Miracle
Jon Bon Jovi; *Blaze Of Glory-ST/Young Guns II* . . . . (Mercury)
Miracle
Suicidal Tendencies; *How Will I Laugh Tomorrow When I Can't Even Smile
Today* . . . .(Epic)
Miracle Cure
Who; *Join Together* . . . .(MCA)
ST/Tommy . . . . (Polydor)
Tommy . . . .(MCA)
Miracle Man
Ozzy Osbourne; *Just Say Ozzy* . . . . (Epic Portrait Assoc.)
No Rest For The Wicked. . . . .(Epic)
Miracle Man
Elvis Costello; *My Aim Is True* . . . . (Columbia)
Miracle Man
Rain People; *Rain People* . . . .(Epic)
Miracles
Jefferson Starship; *Balince-A Collection* . . . . (Rhino)
Jefferson Starship-Gold. . . . . (RCA)
Nipper's Greatest Hits Of The '70s-C . . . . (RCA)
Red Octopus. . . . .(Grunt)
Miracles
Don Williams; *Best Of Don Williams-#3* . . . . (MCA)
Especially For You. . . . . (MCA)
Mister Sandman
Chordettes; *Best Of The Chordettes* . . . . (Rhino)
Emmylou Harris; *Evangeline* . . . .(Warner Bros.)
Profile II-The Best Of Emmylou Harris . . . .(Warner Bros.)
Motorcycle Mystics
Dave Stewart & The Spiritual Cowboys; *Honest* . . . . (Arista)
Music Trance
Ben E. King; *Music Trance.* . . . .(Atlantic)
My Baby Must Be A Magician
Marvelettes; *Marvelettes-The Ultimate Collection.* . . . . (Motown)
Mystic Eyes
Them featuring Van Morrison; *Here Comes The Night* . . . . (Out Of Print)
History Of British Rock-#6-C . . . . (Rhino)
*The Sopranos-Music From The HBO Original
Series* . . . . (Sony Music Soundtrax)
Mystic Rhythms
Rush; *Power Windows* . . . . (Mercury)
Rush-Chronicles. . . . . (Mercury)
Show Of Hands . . . . (Mercury)
Mystic Traveler
Dave Mason; *Let It Flow.* . . . . (Columbia)
Mystical Potato Head Groove Thing
Joe Satriani; *Flying In A Blue Dream* . . . . (Relativity)
Never Saw A Miracle
Curtis Stigers; *Curtis Stigers* . . . . (Arista)
Night Time Magic
Larry Gatlin & The Gatlin Brothers Band; *Larry Gatlin & The Gatlin
Brothers' Greatest Hits* . . . . (Columbia)
Larry Gatlin & The Gatlin Brothers-17 Greatest Hits . . . . (Columbia)
Live At 8:00 . . . . (Capitol)
Oh Brother . . . . (Columbia)
On A Clear Day (You Can See Forever)
Barbra Streisand; *Just For The Record* . . . . (Columbia)
Live Concert At The Forum . . . . (Columbia)
ST/On A Clear Day You Can See Forever . . . . (Columbia Special Prod.)
The Concert . . . . (Columbia)
Roger Williams; *Best Of Roger Williams* . . . .(MCA)
Somewhere In Time . . . . (Bainbridge)
One Small Miracle
Bryan White; *The Right Place* . . . .(Asylum)
One-Trick Pony
Paul Simon; *ST/One-Trick Pony.* . . . .(Warner Bros.)
Open Sesame
Kool & The Gang; *Everything's Kool & The Gang-Greatest Hits
& More* . . . . (Mercury)
Kool & The Gang Spin Their Top Hits . . . . (De-Lite)
ST/Saturday Night Fever . . . . (Polydor)
Open Sesame
Freddie Hubbard; *Best Of Freddie Hubbard.* . . . . (Blue Note)
Open Sesame . . . . (Blue Note)
Pinball Wizard
Elton John; *Elton John's Greatest Hits-#2* . . . . (Polydor)
Pete Townshend; *Another Scoop* . . . . (Atco)
Pete Townshend's Deep End Live! . . . . (Atco)
Rod Stewart; *Best Of Rod Stewart* . . . . (Mercury)
Sing It Again, Rod . . . . (Mercury)
Storyteller/The Complete Anthology: 1964-1990 . . . . . .(Warner Bros.)
Who; *Meaty Beaty Big & Bouncy* . . . .(MCA)
ST/The Kids Are Alright. . . . .(MCA)
ST/Tommy . . . . (Polydor)
Tommy . . . .(MCA)
Who Greatest Hits . . . .(MCA)
Who's Last . . . .(MCA)
Pocketful Of Miracles
Frank Sinatra; *Sinatra's Sinatra* . . . . (Reprise)

Premonition
John Fogerty; *Premonition* . . . . (Reprise)
Psychic Elephant
Shankar; *Vision* . . . .(ECM)
Puff The Magic Dragon
Peter, Paul & Mary; *10 Years Together/The Best Of Peter, Paul
and Mary* . . . . (Warner Bros.)
Moving . . . . (Warner Bros.)
Peter, Paul & Mommy . . . . (Warner Bros.)
Peter, Paul and Mary In Concert . . . . (Warner Bros.)
Rainmaker
Dillards; *There Is A Time-1963-1970* . . . . (Vanguard)
Rainmaker
Traffic; *The Low Spark Of High Heeled Boys* . . . . (Island)
Rope The Moon
John Michael Montgomery; *Kickin' It Up.* . . . .(Atlantic)
Rudy The Magic Crow
Swamp Zombies; *Chicken Vulture Crow* . . . .(Dr. Dream Music Group)
Santeria
Sublime; *Sublime* . . . . (Gasoline Alley)
Semi-Charmed Life
Third Eye Blind; *Jock Rock 2000-C* . . . . (Tommy Boy)
Third Eye Blind . . . . (Elektra)
Seven Wonders
Fleetwood Mac; *Tango In The Night* . . . . (Warner Bros.)
Shaman's Blues
Doors; *Soft Parade* . . . . (Elektra)
Shaman's Song
Shadowfax; *Dreams Of Children* . . . .(Windham Hill)
Shazam
Duane Eddy; *Twang Thang-The Duane Eddy Anthology* . . . . (Rhino)
She's A Miracle
Exile; *19 Hot Country Requests-#3-C* . . . . (Epic)
Exile's Greatest Hits . . . . (Epic)
Kentucky Hearts . . . . (Epic)
Silver Springs
Fleetwood Mac; *1998 Grammy Nominees-C* . . . . (MCA)
25 Years-The Chain . . . . (Warner Bros.)
The Dance . . . . (Reprise)
Snake Charmer
Blackmore's Rainbow; *Ritchie Blackmore's R-A-I-N-B-O-W* . . . .(Polydor)
Snake Charmer
John Hiatt; *ST/White Nights* . . . .(Atlantic)
Snake Charmer
Ted Nugent; *State Of Shock.* . . . . (Epic)
Solsbury Hill
Peter Gabriel; *Peter Gabriel* . . . . (Atco)
Peter Gabriel/Plays Live . . . . (Geffen)
Shaking The Tree-Sixteen Golden Greats. . . . . (Geffen)
Some Enchanted Evening
Jay & The Americans; *Come A Little Bit Closer-Best Of Jay & The
Americans* . . . . (Gold Rush)
Jay & The Americans' All-Time Greatest Hits . . . . (Rhino)
Original Cast; *South Pacific* . . . . (CBS Masterworks)
Perry Como; *Perry Como's All-Time Greatest Hits-#1* . . . . (RCA)
Rosanno Brazzi; *ST/South Pacific* . . . . (RCA)
Willie Nelson; *What A Wonderful World* . . . . (Columbia)
Sorcerer
Stevie Nicks; *Trouble In Shangri-La.* . . . . (Reprise)
Spanish Castle Magic
Jimi Hendrix; *Axis: Bold As Love* . . . . (Reprise)
Lifelines/Jimi Hendrix Story. . . . . (Reprise)
Live At Winterland . . . . (Rykodisc)
Jimi Hendrix Experience; *Radio One* . . . . (Rykodisc)
Spiritual Thang
Eric Benet; *True To Myself* . . . . (Jac-Mac/Warner Bros.)
Spooky
Atlanta Rhythm Section; *Underdog* . . . .(Polydor)
Classics IV; *Ghastly Grooves-C* . . . . (K-Tel)
Good Vibrations (Sounds Of Top 40 Radio: 1964-1967)-C . . . . (Capitol)
Spooky . . . . (Liberty)
Very Best Of The Classics IV . . . . (EMI)
Springtime Magic
Lonnie Liston Smith; *Loveland* . . . . (Columbia)
Stairway To Heaven
Led Zeppelin; *Led Zeppelin IV* . . . .(Atlantic)
Led Zeppelin-Box Set . . . .(Atlantic)
Remasters. . . . .(Atlantic)
ST/The Song Remains The Same. . . . . (Swan Song)
Stanley Jordan; *Best Of Stanley Jordan.* . . . . (Blue Note)
Flying Home . . . . (EMI)
Strange Brew
Cream; *Disraeli Gears* . . . .(Polydor)
Eric Clapton-Crossroads-C . . . .(Polydor)
Strange Brew-Very Best Of Cream. . . . .(Polydor)
Strange Magic
Electric Light Orchestra; *Afterglow.* . . . . (Epic)
Electric Light Orchestra's Greatest Hits . . . .(Jet)
Face The Music . . . .(Jet)

Ole ELO . . . . (Jet)

Supermen
David Bowie; *Hunky Dory* . . . . (Rykodisc)
Man Who Sold The World . . . . (Rykodisc)
Sound + Vision . . . . (Rykodisc)

Supernatural
John Mayall; *London Blues-1964-1969* . . . . (Deram)
John Mayall's Bluesbreakers; *Legends Of Rock Guitar-'60s-#2-C* . . . . . (Rhino)

Supernatural
Army Of Lovers; *Army Of Lovers* . . . . (Giant)

Supernatural
Madonna; *Red Hot + Dance-C* . . . . (Columbia)

Supernatural
New Edition; *Soundtrack Smashes-'80s & More-C* . . . . (MCA)

Supernatural Thing (Part 1)
Ben E. King; *Didn't It Blow Your Mind: Soul Hits Of The '70s-#15-C* . . . (Rhino)
Stand By Me-Best Of Ben E. King . . . . (Atlantic)

Superstition
Stevie Wonder; *20/20-C* . . . . (Motown)
Original Musiquarium . . . . (Motown)
Talking Book . . . . (Motown)

That Old Black Magic
Ella Fitzgerald; *Best Of Ella Fitzgerald* . . . . (MCA)
Big Bands Of The Swinging Years-C . . . . (Everest)
In Rome-Birthday Concert . . . . (Verve)
Frank Sinatra; *Come Swing With Me!* . . . . (Capitol)
Glenn Miller & His Orchestra; *Chattanooga Choo Choo-#1 Hits* . . . . (Bluebird)
Judy Garland; *Best Of Judy Garland* . . . . (MCA)
Louis Prima & Keely Smith; *Memories Are Made Of This-C* . . . . . (Capitol)
Marcels; *Best Of The Marcels* . . . . (Rhino)
Sammy Davis, Jr.; *Hey There-At His Dynamite Greatest* . . . . . (MCA)
Spike Jones; *Best Of Spike Jones-#2* . . . . (RCA)

Theme From "Felix The Cat"
Original Soundtrack; *Television's Greatest Hits-#1-C* . . . . (TVT)

Theme From "I Dream Of Jeannie"
Original Soundtrack; *Television's Greatest Hits-#1-C* . . . . (TVT)

Theme From "Inspector Gadget"
Original Soundtrack; *Television's Greatest Hits-#3-1970s & 1980s-C* . . . (TVT)

Theme From "Outer Limits"
Original Soundtrack; *Television's Greatest Hits-#2-C* . . . . (TVT)

Theme From "Wonder Woman"
Original Soundtrack; *Television's Greatest Hits-#3-1970s & 1980s-C* . . . (TVT)

This Magic Moment
Drifters; *Drifters' Greatest Hits* . . . . (Gusto)
Drifters-Golden Hits . . . . (Atlantic)
Jay & The Americans; *Come A Little Bit Closer-Best Of Jay & The Americans* . . . . (Gold Rush)
Jay & The Americans' All-Time Greatest Hits . . . . (Rhino)
Marvin Gaye; *M.P.G.* . . . . (Motown)

Thriller
Michael Jackson; *Thriller* . . . . (Epic)

Tiki Tiki Tiki Room
Original Music; *Disney Collection-#1-C* . . . . (Disney)

To Make A Miracle
Michael McDonald; *In The Spirit-A Christmas Album* . . . . . . (MCA)

Trick Bag
Blues Brothers; *Red, White & Blues* . . . . (Turnstyle)
Earl King; *Best Of New Orleans Rhythm & Blues-#1-C* . . . . . . (Rhino)
Kevin Eubanks; *Face To Face* . . . . (GRP)
Robert Palmer; *Riptide* . . . . (Island)

Trick Of The Light
Who; *Who Are You* . . . . (MCA)

Trick Of The Tail
Genesis; *Trick Of The Tail* . . . . (Atco)

Trick Rider
McBride & The Ride; *Sacred Ground* . . . . (MCA)

Twilight Zone
Manhattan Transfer; *Best Of The Manhattan Transfer* . . . . . . (Atlantic)
Extensions . . . . (Rhino)
Manhattan Transfer-Anthology-Down In Birdland . . . . (Rhino)

Twilight Zone
Neil Norman & His Cosmic Orchestra; *Elvira Presents Haunted Hits-C* . . . . (Rhino)
Halloween Hits-C . . . . (Rhino)

Twilight Zone
Golden Earring; *Cut* . . . . (21)
Something Heavy Going Down . . . . (21)

Twilight Zone
Iron Maiden; *Killers* . . . . (Capitol)

Under Your Spell
Atlantic Starr; *We're Movin' Up* . . . . (Warner Bros.)

Under Your Spell
Fire Town; *Good Life* . . . . (Atlantic)

Under Your Spell
Mason Ruffner; *Gypsy Blood* . . . . (Epic Portrait Assoc.)

Under Your Spell
Bob Dylan; *Knocked Out Loaded* . . . . (Columbia)

Under Your Spell
Phyllis Hyman; *Under Her Spell-Greatest Hits* . . . . (Arista)

Under Your Spell Again
Buck Owens; *Billboard Top Country Hits-1959-C* . . . . (Rhino)
Buck Owens' All-Time Greatest Hits-#1 . . . . (Curb)

Vanishing Cream
Hunger; *Devil Thumbs A Ride* . . . . (Universal)

Veteran Of The Psychic Wars
Blue Oyster Cult; *Extraterrestrial Live* . . . . (Columbia)
Fire Of Unknown Origin . . . . (Columbia)

Voodoo
Black Sabbath; *Live Evil* . . . . (Warner Bros.)
Mob Rules . . . . (Warner Bros.)

Voodoo
Godsmack; *Godsmack* . . . . (Republic/Universal)

Voodoo
Chris Isaak; *Silvertone* . . . . (Warner Bros.)

Voodoo
Body Count; *Body Count* . . . . (Sire)

Voodoo
Meters; *Good Old Funky Music* . . . . (Rounder)

Voodoo
Neville Brothers; *Yellow Moon* . . . . (A&M)

Voodoo Child
Voodoo Child; *Best Of Techno-#1-C* . . . . (Profile)

Voodoo Chile
Jimi Hendrix; *Concerts* . . . . (Reprise)
Essential Jimi Hendrix . . . . (Reprise)
Kiss The Sky . . . . (Reprise)
Lifelines/Jimi Hendrix Story . . . . (Reprise)
Jimi Hendrix Experience; *Electric Ladyland* . . . . (Reprise)
Stevie Ray Vaughan; *Couldn't Stand The Weather* . . . . (Epic)
Stevie Ray Vaughan and Double Trouble; *Live Alive* . . . . (Epic)

Voodoo Daddy
Lonnie Brooks; *Bayou Lightning* . . . . (Alligator)

Voodoo Doll
Soul Asylum; *Say What You Will* . . . . (Twin-Tone)

Voodoo Jammin'
Dancing Fantasy; *Moonlight Reflections* . . . . (Innovative Comm.)

Voodoo Kiss
Mr. Big; *Lean Into It* . . . . (Atlantic)

Voodoo Medicine Man
Aerosmith; *Pump* . . . . (Geffen)

Voodoo Music
Tuck & Patti; *Dream* . . . . (Windham Hill)

Voodoo Sex Doll
Crisis Party; *Rude Awakening* . . . . (Metal Blade)

Voodoo Village
Bola Sete; *Incomparable* . . . . (Fantasy)

Voodoo Voodoo
LaVern Baker; *Elvira Presents Haunted Hits-C* . . . . (Rhino)

Voodoo Woman
Koko Taylor; *I Got What It Takes* . . . . (Alligator)

Voodoo Woman
Bobby Goldsboro; *Honey-Best Of Bobby Goldsboro* . . . . (EMI)

Walk On The Water
Creedence Clearwater Revival; *1968-1969* . . . . (Fantasy)
Creedence Clearwater Revival . . . . (Fantasy)
Creedence Clearwater Revival-Chronicle-#2 . . . . (Fantasy)

Walk On Water
Neil Diamond; *And The Singer Sings His Song* . . . . (MCA)
Glory Road-1968-1972 . . . . (MCA)
Moods . . . . (MCA)

Walk On Water
T. Graham Brown; *Brilliant Conversationalist* . . . . (Capitol)

Walk On Water
Dio; *Lock Up The Wolves* . . . . (Reprise)

Walk On Water
Marc Cohn; *Marc Cohn* . . . . (Atlantic)

Walk On Water
Marillion; *Six Of One-Half Dozen Of The Other* . . . . (I.R.S.)

Walk On Water
Eddie Money; *Eddie Money's Greatest Hits-Sound Of Money* . . . . (Columbia)
Nothing To Lose . . . . (Columbia)

Wax Ecstatic (To Sell Angeline)
Sponge; *Wax Ecstatic* . . . . (Columbia)

We're Off To See The Wizard
Jewel/Jackson Browne/Ry Cooder; *The Wizard Of Oz In Concert: Dreams Come True-C* . . . . (Rhino)
Judy Garland; *A&E Biography: A Musical Anthology* . . . . (Capitol)
Original Cast; *The Wizard Of Oz* . . . . (TVT)
Original Soundtrack; *The Wizard Of Oz-Selections From The Original Motion Picture Soundtrack* . . . . (Turner Classic Movies)

When The Spell Is Broken
Richard Thompson; *Across A Crowded Room* . . . . (Polydor)
Watching The Dark-History Of Richard Thompson . . . . (Rykodisc)

When You Believe
Mariah Carey & Whitney Houston; *Mariah Carey-#1's* . . . . . . (Columbia)
ST/The Prince Of Egypt . . . . (DreamWorks/SKG)
Whitney Houston & Mariah Carey; *My Love Is Your Love* . . . . . (Arista)

Which Way You Goin' Billy
Poppy Family; *Super Hits Of The '70s-Have A Nice Day-#2-C* . . . . (Rhino)
Wondrous Stories
Yes; *Classic Yes* . . . . (Atlantic)
Going For The One . . . . (Atlantic)
Yesshows . . . . (Atlantic)
Yellow Magic
Yellow Magic Orchestra; *Yellow Magic Orchestra* . . . . (A&M)
You Can Do Magic
America; *America Live* . . . .(Warner Bros.)
Encore-More Greatest Hits . . . . (Rhino)
View From The Ground . . . . (Capitol)
You Do Something To Me
Frank Sinatra; *Concepts* . . . . (Capitol)
Ray Conniff; *Ray Conniff -16 Most Requested Songs.* . . . . (Legacy)
You Make Loving Fun
Fleetwood Mac; *25 Years-The Chain* . . . .(Warner Bros.)
Fleetwood Mac's Greatest Hits . . . .(Warner Bros.)
Rumours . . . .(Warner Bros.)
Jewel; *Legacy-A Tribute To Fleetwood Mac's Rumours-C* . . . . (Lava)
You Never Give Me Your Money
Beatles; *Abbey Road* . . . .(Parlophone)
Beatles-Box Set . . . . (Capitol)
George Benson; *The Best* . . . . (Rebound)
Your Love Amazes Me
John Berry; *John Berry* . . . . (Liberty)
Your Love Is A Miracle
Mark Chesnutt; *Too Cold At Home* . . . . (MCA)
You're Amazing
Robert Palmer; *Don't Explain* . . . . (EMI)

MAIL, Deliveries, Letters, Messages, Notes, Post Office

See Also: **BOOKS (writing), COMMUNICATION (various), COMPUTERS, PAPER, TELEPHONE**

1959
John Anderson; *Country Love Songs-#3-C.* . . . .(Warner Bros.)
John Anderson's Greatest Hits . . . .(Warner Bros.)
26 Cents
Wilkinsons; *Nothing But Love* . . . . (Giant)
4 Page Letter
Aaliyah; *One In A Million.* . . . . (BlackGround Enterp./Atlantic)
49 Bye-Byes
Crosby, Stills & Nash; *Crosby, Stills & Nash* . . . . (Atlantic)
500 Miles Away From Home
Bobby Bare; *500 Miles Away From Home* . . . . (RCA)
Foy Willing; *Cowboy/The New Sound Of American Folk.* . . . . (DRG)
Reba McEntire; *Starting Over* . . . . (MCA)
Air Mail Special
Ella Fitzgerald; *Billie Holiday & Ella Fitzgerald* . . . . (MCA)
Lionel Hampton & His Orchestra; *Best Of Lionel Hampton* . . . . (MCA)
Hamp's Golden Favorites . . . . (MCA)
Quincy Jones; *Great Wide World Of Quincy Jones: Live!* . . . . (Mercury)
All My Loving
Beatles; *Meet The Beatles!* . . . . (Capitol)
The Beatles At The Hollywood Bowl . . . . (Capitol)
The Beatles/1962-1966 . . . . (Capitol)
With The Beatles . . . . (Parlophone)
Amneris' Letter
Shania Twain; *ST/Aida* . . . . (Island)
Another Day (Another Letter)
Boz Scaggs; *Boz Scaggs* . . . . (Atlantic)
Austin
Blake Shelton; *Blake Shelton* . . . . (Giant)
Bad Day
Fuel; *Now That's What I Call Music!-#8-C* . . . . (Virgin)
Something Like Human . . . . (Epic)
Ballad Of The Green Berets
Barry Sadler; *Cruisin'-1966-C* . . . . (Increase)
Hits Of The Sixties-C . . . . (Intercom Music)
More American Graffiti-#4-C . . . . (MCA)
Nipper's Greatest Hits Of The '60s-#2-C . . . . (RCA)
Super Hits-#3-C . . . . (Gusto)
Because I Love You (The Postman Song)
Stevie B; *Because I Love You (The Postman Song)* . . . . (LMR)
Best Of Stevie B . . . . (LMR)
Love & Emotion . . . . (LMR)
Blue Letter
Fleetwood Mac; *Fleetwood Mac* . . . . (Reprise)
Bringin' In The Georgia Mail
Don Reno & Bill Harrell; *Great American Train Songs-C* . . . . . .(C.M.H. Prod.)
Bringing In The Georgia Mail
Norman Blake; *Back Home In Sulphur Springs* . . . . (Rounder)
By The Time I Get To Phoenix
Glen Campbell; *All-Time Country Classics-#1-C.* . . . . (Capitol)
Glen Campbell-Classics Collection. . . . . (Capitol)

Glen Campbell-Live . . . . (Capitol)
Glen Campbell's Greatest Hits. . . . . (Capitol)
Very Best Of Glen Campbell. . . . . (Capitol)
Reba McEntire; *Starting Over* . . . . (MCA)
C.O.D. (I'll Deliver)
Mtume; *You, Me And He* . . . . (Epic)
Calling, The
Yes; *Talk* . . . . (Victory)
Check Yes Or No
George Strait; *Strait Out Of The Box* . . . . (MCA)
Check's In The Mail
Victory; *Don't Get Mad-Get Even* . . . . (Mercenary)
Cindy, Oh Cindy
Beach Boys; *Surfin' Safari-Surfin' Usa (Remasterd With Bonus Tracks).* . . . . (Capitol)
Daddy's Last Letter (Private First Class John H. McCormick)
Tex Ritter; *45-#1267.* . . . . (Capitol)
Dead Flowers
Rolling Stones; *Sticky Fingers* . . . . (Virgin)
Steve Earle & The Dukes; *Shut Up And Die Like An Aviator* . . . . . . (MCA)
Dear Brother
Hank Williams; *I Saw The Light* . . . . (Polydor)
Dear Jean (I'm Nervous)
City Boy; *Young Men Gone West* . . . . (Mercury)
Dear John
Hank Williams With His Drifting Cowboys; *Hank Williams-24 Greatest Hits-#2.* . . . . (Polydor)
Hank Williams-40 Greatest Hits. . . . . (Polydor)
Hey Good Lookin' (December 1950-July 1951). . . . . (Polydor)
Dear John
Joe Walsh; *Confessor* . . . .(Full Moon)
Dear John
Elton John; *Jump Up!* . . . . (MCA)
Dear John
Nazareth; *Nazareth* . . . . (A&M)
Dear John & Marsha Letter
Stan Freberg; *Capitol Collectors Series-Stan Freberg* . . . . (Capitol)
Dear John Letter
Jean Shepard; *Heroes Of Country Music-#4-Legends Of The West Coast-C* . . . . (Rhino)
Jean Shepard & Ferlin Husky; *Classic Duets-C* . . . . (Liberty)
Dear John Letter Lounge
Jerry Jeff Walker; *It's A Good Night For Singin'* . . . . (MCA)
Dear Me
Lorrie Morgan; *Lorrie Morgan's Greatest Hits* . . . . (BNA)
Dear Mrs. Roosevelt
Bob Dylan; *Tribute To Woody Guthrie-C* . . . .(Warner Bros.)
Dear Uncle Sam
Loretta Lynn; *Honky Tonk Girl: The Loretta Lynn Collection* . . . . . . (MCA)
Loretta Lynn's Greatest Hits . . . . (MCA)
Death Letter Blues
Leadbelly; *King Of The Twelve-String Guitar* . . . . (Columbia)
Leadbelly . . . . (Columbia)
Did You Get That Letter
Arthur "Big Boy" Crudup; *Crudup's Mood.* . . . . (Delmark)
Down In The Valley
Elvis Presley; *Reconsider Baby* . . . . (RCA)
Leadbelly; *Defense Blues-Golden Classics-#2* . . . . (Collectables)
Pete Seeger; *American Favorite Ballads-#1* . . . .(Smithsonian Folkways)
Dream Walkin'
Toby Keith; *Dream Walkin'* . . . . (Mercury)
Toby Keith's Greatest Hits, Volume One . . . . (Mercury)
Dust My Broom
Canned Heat; *Uncanned!-Best Of Canned Heat* . . . . (EMI Legends Of Rock 'N' Roll)
Elmore James; *Best Blues Album In The World...Ever!-C* . . . . (Virgin)
Elmore James-Complete Fire & Enjoy Sessions-#1 . . . . (Collectables)
King Of The Slide Guitar . . . . (Capricorn)
Ike & Tina Turner; *Bold Soul Sister-Best Of The Blue Thumb Recordings.* . . . . (Hip-O)
Robert Johnson; *King Of The Delta Blues Singers-#2.* . . . . (Columbia)
ZZ Top; *Deguello* . . . .(Warner Bros.)
E-Bow The Letter
R.E.M.; *New Adventures In Hi-Fi* . . . .(Warner Bros.)
Electric Messengers
220 Volt; *Electric Messengers* . . . . (Epic)
E-Mail My Heart
Britney Spears; *...Baby One More Time* . . . . (Jive)
Epistle To Dippy
Donovan; *Donovan's Greatest Hits* . . . . (Epic)
Faded Love
Bob Wills & His Texas Playboys; *Bob Wills & His Texas Playboys-24 Great Hits* . . . .(Polydor)
For The Last Time . . . . (Capitol)
Tiffany Transcriptions-#2-Best Of The Tiffanys . . . . (Rhino)
Mickey Gilley; *Mickey Gilley's Greatest Hits-#1* . . . . (Epic)
Patsy Cline; *12 Greatest Hits* . . . . (MCA)
Shawn Colvin & Lyle Lovett & Asleep At The Wheel; *Ride With Bob-C* . . . . (DreamWorks/SKG)

Willie Nelson; *Greatest Hits (& Some That Will Be)* . . . . (Columbia)
Fan Mail
Dickies; *Dawn Of* . . . . (A&M)
  Great Dictations (Definitive Collection) . . . . (A&M)
Fan Mail
Blondie; *Plastic Letters* . . . . (Chrysalis)
Few More Memories
Dolly Parton; *The Grass Is Blue* . . . . (Sugar Hill)
Fireball Mail
John McEuen; *String Wizards* . . . . (Vanguard)
Roy Acuff; *Best Of Roy Acuff* . . . . (Liberty)
  Opry Legends-Roy Acuff . . . . (Capitol)
  Roy Acuff's Greatest Hits . . . . (Columbia)
From Me To You
Beatles; *Beatles 1* . . . . (Capitol)
  Past Masters-Volume One . . . . (Parlophone)
  The Beatles/1962-1966 . . . . (Capitol)
  The Beatles-Anthology-#1 . . . . (Capitol)
Get The Message
Electronic; *Electronic* . . . . (Warner Bros.)
Give My Love To Rose
George Jones; *George Jones Sings The Hits Of His Country*
  Cousins . . . . (Razor & Tie)
Johnny Cash; *Johnny Cash-Sun Years* . . . . (Rhino)
Got A Letter From My Kid Today
Asleep At The Wheel; *Tribute To The Music Of Bob Wills And The Texas*
  Playboys-C . . . . (Liberty)
Merle Haggard & The Strangers; *18 Rare Classics* . . . . (Curb)
  Working Man Can't Get Nowhere Today . . . . (Capitol)
Handle With Care
Traveling Wilburys; *Traveling Wilburys-Volume One* . . (Wilbury/Warner Bros.)
He Stopped Loving Her Today
George Jones; *All Time Legends Of Country Music-C* . . . . (Legacy)
  First Time Live! . . . . (Epic)
  George Jones-Anniversary-Ten Years Of Hits . . . . (Epic)
  Greatest Country Hits Of The '80s-1980-C . . . . (Columbia)
  Greatest Hits From The Jukebox-C . . . . (Epic)
  I Am What I Am . . . . (Epic)
Heartbreak Hotel
Whitney Houston Featuring Faith Evans & Kelly Price; *My Love Is*
  Your Love . . . . (Arista)
  Totally Hits-#1-C . . . . (Arista)
  Whitney Houston's Greatest Hits . . . . (Arista)
Heartbreak U.S.A.
Kitty Wells; *I Love Country-Hits Of The '60s-#1-C* . . . . (Priority)
  Kitty Wells' Greatest Songs . . . . (Curb)
  The Country Music Hall Of Fame-Kitty Wells . . . . (MCA Special Prod.)
Hello Muddah, Hello Fadduh
Allan Sherman; *Dr. Demento Presents The Greatest Novelty Records-#3-*
  1960s-C . . . . (Rhino)
  Dr. Demento Presents The Greatest Novelty Records-C . . . . (Rhino)
Hey, Western Union Man
Jerry Butler; *Best Of Jerry Butler* . . . . (Mercury)
  Billboard Top R&B Hits-1968-C . . . . (Rhino)
I Got The Message
Big Jay McNeely; *Swingin'* . . . . (Collectables)
I Got The Message
ZZ Top; *Afterburner* . . . . (Warner Bros.)
I Got The Message
Men Without Hats; *Rhythm Of Youth* . . . . (MCA)
I Thought I'd Write To Juliet
Elvis Costello; *The Juliet Letters* . . . . (Warner Bros.)
I Wrote A Letter
Starz; *Coliseum Rock* . . . . (Capitol)
If I Knew You Were Comin' I'd've Baked A Cake
Bing Crosby; *The Radio Years-#4* . . . . (Crescendo)
Ethel Merman; *The Ethel Merman Collection* . . . . (Razor & Tie)
I'll Be Home
Flamingos; *Alan Freed's Memory Lane-C* . . . . (MCA)
  Best Of The Flamingos . . . . (Rhino)
  Super Oldies Of The '50s-#6-C . . . . (Audio Fidelity)
Platters; *Platters Greatest Hits-#2* . . . . (Curb)
I'm Already Taken
Steve Wariner; *Country Cares For Kids II-C* . . . . (BNA)
  Two Teardrops . . . . (Capitol)
I'm Gonna Sit Right Down And Write Myself A Letter
Billy Williams; *Stardust: The Classic Decca Hits & Standards*
  Collection-C . . . . (Decca)
Fats Waller; *Fats Waller* . . . . (RCA Special Prod.)
Frank Sinatra; *Sinatra-Basie* . . . . (Reprise)
  Songs For Young Lovers & Swing Easy . . . . (Capitol)
Nat "King" Cole; *Just One Of Those Things (& More)* . . . . (Capitol)
  Nat "King" Cole-Gift Set . . . . (Capitol)
Original Cast; *Ain't Misbehavin'* . . . . (RCA)
In A Letter To You
Eddy Raven; *Temporary Sanity* . . . . (Capitol)
In Your Letter
REO Speedwagon; *Hi Infidelity* . . . . (Epic)
  Jane Fonda's Workout . . . . (Columbia)

Indiana Wants Me
R. Dean Taylor; *Hard-To-Find Motown Classics-#2-C* . . . . (Motown)
  Super Hits Of The '70s-Have A Nice Day-#3-C . . . . (Rhino)
  Super Hits-#5-C . . . . (Gusto)
It Came In The Mail
Fuzztones; *In Heat* . . . . (Beggar's Banquet)
I've Gotta Get A Message To You
Bee Gees; *Bee Gees-Gold* . . . . (Polydor)
  Here At Last...Bee Gees...Live . . . . (Polydor)
Junk Mail
Circle Jerks; *Gig* . . . . (Relativity)
  Golden Shower Of Hits . . . . (Avenue)
Keep In Touch
Robert Palmer; *Some People Can Do What They Like* . . . . (Island)
Last Letter
Jack Greene; *Jack Greene Sings His Best* . . . . (Step One)
Ray Price; *Heart Of Country Music* . . . . (Step One)
Last Love Letter
Alison Krauss & Union Station; *Every Time You Say Goodbye* . . . . . . (Rounder)
Last Night's Letter
K-Ci & JoJo; *Love Always* . . . . (MCA)
Letter From America
Proclaimers; *This Is The Story* . . . . (Chrysalis)
Letter From Earth
Black Sabbath; *Dehumanizer* . . . . (Reprise)
Letter From Home
Eddie Jefferson; *Letter From Home* . . . . (Original Jazz Classics)
Letter From Spain
Electric Light Orchestra; *Secret Messages* . . . . (Jet)
Letter From Tina
Ike & Tina Turner; *Best Of Ike & Tina Turner* . . . . (EMI)
  Ike & Tina Turner-Golden Classics . . . . (Collectables)
Letter Full Of Tears
Gladys Knight & The Pips; *Echoes Down The Hall-16 Original Doo-Wop*
  Hits-C . . . . (Arista)
  Gladys Knight & The Pips' Greatest Hits . . . . (Curb)
  Gladys Knight & The Pips-Anthology . . . . (Motown)
Letter Home
Wendy Waldman; *Letters Home* . . . . (Cypress)
Letter Home
Memphis Slim; *All Kinds Of Blues* . . . . (Bluesville)
Letter Home
Forester Sisters; *Forester Sisters' Greatest Hits* . . . . (Warner Bros.)
Letter Home
Elvis Costello & The Brodsky Quartet; *Juliet Letters* . . . . (Warner Bros.)
Letter In The Mail
James Taylor; *Never Die Young* . . . . (Columbia)
Letter Never Sent
R.E.M.; *Reckoning* . . . . (I.R.S.)
Letter To Americans
Albert Brooks; *Star Is Bought* . . . . (Asylum)
Letter To Elise
Cure; *Wish* . . . . (Fiction/Elektra)
Letter To Hermoine
David Bowie; *Space Oddity* . . . . (Rykodisc)
Letter To L.A.
Joe Ely; *Live At Liberty Lunch* . . . . (MCA)
  Lord Of The Highway . . . . (Hightone)
Letter, The
Loretta Lynn & Conway Twitty; *Best Of Conway &*
  Loretta . . . . (MCA Special Prod.)
  Play Guitar Play . . . . (MCA)
  United Talent . . . . (MCA)
  Very Best Of Loretta Lynn & Conway Twitty . . . . (MCA)
Lowell Fulsom; *Let's Go Get Stoned* . . . . (Kent)
  Lowell Fulsom Now . . . . (Kent)
Letter, The
Box Tops; *Billboard Top Rock 'N' Roll Hits-1967-C* . . . . (Rhino)
  Box Tops' Greatest Hits . . . . (Rhino)
  Cruisin'-1967-C . . . . (Increase)
  Oldies But Goodies-#12-C . . . . (Original Sound)
  Rockin' '60s-C . . . . (Priority)
Joe Cocker; *Joe Cocker Live* . . . . (Capitol)
  Joe Cocker-Classics-#4 . . . . (A&M)
  Joe Cocker's Greatest Hits . . . . (A&M)
  Mad Dogs & Englishmen . . . . (A&M)
Vernon Green & The Medallions; *Oldies But Goodies-#1-C* . . . (Original Sound)
  Vernon Green & The Medallions-Golden Classics . . . . (Collectables)
Letter, The
Karla Bonoff; *Restless Nights* . . . . (Columbia)
Letter, The
Macy Gray; *On How Life Is* . . . . (Epic)
Letter, The (That Johnny Walker Read)
Asleep At The Wheel; *Very Best Of Asleep At The Wheel*
  Since 1970 . . . . (Relentless/Madacy)
Letters From The Wasteland
Wallflowers; *Breach* . . . . (Interscope)
Letters To The President
Sly & Robbie; *Silent Assassin* . . . . (Island)

Letting Go
Sozzi; *Songs From Dawson's Creek* . . . . (Sony Music Soundtrax)
Lettres D'Amour
Sweet; *Level-Headed* . . . . (Capitol)
Love Is A Good Thing
Sheryl Crow; *Sheryl Crow* . . . . (A&M)
Love Is The Message
MFSB; *Philadelphia Classics-C.* . . . . (Philadelphia Int'l)
Love Letters
Diana Krall; *The Look Of Love* . . . . (Impulse!)
Elvis Presley; *A Valentine Gift For You* . . . . (RCA)
  Elvis' Gold Records, Volume 4 . . . . (RCA)
  Love Letters From Elvis . . . . (RCA)
Ketty Lester; *Sultry Soul Sisters-Wonder Women-#3-C* . . (Rhino)
Peggy Lee; *Best Of Peggy Lee* . . . . (MCA)
Ronnie Milsap; *Lost In The Fifties Tonight* . . . . (RCA)
Love Letters
Smokey Robinson; *Quiet Storm* . . . . (Motown)
Love Letters
Joe Walsh; *You Bought It-You Name It* . . . . (Warner Bros.)
Love Letters From Old Mexico
Leslie Satcher; *Love Letters* . . . . (Warner Bros.)
Love Letters In The Sand
Mac Wiseman; *24 Greatest Bluegrass Hits-C* . . . . . . (C.M.H. Prod.)
Pat Boone; *Best Of Pat Boone* . . . . (MCA)
  Pat Boone-16 Great Performances . . . . (MCA)
  Vintage Music-#2-C . . . . (MCA)
Ted Black & His Orchestra; *78-#22799* . . . . (Victor)
Love, Me
Collin Raye; *All I Can Be* . . . . (Epic)
  Greatest Country Hits Of The '90s-1992-C . . . . . (Columbia)
Love's In Need Of Love Today
Stevie Wonder featuring Take 6; *America: A Tribute To Heroes-C.* . . . . (Interscope)
Mail Myself To You
Earl Robinson; *Tribute To Woody Guthrie-C* . . . . . . (Warner Bros.)
Mail Order Annie
Harry Chapin; *Gold Medal Collection* . . . . (Elektra)
  Short Stories . . . . (Elektra)
Mail Order Woman
Champion Jack Dupree; *Blues For Everybody* . . . . . (International Mktg. Group)
Mailman Blues
Lloyd Price; *Lloyd Price* . . . . (Specialty)
  Lloyd Price's Greatest Hits . . . . (Curb)
Mailman, Bring Me No More Blues
Beatles; *The Beatles-Anthology-#3* . . . . (Capitol)
Buddy Holly; *Buddy Holly* . . . . (MCA)
Memphis Mail
Eli Owens; *Roosevelt Holts & His Friends* . . . . (Arhoolie)
Message
Gene Loves Jezebel; *House Of Dolls* . . . . (Geffen)
Styx; *Pieces Of Eight* . . . . (A&M)
Message In A Bottle
Police; *Every Breath You Take-The Classics* . . . . . . (A&M)
  Regatta De Blanc . . . . (A&M)
Sting; *The Secret Policeman's Other Ball/The Music* . . (Rhino)
Message Of Love
Pretenders; *Extended Play* . . . . (Sire)
  Pretenders II . . . . (Sire)
  Pretenders-The Singles . . . . (Sire)
Message Of Love
Journey; *Trial By Fire* . . . . (Columbia)
Message Of Love
Jimi Hendrix; *Band Of Gypsys* . . . . (Capitol)
Message To Michael
Dionne Warwick; *Dionne Warwick* . . . . (Everest)
  Dionne Warwick Greatest Hits . . . . (Everest)
  Dionne Warwick-Anthology 1962-1971 . . . . (Rhino)
  Hot! Live & Otherwise . . . . (Arista)
  Original Rock 'N' Roll Hits Of The '60s-C . . . . . (Roulette)
Message To You Rudy
Specials; *Gangsters* . . . . (Chrysalis)
Message, The
Grandmaster Flash & The Furious Five; *Hip Hop Greats-Classic Raps-C* . . . . (Rhino)
  Rap Hall Of Fame-C . . . . (K-Tel)
Mrs. Clara Sullivan's Letter
Pete Seeger; *Best Of Broadside 1962-1968: Anthems Of The American Underground From The Pages Of Broadside Magazine-C* . . . . (Smithsonian Folkways)
Never Ever
All Saints; *All Saints* . . . . (London)
  Now That's What I Call Music!-#1-C . . . . (Virgin)
No Letter Today
Bill Haley & His Comets; *Rock Around The Country* . . (Crescendo)
No Reply
Beatles; *Beatles '65* . . . . (Capitol)
  Beatles-Box Set . . . . (Capitol)
  For Sale . . . . (Capitol)

No Reply At All
Genesis; *Abacab* . . . . (Atlantic)
Not Dark Yet
Bob Dylan; *Time Out Of Mind* . . . . (Columbia)
Note You Never Wrote
Wings; *Wings At The Speed Of Sound* . . . . (Capitol)
One Sweet Letter From You
Benny Goodman; *Roll 'Em* . . . . (Columbia)
Open Letter (To A Landlord)
Living Colour; *Vivid* . . . . (Epic)
Open Letter To George Bush
Wayne Horvitz/The President; *Miracle Mile* . . . . . . (Elektra)
P.S. I Love You
Bette Midler; *ST/For The Boys* . . . . (Atlantic)
Billie Holiday; *Lady Sings The Blues* . . . . (Verve)
Bing Crosby; *Thanks For The Memories Mr. Crosby* . . (J-Bird)
Dion; *Dion-His Best* . . . . (Laurie)
Kay Starr; *Too Marvelous For Words-Capitol Sings Jonny Mercer-C* . . (Capitol)
Mel Torme; *That's All* . . . . (Sony Music Special Prod.)
Rosemary Clooney; *Rosemary Clooney Sings The Lyrics Of Johnny Mercer* . . . . (Concord Jazz)
Tom T. Hall; *Natural Dreams* . . . . (Mercury)
Woody Herman; *Best Of The Big Bands-C* . . . . (Columbia)
P.S. I Love You
Beatles; *Beatles-Box Set* . . . . (Capitol)
  Beatles-Love Songs . . . . (Capitol)
  Introducing...The Beatles . . . . (Vee-Jay)
  Please Please Me . . . . (Parlophone)
  The Early Beatles . . . . (Capitol)
Personally
Karla Bonoff; *Wild Heart Of The Young* . . . . (Columbia)
Picture Postcards From L.A.
Joshua Kadison; *Painted Desert Serenade* . . . . (SBK)
Please Mister Postman
Beatles; *Beatles-Box Set* . . . . (Capitol)
  The Beatles' Second Album . . . . (Capitol)
  With The Beatles . . . . (Parlophone)
Carpenters; *Carpenters-Classics-#2* . . . . (A&M)
  Horizon . . . . (A&M)
  Yesterday Once More . . . . (A&M)
Marvelettes; *Billboard Top Rock 'N' Roll Hits-1961-C* . . (Rhino)
  Marvelettes' Greatest Hits . . . . (Motown)
  Marvelettes-Anthology . . . . (Motown)
  Motown Story-First 25 Years-C . . . . (Motown)
Please Take A Letter Miss Brown
Ink Spots; *Best Of The Ink Spots* . . . . (MCA)
Postcard From India
Rosalie Sorrels; *Travelin' Lady Rides Again* . . . . (Green Linnet)
Postcard From Paris
Jimmy Webb; *Suspending Disbelief* . . . . (Elektra)
Postman Blues
Dinah Washington; *Complete Dinah Washington On Mercury-#1-1946-1949* . . . . (Mercury)
Put The Message In The Box
World Party; *Best Of MTV's 120 Minutes-#1-C* . . . . (Rhino)
  Goodbye Jumbo . . . . (Ensign)
Return Mail Blues
Robert Nighthawk; *Drop Down Mama* . . . . (Chess)
Return To Sender
Elvis Presley; *Girls Girls Girls* . . . . (RCA)
  The Great Performances . . . . (RCA)
  The Top Ten Hits . . . . (RCA)
  Worldwide 50 Gold Award Hits, Vol. 1, Parts 1 & 2 . . (RCA)
Return To Sender
Residents; *The King & Eye* . . . . (Restless)
Riding With Private Malone
David Ball; *Amigo* . . . . (Razor & Tie)
Rock & Roll Love Letter
Bay City Rollers; *Bay City Rollers' Greatest Hits* . . . . (Arista)
  Rock & Roll Love Letters . . . . (Arista)
Roll Over Beethoven
Beatles; *Beatles-Box Set* . . . . (Capitol)
  Rock 'N' Roll Music . . . . (Capitol)
  The Beatles At The Hollywood Bowl . . . . (Capitol)
  The Beatles' Second Album . . . . (Capitol)
  With The Beatles . . . . (Parlophone)
Byrds; *The Byrds* . . . . (Columbia)
Chuck Berry; *Chuck Berry-Golden Hits* . . . . (Mercury)
  Chuck Berry's Greatest Hits . . . . (Everest)
  Cruisin'-1956-C . . . . (Increase)
  Oldies But Goodies-#10-C . . . . (Original Sound)
  The Chess Box-Chuck Berry . . . . (Chess)
Electric Light Orchestra; *Afterglow* . . . . (Epic)
  Ole ELO . . . . (Jet)
Rollin' In My Sweet Baby's Arms
Bill Monroe; *Bean Blossom* . . . . (MCA)
Del McCoury Band; *Appalachian Stomp: Bluegrass Classics-C* . . . (Rhino)
Dillard & Clark; *Fantastic Expedition/Through The Morning* . . . . (Mobile Fidelity Sound Lab)

Flatt & Scruggs; *Flatt & Scruggs At Carnegie Hall!* . . . . (Koch International)
   Flatt & Scruggs-20 Greatest Hits . . . . (Deluxe)
Flying Burrito Brothers; *Close Encounters To The West Coast* . . . . (Relix)
Leon Russell; *Hank Wilson's Back, Vol. 1* . . . . (Right Stuff)
New Lost City Ramblers; *Greatest Folksingers Of The '60s-C* . . . . . . (Vanguard)
Ramblin' Jack Elliott; *Hard Travelin'* . . . . (Fantasy)
Ricky Skaggs and Kentucky Thunder; *History Of The Future* . . (Skaggs Family)
Tony Trischka; *Heartlands* . . . . (Rounder)
Willie Nelson; *Willie & Family Live* . . . . (Columbia)
Sad Letter
Muddy Waters; *Can't Get No Grindin'* . . . . (Chess)
   More Real Folk Blues-Muddy Waters . . . . (Chess)
Scarborough Fair/Canticle
Simon & Garfunkel; *Collected Works* . . . . (Columbia)
   Parsley Sage Rosemary & Thyme . . . . (Columbia)
   Simon & Garfunkel's Greatest Hits . . . . (Columbia)
   ST/The Graduate . . . . (Columbia)
   The Concert In Central Park . . . . (Warner Bros.)
Sealed With A Kiss
Bobby Vinton; *Bobby Vinton's Greatest Hits* . . . . (Curb)
Brian Hyland; *Cruisin'-1962-C* . . . . (Increase)
   Oldies But Goodies-#2-C . . . . (Original Sound)
   Original Rock 'N' Roll Hits Of The '50s-C . . . . (Roulette)
Lettermen; *Best Of The Lettermen-#2* . . . . (Capitol)
   Capitol Collectors Series-The Lettermen . . . . (Capitol)
Secret Messages
Electric Light Orchestra; *Secret Messages* . . . . (Jet)
Send Her My Love
Journey; *Frontiers* . . . . (Columbia)
   Journey's Greatest Hits . . . . (Columbia)
Sensation Communication Together
Albert King; *Truckload Of Lovin'* . . . . (Tomato)
Sex By Mail
Free Hot Lunch; *Penguin Love* . . . . (Flying Fish)
Signed, Sealed, Delivered I'm Yours
Stevie Wonder; *20/20-C* . . . . (Motown)
   Motown Grammy R&B Performances Of The '60s & '70s-C . . . . . . (Motown)
   Stevie Wonder's Greatest Hits-#2 . . . . (Motown)
   Uptight (Everything's Alright) . . . . (Motown)
Soldier's Last Letter
Ernest Tubb; *Legend & The Legacy* . . . . (First Generation)
   Living Legend . . . . (First Generation)
Ernest Tubb & Johnny Cash; *Ernest Tubb Collection-C* . . . . (Step One)
George Jones; *20 Golden Pieces Of George Jones* . . . . (Bulldog)
Merle Haggard; *Capitol Collectors Series-Merle Haggard* . . . . (Capitol)
Stan
Eminem; *The Marshall Mathers LP* . . . . (Aftermath/Interscope)
Strawberry Letter #23
Brothers Johnson; *Brothers Johnson-Classics-#11* . . . . (A&M)
   Right On Time . . . . (A&M)
Tevin Campbell; *T.E.V.I.N.* . . . . (Qwest)
Suicide Note
Pontiac Brothers; *Fuzzy Little Piece Of The World* . . . . (Frontier)
Take A Letter Maria
R.B. Greaves; *Didn't It Blow Your Mind: Soul Hits Of The '70s-#1-C* . . . (Rhino)
Take A Message To Mary
Bob Dylan; *Self Portrait* . . . . (Columbia)
Everly Brothers; *Everly Brothers-All-Time Original Hits* . . . . (Rhino)
   Everly Brothers-Cadence Classics-Their 20 Greatest Hits . . . . (Rhino)
Rockpile; *Seconds Of Pleasure* . . . . (Columbia)
Tear Stained Letter
Jo-el Sonnier; *Best Of Country Rock-C* . . . . (K-Tel)
   Come On Joe . . . . (RCA)
Richard Thompson; *Hand Of Kindness* . . . . (Hannibal)
Teenage Letter
Big Joe Turner; *Rhythm & Blues Years* . . . . (Rhino)
Jerry Lee Lewis; *Jerry Lee Lewis-Original Golden Hits-#1* . . . . (Sun)
Texas Chain Letter Massacre
Pajama Slave Dancers; *Blood Sweat & Beers* . . . . (Restless)
That's All She Wrote
Rick Nelson; *Garden Party* . . . . (MCA Special Prod.)
   Rick Nelson Sings "For You" . . . . (MCA)
That's All She Wrote
Ghetto Girlz; *Ain't Takin' No S@#T* . . . . (Heat Wave)
That's All She Wrote
Marty Robbins; *Come Back To Me* . . . . (Columbia)
That's All She Wrote
Conway Twitty; *Hello Darlin'* . . . . (MCA Special Prod.)
That's All She Wrote
Reba McEntire; *Rumor Has It* . . . . (MCA)
Tie A Yellow Ribbon Round The Ole Oak Tree
Dawn Featuring Tony Orlando; *'70s Party Killers-C* . . . . (Rhino)
   Fantastic-#1-C . . . . (K-Tel)
Frank Sinatra; *Some Nice Things I've Missed* . . . . (Reprise)
Lawrence Welk; *Best Of Lawrence Welk-20 Great Hits* . . . . (Ranwood)
Sonny James & Karla Taylor; *Classic Country Duets-C* . . . . (Curb)
To Whom It May Concern
Nat "King" Cole; *At The Movies* . . . . (Capitol)

Toot Toot Tootsie (Goo'Bye)
Al Jolson; *Al Jolson-Best Of The Decca Years* . . . . (MCA)
   Best Of Al Jolson . . . . (MCA)
Liza Minnelli; *Liza Minnelli-At Carnegie Hall* . . . . (Telarc)
Travelin' Soldier
Bruce Robison; *Bruce Robison* . . . . (Vireo)
Twistin' Postman
Marvelettes; *Compact Command Performances-Marvelettes* . . . . (Motown)
   Marvelettes' Greatest Hits . . . . (Motown)
   Marvelettes-Anthology . . . . (Motown)
Unsent
Alanis Morissette; *Supposed Former Infatuation Junkie* . . . . (Maverick)
Wells Fargo Wagon
Original Broadway Cast; *The Music Man* . . . . (Angel)
Original Cast; *The Music Man* . . . . (Gold Rush)
Western Union
Five Americans; *Back To The '60s-Rock 'N' Roll-C* . . . . (Dominion Entert.)
   Nuggets-#1-The Hits-C . . . . (Rhino)
Western Union
Elvis Presley; *From Nashville To Memphis-The Essential '60s Masters* . . (RCA)
Whispering Pines
Johnny Horton; *Johnny Horton's Greatest Hits* . . . . (Columbia)
Whoever Finds This I Love You
Oak Ridge Boys; *All Our Favorite Songs* . . . . (Columbia)
Why Don't You Write Me
Simon & Garfunkel; *Bridge Over Troubled Water* . . . . (Columbia)
Wish I Were You
Patty Smyth; *ST/Armageddon-The Album* . . . . (Columbia)
Wish You Were Here
Mark Wills; *Wish You Were Here* . . . . (Mercury)
Words By Heart
Billy Ray Cyrus; *It Won't Be The Last* . . . . (Mercury)
Write Me A Few Of Your Lines
Bonnie Raitt; *Takin' My Time* . . . . (Warner Bros.)
Write This Down
George Strait; *Always Never The Same* . . . . (MCA)
XXX's And OOO's
Trisha Yearwood; *Thinkin' About You* . . . . (MCA)
Your Old Love Letters
Ricky Skaggs; *Favorite Country Songs* . . . . (Epic)
   Waitin' For The Sun To Shine . . . . (Epic)

MARRIAGE, Engagement, Honeymoon, Husbands, Weddings, Wives

> *See Also:* **ANNIVERSARY, BEGINNINGS, CHEATING & LIES, COUPLES, DIVORCE, DOMESTIC ABUSE, FAITH, FAMILY *(various)*, GOD, HAPPINESS, HOME, JEWELRY, LIFE, LOVE *(various)*, PARTY, PROMISE, TOGETHERNESS, TRUTH**

(Today I Met) The Boy I'm Gonna Marry
Darlene Love; *Best Of Darlene Love* . . . . (Abkco)
   Phil Spector-Back To Mono 1958-1969-C . . . . (Abkco)
51st Anniversary
Jimi Hendrix Experience; *Are You Experienced?* . . . . (Reprise)
A Mi Esposa Con Amor
Sonny James; *A Mi Esposa Con Amor* . . . . (Columbia)
   American Originals-Sonny James . . . . (Columbia)
Adelaide's Lament
Original Cast; *Guys & Dolls* . . . . (MCA)
   Guys & Dolls . . . . (Motown)
Affirmation
Savage Garden; *Affirmation* . . . . (Columbia)
All I Have To Offer You Is Me
Aaron Tippin; *Essential Aaron Tippin* . . . . (RCA)
Charley Pride; *Charley Pride-Super Hits* . . . . (RCA)
   Essential Charley Pride . . . . (RCA)
Ricky Van Shelton; *Fried Green Tomatoes* . . . . (Audium)
Almost Grown
Chuck Berry; *Berry Is On Top* . . . . (Chess)
   Cruisin'-1959-C . . . . (Increase)
   Roll Over Beethoven . . . . (Allegiance)
   ST/American Graffiti . . . . (MCA)
   The Chess Box-Chuck Berry . . . . (Chess)
Almost Persuaded
David Houston; *Super Hits Of The '60s-C* . . . . (Epic)
Amanda
Don Williams; *Don Williams' Greatest Hits* . . . . (MCA)
   Volume One . . . . (MCA)
Waylon Jennings; *Waylon Jennings' Greatest Hits* . . . . (RCA)
An Acceptable Level Of Ecstasy (The Wedding Song)
Lyle Lovett; *Lyle Lovett* . . . . (MCA)
An Old Fashioned Wedding
Ethel Merman/Bruce Yarnell/Original Cast; *Annie Get
   Your Gun* . . . . (RCA Victor)

Anniversary Song
Al Jolson; *Al Jolson-Best Of The Decca Years* . . . .(MCA)
Cocktail Hour . . . . (Columbia River Entert. Group)
Dinah Shore; *Buttons & Bows.* . . . .(ASV)
Dinah Shore-16 Most Requested Songs-Encore! . . . . (Legacy)
Django Reinhardt; *Verve Jazz Masters 38* . . . . (Verve)
Eva Cassidy; *Time After Time* . . . .(Blix Street)
Guy Lombardo & His Royal Canadians; *Enjoy Yourself, The Hits Of Guy Lombardo* . . . .(MCA)
Arrangement
Joni Mitchell; *Ladies Of The Canyon* . . . . (Reprise)
As We Lay
Kelly Price; *Mirror Mirror* . . . .(Def Soul/IDJMG)
Autumn Of My Life
Bobby Goldsboro; *10th Anniversary Album-#1* . . . .(EMI)
Bobby Goldsboro's Greatest Hits . . . . (Liberty)
Babalu's Wedding Day
Eternals; *Doo-Wop Era-Harlem, New York-40 Hits-C* . . . . (Collectables)
Rockin' & Rollin' Wedding Songs-#1-C . . . . (Rhino)
Baby Please Set A Date
Elmore James; *Elmore James-Complete Fire & Enjoy Sessions-#1* . . . . (Collectables)
George Thorogood & The Destroyers; *Move It On Over* . . . . (Rounder)
Ballad Of John And Yoko
Beatles; *Beatles 1* . . . . (Capitol)
Beatles-Box Set . . . . (Capitol)
Hey Jude . . . . (Capitol)
Past Masters-Volume Two . . . . (Parlophone)
ST/Imagine: John Lennon . . . . (Capitol)
The Beatles/1967-1970 . . . . (Capitol)
Ballad Of Lucy Jordan
Marianne Faithfull; *Blazing Away* . . . . (Island)
Collection Of Her Best Recordings . . . . (Island)
Ballad Of The Green Berets
Barry Sadler; *Cruisin'-1966-C* . . . .(Increase)
Hits Of The Sixties-C . . . .(Intercom Music)
More American Graffiti-#4-C . . . . (MCA)
Nipper's Greatest Hits Of The '60s-#2-C . . . . (RCA)
Super Hits-#3-C . . . . (Gusto)
Band Of Gold
Freda Payne; *Beachbeat Draggin'* . . . .(Dunhill Compact Classics)
Didn't It Blow Your Mind: Soul Hits Of The '70s-#2-C . . . . (Rhino)
Freda Payne's Greatest Hits . . . . (HDH)
Band Of Gold
Don Cherry; *Very Best Of Don Cherry* . . . . (Collector's Choice)
Barber & His Wife
Original Cast/Angela Lansbury; *Sweeney Todd* . . . . (RCA)
Barney Google
Authentic Band Organ; *Catch The Brass Ring-Merry-Go-Round* . . . . . (Klavier)
Firehouse Five Plus Two; *Twenty Years Later* . . . . (Good Time Jazz)
Be My Life's Companion
Mills Brothers; *Best Of The Mills Brothers.* . . . .(MCA)
The Mills Brothers-Best Of The Decca Years. . . . . (Decca)
Rosemary Clooney; *Rosemary Clooney-16 Most Requested Songs* . . . . (Legacy)
Be My Wife
David Bowie; *Low* . . . .(Rykodisc)
Sound + Vision. . . . .(Rykodisc)
The Singles-1969-1993 . . . .(Rykodisc)
Best Day
George Strait; *Latest Greatest Straitest Hits.* . . . .(MCA)
Best Of Intentions
Travis Tritt; *Down The Road I Go* . . . . (Columbia)
Bicycle Built For Two
Kidsongs; *Cars, Boats, Trains, Planes* . . . . (Sony Wonder)
Original Soundtrack; *School Days-Kids Classics.* . . . . (Benson)
Big Bad Bill Is Sweet William Now
Ry Cooder; *Jazz* . . . .(Warner Bros.)
Big Bopper's Wedding
Big Bopper; *Chantilly Lace Starring The Big Bopper* . . . . (Mercury)
Helloo Baby! Best Of The Big Bopper-1954-1959. . . . . (Rhino)
M. Dung's Idiot Classics. . . . . (Rhino)
Billy Don't Be A Hero
Bo Donaldson & The Heywoods; *Super Hits Of The '70s-Have A Nice Day-#13-C* . . . . (Rhino)
Bimbombey
Jimmie Rodgers; *Best Of Jimmie Rodgers* . . . . (Rhino)
Best Of Jimmie Rodgers. . . . . (Curb)
Bird In A Gilded Cage
Joan Morris & William Bolcom; *After The Ball* . . . . (Nonesuch)
Breaking In A Brand New Love
Seals & Crofts; *Takin' It Easy.* . . . .(Warner Bros.)
Bride Of Rain Dog
Tom Waits; *Rain Dogs* . . . . (Island)
Bridge Washed Out
Warner Mack; *Country's Greatest Hits-#3-C.* . . . .(MCA)
MCA Records 30 Years Of Hits-1958-1988-C. . . . . (MCA)
Brilliant Disguise
Bruce Springsteen; *Bruce Springsteen's Greatest Hits.* . . . . (Columbia)

Tunnel Of Love . . . . (Columbia)
Bring Me My Bride
Original Cast; *A Funny Thing Happened On The Way To The Forum.* . . . (Angel)
Bus Stop
Hollies; *Best Of The Hollies* . . . . (EMI)
History Of British Rock-#3-C. . . . . (Rhino)
The Hollies' Greatest Hits . . . . (Epic)
Bus Stop Song, The (Paper Of Pins)
Four Lads; *Moments To Remember-Very Best Of The Four Lads* . . . . . (Taragon)
Buy Me A Rose
Kenny Rogers; *She Rides Wild Horses* . . . .(Dreamcatcher)
By The Book
Michael Peterson; *Michael Peterson.* . . . . (Reprise)
Ceremony, The
George Jones & Tammy Wynette; *George Jones & Tammy Wynette-16 Biggest Hits* . . . .(Epic/Legacy)
George Jones & Tammy Wynette's Greatest Hits. . . . . (Epic)
Chapel Of Love
Dixie Cups; *Girl Groups-Story Of A Sound-C.* . . . . (Rhino)
Jewels-#1-C . . . . (SSS International)
Oldies But Goodies-#11-C . . . .(Original Sound)
Original New York Rock & Roll-C . . . .(Original Sound)
Chapel Of Love/I'm Gonna Get Married
Frankie Avalon; *You're My Life* . . . .(De-Lite)
Chasing Forever
Will Smith; *Big Willie Style.* . . . . (Columbia)
Check Yes Or No
George Strait; *Strait Out Of The Box.* . . . . (MCA)
Cherry Hill Park
Billy Joe Royal; *Billy Joe Royal's Greatest Hits* . . . . (Columbia)
Super Hits Of The '70s-Have A Nice Day-#1-C . . . . (Rhino)
Chime Bells
Elton Britt; *The RCA Years* . . . . (Collector's Choice)
Jody King; *Photographs & Memories* . . . . (Capricorn)
Choppy Water (Rocky Marriage Breakdown)
Connie Kaldor; *Small Cafe* . . . .(Philo)
Church Bells May Ring
Diamonds; *Best Of The Diamonds* . . . . (Rhino)
Willows; *Rockin' & Rollin' Wedding Songs-#1-C* . . . . (Rhino)
ST/A Rage In Harlem . . . . (MCA Special Prod.)
WCBS FM 101 History Of Rock-'50s-#2-C . . . . (Collectables)
Church On Cumberland Road
Shenandoah; *Greatest Country Hits Of The '80s-1989-C* . . . . (Columbia)
Road Not Taken . . . . (Columbia)
Cigarette
Ben Folds Five; *Whatever And Ever Amen* . . . .(Caroline/550)
Could I Have This Dance?
Anne Murray; *Anne Murray's Greatest Hits* . . . . (Capitol)
ST/Urban Cowboy . . . .(Asylum)
Could've Been Me
Billy Ray Cyrus; *Some Gave All* . . . . (Mercury)
Country Bumpkin
Cal Smith; *16 Top Country Hits-#1-C* . . . . (MCA)
Country's Greatest Hits-#2-C . . . . (MCA Special Prod.)
Grand Ole Opry-75 Years-#2-C . . . . (MCA)
Crazy 'Bout That Married Woman
Rockin' Dopsie; *Saturday Night Zydeco* . . . . (Maison De Soul)
Crazy Things I Do
Sammie; *From The Bottom To The Top.* . . . . (Freeworld/Capitol)
Daddy's Money
Ricochet; *Ricochet* . . . . (Columbia)
Dance Little Jean
Nitty Gritty Dirt Band; *Let's Go* . . . . (Warner Bros.)
Twenty Years Of Dirt-Best Of The Nitty Gritty Dirt Band . . . . . (Warner Bros.)
Danny's Song
Anne Murray; *Anne Murray-Country* . . . . (Capitol)
Anne Murray's Greatest Hits . . . . (Capitol)
Danny's Song . . . . (Capitol)
Loggins & Messina; *Loggins & Messina-On Stage.* . . . . (Columbia)
Sittin' In . . . . (Columbia)
The Best Of Friends . . . . (Columbia)
Darlin' Companion
Johnny Cash; *Johnny Cash At Folsom Prison & San Quentin.* . . . . . . (Columbia)
Lovin' Spoonful; *Hums Of The Lovin' Spoonful* . . . . (Kama Sutra)
Lovin' Spoonful-Collector's Edition-#1 . . . . (Platinum Disc)
Lovin' Spoonful's Greatest Hits . . . .(Buddah)
Darling Lorraine
Paul Simon; *You're The One* . . . . (Warner Bros.)
Dear Doctor
Rolling Stones; *Beggars Banquet* . . . .(Abkco)
Diamond Girl
Seals & Crofts; *Diamond Girl* . . . . (Warner Bros.)
Seals & Crofts' Greatest Hits. . . . . (Warner Bros.)
Distant Drums
Jim Reeves; *Best Of The Best Of Jim Reeves* . . . . (King)
Billboard Top Country Hits-1966-C . . . . (Rhino)
Essential Jim Reeves . . . . (RCA)
Do Wah Diddy Diddy
Manfred Mann; *Best Of Manfred Mann* . . . . (EMI Special Markets)

Billboard Top Rock 'N' Roll Hits-1964-C . . . . (Rhino)
History Of British Rock-#2-C . . . . (Rhino)

Do You Hear Wedding Bells
Jive Five; *Jive Five-Their Greatest Hits* . . . . (Collectables)

Do You Love Me?
Original Cast; *Fiddler On The Roof* . . . . (RCA Victor)

Does My Ring Hurt Your Finger
Charley Pride; *Charley Pride-24 Greatest Hits* . . . . (Tee Vee)
Essential Charley Pride . . . . (RCA)

Don't Be Cruel
Cheap Trick; *Cheap Trick's Greatest Hits* . . . . (Epic)
Lap Of Luxury . . . . (Epic)
Elvis Presley; *Billboard Top Rock 'N' Roll Hits-1956-C* . . . . (Rhino)
Nipper's Greatest Hits Of The '50s-#2-C . . . . (RCA)
Number One Hits . . . . (RCA)
The Great Performances . . . . (RCA)
The Top Ten Hits . . . . (RCA)
Judds; *Heartland* . . . . (MCA)

Don't Marry Me
Original Cast; *Flower Drum Song* . . . . (Sony Music Classical)

Don't Pull Your Love
Hamilton, Joe Frank & Reynolds; *'70s Biggest Hits-C* . . . . (MCA Special Prod.)
Hamilton, Joe Frank & Reynolds' Greatest Hits . . . . (MCA Special Prod.)
Rock Around The Oldies-#4-C . . . . (MCA Special Prod.)

Don't Marry The Mormon Boys
Rosalie Sorrels; *Lonesome Roving Wolves-Songs & Ballads Of
The West* . . . . (Green Linnet)

Down The Aisle Of Love
Quin-Tones; *Rockin' & Rollin' Wedding Songs-#2-C* . . . . (Rhino)

Down The Road
Mac McAnally; *Knots* . . . . (MCA)

Drivin' My Wife Away
Pinkard & Bowden; *Great Divorce Songs For Him-C* . . . . (Warner Bros.)

Eddie's First Wife
Gretchen Peters; *Gretchen Peters* . . . . (Purple Crayon Prod.)

Elvira
Murry Kellum; *Country Comedy-20 Country Comedy Hits* . . . . (Plantation)
Oak Ridge Boys; *Fancy Free* . . . . (MCA)
MCA Records 30 Years Of Hits-1958-1988-C . . . . (MCA)
Oak Ridge Boys' Greatest Hits 2 . . . . (MCA)

Fall In Love
Kenny Chesney; *All I Need To Know* . . . . (BNA)
Kenny Chesney's Greatest Hits . . . . (BNA)

Feet Up (Pat Him On The Po-Po)
Guy Mitchell; *Definitive Guy Mitchell* . . . . (Collector's Choice)

Follow Me
John Denver; *John Denver's Greatest Hits* . . . . (RCA)
Take Me Home, Country Roads & Other Hits . . . . (RCA)

Foolish Little Girl
Shirelles; *Shirelles' Greatest Hits* . . . . (Everest)
Shirelles-16 Greatest Hits . . . . (Trip)
Shirelles-Anthology 1959-1964 . . . . (Rhino)

For Me & My Gal
Bing Crosby; *The Radio Years: 25 Songs* . . . . (Crescendo)
Judy Garland & Gene Kelly; *Best Of The Decca Years-#1-Hits!-C* . . . . (Decca)
Nilsson; *A Little Touch Of Schmilsson In The Night* . . . . (RCA)

For You
Kenny Lattimore; *Kenny Lattimore* . . . . (Columbia)
Modern Bride Presents The Wedding Album-C . . . . (Columbia)
Songs From The Heart-C . . . . (Columbia)

For You I Will
Aaron Tippin; *What This Country Needs* . . . . (Lyric Street)

Forever's As Far As I'll Go
Alabama; *Alabama's Greatest Hits-#3* . . . . (RCA)
Alabama-Super Hits . . . . (RCA)
For The Record: 41 Number One Hits . . . . (RCA)
Pass It On Down . . . . (BMG Special Prod.)

Friend, Lover, Wife
Johnny Paycheck; *Johnny Paycheck-16 Biggest Hits* . . . . (Epic)
Johnny Paycheck's Biggest Hits . . . . (Epic)

Froggie Went A Courtin'
Doc Watson; *Essential Doc Watson* . . . . (Vanguard)
Home Again . . . . (Vanguard)

From Here To Eternity
Michael Peterson; *Michael Peterson* . . . . (Reprise)
Wedding Day Music-C . . . . (Reprise)

From This Moment On
Shania Twain & Bryan White; *Come On Over* . . . . (Mercury)

Get Me To The Church On Time
Original Cast; *My Fair Lady* . . . . (Columbia)

Girl That I Marry, The
Dick Haymes; *Best Of Dick Haymes* . . . . (MCA)
Doris Day/Original Cast; *Annie Get Your Gun* . . . . (Columbia)
Original Broadway Cast; *Annie Get Your Gun* . . . . (Angel)
Original Cast; *Annie Get Your Gun* . . . . (MCA)

Give Me A Ring Sometime
Lisa Brokop; *Every Little Girl's Dream* . . . . (Patriot)

Give Me Forever (I Do)
John Tesh featuring James Ingram; *Grand Passion-C* . . . . (GTS)

Give My Love To Rose
George Jones; *George Jones Sings The Hits Of His Country
Cousins* . . . . (Razor & Tie)
Johnny Cash; *Johnny Cash-Sun Years* . . . . (Rhino)

Go On With The Wedding
Patti Page; *Patti Page-Golden Celebration* . . . . (Mercury)

Golden Ring
Emmylou Harris/Linda Ronstadt/Anna & Kate McGarrigle; *Tammy
Wynette...Remembered-C* . . . . (Asylum)
George Jones & Tammy Wynette; *George Jones & Tammy Wynette-16
Biggest Hits* . . . . (Epic/Legacy)
Tammy Wynette & George Jones; *Encore-Tammy Wynette & George
Jones* . . . . (Epic)
Tammy Wynette & George Jones' Greatest Hits . . . . (Epic)
Tammy Wynette-Anniversary-20 Years Of Hits . . . . (Epic)

Goodbye Earl
Dixie Chicks; *Fly* . . . . (Monument)

Grow Old With Me
John Lennon; *The John Lennon Anthology* . . . . (Capitol)
Wonsaponatime . . . . (Capitol)
Mary Chapin Carpenter; *Party Doll And Other Favorites* . . . . (Columbia)

Guy Is A Guy, A
Doris Day; *Doris Day's Greatest Hits* . . . . (Columbia)

Happily Ever After
Case; *Now That's What I Call Music!-#3-C* . . . . (Virgin)
Personal Conversation . . . . (Def Jam/IDJMG)

Happily Married Man
Duane Allman; *Duane Allman-An Anthology-Vol. II* . . . . (Capricorn)

Hard To Be A Husband, Hard To Be A Wife
Chely Wright & Brad Paisley; *Grand Ole Opry-75 Years-#2-C* . . . . . . (MCA)

Harry, Let's Marry
Maxine Brown; *45-#1286* . . . . (Collectables)

Harry's House Centerpiece
Joni Mitchell; *Hissing Of Summer Lawns* . . . . (Asylum)

Hawaiian Wedding Song
Andy Williams; *Andy Williams' Greatest Hits* . . . . (Columbia)
Andy Williams-16 Most Requested Songs . . . . (Legacy)
Jim Reeves; *Jim Reeves-Pure Gold* . . . . (RCA)

He Wasn't Man Enough
Toni Braxton; *The Heat* . . . . (LaFace)
Totally Hits-#3-C . . . . (Atlantic)

Hey Paula
Paul & Paula; *Cruisin'-1963-C* . . . . (Increase)
ST/Animal House . . . . (MCA)
WCBS FM 101 History Of Rock-'60s-#1-C . . . . (Collectables)

High Hopes And Empty Pockets
McBride & The Ride; *McBride & The Ride* . . . . (MCA)

High Noon
Frankie Laine; *Billboard Top Movie Hits-1950-1954-C* . . . . (Rhino)
Tex Ritter; *Heroes Of Country Music-#4-Legends Of The West
Coast-C* . . . . (Rhino)
*The Envelope Please-Academy Award Winning Songs (1946-
1957)-C* . . . . (Rhino)

Holes In The Floor Of Heaven
Steve Wariner; *Burnin' The Roadhouse Down* . . . . (Capitol)

Home
Alan Jackson; *Alan Jackson-The Greatest Hits Collection* . . . . (Arista)
Here In The Real World . . . . (Arista)

Hometown Honeymoon
Alabama; *American Pride* . . . . (RCA)

Honeymoon Hotel
Alice Faye; *Hooray For Hollywood* . . . . (RCA)
Dick Powell; *In Hollywood-1933-1935* . . . . (Legacy)
Ruby Keeler & Dick Powell; *ST/Lullaby Of Broadway-The Best Of Busby
Berkeley At Warner Bros.* . . . . (Rhino)

Honeymoon In Beirut
Rick Springfield; *Rock Of Life* . . . . (RCA)

Honeymoon On Mars
Be Bop Deluxe; *Modern Music* . . . . (Capitol)

Honeymooners
City Boy; *Young Men Gone West* . . . . (Mercury)

Honeymooners
Bruce Springsteen; *Tracks* . . . . (Columbia)

Hour Of Gold
Emmylou Harris; *Red Dirt Girl* . . . . (Nonesuch)

Housewife
Leon Russell; *Americana* . . . . (Paradise)

How Do You Fall In Love
Alabama; *For The Record: 41 Number One Hits* . . . . (RCA)

How Forever Feels
Kenny Chesney; *Everywhere We Go* . . . . (BNA)
Kenny Chesney's Greatest Hits . . . . (BNA)

Husbands And Wives
Brooks & Dunn; *Big Country Hits '99-C* . . . . (K-Tel)
If You See Her . . . . (Arista)
Neil Diamond; *Neil Diamond-Love Songs* . . . . (MCA)
Rainbow . . . . (MCA)
Stones . . . . (MCA)

Roger Miller; *Best Of Roger Miller* .... (Mercury)
Best Of Roger Miller-His Greatest Songs .... (Curb)
Roger Miller-Super Hits .... (Epic)
Roger Miller-The Hits .... (Mercury)

I Cried All The Way To The Altar
Patsy Cline; *20 Golden Pieces Of Patsy Cline* .... (Bulldog)
Patsy Cline .... (Audio Fidelity)
Walkin' Dreams-Her First Recordings-#1 .... (Rhino)

I Do
Paul Brandt; *Calm Before The Storm* .... (Reprise)

I Do
Mila Mason; *That's Enough Of That* .... (Atlantic)

I Do It For Your Love
Paul Simon; *Greatest Hits, Etc.* .... (Columbia)
Still Crazy After All These Years .... (Columbia)

I Don't Even Know Your Name
Alan Jackson; *Alan Jackson-The Greatest Hits Collection* .... (Arista)
Who I Am .... (Arista)

I Don't Want To Have To Marry You
Jim Ed Brown & Helen Cornelius; *Jim Ed Brown & Helen Cornelius'
Greatest Hits* .... (RCA)

I Knew The Bride
Dave Edmunds; *Best Of Dave Edmunds* .... (Swan Song)
Get It .... (Swan Song)
Nick Lowe; *Basher: Best Of* .... (Columbia)

I Lost It
Kenny Chesney; *Kenny Chesney's Greatest Hits* .... (BNA)

I Love To Cry At Weddings
Original Cast; *Sweet Charity* .... (Columbia)

I Married An Angel
George Siravo; *Heritage Of Broadway-Rodgers & Hart* .... (Bainbridge)

I Meant Every Word He Said
Ricky Van Shelton; *Greatest Country Hits Of The '90s-#2-C* ...... (Columbia)
RVS III .... (Columbia)

I Never Will Marry
Bailey Brothers; *Early Days Of Bluegrass-#6* .... (Rounder)
Carter Family; *Wildwood Flower* .... (ASV Living Era)
Linda Ronstadt; *Simple Dreams* .... (Asylum)

I Used To Love Him
Lauryn Hill featuring Mary J. Blige; *The Miseducation Of
Lauryn Hill* .... (Ruffhouse/Columbia)

I Wanna Marry A Lighthouse Keeper
Erika Eigen; *ST/A Clockwork Orange* .... (Warner Bros.)

I Wanna Marry You
Bruce Springsteen; *The River* .... (Columbia)

I Want A Girl (Just Like The Girl)
Al Jolson; *The Al Jolson Story-#1* .... (MCA)
Spike Jones & His City Slickers; *King Of Corn* .... (Glendale)

I Want To Marry You
Del Vikings; *Del Vikings* .... (Collectables)
Rockin' & Rollin' Wedding Songs-#1-C .... (Rhino)

I Went To Your Wedding
Patti Page; *Patti Page-Golden Hits* .... (Mercury)

I Wish That We Were Married
Ronnie and The Hi-Lites; *Rockin' & Rollin' Wedding Songs-#2-C* ..... (Rhino)

I Wonder What The King Is Doing Tonight
Original Cast; *Camelot* .... (Columbia)
Richard Harris; *ST/Camelot* .... (Warner Bros.)

I'd Rather Ride Around With You
Reba McEntire; *What If It's You* .... (MCA)

If I Were A Carpenter
Bobby Darin; *Live At The Desert Inn* .... (Motown)
Four Tops; *Compact Command Performances-Four Tops* ...... (Motown)
Four Tops Reach Out .... (Motown)
Four Tops-Anthology .... (Motown)
Johnny Cash & June Carter; *The Man In Black-His Greatest Hits* ..... (Legacy)
Tim Hardin; *Memorial Album* .... (Polydor)

If Momma Was Married
Cynthia Gibb & Jennifer Beck; *ST/Gypsy* .... (Atlantic)
Original Cast; *Gypsy* .... (Columbia)

If You Ever Have Forever In Mind
Vince Gill; *The Key* .... (MCA)

If You Wanna Be Happy
Jimmy Soul; *Best Of Jimmy Soul* .... (Rhino)
Dick Bartley's One-Hit Wonders Of The '60s-#1-C .... (Rhino)
Son Of Frat Rock!-C .... (Rhino)
ST/Mermaids .... (Geffen)
ST/My Best Friend's Wedding .... (Work/Epic)

I'll Think Of A Reason Later
Lee Ann Womack; *Some Things I Know* .... (Decca)

I'm Already Taken
Steve Wariner; *Country Cares For Kids II-C* .... (BNA)
Two Teardrops .... (Capitol)

I'm Gonna Get Married
Lloyd Price; *Lloyd Price's Greatest Hits* .... (MCA)
Super Oldies Of The '50s-#3-C .... (Audio Fidelity)
Vintage Music-#15-C .... (MCA)

I'm Henry The VIII, I Am
Herman's Hermits; *Herman's Hermits-Their Greatest Hits* .... (Abkco)

Something Good Again .... (Abkco)

I'm In Love Again
George Morgan; *Room Full Of Roses-The George Morgan
Collection* .... (Razor & Tie)

I'm Throwing Rice
Jerry Lee Lewis; *Taste Of Country* .... (Sun)

In The Chapel In The Moonlight
Kitty Kallen; *Those Wonderful Years: Music! Music!
Music!-C* .... (JCI Assoc. Labels)
Patti Page; *Patti Page-16 Most Requested Songs* .... (Legacy)
Shep Fields & His Rippling Rhythm Orchestra; *78-#6640* .... (Bluebird)

Indian Wedding
Roy Orbison; *Legendary Roy Orbison* .... (Sony Music Special Prod.)
Our Love Song .... (Monument)
Roy Orbison-More Greatest Hits .... (Monument)

Ironic
Alanis Morissette; *Jagged Little Pill* .... (Maverick)

It Could've Been Me
Billy Ray Cyrus; *Some Gave All* .... (Mercury)

Jacob's Ladder
Mark Wills; *Mark Wills* .... (Mercury)

James
Huffamoose; *We've Been Had Again* .... (Interscope)

Just Another Day In Paradise
Phil Vassar; *Phil Vassar* .... (Arista)

Just Now It Feels So Right
Jesse Winchester; *Touch On The Rainy Side* .... (Rhino)

Kiss The Bride
Elton John; *Elton John's Greatest Hits-1976-1986* ...... (MCA)
Too Low For Zero .... (MCA)

Kisses Sweeter Than Wine
Jimmie Rodgers; *Best Of Jimmie Rodgers* .... (Rhino)
Cruisin'-1958-C .... (Increase)
Weavers; *Best Of The Weavers* .... (MCA)
Reunion-At Carnegie Hall-1963 .... (Vanguard)
Weavers At Carnegie Hall .... (Vanguard)
Weavers' Greatest Hits .... (Vanguard)

Let's Get Married
Al Green; *Al Green's Greatest Hits* .... (Right Stuff)
Compact Command Performances-Al Green .... (Motown)

Let's Get Married
Jagged Edge; *J.E. Heartbreak* .... (So So Def/Columbia)

Let's Get Married Again
John Conlee; *Friday Night Blues* .... (MCA)

Let's Go All The Way
Norma Jean; *Best Of Norma Jean* .... (Collector's Choice)

Let's Go To Vegas
Faith Hill; *It Matters To Me* .... (Warner Bros.)

Let's Pretend We're Married
Prince; *1999* .... (Warner Bros.)
Tina Turner; *Collected Recordings: Sixties To Nineties* .... (Capitol)

Letter, The (That Johnny Walker Read)
Asleep At The Wheel; *Very Best Of Asleep At The Wheel
Since 1970* .... (Relentless/Madacy)

Lida Rose/Will I Ever Tell You?
Original Broadway Cast; *The Music Man* .... (Angel)
Original Cast; *The Music Man* .... (Gold Rush)
Soundtrack; *ST/The Music Man* .... (Warner Bros.)

Little Band Of Gold
Sonny James; *American Originals-Sonny James* .... (Columbia)
Little Bit South Of Saskatoon .... (Columbia)
Sonny James' Greatest Hits .... (Columbia)

Little Bitty
Alan Jackson; *Everything I Love* .... (Arista)
Tom T. Hall; *Songs From Sopchoppy* .... (Mercury)
Tom T. Hall-The Hits .... (Mercury)

Long Honeymoon
Elvis Costello; *Girls Girls Girls* .... (Columbia)
Elvis Costello & The Attractions; *Imperial Bedroom* .... (Columbia)

Longer
Dan Fogelberg; *Dan Fogelberg/Greatest Hits* .... (Full Moon)
Phoenix .... (Full Moon)

Love And Marriage
Dinah Shore; *45-#6266* .... (RCA)
Frank Sinatra; *Capitol Collectors Series-Frank Sinatra* .... (Capitol)
Sinatra: A Man And His Music .... (Reprise)
The Capitol Years .... (Capitol)
The Reprise Collection .... (Reprise)

Love Is A Golden Ring
Frankie Laine; *Frankie Laine-16 Most Requested Songs* .... (Legacy)

Love Letters From Old Mexico
Leslie Satcher; *Love Letters* .... (Warner Bros.)

Loving You
Elvis Presley; *Elvis' Golden Records* .... (RCA)
Elvis Presley Sings Leiber & Stoller .... (RCA)
Elvis Presley-Pure Gold .... (RCA)
Essential Elvis-The First Movies .... (RCA)
ST/Loving You .... (RCA)

Make Me The Woman That You Go Home To
Gladys Knight & The Pips; *Compact Command Performances-Gladys Knight & The Pips* . . . . (Motown)
Gladys Knight & The Pips-All The Great Hits . . . . (Motown)
Gladys Knight & The Pips-Anthology . . . . (Motown)
Standing Ovation . . . . (S.O.U.L.)

Make My Life With You
Oak Ridge Boys; *Country Classics-#1-C* . . . . (Universal)
MCA #1 Hits Of The '80s-#1-C . . . . (MCA Special Prod.)
Oak Ridge Boys' Greatest Hits 2 . . . . (MCA)

Makin' Whoopie
Art Tatum; *Solo Masterpieces-#5* . . . . (Pablo)
Eddie Cantor; *Nipper's Greatest Hits Of The '20s-C* . . . .(RCA)
Nilsson; *A Little Touch Of Schmilsson In The Night* . . . . (RCA)
Ray Charles; *Ray Charles-His Greatest Hits-#2* . . . . (Dunhill Compact Classics)

Mama Said
Shirelles; *Original Rock 'N' Roll Hits Of The '60s-C* . . . . (Roulette)
Shirelles' Greatest Hits . . . . (Everest)
Shirelles-Anthology 1959-1964 . . . . (Rhino)
Shirelles-Classics . . . . (Bac-Trac)
Super Oldies Of The '60s-#3-C . . . . (Audio Fidelity)

Mandy
Eddie Cantor; *Irving Berlin: A Hundred Years-C* . . . . (Columbia)
Fats Waller; *Breakin' The Ice: The Early Years, Part 1 (1934-1935)* . . . . (Bluebird)
Van & Schenck; *Music From The New York Stage (1890-1920)-#4-1917-1920-C* . . . . (Pearl)

Marriage
Ted Nugent & The Amboy Dukes; *Marriage On The Rocks* . . . . (Polydor)
Rock Bottom . . . . (Polydor)

Marriage Bureau Rendezvouz
10 CC; *Deceptive Bends* . . . . (Mercury)
Live & Let Live . . . . (Mercury)

Marriage License
Chi-Lites; *Chi-Lites* . . . . (Brunswick)

Marriage Made In Heaven
Bob Crewe; *Motivation* . . . . (Elektra)

Marriage On Paper Only
Dramatics; *Anytime Anyplace* . . . . (MCA)

Married
Liza Minnelli; *Liza With A "Z"* . . . . (Columbia)
Original Cast; *Cabaret* . . . . (Columbia)

Married But Not To Each Other
Barbara Mandrell; *Best Of Barbara Mandrell* . . . . (MCA)
Lovers, Friends & Strangers . . . . (MCA)
Midnight Angel . . . . (MCA)

Married Lady
Bill Anderson; *Ladies Choice* . . . . (MCA)

Married Men
Bette Midler; *Thighs And Whispers* . . . . (Atlantic)
Roches; *Bread & Roses Festival Of Acoustic Music-#2-C* . . . . (Fantasy)
Roches . . . . (Warner Bros.)

Married Woman
Frankie Lee Sims; *Lucy Mae Blues* . . . . (Specialty)
This Is How It All Began-#1-C . . . . (Specialty)

Marry Me
Engelbert Humperdinck; *Engelbert* . . . . (Parrot)
Original Cast; *The Rink* . . . . (Polydor)

Marry Me
Neil Diamond; *Tennessee Moon* . . . . (Columbia)
Neil Diamond & Buffy Lawson; *Modern Bride Presents The Wedding Album-C* . . . . (Columbia)

Marry The Man Today
Original Cast; *ST/Guys & Dolls* . . . . (MCA)

Marrying For Love
Original Cast/Dinah Shore; *Call Me Madam* . . . . (RCA)

Matchmaker
Original Cast; *Fiddler On The Roof* . . . . (RCA Victor)

Matrimony: Maybe You
Maxwell; *Embrya* . . . . (Columbia)

Meet In The Middle
Diamond Rio; *Diamond Rio* . . . . (Arista)
Diamond Rio's Greatest Hits . . . . (Arista)

Memories Are Made Of This
Dean Martin; *Billboard Pop Memories-1955-1959-C* . . . . (Rhino)
Dean Martin-Love Songs . . . . (Ranwood)
Dean Martin's All Time Greatest Hits . . . . (Curb)

Midnight Mary
Joey Powers; *Dick Bartley's One-Hit Wonders Of The '60s-#1-C* . . . . . (Rhino)

Moonlight On The Colorado
Sons Of The Pioneers; *Songs Of The Trail* . . . . (Pair)

Mountain Of Love
Charley Pride; *Charley Pride's Greatest Hits-#2* . . . . (RCA)
Solid Country Gold-C . . . . (RCA)
David Houston; *American Originals-David Houston* . . . . (Columbia)
Harold Dorman; *Collectables Presents The History Of Rock-#10-C* . . . . (Collectables)
Johnny Rivers; *Best Of Johnny Rivers* . . . . (EMI)
Johnny Rivers-Anthology 1964-1977 . . . . (Rhino)

Mrs. Steven Rudy
Mark McGuinn; *Mark McGuinn* . . . . (VFR)

My Baby's Coming With A Marriage License
Sunnyland Slim; *Blues Piano Orgy* . . . . (Delmark)

My Kind Of Woman, My Kind Of Man
Patty Loveless; *Patty Loveless-Classics* . . . . (Epic)
Vince Gill with Patty Loveless; *The Key* . . . . (MCA)

My Mother's Wedding Day
Original Cast; *Brigadoon* . . . . (RCA)

My Old Man
Joni Mitchell; *Blue* . . . . (Reprise)

My Only Love
Statler Brothers; *Atlanta Blue* . . . . (Mercury)
Statler Brothers' Greatest Hits . . . . (Mercury)

My Wife
Who; *ST/The Kids Are Alright* . . . . (MCA)
Two's Missing . . . . (MCA)
Who Greatest Hits . . . . (MCA)
Who's next . . . . (MCA)

My Woman, My Woman, My Wife
Marty Robbins; *Lifetime Of Song-1951-1982* . . . . (Columbia)
Marty Robbins' All-Time Greatest Hits . . . . (Columbia)

Never Ending Song Of Love
Conway Twitty & Loretta Lynn; *Lead Me On* . . . . (MCA)
Delaney & Bonnie; *Best Of Delaney & Bonnie* . . . . (Rhino)
Super Hits Of The '70s-Have A Nice Day-#16-C . . . . (Rhino)

Never My Love
Association; *Association Greatest Hits* . . . . (Warner Bros.)
Songs That Made Them Famous . . . . (Pair)
There Is Still Love-Anniversary Songs-C . . . . (Scotti Bros.)

Never Will I Marry
Barbra Streisand; *Third Album* . . . . (Columbia)

New York Mining Disaster 1941 (Mr. Jones)
Bee Gees; *Bee Gees-Gold* . . . . (Polydor)
Here At Last...Bee Gees...Live . . . . (Polydor)
History Of British Rock-#8-C . . . . (Rhino)

No Help Wanted
Carlisles; *Heroes Of Country Music-#3-Legends Of Nashville-C* . . . . . . (Rhino)

No One Said It Would Be Easy
Sheryl Crow; *Tuesday Night Music Club* . . . . (A&M)

Not Too Young To Get Married
Bob B. Soxx/Blue Jeans; *Phil Spector-Back To Mono 1958-1969-C* . . . . (Abkco)
Darlene Love; *Best Of Darlene Love* . . . . (Abkco)

Now And Forever (You And Me)
Anne Murray; *Anne Murray's Greatest Hits-#2* . . . . (Capitol)
Something To Talk About . . . . (Capitol)

Now's The Time To Fall In Love
Eddie Cantor; *The Eddie Cantor Radio Show-1942-1943* . . . . (Original Cast)
Gene Gardos & His Orchestra; *Brother Can You Spare A Dime? Great American Songs Of The Depression-C* . . . . (Pro-Arte)

Ob-La-Di, Ob-La-Da
Beatles; *Beatles-Box Set* . . . . (Capitol)
The Beatles (White Album) . . . . (Capitol)
The Beatles/1967-1970 . . . . (Capitol)

Occasional Wife
Faron Young; *Faron Young-Golden Hits* . . . . (Mercury)

October Wedding
Montreux; *Let Them Say* . . . . (Windham Hill)
Montreux-Windham Hill Retrospective . . . . (Windham Hill)

Oh Promise Me
Liberace; *Piano Magic* . . . . (Sony Music Special Prod.)
Tommy Dorsey; *Tommy Dorsey-1937-1938* . . . . (Classics)

On A Chinese Honeymoon
Mills Brothers; *The Mills Brothers Story* . . . . (Ranwood)

On A Wedding Anniversary
John Cale; *Fragments Of A Rainy Season* . . . . (Hannibal)

On London Bridge
Jo Stafford; *International Hits* . . . . (Corinthian)

On The Other Hand
Randy Travis; *Randy Travis' Greatest Hits-#1* . . . . (Warner Bros.)
Storms Of Life . . . . (Warner Bros.)

One Boy
Ann-Margret; *ST/Bye Bye Birdie* . . . . (RCA)

One Boy, One Girl
Collin Raye; *Best Of Collin Raye-Direct Hits* . . . . (Epic)
I Think About You . . . . (Epic)

One Thousand Dollar Wedding
Gram Parsons; *Grievous Angel* . . . . (Reprise)

One's On The Way (Here In Topeka)
Loretta Lynn; *Loretta Lynn-20 Greatest Hits* . . . . (MCA)
Loretta Lynn-Greatest Hits Live . . . . (K-Tel)
Loretta Lynn's Greatest Hits-#2 . . . . (MCA)
The Country Music Hall Of Fame-Loretta Lynn . . . . (MCA)

Opium Bride
Annabouboula; *Greek Fire* . . . . (Shanachie)

Our Shotgun Wedding Day
Howington Brothers & Tennessee Haymakers; *Long Gone Daddy-C* . . . . (Collectables)

Peggy Sue Got Married
Buddy Holly; *Buddy Holly-20 Golden Greats* ....(MCA)
Rock & Roll Collection ....(MCA)
Pineapple Princess
Annette Funicello; *Frankie Avalon/Annette Funicello* .... (K-Tel)
Pledging My Love
David Allan Coe; *David Allan Coe-17 Greatest Hits* .... (Columbia)
David Allan Coe's Biggest Hits .... (Legacy)
Elvis Presley; *A Touch Of Platinum-#2* .... (RCA)
Moody Blue .... (RCA)
Emmylou Harris; *Great Wedding Songs-C*..................(Warner Bros.)
Profile II-The Best Of Emmylou Harris ....(Warner Bros.)
Freddy Fender; *Freddy Fender-Collection*.................... (Reprise)
Johnny Ace; *Cruisin'-1955-C*....................(Increase)
Duke-Peacock Greatest Hits ....(MCA)
Memorial Album ....(MCA)
Oldies But Goodies-#10-C.................... (Original Sound)
ST/A Rage In Harlem....................(MCA Special Prod.)
Marvin Gaye & Diana Ross; *Diana & Marvin* .... (Motown)
Teresa Brewer; *Best Of Teresa Brewer*.................... (MCA Jazz)
Pocket Full Of Gold
Vince Gill; *Pocket Full Of Gold* ....(MCA)
Prairie Wedding
Mark Knopfler; *Sailing To Philadelphia*....................(Warner Bros.)
Pretty Polly
Judy Collins; *Who Knows Where The Time Goes* .... (Elektra)
Stanley Brothers; *Complete Columbia Stanley Brothers* .... (Legacy)
Folk Classics: Roots Of American Folk Music-C.............. (Columbia)
Long Journey Home....................(Rebel)
Put That Ring On My Finger
Andrews Sisters; *50th Anniversary Collection-#2* ....(MCA)
Woody Herman; *Best Of The Big Bands-C*.................... (Columbia)
Ready Or Not
Jackson Browne; *For Everyman*....................(Asylum)
Rebecca Lynn
Bryan White; *Bryan White* ....(Asylum)
Red Roses For A Blue Lady
Al Martino; *Best Of Al Martino* .... (Capitol)
Capitol Collectors Series-Al Martino .... (Capitol)
Andy Williams; *Andy Williams-16 Most Requested Songs*.......... (Legacy)
Mom & Dads; *Best Of The Mom & Dads* ....(Crescendo)
Roger Whittaker; *All-Time Heart-Touching Favorites*.............. (Capitol)
Roger Whittaker-Classics Collection-#1 .... (Capitol)
Vaughn Monroe; *Best Of Vaughn Monroe* .... (RCA)
Reminiscing
Little River Band; *'70's Super Groups-C* .... (Rhino)
Reminiscing: The Twentieth Anniversary Collection.............. (Rhino)
Ring On Her Finger, Time On Her Hands
Lee Greenwood; *Best Of Lee Greenwood-God Bless America*.......... (Curb)
Inside Out/You've Got A Good Love Comin'....................(MCA)
Lee Greenwood's Greatest Hits....................(MCA)
Lee Greenwood-Super Hits ....(Epic)
Reba McEntire; *Starting Over* ....(MCA)
River, The
Bruce Springsteen; *Bruce Springsteen's Greatest Hits*............ (Columbia)
The River .... (Columbia)
Bruce Springsteen & The E Street Band; *Bruce Springsteen & The E Street Band Live/1975-85* .... (Legacy)
Rose Bouquet
Phil Vassar; *Phil Vassar*.................... (Arista)
Round And Round
Perry Como; *Como's Golden Records* .... (RCA)
Perry Como's All-Time Greatest Hits-#1.................... (RCA)
This Is Perry Como .... (RCA)
Ruby's Golden Wedding
Danny Wilson; *Meet Danny Wilson* .... (Virgin)
Rumor Has It
Clay Walker; *Clay Walker's Greatest Hits*....................(Giant)
Rumor Has It ....(Giant)
Sad Wedding
Marvin Gaye & Tammi Terrell; *United* .... (Motown)
Saigon Bride
Joan Baez; *Contemporary Ballad Book* .... (Vanguard)
Say It
Voices Of Theory; *Voices Of Theory* ....(H.O.L.A./Red Ant)
Secret Marriage
Sting; *...Nothing Like The Sun* .... (A&M)
She Misses Him
Tim Rushlow; *Tim Rushlow* ....(Atlantic)
She Misses Him On Sunday The Most
Diamond Rio; *Diamond Rio IV*.................... (Arista)
Diamond Rio's Greatest Hits.................... (Arista)
She Said Yes
Rhett Akins; *A Thousand Memories*.................... (Decca)
She Wears My Ring
Elvis Presley; *Essential Elvis-#5-Rhythm & Country*.................... (RCA)
Ray Price; *Ray Price-20 Hits* ....(Tee Vee)
Ray Price's Greatest Hits-#1-3 .... (Step One)
She's In Love With The Boy
Trisha Yearwood; *Trisha Yearwood*.................... (MCA)
She's No Lady
Lyle Lovett; *Great Records Of The Decade-'80s Hits-Country-C* .... (Curb)
Pontiac.................... (MCA)
Single Women
Dolly Parton; *Heartbreak Express* ....(RCA)
So In Love With You
U.N.V.; *Universal Nubian Voices*................ (Maverick/Warner Bros.)
So Much In Love
Tymes; *20th Century Rocks-#9-'60's Vocal Groups-I Got Rhythm-C*.................... (Dominion Entert.)
Something In Red
Lorrie Morgan; *Lorrie Morgan's Greatest Hits* ....(BNA)
Something In Red ....(RCA)
To Get To You-Greatest Hits Collection....................(BNA)
Something That We Do
Clint Black; *Country Cares For Kids II-C*....................(BNA)
Nothin' But The Taillights ....(RCA)
Sparrow In The Treetop
Guy Mitchell; *Guy Mitchell-16 Most Requested Songs*............. (Legacy)
Stand By Your Man
Elton John; *Tammy Wynette...Remembered-C* ....(Asylum)
Lyle Lovett and his Large Band; *Lyle Lovett and his Large Band* ....(Curb/MCA)
Tammy Wynette; *Columbia Country Classics-#4-Nashville Sound-C*.................... (Columbia)
ST/Sleepless In Seattle ....(Epic/Sony Music Soundtrax)
Tammy Wynette's Biggest Hits.................... (Epic)
Tears Of Fire-25th Anniversary Collection .... (Epic)
Starting A New Life
Van Morrison; *Tupelo Honey* ....(Polydor)
Stay Together For The Kids
Blink-182; *Take Off Your Pants And Jacket* .... (MCA)
Stop The Wedding
Etta James; *Sweetest Peaches-#1* .... (Chess)
Stress In Marriage
Negativeland; *Escape From Noise* ....(SST)
Strong Enough To Bend
Tanya Tucker; *Strong Enough To Bend*.................... (Liberty)
Tanya Tucker's Greatest Hits.................... (Liberty)
Stupid Marriage
Specials; *Specials* .... (Chrysalis)
Suitelady
Maxwell; *Maxwell's Urban Hang Suite* .... (Columbia)
Sunrise, Sunset
Original Cast; *Fiddler On The Roof* .... (RCA Victor)
Sweet Violets
Mitch Miller; *Sing Along With Mitch* .... (Columbia)
Take Me Back To Tulsa
Asleep At The Wheel; *Route 66* .... (Liberty)
Very Best Of Asleep At The Wheel Since 1970 ....(Relentless/Madacy)
Bob Wills & His Texas Playboys; *All Time Legends Of Country Music-C*.................... (Legacy)
Bob Wills-Anthology .... (Sony Music Special Prod.)
Columbia Country Classics-#1-Golden Age-C .... (Columbia)
Tiffany Transcriptions-#2-Best Of The Tiffanys.................... (Rhino)
Clay Walker & Asleep At The Wheel; *Ride With Bob-C*....(DreamWorks/SKG)
Take Time To Know Her
Percy Sledge; *Best Of Percy Sledge*....................(Atlantic)
It Tears Me Up-Best Of Percy Sledge .... (Rhino)
Ten Commandments Of Love
Bob Marley & The Wailers; *Birth Of A Legend 1963-1966*.................... (Epic Portrait Assoc.)
Harvey & The Moonglows; *Best Of Chess Rock 'N' Roll-#2-C* .... (Chess)
Collectables Presents The History Of Rock-#10-C........... (Collectables)
Cruisin'-1958-C.................... (Increase)
Oldies But Goodies-#11-C....................(Original Sound)
Tennessee Border
Hank Williams; *Alone With His Guitar*.................... (Mercury)
I Ain't Got Nothin' But Time-1946-1947 ....(Polydor)
Red Foley; *Red Foley: The Country Music Hall Of Fame*.................... (MCA Special Prod.)
Sonny Burgess & Dave Alvin; *Tennessee Border*................(Hightone)
Tennessee Ernie Ford; *Best Of Tennessee Ernie Ford-16 Tons Of Boogie* .... (Rhino)
Capitol Collectors Series-Tennessee Ernie Ford.................... (Capitol)
Thank You In Advance
Boyz II Men; *Nathan Michael Shawn Wanya* .... (Universal)
That's The Way I've Always Heard It Should Be
Carly Simon; *Best Of Carly Simon* .... (Elektra)
Carly Simon .... (Elektra)
Theme From "Here Come The Brides"
Original Soundtrack; *Television's Greatest Hits-#5-In Living Color-C* . . . (TVT)
Theme From "Mad About You"
Original Soundtrack; *Television's Greatest Hits-#7-Cable Ready-C* ..... (TVT)
Theme From "The Brady Bunch"
Brady Bunch Kids; *It's A Sunshine Day-Best Of The Brady Bunch Kids* .... (MCA)

Television's Greatest Hits-#2-C . . . . (TVT)
Theme From "The Honeymooners"
Original Soundtrack; *Television's Greatest Hits-#2-C* . . . . (TVT)
Theme From "The Newlywed Game"
Original Soundtrack; *Television's Greatest Hits-#5-In Living Color-C* . . . (TVT)
Theme From "Thirtysomething"
Original Soundtrack; *Television's Greatest Hits-#7-Cable Ready-C* . . . . . (TVT)
Then He Kissed Me
Crystals; *Best Of The Crystals* . . . . (Abkco)
Phil Spector-Back To Mono 1958-1969-C . . . . (Abkco)
There Won't Be A Wedding
Jimmie Davis; *Jimmie Davis-Golden Hits* . . . .(Plantation)
They Just Got Married
Randy Newman; *Born Again* . . . . (Warner Bros.)
Think Of Tomorrow
Chris Isaak; *Baja Sessions* . . . .(Reprise)
This Diamond Ring
Gary Lewis And The Playboys; *Billboard Top Rock 'N' Roll Hits-*
1965-C . . . . (Rhino)
EMI Legends Of Rock & Roll-24 Greatest Hits-C . . . . (EMI)
Golden Years-1965-C . . . . (Dominion Entert.)
Spring Break-#2-Cold Kegs & Tan Legs . . . . (Capitol)
This Is For The Lover In You
Babyface; *The Day* . . . . (Epic)
This Is The Day (A Wedding Song)
Scott Wesley Brown; *I Will Be Here-10 Contemporary Wedding*
Songs . . . . (Sparrow)
Thorny Patch
John Gorka; *After Yesterday* . . . . (Red House)
Three Steps From The Altar
Shep And The Limelites; *Rockin' & Rollin' Wedding Songs-#2-C* . . . . . (Rhino)
To The Aisle
Five Satins; *Collectables Presents The History Of Rock-#7-C* . . . . (Collectables)
Cruisin'-1957-C . . . . (Increase)
Oldies But Goodies-#4-C . . . .(Original Sound)
Rockin' & Rollin' Wedding Songs-#1-C . . . . (Rhino)
ST/American Graffiti . . . . (MCA)
Tomorrow's My Wedding Day
Country Gentlemen; *Country Songs Old & New* . . . . . . (Smithsonian Folkways)
Truck Drivin' Cat With Nine Wives
Charlie Walker; *Truckers' Jukebox-10 All-Time Radio Requests-C* . . . . (Legacy)
Jim Nesbitt; *Truck Driver Boogie Big Rig Hits-1939-1969-C* . . . . (Audium)
Two Sleepy People
Art Garfunkel; *Up 'Til Now* . . . . (Columbia)
Fats Waller; *Fats Waller-Masterpieces-#3* . . . . (EPM)
Jo Sullivan Loesser & Others; *Loesser By Loesser* . . . .(DRG)
Kay Kyser & His Orchestra; *Best Of The Big Bands-C* . . . . (Columbia)
Two Teardrops
Steve Wariner; *Two Teardrops* . . . . (Capitol)
Unbelievable
Diamond Rio; *Unbelievable* . . . . (Arista)
Unwed Fathers
Gail Davies; *Best Of Gail Davies* . . . . (Capitol)
Tammy Wynette; *Best Loved Hits* . . . . (Epic)
Veni-Vidi-Vici (I Came, I Saw, I Conquered)
Gaylords; *Best Of The Gaylords* . . . . (Chronicles)
Vow, The
Flamingos; *Best Of The Flamingos* . . . . (Rhino)
Flamingos . . . . (Chess)
Vows Of Love
Paragons; *Best Of The Paragons* . . . . (Collectables)
Walk Like A Man
Bruce Springsteen; *Tunnel Of Love* . . . . (Columbia)
Wartime Wedding
Original Broadway Cast; *Over Here!* . . . . (Sony Music Classical)
Watermelon Weather
Perry Como; *Yesterday And Today-A Celebration In Song* . . . .(RCA)
We Danced
Brad Paisley; *Who Needs Pictures* . . . . (Arista)
We Got Married
Paul McCartney; *Flowers In The Dirt* . . . . (Capitol)
We Must Be In Love
Pure Soul; *Pure Soul* . . . .(Stepsun/Interscope)
Wedding
Solitaires; *Rockin' & Rollin' Wedding Songs-#1-C* . . . . (Rhino)
Wedding Bell Blues
5th Dimension; *Greatest Hits On Earth* . . . . (Arista)
Rockin' & Rollin' Wedding Songs-#1-C . . . . (Rhino)
ST/My Girl . . . . (Epic)
Wedding Bells
Hank Williams With His Drifting Cowboys; *24 Of Hank Williams'*
Greatest Hits . . . . (Polydor)
Hank Williams-40 Greatest Hits . . . . (Polydor)
Wedding Bells (Are Breaking Up That Old Gang Of Mine)
Four Aces; *Best Of The Four Aces* . . . . (MCA)
Wedding Cake
Jeannie C. Riley; *Things Go Better With Love* . . . .(Plantation)

Wedding Day
UB40; *Labour Of Love II* . . . . (Virgin)
Wedding Day
Paul Young; *Between Two Fires* . . . .(Columbia)
Wedding In Cherokee County
Randy Newman; *Good Old Boys* . . . . (Reprise)
Wedding March
Jesse Crawford; *Wedding Music* . . . . (MCA)
Lawrence Welk; *Music For All Occasions* . . . .(K-Tel)
Richard Ellsasser; *Wedding Album* . . . .(MGM)
Wedding Song
Arlo Guthrie & Shenandoah; *Outlasting The Blues* . . . . (Warner Bros.)
Wedding Song
Smokey Robinson; *Quiet Storm* . . . .(Motown)
Wedding Song
Original Cast; *Threepenny Opera* . . . . (Polydor)
Wedding Song
Bob Dylan And The Band; *Planet Waves* . . . .(Columbia)
Wedding Song
Judy Collins; *Running For My Life* . . . .(Elektra)
Wedding Song (There Is Love)
Captain & Tennille; *Captain & Tennille's Greatest Hits* . . . .(A&M)
Rockin' & Rollin' Wedding Songs-#1-C . . . .(Rhino)
Mary MacGregor; *Modern Bride Presents The Wedding Album-C* . .(Columbia)
Paul Stookey; *45-#196* . . . . (Eric)
Petula Clark; *There Is Love-Wedding Songs-C* . . . . (Scotti Bros.)
Wedding, The
Television Cast; *Cinderella-The CBS Television Network*
Production . . . .(Columbia)
Wedding's Over
Charlie Rich; *Charlie Rich-20 Golden Hits* . . . . (Sun)
Time For Tears-C . . . . (Sun)
We're All The Way
Don Williams; *Lovers & Best Friends* . . . . (MCA)
One Good Well . . . . (RCA)
Eric Clapton; *Slowhand* . . . . (Polydor)
We've Only Just Begun
Barbra Streisand; *Just For The Record* . . . .(Columbia)
Carpenters; *Carpenters-Classics-#2* . . . .(A&M)
Carpenters-The Singles 1969-1973 . . . .(A&M)
Close To You . . . .(A&M)
From The Top . . . .(A&M)
Yesterday Once More . . . .(A&M)
What A Dream
Conway Twitty; *Conway Twitty's Greatest Hits* . . . .(Curb)
Patti Page; *45-#70416* . . . .(Mercury)
Slim Harpo; *Raining In My Heart* . . . . (Hip-O)
When I Said I Do
Clint Black & Lisa Hartman Black; *D'lectrified* . . . . (RCA)
When I'm Sixty-Four
Beatles; *Beatles-Box Set.* . . . .(Capitol)
Sgt. Pepper's Lonely Hearts Club Band . . . .(Capitol)
When The Kids Get Married
Original Broadway Cast; *I Do! I Do!* . . . . (RCA Victor)
When We Get Married
Dreamlovers; *Best Of The Dreamlovers-#1* . . . .(Collectables)
Oldies But Goodies-#5-C . . . . (Original Sound)
Rockin' & Rollin' Wedding Songs-#1-C . . . .(Rhino)
When You Love A Woman
Journey; *Trial By Fire* . . . .(Columbia)
White Trash Wife
Exene Cervenka; *Old Wives' Tales* . . . .(Rhino)
White Wedding
Billy Idol; *Billy Idol* . . . .(Chrysalis)
ST/The Wedding Singer . . . .(Maverick)
Vital Idol . . . .(Chrysalis)
Why Did I Choose You
Barbra Streisand; *Barbra Streisand's Greatest Hits* . . . .(Columbia)
My Name Is Barbra . . . .(Columbia)
Marvin Gaye; *Romantically Yours* . . . .(Columbia)
Michael Crawford; *Michael Crawford With Love* . . . . (Atlantic)
Widow's Walk
Suzanne Vega; *Songs In Red & Gray* . . . .(A&M)
Wife & The Whore
Kristin Lems; *Born A Woman* . . . . (Flying Fish)
Wifey
Next; *Totally Hits-#3-C* . . . . (Atlantic)
Welcome To Nextacy . . . .(Arista)
Wild Week-End
Bill Anderson; *Bill Anderson-Legend* . . . . (Masters)
MCA Records 30 Years Of Hits-1958-1988-C . . . .(MCA)
Still . . . . (MCA Special Prod.)
Will Never Marry
Morrissey; *Bona Drag* . . . . (Sire)
Just Say Yo-#2 Of Just Say Yes-C . . . . (Sire)
Will You Marry Me?
Original Cast; *Pipe Dream* . . . . (RCA)
Paula Abdul; *Spellbound* . . . . (Captive)

Will You Marry Me?
Vonda Shepard; *ST/Songs From ''Ally McBeal'' Featuring Vonda Shepard* . . . . (550/Epic)
With This Ring
Platters; *Enchanted-The Best Of The Platters* . . . . (Rhino)
 Only Their Best For You . . . . (Pair)
 Rockin' & Rollin' Wedding Songs-#2-C . . . . (Rhino)
 The Musicor Years . . . . (Collectables)
 T. Graham Brown; *Best Of T. Graham Brown* . . . . (Liberty)
 T. Graham Brown's All-Time Greatest Hits. . . . . (Curb)
With This Ring
Sawyer Brown; *Six Days On The Road.* . . . . (Curb)
 Wedding Day Music-C . . . . (Reprise)
Wives Are In Connecticut
Carly Simon; *Spoiled Girl* . . . .(Epic)
Worst That Could Happen
Brooklyn Bridge; *Billboard Top Pop Hits-1969-C.* . . . . (Rhino)
 Brooklyn Bridge-Greatest Hits . . . . (Collectables)
Wouldn't It Be Nice
Beach Boys; *Absolutely Best-#2* . . . . (Capitol)
 Made In The U.S.A. . . . . (Capitol)
 Pet Sounds . . . . (Capitol)
 Still Cruisin' . . . . (Capitol)
Wrapped Around
Brad Paisley; *Brad Paisley-Part II* . . . . (Arista)
Yes!
Chad Brock; *Yes!* . . . .(Warner Bros.)
You Ain't Goin' Nowhere
Bob Dylan; *Bob Dylan's Greatest Hits-#2* . . . . (Columbia)
Bob Dylan And The Band; *Basement Tapes* . . . . (Columbia)
Byrds; *Best Of The Byrds-Greatest Hits-#2* . . . . (Columbia)
 Byrds Play Dylan . . . . (Columbia)
 Sweetheart Of The Rodeo. . . . . (Columbia)
 The Byrds . . . . (Columbia)
Chris Hillman & Roger McGuinn; *Will The Circle Be Unbroken-#2-C* . . . . (Uni)
Joan Baez; *The First 10 Years.* . . . . (Vanguard)
You Better Think Twice
Vince Gill; *When Love Finds You* . . . .(MCA)
You Can't Make A Heart Love Somebody
George Strait; *Latest Greatest Straitest Hits* . . . .(MCA)
 Lead On . . . .(MCA)
You Don't Bring Me Flowers
Barbra Streisand; *Songbird* . . . . (Columbia)
Barbra Streisand & Neil Diamond; *Barbra Streisand's Greatest Hits, Volume 2* . . . . (Columbia)
 Just For The Record. . . . . (Columbia)
Neil Diamond; *Hot August Night II* . . . . (Columbia)
Neil Diamond & Barbra Streisand; *12 Greatest Hits-#2.* . . . (Columbia)
 I'm Glad You're Here With Me Tonight. . . . . (Columbia)
 You Don't Bring Me Flowers . . . . (Columbia)
You Make It Easy
James Taylor; *Gorilla* . . . .(Warner Bros.)
You Never Can Tell
Aaron Neville; *The Grand Tour* . . . . (A&M)
Chuck Berry; *Rock 'N' Roll Rarities-20 Magic Tracks.* . . . . (Chess)
 The Chess Box-Chuck Berry . . . . (Chess)
You Send Me
Aretha Franklin; *Aretha's Gold* . . . .(Atlantic)
Manhattans; *Too Hot To Stop It* . . . . (Columbia)
Michael Bolton; *Timeless-Classics.* . . . . (Columbia)
Sam Cooke; *Best Of Sam Cooke* . . . . (RCA)
 ST/American Pop . . . . (MCA)
 The Man And His Music. . . . . (RCA)
You Were Mine
Dixie Chicks; *Big Country Hits '99-C* . . . . (K-Tel)
 Wide Open Spaces . . . . (Monument)
You'll Accomp'ny Me
Bob Seger & The Silver Bullet Band; *Against The Wind* . . . . (Capitol)
 Nine Tonight . . . . (Capitol)
Your Everything
keith urban; *keith urban* . . . . (Capitol)
Your Good Girl's Gonna Go Bad
Billie Jo Spears; *Best Of Billie Jo Spears* . . . . . (CEMA Special Prod.)
 Best Of Billie Jo Spears . . . . (Razor & Tie)
K.T. Oslin; *Tammy Wynette...Remembered-C* . . . . (Asylum)
Tammy Wynette; *Tammy Wynette-Anniversary-20 Years Of Hits* . . . .(Epic)
 Tammy Wynette's Greatest Hits. . . . .(Epic)
 Your Good Girl's Gonna Go Bad. . . . . (Legacy)

MEN: GENERAL, Boys, Guys, Male

See Also: **BOSSES, CELEBRITIES: SPECIFIC, FAMILY (various), GENDER CONFLICT, GENDER STEREOTYPES, KINGS, LOVE (various), MEN'S NAMES: A-Z, PEOPLE, ROYALTY, TEENAGERS**

''Murder'', He Says
Roy Eldridge/Gene Krupa Orchestra/Anita O'Day; *Uptown* . . . . . . (Columbia)

(He's) Some Kind Of Wonderful
Carole King; *Music* . . . . (Epic)
(Man Who Shot) Liberty Valance
Gene Pitney; *Gene Pitney-Anthology 1961-1968* . . . . (Rhino)
 Gene Pitney's Greatest Hits . . . . (Evergreen Music)
 Super Oldies Of The '60s-#9-C . . . . (Audio Fidelity)
Greg Kihn; *Glass House Rock.* . . . . (Beserkley)
(Today I Met) The Boy I'm Gonna Marry
Darlene Love; *Best Of Darlene Love.* . . . .(Abkco)
 Phil Spector-Back To Mono 1958-1969-C . . . .(Abkco)
20th Century Man
Beat Farmers; *Loud & Plowed &...Live!.* . . . .(Curb)
Kinks; *Muswell Hillbillies* . . . . (VelVel)
 One For The Road . . . . (Arista)
24-7 Man
Robert Cray Band; *Take Your Shoes Off* . . . . (Rykodisc)
50 Ways To Leave Your Lover
Paul Simon; *Greatest Hits, Etc.* . . . . (Columbia)
 Negotiations And Love Songs, 1971-1986 . . . . . (Warner Bros.)
 Still Crazy After All These Years. . . . . (Columbia)
Simon & Garfunkel; *The Concert In Central Park* . . . . . (Warner Bros.)
African Shadow Man
Johnny Clegg & Savuka; *Shadow Man* . . . . (Capitol)
All American Boy
Bill Parsons; *History Of Rock-#10-C* . . . . (Collectables)
All American Boy
Statler Brothers; *Son Of The Motherland* . . . . (Mercury)
All American Man
Kiss; *Alive II* . . . .(Casablanca)
All The Good Ones Are Gone
Pam Tillis; *Pam Tillis' Greatest Hits* . . . . (Arista)
All The Man That I Need
Whitney Houston; *I'm Your Baby Tonight* . . . . (Arista)
 Whitney Houston's Greatest Hits . . . . (Arista)
All The Young Dudes
David Bowie; *David Live* . . . . (Rykodisc)
Ian Hunter; *Live/Welcome To The Club.* . . . . (Chrysalis)
Mott The Hoople; *All The Young Dudes* . . . . (Columbia)
 Mott The Hoople-Live . . . . (Columbia)
 Mott The Hoople's Greatest Hits . . . . (Columbia)
 ST/Queen's Logic . . . . (Epic)
All True Man
Alexander O'Neal; *All True Man* . . . . (Tabu)
Alley-Oop
Hollywood Argyles; *American Graffiti-#3-C* . . . . (MCA)
 Collectables Presents The History Of Rock-#5-C. . . . (Collectables)
 M. Dung's Idiot Classics . . . . (Rhino)
Alligator Man
Jimmy C. Newman; *Jimmy C. Newman's Greatest Hits* . . . . . . (Plantation)
 Progressive CC . . . . (Plantation)
 Souvenirs Of Music City U.S.A.-C . . . . (Plantation)
Alpine Milkman
Randy Erwin; *'Til The Cows Come Home/Cowboy Rhythm.* . . . . (Really Outstanding Music)
American Boy
Eddie Rabbitt; *American Music Greatest Hits-C.* . . . . (Curb)
 Eddie Rabbitt-Greatest Country Hits . . . . (Curb)
 Jersey Boy . . . . (Capitol)
American Boys
Deborah Galli; *Radio Active* . . . . (Mercury)
An English Gentleman
Original Broadway Cast; *Me & My Girl* . . . . (MCA)
And Still
Reba McEntire; *Read My Mind.* . . . . (MCA)
 Reba McEntire's Greatest Hits-#3: I'm A Survivor . . . . . (MCA)
Angels Love Bad Men
Barbara Mandrell; *Sure Feels Good* . . . . (EMI)
Barbara Mandrell & Waylon Jennings; *Country Duets Two By Two-C* . . . . (Capitol)
Angry Young Man
Steve Earle & The Dukes; *Exit 0* . . . . (MCA)
Angry Young Man
Billy Joel; *KOHUEPT.* . . . . (Columbia)
 Turnstiles . . . . (Columbia)
Angry Young Man
Corey Hart; *Fields Of Fire* . . . . (EMI)
Animal Boy
Ramones; *Animal Boy* . . . . (Sire)
 Ramones Mania . . . .(Sire)
Another Man Done Gone
Pete Seeger/Memphis Slim/Willie Dixon; *Pete Seeger At The Village Gate.* . . . .(Smithsonian Folkways)
Another Man Done Gone
Jorma Kaukonen & Tom Hobson; *Quah* . . . .(Relix)
Another Night With The Boys
Drifters; *1959-1965-All-Time Greatest Hits And More* . . . . (Atlantic)
Persuasions; *Bread & Roses Festival Of Acoustic Music-#1-C* . . . .(Fantasy)
Ant Man Bee
Captain Beefheart & His Magic Band; *Trout Mask Replica* . . . . (Reprise)

Any Man Of Mine
Shania Twain; *1996 Grammy Nominees-C* . . . . (Columbia)
The Woman In Me . . . . (Mercury)
Snoopy; *Snoopy's Country Classiks On Toys* . . . . (Lightyear)

Armageddon Man
Black Flag; *Family Man* . . . . (SST)

Army Man In Vietnam
Big Joe Williams; *Shake Your Boogie* . . . . (Arhoolie)
Thinking Of What They Did To Me . . . . (Arhoolie)

Astro Boy
Buggles; *Age Of Plastic* . . . . (Island)

Astro Man
Jimi Hendrix; *Cry Of Love* . . . . (Reprise)

Attack Of The Vegetable Men
Active Ingredient; *Extrastrength* . . . . (Bainbridge)

Automatic Man
Michael Sembello; *Bossa Nova Hotel* . . . . (Warner Bros.)

Baby You're A Rich Man
Beatles; *Beatles-Box Set* . . . . (Capitol)
Magical Mystery Tour . . . . (Capitol)

Back Door Man
Doors; *Doors* . . . . (Elektra)
Doors 13 . . . . (Elektra)
Howlin' Wolf; *Best Of Howlin' Wolf-Chess Blues* . . . . (Chess)
Willie Dixon; *I Am The Blues* . . . . (Columbia)

Back Door Man
John Hammond; *Best Of John Hammond* . . . . (Vanguard)

Bad Boy
Beatles; *Beatles VI* . . . . (Capitol)
Beatles-Box Set . . . . (Capitol)
Past Masters-Volume One . . . . (Parlophone)
Rock 'N' Roll Music . . . . (Capitol)

Bad Boy
Ringo Starr; *Bad Boy* . . . . (Epic)

Bad Boy
Miami Sound Machine; *Primitive Love* . . . . (Epic)

Bad Boy
Eddie Money; *Nothing To Lose* . . . . (Columbia)

Bad Boy
Eric Clapton; *Eric Clapton* . . . . (Polydor)

Bad Boy
Eddie Taylor; *Antone's Bringing You The Best In Blues* . . . . (Antone's)

Bad Boy
Ray Parker Jr.; *Ray Parker Jr.'s Greatest Hits* . . . . (Arista)

Bad Boy For Life
P. Diddy & The Bad Boy Family; *The Saga Continues* . . . . (Bad Boy/Arista)
Totally Hits 2001-C . . . . (Arista)

Bad Boy/Having A Party
Luther Vandross; *Best Of Luther Vandross...The Best Of Love* . . . . (Epic)
Forever For Always For Love . . . . (Epic)

Bad Boys
Inner Circle; *Bad Boys* . . . . (Big Beat)

Bad Boys Running Wild
Scorpions; *Love At First Sting* . . . . (Mercury)
Wold Wide Live . . . . (Mercury)

Bad Boyz
Crosby, Stills & Nash; *After The Storm* . . . . (Atlantic)

Bad Boyz
Shyne featuring Levy, Barrington; *Shyne* . . . . (Bad Boy/Arista)

Bad Man
R. Kelly; *I Wish (import EP)* . . . . (Jive)

Ballad Of A Thin Man
Bob Dylan; *Before The Flood* . . . . (Columbia)

Banana Man
Clifton Chenier; *Louisiana Blues & Zydeco* . . . . (Arhoolie)

Banjo Boy Chimes
White Brothers & New Kentucky Colonels; *Live In Sweden* . . . . (Rounder)

Behind Blue Eyes
Who; *Hooligans* . . . . (MCA)
Join Together . . . . (MCA)
Who's Last . . . . (MCA)
Who's next . . . . (MCA)

Belly Up To The Bar, Boys
Debbie Reynolds; *ST/The Unsinkable Molly Brown* . . . . (MCA)
Original Cast; *The Unsinkable Molly Brown* . . . . (EMI-Angel)

Better Man
Clint Black; *Killin' Time* . . . . (RCA)

Better Man
Pearl Jam; *Vitalogy* . . . . (Epic)

Better Man
Warren Brothers; *Beautiful Day In The Cold Cruel World* . . . . (BNA)

Better Man, Better Off
Tracy Lawrence; *The Coast Is Clear* . . . . (Atlantic)

Big Boss Man
B.B. King; *Six Silver Strings* . . . . (MCA)
Elvis Presley; *ST/Clambake* . . . . (RCA)
Grateful Dead; *Grateful Dead (Skull & Roses)* . . . . (Warner Bros.)
Jimmy Reed; *Best Of Jimmy Reed* . . . . (Crescendo)

Oldies But Goodies-#1-C . . . . (Original Sound)
John Hammond; *Best Of John Hammond* . . . . (Vanguard)
So Many Roads . . . . (Vanguard)

Big Boys Don't Cry
Extreme; *Extreme* . . . . (A&M)

Big Butter And Egg Man
Louis Armstrong; *Best Of Louis Armstrong* . . . . (Audio Fidelity)
Hot Fives & Hot Sevens-#2 . . . . (Columbia)
Merle Haggard; *Kern River* . . . . (Epic)
Walking The Line . . . . (Epic)

Big Man
Charlie Daniels Band; *Uneasy Rider* . . . . (Epic)

Big Man In Town
4 Seasons; *4 Seasons' Greatest Hits-#1* . . . . (Rhino)
4 Seasons-Anthology . . . . (Rhino)

Big Rig Rolling Man
Billy Larkin; *Blue Ribbon Country-#2-C* . . . . (Accord)
Johnny Dollar; *Truck Driver Boogie Big Rig Hits-1939-1969-C* . . . . . . (Audium)

Big River, Big Man
Claude King; *American Originals-Claude King* . . . . (Columbia)
Best Of Claude King . . . . (Gusto)

Biggest Thing That Man Has Ever Done (Great Historical Bum)
Tom Paxton; *Tribute To Woody Guthrie-C* . . . . (Warner Bros.)

Birdman Of Alkatrash
Strawberry Alarm Clock; *Strawberry Alarm Clock-Anthology* . . . . . (One Way)

Birthday Boy
Residents; *Duck Stab/Buster & Glenn/Goosebump* . . . . (East Side Digital)

Birthday Boy
Chicago; *Chicago XIV* . . . . (Chicago)

Black Boys On The Corner
Thin Lizzy; *Thin Lizzy-London Collector* . . . . (London)

Black Boys, White Boys
Original Broadway Cast; *Hair* . . . . (RCA)

Black Chick, White Guy
Kid Rock; *Devil Without A Cause* . . . . (Top Dog/Lava/Atlantic)

Black Man
Stevie Wonder; *Songs In The Key Of Life* . . . . (Motown)

Black Man
Alberta Hunter; *Look For The Silver Lining* . . . . (Columbia)

Black Man Can't Get A Cab
U.T.F.O.; *Bag It & Bone It* . . . . (Jive)

Black Sheep Boy
Tim Hardin; *Memorial Album* . . . . (Polydor)

Blind Man
Bobby Bland; *Best Of Bobby Bland* . . . . (MCA)
Introspective Of The Early Years . . . . (MCA)

Blind Man
Champion Jack Dupree; *Back Home In New Orleans* . . . . (Bullseye Blues)

Blind Man
Aerosmith; *Big Ones* . . . . (Geffen)

Blow The Man Down
Paul Clayton; *Bay State Ballads* . . . . (Smithsonian Folkways)

Blue Boy
Jim Reeves; *Best Of Jim Reeves* . . . . (RCA)
Live At The Opry . . . . (Country Music Foundation)

Blue Boy
Joni Mitchell; *Ladies Of The Canyon* . . . . (Reprise)

Blue Collar Man
Styx; *Caught In The Act* . . . . (A&M)
Pieces Of Eight . . . . (A&M)
Styx-Classics-#15 . . . . (A&M)

Blue Jean Boy
Michael Stanley Band; *Ladies' Choice* . . . . (Epic)

Blueboy
John Fogerty; *Blue Moon Swamp* . . . . (Warner Bros.)

Boogie Woogie Bugle Boy
Andrews Sisters; *Andrews Sisters-16 Great Performances* . . . . (MCA)
Best Of The Andrews Sisters . . . . (MCA)
Boogie Woogie Bugle Girls . . . . (MCA)
Rarities . . . . (MCA)
Bette Midler; *Divine Miss M* . . . . (Atlantic)
Live At Last . . . . (Atlantic)
ST/Divine Madness . . . . (Atlantic)

Bowling Green
Everly Brothers; *Walk Right Back: The Everly Brothers On Warner Bros.-
1960-1969* . . . . (Warner Archives)

Boy Blue
Electric Light Orchestra; *Afterglow* . . . . (Epic)
Eldorado . . . . (Jet)
Ole ELO . . . . (Jet)

Boy Blue
Cyndi Lauper; *True Colors* . . . . (Portrait)

Boy Crazy
Tubes; *Tubes* . . . . (A&M)
What Do You Want From Live . . . . (A&M)

Boy From New York City
Ad-Libs; *Jewels-#1-C* . . . . (SSS International)
Oldies But Goodies-#6-C . . . . (Original Sound)

Original Golden Hits Of The Great Groups-#1-C . . . . (SSS International)
Original New York Rock & Roll-#1-C . . . . (SSS International)
Manhattan Transfer; *Best Of The Manhattan Transfer* . . . . (Atlantic)
Mecca For Moderns . . . . (Atlantic)

Boy From Tupelo
Emmylou Harris; *Red Dirt Girl* . . . . (Nonesuch)

Boy In Ohio
Phil Ochs; *Phil Ochs' Greatest Hits* . . . . (A&M)

Boy In The Bubble
Paul Simon; *Graceland* . . . .(Warner Bros.)

Boy Is Mine
Brandy & Monica; *Never Say Never* . . . .(Atlantic)
Monica; *The Boy Is Mine* . . . . (Arista)

Boy Who Wouldn't Hoe Corn
Alison Krauss & Union Station; *New Favorite* . . . . (Rounder)

Boys
Beatles; *Beatles-Box Set* . . . . (Capitol)
Please Please Me . . . . (Parlophone)
Rock 'N' Roll Music . . . . (Capitol)
The Beatles At The Hollywood Bowl . . . . (Capitol)
The Early Beatles . . . . (Capitol)
Shirelles; *Shirelles-Anthology 1959-1964* . . . . (Rhino)

Boys
Britney Spears; *Britney*. . . . . (Jive)

Boys & Me
Sawyer Brown; *Outskirts Of Town* . . . . (Curb)

Boys + Girls
Tony Toni Tone; *Tony Toni Tone-Hits* . . . . (Mercury)

Boys And Me
Sawyer Brown; *Outskirts Of Town* . . . . (Curb)

Boys Are Back In Town
Bon Jovi; *ST/Navy Seals* . . . .(Atlantic)
Thin Lizzy; *'70s Greatest Rock Hits-#14-King Of Rock-C* . . . . (Priority)
Dedication-Very Best Of Thin Lizzy . . . . (Mercury)
Jailbreak . . . . (Mercury)
Live And Dangerous . . . .(Warner Bros.)

Boys Are Back In Town
Gap Band; *The Gap Band II* . . . . (Mercury)

Boys Cry Tough
Bad Company; *Holy Water* . . . . (Atco)

Boys In The Trees
Carly Simon; *Boys In The Trees* . . . . (Elektra)

Boys Of Summer
Don Henley; *Building The Perfect Beast* . . . .(Geffen)

Boys 'R A Drug
Julie Brown; *Trapped In The Body Of A White Girl* . . . . (Sire)

Boyz-N-The-Hood
Dynamite Hack; *Superfast* . . . . (Farm Club/Universal)

Brand New Man
Brooks & Dunn; *Brand New Man*. . . . . (Arista)

Branded Man
Merle Haggard & The Strangers; *For The Record: Merle Haggard-43
Legendary Hits* . . . . (BNA)

Breath Taking Guy
Diana Ross & The Supremes; *Diana Ross & The Supremes-Anthology (1962-
1969)* . . . . (Motown)
Marvelettes; *Marvelettes-Anthology* . . . . (Motown)
Supremes; *Where Did Our Love Go* . . . . (Motown)

Brotherhood Of Man
New Broadway Cast; *How To Succeed In Business Without Really
Trying* . . . .(RCA Victor)
Original Cast; *How To Succeed In Business Without Really Trying* . . . . . . (RCA)

Brown Eyed Handsome Man
Buddy Holly; *Buddy Holly-20 Golden Greats* . . . .(MCA)
For The First Time Anywhere . . . .(MCA)
Rock & Roll Collection . . . .(MCA)
Chuck Berry; *Best Of The Best Of Chuck Berry* . . . . (International Mktg. Group)
Roll Over Beethoven . . . .(Allegiance)
The Chess Box-Chuck Berry . . . . (Chess)
Waylon Jennings; *Essential Waylon Jennings* . . . . (RCA)
Waylon Jennings-Super Hits . . . . (RCA)

Brown Man Do
Small Faces; *78 In The Shade* . . . . (Atlantic)

Busy Man
Billy Ray Cyrus; *Shot Full Of Love* . . . . (Mercury)

California Kid
Beat Farmers; *Tales Of The New West* . . . . (Rhino)

California Man
Cheap Trick; *Heaven Tonight* . . . .(Epic)

Candy Man
Mississippi John Hurt; *Best Of Mississippi John Hurt* . . . . (Vanguard)
Today! . . . . (Vanguard)

Candy Man
Mary Jane Girls; *In My House: The Best Of The Mary Jane Girls* . . . . (Motown)
Mary Jane Girls . . . . (Motown)

Candy Man
Hot Tuna; *Best Of Hot Tuna* . . . . (RCA)
Classic Electric . . . . (Relix)
First Pull Up, Then Pull Down. . . . . (RCA)

John Fahey; *Return Of The Repressed: The John Fahey Anthology* . . . . . (Rhino)
Jorma Kaukonen; *Magic Two* . . . .(Relix)
Reverend Gary Davis; *Pure Religion & Bad
Company* . . . .(Smithsonian Folkways)
Rising Sons; *Rising Sons Featuring Taj Mahal & Ry Cooder* . . . . (Legacy)
Taj Mahal; *Giant Step/De Ole Folks At Home* . . . . (Columbia)

Candy Man
Donovan; *Fairytale* . . . .(Sequel)

Candy Man, The
Mike Curb Congregation; *Mike Curb Congregation's Greatest Hits* . . . . . (Curb)
Sammy Davis, Jr.; *Best Of Sammy Davis, Jr.* . . . . (Curb)
Sammy Davis, Jr.'s Greatest Songs . . . . (Curb)
Super Hits Of The '70s-Have A Nice Day-#8-C . . . . (Rhino)

Candyman
Siouxsie And The Banshees; *Tinderbox* . . . . (Geffen)
Twice Upon A Time-The Singles . . . . (Geffen)

Can't Keep A Good Man Down
38 Special; *Special Delivery* . . . . (A&M)
Alabama; *Alabama-Live* . . . .(RCA)

Carousel Man
Cher; *Cher's Greatest Hits* . . . . (MCA)

Cathy's Clown
Everly Brothers; *Billboard Top Rock 'N' Roll Hits-1960-C* . . . . (Rhino)
Golden Hits Of The Everly Brothers . . . . (Warner Bros.)
The Reunion Concert-Live At Albert Hall 1983 . . . . (Mercury)
Very Best Of The Everly Brothers . . . .(Warner Bros.)
Reba McEntire; *Sweet Sixteen* . . . . (MCA)

Caught A Lite Sneeze
Tori Amos; *Boys For Pele* . . . .(Atlantic)

Chain Of Love
Clay Walker; *Live, Laugh, Love* . . . .(Giant)

Chattanoogie Shoe Shine Boy
Freddy Cannon; *14 Booming Hits* . . . . (Rhino)
Red Foley; *Red Foley: The Country Music Hall
Of Fame* . . . . (MCA Special Prod.)
The Nashville Sound: Owen Bradley-C . . . . (Decca)

Chin Chin Chinaman
James T. Powers; *Music From The New York Stage (1890-1920)-#1-1890-
1908-C* . . . . (Pearl)

China Boy
Benny Goodman; *Carnegie Hall Jazz Concert* . . . . (Columbia)
ST/The Benny Goodman Story . . . . (MCA)
The Benny Goodman Story. (Capitol)

Cigarette Of A Single Man
Squeeze; *Babylon & On* . . . . (A&M)

Comfort Of A Man
Stephanie Mills; *Home* . . . . (MCA)

Common Man
John Conlee; *Best Of John Conlee*. . . . . (Curb)
Busted. . . . . (MCA Special Prod.)
John Conlee-20 Greatest Hits . . . . (MCA)
John Conlee's Greatest Hits . . . .(MCA)

Common Man
Blasters; *Blasters-Collection*. . . . .(Slash)

Company Man
James Taylor; *Flag* . . . . (Columbia)

Country Boy
''Little'' Jimmy Dickens; *Columbia Country Classics-#2-Honky Tonk
Heroes-C* . . . . (Columbia)
Johnny Cash; *Johnny Cash-Original Golden Hits-#3* . . . . (Sun)
Superbilly . . . .(Sun)
The Man-The World-His Music . . . .(Sun)
Ricky Skaggs; *19 Hot Country Requests-#3-C* . . . . (Epic)
Greatest Country Hits Of The '80s-1985-C . . . . (Columbia)
Live In London . . . . (Epic)
Ricky Skaggs-Country Boy . . . .(Epic)

Country Boy (You Got Your Feet In L.A.)
Glen Campbell; *Best Of Glen Campbell* . . . . (Capitol)
Glen Campbell-Classics Collection . . . . (Capitol)
Glen Campbell's Greatest Hits. . . . . (Capitol)

Country Boy Can Survive
Hank Williams, Jr.; *America (The Way I See It)* . . . . (WB/Curb)
Hank Williams, Jr. ''Live''. (WB/Curb)
Hank Williams, Jr.'s Greatest Hits. . . . .(WB/Curb)
ST/Pressure Is On. . . . . (WB/Curb)

Cowboy Man
Lyle Lovett; *Country Classics-#9-1984-1987-C* . . . . (Universal)
ST/Always . . . . (MCA)
Lyle Lovett and his Large Band; *Lyle Lovett and his
Large Band* . . . . (Curb/MCA)

Crab Man's Call
Original Cast; *Porgy & Bess* . . . . (MCA)

Cry For The Bad Man
Lynyrd Skynyrd; *Best Of Lynyrd Skynyrd* . . . . (MCA Special Prod.)
Gimme Back My Bullets . . . . (MCA)

Danger Man
David Bromberg; *Wanted Dead Or Alive* . . . .(Columbia)

Dangerous Man
Dwight Yoakam; *If There Was A Way*. . . . .(Reprise)

Dawgs (Are A Man's Best Friend)
Original Cast; *Dawgs*.....................................(Glendale)
Dead Man
Asleep At The Wheel; *Asleep At The Wheel* ....(Epic)
Dead Man's Hill
Indigo Girls; *Swamp Ophelia* ....(Epic)
Dear Mr. President
4 Non Blondes; *Bigger, Better, Faster, More!* ....(Interscope)
Dear Mr. President
Next Issue; *Next Issue* ....(Epic)
Dear Santa-Bring Me A Man This Christmas
Weather Girls; *Success* ....(Columbia)
Death Of A Ladies' Man
Leonard Cohen; *Death Of A Ladies' Man* ....(Columbia)
Der Kommisar
After The Fire; *Club Epic-#5-C* ....(Epic)
Detective Man
Detective; *Detective* ....(Swan Song)
Diary Of A Madman
Ozzy Osbourne; *Diary Of A Madman* ....(Jet)
Did You See His Name
Kinks; *Kink Kronikles* ....(Reprise)
Difference, The
Wallflowers; *Bringing Down The Horse* ....(Interscope)
Dirty White Boy
Foreigner; *Head Games*.........................(Atlantic)
Records ....(Atlantic)
Do Right Woman, Do Right Man
Aretha Franklin; *Aretha Franklin-30 Greatest Hits*...........(Rhino)
ST/Dead Presidents ....(Capitol)
Commitments; *ST/The Commitments* ....(MCA)
Do You Know Where Your Man Is
Pam Tillis; *Homeward Looking Angel*.....................(Arista)
Does She Love That Man?
Breathe; *Peace Of Mind*................................(A&M)
Don't Mess With My Man
Irma Thomas; *We Got A Party-Best Of Ron Records-#1-C* ....(Rounder)
Don't Pay The Ferryman
Chris DeBurgh; *Getaway*...........................(A&M)
Don't You Get It
Mark Knopfler; *Golden Heart* ....(Warner Bros.)
Don't You Marry The Mormon Boys
Rosalie Sorrels; *Lonesome Roving Wolves-Songs & Ballads Of
The West* ....(Green Linnet)
Donut Man
Rita Coolidge; *The Lady's Not For Sale* ....(A&M)
Down Boys
Warrant; *Dirty Rotten Filthy Stinking Rich* ....(Columbia)
Down Boys
Cars; *Panorama*...................................(Elektra)
Drowning Man
Duran Duran; *Duran Duran (The Wedding Album)*.............(Capitol)
Drowning Man
U2; *War*..(Island)
Drug Store Truck Drivin' Man
Byrds; *Best Of The Byrds-Greatest Hits-#2*...........(Columbia)
Dr. Byrds & Mr. Hyde.............................(Legacy)
The Byrds ....(Columbia)
Gram Parsons & Fallen Angels; *Live 1973* ....(Sierra)
Joan Baez & Jeffrey Shurtleff; *ST/Woodstock*............(Atlantic)
Drunken Hearted Boy
Allman Brothers Band; *Dreams* ....(Polydor)
Drunken Hearted Man
Robert Johnson; *Robert Johnson-Complete Recordings* ....(Columbia)
Dude (Looks Like A Lady)
Aerosmith; *Big Ones*..............................(Geffen)
Permanent Vacation ....(Geffen)
Dutchman
Jerry Jeff Walker; *Hill Country Rain* ....(Rykodisc)
Tommy Makem & Liam Clancy; *Tommy Makem & Liam Clancy-
Collection* ....(Shanachie)
Early To Bed
Morphine; *Like Swimming*......................(DreamWorks/Rykodisc)
El Matador
Kingston Trio; *Capitol Collectors Series-The Kingston Trio* ....(Capitol)
Sold Out/String Along............................(Capitol)
English Boys
Blondie; *The Hunter* ....(Chrysalis)
English Boys (With Guns)
Deaf School; *English Boys/Working Girls* ....(Warner Bros.)
Englishman In New York
Sting; *...Nothing Like The Sun*.........................(A&M)
Fields Of Gold-The Best Of Sting 1984-1994 ....(A&M)
Enlisted Men's Mess
Glenn Miller; *Major Glenn Miller/Army Air Force Band* ....(Bluebird)
Enter Sandman
Metallica; *Metallica* ....(Elektra)

Even The Man In The Moon Is Crying
Mark Collie; *Mark Collie*...........................(MCA)
Every Little Thing He Does Is Magic
Shawn Colvin; *Cover Girl* ....(Columbia)
Every Man A King
Randy Newman; *Good Old Boys* ....(Reprise)
Excitable Boy
Warren Zevon; *Excitable Boy* ....(Asylum)
Quiet Normal Life-Best Of Warren Zevon.................(Asylum)
Stand In The Fire ....(Asylum)
Excuse Me Mr.
No Doubt; *Tragic Kingdom* ....(Trauma)
Fabulous Character
Sarah Vaughan; *Complete Sarah Vaughan On Mercury-#1-Great Jazz Years-
1954-1956* ....(Mercury)
Factory
Bruce Springsteen; *Darkness On The Edge Of Town*............(Columbia)
Family Man
Karyn White; *Karyn White*..........................(Warner Bros.)
Family Man
James Taylor; *In The Pocket* ....(Warner Bros.)
Family Man
Everton Blender; *Live At The White River Reggae Bash* ....(Heartbeat)
Family Man
Black Flag; *Family Man*.............................(SST)
Family Man
Pablo Cruise; *Worlds Away* ....(A&M)
Family Man
Daryl Hall & John Oates; *H2O*.........................(RCA)
Hi Octane-Hard Drivin' Hits-C ....(RCA)
Family Man
Fleetwood Mac; *Tango In The Night* ....(Warner Bros.)
Farmer & The Cowman
Original Broadway Cast; *Oklahoma!* ....(RCA)
Fat Boy
Billy Stewart; *Beach Music Hits-C*.....................(Universal)
One More Time ....(Chess)
One More Time/Chess Years.........................(Chess)
Fat Boy
Max-A-Million; *Club Hitz Of The '90s-#1-C*..................(Beast)
Take Your Time ....(S.O.S./Zoo)
Fat Man
Fats Domino; *Best Of Fats Domino* ....(EMI)
Fats Domino's Greatest Hits ....(MCA)
My Blue Heaven-Best Of Fats Domino-#1 ....(EMI)
Fat Man
Jethro Tull; *20 Years Of Jethro Tull* ....(Chrysalis)
M.U.-The Best Of Jethro Tull ....(Chrysalis)
Stand Up ....(Chrysalis)
Fat Man
Nazareth; *Nazareth* ....(A&M)
Fat Man
Radio Program Theme; *Themes From Old Times* ....(Viva)
Fat Man In The Bathtub
Little Feat; *Dixie Chicken*..........................(Warner Bros.)
Waiting For Columbus ....(Warner Bros.)
Find Yourself A Man
Original Cast; *Funny Girl* ....(Capitol)
Fireman, The
George Strait; *Country Classics-#4-1984-1985-C*.................(Universal)
Does Fort Worth Ever Cross Your Mind ....(MCA)
George Strait's Greatest Hits-#2 ....(MCA)
Five Guys Named Moe
Joe Jackson; *Jumpin' Jive* ....(A&M)
Louis Jordan; *Best Of Louis Jordan* ....(MCA)
Original Decca Recordings-#2 ....(Decca)
Flim Flam Man
Laura Nyro; *The First Songs* ....(Columbia)
Flower & The Young Man
Strawbs; *Grave New World* ....(A&M)
Fly (The Angel Song)
Wilkinsons; *Nothing But Love* ....(Giant)
Fooling Yourself
Styx; *Caught In The Act*.............................(A&M)
Grand Illusion ....(A&M)
Styx-Classics-#15 ....(A&M)
For A Change
Neal McCoy; *You Gotta Love That!* ....(Atlantic)
For He's A Jolly Good Fellow
Good Time Singers; *All Occasions Album* ....(Gateway)
Free Man In Paris
Joni Mitchell; *Court & Spark*.........................(Asylum)
Shadows & Light ....(Asylum)
Freeborn Man
Outlaws; *Bring It Back Alive*.........................(Arista)
Lady In Waiting ....(Arista)
Legends Of Rock Guitar-'70s-C ....(Rhino)

Freshmen, The
Verve Pipe; *Villains* . . . . (RCA)
Fuck You, Man
Pussy Galore; *Right Now!* . . . . (Caroline)
Gambling Man
Bonnie Raitt; *Sweet Forgiveness* . . . . (Warner Bros.)
Garbage Man
Cramps; *Bad Music For Bad People* . . . . (I.R.S.)
Songs The Lord Taught Us . . . . (I.R.S.)
Muddy Waters; *Can't Get No Grindin'* . . . . (Chess)
Gentleman Is A Dope
Jo Stafford; *Jo Stafford's Greatest Hits* . . . . (Curb)
Morgana King; *Another Time Another Space* . . . . (Muse)
Ghost Of A Texas Ladies' Man
Concrete Blonde; *Walking In London* . . . . (I.R.S.)
Gimme Gimme Gimme (A Man After Midnight)
Erasure; *Two Ring Circus* . . . . (Sire)
Girl
Beatles; *Beatles-Box Set* . . . . (Capitol)
Beatles-Love Songs . . . . (Capitol)
Rubber Soul . . . . (Capitol)
The Beatles/1962-1966 . . . . (Capitol)
Girlfriend/Boyfriend
Blackstreet featuring Janet; *Finally* . . . . (Lil' Man/Interscope)
Give Him A Great Big Kiss
Shangri-Las; *Best Of The Girl Groups-#1-C* . . . . (Rhino)
Remember The Shangri-Las At Their Best . . . . (Collectables)
Givin' Water To A Drowning Man
Lee Roy Parnell; *We All Get Lucky Sometimes* . . . . (Career)
Giving Him Something He Can Feel
En Vogue; *Funky Divas* . . . . (East West)
Go To The Mirror Boy
Who; *Tommy* . . . . (MCA)
God Fearing Man
Steppenwolf; *At Your Birthday Party* . . . . (MCA Special Prod.)
God Must Be A Boogie Man
Joni Mitchell; *Mingus* . . . . (Elektra)
Shadows & Light . . . . (Asylum)
Going Out With The Boys
Jimmie Mack; *Jimmie Mack* . . . . (Big Tree)
Golden Boy
Tubes; *Tubes Now* . . . . (A&M)
Good Man Is Hard To Find (Pittsburgh)
Bruce Springsteen; *Tracks* . . . . (Columbia)
Good Ole Boys From Louisiana
Jimmy C. Newman & Cajun Country; *Jimmy C. Newman & Cajun
Country* . . . . (Dot)
Good Time Boy
Buffalo Springfield; *Buffalo Springfield Again* . . . . (Atco)
Good Time Man Like Me Got No Business (Singin' The Blues), A
Jim Croce; *Life & Times* . . . . (Lifesong)
Words And Music . . . . (Dunhill Compact Classics)
Goodnight, Good Night
Collective Soul; *Hints, Allegations And Things Left Unsaid* . . . . (Atlantic)
Gotta Man
Eve; *First Lady Of Ruff Ryders* . . . . (Ruff Ryders/IDJMG)
Gray Haired Young Man
Don Potter; *Over The Rainbow* . . . . (Mirror)
Greatest Man I Never Knew
Reba McEntire; *For My Broken Heart* . . . . (MCA)
Reba McEntire's Greatest Hits Volume Two . . . . (MCA)
Grown Men Don't Cry
Tim McGraw; *Set This Circus Down* . . . . (Curb)
Guitar Man
Elvis Presley; *14 #1 Country Hits-C* . . . . (RCA)
Elvis . . . . (RCA)
Guitar Man . . . . (RCA)
Nipper's Greatest Hits Of The '80s-C . . . . (RCA)
Jerry Reed; *Essential Jerry Reed* . . . . (RCA)
Guitar Man
Bread; *Best Of Bread-#2* . . . . (Elektra)
Bread-Anthology . . . . (Elektra)
Guy Is A Guy, A
Doris Day; *Doris Day's Greatest Hits* . . . . (Columbia)
Guys & Dolls
Original Cast; *ST/Guys & Dolls* . . . . (MCA)
Guys Do It All The Time
Mindy McCready; *Ten Thousand Angels* . . . . (BNA)
Half The Man
Clint Black; *No Time To Kill* . . . . (RCA)
Hands Of A Working Man
Ty Herndon; *Big Hopes* . . . . (Epic)
Handy Man
Del Shannon; *Del Shannon's Greatest Hits* . . . . (Curb)
Del Shannon's Greatest Hits . . . . (Rhino)
James Taylor; *James Taylor-Best Live* . . . . (Columbia)
JT . . . . (Columbia)
Jimmy Jones; *Billboard Top Rock 'N' Roll Hits-1960-C* . . . . (Rhino)

Hard To Find 45s On CD-#1-1955-1960-C . . . . (Eric)
Hangman Jury
Aerosmith; *Permanent Vacation* . . . . (Geffen)
Happily Married Man
Duane Allman; *Duane Allman-An Anthology-Vol. II* . . . . (Capricorn)
Happy Birthday Mr. President
John Southworth; *Mars Pennsylvania* . . . . (Bar/None)
Happy Man
Chicago; *Chicago VII* . . . . (Chicago)
Chicago's Greatest Hits-#2 (1974-81) . . . . (Chicago)
Happy Man
Greg Kihn Band; *Kihnsolidation-Best Of Greg Kihn* . . . . (Rhino)
Hard Drivin' Man
J. Geils Band; *Full House* . . . . (Atlantic)
J. Geils Band . . . . (Atlantic)
Hard Lovin' Woman
Mark Collie; *Unleashed* . . . . (MCA)
Hard Workin' Man
Brooks & Dunn; *Hard Workin' Man* . . . . (Arista)
Hard Workin' Man
Jack Nitzsche; *ST/Blue Collar* . . . . (MCA)
He Ain't Worth Missing
Toby Keith; *Toby Keith* . . . . (Mercury)
He Calls Home
Candlebox; *Candlebox* . . . . (Maverick)
He Don't Love You (Like I Love You)
Tony Orlando & Dawn; *'70s Greatest Rock Hits-#9-#1 Hits-C* . . . . . (Priority)
Behind Closed Doors-'70s Swingers-C . . . . (Rhino)
Best Of Tony Orlando & Dawn . . . . (Rhino)
He Feels Guilty
Bobbie Cryner; *Bobbie Cryner* . . . . (Epic)
He Left A Lot To Be Desired
Ricochet; *Blink Of An Eye* . . . . (Columbia)
He Raped Me
Natas; *Blaz4me* . . . . (Reel Life)
He Stopped Loving Her Today
George Jones; *All Time Legends Of Country Music-C* . . . . (Legacy)
First Time Live! . . . . (Epic)
George Jones-Anniversary-Ten Years Of Hits . . . . (Epic)
Greatest Country Hits Of The '80s-1980-C . . . . (Columbia)
Greatest Hits From The Jukebox-C . . . . (Epic)
I Am What I Am. . . . . (Epic)
He Talks To Me
Lorrie Morgan; *Leave The Light On* . . . . (RCA)
Lorrie Morgan's Greatest Hits . . . . (BNA)
Lorrie Morgan-Super Hits . . . . (RCA)
To Get To You-Greatest Hits Collection . . . . (BNA)
He Thinks He'll Keep Her
Mary Chapin Carpenter; *Come On Come On* . . . . (Columbia)
He Treats Me Like A Dog
St. Louis Bessie; *Barrelhouse Mamas: Born In The Alley, Raised In The
Slums-C* . . . . (Yazoo)
He Was Too Good To Me
Barbara Cook; *Barbara Cook-Live At Carnegie Hall* . . . . (Sony Music Classical)
Bette Midler; *Some People's Lives* . . . . (Atlantic)
Carmen McRae; *Carmen McRae Sings Great American
Songwriters* . . . . (Decca Jazz)
Helen Merrill; *Dream Of You* . . . . (Emarcy)
Jeri Southern; *The Very Thought Of You: The Decca Years-1951-1957* . . . (GRP)
He Wasn't Man Enough
Toni Braxton; *The Heat* . . . . (LaFace)
Totally Hits-#3-C . . . . (Atlantic)
He Went To Paris
Jimmy Buffett; *Songs You Know By Heart-Jimmy Buffett's Greatest
Hit(s)* . . . . (MCA)
White Sport Coat & A Pink Crustacean . . . . (MCA)
You Had To Be There . . . . (MCA)
He Will Break Your Heart
Jerry Butler; *Best Of Jerry Butler* . . . . (Rhino)
He Would Be Sixteen
Michelle Wright; *Now & Then* . . . . (Arista)
He'll Have To Go
Jim Reeves; *60 Years Of Country Music-C* . . . . (RCA)
Best Of Jim Reeves . . . . (RCA)
Billboard Top Country Hits-1960-C . . . . (Rhino)
Great Moments At The Grand Ole Opry-C . . . . (RCA)
Jim Reeves' Greatest Hits. . . . . (RCA)
Nipper's Greatest Hits Of The '50s-#1-C . . . . (RCA)
Ry Cooder; *Chicken Skin Music* . . . . (Reprise)
He'll Never Love You (Like I Do)
Freddie Jackson; *Rock Me Tonight (For Old Time's Sake)* . . . . . (Capitol)
Hello Brother
Louis Armstrong; *What A Wonderful World* . . . . (Decca Jazz)
Her Man
Gary Allan; *Cryin' Lyin' Lovin' & Leavin'-C* . . . . (Universal)
Used Heart For Sale . . . . (Decca)
Waylon Jennings; *The Eagle* . . . . (Epic)
Here Comes A Man
Traffic; *Far From Home* . . . . (Virgin)

He's A Fool For You
Boz Scaggs; *My Time* . . . . (Columbia)
He's A Good Ole Boy
Chely Wright; *Woman In The Moon* . . . .(Polydor Country)
He's A Heartache (Looking For A Place To Happen)
Janie Fricke; *19 Hot Country Requests-C* . . . . (Epic)
  It Ain't Easy . . . . (Columbia)
  Janie Fricke-17 Greatest Hits . . . . (Columbia)
  Very Best Of Janie Fricke . . . . (Columbia)
He's A Rebel
Crystals; *Good Time Rock 'N' Roll-C* . . . . (MCA)
  Phil Spector's Greatest Hits-C . . . . (Spector)
He's A Whore
Cheap Trick; *Cheap Trick* . . . . (Epic)
He's Got You
Brooks & Dunn; *The Greatest Hits Collection* . . . . (Arista)
He's Mine
Mokenstef; *Azz Izz* . . . . (OutBurst/RAL/Island)
  ST/All That . . . . (Loud/RCA)
He's Misstra Know-It-All
Stevie Wonder; *Innervisions* . . . . (Motown)
He's So Fine
Chiffons; *Best Of The Girl Groups-#1-C* . . . . (Rhino)
  Billboard Top Rock 'N' Roll Hits-1963-C . . . . (Rhino)
  Chiffons Greatest Hits . . . . (Right Stuff)
Jody Miller; *Jody Miller's Greatest Hits* . . . . (Epic)
He's The Great Imposter
Fleetwoods; *ST/American Graffiti* . . . . (MCA)
Hey Baby
No Doubt; *Rock Steady* . . . . (Interscope)
Hey Harmonica Man
Stevie Wonder; *Stevie Wonder's Greatest Hits* . . . . (Motown)
Hey Man, Nice Shot
Filter; *Short Bus* . . . .(Reprise)
  ST/Cable Guy . . . . (Work)
Hey, Western Union Man
Jerry Butler; *Best Of Jerry Butler* . . . . (Mercury)
  Billboard Top R&B Hits-1968-C . . . . (Rhino)
High-Tech Redneck
George Jones; *High-Tech Redneck* . . . . (MCA)
Highway Man
Curtis Leach; *Truck Driver Boogie Big Rig Hits-1939-1969-C* . . . . . . (Audium)
Highwayman
Glen Campbell; *Highwayman* . . . . (Capitol)
Johnny Cash with Waylon Jennings, Kris Kristofferson, Willie Nelson; *The Man In Black-His Greatest Hits* . . . . (Legacy)
Waylon Jennings, Willie Nelson, Johnny Cash, Kris Kristofferson; *Columbia Country Classics-#3-Americana-C* . . . . (Columbia)
  Johnny Cash-16 Biggest Hits-#2 . . . . (Legacy)
Willie Nelson; *Greatest Country Hits Of The '80s-1985-C* . . . . (Columbia)
Him
Rupert Holmes; *Partners In Crime* . . . . (MCA)
Hippie Boy
Caroline's Spine; *Monsoon* . . . . (Hollywood)
His Green Eyes
Barbara Fairchild; *Standing In Your Line* . . . . (Columbia)
Home Lovin' Man
Andy Williams; *Andy Williams' Greatest Hits-#2* . . . . (Columbia)
Homeboy
Michael McDonald; *Take It To Heart* . . . . (Reprise)
Homeboy Hawaii
Kerosene; *Teenage Secret* . . . . (Caipirinha)
Honky Tonk Man
Dwight Yoakam; *Guitars, Cadillacs, Etc., Etc.* . . . .(Reprise)
  Just Lookin' For A Hit . . . . (Reprise)
Johnny Horton; *All Time Legends Of Country Music-C* . . . . (Legacy)
  Columbia Country Classics-#2-Honky Tonk Heroes-C . . . . . . (Columbia)
Marty Robbins; *Greatest Country Hits From The Movies-C* . . . . . . (Epic)
Honky Tonk Night Time Man
Lynyrd Skynyrd; *Street Survivors* . . . . (MCA)
Merle Haggard & The Strangers; *Presents His 30th Album.* . . . . . . (Capitol)
  Songs I'll Always Sing . . . . (Capitol)
Honky Tonk Women Love Redneck Men
Ronnie McDowell; *American Music* . . . . (Curb)
Hoochie Coochie Man
Eric Clapton; *From The Cradle* . . . .(Duck/Reprise)
Eric Clapton featuring Buddy Guy; *The Concert For New York City-C* . . . . (Columbia)
Hot Boyz
Missy "Misdemeanor" Elliot; *Da Real World* . . . . (East West)
  Totally Hits-#2-C . . . . (Elektra)
House Of The Rising Sun
Animals; *Animals Greatest Hits* . . . . (Allegiance)
  Best Of The Animals . . . . (Abkco)
  Greatest Hits Live!-Rip It To Shreds. . . . . (I.R.S.)
Hank Williams, Jr.; *Hank Williams, Jr. "Live"* . . . .(WB/Curb)
Ronnie Milsap; *Ronnie Milsap-16 Greatest Hits-#2* . . . . (Trip)

How Can A Poor Man Stand Such Times And Live?
Blind Alfred Reed; *How Can A Poor Man Stand Such Times And Live?* . . . .(Rounder)
Ry Cooder; *Ry Cooder* . . . . (Reprise)
  Show Time . . . . (Warner Bros.)
Hurdy Gurdy Man
Butthole Surfers; *ST/Dumb And Dumber* . . . . (RCA)
Donovan; *Donovan's Greatest Hits* . . . . (Epic)
  Hurdy Gurdy Man . . . . (Epic)
Hymn For The Dudes
Mott The Hoople; *Mott.* . . . .(Columbia)
  Mott The Hoople's Greatest Hits. . . . . (Columbia)
Hymn To Him
Audrey Hepburn; *ST/My Fair Lady* . . . . (Columbia)
Julie Andrews/Original Cast; *My Fair Lady* . . . . (Columbia)
I Am A Man Of Constant Sorrow
Ralph Stanley; *Rebel Records: 35 Years Of The Best In Bluegrass-1960-1995-C* . . . . (Rebel)
Soggy Bottom Boys featuring Dan Tyminski; *ST/O Brother, Where Art Thou?* . . . . (Mercury)
Stanley Brothers; *All Time Legends Of Country Music-C* . . . . (Legacy)
I Am A Simple Man
Ricky Van Shelton; *Backroads* . . . .(Columbia)
I Am That Man
Brooks & Dunn; *Borderline* . . . . (Arista)
I Asked For Water (He Gave Me Gasoline)
Lucinda Williams; *Lucinda Williams* . . . .(Koch International)
I Don't Want Your Millions, Mister
Jim Garland; *Newport Broadside: Newport Folk Festival-1963-C* . . .(Vanguard)
Pete Seeger; *The Prestige/Folklore Years-#4: Singing Out Loud-The Philadelphia Folk-C* . . . . (Prestige)
Tom Rush; *Blues Songs & Ballads* . . . . (Fantasy)
  Tom Rush. . . . . (Fantasy)
I Hate Men
Original Cast; *ST/Kiss Me Kate* . . . .(Rhino)
Original Cast/Patricia Morrison; *Kiss Me Kate* . . . . (Sony Music Classical)
I Just Want To See His Face
Rolling Stones; *Exile On Main Street.* . . . . (Virgin)
I Know What Boys Like
Waitresses; *Best Of The Waitresses* . . . . (Polydor)
  Just Can't Get Enough: New Wave Hits Of The '80s-#5-C . . . . . .(Rhino)
I Love Me Some Him
Toni Braxton; *Secrets.* . . . .(LaFace)
I Met Him On A Sunday
Shirelles; *Shirelles' Greatest Hits* . . . .(Everest)
  Shirelles-16 Greatest Hits . . . . (Trip)
  Shirelles-Anthology 1959-1964. . . . . (Rhino)
  Shirelles-Classics . . . . (Bac-Trac)
I Need A Man To Love
Big Brother & The Holding Company; *Cheap Thrills* . . . .(Columbia)
I Never Loved A Man (The Way I Love You)
Aretha Franklin; *Aretha Franklin-30 Greatest Hits* . . . . (Rhino)
  Golden Age Of Black Music-1960-1970-C . . . . (Atlantic)
  ST/The Commitments . . . . (MCA)
I Saw Him Standing There
Tiffany; *Tiffany* . . . . (MCA)
  Tiffany's Greatest Hits . . . . (Hip-O)
I Wanna Be Your Man
Beatles; *Meet The Beatles!* . . . .(Capitol)
  Rock 'N' Roll Music . . . . (Capitol)
I Wanna Love Him So Bad
Jelly Beans; *Best Of The Girl Groups-#1-C* . . . . (Rhino)
I Want To Be A Dancin' Man
Fred Astaire; *That's Entertainment-The Ultimate Anthology Of MGM Musicals-C* . . . .(Turner Classic Movies)
I Want To Be Your Man
Roger; *Unlimited!* . . . . (Reprise)
I Won't Grow Up
Original Cast/Mary Martin; *Peter Pan-The 1954 Broadway Production* . . . . (RCA Victor)
If He Walked Into My Life
Original Cast; *Mame* . . . .(Columbia)
If I Were A Rich Man
Original Cast; *Fiddler On The Roof* . . . . (RCA Victor)
If It Weren't For Him
Vince Gill & Rosanne Cash; *Collector's Series-Duets-C* . . . . (RCA)
If You See Him/If You See Her
Brooks & Dunn & Reba McEntire; *If You See Her.* . . . .(Arista)
Reba McEntire & Brooks & Dunn; *If You See Him* . . . . (MCA)
  Reba McEntire's Greatest Hits-#3: I'm A Survivor. . . . . (MCA)
If You Were The Only Boy (In The World)
Barbra Streisand; *My Name Is Barbra* . . . . (Columbia)
Illustrated Man
Johnny Winter; *Best Blues Album In The World...Ever!-C* . . . . (Virgin)
I'm A Bad, Bad Man
Ethel Merman/Bruce Yarnell/Original Cast; *Annie Get Your Gun* . . . . (RCA Victor)
I'm A Man
Bo Diddley; *Bo Diddley-His Best.* . . . . (Chess)

Super Blues . . . . (Chess)
The Sopranos-Music From The HBO Original
   Series . . . . (Sony Music Soundtrax)
Yardbirds; Five Live Yardbirds . . . . (Rhino)
   History Of British Rock-#3-C . . . . (Rhino)
   Yardbirds' Greatest Hits-#1 (1964-1966) . . . . (Rhino)

I'm A Man
Spencer Davis Group; Baby Boomer Classics-Rockin'
   Sixties-C . . . . (JCI Assoc. Labels)
   Best Of The Spencer Davis Group . . . .(EMI)

I'm A One- Woman Man
George Jones; Essential George Jones-The Spirit Of Country . . . . (Legacy)
   George Jones-Super Hits . . . .(Epic)
   One Woman Man . . . .(Epic)
   Who's Gonna Fill Their Shoes . . . .(Epic)
Glen Campbell; Still Within The Sound Of My Voice . . . .(MCA)
Johnny Horton; American Originals-Johnny Horton . . . . (Columbia)
   Honky Tonk Man-The Essential Johnny Horton-1956-1960 . . . . (Legacy)

I'm A Real Man
John Hiatt; Warming Up To The Ice Age . . . .(Geffen)

I'm A Steady Rollin' Man
George Thorogood & The Destroyers; The Baddest Of George Thorogood &
   The Destroyers . . . .(EMI)

I'm A Truck Driving Man
Art Gibson; Truck Driver Boogie Big Rig Hits-1939-1969-C . . . .(Audium)

I'm An Ordinary Man
Rex Harrison/Original Cast; My Fair Lady . . . . (Columbia)

I'm Free (Heaven Help The Man)
Kenny Loggins; ST/Footloose . . . . (Columbia)

I'm Gonna Wash That Man Right Outta My Hair
Mitzi Gaynor; ST/South Pacific . . . . (RCA)
Original Cast; South Pacific . . . .(CBS Masterworks)
Weather Girls; Success . . . . (Columbia)

I'm Just A Country Boy
Don Williams; Best Of Don Williams-#2 . . . .(MCA)
   Don Williams-Country Boy . . . .(MCA)

I'm Not A Well Man
Original Cast; I Can Get It For You Wholesale . . . . (Columbia)

I'm Not That Man
10,000 Maniacs; MTV Unplugged-10,000 Maniacs . . . . (Elektra)
   Our Time In Eden . . . . (Elektra)

I'm Not Your Man
Tommy Conwell & The Young Rumblers; Rumble . . . . (Columbia)

I'm The Man Who Murdered Love
XTC; Wasp Star (Apple Venus Volume 2) . . . . (Idea/TVT)

I'm Waiting For The Man
Lou Reed; Lou Reed Live . . . . (RCA)
Velvet Underground; Live MCMXCIII . . . . (Sire)
   The Velvet Underground & Nico . . . . (Verve)

Indian Man
Charlie Daniels Band; Midnight Wind . . . .(Epic)

Invisible Man
98 Degrees; 98 Degrees . . . . (Motown)

Irish Boy
Mark Knopfler; CT/Cal. . . . . (Mercury)

Irishman In Chinatown
Luka Bloom; Riverside . . . . (Reprise)

Iron Man
Black Sabbath; Live Evil . . . .(Warner Bros.)
   Paranoid . . . .(Warner Bros.)
   We Sold Our Soul For Rock 'N' Roll . . . .(Warner Bros.)
Ozzy Osbourne; Tribute . . . .(Epic)

Iron Man
Sir Mix-A-Lot & Metal Church; Swass . . . . (Nastymix)

It Wasn't God Who Made Honky Tonk Angels
Kitty Wells; Grand Ole Opry-75 Years-#1-C . . . .(MCA)
   Kitty Wells' Greatest Hits . . . . (Step One)
   The Kitty Wells Story . . . .(MCA)

It's A Boy
Who; Tommy . . . .(MCA)

It's A Man's Man's Man's World
James Brown; Billboard Top R&B Hits-1966-C . . . . (Rhino)
   James Brown's Greatest Hits . . . . (Rhino)

It's Better With A Union Man
Barbra Streisand; Pins And Needles . . . . (Columbia)

It's In His Kiss (Shoop Shoop Song)
Betty Everett; Billboard Top R&B Hits-1964-C . . . . (Rhino)
   Hits Of The Sixties-C . . . .(Intercom Music)
   More American Graffiti-C . . . .(MCA)
   Oldies But Goodies-#3-C . . . . (Original Sound)
   Very Best Of Betty Everett . . . .(Vee-Jay)
   Wonder Women-History Of Girl Group Sound-C . . . . (Rhino)
Cher; ST/Mermaids. . . . .(Geffen)
Vonda Shepard; ST/Songs From "Ally McBeal" Featuring Vonda
   Shepard . . . . (550/Epic)

It's Raining, It's Pouring
Original Soundtrack; Children's Favorites . . . . (Kid Rhino/Rhino 4 Kids)

Japanese Sandman
Benny Goodman; The Birth Of Swing (1935-1936) . . . . (Bluebird)

Jealous Guy
John Lennon; Lennon . . . . (Capitol)
   ST/Imagine: John Lennon . . . . (Capitol)
John Lennon & Yoko Ono; The John Lennon Collection . . . . (Capitol)
John Lennon/Plastic Ono Band; Imagine . . . . (Capitol)
Roxy Music; Heart Still Beating . . . .(Virgin)
   High Road . . . . (Warner Bros.)
   Street Life-20 Great Hits . . . . (Reprise)

Jealous Hearted Man
Muddy Waters; Hard Again . . . .(Blue Sky)

Jealous Man
Truth; Jump . . . . (I.R.S.)

Jealous Man
Hoyt Axton; Fearless . . . . (A&M)

Journey Man
Jethro Tull; Heavy Horses . . . . (Chrysalis)

Jungle Boy
Bow Wow Wow; I Want Candy . . . . (RCA)

Jungle Boy
John Eddie; John Eddie . . . . (Columbia)

Junk Male
Five Thirty; Bed . . . . (Atco)

Just Good Ol' Boys
Moe Bandy & Joe Stampley; Just Good Ol' Boys . . . . (Columbia)
   Moe Bandy & Joe Stampley's Greatest Hits . . . . (Columbia)
   Trucker's Jukebox-#2-C . . . . (Legacy)

Killing Me Softly With His Song
Fugees; Score . . . .(Ruffhouse)
Luther Vandross; Songs . . . . (Epic)
Roberta Flack; Atlantic Rhythm & Blues 1947-1974-#6 (1966-
   1969)-C . . . .(Atlantic)
   Best Of Roberta Flack . . . .(Atlantic)
   Golden Age Of Black Music-1970-1975-C . . . .(Atlantic)
   Killing Me Softly. . . . .(Atlantic)

Kiss Him Goodbye
Nylons; Happy Together . . . .(Open Air)

Last Game Of The Season (A Blind Man In The Bleachers)
David Geddes; Super Hits Of The '70s-Have A Nice Day-#20-C . . . . (Rhino)

Laughing Boy
Mary Wells; Compact Command Performances-Mary Wells . . . . (Motown)
   Mary Wells' Greatest Hits . . . . (Motown)

Laundry Man
Fenton Robinson; Genuine Houserockin' Music-C . . . .(Alligator)
   Nightflight. . . . .(Alligator)

Leave Him Out Of This
Steve Wariner; I Am Ready . . . . (Arista)

Listen To What The Man Said
Wings; Venus And Mars . . . . (Capitol)
   Wings Over America . . . . (Capitol)

Little Beggar Man
Ian & Sylvia; Ian & Sylvia's Greatest Hits . . . . (Vanguard)
   Northern Journey . . . . (Vanguard)

Little Blue Man
Betty Johnson; 45-#13146 . . . .(Atlantic)

Little Boy Blue
Elegants; Best Of The Elegants . . . . (Collectables)

Little Boy Sad
Johnny Burnette; Best Of Johnny Burnette-You're Sixteen . . . . (Gold Rush)

Little London Boys
Johnny Thunders; Stations Of The Cross . . . . (Roir)

Little Man
Alan Jackson; High Mileage . . . . (Arista)

Little Paper Boy
Hank Williams; Rare Takes & Radio Cuts . . . .(Polydor)

Littlest Cowboy Rides Again
Chris LeDoux; Songbook Of The American West . . . . (Liberty)
   Sounds Of The Western Country . . . . (Liberty)

Living In The Footsteps Of Another Man
Chi-Lites; Chi-Lites Greatest Hits. . . . . (Brunswick)
   Half A Love . . . . (Brunswick)

Lollipop (Candyman)
Aqua; Aquarium . . . . (MCA)

London Boys
David Bowie; David Bowie-London Collector-Starting Point . . . .(London)
   Love You Till Tuesday . . . .(London)

London Leatherboys
Accept; Balls To The Wall . . . . (Portrait)
   Compilation . . . . (Portrait)

Lonely Blue Boy
Conway Twitty; Conway Twitty's Greatest Hits . . . . (Curb)
   Very Best Of Conway Twitty . . . . (MCA)

Long Haired Country Boy
Charlie Daniels Band; A Decade Of Hits . . . . (Epic)
   Fire On The Mountain . . . . (Epic)
   Me & The Boys . . . .(Epic)
   South's Greatest Hits-#2-C . . . . (Capricorn)
   Trucker's Jukebox-#2-C . . . . (Legacy)
   Volunteer Jam 3 & 4. . . . . (Epic)

Long Haired Guys From England
Too Much Joy; *Cereal Killers* . . . . (Giant)
Long Legged Guitar Pickin' Man
Johnny Cash & June Carter; *Johnny Cash's Greatest Hits-#2* . . . . (Columbia)
Looking For A Boy
Eileen Farrell; *I Gotta Right To Sing The Blues* . . . . (Sony Music Classical)
Sarah Vaughan; *Sarah Vaughan Sings George Gershwin Songbook,*
   Vol. 1 . . . . (Emarcy)
Lord Have Mercy On A Country Boy
Don Williams; *True Love* . . . . (RCA)
Lord Have Mercy On The Working Man
Travis Tritt; *T-R-O-U-B-L-E* . . . . (Warner Bros.)
Louisiana Man
Doug Kershaw; *Alive & Pickin'* . . . . (Warner Bros.)
   Best Of Doug Kershaw . . . . (Warner Bros.)
   Louisiana Man . . . . (Warner Bros.)
Louisiana Man
Dave Edmunds; *D.E. 7th* . . . . (Columbia)
Louisiana Woman, Mississippi Man
Loretta Lynn & Conway Twitty; *Louisiana Woman Mississippi Man* . . . . (MCA)
   Very Best Of Loretta Lynn & Conway Twitty . . . . (MCA)
Lover Boy
Billy Ocean; *Billy Ocean's Greatest Hits* . . . . (Jive)
   Suddenly . . . . (Jive)
Lover Boy
Supertramp; *Even In The Quietest Moments* . . . . (A&M)
Lover Man (Oh, Where Can You Be?)
Barbra Streisand; *Simply Streisand* . . . . (Columbia)
Billie Holiday; *Fine & Mellow* . . . . (Collectables)
   History Of The Real Billie Holiday . . . . (Verve)
Blossom Dearie; *Blossom Dearie* . . . . (Verve)
Lena Horne; *Goes Latin & Sings Your Requests* . . . . (DRG)
Sarah Vaughan; *Compact Jazz-Sarah Vaughan* . . . . (Verve)
   Jazz 'Round Midnight-Sarah Vaughan . . . . (Verve)
Sonny Stitt; *Soul Classics* . . . . (Prestige)
Low Spark Of High Heeled Boys
Traffic; *On The Road* . . . . (Island)
   The Low Spark Of High Heeled Boys . . . . (Island)
Lucky Guy
Rickie Lee Jones; *Pirates* . . . . (Warner Bros.)
Lucky Guy
Todd Rundgren; *Hermit Of Mink Hollow* . . . . (Rhino)
Lucky Man
Emerson, Lake & Palmer; *Best Of Emerson, Lake & Palmer* . . . . (Rhino)
   Emerson, Lake & Palmer . . . . (Atlantic)
Lucky Man
Bruce Springsteen; *Tracks* . . . . (Columbia)
Lucky Man
Verve; *Urban Hymns* . . . . (Hut/Virgin)
Mad About The Boy
Dinah Shore; *Dinah Shore-Love Songs* . . . . (Columbia)
Dinah Washington; *Dinah Washington-Golden Hits* . . . . (Mercury)
Madman Across The Water
Elton John; *Live In Australia With The Melbourne Symphony*
   Orchestra . . . . (MCA)
   Madman Across The Water . . . . (Polydor)
Magic Man
Heart; *Dreamboat Annie* . . . . (Capitol)
   Heart's Greatest Hits/Live . . . . (Epic)
Make Love Like A Man
Def Leppard; *Adrenalize* . . . . (Mercury)
Mama He's Crazy
Judds; *Judds* . . . . (RCA)
   Judds' Greatest Hits . . . . (MCA)
   Why Not Me . . . . (MCA)
Mama Let Him Play
Doucette; *Mama Let Him Play* . . . . (Mushroom)
Mama's Never Seen Those Eyes
Forester Sisters; *Forester Sisters* . . . . (Warner Bros.)
Man & The Donkey
Chuck Berry; *Missing Berries-Rarities-#3* . . . . (Chess)
Man At The Top
Bruce Springsteen; *Tracks* . . . . (Columbia)
Man Bites Dog
Plan 9; *Enigma Variations-#2-C* . . . . (Enigma Capitol)
Man Come Into Egypt
Peter, Paul & Mary; *Moving* . . . . (Warner Bros.)
Man For All Seasons
Billy Idol; *Whiplash Smile* . . . . (Chrysalis)
Man For All Seasons
Al Stewart; *Time Passages* . . . . (Arista)
Man From Bowling Green
Johnny Paycheck; *Johnny Paycheck Hits Home* . . (Columbia Special Prod.)
   Take This Job And Shove It . . . . (Epic)
Man From Galilee
Billy Parker; *Average Man* . . . . (Sunshine Country)
Man From Harlem
Cab Calloway & His Orchestra; *Cab Calloway-1932* . . . . (Classics)

Tribute To Black Entertainers-C . . . . (Columbia)
Man From Madrid
John Barry; *The EMI Years-#2-1961* . . . . (Scamp)
Man From Mars
Joni Mitchell; *Taming The Tiger* . . . . (Reprise)
Man From Mars, The
Smokey Wilson; *The Man From Mars* . . . . (Bullseye Blues)
Man From Milwaukee
Hanson; *Live From Albertane* . . . . (Mercury)
   Middle Of Nowhere . . . . (Mercury)
Man From Music Mountain
Gene Autry; *The Singing Cowboy-Chapter Two* . . . . (Varese Sarabande)
Man From New Orleans
Swampwater; *Swampwater* . . . . (One Way)
Man From Out Of Town
Bill Morrissey; *Inside* . . . . (Rounder)
Man From Pakistan
Flaming Lips; *Hear It Is* . . . . (Restless)
Man From Senegal
Mad Professor; *Psychedelic Dub* . . . . (Ariwa)
Man From South Africa
Max Roach; *Percussion Bitter Sweet* . . . . (GRP)
Man From The Moon
Crickets; *Dreams And Wishes* . . . . (Relic)
Man From The South, The
Ted Weems & His Orchestra; *78-#22238* . . . . (Victor)
Man He Was, The
George Jones; *The Rock: Stone Cold Country 2001* . . . . (BNA)
Man Holdin' On (To A Woman Lettin' Go)
Ty Herndon; *Big Hopes* . . . . (Epic)
Man I Love
Benny Goodman; *Carnegie Hall Jazz Concert* . . . . (Columbia)
Betty Carter; *'S Wonderful-Gershwin Songbook* . . . . (Verve)
Billie Holiday; *I Like Jazz-Essence Of Billie Holiday* . . . . (Columbia)
Carmen McRae; *Blue Series-Female Vocals-C* . . . . (Blue Note)
Diana Ross; *ST/Lady Sings The Blues* . . . . (Motown)
Ella Fitzgerald; *Mack The Knife-Ella Fitzgerald In Berlin* . . . . (Verve)
Harry James; *Hollywood Magic-1950s-C* . . . . (Columbia)
Kate Bush; *Glory Of Gershwin Featuring Larry Adler-C* . . . . (Mercury)
Mary Lou Williams; *Best Of Mary Lou Williams* . . . . (Pablo)
Man In Black
Johnny Cash; *Essential Johnny Cash* . . . . (Columbia)
   Patriot . . . . (Columbia)
   The Man In Black-His Greatest Hits . . . . (Legacy)
Man In The Box
Alice In Chains; *Facelift* . . . . (Columbia)
Man In The Corner Shop
Jam; *Snap!* . . . . (Polydor)
Man In The Long Black Coat
Joan Osborne; *Relish* . . . . (Blue Gorilla/Mercury)
Man In The Mirror
Michael Jackson; *Bad* . . . . (Epic)
Man In The Mirror
Jim Glaser; *Man In The Mirror* . . . . (Noble Vision)
Man Loves His Money
Angie Stone; *Black Diamond* . . . . (Arista)
Man Of Me
Gary Allan; *Alright Guy* . . . . (MCA)
Man Of My Word
Collin Raye; *Extremes* . . . . (Epic)
Man Of The World
Fleetwood Mac; *25 Years-The Chain* . . . . (Warner Bros.)
Man On Fire
Wood; *Songs From Stamford Hill* . . . . (Columbia)
Man On The Moon
R.E.M.; *Automatic For The People* . . . . (Warner Bros.)
Man On The Silver Mountain
Blackmore's Rainbow; *Ritchie Blackmore's R-A-I-N-B-O-W* . . . . (Polydor)
Rainbow; *Finyl Vinyl* . . . . (Mercury)
Man Out Of Time
Elvis Costello; *Girls Girls Girls* . . . . (Columbia)
Elvis Costello & The Attractions; *Best Of Elvis Costello & The*
   Attractions . . . . (Columbia)
   Imperial Bedroom . . . . (Columbia)
Man Overboard
Blondie; *Blondie* . . . . (Chrysalis)
Man Overboard
Eric Clapton; *Money And Cigarettes* . . . . (Duck/Reprise)
Man Smart, Woman Smarter
Harry Belafonte; *Harry Belafonte-Pure Gold* . . . . (RCA)
Robert Palmer; *Some People Can Do What They Like* . . . . (Island)
Rosanne Cash; *I Am Woman-C* . . . . (Nick At Nite)
   Right Or Wrong . . . . (Columbia)
Man That I've Become
Nick Lowe; *Dig My Mood* . . . . (Upstart)
Man This Lonely, A
Brooks & Dunn; *Borderline* . . . . (Arista)

Man Who Couldn't Cry
Johnny Cash; *American Recordings* . . . . (American)
Man Who Shot Himself
Tom T. Hall; *Places I've Done Time*. (RCA)
Man Who Sold The World
David Bowie; *Man Who Sold The World* . . . . (Rykodisc)
Sound + Vision. . . . .(Rykodisc)
Nirvana; *MTV Unplugged In New York* . . . . (David Geffen Co.)
Man With The Golden Thumb
Jerry Reed; *Man With The Golden Thumb* . . . . (RCA)
Man With The Lightbulb Head
Robyn Hitchcock & The Egyptians; *Fegmania* . . . . (Slash)
Mannish Boy
Muddy Waters; *Electric Mud* . . . . (Chess)
King Of The Electric Blues. . . . . (Legacy)
The Best Blues Album In The World...Ever!-C . . . . (Virgin)
Married Man's A Fool
Blind Willie McTell; *Last Session* . . . . (Prestige)
Ry Cooder; *Paradise And Lunch* . . . . (Reprise)
Married Men
Bette Midler; *Thighs And Whispers* . . . . (Atlantic)
Roches; *Bread & Roses Festival Of Acoustic Music-#2-C* . . . . (Fantasy)
Roches . . . .(Warner Bros.)
Marry The Man Today
Original Cast; *ST/Guys & Dolls* . . . .(MCA)
Maybe He'll Notice Her Now
Mindy McCready; *Ten Thousand Angels* . . . . (BNA)
Maybe It Was Memphis
Pam Tillis; *Pam Tillis' Greatest Hits* . . . . (Arista)
Pam Tillis-Collection. . . . .(Warner Bros.)
Put Yourself In My Place . . . . (Arista)
Me & Fat Boy
Mac Davis; *Texas In My Rear View Mirror* . . . . (Casablanca)
Medicine Man
George Benson; *Absolute Benson*. . . . . (GRP/VMG)
Meet De Boys On The Battlefront
Wild Tchoupitoulas; *Treacherous: A History Of The Neville Brothers* . . (Rhino)
Wild Tchoupitoulas . . . . (Island)
Men
Charly McClain; *Charly McClain's Greatest Hits* . . . .(Epic)
Forester Sisters; *Talkin' 'Bout Men* . . . .(Warner Bros.)
Men
Madge Crichton; *Music From The New York Stage (1890-1920)-#1-1890-1908-C* . . . . (Pearl)
Men
Gladys Knight; *Good Woman*. . . . .(MCA)
Men In Black
Will Smith; *Big Willie Style* . . . . (Columbia)
ST/Men In Black. . . . . (Columbia)
Men Of Ohio
Ohio State University Marching Band; *Foot Tappers* . . . .(Fidelity Sound)
Mercedes Boy
Pebbles; *Pebbles*. . . . .(MCA)
Midnight Man
James Gang; *Best Of The James Gang* . . . .(MCA)
James Gang-16 Greatest Hits . . . .(MCA)
Midnight Man
Rita Remington; *My Melody Of Love* . . . . (Plantation)
Midnight Man
Allman Brothers Band; *Shades Of Two Worlds* . . . .(Epic)
Minnesota Man Claims Monkey Bowled Perfect Game
Jad Fair; *Strange But True* . . . . (Matador)
Minstrel Boy
Boston Pops Orchestra/Arthur Fiedler; *Irish Album* . . . . (RCA)
Irish Night At The Pops . . . . (RCA)
John McDermott; *Battlefields Of Green-Songs Of Love & Loss* . . . . (Angel)
Miracle Man
Ozzy Osbourne; *Just Say Ozzy* . . . . (Epic Portrait Assoc.)
No Rest For The Wicked. . . . .(Epic)
Miracle Man
Elvis Costello; *My Aim Is True* . . . . (Columbia)
Miracle Man
Rain People; *Rain People* . . . .(Epic)
Mirror Man
Captain Beefheart & His Magic Band; *Mirror Man* . . . .(One Way)
Mirror Man
Prism; *Armageddon* . . . . (Capitol)
Mirror Man
Human League; *Human League's Greatest Hits* . . . . (A&M)
Mirror Man
Talk Talk; *Party's Over* . . . .(EMI)
Mirror Man
Pere Ubu; *Worlds In Collision* . . . . (Fontana)
Missionary Man
Eurythmics; *Eurythmics' Greatest Hits* . . . . (Arista)
Revenge . . . . (RCA)
Mister & Mississippi
Patti Page; *Patti Page's Greatest Hits* . . . . (Columbia)

Mister Big Time
Jon Bon Jovi; *ST/Armageddon-The Album* . . . . (Columbia)
Mister Please
Damn Yankees; *Don't Tread*. . . . . (Warner Bros.)
Monkey Man
Toots & The Maytals; *Toots & The Maytals-Live* . . . . (Mango)
Monkey Man
Rolling Stones; *Let It Bleed*. . . . .(Abkco)
Morning Man
Joy; *Joy*. . . . . (Fantasy)
Morning Side Of The Mountain, The
Tommy Edwards; *It's All In The Game-The Complete Hits Of Tommy Edwards*. . . . .(Eric)
Most Happy Fella
Broadway Cast; *Most Happy Fella* . . . . (RCA)
Original Broadway Cast; *Most Happy Fella* . . . .(Sony Music Classical)
Most Peculiar Man
Simon & Garfunkel; *Sounds Of Silence*. . . . . (Columbia)
Motorcycle Boys
Bill Molenhof; *All Pass By* . . . . (Cexton)
Mr. Man
Alicia Keys with Jimmy Cozier; *Songs In A Minor*. . . . . (J)
Muffin Man
Zappa/Beefheart; *Bongo Fury*. . . . . (Rykodisc)
Music Man
REO Speedwagon; *A Decade Of Rock And Roll 1970 To 1980* . . . . (Epic)
REO Speedwagon Live/You Get What You Play For . . . . (Epic)
Music Man
Cat Stevens; *Buddha & The Chocolate Box* . . . .(A&M)
Music Man
Cleo Laine; *Cleo Laine-Live At Carnegie Hall* . . . . (RCA)
I Am A Song . . . . (RCA)
Music Man
James Taylor; *Gorilla* . . . . (Warner Bros.)
Music Man
Exile; *Hang On To Your Heart* . . . .(Epic)
Music To Watch Girls By
Andy Williams; *Andy Williams' Greatest Hits-#2* . . . . (Columbia)
My Boo
Ghost Town DJ's; *So So Def Bass All-Stars-#2-C*. . . . . . . (So So Def/Columbia)
So So Def Bass All-Stars-C. . . . . (So So Def/Columbia)
Total Dance Explosion-C . . . . (Columbia)
My Boyfriend's Back
Angels; *Billboard Top Rock 'N' Roll Hits-1963-C* . . . . (Rhino)
Girl Groups-Story Of A Sound-C . . . . (Rhino)
My Boyfriend's Back . . . . (Collectables)
Oldies But Goodies-#11-C . . . . (Original Sound)
ST/The Wanderers . . . .(Warner Bros.)
Wonder Women-#2-History Of Girl Group-C . . . . (Rhino)
My Daddy Was A Milkman
Kentucky HeadHunters; *Pickin' On Nashville* . . . . (Mercury)
My Guy
Mary Wells; *Mary Wells' Greatest Hits* . . . . (Motown)
My Guy . . . . (Motown)
Oldies But Goodies-#11-C . . . . (Original Sound)
My Jamaican Guy
Grace Jones; *Island Life* . . . . (Island)
My Little Marine
Jamie Horton; *45-#118* . . . .(Eric)
My Lover Man
Bruce Springsteen; *Tracks* . . . . (Columbia)
My Man
Regina Belle; *Passion* . . . . (Columbia)
My Man
Jeannie C. Riley; *Jeannie C. Riley's Greatest Hits* . . . . (Plantation)
My Man
Barbra Streisand; *Barbra Streisand's Greatest Hits* . . . . (Columbia)
Live Concert At The Forum . . . . (Columbia)
My Name Is Barbra . . . . (Columbia)
ST/Funny Girl. . . . . (Columbia)
Billie Holiday; *Billie Holiday-Live* . . . . (Verve)
Essential Billie Holiday-Carnegie Hall Concert . . . . (Verve)
Diana Ross; *Evening With Diana Ross* . . . . (Motown)
ST/Lady Sings The Blues . . . . (Motown)
Ella Fitzgerald & Tommy Flanagan Trio; *Montreux '77-C*. . . . . (Pablo)
Peggy Lee; *Peggy Lee's All-Time Greatest Hits* . . . . (Curb)
Sarah Vaughan; *Jazz 'Round Midnight-Sarah Vaughan* . . . . (Verve)
My Man's Gone Now
Ella Fitzgerald & Louis Armstrong; *Porgy & Bess* . . . . (Verve)
Nina Simone; *Vocalists-Jazz Masters-C* . . . . (Bluebird)
Original Cast; *Porgy & Bess* . . . .(MCA)
Sarah Vaughan & L.A. Philharmonic; *Gershwin Live*. . . . . (Columbia)
Sinead O'Connor; *Glory Of Gershwin Featuring Larry Adler-C* . . . . (Mercury)
My Melancholy Baby
Barbra Streisand; *Third Album* . . . . (Columbia)
Bing Crosby; *Hits Of 1939-C* . . . . (Living Era)
Coleman Hawkins; *Genius Of Coleman Hawkins*. . . . . (Verve)
Dorothy Loudon; *Saloon*. . . . . (DRG)

Frank Sinatra; *Voice: The Columbia Years-1943-1952* . . . . (Columbia)
Gene Austin; *78-#21015* . . . .(Victor)
Jan Garber & His Orchestra; *Jan Garber & His Orchestra Play 22 Original*
   Big Band Favorites . . . . (Hindsight)
Kate Smith; *Kate Smith-16 Most Requested Songs* . . . . (Columbia)
Leon Redbone; *Double Time* . . . . (Warner Bros.)
Marcels; *Best Of The Marcels* . . . . (Rhino)

My Rock & Roll Man
Rita Coolidge; *It's Only Love* . . . . (A&M)

Na Na Hey Hey Kiss Him Goodbye
Steam; *Billboard Top Rock 'N' Roll Hits-1969-C* . . . . (Rhino)
   Super Hits Of The '70s-Have A Nice Day-#1-C . . . . (Rhino)
   Toga Rock-C . . . . (Dunhill Compact Classics)

Nature Boy
George Benson; *George Benson-Collection* . . . . (Warner Bros.)
Jose Feliciano; *Encore-Jose Feliciano* . . . .(RCA)
Nat "King" Cole; *Blossom Fell* . . . . (Capitol)
   The Nat "King" Cole Story . . . . (Capitol)

Neanderthal Man
Hotlegs; *Rock Radio Vietnam-C* . . . . (K-Tel)
   Super Hits Of The '70s-Have A Nice Day-#3-C . . . . (Rhino)

Never Kill Another Man
Steve Miller Band; *Steve Miller Band-Anthology* . . . . (Capitol)
   Steve Miller Band-Number 5 . . . . (Capitol)

New World Man
Rush; *Rush-Chronicles* . . . . (Mercury)
   Signals . . . . (Mercury)
   Three Decades Of Rock ('60s, '70s, '80s)-C . . . . (Priority)

New York Boy
Neil Diamond; *Glory Road-1968-1972* . . . . (MCA)
   Touching You Touching Me . . . . (MCA)

New York's A Lonely Town
Tradewinds; *Beach Classics-All Original*
   Recordings-C . . . . (Dunhill Compact Classics)
   Original Golden Hits Of The Great Groups-#1-C . . . . (SSS International)
   Surfin' Hits-C . . . . (Rhino)

No Man's Land
Billy Joel; *River Of Dreams* . . . . (Columbia)

No Man's Land
John Michael Montgomery; *John Michael Montgomery* . . . . (Atlantic)

No Man's Woman
Sinead O'Connor; *Faith & Courage* . . . . (Atlantic)

No Scrubs
TLC; *Fanmail* . . . . (LaFace)
   Totally Hits-#1-C . . . . (Arista)

Northern Lad
Tori Amos; *From The Choirgirl Hotel* . . . . (Atlantic)

Nowhere Man
Beatles; *"Yesterday"...And Today* . . . . (Capitol)
   Beatles-Box Set . . . . (Capitol)
   Compact Disc Singles Collection . . . . (Capitol)
   The Beatles/1962-1966 . . . . (Capitol)

O Lucky Man
Alan Price; *ST/O Lucky Man* . . . . (Warner Bros.)
Animals; *Greatest Hits Live!-Rip It To Shreds* . . . . (I.R.S.)

Oklahoma Boy
Dewayne Boyd & The Silver Dollar Band;
   45-#162 . . . .(Nationwide Sound Distrib.)

Old Man
Neil Young; *Decade* . . . .(Reprise)
   Harvest . . . .(Reprise)

Old Man
Alabama; *Just Us* . . . .(RCA)

Old Man
Randy Newman; *Sail Away* . . . .(Reprise)

Old Man
ZZ Top; *Six Pack* . . . . (Warner Bros.)
   ZZ Top . . . . (Warner Bros.)

Old Man & Me
J.J. Cale; *Okie* . . . . (MCA)

Old Man And Me
Hootie & The Blowfish; *Fairweather Johnson* . . . . (Atlantic)

Old Man Down The Road
John Fogerty; *Centerfield* . . . . (Warner Bros.)

Old Man From The Mountain
Merle Haggard & The Strangers; *For The Record: Merle Haggard-43*
   Legendary Hits . . . . (BNA)

Old Man On The Farm
Randy Newman; *Little Criminals* . . . . (Warner Bros.)

One And Only Man
Steve Winwood; *Refugees Of The Heart* . . . .(Virgin)

One Boy
Ann-Margret; *ST/Bye Bye Birdie* . . . .(RCA)

One Boy, One Girl
Collin Raye; *Best Of Collin Raye-Direct Hits* . . . . (Epic)
   I Think About You . . . . (Epic)

One Good Man
Michelle Wright; *The Reasons Why* . . . . (Arista)

One Man Army
Our Lady Peace; *Happiness...Is Not A Fish That You Can Catch* . . . .(Columbia)

One Man Band
Moe Bandy; *Moe Bandy's Greatest Hits* . . . .(Curb)
   You Haven't Heard The Last Of Me . . . . (MCA)

One Man Band
Roger Daltrey; *Daltrey* . . . . (MCA)

One Man Band
Three Dog Night; *Joy To The World-Greatest Hits* . . . . (MCA)

One Man Woman
Judds; *Judds-Collection 1983-1990* . . . . (RCA)
   River Of Time . . . . (RCA)

One Woman Man
Dave Hollister; *Chicago '85 The Movie* . . . .(Def Squad/DreamWorks)

Only Living Boy In New York
Simon & Garfunkel; *Bridge Over Troubled Water* . . . .(Columbia)
   Collected Works . . . .(Columbia)

Ordinary Average Guy
Joe Walsh; *Ordinary Average Guy.* . . . .(Epic Portrait Assoc.)

Other Guy
Little River Band; *Little River Band's Greatest Hits* . . . . (Capitol)

Other Man's Grass Is Always Greener
Petula Clark; *Petula Clark's Greatest Hits* . . . . (Crescendo)

Outlaw Man
Eagles; *Desperado* . . . . (Asylum)

Pale September
Fiona Apple; *Tidal* . . . . (Clean Slate/Work)

Part Man, Part Monkey
Bruce Springsteen; *Tracks* . . . .(Columbia)

Peppermint Man
Dick Dale And The Del-Tones; *Dick Dale And The Del-Tones'*
   Greatest Hits . . . . (Crescendo)

Phone Booth Man
Tuff Darts; *Tuff Darts.* . . . . (Sire)

Piano Lesson & If You Don't Mind My Saying So
Shirley Jones; *ST/The Music Man* . . . .(Warner Bros.)

Piano Man
Billy Joel; *Billy Joel-Greatest Hits, Volume I & Volume II* . . . .(Columbia)
   Piano Man . . . .(Columbia)
   Rock Classics Of The '70s-C . . . .(Columbia)

Piano Man
Thelma Houston; *Motown Superstar Series-#20-Thelma Houston* . . . .(Motown)

Pickup Man
Joe Diffie; *Third Rock From The Sun* . . . . (Epic)

Pictures Of Matchstick Men
Camper Van Beethoven; *Edge Of Rock-C* . . . . (Era)
   Key Lime Pie . . . . (Virgin)
Status Quo; *History Of British Rock-#8-C* . . . .(Rhino)
   Sixties Rule! Chapter 1-C . . . . (One Way)

Please Mr. Jailer
Wynona Carr; *Jump Jack Jump!* . . . . (Specialty)

Please Mr. Please
Olivia Newton-John; *Back To Basics-Essential Collection 1971-1992* . . (Geffen)

Poetry Man
Phoebe Snow; *Best Of Phoebe Snow* . . . . (Columbia)
   Phoebe Snow . . . . (MCA)

Policeman
Chicago; *Chicago XI* . . . . (Chicago)

Pony Boy
Allman Brothers Band; *Brothers & Sisters* . . . . (Polydor)

Pony Boy
Bruce Springsteen; *Human Touch* . . . .(Columbia)

Pony Man
Gordon Lightfoot; *Gord's Gold-#2* . . . .(Warner Bros.)
   If You Could Read My Mind . . . . (Reprise)
   Sit Down Young Stranger . . . . (Reprise)

Poor Boy
Howlin' Wolf; *Real Folk Blues-C* . . . .(Chess)

Poor Boy
Royaltones; *Rock Instrumental Classics-#1-'50s-C.* . . . .(Rhino)

Poor Boy
Woody Guthrie; *Legendary Woody Guthrie* . . . . (Tradition)
   Woody Guthrie . . . .(Everest)
   Worried Man Blues-Golden Classics-#1 . . . .(Collectables)

Poor Boy
Elvis Presley; *Essential Elvis-The First Movies* . . . . (RCA)
   For LP Fans Only . . . . (RCA)

Poor Boy
Split Enz; *History Never Repeats-Best Of Split Enz* . . . .(A&M)
   True Colours . . . .(A&M)

Poor Boy
Nick Drake; *Bryter Layter* . . . . (Hannibal)
   Fruit Tree . . . . (Hannibal)

Poor Boy
Champion Jack Dupree; *Forever & Ever* . . . .(Bullseye Blues)

Poor Boy
Supertramp; *Crisis? What Crisis?* . . . .(A&M)

Poor Boy
Fabulous Thunderbirds; *T-Bird Rhythm* . . . .(Chrysalis)
Poor Boy Blues
Chet Atkins & Mark Knopfler; *Neck And Neck*. . . . . (Columbia)
Poor Boy Shuffle
Creedence Clearwater Revival; *1969* . . . . (Fantasy)
Willy & The Poor Boys. . . . . (Fantasy)
Poor Little Orphaned Boy
Carter Family; *Their Complete Victor Recordings-Gold Watch And Chain-*
1933-1934 . . . . (Rounder)
Poor Man
Tom Rush; *Tom Rush* . . . . (Elektra)
Poor Man's Roses (Or A Rich Man's Gold)
Patsy Cline; *Best Of Patsy Cline*. . . . . (Curb)
Forever & Always . . . .(Epic)
Stop, Look & Listen . . . .(MCA)
The Patsy Cline Story . . . .(MCA)
Reba McEntire; *Feel The Fire* . . . . (Mercury)
Poor Man's Son
Rockin' Berries; *History Of British Rock-#2-C* . . . . (Rhino)
Postman Blues
Dinah Washington; *Complete Dinah Washington On Mercury-#1-1946-*
1949 . . . . (Mercury)
Potential New Boyfriend
Dolly Parton; *Best Of Dolly Parton-#3* . . . . (RCA)
Pow Wow The Indian Boy
Hot Rize; *Hot Rize* . . . . (Flying Fish)
Power Of Love
Celine Dion; *All The Way...A Decade Of Song*. . . . .(550 Music)
The Colour Of My Love . . . .(550 Music)
Powerman
Kinks; *Lola Versus Powerman And The Moneygoround, Part One* . . . . (Reprise)
Preacher Man
Bananarama; *Pop Life*. . . . . (London)
Preacher Man
Bananarama; *Pop Life*. . . . . (London)
Pretty Fly (For A White Guy)
Offspring; *Americana*. . . . . (Columbia)
Pretzel Man
Harry Chapin; *Legends Of The Lost & Found*. . . . . (Elektra)
Pride Of Man
Quicksilver Messenger Service; *Quicksilver Messenger Service* . . . . . . (Capitol)
Quicksilver Messenger Service-Anthology . . . . (Capitol)
San Francisco Nights-C. . . . . (Rhino)
Sons Of Mercury . . . . (Rhino)
Private Conversation
Lyle Lovett; *The Road To Ensenada*. . . . .(MCA)
Promised Land
Bruce Springsteen; *Darkness On The Edge Of Town* . . . . (Columbia)
Bruce Springsteen & The E Street Band; *Bruce Springsteen & The E Street*
Band Live/1975-85 . . . . (Legacy)
Psycho Man
Black Sabbath; *Reunion* . . . .(Epic)
Puppet Man
5th Dimension; *Greatest Hits On Earth* . . . . (Arista)
Pusherman
Curtis Mayfield; *Pimps, Players & Private Eyes-C* . . . . (Sire)
Radio M.U.S.I.C. Man
Womack & Womack; *Radio M.U.S.I.C. Man* . . . . (Elektra)
Radio Man
World's Famous Supreme Team; *45-#99683* . . . . (Island)
Railroad Boy
Joan Baez; *Ballad Book-#2*. . . . . (Vanguard)
Joan Baez, Vol. 2 . . . . (Vanguard)
Very Best Of Joan Baez . . . . (Vanguard)
Rainy Day Man
Bonnie Raitt; *Streetlights* . . . .(Warner Bros.)
James Taylor; *Flag* . . . . (Columbia)
James Taylor . . . . (Capitol)
Tom Rush; *Tom Rush* . . . . (Columbia)
Ramblin' Boy
Tom Paxton; *Greatest Folksingers Of The '60s-C* . . . . (Vanguard)
Newport Broadside: Newport Folk Festival-1963-C. . . . . (Vanguard)
Ramblin' Boy. . . . . (Elektra)
Troubadours Of The Folk Era-#2-C . . . . (Rhino)
Ramblin' Gamblin' Man
Bob Seger; *Live Bullet* . . . . (Capitol)
Ramblin' Man
Allman Brothers Band; *Best Of The Allman Brothers Band* . . . . (Polydor)
Billboard Top Rock 'N' Roll Hits-1973-C . . . . (Rhino)
Brothers & Sisters . . . . (Polydor)
Decade Of Hits-1969-1979 . . . . (Polydor)
Dreams . . . . (Polydor)
Rock Classics-C . . . . (K-Tel)
South's Greatest Hits-C . . . . (Capricorn)
The Road Goes On Forever, A Collection Of Their Greatest
Recordings . . . . (Polydor)
Wipe The Windows-Check The Oil-Dollar Gas . . . . (Capricorn)

Ramblin' Man
Hank Williams; *24 Of Hank Williams' Greatest Hits* . . . .(Polydor)
Hank Williams-16 Great Hits. . . . . (Everest)
Hank Williams-40 Greatest Hits. . . . . (Polydor)
Hank Williams, Jr.; *Rowdy* . . . . (WB/Curb)
ST/Your Cheatin' Heart . . . .(Sony Music Special Prod.)
Kieran Kane; *Steel Rails-Classic Railroad Songs-#1-C* . . . . (Rounder)
Rambling Irishman
De Danann; *Best Of De Danann* . . . .(Shanachie)
Rastaman Chant
Wailers; *Burnin'* . . . .(Tuff Gong)
Real Man
Todd Rundgren; *Back To The Bars* . . . . (Rhino)
Todd Rundgren-Anthology 1968-1985 . . . . (Rhino)
Real Man
Bruce Springsteen; *Human Touch*. . . . . (Columbia)
Real Man
Bonnie Raitt; *Nick Of Time* . . . . (Capitol)
Red Headed Irishman
J.P. Fraley & Annadeene; *Wild Rose Of The Mountain* . . . . (Rounder)
Redneck Fiddlin' Man
Charlie Daniels Band; *Greatest Fiddlin' Licks* . . . . (Epic)
Midnight Wind . . . . (Epic)
Rhumba Man
Jesse Winchester; *Best Of Jesse Winchester* . . . . (Rhino)
Nothing But The Breeze . . . . (Rhino)
Rich Man
Great Plains; *Great Plains*. . . . . (Columbia)
Rich Man Poor Man
Peter, Paul & Mary; *Late Again*. . . . . (Warner Bros.)
Rich Man, Poor Boy
Joe Ely; *Dig All Night* . . . .(Hightone)
Rich Man's Frug
Original Cast; *Sweet Charity*. . . . . (Columbia)
Rich Man's Spiritual
Gordon Lightfoot; *Lightfoot* . . . . (EMI)
Richest Man In Bogota
Gil Melle; *Mindscape* . . . . (Blue Note)
Richest Man On Earth
Paul Overstreet; *Sowin' Love* . . . . (RCA)
Ricky Wants A Man Of Her Own
Bruce Springsteen; *Tracks* . . . . (Columbia)
Riflemen Of Bennington
Jim Burroughs; *Songs Of Rebellion*. . . . . (Audio Fidelity)
Right Hand Man
Eddy Raven; *Best Of Eddy Raven* . . . . (RCA)
Right Hand Man . . . . (RCA)
River And The Highway
Pam Tillis; *All Of This Love* . . . . (Arista)
Pam Tillis' Greatest Hits . . . . (Arista)
River Boy
Willie Nelson; *There'll Be No Teardrops Tonight* . . . .(United Artists)
Road Of Broken Hearted Men
Bobby Bland; *Introspective Of The Early Years* . . . . (MCA)
Touch Of The Blues . . . . (MCA)
Robot Man
Scorpions; *Best Of The Scorpions* . . . . (RCA)
In Trance . . . . (RCA)
Tokyo Tapes . . . . (RCA)
Robot Man
Connie Francis; *Rocksides-1957-1964* . . . .(Polydor)
Rock & Roll Man
Kenny Rogers; *Daytime Friends*. . . . . (EMI)
Rock & Roll Man
Savoy Brown; *Savage Return* . . . . (London)
Rocket Man
Elton John; *Elton John's Greatest Hits* . . . .(Polydor)
Here And There . . . . (Rocket)
Honky Chateau . . . . (Rocket)
Kate Bush; *Two Rooms-Celebrating The Songs Of Elton John & Bernie*
Taupin-C . . . . (Polydor)
Rockit Man
J.T.; *Kick The Funk* . . . . (East West)
Rootsman Skanking
Bunny Wailer; *Rootsman Skanking*. . . . .(Shanachie)
Rough Boy
ZZ Top; *Afterburner* . . . . (Warner Bros.)
ZZ Top's Greatest Hits . . . . (Warner Bros.)
Rough Boys
Pete Townshend; *Classic Rock 1966-1988-C* . . . .(Atlantic)
Empty Glass . . . . (Atco)
Who; *Join Together* . . . . (MCA)
Rubberband Man
Spinners; *Best Of The Spinners* . . . .(Atlantic)
Mega Hits Dance Classics-#9-C . . . . (Priority)
One Of A Kind Love Affair-Anthology . . . . (Rhino)

Rude Boy Train
Desmond Dekker & The Aces; *Rockin' Steady-Best Of Desmond Dekker & The Aces*. . . . . (Rhino)
Sailor Boy
Chiffons; *Best Of The Chiffons* . . . .(Laurie)
Satisfied Man
Molly Hatchet; *Double Trouble-Live* . . . . (Epic)
The Deed Is Done . . . . (Epic)
Saturday Boy
Billy Bragg; *Back To Basics* . . . . (Elektra)
Say Man
Bo Diddley; *Bo Diddley-His Best* . . . . (Chess)
Cruisin'-1959-C . . . . (Increase)
School Boy Crush
Average White Band; *Cut The Cake* . . . . (Atlantic)
Person To Person . . . . (Atlantic)
Scotsman
Bryan Bowers; *Dr. Demento Presents The Greatest Novelty Records-#5-1980s-C* . . . . (Rhino)
Dr. Demento: 20th Anniversary Collection-C . . . . (Rhino)
Home Home On The Road . . . . (Flying Fish)
Secret Agent Man
Devo; *Duty Now For The Future* . . . . (Warner Bros.)
Johnny Rivers; *Best Of Johnny Rivers* . . . . (EMI)
Johnny Rivers-Anthology 1964-1977 . . . . (Rhino)
Television's Greatest Hits-#1-C . . . . (TVT)
Very Best Of Johnny Rivers . . . . (EMI)
See You In Hell, Blind Boy
Ry Cooder; *ST/Crossroads* . . . . (Warner Bros.)
Self Made Man
Montgomery Gentry; *Tattoos & Scars* . . . . (Columbia)
Sense Of Purpose
Pretenders; *Isle Of View* . . . . (Warner Bros.)
Packed . . . .(Sire)
Sensitive New Age Guys
Christine Lavin; *Attainable Love* . . . .(Philo)
Shadow Of A Lonely Man
Alan Parsons Project; *Pyramid* . . . . (Arista)
Sharp Dressed Man
ZZ Top; *Eliminator* . . . . (Warner Bros.)
ZZ Top's Greatest Hits . . . . (Warner Bros.)
She Gave Her Heart To A Soldier Boy
Roy Rogers; *The Country Music Hall Of Fame-Roy Rogers* . . . . (MCA)
She Misses Him
Tim Rushlow; *Tim Rushlow* . . . . (Atlantic)
She's In Love With A Rodeo Man
Chris LeDoux; *Songs Of Rodeo & Country* . . . . (Liberty)
Don Williams; *Don Williams' Greatest Hits* . . . . (MCA)
She's In Love With The Boy
Trisha Yearwood; *Trisha Yearwood* . . . . (MCA)
Shoe Salesman
Alice Cooper; *Easy Action* . . . . (Bizarre/Straight)
Shoeshine Boy
Count Basie & His Kansas City 7; *Count Basie & His Kansas City 7* . . . . (MCA/Impulse)
Eddie Kendricks; *Eddie Kendricks-At His Best* . . . . (Motown)
Motown Superstar Series-#19-Eddie Kendricks . . . . (Motown)
Shoeshine Man
Tom T. Hall; *Tom T. Hall's Greatest Hits-#1* . . . . (Mercury)
Shoot Him
Sugarcubes; *Here Today, Tomorrow Next Week!* . . . . (Elektra)
Showman's Life
Jesse Winchester; *Best Of Jesse Winchester* . . . . (Rhino)
Touch On The Rainy Side . . . . (Rhino)
Shy Guy
Diana King; *ST/Bad Boys* . . . . (Work)
Tougher Than Love . . . . (Work)
Silver Girl
Survivor; *Eye Of The Tiger* . . . . (Scotti Bros.)
Simple Man
Confederate Railroad; *Skynyrd Frynds-C* . . . . (MCA)
Hank Williams, Jr.; *Pure Hank* . . . . (WB/Curb)
Lynyrd Skynyrd; *Gold & Platinum* . . . . (MCA)
Lynyrd Skynyrd-Legend . . . . (MCA)
Pronounced Leh-nerd Skin-nerd. . . . . (MCA)
What's Your Name . . . . (MCA Special Prod.)
Simple Man
Crosby, Stills & Nash; *CSN.* . . . . (Atlantic)
Graham Nash; *Songs For Beginners* . . . . (Atlantic)
Simple Man
Barbra Streisand; *Butterfly.* . . . . (Columbia)
Simple Man
Junkyard; *Junkyard* . . . . (Geffen)
Simple Man
Bad Company; *Run With The Pack* . . . . (Swan Song)
Simple Man
Charlie Daniels; *Charlie Daniels' All-Time Greatest Hits* . . . . (Epic)
Country Greatest Hits-#3-C . . . . (Priority)

Charlie Daniels Band; *Simple Man* . . . . (Epic)
Simple Man Simple Dream
John David Souther; *Black Rose* . . . . (Asylum)
Linda Ronstadt; *Simple Dreams.* . . . . (Asylum)
Sixty Minute Man
Billy Ward & His Dominoes; *Rock & Roll Show-C* . . . . (Gusto)
Dominos; *Oldies But Goodies-#5-C.* . . . . (Original Sound)
Rufus Thomas & Carla Thomas; *Rufus Thomas & Carla Thomas-Chronicle* . . . . (Stax)
Skinny Boy
Chicago; *Chicago VII.* . . . . (Chicago)
Group Portrait . . . . (Chicago)
Sleep Tight, Good Night Man
Kenny Rogers; *The Gambler* . . . . (EMI)
Smashing Young Man
Collective Soul; *Collective Soul.* . . . . (Atlantic)
Smokin' In The Boy's Room
Brownsville Station; *Hit Singles-1958-1977-C* . . . . (Atlantic)
Legends Of Rock Guitar-'70s-C . . . . (Rhino)
ST/Rock 'N' Roll High School . . . . (Sire)
Motley Crue; *Decade Of Decadence* . . . . (Elektra)
Theatre Of Pain . . . . (Elektra)
Snake Man
Doobie Brothers; *Toulouse Street* . . . . (Warner Bros.)
Soldier Boy
Shirelles; *Billboard Top Rock 'N' Roll Hits-1962-C* . . . . (Rhino)
Oldies But Goodies-#4-C . . . . (Original Sound)
Shirelles-Anthology 1959-1964. . . . . (Rhino)
ST/The Wanderers. . . . . (Warner Bros.)
Soldier Boy
Small Faces; *78 In The Shade.* . . . . (Atlantic)
Soldier Boy
Elvis Presley; *A Golden Celebration* . . . . (RCA)
Elvis Is Back!. . . . . (RCA)
From Nashville To Memphis-The Essential '60s Masters . . . . . . (RCA)
Solitary Man
Chris Isaak; *San Francisco Days* . . . . (Reprise)
Neil Diamond; *Glory Road-1968-1972* . . . . (MCA)
Hot August Night. . . . . (MCA)
Neil Diamond-Classics (Early Years) . . . . (Columbia)
Neil Diamond-Gold. . . . . (MCA)
Neil Diamond's Greatest Hits-1966-1992. . . . . (Columbia)
Some Girls Do
Sawyer Brown; *Dirt Road* . . . . (Curb)
Some Guys Have All The Love
Little Texas; *First Time For Everything.* . . . . (Warner Bros.)
Some Guys Have All The Luck
Maxi Priest; *Best Of Me* . . . . (Charisma)
Maxi . . . . (Virgin)
Robert Palmer; *Addictions-#1* . . . . (Island)
Rod Stewart; *Camouflage* . . . . (Warner Bros.)
Storyteller/The Complete Anthology: 1964-1990 . . . . . (Warner Bros.)
Somebody Else's Guy
Jocelyn Brown; *Somebody Else's Guy* . . . . (Vinyl Dreams)
Somebody's Knockin'
Terri Gibbs; *Best Of Terri Gibbs* . . . . (MCA)
Country Gold-C. . . . . (Priority)
Country Music Classics-#6-1980-1985-C. . . . . (K-Tel)
Someday Soon
Chris LeDoux; *Rodeo Songs Old & New* . . . . (Liberty)
Ian & Sylvia; *Ian & Sylvia's Greatest Hits* . . . . (Vanguard)
Northern Journey . . . . (Vanguard)
Judy Collins; *Colors Of The Day-The Best Of Judy Collins* . . . . (Elektra)
Who Knows Where The Time Goes . . . . (Elektra)
Moe Bandy; *Moe Bandy's Greatest Hits* . . . . (Columbia)
Rodeo Romeo . . . . (Columbia)
Suzy Bogguss; *Aces* . . . . (Liberty)
Suzy Bogguss' Greatest Hits . . . . (Liberty)
Son Of A Poor Man
REO Speedwagon; *A Decade Of Rock And Roll 1970 To 1980* . . . . (Epic)
REO Speedwagon Live/You Get What You Play For . . . . (Epic)
Ridin' The Storm Out. . . . . (Epic)
Son Of A Preacher Man
Dusty Springfield; *Dusty Springfield* . . . . (Rhino)
Dusty Springfield-Anthology. . . . . (Mercury)
Song Of The Volga Boatmen
Glenn Miller; *Best Of Glenn Miller* . . . . (RCA)
Chattanooga Choo Choo-#1 Hits . . . . (Bluebird)
Glenn Miller-A Legendary Performer-#1 & 2. . . . . (Bluebird)
Memorial-1944-1969 . . . . (Bluebird)
This Is Glenn Miller. . . . . (RCA)
Tuxedo Junction; *Tuxedo Junction.* . . . . (Butterfly)
Soul Man
Blues Brothers; *Best Of The Blues Brothers.* . . . . (Atlantic)
Blues Brothers-The Definitive Collection . . . . (Atlantic)
Briefcase Full Of Blues . . . . (Atlantic)
Sam & Dave; *Best Of Sam & Dave.* . . . . (Atlantic)
Golden Age Of Black Music-1960-1970-C . . . . (Atlantic)
Soul Men. . . . . (Rhino)

Spaceboy
Smashing Pumpkins; *Siamese Dream* . . . . (Virgin)
Spaceman
Journey; *Journey-In The Beginning* . . . . (Columbia)
Next . . . . (Columbia)
Spaceman
Nilsson; *Son Of Schmilsson* . . . . (RCA)
Songwriter . . . . (RCA)
Spilled Perfume
Pam Tillis; *Sweetheart's Dance* . . . . (Arista)
Spirit Of A Boy, Wisdom Of A Man
Randy Travis; *Big Country Hits '99-C* . . . . (K-Tel)
You And You Alone . . . . (DreamWorks/SKG)
Stand Beside Me
Jo Dee Messina; *Big Country Hits '99-C* . . . . (K-Tel)
I'm Alright . . . . (Curb)
Stand By Your Man
Elton John; *Tammy Wynette...Remembered-C* . . . . (Asylum)
Lyle Lovett and his Large Band; *Lyle Lovett and his Large Band* . . . . (Curb/MCA)
Tammy Wynette; *Columbia Country Classics-#4-Nashville Sound-C* . . . . (Columbia)
ST/Sleepless In Seattle . . . . (Epic/Sony Music Soundtrax)
Tammy Wynette's Biggest Hits . . . . (Epic)
Tears Of Fire-25th Anniversary Collection . . . .(Epic)
Starman
David Bowie; *Changestwobowie* . . . . (RCA)
Fame & Fashion . . . . (RCA)
Rise & Fall Of Ziggy Stardust And The Spiders From Mars . . . . . . (Rykodisc)
The Singles-1969-1993 . . . . (Rykodisc)
Station Man
Fleetwood Mac; *25 Years-The Chain* . . . . (Warner Bros.)
Kiln House . . . . (Reprise)
Stone Cold Gentleman
Ralph Tresvant; *Ralph Tresvant* . . . . (MCA)
Stories For Boys
U2; *Boy* . . . . (Island)
Stout-Hearted Men
Barbra Streisand; *Simply Streisand* . . . . (Columbia)
Strawberry Wine
Deana Carter; *Did I Shave My Legs For This?* . . . . (Capitol)
Street Fighting Man
Rod Stewart; *Best Of Rod Stewart* . . . . (Mercury)
Sing It Again, Rod . . . . (Mercury)
Storyteller/The Complete Anthology: 1964-1990 . . . . . .(Warner Bros.)
Rolling Stones; *Beggars Banquet* . . . . (Abkco)
Get Yer Ya-Ya's Out! . . . . (Abkco)
Hot Rocks 1964-1971 . . . . (Abkco)
Singles Collection-The London Years . . . . (Abkco)
Through The Past, Darkly (Big Hits Vol. 2) . . . . (Abkco)
String Man
Mamas & The Papas; *Deliver* . . . .(MCA)
Stringman
Neil Young; *Neil Young-Unplugged* . . . . (Reprise)
Strong Enough
Sheryl Crow; *Tuesday Night Music Club* . . . . (A&M)
Struggling Man
Jimmy Cliff; *In Concert-Best Of Jimmy Cliff* . . . . (Reprise)
Struggling Man . . . . (Island)
Stubborn Kind Of Fellow
Marvin Gaye; *Marvin Gaye-Anthology* . . . . (Motown)
Marvin Gaye's Greatest Hits . . . . (Motown)
Superhits . . . . (Motown)
Suicidal Man
Uriah Heep; *Wonderworld* . . . . (Sequel)
Summer Boy
Buffy Sainte-Marie; *Best Of Buffy Sainte-Marie* . . . . . . (Vanguard)
Sun Hasn't Set On This Boy Yet
Nils Lofgren; *Nils Lofgren* . . . . (Rykodisc)
Nils Lofgren-Classics-#13 . . . . (A&M)
Superman (It's Not Easy)
Five For Fighting; *America Town* . . . .(Aware/C2/Columbia)
The Concert For New York City-C . . . . (Columbia)
Supermen
David Bowie; *Hunky Dory* . . . . (Rykodisc)
Man Who Sold The World . . . . (Rykodisc)
Sound + Vision . . . . (Rykodisc)
Sure The Boy Was Green
Horslips; *Aliens* . . . . (DJM)
Sweet Gingerbread Man
Mike Curb Congregation; *Mike Curb Congregation's Greatest Hits* . . . . . (Curb)
Sweet Lover Man
Pointer Sisters; *Best Of The Pointer Sisters 1978-1981* . . . . (RCA)
Sweet & Soulful . . . . (RCA)
Sweet Man
Jelly Roll Morton; *The Piano Rolls* . . . . (Nonesuch)
Sweet Music Man
Dolly Parton; *Here You Come Again* . . . .(Dunhill Compact Classics)

Kenny Rogers; *Daytime Friends* . . . . (EMI)
Reba McEntire; *Reba McEntire's Greatest Hits-#3: I'm A Survivor* . . . . . (MCA)
Sweet Music Man
Millie Jackson; *Get It Out'cha System* . . . . (Spring)
Live & Uncensored . . . . (Spring)
Sweet Music Man
Nana Mouskouri; *Song For Liberty* . . . . (Mercury)
Sweet Talkin' Guy
Chiffons; *Best Of The Chiffons* . . . . (Laurie)
Chiffons-Golden Classics . . . . (Collectables)
Collectables Presents The History Of Rock-#1-C . . . . . (Collectables)
Everything You Always Wanted . . . . (Laurie)
Swiss Boy
Michigan Dutchmen; *German Polka Favorites* . . . . (Jay Jay)
Swiss Boy Waltz
Michigan Dutchmen; *German Polka Favorites* . . . . (Jay Jay)
Take Him Back, Rachel
Basia; *London Warsaw New York* . . . . (Epic)
Take It Like A Man
Michelle Wright; *Now & Then* . . . . (Arista)
Today's Top Country-C . . . . (K-Tel)
Taker, The
Kris Kristofferson; *The Silver Tongued Devil And I* . . . . (Columbia)
Waylon Jennings; *Essential Waylon Jennings* . . . . (RCA)
Only Daddy That'll Walk The Line-The RCA Years . . . . . (RCA)
Tattoos & Scars
Montgomery Gentry; *Tattoos & Scars* . . . . (Columbia)
Taxman
Beatles; *Beatles-Box Set* . . . . (Capitol)
Revolver . . . . (Capitol)
Rock 'N' Roll Music . . . . (Capitol)
George Harrison; *Best Of George Harrison* . . . . (Capitol)
Live In Japan . . . . (Dark Horse)
Taxman Mr. Thief
Cheap Trick; *Cheap Trick* . . . . (Epic)
Telephone Man
Meri Wilson; *First Take* . . . . (GRT)
Super Hits Of The '70s-Have A Nice Day-#21-C . . . . . . (Rhino)
Television Man
Talking Heads; *Little Creatures* . . . . (Sire)
Tell Him
Barbra Streisand & Celine Dion; *Higher Ground* . . . . . (Columbia)
Celine Dion & Barbra Streisand; *Let's Talk About Love-C* . . . . .(550 Music)
Tell Him
Exciters; *Best Of The Girl Groups-#2-C* . . . . (Rhino)
ST/Big Chill . . . . (Motown)
ST/My Best Friend's Wedding . . . . (Work/Epic)
Tell Him . . . . (Collectables)
Patti Drew; *Tell Him-Golden Classics* . . . . (Collectables)
Vonda Shepard; *ST/Songs From ''Ally McBeal'' Featuring Vonda Shepard* . . . . (550/Epic)
Ten Cents A Dance
Eileen Farrell; *I Gotta Right To Sing The Blues* . . . . . .(Sony Music Classical)
Ella Fitzgerald; *Rodgers & Hart Songbook* . . . . (Verve)
Ten Dollar Man
ZZ Top; *Six Pack* . . . . (Warner Bros.)
Tejas . . . . (Warner Bros.)
Tennessee Flat Top Box
Johnny Cash; *Classic Cash-Hall Of Fame Series* . . . . . (Mercury)
Columbia Country Classics-#3-Americana-C . . . . (Columbia)
Essential Johnny Cash . . . . (Columbia)
The Man In Black-His Greatest Hits . . . . (Legacy)
Rosanne Cash; *30 Years Of #1 Hits-#17-C* . . . . (Columbia)
Hits-1979-1989 . . . . (Columbia)
King's Record Shop . . . . (Columbia)
Testosterone
Bush; *Sixteen Stone* . . . . (Trauma)
Texaco Star Theme
Original Soundtrack; *TeeVee Toons-The Commercials-#1-C* . . . . . (TVT)
Texas Fiddle Man
Asleep At The Wheel; *Keepin' Me Up Nights* . . . . (Arista)
Thank God I'm A Country Boy
John Denver; *Back Home Again* . . . . (RCA)
Evening With John Denver . . . . (RCA)
John Denver's Greatest Hits-#2 . . . . (RCA)
Thank You Boys
Jane's Addiction; *Nothing's Shocking* . . . . (Warner Bros.)
That Boy Could Dance
''Weird Al'' Yankovic; *In 3-D* . . . . (Scotti Bros.)
That Man From New York City
Lightnin' Hopkins; *Lost Texas Tapes-#1* . . . . (Collectables)
That Mister Man Of Mine
Original Off-Broadway Cast; *Dames At Sea* . . . . (Sony Music Classical)
That Rhythm Man
Louis Armstrong & His Orchestra; *Louis Armstrong & The Big Bands* . . . . (Disques Swing)
That's A Man's Way
Wilson Pickett; *A Man & A Half-Best Of Wilson Pickett* . . . . . . (Rhino)

In The Midnight Hour . . . . (Rhino)
That's My Baby
Lari White; *Wishes* . . . . (RCA)
That's The Way Boys Are
Lesley Gore; *Golden Hits Of Lesley Gore* . . . . (Mercury)
That's What He Said
Reba McEntire; *My Kind Of Country* . . . . (MCA)
That's What My Man Is For
Delaney & Bonnie; *Best Of Delaney & Bonnie* . . . . (Rhino)
Delaney & Bonnie & Friends On Tour With Eric Clapton . . . . (Rhino)
Theme From "The Man From U.N.C.L.E."
Challengers; *25 Greatest Instrumental Hits-C* . . . . (Crescendo)
Original Soundtrack; *Television's Greatest Hits-#1-C* . . . . (TVT)
The Man From U.N.C.L.E.: The Music From U.N.C.L.E. . . . . . . (Razor & Tie)
TV Classic Themes: 25th Anniversary Edition-C . . . . (Breakable)
Theme From "The Men"
Isaac Hayes; *Isaac Hayes' Greatest Hit Singles* . . . . (Stax)
Theme From "The Rifleman"
Cincinnati Pops Orchestra/Erich Kunzel; *Round-Up* . . . . (Telarc)
Original Soundtrack; *Television's Greatest Hits-#1-C* . . . . (TVT)
Theme From "The Single Guy"
Original Soundtrack; *Television's Greatest Hits-#7-Cable Ready-C* . . . . . (TVT)
Theme From "The Six Million Dollar Man"
Original Soundtrack; *Television's Greatest Hits-#5-In Living Color-C* . . . (TVT)
Then He Kissed Me
Crystals; *Best Of The Crystals* . . . . (Abkco)
Phil Spector-Back To Mono 1958-1969-C . . . . (Abkco)
There He Is (At My Door)
Martha Reeves & The Vandellas; *Live Wire! Singles-1962-1972* . . . . . (Motown)
Martha Reeves & The Vandellas-Anthology . . . . (Motown)
There Once Was A Man
Original Cast; *Pajama Game* . . . . (Columbia)
ST/Pajama Game . . . . (Collectables)
There's A Fella Waitin' In Poughkeepsie
Pied Pipers; *Capitol Collectors Series-Pied Pipers* . . . . (Capitol)
There's A Whole Lot About A Woman (A Man Don't Know)
Jack Greene; *45-#32823* . . . . (Decca)
They Call Me The Popcorn Man
Luther Johnson; *Lonesome In My Bedroom* . . . . (Evidence Music)
Third Man Theme (Harry Lime Theme)
Band; *Moondog Matinee* . . . . (Capitol)
Dukes Of Dixieland; *Dukes Of Dixieland's Greatest Hits* . . . . (MCA)
Guy Lombardo & His Royal Canadians; *Best Of Guy Lombardo* . . . . (Curb)
This Boy
Beatles; *Beatles-Box Set* . . . . (Capitol)
Beatles-Love Songs . . . . (Capitol)
Meet The Beatles! . . . . (Capitol)
Past Masters-Volume One . . . . (Parlophone)
The Beatles-Anthology-#1 . . . . (Capitol)
This Boy Needs To Rock
Night Ranger; *7 Wishes* . . . . (MCA)
ST/Explorers . . . . (Varese Sarabande)
This Guy's In Love With You
Burt Bacharach; *Burt Bacharach-Classics-#23* . . . . (A&M)
Burt Bacharach's Greatest Hits . . . . (A&M)
Herb Alpert & The Tijuana Brass; *Herb Alpert & The Tijuana Brass-Greatest Hits-#2* . . . . (A&M)
This Old Man
Dana; *Dana's Best Sing & Play-Along Tunes!* . . . . (Real Music For Kidz)
Original Soundtrack; *Children's Favorites* . . . . (Kid Rhino/Rhino 4 Kids)
This Woman And This Man
Clay Walker; *If I Could Make A Living* . . . . (Giant)
Thoroughly African Man
Red Clay Ramblers; *Chuckin' The Frizz* . . . . (Flying Fish)
Tin Man, The
Kenny Chesney; *In My Wildest Dreams* . . . . (Capricorn)
To Ev'ry Girl-To Ev'ry Boy (The Meaning Of Love)
Johnnie Ray; *45-#40252* . . . . (Columbia)
To Sir With Love
Lulu; *History Of British Rock-#6-C* . . . . (Rhino)
Hollywood Magic-1960s-C . . . . (Columbia)
Rock Artifacts-From The Vaults-#3-C . . . . (Columbia)
Torn
Natalie Imbruglia; *Left Of The Middle* . . . . (RCA)
Train Man
Bob Seger System; *Ramblin' Gamblin' Man* . . . . (Capitol)
Trash Man
Jimi Hendrix; *Midnight Lightning* . . . . (Reprise)
Trashmen
Phantom Opera; *Phantom Opera* . . . . (New Allegiance)
Travelin' Man
Lynyrd Skynyrd; *Live From Steel Town* . . . . (CMC Int'l)
One More From The Road . . . . (MCA)
Travelin' Man
Ricky Nelson; *Best Of Ricky Nelson* . . . . (EMI)
Rick Nelson's Greatest Hits . . . . (Rhino)
Travelin' Man
Doobie Brothers; *Doobie Brothers* . . . . (Warner Bros.)

Travelin' Man
Albert King; *I Wanna Get Funky* . . . . (Stax)
Travelin' Man
Bob Seger; *Beautiful Loser* . . . . (Capitol)
Live Bullet . . . . (Capitol)
Travelin' Man
Jacky Ward; *45-#47424* . . . . (Asylum)
Travelin' Man
Stevie Wonder; *Stevie Wonder's Greatest Hits-#2* . . . . (Motown)
Traveling Man
Dolly Parton; *Best Of Dolly Parton* . . . . (RCA)
Coat Of Many Colors . . . . (RCA)
Travelling Man
Simple Minds; *Real Life* . . . . (A&M)
Trouble Man
Grover Washington, Jr.; *Grover Washington, Jr.-Anthology* . . . . (Motown)
Soul Box-#1 . . . . (Motown)
Marvin Gaye; *Every Great Motown Hit Of Marvin Gaye* . . . . (Motown)
Marvin Gaye Live At The London Palladium . . . . (Motown)
Marvin Gaye-Anthology . . . . (Motown)
Marvin Gaye's Greatest Hits . . . . (Motown)
ST/Trouble Man . . . . (Motown)
Truck Drivin' Man
Commander Cody & His Lost Planet Airmen; *Hot Licks, Cold Steel & Trucker's Favorites* . . . . (MCA)
Too Much Fun-Best Of Commander Cody & His Lost Planet Airmen . . . (MCA)
J. Geils Band; *Blow Your Face Out* . . . . (Rhino)
Truck Drivin' Man
Flying Burrito Brothers; *Close Encounters To The West Coast* . . . . (Relix)
Truck Drivin' Man
Hank Wilson; *Hank Wilson's Back, Vol. 1* . . . . (Right Stuff)
Truck Drivin' Man
Larry Scott; *Keep On Truckin'* . . . . (Exact)
Truck Drivin' Man
Lynyrd Skynyrd; *Lynyrd Skynyrd-Legend* . . . . (MCA)
Truck Drivin' Man
Charlie Walker; *Trucker's Jukebox-#2-C* . . . . (Legacy)
Truck Drivin' Son Of A Gun
Boxcar Willie; *Truck Driving Favorites* . . . . (Madacy)
Dave Dudley; *20 Golden Souvenirs Of Music City U.S.A.-C* . . . . . (Plantation)
Billboard Top Country Hits-1965-C . . . . (Rhino)
Truck Driving Man
Terry Fell & The Fellers; *Truck Driver Boogie Big Rig Hits-1939-1969-C* . . . . (Audium)
Truckdrivin' Man
Boxcar Willie; *Truck Driving Favorites* . . . . (Madacy)
True Men Don't Kill Coyotes
Red Hot Chili Peppers; *Abbey Road E.P.* . . . . (EMI)
Red Hot Chili Peppers . . . . (EMI)
What Hits!? . . . . (EMI)
Try To Find Another Man
Righteous Brothers; *Righteous Brothers-Anthology 1962-1974* . . . . . . (Rhino)
TV Preacher Man Blues
Glenn Sutton; *Close Encounters Of The Sutton Kind* . . . . (Mercury)
Tweeter & The Monkey Man
Traveling Wilburys; *The Traveling Wilburys* . . . . (Wilbury/Warner Bros.)
Twelve Volt Man
Jimmy Buffett; *Boats Beaches Bars & Ballads* . . . . (Margaritaville)
One Particular Harbour . . . . (MCA)
Twelve Year Old Boy
Elmore James; *Collectables Blues Collection-#1-C* . . . . (Collectables)
Golden Classics-Elmore James . . . . (Collectables)
The Sky Is Crying-History Of Elmore James . . . . (Rhino)
Twentieth Century Man
Scorpions; *Animal Magnetism* . . . . (Mercury)
Twenty-First Century Schizoid Man
King Crimson; *Abbreviated* . . . . (Editions E.G.)
Compact . . . . (Editions E.G.)
In The Court Of The Crimson King-An Observation By King Crimson . . . . (Editions E.G.)
Two Gentlemen Of Peru
Simon & Bard Group; *Enormous Radio* . . . . (Flying Fish)
Two Headed Man
Lonnie Brooks; *Genuine Houserockin' Music-#3-C* . . . . (Alligator)
Two Lovers
Mary Wells; *Hitsville USA-The Motown Singles Collection-1959-1971-C* . . . . (Motown)
Mary Wells' Greatest Hits . . . . (Motown)
Two-Bit Man Child
Neil Diamond; *Glory Road-1968-1972* . . . . (MCA)
Velvet Gloves & Spit . . . . (MCA Special Prod.)
Typical Male
Tina Turner; *Break Every Rule* . . . . (Capitol)
Hot Ladies Of The '80s-C . . . . (K-Tel)
Live In Europe . . . . (Capitol)
Simply The Best . . . . (Capitol)
U.S. Male
Jerry Reed; *Best Of Jerry Reed* . . . . (RCA)

Umbrella Man
Kay Kyser & His Orchestra; *Sentimental Favorites* . . . . (Columbia)
Undercover Man
Edgar Winter Group; *They Only Come Out At Night* . . . .(Epic)
Understand Your Man
Johnny Cash; *Billboard Top Country Hits-1964-C*. . . . . (Rhino)
Johnny Cash's Greatest Hits . . . . (Columbia)
The Man In Black-His Greatest Hits . . . . (Legacy)
Unsent
Alanis Morissette; *Supposed Former Infatuation Junkie* . . . .(Maverick)
Up And Gone
McCarters; *Better Be Home Soon* . . . .(Warner Bros.)
Use The Man
Megadeth; *Cryptic Writings* . . . . (Capitol)
Vigilante Man
Bruce Springsteen; *Folkways: A Vision Shared-C* . . . . (Columbia)
Ry Cooder; *Into The Purple Valley* . . . . (Reprise)
Woody Guthrie; *Dust Bowl Ballads* . . . . (Rounder)
Virginia Boys
Country Gazette; *Hello Operator...This Is Country Gazette* . . . . . . (Flying Fish)
Strictly Instrumental . . . . (Flying Fish)
Voodoo Medicine Man
Aerosmith; *Pump* . . . .(Geffen)
Walk Like A Man
4 Seasons; *4 Seasons' Greatest Hits-#1* . . . . (Rhino)
4 Seasons-Anthology . . . . (Rhino)
Billboard Top Rock 'N' Roll Hits-1963-C . . . . (Rhino)
ST/The Wanderers . . . .(Warner Bros.)
Walk Like A Man
Bruce Springsteen; *Tunnel Of Love* . . . . (Columbia)
Walk Like A Man
Grand Funk Railroad; *We're An American Band* . . . . (Capitol)
Walking Dream
Patsy Cline; *Forever & Always*. . . . .(Epic)
Here's Patsy Cline. . . . .(MCA)
Walking Man
James Taylor; *James Taylor's Greatest Hits* . . . .(Warner Bros.)
Walking Man . . . .(Warner Bros.)
Wanted Man
Johnny Cash; *Essential Johnny Cash* . . . . (Columbia)
Johnny Cash At Folsom Prison & San Quentin . . . . (Columbia)
Wanted Man
George Thorogood & The Destroyers; *Bad To The Bone* . . . .(EMI)
Wanted Man
Ratt; *Out Of The Cellar*. . . . . (Atlantic)
Ratt & Roll 8191 . . . . (Atlantic)
War Of Man
Neil Young; *Harvest Moon*. . . . . (Reprise)
Water Boy
Roger Whittaker; *Last Farewell & Other Hits* . . . . (RCA)
New World In The Morning . . . . (RCA)
Water Boy
John Lee Hooker; *Country Blues Of John Lee Hooker* . . . .(Riverside)
Water Boy
Paul Robeson; *Historic Paul Robeson-Golden Classics-#3* . . . . . . (Collectables)
Waterfalls
TLC; *1996 Grammy Nominees-C* . . . . (Columbia)
CrazySexyCool . . . . (LaFace)
Watermelon Man
Albert King; *Wednesday Night In San Francisco* . . . .(Stax)
Buddy Guy; *Hold That Plane* . . . . (Vanguard)
Herbie Hancock; *Best Of Herbie Hancock-The Blue Note Years* . . . . (Blue Note)
Head Hunters . . . . (Columbia)
Takin' Off. . . . . (Blue Note)
Johnny Taylor; *Wanted One Soul Singer* . . . . (Atlantic)
Mongo Santamaria; *Mongo Santamaria's Greatest Hits* . . . . (Fantasy)
Mongo Santamaria's Greatest Hits . . . . (Columbia)
New Grass Revival; *Too Late To Turn Back Now* . . . . (Flying Fish)
Watermelon Man
Gun Club; *Miami* . . . .(I.R.S.)
Way He Makes Me Feel
Barbra Streisand; *Collection-Greatest Hits...And More*. . . . . (Columbia)
ST/Yentl . . . . (Columbia)
We Are Hungry Men
David Bowie; *David Bowie-London Collector-Starting Point* . . . . (London)
Starting Point. . . . . (Deram)
Well Fed Slave/Hungry Free Man
Lucky Dube; *Taxman* . . . . (Shanachie)
Well Respected Man
Kinks; *History Of British Rock-#4-C* . . . . (Rhino)
Kinks' Greatest Hits . . . . (Rhino)
Kinks-Size Kinkdom. . . . . (Rhino)
West Virginia Man
David Allan Coe; *20 Great Hits-C* . . . . (Plantation)
Willie Nelson; *Longhorn Jamboree* . . . . (Plantation)
Willie Nelson & His Friends . . . . (Plantation)
What Does A Woman See In A Man
Jimmy Webb; *Suspending Disbelief* . . . . (Elektra)

What Kind Of Man Would I Be
Mint Condition; *Definition Of A Band*. . . . . (Perspective/A&M)
What Kind Of Man Would I Be?
Chicago; *Chicago 19*. . . . . (Reprise)
Chicago's Greatest Hits-1982-1989 . . . .(Full Moon)
Whatta Man
Salt-N-Pepa featuring En Vogue; *Very
Necessary* . . . .(Next Plateau/London/Island)
When A Man Loves A Woman
Bette Midler; *ST/The Rose*. . . . .(Atlantic)
Michael Bolton; *Time, Love & Tenderness* . . . . (Columbia)
Percy Sledge; *Atlantic Rhythm & Blues 1947-1974-#5 (1962-
1966)-C* . . . .(Atlantic)
Atlantic Soul Classics-C. . . . . (Warner Special Prod.)
Best Of Percy Sledge . . . . (Atlantic)
Golden Age Of Black Music-1960-1970-C. . . . . (Atlantic)
ST/Platoon . . . . (Atlantic)
When A Man Loves A Woman
Barbara Mandrell; *Best Of Barbara Mandrell*. . . . . (Liberty)
Key's In The Mailbox . . . . (Capitol)
When A Woman Loves A Man
Lee Roy Parnell; *We All Get Lucky Sometimes* . . . .(Career)
When Boy Meets Girl
Terri Clark; *Terri Clark*. . . . . (Mercury)
When He Shines
Sheena Easton; *Sheena Easton's Greatest Hits* . . . . (EMI Special Markets)
The World Of Sheena Easton: The Singles Collection-C . . . . (EMI)
When I Grow Up (To Be A Man)
Beach Boys; *Absolute Best-#1*. . . . . (Capitol)
Beach Boys-Gift Set . . . . (Capitol)
Dance Dance Dance . . . . (Capitol)
Made In The U.S.A. . . . . (Capitol)
Spirit Of America . . . . (Capitol)
White Boys
Original Cast; *ST/Hair* . . . . (RCA)
White Man
Queen; *Day At The Races* . . . . (Hollywood)
White Man In Hammersmith Palais
Clash; *On Broadway* . . . . (Epic)
The Clash . . . . (Epic)
The Story Of The Clash, Volume 1 . . . . (Epic)
White Man/Black Man
James Gang; *James Gang-16 Greatest Hits* . . . . (MCA)
Thirds . . . . (One Way)
Who Is He And What Is He To You
Me'Shell Ndegeocello; *Peace Beyond Passion*. . . . . (Maverick)
Who Put The Bomp (In The Bomp, Bomp, Bomp)
Barry Mann; *Goofy Greats-C* . . . . (K-Tel)
Sixties Rule! Chapter Two-C . . . . (One Way)
Who's That Man
Toby Keith; *Boomtown* . . . .(Polydor Country)
Wild Boys
Duran Duran; *Arena* . . . . (Capitol)
Decade . . . . (Capitol)
Wild Eyed Boy From Freecloud
David Bowie; *Sound + Vision*. . . . . (Rykodisc)
Space Oddity . . . . (Rykodisc)
ST/Ziggy Stardust-The Motion Picture. . . . . (Rykodisc)
Wild Man
Ricky Van Shelton; *Ricky Van Shelton's Greatest Hits Plus* . . . . . . (Columbia)
Steppin' Country-C . . . . (Columbia)
Wild Man
J. Geils Band; *Flashback-Best Of The J. Geils Band*. . . . . (EMI)
Wild Man Blues
Jelly Roll Morton; *Jelly's Last Jam & Other Morton Classics* . . . . . . (Bluebird)
Louis Armstrong; *Louis Armstrong-Best Of The Decca Years-#2-The
Composer-C* . . . . (MCA)
Wild-Eyed Southern Boys
38 Special; *Wild-Eyed Southern Boys* . . . . (A&M)
Will You Be Loving Another Man
Bill Monroe & His Blue Grass Boys; *Essential Bill Monroe & His Blue
Grass Boys*. . . . . (Legacy)
Essential Bill Monroe-1945-1949 . . . . (Columbia)
Winter Boy
Buffy Sainte-Marie; *Best Of Buffy Sainte-Marie*. . . . . (Vanguard)
Little Wheel Spin & Spin. . . . . (Vanguard)
Without Expression
John Mellencamp; *Best That I Could Do-1978-1988* . . . . (Mercury)
Woman Behind The Man Behind The Wheel
Red Sovine; *Truckin' On-C*. . . . . (Hollywood)
Woman In Me (Needs The Man In You)
Shania Twain; *Woman In Me* . . . . (Mercury)
Woman's Worth, A
Alicia Keys; *Songs In A Minor* . . . . (J)
Wonderful Guy, A
Original Cast; *South Pacific* . . . . (CBS Masterworks)
Worker Man
PAtra; *Queen Of The Pack* . . . . (Epic)

Workin' Man
Creedence Clearwater Revival; *1968-1969* . . . .(Fantasy)
Creedence Clearwater Revival . . . .(Fantasy)
Workin' Man Blues
Diamond Rio/Lee Roy Parnell/Steve Wariner; *Mama's Hungry Eyes-Merle Haggard Tribute-C* . . . .(Arista)
Gary Morris; *These Days* . . . .(Capitol)
Merle Haggard & The Strangers; *Best Of Country Blues* . . . .(Curb)
Capitol Collectors Series-Merle Haggard & The Strangers . . . .(Capitol)
For The Record: Merle Haggard-43 Legendary Hits . . . .(BNA)
Okie From Muskogee . . . .(Capitol)
Songs I'll Always Sing . . . .(Capitol)
Ricky Van Shelton; *Wild-Eyed Dream* . . . .(Columbia)
Working Class Man
Jimmy Barnes; *Jimmy Barnes* . . . .(Geffen)
Lacy J. Dalton; *Highway Diner* . . . .(Columbia)
Working For The Man
Roy Orbison; *For The Lonely: A Roy Orbison Anthology 1959-1965* . . . . (Rhino)
In Dreams-Greatest Hits . . . .(Orbison)
Roy Orbison-More Greatest Hits . . . .(Monument)
Roy Orbison's All-Time Greatest Hits-#1 & 2 . . . .(Monument)
Working Man
Rush; *All The World's A Stage* . . . .(Mercury)
Archives . . . .(Mercury)
Rush . . . .(Mercury)
Rush-Chronicles . . . .(Mercury)
Working Man
John Conlee; *Blue Highway* . . . .(MCA)
John Conlee-20 Greatest Hits . . . .(MCA)
Songs For The Working Man . . . .(MCA)
Working Man
Otis Rush; *Mourning In The Morning* . . . . (Atlantic)
Working Man
Glenn Frey; *Soul Searchin'* . . . .(MCA)
Working Man Can't Get Nowhere Today
Merle Haggard; *18 Rare Classics* . . . .(Curb)
Merle Haggard & The Strangers; *Working Man Can't Get Nowhere Today* . . . .(Capitol)
Working Man's Ph.D.
Aaron Tippin; *Call Of The Wild* . . . .(RCA)
Would They Love Him Down In Shreveport
George Jones; *Hallelujah Weekend* . . . .(Epic)
Oak Ridge Boys; *Bobbie Sue* . . . .(MCA)
Yellow Man
Randy Newman; *12 Songs* . . . .(Reprise)
Randy Newman/Live . . . . (Warner Archives)
Yo Mister
Patti LaBelle; *Be Yourself* . . . .(MCA)
You And Me
Lorrie Morgan; *Tammy Wynette...Remembered-C* . . . .(Asylum)
Tammy Wynette; *Tammy Wynette-16 Biggest Hits* . . . .(Legacy)
Tammy Wynette-Anniversary-20 Years Of Hits . . . .(Epic)
Tammy Wynette-Super Hits . . . .(Epic)
You Can't Fool The Fat Man
Randy Newman; *Little Criminals* . . . . (Warner Bros.)
You Can't Get A Man With A Gun
Ethel Merman/Ray Middleton/Original Cast; *Annie Get Your Gun* . . . . . . (MCA)
Original Broadway Cast; *Annie Get Your Gun* . . . . (Angel)
You Made A Wanted Man Of Me
Ronnie McDowell; *19 Hot Country Requests-#2-C* . . . .(Epic)
Country Boy's Heart . . . .(Epic)
Older Women & Other Greatest Hits . . . .(Epic)
You Make Me Feel Like A Man
Ricky Skaggs; *Live In London* . . . .(Epic)
You Wouldn't Believe
311; *From Chaos* . . . . (Volcano Entertainment)
Young Man Blues
Who; *Live At Leeds* . . . .(MCA)
ST/The Kids Are Alright . . . .(MCA)
Young Man, Older Woman
Millie Jackson; *Very Best Of Millie Jackson* . . . .(Jive)
You're A Man Of Words, I'm A Woman
Betty LaVette; *Lost Soul-#1-C* . . . .(Epic)
You're My Man
Lynn Anderson; *Country Music Classics-#11-Early '70s-C* . . . .(K-Tel)
Lynn Anderson Anthology: The Columbia Years . . . .(Renaissance)
You're Still A Young Man
Tower Of Power; *Bump City* . . . .(Warner Bros.)
Live & In Living Color . . . .(Warner Bros.)

MEN'S NAMES: A

See Also: **CELEBRITIES: SPECIFIC, FAMILY (various), MEN: GENERAL**

Abraham, Martin And John
Dion; *Collectables Presents The History Of Rock-#3-C* . . . .(Collectables)

Dion-24 Original Classics . . . .(Arista)
Songs Of Protest-C . . . .(Rhino)
WCBS FM 101 History Of Rock-'60s-#2-C . . . .(Collectables)
Harry Belafonte; *Harry Belafonte's All Time Greatest Hits-#1* . . . . (RCA)
Smokey Robinson & The Miracles; *Smokey Robinson & The Miracles' Anthology* . . . .(Motown)
Time Out For Smokey Robinson & The Miracles/Special Occasion . . . .(Motown)
Adam Raised A Cain
Bruce Springsteen; *Darkness On The Edge Of Town* . . . .(Columbia)
Adam's Song
Blink-182; *Enema Of The State* . . . .(MCA)
Adrian
Jewel; *Pieces Of You* . . . . (Atlantic)
Ahab The Arab
Ray Stevens; *Best Of Ray Stevens* . . . .(Rhino)
Gitarzan . . . .(Barnaby)
Very Best Of Ray Stevens . . . .(Barnaby)
Alan's Psychedelic Breakfast
Pink Floyd; *Atom Heart Mother* . . . .(Capitol)
Alexander's Ragtime Band
Al Jolson & Bing Crosby; *Al Jolson Story-#1* . . . .(MCA)
Immortal Al Jolson . . . .(MCA)
Alfie
Barbra Streisand; *What About Today* . . . .(Columbia)
Dionne Warwick; *Dionne Warwick Greatest Hits* . . . .(Everest)
Dionne Warwick-Anthology 1962-1971 . . . .(Rhino)
Alvin For President
Alvin & The Chipmunks; *Greatest Hits: Still Squeaky After All These Years* . . . .(Capitol)
Amos Moses
Jerry Reed; *Best Of Jerry Reed* . . . . (RCA)
Nipper's Greatest Hits Of The '70s-C . . . . (RCA)
Super Hits Of The '70s-Have A Nice Day-#3-C . . . .(Rhino)
Andy's Birthday
Original Soundtrack; *ST/Toy Story* . . . . (Disney)
Arnold Layne
Pink Floyd; *Relics* . . . .(Capitol)
Works . . . .(Capitol)
Arthur
Hoodoo Gurus; *Stoneage Romeos* . . . .(A&M)
Arthur
Kinks; *Arthur Or The Decline And Fall Of The British Empire* . . . . (Reprise)
Arthur
Badfinger; *Magic Christian Music* . . . .(Capitol)
Arthur In The Afternoon
Liza Minnelli/Original Cast; *The Act* . . . . (DRG)
Arthur's Theme (Best That You Can Do)
Christopher Cross; *ST/Arthur* . . . .(Warner Bros.)
Brother, Can You Spare A Dime
Bing Crosby; *Bing Crosby-16 Most Requested Songs* . . . .(Legacy)
Odetta/Dr. John/John Campbell/Rufus Reid; *Strike A Deep Chord-Blues For The Homeless-C* . . . .(Justice)
Peter, Paul & Mary; *See What Tomorrow Brings* . . . .(Warner Bros.)
Weavers; *Weavers' Greatest Hits* . . . .(Vanguard)
Connecticut Yankee In The Court Of King Arthur
Robert Fripp & The League Of Crafty Guitarists; *Show Of Hands* . . . . (Editions E.G.)
Elvis And Andy
Confederate Railroad; *Confederate Railroad's Greatest Hits* . . . . (Atlantic)
Notorious . . . . (Atlantic)
Garden Of Allah
Don Henley; *Actual Miles: Henley's Greatest Hits* . . . . (Geffen)
Joe Avery
Preservation Hall Jazz Band; *Best Of The Preservation Hall Jazz Band* . . . .(Columbia)
Me & Little Andy
Dolly Parton; *Collector's Series-Dolly Parton* . . . . (RCA)
Dolly Parton's Greatest Hits . . . . (RCA)
Here You Come Again . . . . (Dunhill Compact Classics)
Night The Lights Went Out In Georgia (Andy)
Lynn Anderson; *Top Of The World* . . . .(Columbia)
Reba McEntire; *For My Broken Heart* . . . . (MCA)
Reba McEntire's Greatest Hits-#3: I'm A Survivor . . . . (MCA)
Vicki Lawrence; *Super Hits Of The '70s-Have A Nice Day-#10-C* . . . . . .(Rhino)
Poland Whole/Madam I'm Adam
Tubes; *Young And Rich* . . . .(A&M)
Rock Me Amadeus
Falco; *Falco 3* . . . .(A&M)
Remix Hit Collection . . . . (Sire)
Song For Adam
Jackson Browne; *Jackson Browne* . . . .(Asylum)
St. Alphonzo's Pancake Breakfast
Frank Zappa; *Apostrophe/Overnite Sensation* . . . .(Rykodisc)
Temporary Like Achilles
Bob Dylan; *Blonde On Blonde* . . . .(Columbia)
Theme From "Alfred Hitchcock Presents"
Original Soundtrack; *Alfred Hitchcock Presents Signature In Suspense* . . . . (Hip-O)

CBS: The First 50 Years. . . . . (TVT)
Television's Greatest Hits-#1-C . . . . (TVT)

Theme From "Augie Doggie"
Original Soundtrack; Hanna-Barbera Classics-#1-Original Recordings Of
The World's Most Famous Cartoon Themes &
Scores . . . . (Kid Rhino/Rhino 4 Kids)
Hanna-Barbera Pic-A-Nic Basket Of Cartoon
Classics . . . . (Kid Rhino/Rhino 4 Kids)

Theme From "Fat Albert And The Cosby Kids"
Original Soundtrack; Television's Greatest Hits-#3-1970s & 1980s-C . . . (TVT)

Theme From "The Alvin Show"
Original Soundtrack; Television's Greatest Hits-#3-1970s & 1980s-C . . . (TVT)

Theme From "The Andy Griffith Show"
Original Soundtrack; CBS: The First 50 Years . . . . (TVT)
Television's Greatest Hits-#1-C . . . . (TVT)

Theme From "The Archies"
Original Soundtrack; Television's Greatest Hits-#3-1970s & 1980s-C . . . (TVT)

Trouble With Andre
Sheakespear's Sister; Hormonally Yours . . . . (London)

Uncle Albert/Admiral Halsey
Paul And Linda McCartney; RAM . . . . (Capitol)
Paul McCartney; All The Best! . . . . (Capitol)
Paul McCartney-Gift Set . . . . (Capitol)
Wings; Wings Greatest . . . . (Capitol)

You Can Call Me Al
Paul Simon; Concert In The Park-August 15 1991 . . . . (Warner Bros.)
Graceland . . . . (Warner Bros.)
Negotiations And Love Songs, 1971-1986 . . . . (Warner Bros.)

MEN'S NAMES: B

See Also: **CELEBRITIES: SPECIFIC, FAMILY (various),**
MEN: GENERAL

Bach, Beethoven, Mozart & Me
Phil Ochs; Phil Ochs' Greatest Hits . . . . (A&M)

Ballad Of Ben Gay
Ben Gay & His Silly Savages; Dr. Demento's Delights-C . . . . . (Warner Bros.)

Ballad Of Billy The Kid
Billy Joel; Piano Man . . . . (Columbia)
Songs In The Attic . . . . (Columbia)

Barney Google
Authentic Band Organ; Catch The Brass Ring-Merry-Go-Round . . . . . (Klavier)
Firehouse Five Plus Two; Twenty Years Later . . . . (Good Time Jazz)

Beau's All Night Radio Love Line
Joshua Kadison; Painted Desert Serenade . . . . (SBK)

Ben
Michael Jackson; Best Of Michael Jackson . . . . (Motown)
Jackson 5-16 Greatest Hits . . . . (Motown)
Jackson 5-Anthology . . . . (Motown)
Jacksons Live . . . . (Epic)
Michael Jackson-Anthology . . . . (Motown)
Motown Superstar Series-#7-Michael Jackson . . . . (Motown)

Bennie And The Jets
Elton John; Billboard Top Rock 'N' Roll Hits-1974-C . . . . (Rhino)
Classic Rock-#1-C . . . . (MCA)
Elton John's Greatest Hits . . . . (Polydor)
Goodbye Yellow Brick Road . . . . (Polydor)
Here And There . . . . (Rocket)

Big Bad Bill Is Sweet William Now
Ry Cooder; Jazz . . . . (Warner Bros.)

Big Bopper's Wedding
Big Bopper; Chantilly Lace Starring The Big Bopper . . . . (Mercury)
Helloo Baby! Best Of The Big Bopper-1954-1959 . . . . (Rhino)
M. Dung's Idiot Classics . . . . (Rhino)

Biko
Peter Gabriel; Peter Gabriel . . . . (Geffen)
Peter Gabriel/Plays Live . . . . (Geffen)
Shaking The Tree-Sixteen Golden Greats . . . . (Geffen)

Bill
Ava Gardner; ST/Show Boat . . . . (Sony Music Special Prod.)
Original Cast; Show Boat . . . . (RCA Victor)

Bill Bailey
Louis Armstrong; Essential Louis Armstrong. . . . . (Vanguard)
Louis Armstrong . . . . (Audio Fidelity)
Pearl Bailey; Echoes Of An Era-Pearl Bailey . . . . (Roulette)
Preservation Hall Jazz Band; New Orleans-#1 . . . . (Columbia)

Billy 1, 2 & 7
Bob Dylan; ST/Pat Garrett & Billy The Kid . . . . (Columbia)

Billy Dale
Asleep At The Wheel featuring Dolly Parton; Tribute To The Music Of Bob
Wills And The Texas Playboys-C . . . . (Liberty)

Billy Dee
Kris Kristofferson; The Silver Tongued Devil And I . . . . (Columbia)

Billy Don't Be A Hero
Bo Donaldson & The Heywoods; Super Hits Of The '70s-Have A Nice
Day-#13-C . . . . (Rhino)

Billy Get Me A Woman
Joe Stampley; Joe Stampley's Biggest Hits . . . . (Epic)

Billy Got Some Bad News Today
Tom Paxton; It Ain't Easy . . . . (Flying Fish)

Billy The Kid
Charlie Daniels Band; High Lonesome . . . . (Epic)

Billy The Kid
Marty Robbins; Gunfighter Ballads & Trail Songs . . . . (Legacy)

Billy The Kid
Ry Cooder; Into The Purple Valley . . . . (Reprise)

Billy The Kid (I Miss...)
Billy Dean; Billy Dean . . . . (Liberty)

Bo Diddley
Bo Diddley; Good Time Rock 'N' Roll-C . . . . (MCA)
History Of Rock-#5-C . . . . (Collectables)
Oldies But Goodies-#10-C . . . . (Original Sound)
ST/Rage In Harlem . . . . (Sire)
Buddy Holly; Buddy Holly-20 Golden Greats . . . . (MCA)
For The First Time Anywhere . . . . (MCA)

Bo Diddley Is Jesus
Jesus & Mary Chain; Barbed Wire Kisses . . . . (Warner Bros.)

Bob Dylan's 115th Dream
Bob Dylan; Bringing It All Back Home . . . . (Columbia)

Bob Dylan's Dream
Bob Dylan; Freewheelin' . . . . (Columbia)
Peter, Paul & Mary; Album 1700 . . . . (Warner Bros.)

Bobby Orr Breakaway
Kirk Elliott; No Fixed Address . . . . (Boot)

Bobby's Girl
Marcie Blaine; Collectables Presents The History Of Rock-#5-C . . (Collectables)
Million-Dollar Memories-#2-C . . . . (RCA)
WCBS FM 101 History Of Rock-'60s-#5-C . . . . (Collectables)

Bobby's In Vicksburg
Sylvia; Snapshot . . . . (RCA)

Bonaparte's Retreat
Chieftains; Bonaparte's Retreat . . . . (Shanachie)
Glen Campbell; Glen Campbell-Classics Collection . . . . (Capitol)
Kay Starr; Kay Starr's Greatest Hits . . . . (Curb)
Sons Of The Pioneers; Country & Western Memories . . . . (Pair)

Boris The Spider
Who; Happy Jack . . . . (MCA)
Meaty Beaty Big & Bouncy . . . . (MCA)
Who's Last . . . . (MCA)

Brian Wilson
Barenaked Ladies; Gordon . . . . (Reprise)
Rock Spectacle . . . . (Reprise)

Brian's Song
Johnny Mathis; First Time Ever I Saw Your Face . . . . (Columbia)
Michel Legrand; Michel Plays Legrand . . . . (Laserlight)

Bubba Hyde
Diamond Rio; Diamond Rio's Greatest Hits . . . . (Arista)
Love A Little Stronger . . . . (Arista)

Bubba Shot The Jukebox
Mark Chesnutt; Longnecks & Short Stories . . . . (MCA)

Buck Rogers In The 25th Century
Neil Norman & His Cosmic Orchestra; Greatest Science Fiction
Hits-#2 . . . . (Crescendo)

Bud The Spud
Stompin' Tom Connors; Bud The Spud . . . . (EMI)

Buddy Holly
Weezer; Weezer . . . . (David Geffen Co.)

Candyman (Mr. Benson)
Grateful Dead; American Beauty . . . . (Warner Bros.)
Dead Set . . . . (Arista)

Captain Bligh
Filter; Title Of Record . . . . (Reprise)

Colonel Buffalo Bill
Ethel Merman/Bruce Yarnell/Original Cast; Annie Get
Your Gun . . . . (RCA Victor)

Continuing Story Of Bungalow Bill, The
Beatles; The Beatles (White Album) . . . . (Capitol)

Cowboy Bill
Garth Brooks; Garth Brooks . . . . (Liberty)

Da Doo Ron Ron (When He Walked Me Home) [Bill]
Crystals; Best Of The Crystals . . . . (Abkco)
Good Time Rock 'N' Roll-C . . . . (MCA)
Hits Of The Sixties-C . . . . (Intercom Music)
Phil Spector's Greatest Hits-C . . . . (Spector)
Shaun Cassidy; Shaun Cassidy's Greatest Hits . . . . (Curb)

Did Beethoven Do The Dishes
Reilly & Maloney; Profiles . . . . (Freckle)

Do The Bartman
Bart Simpson; Simpsons Sing The Blues . . . . (Geffen)

Done With Bonaparte
Mark Knopfler; Golden Heart . . . . (Warner Bros.)

Don't Forget The Coffee Billy Joe
Tom T. Hall; Essential Tom T. Hall-20th Anniversary Collection . . (Mercury)

Don't Mess With Bill
Marvelettes; *Compact Command Performances-Marvelettes* . . . . (Motown)
Marvelettes' Greatest Hits . . . . (Motown)
Marvelettes-Anthology . . . . (Motown)
Top 10 With A Bullet-Motown Girl Groups-C . . . . (Motown)
Don't Take Your Guns To Town (Billy Joe)
Johnny Cash; *The Man In Black-His Greatest Hits* . . . . (Legacy)
Graduation (Friends Forever) (Bobby)
Vitamin C; *Totally Hits-#3-C* . . . . (Atlantic)
Vitamin C . . . . (Elektra)
Hey Bobby
K.T. Oslin; *This Woman* . . . . (RCA)
Hey, Mr. Bluebird
Ernest Tubb & Wilburn Brothers; *More Great Country Duets-C* . . . . (MCA Special Prod.)
Hobo Bill's Last Ride
Merle Haggard & The Strangers; *Okie From Muskogee* . . . . (Capitol)
Same Train Different Time . . . . (Capitol)
Train Whistle Blues . . . . (Rounder)
If Bubba Can Dance (I Can Too)
Shenandoah; *Under The Kudzu* . . . . (RCA)
In Buddy's Eyes
Jane Harvey; *Other Side Of Sondheim* . . . . (Atlantic)
In Walked Bud
Art Blakey & Thelonius Monk; *Great Moments In Jazz-C* . . . . (Atlantic)
Thelonius Monk; *Best Of Thelonius Monk* . . . . (Blue Note)
Genius Of Modern Music-#1 . . . . (Blue Note)
It's All About The Benjamins
Puff Daddy & The Family; *No Way Out* . . . . (Bad Boy/Arista)
John Deere Green (Billy Bob)
Joe Diffie; *A Thousand Winding Roads* . . . . (Epic)
Lilies Of The Field (Billy)
Gretchen Peters; *Gretchen Peters* . . . . (Purple Crayon Prod.)
Lone Star Beer & Bob Wills Music
Red Steagall; *Lone Star Beer & Bob Wills Music* . . . . (MCA)
Texas Country . . . . (MCA)
Me And Bobby McGee
Grateful Dead; *Grateful Dead (Skull & Roses)* . . . . (Warner Bros.)
Janis Joplin; *Janis* . . . . (Legacy)
Janis Joplin's Greatest Hits . . . . (Columbia)
Pearl . . . . (Legacy)
Rock Classics Of The '70s-C . . . . (Columbia)
Willie Nelson; *Willie Nelson Sings Kristofferson* . . . . (Columbia)
Mr. Big Stuff
Jean Knight; *'70s Hit(s) Back Again-C* . . . . (Hip-O)
Have A Nice Decade-The '70s Pop Culture Box-C . . . . (Rhino)
Mr. Blue
Fleetwoods; *Best Of The Fleetwoods* . . . . (Rhino)
Timmy & The Tulips; *ST/American Hot Wax* . . . . (A&M)
Mr. Blue
Garth Brooks; *No Fences* . . . . (Capitol)
Mr. Blue
Michael Franks; *Art Of Tea* . . . . (Reprise)
Mr. Blue Sky
Electric Light Orchestra; *Afterglow* . . . . (Epic)
Electric Light Orchestra's Greatest Hits . . . . (Jet)
Out Of The Blue . . . . (Jet)
Mr. Bojangles
David Bromberg; *Out Of The Blues-Best Of David Bromberg* . . . . (Columbia)
Jerry Jeff Walker; *A Man Must Carry On* . . . . (MCA)
Best Of Jerry Jeff Walker . . . . (MCA)
Gypsy Songman . . . . (Rykodisc)
Mr. Bojangles . . . . (Bainbridge)
Nitty Gritty Dirt Band; *Best Of The Nitty Gritty Dirt Band* . . . . (Liberty)
On The Road Again . . . . (Capitol)
Super Hits Of The '70s-Have A Nice Day-#4-C . . . . (Rhino)
Twenty Years Of Dirt-Best Of The Nitty Gritty Dirt Band . . . . (Warner Bros.)
Uncle Charlie And His Dog Teddy . . . . (Liberty)
My Attorney Bernie
David Frishberg; *Can't Take You Nowhere* . . . . (Fantasy)
David Frishberg-Classics . . . . (Concord Jazz)
My Name Is Bocephus
Hank Williams, Jr.; *Hank Williams, Jr. ''Live''* . . . . (WB/Curb)
Hank Williams, Jr.'s Greatest Hits III . . . . (Curb)
Montana Cafe . . . . (WB/Curb)
November In The Snow/Lord Buckley
Mark Murphy; *Kerouac Then & Now* . . . . (Muse)
Ode To Billy Joe
Bobbi Gentry; *All-Time Country Classics-#1-C* . . . . (Capitol)
Old Count Basie Is Gone (Old Piney Brown Is Gone)
Tony Bennett; *Playin' With My Friends-Bennett Sings The Blues-C* . . . . (Columbia)
Pretty Fly For A Rabbi (Bernie)
''Weird Al'' Yankovic; *Running With Scissors* . . . . (Volcano Entertainment)
Railroad Bill
Etta Baker; *One-Dime Blues* . . . . (Rounder)
Ramblin' Jack Elliott; *Hard Travelin'* . . . . (Fantasy)
Ramblin' Jack Elliott . . . . (Prestige)
Reverend Mr. Black
Johnny Cash; *Johnny Cash's Biggest Hits* . . . . (Columbia)
Kingston Trio; *Capitol Collectors Series-The Kingston Trio* . . . . (Capitol)
Roll Over Beethoven
Beatles; *Beatles-Box Set* . . . . (Capitol)
Rock 'N' Roll Music . . . . (Capitol)
The Beatles At The Hollywood Bowl . . . . (Capitol)
The Beatles' Second Album . . . . (Capitol)
With The Beatles . . . . (Parlophone)
Byrds; *The Byrds* . . . . (Columbia)
Chuck Berry; *Chuck Berry-Golden Hits* . . . . (Mercury)
Chuck Berry's Greatest Hits . . . . (Everest)
Cruisin'-1956-C . . . . (Increase)
Oldies But Goodies-#10-C . . . . (Original Sound)
The Chess Box-Chuck Berry . . . . (Chess)
Electric Light Orchestra; *Afterglow* . . . . (Epic)
Ole ELO . . . . (Jet)
Sgt. Pepper's Lonely Hearts Club Band
Beatles; *Beatles-Box Set* . . . . (Capitol)
The Beatles/1967-1970 . . . . (Capitol)
Jimi Hendrix; *Stages-Stockholm/Paris/San Diego/Atlanta* . . . . (Reprise)
Son Of A Preacher Man (Billy Ray)
Dusty Springfield; *Dusty Springfield* . . . . (Rhino)
Dusty Springfield-Anthology . . . . (Mercury)
Stagger Lee
Dion; *Dion-His Best* . . . . (Laurie)
Huey Lewis and the News; *Four Chords & Several Years Ago* . . . . (Elektra)
Ike & Tina Turner; *Best Of Ike & Tina Turner* . . . . (EMI)
Lloyd Price; *Billboard Top Rock 'N' Roll Hits-1959-C* . . . . (Rhino)
Collectables Presents The History Of Rock-#5-C . . . . (Collectables)
Lloyd Price's Greatest Hits . . . . (MCA)
Oldies But Goodies-#1-C . . . . (Original Sound)
Professor Longhair; *Rock 'N' Roll Gumbo* . . . . (Dancing Cat)
Wilson Pickett; *A Man & A Half-Best Of Wilson Pickett* . . . . (Rhino)
Story Of Bo Diddley
Animals; *Best Of The Animals* . . . . (Abkco)
Bo Diddley; *In The Spotlight* . . . . (Chess)
Theme From ''B.J. And The Bear''
Original Soundtrack; *Television's Greatest Hits-#6-Remote Control-C* . . . (TVT)
Theme From ''Baretta''
Original Soundtrack; *Television's Greatest Hits-#3-1970s & 1980s-C* . . . . (TVT)
Theme From ''Barnaby Jones''
Original Soundtrack; *CBS: The First 50 Years* . . . . (TVT)
Television's Greatest Hits-#3-1970s & 1980s-C . . . . (TVT)
Theme From ''Barney And Friends''
Original Soundtrack; *Television's Greatest Hits-#7-Cable Ready-C* . . . . . . (TVT)
Theme From ''Barney Miller''
Original Soundtrack; *Television's Greatest Hits-#3-1970s & 1980s-C* . . . . (TVT)
Theme From ''Bat Masterson''
Original Soundtrack; *Television's Greatest Hits-#2-C* . . . . (TVT)
Theme From ''Batman''
Original Soundtrack; *Television's Greatest Hits-#1-C* . . . . (TVT)
Theme From ''Ben Casey''
Original Soundtrack; *Television's Greatest Hits-#2-C* . . . . (TVT)
Theme From ''Ben Hur''
BBC Concert Orchestra; *Golden Cinema Classics-#1-The Adventure Film* . . . . (Bainbridge)
Theme From ''Benson''
Original Soundtrack; *Television's Greatest Hits-#6-Remote Control-C* . . . (TVT)
Theme From ''Bronco''
Original Soundtrack; *Television's Greatest Hits-#4-Black & White Classics-C* . . . . (TVT)
Theme From ''Bugs Bunny Overture''
Original Soundtrack; *Television's Greatest Hits-#1-C* . . . . (TVT)
Theme From ''Burke's Law''
Original Soundtrack; *Television's Greatest Hits-#4-Black & White Classics-C* . . . . (TVT)
Theme From ''Leave It To Beaver''
Original Soundtrack; *CBS: The First 50 Years* . . . . (TVT)
Television's Greatest Hits-#1-C . . . . (TVT)
Theme From ''Mr. Belvedere'' (According To Our New Arrivals)
Leon Redbone; *Television's Greatest Hits-#6-Remote Control-C* . . . . (TVT)
Theme From ''The Beany & Cecil Show''
Original Soundtrack; *Television's Greatest Hits-#4-Black & White Classics-C* . . . . (TVT)
Theme From ''The Bob Hope Show'' (Thanks For The Memories)
Original Soundtrack; *Television's Greatest Hits-#4-Black & White Classics-C* . . . . (TVT)
Theme From ''The Bob Newhart Show''
Original Soundtrack; *CBS: The First 50 Years* . . . . (TVT)
Television's Greatest Hits-#3-1970s & 1980s-C . . . . (TVT)
Theme From ''The Brady Bunch''
Brady Bunch Kids; *It's A Sunshine Day-Best Of The Brady Bunch Kids* . . . . (MCA)
Television's Greatest Hits-#2-C . . . . (TVT)
Which Way You Goin' Billy
Poppy Family; *Super Hits Of The '70s-Have A Nice Day-#2-C* . . . . (Rhino)
Wild Bill Jones
Hot Rize; *Radio Boogie* . . . . (Flying Fish)

Kentucky Colonels; *Appalachian Swing!* . . . . (Rounder)
Wild Bill's Blues
Country Gazette; *Strictly Instrumental* . . . . (Flying Fish)
Wild Billy's Circus Story
Bruce Springsteen; *The Wild, The Innocent & The E Street Shuffle* . . (Columbia)

MEN'S NAMES: C

See Also: **CELEBRITIES: SPECIFIC, FAMILY (various), MEN: GENERAL**

Adam Raised A Cain
Bruce Springsteen; *Darkness On The Edge Of Town* . . . . (Columbia)
Ballad Of Bonnie And Clyde
Georgie Fame; *History Of British Rock-#8-C* . . . . (Rhino)
Band Played On, The (Casey)
Guy Lombardo & His Royal Canadians; *Guy Lombardo-All Time Favorites* . . . . (MCA Special Prod.)
C.C. Waterback
Merle Haggard & George Jones; *By Request* . . . . (Epic)
Greatest Country Duets-C . . . . (Epic)
His Epic Hits-First 11 To Be Continued-C . . . . (Epic)
Taste Of Yesterday's Wine . . . . (Epic)
Carey
Joni Mitchell; *Blue* . . . . (Reprise)
Joni Mitchell with Tom Scott & The L.A. Express; *Miles Of Aisles* . . . . (Asylum)
Casanova
Levert; *Big Throwdown* . . . . (Atlantic)
Golden Age Of Black Music-1977-1988-C . . . . (Atlantic)
ST/Fatal Beauty . . . . (Atlantic)
Casanova
Bryan Ferry; *Let's Stick Together* . . . . (Virgin)
Roxy Music; *Country Life* . . . . (Atco)
Casey Jones
Grateful Dead; *Best Of The Grateful Dead-Skeletons From The Closet* . . . . (Warner Bros.)
Bill Graham Presents The Last Days Of The Fillmore-C . . . . (Epic Portrait Assoc.)
Workingman's Dead . . . . (Warner Bros.)
Jerry Garcia Acoustic Band; *Almost Acoustic* . . . . (Grateful Dead)
Casey Jones
Fred McDowell; *Fred McDowell & Furry Lewis: When I Lay My Burden Down* . . . . (Biograph)
Casey's Last Ride
Johnny Cash; *Rainbow* . . . . (Columbia)
Catfish John
Johnny Russell; *Johnny Russell's Greatest Hits* . . . . (Dominion Entert.)
Charlie Brown
Coasters; *Billboard Top Rock 'N' Roll Hits-1957-C* . . . . (Rhino)
Coasters' Greatest Hits . . . . (Atco)
Coasters-Their Greatest Recordings-Early Years . . . . (Atco)
Cruisin'-1959-C . . . . (Increase)
Super Oldies Of The '50s-#7-C . . . . (Audio Fidelity)
Young Blood . . . . (Atlantic)
Charlie Brown's Parents
Dishwalla; *Pet Your Friends* . . . . (A&M)
Charlie Don't Surf
Clash; *Sandinista* . . . . (Epic)
Charlie Dunn
Jerry Jeff Walker; *Gypsy Songman* . . . . (Rykodisc)
Jerry Jeff Walker . . . . (MCA)
Charlie's Shoes
Billy Walker; *Best Of Billy Walker* . . . . (Deluxe)
Columbia Country Classics-#4-Nashville Sound-C . . . . (Columbia)
Chubbster
Chubb Rock; *Beats & Rhymes: Hip-Hop Of The '90s, Part 2-C* . . . . . . (Rhino)
Chuck E.'s In Love
Rickie Lee Jones; *Rickie Lee Jones* . . . . (Warner Bros.)
Cisco Kid
War; *All Day Music* . . . . (MCA)
Best Of War...And More . . . . (Avenue)
War Live! . . . . (Avenue)
Clap Hands, Here Comes Charlie
Barbra Streisand; *ST/Funny Lady* . . . . (Arista)
Charlie Barnet; *Big Band-1967* . . . . (Mobile Fidelity Sound Lab)
Clap Hands, Here Comes Charlie . . . . (Bluebird)
Complete Charlie Barnet-#6 . . . . (RCA)
Clyde
Waylon Jennings; *Music Man* . . . . (RCA)
Cocaine Charlie
Atlanta Rhythm Section; *Boys From Doraville* . . . . (Polydor)
Cortez The Killer
Neil Young & Crazy Horse; *Decade* . . . . (Reprise)
Live Rust . . . . (Reprise)
Zuma . . . . (Reprise)
Cosmic Charlie
Grateful Dead; *Aoxomoxoa* . . . . (Warner Bros.)

What A Long Strange Trip It's Been: The Best Of The Grateful Dead . . . . (Warner Bros.)
Curly Shuffle
Jump 'N The Saddle Band; *Dr. Demento Presents The Greatest Novelty Records-#5-1980s-C* . . . . (Rhino)
Danny's All-Star Joint (Cecil)
Rickie Lee Jones; *Rickie Lee Jones* . . . . (Warner Bros.)
Day That Curly Bill Shot Down Crazy Sam
Hollies; *Hollies* . . . . (Epic)
Diesel Cecil
Larry Scott; *Keep On Truckin'* . . . . (Exact)
General Custer
Tom Paxton; *How Come The Sun* . . . . (Out Of Print)
Good Time Charlie's Got The Blues
Danny O'Keefe; *Breezy Stories* . . . . (Atlantic)
Seattle Tapes . . . . (First Warning)
Willie Nelson; *City Of New Orleans* . . . . (Columbia)
Hang On St. Christopher
Tom Waits; *Frank's Wild Years-Un Operachi Romantico* . . . . (Island)
I Remember Clifford
Lee Morgan; *Best Of Lee Morgan* . . . . (Blue Note)
Pieces Of A Dream & Manhattan Transfer; *In Performance At The Playboy Jazz Festival* . . . . (Elektra)
Jukebox Charlie
Johnny Paycheck; *Johnny Paycheck Sings Jukebox Charlie And Other Songs That Make The Jukebox Play* . . . . (Little Darlin')
Kid Charlemagne
Steely Dan; *Steely Dan's Greatest Hits* . . . . (MCA)
The Royal Scam . . . . (MCA)
Legend Of Bonnie And Clyde
Merle Haggard & The Strangers; *For The Record: Merle Haggard-43 Legendary Hits* . . . . (BNA)
M.T.A. (Charlie)
Kingston Trio; *25 Years Non-Stop* . . . . (Xeres)
Best Of The Kingston Trio . . . . (Capitol)
Capitol Collectors Series-The Kingston Trio . . . . (Capitol)
Scarlet Ribbons . . . . (Capitol)
Very Best Of The Kingston Trio . . . . (Capitol)
Mr. Clean, Mr. Clean
Original Soundtrack; *TeeVee Toons-The Commercials-#1-C* . . . . (TVT)
Mr. Custer
Larry Verne; *Collectables Presents The History Of Rock-#10-C* . . (Collectables)
Dr. Demento Presents The Greatest Novelty Records-#3-1960s-C . . . . (Rhino)
Wacky Weirdos-C . . . . (K-Tel)
Nowadays Clancy Can't Even Sing
Buffalo Springfield; *Buffalo Springfield* . . . . (Atco)
Buffalo Springfield-Retrospective . . . . (Atco)
Old King Cole
Original Soundtrack; *Children's Favorites* . . . . (Kid Rhino/Rhino 4 Kids)
Please Mr. Custer
Ray Stevens; *Gitarzan* . . . . (Barnaby)
Prince Charming
Adam Ant; *Antics In The Forbidden Zone* . . . . (Epic)
Prince Charming . . . . (Epic)
Salute To Charlie Christian
Barney Kessel; *"Guitar Player" Presents Guitar Classics* . . . . (Prestige)
Theme From "Captain Kangaroo"
Original Soundtrack; *CBS: The First 50 Years* . . . . (TVT)
Television's Greatest Hits-#1-C . . . . (TVT)
Theme From "Casper The Friendly Ghost"
Original Soundtrack; *Television's Greatest Hits-#1-C* . . . . (TVT)
Theme From "Charles In Charge"
Shandi; *Television's Greatest Hits-#6-Remote Control-C* . . . . (TVT)
Tube Tunes-#3-The '70s & '80s-C . . . . (Rhino)
Theme From "Charlie's Angels"
Original Soundtrack; *Television's Greatest Hits-#3-1970s & 1980s-C* . . . (TVT)
TV Classic Themes: 25th Anniversary Edition-C . . . . (Breakable)
Theme From "Cheyenne"
Original Soundtrack; *Television's Greatest Hits-#4-Black & White Classics-C* . . . . (TVT)
Theme From "Chico And The Man"
Original Soundtrack; *Television's Greatest Hits-#5-In Living Color-C* . . . (TVT)
Theme From "Cosby"
Original Soundtrack; *CBS: The First 50 Years* . . . . (TVT)
Theme From "Lois And Clark: The New Adventures Of Superman"
Original Soundtrack; *Television's Greatest Hits-#7-Cable Ready-C* . . . . . (TVT)
Theme From "The Cosby Show"
Original Soundtrack; *Television's Greatest Hits-#7-Cable Ready-C* . . . . . (TVT)
Trash Can Charlie
Billy Goat; *Bush Roaming Mammals* . . . . (Third Rail)
TV Caesar
Procol Harum; *Grand Hotel* . . . . (Chrysalis)
Uncle Clooney Played The Banjo
Country Gazette; *Hello Operator...This Is Country Gazette* . . . . (Flying Fish)
Out To Lunch . . . . (Flying Fish)
Utah Caroi
Harry K. McClintock; *Cowboy Songs On Folkways-C* . . . . (Smithsonian Folkways)

Marty Robbins; *Gunfighter Ballads & Trail Songs* . . . . (Legacy)
Wolverton Mountain (Clifton Clowers)
Claude King; *American Originals-Claude King* . . . . (Columbia)
Best Of Claude King . . . . (Gusto)
Billboard Top Country Hits-1962-C . . . . (Rhino)
Super Hits Of The '60s-C . . . . (Epic)
You're A Good Man, Charlie Brown
Original Cast; *You're A Good Man, Charlie Brown* . . . . (Polydor)

MEN'S NAMES: D

See Also: **CELEBRITIES: SPECIFIC, FAMILY (various), MEN: GENERAL**

Ballad Of Danny Bailey
Elton John; *Goodbye Yellow Brick Road* . . . . (Polydor)
Ballad Of Davy Crockett
Bill Hayes; *Songs Of The West-#4-Movie & Television Themes-C* . . . . . . (Rhino)
Fess Parker; *16 Most Requested Songs Of The '50s-#1-C* . . . . (Legacy)
Columbia Country Classics-#3-Americana-C . . . . (Columbia)
Hollywood Magic-1950s-C . . . . (Columbia)
Kentucky HeadHunters; *Electric Barnyard* . . . . (Mercury)
Mac Wiseman; *45-#1240.* . . . . (Dot)
Original Soundtrack; *Television's Greatest Hits-#4-Black & White Classics-C* . . . . (TVT)
Tennessee Ernie Ford; *Capitol Collectors Series-Tennessee Ernie Ford* . . . . (Capitol)
Black Jack David
Alice Stuart; *All The Good Times* . . . . (Arhoolie)
Steeleye Span; *All Around My Hat* . . . . (Chrysalis)
The Steeleye Span Story . . . . (Chrysalis)
Warren Smith; *45-#11* . . . . (Sun)
Dancing With Mr. D
Rolling Stones; *Goats Head Soup* . . . . (Rolling Stones)
Daniel
Elton John; *Don't Shoot Me I'm Only The Piano Player* . . . . (Polydor)
Elton John's Greatest Hits . . . . (Polydor)
Wilson Phillips; *Two Rooms-Celebrating The Songs Of Elton John & Bernie Taupin-C* . . . . (Polydor)
Daniel & The Sacred Harp
Band; *Stage Fright* . . . . (Capitol)
The Band-Anthology-#1 . . . . (Capitol)
To Kingdom Come-The Definitive Collection . . . . (Capitol)
Daniel Prayed
Patty Loveless; *Mountain Soul* . . . . (Epic)
Stanley Brothers; *Stanley Brothers-On Radio* . . . . (Rebel)
Danny Boy
Bill Evans; *Bill Evans-Complete Riverside Recordings* . . . . (Riverside)
Bing Crosby; *When Irish Eyes Are Smiling* . . . . (MCA)
Conway Twitty; *Conway Twitty-Classics-#1* . . . . (Warner Bros.)
Very Best Of Conway Twitty . . . . (MCA)
Tony Bennett; *Jazz* . . . . (Columbia)
Danny's All-Star Joint
Rickie Lee Jones; *Rickie Lee Jones* . . . . (Warner Bros.)
Danny's Song
Anne Murray; *Anne Murray-Country* . . . . (Capitol)
Anne Murray's Greatest Hits . . . . (Capitol)
Danny's Song . . . . (Capitol)
Loggins & Messina; *Loggins & Messina-On Stage* . . . . (Columbia)
Sittin' In . . . . (Columbia)
The Best Of Friends . . . . (Columbia)
David & Me
Jerry Jeff Walker; *Jerry Jeff Walker* . . . . (MCA)
David Duchovny
Bree Sharp; *Cheap & Evil Girl* . . . . (Trauma)
David Watts
Kinks; *Kink Kronikles* . . . . (Reprise)
Something Else . . . . (Reprise)
Davy Crockett
Hermes Nye; *Ballads Of The Civil War-#1 & 2* . . . . (Smithsonian Folkways)
Davy The Fat Boy
Randy Newman; *Randy Newman* . . . . (Warner Archives)
Randy Newman/Live . . . . (Warner Archives)
Davy's Dinghy
Ruth Wallis; *Dr. Demento Presents The Greatest Novelty Records-#2-1950s-C* . . . . (Rhino)
Dr. Demento's Dementia Royale-C . . . . (Rhino)
Denis
Blondie; *Blonde And Beyond-Rarities & Oddities* . . . . (Gold Rush)
Once More Into The Bleach . . . . (Gold Rush)
Plastic Letters . . . . (Chrysalis)
The Platinum Collection . . . . (Chrysalis)
Dexter Digs In
Eddie Jefferson; *Come Along With Me* . . . . (Prestige)
There I Go Again . . . . (Prestige)
Dickie's Such An Asshole
Frank Zappa; *Broadway The Hard Way* . . . . (Rykodisc)

You Can't Do That On Stage Anymore-#3 . . . . (Rykodisc)
Dillon's Store
Lightnin' Hopkins; *Prison Blues-Golden Classics-#2* . . . . (Collectables)
Dinner With Gershwin
Brenda Russell; *Kiss Me With The Wind* . . . .(A&M)
Donna Summer; *All Systems Go.* . . . . (Geffen)
Django
Chet Baker; *My Favourite Songs-#1-Last Great Concert* . . . . (Enja)
John Lewis; *Garden Of Delight-Delaunay's Dilemma* . . . . (Emarcy)
Midnight In Paris . . . . (Emarcy)
Modern Jazz Quartet; *Artistry Of The Modern Jazz Quartet* . . . . (Prestige)
Django. . . . . (Prestige)
Modern Jazz Quartet . . . . (Prestige)
Stephane Grappelli; *Feeling Plus Finesse Equals Jazz* . . . . (Atlantic)
Vince Guaraldi Trio; *Vince Guaraldi Trio* . . . . (Fantasy)
Wynton Marsalis; *Hot House Flowers* . . . . (Columbia)
Dogman
King's X; *Dogman.* . . . . (Atlantic)
Don Jose Of Sevilla
W.H. MacDonald & Jessie Bartlett Davis; *Music From The New York Stage (1890-1920)-#1-1890-1908-C* . . . . (Pearl)
Donald And Lydia
John Prine; *John Prine* . . . . (Atlantic)
John Prine-Souvenirs . . . . (Oh Boy)
Prime Prine-The Best Of John Prine . . . . (Atlantic)
Doolin Dalton
Eagles; *Desperado* . . . . (Asylum)
Eagles Live . . . . (Asylum)
Dream Merchant
New Birth; *Smooth Grooves-A Sensual Collection-#5-C.* . . . . (Rhino)
Duncan
Paul Simon; *Greatest Hits, Etc.* . . . . (Columbia)
Paul Simon . . . . (Columbia)
Paul Simon In Concert/Live Rhymin' . . . . (Columbia)
Dupree's Diamond Blues
Grateful Dead; *Aoxomoxoa* . . . . (Warner Bros.)
King David
Judy Collins; *Bread & Roses* . . . . (Elektra)
Lion's Den (Daniel)
Bruce Springsteen; *Tracks* . . . . (Columbia)
Mr. Dream Merchant
Jerry Butler; *Best Of Jerry Butler* . . . . (Rhino)
Soul Shots-#2-The "In" Crowd-Sweet Soul-C . . . . (Rhino)
Ob-La-Di, Ob-La-Da (Desmond & Molly Jones)
Beatles; *Beatles-Box Set.* . . . . (Capitol)
The Beatles (White Album) . . . . (Capitol)
The Beatles/1967-1970 . . . . (Capitol)
Old Dan Tucker
Original Soundtrack; *Children's Favorites* . . . . (Kid Rhino/Rhino 4 Kids)
Rocky Raccoon
Beatles; *Beatles-Box Set.* . . . . (Capitol)
The Beatles (White Album) . . . . (Capitol)
Sailing To Philadelphia (Mason-Dixon)
Mark Knopfler; *Sailing To Philadelphia* . . . . (Warner Bros.)
Sir Duke
Stevie Wonder; *Original Musiquarium* . . . . (Motown)
Songs In The Key Of Life . . . . (Motown)
Sixty Minute Man
Billy Ward & His Dominoes; *Rock & Roll Show-C* . . . . (Gusto)
Dominos; *Oldies But Goodies-#5-C.* . . . . (Original Sound)
Rufus Thomas & Carla Thomas; *Rufus Thomas & Carla Thomas-Chronicle* . . . . (Stax)
Somebody Killed Dewey Jones' Daughter
Lacy J. Dalton; *Takin' It Easy* . . . . (Columbia)
Stone Outside Dan Murphy's Door
Anna McGoldrick; *Ireland On My Mind* . . . . (Rego Irish)
Street Man Named Desire
Pirates Of The Mississippi; *Street Man Named Desire* . . . . (Liberty)
Surfer Dan
Turtles; *Turtle Wax-Best Of The Turtles-#2* . . . . (Rhino)
Theme From "Daniel Boone"
Original Soundtrack; *Television's Greatest Hits-#1-C* . . . .(TVT)
Theme From "Dastardly & Muttley In Their Flying Machine"
Original Soundtrack; *Hanna-Barbera Pic-A-Nic Basket Of Cartoon Classics* . . . . (Kid Rhino/Rhino 4 Kids)
Television's Greatest Hits-#3-1970s & 1980s-C. . . . . (TVT)
Theme From "Dennis The Menace"
Original Soundtrack; *Television's Greatest Hits-#1-C* . . . .(TVT)
Theme From "Doogie Howser, M.D."
Original Soundtrack; *Television's Greatest Hits-#7-Cable Ready-C* . . . . .(TVT)
Theme From "Dudley-Do-Right"
Original Soundtrack; *Television's Greatest Hits-#3-1970s & 1980s-C* . . . .(TVT)
Theme From "The Dick Van Dyke Show"
Original Soundtrack; *CBS: The First 50 Years.* . . . .(TVT)
Television's Greatest Hits-#1-C . . . . (TVT)
Theme From "The Dukes Of Hazzard"
Waylon Jennings; *Only Daddy That'll Walk The Line-The RCA Years* . . . (RCA)
Television's Greatest Hits-#6-Remote Control-C . . . .(TVT)

Waylon Jennings' Greatest Hits-#2 .... (RCA)
Theme From "The Late Show With David Letterman"
Original Soundtrack; *CBS: The First 50 Years* .... (TVT)
Television's Greatest Hits-#7-Cable Ready-C .... (TVT)
Theme From "The Many Loves Of Dobie Gillis"
Original Soundtrack; *CBS: The First 50 Years* .... (TVT)
Television's Greatest Hits-#1-C .... (TVT)
TV Classic Themes: 25th Anniversary Edition-C .... (Breakable)
Tom, Dick Or Harry
Original Cast; *Kiss Me Kate* .... (Sony Music Classical)
Trudy & Dave
John Hiatt; *Slow Turning* .... (A&M)
Turn Me On "Mr. Deadman"
Union Underground; *...An Education In Rebellion* .... (Portrait)
Uncle Dave's Travels-Misery In Arkansas
Uncle Dave Macon; *The Country Music Hall Of Fame-Uncle Dave Macon* .... (MCA)

MEN'S NAMES: E

See Also: **CELEBRITIES: SPECIFIC, ELVIS, FAMILY (various), MEN: GENERAL**

Ballad Of Fast Eddie
Rodney Crowell; *Street Language* .... (Columbia)
Careful With That Axe Eugene
Pink Floyd; *Relics* .... (Capitol)
Ummagumma .... (Capitol)
Charlie Brown's Parents
Dishwalla; *Pet Your Friends* .... (A&M)
Eddie My Love
Fontane Sisters; *History Of Dot-#1-Young Love-C* .... (Varese Sarabande)
Eddie's First Wife
Gretchen Peters; *Gretchen Peters* .... (Purple Crayon Prod.)
Einstein At The Pool Hall
Pat McDonald & The Essentials; *Lowdown* .... (Mountain Railroad)
Einstein On The Beach
Counting Crows; *August And Everything After* .... (David Geffen Co.)
Eisenhower
John Scofield; *Meant To Be* .... (Blue Note)
Eisenhower Blues
J.B. Lenoir; *Best Of Chess Blues-C* .... (Chess)
Natural Man .... (Chess)
Eisenhower Blues
Costello Show (Featuring Elvis Costello); *King Of America* ...... (Columbia)
Eli's Comin'
Laura Nyro; *Eli And The Thirteenth Confession* .... (Columbia)
Three Dog Night; *Best Of Three Dog Night* .... (MCA)
Rockin' '60s-C .... (Priority)
Elmer's Tune
Glenn Miller; *Best Of Glenn Miller* .... (RCA)
Best Of Glenn Miller-#2 .... (RCA)
Glenn Miller-A Legendary Performer-#1 & 2 .... (Bluebird)
Memorial-1944-1969 .... (Bluebird)
Glenn Miller & His Orchestra; *Complete Glenn Miller & His Orchestra-#7* .... (Bluebird)
Peggy Lee; *Peggy Lee Sings With Benny Goodman* .... (Columbia)
Peggy Lee & Benny Goodman & His Orchestra; *Miss Peggy Lee* ... (Columbia)
Eric's Dream
Ken Navarro; *Brighter Days* .... (Positive)
Eugene You Genius
Bryan White; *Bryan White* .... (Asylum)
Goodbye Earl
Dixie Chicks; *Fly* .... (Monument)
My True Story (Earl)
Jive Five; *Back Seat Jams-C* .... (Dunhill Compact Classics)
Billboard Top R&B Hits-1961-C .... (Rhino)
Cruisin'-1961-C .... (Increase)
Jive Five-Their Greatest Hits .... (Collectables)
Oldies But Goodies-#4-C .... (Original Sound)
Queen Of My Double Wide Trailer (Earl)
Sammy Kershaw; *Haunted Heart* .... (Mercury)
Spanish Eddie
Laura Branigan; *Hold Me* .... (Atlantic)
Speedoo (Mr. Earl)
Cadillacs; *Best Of The Cadillacs* .... (Rhino)
Echoes Of A Rock Era-Early Years-C .... (Roulette)
More American Graffiti-C .... (MCA)
Original Rock 'N' Roll Hits Of The '50s-C .... (Roulette)
ST/Goodfellas .... (Atlantic)
Ry Cooder; *Borderline* .... (Warner Bros.)
Stupid Einstein
Three O'Clock; *Sixteen Tambourines* .... (Frontier)
Theme From "Mr. Ed"
Original Soundtrack; *Television's Greatest Hits-#1-C* .... (TVT)
Theme From "Siskel And Ebert"
Original Soundtrack; *Television's Greatest Hits-#6-Remote Control-C* .. (TVT)

Theme From "The Courtship Of Eddie's Father" (Best Friend)
Nilsson; *Television's Greatest Hits-#2-C* .... (TVT)
Theme From "The Ed Sullivan Show"
Original Soundtrack; *CBS: The First 50 Years* .... (TVT)
Wreck Of The Edmund Fitzgerald
Gordon Lightfoot; *Gord's Gold-#2* .... (Warner Bros.)
Summertime Dream .... (Reprise)

MEN'S NAMES: F

See Also: **CELEBRITIES: SPECIFIC, FAMILY (various), MEN: GENERAL**

Axel F
Harold Faltermeyer; *'80s Mega Hits-C* .... (K-Tel)
ST/Beverly Hills Cop .... (MCA)
Ballad Of Frankie Lee & Judas Priest
Bob Dylan; *John Wesley Harding* .... (Columbia)
Captain Fantastic And The Brown Dirt Cowboy
Elton John; *Captain Fantastic And The Brown Dirt Cowboy* .... (Polydor)
Daddy Frank (The Guitar Man)
Merle Haggard; *Best Of Merle Haggard* .... (Capitol)
Capitol Collectors Series-Merle Haggard .... (Capitol)
Merle Haggard & The Strangers; *For The Record: Merle Haggard-43 Legendary Hits* .... (BNA)
Songs I'll Always Sing .... (Capitol)
Dear Mr. Fantasy
Traffic; *Best Of Traffic* .... (Island)
Dear Mr. Fantasy .... (Island)
Welcome To The Canteen .... (Island)
Do The Freddy
Chubby Checker; *Chubby Checker's Greatest Hits* .... (Abkco)
F. Lee Bailey Blues
Sugar Ray & The Bluetones; *Don't Stand In My Way* .... (Bullseye Blues)
Fernando
Abba; *Abba Live* .... (Atlantic)
Abba's Greatest Hits .... (Atlantic)
Gold-Greatest Hits .... (Polydor)
I Love Abba .... (Atlantic)
The Singles-First 10 Years .... (Atlantic)
Forrest Gump Suite
Alan Silvestri; *ST/Forrest Gump* .... (Epic/Sony Music Soundtrax)
Frankie
Sister Sledge; *When The Boys Meet The Girls* .... (Atlantic)
Frankie
Connie Francis; *Very Best Of Connie Francis* .... (Polydor)
Franklin D. Roosevelt's Back Again
New Lost City Ramblers; *New Lost City Ramblers-Early Years-1958-1962* .... (Smithsonian Folkways)
Fred Jones Part 2
Ben Folds; *Rockin' The Suburbs* .... (Epic)
Freddie's Dead
Curtis Mayfield; *Very Best Of Curtis Mayfield* .... (Rhino)
Fishbone; *Truth & Soul* .... (Columbia)
Froggie Went A Courtin'
Doc Watson; *Essential Doc Watson* .... (Vanguard)
Home Again .... (Vanguard)
Go On With The Wedding (Fred)
Patti Page; *Patti Page-Golden Celebration* .... (Mercury)
Lord, Mr. Ford
Jerry Reed; *Best Of A Great Year-#3-C* .... (RCA)
Jerry Reed In Concert .... (RCA)
New Timer (Frank)
Bruce Springsteen; *The Ghost Of Tom Joad* .... (Columbia)
Pretty Boy Floyd
Arlo Guthrie & Pete Seeger; *Precious Friend* .... (Warner Bros.)
Bob Dylan; *Folkways: A Vision Shared-C* .... (Columbia)
Byrds; *Sweetheart Of The Rodeo* .... (Columbia)
The Byrds .... (Columbia)
Joan Baez; *Greatest Songs Of Woody Guthrie-C* .... (Vanguard)
Woody Guthrie; *Dust Bowl Ballads* .... (Rounder)
Legendary Woody Guthrie .... (Tradition)
Struggle .... (Smithsonian Folkways)
Woody Guthrie .... (Everest)
Worried Man Blues-Golden Classics-#1 .... (Collectables)
Seven Little Girls Sitting In The Back Seat (Fred)
Paul Evans; *Music To Remember-C* .... (Dominion Entert.)
Theme From "Felix The Cat"
Original Soundtrack; *Television's Greatest Hits-#1-C* .... (TVT)
Theme From "Flash Gordon"
Neil Norman; *Greatest Science Fiction Hits-#3-C* .... (Crescendo)
Theme From "The Flintstones"
Original Soundtrack; *Hanna-Barbera Classics-#1-Original Recordings Of The World's Most Famous Cartoon Themes & Scores* .... (Kid Rhino/Rhino 4 Kids)
Hanna-Barbera Pic-A-Nic Basket Of Cartoon Classics .... (Kid Rhino/Rhino 4 Kids)

Television's Greatest Hits-#1-C . . . . (TVT)
Steve Hobbs; *Escape* . . . . (Cexton)
Where Did Robinson Crusoe Go With Friday On Saturday Night
Ian Whitcomb; *You Turn Me On-The Very Best Of Ian Whitcomb* . . . . (Varese Sarabande)
Whiskey In The Jar (Capt. Farrell)
Metallica; *Garage Inc* . . . . (Elektra)

MEN'S NAMES: G

See Also: **CELEBRITIES: SPECIFIC, FAMILY (various),**
MEN: GENERAL

Gabriel's Mother's Hiway Ballad 16 Blues
Arlo Guthrie; *Best Of Arlo Guthrie* . . . . (Warner Bros.)
Georgy Porgy
Eric Benet featuring Faith Evans; *A Day In The Life* . . . . (Warner Bros.)
Toto; *Past To Present 1977-1990* . . . . (Columbia)
Toto . . . . (Columbia)
Gitarzan
Ray Stevens; *Dr. Demento Presents The Greatest Novelty Records-#3-1960s-C* . . . . (Rhino)
Ray Stevens' Greatest Hits . . . . (RCA)
Ray Stevens' Greatest Hits . . . . (MCA)
Goldfinger
Shirley Bassey; *13 Original James Bond Themes-C* . . . . (EMI)
Best Of Shirley Bassey . . . . (EMI)
Great Performances . . . . (Liberty)
Shirley Bassey-Live At Carnegie Hall . . . . (United Artists)
Shirley Bassey's Greatest Hits . . . . (EMI)
ST/Goldfinger . . . . (United Artists)
Just Like Gene Autry
Moby Grape; *Very Best Of Moby Grape-Vintage* . . . . (Columbia)
Killing Of Georgie
Rod Stewart; *Night On The Town* . . . . (Warner Bros.)
Rod Stewart's Greatest Hits . . . . (Warner Bros.)
Mr. Goldstone
Original Cast; *ST/Gypsy* . . . . (Columbia)
Open Letter To George Bush
Wayne Horvitz/The President; *Miracle Mile* . . . . (Elektra)
Perfumed Garden of Gulliver Smith
Marc Bolan; *T. Rex Classics* . . . . (Cleopatra)
President Garfield
Jerry Holland; *Jerry Holland* . . . . (Rounder)
Same Ol' G
Ginuwine; *ST/Dr. Dolittle* . . . . (Atlantic)
Shorty George
Count Basie; *Best Of Count Basie* . . . . (MCA)
Command Performances . . . . (Accord)
Country Party . . . . (Accord)
Sing Along With Count Basie . . . . (Roulette)
Leadbelly; *King Of The 12-String Guitar* . . . . (Legacy)
Take This Hammer . . . . (Smithsonian Folkways)
St. George & The Dragonet
Stan Freberg; *Greatest Hits-Stan Freberg* . . . . (Curb)
Tip Of The Freberg: The Stan Freberg Collection-1951-1998 . . . . (Rhino)
Sunday In The Park With George
Original Cast; *Sunday In The Park With George* . . . . (RCA Victor)
Theme From "George Of The Jungle"
Original Soundtrack; *Television's Greatest Hits-#2-C* . . . . (TVT)
Theme From "Gilligan's Island"
Original Soundtrack; *CBS: The First 50 Years* . . . . (TVT)
Television's Greatest Hits-#1-C . . . . (TVT)
Theme From "Gomer Pyle, U.S.M.C."
Original Soundtrack; *Television's Greatest Hits-#2-C* . . . . (TVT)
Theme From "Inspector Gadget"
Original Soundtrack; *Television's Greatest Hits-#3-1970s & 1980s-C* . . . (TVT)
Theme From "It's Garry Shandling's Show"
Original Soundtrack; *Television's Greatest Hits-#7-Cable Ready-C* . . . . . (TVT)
Theme From "The Gumby Show"
Original Soundtrack; *Television's Greatest Hits-#4-Black & White Classics-C* . . . . (TVT)

MEN'S NAMES: H

See Also: **CELEBRITIES: SPECIFIC, FAMILY (various),**
MEN: GENERAL

Are You Sure Hank Done It This Way
Hank Williams, Jr.; *Rowdy* . . . . (WB/Curb)
Waylon Jennings; *Waylon Jennings' Greatest Hits* . . . . (RCA)
Captain Hook's Waltz
Original Cast/Cyril Ritchard; *Peter Pan-The 1954 Broadway Production* . . . . (RCA Victor)

Cousin Henry
Bobby Womack; *Back To My Roots* . . . . (Right Stuff)
Death Of Hank Williams
Jack Cardwell; *Super Country Hits Of The '50s-C* . . . . (Gusto)
Death Of Harry Simms
Pete Seeger; *Essential Pete Seeger* . . . . (Vanguard)
Der Fuehrer's Face
Spike Jones & His City Slickers; *Best Of Spike Jones & His City Slickers* . . . . (RCA)
Diary Of Horace Wimp
Electric Light Orchestra; *Discovery* . . . . (Jet)
Don'tcha Tell Henry
Bob Dylan And The Band; *Basement Tapes* . . . . (Columbia)
Dr. Heckyll & Mr. Jive
Men At Work; *Cargo* . . . . (Columbia)
Dr. Jeckyll & Mr. Hyde
Who; *Magic Bus-The Who On Tour* . . . . (MCA)
Harrigan
Mickey Finn; *Mickey Finn's Music* . . . . (Crescendo)
Harry
Big Brother & The Holding Company; *Big Brother & The Holding Company Live* . . . . (Rhino)
Farewell Song . . . . (Columbia)
Harry
Macy Gray; *The Id* . . . . (Epic)
Harry The Hairy Ape
Ray Stevens; *Best Of Ray Stevens* . . . . (Mercury)
Harry The Hippie
Bobby Womack; *Bobby Womack Greatest Hits* . . . . (Liberty)
Soul Survivor . . . . (EMI)
Harry, Let's Marry
Maxine Brown; *45-#1286* . . . . (Collectables)
Harry's House Centerpiece
Joni Mitchell; *Hissing Of Summer Lawns* . . . . (Asylum)
Henry
New Riders Of The Purple Sage; *Best Of New Riders Of The Purple Sage* . . . . (Columbia)
Bill Graham Presents The Last Days Of The Fillmore-C . . . . (Epic Portrait Assoc.)
Home Home On The Road . . . . (Columbia)
New Riders Of The Purple Sage . . . . (Columbia)
Henry Martin
Joan Baez; *Jack Orion* . . . . (Vanguard)
Joan Baez . . . . (Vanguard)
The Joan Baez Ballad Book . . . . (Vanguard)
Henry's Got Flat Feet (Can't Dance No More)
Hank Ballard And The Midnighters; *Sexy Ways: The Best Of Hank Ballard & The Midnighters* . . . . (Rhino)
Hernando's Hideaway
Original Cast; *Pajama Game* . . . . (Columbia)
ST/Pajama Game . . . . (Collectables)
Hey, Herman
Original Broadway Cast; *The Most Happy Fella* . . . . (Sony Music Classical)
Hook's Tango
Original Cast/Cyril Ritchard; *Peter Pan-The 1954 Broadway Production* . . . . (RCA Victor)
Howard's Dead & Gone
Weavers; *Weavers-Classics* . . . . (Vanguard)
Hurricane
Bob Dylan; *Desire* . . . . (Columbia)
Hymn To Hymie
Original Cast; *Milk & Honey* . . . . (RCA Victor)
I'm Henry The VIII, I Am
Herman's Hermits; *Herman's Hermits-Their Greatest Hits* . . . . (Abkco)
Something Good Again . . . . (Abkco)
Just You Wait (Henry Higgins)
Julie Andrews/Original Cast; *My Fair Lady* . . . . (Columbia)
Little Hitler
Nick Lowe; *Pure Pop For Now People* . . . . (Columbia)
Open The Door, Homer
Bob Dylan And The Band; *Basement Tapes* . . . . (Columbia)
Thunderclap Newman; *Hollywood Dream* . . . . (MCA)
Over At Herbie's Juke Joint
Donald Brown; *People Music* . . . . (Muse)
Poor Howard
Leadbelly; *Gwine Dig A Hole To Put The Devil In* . . . . (Rounder)
Leadbelly . . . . (Everest)
Leadbelly . . . . (Fantasy)
Memorial-#4 . . . . (Stinson)
President Hayes
Sonny Rollins; *Don't Stop The Carnival* . . . . (Milestone)
Save The Bones For Henry
Ray Charles; *Just Between Us* . . . . (Columbia)
Springtime For Hitler
Mel Brooks; *ST/High Anxiety* . . . . (Asylum)
Original Broadway Cast; *The Producers* . . . . (Sony Music Classical)
Theme From "Hardcastle And McCormick"
Original Soundtrack; *Television's Greatest Hits-#6-Remote Control-C* . . . (TVT)

Theme From "Hart To Hart"
Original Soundtrack; *Television's Greatest Hits-#3-1970s & 1980s-C* . . . (TVT)
Theme From "Hogan's Heroes"
Original Soundtrack; *CBS: The First 50 Years* . . . . (TVT)
Television's Greatest Hits-#2-C . . . . (TVT)
Theme From "Hopalong Cassidy"
Original Soundtrack; *Television's Greatest Hits-#4-Black & White*
Classics-C . . . . (TVT)
Theme From "Howdy Doody"
Original Soundtrack; *Television's Greatest Hits-#1-C* . . . . (TVT)
Theme From "Huckleberry Hound"
Original Soundtrack; *Hanna-Barbera Classics-#1-Original Recordings Of*
The World's Most Famous Cartoon Themes &
Scores . . . . (Kid Rhino/Rhino 4 Kids)
Hanna-Barbera Pic-A-Nic Basket Of Cartoon
Classics . . . . (Kid Rhino/Rhino 4 Kids)
Television's Greatest Hits-#2-C . . . . (TVT)
Theme From "Hunter"
Original Soundtrack; *Television's Greatest Hits-#6-Remote Control-C* . . (TVT)
Theme From "Starsky & Hutch"
Original Soundtrack; *Television's Greatest Hits-#3-1970s & 1980s-C* . . . (TVT)
Theme From "The Mighty Hercules"
Original Soundtrack; *Television's Greatest Hits-#4-Black & White*
Classics-C . . . . (TVT)
Tom, Dick Or Harry
Original Cast; *Kiss Me Kate* . . . . (Sony Music Classical)
Uncle Albert/Admiral Halsey
Paul And Linda McCartney; *RAM* . . . . (Capitol)
Paul McCartney; *All The Best!* . . . . (Capitol)
Paul McCartney-Gift Set . . . . (Capitol)
Wings; *Wings Greatest* . . . . (Capitol)
Voice Of Harold
R.E.M.; *Dead Letter Office* . . . .(I.R.S.)
Wallflower, The (Henry)
Etta James and "The Peaches"; *Collectables Presents The History Of*
Rock-#1-C . . . . (Collectables)
Oldies But Goodies-#1-C . . . . (Original Sound)
We'd Like To Thank You Herbert Hoover
Original Broadway Cast; *Annie* . . . . (Columbia)

MEN'S NAMES: I

See Also: **CELEBRITIES: SPECIFIC, FAMILY (various),**
MEN: GENERAL

Ballad Of Ira Hayes, The
Johnny Cash; *The Man In Black-His Greatest Hits.* . . . . (Legacy)
Peter La Farge; *Best Of Broadside 1962-1968: Anthems Of The American*
Underground From The Pages Of Broadside
Magazine-C . . . . (Smithsonian Folkways)
Theme From "Ironside"
Original Soundtrack; *Television's Greatest Hits-#1-C* . . . . (TVT)
Uncle Isak Goes To Africa
Tom Wasinger; *Rock Music* . . . . (Invincible)

MEN'S NAMES: J

See Also: **CELEBRITIES: SPECIFIC, GOD (Jesus), FAMILY**
(various), MEN: GENERAL

Abraham, Martin And John
Dion; *Collectables Presents The History Of Rock-#3-C* . . . . (Collectables)
Dion-24 Original Classics . . . . (Arista)
Songs Of Protest-C . . . . (Rhino)
WCBS FM 101 History Of Rock-'60s-#2-C . . . . (Collectables)
Harry Belafonte; *Harry Belafonte's All Time Greatest Hits-#1* . . . . (RCA)
Smokey Robinson & The Miracles; *Smokey Robinson & The Miracles'*
Anthology . . . . (Motown)
Time Out For Smokey Robinson & The Miracles/Special
Occasion . . . . (Motown)
Angry Johnny
Poe; *Hello* . . . . (Modern)
Are You Jimmy Ray?
Jimmy Ray; *Jimmy Ray* . . . .(Epic)
Ballad Of A Thin Man (Mr. Jones)
Bob Dylan; *Before The Flood* . . . . (Columbia)
Ballad Of Frankie Lee & Judas Priest
Bob Dylan; *John Wesley Harding* . . . . (Columbia)
Ballad Of Jed Clampett
Flatt & Scruggs; *Columbia Country Classics-#3-Americana-C* . . . . . (Columbia)
On Foggy Mountain . . . . (Fifty One West)
Ballad Of John And Yoko
Beatles; *Beatles 1* . . . . (Capitol)
Beatles-Box Set . . . . (Capitol)
Hey Jude . . . . (Capitol)
Past Masters-Volume Two . . . . (Parlophone)

ST/Imagine: John Lennon . . . .(Capitol)
The Beatles/1967-1970. . . . .(Capitol)
Be Good Johnny
Men At Work; *Business As Usual* . . . . (Columbia)
Big Bad John
Jimmy Dean; *American Originals-Jimmy Dean* . . . . (Columbia)
Billboard Top Country Hits-1961-C . . . . (Rhino)
Columbia Country Classics-#3-Americana-C . . . . (Columbia)
Jimmy Dean's Greatest Hits . . . . (Columbia)
Big Joe & Phantom 309
Tom Waits; *Double Live* . . . . (Asylum)
Nighthawks At The Diner . . . . (Asylum)
Big John
Shirelles; *Shirelles-16 Greatest Hits* . . . .(Trip)
Shirelles-Anthology 1959-1964 . . . . (Rhino)
Shirelles-Classics . . . . (Bac-Trac)
Super Oldies Of The '60s-#10-C . . . . (Audio Fidelity)
Captain Jack
Billy Joel; *Billy Joel-Greatest Hits, Volume I & Volume II* . . . . (Columbia)
Piano Man . . . . (Columbia)
Songs In The Attic . . . . (Columbia)
Choo Choo Ch'Boogie (Jack)
Asleep At The Wheel; *All Time Legends Of Country Music-C* . . . . . . (Legacy)
Asleep At The Wheel . . . . (Epic)
Hot Tracks-Train Super Hits-C . . . . (Epic)
Served Live . . . . (Capitol)
Very Best Of Asleep At The Wheel Since 1970 . . . . (Relentless/Madacy)
Beach Boys; *Ten Years Of Harmony* . . . .(Caribou)
Clifton Chenier; *Alligator Stomp-#2-C* . . . . (Rhino)
Louis Jordan; *Best Of Louis Jordan* . . . . (MCA)
Quincy Jones; *Birth Of A Band-#2* . . . . (Mercury)
Cotton Eyed Joe
Bob Wills; *Columbia Historic Edition-Bob Wills* . . . . (Columbia)
Carlton Moody & The Moody Brothers; *Carlton Moody & The Moody*
Brothers. . . . . (Lamon)
Daddy's Last Letter (Private First Class John H. McCormick)
Tex Ritter; *45-#1267* . . . . (Capitol)
Dear John
Hank Williams With His Drifting Cowboys; *Hank Williams-24 Greatest*
Hits-#2. . . . .(Polydor)
Hank Williams-40 Greatest Hits. . . . .(Polydor)
Hey Good Lookin' (December 1950-July 1951). . . . .(Polydor)
Dear John
Joe Walsh; *Confessor* . . . . (Full Moon)
Dear John
Elton John; *Jump Up!* . . . . (MCA)
Dear John
Nazareth; *Nazareth* . . . . (A&M)
Dear John & Marsha Letter
Stan Freberg; *Capitol Collectors Series-Stan Freberg* . . . . (Capitol)
Dear John Letter
Jean Shepard; *Heroes Of Country Music-#4-Legends Of The West*
Coast-C . . . . (Rhino)
Jean Shepard & Ferlin Husky; *Classic Duets-C* . . . . (Liberty)
Dear John Letter Lounge
Jerry Jeff Walker; *It's A Good Night For Singin'* . . . . (MCA)
Devil Comes Back To Georgia (Johnny)
Marc O'Connor; *Heroes* . . . . (Warner Bros.)
Devil Went Down To Georgia (Johnny)
Charlie Daniels Band; *A Decade Of Hits.* . . . . (Epic)
Billboard Top Hits-1979-C . . . . (Rhino)
Me & The Boys . . . . (Epic)
Million Mile Reflections . . . . (Epic)
ST/Urban Cowboy . . . .(Asylum)
Diamond Joe
Tom Rush; *Mind Ramblin'* . . . .(Prestige)
Tom Rush . . . . (Fantasy)
Did You See Jackie Robinson Hit That Ball?
Count Basie; *RCA Victor Blues & Rhythm Revue-C* . . . . (RCA)
Count Basie & His Orchestra; *Baseball's Greatest Hits-C* . . . . (Rhino)
Dinner For One Please James
Nat "King" Cole; *Blossom Fell* . . . . (Capitol)
Nat "King" Cole-Gift Set . . . . (Capitol)
D-I-V-O-R-C-E
Rosanne Cash; *Tammy Wynette...Remembered-C* . . . .(Asylum)
Tammy Wynette; *Super Hits Of The '60s-C* . . . . (Epic)
Tammy Wynette-Anniversary-20 Years Of Hits . . . . (Epic)
Tammy Wynette's Biggest Hits . . . . (Epic)
Tammy Wynette's Greatest Hits . . . . (Epic)
Don't Cry Joe (Let Her Go, Let Her Go)
Frank Sinatra; *Sinatra Swings* . . . . (Reprise)
Down At Papa Joe's
Dixiebelles; *WCBS FM 101 History Of Rock-'60s-#3-C.* . . . . (Collectables)
Dr. Heckyll & Mr. Jive
Men At Work; *Cargo* . . . . (Columbia)
Dr. Jeckyll & Mr. Hyde
Who; *Magic Bus-The Who On Tour* . . . . (MCA)
Dr. Jimmy
Who; *ST/Quadrophenia* . . . . (MCA)

El Macho (Jerry)
Mark Knopfler; *Sailing To Philadelphia* . . . . (Warner Bros.)

Empty Garden (Hey Hey Johnny)
Elton John; *Elton John's Greatest Hits-1976-1986* . . . . (MCA)
   Jump Up! . . . . (MCA)

Farmer John
Premiers; *Frat Rock!-#2-C* . . . . (Rhino)
   History Of Latino Rock-#1-C . . . . (Rhino)

Farmer John
Neil Young & Crazy Horse; *Ragged Glory* . . . . (Reprise)

Fat Jack
Steppenwolf; *Steppenwolf 7* . . . . (MCA)

Feed Jake
Pirates Of The Mississippi; *Pirates Of The Mississippi* . . . . (Liberty)

Frankie & Johnny
Brook Benton; *Endlessly-The Best Of Brook Benton* . . . . (Rhino)
Doc Watson; *Favorites-Doc Watson* . . . . (Liberty)
Jerry Lee Lewis; *Jerry Lee's Greatest!* . . . . (Rhino)

Frankie & Johnny Blues
Glenn Yarbrough; *Best Of Glenn Yarbrough.* . . . . (RCA)
Kay Starr; *Kay Starr-Country* . . . . (Crescendo)

Frere Jacques
Original Soundtrack; *Toddler Favorites* . . . . (Kid Rhino/Rhino 4 Kids)

Gentleman Jim
Joe Hackney; *Heavy Hitter* . . . . (Happy Hour Music)

Get Back (Jo Jo)
Beatles; *Beatles 1.* . . . . (Capitol)
   Beatles-20 Greatest Hits . . . . (Capitol)
   Beatles-Box Set . . . . (Capitol)
   Let It Be. . . . . (Capitol)
   Past Masters-Volume Two . . . . (Parlophone)
   Reel Music . . . . (Capitol)
   Rock 'N' Roll Music . . . . (Capitol)
   The Beatles/1967-1970. . . . . (Capitol)

Get Up John
Ricky Skaggs and Kentucky Thunder; *Bluegrass Rules!.* . . . . (Rounder)

Go Jimmy Go
Jimmy Clanton; *Super Oldies Of The '50s-#2-C* . . . . (Audio Fidelity)

Go On With The Wedding (Jim)
Patti Page; *Patti Page-Golden Celebration* . . . . (Mercury)

Goodbye Jimmy Goodbye
Kathy Linden; *Rock 'N Roll Relix: 1954-1959-C* . . . . (Eclipse)

Great Joe Bob (A Regional Tragedy)
Country Gazette; *Hello Operator...This Is Country Gazette* . . . . . . (Flying Fish)

Happy Birthday, John (Happy Trails)
Janis Joplin; *Janis* . . . . (Legacy)

Happy Jack
Who; *Happy Jack* . . . . (MCA)
   Meaty Beaty Big & Bouncy . . . . (MCA)
   ST/The Kids Are Alright . . . . (MCA)
   Who Greatest Hits. . . . . (MCA)

Haul Away, Joe
Burl Ives; *Best Of Burl Ives* . . . . (MCA)
Clancy Brothers; *Clancy Brothers Greatest Hits.* . . . . (Vanguard)

Hey Joe
Jimi Hendrix; *Essential Jimi Hendrix, Volume 2* . . . . (Reprise)
   Live At Winterland . . . . (Rykodisc)
Jimi Hendrix Experience; *Are You Experienced?* . . . . (Reprise)
   Smash Hits . . . . (Reprise)
Love; *Best Of Love* . . . . (Rhino)

Hey Joe!
Carl Smith; *All Time Legends Of Country Music-C* . . . . (Legacy)

Hey Joe, Hey Moe
Moe Bandy & Joe Stampley; *Hey Joe, Hey Moe* . . . . (Columbia)
   Live At Bad Bob's . . . . (Columbia)
   Moe Bandy & Joe Stampley's Greatest Hits . . . . (Columbia)

Hey Jude
Beatles; *Beatles 1.* . . . . (Capitol)
   Beatles-20 Greatest Hits. . . . . (Capitol)
   Past Masters-Volume Two . . . . (Parlophone)
   The Beatles/1967-1970. . . . . (Capitol)
Paul McCartney; *Knebworth-The Album-C* . . . . (Polydor)
Wilson Pickett; *Wilson Pickett's Greatest Hits* . . . . (Atlantic)

Hit The Road Jack
Ray Charles; *Ray Charles' Greatest Hits* . . . . (Rhino)
   Ray Charles-Anthology . . . . (Rhino)
   Ray Charles-His Greatest Hits-#2 . . . . (Dunhill Compact Classics)

House That Jack Built
Aretha Franklin; *Aretha Franklin-30 Greatest Hits.* . . . . (Rhino)
   Aretha's Gold . . . . (Atlantic)

I Just Shot John Lennon
Cranberries; *To The Faithful Departed* . . . . (Island)

In Memoriam-John F. & Robert F. Kennedy
Clare Fischer; *'Twas Only Yesterday.* . . . . (Discovery)

I've Been Watching You (Jamie's Girl)
Randy Hall; *I Belong To You* . . . . (MCA)

J.A.R. (Jason Andrew Relva)
Green Day; *ST/Angus* . . . . (Reprise)

Jack & Diane
John Cougar; *American Fool* . . . . (Riva)

Jack And Jill
Ray Parker Jr.; *Chartbusters* . . . . (Arista)
   Ray Parker Jr.'s Greatest Hits . . . . (Arista)
Raydio; *Raydio.* . . . . (Arista)

Jack Daniel And Mr. Jim Beam
Philip Claypool; *Perfect World* . . . . (Curb)

Jack Daniel's If You Please
David Allan Coe; *David Allan Coe-Super Hits* . . . . (Columbia)
   For The Record-The First 10 Years. . . . . (Columbia)

Jack Daniel's Kind Of Day
Johnny Winter; *Lone Star Kind Of Day* . . . . (Relix)

Jack Daniel's Old No. 7
Jerry Lee Lewis; *Killer Country* . . . . (Mercury)

Jack Daniels, You Lied To Me Again
Ray Stevens; *20 Comedy Hits Special Collection* . . . . (Curb)

Jack Straw
Bruce Hornsby & The Range; *Deadicated-C* . . . . (Arista)
Grateful Dead; *Europe '72.* . . . . (Warner Bros.)
   What A Long Strange Trip It's Been: The Best Of The
   Grateful Dead. . . . . (Warner Bros.)

Jack You're Dead
Joe Jackson; *Jumpin' Jive* . . . . (A&M)
Louis Jordan; *Jazz Heritage-Greatest Hits-#2-1941-1947* . . . . (MCA)

Jackhammer John
Richie Havens & Pete Seeger; *Tribute To Woody Guthrie-C* . . . . (Warner Bros.)

Jackie Brown
John Cougar Mellencamp; *Big Daddy* . . . . (Mercury)

Jackie Wilson Said (I'm In Heaven When You Smile)
Van Morrison; *Best Of Van Morrison* . . . . (Polydor)
   St. Dominic's Preview . . . . (Warner Bros.)
   ST/Queen's Logic . . . . (Epic)

Jacob's Ladder
Rush; *Exit...Stage Left* . . . . (Mercury)
   Permanent Waves . . . . (Mercury)

Jacob's Ladder
Mark Wills; *Mark Wills* . . . . (Mercury)

Jacob's Ladder
Huey Lewis and the News; *Fore!.* . . . . (Chrysalis)

Jacob's Ladder
Bruce Hornsby & The Range; *Scenes From The Southside* . . . . (RCA)

Jambalaya (On The Bayou) (Joe)
Blue Ridge Rangers; *Blue Ridge Rangers* . . . . (Fantasy)
Fats Domino; *Fats Domino's Greatest Hits* . . . . (MCA)
Hank Williams With His Drifting Cowboys; *24 Of Hank Williams'*
   Greatest Hits . . . . (Polydor)
   Hank Williams-16 Great Hits . . . . (Everest)
   Hank Williams-40 Greatest Hits . . . . (Polydor)
Hank Williams, Jr.; *ST/Your Cheatin' Heart* . . . . (Sony Music Special Prod.)
Jerry Lee Lewis; *Twenty Classic Hits* . . . . (Sun)
Nitty Gritty Dirt Band; *All The Good Times* . . . . (United Artists)
   Stars And Stripes Forever . . . . (Capitol)

James
Huffamoose; *We've Been Had Again.* . . . . (Interscope)

James Dean
Eagles; *On The Border.* . . . . (Elektra)

Jeremy
Pearl Jam; *Ten* . . . . (Epic Portrait Assoc.)

Jesse
Roberta Flack; *Best Of Roberta Flack* . . . . (Atlantic)
   Killing Me Softly . . . . (Atlantic)

Jesse
Carly Simon; *Come Upstairs* . . . . (Warner Bros.)

Jesse
Stephanie Mills; *If I Were Your Woman* . . . . (MCA)

Jesse
Joan Baez; *Joan Baez-Classics-#8.* . . . . (A&M)

Jesse
Joan Armatrading; *Sleight Of Hand* . . . . (A&M)

Jesse James
Country Joe McDonald; *Country Joe* . . . . (Vanguard)
   Essential Country Joe McDonald . . . . (Vanguard)

Jesse James
Sam McGee; *Granddad Of The Country Guitar Pickers* . . . . (Arhoolie)

Jesse James
Bob Seger; *Smokin' O.P.'s.* . . . . (Capitol)

Jessie's Girl
Rick Springfield; *Nipper's Greatest Hits Of The '80s-C* . . . . (RCA)
   Rick Springfield's Greatest Hits . . . . (RCA)
   Working Class Dog . . . . (RCA)

Jim
Big Maybelle; *Ladies Sing The Blues-#2-C* . . . . (Savoy)

Jim Dandy
Black Oak Arkansas; *Best Of Black Oak Arkansas* . . . . (Atco)
   Super Hits Of The '70s-Have A Nice Day-#12-C . . . . (Rhino)
LaVern Baker; *Atlantic Rhythm & Blues 1947-1974-#3 (1955-*
   1958)-C . . . . (Atlantic)

Jim Dean Of Indiana
Phil Ochs; *Chords Of Fame* . . . . (A&M)
Phil Ochs' Greatest Hits . . . . (A&M)
The War Is Over-Best Of Phil Ochs . . . . (A&M)
Jim, What's Wrong With Him
Dramatics; *Dramatic Experience* . . . .(Stax)
Jimmie The Kid
Jimmie Rodgers; *Steel Town* . . . . (Flying Fish)
Jimmy Jazz
Clash; *London Calling* . . . .(Epic)
Jimmy Lee
Aretha Franklin; *Aretha* . . . . (Arista)
Jimmy Mack
Martha & The Vandellas; *Billboard Top R&B Hits-1967-C* . . . . (Rhino)
Compact Command Performances-Martha Reeves & The Vandellas . . . . (Motown)
Martha Reeves & The Vandellas-Anthology . . . . (Motown)
Motown Story-First 25 Years-C . . . . (Motown)
Motown Superstar Series-#11-Martha Reeves & The Vandellas . . . . (Motown)
Top 10 With A Bullet-Motown Girl Groups-C . . . . (Motown)
Jimmy Olsen's Blues
Spin Doctors; *Pocket Full Of Kryptonite* . . . . (Epic Portrait Assoc.)
Jimmy, Jimmy
Madonna; *True Blue* . . . . (Sire)
Jo Jo
Boz Scaggs; *Boz Scaggs-Hits!* . . . . (Columbia)
Middle Man . . . . (Columbia)
Jody's Got Your Girl & Gone
Johnnie Taylor; *Johnnie Taylor-Super Hits* . . . .(Stax)
Joe Hill
Arlo Guthrie & Pete Seeger; *Together In Concert* . . . . (Reprise)
Joan Baez; *Carry It On* . . . . (Vanguard)
From Every Stage . . . . (A&M)
One Day At A Time . . . . (Vanguard)
ST/Woodstock . . . .(Atlantic)
Joe Knows How To Live
Eddy Raven; *Best Of Eddy Raven* . . . . (RCA)
Nitty Gritty Dirt Band; *Hold On* . . . .(Warner Bros.)
Joe Slam And The Spaceship
Harry Connick, Jr.; *She* . . . . (Columbia)
Joey
Bob Dylan; *Desire* . . . . (Columbia)
Bob Dylan & The Grateful Dead; *Bob Dylan & The Grateful Dead* . . . . (Columbia)
Joey
Concrete Blonde; *Bloodletting* . . . .(I.R.S.)
Joey, Joey, Joey
Al Jarreau; *1965* . . . . (Bainbridge)
Broadway Cast; *Most Happy Fella* . . . . (RCA)
Judy Garland; *Judy Garland-Live* . . . . (Capitol)
One & Only . . . . (Capitol)
Joey's On The Streets Again
Boomtown Rats; *Boomtown Rats' Greatest Hits* . . . . (Columbia)
Ratrospective . . . . (Columbia)
Tonic For The Troops . . . . (Columbia)
John 3:16
Wyclef; *Muggs Presents...The Soul Assassins-C* . . . . (Columbia)
John Barleycorn
Traffic; *John Barleycorn Must Die* . . . . (Island)
John Brown's Body
Pete Seeger; *American Favorite Ballads-#3* . . . . (Smithsonian Folkways)
Sonny Terry & Brownie McGhee; *Every Tone A Testimony-C* . . . . (Smithsonian Folkways)
John Doe No. 24
Mary Chapin Carpenter; *Stones In The Road* . . . . (Columbia)
John Hardy
Leadbelly; *Bourgeois Blues-Golden Classics-#1* . . . . (Collectables)
Leadbelly . . . . (Fantasy)
Legend Of Leadbelly . . . . (Tradition)
Pete Seeger; *Essential Pete Seeger* . . . . (Vanguard)
John Henry
''Little'' Jimmy Dickens; *Columbia Historic Edition-''Little'' Jimmy Dickens* . . . . (Columbia)
Harry Belafonte; *Harry Belafonte-At Carnegie Hall* . . . . (RCA)
Harry Belafonte-Legendary Performer . . . . (RCA)
Harry Belafonte's All Time Greatest Hits-#1 . . . . (RCA)
Merle Travis; *Great American Train Songs-C* . . . .(C.M.H. Prod.)
Odetta; *Essential Odetta* . . . . (Vanguard)
Greatest Folksingers Of The '60s-C . . . . (Vanguard)
Woody Guthrie; *Immortal Woody Guthrie-Golden Classics-#2* . . . (Collectables)
Legendary Woody Guthrie . . . .(Tradition)
John I'm Only Dancing
David Bowie; *Changesbowie* . . . .(Rykodisc)
Sound + Vision . . . .(Rykodisc)
The Singles-1969-1993 . . . .(Rykodisc)
John Lee Hooker
Johnny Rivers; *Johnny Rivers-Golden Hits* . . . . (Imperial)
John Peel
Hermes Nye; *Anglo-American Songs* . . . . (Smithsonian Folkways)

Johnny 99
Bruce Springsteen; *Nebraska* . . . . (Columbia)
Bruce Springsteen & The E Street Band; *Bruce Springsteen & The E Street Band Live/1975-85* . . . . (Legacy)
Johnny Cash; *Cover Me (Bruce Springsteen Tribute)-C* . . . . (Rhino)
Johnny Angel
Shelley Fabares; *Billboard Top Rock 'N' Roll Hits-1962-C* . . . . (Rhino)
ST/Mermaids . . . . (Geffen)
Johnny B
Hooters; *One Way Home* . . . . (Columbia)
Johnny B. Goode
Chuck Berry; *Chuck Berry's Greatest Hits* . . . . (Everest)
Classic Rock-#2-C . . . . (MCA)
Roll Over Beethoven . . . . (Allegiance)
ST/American Graffiti . . . . (MCA)
The Chess Box-Chuck Berry . . . . (Chess)
Elvis Presley; *Elvis In Concert* . . . . (RCA)
From Memphis To Vegas/From Vegas To Memphis . . . . (RCA)
Grateful Dead; *Bill Graham Presents The Last Days Of The Fillmore-C* . . . . (Epic Portrait Assoc.)
Johnny Winter; *Live/Johnny Winter And* . . . . (Columbia)
Second Winter . . . . (Columbia)
Johnny Bye-Bye
Bruce Springsteen; *Tracks* . . . . (Columbia)
Johnny Can't Read
Don Henley; *I Can't Stand Still* . . . .(Asylum)
Johnny Get Angry
Joanie Sommers; *Best Of The Girl Groups-#2-C* . . . . (Rhino)
Johnny Has Gone For A Soldier
Jo Stafford; *American Folk Songs* . . . . (Corinthian)
Johnny Have You Seen Her?
Rembrandts; *United* . . . . (Atco)
Johnny I Love You
Booker T. & The M.G.s; *Booker T. & The M.G.s' Greatest Hits* . . . . (Stax)
Johnny Needs A Fast Car
Chris Rea; *Espresso Logic* . . . . (East West)
Johnny One Note
Judy Garland; *Best Of Judy Garland-From MGM Classic Films* . . . . (MCA)
Original Cast/Mary Martin; *Babes In Arms* . . . . (Sony Music Special Prod.)
Johnny Porter
Persuasions; *Chirpin'* . . . . (Elektra)
Ry Cooder; *Borderline* . . . . (Warner Bros.)
Johnny Strikes Up The Band
Warren Zevon; *Excitable Boy* . . . .(Asylum)
Quiet Normal Life-Best Of Warren Zevon . . . .(Asylum)
Johnny The Fox Meets Jimmy The Weed
Thin Lizzy; *Live And Dangerous* . . . . (Warner Bros.)
Johnny Thunder
Kinks; *Are The Village Green Preservation Society* . . . . (Reprise)
Johnny Too Bad
Slickers; *ST/The Harder They Come* . . . . (Mango)
Taj Mahal; *Best Of Taj Mahal* . . . . (Columbia)
Mo' Roots . . . . (Legacy)
UB40; *Labour Of Love* . . . . (A&M)
Live In Moscow . . . . (A&M)
Johnny, My Love (Grandma's Diary)
Wilma Lee & Stoney Cooper; *45-#1118* . . . . (Hickory)
Johnny's Garden
Stephen Stills; *Manassas* . . . .(Atlantic)
John's Back In Town
Gene Watson; *Best Of Gene Watson* . . . . (Capitol)
John's Idea
Count Basie; *Basie Reunions* . . . .(Prestige)
Best Of Count Basie . . . . (MCA)
One O'Clock Jump . . . . (MCA)
Joker James
Brian Hyland; *Brian Hyland's Greatest Hits* . . . . (Rhino)
Joltin' Joe DiMaggio
Les Brown & His Orchestra; *Baseball's Greatest Hits-C* . . . . (Rhino)
Words & Music Of World War II-C . . . . (Columbia)
Jones On The Jukebox
Becky Hobbs; *All Keyed Up* . . . . (RCA)
Joshua Fought The Battle Of Jericho
Elvis Presley; *His Hand In Mine* . . . . (RCA)
Jordanaires; *Tribute To Elvis' Favorite Spirituals* . . . . (Step One)
New Messengers Of Happiness; *Swinging Gospel* . . . . (Alshire)
Pete Seeger; *20 Golden Pieces Of Pete Seeger* . . . . (Bulldog)
Sister Rosetta Tharpe; *Live At The Hot Club De France* . . . . (Milan)
Judy's Turn To Cry (Johnny)
Lesley Gore; *'60s Dance Party-#2-C* . . . . (Dominion Entert.)
Golden Hits Of Lesley Gore . . . . (Mercury)
Lesley Gore-Anthology . . . . (Rhino)
Jumpin' Jack Flash
Aretha Franklin; *Aretha* . . . . (Arista)
Johnny Winter; *Live/Johnny Winter And* . . . . (Columbia)
Peter Frampton; *Frampton Comes Alive* . . . . (A&M)
Rolling Stones; *Flashpoint* . . . . (Virgin)
Get Yer Ya-Ya's Out! . . . .(Abkco)
Hot Rocks 1964-1971 . . . .(Abkco)

Love You Live . . . .(Virgin)
ST/Jumpin' Jack Flash . . . . (Mercury)
Through The Past, Darkly (Big Hits Vol. 2) . . . . (Abkco)

Junior's Farm
Paul McCartney; *All The Best!* . . . . (Capitol)
Wings; *Wings Greatest* . . . . (Capitol)

Just Like Jesse James
Cher; *Heart Of Stone* . . . . (Geffen)

Just Tell Her Jim Said Hello
Elvis Presley; *Collector's Gold* . . . .(RCA)
Elvis' Gold Records, Volume 4 . . . .(RCA)
The Other Sides-Worldwide Gold Award Hits, Vol. 2 . . . . . .(RCA)

Killer Joe
Quincy Jones; *I Heard That!* . . . . (A&M)
Quincy Jones-Classics-#3 . . . . (A&M)
Quincy Jones-The Best . . . . (A&M)
ST/Listen Up-The Lives Of Quincy Jones . . . . (Qwest)
Walking In Space . . . . (A&M)

Killer Joe
Rocky Fellers; *Scepter Records Story-C* . . . . (Capricorn)

Late Great Johnny Ace, The
Paul Simon; *Hearts & Bones* . . . . (Warner Bros.)

Leader Of The Pack (Jimmy)
Bette Midler; *Divine Miss M* . . . . (Atlantic)
ST/Divine Madness . . . . (Atlantic)
Original Cast; *Leader Of The Pack* . . . . (Elektra)
Shangri-Las; *21 Number One Hits-C* . . . .(Original Sound)
Billboard Top Rock 'N' Roll Hits-1964-C . . . . (Rhino)
Girl Groups-Story Of A Sound-C . . . . (Rhino)
Golden Hits Of The Shangri-Las . . . . (Mercury)
Oldies But Goodies-#15-C . . . .(Original Sound)
Radio Active Hits-#2-C . . . . (Accord)
Remember The Shangri-Las At Their Best . . . . (Collectables)

Letter, The (That Johnny Walker Read)
Asleep At The Wheel; *Very Best Of Asleep At The Wheel*
Since 1970 . . . .(Relentless/Madacy)

Little Joe From Chicago
Mary Lou Williams; *Best Of Mary Lou Williams* . . . . (Pablo)
Nat ''King'' Cole; *Straighten Up And Fly Right* . . . . (Pro-Arte)

Little Joe The Wrangler
Goebel Reeves; *Songs Of Old West* . . . . (Glendale)
Texas Drifter . . . . (Glendale)

Little Joe The Wrangler's Sister Nell
Skip Gorman; *A Cowboy's Wild Song To His Herd* . . . . (Rounder)

Little John Of God
Los Lobos; *The Neighborhood* . . . . (Slash)

Long Gone John From Bowling Green
Red Knuckles & The Trailblazers; *Red Knuckles & The*
Trailblazers . . . . (Flying Fish)

Long Live Our Love (Johnny)
Shangri-Las; *Best Of The Shangri-Las* . . . . (Mercury)

Long Tall Sally
Beatles; *Past Masters-Volume One* . . . .(Parlophone)
Rock 'N' Roll Music . . . . (Capitol)
The Beatles At The Hollywood Bowl . . . . (Capitol)
The Beatles' Second Album . . . . (Capitol)
Little Richard; *Billboard Top R&B Hits-1956-C* . . . . (Rhino)
Here's Little Richard . . . . (Specialty)
Little Richard-18 Greatest Hits . . . . (Rhino)
Little Richard's Greatest Hits . . . . (Everest)
Oldies But Goodies-#3-C . . . .(Original Sound)
ST/Heaven Help Us . . . . (EMI)
Super Oldies Of The '50s-#3-C . . . . (Audio Fidelity)
Tutti Frutti . . . . (Accord)

Long Tall Sally (John)
Beatles; *Past Masters-Volume One* . . . .(Parlophone)
Rock 'N' Roll Music . . . . (Capitol)
The Beatles At The Hollywood Bowl . . . . (Capitol)
The Beatles' Second Album . . . . (Capitol)
Little Richard; *Billboard Top R&B Hits-1956-C* . . . . (Rhino)
Here's Little Richard . . . . (Specialty)
Little Richard-18 Greatest Hits . . . . (Rhino)
Little Richard's Greatest Hits . . . . (Everest)
Oldies But Goodies-#3-C . . . .(Original Sound)
ST/Heaven Help Us . . . . (EMI)
Super Oldies Of The '50s-#3-C . . . . (Audio Fidelity)
Tutti Frutti . . . . (Accord)

Lost John
Doc Watson; *On Stage (Featuring Merle Watson)* . . . . . . (Vanguard)
Reverend Gary Davis; *Legendary Rev. Gary Davis-#1* . . . . (Biograph)
Woody Guthrie; *Woody Guthrie-Early Years* . . . . (Tradition)

Lost John Boogied His Way Into Mexico
Maddox Brothers & Rose; *On The Air-#1 & 2* . . . .(Arhoolie)

Louisiana Joe
Joe Douglas; *45-#1005* . . . . (Bellaire)

Louisiana Lou & Three-Card Monty John
Allman Brothers Band; *Win, Lose Or Draw* . . . . (Polydor)

Manny, Moe & Jack
Dickies; *10 Roir Years-Anthology-C* . . . . (Roir)

We Aren't The World! . . . . (Roir)

Master Jack
Four Jacks & A Jill; *Dick Bartley Presents Collectors Essentials-#1-*
'60s-C . . . . (VSI)

Me And Julio Down By The Schoolyard
Paul Simon; *Greatest Hits, Etc.* . . . .(Columbia)
Negotiations And Love Songs, 1971-1986 . . . . (Warner Bros.)
Paul Simon . . . . (Columbia)
Paul Simon In Concert/Live Rhymin' . . . . (Columbia)
Simon & Garfunkel; *The Concert In Central Park* . . . . . . (Warner Bros.)

Mr. Jones
Grass Roots; *Grass Roots-Anthology (1966-1975)* . . . . (Rhino)

Mr. Jones
Counting Crows; *August And Everything After* . . . . . . (David Geffen Co.)

Mr. Jones
Talking Heads; *Naked* . . . . (Fly/Sire)

New Kid In Town (Johnny Come Lately)
Eagles; *Eagles Greatest Hits, Volume 2* . . . . (Asylum)
Eagles Live . . . . (Asylum)
Hotel California . . . . (Asylum)
Trisha Yearwood; *Common Thread-Songs Of The Eagles-C* . . . . . (Giant)

New York Mining Disaster 1941 (Mr. Jones)
Bee Gees; *Bee Gees-Gold* . . . . (Polydor)
Here At Last...Bee Gees...Live . . . . (Polydor)
History Of British Rock-#8-C . . . . (Rhino)

Nightshift (Jackie)
Commodores; *Nightshift* . . . . (Motown)

No Way Jose
Ray Kennedy; *Guitar Man* . . . . (Atlantic)

Oh Johnny, Oh Johnny, Oh!
Andrews Sisters; *Andrews Sisters' All-Time Greatest Hits* . . . .(Decca)
Boogie Woogie Bugle Boy . . . . (Pro-Arte)

Old Joe Clark
Dillards; *Bluegrass Breakdown* . . . .(Vanguard)
Eric Weissberg; *ST/Deliverance* . . . . (Warner Bros.)

Old Judge Jones
Les Dudek; *Say No More* . . . .(Columbia)

Over There (Johnny)
Glenn Miller; *Original Recordings-#3-Army/Air Force Band* . . . . . . (Pair)
Glenn Miller & His Army/Air Force Band; *Glenn Miller-A Legendary*
Performer-#3 . . . .(Bluebird)
Mormon Tabernacle Choir; *God Bless America* . . . . . . (Sony Music Classical)

Over Yonder (Jonathan's Song)
Steve Earle; *Transcendental Blues* . . . . (Artemis)

Please Mr. Junkman
Penguins; *Oldies-C* . . . .(Dooto)

Poor Little Jimmie
Burl Ives; *Best Of Burl Ives-#2* . . . . (MCA)

Poor, Poor Joseph
Original Cast; *Joseph & The Amazing Technicolor Dreamcoat* . . . . . . (Polydor)

Pore Jud Is Daid
Original Cast; *Oklahoma!* . . . . (MCA)

Puff The Magic Dragon (Johnny Paper)
Peter, Paul & Mary; *10 Years Together/The Best Of Peter, Paul*
and Mary . . . . (Warner Bros.)
Moving . . . . (Warner Bros.)
Peter, Paul & Mommy . . . . (Warner Bros.)
Peter, Paul and Mary In Concert . . . . (Warner Bros.)

Ragtime Cowboy Joe
Jo Stafford; *Capitol Collectors Series-Jo Stafford* . . . . (Capitol)
Spike Jones & His City Slickers; *King Of Corn* . . . . (Glendale)

Ramblin' Jack (A Lonesome Hobo)
Skip Gorman; *A Cowboy's Wild Song To His Herd* . . . . (Rounder)

Ravishing Ruby (Smilin' Jack)
Tom T. Hall; *Essential Tom T. Hall-20th Anniversary Collection* . . . . (Mercury)
Tom T. Hall's Greatest Hits-#2 . . . . (Mercury)

Rebel-Johnny Yuma
Johnny Cash; *The Man In Black-His Greatest Hits* . . . . (Legacy)

Reverend Jack & His Roamin' Cadillac Church
Timbuk 3; *Eden Alley* . . . . (I.R.S.)

Row Jimmy
Grateful Dead; *Wake Of The Flood* . . . . (Grateful Dead)

Roxanna Waltz & Scotland Calling Jesse
Jay Ungar & Others; *Fiddle Fever* . . . . (Flying Fish)

Run Joe
Louis Jordan; *Best Of Louis Jordan* . . . . (MCA)
Neville Brothers; *Fiyo On The Bayou* . . . .(A&M)

Run Joey Run
David Geddes; *Super Hits Of The '70s-Have A Nice Day-#15-C* . . . . .(Rhino)

Sailing, Sailing (Jack)
Original Soundtrack; *Children's Favorites* . . . . (Kid Rhino/Rhino 4 Kids)

Saint Joe On The School Bus
Marcy Playground; *Marcy Playground* . . . .(Capitol)

Say It Isn't So Joe
Roger Daltrey; *Best Bits* . . . . (MCA)
One Of The Boys . . . . (MCA)

Say It's Alright Joe
Genesis; *And Then There Were Three* . . . . (Atlantic)

Set 'Em Up Joe
Vern Gosdin; *Chiseled In Stone* . . . . (Columbia)
Greatest Country Hits Of The '80s-1988-C . . . . (Columbia)
Set Up Two Glasses, Joe
Ernest Tubb/Ferlin Husky/Simon Crum; *Ernest Tubb Collection-C* . . (Step One)
She Gave Her Heart To Jethro
Tom T. Hall; *Essential Tom T. Hall-20th Anniversary Collection* . . (Mercury)
She Thinks His Name Was John
Reba McEntire; *Read My Mind* . . . .(MCA)
Reba McEntire's Greatest Hits-#3: I'm A Survivor . . . .(MCA)
Shoeless Joe From Hannibal, Mo.
Original Broadway Cast; *Damn Yankees* . . . . (RCA)
Skid Row Joe
Porter Wagoner; *Best Of Porter Wagoner-#1* . . . . (RCA)
Porter Wagoner's Greatest . . . . (Tudor)
Sloop John B
Beach Boys; *Absolute Best-#2* . . . . (Capitol)
Beach Boys '69 (The Beach Boys Live In London) . . . . (Capitol)
Beach Boys-Gift Set . . . . (Capitol)
Best Of (Good Vibrations) . . . . (Reprise)
Made In The U.S.A. . . . . (Capitol)
Pet Sounds . . . . (Capitol)
ST/Forrest Gump . . . . (Epic/Sony Music Soundtrax)
The Pet Sounds Sessions: A 30th Anniversary Collection . . . . . . (Capitol)
Smackwater Jack
Carole King; *Carole King's Greatest Hits* . . . .(Epic)
Tapestry . . . .(Epic)
Smokey Joe's Cafe
Coasters; *Coasters-Their Greatest Recordings-Early Years* . . . . . (Atco)
Young Blood . . . .(Atlantic)
Loudon Wainwright III; *Album III* . . . . (Columbia)
Stagedoor Johnny
Donnie Iris; *Fortune 410* . . . .(MCA)
Surabaya Johnny
Bette Midler; *Bette Midler* . . . .(Atlantic)
Dagmar Krause; *Lost In The Stars-Music Of Kurt Weill-C* . . . . (A&M)
Surfer Joe
Surfaris; *Surfin' Hits-C* . . . . (Rhino)
Surfin' Sixties-C . . . . (JCI Assoc. Labels)
Sweet Baby James
James Taylor; *James Taylor's Greatest Hits* . . . .(Warner Bros.)
Sweet Baby James . . . . (Warner Bros.)
Sweet Baby James
Highway 101; *Paint The Town* . . . . (Warner Bros.)
Theme From "James At 15"
Original Soundtrack; *Television's Greatest Hits-#6-Remote Control-C* . . (TVT)
Theme From "James Bond"
John Barry Orchestra; *Best Of James Bond-30th Anniversary-C* . . . .(EMI)
London Symphony Orchestra; *From London With Love-Music Of
James Bond* . . . . (Pro-Arte)
Theme From "John Larroquette Show"
Original Soundtrack; *Television's Greatest Hits-#7-Cable Ready-C* . . . . . (TVT)
Theme From "Johnny Quest"
Original Soundtrack; *Hanna-Barbera Pic-A-Nic Basket Of Cartoon
Classics* . . . . (Kid Rhino/Rhino 4 Kids)
Television's Greatest Hits-#2-C . . . . (TVT)
Theme From "Judd For The Defense"
Original Soundtrack; *Television's Greatest Hits-#5-In Living Color-C* . . . (TVT)
Theme From "The Jackie Gleason Show"
Original Soundtrack; *CBS: The First 50 Years* . . . . (TVT)
Television's Greatest Hits-#2-C . . . . (TVT)
Theme From "The Jeffersons"
Original Soundtrack; *CBS: The First 50 Years* . . . . (TVT)
Television's Greatest Hits-#3-1970s & 1980s-C . . . . (TVT)
Theme From "The Jetsons"
Original Soundtrack; *Hanna-Barbera Pic-A-Nic Basket Of Cartoon
Classics* . . . . (Kid Rhino/Rhino 4 Kids)
Television's Greatest Hits-#1-C . . . . (TVT)
Stunners; *ST/Jetsons-The Movie* . . . .(MCA)
Theme From "The Legend Of Jesse James"
Original Soundtrack; *Television's Greatest Hits-#4-Black & White
Classics-C* . . . . (TVT)
Theme From "Tom & Jerry"
Henry Mancini; *ST/Tom & Jerry-The Movie* . . . .(MCA)
Theme From Jack Johnson
Miles Davis; *Agharta* . . . . (Columbia)
They Were Doin' The Mambo (Joe)
Vaughn Monroe; *Very Best Of Vaughn Monroe* . . . .(Taragon)
This Is The Army, Mr. Jones
Irving Berlin; *V-E Day 50th Anniversary-The Musical
Memories-C* . . . .(Living Era)
Mel Torme & George Shearing; *Mel & George Do World
War II* . . . . (Concord Jazz)
Mormon Tabernacle Choir; *God Bless America* . . . . (Sony Music Classical)
Three Bells, The (Jimmy Brown)
Browns; *Billboard Top Country Hits-1959-C* . . . . (Rhino)
Nipper's Greatest Hits Of The '50s-#1-C . . . . (RCA)
Tokyo Joe
Bryan Ferry; *In Your Mind* . . . . (Reprise)

Top Jimmy
Van Halen; *1984* . . . . (Warner Bros.)
Uncle Jack
Spirit; *Best Of Spirit* . . . . (Epic)
Spirit . . . . (Epic)
Spirit Of '84 . . . . (Mercury)
Time Circle . . . . (Epic)
Uncle John's Band
Grateful Dead; *Best Of/Skeletons From The Closet* . . . . (Warner Bros.)
Workingman's Dead . . . . (Warner Bros.)
Indigo Girls; *Deadicated-C* . . . . (Arista)
Under African Skies (Joseph)
Paul Simon; *Graceland* . . . . (Warner Bros.)
Walkaway Joe
Trisha Yearwood; *Hearts In Armor* . . . . (MCA)
Songbook-A Collection Of Hits . . . . (MCA)
When Johnny Comes Marching Home
Marilyn Horne; *Beautiful Dreamer-Great American Songbook* . . . .(London)
Mormon Tabernacle Choir; *Songs Of The Civil War And Stephen Foster
Favorites* . . . . (Sony Music Classical)
United States Military Academy Band; *Songs Of The Civil War-C* . . . (Columbia)
Who's Johnny
El DeBarge; *El DeBarge* . . . . (Motown)
You Don't Mess Around With Jim
Jim Croce; *Down The Highway* . . . .(Atlantic)
Photographs & Memories/His Greatest Hits . . . .(Atlantic)

MEN'S NAMES: K

See Also: **CELEBRITIES: SPECIFIC, FAMILY (various),
MEN: GENERAL**

Barbie & Ken
Weathermen; *Black Album According To The
Weathermen* . . . .(Play It Again Sam)
Barbie & Ken Ferrari
John Hiatt; *Perfectly Good Guitar* . . . . (A&M)
Being For The Benefit Of Mr. Kite
Beatles; *Beatles-Box Set* . . . . (Capitol)
Sgt. Pepper's Lonely Hearts Club Band . . . . (Capitol)
Cousin Kevin
Original Cast; *Tommy* . . . . (RCA Victor)
Who; *Join Together* . . . . (MCA)
Odds & Sods . . . . (MCA)
ST/Tommy . . . .(Polydor)
Tommy . . . . (MCA)
Gee, Officer Krupke!
Original Cast; *ST/West Side Story* . . . . (Sony Broadway)
He's Misstra Know-It-All
Stevie Wonder; *Innervisions* . . . . (Motown)
Kaw-Liga
Hank Williams; *Alone With His Guitar* . . . . (Mercury)
Hank Williams-40 Greatest Hits . . . .(Polydor)
Hank Williams-The Hits-#2 . . . . (Mercury)
Keith Don't Go (Ode To The Glimmer Twin)
Nils Lofgren; *Best Of Nils Lofgren* . . . . (A&M)
Night After Night . . . . (A&M)
Nils Lofgren . . . . (Rykodisc)
Nils Lofgren-Classics-#13 . . . . (A&M)
Kevorkian
Public Enemy; *There's A Poison Goin On* . . . . (Atomic Pop)
King Holiday
King Dream Chorus & The Holiday Crew; *45-#884442-7* . . . . (Mercury)
Kookie, Kookie (Lend Me Your Comb)
Edd Byrnes & Connie Stevens Taylor; *Wacky Weirdos-C* . . . . (K-Tel)
Machine Gun Kelly
James Taylor; *Mud Slide Slim And The Blue Horizon* . . . . (Warner Bros.)
President Kennedy
Son House; *Father Of The Delta Blues-1965 Sessions* . . . . (Columbia)
President Kennedy
Ry Cooder; *Boomer's Story* . . . . (Reprise)
President Kennedy March
Lawrence Welk; *10th Anniversary Television Show* . . . . (Ranwood)
President Kennedy Stayed Away Too Long
Sleepy John Estes; *Electric Sleep* . . . . (Delmark)
Kings Of Country Blues-#1 . . . . (Arhoolie)
President Kennedy's Mile
Screaming Blue Messiahs; *Gun-Shy* . . . . (Elektra)
Theme From "Dr. Kildare" (Three Stars Will Shine Tonight)
Betty Carter; *'Round Midnight* . . . .(Atlantic)
Original Soundtrack; *Television's Greatest Hits-#4-Black & White
Classics-C* . . . . (TVT)
Theme From "Kojak"
Henry Mancini; *Cop Show Themes* . . . . (RCA)
John Gregory; *TV's Greatest Detective Hits* . . . . (Mercury)
Original Soundtrack; *Television's Greatest Hits-#3-1970s & 1980s-C* . . . (TVT)

Theme From "Welcome Back, Kotter"
John Sebastian; *Best Of John Sebastian*. . . . . (Rhino)
Original Soundtrack; *Television's Greatest Hits-#3-1970s & 1980s-C*. . . . (TVT)
What's The Frequency, Kenneth?
R.E.M.; *Monster* . . . . (Warner Bros.)

MEN'S NAMES: L

See Also: **CELEBRITIES: SPECIFIC, FAMILY (various), MEN: GENERAL**

(Man Who Shot) Liberty Valance
Gene Pitney; *Gene Pitney-Anthology 1961-1968* . . . . (Rhino)
Gene Pitney's Greatest Hits . . . . (Evergreen Music)
Super Oldies Of The '60s-#9-C . . . . (Audio Fidelity)
Greg Kihn; *Glass House Rock* . . . . (Beserkley)
Bad, Bad Leroy Brown
Jim Croce; *Billboard Top Rock 'N' Roll Hits-1973-C* . . . . (Rhino)
Down The Highway . . . . (Atlantic)
Life & Times . . . . (Lifesong)
Photographs & Memories/His Greatest Hits . . . . (Atlantic)
Blue Lou
Benny Carter; *1933* . . . . (Prestige)
Ella Fitzgerald; *Best Of Ella Fitzgerald-#2* . . . . (MCA)
Ella Sings/Chick Swings . . . . (Olympic)
Brother Louie
Stories; *Billboard Top Rock 'N' Roll Hits-1973-C* . . . . (Rhino)
Brother Love's Traveling Salvation Show
Neil Diamond; *Hot August Night*. . . . . (MCA)
Love At The Greek . . . . (Columbia)
Neil Diamond-Gold . . . . (MCA)
Neil Diamond-His 12 Greatest Hits . . . . (MCA)
Sweet Caroline . . . . (MCA)
Calling Dr. Love
Kiss; *Alive II* . . . . (Casablanca)
Double Platinum. . . . . (Mercury)
Rock & Roll Over . . . . (Casablanca)
Smashes, Thrashes & Hits . . . . (Mercury)
Chop Suey Louie
Jimmy Preston; *Rock The Joint-#2-C* . . . . (Collectables)
Cincinnati Lou
Merle Travis; *Best Of Merle Travis* . . . . (Rhino)
Death Of Louis
Champion Jack Dupree; *Happy To Be Free*. . . . . (Crescendo)
Hats Off To Larry
Del Shannon; *Runaway Hits!*. . . . . (Rhino)
Super Oldies Of The '60s-#2-C. . . . . (Audio Fidelity)
WCBS FM 101 History Of Rock-'60s-#3-C . . . . (Collectables)
Lee Harvey Oswald
Skatalites; *Stretching Out* . . . . (Roir)
Levon
Elton John; *Elton John's Greatest Hits-#2* . . . . (Polydor)
Madman Across The Water. . . . . (Polydor)
Lido Shuffle
Boz Scaggs; *Hits!* . . . . (Columbia)
Silk Degrees . . . . (Columbia)
ST/FM . . . . (MCA)
Lightning's Girl
Nancy Sinatra; *How Does That Grab You?* . . . . (Sundazed Music)
Lollipop
Chordettes; *Best Of The Chordettes*. . . . . (Rhino)
Chordettes Greatest Hits . . . . (Everest)
Jukebox Classics-#2-C . . . . (Rhino)
Lil' Bit Of Gold 3'' CD Series-C. . . . . (Rhino)
ST/Stand By Me . . . . (Atlantic)
Longfellow Serenade
Neil Diamond; *12 Greatest Hits-#2*. . . . . (Columbia)
Love At The Greek . . . . (Columbia)
On The Way To The Sky . . . . (Columbia)
Serenade . . . . (Columbia)
Louie Louie
Pretenders; *Pretenders II* . . . . (Sire)
Louisiana Lou & Three-Card Monty John
Allman Brothers Band; *Win, Lose Or Draw* . . . . (Polydor)
Louisville Lou
Johnny Mercer; *The Uncollected Johnny Mercer-1944*. . . . . (Hindsight)
Meet Me In St. Louis, Louis
Judy Garland; *Best Of Judy Garland* . . . . (MCA)
Mr. Lee
Bobbettes; *Billboard Top R&B Hits-1957-C* . . . . (Rhino)
ST/Stand By Me. . . . . (Atlantic)
Pointer Sisters; *Rock Rhythm & Blues-C* . . . . (Warner Bros.)
Mr. Lincoln
Hank Williams, Jr.; *America (The Way I See It)* . . . . (WB/Curb)

Major Moves . . . . (WB/Curb)
Mr. Lonely
Bobby Vinton; *Bobby Vinton-16 Most Requested Songs* . . . . (Legacy)
Bobby Vinton's All-Time Greatest Hits . . . . (Epic)
Mr. Lucky
John Lee Hooker; *Mr. Lucky* . . . . (Point Blank/Virgin)
Urban Blues . . . . (MCA)
Mr. Lucky
Henry Mancini; *Henry Mancini-Pure Gold* . . . . (RCA)
Peter Gunn . . . . (RCA)
My Boy Lollipop
Millie Small; *The Island Story-1962-1987-25th Anniversary-C* . . . .(Island)
My Name Is Larry
Wild Man Fischer; *Dr. Demento's Dementia Royale-C* . . . . (Rhino)
N.I.B. (Lucifer)
Primus with Ozzy; *Nativity In Black II: Tribute To Black Sabbath-C*. . . . . (Divine/Priority)
One Hit Wonder (Loopy)
Everclear; *So Much For The Afterglow* . . . .(Capitol)
Pancho And Lefty
Merle Haggard; *For The Record: Merle Haggard-43 Legendary Hits*. . . . (BNA)
Merle Haggard & Willie Nelson; *19 Hot Country Requests-C*. . . . . . .(Epic)
All Time Legends Of Country Music-C . . . .(Legacy)
Columbia Country Classics-#3-Americana-C . . . . (Columbia)
His Epic Hits-First 11 To Be Continued-C . . . .(Epic)
Pancho And Lefty . . . .(Epic)
Townes Van Zandt; *Live & Obscure* . . . . (Sugar Hill)
Po Lazarus
James Carter & The Prisoners; *ST/O Brother, Where Art Thou?* . . . . . .(Mercury)
Sinaloa Cowboys (Miguel, Louis)
Bruce Springsteen; *The Ghost Of Tom Joad*. . . . .(Columbia)
Sneaky Private Lee
Paice/Ashton/Lord; *Malice In Wonderland* . . . . (Warner Bros.)
Swap Meet Louie
Sir Mix-A-Lot; *Mack Daddy* . . . . (Def American)
Theme From "Lawrence Of Arabia"
BBC Concert Orchestra; *Golden Cinema Classics-#1-The Adventure Film*. . . . .(Bainbridge)
Cincinnati Pops Orchestra/Erich Kunzel; *Hollywood's Greatest Hits-#1* . . . . (Telarc)
Theme From "Mr. Lucky"
Original Soundtrack; *Television's Greatest Hits-#4-Black & White Classics-C* . . . .(TVT)

MEN'S NAMES: M

See Also: **CELEBRITIES: SPECIFIC, FAMILY (various), MEN: GENERAL**

Abraham, Martin And John
Dion; *Collectables Presents The History Of Rock-#3-C* . . . .(Collectables)
Dion-24 Original Classics . . . .(Arista)
Songs Of Protest-C . . . .(Rhino)
WCBS FM 101 History Of Rock-'60s-#2-C. . . . .(Collectables)
Harry Belafonte; *Harry Belafonte's All Time Greatest Hits-#1* . . . . (RCA)
Smokey Robinson & The Miracles; *Smokey Robinson & The Miracles' Anthology*. . . . .(Motown)
Time Out For Smokey Robinson & The Miracles/Special Occasion. . . . . (Motown)
Bach, Beethoven, Mozart & Me
Phil Ochs; *Phil Ochs' Greatest Hits*. . . . .(A&M)
Blue Monk
Bill Evans; *Conversations With Myself* . . . .(Verve)
Thelonius Monk; *Alone In San Francisco* . . . . (Riverside)
Thelonius Monk-Composer. . . . . (Columbia)
Brand New Mister Me
Mel Tillis & The Statesiders; *The Ultimate Mel Tillis* . . . . (Bransounds)
Crazy Man Michael
Fairport Convention; *Fairport Convention-Chronicles*. . . . .(A&M)
In Real Time-Live '87 . . . .(Island)
Liege & Lief . . . .(A&M)
Dear Michael
Michael Jackson; *Michael Jackson-Anthology* . . . .(Motown)
One Day In Your Life . . . .(Motown)
Exhuming McCarthy
R.E.M.; *Document* . . . . (EMI-Capitol Entert. Properties)
Five Guys Named Moe
Joe Jackson; *Jumpin' Jive* . . . .(A&M)
Louis Jordan; *Best Of Louis Jordan* . . . . (MCA)
Original Decca Recordings-#2 . . . .(Decca)
Go Down Moses
Arlo Guthrie; *Arlo Guthrie* . . . . (Rising Son)
Fats Waller; *Ain't Misbehavin'* . . . . (Laserlight)
Paul Robeson; *Ballad For Americans* . . . .(Vanguard)

The Power & The Glory. . . . . (Columbia)
Simon Estes; *Spirituals*. . . . .(Philips)
Hey Joe, Hey Moe
Moe Bandy & Joe Stampley; *Hey Joe, Hey Moe*. . . . . (Columbia)
Live At Bad Bob's . . . . (Columbia)
Moe Bandy & Joe Stampley's Greatest Hits . . . . (Columbia)
House Of Marcus Lycus
George Hearn, Bob Gunton & Women; *Collector's Sondheim-C* . . . . (RCA)
Stephen Sondheim; *Collector's Sondheim-C* . . . . (RCA)
I Love Mickey
Mickey Mantle & Teresa Brewer; *Baseball's Greatest Hits-C*. . . . . (Rhino)
King Midas In Reverse
Hollies; *Best Of The Hollies-#2* . . . . (EMI)
Hollies-Epic Anthology From The Original Master Tapes . . . .(Epic)
The Hollies' Greatest Hits . . . .(Epic)
Mack The Bomb
Pete Seeger; *Best Of Broadside 1962-1968: Anthems Of The American*
  Underground From The Pages Of Broadside
  Magazine-C . . . . (Smithsonian Folkways)
Mack The Knife
Bobby Darin; *Bobby Darin-At The Copa* . . . . (Bainbridge)
Hit Singles-1958-1977-C . . . .(Atlantic)
The Bobby Darin Story . . . .(Atlantic)
Frank Sinatra; *The Reprise Collection* . . . . (Reprise)
Louis Armstrong; *Best Of Louis Armstrong* . . . . (Vanguard)
Magic Johnson
Red Hot Chili Peppers; *Mother's Milk* . . . .(EMI)
Manny, Moe & Jack
Dickies; *10 Roir Years-Anthology-C* . . . . (Roir)
We Aren't The World! . . . .(Roir)
Marvin I Love You
Marvin The Paranoid Android; *Dr. Demento Presents The Greatest Novelty*
  Records-#5-1980s-C . . . . (Rhino)
Matty Groves
Fairport Convention; *Fairport Convention-Chronicles* . . . . (A&M)
Liege & Lief . . . . (A&M)
Maxwell's Silver Hammer
Beatles; *Abbey Road*. . . . . (Parlophone)
Mean Mr. Mustard
Beatles; *Abbey Road*. . . . . (Parlophone)
Mellow Yellow
Donovan; *Donovan's Greatest Hits* . . . .(Epic)
Seems Like Yesterday-#5-Mid '60s-C . . . . (K-Tel)
Memphis Slim U.S.A.
Memphis Slim; *Blue This Evening* . . . . (Black Lion)
Message To Michael
Dionne Warwick; *Dionne Warwick* . . . . (Everest)
Dionne Warwick Greatest Hits . . . . (Everest)
Dionne Warwick-Anthology 1962-1971 . . . . (Rhino)
Hot! Live & Otherwise . . . . (Arista)
Original Rock 'N' Roll Hits Of The '60s-C . . . . (Roulette)
Michael
Highwaymen; *Billboard Top Pop Hits-1961-C* . . . . (Rhino)
Michael
Prefab Sprout; *Jordan-The Comeback* . . . .(Epic)
Michael Row The Boat Ashore
Joe & Eddie; *Best Of Joe & Eddie*. . . . . (Crescendo)
Gospel Truth . . . . (Crescendo)
Weavers; *Weavers' Greatest Hits* . . . . (Vanguard)
Michelangelo
Emmylou Harris; *Red Dirt Girl* . . . . (Nonesuch)
Mickey
Toni Basil; *Word Of Mouth*. . . . .(Chrysalis)
Mickey's Monkey
Miracles; *Greatest Hits From The Beginning* . . . . (Motown)
Smokey Robinson & The Miracles; *Compact Command Performances-*
  Smokey Robinson & The Miracles . . . . (Motown)
Great Songs & Performances That Inspired The Motown 25th Anniversary
  Television Special-C . . . . (Motown)
Motown Story-First 25 Years-C . . . . (Motown)
Smokey Robinson & The Miracles' Anthology. . . . . (Motown)
Mohammed's Radio
Linda Ronstadt; *Living In The USA* . . . . (Asylum)
Warren Zevon; *Quiet Normal Life-Best Of Warren Zevon* . . . . (Asylum)
Stand In The Fire . . . . (Asylum)
Warren Zevon . . . . (Asylum)
Morrisey & The Russian Sailor
Tom Dahill; *Irish Music From St. Paul To Donegal* . . . . (Flying Fish)
Mr. Melody
Natalie Cole; *Natalie* . . . . (Capitol)
Natalie Cole-Collection . . . . (Capitol)
Natalie Cole-Live . . . . (Capitol)
Mr. Midnight
Garth Brooks; *Scarecrow* . . . . (Capitol)
Mr. Mistofelees
Original Broadway Cast; *Cats* . . . .(Geffen)

Original London Cast; *Cats*. . . . . (Geffen)
Mr. Moonlight
Beatles; *Beatles '65*. . . . .(Capitol)
Beatles-Box Set. . . . . (Capitol)
For Sale . . . .(Capitol)
Murphy's Law
Murphy's Law; *Murphy's Law* . . . .(Rock Hotel)
Murphy's Law
Cheri; *Best Disco In Town-#1-C* . . . .(Hip-O)
Murphy's Law
Al Jarreau; *High Crime* . . . . (Warner Bros.)
Nightshift (Marvin)
Commodores; *Nightshift* . . . . (Motown)
Old MacDonald Had A Farm
Original Soundtrack; *Toddler Favorites* . . . .(Kid Rhino/Rhino 4 Kids)
On The Rock Where Moses Stood
Carter Family; *Worried Man Blues: Their Complete Victor Recordings-*
  1930. . . . . (Rounder)
Flatt & Scruggs; *Songs Of The Famous Carter Family* . . . . (Legacy)
Return Of The Mack
Mark Morrison; *Return Of The Mack* . . . .(Atlantic)
Riding With Private Malone
David Ball; *Amigo*. . . . . (Razor & Tie)
Sailing To Philadelphia (Mason-Dixon)
Mark Knopfler; *Sailing To Philadelphia* . . . . (Warner Bros.)
Saturday Miles
Miles Davis; *Miles Davis At Fillmore* . . . . (Columbia)
Sinaloa Cowboys (Miguel, Louis)
Bruce Springsteen; *The Ghost Of Tom Joad* . . . . (Columbia)
Theme From "Hardcastle And McCormick"
Original Soundtrack; *Television's Greatest Hits-#6-Remote Control-C* . . . (TVT)
Theme From "Magilla Gorilla"
Original Soundtrack; *Hanna-Barbera Classics-#1-Original Recordings Of*
  The World's Most Famous Cartoon Themes &
  Scores . . . .(Kid Rhino/Rhino 4 Kids)
Hanna-Barbera Pic-A-Nic Basket Of Cartoon
  Classics . . . .(Kid Rhino/Rhino 4 Kids)
Television's Greatest Hits-#1-C . . . . (TVT)
Theme From "Magnum P.I."
Original Soundtrack; *Television's Greatest Hits-#3-1970s & 1980s-C* . . . (TVT)
Theme From "Mannix"
Original Soundtrack; *CBS: The First 50 Years* . . . . (TVT)
Television's Greatest Hits-#1-C . . . . (TVT)
San Diego Symphony & Lalo Schifrin; *Hitchcock-Master Of*
  Mayhem . . . . (Pro-Arte)
Theme From "Marcus Welby, M.D."
Original Soundtrack; *Television's Greatest Hits-#3-1970s & 1980s-C* . . . (TVT)
Theme From "Matt Houston"
Original Soundtrack; *Television's Greatest Hits-#6-Remote Control-C* . . . (TVT)
Theme From "Maverick"
Original Soundtrack; *Television's Greatest Hits-#2-C* . . . . (TVT)
Theme From "Max Headroom"
Original Soundtrack; *Television's Greatest Hits-#7-Cable Ready-C* . . . . (TVT)
Theme From "McHale's Navy"
Original Soundtrack; *Television's Greatest Hits-#1-C* . . . . (TVT)
Theme From "Monty Python's Flying Circus"
Original Soundtrack; *Television's Greatest Hits-#2-C* . . . . (TVT)
Theme From "Mork & Mindy"
Original Soundtrack; *Television's Greatest Hits-#6-Remote Control-C* . . . (TVT)
Theme From "Mr. Magoo"
Original Soundtrack; *Television's Greatest Hits-#3-1970s & 1980s-C* . . . (TVT)
Theme From "The Real McCoys"
Original Soundtrack; *Television's Greatest Hits-#4-Black & White*
  Classics-C . . . . (TVT)

MEN'S NAMES: N

See Also: CELEBRITIES: SPECIFIC, FAMILY (various),
MEN: GENERAL

Free Nelson Mandela
Special AKA; *In The Studio* . . . . (Chrysalis)
Here's To The State Of Nixon
Phil Ochs; *Chords Of Fame*. . . . . (A&M)
Nathan Jones
Bananarama; *ST/Rain Man* . . . . (Capitol)
Supremes; *Top 10 With A Bullet-Motown Girl Groups-C* . . . . (Motown)
Neal's Fandango
Doobie Brothers; *Stampede*. . . . . (Warner Bros.)
Nolan Ryan (He's A Hero To Us All)
Jerry Jeff Walker; *Navajo Rug* . . . . (Rykodisc)
Oldest Established (Permanent Floating Crap Game In New York)
(Nathan Detroit)
Original Cast; *ST/Guys & Dolls* . . . . (MCA)

Rain, Rain, Rain
Frankie Laine; *Frankie Laine-16 Most Requested Songs* . . . . (Legacy)

MEN'S NAMES: O

See Also: **CELEBRITIES: SPECIFIC, FAMILY (various), MEN: GENERAL**

Black Orpheus
Roger Williams; *Best Of Roger Williams* . . . . (MCA)
Vince Guaraldi & Bola Sete; *Live At El Matador* . . . .(Fantasy)
Oklahoma Joe
Chris LeDoux; *Songs Of Rodeo & Country* . . . . (Liberty)
Oliver's Army
Elvis Costello; *Girls Girls Girls* . . . . (Columbia)
Elvis Costello & The Attractions; *Armed Forces* . . . . (Rykodisc)
Best Of Elvis Costello & The Attractions . . . . (Columbia)
Oney
Johnny Cash; *Johnny Cash-16 Biggest Hits-#2* . . . .(Legacy)
Operaman
Adam Sandler; *The Concert For New York City-C* . . . . (Columbia)
O'Reilly At The Bar
Dan Hicks & His Hot Licks; *Striking It Rich!* . . . . (MCA)
Rock Around With Ollie Vee
Buddy Holly; *Legend-From The Original Master Tapes* . . . . (MCA)
Samba De Orfeu (Orpheus)
Pablo All-Stars Jam; *Montreux '77-C* . . . . (Pablo)
Vince Guaraldi; *Vince Guaraldi's Greatest Hits* . . . .(Fantasy)
Vince Guaraldi Trio; *Jazz Impressions Of Black Orpheus* . . . .(Fantasy)
Theme From "Kukla, Fran And Ollie" ("Here We Are, Hop, Hop, Hop")
Original Soundtrack; *Television's Greatest Hits-#4-Black & White Classics-C* . . . . (TVT)
Theme From "The Adventures Of Ozzie And Harriet"
Original Soundtrack; *Television's Greatest Hits-#4-Black & White Classics-C* . . . . (TVT)

MEN'S NAMES: P

See Also: **CELEBRITIES: SPECIFIC, FAMILY (various), MEN: GENERAL**

Black Peter
Grateful Dead; *History Of The Grateful Dead-Vol. 1 (Bear's Choice)* . . . . (Warner Bros.)
What A Long Strange Trip It's Been: The Best Of The Grateful Dead . . . . (Warner Bros.)
Workingman's Dead . . . . (Warner Bros.)
Check Mr. Popeye
Eddie Bo; *Carnival Time-Best Of Ric Records-#1-C* . . . . (Rounder)
Check Mr. Popeye . . . . (Rounder)
Southside Johnny And The Asbury Jukes; *This Time It's For Real* . . . . . . (Epic)
I Loves You Porgy
Original Cast; *Porgy & Bess* . . . . (MCA)
I Loves You Porgy/Porgy, I's Your Woman
Barbra Streisand; *The Broadway Album* . . . . (Columbia)
I'm Popeye The Sailor Man
Billy Costello; *Dr. Demento Presents The Greatest Novelty Records-#1-1940s & Before-C* . . . . (Rhino)
Me And Paul
Willie Nelson; *Best Of Willie* . . . . (RCA)
Nite Life-Greatest Hits & Rare Tracks . . . . (Rhino)
The Outlaws . . . . (RCA)
What A Wonderful World . . . . (Columbia)
Willie . . . . (RCA)
Mr. Pharmacist
Other Half; *Nuggets-#12-Punk-#3-C* . . . . (Rhino)
Mr. Policeman
Rick James; *Street Songs* . . . . (Motown)
Mr. Pollution
P'Cock; *Burning Beach* . . . . (Innovative Comm.)
Mr. President (Have Pity On The Working Man)
Randy Newman; *Good Old Boys* . . . .(Reprise)
ST/Forrest Gump . . . . (Epic/Sony Music Soundtrax)
Oh Mr. Possum
Jimmy Preston; *Jimmy Preston* . . . . (Collectables)
Paddy Doyle's Boots
Clancy Brothers & Tommy Makem; *Best Of Clancy Brothers & Tommy Makem* . . . . (Tradition)
Paddy Goes To Nashville
Adrian Legg; *Mrs. Crowe's Blue Waltz* . . . . (Relativity)
Paddy Kelly's Brew
Tommy Makem; *Evening With Tommy Makem* . . . .(Shanachie)
Paddy McGinty's Coat
Pat Harrington; *St. Patrick's Day Celebration* . . . . (Columbia)

Paddy On The Railway
Barley Bree; *Castles In The Air* . . . . (Shanachie)
Paddy Ryan's Dream
Matt Molloy; *Stony Steps* . . . . (Green Linnet)
Paddy Won't You Drink Some Cider
Red Clay Ramblers; *Chuckin' The Frizz* . . . . (Flying Fish)
Paddy Works On The Railway
Pete Seeger; *Concert Folk Songs And Ballads* . . . .(Collectables)
Paddy's Green Shamrock Shore
Chieftains; *Another Country* . . . . (RCA)
Pancho And Lefty
Merle Haggard; *For The Record: Merle Haggard-43 Legendary Hits* . . . . (BNA)
Merle Haggard & Willie Nelson; *19 Hot Country Requests-C* . . . .(Epic)
All Time Legends Of Country Music-C . . . .(Legacy)
Columbia Country Classics-#3-Americana-C . . . . (Columbia)
His Epic Hits-First 11 To Be Continued-C . . . .(Epic)
Pancho And Lefty . . . .(Epic)
Townes Van Zandt; *Live & Obscure* . . . . (Sugar Hill)
Parker's Band
Steely Dan; *Pretzel Logic* . . . . (MCA)
Patches
Clarence Carter; *Atlantic Rhythm & Blues 1947-1974-#7 (1969-1974)-C* . . . . (Atlantic)
Snatching It Back-The Best Of Clarence Carter . . . .(Rhino)
Super Hits-#1-C . . . . (Gusto)
Dickey Lee; *Teenage Tragedies-C* . . . .(Rhino)
George Jones & B.B. King; *Rhythm Country And Blues-C* . . . .(MCA)
Paul Revere
Beastie Boys; *Licensed To Ill* . . . . (Def Jam)
Rap Rap Rap-C . . . . (K-Tel)
Paul Revere
Johnny Cash; *Patriot* . . . . (Columbia)
Paul Wants A Pig
John Jarvis; *Whatever Works* . . . . (MCA)
Pepe
Duane Eddy; *Duane Eddy-16 Greatest Hits* . . . . (Jamie)
Pepino The Italian Mouse
Lou Monte; *Pepino The Italian Mouse & Other Songs* . . . . (Reprise)
Percy's Song
Arlo Guthrie; *Washington County* . . . . (Reprise)
Bob Dylan; *Biograph* . . . .(Columbia)
Perry Mason
Ozzy Osbourne; *Ozzmosis* . . . . (Epic)
Peter And The Wolf
Dave Van Ronk; *Peter And The Wolf* . . . .(Alacazam)
Original Soundtrack; *Beethoven Wrote It...But It Swings* . . . . (Sony Music Classical)
Peter Gunn
Duane Eddy; *Duane Eddy-16 Greatest Hits* . . . . (Jamie)
Henry Mancini; *Best Of Henry Mancini* . . . . (RCA)
Henry Mancini-Legendary Performer . . . . (RCA)
Henry Mancini-Pure Gold . . . . (RCA)
Peter Gunn . . . . (RCA)
Television's Greatest Hits-#2-C . . . .(TVT)
Ray Anthony; *Capitol Collectors Series-Ray Anthony* . . . . (Capitol)
Picasso's Last Words
Paul McCartney & Wings; *Band On The Run* . . . .(Capitol)
Wings; *Wings Over America* . . . . (Capitol)
Pilate & Christ
Original London Cast; *Jesus Christ Superstar* . . . . (MCA)
Pilate's Dream
Original London Cast; *Jesus Christ Superstar* . . . . (MCA)
Please Mister Postman
Beatles; *Beatles-Box Set* . . . .(Capitol)
The Beatles' Second Album . . . .(Capitol)
With The Beatles . . . . (Parlophone)
Carpenters; *Carpenters-Classics-#2* . . . .(A&M)
Horizon . . . .(A&M)
Yesterday Once More . . . .(A&M)
Marvelettes; *Billboard Top Rock 'N' Roll Hits-1961-C* . . . .(Rhino)
Marvelettes' Greatest Hits . . . .(Motown)
Marvelettes-Anthology . . . . (Motown)
Motown Story-First 25 Years-C . . . .(Motown)
Pow Wow The Indian Boy
Hot Rize; *Hot Rize* . . . . (Flying Fish)
Remember Pat Boone
David Steinberg; *Booga! Booga!* . . . .(Columbia)
Roll 'Em Pete
Big Joe Turner; *Atlantic Blues-Piano-C* . . . . (Atlantic)
Boss Of The Blues . . . . (Atlantic)
Count Basie & Big Joe Turner; *The Bosses* . . . . (Pablo)
Sgt. Pepper's Lonely Hearts Club Band
Beatles; *Beatles-Box Set* . . . .(Capitol)
The Beatles/1967-1970 . . . . (Capitol)
Jimi Hendrix; *Stages-Stockholm/Paris/San Diego/Atlanta* . . . . (Reprise)
Tall Paul
Annette with the Afterbeats; *Best Of Annette Funicello* . . . .(Rhino)
Sherman Brothers . . . . (Disney)
Too Cute-C . . . .(Dunhill Compact Classics)

Theme From "Adventures Of Pete And Pete"
Original Soundtrack; *Television's Greatest Hits-#7-Cable Ready-C* . . . . . (TVT)
Theme From "Have Gun Will Travel" (Ballad Of Paladin)
Duane Eddy; *Duane Eddy-Pure Gold* . . . . (RCA)
Johnny Western; *Columbia Country Classics-#3-Americana-C* . . . . (Columbia)
Television's Greatest Hits-#7-Cable Ready-C . . . . (TVT)
Theme From "Perry Mason"
Blues Brothers; *Made In America* . . . .(Atlantic)
Jerry Goodman; *It's Alive* . . . . (Private Music)
Original Soundtrack; *CBS: The First 50 Years* . . . . (TVT)
Television's Greatest Hits-#1-C . . . . (TVT)
TV Theme Sing-Along Album . . . . (Rhino)
Theme From "Popeye"
Original Soundtrack; *Television's Greatest Hits-#1-C* . . . . (TVT)
Theme From "The Partridge Family"
Original Soundtrack; *Television's Greatest Hits-#2-C* . . . . (TVT)
Trial Before Pilate
Original London Cast; *Jesus Christ Superstar* . . . .(MCA)
Uncle Pen
Bill Monroe; *Bean Blossom* . . . .(MCA)
Best Of Bill Monroe & His Blue Grass Boys . . . .(MCA)
Ricky Skaggs; *19 Hot Country Requests-#2-C* . . . .(Epic)
Bluegrass Super Hits-C . . . . (Columbia)
Columbia Country Classics-#5-A New Tradition-C . . . . (Columbia)
Don't Cheat In Our Hometown . . . .(Epic)
Live In London . . . .(Epic)

MEN'S NAMES: Q

See Also: **CELEBRITIES: SPECIFIC, FAMILY (various),**
MEN: GENERAL

Don Quixote
Gordon Lightfoot; *Gord's Gold* . . . . (Reprise)
Don Quixote
Nik Kershaw; *The Riddle* . . . .(MCA)
Man Of La Mancha (Don Quixote)
Original Cast; *Lost In The Stars* . . . .(MCA)
Original London Cast; *Man Of La Mancha* . . . .(MCA)
Mighty Quinn (Quinn The Eskimo)
Bob Dylan; *Biograph* . . . . (Columbia)
Bob Dylan's Greatest Hits-#2 . . . . (Columbia)
Self Portrait . . . . (Columbia)
Ian & Sylvia; *Ian & Sylvia's Greatest Hits* . . . . (Vanguard)
Manfred Mann; *Chapter Two-The Best Of The Fontana Years* . . . .(Fontana)
Theme From "Quincy, M.E."
Original Soundtrack; *Television's Greatest Hits-#3-1970s & 1980s-C* . . . (TVT)

MEN'S NAMES: R

See Also: **CELEBRITIES: SPECIFIC, FAMILY (various),**
MEN: GENERAL

(Just Like) Romeo & Juliet
Reflections; *'60s Dance Party-C* . . . . (Dominion Entert.)
Sensational '60s-#1-C . . . . (Dominion Entert.)
Ballad Of Richard Nixon
John Denver; *Rhymes & Reasons* . . . . (RCA)
Black Uncle Remus
Loudon Wainwright III; *Loudon Wainwright III* . . . .(Atlantic)
Blue Monday At Kansas City Red's
Cary Bell; *Blues Harp* . . . . (Delmark)
Dear Mrs. Roosevelt
Bob Dylan; *Tribute To Woody Guthrie-C* . . . .(Warner Bros.)
Dr. Robert
Beatles; *"Yesterday"...And Today* . . . . (Capitol)
Revolver . . . . (Capitol)
In Memoriam-John F. & Robert F. Kennedy
Clare Fischer; *'Twas Only Yesterday* . . . . (Discovery)
Joy (Roy)
Nilsson; *Son Of Schmilsson* . . . . (RCA)
Last Time I Saw Richard
Joni Mitchell; *Blue* . . . . (Reprise)
Love Theme From "Romeo & Juliet"
101 Strings Orchestra; *World's Greatest Standards* . . . . (Alshire)
Andre Kostelanetz; *Andre Kostelanetz-16 Most Requested Songs* . . . (Columbia)
Andy Williams & The Royal Philharmonic Orchestra; *Greatest Love*
Classics . . . . (Capitol)
Percy Faith & His Orchestra; *Percy Faith & His Orchestra-16 Most*
Requested Songs . . . . (Columbia)
Message To You Rudy
Specials; *Gangsters* . . . .(Chrysalis)
Mr. Radio
Electric Light Orchestra; *Afterglow* . . . .(Epic)
No Answer . . . .(Jet)

Mr. Record Man
Willie Nelson; *Best Of Willie Nelson* . . . . (Capitol)
Horse Called Music . . . . (Columbia)
Willie & Family Live . . . . (Columbia)
Mr. Roboto
Styx; *Caught In The Act* . . . . (A&M)
Kilroy Was Here . . . . (A&M)
Styx-Classics-#15 . . . . (A&M)
My Name Is Not Susan (Romeo)
Whitney Houston; *I'm Your Baby Tonight* . . . . (Arista)
Oh King Richard
Rodney Crowell; *Hot Country Rock-#2-C* . . . . (Epic)
Street Language . . . . (Columbia)
Open The Door, Richard
Louis Jordan; *Jazz Heritage-Greatest Hits-#2-1941-1947* . . . . (MCA)
President Roosevelt
Big Joe Williams; *Shake Your Boogie* . . . . (Arhoolie)
Tough Times . . . . (Arhoolie)
Ray's Dad Cadillac
Joni Mitchell; *Night Ride Home* . . . . (Geffen)
Reagonomics
D.R.I.; *Dealing With It* . . . . (Metal Blade)
Johnnie Taylor; *Just Ain't Good Enough* . . . . (Beverly Glen)
Redneck Romeo
Confederate Railroad; *Notorious* . . . .(Atlantic)
Reuben's Train
Doc Watson & Family; *Treasures Untold-C* . . . . (Vanguard)
Rex Bob Lowenstein
Mark Germino; *Rank & File* . . . . (Winter Harvest Entert.)
Richard Cory
Simon & Garfunkel; *Collected Works* . . . . (Columbia)
Sounds Of Silence . . . . (Columbia)
Wings; *Wings Over America* . . . . (Capitol)
Richard Cory Cries
Midnight Reign; *Mountain Of Metal* . . . . (Mountain)
Richard Hung Himself
D.I.; *Team Goon* . . . . (Triple X Entert.)
Richard Nixon
Christmas; *Ultraprophets Of Thee Psykick Revolution* . . . . (I.R.S.)
Robin And Marian
Nickel Creek; *Nickel Creek* . . . .(Sugar Hill)
Robin Hood
38 Special; *Rockin' Into The Night* . . . . (A&M)
Robinson Crusoe
Art Of Noise; *Ambient Collection* . . . .(Polydor)
Below The Waste . . . . (China)
Robinson Crusoe
Cud; *Cub Band E.P.* . . . . (A&M)
Robinson Crusoe In New York
Silencers; *Dance To The Holy Man* . . . .(RCA)
Rocky Raccoon
Beatles; *Beatles-Box Set* . . . . (Capitol)
The Beatles (White Album) . . . . (Capitol)
Rodeo Romeo
Moe Bandy; *Moe Bandy's Greatest Hits* . . . . (Columbia)
Rodney On The ROQ
Target 13; *Rodney On The ROQ-#2-C* . . . . (Posh Boy)
Roger's Bumble Bee (Latter Day)
Roger Williams; *Best Of Roger Williams* . . . . (MCA)
Roger Williams-Golden Hits . . . . (MCA)
Roland The Headless Thompson Gunner
Warren Zevon; *Excitable Boy* . . . .(Asylum)
Quiet Normal Life-Best Of Warren Zevon . . . .(Asylum)
Romeo
Dino; *Swingin'* . . . .(Polydor)
Romeo
Cadillacs; *Best Of The Cadillacs* . . . . (Rhino)
Romeo
Jamaica Boys; *Jamaica Boys* . . . . (Warner Bros.)
Romeo
Donna Summer; *ST/Flashdance* . . . .(Casablanca)
Romeo
Times Two; *X2* . . . . (Reprise)
Romeo & Juliet
Chambers Brothers; *The Time Has Come* . . . . (Columbia)
Romeo & Juliet
Dire Straits; *Live-Alchemy* . . . . (Warner Bros.)
Making Movies . . . . (Warner Bros.)
Money For Nothing . . . . (Warner Bros.)
Indigo Girls; *Rites Of Passage* . . . . (Epic)
Romeo's Tune
Steve Forbert; *Jackrabbit Slim* . . . .(Nemperor)
Ronnie, Talk To Russia
Prince; *Controversy* . . . . (Warner Bros.)
Ronny Zamora (My Friend Ron)
Deaf School; *English Boys/Working Girls* . . . . (Warner Bros.)
Roy Rogers
Elton John; *Goodbye Yellow Brick Road* . . . .(Polydor)

Ruben James
Conway Twitty; *Hello Darlin'* . . . . (MCA Special Prod.)
Kenny Rogers; *Kenny Rogers' Greatest Hits* . . . . (EMI)
   Kenny Rogers-Twenty Greatest Hits . . . . (EMI)
   Ten Years Of Gold . . . . (EMI)
Kenny Rogers And The First Edition; *Best Of Kenny Rogers And The First*
   Edition . . . . (K-Tel)
White Mountain Singers; *Best Of The White Mountain Singers* . . . . . . (Folk Era)
Rudiger
Mark Knopfler; *Golden Heart* . . . . (Warner Bros.)
Rudy
Supertramp; *Crime Of The Century* . . . . (A&M)
   Paris . . . . (A&M)
   Supertramp-Classics-#9 . . . . (A&M)
Running Bear
Johnny Preston; *45s On CD-#1-1956-1959-C* . . . . (Mercury)
   Billboard Top Rock 'N' Roll Hits-1960-C . . . . (Rhino)
   Cruisin'-1960-C . . . . (Increase)
Sonny James; *All-Time Country Classics-#1-C* . . . . (Capitol)
Theme From "Everybody Loves Raymond"
Original Soundtrack; *CBS: The First 50 Years* . . . . (TVT)
Theme From "Mr. Rogers' Neighborhood"
Original Soundtrack; *Television's Greatest Hits-#2-C* . . . . (TVT)
Theme From "Rockford Files"
Original Soundtrack; *Television's Greatest Hits-#3-1970s & 1980s-C* . . . . (TVT)
Theme From "Roger Ramjet"
Original Soundtrack; *Television's Greatest Hits-#4-Black & White*
   Classics-C . . . . (TVT)
Theme From "The Adventures Of Robin Hood"
Original Soundtrack; *Television's Greatest Hits-#2-C* . . . . (TVT)
Theme From "The Red Skelton Show"
Original Soundtrack; *CBS: The First 50 Years* . . . . (TVT)
This Romeo Ain't Got Julie Yet
Diamond Rio; *Close To The Edge* . . . . (Arista)
Tore Down A La Rimbaud
Van Morrison; *A Sense Of Wonder* . . . . (Mercury)
Vic And Ray
Mark Knopfler; *Golden Heart* . . . . (Warner Bros.)
Waiting For The Robert E. Lee
Al Jolson; *My Mammy* . . . . (MCA Special Prod.)
Eddie Cantor; *Centennial Celebration* . . . . (RCA)
Where Did Robinson Crusoe Go With Friday On Saturday Night
Ian Whitcomb; *You Turn Me On-The Very Best Of Ian*
   Whitcomb . . . . (Varese Sarabande)
Write Your Own Songs (Mr. Record Executive)
Asleep At The Wheel; *Asleep At The Wheel* . . . . (MCA Special Prod.)
Waylon Jennings & Willie Nelson; *WWII* . . . . (RCA)
Willie Nelson; *Revolutions In Time-The Journey-1975-1993* . . . . (Legacy)
Willie Nelson & Kris Kristofferson; *Music From "Songwriter"* . . . . (Columbia)

MEN'S NAMES: S

   See Also: **CELEBRITIES: SPECIFIC, FAMILY (various),**
    MEN: GENERAL

Ballad Of Spiro Agnew
John Denver; *Rhymes & Reasons* . . . . (RCA)
Boogie With Stu
Led Zeppelin; *Physical Graffiti* . . . . (Swan Song)
Boy Named Sue
Johnny Cash; *Columbia Country Classics-#3-Americana-C* . . . . (Columbia)
   Johnny Cash's Biggest Hits . . . . (Columbia)
   Johnny Cash's Greatest Hits-#2 . . . . (Columbia)
   The Man In Black-His Greatest Hits . . . . (Legacy)
Brush Up Your Shakespeare
Dick Hyman; *Cole Porter- All Through The Night* . . . . (Musicmasters)
Keenan Wynn & James Whitmore; *ST/Kiss Me Kate* . . . . (MCA)
Original Cast; *Kiss Me Kate* . . . . (Sony Music Classical)
Cut Across Shorty
Eddie Cochran; *Eddie Cochran-Legendary Masters* . . . . (EMI)
Rod Stewart; *Best Of Rod Stewart* . . . . (Mercury)
   Faces Live . . . . (Mercury)
   Gasoline Alley . . . . (Mercury)
   Storyteller/The Complete Anthology: 1964-1990 . . . . (Warner Bros.)
   Unplugged...And Seated . . . . (Warner Bros.)
   Vintage Rod Stewart . . . . (Mercury)
Day That Curly Bill Shot Down Crazy Sam
Hollies; *Hollies* . . . . (Epic)
Dear Uncle Sam
Loretta Lynn; *Honky Tonk Girl: The Loretta Lynn Collection* . . . . (MCA)
   Loretta Lynn's Greatest Hits . . . . (MCA)
Don't Step On The Grass, Sam
Steppenwolf; *Live Steppenwolf* . . . . (MCA)
   The Second . . . . (MCA)
Father Of A Boy Named Sue
Shel Silverstein; *Songs & Stories* . . . . (Parachute)

Hooray For Captain Spaulding
Groucho Marx; *Dr. Demento Presents The Greatest Novelty Records-#1-*
   1940s & Before-C . . . . (Rhino)
   Dr. Demento Presents The Greatest Novelty Records-C . . . . (Rhino)
Original Soundtrack; *Television's Greatest Hits-#6-Remote Control-C* . . . (TVT)
Just A Pimp (Sammy)
Angie Stone; *Black Diamond* . . . . (Arista)
Key West Intermezzo (I Saw You First) (Gypsy Scotty)
John Mellencamp; *Mr. Happy Go Lucky* . . . . (Mercury)
Lord Stanley's Cup
Zamboni Brothers; *The Hockey Zone-C* . . . . (Sportsongs)
Mister Sandman
Chordettes; *Best Of The Chordettes* . . . . (Rhino)
Emmylou Harris; *Evangeline* . . . . (Warner Bros.)
   Profile II-The Best Of Emmylou Harris . . . . (Warner Bros.)
Mohair Sam
Derailers; *Here Come The Derailers* . . . . (Lucky Dog)
Mr. Shorty
Marty Robbins; *The Drifter* . . . . (Koch International)
Mr. Skin
Spirit; *12 Dreams Of Dr. Sardonicus* . . . . (Epic)
   Best Of Spirit . . . . (Epic)
   Spirit Of '84 . . . . (Mercury)
   Time Circle . . . . (Epic)
Mr. Spaceman
Byrds; *Original Singles-#1-1965-1967* . . . . (Columbia)
   The Byrds . . . . (Columbia)
   The Byrds (Untitled) . . . . (Legacy)
   The Byrds' Greatest Hits . . . . (Columbia)
Mr. Sunday
Simon Townshend; *Sweet Sound* . . . . (21)
Mrs. Steven Rudy
Mark McGuinn; *Mark McGuinn* . . . . (VFR)
Nevada Smith
Mystic Moods Orchestra; *Nighttide* . . . . (Bainbridge)
North To Alaska (Sam)
Dwight Yoakam; *Under The Covers* . . . . (Reprise)
Johnny Horton; *American Originals-Johnny Horton* . . . . (Columbia)
   Billboard Top Country Hits-1961-C . . . . (Rhino)
   Johnny Horton's Greatest Hits . . . . (Columbia)
   Super Hits Of The '60s-C . . . . (Epic)
Please Mr. Sun
Johnnie Ray; *Back To The Early '50s* . . . . (Dominion Entert.)
   Johnnie Ray-16 Most Requested Songs . . . . (Legacy)
Vogues; *Vogues' Greatest Hits* . . . . (Rhino)
Real Slim Shady
Eminem; *The Marshall Mathers LP* . . . . (Aftermath/Interscope)
Road Goes On Forever, The (Sonny)
Joe Ely; *Love & Danger* . . . . (MCA)
Run Samson Run
Neil Sedaka; *Neil Sedaka Sings His Greatest Hits* . . . . (RCA)
   Neil Sedaka-Pure Gold . . . . (RCA)
   Neil Sedaka's All-Time Greatest Hits . . . . (RCA)
Sabu Visits The Twin Cities Alone
John Prine; *Bruised Orange* . . . . (Oh Boy)
Sam
Olivia Newton-John; *Back To Basics-Essential Collection 1971-1992* . . (Geffen)
   Don't Stop Believin' . . . . (MCA)
Sam & Delilah
Original Cast; *Girl Crazy* . . . . (Sony Music Special Prod.)
Sam Hall
Tex Ritter; *The Country Music Hall Of Fame-Tex Ritter* . . . . (MCA)
Sam Stone
John Prine; *John Prine* . . . . (Atlantic)
   John Prine-Souvenirs . . . . (Oh Boy)
   Prime Prine-The Best Of John Prine . . . . (Atlantic)
Sam, The Old Accordion Man
Doris Day & James Cagney; *ST/Love Me Or*
   Leave Me . . . . (Sony Music Special Prod.)
Sam, You Made The Pants Too Long
Barbra Streisand; *Barbra Streisand's Greatest Hits* . . . . (Columbia)
   Color Me Barbra . . . . (Columbia)
Sam's Place
Buck Owens & The Buckaroos; *Billboard Top Country Hits-1967-C* . . . (Rhino)
Samson & Delilah
Blind Gary Davis; *Harlem Street Singer* . . . . (Bluesville)
Reverend Gary Davis; *From Blues To Gospel* . . . . (Biograph)
Samson & Delilah
Blasters; *Blasters-Collection* . . . . (Slash)
Samson & Delilah
Grateful Dead; *Dead Set* . . . . (Arista)
   Terrapin Station . . . . (Arista)
Sam-The Hot Dog Man
Lil Johnson; *Raunchy Business-Hot Nuts & Lollypops-C* . . . . (Legacy)
Shakespeare Stole My Baby
Eye To Eye; *Shakespeare Stole My Baby* . . . . (Warner Bros.)
Shakespeare's Sister
Smiths; *Louder Than Bombs* . . . . (Sire)

Shine (Samuel, "Shine")
Ry Cooder; *Jazz* . . . .(Warner Bros.)
Shorty Falls In Love
Dan Hicks & His Hot Licks; *Where's The Money?*. . . . .(MCA)
Simon Says
1910 Fruitgum Company; *Best Of The 1910 Fruitgum Company-#2-C* . . (Rhino)
Bubblegum's Greatest Hits-#2-C. . . . . (Accord)
Fabulous Bubblegum Years-C. . . . . (Fifty One West)
Simon Smith & His Amazing Dancing Bear
Randy Newman; *Sail Away* . . . . (Reprise)
Slim Carter
Nitty Gritty Dirt Band; *All The Good Times* . . . . (United Artists)
Slim Jenkins' Place
Booker T. & The M.G.s; *Best Of Booker T. & The M.G.s* . . . .(Atlantic)
Hip Hug-Her . . . . (Rhino)
Speedoo
Cadillacs; *Best Of The Cadillacs*. . . . . (Rhino)
Echoes Of A Rock Era-Early Years-C . . . . (Roulette)
More American Graffiti-C . . . . (MCA)
Original Rock 'N' Roll Hits Of The '50s-C . . . . (Roulette)
ST/Goodfellas . . . .(Atlantic)
Ry Cooder; *Borderline* . . . . (Warner Bros.)
Speedy Gonzales
Pat Boone; *Best Of Pat Boone* . . . . (MCA)
Speedy's Coming
Scorpions; *Best Of The Scorpions*. . . . . (RCA)
Fly To The Rainbow . . . . (RCA)
Tokyo Tapes . . . . (RCA)
Spoonman
Soundgarden; *Superunknown* . . . . (A&M)
St. Stephen
Grateful Dead; *Aoxomoxoa*. . . . .(Warner Bros.)
Best Of/Skeletons From The Closet. . . . .(Warner Bros.)
Live/Dead . . . .(Warner Bros.)
Two From The Vault . . . . (Grateful Dead)
*What A Long Strange Trip It's Been: The Best Of The
Grateful Dead* . . . .(Warner Bros.)
Stagger Lee
Dion; *Dion-His Best* . . . . (Laurie)
Huey Lewis and the News; *Four Chords & Several Years Ago* . . . . . . (Elektra)
Ike & Tina Turner; *Best Of Ike & Tina Turner* . . . .(EMI)
Lloyd Price; *Billboard Top Rock 'N' Roll Hits-1959-C* . . . . (Rhino)
Collectables Presents The History Of Rock-#5-C . . . . (Collectables)
Lloyd Price's Greatest Hits . . . . (MCA)
Oldies But Goodies-#1-C. . . . . (Original Sound)
Professor Longhair; *Rock 'N' Roll Gumbo* . . . . (Dancing Cat)
Wilson Pickett; *A Man & A Half-Best Of Wilson Pickett* . . . . (Rhino)
Stan
Eminem; *The Marshall Mathers LP* . . . . (Aftermath/Interscope)
Steven's Last Night In Town
Ben Folds Five; *Whatever And Ever Amen*. . . . . (Caroline/550)
Streak, The
Ray Stevens; *Ray Stevens' Greatest Hits* . . . . (RCA)
Ray Stevens' Greatest Hits. . . . . (MCA)
Ray Stevens-All-Time Greatest Comic Hits . . . . (Curb)
Super Hits Of The '70s-Have A Nice Day-#12-C . . . . (Rhino)
Sugarfoot
Wallflowers; *The Wallflowers*. . . . . (Virgin)
Sullivan
Caroline's Spine; *Monsoon*. . . . . (Hollywood)
Theme From "Get Smart"
Original Soundtrack; *Television's Greatest Hits-#1-C* . . . . (TVT)
Theme From "Sanford & Son"
Original Soundtrack; *Television's Greatest Hits-#3-1970s & 1980s-C* . . . (TVT)
Theme From "Schindler's List"
John Williams & Itzhak Perlman; *ST/Schindler's List* . . . .(MCA)
Theme From "Seinfeld"
Original Soundtrack; *Television's Greatest Hits-#7-Cable Ready-C* . . . . . (TVT)
Theme From "Shaft"
Isaac Hayes; *Isaac Hayes' Greatest Hit Singles* . . . .(Stax)
Pimps, Players & Private Eyes-C . . . . (Sire)
Top Of The Stax-Twenty Greatest Hits-C . . . .(Stax)
Theme From "Simon And Simon"
Original Soundtrack; *Television's Greatest Hits-#3-1970s & 1980s-C* . . (TVT)
Theme From "Siskel And Ebert"
Original Soundtrack; *Television's Greatest Hits-#6-Remote Control-C* . . (TVT)
Theme From "Sledge Hammer"
Original Soundtrack; *Television's Greatest Hits-#7-Cable Ready-C* . . . . (TVT)
Theme From "Snagglepuss"
Original Soundtrack; *Hanna-Barbera Classics-#1-Original Recordings Of
The World's Most Famous Cartoon Themes &
Scores* . . . . (Kid Rhino/Rhino 4 Kids)
*Hanna-Barbera Pic-A-Nic Basket Of Cartoon
Classics*. . . . . (Kid Rhino/Rhino 4 Kids)
*Toon Tunes: 50 Favorite Classic Cartoon
Songs-C* . . . . (Kid Rhino/Rhino 4 Kids)
Theme From "Speed Racer"
Original Soundtrack; *Television's Greatest Hits-#3-1970s & 1980s-C* . . (TVT)

Theme From "Spiderman"
Original Soundtrack; *Television's Greatest Hits-#2-C* . . . . (TVT)
Theme From "Starsky & Hutch"
Original Soundtrack; *Television's Greatest Hits-#3-1970s & 1980s-C* . . . (TVT)
Theme From "Superman"
London Symphony Orchestra & John Williams; *ST/Superman-The
Movie*. . . . . (Warner Bros.)
Neil Norman; *Greatest Science Fiction Hits* . . . .(Crescendo)
Original Soundtrack; *Television's Greatest Hits-#1-C* . . . . (TVT)
Theme From "The Simpsons"
Original Soundtrack; *Television's Greatest Hits-#7-Cable Ready-C* . . . . . (TVT)
Theme From "The Smothers Brothers Comedy Hour"
Original Soundtrack; *Television's Greatest Hits-#2-C* . . . . (TVT)
Theme From "The Smurfs"
Original Soundtrack; *Television's Greatest Hits-#3-1970s & 1980s-C* . . . (TVT)
Theme From "The Soupy Sales Show"
Original Soundtrack; *Television's Greatest Hits-#4-Black & White
Classics-C* . . . . (TVT)
Watching Scotty Grow
Bobby Goldsboro; *Bobby Goldsboro's All-Time Greatest Hits* . . . . (Curb)
Honey-Best Of Bobby Goldsboro . . . . (EMI)
Mac Davis; *Mac Davis' Greatest Hits*. (Columbia)

MEN'S NAMES: T

See Also: **CELEBRITIES: SPECIFIC, FAMILY (various),
MEN: GENERAL**

Belgian Tom's Hat Trick
Whitesnake; *Trouble* . . . . (Geffen)
Big Iron (Texas Red)
Marty Robbins; *Columbia Country Classics-#3-Americana-C* . . . . . (Columbia)
Gunfighter Ballads & Trail Songs . . . . (Legacy)
Marty Robbins' All-Time Greatest Hits . . . . (Columbia)
Marty Robbins-More Greatest Hits . . . . (Columbia)
Fort Worth Blues (Townes Van Zandt)
Guy Clark; *Cold Dog Soup* . . . . (Sugar Hill)
From The Vine Came The Grape (Tony)
Gaylords; *X-tra Cheese-Originals By The Originals-C*. . . . . (Compose)
Ghost Of Tom Joad
Bruce Springsteen; *The Ghost Of Tom Joad* . . . . (Columbia)
Just Like Tom Thumb's Blues
Bob Dylan; *Highway 61 Revisited*. . . . . (Columbia)
Grateful Dead; *Terrapin Station* . . . . (Arista)
Judy Collins; *In My Life* . . . . (Elektra)
Linda Ronstadt; *We Ran* . . . . (Elektra)
King Tut
Steve Martin & Toot Uncommons; *Dr. Demento Presents The Greatest
Novelty Records-#4-1970s-C* . . . . (Rhino)
Dr. Demento Presents The Greatest Novelty Records-C . . . . (Rhino)
Livin' On A Prayer (Tommy)
Bon Jovi; *America: A Tribute To Heroes-C* . . . .(Interscope)
Cross Road-14 Classic Grooves. . . . . (Mercury)
Slippery When Wet . . . .(Jambco)
The Concert For New York City-C . . . . (Columbia)
Major Tom (Coming Home)
Peter Schilling; *Different Story (World Of Lust & Crime)*. . . . . (Elektra)
Error In The The System. . . . . (Elektra)
Mister Touchdown U.S.A.
Original Soundtrack; *Top Ten College Fight Songs* . . . . (K-Tel)
University Of Michigan Band; *Greatest College Football Marches*. . (Vanguard)
Mr. Tambourine Man
Bob Dylan; *Biograph* . . . . (Columbia)
Bob Dylan At Budokan . . . . (Columbia)
Bob Dylan's Greatest Hits . . . . (Columbia)
Bringing It All Back Home . . . . (Columbia)
Byrds; *Billboard Top Rock 'N' Roll Hits-1965-C* . . . . (Rhino)
Original Singles-#1-1965-1967 . . . . (Columbia)
The Byrds' Greatest Hits . . . . (Columbia)
The Original Singles-1965-1967 . . . . (Columbia)
Turn! Turn! Turn!. . . . . (Legacy)
Mr. Telephone Man
New Edition; *New Edition*. . . . . (MCA)
New Edition's Greatest Hits, Vol. 1 . . . . (MCA)
Mr. Too Damn Good
Gerald Levert; *G* . . . . (East West)
Only Living Boy In New York (Tom)
Simon & Garfunkel; *Bridge Over Troubled Water* . . . . (Columbia)
Collected Works . . . . (Columbia)
Ready Teddy
Buddy Holly; *Buddy Holly* . . . . (MCA)
Rock & Roll Collection. . . . . (MCA)
Elvis Presley; *Elvis* . . . . (RCA)
Rocker . . . . (RCA)
The Great Performances . . . . (RCA)
Little Richard; *Georgia Peach* . . . .(Specialty)

Grooviest 17 Original Hits . . . . (Specialty)
More American Graffiti . . . . (MCA)
She's In Love With The Boy (Tommy)
Trisha Yearwood; *Trisha Yearwood* . . . . (MCA)
Tar Top
Alabama; *Just Us* . . . . (RCA)
Tarzan & Jane
Sparks; *Angst In My Pants* . . . . (Atlantic)
Tarzan Boy
Baltimora; *Living In The Background* . . . . (Manhattan)
Tarzan Was A Bluesman
Timbuk 3; *Eden Alley* . . . . (I.R.S.)
Tarzan's Nuts
Madness; *One Step Beyond* . . . . (Sire)
Ted, Just Admit It
Jane's Addiction; *Nothing's Shocking* . . . . (Warner Bros.)
Teddy Boy
Beatles; *The Beatles-Anthology-#3* . . . . (Capitol)
Paul McCartney; *McCartney* . . . . (Capitol)
Tennessee Jed
Grateful Dead; *Europe '72* . . . . (Warner Bros.)
What A Long Strange Trip It's Been: The Best Of The
Grateful Dead . . . . (Warner Bros.)
Terence's Farewell To Kathleen
John McCormack; *Ireland Of Treasures-Voices & Melodies-C* . . . . . . (Capitol)
Theme From "T.J. Hooker"
Original Soundtrack; *Television's Greatest Hits-#6-Remote Control-C* . . . (TVT)
Theme From "Tarzan"
Original Soundtrack; *Television's Greatest Hits-#2-C* . . . . (TVT)
Theme From "Ted Mack's Original Amateur Hour"
Original Soundtrack; *Television's Greatest Hits-#4-Black & White*
Classics-C . . . . (TVT)
Theme From "Tennessee Tuxedo"
Original Soundtrack; *Television's Greatest Hits-#4-Black & White*
Classics-C . . . . (TVT)
Theme From "Tom & Jerry"
Henry Mancini; *ST/Tom & Jerry-The Movie* . . . . (MCA)
Theme From "Trapper John, M.D."
Original Soundtrack; *Television's Greatest Hits-#6-Remote Control-C* . . . (TVT)
Timmy Is An Arsonist
Plow; *Shreds-#2: American Underground 1994-C* . . . . (Shredder)
Timothy
Buoys; *Scepter Records Story-C* . . . . (Capricorn)
Super Hits Of The '70s-Have A Nice Day-#6-C . . . . (Rhino)
Tom & Jerry
Hot Rize; *Radio Boogie* . . . . (Flying Fish)
Mark O'Connor; *Championship Years* . . . . (Country Music Foundation)
Tom Dooley
Doc Watson; *Doc Watson* . . . . (Vanguard)
Essential Doc Watson . . . . (Vanguard)
Out In The Country . . . . (Intermedia)
Kingston Trio; *Capitol Collectors Series-The Kingston Trio* . . . . (Capitol)
From The Hungry i . . . . (Capitol)
Kingston Trio's Greatest Hits . . . . (Curb)
Tom Dooley . . . . (Capitol)
Troubadours Of The Folk Era-#3-C . . . . (Rhino)
Tom Sawyer
Rush; *Exit...Stage Left* . . . . (Mercury)
Moving Pictures . . . . (Mercury)
Rush-Chronicles . . . . (Mercury)
Tom Thumb
Wayne Shorter; *Best Of Wayne Shorter-TheBlue Note Years* . . . . . . (Blue Note)
Tom, Dick Or Harry
Original Cast; *Kiss Me Kate* . . . . (Sony Music Classical)
Tommy Can You Hear Me
Who; *Join Together* . . . . (MCA)
ST/The Kids Are Alright . . . . (MCA)
ST/Tommy . . . . (Polydor)
Tommy . . . . (MCA)
Tom's Diner
D.N.A. Featuring Suzanne Vega; *Solitude Standing* . . . . (A&M)
Tom's Album . . . . (A&M)
Tranquillo (Melt My Heart)
Carly Simon; *Boys In The Trees* . . . . (Elektra)
Tyrone
Erykah Badu; *Erykah Badu-Live* . . . . (Kedar Entert./Universal)

MEN'S NAMES: U

See Also: **CELEBRITIES: SPECIFIC, FAMILY (various),**
MEN: GENERAL

Tales Of Brave Ulysses
Cream; *Disraeli Gears* . . . . (Polydor)
Eric Clapton-Crossroads-C . . . . (Polydor)
Live Cream-#2 . . . . (Polydor)

Utah Carroll
Skip Gorman; *A Cowboy's Wild Song To His Herd* . . . . (Rounder)

MEN'S NAMES: V

See Also: **CELEBRITIES: SPECIFIC, FAMILY (various),**
MEN: GENERAL

Mr. Vain
Culture Beat; *Serenity* . . . . (550 Music)
Night Of Van Gogh
Boz Scaggs; *Other Roads* . . . . (Columbia)
Van Gogh's Left Ear
Kenny Garrett; *Black Hope* . . . . (Warner Bros.)
Vic And Ray
Mark Knopfler; *Golden Heart* . . . . (Warner Bros.)
Viking
Los Lobos; *The Sopranos-Music From The HBO Original*
Series . . . . (Sony Music Soundtrax)
Vincent
Don McLean; *American Pie* . . . . (EMI)
Best Of Don McLean . . . . (EMI)
Greatest Hits Then & Now . . . . (EMI)
Walk In The Sun (Vernon James)
Bruce Hornsby; *Hot House* . . . . (RCA)

MEN'S NAMES: W

See Also: **CELEBRITIES: SPECIFIC, FAMILY (various),**
MEN: GENERAL

Ballad Of William Worthy
Phil Ochs; *Best Of Broadside 1962-1968: Anthems Of The American*
Underground From The Pages Of Broadside
Magazine-C . . . . (Smithsonian Folkways)
Beautiful Brown Eyes (Willie)
Rosemary Clooney; *Songs From The Girl Singer-A Musical*
Autobiography . . . . (Concord Jazz)
Big Bad Bill Is Sweet William Now
Ry Cooder; *Jazz* . . . . (Warner Bros.)
Big Willie Style
Will Smith featuring Left Eye; *Big Willie Style* . . . . (Columbia)
Calling Mr. Welfare
Big Daddy Kane; *It's A Big Daddy Thing* . . . . (Cold Chillin')
Carroll County Accident (Walter Browning)
Porter Wagoner; *Essential Porter Wagoner* . . . . (RCA)
Porter Wagoner-Greatest Songs . . . . (Curb)
Doctor Wu
Steely Dan; *Katy Lied* . . . . (MCA)
Steely Dan's Greatest Hits . . . . (MCA)
Good Evening Mr. Waldheim
Lou Reed; *New York* . . . . (Sire)
Little Willie
Sweet; *Best Of The 1910 Fruitgum Company-#2-C* . . . . (Rhino)
Mr. Wendal
Arrested Development; *3 Years 5 Months 2 Days In The Life Of* . . . . . (Chrysalis)
Arrested Development-Unplugged . . . . (Chrysalis)
Poor Will & The Jolly Hangman
Richard Thompson; *Guitar/Vocal* . . . . (Hannibal)
Rambling, Gambling Willie
Bob Dylan; *The Bootleg Series-Volumes 1-3 [Rare & Unreleased]* . . (Columbia)
Say Hey (The Willie Mays Song)
Treniers; *Baseball's Greatest Hits-C* . . . . (Rhino)
Shotgun Willie
Willie Nelson; *Shotgun Willie* . . . . (Atlantic)
Theme From "The Life And Legend Of Wyatt Earp"
Original Soundtrack; *Television's Greatest Hits-#4-Black & White*
Classics-C . . . . (TVT)
Theme From "The Waltons"
Original Soundtrack; *CBS: The First 50 Years* . . . . (TVT)
Television's Greatest Hits-#3-1970s & 1980s-C . . . . (TVT)
Theme From "The Woody Woodpecker Show"
Original Soundtrack; *Television's Greatest Hits-#1-C* . . . . (TVT)
Theme From "Walker, Texas Ranger"
Original Soundtrack; *CBS: The First 50 Years* . . . . (TVT)
Theme From "Wally Gator"
Original Soundtrack; *Hanna-Barbera Classics-#1-Original Recordings Of*
The World's Most Famous Cartoon Themes &
Scores . . . . (Kid Rhino/Rhino 4 Kids)
Hanna-Barbera Pic-A-Nic Basket Of Cartoon
Classics . . . . (Kid Rhino/Rhino 4 Kids)
Theme From "Walt Disney's Wonderful World Of Color"
Original Soundtrack; *Television's Greatest Hits-#4-Black & White*
Classics-C . . . . (TVT)

Theme From "Wayne's World"
  Mike Myers & Dana Carvey; *ST/Wayne's World* . . . . (Reprise)
Theme From "Webster" (Then Came You)
  Original Soundtrack; *Television's Greatest Hits-#6-Remote Control-C* . . (TVT)
W.S. Walcott Medicine Show
  Band; *Rock Of Ages* . . . . (Capitol)
    Stage Fright . . . . (Capitol)
    To Kingdom Come-The Definitive Collection . . . . (Capitol)
Waldo P. Emerson Jones
  Archies; *Grooviest Hits Of The Archies* . . . . (Bac-Trac)
Waldo's Discount Donuts
  Red Knuckles & The Trailblazers; *Hot Rize Presents.* . . . . (Flying Fish)
Waltz Me Around Again Willie
  Joan Morris & William Bolcom; *After The Ball* . . . . (Nonesuch)
Warren Harding
  Al Stewart; *Past, Present & Future* . . . . (Rhino)
Washington's Birthday
  Bob Hope; *Thanks For The Memories* . . . . (Collectables)
Wild Little Willy
  Ronnie Hawkins and The Hawks; *Best Of Ronnie Hawkins and The*
    Hawks . . . . (Rhino)
Wild Wild West
  Will Smith; *Willenium* . . . . (Columbia)
Will 2K
  Will Smith; *Willenium* . . . . (Columbia)
Willie & The Hand Jive
  Eric Clapton; *461 Ocean Boulevard* . . . . (Polydor)
    Time Pieces-#1-The Best Of Eric Clapton . . . . (Polydor)
  George Thorogood & The Destroyers; *Maverick* . . . .(EMI)
  Johnny Otis; *All-Time Greatest Hits Of Rock 'N' Roll-C* . . . . (Curb)
    Capitol Years-Johnny Otis . . . . (Capitol)
    Let The Good Times Roll-C . . . . (Capitol)
Willie Jones
  Charlie Daniels Band; *Night Rider* . . . .(Epic)
    Renegade . . . .(Epic)
Willie Short
  Mary Chapin Carpenter; *Red Hot + Country-C* . . . . (Mercury)
Willie The Pimp
  Frank Zappa; *Hot Rats* . . . .(Rykodisc)
    You Can't Do That On Stage Anymore-#4 . . . .(Rykodisc)
  Mothers Of Invention; *Fillmore East-June 1971* . . . . (Reprise)

MEN'S NAMES: Y

See Also: **CELEBRITIES: SPECIFIC, FAMILY (various),**
MEN: GENERAL

Theme From "Yogi Bear"
  Original Soundtrack; *Hanna-Barbera Classics-#1-Original Recordings Of*
    The World's Most Famous Cartoon Themes &
    Scores . . . . (Kid Rhino/Rhino 4 Kids)
    Hanna-Barbera Pic-A-Nic Basket Of Cartoon
    Classics . . . . (Kid Rhino/Rhino 4 Kids)
    Television's Greatest Hits-#1-C . . . . (TVT)
Yankee Doodle
  Boston Pops Orchestra/Arthur Fiedler; *Fiedler's Favorite Marches* . . . . (RCA)
    Music For All Occasions . . . . (RCA)
Young Blood
  Rickie Lee Jones; *Naked Songs Live And Acoustic* . . . . (Reprise)
    Rickie Lee Jones . . . .(Warner Bros.)

MEN'S NAMES: Z

See Also: **CELEBRITIES: SPECIFIC, FAMILY (various),**
MEN: GENERAL

Theme From "Doctor Zhivago"
  101 Strings Orchestra; *Music From Doctor Zhivago & Others* . . . . (Alshire)
Theme From "Zorba The Greek"
  Cincinnati Pops Orchestra/Erich Kunzel; *Hollywood's Greatest*
    Hits-#2 . . . . (Telarc)
Theme From "Zorro"
  Original Soundtrack; *Disney Collection-#2-C* . . . .(Disney)
To Zion
  Lauryn Hill featuring Carlos Santana; *The Miseducation Of*
    Lauryn Hill . . . . (Ruffhouse/Columbia)
War Baby Son Of Zorro
  Daryl Hall & John Oates; *War Babies* . . . .(Atlantic)
Zak And Sara
  Ben Folds; *Rockin' The Suburbs.* . . . .(Epic)
Zero And Blind Terry
  Bruce Springsteen; *Tracks* . . . . (Columbia)
Ziggy Stardust
  David Bowie; *Changesbowie* . . . .(Rykodisc)
    Rise & Fall Of Ziggy Stardust And The Spiders From Mars . . . . . . (Rykodisc)

    Sound + Vision . . . . (Rykodisc)
    ST/Ziggy Stardust-The Motion Picture . . . . (Rykodisc)
    Stage . . . . (Rykodisc)
    The Singles-1969-1993 . . . . (Rykodisc)

MIDNIGHT

See Also: **AFTERNOON, DAYS OF THE WEEK (various),**
MORNING, NIGHT, TIME: GENERAL, TIME: SPECIFIC

After Midnight
  Eric Clapton; *Eric Clapton* . . . .(Polydor)
    Eric Clapton-Crossroads-C . . . .(Polydor)
    Just One Night . . . .(Polydor)
    Time Pieces-#1-The Best Of Eric Clapton . . . .(Polydor)
  J.J. Cale; *Naturally* . . . . (MCA)
At Midnight
  Mighty Lemon Drops; *Laughter* . . . .(Sire)
At Midnight (My Love Will Lift You Up)
  Rufus Featuring Chaka Khan; *Ask Rufus.* . . . . (MCA)
    Live-Stompin' At The Savoy . . . . (Warner Bros.)
Brown Sugar
  Rolling Stones; *Classic Rock 1966-1988-C* . . . .(Atlantic)
    Hot Rocks 1964-1971 . . . .(Abkco)
    Made In The Shade . . . . (Rolling Stones)
    Sticky Fingers . . . .(Virgin)
Burnin' The Midnight Oil
  Foghat; *Night Shift* . . . . (Rhino)
Burning Of The Midnight Lamp
  Jimi Hendrix; *Essential Jimi Hendrix* . . . . (Reprise)
    Lifelines/Jimi Hendrix Story . . . . (Reprise)
  Jimi Hendrix Experience; *Electric Ladyland* . . . . (Reprise)
    Radio One . . . . (Rykodisc)
  Living Colour; *Biscuits* . . . . (Epic)
California Nights
  Lesley Gore; *Summer & Sun-C* . . . . (Rhino)
Caravan To Midnight
  Robin Trower; *Caravan To Midnight* . . . . (Chrysalis)
Celery Stalks At Midnight
  Will Bradley; *Swing Time! Fabulous Big Band Era-1925-1955-C* . . . (Columbia)
Coffee At Midnite
  Bluegrass Parlor Band; *Two Colors* . . . . (Pinecastle)
Confessin' Midnight
  Robin Trower; *For Earth Below* . . . . (Chrysalis)
Down In The Tube Station At Midnight
  Jam; *Snap!.* . . . .(Polydor)
    The Jam's Greatest Hits . . . .(Polydor)
Fire At Midnight
  Jethro Tull; *Songs From The Wood* . . . . (Chrysalis)
Gimme Gimme Gimme (A Man After Midnight)
  Erasure; *Two Ring Circus* . . . .(Sire)
In The Midnight Hour
  Rascals; *Classic Rock 1966-1988-C* . . . .(Atlantic)
    ST/More Songs From "The Big Chill" . . . . (Motown)
    Time Peace/The Rascals' Greatest Hits . . . .(Atlantic)
  Roxy Music; *Flesh + Blood* . . . . (Atco)
    Street Life-20 Great Hits . . . . (Reprise)
  Wilson Pickett; *Atlantic Rhythm & Blues 1947-1974-#5 (1962-*
    1966)-C . . . .(Atlantic)
    Best Of Wilson Pickett . . . .(Atlantic)
    Frat Rock!-#4-C . . . . (Rhino)
    Golden Soul-C . . . .(Atlantic)
    Soul Years-C . . . .(Atlantic)
    Wilson Pickett's Greatest Hits . . . .(Atlantic)
Isn't It Midnight
  Fleetwood Mac; *25 Years-The Chain* . . . . (Warner Bros.)
    Tango In The Night. . . . . (Warner Bros.)
It Gets Lonely In A Small Town
  Greg Brown; *One More Goodnight Kiss* . . . . (Red House)
It's Midnight Cinderella
  Garth Brooks; *Fresh Horses* . . . . (Capitol)
    Limited Series Box . . . . (Capitol)
London After Midnight
  Wrathchild America; *Climbin' The Walls* . . . .(Atlantic)
Love In The Midnight
  Styx; *Cornerstone* . . . . (A&M)
Mdnite Special
  Paul Evans; *Super Oldies Of The '60s-#2-C* . . . . (Audio Fidelity)
Midnight
  Ice-T; *O.G. Original Gangster* . . . .(Sire)
Midnight
  Altered Images; *Happy Birthday.* . . . .(Portrait)
Midnight
  Maze featuring Frankie Beverly; *Silky Soul* . . . . (Warner Bros.)
Midnight Angel
  Barbara Mandrell; *Best Of Barbara Mandrell* . . . . (MCA)

Midnight Angel .... (MCA)
Midnight Angel
  Highway 101; *Paint The Town* .... (Warner Bros.)
Midnight At The Oasis
  Maria Muldaur; *Maria Muldaur* ....(Reprise)
  Super Hits Of The '70s-Have A Nice Day-#13-C .... (Rhino)
Midnight Blue
  Melissa Manchester; *Melissa*...........................(Arista)
  Melissa Manchester's Greatest Hits......................(Arista)
Midnight Blue
  Electric Light Orchestra; *Afterglow*............................(Epic)
  Discovery ....(Jet)
Midnight Blue
  King Curtis; *Enjoy...Best Of* ....(Collectables)
  Soul Twist & Other Golden Classics...................(Collectables)
Midnight Blue
  Lou Gramm; *Ready or Not* .... (Atlantic)
Midnight Blue
  Johnny Mathis; *Feelings* ....(Columbia)
Midnight Blue
  Louise Tucker; *Midnight Blue* ....(Arista)
Midnight Blue
  Seals & Crofts; *Takin' It Easy* .... (Warner Bros.)
Midnight Blue
  Foreigner; *Jukebox Heroes-Anthology* .... (Rhino)
Midnight Blues
  Charlie Daniels Band; *Original Charlie Daniels Band* ....(Sun)
  Time For Tears-C ....(Sun)
Midnight Blues
  Allman Brothers Band; *An Evening With The Allman Brothers Band-*
   First Set .... (Epic)
Midnight Blues
  Bessie Smith; *Bessie Smith-The Complete Recordings-#1* ....(Legacy)
Midnight Blues
  Gary Moore; *Still Got The Blues* .... (Charisma)
Midnight Blues
  Memphis Slim; *Traveling With The Blues* .... (Storyville)
Midnight Bus
  Jesse Winchester; *Third Down 110 To Go* .... (Rhino)
Midnight Carnival
  Chris Mars; *Horseshoes & Hand Grenades*.............. (Smash)
Midnight Confessions
  Grass Roots; *Grass Roots-Anthology (1966-1975)* .... (Rhino)
  Original Rock 'N' Roll Hits Of The '60s-C .... (Roulette)
  Vintage Music-#9-C .... (MCA)
Midnight Creeper
  Elton John; *Don't Shoot Me I'm Only The Piano Player* .... (Polydor)
Midnight Dreamer
  Journey; *Look Into The Future* ....(Columbia)
Midnight Fire
  Steve Wariner; *Best Of Steve Wariner* ....(RCA)
  Steve Wariner's Greatest Hits ....(RCA)
Midnight Flyer
  Eagles; *On The Border* .... (Elektra)
  Osborne Brothers; *Essential Bluegrass Album* .... (C.M.H. Prod.)
  Osborne Brothers & Mac Wiseman; *Great American Train*
   Songs-C .... (C.M.H. Prod.)
Midnight Girl/Sunset Town
  Sweethearts Of The Rodeo; *Sweethearts Of The Rodeo* .... (Columbia)
Midnight Hauler
  Razzy Bailey; *Razzy Bailey's Greatest Hits* ....(RCA)
Midnight In Memphis
  Bette Midler; *ST/The Rose*........................... (Atlantic)
  Hoyt Axton; *Where Did The Money Go*....................(Jeremiah)
  Meri Wilson; *First Take* ....(GRT)
Midnight In Montgomery
  Alan Jackson; *Don't Rock The Jukebox*................. (Arista)
Midnight In Morocco
  Michael Powers; *Perpetual Motion*....................(Nastymix)
Midnight In Moscow
  Dukes Of Dixieland; *Dixieland's Greatest Hits* .... (MCA)
  Kenny Ball; *Billboard Top Pop Hits-1962-C* .... (Rhino)
Midnight In Old Amarillo
  Buddy Emmons & Ray Pennington; *Swing & Other Things* ....(Step One)
Midnight In Paris
  Michael Hurley & The Unholy Modal Rounders; *Have Moicy* .... (Rounder)
Midnight In Paris
  Stephen Stills; *Illegal Stills* .... (Columbia)
Midnight In San Juan
  Earl Klugh; *Midnight In San Juan* .... (Warner Bros.)
Midnight In Tokyo
  Y & T; *Best Of '81 To '85* ....(A&M)
  Mean Streak ....(A&M)
  Yesterday & Today Live .... (Metal Blade)
Midnight Light
  Le Blanc & Carr; *Midnight Light* .... (Big Tree)
Midnight Lover
  Leon Russell; *Americana*............................ (Paradise)

Midnight Madness
  Clockwork; *Made In The U.S. Of Japan*......................(Mercury)
Midnight Madness
  Foghat; *Stone Blue* ....(Rhino)
Midnight Magic
  38 Special; *Rock & Roll Strategy* ....(A&M)
Midnight Magic
  Commodores; *Midnight Magic*..........................(Motown)
Midnight Man
  James Gang; *Best Of The James Gang* .... (MCA)
  James Gang-16 Greatest Hits .... (MCA)
Midnight Man
  Rita Remington; *My Melody Of Love* .... (Plantation)
Midnight Man
  Allman Brothers Band; *Shades Of Two Worlds* ....(Epic)
Midnight Maniac
  Krokus; *Blitz* ....(Arista)
Midnight Mary
  Joey Powers; *Dick Bartley's One-Hit Wonders Of The '60s-#1-C* ......(Rhino)
Midnight Moodies
  Joe Walsh; *The Smoker You Drink The Player You Get* .... (MCA)
Midnight 'N Peru
  Ken Tamplin; *Soul Survivor*.........................(Intense)
Midnight On Mars
  Ashra; *Blackouts* .... (Blue Plate)
Midnight On The Bay
  Stills/Young Band; *Long May You Run* .... (Reprise)
Midnight On The Radio
  Mike Bloomfield; *Try It Before You Buy It*................ (One Way)
Midnight On The Water/Dry And Dusty
  Skip Gorman; *A Cowboy's Wild Song To His Herd* ....(Rounder)
Midnight Prowl
  John David Souther; *Black Rose* ....(Asylum)
Midnight Rambler
  Rolling Stones; *Get Yer Ya-Ya's Out!* .... (Abkco)
  Hot Rocks 1964-1971 .... (Abkco)
  Let It Bleed .... (Abkco)
Midnight Ravers
  Bob Marley & The Wailers; *Catch A Fire* .... (Tuff Gong)
Midnight Rendezvous
  Babys; *Babys-Anthology* .... (Chrysalis)
  Union Jacks.. (Chrysalis)
Midnight Rendezvous
  Jacksons; *2300 Jackson Street* .... (Epic)
Midnight Rider
  Allman Brothers Band; *Beginnings* .... (Polydor)
  Best Of The Allman Brothers Band .... (Polydor)
  Decade Of Hits-1969-1979 .... (Polydor)
  Idlewild South .... (Polydor)
  The Road Goes On Forever, A Collection Of Their Greatest
   Recordings .... (Polydor)
  Duane Allman; *Duane Allman-An Anthology-Vol. II*.........(Capricorn)
  Gregg Allman; *Laid Back*........................... (Polydor)
  South's Greatest Hits-C ....(Capricorn)
  Willie Nelson; *ST/The Electric Horseman* ....(Columbia)
Midnight Rocks
  Al Stewart; *24 Carrots* ....(Arista)
Midnight Rodeo
  Leon Everette; *45-#12355* .... (RCA)
Midnight Shift
  Commander Cody & His Lost Planet Airmen; *Lost In The Ozone* .... (MCA)
Midnight Sky
  Isley Brothers; *Live It Up* .... (T-Neck/Columbia)
  The Isley Brothers Story-#2-The T-Neck Years-1969-1985..........(Rhino)
Midnight Special
  Creedence Clearwater Revival; *1969*...................... (Fantasy)
  Creedence Clearwater Revival-Chronicle-#2.............. (Fantasy)
  Creedence Clearwater Revival-Gold .... (Fantasy)
  Movie Album .... (Fantasy)
  Willy & The Poor Boys .... (Fantasy)
  Johnny Rivers; *Johnny Rivers-Anthology 1964-1977* ....(Rhino)
  Very Best Of Johnny Rivers .... (EMI)
Midnight Special Train
  Big Joe Turner; *Atlantic Rhythm & Blues 1947-1974-#3 (1955-*
   1958)-C .... (Atlantic)
  Joe Turner's Greatest Hits .... (Atlantic)
Midnight Sun
  Brian Culbertson; *Modern Life*.................. (Mesa/Bluemoon)
  Ella Fitzgerald; *In Rome-Birthday Concert* ....(Verve)
  Ella Fitzgerald & Oscar Peterson; *Ella & Oscar* ....(Pablo)
  Sarah Vaughan; *Best Of Sarah Vaughan* ....(Pablo)
  How Long Has This Been Going On? .... (Pablo)
Midnight Tennessee Woman
  Jack Greene; *Jack Greene Sings His Best*................. (Step One)
Midnight Train
  Jim & Jesse; *Great American Train Songs-C* .... (C.M.H. Prod.)
Midnight Train To Georgia
  Gladys Knight & The Pips; *Billboard Top Rock 'N' Roll Hits-1973-C* ...(Rhino)

Gladys Knight & The Pips' Greatest Hits . . . . (Buddah)
Imagination . . . . (Right Stuff)
On & On. . . . . (Fifty One West)
Radio Active Hits-C . . . . (Accord)
Train Trax-C . . . . (Sony Music Special Prod.)
Very Best Of Gladys Knight & The Pips. . . . . (Buddah)

Midnight Wind
Charlie Daniels Band; *Midnight Wind* . . . .(Epic)

Midnight Wind
John Stewart; *Bombs Away Dream Babies* . . . . (RSO)

Midnight, Me & The Blues
Mel Tillis & The Statesiders; *Best Of Mel Tillis & The Statesiders* . . (MGM)
Mel Tillis & The Statesiders' Greatest Hits . . . . (MGM)
Mel Tillis & The Statesiders-24 Great Hits . . . . (MGM)

Midnite Cruiser
Steely Dan; *Can't Buy A Thrill* . . . .(MCA)

Mr. Midnight
Garth Brooks; *Scarecrow* . . . . (Capitol)

New York City Serenade
Bruce Springsteen; *The Wild, The Innocent & The E Street Shuffle* . . (Columbia)

Private Life
Pretenders; *Pretenders* . . . . (Sire)

Rainbow At Midnight
Carlisle Brothers; *45-#535* . . . . (King)
Ernest Tubb; *Ernest Tubb Collection-C* . . . . (Step One)
Ernest Tubb-Retrospective-#1 . . . .(MCA Special Prod.)
The Ernest Tubb Story . . . . (MCA)

Ridin' That Midnight Train
Ricky Skaggs and Kentucky Thunder; *Bluegrass Rules!* . . . . (Rounder)

Riding That Midnight Train
Doc Watson; *Riding That Midnight Train* . . . . (Sugar Hill)

Rockin' After Midnight
Marvin Gaye; *Midnight Love* . . . . (Columbia)

Rockin' At Midnight
Honeydrippers; *Little By Little-Collector's Edition* . . . .(Es Paranza)
Volume One . . . .(Es Paranza)

Round About Way
George Strait; *Carrying Your Love With Me.* . . . .(MCA)
Latest Greatest Straitest Hits . . . .(MCA)

'Round Midnight
Carmen McRae; *Carmen Sings Monk.* . . . . (Novus)
Ella Fitzgerald; *Fine And Mellow* . . . . (Pablo)
Newport Jazz Festival . . . . (Columbia)
Ella Fitzgerald & Count Basie; *Perfect Match* . . . . (Pablo)
John Lewis; *Midnight In Paris* . . . . (Emarcy)
Private Concert . . . . (Emarcy)
Miles Davis; *Live At The Plugged Nickel* . . . . (Columbia)
Miles Davis . . . .(Philips)
Miles Davis' Greatest Hits . . . . (Columbia)
Miles Davis-Collector's Items . . . . (Prestige)
Miles Davis Quintet; *Round About Midnight* . . . . (Columbia)
Sarah Vaughan; *Roulette Years* . . . . (Roulette)
Thelonius Monk; *At The It Club* . . . . (Columbia)
Best Of Thelonius Monk. . . . . (Blue Note)
I Like Jazz-Essence Of Thelonius Monk. . . . . (Columbia)
'Round Midnight . . . . (Milestone)
Thelonius Monk . . . . (Crescendo)
Wynton Marsalis; *All-American Hero* . . . . (Who's Who In Jazz)

Saturday At Midnight
Cheap Trick; *One On One.* . . . .(Epic)

South City Midnight Lady
Doobie Brothers; *Best Of The Doobies* . . . .(Warner Bros.)
Captain & Me . . . .(Warner Bros.)

Theme From "Midnight Caller"
Original Soundtrack; *Television's Greatest Hits-#7-Cable Ready-C* . . . . . (TVT)

Theme From "Midnight Cowboy"
Cincinnati Pops Orchestra/Erich Kunzel; *Hollywood's Greatest Hits-#2* . . . . (Telarc)

Tired Of Midnight Blue
George Harrison; *Extra Texture* . . . . (Capitol)

Two Minutes To Midnight
Iron Maiden; *A Real Dead One* . . . . (Capitol)
Live After Death-World Slavery Tour . . . . (Capitol)
Powerslave . . . . (Capitol)

Two More Bottles Of Wine
Delbert McClinton; *Honky Tonkin'-I Done Me Some.* . . . . (Alligator)
Emmylou Harris; *Honky Tonk Country-C* . . . .(Warner Bros.)
Profile/Best Of Emmylou Harris . . . .(Warner Bros.)
Quarter Moon In A Ten Cent Town . . . .(Warner Bros.)
Martina McBride; *Wild Angels* . . . . (RCA)

Walkin' After Midnight
Garth Brooks; *The Chase* . . . . (Liberty)
Loretta Lynn; *I Remember Patsy* . . . .(MCA)
Oak Ridge Boys; *Unstoppable* . . . . (RCA)
Patsy Cline; *20 Golden Pieces Of Patsy Cline* . . . . (Bulldog)
Let The Teardrops Fall . . . . (Accord)
Live At The Opry . . . .(MCA)
Patsy Cline. . . . .(MCA)
Patsy Cline's Greatest Hits . . . .(MCA)

The Patsy Cline Story . . . . (MCA)

We Just Couldn't Say Goodbye
Guy Lombardo & His Royal Canadians; *Guy Lombardo-16 Most Requested Songs* . . . . (Legacy)

When The Midnight Choo Choo Leaves For Alabam'
Andrews Sisters; *Best Of The Andrews Sisters-#2.* . . . . (MCA)
Judy Garland & Fred Astaire; *ST/Easter Parade.* . . . . (Rhino)

Young Blood
Bad Company; *Run With The Pack* . . . . (Swan Song)
Coasters; *Coasters' Greatest Hits* . . . . (Atco)
Coasters-Their Greatest Recordings-Early Years . . . . (Atco)
The Ultimate Coasters . . . .(Warner Special Prod.)

MINING

See Also: **DANGER & DISASTER, ENERGY, GOLD, MOUNTAINS, NATURE, POLITICS: SOCIAL INJUSTICE, POVERTY, SILVER, WORK**

1913 Massacre
Arlo Guthrie; *Hobo's Lullaby* . . . . (Reprise)
Jack Elliot; *Tribute To Woody Guthrie-C* . . . . (Warner Bros.)
Ramblin' Jack Elliott; *Greatest Songs Of Woody Guthrie-C.* . . . . . . (Vanguard)
Woody Guthrie; *Struggle* . . . . (Smithsonian Folkways)

Aberfan Coal Tip Tragedy
Thom Parrott; *Best Of Broadside 1962-1968: Anthems Of The American Underground From The Pages Of Broadside Magazine-C* . . . .(Smithsonian Folkways)

Big Bad John
Jimmy Dean; *American Originals-Jimmy Dean* . . . . (Columbia)
Billboard Top Country Hits-1961-C. . . . . (Rhino)
Columbia Country Classics-#3-Americana-C . . . . (Columbia)
Jimmy Dean's Greatest Hits . . . . (Columbia)

Blackleg Miner
Steeleye Span; *Hark The Village Wait.* . . . . (Chrysalis)
The Steeleye Span Story . . . . (Chrysalis)

Blue Sky Mine
Midnight Oil; *Blue Sky Mining* . . . . (Columbia)

Canary In A Coal Mine
Police; *Zenyatta Mondatta* . . . . (A&M)

Clementine
Bobby Darin; *Bobby Darin-At The Copa* . . . . (Bainbridge)
The Bobby Darin Story . . . .(Atlantic)
Original Soundtrack; *Children's Favorites* . . . .(Kid Rhino/Rhino 4 Kids)

Coal Miner's Daughter
Loretta Lynn; *Coal Miner's Daughter* . . . . (MCA)
Coal Miner's Daughter . . . . (MCA)
Loretta Lynn-20 Greatest Hits . . . . (MCA)
Loretta Lynn-Greatest Hits Live. . . . . (K-Tel)
Loretta Lynn's Greatest Hits-#2. . . . . (MCA)
The Country Music Hall Of Fame-Loretta Lynn. . . . . (MCA)

Diamond Mine
Hank Williams, Jr.; *Out Of Left Field* . . . . (Capricorn)

Diamond Mine
Blue Rodeo; *Diamond Mine* . . . .(Atlantic)

Dirty Business
New Riders Of The Purple Sage; *New Riders Of The Purple Sage* . . . (Columbia)

Don't Give Up
Peter Gabriel; *Shaking The Tree-Sixteen Golden Greats.* . . . . (Geffen)
So . . . . (Geffen)

Dying Miner
Woody Guthrie; *Struggle* . . . .(Smithsonian Folkways)

Explosion In The Fairmount Mines
Blind Alfred Reed; *How Can A Poor Man Stand Such Times And Live?* . . . . (Rounder)

Heart Of Gold
Neil Young; *Decade* . . . . (Reprise)
Harvest. . . . . (Reprise)

I Ain't Goin' Down
Nashville Bluegrass Band; *Waitin' For The Hard Times To Go* . . . . .(Sugar Hill)

Miner's Blues
Frank Hutchison; *Train That Carried My Girl From Town.* . . . . (Rounder)

Miner's Life
Tom Juravich; *Out Of Darkness (Mine Workers' Story)* . . . . (Flying Fish)
Weavers; *Reunion-At Carnegie Hall-1963-#2* . . . . (Vanguard)

Miner's Lifeguard
Almanac Singers/Peter Seeger/Chorus; *Talking Union & Other Union Songs* . . . .(Smithsonian Folkways)

Miner's Prayer
Dwight Yoakam; *Guitars, Cadillacs, Etc., Etc.* . . . . (Reprise)

Mining Camp Blues
Fletcher Henderson & Trixie Smith; *Fletcher Henderson & His Orchestra-1923-1927* . . . .(Biograph)

Mining For Coal
Randy Travis; *No Holdin' Back* . . . . (Warner Bros.)

Mining For Gold
Cowboy Junkies; *Trinity Session.* . . . . (RCA)

Mrs. Clara Sullivan's Letter
Pete Seeger; *Best Of Broadside 1962-1968: Anthems Of The American
Underground From The Pages Of Broadside
Magazine*-C ....(Smithsonian Folkways)

New York Mining Disaster 1941 (Mr. Jones)
Bee Gees; *Bee Gees-Gold* ....(Polydor)
Here At Last...Bee Gees...Live ....(Polydor)
History Of British Rock-#8-C ....(Rhino)

One Miner's Life-The Image Of God
Battlefield Band; *There's A Buzz* ....(Flying Fish)

Open Pit Mine
Nashville Bluegrass Band; *Waitin' For The Hard Times To Go* .....(Sugar Hill)

Saginaw, Michigan
Lefty Frizzell; *American Originals-Lefty Frizzell* ....(Columbia)
Billboard Top Country Hits-1964-C ....(Rhino)
Columbia Country Classics-#3-Americana-C ....(Columbia)
Lefty Frizzell's Greatest Hits ....(Columbia)

Sixteen Tons
Cactus Brothers; *Cactus Brothers* ....(Liberty)
Tennessee Ernie Ford; *Best Of Tennessee Ernie Ford-16 Tons Of
Boogie* ....(Rhino)
Capitol Collectors Series-Tennessee Ernie Ford ....(Capitol)
When AM Was King-C ....(Capitol)
Weavers; *Weavers' Greatest Hits* ....(Vanguard)

Stripmining
James; *Strip-Mine* ....(Sire)

There's A Gold Mine In The Sky
Jimmy C. Newman; *Cajun Cowboy* ....(Plantation)
Pat Boone; *Love Letters In The Sand* ....(MCA Special Prod.)

We Work The Black Seam
Sting; *Bring On The Night* ....(A&M)
Dream Of The Blue Turtles ....(A&M)

Work In The Mines
Bill Shute & Lisa Null; *American Primitive* ....(Green Linnet)

Working In The Coal Mine
Devo; *Best Of Devo-Greatest Hits* ....(Warner Bros.)
Devo's Greatest Hits ....(Warner Bros.)
New Traditionalists ....(Warner Bros.)
Now It Can Be Told (Devo At The Palace) ....(Enigma)
ST/Heavy Metal ....(Asylum)
Judds; *Collection-1983-1990* ....(RCA)
Rockin' With The Rhythm ....(MCA)
Lee Dorsey; *Best Of New Orleans Rhythm & Blues-#2*-C .....(Rhino)
Golden Classics-Lee Dorsey ....(Collectables)
History Of New Orleans R&B-#3-1962-1970-C ....(Rhino)
Holy Cow ....(Arista)
New Orleans Jazz & Heritage Festival-1976-C ....(Rhino)

You'll Never Leave Harlan Alive
Patty Loveless; *Mountain Soul* ....(Epic)

MISTAKES

See Also: **ADVICE, BAD, DIVORCE, ENDINGS, FOOLS, FORGIVE,
GUILT, INSULTS, LOVE (various), LOW SELF-ESTEEM,
WARNINGS, WRONG**

(Lost His Love) On Our Last Date
Emmylou Harris; *Profile II-The Best Of Emmylou Harris* ....(Warner Bros.)

...Baby One More Time
Britney Spears; *...Baby One More Time* ....(Jive)
Now That's What I Call Music!-#2-C ....(Virgin)

Adia
Sarah McLachlan; *Mirrorball* ....(Arista)
Surfacing ....(Arista)

Amigone
Goo Goo Dolls; *Dizzy Up The Girl* ....(Warner Sunset/Reprise)

Angels Of The Silences
Counting Crows; *Recovering The Satellites* ....(David Geffen Co.)

Been There
Clint Black with Steve Wariner; *D'lectrified* ....(RCA)

Before You Walk Out Of My Life
Monica; *Miss Thang* ....(Rowdy/Arista)

Best Man I Can Be
Ginuwine, R.L., Tyrese, Case; *ST/The Best Man* ......(Sony Music Soundtrax)

Blame It On Your Heart
Patty Loveless; *Only What I Feel* ....(Epic)
Patty Loveless-Classics ....(Epic)

Blood Is Thicker Than Water
Wyclef Jean featuring G&B (The Product); *The Sopranos-Music From The
HBO Original Series* ....(Sony Music Soundtrax)

Breathe
Nickelback; *State* ....(Roadrunner)

Bullet Proof
Goo Goo Dolls; *Dizzy Up The Girl* ....(Warner Sunset/Reprise)

Careless Whisper
Dave Koz featuring Montell Jordan; *Dance* ....(Capitol)

Wham! Featuring George Michael; *Make It Big* ....(Columbia)
Music For The Miracle-C ....(Epic Portrait Assoc.)

Computers Don't Blunder
Exploited; *The Singles Collection* ....(Cleopatra)

Couldn't Last A Moment
Collin Raye; *Tracks* ....(Epic)

Crazy
Jimmie Dale Gilmore with Willie Nelson; *Red Hot + Country*-C .....(Mercury)
Kenny Rogers; *Kenny Rogers' Greatest Hits* ....(RCA)
What About Me? ....(RCA)
Linda Ronstadt; *Hasten Down The Wind* ....(Asylum)
Patsy Cline; *Songwriter's Tribute* ....(MCA)
ST/Sweet Dreams ....(MCA)
The Patsy Cline Story ....(MCA)
Ray Price; *Ray Price's Greatest Hits-#2* ....(Step One)
Willie Nelson; *Best Of Willie* ....(RCA)
Healing Hands Of Time ....(Liberty)
Nite Life-Greatest Hits & Rare Tracks ....(Rhino)
Willie & Family Live ....(Columbia)

Detour (Devil Took A)
Patti Page; *Patti Page-Golden Hits* ....(Mercury)

Didn't Cha Know
Erykah Badu; *Mama's Gun* ....(Motown)

Diving To Be Deeper
Sinead Lohan; *No Mermaid* ....(Grapevine)

Do Right
Jimmie's Chicken Shack; *Bring Your Own Stereo* ....(Rocket)

Do Your Thing
7 Mile; *7 Mile* ....(Crave)

Don't Let Me Be Misunderstood
Animals; *Greatest Hits Live!-Rip It To Shreds* ....(I.R.S.)
Sullivan Years-British Invasion ....(TVT)
Joe Cocker; *With A Little Help From My Friends* ....(A&M)

Evaporated
Ben Folds Five; *Whatever And Ever Amen* ....(Caroline/550)

Everything I Love
Alan Jackson; *Everything I Love* ....(Arista)

Expressway To Your Heart
Blues Brothers; *Best Of The Blues Brothers* ....(Atlantic)
Soul Survivors; *Dick Bartley's One-Hit Wonders Of The '60s-#2*-C .....(Rhino)
Oldies But Goodies-#11-C ....(Original Sound)
Super Oldies Of The '60s-#6-C ....(Audio Fidelity)
When The Whistle Blows Anything Goes ....(Collectables)

Fool
Sanford Clark; *Billboard Top Rock 'N' Roll Hits-1956*-C ....(Rhino)
Original Classic Oldies Of The '50s & '60s-#17-C ....(MCA)

Foolish Little Girl
Shirelles; *Shirelles' Greatest Hits* ....(Everest)
Shirelles-16 Greatest Hits ....(Trip)
Shirelles-Anthology 1959-1964 ....(Rhino)

God's Gonna Get'cha (For That)
George Jones & Tammy Wynette; *George Jones & Tammy Wynette-16
Biggest Hits* ....(Epic/Legacy)
George Jones & Tammy Wynette's Greatest Hits ....(Epic)

Higher Ground
Stevie Wonder; *Innervisions* ....(Motown)
Original Musiquarium ....(Motown)

Hit Or Miss (Waited Too Long)
New Found Glory; *New Found Glory* ....(Drive-Thru)

I Don't Make Promises (I Can't Break)
Shannon Curfman; *Loud Guitars Big Suspicions* ....(Arista)

I Drive Myself Crazy
'N Sync; *'N Sync* ....(RCA)
Totally Hits-#2-C ....(Elektra)

I Want It That Way
Backstreet Boys; *Millennium* ....(Jive)

I Won't Let You Do That To Me
Luther Vandross; *One Night With You-The Best Of Love-#2* ....(LV/Epic)

If I Could Turn Back The Hands Of Time
R. Kelly; *Now That's What I Call Music!-#3*-C ....(Virgin)
R. ....(Jive)

I'm Sorry
Brenda Lee; *Billboard Top Pop Hits-1960*-C ....(Rhino)
Brenda Lee-Anthology-#1 & #2 ....(MCA)
The Brenda Lee Story-Her Greatest Hits ....(MCA)
Platters; *Enchanted-The Best Of The Platters* ....(Rhino)
Magic Touch-An Anthology ....(Mercury)

It's Too Late
Derek And The Dominos; *Layla* ....(Polydor)

Lessons To Be Learned
Barbra Streisand; *Higher Ground* ....(Columbia)

Lost Ones
Lauryn Hill; *The Miseducation Of Lauryn Hill* ....(Ruffhouse/Columbia)

Mississippi
Bob Dylan; *"Love And Theft"* ....(Columbia)
Sheryl Crow; *The Globe Sessions* ....(A&M)

Mistake No. 3
Culture Club; *Waking Up With The House On Fire* ....(Virgin)

Mistakes
Mandy Barnett; *I've Got A Right To Cry* . . . . (Sire)
My Favorite Mistake
Sheryl Crow; *Now That's What I Call Music!-#2-C* . . . . (Virgin)
The Globe Sessions . . . . (A&M)
Never Again, Again
Lee Ann Womack; *Lee Ann Womack* . . . . (Decca)
Nietzche's Eyes
Paula Cole; *This Fire* . . . . (Imago)
Nineteen
Old 97's; *Fight Songs* . . . . (Elektra)
One Piece At A Time
Johnny Cash; *The Man In Black-His Greatest Hits* . . . . (Legacy)
Only Sixteen
Dr. Hook; *Bankrupt* . . . . (Capitol)
Dr. Hook-Greatest Hits & More . . . . (Capitol)
Great Records Of The Decade-'70s Hits-#2-C . . . . (Curb)
Little Bit More . . . . (Capitol)
Sam Cooke; *Best Of Sam Cooke* . . . . (RCA)
The Man And His Music . . . . (RCA)
This Is Sam Cooke . . . . (RCA)
Ooh Baby Baby
Linda Ronstadt; *Linda Ronstadt's Greatest Hits, Volume Two* . . . . . . (Asylum)
Living In The USA . . . . (Asylum)
Miracles; *Best Of Smokey Robinson & The Miracles-Anthology* . . . . (Motown)
Smokey Robinson's Greatest Hits-#2 . . . . (Motown)
Oops!...I Did It Again
Britney Spears; *Oops!...I Did It Again* . . . . (Jive)
Pack Up Your Sins And Go To The Devil
Dorothy Loudon; *Broadway Baby* . . . . (DRG)
Ella Fitzgerald & Chick Webb; *The Early Years-#1: With Chick Webb & His Orchestra-1935-1938* . . . . (GRP)
Prayin' For Daylight
Rascal Flatts; *Rascal Flatts* . . . . (Lyric Street)
Rollin' Stoned
Great White; *Can't Get There From Here* . . . . (Portrait)
Roving Kind, The
Guy Mitchell; *Guy Mitchell-16 Most Requested Songs* . . . . (Legacy)
Send In The Clowns
Barbra Streisand; *The Broadway Album* . . . . (Columbia)
Carmen McRae; *Sarah-Dedicated To You* . . . . (Novus)
Frank Sinatra; *The Reprise Collection* . . . . (Reprise)
Judy Collins; *Judith* . . . . (Elektra)
So Early In The Spring, The First 15 Years . . . . (Elektra)
Original Cast; *Little Night Music* . . . . (Columbia)
Should've Asked Her Faster
Ty England; *Ty England* . . . . (RCA)
Somebody To Love
Jefferson Airplane; *2400 Fulton Street-An Anthology* . . . . (RCA)
Loves You . . . . (RCA)
Nipper's Greatest Hits Of The '60s #1-C . . . . (RCA)
Surrealistic Pillow . . . . (RCA)
The Worst Of Jefferson Airplane . . . . (RCA)
Someday We'll Be Together
Diana Ross & The Supremes; *20/20-C* . . . . (Motown)
Diana Ross & The Supremes' Greatest Hits-#3 . . . . (Motown)
Diana Ross & The Supremes-Anthology (1962-1969) . . . . (Motown)
Evening With Diana Ross . . . . (Motown)
Motown Story-First 25 Years-C . . . . (Motown)
Motown Superstar Series-#1-Diana Ross & The Supremes . . . . . (Motown)
Special
Garbage; *Now That's What I Call Music!-#3-C* . . . . (Virgin)
Version 2.0 . . . . (Almo Sounds)
Still
Commodores; *Best Of The Commodores-Anthology* . . . . (Motown)
Commodores-All The Great Hits . . . . (Motown)
Commodores-The Ultimate Collection . . . . (Motown)
Lionel Richie; *Back To Front* . . . . (Motown)
Truly-The Love Songs . . . . (Motown)
Straight Lines
Wood; *Songs From Stamford Hill* . . . . (Columbia)
Sweet Sixteen
Destiny's Child; *The Writing's On The Wall* . . . . (Columbia)
Then What
Clay Walker; *Clay Walker's Greatest Hits* . . . . (Giant)
There's Your Trouble
Dixie Chicks; *Wide Open Spaces* . . . . (Monument)
Waist Deep In The Big Muddy
Pete Seeger; *Best Of Broadside 1962-1968: Anthems Of The American Underground From The Pages Of Broadside Magazine-C* . . . . (Smithsonian Folkways)
When The Fallen Angels Fly
Patty Loveless; *When Fallen Angels Fly* . . . . (Epic)
Why Would I Say Goodbye
Brooks & Dunn; *Borderline* . . . . (Arista)
Wide Open Spaces
Dixie Chicks; *Big Country Hits '99-C* . . . . (K-Tel)
Wide Open Spaces . . . . (Monument)

Wildest Times Of The World
Vonda Shepard; *ST/Songs From "Ally McBeal" Featuring Vonda Shepard* . . . . (550/Epic)
Woke Up This Morning
A3; *Exile On Coldharbour Lane* . . . . (C2/Columbia)
The Sopranos-Music From The HBO Original Series . . . . (Sony Music Soundtrax)
World Leader Pretend
R.E.M.; *Green* . . . . (Warner Bros.)
Wrong Way
Sublime; *Sublime* . . . . (Gasoline Alley)
You Learn
Alanis Morissette; *Jagged Little Pill* . . . . (Maverick)
You Should've Told Me
Kelly Price; *Mirror Mirror* . . . . (Def Soul/IDJMG)

MISTREATMENT, Be Cruel, Treat Badly
See Also: BAD, CHEATING & LIES, DIVORCE, GUILT, LOVE (various), PAIN & HEALING, REVENGE, WRONG

Abuse Me
Silverchair; *Freak Show* . . . . (Epic)
All Cried Out
Allure; *Allure* . . . . (Track Masters/Crave)
Boom! 17 Explosive Hits-C . . . . (Simitar)
Lisa Lisa; *Lisa Lisa & Cult Jam With Full Force* . . . . (Columbia)
Lisa Lisa-Super Hits . . . . (Columbia)
Past, Present & Future . . . . (TMP)
Bad To Me
Billy J. Kramer With The Dakotas; *History Of British Rock-#1-C* . . . . . (Rhino)
Rock Is Dead But It Won't Lie Down-C . . . . (Gold Rush)
Big Boss Man
B.B. King; *Six Silver Strings* . . . . (MCA)
Elvis Presley; *ST/Clambake* . . . . (RCA)
Grateful Dead; *Grateful Dead (Skull & Roses)* . . . . (Warner Bros.)
Jimmy Reed; *Best Of Jimmy Reed* . . . . (Crescendo)
Oldies But Goodies-#1-C . . . . (Original Sound)
John Hammond; *Best Of John Hammond* . . . . (Vanguard)
So Many Roads . . . . (Vanguard)
Blame It On Your Heart
Patty Loveless; *Only What I Feel* . . . . (Epic)
Patty Loveless-Classics . . . . (Epic)
Blistering
Machine Head; *The More Things Change...* . . . . (Roadrunner)
Blue Suede Shoes
Carl Perkins; *Blue Suede Shoes* . . . . (Sun)
Carl Perkins-Original Sun Greatest Hits . . . . (Rhino)
Cruisin'-1956-957-C . . . . (Dunhill Compact Classics)
Oldies But Goodies-#4-C . . . . (Original Sound)
Elvis Presley; *Aloha from Hawaii via Satellite* . . . . (RCA)
Elvis Presley . . . . (RCA)
Elvis-A Legendary Performer, Volume 2 . . . . (RCA)
From Memphis To Vegas/From Vegas To Memphis . . . . (RCA)
ST/G.I. Blues . . . . (RCA)
Born A Woman
Sandy Posey; *Best Of Sandy Posey-With Skeeter Davis* . . . . (Gusto)
Best Of Town & Country-#3-C . . . . (Gusto)
Cruisin'-1966-C . . . . (Increase)
Sandy Posey/Skeeter Davis/Wanda Jackson . . . . (Gusto)
Super Hits-#5-C . . . . (Gusto)
Born In The U.S.A.
Bruce Springsteen; *Born In The U.S.A.* . . . . (Columbia)
Bruce Springsteen's Greatest Hits . . . . (Columbia)
Tracks . . . . (Columbia)
Bruce Springsteen & The E Street Band; *Bruce Springsteen & The E Street Band Live/1975-85* . . . . (Legacy)
Boyz-N-The-Hood
Dynamite Hack; *Superfast* . . . . (Farm Club/Universal)
Broken Wing
Martina McBride; *Evolution* . . . . (RCA)
Bully, The
May Irwin; *Music From The New York Stage (1890-1920)-#1-1890-1908-C* . . . . (Pearl)
Can I Get A...
Jay-Z featuring Amil & Ja Rule; *Vol. 2-Hard Knock Life* . . . . (Def Jam)
Captain Bligh
Filter; *Title Of Record* . . . . (Reprise)
Chains
Patty Loveless; *Honky Tonk Angel* . . . . (MCA)
Patty Loveless' Greatest Hits . . . . (MCA)
Chante's Got A Man
Chante Moore; *Now That's What I Call Music!-#3-C* . . . . (Virgin)
This Moment Is Mine . . . . (Silas)
Criminal
Fiona Apple; *1998 Grammy Nominees-C* . . . . (MCA)

Tidal . . . .(Clean Slate/Work)

Cruel Summer
Ace Of Base; *Cruel Summer* . . . . (Arista)
Bananarama; *Bananarama* . . . .(London)

Do Right
Jimmie's Chicken Shack; *Bring Your Own Stereo* . . . . (Rocket)

Don't Be Cruel
Cheap Trick; *Cheap Trick's Greatest Hits* . . . . (Epic)
Lap Of Luxury . . . . (Epic)
Elvis Presley; *Billboard Top Rock 'N' Roll Hits-1956-C* . . . . (Rhino)
Nipper's Greatest Hits Of The '50s-#2-C . . . . (RCA)
Number One Hits . . . . (RCA)
The Great Performances . . . . (RCA)
The Top Ten Hits . . . . (RCA)
Judds; *Heartland* . . . . (MCA)

Don't Be Cruel
Bobby Brown; *Chart Toppers-R&B Hits Of The '80s-C* . . . .(Priority)

Don't Leave Me This Way
Thelma Houston; *Billboard Top Rock 'N' Roll Hits-1977-C* . . . .(Rhino)
Disco Nights-#6-C . . . .(Rebound)
Motown's Leading Ladies-C . . . . (Motown)

Easy To Be Hard
Original Broadway Cast; *Hair* . . . .(RCA)
Original Cast; *ST/Hair* . . . .(RCA)
Three Dog Night; *Best Of Three Dog Night* . . . . (MCA)
Captured Live At The Forum . . . . (MCA)
Celebrate-The Three Dog Night Story . . . . (MCA)

Free Girl Now
Tom Petty And The Heartbreakers; *Echo* . . . . (Warner Bros.)

Friday Night Blues
John Conlee; *John Conlee-Live At Billy Bob's* . . . . (Razor & Tie)
John Conlee's Greatest Hits . . . . (MCA)
Sonny Throckmorton; *45-#57018* . . . . (Mercury)

Goodbye Cruel World
James Darren; *Best Of James Darren* . . . . (Rhino)
Billboard Top Rock 'N' Roll Hits-1961-C . . . . (Rhino)

Happy Jack
Who; *Happy Jack* . . . . (MCA)
Meaty Beaty Big & Bouncy . . . . (MCA)
ST/The Kids Are Alright . . . . (MCA)
Who Greatest Hits . . . . (MCA)

He Treats Me Like A Dog
St. Louis Bessie; *Barrelhouse Mamas: Born In The Alley, Raised In The
Slums-C* . . . . (Yazoo)

Heartbreak Hotel
Whitney Houston Featuring Faith Evans & Kelly Price; *My Love Is
Your Love* . . . . (Arista)
Totally Hits-#1-C . . . . (Arista)
Whitney Houston's Greatest Hits . . . . (Arista)

Heartbreak Town
Dixie Chicks; *Fly* . . . . (Monument)

Hit The Road Jack
Ray Charles; *Ray Charles' Greatest Hits* . . . . (Rhino)
Ray Charles-Anthology . . . . (Rhino)
Ray Charles-His Greatest Hits-#2 . . . . (Dunhill Compact Classics)

I Asked For Water (He Gave Me Gasoline)
Lucinda Williams; *Lucinda Williams* . . . . (Koch International)

I Asked For Water (She Gave Me Gasoline)
Howlin' Wolf; *Howlin' Wolf-His Best* . . . . (Chess)
The Blues-#3-C . . . . (Chess)

I Can Make It Better
Luther Vandross; *Your Secret Love* . . . . (LV/Epic)

I Know One
Charley Pride; *Charley Pride-Super Hits* . . . .(RCA)
Garth Brooks; *Garth Brooks* . . . .(Liberty)
Jim Reeves; *Essential Jim Reeves* . . . .(RCA)

If You're Gone
Matchbox Twenty; *Mad Season By Matchbox Twenty* . . . .(Lava)

I'll Stick Around
Foo Fighters; *Foo Fighters* . . . .(Roswell/RCA)

Indian Reservation (The Lament Of The Cherokee Reservation Indian)
Don Fardon; *45-#408.* . . . .(GNP/Crescendo)
Raiders; *Billboard Top Rock 'N' Roll Hits-1971-C* . . . .(Rhino)
Legend Of Paul Revere And The Raiders . . . .(Columbia)
Pop Classics Of The '70s-C . . . .(Columbia)
Super Hits Of The '70s-Have A Nice Day-#5-C . . . . (Rhino)

It Isn't Right
Platters; *Enchanted-The Best Of The Platters* . . . . (Rhino)
Magic Touch-An Anthology . . . . (Mercury)

Keep Searchin' (We'll Follow The Sun)
Del Shannon; *Del Shannon's Greatest Hits* . . . . (Rhino)
Del Shannon's Greatest Hits . . . . (Curb)

Last Fair Deal Gone Down
Keb' Mo'; *Just Like You* . . . . (Okeh)

Love Me
Elvis Presley; *24 Karat Hits!* . . . . (Dunhill Compact Classics)

Make Em Say Uhh #2
Master P; *MP Da Last Don* . . . .(No Limit/Priority)

May The Bird Of Paradise Fly Up Your Nose
"Little" Jimmy Dickens; *Columbia Country Classics-#3-
Americana-C* . . . .(Columbia)
Super Hits Of The '60s-C . . . . (Epic)
Harlow Wilcox and the Oakies; *Cripple Cricket* . . . . (Plantation)

Mommy Can I Come Home
Keb' Mo'; *The Door* . . . . (550/Epic/Okeh)

One Angry Dwarf And 200 Solemn Faces
Ben Folds Five; *Whatever And Ever Amen.* . . . . (Caroline/550)

One Of These Days
Tim McGraw; *Everywhere.* . . . .(Curb)

Out Of My Head
Fastball; *All The Pain Money Can Buy* . . . .(Hollywood)
Now That's What I Call Music!-#3-C . . . . (Virgin)

Push
Matchbox Twenty; *Yourself Or Someone Like You* . . . .(Lava)

Red Football
Sinead O'Connor; *Universal Mother* . . . .(Ensign)

Shadowboxer
Fiona Apple; *Tidal* . . . . (Clean Slate/Work)

She's A Fool
Lesley Gore; *Golden Hits Of Lesley Gore* . . . .(Mercury)
Lesley Gore-Anthology . . . .(Rhino)

Somebody Like Me
Eddy Arnold; *Best Of Eddy Arnold-#2* . . . . (Dunhill Compact Classics)

Someone You Use
Vonda Shepard; *ST/Songs From "Ally McBeal" Featuring Vonda
Shepard* . . . .(550/Epic)

Sweet Dreams (Are Made Of This)
Eurythmics; *Eurythmics' Greatest Hits* . . . .(Arista)
Sweet Dreams (Are Made Of This) . . . . (RCA)
Marilyn Manson; *Smells Like Children* . . . .(Interscope)

That's The Way Boys Are
Lesley Gore; *Golden Hits Of Lesley Gore* . . . .(Mercury)

'Til You Do Me Right
After 7; *Rock On 1995-C* . . . . (Madacy)
Very Best Of After 7. . . . . (Virgin)

Trash
Korn; *Issues* . . . .(Immortal/Epic)

What Goes On
Beatles; *"Yesterday"...And Today* . . . .(Capitol)

Wrong Way
Sublime; *Sublime* . . . .(Gasoline Alley)

You Don't Know What You've Got (Until You Lose It)
Ral Donner; *You Don't Know What You've Got (Until You
Lose It)* . . . .(Collectables)

You Keep Me Hangin' On
Diana Ross; *Evening With Diana Ross.* . . . .(Motown)
Diana Ross & The Supremes; *Diana Ross & The Supremes-Anthology (1962-
1969)* . . . .(Motown)
Motown Story-First 25 Years-C . . . . (Motown)
Kim Wilde; *Another Step* . . . .(MCA)
Reba McEntire; *Starting Over* . . . . (MCA)
Supremes; *Billboard Top R&B Hits-1965-C* . . . . (Rhino)
Diana Ross & The Supremes' Greatest Hits-#2 . . . .(Motown)
Vanilla Fudge; *Best Of Vanilla Fudge* . . . . (Atco)
Vanilla Fudge . . . . (Atco)
Wilson Pickett; *A Man & A Half-Best Of Wilson Pickett* . . . .(Rhino)
Wilson Pickett's Greatest Hits. . . . . (Atlantic)

MONEY, Cash, Getting Paid, Rich, Taxes, Wealth

*See Also: BUSINESS & INDUSTRY, CARS (various), GAMBLING,
GOLD, GREED, HARD CITY LIFE, JEWELRY, KINGS, LOSING &
LOSS, LOVE: LOVE & MONEY, LUCK, POVERTY, QUEENS,
ROYALTY, SHOPPING, SILVER, SOCIAL CLASS: GENERAL,
SOCIAL CLASS: RURAL, TRAINS, WINNING, WORK*

(It's Just) The Way That You Love Me
Paula Abdul; *Forever Your Girl.* . . . . (Virgin)
Shut Up And Dance (The Dance Mixes) . . . . (Virgin)

(Just Like) Romeo & Juliet
Reflections; *'60s Dance Party-C* . . . .(Dominion Entert.)
Sensational '60s-#1-C . . . .(Dominion Entert.)

(We're Not) The Jet Set
George Jones & Tammy Wynette; *George Jones & Tammy Wynette-16
Biggest Hits* . . . . (Epic/Legacy)

1040 Blues
Robert Cray Band; *Shame + Sin.* . . . .(Mercury)

1st Of Tha Month
Bone Thugs-N-Harmony; *E. 1999 Eternal* . . . . (Ruthless/Relativity)

26 Cents
Wilkinsons; *Nothing But Love* . . . . (Giant)

90 Days (Same As Cash)
Midnight Star; *Midnight Star.* . . . . (Solar)

Addicted To A Dollar
Doug Stone; *More Love* . . . .(Epic)
Affirmation
Savage Garden; *Affirmation* . . . . (Columbia)
Ain't Got No Money
Bob Seger & The Silver Bullet Band; *Stranger In Town* . . . . (Capitol)
Ain't No Fun (Waiting Round To Be A Millionaire)
AC/DC; *Dirty Deeds Done Dirt Cheap* . . . .(Atlantic)
Ain't No Money
Rosanne Cash; *Somewhere In The Stars* . . . . (Columbia)
All I Have To Give
Backstreet Boys; *Backstreet Boys* . . . . (Jive)
    Now That's What I Call Music!-#3-C . . . . (Virgin)
All N My Grill
Missy "Misdemeanor" Elliot; *Da Real World* . . . . (East West)
Always True To You In My Fashion
Blossom Dearie; *ST/Day-Cole Porter Songbook-C* . . . . (Verve)
    Original Cast; *Kiss Me Kate* . . . . (EMI-Angel)
    Peggy Lee & George Shearing; *Anything Goes-Capitol Sings Cole Porter-C* . . . . (Capitol)
Another Day Another Dollar
Alison Krauss & Union Station; *Every Time You Say Goodbye* . . . . . . (Rounder)
Another Saturday Night
Cat Stevens; *Cat Stevens Greatest Hits* . . . . (A&M)
    Jimmy Buffett; *Margaritaville Cafe Late Night Menu* . . . (Margaritaville)
    Sam Cooke; *The Man And His Music* . . . . (RCA)
    This Is Sam Cooke . . . . (RCA)
Any Bonds Today?
Andrews Sisters; *Swing Out To Victory: Songs Of World War II-C* . . . . (ISD/Intersound)
    Barry Wood; *78-#27478* . . . . (Victor)
    Bing Crosby; *Original Soundtrack Sessions* . . . . (Vintage Jazz Classics)
Any Lucky Penny
Nikki Hassman; *Songs From Dawson's Creek* . . . . (Sony Music Soundtrax)
Anything For Money
DV8; *ST/Far Out Man* . . . . (Chameleon)
    ST/Halloween V-Revenge Of Michael Myers . . . . (Varese Sarabande)
Are The Good Times Really Over (I Wish A Buck Was Still Silver)
Merle Haggard; *Big City* . . . .(Epic)
    For The Record: Merle Haggard-43 Legendary Hits . . . . (BNA)
    Greatest Country Hits Of The '80s-1982-C . . . . (Columbia)
    His Epic Hits-First 11 To Be Continued-C . . . .(Epic)
As Tears Go By
Marianne Faithfull; *Marianne Faithfull's Greatest Hits* . . . . . . (Abkco)
    Strange Weather . . . . (Island)
    Rolling Stones; *Big Hits (High Tide & Green Grass)* . . . . (Abkco)
    December's Children (and everybody's) . . . . (Abkco)
    Hot Rocks 1964-1971 . . . . (Abkco)
    Singles Collection-The London Years . . . . (Abkco)
Atlantic City
Bruce Springsteen; *Bruce Springsteen's Greatest Hits* . . . . (Columbia)
    Nebraska . . . . (Columbia)
Baby You're A Rich Man
Beatles; *Beatles-Box Set* . . . . (Capitol)
    Magical Mystery Tour . . . . (Capitol)
Back That Azz Up
Juvenile; *Back That Azz Up (single)* . . . . (Cash Money/Universal)
Ballad Of Forty Dollars
Johnny Cash & Waylon Jennings; *Heroes* . . . . (Columbia)
    Tom T. Hall; *Essential Tom T. Hall-20th Anniversary Collection* . . . . (Mercury)
    Tom T. Hall's Greatest Hits-#1 . . . . (Mercury)
Ballad Of Jed Clampett
Flatt & Scruggs; *Columbia Country Classics-#3-Americana-C* . . . . . . (Columbia)
    On Foggy Mountain . . . . (Fifty One West)
Bankrobber
Clash; *On Broadway* . . . .(Epic)
    The Story Of The Clash, Volume 1 . . . .(Epic)
Bankrobber/Robber Dub
Clash; *Black Market Clash* . . . .(Epic)
    Rhythm Come Forward: Volume III-C . . . . (Columbia)
Best Things In Life Are Free
June Allyson; *ST/Good News* . . . . (Sony Music Special Prod.)
    Luther Vandross & Janet Jackson; *ST/Mo' Money* . . . . (Bluebird)
    Mel Torme; *Easy To Remember* . . . . (Glendale)
    Sam Cooke; *Sam Cooke-At The Copa* . . . . (RCA)
Big Money
Rush; *Power Windows* . . . . (Mercury)
    Show Of Hands . . . . (Mercury)
Big Money
Garth Brooks; *Scarecrow* . . . . (Capitol)
Big Spender (Muriel Cigars)
Original Soundtrack; *TeeVee Toons-The Commercials-#1-C* . . . . (TVT)
Big Willie Style
Will Smith featuring Left Eye; *Big Willie Style* . . . . (Columbia)
Billion Dollar Babies
Alice Cooper; *Alice Cooper's Greatest Hits* . . . .(Warner Bros.)
    Billion Dollar Babies . . . .(Warner Bros.)
    The Alice Cooper Show . . . .(Warner Bros.)

Bills, Bills, Bills
Destiny's Child; *The Writing's On The Wall* . . . . (Columbia)
Bitch Betta Have My Money
AMG; *Give A Dog A Bone* . . . . (Select)
Bitter Sweet Symphony
Verve; *Urban Hymns* . . . . (Hut/Virgin)
Black Money
Vinnie James; *All-American Boy* . . . .(RCA)
Bling Bling
B.G.; *Chopper City In The Ghetto* . . . .(Cash Money/Universal)
Blue Money
Van Morrison; *His Band And The Street Choir* . . . . (Warner Bros.)
Bring It All To Me
Blaque; *Blaque* . . . . (Track Masters/Columbia)
Brother, Can You Spare A Dime
Bing Crosby; *Bing Crosby-16 Most Requested Songs* . . . . (Legacy)
    Odetta/Dr. John/John Campbell/Rufus Reid; *Strike A Deep Chord-Blues For The Homeless-C* . . . .(Justice)
    Peter, Paul & Mary; *See What Tomorrow Brings* . . . . (Warner Bros.)
    Weavers; *Weavers' Greatest Hits* . . . . (Vanguard)
Burn Your Money!
Mojo Nixon & Skid Roper; *Root Hog Or Die* . . . . (I.R.S.)
Bus Fare Home
Spaniels; *Heart & Soul-#2-C* . . . . (Vee-Jay)
Busted
Harlan Howard; *All-Time Favorite Country Songwriter* . . . (Koch International)
    John Conlee; *John Conlee's Greatest Hits* . . . . (MCA)
    Songs For The Working Man . . . . (MCA)
    Johnny Cash; *Johnny Cash-16 Biggest Hits-#2* . . . . (Legacy)
    Ray Charles; *Ray Charles' Greatest Hits* . . . . (Rhino)
    Ray Charles-His Greatest Hits-#2 . . . . . . (Dunhill Compact Classics)
Buy Me A Million Dollars
Love Tractor; *Love Tractor/'Til The Cows Come Home* . . . . (DB)
Buying My Way Into Heaven
Sammy Hagar; *Unboxed* . . . . (Geffen)
Can I Get A…
Jay-Z featuring Amil & Ja Rule; *Vol. 2-Hard Knock Life* . . . . (Def Jam)
Can I Have My Money Back
Gerry Rafferty; *Can I Have My Money Back* . . . . (MCA)
Can't Buy Me Love
Beatles; *Beatles 1* . . . . (Capitol)
    Hey Jude . . . . (Capitol)
    Reel Music . . . . (Capitol)
    ST/A Hard Day's Night . . . . (Capitol)
    The Beatles At The Hollywood Bowl . . . . (Capitol)
    The Beatles/1962-1966 . . . . (Capitol)
Can't Nobody Hold Me Down
Puff Daddy; *No Way Out* . . . .(Bad Boy/Arista)
Cash For Your Trash
Original Cast; *Ain't Misbehavin'* . . . . (RCA)
Casual Affair
Tonic; *Lemon Parade* . . . .(Polydor)
Change
Keb' Mo'; *The Door* . . . . (550/Epic/Okeh)
Chasing Forever
Will Smith; *Big Willie Style* . . . . (Columbia)
Check's In The Mail
Victory; *Don't Get Mad-Get Even* . . . . (Mercenary)
Cold Hard Cash
Greg Kihn; *Next Of Kihn* . . . . (Beserkley)
Come And Get It
Badfinger; *Best Of Badfinger* . . . . (Capitol)
    Beatles; *The Beatles-Anthology-#3* . . . . (Capitol)
Country Grammar (Hot Sh*t)
Nelly; *Country Grammar* . . . .(Fo' Reel/Universal)
Daddy Never Was The Cadillac Kind
Confederate Railroad; *Notorious* . . . .(Atlantic)
Daddy's Money
Ricochet; *Ricochet* . . . . (Columbia)
Dance Tonight
Lucy Pearl; *Lucy Pearl* . . . . (Overbrook/Pookie/Beyond)
Dangerous
Busta Rhymes; *When Disaster Strikes* . . . . (Elektra)
Deep Inside
Mary J. Blige; *Mary* . . . . (MCA)
Diamonds On The Soles Of Her Shoes
Paul Simon; *Concert In The Park-August 15 1991* . . . . (Warner Bros.)
    Graceland . . . .(Warner Bros.)
    Negotiations And Love Songs, 1971-1986 . . . . (Warner Bros.)
Did You Ever Think
R. Kelly; *R.* . . . .(Jive)
Did You Steal My Money
Who; *Face Dances* . . . . (MCA)
Dime At A Time
Del Reeves; *Super Country Hits Of The '60s-C* . . . . (Gusto)
Dime Store Mystery
Lou Reed; *New York* . . . .(Sire)

Ding Dong Dollar
Glasgow Song Guild; *Best Of Broadside 1962-1968: Anthems Of The American Underground From The Pages Of Broadside Magazine-C* ....(Smithsonian Folkways)

Dirty Cash (Money Talks)
Adventures Of Stevie V; *Best Of '90s Dance Music-#1-Hip House-C* ....(PWL America)
Dirty Cash (Money Talks) ....(Mercury)

Do Re Mi
Arlo Guthrie; *Tribute To Woody Guthrie-C* ....(Warner Bros.)
John Cougar Mellencamp; *Folkways: A Vision Shared-C* ....(Columbia)
Ry Cooder; *Ry Cooder* ....(Reprise)
Show Time ....(Warner Bros.)
Woody Guthrie; *Dust Bowl Ballads* ....(Rounder)

Doggie In The Window
Patti Page; *Patti Page-16 Most Requested Songs* ....(Legacy)
Patti Page-Golden Hits ....(Mercury)
Patti Page's Greatest Hits ....(Columbia)

Dollar Bill
Screaming Trees; *Sweet Oblivion* .... (Epic)

Dollar's Worth Of Gasoline
Tom Russell; *Hurricane Season* ....(Philo)

Don't Bet Money
Whispers; *Best Of The Whispers* ....(Solar)
Don't Bet Money ....(Solar)

Don't Pay The Ferryman
Chris DeBurgh; *Getaway* .... (A&M)

Don't Put A Tax On The Beautiful Girls
Eddie Cantor; *Rare Early Recordings-1919-1921* .... (Biograph)

Don't Want Money
Jasmine Guy; *Jasmine Guy* ....(Warner Bros.)

Do-Wacka-Do
Roger Miller; *Best Of Roger Miller-His Greatest Songs* ....(Curb)
Dumb Ditties-C ....(K-Tel)

Easy Money
Benny Carter; *The King* .... (Pablo)
Benny Carter All-Star Sax Ensemble; *Over The Rainbow* ....(Musicmasters)

Easy Money
King Crimson; *Lark's Tongues In Aspic* .... (Editions E.G.)

Easy Money
Billy Joel; *Innocent Man* .... (Columbia)

Easy Money
Rickie Lee Jones; *Rickie Lee Jones* .... (Warner Bros.)

Easy Money
James O'Gwynn; *James O'Gwynn's Greatest Hits* ....(Plantation)

Easy Money
REO Speedwagon; *Nine Lives* ....(Epic)
You Can Tune A Piano But You Can't Tuna Fish ....(Epic)

Eat The Rich
Aerosmith; *Get A Grip* .... (Geffen)

Ends
Everlast; *Whitey Ford Sings The Blues* ....(Tommy Boy)

Even It Up
Heart; *Bebe Le Strange* .... (Epic)
Heart's Greatest Hits/Live .... (Epic)

Everything For Free
K's Choice; *Cocoon Choice* .... (550 Music)

Fame And Fortune
Bad Company; *Fame & Fortune* .... (Atlantic)

Fame And Fortune
Elvis Presley; *A Valentine Gift For You* ....(RCA)
Elvis' Golden Records, Volume 3 ....(RCA)
Elvis-A Legendary Performer, Volume 3 ....(RCA)

Fancy
Bobbi Gentry; *All-Time Country Classics-#1-C* ....(Capitol)
Reba McEntire; *Rumor Has It* .... (MCA)

Father Christmas
Kinks; *Billboard Rock 'N Roll Christmas-C* ....(Rhino)
Come Dancing With The Kinks-Best Of The Kinks 1977-1986 ....(Arista)

Final Hour
Lauryn Hill; *The Miseducation Of Lauryn Hill* .... (Ruffhouse/Columbia)

First I Look At The Purse
Contours; *25 Hard-To-Find Motown Classics-#3-C* ....(Motown)
Do You Love Me (Now That I Can Dance) ....(Motown)
J. Geils Band; *Best Of The J. Geils Band* ....(Atlantic)
Full House ....(Atlantic)
J. Geils Band ....(Atlantic)

Fool & His Money
Wang Chung; *Mosaic* .... (Geffen)

Fool With My Money
Special Forces; *Special Forces* ....(Empire Recording Comm.)

For The Love Of Money
O'Jays; *Didn't It Blow Your Mind: Soul Hits Of The '70s-#14-C* ....(Rhino)
O'Jays-Collector's Item ....(Philadelphia Int'l)
Ship Ahoy ....(Philadelphia Int'l)

Forgive Them Father
Lauryn Hill featuring Shelly Thunder; *The Miseducation Of Lauryn Hill* ....(Ruffhouse/Columbia)

Friends In Low Places
Garth Brooks; *Garth Brooks-Double Live* ....(Capitol)
No Fences ....(Capitol)

Gimme A Quarter, 25 Cents For The Bus
October Faction; *October Faction* ....(SST)

God Bless The Child
Billie Holiday; *Billie Holiday's Greatest Hits* ....(Decca Jazz)
Billie Holiday's Greatest Hits ....(Legacy)
From The Original Decca Masters ....(MCA)
Songbook ....(Verve)
The Billie Holiday Story-#2 ....(Columbia)
Blood, Sweat & Tears; *Blood, Sweat & Tears* ....(Columbia)
Blood, Sweat & Tears Greatest Hits ....(Columbia)
Diana Ross; *ST/Lady Sings The Blues* ....(Motown)
Liza Minnelli; *4-Sider* ....(Cypress)
ST/Liza With A "Z" ....(Columbia)
Lou Rawls; *Best From Lou Rawls* ....(Capitol)

Gold Diggers' Song (We're In The Money)
Ginger Rogers; *Lullaby Of Broadway-The Best Of Busby Berkeley At Warner Brothers* ....(Rhino)

Golden Coins
Elvis Presley; *ST/Harum Scarum* .... (RCA)

Got To Get It
Sisqo; *Got To Get It (single)* .... (Dragon/Def Soul/IDJMG)

Got Your Money
Ol' Dirty Bastard; *Nigga Please* ....(Elektra)

Gotta Get The Money
Levert; *Just Coolin'* .... (Atlantic)

Green Christmas
Stan Freberg; *Capitol Collectors Series-Stan Freberg* ....(Capitol)
Christmas Comedy Classics-C .... (Priority)
Dr. Demento Presents The Greatest Novelty Records-#6-Christmas-C ....(Rhino)
Dr. Demento's Greatest Christmas CD-C ....(Rhino)

Greenback Dollar
Kingston Trio; *Best Of The Best Of The Kingston Trio* ....(Pro-Arte)
Capitol Collectors Series-The Kingston Trio ....(Capitol)
Very Best Of The Kingston Trio ....(Capitol)

Grey Goose/Sixpenny Money
Joe Burke; *Traditional Music Of Ireland* .... (Green Linnet)

Handful Of Dust
Patty Loveless; *When Fallen Angels Fly* .... (Epic)

Have A Cigar
Pink Floyd; *Wish You Were Here* ....(Columbia)

Heads Carolina, Tails California
Jo Dee Messina; *Greatest Hits Of Country Dance-C* ....(Curb)
Jo Dee Messina ....(Curb)

Heartspark Dollarsign
Everclear; *Sparkle And Fade* ....(Capitol)

Here's A Quarter (Call Someone Who Cares)
Travis Tritt; *It's All About To Change* ....(Warner Bros.)

Hidden Treasure
Traffic; *The Low Spark Of High Heeled Boys* ....(Island)

Hissing Of Summer Lawns
Joni Mitchell; *Hissing Of Summer Lawns* .... (Asylum)

Hit 'Em Up Style (Oops!)
Blu Cantrell; *So Blu* ....(Arista)
Totally Hits 2001-C ....(Arista)

Hopeless
Dionne Farris; *ST/Love Jones* ....(Columbia)

Horse & Carriage
Cam'ron featuring Mase; *Confessions Of Fire* ....(Untertainment/Epic)

Hot Boyz
Missy "Misdemeanor" Elliot; *Da Real World* ....(East West)
Totally Hits-#2-C ....(Elektra)

I Don't Want Your Millions, Mister
Jim Garland; *Newport Broadside: Newport Folk Festival-1963-C* ...(Vanguard)
Pete Seeger; *The Prestige/Folklore Years-#4: Singing Out Loud-The Philadelphia Folk-C* .... (Prestige)
Tom Rush; *Blues Songs & Ballads* ....(Fantasy)
Tom Rush .... (Fantasy)

I Don't Want Your Money
Chicago; *Chicago At Carnegie Hall* ....(Chicago)
Chicago III ....(Chicago)

I Found A Million-Dollar Baby (In A Five-And-Ten-Cent Store)
Barbra Streisand; *ST/Funny Girl* ....(Columbia)
Bing Crosby; *Pennies From Heaven* ....(Pro-Arte)
Fred Waring's Pennsylvanians; *78-#22707* ....(Victor)
Nat "King" Cole; *Nat "King" Cole-Gift Set* ....(Capitol)

I Got The Sun In The Morning
Ethel Merman/Bruce Yarnell/Original Cast; *Annie Get Your Gun* ....(RCA Victor)
Ethel Merman/Ray Middleton/Original Cast; *Annie Get Your Gun* ......(MCA)
Original Broadway Cast; *Annie Get Your Gun* ....(Angel)

I Left My Wallet In El Segundo
Tribe Called Quest; *People's Instinctive Travels And The Paths Of Rhythm* .... (Jive)
Rap: Most Valuable Players-C ....(K-Tel)

I Love Robbing Banks
Greg Austin Band; *Midnight Driver* . . . .(Xeres)
I Spent My Last Ten Dollars (On Birth Control And Beer)
Two Nice Girls; *Lesbian Favorites-Women Like Us-C* . . . . (Rhino)
I Wanna Be Rich
Original Broadway Cast; *Stop The World I Want To Get Off* . . . . (Polydor)
I Wanna Be Rich
Calloway; *Shut Up And Dance! The '90s-#1-C* . . . . (Priority)
I Will Buy You A New Life
Everclear; *Now That's What I Call Music!-#1-C* . . . . (Virgin)
So Much For The Afterglow . . . . (Capitol)
I.O.U.
Lee Greenwood; *Lee Greenwood's Greatest Hits* . . . .(MCA)
MCA Records 30 Years Of Hits-1958-1988-C . . . .(MCA)
Somebody's Gonna Love You . . . .(MCA)
If Dirt Were Dollars
Don Henley; *End Of The Innocence* . . . . (Geffen)
If I Could Make A Living
Clay Walker; *Clay Walker's Greatest Hits* . . . .(Giant)
If I Could Make A Living . . . . (Giant)
If I Didn't Have A Dime (To Play The Jukebox)
Gene Pitney; *Gene Pitney-Anthology 1961-1968* . . . . (Rhino)
Gene Pitney's Greatest Hits . . . .(Evergreen Music)
If I Had A $1,000,000
Barenaked Ladies; *Disc One 1991-2001-All Their Greatest Hits* . . . . . . (Reprise)
If I Had No Loot
Tony Toni Tone; *Sons Of Soul* . . . . (Wing)
If I Lose
Ricky Skaggs and Kentucky Thunder; *Bluegrass Rules!* . . . . (Rounder)
If I Were A Rich Man
Original Cast; *Fiddler On The Roof* . . . .(RCA Victor)
If You've Got The Money I've Got The Time
Lefty Frizzell; *American Originals-Lefty Frizzell* . . . . (Columbia)
Columbia Country Classics-#2-Honky Tonk Heroes-C . . . . (Columbia)
Lefty Frizzell's Greatest Hits . . . . (Columbia)
Willie Nelson; *Greatest Hits (& Some That Will Be)* . . . . (Columbia)
Sound In Your Mind . . . . (Columbia)
Willie & Family Live . . . . (Columbia)
If You've Got Trouble
Beatles; *The Beatles-Anthology-#2* . . . . (Capitol)
I'm Payin' Taxes, What Am I Buyin'
JB's; *Funky Good Time-The Anthology* . . . . (Polydor)
Incomplete
Sisqo; *Now That's What I Call Music!-#5-C* . . . . (Virgin)
Unleash The Dragon . . . . (Dragon/Def Soul/IDJMG)
Independent Women Pt.1
Destiny's Child; *Now That's What I Call Music!-#6-C* . . . . (Virgin)
ST/Charlie's Angels . . . . (Columbia)
It's All About The Benjamins
Puff Daddy & The Family; *No Way Out* . . . .(Bad Boy/Arista)
It's Money That Matters
Randy Newman; *Land Of Dreams* . . . . (Reprise)
It's Your Money
James Brown; *I'm Real* . . . . (Scotti Bros.)
I've Committed Murder
Macy Gray; *On How Life Is* . . . .(Epic)
I've Got Five Dollars
Bobby Short; *50 By Bobby Short* . . . .(Atlantic)
Ella Fitzgerald; *Rodgers & Hart Songbook* . . . . (Verve)
Tony Bennett; *Rodgers & Hart Songbook* . . . . (DRG)
I've Got Five Dollars And It's Saturday Night
Faron Young; *Faron Young's Greatest Hits* . . . . (CEMA Special Prod.)
George & Gene; *Gene Pitney-Anthology 1961-1968* . . . . (Rhino)
George Jones; *Best Of George Jones-1955-1967* . . . . (Rhino)
I've Got Sixpence
Mitch Miller; *Mitch Miller-16 Most Requested Songs* . . . . (Columbia)
Sing Along With Mitch . . . . (Columbia)
Just Be Straight With Me
Silkk The Shocker; *Charge It 2 Da Game* . . . . (No Limit/Priority)
Just Got Paid
ZZ Top; *Best Of ZZ Top* . . . .(Warner Bros.)
Rio Grande Mud . . . .(Warner Bros.)
Six Pack . . . .(Warner Bros.)
Just Got Paid
'N Sync; *No Strings Attached* . . . . (Jive)
King Of New Orleans
Better Than Ezra; *Friction, Baby* . . . . (Swell/Elektra)
King Of The Dollar
School Of Fish; *School Of Fish* . . . . (Capitol)
Last Night On Earth
U2; *Pop* . . . . (Island)
Lawyers, Guns & Money
Warren Zevon; *Excitable Boy* . . . .(Asylum)
Quiet Normal Life-Best Of Warren Zevon . . . .(Asylum)
Stand In The Fire . . . . (Asylum)
Let's Go Spend Your Money Honey
Evangeline; *French Quarter Moon* . . . . (Margaritaville)

Life Is A Lemon And I Want My Money Back
Meat Loaf; *Bat Out Of Hell II: Back Into Hell* . . . . (MCA)
Life Is Just A Bowl Of Cherries
Ethel Merman; *The Ethel Merman Collection* . . . . (Razor & Tie)
Jaye P. Morgan; *The Jaye P. Morgan Story* . . . .(Simitar)
Original Cast; *Fosse* . . . . (RCA Victor)
Rudy Vallee & His Connecticut Yankees; *As Time
Goes By* . . . .(Varese Sarabande)
Life's Been Good
Eagles; *Eagles Live* . . . . (Asylum)
Joe Walsh; *But Seriously Folks* . . . .(Asylum)
ST/FM . . . . (MCA)
Lifestyles Of The Not-So-Rich & Famous
Tracy Byrd; *No Ordinary Man* . . . . (MCA)
Like A Rolling Stone
Bob Dylan; *Biograph* . . . . (Columbia)
Bob Dylan At Budokan . . . . (Columbia)
Bob Dylan's Greatest Hits . . . . (Columbia)
Highway 61 Revisited . . . . (Columbia)
More American Graffiti-#4-C . . . . (MCA)
Self Portrait . . . . (Columbia)
Bob Dylan And The Band; *Before The Flood* . . . . (Columbia)
Jimi Hendrix; *ST/Jimi Plays Monterey* . . . . (Reprise)
Jimi Hendrix Experience; *Jimi Hendrix Experience* . . . .(Reprise)
Rolling Stones; *Stripped* . . . .(Virgin)
Loan Me A Dime
Boz Scaggs; *Boz Scaggs* . . . .(Atlantic)
Duane Allman-An Anthology . . . . (Capricorn)
Lookin' In The Same Direction
Ken Mellons; *Ken Mellons* . . . . Epic)
Loose Change
Bruce Springsteen; *Tracks* . . . . (Columbia)
Losing A Whole Year
Third Eye Blind; *Third Eye Blind* . . . . (Elektra)
Love At The Five & Dime
Kathy Mattea; *Collection Of Hits* . . . . (Mercury)
Fourteen Country Favorites-C . . . . (Mercury)
Walk The Way The Wind Blows . . . . (Mercury)
Nanci Griffith; *Last Of The True Believers* . . . . (Philo)
One Fair Summer Evening . . . . (MCA)
Love Don't Cost A Thing
Jennifer Lopez; *J. Lo* . . . .(Epic)
Now That's What I Call Music!-#6-C . . . . (Virgin)
Love Me
112 Featuring Mase; *Room 112* . . . .(Bad Boy/Arista)
Luv 2 Luv You
Timbaland & Magoo; *Welcome To Our World* . . (BlackGround Enterp./Atlantic)
Make Em Say Uhh #2
Master P; *MP Da Last Don* . . . . (No Limit/Priority)
Making Music For Money
Kenny Rogers; *The Gambler* . . . . (EMI)
Making Music For Money
Jimmy Buffett; *A1A* . . . . (MCA)
Mama Can't Buy You Love
Elton John; *Complete Thom Bell Sessions* . . . . (MCA)
Elton John's Greatest Hits-1976-1986 . . . . (MCA)
Man Loves His Money
Angie Stone; *Black Diamond* . . . . (Arista)
Mansion In The Slums
Crowded House; *Temple Of Low Men* . . . . (Capitol)
Mansion On The Hill
Hank Williams With His Drifting Cowboys; *Hank Williams-40
Greatest Hits* . . . .(Polydor)
Lovesick Blues . . . . (Polydor)
Mansion On The Hill
Bruce Springsteen; *Nebraska* . . . . (Columbia)
Emmylou Harris & The Nash Ramblers; *At The Ryman* . . . .(Reprise)
Mansion On The Hill
Neil Young & Crazy Horse; *Ragged Glory* . . . . (Reprise)
WELD . . . . (Reprise)
Material Girl
Madonna; *Immaculate Collection* . . . . (Sire)
Like A Virgin . . . . (Sire)
Royal Box . . . . (Sire)
Material Thangz
Deele; *Material Thangz* . . . .(Solar)
Me & The I.R.S.
Johnny Paycheck; *Johnny Paycheck's Greatest Hits-#2* . . . . (Epic)
Me And My Uncle
Grateful Dead; *Grateful Dead (Skull & Roses)* . . . .(Warner Bros.)
Hundred Year Hall . . . . (Grateful Dead)
*What A Long Strange Trip It's Been: The Best Of The
Grateful Dead* . . . . (Warner Bros.)
Mean Mr. Mustard
Beatles; *Abbey Road* . . . . (Parlophone)
Midnight Rider
Allman Brothers Band; *Beginnings* . . . .(Polydor)
Best Of The Allman Brothers Band . . . . (Polydor)

Decade Of Hits-1969-1979. . . . . (Polydor)
Idlewild South . . . . (Polydor)
The Road Goes On Forever, A Collection Of Their Greatest
Recordings . . . . (Polydor)
Duane Allman; *Duane Allman-An Anthology-Vol. II* . . . . (Capricorn)
Gregg Allman; *Laid Back* . . . . (Polydor)
South's Greatest Hits-C . . . . (Capricorn)
Willie Nelson; *ST/The Electric Horseman* . . . . (Columbia)

Million Dollar Bash
Bob Dylan; *Biograph*. . . . . (Columbia)
Bob Dylan And The Band; *Basement Tapes* . . . . (Columbia)

Millionaire
ABC; *How To Be A Zillionaire* . . . . (Mercury)

Minimum Wage
They Might Be Giants; *Flood* . . . . (Elektra)

Mo Money Mo Problems
Notorious B.I.G.; *Jock Jams-#4-C*. (Tommy Boy)
Life After Death . . . . (Bad Boy/Arista)
The Ultimate Dance Party-1998-C . . . . (Arista)

Money
Clifton Chenier; *King Of Zydeco* . . . . (Arhoolie)
King Of Zydeco Live At Montreux. . . . . (Arhoolie)

Money
Pink Floyd; *Collection Of Great Dance Songs* . . . . (Columbia)
Dark Side Of The Moon . . . . (Capitol)
Delicate Sound Of Thunder . . . . (Columbia)
Pink Floyd-Gift Set . . . . (Capitol)

Money
Cameo; *Emotional Violence* . . . . (Reprise)

Money
Charlie Daniels Band; *Full Moon* . . . . (Epic)

Money
Peter Frampton; *Frampton* . . . . (A&M)
Frampton Comes Alive . . . . (A&M)

Money
Laura Nyro; *Smile* . . . . (Columbia)

Money
Bros; *The Time*. . . . . (Epic)

Money
K.T. Oslin; *This Woman* . . . . (RCA)

Money
Yes; *Yesyears* . . . . (Atco)

Money (That's What I Want)
Barrett Strong; *Motown Story-First 25 Years-C* . . . . (Motown)
Oldies But Goodies-#4-C . . . . (Original Sound)
Beatles; *Beatles-Box Set* . . . . (Capitol)
Rock 'N' Roll Music . . . . (Capitol)
The Beatles' Second Album . . . . (Capitol)
Buddy Guy; *Man & The Blues* . . . . (Vanguard)
Diana Ross & The Supremes; *Diana Ross & The Supremes Sing*
Motown . . . . (Motown)
Jerry Lee Lewis; *Jerry Lee's Greatest!* . . . . (Rhino)
John Lennon; *Lennon* . . . . (Capitol)
Junior Walker & The All Stars; *Junior Walker & The All Stars'*
Greatest Hits . . . . (S.O.U.L.)
Junior Walker & The All Stars-Anthology . . . . (Motown)
Rolling Stones; *More Hot Rocks (big hits & fazed cookies)* . . . . . (Abkco)
Ronnie Milsap; *Lost In The Fifties Tonight* . . . . (RCA)
Todd Rundgren; *Something/Anything?* . . . . (Rhino)

Money Ain't A Thang
Jermaine Dupri featuring Jay-Z; *Presents Life In 1472-Original*
Soundtrack . . . . (So So Def/Columbia)

Money Burns A Hole In My Pocket
Dean Martin; *Capitol Collectors Series-Dean Martin*. . . . . (Capitol)

Money Can't Buy It
Annie Lennox; *Diva* . . . . (Arista)

Money Don't Matter 2 Night
Prince And The New Power Generation; *Diamonds And Pearls* . . . (Paisley Park)

Money For Nothing
Dire Straits; *Brothers In Arms* . . . . (Warner Bros.)
Money For Nothing . . . . (Warner Bros.)

Money Honey
38 Special; *Rockin' Into The Night* . . . . (A&M)
Drifters; *Drifters' Greatest Hits 1953-1958* . . . . (Atlantic)
Drifters-Their Greatest Recordings . . . . (Atco)
Soul Years-C . . . . (Atlantic)
Elvis Presley; *Rocker*. . . . . (RCA)
Little Richard; *Little Richard's Greatest Hits* . . . . (Everest)

Money Honey
Bay City Rollers; *Bay City Rollers' Greatest Hits*. . . . . (Arista)
Rock & Roll Love Letters . . . . (Arista)

Money In The Bank
John Anderson; *On Solid Ground* . . . . (BNA)

Money Machine
James Taylor; *In The Pocket* . . . . (Warner Bros.)

Money Song
Original Cast; *Cabaret*. . . . . (Columbia)

Money Talk
Pretenders; *Last Of The Independents* . . . . (Sire)

Money Talks
Living Colour; *Biscuits* . . . . (Epic)

Money Talks
Gang Of Four; *Mall* . . . . (Polydor)

Money Talks
J.J. Cale; *Number 8*. . . . . (Mercury)
Special Edition . . . . (Mercury)

Money Talks
Bar-Kays; *Money Talks* . . . . (Stax)

Money Talks
Rick James; *Throwin' Down* . . . . (Motown)

Money, Money, Money
Abba; *Abba's Greatest Hits-#2* . . . . (Atlantic)
Arrival . . . . (Polydor)
The Singles-First 10 Years . . . . (Atlantic)

Moneytalks
AC/DC; *Razor's Edge* . . . . (Atco)

More Than A Paycheck
Sweet Honey In The Rock; *We All...Every One Of Us*. . . . . (Flying Fish)

Mr. Big Stuff
Jean Knight; *'70s Hit(s) Back Again-C* . . . . (Hip-O)
Have A Nice Decade-The '70s Pop Culture Box-C . . . . (Rhino)

Mr. Goldstone
Original Cast; *ST/Gypsy*. . . . . (Columbia)

Ms. Jackson
Outkast; *Stankonia* . . . . (LaFace/Arista)

Music For Money
Nick Lowe; *Pure Pop For Now People* . . . . (Columbia)

Music! Music! Music!
Teresa Brewer; *Best Of Teresa Brewer* . . . . (MCA Jazz)

My Baby Just Cares For Me
Frank Sinatra; *Strangers In The Night* . . . . (Reprise)

New Greenback Dollar
Roy Acuff; *Columbia Historic Edition-Roy Acuff* . . . . (Columbia)

Nickel & Dime
Journey; *Next* . . . . (Columbia)
Time Cubed (Box) . . . . (Columbia)

Nickel Bags
Digable Planets; *Reachin'-New Refutation Of Time & Space* . . . . . (Pendulum)

Nickel Dreams
Nanci Griffith; *Lone Star State Of Mind*. . . . . (MCA)

Nickel For The Fiddler
Guy Clark; *Old No. 1* . . . . (Sugar Hill)

Nickel In The Well
Shenandoah; *Under The Kudzu* . . . . (RCA)

Nickel Song
Melanie; *Best Of Melanie* . . . . (Rhino)

Nickels & Dimes
Plimsouls; *...Plus* . . . . (Rhino)

Nickels & Dimes & Love
John Michael Montgomery; *Life's A Dance* . . . . (Atlantic)
Vern Gosdin; *Nickels & Dimes & Love* . . . . (Columbia)

No Cheap Thrill
Suzanne Vega; *Nine Objects Of Desire* . . . . (A&M)

No Guarantee
Chico DeBarge; *Long Time No See* . . . . (Kedar Entert./Universal)
MTV Jams-C . . . . (Kedar Entert./Universal)
ST/Hoodlum . . . . (Interscope)

No Matter What They Say
Lil' Kim; *Notorious K.I.M.* . . . . (Queen Bee/Undeas/Atlantic)

No Money Down
Chuck Berry; *The Chess Box-Chuck Berry* . . . . (Chess)
John Hammond; *Best Of John Hammond* . . . . (Vanguard)
Blues Explosion . . . . (Atlantic)

No Scrubs
TLC; *Fanmail* . . . . (LaFace)
Totally Hits-#1-C . . . . (Arista)

Not Everyone's As Rich As Your Parents
Doctor Nerve; *Armed Observation*. (Cuneiform)

Not Tonight
Lil' Kim; *Hard Core* . . . . (Atlantic)

Nothin' To Somethin'
Gerald Levert; *G* . . . . (East West)

Offshore Banking Business
Members; *At The 1980 Chelsea Night Club* . . . . (Blue Plate)
ST/Urgh! A Music War . . . . (A&M)

One For The Money
T.G. Sheppard; *Greatest Country Hits Of The '80s-1987-C* . . . . . . (Columbia)
T.G. Sheppard's Biggest Hits . . . . (Columbia)

One For The Money
Whispers; *Best Of The Whispers* . . . . (Solar)
One For The Money. . . . . (Soul Train)

One More Payment
Clint Black; *Put Yourself In My Shoes* . . . . (RCA)

One Thousand Dollar Wedding
Gram Parsons; *Grievous Angel* . . . . (Reprise)

Opportunities (Let's Make Lots Of Money)
Pet Shop Boys; *Disco*. . . . . (EMI)

    Discography-Complete Singles Collection . . . .(EMI)
    Please . . . .(EMI)
Over Now
    Alice In Chains; *Alice In Chains* . . . . (Columbia)
Paper Rosie (10 Cents)
    Gene Watson; *Gene Watson's Greatest Hits* . . . . (Curb)
Party Continues
    Jermaine Dupri; *Presents Life In 1472-Original
      Soundtrack* . . . . (So So Def/Columbia)
Party 'Till The Money Runs Out
    Radiators; *Total Evaporation* . . . .(Epic)
Pay It Back
    Elvis Costello; *My Aim Is True* . . . . (Columbia)
Pay Me Alimony
    Maddox Brothers & Rose; *America's Most Colorful Hillbilly Band* . . (Arhoolie)
Pay You Back With Interest
    Hollies; *Best Of The Hollies* . . . .(EMI)
    History Of British Rock-#4-C . . . . (Rhino)
    The Hollies' Greatest Hits . . . .(Epic)
Payday/Mine 'Til Monday
    Original Broadway Cast; *Tree Grows In Brooklyn* . . . . . . (Sony Music Classical)
Pennies From Heaven
    Billie Holiday; *Billie Holiday-16 Most Requested Songs* . . . . (Legacy)
    Bing Crosby; *Pennies From Heaven* . . . . (Pro-Arte)
    Frank Sinatra & Nelson Riddle Orchestra; *songs for swingin'
      Lovers!* . . . . (Capitol)
    Lester Young; *Birdland All-Stars At Carnegie Hall* . . . . (Roulette)
    Louis Armstrong; *RCA Victor Jazz: First Half-Century-C* . . . . (RCA)
    Mandy Patinkin; *Mandy Patinkin* . . . . (Columbia)
    Skyliners; *Skyliners' Greatest Hits* . . . . (Original Sound)
    Stan Getz; *Essential Stan Getz Songbook* . . . . (Verve)
    Stephane Grappelli; *Satin Doll-#1-Best Of Stephane Grappelli* . . . . . (Vanguard)
Penny
    Joe Stampley; *Best Of Joe Stampley* . . . . (Varese Sarabande)
Penny For Your Thoughts
    Peter Frampton; *Frampton Comes Alive* . . . . (A&M)
    Shine On-Collection . . . . (A&M)
Penny For Your Thoughts
    Tavares; *Slow Jams-The Timeless Collection-#3-C* . . . . (Right Stuff)
Penny For Your Thoughts
    Willie Nelson; *Sound In Your Mind* . . . . (Columbia)
Penny Lover
    Lionel Richie; *Back To Front* . . . . (Motown)
    Can't Slow Down . . . . (Motown)
Pleasant Valley Sunday
    Monkees; *Listen To The Band* . . . . (Rhino)
    Monkees' Greatest Hits . . . . (Rhino)
    Nuggets-Classic Collection From The Psychedelic '60s-C . . . . . . (Rhino)
Pocket Change
    Chuck Loeb; *In A Heartbeat* . . . . (Shanachie)
Pocket Full Of Gold
    Vince Gill; *Pocket Full Of Gold* . . . .(MCA)
Poor Little Rich Girl
    Count Basie & Tony Bennett; *Basie Swings Bennett Sings* . . . . (Roulette)
    Judy Garland; *Best Of Judy Garland* . . . .(MCA)
Poor Little Rich Girl
    Uriah Heep; *Equator* . . . . (Columbia)
Poor Little Rich Girl
    Romantics; *National Breakout* . . . . (Nemperor)
Poor Man's Roses (Or A Rich Man's Gold)
    Patsy Cline; *Best Of Patsy Cline* . . . . (Curb)
    Forever & Always . . . .(Epic)
    Stop, Look & Listen . . . .(MCA)
    The Patsy Cline Story . . . .(MCA)
    Reba McEntire; *Feel The Fire* . . . . (Mercury)
Pound Is Sinking
    Paul McCartney; *Tug Of War* . . . . (Gold Rush)
Price I Pay
    Emmylou Harris; *Cimarron* . . . . (Warner Bros.)
    Emmylou Harris & Desert Rose Band; *Classic Country Duets-C* . . (Curb)
Price Of Paradise
    Minutemen; *3-Way Tie (For Last)* . . . . (SST)
    Ballot Result . . . . (SST)
Price To Pay
    Lucinda Williams; *Lucinda Williams* . . . . (Koch International)
Price You Pay
    Bruce Springsteen; *The River* . . . . (Columbia)
Private Dancer
    Tina Turner; *Live In Europe* . . . . (Capitol)
    Private Dancer . . . . (Capitol)
    Simply The Best . . . . (Capitol)
Put A Nickel In The Jukebox
    Sharon McNight; *Another Side Of Sharon McNight* . . . . (Glendale)
    Presenting Sharon McNight . . . . (Glendale)
Put A Quarter In The Jukebox
    Barry Manilow; *Barry Manilow's Greatest Hits-#2* . . . . (Arista)
Put A Quarter In The Jukebox
    Buck Owens; *Hot Dog!* . . . . (Capitol)

Put The Money Down
    Who; *Odds & Sods* . . . . (MCA)
Puttin' On The Ritz
    Ella Fitzgerald; *Silver Collection-Songbooks* . . . . (Verve)
    Fred Astaire; *Irving Berlin Always-C* . . . . (Verve)
    Irving Berlin Songbook . . . . (Verve)
    Harry Richman; *Hollywood Sings-C* . . . . (Living Era)
    Those Wonderful Years: Puttin' On The Ritz-C . . . . (JCI Assoc. Labels)
    Judy Garland; *One & Only* . . . . (Capitol)
    Mandy Patinkin; *Mandy Patinkin* . . . . (Columbia)
    Taco; *After Eight* . . . . (RCA)
    Nipper's Greatest Hits Of The '80s-C . . . . (RCA)
Queen Of The Silver Dollar
    Dave & Sugar; *Dave & Sugar's Greatest Hits* . . . . (RCA)
    Dr. Hook; *Dr. Hook & The Medicine Show Revisited* . . . . (Columbia)
    Emmylou Harris; *Pieces Of The Sky* . . . . (Reprise)
Radar Gun
    Bottle Rockets; *The Brooklyn Side* . . . . (East Side Digital)
Rags To Riches
    Kool & The Gang; *Everything Is-Greatest Hits* . . . . (Mercury)
Rags To Riches
    Tony Bennett; *Tony Bennett-16 Most Requested Songs* . . . . (Legacy)
    Tony Bennett's All-Time Greatest Hits . . . . (Columbia)
    Tony Bennett & Percy Faith & His Orchestra; *Radio Classics Of The
      '50s-C* . . . . (Columbia)
Rags To Riches
    Electric Boys; *Funk-O-Metal Carpet Ride* . . . . (Atco)
Rags To Riches
    John Scofield; *Shinola* . . . . (Enja)
Ragtop Cadillac
    Lonestar; *Lonestar* . . . . (BNA)
Reagonomics
    D.R.I.; *Dealing With It* . . . . (Metal Blade)
    Johnnie Taylor; *Just Ain't Good Enough* . . . . (Beverly Glen)
Red Money
    David Bowie; *Lodger* . . . . (Rykodisc)
Rich & Poor
    Randy Crawford; *Rich & Poor* . . . . (Warner Bros.)
Rich Bitch
    D.O.A.; *War On 45/Bloodied But Unbowed* . . . . (Restless)
Rich Don't Rock
    Vamp; *Rich Don't Rock* . . . . (Atlantic)
Rich Get Richer
    O'Jays; *Survival* . . . . (Philadelphia Int'l)
Rich Girl
    Daryl Hall & John Oates; *Bigger Than Both Of Us* . . . . (RCA)
    Billboard Top Rock 'N' Roll Hits-1977-C . . . . (Rhino)
    Livetime . . . . (RCA)
    Nipper's Greatest Hits Of The '70s-C . . . . (RCA)
    Rock 'N Soul, Part 1 . . . . (RCA)
    Soulful Sounds . . . . (RCA)
Rich Kind Of Poverty
    Sam & Dave; *Soul Men* . . . . (Rhino)
Rich Little Bitch
    Dash Rip Rock; *Boiled Alive!* . . . . (Mammoth)
    Not Of This World . . . . (Mammoth)
Rich Man
    Great Plains; *Great Plains* . . . . (Columbia)
Rich Man Poor Man
    Peter, Paul & Mary; *Late Again* . . . . (Warner Bros.)
Rich Man, Poor Boy
    Joe Ely; *Dig All Night* . . . . (Hightone)
Rich Man's Frug
    Original Cast; *Sweet Charity* . . . . (Columbia)
Rich Man's Spiritual
    Gordon Lightfoot; *Lightfoot* . . . . (EMI)
Rich Woman
    Fabulous Thunderbirds; *Fabulous Thunderbirds* . . . . (Chrysalis)
Rich, The
    Original Broadway Cast; *Carnival* . . . . (Polydor)
Richest Man In Bogota
    Gil Melle; *Mindscape* . . . . (Blue Note)
Richest Man On Earth
    Paul Overstreet; *Sowin' Love* . . . . (RCA)
Ride Wit Me
    Nelly; *Country Grammar* . . . . (Fo' Reel/Universal)
    Now That's What I Call Music!-#7-C . . . . (Virgin)
Right On
    Marvin Gaye; *What's Going On* . . . . (Motown)
Right On The Money
    Alan Jackson; *Big Country Hits '99-C* . . . . (K-Tel)
    High Mileage . . . . (Arista)
Rip It Up
    Elvis Presley; *Elvis* . . . . (RCA)
    Rocker . . . . (RCA)
    Little Richard; *Big Hits* . . . . (Crescendo)
    Grooviest 17 Original Hits . . . . (Specialty)
    Little Richard-18 Greatest Hits . . . . (Rhino)
    Little Richard's Greatest Hits . . . . (Everest)

Road To My Riches
Vanilla Ice; *Extremely Live* . . . . (SBK)
Rockin' Chair Money
Hank Williams; *Alone With His Guitar* . . . . (Mercury)
Roll Out (My Business)
Ludacris; *Word Of Mouf* . . . . (Murder Inc./Def Jam/IDJMG)
Run Away
Real McCoy; *Another Night* . . . . (Arista)
Saginaw, Michigan
Lefty Frizzell; *American Originals-Lefty Frizzell* . . . . (Columbia)
Billboard Top Country Hits-1964-C . . . . (Rhino)
Columbia Country Classics-#3-Americana-C . . . . (Columbia)
Lefty Frizzell's Greatest Hits . . . . (Columbia)
Sales Tax On The Woman
New Lost City Ramblers; *New Lost City Ramblers-Early Years-1958-
1962* . . . . (Smithsonian Folkways)
Send Me Your Money
Suicidal Tendencies; *Lights...Camera...Revolution* . . . . (Epic)
Seven-And-A-Half Cents
John Raitt; *ST/Pajama Game* . . . . (Collectables)
Original Cast; *Pajama Game* . . . . (Columbia)
Shake Your Money Maker
Elmore James; *King Of The Slide Guitar* . . . . (Capricorn)
Fleetwood Mac; *Vintage Years* . . . . (Sire)
George Thorogood & The Destroyers; *Born To Be Bad* . . . . (Gold Rush)
Paul Butterfield Blues Band; *Golden Butter* . . . . (Elektra)
Paul Butterfield Blues Band . . . . (Elektra)
She Put Her Hand Where My Money Was
John Lee; *Down At The Depot* . . . . (Rounder)
She Works Hard For The Money
Donna Summer; *I Am Woman-C* . . . . (Nick At Nite)
She Works Hard For The Money . . . . (Mercury)
Summer Collection . . . . (Mercury)
Shut Up
Trick Daddy; *Book Of Thugs-Chapter AK Verse 47* . . . . (Slip 'N Slide)
Silver Dollar
Lee Greenwood; *If There's Any Justice* . . . . (Panorama)
Silver Dollar
April Wine; *First Glance* . . . . (Capitol)
Simply Irresistible
Robert Palmer; *Super Nova* . . . . (Island)
Sing A Song Of Sixpence
Original Soundtrack; *Children's Favorites* . . . . (Kid Rhino/Rhino 4 Kids)
Sold My Fortune
Sugartooth; *Sugartooth* . . . . (Geffen)
Soldier Of Fortune
Joe Perry Project; *I've Got The Rock 'N' Rolls Again* . . . . (Columbia)
Soldier Of Fortune
Alan O'Day; *Appetizers* . . . . (Pacific)
Soldier Of Fortune
Thin Lizzy; *Bad Reputation* . . . . (Mercury)
Soldier Of Fortune
Manhattan Transfer; *Bodies & Souls* . . . . (Atlantic)
Soldier Of Fortune
Deep Purple; *Stormbringer* . . . . (Warner Bros.)
Some Girls
Rolling Stones; *Some Girls* . . . . (Virgin)
Somebody Else's Money
Wallflowers; *The Wallflowers* . . . . (Virgin)
Song For The Dumped
Ben Folds Five; *Naked Baby Photos* . . . . (Caroline)
ST/Mr. Wrong . . . . (Hollywood)
Whatever And Ever Amen . . . . (Caroline/550)
Squeeze Me In
Garth Brooks; *Scarecrow* . . . . (Capitol)
Standing Outside A Broken Phone Booth With Money In My Hand
Primitive Radio Gods; *MTV Best Of The Buzz Bin-#2-C* . . . . (Mammoth)
Rocket . . . . (Ergo)
Stop On A Dime
Little Texas; *Big Time* . . . . (Warner Bros.)
Straight To The Bank
Kid Frost; *Hispanic Causing Panic* . . . . (Virgin)
Strange Currencies
R.E.M.; *Monster* . . . . (Warner Bros.)
Stranger To Himself
Sandy Denny; *Best Of Sandy Denny* . . . . (Hannibal)
Who Knows Where The Time Goes . . . . (Hannibal)
Sugar Daddy
Bellamy Brothers; *Bellamy Brothers' Greatest Hits* . . . . (MCA)
You Can Get Crazy . . . . (WB/Curb)
Sugar Daddy
Thompson Twins; *Big Trash* . . . . (Red Eye)
Sugar Daddy
Fleetwood Mac; *Fleetwood Mac* . . . . (Reprise)
Sugar Daddy
Michigan & Smiley; *Sugar Daddy* . . . . (Real Authentic Sound)
Sugar Daddy
Jackson 5; *Jackson 5-Anthology* . . . . (Motown)

Jackson 5's Greatest Hits . . . . (Motown)
Summertime Blues
Alan Jackson; *Who I Am* . . . . (Arista)
Blue Cheer; *Good Times Are So Hard To Find-History Of Blue
Cheer* . . . . (Mercury)
Louder Than God-Best Of Blue Cheer . . . . (Rhino)
San Francisco Nights-C . . . . (Rhino)
Brian Setzer; *ST/La Bamba* . . . . (Slash)
Eddie Cochran; *Eddie Cochran-Legendary Masters* . . . . (EMI)
Eddie Cochran's Greatest Hits . . . . (Curb)
EMI Legends Of Rock & Roll-24 Greatest Hits-C . . . . (EMI)
Joan Jett & The Blackhearts; *I Love Rock 'n' Roll* . . . . (Blackheart)
Who; *Hooligans* . . . . (MCA)
Live At Leeds . . . . (MCA)
Who's Last . . . . (MCA)
Take That To The Bank
Shalamar; *Shalamar's Greatest Hits* . . . . (Solar)
Take The Money & Run
Steve Miller Band; *Fly Like An Eagle* . . . . (Capitol)
Steve Miller Band-Gift Set . . . . (Capitol)
Steve Miller Band-Live . . . . (Capitol)
Steve Miller Band's Greatest Hits-1974-78 . . . . (Capitol)
Taxes On The Farmer Feeds Us All
Ry Cooder; *Into The Purple Valley* . . . . (Reprise)
Taxman
Beatles; *Beatles-Box Set* . . . . (Capitol)
Revolver . . . . (Capitol)
Rock 'N' Roll Music . . . . (Capitol)
George Harrison; *Best Of George Harrison* . . . . (Capitol)
Live In Japan . . . . (Dark Horse)
Taxman Mr. Thief
Cheap Trick; *Cheap Trick* . . . . (Epic)
Ten Cents A Chop
Phil Ochs; *Phil Ochs' Greatest Hits* . . . . (A&M)
Ten Cents A Dance
Eileen Farrell; *I Gotta Right To Sing The Blues* . . . . (Sony Music Classical)
Ella Fitzgerald; *Rodgers & Hart Songbook* . . . . (Verve)
Ten Dollar Man
ZZ Top; *Six Pack* . . . . (Warner Bros.)
Tejas . . . . (Warner Bros.)
Thank God For You
Sawyer Brown; *Outskirts Of Town* . . . . (Curb)
Sawyer Brown's Greatest Hits 1990-1995 . . . . (Curb)
That's The Way I Made My Millions
Charlie King; *Food Phone Gas Lodging* . . . . (Flying Fish)
That's Where My Money Goes
Loverboy; *Wildside* . . . . (Columbia)
That's Where My Money Goes
101 Strings Orchestra; *Beer Drinkin' Sing Alongs!!* . . . . (Alshire)
Theme From "Dynasty"
Original Soundtrack; *Television's Greatest Hits-#3-1970s & 1980s-C* . . . . (TVT)
Theme From "Lifestyles Of The Rich And Famous"
Original Soundtrack; *Television's Greatest Hits-#6-Remote Control-C* . . . (TVT)
Theme From "The Beverly Hillbillies"
Original Soundtrack; *CBS: The First 50 Years* . . . . (TVT)
Television's Greatest Hits-#1-C . . . . (TVT)
Theme From "The Price Is Right"
Original Soundtrack; *Television's Greatest Hits-#6-Remote Control-C* . . . (TVT)
Theme From "The Six Million Dollar Man"
Original Soundtrack; *Television's Greatest Hits-#5-In Living Color-C* . . . (TVT)
They Want Money
Kool Moe Dee; *Knowledge Is King* . . . . (Jive)
Kool Moe Dee's Greatest Hits . . . . (Jive)
Nasty Wax-C . . . . (K-Tel)
This Money Is Yours
Original London Cast; *Miss Saigon* . . . . (Geffen)
Three Coins In The Fountain
Andy Williams; *Moon River & Other Great Movie Themes* . . . . . . (Columbia)
Doris Day & Frank De Vol Orchestra; *Hooray For
Hollywood-#2-C* . . . . (Columbia)
Four Aces; *Billboard Top Movie Hits-1950-1954-C* . . . . (Rhino)
Four Aces' Greatest Hits . . . . (MCA)
Frank Sinatra; *At The Movies* . . . . (Capitol)
Capitol Collectors Series-Frank Sinatra . . . . (Capitol)
Harry James; *Harry James Plays The Songs That Sold A Million* . . . . (Columbia)
Julius LaRosa; *The Envelope Please-Academy Award Winning Songs-#2
(1946-1957)-C* . . . . (Rhino)
Three Nickels & A Dime
Ricky Lynn Gregg; *Ricky Lynn Gregg* . . . . (Liberty)
'Till The Money Runs Out
Tom Waits; *Heartattack & Vine* . . . . (Asylum)
Time Ain't Money
Huey Lewis and the News; *Hard At Play* . . . . (EMI)
Tomorrow
Silverchair; *Frogstomp* . . . . (Epic)
Too High A Price
Doobie Brothers; *Cycles* . . . . (Warner Bros.)
Too Much Candy For A Dime
Eddy Raven; *Best Of Eddy Raven* . . . . (Liberty)

Right For The Flight . . . . (Liberty)
Too Much Month At The End Of The Money
Billy Hill; *I Am Just A Rebel* . . . . (Reprise)
Top Of The World
Brandy featuring Mase; *Never Say Never* . . . . (Atlantic)
Turn Me On ''Mr. Deadman''
Union Underground; *...An Education In Rebellion* . . . . (Portrait)
TV Movie
Bruce Springsteen; *Tracks* . . . . (Columbia)
Two Dollars In The Jukebox
Eddie Rabbitt; *Best Of Eddie Rabbitt/Greatest Hits-II* . . . .(Warner Bros.)
Eddie Rabbitt's All-Time Greatest Hits . . . . (Warner Bros.)
Rocky Mountain Music . . . . (Elektra)
Ten Years Of Greatest Hits . . . . (Capitol)
Two Plays For A Quarter
Kathy Hart & The Bluestars; *Tonight I Want It All* . . . .(Biograph)
Two Story House
George Jones & Tammy Wynette; *George Jones & Tammy Wynette-16*
Biggest Hits . . . . (Epic/Legacy)
Tyrone
Erykah Badu; *Erykah Badu-Live* . . . . (Kedar Entert./Universal)
Unbelievable
Diamond Rio; *Unbelievable* . . . . (Arista)
Uptown Girl
Billy Joel; *An Innocent Man* . . . . (Columbia)
Billy Joel-Greatest Hits, Volume I & Volume II . . . . (Columbia)
KOHUEPT . . . . (Columbia)
Wages Of Sin
Bruce Springsteen; *Tracks* . . . . (Columbia)
Wall Street Shuffle
10 CC; *10 CC's Greatest Hits-1972-1978* . . . . (Polydor)
Live & Let Live . . . . (Mercury)
Welcome To The Boomtown
David & David; *Boomtown* . . . . (A&M)
We're In The Money
Fred Astaire; *Nipper's Greatest Hits Of The '30s-#2-C* . . . . (RCA)
Original Broadway Cast; *42nd Street* . . . . (RCA Victor)
What I Got
Sublime; *Now That's What I Call Music!-#2-C* . . . . (Virgin)
Sublime . . . . (Gasoline Alley)
What You Want
Mase Featuring Total; *Harlem World* . . . . (Bad Boy/Arista)
Wheel Of Fortune
Cardinals; *Atlantic Rhythm & Blues 1947-1974-box-C* . . . . (Atlantic)
Kay Starr; *Capitol Collectors Series-Kay Starr* . . . . (Capitol)
Wheels Of Fortune
Doobie Brothers; *Takin' It To The Streets* . . . .(Warner Bros.)
White Trash With Cash
Southgang; *Group Therapy* . . . . (Charisma)
Whoa
Black Rob; *Life Story* . . . . (Bad Boy/Arista)
Why Don't You Do Right
Benny Goodman; *Benny Goodman-16 Most Requested Songs* . . . . . . (Columbia)
Ella Fitzgerald & Joe Pass; *Easy Living* . . . . (Pablo)
Peggy Lee; *Capitol Collectors Series-Peggy Lee-#1-Early Years* . . . . . (Capitol)
Peggy Lee's All-Time Greatest Hits . . . . (Curb)
Why Don't You Get A Job?
Offspring; *Americana* . . . . (Columbia)
With Plenty Of Money & You
Ink Spots; *If I Didn't Care* . . . . (Pro-Arte)
Tony Bennett & Count Basie; *Some Pair* . . . . (Pair)
Workin' For The Weekend
Ken Mellons; *Ken Mellons* . . . .(Epic)
Steppin' Country-#2-C . . . . (Columbia)
Wurlitzer Prize (I Don't Want To Get Over You)
Waylon Jennings; *Waylon & Willie* . . . . (RCA)
You Don't Count The Cost
Billy Dean; *Billy Dean* . . . . (Liberty)
Ricky Skaggs; *My Father's Son* . . . .(Epic)
You Never Give Me Your Money
Beatles; *Abbey Road* . . . . (Parlophone)
Beatles-Box Set . . . . (Apple)
George Benson; *The Best* . . . . (Rebound)
You Owe Me
NaS featuring Ginuwine; *NaStradamus* . . . . (Columbia)
Your Cash Ain't Nothin' But Trash
Clovers; *Down In The Alley* . . . . (Rhino)
Huey Lewis and the News; *Four Chords & Several Years Ago* . . . . . . (Elektra)
Steve Miller Band; *The Joker* . . . . (Capitol)

MONSTERS, Dragons, Halloween, Vampires
See Also: **DANGER & DISASTER, DEVILS, HELL, MAGIC,**
SPIRITS, UFO'S

Amazing Bigfoot Diet
Mojo Nixon & Skid Roper; *Frenzy/Get Out Of My Way* . . . .(I.R.S.)

Apeman
Kinks; *Kink Kronikles* . . . . (Reprise)
Lola Versus Powerman And The Moneygoround, Part One . . . . (Reprise)
The Road . . . . (MCA)
Attack Of The Fifty-Foot Woman
Tubes; *Best Of The Tubes* . . . . (Gold Rush)
Completion Backward Principle . . . . (Capitol)
Elvira Presents Haunted Hits-C . . . . (Rhino)
Attack Of The Killer Beers
Murphy's Law; *Back With A Bong!* . . . .(Profile)
Attack Of The Killer Tomatoes
Lewis Lee; *Elvira Presents Haunted Hits-C* . . . . (Rhino)
Halloween Hits-C . . . . (Rhino)
Attack Of The Radioactive Hamsters
''Weird Al'' Yankovic; *ST/UHF & Other Stuff* . . . .(Scotti Bros.)
Attack Of The Vegetable Men
Active Ingredient; *Extrastrength.* . . . . (Bainbridge)
Attacked By Monsters
Meat Puppets; *Monsters* . . . . (Rykodisc)
No Strings Attached . . . .(SST)
Beast
Blondie; *The Hunter* . . . . (Chrysalis)
Beast
Only Ones; *Special View* . . . . (Epic)
Beast
Twisted Sister; *Stay Hungry* . . . .(Atlantic)
Beast In Me
Johnny Cash; *American Recordings* . . . . (American)
Nick Lowe; *The Impossible Bird* . . . . (Upstart)
The Sopranos-Music From The HBO Original
Series . . . . (Sony Music Soundtrax)
Beast In Me
Bonnie Pointer; *ST/Heavenly Bodies* . . . . (Private I)
Beast Of Burden
Bette Midler; *No Frills* . . . .(Atlantic)
Rolling Stones; *Rewind (1971-1984)* . . . . (Rolling Stones)
Some Girls . . . . (Virgin)
Sucking In The Seventies . . . . (Rolling Stones)
Beast Within
Southside Johnny And The Asbury Jukes; *Trash It Up* . . . . (Mirage)
Beastie
Jethro Tull; *The Broadsword And The Beast* . . . . (Chrysalis)
Beauty And The Beast
Celine Dion & Peabo Bryson; *All The Way...A Decade Of Song.* . . . . .(550 Music)
Celine Dion . . . . (Epic)
ST/Beauty And The Beast . . . . (Disney)
Blob, The
Five Blobs; *Elvira Presents Haunted Hits-C* . . . . (Rhino)
Halloween Hits-C . . . . (Rhino)
Little Stevie & The McQueens; *Horror Rock Classics-#2-C* . . . . (Rhino)
Clap For The Wolfman
Guess Who; *Only Dance 1970-1974-C* . . . . (Rhino)
Cockroach That Ate Cincinnati
Possum; *Dr. Demento's Delights-C* . . . . (Warner Bros.)
Rose & The Arrangement; *Dr. Demento Presents The Greatest Novelty*
Records-#4-1970s-C . . . . (Rhino)
Creature Feature
Uptown Express; *45-#2* . . . .(Sutra)
Creature From The Black Lagoon
Dave Edmunds; *Best Of Dave Edmunds* . . . . (Swan Song)
Elvira Presents Haunted Hits-C . . . . (Rhino)
Repeat When Necessary . . . . (Swan Song)
Creatures Of The Night
Kiss; *Creatures Of The Night* . . . . (Casablanca)
Dance With The Dragon
Jefferson Starship; *Spitfire* . . . . (Grunt)
Dinner With Drac
Zacherle; *Rock-O-Rama-#2-C* . . . .(Abkco)
Dr. Funkenstein
Parliament; *Parliament Live/P. Funk Earth Tour* . . . . (Casablanca)
The Clones Of Dr. Funkenstein . . . . (Casablanca)
Dracula Moon
Joan Osborne; *Relish* . . . .(Blue Gorilla/Mercury)
Dracula's Dance
Flip Phillips; *Flipenstein* . . . .(Progressive)
Dragon Lady
Blue Oyster Cult; *Revolution By Night* . . . . (Columbia)
Dragon Lady
Germs; *Germs* . . . .(Slash)
Dragon Lady
Bob Dylan; *Infidels* . . . . (Columbia)
Eggplant That Ate Chicago
Dr. West's Medicine Show & Junk Band; *Dr. Demento Presents The*
Greatest Novelty Records-#3-1960s-C . . . . (Rhino)
Eye Of The Zombie
John Fogerty; *Eye Of The Zombie* . . . . (Warner Bros.)
Female Of The Species
Space; *Spiders* . . . .(Gut/Universal)

Frankenstein
Edgar Winter Group; *Billboard Top Rock 'N' Roll Hits-1973-C* . . . . (Rhino)
  Edgar Winter Group-Anthology . . . . (Bac-Trac)
  Edgar Winter Group-Collection . . . . (Rhino)
  They Only Come Out At Night . . . . (Epic)
Frankenstein
New York Dolls; *Lipstick Killers* . . . . (Roir)
  New York Dolls . . . . (Mercury)
Godzilla
Blue Oyster Cult; *Career Of Evil* . . . . (Columbia)
  Extraterrestrial Live . . . . (Columbia)
  Some Enchanted Evening . . . . (Columbia)
  Spectres . . . . (Columbia)
Godzilla Stomp
Wedge; *Big Bad Boss Beat Of The Wedge* . . . . (Rhino)
Goonies 'R' Good Enough
Cyndi Lauper; *ST/The Goonies* . . . . (Epic)
Halloween Parade
Lou Reed; *New York* . . . . (Sire)
I Was A Teenage Werewolf
Cramps; *Elvira Presents Haunted Hits-C* . . . . (Rhino)
  Songs The Lord Taught Us . . . . (I.R.S.)
King Kong
Frank Zappa; *Uncle Meat* . . . . (Barking Pumpkin)
  You Can't Do That On Stage Anymore-#3 . . . . (Rykodisc)
King Kong
Kinks; *Kink Kronikles* . . . . (Reprise)
Living Dead Girl
Rob Zombie; *Hellbilly Deluxe* . . . . (Geffen)
Loopzilla
George Clinton; *Computer Games* . . . . (Capitol)
Maneater
Daryl Hall & John Oates; *H2O* . . . . (RCA)
  Nipper's Greatest Hits Of The '80s-C . . . . (RCA)
  Rock 'N Soul, Part 1 . . . . (RCA)
March Of The Meanies
Beatles; *Yellow Submarine* . . . . (Capitol)
Mole People
Michael Feinstein; *Pure Imagination* . . . . (Elektra)
Monster
Steppenwolf; *Live Steppenwolf* . . . . (MCA)
  Steppenwolf-16 Greatest Hits . . . . (MCA)
Monster Mash
Beach Boys; *Concert/'69-Live In London* . . . . (Capitol)
Big O; *ST/Return Of The Living Dead, Part 2* . . . . (Island)
Bobby "Boris" Pickett & The Crypt-Kickers; *Dr. Demento Presents The
  Greatest Novelty Records-#3-1960s-C* . . . . (Rhino)
  Dr. Demento: 20th Anniversary Collection-C . . . . (Rhino)
  Halloween Hits-C . . . . (Rhino)
  Horror Rock Classics-#2-C . . . . (Rhino)
Monster Surfing Time
Halibuts; *Halibut Beach* . . . . (Waterhouse)
Monsterside
Addict; *Stones* . . . . (Big Cat)
More Human Than Human
White Zombie; *Astro-Creep: 2000 Songs Of Love* . . . . (Geffen)
Mutants Of The Monster
Black Oak Arkansas; *Hot & Nasty-Best Of Black Oak Arkansas* . . . . . . (Rhino)
  Raunch 'N' Roll . . . . (Atco)
Night Creatures
Melissa Manchester; *Mathematics* . . . . (MCA)
Night Of The Vampire
Roky Erickson; *You're Gonna Miss Me-Best Of Roky Erickson* . . . . . . (Restless)
Night Of The Vampire
Grim Reaper; *Rock You To Hell* . . . . (RCA)
No More "I Love You's"
Annie Lennox; *Medusa* . . . . (Arista)
November Spawned A Monster
Morrissey; *Bona Drag* . . . . (Sire)
  Just Say Da-#4 Of Just Say Yes-C . . . . (Sire)
Over At The Frankenstein Place
Original London Cast; *Rocky Horror Show* . . . . (Rhino)
Tim Curry & Original Roxy Cast; *Rocky Horror Show* . . . . . . (Rhino)
Possum Kingdom
Toadies; *ESPN Presents X Games-#1-C* . . . . (Tommy Boy)
  Rubberneck . . . . (Interscope)
Prelude To King Kong
Frank Zappa; *Uncle Meat* . . . . (Barking Pumpkin)
Pride Of Frankenstein
Too Much Joy; *Cereal Killers* . . . . (Giant)
Puff The Magic Dragon
Peter, Paul & Mary; *10 Years Together/The Best Of Peter, Paul
  and Mary* . . . . (Warner Bros.)
  Moving . . . . (Warner Bros.)
  Peter, Paul & Mommy . . . . (Warner Bros.)
  Peter, Paul and Mary In Concert . . . . (Warner Bros.)
Purple People Eater
Sheb Wooley; *45s On CD-#1-1956-1959-C* . . . . (Mercury)

Dr. Demento: 20th Anniversary Collection-C . . . . (Rhino)
  Halloween Hits-C . . . . (Rhino)
  Horror Rock Classics-#2-C . . . . (Rhino)
  Super Hits-#4-C . . . . (Gusto)
Purple People Eater Meets The Witch Doctor
Big Bopper; *Helloo Baby! Best Of The Big Bopper-1954-1959* . . . . . . (Rhino)
Return Of The Giant Hogweed
Genesis; *Genesis-Live* . . . . (Atlantic)
  Nursery Cryme . . . . (Atlantic)
Road Mutants
Death Angel; *Frolic Through The Park* . . . . (Enigma Capitol)
  Speed Metal-C . . . . (Priority)
Scary Monsters
David Bowie; *Golden Years* . . . . (Rykodisc)
  Scary Monsters . . . . (Rykodisc)
  The Singles-1969-1993 . . . . (Rykodisc)
Sea Of Monsters
Beatles; *Beatles-Box Set* . . . . (Capitol)
  Yellow Submarine . . . . (Capitol)
Smiling Up The Frown
Agents Of Good Roots; *One By One* . . . . (RCA)
  Where'd You Get That Vibe? . . . . (RCA)
Suck On The Jugular
Rolling Stones; *Voodoo Lounge* . . . . (Virgin)
Tattoo Vampire
Blue Oyster Cult; *Agents Of Fortune* . . . . (Columbia)
Tears Of The Dragon
Bruce Dickinson; *Balls To Picasso* . . . . (Mercury)
Teenage Frankenstein
Alice Cooper; *Constrictor* . . . . (MCA)
  Prince Of Darkness . . . . (MCA)
Theme From "Beetlejuice"
Alshire Hollywood Pops Orchestra; *20 Greatest Movie Hits-C* . . . . . . (Alshire)
Roy Shakked; *Fright Night Delight* . . . . (Laserlight)
**Theme From "Kukla, Fran And Ollie" ("Here We Are, Hop,
  Hop, Hop")**
Original Soundtrack; *Television's Greatest Hits-#4-Black & White
  Classics-C* . . . . (TVT)
Theme From "The Addams Family"
Original Soundtrack; *Television's Greatest Hits-#1-C* . . . . (TVT)
Vic Mizzy; *Elvira Presents Haunted Hits-C* . . . . (Rhino)
  Haunted Hits-C . . . . (Rhino)
  Original Music From "The Addams Family" . . . . (RCA)
Theme From "The Beany & Cecil Show"
Original Soundtrack; *Television's Greatest Hits-#4-Black & White
  Classics-C* . . . . (TVT)
Theme From "The Munsters"
Original Soundtrack; *Television's Greatest Hits-#1-C* . . . . (TVT)
Thing That Only Eats Hippies
Dead Milkmen; *Eat Your Paisley* . . . . (Restless)
  Enigma Variations-#2-C . . . . (Enigma Capitol)
This Is Halloween
Danny Elfman & Citizens Of Halloween; *ST/Nightmare Before
  Christmas* . . . . (Disney)
Thriller
Michael Jackson; *Thriller* . . . . (Epic)
Two Thousand Pound Bee
Ventures; *Radical Guitars* . . . . (Iloki)
  ST/Wired . . . . (Varese Sarabande)
Vampire
Blood Feast; *Face Fate* . . . . (New Renaissance)
  Kill For Pleasure . . . . (New Renaissance)
Vampire
Buffy Sainte-Marie; *Best Of Buffy Sainte-Marie* . . . . (Vanguard)
Vampire
Peter Tosh; *No Nuclear War* . . . . (EMI)
Vampire
Black Uhuru; *Sinsemilla* . . . . (Mango)
Vampire Bat
Twisters; *Twisters* . . . . (Rhino)
Vampire Blues
Loudon Wainwright III; *More Love Songs* . . . . (Rounder)
Vampire Blues
Neil Young; *On The Beach* . . . . (Reprise)
Vampire Cows On Parade
Simon & Bard Group; *Enormous Radio* . . . . (Flying Fish)
Vampire Planet
Neil Norman & His Cosmic Orchestra; *Greatest Science Fiction
  Hits-#2* . . . . (Crescendo)
Vlad The Impaler
Gwar; *Scumdogs Of The Universe* . . . . (Metal Blade)
Werewolves Of London
Warren Zevon; *Excitable Boy* . . . . (Asylum)
  Quiet Normal Life-Best Of Warren Zevon . . . . (Asylum)
  ST/Color Of Money . . . . (MCA)
  Stand In The Fire . . . . (Asylum)
Woke Up With A Monster
Cheap Trick; *Woke Up With A Monster* . . . . (Warner Bros.)

Zomby Woof
Frank Zappa/Mothers Of Invention; *Apostrophe/Overnite Sensation* .(Rykodisc)

MONTHS & DATES: APRIL

See Also: FOOLS, SEASONS: SPRING

Abril En Portugal
Julio Iglesias; *Libra* . . . . (Columbia)
April
Dave Mallett; *Vital Signs* . . . . (Flying Fish)
April
Brand X; *Project*. . . . . (Passport)
April
Sarah Vaughan; *Singles Sessions* . . . . (Roulette)
April 2031
Warrant; *Dog Eat Dog* . . . . (Columbia)
April 24, 1981
Rick Springfield; *Success Hasn't Spoiled Me Yet* . . . . (RCA)
April 5th
Talk Talk; *Colour Of Spring* . . . .(EMI)
April Afternoon
Joan Amalbert Latin Jazz Quintet; *Hot Sauce* . . . .(Prestige)
April Avenue
Crickets; *Liberty Years* . . . .(EMI)
April Come She Will
Simon & Garfunkel; *Collected Works* . . . . (Columbia)
Sounds Of Silence . . . . (Columbia)
ST/The Graduate . . . . (Columbia)
The Concert In Central Park . . . .(Warner Bros.)
April Fool
Pete Townshend & Ronnie Lane; *Rough Mix* . . . .(Atlantic)
April Fool
Soul Asylum; *Grave Dancers Union* . . . . (Columbia)
April Fool
Eric Dolphy; *Here & There*. . . . .(Prestige)
April Fools
Dionne Warwick; *Dionne Warwick-Anthology 1962-1971* . . . . (Rhino)
April Fools
Earl Klugh; *Living Inside Your Love*. . . . .(EMI)
April Fools
Aretha Franklin; *Young, Gifted And Black* . . . . (Atlantic & Atco Remasters)
April Fool's Day Morn
Loudon Wainwright III; *Career Moves* . . . . (Virgin)
Fame & Wealth . . . . (Rounder)
April Give Me One More Day
Sarah Vaughan; *Complete Sarah Vaughan On Mercury-#2* . . . . (Mercury)
April In Cambridge
Peter Walker; *Rainy Day Raga* . . . . (Vanguard)
April In My Heart
Billie Holiday; *Quintessential-#6-1938* . . . . (Columbia)
April In Paris
Charlie Parker; *Charlie Parker With Strings* . . . . (Verve)
Verve Years-1950-1951. . . . . (Verve)
Ella Fitzgerald & Oscar Peterson; *Ella & Oscar*. . . . . (Pablo)
Frank Sinatra; *Come Fly With Me*. . . . . (Capitol)
Mel Torme; *Mel Torme*. . . . . (Glendale)
Sarah Vaughan; *Complete Sarah Vaughan On Mercury-#1-Great Jazz Years-1954-1956*. . . . . (Mercury)
Sarah Vaughan . . . . (Emarcy)
Wynton Marsalis; *Marsalis Standard Time-#1*. . . . . (Columbia)
Perspectives: Columbia Jazz Sampler. . . . . (Columbia)
April In Portugal
Eartha Kitt; *Best Of Eartha Kitt* . . . .(MCA)
April Joy
Pat Metheny Group; *Pat Metheny Group* . . . . (ECM)
April Love
Pat Boone; *Best Of Pat Boone*. . . . .(MCA)
Pat Boone's Greatest Hits . . . . (Curb)
April Love
L.T.D.; *L.T.D.-Classics-#27 (Featuring Jeffrey Osborne)* . . . . (A&M)
April Mist
Tom Harrell; *Visions*. . . . .(Contemporary)
April Seventh
Larry Coryell & John Scofield & Joe Beck; *Tributaries* . . . . (Novus)
April Skies
Wardell Gray; *Memorial-#2* . . . .(Prestige)
April Skies
Jesus & Mary Chain; *Darklands* . . . .(Warner Bros.)
April Sky
Vinnie Moore; *Time Odyssey* . . . . (Mercury)
April Snow
Northern Lights; *Take You To The Sky* . . . . (Flying Fish)
April Snow
Hi-Lo's; *Cherries & Other Delights* . . . .(Hindsight)
April Song
John Tesh; *Monterey Nights* . . . . (GTS)

The Games . . . . (GTS)
April The 14th, Part 1
Gillian Welch; *Time (The Revelator)* . . . .(Acony)
April Waltz
Critton Hollow; *Great Dreams* . . . . (Flying Fish)
April Was The Month
Chris Farlowe; *Chris Farlowe-Collection*. . . . . (Sony Music Special Prod.)
Aprilling
Lee Konitz & Gil Evans; *Heroes*. . . . . (Verve)
April's Fool
Ray Price; *Ray Price's Greatest Hits-#4-By Request* . . . .(Step One)
April's Fool
Mark Chesnutt; *Almost Goodbye*. . . . .(MCA)
April's Fool
Tracy Lawrence; *Sticks & Stones* . . . .(Atlantic)
Calendar Girl
Neil Sedaka; *Neil Sedaka Sings His Greatest Hits* . . . . (RCA)
Neil Sedaka-Greatest Hits Live . . . . (K-Tel)
Neil Sedaka's All-Time Greatest Hits . . . . (RCA)
Girl With April In Her Eyes
Chris DeBurgh; *Crusader* . . . . (A&M)
I'll Remember April
Cal Tjader; *Mambo With Cal Tjader* . . . .(Fantasy)
Charlie Parker; *Charlie Parker With Strings*. . . . . (Verve)
Chet Baker; *Chet Baker*. . . . .(Emarcy)
Cleo Laine; *Cleo's Choice*. . . . .(Crescendo)
Doris Day & The Frank DeVol Orchestra; *Hooray For Hollywood-#1-C* . . . . (Columbia)
Erroll Garner; *Erroll Garner-Concert By The Sea* . . . . (Columbia)
Frank Sinatra; *Point Of No Return* . . . . (Capitol)
June Christy; *June Christy-#2-1957* . . . . (Hindsight)
Modern Jazz Quartet; *Concorde* . . . .(Prestige)
Modern Jazz Quartet . . . .(Prestige)
Stephane Grappelli & Martin Taylor; *Just One Of Those Things* . . . . (Angel)
Wynton Marsalis; *Standard Time-#2-Intimacy Calling* . . . . (Columbia)
Let's Have Another Cup Of Coffee
Glenn Miller; *Complete Glenn Miller & His Orchestra-#8*. . . . . (Bluebird)
Michael Feinstein; *Remember-Michael Feinstein Sings Irving Berlin* . . (Elektra)
Lost April
Nat "King" Cole; *Nat "King" Cole (Box Set)* . . . . (Capitol)
Unforgettable . . . . (Capitol)
March Winds And April Showers
Wingy Manone; *Wingy Manone Collection-#3-1934-1935*. . . . . (Collector's Classics)
When April Comes Again
Paul Weston & His Orchestra; *Music For Easy Listening*. . . . . (Corinthian)

MONTHS & DATES: AUGUST

See Also: SEASONS: SUMMER

August
Lyle Mays; *Street Dreams*. . . . . (Geffen)
August
Anthony Phillips; *Private Parts & Pieces V-Twelve* . . . . (PVC)
August & September
The The; *Mind Bomb* . . . . (Epic)
August 19
Ralph Simon; *Time Being* . . . .(Gramavision)
August 1967
Holy Modal Rounders; *Last Round* . . . .(Adelphi)
August Afternoon
Mulgrew Miller; *The Countdown* . . . .(Landmark)
August Blues
Dexter Gordon; *Tangerine* . . . .(Prestige)
August Day
Daryl Hall & John Oates; *Along The Red Ledge* . . . . (RCA)
August Freeze
Grace Pool; *Where We Live* . . . . (Reprise)
August In Forest City
Carol Montag; *Song For Carrie* . . . .(Salek)
August Moon
Ottmar Liebert & Luna Negra; *Borrasca*. . . . . (Higher Octave)
August Rain
Murray Attaway; *In Thrall* . . . .(David Geffen Co.)
August Tides
Woody Simmons; *Woody Simmons*. . . . . (Deep River)
August Was A Heavy Month
Bob Geldof; *Deep In The Heart Of Nowhere* . . . .(Atlantic)
Bus Stop
Hollies; *Best Of The Hollies* . . . . (EMI)
History Of British Rock-#3-C . . . . (Rhino)
The Hollies' Greatest Hits . . . . (Epic)
Calendar Girl
Neil Sedaka; *Neil Sedaka Sings His Greatest Hits* . . . . (RCA)
Neil Sedaka-Greatest Hits Live . . . . (K-Tel)

Neil Sedaka's All-Time Greatest Hits . . . . (RCA)
Cold Wind In August
Van Morrison; *Period Of Transition* . . . . (Warner Bros.)
Either End Of August
Bill Bruford; *Feels Good To Me* . . . . (Editions E.G.)
First Day In August
Carole King; *Rhymes & Reasons* . . . . (Legacy)
Goin' Through The Big D
Mark Chesnutt; *What A Way To Live* . . . . (Decca)
Rainmaker
Nilsson; *Harry* . . . . (Dunhill Compact Classics)
Second Sunday In August
Weather Report; *I Sing The Body Electric* . . . . (Columbia)
Someday, August 29, 1968
Chicago; *Chicago Transit Authority* . . . . (Chicago)
Wonderful Guy, A
Original Cast; *South Pacific* . . . . (CBS Masterworks)

MONTHS & DATES: DECEMBER

See Also: **CHRISTMAS, COLD, SEASONS: WINTER, SNOW**

Anos Dourados (Looks Like December)
Antonio Carlos Jobim & His New Band; *Passarim* . . . . (Verve)
Joanne Brackeen; *Breath Of Brazil* . . . . (Concord Picante Jazz)
Calendar Girl
Neil Sedaka; *Neil Sedaka Sings His Greatest Hits* . . . . (RCA)
Neil Sedaka-Greatest Hits Live . . . . (K-Tel)
Neil Sedaka's All-Time Greatest Hits . . . . (RCA)
Cold Day In December
George Jones; *You Oughta Be Here With Me* . . . . (Epic)
Cold December
Mike Auldridge; *Mike Auldridge & Old Dog* . . . . (Flying Fish)
December
Robert Vaughan & The Shadows; *Love & War* . . . . (Exit)
December
Collective Soul; *Collective Soul* . . . . (Atlantic)
December
Expose; *Exposure* . . . . (Arista)
December
Anthony Phillips; *Private Parts & Pieces V-Twelve* . . . . (PVC)
December
Waterboys; *Waterboys* . . . . (Ensign)
December African Rain
Juluka; *Best Of Juluka* . . . . (Rhythm Safari)
Stand Your Ground . . . . (Warner Bros.)
December Days
Willie Nelson; *Love & Pain* . . . . (Aura)
Sweet Memories . . . . (RCA)
December Will Be Magic Again
Kate Bush; *December Will Be Magic Again-12''* . . . . (EMI)
December, 1963 (Oh, What A Night)
4 Seasons; *25th Anniversary Collection* . . . . (Rhino)
4 Seasons-Anthology . . . . (Rhino)
Oh What A Night . . . . (Curb)
December's Boudoir
Laura Nyro; *Eli And The Thirteenth Confession* . . . . (Columbia)
Gloomy December
Jean Redpath; *Songs Of Robert Burns-#6* . . . . (Philo)
I Am A Rock
Simon & Garfunkel; *Collected Works* . . . . (Columbia)
Simon & Garfunkel's Greatest Hits . . . . (Columbia)
Sounds Of Silence . . . . (Columbia)
I Just Shot John Lennon
Cranberries; *To The Faithful Departed* . . . . (Island)
If We Make It Through December
Merle Haggard; *A Christmas Present* . . . . (Curb)
Eleven Winners . . . . (Capitol)
Goin' Home For Christmas . . . . (Sony Music Special Prod.)
Merle Haggard-Christmas Gift . . . . (Curb)
Very Best Of Merle Haggard . . . . (Capitol)
Long December
Counting Crows; *Recovering The Satellites* . . . . (David Geffen Co.)
Magic In December
Tom Barabas; *Incredible Invincible Sampler* . . . . (Invincible)
Same Old Lang Syne
Dan Fogelberg; *Dan Fogelberg/Greatest Hits* . . . . (Full Moon)
Innocent Age . . . . (Full Moon)
Live-Greetings From The West . . . . (Full Moon)

MONTHS & DATES: FEBRUARY

See Also: **HEART, PRESIDENTS, SEASONS: WINTER**

Calendar Girl
Neil Sedaka; *Neil Sedaka Sings His Greatest Hits* . . . . (RCA)

Neil Sedaka-Greatest Hits Live . . . . (K-Tel)
Neil Sedaka's All-Time Greatest Hits . . . . (RCA)
February
Anthony Phillips; *Private Parts & Pieces V-Twelve* . . . . (PVC)
Jennifer Hall; *Fortune & Men's Eyes* . . . . (Warner Bros.)
February In My Heart
Osborne Brothers; *Some Things I Want To Sing About* . . . . (Sugar Hill)
February Ingenue
Don Dixon; *Romeo At Juilliard* . . . . (Enigma)
February March
Lou & Peter Berryman; *February March* . . . .(Cornbelt)
February Moment
Herbie Hancock & Chick Corea; *Evening With Herbie Hancock & Chick Corea* . . . .(Columbia)
February Sea
George Winston; *Winter Into Spring* . . . . (Windham Hill)
February Song
Barbi Benton & Jamii Szmadzinski; *Kinetic Voyage* . . . . (Takoma)
February Song
Blazing Redheads & Patricia Thumas; *Blazing Redheads* . . . . (Reference)
Getaway (February)
Jen Trynin; *Gun Shy Trigger Happy* . . . . (Squint/Columbia)
Two Days In February
Goo Goo Dolls; *Hold Me Up* . . . . (Metal Blade)
ST/Freddy's Dead-The Final Nightmare . . . .(Metal Blade)

MONTHS & DATES: JANUARY

See Also: **BEGINNINGS, CHRISTMAS, SEASONS: WINTER**

Back In January
Angst; *Mystery Spot* . . . . (SST)
Calendar Girl
Neil Sedaka; *Neil Sedaka Sings His Greatest Hits* . . . . (RCA)
Neil Sedaka-Greatest Hits Live . . . .(K-Tel)
Neil Sedaka's All-Time Greatest Hits . . . . (RCA)
Don't Get Me Started
Rhett Akins; *Somebody New* . . . .(Decca)
Eighth Of January
Eric Weissberg; *ST/Deliverance* . . . . (Warner Bros.)
Jan In January
Warren Bernhardt; *Hands On* . . . . (Digital Music Prod.)
January
Anthony Phillips; *Private Parts & Pieces V-Twelve* . . . . (PVC)
January
Mose Allison; *Back Country Suite* . . . . (Prestige)
January
Painted Willie; *Mind Bowling* . . . . (SST)
January 23-30, 1978
Steve Forbert; *Jackrabbit Slim* . . . . (Nemperor)
January Friend
Goo Goo Dolls; *Dizzy Up The Girl* . . . . (Warner Sunset/Reprise)
January Rain
Hunters & Collectors; *Living Daylight* . . . . (I.R.S.)
January Stars
George Winston; *Winter Into Spring* . . . . (Windham Hill)
January Wind
Erica Wheeler; *Three Wishes* . . . . (Signature)
June In January
Bing Crosby; *Best Of Bing Crosby* . . . . (MCA)
Dean Martin; *Best Of Dean Martin* . . . . (CEMA Special Prod.)
Month Of January
June Tabor; *Abyssinians* . . . . (Shanachie)
Sally Ann 28th Of January
Fuzzy Mountain String Band; *Fuzzy Mountain String Band* . . . .(Rounder)
Turnaround, January Thaw
Priscilla Herdmann; *Forgotten Dreams* . . . . (Flying Fish)

MONTHS & DATES: JULY

See Also: **COUNTRIES: AMERICA, FREEDOM, HOT, PATRIOTISM, SEASONS: SUMMER**

4th Of July
U2; *Unforgettable Fire* . . . .(Island)
4th Of July, Asbury Park (Sandy)
Bruce Springsteen; *The Wild, The Innocent & The E Street Shuffle* . . .(Columbia)
Bruce Springsteen & The E Street Band; *Bruce Springsteen & The E Street Band Live/1975-85* . . . .(Legacy)
Black Day In July
Gordon Lightfoot; *Best Of Gordon Lightfoot* . . . . (EMI)
Did She Mention My Name . . . . (United Artists)
Lightfoot . . . . (EMI)

Calendar Girl
Neil Sedaka; *Neil Sedaka Sings His Greatest Hits* . . . . (RCA)
  Neil Sedaka-Greatest Hits Live . . . . (K-Tel)
  Neil Sedaka's All-Time Greatest Hits . . . . (RCA)
Cold Day In July
Dixie Chicks; *Fly* . . . . (Monument)
Joy White; *Between Midnight & Hindsight* . . . . (Columbia)
Ray Price; *For The Good Times/I Won't Mention It Again* . . . . (Columbia)
Suzy Bogguss; *Voices In The Wind.* . . . . (Liberty)
Darlington County
Bruce Springsteen; *Born In The U.S.A.* . . . . (Columbia)
Fifth Of July
Terry Reid; *The Driver* . . . .(Warner Bros.)
Fourth Of July
X; *See How We Are* . . . . (Elektra)
Fourth Of July
Mariah Carey; *Butterfly* . . . . (Columbia)
Fourth Of July
Linda Waterfall; *Body English* . . . . (Flying Fish)
Fourth Of July
Rosalie Sorrels; *Lonesome Roving Wolves-Songs & Ballads Of
  The West* . . . . (Green Linnet)
Fourth Of July
Dave Alvin; *Romeo's Escape* . . . .(Epic)
Fourth Of July At A County Fair
Red Clay Ramblers; *Chuckin' The Frizz.* . . . . (Flying Fish)
Independence Day
Martina McBride; *The Way That I Am* . . . . (RCA)
July
Al DiMeola; *Soaring Through A Dream.* . . . .(Manhattan)
July
Vienna; *Guess What* . . . .(Warner Bros.)
July
Anthony Phillips; *Private Parts & Pieces V-Twelve.* . . . . (PVC)
July Morning
Uriah Heep; *Best Of Uriah Heep* . . . . (Mercury)
  Uriah Heep-Live . . . . (Mercury)
June 25 At The Fourth Of July
Shel Silverstein; *Great Conch Train Robbery* . . . . (Flying Fish)
Lake Of Fire
Nirvana; *MTV Unplugged In New York* . . . . (David Geffen Co.)
London In July
Corky Hale; *Corky Hale Plays George Gershwin & Vernon Duke* . . . (Crescendo)
Nonstop July (Seemingly)
A-Ha; *East Of The Sun-West Of The Moon* . . . .(Warner Bros.)
Saturday In The Park (July 4)
Chicago; *Chicago IX-Chicago's Greatest Hits* . . . .(Chicago)
  Chicago V . . . .(Chicago)
  Group Portrait . . . .(Chicago)
  If You Leave Me Now . . . .(Chicago)
  ST/My Girl . . . .(Epic)
See You In July
Jazzmasters; *Jazzmasters* . . . .(JVC Musical Industries)
Strawberry Wine
Deana Carter; *Did I Shave My Legs For This?* . . . . (Capitol)
Third Of July
Jody Grind; *Lefty's Deceiver* . . . . (DB)
Watermelon Crawl
Tracy Byrd; *No Ordinary Man* . . . .(MCA)

MONTHS & DATES: JUNE

See Also: **SCHOOL, SEASONS: SUMMER**

3rd Of June
Yello; *Flag* . . . . (Mercury)
Atlanta June
Pablo Cruise; *A Place In The Sun* . . . . (A&M)
By The Light Of The Silvery Moon
Al Jolson; *The Al Jolson Story-#1* . . . .(MCA)
Doris Day; *Day At The Movies* . . . . (Columbia)
Julie Andrews; *A Little Bit Of Broadway* . . . . (Columbia)
Mitch Miller; *34 All-Time Great Sing-Along Selections-C.* . . . . (Columbia)
  Sing Along With Mitch . . . . (Columbia)
Calendar Girl
Neil Sedaka; *Neil Sedaka Sings His Greatest Hits* . . . . (RCA)
  Neil Sedaka-Greatest Hits Live . . . . (K-Tel)
  Neil Sedaka's All-Time Greatest Hits . . . . (RCA)
Desiree (June 3)
Neil Diamond; *12 Greatest Hits-#2* . . . . (Columbia)
  I'm Glad You're Here With Me Tonight. . . . . (Columbia)
Dream In June
Tom Harrell; *Sail Away* . . . .(Contemporary)
Goin' Through The Big D
Mark Chesnutt; *What A Way To Live* . . . . (Decca)
June
Adventure Babies; *Laugh* . . . . (London)

June 25 At The Fourth Of July
Shel Silverstein; *Great Conch Train Robbery.* . . . . (Flying Fish)
June Bug
Leo Kottke; *Best Of Leo Kottke* . . . . (Capitol)
  Did You Hear Me . . . . (Capitol)
  Mudlark . . . . (Capitol)
  My Feet Are Smiling . . . . (Capitol)
June Bug
Lester Young; *Lester Young-Complete Savoy Recordings* . . . . (Savoy)
  Master Takes . . . . (Savoy)
June In January
Bing Crosby; *Best Of Bing Crosby* . . . . (MCA)
Dean Martin; *Best Of Dean Martin* . . . . (CEMA Special Prod.)
June Is Bustin' Out All Over
Original Cast; *Carousel* . . . . (MCA)
June Night
Betty Everett; *Very Best Of Betty Everett* . . . . (Vee-Jay)
June Parade
Vic Shine; *Far & Distant Shore* . . . .(RCA)
June The 15, 1967
Gary Burton; *Artist's Choice* . . . . (Bluebird)
Juneteenth
Anthony Rivers & Others; *I've Known Rivers.* . . . .(Gramavision)
Memphis In June
Eddie Miller & His Orchestra; *The Uncollected Eddie Miller & His
  Orchestra-1944-1945* . . . . (Hindsight)
Hoagy Carmichael; *Hoagy Sings Carmichael.* . . . . (Pausa)
  Hoagy Sings Carmichael . . . . (EMI)
Ninety Nine Years (Dead Or Alive)
Guy Mitchell; *Definitive Guy Mitchell* . . . . (Collector's Choice)

MONTHS & DATES: MARCH

See Also: **COUNTRIES: IRELAND, SEASONS: SPRING**

23rd Of March
Gene Pitney; *Many Sides Of Gene Pitney* . . . . (Out Of Print)
Calendar Girl
Neil Sedaka; *Neil Sedaka Sings His Greatest Hits* . . . . (RCA)
  Neil Sedaka-Greatest Hits Live . . . . (K-Tel)
  Neil Sedaka's All-Time Greatest Hits . . . . (RCA)
March 19th Blues
Duke Ellington; *Duke Ellington-Vol. 1-Studio Sessions-Chicago-1956* . . . .(Saja)
March 7th
Leaving Trains; *Well Down Blue Highway* . . . . (Enigma)
March Sky
Alex DeGrassi; *Slow Circle.* . . . .(Windham Hill)
March Winds And April Showers
Wingy Manone; *Wingy Manone Collection-#3-1934-
  1935.* . . . . (Collector's Classics)
March Winds Gonna Blow My Blues All Away
Carter Family; *Longing For Old Virginia: Their Complete Victor Recordings-
  1934.* . . . . (Rounder)
One Day In March I Go Down To The Sea And Listen
Jan Garbarek Group; *It's OK To Listen To The Gray Voice.* . . . .(ECM)
Prague In March
Hendrik Meurkens; *Sambahia.* . . . . (Concord Picante Jazz)
Waters Of March
Art Garfunkel; *Breakaway* . . . . (Columbia)
Winds Of March
Journey; *Infinity.* . . . . (Columbia)

MONTHS & DATES: MAY

See Also: **PATRIOTISM, SEASONS: SPRING, WAR**

April Showers
Al Jolson; *Best Of Al Jolson* . . . . (MCA)
  The Al Jolson Story-#2 . . . . (MCA)
Judy Garland; *Hits Of Judy Garland* . . . . (Capitol)
  Judy . . . . (Capitol)
Autumn To May
Peter, Paul & Mary; *Peter, Paul and Mary* . . . . (Warner Bros.)
Blues For The Month Of May
Stan Getz & Others; *Tenors Anyone?* . . . .(Biograph)
Calendar Girl
Neil Sedaka; *Neil Sedaka Sings His Greatest Hits* . . . . (RCA)
  Neil Sedaka-Greatest Hits Live . . . . (K-Tel)
  Neil Sedaka's All-Time Greatest Hits . . . . (RCA)
Drunken May (May 20)
Ricky Skaggs and Kentucky Thunder; *Bluegrass Rules!* . . . . . . (Rounder)
First Day Of May
James Taylor; *Never Die Young* . . . . (Columbia)
First Of May
Bee Gees; *Odessa* . . . . (RSO)

First Of May
So; *Horseshoe In The Glove* . . . . (EMI)
In The Middle Of May
Pied Pipers; *Capitol Collectors Series-Pied Pipers* . . . . (Capitol)
In The Still Of The Nite
Dion; *Dion Sings The 15 Million Sellers* . . . . (Laurie)
Dion's Greatest Hits . . . . (Laurie)
Dion And The Belmonts; *Wish Upon A Star With Dion And The
Belmonts* . . . . (Collectables)
Five Satins; *Billboard Top R&B Hits-1956-C* . . . . (Rhino)
Cruisin'-1956-C . . . . (Increase)
Five Satins Sing Their Greatest Hits . . . . (Collectables)
In The Still Of The Night . . . . (Capitol)
ST/Dirty Dancing . . . . (RCA)
Johnny Mathis; *In The Still Of The Night* . . . . (Columbia)
Lusty Month Of May
Julie Andrews; *A Little Bit Of Broadway* . . . . (Columbia)
Original 1982 London Cast; *Camelot* . . . . (Varese Sarabande)
Original Cast; *Camelot* . . . . (Columbia)
Various Artists; *ST/Camelot* . . . . (Warner Bros.)
May
Anthony Phillips; *Private Parts & Pieces V-Twelve* . . . . (PVC)
My Girl
Mamas & The Papas; *Best Of The Mamas & The Papas* . . . . (MCA)
Otis Redding; *Best Of Otis Redding* . . . . (Atco)
Rolling Stones; *Flowers* . . . . (Abkco)
Temptations; *All The Million-Sellers* . . . . (Motown)
ST/Big Chill . . . . (Motown)
Temptations' Greatest Hits-#1 . . . . (Motown)
Temptations-25th Anniversary . . . . (Motown)
Temptations-Anthology-The Best Of The Temptations . . . . (Motown)
Night On The 4th Of May
Al Stewart; *Al Stewart-Early Years* . . . . (Janus)
One Morning In May
Charlie Byrd Trio; *Isn't It Romantic?* . . . . (Concord Jazz)
Jean Ritchie; *Love Is Teasin'* . . . . (Elektra)
Seven Days Of May
Testament; *Souls Of Black* . . . . (Megaforce)
Sweet And Lovely
Bing Crosby; *Pennies From Heaven* . . . . (Pro-Arte)
Thelonius Monk; *Monk's Dream* . . . . (Columbia)
Woody Herman; *Essential Big Bands-C* . . . . (Verve)
Then Came The Last Days Of May
Blue Oyster Cult; *Blue Oyster Cult* . . . . (Columbia)
On Your Feet Or On Your Knees . . . . (Columbia)

MONTHS & DATES: NOVEMBER

See Also: **GRATITUDE, SEASONS: AUTUMN, WAR**

Calendar Girl
Neil Sedaka; *Neil Sedaka Sings His Greatest Hits* . . . . (RCA)
Neil Sedaka-Greatest Hits Live . . . . (K-Tel)
Neil Sedaka's All-Time Greatest Hits . . . . (RCA)
Cold November
John O'Connor; *Songs For Our Times* . . . . (Flying Fish)
Gone Till November
Wyclef Jean featuring The Refugee Allstars; *Presents The Carnival F/
Refugee Allstars* . . . . (Ruffhouse/Columbia)
November
Paul Greaver; *Joy* . . . . (Global Pacific)
November
Chyld; *Chyld* . . . . (New Renaissance)
November
Duncan Sheik; *Duncan Sheik* . . . . (Atlantic)
November
Anthony Phillips; *Private Parts & Pieces V-Twelve* . . . . (PVC)
November 22, 1963
Original Cast; *Assassins* . . . . (RCA)
November 68th
Chick Corea; *CTI Masters Of The Keyboard* . . . . (CBS Associated)
Joe Farrell; *Outback* . . . . (CTI)
November Afternoon
Dizzy Gillespie; *Composer's Concepts* . . . . (Emarcy)
James Moody; *Moving Forward* . . . . (Novus)
Paul Christopher; *Lavender* . . . . (Arylis)
November Cotillion
Country Cooking; *Barrel Of Fun* . . . . (Rounder)
November Day
Rob Mullins; *Nite Street* . . . . (RMC)
November Days
Origin; *Origin* . . . . (Virgin)
November Girl
Carmen McRae; *November Girl* . . . . (Jazz Man)
November In The Snow/Lord Buckley
Mark Murphy; *Kerouac Then & Now* . . . . (Muse)

November Mood
Larry Coryell; *Toku Do* . . . . (Muse)
November Nights
Flim & The BB's; *Tunnel* . . . . (Digital Music Prod.)
November Rain
Guns N' Roses; *Use Your Illusion I* . . . . (Geffen)
November Song
Norrie Paramor; *Autumn* . . . . (Angel)
November Song
Didier Lockwood; *Out Of The Blue* . . . . (Gramavision)
November Spawned A Monster
Morrissey; *Bona Drag* . . . . (Sire)
Just Say Da-#4 Of Just Say Yes-C . . . . (Sire)
November Winds
Friedemann; *Indian Summer* . . . . (Narada)
Narada Equinox Sampler One-C . . . . (Narada)
Novembering
Claudia Schmidt; *Big Earful* . . . . (Red House)
November's Eve
Tim Story; *Untitled* . . . . (Lost Lake Arts)
Wreck Of The Edmund Fitzgerald
Gordon Lightfoot; *Gord's Gold-#2* . . . . (Warner Bros.)
Summertime Dream . . . . (Reprise)

MONTHS & DATES: OCTOBER

See Also: **MONSTERS, SEASONS: AUTUMN**

Calendar Girl
Neil Sedaka; *Neil Sedaka Sings His Greatest Hits* . . . . (RCA)
Neil Sedaka-Greatest Hits Live . . . . (K-Tel)
Neil Sedaka's All-Time Greatest Hits . . . . (RCA)
Grey October Clouds
Tommy Makem & Liam Clancy; *Two For The Early Dew* . . . . (Shanachie)
Leaving October
Sons Of The Desert; *Whatever Comes First* . . . . (Epic)
Moondance
Van Morrison; *Best Of Van Morrison* . . . . (Polydor)
Moondance . . . . (Warner Bros.)
My October Symphony
Pet Shop Boys; *Behavior* . . . . (EMI)
October
Borghesia; *Resistance* . . . . (Play It Again Sam)
October
Terry Garland; *Edge Of The Valley* . . . . (First Warning)
October
Paul Desmond; *From The Hot Afternoon* . . . . (A&M)
October
Warren Bernhardt; *Hands On* . . . . (Digital Music Prod.)
October
U2; *October* . . . . (Island)
October
Danny Wright; *Phantasys* . . . . (Moulin D'Or)
October
Larry McNeely; *Power Play* . . . . (Flying Fish)
October
Anthony Phillips; *Private Parts & Pieces V-Twelve* . . . . (PVC)
October
A-Ha; *Scoundrel Days* . . . . (Warner Bros.)
October
Leif Strand; *The Year* . . . . (Innovative Comm.)
October & The Frost Is Early
Dusing Singers; *Cool Of The Day-Music Of Jean Ritchie* . . . . (Green Hays)
October 17, 1988
Keith Jarrett; *Paris Concert* . . . . (ECM)
October 7
Mitch Watkins; *Strings With Wings* . . . . (Enja)
October Anywhere
Giant Sand; *Valley Of Rain* . . . . (Enigma)
October Ballad
Chick Corea; *Griffith Park-#2: The Concert* . . . . (Elektra)
October Country
October Country; *Nuggets-#3-Pop-C* . . . . (Rhino)
October Fool
Charlie Shoemaker & Bill Holman; *Collaboration* . . . . (Pausa)
October Impressions (No. 38)
Mark O'Connor; *Elysian Forest* . . . . (Warner Bros.)
October In September
John Nilsen; *October In September* . . . . (Magic Wind)
October Morning
Fourplay; *Fourplay* . . . . (Warner Bros.)
October Night
Cliff Sarde; *Every Bit Better/Waiting* . . . . (MCA)
Waiting . . . . (MCA)
October Nights
Stone Soup; *October Nights* . . . . (Windchime)

October Sigh
Phil Sheeran; *Breaking Through*. (Sonic Atmospheres)
October Song
Pat Kilbride; *Rock & More Roses* . . . . (Temple)
October Sunshine
First Brass; *First Brass* . . . . (M-A Music Int'l)
    Jazz Horizons-Best Of M-A Music-#1-C . . . . (M-A Music Int'l)
October Thorns
Flotsam & Jetsam; *When The Storm Comes Down* . . . . (MCA)
October Wedding
Montreux; *Let Them Say*. . . . . (Windham Hill)
    Montreux-Windham Hill Retrospective . . . . (Windham Hill)
October Winds
Bela Fleck; *Natural Bridge*. . . . . (Rounder)
October-Love Song
Chris & Cosey; *Funky Alternatives-18 Techno Remixes-C* . . . . (Roir)
October's Child
Elvin Jones; *Brother John*. . . . . (Palo Alto Jazz)
Tell Me I'm October
Porn Orchard; *Urges & Angers*. . . . . (C/Z)
When October Goes
Barry Manilow; *2 AM Paradise Cafe* . . . . (Arista)
Rosemary Clooney; *Rosemary Clooney Sings The Lyrics Of Johnny*
    Mercer . . . .(Concord Jazz)

MONTHS & DATES: SEPTEMBER

See Also: SCHOOL, SEASONS: AUTUMN, WORK

And Then Comes September
Doris Day; *Duet* . . . . (DRG)
Sacha Distel; *Amour Tout Court*. . . . . (DRG)
August & September
The The; *Mind Bomb* . . . .(Epic)
Biko (September 1977)
Peter Gabriel; *Peter Gabriel*. . . . .(Geffen)
    Peter Gabriel/Plays Live . . . .(Geffen)
    Shaking The Tree-Sixteen Golden Greats . . . .(Geffen)
Calendar Girl
Neil Sedaka; *Neil Sedaka Sings His Greatest Hits* . . . . (RCA)
    Neil Sedaka-Greatest Hits Live . . . . (K-Tel)
    Neil Sedaka's All-Time Greatest Hits . . . . (RCA)
Don't Happen Twice
Kenny Chesney; *Kenny Chesney's Greatest Hits* . . . . (BNA)
It Might As Well Rain Until September
Carole King; *More American Graffiti-C* . . . .(MCA)
Leaving October
Sons Of The Desert; *Whatever Comes First* . . . .(Epic)
Maybe September
Tony Bennett; *Forty Years-The Artistry Of Tony Bennett*. . . . . (Columbia)
    The Movie Song Album . . . . (Columbia)
October In September
John Nilsen; *October In September* . . . . (Magic Wind)
Pale September
Fiona Apple; *Tidal* . . . . (Clean Slate/Work)
Papa Was A Rollin' Stone (September 3)
Temptations; *20/20-C*. . . . . (Motown)
    25 #1 Hits From 25 Years-C . . . . (Motown)
    All The Million-Sellers. . . . . (Motown)
    Billboard Top Rock 'N' Roll Hits-1972-C . . . . (Rhino)
    Compact Command Performances-Temptations. . . . . (Motown)
    Temptations-Anthology-The Best Of The Temptations . . . . (Motown)
Sealed With A Kiss
Bobby Vinton; *Bobby Vinton's Greatest Hits* . . . . (Curb)
Brian Hyland; *Cruisin'-1962-C* . . . .(Increase)
    Oldies But Goodies-#2-C . . . . (Original Sound)
    Original Rock 'N' Roll Hits Of The '50s-C . . . . (Roulette)
Lettermen; *Best Of The Lettermen-#2*. . . . .(Capitol)
    Capitol Collectors Series-The Lettermen. . . . . (Capitol)
See You In September
Chiffons; *Best Of The Chiffons* . . . . (Laurie)
Happenings; *ST/Purple People Eater* . . . . (AJK Music)
Tempos; *Cruisin'-1960-C* . . . .(Increase)
    ST/American Graffiti . . . .(MCA)
September
Michael Urbaniak; *Folk Songs, Children's Melodies, Jazz Tunes &*
    Others . . . .(Antilles)
September
Earth, Wind & Fire; *Best Of Earth, Wind & Fire-#1* . . . . (Legacy)
    Eternal Dance . . . . (Columbia)
    Mega Hits Dance Classics-#7-C . . . . (Priority)
September
Nashville Rhythm Section; *Keep On Dancing* . . . . (Koala)
September
Vladislav Sendecki; *Men From Wilnau* . . . . (Antilles)

September
Anthony Phillips; *Private Parts & Pieces V-Twelve* . . . . (PVC)
September
David Sylvian; *Secrets Of The Beehive* . . . .(Virgin)
September 13
Deodato; *Live At The Felt Forum-2001 Concert* . . . . (CBS Associated)
    Prelude . . . . (CBS Associated)
September 1979
Bill Barron; *Variations In Blue* . . . .(Muse)
September Blue
Chris Rea; *Dancing With The Strangers* . . . . (Motown)
September Fifteenth
Mark Murphy; *September Ballads* . . . . (Milestone)
Pat Metheny & Lyle Mays; *As Falls Wichita, So Falls Wichita Falls* . . . . .(ECM)
September Girls
Bangles; *Different Light* . . . . (Columbia)
September Girls
Big Star; *Big Star Live* . . . . (Rykodisc)
September In The Rain
Chad & Jeremy; *Capitol Gold-Best Of Chad & Jeremy* . . . . (Capitol)
    The Soft Sound Of Chad & Jeremy . . . . (K-Tel)
Dinah Washington; *Dinah Washington-Golden Hits* . . . . (Mercury)
    This Is My Story . . . . (Mercury)
Doris Day; *Doris Day Sings 22 Great Songs-Original Big Band* . . . . (Hindsight)
Duprees; *Best Of The Duprees* . . . .(Rhino)
Frank Sinatra; *Round #1* . . . . (Capitol)
    Sinatra's Swingin' Session!!! . . . . (Capitol)
Joe Williams; *Swingin'...At Birdland* . . . . (Roulette)
Marty Robbins; *Essential Marty Robbins-1951-1982* . . . . (Columbia)
Peggy Lee; *You Can Depend On Me* . . . . (Glendale)
September Love
Kool & The Gang; *In The Heart* . . . .(De-Lite)
September Morn
Mark Masters Jazz Composer Orchestra; *Early Start* . . . . (Sea Breeze)
Neil Diamond; *12 Greatest Hits-#2*. (Columbia)
    Hot August Night II. . . . . (Columbia)
    September Morn. . . . . (Columbia)
September Night
Van Morrison; *Inarticulate Speech Of The Heart* . . . . (Warner Bros.)
September Of My Years
Frank Sinatra; *At The Sands* . . . .(Reprise)
    Frank Sinatra Sings The Songs Of Van Heusen & Cahn . . . .(Reprise)
    Frank Sinatra's Greatest Hits-#2 . . . .(Reprise)
    September Of My Years . . . .(Reprise)
    Sinatra: A Man And His Music . . . .(Reprise)
September Rain
Full Swing; *Full Swing* . . . .(Cypress)
George Howard; *Love Will Follow* . . . . (GRP)
September Snow
Danny Heines; *Aqua Touch*. . . . . (Silver Wave)
September Song
Boston Pops Orchestra/Arthur Fiedler; *Greatest Hits Of The '30s* . . . . . . (RCA)
    Mister Music U.S.A. . . . . (Deutsche Grammophon)
    Music For Every Mood-Yesterday . . . . (RCA)
Eddy Duchin & Stanley Worth; *Best Of The Big Bands-C* . . . . (Columbia)
Eydie Gorme; *Best Of Eydie Gorme* . . . . (Curb)
Flamingos & Moonglows; *On The Dusty Road Of Hits*. . . . .(Vee-Jay)
Frank Sinatra; *A Lovely Way To Spend An Evening*. . . . .(ASV)
    Point Of No Return . . . . (Capitol)
    September Of My Years . . . .(Reprise)
Kate Wolf; *Safe At Anchor* . . . . (Kaleidoscope)
Lindsey Buckingham; *Law And Order* . . . . (Asylum)
Lou Reed; *Lost In The Stars-Music Of Kurt Weill-C* . . . . (A&M)
Roger Williams; *Roger Williams' Greatest Hits* . . . . (MCA)
Roy Clark; *Best Of Roy Clark* . . . . (MCA)
Sarah Vaughan & Clifford Brown; *Sarah Vaughan & Clifford*
    Brown . . . . (Emarcy)
Stan Kenton; *Comprehensive Stan Kenton* . . . . (Capitol)
    Retrospective-Capitol Years. . . . . (Blue Note)
Tony Bennett; *Forty Years-The Artistry Of Tony Bennett* . . . . (Columbia)
Willie Nelson; *Stardust*. . . . . (Legacy)
Sweet September
Buddy Merrill; *Best Of Buddy Merrill*. . . . . (Accent)
    Holiday For Guitars. . . . . (Accent)
Sweet September Morning
Buffy Sainte-Marie; *She Used To Wanna Be A Ballerina* . . . . (Vanguard)
Till There Was You
Beatles; *Beatles-Box Set* . . . . (Capitol)
    Meet The Beatles!. . . . . (Capitol)
    With The Beatles. . . . . (Parlophone)
Original Cast; *ST/The Music Man* . . . . (Warner Bros.)
To Be With You
Mavericks; *Trampoline* . . . . (MCA)
Try To Remember
Original Cast; *Fantasticks* . . . .(Polydor)
Where Were You (When The World Stopped Turning) [September 11]
Alan Jackson; *Alan Jackson-Drive* . . . . (Arista)

MOON, Moonlight

See Also: **NIGHT, SPACE, STARS, SUN**

(They Long To Be) Close To You
Carpenters; *Carpenters-Classics-#2* . . . . (A&M)
  Carpenters-Love Songs . . . . (A&M)
  Carpenters-The Singles 1969-1973 . . . . (A&M)
  From The Top . . . . (A&M)
All At Once You Love Her
Perry Como; *Perry Como's Greatest Hits* . . . . (RCA)
Allegheny Moon
Patti Page; *Patti Page-Golden Hits* . . . . (Mercury)
  Patti Page's Greatest Hits . . . . (Columbia)
Arizona Moon
Ranch Romance; *Blue Blazes* . . . . (Sugar Hill)
Arizona Moon
Flying Burrito Brothers; *Eye Of A Hurricane* . . . . (One Way)
Arthur's Theme (Best That You Can Do)
Christopher Cross; *ST/Arthur* . . . . (Warner Bros.)
Au Clair De La Lune
Maurice Andre; *Children's Songs* . . . . (CBS Masterworks)
August Moon
Ottmar Liebert & Luna Negra; *Borrasca* . . . . (Higher Octave)
Bad Moon Rising
Creedence Clearwater Revival; *1969* . . . . (Fantasy)
  Creedence Clearwater Revival-Chronicle . . . . (Fantasy)
  Creedence Clearwater Revival-Gold . . . . (Fantasy)
  Green River . . . . (Fantasy)
  Live In Europe . . . . (Fantasy)
Bad Side Of The Moon
Elton John; *11-17-70* . . . . (Polydor)
Banging My Head Against The Moon
John David Souther; *Black Rose* . . . . (Asylum)
Bark At The Moon
Ozzy Osbourne; *Bark At The Moon* . . . . (CBS Associated)
  The Ozzman Cometh . . . . (Epic)
Bayou Girl
Bob Woodruff; *Dreams & Saturday Nights* . . . . (Asylum)
Big Wheels In The Moonlight
Dan Seals; *Dan Seals' Greatest Hits* . . . . (Liberty)
  Dan Seals-Classics Collection-#2 . . . . (Liberty)
  Rage On . . . . (Capitol)
Black Moonlight
Bing Crosby; *Pennies From Heaven* . . . . (Pro-Arte)
Black Water
Doobie Brothers; *Best Of The Doobies* . . . . (Warner Bros.)
  What Were Once Vices Are Now Habits . . . . (Warner Bros.)
Blow Out The Stars, Turn Off The Moon
Nitty Gritty Dirt Band; *Rest Of The Dream* . . . . (MCA)
Blue Kentucky Girl
Emmylou Harris; *Blue Kentucky Girl* . . . . (Warner Bros.)
  Profile II-The Best Of Emmylou Harris . . . . (Warner Bros.)
Loretta Lynn; *Loretta Lynn's Greatest Hits* . . . . (MCA)
Blue Moon
Billie Holiday; *Billie's Blues* . . . . (Blue Note)
  First Verve Sessions . . . . (Verve)
  History Of Billie Holiday . . . . (Verve)
Elvis Presley; *Elvis Presley* . . . . (RCA)
  The Sun Sessions . . . . (RCA)
Marcels; *Best Of The Marcels* . . . . (Rhino)
  Billboard Top Rock 'N' Roll Hits-1961-C . . . . (Rhino)
Blue Moon Of Kentucky
Bill Monroe; *American Originals-Bill Monroe* . . . . (Columbia)
  Bean Blossom . . . . (MCA)
  Best Of Bill Monroe & His Blue Grass Boys . . . . (MCA)
Bill Monroe & His Blue Grass Boys; *Bluegrass Super Hits-C* . . (Columbia)
Elvis Presley; *A Date With Elvis* . . . . (RCA)
  A Golden Celebration . . . . (RCA)
  The Sun Sessions . . . . (RCA)
Blue Moon With Heartache
Rosanne Cash; *19 Hot Country Requests-#2-C* . . . . (Epic)
  Rosanne Cash-Hits-1979-1989 . . . . (Columbia)
  Seven Year Ache . . . . (Columbia)
Born With The Moon In Virgo
Michael Franks; *Previously Unavailable* . . . . (DRG)
Bring Down The Moon
Pamela Rose; *Morpheus* . . . . (Grace)
Brother Wolf, Sister Moon
Cult; *Love* . . . . (Sire)
Buicks To The Moon
Alan Jackson; *Everything I Love* . . . . (Arista)
By The Light Of The Silvery Moon
Al Jolson; *The Al Jolson Story-#1* . . . . (MCA)
Doris Day; *Day At The Movies* . . . . (Columbia)
Julie Andrews; *A Little Bit Of Broadway* . . . . (Columbia)
Mitch Miller; *34 All-Time Great Sing-Along Selections-C* . . . (Columbia)
  Sing Along With Mitch . . . . (Columbia)

Cajun Moon
J.J. Cale; *Okie* . . . . (MCA)
Randy Crawford; *Best Of Randy Crawford* . . . . (Warner Bros.)
  Naked And True . . . . (Blue Moon)
Cajun Moon
Ricky Skaggs; *Greatest Country Hits Of The '80s-1986-C* . . . (Columbia)
  Live In London . . . . (Epic)
Cajun Moon
Rosanne Cash; *19 Hot Country Requests-#3-C* . . . . (Epic)
Can't Fight The Moonlight
LeAnn Rimes; *ST/Coyote Ugly* . . . . (London Sire/Curb)
Carolina Moon
Thelonius Monk; *Genius Of Modern Music-#2* . . . . (Blue Note)
Carolina Moon
Slim Whitman; *Ghost Riders In The Sky* . . . . (Liberty)
Chattahoochee
Alan Jackson; *A Lot About Livin' (And A Little 'Bout Love)* . . (Arista)
Child Of The Moon
Rolling Stones; *More Hot Rocks (big hits & fazed cookies)* . . . . (Abkco)
Come To My Window
Melissa Etheridge; *The Concert For New York City-C* . . . . . (Columbia)
  Yes I Am . . . . (Island)
Dance By The Light Of The Moon
Olympics; *Meet The Marathons* . . . . (Collectables)
Dancing In The Moonlight
Thin Lizzy; *Bad Reputation* . . . . (Mercury)
  Live And Dangerous . . . . (Warner Bros.)
  Lizzy Lives! (1976-1984) . . . . (Gland Slamm)
Dancing In The Moonlight
King Harvest; *Have A Nice Night-Romantic Hits Of The '70s-C* . . (Rhino)
  Super Hits Of The '70s-Have A Nice Day-#17-C . . . . (Rhino)
Dancing In The Moonlight
Be Bop Deluxe; *Modern Music* . . . . (Capitol)
Dancing In The Moonlight
Liza Minnelli; *Singer* . . . . (Columbia)
Desert Moon
Great White; *Hooked* . . . . (Capitol)
Desert Moon
Dennis DeYoung; *Desert Moon* . . . . (A&M)
Does That Blue Moon Ever Shine On You
Toby Keith; *Blue Moon* . . . . (Polydor Country)
  Toby Keith's Greatest Hits, Volume One . . . . (Mercury)
Don't Fence Me In
Andrews Sisters; *Andrews Sisters' All-Time Greatest Hits* . . . (Decca)
Bing Crosby; *Best Of Bing Crosby* . . . . (MCA)
David Byrne; *Red Hot + Blue-Tribute To Cole Porter-C* . . . (Chrysalis)
Ella Fitzgerald; *Cole Porter Songbook* . . . . (Verve)
Lari White/Shelby Lynne/Trisha Yearwood; *Don't Fence Me In* . . (RCA)
Willie Nelson & Leon Russell; *Cowboy Super Hits-C* . . . . . (Columbia)
Don't Let The Stars Get In Your Eyes
Perry Como; *Como's Golden Records* . . . . (RCA)
  Perry Como-Pure Gold . . . . (RCA)
  Perry Como's All-Time Greatest Hits-#1 . . . . (RCA)
  This Is Perry Como . . . . (RCA)
Dracula Moon
Joan Osborne; *Relish* . . . . (Blue Gorilla/Mercury)
Dreamy Georgiana Moon
Asa Martin; *Dr. Ginger Blue* . . . . (Rounder)
Drunk On The Moon
Tom Waits; *The Heart Of Saturday Night* . . . . (Asylum)
East Of The Sun & West Of The Moon
Al Cohn & Zoot Sims; *RCA Victor Jazz: First Half-Century-C* . . (RCA)
Billie Holiday; *Billie's Best* . . . . (Verve)
Diana Krall; *When I Look In Your Eyes* . . . . (GRP)
Tommy Dorsey & Frank Sinatra; *Stardust* . . . . (Bluebird)
Eldorado To The Moon
Michael Nesmith; *Newer Stuff* . . . . (Rhino)
Electrolite
Michael Stipe/Mike Mills; *Tibetan Freedom Concert* . . . . . . (Capitol)
R.E.M.; *New Adventures In Hi-Fi* . . . . (Warner Bros.)
Even The Man In The Moon Is Crying
Mark Collie; *Mark Collie* . . . . (MCA)
Everyone's Gone To The Moon
Jonathan King; *British Rock-#3-C* . . . . (Original Sound)
  History Of British Rock-#7-C . . . . (Rhino)
Fishin' In The Dark
Nitty Gritty Dirt Band; *Billboard Top Country Hits-1987-C* . . (Rhino)
  Hold On . . . . (Warner Bros.)
  More Great Dirt-Best Of Nitty Gritty Dirt Band . . . . . (Warner Bros.)
Fly Me To The Moon
Frank Sinatra; *At The Sands* . . . . (Reprise)
  It Might As Well Be Swing . . . . (Reprise)
  Sinatra: A Man And His Music . . . . (Reprise)
  The Reprise Collection . . . . (Reprise)
For You I Will
Monica; *The Boy Is Mine* . . . . (Arista)
Free Trade And A Misty Moon
Greek Evans & Ensemble; *Music From The New York Stage (1890-1920)-#4-1917-1920-C* . . . . (Pearl)

Full Forever
Goo Goo Dolls; *Dizzy Up The Girl* . . . . (Warner Sunset/Reprise)
Full Moon
Kinks; *Sleepwalker*. . . . . (Arista)
Full Moon
John Hiatt; *Hangin' Around The Observatory* . . . .(Epic)
Full Moon And Empty Arms
Frank Sinatra; *A Lovely Way To Spend An Evening* . . . . (ASV)
Sarah Vaughan; *Slightly Classical* . . . . (Roulette)
Goodnight Moon
Shivaree; *I Oughtta Give You A Shot*. . . . . (Capitol)
Hard To Explain
Cowboy Junkies; *Pale Sun, Crescent Moon* . . . . (RCA)
Harvest Moon
Neil Young; *Harvest Moon*. . . . . (Reprise)
Havana Moon
Carlos Santana; *Havana Moon* . . . . (Columbia)
Chuck Berry; *After School Session* . . . . (Chess)
Rockit. . . . . (Atco)
The Chess Box-Chuck Berry . . . . (Chess)
Here Comes The Moon
George Harrison; *Best Of Dark Horse 1976-1989* . . . . (Dark Horse)
George Harrison . . . . (Dark Horse)
Homeless
Paul Simon; *Graceland*. . . . .(Warner Bros.)
Honky Tonk Moon
Randy Travis; *Old 8 X 10* . . . .(Warner Bros.)
Randy Travis' Greatest Hits-#1 . . . .(Warner Bros.)
Rosie Flores; *Once More With Feeling*. . . . . (Hightone)
How High The Moon
Duke Ellington; *1954 Los Angeles Concert* . . . .(Crescendo)
Ella Fitzgerald; *Best Of Ella Fitzgerald* . . . .(MCA)
Les Paul & Mary Ford; *Memories Are Made Of This-C* . . . . (Capitol)
Sarah Vaughan; *Compact Jazz-Best Of The Compact Jazz Vocalists-C* . . (Verve)
Complete Sarah Vaughan On Mercury-#3. . . . . (Mercury)
Stephane Grappelli & Martin Taylor; *Just One Of Those Things* . . . . . . (Angel)
How Many Moons
Whites; *A Lifetime In The Making* . . . . (Ceili Music)
Howlin' At The Moon
Hank Williams; *Hank Williams-24 Greatest Hits-#2* . . . . (Polydor)
Hank Williams-40 Greatest Hits . . . . (Polydor)
Hey Good Lookin' (December 1950-July 1951) . . . . (Polydor)
Howlin' At The Moon
Chenille Sisters; *Haute Chenille: A Retrospective* . . . . (Red House)
House On Fire: An Urban Folk Collection-C . . . . (Red House)
Hypnotize The Moon
Clay Walker; *Hypnotize The Moon*. . . . . (Giant)
I Got The Sun In The Morning
Ethel Merman/Bruce Yarnell/Original Cast; *Annie Get
Your Gun*. . . . .(RCA Victor)
Ethel Merman/Ray Middleton/Original Cast; *Annie Get Your Gun* . . . . . (MCA)
Original Broadway Cast; *Annie Get Your Gun* . . . . (Angel)
I Wished On The Moon
Billie Holiday; *Billie Holiday-Live* . . . . (Verve)
Stormy Blues . . . . (Verve)
Ella Fitzgerald; *Best Of Ella Fitzgerald* . . . .(MCA)
I'll Be Home
Flamingos; *Alan Freed's Memory Lane-C* . . . . (MCA)
Best Of The Flamingos. . . . . (Rhino)
Super Oldies Of The '50s-#6-C . . . .(Audio Fidelity)
Platters; *Platters Greatest Hits-#2* . . . . (Curb)
I'm Gonna Knock On Your Door
Eddie Hodges; *History Of Cadence Records-#1-C*. . . . . (Varese Vintage)
In The Chapel In The Moonlight
Kitty Kallen; *Those Wonderful Years: Music! Music!
Music!-C* . . . . (JCI Assoc. Labels)
Patti Page; *Patti Page-16 Most Requested Songs* . . . . (Legacy)
Shep Fields & His Rippling Rhythm Orchestra; *78-#6640* . . . . (Bluebird)
It's Only A Paper Moon
Art Blakey & His Jazz Messengers; *Big Beat* . . . . (Blue Note)
Bing Crosby; *The Radio Years-#2* . . . .(Crescendo)
David Rose & His Orchestra; *Music Of The 1930s-C* . . . .(MCA)
Ella Fitzgerald; *Harold Arlen Songbook-#2* . . . . (Verve)
Frank Sinatra; *Round #1* . . . . (Capitol)
Mystics; *Mystics-16 Golden Classics* . . . . (Collectables)
Nat ''King'' Cole; *Capitol Sings Harold Arlen: Over The
Rainbow-C* . . . .(Gold Rush)
The Nat ''King'' Cole Story. . . . . (Capitol)
Sammy Kaye & His Orchestra; *Sammy Kaye & His Orchestra Play 22
Original Big Band Recordings* . . . . (Hindsight)
Just To Hear You Say That You Love Me
Faith Hill & Tim McGraw; *Faith* . . . .(Warner Bros.)
Just You And I And The Moon
Jose Collins; *Music From The New York Stage (1890-1920)-#3-1913-
1917-C* . . . . (Pearl)
Killing Moon
Echo & The Bunnymen; *Ocean Rain* . . . . (Sire)
Songs To Learn & Sing-The Hits . . . . (Sire)

Kiss Me
Sixpence None The Richer; *Sixpence None The Richer* . . . . . (Squint/Columbia)
Songs From Dawson's Creek . . . .(Sony Music Soundtrax)
Lasso The Moon
Gary Morris; *Gary Morris-Hits*. (Warner Bros.)
Letter, The
Macy Gray; *On How Life Is* . . . . (Epic)
Lucky Moon
Oak Ridge Boys; *Unstoppable* . . . . (RCA)
Luna
Tom Petty And The Heartbreakers; *Tom Petty & The
Heartbreakers* . . . .(Gone Gator)
Luna
Smashing Pumpkins; *Siamese Dream* . . . .(Virgin)
Lying To The Moon
Matraca Berg; *Lying To The Moon And Other Stories*. . . . . (RCA)
Magic Moon
Peter Frampton; *Something's Happening* . . . . (A&M)
Magnolia Moon
Seals & Crofts; *Takin' It Easy* . . . . (Warner Bros.)
Man From The Moon
Crickets; *Dreams And Wishes* . . . .(Relic)
Man On The Moon
R.E.M.; *Automatic For The People*. . . . . (Warner Bros.)
Mississippi Moon
Jimmie Rodgers; *Down The Old Road-1931-1932* . . . . (Rounder)
Jimmie Rodgers-Early Years-1928-1929 . . . . (Rounder)
Mississippi Moon
Jerry Garcia; *Compliments* . . . .(Grateful Dead)
Mississippi Moon
Seatrain; *Marblehead Messenger* . . . . (One Way)
Mississippi Moon
Greg Brown; *One More Goodnight Kiss* . . . . (Red House)
Moon At The Window
Joni Mitchell; *Wild Things Run Fast* . . . . (Geffen)
Moon Is Still Over Her Shoulder
Michael Johnson; *Best Of Michael Johnson* . . . . (RCA)
Country Love Songs-C . . . . (Warner Bros.)
That's That . . . . (RCA)
Wings . . . . (RCA)
Moon Is Up
Rolling Stones; *Voodoo Lounge* . . . .(Virgin)
Moon Love
Frank Sinatra; *Moonlight Sinatra* . . . . (Reprise)
Glenn Miller; *Essential Glenn Miller* . . . .(Bluebird)
Glenn Miller's Greatest Hits . . . . (RCA Victor)
Moon Of Kentucky
Elvis Presley; *A Golden Celebration* . . . .(RCA)
Moon Over Bourbon Street
Sting; *Bring On The Night* . . . . (A&M)
Dream Of The Blue Turtles . . . . (A&M)
Moon Over Brooklyn
Anne Murray; *Somebody's Waiting* . . . . (Capitol)
Moon Over Cuba
Duke Ellington; *Duke Ellington & The Blanton-Webster Band* . . . . . . (Bluebird)
Moon Over Georgia
Shenandoah; *Extra Mile* . . . . (Columbia)
Shenandoah's Greatest Hits. . . . . (Columbia)
Moon Over Miami
Bourbon Street Stompers; *I Like Dixieland*. . . . . (Bainbridge)
Vaughn Monroe; *This Is Vaughn Monroe/Decade Of The '40s*. . . . . (RCA)
Moon Over Naples
Billy Vaughn; *Best Of Billy Vaughn* . . . . (MCA)
Moon Over Palmilla
Greg Adams; *Hidden Agenda* . . . . (Epic)
Moon Over Venice
Thom Rotella; *Home Again* . . . . (Digital Music Prod.)
Moon River
Andy Williams; *Andy Williams' Greatest Hits* . . . . (Columbia)
Andy Williams-16 Most Requested Songs. . . . . (Legacy)
More American Graffiti-#4-C . . . . (MCA)
Henry Mancini; *Henry Mancini-Pure Gold* . . . . (RCA)
Peter Gunn . . . . (RCA)
Jerry Butler; *Best Of Jerry Butler* . . . . (Rhino)
Moon Shadow
Cat Stevens; *Cat Stevens Greatest Hits* . . . . (A&M)
Cat Stevens-Classics-#24 . . . . (A&M)
Teaser And The Firecat . . . . (A&M)
Moon Song (That Wasn't Meant For Me)
Art Tatum; *Solo Masterpieces-#7* . . . . (Pablo)
Frank Sinatra; *Moonlight Sinatra* . . . . (Reprise)
Moon Tears
Nils Lofgren; *Best Of Grin* . . . . (Epic)
Grin . . . . (Epic Portrait Assoc.)
Night After Night . . . . (A&M)
Nils Lofgren-Classics-#13 . . . . (A&M)
Moon Was Yellow
Frank Sinatra; *Moonlight Sinatra* . . . . (Reprise)

Moon, Turn The Tides...Gently Gently Away
Jimi Hendrix Experience; *Electric Ladyland*....................(Reprise)
Moonage Daydream
David Bowie; *David Live*...........................(Rykodisc)
Man Who Sold The World..........................(Rykodisc)
Rise & Fall Of Ziggy Stardust And The Spiders From Mars .....(Rykodisc)
Sound + Vision...............................(Rykodisc)
ST/Ziggy Stardust-The Motion Picture................(Rykodisc)
Moonchild
King Crimson; *In The Court Of The Crimson King-An Observation By King Crimson*...................... (Editions E.G.)
Moonchild
Shakespear's Sister; *Hormonally Yours* ....(London)
Moonchild
Iron Maiden; *Seventh Son Of A Seventh Son* ....(Capitol)
Moondance
Van Morrison; *Best Of Van Morrison* ....(Polydor)
Moondance...............................(Warner Bros.)
Moon-Faced, Starry-Eyed
Benny Goodman; *Jazz Collector Edition* ....(Laserlight)
Moonflower
Santana; *Moonflower*..........................(Columbia)
Moonglow
Art Tatum; *Solo Masterpieces-#1* ....(Pablo)
Billie Holiday; *First Verve Sessions* ....(Verve)
Count Basie; *The Standards* ....(Verve)
Moonlight
Bob Dylan; *"Love And Theft"* ....(Columbia)
Moonlight Bay
Beatles; *The Beatles-Anthology-#1* ....(Capitol)
Bing Crosby; *The Radio Years-#4* ....(Crescendo)
The Radio Years: 20 Songs ....(Crescendo)
Drifters; *Clyde McPhatter & The Drifters-Rockin' & Driftin'* ....(Collectables)
Glenn Miller; *Big Bands-#1-C*......................(Universal)
Moonlight Becomes You
Frank Sinatra; *Frank Sinatra Sings The Songs Of Van Heusen & Cahn*...........................(Reprise)
Moonlight Sinatra...........................(Reprise)
Moonlight Cocktail
Glenn Miller; *Best Of Glenn Miller-#2* ....(RCA)
Memorial-1944-1969 ....(Bluebird)
Nipper's Greatest Hits Of The '40s-#1-C ....(RCA)
Glenn Miller & His Orchestra; *Complete Glenn Miller & His Orchestra-#8* ....(Bluebird)
Rivieras; *45-#1134* ....(Collectables)
Moonlight Cocktails ....(Collectables)
Moonlight Drive
Doors; *Alive She Cried* ....(Elektra)
Doors 13 ....(Elektra)
Strange Days ....(Elektra)
Moonlight Feels Right
Starbuck; *Super Hits Of The '70s-Have A Nice Day-#18-C* ......(Rhino)
Moonlight Gambler
Frankie Laine; *Frankie Laine-16 Most Requested Songs* ....(Legacy)
Frankie Laine's Greatest Hits ....(Columbia)
Moonlight In Marrakesh
Otto Cesana; *Otto Cesana-Vol. 2* ....(Tudor)
Moonlight In Vermont
Cal Tjader; *Latin Kick* ....(Fantasy)
Captain Beefheart & His Magic Band; *Trout Mask Replica* ....(Reprise)
Frank Sinatra; *Come Fly With Me* ....(Capitol)
Frank Sinatra-Gift Set ....(Capitol)
Sarah Vaughan; *Complete Sarah Vaughan On Mercury-#3* ....(Mercury)
Sarah Vaughan-Golden Hits.....................(Mercury)
Moonlight Lady
Julio Iglesias; *1100 Bel Air Place* ....(Columbia)
Moonlight Mile
Rolling Stones; *Sticky Fingers*.......................(Virgin)
Moonlight Montreal
Peter White; *Reveillez-Vous* ....(Chase Music Group)
Moonlight Motel
Gun Club; *Las Vegas Story* ....(I.R.S.)
Moonlight On The Colorado
Sons Of The Pioneers; *Songs Of The Trail*....................(Pair)
Moonlight On The Ganges
Frank Sinatra; *Sinatra Swings* ....(Reprise)
Glenn Miller; *Best Of The Big Bands-C*................ (Columbia)
Moonlight Savings Time (There Ought To Be A)
Guy Lombardo & His Royal Canadians; *Auld Lang Syne* ....(Pro-Arte)
Moonlight Serenade
Frank Sinatra; *Moonlight Sinatra* ....(Reprise)
The Reprise Collection ....(Reprise)
Glenn Miller; *Best Of Glenn Miller-#2* ....(RCA)
Glenn Miller-A Legendary Performer-#1 & 2 ....(Bluebird)
Memorial-1944-1969 ....(Bluebird)
Nipper's Greatest Hits Of The '30s-#1-C ....(RCA)
The Glenn Miller Story ....(RCA)
Glenn Miller & His Orchestra; *Glenn Miller & His Orchestra-Pure Gold*.............................(Bluebird)

Moonlight Sonata
Glenn Miller; *Glenn Miller-A Legendary Performer-#1 & 2* ....(Bluebird)
Liberace; *Liberace's Greatest Hits* ....(Columbia)
Moons Of Jupiter
Paul Halley; *Pianosong* ....(Living Music)
Moonshadow Road
T. Graham Brown; *Best Of T. Graham Brown* ....(Liberty)
Mountains Of The Moon
Grateful Dead; *Aoxomoxoa* ....(Warner Bros.)
Mr. Moonlight
Beatles; *Beatles '65* ....(Capitol)
Beatles-Box Set ....(Capitol)
For Sale ....(Capitol)
Mr. Too Damn Good
Gerald Levert; *G* ....(East West)
Nashville Moon
Charlie Daniels Band; *Windows* ....(Epic)
Ronnie Milsap; *Lost In The Fifties Tonight* ....(RCA)
Neon Moon
Brooks & Dunn; *Brand New Man* ....(Arista)
Neon Moonlight
Rosco Martinez; *Neon Moonlight (Single)*.................. (Zoo)
New Blue Moon
Traveling Wilburys; *Traveling Wilburys-Vol. 3* ....(Wilbury/Warner Bros.)
New Moon On Monday
Duran Duran; *After The Hurricane* ....(Chrysalis)
Seven And The Ragged Tiger ....(Capitol)
New San Antonio Rose
Bob Wills & His Texas Playboys; *Bob Wills & His Texas Playboys-Greatest Hits* ....(Curb)
Columbia Country Classics-#1-Golden Age-C ....(Columbia)
Essential Bob Wills & His Texas Playboys-1935-1973 ....(Legacy)
Dwight Yoakam & Asleep At The Wheel; *Ride With Bob-C* ....(DreamWorks/SKG)
No Moon At All
Anita O'Day; *In A Mellow Tone* ....(DRG)
Billy Stritch; *Billy Stritch* ....(DRG)
Nothin' But The Taillights
Clint Black; *Nothin' But The Taillights* ....(RCA)
Nothin' New Under The Moon
LeAnn Rimes; *Sittin' On Top Of The World* ....(Curb)
Oh You Crazy Moon
Frank Sinatra; *Frank Sinatra Sings The Songs Of Van Heusen & Cahn*...........................(Reprise)
Moonlight Sinatra...........................(Reprise)
Mark Murphy; *Mark Murphy Sings Nat's Choice-Nat "King" Cole Songbook-#1*.............................(Muse)
Old Devil Moon
Anita O'Day; *Anita Sings The Most*....................(Verve)
Frank Sinatra & Nelson Riddle Orchestra; *songs for Swingin' Lovers!*.............................(Capitol)
John Raitt; *Highlights Of Broadway-Under Open Skies* ....(Capitol)
Lena Horne; *The Lady* ....(Dunhill Compact Classics)
Michael Feinstein; *Michael Feinstein Sings The Burton Lane Songbook-#1*...........................(Nonesuch)
Miles Davis; *Blue Haze* ....(Prestige)
Original Cast; *Finian's Rainbow* ....(Columbia)
Tony Bennett; *Forty Years-The Artistry Of Tony Bennett* ....(Columbia)
Once In A Blue Moon
Earl Thomas Conley; *Earl Thomas Conley's Greatest Hits* .... (RCA)
Hits Of '86-C .... (RCA)
Once In A Very Blue Moon
Nanci Griffith; *One Fair Summer Evening*....................(MCA)
Steal This Disc-C...........................(Rykodisc)
Pat Alger; *True Love & Other Short Stories-C*............. (Sugar Hill)
Pale Moon
Tommy Dorsey & Frank Sinatra; *Tommy Dorsey & Frank Sinatra's All-Time Greatest Hits-#4* ....(Bluebird)
Phone Call From The Moon
Adrian Belew; *Young Lions* ....(Atlantic)
Polka Dots & Moonbeams
Charlie Parker/Dizzy Gillespie/Charles Mingus/Others; *Greatest Jazz Concert Ever* ....(Prestige)
Ella Fitzgerald; *Fine And Mellow* ....(Pablo)
Frank Sinatra; *Frank Sinatra Sings The Songs Of Van Heusen & Cahn*...........................(Reprise)
I Remember Tommy..........................(Reprise)
Sinatra: A Man And His Music ....(Reprise)
Quarter Moon
Kathy Mattea; *Time Passes By*......................(Mercury)
Quarter Moon
Cheryl Wheeler; *Cheryl Wheeler* ....(North Star)
Rabbit In The Moon
Aztec Two-Step; *See It Was Like This...Acoustic Retrospective* ... (Flying Fish)
Peter Erskine; *Transition* ....(Denon)
Racing With The Moon
Vaughn Monroe; *Best Of Vaughn Monroe* ....(RCA)
Best Of Vaughn Monroe ....(MCA)
Decade Of The '40s-C..........................(RCA)

This Is Vaughn Monroe/Decade Of The '40s . . . . (RCA)

Rainbow
Russ Hamilton; *45-#184* . . . . (Kapp)

Reaching For The Moon
Ella Fitzgerald; *The Irving Berlin Songbook-#2* . . . . (Verve)
Frank Sinatra; *Moonlight Sinatra* . . . . (Reprise)

Red Moon Over Boston
Romanovsky & Phillips; *Be Political Not Polite* . . . .(Fresh Fruit)

Rock On The Moon
Cramps; *Songs The Lord Taught Us* . . . . (I.R.S.)

Rockin' Chair On The Moon
Bill Haley & His Comets; *King Of Rock & Roll* . . . . (Alshire)

Roll Along, Kentucky Moon
Jimmie Rodgers; *Down The Old Road-1931-1932* . . . . (Rounder)
Leon Redbone; *Sugar* . . . . (Private Music)

Rooty Toot Toot For The Moon
Greg Brown; *All-Ears Review-#3-Songwriters For The
'90s-C* . . . . (Really Outstanding Music)

Rope The Moon
John Michael Montgomery; *Kickin' It Up* . . . . (Atlantic)

Sad Lookin' Moon
Alabama; *Dancin' On The Boulevard* . . . . (RCA)
For The Record: 41 Number One Hits . . . . (RCA)

Sail Along, Silv'ry Moon
Andy Williams; *Unchained Melody-Greatest Songs* . . . . (Curb)
Billy Vaughn; *Best Of Billy Vaughn* . . . . (MCA)
Billy Vaughn's Greatest Hits . . . . (Curb)
Billy Vaughn & His Orchestra; *Billy Vaughn & His Orchestra Play 22 Of
His Greatest Hits* . . . .(Ranwood)

Sail On White Moon
Boz Scaggs; *Slow Dancer* . . . . (Columbia)

Sailboat In The Moonlight
Billie Holiday; *Billie Holiday's Greatest Hits* . . . . (Legacy)
Lady Day . . . . (Columbia)
Legacy Box-1933-1958 . . . . (Columbia)
Quintessential-#4-1937 . . . . (Columbia)

Same Moon
Maureen McGovern; *State Of The Heart* . . . . (Columbia)

Seventh Avenue
Rosanne Cash; *The Wheel* . . . . (Columbia)

Shadow On A Harvest Moon
Everything But The Girl; *Idlewild* . . . . (Sire)

Shadows In The Moonlight
Anne Murray; *15 Of The Best* . . . . (Liberty)
Anne Murray's Greatest Hits . . . . (Capitol)
New Kind Of Feeling . . . . (Capitol)

Shame On The Moon
Bob Seger & The Silver Bullet Band; *The Distance* . . . . (Capitol)
Mac Davis; *Mac Davis-Very Best & More* . . . . (Casablanca)
Rodney Crowell; *Rodney Crowell-Collection* . . . .(Warner Bros.)

She Hung The Moon
George Jones; *Shine On* . . . .(Epic)

Shine On Harvest Moon
Dorsey Brothers; *I'm Getting Sentimental Over You* . . . . (Pro-Arte)
Jimmy Dorsey & His Orchestra; *Then & Now-Fabulous New Jimmy Dorsey
& His Orchestra* . . . . (Atlantic)
Leon Redbone; *Double Time* . . . .(Warner Bros.)
Mitch Miller; *Mitch Miller-16 Most Requested Songs* . . . . (Columbia)

Shine On Moon
Lightnin' Hopkins; *Collectables Blues Collection-#3-C* . . . . (Collectables)
Mojo Hand . . . . (Collectables)

Shinin' Moon
Cowboy Junkies; *Whites Off Earth Now!!* . . . . (RCA)
Lightnin' Hopkins; *Drinkin' In The Blues-Golden Classics-#1* . . . (Collectables)
Gold Star Sessions-#2 . . . . (Arhoolie)

Shoot Down The Moon
Elton John; *Ice On Fire* . . . . (MCA)

Shoot For The Moon
Poco; *Ghost Town & Inamorata* . . . . (Rhino)
Ultimate Collection . . . . (Hip-O)

Shy Of The Moon
Wallflowers; *The Wallflowers* . . . . (Virgin)

Silver Moon
Lawrence Welk; *22 Great Waltzes* . . . .(Ranwood)
Mom & Dads; *Mom & Dads-20 Favorite Waltzes* . . . . (Crescendo)

Silver Moon
David Sylvian; *Gone To Earth* . . . . (Virgin)

Silver Moon
Kitaro; *In Person* . . . . (Gramavision)
My Best . . . . (Gramavision)
Silk Road II . . . . (Gramavision)

Silver Moon
Michael Nesmith; *Older Stuff* . . . . (Rhino)

Sister Moonshine
Supertramp; *Crisis? What Crisis?* . . . . (A&M)

Sisters Of The Moon
Fleetwood Mac; *25 Years-The Chain* . . . .(Warner Bros.)
Tusk . . . .(Warner Bros.)

Somebody Else's Moon
Collin Raye; *In This Life* . . . . (Epic)

Spanish Moon
Little Feat; *Feats Don't Fail Me Now* . . . . (Warner Bros.)
Waiting For Columbus . . . . (Warner Bros.)
Robert Palmer; *Some People Can Do What They Like* . . . . (Island)

Standing On The Corner
Broadway Cast; *Most Happy Fella* . . . . (RCA)
Dean Martin; *Best Of Dean Martin* . . . . (CEMA Special Prod.)
Four Lads; *Four Lads-16 Most Requested Songs* . . . . (Legacy)
Original Broadway Cast; *Most Happy Fella* . . . . (Sony Music Classical)

Stars Over Texas
Tracy Lawrence; *Best Of Tracy Lawrence* . . . .(Atlantic)
Time Marches On . . . .(Atlantic)

Strawberry Wine
Deana Carter; *Did I Shave My Legs For This?* . . . . (Capitol)

Sugar Moon
Bob Wills & His Texas Playboys; *Essential Bob Wills & His Texas
Playboys-1935-1973* . . . . (Legacy)
k.d. lang; *Shadowland* . . . .(Sire)

Sugar Moon
Pat Boone; *Best Of Pat Boone* . . . . (MCA)

Sun & Moon
Original London Cast; *Miss Saigon* . . . . (Geffen)

Sun On The Moon
James Taylor; *Never Die Young* . . . . (Columbia)

Sun, Moon & Stars
Nanci Griffith; *Late Night Grande Hotel* . . . . (MCA)

Swinging On A Star
Bing Crosby; *All-Time Best* . . . . (Curb)
Best Of Bing Crosby . . . . (MCA)
Dion And The Belmonts; *Dion And The Belmonts-Their Best* . . . . (Laurie)
Frank Sinatra; *Frank Sinatra Sings The Songs Of Van Heusen
& Cahn* . . . . (Reprise)

Tahitian Moon
Michael Franks; *Objects Of Desire* . . . . (Warner Bros.)

Tahitian Moon
Porno For Pyros; *Good God's Urge* . . . . (Warner Bros.)

Talkin' To The Moon
Gatlin Brothers; *Best Of The Gatlins-All The Gold In California* . . . . . (Legacy)
Larry Gatlin & The Gatlin Brothers Band; *Live At 8:00* . . . . (Capitol)
More Hot Country Requests-#2-C . . . . (Epic)
Partners . . . . (Columbia)
The Gatlin Brothers' Biggest Hits . . . . (Columbia)

Talkin' To The Moon
Charlie Daniels Band; *Me & The Boys* . . . . (Epic)

Talking To A Tennessee Moon
Candace Anderson; *Talking To A Tennessee Moon* . . . .(Adobe)

Tennessee Moon
Neil Diamond; *Tennessee Moon* . . . . (Columbia)

Tennessee Moon
Cowboy Copas; *45-#714* . . . . (King)

That's Amore
Dean Martin; *Best Of Dean Martin* . . . . (CEMA Special Prod.)
Dean Martin's All Time Greatest Hits . . . . (Curb)
Dean Martin's Greatest Hits . . . . (EMI)
The Capitol Years-Dean Martin . . . . (Capitol)

Theme From "Moonlighting"
Al Jarreau; *ST/Moonlighting* . . . . (MCA)
Television's Greatest Hits-#6-Remote Control-C . . . . (TVT)

Theme From "Moonraker"
John Barry & Shirley Bassey; *ST/Moonraker* . . . . (EMI)
Shirley Bassey; *Best Of James Bond-30th Anniversary-C* . . . . (EMI)

There's A Moon Out Tonight
Capris; *20 Top 10 Hits Of The '50s & '60s-C* . . . . (Laurie)
22 Leaders Of The Pack-#2-C . . . . (Laurie)
Collectables Presents The History Of Rock-#3-C . . . . (Collectables)
There's A Moon Out Tonight . . . . (Collectables)

There's A New Moon Over My Shoulder
Gene Autry; *Columbia Historic Edition-Gene Autry* . . . . (Columbia)
Jimmie Davis; *Best Of Jimmie Davis* . . . . (MCA)
Jimmie Davis-Golden Hits . . . . (Plantation)
The Country Music Hall Of Fame-Jimmie Davis . . . . (MCA)
Tex Ritter; *Tex Ritter's Greatest Hits* . . . . (Curb)

Tijuana Moon
Tim Buckley; *Look At The Fool* . . . . (Bizarre/Straight)

To The Moon And Back
Savage Garden; *Savage Garden* . . . . (Columbia)

Tropic Moon
Bruce Cockburn; *Trouble With Normal* . . . . (Columbia)

Tubas In The Moonlight
Bonzo Dog Band; *Tadpoles* . . . . (Liberty)

Under A Raging Moon
Roger Daltrey; *Under A Raging Moon* . . . .(Atlantic)

Under The Harlem Moon
Fletcher Henderson & His Orchestra; *Fletcher Henderson & His
Orchestra* . . . . (ASV)

Under The Moon Of Love
Curtis Lee; *Phil Spector-Back To Mono 1958-1969-C* . . . . (Abkco)

Underneath The Harlem Moon
Randy Newman; *12 Songs*...........................(Reprise)
Waiting For The Moon
Bruce Cockburn; *Trouble With Normal*......................(Columbia)
Walkin' After Midnight
Garth Brooks; *The Chase*.............................(Liberty)
Loretta Lynn; *I Remember Patsy*...............................(MCA)
Oak Ridge Boys; *Unstoppable*...............................(RCA)
Patsy Cline; *20 Golden Pieces Of Patsy Cline*..............(Bulldog)
  Let The Teardrops Fall...............................(Accord)
  Live At The Opry...................................(MCA)
  Patsy Cline.......................................(MCA)
  Patsy Cline's Greatest Hits.........................(MCA)
  The Patsy Cline Story.............................(MCA)
Was It Just The Moonlight
Timothy B. Schmit; *Tell Me The Truth* .... (MCA)
Watch The Moon Come Down
Graham Parker And The Rumour; *Stick To Me* ....(Mercury)
  The Parkerilla....................................(Mercury)
Water From The Moon
Lee Ritenour; *Earth Run* ....(GRP)
Water From The Moon
Celine Dion; *Celine Dion* .... (Epic)
What A Little Moonlight Can Do
Billie Holiday; *Billie Holiday's Greatest Hits*...............(Legacy)
  Billie's Best.......................................(Verve)
  First Verve Sessions ....(Verve)
  History Of The Real Billie Holiday....................(Verve)
  Songbook...(Verve)
Diana Ross; *ST/Lady Sings The Blues* ....(Motown)
Whatever It Takes
Sinead Lohan; *No Mermaid* . ... (Grapevine)
When My Blue Moon Turns To Gold Again
Elvis Presley; *A Golden Celebration* ....(RCA)
  Elvis..(RCA)
  The Other Sides-Worldwide Gold Award Hits, Vol. 2.......(RCA)
Merle Haggard; *Merle Haggard-His Best* ....(MCA)
  Ramblin' Fever....................................(MCA)
When The Golden Leaves Begin To Fall
Joe Val & The New England Bluegrass Boys; *Diamond Joe*........(Rounder)
  Joe Val & The New England Bluegrass Boys-Vol. 2...........(Rounder)
When The Moon Comes Over The Mountain
Kate Smith; *Best Of Kate Smith*........................(RCA)
  Kate Smith-16 Most Requested Songs..................(Columbia)
When The Moon Shines On The Moonshine
Bert Williams; *Music From The New York Stage (1890-1920)-#4-1917-1920-C*....................................(Pearl)
When You Love Someone
Bryan Adams; *MTV Unplugged-Bryan Adams* ....(A&M)
Where You Are
Jessica Simpson featuring Nick Lachey; *Sweet Kisses* ....(Columbia)
Whitey On The Moon
Gil Scott-Heron; *Whitey On The Moon* ....(Bluebird)
Whole Of The Moon
Jennifer Warnes; *The Hunter*.......................(Private Music)
Terry Reid; *The Driver* ....(Warner Bros.)
Waterboys; *Greenpeace/Rainbow Warriors-C*..............(Geffen)
  This Is The Sea ....(Chrysalis)
Wild Dog Moon
Drivin' N' Cryin'; *Mystery Road*.........................(Island)
Wishing On The Moon
Dan Fogelberg; *Phoenix* . ... (Full Moon)
Woke Up This Morning
A3; *Exile On Coldharbour Lane* ....(C2/Columbia)
  The Sopranos-Music From The HBO Original Series.........(Sony Music Soundtrax)
Wrong Side Of The Moon
Squeeze; *Argybargy* ....(A&M)

MORNING, Dawn, Good Morning, Sunrise

See Also: **AFTERNOON, BEGINNINGS, DAYS OF THE WEEK (various), DAYS: GENERAL, MIDNIGHT, NIGHT, SLEEP, SUN, TIME: GENERAL, TIME: SPECIFIC**

(It's A) Beautiful Morning
Rascals; *Rascals' Greatest Hits*.......................(Atlantic)
100% Chance Of Rain
Gary Morris; *Anything Goes* ....(Warner Bros.)
  Gary Morris-Hits.................................(Warner Bros.)
3am
Matchbox Twenty; *Yourself Or Someone Like You*...............(Lava)
59th Street Bridge Song (Feelin' Groovy)
Harper's Bizarre; *Baby Boomer Classics-More Mellow Sixties-C*.......................(JCI Assoc. Labels)
  Better Days-C.....................................(Rhino)

Simon & Garfunkel; *Collected Works* ....(Columbia)
  Parsley Sage Rosemary & Thyme ....(Columbia)
  Simon & Garfunkel's Greatest Hits....................(Columbia)
  The Concert In Central Park ....(Warner Bros.)
Ain't Going Down (Til The Sun Comes Up)
Garth Brooks; *In Pieces*.............................(Liberty)
All Mixed Up
311; *311*..(Capricorn)
Almost Dawn In Denver
Faron Young; *Faron Young's Greatest Hits-#3* .... (Step One)
Amarillo By Morning
George Strait; *George Strait's Greatest Hits* .... (MCA)
  Strait From The Heart.............................(MCA)
Angel Of The Morning
Juice Newton; *All-Time Country Classics-#2-C*...............(Capitol)
  Juice ....(Capitol)
  Juice Newton-Greatest Hits & More...................(Capitol)
  Juice Newton's Greatest Hits ....(Gold Rush)
Merrilee Rush; *Dick Bartley's One-Hit Wonders Of The '60s-#2-C* .....(Rhino)
  Mellow '60s-C...................................(Priority)
Another Dawn Breaking Over Georgia
David Frizzell & Shelly West; *Our Best To You*.............(Warner Bros.)
Another Grey Morning
James Taylor; *JT* ....(Columbia)
Another Nine Minutes
Yankee Grey; *Untamed* ....(Monument)
April Fool's Day Morn
Loudon Wainwright III; *Career Moves* .... (Virgin)
  Fame & Wealth...................................(Rounder)
As I Went Out One Morning
Bob Dylan; *John Wesley Harding* ....(Columbia)
As We Lay
Kelly Price; *Mirror Mirror*......................(Def Soul/IDJMG)
At 4 A.M.
Tom Verlaine; *Flash Light*............................(I.R.S.)
Before Dawn
Joyce Cooling; *Keeping Cool* ....(Heads Up Records Int'l)
Best I Ever Had (Grey Sky Morning)
Vertical Horizon; *Everything You Want*...................(RCA)
Bloody Mary Morning
Willie Nelson; *Best Of Willie* ....(RCA)
  Phases & Stages .... (Atlantic)
  ST/Honeysuckle Rose ....(Columbia)
  Willie & Family Live ....(Columbia)
Blue Morning Blue Day
Foreigner; *Double Vision* .... (Atlantic)
Blues Before Sunrise
Eric Clapton; *From The Cradle* ....(Duck/Reprise)
Brand New Day
Frankie Laine; *Frankie Laine's 16 Greatest Hits* .... (Trip)
Brand New Day
Van Morrison; *Moondance* ....(Warner Bros.)
Can I See You In The Morning
Jackson 5; *Third Album*............................(Motown)
Carolina In The Morning
Al Jolson; *Best Of Al Jolson* .... (MCA)
  The Al Jolson Story-#2 ....(MCA)
Chelsea Morning
Joni Mitchell; *Clouds* .... (Reprise)
Judy Collins; *New York Songs-C*........................(Rhino)
Neil Diamond; *Rainbow*.............................(MCA)
  Stones..(MCA)
City Of New Orleans
Arlo Guthrie; *Best Of Arlo Guthrie* ....(Warner Bros.)
  Hobo's Lullaby .... (Reprise)
  Together In Concert .... (Reprise)
HARP; *HARP*......................................(Redwood)
Willie Nelson; *19 Hot Country Requests-#2-C* .... (Epic)
  City Of New Orleans ....(Columbia)
  Greatest Country Hits Of The '80s-#4-C...............(Columbia)
  Hot Tracks-Train Super Hits-C ....(Epic)
  Train Trax-C ....(Sony Music Special Prod.)
Cloudy Morning
Carmen McRae & George Shearing; *Two For The Road* ....(Concord Jazz)
Come Early Morning
Don Williams; *Don Williams' Greatest Hits* .... (MCA)
  Don Williams-20 Greatest Hits........................(MCA)
  Some Broken Hearts Never Mend .... (MCA Special Prod.)
Come Saturday Morning
Sandpipers; *Four Sider* ....(A&M)
  Super Hits Of The '70s-Have A Nice Day-#1-C ....(Rhino)
Crying In The Morning
Billy Tate; *Crying In The Morning-Anthology Of Postwar Blues* ....(Muse)
  Southern Blues ....(Savoy)
Crystal Blue Persuasion
Tommy James And The Shondells; *Best Of Tommy James And The Shondells*..................................(Roulette)
  Tommy James And The Shondells-Anthology ....(Rhino)

Dawn In Malaysia
Kitaro; *Asia*. . . . .(Geffen)
Dawn Of Correction
Spokesmen; *Sixties Rule! Chapter 1-C*. . . . . (One Way)
Dawning Is The Day
Moody Blues; *A Question Of Balance* . . . . (Polydor)
Daybreak
Barry Manilow; *Barry Manilow/Live*. . . . . (Arista)
   Barry Manilow's Greatest Hits-#1 . . . . (Arista)
   This One's For You . . . . (Arista)
Daybreak
Special EFX; *Global Village* . . . . (GRP)
   Special EFX . . . . (GRP)
Daybreak
Acoustic Alchemy; *Early Alchemy*. . . . . (GRP)
Daybreak
Pat Metheny; *New Chautauqua* . . . . (ECM)
Daybreak
Robin Trower; *Robin Trower-Live* . . . .(Chrysalis)
Daybreak
Steve Wariner; *Steve Wariner*. . . . . (RCA)
Daybreak
Chet Baker; *Let's Get Lost-Best Of Chet Baker Sings*. . . . (Blue Note)
Tommy Dorsey & Frank Sinatra; *Tommy Dorsey & Frank Sinatra's All-Time
   Greatest Hits-#4* . . . . (Bluebird)
Daydream Believer
Anne Murray; *Anne Murray's Greatest Hits* . . . . (Capitol)
   I'll Always Love You . . . . (Capitol)
Monkees; *Billboard Top Rock 'N' Roll Hits-1967-C* . . . . (Rhino)
   Mellow '60s-C . . . . (Priority)
   Monkees' Greatest Hits . . . . (Rhino)
Dolphin Morning
Paul Winter Consort; *Sun Singer* . . . .(Living Music)
Draft Morning
Byrds; *Notorious Byrd Brothers*. . . . . (Columbia)
   The Byrds. . . . . (Columbia)
Dutch Morning
Phil Woods & Jim McNeely; *Flowers For Hodges* . . . .(Concord Jazz)
Early In The Morning
Gap Band; *12'' Collection* . . . . (Mercury)
   Gap Band IV . . . . (Mercury)
   Gap Gold/Best Of The Gap Band. . . . . (Mercury)
Early In The Morning
Bad Company; *Desolation Angels* . . . . (Swan Song)
Early In The Morning
Robert Palmer; *Heavy Nova* . . . .(EMI)
Early In The Morning
Peter, Paul & Mary; *Peter, Paul and Mary* . . . .(Warner Bros.)
Early Morning Blues
Jimmy Preston; *Jimmy Preston*. . . . . (Collectables)
Muddy Waters; *More Real Folk Blues-Muddy Waters* . . . . (Chess)
Early One Morning
Elmore James; *King Of The Slide Guitar* . . . . (Capricorn)
John Lee Hooker; *Jealous*. (Chase Music Group)
Easy
Commodores; *20 Greatest Songs In Motown History-C*. . . . . (Motown)
   All The Great Love Songs-Commodores . . . . (Motown)
   Commodores . . . . (Motown)
   Commodores Greatest Hits . . . . (Motown)
   Compact Command Performances-Commodores . . . . (Motown)
   Composer-Great Love Songs By Lionel Richie . . . . . (Motown)
Lionel Richie; *Back To Front* . . . . (Motown)
Every Morning
Sugar Ray; *14:59* . . . . (Lava)
Every Morning
Keb' Mo'; *Keb' Mo'*. . . . .(Okeh)
Fever
Buddy Guy; *This Is Buddy Guy*. . . . . (Vanguard)
Elvis Presley; *A Valentine Gift For You* . . . .(RCA)
   Aloha from Hawaii via Satellite. . . . . (RCA)
   Elvis Presley-Pure Gold . . . . (RCA)
Little Willie John; *Best Of Little Willie John-Fever*. . . . . (Rhino)
Peggy Lee; *Memories Are Made Of This-C* . . . . (Capitol)
Rita Coolidge; *Rita Coolidge-Classics-#5* . . . . (A&M)
   Rita Coolidge's Greatest Hits . . . . (A&M)
Fine Spring Morning
Blossom Dearie; *Blossom Dearie* . . . . (Verve)
Fire In The Morning
Melissa Manchester; *Melissa Manchester*. . . . . (Arista)
For No One
Beatles; *Beatles-Box Set* . . . . (Capitol)
   Beatles-Love Songs . . . . (Capitol)
   Revolver. . . . . (Capitol)
Emmylou Harris; *Pieces Of The Sky* . . . . (Reprise)
Four In The Morning
Night Ranger; *7 Wishes* . . . . (MCA)
   Night Ranger's Greatest Hits. . . . . (Camel)
Four In The Morning
Faron Young; *Faron Young's Greatest Hits-#3* . . . . (Step One)

Frere Jacques
Original Soundtrack; *Toddler Favorites* . . . .(Kid Rhino/Rhino 4 Kids)
Good Day Sunshine
Beatles; *Beatles-Box Set* . . . . (Capitol)
   Revolver . . . . (Capitol)
Good Morning
Gene Kelly/Debbie Reynolds/Donald O'Connor; *ST/Singin' In
   The Rain* . . . . (Sony Music Special Prod.)
Good Morning Beautiful
Steve Holy; *Blue Moon* . . . . (Curb)
Good Morning Girl
Journey; *Departure* . . . . (Columbia)
Good Morning Good Morning
Beatles; *Beatles-Box Set* . . . . (Capitol)
   Sgt. Pepper's Lonely Hearts Club Band . . . . (Capitol)
Good Morning Heartache
Billie Holiday; *All Or Nothing At All*. . . . . (Verve)
   Billie Holiday's Greatest Hits . . . . (Decca Jazz)
   From The Original Decca Masters . . . . (MCA)
   History Of Billie Holiday . . . . (Verve)
Diana Ross; *Diana Ross-Anthology* . . . . (Motown)
   ST/Lady Sings The Blues. . . . . (Motown)
Tony Bennett with Sheryl Crow; *Playin' With My Friends-Bennett Sings The
   Blues-C* . . . . (Columbia)
Good Morning Judge
10 CC; *10 CC's Greatest Hits-1972-1978.* . . . .(Polydor)
   Deceptive Bends. . . . . (Mercury)
   Jailhouse Rock (Hits From The Big House)-C . . . . (Sony Music Special Prod.)
   Live & Let Live . . . . (Mercury)
Good Morning Starshine
Oliver; *'60s Rock Classics-#3-C* . . . . (Rhino)
Original Broadway Cast; *Hair*. . . . . (RCA)
Good Morning To You
Steve Miller Band; *Number 5* . . . . (Capitol)
Got To Be There
Michael Jackson; *Best Of Michael Jackson*. . . . . (Motown)
   Michael Jackson-Anthology. . . . . (Motown)
Gotta Get Up
Nilsson; *Nilsson Schmilsson* . . . .(RCA)
Happier Than The Morning Sun
Stevie Wonder; *Music Of My Mind* . . . . (Motown)
Here Comes The Sun
Beatles; *Abbey Road* . . . .(Parlophone)
   The Beatles/1967-1970. . . . . (Capitol)
George Benson; *Best Of George Benson* . . . .(A&M)
   George Benson-Collection . . . . (Warner Bros.)
George Harrison; *Bangladesh* . . . . (Capitol)
   Best Of George Harrison . . . . (Capitol)
Here Comes Yet Another Day
Kinks; *Everybody's In Show-Biz*. . . . . (Rhino)
Hold Me 'Til The Mornin' Comes
Paul Anka; *Paul Anka-Live* . . . . (Columbia)
   Walk A Fine Line . . . . (Columbia)
Hopeless
Dionne Farris; *ST/Love Jones* . . . . (Columbia)
How Do You Like Your Eggs In The Morning?
Jane Powell/Vic Damone/Four Freshmen; *ST/Romantic Duets From MGM
   Classics-C* . . . . (Turner Classic Movies)
I Got The Sun In The Morning
Ethel Merman/Bruce Yarnell/Original Cast; *Annie Get
   Your Gun* . . . . (RCA Victor)
Ethel Merman/Ray Middleton/Original Cast; *Annie Get Your Gun* . . . . . (MCA)
Original Broadway Cast; *Annie Get Your Gun* . . . . (Angel)
I'll Fly Away
Gillian Welch & Alison Krauss; *ST/O Brother, Where Art Thou?* . . . . (Mercury)
Illinois Dawn
Skyline; *Late To Work*. . . . . (Flying Fish)
I'm Gonna Miss You In The Morning
Quincy Jones; *Quincy Jones-Classics-#3* . . . . (A&M)
   Quincy Jones-The Best. (A&M)
   Sounds... And Stuff Like That!! . . . . (A&M)
In The Morning Time
Tramaine; *45-#2805* . . . . (A&M)
In The Wee Small Hours Of The Morning
Frank Sinatra; *In The Wee Small Hours.* . . . . (Capitol)
   Sinatra: A Man And His Music . . . . (Reprise)
   Sinatra's Sinatra . . . . (Reprise)
   The Capitol Years . . . . (Capitol)
It's Been A Great Afternoon
Merle Haggard; *For The Record: Merle Haggard-43 Legendary Hits* . . . .(BNA)
   I'm Always On A Mountain When I Fall. . . . . (MCA)
   Merle Haggard's Greatest Hits . . . . (MCA)
   More Of The Best . . . . (Rhino)
It's Four In The Morning
Faron Young; *Faron Young-Golden Hits* . . . . (Mercury)
   Faron Young-The Hits . . . . (Mercury)
It's Late
Ricky Nelson; *Lonesome Town*. . . . . (CEMA Special Prod.)

Ricky Nelson Volume 1 . . . . (Gold Rush)
Jam On Monday Morning
Buddy Guy; *Man & The Blues* . . . . (Vanguard)
Jamaica Sunday Morning
Kim Carnes; *St. Vincent's Court* . . . . (Out Of Print)
Jets At Dawn
Be Bop Deluxe; *Axe Victim* . . . . (Capitol)
Joy Comes In The Morning
Oak Ridge Boys; *All Our Favorite Songs* . . . . (Columbia)
July Morning
Uriah Heep; *Best Of Uriah Heep* . . . . (Mercury)
Uriah Heep-Live . . . . (Mercury)
Just A Little Lovin' (Early In The Mornin')
Barbra Streisand; *Stoney End* . . . . (Columbia)
Dusty Springfield; *Dusty In Memphis* . . . . (Rhino)
Kiss An Angel Good Mornin'
Charley Pride; *Charley Pride-24 Greatest Hits* . . . . (Tee Vee)
Pride! My 6 Latest And 6 Greatest . . . . (ISD/Intersound)
The Ultimate Charley Pride . . . . (Bransounds)
Long Time Gone
Crosby, Stills & Nash; *Crosby, Stills & Nash* . . . . (Atlantic)
CSN. . . . . (Atlantic)
Crosby, Stills, Nash & Young; *4 Way Street* . . . . (Atlantic)
Loving You Sunday Morning
Scorpions; *Lovedrive* . . . . (Mercury)
World Wide Live . . . . (Mercury)
Marie
Tommy Dorsey & His Orchestra; *Seventeen Number Ones* . . . . (RCA)
Mary In The Morning
Al Martino; *Al Martino's Greatest Hits* . . . . (EMI Special Markets)
Massachusetts Morning
Peter Gordon; *The Long Way Home* . . . . (Positive)
Meet Me In The Morning
Bob Dylan; *Blood On The Tracks* . . . . (Columbia)
Mona Lisas And Mad Hatters
Elton John; *Honky Chateau* . . . . (Rocket)
Reg Strikes Back . . . . (MCA)
The Concert For New York City-C . . . . (Columbia)
Monday Mornin' Keep A Hurtin' Blues
Sonny James; *Little Bit Of Saskatoon* . . . . (Columbia)
Monday Morning
Fleetwood Mac; *25 Years-The Chain* . . . . (Warner Bros.)
Fleetwood Mac . . . . (Reprise)
Fleetwood Mac Live . . . . (Warner Bros.)
Monday Morning
Church; *Gold Afternoon Fix* . . . . (Arista)
Monday Morning
Peter, Paul & Mary; *Song Will Rise* . . . . (Warner Bros.)
Monday Morning Blues
Mississippi John Hurt; *Best Of Mississippi John Hurt* . . . . (Vanguard)
Candy Man . . . . (Intermedia)
Monday Morning Blues
Breathe; *All That Jazz* . . . . (A&M)
Monday Morning In Paradise
Tom Paxton; *One Million Lawyers & Other Disasters* . . . . (Flying Fish)
Monday Morning Quarterback
Frank Sinatra; *She Shot Me Down* . . . . (Reprise)
Monday Morning Rock
Marshall Crenshaw; *Field Day* . . . . (Warner Bros.)
Monday Morning Secretary
Statler Brothers; *Statler Brothers* . . . . (Mercury)
Mornin'
Al Jarreau; *Jarreau* . . . . (Warner Bros.)
Morning
Jim Ed Brown; *Best Of Jim Ed Brown* . . . . (RCA)
Stars Of The Grand Ole Opry-1926-1974-C . . . . (RCA)
Morning
Brigette McWilliams; *Too Much Woman* . . . . (Virgin)
Morning
Call; *Reconciled* . . . . (Elektra)
Morning After
Maureen McGovern; *Super Hits Of The '70s-Have A Nice Day-#11-C.* . . (Rhino)
Morning After
Alexander O'Neal; *All True Man* . . . . (Tabu)
Morning After
Ratt; *Out Of The Cellar* . . . . (Atlantic)
Morning After
Faith No More; *Real Thing* . . . . (Slash)
Morning After
Barbra Streisand; *What About Today* . . . . (Columbia)
Morning Coffee
Joe King Carrasco & The Crowns; *Tales From The Crypt-Basement Tapes-1979* . . . . (Roir)
Morning Comes Too Early
Jim Ed Brown & Helen Cornelius; *Jim Ed Brown & Helen Cornelius' Greatest Hits* . . . . (RCA)
Morning Dance
Spyro Gyra; *Access All Areas* . . . . (MCA)

Morning Dance . . . . (MCA)
Spyro Gyra-Collection . . . . (GRP)
Morning Desire
Kenny Rogers; *Kenny Rogers' Greatest Hits* . . . . (RCA)
Morning Dew
Jeff Beck Group; *Truth.* . . . . (Epic)
Morning Dew
Bonnie Dobson; *Troubadours Of The Folk Era-#1-C* . . . . (Rhino)
Grateful Dead; *Europe '72* . . . . (Warner Bros.)
Morning Dew
Lulu; *From Crayons To Perfume: The Best Of Lulu.* . . . . (Rhino)
Morning Dew
Nazareth; *Nazareth* . . . . (A&M)
Morning Dew
Blackfoot; *Vertical Smiles* . . . . (Atco)
Morning Glory
Oasis; *(What's The Story) Morning Glory* . . . . (Epic)
Morning Has Broken
Cat Stevens; *Cat Stevens Greatest Hits* . . . . (A&M)
Cat Stevens-Classics-#24 . . . . (A&M)
Teaser And The Firecat . . . . (A&M)
Morning In Paris
John Lewis; *Private Concert* . . . . (Emarcy)
Morning Man
Joy; *Joy* . . . . (Fantasy)
Morning Morgantown
Joni Mitchell; *Ladies Of The Canyon* . . . . (Reprise)
Morning Papers
Prince And The New Power Generation; *Love Symbol Album* . . . . (Paisley Park)
Morning Side
Neil Diamond; *Hot August Night* . . . . (MCA)
Moods . . . . (MCA)
Morning Side Of The Mountain, The
Tommy Edwards; *It's All In The Game-The Complete Hits Of Tommy Edwards* . . . . (Eric)
Morning Sky
Dan Fogelberg; *Dan Fogelberg-Souvenirs* . . . . (Full Moon)
Morning Sun
Jesse Colin Young; *Best Of Jesse Colin Young-Solo Years* . . . . (Rhino)
Song For Juli. . . . . (Warner Bros.)
Morning Sun
Bad Company; *Burnin' Sky* . . . . (Swan Song)
Morning Train (Nine To Five)
Sheena Easton; *Sheena Easton.* . . . . (EMI)
Morning Will Come
Spirit; *12 Dreams Of Dr. Sardonicus* . . . . (Epic)
Best Of Spirit . . . . (Epic)
Time Circle . . . . (Epic)
Most Beautiful Girl
Charlie Rich; *Behind Closed Doors* . . . . (Epic)
Charlie Rich's Greatest Hits . . . . (Epic)
Columbia Country Classics-#4-Nashville Sound-C . . . . (Columbia)
New Day For You
Basia; *Time And Tide* . . . . (Epic)
New Morning
Bob Dylan; *New Morning* . . . . (Columbia)
New World In The Morning
Roger Whittaker; *Best Of Roger Whittaker* . . . . (RCA)
Last Farewell & Other Hits . . . . (RCA)
Live In Concert . . . . (RCA)
New World In The Morning . . . . (RCA)
Nobody Knows The Way I Feel This Morning
Aretha Franklin; *Aretha Franklin Sings The Blues* . . . . (Columbia)
Ernest "Punch" Miller; *Atlantic Jazz-New Orleans-C* . . . . (Atlantic)
North Dakota Sunrise
Metamora; *Metamora* . . . . (Sugar Hill)
October Morning
Fourplay; *Fourplay* . . . . (Warner Bros.)
Of A Summer Morn
Nightnoise; *At The End Of The Evening.* . . . . (Windham Hill)
Oh! How I Hate To Get Up In The Morning
Irving Berlin; *American Songbook Series-Irving Berlin* . . . . (Smithsonian Collection)
War Years-C . . . . (ISD/Intersound)
Soundtrack; *American Musical Theater-#2* . . . . (Smithsonian Collection)
Oh, What A Beautiful Morning
Original Broadway Cast; *Oklahoma!* . . . . (RCA)
Original Cast; *Oklahoma!* . . . . (MCA)
One Morning In May
Charlie Byrd Trio; *Isn't It Romantic?* . . . . (Concord Jazz)
Jean Ritchie; *Love Is Teasin'* . . . . (Elektra)
One Too Many Mornings
Beau Brummels; *Best Of The Beau Brummels* . . . . (Rhino)
Bob Dylan; *Hard Rain* . . . . (Columbia)
The Times They Are A-Changin' . . . . (Columbia)
Johnny Cash & Waylon Jennings; *Heroes* . . . . (Columbia)
Kingston Trio; *American Troubadours* . . . . (Pair)

Ordinary Morning
Sheryl Crow; *Sheryl Crow* . . . . (A&M)
Our Sunday Morning
Yoshio "Chin" Suzuki; *Morning Picture* . . . .(JVC Musical Industries)
Prayin' For Daylight
Rascal Flatts; *Rascal Flatts*. . . . . (Lyric Street)
Princess Of The Dawn
Accept; *Compilation*. . . . . (Portrait)
Restless & Wild . . . . (Portrait)
Staying A Life . . . .(Epic)
Promise Of A New Day
Paula Abdul; *Spellbound* . . . . (Captive)
Pure Love
Ronnie Milsap; *Ronnie Milsap's Greatest Hits* . . . . (RCA)
Ronnie Milsap-Super Hits . . . . (RCA)
Pure Morning
Placebo; *Without You I'm Nothing* . . . . (Virgin)
Quite Early Morning
Pete Seeger; *Essential Pete Seeger* . . . . (Vanguard)
Race You To The Top Of The Morning
Original Broadway Cast; *Secret Garden*. . . . . (Columbia)
Red Rubber Ball
Cyrkle; *Even More Nuggets-C* . . . . (Rhino)
Pop Classics Of The '60s-C . . . . (Columbia)
Red Rubber Ball (A Collection) . . . . (Columbia)
Rise 'N' Shine
Kool Moe Dee with KRS-One & Chuck D; *Funke Funke Wisdom*. . . . . . . (Jive)
Saturday Morning
Harry Chapin; *Greatest Stories-Live* . . . . (Elektra)
Saturday Morning
Joe Higgs; *Black Man Know Yourself*. . . . . (Shanachie)
Saturday Morning
Tom Chapin; *In The City Of Mercy*. . . . . (Spector)
Saturday Morning
Meat Puppets; *Meat Puppets*. . . . . (SST)
Saturday Morning Cartoons
Sergio Salvatore; *Sergio Salvatore*. . . . . (GRP)
Saturday Morning Confusion
Bobby Russell; *Super Hits Of The '70s-Have A Nice Day-#6-C*. . . . . . . (Rhino)
Saturday Morning Fever
Loudon Wainwright III; *Fame & Wealth* . . . . (Rounder)
Saturday Morning Movies
Bonnie Koloc; *Bonnie Koloc* . . . .(Ovation)
Bonnie Koloc-At Her Best . . . .(Ovation)
Saturday Night & Sunday Morning
Phil Collins; *...But Seriously* . . . .(Atlantic)
Save A Prayer
Duran Duran; *Arena* . . . . (Capitol)
Decade . . . . (Capitol)
Rio . . . . (Capitol)
Secret Policeman's Third Ball-The Music-C . . . . (Virgin)
Seattle Morning
David Benoit; *Urban Daydreams* . . . . (GRP)
September Morn
Mark Masters Jazz Composer Orchestra; *Early Start* . . . . . . (Sea Breeze)
Neil Diamond; *12 Greatest Hits-#2* . . . . (Columbia)
Hot August Night II . . . . (Columbia)
September Morn. . . . . (Columbia)
Shake Me Wake Me
Barbra Streisand; *Lazy Afternoon*. . . . . (Columbia)
Four Tops; *Four Tops' Greatest Hits* . . . . (Motown)
Four Tops-Anthology. . . . . (Motown)
Motown Superstar Series-#14-Four Tops . . . . (Motown)
Shake, Rattle And Roll
Big Joe Turner; *Big Joe Turner's Greatest Hits* . . . .(Atlantic)
Every Day I Have The Blues . . . .(Pablo)
Oldies But Goodies-#2-C. . . . . (Original Sound)
Soul Years-C . . . . (Atlantic)
Bill Haley & His Comets; *Bill Haley & His Comets' Greatest Hits* . . . . . .(MCA)
Bill Haley & His Comets-Golden Hits . . . . (MCA)
Elvis Presley; *For LP Fans Only* . . . . (RCA)
Rocker . . . . (RCA)
ST/This Is Elvis . . . . (RCA)
Fats Domino; *Fats Domino's Greatest Hits* . . . .(MCA)
Huey Lewis and the News; *Four Chords & Several Years Ago* . . . . . . (Elektra)
NRBQ; *At Yankee Stadium* . . . . (Mercury)
Vern Gosdin; *Best Of Vern Gosdin*. . . . .(Warner Bros.)
She's Leaving Home
Al Jarreau; *All Fly Home*. . . . .(Warner Bros.)
Beatles; *Beatles-Box Set* . . . . (Capitol)
Beatles-Love Songs . . . . (Capitol)
Sgt. Pepper's Lonely Hearts Club Band . . . . (Capitol)
Silver Morning
Kenny Rankin; *Silver Morning*. . . . .(Little David)
Six O'Clock
Lovin' Spoonful; *Lovin' Spoonful-Anthology* . . . . (Rhino)
Six-Thirty Sunday Morning
Peter Allen; *Taught By Experts*. . . . . (A&M)

Skating Away On The Thin Ice Of A New Day
Jethro Tull; *"M.U."-Best Of*. (Chrysalis)
Bursting Out. . . . . (Chrysalis)
Original Masters . . . . (Chrysalis)
War Child . . . . (Chrysalis)
Slide
Goo Goo Dolls; *Dizzy Up The Girl* . . . .(Warner Sunset/Reprise)
Slow Train To Dawn
The The & Neneh Cherry; *Infected* . . . . (Epic)
Softly, As In A Morning Sunrise
Artie Shaw; *Artie Shaw Plays 22 Original Big Band Recordings-1938-1939*. . . . . (Hindsight)
Big Bands In Hi-Fi-#1-Let's Dance-C . . . . (Capitol)
Bing Crosby; *Bing: His Legendary Years-1931-1957*. . . . . . (MCA)
Bobby Darin; *That's All* . . . .(Atlantic)
Dianne Reeves; *I Remember* . . . .(Blue Note)
Sonny Rollins; *Best Of Sonny Rollins-The Blue Note Years* . . . .(Blue Note)
Some Beautiful Morning
Al Jolson; *Music From The New York Stage (1890-1920)-#4-1917-1920-C*. . . . . (Pearl)
Sun Comes Up, It's Tuesday
Cowboy Junkies; *Caution Horses* . . . . (RCA)
Sunday Morning
Velvet Underground; *Live At Max's Kansas City* . . . . . . (Collectables)
Sunday Morning Blues
Big Joe Turner; *Big Joe Is Here*. . . . . (Savoy)
Have No Fear Big Joe Is Here . . . . (Savoy)
Sunday Morning Coming Down
Johnny Cash; *Classic Cash-Hall Of Fame Series* . . . . (Mercury)
Johnny Cash's Greatest Hits-#2. . . . . (Columbia)
The Man In Black-His Greatest Hits. . . . . (Legacy)
Kris Kristofferson; *Me & Bobby McGee* . . . . (Columbia)
Songs Of Kris Kristofferson . . . . (Columbia)
Vikki Carr; *Best Of Vikki Carr* . . . . (EMI)
Willie Nelson; *Willie* . . . . (RCA)
Willie Nelson Sings Kristofferson. . . . . (Columbia)
Sunday Morning Fool
Michael Dinner; *Great Pretenders* . . . .(Fantasy)
Sunday Morning Movies
Bonnie Koloc; *Bonnie Koloc*. . . . .(Ovation)
Bonnie Koloc-At Her Best . . . .(Ovation)
Sunday Morning Radio
Sha Na Na; *Sh-Boom* . . . . (Accord)
Sunday Morning Sunshine
Harry Chapin; *Harry Chapin-Anthology*. . . . . (Elektra)
Sunday Sunrise
Brenda Lee; *Brenda Lee-Greatest Country Hits* . . . . (MCA)
Sunflower
Glen Campbell; *Best Of Glen Campbell* . . . . (Capitol)
Glen Campbell-Live . . . . (Capitol)
Southern Nights . . . . (Capitol)
Sunrise
White Mountain Singers; *Best Of The White Mountain Singers* . . . . . . (Folk Era)
Memories-Live! . . . . (Folk Era)
Sunrise . . . . (Takoma)
Sunrise
Jay Beckenstein; *Eye Contact* . . . .(Windham Hill)
Sunrise
Triplets; *...Thicker Than Water*. . . . . (Mercury)
Sunrise
Uriah Heep; *Best Of Uriah Heep*. . . . . (Mercury)
Magician's Birthday. . . . . (Mercury)
Sunrise
Paul Kantner/Jefferson Starship; *Blows Against The Empire* . . . .(RCA)
Sunrise
Joe Sample; *Carmel* . . . . (MCA)
Joe Sample-Collection . . . . (GRP)
Sunrise
Jimmy Cliff; *Cliff Hanger* . . . . (Columbia)
Sunrise
Eric Carmen; *Eric Carmen-The Definitive Collection*. . . . . . . (Arista)
Sunrise
New Order; *Low-Life* . . . . (Qwest)
Sunrise
Originals; *Motown Superstar Series-#10-Originals* . . . . (Motown)
Sunrise
Chet Atkins & George Benson; *Stay Tuned*. . . . . (Columbia)
Sunrise
Seals & Crofts; *Takin' It Easy* . . . . (Warner Bros.)
Sunrise
Grateful Dead; *Terrapin Station* . . . . (Arista)
Sunrise In La Jolla
Kilauea; *Antigua Blue* . . . .(Brainchild)
Sunrise In Mexico
Clifford Jordan; *Starting Time*. . . . . (Jazz Land)
Sunrise Over Haleakala
Merl Saunders & Jerry Garcia; *Blues From The Rainforest-A Musical Suite* . . . . (Sumertone)

Sunrise Serenade
Frankie Carle & His Orchestra; *Big Band Instrumentals-16 Most Requested*. . . . . (Columbia)
Glenn Miller; *Best Of Glenn Miller* . . . . (Bluebird)
Glenn Miller-A Legendary Performer-#1 & 2 . . . . (Bluebird)
Glenn Miller & His Orchestra; *Glenn Miller & His Orchestra-Pure Gold* . . . . (Bluebird)

Sunrise, Sunset
Original Cast; *Fiddler On The Roof*. . . . . (RCA Victor)

Sunset To Sunrise
Duprees; *Best Of The Duprees*. . . . . (Rhino)

Sunshine Saturday Morning
Jim Aikin; *Light's Broken Speech Revived* . . . . (Linden)

Sweet September Morning
Buffy Sainte-Marie; *She Used To Wanna Be A Ballerina* . . . . . . (Vanguard)

Sweet Tuesday Morning
Badfinger; *Straight Up*. . . . . (Apple)

Tears In The Morning
Beach Boys; *Sunflower* . . . . (Caribou)

Tell Me I Was Dreaming
Travis Tritt; *Ten Feet Tall And Bulletproof* . . . . . (Warner Bros.)
Travis Tritt's Greatest Hits-From The Beginning. . . . . (Warner Bros.)

Tequila Sunrise
Alan Jackson; *Common Thread-Songs Of The Eagles-C*. . . . . . . (Giant)
Eagles; *Desperado*. . . . . (Asylum)
Eagles/Their Greatest Hits 1971-1975 . . . . (Asylum)
Hell Freezes Over . . . . (Geffen)

Texas Morning
Michael Nesmith & The First National Band; *Complete Michael Nesmith* . . . . (Pacific Arts)

Then The Morning Comes
Smash Mouth; *Astro Lounge* . . . . (Interscope)
Now That's What I Call Music!-#4-C . . . . (Virgin)

Thursday Morning Garden Club
Buddy Winfield; *45-#167* . . . . (Nationwide Sound Distrib.)

Till The Morning Comes
Grateful Dead; *American Beauty*. . . . . (Warner Bros.)
Neil Young; *After The Gold Rush* . . . . (Reprise)

To Raise The Morning Star
Bruce Cockburn; *Stealing Fire* . . . . (Columbia)

To The Morning
Dan Fogelberg; *Home Free* . . . . (Columbia)

Too Many Mornings
Original Broadway Cast; *Follies* . . . . (Capitol)

Touch Me In The Morning
Diana Ross; *12 #1 Hits From The '70s-C* . . . . (Motown)
20 Greatest Songs In Motown History-C . . . . (Motown)
Diana Ross-All The Great Hits . . . . (Motown)
Diana Ross-Anthology . . . . (Motown)
Diana Ross-The Ultimate Collection . . . . (Motown)
Evening With Diana Ross . . . . (Motown)
Touch Me In The Morning . . . . (Motown)

Touch The Morning
Don Gibson; *Best Of Don Gibson-#1* . . . . (Curb)
Don Gibson-18 Greatest Hits . . . . (Curb)

Train Leaves Here This Morning
Eagles; *Eagles* . . . . (Asylum)

Two O'Clock In The Morning
Stuart Duncan; *Stuart Duncan*. . . . . (Rounder)

Violets Of Dawn
Blues Project; *No Time Like The Right Time-Best Of The Blues Project* . . . . (Rhino)
Eric Andersen; *Best Of Eric Andersen*. . . . . (Vanguard)
Troubadours Of The Folk Era-#1-C . . . . (Rhino)

Wake Up Morning
Rex Allen, Jr.; *Country Comfort* . . . . (Plantation)
Today's Generation . . . . (SSS International)

Wake Up Sunshine
Chicago; *Chicago II*. . . . . (Chicago)

Wednesday Morning, 3 AM
Simon & Garfunkel; *Collected Works*. . . . . (Columbia)
Wednesday Morning 3 A.M. . . . . (Columbia)

When The Morning Comes
Daryl Hall & John Oates; *Abandoned Luncheonette* . . . . (Atlantic)
No Goodbyes . . . . (Atlantic)

When The Morning Comes
Bryan Adams; *Bryan Adams* . . . . (A&M)

Where The Blue Of The Night Meets The Gold Of The Day
Bing Crosby; *All-Time Best Of* . . . . (Curb)
Best Of Bing Crosby . . . . (MCA)
Where The Blue Of The Night Meets The Gold Of The Day . . . . . . (Biograph)

Who Will Buy?
Barbra Streisand; *The Second Barbra Streisand Album* . . . . . (Columbia)
Original Broadway Cast; *Oliver!*. . . . . (RCA Victor)
Original London Cast; *Oliver!*. . . . . (EMI-Angel)

Will It Be Love By Morning
Michael Martin Murphey; *Best Of Michael Martin Murphey* . . . . . (Liberty)
Heart Never Lies . . . . (Liberty)

Will You Be There (In The Morning)
Heart; *Desire Walks On* . . . . (Capitol)

Woke Up In Love
Exile; *Exile*. . . . . (Epic)
Exile's Greatest Hits . . . . (Epic)

Woke Up This Morning
A3; *Exile On Coldharbour Lane* . . . . (C2/Columbia)
The Sopranos-Music From The HBO Original Series . . . . (Sony Music Soundtrax)

World Is Waiting For The Sunrise
Benny Goodman; *I Like Jazz-Essence Of Benny Goodman* . . . . . . (Columbia)
Benny Goodman Orchestra & Quartet; *Let's Dance* . . . . (Laserlight)
Les Paul & Mary Ford; *The World Is Waiting For The Sunrise* . . . . (Laserlight)
Roy Clark & Buck Trent; *Banjo Bandit* . . . . (MCA)

You Don't Have To Cry
Crosby, Stills & Nash; *Crosby, Stills & Nash*. . . . . (Atlantic)

You Were Meant For Me
Jewel; *Pieces Of You* . . . . (Atlantic)

You Were On My Mind
We Five; *Baby Boomer Classics-Folk Sixties-C* . . . . . (JCI Assoc. Labels)
Billboard Top Pop Hits-1965-C . . . . (Rhino)

MOTIVATION, Ambition, Determination, Encouragement, Inspiration, Try

> See Also: **ADVICE, BACK ON MY FEET, DESIRE, EGO, FAITH, FEAR & COURAGE, FRIENDS, GOD, HELP, HOLDING ON, LIFE, OPTIMISM, STRONG**

(Everything I Do) I Do It For You
Bryan Adams; *ST/Robin Hood: Prince Of Thieves* . . . . (Morgan Creek)
Waking Up The Neighbours . . . . (A&M)

(Your Love Keeps Lifting Me) Higher And Higher
Bette Midler; *Bette Midler* . . . . (Atlantic)
Bonnie Bramlett; *It's Time* . . . . (Capricorn)
Jackie Wilson; *Billboard Top R&B Hits-1967-C* . . . . (Rhino)
Jackie Wilson's Greatest Hits . . . . (Brunswick)
Jackie Wilson's Greatest Hits-#2 . . . . (Brunswick)
Reet Petite-Best Of Jackie Wilson . . . . (Columbia)
The Jackie Wilson Story . . . . (Epic)
Very Best Of Jackie Wilson . . . . (Rhino)
Rita Coolidge; *Anytime...Anywhere*. . . . . (A&M)
Havana Jam . . . . (Columbia)
Rita Coolidge-Classics-#5 . . . . (A&M)
Rita Coolidge's Greatest Hits . . . . (A&M)

10 Miles To Go On A 9 Mile Road
Jim White; *No Such Place* . . . . (Luaka Bop)

10,000 Horses
Candlebox; *Happy Pills* . . . . (Maverick)

Against The Wind
Bob Seger & The Silver Bullet Band; *Against The Wind* . . . . . . (Capitol)
Nine Tonight . . . . (Capitol)
ST/Forrest Gump. . . . . (Epic/Sony Music Soundtrax)

Ain't No Stoppin' Us Now
McFadden & Whitehead; *Ten Years Of #1 Hits-C* . . . . (Philadelphia Int'l)

All For You
Sister Hazel; *Somewhere More Familiar* . . . . (Universal)
Sister Hazel. . . . . (Universal)

All My Friends
Counting Crows; *This Desert Life* . . . . (David Geffen Co.)

All Star
Smash Mouth; *Astro Lounge* . . . . (Interscope)
Now That's What I Call Music!-#3-C . . . . (Virgin)

All The Way To Reno (You're Gonna Be A Star)
R.E.M.; *Reveal* . . . . (Warner Bros.)

Almost Home
Mary Chapin Carpenter; *Party Doll And Other Favorites* . . . . . (Columbia)

Amigone
Goo Goo Dolls; *Dizzy Up The Girl* . . . . (Warner Sunset/Reprise)

Another Op'nin', Another Show
Original Cast; *Kiss Me Kate* . . . . (Sony Music Classical)
Kiss Me Kate . . . . (MCA)
Kiss Me Kate . . . . (EMI-Angel)
There's No Business Like Show Business: Broadway Showstoppers-C . . . . (Sony Broadway)

Another Try
America; *Encore-More Greatest Hits* . . . . (Rhino)

April Showers
Al Jolson; *Best Of Al Jolson* . . . . (MCA)
The Al Jolson Story-#2 . . . . (MCA)
Judy Garland; *Hits Of Judy Garland* . . . . (Capitol)
Judy . . . . (Capitol)

At The Same Time
Barbra Streisand; *Higher Ground* . . . . (Columbia)

Auctioneer, The
Leroy Van Dyke; *Deep In The Heart Of Country-C*. . . . . (Drive)

Babylon
David Gray; *White Ladder* . . . . (ATO/RCA)
Back On Top
Van Morrison; *Back On Top* . . . . (Point Blank/Virgin)
Bad Boy For Life
P. Diddy & The Bad Boy Family; *The Saga Continues* . . . . (Bad Boy/Arista)
Totally Hits 2001-C . . . . (Arista)
Badlands
Bruce Springsteen; *Bruce Springsteen's Greatest Hits* . . . . (Columbia)
Darkness On The Edge Of Town . . . . (Columbia)
Bruce Springsteen & The E Street Band; *Bruce Springsteen & The E Street Band Live/1975-85* . . . . (Legacy)
Be Your Own Girl
Wallflowers; *The Wallflowers* . . . . (Virgin)
Beautiful
Carole King; *Tapestry* . . . . (Epic)
Beautiful Day
U2; *All That You Can't Leave Behind* . . . . (Interscope)
Now That's What I Call Music!-#6-C . . . . (Virgin)
Beautiful Life
Ace Of Base; *Bridge* . . . . (Arista)
MTV Party To Go-#9-C . . . . (Tommy Boy)
Because You Loved Me
Celine Dion; *All The Way...A Decade Of Song* . . . . (550 Music)
Diana, Princess Of Wales-Tribute-C . . . . (Columbia)
Falling Into You . . . . (550 Music)
Before I Go
John Hiatt; *Crossing Muddy Waters* . . . . (Vanguard)
Bend It Until It Breaks
John Anderson; *John Anderson's Greatest Hits* . . . . (BNA)
Best Man I Can Be
Ginuwine, R.L., Tyrese, Case; *ST/The Best Man* . . . . . . (Sony Music Soundtrax)
Blackbird
Beatles; *Beatles-Box Set* . . . . (Capitol)
The Beatles (White Album) . . . . (Capitol)
Crosby, Stills & Nash; *CSN* . . . . (Atlantic)
Paul McCartney; *Unplugged (The Official Bootleg)* . . . . (Capitol)
Wings; *Wings Over America* . . . . (Capitol)
Bleeders
Wallflowers; *Bringing Down The Horse* . . . . (Interscope)
Bleeding Me
Metallica; *Load* . . . . (Elektra)
Boxer, The
Simon & Garfunkel; *Bridge Over Troubled Water* . . . . (Columbia)
Collected Works . . . . (Columbia)
Simon & Garfunkel's Greatest Hits . . . . (Columbia)
The Concert In Central Park . . . . (Warner Bros.)
Brand New Day
Sting; *Brand New Day* . . . . (A&M)
Brass In Pocket (I'm Special)
Pretenders; *Pretenders* . . . . (Sire)
Pretenders-The Singles . . . . (Sire)
Bridge Over Troubled Water
Aretha Franklin; *Aretha Franklin-30 Greatest Hits* . . . . (Rhino)
Aretha Franklin's Greatest Hits . . . . (Atlantic)
Live At Fillmore West . . . . (Atlantic)
Paul Simon; *America: A Tribute To Heroes-C* . . . . (Interscope)
Concert In The Park-August 15 1991 . . . . (Warner Bros.)
Paul Simon In Concert/Live Rhymin' . . . . (Columbia)
Simon & Garfunkel; *Bridge Over Troubled Water* . . . . (Columbia)
Collected Works . . . . (Columbia)
God Bless America-C . . . . (Columbia)
Simon & Garfunkel's Greatest Hits . . . . (Columbia)
The Concert In Central Park . . . . (Warner Bros.)
Bring On The Rain
Jo Dee Messina with Tim McGraw; *Burn* . . . . (Curb)
Broken Wing
Martina McBride; *Evolution* . . . . (RCA)
Brother, Brother
Carole King; *Music* . . . . (Epic)
Burn
Jo Dee Messina; *Burn* . . . . (Curb)
Can't Take That Away (Mariah's Theme)
Mariah Carey; *Rainbow* . . . . (Columbia)
Can't We Try
Dan Hill; *Dan Hill* . . . . (Columbia)
Greatest Hits And More...Let Me Show You . . . . (Spontaneous)
Dan Hill & Vonda Shepherd; *Chicken Soup For The Couples Soul-C* . . . (Rhino)
Caravan Of Love
Isley, Jasper, Isley; *Caravan Of Love* . . . . (CBS Associated)
Carol
Chuck Berry; *Berry Is On Top* . . . . (Chess)
Chuck Berry-Golden Hits . . . . (Mercury)
Chuck Berry's Greatest Hits . . . . (Everest)
Roll Over Beethoven . . . . (Allegiance)
Rolling Stones; *England's Newest Hit Makers/The Rolling Stones* . . . . . (Abkco)
Get Yer Ya-Ya's Out! . . . . (Abkco)
Change The World
Eric Clapton; *ST/Phenomenon* . . . . (Reprise)

Change Your Mind
Sister Hazel; *Fortress* . . . . (Universal)
Changes
2Pac; *2Pac Greatest Hits* . . . . (Amaru/Death Row/Interscope)
Chante's Got A Man
Chante Moore; *Now That's What I Call Music!-#3-C* . . . . (Virgin)
This Moment Is Mine . . . . (Silas)
Chestnut Mare
Byrds; *Best Of The Byrds-Greatest Hits-#2* . . . . (Columbia)
Rock Classics Of The '70s-C . . . . (Columbia)
The Byrds . . . . (Columbia)
The Byrds (Untitled) . . . . (Legacy)
Child Should Live Forever (Theme For The Eddie Cantor Fund For Children With AIDS)
Original Off-Broadway Cast; *A Hard Time To Be Single* . . . . . . (Original Cast)
Climb Ev'ry Mountain
Mormon Tabernacle Choir; *Climb Ev'ry Mountain* . . . . (Columbia)
Original Cast/Mary Martin; *The Sound Of Music* . . . . (Sony Broadway)
Trapp Family Singers; *The Sound Of Music* . . . . (Warner Bros.)
Climb That Hill
Tom Petty And The Heartbreakers; *ST/She's The One* . . . . . . (Warner Bros.)
Color Of Roses
Beth Nielsen Chapman; *Sand And Water* . . . . (Reprise)
Come On Over
Shania Twain; *Come On Over* . . . . (Mercury)
Coming Out Of The Dark
Gloria Estefan; *Gloria Estefan's Greatest Hits* . . . . (Epic)
God Bless America-C . . . . (Columbia)
Hot #1 Hits-C . . . . (Foundation)
Into The Light . . . . (Epic)
Constant Craving
k.d. lang; *Ingenue* . . . . (Sire)
Count On Me
Whitney Houston and CeCe Winans; *ST/Waiting To Exhale* . . . . (Arista)
Crash And Burn
Savage Garden; *Affirmation* . . . . (Columbia)
Cup Of Life
Ricky Martin; *Ricky Martin* . . . . (Columbia)
Cynthia
Bruce Springsteen; *Tracks* . . . . (Columbia)
Dance Into The Light
Phil Collins; *Dance Into The Light* . . . . (Atlantic)
Dance Little Sister
Terence Trent D'Arby; *Introducing The Hardline According To Terence Trent D'Arby* . . . . (Columbia)
Dancing In The Dark
Bruce Springsteen; *Born In The U.S.A.* . . . . (Columbia)
Bruce Springsteen's Greatest Hits . . . . (Columbia)
Defy You
Offspring; *Defy You-CD Single* . . . . (Columbia)
Desperately Wanting
Better Than Ezra; *Friction, Baby* . . . . (Swell/Elektra)
Didn't Cha Know
Erykah Badu; *Mama's Gun* . . . . (Motown)
Dig In
Lenny Kravitz; *Lenny* . . . . (Virgin)
Do Something
Macy Gray; *On How Life Is* . . . . (Epic)
ST/Music Of The Heart . . . . (Epic/Sony Music Soundtrax)
Do What You Do
Martina McBride; *Emotion* . . . . (RCA)
Do What You Gotta Do
Garth Brooks; *Sevens* . . . . (Capitol)
Don't Give Up
Peter Gabriel; *Shaking The Tree-Sixteen Golden Greats* . . . . . . (Geffen)
So . . . . (Geffen)
Don't Stop
Elton John; *Legacy-A Tribute To Fleetwood Mac's Rumours-C* . . . . . (Lava)
Fleetwood Mac; *25 Years-The Chain* . . . . (Warner Bros.)
Fleetwood Mac Live . . . . (Warner Bros.)
Fleetwood Mac's Greatest Hits . . . . (Warner Bros.)
Rumours . . . . (Warner Bros.)
Don't Think About Her When You're Trying To Drive
Little Village; *Little Village* . . . . (Reprise)
Don't Try So Hard
Queen; *Innuendo* . . . . (Hollywood)
Don't Try Suicide
Queen; *The Game* . . . . (Hollywood)
Don't Try To Make Me Real
Pete Townshend; *PsychoDerelict* . . . . (Atlantic)
Don't Try To Play Me Homey
Dat Nigga Daz; *ST/Gridlock'd* . . . . (Death Row)
Down In The Boondocks
Billy Joe Royal; *Billy Joe Royal's Greatest Hits* . . . . (Columbia)
Rock Classics Of The '60s-C . . . . (Columbia)
Drive
Incubus; *Make Yourself* . . . . (Immortal/Epic)
Now That's What I Call Music!-#6-C . . . . (Virgin)

Duck And Run
3 Doors Down; *Better Life* . . . . (Republic/Universal)
Enjoy Yourself
Kylie Minogue; *Enjoy Yourself* . . . . (Geffen)
Every Time I Try
Spain; *She Haunts My Dreams* . . . . (Restless)
Every Time I Try
That Dog; *Retreat From The Sun* . . . . (David Geffen Co.)
Everybody Hurts
R.E.M.; *Automatic For The People* . . . . (Warner Bros.)
Diana, Princess Of Wales-Tribute-C . . . . (Columbia)
Everybody's Trying
Poi Dog Pondering; *Wishing Like A Mountain & Thinking Like*
The Sea . . . . (Columbia)
Everybody's Trying To Be My Baby
Beatles; *Beatles '65* . . . . (Capitol)
For Sale . . . . (Capitol)
The Beatles-Anthology-#2 . . . . (Capitol)
Carl Perkins; *Blue Suede Shoes: The Very Best Of Carl Perkins* . . . (Collectables)
Carl Perkins' Greatest Hits/Finest Performances . . . . (Sun)
Carl Perkins-Original Sun Greatest Hits . . . . (Rhino)
Everything Is Everything
Lauryn Hill; *The Miseducation Of Lauryn Hill* . . . . (Ruffhouse/Columbia)
Everything's Coming Up Roses
Ethel Merman; *Broadway Magic-The 1960s-C* . . . . (Columbia)
Original Cast; *Gypsy* . . . . (Columbia)
Original London Cast; *Gypsy* . . . . (RCA)
Exhale (Shoop Shoop)
Whitney Houston; *ST/Waiting To Exhale* . . . . (Arista)
Whitney Houston's Greatest Hits . . . . (Arista)
Eye Of The Tiger
Survivor; *Eye Of The Tiger* . . . . (Scotti Bros.)
Frankenstein & Other Rock Monsters-C . . . . (CBS Associated)
Rocky Story-C . . . . (Scotti Bros.)
ST/Rocky III . . . . (EMI)
Faith Of The Heart
Rod Stewart; *ST/Patch Adams* . . . . (Universal)
Fill Her Up
Earl Scruggs & Sting; *Earl Scruggs And Friends-C* . . . . (MCA)
Finer Things, The
Steve Winwood; *Back In The High Life* . . . . (Island)
First Taste
Fiona Apple; *Tidal* . . . . (Clean Slate/Work)
Flashdance...What A Feeling
Irene Cara; *ST/Flashdance* . . . . (Casablanca)
Followin' A Feelin'
Sherrie Austin; *Followin' A Feelin'* . . . . (We/Madacy)
Forty Six & 2
Tool; *Aenima* . . . . (Freeworld/Capitol)
From A Distance
Bette Midler; *Some People's Lives* . . . . (Atlantic)
Byrds; *20 Essential Tracks From The Box Set* . . . . (Columbia)
The Byrds . . . . (Columbia)
Judy Collins; *Fires Of Eden* . . . . (Columbia)
Kathy Mattea; *Time Passes By* . . . . (Mercury)
Nanci Griffith; *Lone Star State Of Mind* . . . . (MCA)
One Fair Summer Evening . . . . (MCA)
From The Ashes
Martina McBride; *Emotion* . . . . (RCA)
From The Ashes
Rosanne Cash; *The Wheel* . . . . (Columbia)
Galilee Road
Marcus Hummon; *Looking For The Child* . . . . (Velvet Armadillo)
Get Happy
Benny Goodman; *Benny Goodman's Greatest Hits* . . . . (RCA Victor)
Ella Fitzgerald; *Harold Arlen Songbook-#2* . . . . (Verve)
Judy Garland; *Best Of Judy Garland In Hollywood* . . . . . (Turner Classic Movies)
Nat Shilkret & The Victor Orchestra; *78-#22444* . . . . (Victor)
Get Ready
Rare Earth; *Earth Tones-Essential* . . . . (Motown)
Very Best Of Rare Earth . . . . (Motown)
Temptations; *Temptations-Anthology-The Best Of The Temptations* . . (Motown)
Temptations-The Ultimate Collection . . . . (Motown)
Getaway
Earth, Wind & Fire; *Best Of Earth, Wind & Fire-#1* . . . . (Legacy)
Spirit . . . . (Columbia)
Giving You The Best That I Got
Anita Baker; *Giving You The Best That I Got* . . . . (Elektra)
Go The Distance
Michael Bolton; *All That Matters* . . . . (Columbia)
Gonna Get A Life
Mark Chesnutt; *Mark Chesnutt's Greatest Hits* . . . . (Decca)
What A Way To Live . . . . (Decca)
Got A Lot O' Livin' To Do!
Elvis Presley; *Loving You* . . . . (RCA)
The Great Performances . . . . (RCA)
The Other Sides-Worldwide Gold Award Hits, Vol. 2 . . . . (RCA)
Got To Be Strong
Maysa; *All My Life* . . . . (Rice/N-Coded)

Gotham City
R. Kelly; *ST/Batman & Robin-Music From And Inspired By The Motion*
Picture . . . . (Jive)
Greatest Love Of All
George Benson; *George Benson-Collection* . . . . (Warner Bros.)
ST/The Greatest . . . . (Arista)
Weekend In L.A. . . . . (Warner Bros.)
Whitney Houston; *Whitney Houston* . . . . (Arista)
Whitney Houston's Greatest Hits . . . . (Arista)
Greatest, The
Kenny Rogers; *She Rides Wild Horses* . . . . (Dreamcatcher)
Half Way Up
Clint Black; *Clint Black-The Greatest Hits* . . . . (RCA)
Hands
Jewel; *Spirit* . . . . (Atlantic)
Happiness
Vanessa Williams; *Next* . . . . (Mercury)
Hard Times Come Easy
Richie Sambora; *Undiscovered Soul* . . . . (Mercury)
He Will, She Knows
Kenny Rogers; *There You Go Again* . . . . (Dreamcatcher)
Healing Hands
Elton John; *Sleeping With The Past* . . . . (MCA)
Hello Brother
Louis Armstrong; *What A Wonderful World* . . . . (Decca Jazz)
Hero
Mariah Carey; *America: A Tribute To Heroes-C* . . . . (Interscope)
Diana, Princess Of Wales-Tribute-C . . . . (Columbia)
God Bless America-C . . . . (Columbia)
Mariah Carey-#1's . . . . (Columbia)
Music Box . . . . (Columbia)
He's So Fine
Chiffons; *Best Of The Girl Groups-#1-C* . . . . (Rhino)
Billboard Top Rock 'N' Roll Hits-1963-C . . . . (Rhino)
Chiffons Greatest Hits . . . . (Right Stuff)
Jody Miller; *Jody Miller's Greatest Hits* . . . . (Epic)
Hey Jude
Beatles; *Beatles 1* . . . . (Capitol)
Beatles-20 Greatest Hits . . . . (Capitol)
Past Masters-Volume Two . . . . (Parlophone)
The Beatles/1967-1970 . . . . (Capitol)
Paul McCartney; *Knebworth-The Album-C* . . . . (Polydor)
Wilson Pickett; *Wilson Pickett's Greatest Hits* . . . . (Atlantic)
Hey Young World II
Macy Gray featuring Slick Rick; *The Id* . . . . (Epic)
High Hopes
Pink Floyd; *The Division Bell* . . . . (Columbia)
High Hopes
Doris Day; *The Envelope Please-Academy Award Winning Songs (1934-*
1993)-C . . . . (Rhino)
Frank Sinatra; *Best Of The Capitol Years* . . . . (Capitol)
ST/Sinatra-CBS Mini-Series . . . . (Reprise)
High Hopes
Sammy Hagar; *Unboxed* . . . . (Geffen)
Higher
Creed; *Human Clay* . . . . (Wind-up)
Higher Ground
Stevie Wonder; *Innervisions* . . . . (Motown)
Original Musiquarium . . . . (Motown)
Higher Ground
Barbra Streisand; *Higher Ground* . . . . (Columbia)
Hold On
Jamie Walters; *Jamie Walters* . . . . (Atlantic)
Hold On (Change Is Comin')
Sounds Of Blackness; *Time For Healing* . . . . (Perspective/A&M)
Hold On To Your Dream
Stevie Wonder; *Song Review-A Greatest Hits Collection* . . . . . (Motown)
ST/The Adventures Of Pinocchio . . . . (London)
Hymn To Her
Pretenders; *Diana, Princess Of Wales-Tribute-C* . . . . . . (Columbia)
Get Close . . . . (Sire)
The Isle Of View . . . . (Warner Bros.)
I Am Woman
Helen Reddy; *Helen Reddy's Greatest Hits* . . . . (Capitol)
I Am Woman . . . . (Capitol)
I Am Woman-C . . . . (Nick At Nite)
I Don't Know How To Love Him . . . . (Capitol)
I Can See Clearly Now
Gladys Knight & The Pips; *Gladys Knight & The Pips'*
Greatest Hits . . . . (Buddah)
Imagination . . . . (Right Stuff)
On & On . . . . (Fifty One West)
Johnny Nash; *Billboard Top Rock 'N' Roll Hits-1972-C* . . . . (Rhino)
Rock Artifacts-From The Vaults-#2-C . . . . (Legacy)
I Can't Stop Loving You (Though I Try)
Leo Sayer; *Leo Sayer* . . . . (Warner Bros.)
I Didn't Know My Own Strength
Lorrie Morgan; *Lorrie Morgan's Greatest Hits* . . . . (BNA)

Reflections-Limited Edition Greatest Hits . . . . (BNA)

I Don't Want To Wait

Paula Cole; *Live On Letterman-From The Late Show* . . . . (Reprise)
Songs From Dawson's Creek . . . . (Sony Music Soundtrax)
This Fire . . . . (Imago)

I Gotta Try

Kenny Loggins; *High Adventure* . . . . (Columbia)

I Guess That's Why They Call It The Blues

Elton John; *Elton John's Greatest Hits-1976-1986* . . . . (MCA)
Too Low For Zero . . . . (MCA)

I Hope You Dance

Lee Ann Womack; *I Hope You Dance* . . . . (MCA)

I Shall Not Be Moved

Charley Patton; *King Of The Delta Blues: The Music Of Charley Patton* . . . . (Yazoo)
Mississippi John Hurt; *Best Of Mississippi John Hurt* . . . . . . (Vanguard)
Pops Staples; *Best Blues Album In The World...Ever!-C* . . . . . . (Virgin)

I Try

Macy Gray; *Now That's What I Call Music!-#4-C* . . . . (Virgin)
On How Life Is . . . . (Epic)

I Try To Think About Elvis

Patty Loveless; *Patty Loveless-Classics* . . . . (Epic)
When Fallen Angels Fly . . . . (Epic)

I Turn To You

Christina Aguilera; *Christina Aguilera* . . . . (RCA)

I Want To Take You Higher

Ike & Tina Turner; *Proud Mary-Best Of Ike & Tina Turner* . . . . . . (EMI)
Sly & The Family Stone; *Sly & The Family Stone-Anthology* . . . . . . (Epic)
Sly & The Family Stone's Greatest Hits . . . . (Epic)

I Whistle A Happy Tune

Barbara Cook; *My Little Broadway* . . . . (Sony Wonder)
Frank Sinatra; *Frank Sinatra Sings Rodgers & Hammerstein* . . . . . . (Columbia)
Micky Dolenz; *Broadway Micky* . . . . (Kid Rhino/Rhino 4 Kids)
Original Broadway Cast; *The King And I* . . . . (RCA Victor)
Original Cast; *The King And I* . . . . (MCA)

I Will Get There

Boyz II Men; *ST/The Prince Of Egypt-Inspirational* . . . . . . (DreamWorks/SKG)

I Will Love Again

Lara Fabian; *Lara Fabian* . . . . (Columbia)

I Will Survive

Gloria Gaynor; *Billboard Top Hits-1979-C* . . . . (Rhino)
I Am Woman-C . . . . (Nick At Nite)
Love Tracks . . . . (Polydor)
The Disco Years-#2-On The Beat-1978-1982-C . . . . (Rhino)

I Won't Back Down

Tom Petty; *America: A Tribute To Heroes-C* . . . . (Interscope)
Full Moon Fever . . . . (MCA)

If I Could

Barbra Streisand; *Higher Ground* . . . . (Columbia)

If I Were You

Collin Raye; *All I Can Be* . . . . (Epic)
Best Of Collin Raye-Direct Hits . . . . (Epic)

If We Make It Through December

Merle Haggard; *A Christmas Present* . . . . (Curb)
Eleven Winners . . . . (Capitol)
Goin' Home For Christmas . . . . (Sony Music Special Prod.)
Merle Haggard-Christmas Gift . . . . (Curb)
Very Best Of Merle Haggard . . . . (Capitol)

If We Try

Carpenters; *Lovelines* . . . . (A&M)
Voice Of The Heart . . . . (A&M)

If We Try

Don McLean; *Favorites & Rarities* . . . . (Gold Rush)

I'll Be Around

Rappin' 4-Tay; *Don't Fight The Feelin'* . . . . (Rag Top/EMI)

I'll Get You

Beatles; *Past Masters-Volume One* . . . . (Parlophone)
The Beatles' Second Album . . . . (Capitol)

I'll Keep Tryin'

Ugly Kid Joe; *America's Least Wanted* . . . . (Stardog)

I'll Try

Alan Jackson; *Alan Jackson-The Greatest Hits Collection* . . . . . . (Arista)

I'm A Survivor

Reba McEntire; *Reba McEntire's Greatest Hits-#3: I'm A Survivor* . . . . (MCA)

I'm Flying

Original Cast/Mary Martin; *Peter Pan-The 1954 Broadway Production* . . . . (RCA Victor)

I'm Gonna Be Somebody

Travis Tritt; *Country Club* . . . . (Warner Bros.)

I'm Gonna Get You

Eddy Raven; *Best Of Eddy Raven* . . . . (Curtom)
Eddy Raven-Greatest Country Hits . . . . (Curb)

I'm Gonna Knock On Your Door

Eddie Hodges; *History Of Cadence Records-#1-C* . . . . (Varese Vintage)

I'm Gonna Make You Love Me

Diana Ross; *Diana Ross-Anthology* . . . . (Motown)
Diana Ross-The Ultimate Collection . . . . (Motown)
Temptations; *Temptations-Anthology-The Best Of The Temptations* . . (Motown)

I'm Gonna Make You Love Me

Jayhawks; *Smile* . . . . (American/Columbia)

I'm Gonna Make You Mine

Lou Christie; *Enlightnin'ment-Best Of Lou Christie* . . . . (Rhino)

I'm Gonna Try

Monkees; *Birds Bees & The Monkees* . . . . (Rhino)

I'm Just An Old Chunk Of Coal (But I'm Gonna Be A Diamond Someday)

Billy Joe Shaver; *Restless Wind-The Legendary Billy Joe Shaver-1973-1987* . . . . (Razor & Tie)
John Anderson; *John Anderson's Greatest Hits* . . . . . . (Warner Bros.)

I'm Tryin'

Trace Adkins; *Chrome* . . . . (Capitol)

I'm Willing To Try

Joe Diffie; *Life's So Funny* . . . . (Epic)

I'm Your Angel

Celine Dion & R. Kelly; *All The Way...A Decade Of Song* . . . . . . (550 Music)
These Are Special Times . . . . (550 Music)
R. Kelly & Celine Dion; *R.* . . . . (Jive)

Imitation Of Life

R.E.M.; *Reveal* . . . . (Warner Bros.)

Impossible Dream

Andy Williams; *Andy Williams' Greatest Hits-#2* . . . . (Columbia)
Andy Williams-16 Most Requested Songs . . . . (Legacy)
Impossible Dream . . . . (Columbia)
Ed Ames; *Best Of Ed Ames* . . . . (RCA)
Ed Ames-Pure Gold . . . . (RCA)
Impossible Dream . . . . (RCA)
This Is Ed Ames . . . . (RCA)
Jack Jones; *Best Of Jack Jones* . . . . (MCA)
Kate Smith; *Best Of Kate Smith* . . . . (RCA)
Kate Smith-Legendary Performer . . . . (RCA)
Luther Vandross; *Songs* . . . . (Epic)
Original London Cast; *Man Of La Mancha* . . . . (MCA)
Robert Goulet; *Robert Goulet's Greatest Hits* . . . . (Columbia)

Impossible!; It's Possible!

Celeste Holm & Lesley Ann Warren; *Cinderella-The CBS Television Network Production* . . . . (Columbia)

In The House Of Stone And Light

Martin Page; *In The House Of Stone And Light* . . . . (Mercury)

Indian Reservation (The Lament Of The Cherokee Reservation Indian)

Don Fardon; *45-#408* . . . . (GNP/Crescendo)
Raiders; *Billboard Top Rock 'N' Roll Hits-1971-C* . . . . (Rhino)
Legend Of Paul Revere And The Raiders . . . . (Columbia)
Pop Classics Of The '70s-C . . . . (Columbia)
Super Hits Of The '70s-Have A Nice Day-#5-C . . . . (Rhino)

Infinite Possibilities

Amel Larrieux; *Infinite Possibilities* . . . . (Epic)

Inside Of Me

Little Steven & The Disciples Of Soul; *The Sopranos-Music From The HBO Original Series* . . . . (Sony Music Soundtrax)

It's My Life

Bon Jovi; *Crush* . . . . (Island/IDJMG)
Now That's What I Call Music!-#5-C . . . . (Virgin)
The Concert For New York City-C . . . . (Columbia)

It's My Time

Martina McBride; *Emotion* . . . . (RCA)

It's Not Where You Start (It's Where You Finish)

Barbara Cook; *Dorothy Fields-Close As Pages In A Book* . . . . . . (DRG)
Original Broadway Cast; *See Saw* . . . . (DRG)

It's Wonderful

Rascals; *Nuggets-#8-Acid Rock-C* . . . . (Rhino)
Once Upon A Time . . . . (Rhino)
Rascals' Greatest Hits . . . . (Atlantic)

Jump

Van Halen; *1984* . . . . (Warner Bros.)
Best Of Van Halen-#1 . . . . (Warner Bros.)
LIVE: Right here, right now. . . . . (Warner Bros.)

Jumper

Third Eye Blind; *Third Eye Blind* . . . . (Elektra)
Totally Hits-#1-C . . . . (Arista)

Just A Little Bit Of Love

Celine Dion; *Let's Talk About Love-C* . . . . (550 Music)

Just The Two Of Us

Will Smith; *Big Willie Style* . . . . (Columbia)

Just The Two Of Us

Grover Washington, Jr. & Bill Withers; *Billboard Top R&B Hits-1981-C* . . . . (Rhino)
Grover Washington, Jr.-Anthology . . . . (Elektra)
Grover Washington, Jr.-Winelight . . . . (Elektra)

Just Trying To Be

Jethro Tull; *Living In The Past* . . . . (Chrysalis)

Keep On Pushing

Curtis Mayfield & The Impressions; *Curtis Mayfield-The Anthology-1961-1977* . . . . (MCA)
Impressions; *Very Best Of The Impressions* . . . . (Rhino)

Keep Tryin'

Groove Theory; *Groove Theory* . . . . (Epic)

Keep Your Head To The Sky
Earth, Wind & Fire; *Best Of Earth, Wind & Fire-#2* .... (Columbia)
Elements Of Love: The Ballads .... (Legacy)
Head To The Sky .... (Columbia)
Keepin' Up
Alabama; *For The Record: 41 Number One Hits* .... (RCA)
King Herod's Song
Original London Cast; *Jesus Christ Superstar* .... (MCA)
Land Of Hope And Dreams
Bruce Springsteen & The E Street Band; *God Bless America-C* ..... (Columbia)
Live In New York City .... (Columbia)
Land Of The Living
Pam Tillis; *Pam Tillis' Greatest Hits* .... (Arista)
Last Day, The
Marilyn Scott; *Avenues Of Love* .... (Warner Bros.)
Lateralus
Tool; *Lateralus* .... (Volcano Entertainment)
Lean On Me
Kirk Franklin; *The Nu Nation Project* .... (Gospo Centric/Interscope)
Leaving Town
Dexter Freebish; *Life Of Saturdays* .... (Capitol)
Let A Smile Be Your Umbrella
Sammy Kaye & His Orchestra; *Best Of Sammy Kaye & His Orchestra* .. (MCA)
Let Me Try
Randy Travis; *High Lonesome* .... (Warner Bros.)
Let Me Try Again
Frank Sinatra; *Ol' Blue Eyes Is Back* .... (Reprise)
Let The River Run
Carly Simon; *Coming Around Again* .... (Arista)
ST/Working Girl .... (Arista)
Let Your Soul Be Your Pilot
Sting; *Mercury Falling* .... (A&M)
Let's Try It Again
New Kids On The Block; *Step By Step* .... (Columbia)
Letting The Cables Sleep
Bush; *Science Of Things* .... (Trauma)
Life Is Sweet
Natalie Merchant; *Ophelia* .... (Elektra)
Life's Highway
Steve Wariner; *Country Classics-#2-Today's Country Classics-C* ... (Universal)
Grand Ole Opry-75 Years-#2-C .... (MCA)
Life's Highway .... (MCA)
Lifetime
Maxwell; *Now* .... (Columbia)
Light In Your Eyes
LeAnn Rimes; *Blue* .... (MCG/Curb)
Like The Rain
Clint Black; *Clint Black-The Greatest Hits* .... (RCA)
Little Bit Of Soul
Music Explosion; *Best Of Ohio Express & Other Bubblegum*
Smashes-#1-C .... (Rhino)
Cruisin'-1967-C .... (Increase)
Million-Dollar Memories-#1-C .... (RCA)
Little White Cloud That Cried
Johnnie Ray; *Best Of Johnnie Ray* .... (Columbia)
Best Of Johnnie Ray .... (Exact)
Johnnie Ray's Greatest Hits .... (Sony Music Special Prod.)
Livin' On A Prayer
Bon Jovi; *America: A Tribute To Heroes-C* .... (Interscope)
Cross Road-14 Classic Grooves .... (Mercury)
Slippery When Wet .... (Jambco)
The Concert For New York City-C .... (Columbia)
Lock And Load
Bob Seger; *It's A Mystery* .... (Capitol)
Look For The Silver Lining
Alberta Hunter; *Look For The Silver Lining* .... (Columbia)
Chet Baker; *Let's Get Lost-Best Of Chet Baker Sings* .... (Blue Note)
Dave Brubeck Quartet; *Stardust* .... (Fantasy)
Judy Garland; *Best Of Judy Garland In Hollywood* ..... (Turner Classic Movies)
Marion Harris; *78-#3367* .... (Columbia)
Love A Little Stronger
Diamond Rio; *'90s Hot Country-C* .... (K-Tel)
Diamond Rio's Greatest Hits .... (Arista)
Diamond Rio-Super Hits .... (Arista)
Hit Country '96-C .... (K-Tel)
Love A Little Stronger .... (Arista)
Love Can Build A Bridge
Judds; *Love Can Build A Bridge* .... (MCA)
Love Can Move Mountains
Celine Dion; *All The Way...A Decade Of Song* .... (550 Music)
Celine Dion .... (Epic)
Love Is The Power
Michael Bolton; *This Is The Time-The Christmas Album* .... (Columbia)
Love Will Find Its Way To You
Reba McEntire; *Last One To Know* .... (MCA)
Reba McEntire's Greatest Hits Volume Two .... (MCA)
Maggie May
Rod Stewart; *Absolutely Live* .... (Warner Bros.)

Best Of Rod Stewart .... (Mercury)
Billboard Top Rock 'N' Roll Hits-1971-C .... (Rhino)
Every Picture Tells A Story .... (Mercury)
Rod Stewart's Greatest Hits .... (Warner Bros.)
Sing It Again, Rod .... (Mercury)
Storyteller/The Complete Anthology: 1964-1990 ...... (Warner Bros.)
Make It Right
Econoline Crush; *Brand New History* .... (Restless)
Mama Tried
Grateful Dead; *Grateful Dead (Skull & Roses)* .... (Warner Bros.)
John Anderson & Marty Stuart; *Mama's Hungry Eyes-Merle Haggard*
Tribute-C .... (Arista)
Merle Haggard; *Jailhouse Rock (Hits From The Big*
House)-C .... (Sony Music Special Prod.)
Merle Haggard & The Strangers; *Best Of Merle Haggard & The*
Strangers .... (Capitol)
For The Record: Merle Haggard-43 Legendary Hits .... (BNA)
Okie From Muskogee .... (Capitol)
Songs I'll Always Sing .... (Capitol)
Very Best Of Merle Haggard .... (Capitol)
Me
Paula Cole; *This Fire* .... (Imago)
Milk & Honey
Original Cast; *Milk & Honey* .... (RCA Victor)
Million Miles
Bob Dylan; *Time Out Of Mind* .... (Columbia)
Miseducation Of Lauryn Hill
Lauryn Hill; *The Miseducation Of Lauryn Hill* .... (Ruffhouse/Columbia)
Moment To Myself
Macy Gray; *On How Life Is* .... (Epic)
More We Try, The
Kenny Loggins; *High Adventure* .... (Columbia)
Most Precarious
Blues Traveler; *Straight On Till Morning* .... (A&M)
New Attitude
Patti LaBelle; *Classic Soul-C* .... (MCA)
I Am Woman-C .... (Nick At Nite)
Soundtrack Smashes-'80s & More-C .... (MCA)
ST/Beverly Hills Cop .... (MCA)
Next Voice You Hear
Jackson Browne; *The Next Voice You Hear-Best Of Jackson Browne* ... (Elektra)
No Fear
Terri Clark; *Fearless* .... (Mercury)
No Good Trying
Syd Barrett; *Madcap Laughs, The* .... (Capitol)
Norma Jean Riley
Diamond Rio; *Diamond Rio* .... (Arista)
Diamond Rio's Greatest Hits .... (Arista)
Of Thee I Sing
Sarah Vaughan; *Sarah Vaughan Sings George Gershwin* .... (Verve)
On My Own
Patti LaBelle & Michael McDonald; *Chicken Soup For The Couples*
Soul-C .... (Rhino)
Patti LaBelle's Greatest Hits .... (MCA)
Winner In You .... (MCA)
On My Own
Reba McEntire; *Starting Over* .... (MCA)
On The Side Of Angels
LeAnn Rimes; *You Light Up My Life-Inspirational Songs* .... (Curb)
On The Sunny Side Of The Street
Diana Krall; *Stepping Out* .... (Justin Time)
Frank Sinatra; *Come Swing With Me!* .... (Capitol)
One More For The Road .... (Capitol)
Sentimental Journey .... (Capitol)
The Capitol Years .... (Capitol)
Judy Garland; *Best Of Judy Garland* .... (MCA)
Louis Armstrong; *Best Of Louis Armstrong* .... (MCA)
Chicago Concert 1956 .... (Columbia)
Jazz Club-Vocal .... (Verve)
Music Autobiography .... (MCA)
Ted Lewis & His Orchestra; *Charming Gents Of Stage & Screen-C* .... (Legacy)
Those Wonderful Years: Puttin' On The Ritz-C .... (JCI Assoc. Labels)
One Headlight
Wallflowers; *Bringing Down The Horse* .... (Interscope)
One More Try
Divine; *Fairy Tales* .... (Pendulum)
One More Try
George Michael; *Faith* .... (Columbia)
One More Try
Richard Marx; *Paid Vacation* .... (Capitol)
One More Try
Rolling Stones; *Out Of Our Heads* .... (Abkco)
One More Try
Kristine W.; *Dance Mix USA-#6-C* .... (Warlock)
Land Of The Living .... (RCA)
One More Try
Timmy T; *Time After Time* .... (Quality)
One Step At A Time
Brenda Lee; *Brenda Lee-Anthology-#1 & #2* .... (MCA)

Only In America
Brooks & Dunn; *Steers & Stripes* . . . . (Arista)
Only The Strong Survive
Elvis Presley; *From Elvis In Memphis* . . . . (RCA)
 Memphis Record . . . . (RCA)
Jerry Butler; *Best Of Jerry Butler* . . . . (Mercury)
 Best Of Jerry Butler . . . . (Rhino)
O-o-h Child
Five Stairsteps; *Didn't It Blow Your Mind: Soul Hits Of The
 '70s-#2-C* . . . . (Rhino)
 Five Stairsteps' Greatest Hits . . . . (Collectables)
 Radio Active Hits-#2-C . . . . (Accord)
Spinners; *Best Of The Spinners* . . . . (Motown)
Valerie Carter; *Just A Stone's Throw Away* . . . . (Columbia)
 ST/Over The Edge . . . . (Warner Bros.)
Open Your Eyes
Yes; *Open Your Eyes* . . . . (Beyond)
Optimistic
Radiohead; *Kid A* . . . . (Capitol)
Original Prankster
Offspring; *Conspiracy Of One* . . . . (Columbia)
Over There
Glenn Miller; *Original Recordings-#3-Army/Air Force Band* . . . . (Pair)
Glenn Miller & His Army/Air Force Band; *Glenn Miller-A Legendary
 Performer-#3* . . . . (Bluebird)
Mormon Tabernacle Choir; *God Bless America* . . . . (Sony Music Classical)
Paperback Writer
Beatles; *Beatles 1* . . . . (Capitol)
 Beatles-20 Greatest Hits . . . . (Capitol)
 Beatles-Box Set . . . . (Capitol)
 Hey Jude . . . . (Capitol)
 Past Masters-Volume Two . . . . (Parlophone)
 The Beatles/1962-1966 . . . . (Capitol)
Paul McCartney; *Paul Is Live* . . . . (Capitol)
Piano & I
Alicia Keys; *Songs In A Minor* . . . . (J)
Pick Yourself Up
Diana King; *When I Look In Your Eyes* . . . . (GRP)
Frank Sinatra; *Sinatra and Swingin' Brass* . . . . (Reprise)
Fred Astaire; *Starring Fred Astaire* . . . . (Columbia)
 That's Dancing . . . . (EMI)
Pinch Me
Barenaked Ladies; *Maroon* . . . . (Reprise)
 Totally Hits-#3-C . . . . (Atlantic)
Place In The Sun
Stevie Wonder; *Looking Back* . . . . (Motown)
 Stevie Wonder's Greatest Hits . . . . (Motown)
Please Please Me
Beatles; *Beatles-Box Set* . . . . (Capitol)
 Please Please Me . . . . (Parlophone)
 The Beatles/1962-1966 . . . . (Capitol)
 The Early Beatles . . . . (Capitol)
Pop Ya Collar
Usher; *All About U* . . . . (LaFace)
Pretend
Nat "King" Cole; *Capitol Collectors Series-Nat "King" Cole* . . . . . . (Capitol)
 The Nat "King" Cole Story . . . . (Capitol)
 Unforgettable . . . . (Capitol)
Promise
Eve 6; *Horrorscope* . . . . (RCA)
Promise Me You'll Try
Jennifer Lopez; *On The 6* . . . . (Work)
Promise To Try
Madonna; *Like A Prayer* . . . . (Sire)
Promised Land
Bruce Springsteen; *Darkness On The Edge Of Town* . . . . (Columbia)
Bruce Springsteen & The E Street Band; *Bruce Springsteen & The E Street
 Band Live/1975-85* . . . . (Legacy)
Prove It All Night
Bruce Springsteen; *Darkness On The Edge Of Town* . . . . (Columbia)
Pump The Bass
D.J. Jazzy Jeff & The Fresh Prince; *He's The D.J. I'm The Rapper* . . . . . . (Jive)
Pump Up The Jam
Technotronic; *Pump Up The Jam-The Album* . . . . (SBK)
 Rock The First-#3-C . . . . (Priority)
Pump Up The Volume
M/A/R/R/S; *ST/Bright Lights Big City* . . . . (Warner Bros.)
Racing In The Street
Bruce Springsteen; *Darkness On The Edge Of Town* . . . . (Columbia)
Bruce Springsteen & The E Street Band; *Bruce Springsteen & The E Street
 Band Live/1975-85* . . . . (Legacy)
Reach
Gloria Estefan; *Destiny* . . . . (Epic)
Reach For The Light
Steve Winwood; *ST/Balto* . . . . (MCA)
Recover Your Soul
Elton John; *The Big Picture* . . . . (Rocket)
Relentless
Brian Bromberg; *Oasis Smooth Jazz Awards Collection* . . . . . (Native Language)

River, The
Garth Brooks; *Ropin' The Wind* . . . . (Liberty)
 The Limited Series . . . . (Capitol)
Roll With It
Steve Winwood; *Rock The First-#2-C* . . . . (Sandstone Music)
 Roll With It . . . . (Virgin)
 ST/Nuns On The Run . . . . (Mercury)
Rose Is Still A Rose
Aretha Franklin; *A Rose Is Still A Rose* . . . . (Arista)
Sailin' Shoes
Little Feat; *Sailin' Shoes* . . . . (Warner Bros.)
 Waiting For Columbus . . . . (Warner Bros.)
Save The Children
Diana Ross; *Diana Ross-Anthology* . . . . (Motown)
 Touch Me In The Morning . . . . (Motown)
Gil Scott-Heron; *Gil Scott-Heron* . . . . (Bluebird)
 Revolution Will Not Be Televised . . . . (Flying Dutchman)
Marvin Gaye; *Marvin Gaye Live At The London Palladium* . . . . (Motown)
 Marvin Gaye-Anthology . . . . (Motown)
 Musical Testament 1964-1984 . . . . (Motown)
 What's Going On . . . . (Motown)
Say You, Say Me
Lionel Richie; *Back To Front* . . . . (Motown)
 Dancing On The Ceiling . . . . (Motown)
Scary Kisses
Voice Of The Beehive; *Sex And Misery* . . . . (Discovery)
Searchin' My Soul
Vonda Shepard; *ST/Songs From "Ally McBeal" Featuring Vonda
 Shepard* . . . . (550/Epic)
 The Radical Light . . . . (Vesperally)
Send It On
D'Angelo; *Voodoo* . . . . (Cheeba Sound/Virgin)
Sending Me Angels
Kathy Mattea; *Love Travels* . . . . (Mercury)
Sense Of Purpose
Pretenders; *Isle Of View* . . . . (Warner Bros.)
 Packed . . . . (Sire)
Shackles (Praise You)
Mary Mary; *Thankful* . . . . (C2/Columbia)
She's Gonna Make It
Garth Brooks; *Sevens* . . . . (Capitol)
Shining Star
Earth, Wind & Fire; *Best Of Earth, Wind & Fire-#1* . . . . (Legacy)
 Eternal Dance . . . . (Columbia)
 Gratitude . . . . (Legacy)
 That's The Way Of The World . . . . (Legacy)
Shoes You're Wearing
Clint Black; *Nothin' But The Taillights* . . . . (RCA)
Smile
Dexter Gordon; *Best Of Dexter Gordon* . . . . (Blue Note)
Lyle Lovett; *ST/Hope Floats* . . . . (Capitol)
Nat "King" Cole; *The Nat "King" Cole Story* . . . . (Capitol)
Natalie Cole; *Unforgettable With Love* . . . . (Elektra)
Tony Bennett; *The Movie Song Album* . . . . (Columbia)
 Tony Bennett's All-Time Greatest Hits . . . . (Columbia)
Some People
Original Cast; *ST/Gypsy* . . . . (Columbia)
Somebody's Trying To Tell Me Something
Midnight Oil; *10-9-8-7-6-5-4-3-2-1* . . . . (Columbia)
Someday
Steve Earle & The Dukes; *Guitar Town* . . . . (MCA)
 Shut Up And Die Like An Aviator . . . . (MCA)
Someday We'll All Be Free
Alicia Keys; *America: A Tribute To Heroes-C* . . . . (Interscope)
Donny Hathaway; *Best Of Donny Hathaway* . . . . (Atco)
James Ingram; *It's Real* . . . . (Warner Bros.)
Somehow, Somewhere, Someway
Kenny Wayne Shepherd; *Trouble Is...* . . . . (Revolution)
Someone Else's Dream
Faith Hill; *It Matters To Me* . . . . (Warner Bros.)
Sometimes
Strokes; *Is This It* . . . . (RCA)
Somewhere
Aretha Franklin; *Aretha's Jazz* . . . . (Rhino)
Barbra Streisand; *The Broadway Album* . . . . (Columbia)
Dave Brubeck; *Music From West Side Story* . . . . (Columbia)
Jose Carreras; *Amigos Para Siempre-Friends For Life* . . . . (Atlantic)
Original Cast; *ST/West Side Story* . . . . (Sony Broadway)
Tom Waits; *Tom Waits-Anthology* . . . . (Asylum)
Stand Up
Keb' Mo'; *The Door* . . . . (550/Epic/Okeh)
Start The Commotion
Wiseguys; *Now That's What I Call Music!-#8-C* . . . . (Virgin)
 The Antidote . . . . (Mammoth)
Stayin' Alive
Bee Gees; *Bee Gees' Greatest* . . . . (Polydor)
 ST/Saturday Night Fever . . . . (Polydor)
 ST/Stayin' Alive . . . . (Polydor)

Step By Step
Whitney Houston; *ST/The Preacher's Wife* . . . . (Arista)
Step Into The Light
Dust For Life; *Dust For Life* . . . .(Wind-up)
Stepping Stone
Lari White; *Stepping Stone* . . . . (Lyric Street)
Straight Lines
Wood; *Songs From Stamford Hill* . . . .(Columbia)
Stuck In A Moment You Can't Get Out Of
U2; *All That You Can't Leave Behind* . . . . (Interscope)
Sunny Side To Every Situation
Original Broadway Cast; *42nd Street* . . . . (RCA Victor)
Superstar
Lauryn Hill; *The Miseducation Of Lauryn Hill* . . . . (Ruffhouse/Columbia)
Survivor
Destiny's Child; *Now That's What I Call Music!-#7-C* . . . .(Virgin)
Survivor . . . . (Columbia)
Sweet Dreams (Are Made Of This)
Eurythmics; *Eurythmics' Greatest Hits* . . . . (Arista)
Sweet Dreams (Are Made Of This) . . . .(RCA)
Marilyn Manson; *Smells Like Children* . . . . (Interscope)
Sweet Inspiration
Sweet Inspirations; *Best Of The Sweet Inspirations* . . . . (Soul Classics)
Great R&B Female Groups-Hits Of The '60s-C . . . . (K-Tel)
Swim
Madonna; *Ray Of Light* . . . . (Maverick)
Swinging On A Star
Bing Crosby; *All-Time Best* . . . .(Curb)
Best Of Bing Crosby . . . . (MCA)
Dion And The Belmonts; *Dion And The Belmonts-Their Best* . . . .(Laurie)
Frank Sinatra; *Frank Sinatra Sings The Songs Of Van Heusen
& Cahn* . . . .(Reprise)
Take It To The Limit
Eagles; *Eagles Live* . . . . (Asylum)
Eagles/Their Greatest Hits 1971-1975 . . . . (Asylum)
One Of These Nights . . . . (Asylum)
Takes A Little Time
Amy Grant; *Behind The Eyes* . . . .(A&M)
Tell Him
Exciters; *Best Of The Girl Groups-#2-C* . . . .(Rhino)
ST/Big Chill . . . . (Motown)
ST/My Best Friend's Wedding . . . . (Work/Epic)
Tell Him . . . . (Collectables)
Patti Drew; *Tell Him-Golden Classics* . . . . (Collectables)
Vonda Shepard; *ST/Songs From ''Ally McBeal'' Featuring Vonda
Shepard* . . . .(550/Epic)
Tell Me It's Real
K-Ci & JoJo; *It's Real* . . . . (Rock Land/Interscope)
Now That's What I Call Music!-#3-C . . . .(Virgin)
That's How You Know It's Love
Deana Carter; *Did I Shave My Legs For This?* . . . .(Capitol)
That's Life
David Lee Roth; *Eat 'Em & Smile* . . . . (Warner Bros.)
Frank Sinatra; *Frank Sinatra's Greatest Hits!* . . . . (Reprise)
Frank Sinatra-The Reprise Collection . . . . (Reprise)
Sinatra Reprise-The Very Good Years . . . . (Reprise)
That's Life . . . .(Reprise)
That's The Way (I'm Only Trying To Help You)
Culture Club; *Colour By Numbers* . . . .(Virgin)
That's The Way It Is
Celine Dion; *All The Way...A Decade Of Song* . . . . (550 Music)
Collector's Series-Celine Dion-#1 . . . . (550 Music)
That's The Way Love Is
Marvin Gaye; *M.P.G.* . . . . (Motown)
Marvin Gaye-Anthology . . . . (Motown)
Marvin Gaye-Super Hits . . . . (Motown)
That's The Way Of The World
Earth, Wind & Fire; *Best Of Earth, Wind & Fire-#1* . . . . (Legacy)
Eternal Dance . . . . (Columbia)
Love Shouldn't Hurt-C . . . . (Qwest)
Pop Classics Of The '70s-C . . . . (Columbia)
That's The Way Of The World . . . . (Legacy)
Theme From ''Gimme A Break''
Original Soundtrack; *Television's Greatest Hits-#3-1970s & 1980s-C* . . .(TVT)
There Will Come A Day
Faith Hill; *America: A Tribute To Heroes-C* . . . . (Interscope)
Breathe . . . . (Warner Bros.)
There's A Hero
Billy Gilman; *God Bless America-C* . . . . (Columbia)
There's Gotta Be Something Better Than This
Original Cast/Gwen Verdon; *Sweet Charity* . . . . (Columbia)
They All Laughed
Carmen McRae; *Setting Standards* . . . .(Pair)
Ella Fitzgerald & Louis Armstrong & Oscar Peterson Trio; *Great American
Songwriters-#1George & Ira Gershwin-C* . . . . (Rhino)
Fred Astaire; *Starring Fred Astaire* . . . . (Columbia)
Sarah Vaughan; *Sarah Vaughan Sings George Gershwin Songbook,
Vol. 1* . . . . (Emarcy)

Tony Bennett; *Steppin' Out* . . . .(Columbia)
Thirty-Three
Smashing Pumpkins; *Mellon Collie And The Infinite Sadness* . . . . (Virgin)
This Land Is Your Land
Bruce Springsteen & The E Street Band; *Bruce Springsteen & The E Street
Band Live/1975-85* . . . .(Legacy)
Glen Campbell; *All American* . . . . (Liberty)
Lee Greenwood; *American Patriot* . . . . (Capitol)
Odetta, Arlo Guthrie & Company; *Tribute To Woody
Guthrie-C* . . . . (Warner Bros.)
Pete Seeger; *God Bless America-C* . . . . (Columbia)
Pete Seeger Sings Woody Guthrie . . . . (Smithsonian Folkways)
Pete Seeger-Complete Carnegie Hall Concert-1963 . . . .(Columbia)
Weavers; *Weavers' Greatest Hits* . . . . (Vanguard)
Woody Guthrie; *Greatest Songs Of Woody Guthrie-C* . . . . (Vanguard)
Troubadours Of The Folk Era-#1-C . . . .(Rhino)
Woody Guthrie . . . . (Vanguard)
Through Your Hands
Don Henley; *ST/Michael* . . . . (Revolution)
Thunder Road
Bruce Springsteen; *Born To Run* . . . .(Columbia)
Bruce Springsteen's Greatest Hits . . . . (Columbia)
Bruce Springsteen & The E Street Band; *Bruce Springsteen & The E Street
Band Live/1975-85* . . . .(Legacy)
'Til I Get It Right
Tammy Wynette; *Tammy Wynette's Biggest Hits* . . . . (Epic)
Tammy Wynette's Greatest Hits-#3 . . . . (Epic)
Tears Of Fire-25th Anniversary Collection . . . . (Epic)
Trisha Yearwood; *Tammy Wynette...Remembered-C* . . . . (Asylum)
Till You Love Me
Reba McEntire; *Read My Mind* . . . . (MCA)
To Be Loved By You
Wynonna; *Revelations* . . . . (Curb/MCA)
Wynonna-Collection . . . .(Curb)
To Beat The Devil
Johnny Cash; *Johnny Cash-16 Biggest Hits-#2* . . . . (Legacy)
To Try For The Sun
Donovan; *Sunshine Superman* . . . . (Epic)
Trouble Man
Angie Stone; *Black Diamond* . . . .(Arista)
Try
Pennywise; *About Time* . . . . (Epitaph)
Try
Billy Pilgrim; *Billy Pilgrim* . . . . (Atlantic)
Try (A Little Harder)
Aaron Neville; *The Tattooed Heart* . . . .(A&M)
Try (Just A Little Bit Harder)
Janis Joplin; *I Got Dem Ol' Kozmic Blues Again Mama* . . . .(Columbia)
Try A Little Harder
Rolling Stones; *Singles Collection-The London Years* . . . . (Abkco)
Try A Little Kindness
Glen Campbell; *Best Of Glen Campbell* . . . .(Capitol)
Glen Campbell-Best Of The Early Years . . . . (Curb)
Glen Campbell's Greatest Hits . . . . (Capitol)
Try A Little Tenderness
Aretha Franklin; *Sweet Bitter Love* . . . . (Columbia)
David Sanborn; *ST/The Mirror Has Two Faces* . . . . (Columbia)
Otis Redding; *Best Of Otis Redding* . . . .(Atco)
Best Of Otis Redding . . . . (Atlantic)
Live In Europe . . . . (Atco)
The Otis Redding Story . . . . (Atlantic)
Very Best Of Otis Redding . . . . (Rhino)
Three Dog Night; *Best Of Three Dog Night* . . . . (MCA)
Try A Little Tenderness
Rod Stewart; *Out Of Order* . . . . (Warner Bros.)
Try Again
Aaliyah; *Now That's What I Call Music!-#4-C* . . . .(Virgin)
ST/Romeo Must Die . . . .(BlackGround Enterp./Atlantic)
Try Again
Big Star; *Number 1 Record-Radio City* . . . . (Stax)
Try Again
Sugar; *Besides* . . . . (Rykodisc)
Try All You Want
Electronic; *Electronic* . . . . (Warner Bros.)
Try And Love Again
Eagles; *Hotel California* . . . . (Asylum)
Try It Baby
Marvin Gaye; *20th Century Masters-The Millennium Collection-The Best Of
Marvin Gaye-#1 (The '60s)* . . . . (Motown)
Marvin Gaye-Anthology . . . . (Motown)
Motown Classic Hits-#5-C . . . . (Motown)
Try It One More Time
Allman Brothers Band; *Enlightened Rogues* . . . . (Polydor)
Try Me
Bob Marley & The Wailers; *Best Of Bob Marley* . . . . (Madacy)
Try Me Again
Linda Ronstadt; *Hasten Down The Wind* . . . . (Asylum)
Try Me I Know We Can Make It
Donna Summer; *Love Trilogy* . . . . (Casablanca)

Try Me On, I'm Very You
Deee-Lite; *World Clique*. . . . . (Elektra)
Try Me One More Time
Charmers; *Dynamite Ska-#3* . . . . (Eclipse)
Try Not To Breathe
R.E.M.; *Automatic For The People* . . . .(Warner Bros.)
Try So Hard
Tesla; *Bust A Nut* . . . . (Geffen)
Try Some, Buy Some
George Harrison; *Living In The Material World*. . . . . (Capitol)
Try The Love
Nanci Griffith; *Other Voices, Too (A Trip Back To Bountiful)* . . . . . . (Elektra)
Try This For Sighs
Adam Ant; *Friend Or Foe* . . . . (Epic)
Try To Believe
Oingo Boingo; *Dark At The End Of The Tunnel* . . . . (MCA Special Prod.)
Try To Conform
Pennywise; *Unknown Road* . . . . (Epitaph)
Try To Remember
Original Cast; *Fantasticks* . . . . (Polydor)
Try To See It My Way
Bryan Adams; *Bryan Adams*. . . . . (A&M)
Try Too Hard
Dave Clark Five; *History Of The Dave Clark Five* . . . . (Hollywood)
Try Try Try
Julian Cope; *20 Mothers* . . . . (American)
Try Whistling This
Neil Finn; *Try Whistling This* . . . .(Work)
Try Your Love Again
James Ingram; *It's Your Night-C* . . . . (Qwest)
Tryin'
Eagles; *Eagles* . . . . (Asylum)
Tryin' To Get Over You
Vince Gill; *I Still Believe In You* . . . .(MCA)
Tryin' To Get To Heaven
Bob Dylan; *Time Out Of Mind* . . . . (Columbia)
Tryin' To Get To You
Elvis Presley; *Elvis Recorded Live On Stage In Memphis* . . . . . . (RCA)
Tryin' To Grow A Chin
Frank Zappa; *Sheik Yerbouti*. . . . . (Zappa)
Tryin' To Throw Your Arms Around The World
U2; *Achtung Baby*. . . . . (Island)
Trying Not To Think About It
Juliana Hatfield; *Please Do Not Disturb* . . . . (Bar/None)
Trying So Hard To Forget
Fleetwood Mac; *Complete Blue Horizon Sessions 1967-1969* . . . . (Sire)
Trying Times
Boyz II Men; *Boyz II Men II* . . . . (Motown)
Trying To Cry
Joe Jackson; *Laughter And Lust* . . . . (Virgin)
Trying To Find Purpose
Vertical Horizon; *There And Back Again* . . . . (RCA)
Trying To Get Away
Grand Funk Railroad; *Phoenix* . . . . (Capitol)
Trying To Get Through
Hothouse Flowers; *Home* . . . . (London)
Trying To Get To Heaven Before They Close The Door
Bob Dylan; *Time Out Of Mind* . . . . (Columbia)
Trying To Love Two Women
Oak Ridge Boys; *Oak Ridge Boys' Greatest Hits* . . . .(MCA)
Oak Ridge Boys-Collection . . . .(MCA)
Together. . . . .(MCA)
Tryouts For The Human Race
Sparks; *Profile-The Ultimate Sparks Collection* . . . . (Rhino)
Tubthumping
Chumbawamba; *Tubthumper* . . . . (Universal)
Two Story House
George Jones & Tammy Wynette; *George Jones & Tammy Wynette-16
Biggest Hits*. . . . . (Epic/Legacy)
Unbreakable
Michael Jackson; *Invincible* . . . .(Epic)
Union Maid
Judy Collins; *Tribute To Woody Guthrie-C* . . . .(Warner Bros.)
Up Where We Belong
Joe Cocker; *Joe Cocker Live* . . . . (Capitol)
Joe Cocker & Jennifer Warnes; *ST/An Officer And A Gentleman* . . . . (Island)
The Island Story-1962-1987-25th Anniversary-C . . . . (Island)
Use The Force
Jamiroquai; *Traveling Without Moving* . . . . (Work/Epic)
Vaya Con Dios
Bing Crosby; *The Radio Years-#2* . . . .(Crescendo)
Freddy Fender; *Freddy Fender-Collection* . . . . (Reprise)
Les Paul & Mary Ford; *Memories Are Made Of This-C* . . . . (Capitol)
Roger Whittaker; *All-Time Heart-Touching Favorites*. . . . . (Capitol)
Voice Of The Heart
Diana Ross; *Take Me Higher* . . . . (Motown)
Walk Away
Cool For August; *Grand World* . . . .(Warner Bros.)

Walk Hand In Hand
Andy Williams; *I Like Your Kind Of Love-The Best Of The Cadence
Years* . . . .(Varese Vintage)
Walk On
U2; *America: A Tribute To Heroes-C* . . . .(Interscope)
Now That's What I Call Music!-#8-C . . . .(Virgin)
Wash It Away
Black Lab; *Your Body Above Me* . . . .(David Geffen Co.)
Way It Is
Bruce Hornsby & The Range; *Heart Of Rock-C* . . . . (Columbia)
Nipper's Greatest Hits Of The '80s-C . . . . (RCA)
The Way It Is . . . . (RCA)
We Ain't Got Nothin' Yet
Blues Magoos; *Billboard Top Pop Hits-1967-C* . . . . (Rhino)
We Are Family
Sister Sledge; *Atlantic Records 50 Years-The Gold Anniversary
Collection-C* . . . .(Atlantic)
Best Of Sister Sledge-1973-1985 . . . . (Rhino)
Chicken Soup For The Soul: I'll Be There For You-Songs Of Friendship,
Brotherhood And Sisterhood-C. . . . . (Rhino)
ST/The Full Monty . . . . (RCA Victor)
We Are Family . . . . (Rhino)
We Are The Champions
Big Blue Wrecking Crew; *Baseball's Greatest Hits-C* . . . . (Rhino)
Queen; *Billboard Top Rock 'N' Roll Hits-1978-C*. . . . . (Rhino)
Live At Wembley '86 . . . . (Hollywood)
Live Killers . . . . (Hollywood)
News Of The World. . . . . (Hollywood)
Queen's Greatest Hits I & II . . . . (Hollywood)
We Gotta Get Out Of This Place
Animals; *Best Of The Animals*. . . . .(Abkco)
Greatest Hits Live!-Rip It To Shreds. . . . . (I.R.S.)
Sullivan Years-British Invasion . . . . (TVT)
Fear; *The Record* . . . .(Slash)
We Shall Overcome
Bruce Springsteen; *Where Have All The Flowers Gone: The Songs Of Pete
Seeger* . . . .(Appleseed)
James Cleveland & The Troubadors; *James Cleveland & The
Troubadors* . . . . (Savoy)
Joan Baez; *Carry It On* . . . . (Vanguard)
Joan Baez In Concert, Part 2 . . . . (Vanguard)
Mahalia Jackson; *God Bless America-C* . . . . (Columbia)
Pete Seeger; *Bitter & The Sweet* . . . .(Mobile Fidelity Sound Lab)
Pete Seeger's Greatest Hits . . . . (Columbia)
We Trying To Stay Alive
Wyclef Jean; *Carnival* . . . . (Refugee)
We Will Rock You
Queen; *Live At Wembley '86* . . . . (Hollywood)
Live Killers . . . . (Hollywood)
News Of The World. . . . . (Hollywood)
Queen's Greatest Hits I & II . . . . (Hollywood)
ST/FM. . . . . (MCA)
Weather
Amel Larrieux; *Infinite Possibilities* . . . . (Epic)
Welcome To Try
Gordon Lightfoot; *Waiting For You* . . . . (Reprise)
We'll Meet Again
Vera Lynn; *ST/Dr. Strangelove: Music From The Films Of Stanley
Kubrick* . . . .(Silva Classics)
We'll Meet Again . . . . (Living Era)
We'll Never Turn Back
Freedom Singers; *Best Of Broadside 1962-1968: Anthems Of The
American Underground From The Pages Of Broadside
Magazine-C*. . . . .(Smithsonian Folkways)
Well, Alright!
CeCe Winans; *Everlasting Love* . . . .(PMG/Atlantic)
Wow Gospel 1999-C. . . . .(Verity/BMG)
We're Gonna Hold On
George Jones & Tammy Wynette; *George Jones & Tammy Wynette-16
Biggest Hits*. . . . . (Epic/Legacy)
We're In This Together
Nine Inch Nails; *The Fragile*. . . . . (Nothing)
What About Now
Lonestar; *Lonely Grill* . . . .(BNA)
What If
Reba McEntire; *CD Single-#72026*. . . . . (MCA)
When You Believe
Mariah Carey & Whitney Houston; *Mariah Carey-#1's* . . . . (Columbia)
ST/The Prince Of Egypt . . . .(DreamWorks/SKG)
Whitney Houston & Mariah Carey; *My Love Is Your Love* . . . . (Arista)
When You're Smiling (The Whole World Smiles With You)
Frank Sinatra; *Sinatra's Swingin' Session!!!* . . . . (Capitol)
Judy Garland; *Judy Garland-At Carnegie Hall*. . . . . (Capitol)
Judy Garland's Greatest Hits. . . . .(Curb)
One & Only . . . . (Capitol)
Louis Armstrong; *Best Of Louis Armstrong* . . . . (MCA)
Louis Armstrong-Vol. 4-In New York . . . . (Columbia)
Musical Autobiography-#2. . . . . (MCA)

Whole New You
Shawn Colvin; *Whole New You* . . . . (Columbia)
Wholy Holy
Aretha Franklin; *Aretha Franklin-30 Greatest Hits* . . . . (Rhino)
Marvin Gaye; *Musical Testament 1964-1984* . . . . (Motown)
What's Going On . . . . (Motown)
Why Don't We Try Again
Brian May; *Another World* . . . . (Hollywood)
Why Don't You Try
Leonard Cohen; *New Skin For The Old Ceremony* . . . . (Columbia)
Why Don't You Try Me
Ry Cooder; *Borderline* . . . . (Warner Bros.)
Why Try To Change Me Now
Frank Sinatra; *Best Of The Columbia Years-1943-1952* . . . . (Columbia)
Concepts . . . . (Capitol)
I've Got A Crush On You . . . . (Legacy)
Wild Angels
Martina McBride; *Angels Among Us-C* . . . . (RCA)
Wild Angels . . . . (RCA)
Wild One
Faith Hill; *Take Me As I Am* . . . . (Warner Bros.)
Wind Beneath My Wings
Bette Midler; *ST/Beaches* . . . . (Atlantic)
Gary Morris; *Chicken Soup For The Soul: I'll Be There For You-Songs Of
Friendship, Brotherhood And Sisterhood-C* . . . . (Rhino)
Country Love Songs-C . . . . (Warner Bros.)
Gary Morris-Hits . . . . (Warner Bros.)
Why Lady Why . . . . (Warner Bros.)
James Galway; *Wind Beneath My Wings* . . . . (RCA)
Lee Greenwood; *Somebody's Gonna Love You* . . . . (MCA)
Lou Rawls; *When The Night Comes* . . . . (Epic)
Roger Whittaker; *Roger Whittaker Greatest Hits* . . . . (RCA)
Wind Beneath My Wings . . . . (RCA)
Willie Nelson; *City Of New Orleans* . . . . (Columbia)
Windows Of The World
Burt Bacharach; *One Amazing Night* . . . . (N2K)
Dionne Warwick; *Dionne Warwick Collection-Her All-Time
Greatest Hits* . . . . (Rhino)
Dionne Warwick-Definitive Collection . . . . (Arista)
Isaac Hayes; *Live At The Sahara Tahoe* . . . . (Stax)
Mormon Tabernacle Choir; *Voices In Harmony* . . . . (CBS Masterworks)
Pretenders; *ST/1969* . . . . (Polydor)
With A Little Luck
Paul McCartney; *All The Best!* . . . . (Capitol)
Wings; *London Town* . . . . (Capitol)
Wings Greatest . . . . (Capitol)
Without You
Van Halen; *Van Halen 3* . . . . (Warner Bros.)
Wolverton Mountain
Claude King; *American Originals-Claude King* . . . . (Columbia)
Best Of Claude King . . . . (Gusto)
Billboard Top Country Hits-1962-C . . . . (Rhino)
Super Hits Of The '60s-C . . . . (Epic)
Woman In Me
Jessica Simpson featuring Destiny's Child; *Sweet Kisses* . . . . (Columbia)
World's Greatest, The
R. Kelly; *ST/Ali* . . . . (Interscope)
Wrong Side Of Memphis
Matraca Berg; *Bittersweet Surrender* . . . . (RCA)
Trisha Yearwood; *Grand Ole Opry-75 Years-#1-C* . . . . (MCA)
Hearts In Armor . . . . (MCA)
XXX's And OOO's
Trisha Yearwood; *Thinkin' About You* . . . . (MCA)
You Can Get It If You Really Want
Jimmy Cliff; *In Concert-Best Of Jimmy Cliff* . . . . (Reprise)
ST/The Harder They Come . . . . (Mango)
You Can Make It If You Try
Sly & The Family Stone; *Sly & The Family Stone-Anthology* . . . . (Epic)
Sly & The Family Stone's Greatest Hits . . . . (Epic)
Stand! . . . . (Epic)
You Can Make It If You Try
Rolling Stones; *England's Newest Hit Makers/The Rolling Stones* . . . . . (Abkco)
You Can't Be A Beacon (If Your Light Don't Shine)
Donna Fargo; *Country Gospel-#4-C* . . . . (Platinum Disc)
The Happiest Girl In The Whole U.S.A. . . . . (Universal)
You Didn't Try To Call Me
Frank Zappa/Mothers Of Invention; *Cruising With Ruben &
The Jets* . . . . (Barking Pumpkin)
You Get What You Give
New Radicals; *Maybe You've Been Brainwashed Too* . . . . (MCA)
Now That's What I Call Music!-#2-C . . . . (Virgin)
You Gotta Be
Des'ree; *Diana, Princess Of Wales-Tribute-C* . . . . (Columbia)
I Ain't Movin' . . . . (550 Music)
You Gotta Love That
Neal McCoy; *Neal McCoy's Greatest Hits* . . . . (Atlantic)
Today's Country Love-C . . . . (K-Tel)
You Gotta Love That! . . . . (Atlantic)

You'll Be In My Heart
Phil Collins; *ST/Tarzan* . . . . (Hollywood)
You'll Never Walk Alone
Andy Williams; *Unchained Melody-Greatest Songs* . . . . (Curb)
Jim Nabors; *Jim Nabors-16 Most Requested Songs* . . . . (Legacy)
Judy Garland; *Best Of The Capitol Masters-One & Only Box* . . . . . . (Capitol)
Mormon Tabernacle Choir; *Climb Ev'ry Mountain* . . . . (Columbia)
Original Broadway Cast; *Carousel* . . . . (Angel)
Original Cast; *Carousel* . . . . (MCA)
Pink Floyd; *Meddle* . . . . (Capitol)
Your Life Is Now
John Mellencamp; *John Mellencamp* . . . . (Columbia)
You're Not Alone
Chicago; *Chicago 19* . . . . (Reprise)

MOTORCYCLES

See Also: **CARS: GENERAL, GAS STATIONS, ROAD, ROAD
ACCIDENTS, TRAVELING**

1952 Vincent Black Lightning
Richard Thompson; *Richard Thompson-Best Of Capitol Years* . . . . . . (Capitol)
Angel On My Bike
Wallflowers; *Bringing Down The Horse* . . . . (Interscope)
Black Denim Trousers & Motorcycle Boots
Cheers; *Monster Summer Hits-Drag City-C* . . . . (Capitol)
Blue Motorcycle Eyes
Havana 3 A.M.; *Havana 3 A.M.* . . . . (I.R.S.)
Born To Run
Bruce Springsteen; *Born To Run* . . . . (Columbia)
Chimes Of Freedom . . . . (Columbia)
Bruce Springsteen & The E Street Band; *Bruce Springsteen & The E Street
Band Live/1975-85* . . . . (Legacy)
Melissa Etheridge; *The Concert For New York City-C* . . . . (Columbia)
It's A Great Day To Be Alive
Travis Tritt; *Down The Road I Go* . . . . (Columbia)
Leader Of The Pack
Bette Midler; *Divine Miss M* . . . . (Atlantic)
ST/Divine Madness . . . . (Atlantic)
Original Cast; *Leader Of The Pack* . . . . (Elektra)
Shangri-Las; *21 Number One Hits-C* . . . . (Original Sound)
Billboard Top Rock 'N' Roll Hits-1964-C . . . . (Rhino)
Girl Groups-Story Of A Sound-C . . . . (Rhino)
Golden Hits Of The Shangri-Las . . . . (Mercury)
Oldies But Goodies-#15-C . . . . (Original Sound)
Radio Active Hits-#2-C . . . . (Accord)
Remember The Shangri-Las At Their Best . . . . (Collectables)
Lilies Of The Field
Gretchen Peters; *Gretchen Peters* . . . . (Purple Crayon Prod.)
Little Honda
Beach Boys; *Absolute Best-#1* . . . . (Capitol)
All Summer Long . . . . (Capitol)
Best Of The Beach Boys . . . . (Capitol)
Spirit Of America . . . . (Capitol)
Hondells; *Beach Classics-All Original
Recordings-C* . . . . (Dunhill Compact Classics)
Cruisin'-1964-C . . . . (Increase)
Motor-bike In Afrika
Peter Hammill; *The Future Now* . . . . (Blue Plate)
Motorcycle
Love And Rockets; *Love And Rockets* . . . . (Beggar's Banquet)
Motorcycle Boys
Bill Molenhof; *All Pass By* . . . . (Cexton)
Motorcycle Cowboy
Merle Haggard; *Merle Haggard-Live At Billy Bob's* . . . . (Razor & Tie)
Motorcycle Driver
Joe Satriani; *The Extremist* . . . . (Relativity)
Motorcycle Emptiness
Manic Street Preachers; *Generation Terrorists* . . . . (Columbia)
Motorcycle Mama
Sailcat; *Back To The '70s-#2-C* . . . . (Dominion Entert.)
Super Hits Of The '70s-Have A Nice Day-#8-C . . . . (Rhino)
Motorcycle Mama
Neil Young; *Comes A Time* . . . . (Reprise)
Motorcycle Mystics
Dave Stewart & The Spiritual Cowboys; *Honest* . . . . (Arista)
Motorcycle Song
Arlo Guthrie; *Alice's Restaurant* . . . . (Reprise)
Best Of Arlo Guthrie . . . . (Warner Bros.)
Motorcycle Song
Soul Brothers; *Three Hour Tour* . . . . (Scheming Intelligentsia)
My White Bicycle
Nazareth; *Hot Tracks* . . . . (A&M)
Nazareth-Classics-#16 . . . . (A&M)
Roll Me Away
Bob Seger & The Silver Bullet Band; *ST/Armageddon-The Album* . . (Columbia)

Theme From "CHiPs"
Original Soundtrack; *Television's Greatest Hits-#6-Remote Control-C* . . (TVT)

MOUNTAINS, Cliffs, Highlands, Hills, Valleys, Volcanoes
See Also: CLIMBING, DIFFICULT, MINING, NATURE, RIVERS, STONES

Ain't No Mountain High Enough
Diana Ross; *20/20-C* . . . . (Motown)
25 #1 Hits From 25 Years-C . . . . (Motown)
Diana Ross . . . . (Motown)
Diana Ross-The Ultimate Collection . . . . (Motown)
Every Great Motown Song-First 25 Years-C . . . . (Motown)
Greatest Songs By Ashford & Simpson . . . . (Motown)
Motown Legends-Diana Ross . . . . (Motown)
Motown Story-First 25 Years-C . . . . (Motown)
Motown's Biggest Pop Hits-C . . . . (Motown)
TV ST/Diana-C . . . . (Motown)
Marvin Gaye & Tammi Terrell; *20 Greatest Songs In Motown History-C* . . . . (Motown)
Classic Duets-Marvin Gaye & His Women-C . . . . (Motown)
Marvin Gaye & Tammi Terrell's Greatest Hits . . . . (Motown)
Marvin Gaye Live At The London Palladium . . . . (Motown)
Motown Grammy R&B Performances Of The '60s & '70s-C . . (Motown)
Performances Of The '60s & '70s-C . . . . (Motown)
United . . . . (Motown)
Allegheny Moon
Patti Page; *Patti Page-Golden Hits* . . . . (Mercury)
Patti Page's Greatest Hits . . . . (Columbia)
Alpine Milkman
Randy Erwin; *'Til The Cows Come Home/Cowboy Rhythm* . . . . (Really Outstanding Music)
Appalachian Dream
Diamond Rio; *Love A Little Stronger* . . . . (Arista)
Away Out On The Mountain
Jimmie Rodgers; *Best Of Jimmie Rodgers-Legendary Master Series* . . . . . (RCA)
Essential Jimmie Rodgers . . . . (RCA)
First Sessions-1927-1928-#1 . . . . (Rounder)
My Rough & Rowdy Ways . . . . (RCA)
This Is Jimmie Rodgers . . . . (RCA)
Skip Gorman; *A Cowboy's Wild Song To His Herd* . . . . (Rounder)
Tim & Mollie O'Brien; *Away Out On The Mountain* . . . . (Sugar Hill)
Banjo In The Hills
Stanley Brothers/Carl Story/Jim & Jesse; *Banjo In The Hills* . . . . (Starday)
Banjo On The Mountain
Doug Dillard Band; *Heartbreak Hotel* . . . . (Flying Fish)
Barstool Mountain
Moe Bandy; *Moe Bandy's Greatest Hits* . . . . (Columbia)
Wayne Carson; *45-#45358* . . . . (Elektra)
Bear Went Over The Mountain, The
Original Soundtrack; *Children's Favorites* . . . . (Kid Rhino/Rhino 4 Kids)
Beautiful Hills Of Galilee
Hazel Dickens; *Old-Timey Gospel Music* . . . . (Rounder)
Big Rock Candy Mountain
Burl Ives; *Burl Ives' Greatest Hits* . . . . (MCA)
Poor Wayfaring Stranger . . . . (Flapper)
Harry McClintock; *ST/O Brother, Where Art Thou?* . . . . (Mercury)
John Hartford; *ST/Down From The Mountain* . . . (Lost Highway/IDJMG)
Pete Seeger; *20 Golden Pieces Of Pete Seeger* . . . . (Bulldog)
Tex Ritter; *Capitol Collectors Series-Tex Ritter* . . . . (Capitol)
Bimbombey
Jimmie Rodgers; *Best Of Jimmie Rodgers* . . . . (Rhino)
Best Of Jimmie Rodgers . . . . (Curb)
Black Mountain Blues
Bessie Smith; *Bessie Smith-The Collection* . . . . (Legacy)
Janis Joplin; *ST/Janis* . . . . (Columbia)
Black Mountain Breakdown
Youngbloods; *Youngbloods* . . . . (RCA)
Black Mountain Rag
Doc Watson; *Doc Watson* . . . . (Vanguard)
Essential Doc Watson-#2 . . . . (Vanguard)
Newport Country Music & Blues . . . . (Vanguard)
Doc Watson/Hot Rize/Dan Crary/Peter Rowan; *Tellulive* . . . . . (Flying Fish)
Nitty Gritty Dirt Band; *Will The Circle Be Unbroken* . . . . (EMI)
Black Mountain Side
Led Zeppelin; *Led Zeppelin* . . . . (Atlantic)
Led Zeppelin-Box Set . . . . (Atlantic)
Blue Canadian Rockies
Byrds; *Sweetheart Of The Rodeo* . . . . (Columbia)
Gene Autry; *50th Anniversary* . . . . (Republic/Universal)
Live From Madison Square Garden . . . . (Republic/Universal)
Jimmy C. Newman; *Cajun Cowboy* . . . . (Plantation)
Blue Ridge Mountain Blues
Blue Ridge Rangers; *Blue Ridge Rangers* . . . . (Fantasy)
Doc Watson; *Essential Doc Watson* . . . . (Vanguard)
Earl Scruggs & John Fogerty; *Earl Scruggs And Friends-C* . . . . (MCA)

Norman Blake; *Directions* . . . . (Takoma)
Blue Ridge Mountain Sky
Marshall Tucker Band; *New Life* . . . . (AJK Music)
Blue Ridge Mountains Turnin' Green
Charley Pride; *Amazing Love* . . . . (RCA)
Blueberry Hill
Elvis Presley; *Elvis Recorded Live On Stage In Memphis* . . . . (RCA)
Loving You . . . . (RCA)
Fats Domino; *Fats Domino's Greatest Hits* . . . . (Everest)
Fats Domino's Greatest Hits . . . . (MCA)
My Blue Heaven-Best Of Fats Domino-#1 . . . . (EMI)
Little Richard; *Big Hits* . . . . (Crescendo)
Louis Armstrong; *Best Of Louis Armstrong* . . . . (MCA)
Essential Louis Armstrong . . . . (Vanguard)
I Like Jazz-Essence Of Louis Armstrong . . . . (Columbia)
Bluebirds Over the Mountain
Beach Boys; *Absolute Best-#2* . . . . (Capitol)
Beach Boys '69 (The Beach Boys Live In London) . . . . (Capitol)
Friends-20/20 . . . . (Capitol)
Sunshine Dream . . . . (Capitol)
Ritchie Valens; *Best Of Ritchie Valens* . . . . (Rhino)
History Of Ritchie Valens . . . . (Rhino)
Ritchie Valens . . . . (Rhino)
Cabin Home On The Hill
Ricky Skaggs; *Sweet Temptation* . . . . (Sugar Hill)
Cabin On A Mountain
Country Gazette; *Bluegrass Tonight* . . . . (Flying Fish)
Cabin On The Hill
Flatt & Scruggs; *Columbia Historic Edition-Flatt & Scruggs* . . . . . . (Columbia)
Lester Flatt & Earl Scruggs; *Bluegrass Super Hits-C* . . . . . . (Columbia)
Car On A Hill
Joni Mitchell; *Court & Spark* . . . . (Asylum)
Chapel On The Hill
Mello-Kings; *Mello-Kings' Greatest Hits* . . . . (Collectables)
Chestnut Mare
Byrds; *Best Of The Byrds-Greatest Hits-#2* . . . . (Columbia)
Rock Classics Of The '70s-C . . . . (Columbia)
The Byrds . . . . (Columbia)
The Byrds (Untitled) . . . . (Legacy)
Child In These Hills
Jackson Browne; *Jackson Browne* . . . . (Asylum)
Chime Bells
Elton Britt; *The RCA Years* . . . . (Collector's Choice)
Jody King; *Photographs & Memories* . . . . (Capricorn)
Cliffs Of Dover
Eric Johnson; *Ah Via Musicom* . . . . (Capitol)
Climb Ev'ry Mountain
Mormon Tabernacle Choir; *Climb Ev'ry Mountain* . . . . (Columbia)
Original Cast/Mary Martin; *The Sound Of Music* . . . . (Sony Broadway)
Trapp Family Singers; *The Sound Of Music* . . . . (Warner Bros.)
Climb That Hill
Tom Petty And The Heartbreakers; *ST/She's The One* . . . . (Warner Bros.)
Cowboy Love Song (Red River Valley)
Skip Gorman; *A Cowboy's Wild Song To His Herd* . . . . (Rounder)
Cumberland Blues
Grateful Dead; *Europe '72* . . . . (Warner Bros.)
What A Long Strange Trip It's Been: The Best Of The Grateful Dead . . . . (Warner Bros.)
Workingman's Dead . . . . (Warner Bros.)
Cumberland Gap
Woody Guthrie; *Woody Guthrie-Early Years* . . . . (Tradition)
Woody Guthrie & Cisco Houston; *Folk Songs* . . . . (Stinson)
Cumberland Mountain #9
Charlie Daniels Band; *Saddle Tramp* . . . . (Epic)
Volunteer Jam 3 & 4 . . . . (Epic)
Dance On A Volcano
Genesis; *Seconds Out* . . . . (Atlantic)
Trick Of The Tail . . . . (Atco)
Dead Man's Hill
Indigo Girls; *Swamp Ophelia* . . . . (Epic)
Diamond Head
Beach Boys; *Friends-20/20* . . . . (Capitol)
Down In The Valley
Elvis Presley; *Reconsider Baby* . . . . (RCA)
Leadbelly; *Defense Blues-Golden Classics-#2* . . . . (Collectables)
Pete Seeger; *American Favorite Ballads-#1* . . . . (Smithsonian Folkways)
Down To The Valley
Nilsson; *Everybody's Talkin': The Encore Collection* . . . . (BMG Special Prod.)
East Kentucky Mountains
Anne Hills; *Don't Panic (Panic Is On/Don't Explain)* . . . . (Hogeye)
Eruption
Van Halen; *Van Halen* . . . . (Warner Bros.)
Fire On The Mountain
Marshall Tucker Band; *Marshall Tucker Band's Greatest Hits* . . . . . (Capricorn)
Searchin' For A Rainbow . . . . (AJK Music)
South's Greatest Hits-C . . . . (Capricorn)
Fire On The Mountain
Bill Monroe & His Blue Grass Boys; *Kentucky Bluegrass* . . . . (MCA)

Fire On The Mountain
Grateful Dead; *Dead Set* . . . .(Arista)
  Shakedown Street . . . .(Arista)

Flint Hill Special
Flatt & Scruggs; *Golden Era* . . . .(Rounder)
Nitty Gritty Dirt Band; *Will The Circle Be Unbroken* . . . . (EMI)

Foggy Mountain Breakdown
Earl Scruggs & Friends; *Earl Scruggs And Friends-C* . . . .(MCA)
Flatt & Scruggs; *20 All-Time Great Recordings* . . . . (Columbia)
  Truckers' Jukebox-10 All-Time Radio Requests-C . . . . (Legacy)
Lester Flatt; *Foggy Mountain Breakdown* . . . .(RCA)
  Live Bluegrass Festival . . . .(RCA)
Tony Trischka; *Banjoland* . . . .(Rounder)

Folks Who Live On The Hill
Diana Krall; *Only Trust Your Heart* . . . .(GRP)

Fool On The Hill
Beatles; *Beatles-Box Set* . . . .(Capitol)
  Magical Mystery Tour . . . .(Capitol)
  The Beatles/1967-1970 . . . .(Capitol)

From The Indies To The Andies In His Undies
Hoosier Hot Shots; *All Time Legends Of Country Music-C* . . . .(Legacy)

Go Rest High On That Mountain
Vince Gill; *When Love Finds You* . . . .(MCA)

Go Tell It On The Mountain
Bobby Darin; *Bobby Darin-25th Day Of December* . . . .(Atco)
Bruce Cockburn; *Christmas* . . . . (Columbia)
Dolly Parton; *Home For Christmas* . . . .(Columbia)
Don McLean; *Christmas* . . . . (Curb)
Garth Brooks; *Beyond The Season* . . . .(Liberty)
Simon & Garfunkel; *Collected Works* . . . .(Columbia)
  Wednesday Morning 3 A.M. . . . .(Columbia)
Weavers; *On Tour* . . . .(Vanguard)

Gonna Build A Mountain
Monkees; *Monkees-Live-1967* . . . .(Rhino)
Original Broadway Cast; *Stop The World I Want To Get Off* . . . . (Polydor)
Sammy Davis, Jr.; *Sammy Davis, Jr.'s Greatest Songs* . . . .(Curb)

Green Rolling Hills
Bottle Hill; *Rumor In Their Own Time-#1* . . . . (Biograph)
Emmylou Harris; *Quarter Moon In A Ten Cent Town* . . . . (Warner Bros.)

Happy Wanderer
Frank Weir & His Orchestra; *Hits To Remember-C* . . . .(PolyGram Special Prod.)
Joey Miskulin; *Hooked On Polkas* . . . . (K-Tel)
Original Soundtrack; *Disney Travel Songs-C* . . . .(Disney)

Heather On The Hill
Gene Kelly; *ST/Brigadoon* . . . .(MCA)
Original Cast; *Brigadoon* . . . .(Columbia Special Prod.)

Henry
New Riders Of The Purple Sage; *Best Of New Riders Of The*
  Purple Sage . . . .(Columbia)
  Bill Graham Presents The Last Days Of The
  Fillmore-C . . . . (Epic Portrait Assoc.)
  Home Home On The Road . . . .(Columbia)
  New Riders Of The Purple Sage . . . .(Columbia)

High Country Snows
Dan Fogelberg; *High Country Snows* . . . . (Full Moon)

High On A Hill Top
Merle Haggard & The Strangers; *Best Of Merle Haggard & The*
  Strangers . . . .(Capitol)
  High On A Hill Top . . . .(Capitol)

High Sierra
Keith Carradine; *I'm Easy* . . . . (Asylum)

Higher Ground
Stevie Wonder; *Innervisions* . . . .(Motown)
  Original Musiquarium . . . .(Motown)

Higher Ground
Barbra Streisand; *Higher Ground* . . . .(Columbia)

Higher Place
Tom Petty; *Wildflowers* . . . .(Warner Bros.)

Highlands
Bob Dylan; *Time Out Of Mind* . . . .(Columbia)

Hill Where The Lord Hides
Chuck Mangione; *Best Of Chuck Mangione* . . . .(Mercury)
  Best Of Chuck Mangione . . . .(A&M)
  Chuck Mangione-Classics-#6 . . . .(A&M)
  Evening Of Magic . . . .(A&M)
  Friends & Love . . . .(Mercury)
  Together . . . .(Mercury)

Hills Of Alabam'
Kathy Mattea; *Willow In The Wind* . . . .(Mercury)

Hills Of Arkansas
Black Oak Arkansas; *Black Oak Arkansas* . . . .(Atco)

Hills Of Kentucky
Debby McClatchy & The Red Clay Ramblers; *Debby McClatchy & The Red*
  Clay Ramblers . . . . (Green Linnet)
Kendalls; *Kendalls* . . . . (Gusto)

Hills Of Old Wyomin'
Sons Of The Pioneers; *The Country Music Hall Of Fame-Sons Of The*
  Pioneers . . . .(MCA)
Tex Ritter; *The Country Music Hall Of Fame-Tex Ritter* . . . .(MCA)

House On The Hill
Turtles; *Turtle Soup* . . . .(Rhino)
  Turtle Wax-Best Of The Turtles-#2 . . . .(Rhino)

House On The Hill
Stevie Wonder; *For Once In My Life* . . . .(Motown)

House Upon A Hill
Paul Anka; *She's A Lady* . . . .(RCA)
  Very Best Of Paul Anka . . . .(Ranwood)

I Like Mountain Music
Roy Acuff; *Grand Ole Opry-75 Years-#1-C* . . . .(MCA)

If You've Got Love
John Michael Montgomery; *Kickin' It Up* . . . .(Atlantic)

I'm Always On A Mountain When I Fall
Merle Haggard; *For The Record: Merle Haggard-43 Legendary Hits* . . . . (BNA)

I'm Tryin'
Trace Adkins; *Chrome* . . . .(Capitol)

In The Hall Of The Mountain King
Duke Ellington; *Three Suites* . . . .(Columbia)
Electric Light Orchestra; *On The Third Day* . . . . (Jet)
Sounds Incorporated; *History Of British Rock-#3-C* . . . .(Rhino)

In The Valley
Marty Robbins; *Gunfighter Ballads & Trail Songs* . . . .(Legacy)

Kentucky Hills Of Tennessee
Commander Cody & His Lost Planet Airmen; *Hot Licks, Cold Steel &*
  Trucker's Favorites . . . .(MCA)

Kern River
Merle Haggard; *For The Record: Merle Haggard-43 Legendary Hits* . . . (BNA)
  Kern River . . . .(Epic)

Kilimanjaro
Juluka; *Stand Your Ground* . . . .(Warner Bros.)

King Of The Hill
Minutemen; *Ballot Result* . . . . (SST)
  Project: Mersh . . . .(SST)

King Of The Hill
Roger McGuinn; *Back From Rio* . . . .(Arista)

King Of The Hill
Quiet Riot; *Quiet Riot* . . . .(Pasha)

King Of The Mountain
Bon Jovi; *7800 Degrees Fahrenheit* . . . .(Mercury)

King Of The Mountain
George Strait; *Blue Clear Sky* . . . .(MCA)
  Latest Greatest Straitest Hits . . . .(MCA)

Ladies Of The Canyon
Joni Mitchell; *Ladies Of The Canyon* . . . .(Reprise)

Landslide
Fleetwood Mac; *25 Years-The Chain* . . . .(Warner Bros.)
  Fleetwood Mac . . . .(Reprise)
  Fleetwood Mac Live . . . .(Warner Bros.)
  The Dance . . . .(Reprise)
Smashing Pumpkins; *Pisces Iscariot* . . . . (Virgin)

Landslide
AC/DC; *Flick Of The Switch* . . . . (Atlantic)

Little Green Valley
Marty Robbins; *Gunfighter Ballads & Trail Songs* . . . .(Legacy)

Lonesome Valley
Fairfield Four; *ST/O Brother, Where Art Thou?* . . . .(Mercury)

Lost You In The Canyon
Marc Cohn; *Burning The Daze* . . . .(Atlantic)

Love Can Move Mountains
Celine Dion; *All The Way...A Decade Of Song* . . . . (550 Music)
Celine Dion . . . .(Epic)

Man From Music Mountain
Gene Autry; *The Singing Cowboy-Chapter Two* . . . . (Varese Sarabande)

Man On The Silver Mountain
Blackmore's Rainbow; *Ritchie Blackmore's R-A-I-N-B-O-W* . . . .(Polydor)
Rainbow; *Finyl Vinyl* . . . .(Mercury)

Mansion On The Hill
Hank Williams With His Drifting Cowboys; *Hank Williams-40*
  Greatest Hits . . . .(Polydor)
  Lovesick Blues . . . .(Polydor)

Mansion On The Hill
Bruce Springsteen; *Nebraska* . . . .(Columbia)
Emmylou Harris & The Nash Ramblers; *At The Ryman* . . . .(Reprise)

Mansion On The Hill
Neil Young & Crazy Horse; *Ragged Glory* . . . .(Reprise)
  WELD . . . .(Reprise)

Maybelline
Chuck Berry; *Chuck Berry-Golden Hits* . . . .(Mercury)
  Chuck Berry's Greatest Hits . . . .(Everest)
  Cruisin'-1955-C . . . .(Increase)
  Oldies But Goodies-#11-C . . . .(Original Sound)
  Super Oldies Of The '50s-#5-C . . . .(Audio Fidelity)
Johnny Rivers; *Johnny Rivers-Anthology 1964-1977* . . . .(Rhino)
  Very Best Of Johnny Rivers . . . .(EMI)

Mocking Bird Hill
Patti Page; *Patti Page-16 Most Requested Songs* . . . .(Legacy)
  Patti Page-Golden Hits . . . .(Mercury)
  Patti Page's Greatest Hits . . . .(Columbia)

Russ Morgan; *Best Of Russ Morgan* . . . .(MCA)
Morning Side Of The Mountain, The
Tommy Edwards; *It's All In The Game-The Complete Hits Of Tommy
Edwards* . . . . (Eric)
Mountain Blues
Sonny Terry; *From Spirituals To Swing* . . . . (Vanguard)
Great Blues Men-C . . . . (Vanguard)
Mountain Dew
Charlie Daniels Band; *Volunteer Jam-C* . . . . (Capricorn)
Clancy Brothers; *Clancy Brothers Greatest Hits* . . . . (Vanguard)
Doc Watson; *Old Timey Concert* . . . . (Vanguard)
Eric Weissberg; *ST/Deliverance* . . . .(Warner Bros.)
Stanley Brothers; *Stanley Series-Vol. 1-#2* . . . . (Copper Creek)
Stanley Series-Vol. 2-#2 . . . . (Copper Creek)
Mountain Greenery
Ella Fitzgerald; *Rodgers & Hart Songbook* . . . . (Verve)
Tony Bennett; *Rodgers & Hart Songbook* . . . . (DRG)
Tony Bennett Sings More Great Rodgers & Hart. . . . . (Improv)
Mountain Jam
Allman Brothers Band; *Eat A Peach.* . . . . (Polydor)
Mountain Music
Alabama; *Alabama's Greatest Hits* . . . . (RCA)
Mountain Music . . . . (RCA)
Mountain Of Love
Charley Pride; *Charley Pride's Greatest Hits-#2* . . . . (RCA)
Solid Country Gold-C . . . . (RCA)
David Houston; *American Originals-David Houston.* . . . . (Columbia)
Harold Dorman; *Collectables Presents The History Of
Rock-#10-C.* . . . . (Collectables)
Johnny Rivers; *Best Of Johnny Rivers* . . . .(EMI)
Johnny Rivers-Anthology 1964-1977. . . . . (Rhino)
Mountains
Prince and the Revolution; *Parade-Music From ''Under The Cherry
Moon''* . . . . (Paisley Park)
Mountains
Rita Coolidge; *Rita Coolidge* . . . . (A&M)
Mountain's High
Dick & Dee Dee; *'Til My Dreamin' Comes True-C* . . . . (Capitol)
Mountains Of Burma
Midnight Oil; *Blue Sky Mining* . . . . (Columbia)
Mountains Of The Moon
Grateful Dead; *Aoxomoxoa.* . . . .(Warner Bros.)
Mountainside
Sweet Vine; *Sweet Vine* . . . . (Columbia)
My Swiss Mountain Lullaby
Montana Slim; *60 Years Of Country Music-C* . . . . (RCA)
My Tennessee Mountain Home
Dolly Parton; *Best Of A Great Year-#3-C.* . . . . (RCA)
Best Of Dolly Parton . . . . (RCA)
My Tennessee Mountain Home . . . . (RCA)
Rose Maddox; *Reckless Love & Bold Adventure* . . . .(Takoma)
No Matter How High
Oak Ridge Boys; *American Dreams* . . . .(MCA)
No Mountains In The State Of Kansas
Reilly & Maloney; *Everyday* . . . . (Freckle)
Oklahoma Hills
Arlo Guthrie; *Tribute To Woody Guthrie-C* . . . .(Warner Bros.)
Hank Thompson; *Hank Thompson's All-Time Greatest Hits* . . . . (Curb)
Jack Guthrie and his Oklahomans; *Birth Of A Dream-Capitol's Early
Hits-C* . . . . (Capitol)
Great Records Of The Decade-'40s-Country-C. . . . . (Curb)
Kay Starr; *Kay Starr-Country.* . . . .(Crescendo)
Old Man From The Mountain
Merle Haggard & The Strangers; *For The Record: Merle Haggard-43
Legendary Hits* . . . . (BNA)
On Squirrel Hill
Ian Matthews; *Legacy-Collection Of New Folk Music-C* . . . . (Windham Hill)
Walking A Changing Line . . . . (Windham Hill)
On Top Of Old Smokey
Bing Crosby; *The Radio Years-#3* . . . .(Crescendo)
Weavers; *Best Of The Weavers.* . . . .(MCA)
Reunion-At Carnegie Hall-1963-#2. . . . . (Vanguard)
Weavers' Greatest Hits . . . . (Vanguard)
Oregon Hill
Cowboy Junkies; *Black Eyed Man* . . . . (RCA)
Oregon Hills
Martin Oberschelp; *Nightingale Lightdance* . . . .(Higher Octave)
Oregon Mountains
Woody Simmons; *Oregon Mountains* . . . . (Deep River)
Over The Mountain
Ozzy Osbourne; *The Ozzman Cometh* . . . .(Epic)
Over The Next Hill
Johnny Cash with The Carter Family; *Johnny Cash-16 Biggest
Hits-#2* . . . . (Legacy)
Ozark Mountain Jubilee
Oak Ridge Boys; *Deliver* . . . .(MCA)
Oak Ridge Boys' Greatest Hits 2 . . . .(MCA)
Ozark Mountain Jubilee. . . . .(MCA Special Prod.)

Peace In The Valley
Elvis Presley; *A Golden Celebration.* . . . . (RCA)
Elvis-A Legendary Performer, Volume 1 . . . . (RCA)
Million-Dollar Quartet. . . . . (RCA)
Johnny Cash; *At San Quentin* . . . . (Columbia)
Classic Cash-Hall Of Fame Series . . . . (Mercury)
J.L. Lewis/Carl Perkins-The Survivors. . . . . (Columbia)
Red Foley; *Grand Ole Opry-75 Years-#1-C* . . . . (MCA)
Purple Mountain
Scott Cossu; *Wind Dance* . . . .(Windham Hill)
Windham Hill Retrospective-C. . . . .(Windham Hill)
Rattlesnake Mountain
Patrick Sky; *Patrick Sky* . . . . (Vanguard)
Red River Valley
Gene Autry; *Cowboy Hall Of Fame* . . . . (Republic/Universal)
*The Country Music Hall Of Fame-Gene Autry-15 Of His All-Time
Greatest Hits* . . . . (Columbia)
Western Classics . . . . (Columbia)
Pete Seeger; *American Favorite Ballads-#5* . . . .(Smithsonian Folkways)
Redwood Hill
Vassar Clements; *Westport Drive* . . . . (Mind Dust Music)
Ridge Running Roan
Skip Gorman; *A Cowboy's Wild Song To His Herd.* . . . . (Rounder)
Ridgetop
Jesse Colin Young; *Best Of Jesse Colin Young-Solo Years* . . . . (Rhino)
On The Road. . . . . (Warner Bros.)
Song For Juli. . . . . (Warner Bros.)
Ridin' Down The Canyon
Gene Autry; *Columbia Historic Edition-Gene Autry* . . . . (Columbia)
Western Classics . . . . (Columbia)
Riders In The Sky; *Cowboy Way.* . . . . (MCA)
Willie Nelson & Leon Russell; *One For The Road* . . . . (Columbia)
River Deep, Mountain High
Celine Dion; *Falling Into You* . . . .(550 Music)
Erasure; *Innocents.* . . . . (Sire)
Four Tops; *Four Tops-Anthology* . . . . (Motown)
Ike & Tina Turner; *Best Of Ike & Tina Turner* . . . . (EMI)
Phil Spector's Greatest Hits-C . . . . (Spector)
Proud Mary-Best Of Ike & Tina Turner . . . . (EMI)
Tina Turner; *Simply The Best* . . . . (Capitol)
Rocky Mountain Blues
Billie Holiday; *Billie's Blues.* . . . .(Blue Note)
Duke Ellington; *Okeh Ellington* . . . . (Columbia)
Lightnin' Hopkins; *Double Blues* . . . . (Fantasy)
Soul Blues. . . . .(Prestige)
Lightnin' Hopkins & Sonny Terry; *Gotta Move Your Baby* . . . .(Prestige)
Rocky Mountain Breakdown
Poco; *Forgotten Trail-1969-1974* . . . . (Epic)
Ride The Country . . . . (Epic)
Very Best Of Poco. . . . . (Epic)
Rocky Mountain High
John Denver; *Evening With John Denver* . . . . (RCA)
John Denver's Greatest Hits . . . . (RCA)
Rocky Mountain High. . . . . (RCA)
Take Me Home, Country Roads & Other Hits . . . . (RCA)
Rocky Mountain Music
Eddie Rabbitt; *Best Of Eddie Rabbitt/Greatest Hits-II* . . . . (Warner Bros.)
Eddie Rabbitt's All-Time Greatest Hits . . . . (Warner Bros.)
Rocky Mountain Music . . . .(Elektra)
Ten Years Of Greatest Hits . . . . (Capitol)
Rocky Mountain Suite
John Denver; *Evening With John Denver* . . . . (RCA)
Farewell Andromeda . . . . (RCA)
Rocky Mountain Way
Joe Walsh; *Best Of Joe Walsh* . . . . (MCA)
Classic Rock-#1-C. . . . . (MCA)
Heavy Metal Memories-C. . . . . (Rhino)
The Smoker You Drink The Player You Get . . . . (MCA)
You Can't Argue With A Sick Mind. . . . . (MCA)
Rocky Top
Conway Twitty; *Hello Darlin'* . . . . (MCA Special Prod.)
Flying Burrito Brothers; *Close Encounters To The West Coast.* . . . . (Relix)
Osborne Brothers; *Best Of The Osborne Brothers.* . . . . (MCA)
Yesterday, Today & The Osborne Brothers . . . . (MCA)
Roy Clark; *Roy Clark In Concert* . . . . (MCA)
White Mountain Singers; *Best Of The White Mountain Singers* . . . . . . (Folk Era)
'Round About The Mountain
Kingston Trio; *At Large/Here We Go Again!* . . . . (Capitol)
Running Up That Hill
Kate Bush; *Hounds Of Love* . . . . (EMI)
The Whole Story. . . . . (EMI)
Kate Bush & David Gilmour; *Secret Policeman's Third Ball-The
Music-C.* . . . . (Virgin)
Secret Mountain Hideout
Michael Martin Murphey; *Blue Sky-Night Thunder* . . . . (Epic)
Secret Of The Andes
Victor Feldman; *Secret Of The Andes.* . . . .(Palo Alto Jazz)

Victor Feldman/Generation Band; *Best Of Victor Feldman/ Generation Band* . . . . (Nova)

She'll Be Coming 'Round The Mountain
Four Freshmen & Stan Kenton & Orchestra; *Live At Butler University* . . . .(Creative World)
Mormon Tabernacle Choir; *This Land Is Your Land* . . . . (Columbia)
Original Soundtrack; *Children's Favorites* . . . . (Kid Rhino/Rhino 4 Kids)
School Days-Kids Classics . . . .(Benson)

She's My Rock
George Jones; *19 Hot Country Requests-#2-C* . . . . (Epic)
First Time Live! . . . . (Epic)
Ladies Choice . . . . (Epic)

Shine On Ruby Mountain
Kenny Rogers And The First Edition; *Best Of Kenny Rogers And The First Edition* . . . . (K-Tel)
Kenny Rogers And The First Edition's All-Time Greatest Hits-#2 . . . . (MCA Special Prod.)

Silverthorn Mountain
Merle Haggard; *Friend In California* . . . . (Epic)

Singing Hills
Gene Autry; *50th Anniversary* . . . . (Republic/Universal)
Slim Whitman; *Best Of Slim Whitman 1952-1972* . . . . (Rhino)
Una Paloma Blanca-Best Of Slim Whitman . . . . (EMI)

Small Hills Of Offaly
Irish Tradition; *Times We've Had* . . . . (Green Linnet)

Smokey Mountain Rain
Ronnie Milsap; *Ronnie Milsap's Greatest Hits* . . . . (RCA)

Solid
Ashford & Simpson; *Chicken Soup For The Couples Soul-C* . . . . (Rhino)
Solid . . . . (Capitol)
Solid Plus Seven . . . . (Capitol)

Solsbury Hill
Peter Gabriel; *Peter Gabriel* . . . . (Atco)
Peter Gabriel/Plays Live . . . . (Geffen)
Shaking The Tree-Sixteen Golden Greats . . . . (Geffen)

Song From Half Mountain
Dan Fogelberg; *Dan Fogelberg-Souvenirs* . . . . (Full Moon)

Stony Mountain, West Virginia
Jim & Jesse; *In The Tradition* . . . . (Rounder)

Suddenly There's A Valley
Reba McEntire; *Feel The Fire* . . . . (Mercury)

Sugar Hill Saturday Night
Charlie Daniels Band; *Midnight Wind* . . . . (Epic)

Sugar Mountain
Neil Young; *Decade* . . . . (Reprise)
Neil Young & Crazy Horse; *Live Rust* . . . . (Reprise)

Sunny Hills
Bobby Caldwell; *Carry On* . . . . (Sin-Drome)

Sunny Side Of The Mountain
Bill Monroe; *Bean Blossom* . . . . (MCA)
Jimmy Martin and the Sunny Mountain Boys; *Best Of Bluegrass-C* . . . . . (K-Tel)
Nitty Gritty Dirt Band; *Will The Circle Be Unbroken* . . . . (EMI)

Sunrise Over Haleakala
Merl Saunders & Jerry Garcia; *Blues From The Rainforest-A Musical Suite* . . . . (Sumertone)

Swingtime In The Rockies
Benny Goodman; *Birth Of Swing* . . . . (Bluebird)
Carnegie Hall Jazz Concert . . . . (Columbia)
ST/Swing Kids . . . . (Hollywood)

Take Me Home, Country Roads
John Denver; *Evening With John Denver* . . . . (RCA)
John Denver's Greatest Hits . . . . (RCA)
Poems, Prayers & Promises . . . . (RCA)
Take Me Home, Country Roads & Other Hits . . . . (RCA)
Toots & The Maytals; *Brand New Second-Hand* . . . . (Rykodisc)

Tales Of Kilimanjaro
Carlos Santana; *Havana Moon* . . . . (Columbia)
Santana; *Zebop!* . . . . (Columbia)

Texas Hills
Sons Of The Pioneers; *Western Country* . . . . (Granite)

That Ain't No Mountain
Stacy Dean Campbell; *Lonesome Wins Again* . . . . (Columbia)

That's Just About Right
BlackHawk; *BlackHawk* . . . . (Arista)
The Hits-Love & Gravity . . . . (Arista)

Theme From "The Waltons"
Original Soundtrack; *CBS: The First 50 Years* . . . . (TVT)
Television's Greatest Hits-#3-1970s & 1980s-C . . . . (TVT)

There Goes The Mountain
Tom Paxton; *Heroes* . . . . (Vanguard)
New Songs From The Briarpatch . . . . (Vanguard)

There Is A Mountain
Donovan; *Donovan's Greatest Hits* . . . . (Epic)
Troubadour-Definitive Collection . . . . (Epic)

Third Stone From The Sun
Jimi Hendrix; *Essential Jimi Hendrix* . . . . (Reprise)

Kiss The Sky . . . . (Reprise)
Jimi Hendrix Experience; *Are You Experienced?* . . . . (Reprise)

Three Bells, The
Browns; *Billboard Top Country Hits-1959-C* . . . .(Rhino)
Nipper's Greatest Hits Of The '50s-#1-C . . . . (RCA)

Through Your Hands
Don Henley; *ST/Michael* . . . .(Revolution)

To Be Loved By You
Wynonna; *Revelations* . . . . (Curb/MCA)
Wynonna-Collection . . . .(Curb)

Truly Madly Deeply
Savage Garden; *Savage Garden* . . . .(Columbia)

Twelve Thirty (Young Girls Are Coming To The Canyon)
Mamas & The Papas; *Best Of The Mamas & The Papas* . . . . (MCA)
Mamas & The Papas-16 Of Their Greatest Hits . . . . (MCA)
The Papas & The Mamas . . . . (MCA)

Up Where We Belong
Joe Cocker; *Joe Cocker Live* . . . . (Capitol)
Joe Cocker & Jennifer Warnes; *ST/An Officer And A Gentleman* . . . . . . (Island)
The Island Story-1962-1987-25th Anniversary-C . . . . (Island)

Valley Of Tears
Buddy Holly; *Buddy Holly* . . . . (MCA)
Fats Domino; *Antoine "Fats" Domino* . . . .(Rhino)
My Blue Heaven-Best Of Fats Domino-#1 . . . . (EMI)

Valley Road
Bruce Hornsby & The Nitty Gritty Dirt Band; *Will The Circle Be Unbroken-#2-C* . . . .(Uni)
Bruce Hornsby & The Range; *Scenes From The Southside* . . . . (RCA)

Visionary Mountains
Joan Armatrading; *Whatever's For Us* . . . .(A&M)

Volcano
Jimmy Buffett; *Boats Beaches Bars & Ballads* . . . . (Margaritaville)
Songs You Know By Heart-Jimmy Buffett's Greatest Hit(s) . . . . (MCA)
Volcano . . . . (MCA)

Volcano
Band; *Cahoots* . . . .(Capitol)

Volcano
Count Basie; *Essential Count Basie-#2* . . . .(Columbia)

Volcano
Rupture; *Hardness Of The World* . . . . (Cotillion)
Slave . . . . (Cotillion)

Volcano Girls
Veruca Salt; *Eight Arms To Hold You* . . . . (Geffen)

Warm Valley
Duke Ellington; *Money Jungle* . . . . (Blue Note)
Paul Desmond; *Pure Desmond* . . . .(CBS Associated)

When The Golden Leaves Begin To Fall
Joe Val & The New England Bluegrass Boys; *Diamond Joe* . . . .(Rounder)
Joe Val & The New England Bluegrass Boys-Vol. 2 . . . .(Rounder)

When The Moon Comes Over The Mountain
Kate Smith; *Best Of Kate Smith* . . . . (RCA)
Kate Smith-16 Most Requested Songs . . . .(Columbia)

White Cliffs Of Dover
Kay Kyser & His Orchestra; *16 Most Requested Songs Of The '40s-#1-C* . . . .(Legacy)
Lee Andrews And The Hearts; *Lee Andrews And The Hearts' Biggest Hits* . . . .(Collectables)
Mystics; *Mystics-16 Golden Classics* . . . .(Collectables)
Righteous Brothers; *Righteous Brothers' Greatest Hits* . . . .(Verve)
Righteous Brothers-Anthology 1962-1974 . . . . (Rhino)
Rosemary Clooney; *For The Duration* . . . .(Concord Jazz)

White Mountain
Genesis; *Trespass* . . . . (MCA)

Wild Mountain Honey
Steve Miller Band; *Fly Like An Eagle* . . . .(Capitol)
Steve Miller Band's Greatest Hits-1974-78 . . . . (Capitol)

Wild Mountain Thyme
Armstrong Family; *Wheel Of The Year-Thirty Years With The Armstrong Family* . . . . (Flying Fish)
Byrds; *Fifth Dimension* . . . .(Columbia)
Joan Baez; *Farewell Angelina* . . . .(Vanguard)

Wolverton Mountain
Claude King; *American Originals-Claude King* . . . .(Columbia)
Best Of Claude King . . . . (Gusto)
Billboard Top Country Hits-1962-C . . . .(Rhino)
Super Hits Of The '60s-C . . . . (Epic)

World's Greatest, The
R. Kelly; *ST/Ali* . . . . (Interscope)

You Gave Me A Mountain
Elvis Presley; *Aloha from Hawaii via Satellite* . . . . (RCA)
Always On My Mind . . . . (RCA)
Elvis In Concert . . . . (RCA)
Marty Robbins; *Essential Marty Robbins-1951-1982* . . . .(Columbia)
Marty Robbins' All-Time Greatest Hits . . . .(Columbia)
Marty Robbins' Biggest Hits . . . .(Columbia)

You Made A Rock Of A Rolling Stone
Oak Ridge Boys; *Seasons* . . . . (MCA)

MOVIES, Actors, Actresses, Movie Theaters

See Also: *CELEBRITIES: SPECIFIC, ELVIS, HOLLYWOOD, SHOW BIZ, TELEVISION*

"B" Movie Box Car Blues
Blues Brothers; *Best Of The Blues Brothers* ....(Atlantic)
  Briefcase Full Of Blues ....(Atlantic)
Delbert McClinton; *Live From Austin* ....(Alligator)

35 Millimeter Dreams
Garland Jeffreys; *Ghost Rider* ....(A&M)
  Ghost Writer ....(A&M)

Act Naturally
Beatles; *"Yesterday"...And Today* ....(Capitol)
Buck Owens; *Beatles Originals* ....(Rhino)
Buck Owens & Ringo Starr; *Act Naturally* ....(Capitol)
Buck Owens & The Buckaroos; *Buck Owens & The Buckaroos-Live At Carnegie Hall* ....(Country Music Foundation)
Charley Pride; *Country Pride* ....(RCA)
Johnny Russell; *20 Great Country Hits-C* ....(RCA)

Action! Not Words
Def Leppard; *Pyromania* ....(Mercury)

Alone At A Drive In Movie
Olivia Newton-John & John Travolta; *ST/Grease* ......(Polydor)
Original Broadway Cast; *Grease* ....(Polydor)

Another Cheap Western/Western Movies
Michael Murphey; *Peaks Valleys Honky Tonks & Alleys* .....(Epic)

At The Movies
Bad Brains; *Rock For Light* ....(Caroline)
  The Youth Are Getting Restless-Paradiso-1987 ......(Caroline)

B Movie
Elvis Costello & The Attractions; *Get Happy!* ....(Rykodisc)

B Movie
Delbert McClinton; *Second Wind* ....(Capricorn)

B Movies
Fabulous Poodles; *Mirror Stars* ....(Epic)

Back It Up
Nils Lofgren; *Best Of Nils Lofgren* ....(A&M)
  Night After Night ....(A&M)
  Nils Lofgren ....(Rykodisc)
  Nils Lofgren-Classics-#13 ....(A&M)

Ballad Of A Teenage Queen
Johnny Cash; *Johnny Cash* ....(Sun)
  Johnny Cash-Original Golden Hits-#2 ....(Sun)
  Johnny Cash-Sun Years ....(Rhino)
  ST/Harper Valley PTA ....(Sun)
  The Legend ....(Plantation)
  The Man In Black-His Greatest Hits ....(Legacy)

Barrel Of A Gun (4,3,2,1)
Guster; *Lost & Gone Forever* ....(Hybrid/Sire)

Be True
Bruce Springsteen; *Tracks* ....(Columbia)

Breakfast At Tiffany's
Deep Blue Something; *Home* ....(RainMaker/Interscope)

Burn Hollywood Burn
Chuck D/The Roots/Zack De La Rocha; *ST/Bamboozled* ......(Motown)
Public Enemy; *Fear Of A Black Planet* ....(Def Jam)

Camera One
Josh Joplin Group; *Useful Music* ....(Artemis)

Can I Have My Money Back
Gerry Rafferty; *Can I Have My Money Back* ....(MCA)

Celluloid Heroes
Joan Jett; *The Hit List* ....(Epic)
Kinks; *Come Dancing With The Kinks-Best Of The Kinks 1977-1986* ... (Arista)
  Everybody's In Show-Biz ....(Rhino)
  The Kinks' Greatest-Celluloid Heroes ....(RCA)

Cinema Show
Genesis; *Seconds Out* ....(Atlantic)

Cool For Cats
Squeeze; *Cool For Cats* ....(A&M)
  Singles-45's and under ....(A&M)
  Squeeze-Classics-#25 ....(A&M)

Cowboy Heaven
Roy Rogers; *Peace In The Valley* ....(Pair)

Cowboy Movie
David Crosby; *If I Could Only Remember My Name* .....(Atlantic)

Creature Feature
Uptown Express; *45-#026* ....(Sutra)

Dirty Movies
Van Halen; *Fair Warning* ....(Warner Bros.)

Drive-In Movies & Dashboard Lights
Nanci Griffith; *Storms* ....(MCA)

Elvis & Marilyn
Leon Russell; *Americana* ....(Paradise)

Emma
Hot Chocolate; *Super Hits Of The '70s-Have A Nice Day-#14-C* ....(Rhino)

Face On The Cutting Room Floor
Nitty Gritty Dirt Band; *Live Two Five* ....(Capitol)

  More Great Dirt-Best Of Nitty Gritty Dirt Band ....(Warner Bros.)

Here In The Real World
Alan Jackson; *Here In The Real World* ....(Arista)

Hollywood Movie Girls
Dusty Springfield; *It Begins Again* ....(United Artists)

Honey Pie
Beatles; *The Beatles (White Album)* ....(Capitol)
  The Beatles-Anthology-#3 ....(Capitol)

It's All In The Movies
Merle Haggard & The Strangers; *Country's Greatest Hits-#6-Superstars-C* ....(Priority)
  For The Record: Merle Haggard-43 Legendary Hits ....(BNA)

I've Seen That Movie Too
Elton John; *Goodbye Yellow Brick Road* ....(Polydor)

James Dean
Eagles; *On The Border* ....(Elektra)

Just Like In The Movies
Joan Jett & The Blackhearts; *Up Your Alley* .....(Epic Portrait Assoc.)

Just Like In The Movies
Upbeats; *45-#4010* ....(Swan)

Key Largo
Bertie Higgins; *Just Another Day In Paradise* ....(Kat Family)

King Of The Silver Screen
Alice Cooper; *Lace And Whiskey* ....(Warner Bros.)

Lady Picture Show
Stone Temple Pilots; *Tiny Music...Songs From The Vatican Gift Shop* ....(Atlantic)

Late Late Late Show
Stella Parton; *Stella Parton* ....(Elektra)

Late Late Show
Dakota Station; *Spotlight On...* ....(Capitol)
Nat "King" Cole; *Big Band Cole* ....(Blue Note)

Like A Movie
Troy Shondell; *45-#31* ....(Commercial)

Like A Movie
Climax Blues Band; *Shine On* ....(Sire)

Love Scene
Joe; *All That I Am* ....(Jive)

Mann's Chinese
Naked; *Naked* ....(Red Ant)

Mary Lou
Bruce Springsteen; *Tracks* ....(Columbia)

Moonlight Drive-In
Turner Nichols; *Moonlight Drive-In* ....(BNA)

Motion Pictures
Neil Young; *On The Beach* ....(Reprise)

Movie
Doors; *An American Prayer-Jim Morrison* ....(Elektra)
Jim Morrison; *ST/The Doors* ....(Elektra)

Movie
Aerosmith; *Permanent Vacation* ....(Geffen)

Movie Buff
Glenn Sutton; *Close Encounters Of The Sutton Kind* ....(Mercury)

Movie In My Mind
Original London Cast; *Miss Saigon* ....(Geffen)

Movie Magg
Carl Perkins; *Blue Suede Shoes* ....(Sun)
  Carl Perkins-Original Sun Greatest Hits ....(Rhino)

Movie Pictures
Kinks; *Low Budget* ....(Arista)

Movie Queen
Bill Anderson; *Scorpio* ....(MCA)

Movie, The
Tom Waits; *Devout Catalyst* ....(Grateful Dead)

Movieola
Country Joe McDonald; *Paris Sessions* ....(Vanguard)

Movies
Statler Brothers; *Best Of The Statler Brothers-Rides Again-#2* ....(Mercury)
  Country American Loves ....(Mercury)

Movies
Hothouse Flowers; *Home* ....(London)

Movies
Steely Dan; *Katy Lied* ....(MCA)

Movies
Miami Sound Machine; *Primitive Love* ....(Epic)

Movies Are A Mother To Me
Loudon Wainwright III; *Loudon Wainwright III* ....(Atlantic)

Mrs. Potter's Lullaby
Counting Crows; *This Desert Life* ....(David Geffen Co.)

Optimistic Voices
Bette Midler; *Bette Midler* ....(Atlantic)

Pencil Thin Mustache
Jimmy Buffett; *Boats Beaches Bars & Ballads* ....(Margaritaville)
  Living & Dying In 3/4 Time ....(MCA)
  Songs You Know By Heart-Jimmy Buffett's Greatest Hit(s) ....(MCA)
  You Had To Be There ....(MCA)

Picture Show
John Prine; *The Missing Years* ....(Oh Boy)

Put Me In The Movies
Daryle Ryce; *Carolina Blue* . . . . (Rounder)
Riding With A Movie Star
L7; *Hungry For Stink*. . . . . (Slash)
Road Movie To Berlin
They Might Be Giants; *Flood* . . . . (Elektra)
Roy Rogers
Elton John; *Goodbye Yellow Brick Road* . . . . (Polydor)
Sad Movies (Make Me Cry)
Sue Thompson; *Collectables Presents The History Of Rock-#10-C* . . . . (Collectables)
Sue Thompson's Greatest Hits . . . . (Curb)
Same Script, Different Cast
Whitney Houston & Deborah Cox; *Whitney Houston's Greatest Hits* . . . (Arista)
Saturday Matinee
Gordon Brisker; *About Charlie* . . . .(Discovery)
Saturday Morning Movies
Bonnie Koloc; *Bonnie Koloc* . . . . (Ovation)
Bonnie Koloc-At Her Best. (Ovation)
Saturday Night At The Movies
Drifters; *1959-1965-All-Time Greatest Hits And More* . . . . (Atlantic)
Drifters-16 Greatest Hits . . . . (Trip)
Drifters-Golden Hits . . . . (Atlantic)
Save The Last Dance For Me . . . .(Fifty One West)
Silent Movies
Neil Sedaka; *Singer- Songwriter-Melody Maker*. . . . . (Accord)
Solitaire . . . . (Fifty One West)
Superbird . . . . (Intermedia)
Silver Screen
Little Feat; *Representing The Mambo* . . . . (Warner Bros.)
Sittin' In The Balcony
Eddie Cochran; *Eddie Cochran's Greatest Hits* . . . . (Curb)
Singin' To My Baby/Never To Be Forgotten . . . . (EMI)
Somethin' Else: The Fine Lookin' Hits Of Eddie Cochran . . . (Razor & Tie)
Song Of The South (Gone With The Wind)
Alabama; *Alabama's Greatest Hits-#2* . . . . (RCA)
Southern Star . . . . (RCA)
Stupid War Movies
Paleface; *Paleface* . . . . (Polydor)
Sunday Morning Movies
Bonnie Koloc; *Bonnie Koloc*. . . . . (Ovation)
Bonnie Koloc-At Her Best. (Ovation)
That's Why God Made The Movies
Paul Simon; *ST/One-Trick Pony* . . . . (Warner Bros.)
Theme From "Cinema Paradiso"
Original Soundtrack; *Ennio Morricone With Love* . . . . (DRG)
Theme From "Siskel And Ebert"
Original Soundtrack; *Television's Greatest Hits-#6-Remote Control-C* . . . (TVT)
Theme From "Tarzan"
Original Soundtrack; *Television's Greatest Hits-#2-C* . . . . (TVT)
Thriller
Michael Jackson; *Thriller* . . . . (Epic)
True Western Movie
Chris LeDoux; *Songs Of Rodeo & Country* . . . . (Liberty)
TV Movie
Bruce Springsteen; *Tracks*. . . . . (Columbia)
Wake Up Little Susie
Everly Brothers; *All They Had To Do Was Dream* . . . . . . (Rhino)
American Graffiti-#3-C . . . . (MCA)
Everly Brothers . . . . (Rhino)
Everly Brothers' All-Time Greatest Hits. . . . . (Curb)
Oldies But Goodies-#7-C . . . .(Original Sound)
Very Best Of The Everly Brothers . . . . (Warner Bros.)
Grateful Dead; *History Of The Grateful Dead-Vol. 1 (Bear's Choice)* . . . . (Warner Bros.)
Simon & Garfunkel; *The Concert In Central Park* . . . . (Warner Bros.)
Western Movies (My Baby Loves)
Olympics; *All-Time Greatest Hits Of Rock 'N' Roll-C* . . . . . . (Curb)
American Graffiti-#3-C . . . . (MCA)
Best Of The Olympics . . . . (Vee-Jay)
Jumpin' Jive '50s-C . . . . (Priority)
Wide Screen
Barbra Streisand; *Lazy Afternoon* . . . . (Columbia)
You Oughta Be In Pictures
Doris Day; *Sentimental Journey* . . . . (Hindsight)
Jackie Gleason; *The Romantic Moods Of Jackie Gleason* . . . . (Capitol)
Rudy Vallee & His Connecticut Yankees; *78-#24580*. . . . . (Victor)

MUSIC, Bands, Musicians, Playing Music, Singing, Songs
See Also: BARS, COUNTRY, DANCE, FUN, JUKEBOX, MUSICAL INSTRUMENTS (various), PARTY, RADIO, RECORD BUSINESS, RHYTHM, ROCK & ROCKING, SHOW BIZ, TELEVISION

(All Of A Sudden) My Heart Sings
Paul Anka; *Paul Anka Sings His Big 15, Vol. 2* . . . . (RCA)
Paul Anka-30th Anniversary Anthology . . . . (Rhino)

(Hey Won't You Play) Another Somebody Done Somebody Wrong Song
B.J. Thomas; *Class Of Country-1975-1979-C* . . . . (Hip-O)
33 R.P.M. Soul
Michelle Shocked; *Arkansas Traveler* . . . .(Mercury)
Say What U Want-Rock The Vote-C . . . .(Mercury)
33, 45, 78 (Record Time)
Kathy Mattea; *Lonesome Standard Time* . . . .(Mercury)
A Little Night Music
Original Cast; *Little Night Music* . . . .(Columbia)
Add Some Music To Your Day
Beach Boys; *Best Of (Good Vibrations)*. . . . . (Reprise)
Sunflower. . . . . (Caribou)
Ten Years Of Harmony . . . . (Caribou)
Aeroplane
Red Hot Chili Peppers; *One Hot Minute* . . . . (Warner Bros.)
Alexander's Ragtime Band
Al Jolson & Bing Crosby; *Al Jolson Story-#1* . . . . (MCA)
Immortal Al Jolson . . . . (MCA)
All Day Music
War; *All Day Music* . . . . (MCA)
Best Of War...And More . . . . (Avenue)
War Live!. . . . . (Avenue)
All Night Long
Asleep At The Wheel featuring Leon Rausch; *Tribute To The Music Of Bob Wills And The Texas Playboys-C* . . . .(Liberty)
All Our Favorite Songs
Oak Ridge Boys; *All Our Favorite Songs*. . . . .(Columbia)
All The Children Sing
Todd Rundgren; *Hermit Of Mink Hollow* . . . .(Rhino)
Todd Rundgren-Anthology 1968-1985 . . . .(Rhino)
All The Rage In Paris
Derailers; *Here Come The Derailers* . . . .(Lucky Dog)
All Those Years Ago
George Harrison; *Best Of Dark Horse 1976-1989* . . . . (Dark Horse)
Somewhere In England . . . . (Dark Horse)
Ambush
Nilsson; *Son Of Schmilsson* . . . . (RCA)
American Music
Blasters; *Blasters* . . . . (Slash)
Blasters-Collection . . . . (Slash)
American Music
Violent Femmes; *Why Do Birds Sing?*. . . . . (Slash)
American Music
Pointer Sisters; *So Excited* . . . . (Planet)
American Pie
Don McLean; *American Pie* . . . . (EMI)
Best Of Don McLean . . . . (EMI)
Greatest Hits Then & Now . . . . (EMI)
ST/Born On The Fourth Of July . . . . (MCA)
Madonna; *ST/The Next Big Thing* . . . . (Maverick)
American Tune
Paul Simon; *Paul Simon In Concert/Live Rhymin'* . . . . (Columbia)
There Goes Rhymin' Simon . . . . (Columbia)
Simon & Garfunkel; *The Concert In Central Park*. . . . (Warner Bros.)
And The Angels Sing
Ella Fitzgerald; *Lady Time* . . . . (Pablo)
And Your Bird Can Sing
Beatles; *"Yesterday"...And Today* . . . .(Capitol)
Revolver . . . . (Capitol)
Angel Band
Emmylou Harris; *Angel Band* . . . . (Warner Bros.)
Stanley Brothers; *ST/O Brother, Where Art Thou?* . . . .(Mercury)
Stanley Brothers & The Clinch Mountain Boys; *Best Of Bluegrass-#1-Standards-C* . . . .(Mercury)
Angel's Son
Strait Up featuring Lajon of Sevendust; *Strait Up-C* . . . . (Immortal/Virgin)
Another Lonely Song
Tammy Wynette; *Tammy Wynette-16 Biggest Hits* . . . .(Legacy)
Tammy Wynette-Anniversary-20 Years Of Hits. . . . .(Epic)
Tammy Wynette-Super Hits . . . .(Epic)
Tears Of Fire-25th Anniversary Collection. . . . .(Epic)
Another Sad Love Song
Toni Braxton; *Toni Braxton* . . . .(LaFace)
Anyone Can Whistle
Cleo Laine; *Cleo Laine Sings Sondheim* . . . . (RCA)
Original Broadway Cast; *Anyone Can Whistle*. . . . .(Columbia)
Are You Sure Hank Done It This Way
Hank Williams, Jr.; *Rowdy*. . . . .(WB/Curb)
Waylon Jennings; *Waylon Jennings' Greatest Hits* . . . . (RCA)
Army
Ben Folds Five; *The Unauthorized Biography Of Reinhold Messner* . . . . (550 Music)
Around The World (La La La...)
ATC; *Now That's What I Call Music!-#6-C*. . . . . (Virgin)
Planet Pop. . . . .(Republic/Universal)
At The Hop
Danny & The Juniors; *Billboard Top Rock 'N' Roll Hits-1958-C* . . . . . .(Rhino)
Cruisin'-1958-C . . . . (Increase)
Oldies But Goodies-#2-C . . . . (Original Sound)

Rockin' With Danny & The Juniors . . . .(MCA Special Prod.)
Super Oldies Of The '50s-#6-C . . . . (Audio Fidelity)
Sha Na Na; ST/Woodstock . . . .(Atlantic)

Autumn Serenade
Harry James & His Orchestra; 70 Ounces Of Big Band-
Instrumentals-C . . . .(Compose)
John Coltrane & Johnny Hartman; John Coltrane & Johnny Hartman. . . . (GRP)
Mel Torme; Velvet & Brass . . . .(Concord Jazz)

Bach, Beethoven, Mozart & Me
Phil Ochs; Phil Ochs' Greatest Hits . . . . (A&M)

Bad Boy
Beatles; Beatles VI . . . . : (Capitol)
Beatles-Box Set . . . . (Capitol)
Past Masters-Volume One . . . . (Parlophone)
Rock 'N' Roll Music . . . . (Capitol)

Bad Boy
Ringo Starr; Bad Boy . . . .(Epic)

Bailamos
Enrique Iglesias; Bailamos Greatest Hits . . . .(Overbrook/Interscope)
Enrique . . . .(Overbrook/Interscope)
Now That's What I Call Music!-#3-C . . . . (Virgin)

Band From Chicago
Max Creek; Windows . . . . (Relix)

Band On The Run
Paul McCartney; All The Best! . . . . (Capitol)
Paul McCartney & Wings; Band On The Run . . . .(Capitol)
Wings; Wings Greatest . . . .(Capitol)
Wings Over America . . . .(Capitol)

Barroom Country Singer
Roger Whittaker; Roger Whittaker Greatest Hits . . . . (RCA)

Beat Goes On, The
Sonny & Cher; Best Of Sonny & Cher . . . . (Atco)
Hit Singles-1958-1977-C . . . .(Atlantic)
Sonny & Cher-Live . . . . (MCA)
The Beat Goes On-Best Of Sonny & Cher . . . . (Rhino)
Two Of Us . . . . (Atco)

Bebe Le Strange
Heart; Bebe Le Strange . . . .(Epic)
Heart's Greatest Hits/Live . . . .(Epic)

Be-Bop Baby
Rick Nelson; Rick Nelson's Greatest Hits . . . . (Rhino)
Ricky Nelson-Legendary Masters . . . .(EMI)
Ricky Nelson; Best Of Ricky Nelson . . . .(EMI)

Beer And Bones
John Michael Montgomery; John Michael Montgomery's
Greatest Hits . . . .(Atlantic)
Life's A Dance . . . .(Atlantic)

Begin The Beguine
Art Tatum; Solos-1940 . . . .(MCA)
Ella Fitzgerald; Cole Porter Songbook . . . . (Verve)
Johnny Mathis; Best Days Of My Life . . . .(Columbia)
First 25 Years-Silver Anniversary Album . . . . (Columbia)
Johnny Mathis-Live . . . .(Columbia)
Tony Bennett; Forty Years-The Artistry Of Tony Bennett. . . . .(Columbia)

Bennie And The Jets
Elton John; Billboard Top Rock 'N' Roll Hits-1974-C . . . . (Rhino)
Classic Rock-#1-C . . . .(MCA)
Elton John's Greatest Hits . . . .(Polydor)
Goodbye Yellow Brick Road . . . . (Polydor)
Here And There . . . .(Rocket)

Big Music
Waterboys; Pagan Place . . . .(Chrysalis)

Bitter Sweet Symphony
Verve; Urban Hymns . . . . (Hut/Virgin)

Black Velvet
Alannah Myles; Alannah Myles . . . .(Atlantic)
Robin Lee; Black Velvet . . . .(Atlantic)

Blackbird
Beatles; Beatles-Box Set . . . . (Capitol)
The Beatles (White Album) . . . . (Capitol)
Crosby, Stills & Nash; CSN . . . .(Atlantic)
Paul McCartney; Unplugged (The Official Bootleg). . . . . .(Capitol)
Wings; Wings Over America . . . . (Capitol)

Blue Must Be The Color Of The Blues
Willie Nelson; There'll Be No Teardrops Tonight . . . . (United Artists)

Bob Wills Is Still The King
Clint Black & Asleep At The Wheel; Ride With Bob-C . . . . (DreamWorks/SKG)

Boomin' System
L.L. Cool J; Mama Said Knock You Out . . . .(Def Jam)

Born With A Broken Heart
Kenny Wayne Shepherd; Ledbetter Heights. . . . .(Giant)

Brand New Country Star
Jimmy Buffett; Living & Dying In 3/4 Time . . . .(MCA)

Brass Band In African Chimes
Simple Minds; 45-#2703 . . . . (A&M)

Break Ya Neck
Busta Rhymes; Genesis . . . . (J)

Brian Wilson
Barenaked Ladies; Gordon . . . . (Reprise)

Rock Spectacle . . . . (Reprise)

Bright Lights And Country Music
Bill Anderson; Bill Anderson's Greatest Hits . . . . (MCA)

Brimful Of Asha
Cornershop; Target . . . . (Luaka Bop)

Bringing Out The Elvis
Faith Hill; Breathe. . . . . (Warner Bros.)

Brokedown Palace
Grateful Dead; American Beauty. . . . . (Warner Bros.)
Persuasions; Might As Well...The Persuasions Sing
Grateful Dead . . . .(Grateful Dead)

Brown Eyed Girl
Isley Brothers; Live It Up . . . . (T-Neck/Columbia)
Jimmy Buffett; One Particular Harbour. . . . . (MCA)
Van Morrison; Bang Masters . . . . (Epic)
Best Of Van Morrison . . . .(Polydor)
ST/Born On The Fourth Of July . . . . (MCA)
ST/Sleeping With The Enemy . . . . (Columbia)
Wonder Years-Music From Emmy Shows/Era-C . . . .(Atlantic)

Buddy Holly
Weezer; Weezer. . . . . (David Geffen Co.)

Bumble Boogie
Freddy Martin; Big Band In Hi Fi-#1-Let's Dance . . . . (Capitol)

Bumble Boogie
Jo Ann Castle; Legends Of Accordion-C . . . . (Rhino)

Burnin' The Roadhouse Down
Steve Wariner & Garth Brooks; Burnin' The Roadhouse Down . . . (Capitol)

But Not For Me
Billie Holiday; Silver Collection . . . . (Verve)
Chet Baker; Let's Get Lost-Best Of Chet Baker Sings . . . .(Blue Note)
Ella Fitzgerald; Ella Sings Jazz . . . .(MCA Jazz)
Elvis Costello; Glory Of Gershwin Featuring Larry Adler-C . . . . .(Mercury)
Harry Connick, Jr.; ST/When Harry Met Sally . . . .(Columbia)
Judy Garland; Best Of Judy Garland . . . . (MCA)
Original London Cast; Crazy For You . . . .(RCA)
Original Soundtrack; Manhattan. . . . .(CBS Masterworks)
Sarah Vaughan; Sarah Vaughan Sings George Gershwin Songbook,
Vol. 2 . . . .(Emarcy)

Caged Bird
Alicia Keys; Songs In A Minor . . . . (J)

Can You Hear The Music?
Rolling Stones; Goats Head Soup . . . . (Rolling Stones)

Canned Heat
Jamiroquai; Synkronized . . . . (Work/Epic)

Canned Music
Dan Hicks & His Hot Licks; Striking It Rich! . . . . (MCA)

Can't Stop The Music
Daryl Hall & John Oates; No Goodbyes . . . .(Atlantic)
War Babies . . . .(Atlantic)

Can't Stop The Music
Village People; Can't Stop The Music . . . .(Casablanca)
Village People's Greatest Hits . . . . (Rhino)

Champagne Jam
Atlanta Rhythm Section; Are You Ready! . . . .(Polydor)
Champagne Jam . . . .(Polydor)

Chanel No. Fever
De La Soul; ST/Men In Black . . . . (Columbia)

Changing Partners
Bing Crosby; Bing Crosby. . . . . (MCA Special Prod.)
Kay Starr; Capitol Collectors Series-Kay Starr . . . . (Capitol)
Patti Page; Patti Page-Golden Hits . . . .(Mercury)

Chattanoogie Shoe Shine Boy
Freddy Cannon; 14 Booming Hits . . . . (Rhino)
Red Foley; Red Foley: The Country Music Hall
Of Fame . . . . (MCA Special Prod.)
The Nashville Sound: Owen Bradley-C . . . .(Decca)

Cheap Shot
John Cougar; Nothin' Matters And What If It Did . . . . (Riva)
John Cougar Mellencamp; John Cougar Mellencamp-Early Years . . . . . (Rhino)
Kid Inside . . . . (Rhino)

Chords Of Fame
Phil Ochs; Chords Of Fame . . . . (A&M)
Phil Ochs' Greatest Hits. (A&M)
The War Is Over-Best Of Phil Ochs . . . . (A&M)

Chorus
Erasure; Chorus. . . . .(Sire)

Click Click Boom
Saliva; Every Six Seconds . . . . (Island/IDJMG)

Club At The End Of The Street
Elton John; Sleeping With The Past . . . . (MCA)

Come And Get With Me
Keith Sweat featuring Snoop Dogg; Still In The Game . . . . (Elektra)

Come From The Heart
Don Williams; Traces . . . . (Capitol)
Kathy Mattea; Willow In The Wind . . . .(Mercury)

Come Original
311; Soundsystem . . . . (Capricorn)

Country In My Jeans
Loretta Lynn; Still Country . . . . (Audium)

Cowboy Band
Billy Dean; *Men'll Be Boys* . . . . (Liberty)
Cowboy Singer
Sonny Curtis; *Love Is All Around* . . . . (Elektra)
Sonny Curtis . . . . (Elektra)
Cowboy's Wild Song To His Herd
Skip Gorman; *A Cowboy's Wild Song To His Herd*. . . . . (Rounder)
Cracklin' Rosie
Neil Diamond; *Hot August Night*. . . . . (MCA)
Hot August Night II. . . . . (Columbia)
Neil Diamond-His 12 Greatest Hits . . . . (MCA)
Tap Root Manuscript . . . . (MCA)
Crazy Man Crazy
Bill Haley; *Still Rockin' Around The Clock* . . . . (BMG Special Prod.)
Creeque Alley
Mamas & The Papas; *Best Of The Mamas & The Papas* . . . . (MCA)
Mamas & The Papas' Greatest Hits . . . . (MCA)
Mamas & The Papas-16 Of Their Greatest Hits . . . . (MCA)
Cruisin'
D'Angelo; *Brown Sugar* . . . . (EMI)
Huey Lewis and Gwyneth Paltrow; *ST/Duets* . . . . (Hollywood)
Smokey Robinson; *Compact Command Performances-Smokey
    Robinson* . . . . (Motown)
Motown Love Songs-C . . . . (Motown)
Motown Story-First 25 Years-C . . . . (Motown)
Where There's Smoke . . . . (Motown)
Cuban Love Song
George Shearing; *Best Of George Shearing* . . . . (Capitol)
Cum On Feel The Noise
Quiet Riot; *Metal Health* . . . . (Pasha)
Daddy Sang Bass
Johnny Cash; *Columbia Country Classics-#5-A New Tradition-C* . . . (Columbia)
Johnny Cash's Greatest Hits-#2 . . . . (Columbia)
The Man In Black-His Greatest Hits . . . . (Legacy)
Dance To The Music
Sly & The Family Stone; *Frat Rock!-#2-C* . . . . (Rhino)
Frat Rock!-C . . . . (Rhino)
Sly & The Family Stone-Anthology . . . . (Epic)
Sly & The Family Stone's Greatest Hits . . . . (Epic)
Dancing In The Street
David Bowie & Mick Jagger; *Bowie-The Singles-1969-1993* . . . . . . (Rykodisc)
Grateful Dead; *Terrapin Station* . . . . (Arista)
Martha & The Vandellas; *20 Greatest Songs In Motown History-C* . . . (Motown)
*Compact Command Performances-Martha Reeves & The
    Vandellas* . . . . (Motown)
Motown Story-First 25 Years-C . . . . (Motown)
Oldies But Goodies-#14-C . . . . (Original Sound)
Van Halen; *Diver Down* . . . . (Warner Bros.)
Days Of Our Livez
Bone Thugs-N-Harmony; *The Collection-#1* . . . . (Ruthless)
Dazz
Brick; *Good High* . . . . (Bang)
Dear Mr. Fantasy
Traffic; *Best Of Traffic*. . . . . (Island)
Dear Mr. Fantasy . . . . (Island)
Welcome To The Canteen . . . . (Island)
Dedicated To The One I Love
Mamas & The Papas; *Best Of The Mamas & The Papas* . . . . (MCA)
Farewell To The First Golden Era . . . . (MCA)
Original Classic Oldies Of The '50s & '60s-#13-C . . . . (MCA)
Shirelles; *Oldies But Goodies-#10-C*. . . . . (Original Sound)
Shirelles' Greatest Hits. . . . . (Everest)
Shirelles-Anthology 1959-1964 . . . . (Columbia)
Super Oldies Of The '50s-#4-C. . . . . (Audio Fidelity)
Deja Vu (Uptown Baby)
Lord Tariq & Peter Gunz; *Deja Vu* . . . . (Codeine/Columbia)
Devil Comes Back To Georgia
Marc O'Connor; *Heroes* . . . . (Warner Bros.)
Devil Went Down To Georgia
Charlie Daniels Band; *A Decade Of Hits* . . . . (Epic)
Billboard Top Hits-1979-C . . . . (Rhino)
Me & The Boys . . . . (Epic)
Million Mile Reflections . . . . (Epic)
ST/Urban Cowboy . . . . (Asylum)
Dim Lights Thick Smoke & Loud Loud Music
Flatt & Scruggs; *Golden Era* . . . . (Rounder)
Flying Burrito Brothers; *Close Encounters To The West Coast*. . . . . . . (Relix)
Farther Along-Best Of The Flying Burrito Brothers . . . . (A&M)
Ricky Skaggs and Kentucky Thunder; *History Of The Future* . . (Skaggs Family)
Discotheque
U2; *Pop* . . . . (Island)
Distant Melody
Original Cast/Mary Martin; *Peter Pan-The 1954 Broadway
    Production* . . . . (RCA Victor)
Do America
Mark Knopfler; *Sailing To Philadelphia* . . . . (Warner Bros.)
Do I Hear A Waltz?
Elizabeth Allen; *Broadway Magic-The 1960s-C* . . . . (Columbia)
Original Broadway Cast; *Do I Hear A Waltz?* . . . . (Sony Music Classical)

Do Re Mi
Julie Andrews; *ST/The Sound Of Music* . . . . (RCA)
Original Cast; *The Sound Of Music* . . . . (Sony Broadway)
Do Wah Diddy Diddy
Manfred Mann; *Best Of Manfred Mann* . . . . (EMI Special Markets)
Billboard Top Rock 'N' Roll Hits-1964-C. . . . . (Rhino)
History Of British Rock-#2-C . . . . (Rhino)
Do You Believe In Magic
Lovin' Spoonful; *Lovin' Spoonful-Anthology* . . . . (Rhino)
Do You Know You Are My Sunshine
Statler Brothers; *Statler Brothers-30th Anniversary Celebration* . . . . . (Mercury)
Don't Leave Your Records In The Sun
John Hartford; *Mark Twang* . . . . (Flying Fish)
Don't Play That Song
Aretha Franklin; *Aretha Franklin-30 Greatest Hits* . . . . (Rhino)
Aretha Franklin's Greatest Hits . . . . (Atlantic)
Live At Fillmore West . . . . (Atlantic)
Ben E. King; *Atlantic Rhythm & Blues 1947-1974-#4 (1958-
    1962)-C* . . . . (Atlantic)
Ben E. King's Greatest Hits. . . . . (Atco)
Stand By Me-Best Of Ben E. King . . . . (Atlantic)
Don't Play That Song (You Lied)
Aretha Franklin; *Aretha Franklin-30 Greatest Hits* . . . . (Rhino)
Aretha Franklin's Greatest Hits . . . . (Atlantic)
Golden Age Of Black Music-1970-1975-C . . . . (Atlantic)
Don't Rock The Jukebox
Alan Jackson; *Alan Jackson-The Greatest Hits Collection* . . . . (Arista)
Don't Rock The Jukebox . . . . (Arista)
Don't Sing A Song About Texas
Charlie Walker; *Texas Gold* . . . . (Plantation)
Don't Stop The Music
Yarbrough & Peoples; *Two Of Us* . . . . (Mercury)
Downtown
Neil Young; *Mirror Ball* . . . . (Reprise)
Dr. Music
Blue Oyster Cult; *Extraterrestrial Live* . . . . (Columbia)
Mirrors . . . . (Columbia)
Dream On
Aerosmith; *Aerosmith* . . . . (Columbia)
Aerosmith-Classics Live . . . . (Columbia)
Aerosmith's Greatest Hits . . . . (Columbia)
Live! Bootleg . . . . (Columbia)
Drift Away
Dobie Gray; *Classic Rock-#1-C*. . . . . (MCA)
Oldies But Goodies-#10-C . . . . (Original Sound)
Oldies But Goodies-#3-C . . . . (Original Sound)
Super Hits Of The '70s-Have A Nice Day-#10-C . . . . (Rhino)
Michael Bolton; *Timeless-Classics* . . . . (Columbia)
Rod Stewart; *Atlantic Crossing* . . . . (Warner Bros.)
Duchess
Genesis; *Duke* . . . . (Atlantic)
Three Sides Live . . . . (Atlantic)
Dusic
Brick; *Brick* . . . . (Bang)
Edge Of Seventeen
Stevie Nicks; *Bella Donna* . . . . (Modern)
Emma Jean's Guitar
Chely Wright; *Let Me In*. . . . . (MCA)
Empty Garden (Hey Hey Johnny)
Elton John; *Elton John's Greatest Hits-1976-1986* . . . . (MCA)
Jump Up! . . . . (MCA)
Euphonius Whale
Dan Hicks & His Hot Licks; *Last Train To Hicksville* . . . . (MCA)
Every Long Song
Greg Kihn Band; *Kihntinued* . . . . (Beserkley)
Everything Is Everything
Lauryn Hill; *The Miseducation Of Lauryn Hill* . . . . (Ruffhouse/Columbia)
Face The Music
RTZ; *Return To Zero* . . . . (Giant)
Famous Groupies
Wings; *London Town* . . . . (Capitol)
Follow The Music
Harry Connick, Jr.; *She* . . . . (Columbia)
Follow The Music Further
Harry Connick, Jr.; *She* . . . . (Columbia)
Forever
Kid Rock; *Cocky* . . . . (Top Dog/Lava/Atlantic)
Free Man In Paris
Joni Mitchell; *Court & Spark* . . . . (Asylum)
Shadows & Light . . . . (Asylum)
Funiculi, Funicula
Mario Lanza; *Legendary Tenor* . . . . (RCA)
Funky Music Sho Nuff Turns Me On
Temptations; *Temptations-Anthology-The Best Of The Temptations*. . . (Motown)
Gang That Sang "Heart Of My Heart"
Four Aces; *Best Of The Four Aces* . . . . (MCA)
Georgia On My Mind
Billie Holiday; *God Bless The Child* . . . . (Columbia)

The Billie Holiday Story-#2 .... (Columbia)
Hoagy Carmichael; *Hoagy Carmichael-Legendary Performer* .... (RCA)
   Hoagy Sings Carmichael .... (EMI)
Mildred Bailey; *Harlem Lullaby* .... (ASV)
Preservation Hall Jazz Band; *Best Of The Preservation Hall*
   Jazz Band .... (Columbia)
Ray Charles; *Ray Charles' Greatest Hits-#2* .... (Rhino)
   Ray Charles-Anthology .... (Rhino)
Willie Nelson; *Greatest Hits (& Some That Will Be)* .... (Columbia)
   Stardust .... (Legacy)
   Willie & Family Live .... (Columbia)

Get Ready For This
2 Unlimited; *Get Ready* .... (Critique)
   Greatest Sports Rock And Jams-C .... (Cold Front)

Get Rhythm
Johnny Cash; *Johnny Cash-Sun Years* .... (Rhino)
Ry Cooder; *Get Rhythm* ....(Warner Bros.)

Getting In Tune
Who; *Who's next.* ....(MCA)

Ghetto Supastar (That Is What You Are)
Pras Michel featuring Old Dirty Bastard & Mya; *ST/Bulworth* ... (Interscope)

God's Own Singer
Flying Burrito Brothers; *Burrito Deluxe* .... (A&M)
   Close Up The Honky Tonks .... (A&M)
   Farther Along-Best Of The Flying Burrito Brothers .... (A&M)

Golden Slumbers
Beatles; *Abbey Road* .... (Parlophone)
   Beatles-Box Set .... (Capitol)

Good Time Man Like Me Got No Business (Singin' The Blues), A
Jim Croce; *Life & Times* .... (Lifesong)
   Words And Music ....(Dunhill Compact Classics)

Good Woman Blues
Mel Tillis; *Mel Tillis' Greatest Hits* .... (Curb)

Grandma's Song
Gail Davies; *Gail Davies' Greatest Hits* .... (Little Chickadee)

Grandmother Song
Steve Martin; *Let's Get Small* ....(Warner Bros.)

Green Tambourine
Lemon Pipers; *Best Of Ohio Express & Other Bubblegum*
   Smashes-#1-C .... (Rhino)
   Billboard Top Rock 'N' Roll Hits-1968-C .... (Rhino)
   Bubblegum's Greatest Hits-#3-C .... (Accord)
   Fabulous Bubblegum Years-C .... (Fifty One West)

Groove Line, The
Heatwave; *Club Epic-#1-C* .... (Legacy)
   Disco Super Hits-C .... (Epic Dance)
   The Funky Sounds Of The Soul '70s-C ....(Sony Music Special Prod.)

Happy Days Are Here Again
Barbra Streisand; *A Happening In Central Park* .... (Columbia)
   Barbra Streisand's Greatest Hits .... (Columbia)
   One Voice .... (Columbia)
   The Barbra Streisand Album .... (Columbia)
Leo Reisman & His Orchestra; *Nipper's Greatest Hits Of The*
   '30s-#1-C .... (RCA)

Happy Wanderer
Frank Weir & His Orchestra; *Hits To Remember-C* ... (PolyGram Special Prod.)
Joey Miskulin; *Hooked On Polkas* .... (K-Tel)
Original Soundtrack; *Disney Travel Songs-C* ....(Disney)

Hard Knock Life (Ghetto Anthem)
Jay-Z; *Now That's What I Call Music!-#2-C* .... (Virgin)
   Vol. 2-Hard Knock Life .... (Def Jam)

Hard To Be A Husband, Hard To Be A Wife
Chely Wright & Brad Paisley; *Grand Ole Opry-75 Years-#2-C* ....(MCA)

Harmony
John Conlee; *45-#13-08398* .... (Columbia)

Harmony
Bar-Kays; *Coldblooded* ....(Stax)

Harmony
Elton John; *Goodbye Yellow Brick Road* .... (Polydor)

Harmony
Take 6 (featuring Queen Latifah); *Join The Band-C* .... (Reprise)

Harmony
Limeliters; *Live In Concert* ....(Crescendo)

Harmony
Happy Mondays; *Pills 'N' Thrills & Bellyaches* .... (Elektra)

Having A Party
Norma Jean; *Norma Jean* .... (Bearsville)
Pointer Sisters; *Having A Party* ....(MCA)
Rod Stewart & Ronnie Wood; *Unplugged...And Seated* ....(Warner Bros.)
Sam Cooke; *Best Of Sam Cooke* .... (RCA)
   Feel It. .... (RCA)
   Live At The Harlem Square Club .... (RCA)
   This Is Sam Cooke .... (RCA)
Southside Johnny And The Asbury Jukes; *Havin' A Party With Southside*
   Johnny And The Asbury Jukes. ....(Epic)

Healing Game
Van Morrison; *The Healing Game* .... (A&M)

Hear Me In The Harmony
Harry Connick, Jr.; *Star Turtle* .... (Columbia)

Heavy Traffic Ahead
Bill Monroe & His Blue Grass Boys; *The Father Of Bluegrass: The Early*
   Years-1940-1947. ....(ASV)
Ricky Skaggs with Steve Wariner; *Big Mon: The Songs Of Bill*
   Monroe-C .... (Skaggs Family)

Here We Go Again
Aretha Franklin; *A Rose Is Still A Rose* .... (Arista)

Hey Baby (They're Playing Our Song)
Buckinghams; *Mercy, Mercy, Mercy* ....(Legacy Rock Artifacts Series)

Hey Jude
Beatles; *Beatles 1* .... (Capitol)
   Beatles-20 Greatest Hits .... (Capitol)
   Past Masters-Volume Two .... (Parlophone)
   The Beatles/1967-1970. .... (Capitol)
Paul McCartney; *Knebworth-The Album-C* ....(Polydor)
Wilson Pickett; *Wilson Pickett's Greatest Hits* ....(Atlantic)

High Lonesome Sound
Vince Gill; *Bluegrass Essentials-C* .... (Hip-O)
   High Lonesome Sound .... (MCA)
Vince Gill with Alison Krauss & Union Station; *Grand Ole Opry-75*
   Years-#1-C .... (MCA)

Hi-Lili, Hi-Lo
Anne Murray; *There's A Hippo In My Tub* .... (Capitol)
Ray Conniff; *Encore! 16 Most Requested Songs* .... (Legacy)

Hillbilly Rock
Marty Stuart; *Hillbilly Rock* .... (MCA)
   Marty Party Hit Pack .... (MCA)

His Eye Is On The Sparrow
Carmen McRae; *Greatest Of Carmen McRae* .... (MCA)
Marvin Gaye; *Musical Testament 1964-1984* .... (Motown)
Preservation Hall Jazz Band; *Best Of The Preservation Hall*
   Jazz Band. .... (Columbia)
Soundtrack; *Streetcar Named Desire* .... (Allegiance)

Homeward Bound
Paul Simon; *Paul Simon In Concert/Live Rhymin'* .... (Columbia)
Paul Simon & George Harrison; *Nobody's Child-Romanian Angel*
   Appeal-C .... (Warner Bros.)
Simon & Garfunkel; *Collected Works* .... (Columbia)
   Parsley Sage Rosemary & Thyme. .... (Columbia)
   Simon & Garfunkel's Greatest Hits .... (Columbia)
   The Concert In Central Park .... (Warner Bros.)
Willie Nelson & Waylon Jennings; *Take It To The Limit* .... (Columbia)

Homey Don't Play Dat
Terminator X; *Terminator X & The Valley Of The Jeep*
   Beets .... (P.R.O. Division)

Honky Tonk Song
Webb Pierce; *Best Of Webb Pierce* .... (MCA)
   Webb Pierce-Golden Hits-#2 .... (Plantation)

Hooked On Music
Pat Travers; *Go For What You Know* ....(Polydor)
   Makin' Magic ....(Polydor)

Hooked On Music
Mac Davis; *Best Of Country Rock-C* .... (K-Tel)
   Mac Davis-Very Best & More .... (Casablanca)

Hook's Tango
Original Cast/Cyril Ritchard; *Peter Pan-The 1954 Broadway*
   Production .... (RCA Victor)

Hoop-Dee-Doo
Perry Como; *Perry Como's Greatest Hits* ....(RCA)

How Do You Keep The Music Playing
James Ingram & Patti Austin; *It's Your Night-C* .... (Qwest)
   ST/Listen Up-The Lives Of Quincy Jones .... (Qwest)

How High The Moon
Duke Ellington; *1954 Los Angeles Concert* ....(Crescendo)
Ella Fitzgerald; *Best Of Ella Fitzgerald* .... (MCA)
Les Paul & Mary Ford; *Memories Are Made Of This-C* .... (Capitol)
Sarah Vaughan; *Compact Jazz-Best Of The Compact Jazz Vocalists-C* .. (Verve)
   Complete Sarah Vaughan On Mercury-#3 .... (Mercury)
Stephane Grappelli & Martin Taylor; *Just One Of Those Things* .... (Angel)

How To Be A Country Star
Statler Brothers; *Best Of The Statler Brothers-Rides Again-#2* .... (Mercury)

Humming Song
Martin Mull; *I'm Everyone I Ever Loved.* .... (MCA)

Hurdy Gurdy Man
Butthole Surfers; *ST/Dumb And Dumber* .... (RCA)
Donovan; *Donovan's Greatest Hits* .... (Epic)
   Hurdy Gurdy Man .... (Epic)

Hymn
James Taylor; *One Man Dog* .... (Warner Bros.)

Hymn
Patti Smith Group; *Wave* .... (Arista)

Hymn
Peter, Paul & Mary; *Late Again.* .... (Warner Bros.)

Hymn 43
Jethro Tull; *Aqualung* .... (Chrysalis)
   Living In The Past. .... (Chrysalis)

Hymn For The Dudes
Mott The Hoople; *Mott* .... (Columbia)
   Mott The Hoople's Greatest Hits .... (Columbia)

Hymn To Her
Pretenders; *Diana, Princess Of Wales-Tribute-C* (Columbia)
Get Close (Sire)
The Isle Of View (Warner Bros.)
Hymn To Me
Brinsley Schwarz; *Brinsley Schwarz* (Capitol)
Hymn To The Sea
James Horner; *ST/Titanic* (Sony Music Classical)
I Am Looking At Music
Nia Long; *ST/Love Jones* (Columbia)
I Can Hear Music
Beach Boys; *Friends-20/20* (Capitol)
Sunshine Dream (Capitol)
Beach Boys & Kathy Troccoli; *Stars And Stripes-#1* (River North)
I Dig Rock & Roll Music
Peter, Paul & Mary; *10 Years Together/The Best Of Peter, Paul and Mary* (Warner Bros.)
1700 (Warner Bros.)
I Don't Want To
Toni Braxton; *Secrets* (LaFace)
I Feel Like Singing
Dan Hicks & His Hot Licks; *Where's The Money?* (MCA)
I Got Rhythm
Ella Fitzgerald; *George & Ira Gershwin Songbook* (Verve)
Ethel Waters; *I Got Rhythm: The Smithsonian George Gershwin Collection-C* (Smithsonian Collection)
Happenings; *'60s Rock Classics-#1-C* (Rhino)
Judy Garland; *Judy Garland-Collector's Items-1936-1945* (MCA)
Louis Armstrong; *Essential Louis Armstrong* (Verve)
Original Cast; *Girl Crazy* (Nonesuch)
Original London Cast; *Crazy For You* (RCA)
Robert Palmer; *Glory Of Gershwin Featuring Larry Adler-C* (Mercury)
I Gotta Have A Song
Stevie Wonder; *Looking Back* (Motown)
Signed Sealed & Delivered (Motown)
I Guess That's Why They Call It The Blues
Elton John; *Elton John's Greatest Hits-1976-1986* (MCA)
Too Low For Zero (MCA)
I Hear A Rhapsody
John Coltrane; *Lush Life* (Prestige)
More Lasting Than Bronze (Prestige)
Prestige Twofer Giants-#2 (Prestige)
I Hear A Symphony
Diana Ross & The Supremes; *16 #1 Hits From The Early '60s-C* (Motown)
Diana Ross & The Supremes' Greatest Hits (Motown)
Diana Ross & The Supremes-25th Anniversary (Motown)
Diana Ross & The Supremes-Anthology (1962-1969) (Motown)
Evening With Diana Ross (Motown)
Every Great #1 Hit (Motown)
Good Feeling Music Of The Big Chill Generation-#2-C (Motown)
Motown Story-First 25 Years-C (Motown)
Supremes; *I Hear A Symphony* (Motown)
I Hear Music
Anita O'Day; *Big Band Session* (Verve)
Live At Mingos (Emily)
I Hear Music
Billie Holiday; *Billie Holiday-Golden Year-#2* (Columbia)
Quintessential-#8-1939-1940 (Legacy)
The Billie Holiday Story-#3 (Columbia)
I Know A Place
Petula Clark; *History Of British Rock-#7-C* (Rhino)
Petula Clark's Greatest Hits (Crescendo)
I Let A Song Go Out Of My Heart
Bill Jennings; *Stompin' With Bill* (Collectables)
Duke Ellington; *Braggin' In Brass-Immortal 1938 Year* (Portrait)
Joe Pass; *Portraits Of Duke Ellington* (Pablo)
Teresa Brewer; *Sophisticated Lady* (Columbia)
Tony Bennett; *Jazz* (Columbia)
I Like Mountain Music
Roy Acuff; *Grand Ole Opry-75 Years-#1-C* (MCA)
I Love Music
O'Jays; *Family Reunion* (Philadelphia Int'l)
O'Jays-Collector's Item (Philadelphia Int'l)
Philadelphia Classics-C (Philadelphia Int'l)
Ten Years Of #1 Hits-C (Philadelphia Int'l)
Rozalla; *ST/Carlito's Way* (Epic/Sony Music Soundtrax)
I Love New Orleans Music
Ronnie Milsap; *Inside Ronnie Milsap* (RCA)
I Sang Dixie
Dwight Yoakam; *Buenas Noches From A Lonely Room* (Reprise)
Just Lookin' For A Hit (Reprise)
I Try To Think About Elvis
Patty Loveless; *Patty Loveless-Classics* (Epic)
When Fallen Angels Fly (Epic)
I Walk The Line (Revisited)
Rodney Crowell; *The Houston Kid* (Sugar Hill)
I Want To Hear A Yankee Doodle Tune
George M. Cohan; *Music From The New York Stage (1890-1920)-#1-1890-1908-C* (Pearl)
I Want To Sing That Rock And Roll
Gillian Welch; *Time (The Revelator)* (Acony)
I Was Country When Country Wasn't Cool
Barbara Mandrell; *Barbara Mandrell Live* (MCA)
Barbara Mandrell's Greatest Hits (MCA)
I Watched It All (On My Radio)
Lionel Cartwright; *I Watched It All On The Radio* (MCA)
I Whistle A Happy Tune
Barbara Cook; *My Little Broadway* (Sony Wonder)
Frank Sinatra; *Frank Sinatra Sings Rodgers & Hammerstein* (Columbia)
Micky Dolenz; *Broadway Micky* (Kid Rhino/Rhino 4 Kids)
Original Broadway Cast; *The King And I* (RCA Victor)
Original Cast; *The King And I* (MCA)
I Write The Songs
Barry Manilow; *Barry Manilow/Live* (Arista)
Barry Manilow's Greatest Hits-#2 (Arista)
Tryin' To Get The Feeling (Arista)
I'd Like To Teach The World To Sing (In Perfect Harmony)
New Seekers; *Chicken Soup For The Soul-Celebrating Life-C* (Rhino)
If I Could Sing Something In Spanish
Shelly West; *Don't Make Me Wait On The Moon* (Viva)
If I Had A Hammer (The Hammer Song)
Pete Seeger; *Sing-A-Long-Live At Sanders Theatre 1980* (Smithsonian Folkways)
Peter, Paul & Mary; *10 Years Together/The Best Of Peter, Paul and Mary* (Warner Bros.)
Peter, Paul and Mary (Warner Bros.)
Peter, Paul and Mary In Concert (Warner Bros.)
Trini Lopez; *Best Of Trini Lopez* (Exact)
Weavers; *Weavers' Greatest Hits* (Vanguard)
If I Knew You Were Comin' I'd've Baked A Cake
Bing Crosby; *The Radio Years-#4* (Crescendo)
Ethel Merman; *The Ethel Merman Collection* (Razor & Tie)
If You're Gonna Play In Texas
Alabama; *Alabama-Live* (RCA)
Roll On (RCA)
Stars Are Out In Texas-C (RCA)
I'll Always Remember That Song
Charlie Daniels Band; *Whiskey* (Epic)
I'll Have To Say I Love You In A Song
Jim Croce; *Baby Boomer Classics-Love Seventies-C* (JCI Assoc. Labels)
Billboard Top Soft Rock Hits-1974-C (Rhino)
Dim The Lights-C (K-Tel)
I'll Play For You
Seals & Crofts; *I'll Play For You* (Warner Bros.)
Seals & Crofts' Greatest Hits (Warner Bros.)
I'll Play The Blues For You
Albert King; *16 Original Big Hits-#2-C* (Stax)
Albert King Live (Tomato)
Albert King-Chronicle (Stax)
I'll Play The Blues For You (Stax)
Superblues-#1-All-Time Classic Blues-C (Stax)
I'll Write A Song For You
Earth, Wind & Fire; *All 'N All* (Columbia)
I'm Just A Singer In A Rock & Roll Band
Moody Blues; *Seventh Sojourn* (Polydor)
This Is The Moody Blues (Polydor)
Voices In The Sky-The Best Of The Moody Blues (Threshold)
I'm My Own Walkman
Bobby McFerrin; *The Voice* (Elektra)
I'm Playing For You
Ronnie Milsap; *True Believer* (Liberty)
Immigrant Song
Led Zeppelin; *Led Zeppelin III* (Atlantic)
Led Zeppelin-Box Set (Atlantic)
In The Mood
Robert Plant; *Principle Of Moments* (Es Paranza)
Innamorata
Dean Martin; *Capitol Collectors Series-Dean Martin* (Capitol)
Dean Martin's All Time Greatest Hits (Curb)
Jerry Vale; *Essence Of Jerry Vale* (Legacy)
Jerry Vale-17 Most Requested Songs (Legacy)
Jerry Vale's Greatest Hits (Columbia)
Intergalactic
Beastie Boys; *Hello Nasty* (Grand Royal)
It Don't Hurt
Sheryl Crow; *The Globe Sessions* (A&M)
It Don't Mean A Thing If It Ain't Got That Swing
Duke Ellington; *Carnegie Hall Concert* (Prestige)
Duke Ellington & Teresa Brewer; *It Don't Mean A Thing If It Ain't Got That Swing* (Columbia)
Ella Fitzgerald; *Ella Fitzgerald In London* (Pablo)
Ella Fitzgerald & Duke Ellington; *At The Cote D'Azur* (Verve)
It Was Almost Like A Song
Ronnie Milsap; *60 Years Of Country Music-C* (RCA)
Lost In The Fifties Tonight (RCA)
Ronnie Milsap's Greatest Hits (RCA)
It's Alright
Candlebox; *Happy Pills* (Maverick)

It's The Same Old Song
Four Tops; *Billboard Top R&B Hits-1965-C* . . . (Rhino)
Compact Command Performances-Four Tops . . . (Motown)
Four Tops' Greatest Hits . . . (Motown)
Four Tops-Anthology . . . (Motown)
It's Your Song
Garth Brooks; *Big Country Hits '99-C* . . . (K-Tel)
Garth Brooks-Double Live . . . (Capitol)
I've Got A Right To Sing The Blues
Tony Bennett with Bonnie Raitt; *Playin' With My Friends-Bennett Sings The Blues-C* . . . (Columbia)
Jam
Michael Jackson; *Dangerous* . . . (Epic)
Jamming
Bob Marley & The Wailers; *Babylon By Bus* . . . (Tuff Gong)
Exodus . . . (Tuff Gong)
Legend: The Best Of Bob Marley & The Wailers . . . (Island)
Jody Like A Melody
David Allan Coe; *David Allan Coe-17 Greatest Hits* . . . (Columbia)
For The Record-The First 10 Years . . . (Columbia)
Johnny B. Goode
Chuck Berry; *Chuck Berry's Greatest Hits* . . . (Everest)
Classic Rock-#2-C . . . (MCA)
Roll Over Beethoven . . . (Allegiance)
ST/American Graffiti . . . (MCA)
The Chess Box-Chuck Berry . . . (Chess)
Elvis Presley; *Elvis In Concert* . . . (RCA)
From Memphis To Vegas/From Vegas To Memphis . . . (RCA)
Grateful Dead; *Bill Graham Presents The Last Days Of The Fillmore-C* . . . (Epic Portrait Assoc.)
Johnny Winter; *Live/Johnny Winter And* . . . (Columbia)
Second Winter . . . (Columbia)
Johnny One Note
Judy Garland; *Best Of Judy Garland-From MGM Classic Films* . . . (MCA)
Original Cast/Mary Martin; *Babes In Arms* . . . (Sony Music Special Prod.)
Johnny Strikes Up The Band
Warren Zevon; *Excitable Boy* . . . (Asylum)
Quiet Normal Life-Best Of Warren Zevon . . . (Asylum)
Jones On The Jukebox
Becky Hobbs; *All Keyed Up* . . . (RCA)
Julia
Beatles; *Beatles-Box Set* . . . (Capitol)
ST/Imagine: John Lennon . . . (Capitol)
The Beatles (White Album) . . . (Capitol)
Jump Jive An' Wail
Brian Setzer Orchestra; *Dirty Boogie* . . . (Interscope)
Now That's What I Call Music!-#1-C . . . (Virgin)
Louis Prima; *Capitol Collectors Series-Louis Prima* . . . (Capitol)
Ultra-Lounge-#5-Wild, Cool & Swingin'-C . . . (Capitol)
Jungleland
Bruce Springsteen; *Born To Run* . . . (Columbia)
Junkie For My Music
Lonnie Jordan; *Different Moods Of Me* . . . (MCA)
Just A Song Before I Go
Crosby, Stills & Nash; *CSN* . . . (Atlantic)
Replay . . . (Atlantic)
Just Push Play
Aerosmith; *Just Push Play* . . . (Columbia)
Keep On Singing
Helen Reddy; *Helen Reddy's Greatest Hits* . . . (Capitol)
Love Song For Jeffrey . . . (Capitol)
Keep Their Heads Ringin'
Dr. Dre; *Hip Hop's Most Wanted-C* . . . (Priority)
ST/Friday . . . (Priority)
Key West Intermezzo (I Saw You First)
John Mellencamp; *Mr. Happy Go Lucky* . . . (Mercury)
Killing Me Softly With His Song
Fugees; *Score* . . . (Ruffhouse)
Luther Vandross; *Songs* . . . (Epic)
Roberta Flack; *Atlantic Rhythm & Blues 1947-1974-#6 (1966-1969)-C* . . . (Atlantic)
Best Of Roberta Flack . . . (Atlantic)
Golden Age Of Black Music-1970-1975-C . . . (Atlantic)
Killing Me Softly . . . (Atlantic)
King Creole
Elvis Presley; *Hits Like Never Before-Essential-#3* . . . (RCA)
ST/King Creole . . . (RCA)
The Great Performances . . . (RCA)
The Other Sides-Worldwide Gold Award Hits, Vol. 2 . . . (RCA)
Lady Sings The Blues
Billie Holiday; *All Or Nothing At All* . . . (Verve)
Essential Billie Holiday-Carnegie Hall Concert . . . (Verve)
History Of The Real Billie Holiday . . . (Verve)
Lady Sings The Blues . . . (Verve)
Large Time
Atlanta Rhythm Section; *Are You Ready!* . . . (Polydor)
Champagne Jam . . . (Polydor)
Last Love Song
Hank Williams, Jr.; *Hank Williams, Jr.-14 Greatest Hits* . . . (Polydor)
Standing In The Shadows . . . (Polydor)
Last Love Song
Cat Stevens; *Back To Earth* . . . (A&M)
Last Of The Singing Cowboys
Marshall Tucker Band; *Running Like The Wind* . . . (Warner Bros.)
Late In The Evening
Paul Simon; *Negotiations And Love Songs, 1971-1986* . . . (Warner Bros.)
One-Trick Pony . . . (Warner Bros.)
Simon & Garfunkel; *The Concert In Central Park* . . . (Warner Bros.)
Lay Down Your Weary Tune
Ashley Hutchings; *The Guv'nor* . . . (Wildcat)
Bob Dylan; *Biograph* . . . (Columbia)
Byrds; *The Byrds* . . . (Columbia)
Turn! Turn! Turn! . . . (Legacy)
Tim O'Brien; *Red On Blonde* . . . (Sugar Hill)
Leader Of The Band
Dan Fogelberg; *Dan Fogelberg/Greatest Hits* . . . (Full Moon)
Innocent Age . . . (Full Moon)
Legend Of A Cowgirl
Imani Coppola; *Chupacapra* . . . (Columbia)
Let Me Blow Ya Mind
Eve featuring Gwen Stefani; *Now That's What I Call Music!-#7-C* . . . (Virgin)
Scorpion . . . (Ruff Ryders/IDJMG)
Let Me In
Bonnie Raitt; *Takin' My Time* . . . (Warner Bros.)
Sensations; *Billboard Top R&B Hits-1962-C* . . . (Rhino)
Chess Rhythm & Roll Box-C . . . (Chess)
Cruisin'-1962-1963-C . . . (Dunhill Compact Classics)
Vintage Music-#6-C . . . (MCA)
Let Me Sing & I'm Happy
Al Jolson; *Best Of Al Jolson* . . . (MCA)
The Al Jolson Story-#3 . . . (MCA)
Let Me Sing For You
Kenny Rogers; *Daytime Friends* . . . (EMI)
Let Me Sing Your Blues Away
Grateful Dead; *Wake Of The Flood* . . . (Grateful Dead)
Let There Be Music
Orleans; *Before The Dance* . . . (Elektra)
Let There Be Music . . . (Elektra)
Let's Face The Music And Dance
Diana Krall; *When I Look In Your Eyes* . . . (GRP)
Ella Fitzgerald; *Irving Berlin Always-C* . . . (Verve)
Tony Bennett; *Bennett/Berlin* . . . (Columbia)
Jazz . . . (Columbia)
Life In A Song
Marshall Tucker Band; *Carolina Dreams* . . . (Capricorn)
Life Is A Long Song
Jethro Tull; *Living In The Past* . . . (Chrysalis)
Life Is A Song Worth Singing
Johnny Mathis; *I'm Coming Home* . . . (Columbia)
Teddy Pendergrass; *Life Is A Song Worth Singing* . . . (Philadelphia Int'l)
Life's A Song
Kool & The Gang; *Force* . . . (De-Lite)
Life's Been Good
Eagles; *Eagles Live* . . . (Asylum)
Joe Walsh; *But Seriously Folks* . . . (Asylum)
ST/FM . . . (MCA)
Lights
Styx; *Cornerstone* . . . (A&M)
Listen To A Country Song
Loggins & Messina; *Loggins & Messina-On Stage* . . . (Columbia)
Sittin' In . . . (Columbia)
Lynn Anderson; *Country Chartbusters-#2* . . . (Columbia)
Lynn Anderson's Greatest Hits . . . (Columbia)
Listen To The Band
Monkees; *Monkees' Greatest Hits* . . . (Rhino)
Present . . . (Rhino)
Listen To The Music
Doobie Brothers; *Best Of The Doobies* . . . (Warner Bros.)
Farewell Tour . . . (Warner Bros.)
Toulouse Street . . . (Warner Bros.)
Little Bit Of Soul
Music Explosion; *Best Of Ohio Express & Other Bubblegum Smashes-#1-C* . . . (Rhino)
Cruisin'-1967-C . . . (Increase)
Million-Dollar Memories #1-C . . . (RCA)
Live For The Music
Bad Company; *10 From 6* . . . (Atlantic)
Run With The Pack . . . (Swan Song)
Livingston Saturday Night
Jimmy Buffett; *Son Of A Son Of A Sailor* . . . (MCA)
ST/FM . . . (MCA)
Load Out/Stay
Jackson Browne; *Running On Empty* . . . (Asylum)
Lodi
Creedence Clearwater Revival; *1969* . . . (Fantasy)
Creedence Clearwater Revival-Chronicle . . . (Fantasy)
Creedence Country . . . (Fantasy)
Green River . . . (Fantasy)

Live In Europe . . . .(Fantasy)
More Creedence Gold. . . . .(Fantasy)
Travelin' Band . . . .(Fantasy)

Londonderry Air
Mormon Tabernacle Choir; *Lord's Prayer* . . . .(Columbia)
Mormon Tabernacle Choir's Greatest Hits-#2 . . . .(Columbia)
The Mormon Tabernacle Choir Album . . . .(Columbia)

Lone Star Beer & Bob Wills Music
Red Steagall; *Lone Star Beer & Bob Wills Music* . . . . (MCA)
Texas Country . . . . (MCA)

Longfellow Serenade
Neil Diamond; *12 Greatest Hits-#2* . . . .(Columbia)
Love At The Greek . . . .(Columbia)
On The Way To The Sky . . . .(Columbia)
Serenade . . . .(Columbia)

Lookin' At Me
Mase Featuring Puff Daddy; *Harlem World* . . . . (Bad Boy/Arista)

Losing My Religion
R.E.M.; *Out Of Time* . . . . (Warner Bros.)

Lost In The Fifties Tonight
Ronnie Milsap; *Lost In The Fifties Tonight* . . . .(RCA)
Ronnie Milsap's Greatest Hits-#2 . . . .(RCA)

Louisiana Cajun Band
Jimmy C. Newman; *Backstage At The Grand Ole Opry-C* . . . .(RCA)
Cajun Country . . . .(Delmark)

Louisiana Cajun Rock Band
Carol Channing & Jimmy C. Newman; *Carol Channing & Her Country
Friends* . . . .(Plantation)

Love At The Five & Dime
Kathy Mattea; *Collection Of Hits* . . . .(Mercury)
Fourteen Country Favorites-C . . . .(Mercury)
Walk The Way The Wind Blows . . . .(Mercury)
Nanci Griffith; *Last Of The True Believers* . . . .(Philo)
One Fair Summer Evening . . . . (MCA)

Love Song
Kenny Rogers; *Kenny Rogers-Twenty Greatest Hits* . . . . (EMI)
Love Will Turn You Around . . . . (EMI)

Love Song
Oak Ridge Boys; *American Made* . . . . (MCA)
Oak Ridge Boys' Greatest Hits 2 . . . . (MCA)

Love Song
Anne Murray; *Anne Murray's Greatest Hits* . . . . (Capitol)
Love Song . . . . (Capitol)
Loggins & Messina; *Full Sail* . . . .(Columbia)

Love Song
Original Cast; *Pippin* . . . .(Motown)
Threepenny Opera . . . .(Polydor)

Love Song
Cure; *Disintegration* . . . .(Elektra)
Mixed Up . . . .(Elektra)

Love Song
Madonna; *Like A Prayer* . . . .(Sire)

Love Song
Damned; *Final Damnation* . . . .(Restless)
Light At The End Of The Tunnel . . . . (MCA)

Love Song
Elton John; *Here And There* . . . .(Rocket)
Tumbleweed Connection . . . .(Polydor)

Love Song
Tesla; *Five Man Acoustical Jam* . . . .(Geffen)
Great Radio Controversy . . . .(Geffen)

Love Song
Lee Greenwood; *Inside Out/You've Got A Good Love Comin'* . . . . (MCA)

Luckenbach Texas (Back To The Basics Of Love)
Waylon Jennings; *Ol' Waylon* . . . .(RCA)
Stars Are Out In Texas-C . . . .(RCA)
Waylon Jennings' Greatest Hits . . . .(RCA)

Lullaby
Shawn Mullins; *Soul's Core* . . . .(Columbia)

Lullaby Of Birdland
Ella Fitzgerald; *Best Of Ella Fitzgerald-#2* . . . . (MCA)
Ella Fitzgerald With Billie Holiday . . . . (MCA)
Four Freshmen; *Greatest Hits-Four Freshman* . . . .(Curb)
Mel Torme; *Songs Of New York* . . . .(Rhino)
Sarah Vaughan; *Sarah Vaughan-Golden Hits* . . . .(Mercury)
Tito Puente & His Latin Ensemble; *Mambo Diablo* . . . .(Concord Jazz)

Lullaby Of Broadway
Andrews Sisters; *Best Of The Andrews Sisters-#2* . . . . (MCA)
Bette Midler; *Bette Midler* . . . .(Atlantic)
Live At Last . . . .(Atlantic)
Original Broadway Cast; *42nd Street* . . . .(RCA Victor)
Tony Bennett; *Jazz* . . . .(Columbia)

Lullaby Of The Leaves
Various Artists; *Birdlanders-#1-C* . . . . (Original Jazz Classics)

Make It Funky (Part 1)
James Brown; *In Yo' Face!-History Of Funk-#2-C* . . . .(Rhino)
James Brown's 20 All Time Greatest Hits! . . . .(Polydor)

Make Love To The Music
Maria Muldaur; *Southern Winds* . . . . (Warner Bros.)

Make The Music Magic
Be Bop Deluxe; *Modern Music* . . . .(Capitol)

Making Music For Money
Kenny Rogers; *The Gambler* . . . . (EMI)

Making Music For Money
Jimmy Buffett; *A1A* . . . . (MCA)

Mama Let Him Play
Doucette; *Mama Let Him Play* . . . .(Mushroom)

Mama Sang A Song
Bill Anderson; *Bill Anderson's Greatest Hits* . . . . (Varese Sarabande)
Country Music Classics-#17-C . . . .(K-Tel)

Mama's Opry
Iris DeMent; *Infamous Angel* . . . . (Warner Bros.)

Man From Music Mountain
Gene Autry; *The Singing Cowboy-Chapter Two* . . . . (Varese Sarabande)

Manic Depression
Jimi Hendrix Experience; *Are You Experienced?* . . . . (Reprise)

Maryland
Vonda Shepard; *ST/Songs From "Ally McBeal" Featuring Vonda
Shepard* . . . . (550/Epic)

Master Blaster (Jammin')
Stevie Wonder; *Hotter Than July* . . . .(Motown)
Original Musiquarium . . . .(Motown)

Melody
David Crosby; *Oh Yes I Can* . . . .(A&M)

Melody
Rolling Stones; *Black And Blue* . . . .(Rolling Stones)

Memphis Soul Stew
King Curtis; *Atlantic Jazz-Soul-C* . . . . (Atlantic)
Atlantic Rhythm & Blues 1947-1974-#6 (1966-1969)-C . . . . (Atlantic)
Best Of King Curtis . . . . (Atlantic)
Golden Soul-C . . . . (Atlantic)
Live At The Fillmore West . . . . (Atlantic)

Mercury Poisoning
Graham Parker And The Rumour; *Live Sparks* . . . .(Arista)

Minstrel Boy
Boston Pops Orchestra/Arthur Fiedler; *Irish Album* . . . . (RCA)
Irish Night At The Pops . . . . (RCA)
John McDermott; *Battlefields Of Green-Songs Of Love & Loss* . . . .(Angel)

Minstrel In The Gallery
Jethro Tull; *20 Years Of Jethro Tull* . . . .(Chrysalis)
Bursting Out . . . .(Chrysalis)
Original Masters . . . .(Chrysalis)
Repeat-The Best Of Jethro Tull, Vol. II . . . .(Chrysalis)
Too Old To Rock 'N' Roll: Too Young To Die! . . . .(Chrysalis)

Modern Music
Be Bop Deluxe; *Best Of Be Bop Deluxe-Raiding The Divine Archive* . . .(Capitol)
Modern Music . . . .(Capitol)

Moonlight Bay
Beatles; *The Beatles-Anthology-#1* . . . .(Capitol)
Bing Crosby; *The Radio Years-#4* . . . .(Crescendo)
The Radio Years: 20 Songs . . . .(Crescendo)
Drifters; *Clyde McPhatter & The Drifters-Rockin' & Driftin'* . . . . .(Collectables)
Glenn Miller; *Big Bands-#1-C* . . . .(Universal)

Mother Nature's Son
Beatles; *Beatles-Box Set* . . . .(Capitol)
The Beatles (White Album) . . . .(Capitol)
John Denver; *Evening With John Denver* . . . . (RCA)
Rocky Mountain High . . . . (RCA)

Motown Song
Larry John McNally; *Fade To Black* . . . .(Atco)
Rod Stewart; *Vagabond Heart* . . . . (Warner Bros.)

Motownphilly
Boyz II Men; *Cooleyhighharmony* . . . .(Motown)

Mountain Music
Alabama; *Alabama's Greatest Hits* . . . . (RCA)
Mountain Music . . . . (RCA)

Mr. Melody
Natalie Cole; *Natalie* . . . .(Capitol)
Natalie Cole-Collection . . . .(Capitol)
Natalie Cole-Live . . . .(Capitol)

Mr. Record Man
Willie Nelson; *Best Of Willie Nelson* . . . .(Capitol)
Horse Called Music . . . .(Columbia)
Willie & Family Live . . . .(Columbia)

Mr. Tambourine Man
Bob Dylan; *Biograph* . . . .(Columbia)
Bob Dylan At Budokan . . . .(Columbia)
Bob Dylan's Greatest Hits . . . .(Columbia)
Bringing It All Back Home . . . .(Columbia)
Byrds; *Billboard Top Rock 'N' Roll Hits-1965-C* . . . .(Rhino)
Original Singles-#1-1965-1967 . . . .(Columbia)
The Byrds' Greatest Hits . . . .(Columbia)
The Original Singles-1965-1967 . . . .(Columbia)
Turn! Turn! Turn! . . . .(Legacy)

Mr. Too Damn Good
Gerald Levert; *G* . . . .(East West)

Mud Shark, The
Mothers Of Invention; *Fillmore East-June 1971* . . . . (Reprise)

Murder On Music Row
George Strait & Alan Jackson; *Latest Greatest Straitest Hits* . . . . (MCA)
Music
Madonna; *GHV2* . . . . (Warner Bros.)
   Music . . . . (Maverick)
   Totally Hits-#3-C . . . . (Atlantic)
Music
Erick Sermon featuring Marvin Gaye; *Music* . . . . (J)
   ST/What's The Worst That Can Happen? . . . . (Bad Boy/Arista)
Music Band
War; *The Music Band* . . . . (MCA)
Music For Money
Nick Lowe; *Pure Pop For Now People* . . . . (Columbia)
Music In Dreamland
Be Bop Deluxe; *Best Of And The Rest Of Be Bop Deluxe* . . . . . (Capitol)
   Best Of Be Bop Deluxe-Raiding The Divine Archive . . . . (Capitol)
   Futurama . . . . (Harvest)
Music Is You
John Denver; *Back Home Again* . . . . (RCA)
   Evening With John Denver . . . . (RCA)
Music Makin' Mama From Memphis
Hank Snow; *Best Of Hank Snow* . . . . (RCA)
Music Man
REO Speedwagon; *A Decade Of Rock And Roll 1970 To 1980* . . (Epic)
   REO Speedwagon Live/You Get What You Play For . . . . (Epic)
Music Man
Cat Stevens; *Buddha & The Chocolate Box* . . . . (A&M)
Music Man
Cleo Laine; *Cleo Laine-Live At Carnegie Hall* . . . . (RCA)
   I Am A Song . . . . (RCA)
Music Man
James Taylor; *Gorilla* . . . . (Warner Bros.)
Music Man
Exile; *Hang On To Your Heart* . . . . (Epic)
Music Must Change
Who; *Who Are You* . . . . (MCA)
Music Never Stopped
Grateful Dead; *Blues For Allah* . . . . (Grateful Dead)
   One From The Vault . . . . (Grateful Dead)
Music Of The Night
Michael Crawford; *Premiere Collection-Best Of Andrew Lloyd
   Webber-C* . . . . (MCA)
Original London Cast; *Phantom Of The Opera* . . . . (Polydor)
Music That Makes Me Dance
Barbra Streisand/Original Cast; *Funny Girl* . . . . (Capitol)
Michael Feinstein & Jule Styne; *M. Feinstein Sings Jule Styne
   Songbook* . . . . (Elektra)
Music To Watch Girls By
Andy Williams; *Andy Williams' Greatest Hits-#2* . . . . (Columbia)
Music Trance
Ben E. King; *Music Trance* . . . . (Atlantic)
Music! Music! Music!
Teresa Brewer; *Best Of Teresa Brewer* . . . . (MCA Jazz)
Musical Box
Genesis; *Genesis-Live* . . . . (Atlantic)
   Live/The Way We Walk-Volume Two: The Longs . . . . (Atlantic)
   Nursery Cryme . . . . (Atlantic)
   Seconds Out . . . . (Atlantic)
Muskrat Ramble
Dukes Of Dixieland; *Digital Dixieland* . . . . (Pro Jazz)
Kid Ory's Creole Jazz Band; *Kid Ory's Creole Jazz Band-
   1954* . . . . (Good Time Jazz)
Louis Armstrong; *Essential Louis Armstrong* . . . . (Vanguard)
   Louis Armstrong's Greatest Hits . . . . (Curb)
McGuire Sisters; *McGuire Sisters' Greatest Hits* . . . . (MCA)
Pete Fountain; *High Society* . . . . (Bluebird)
My Melody Of Love
Frank Sinatra & Ray Anthony; *Capitol Collectors Series-Frank
   Sinatra* . . . . (Capitol)
My Music
Loggins & Messina; *Best Of Friends* . . . . (Columbia)
   Full Sail . . . . (Columbia)
My Song
Jerry Cantrell; *Boggy Depot* . . . . (Columbia)
Nashville Cats
Del McCoury Band; *The Family* . . . . (Ceili Music)
Lovin' Spoonful; *Lovin' Spoonful-Anthology* . . . . (Rhino)
Nashville Pickin'
Doc Watson; *Southbound* . . . . (Vanguard)
Never Ending
Wood; *Songs From Stamford Hill* . . . . (Columbia)
Never Ending Song Of Love
Conway Twitty & Loretta Lynn; *Lead Me On* . . . . (MCA)
Delaney & Bonnie; *Best Of Delaney & Bonnie* . . . . (Rhino)
   Super Hits Of The '70s-Have A Nice Day-#16-C . . . . (Rhino)
New San Antonio Rose
Bob Wills & His Texas Playboys; *Bob Wills & His Texas Playboys-
   Greatest Hits* . . . . (Curb)

   Columbia Country Classics-#1-Golden Age-C . . . . (Columbia)
   Essential Bob Wills & His Texas Playboys-1935-1973 . . . . . . (Legacy)
Dwight Yoakam & Asleep At The Wheel; *Ride With
   Bob-C* . . . . (DreamWorks/SKG)
Nickel For The Fiddler
Guy Clark; *Old No. 1* . . . . (Sugar Hill)
Nightclubbing
Grace Jones; *Nightclubbing* . . . . (Island)
Iggy Pop; *Idiot* . . . . (RCA)
   TV Eye/1977 Live . . . . (RCA)
Nightfly, The
Donald Fagen; *The Nightfly* . . . . (Warner Bros.)
Nightshift
Commodores; *Nightshift* . . . . (Motown)
No Matter What They Say
Lil' Kim; *Notorious K.I.M.* . . . . (Queen Bee/Undeas/Atlantic)
No More Songs
Phil Ochs; *Chords Of Fame* . . . . (A&M)
   No More Songs . . . . (A&M)
   Phil Ochs' Greatest Hits . . . . (A&M)
   The War Is Over-Best Of Phil Ochs . . . . (A&M)
Norwegian Aire
Magical Strings; *Crossing To Skellig* . . . . (Flying Fish)
November Song
Norrie Paramor; *Autumn* . . . . (Angel)
November Song
Didier Lockwood; *Out Of The Blue* . . . . (Gramavision)
Now That's Country
Marty Stuart; *This One's Gonna Hurt You* . . . . (MCA)
Now They Call It Swing
Billie Holiday; *Golden Years-#1* . . . . (Columbia)
   Quintessential-#5-1937-1938 . . . . (Columbia)
   The Billie Holiday Story-#3 . . . . (Columbia)
Nowadays Clancy Can't Even Sing
Buffalo Springfield; *Buffalo Springfield* . . . . (Atco)
   Buffalo Springfield-Retrospective . . . . (Atco)
Ob-La-Di, Ob-La-Da
Beatles; *Beatles-Box Set* . . . . (Capitol)
   The Beatles (White Album) . . . . (Capitol)
   The Beatles/1967-1970 . . . . (Capitol)
Of Thee I Sing
Sarah Vaughan; *Sarah Vaughan Sings George Gershwin* . . . . . . (Verve)
Oh Baby Doll
Chuck Berry; *The Chess Box-Chuck Berry* . . . . (Chess)
Oh Yeah
Roxy Music; *Flesh + Blood* . . . . (Atco)
   Street Life-20 Great Hits . . . . (Reprise)
Old Fashioned Love Song
Three Dog Night; *Harmony-C* . . . . (MCA Special Prod.)
   Joy To The World-Greatest Hits . . . . (MCA)
Old Songs
Barry Manilow; *Barry Manilow's Greatest Hits-#3* . . . . (Arista)
   If I Should Love Again . . . . (Arista)
One Man Band
Moe Bandy; *Moe Bandy's Greatest Hits* . . . . (Curb)
   You Haven't Heard The Last Of Me . . . . (MCA)
One Man Band
Roger Daltrey; *Daltrey* . . . . (MCA)
One Man Band
Three Dog Night; *Joy To The World-Greatest Hits* . . . . (MCA)
One More Goodtime Band In Texas
Leon Rausch; *Rausch Touch* . . . . (Southland)
One Of Those Love Songs
Xscape; *Traces Of My Lipstick* . . . . (So So Def/Columbia)
One On The Right Is On The Left, The
Johnny Cash; *Johnny Cash-16 Biggest Hits-#2* . . . . (Legacy)
Only A Northern Song
Beatles; *The Beatles-Anthology-#2* . . . . (Capitol)
   Yellow Submarine . . . . (Capitol)
Painted Perfect
One Way Ride; *Strait Up!* . . . . (Refuge/MCA)
Papa's Got A Brand New Bag
James Brown; *21 Legendary Superstars-C* . . . . (Original Sound)
   Everybody's Doin' The Hustle & Dead On The Double Bump . . . . . (Polydor)
   James Brown's Greatest Hits . . . . (Rhino)
   Live-Hot On The One . . . . (Polydor)
Otis Redding; *The Otis Redding Story* . . . . (Atlantic)
   Unlimited! . . . . (Reprise)
Parker's Band
Steely Dan; *Pretzel Logic* . . . . (MCA)
Phantom Of The Opera
Iron Maiden; *Iron Maiden* . . . . (Capitol)
   Live After Death-World Slavery Tour . . . . (Capitol)
Phantom Of The Opera
Original London Cast; *Phantom Of The Opera* . . . . (Polydor)
Piano Man
Billy Joel; *Billy Joel-Greatest Hits, Volume I & Volume II* . . . . . . (Columbia)
   Piano Man . . . . (Columbia)

Rock Classics Of The '70s-C . . . . (Columbia)

Play
Jennifer Lopez; *J. Lo* . . . . (Epic)
Now That's What I Call Music!-#7-C . . . .(Virgin)

Play A Simple Melody
Bing Crosby; *Best Of Bing Crosby* . . . . (MCA)

Play It All Night Long
Warren Zevon; *Bad Luck Streak In Dancing School* . . . . (Asylum)
Quiet Normal Life-Best Of Warren Zevon . . . . (Asylum)

Play Me The Waltz Of The Angels
Derailers featuring Buck Owens; *Full Western Dress* . . . .(Sire)

Play That Funky Music
Vanilla Ice; *Extremely Live* . . . . (SBK)
To The Extreme . . . . (SBK)
Wild Cherry; *Billboard Top Rock 'N' Roll Hits-1978-C* . . . . . . (Rhino)
ST/Queen's Logic . . . . (Epic)
Wild Cherry . . . . (Epic)

Play Those Oldies Mr. DJ
Anthony And The Sophomores; *WCBS FM 101 History Of Rock-Doo-Wop-#2-C* . . . . (Collectables)

Polly-Wolly-Doodle
Leon Redbone; *Live!* . . . .(Pair)
On The Track . . . . (Warner Bros.)
Mance Lipscomb; *Mance Lipscomb-Vol. 3-Texas Songster In A Live Performance* . . . . (Arhoolie)
Pete Seeger/Woody Guthrie/Cisco Houston; *Lonesome Valley* . . . .(Smithsonian Folkways)

Poor People Of Paris
Les Baxter & His Orchestra; *Memories Are Made Of This-C* . . . . (Capitol)

Pop
'N Sync; *Celebrity* . . . .(Jive)
Now That's What I Call Music!-#8-C . . . .(Virgin)

Pop Goes The Weasel
Bing Crosby; *Where The Blue Of The Night Meets The Gold Of The Day* . . . . (Biograph)
Boston Pops Orchestra/Arthur Fiedler; *Forever Fiedler* . . . .(RCA)
Merry Macs; *Small Fry-Capitol Sings Kids Songs For Grownups-C* . . . (Capitol)

Pop Muzik
M; *Just Say Yesterday-#6 Of Just Say Yes-C* . . . . (Sire)
Mega Hits Dance Classics-#10-C . . . .(Priority)

Pop Singer
John Cougar Mellencamp; *Big Daddy* . . . . (Mercury)

Preaching, Praying, Singing
Bluegrass Album Band; *Bluegrass Class Of 1990* . . . . (Rounder)
Lester Flatt, Earl Scruggs & The Foggy Mountain Boys; *Lester Flatt, Earl Scruggs & The Foggy Mountain Boys-Complete Mercury Sessions* . . . . (Mercury)

Pretty Girl Is Like A Melody, A
John Steel; *Music From The New York Stage (1890-1920)-#4-1917-1920-C* . . . . (Pearl)

Private Conversation
Lyle Lovett; *The Road To Ensenada* . . . . (MCA)

Pump Up The Bass
D.J. Jazzy Jeff & The Fresh Prince; *He's The D.J. I'm The Rapper* . . . .(Jive)

Pump Up The Jam
Technotronic; *Pump Up The Jam-The Album* . . . . (SBK)
Rock The First-#3-C . . . . (Priority)

Pump Up The Volume
M/A/R/R/S; *ST/Bright Lights Big City* . . . . (Warner Bros.)

R&B Skeletons (In The Closet)
George Clinton; *R&B Skeletons (In The Closet)* . . . . (Capitol)

Radio M.U.S.I.C. Man
Womack & Womack; *Radio M.U.S.I.C. Man* . . . . (Elektra)

Ragtime Annie
Byron Berline; *Dad's Favorites* . . . . (Rounder)
Mason Williams; *Fresh Fish-C* . . . .(Flying Fish)

Ragtime Cowboy Joe
Jo Stafford; *Capitol Collectors Series-Jo Stafford* . . . . (Capitol)
Spike Jones & His City Slickers; *King Of Corn* . . . . (Glendale)

Ragtime Dance
Jean-Pierre Rampal; *Jean-Pierre Rampal Plays Scott Joplin* . . . . . . (Columbia)
Richard Zimmerman; *Scott Joplin-His Greatest Hits* . . . . (Everest)
Scott Joplin; *The Entertainer* . . . . (Biograph)

Ragtime Nightingale
Max Morath; *Max Morath Plays The Best Of Scott Joplin And Other Rags* . . . . (Vanguard)

Ragtime Oriole
Max Morath; *The World Of Scott Joplin* . . . . (Vanguard)

Ready Or Not
Fugees; *The Score* . . . . (Ruffhouse)
The Score-Edit . . . . (Columbia)

Ready Teddy
Buddy Holly; *Buddy Holly* . . . . (MCA)
Rock & Roll Collection . . . . (MCA)
Elvis Presley; *Elvis* . . . .(RCA)
Rocker . . . . (RCA)
The Great Performances . . . . (RCA)
Little Richard; *Georgia Peach* . . . . (Specialty)

Grooviest 17 Original Hits . . . . (Specialty)
More American Graffiti-C . . . . (MCA)

Real American Folk Song (Is A Rag)
Marni Nixon & Lincoln Mayorga; *Marni Nixon Sings Gershwin* . . . (Reference)

Rebel Music
Bob Marley & The Wailers; *Babylon By Bus* . . . . (Tuff Gong)
Natty Dread . . . . (Tuff Gong)
Rebel Music . . . . (Tuff Gong)

Redemption Song
Bob Marley & The Wailers; *Legend: The Best Of Bob Marley & The Wailers* . . . . (Island)
Uprising . . . . (Island)
Wyclef Jean; *America: A Tribute To Heroes-C* . . . . (Interscope)

Redneck Jazz
Danny Gatton; *Hot Rod Guitar: The Danny Gatton Anthology* . . . .(Rhino)

Redneck Rhythm & Blues
Brooks & Dunn; *Borderline* . . . . (Arista)

Remember
Jimi Hendrix Experience; *Are You Experienced?* . . . . (Reprise)

Renegades Of Funk
Rage Against The Machine; *Renegades* . . . .(Epic)

Rhumba Man
Jesse Winchester; *Best Of Jesse Winchester* . . . .(Rhino)
Nothing But The Breeze . . . .(Rhino)

Rhythm Divine
Enrique Iglesias; *Enrique* . . . . (Overbrook/Interscope)

Riding With The King
B.B. King & Eric Clapton; *Riding With The King* . . . .(Duck/Reprise)

Ritmo Africano
Cal Tjader; *Cal Tjader's Greatest Hits-#2* . . . . (Fantasy)
Ritmos Calientes . . . . (Fantasy)

R-O-C-K
Bill Haley & His Comets; *Bill Haley & His Comets-Golden Hits* . . . . (MCA)
R-O-C-K . . . . (Sun)

Rock & Soul Music
Country Joe & The Fish; *ST/Woodstock* . . . . (Atlantic)

Rock A Bye Your Baby With A Dixie Melody
Al Jolson; *Best Of Al Jolson* . . . . (MCA)
Jolson Sang 'Em . . . . (Biograph)
Music From The New York Stage (1890-1920)-#4-1917-1920-C . . . . . (Pearl)
The Al Jolson Story-#1 . . . . (MCA)
Jerry Lewis; *Just Sings* . . . .(Razor & Tie)
Judy Garland; *Judy Garland-At Carnegie Hall* . . . . (Capitol)
Miss Show Business . . . . (Capitol)
One & Only . . . . (Capitol)

Rock And Roll Music
Beach Boys; *15 Big Ones* . . . . (Brother)
Beach Boys-Gift Set . . . . (Capitol)
Made In The U.S.A. . . . .(Capitol)
Ten Years Of Harmony . . . . (Caribou)
Beatles; *Beatles '65* . . . . (Capitol)
Beatles-Box Set . . . .(Capitol)
For Sale . . . . (Capitol)
Rock 'N' Roll Music . . . . (Capitol)
Chuck Berry; *Chuck Berry-Golden Hits* . . . . (Mercury)
Chuck Berry's Greatest Hits . . . . (Everest)
Cruisin'-1958-C . . . . (Increase)
The Chess Box-Chuck Berry . . . . (Chess)
REO Speedwagon; *Nine Lives* . . . . (Epic)

Rock And Roll Waltz
Kay Starr; *Capitol Collectors Series-Kay Starr* . . . . (Capitol)

Rock Is My Life And This Is My Song
Bachman-Turner Overdrive; *Not Fragile* . . . .(Mercury)

Rock Me Amadeus
Falco; *Falco 3* . . . .(A&M)
Remix Hit Collection . . . . (Sire)

Rock Show, The
Blink-182; *Now That's What I Call Music!-#8-C* . . . . (Virgin)
Take Off Your Pants And Jacket . . . . (MCA)

Rockabilly Blues (Texas 1955)
Johnny Cash; *Texas Super Hits-C* . . . .(Columbia)

Rocky Mountain Music
Eddie Rabbitt; *Best Of Eddie Rabbitt/Greatest Hits-II* . . . . (Warner Bros.)
Eddie Rabbitt's All-Time Greatest Hits . . . . (Warner Bros.)
Rocky Mountain Music . . . . (Elektra)
Ten Years Of Greatest Hits . . . .(Capitol)

Roll Over Beethoven
Beatles; *Beatles-Box Set* . . . .(Capitol)
Rock 'N' Roll Music . . . . (Capitol)
The Beatles At The Hollywood Bowl . . . . (Capitol)
The Beatles' Second Album . . . .(Capitol)
With The Beatles . . . . (Parlophone)
Byrds; *The Byrds* . . . . (Columbia)
Chuck Berry; *Chuck Berry-Golden Hits* . . . . (Mercury)
Chuck Berry's Greatest Hits . . . . (Everest)
Cruisin'-1956-C . . . . (Increase)
Oldies But Goodies-#10-C . . . . (Original Sound)
The Chess Box-Chuck Berry . . . . (Chess)
Electric Light Orchestra; *Afterglow* . . . .(Epic)

Ole ELO . . . . (Jet)

Rope Song, The
Devo; *Hardcore-#2 (1974-1977)* . . . . (Rykodisc)

Rosalita
Bruce Springsteen; *The Wild, The Innocent & The E Street Shuffle* . . (Columbia)
Bruce Springsteen & The E Street Band; *Bruce Springsteen & The E Street Band Live/1975-85* . . . . (Legacy)

Russian Bandstand
Spencer & Spencer; *Dr. Demento Presents The Greatest Novelty Records-#2-1950s-C* . . . . (Rhino)

Sad Song
Lou Reed; *Between Thought & Expression-Anthology* . . . . (RCA)
Lou Reed Live . . . . (RCA)

Sad Song
Rachel Sweet; *Fool Around* . . . . (Rhino)

Sad Song
Joe Williams; *Joe Williams-Live* . . . . (Fantasy)

Sad Songs
Olivia Newton-John; *Making A Good Thing Better* . . . .(MCA)

Sad Songs (Say So Much)
Elton John; *Breaking Hearts* . . . .(MCA)
Elton John's Greatest Hits-1976-1986 . . . .(MCA)
Knebworth-The Album-C . . . . (Polydor)

Saints Rock 'n Roll, The
Bill Haley & His Comets; *Twentieth Century Masters-Millenium Collection-Bill Haley & His Comets* . . . .(MCA)

Same Old Song & Dance
Aerosmith; *Aerosmith-Classics Live 2* . . . . (Columbia)
Aerosmith's Greatest Hits . . . . (Columbia)
Get Your Wings . . . . (Columbia)
Pandora's Box . . . . (Columbia)

Sam's Place
Buck Owens & The Buckaroos; *Billboard Top Country Hits-1967-C* . . . (Rhino)

San Antonio Rose To You
Rick Trevino; *Texas Super Hits-C* . . . . (Columbia)

Satan's Choir
Red Clay Ramblers; *It Ain't Right* . . . . (Flying Fish)

Saturday Gigs
Mott The Hoople; *Mott The Hoople's Greatest Hits* . . . . (Columbia)
The Ballad Of Mott: A Retrospective . . . . (Columbia)

Save Black Music
Steel Pulse; *Babylon The Bandit* . . . . (Elektra)

School Days
Chuck Berry; *Best Of Chuck Berry* . . . . (Gusto)
Billboard Top Rock 'N' Roll Hits-1957-C . . . . (Rhino)
Chuck Berry-Golden Hits . . . . (Mercury)
ST/Rock 'N' Roll High School . . . . (Sire)

Scottish Air
Carl MacKenzie; *Welcome To Your Feet Again* . . . . (Rounder)

Serenade
Steve Miller Band; *Fly Like An Eagle* . . . . (Capitol)
Steve Miller Band-Gift Set . . . . (Capitol)
Steve Miller Band's Greatest Hits-1974-78 . . . . (Capitol)

Serenade
Liberace; *Best Of Liberace* . . . .(MCA)
Mario Lanza; *Best Of Mario Lanza* . . . . (RCA)

Set 'Em Up Joe
Vern Gosdin; *Chiseled In Stone* . . . . (Columbia)
Greatest Country Hits Of The '80s-1988-C . . . . (Columbia)

Set The Night To Music
Roberta Flack & Maxi Priest; *Set The Night To Music* . . . . (Atlantic)

Set The Night To Music
Starship; *No Protection* . . . .(Grunt)

Sexy Music
Meat Puppets; *Huevos* . . . . (SST)

Sgt. Pepper's Lonely Hearts Club Band
Beatles; *Beatles-Box Set* . . . . (Capitol)
The Beatles/1967-1970 . . . . (Capitol)
Jimi Hendrix; *Stages-Stockholm/Paris/San Diego/Atlanta* . . . . (Reprise)

She Believes In Me
Kenny Rogers; *Kenny Rogers-20 Great Years* . . . . (Reprise)

She Put The Sad In All His Songs
Alabama; *Closer You Get* . . . . (RCA)

She's Got The Rhythm (And I Got The Blues)
Alan Jackson; *A Lot About Livin' (And A Little 'Bout Love)* . . . (Arista)

She's Just A Groupie
Bobby Nunn; *Second To Nunn* . . . . (Motown)

Side By Side
Kay Starr; *Kay Starr's Greatest Hits* . . . . (Curb)
Mitch Miller; *Mitch Miller-16 Most Requested Songs* . . . . (Columbia)

Silly Love Songs
Paul McCartney; *All The Best!* . . . . (Capitol)
ST/Give my regards to Broad Street . . . . (Columbia)
Wings; *Wings At The Speed Of Sound* . . . . (Capitol)
Wings Greatest . . . . (Capitol)
Wings Over America . . . . (Capitol)

Simple Song Of Freedom
Tim Hardin; *Simple Songs Of Freedom: The Tim Hardin Collection* . . . (Legacy)

Sing
Carpenters; *Carpenters-Classics-#2* . . . . (A&M)
Carpenters-The Singles 1969-1973 . . . . (A&M)
Now & Then . . . . (A&M)
Yesterday Once More . . . . (A&M)

Sing
Original Cast; *A Chorus Line* . . . . (Columbia)

Sing
Barbra Streisand; *Live Concert At The Forum* . . . . (Columbia)

Sing
Travis; *Invisible Band* . . . . (Independiente/Epic)

Sing A Happy Song
Taj Mahal; *Evolution* . . . . (Warner Bros.)

Sing A Happy Song
O'Jays; *Identify Yourself* . . . . (Philadelphia Int'l)

Sing A Mean Tune Kid
Chicago; *Chicago At Carnegie Hall* . . . . (Chicago)
Chicago III . . . . (Chicago)

Sing A Sad Song
Merle Haggard; *Epic Collection-Recorded Live* . . . . (Epic)
For The Record: Merle Haggard-43 Legendary Hits . . . .(BNA)
More Of The Best . . . . (Rhino)
Sing A Sad Song . . . . (Capitol)
Merle Haggard & The Strangers; *Songs I'll Always Sing* . . . . (Capitol)

Sing A Simple Song
Sly & The Family Stone; *Sly & The Family Stone-Anthology* . . . . (Epic)
Sly & The Family Stone's Greatest Hits . . . . (Epic)

Sing A Song
Earth, Wind & Fire; *Best Of Earth, Wind & Fire-#1* . . . . (Legacy)
Eternal Dance . . . . (Columbia)
Gratitude . . . . (Legacy)

Sing A Song Of Sixpence
Original Soundtrack; *Children's Favorites* . . . .(Kid Rhino/Rhino 4 Kids)

Sing About Love
Lynn Anderson; *Lynn Anderson's Greatest Hits-#2* . . . . (Columbia)
Top Of The World . . . . (Columbia)

Sing Baby Sing
Stylistics; *Best Of The Stylistics-#2* . . . . (Amherst)
Thank You Baby . . . .(H&L)

Sing C'Est La Vie
Sonny & Cher; *Beat Goes On* . . . . (Atco)
Best Of Sonny & Cher . . . . (Atco)
Two Of Us . . . . (Atco)

Sing Child
Heart; *Dreamboat Annie* . . . . (Capitol)

Sing For The Day
Styx; *Pieces Of Eight* . . . . (A&M)

Sing Me A Love Song To Baby
Billy Walker; *45-#11422* . . . . (MGM)

Sing Me A Song With Social Significance
Barbra Streisand; *Pins And Needles* . . . . (Columbia)

Sing Me Back Home
Alabama; *Mama's Hungry Eyes-Merle Haggard Tribute-C* . . . . (Arista)
Flying Burrito Brothers; *Farther Along-Best Of The Flying Burrito Brothers* . . . . (A&M)
Merle Haggard & The Strangers; *Best Of Merle Haggard & The Strangers* . . . . (Capitol)
Capitol Collectors Series-Merle Haggard & The Strangers . . . . (Capitol)
For The Record: Merle Haggard-43 Legendary Hits . . . .(BNA)
Okie From Muskogee . . . . (Capitol)
Songs I'll Always Sing . . . . (Capitol)

Sing My Heart Out
O'Jays; *So Full Of Love* . . . . (Philadelphia Int'l)

Sing My Song To Me
Jackson Browne; *For Everyman* . . . .(Asylum)

Sing Sing Sing
Benny Goodman; *Benny Goodman Today* . . . .(London)
Benny Goodman-Live At Carnegie Hall . . . .(London)
Benny Goodman-Pure Gold . . . . (RCA)
Benny Goodman's Greatest Hits . . . . (Columbia)
Carnegie Hall Jazz Concert . . . . (Columbia)
Complete Benny Goodman-#4 . . . . (RCA)
Nipper's Greatest Hits Of The '30s-#2-C . . . . (RCA)
Stompin' At The Savoy . . . . (Bluebird)

Sing Sing Sing
Country Joe & The Fish; *C.J. Fish* . . . . (Vanguard)
Life & Times Of Country Joe & The Fish . . . . (Vanguard)

Sing Something Simple
June Christy; *The Misty Miss Christy* . . . . (Capitol)

Sing This All Together
Rolling Stones; *Their Satanic Majesties Request* . . . .(Abkco)

Sing To Me
REO Speedwagon; *You Can Tune A Piano But You Can't Tuna Fish* . . . . . (Epic)

Sing You Sinners
Sammy Davis, Jr./Original Cast; *Mr. Wonderful* . . . . (MCA)
Tony Bennett; *Forty Years-The Artistry Of Tony Bennett* . . . . (Columbia)
Tony Bennett At Carnegie Hall . . . . (Sony Music Special Prod.)
Tony Bennett's All-Time Greatest Hits . . . . (Columbia)

Singer Not The Song
Rolling Stones; *December's Children (and everybody's)* (Abkco)
Singles Collection-The London Years (Abkco)
Singin' In The Rain
Gene Kelly; *ST/A Clockwork Orange* (Warner Bros.)
ST/Singin' In The Rain (Sony Music Special Prod.)
ST/Those Glorious MGM Musicals (MGM)
Singin' The Blues
Kentucky HeadHunters; *Stompin' Ground* (BNA)
Singing All Day
Jethro Tull; *Living In The Past* (Chrysalis)
Singing Bridge Of Memphis Tennessee
John Fahey; *Essential John Fahey* (Vanguard)
Singing From My Soul
Melissa Manchester; *Don't Cry Out Loud* (Arista)
Help Is On The Way (Arista)
Singing Hills
Gene Autry; *50th Anniversary* (Republic/Universal)
Slim Whitman; *Best Of Slim Whitman 1952-1972* (Rhino)
Una Paloma Blanca-Best Of Slim Whitman (EMI)
Singing In My Sleep
Semisonic; *Feeling Strangely Fine* (MCA)
Singing My Song
Guy & Ralna; *22 Golden Country Classics* (Ranwood)
Lovelight (Ranwood)
Tammy Wynette; *Tammy Wynette-Anniversary-20 Years Of Hits* (Epic)
Tammy Wynette's Greatest Hits (Epic)
Singing Rhymes
Marshall Tucker Band; *Together Forever* (AJK Music)
Singing The Blues
Guy Mitchell; *CBS Classics-Radio Classics Of The '50s-C* (Columbia)
Guy Mitchell-16 Most Requested Songs (Legacy)
Singing Tree
Elvis Presley; *ST/Clambake* (RCA)
Sir Duke
Stevie Wonder; *Original Musiquarium* (Motown)
Songs In The Key Of Life (Motown)
Soft Lights And Hard Country Music
Moe Bandy; *Honky Tonk Amnesia-The Hard Country Sound Of Moe Bandy* (Razor & Tie)
Soft Lights And Sweet Music
John Coltrane; *John Coltrane And The Jazz Giants* (Fantasy)
Victor Young & The Brunswick Orchestra with Bing Crosby; *Irving Berlin: A Hundred Years-C* (Columbia)
Someone's Final Song
Elton John; *Blue Moves* (MCA)
Song & Emotion
Tesla; *Psychotic Supper* (Geffen)
Song A Day In Nashville
John Sebastian; *Welcome Back* (Reprise)
Song For The Asking
Simon & Garfunkel; *Bridge Over Troubled Water* (Columbia)
Song For The Dumped
Ben Folds Five; *Naked Baby Photos* (Caroline)
ST/Mr. Wrong (Hollywood)
Whatever And Ever Amen (Caroline/550)
Song For The Life
Alan Jackson; *Who I Am* (Arista)
Alison Krauss; *Too Late To Cry* (Rounder)
Jerry Jeff Walker; *A Man Must Carry On* (MCA)
John Denver; *Country Roads Collection* (RCA)
Kathy Mattea; *Walk The Way The Wind Blows* (Mercury)
Rodney Crowell; *Ain't Living Long Like This* (Warner Bros.)
Song I Can Sing
Donna Fargo; *Best Of Donna Fargo* (MCA)
Song I See You Three
Doobie Brothers; *What Were Once Vices Are Now Habits* (Warner Bros.)
Song Is Over
Who; *Hooligans* (MCA)
Who's next (MCA)
Song Is You
Charlie Parker; *Compact Jazz-Charlie Parker* (Verve)
Chet Baker; *Once Upon A Summertime* (Galaxy)
Frank Sinatra; *Come Dance With Me!* (Capitol)
The Capitol Years (Capitol)
The Reprise Collection (Reprise)
Tommy Dorsey & Frank Sinatra; *Dorsey/Sinatra Radio Years-1940-1942* (RCA)
Song Of A Cowboy
Skip Gorman; *A Cowboy's Wild Song To His Herd* (Rounder)
Song Of A Summer Night
Original Broadway Cast; *The Most Happy Fella* (Sony Music Classical)
Song Of Freedom
Bing Crosby; *Original Soundtrack Sessions* (Vintage Jazz Classics)
Song Of The South
Alabama; *Alabama's Greatest Hits-#2* (RCA)
Southern Star (RCA)
Song On The Radio
Al Stewart; *Best Of Al Stewart* (Arista)
Time Passages (Arista)
Jane Gillman; *Jane Gillman* (Green Linnet)
Song Remembers When
Trisha Yearwood; *The Song Remembers When* (MCA)
Song Sung Blue
Neil Diamond; *Glory Road-1968-1972* (MCA)
Hot August Night (MCA)
Love At The Greek (Columbia)
Moods (MCA)
Neil Diamond-His 12 Greatest Hits (MCA)
Songbird
Barbra Streisand; *Barbra Streisand's Greatest Hits, Volume 2* (Columbia)
Lazy Afternoon (Columbia)
Songbird
Duncan Sheik; *Legacy-A Tribute To Fleetwood Mac's Rumours-C* (Lava)
Fleetwood Mac; *25 Years-The Chain* (Warner Bros.)
Rumours (Warner Bros.)
Songbird
Kenny G; *Duotones* (Arista)
Kenny G-Live (Arista)
Songbird
Jesse Colin Young; *Songbird* (Warner Bros.)
Songs From The Wood
Jethro Tull; *20 Years Of Jethro Tull* (Chrysalis)
Bursting Out (Chrysalis)
Original Masters (Chrysalis)
Too Old To Rock 'N' Roll: Too Young To Die! (Chrysalis)
Songs Of Freedom
Santana; *Freedom* (Columbia)
Soul Singing
Black Crowes; *Lions* (V2)
Sound Of Music
Mormon Tabernacle Choir; *Mormon Tabernacle Choir's Greatest Hits-22 Best-Loved Favorites* (Sony Masterworks)
Original Cast; *The Sound Of Music* (Sony Broadway)
South Street
Orlons; *South Street* (Cameo)
South's Gonna Do It Again
Charlie Daniels; *Charlie Daniels-Super Hits* (Columbia)
Charlie Daniels Band; *A Decade Of Hits* (Epic)
Fire On The Mountain (Epic)
Spanish Guitar
Toni Braxton; *The Heat* (LaFace)
Stardust
Artie Shaw; *Begin The Beguine* (Bluebird)
Artie Shaw & His Orchestra; *22 Original Big Band Recordings-C* (Hindsight)
Nipper's Greatest Hits Of The '40s-#1-C (RCA)
Benny Goodman; *Benny Goodman Sextet featuring Charlie Christian-1939-1941* (Columbia)
Benny Goodman-Live At Carnegie Hall (London)
Carly Simon; *Come Upstairs* (Warner Bros.)
Coleman Hawkins; *Hollywood Stampede* (Capitol)
Dave Brubeck; *Art Of Dave Brubeck* (Atlantic)
Greatest Hits From The Fantasy Years (Fantasy)
Dave Brubeck Quartet; *Jazz At Oberlin* (Fantasy)
Stardust (Fantasy)
Frank Sinatra; *Sinatra & Strings* (Reprise)
Harry Connick, Jr.; *25* (Columbia)
Hoagy Carmichael; *Nipper's Greatest Hits Of The '30s-#1-C* (RCA)
Stardust Road (MCA)
Johnny Mathis; *Feelings* (Columbia)
First 25 Years-Silver Anniversary Album (Columbia)
Nat "King" Cole; *The Nat "King" Cole Story* (Capitol)
Rob Wasserman & Aaron Neville; *Duets-C* (MCA)
Roger Williams; *Best Of Roger Williams* (MCA)
Tommy Dorsey; *Best Of Tommy Dorsey* (Bluebird)
This Is Tommy Dorsey (RCA)
Tommy Dorsey & Frank Sinatra; *Stardust* (Bluebird)
Wayne King & His Orchestra; *78-#22656* (Victor)
State Of Mind
Clint Black; *No Time To Kill* (RCA)
Stone Cold Country
Gibson/Miller Band; *Where There's Smoke* (Epic)
Story Of Bo Diddley
Animals; *Best Of The Animals* (Abkco)
Bo Diddley; *In The Spotlight* (Chess)
Strange Music
John Raitt; *Highlights Of Broadway-Under Open Skies* (Capitol)
Strange Music
Dave Frishberg; *Let's Eat Home* (Concord Jazz)
Strike Up The Band
Boston Pops Orchestra/Arthur Fiedler; *Gershwin-Greatest Hits* (RCA)
Count Basie & His Orchestra; *Fancy Pants* (Pablo)
Ella Fitzgerald; *Ella Fitzgerald Sings The George & Ira Gershwin Songbook* (Verve)
Rosemary Clooney; *Rosemary Clooney Sings The Lyrics Of Ira Gershwin* (Concord Jazz)
Tony Bennett; *Fascinatin' Rhythm-Capitol Sings Gershwin-C* (Capitol)

Stupid Texas Song
Austin Lounge Lizards; *Employee Of The Month* . . . . (Sugar Hill)
Sultans Of Swing
Dire Straits; *Dire Straits* . . . .(Warner Bros.)
Live-Alchemy . . . .(Warner Bros.)
Money For Nothing . . . .(Warner Bros.)
Summer Of '69
Bryan Adams; *Reckless* . . . . (A&M)
Sun Singer
Paul Winter; *Anthems* . . . . (Living Music)
Paul Winter Consort; *Sun Singer* . . . . (Living Music)
Superstar
Lauryn Hill; *The Miseducation Of Lauryn Hill* . . . . (Ruffhouse/Columbia)
Swamp Music
Lynyrd Skynyrd; *Second Helping* . . . . (MCA)
Skynyrd's Innards-Their Greatest Hits . . . . (MCA)
Southern By The Grace Of God-Tribute '87 . . . . (MCA)
Swayin' To The Music
Johnny Rivers; *Johnny Rivers-Anthology 1964-1977* . . . . (Rhino)
Sweet Country Music
Atlanta; *Pictures* . . . .(MCA)
Today's Country Classics-C . . . . (MCA Special Prod.)
Sweet Little Rock & Roller
Chuck Berry; *Chuck Berry Is On Top* . . . . (Chess)
The Chess Box-Chuck Berry . . . . (Chess)
Richard Thompson; *Guitar/Vocal* . . . . (Hannibal)
Rod Stewart; *Absolutely Live* . . . .(Warner Bros.)
Best Of Rod Stewart . . . . (Mercury)
Storyteller/The Complete Anthology: 1964-1990 . . . . (Warner Bros.)
Sweet Music Man
Dolly Parton; *Here You Come Again* . . . . (Dunhill Compact Classics)
Kenny Rogers; *Daytime Friends* . . . .(EMI)
Reba McEntire; *Reba McEntire's Greatest Hits-#3: I'm A Survivor* . . . . .(MCA)
Sweet Music Man
Millie Jackson; *Get It Out'cha System* . . . . (Spring)
Live & Uncensored . . . . (Spring)
Sweet Music Man
Nana Mouskouri; *Song For Liberty* . . . . (Mercury)
Sweet Sixteen Bars
Earl Gray; *Best Of Earl Gray* . . . . (MCA)
Ray Charles; *Atlantic Jazz-Piano-C* . . . . (Atlantic)
Best Of Ray Charles . . . . (Atlantic)
Great Ray Charles . . . . (Atlantic)
Sweet Soul Music
Arthur Conley; *Atlantic Soul Classics-C* . . . . (Warner Special Prod.)
Golden Age Of Black Music-1960-1970-C . . . . (Atlantic)
Sweet Surf Music
Malibooz; *Malibooz Rule* . . . . (Rhino)
Sweetest Sounds
Art Pepper; *Goin' Home* . . . . (Galaxy)
Barbra Streisand; *Barbra Streisand...and other musical
instruments* . . . . (Columbia)
Original Broadway Cast; *No Strings* . . . . (Angel)
Rosemary Clooney; *Rosemary Clooney Sings Rodgers, Hart &
Hammerstein* . . . .(Concord Jazz)
Sarah Vaughan; *Compact Jazz-Sarah Vaughan* . . . . (Verve)
Swing That Music
Dukes Of Dixieland; *Tiger Rag* . . . .(Pro Jazz)
Louis Armstrong; *Louis Armstrong-Vol. 2-1936-1938-Heart Full Of
Rhythm* . . . . (GRP)
Swingin'
Tom Petty And The Heartbreakers; *Echo* . . . .(Warner Bros.)
Swingin' On The Campus
Duke Ellington And Johnny Hodges & His Orchestra; *Duke's Men-Small
Groups-#2-C* . . . . (Columbia)
Swingtime In Honolulu
Duke Ellington/Cootie Williams/R. Cutters; *Duke's Men-Small
Groups-#2-C* . . . . (Columbia)
Swingtime In The Rockies
Benny Goodman; *Birth Of Swing* . . . . (Bluebird)
Carnegie Hall Jazz Concert . . . . (Columbia)
ST/Swing Kids . . . . (Hollywood)
Take 54
Nilsson; *Son Of Schmilsson* . . . . (RCA)
Take It Away
Paul McCartney; *Tug Of War* . . . .(Gold Rush)
Tarzan Was A Bluesman
Timbuk 3; *Eden Alley* . . . .(I.R.S.)
Teenage Dirtbag
Wheatus; *Wheatus* . . . . (Columbia)
Ten Cents A Dance
Eileen Farrell; *I Gotta Right To Sing The Blues* . . . . (Sony Music Classical)
Ella Fitzgerald; *Rodgers & Hart Songbook* . . . . (Verve)
Tennessee Waltz
Cowboy Copas; *45-#696* . . . . (King)
Emmylou Harris; *Cimarron* . . . .(Warner Bros.)
Country's Greatest Hits-#5-C . . . .(Warner Bros.)
New Tradition Sings The Old Tradition-C . . . .(Warner Bros.)

Guy Lombardo & His Royal Canadians; *Best Of Guy Lombardo* . . . . (Curb)
Hank Williams, Jr.; *Living Proof-MGM Recordings 1963-1975* . . . . . (Mercury)
Lacy J. Dalton; *Lacy J. Dalton's Greatest Hits* . . . . (Columbia)
Les Paul & Mary Ford; *Les Paul-Selections From Legend & Legacy* . . . (Capitol)
Patti Page; *Patti Page-Golden Hits* . . . . (Mercury)
Patti Page's Greatest Hits . . . . (Columbia)
Roy Acuff; *Essential Roy Acuff-1936-1949* . . . . (Legacy)
Roy Acuff's Greatest Hits . . . . (Columbia)
Roy Rogers; *Best Of Roy Rogers* . . . . (Curb)
Sammy Kaye & His Orchestra; *Best Of The Big Bands-C* . . . . (Columbia)
Spike Jones & His City Slickers; *Best Of Spike Jones & His City
Slickers* . . . . (RCA)
Tenth Avenue Freeze-Out
Bruce Springsteen; *Born To Run* . . . . (Columbia)
Bruce Springsteen & The E Street Band; *Bruce Springsteen & The E Street
Band Live/1975-85* . . . . (Legacy)
Terrific Band & A Real Nice Crowd
Original Broadway Cast; *Ballroom* . . . .(Sony Music Classical)
Texas Playboy Rag
Bob Wills & His Texas Playboys; *Essential Bob Wills & His Texas
Playboys-1935-1973* . . . . (Legacy)
Thank You For The Music
Abba; *Gold-Greatest Hits* . . . .(Polydor)
That Girl Could Sing
Jackson Browne; *Hold Out* . . . .(Asylum)
That Old Song
Ray Parker Jr.; *Ray Parker Jr.'s Greatest Hits* . . . . (Arista)
Ray Parker Jr./Raydio; *A Woman Needs Love* . . . . (Arista)
That Song About The Midway
Bonnie Raitt; *Streetlights* . . . . (Warner Bros.)
Joni Mitchell; *Clouds* . . . . (Reprise)
That Song Is Driving Me Crazy
Tom T. Hall; *Tom T. Hall's Greatest Hits-#2* . . . . (Mercury)
That's Another Song
Bryan White; *Between Now And Forever* . . . .(Asylum)
That's The Tune
Vogues; *Vogues' Greatest Hits* . . . . (Rhino)
That's Where I Belong
Paul Simon; *You're The One* . . . . (Warner Bros.)
Theme From "American Bandstand" (Bandstand Boogie)
Barry Manilow; *Barry Manilow's Greatest Hits-#1* . . . . (Arista)
Trying To Get The Feeling . . . . (Arista)
Original Soundtrack; *Television's Greatest Hits-#3-1970s & 1980s-C* . . . (TVT)
Theme From "Josie & The Pussycats"
Original Soundtrack; *Hanna-Barbera Pic-A-Nic Basket Of Cartoon
Classics* . . . .(Kid Rhino/Rhino 4 Kids)
Television's Greatest Hits-#3-1970s & 1980s-C . . . . (TVT)
Theme From "Looney Tunes"
Original Soundtrack; *Television's Greatest Hits-#2-C* . . . . (TVT)
Theme From "Merrie Melodies"
Original Soundtrack; *Television's Greatest Hits-#2-C* . . . . (TVT)
Theme From "Solid Gold"
Original Soundtrack; *Television's Greatest Hits-#3-1970s & 1980s-C* . . . (TVT)
Theme From "The Archies"
Original Soundtrack; *Television's Greatest Hits-#3-1970s & 1980s-C* . . . (TVT)
Theme From "The Bodyguard"
Original Soundtrack; *ST/The Bodyguard* . . . . (Arista)
Theme From "The Monkees"
Monkees; *Monkees' Greatest Hits* . . . . (Rhino)
Original Soundtrack; *Television's Greatest Hits-#2-C* . . . . (TVT)
Theme From "The Partridge Family"
Original Soundtrack; *Television's Greatest Hits-#2-C* . . . . (TVT)
There Ain't No Country Music On This Jukebox
Tom T. Hall; *Storyteller, Poet, Philospher* . . . . (Mercury)
There Goes Another Love Song
Outlaws; *Bring It Back Alive* . . . . (Arista)
Greatest Hits Of The Outlaws-High Tides Forever . . . . (Arista)
Southern Fried Rock . . . . (K-Tel)
There Won't Be No Country Music (There Won't Be No Rock 'N' Roll)
C.W. McCall; *C.W. McCall's Greatest Hits* . . . .(Polydor)
There'll Be Sad Songs (To Make You Cry)
Billy Ocean; *Billy Ocean's Greatest Hits* . . . . (Jive)
Love Zone . . . . (Jive)
There's A Red-Neck In The Soul Band
Latimore; *Straighten It Out: The Best Of Latimore* . . . . (Rhino)
There's A Song On The Jukebox
David Wills; *Columbia Country Classics-#5-A New Tradition-C* . . . . (Columbia)
They Pass By Singin'
Cleo Laine & Ray Charles; *Porgy & Bess* . . . . (RCA)
They're Playin' Our Song
Neal McCoy; *Neal McCoy's Greatest Hits* . . . .(Atlantic)
You Gotta Love That! . . . .(Atlantic)
They're Playing Our Song
Original Cast; *They're Playing Our Song* . . . . (Casablanca)
Third Man Theme (Harry Lime Theme)
Band; *Moondog Matinee* . . . . (Capitol)
Dukes Of Dixieland; *Dukes Of Dixieland's Greatest Hits* . . . . (MCA)
Guy Lombardo & His Royal Canadians; *Best Of Guy Lombardo* . . . . (Curb)

This Ain't A Love Song
Bon Jovi; *These Days* . . . . (Mercury)
This Is My Song
Engelbert Humperdinck; *Release Me* . . . . (Mercury)
This Is My Song
Petula Clark; *Greatest Hits Of Petula Clark* . . . . (Crescendo)
This Old Man
Dana; *Dana's Best Sing & Play-Along Tunes!* . . . . (Real Music For Kidz)
Original Soundtrack; *Children's Favorites* . . . . (Kid Rhino/Rhino 4 Kids)
This Song
George Harrison; *33 1/3* . . . . (Dark Horse)
This Song Has No Title
Elton John; *Goodbye Yellow Brick Road* . . . . (Polydor)
This Song Will Last Forever
Lou Rawls; *All Things In Time* . . . . (Right Stuff)
Lou Rawls-Live (Right Stuff) . . . . (Right Stuff)
Those Good Old Sun Records
Sun Rhythm Section; *Old Time Rock 'N Roll* . . . . (Flying Fish)
Those Oldies But Goodies (Remind Me Of You)
John Cafferty And The Beaver Brown Band; *ST/Eddie & The Cruisers* . . . . (Scotti Bros.)
Little Caesar and The Romans; *Best Love Songs-C* . . . . (Original Sound)
Collectables Presents The History Of Rock-#2-C . . . . . . (Collectables)
Cruisin'-1961-C . . . . (Increase)
Oldies But Goodies-#6-C . . . . (Original Sound)
Till There Was You
Beatles; *Beatles-Box Set* . . . . (Capitol)
Meet The Beatles! . . . . (Capitol)
With The Beatles . . . . (Parlophone)
Original Cast; *ST/The Music Man* . . . . (Warner Bros.)
To Beat The Devil
Johnny Cash; *Johnny Cash-16 Biggest Hits-#2* . . . . (Legacy)
To Cry You A Song
Jethro Tull; *Benefit* . . . . (Chrysalis)
Repeat-The Best Of Jethro Tull, Vol. II . . . . (Chrysalis)
Today I Sing The Blues
Aretha Franklin; *Aretha Sings The Blues* . . . . (Columbia)
Aretha's Jazz . . . . (Rhino)
Jazz To Soul . . . . (Columbia)
Top Of The Pops
Kinks; *Everybody's In Show-Biz* . . . . (Rhino)
Lola Versus Powerman And The Moneygoround, Part One . . . . (Reprise)
Top Of The Pops
Smithereens; *Blow Up* . . . . (Capitol)
Torn And Frayed
Rolling Stones; *Exile On Main Street* . . . . (Virgin)
Travelin' Band
Creedence Clearwater Revival; *1970* . . . . (Fantasy)
Cosmo's Factory . . . . (Fantasy)
Creedence Clearwater Revival-Chronicle . . . . (Fantasy)
Live In Europe . . . . (Fantasy)
Royal Albert Hall Concert . . . . (Fantasy)
Tropicalia
Beck; *Mutations* . . . . (David Geffen Co.)
Trudy Sings The Blues
Trudy Lynn; *Trudy Sings The Blues* . . . . (Ichiban Int'l)
Tubthumping
Chumbawamba; *Tubthumper* . . . . (Universal)
Tune Up
Miles Davis; *Blue Haze* . . . . (Prestige)
Philly Joe Jones Sextet; *Blues For Dracula* . . . . (Riverside)
Sonny Stitt; *Tune Up* . . . . (Muse)
Wes Montgomery With Strings; *Fusion* . . . . (Riverside)
Turn It Up
Busta Rhymes; *When Disaster Strikes* . . . . (Elektra)
Turn It Up Or Turn It Off
Drivin' N' Cryin'; *Smoke* . . . . (Island)
Turn On Your Radio
Nilsson; *Son Of Schmilsson* . . . . (RCA)
Turn The Beat Around
Gloria Estefan; *Hold Me, Thrill Me, Kiss Me* . . . . (Epic)
ST/The Specialist . . . . (Epic/Sony Music Soundtrax)
Vicki Sue Robinson; *Dance Floor Divas-The '70s-C* . . . . . . (Rhino)
Never Gonna Let You Go . . . . (RCA)
Nipper's Greatest Hits Of The '70s-C . . . . (RCA)
Turn Up The Music
Sammy Hagar; *All Night Long* . . . . (One Way)
Best Of Sammy Hagar . . . . (Capitol)
Musical Chairs . . . . (Capitol)
Uncle John's Band
Grateful Dead; *Best Of/Skeletons From The Closet* . . . . . (Warner Bros.)
Workingman's Dead . . . . (Warner Bros.)
Indigo Girls; *Deadicated-C* . . . . (Arista)
Uncle Pen
Bill Monroe; *Bean Blossom* . . . . (MCA)
Best Of Bill Monroe & His Blue Grass Boys . . . . (MCA)
Ricky Skaggs; *19 Hot Country Requests-#2-C* . . . . (Epic)
Bluegrass Super Hits-C . . . . (Columbia)

Columbia Country Classics-#5-A New Tradition-C . . . . (Columbia)
Don't Cheat In Our Hometown . . . . (Epic)
Live In London . . . . (Epic)
Unheard Music
X; *Live At The Whisky A Go-Go* . . . . (Elektra)
Los Angeles/Wild Gift . . . . (Slash)
Voice Of Harold
R.E.M.; *Dead Letter Office* . . . . (I.R.S.)
Volare
Bobby Rydell; *'60s Rock 'N' Roll-#1-It's My Party-C* . . . . . (Dominion Entert.)
Voodoo Music
Tuck & Patti; *Dream* . . . . (Windham Hill)
Warning Labels
Doug Stone; *From The Heart* . . . . (Epic)
We Danced
Brad Paisley; *Who Needs Pictures* . . . . (Arista)
We Danced Anyway
Deana Carter; *Did I Shave My Legs For This?* . . . . (Capitol)
We'll Sing In The Sunshine
Gale Garnett; *21 Country Rock & Love Songs Of The '50s & '60s-#1-C* . . . . (Laurie)
Nipper's Greatest Hits Of The '60s-#1-C . . . . (RCA)
We're An American Band
Grand Funk Railroad; *Capitol Collectors Series-Grand Funk Railroad* . . . . (Capitol)
Caught In The Act . . . . (Capitol)
ST/Spirit Of '76 . . . . (Rhino)
We're An American Band . . . . (Capitol)
When AM Was King-C . . . . (Capitol)
Westside
TQ; *They Never Saw Me Coming* . . . . (ClockWork/Epic)
What Do The Simple Folk Do?
Julie Andrews; *Best Of Julie Andrews* . . . . (Rhino)
Julie Andrews & Richard Burton; *Camelot* . . . . (Columbia)
Original Soundtrack; *Camelot* . . . . (Warner Bros.)
What's It Gonna Be
Busta Rhymes Featuring Janet Jackson; *E.L.E.* . . . . (Elektra)
When I Think About Angels
Jamie O'Neal; *Shiver* . . . . (Mercury)
When Smokey Sings
ABC; *Alphabet City* . . . . (Mercury)
When The Music Stops
Roger Daltrey; *Daltrey* . . . . (MCA)
When The Music's Over
Doors; *Absolutely Live* . . . . (Elektra)
Best Of The Doors . . . . (Elektra)
ST/The Doors . . . . (Elektra)
Strange Days . . . . (Elektra)
Weird Scenes Inside The Gold Mine . . . . (Elektra)
When The Saints Go Marching In
Al Hirt; *Best Of Al Hirt* . . . . (RCA)
Our Man-In New Orleans . . . . (Novus)
Jerry Lee Lewis; *Jerry Lee Lewis* . . . . (Rhino)
Louis Armstrong; *At The Crescendo* . . . . (MCA)
Big Bands Of The Swinging Years-#1-C . . . . (Collectables)
C'Est Si Bon . . . . (Rhino)
Essential Louis Armstrong . . . . (Vanguard)
Louis Armstrong Of New Orleans . . . . (MCA)
Original Soundtrack; *Children's Favorites* . . . . (Kid Rhino/Rhino 4 Kids)
Pete Fountain; *Best Of Pete Fountain* . . . . (MCA)
Down On Rampart Street . . . . (Intermedia)
Pete Fountain's New Orleans . . . . (MCA)
Preservation Hall Jazz Band; *Best Of The Preservation Hall Jazz Band* . . . . (Columbia)
Where It's At
Beck; *Odelay* . . . . (David Geffen Co.)
Where The Bands Are
Bruce Springsteen; *Tracks* . . . . (Columbia)
Where The Blues Were Born In New Orleans
Louis Armstrong; *Louis Armstrong Sings The Blues* . . . . (Bluebird)
Pops: 1940s Small Band Sides . . . . (Bluebird)
Whistle While You Work
NRBQ; *Peek-A-Boo-Best Of-1969-1989* . . . . (Rhino)
Whistle While You Work/Heigh Ho
Adriana Caselotti; *Disney Collection-#1-C* . . . . (Disney)
Mormon Tabernacle Choir & Columbia Symphony Orchestra; *When You Wish Upon A Star-A Tribute To Walt Disney* . . . . (CBS Masterworks)
White Noise
Jay Ferguson; *White Noise* . . . . (Capitol)
White Rhythm & Blues
J.D. Souther; *You're Only Lonely* . . . . (Legacy)
Linda Ronstadt; *Living In The USA* . . . . (Asylum)
Who Put The Bomp (In The Bomp, Bomp, Bomp)
Barry Mann; *Goofy Greats-C* . . . . (K-Tel)
Sixties Rule! Chapter Two-C . . . . (One Way)
Who's Gonna Fill Their Shoes
George Jones; *George Jones-Super Hits* . . . . (Epic)
Greatest Country Hits Of The '80s-1985-C . . . . (Columbia)

Who's Gonna Fill Their Shoes . . . .(Epic)
Why It Is I Sing The Blues
B.B. King; *Best Of B.B. King* . . . . (MCA)
Live & Well . . . . (MCA)
Why It Is I Sing The Blues . . . .(MCA Special Prod.)
Wish, The
Bruce Springsteen; *Tracks* . . . . (Columbia)
With A Little Help From My Friends
Beatles; *Beatles-Box Set* . . . . (Capitol)
Rarities . . . . (Capitol)
Sgt. Pepper's Lonely Hearts Club Band. . . . . (Capitol)
The Beatles/1967-1970 . . . . (Capitol)
Joe Cocker; *History Of British Rock-#9-C* . . . . (Rhino)
Joe Cocker-Classics-#4 . . . . (A&M)
Joe Cocker's Greatest Hits . . . . (A&M)
ST/Woodstock . . . . (Atlantic)
With A Little Help From My Friends . . . . (A&M)
Ringo Starr & His All-Star Band; *Nobody's Child-Romanian Angel*
Appeal-C . . . .(Warner Bros.)
With A Song In My Heart
Ella Fitzgerald; *Rodgers & Hart Songbook* . . . . (Verve)
Jerry Vale; *Standing Ovation!-Carnegie Hall Concert.* . . . . (Columbia)
Jose Carreras; *The 3 Tenors In Concert 1994* . . . . (Teldec)
Mario Lanza; *Be My Love* . . . . (RCA)
Stevie Wonder; *Uptight (Everything's Alright)* . . . . (Motown)
Without A Song
Duke Ellington; *Great Ellington Units* . . . . (Bluebird)
Frank Sinatra; *My Kind Of Broadway.* . . . . (Reprise)
James Ray; *Golden Classics-James Ray.* . . . . (Collectables)
Supremes; *I Hear A Symphony* . . . . (Motown)
Tommy Dorsey & Frank Sinatra; *Tommy Dorsey & Frank Sinatra's All-Time*
Greatest Hits-#1 . . . . (Bluebird)
Willie Nelson; *What A Wonderful World* . . . . (Columbia)
Woodstock
Crosby, Stills & Nash; *CSN* . . . . (Atlantic)
Crosby, Stills, Nash & Young; *Deja Vu* . . . . (Atlantic)
So Far . . . . (Atlantic)
Joni Mitchell; *Ladies Of The Canyon* . . . . (Reprise)
Shadows & Light . . . . (Asylum)
Joni Mitchell with Tom Scott & The L.A. Express; *Miles Of Aisles* . . . . (Asylum)
Working For MCA
Hank Williams, Jr.; *Hank Williams, Jr. "Live"* . . . . (WB/Curb)
Lynyrd Skynyrd; *Best Of The Rest Of Lynyrd Skynyrd* . . . .(MCA)
One More From The Road . . . .(MCA)
Second Helping . . . .(MCA)
World Is A Concerto
Barbra Streisand; *Barbra Streisand...and other musical*
instruments . . . . (Columbia)
World Needs A Melody
George Jones & Tammy Wynette; *George Jones' Greatest Hits-#2* . . . . . .(Epic)
Kenny Rogers; *Love Lifted Me* . . . .(EMI)
Wrote A Song For Everyone
Creedence Clearwater Revival; *1969* . . . . (Fantasy)
Creedence Clearwater Revival-Chronicle-#2 . . . . (Fantasy)
Creedence Country . . . . (Fantasy)
Green River . . . . (Fantasy)
Yes, Yes Y'all
Will Smith; *Big Willie Style* . . . . (Columbia)
Yesterday's Songs
Neil Diamond; *12 Greatest Hits-#2* . . . . (Columbia)
On The Way To The Sky . . . . (Columbia)
Yodeling Hobo
Gene Autry; *Gene Autry: Blues Singer-1929-1933* . . . . (Legacy)
You Are My Music, You Are My Song
Charly McClain & Wayne Massey; *Radio Heart* . . . . (Epic)
You Can All Join In
Traffic; *Best Of Traffic* . . . . (Island)
Traffic . . . . (Island)
You Get What You Give
New Radicals; *Maybe You've Been Brainwashed Too* . . . .(MCA)
Now That's What I Call Music!-#2-C . . . . (Virgin)
You Sang To Me
Marc Anthony; *Marc Anthony* . . . . (Columbia)
You Spin Me Around (Like A Record)
Dead Or Alive; *Rip It Up* . . . .(Epic)
Youthquake . . . .(Epic)
Your Mother Should Know
Beatles; *Beatles-Box Set* . . . . (Capitol)
Magical Mystery Tour . . . . (Capitol)
Your Song
Elton John; *Elton John* . . . . (Polydor)
Elton John's Greatest Hits . . . . (Polydor)
Live In Australia With The Melbourne Symphony Orchestra. . . . .(MCA)
Rod Stewart; *Two Rooms-Celebrating The Songs Of Elton John & Bernie*
Taupin-C . . . . (Polydor)
Zak And Sara
Ben Folds; *Rockin' The Suburbs* . . . .(Epic)

MUSICAL INSTRUMENTS: BANJOS
See Also: **COUNTRY, MUSIC, MUSICAL INSTRUMENTS**
(various)

At The Banjo Cafe
Pat Cloud; *Higher Power* . . . . (Flying Fish)
Banjo
Kaleidoscope; *Egyptian Candy-Collection* . . . . (Epic)
Banjo Bounce
Allen Shelton; *Rounder Bluegrass-#1-C* . . . . (Rounder)
Banjo Kings; *Banjo Kings* . . . . (Good Time Jazz)
Banjo Boy Chimes
White Brothers & New Kentucky Colonels; *Live In Sweden.* . . . . (Rounder)
Banjo Breakdown
Stanley Brothers/Carl Story/Jim & Jesse; *Banjo In The Hills* . . . . (Starday)
Banjo In The Hills
Stanley Brothers/Carl Story/Jim & Jesse; *Banjo In The Hills* . . . . (Starday)
Banjo In The Hollow
Dillards; *Bluegrass Breakdown.* . . . . (Vanguard)
Banjo On The Mountain
Doug Dillard Band; *Heartbreak Hotel* . . . . (Flying Fish)
Banjo Picking Girl
Lamar Grier; *Rounder Banjo-C.* . . . . (Rounder)
Banjo Signal
John Hickman; *Don't Mean Maybe.* . . . . (Rounder)
Banjo Story
Elizabeth Cotten; *Elizabeth Cotten-Live* . . . . (Arhoolie)
Banjos
Original Broadway Cast; *Meet Me In St. Louis* . . . .(DRG)
Crowe On The Banjo
Jimmy Martin; *You Don't Know My Mind-1956-1966* . . . . (Rounder)
Dueling Banjos
Eric Weissberg & Steve Mandell; *ST/Deliverance* . . . . (Warner Bros.)
Hippie With A Banjo
Those Darn Accordions!; *Clownhead* . . . . (Globe)
Key To Life, The
Vince Gill; *The Key* . . . . (MCA)
Little Maggie
Kingston Trio; *Tom Dooley.* . . . . (Capitol)
Ricky Skaggs and Kentucky Thunder; *Bluegrass Rules!* . . . . (Rounder)
Oh, Susanna
Disneyland Cast; *Children's Favorite Songs-#1* . . . . (Disney)
James Taylor; *Sweet Baby James* . . . . (Warner Bros.)
Myron Floren; *Best Of The Wurstfest* . . . . (Ranwood)
Myron Floren . . . . (Ranwood)
Sad Banjo
Shrimp Boat; *Duende* . . . . (Bar/None)
That Banjo Rag
Banjo Kings; *Banjo Kings* . . . . (Good Time Jazz)
Uncle Clooney Played The Banjo
Country Gazette; *Hello Operator...This Is Country Gazette* . . . . (Flying Fish)
Out To Lunch . . . . (Flying Fish)

MUSICAL INSTRUMENTS: BRASS
See Also: **MUSIC, MUSICAL INSTRUMENTS (various)**

76 Trombones
Original Cast; *The Music Man.* . . . . (Gold Rush)
Boogie Woogie Bugle Boy
Andrews Sisters; *Andrews Sisters-16 Great Performances.* . . . . (MCA)
Best Of The Andrews Sisters . . . . (MCA)
Boogie Woogie Bugle Girls . . . . (MCA)
Rarities . . . . (MCA)
Bette Midler; *Divine Miss M* . . . .(Atlantic)
Live At Last. . . . .(Atlantic)
ST/Divine Madness. . . . .(Atlantic)
Bugle Call Rag
Benny Goodman; *Stompin' At The Savoy* . . . . (Bluebird)
Enoch Light & His Light Brigade; *Big Band Hits Of The '30s-#2* . . . . . (Project 3)
New Orleans Rhythm Kings; *New Orleans Rhythm Kings* . . . . (Milestone)
Doo Wa Ditty (Blow That Thing)
Zapp; *Zapp II.* . . . . (Warner Bros.)
Holiday For Trumpet
Al Hirt; *Best Of Al Hirt* . . . . (RCA)
Oh, How I Hate To Get Up In The Afternoon
Harry "Sweets" Edison; *Swing Trumpet Kings-C* . . . . (Verve)
Sax & Violins
Talking Heads; *ST/Until The End Of The World* . . . . (Warner Bros.)
Saxafunk
Neville Brothers; *Family Groove* . . . . (A&M)
Saxophone Song
Kate Bush; *Kick Inside* . . . . (EMI)
Saxophones
Jimmy Buffett; *Living & Dying In 3/4 Time* . . . . (MCA)

Say It With Trumpets
Maynard Ferguson; *Birdland Dreamband*....................(Bluebird)
That Mellow Saxophone
Roy Montrell; *Best Of New Orleans Rhythm & Blues-#2-C* ...(Rhino)
There Won't Be Trumpets
Barbra Streisand; *Just For The Record* ....(Columbia)
Original Broadway Cast; *Anyone Can Whistle* ....(Columbia)
Original Cast; *Marry Me A Little*...........................(RCA)
Trombone Butter
Dinah Washington; *Bessie Smith Songbook* ....(Emarcy)
Trombone Cholly
Bessie Smith; *Bessie Smith-The Complete Recordings-#3* ....(Legacy)
Teresa Brewer & Count Basie; *Songs Of Bessie Smith* ....(Doctor Jazz)
Trombone Dixie
Beach Boys; *Pet Sounds* ....(Capitol)
Trombone Rag
Turk Murphy's San Francisco Jazz Band; *Turk Murphy's San Francisco Jazz Band*........................(Good Time Jazz)
Trumpet
Chuck Mangione; *Children Of Sanchez* ....(A&M)
Trumpet Blues & Cantabile
Harry James; *Best Of The Big Bands-C*....................(Columbia)
Trumpet Boogie
Ray Anthony; *Young Man With A Horn-1952-1954--22 Original Big Band Recordings*.............................(Hindsight)
Trumpet Player's Lament
Louis Armstrong; *Jazz Heritage-Satchmo's Discoveries* ....(MCA)
Trumpeter Blow Your Golden Horn
Michael Tilson Thomas; *Of Thee I Sing/Let 'Em Eat Cake* ....(Columbia)
Trumpeter's Lullaby
Utah Symphony Orchestra; *Fiddle Faddle* ....(Vanguard)
Trumpets
Waterboys; *This Is The Sea* ....(Chrysalis)
Tubas In The Moonlight
Bonzo Dog Band; *Tadpoles*...............................(Liberty)
Two Bass Hit
Dizzy Gillespie; *Dizziest* ....(Bluebird)
Miles Davis; *Milestones* ....(Columbia)
Sonny Clark; *Blue Piano-#2* ....(Blue Note)

MUSICAL INSTRUMENTS: DRUMS & PERCUSSION

See Also: **MUSIC, MUSICAL INSTRUMENTS (various), RHYTHM, ROCK & ROCKING**

Bang The Drum All Day
Todd Rundgren; *Popular Tortured Artist Effect* ....(Rhino)
Todd Rundgren-Anthology 1968-1985 ....(Rhino)
Bang The Drum Slowly
Emmylou Harris; *Red Dirt Girl* ....(Nonesuch)
Beat Goes On, The
Sonny & Cher; *Best Of Sonny & Cher*......................(Atco)
Hit Singles-1958-1977-C ....(Atlantic)
Sonny & Cher-Live ....(MCA)
The Beat Goes On-Best Of Sonny & Cher...................(Rhino)
Two Of Us..(Atco)
Born With A Broken Heart
Kenny Wayne Shepherd; *Ledbetter Heights* ....(Giant)
Conga
Leonard Bernstein; *Songbook* ....(Columbia)
Conga
Miami Sound Machine; *Primitive Love*.......................(Epic)
Different Drum
Linda Ronstadt; *Different Drum* ....(Capitol)
Linda Ronstadt-Retrospective ....(Capitol)
Linda Ronstadt's Greatest Hits ....(Asylum)
Stone Poneys Featuring Linda Ronstadt; *Baby Boomer Classics-Mellow '60s-C*..............................(JCI Assoc. Labels)
On The Road Again-Rock's New Frontiers-C ....(Capitol)
The Stone Poneys Featuring Linda Ronstadt ....(EMI)
Victoria Shaw; *Victoria Shaw* ....(Reprise)
Distant Drums
Jim Reeves; *Best Of The Best Of Jim Reeves* ....(King)
Billboard Top Country Hits-1966-C ....(Rhino)
Essential Jim Reeves ....(RCA)
Drum Boogie
Gene Krupa; *Big Bands' Greatest Hits-#1-C*................(Columbia)
Gene Krupa & Buddy Rich; *Original Drum Battle* ....(Verve)
Drum Song
Earth, Wind & Fire; *Open Our Eyes* ....(Columbia)
Drum Stomp
Sandy Nelson; *Collector's Gems-#2* ....(Liberty)
Drums
Tubes; *Outside/Inside* ....(Capitol)
Fiddle & The Drum
Joni Mitchell; *Clouds*...................................(Reprise)

Get It On (Bang A Gong)
Power Station; *Power Station*............................(Capitol)
T. Rex; *Electric Warrior* ....(Reprise)
Green Tambourine
Lemon Pipers; *Best Of Ohio Express & Other Bubblegum Smashes-#1-C*.......................................(Rhino)
Billboard Top Rock 'N' Roll Hits-1968-C...................(Rhino)
Bubblegum's Greatest Hits-#3-C ....(Accord)
Fabulous Bubblegum Years-C ....(Fifty One West)
Hillbilly Rock
Marty Stuart; *Hillbilly Rock*...........................(MCA)
Marty Party Hit Pack ....(MCA)
Japanese Drums
Kitaro; *Asia* ....(Geffen)
Jungle Drums
Artie Shaw; *Begin The Beguine* ....(Pro-Arte)
This Is Artie Shaw ....(Bluebird)
Let Me Bang Your Box
Toppers; *Risque Rhythms: Nasty '50s R&B-C*...............(Rhino)
Listen To A Country Song
Loggins & Messina; *Loggins & Messina-On Stage* ....(Columbia)
Sittin' In..(Columbia)
Lynn Anderson; *Country Chartbusters-#2*..................(Columbia)
Lynn Anderson's Greatest Hits ....(Columbia)
Mr. Tambourine Man
Bob Dylan; *Biograph*..................................(Columbia)
Bob Dylan At Budokan ....(Columbia)
Bob Dylan's Greatest Hits..............................(Columbia)
Bringing It All Back Home ....(Columbia)
Byrds; *Billboard Top Rock 'N' Roll Hits-1965-C* ....(Rhino)
Original Singles-#1-1965-1967 ....(Columbia)
The Byrds' Greatest Hits ....(Columbia)
The Original Singles-1965-1967 ....(Columbia)
Turn! Turn! Turn! ....(Legacy)
Sex Cymbal
Sheila E.; *Sex Cymbal* ....(Warner Bros.)
She Bangs The Drums
Stone Roses; *The Stone Roses* ....(Silvertone)
Sloth (Drums)
Fairport Convention; *Fairport Convention-Chronicles*...............(A&M)
Full House..(Carthage)
Tambourine
Prince and the Revolution; *Around The World In A Day* ....(Paisley Park)
Tambourine
Electric Boys; *Groovus Maximus*..........................(Atco)
Tambourine
Book Of Love; *Lovebubble* ....(Sire)
Tin Drum
Toni Childs; *Union*....................................(A&M)
Tin Drum
Big Pig; *Bonk*.......................................(A&M)
Whistle Song
Frankie Knuckles; *Beyond The Mix* ....(Virgin)

MUSICAL INSTRUMENTS: FIDDLES & VIOLINS

See Also: **COUNTRY, MUSIC, MUSICAL INSTRUMENTS (various)**

Arkansas Traveler
Albert Lee; *Speechless*.................................(MCA)
Fiddlin' Red Herron; *Red, White & Bluegrass-C*.............(C.M.H. Prod.)
Floyd Cramer; *Country Gold-Floyd Cramer* ....(Step One)
Mark O'Connor; *Championship Years*..........(Country Music Foundation)
Michelle Shocked; *Arkansas Traveler*......................(Mercury)
Sam Hinton; *Newport Broadside: Newport Folk Festival-1963-C* ...(Vanguard)
Cherokee Fiddle
Johnny Lee; *Johnny Lee's Greatest Hits* ....(Full Moon/Asylum)
ST/Urban Cowboy....................................(Asylum)
Michael Martin Murphey; *Best Of Michael Martin Murphey* ....(Liberty)
Flowing Free Forever ....(EMI)
Devil Comes Back To Georgia
Marc O'Connor; *Heroes* ....(Warner Bros.)
Devil Went Down To Georgia
Charlie Daniels Band; *A Decade Of Hits* ....(Epic)
Billboard Top Hits-1979-C ....(Rhino)
Me & The Boys ....(Epic)
Million Mile Reflections ....(Epic)
ST/Urban Cowboy....................................(Asylum)
Fiddle & The Drum
Joni Mitchell; *Clouds*..................................(Reprise)
Fiddle About
Who; *Join Together* ....(MCA)
ST/Tommy ....(Polydor)
Fiddlin' Around
Johnny Gimble; *ST/Honeysuckle Rose* ....(Columbia)
Still Fiddlin' Around ....(MCA)

Fit As A Fiddle (and Ready For Love)
Fred Waring's Pennsylvanians; *The Fred Waring Memorial Album* . . . . (Viper's Nest)
Very Best Of Fred Waring & The Pennsylvanians . . . . (Reader's Digest Music)
Gene Kelly/Donald O'Connor/The MGM Studio Orchestra; *ST/Singin' In The Rain* . . . . (Turner Classic Movies)

Holiday For Strings
Boston Pops Orchestra/Arthur Fiedler; *Greatest Hits Of The '40s-#2* . . . . (RCA)
David Rose & His Orchestra; *Nipper's Greatest Hits Of The '40s-#1-C* . . (RCA)

My Father's Fiddle
Dave Loggins; *Apprentice (In A Musical Workshop)* . . . .(Epic)

Nickel For The Fiddler
Guy Clark; *Old No. 1* . . . . (Sugar Hill)

Old Kentucky Fiddle
Hoot Hester; *45-#114* . . . . (Nationwide Sound Distrib.)

Old King Cole
Original Soundtrack; *Children's Favorites* . . . . (Kid Rhino/Rhino 4 Kids)

Prologue (Tradition)
Original Cast; *Fiddler On The Roof* . . . .(RCA Victor)

Redneck Fiddlin' Man
Charlie Daniels Band; *Greatest Fiddlin' Licks* . . . .(Epic)
Midnight Wind . . . .(Epic)

Robbery With Violins
Steeleye Span; *Parcel Of Rogues* . . . .(Chrysalis)

Sax & Violins
Talking Heads; *ST/Until The End Of The World* . . . .(Warner Bros.)

Second Fiddle
Kay Starr; *Essential RCA Singles Collection* . . . .(Taragon)

Texas Fiddle Man
Asleep At The Wheel; *Keepin' Me Up Nights* . . . . (Arista)

Texas Fiddle Song
Merle Haggard; *Big City* . . . .(Epic)

Uncle Pen
Bill Monroe; *Bean Blossom* . . . .(MCA)
Best Of Bill Monroe & His Blue Grass Boys . . . .(MCA)
Ricky Skaggs; *19 Hot Country Requests-#2-C* . . . .(Epic)
Bluegrass Super Hits-C . . . . (Columbia)
Columbia Country Classics-#5-A New Tradition-C . . . . (Columbia)
Don't Cheat In Our Hometown . . . .(Epic)
Live In London . . . .(Epic)

Violin
Kate Bush; *Never For Ever* . . . .(EMI)

Violin Walk
Laurie Anderson; *United States Live* . . . .(Warner Bros.)

MUSICAL INSTRUMENTS: GUITARS

See Also: **COUNTRY, MUSIC, MUSICAL INSTRUMENTS (various), ROCK & ROCKING**

Born With A Broken Heart
Kenny Wayne Shepherd; *Ledbetter Heights* . . . .(Giant)

Boss Guitar
Duane Eddy; *Twang Thang-The Duane Eddy Anthology* . . . . (Rhino)

Daddy Frank (The Guitar Man)
Merle Haggard; *Best Of Merle Haggard* . . . .(Capitol)
Capitol Collectors Series-Merle Haggard . . . . (Capitol)
Merle Haggard & The Strangers; *For The Record: Merle Haggard-43 Legendary Hits* . . . . (BNA)
Songs I'll Always Sing . . . . (Capitol)

Doc's Guitar
Doc Watson; *Doc Watson* . . . . (Vanguard)
On Stage (Featuring Merle Watson) . . . . (Vanguard)
Out In The Country . . . .(Intermedia)

Emma Jean's Guitar
Chely Wright; *Let Me In* . . . .(MCA)

Free Form Guitar
Chicago; *Chicago Transit Authority* . . . .(Chicago)

Girls With Guitars
Wynonna; *Tell Me Why* . . . .(MCA)

Gitarzan
Ray Stevens; *Dr. Demento Presents The Greatest Novelty Records-#3-1960s-C* . . . . (Rhino)
Ray Stevens' Greatest Hits . . . .(RCA)
Ray Stevens' Greatest Hits . . . .(MCA)

Golden Guitar
Bill Anderson; *Bill Anderson's Greatest Hits* . . . .(MCA)
The Bill Anderson Story . . . .(MCA)

Guitar & Pen
Who; *Who Are You* . . . .(MCA)

Guitar Boogie Shuffle
Virtues; *Legends Of Rock Guitar-'50s-#1-C* . . . . (Rhino)

Guitar Heaven
Neil Diamond; *On The Way To The Sky* . . . . (Columbia)

Guitar Man
Elvis Presley; *14 #1 Country Hits-C* . . . .(RCA)
Elvis . . . .(RCA)

Guitar Man *(continued)*
Guitar Man . . . .(RCA)
Nipper's Greatest Hits Of The '80s-C . . . .(RCA)
Jerry Reed; *Essential Jerry Reed* . . . .(RCA)

Guitar Man
Bread; *Best Of Bread-#2* . . . . (Elektra)
Bread-Anthology . . . . (Elektra)

Guitar Picker From Rody, Wyoming
Joey Davis; *45-#2248* . . . .(MRC)

Guitar Town
Steve Earle & The Dukes; *Country Classics-#8-1986-1987-C* . . . . . . (Universal)
Guitar Town . . . . (MCA)

Guitars, Cadillacs
Dwight Yoakam; *Guitars, Cadillacs, Etc., Etc.* . . . . (Reprise)
Just Lookin' For A Hit . . . .(Reprise)

Johnny B. Goode
Chuck Berry; *Chuck Berry's Greatest Hits* . . . . (Everest)
Classic Rock-#2-C . . . . (MCA)
Roll Over Beethoven . . . . (Allegiance)
ST/American Graffiti . . . . (MCA)
The Chess Box-Chuck Berry . . . .(Chess)
Elvis Presley; *Elvis In Concert* . . . .(RCA)
From Memphis To Vegas/From Vegas To Memphis . . . .(RCA)
Grateful Dead; *Bill Graham Presents The Last Days Of The Fillmore-C* . . . . (Epic Portrait Assoc.)
Johnny Winter; *Live/Johnny Winter And* . . . . (Columbia)
Second Winter . . . . (Columbia)

King Creole
Elvis Presley; *Hits Like Never Before-Essential-#3* . . . . (RCA)
ST/King Creole . . . .(RCA)
The Great Performances . . . .(RCA)
The Other Sides-Worldwide Gold Award Hits, Vol. 2 . . . .(RCA)

King Of The Surf Guitar
Dick Dale And The Del-Tones; *Beach Classics-All Original Recordings-C* . . . . (Dunhill Compact Classics)
Dick Dale And The Del-Tones' Greatest Hits . . . .(Crescendo)
Tigers Loose . . . . (Rhino)

Little Guitars
Van Halen; *Diver Down* . . . . (Warner Bros.)

Long Legged Guitar Pickin' Man
Johnny Cash & June Carter; *Johnny Cash's Greatest Hits-#2* . . . . (Columbia)

Maria Maria
Santana; *Supernatural* . . . . (Arista)
Totally Hits-#2-C . . . . (Elektra)

My Guitar Sings The Blues
B.B. King; *Six Silver Strings* . . . . (MCA)

My Guitar Wants To Kill Your Mama
Frank Zappa; *You Can't Do That On Stage Anymore-#4* . . . . (Rykodisc)
Mothers Of Invention; *Weasels Ripped My Flesh* . . . . (Bizarre/Straight)

Nashville Cats
Del McCoury Band; *The Family* . . . .(Ceili Music)
Lovin' Spoonful; *Lovin' Spoonful-Anthology* . . . .(Rhino)

On Broadway
Drifters; *Drifters-16 Greatest Hits* . . . .(Trip)
Drifters-Golden Hits . . . .(Atlantic)
George Benson; *George Benson-Collection* . . . . (Warner Bros.)
ST/All That Jazz . . . .(Casablanca)
Weekend In L.A. . . . . (Warner Bros.)

Orange Guitars
Jimmy Haslip; *Arc* . . . . (GRP)

Perfectly Good Guitar
John Hiatt; *Perfectly Good Guitar* . . . .(A&M)

Play Guitar
John Cougar Mellencamp; *Uh-Huh* . . . . (Riva)

Play, Guitar, Play
Conway Twitty; *Classic Conway* . . . . (MCA)
Very Best Of Conway Twitty . . . .(MCA)

Rhythm Guitar
Emmylou Harris; *Ballad Of Sally Rose* . . . . (Warner Bros.)
Johnny Paycheck; *Johnny Paycheck's Greatest Hits-#2* . . . . (Epic)
Oak Ridge Boys; *All Our Favorite Songs* . . . .(Columbia)
Best Of The Oak Ridge Boys . . . . (Columbia)

Riding With The King
B.B. King & Eric Clapton; *Riding With The King* . . . . (Duck/Reprise)

Spanish Guitar
Squeeze; *Picadilly Collection* . . . .(A&M)

Spanish Guitar
Toni Braxton; *The Heat* . . . . (LaFace)

Ten Guitars
Engelbert Humperdinck; *Release Me* . . . . (Mercury)

Tennessee Flat Top Box
Johnny Cash; *Classic Cash-Hall Of Fame Series* . . . . (Mercury)
Columbia Country Classics-#3-Americana-C . . . . (Columbia)
Essential Johnny Cash . . . . (Columbia)
The Man In Black-His Greatest Hits . . . . (Legacy)
Rosanne Cash; *30 Years Of #1 Hits-#17-C* . . . . (Columbia)
Hits-1979-1989 . . . . (Columbia)
King's Record Shop . . . . (Columbia)

Texas Guitar Stomp
Maddox Brothers & Rose; *1946-1951-#2* . . . .(Arhoolie)

That Old Beat Up Guitar
Jerry Jeff Walker; *Jerry Jeff Walker* . . . . (MCA)
There Goes That Old Steel Guitar
Tammy Wynette; *Tammy Wynette's Greatest Hits-#3* . . . . (Epic)
This Old Guitar
John Denver; *Back Home Again* . . . . (RCA)
  Evening With John Denver . . . . (RCA)
  John Denver's Greatest Hits-#2 . . . . (RCA)
Three Guitar Special
Bob Wills & His Texas Playboys; *Bob Wills & His Texas Playboys-
  Anthology 1935-1973* . . . . (Rhino)
While My Guitar Gently Weeps
Beatles; *Beatles-Box Set* . . . . (Capitol)
  The Beatles (White Album) . . . . (Capitol)
  The Beatles/1967-1970 . . . . (Capitol)
George Harrison; *Best Of George Harrison* . . . . (Capitol)
  Concert For Bangladesh-C . . . . (Capitol)
  Live In Japan . . . . (Dark Horse)
Wish, The
Bruce Springsteen; *Tracks* . . . . (Columbia)
Won't Get Fooled Again
Van Halen; *LIVE: Right here, right now..* . . . . (Warner Bros.)
Who; *ST/The Kids Are Alright* . . . . (MCA)
  The Concert For New York City-C . . . . (Columbia)
  Who Greatest Hits . . . . (MCA)
  Who's Last . . . . (MCA)
  Who's next . . . . (MCA)
Wood And Wire
George Jones; *The Rock: Stone Cold Country 2001* . . . . (BNA)
You Gotta Love That
Neal McCoy; *Neal McCoy's Greatest Hits* . . . . (Atlantic)
  Today's Country Love-C . . . . (K-Tel)
  You Gotta Love That! . . . . (Atlantic)

MUSICAL INSTRUMENTS: MANDOLINS

See Also: **COUNTRY, MUSIC, MUSICAL INSTRUMENTS
(various)**

Kentucky Mandolin
Bill Monroe & His Blue Grass Boys; *Best Of Bill Monroe & His Blue
  Grass Boys* . . . . (MCA)
  Kentucky Bluegrass . . . . (MCA)
Mandolin Rain
Bruce Hornsby & The Range; *The Way It Is* . . . . (RCA)
Mandolin Wind
Rod Stewart; *Best Of Rod Stewart-#2* . . . . (Mercury)
  Every Picture Tells A Story . . . . (Mercury)
  Sing It Again, Rod . . . . (Mercury)
  Storyteller/The Complete Anthology: 1964-1990 . . . . (Warner Bros.)
Orange Blossom Mandolin
Northeast Winds; *Northeast Winds In Concert* . . . . (Folk Era)
Something So Feminine About A Mandolin
Jimmy Buffett; *Havana Daydreamin'* . . . . (MCA)
Third Man Theme (Harry Lime Theme)
Band; *Moondog Matinee* . . . . (Capitol)
Dukes Of Dixieland; *Dukes Of Dixieland's Greatest Hits* . . . . (MCA)
Guy Lombardo & His Royal Canadians; *Best Of Guy Lombardo* . . . . . . (Curb)
Wildwood Mandolin
Jack Tottle; *Rounder Bluegrass-#1-C* . . . . (Rounder)

MUSICAL INSTRUMENTS: MISCELLANEOUS

See Also: **COUNTRY, MUSIC, MUSICAL INSTRUMENTS
(various), ROCK & ROCKING**

Belfast Hornpipe
James Galway; *James Galway's Greatest Hits* . . . . (RCA)
Bo Diddley
Bo Diddley; *Good Time Rock 'N' Roll-C* . . . . (MCA)
  History Of Rock-#5-C . . . . (Collectables)
  Oldies But Goodies-#10-C . . . . (Original Sound)
  ST/Rage In Harlem . . . . (Sire)
Buddy Holly; *Buddy Holly-20 Golden Greats* . . . . (MCA)
  For The First Time Anywhere . . . . (MCA)
Brazilian Ukelele
Buddy Merrill; *Best Of Buddy Merrill* . . . . (Accord)
  Latin Festival . . . . (Accord)
Cello Solo
Laurie Anderson; *United States Live* . . . . (Warner Bros.)
Daddy Sang Bass
Johnny Cash; *Columbia Country Classics-#5-A New Tradition-C* . . . (Columbia)
  Johnny Cash's Greatest Hits-#2 . . . . (Columbia)
  The Man In Black-His Greatest Hits . . . . (Legacy)

Daniel & The Sacred Harp
Band; *Stage Fright* . . . . (Capitol)
  The Band-Anthology-#1 . . . . (Capitol)
  To Kingdom Come-The Definitive Collection . . . . (Capitol)
Happy Organ
Dave ''Baby'' Cortez; *Billboard Top Rock 'N' Roll Hits-1959-C* . . . . . (Rhino)
  History Of Rock Instrumentals-#1-C . . . . (Rhino)
  Super Oldies Of The '50s-#7-C . . . . (Audio Fidelity)
Hey Harmonica Man
Stevie Wonder; *Stevie Wonder's Greatest Hits* . . . . (Motown)
Hoop-Dee-Doo
Perry Como; *Perry Como's Greatest Hits* . . . . (RCA)
I Love To Bass
Bardeux; *Free To Be-#8-C* . . . . (Right Stuff)
Memphis Soul Stew
King Curtis; *Atlantic Jazz-Soul-C* . . . . (Atlantic)
  Atlantic Rhythm & Blues 1947-1974-#6 (1966-1969)-C . . . . . . (Atlantic)
  Best Of King Curtis . . . . (Atlantic)
  Golden Soul-C . . . . (Atlantic)
  Live At The Fillmore West . . . . (Atlantic)
Oh! How I Hate To Get Up In The Morning (bugle)
Irving Berlin; *American Songbook Series-Irving
  Berlin* . . . . (Smithsonian Collection)
  War Years-C . . . . (ISD/Intersound)
Pineapple Princess (ukelele)
Annette Funicello; *Frankie Avalon/Annette Funicello* . . . . (K-Tel)
Play The Bass
Stanley Clarke; *Let Me Know You* . . . . (Epic)
  Time Exposure . . . . (Epic)
Sam, The Old Accordion Man
Doris Day & James Cagney; *ST/Love Me Or
  Leave Me* . . . . (Sony Music Special Prod.)
Squeezebox
Who; *By Numbers* . . . . (MCA)
  Hooligans . . . . (MCA)
  Who Greatest Hits . . . . (MCA)
Zak And Sara
Ben Folds; *Rockin' The Suburbs* . . . . (Epic)

MUSICAL INSTRUMENTS: PIANOS

See Also: **MUSIC, MUSICAL INSTRUMENTS (various), ROCK
& ROCKING**

Baby Grand
Billy Joel; *KOHUEPT* . . . . (Columbia)
Ebony And Ivory
Paul McCartney & Stevie Wonder; *All The Best!* . . . . (Capitol)
  Tug Of War . . . . (Gold Rush)
Great Beyond, The
R.E.M.; *Man On The Moon* . . . . (Warner Bros.)
  Totally Hits-#2-C . . . . (Elektra)
Green Door
Jim Lowe; *Billboard Top Rock 'N' Roll Hits-1956-C* . . . . (Rhino)
  Super Hits-#4-C . . . . (Gusto)
Kitten On The Keys
Claude Bolling; *Original Ragtime* . . . . (Columbia)
Dick Hyman; *Flip Side Of Red Seal* . . . . (RCA)
  Kitten On The Keys . . . . (RCA)
Liberace; *Liberace-16 Most Requested Songs* . . . . (Columbia)
My Old Piano
Diana Ross; *Diana* . . . . (Motown)
  Diana Ross-All The Great Hits . . . . (Motown)
  Diana Ross-Anthology . . . . (Motown)
Piano & I
Alicia Keys; *Songs In A Minor* . . . . (J)
Piano Has Been Drinking
Tom Waits; *Small Change* . . . . (Asylum)
  Tom Waits-Anthology . . . . (Asylum)
Piano In The Dark
Brenda Russell; *Brenda Russell's Greatest Hits* . . . . (A&M)
  Get Here . . . . (A&M)
  Making Love-C . . . . (Priority)
  Slow Dancin'-C . . . . (K-Tel)
Piano Lesson & If You Don't Mind My Saying So
Shirley Jones; *ST/The Music Man* . . . . (Warner Bros.)
Piano Man
Billy Joel; *Billy Joel-Greatest Hits, Volume I & Volume II* . . . . . . (Columbia)
  Piano Man . . . . (Columbia)
  Rock Classics Of The '70s-C . . . . (Columbia)
Piano Man
Thelma Houston; *Motown Superstar Series-#20-Thelma Houston* . . . (Motown)
Sweet Man
Jelly Roll Morton; *The Piano Rolls* . . . . (Nonesuch)
This Old Piano
Mike Gray; *This Old Piano* . . . . (Twin-Tone)

Who's Gonna Play This Old Piano
Jerry Lee Lewis; *Best Of Jerry Lee Lewis-#2* . . . . (Mercury)
Milestones . . . . (Rhino)

NAMES: GENERAL

See Also: **CELEBRITIES: SPECIFIC, FAMILY (various), MEN'S NAMES: A-Z, PEOPLE, PRESIDENTS, WOMEN'S NAMES: A-Z**

50,000 Names
George Jones; *The Rock: Stone Cold Country 2001* . . . . (BNA)
Already Home
Marc Cohn; *Burning The Daze* . . . . (Atlantic)
Baby Driver
Simon & Garfunkel; *Bridge Over Troubled Water* . . . . (Columbia)
Collected Works . . . . (Columbia)
Believe In Me
Eric Clapton; *Reptile* . . . . (Duck/Reprise)
Big Poppa
Notorious B.I.G.; *MTV Party To Go-#8-C* . . . . (Tommy Boy)
Ready To Die . . . . (Bad Boy/Arista)
Bow Wow (That's My Name)
Lil Bow Wow; *Beware Of Dog* . . . . (So So Def/Columbia)
Boy Named Sue
Johnny Cash; *Columbia Country Classics-#3-Americana-C* . . . . . . (Columbia)
Johnny Cash's Biggest Hits . . . . (Columbia)
Johnny Cash's Greatest Hits-#2 . . . . (Columbia)
The Man In Black-His Greatest Hits . . . . (Legacy)
Bullet Proof
Goo Goo Dolls; *Dizzy Up The Girl* . . . . (Warner Sunset/Reprise)
Cockeyed Optimist
Mitzi Gaynor; *ST/South Pacific* . . . . (RCA)
Original Cast; *South Pacific* . . . . (CBS Masterworks)
Damn Thing Called Love
After 7; *Reflections* . . . . (Virgin)
Deportee (Plane Wreck At Los Gatos)
Arlo Guthrie & Pete Seeger; *Together In Concert* . . . . (Reprise)
Byrds; *The Byrds* . . . . (Columbia)
Cisco Houston; *Greatest Songs Of Woody Guthrie-C* . . . . (Vanguard)
Gene Clark & Carla Olson; *So Rebellious A Lover* . . . . (Rhino)
Judy Collins; *Tribute To Woody Guthrie-C* . . . . (Warner Bros.)
Waylon Jennings, Willie Nelson, Johnny Cash, Kris Kristofferson;
Highwayman . . . . (Columbia)
El Macho
Mark Knopfler; *Sailing To Philadelphia* . . . . (Warner Bros.)
Father Of Mine
Everclear; *Now That's What I Call Music!-#2-C* . . . . (Virgin)
So Much For The Afterglow . . . . (Capitol)
Fearless Boogie
ZZ Top; *XXX* . . . . (RCA)
Feels Like Love
Vince Gill; *Let's Make Sure We Kiss Goodbye* . . . . (MCA)
Gave It A Name
Bruce Springsteen; *Tracks* . . . . (Columbia)
Hell On High Heels
Motley Crue; *New Tattoo* . . . . (Motley/Beyond)
Hymn To Her
Pretenders; *Diana, Princess Of Wales-Tribute-C* . . . . (Columbia)
Get Close . . . . (Sire)
The Isle Of View . . . . (Warner Bros.)
I Call Your Name
Beatles; *Past Masters-Volume One* . . . . (Parlophone)
Rock 'N' Roll Music . . . . (Capitol)
The Beatles' Second Album . . . . (Capitol)
I Don't Even Know Your Name
Mavericks; *Trampoline* . . . . (MCA)
I'm Still Wearing Your Name
Ann Nesby; *I'm Here For You* . . . . (Perspective/A&M)
It's In Your Eyes (Any Time At All)
Phil Collins; *Dance Into The Light* . . . . (Atlantic)
Jigga My Nigga
Jay-Z; *Ruff Ryders: Ride Or Die-#1* . . . . (Ruff Ryders/IDJMG)
Just Another Girl
Monica; *ST/Down To Earth* . . . . (Epic)
Just Friends (Sunny)
Musiq Soulchild; *Aijuswanaseing* . . . . (Def Soul/IDJMG)
Keep The Ball Rollin'
Jay And The Techniques; *Bubblegum Classics-#4-C* . . . . (Varese Vintage)
Love Child
Diana Ross & The Supremes; *Billboard Top Rock 'N' Roll Hits-
1968-C* . . . . (Rhino)
Diana Ross & The Supremes' Greatest Hits-#3 . . . . (Motown)
Diana Ross & The Supremes-Anthology (1962-1969) . . . . (Motown)
Every Great #1 Hit . . . . (Motown)
Motown Story-First 25 Years-C . . . . (Motown)
Motown's Biggest Pop Hits-C . . . . (Motown)

Sweet Sensation; *Love Child* . . . . (Atco)
Love Will Be Waiting
Kevon Edmonds; *24/7* . . . . (RCA)
Master's Call
Marty Robbins; *Gunfighter Ballads & Trail Songs* . . . . (Legacy)
Oh, My Mysterious Lady
Original Cast; *Peter Pan-The 1954 Broadway Production* . . . . (RCA Victor)
On & On
Erykah Badu; *Baduizm* . . . . (Kedar Entert./Universal)
People Are Strange
Doors; *Best Of The Doors* . . . . (Elektra)
Ruby Tuesday
Rolling Stones; *Between The Buttons* . . . . (Abkco)
Flashpoint . . . . (Virgin)
Flowers . . . . (Abkco)
Hot Rocks 1964-1971 . . . . (Abkco)
Singles Collection-The London Years . . . . (Abkco)
Through The Past, Darkly (Big Hits Vol. 2) . . . . (Abkco)
Say My Name
Destiny's Child; *The Writing's On The Wall* . . . . (Columbia)
Stop! In The Name Of Love
Diana Ross & The Supremes; *16 #1 Hits From The Early '60s-C* . . . . . (Motown)
Diana Ross & The Supremes' Greatest Hits . . . . (Motown)
Diana Ross & The Supremes-Anthology (1962-1969) . . . . (Motown)
Evening With Diana Ross . . . . (Motown)
Girl Groups-Story Of A Sound-C . . . . (Rhino)
Motown Superstar Series-#1-Diana Ross & The Supremes . . . . (Motown)
Hollies; *45-#89819* . . . . (Atlantic)
Supremes; *Billboard Top Pop Hits-1965-C* . . . . (Rhino)
Sympathy For The Devil
Bryan Ferry; *These Foolish Things* . . . . (Reprise)
Jane's Addiction; *Jane's Addiction* . . . . (Triple X Entert.)
Rolling Stones; *Beggars Banquet* . . . . (Abkco)
Flashpoint . . . . (Virgin)
Get Yer Ya-Ya's Out! . . . . (Abkco)
Hot Rocks 1964-1971 . . . . (Abkco)
Love You Live . . . . (Virgin)
Tell Me (I'll Be Around)
Shades; *110% Love Jams-C* . . . . (Simitar)
Shades . . . . (Motown)
Theme From "Cheers"
Gary Portnoy; *Tube Tunes-#3-The '70s & '80s-C* . . . . (Rhino)
Original Soundtrack; *Television's Greatest Hits-#3-1970s & 1980s-C* . . . (TVT)
Untitled Protest
Country Joe & The Fish; *Life & Times Of Country Joe &
The Fish* . . . . (Vanguard)
Together . . . . (Vanguard)
What's Your Name
Don & Juan; *WCBS FM 101 History Of Rock-For Lovers-#2-C* . . . (Collectables)
When I Call Your Name
Vince Gill; *When I Call Your Name* . . . . (MCA)
Why They Call It Falling
Lee Ann Womack; *I Hope You Dance* . . . . (MCA)
You Give Love A Bad Name
Bon Jovi; *7800 Degrees Fahrenheit* . . . . (Mercury)
Cross Road-14 Classic Grooves . . . . (Mercury)
You Know My Name (Look Up My Number)
Beatles; *Beatles-Box Set* . . . . (Capitol)
Past Masters-Volume Two . . . . (Parlophone)
Rarities . . . . (Capitol)
You Were Mine
Dixie Chicks; *Big Country Hits '99-C* . . . . (K-Tel)
Wide Open Spaces . . . . (Monument)
You've Got A Friend
Barbra Streisand; *Barbra Joan Streisand* . . . . (Columbia)
Carole King; *Tapestry* . . . . (Epic)
Donny Hathaway & Roberta Flack; *Best Of Donny Hathaway* . . . . . . (Atco)
Jamaica Boys; *J Boys* . . . . (Reprise)
James Taylor; *James Taylor's Greatest Hits* . . . . (Warner Bros.)
Mud Slide Slim And The Blue Horizon . . . . (Warner Bros.)
Michael Jackson; *Got To Be There* . . . . (Motown)
Original Soul Of Michael Jackson . . . . (Motown)
Roberta Flack & Donny Hathaway; *Best Of Roberta Flack* . . . . . . (Atlantic)
Roberta Flack & Donny Hathaway . . . . (Atlantic)

NATIVE AMERICANS, North American Indians

See Also: **AMERICAN WEST, COWBOYS**

Across The Alley From The Alamo
Asleep At The Wheel featuring Johnny Rodriguez; *Tribute To The Music Of
Bob Wills And The Texas Playboys-C* . . . . (Liberty)
Bob Wills & His Texas Playboys; *Best Of Bob Wills & His Texas
Playboys* . . . . (MCA)
Tiffany Transcriptions-#4-You're From Texas . . . . (Rhino)
Alcatraz
Leon Russell; *Leon Russell & The Shelter People* . . . . (MCA)

Nazareth; *Razamanaz* . . . . (A&M)

Along The Navajo Trail
Riders In The Sky; *Riders Go Commercial* . . . . (MCA)
Roy Rogers; *Hooray For Hollywood* . . . . (RCA)

Apache
Jorgen Ingmann & His Guitar; *Billboard Top Pop Hits-1961-C* . . . . (Rhino)
Shadows; *Legends Of Rock Guitar-'60s-#1-C* . . . . (Rhino)
Sonny James; *Great Moments At The Grand Ole Opry-C* . . . . (RCA)

Apache Dance
Woody Herman & His Orchestra; *The Uncollected Woody Herman & His Orchestra* . . . . (Hindsight)

Apache Woman
Rolling Stones; *Made In The Shade* . . . . (Rolling Stones)

Arizona Indian Doll
Faster Pussycat; *Wake Me When It's Over* . . . . (Elektra)

Ballad Of Davy Crockett
Bill Hayes; *Songs Of The West-#4-Movie & Television Themes-C* . . . . . . (Rhino)
Fess Parker; *16 Most Requested Songs Of The '50s-#1-C* . . . . . (Legacy)
Columbia Country Classics-#3-Americana-C . . . . (Columbia)
Hollywood Magic-1950s-C . . . . (Columbia)
Kentucky HeadHunters; *Electric Barnyard* . . . . (Mercury)
Mac Wiseman; *45-#1240* . . . . (Dot)
Original Soundtrack; *Television's Greatest Hits-#4-Black & White Classics-C* . . . . (TVT)
Tennessee Ernie Ford; *Capitol Collectors Series-Tennessee Ernie Ford* . . . . (Capitol)

Ballad Of Ira Hayes, The
Johnny Cash; *The Man In Black-His Greatest Hits* . . . . (Legacy)
Peter La Farge; *Best Of Broadside 1962-1968: Anthems Of The American Underground From The Pages Of Broadside Magazine-C* . . . . (Smithsonian Folkways)

Big Chief
Dr. John; *Dr. John's Gumbo* . . . . (Alligator)
Neville Brothers; *Live At Tipitina's-#1-Nevillization* . . . . (Spindletop)
Professor Longhair; *Crawfish Fiesta* . . . . (Alligator)
Mardi Gras Party . . . . (Rounder)
New Orleans Party Classics-C . . . . (Rhino)

Big Chief From New Orleans
Mike Bloomfield; *Between The Hard Place & The Ground* . . . . (Takoma)

Brave Heart
Bill Miller; *Raven In The Snow* . . . . (Reprise)

Buffalo Gun
Michael Murphey; *Swans Against The Sun* . . . . (Epic)

Chant: 13th Hour
Redbone; *Best Of Redbone* . . . . (Epic)

Cherokee
Charlie Barnet; *Big Bands Of The Swinging Years-#1-C* . . . . (Collectables)
Nipper's Greatest Hits Of The '30s-#2-C . . . . (RCA)
Swing's The Thing-C . . . . (Capitol)

Cherokee
Europe; *Final Countdown* . . . . (Epic)

Cherokee
Sarah Vaughan; *Complete Sarah Vaughan On Mercury-#1-Great Jazz Years-1954-1956* . . . . (Mercury)
In The Land Of Hi-Fi . . . . (Emarcy)

Cherokee
Stephen Stills; *Stephen Stills* . . . . (Atlantic)

Cherokee
White Lion; *Fight To Survive* . . . . (Gland Slamm)

Cherokee
Wynton Marsalis; *Marsalis Standard Time-#1* . . . . (Columbia)
Wynton Marsalis Quartet; *Wynton Marsalis Quartet-Live At Blues Alley* . . . . (Columbia)

Cherokee Fiddle
Johnny Lee; *Johnny Lee's Greatest Hits* . . . . (Full Moon/Asylum)
ST/Urban Cowboy . . . . (Asylum)
Michael Martin Murphey; *Best Of Michael Martin Murphey* . . . . (Liberty)
Flowing Free Forever . . . . (EMI)

Cherokee Maiden
Asleep At The Wheel; *Ride With Bob-C* . . . . (DreamWorks/SKG)
Merle Haggard; *All Time Greatest Hits Of Country-C* . . . . (Curb)
Capitol Collectors Series-Merle Haggard . . . . (Capitol)

Cherokee Mist
Jimi Hendrix; *Lifelines/Jimi Hendrix Story* . . . . (Reprise)

Cowboys & Indians
Billy Strange; *Great Western Themes* . . . . (Crescendo)

Cowboys & Indians
Rita Coolidge; *Fall Into Spring* . . . . (A&M)

Crow
Dan Fogelberg; *Captured Angel* . . . . (Full Moon)

Dreams Of Wounded Knee
Bill Miller; *The Red Road* . . . . (Warner Western)

General Custer
Tom Paxton; *How Come The Sun* . . . . (Out Of Print)

Georgia Pineywoods
Osborne Brothers; *Best Of The Osborne Brothers* . . . . (MCA)
Country Bluegrass . . . . (MCA Special Prod.)
Red, White & Bluegrass-C . . . . (C.M.H. Prod.)

Give It Back To The Indians
Ella Fitzgerald; *Rodgers & Hart Songbook* . . . . (Verve)

Give It Back To The Indians (New York)
Ella Fitzgerald; *Rodgers & Hart Songbook* . . . . (Verve)

Half-Breed
Cher; *Cher's Greatest Hits* . . . . (MCA)
Half-Breed . . . . (MCA Special Prod.)

I Want To Live In A Wigwam
Cat Stevens; *Footsteps In The Dark-Greatest Hits-#2* . . . . (A&M)

I'm An Indian
Fanny Brice; *Music From The New York Stage (1890-1920)-#4-1917-1920-C* . . . . (Pearl)

I'm An Indian Too
Ethel Merman/Bruce Yarnell/Original Cast; *Annie Get Your Gun* . . . . (RCA Victor)
Ethel Merman/Ray Middleton/Original Cast; *Annie Get Your Gun* . . . . . . (MCA)
Original Broadway Cast; *Annie Get Your Gun* . . . . (Angel)
Original Cast/Doris Day; *Annie Get Your Gun* . . . . (Columbia)

In Every Corner Of The Forest (Parts 1-3)
Bill Miller; *Raven In The Snow* . . . . (Reprise)

In God We Trust
Barefoot Jerry; *Barefoot Jerry's Grocery* . . . . (Monument)

Indian Girl
Rolling Stones; *Emotional Rescue* . . . . (Rolling Stones)

Indian Girl
Hollies; *Hollies-Epic Anthology From The Original Master Tapes* . . . . (Epic)

Indian Girl
Capris; *There's A Moon Out Tonight* . . . . (Collectables)

Indian Giver
1910 Fruitgum Company; *Best Of 1910 Fruitgum Company & Other Bubblegum Smashes-#2-C* . . . . (Rhino)

Indian Lady
Roger Whittaker; *Reflections Of Love* . . . . (RCA)

Indian Lake
Freddy Weller; *Freddy Weller's Greatest Hits* . . . . (Columbia)

Indian Love Call
Jeanette MacDonald & Nelson Eddy; *Jeanette MacDonald & Nelson Eddy-Legendary Performer* . . . . (RCA)
Ray Stevens; *Misty* . . . . (Barnaby)
Very Best Of Ray Stevens . . . . (Barnaby)
Slim Whitman; *Best Of Slim Whitman 1952-1972* . . . . (Rhino)
Paloma Blanca-Best Of Slim Whitman-Legendary Masters . . . . (EMI)

Indian Man
Charlie Daniels Band; *Midnight Wind* . . . . (Epic)

Indian Outlaw
Tim McGraw; *Not A Moment Too Soon* . . . . (Curb)
Tim McGraw's Greatest Hits . . . . (Curb)

Indian Red
Wild Tchoupitoulas; *Wild Tchoupitoulas* . . . . (Island)

Indian Reservation (The Lament Of The Cherokee Reservation Indian)
Don Fardon; *45-#408* . . . . (GNP/Crescendo)
Raiders; *Billboard Top Rock 'N' Roll Hits-1971-C* . . . . (Rhino)
Legend Of Paul Revere And The Raiders . . . . (Columbia)
Pop Classics Of The '70s-C . . . . (Columbia)
Super Hits Of The '70s-Have A Nice Day-#5-C . . . . (Rhino)

Indian Summer
Ella Fitzgerald; *Newport Jazz Festival* . . . . (Columbia)
Frank Sinatra; *The Reprise Collection* . . . . (Reprise)
Glenn Miller; *Memorial-1944-1969* . . . . (Bluebird)
Stan Getz; *Stan Getz's Greatest Hits* . . . . (Prestige)

Indian Summer
Joe Walsh; *But Seriously Folks* . . . . (Asylum)

Indian Summer
Poco; *Indian Summer* . . . . (MCA)

Indian Summer
Roy Orbison & The Gatlin Brothers; *Legendary Roy Orbison* . . . . (Sony Music Special Prod.)

Indian Summer
Doors; *Morrison Hotel/Hard Rock Cafe* . . . . (Elektra)

Indian Summer Love
Con Funk Shun; *Secrets* . . . . (Mercury)

Indian Sunset
Elton John; *Madman Across The Water* . . . . (Polydor)

Indian War Whoop
John Hartford; *ST/O Brother, Where Art Thou?* . . . . (Mercury)

Indian Wedding
Roy Orbison; *Legendary Roy Orbison* . . . . (Sony Music Special Prod.)
Our Love Song . . . . (Monument)
Roy Orbison-More Greatest Hits . . . . (Monument)

Indian Woman
Sons Of The Pioneers; *Western Country* . . . . (Granite)

Indian Woman
Dan Hill; *Frozen In The Night* . . . . (20th Century Fox)

Indians
Original Cast; *Peter Pan-The 1954 Broadway Production* . . . . (RCA Victor)

Indians
Anthrax; *Among The Living* . . . . (Island)

Indians Here Dey Come
Wild Tchoupitoulas; *Wild Tchoupitoulas* . . . . (Island)
Inter-Tribal Pow Wow Song
Bill Miller; *The Red Road* . . . . (Warner Western)
Kaw-Liga
Hank Williams; *Alone With His Guitar* . . . . (Mercury)
Hank Williams-40 Greatest Hits . . . . (Polydor)
Hank Williams-The Hits-#2 . . . . (Mercury)
Land Of The Navajo
Peter Rowan; *New Grass Revival-Festival Tapes* . . . . (Flying Fish)
Peter Rowan . . . . (Flying Fish)
Lonesome Indian
Country Gazette; *American & Clean* . . . . (Flying Fish)
Lost Indian
Clark Kessinger & Gene Meade; *Clark Kessinger & Gene Meade* . . . . (Rounder)
Norman Blake & Tony Rice; *Norman Blake & Tony Rice-Vol. 2* . . . . . (Rounder)
Massacre
Thin Lizzy; *Johnny The Fox* . . . .(Warner Bros.)
Live And Dangerous . . . .(Warner Bros.)
Mighty Quinn (Quinn The Eskimo)
Bob Dylan; *Biograph* . . . . (Columbia)
Bob Dylan's Greatest Hits-#2 . . . . (Columbia)
Self Portrait . . . . (Columbia)
Ian & Sylvia; *Ian & Sylvia's Greatest Hits* . . . . (Vanguard)
Manfred Mann; *Chapter Two-The Best Of The Fontana Years* . . . . . . (Fontana)
My People
Bill Miller; *The Red Road* . . . . (Warner Western)
Native North American Child (Entire LP)
Buffy Sainte-Marie; *Native North American Child* . . . . (Vanguard)
Native Son
Bryan Adams; *Into The Fire* . . . . (A&M)
Navajo Know
Pixies; *Trompe Le Monde* . . . . (Elektra)
Navajo Land Blessing
Peter Kater & Carlos Nakai; *How The West Was Lost* . . . . (Silver Wave)
Navajo Rug
Ian Tyson; *Cowboyography* . . . . (Sugar Hill)
Navajo Sky
James Asher; *Globalarium* . . . . (Silver Wave)
Navajo Trail
Michael Nesmith; *From A Radio Engine To The Photon Wing* . . . . (Pacific Arts)
Navajo Wrangler
Chris LeDoux; *Western Tunesmith* . . . . (Liberty)
Now That The Buffalo's Gone
Buffy Sainte-Marie; *American Child* . . . . (Vanguard)
Best Of Buffy Sainte-Marie . . . . (Vanguard)
Greatest Folksingers Of The '60s-C . . . . (Vanguard)
I'm Gonna Be A Country Child . . . . (Vanguard)
Oklahoma Hills
Arlo Guthrie; *Tribute To Woody Guthrie-C* . . . .(Warner Bros.)
Hank Thompson; *Hank Thompson's All-Time Greatest Hits* . . . . (Curb)
Jack Guthrie and his Oklahomans; *Birth Of A Dream-Capitol's Early
Hits-C* . . . . (Capitol)
Great Records Of The Decade-'40s-Country-C . . . . (Curb)
Kay Starr; *Kay Starr-Country* . . . .(Crescendo)
Please Mr. Custer
Ray Stevens; *Gitarzan* . . . . (Barnaby)
Pow Wow The Indian Boy
Hot Rize; *Hot Rize* . . . . (Flying Fish)
Pretty Little Indian
Dan Crary; *Lady's Fancy* . . . . (Rounder)
Primitive People
Country Joe McDonald; *Goodbye Blues* . . . . (Fantasy)
Raven In The Snow
Bill Miller; *Raven In The Snow* . . . . (Reprise)
Reservation Road
Bill Miller; *The Red Road* . . . . (Warner Western)
Running Bear
Johnny Preston; *45s On CD-#1-1956-1959-C* . . . . (Mercury)
Billboard Top Rock 'N' Roll Hits-1960-C . . . . (Rhino)
Cruisin'-1960-C . . . . (Increase)
Sonny James; *All-Time Country Classics-#1-C* . . . . (Capitol)
Seminole Wind
John Anderson; *Seminole Wind* . . . . (BNA)
Shenandoah
Bob Dylan; *Down In The Groove* . . . . (Columbia)
Harry Belafonte; *Harry Belafonte-Legendary Performer* . . . . (RCA)
James Galway; *James Galway's Greatest Hits* . . . . (RCA)
Leontyne Price; *God Bless America* . . . . (RCA)
Van Morrison & The Chieftains; *ST/Long Journey Home: The Irish In
America* . . . .(RCA Victor)
Vienna Boys Choir; *International Folk Songs: Around The World With The
Vienna Boys' Choir* . . . .(Philips)
Smoke Signal
Band; *Cahoots* . . . . (Capitol)
Song Of Crazy Horse
J.D. Blackfoot; *Song Of Crazy Horse* . . . . (Fantasy)
Squaws Along The Yukon
Hank Thompson; *Capitol Collectors Series-Hank Thompson* . . . . (Capitol)

Hank Thompson's Greatest Hits-#2 . . . .(Step One)
Straight Brother
Leon Russell & Marc Benno; *Asylum Choir II* . . . . (MCA)
Sundancing (For The Hopi/Navajo Energy)
Jon Anderson; *In The City Of Angels* . . . . (Columbia)
Ten Little Indians
Beach Boys; *Surfin' Safari* . . . . (Capitol)
Ten Little Indians
Nilsson; *Pandemonium Shadow Show* . . . . (RCA)
Theme From "Dances With Wolves"
John Barry; *Moviola* . . . . (Epic)
Theme From "The Last Of The Mohicans"
Twentieth Century Fox Orchestra; *ST/The Last Of The
Mohicans* . . . . (Morgan Creek)
Theme From "The Lone Ranger" (William Tell Overture)
Boston Pops Orchestra; *TV Classics-C* . . . . (RCA)
Boston Pops Orchestra/Arthur Fiedler; *Fiedler-Greatest Hits* . . . . (RCA)
Original Soundtrack; *Television's Greatest Hits-#7-Cable Ready-C* . . . . . (TVT)
Spike Jones & His City Slickers; *Best Of Spike Jones & His City
Slickers* . . . . (RCA)
Trader
Beach Boys; *10 Years Of Harmony* . . . .(Caribou)
Holland . . . . (Brother)
Trail Of Freedom
Bill Miller; *The Red Road* . . . . (Warner Western)
Ugg-a-Wugg
Original Cast; *Peter Pan-The 1954 Broadway Production* . . . . (RCA Victor)
Various Tracks
Joyce Yarrow; *"Jumping Mouse"* . . . .(Pacific Arts)
Voice Of The Eagle
Robbie Basho; *Voice Of The Eagle* . . . . (Vanguard)
Wedding In Cherokee County
Randy Newman; *Good Old Boys* . . . .(Reprise)
Wigwam
Bob Dylan; *Self Portrait* . . . . (Columbia)
Wild Injuns
Neville Brothers; *Yellow Moon* . . . . (A&M)
Wind In The Wire
Randy Travis; *Wind In The Wire* . . . . (Warner Bros.)
Witchi Tai To
Jim Pepper; *Comin' & Goin'* . . . .(Antilles)
Oregon; *Out Of The Woods* . . . . (Elektra)
Winter Light . . . . (Vanguard)
With God On Our Side
Bob Dylan; *The Times They Are A-Changin'* . . . . (Columbia)
Joan Baez; *The First 10 Years* . . . . (Vanguard)
Manfred Mann; *Songs Of Protest-C* . . . . (Rhino)
Neville Brothers; *Uptown Rulin': The Best Of The Neville Brothers* . . . . (A&M)
Yellow Moon . . . . (A&M)
Wire Train; *Best Of 415 Records-C* . . . .(Legacy)
Wooden Indian
John Denver; *Poems, Prayers & Promises* . . . . (RCA)
Wounded Knee Soliloquy
Robbie Basho; *Voice Of The Eagle* . . . . (Vanguard)
Wreck Of The Edmund Fitzgerald
Gordon Lightfoot; *Gord's Gold-#2* . . . .(Warner Bros.)
Summertime Dream . . . . (Reprise)
Your Squaw Is On The Warpath
Loretta Lynn; *Loretta Lynn's Greatest Hits-#2* . . . . (MCA)

NATURE, Ecology, Environment, Natural, Outdoors, Pollution, Wilderness

See Also: AIR, ANIMALS: A-Z, BUSINESS & INDUSTRY, COUNTRY, EARTH, ENERGY, FARMS, FLOWERS: GENERAL, FLOWERS: ROSES, JUNGLES, MOON, MOUNTAINS, NUCLEAR ENERGY, OCEAN, POLITICS (various), PROTEST, RAIN, RIVERS, SKY, SPACE, STARS, SUN, TREES, WILD, WIND, WORLD

Acid Rain
John Martyn; *Sapphire* . . . . (Island)
Acid Rain
Saigon Kick; *Saigon Kick* . . . .(Third Stone)
After The Goldrush
Emmylou Harris/Dolly Parton/Linda Ronstadt; *Trio II* . . . .(Asylum)
Neil Young; *After The Gold Rush* . . . . (Reprise)
Decade . . . . (Reprise)
Neil Young & Crazy Horse; *Live Rust* . . . . (Reprise)
Balance Of Nature
Dionne Warwick; *Dionne* . . . . (Warner Bros.)
Beauty Of Nature
Edmund Sylvers; *Have You Heard* . . . .(Casablanca)
Before The Deluge
Jackson Browne; *Late For The Sky* . . . .(Asylum)
Joan Baez; *Honest Lullaby* . . . . (Portrait)

Big Yellow Taxi
Amy Grant; *House Of Love* . . . . (A&M)
Joni Mitchell; *Ladies Of The Canyon* . . . . (Reprise)
Joni Mitchell with Tom Scott & The L.A. Express; *Miles Of Aisles* . . . (Asylum)

Birds And The Bees
Jewel Akens; *American Graffiti-#3-C* . . . . (MCA)
Collectables Presents The History Of Rock-#4-C . . . . (Collectables)
Cruisin'-1965-C . . . . (Increase)
Oldies But Goodies-#9-C . . . . (Original Sound)
Super Hits-#3-C . . . . (Gusto)

Blue Sky Mine
Midnight Oil; *Blue Sky Mining* . . . . (Columbia)

Blue White Planet
Raffi; *Country Goes Raffi-C* . . . . (Rounder)

Blues From The Rainforest
Merl Saunders; *Blues From The Rainforest-A Musical Suite* . . . . . . (Sumertone)

Burn On
Randy Newman; *Sail Away* . . . . (Reprise)

Colors Of The Wind
Judy Kuhn; *Princess Collection* . . . . (Disney)
Vanessa Williams; *ST/Pocahontas* . . . . (Hollywood)
Vanessa Williams' Greatest Hits-The First Ten Years . . . . (Mercury)

Death Of Mother Nature
Kansas; *Kansas* . . . . (Kirshner)

Do The Evolution
Pearl Jam; *Yield* . . . . (Epic)

Do You Want My Job
Little Village; *Little Village* . . . . (Reprise)

Don't Drop That Bomb On Me
Bryan Adams; *Waking Up The Neighbours* . . . . (A&M)

Don't Go Near The Water
Beach Boys; *10 Years Of Harmony* . . . . (Caribou)
Surf's Up . . . . (Caribou)

Ecology Poem
Mutabaruka; *Blakk Wi Blak...k...k* . . . . (Shanachie)

Ecology Song
Stephen Stills; *Stephen Stills 2* . . . . (Atlantic)

Every Natural Think
Aretha Franklin; *Let Me In Your Life* . . . . (Out Of Print)

Faith In You
Steve Wariner; *Faith In You* . . . . (Capitol)

Flesh And Blood
Johnny Cash; *Johnny Cash's Biggest Hits* . . . . (Columbia)
The Man In Black-His Greatest Hits . . . . (Legacy)

For The Beauty Of The Earth
Paul Winter Consort; *Missa Gaia (Earth Mass)* . . . . (Living Music)

Fresh Air
Quicksilver Messenger Service; *Quicksilver Messenger Service-*
Anthology . . . . (Capitol)
Sons Of Mercury . . . . (Rhino)

Garden Of Eden
New Riders Of The Purple Sage; *New Riders Of The Purple Sage* . . . (Columbia)

Green, Green
New Christy Minstrels; *New Christy Minstrels' Greatest Hits* . . . . . . (Columbia)

Hand Me Down World
Guess Who; *Best Of The Guess Who* . . . . (RCA)
Greatest Of The Guess Who . . . . (RCA)

Hiroshima Hole
Barefoot Jerry; *Barefootin'* . . . . (Monument)

Honeysuckle Honey
Commander Cody & His Lost Planet Airmen; *Country Casanova* . . . . (MCA)

Hundred Million Miracles
Original Cast; *Flower Drum Song* . . . . (Sony Music Classical)

In Every Corner Of The Forest (Parts 1-3)
Bill Miller; *Raven In The Snow* . . . . (Reprise)

Lazy Day
Spanky & Our Gang; *Best Of Spanky & Our Gang* . . . . (Rhino)

Let Old Mother Nature Have Her Way
Carl Smith; *Columbia Country Classics-#2-Honky Tonk Heroes-C* . . (Columbia)
Essential Carl Smith-1950-1956 . . . . (Legacy)
Seldom Scene; *After Midnight* . . . . (Sugar Hill)

Let's Make The Water Turn Black
Mothers Of Invention; *Lumpy Gravy* . . . . (Rykodisc)

Looking East
Jackson Browne; *Looking East* . . . . (Elektra)

Love & Maple Syrup
Gordon Lightfoot; *Summer Side Of Life* . . . . (Reprise)

Mercy Mercy Me (The Ecology)
Marvin Gaye; *Every Great Motown Hit Of Marvin Gaye* . . . . (Motown)
Marvin Gaye-Anthology . . . . (Motown)
Marvin Gaye's Greatest Hits . . . . (Motown)
What's Going On . . . . (Motown)
Robert Palmer; *Don't Explain* . . . . (EMI)

Miracle Of Love
Eileen Rodgers; *Hard To Find 45s On CD-#3-The Mid '50s-C* . . . . . . (Eric)

Mocking Bird Hill
Patti Page; *Patti Page-16 Most Requested Songs* . . . . (Legacy)
Patti Page-Golden Hits . . . . (Mercury)

Patti Page's Greatest Hits . . . . (Columbia)
Russ Morgan; *Best Of Russ Morgan* . . . . (MCA)

Mother Nature
Temptations; *Temptations-Anthology-The Best Of The Temptations* . . . (Motown)

Mother Nature's Son
Beatles; *Beatles-Box Set* . . . . (Capitol)
The Beatles (White Album) . . . . (Capitol)
John Denver; *Evening With John Denver* . . . . (RCA)
Rocky Mountain High . . . . (RCA)

Mr. Pollution
P'Cock; *Burning Beach* . . . . (Innovative Comm.)

Naturally
Marty Stuart; *Country Goes Raffi-C* . . . . (Rounder)

Nature Avenue
John Lodge; *Nature Avenue* . . . . (London)

Nature Boy
George Benson; *George Benson-Collection* . . . . (Warner Bros.)
Jose Feliciano; *Encore-Jose Feliciano* . . . . (RCA)
Nat "King" Cole; *Blossom Fell* . . . . (Capitol)
The Nat "King" Cole Story . . . . (Capitol)

Nature Lover
Mass Production; *Massterpiece* . . . . (Cotillion)

Nature Planned It
Four Tops; *Four Tops-Anthology* . . . . (Motown)
Nature Planned It . . . . (Motown)

Nature Trail To Hell
"Weird Al" Yankovic; *In 3-D* . . . . (Scotti Bros.)

Nature's Child
Triumph; *Progressions Of Power* . . . . (MCA)

Nature's Creation
Valentines; *Best Of The Valentines* . . . . (Collectables)

Nature's Disappearing
John Mayall; *Room To Move-1969-1974-Chronicle Series* . . . . (Polydor)
Wake Up Call . . . . (Silvertone)

Nature's Way
Spirit; *12 Dreams Of Dr. Sardonicus* . . . . (Epic)
Best Of Spirit . . . . (Epic)
Time Circle . . . . (Epic)

New Mother Nature
Guess Who; *American Woman* . . . . (RCA)
Best Of The Guess Who . . . . (RCA)

New Pollution
Beck; *Odelay* . . . . (David Geffen Co.)

Nine Types Of Industrial Pollution
Frank Zappa; *Uncle Meat* . . . . (Barking Pumpkin)
Mothers Of Invention; *Legends Of Rock Guitar-'60s-#1-C* . . . . (Rhino)

Northern Lights
Val Gardena; *On The Bridge* . . . . (Mercury)

Northern Lights
Bruce Cockburn; *Dancing In The Dragon's Jaws* . . . . (Columbia)

Northern Lights
Duke Ellington; *The Ellington Suites* . . . . (Original Jazz Classics)

Northern Lights
Rippingtons; *Kilimanjaro* . . . . (GRP)

On A Clear Day (You Can See Forever)
Barbra Streisand; *Just For The Record* . . . . (Columbia)
Live Concert At The Forum . . . . (Columbia)
ST/On A Clear Day You Can See Forever . . . . . . (Columbia Special Prod.)
The Concert . . . . (Columbia)
Roger Williams; *Best Of Roger Williams* . . . . (MCA)
Somewhere In Time . . . . (Bainbridge)

Once A Forest
Grace Pool; *Where We Live* . . . . (Reprise)

Ozone Alert
Special EFX; *Global Village* . . . . (GRP)

Ozone Layer
Augustus Pablo; *Rockers International Showcase-C* . . . . (Rykodisc)

Ozone Layer
Black Uhuru; *Mystical Truth* . . . . (Mesa)

Pass It On Down
Alabama; *Pass It On Down* . . . . (BMG Special Prod.)

Pollution
Tom Lehrer; *That Was The Year That Was* . . . . (Reprise)

Power
John Hall; *Power* . . . . (Columbia)
John Hall/Doobie Brothers/James Taylor; *No Nukes* . . . . (Asylum)

Red Rain
Peter Gabriel; *Greenpeace/Rainbow Warriors-C* . . . . (Geffen)
Secret World Live . . . . (Geffen)
Shaking The Tree-Sixteen Golden Greats . . . . (Geffen)
So . . . . (Geffen)

River Song
Beach Boys; *10 Years Of Harmony* . . . . (Caribou)

Rockin' In The Free World
Bon Jovi; *One Wild Night: Live 1985-2001* . . . . (Island)
Neil Young; *Freedom* . . . . (Reprise)
Neil Young & Crazy Horse; *WELD* . . . . (Reprise)
Pearl Jam; *8/12/00: Tampa, Florida* . . . . (Epic)

Save Mother Earth
Merl Saunders; *Heavy Turbulence* . . . . (Fantasy)
Merl Saunders & Friends; *Fire Up* . . . . (Fantasy)
Merl Saunders & The Rainforest Band; *Save The Planet* . . . . (Sumertone)
Save The Planet
Edgar Winter's White Trash; *Edgar Winter's White Trash* . . . . (Epic)
Roadwork. . . . .(Epic)
Seminole Wind
John Anderson; *Seminole Wind* . . . . (BNA)
Skellig
Loreena McKennitt; *The Book Of Secrets.* . . . . (Quinlan Rd./Warner Bros.)
Sky Is A Poisonous Garden
Concrete Blonde; *Bloodletting* . . . .(I.R.S.)
Smog
Miracles; *City Of Angels.* . . . . (Tamla)
Sparrow
Simon & Garfunkel; *Wednesday Morning 3 A.M.* . . . . (Columbia)
Thanks A Lot
Raul Malo; *Country Goes Raffi-C* . . . . (Rounder)
There's A Moon Out Tonight
Capris; *20 Top 10 Hits Of The '50s & '60s-C* . . . . (Laurie)
22 Leaders Of The Pack-#2-C . . . . (Laurie)
Collectables Presents The History Of Rock-#3-C . . . . (Collectables)
There's A Moon Out Tonight . . . . (Collectables)
Tree Hugger
Rugburns; *Taking The World By Donkey* . . . . (Priority)
Victims Of Comfort
Keb' Mo'; *Keb' Mo'.* . . . . (Okeh)
Weather
Amel Larrieux; *Infinite Possibilities.* . . . .(Epic)
Where The Blacktop Ends
keith urban; *keith urban.* . . . . (Capitol)
Will The Wolf Survive
Los Lobos; *How Will The Wolf Survive* . . . . (Slash)
Waylon Jennings; *Country Classics-#6-1985-1986-C* . . . . . . (Universal)
New Classic Waylon . . . . (MCA)
Will The Wolf Survive . . . .(MCA)

NEW

See Also: BEGINNINGS, ENDINGS, MORNING, MOTIVATION

1,2,3,4 (Sumpin' New)
Coolio; *ESPN Presents Jock Jams-#2-C.* . . . . (Tommy Boy)
MTV Party To Go-#9-C . . . . (Tommy Boy)
Tommy Boy's Greatest Beats-#2-C . . . . (Tommy Boy)
Another Girl
Beatles; *Beatles-Box Set* . . . . (Capitol)
ST/Help! . . . . (Capitol)
Beginning, The
Keb' Mo'; *The Door.* . . . . (550/Epic/Okeh)
Brand New Amerika
Poorboys; *Pardon Me* . . . . (Hollywood)
Brand New Cadillac
Clash; *London Calling* . . . .(Epic)
On Broadway. . . . .(Epic)
Brand New Car
Rolling Stones; *Voodoo Lounge* . . . . (Virgin)
Brand New Convertible Car
Die Warzau; *Big Electric Metal Bass Face.* . . . . (Atlantic)
Brand New Country Star
Jimmy Buffett; *Living & Dying In 3/4 Time* . . . .(MCA)
Brand New Dance
Emmylou Harris; *Brand New Dance* . . . . (Reprise)
Brand New Day
Frankie Laine; *Frankie Laine's 16 Greatest Hits* . . . . (Trip)
Brand New Day
Van Morrison; *Moondance.* . . . .(Warner Bros.)
Brand New Day
Sting; *Brand New Day* . . . . (A&M)
Brand New Heartache
Everly Brothers; *Everly Brothers* . . . . (Rhino)
Everly Brothers-Cadence Classics-Their 20 Greatest Hits . . . . (Rhino)
Brand New Key
Deana Carter; *Everything's Gonna Be Alright* . . . . (Capitol)
Melanie; *Best Of Melanie* . . . . (Rhino)
Super Hits Of The '70s-Have A Nice Day-#7-C . . . . (Rhino)
Brand New Man
Brooks & Dunn; *Brand New Man* . . . . (Arista)
Brand New Me
Dusty Springfield; *Brand New Me* . . . . (Rhino)
Brand New Mister Me
Mel Tillis & The Statesiders; *The Ultimate Mel Tillis* . . . . (Bransounds)
Brand New Tennessee Waltz
Jesse Winchester; *Best Of Jesse Winchester* . . . . (Rhino)
Jesse Winchester . . . . (Rhino)

Joan Baez; *Country Music Album* . . . . (Vanguard)
Brand New Toy
Hot Tuna; *Pair A Dice Found* . . . . (Epic)
Brand New Whiskey
Gary Stewart; *Brand New* . . . .(Hightone)
Gary's Greatest . . . .(Hightone)
Brave New World
Steve Miller Band; *Brave New World* . . . . (Capitol)
Brave New World
Public Image Ltd.; *9* . . . .(Virgin)
Brave New World
Choirboys; *Big Bad Noise* . . . . (WTG)
Burnin' Old Memories With A Brand New Flame
Kathy Mattea; *Country Hits 4: Sweet Country-C* . . . .(Priority)
Willow In The Wind . . . . (Mercury)
Change Partners
Rosanne Cash; *The Wheel.* . . . . (Columbia)
Cupid's Got A Brand New Gun
Michael Penn; *March* . . . . (RCA)
Got A Bran' New Suit
Louis Armstrong; *Jazz Heritage-Back In New York* . . . . (MCA)
I Almost Lost My Mind
Eddy Arnold; *World Of Hits* . . . .(MGM)
Fats Domino; *Fats Domino's Greatest Hits* . . . . (MCA)
Ivory Joe Hunter; *Since I Met You Baby* . . . . (Mercury)
Pat Boone; *Pat Boone's Greatest Hits.* . . . . (Curb)
I Will Buy You A New Life
Everclear; *Now That's What I Call Music!-#1-C.* . . . .(Virgin)
So Much For The Afterglow . . . . (Capitol)
I've Found A New Baby
Benny Goodman; *Benny Goodman-Live At Carnegie Hall.* . . . .(London)
Benny Goodman-On Stage . . . . (London)
Complete Benny Goodman-#2 . . . . (RCA)
I've Got A New Heartache
Ray Price; *Ray Price's Greatest Hits.* . . . . (Columbia)
Ricky Skaggs; *Live In London.* . . . . (Epic)
More Hot Country Requests-C . . . . (Epic)
Like A Virgin
Madonna; *Immaculate Collection* . . . .(Sire)
Like A Virgin . . . .(Sire)
Royal Box . . . .(Sire)
Looking For A New Love
Jody Watley; *Do You Wanna Dance With Me?* . . . . (MCA)
Jody Watley . . . . (MCA)
Love Will Be Waiting
Kevon Edmonds; *24/7.* . . . . (RCA)
Nadine (Is It You?)
Chuck Berry; *Rock & Roll Rarities* . . . . (Chess)
New Africa
Youssou N'Dour; *Eyes Open* . . . . (40 Acres & A Mule Musicworks)
New African Blues
Cassandra Wilson; *She Who Weeps* . . . .(Jazz Music Today)
New African Whistler
Roger Whittaker; *Live In Concert* . . . . (RCA)
New Age In America
Larry Coryell; *American Odyssey* . . . .(DRG)
New America
Flim & The BB's; *Big Notes* . . . . (Digital Music Prod.)
New Argentina
Original Cast; *Evita.* . . . . (MCA)
New Attitude
Patti LaBelle; *Classic Soul-C* . . . . (MCA)
I Am Woman-C. . . . .(Nick At Nite)
Soundtrack Smashes-'80s & More-C . . . . (MCA)
ST/Beverly Hills Cop . . . . (MCA)
New Beginning
Tracy Chapman; *New Beginning.* . . . . (Elektra)
New Beginning
Stir; *Holy Dogs* . . . .(Capitol)
New Blue Moon
Traveling Wilburys; *Traveling Wilburys-Vol. 3* . . . . (Wilbury/Warner Bros.)
New Career In A New Town
David Bowie; *Low.* . . . . (Rykodisc)
New Cut Road
Bobby Bare; *Bare Tracks* . . . . (Koch International)
New Day Yesterday, A
Jethro Tull; *Best Of Jethro Tull-The Anniversary Collection* . . . . . .(Chrysalis)
Stand Up . . . . (Chrysalis)
New East St. Louis Toodle-oo
Duke Ellington; *Reminiscing In Tempo.* . . . . (Columbia)
New Faces
Rolling Stones; *Voodoo Lounge* . . . .(Virgin)
New Favorite
Alison Krauss & Union Station; *New Favorite* . . . . (Rounder)
New Frisco Train
Washington White; *Mississippi Moaners-1927-1942* . . . . (Yazoo)
New Frontier
Donald Fagen; *The Nightfly.* . . . . (Warner Bros.)

New Girl In School
Jan & Dean; *Jan & Dean-Legendary Masters* . . . . (EMI)
   Surf City-Best Of Jan & Dean . . . . (EMI)
New Gods
Meat Puppets; *Meat Puppets II* . . . . (SST)
   No Strings Attached . . . . (SST)
New Gold Dream
Simple Minds; *New Gold Dream* . . . . (A&M)
   Simple Minds Live: In The City Of Light . . . . (A&M)
New Gold Dream
Utah Saints; *Utah Saints* . . . . (London)
New Grey Bonnet
Johnny Gimble; *Still Fiddlin' Around* . . . . (MCA)
New Hawaiian Boogie
George Thorogood & The Destroyers; *Move It On Over* . . . . (Rounder)
New Huntsville Jail
Joe Evans & John Dilleshaw; *Early Country Music* . . . . (Historical)
New Jerusalem
Word Of Mouth Chorus; *Rivers Of Delight* . . . . (Nonesuch)
New Jerusalem
Tom Gavornik; *High Places* . . . . (August Prod.)
New Lee Highway Blues
David Bromberg; *Out Of The Blues-Best Of David Bromberg* . . . . . . (Columbia)
   Wanted Dead Or Alive . . . . (Columbia)
New Machine Pt. 1
Pink Floyd; *Momentary Lapse Of Reason* . . . . (Columbia)
   Shine On . . . . (Columbia)
New Machine Pt. 2
Pink Floyd; *Momentary Lapse Of Reason* . . . . (Columbia)
   Shine On . . . . (Columbia)
New Math
Tom Lehrer; *That Was The Year That Was* . . . . (Reprise)
New Moon On Monday
Duran Duran; *After The Hurricane* . . . . (Chrysalis)
   Seven And The Ragged Tiger . . . . (Capitol)
New Morning
Bob Dylan; *New Morning* . . . . (Columbia)
New Mother Nature
Guess Who; *American Woman* . . . . (RCA)
   Best Of The Guess Who . . . . (RCA)
New Pollution
Beck; *Odelay* . . . . (David Geffen Co.)
New Pony
Bob Dylan; *Street Legal* . . . . (Columbia)
New River Train
Doc & Merle Watson; *Remembering Merle* . . . . (Sugar Hill)
   White Brothers & New Kentucky Colonels; *Live In Sweden* . . . . (Rounder)
New Soldiers Joy
Kentucky Colonels featuring Roland & Clarence White; *1965-1967* . . (Rounder)
New Spanish Two-Step
Bob Wills & His Texas Playboys; *Country Music Classics-#14-
   1940s-C* . . . . (K-Tel)
   Essential Bob Wills & His Texas Playboys-1935-1973 . . . . (Legacy)
New St. Louis Blues
Johnny Dodds; *South Side Chicago Jazz* . . . . (MCA)
New Way (To Light Up An Old Flame)
Joe Diffie; *A Thousand Winding Roads* . . . . (Epic)
New World
X; *Live At The Whisky A Go-Go* . . . . (Elektra)
   More Fun In The New World . . . . (Elektra)
New World
Cause & Effect; *Another Minute* . . . . (Zoo)
New World
Strawbs; *Grave New World* . . . . (A&M)
New World
Saigon Kick; *Saigon Kick* . . . . (Third Stone)
New World
Boston; *Third Stage* . . . . (MCA)
New World In The Morning
Roger Whittaker; *Best Of Roger Whittaker* . . . . (RCA)
   Last Farewell & Other Hits . . . . (RCA)
   Live In Concert . . . . (RCA)
   New World In The Morning . . . . (RCA)
New World Man
Rush; *Rush-Chronicles* . . . . (Mercury)
   Signals . . . . (Mercury)
   Three Decades Of Rock ('60s, '70s, '80s)-C . . . . (Priority)
New World Order
Curtis Mayfield; *New World Order* . . . . (Warner Bros.)
New World Rising
Electric Light Orchestra; *On The Third Day* . . . . (Jet)
Nothin' New Under The Moon
LeAnn Rimes; *Sittin' On Top Of The World* . . . . (Curb)
Old Flames Have New Names
Mark Chesnutt; *Longnecks & Short Stories* . . . . (MCA)
P.S. I Love You
Bette Midler; *ST/For The Boys* . . . . (Atlantic)
   Billie Holiday; *Lady Sings The Blues* . . . . (Verve)

Bing Crosby; *Thanks For The Memories Mr. Crosby* . . . . (J-Bird)
Dion; *Dion-His Best* . . . . (Laurie)
Kay Starr; *Too Marvelous For Words-Capitol Sings Jonny Mercer-C* . . (Capitol)
Mel Torme; *That's All* . . . . (Sony Music Special Prod.)
Rosemary Clooney; *Rosemary Clooney Sings The Lyrics Of Johnny
   Mercer* . . . . (Concord Jazz)
Tom T. Hall; *Natural Dreams* . . . . (Mercury)
Woody Herman; *Best Of The Big Bands-C* . . . . (Columbia)
Papa's Got A Brand New Bag
James Brown; *21 Legendary Superstars-C* . . . . (Original Sound)
   Everybody's Doin' The Hustle & Dead On The Double Bump . . . . . . (Polydor)
   James Brown's Greatest Hits . . . . (Rhino)
   Live-Hot On The One . . . . (Polydor)
Otis Redding; *The Otis Redding Story* . . . . (Atlantic)
   Unlimited! . . . . (Reprise)
Potential New Boyfriend
Dolly Parton; *Best Of Dolly Parton-#3* . . . . (RCA)
Ride My New Car With Me
Big Joe Williams; *Dark Muddy Bottom Blues-C* . . . . (Specialty)
Rock And Roll Waltz
Kay Starr; *Capitol Collectors Series-Kay Starr* . . . . (Capitol)
Skating Away On The Thin Ice Of A New Day
Jethro Tull; *"M.U."-Best Of* . . . . (Chrysalis)
   Bursting Out . . . . (Chrysalis)
   Original Masters . . . . (Chrysalis)
   War Child . . . . (Chrysalis)
Somebody New
Billy Ray Cyrus; *It Won't Be The Last* . . . . (Mercury)
Start A New Life
REO Speedwagon; *Ridin' The Storm Out* . . . . (Epic)
Starting A New Life
Van Morrison; *Tupelo Honey* . . . . (Polydor)
There's A New Moon Over My Shoulder
Gene Autry; *Columbia Historic Edition-Gene Autry* . . . . (Columbia)
Jimmie Davis; *Best Of Jimmie Davis* . . . . (MCA)
   Jimmie Davis-Golden Hits . . . . (Plantation)
   The Country Music Hall Of Fame-Jimmie Davis . . . . (MCA)
Tex Ritter; *Tex Ritter's Greatest Hits* . . . . (Curb)
Times They Are A-Changin'
Billy Joel; *KOHUEPT* . . . . (Columbia)
Bob Dylan; *Biograph* . . . . (Columbia)
   Bob Dylan At Budokan . . . . (Columbia)
   Bob Dylan's Greatest Hits . . . . (Columbia)
   The Bootleg Series-Volumes 1-3 [Rare & Unreleased] . . . . (Columbia)
   The Times They Are A-Changin' . . . . (Columbia)
Byrds; *The Byrds* . . . . (Columbia)
   Turn! Turn! Turn! . . . . (Legacy)
Peter, Paul & Mary; *Peter, Paul and Mary In Concert* . . . . (Warner Bros.)
Simon & Garfunkel; *Collected Works* . . . . (Columbia)
   Wednesday Morning 3 A.M. . . . . (Columbia)
What's New In Baltimore?
Frank Zappa; *Meets The Mothers Of Prevention* . . . . (Rykodisc)
   You Can't Do That On Stage Anymore-#5 . . . . (Rykodisc)
What's New Pussycat
Tom Jones; *Tom Jones-London Collector-Greatest Hits* . . . . (London)
Whole New World (Aladdin's Theme)
Peabo Bryson & Regina Belle; *ST/Aladdin* . . . . (Disney)
Regina Belle & Peabo Bryson; *Passion* . . . . (Columbia)
Whole New You
Shawn Colvin; *Whole New You* . . . . (Columbia)
Woman On The Tier (I'll See You Through)
Suzanne Vega; *ST/Dead Man Walking* . . . . (Columbia)
You Brought A New Kind Of Love To Me
Ella Fitzgerald; *Ella Swings Lightly* . . . . (Verve)

NEWS, Magazines, Newspapers

**See Also: BOOKS, COMMUNICATION (various), COMPUTERS,
GOSSIP, MOVIES, PAPER, MUSIC, RADIO, SHOPPING,
TELEPHONE, TELEVISION**

Ain't That Good News
David "Fathead" Newman; *Bigger & Better-Many Facets Of David
   "Fathead" Newman* . . . . (Rhino)
Ain't That News?
Broadside Singers & Tom Paxton; *Best Of Broadside 1962-1968: Anthems
   Of The American Underground From The Pages Of Broadside
   Magazine-C* . . . . (Smithsonian Folkways)
Attractive Female Wanted
Rod Stewart; *Blondes Have More Fun* . . . . (Warner Bros.)
Bad News
Johnny Winter; *About Blues* . . . . (Janus)
   Before The Storm . . . . (Janus)
Bad News
Emmylou Harris; *Ballad Of Sally Rose* . . . . (Warner Bros.)
Bad News Travels Fast
Bachman-Turner Overdrive; *Live Live Live* . . . . (MCA)

Bad News Travels Fast
Walter Egan; *Hi-Fi* . . . . (Columbia)
Bad News Travels Fast
Player; *Room With A View* . . . . (Casablanca)
Billy Got Some Bad News Today
Tom Paxton; *It Ain't Easy* . . . . (Flying Fish)
Boy Wanted
Original Cast; *My One And Only* . . . . (Atlantic)
Breakfast In Mayfair
Fairport Convention; *Babbacombe Lee* . . . . (A&M)
Fairport Convention-Chronicles . . . . (A&M)
Carlene
Phil Vassar; *Phil Vassar* . . . . (Arista)
Centerfold
J. Geils Band; *Flashback-Best Of The J. Geils Band* . . . . (EMI)
Freeze-Frame . . . . (EMI)
Showtime . . . . (EMI)
Cover Of Rolling Stone
Dr. Hook & The Medicine Show; *Dr. Hook & The Medicine Show's*
Greatest Hits . . . . (Capitol)
Revisited . . . . (Columbia)
Day In The Life, A
Beatles; *Sgt. Pepper's Lonely Hearts Club Band* . . . . (Capitol)
ST/Imagine: John Lennon . . . . (Capitol)
The Beatles/1967-1970 . . . . (Capitol)
Digging In The Dirt
Peter Gabriel; *Us* . . . . (Geffen)
Ding Dong The Witch Is Dead
Fifth Estate; *Dick Bartley's One-Hit Wonders Of The '60s-#2-C* . . . (Rhino)
Meco; *The Wizard Of Oz* . . . . (Millennium)
MGM Studio Orchestra; *ST/The Wizard Of Oz* . . . . . . (Sony Music Special Prod.)
Dirty Laundry
Don Henley; *I Can't Stand Still* . . . . (Asylum)
Don't Give Me Bad News
Bobby Caldwell; *Stuck On You* . . . . (Sin-Drome)
Don't Nobody Bring Me No Bad News
Mabel King; *ST/The Wiz* . . . . (MCA)
Don't Take My Sunday Paper
Holly Near & Jeff Langley; *You Can Know All I Am* . . . . (Redwood)
Escape (Pina Colada Song)
Rupert Holmes; *Billboard Top Hits-1979-C* . . . . (Rhino)
Partners In Crime . . . . (MCA)
Front Page News
Little Feat; *Down On The Farm* . . . . (Warner Bros.)
Hoy-Hoy! . . . . (Warner Bros.)
Front Page News
Angel City; *Two-Minute Warning* . . . . (Metal Blade)
Front Page Story
Neil Diamond; *Heartlight* . . . . (Columbia)
God Trying To Get Your Attention
Keb' Mo'; *Slow Down* . . . . (550/Epic/Okeh)
Good News
Muddy Waters; *The Chess Box-Muddy Waters* . . . . (Chess)
Good News
Melissa Manchester; *Better Days & Happy Endings* . . . . (Arista)
Essence Of Melissa Manchester . . . . (Arista)
Good News
Attitudes; *Good News* . . . . (Dark Horse)
Good News
Red Rider; *Don't Fight It* . . . . (Capitol)
Good News
King Curtis; *Best Of King Curtis* . . . . (Collectables)
Good News
Kingston Trio; *Scarlet Ribbons* . . . . (Capitol)
Mary Travers; *It's In Every One Of Us* . . . . (Chrysalis)
Sweet Honey In The Rock; *Good News* . . . . (Flying Fish)
Good News
Staple Singers; *Swing Low Sweet Chariot* . . . . (Collectables)
Good News Travels Fast
Jerry Lee Lewis; *When Two Worlds Collide* . . . . (Elektra)
Good News, Bad News
Eddy Raven; *Eddy Raven-Greatest Country Hits* . . . . (Curb)
Have You Heard The News
Ben Sidran; *Puttin' In Time On Planet Earth* . . . . (MCA)
Vikki Carr; *Live At The Greek Theatre* . . . . (Columbia)
Headlines
Midnight Star; *Headlines* . . . . (Solar)
Headlines
John Fogerty; *Eye Of The Zombie* . . . . (Warner Bros.)
I Got The News
Steely Dan; *Aja* . . . . (MCA)
In The Want Ads
Mickey Gilley; *Mickey Gilley* . . . . (Paula)
It's Good News Week
Hedgehoppers Anonymous; *Songs Of Protest-C* . . . . (Rhino)
Little Good News
Anne Murray; *Anne Murray's Greatest Hits-#2* . . . . (Capitol)
Little Good News . . . . (Capitol)

Little Paper Boy
Hank Williams; *Rare Takes & Radio Cuts* . . . . (Polydor)
Magazine
Rickie Lee Jones; *The Magazine* . . . . (Warner Bros.)
Magazine
Heart; *Magazine* . . . . (Capitol)
Magazine Lover
Pieces; *Pieces* . . . . (United Artists)
More News At 11
Public Enemy; *Apocalypse 91...The Enemy Strikes Black* . . (Def Jam/Columbia)
More Trouble Every Day
Zappa/Mothers; *Roxy & Elsewhere* . . . . (Rykodisc)
Morning Papers
Prince And The New Power Generation; *Love Symbol Album* . . . . (Paisley Park)
News
Jimmy Cliff; *Follow My Mind* . . . . (Reprise)
News
Dire Straits; *Communique* . . . . (Warner Bros.)
News At Ten
Vapors; *New Clear Days* . . . . (Liberty)
News For You Baby
Sonny Terry; *Sonny Terry* . . . . (Collectables)
T-Bone Walker; *T-Bone Walker* . . . . (Blue Note)
News From Spain
Al Stewart; *Al Stewart-Early Years* . . . . (Janus)
News From Up The Street
Dan Hicks & His Hot Licks; *Where's The Money?* . . . . (MCA)
Newspapers
Stan Ridgway; *Mosquitos* . . . . (Geffen)
Newspapers
Automatic Man; *Automatic Man* . . . . (Island)
Newsreel Babies
INXS; *INXS* . . . . (Atco)
No News
Lonestar; *Lonestar* . . . . (BNA)
Nothing's News
Clint Black; *Killin' Time* . . . . (RCA)
ST/My Heroes Have Always Been Cowboys . . . . (RCA)
Ode To Billy Joe
Bobbi Gentry; *All-Time Country Classics-#1-C* . . . . (Capitol)
One Reporter's Opinion
Minutemen; *Double Nickels On The Dime* . . . . (SST)
Pigs, Sheep & Wolves
Paul Simon; *You're The One* . . . . (Warner Bros.)
Power Of The Press
Angelic Upstarts; *Brighton Bomb* . . . . (Charisma)
Pump It Up (Here's The News)
M.C. Hammer; *Let's Get It Started* . . . . (Capitol)
Reader's Digest
Betty Comden & Adolph Green; *Party With Betty Comden & Adolph*
Green . . . . (DRG)
Richard Cory
Simon & Garfunkel; *Collected Works* . . . . (Columbia)
Sounds Of Silence . . . . (Columbia)
Wings; *Wings Over America* . . . . (Capitol)
Rockabilly Blues (Texas 1955)
Johnny Cash; *Texas Super Hits-C* . . . . (Columbia)
Roll Over Beethoven
Beatles; *Beatles-Box Set* . . . . (Capitol)
Rock 'N' Roll Music . . . . (Capitol)
The Beatles At The Hollywood Bowl . . . . (Capitol)
The Beatles' Second Album . . . . (Capitol)
With The Beatles . . . . (Parlophone)
Byrds; *The Byrds* . . . . (Columbia)
Chuck Berry; *Chuck Berry-Golden Hits* . . . . (Mercury)
Chuck Berry's Greatest Hits . . . . (Everest)
Cruisin'-1956-C . . . . (Increase)
Oldies But Goodies-#10-C . . . . (Original Sound)
The Chess Box-Chuck Berry . . . . (Chess)
Electric Light Orchestra; *Afterglow* . . . . (Epic)
Ole ELO . . . . (Jet)
Sad News From Korea
Lightnin' Hopkins; *Houston's King of the blues-1952-1953* . . . (Blues Classics)
Second Hand News
Fleetwood Mac; *25 Years-The Chain* . . . . (Warner Bros.)
Rumours . . . . (Warner Bros.)
Tonic; *Legacy-A Tribute To Fleetwood Mac's Rumours-C* . . . . (Lava)
Seven O'Clock News
Simon & Garfunkel; *Collected Works* . . . . (Columbia)
Parsley Sage Rosemary & Thyme . . . . (Columbia)
Single White Female
Chely Wright; *Single White Female* . . . . (MCA)
Six O'Clock News
John Prine; *John Prine* . . . . (Atlantic)
John Prine-Souvenirs . . . . (Oh Boy)
Stayin' Alive
Bee Gees; *Bee Gees' Greatest* . . . . (Polydor)
ST/Saturday Night Fever . . . . (Polydor)

ST/*Stayin' Alive* .... (Polydor)

Sunday Papers
Joe Jackson; *Live 1980/86* .... (A&M)
   Look Sharp! .... (A&M)
   No Wave .... (A&M)

Swimsuit Issue
Sonic Youth; *Dirty*.................... (David Geffen Co.)

Tell Me What The Papers Say
Elton John; *Ice On Fire* .... (MCA)

Tennessee Newsboy (Newsboy Blues)
Frank Sinatra; *Columbia Years-1943-1952-Complete Recordings* ..... (Legacy)

Theme From "Max Headroom"
Original Soundtrack; *Television's Greatest Hits-#7-Cable Ready-C* ..... (TVT)

Theme From "Murphy Brown"
Original Soundtrack; *CBS: The First 50 Years* .... (TVT)

Tom's Diner
D.N.A. Featuring Suzanne Vega; *Solitude Standing* .... (A&M)
   Tom's Album.. (A&M)

Trainwreck Of Emotion
Lorrie Morgan; *Essential Lorrie Morgan* .... (RCA)
   Leave The Light On............................... (RCA)
   To Get To You-Greatest Hits Collection .... (BNA)

Turn On The News
Husker Du; *Zen Arcade* .... (SST)

Vogue
Madonna; *I'm Breathless-Music From Dick Tracy* .... (Sire)
   Immaculate Collection .... (Sire)
   Royal Box .... (Sire)

Want Ad Blues
John Lee Hooker; *Best Of John Lee Hooker* .... (Crescendo)
   John Lee Hooker............................... (Everest)
   World's Greatest Blues Singer .... (Vee-Jay)

Want Ads
Honey Cone; *Honey Cone's Greatest Hits* .... (HDH)

Yesterday's News Just Hit Home Today
Johnny Paycheck; *Johnny Paycheck's Biggest Hits* .... (Epic)

Yesterday's Paper
Tish Hinojosa; *Destiny's Gate*.............. (Warner Bros.)

Yesterday's Papers
Rolling Stones; *Between The Buttons* .... (Abkco)

Your Picture In The Paper
Statler Brothers; *Best Of The Statler Brothers-Rides Again-#2* .... (Mercury)
   Harold Lew Phil & Don .... (Mercury)

NIGHT, Dark, Evening, Goodnight, Tonight

See Also: **BARS, DAYS OF THE WEEK (various), DAYS:
GENERAL, LATE, LIGHT, MIDNIGHT, MOON, PARTY, SEX,
SHADOWS, STARS, SUN, TIME: GENERAL, TIME:
SPECIFIC, WEEKEND**

(There's A) Fire In The Night
Alabama; *Roll On* ....(RCA)

(Turn Out The Light And) Love Me Tonight
Don Williams; *Best Of Don Williams-#2*......................... (MCA)
   Don Williams-20 Greatest Hits..................... (MCA)

(We're Gonna) Rock Around The Clock
Bill Haley & His Comets; *Bill Haley & His Comets' Greatest Hits*...... (MCA)
   Bill Haley & His Comets' Greatest Hits ....(Everest)
   Bill Haley & His Comets-Golden Hits .... (MCA)
   Billboard Top Rock 'N' Roll Hits-1955-C .... (Rhino)
   ST/American Graffiti .... (MCA)

2 Become 1
Spice Girls; *Spice*.................................(Virgin)

3am
Matchbox Twenty; *Yourself Or Someone Like You*.................... (Lava)

A Little Night Music
Original Cast; *Little Night Music*.................. (Columbia)

About A Quarter To Nine
Original Broadway Cast; *42nd Street* .... (RCA Victor)

Absolutely Sweet Marie
Bob Dylan; *Blonde On Blonde* .... (Columbia)

African Night Flight
David Bowie; *Lodger* .... (Rykodisc)

After Tonight
Mariah Carey; *Rainbow*.......................... (Columbia)

Again Tonight
John Mellencamp; *Whenever We Wanted* .... (Mercury)

Ain't Going Down (Til The Sun Comes Up)
Garth Brooks; *In Pieces*........................... (Liberty)

Alaskan Nights
David Schwartz; *ST/Music From "Northern Exposure"* .... (MCA)

All At Once You Love Her
Perry Como; *Perry Como's Greatest Hits* .... (RCA)

All Day And All Of The Night
Kinks; *British Rock-#1-C* ....(Original Sound)

God Save The Kinks! .... (Castle Music America)
   History Of British Rock-#2-C ....(Rhino)

All I Want
Toad The Wet Sprocket; *Fear* .... (Columbia)
   P.S. (A Toad Retrospective) .... (Columbia)

All My Rowdy Friends Are Coming Over Tonight
Hank Williams, Jr.; *Great Divorce Songs For Him-C* ..... (Warner Bros.)
   Hank Williams, Jr.'s Greatest Hits-#2 ....(WB/Curb)
   Major Moves ....(WB/Curb)

All Night
Entouch Featuring Keith Sweat; *All Nite* .... (Vintertainment)

All Night
Keith Washington; *Make Time For Love* .... (Qwest)

All Night Juke
Lloyd Green; *Lloyd's Of Nashville*.....................(Boot)

All Night Laundromat Blues
Joe Walsh; *So What* .... (MCA)

All Night Long
Joe Houston; *20 Super Rhythm & Blues Hits-C* ....(Kent)
   Rock & Roll Festival-#1-C ....(Kent)

All Night Long
Faith Evans featuring Puff Daddy; *Keep The Faith* .... (Bad Boy/Arista)

All Night Long
Montgomery Gentry; *Tattoos & Scars* ....(Columbia)

All Night Long
Boney James; *Body Language* .... (Warner Bros.)

All Night Long
Jerry Lee Lewis; *18 Original Sun Greatest Hits*..............(Rhino)
   Milestones ....(Rhino)

All Night Long
Billy Squier; *Signs Of Life* ....(Capitol)

All Night Long
Eagles; *Eagles Live* .... (Asylum)
Joe Walsh; *ST/Urban Cowboy* .... (Asylum)

All Night Long
Little Richard; *Fabulous Little Richard* .... (Specialty)
   Well Alright! .... (Specialty)

All Night Long
Asleep At The Wheel featuring Leon Rausch; *Tribute To The Music Of Bob
Wills And The Texas Playboys-C* ....(Liberty)

All Night Long (All Night)
Lionel Richie; *Can't Slow Down* .... (Motown)
   Motown Story-First 25 Years-C .... (Motown)

All Night Television
3-D; *3-D* .... (Polydor)

All Quiet Along The Potomac Tonight
Hermes Nye; *Ballads Of The Civil War-#1 & 2* .... (Smithsonian Folkways)

All Through The Night
Original Broadway Cast; *Anything Goes* .... (RCA Victor)

All Through The Night
Cyndi Lauper; *She's So Unusual* ....(Portrait)
   Twelve Deadly Cyns...And Then Some .... (Epic)
Jules Shear; *Horse Of A Different Color: The Jules Shear Collection-1976-
1989* ....(Razor & Tie)

All Through The Night
Judy Collins; *Baby's Bedtime*...................(Lightyear)

And I Love You So
Perry Como; *Perry Como's Greatest Hits* .... (RCA)

And We Bid You Goodnight
Grateful Dead; *Live/Dead* .... (Warner Bros.)

Angel
Aerosmith; *Permanent Vacation* .... (Geffen)

Angel Of The Night
Angela Bofill; *Angel Of The Night* ....(GRP)
   Best Of Angela Bofill .... (Arista)

Anniversary Song
Al Jolson; *Al Jolson-Best Of The Decca Years*.................... (MCA)
   Cocktail Hour .... (Columbia River Entert. Group)
Dinah Shore; *Buttons & Bows* ....(ASV)
   Dinah Shore-16 Most Requested Songs-Encore! .... (Legacy)
Django Reinhardt; *Verve Jazz Masters 38* ....(Verve)
Eva Cassidy; *Time After Time* .... (Blix Street)
Guy Lombardo & His Royal Canadians; *Enjoy Yourself, The Hits Of Guy
Lombardo* .... (MCA)

Another Honky Tonk Night On Broadway
David Frizzell & Shelly West; *Golden Duets*....................(Viva)
   The David Frizzell & Shelly West Album.............. (Warner Bros.)

Another Night
Hollies; *Best Of The Hollies-#2* .... (EMI)
   Hollies-Epic Anthology From The Original Master Tapes .... (Epic)

Another Night
Real McCoy; *Another Night*....................... (Arista)

Another Night
Ricky Skaggs and Kentucky Thunder; *Bluegrass Rules!* .... (Rounder)

Another Night
Dionne Warwick; *Dionne Warwick-Anthology 1962-1971* .... (Rhino)

Another Night
Aretha Franklin; *Who's Zoomin' Who?* ....(Arista)

Another Night In Tunisia
Bobby McFerrin; *Spontaneous Inventions* . . . . (Blue Note)
Manhattan Transfer; *Vocalese* . . . . (Atlantic)
Another Night With The Boys
Drifters; *1959-1965-All-Time Greatest Hits And More* . . . . (Atlantic)
Persuasions; *Bread & Roses Festival Of Acoustic Music-#1-C* . . . . (Fantasy)
Another One In The Dark
Wallflowers; *The Wallflowers* . . . . (Virgin)
Another Rainy Night
Queensryche; *Empire* . . . .(EMI)
Another Sleepless Night
Anne Murray; *Anne Murray-Country Hits* . . . . (Capitol)
   Anne Murray's Greatest Hits . . . . (Capitol)
   Where Do You Go When You Dream . . . . (Capitol)
Another Sleepless Night
Shawn Christopher; *Divas Of Dance-#2-C* . . . .(Dunhill Compact Classics)
Apartment #9
Melissa Etheridge; *Tammy Wynette...Remembered-C* . . . . (Asylum)
Tammy Wynette; *Tammy Wynette-Anniversary-20 Years Of Hits* . . . .(Epic)
   Tammy Wynette's Greatest Hits . . . .(Epic)
Arabian Nights
Bruce Adler; *ST/Aladdin* . . . .(Disney)
Are You Lonesome To-night?
Elvis Presley; *A Valentine Gift For You* . . . . (RCA)
   Elvis' Golden Records, Volume 3 . . . . (RCA)
   From Memphis To Vegas/From Vegas To Memphis . . . . (RCA)
   Worldwide 50 Gold Award Hits, Vol. 1, Parts 1 & 2 . . . . (RCA)
Arubian Nights
Larry Coryell & Emily Remler; *Together* . . . .(Concord Jazz)
As Tears Go By
Marianne Faithfull; *Marianne Faithfull's Greatest Hits* . . . . (Abkco)
   Strange Weather . . . . (Island)
Rolling Stones; *Big Hits (High Tide & Green Grass)* . . . . (Abkco)
   December's Children (and everybody's) . . . . (Abkco)
   Hot Rocks 1964-1971 . . . . (Abkco)
   Singles Collection-The London Years . . . . (Abkco)
As We Kiss Goodnight
Iguanas; *Nuevo Boogaloo* . . . .(Margaritaville)
At Night
Cure; *Seventeen Seconds* . . . . (Elektra)
At Night
See No Evil; *See No Evil* . . . . (Epic Portrait Assoc.)
At Night She Sleeps
Night Ranger; *Dawn Patrol* . . . . (Camel)
Atlantic City
Bruce Springsteen; *Bruce Springsteen's Greatest Hits* . . . . (Columbia)
   Nebraska . . . . (Columbia)
Autumn Nocturne
Sonny Rollins; *Don't Stop The Carnival* . . . . (Milestone)
Baby
Robert Bradley's Blackwater Surprise; *Time To Discover* . . . . (RCA)
Baby, Come Over (This Is Our Night)
Samantha Mumba; *Gotta Tell You* . . . . (Wildcard/Polydor/Interscope)
Baby, It's Tonight
Jude Cole; *View From Third Street* . . . . (Reprise)
Back To The Night
Joan Armatrading; *Back To The Night* . . . . (A&M)
   Joan Armatrading-Classics-#21 . . . . (A&M)
Bad Moon Rising
Creedence Clearwater Revival; *1969* . . . . (Fantasy)
   Creedence Clearwater Revival-Chronicle . . . . (Fantasy)
   Creedence Clearwater Revival-Gold . . . . (Fantasy)
   Green River . . . . (Fantasy)
   Live In Europe . . . . (Fantasy)
Bailamos
Enrique Iglesias; *Bailamos Greatest Hits* . . . .(Overbrook/Interscope)
   Enrique . . . .(Overbrook/Interscope)
   Now That's What I Call Music!-#3-C . . . . (Virgin)
Banana Boat (Day-O)
Harry Belafonte; *Belafonte '89* . . . . (EMI)
   Nipper's Greatest Hits Of The '50s-#1-C . . . . (RCA)
Kinks; *Everybody's In Show-Biz* . . . . (Rhino)
Be Mine (Tonight)
Grover Washington, Jr.; *Come Morning* . . . . (Elektra)
   Grover Washington, Jr.-Anthology . . . . (Elektra)
Be Mine Tonight
Neil Diamond; *On The Way To The Sky* . . . . (Columbia)
Be My Baby Tonight
John Michael Montgomery; *John Michael Montgomery's*
   Greatest Hits . . . .(Atlantic)
   Kickin' It Up . . . .(Atlantic)
Beau's All Night Radio Love Line
Joshua Kadison; *Painted Desert Serenade* . . . . (SBK)
Because The Night
10,000 Maniacs; *MTV's Unplugged* . . . . (Elektra)
Bruce Springsteen & The E Street Band; *Bruce Springsteen & The E Street*
   Band Live/1975-85 . . . . (Legacy)
Patti Smith Group; *Cover Me (Bruce Springsteen Tribute)-C* . . . . (Rhino)

   Easter . . . . (Arista)
Before Dawn
Joyce Cooling; *Keeping Cool* . . . . (Heads Up Records Int'l)
Berlin Tonight
Bruce Cockburn; *World Of Wonders* . . . . (Columbia)
Betty Lou's Gettin' Out Tonight
Bob Seger & The Silver Bullet Band; *Against The Wind* . . . . (Capitol)
   Nine Tonight . . . . (Capitol)
Beware Of Darkness
George Harrison; *All Things Must Pass* . . . .(Parlophone)
   Concert For Bangladesh-C . . . . (Capitol)
Big City Nights
Scorpions; *Best Of Rockers 'N' Ballads* . . . . (Mercury)
   Love At First Sting . . . . (Mercury)
   World Wide Live . . . . (Mercury)
Black Is The Night
Sandy Posey; *45-#49104* . . . . (Warner Bros.)
Black Night
Deep Purple; *Deepest Purple/The Very Best Of Deep Purple* . . . . (Warner Bros.)
   Nobody's Perfect . . . . (Mercury)
Black Night
Dr. John; *In A Sentimental Mood* . . . . (Warner Bros.)
Black Night
Bob Seger; *Beautiful Loser* . . . . (Capitol)
Black Night
Muddy Waters; *The Chess Box-Muddy Waters* . . . . (Chess)
Black Nights
Bobby Bland; *Ain't Nothing You Can Do* . . . . (MCA)
   Introspective Of The Early Years . . . . (MCA)
Black Nights
Charles Brown; *Best Of Charles Brown-Driftin' Blues* . . . . (Collectables)
Black Water
Doobie Brothers; *Best Of The Doobies* . . . . (Warner Bros.)
   What Were Once Vices Are Now Habits . . . . (Warner Bros.)
Blackbird
Beatles; *Beatles-Box Set* . . . . (Capitol)
   The Beatles (White Album) . . . . (Capitol)
Crosby, Stills & Nash; *CSN* . . . .(Atlantic)
Paul McCartney; *Unplugged (The Official Bootleg)* . . . . (Capitol)
Wings; *Wings Over America* . . . . (Capitol)
Blinded By The Light
Bruce Springsteen; *Greetings From Asbury Park, N.J.* . . . . (Columbia)
Manfred Mann's Earth Band; *Roaring Silence* . . . . (Warner Bros.)
Blues In The Night
Benny Goodman; *Small Groups-1941-1945* . . . . (Columbia)
Bobby Bland; *Introspective Of The Early Years* . . . . (MCA)
Dinah Shore; *Nipper's Greatest Hits Of The '40s-#1-C* . . . . (RCA)
Doc Severinsen; *Best Of Doc Severinsen* . . . . (MCA)
Frank Sinatra; *Frank Sinatra sings for Only The Lonely* . . . . (Capitol)
Jimmie Lunceford & His Orchestra; *Warner Bros.' 75 Years Entertaining*
   The World-Film Music-C . . . . (Rhino)
Mel Torme; *Torme* . . . . (Verve)
Robins; *Best Of The Robins* . . . .(Crescendo)
Rosemary Clooney; *Rosemary Clooney-16 Most Requested Songs* . . . . (Legacy)
Tony Bennett; *Playin' With My Friends-Bennett Sings The*
   Blues-C . . . . (Columbia)
Woody Herman; *Blues On Parade* . . . . (GRP)
   Woody Herman-Best Of The Decca Years . . . . (Decca)
Woody Herman & His Orchestra; *Big Bands Greatest*
   Hits-#3-C . . . . (MCA Special Prod.)
Bluest Eyes In Texas
Restless Heart; *Big Dreams In A Small Town* . . . .(RCA)
Boogie Nights
Heatwave; *Heatwave's Greatest Hits* . . . . (Epic)
   Skatetown U.S.A.-C . . . . (Columbia)
   Too Hot To Handle . . . . (Epic)
Bordello Night
City Boy; *Young Men Gone West* . . . . (Mercury)
Born In The Dark
Doug Stone; *Faith In Me Faith In You* . . . . (Columbia)
   Steppin' Country-#2-C . . . . (Columbia)
Bossanovanight
Judson Spence; *I Guess I Love It* . . . .(Pioneer)
Bring On The Night
Bruce Springsteen; *Tracks* . . . . (Columbia)
Brother To The Night
Larenz Tate; *ST/Love Jones* . . . . (Columbia)
Buenos Noches From A Lonely Room
Dwight Yoakam; *Buenas Noches From A Lonely Room* . . . . (Reprise)
But I Might Die Tonight
Cat Stevens; *Tea For The Tillerman* . . . . (A&M)
By The Time This Night Is Over
Kenny G & Peabo Bryson; *Breathless* . . . . (Arista)
California Nights
Sweet; *Level-Headed* . . . . (Capitol)
California Nights
Lesley Gore; *Summer & Sun-C* . . . . (Rhino)
Can I See You Tonight
Tanya Tucker; *Best Of Tanya Tucker* . . . . (MCA)

Tanya Tucker Live . . . . (MCA Special Prod.)

Can You Feel The Love Tonight
Elton John; *ST/The Lion King* . . . .(Walt Disney)
John Tesh; *Sax On The Beach* . . . . (GTS)

Candy's Room
Bruce Springsteen; *Darkness On The Edge Of Town*. . . . .(Columbia)
Bruce Springsteen & The E Street Band; *Bruce Springsteen & The E Street Band Live/1975-85* . . . . (Legacy)

Caravan
Duke Ellington; *Best Of Duke Ellington* . . . . (Capitol)
Money Jungle . . . .(Blue Note)
Ella Fitzgerald; *Montreux '75* . . . . (Pablo)
Johnny Mathis; *In A Sentimental Mood-Johnny Mathis Sings Ellington* . . . . (Columbia)
Wynton Marsalis; *Marsalis Standard Time-#1* . . . . (Columbia)

Cheat The Night
Deborah Allen; *Cheat The Night* . . . . (RCA)

Children Of Darkness
Joan Baez; *Contemporary Ballad Book* . . . . (Vanguard)

Children Of The Night
Richard Marx; *Repeat Offender* . . . . (EMI)

Chug All Night
Eagles; *Eagles* . . . . (Asylum)

City Of Night
Peter Schilling; *Different Story (World Of Lust & Crime)* . . . . (Elektra)

Clock Strikes Ten
Cheap Trick; *Cheap Trick At Budokan* . . . . (Epic)
In Color . . . . (Epic)

Colder Are My Nights
Isley Brothers; *45-#28860* . . . . (Warner Bros.)

Color Of The Night
Lauren Christy; *ST/Color Of Night* . . . . (Mercury)

Come Down, Ma' Evenin' Star
Lillian Russell; *Music From The New York Stage (1890-1920)-#1-1890-1908-C* . . . . (Pearl)

Coming Out Of The Dark
Gloria Estefan; *Gloria Estefan's Greatest Hits-C* . . . . (Epic)
God Bless America-C . . . . (Columbia)
Hot #1 Hits-C . . . .(Foundation)
Into The Light . . . . (Epic)

Cool Night
Paul Davis; *Cool Night* . . . . (Arista)

Could've Been
Tiffany; *Tiffany* . . . . (MCA)
Tiffany's Greatest Hits . . . . (Hip-O)

Cowboy Night Herd Song
Roy Rogers & Sons Of The Pioneers; *Cowboy Super Hits-C* . . . . (Columbia)

Cowboy's Wild Song To His Herd
Skip Gorman; *A Cowboy's Wild Song To His Herd* . . . . (Rounder)

Crawling In The Dark
Hoobastank; *Hoobastank* . . . . (Island/IDJMG)

Creatures Of The Night
Kiss; *Creatures Of The Night* . . . .(Casablanca)

Cryin' Through The Night
Stevie Wonder; *Characters* . . . . (Motown)

Crying In The Night
Melba Moore; *Soul Exposed* . . . . (Capitol)

Dance The Night Away
Van Halen; *Van Halen II* . . . . (Warner Bros.)

Dance The Night Away
Mavericks; *Trampoline* . . . . (MCA)

Dance The Night Away
Cream; *Disraeli Gears* . . . . (Polydor)

Dance The Night Away
Europe; *Wings Of Tomorrow* . . . . (Epic)

Dance Tonight
Lucy Pearl; *Lucy Pearl* . . . . (Overbrook/Pookie/Beyond)

Dance With Me
Debelah Morgan; *Dance With Me* . . . . (Atlantic)
Totally Hits-#3-C . . . . (Atlantic)

Dancing In The Dark
Barbara Cook; *Barbara Cook-Live At Carnegie Hall* . . . .(Sony Music Classical)
Diana Krall; *The Look Of Love* . . . .(Impulse!)
Fred Waring's Pennsylvanians; *78-#22708* . . . . (Victor)
Tony Bennett; *Forty Years-The Artistry Of Tony Bennett* . . . . (Columbia)
Jazz . . . . (Columbia)

Dancing In The Dark
Bruce Springsteen; *Born In The U.S.A.* . . . . (Columbia)
Bruce Springsteen's Greatest Hits . . . . (Columbia)

Dark End Of The Street
Commitments; *ST/The Commitments* . . . . (MCA)
James Carr; *Essential James Carr* . . . . (Razor & Tie)
Linda Ronstadt; *Heart Like A Wheel* . . . . (Capitol)
Percy Sledge; *Best Of Percy Sledge* . . . . (Atlantic)

Darkness On The Edge Of Town
Bruce Springsteen; *Darkness On The Edge Of Town* . . . . (Columbia)
Bruce Springsteen & The E Street Band; *Bruce Springsteen & The E Street Band Live/1975-85* . . . . (Legacy)

Daydreams About Night Things
Ronnie Milsap; *Collector's Series-Ronnie Milsap* . . . . (RCA)
Night Things . . . . (RCA)
Ronnie Milsap-Live . . . . (RCA)
Ronnie Milsap's Greatest Hits . . . . (RCA)

Daylight Fading
Counting Crows; *Recovering The Satellites* . . . . (David Geffen Co.)

Daysleeper
R.E.M.; *Up* . . . . (Warner Bros.)

Daytime Nightime Suffering
Wings; *Back To The Egg* . . . .(Capitol)

Dead Of The Night
Shawn Colvin; *Steady On* . . . .(Columbia)

Dead Of The Night
Bad Company; *Holy Water* . . . .(Atco)

December, 1963 (Oh, What A Night)
4 Seasons; *25th Anniversary Collection* . . . .(Rhino)
4 Seasons-Anthology . . . .(Rhino)
Oh What A Night . . . .(Curb)

Dedicated To The One I Love
Mamas & The Papas; *Best Of The Mamas & The Papas* . . . . (MCA)
Farewell To The First Golden Era . . . . (MCA)
Original Classic Oldies Of The '50s & '60s-#13-C . . . . (MCA)
Shirelles; *Oldies But Goodies-#10-C* . . . . (Original Sound)
Shirelles' Greatest Hits . . . .(Everest)
Shirelles-Anthology 1959-1964 . . . .(Rhino)
Super Oldies Of The '50s-#4-C . . . . (Audio Fidelity)

Deeper Than The Night
Olivia Newton-John; *Totally Hot* . . . . (MCA)

Dim All The Lights
Donna Summer; *Bad Girls* . . . . (Casablanca)
Dance Collection . . . . (Casablanca)
Donna Summer's Greatest Hits . . . . (Casablanca)
On The Radio-Greatest Hits-Volumes I & II . . . . (Casablanca)

Dimming Of The Day
Bonnie Raitt; *Longing In Their Hearts* . . . .(Capitol)

Does Your Chewing Gum Lose Its Flavor (On The Bedpost Overnight)
Lonnie Donegan; *Dr. Demento Presents The Greatest Novelty Records-#3-1960s-C* . . . .(Rhino)
Dr. Demento Presents The Greatest Novelty Records-C . . . .(Rhino)

Don't Crash The Car Tonight
Mary's Danish; *Experience (Live + Foxey Lady)* . . . . (Chameleon)
There Goes The Wondertruck . . . . (Chameleon)

Don't Let Me Be Lonely Tonight
James Taylor; *James Taylor's Greatest Hits* . . . . (Warner Bros.)
One Man Dog . . . . (Warner Bros.)

Don't Let The Stars Get In Your Eyes
Perry Como; *Como's Golden Records* . . . . (RCA)
Perry Como-Pure Gold . . . . (RCA)
Perry Como's All-Time Greatest Hits-#1 . . . . (RCA)
This Is Perry Como . . . . (RCA)

Don't Say Goodnight
Valentines; *Original Rock 'N' Roll Hits Of The '50s-C* . . . . (Roulette)

Don't Say No Tonight
Eugene Wilde; *The Glory Of Love-'80s Sweet & Soulful Love Songs-C* . . . . (Hip-O)

Don't Sleep In The Subway
Frank Sinatra; *Frank Sinatra* . . . . (Reprise)
Petula Clark; *Petula Clark's Greatest Hits* . . . . (Crescendo)
Summer Of Love-#1-C . . . .(Rhino)

Don't You Know What The Night Can Do?
Steve Winwood; *Roll With It* . . . . (Virgin)

Don't Your Mem'ry Ever Sleep At Night
Ronnie Milsap; *Keyed Up* . . . . (RCA)
Steve Wariner; *Best Of Steve Wariner* . . . . (RCA)

Down That Road Tonight
Nitty Gritty Dirt Band; *More Great Dirt-Best Of Nitty Gritty Dirt Band* . . . . (Warner Bros.)
Workin' Band . . . . (Warner Bros.)

Down The Road Tonight
Bruce Hornsby & The Range; *The Way It Is* . . . . (RCA)

Downtown
Neil Young; *Mirror Ball* . . . . (Reprise)

Dream A Little Dream Of Me
Ella Fitzgerald; *All That Jazz* . . . . (Pablo)
Mama Cass; *Mama's Big Ones-Her Greatest Hits* . . . . (MCA)
Mama Cass With The Mamas & The Papas; *Best Of The Mamas & The Papas* . . . . (MCA)
Mamas & The Papas-20 Golden Hits . . . . (MCA)
Wayne King & His Orchestra; *78-#22643* . . . . (Victor)

Dreaming Of You
Selena; *Dreaming Of You* . . . . (EMI Latin)

Drifting Like Whales In The Darkness
Sven Vath; *Accident In Paradise* . . . . (Warner Bros.)

Drive
Cars; *Heartbeat City* . . . .(Elektra)
MTV's Rock 'N' Roll To Go-C . . . .(Elektra)
The Cars' Greatest Hits . . . .(Elektra)

Drive All Night
Bruce Springsteen; *The River* . . . . (Columbia)
Driving At Night
Delevantes; *Long About That Time* . . . . (Rounder)
Early To Bed
Morphine; *Like Swimming* . . . . (DreamWorks/Rykodisc)
Easy Tonight
Five For Fighting; *America Town* . . . . (Aware/C2/Columbia)
Eclipse
Pink Floyd; *Dark Side Of The Moon* . . . . (Capitol)
Works . . . . (Capitol)
End Of The Night
Doors; *Doors* . . . . (Elektra)
Weird Scenes Inside The Gold Mine . . . . (Elektra)
Endless Night
Graham Parker And The Rumour; *Up Escalator* . . . . (Razor & Tie)
Endless Summer Nights
Richard Marx; *Richard Marx* . . . . (Capitol)
Richard Marx's Greatest Hits . . . . (Capitol)
Even The Nights Are Better
Air Supply; *Air Supply's Greatest Hits* . . . . (Arista)
Now & Forever . . . . (Arista)
Evenin'
Tony Bennett with Ray Charles; *Playin' With My Friends-Bennett Sings The Blues-C* . . . . (Columbia)
Evening Falls
Enya; *Watermark* . . . . (Reprise)
Evening In Casablanca
Art Farmer Quintet; *Art Farmer Quintet* . . . . (Prestige)
Evening Rainbow
Sylvia St. James; *Echoes & Images* . . . . (Elektra)
Evening Star
Gene Loves Jezebel; *Kiss Of Life* . . . . (Geffen)
Evening Star
Kenny Rogers; *Eyes That See In The Dark* . . . . (RCA)
Evening Star
Judas Priest; *Hell Bent For Leather* . . . . (Columbia)
Every Light In The House
Trace Adkins; *Dreamin' Out Loud* . . . . (Capitol)
Every Night
Paul McCartney; *McCartney* . . . . (Capitol)
Unplugged (The Official Bootleg) . . . . (Capitol)
Paul McCartney & Wings; *Kampuchea-C* . . . . (Atlantic)
Phoebe Snow; *Best Of Phoebe Snow* . . . . (Columbia)
Every Night
Joe Williams; *Every Night-Live At Vine St.* . . . . (Verve)
Every Night
Chantels; *For Collectors Only* . . . . (Collectables)
Every Night
Weavers; *Weavers-Classics* . . . . (Vanguard)
Every Night When The Sun Goes In
Jo Stafford; *Jo Plus Blues* . . . . (Corinthian)
Everybody Have Fun Tonight
Wang Chung; *Mosaic* . . . . (Geffen)
Father Of Night
Bob Dylan; *New Morning* . . . . (Columbia)
Fever
Buddy Guy; *This Is Buddy Guy* . . . . (Vanguard)
Elvis Presley; *A Valentine Gift For You* . . . . (RCA)
Aloha from Hawaii via Satellite . . . . (RCA)
Elvis Presley-Pure Gold . . . . (RCA)
Little Willie John; *Best Of Little Willie John-Fever* . . . . (Rhino)
Peggy Lee; *Memories Are Made Of This-C* . . . . (Capitol)
Rita Coolidge; *Rita Coolidge-Classics-#5* . . . . (A&M)
Rita Coolidge's Greatest Hits . . . . (A&M)
First Night
Monica; *The Boy Is Mine* . . . . (Arista)
Fishin' In The Dark
Nitty Gritty Dirt Band; *Billboard Top Country Hits-1987-C* . . . . (Rhino)
Hold On . . . . (Warner Bros.)
More Great Dirt-Best Of Nitty Gritty Dirt Band . . . . . . (Warner Bros.)
Flowers Of The Night
Paul Kantner, Grace Slick & David Freiberg; *Baron Von Tollbooth & The Chrome Nun* . . . . (Grunt)
Fly By Night
Rush; *All The World's A Stage* . . . . (Mercury)
Archives . . . . (Mercury)
Fly By Night . . . . (Mercury)
Fly Into Night
Charly McClain; *Charly McClain's Biggest Hits* . . . . (Epic)
Paradise . . . . (Epic)
Fly Into This Night
Gino Vannelli; *Best Of Gino Vannelli* . . . . (A&M)
Gino Vannelli-Classics-#7 . . . . (A&M)
Gist Of The Gemini . . . . (A&M)
Forever Tonight
Peter Cetera & Crystal Bernard; *One Clear Voice* . . . . (River North)

Freek'n You
Jodeci; *MTV Party To Go-#7-C* . . . . (Tommy Boy)
The Show, The After-Party, The Hotel . . . . (Uptown/MCA)
Friday Night Blues
John Conlee; *John Conlee-Live At Billy Bob's* . . . . (Razor & Tie)
John Conlee's Greatest Hits . . . . (MCA)
Sonny Throckmorton; *45-#57018* . . . . (Mercury)
Gardening At Night
R.E.M.; *Chronic Town* . . . . (I.R.S.)
Eponymous . . . . (I.R.S.)
Get Down Tonight
KC And The Sunshine Band; *Best Of KC And The Sunshine Band* . . . . . (Rhino)
Billboard Top Hits-1975-C . . . . (Rhino)
Get Down Tonight! Best Of T.K. Records-C . . . . (Rhino)
Get It On Tonite
Montell Jordan; *Get It On...Tonite* . . . . (Def Soul/IDJMG)
Now That's What I Call Music!-#4-C . . . . (Virgin)
Get Up! (Before The Night Is Over)
Technotronic; *Pump Up The Jam-The Album* . . . . (SBK)
Ghost Of You And Me
BBMak; *Sooner Or Later* . . . . (Hollywood)
Girls Night Out
Judds; *Judds' Greatest Hits* . . . . (MCA)
Why Not Me . . . . (MCA)
Girls Nite Out
Tyler Collins; *Girls Nite Out* . . . . (RCA)
Give Me All Night
Carly Simon; *Coming Around Again* . . . . (Arista)
Give Me Just One Night (Una Noche)
98 Degrees; *Now That's What I Call Music!-#5-C* . . . . (Virgin)
Revelation . . . . (Universal)
Give Me The Night
George Benson; *George Benson-Collection* . . . . (Warner Bros.)
Give Me The Night . . . . (Warner Bros.)
Give Me Tonight
Shannon; *Let The Music Play* . . . . (Mirage)
Go All Night
Pat Travers; *Boom Boom...The Best Of* . . . . (Polydor)
Go For What You Know . . . . (Polydor)
Heat In The Street . . . . (Polydor)
Going Out Tonight
Mary Chapin Carpenter; *Shooting Straight In The Dark* . . . . (Columbia)
Gonna Go Huntin' Tonight
Hank Williams, Jr.; *Hank Williams, Jr.'s Greatest Hits-#2* . . . . . . (WB/Curb)
Strong Stuff . . . . (Warner Bros.)
Good Evening Mr. Waldheim
Lou Reed; *New York* . . . . (Sire)
Good Morning Beautiful
Steve Holy; *Blue Moon* . . . . (Curb)
Good Rockin' Tonight
Elvis Presley; *A Date With Elvis* . . . . (RCA)
Sun Story-C . . . . (Rhino)
The Sun Sessions . . . . (RCA)
Jerry Lee Lewis; *20 Classic Jerry Lee Lewis Hits* . . . . (Original Sound)
Trio Plus . . . . (Sun)
Jimmy Witherspoon; *Best Of Jimmy Witherspoon* . . . . (Prestige)
'Spoon Concerts . . . . (Fantasy)
Goodnight
Roy Orbison; *For The Lonely: A Roy Orbison Anthology 1959-1965* . . . . (Rhino)
Legendary Roy Orbison . . . . (Sony Music Special Prod.)
Our Love Song . . . . (Monument)
Goodnight
Original Broadway Cast; *I Do! I Do!* . . . . (RCA Victor)
Goodnight
Rembrandts; *Rembrandts* . . . . (Atco)
Goodnight
Beatles; *The Beatles (White Album)* . . . . (Capitol)
Goodnight Dallas
Carlene Carter; *I Fell In Love* . . . . (Reprise)
Goodnight Irene
Jim Reeves; *Jim Reeves-Pure Gold* . . . . (RCA)
Johnny Cash; *Rough Cut King Of Country Music* . . . . (Sun)
The Man-The World-His Music . . . . (Sun)
Ry Cooder; *Chicken Skin Music* . . . . (Reprise)
Weavers; *Best Of The Weavers* . . . . (MCA)
Weavers At Carnegie Hall . . . . (Vanguard)
Weavers' Greatest Hits . . . . (Vanguard)
Goodnight Moon
Shivaree; *I Oughtta Give You A Shot* . . . . (Capitol)
Goodnight My Love
Benny Goodman; *Benny Goodman-Pure Gold* . . . . (RCA)
Best Of Benny Goodman . . . . (RCA)
Complete Benny Goodman-#4 . . . . (RCA)
This Is Benny Goodman . . . . (RCA)
Sarah Vaughan; *Divine Sarah Vaughan-Columbia Years-1949-1953* . . . . (Columbia)
Goodnight My Love (Pleasant Dreams)
Fleetwoods; *Best Of The Fleetwoods* . . . . (Rhino)

Fleetwoods' Greatest Hits . . . . (CEMA Special Prod.)
Jesse Belvin; *Collectables Presents The History Of Rock-#9-C* . . . (Collectables)
Oldies But Goodies-#2-C . . . . (Original Sound)

Goodnight My Someone
Shirley Jones; *ST/The Music Man* . . . . (Warner Bros.)

Goodnight Now
Cheap Trick; *Cheap Trick At Budokan* . . . . (Epic)

Goodnight Saigon
Billy Joel; *Billy Joel-Greatest Hits, Volume I & Volume II* . . . . (Columbia)
KOHUEPT . . . . (Columbia)
Nylon Curtain . . . . (Columbia)

Goodnight Sweetheart
David Kersh; *Goodnight Sweetheart* . . . . (Curb)

Goodnight Sweetheart
Guy Lombardo & His Royal Canadians; *Guy Lombardo-All Time
Favorites* . . . . (MCA Special Prod.)

Goodnight Tonight (Don't Say It)
Paul McCartney & Wings; *All The Best!* . . . . (Capitol)

Goodnight Vienna
Ringo Starr; *Goodnight Vienna* . . . . (Capitol)

Goodnight, Good Guy
Collective Soul; *Hints, Allegations And Things Left Unsaid* . . . . (Atlantic)

Goodnight, Sweetheart
Flamingos; *Best Of The Flamingos* . . . . (Rhino)
Spaniels; *Cruisin'-1957-C* . . . . (Increase)
Doo-Wop Ballads-#2-C . . . . (Rhino)
Lovin' '50s-C . . . . (Priority)

Goodnight, Sweetheart, Goodnight
McGuire Sisters; *McGuire Sisters-Anthology* . . . . (MCA)

Goodnight, Well It's Time To Go
Chuck Berry; *Chuck Berry's Greatest Hits* . . . . (Everest)
Spaniels; *Goodnight, Well It's Time To Go* . . . . (Vee-Jay)
Hits From The Legendary Vee-Jay Records-C . . . . (Motown)
ST/American Graffiti . . . . (MCA)

Gotta Get You Home Tonight
Eugene Wilde; *Eugene Wilde* . . . . (Phil World)

Gotta Tell You
Samantha Mumba; *Gotta Tell You* . . . . (Wildcard/Polydor/Interscope)
Now That's What I Call Music!-#6-C . . . . (Virgin)

Green Door
Jim Lowe; *Billboard Top Rock 'N' Roll Hits-1956-C* . . . . . . (Rhino)
Super Hits-#4-C . . . . (Gusto)

Hard Day's Night, A
Beatles; *Beatles 1* . . . . (Capitol)
Beatles-20 Greatest Hits . . . . (Capitol)
ST/A Hard Day's Night . . . . (Capitol)
The Beatles At The Hollywood Bowl . . . . (Capitol)
The Beatles/1962-1966 . . . . (Capitol)

Hardest Part Is The Night, The
Bon Jovi; *7800 Degrees Fahrenheit* . . . . (Mercury)

Harlem Nocturne
Mel Torme; *Songs Of New York* . . . . (Rhino)
Viscounts; *Soul Shots-#3-Soul Twist-C* . . . . (Rhino)

Harmless
Mulberry Lane; *Run Your Own Race* . . . . (Refuge/MCA)

Havana For A Night
Mae West; *Fabulous Mae West* . . . . (MCA)

Have You Seen The Stars Tonight
Jefferson Airplane; *Flight Log (1966-1976)* . . . . (Grunt)
Paul Kantner/Jefferson Starship; *Blows Against The Empire* . . . . . . (RCA)

Hawaiian Nights
Kingston Trio; *Looking For The Sunrise* . . . . (Xeres)

Hazard (The River)
Richard Marx; *Rush Street* . . . . (Capitol)

Headache Tomorrow (Or A Heartache Tonight)
Mickey Gilley; *Mickey Gilley's Biggest Hits* . . . . (Epic)
Ten Years Of Hits . . . . (Epic)
That's All That Matters To Me . . . . (Epic)

Healing Hands
Elton John; *Sleeping With The Past* . . . . (MCA)

Heart Of The Night
Juice Newton; *Juice Newton-Greatest Hits & More* . . . . (Capitol)
Juice Newton's Greatest Hits . . . . (Gold Rush)
Quiet Lies . . . . (Capitol)

Heart Of The Night
Poco; *Backtracks* . . . . (MCA)
Poco-Legend . . . . (MCA)

Heartache Tonight
Conway Twitty; *Latest Greatest Hits-#1* . . . . (Warner Bros.)
Lost In The Feeling . . . . (Warner Bros.)
Eagles; *Eagles Greatest Hits, Volume 2* . . . . (Asylum)
Eagles Live . . . . (Asylum)
Long Run . . . . (Asylum)
John Anderson; *Common Thread-Songs Of The Eagles-C* . . . . (Giant)

Heartbeat In The Darkness
Don Williams; *New Moves* . . . . (Capitol)
Prime Cuts . . . . (Capitol)

Heat Of The Night
Jay Ferguson; *White Noise* . . . . (Capitol)

Heat Of The Night
Bryan Adams; *Into The Fire* . . . . (A&M)

Heaven Tonight
Cheap Trick; *Heaven Tonight* . . . . (Epic)

Help Me Make It Through The Night
Bryan Ferry; *Another Time Another Place* . . . . (Reprise)
Gladys Knight & The Pips; *Compact Command Performances-Gladys Knight
& The Pips* . . . . (Motown)
Gladys Knight & The Pips-Anthology . . . . (Motown)
Joan Baez; *Blessed Are* . . . . (Vanguard)
Hits/Greatest & Others . . . . (Vanguard)
Sammi Smith; *Super Hits Of The '70s-Have A Nice Day-#4-C* . . . . (Rhino)
Willie Nelson; *Greatest Hits (& Some That Will Be)* . . . . (Columbia)
Sweet Memories . . . . (RCA)
Willie Nelson Sings Kristofferson . . . . (Columbia)

Here Comes The Night
Van Morrison; *It's Too Late To Stop Now* . . . . (Warner Bros.)
Van Morrison & Them; *Best Of Van Morrison* . . . . (Polydor)
Featuring Van Morrison . . . . (Parrot)

Here Comes The Night
David Bowie; *Bowie Pin Ups* . . . . (Rykodisc)

Here Comes The Night
3rd Force; *Force Of Nature* . . . . (Higher Octave)

Here Comes The Night
Beach Boys; *L.A.-The Light Album* . . . . (Caribou)
Smiley Smile/Wild Honey . . . . (Capitol)

Here's To Good Friends (Lowenbrau Beer)
Original Soundtrack; *TeeVee Toons-The Commercials-#1-C* . . . . (TVT)

Here's To The Night
Eve 6; *Horrorscope* . . . . (RCA)
Totally Hits 2001-C . . . . (Arista)

Hey Nineteen
Steely Dan; *Gaucho* . . . . (MCA)
Steely Dan-Gold . . . . (MCA)

High School Nights
Dave Edmunds; *Dave Edmunds-Anthology-1968-1990* . . . . (Rhino)
ST/Porky's Revenge . . . . (Columbia)

Hold Back The Night
Trammps; *Best Of The Trammps-This Is Where The Happy
People Go* . . . . (Rhino)
Trammps-Golden Classics . . . . (Collectables)

Hold Back The Night
Graham Parker; *Pourin' It All Out-Mercury Years* . . . . (Mercury)

Hold Me Tight
Beatles; *Meet The Beatles!* . . . . (Capitol)

Hold On To The Nights
Richard Marx; *Richard Marx* . . . . (Capitol)

Hollywood Nights
Bob Seger & The Silver Bullet Band; *Nine Tonight* . . . . (Capitol)
Stranger In Town . . . . (Capitol)

Home Sweet Home
Motley Crue; *Theatre Of Pain* . . . . (Elektra)

Homeless
Paul Simon; *Graceland* . . . . (Warner Bros.)

Honky Tonk Night Time Man
Lynyrd Skynyrd; *Street Survivors* . . . . (MCA)
Merle Haggard & The Strangers; *Presents His 30th Album* . . . . (Capitol)
Songs I'll Always Sing . . . . (Capitol)

Hot Night In New York City
Bonnie Koloc; *With You On My Side* . . . . (Flying Fish)

Hot Nite In Dallas
Moon Martin; *Shots From A Cold Nightmare* . . . . (Capitol)

Hot Summer Nights
Rick James; *Wonderful* . . . . (Reprise)

Hot Summer Nights
Walter Egan; *Not Shy* . . . . (Columbia)

Hot Summer Nights
Miami Sound Machine; *ST/Top Gun* . . . . (Columbia)

Hot Texas Night
Mac Davis; *Texas In My Rear View Mirror* . . . . (Casablanca)

How Do You Sleep At Night
Wade Hayes; *When The Wrong One Loves You Right* . . . . (Columbia/DKC)

Hymn For A Sunday Evening
Original Cast; *Bye Bye Birdie* . . . . (Columbia)

I Ain't Gonna Cry Tonight
Barbra Streisand; *Wet* . . . . (Columbia)

I Could Have Danced All Night
Frank Sinatra; *Concepts* . . . . (Capitol)
Julie Andrews/Original Cast; *My Fair Lady* . . . . (Columbia)
Rosemary Clooney; *Rosemary Clooney-16 Most Requested Songs* . . . . . (Legacy)

I Couldn't Sleep A Wink Last Night
Frank Sinatra; *A Lovely Way To Spend An Evening* . . . . (ASV)
Voice: The Columbia Years-1943-1952 . . . . (Columbia)
Mello Moods; *Great Groups Of The '50s-#3-C* . . . . (Collectables)

I Cried Last Night
Charles Brown; *One More For The Road* . . . . (Allegiance)

I Dreamed About Mama Last Night
Hank Williams; *Complete Hank Williams* . . . . (Mercury)

Johnny Cash; *Timeless: Hank Williams Tribute-C* . . . . . (Lost Highway/IDJMG)

I Drove All Night
Cyndi Lauper; *Night To Remember* . . . .(Epic)

I Fell In Love Again Last Night
Forester Sisters; *Country Love Songs-C* . . . .(Warner Bros.)
Forester Sisters . . . .(Warner Bros.)
Forester Sisters' Greatest Hits . . . .(Warner Bros.)

I Got Dreams
Steve Wariner; *I Got Dreams* . . . .(MCA)

I Got The Sun In The Morning
Ethel Merman/Bruce Yarnell/Original Cast; *Annie Get
Your Gun* . . . .(RCA Victor)
Ethel Merman/Ray Middleton/Original Cast; *Annie Get Your Gun* . . . . .(MCA)
Original Broadway Cast; *Annie Get Your Gun* . . . . (Angel)

I Had A Dream
John Sebastian; *ST/Woodstock* . . . . (Atlantic)

I Had Too Much To Dream (Last Night)
Electric Prunes; *Even More Nuggets-C* . . . . (Rhino)
Nuggets-#1-The Hits-C . . . . (Rhino)
Summer Of Love-#1-C . . . . (Rhino)

I Love A Rainy Night
Eddie Rabbitt; *Eddie Rabbitt's All-Time Greatest Hits* . . .(Warner Bros.)
Eddie Rabbitt's Greatest Hits-#2 . . . .(Warner Bros.)
Horizon . . . . (Elektra)
Number 1's . . . .(Warner Bros.)
Ten Years Of Greatest Hits . . . .(Capitol)

I Love The Night
Blue Oyster Cult; *Spectres* . . . . (Columbia)

I Love The Night
Joe Cocker; *Civilized Man* . . . . (Capitol)

I Love The Night Life
Alicia Bridges; *Alicia Bridges* . . . . (Polydor)
Night At Studio 54-C . . . . (Casablanca)
Oldies But Goodies-#14-C . . . . (Original Sound)
Polydor Dance Classics-C . . . . (Polydor)

I Need Your Love Tonight
Elvis Presley; *50,000,000 Elvis Fans Can't Be Wrong-Elvis' Gold Records-
Volume 2* . . . . (RCA)
The Top Ten Hits . . . . (RCA)

I Saw Her Again
Mamas & The Papas; *Best Of The Mamas & The Papas* . . . .(MCA)
Farewell To The First Golden Era . . . .(MCA)
Mamas & The Papas . . . .(MCA)

I Saw The Light
Hank Williams; *Hank Williams-24 Greatest Hits-#2* . . . . (Polydor)
Hank Williams-40 Greatest Hits . . . . (Polydor)
I Ain't Got Nothin' But Time-1946-1947 . . . . (Polydor)
Legend In Song-With Hank Williams, Jr. . . . . (Polydor)
Rare Takes & Radio Cuts . . . . (Polydor)

I Think We're Alone Now
Tiffany; *Tiffany* . . . .(MCA)
Tiffany's Greatest Hits . . . .(Hip-O)
Tommy James And The Shondells; *Best Of Tommy James And The
Shondells* . . . . (Roulette)
Billboard Top Rock 'N' Roll Hits-1967-C . . . . (Rhino)
Tommy James And The Shondells-Anthology . . . . (Rhino)

I Want You Tonight
Pablo Cruise; *Want You Tonight* . . . . (Universal Special Mkts.)

I Watched It All (On My Radio)
Lionel Cartwright; *I Watched It All On The Radio* . . . .(MCA)

I Will Get There
Boyz II Men; *ST/The Prince Of Egypt-Inspirational* . . . . . . (DreamWorks/SKG)

I Wish I Was In Texas Tonight
Patti Ford; *45-#25* . . . . (Nationwide Sound Distrib.)

I Wish You Were Here Tonight
Ray Charles; *Greatest Hits Of Country Blues-C* . . . . (Columbia)
I Wish You Were Here Tonight . . . . (Columbia)

I Wonder Where We'd Be Tonight
Vern Gosdin; *Truly Greatest Hits Of Vern Gosdin* . . . . (American Harvest)

I Wonder Where You Are Tonight
Bill Monroe; *Bean Blossom* . . . .(MCA)
Jerry Lee Lewis; *Country Music Hall Of Fame Hits* . . . . (Smash)
Keith Whitley; *L.A. To Miami* . . . . (RCA)

I Wonder Who's Holding My Baby
Whites; *Whites' Greatest Hits* . . . . (Curb)

I Won't Be Home Tonight
Tony Carey; *Tony Carey* . . . .(Rocket)

I'd Really Love To See You Tonight
England Dan & John Ford Coley; *Best Of England Dan & John Ford
Coley* . . . . (Big Tree)
Hit Singles-1958-1977-C . . . . (Atlantic)
Nights Are Forever Without You . . . . (Big Tree)

If I Could Be With You
Helen Humes; *Ladies Sing The Blues-#2-C* . . . . (Savoy)
Louis Armstrong; *Best Of Louis Armstrong* . . . .(MCA)
Satchmo-Musical Autobiography-#2 . . . .(MCA)
The Louis Armstrong Story-#4 . . . . (Columbia)

If I Could Have Her Tonight
Neil Young; *Neil Young* . . . . (Reprise)

If I Should Die Tonight
Marvin Gaye; *Let's Get It On* . . . . (Motown)
Musical Testament 1964-1984 . . . . (Motown)

If We Fall In Love Tonight
Rod Stewart; *If We Fall In Love Tonight* . . . . (Warner Bros.)

If You Leave Me Tonight I'll Cry
Jerry Wallace; *From The Vaults: Decca Country Classics-1934-
1973-C* . . . .(Decca)
Jerry Wallace's Greatest Hits . . . .(Curb)

If You Think You're Lonely Now
Bobby Womack; *The Poet* . . . . (Razor & Tie)
K-Ci Hailey; *ST/Jason's Lyric* . . . .(Mercury)

If Your Heart Ain't Busy Tonight
Tanya Tucker; *What Do I Do With Me* . . . . (Capitol)

I'll Be With You Tonight
Cheap Trick; *Dream Police* . . . . (Epic)

I'll Be Your Baby Tonight
Bob Dylan; *Biograph* . . . . (Columbia)
Bob Dylan's Greatest Hits-#2 . . . . (Columbia)
Columbia Country Classics-#5-A New Tradition-C . . . . (Columbia)
John Wesley Harding . . . . (Columbia)
Linda Ronstadt; *Different Drum* . . . . (Capitol)
Hand Sown Home Grown . . . . (Capitol)
Linda Ronstadt-Retrospective . . . . (Capitol)

I'll Be Your Jukebox Tonight
Barbara Mandrell; *I'll Be Your Jukebox Tonight* . . . . (Capitol)

I'll Make Love To You
Boyz II Men; *Boyz II Men II* . . . . (Motown)

I'm Gonna Knock On Your Door
Eddie Hodges; *History Of Cadence Records-#1-C* . . . . (Varese Vintage)

I'm Just Talkin' About Tonight
Toby Keith; *Pull My Chain* . . . .(DreamWorks/SKG)

I'm Missing Texas Tonight
Kim Grayson; *45-#4800* . . . . (Soundwaves)

I'm Not Gonna Let It Bother Me Tonight
Atlanta Rhythm Section; *Are You Ready!* . . . .(Polydor)
Champagne Jam . . . .(Polydor)

I'm Thinking Tonight Of My Blue Eyes
Gene Autry; *All Time Legends Of Country Music-C* . . . . (Legacy)

I'm Your Baby Tonight
Whitney Houston; *I'm Your Baby Tonight* . . . . (Arista)
Whitney Houston's Greatest Hits . . . . (Arista)

I'm Your Late Night Evening Prostitute
Tom Waits; *Tom Waits-Early Years-Volume One* . . . .(Planet 3)

In The Air Tonight
Phil Collins; *Classic Rock 1966-1988-C* . . . .(Atlantic)
Face Value . . . .(Atlantic)
Miami Vice-C . . . .(MCA)
Prince's Trust 10th Anniversary Party-C . . . .(A&M)
Serious Hits...Live! . . . .(Atlantic)
The Secret Policeman's Other Ball/The Music . . . . (Rhino)

In The Cool, Cool, Cool Of The Evening
Bing Crosby; *Best Of Bing Crosby* . . . . (MCA)
Frank Sinatra; *Days Of Wine And Roses, Moon River, And Other Academy
Award Winners* . . . . (Reprise)
Rosemary Clooney; *Rosemary Clooney-16 Most Requested Songs* . . . . (Legacy)

In The Dark
Roy Ayers; *In The Dark* . . . . (Columbia)

In The Dark
Lonnie Brooks; *Bayou Lightning* . . . .(Alligator)

In The Dark
Billy Squier; *Don't Say No* . . . . (Capitol)

In The Evening
Led Zeppelin; *In Through The Out Door* . . . . (Swan Song)
Led Zeppelin-Box Set . . . .(Atlantic)

In The Evening
Big Joe Turner; *In The Evening* . . . . (Pablo)
Joe Williams; *Everyday I Have The Blues* . . . .(Savoy)

In The Evening When The Sun Goes Down
Ella Fitzgerald; *These Are The Blues* . . . . (Verve)
Mel Torme; *Duke Ellington & Count Basie Songbook* . . . . (Verve)
Pete Seeger; *20 Golden Pieces Of Pete Seeger* . . . .(Bulldog)
Pete Seeger Sings Folk Music Of The World . . . .(Tradition)

In The Heat Of The Night
Ray Charles; *Ray Charles-His Greatest Hits-#2* . . . . (Dunhill Compact Classics)
ST/In The Heat Of The Night . . . .(United Artists)

In The Heat Of The Night
Pat Benatar; *In The Heat Of The Night* . . . . (Chrysalis)

In The Middle Of The Night
Mel Tillis; *45-#52182* . . . .(MCA)

In The Still Of The Nite
Dion; *Dion Sings The 15 Million Sellers* . . . .(Laurie)
Dion's Greatest Hits . . . .(Laurie)
Dion And The Belmonts; *Wish Upon A Star With Dion And The
Belmonts* . . . . (Collectables)
Five Satins; *Billboard Top R&B Hits-1956-C* . . . . (Rhino)
Cruisin'-1956-C . . . . (Increase)
Five Satins Sing Their Greatest Hits . . . . (Collectables)

In The Still Of The Night . . . . (Capitol)
   ST/Dirty Dancing . . . . (RCA)
Johnny Mathis; *In The Still Of The Night* . . . . (Columbia)
In The Still Of The Nite (I'll Remember)
   Boyz II Men; *Cooleyhighharmony* . . . . (Motown)
Into The Night
   B.B. King; *Six Silver Strings* . . . . (MCA)
   Soundtrack Smashes-'80s & More-C . . . . (MCA)
   ST/Into The Night . . . . (MCA)
Into The Night
   Benny Mardones; *Benny Mardones.* . . . . (Curb)
   Never Run Never Hide . . . . (Polydor)
Into The Night
   Julee Cruise; *Floating Into The Night* . . . . (Warner Bros.)
   Twin Peaks . . . . (Warner Bros.)
Into The Night
   Sweet; *Desolation Boulevard* . . . . (Capitol)
Irish Have A Great Day Tonight, The
   Vernon Stiles Quartet; *Music From The New York Stage (1890-1920)-#4-*
   1917-1920-C . . . . (Pearl)
It's 3 O'Clock In The Morning
   Mom & Dads; *Blue Hawaii* . . . . (Crescendo)
It's All About Me
   Mya featuring Sisqo of Dru Hill; *Mya* . . . . . . (University/Interscope)
It's All Coming Down Tonight
   Frankie Miller; *Standing On The Edge* . . . . (Capitol)
It's All Coming Down Tonight
   Barbusters; *ST/Light Of Day* . . . . (CBS Associated)
It's Four In The Morning
   Faron Young; *Faron Young-Golden Hits* . . . . (Mercury)
   Faron Young-The Hits . . . . (Mercury)
It's Late
   Ricky Nelson; *Lonesome Town* . . . . (CEMA Special Prod.)
   Ricky Nelson Volume 1 . . . . (Gold Rush)
It's On Tonight
   Sam Salter; *It's On Tonight* . . . . (LaFace)
It's Time For Love
   Chi-Lites; *Chi-Lites' Greatest Hits-#2* . . . . (Rhino)
I've Got My Eyes On You
   Jessica Simpson; *Sweet Kisses* . . . . (Columbia)
Jam Tonight
   Freddie Jackson; *Just Like The First Time* . . . . (Capitol)
Jumpin, Jumpin
   Destiny's Child; *Now That's What I Call Music!-#5-C* . . . .(Virgin)
   The Writing's On The Wall . . . . (Columbia)
June Night
   Betty Everett; *Very Best Of Betty Everett* . . . . (Vee-Jay)
Just Another Night
   Ian Hunter; *You're Never Alone With A Schizophrenic* . . . . (Razor & Tie)
Just Another Night
   Mick Jagger; *She's The Boss* . . . . (Columbia)
Just For Tonight
   Vanessa Williams; *The Comfort Zone* . . . . (Wing)
Just Got Paid
   'N Sync; *No Strings Attached* . . . .(Jive)
Just One Night
   McBride & The Ride; *Sacred Ground* . . . . (MCA)
Justice Tonight/Rock It Over
   Clash; *Black Market Clash* . . . . (Epic)
Keep It Dark
   Genesis; *Abacab* . . . . (Atlantic)
Key West Intermezzo (I Saw You First)
   John Mellencamp; *Mr. Happy Go Lucky* . . . . (Mercury)
Kindly Keep It Country
   Vince Gill; *The Key* . . . . (MCA)
King Of The Night Time World
   Kiss; *Alive II* . . . . (Casablanca)
   Destroyer . . . . (Casablanca)
Ladies Night
   Kool & The Gang; *Ladies Night* . . . .(De-Lite)
Ladies Night In Buffalo
   David Lee Roth; *Eat 'Em & Smile* . . . . (Warner Bros.)
Ladies Of The Night
   Leon Russell; *Americana.* . . . . (Paradise)
Lady Marmalade
   Christina Aguilera, Lil' Kim, Mya & Pink; *ST/Moulin Rouge* . . . . . . (Interscope)
   Labelle; *Nightbirds* . . . . (Epic)
   Patti LaBelle; *Best Of Patti LaBelle.* . . . . (Epic)
   Sheila E.; *Sex Cymbal* . . . . (Warner Bros.)
Last Night
   Mar-Keys; *Atlantic Rhythm & Blues 1947-1974-#4 (1958-1962)-C* . . . . (Atlantic)
   Soul Shots-#3-Soul Twist-C . . . . (Rhino)
Last Night
   Az Yet; *Az Yet* . . . . (LaFace)
Last Night
   Al Jarreau; *Tomorrow Today.* . . . . (GRP/VMG)
Last Night
   Buddy Holly/The Crickets; *Chirping Crickets* . . . . (MCA)

Last Night
   Stephanie Mills; *Tantalizingly Hot.* . . . . (Casablanca)
Last Night
   Traveling Wilburys; *Traveling Wilburys-Volume One* . .(Wilbury/Warner Bros.)
Last Night A D.J. Saved My Life
   Indeep; *Last Night A D.J. Saved My Life* . . . . (Sound Of New York)
   The Disco Years-#2-On The Beat-1978-1982-C . . . .(Rhino)
Last Night I Didn't Get To Sleep At All
   5th Dimension; *Greatest Hits On Earth* . . . .(Arista)
Last Night I Had A Dream
   Randy Newman; *Randy Newman/Live* . . . . (Warner Archives)
   Sail Away. . . . . (Reprise)
Last Night I Had The Strangest Dream
   Simon & Garfunkel; *Collected Works* . . . .(Columbia)
   Wednesday Morning 3 A.M. . . . .(Columbia)
Last Night Of The World
   Bruce Cockburn; *Breakfast In New Orleans, Dinner In Timbuktu* . . . . (Rykodisc)
Last Night On Earth
   U2; *Pop* . . . . (Island)
Last Night's Letter
   K-Ci & JoJo; *Love Always* . . . . (MCA)
Last Worthless Evening
   Don Henley; *End Of The Innocence* . . . . (Geffen)
Late In The Evening
   Paul Simon; *Negotiations And Love Songs, 1971-1986* . . . . (Warner Bros.)
   One-Trick Pony. . . . . (Warner Bros.)
   Simon & Garfunkel; *The Concert In Central Park.* . . . . (Warner Bros.)
Late Night Radio
   John Denver; *Windsong* . . . . (RCA)
Left In The Dark
   Barbra Streisand; *Emotion* . . . .(Columbia)
Let It Roll
   Little Feat; *Let It Roll* . . . . (Warner Bros.)
Let Me Love You Tonight
   Pure Prairie League; *Firin' Up* . . . . (Casablanca)
   Let Me Love You Tonight & Other Hits . . . . (RCA)
Let Me Take You Home Tonight
   Boston; *Boston.* . . . . (Epic)
Let The Good Times Roll
   Barbra Streisand; *Butterfly* . . . .(Columbia)
   Betty Everett & Jerry Butler; *Delicious Together* . . . . (Vee-Jay)
   Starring Betty Everett . . . . (Tradition)
   Bobby Bland & B.B. King; *Together Again Live* . . . . (MCA)
   Jerry Lee Lewis; *Golden Rock & Roll* . . . . (Sun)
   Louis Jordan; *Best Of Louis Jordan* . . . . (MCA)
   Molly Hatchet; *Flirtin' With Disaster* . . . . (Epic)
   Nilsson; *Nilsson Schmilsson* . . . . (RCA)
   Phoebe Snow; *Phoebe Snow* . . . . (MCA)
   Ray Charles; *Genius Of Ray Charles* . . . . (Atlantic)
   Shirley & Lee; *Billboard Top R&B Hits-1956-C* . . . . (Rhino)
   History Of New Orleans R&B-#1-1950-1958-C . . . . (Rhino)
   ST/Stand By Me. . . . . (Atlantic)
   Super Oldies Of The '50s-#4-C . . . . (Audio Fidelity)
   Tony Bennett with B.B. King; *Playin' With My Friends-Bennett Sings The*
   Blues-C. . . . .(Columbia)
Let's Go
   Cars; *Candy-O* . . . .(Elektra)
   The Cars' Greatest Hits. . . . .(Elektra)
Let's Groove
   Earth, Wind & Fire; *Best Of Earth, Wind & Fire-#1* . . . .(Legacy)
   Raise. . . . .(Columbia)
Let's Make A Night To Remember
   Bryan Adams; *18 Til I Die* . . . .(A&M)
Let's Make Love
   Faith Hill & Tim McGraw; *Breathe* . . . . (Warner Bros.)
   Tim McGraw & Faith Hill; *Tim McGraw's Greatest Hits* . . . . . . (Curb)
Let's Spend The Night Together
   David Bowie; *Aladdin Sane* . . . . (Rykodisc)
   ST/Ziggy Stardust-The Motion Picture . . . . (Rykodisc)
   Rolling Stones; *"Still Life" (American Concert 1981)* . . . . (Virgin)
   Between The Buttons . . . . (Abkco)
   Flowers . . . . (Abkco)
   Hot Rocks 1964-1971 . . . . (Abkco)
   Through The Past, Darkly (Big Hits Vol. 2) . . . . (Abkco)
Let's Take All Night (To Say Goodbye)
   Barry Manilow; *If I Should Love Again* . . . .(Arista)
Light My Fire
   Doors; *Best Of The Doors* . . . .(Elektra)
   Doors. . . . .(Elektra)
   Doors 13 . . . .(Elektra)
   Doors' Greatest Hits . . . .(Elektra)
   ST/The Doors . . . .(Elektra)
   Jose Feliciano; *Encore-Jose Feliciano.* . . . . (RCA)
   Jose Feliciano's All-Time Greatest Hits . . . . (RCA)
Light Up The Night
   Brothers Johnson; *Brothers Johnson-Classics-#11* . . . .(A&M)
   Light Up The Night . . . .(A&M)
Like No Other Night
   38 Special; *Flashback-Best Of 38 Special* . . . .(A&M)

Strength In Numbers .... (A&M)
Little More Love
Vince Gill; *High Lonesome Sound* .... (MCA)
Little Night Dancin'
John Cougar; *John Cougar* .... (Riva)
Little White Lies
Dick Haymes with Gordon Jenkins & His Orchestra; *Sentimental Journey: Pop Vocal Classics-#2-1947-1950-C* .... (Rhino)
Dinah Shore; *Dinah Shore-16 Most Requested Songs-Encore!* .... (Legacy)
Fred Waring's Pennsylvanians featuring Clare Hanlon; *Very Best Of Fred Waring & The Pennsylvanians* .... (Reader's Digest Music)
Tommy Dorsey; *Best Of Tommy Dorsey* .... (Bluebird)
Complete Tommy Dorsey-#6 .... (RCA)
Living On The Edge Of The World
Bruce Springsteen; *Tracks* .... (Columbia)
London By Night
Frank Sinatra; *Come Fly With Me* .... (Capitol)
Sinatra Rarities-Columbia Years .... (Columbia)
Loneliness Of Evening
Stuart Damon; *Cinderella-The CBS Television Network Production* .... (Columbia)
Lonely Days
Bee Gees; *Bee Gees-Gold* .... (Polydor)
Here At Last...Bee Gees...Live .... (Polydor)
One Night Only .... (Polydor)
Lonely Is The Night
Billy Squier; *Don't Say No* .... (Capitol)
Lonely Nights
Mickey Gilley; *Greatest Country Hits Of The '80s-1982-C* .... (Columbia)
Mickey Gilley's Biggest Hits .... (Epic)
Ten Years Of Hits .... (Epic)
You Don't Know Me .... (Epic)
Lonely Nights
White Lion; *Pride* .... (Atlantic)
Lonely Nights
Bryan Adams; *You Want It, You Got It* .... (A&M)
Lonely Ol' Night
John Cougar Mellencamp; *Scarecrow* .... (Riva)
Long Hot Summer Night
Jimi Hendrix Experience; *Electric Ladyland* .... (Reprise)
Long Tall Sally
Beatles; *Past Masters-Volume One* .... (Parlophone)
Rock 'N' Roll Music .... (Capitol)
The Beatles At The Hollywood Bowl .... (Capitol)
The Beatles' Second Album .... (Capitol)
Little Richard; *Billboard Top R&B Hits-1956-C* .... (Rhino)
Here's Little Richard .... (Specialty)
Little Richard-18 Greatest Hits .... (Rhino)
Little Richard's Greatest Hits .... (Everest)
Oldies But Goodies-#3-C .... (Original Sound)
ST/Heaven Help Us .... (EMI)
Super Oldies Of The '50s-#3-C .... (Audio Fidelity)
Tutti Frutti .... (Accord)
Long Walk, A
Jill Scott; *Who Is Jill Scott? Words And Sounds-#1* .... (Hidden Beach/Epic)
Lost In The Fifties Tonight
Ronnie Milsap; *Lost In The Fifties Tonight* .... (RCA)
Ronnie Milsap's Greatest Hits-#2 .... (RCA)
Love Is Alright Tonight
Rick Springfield; *Rick Springfield's Greatest Hits* ...... (RCA)
Working Class Dog .... (RCA)
Love On My Mind Tonight
Temptations; *45-#1666* .... (Gordy)
Lovely Night, A
Julie Andrews; *A Little Bit Of Broadway* .... (Columbia)
Julie Andrews/Original Cast; *Cinderella-The CBS Television Production* .... (Columbia)
Lover Who Rocks You (All Night)
India; *Breaking Out* .... (Jellybean Prod.)
Lovers In The Night
Toto; *Toto IV.* .... (Columbia)
Love's Gonna Fall Here Tonight
Razzy Bailey; *Anthology* .... (Renaissance)
Lovin' All Night
Rodney Crowell; *Greatest Country Hits Of The '90s-#2-C* .... (Columbia)
Life Is Messy .... (Columbia)
Low Light
Pearl Jam; *Yield* .... (Epic)
Luck Be A Lady
Frank Sinatra; *Sinatra Reprise-The Very Good Years* ...... (Reprise)
The Reprise Collection .... (Reprise)
Original Cast; *Guys & Dolls* .... (MCA)
Lucky
Britney Spears; *Now That's What I Call Music!-#5-C* .... (Virgin)
Oops!...I Did It Again .... (Jive)
Lucky 4 You (Tonight I'm Just Me)
SHeDAISY; *The Whole Shebang* .... (Lyric Street)

Maybe Not Tonight
Lorrie Morgan & Sammy Kershaw; *To Get To You-Greatest Hits Collection* .... (BNA)
Maybe We Should Just Sleep On It
Tim McGraw; *All I Want* .... (Curb)
Tim McGraw's Greatest Hits .... (Curb)
Me Against The Night
Crystal Gayle; *Cage The Songbird* .... (Warner Bros.)
Meet Me Tonight By My Old Kentucky Home
Joe Val & The New England Bluegrass Boys; *Joe Val & The New England Bluegrass Boys-Vol. 2* .... (Rounder)
Memory
Original Broadway Cast; *Cats* .... (Geffen)
Michelangelo
Emmylou Harris; *Red Dirt Girl* .... (Nonesuch)
Middle Of The Night
Divine Horsemen; *Devil's River* .... (SST)
Middle Of The Night .... (SST)
Missing The War
Ben Folds Five; *Whatever And Ever Amen* .... (Caroline/550)
Mommy, Can I Go Out & Kill Tonight
Misfits; *Walk Among Us* .... (Ruby)
Mona Lisas And Mad Hatters
Elton John; *Honky Chateau* .... (Rocket)
Reg Strikes Back .... (MCA)
The Concert For New York City-C .... (Columbia)
Monday Night
Golden Palominos; *Golden Palominos* .... (Celluloid)
History-1982-1986 .... (Metrotone)
Monday Night
Pere Ubu; *Cloudland* .... (Fontana)
Money Don't Matter 2 Night
Prince And The New Power Generation; *Diamonds And Pearls* ... (Paisley Park)
Morning Side Of The Mountain, The
Tommy Edwards; *It's All In The Game-The Complete Hits Of Tommy Edwards* .... (Eric)
Moroccan Nights
John Tropea; *NY Cats Direct* .... (Digital Music Prod.)
Moscow Nights
Feelies; *Crazy Rhythms* .... (A&M)
Murder, Tonight, In The Trailer Park
Cowboy Junkies; *Black-Eyed Man* .... (RCA)
Music Of The Night
Michael Crawford; *Premiere Collection-Best Of Andrew Lloyd Webber-C* .... (MCA)
Original London Cast; *Phantom Of The Opera* .... (Polydor)
My All
Mariah Carey; *Butterfly* .... (Columbia)
Mariah Carey-#1's .... (Columbia)
VH-1 Divas Live-C .... (Epic)
My First Night Alone Without You
Bonnie Raitt; *Bonnie Raitt-Collection* .... (Warner Bros.)
Home Plate .... (Warner Bros.)
Jane Olivor; *First Night* .... (Columbia)
My First Night With You
Mya; *Mya* .... (University/Interscope)
My First Night Without You
Cyndi Lauper; *Night To Remember* .... (Epic)
My Night To Howl
Lorrie Morgan; *War Paint* .... (BNA)
Nashville 1 A.M.
Harvey Mandel; *Cristo Redentor* .... (Editions E.G.)
Need You Tonight
INXS; *Hit Singles-1980-1988-C* .... (Atlantic)
Kick .... (Atlantic)
Live Baby Live .... (Atlantic)
Need Your Loving Tonight
Queen; *The Game* .... (Hollywood)
Neon Rainbow
Box Tops; *Box Tops' Greatest Hits* .... (Rhino)
Nicaragua Night
Holly Near; *All-Ears Review-#7-Still Amazing...-C* .... (Really Outstanding Music)
Night
Jackie Wilson; *Mr. Excitement* .... (Rhino)
My Golden Favorites .... (Brunswick)
Night
Bruce Springsteen; *Born To Run* .... (Columbia)
Night (Feel Like Getting Down)
Billy Ocean; *Night (Feel Like Getting Down)* .... (Epic)
Night And Day
Bette Midler; *Some People's Lives* .... (Atlantic)
Billie Holiday; *Legacy Box-1933-1958.* .... (Columbia)
Ella Fitzgerald; *Cole Porter Songbook* .... (Verve)
Frank Sinatra; *Nipper's Greatest Hits Of The '40s-#1-C* ... (RCA)
Sinatra & Strings .... (Reprise)
Sinatra Reprise-The Very Good Years .... (Reprise)
Sinatra: A Man And His Music .... (Reprise)

The Capitol Years . . . . (Capitol)
The Reprise Collection . . . . (Reprise)
Fred Astaire; *Cheek To Cheek* . . . . (Pro-Arte)
Steppin' Out-Astaire Sings . . . . (Verve)
Tony Bennett; *Perfectly Frank* . . . . (Columbia)
U2; *Red Hot + Blue-Tribute To Cole Porter-C* . . . . (Chrysalis)

Night Before
Beatles; *Beatles-Box Set* . . . . (Capitol)
Rock 'N' Roll Music . . . . (Capitol)
ST/Help! . . . . (Capitol)

Night Bird Flying
Jimi Hendrix; *Cry Of Love* . . . . (Reprise)
Lifelines/Jimi Hendrix Story . . . . (Reprise)

Night Blooming Jasmine
Charles Lloyd Quartet; *Night In Copenhagen* . . . . (Blue Note)

Night Boat To Cairo
Madness; *One Step Beyond* . . . . (Sire)
ST/Dance Craze . . . . (Chrysalis)

Night By Night
Steely Dan; *Pretzel Logic* . . . . (MCA)

Night By Night
Dokken; *Back For The Attack* . . . . (Elektra)

Night By Night
Heather Mullen; *Heather Mullen* . . . . (East West)

Night Chicago Died
Paper Lace; *Back To The '70s-#3-C* . . . . (Dominion Entert.)
Super Hits Of The '70s-Have A Nice Day-#13-C . . . . (Rhino)

Night Comes Down
Queen; *Queen* . . . . (Hollywood)

Night Comes Down
Judas Priest; *Defenders Of The Faith* . . . . (Columbia)

Night Creatures
Melissa Manchester; *Mathematics* . . . . (MCA)

Night Fever
Bee Gees; *Bee Gees' Greatest* . . . . (Polydor)
ST/Saturday Night Fever . . . . (Polydor)

Night Flight
Buddy Guy; *Buddy Guy-Complete Chess Studio Recordings* . . . . (Chess)

Night Flight
Led Zeppelin; *Physical Graffiti* . . . . (Swan Song)

Night Game
Paul Simon; *Still Crazy After All These Years* . . . . (Columbia)

Night Games
Charley Pride; *Charley Pride* . . . . (RCA)
Charley Pride's Greatest Hits-#2 . . . . (RCA)
Night Games . . . . (RCA)

Night Games
Gregg Allman Band; *Just Before The Bullets Fly* . . . . (Epic)

Night Has A Thousand Eyes
Anita O'Day; *Night Has A Thousand Eyes* . . . . (Emily)
Bobby Vee; *Best Of Bobby Vee* . . . . (EMI)
Bobby Vee-Legendary Masters . . . . (EMI)
Golden Years-1962-C . . . . (Dominion Entert.)

Night I Called The Old Man Out
Garth Brooks; *In Pieces* . . . . (Liberty)

Night In Buenos Aires
101 Strings Orchestra; *Best Of Latin* . . . . (Alshire)

Night In London
Poncho Sanchez; *Chile Con Soul* . . . . (Concord Picante Jazz)

Night In My Veins
Pretenders; *Last Of The Independents* . . . . (Sire)

Night In Oklahoma
Larry McNeely; *Power Play* . . . . (Flying Fish)

Night In Summer Long Ago
Mark Knopfler; *Golden Heart* . . . . (Warner Bros.)

Night In The City
Joni Mitchell; *Joni Mitchell* . . . . (Reprise)

Night In Tunisia
Charlie Parker; *Bird On 52nd St.* . . . . (Fantasy)
Charlie Parker . . . . (Prestige)
One Night In Birdland . . . . (Columbia)
Very Best Of Bird . . . . (Warner Bros.)
Dizzy Gillespie; *Electrifying Evening* . . . . (Verve)
Jazz At Massey Hall . . . . (Fantasy)
Musician Composer Raconteur . . . . (Pablo)
Nipper's Greatest Hits Of The '40s-#2-C . . . . (RCA)
Tuxedo Junction; *Take The "A" Train* . . . . (Butterfly)

Night Is Fallin' In My Heart
Diamond Rio; *Diamond Rio's Greatest Hits* . . . . (Arista)
Love A Little Stronger . . . . (Arista)

Night Is Still Young
Billy Joel; *Billy Joel-Greatest Hits, Volume I & Volume II* . . . . (Columbia)

Night Life
Willie Nelson; *Country Willie* . . . . (United Artists)
Healing Hands Of Time . . . . (Liberty)
Souvenirs Of Music City U.S.A.-C . . . . (Plantation)
Willie . . . . (RCA)
Willie & Family Live . . . . (Columbia)

Night Life
Miracles; *Miracles' Greatest Hits* . . . . (Motown)

Night Life
Thin Lizzy; *Night Life* . . . . (Mercury)

Night Life
Ray Price; *Ray Price's Greatest Hits-#2* . . . . (Step One)

Night Life
Charlie Daniels Band & Friends; *Volunteer Jam 3 & 4* . . . . (Epic)

Night Life In Pompeii
Earl "Fatha" Hines; *Earl "Fatha" Hines* . . . . (Crescendo)

Night Lights
Nat "King" Cole; *Night Lights* . . . . (Capitol/EMI)

Night Moves
Bob Seger; *Night Moves* . . . . (Capitol)
ST/FM . . . . (MCA)
Bob Seger & The Silver Bullet Band; *Nine Tonight* . . . . . (Capitol)

Night Moves
Marilyn Martin; *Marilyn Martin* . . . . (Atlantic)

Night Of My Nights
Original Cast; *Kismet* . . . . (Columbia)
Vic Damone; *ST/Kismet* . . . . (Sony Music Special Prod.)

Night Of The Thumpasorus Peoples
Parliament; *Mothership Connection* . . . . (Casablanca)
Parliament Live/P. Funk Earth Tour . . . . (Casablanca)

Night Of The Vampire
Roky Erickson; *You're Gonna Miss Me-Best Of Roky Erickson* . . . . . . (Restless)

Night Of The Vampire
Grim Reaper; *Rock You To Hell* . . . . (RCA)

Night Of Van Gogh
Boz Scaggs; *Other Roads* . . . . (Columbia)

Night On The 4th Of May
Al Stewart; *Al Stewart-Early Years* . . . . (Janus)

Night On The Town
Bruce Hornsby & The Range; *Night On The Town* . . . . (RCA)

Night Owl
Carly Simon; *Best Of Carly Simon* . . . . (Elektra)
No Secrets . . . . (Elektra)

Night Owls
Little River Band; *Little River Band's Greatest Hits* . . . . (Capitol)
Time Exposure . . . . (Capitol)

Night Prowler
AC/DC; *Highway To Hell* . . . . (Atco)

Night Ride Out Of Phoenix
Gillan; *Future Shock* . . . . (Metal Blade)

Night Rider
Elvis Presley; *Collector's Gold* . . . . (RCA)
Live In Nashville . . . . (RCA)
ST/Pot Luck . . . . (RCA)

Night Rider
Electric Light Orchestra; *Face The Music* . . . . (Jet)

Night Rider's Lament
Chris LeDoux; *Chris LeDoux & The Saddle Boogie Band* . . . . . . (Liberty)
Old Cowboy Classics . . . . (Capitol)
Paint Me Back Home In Wyoming . . . . (Liberty)
Garth Brooks; *The Chase* . . . . (Liberty)
Jerry Jeff Walker; *Ridin' High* . . . . (MCA)
Nanci Griffith; *Other Voices Other Rooms* . . . . (Elektra)
Suzy Bogguss; *Somewhere Between* . . . . (Capitol)

Night Shift
Bob Marley & The Wailers; *Rastaman Vibration* . . . . . . (Tuff Gong)
Foghat; *Best Of Foghat* . . . . (Rhino)
Night Shift . . . . (Rhino)

Night The Carousel Burned Down
Todd Rundgren; *Something/Anything?* . . . . (Rhino)

Night The Lights Went Out
Trammps; *Best Of The Trammps* . . . . (Atlantic)
Trammps III . . . . (Atlantic)

Night The Lights Went Out In Georgia
Lynn Anderson; *Top Of The World* . . . . (Columbia)
Reba McEntire; *For My Broken Heart* . . . . (MCA)
Reba McEntire's Greatest Hits-#3: I'm A Survivor . . . . . . (MCA)
Vicki Lawrence; *Super Hits Of The '70s-Have A Nice Day-#10-C* . . . . . . (Rhino)

Night They Drove Old Dixie Down
Band; *Best Of The Band* . . . . (Capitol)
Rock Of Ages . . . . (Capitol)
The Band . . . . (Capitol)
The Band-Anthology-#1 . . . . (Capitol)
The Band-Gift Set . . . . (Capitol)
The Last Waltz . . . . (Warner Bros.)
Bob Dylan And The Band; *Before The Flood* . . . . (Columbia)
Joan Baez; *Country Music Album* . . . . (Vanguard)
From Every Stage . . . . (A&M)
Hits/Greatest & Others . . . . (Vanguard)
Joan Baez-Classics-#8 . . . . (A&M)

Night They Invented Champagne
Betty Wand/Louis Jordan/Others; *ST/Gigi* . . . . (Sony Music Special Prod.)
Original Cast; *Gigi* . . . . (RCA Victor)

Night Time
Ted Nugent & The Amboy Dukes; *Greatest
    Collection Ever* . . . .(Dunhill Compact Classics)
Night Time
J. Geils Band; *Love Stinks* . . . .(EMI)
Night Time In The Switching Yard
Warren Zevon; *Excitable Boy* . . . . (Asylum)
Night Time Is Cry Time
Jimmy C. Newman; *Jimmy C. Newman's Greatest Hits* . . . . (Plantation)
Night Time Is The Right Time
Creedence Clearwater Revival; *1969* . . . . (Fantasy)
    Creedence Clearwater Revival-Chronicle-#2 . . . . (Fantasy)
    Green River . . . . (Fantasy)
Ray Charles; *Ray Charles-Complete Atlantic R&B Recordings-1952-
    1959* . . . . (Atlantic)
Night Time Magic
Larry Gatlin & The Gatlin Brothers Band; *Larry Gatlin & The Gatlin
    Brothers' Greatest Hits* . . . . (Columbia)
    Larry Gatlin & The Gatlin Brothers-17 Greatest Hits . . . . (Columbia)
    Live At 8:00 . . . . (Capitol)
    Oh Brother . . . . (Columbia)
Night To Remember
Joe Diffie; *A Night To Remember* . . . .(Epic)
Night To Remember
Shalamar; *Friends* . . . . (Solar)
    Mega Hits Dance Classics-#5-C . . . . (Priority)
    Shalamar's Greatest Hits . . . . (Solar)
Night To Remember
Jody Watley; *Beginnings* . . . . (Solar)
Night To Remember
Foreigner; *Inside Information* . . . . (Atlantic)
Night To Remember
Cyndi Lauper; *Night To Remember* . . . .(Epic)
Night Train
James Brown; *Train Trax-C* . . . . (Sony Music Special Prod.)
James Brown And The Famous Flames; *Soul Shots-C* . . . . (Rhino)
    ST/Quadrophenia . . . .(MCA)
Night Train
Jimmy Forrest; *Heart Of The Forest* . . . .(Palo Alto Jazz)
    Night Train . . . . (Delmark)
Night Train
U2; *The Island Story-1962-1987-25th Anniversary-C* . . . . (Island)
Night Train
Steve Winwood; *Arc Of A Diver* . . . . (Island)
Night Train
Lionel Richie; *Dancing On The Ceiling* . . . . (Motown)
Night Train
Paul Revere And The Raiders; *Legend Of Paul Revere And The
    Raiders* . . . . (Columbia)
Night Train
Rickie Lee Jones; *Rickie Lee Jones* . . . .(Warner Bros.)
Night Train To Madrid
Bertram Levy; *That Old Gut Feeling* . . . . (Flying Fish)
Night Train To Memphis
Jerry Lee Lewis; *Rare Tracks* . . . . (Rhino)
    Taste Of Country . . . . (Sun)
Joe Maphis; *Great American Train Songs-C* . . . .(C.M.H. Prod.)
Roy Acuff; *Best Of Roy Acuff* . . . . (Liberty)
    Essential Roy Acuff-1936-1949 . . . . (Legacy)
    Roy Acuff's Greatest Hits . . . . (Columbia)
Night Watch
Fleetwood Mac; *Penguin* . . . . (Reprise)
Night We Called It A Day
Diana Krall; *The Look Of Love* . . . . (Impulse!)
Frank Sinatra; *Night We Called It A Day* . . . . (Capitol)
    Where Are You? . . . . (Capitol)
Tommy Dorsey & Frank Sinatra; *Radio Years 1940-1942* . . . . (RCA)
Nightclubbing
Grace Jones; *Nightclubbing* . . . . (Island)
Iggy Pop; *Idiot* . . . . (RCA)
    TV Eye/1977 Live . . . . (RCA)
Nightfly, The
Donald Fagen; *The Nightfly* . . . .(Warner Bros.)
Nightingale Sang In Berkeley Square
Harry Connick, Jr.; *We Are In Love* . . . . (Columbia)
Manhattan Transfer; *Best Of The Manhattan Transfer* . . . . (Atlantic)
    Mecca For Moderns . . . . (Atlantic)
Tony Bennett; *Perfectly Frank* . . . . (Columbia)
Nightmare
Artie Shaw; *Begin The Beguine* . . . . (Bluebird)
    Best Of The Big Bands-C . . . . (Columbia)
Nightmare
Black Sabbath; *Eternal Idol* . . . .(Warner Bros.)
Nightmare
Slaughterhouse; *Face Reality* . . . .(Metal Blade)
Nightmare
Eddie Money; *Life For The Taking* . . . . (Columbia)
Nightmare
Stevie Nicks; *Rock A Little* . . . . (Modern)

Nightmares
A Flock Of Seagulls; *Best Of A Flock Of Seagulls* . . . . (Jive)
    Listen . . . . (Jive)
Nightmares
J. Geils Band; *Nightmares* . . . .(Atlantic)
Nightmares
Omen; *Nightmares* . . . . (Metal Blade)
Nightmares
Dana Dane; *Rap Hall Of Fame-C* . . . . (K-Tel)
    With Fame . . . . (Profile)
Nightmares
Violent Femmes; *Violent Femmes 3* . . . .(Slash)
Nights
Ed Bruce; *Night Things* . . . . (RCA)
Nights Are Forever
Jennifer Warnes; *ST/Twilight Zone-The Movie* . . . . (Warner Bros.)
Nights Are Forever Without You
England Dan & John Ford Coley; *Best Of England Dan & John Ford
    Coley* . . . . (Big Tree)
    Nights Are Forever Without You . . . . (Big Tree)
Nights In Harlem
Luther Vandross; *I Know* . . . .(LV/Virgin)
Nights In White Satin
Moody Blues; *Billboard Top Rock 'N' Roll Hits-1972-C* . . . . Rhino)
    Caught Live Plus Five . . . .(Polydor)
    Days Of Future Passed . . . .(Polydor)
    History Of British Rock-#8-C . . . . (Rhino)
    This Is The Moody Blues . . . .(Polydor)
Nights Like This
Stacey Q; *Nights Like This* . . . .(Atlantic)
Nights On Broadway
Bee Gees; *Bee Gees' Greatest* . . . .(Polydor)
    Here At Last...Bee Gees...Live . . . .(Polydor)
    Main Course . . . . (RSO)
Nights Over Egypt
Jones Girls; *Get As Much Love As You Can* . . . . (Philadelphia Int'l)
Nights Over Egypt
Rastine; *Afrodisiac* . . . .(Zoo)
Night's Too Long
Patty Loveless; *On Down The Line* . . . . (MCA)
Nighttrain
Public Enemy; *Apocalypse 91...The Enemy Strikes Black* . .(Def Jam/Columbia)
    Stanley Son Of Theodore-Music Sampler . . . . (Epic)
Nighttrain
Guns N' Roses; *Appetite For Destruction* . . . . (Geffen)
Nightwatch
Kenny Loggins; *Nightwatch* . . . . (Columbia)
Nightwatchman
Tom Petty And The Heartbreakers; *Hard Promises* . . . . (MCA)
Nine Tonight
Bob Seger & The Silver Bullet Band; *Nine Tonight* . . . . (Capitol)
    ST/Urban Cowboy . . . .(Asylum)
Nite And Day
Al B. Sure!; *In Effect Mode* . . . . (Warner Bros.)
No Moon At All
Anita O'Day; *In A Mellow Tone* . . . .(DRG)
Billy Stritch; *Billy Stritch* . . . .(DRG)
No More Lonely Nights
Paul McCartney; *All The Best!* . . . . (Capitol)
    ST/Give my regards to Broad Street . . . . (Columbia)
No More, No Less
Collective Soul; *Dosage* . . . .(Atlantic)
No Sugar Tonight
Guess Who; *American Woman* . . . .(RCA)
    Best Of The Guess Who . . . .(RCA)
    Track Record-Collection . . . .(RCA)
North Won The War Again Last Night, The
Cal Smith; *Cal Smith* . . . . (First Generation)
Not Dark Yet
Bob Dylan; *Time Out Of Mind* . . . . (Columbia)
Not Enough Hours In The Night
Doug Supernaw; *You Still Got Me* . . . .(Giant)
Not Tonight
Lil' Kim; *Hard Core* . . . .(Atlantic)
Nothin' But The Taillights
Clint Black; *Nothin' But The Taillights* . . . .(RCA)
Nothin' But The Wheel
Patty Loveless; *Only What I Feel* . . . .(Epic)
    Patty Loveless-Classics . . . .(Epic)
November Nights
Flim & The BB's; *Tunnel* . . . . (Digital Music Prod.)
October Night
Cliff Sarde; *Every Bit Better/Waiting* . . . . (MCA)
    Waiting . . . . (MCA)
October Nights
Stone Soup; *October Nights* . . . .(Windchime)
Oh, What A Night
Dells; *Billboard Top R&B Hits-1965-1969-C* . . . . (Rhino)

Collectables Presents The History Of Rock-#9-C . . . . (Collectables)
Cruisin'-1956-C . . . . (Increase)
Oh, What A Night . . . . (Vee-Jay)
Oldies But Goodies-#3-C . . . . (Original Sound)
Oh, What A Night For Dancing
Barry White; *Barry White Sings For Someone You Love* . . . . . (20th Century Fox)
Barry White's All-Time Greatest Hits . . . . (Mercury)
On A Good Night
Wade Hayes; *On A Good Night* . . . . (Columbia)
Super Hits Of 1996-C . . . . (Epic)
On A Night Like This
Bob Dylan; *Biograph* . . . . (Columbia)
Bob Dylan And The Band; *Planet Waves* . . . . (Columbia)
On The Dark Side
John Cafferty And The Beaver Brown Band; *ST/Eddie & The
Cruisers* . . . . (Scotti Bros.)
On The Verge
Collin Raye; *I Think About You* . . . . (Epic)
One Lonely Night
REO Speedwagon; *REO Speedwagon-The Hits* . . . . (Epic)
Wheels Are Turnin' . . . . (Epic)
One More Night
Phil Collins; *No Jacket Required* . . . . (Atlantic)
Serious Hits...Live! . . . . (Atlantic)
One More Night
Stephen Bishop; *Best Of Bish* . . . . (Rhino)
One More Night
Corbin/Hanner Band; *Black & White Photograph* . . . . (Mercury)
One More Night
Bobby Brown; *Bobby* . . . . (MCA)
One More Night
Fleetwood Mac; *Fleetwood Mac Live* . . . . (Warner Bros.)
One More Night
Bob Dylan; *Nashville Skyline* . . . . (Columbia)
One More Night
Barbra Streisand; *Songbird* . . . . (Columbia)
One Night
Albert King; *Blues For Elvis* . . . . (Stax)
Elvis Presley; *50,000,000 Elvis Fans Can't Be Wrong-Elvis' Gold Records-
Volume 2* . . . . (RCA)
Reconsider Baby . . . . (RCA)
The Other Sides-Worldwide Gold Award Hits, Vol. 2 . . . . (RCA)
The Top Ten Hits . . . . (RCA)
Ronnie Milsap; *Heart & Soul* . . . . (RCA)
One Night A Day
Garth Brooks; *In Pieces* . . . . (Liberty)
One Night At A Time
George Strait; *Carrying Your Love With Me* . . . . (MCA)
Latest Greatest Straitest Hits . . . . (MCA)
One Night In Bangkok
Murray Head; *Chess Pieces* . . . . (RCA)
Original Broadway Cast; *Chess* . . . . (RCA)
One Night In Paris
John Boswell; *Count Me In* . . . . (Hearts Of Space)
One Night In The Hotel
Michel Petrucciani; *Promenade With Duke* . . . . (Blue Note)
One Night In Trinidad
Earl "Fatha" Hines; *Lionel Hampton Presents Earl "Fatha"
Hines* . . . . (Who's Who In Jazz)
One Night In Vienna
Schoenerz & Scott; *One Night In Vienna* . . . . (Windham Hill)
One Night Love Affair
Bryan Adams; *Reckless* . . . . (A&M)
One Night Stand
Janis Joplin; *Farewell Song* . . . . (Columbia)
Janis Joplin-Super Hits . . . . (Epic)
One Night Stands
Hank Williams, Jr.; *Hank Williams, Jr.-Early Years* . . . . (WB/Curb)
One Night Stands . . . . (Warner Bros.)
One O'clock Jump
Count Basie & His Orchestra; *Swingingest Sounds Ever Heard-C* . . . . . . (Hip-O)
One Of These Nights
Eagles; *Eagles/Their Greatest Hits 1971-1975* . . . . (Asylum)
One Of These Nights . . . . (Asylum)
One Of Those Love Songs
Xscape; *Traces Of My Lipstick* . . . . (So So Def/Columbia)
One Of Those Nights
Lisa Brokop; *Every Little Girl's Dream* . . . . (Patriot)
One Of Those Nights Tonight
Lorrie Morgan; *Shakin' Things Up* . . . . (BNA)
To Get To You-Greatest Hits Collection . . . . (BNA)
One On One
Daryl Hall & John Oates; *H2O* . . . . (RCA)
Live At The Apollo . . . . (RCA)
Rock 'N Soul, Part 1 . . . . (RCA)
Soulful Sounds . . . . (RCA)
One Sad Night In Kerrville
Tom Kell; *Sad Night* . . . . (Warner Bros.)

One Summer Night
Danleers; *Mercury Vocal Group Collection-C* . . . . (Mercury)
More American Graffiti-C . . . . (MCA)
Remember When-C . . . . (Garland)
Super Oldies Of The '50s-#1-C . . . . (Audio Fidelity)
WCBS FM 101 History Of Rock-'50s-#1-C . . . . (Collectables)
One Summer Night In Brazil
Rippingtons; *Tourist In Paradise* . . . . (GRP)
One Time, One Night
Los Lobos; *By The Light Of The Moon* . . . . (Slash)
Open All Night
Bruce Springsteen; *Nebraska* . . . . (Columbia)
Open All Night
Daryl Hall & John Oates; *H2O* . . . . (RCA)
Out Of Your Shoes
Lorrie Morgan; *Essential Lorrie Morgan* . . . . (RCA)
Leave The Light On . . . . (RCA)
Lorrie Morgan-Super Hits . . . . (RCA)
Overnight Angels
Ian Hunter & Mott The Hoople; *Shades Of Ian Hunter* . . . . (Chrysalis)
Overnight Cafe
Chicago; *Chicago XIV* . . . . (Chicago)
Overnight Sensation
Tina Turner; *Break Every Rule* . . . . (Capitol)
Overnight Sensation
Mickey Gilley; *Mickey Gilley's Greatest Hits-#2* . . . . (Epic)
Overnight Sensation (Hit Record)
Eric Carmen; *Eric Carmen-The Definitive Collection* . . . . (Arista)
Raspberries; *Raspberries' Best Featuring Eric Carmen* . . . . . (Capitol)
Overnight Success
George Strait; *Beyond The Blue Neon* . . . . (MCA)
Ten Strait Hits . . . . (MCA)
Paradise Tonight
Charly McClain & Mickey Gilley; *19 Hot Country Requests-C* . . . . (Epic)
Charly McClain's Biggest Hits . . . . (Epic)
It Takes Believers . . . . (Epic)
Paradise . . . . (Epic)
Ten Year Anniversary . . . . (Epic)
Party All Night
Quiet Riot; *Condition Critical* . . . . (Epic Portrait Assoc.)
Winners Take All . . . . (Sony Music Special Prod.)
Party Night
Curtis Mayfield; *Do It All Night* . . . . (Curtom)
Give, Get, Take And Have . . . . (Curtom)
Party Night
Isley Brothers; *Grand Slam* . . . . (T-Neck/Columbia)
Peace Tonight
Indigo Girls; *Come On Now Social* . . . . (Epic)
Pilots Of Purple Twilight
Tangerine Dream; *Exit* . . . . (Elektra)
Play
Jennifer Lopez; *J. Lo* . . . . (Epic)
Now That's What I Call Music!-#7-C . . . . (Virgin)
Play It All Night Long
Warren Zevon; *Bad Luck Streak In Dancing School* . . . . (Asylum)
Quiet Normal Life-Best Of Warren Zevon . . . . (Asylum)
Play The Game Tonight
Kansas; *Best Of Kansas* . . . . (CBS Associated)
Vinyl Confessions . . . . (Kirshner)
Play The Game Tonight
Neil Diamond; *On The Way To The Sky* . . . . (Columbia)
Prayin' For Daylight
Rascal Flatts; *Rascal Flatts* . . . . (Lyric Street)
Pretty Girl
Jon B.; *Bonafide* . . . . (Yab Yum/550)
Pretty Little Adriana
Vince Gill; *High Lonesome Sound* . . . . (MCA)
Prince Of Darkness
Nylons; *Best Of The Nylons* . . . . (Open Air)
One Size Fits All . . . . (Open Air)
Prince Of Darkness
Indigo Girls; *Back On The Bus Y'All* . . . . (Epic)
Indigo Girls . . . . (Epic)
Prince Of Darkness
Big Daddy Kane; *Prince Of Darkness* . . . . (Cold Chillin')
Prince Of Darkness
Alice Cooper; *Raise Your Fist And Yell* . . . . (MCA)
Prince Of Darkness
Miles Davis; *Sorcerer* . . . . (Columbia)
Promises In The Dark
Pat Benatar; *Best Shots* . . . . (Chrysalis)
Live From Earth . . . . (Chrysalis)
Precious Time . . . . (Chrysalis)
Queen Of The Night
Whitney Houston; *ST/The Bodyguard* . . . . (Arista)
Quiet Nights Of Quiet Stars
Antonio Carlos Jobim; *Terra Brasilis* . . . . (Warner Bros.)
Shirley Horn; *I Thought About You-Live At Vine Street* . . . . (Verve)

Racing In The Street
Bruce Springsteen; *Darkness On The Edge Of Town* . . . . (Columbia)
Bruce Springsteen & The E Street Band; *Bruce Springsteen & The E Street Band Live/1975-85* . . . . (Legacy)

Rainy Night House
Joni Mitchell; *Ladies Of The Canyon* . . . . (Reprise)
Joni Mitchell with Tom Scott & The L.A. Express; *Miles Of Aisles* . . . . (Asylum)

Rainy Night In Georgia
Brook Benton; *Atlantic Rhythm & Blues 1947-1974-#6 (1966-1969)-C* . . . . (Atlantic)
Brook Benton Today . . . . (Cotillion)
Brook Benton-Anthology . . . . (Rhino)
Golden Age Of Black Music-1960-1970-C . . . . (Atlantic)
Pick Of Brook Benton . . . . (Fifty One West)
Soul Years-C . . . . (Atlantic)
Hank Williams, Jr.; *Hank Williams, Jr.-14 Greatest Hits* . . . . (Polydor)
Sam Moore & Conway Twitty; *Rhythm Country And Blues* . . . . (MCA)

Rainy Night In Rio
Susannah McCorkle; *Thanks For The Memory* . . . . (Pausa)

Rainy Night In Tokyo
Michael Franks; *Passionfruit* . . . . (Warner Bros.)

Ramrod
Bruce Springsteen; *The River* . . . . (Columbia)

Reach Out Of The Darkness
Friend And Lover; *Chicken Soup For The Soul: I'll Be There For You-Songs Of Friendship, Brotherhood And Sisterhood-C* . . . . (Rhino)
Flower Power-Psychedelic Rock Classics-C . . . . (K-Tel)

Reason, The
Celine Dion with Carole King; *Let's Talk About Love-C* . . . . (550 Music)

Red Neckin' Love Makin' Night
Conway Twitty; *Classic Conway* . . . . (MCA)
Conway Twitty-Legends . . . . (MCA)
Mr. T . . . . (MCA)
Night With Conway Twitty . . . . (MCA)

Remember The Night
Johnny Law; *Johnny Law* . . . . (Metal Blade)
ST/Freddy's Dead-The Final Nightmare . . . . (Metal Blade)

Remember The Night
Loungers; *Harlem Holiday-New York Rhythm & Blues-#6-C* . . . . (Collectables)

Remember The Nights
Motels; *Best Of The Motels-No Vacancy* . . . . (Capitol)
Little Robbers . . . . (Capitol)

Rendezvous
Bruce Springsteen; *Tracks* . . . . (Columbia)
Gary U.S. Bonds; *Best Of Gary U.S. Bonds* . . . (EMI Legends Of Rock 'N' Roll)
Greg Kihn; *Kihnsolidation-Best Of Greg Kihn* . . . . (Rhino)
Greg Kihn Band; *Cover Me (Bruce Springsteen Tribute)-C* . . . . (Rhino)

Rest Of The Night
Natalie Cole; *Good To Be Back* . . . . (Elektra)

Restless Nights
Bruce Springsteen; *Tracks* . . . . (Columbia)
Rocking Chairs; *One Step Up/Two Steps Back-The Songs Of Bruce Springsteen-C* . . . . (Right Stuff)

Rhythm Of The Night
Corona; *Hot Luv-Ultimate Dance Songs Collection-C* . . . . (EMI)
Rhythm Of The Night . . . . (East West)
DeBarge; *DeBarge's Greatest Hits* . . . . (Motown)
Motown Story-First 25 Years-C . . . . (Motown)
Rhythm Of The Night . . . . (Motown)

Right Time Of The Night
Jennifer Warnes; *Best Of Jennifer Warnes* . . . . (Arista)
Jennifer Warnes . . . . (Arista)

River Of Dreams
Billy Joel; *River Of Dreams* . . . . (Columbia)

Rock & Roll Tonight
Grim Reaper; *Fear No Evil* . . . . (RCA)

Rock And Roll All Nite
Kiss; *Alive!* . . . . (Mercury)
Double Platinum . . . . (Mercury)
Dressed To Kill . . . . (Mercury)
Heavy Metal Memories-C . . . . (Rhino)
Smashes, Thrashes & Hits . . . . (Mercury)
The Originals . . . . (Casablanca)

Rock Me Tonight (For Old Time's Sake)
Freddie Jackson; *Rock Me Tonight (For Old Time's Sake)* . . . . (Capitol)

Rock Me Tonite
Billy Squier; *Signs Of Life* . . . . (Capitol)

Rock 'N' Roll Tonight
Cheap Trick; *Busted* . . . . (Epic)

Rock Steady
Aretha Franklin; *Aretha Franklin-30 Greatest Hits* . . . . (Rhino)
Best Of Aretha Franklin . . . . (Atlantic)
Ten Years Of Gold . . . . (Atlantic)
Young, Gifted And Black . . . . (Atlantic & Atco Remasters)

Rock Steady
Whispers; *Just Gets Better With Time* . . . . (Solar)

Rock The Night
Europe; *Final Countdown* . . . . (Epic)

Rock With You
Jacksons; *Jacksons Live* . . . . (Epic)
Michael Jackson; *Off The Wall* . . . . (Epic)

Rockaway The Days
Bruce Springsteen; *Tracks* . . . . (Columbia)

Rockin' Every Night
Gary Moore; *Gary Moore-Early Years* . . . . (WTG)

Rockin' Into The Night
38 Special; *Flashback-Best Of 38 Special* . . . . (A&M)
Rockin' Into The Night . . . . (A&M)

Room At The Top
Tom Petty And The Heartbreakers; *Echo* . . . . (Warner Bros.)

Running With The Night
Lionel Richie; *Back To Front* . . . . (Motown)
Can't Slow Down . . . . (Motown)
Music For The Miracle-C . . . . (Epic Portrait Assoc.)

Sable On Blond
Stevie Nicks; *Wild Heart* . . . . (Modern)

Sailing Nights
Bob Seger; *Beautiful Loser* . . . . (Capitol)

Sambuca Nights
Special EFX; *Special EFX* . . . . (GRP)

San Antonio Nights
Eddy Raven; *Eddy Raven's Greatest Hits* . . . . (Warner Bros.)

San Franciscan Nights
Eric Burdon & The Animals; *Eric Burdon & The Animals' Greatest Hits* . . . . (MGM)
History Of British Rock-#8-C . . . . (Rhino)

San Francisco Days
Chris Isaak; *San Francisco Days* . . . . (Reprise)

Saturday Night
Bay City Rollers; *Bay City Rollers* . . . . (Arista)
Bay City Rollers' Greatest Hits . . . . (Arista)
Billboard Top Rock 'N' Roll Hits-1976-C . . . . (Rhino)
Super Hits Of The '70s-Have A Nice Day-#15-C . . . . (Rhino)

Saturday Night
Ten Years After; *About Time* . . . . (Chrysalis)

Saturday Night
Schoolly D; *Adventures Of Schoolly D* . . . . (Rykodisc)

Saturday Night
Eagles; *Desperado* . . . . (Asylum)
Eagles Live . . . . (Asylum)

Saturday Night
Bobby Fuller Four; *Best Of The Bobby Fuller Four* . . . . (Rhino)

Saturday Night
Count Basie; *Compact Jazz-Count Basie-Standards* . . . . (Verve)

Saturday Night
Red Norvo Quintet; *Forward Look* . . . . (Reference)

Saturday Night
Herman Brood; *Herman Brood & His Wild Romance* . . . . (Ariola America)

Saturday Night
Commodores; *In The Pocket* . . . . (Motown)

Saturday Night
Original Cast; *Marry Me A Little* . . . . (RCA)

Saturday Night
Bunny Wailer; *Rule Dance Hall* . . . . (Shanachie)

Saturday Night
John Waite; *No Brakes* . . . . (EMI)

Saturday Night
Maynard Ferguson; *Maynard '61* . . . . (Roulette)

Saturday Night
Kay Starr; *Kay Starr-Country* . . . . (Crescendo)

Saturday Night
Blue Nile; *Hats* . . . . (A&M)

Saturday Night
Buddy Blue; *Guttersnipes 'N' Zealots* . . . . (Rhino)

Saturday Night
Bobby King & Terry Evans; *Live & Let Live* . . . . (Rounder)

Saturday Night Jag
Clarence Williams & His Orchestra; *Clarence Williams & His Orchestra-#1 (1927-1929)* . . . . (Biograph)

Saturday Night's Alright For Fighting
Elton John; *Elton John's Greatest Hits* . . . . (Polydor)
Goodbye Yellow Brick Road . . . . (Polydor)
Knebworth-The Album-C . . . . (Polydor)
Rock Classics-C . . . . (K-Tel)
Who; *Two Rooms-Celebrating The Songs Of Elton John & Bernie Taupin-C* . . . . (Polydor)

Sausalito Summernight
Diesel; *Watts In A Tank* . . . . (Regency/Atco)

Savannah Nights
Tom Johnston; *Everything You've Heard Is True* . . . . (Warner Bros.)

Save Tonight
Eagle-Eye Cherry; *Desireless* . . . . (Work)

Save Your Nights For Me
Placido Domingo; *Save Your Nights For Me* . . . . (Columbia)

Screaming In The Night
Krokus; *Headhunter* . . . . (Arista)

Stayed Awake All Night-Best Of Krokus . . . . (Arista)
Screaming Night Hog
Steppenwolf; *Steppenwolf-16 Greatest Hits* . . . . (MCA)
Searchin' My Soul
Vonda Shepard; *ST/Songs From ''Ally McBeal'' Featuring Vonda
Shepard* . . . .(550/Epic)
The Radical Light . . . . (Vesperally)
Seaside Bar Song
Bruce Springsteen; *Tracks* . . . .(Columbia)
Little Bob Story; *One Step Up/Two Steps Back-The Songs Of Bruce
Springsteen-C* . . . . (Right Stuff)
September Night
Van Morrison; *Inarticulate Speech Of The Heart* . . . . (Warner Bros.)
Set The Night To Music
Roberta Flack & Maxi Priest; *Set The Night To Music* . . . . (Atlantic)
Set The Night To Music
Starship; *No Protection* . . . . (Grunt)
Shadows Of The Night
Pat Benatar; *Best Shots* . . . . (Chrysalis)
Get Nervous . . . . (Chrysalis)
Shake It Up Tonight
Cheryl Lynn; *Club Columbia-C* . . . . (Columbia)
In The Night . . . . (Columbia)
Sharin' The Night Together
Dr. Hook; *Dr. Hook-Greatest Hits & More* . . . . (Capitol)
Pleasure & Pain . . . . (Capitol)
Sherry
4 Seasons; *4 Seasons' Greatest Hits-#1* . . . . (Rhino)
4 Seasons-Anthology . . . . (Rhino)
ST/The Wanderers . . . . (Warner Bros.)
She's My Girl
Turtles; *'60s Sound Explosion-C* . . . . (K-Tel)
Nuggets-#9-Acid Rock-C . . . . (Rhino)
Turtles-20 Greatest Hits . . . . (Rhino)
Ships
Barry Manilow; *Barry Manilow's Greatest Hits-#3* . . . . (Arista)
One Voice . . . . (Arista)
Ships Don't Disappear In The Night
10 CC; *Live & Let Live* . . . . (Mercury)
Ships In The Night
Be Bop Deluxe; *Best Of Be Bop Deluxe-Raiding The Divine Archive* . . . (Capitol)
Live! In The Air Age . . . . (Harvest)
Sunburst Finish . . . . (Capitol)
Shot In The Dark
Ozzy Osbourne; *The Ozzman Cometh* . . . . (Epic)
Ultimate Sin . . . . (CBS Associated)
Shot In The Dark
Utopia; *Adventures In Utopia* . . . . (Rhino)
Silver Bells (That Ring In The Night)
Bob Wills; *Best Of Bob Wills & His Texas Playboys* . . . . (MCA)
Best Of Bob Wills-#2 . . . . (MCA)
Bob Wills-Anthology . . . . (Sony Music Special Prod.)
Silver Dew On The Bluegrass Tonight
Johnnie Lee Wills; *Tulsa Swing* . . . . (Rounder)
Six Days On The Road
Boxcar Willie; *Truck Driving Favorites* . . . . (Madacy)
Dave Dudley; *Billboard Top Country Hits-1963-C* . . . . (Rhino)
Country Music Classics-#2-1960-1965-C . . . . (K-Tel)
Legends Of Country Guitar-#2-C . . . . (Rhino)
Truck Driver Boogie Big Rig Hits-1939-1969-C . . . . (Audium)
Flying Burrito Brothers; *Cabin Fever* . . . . (Relix)
Farther Along-Best Of The Flying Burrito Brothers . . . . (A&M)
Last Of The Red Hot Burritos . . . . (A&M)
Sawyer Brown; *Six Days On The Road* . . . . (Curb)
Taj Mahal; *Giant Step/De Ole Folks At Home* . . . . (Columbia)
Legends Of Rock Guitar-'60s-#2-C . . . . (Rhino)
Sleep Tight, Good Night Man
Kenny Rogers; *The Gambler* . . . . (EMI)
Sleepless Night
Dokken; *Back For The Attack* . . . . (Elektra)
Beast From The East . . . . (Elektra)
Sleepless Night
John Lennon & Yoko Ono; *Milk & Honey* . . . . (Polydor)
Sleepless Night
Kinks; *Sleepwalker* . . . . (Arista)
Sleepless Nights
Emmylou Harris; *Pieces Of The Sky* . . . . (Reprise)
Gram Parsons & The Flying Burrito Brothers; *Sleepless Nights* . . . . . . (A&M)
Judds; *Collector's Series-The Judds* . . . . (RCA)
River Of Time . . . . (RCA)
Slippin' Into Darkness
War; *All Day Music* . . . . (MCA)
Best Of War...And More . . . . (Avenue)
ST/American Me . . . . (Virgin)
Super Bad-C . . . . (K-Tel)
Smoke Rings In The Dark
Gary Allan; *Smoke Rings In The Dark* . . . . (MCA)
Snakes Crawl At Night
Charley Pride; *Best Of Charley Pride* . . . . (RCA)

Some Enchanted Evening
Jay & The Americans; *Come A Little Bit Closer-Best Of Jay & The
Americans* . . . . (Gold Rush)
Jay & The Americans' All-Time Greatest Hits . . . .(Rhino)
Original Cast; South Pacific . . . . (CBS Masterworks)
Perry Como; Perry Como's All-Time Greatest Hits-#1 . . . . (RCA)
Rosanno Brazzi; ST/South Pacific . . . . (RCA)
Willie Nelson; What A Wonderful World . . . . (Columbia)
Somebody Else's Moon
Collin Raye; *In This Life* . . . . (Epic)
Somebody's Somebody
''AFKAP''; *Emancipation* . . . .(NPG)
Somehow Tonight
Ricky Skaggs and Kentucky Thunder; *Bluegrass Rules!* . . . .(Rounder)
Someone Could Lose A Heart Tonight
Eddie Rabbitt; *Best Of Eddie Rabbitt/Greatest Hits-II* . . . . (Warner Bros.)
Number 1's . . . . (Warner Bros.)
Step By Step . . . . (Liberty)
Someone Saved My Life Tonight
Elton John; *Captain Fantastic And The Brown Dirt Cowboy* . . . . (Polydor)
Elton John's Greatest Hits-#2 . . . . (Polydor)
Something About The Way You Look Tonight
Elton John; *The Big Picture* . . . . (Rocket)
Something In The Night
Bruce Springsteen; *Darkness On The Edge Of Town* . . . . (Columbia)
Somewhere In The Night
Barry Manilow; *Barry Manilow's Greatest Hits-#2* . . . . (Arista)
Even Now . . . . (Arista)
Somewhere Other Than The Night
Garth Brooks; *The Chase* . . . . (Liberty)
Somewhere Tonight
Highway 101; *Featuring Paulette Carlson* . . . . (Warner Bros.)
Highway 101's Greatest Hits . . . . (Warner Bros.)
Somewhere Tonight
Toto; *Fahrenheit* . . . .(Columbia)
Somewhere Tonight
Bob Seger & The Silver Bullet Band; *Like A Rock* . . . .(Capitol)
Song For A Winter's Night
Gordon Lightfoot; *Gord's Gold* . . . . (Reprise)
The Way I Feel . . . . (United Artists)
Song Of A Summer Night
Original Broadway Cast; *The Most Happy Fella* . . . . (Sony Music Classical)
Sound Of Silence, The
Paul Simon; *Paul Simon In Concert/Live Rhymin'* . . . .(Columbia)
Simon & Garfunkel; *Collected Works* . . . .(Columbia)
More American Graffiti-#4-C . . . . (MCA)
Simon & Garfunkel's Greatest Hits . . . . (Columbia)
Sounds Of Silence . . . . (Columbia)
ST/The Graduate . . . . (Columbia)
The Concert In Central Park . . . . (Warner Bros.)
Southern Nights
Chet Atkins & Allen Toussaint; *Rhythm Country And Blues-C* . . . . (MCA)
Glen Campbell; *Best Of Glen Campbell* . . . . (Capitol)
Glen Campbell-Classics Collection . . . . (Capitol)
Glen Campbell-Live . . . . (Capitol)
Southern Nights . . . . (Capitol)
ST/Convoy . . . . (Polydor)
Southside
Moby featuring Gwen Stefani; *12'' Maxi Single* . . . . (V2)
Play . . . . (V2)
Spanish Guitar
Toni Braxton; *The Heat* . . . .(LaFace)
Spend Another Night In Houston
Sonny James; *Sonny's Side Of The Street* . . . .(Monument)
Spend The Night
Rahsaan Patterson; *Rahsaan Patterson* . . . . (MCA)
Spirit In The Dark
Aretha Franklin; *Aretha Franklin-30 Greatest Hits* . . . .(Rhino)
Live At Fillmore West . . . . (Atlantic)
Spirit In The Dark . . . . (Atlantic)
Spirit In The Night
Bruce Springsteen; *Greetings From Asbury Park, N.J.* . . . .(Columbia)
Bruce Springsteen & The E Street Band; *Bruce Springsteen & The E Street
Band Live/1975-85* . . . . (Legacy)
Manfred Mann's Earth Band; *Nightingales & Bombers* . . . . (Warner Bros.)
Roaring Silence . . . . (Warner Bros.)
Stay
Temptations; *Phoenix Rising* . . . .(Motown)
Stay A Little Longer
Bob Wills; *Sounds Of Texas* . . . . (Capitol)
Bob Wills & His Texas Playboys; *Bob Wills & His Texas Playboys-
Anthology 1935-1973* . . . .(Rhino)
Tiffany Transcriptions-#2-Best Of The Tiffanys . . . . (Rhino)
Willie Nelson; Greatest Hits (& Some That Will Be) . . . . (Columbia)
Willie & Family Live . . . . (Columbia)
Stay All Night (Stay A Little Longer)
Backwoods Banjo; *Jes' Fine* . . . . (Rounder)
Mark Chesnutt & Asleep At The Wheel; *Ride With
Bob-C* . . . . (DreamWorks/SKG)

Willie Nelson; *Willie & Family Live*. . . . . (Columbia)

Stay The Night
Chicago; *Chicago 17* . . . .(Warner Bros.)
Chicago's Greatest Hits-1982-1989 . . . . (Full Moon)

Stay The Night
Jane Olivor; *Jane Olivor In Concert*. . . . . (Columbia)
Stay The Night . . . . (Columbia)

Stay The Night
IMx; *IMx*. . . . .(MCA)

Stay The Night
Benjamin Orr; *The Lace* . . . . (Elektra)

Stay With Me Tonight
Dave Edmunds; *Closer To The Flame* . . . . (Capitol)
Jeffrey Osborne; *Stay With Me Tonight* . . . . (A&M)

Stay With Me Tonight
Dave Edmunds; *Closer To The Flame* . . . . (Capitol)

Steal The Night Away
Stevie Woods; *Stevie Woods* . . . . (Cotillion)

Step Into The Light
Dust For Life; *Dust For Life* . . . . (Wind-up)

Steppin' Out With My Baby
Fred Astaire; *Cheek To Cheek: The Irving Berlin Songbook-C* . . . . (Verve)
Fred Astaire At MGM . . . . (Rhino)
ST/Easter Parade. . . . . (Rhino)
Steppin' Out-Astaire Sings. . . . . (Verve)
Tony Bennett; *MTV Unplugged-Tony Bennett* . . . . (Columbia)
Steppin' Out . . . . (Columbia)

Steven's Last Night In Town
Ben Folds Five; *Whatever And Ever Amen* . . . .(Caroline/550)

Stillness Of The Night
REO Speedwagon; *Good Trouble* . . . .(Epic)

Stolen Car
Bruce Springsteen; *The River* . . . . (Columbia)
Tracks . . . . (Columbia)
Elliott Murphy; *One Step Up/Two Steps Back-The Songs Of Bruce
Springsteen-C* . . . . (Right Stuff)

Straight Tequila Night
John Anderson; *Seminole Wind* . . . . (BNA)
Today's Hot Country-C . . . . (K-Tel)

Strange Night
Heart; *Bebe Le Strange* . . . .(Epic)

Stranger In Our House Tonight
Gene Watson; *Memories To Burn*. . . . .(Epic)

Strangered In The Night
Tom Petty And The Heartbreakers; *Tom Petty & The
Heartbreakers* . . . . (Gone Gator)

Strangers In The Night
Frank Sinatra; *Frank Sinatra's Greatest Hits!* . . . . (Reprise)
Sinatra Reprise-The Very Good Years . . . . (Reprise)
Strangers In The Night . . . . (Reprise)

Streets Of Fire
Bruce Springsteen; *Darkness On The Edge Of Town* . . . . (Columbia)

Such A Night
Elvis Presley; *From Nashville To Memphis-The Essential '60s Masters* . . (RCA)

Such A Night
Dr. John; *Very Best Of Dr. John* . . . . (Rhino)
Dr. John & Chris Barber; *On A Mardi Gras Day* . . . . (Great Southern)
Dr. John & The Band; *The Last Waltz* . . . .(Warner Bros.)

Summer Nights
Olivia Newton-John & John Travolta; *Back To Basics-Essential Collection
1971-1992*. . . . .(Geffen)
ST/Grease . . . . (Polydor)
Original Broadway Cast; *Grease* . . . . (Polydor)

Summer Nights
Marianne Faithfull; *Marianne Faithfull's Greatest Hits*. . . . . (Abkco)

Summer Nights
Van Halen; *5150*. . . . .(Warner Bros.)

Summer Nights
Earl Klugh; *Whispers & Promises* . . . .(Warner Bros.)

Summer Song
Chad & Jeremy; *Best Of Chad & Jeremy* . . . . (K-Tel)
Capitol Gold-Best Of Chad & Jeremy . . . . (Capitol)
History Of British Rock-#2-C . . . . (Rhino)

Sunday Night In San Fernando
Mel Torme & The Mel-Tones; *California Suite* . . . . (Discovery)

Sunglasses At Night
Corey Hart; *First Offense* . . . .(EMI)
The Singles. . . . .(EMI)

Sunrise, Sunset
Original Cast; *Fiddler On The Roof* . . . .(RCA Victor)

Sweet Dreams
La Bouche; *Sweet Dreams* . . . . (RCA)
The Ultimate Dance Party-1998-C . . . . (Arista)

Sweetwater Nights
Dave Grusin; *Out Of The Shadows* . . . . (GRP)

Sydney By Night
James Morrison; *Postcards From Down Under* . . . .(Atlantic)

Take Me Home Tonight
Eddie Money; *Can't Hold Back* . . . . (Columbia)
Eddie Money's Greatest Hits-Sound Of Money . . . . (Columbia)

Talking Back To The Night
Steve Winwood; *Steve Winwood-Chronicles* . . . . (Island)
Talking Back To The Night. . . . . (Island)

Tango In The Night
Fleetwood Mac; *Tango In The Night*. . . . . (Warner Bros.)

Teach Me Tonight
Al Jarreau; *Al Jarreau In London* . . . . (Warner Bros.)
Breakin' Away . . . . (Warner Bros.)
Diane Schuur; *Diane Schuur-Collection* . . . . (GRP)
Ella Fitzgerald; *Montreux '75* . . . . (Pablo)
Phoebe Snow; *Best Of Phoebe Snow* . . . . (Columbia)
It Looks Like Snow . . . . (Columbia)
Sarah Vaughan; *How Long Has This Been Going On?* . . . . (Pablo)

Teenage Good Night
Chordettes; *Best Of The Chordettes* . . . . (Rhino)

Ten Thousand Angels
Mindy McCready; *Ten Thousand Angels* . . . . (BNA)

Tender Is The Night
Andy Williams; *Moon River & Other Great Movie Themes* . . . . . (Columbia)
Tony Bennett; *I Left My Heart In San Francisco*. . . . . (Columbia)
Tony Bennett-16 Most Requested Songs. . . . . (Legacy)

Tender Is The Night
Jackson Browne; *Lawyers In Love* . . . .(Asylum)

Tennessee Nights
Pam Tillis; *Pam Tillis-Collection* . . . . (Warner Bros.)

Tennessee Waltz
Cowboy Copas; *45-#696* . . . . (King)
Emmylou Harris; *Cimarron* . . . . (Warner Bros.)
Country's Greatest Hits-#5-C . . . . (Warner Bros.)
New Tradition Sings The Old Tradition-C . . . . (Warner Bros.)
Guy Lombardo & His Royal Canadians; *Best Of Guy Lombardo* . . . . . . (Curb)
Hank Williams, Jr.; *Living Proof-MGM Recordings 1963-1975*. . . . . (Mercury)
Lacy J. Dalton; *Lacy J. Dalton's Greatest Hits* . . . . (Columbia)
Les Paul & Mary Ford; *Les Paul-Selections From Legend & Legacy* . . . (Capitol)
Patti Page; *Patti Page-Golden Hits* . . . . (Mercury)
Patti Page's Greatest Hits . . . . (Columbia)
Roy Acuff; *Essential Roy Acuff-1936-1949* . . . . (Legacy)
Roy Acuff's Greatest Hits . . . . (Columbia)
Roy Rogers; *Best Of Roy Rogers*. . . . . (Curb)
Sammy Kaye & His Orchestra; *Best Of The Big Bands-C* . . . . . . (Columbia)
Spike Jones & His City Slickers; *Best Of Spike Jones & His City
Slickers* . . . . (RCA)

Texas On A Saturday Night
Willie Nelson; *Taste Of Texas-Songs 'Bout Texas By Texans-C* . . . . (Columbia)
Willie Nelson & Mel Tillis; *Half Nelson-C*. . . . . (Columbia)

Thank The Lord For The Night Time
Neil Diamond; *Glory Road-1968-1972*. . . . . (MCA)
Hot August Night II. . . . . (Columbia)
Neil Diamond-Classics (Early Years) . . . . (Columbia)
Neil Diamond-Gold . . . . (MCA)
Neil Diamond's Greatest Hits-1966-1992 . . . . (Columbia)

That Night In Las Vegas
Ennio Morricone; *ST/Bugsy* . . . . (Epic)

Theme From "Dark Shadows"
Original Soundtrack; *Television's Greatest Hits-#2-C* . . . . (TVT)

Theme From "Dr. Kildare" (Three Stars Will Shine Tonight)
Betty Carter; *'Round Midnight* . . . .(Atlantic)
Original Soundtrack; *Television's Greatest Hits-#4-Black & White
Classics-C* . . . . (TVT)

Theme From "Entertainment Tonight"
Original Soundtrack; *Television's Greatest Hits-#3-1970s & 1980s-C* . . . (TVT)

Theme From "Evening Shade"
Original Soundtrack; *Television's Greatest Hits-#7-Cable Ready-C* . . . . (TVT)

Theme From "In The Heat Of The Night"
Original Soundtrack; *Television's Greatest Hits-#7-Cable Ready-C* . . . . (TVT)

Theme From "Monday Night Football"
Original Soundtrack; *Television's Greatest Hits-#6-Remote Control-C* . . . (TVT)

Theme From "Night Court"
Original Soundtrack; *Television's Greatest Hits-#6-Remote Control-C* . . . (TVT)

Theme From "The Days And Nights Of Molly Dodd"
Original Soundtrack; *Television's Greatest Hits-#7-Cable Ready-C* . . . . (TVT)

Theme From "The Late Late Show"
Original Soundtrack; *Television's Greatest Hits-#1-C* . . . . (TVT)

Theme From "The Tonight Show"
Original Soundtrack; *Television's Greatest Hits-#1-C* . . . . (TVT)

There Ain't No Santa Claus On The Evenin' Stage
Captain Beefheart; *The Spotlight Kid* . . . . (Reprise)

There Ain't S... On T.V. Tonight
Minutemen; *Double Nickels On The Dime* . . . . (SST)

There Goes My Baby
Trisha Yearwood; *Where Your Road Leads* . . . . (MCA)

There Will Never Be Another Tonight
Bryan Adams; *Waking Up The Neighbours*. . . . . (A&M)

There'll Be A Hot Time In The Old Town Tonight
Bessie Smith; *Bessie Smith-The Complete Recordings-#3* . . . . (Legacy)
Louis Armstrong; *Best Of Louis Armstrong* . . . . (Audio Fidelity)

Turk Murphy's San Francisco Jazz Band; *Turk Murphy's San Francisco Jazz Band* .... (Good Time Jazz)
Woody Herman; *The Uncollected Woody Herman & His First Herd* .... (Hindsight)

There'll Be No Teardrops Tonight
Anita Carter; *Hank Williams Songbook-C* .... (Columbia)
Hank Williams; *24 Of Hank Williams' Greatest Hits* .... (Polydor)
Hank Williams' Greatest Hits .... (Polydor)

There's A Kind Of Hush (All Over The World)
Carpenters; *A Kind Of Hush* .... (A&M)
Carpenters-Classics-#2 .... (A&M)
Yesterday Once More .... (A&M)
Herman's Hermits; *Herman's Hermits-Their Greatest Hits* .... (Abkco)

There's A Moon Out Tonight
Capris; *20 Top 10 Hits Of The '50s & '60s-C* .... (Laurie)
22 Leaders Of The Pack-#2-C .... (Laurie)
Collectables Presents The History Of Rock-#3-C .... (Collectables)
There's A Moon Out Tonight .... (Collectables)

They're Hanging Me Tonight
Marty Robbins; *Gunfighter Ballads & Trail Songs* .... (Legacy)

This Could Be The Night
Loverboy; *Big Ones* .... (Columbia)
Lovin' Every Minute Of It .... (Columbia)

This Flight Tonight
Nazareth; *Hot Tracks* .... (A&M)
Nazareth-Classics-#16 .... (A&M)

This Flight Tonight
Joni Mitchell; *Blue* .... (Reprise)

This Heartache Never Sleeps
Mark Chesnutt; *I Don't Want To Miss A Thing* .... (MCA)

This Is My Night
Chaka Khan; *I Feel For You* .... (Warner Bros.)
Life Is A Dance/The Remix Project .... (Warner Bros.)

This Is Your Night
Amber; *ESPN Presents Jock Jams-#2-C* .... (Tommy Boy)
This Is Your Night .... (Tommy Boy)

This Night Won't Last Forever
Bill LaBounty; *The Right Direction* .... (Noteworthy)
This Night Won't Last Forever .... (Warner Bros.)
Michael Johnson; *Dialogue* .... (EMI)
Have A Nice Night-Romantic Hits Of The '70s-C .... (Rhino)
Radio Daze-Pop Hits Of The '80s-#1-C .... (Rhino)
Then & Now .... (ISD/Intersound)
Moe Bandy; *Many Mansions* .... (Curb)
Sawyer Brown; *Six Days On The Road* .... (Curb)

Thunder Rolls, The
Garth Brooks; *Garth Brooks-Double Live* .... (Capitol)
No Fences .... (Capitol)

Thursday Night Fever
Legendary Pink Dots; *Legendary Pink Dots* .... (Play It Again Sam)

Tokyo Nights
Bee Gees; *One* .... (Warner Bros.)

Tokyo Nights
Rob Mullins; *Tokyo Nights* .... (Nova)

Tomorrow & Tonight
Kiss; *Alive II* .... (Casablanca)
Love Gun .... (Casablanca)

Tomorrow Doesn't Matter Tonight
Starship; *Knee Deep In The Hoopla* .... (Grunt)

Tomorrow Night
Elvis Presley; *For Everyone* .... (RCA)
Reconsider Baby .... (RCA)
Sun's Greatest Hits-C .... (RCA)
The Sun Sessions .... (RCA)
LaVern Baker; *Atlantic Rhythm & Blues 1947-1974-#2 (1952-1955)-C* .... (Atlantic)
Soul On Fire .... (Atlantic)

Tomorrow Night
Barbra Streisand; *ST/Yentl* .... (Columbia)

Tomorrow Night
Bob Dylan; *Good As I Been To You* .... (Columbia)

Tomorrow Night In Baltimore
Roger Miller; *Best Of Roger Miller* .... (Mercury)
More Golden Hits .... (Smash)

Tonight
Larry Graham & Graham Central Station; *Star Walk* .... (Warner Bros.)

Tonight
Marc Nelson; *chocolate mood* .... (Columbia)

Tonight
Def Leppard; *Adrenalize* .... (Mercury)
Retro Active .... (Mercury)

Tonight
Ringo Starr; *Bad Boy* .... (Epic)

Tonight
Barbara Mandrell; *Best Of Barbara Mandrell* .... (MCA)
Love Ups & Downs .... (MCA)

Tonight
Raspberries; *Best Of The Raspberries* .... (Capitol)
Capitol Collectors Series-The Raspberries .... (Capitol)

Tonight
Elton John; *Blue Moves* .... (MCA)
Live In Australia With The Melbourne Symphony Orchestra .... (MCA)

Tonight
Kool & The Gang; *In The Heart* .... (De-Lite)

Tonight
Whispers; *Love For Love* .... (Solar)

Tonight
Iggy Pop; *Lust For Life* .... (Virgin)

Tonight
John Cougar; *Nothin' Matters And What If It Did* .... (Riva)

Tonight
Nick Lowe; *Pure Pop For Now People* .... (Columbia)

Tonight
REO Speedwagon; *R.E.O.* .... (Epic)

Tonight
Ready For The World; *Ready For The World* .... (MCA)

Tonight
Rude Boys; *Rude House* .... (Atlantic)

Tonight
Original Cast; *ST/West Side Story* .... (Sony Broadway)

Tonight
New Kids On The Block; *Step By Step* .... (Columbia)

Tonight
Rick Springfield; *Success Hasn't Spoiled Me Yet* .... (RCA)

Tonight
Timothy B. Schmit; *Tell Me The Truth* .... (MCA)

Tonight
George Michael; *Two Rooms-Celebrating The Songs Of Elton John & Bernie Taupin-C* .... (Polydor)

Tonight
Bryan Adams; *You Want It, You Got It* .... (A&M)

Tonight Carmen
Marty Robbins; *American Originals-Marty Robbins* .... (Columbia)
Essential Marty Robbins-1951-1982 .... (Columbia)
Marty Robbins' All-Time Greatest Hits .... (Columbia)

Tonight I Climbed The Wall
Alan Jackson; *A Lot About Livin' (And A Little 'Bout Love)* .... (Arista)

Tonight I Feel Like Texas
Barbara Lamb; *Tonight I Feel Like Texas* .... (Sugar Hill)

Tonight I Give In
Angela Bofill; *Best Of Angela Bofill* .... (Arista)
Too Tough .... (Arista)

Tonight I Shall Sleep With A Smile On My Face
Duke Ellington; *Black, Brown & Beige: 1944-1946 Band Recordings* .... (Bluebird)
Sarah Vaughan; *Duke Ellington Songbook Two* .... (Pablo)

Tonight I'll Be Staying Here With You
Bob Dylan; *Bob Dylan's Greatest Hits-#2* .... (Columbia)
Nashville Skyline .... (Columbia)

Tonight I'm Yours
Rod Stewart; *Absolutely Live* .... (Warner Bros.)
Storyteller/The Complete Anthology: 1964-1990 .... (Warner Bros.)
Tonight I'm Yours .... (Warner Bros.)

Tonight Is So Right For Love
Elvis Presley; *ST/G.I. Blues* .... (RCA)

Tonight Is The Night
Betty Wright; *Best Of Betty Wright* .... (Rhino)
Betty Wright Live .... (Rhino)
Danger High Voltage .... (Alston)

Tonight Is The Night I Fell Asleep At The Wheel
Barenaked Ladies; *Maroon* .... (Reprise)

Tonight It's You
Cheap Trick; *Cheap Trick's Greatest Hits* .... (Epic)
Standing On The Edge .... (Epic)

Tonight My Baby's Coming Home
Barbara Mandrell; *Best Of Barbara Mandrell* .... (Columbia)

Tonight My Love Tonight
Paul Anka; *Paul Anka-30th Anniversary Anthology* .... (Rhino)
Paul Anka's 21 Golden Hits .... (RCA)

Tonight She Comes
Cars; *The Cars' Greatest Hits* .... (Elektra)

Tonight Someone's Falling In Love
Johnny Carver; *Afternoon Delight* .... (MCA Special Prod.)
Best Of Johnny Carver .... (MCA)

Tonight The Bottle Let Me Down
Brooks & Dunn; *Mama's Hungry Eyes-Merle Haggard Tribute-C* .... (Arista)
Elvis Costello & The Attractions; *Almost Blue* .... (Columbia)
Gram Parsons & The Flying Burrito Brothers; *Sleepless Nights* .... (A&M)
Merle Haggard; *Swinging Doors* .... (Out Of Print)

Tonight The Heartache's On Me
Dixie Chicks; *Wide Open Spaces* .... (Monument)

Tonight Tonight
Dion; *Dion-His Best* .... (Laurie)
Mello-Kings; *Cruisin'-1956-C* .... (Increase)
Mello-Kings' Greatest Hits .... (Collectables)

Tonight We Just Might Fall In Love Again
Hal Ketchum; *Every Little Word* .... (Curb)

Tonight We're Gonna Tear Down The Walls
Randy Travis; *Always & Forever* . . . .(Warner Bros.)
Tonight You Belong To Me
Patience & Prudence; *Great Jukebox Hits Of The*
'50s-#2-C . . . . (CEMA Special Prod.)
Tonight, I Celebrate My Love
Peabo Bryson; *Tonight I Celebrate My Love* . . . . (Capitol)
Peabo Bryson & Roberta Flack; *Born To Love* . . . . (Capitol)
Quiet Storms 2-C . . . . (MCA)
The Peabo Bryson Collection . . . . (Capitol)
Roberta Flack; *Softly With These Songs-The Best Of Roberta Flack* . . .(Atlantic)
Tonight, Tonight
Smashing Pumpkins; *Mellon Collie And The Infinite Sadness* . . . . (Virgin)
Tonight, Tonight, Tonight
Genesis; *Invisible Touch* . . . .(Atlantic)
Live/The Way We Walk-Volume One: The Shorts . . . .(Atlantic)
Tonight's All Right For Love
Elvis Presley; *Elvis-A Legendary Performer, Volume 1* . . . . (RCA)
Tonight's Tha Night
Kris Kross; *Ruffhouse Records Greatest Hits-C* . . . . (Ruffhouse)
Young Rich & Dangerous . . . . (Ruffhouse)
Tonight's The Night
Neil Young; *Decade* . . . . (Reprise)
Tonight's The Night . . . . (Reprise)
Neil Young & Crazy Horse; *Live Rust* . . . . (Reprise)
Tonight's The Night
Blackstreet; *Blackstreet* . . . . (Interscope)
Tonight's The Night
Kool & The Gang; *Ladies Night* . . . . (De-Lite)
Tonight's The Night
Shirelles; *Shirelles-16 Greatest Hits* . . . . (Trip)
Shirelles-Anthology 1959-1964 . . . . (Rhino)
Tonight's The Night (Gonna Be All Right)
Rod Stewart; *Absolutely Live* . . . .(Warner Bros.)
Downtown Train-Selections From The Storyteller Anthology . . .(Warner Bros.)
Night On The Town . . . .(Warner Bros.)
Rod Stewart's Greatest Hits . . . .(Warner Bros.)
Tonite
A Few Good Men; *Take A Dip* . . . .(LaFace/Arista)
Tonite
Boys; *Saga Continues* . . . . (Motown)
Tonite (Falling For Ya)
Jay Ferguson; *White Noise* . . . . (Capitol)
Too Broke To Spend The Night
Buddy Guy; *Damn Right, I've Got The Blues* . . . . (Silvertone)
Touch Me (All Night Long)
Cathy Dennis; *Move To This* . . . . (Polydor)
Touch The Night
Neil Young; *Landing On Water* . . . .(Geffen)
Train Wreck On Prom Night
Pajama Slave Dancers; *Blood Sweat & Beers* . . . .(Restless)
Truck Drivers Night Run Blues
Joe ''Cannonball'' Lewis; *Truck Driver Boogie Big Rig Hits-1939-*
1969-C . . . .(Audium)
Trying To Sleep Tonight
Clarence Carter; *Hooked On Love* . . . . (Ichiban Int'l)
The Dr.'s Greatest Prescriptions-Best Of Clarence Carter . . . . . (Ichiban Int'l)
Turn Off The Light
Nelly Furtado; *Whoa Nelly!* . . . .(DreamWorks/SKG)
Turn On Your Radio
Nilsson; *Son Of Schmilsson* . . . . (RCA)
Twilight
Electric Light Orchestra; *Time* . . . . (Jet)
Twilight
Band; *Best Of The Band* . . . . (Capitol)
Twilight
Paragons; *Best Of The Paragons*. . . . . (Collectables)
Twilight
Shawn Colvin; *Cover Girl* . . . . (Columbia)
Twilight
Neil Young; *This Note's For You* . . . . (Reprise)
Twilight
Wynton Marsalis; *Wynton Marsalis* . . . . (Columbia)
Twilight In Boston
Jonathan Richman; *I Jonathan* . . . . (Rounder)
Twilight In Turkey
Raymond Scott; *Reckless Nights & Turkish Twilights* . . . . (Columbia)
Twilight On The Trail
Michael Nesmith; *Tropical Campfires* . . . . (Pacific Arts)
Twilight Time
Platters; *Pick Of The Platters* . . . . (Fifty One West)
Platters . . . . (Everest)
Platters-16 Greatest Hits . . . . (Trip)
Platters-Anthology . . . . (Rhino)
Sold Out . . . . (Fifty One West)
Willie Nelson; *What A Wonderful World* . . . . (Columbia)
Twilight Time
Moody Blues; *Days Of Future Passed* . . . . (Polydor)

Twistin' The Night Away
Rod Stewart; *Best Of Rod Stewart-#2* . . . . (Mercury)
Never A Dull Moment . . . . (Mercury)
Sing It Again, Rod . . . . (Mercury)
Storyteller/The Complete Anthology: 1964-1990 . . . . (Warner Bros.)
Sam Cooke; *Best Of Sam Cooke* . . . . (RCA)
Dance Music . . . .(RCA)
Nipper's Greatest Hits Of The '60s-#2-C . . . . (RCA)
Sam Cooke-At The Copa . . . . (RCA)
ST/Animal House . . . . (MCA)
The Man And His Music . . . . (RCA)
Two Hot Girls (On A Hot Summer Night)
Carly Simon; *Carly Simon-Greatest Hits Live* . . . . (Arista)
Coming Around Again . . . . (Arista)
Two Sleepy People
Art Garfunkel; *Up 'Til Now* . . . . (Columbia)
Fats Waller; *Fats Waller-Masterpieces-#3* . . . . (EPM)
Jo Sullivan Loesser & Others; *Loesser By Loesser* . . . . (DRG)
Kay Kyser & His Orchestra; *Best Of The Big Bands-C* . . . . (Columbia)
Undercover Of The Night
Rolling Stones; *Rewind (1971-1984)* . . . . (Rolling Stones)
Undercover . . . . (Rolling Stones)
Until The Night
Billy Joel; *52nd Street* . . . . (Columbia)
Vincent
Don McLean; *American Pie* . . . . (EMI)
Best Of Don McLean . . . . (EMI)
Greatest Hits Then & Now . . . . (EMI)
Waiting For Tonight
Jennifer Lopez; *Now That's What I Call Music!-#4-C* . . . .(Virgin)
On The 6 . . . . (Work)
Waiting For Tonight
Tom Petty; *Playback* . . . . (MCA)
Walk In The Night
Junior Walker & The All Stars; *Junior Walker & The All Stars-All The*
Great Hits . . . . (Motown)
Junior Walker & The All Stars-Anthology . . . . (Motown)
Motown Superstar Series-#5-Junior Walker & The All Stars . . . . (Motown)
Walkin' All Night
Little Feat; *Dixie Chicken* . . . . (Warner Bros.)
Warm Machine
Bush; *Science Of Things* . . . . (Trauma)
Was
Kenny Wayne Shepherd Band; *Live On* . . . .(Giant)
Wasted Days And Wasted Nights
Freddy Fender; *Before The Next Teardrop Falls* . . . . (Universal)
Best Of Freddy Fender . . . . (MCA)
Country Comes To Carnegie Hall-C . . . . (MCA)
Happy Trails . . . . (United Artists)
Texas Country . . . . (United Artists)
The Freddy Fender Collection . . . . (MCA)
Watchdogs Of The Night
UB40; *Live In Moscow* . . . . (A&M)
Rat In The Kitchen . . . . (A&M)
Way You Look Tonight, The
Billie Holiday; *Quintessential-#2-1936* . . . . (Columbia)
Erroll Garner; *Body And Soul* . . . . (Legacy)
Frank Sinatra; *Days Of Wine And Roses, Moon River, And Other Academy*
Award Winners . . . . (Reprise)
Sinatra Reprise-The Very Good Years . . . . (Reprise)
The Reprise Collection . . . . (Reprise)
Fred Astaire; *Steppin' Out-Astaire Sings* . . . . (Verve)
Lettermen; *Best Of The Lettermen-All Original Recordings* . . . . (Curb)
Capitol Collectors Series-The Lettermen . . . . (Capitol)
The Lettermen's All-Time Greatest Hits . . . . (Capitol)
Tony Bennett; *ST/My Best Friend's Wedding* . . . . (Work/Epic)
We Belong
Pat Benatar; *Best Shots* . . . . (Chrysalis)
Tropico . . . . (Chrysalis)
We Belong To The Night
UFO; *Mechanix* . . . . (Chrysalis)
We Were In Love
Toby Keith; *Dream Walkin'* . . . . (Mercury)
Toby Keith's Greatest Hits, Volume One . . . . (Mercury)
Wednesday Evening Blues
John Lee Hooker; *Black Snake* . . . . (Fantasy)
John Lee Hooker . . . . (Everest)
That's My Story . . . . (Riverside)
World's Greatest Blues Singer . . . . (Vee-Jay)
Well All Right (Tonight's The Night)
Andrews Sisters; *50th Anniversary Collection-#2* . . . . (MCA)
Capitol Collectors Series-The Andrews Sisters . . . . (Capitol)
We'll Be Together
Sting; *...Nothing Like The Sun* . . . . (A&M)
Fields Of Gold-The Best Of Sting 1984-1994 . . . . (A&M)
We're Goin' Out Tonight
Cameo; *Cameosis* . . . .(Casablanca)
We've Got Tonight
Bob Seger & The Silver Bullet Band; *Nine Tonight* . . . . (Capitol)

Stranger In Town . . . . (Capitol)
Kenny Rogers & Sheena Easton; *Kenny Rogers/Kim Carnes/Sheena Easton/
Dottie West* . . . . (EMI)
Kenny Rogers-25 Greatest Hits . . . . (EMI)
Kenny Rogers-Greatest Country Hits . . . . (Curb)
Kenny Rogers-Twenty Greatest Hits . . . . (EMI)
We've Got Tonight . . . . (Razor & Tie)
What About Now
Lonestar; *Lonely Grill* . . . .(BNA)
What It Is
Mark Knopfler; *Sailing To Philadelphia* . . . . (Warner Bros.)
Whatever Gets You Thru The Night
John Lennon; *Lennon* . . . . (Capitol)
Walls And Bridges . . . . (Capitol)
John Lennon & Yoko Ono; *The John Lennon Collection* . . . . . . (Capitol)
John Lennon/Plastic Ono Band; *Shaved Fish* . . . . (Capitol)
What's On Tonight
Montell Jordan; *More.* . . . . (Mercury)
When Day Is Done
Coleman Hawkins; *Body And Soul* . . . . (Bluebird)
Helen Humes; *Swingin' With Humes* . . . . (Contemporary)
Mormon Tabernacle Choir & Columbia Symphony Orchestra; *Songs America
Loves Best-Memories* . . . . (Columbia)
When She Cries
Restless Heart; *Big Iron Horses* . . . . (RCA)
Restless Heart's Greatest Hits . . . . (RCA)
Today's Number One Country-C . . . . (K-Tel)
When The Lights Go Out
Bruce Springsteen; *Tracks.* . . . . (Columbia)
When The Lights Go Out
Five; *5* . . . . (Arista)
Totally Hits-#1-C . . . . (Arista)
When The Night
Paul McCartney; *Paul McCartney-Gift Set* . . . . (Capitol)
Wings; *Red Rose Speedway.* . . . . (Capitol)
When The Night Comes
Joe Cocker; *Best Of Joe Cocker.* . . . . (Capitol)
Joe Cocker Live . . . . (Capitol)
One Night Of Sin . . . . (Capitol)
When The Night Comes Falling From The Sky
Bob Dylan; *Empire Burlesque* . . . . (Columbia)
The Bootleg Series-Volumes 1-3 [Rare & Unreleased] . . . . (Columbia)
Jeff Healey Band; *ST/Road House.* . . . . (Arista)
When The Night Falls
Eyes; *History Of British Rock-#6-C* . . . . (Rhino)
When The Sun Goes Down
Mark Collie; *Born & Raised In Black & White* . . . . (MCA)
When The Sun Goes Down
Fleetwood Mac; *Behind The Mask* . . . . (Warner Bros.)
When The Sun Goes Down
Count Basie & Joe Williams; *Count Basie Swings Joe Williams Sings* . . . (Verve)
When The Sun Goes Down
T-Bone Walker; *T-Bone Walker-Complete Imperial Recordings-1950-
1954.* . . . . (EMI)
When The Sun Goes Down
Marty Stuart; *Hillbilly Rock.* . . . . (MCA)
When The Sun Goes Down In The South
Original Broadway Cast; *Big River-The Adventures Of
Huckleberry Finn.* . . . . (MCA)
Where Do The Nights Go
Ronnie Milsap; *Heart & Soul* . . . . (RCA)
Ronnie Milsap's Greatest Hits-#3 . . . . (RCA)
Where The Blue Of The Night Meets The Gold Of The Day
Bing Crosby; *All-Time Best Of* . . . . (Curb)
Best Of Bing Crosby . . . . (MCA)
Where The Blue Of The Night Meets The Gold Of The Day . . . . . . (Biograph)
While You Loved Me
Rascal Flatts; *Rascal Flatts* . . . . (Lyric Street)
Whisper In The Dark
Dionne Warwick; *Friends.* . . . . (Arista)
Why Don't You Spend The Night
Ronnie Milsap; *Milsap Magic* . . . . (RCA)
Wild Night
John Mellencamp & Me'shell Ndegeocello; *Dance Naked* . . . . . . (Mercury)
Rough Harvest . . . . (Mercury)
Martha Reeves; *ST/Thelma & Louise* . . . . (MCA)
Van Morrison; *Best Of Van Morrison* . . . . (Polydor)
Tupelo Honey . . . . (Polydor)
Wild Night In Odessa
Klezmorim; *Metropolis* . . . . (Flying Fish)
Wild Nights, Hot & Crazy Days
Judas Priest; *Metal Works-1973-1993.* . . . . (Columbia)
Turbo . . . . (Columbia)
Wimoweh (Mbube)-The Lion Sleeps Tonight
Chet Atkins; *RCA Years* . . . . (RCA)
Kingston Trio; *Kingston Trio/From The Hungry i.* . . . . (Capitol)
Nylons; *Seamless.* . . . . (Open Air)
Pete Seeger; *Pete Seeger's Greatest Hits* . . . . (Columbia)

Tokens; *Billboard Top Rock 'N' Roll Hits-1961-C* . . . . (Rhino)
Nipper's Greatest Hits Of The '60s-#1-C . . . . (RCA)
Weavers; *Weavers' Greatest Hits* . . . .(Vanguard)
Wired All Night
Mick Jagger; *Wandering Spirit* . . . . (Atlantic)
Wishing On The Moon
Dan Fogelberg; *Phoenix.* . . . . (Full Moon)
With Me Tonight
Beach Boys; *Smiley Smile/Wild Honey* . . . . (Capitol)
Without You (Not Another Lonely Night)
Frankie & The Knockouts; *Below The Belt* . . . . (Millennium)
Woman Tonight
America; *Hearts.* . . . .(Warner Bros.)
History-Greatest Hits . . . . (Warner Bros.)
Wonderful Tonight
Eric Clapton; *24 Nights* . . . .(Duck/Reprise)
Eric Clapton-Crossroads-C . . . . (Polydor)
Just One Night . . . . (Polydor)
Slowhand. . . . . (Polydor)
Time Pieces-#1-The Best Of Eric Clapton. . . . . (Polydor)
Won'tcha Come Out Tonight
Beach Boys; *M.I.U. Album.* . . . . (Brother)
Working Day & Night
Michael Jackson; *Off The Wall.* . . . .(Epic)
World Tonight
Paul McCartney; *Flaming Pie* . . . .(Capitol)
Wrong Night
Reba McEntire; *If You See Him* . . . . (MCA)
You Alone
Perry Como; *Perry Como's Greatest Hits* . . . . (RCA)
You Belong To The City
Glenn Frey; *'80s Greatest Rock Hits-#1-Passion & Power-C* . . . . . . (Priority)
Soundtrack Smashes-'80s & More-C . . . . (MCA)
ST/Miami Vice. . . . . (MCA)
You Don't Have To Go Home Tonight
Triplets; *...Thicker Than Water* . . . .(Mercury)
You Need A Woman Tonight
Captain & Tennille; *Dreams* . . . . (A&M)
You Shook Me All Night Long
AC/DC; *Back In Black* . . . .(Atco)
Who Made Who . . . . (Atlantic)
You Were Meant For Me
Jewel; *Pieces Of You* . . . . (Atlantic)
You'll Be Back (Every Night In My Dreams)
Statler Brothers; *Years Ago* . . . .(Mercury)
Young Blood
Rickie Lee Jones; *Naked Songs Live And Acoustic* . . . . (Reprise)
Rickie Lee Jones . . . . (Warner Bros.)
Young Turks
Rod Stewart; *Absolutely Live* . . . . (Warner Bros.)
Downtown Train-Selections From The Storyteller Anthology. . . (Warner Bros.)
Storyteller/The Complete Anthology: 1964-1990 . . . . (Warner Bros.)
Tonight I'm Yours . . . . (Warner Bros.)
Your Love
Boyz II Men; *Cooleyhighharmony.* . . . . (Motown)
You're All I've Got Tonight
Cars; *The Cars* . . . . (Elektra)
You're Not Leaving Here Tonight
Ed Bruce; *Ed Bruce's Greatest Hits* . . . . (MCA)
You're Not Leaving Here Tonight . . . . (MCA)
You're Welcome To Tonight
Gary Morris & Lynn Anderson; *Gary Morris' Greatest
Hits-#2* . . . . (Warner Bros.)
Lynn Anderson & Gary Morris; *Back* . . . . (Permian)

NONSENSE WORDS

11 O'Clock Tick Tock
U2; *Under A Blood Red Sky* . . . .(Island)
A Tisket, A Tasket
Ella Fitzgerald; *Best Of Ella Fitzgerald* . . . . (MCA)
Ella Fitzgerald . . . . (Laserlight)
Glenn Miller & His Army/Air Force Band; *Glenn Miller & His Army/Air
Force Band.* . . . . (Laserlight)
Tommy Dorsey; *Complete Tommy Dorsey-#7.* . . . . (RCA)
Aba Daba Honeymoon
Debbie Reynolds; *Debbie Reynolds' Greatest Hits* . . . .(Curb)
Abacab
Genesis; *Abacab.* . . . . (Atlantic)
Three Sides Live . . . . (Atlantic)
Turn It On Again: The Hits . . . . (Atlantic)
Abracadabra
Steve Miller Band; *Abracadabra* . . . .(Capitol)
Steve Miller Band-Live . . . . (Capitol)
Abra-Ca-Dabra
De Franco Family; *The DeFranco Family* . . . . (DeFranco Entert.)

Ain't It Great To Be Crazy
Wonder Kids; *Really Silly Songs* .... (Madacy)
Alabambama
Willie Nelson & Roger Miller; *Old Friends* .... (Columbia)
Alley-Oop
Hollywood Argyles; *American Graffiti-#3-C* .... (MCA)
Collectables Presents The History Of Rock-#5-C .... (Collectables)
M. Dung's Idiot Classics .... (Rhino)
Ally Ally Oxen Free
Kingston Trio; *Capitol Collectors Series-The Kingston Trio* .... (Capitol)
Made In The U.S.A. .... (Pair)
Alphabet Song
Three Stooges; *ST/Violent Is The Word For Curlee* .... (Out Of Print)
Apples And Bananas
keith urban; *Country Goes Raffi-C* .... (Rounder)
Assorted Glugs, Pbrts & Skks
Spike Jones; *Dinner Music...For People Who Aren't Very Hungry!* .... (Rhino)
A-Ting A Ling
Stan Kenton; *Lighter Side* .... (Creative World)
Ba Doom
Nick Lowe; *Nick The Knife* .... (Columbia)
Baby Talk
Jan & Dean; *Best Of Jan & Dean* .... (EMI)
Collectables Presents The History Of Rock-#9-C .... (Collectables)
One Summer Night-Live .... (Rhino)
Bang Bang
Cher; *Cher* .... (Geffen)
EMI Legends Of Rock & Roll-24 Greatest Hits-C ....(EMI)
Bawitdaba
Kid Rock; *Devil Without A Cause* ....(Top Dog/Lava/Atlantic)
Totally Hits-#1-C .... (Arista)
Be Bop/Drop
Daryl Hall & John Oates; *X-Static* .... (RCA)
Be-Bop Baby
Rick Nelson; *Rick Nelson's Greatest Hits* .... (Rhino)
Ricky Nelson-Legendary Masters ....(EMI)
Ricky Nelson; Best Of Ricky Nelson ....(EMI)
Be-Bop-A-Lula
Everly Brothers; *Everly Brothers* .... (Rhino)
Gene Vincent and His Blue Caps; *Billboard Top Rock 'N' Roll Hits-*
1956-C .... (Rhino)
ST/Wild At Heart .... (Polydor)
Jerry Lee Lewis; *Monsters* .... (Sun)
Trio Plus .... (Sun)
John Lennon; *Rock 'N' Roll* .... (Capitol)
Beep A Freak
Gap Band; *Gap Band VI* ....(Total Experience)
Beep Beep
Playmates; *Dr. Demento: 20th Anniversary Collection-C* .... (Rhino)
Beep Beep Beep
Bobby Day; *Best Of Bobby Day* .... (Rhino)
Betcha By Golly, Wow
"AFKAP"; *Emancipation* .... (NPG)
Johnny Mathis; *First Time Ever I Saw Your Face* .... (Columbia)
Stylistics; *Best Of The Stylistics* .... (Amherst)
Bibbidi-Bobbidi-Boo
Mormon Tabernacle Choir & Columbia Symphony Orchestra; *When You*
Wish Upon A Star-A Tribute To Walt Disney .... (CBS Masterworks)
Original Soundtrack; *Cinderella* .... (Disney)
Verna Felton/Ilene Woods/Disney Chorus; *Disney Collection-#1-C* .... (Disney)
Bing Bang Boom
Highway 101; *Bing Bang Boom* ....(Warner Bros.)
Bip Bam Thank You Ma'am
Ann Peebles; *Fill This World With Love* .... (Bullseye Blues)
Bip Bop
Wings; *Wild Life* .... (Capitol)
Blue (Da Ba Dee)
Eiffel 65; *Europop* ....(Republic/Universal)
Now That's What I Call Music!-#4-C .... (Virgin)
Body Bumpin'-Yippie-Yi-Yo
Public Announcement; *All Work, No Play* .... (A&M)
Bony Moronie
John Lennon; *Rock 'N' Roll* .... (Capitol)
Larry Williams; *Cruisin'-1957-C* .... (Increase)
Let The Good Times Roll-C .... (Capitol)
Original Rock Oldies-Golden Hits-#2-C .... (Specialty)
ST/Christine .... (Motown)
This Is Larry Williams-How It All Began-#2 .... (Specialty)
Boogaloo Down Broadway
Fantastic Johnny C; *Dick Bartley Presents On The Radio-#7-C* .... (VSI)
Boogie Oogie Oogie
Taste Of Honey; *Taste Of Honey* .... (Capitol)
The Disco Years-#1-Turn The Beat Around-1974-1978-C .... (Rhino)
Boo-Hoo-Hoo-Hoo
Little Richard; *Grooviest 17 Original Hits* .... (Specialty)
Little Richard-His Biggest Hits .... (Specialty)
Boom Boom Boom
Iguanas; *Nuevo Boogaloo* ....(Margaritaville)

Bop
Dan Seals; *Best Of Dan Seals* .... (Capitol)
Dan Seals' Greatest Hits .... (Liberty)
Won't Be Blue Anymore ....(EMI)
Buzz Buzz A Diddle-It
Freddy Cannon; *Big Blast From Boston: The Best Of Freddy "Boom Boom"*
Cannon .... (Rhino)
Can't Let You Go (The Sha La Song)
Dave Koz; *Dance* .... (Capitol)
Chick-A-Boom (Don't Ya Jes' Love It)
Daddy Dewdrop; *'70s Smash Hits-#4-C* .... (Rhino)
Super Hits Of The '70s-Have A Nice Day-#5-C .... (Rhino)
Chickery Chick
Sammy Kaye & His Orchestra; *Dance To My Golden Favorites* .... (MCA)
Chim Chim Cheree
Julie Andrews & Dick Van Dyke; *ST/Mary Poppins* .... (Disney)
Ching-A-Ring-Ching-Chaw
Marilyn Horne; *Beautiful Dreamer-Great American Songbook* .... (London)
Chitty Chitty Bang Bang
Myron Floren; *22 Of The Greatest Polkas* .... (Ranwood)
Choo Choo Charlie (Good & Plenty)
Original Soundtrack; *TeeVee Toons-The Commercials-#1-C* .... (TVT)
Choo Choo Ch'Boogie (Jack)
Asleep At The Wheel; *All Time Legends Of Country Music-C* .... (Legacy)
Asleep At The Wheel .... (Epic)
Hot Tracks-Train Super Hits-C .... (Epic)
Served Live .... (Capitol)
Very Best Of Asleep At The Wheel Since 1970 ....(Relentless/Madacy)
Beach Boys; *Ten Years Of Harmony* .... (Caribou)
Clifton Chenier; *Alligator Stomp-#2-C* .... (Rhino)
Louis Jordan; *Best Of Louis Jordan* .... (MCA)
Quincy Jones; *Birth Of A Band-#2* .... (Mercury)
Chug-A-Lug
Roger Miller; *Billboard Top Country Hits-1964-C* .... (Rhino)
Frat Rock!-#3-Grandson Of Frat Rock!-C .... (Rhino)
Click Click Boom
Saliva; *Every Six Seconds* .... (Island/IDJMG)
Click-Clack
Dicky Doo And The Don'ts; *Greatest Hit Singles Collection-C* ..... (Laserlight)
Come Go With Me
Del Vikings; *1956 Audition Tapes* .... (Collectables)
Billboard Top R&B Hits-1957-C .... (Rhino)
Oldies But Goodies-#3-C ....(Original Sound)
ST/American Graffiti .... (MCA)
ST/Stand By Me .... (Atlantic)
Curly Shuffle
Jump 'N The Saddle Band; *Dr. Demento Presents The Greatest Novelty*
Records-#5-1980s-C .... (Rhino)
Da Doo Ron Ron (When He Walked Me Home)
Crystals; *Best Of The Crystals* ....(Abkco)
Good Time Rock 'N' Roll-C .... (MCA)
Hits Of The Sixties-C .... (Intercom Music)
Phil Spector's Greatest Hits-C ....(Spector)
Shaun Cassidy; *Shaun Cassidy's Greatest Hits* ....(Curb)
Dah Dee Dah (Sexy Thing)
Alicia Keys; *ST/Men In Black* .... (Columbia)
De Doo Doo Doo, De Da Da Da
Police; *Every Breath You Take-The Classics* .... (A&M)
Zenyatta Mondatta .... (A&M)
Diddley Daddy
Bo Diddley; *Bo Diddley-His Best* .... (Chess)
Bo Knows Bo .... (MCA Special Prod.)
Chris Isaak; *Heart Shaped World* .... (Reprise)
Diga Diga Doo
Duke Ellington; *Okeh Ellington* .... (Columbia)
Ella Fitzgerald; *Ella Sings/Chick Swings* .... (Olympic)
Diggy Diggy Lo
Commander Cody; *Hot Licks, Cold Steel & Trucker's Favorites* .... (MCA)
Live From Deep In The Heart Of Texas .... (MCA)
Doug Kershaw; *Best Of Doug Kershaw* ....(Warner Bros.)
Cajun Way ....(Warner Bros.)
Guy & Ralna; *Best Of Cajun Country-C* .... (Era)
Lovelight .... (Ranwood)
Ding Dong
Echoes; *Spotlite Series-Gee Records-#1-C* ....(Collectables)
Dippity-Do, Dippity-Do (Styling Gel)
Original Soundtrack; *TeeVee Toons-The Commercials-#1-C* .... (TVT)
Ditty Wa Ditty
Ry Cooder; *Paradise And Lunch* .... (Reprise)
Do Wah Diddy Diddy
Manfred Mann; *Best Of Manfred Mann* ....(EMI Special Markets)
Billboard Top Rock 'N' Roll Hits-1964-C .... (Rhino)
History Of British Rock-#2-C .... (Rhino)
Don't You Just Know It
Huey "Piano" Smith; *New Orleans Party Classics-C* .... (Rhino)
Huey "Piano" Smith And The Clowns; *Oldies But*
Goodies-#3-C ....(Original Sound)
Doo Doo Doo Doo Doo
Rolling Stones; *Goats Head Soup* .... (Rolling Stones)

Made In The Shade . . . . (Rolling Stones)
Rewind (1971-1984) . . . . (Rolling Stones)

Doo Wa Ditty (Blow That Thing)
Zapp; *Zapp II* . . . . (Warner Bros.)

Doobie Wah
Peter Frampton; *Frampton Comes Alive* . . . . (A&M)
Peter Frampton-Classics-#12 . . . . (A&M)

Dooby Dooby Wah
Ritchie Valens; *History Of Ritchie Valens* . . . . (Rhino)
Ritchie Valens . . . . (Rhino)

Doodle De Doo Song
Maury Finney; *45-#4637* . . . . (Soundwaves)

Doodle Dee Doo
Sammy Kaye & His Orchestra; *Best Of Sammy Kaye & His Orchestra* . . (MCA)

Doo-Wah Days
Mickey Gilley; *Back To Basics* . . . . (Epic)
More Hot Country Requests-C . . . . (Epic)
One & Only . . . . (Epic)

Do-Wacka-Do
Roger Miller; *Best Of Roger Miller-His Greatest Songs* . . . . (Curb)
Dumb Ditties-C . . . . (K-Tel)

Dum Dum
Brenda Lee; *Brenda Lee-Anthology-#1 & #2* . . . . (MCA)

Eeny Meeny Miney Mo
Benny Goodman; *Birth Of Swing* . . . . (Bluebird)
Billie Holiday; *Quintessential-#1-1933-1935* . . . . (Columbia)

Exhale (Shoop Shoop)
Whitney Houston; *ST/Waiting To Exhale* . . . . (Arista)
Whitney Houston's Greatest Hits . . . . (Arista)

Fa (Never Be The Same Again)
Guster; *Lost & Gone Forever* . . . . (Hybrid/Sire)

Fa Fa Fa Fa Fa
Otis Redding; *Best Of Otis Redding* . . . . (Atlantic)
Live In Europe . . . . (Atco)
Otis Redding-History . . . . (Atco)
The Otis Redding Story . . . . (Atlantic)

Fee Fi Fo Fum
Artie Shaw; *Best Of The Big Bands-C* . . . . (Columbia)
Free For All . . . . (Portrait)

Fiddle Faddle
Boston Pops Orchestra/Arthur Fiedler; *Fiddle Faddle* . . . . (RCA)
Rochester Pops Orchestra; *Syncopated Clock* . . . . (Pro-Arte)

Fi-Li-Mi-Oo-Re-Ay
Weavers; *On Tour* . . . . (Vanguard)

Flim Flam Man
Laura Nyro; *The First Songs* . . . . (Columbia)

Fo Fi Fo
Pieces Of A Dream; *Imagine This* . . . . (Elektra)

Frim Fram Sauce
Diana Krall; *Stepping Out* . . . . (Justin Time)
Nat "King" Cole; *V-Disc Recordings-Nat "King" Cole* . . . (Collector's Choice)

Funky Dunky
Harry Connick, Jr.; *She* . . . . (Columbia)

Gee Whiz
Kathy Young with The Innocents; *45-#6019* . . . . (Virgo)

Gee Whiz (Look At His Eyes)
Carla Thomas; *Gee Whiz: The Best Of Carla Thomas* . . . . (Rhino)

Get A Job
Sha Na Na; *Best Of Sha Na Na* . . . . (Pair)
Silhouettes; *Best Of Doo Wop Uptempo-#1-C* . . . . (Rhino)
Billboard Top Rock 'N' Roll Hits-1958-C . . . . (Rhino)
ST/American Graffiti . . . . (MCA)
ST/Stand By Me . . . . (Atlantic)

Gobbledygook
Wendys; *Gobbledygook* . . . . (East West)

Gypsy Woman (She's Homeless)
Crystal Waters; *Red Hot + Dance-C* . . . . (Columbia)
Surprise . . . . (Mercury)

Hanky Panky
Tommy James And The Shondells; *Billboard Top Rock 'N' Roll Hits-
1966-C* . . . . (Rhino)
Tommy James And The Shondells-Anthology . . . . (Rhino)

Hanky Panky
Chicago; *Chicago VII* . . . . (Chicago)

Hanky Panky
Madonna; *I'm Breathless-Music From Dick Tracy* . . . . (Sire)

Hanky Panky
Lou Reed; *Transformer* . . . . (RCA)

Hey Ba Ba Re Bop
Lionel Hampton & His Orchestra; *Best Of Lionel Hampton* . . . . . . (MCA)
Hamp's Big Band . . . . (Audio Fidelity)

Hey Diddle Diddle
Marvin Gaye; *Moods Of Marvin Gaye/That's The Way Love Is* . . . . . . (Motown)
Motown Legends-Marvin Gaye . . . . (Motown)

Hey Pocky Way
Meters; *Uptown Rulers-Live On The Queen Mary* . . . . (Rhino)
Neville Brothers; *Fiyo On The Bayou* . . . . (A&M)
New Orleans Party Classics-C . . . . (Rhino)

Treacherous: A History Of The Neville Brothers . . . . (Rhino)

Hi De Hi, Hi De Ho
Kool & The Gang; *As One* . . . . (De-Lite)

Hi De Ho (That Old Sweet Roll)
Bobby Darin; *Live At The Desert Inn* . . . . (Motown)

Hi-De-Ho
Blood, Sweat & Tears; *Blood, Sweat & Tears Greatest Hits* . . . . (Columbia)

Hi-Diddle-Diddle
Fletcher Henderson & The Dixie Stompers; *Fletcher Henderson & The Dixie
Stompers-1925-1928* . . . . (Disques Swing)

Hi-Lili, Hi-Lo
Anne Murray; *There's A Hippo In My Tub* . . . . (Capitol)
Ray Conniff; *Encore! 16 Most Requested Songs* . . . . (Legacy)

Hokey Pokey
Original Soundtrack; *Children's Favorites* . . . . (Kid Rhino/Rhino 4 Kids)
School Days-Kids Classics . . . . (Benson)
Ray Anthony; *Capitol Collectors Series-Ray Anthony* . . . . (Capitol)

Hold Tight, Hold Tight (Sea Food)
Andrews Sisters; *Andrews Sisters-16 Great Performances* . . . . (MCA)
Best Of The Andrews Sisters . . . . (MCA)
Boogie Woogie Bugle Girls . . . . (MCA)

Hoochie Coochie Man
Eric Clapton; *From The Cradle* . . . . (Duck/Reprise)
Eric Clapton featuring Buddy Guy; *The Concert For New York
City-C* . . . . (Columbia)

Hoop-Dee-Doo
Perry Como; *Perry Como's Greatest Hits* . . . . (RCA)

Hot Diggity (Dog Ziggity Boom)
Perry Como; *Como's Golden Records* . . . . (RCA)
Nipper's Greatest Hits Of The '50s-#2-C . . . . (RCA)
Perry Como-Pure Gold . . . . (RCA)
Perry Como's All-Time Greatest Hits-#1 . . . . (RCA)
This Is Perry Como . . . . (RCA)

Howdido
Jack Elliot; *Tribute To Woody Guthrie-C* . . . . (Warner Bros.)

I Ride An Old Paint/Whoopee Ti-Yi-Yo/Git Along Little Doggies
Michael Martin Murphey; *Cowboy Songs* . . . . (Warner Western)

Iko Iko
Cyndi Lauper; *True Colors* . . . . (Portrait)
Dixie Cups; *Best Of The Dixie Cups* . . . . (Bac-Trac)
Wonder Women-History Of Girl Group Sound-C . . . . (Rhino)
Dr. John; *Dr. John's Gumbo* . . . . (Alligator)
New Orleans Party Classics-C . . . . (Rhino)

In-A-Gadda-Da-Vida
Iron Butterfly; *Atlantic Records Classic Rock 1966-1988-C* . . . . (Atlantic)
In-A-Gadda-Da-Vida . . . . (Atco)
Iron Butterfly-Live . . . . (Atco)
Nuggets-#9-Acid Rock-C . . . . (Rhino)
ST/Manhunter . . . . (MCA)

Inka-Dinka Doo
Jimmy Durante; *Dr. Demento Presents The Greatest Novelty Records-#1-
1940s & Before-C* . . . . (Rhino)

Itchycoo Park
Small Faces; *Baby Boomer Classics-British Sixties-C* . . . . . . (JCI Assoc. Labels)

It's In His Kiss (Shoop Shoop Song)
Betty Everett; *Billboard Top R&B Hits-1964-C* . . . . (Rhino)
Hits Of The Sixties-C . . . . (Intercom Music)
More American Graffiti-C . . . . (MCA)
Oldies But Goodies-#3-C . . . . (Original Sound)
Very Best Of Betty Everett . . . . (Vee-Jay)
Wonder Women-History Of Girl Group Sound-C . . . . (Rhino)
Cher; *ST/Mermaids* . . . . (Geffen)
Vonda Shepard; *ST/Songs From "Ally McBeal" Featuring Vonda
Shepard* . . . . (550/Epic)

Jeepers Creepers
Frank Sinatra; *Frank Sinatra-Gift Set* . . . . (Capitol)
Louis Armstrong; *20 Golden Pieces Of Louis Armstrong & Friends* . . . (Bulldog)
At The Crescendo . . . . (MCA)
Hello Dolly! & Other Hits . . . . (MCA)

Jingle Jangle
Archies; *Grooviest Hits Of The Archies* . . . . (Bac-Trac)
Penguins; *Doo-Wop Christmas-C* . . . . (Rhino)

Jingle Jangle Jingle (I've Got Spurs)
Kay Kyser & His Orchestra; *Best Of The Big Bands-C* . . . . (Columbia)
Golden Hits Of The '40s-C . . . . (Columbia Special Prod.)
Sentimental Favorites . . . . (Columbia)
Tex Ritter; *Opry Legends-Tex Ritter* . . . . (Capitol)
Out West-C . . . . (Capitol)

Jocko Homo
Devo; *Best Of Devo-Greatest Hits* . . . . (Warner Bros.)
Q: Are We Not Men? A: We Are Devo! . . . . (Warner Bros.)
Rest Of Devo-Greatest Misses . . . . (Warner Bros.)

Jockomo Jockomo
James "Sugar Boy" Crawford; *History Of New Orleans R&B-#1-1950-
1958-C* . . . . (Rhino)

La La La
Cavedogs; *Joyrides For Shut-Ins* . . . . (Enigma)

La La La La
Blendells; *Frat Rock!-#2-C* . . . . (Rhino)

History Of Latino Rock-#1-C (Rhino)
Son Of Frat Rock!-C (Rhino)
Toga Rock-C (Dunhill Compact Classics)
Stevie Wonder; *12-Year-Old Genius* (Motown)

La La Means I Love You
Delfonics; *Billboard Top R&B Hits-1968-C* (Rhino)
Lovin' '60s-C (Priority)
Oldies But Goodies-#12-C (Original Sound)
Soul Shots-#5-La-La Means I Love You-C (Rhino)
Todd Rundgren; *A Wizard A True Star* (Rhino)
Back To The Bars (Rhino)

Land Of 1000 Dances
Cannibal & The Headhunters; *History Of Latino Rock-#1-C* (Rhino)
Super Oldies Of The '60s-#8-C (Audio Fidelity)
Toga Rock-C (Dunhill Compact Classics)
Wilson Pickett; *Atlantic Rhythm & Blues 1947-1974-#6 (1966-1969)-C* (Atlantic)
Best Of Wilson Pickett (Atlantic)
ST/Forrest Gump (Epic/Sony Music Soundtrax)
Wilson Pickett's Greatest Hits (Atlantic)

Language Of Love
John D. Loudermilk; *45-#47-7938* (RCA)

Ling, Ting, Tong
Buddy Knox; *Best Of Buddy Knox* (Rhino)
Five Keys; *Golden Classics-Five Keys* (Collectables)

Little Latin Lupe Lu
Mitch Ryder And The Detroit Wheels; *Mitch Ryder And The Detroit Wheels' Greatest Hits* (Roulette)
Rev Up-Best Of Mitch Ryder (Rhino)
Righteous Brothers; *Righteous Brothers-Anthology 1962-1974* (Rhino)

Little Rootie Tootie
Thelonius Monk; *High Priest* (Prestige)
In Person (Milestone)
Memorial Album (Milestone)
Piano Giants (Prestige)
Reflections #1 (Prestige)
Thelonius Monk (Milestone)
Thelonius Monk Trio (Prestige)

Lodi Dodi
Snoop Doggy Dogg; *Doggystyle* (Death Row)

Mairzy Doats
Merry Macs; *G.I. Jukebox-Songs From World War II-C* (Hip-O)

Makin' Whoopie
Art Tatum; *Solo Masterpieces-#5* (Pablo)
Eddie Cantor; *Nipper's Greatest Hits Of The '20s-C* (RCA)
Nilsson; *A Little Touch Of Schmilsson In The Night* (RCA)
Ray Charles; *Ray Charles-His Greatest Hits-#2* (Dunhill Compact Classics)

Mama-Oom-Mow-Mow
Rivingtons; *Liberty Years-Legends Of Rock & Roll* (EMI)

Minnie The Moocher
Cab Calloway; *Best Of The Big Bands-C* (Columbia)
Cab Calloway (Glendale)
Dr. Demento Presents The Greatest Novelty Records-#1-1940s & Before-C (Rhino)
Jazz Heritage: Mr. Hi-De-Ho (MCA)
ST/The Blues Brothers (Atlantic)

Mmm Bop
Hanson; *1998 Grammy Nominees-C* (MCA)
Middle Of Nowhere (Mercury)
Now That's What I Call Music!-#1-C (Virgin)
Three Car Garage: The Independent Recordings (Mercury)

MMM MMM MMM MMM
Crash Test Dummies; *God Shuffled His Feet* (Arista)

Moomba
Richard Elliot; *Chill Factor* (Blue Note)

Mumbo Jumbo
Original Broadway Cast; *Stop The World I Want To Get Off* (Polydor)

Mumbo Jumbo
Squeeze; *East Side Story* (A&M)

My Ding-A-Ling
Chuck Berry; *Best Of The Best Of Chuck Berry* (International Mktg. Group)
Billboard Top Rock 'N' Roll Hits-1972-C (Rhino)
Roll Over Beethoven (Allegiance)
The Chess Box-Chuck Berry (Chess)
Toronto Rock 'N' Roll Revival-#2-C (Accord)

My My Hey Hey
Neil Young & Crazy Horse; *Live Rust* (Reprise)
Rust Never Sleeps (Reprise)

My Toot Toot
Fats Domino; *Fats Domino's Greatest Hits* (MCA)
Fats Domino & Doug Kershaw; *Alligator Stomp-#2-C* (Rhino)
Rockin' Sidney; *19 Hot Country Requests-#3-C* (Epic)
Alligator Stomp-#1-C (Rhino)

Na Na Hey Hey Kiss Him Goodbye
Steam; *Billboard Top Rock 'N' Roll Hits-1969-C* (Rhino)
Super Hits Of The '70s-Have A Nice Day-#1-C (Rhino)
Toga Rock-C (Dunhill Compact Classics)

Name Game
Shirley Ellis; *Cruisin'-1965-C* (Increase)

Ob-La-Di, Ob-La-Da
Beatles; *Beatles-Box Set* (Capitol)
The Beatles (White Album) (Capitol)
The Beatles/1967-1970 (Capitol)

Oh Gee, Oh Gosh
Kodaks; *Great Groups Of The '50s-#1-C* (Collectables)
Lewis Lymon/Teen Chords Meet The Kodaks (Collectables)

Oke-She-Moke-She-Pop
Big Joe Turner; *Atlantic Blues-Vocalists-C* (Atlantic)
Big Joe Turner's Greatest Hits (Atlantic)

Oo Poo Pah Doo
Paul Revere And The Raiders; *Here They Come!* (Columbia)
Legend Of Paul Revere And The Raiders (Columbia)

Oo Shoo Be Doo Be
Sammy Davis, Jr.; *Hey There-At His Dynamite Greatest* (MCA)

Ooby Dooby
Creedence Clearwater Revival; *1970* (Fantasy)
Cosmo's Factory (Fantasy)
Creedence Country (Fantasy)
Roy Orbison; *Best Of Roy Orbison* (Curb)
In Dreams-Greatest Hits (Orbison)
Original Sound Of Roy Orbison (Sun)
Roy Orbison-The Sun Years (Rhino)
Sun's Greatest Hits-C (RCA)

Oogum Boogum Song
Brenton Wood; *Collectables Presents The History Of Rock-#9-C* (Collectables)
Oldies But Goodies-#7-C (Original Sound)
Soul Shots-#2-The "In" Crowd-Sweet Soul-C (Rhino)

Ooh La La
Frankie Avalon; *45-#1011* (Chancellor)

Ooh La La
Coolio; *MTV Party To Go '98-C* (Tommy Boy)
My Soul (Tommy Boy)
David Hallyday; *Rock 'N' Heart* (Scotti Bros.)
ST/Baywatch (Scotti Bros.)

Ooh La La
Rod Stewart; *When We Were The New Boys* (Warner Bros.)

Ooh La La La
Linear; *Caught In The Middle* (Atlantic)

Ooh Ooh Song
Pat Benatar; *Tropico* (Chrysalis)

Ooh Poo Pah Doo
Etta James; *Rocks The House* (Chess)
Freddy Fender; *All-Star Chartbusters* (Intermedia)
Let The Good Times Roll (Fifty One West)
Ike & Tina Turner; *Best Of Ike & Tina Turner* (EMI)
Jessie Hill; *Golden Classics-Ooh Poo Pah Doo* (Collectables)
History Of New Orleans R&B-#2-1959-1962-C (Rhino)
ST/Everybody's All-American (Capitol)
Rufus Thomas; *Walking The Dog* (Atlantic)

Ooh, Aah, Nah-Nah-Nah
Big Daddy Kane; *Prince Of Darkness* (Cold Chillin')

Ooh-Eee
Ric Cartey; *Get Hot Or Go Home-Vintage Rockabilly-C* (Country Music Foundation)

Ooh-Wakka-Doo-Wakka-Day
Gilbert O'Sullivan; *Best Of Gilbert O'Sullivan* (Rhino)

Ookey Ook
Penguins; *Golden Classics-Penguins* (Collectables)

Ool-Ya-Koo
Dizzy Gillespie; *Dizzy's Diamonds-Best Of The Verve Years* (Verve)
Dizzy Gillespie & Sarah Vaughan; *Body And Soul* (Intermedia)

Oom Pah Pah
Original Broadway Cast; *Oliver!* (RCA Victor)
Original London Cast; *Oliver!* (EMI-Angel)

Ooo Baba Leba
Helen Humes; *Let The Good Times Roll* (Classic Jazz)

Ooo La La La
Teena Marie; *Naked To The World* (Epic)
Teena Marie's Greatest Hits (Epic)

Ooo Wee
Louis Jordan; *One Guy Named Louis* (Blue Note)

Oooh-Whee Baby
Art Neville; *His Specialty Recordings-1956-1958* (Specialty)
Tracherous Too!-Neville Brothers-#2 (Rhino)

Oop Boopy Oop
Don Julian & The Meadowlarks; *Don Julian & The Meadowlarks-Golden Classics* (Collectables)

Oop-Bop Sh-Bam
Charlie Parker; *Charlie Parker-Vol. 3* (Everest)
Kenny Clarke & The 52nd Street Boys; *Beat Generation* (Rhino)

Oo-Shoo-Be-Doo-Be
Dizzy Gillespie; *Paris Concert* (Crescendo)
Sammy Davis, Jr.; *Hey There-At His Dynamite Greatest* (MCA)

Oo-Wee
Sasm "The Man" Taylor; *Blues Masters-#13-New York City Blues-C* (Rhino)

Oo-Wee Baby
Ivy Tones; *Doo-Wop Era-Harlem, New York-40 Hits-C* (Collectables)

Papa-Oom-Mow-Mow
Rivingtons; *Cruisin'-1962-C*.....................................(Increase)
EMI Legends Of Rock & Roll-24 Greatest Hits-C ....(EMI)
In The Still Of The Night.....................................(Capitol)
Kahuna Classics-A Collection Of Surf Music-C...............(K-Tel)
Monster Summer Hits-Wild Surf-C.......................(Capitol)

Plop, Plop, Fizz, Fizz (Alka-Seltzer)
Original Soundtrack; *TeeVee Toons-The Commercials-#1-C*..........(TVT)

Polly-Wolly-Doodle
Leon Redbone; *Live!*...(Pair)
On The Track..(Warner Bros.)
Mance Lipscomb; *Mance Lipscomb-Vol. 3-Texas Songster In A Live Performance*.....................................(Arhoolie)
Pete Seeger/Woody Guthrie/Cisco Houston; *Lonesome Valley*.....................................(Smithsonian Folkways)

Pop Pop Pop-Pie
Sherrys; *Golden Age Of American Rock-C*......................(Ace)

Rackety Coo
Sam Ash; *Music From The New York Stage (1890-1920)-#3-1913-1917-C*.....................................(Pearl)

Rama Lama Ding Dong
Edsels; *Legends Of Doo-Wop-#2-C*...............(Juke Box Treasures)
Rubber Biscuits & Rama Lama Ding Dong: Doo Wop For Kids-C.....................................(Kid Rhino/Rhino 4 Kids)

Razzamatazz
Quincy Jones; *Best Of Quincy Jones-#2*......................(A&M)
Quincy Jones-Classics-#3 ....(A&M)
The Dude ....(A&M)

Razzle Dazzle
Bill Haley & His Comets; *Bill Haley & His Comets*..........(Everest)
Bill Haley & His Comets' Greatest Hits...................(MCA)
Bill Haley & His Comets' Greatest Hits.................(Everest)
Bill Haley & His Comets-Golden Hits....................(MCA)
Rockin' & Rollin'......................................(Accord)

Re-Doo-Wopp-Little Star
Tokens; *Re-Doo-Wopp-Little Star*............................(RCA)

Riff Raff
AC/DC; *If You Want Blood You've Got It* ....(Atlantic)
Powerage..(Atlantic)

Riki Tiki Tavi
Donovan; *Donovan's Greatest Hits*.............................(Epic)

Ring-A-Ling-A-Ling
Isley Brothers; *Shout* ....(Collectables)

Rock And Roll, Hoochie Koo
Edgar Winter's White Trash; *Roadwork* ....(Epic)
Johnny Winter; *Johnny Winter And*.......................(Columbia)
Rock Classics-C.......................................(K-Tel)
Johnny Winter & Rick Derringer; *Metal Age-Roots Of Metal-C*...(Rhino)
Rick Derringer; *All American Boy* ....(Blue Sky)
Legends Of Rock Guitar-'70s-C.........................(Rhino)
Super Hits Of The '70s-Have A Nice Day-#12-C...........(Rhino)

Roly Poly
Asleep At The Wheel; *Western Standard Time* ....(Epic)
Bob Wills & His Texas Playboys; *Bob Wills & His Texas Playboys-Anthology 1935-1973*.....................................(Rhino)
Dixie Chicks & Asleep At The Wheel; *Ride With Bob-C* ..(DreamWorks/SKG)
Hank Williams; *I Ain't Got Nothin' But Time-1946-1947*..........(Polydor)
Joey Dee & the Starliters; *Hey Let's Twist! Best Of Joey Dee & The Starliters* ....(Rhino)

Roly Poly
Terence Trent D'Arby; *Neither Fish Nor Flesh*.............(Columbia)

Rootie Tootie
Hank Williams; *Lovesick Blues* ....(Polydor)

Rooty Toot Toot
John Cougar Mellencamp; *The Lonesome Jubilee*............(Mercury)

Rooty Toot Toot For The Moon
Greg Brown; *All-Ears Review-#3-Songwriters For The '90s-C*.....................................(Really Outstanding Music)

Rubber Biscuit
Blues Brothers; *Best Of The Blues Brothers* ....(Atlantic)
Briefcase Full Of Blues................................(Atlantic)

Say La La
Pieces Of A Dream; *45-#50038*.........................(Manhattan)

Scooba Doo
Moses Rascoe; *Blues*..................................(Flying Fish)

Sha La La La Lee
Small Faces; *History Of British Rock-#6-C*.................(Rhino)

Sha La La Means I Love You
Barry White; *The Man*..................................(Mercury)

Sha-La-La
Manfred Mann; *History Of British Rock-#3-C* ....(Rhino)
Shirelles; *Scepter Records Story-C*.....................(Capricorn)
Shirelles-Anthology 1959-1964 ....(Rhino)

Sha-La-La (Make Me Happy)
Al Green; *Al Green Explores Your Mind*.....................(Motown)
Al Green's Greatest Hits-#2 ....(Motown)
Tokyo...Live ....(Right Stuff)

Shama Lama Ding Dong
Otis Day & The Knights; *Shout* ....(MCA)

ST/Animal House......................................(MCA)

Shang A Lang
Bay City Rollers; *Bay City Rollers*.......................(Arista)

Shazam
Duane Eddy; *Twang Thang-The Duane Eddy Anthology*..........(Rhino)

Sh-Boom
Chords; *Atlantic Rhythm & Blues 1947-1974-#2 (1952-1955)-C* .....(Atlantic)
Crew-Cuts; *Partytime '50s-C*............................(Priority)
Stan Freberg; *Capitol Collectors Series-Stan Freberg*..........(Capitol)

She Bop
Cyndi Lauper; *Music For The Miracle-C*..........(Epic Portrait Assoc.)
She's So Unusual......................................(Portrait)

She Say (Oom Dooby Doom)
Diamonds; *Best Of The Diamonds* ....(Rhino)

Sheela-Na-Gig
PJ Harvey; *Dry*...(Indigo)

She's A Hum Dum Dinger
Jimmie Davis; *The Roots Of Rap-Classic Recordings-C* ....(Yazoo)

Shim Sham Shimmy
Dorsey Brothers; *Best Of The Big Bands-C* ....(Columbia)
I'm Getting Sentimental Over You........................(Pro-Arte)

Shim, Sham Shimmy On The St. Louis Blues
Dizzy Gillespie; *Best Of Dizzy Gillespie* ....(Pablo)

Shimmy Shimmy Ko Ko Bop
Little Anthony And The Imperials; *American Graffiti-#2-C* ....(MCA)
Best Of Little Anthony And The Imperials.................(Rhino)
Forever Yours ....(Roulette)

Shipoopi
Original Broadway Cast; *The Music Man* ....(Angel)
Original Cast; *The Music Man* ....(Gold Rush)

Shoo Be Doo
Blue Riddim Band; *Restless Spirit* ....(Flying Fish)
Cars; *Candy-O*...(Elektra)

Shoo Be Doo Be Doo Da Day
Michael Jackson; *Ben*..................................(Motown)
Stevie Wonder; *For Once In My Life* ....(Motown)
Good Feeling Music Of The Big Chill Generation-#1-C.........(Motown)
Looking Back....(Motown)
Stevie Wonder-20 Classic Hits ....(Motown)
Stevie Wonder's Greatest Hits-#2 ....(Motown)

Shoo Shoo Baby
Andrews Sisters; *Capitol Collectors Series-The Andrews Sisters* ......(Capitol)
Sentimental Journey: Capitol's Great Ladies Of Song-C ....(Gold Rush)

Shoo Shoo Boogiesboo
Big Joe Turner; *Blues Boss Live*.......................(Intermedia)

Shoo Shoo Wah
World; *Break The Silence.*...............................(Elektra)

Shoop
Salt-N-Pepa; *Very Necessary* ....(Next Plateau/London/Island)

Shoop Shoop, Diddy Wop, Cumma Cumma
Monte Video & The Cassettes; *Monte Video* ....(Geffen)

Shoorah Shoorah
Allen Toussaint; *New Orleans Jazz-C*....................(Arhoolie)
Betty Wright; *Get Down Tonight! Best Of T.K. Records-C* ....(Rhino)
Phoebe Snow; *Rock Away*.................................(Mirage)

Shout Bamalama
Mickey Murray; *Jewels-#2-C*.....................(SSS International)
Soul Gold-#1 ....(SSS International)
Wet Willie; *Southern Rock*.............................(K-Tel)
Wet Willie's Greatest Hits............................(Polydor)

Shu Ba Da Du Ma Ma Ma Ma
Steve Miller Band; *Best Of Steve Miller 1968-1973*.........(Capitol)
Joker...(Capitol)

Slick Titty Boom
Elvin Bishop; *Struttin' My Stuff* ....(Capricorn)

Snookeroo
Ringo Starr; *Goodnight Vienna* ....(Capitol)

Solar Prestige A Gammon
Elton John; *Caribou* ....(Rocket)

Sookie Sookie
Steppenwolf; *Live Steppenwolf* ....(MCA)
Steppenwolf. ....(MCA)
Steppenwolf Gold/Their Great Hits.......................(MCA)
Steppenwolf-16 Greatest Hits ....(MCA)

Space Cowboy (Yippie-Yi-Yay)
'N Sync featuring Lisa "Left Eye" Lopes; *No Strings Attached* ....(Jive)

Supercalifragilisticexpialidocious
Julie Andrews; *ST/Mary Poppins*..........................(Disney)

Ta-Ra-Ra-Boom-De-Ay
Walt Solek; *16 Most Requested Polkas-C*..................(Legacy)

Tenderoni
Leon Haywood; *45-#99708* ....(Modern)

Te-Ni-Nee-Ni-Nu
Slim Harpo; *Best Of Slim Harpo* ....(Rhino)

Thing, The
Phil Harris; *The Thing About Phil Harris*.................(Living Era)

Tico Tico
Andrews Sisters; *Best Of The Andrews Sisters* ....(MCA)

Desi Arnaz & Rene Touzet; *Best Of Desi Arnaz-The Mambo King* . . . . . . (RCA)
Stan Kenton & His Orchestra; *Live At Redlands University* . . . . (Creative World)
Ting-A-Ling
Shabba Ranks; *X-Tra Naked*. . . . .(Epic)
Ting-A-Ling
Clovers; *Down In The Alley* . . . . (Rhino)
Tom's Diner
D.N.A. Featuring Suzanne Vega; *Solitude Standing* . . . . (A&M)
Tom's Album . . . . (A&M)
Too Ra Loo Ra Loo Ral
Band; *The Last Waltz* . . . .(Warner Bros.)
Bing Crosby; *Best Of Bing Crosby* . . . .(MCA)
When Irish Eyes Are Smiling . . . .(MCA)
Toot Toot Tootsie (Goo'Bye)
Al Jolson; *Al Jolson-Best Of The Decca Years* . . . .(MCA)
Best Of Al Jolson . . . .(MCA)
Liza Minnelli; *Liza Minnelli-At Carnegie Hall*. . . . . (Telarc)
Tra La La La La
Ike & Tina Turner; *Ike & Tina Turner-Golden Classics* . . . . (Collectables)
Proud Mary-Best Of Ike & Tina Turner. . . . .(EMI)
Workin' It Out . . . . (Pair)
Tra La La La Suzy
Dean & Jean; *22 Leaders Of The Pack-#1-C* . . . . (Laurie)
Classic Old & Gold-C . . . . (Laurie)
Tutti Frutti
Elvis Presley; *Elvis Presley* . . . . (RCA)
Rocker . . . . (RCA)
Little Richard; *Greatest Hits Recorded Live* . . . .(Epic)
Little Richard . . . . (Specialty)
Little Richard-18 Greatest Hits . . . . (Rhino)
More American Graffiti-C . . . .(MCA)
This Is How It All Began-#2-C . . . . (Specialty)
Tribute To Black Entertainers-C . . . . (Columbia)
Queen; *Live At Wembley '86* . . . . (Hollywood)
Tweedlee Dee
Ike & Tina Turner; *Ike & Tina Turner's Greatest Hits-#3* . . . . (Saja)
LaVern Baker; *20 Million-Dollar Memories-#1-C* . . . . (Laurie)
Billboard Top Rock 'N' Roll Hits-1955-C . . . . (Rhino)
Ugg-a-Wugg
Original Cast; *Peter Pan-The 1954 Broadway Production* . . . .(RCA Victor)
Uhh Ahh
Boyz II Men; *Cooleyhighharmony* . . . . (Motown)
Um, Um, Um, Um, Um, Um (Curious Mind)
Major Lance; *Seems Like Yesterday-#5-Mid '60s-C* . . . . (K-Tel)
Wah Diddy Wah
Little David & The Harps; *Vocal Group Album* . . . . (Savoy)
Wang Dang Doodle
Koko Taylor; *Atlantic Blues-Chicago-C* . . . . (Atlantic)
Best Blues Album In The World...Ever!-C. . . . . (Virgin)
Greatest Blues Legends-C . . . .(MCA Special Prod.)
Koko Taylor . . . . (Chess)
Superblues-#1-All-Time Classic Blues-C . . . . (Stax)
Savoy Brown; *Best Of Savoy Brown-London Collector* . . . . (London)
Live & Kickin' . . . . (Crescendo)
Street Corner Talking . . . . (Deram)
Willie Dixon; *Blues Deluxe* . . . . (Alligator)
Wang Dang Sweet Poontang
Ted Nugent; *Cat Scratch Fever* . . . .(Epic)
Double Live Gonzo . . . .(Epic)
Wang Wang Blues
Benny Goodman; *Small Groups-1941-1945* . . . . (Columbia)
Fletcher Henderson & The Dixie Stompers; *1925-1928*. . . . . . . (Disques Swing)
Who Put The Bomp (In The Bomp, Bomp, Bomp)
Barry Mann; *Goofy Greats-C* . . . . (K-Tel)
Sixties Rule! Chapter Two-C . . . . (One Way)
Whoopee Ti Yi Yo
Burl Ives; *Best Of Burl Ives*. . . . .(MCA)
David Bromberg; *How Late'll Ya Play 'Til?* . . . . (Fantasy)
Roy Rogers & Sons Of The Pioneers; *Roy Rogers & Sons Of The
Pioneers* . . . . (Varese Sarabande)
Woody Guthrie & Cisco Houston; *Cowboy Songs On
Folkways-C*. . . . . (Smithsonian Folkways)
Witch Doctor
Chipmunks; *Rockin' Through The Decades*. . . . .(EMI)
David Seville; *Dr. Demento: 20th Anniversary Collection-C* . . . . . . (Rhino)
Wacky Weirdos-C . . . . (K-Tel)
Wooly Bully
Sam The Sham and The Pharaohs; *Best Of Sam The Sham and The
Pharaohs*. . . . . (Polydor)
Billboard Top Rock 'N' Roll Hits-1965-C . . . . (Rhino)
Cruisin'-1965-C . . . . (Increase)
Oldies But Goodies-#10-C . . . . (Original Sound)
ST/Full Metal Jacket . . . .(Warner Bros.)
Smithereens; *ST/Encino Man* . . . . (Hollywood)
Wynkin', Blinkin' & Nod
Doobie Brothers; *In Harmony-Sesame Street-C* . . . . (Columbia)
Irish Rovers; *Irish Rovers' Greatest Hits* . . . .(MCA)
Simon Sisters; *Troubadours Of The Folk Era-#2-C* . . . . (Rhino)

Ya Ba Da Ba Do (So Are You)
George Jones; *One Woman Man* . . . .(Epic)
Ya Ya
Ike & Tina Turner; *Ike & Tina Turner's Greatest Hits* . . . .(Saja)
John Lennon; *Rock 'N' Roll* . . . . (Capitol)
Walls And Bridges . . . . (Capitol)
Lee Dorsey; *Cruisin'-1961-C* . . . . (Increase)
ST/American Graffiti . . . .(MCA)
ST/The Wanderers . . . .(Warner Bros.)
Rufus Thomas; *Walking The Dog* . . . . (Atlantic)
Steve Miller; *Born 2 B Blue* . . . . (Gold Rush)
Yaaka, Hoola, Hickey Doola
Al Jolson; *Music From The New York Stage (1890-1920)-#3-1913-
1917-C* . . . . (Pearl)
Yale Boola
All-Star Inter-Conference Band; *College Marches At Halftime* . . . . . . (Alshire)
You Should Be Mine (The Woo Woo Song)
Jeffrey Osborne; *Emotional* . . . . (A&M)
Zing Zing Zing
Dells; *Oh, What A Night* . . . . (Vee-Jay)
Zip A Dee Doo Dah
Barbara Cook; *Disney Album* . . . . (Disney)
Bing Crosby; *The Radio Years: 25 Songs* . . . .(Crescendo)
Jackson 5; *Motown Legends-Jackson 5* . . . . (Motown)
Johnny Mercer; *Capitol Collectors Series-Johnny Mercer* . . . . (Capitol)
Kelly Stevens & Carnival; *When You Wish Upon A Star* . . . . (American Variety)
Mormon Tabernacle Choir & Columbia Symphony Orchestra; *When You
Wish Upon A Star-A Tribute To Walt Disney*. . . . . (CBS Masterworks)
Ric Ocasek; *Simply Mad About The Mouse-C*. . . . . (Columbia)
Steve Miller; *Born 2 B Blue*. . . . . (Gold Rush)
Zip Boom
Supremes; *Spotlight On Old Town Records-#4-C* . . . . (Collectables)

NUCLEAR ENERGY, Nuclear War, Nuclear Weapons, Radioactive

See Also: ENERGY, NATURE, PEACE, POLITICS: POLITICAL CLASSICS, PROTEST, WAR

Atom Tan
Clash; *Combat Rock* . . . .(Epic)
Atomic
Blondie; *Best Of Blondie* . . . . (Chrysalis)
Eat To The Beat . . . . (Chrysalis)
Atomic Bombs
Kix; *Kix* . . . .(Atlantic)
Atomic Cafe
Motels; *Motels*. . . . . (Capitol)
Atomic Dog
George Clinton; *Best Of George Clinton* . . . . (Capitol)
Computer Games . . . . (Capitol)
Atomic Flash Deluxe
Nina Hagen; *In Ekstasy* . . . . (Columbia)
Atomic Funk
Undisputed Truth; *Smokin'* . . . . (Whitfield)
Atomic Funk
Nytro; *Nytro* . . . . (Whitfield)
Atomic Power
Uncle Tupelo; *March 16-20 1992* . . . . (Rockville)
Atomic Punk
Van Halen; *Van Halen*. . . . . (Warner Bros.)
Atomic Tests
John Trubee & The Ugly Janitors Of America; *Communists Are Coming To
Kill Us* . . . . (Enigma)
Atomic Waste
Peter Alsop; *Draw The Line* . . . . (Flying Fish)
Attack Of The Radioactive Hamsters
"Weird Al" Yankovic; *ST/UHF & Other Stuff* . . . .(Scotti Bros.)
Baby's Got A Neutron Bomb
Army Of Lovers; *Army Of Lovers* . . . .(Giant)
Crown Of Creation
Jefferson Airplane; *2400 Fulton Street-An Anthology*. . . . . (RCA)
30 Seconds Over Winterland . . . . (RCA)
Crown Of Creation . . . . (RCA)
The Worst Of Jefferson Airplane . . . . (RCA)
Dancing On Ground Zero
Carol Nethen; *Narada Mystique Sampler One-C* . . . . (Narada)
View From The Bridge . . . . (Narada)
Do You Want My Job
Little Village; *Little Village*. . . . . (Reprise)
Enola Gay
Orchestral Manoeuvres In The Dark; *in the dark/the best of OMD* . . . . . (A&M)
Organization . . . .(Virgin)
ST/Urgh! A Music War . . . . (A&M)
Eve Of Destruction
Barry McGuire; *Billboard Top Rock 'N' Roll Hits-1965-C* . . . . (Rhino)

Cruisin'-1965-C . . . . (Increase)
Good Feeling Music Of The Big Chill Generation-#3-C . . . . (Motown)
Songs Of Protest-C . . . . (Rhino)
Vintage Music-#9 & 10-C . . . . (MCA)
Dickies; *Great Dictations (Definitive Collection)* . . . . (A&M)
Incredible Shrinking Dickies . . . . (A&M)
Turtles; *Turtle Wax-Best Of The Turtles-#2* . . . . (Rhino)
Turtlesized . . . . (Rhino)

Face The Fire
Dan Fogelberg; *Phoenix* . . . . (Full Moon)

Ground Zero Brooklyn
Carnivore; *Retaliation* . . . . (Roadrunner)

Hard Rain's Gonna Fall
Bob Dylan; *Bob Dylan's Greatest Hits-#2* . . . . (Columbia)
Concert For Bangladesh-C . . . . (Capitol)
Freewheelin' . . . . (Columbia)
Bryan Ferry; *Street Life-20 Great Hits* . . . . (Reprise)
These Foolish Things . . . . (Reprise)
Edie Brickell & New Bohemians; *ST/Born On The Fourth Of July* . . . . . . (MCA)
Joan Baez; *Farewell Angelina* . . . . (Vanguard)
The First 10 Years . . . . (Vanguard)

Hiroshima, Nagasaki Russian Roulette
Jim Page; *Best Of Broadside 1962-1968: Anthems Of The American
Underground From The Pages Of Broadside
Magazine-C* . . . . (Smithsonian Folkways)

It's A Mistake
Men At Work; *Cargo* . . . . (Columbia)

Masters Of War
Bob Dylan; *Biograph* . . . . (Columbia)
Freewheelin' . . . . (Columbia)
Real Live . . . . (Columbia)

Morning Dew
Bonnie Dobson; *Troubadours Of The Folk Era-#1-C* . . . . (Rhino)
Grateful Dead; *Europe '72* . . . . (Warner Bros.)

Neutron Bomb
Arlo Guthrie & Pete Seeger; *Precious Friend* . . . . (Warner Bros.)
Weirdos; *Weird World-#1* . . . . (Frontier)

Neutron Dance
Pointer Sisters; *Break Out* . . . . (Planet)
Pointer Sisters' Greatest Hits . . . . (RCA)
ST/Beverly Hills Cop . . . . (MCA)

New Frontier
Donald Fagen; *The Nightfly* . . . . (Warner Bros.)

Nuclear Apathy
Crack The Sky; *Safety In Numbers* . . . . (Lifesong)

Nuclear Attack
Gary Moore; *Dirty Fingers* . . . . (Roadracer)
Rockin' Every Night-Live In Japan . . . . (Virgin)
Greg Lake; *Greg Lake* . . . . (Chrysalis)

Nuclear Burn
Brand X; *Unorthodox Behaviour* . . . . (Blue Plate)

Nuclear Device
Stranglers; *Stranglers IV* . . . . (I.R.S.)

Nuclear Funeral
D.I.; *Team Goon* . . . . (Triple X Entert.)

Nuclear Hayride
Johnny J. & The Hitmen; *Nuclear Hayride* . . . . (Great Southern)

Nuclear Mishap
Lenny Hat; *Place In The Sun* . . . . (Terra Firma)

Nuclear War
Brian Ritchie; *The Blend* . . . . (SST)

Nuclear War
Jimmy Cliff; *Cliff Hanger* . . . . (Columbia)

Nuclear Waste
Tuff Darts; *Tuff Darts* . . . . (Sire)

Oh Lord Don't Let Them Drop That...
Charles Mingus; *Oh Yeah-Jazzlore-#38* . . . . (Atlantic)

Party At Ground Zero
Fishbone; *Fishbone* . . . . (Columbia)
Richard Blade's Flashback Favorites-C . . . . (Oglio)

Plutonium Is Forever
John Hall; *ST/No Nukes-Muse Concerts* . . . . (Asylum)

Political Science
Randy Newman; *Sail Away* . . . . (Reprise)

Power
John Hall; *Power* . . . . (Columbia)
John Hall/Doobie Brothers/James Taylor; *No Nukes* . . . . (Asylum)

Radiation Day
Pandemonium; *Heavy Metal Soldiers* . . . . (Metal Blade)

Radiation Ranch
Brian Setzer; *Knife Feels Like Justice* . . . . (EMI)

Radiation Vibe
Fountains Of Wayne; *Fountains Of Wayne* . . . . (Tag/Atlantic)

Radioactive
Gene Simmons; *Gene Simmons* . . . . (Casablanca)

Radioactive
Firm; *Firm* . . . . (Atlantic)

Radium Rain
Bruce Cockburn; *Big Circumstance* . . . . (Columbia)

Roulette
Bruce Springsteen; *Tracks* . . . . (Columbia)

Russians
Sting; *Dream Of The Blue Turtles* . . . . (A&M)
Fields Of Gold-The Best Of Sting 1984-1994 . . . . (A&M)

S.O.S. Fire In The Sky
Deodato; *Motion* . . . . (Warner Bros.)

Shades Of '45
Gary O'; *Strange Behavior* . . . . (RCA)

Thermonuclear War
Carnivore; *Carnivore* . . . . (Roadrunner)

Three Mile Island
Pinkard & Bowden; *Writers In Disguise* . . . . (Warner Bros.)

Three Mile Smile
Aerosmith; *Night In The Ruts* . . . . (Columbia)
Pandora's Box . . . . (Columbia)

Uranium Rock
Cramps; *Bad Music For Bad People* . . . . (I.R.S.)

We Got The Neutron Bombs
Weirdos; *D.I.Y.-#6-L.A. Scene-1976-1979-C* . . . . (Rhino)

We Work The Black Seam
Sting; *Bring On The Night* . . . . (A&M)
Dream Of The Blue Turtles . . . . (A&M)

What Have They Done To The Rain
Malvina Reynolds; *Best Of Broadside 1962-1968: Anthems Of The
American Underground From The Pages Of Broadside
Magazine-C* . . . . (Smithsonian Folkways)
ST/Dogfight . . . . (Nouveau)
Searchers; *Searchers' Greatest Hits* . . . . (Rhino)

NUMBERS: 1, First, Once

*See Also: AGES (various), BEGINNINGS, COUNTING SONGS,
LONELY, MONTHS & DATES (various), NUMBERS (various),
SOLITUDE, TIME: SPECIFIC*

#1
Nelly; *Soundtrack Single* . . . . (Priority)

#1 Crush
Garbage; *ST/William Shakespeare's Romeo & Juliet* . . . . (Capitol)

#1 Stunna
Big Tymers; *I Got That Work* . . . . (Cash Money/Universal)

...Baby One More Time
Britney Spears; *...Baby One More Time* . . . . (Jive)
Now That's What I Call Music!-#2-C . . . . (Virgin)

1+2<2
Classic Ruins; *D.I.Y.-Mass Ave.-The Boston Scene-1979-1983-C* . . . . . . (Rhino)

1-2-3
Gloria Estefan; *Gloria Estefan's Greatest Hits* . . . . (Epic)
Gloria Estefan and Miami Sound Machine; *Let It Loose* . . . . (Epic)

1-2-3
Len Barry; *24 Of The Grooviest Hits Of All Time! The '60s Ultimate
Collection-#1-C* . . . . (Sundazed Music)

1970 #1 Song Cadillac
Terry Radigan; *Pawnbroker's Daughter* . . . . (Asylum)

1st Of Tha Month
Bone Thugs-N-Harmony; *E. 1999 Eternal* . . . . (Ruthless/Relativity)

2 Become 1
Spice Girls; *Spice* . . . . (Virgin)

A-1 On The Jukebox
Dave Edmunds; *Best Of Dave Edmunds* . . . . (Swan Song)
Tracks On Wax 4 . . . . (Swan Song)

Am I The Only One
Marc Anthony; *Marc Anthony* . . . . (Columbia)

Back At One
Brian McKnight; *Back At One* . . . . (Motown)
Mark Wills; *Permanently* . . . . (Mercury)

Barrel Of A Gun
Depeche Mode; *The Singles-1986-1998* . . . . (Mute/Reprise)
Ultra . . . . (Mute/Reprise)

Be Like That
3 Doors Down; *Better Life* . . . . (Republic/Universal)
Now That's What I Call Music!-#8-C . . . . (Virgin)

Be One Now
Little Feat; *Down On The Farm* . . . . (Warner Bros.)

Beautiful Ones
Mariah Carey; *Butterfly* . . . . (Columbia)

Betcha Can't Cry Just One
David Frizzell & Shelly West; *In Session* . . . . (Viva)

Billie Jean
Michael Jackson; *Thriller* . . . . (Epic)

Billy 1, 2 & 7
Bob Dylan; *ST/Pat Garrett & Billy The Kid* . . . . (Columbia)

Blue Yodel #1
Bob Wills; *Bob Wills-Anthology* . . . . (Sony Music Special Prod.)
Lynyrd Skynyrd; *Best Of The Rest Of Lynyrd Skynyrd* . . . . (MCA)

One More From The Road . . . .(MCA)
Burn One Down
Clint Black; *The Hard Way* . . . . (RCA)
Camera One
Josh Joplin Group; *Useful Music* . . . .(Artemis)
Can't Wait One Minute More
CIV; *Box Presents Big Ones Of Alternative Rock-#1-C* . . . .(Box Tunes)
Set Your Goals . . . . (Lava)
Capital Radio One
Clash; *The Story Of The Clash, Volume 1* . . . .(Epic)
Circle Of One
Oleta Adams; *Circle Of One* . . . .(Fontana)
Cluster One
Pink Floyd; *The Division Bell* . . . .(Columbia)
Computer One
Dear Enemy; *Ransom Notes* . . . . (Capitol)
Cry One More Time
Gram Parsons; *GP/Grievous Angel* . . . . (Reprise)
Gram Parsons/Fallen Angels Live-1973 . . . . (Sierra)
Cry One More Time
J. Geils Band; *Best Of The J. Geils Band* . . . . (Atlantic)
Day Tripper
Beatles; *"Yesterday"...And Today* . . . . (Capitol)
Beatles 1 . . . . (Capitol)
Beatles-Box Set . . . . (Capitol)
Past Masters-Volume Two . . . . (Parlophone)
The Beatles/1962-1966 . . . . (Capitol)
Jimi Hendrix Experience; *Radio One* . . . .(Rykodisc)
Otis Redding; *Dictionary Of Soul* . . . . (Atco)
The Otis Redding Story . . . . (Atlantic)
Sergio Mendes & Brasil '66; *Sergio Mendes & Brasil '66's
Greatest Hits* . . . . (A&M)
Dinner For One Please James
Nat "King" Cole; *Blossom Fell* . . . . (Capitol)
Nat "King" Cole-Gift Set . . . . (Capitol)
Dollar's Worth Of Gasoline
Tom Russell; *Hurricane Season* . . . . (Philo)
Don't Happen Twice
Kenny Chesney; *Kenny Chesney's Greatest Hits* . . . . (BNA)
Early One Morning
Elmore James; *King Of The Slide Guitar* . . . . (Capricorn)
John Lee Hooker; *Jealous* . . . . (Chase Music Group)
Eddie's First Wife
Gretchen Peters; *Gretchen Peters* . . . . (Purple Crayon Prod.)
Ellis Unit One
Steve Earle; *Johnny Too Bad* . . . . (E Squared)
ST/Dead Man Walking . . . . (Columbia)
Every 1's A Winner
Hot Chocolate; *Every 1's A Winner* . . . . (Infinity)
Falling For The First Time
Barenaked Ladies; *Maroon* . . . . (Reprise)
First Day In August
Carole King; *Rhymes & Reasons* . . . . (Legacy)
First Day Of May
James Taylor; *Never Die Young* . . . . (Columbia)
First I Look At The Purse
Contours; *25 Hard-To-Find Motown Classics-#3-C* . . . . (Motown)
Do You Love Me (Now That I Can Dance) . . . . (Motown)
J. Geils Band; *Best Of The J. Geils Band* . . . . (Atlantic)
Full House . . . . (Atlantic)
J. Geils Band . . . . (Atlantic)
First Night
Monica; *The Boy Is Mine* . . . . (Arista)
First Of May
Bee Gees; *Odessa* . . . . (RSO)
First Of May
So; *Horseshoe In The Glove* . . . .(EMI)
First Taste
Fiona Apple; *Tidal* . . . . (Clean Slate/Work)
First Time
Surface; *3 Deep* . . . . (Columbia)
First Time Ever I Saw Your Face
Celine Dion; *All The Way...A Decade Of Song* . . . .(550 Music)
Roberta Flack; *Atlantic Rhythm & Blues 1947-1974-#6 (1966-
1969)-C* . . . . (Atlantic)
Best Of Roberta Flack . . . . (Atlantic)
First Take . . . . (Atlantic)
First Train Heading South
Johnny Horton; *Between The Rails: America's Train Songs-C* . . . . .(Crescendo)
First Train To California
Cryan' Shames; *Best Of The Cryan' Shames* . . . .(Bac-Trac)
First We Take Manhattan
Jennifer Warnes; *Critics Choice-C* . . . .(Cypress)
Famous Blue Raincoat . . . . (Private Music)
Leonard Cohen; *I'm Your Man* . . . . (Columbia)
R.E.M.; *I'm Your Fan-Songs Of Leonard Cohen* . . . . (Atlantic)
First Week, Last Week Carefree
Talking Heads; *'77* . . . . (Sire)

First Year Blues
Hank Williams; *Alone With His Guitar* . . . . (Mercury)
Fool #1
Brenda Lee; *The Brenda Lee Story-Her Greatest Hits* . . . . (MCA)
Joe Stampley/The Uniques; *Joe Stampley-Golden Hits* . . . .(Paula)
Fool #1
Mavericks; *Trampoline* . . . . (MCA)
For Once In My Life
Gladys Knight & The Pips; *Gladys Knight & The Pips-Anthology* . . . . (Motown)
Motown Superstar Series-#13-Gladys Knight & The Pips . . . . . (Motown)
Neither One Of Us . . . . (Motown)
Stevie Wonder; *Motown Story-First 25 Years-C* . . . . (Motown)
Stevie Wonder-Love Songs-20 Classic Hits . . . . (Motown)
Stevie Wonder's Greatest Hits-#2 . . . . (Motown)
Tony Bennett; *Tony Bennett's All-Time Greatest Hits* . . . . (Columbia)
Vikki Carr; *Best Of Vikki Carr* . . . . (EMI)
For Once In Our Lives
Paul Carrack; *Blue Views* . . . . (Ark 21)
For The First Time
Kenny Loggins; *ST/One Fine Day* . . . . (Columbia)
Forever
Mariah Carey; *Daydream* . . . . (Columbia)
Forever More (I'll Be The One)
James Ingram; *Forever More (Love Songs, Hits & Duets)* . . . . . (Private Music)
John Tesh featuring James Ingram; *One World* . . . . (GTS)
Give Me Just One Night (Una Noche)
98 Degrees; *Now That's What I Call Music!-#5-C* . . . .(Virgin)
Revelation . . . . (Universal)
Give Me One More Shot
Alabama; *Alabama's Greatest Hits-#3* . . . . (RCA)
Give Me One Reason
Tracy Chapman; *New Beginning* . . . . (Elektra)
Give One Heart
Linda Ronstadt; *Hasten Down The Wind* . . . .(Asylum)
Grease Megamix
Grease Megamix; *Pure Disco* . . . . (A&M)
Halfway Home Cafe
Ricky Skaggs and Kentucky Thunder; *History Of The Future* . . (Skaggs Family)
Helplessly Hoping
Crosby, Stills & Nash; *Crosby, Stills & Nash* . . . .(Atlantic)
CSN . . . .(Atlantic)
Crosby, Stills, Nash & Young; *So Far* . . . .(Atlantic)
Here In My Heart
Chicago; *The Heart Of Chicago-1967-1997* . . . . (Reprise)
Highway One
B.W. Stevenson; *B.W. Stevenson* . . . . (RCA)
How Do You Tell The One
After 7; *Reflections* . . . .(Virgin)
I Know One
Charley Pride; *Charley Pride-Super Hits* . . . .(RCA)
Garth Brooks; *Garth Brooks* . . . . (Liberty)
Jim Reeves; *Essential Jim Reeves* . . . . (RCA)
I Want To Be The One
Lonestar; *I'm Already There* . . . . (BNA)
I Was The One
Elvis Presley; *Elvis' Golden Records* . . . . (RCA)
If I Could Be With You
Helen Humes; *Ladies Sing The Blues-#2-C* . . . .(Savoy)
Louis Armstrong; *Best Of Louis Armstrong* . . . . (MCA)
Satchmo-Musical Autobiography-#2 . . . . (MCA)
The Louis Armstrong Story-#4 . . . . (Columbia)
If I'd Been The One
38 Special; *Flashback-Best Of 38 Special* . . . . (A&M)
Tour De Force . . . . (A&M)
I'll Always Be Right There
Bryan Adams; *18 Til I Die* . . . . (A&M)
MTV Unplugged-Bryan Adams . . . . (A&M)
I'm A One- Woman Man
George Jones; *Essential George Jones-The Spirit Of Country* . . . . (Legacy)
George Jones-Super Hits . . . . (Epic)
One Woman Man . . . . (Epic)
Who's Gonna Fill Their Shoes . . . . (Epic)
Glen Campbell; *Still Within The Sound Of My Voice* . . . . (MCA)
Johnny Horton; *American Originals-Johnny Horton* . . . . (Columbia)
Honky Tonk Man-The Essential Johnny Horton-1956-1960 . . . . (Legacy)
I'm Holdin' On To Love (To Save My Life)
Shania Twain; *Come On Over* . . . . (Mercury)
I'm Putting All My Eggs In One Basket
Carmen McRae; *Greatest Of Carmen McRae* . . . . (MCA)
Fred Astaire; *Irving Berlin Songbook* . . . . (Verve)
Irving Berlin; *American Songbook Series-Irving
Berlin* . . . . (Smithsonian Collection)
I'm The One
Roberta Flack; *I'm The One* . . . .(Atlantic)
I'm The Only One
Melissa Etheridge; *Yes I Am* . . . . (Island)
Imagine
Diana Ross; *Best Of The Beatles Songs-C* . . . . (Motown)
Diana Ross-Anthology . . . . (Motown)

Touch Me In The Morning .... (Motown)
Joan Baez; *Best Of Joan Baez* .... (A&M)
  Come From The Shadows .... (A&M)
John Lennon; *Lennon* .... (Capitol)
  Live In New York City .... (Capitol)
  ST/Imagine: John Lennon .... (Capitol)
John Lennon & Yoko Ono; *The John Lennon Collection* .... (Capitol)
John Lennon/Plastic Ono Band; *Imagine* .... (Capitol)
  Shaved Fish .... (Capitol)
Neil Young; *America: A Tribute To Heroes-C* .... (Interscope)

Inside My Love
Trina Broussard; *ST/Love Jones* .... (Columbia)

It Takes Two
Marvin Gaye & Kim Weston; *Hitsville USA-The Motown Singles Collection-1959-1971-C* .... (Motown)

It's Been A Long, Long Time
Bing Crosby; *Best Of Bing Crosby* .... (MCA)
Harry James & His Orchestra; *Words & Music Of World War II-C* .... (Columbia)
Harry James & Kitty Kallen; *Best Of The Big Bands-C* .... (Columbia)
Jan Garber & His Orchestra; *Best Of Jan Garber* .... (MCA)
Louis Armstrong; *Hello Dolly! & Other Hits* .... (MCA)

Just Once
David Lee Murphy; *ST/8 Seconds* .... (MCA)

Just Once
James Ingram; *Forever More (Love Songs, Hits & Duets)* .... (Private Music)

Just One Night
McBride & The Ride; *Sacred Ground* .... (MCA)

Just One Of Those Things
Bobby Short; *Loves Cole Porter* .... (Atlantic)
Ella Fitzgerald; *Best Of The Song Books: Love Songs* ...... (Verve)
Frank Sinatra; *Timeless* .... (Pair)
Lena Horne; *American Songbook Series-Cole Porter* .. (Smithsonian Collection)
Lester Lanin; *Best Of The Big Bands-C* .... (Columbia)
Louis Armstrong; *Jazz Masters-#1-Louis Armstrong* .... (Verve)
Peggy Lee; *Peggy Lee Sings For You* .... (Avid)
Sarah Vaughan; *Essential Sarah Vaughan-The Great Songs* ..... (Verve)

Just One Victory
Todd Rundgren; *A Wizard A True Star* .... (Rhino)
  Todd Rundgren-Anthology 1968-1985 .... (Rhino)
Utopia; *Another Live* .... (Rhino)

Key West Intermezzo (I Saw You First)
John Mellencamp; *Mr. Happy Go Lucky* .... (Mercury)

Kiss Off
Violent Femmes; *Violent Femmes* .... (Slash)

Let Me Be The One
Blessid Union Of Souls; *Home* .... (EMI)

Let Me Be The One
Mint Condition; *Definition Of A Band* .... (Perspective/A&M)
  Mint Condition-Collection (1991-1998) .... (Perspective/A&M)

Letters From The Wasteland
Wallflowers; *Breach* .... (Interscope)

Life In One Day
Howard Jones; *Dream Into Action* .... (Elektra)

Life's In One Day
Howard Jones; *Dream Into Action* .... (Elektra)

Like A Virgin
Madonna; *Immaculate Collection* .... (Sire)
  Like A Virgin .... (Sire)
  Royal Box .... (Sire)

Linda Let Me Be The One
Bruce Springsteen; *Tracks* .... (Columbia)

Little Bitty Pretty One
Huey Lewis and the News; *Four Chords & Several Years Ago* .... (Elektra)
Jackson 5; *Jackson 5-16 Greatest Hits* .... (Motown)
  Jackson 5-Anthology .... (Motown)
  Lookin' Through The Windows .... (Motown)
  Motown Legends-Jackson 5 .... (Motown)
  Top 10 With A Bullet-Motown Male Groups-C .... (Motown)
Thurston Harris; *Billboard Top R&B Hits-1957-C* .... (Rhino)
  Collectables Presents The History Of Rock-#2-C ..... (Collectables)

Little White Lie
Sammy Hagar; *Marching To Mars* .... (MCA)

Lookin' After #1
Boomtown Rats; *Boomtown Rats* .... (Mercury)

Looking For The Right One
Stephen Bishop; *Best Of Bish* .... (Rhino)
  Bish .... (MCA)

Looking For The Right One
Art Garfunkel; *Breakaway* .... (Columbia)

Looking Out For Number One
Travis Tritt; *T-R-O-U-B-L-E* .... (Warner Bros.)

Lord Loves The One
George Harrison; *Living In The Material World* .... (Capitol)

Lost Ones
Lauryn Hill; *The Miseducation Of Lauryn Hill* .... (Ruffhouse/Columbia)

Love In The First Degree
Alabama; *Alabama-Live* .... (RCA)
  Alabama's Greatest Hits .... (RCA)

  Feels So Right .... (RCA)
  Nipper's Greatest Hits Of The '80s-C .... (RCA)

Love The One You're With
Crosby, Stills & Nash; *Replay* .... (Atlantic)
Crosby, Stills, Nash & Young; *4 Way Street* .... (Atlantic)
Luther Vandross; *Songs* .... (Epic)
Stephen Stills; *Hit Singles-1958-1977-C* .... (Atlantic)
  Stephen Stills .... (Atlantic)
  Still .... (Atlantic)

Lucky One
Laura Branigan; *Best Of Branigan* .... (Atlantic)
  Self Control .... (Atlantic)

Lucky One
Amy Grant; *House Of Love* .... (A&M)

Lucky One
Alison Krauss & Union Station; *New Favorite* .... (Rounder)

Margie
Cab Calloway; *More Big Band Greatest Hits-C* .... (RCA Victor)
Eddie Cantor; *Eddie Cantor-The Columbia Years: 1922-1940* .... (Legacy)
Jimmy Lunceford; *Big Bands Of The Swinging Years-#2-C* ..... (Collectables)

Memories Are Made Of This
Dean Martin; *Billboard Pop Memories-1955-1959-C* .... (Rhino)
  Dean Martin-Love Songs .... (Ranwood)
  Dean Martin's All Time Greatest Hits .... (Curb)

Monkey Wrench
Foo Fighters; *The Colour And The Shape* .... (Roswell/RCA)

More Pretty Girls Than One
Tom Rush; *Blues Songs & Ballads* .... (Fantasy)
Woody Guthrie; *One Of A Kind* .... (Pair)

Murder Of One
Counting Crows; *August And Everything After* .... (David Geffen Co.)

Murder One
Awesome Dre & The Hardcore Committee; *You Can't Hold Me Back* .... (Priority)

My All
Mariah Carey; *Butterfly* .... (Columbia)
  Mariah Carey-#1's .... (Columbia)
  VH-1 Divas Live-C .... (Epic)

My First Love
Avant; *My Thoughts* .... (MCA)

My First Night Alone Without You
Bonnie Raitt; *Bonnie Raitt-Collection* .... (Warner Bros.)
  Home Plate .... (Warner Bros.)
Jane Olivor; *First Night* .... (Columbia)

My First Night Without You
Cyndi Lauper; *Night To Remember* .... (Epic)

My One And Only Heart
Perry Como; *Sing Just For You* .... (RCA)

My One True Friend
Bette Midler; *Bathhouse Betty* .... (Warner Bros.)

Nashville 1 A.M.
Harvey Mandel; *Cristo Redentor* .... (Editions E.G.)

Natural One
Folk Implosion; *MTV Best Of The Buzz Bin-#2-C* .... (Mammoth)
  ST/Kids .... (London)

Never Going Back Again
Fleetwood Mac; *25 Years-The Chain* .... (Warner Bros.)
  Fleetwood Mac Live .... (Warner Bros.)
  Rumours .... (Warner Bros.)
Matchbox Twenty; *Legacy-A Tribute To Fleetwood Mac's Rumours-C* ...(Lava)

Night And Day
Bette Midler; *Some People's Lives* .... (Atlantic)
Billie Holiday; *Legacy Box-1933-1958* .... (Columbia)
Ella Fitzgerald; *Cole Porter Songbook* .... (Verve)
Frank Sinatra; *Nipper's Greatest Hits Of The '40s-#1-C* .... (RCA)
  Sinatra & Strings .... (Reprise)
  Sinatra Reprise-The Very Good Years .... (Reprise)
  Sinatra: A Man And His Music .... (Reprise)
  The Capitol Years .... (Capitol)
  The Reprise Collection .... (Reprise)
Fred Astaire; *Cheek To Cheek* .... (Pro-Arte)
  Steppin' Out-Astaire Sings .... (Verve)
Tony Bennett; *Perfectly Frank* .... (Columbia)
U2; *Red Hot + Blue-Tribute To Cole Porter-C* .... (Chrysalis)

No One Is To Blame
Howard Jones; *Best Of Howard Jones 1983-1993* .... (Elektra)
  Dream Into Action .... (Elektra)

Nobody's Got The Gun
Mark Knopfler; *Golden Heart* .... (Warner Bros.)

Not The Only One
Bonnie Raitt; *Luck Of The Draw* .... (Capitol)

On The One For Fun
Dazz Band; *Dazz Band's Greatest Hits* .... (Motown)

Once A Day
Connie Smith; *Billboard Top Country Hits-1964-C* .... (Rhino)
  Connie Smith-Super Hits .... (RCA)
  Essential Connie Smith .... (RCA)

Once In A Lifetime
Michael Bolton; *ST/Only You* .... (Columbia)

Once-A-Year Day!
Original Cast; *ST/Pajama Game* . . . . (Collectables)
One
Metallica; *...And Justice For All* . . . . (Elektra)
One
Creed; *My Own Prison* . . . . (Wind-up)
One
Nilsson; *Aerial Ballet* . . . . (RCA)
Everybody's Talkin': The Encore Collection . . . . (BMG Special Prod.)
Nilsson-All-Time Greatest Hits . . . . (RCA)
Three Dog Night; *Best Of Three Dog Night* . . . . (MCA)
Captured Live At The Forum . . . . (MCA)
Joy To The World-Greatest Hits . . . . (MCA)
One
George Jones & Tammy Wynette; *George Jones Collection* . . . . (MCA)
Grand Ole Opry-75 Years-#2-C . . . . (MCA)
One . . . . (MCA)
One
Original Broadway Cast; *A Chorus Line* . . . . (Columbia)
One
U2; *Achtung Baby* . . . . (Island)
One
Bee Gees; *One* . . . . (Warner Bros.)
One After 909
Beatles; *Let It Be* . . . . (Capitol)
The Beatles-Anthology-#1 . . . . (Capitol)
One And One Does Not Make Three
Ides Of March; *Ideology* . . . . (Sundazed Music)
One And One Is Five
Ben Aiken; *Ben Aiken & Friends* . . . . (Collectables)
Delfonics; *Forever New* . . . . (Volt)
One And One Make Two
Sesame Street; *Numbers* . . . . (Sony Wonder)
One And Only Man
Steve Winwood; *Refugees Of The Heart* . . . . (Virgin)
One Angel
Stir; *Stir* . . . . (Aware/C2/Columbia)
One Angry Dwarf And 200 Solemn Faces
Ben Folds Five; *Whatever And Ever Amen* . . . . (Caroline/550)
One Bad Apple
Osmonds; *Billboard Top Rock 'N' Roll Hits-1971-C* . . . . (Rhino)
One Bad Elephant
Brian Slawson; *Distant Drums* . . . . (Columbia)
One Belief Away
Bonnie Raitt; *Fundamental* . . . . (Capitol)
One Big Love
Emmylou Harris; *Red Dirt Girl* . . . . (Nonesuch)
Patty Griffin; *Flaming Red* . . . . (A&M)
One Bourbon One Scotch One Beer
George Thorogood & The Destroyers; *George Thorogood & The Destroyers* . . . . (Rounder)
George Thorogood & The Destroyers-Live . . . . (EMI)
John Lee Hooker; *Best Of Chess Blues-C* . . . . (Chess)
John Lee Hooker-The Ultimate Collection-1948-1990 . . . . (Rhino)
Real Folk Blues-C . . . . (Chess)
One Boy, One Girl
Collin Raye; *Best Of Collin Raye-Direct Hits* . . . . (Epic)
I Think About You . . . . (Epic)
One Broken Heart For Sale
Elvis Presley; *Collector's Gold* . . . . (RCA)
It Happened At The World's Fair . . . . (RCA)
Worldwide 50 Gold Award Hits, Vol. 1, Parts 1 & 2 . . . . (RCA)
One Brown Mouse
Jethro Tull; *Bursting Out* . . . . (Chrysalis)
Heavy Horses . . . . (Chrysalis)
One By One
Enya; *A Day Without Rain* . . . . (Reprise)
One Chain
Santana; *Inner Secrets* . . . . (Columbia)
One Chain
Doobie Brothers; *Cycles* . . . . (Warner Bros.)
One Child China
Ecoteur; *Decorated Life* . . . . (Dali)
One Cup Of Coffee
Bob Marley & The Wailers; *Songs Of Freedom* . . . . (Tuff Gong)
One Day At A Time
John Lennon; *Lennon* . . . . (Capitol)
Mind Games . . . . (Capitol)
One Day At A Time
Cristy Lane; *Cristy Lane-At Her Best* . . . . (EMI)
One Day At A Time
Willie Nelson; *Me & Paul* . . . . (Columbia)
Willie . . . . (RCA)
Willie & Family Live . . . . (Columbia)
One Emotion
Clash; *Clash On Broadway* . . . . (Legacy)
One Emotion
Clint Black; *One Emotion* . . . . (RCA)

One Fine Day
Carpenters; *From The Top* . . . . (A&M)
Now & Then . . . . (A&M)
Chiffons; *Best Of The Chiffons* . . . . (Laurie)
Chiffons-Golden Classics . . . . (Collectables)
Collectables Presents The History Of Rock-#9-C . . . . (Collectables)
Oldies But Goodies-#12-C . . . . (Original Sound)
One Good Woman
Billy Squier; *Emotions In Motion* . . . . (Capitol)
One Headlight
Wallflowers; *Bringing Down The Horse* . . . . (Interscope)
One Hit (To The Body)
Rolling Stones; *Dirty Work* . . . . (Virgin)
One Hit Wonder
Everclear; *So Much For The Afterglow* . . . . (Capitol)
One Honest Heart
Reba McEntire; *If You See Him* . . . . (MCA)
Reba McEntire's Greatest Hits-#3: I'm A Survivor . . . . (MCA)
One Horse Town
Bobby Bland; *Introspective Of The Early Years* . . . . (MCA)
Touch Of The Blues . . . . (MCA)
One Horse Town
Elton John; *Blue Moves* . . . . (MCA)
One Horse Town
David Frishberg; *Live At Vine Street* . . . . (Original Jazz Classics)
One Horse Town
Rembrandts; *Untitled* . . . . (Atco)
One Hour With You
Nelson Eddy; *When I'm Calling You* . . . . (Living Era)
One In A Million
Aaliyah; *One In A Million* . . . . (BlackGround Enterp./Atlantic)
One In A Million
Platters; *Magic Touch-An Anthology* . . . . (Mercury)
One In The Sun
Lynyrd Skynyrd; *Lynyrd Skynyrd-Legend* . . . . (MCA)
Steve Gaines; *Rockin' Southern Style-C* . . . . (MCA Special Prod.)
One Is A Lonely Number
George Jones; *Truckin' On-C* . . . . (Hollywood)
One Jungle
Fixx; *Ink* . . . . (Impact)
One Lane Bridge
Kim Pensyl; *Eyes Of Wonder* . . . . (GRP)
One Less Bell To Answer
5th Dimension; *5th Dimension-Anthology 1967-1973* . . . . (Rhino)
Greatest Hits On Earth . . . . (Arista)
Barbra Streisand; *Barbra Joan Streisand* . . . . (Columbia)
Gladys Knight & The Pips; *Gladys Knight & The Pips-Anthology* . . . . (Motown)
If I Were Your Woman . . . . (Motown)
One Little Coyote
Riders In The Sky; *Harmony Ranch* . . . . (Columbia)
One Lonely Night
REO Speedwagon; *REO Speedwagon-The Hits* . . . . (Epic)
Wheels Are Turnin' . . . . (Epic)
One Love At A Time
Tanya Tucker; *Tanya Tucker's Greatest Hits* . . . . (Liberty)
One Love In My Lifetime
Diana Ross; *Diana Ross* . . . . (Motown)
Diana Ross-Anthology . . . . (Motown)
One Man Army
Our Lady Peace; *Happiness...Is Not A Fish That You Can Catch* . . . . (Columbia)
One Man Band
Moe Bandy; *Moe Bandy's Greatest Hits* . . . . (Curb)
You Haven't Heard The Last Of Me . . . . (MCA)
One Man Band
Roger Daltrey; *Daltrey* . . . . (MCA)
One Man Band
Three Dog Night; *Joy To The World-Greatest Hits* . . . . (MCA)
One Man Woman
Judds; *Judds-Collection 1983-1990* . . . . (RCA)
River Of Time . . . . (RCA)
One Meat Ball
Ry Cooder; *Ry Cooder* . . . . (Reprise)
One Meatball
Roy Bookbinder; *Hillbilly Blues Cats* . . . . (Rounder)
One Million Billionth Of A Millisecond On A Sunday Morning
Flaming Lips; *Oh My Gawd The Flaming Lips* . . . . (Restless)
One Million Lawyers
Tom Paxton; *One Million Lawyers & Other Disasters* . . . . . . (Flying Fish)
One Mint Julep
Clovers; *Down In The Alley* . . . . (Rhino)
Love Potion No. 9 . . . . (EMI)
Ray Charles; *Ray Charles-His Greatest Hits-#1* . . . . (Dunhill Compact Classics)
One Minute Man
Missy ''Misdemeanor'' Elliot; *Miss E...So Addictive* . . . . (Gold Mind/East West/EEG)
One Moment In Time
Whitney Houston; *1984 Olympics Album-C* . . . . (Arista)
Whitney Houston's Greatest Hits . . . . (Arista)

One More Astronaut
I Mother Earth; *Scenery And Fish* . . . . (Capitol)
One More Chance
Notorious B.I.G.; *Ready To Die* . . . . (Bad Boy/Arista)
One More Cup Of Coffee
Bob Dylan; *Bob Dylan At Budokan* . . . . (Columbia)
Desire . . . . (Columbia)
One More Day
Diamond Rio; *One More Day* . . . . (Arista)
One More For The Rodeo
UFO; *Obsession* . . . . (Chrysalis)
One More Goodtime Band In Texas
Leon Rausch; *Rausch Touch* . . . . (Southland)
One More Kiss
Original Broadway Cast; *Follies* . . . . (Capitol)
Follies . . . . (Capitol)
One More Kiss
Paul McCartney; *Paul McCartney-Gift Set* . . . . (Capitol)
One More Last Chance
Vince Gill; *I Still Believe In You* . . . . (MCA)
The Ultimate Country Party-C . . . . (Arista)
Vince Gill-Souvenirs . . . . (MCA)
One More Mile
Clarence "Gatemouth" Brown; *One More Mile* . . . . (Rounder)
Paul Butterfield Blues Band; *Golden Butter* . . . . (Elektra)
One More Night
Phil Collins; *No Jacket Required* . . . . (Atlantic)
Serious Hits...Live! . . . . (Atlantic)
One More Night
Stephen Bishop; *Best Of Bish* . . . . (Rhino)
One More Night
Corbin/Hanner Band; *Black & White Photograph* . . . . (Mercury)
One More Night
Bobby Brown; *Bobby* . . . . (MCA)
One More Night
Fleetwood Mac; *Fleetwood Mac Live* . . . . (Warner Bros.)
One More Night
Bob Dylan; *Nashville Skyline* . . . . (Columbia)
One More Night
Barbra Streisand; *Songbird* . . . . (Columbia)
One More River
Soul Stirrers featuring Sam Cooke; *The Specialty Story* . . . . (Specialty)
One More River
Alan Parsons Project; *Pyramid* . . . . (Arista)
One More River
Max Carl And Big Dance; *One Planet, One Groove* . . . . (Mission)
One More Saturday Night
Bob Weir; *Ace* . . . . (Grateful Dead)
Grateful Dead; *Best Of/Skeletons From The Closet* . . . . . (Warner Bros.)
Europe '72 . . . . (Warner Bros.)
Without A Net . . . . (Arista)
One More Time
Seals & Crofts; *Takin' It Easy* . . . . (Warner Bros.)
One More Time
Corey Stevens; *Road To Zen* . . . . (Eureka)
One More Time Around Rosie
Manhattan Transfer; *Jukin'* . . . . (Capitol)
One More Try
George Michael; *Faith* . . . . (Columbia)
One Night
Albert King; *Blues For Elvis* . . . . (Stax)
Elvis Presley; *50,000,000 Elvis Fans Can't Be Wrong-Elvis' Gold Records-
Volume 2* . . . . (RCA)
Reconsider Baby . . . . (RCA)
The Other Sides-Worldwide Gold Award Hits, Vol. 2 . . . . (RCA)
The Top Ten Hits . . . . (RCA)
Ronnie Milsap; *Heart & Soul* . . . . (RCA)
One Night In Bangkok
Murray Head; *Chess Pieces* . . . . (RCA)
Original Broadway Cast; *Chess* . . . . (RCA)
One Night In Paris
John Boswell; *Count Me In* . . . . (Hearts Of Space)
One Night In The Hotel
Michel Petrucciani; *Promenade With Duke* . . . . (Blue Note)
One Night In Trinidad
Earl "Fatha" Hines; *Lionel Hampton Presents Earl "Fatha"
Hines* . . . . (Who's Who In Jazz)
One Night In Vienna
Schoenerz & Scott; *One Night In Vienna* . . . . (Windham Hill)
One Night Love Affair
Bryan Adams; *Reckless* . . . . (A&M)
One Night Stand
Janis Joplin; *Farewell Song* . . . . (Columbia)
Janis Joplin-Super Hits . . . . (Epic)
One Night Stands
Hank Williams, Jr.; *Hank Williams, Jr.-Early Years* . . . . (WB/Curb)
One Night Stands . . . . (Warner Bros.)

One O'clock Jump
Count Basie & His Orchestra; *Swingingest Sounds Ever Heard-C* . . . . . (Hip-O)
One Of A Kind Pair Of Fools
Barbara Mandrell; *Barbara Mandrell-Greatest Country Hits* . . . . (Curb)
Barbara Mandrell's Greatest Hits . . . . (MCA)
Spun Gold . . . . (MCA)
One Of Our Submarines
Thomas Dolby; *Golden Age Of Wireless* . . . . (Capitol)
One Of The Living
Tina Turner; *ST/Beyond Thunderdome* . . . . (Capitol)
One Of The Survivors
Kinks; *Preservation Act 1* . . . . (Rhino)
The Kinks' Greatest-Celluloid Heroes . . . . (RCA)
One Of These Days
John Lee Hooker; *That's My Story* . . . . (Riverside)
One Of These Days
Tim McGraw; *Everywhere* . . . . (Curb)
One Of These Days
Pink Floyd; *Collection Of Great Dance Songs* . . . . (Columbia)
Delicate Sound Of Thunder . . . . (Columbia)
Meddle . . . . (Capitol)
Pink Floyd-Gift Set . . . . (Capitol)
Works . . . . (Capitol)
One Of These Days
Emmylou Harris; *Elite Hotel* . . . . (Reprise)
Profile/Best Of Emmylou Harris . . . . (Warner Bros.)
One Of These Days
Neil Young; *Harvest Moon* . . . . (Reprise)
One Of These Days
Nanci Griffith; *Last Of The True Believers* . . . . (Philo)
One Of These Days
Camper Van Beethoven; *Our Beloved Revolutionary Sweetheart* . . . . . (Virgin)
One Of These Days
Ten Years After; *A Space In Time* . . . . (Columbia)
One Of These Days
Ronnie Hawkins and The Hawks; *Best Of Ronnie Hawkins and The
Hawks* . . . . (Rhino)
One Of These Days
Matthews, Wright & King; *Dream Seekers* . . . . (Columbia)
One Of These Days
Tom Grant; *Just The Right Moment* . . . . (Verve/Forecast)
One Of These Days
Marvin Gaye; *Marvin Gaye's Greatest Hits* . . . . (Motown)
One Of These Days
Velvet Underground; *V.U.* . . . . (Verve)
One Of These Nights
Eagles; *Eagles/Their Greatest Hits 1971-1975* . . . . (Asylum)
One Of These Nights . . . . (Asylum)
One Of Those Love Songs
Xscape; *Traces Of My Lipstick* . . . . (So So Def/Columbia)
One Of Those Nights Tonight
Lorrie Morgan; *Shakin' Things Up* . . . . (BNA)
To Get To You-Greatest Hits Collection . . . . (BNA)
One Of Those Things
Pam Tillis; *Put Yourself In My Place* . . . . (Arista)
One Of Those Things
Pride 'N Politix; *Changes* . . . . (East West)
One Of Those Things
Janie Fricke; *Labor Of Love* . . . . (Columbia)
One Of Us
Joan Osborne; *Relish* . . . . (Blue Gorilla/Mercury)
One On One
Daryl Hall & John Oates; *H2O* . . . . (RCA)
Live At The Apollo . . . . (RCA)
Rock 'N Soul, Part 1 . . . . (RCA)
Soulful Sounds . . . . (RCA)
One On The Right Is On The Left, The
Johnny Cash; *Johnny Cash-16 Biggest Hits-#2* . . . . (Legacy)
One Owner Heart
T.G. Sheppard; *One Owner Heart* . . . . (WB/Curb)
T.G. Sheppard's Greatest Hits-#2 . . . . (WB/Curb)
One Paper Kid
Emmylou Harris; *Quarter Moon In A Ten Cent Town* . . . . (Warner Bros.)
One Plus One
Chris Smither; *It Ain't Easy* . . . . (Adelphi)
One Plus One
Grant McLennan; *In Your Bright Ray* . . . . (Beggar's Banquet)
One Plus One
Ace Frehley; *Loaded Deck* . . . . (Megaforce)
One Plus One Equals Three
Original Cast; *Side Show* . . . . (Sony Music Classical)
One Potato
Sesame Street; *The Count's Countdown* . . . . (Sony Wonder)
One Potato Two
Music Explosion; *Super K Kollection-#2-C* . . . . (Collectables)
One Potato, Two Potato
Westside Children's Singers; *Play Time: 25 Favorite Play And Party
Songs* . . . . (EMI Special Markets)

One Promise Too Late
Reba McEntire; *Country Classics-#10-1987-C* . . . . (Universal)
Reba McEntire's Greatest Hits . . . .(MCA)
What Am I Gonna Do About You . . . .(MCA)
One Red Rose
John Prine; *Great Days-Anthology* . . . . (Rhino)
Storm Windows . . . . (Asylum)
One Reporter's Opinion
Minutemen; *Double Nickels On The Dime* . . . .(SST)
One Rock & Roll Too Many
Marc Cohn; *ST/Starlight Express* . . . .(MCA)
One Room Country Shack
Buddy Guy; *Man & The Blues* . . . . (Vanguard)
My Time After Awhile . . . . (Vanguard)
Mercy Dee Walton; *Mercy's Troubles* . . . . (Arhoolie)
One Room Country Shack . . . .(Specialty)
Pity & A Shame . . . .(Prestige)
Mose Allison; *Mose Allison's Greatest Hits* . . . .(Prestige)
One Rose (That's Left In My Heart)
Bing Crosby; *Best Of Bing Crosby* . . . .(MCA)
Leon Redbone; *Champagne Charlie* . . . . (Warner Bros.)
One Sad Night In Kerrville
Tom Kell; *Sad Night* . . . .(Warner Bros.)
One Shirt, Soulless Shoes
Latimore; *I'll Do Anything For You* . . . . (Malaco)
One Small Boat
Altered State; *Altered State* . . . .(Warner Bros.)
One Step At A Time
Brenda Lee; *Brenda Lee-Anthology-#1 & #2* . . . .(MCA)
One Step Closer
Doobie Brothers; *Best Of The Doobies, Volume II* . . . .(Warner Bros.)
One Step Closer . . . .(Warner Bros.)
One Step Closer
Linkin Park; *Hybrid Theory* . . . .(Warner Bros.)
One Step Closer
Highway 101; *Highway 101* . . . .(Warner Bros.)
One Step Closer To You
Gavin Christopher; *One Step Closer* . . . .(Manhattan)
One Step Up
Bruce Springsteen; *Tunnel Of Love* . . . . (Columbia)
One Summer Dream
Electric Light Orchestra; *Afterglow* . . . .(Epic)
Face The Music . . . . (Jet)
One Sweet Day
Mariah Carey; *Daydream* . . . . (Columbia)
Mariah Carey & Boyz II Men; *1996 Grammy Nominees-C* . . . . (Columbia)
One Sweet Letter From You
Benny Goodman; *Roll 'Em* . . . . (Columbia)
One That You Love, The
Air Supply; *Air Supply-The Definitive Collection* . . . . (Arista)
One Thing Leads To Another
Fixx; *One Thing Leads To Another-Greatest Hits* . . . .(MCA)
Reach The Beach . . . .(MCA)
One Tin Soldier
Coven; *Super Hits Of The '70s-Have A Nice Day-#7-C* . . . . (Rhino)
One Toke Over The Line
Brewer & Shipley; *'70s Greatest Rock Hits-#10-C* . . . . (Priority)
Super Hits Of The '70s-Have A Nice Day-#4-C . . . . (Rhino)
One Vision
Queen; *A Kind Of Magic* . . . . (Hollywood)
Classic Queen . . . . (Hollywood)
Live At Wembley '86 . . . . (Hollywood)
One Way Bus
New Birth; *Golden Classics-New Birth* . . . . (Collectables)
One Way Ticket (Because I Can)
LeAnn Rimes; *Blue* . . . . (MCG/Curb)
One Week
Barenaked Ladies; *Stunt* . . . . (Reprise)
Totally Hits-#1-C . . . . (Arista)
One Wish
Hiroshima; *Another Place* . . . .(Epic)
One Woman Man
Dave Hollister; *Chicago '85 The Movie* . . . .(Def Squad/DreamWorks)
One World
Utopia; *Swing To The Right* . . . . (Rhino)
Utopia-Anthology 1974-1985 . . . . (Rhino)
One World
Anthrax; *Among The Living* . . . . (Island)
One World
Dire Straits; *Brothers In Arms* . . . .(Warner Bros.)
One World
John Denver; *One World* . . . . (RCA)
One, The
Elton John; *Elton John-Love Songs* . . . .(MCA)
The One . . . .(MCA)
One, The
Backstreet Boys; *Millennium* . . . . (Jive)

One, Two, Button Your Shoe
Artie Shaw & Tony Pastor; *Best Of The Big Bands-C* . . . . (Columbia)
Billie Holiday; *Quintessential-#2-1936* . . . . (Columbia)
One-Eyed Jack
Garland Jeffreys; *Matador & More* . . . . (A&M)
One-Eyed Jack . . . . (A&M)
One-Trick Pony
Paul Simon; *ST/One-Trick Pony* . . . . (Warner Bros.)
Only Child
Jackson Browne; *The Pretender* . . . .(Asylum)
Only Love
Wynonna; *Tell Me Why* . . . . (MCA)
Only One Road
Celine Dion; *The Colour Of My Love* . . . .(550 Music)
Only One Way To Rock
Sammy Hagar; *Standing Hampton* . . . . (Geffen)
Only One You
T.G. Sheppard; *Best Of T.G. Sheppard* . . . .(Curb)
T.G. Sheppard's All-Time Greatest Hits . . . . (Warner Bros.)
Only One, The
Chicago; *The Heart Of Chicago-1967-1997* . . . .(Reprise)
Opus 1
Gene Krupa; *Drummer Man* . . . . (Verve)
Mills Brothers; *Best Of The Decca Years-Mills Brothers* . . . . (MCA)
Tommy Dorsey; *Best Of Tommy Dorsey* . . . . (Bluebird)
Tommy Dorsey 's Greatest Hits . . . . (Victor Jazz/RCA Victor)
Rolled Into One
Anna Wheaton; *Music From The New York Stage (1890-1920)-#4-1917-1920-C* . . . . (Pearl)
Say I'm Your Number One
Princess; *45-#50035* . . . .(Next Plateau/London/Island)
Second Fiddle
Kay Starr; *Essential RCA Singles Collection* . . . . (Taragon)
She's The One
Bruce Springsteen; *Born To Run* . . . . (Columbia)
Sole Survivor
Asia; *Asia* . . . . (Geffen)
Live In Moscow . . . . (Rhino)
Solitaire
Elvis Presley; *Always On My Mind* . . . .(RCA)
From Elvis Presley Boulevard, Memphis, Tennessee . . . .(RCA)
Solitaire
Laura Branigan; *Branigan 2* . . . .(Atlantic)
Solitaire
Stan Kenton; *Artistry In Voices & Brass* . . . .(Creative World)
Solitaire
Johnny Mathis; *Feelings* . . . . (Columbia)
Solitaire
Carpenters; *From The Top* . . . . (A&M)
Horizon . . . . (A&M)
Solitaire
Neil Sedaka; *I'm A Song* . . . . (Fifty One West)
Solitaire . . . . (Fifty One West)
Solitaire
Jerry Vale; *Jerry Vale's Greatest Hits* . . . . (Columbia)
Solitaire
Erroll Garner; *Other Voices* . . . . (Columbia)
Solitaire
Jane Olivor; *Stay The Night* . . . . (Columbia)
Solitaire
Public Image Ltd.; *Live In Tokyo* . . . . (Elektra)
This Is What You Want...Is What You Get . . . . (Elektra)
Soup For One
Chic; *Dance Dance Dance-Best Of* . . . .(Atlantic)
Still The One
Orleans; *Dance With Me* . . . . (Rhino)
Still The One . . . . (Elektra)
Super Hits Of The '70s-Have A Nice Day-#19-C . . . . (Rhino)
Stomp Dance (Unity)
Robbie Robertson featuring The Six Nations Women Singers; *Contact From The Underworld Of Redboy* . . . . (Capitol)
Strollin' Beale No. 1
Rufus Thomas; *Can't Get Away From This Dog* . . . . (Stax)
Stupify
Disturbed; *The Sickness* . . . .(Giant)
Tea For One
Led Zeppelin; *Presence* . . . . (Swan Song)
Texas Heartache #1
Mickey Gilley; *Put Your Dreams Away* . . . . (Epic)
Theme From "One Day At A Time"
Original Soundtrack; *CBS: The First 50 Years* . . . . (TVT)
Theme From "One Life To Live"
Rosemary Joyce & Bill Bartholomew; *Soap Opera Themes* . . . .(Crescendo)
There Is Only One Paris For That
Original Cast; *Irma La Douce* . . . . (Sony Music Special Prod.)
There's Only One Way To Rock
Sammy Hagar; *Standing Hampton* . . . . (Geffen)
The Ultimate Rock Album-C . . . .(Foundation)

Van Halen; *LIVE: Right here, right now* .... (Warner Bros.)

This Could Be The One
Bad Company; *Here Comes Trouble* .... (Atco)

Till We Two Are One
Eddy Howard; *Best Of Eddy Howard-The Mercury Years* .... (Mercury)
Georgie Shaw; *45-#28937* .... (Decca)
Louis Jordan; *One Guy Named Louis* .... (Blue Note)

Together
Nilsson; *Aerial Ballet* .... (RCA)

Travelin' Light
Eric Clapton; *Reptile* .... (Duck/Reprise)

Two Different Worlds
Robert Goulet; *My Love Forgive Me-Sincerely Yours Robert
    Goulet* .... (Collector's Choice)

Two For The Road
Bruce Springsteen; *Tracks* .... (Columbia)

Two Hearts Beat As One
U2; *War* .... (Island)

Unison
Bjork; *Vespertine* .... (Elektra)

Uno Mundo
Buffalo Springfield; *Buffalo Springfield* .... (Atco)

Walkin' One & Only
Maria Muldaur; *Bread & Roses Festival Of Acoustic Music-#1-C* ..... (Fantasy)
    Maria Muldaur .... (Reprise)

Whatever Comes First
Sons Of The Desert; *Whatever Comes First* .... (Epic)

Where Are You Now
Trisha Yearwood; *Real Live Woman* .... (MCA)

Wild One
Faith Hill; *Take Me As I Am* .... (Warner Bros.)

Wild One, Forever
Tom Petty And The Heartbreakers; *Tom Petty & The
    Heartbreakers* .... (Gone Gator)

You Are The Only One
God's Property; *God's Property* .... (Interscope)

You Win My Love
Shania Twain; *The Woman In Me* .... (Mercury)

Young Love
Sonny James; *Golden Jukebox Favorites* .... (Capitol)
    Opry Legends-Sonny James .... (Capitol)
    Stars Of The Grand Ole Opry-1926-1974-C .... (RCA)
    Traditions In Country Music-C .... (Capitol)
Tab Hunter; *Fonzie's Make-Out Music-C* .... (Nick At Nite)
    Teen Idols-C .... (Universal)

You're Still The One
Shania Twain; *Come On Over* .... (Mercury)

You're The One
Oak Ridge Boys; *American Made* .... (MCA)
    Oak Ridge Boys' Greatest Hits .... (MCA)
    Oak Ridge Boys-Collection .... (MCA)
    Y'All Come Back Saloon .... (MCA)

You're The One
Vogues; *Back To The '60s-#2-C* .... (Dominion Entert.)
    Vogues' Greatest Hits .... (Rhino)

You're The One
Paul Simon; *You're The One* .... (Warner Bros.)

You're The One
SWV; *MTV Party To Go-#10-C* .... (Tommy Boy)
    New Beginning .... (RCA)
    SWV's Greatest Hits .... (Beast)

You're The One
Roches; *A Dove* .... (MCA)

You're The One
Hank Crawford; *Atlantic Jazz-Soul-C* .... (Atlantic)

You're The One
Dwight Yoakam; *If There Was A Way* .... (Reprise)

You're The One
Champion Jack Dupree; *Legacy Of The Blues-#3* .... (Crescendo)

You're The One
Carpenters; *Lovelines* .... (A&M)

You're The One
Marvelettes; *Marvelettes-Anthology* .... (Motown)

You're The One
Neville Brothers; *Uptown* .... (EMI)

NUMBERS: 10

See Also: *AGES (various), COUNTING SONGS, MONTHS &
DATES (various), NUMBERS (various), TIME: SPECIFIC*

10 Days Late
Third Eye Blind; *Blue* .... (Elektra)

10 Miles To Go On A 9 Mile Road
Jim White; *No Such Place* .... (Luaka Bop)

10-4 (Calling All Cars)
Benny Spellman; *Fortune Teller-Golden Classics* .... (Collectables)

Dance: Ten; Looks: Three
Original Cast; *A Chorus Line* .... (Columbia)

Heaven Is 10 Zillion Light Years Away
Stevie Wonder; *Fulfillingness' First Finale* .... (Motown)

I Found A Million-Dollar Baby (In A Five-And-Ten-Cent Store)
Barbra Streisand; *ST/Funny Girl* .... (Columbia)
Bing Crosby; *Pennies From Heaven* .... (Pro-Arte)
Fred Waring's Pennsylvanians; *78-#22707* .... (Victor)
Nat "King" Cole; *Nat "King" Cole-Gift Set* .... (Capitol)

I Spent My Last Ten Dollars (On Birth Control And Beer)
Two Nice Girls; *Lesbian Favorites-Women Like Us-C* .... (Rhino)

Lucky 4 You (Tonight I'm Just Me)
SHeDAISY; *The Whole Shebang* .... (Lyric Street)

Monkey Wrench
Foo Fighters; *The Colour And The Shape* .... (Roswell/RCA)

News At Ten
Vapors; *New Clear Days* .... (Liberty)

Paper Rosie (10 Cents)
Gene Watson; *Gene Watson's Greatest Hits* .... (Curb)

Question Everything
8Stops7; *In Moderation* .... (Reprise)

Ten Cents A Chop
Phil Ochs; *Phil Ochs' Greatest Hits* .... (A&M)

Ten Cents A Dance
Eileen Farrell; *I Gotta Right To Sing The Blues* .... (Sony Music Classical)
Ella Fitzgerald; *Rodgers & Hart Songbook* .... (Verve)

Ten Commandments Of Love
Bob Marley & The Wailers; *Birth Of A Legend 1963-
    1966* .... (Epic Portrait Assoc.)
Harvey & The Moonglows; *Best Of Chess Rock 'N' Roll-#2-C* .... (Chess)
    Collectables Presents The History Of Rock-#10-C .... (Collectables)
    Cruisin'-1958-C .... (Increase)
    Oldies But Goodies-#11-C .... (Original Sound)

Ten Degrees & Gettin' Colder
Nanci Griffith; *Other Voices Other Rooms* .... (Elektra)

Ten Dollar Man
ZZ Top; *Six Pack* .... (Warner Bros.)
    Tejas .... (Warner Bros.)

Ten Feet Tall And Bulletproof
Travis Tritt; *Ten Feet Tall And Bulletproof* .... (Warner Bros.)

Ten Girls Ago
Graham Parker; *Best Of Graham Parker 1988-1991* .... (RCA)

Ten Guitars
Engelbert Humperdinck; *Release Me* .... (Mercury)

Ten Little Indians
Beach Boys; *Surfin' Safari* .... (Capitol)

Ten Little Indians
Nilsson; *Pandemonium Shadow Show* .... (RCA)

Ten Little Numbers
Hank Williams; *Complete Hank Williams* .... (Mercury)

Ten Minutes Ago
Julie Andrews & Jon Cypher; *Cinderella-The CBS Television
    Production* .... (Columbia)
Stuart Damon & Lesley Ann Warren; *Cinderella-The CBS Television
    Network Production* .... (Columbia)

Ten O'Clock In Toronto
Christine Lavin; *Compass* .... (Philo)

Ten Pound Hammer
Aaron Tippin; *Tool Box* .... (RCA)

Ten Tall Giraffes
Liquid Pink; *Liquid Pink* .... (Atomic)

Ten Thousand Angels
Mindy McCready; *Ten Thousand Angels* .... (BNA)

Ten Thousand Angels Cried
LeAnn Rimes; *You Light Up My Life-Inspirational Songs* .... (Curb)

Tenth Avenue Freeze-Out
Bruce Springsteen; *Born To Run* .... (Columbia)
Bruce Springsteen & The E Street Band; *Bruce Springsteen & The E Street
    Band Live/1975-85* .... (Legacy)

Tuesday At Ten
Count Basie; *Essential Count Basie-#3* .... (Columbia)

NUMBERS: 11-99

See Also: *AGES (various), MONTHS & DATES (various),
NUMBERS (various), TEENAGERS, TIME: SPECIFIC, YEARS:
SPECIFIC*

11 O'Clock Tick Tock
U2; *Under A Blood Red Sky* .... (Island)

15 Minutes
Marc Nelson; *chocolate mood* .... (Columbia)

16 Candles
Crests; *Alan Freed's Memory Lane-C* .... (MCA)
    Billboard Top Rock 'N' Roll Hits-1959-C .... (Rhino)
    Crests Greatest Hits .... (Collectables)

Cruisin'-1959-C . . . . (Increase)
Oldies But Goodies-#14-C . . . . (Original Sound)
Rock & Roll U.S.A.-21 Rock & Roll Favorites-#2-C . . . . . . (Laurie)
ST/American Graffiti . . . . (MCA)

16th Avenue
Lacy J. Dalton; *19 Hot Country Requests-#2-C* . . . . (Epic)
Greatest Country Hits Of The '80s-1982-C . . . . (Columbia)
Lacy J. Dalton's Greatest Hits . . . . (Columbia)

17 Again
Eurythmics; *Peace* . . . . (Arista)

18 Miles To Memphis
Stray Cats; *Rant 'N' Rave With The Stray Cats* . . . . (EMI)

19th Nervous Breakdown
Rolling Stones; *Big Hits (High Tide & Green Grass)* . . . . . . (Abkco)
got Live if you want it! . . . . (Abkco)
Hot Rocks 1964-1971 . . . . (Abkco)
Singles Collection-The London Years . . . . (Abkco)

20th Century Man
Beat Farmers; *Loud & Plowed &...Live!* . . . . (Curb)
Kinks; *Muswell Hillbillies* . . . . (VelVel)
One For The Road . . . . (Arista)

21 Days In Jail
Magic Sam; *Chicago Boss Guitar* . . . . (Paula)

21st Century Sha La La La Girl
Def Leppard; *Euphoria* . . . . (Mercury)

23rd Of March
Gene Pitney; *Many Sides Of Gene Pitney* . . . . (Out Of Print)

24 Hours From Tulsa
Gene Pitney; *45-#3015* . . . . (Collectables)
Double Gold-Gene Pitney . . . . (Mustcor)
Ian & Sylvia; *Best Of Ian & Sylvia* . . . . (Vanguard)
Ian & Sylvia's Greatest Hits . . . . (Vanguard)
Play One More . . . . (Vanguard)

24/7
Kevon Edmonds; *24/7* . . . . (RCA)

24-7 Man
Robert Cray Band; *Take Your Shoes Off* . . . . (Rykodisc)

25th Floor
Patti Smith Group; *Easter* . . . . (Arista)

26 Cents
Wilkinsons; *Nothing But Love* . . . . (Giant)

29 Palms
Robert Plant; *Fate Of Nations* . . . . (Es Paranza)

30 Years In The Bathroom
Wonderstuff; *Hup!* . . . . (Polydor)

317 East 32nd
Lennie Tristano; *Continuity* . . . . (Jazz)
Live In Toronto 1952 . . . . (Jazz)

32 Flavors
Alana Davis; *Blame It On Me* . . . . (Elektra)
Ani DiFranco; *Living In Clip* . . . . (Righteous Babe)
Not A Pretty Girl . . . . (Righteous Babe)

33 R.P.M. Soul
Michelle Shocked; *Arkansas Traveler* . . . . (Mercury)
Say What U Want-Rock The Vote-C . . . . (Mercury)

36-22-36
Bobby Bland; *Best Of Bobby Bland-#2* . . . . (MCA)
Bobby Bland . . . . (MCA)
Here's The Man . . . . (MCA)

38 Pistol Blues
Big Joe Williams; *Walkin' Blues* . . . . (Fantasy)

42nd Street
Diana Krall; *Stepping Out* . . . . (Justin Time)
Hal Kemp; *Best Of The Big Bands-C* . . . . (Columbia)
Mel Torme; *Cocktail Mix-#3-Swingin' Singles-C* . . . . (Rhino)
Original Broadway Cast; *42nd Street* . . . . (RCA Victor)

48 Hours Till Monday
Sawyer Brown; *Buick* . . . . (Curb)

49 Bye-Byes
Crosby, Stills & Nash; *Crosby, Stills & Nash* . . . . (Atlantic)

50 Ways To Leave Your Lover
Paul Simon; *Greatest Hits, Etc.* . . . . (Columbia)
Negotiations And Love Songs, 1971-1986 . . . . (Warner Bros.)
Still Crazy After All These Years . . . . (Columbia)
Simon & Garfunkel; *The Concert In Central Park* . . . . . . (Warner Bros.)

51 Beers
Claude King; *Hi-Tone Poppa* . . . . (Collectables)

51st Anniversary
Jimi Hendrix Experience; *Are You Experienced?* . . . . (Reprise)

53 Miles West Of Venus
B-52's; *Wild Planet* . . . . (Warner Bros.)

57 Channels (And Nothin' On)
Bruce Springsteen; *Human Touch* . . . . (Columbia)

59 Chevy
Geronimo Black; *Geronimo Black* . . . . (One Way)

59th Street Bridge Song (Feelin' Groovy)
Harper's Bizarre; *Baby Boomer Classics-More Mellow
    Sixties-C* . . . . (JCI Assoc. Labels)

Better Days-C . . . . (Rhino)
Simon & Garfunkel; *Collected Works* . . . . (Columbia)
Parsley Sage Rosemary & Thyme . . . . (Columbia)
Simon & Garfunkel's Greatest Hits . . . . (Columbia)
The Concert In Central Park . . . . (Warner Bros.)

6, 8, 12
Brian McKnight; *Back At One* . . . . (Motown)

'70s TV
Dramarama; *Stuck In Wonderamaland* . . . . (Chameleon)

7-11 (A Winner)
Li'l Wally; *Polish Carnival* . . . . (Jay Jay)

76 Trombones
Original Cast; *The Music Man* . . . . (Gold Rush)

80's Ladies
K.T. Oslin; *80's Ladies* . . . . (RCA)
K.T. Oslin's Greatest Hits: Songs From An Aging Sex Bomb . . . . (RCA)
Nipper's Greatest Hits Of The '80s-C . . . . (RCA)

90 Minute Cigarette
John Hart; *Blue Guitar* . . . . (Blue Note)

96 Miles To Birmingham
Dick Silveras; *Negro Folk Songs & Ballads* . . . . (Stinson)

96 Tears
? & The Mysterians; *? & The Mysterians* . . . . (Collectables)
Ten Roir Years . . . . (Roir)

99 Luftballons (99 Red Balloons)
Nena; *99 Luftballons* . . . . (Epic)

A-11
Buck Owens; *Buck Owens Collection-1959-1990* . . . . (Rhino)
Johnny Paycheck; *Johnny Paycheck-20 Greatest Hits* . . . . . . (Deluxe)

After 12, Before 6
Sam Salter; *It's On Tonight* . . . . (LaFace)

Almost Eighteen
Roy Orbison; *Get Hot Or Go Home-Vintage
    Rockabilly-C* . . . . (Country Music Foundation)
Legendary Roy Orbison . . . . (Sony Music Special Prod.)

American Beat '84
Fleshtones; *Living Legends* . . . . (I.R.S.)

American Skin (41 Shots)
Bruce Springsteen & The E Street Band; *Live In New York City* . . . . (Columbia)

Anti-Sex Backlash Of The '80s
Roches; *Speak* . . . . (MCA)

Apollo XI
Orchestral Manoeuvres In The Dark; *Sugar Tax* . . . . (Virgin)

April 24, 1981
Rick Springfield; *Success Hasn't Spoiled Me Yet* . . . . (RCA)

April The 14th, Part 1
Gillian Welch; *Time (The Revelator)* . . . . (Acony)

Around The World In Eighty Days
Boston Pops Orchestra/Arthur Fiedler; *Greatest Hits Of The '50s-#2* . . (RCA)
Frank Sinatra; *Come Fly With Me* . . . . (Capitol)
Roger Williams; *Roger Williams' Greatest Hits* . . . . (MCA)
Victor Young & His Singing Strings; *Hollywood's Greatest Hits-#2* . . . (Telarc)

At Seventeen
Janis Ian; *Between The Lines* . . . . (Columbia)
Super Hits Of The '70s-Have A Nice Day-#15-C . . . . (Rhino)

August 19
Ralph Simon; *Time Being* . . . . (Gramavision)

Back When Gas Was Thirty Cents A Gallon
Tom T. Hall; *Soldier Of Fortune* . . . . (RCA)

Ballad Of Forty Dollars
Johnny Cash & Waylon Jennings; *Heroes* . . . . (Columbia)
Tom T. Hall; *Essential Tom T. Hall-20th Anniversary Collection* . . . (Mercury)
Tom T. Hall's Greatest Hits-#1 . . . . (Mercury)

Bermuda Triangle Blues (Flight 45)
Blondie; *Plastic Letters* . . . . (Chrysalis)

Brimful Of Asha (45)
Cornershop; *Target* . . . . (Luaka Bop)

Buck Rogers In The 25th Century
Neil Norman & His Cosmic Orchestra; *Greatest Science Fiction
    Hits-#2* . . . . (Crescendo)

Buick '55
Johnny & The Distractions; *My Desire* . . . . (Burnside)

Buick '59
Vernon Green & The Medallions; *Best Vocal Group In Rhythm &
    Blues* . . . . (Dooto)
Vernon Green & The Medallions . . . . (Dooto)
Vernon Green & The Medallions-Golden Classics . . . . . . (Collectables)

Chant: 13th Hour
Redbone; *Best Of Redbone* . . . . (Epic)

Christine 16
Kiss; *Alive II* . . . . (Casablanca)
Love Gun . . . . (Casablanca)

Class Of '57
Statler Brothers; *Best Of The Statler Brothers* . . . . (Mercury)

Cold Irons Bound
Bob Dylan; *Time Out Of Mind* . . . . (Columbia)

Cowboy's Dream No. 19
Dan Hicks & His Hot Licks; *Last Train To Hicksville* . . . . (MCA)

December, 1963 (Oh, What A Night)
4 Seasons; *25th Anniversary Collection* . . . . (Rhino)
4 Seasons-Anthology . . . . (Rhino)
Oh What A Night . . . . (Curb)
Does This Bus Stop At 82nd Street?
Bruce Springsteen; *Greetings From Asbury Park, N.J.* . . . . . . (Columbia)
Tracks . . . . (Columbia)
Drunken Driver (May 20)
Ricky Skaggs and Kentucky Thunder; *Bluegrass Rules!* . . . . (Rounder)
Easter '88
Urge Overkill; *Americruiser/Jesus Urge Superstar* . . . . . . (Touch & Go)
Edge Of Seventeen
Stevie Nicks; *Bella Donna* . . . . (Modern)
Eighteen Wheels And A Dozen Roses
Kathy Mattea; *Collection Of Hits* . . . . (Mercury)
Untasted Honey . . . . (Polydor Country)
Eleven Roses
Hank Williams, Jr.; *Eleven Roses* . . . . (Polydor)
Hank Williams, Jr.-14 Greatest Hits . . . . (Polydor)
Number One Country Hits: '50s Through The '80s-C . . . . (Universal)
Standing In The Shadows . . . . (Polydor)
Erie Canal
Burl Ives; *Best Of Burl Ives* . . . . (MCA)
Weavers; *Greatest Folksingers Of The '60s-C* . . . . (Vanguard)
Weavers' Greatest Hits . . . . (Vanguard)
Weavers-Classics . . . . (Vanguard)
Everybody Knows (32)
Trisha Yearwood; *Everybody Knows* . . . . (MCA)
Everybody's Trying To Be My Baby (19)
Beatles; *For Sale* . . . . (Capitol)
The Beatles-Anthology-#2 . . . . (Capitol)
Carl Perkins; *Blue Suede Shoes: The Very Best Of Carl Perkins* . . (Collectables)
Carl Perkins' Greatest Hits/Finest Performances . . . . (Sun)
Carl Perkins-Original Sun Greatest Hits . . . . (Rhino)
Fifteen Beers
Johnny Paycheck; *Johnny Paycheck's Biggest Hits* . . . . (Epic)
Fifteen Miles To Birmingham
Happy & Artie Traum/Others; *Mud Acres* . . . . (Rounder)
Fifty Miles Of Elbow Room
Iris DeMent; *Infamous Angel* . . . . (Warner Bros.)
Norman & Nancy Blake; *Blind Dog* . . . . (Rounder)
Red Clay Ramblers; *Twisted Laurel* . . . . (Flying Fish)
Fifty-Fifty Love
Lee Roy Parnell; *Lee Roy Parnell* . . . . (Arista)
Two Steppin' Country-#1-C . . . . (Priority)
Flood Of '57
Stanley Brothers & The Clinch Mountain Boys; *Classic Bluegrass-Stanley Brothers & The Clinch Mountain Boys* . . . . (Rebel)
Forty Acres
Boxcar Willie; *Truck Driving Favorites* . . . . (Madacy)
Forty Again
John Berry; *Faces* . . . . (Capitol)
Forty Hour Week (For A Livin')
Alabama; *Alabama's Greatest Hits* . . . . (RCA)
Forty Hour Week . . . . (RCA)
Forty Miles Of Bad Road
Duane Eddy; *Compact Command Performances-Duane Eddy* . . . . . . (Motown)
Duane Eddy-16 Greatest Hits . . . . (Jamie)
Roy Clark; *Hookin' It* . . . . (MCA)
My Music & Me . . . . (MCA)
Forty Six & 2
Tool; *Aenima* . . . . (Freeworld/Capitol)
Fourteen Karat Mind
Gene Watson; *Gene Watson's Greatest Hits* . . . . (MCA)
Old Loves Never Die . . . . (MCA)
Fourteen Minutes Old
Doug Stone; *Doug Stone* . . . . (Epic)
Friday The 13th
Alvin Lee; *Rocket Fuel* . . . . (RSO)
Friday The 13th Child
David Clayton-Thomas; *Clayton* . . . . (MCA)
Gabriel's Mother's Hiway Ballad 16 Blues
Arlo Guthrie; *Best Of Arlo Guthrie* . . . . (Warner Bros.)
Gimme A Quarter, 25 Cents For The Bus
October Faction; *October Faction* . . . . (SST)
He Would Be Sixteen
Michelle Wright; *Now & Then* . . . . (Arista)
Hero #99
Gene Ryder; *Last Cigarette & A Blindfold* . . . . (Mercury)
Hey Nineteen
Steely Dan; *Gaucho* . . . . (MCA)
Steely Dan-Gold . . . . (MCA)
Highway 28
Paul Butterfield's Better Days; *Better Days* . . . . (Rhino)
Highway 29
Bruce Springsteen; *The Ghost Of Tom Joad* . . . . (Columbia)
Highway 40 Blues
Ricky Skaggs; *19 Hot Country Requests-C* . . . . (Epic)

Greatest Country Hits Of The '80s-1983-C . . . . (Columbia)
Highways & Heartaches . . . . (Epic)
Live In London . . . . (Epic)
Highway 61 Revisited
Bob Dylan; *Highway 61 Revisited* . . . . (Columbia)
Real Live . . . . (Columbia)
Bob Dylan And The Band; *Before The Flood* . . . . (Columbia)
James Taylor; *Mud Slide Slim And The Blue Horizon* . . . (Warner Bros.)
Johnny Winter; *Johnny Winter-Anthology* . . . . (Bac-Trac)
Second Winter . . . . (Columbia)
Homecoming '63
Keith Whitley; *L.A. To Miami* . . . . (RCA)
Hotel 49
Chet Baker; *In New York* . . . . (Riverside)
Hymn 43
Jethro Tull; *Aqualung* . . . . (Chrysalis)
Living In The Past . . . . (Chrysalis)
I Can't Drive 55
Sammy Hagar; *VOA* . . . . (Geffen)
I Saw Her Standing There (17)
Beatles; *Please Please Me* . . . . (Parlophone)
The Beatles-Anthology-#1 . . . . (Capitol)
Paul McCartney; *Tripping The Live Fantastic-Highlights!* . . . . (Capitol)
I Saw Him Standing There (17)
Tiffany; *Tiffany* . . . . (MCA)
Tiffany's Greatest Hits . . . . (Hip-O)
I'll Be Your .44
Dr. Blue; *Salt City Blues-C* . . . . (Blue Wave)
Incident On 57th Street
Bruce Springsteen; *The Wild, The Innocent & The E Street Shuffle* . . . (Columbia)
Ireland's 32
Paddy Noonan; *Happy Hours* . . . . (Rego Irish)
Johnny 99
Bruce Springsteen; *Nebraska* . . . . (Columbia)
Bruce Springsteen & The E Street Band; *Bruce Springsteen & The E Street Band Live/1975-85* . . . . (Legacy)
Johnny Cash; *Cover Me (Bruce Springsteen Tribute)-C* . . . . (Rhino)
June 25 At The Fourth Of July
Shel Silverstein; *Great Conch Train Robbery* . . . . (Flying Fish)
June The 15, 1967
Gary Burton; *Artist's Choice* . . . . (Bluebird)
Live Through This (Fifteen Stories)
Mighty Joe Plum; *Happiest Dogs* . . . . (Atlantic)
Lucky 4 You (Tonight I'm Just Me)
SHeDAISY; *The Whole Shebang* . . . . (Lyric Street)
March 19th Blues
Duke Ellington; *Duke Ellington-Vol. 1-Studio Sessions-Chicago-1956* . . . (Saja)
Molly (16)
Sponge; *Rotting Pinata* . . . . (Work)
Mr. Shorty (44)
Marty Robbins; *The Drifter* . . . . (Koch International)
My Next Thirty Years
Tim McGraw; *A Place In The Sun* . . . . (Curb)
Tim McGraw's Greatest Hits . . . . (Curb)
Nineteen
Old 97's; *Fight Songs* . . . . (Elektra)
Ninety Nine
Toto; *Hydra* . . . . (Columbia)
Ninety Nine Years (Dead Or Alive)
Guy Mitchell; *Definitive Guy Mitchell* . . . . (Collector's Choice)
Ninety-Nine
Bill Anderson; *45-#30914* . . . . (Decca)
November 22, 1963
Original Cast; *Assassins* . . . . (RCA)
November 68th
Chick Corea; *CTI Masters Of The Keyboard* . . . . (CBS Associated)
Joe Farrell; *Outback* . . . . (CTI)
October 17, 1988
Keith Jarrett; *Paris Concert* . . . . (ECM)
October Impressions (No. 38)
Mark O'Connor; *Elysian Forest* . . . . (Warner Bros.)
Ol' '55
Eagles; *On The Border* . . . . (Elektra)
Tom Waits; *Tom Waits-Anthology* . . . . (Asylum)
Only 12 Years Old
Tony Adolescent & The Flower Leperds; *Dirges In The Dark* . . . . (Triple X Entert.)
Only Sixteen
Dr. Hook; *Bankrupt* . . . . (Capitol)
Dr. Hook-Greatest Hits & More . . . . (Capitol)
Great Records Of The Decade-'70s Hits-#2-C . . . . (Curb)
Little Bit More . . . . (Capitol)
Sam Cooke; *Best Of Sam Cooke* . . . . (RCA)
The Man And His Music . . . . (RCA)
This Is Sam Cooke . . . . (RCA)
Page 43
Crosby, Stills & Nash; *CSN* . . . . (Atlantic)
David Crosby & Graham Nash; *David Crosby & Graham Nash* . . . . . . (Atlantic)

Pass The 40 Ounce
Jena Si Qua; *Conquest Of A Nation* . . . .(Conquest)
Please Mr. Please (B17)
Olivia Newton-John; *Back To Basics-Essential Collection 1971-1992* . .(Geffen)
Poem 58
Chicago; *Chicago Transit Authority* . . . .(Chicago)
Group Portrait . . . .(Chicago)
Questions 67 & 68
Chicago; *Chicago At Carnegie Hall* . . . .(Chicago)
Chicago Transit Authority . . . .(Chicago)
Chicago's Greatest Hits-#2 (1974-81) . . . .(Chicago)
Group Portrait . . . .(Chicago)
Race The K-12
Rupert Hine; *ST/Better Off Dead* . . . . (A&M)
Rainy Day Women #12 & 35
Bob Dylan; *Blonde On Blonde* . . . . (Columbia)
Bob Dylan's Greatest Hits . . . . (Columbia)
Rock Classics Of The '60s-C . . . . (Columbia)
ST/Forrest Gump . . . .(Epic/Sony Music Soundtrax)
Bob Dylan And The Band; *Before The Flood* . . . . (Columbia)
Red House (99½)
Jimi Hendrix; *Concerts* . . . . (Reprise)
Kiss The Sky . . . . (Reprise)
Lifelines/Jimi Hendrix Story . . . . (Reprise)
Live At Winterland . . . . (Rykodisc)
ST/Jimi Hendrix . . . . (Reprise)
Jimi Hendrix Experience; *Are You Experienced?* . . . . (Reprise)
Smash Hits . . . . (Reprise)
Redneck 12 Days Of Christmas
Jeff Foxworthy; *Crank It Up: The Music Album* . . . .(Warner Bros.)
Jeff Foxworthy's Greatest Bits . . . .(Warner Bros.)
Rock Radio Into The Nineties & Beyond
KLF; *Chill Out* . . . . (Wax Trax)
Roll On (Eighteen Wheeler)
Alabama; *Alabama's Greatest Hits-#2* . . . . (RCA)
Roll On . . . . (RCA)
Route 66
Asleep At The Wheel; *Served Live* . . . . (Capitol)
Very Best Of Asleep At The Wheel Since 1970 . . . . (Relentless/Madacy)
Wheelin' & Dealin' . . . . (Capitol)
Depeche Mode; *ST/Earth Girls Are Easy* . . . . (Sire)
George Maharis; *45-#15-2227* . . . . (Epic)
Manhattan Transfer; *Bop doo-wopp* . . . .(Atlantic)
Nat "King" Cole; *Capitol Collectors Series-Nat "King" Cole* . . . . . . (Capitol)
The Nat "King" Cole Story . . . . (Capitol)
Natalie Cole; *Unforgettable With Love* . . . .(Elektra)
Rolling Stones; *December's Children (and everybody's)* . . . .(Abkco)
England's Newest Hit Makers/The Rolling Stones . . . .(Abkco)
Sally Ann 28th Of January
Fuzzy Mountain String Band; *Fuzzy Mountain String Band* . . . . (Rounder)
Send Me An Angel '89
Real Life; *Send Me An Angel '89* . . . . (Curb)
Send One Your Love (Dozen)
Stevie Wonder; *Journey Through The Secret Life Of Plants* . . . . (Motown)
Original Musiquarium . . . . (Motown)
September 13
Deodato; *Live At The Felt Forum-2001 Concert* . . . . (CBS Associated)
Prelude . . . . (CBS Associated)
September Fifteenth
Mark Murphy; *September Ballads* . . . . (Milestone)
Pat Metheny & Lyle Mays; *As Falls Wichita, So Falls Wichita Falls* . . . . .(ECM)
Set 'Em Up Joe (B24)
Vern Gosdin; *Chiseled In Stone* . . . . (Columbia)
Greatest Country Hits Of The '80s-1988-C . . . . (Columbia)
Seven Come Eleven
Benny Goodman; *Benny Goodman-Live At Carnegie Hall* . . . . (London)
Charlie Christian; *Genius Of The Electric Guitar* . . . . (Columbia)
Herb Ellis & Joe Pass; *Seven Come Eleven* . . . .(Concord Jazz)
Two For The Road . . . . (Pablo)
Seven Eleven
Commander Cody; *Midnight Man* . . . . (Out Of Print)
Seventeen
Bobby Brown; *Dance!...Ya Know It!* . . . .(MCA)
King Of Stage . . . .(MCA)
Seventeen
Chambers Brothers; *Best Of The Chambers Brothers* . . . . (Fantasy)
Seventeen
Foreigner; *Head Games* . . . . (Atlantic)
Seventeen
Sex Pistols; *Never Mind The Bollocks, Here's The Sex Pistols* . . . .(Warner Bros.)
Seventeen
Rusty Draper; *Rusty Draper's Greatest Hits* . . . . (Monument)
Seventeen
Winger; *Winger* . . . .(Atlantic)
Seventeen
Chris LeDoux; *Radio & Rodeo Hits* . . . . (Liberty)
Seventeen Come Sunday
John Wright & Catherine Perrier; *Traditional Music Of*
Ireland . . . .(Green Linnet)

Seventeen Goin' On 21
Brian Elliot; *Brian Elliot* . . . . (Warner Bros.)
Sex In The '90s
Gloria Estefan; *Into The Light* . . . . (Epic)
Sexy + 17
Stray Cats; *Best Of Stray Cats-Rock This Town* . . . . (EMI)
Rant 'N' Rave With The Stray Cats . . . . (EMI)
Shakespeare's Sonnet No. 18
Bryan Ferry; *Diana, Princess Of Wales-Tribute-C* . . . . (Columbia)
She Is Always Seventeen
Harry Chapin; *Greatest Stories-Live* . . . .(Elektra)
Harry Chapin-Anthology . . . .(Elektra)
She Was Only Seventeen (He Was One Year More)
Marty Robbins; *American Originals-Marty Robbins* . . . . (Columbia)
Marty Robbins' Greatest Hits . . . . (Columbia)
She's A Little Past Forty
Ronnie McDowell; *Best Of Ronnie McDowell* . . . . (Curb)
She's Got a 60 Cycle Brain
Paul Buff Organization; *45-#55* . . . .(Original Sound)
She's Nineteen Years Old
Muddy Waters; *Best Of Blues-#1-C* . . . . (MCA Special Prod.)
The Chess Box-Muddy Waters . . . . (Chess)
Sing A Song Of Sixpence (24)
Original Soundtrack; *Children's Favorites* . . . .(Kid Rhino/Rhino 4 Kids)
Six Times Six Is Thirty-Six
Frances White; *Music From The New York Stage (1890-1920)-#4-1917-*
1920-C . . . . (Pearl)
Sixteen Going On Seventeen
Original Cast; *The Sound Of Music* . . . . (Sony Broadway)
Sixteen Reasons
Connie Stevens; *Only Rock 'N Roll-1960-1964-#1 Radio Hits-C* . . . . . . (Rhino)
Sixty Minute Man
Billy Ward & His Dominoes; *Rock & Roll Show-C* . . . . (Gusto)
Dominos; *Oldies But Goodies-#5-C* . . . .(Original Sound)
Rufus Thomas & Carla Thomas; *Rufus Thomas & Carla Thomas-*
Chronicle . . . . (Stax)
Someday, August 29, 1968
Chicago; *Chicago Transit Authority* . . . .(Chicago)
Spirit Of A Boy, Wisdom Of A Man (16)
Randy Travis; *Big Country Hits '99-C* . . . . (K-Tel)
Star 69
R.E.M.; *Monster* . . . . (Warner Bros.)
Stompin' In The '90s
Yo-Yo; *Make Way For The Motherlode* . . . . (East West)
Strawberry Letter #23
Brothers Johnson; *Brothers Johnson-Classics-#11* . . . . (A&M)
Right On Time . . . . (A&M)
Tevin Campbell; *T.E.V.I.N.* . . . .(Qwest)
Strawberry Wine (17)
Deana Carter; *Did I Shave My Legs For This?* . . . . (Capitol)
Summer Of '69
Bryan Adams; *Reckless* . . . . (A&M)
Sun Of '79
Des'ree; *Mind Adventures* . . . .(550 Music)
Superstition
Stevie Wonder; *20/20-C* . . . . (Motown)
Original Musiquarium . . . . (Motown)
Talking Book . . . . (Motown)
Sweet Little '66
Steve Earle & The Dukes; *Exit 0* . . . .(MCA)
Sweet Little Sixteen
Beatles; *45-#1502* . . . . (Collectables)
Chuck Berry; *Best Of The Best Of Chuck Berry* . . . . (International Mktg. Group)
Chuck Berry-Golden Hits . . . . (Mercury)
Chuck Berry-Greatest Hits Live . . . .(Quicksilver)
Cruisin'-1965-C . . . . (Increase)
Oldies But Goodies-#12-C . . . .(Original Sound)
Jerry Lee Lewis; *Jerry Lee Lewis-Original Golden Hits-#3* . . . . (Sun)
Jerry Lee Lewis & Friends; *Jerry Lee Lewis & Friends-Duets* . . . . (Sun)
John Lennon; *Lennon* . . . . (Capitol)
Rock 'N' Roll . . . . (Capitol)
Sweet Sixteen
B.B. King; *Back In The Alley* . . . .(MCA)
Best Of B.B. King . . . .(MCA)
Electric B.B. King-His Best . . . .(MCA)
Live In Cook County Jail . . . .(MCA)
Sweet Sixteen
Destiny's Child; *The Writing's On The Wall* . . . . (Columbia)
Sweet Sixteen
Judy Garland; *Best Of Judy Garland* . . . .(MCA)
Sweet Sixteen
Big Joe Turner; *Big Joe Turner's Greatest Hits* . . . .(Atlantic)
Sweet Sixteen
Chuck Berry; *Chuck Berry's Greatest Hits* . . . .(Everest)
Sweet Sixteen Bars
Earl Gray; *Best Of Earl Gray* . . . .(MCA)
Ray Charles; *Atlantic Jazz-Piano-C* . . . .(Atlantic)
Best Of Ray Charles . . . . (Atlantic)

Great Ray Charles . . . . (Atlantic)
Take 54
Nilsson; *Son Of Schmilsson* . . . . (RCA)
The 13th
Cure; *Wild Mood Swings* . . . . (Elektra)
Theme From ''21 Jump Street''
Original Soundtrack; *Television's Greatest Hits-#7-Cable Ready-C* . . . . . (TVT)
Theme From ''77 Sunset Strip''
Original Soundtrack; *Television's Greatest Hits-#1-C* . . . . (TVT)
TV Classic Themes: 25th Anniversary Edition-C . . . . (Breakable)
Theme From ''Adam-12''
Original Soundtrack; *Television's Greatest Hits-#1-C* . . . . (TVT)
Theme From ''Car 54, Where Are You?''
Original Soundtrack; *Television's Greatest Hits-#2-C* . . . . (TVT)
Theme From ''Colt .45''
Original Soundtrack; *Television's Greatest Hits-#4-Black & White
Classics-C* . . . . (TVT)
Theme From ''Hawaii Five-O''
Original Soundtrack; *CBS: The First 50 Years* . . . . (TVT)
Television's Greatest Hits-#1-C . . . . (TVT)
Ventures; *Billboard Top Pop Hits-1969-C* . . . . (Rhino)
Drew's Famous Luau Party Music-C . . . . (Turn Up The Music)
Theme From ''James At 15''
Original Soundtrack; *Television's Greatest Hits-#6-Remote Control-C* . . . (TVT)
Theme From ''Route 66''
Nelson Riddle & His Orchestra; *Beat Generation* . . . . (Rhino)
Television's Greatest Hits-#2-C . . . . (TVT)
Original Soundtrack; *CBS: The First 50 Years* . . . . (TVT)
Theme From ''The Twenty-First Century''
Original Soundtrack; *Television's Greatest Hits-#4-Black & White
Classics-C* . . . . (TVT)
Theme From ''Twelve O'Clock High''
Original Soundtrack; *Television's Greatest Hits-#2-C* . . . . (TVT)
Thirteen
Johnny Cash; *American Recordings* . . . . (American)
Thirteen Years In Prison
Big Leon Brooks' Blues Harp Band; *Living Chicago Blues-#4* . . . . . . (Alligator)
Thirty Days (To Come Back Home)
Chuck Berry; *Blues-#2-C* . . . . (Chess)
Chuck Berry-Golden Hits . . . . (Mercury)
Johnny Winter; *Rock N' Roll Collection-C* . . . . (Columbia)
Thirty Days In The Hole
Gov't Mule; *Live With A Little Help From Our Friends-Collector's
Edition* . . . . (Capricorn)
Humble Pie; *Best Of Humble Pie* . . . . (A&M)
Humble Pie-Classics-#14 . . . . (A&M)
Rock This Way Live-#1-C . . . . (BMG Special Prod.)
Smokin' . . . . (A&M)
Mr. Big; *Mr. Big* . . . . (Atlantic)
Thirty Dirty Birds
Red Hot Chili Peppers; *Freaky Styley* . . . . (EMI)
Thirty Nine Miles To Mobile
Charlie Daniels Band; *Charlie Daniels Band* . . . . (Capitol)
Thirty Years Of Tears
John Hiatt; *Stolen Moments* . . . . (A&M)
Thirty-Three
Smashing Pumpkins; *Mellon Collie And The Infinite Sadness* . . . . (Virgin)
Top 40 Radio (The History Of Rock)
Joey Welz; *Return Of Haley's Comet* . . . . (Caprice Int'l)
Train 45
Bill Monroe; *Bean Blossom* . . . . (MCA)
Mac Wiseman; *Great American Train Songs-C* . . . . (C.M.H. Prod.)
Train 45 & A Half
Mike Auldridge; *Critic's Choice-C* . . . . (Takoma)
Dobro/Blues & Bluegrass . . . . (Takoma)
Dobro/Blues & Bluegrass . . . . (Takoma)
TVC 15
David Bowie; *Fame & Fashion* . . . . (RCA)
Sound + Vision . . . . (Rykodisc)
ST/Chrisiane F. . . . . (RCA)
Stage . . . . (Rykodisc)
Station To Station . . . . (Rykodisc)
The Singles-1969-1993 . . . . (Rykodisc)
Twelve Days Of Christmas
Allan Sherman; *Christmas Comedy Classics-#2-C* . . . . (Priority)
*Dr. Demento Presents The Greatest Novelty Records-#6-
Christmas-C* . . . . (Rhino)
Andrews Sisters; *Andrews Sisters-Christmas* . . . . (MCA Special Prod.)
Bing Crosby; *That Christmas Feeling* . . . . (MCA Special Prod.)
Bob & Doug McKenzie; *Dr. Demento's Greatest Christmas CD-C* . . . . . (Rhino)
David Seville & The Chipmunks; *Christmas With The Chipmunks-#2* . . . . (EMI)
Frank Sinatra; *Sinatra Christmas Album* . . . . (Reprise)
Fred Waring's Pennsylvanians; *Now Is The Caroling Season* . . . . (Capitol)
Garrison Keillor; *Now It Is Christmas Again* . . . . (Angel)
Harry Belafonte; *Christmas Classics-#2* . . . . (RCA)
Joan Sutherland; *Christmas Stars-C* . . . . (London)
John Denver; *A Christmas Together* . . . . (Laserlight)
Kiri Te Kanawa; *Christmas With Kiri Te Kanawa* . . . . (London)
Ray Conniff; *Christmas Wonderland* . . . . (Sony Music Special Prod.)

Twelve Days To Christmas
Original Cast; *She Loves Me* . . . . (Polydor)
Twelve Volt Man
Jimmy Buffett; *Boats Beaches Bars & Ballads* . . . . (Margaritaville)
One Particular Harbour . . . . (MCA)
Twentieth Century Drifter
Marty Robbins; *Best Of Marty Robbins* . . . . (Curb)
Twentieth Century Fox
Doors; *Doors* . . . . (Elektra)
Twentieth Century Man
Scorpions; *Animal Magnetism* . . . . (Mercury)
Twenty-First Century Schizoid Man
King Crimson; *Abbreviated* . . . . (Editions E.G.)
Compact . . . . (Editions E.G.)
*In The Court Of The Crimson King-An Observation By King
Crimson* . . . . (Editions E.G.)
Twenty-Five Miles
Edwin Starr; *Motown Superstar Series-#3-Edwin Starr* . . . . (Motown)
Michael Jackson; *Original Soul Of Michael Jackson* . . . . (Motown)
Twenty-Five Minutes To Go
Johnny Cash; *Essential Johnny Cash* . . . . (Columbia)
Johnny Cash At Folsom Prison & San Quentin . . . . (Columbia)
True West . . . . (Columbia)
Twenty-Four Hours From Tulsa
Burt Bacharach; *Walk On By* . . . . (MCA Special Prod.)
Gene Pitney; *Best Of Gene Pitney* . . . . (K-Tel)
Twenty-Nine Ways (To My Baby's Door)
Koko Taylor; *Koko Taylor* . . . . (Chess)
South Side Lady . . . . (Evidence Music)
Marc Cohn; *Marc Cohn* . . . . (Atlantic)
Willie Dixon; *The Chess Box-Willie Dixon* . . . . (Chess)
Two Dozen Roses
Shenandoah; *30 Years Of #1 Hits-#20-C* . . . . (Columbia)
Road Not Taken . . . . (Columbia)
Shenandoah's Greatest Hits . . . . (Columbia)
Way Down The Line (17)
Offspring; *Ixnay On The Hombre* . . . . (Columbia)
What A Diff'rence A Day Makes (24)
Dinah Washington; *What A Diff'rence A Day Makes* . . . . (Mercury)
Whatcha Gone Do? (69)
Link; *Sex Down* . . . . (Relativity)
What's My Age Again? (23)
Blink-182; *Enema Of The State* . . . . (MCA)
Now That's What I Call Music!-#3-C . . . . (Virgin)
When I'm Sixty-Four
Beatles; *Beatles-Box Set* . . . . (Capitol)
Sgt. Pepper's Lonely Hearts Club Band . . . . (Capitol)
When It's Springtime In Alaska (40)
Johnny Horton; *American Originals-Johnny Horton* . . . . (Columbia)
Johnny Horton's Greatest Hits . . . . (Columbia)
When You Are Sixty-Five
Statler Brothers; *Entertainers...On And Off The Record* . . . . (Mercury)
Wreck Of The Old '97
Johnny Cash; *Johnny Cash At Folsom Prison & San Quentin* . . . . . (Columbia)
Johnny Cash-Original Golden Hits-#3 . . . . (Sun)
Story Songs Of The Trains & Rivers . . . . (Sun)
Superbilly . . . . (Sun)
The Man-The World-His Music . . . . (Sun)
Yo Ho Ho And A Bottle Of Rum (15)
Original Cast; *Rugrats Sing-Along* . . . . (Interscope)
You're Sixteen
Johnny Burnette; *ST/American Graffiti* . . . . (MCA)
Ringo Starr; *Blast From Your Past* . . . . (Gold Rush)
Ringo . . . . (Capitol)

NUMBERS: 2

*See Also: **AGES (various), COUNTING SONGS, COUPLES,
MONTHS & DATES (various), NUMBERS (various), TIME:
SPECIFIC, TOGETHERNESS***

1+2<2
Classic Ruins; *D.I.Y.-Mass Ave.-The Boston Scene-1979-1983-C* . . . . . (Rhino)
1-2-3
Gloria Estefan; *Gloria Estefan's Greatest Hits* . . . . (Epic)
Gloria Estefan and Miami Sound Machine; *Let It Loose* . . . . (Epic)
1-2-3
Len Barry; *24 Of The Grooviest Hits Of All Time! The '60s Ultimate
Collection-#1-C* . . . . (Sundazed Music)
2 Become 1
Spice Girls; *Spice* . . . . (Virgin)
After All (Love Theme From Chances Are)
Cher; *Heart Of Stone* . . . . (Geffen)
All I Want For Christmas (Is My Two Front Teeth)
David Seville & The Chipmunks; *Christmas With The Chipmunks-#2* . . . . (EMI)
Nat ''King'' Cole; *Let It Snow!-Cuddly Christmas Classics* . . . . (Capitol)

Spike Jones; *Dr. Demento Presents The Greatest Novelty Records-#6-
Christmas-C* .... (Rhino)
   Spike Jones-Christmas .... (Rhino)

Between Two Fires
Gary Morris; *Faded Blue* .... (Warner Bros.)
   Gary Morris'-Greatest Hits-#2 .... (Warner Bros.)

Bicycle Built For Two
Kidsongs; *Cars, Boats, Trains, Planes* .... (Sony Wonder)
Original Soundtrack; *School Days-Kids Classics* .... (Benson)

Billy 1, 2 & 7
Bob Dylan; *ST/Pat Garrett & Billy The Kid* .... (Columbia)

Cocktails For Two
Duke Ellington & His Orchestra; *No. 1 Hits Greatest Hits-C* ..... (RCA Victor)
Spike Jones; *Dinner Music...For People Who Aren't Very Hungry!* .... (Rhino)
   *Dr. Demento Presents The Greatest Novelty Records-#1-1940s &
Before-C* .... (Rhino)
   Dr. Demento: 20th Anniversary Collection-C .... (Rhino)
   Nipper's Greatest Hits Of The '40s-#1-C .... (RCA)
Spike Jones & His City Slickers; *Best Of Spike Jones & His City
Slickers* .... (RCA)

Death On Two Legs
Queen; *A Night At The Opera* .... (Hollywood)
   Live Killers .... (Hollywood)

Deuce
Lenny Kravitz; *Kiss My Ass-C* .... (Mercury)

Don't Happen Twice
Kenny Chesney; *Kenny Chesney's Greatest Hits* .... (BNA)

Don't Think Twice, It's All Right
Bob Dylan; *Before The Flood* .... (Columbia)
   Bob Dylan's Greatest Hits-#2 .... (Columbia)
   Freewheelin' .... (Columbia)
Joan Baez; *The First 10 Years* .... (Vanguard)
Wonder Who?; *Anniversary* .... (Rhino)

Doubleback
ZZ Top; *Recycler* .... (Warner Bros.)

Every Time Two Fools Collide
Kenny Rogers & Dottie West; *Every Time Two Fools Collide* .... (EMI)
   Kenny Rogers' Greatest Hits .... (EMI)

Feels Like Love
Vince Gill; *Let's Make Sure We Kiss Goodbye* .... (MCA)

Fire Of Two Old Flames
Roy Head; *In Our Room* .... (Elektra)

Forty Six & 2
Tool; *Aenima* .... (Freeworld/Capitol)

Get Off Of My Cloud
Rolling Stones; *Big Hits (High Tide & Green Grass)* .... (Abkco)
   December's Children (and everybody's) .... (Abkco)
   got Live if you want it! .... (Abkco)
   Hot Rocks 1964-1971 .... (Abkco)
   Singles Collection-The London Years .... (Abkco)

Goody Two Shoes
Adam Ant; *Antics In The Forbidden Zone* .... (Epic)
   Friend Or Foe .... (Epic)

Ground Beneath Her Feet, The
U2; *ST/The Million Dollar Hotel* .... (Interscope)

Helplessly Hoping
Crosby, Stills & Nash; *Crosby, Stills & Nash* .... (Atlantic)
   CSN .... (Atlantic)
Crosby, Stills, Nash & Young; *So Far* .... (Atlantic)

Husbands And Wives
Brooks & Dunn; *Big Country Hits '99-C* .... (K-Tel)
   If You See Her .... (Arista)
Neil Diamond; *Neil Diamond-Love Songs* .... (MCA)
   Rainbow .... (MCA)
   Stones .... (MCA)
Roger Miller; *Best Of Roger Miller* .... (Mercury)
   Best Of Roger Miller-His Greatest Songs .... (Curb)
   Roger Miller-Super Hits .... (Epic)
   Roger Miller-The Hits .... (Mercury)

I Second That Emotion
Smokey Robinson & The Miracles; *Smokey Robinson & The Miracles'
Anthology* .... (Motown)
   Smokey Robinson-The Ultimate Collection .... (Motown)
Tammy Wynette & Smokey Robinson; *Without Walls-C* .... (Epic)

Inside My Love
Trina Broussard; *ST/Love Jones* .... (Columbia)

It Takes Two
Marvin Gaye & Kim Weston; *Hitsville USA-The Motown Singles Collection-
1959-1971-C* .... (Motown)

It's 2 A.M.
Shemekia Copeland; *Wicked* .... (Alligator)

It's Been A Long, Long Time
Bing Crosby; *Best Of Bing Crosby* .... (MCA)
Harry James & His Orchestra; *Words & Music Of World
War II-C* .... (Columbia)
Harry James & Kitty Kallen; *Best Of The Big Bands-C* .... (Columbia)
Jan Garber & His Orchestra; *Best Of Jan Garber* .... (MCA)
Louis Armstrong; *Hello Dolly! & Other Hits* .... (MCA)

Just The Two Of Us
Will Smith; *Big Willie Style* .... (Columbia)

Just The Two Of Us
Grover Washington, Jr. & Bill Withers; *Billboard Top R&B Hits-
1981-C* .... (Rhino)
   Grover Washington, Jr.-Anthology .... (Elektra)
   Grover Washington, Jr.-Winelight .... (Elektra)

Knock Three Times
Tony Orlando & Dawn; *Best Of Tony Orlando & Dawn* .... (Rhino)

Letters From The Wasteland
Wallflowers; *Breach* .... (Interscope)

Little Darlin'
Diamonds; *Best Of The Diamonds* .... (Rhino)
   Billboard Top Rock 'N' Roll Hits-1957-C .... (Rhino)
   Cruisin'-1957-C .... (Increase)
   Good Time Rock 'N' Roll-C .... (MCA)
   Oldies But Goodies-#11-C .... (Original Sound)
   ST/American Graffiti .... (MCA)

Little White Lie
Sammy Hagar; *Marching To Mars* .... (MCA)

Louisiana Two-Step
Clifton Chenier; *King Of Zydeco Live At Montreux* .... (Arhoolie)
   Out West .... (Arhoolie)

Love Scene
Joe; *All That I Am* .... (Jive)

My Second Home
Tracy Lawrence; *Alibis* .... (Atlantic)

Never Going Back Again
Fleetwood Mac; *25 Years-The Chain* .... (Warner Bros.)
   Fleetwood Mac Live .... (Warner Bros.)
   Rumours .... (Warner Bros.)
Matchbox Twenty; *Legacy-A Tribute To Fleetwood Mac's Rumours-C* ... (Lava)

No Two Ways About It
Jeff Golub featuring Peter White; *Dangerous Curves* .... (GRP/VMG)

Not A Second Time
Beatles; *With The Beatles* .... (Parlophone)

On Second Thought
Eddie Rabbitt; *Country's Greatest Hits-#8-Lonely Hearts-C* .... (Priority)
   Jersey Boy .... (Capitol)
   Ten Years Of Greatest Hits .... (Capitol)

One
Nilsson; *Aerial Ballet* .... (RCA)
   Everybody's Talkin': The Encore Collection .... (BMG Special Prod.)
   Nilsson-All-Time Greatest Hits .... (RCA)
Three Dog Night; *Best Of Three Dog Night* .... (MCA)
   Captured Live At The Forum .... (MCA)
   Joy To The World-Greatest Hits .... (MCA)

One
George Jones & Tammy Wynette; *George Jones Collection* .... (MCA)
   Grand Ole Opry-75 Years-#2-C .... (MCA)
   One .... (MCA)

One And One Make Two
Sesame Street; *Numbers* .... (Sony Wonder)

One Hundred And Two
Judds; *Judds-Collection 1983-1990* .... (RCA)
   Love Can Build A Bridge .... (MCA)

One Of A Kind Pair Of Fools
Barbara Mandrell; *Barbara Mandrell-Greatest Country Hits* .... (Curb)
   Barbara Mandrell's Greatest Hits .... (MCA)
   Spun Gold .... (MCA)

One Potato Two
Music Explosion; *Super K Kollection-#2-C* .... (Collectables)

One Potato, Two Potato
Westside Children's Singers; *Play Time: 25 Favorite Play And Party
Songs* .... (EMI Special Markets)

One Week
Barenaked Ladies; *Stunt* .... (Reprise)
   Totally Hits-#1-C .... (Arista)

One, Two, Button Your Shoe
Artie Shaw & Tony Pastor; *Best Of The Big Bands-C* .... (Columbia)
Billie Holiday; *Quintessential-#2-1936* .... (Columbia)

Pair Of Old Sneakers
George Jones; *George Jones & Tammy Wynette-16
Biggest Hits* .... (Epic/Legacy)

Power Of Two
Indigo Girls; *Swamp Ophelia* .... (Epic)

Remember
Jimi Hendrix Experience; *Are You Experienced?* .... (Reprise)

Rude Awakening No. 2
Creedence Clearwater Revival; *1970* .... (Fantasy)
   Pendulum .... (Fantasy)

Second Chance
Reivers; *Pop Beloved* .... (DB)

Second Chance
38 Special; *Rock & Roll Strategy* .... (A&M)

Second Class Wait Here
Slim Dusty; *Australia Is His Name* .... (Philo)

Second Fiddle
Kay Starr; *Essential RCA Singles Collection* .... (Taragon)

Second Hand News
Fleetwood Mac; *25 Years-The Chain* . . . . (Warner Bros.)
Rumours . . . . (Warner Bros.)
Tonic; *Legacy-A Tribute To Fleetwood Mac's Rumours-C* . . . . (Lava)
Second Hand Store
Joe Walsh; *But Seriously Folks* . . . . (Asylum)
Second Home By The Sea
Genesis; *Genesis* . . . . (Atlantic)
Second Sunday In August
Weather Report; *I Sing The Body Electric* . . . . (Columbia)
Second Wind
Darryl Worley; *Hard Rain Don't Last* . . . . (DreamWorks/SKG)
Second-Hand Woman
Steve Winwood; *Arc Of A Diver* . . . . (Island)
Ships
Barry Manilow; *Barry Manilow's Greatest Hits-#3* . . . . (Arista)
One Voice . . . . (Arista)
So Much In Love
Tymes; *20th Century Rocks-#9-'60's Vocal Groups-I Got
Rhythm-C* . . . . (Dominion Entert.)
Tea For Two
Fred Waring's Pennsylvanians; *Nipper's Greatest Hits Of The
'30s-#2-C* . . . .(RCA)
Julie Andrews; *Love Julie* . . . . (USA Music Group)
Leigh Kaplan & Lincoln Mayorga; *Dizzy Fingers* . . . . (Cambria)
Original Cast/Ruby Keeler; *No No Nanette* . . . . (Columbia)
Tommy Dorsey & His Orchestra; *Best Of Tommy Dorsey & His
Orchestra* . . . . (Curb)
Texas Two Step
Bob Wills; *The Country Music Hall Of Fame-Bob Wills* . . . . (Universal)
Theme From "My Two Dads"
Original Soundtrack; *Television's Greatest Hits-#7-Cable Ready-C* . . . . (TVT)
There's Your Trouble
Dixie Chicks; *Wide Open Spaces* . . . . (Monument)
Think Twice
Brook Benton; *Best Of Brook Benton* . . . . (Mercury)
Till We Two Are One
Eddy Howard; *Best Of Eddy Howard-The Mercury Years* . . . .(Mercury)
Georgie Shaw; *45-#28937* . . . .(Decca)
Louis Jordan; *One Guy Named Louis* . . . . (Blue Note)
Together
Nilsson; *Aerial Ballet* . . . .(RCA)
Torn Between Two Lovers
Mary McGregor; *'70s Greatest Rock Hits-#9-#1 Hits-C* . . . .(Priority)
Travelin' Light
Eric Clapton; *Reptile* . . . . (Duck/Reprise)
Tryin' To Love Two
William Bell; *Coming Back For More* . . . . (Razor & Tie)
Trying To Love Two Women
Oak Ridge Boys; *Oak Ridge Boys' Greatest Hits* . . . . (MCA)
Oak Ridge Boys-Collection . . . . (MCA)
Together . . . . (MCA)
Twice As Hard
Black Crowes; *Shake Your Money Maker* . . . .(Def American)
Twice In A Lifetime
Michael Lington; *Vivid* . . . . (Samson)
Two Bass Hit
Dizzy Gillespie; *Dizziest* . . . .(Bluebird)
Miles Davis; *Milestones* . . . .(Columbia)
Sonny Clark; *Blue Piano-#2* . . . . (Blue Note)
Two Beers Away
Moe Bandy & Joe Stampley; *Moe Bandy & Joe Stampley's
Greatest Hits* . . . . (Columbia)
Two Bullets & A Gun
Stevie Salas Colorcode; *Stevie Salas Colorcode* . . . . (Island)
Two Chinese Songs
Pete Seeger; *Banks Of Marble* . . . .(Smithsonian Folkways)
Two Cigarettes In The Dark
Alberta Hunter; *Legendary Alberta Hunter-London Sessions* . . . .(DRG)
Betty Carter; *'Round Midnight* . . . . (Atlantic)
Two Days In February
Goo Goo Dolls; *Hold Me Up* . . . . (Metal Blade)
ST/Freddy's Dead-The Final Nightmare . . . . (Metal Blade)
Two Different Worlds
Robert Goulet; *My Love Forgive Me-Sincerely Yours Robert
Goulet* . . . . (Collector's Choice)
Two Dollars In The Jukebox
Eddie Rabbitt; *Best Of Eddie Rabbitt/Greatest Hits-II* . . . . (Warner Bros.)
Eddie Rabbitt's All-Time Greatest Hits . . . . (Warner Bros.)
Rocky Mountain Music . . . .(Elektra)
Ten Years Of Greatest Hits . . . .(Capitol)
Two Doors Down
Dolly Parton; *Collector's Series-Dolly Parton* . . . .(RCA)
Dolly Parton's Greatest Hits . . . .(RCA)
Here You Come Again . . . . (Dunhill Compact Classics)
Two Dozen Roses
Shenandoah; *30 Years Of #1 Hits-#20-C* . . . .(Columbia)
Road Not Taken . . . .(Columbia)

Shenandoah's Greatest Hits . . . .(Columbia)
Two Faces
Bruce Springsteen; *Tunnel Of Love* . . . .(Columbia)
Two Faces Have I
Lou Christie; *Back To The '60s-#4-C* . . . .(Dominion Entert.)
Enlightnin'ment-Best Of Lou Christie . . . .(Rhino)
Two Fairy Tales
Mark Lambert & Victoria Mallory; *Sondheim-A Musical Tribute* . . . . (RCA)
Original Cast; *Marry Me A Little* . . . . (RCA)
Two For The Road
Henry Mancini; *Henry Mancini-Legendary Performer* . . . . (RCA)
Peter Gunn . . . . (RCA)
James Galway; *James Galway's Greatest Hits-#2* . . . . (RCA)
Two Gentlemen Of Peru
Simon & Bard Group; *Enormous Radio* . . . . (Flying Fish)
Two Headed Cow
Ennui; *Olive* . . . .(Slamdek)
Two Headed Dog (Red Temple Prayer)
Roky Erickson; *You're Gonna Miss Me-Best Of Roky Erickson* . . . . . . (Restless)
Two Headed Man
Lonnie Brooks; *Genuine Houserockin' Music-#3-C* . . . . (Alligator)
Two Headed Sex Change
Cramps; *Look Mom No Head!* . . . . (Restless)
Two Hearts
Bruce Springsteen; *The River* . . . .(Columbia)
Bruce Springsteen & The E Street Band; *Bruce Springsteen & The E Street
Band Live/1975-85* . . . .(Legacy)
Two Hearts
Stephanie Mills; *Greatest Hits In My Life* . . . . (Casablanca)
Two Hearts
K.T. Oslin; *Love In A Small Town* . . . . (RCA)
Two Hearts
Pebbles; *Pebbles* . . . .(MCA)
Two Hearts
Chris Isaak; *San Francisco Days* . . . . (Reprise)
Two Hearts
Phil Collins; *Serious Hits...Live!* . . . . (Atlantic)
Two Hearts Beat As One
U2; *War* . . . .(Island)
Two Hits And The Joint Turned Brown
Pfaff Family Dog; *Marijuana's Greatest Hits Revisited-C* . . . .(Rehash)
Rodney & Doug Dillard and John Hartford; *Glitter Grass From The
Nashwood Hollyville Strings & Permanent Wave* . . . . (Flying Fish)
Two Hot Girls (On A Hot Summer Night)
Carly Simon; *Carly Simon-Greatest Hits Live* . . . .(Arista)
Coming Around Again . . . .(Arista)
Two Kinds Of Teardrops
Del Shannon; *Del Shannon's Greatest Hits* . . . .(Rhino)
Two Ladies
Original Cast; *Cabaret* . . . .(Columbia)
Two Lane Highway
Pure Prairie League; *Two Lane Highway* . . . . (RCA)
Two Left Feet
Richard Thompson; *Hand Of Darkness* . . . . (Hannibal)
Watching The Dark-History Of Richard Thompson . . . . (Rykodisc)
Two Less Lonely People In The World
Air Supply; *Now & Forever* . . . .(Arista)
Two Little Bees
Hollywood Flames; *Hollywood Flames* . . . . (Specialty)
Two Little Girls
Ani DiFranco; *Little Plastic Castle* . . . . (Righteous Babe)
Two Lives
Bonnie Raitt; *Sweet Forgiveness* . . . .(Warner Bros.)
Carpenters; *Voice Of The Heart* . . . .(A&M)
Randy Crawford; *Secret Combination* . . . .(Warner Bros.)
Two Lovers
Mary Wells; *Hitsville USA-The Motown Singles Collection-1959-
1971-C* . . . .(Motown)
Mary Wells' Greatest Hits . . . .(Motown)
Two Minutes Till Lunch
Wall Of Voodoo; *Dark Continent* . . . .(A&M)
Two Minutes To Midnight
Iron Maiden; *A Real Dead One* . . . .(Capitol)
Live After Death-World Slavery Tour . . . .(Capitol)
Powerslave . . . .(Capitol)
Two Moose In A Caboose
Stan Kenton & His Orchestra; *The Uncollected Stan Kenton & His
Orchestra-#5-1945-1947* . . . .(Hindsight)
Two More Bottles Of Wine
Delbert McClinton; *Honky Tonkin'-I Done Me Some* . . . . (Alligator)
Emmylou Harris; *Honky Tonk Country-C* . . . .(Warner Bros.)
Profile/Best Of Emmylou Harris . . . .(Warner Bros.)
Quarter Moon In A Ten Cent Town . . . .(Warner Bros.)
Martina McBride; *Wild Angels* . . . . (RCA)
Two O'Clock In The Morning
Stuart Duncan; *Stuart Duncan* . . . .(Rounder)
Two O'Clock Jump
Harry James; *All-Time Favorites By Harry James* . . . (Sony Music Special Prod.)

Harry James' Greatest Hits . . . . (Columbia)
Two O'Clock Jump . . . . (Pro-Arte)

Two Of A Kind, Workin' On A Full House
Garth Brooks; *No Fences* . . . . (Capitol)

Two Of Hearts
Stacey Q; *Better Than Heaven* . . . . (Atlantic)
Dance Traxx-#2-C . . . . (Atlantic)

Two Of Us
Beatles; *Beatles-Box Set* . . . . (Capitol)
Let It Be . . . . (Capitol)

Two Old Cats Like Us
Hank Williams, Jr. & Ray Charles; *Hank Williams, Jr.'s Greatest*
Hits-#2 . . . . (WB/Curb)
Ray Charles & Hank Williams, Jr.; *Friendship-C* . . . . (Columbia)
Seven Spanish Angels & Other Hits . . . . (Columbia)

Two Out Of Three Ain't Bad
Meat Loaf; *Bat Out Of Hell* . . . . (Epic)
Hits Out Of Hell . . . . (Epic)

Two People Fell In Love
Brad Paisley; *Brad Paisley-Part II* . . . . (Arista)

Two Pina Coladas
Garth Brooks; *Sevens* . . . . (Capitol)

Two Plays For A Quarter
Kathy Hart & The Bluestars; *Tonight I Want It All* . . . . (Biograph)

Two Princes
Spin Doctors; *Pocket Full Of Kryptonite* . . . . (Epic Portrait Assoc.)

Two Pump Texaco
Diamond Rio; *Unbelievable* . . . . (Arista)

Two Purple Shadows
Jerry Vale; *Jerry Vale-17 Most Requested Songs* . . . . (Legacy)
Jerry Vale's All-Time Greatest Hits . . . . (Columbia)

Two Rivers In Montana
Gove Scrivenor; *Coconut Gove* . . . . (Flying Fish)

Two Scoops Of Raisins
Common Sense; *Can I Borrow A Dollar?* . . . . (Relativity)

Two Shades Of Autumn
Stan Kenton; *Rendezvous With Stan Kenton* . . . . (Creative World)

Two Silhouettes
Dinah Shore; *Dinah Shore-16 Most Requested Songs* . . . . (Legacy)

Two Silhouettes
Sha Na Na; *Best Of Sha Na Na* . . . . (Pair)

Two Sleepy People
Art Garfunkel; *Up 'Til Now* . . . . (Columbia)
Fats Waller; *Fats Waller-Masterpieces-#3* . . . . (EPM)
Jo Sullivan Loesser & Others; *Loesser By Loesser* . . . . (DRG)
Kay Kyser & His Orchestra; *Best Of The Big Bands-C* . . . . . . (Columbia)

Two Sparrows In A Hurricane
Tanya Tucker; *Can't Run From Yourself* . . . . (Liberty)
Tanya Tucker's Greatest Hits-1990-1992 . . . . (Capitol)

Two Step
Dave Matthews Band; *Crash* . . . . (RCA)

Two Steps Behind
Def Leppard; *ST/Last Action Hero* . . . . (Columbia)

Two Story House
George Jones & Tammy Wynette; *George Jones & Tammy Wynette-16*
Biggest Hits . . . . (Epic/Legacy)

Two Teardrops
Steve Wariner; *Two Teardrops* . . . . (Capitol)

Two Tickets To Paradise
Eddie Money; *Eddie Money* . . . . (Columbia)
Eddie Money's Greatest Hits-Sound Of Money . . . . (Columbia)
Unplug It In . . . . (Columbia)

Two To Make It Right
Seduction; *100% Pure Dance-C* . . . . (Mercury)

Two To Tango
Bing Crosby; *The Radio Years: 20 Songs* . . . . (Crescendo)

Two Trains
Little Feat; *Dixie Chicken* . . . . (Warner Bros.)
Hoy-Hoy! . . . . (Warner Bros.)
Lowell George; *Thanks I'll Eat It Here* . . . . (Warner Bros.)

Two Trains Running
Blues Project; *No Time Like The Right Time-Best Of The Blues*
Project . . . . (Rhino)
Projections . . . . (Polydor)
Paul Butterfield Blues Band; *East-West* . . . . (Elektra)

Two Tribes
Frankie Goes To Hollywood; *Welcome To The Pleasuredome* . . . . (Island)

Two Triple Cheese, Side Order Of Fries
Commander Cody & His Lost Planet Airmen; *Aces High* . . . . (Relix)

Two Weeks Last Summer
Sandy Denny; *Who Knows Where The Time Goes* . . . . (Hannibal)
Sandy Denny & The Strawbs; *Sandy Denny & The Strawbs* . . . . (Hannibal)

Two White Horses
John Lee Hooker; *That's Where It's At* . . . . (Stax)

Two Years In Chicago
Robin Trower; *1st Dibs* . . . . (Flying Fish)

Two Years Of Torture
Lou Rawls; *Lou Rawls-At Last* . . . . (Blue Note)

Percy Mayfield; *Please Send Me Someone To Love* . . . . (Intermedia)

Two-Car Garage
B.J. Thomas; *19 Hot Country Requests-#2-C* . . . . (Epic)
Great American Dream . . . . (Cleveland International)
Greatest Country Hits Of The '80s-1984-C . . . . (Columbia)

Two-Story House
George Jones & Tammy Wynette; *20 Years Of Hits/First Lady Of*
Country . . . . (Epic)
George Jones' Greatest Hits-#2 . . . . (Epic)
Tears Of Fire-25th Anniversary Collection . . . . (Epic)
Tammy Wynette & George Jones; *Encore-Tammy Wynette & George*
Jones . . . . (Epic)

Two-Timin' Me
Remingtons; *Blue Frontier* . . . . (BNA)

Two-Tone Shoes
Homer & Jethro; *Get Hot Or Go Home-Vintage*
Rockabilly-C . . . . (Country Music Foundation)

When Two Worlds Collide
Rex Allen, Jr.; *20 Golden Souvenirs Of Music City U.S.A.-C* . . . . (Plantation)
Roger Miller; *Best Of Roger Miller-His Greatest Songs* . . . . (Curb)

Where Are You Now
Trisha Yearwood; *Real Live Woman* . . . . (MCA)

Where It's At
Beck; *Odelay* . . . . (David Geffen Co.)

Without You
Dixie Chicks; *Fly* . . . . (Monument)

You Better Think Twice
Vince Gill; *When Love Finds You* . . . . (MCA)

NUMBERS: 3

*See Also: **AGES (various), COUNTING SONGS, MONTHS &***
DATES (various), NUMBERS (various), TIME: SPECIFIC

1-2-3
Gloria Estefan; *Gloria Estefan's Greatest Hits* . . . . (Epic)
Gloria Estefan and Miami Sound Machine; *Let It Loose* . . . . (Epic)

1-2-3
Len Barry; *24 Of The Grooviest Hits Of All Time! The '60s Ultimate*
Collection-#1-C . . . . (Sundazed Music)

3 A.M. Eternal
KLF; *MTV Party To Go-#2-C* . . . . (Tommy Boy)
The White Room . . . . (Arista)

3 A.M. Somewhere Out Of Beaumont
KLF; *Chill Out* . . . . (Wax Trax)

3 Chains O' Gold
Prince And The New Power Generation; *Love Symbol Album* . . . . (Paisley Park)

3 Martini Lunch
Graham Parker; *Best Of Graham Parker 1988-1991* . . . . (RCA)

3 O'Clock...School's Out!
Full Force; *Guess Who's Comin' To The Crib?* . . . . (Columbia)

3 Strange Days
School Of Fish; *School Of Fish* . . . . (Capitol)

3am
Matchbox Twenty; *Yourself Or Someone Like You* . . . . (Lava)

3rd Of June
Yello; *Flag* . . . . (Mercury)

African Trilogy
Neil Diamond; *Tap Root Manuscript* . . . . (MCA)

Austin
Blake Shelton; *Blake Shelton* . . . . (Giant)

Baa Baa Black Sheep
Original Soundtrack; *Toddler Favorites* . . . . (Kid Rhino/Rhino 4 Kids)

Book, The
Sheryl Crow; *Sheryl Crow* . . . . (A&M)

Dance: Ten; Looks: Three
Original Cast; *A Chorus Line* . . . . (Columbia)

Door Number Three
Jimmy Buffett; *A1A* . . . . (MCA)

Gimme Three Steps
Lynyrd Skynyrd; *Gold & Platinum* . . . . (MCA)
One More From The Road . . . . (MCA)
Pronounced Leh-nerd Skin-nerd . . . . (MCA)

Halfway Home Cafe
Ricky Skaggs and Kentucky Thunder; *History Of The Future* . . (Skaggs Family)

Helplessly Hoping
Crosby, Stills & Nash; *Crosby, Stills & Nash* . . . . (Atlantic)
CSN . . . . (Atlantic)
Crosby, Stills, Nash & Young; *So Far* . . . . (Atlantic)

It's 3 O'Clock In The Morning
Mom & Dads; *Blue Hawaii* . . . . (Crescendo)

John 3:16
Wyclef; *Muggs Presents...The Soul Assassins-C* . . . . (Columbia)

Knock Three Times
Tony Orlando & Dawn; *Best Of Tony Orlando & Dawn* . . . . (Rhino)

Louisiana Lou & Three-Card Monty John
Allman Brothers Band; *Win, Lose Or Draw* . . . . (Polydor)

Mistake No. 3
Culture Club; *Waking Up With The House On Fire* . . . .(Virgin)
Old King Cole
Original Soundtrack; *Children's Favorites* . . . . (Kid Rhino/Rhino 4 Kids)
One And One Does Not Make Three
Ides Of March; *Ideology* . . . .(Sundazed Music)
One Plus One Equals Three
Original Cast; *Side Show* . . . .(Sony Music Classical)
One Week
Barenaked Ladies; *Stunt* . . . .(Reprise)
Totally Hits-#1-C . . . .(Arista)
Pigs (Three Different Ones)
Pink Floyd; *Animals* . . . .(Columbia)
Shine On . . . .(Columbia)
Quarter To Three
Gary U.S. Bonds; *Best Of Gary U.S. Bonds* . . . .(Rhino)
Best Of Gary U.S. Bonds . . . .(EMI Legends Of Rock 'N' Roll)
Song I See You Three
Doobie Brothers; *What Were Once Vices Are Now Habits* . . . . . . (Warner Bros.)
Sucker In A 3-Piece Suit
Van Halen; *OU812* . . . . (Warner Bros.)
Thee Cool Cats
Beatles; *The Beatles-Anthology-#1* . . . . (Capitol)
Theme From "Close Encounters Of The Third Kind"
John Williams; *Billboard Top Movie Hits-1970s-C* . . . .(Rhino)
ST/Close Encounters Of The Third Kind . . . .(Varese Sarabande)
Original Soundtrack; *Sci-Fi's Greatest Hits-#3-The Uninvited* . . . . (TVT)
Walter Murphy; *Themes From E.T.* . . . . (MCA)
Theme From "Dr. Kildare" (Three Stars Will Shine Tonight)
Betty Carter; *'Round Midnight* . . . . (Atlantic)
Original Soundtrack; *Television's Greatest Hits-#4-Black & White
Classics-C* . . . . (TVT)
Theme From "My Three Sons"
Original Soundtrack; *CBS: The First 50 Years* . . . . (TVT)
Television's Greatest Hits-#1-C . . . . (TVT)
Theme From "The Three Stooges"
Original Soundtrack; *Television's Greatest Hits-#2-C* . . . . (TVT)
Theme From "Three's Company"
Original Soundtrack; *Television's Greatest Hits-#3-1970s & 1980s-C* . . . . (TVT)
Third Degree
Eric Clapton; *From The Cradle* . . . .(Duck/Reprise)
Third Man Theme (Harry Lime Theme)
Band; *Moondog Matinee* . . . .(Capitol)
Dukes Of Dixieland; *Dukes Of Dixieland's Greatest Hits* . . . . (MCA)
Guy Lombardo & His Royal Canadians; *Best Of Guy Lombardo* . . . . . .(Curb)
Third Of July
Jody Grind; *Lefty's Deceiver* . . . . (DB)
Third Rate Romance
Amazing Rhythm Aces; *Stacked Deck* . . . . (MCA)
Rosanne Cash; *Somewhere In The Stars* . . . .(Columbia)
Sammy Kershaw; *Cryin' Lyin' Lovin' & Leavin'-C* . . . .(Universal)
Feelin' Good Train . . . .(Mercury)
The Hits-Chapter 1 . . . .(Mercury)
Third Rock From The Sun
Joe Diffie; *A Thousand Winding Roads* . . . . (Epic)
Third Stone From The Sun
Jimi Hendrix; *Essential Jimi Hendrix* . . . .(Reprise)
Kiss The Sky . . . .(Reprise)
Jimi Hendrix Experience; *Are You Experienced?* . . . .(Reprise)
Third Time Lucky
Foghat; *Best Of Foghat* . . . .(Rhino)
Boogie Motel . . . .(Rhino)
Third World Child
Johnny Clegg & Savuka; *Sounds Of Soweto* . . . .(Capitol)
Third World Child . . . .(Capitol)
Three Base Hit
Pat Martino; *Exit* . . . . (Muse)
Three Bells, The
Browns; *Billboard Top Country Hits-1959-C* . . . .(Rhino)
Nipper's Greatest Hits Of The '50s-#1-C . . . . (RCA)
Three Blind Mice
Van Alexander; *Small Fry-Capitol Sings Kids Songs For
Grownups-C* . . . .(Capitol)
Three Cigarettes In An Ashtray
k.d. lang; *New Tradition Sings The Old Tradition-C* . . . .(Warner Bros.)
k.d. lang and The Reclines; *Angel With A Lariat* . . . .(Sire)
Patsy Cline; *20 Golden Pieces Of Patsy Cline* . . . .(Bulldog)
Patsy Cline . . . . (MCA)
Stop Look & Listen . . . . (MCA)
Walkin' Dreams-Her First Recordings-#1 . . . .(Rhino)
Three Coins In The Fountain
Andy Williams; *Moon River & Other Great Movie Themes* . . . .(Columbia)
Doris Day & Frank De Vol Orchestra; *Hooray For
Hollywood-#2-C* . . . .(Columbia)
Four Aces; *Billboard Top Movie Hits-1950-1954-C* . . . .(Rhino)
Four Aces' Greatest Hits . . . . (MCA)
Frank Sinatra; *At The Movies* . . . .(Capitol)
Capitol Collectors Series-Frank Sinatra . . . .(Capitol)

Harry James; *Harry James Plays The Songs That Sold A Million* . . . .(Columbia)
Julius LaRosa; *The Envelope Please-Academy Award Winning Songs-#2
(1946-1957)-C* . . . .(Rhino)
Three Drunk Newts
Barnes & Barnes; *Dr. Demento's Dementia Royale-C* . . . .(Rhino)
Three Drunken Maidens
Maddy Prior & Tim Hart; *Summer Solstice* . . . . (Shanachie)
Three Flowers
McCoy Tyner; *Soliloquy* . . . . (Blue Note)
Today & Tomorrow . . . . (Blue Note)
Three Flowers
Richard Hayward; *Ireland Of Treasures-Voices & Melodies-C* . . . .(Capitol)
Three Girls From Detroit
Will & The Bushmen; *Will & The Bushmen* . . . .(SBK)
Three Guitar Special
Bob Wills & His Texas Playboys; *Bob Wills & His Texas Playboys-
Anthology 1935-1973* . . . .(Rhino)
Three Hearts In A Tangle
Roy Drusky; *45-#31193* . . . .(Decca)
Three Little Birds
Bob Marley & The Wailers; *Exodus* . . . . (Tuff Gong)
Legend: The Best Of Bob Marley & The Wailers . . . .(Island)
Songs Of Freedom . . . . (Tuff Gong)
Three Little Fishes
Andrews Sisters; *Boogie Woogie Bugle Girls* . . . . (MCA)
Kay Kyser & His Orchestra; *Dr. Demento Presents The Greatest Novelty
Records-#1-1940s & Before-C* . . . .(Rhino)
Sentimental Favorites . . . .(Columbia)
Three Little Pigs
Lloyd Price; *Lloyd Price's Greatest Hits* . . . . (MCA)
Three Little Words
Carmen McRae; *Great American Songbook* . . . . (Atlantic)
Duke Ellington & His Orchestra; *Nipper's Greatest Hits Of The
'30s-#2-C* . . . . (RCA)
Nat "King" Cole; *L-O-V-E* . . . .(Capitol)
Three Marlenas
Wallflowers; *Bringing Down The Horse* . . . . (Interscope)
Three Mile Island
Pinkard & Bowden; *Writers In Disguise* . . . .(Warner Bros.)
Three Mile Smile
Aerosmith; *Night In The Ruts* . . . .(Columbia)
Pandora's Box . . . .(Columbia)
Three O'Clock Blues
B.B. King; *Best Blues Album In The World...Ever!-C* . . . .(Virgin)
Chart Toppers-R&B Hits Of The '50s-C . . . .(Priority)
Three Ravens
Peter, Paul & Mary; *Peter, Paul and Mary In Concert* . . . .(Warner Bros.)
Three Seasons Of Winter
Joel Mabus; *Fairies & Fools* . . . . (Flying Fish)
Three Steps From The Altar
Shep And The Limelites; *Rockin' & Rollin' Wedding Songs-#2-C* . . . . .(Rhino)
Three Steps To Heaven
Eddie Cochran; *Eddie Cochran-Legendary Masters* . . . . (EMI)
Eddie Cochran's Greatest Hits . . . .(Curb)
Three Sunrises
U2; *Unforgettable Fire* . . . .(Island)
Wide Awake In America . . . .(Island)
Three Times A Lady
Commodores; *All The Great Love Songs-Commodores* . . . .(Motown)
Commodores Greatest Hits . . . .(Motown)
Commodores-All The Great Hits . . . .(Motown)
Endless Love-Motown's Greatest Love Songs-C . . . .(Motown)
Natural High . . . .(Motown)
Three Window Coupe
Rip Chords; *Rock Artifacts-From The Vaults-#4-C* . . . .(Columbia)
Triplets
Fred Astaire/Nanette Fabray/Jack Buchanan; *ST/Band Wagon* . . . . (MCA)
Original Cast; *Forbidden Broadway* . . . .(DRG)
Two Out Of Three Ain't Bad
Meat Loaf; *Bat Out Of Hell* . . . . (Epic)
Hits Out Of Hell . . . . (Epic)

NUMBERS: 4

See Also: **AGES (various), COUNTING SONGS, COUNTRIES:
AMERICA (4th of July), MONTHS & DATES (various), NUMBERS
(various), TIME: SPECIFIC**

10-4 (Calling All Cars)
Benny Spellman; *Fortune Teller-Golden Classics* . . . .(Collectables)
4 A.M. In Texas
7 Seconds; *Soulforce Revolution* . . . . (Restless)
4 Miles
Take 6; *Join The Band-C* . . . . (Reprise)
4 Page Letter
Aaliyah; *One In A Million* . . . .(BlackGround Enterp./Atlantic)

4 Seasons Of Loneliness
Boyz II Men; *Evolution* . . . . (Motown)
4th Of July
U2; *Unforgettable Fire* . . . . (Island)
4th Of July, Asbury Park (Sandy)
Bruce Springsteen; *The Wild, The Innocent & The E Street Shuffle* . . (Columbia)
Bruce Springsteen & The E Street Band; *Bruce Springsteen & The E Street
    Band Live/1975-85* . . . . (Legacy)
All 4 Love
Color Me Badd; *C.M.B.* . . . .(Giant)
MTV Party To Go-#2-C . . . . (Tommy Boy)
At 4 A.M.
Tom Verlaine; *Flash Light* . . . .(I.R.S.)
Big Four Poster Bed
Brenda Lee; *Brenda Lee-Anthology-#1 & #2* . . . . (MCA)
Blue Yodel #4 (California Blues)
Bill Monroe; *Columbia Historic Edition-Bill Monroe* . . . . (Columbia)
Jimmie Rodgers; *Jimmie Rodgers-Early Years-1928-1929* . . . . (Rounder)
Never No Mo' Blues . . . . (RCA)
This Is Jimmie Rodgers . . . . (RCA)
Merle Haggard & The Strangers; *Train Whistle Blues* . . . . (Rounder)
Double Dealin' Four Flusher
Doobie Brothers; *Stampede* . . . .(Warner Bros.)
Four In The Morning
Night Ranger; *7 Wishes* . . . .(MCA)
Night Ranger's Greatest Hits . . . . (Camel)
Four In The Morning
Faron Young; *Faron Young's Greatest Hits-#3* . . . . (Step One)
Four Leaf Clover
Abra Moore; *Strangest Places* . . . .(Arista Austin)
Four Percent Pantomime
Band; *Cahoots* . . . . (Capitol)
To Kingdom Come-The Definitive Collection . . . . (Capitol)
Four Strong Winds
Ian & Sylvia; *Best Of Ian & Sylvia* . . . . (Vanguard)
Ian & Sylvia's Greatest Hits . . . . (Vanguard)
Neil Young; *Comes A Time* . . . . (Reprise)
Four Wheel Drive
C.W. McCall; *C.W. McCall's Greatest Hits* . . . . (Polydor)
Wolf Creek Pass . . . . (MGM)
Four Wheels
38 Special; *38 Special* . . . . (A&M)
Fourth Of July
X; *See How We Are* . . . . (Elektra)
Fourth Of July
Mariah Carey; *Butterfly* . . . . (Columbia)
Fourth Of July
Linda Waterfall; *Body English* . . . . (Flying Fish)
Fourth Of July
Rosalie Sorrels; *Lonesome Roving Wolves-Songs & Ballads Of
    The West* . . . . (Green Linnet)
Fourth Of July
Dave Alvin; *Romeo's Escape* . . . .(Epic)
Fourth Of July At A County Fair
Red Clay Ramblers; *Chuckin' The Frizz* . . . . (Flying Fish)
Fourth Time Around
Bob Dylan; *Blonde On Blonde* . . . . (Columbia)
Girl Inside My Head
Blues Traveler; *Bridge* . . . . (A&M)
Helplessly Hoping
Crosby, Stills & Nash; *Crosby, Stills & Nash* . . . . (Atlantic)
CSN . . . .(Atlantic)
Crosby, Stills, Nash & Young; *So Far* . . . . (Atlantic)
House Of Four Doors
Moody Blues; *In Search Of The Lost Chord* . . . . (Polydor)
I'm Looking Over A Four Leaf Clover
Al Jolson; *Best Of Al Jolson* . . . .(MCA)
Rainbow 'Round My Shoulder . . . .(MCA Special Prod.)
Jerry Lee Lewis; *I Am What I Am* . . . . (MCA)
It's Four In The Morning
Faron Young; *Faron Young-Golden Hits* . . . . (Mercury)
Faron Young-The Hits . . . . (Mercury)
June 25 At The Fourth Of July
Shel Silverstein; *Great Conch Train Robbery* . . . . (Flying Fish)
Let The Four Winds Blow
Fats Domino; *Best Of Fats Domino* . . . .(EMI)
Billboard Top R&B Hits-1961-C . . . . (Rhino)
Roy Brown; *Best Of New Orleans Rhythm & Blues-#1-C* . . . . (Rhino)
Lucky 4 You (Tonight I'm Just Me)
SHeDAISY; *The Whole Shebang* . . . . (Lyric Street)
Positively 4th Street
Bob Dylan; *Biograph* . . . . (Columbia)
Bob Dylan's Greatest Hits . . . . (Columbia)
Byrds; *The Byrds* . . . . (Columbia)
The Byrds (Untitled) . . . . (Legacy)
Radio 4
Public Image Ltd.; *Second Edition* . . . . (Island)

Touch A Four Leaf Clover
Atlantic Starr; *Atlantic Starr-Classics-#10* . . . . (A&M)
Secret Lovers: Best Of Atlantic Starr . . . . (A&M)
Yours Forever . . . . (A&M)

NUMBERS: 5

*See Also: **AGES (various), COUNTING SONGS, MONTHS &
DATES (various), NUMBERS (various), TIME: SPECIFIC***

5 Miles To Empty
Brownstone; *Still Climbing* . . . . (MJJ Music/Work)
5 Steps
Dru Hill; *Dru Hill* . . . . (Island)
9 To 5
Dolly Parton; *9 To 5 And Odd Jobs* . . . . (RCA)
Best There Is . . . . (RCA)
Dolly Parton's Greatest Hits . . . . (RCA)
I Am Woman-C . . . . (Nick At Nite)
Nipper's Greatest Hits Of The '80s-C . . . . (RCA)
April 5th
Talk Talk; *Colour Of Spring* . . . . (EMI)
Easter Parade (Fifth Avenue)
Andy Russell; *Puttin' On The Ritz-Capitol Sings Berlin-C* . . . . (Capitol)
Bing Crosby; *All Time Best Of Bing Crosby* . . . . (Curb)
Judy Garland & Fred Astaire; *ST/Easter Parade* . . . . (Rhino)
Sarah Vaughan; *Complete Sarah Vaughan On Mercury-#2* . . . . (Mercury)
Fifth Of July
Terry Reid; *The Driver* . . . . (Warner Bros.)
Five Feet High And Rising
Johnny Cash; *The Man In Black-His Greatest Hits* . . . . (Legacy)
Five Foot Two, Eyes Of Blue
Mom & Dads; *Very Best Of The Mom & Dads* . . . .(Crescendo)
Five Guys Named Moe
Joe Jackson; *Jumpin' Jive* . . . . (A&M)
Louis Jordan; *Best Of Louis Jordan* . . . . (MCA)
Original Decca Recordings-#2 . . . . (Decca)
Five Long Years
Eric Clapton; *From The Cradle* . . . .(Duck/Reprise)
Five Miles To Texas
Stockton & Johnson; *Born By The River* . . . . (Out Of Print)
Five Minutes
Lorrie Morgan; *Lorrie Morgan's Greatest Hits* . . . .(BNA)
Lorrie Morgan-Super Hits . . . . (RCA)
Pam Tillis; *Pam Tillis-Collection* . . . . (Warner Bros.)
Five O'Clock World
Hal Ketchum; *Past The Point Of Rescue* . . . . (Curb)
Vogues; *ST/Good Morning, Vietnam* . . . . (A&M)
Vogues' Greatest Hits . . . . (SSS International)
Vogues' Greatest Hits . . . . (Rhino)
Five Planets In Leo
Brew Moore Quintet; *Brew Moore Quintet* . . . .(Fantasy)
High Five
Chuck Loeb; *Listen* . . . .(Shanachie)
I Found A Million-Dollar Baby (In A Five-And-Ten-Cent Store)
Barbra Streisand; *ST/Funny Girl* . . . . (Columbia)
Bing Crosby; *Pennies From Heaven* . . . . (Pro-Arte)
Fred Waring's Pennsylvanians; *78-#22707* . . . . (Victor)
Nat "King" Cole; *Nat "King" Cole-Gift Set* . . . . (Capitol)
I Got 5 On It
Luniz; *Operation Stackola* . . . . (Noo Trybe)
I'll Be There For You
Bon Jovi; *New Jersey* . . . . (Jambco)
I've Got Five Dollars
Bobby Short; *50 By Bobby Short* . . . .(Atlantic)
Ella Fitzgerald; *Rodgers & Hart Songbook* . . . . (Verve)
Tony Bennett; *Rodgers & Hart Songbook* . . . . (DRG)
I've Got Five Dollars And It's Saturday Night
Faron Young; *Faron Young's Greatest Hits* . . . . (CEMA Special Prod.)
George & Gene; *Gene Pitney-Anthology 1961-1968* . . . . (Rhino)
George Jones; *Best Of George Jones-1955-1967* . . . . (Rhino)
Lucky 4 You (Tonight I'm Just Me)
SHeDAISY; *The Whole Shebang* . . . .(Lyric Street)
Mach 5
Presidents Of The United States Of America; *Presidents Of The United States
    Of America II* . . . . (Columbia)
Mambo No. 5 (A Little Bit Of...)
Lou Bega; *A Little Bit Of Mambo* . . . .(RCA)
Totally Hits-#2-C . . . . (Elektra)
Morning Train (Nine To Five)
Sheena Easton; *Sheena Easton* . . . . (EMI)
Next Plane To London
Rose Garden; *Only Love-1965-1969-C* . . . .(JCI Assoc. Labels)
Obviously Five Believers
Bob Dylan; *Blonde On Blonde* . . . . (Columbia)
One And One Is Five
Ben Aiken; *Ben Aiken & Friends* . . . . (Collectables)

Delfonics; *Forever New.* . . . . (Volt)
One Week
Barenaked Ladies; *Stunt* . . . .(Reprise)
Totally Hits-#1-C . . . . (Arista)
Rollin' In My 5.0
Vanilla Ice; *Extremely Live* . . . . (SBK)
Space Station #5
Montrose; *Montrose* . . . . (Warner Bros.)
Sullivan
Caroline's Spine; *Monsoon* . . . .(Hollywood)
Theme From "Fireball XL-5"
Original Soundtrack; *Television's Greatest Hits-#1-C* . . . . (TVT)

NUMBERS: 6

See Also: **AGES (various), COUNTING SONGS, MONTHS & DATES (various), NUMBERS (various), TIME: SPECIFIC**

6 Underground
Sneaker Pimps; *Becoming X* . . . .(Virgin)
6, 8, 12
Brian McKnight; *Back At One* . . . . (Motown)
After 12, Before 6
Sam Salter; *It's On Tonight* . . . . (LaFace)
From A Buick 6
Bob Dylan; *Highway 61 Revisited* . . . . (Columbia)
If 6 Was 9
Jimi Hendrix; *Axis: Bold As Love* . . . . (Reprise)
Essential Jimi Hendrix . . . . (Reprise)
She'll Be Coming 'Round The Mountain
Four Freshmen & Stan Kenton & Orchestra; *Live At Butler University* . . . .(Creative World)
Mormon Tabernacle Choir; *This Land Is Your Land* . . . . (Columbia)
Original Soundtrack; *Children's Favorites* . . . . (Kid Rhino/Rhino 4 Kids)
School Days-Kids Classics . . . . (Benson)
Sing A Song Of Sixpence
Original Soundtrack; *Children's Favorites* . . . . (Kid Rhino/Rhino 4 Kids)
Six Days On The Road
Boxcar Willie; *Truck Driving Favorites* . . . . (Madacy)
Dave Dudley; *Billboard Top Country Hits-1963-C* . . . . (Rhino)
Country Music Classics-#2-1960-1965-C . . . . (K-Tel)
Legends Of Country Guitar-#2-C . . . . (Rhino)
Truck Driver Boogie Big Rig Hits-1939-1969-C . . . . . . (Audium)
Flying Burrito Brothers; *Cabin Fever* . . . . (Relix)
Farther Along-Best Of The Flying Burrito Brothers . . . . (A&M)
Last Of The Red Hot Burritos . . . . (A&M)
Sawyer Brown; *Six Days On The Road* . . . . (Curb)
Taj Mahal; *Giant Step/De Ole Folks At Home* . . . . (Columbia)
Legends Of Rock Guitar-'60s-#2-C . . . . (Rhino)
Six Feet Of Snow
Little Feat; *Down On The Farm* . . . . (Warner Bros.)
Six O'Clock News
John Prine; *John Prine* . . . . (Atlantic)
John Prine-Souvenirs . . . .(Oh Boy)
Six Pack To Go, A
Hank Thompson and His Brazos Valley Boys; *Best Of The Best Of Hank Thompson* . . . . (Gusto)
Capitol Collectors Series-Hank Thompson . . . . (Capitol)
Country Comes To Carnegie Hall-C . . . . (MCA)
Hank Thompson . . . . (Dot)
Hank Thompson's Greatest Hits-#2 . . . .(Step One)
Six Times Six Is Thirty-Six
Frances White; *Music From The New York Stage (1890-1920)-#4-1917-1920-C* . . . .(Pearl)
Six-Pack Summer
Phil Vassar; *Phil Vassar* . . . . (Arista)
Theme From "Surfside 6"
Original Soundtrack; *Television's Greatest Hits-#1-C* . . . . (TVT)
Theme From "The Six Million Dollar Man"
Original Soundtrack; *Television's Greatest Hits-#5-In Living Color-C* . . (TVT)

NUMBERS: 7

See Also: **AGES (various), COUNTING SONGS, MONTHS & DATES (various), NUMBERS (various), TIME: SPECIFIC**

24/7
Kevon Edmonds; *24/7* . . . .(RCA)
24-7 Man
Robert Cray Band; *Take Your Shoes Off* . . . . (Rykodisc)
7
Prince And The New Power Generation; *Love Symbol Album* . . . . (Paisley Park)
7
James; *7* . . . . (Fontana)
7 Chinese Bros.
R.E.M.; *Reckoning* . . . . (I.R.S.)

7 Deadly Sins
Traveling Wilburys; *Traveling Wilburys-Vol. 3* . . . .(Wilbury/Warner Bros.)
7 Deadly Sins
Mary's Danish; *Circa* . . . . (Morgan Creek)
7 Dee Jays
Boogie Down Productions; *Edutainment (Education + Entertainment)* . . . (Jive)
7 Sign (Bizzy)
Bone Thugs-N-Harmony; *Art Of War* . . . . (Ruthless/Relativity)
7 Things To Do On Speed
God's Acre; *Ten Gospel Greats* . . . .(Wax Trax)
7-11 (A Winner)
Li'l Wally; *Polish Carnival* . . . .(Jay Jay)
April Seventh
Larry Coryell & John Scofield & Joe Beck; *Tributaries.* . . . . (Novus)
Billy 1, 2 & 7
Bob Dylan; *ST/Pat Garrett & Billy The Kid* . . . .(Columbia)
Game Seven
Chuck Brown & The Soul Searchers; *Bustin' Loose* . . . . (Source)
Halfway Home Cafe
Ricky Skaggs and Kentucky Thunder; *History Of The Future* . . .(Skaggs Family)
Heaven On The 7th Floor
Paul Nicholas; *Super Hits Of The '70s-Have A Nice Day-#24-C* . . . .(Rhino)
Hoochie Coochie Man
Eric Clapton; *From The Cradle* . . . .(Duck/Reprise)
Eric Clapton featuring Buddy Guy; *The Concert For New York City-C* . . . .(Columbia)
Jack Daniel's Old No. 7
Jerry Lee Lewis; *Killer Country* . . . .(Mercury)
Just Seven Numbers
Four Tops; *Compact Command Performances-Four Tops* . . . . (Motown)
Four Tops-Anthology . . . . (Motown)
Love Is The Seventh Wave
Sting; *Dream Of The Blue Turtles* . . . .(A&M)
Greenpeace/Rainbow Warriors-C . . . . (Geffen)
Lucky 4 You (Tonight I'm Just Me)
SHeDAISY; *The Whole Shebang* . . . . (Lyric Street)
March 7th
Leaving Trains; *Well Down Blue Highway* . . . . (Enigma)
More Than Seven Dwarfs In Penis-Land
Ron Geesin; *ST/The Body.* . . . . (Restless)
October 7
Mitch Watkins; *Strings With Wings* . . . . (Enja)
Seven Angels
Bruce Springsteen; *Tracks* . . . .(Columbia)
Seven Bridges Road
Eagles; *Eagles Greatest Hits, Volume 2* . . . . (Asylum)
Eagles Live . . . . (Asylum)
Steve Young; *Seven Bridges Road* . . . .(Rounder)
Seven Come Eleven
Benny Goodman; *Benny Goodman-Live At Carnegie Hall* . . . . (London)
Charlie Christian; *Genius Of The Electric Guitar* . . . .(Columbia)
Herb Ellis & Joe Pass; *Seven Come Eleven* . . . .(Concord Jazz)
Two For The Road . . . . (Pablo)
Seven Days
Mary J. Blige; *Share My World* . . . . (MCA)
The Tour . . . . (MCA)
Seven Days Come Sunday
Rodney Lay; *Silent Partners* . . . . (Sun)
Seven Days Of May
Testament; *Souls Of Black* . . . .(Megaforce)
Seven Deadly Sins
Bryan Ferry; *Bete Noire* . . . . (Reprise)
Seven Deadly Virtues
Original Cast; *Camelot.* . . . .(Columbia)
Seven Doors Hotel
Europe; *Europe* . . . . (Epic)
Seven Dwarfs
Airto Moreira; *Struck By Lightning* . . . . (Venture)
Seven Eleven
Commander Cody; *Midnight Man* . . . .(Out Of Print)
Seven Little Girls Sitting In The Back Seat
Paul Evans; *Music To Remember-C* . . . .(Dominion Entert.)
Seven Rooms Of Gloom
Four Tops; *Four Tops' Greatest Hits* . . . .(Motown)
Four Tops Reach Out . . . .(Motown)
Four Tops-Anthology . . . . (Motown)
Seven Seas
Babyface; *The Day* . . . . (Epic)
Seven Spanish Angels
Willie Nelson & Ray Charles; *19 Hot Country Requests-#3-C* . . . . (Epic)
Friendship-C . . . .(Columbia)
Greatest Country Hits Of The '80s-1985-C . . . .(Columbia)
Half Nelson-C . . . .(Columbia)
Seven Steps To Heaven
Miles Davis; *Miles Davis' Greatest Hits* . . . .(Columbia)
Seven Steps To Heaven . . . .(Columbia)
Seven Sundays
Extreme; *III Sides To Every Story* . . . .(A&M)

Seven Wonders
Fleetwood Mac; *Tango In The Night* . . . .(Warner Bros.)
Seven Year Ache
Rosanne Cash; *Columbia Country Classics-#5-A New Tradition-C* . . (Columbia)
   Greatest Country Hits Of The '80s-1981-C . . . . (Columbia)
   Hits-1979-1989 . . . . (Columbia)
   Seven Year Ache . . . . (Columbia)
Seven-And-A-Half Cents
John Raitt; *ST/Pajama Game* . . . . (Collectables)
Original Cast; *Pajama Game* . . . . (Columbia)
Seventh Avenue
Rosanne Cash; *The Wheel.* . . . . (Columbia)
Sweet Dreams (Are Made Of This)
Eurythmics; *Eurythmics' Greatest Hits* . . . . (Arista)
   Sweet Dreams (Are Made Of This) . . . . (RCA)
Marilyn Manson; *Smells Like Children* . . . . (Interscope)
Theme From "The Magnificent Seven"
BBC Concert Orchestra; *Golden Cinema Classics-#1-The
Adventure Film* . . . . (Bainbridge)

NUMBERS: 8

*See Also: **AGES (various), COUNTING SONGS, MONTHS &
DATES (various), NUMBERS (various), TIME: SPECIFIC***

"8" Ball
Slammin' Watusis; *Super Oldies Of The '60s-#7-C* . . . .(Audio Fidelity)
"8" Ball
Herb Alpert; *Wild Romance* . . . . (A&M)
6, 8, 12
Brian McKnight; *Back At One* . . . . (Motown)
Amarillo By Morning
George Strait; *George Strait's Greatest Hits* . . . . (MCA)
   Strait From The Heart . . . . (MCA)
Boogie Back To Texas
Asleep At The Wheel; *Asleep At The Wheel-10* . . . . (Epic)
   Swinging Best Of Asleep At The Wheel . . . . (Epic)
   Texas Super Hits-C . . . . (Columbia)
   Very Best Of Asleep At The Wheel Since 1970 . . . . (Relentless/Madacy)
Eight Days A Week
Beatles; *Beatles 1* . . . . (Capitol)
   Beatles VI . . . . (Capitol)
   Beatles-20 Greatest Hits . . . . (Capitol)
   The Beatles/1962-1966 . . . . (Capitol)
Eight Days On The Road
Foghat; *Best Of Foghat.* . . . . (Rhino)
   Rock & Roll Outlaws . . . . (Rhino)
Eight Line Poem
David Bowie; *Hunky Dory* . . . . (Rykodisc)
Eight Miles High
Byrds; *Fifth Dimension.* . . . . (Columbia)
   Original Singles-#1-1965-1967 . . . . (Columbia)
   The Byrds . . . . (Columbia)
   The Byrds (Untitled) . . . . (Legacy)
   The Byrds' Greatest Hits . . . . (Columbia)
Leo Kottke; *Best Of Leo Kottke* . . . . (Capitol)
   Mudlark . . . . (Capitol)
Roxy Music; *Flesh + Blood* . . . . (Atco)
Eight More Miles
Kieran Kane/Kevin Welch; *11/12/13: Live In Melbourne,
Australia* . . . . (Dead Reckoning)
Eight More Miles To Louisville
Eric Weissberg; *Dueling Banjos From "Deliverance"* . . . .(Warner Bros.)
Grandpa Jones; *Truckin' On-C* . . . . (Hollywood)
Mike Auldridge; *Dobro/Blues & Bluegrass* . . . .(Takoma)
Reno & Smiley; *1983 Collector's Edition-#3* . . . . (Gusto)
   Best Of Reno & Smiley . . . . (Starday)
Eighth Avenue Shuffle
Doobie Brothers; *Takin' It To The Streets* . . . .(Warner Bros.)
Eight'r From Decatur
Bob Wills; *Best Of Bob Wills-#2.* . . . . (MCA)
I'm Henry The VIII, I Am
Herman's Hermits; *Herman's Hermits-Their Greatest Hits.* . . . . (Abkco)
   Something Good Again . . . . (Abkco)
Ride To A Funeral In A V-8
Dan Pickett; *1949 Country Blues* . . . . (Collectables)
Theme From "Eight Is Enough"
Original Soundtrack; *Television's Greatest Hits-#6-Remote Control-C* . . (TVT)

NUMBERS: 9

*See Also: **AGES (various), COUNTING SONGS, MONTHS &
DATES (various), NUMBERS (various), TIME: SPECIFIC***

10 Miles To Go On A 9 Mile Road
Jim White; *No Such Place.* . . . . (Luaka Bop)

9 To 5
Dolly Parton; *9 To 5 And Odd Jobs* . . . . (RCA)
   Best There Is . . . . (RCA)
   Dolly Parton's Greatest Hits . . . . (RCA)
   I Am Woman-C . . . . (Nick At Nite)
   Nipper's Greatest Hits Of The '80s-C . . . . (RCA)
Angel Number Nine
Pure Prairie League; *Bustin' Out* . . . . (RCA)
Another Nine Minutes
Yankee Grey; *Untamed* . . . . (Monument)
Apartment #9
Melissa Etheridge; *Tammy Wynette...Remembered-C* . . . .(Asylum)
Tammy Wynette; *Tammy Wynette-Anniversary-20 Years Of Hits* . . . . . . (Epic)
   Tammy Wynette's Greatest Hits . . . . (Epic)
Apollo 9
Adam Ant; *Antics In The Forbidden Zone.* . . . . (Epic)
Cloud 9
George Harrison; *Best Of Dark Horse 1976-1989.* . . . .(Dark Horse)
   Cloud Nine . . . . (Dark Horse)
Cloud Nine
Temptations; *25 Years Of Grammy Greats-C* . . . . (Motown)
   Cloud Nine . . . . (Motown)
   Motown Grammy R&B Performances Of The '60s & '70s-C . . . . . . (Motown)
   Motown Story-First 25 Years-C . . . . (Motown)
   Temptations' Greatest Hits-#2 . . . . (Motown)
Cumberland Mountain #9
Charlie Daniels Band; *Saddle Tramp* . . . . (Epic)
   Volunteer Jam 3 & 4. . . . . (Epic)
Engine #9
Midnight Star; *Headlines* . . . . (Solar)
Engine Engine #9
Roger Miller; *Best Of Roger Miller-#2-King Of The Road* . . . . . . (Mercury)
   Best Of Roger Miller-His Greatest Songs. . . . . (Curb)
   King Of The Road-Genius Of Roger Miller . . . . (Mercury)
   Roger Miller-Golden Hits . . . . (Smash)
   Roger Miller-The Hits . . . . (Mercury)
   Train Trax-C . . . . (Sony Music Special Prod.)
Game Number 9
Ray Charles; *True To Life* . . . . (Atlantic)
If 6 Was 9
Jimi Hendrix; *Axis: Bold As Love* . . . . (Reprise)
   Essential Jimi Hendrix . . . . (Reprise)
Karn Evil 9
Emerson, Lake & Palmer; *Best Of Emerson, Lake & Palmer* . . . . (Rhino)
   Brain Salad Surgery . . . . (Rhino)
   *Welcome back, my friends, to the show that never ends-Ladies and
Gentlemen* . . . . (Manticore)
Life #9
Martina McBride; *The Way That I Am.* . . . . (RCA)
Love Potion Number 9
Clovers; *ST/American Graffiti.* . . . . (MCA)
   Super Oldies Of The '50s-#7-C . . . . (Audio Fidelity)
Herb Alpert & The Tijuana Brass; *Herb Alpert & The Tijuana Brass'
Greatest Hits* . . . . (A&M)
   Herb Alpert & The Tijuana Brass-Classics-#1 . . . . (A&M)
Searchers; *History Of British Rock-#3-C* . . . . (Rhino)
   Searchers' Greatest Hits . . . . (Rhino)
Morning Train (Nine To Five)
Sheena Easton; *Sheena Easton* . . . . (EMI)
Nine Below Zero
Muddy Waters; *King Of The Electric Blues* . . . . (Legacy)
Snooky Pryor; *Blind Pig Sampler: Prime Chops-#1-C* . . . . (Blind Pig)
Sonny Boy Williamson; *More Real Folk Blues-Sonny Boy Williamson* . . (Chess)
Nine Lives
Aerosmith; *Nine Lives.* . . . . (Columbia)
Nine Pound Hammer
David Grisman with Doc Watson and Alan O'Bryant; *Steel Rails-Classic
Railroad Songs-#1-C* . . . . (Rounder)
Merle Travis; *Great American Train Songs-C* . . . . (C.M.H. Prod.)
Nine Pound Steel
Joe Simon; *Jailhouse Rock (Hits From The Big
House)-C* . . . . (Sony Music Special Prod.)
Nine Tonight
Bob Seger & The Silver Bullet Band; *Nine Tonight* . . . . (Capitol)
   ST/Urban Cowboy . . . . (Asylum)
Nine Types Of Industrial Pollution
Frank Zappa; *Uncle Meat* . . . . (Barking Pumpkin)
Mothers Of Invention; *Legends Of Rock Guitar-'60s-#1-C* . . . . (Rhino)
Number 9 Dream
John Lennon; *Lennon* . . . . (Capitol)
   The John Lennon Collection. . . . . (Capitol)
   Walls And Bridges . . . . (Capitol)
John Lennon/Plastic Ono Band; *Shaved Fish* . . . . (Capitol)
Peas, Porridge Hot
Original Soundtrack; *Toddler Favorites* . . . . (Kid Rhino/Rhino 4 Kids)
Revolution 9
Beatles; *The Beatles (White Album)* . . . . (Capitol)
Riot In Cell Block #9
Blues Brothers; *Made In America* . . . .(Atlantic)

Coasters; *Very Best Of The Coasters* . . . . (Rhino)
Commander Cody & His Lost Planet Airmen; *Live From Deep In The Heart
   Of Texas. . . . . (MCA)
Robins; *50 Coastin' Classics-C*. . . . . (Rhino)
   There's A Riot Goin' On! Rock Classics-C. . . . . (Rhino)
Wanda Jackson; *Rockin' In The Country-Best Of Wanda Jackson* . . . . . (Rhino)

This Black Cat Has 9 Lives
Louis Armstrong; *What A Wonderful World* . . . . (Bluebird)

Truck Drivin' Cat With Nine Wives
Charlie Walker; *Truckers' Jukebox-10 All-Time Radio Requests-C* . . . . (Legacy)
Jim Nesbitt; *Truck Driver Boogie Big Rig Hits-1939-1969-C*. . . . . . . (Audium)

NUMBERS: HUNDREDS

See Also: NUMBERS (various)

.357-Break It On Down
L.L. Cool J; *Bigger & Deffer* . . . . (Def Jam/Columbia)
100 Years From Now
Huey Lewis and the News; *Time Flies...Best Of Huey Lewis and
   the News* . . . . (Elektra)
100%
Sonic Youth; *Dirty*. . . . . (David Geffen Co.)
100% Chance Of Rain
Gary Morris; *Anything Goes* . . . . (Warner Bros.)
   Gary Morris-Hits . . . . (Warner Bros.)
100% Pure Love
Crystal Waters; *Storyteller* . . . . (Mercury)
317 East 32nd
Lennie Tristano; *Continuity*. . . . . (Jazz)
   Live In Toronto 1952 . . . . (Jazz)
409
Beach Boys; *Beach Boys' Greatest Hits* . . . . (Gusto)
   Best Of The Beach Boys . . . . (Capitol)
   Made In The U.S.A. . . . . (Capitol)
   Spirit Of America . . . . (Capitol)
455 Rocket
Kathy Mattea; *Love Travels*. . . . . (Mercury)
500 Miles Away From Home
Bobby Bare; *500 Miles Away From Home* . . . . (RCA)
Foy Willing; *Cowboy/The New Sound Of American Folk* . . . . (DRG)
Reba McEntire; *Starting Over*. . . . . (MCA)
800 Pound Jesus
Sawyer Brown; *Drive Me Wild* . . . . (Curb)
808
Blaque; *Blaque* . . . . (Track Masters/Columbia)
911
Wyclef Jean featuring Mary J. Blige; *The Ecleftic-2 Sides II
   A Book* . . . . (Ruffhouse/Columbia)
911 Is A Joke
Public Enemy; *Fear Of A Black Planet* . . . . (Def Jam)
   Yo! MTV Raps-C . . . . (Def Jam)
977
Pretenders; *Last Of The Independents* . . . .(Sire)
Beep Me 911
Missy ''Misdemeanor'' Elliot; *Supa Dupa Fly* . . . . (East West)
Big Joe & Phantom 309
Tom Waits; *Double Live* . . . . (Asylum)
   Nighthawks At The Diner . . . . (Asylum)
Bob Dylan's 115th Dream
Bob Dylan; *Bringing It All Back Home* . . . . (Columbia)
City Of New Orleans (500)
Arlo Guthrie; *Best Of Arlo Guthrie* . . . . (Warner Bros.)
   Hobo's Lullaby . . . . (Reprise)
   Together In Concert . . . .(Reprise)
HARP; *HARP* . . . . (Redwood)
Willie Nelson; *19 Hot Country Requests-#2-C* . . . . (Epic)
   City Of New Orleans . . . . (Columbia)
   Greatest Country Hits Of The '80s-#4-C . . . . (Columbia)
   Hot Tracks-Train Super Hits-C . . . . (Epic)
   Train Trax-C . . . . (Sony Music Special Prod.)
Detroit 442
Blondie; *Plastic Letters* . . . . (Chrysalis)
Don't Pull Your Love (100)
Hamilton, Joe Frank & Reynolds; *'70s Biggest Hits-C* . . . . (MCA Special Prod.)
   Hamilton, Joe Frank & Reynolds' Greatest Hits . . . . (MCA Special Prod.)
   Rock Around The Oldies-#4-C . . . . (MCA Special Prod.)
Down (311)
311; *311*. . . . . (Capricorn)
Engine 143
Joan Baez; *Joan Baez, Vol. 2* . . . . (Vanguard)
Engine 999
Hooters; *One Way Home* . . . . (Columbia)
Flight 309 To Tennessee
Shelly West; *West By West* . . . . (Viva)
Flight 602
Chicago; *Chicago At Carnegie Hall* . . . . (Chicago)

   Chicago III . . . . (Chicago)
   Group Portrait . . . . (Chicago)
Ghost Of Flight 401
Bob Welch; *Three Hearts*. . . . .(Capitol)
Hundred And Sixty Acres
Marty Robbins; *Gunfighter Ballads & Trail Songs* . . . .(Legacy)
Hundred Million Miracles
Original Cast; *Flower Drum Song* . . . . (Sony Music Classical)
I'm A Hundred Percent For You
Fats Waller; *Breakin' The Ice: The Early Years, Part 1 (1934-
   1935)* . . . .(Bluebird)
I'm Gonna Be (500 Miles)
Proclaimers; *ST/Benny & Joon.* . . . .(BMG)
   Sunshine On Leith . . . . (Chrysalis)
It's In The Book (Parts 1 & 2)
Johnny Standley; *Dr. Demento Gooses Mother-C* . . . . (Kid Rhino/Rhino 4 Kids)
Last Cowboy Song
Ed Bruce; *16 Top Country Hits-#2-C* . . . . (MCA)
   Ed Bruce's Greatest Hits . . . . (MCA)
Waylon Jennings, Willie Nelson, Johnny Cash, Kris Kristofferson; *Cowboy
   Super Hits-C* . . . . (Columbia)
   Highwayman . . . . (Columbia)
Memphis #999
Graveyard Train; *Graveyard Train* . . . . (Geffen)
Mighty K.C.
For Squirrels; *Example.* . . . . (550 Music)
More Love (100)
Kim Carnes; *Gypsy Honeymoon-The Best Of Kim Carnes*. . . . . (Gold Rush)
Smokey Robinson; *Smokey Robinson-The Ultimate Collection* . . . . .(Motown)
Smokey Robinson & The Miracles; *Smokey Robinson & The Miracles'
   Anthology* . . . .(Motown)
Muskrat Ramble
Dukes Of Dixieland; *Digital Dixieland* . . . . (Pro Jazz)
Kid Ory's Creole Jazz Band; *Kid Ory's Creole Jazz Band-
   1954* . . . . (Good Time Jazz)
Louis Armstrong; *Essential Louis Armstrong* . . . .(Vanguard)
   Louis Armstrong's Greatest Hits . . . .(Curb)
McGuire Sisters; *McGuire Sisters' Greatest Hits* . . . . (MCA)
Pete Fountain; *High Society* . . . .(Bluebird)
Nashville Cats (1352)
Del McCoury Band; *The Family* . . . . (Ceili Music)
Lovin' Spoonful; *Lovin' Spoonful-Anthology* . . . . (Rhino)
Northwest 222
Harry Chapin; *Remember When The Music* . . . . (Dunhill Compact Classics)
Oddfellows Local 151
R.E.M.; *Document* . . . . (EMI-Capitol Entert. Properties)
One After 909
Beatles; *Let It Be* . . . .(Capitol)
   The Beatles-Anthology-#1. . . . .(Capitol)
One Angry Dwarf And 200 Solemn Faces
Ben Folds Five; *Whatever And Ever Amen.* . . . . (Caroline/550)
One Hundred And Two
Judds; *Judds-Collection 1983-1990*. . . . . (RCA)
   Love Can Build A Bridge . . . . (MCA)
Phantom 309
Boxcar Willie; *Truck Driving Favorites* . . . . (Madacy)
Red Sovine; *Best Of Red Sovine*. . . . . (Starday)
Room 317
Original London Cast; *Miss Saigon* . . . . (Geffen)
Room 608
Horace Silver; *Best Of Horace Silver-The Blue Note Years* . . . . (Blue Note)
RU 486
Pain Teens; *Destroy Me, Lover* . . . .(Trance Syndicate)
Theme From ''Room 222''
Original Soundtrack; *Television's Greatest Hits-#3-1970s & 1980s-C* . . . .(TVT)
Three Hundred Pounds Of Heavenly Joy
Big Twist & The Mellow Fellows; *Alligator Records 20th Anniversary
   Collection-C* . . . . (Alligator)
Howlin' Wolf; *The Chess Box-Howlin' Wolf* . . . .(Chess)
Two Little Girls (911)
Ani DiFranco; *Little Plastic Castle* . . . . (Righteous Babe)

NUMBERS: MILLIONS

See Also: NUMBERS (various)

Ain't No Fun (Waiting Round To Be A Millionaire)
AC/DC; *Dirty Deeds Done Dirt Cheap* . . . . (Atlantic)
Billion Dollar Babies
Alice Cooper; *Alice Cooper's Greatest Hits* . . . . (Warner Bros.)
   Billion Dollar Babies . . . . (Warner Bros.)
   The Alice Cooper Show . . . . (Warner Bros.)
Bitter Sweet Symphony
Verve; *Urban Hymns* . . . . (Hut/Virgin)
Can't You Hear Me Callin'?
Ricky Skaggs; *Bluegrass Super Hits-C* . . . .(Columbia)

Favorite Country Songs . . . .(Epic)
Highway & Heartaches . . . .(Epic)
Hundred Million Miracles
Original Cast; *Flower Drum Song* . . . . (Sony Music Classical)
I Found A Million-Dollar Baby (In A Five-And-Ten-Cent Store)
Barbra Streisand; *ST/Funny Girl* . . . . (Columbia)
Bing Crosby; *Pennies From Heaven.* . . . . (Pro-Arte)
Fred Waring's Pennsylvanians; *78-#22707* . . . . (Victor)
Nat ''King'' Cole; *Nat ''King'' Cole-Gift Set* . . . . (Capitol)
If I Had A $1,000,000
Barenaked Ladies; *Disc One 1991-2001-All Their Greatest Hits* . . . . . . (Reprise)
I'll Trade (A Million Bucks)
Keith Sweat featuring Lil' Mo; *Didn't See Me Coming* . . . . (Elektra)
I'm Gonna Make You Love Me
Jayhawks; *Smile* . . . . (American/Columbia)
Million Dollar Bash
Bob Dylan; *Biograph* . . . . (Columbia)
Bob Dylan And The Band; *Basement Tapes* . . . . (Columbia)
Million Miles
Bob Dylan; *Time Out Of Mind* . . . . (Columbia)
My Mammy
Al Jolson; *Best Of Al Jolson* . . . .(MCA)
Let Me Sing And I'm Happy . . . . (Turner Classic Movies)
The '20s-From Broadway To Hollywood-#3-C . . . . (Flapper)
Happenings; *Happenings-Golden Hits!* . . . . (B.T. Puppy)
Old Man And Me
Hootie & The Blowfish; *Fairweather Johnson.* . . . .(Atlantic)
One In A Million
Aaliyah; *One In A Million.* . . . . (BlackGround Enterp./Atlantic)
One In A Million
Platters; *Magic Touch-An Anthology* . . . . (Mercury)
Perfect Day
Collective Soul; *Blender.* . . . .(Atlantic)
Space Lord
Monster Magnet; *Powertrip* . . . . (A&M)
Theme From ''The Six Million Dollar Man''
Original Soundtrack; *Television's Greatest Hits-#5-In Living Color-C* . . . (TVT)
They're Playin' Our Song
Neal McCoy; *Neal McCoy's Greatest Hits.* . . . .(Atlantic)
You Gotta Love That! . . . .(Atlantic)

NUMBERS: THOUSANDS

See Also: **MONTHS & DATES** *(various),* **NUMBERS** *(various),*
YEARS: SPECIFIC

10,000 Horses
Candlebox; *Happy Pills* . . . .(Maverick)
10,432 Sheep
Doris Day Quartet & The Frank Comstock Orchestra; *Day At The*
Movies. . . . . (Columbia)
1040 Blues
Robert Cray Band; *Shame + Sin* . . . . (Mercury)
1952 Vincent Black Lightning
Richard Thompson; *Richard Thompson-Best Of Capitol Years* . . . . (Capitol)
1959
John Anderson; *Country Love Songs-#3-C.* . . . .(Warner Bros.)
John Anderson's Greatest Hits . . . .(Warner Bros.)
1970 #1 Song Cadillac
Terry Radigan; *Pawnbroker's Daughter* . . . . (Asylum)
1979
Smashing Pumpkins; *Mellon Collie And The Infinite Sadness* . . . . (Virgin)
The Aeroplane Flies High . . . . (Virgin)
1984
David Bowie; *Changestwobowie* . . . . (RCA)
David Live . . . .(Rykodisc)
Diamond Dogs. . . . .(Rykodisc)
Fame & Fashion . . . . (RCA)
Tina Turner; *Private Dancer* . . . . (Capitol)
1984
Spirit; *Best Of Spirit* . . . .(Epic)
Spirit Of '84 . . . . (Mercury)
1984
Van Halen; *1984.* . . . .(Warner Bros.)
1999
Prince; *1999* . . . .(Warner Bros.)
2,000 Light Years From Home
Rolling Stones; *More Hot Rocks (big hits & fazed cookies)* . . . .(Abkco)
Singles Collection-The London Years . . . .(Abkco)
Their Satanic Majesties Request . . . .(Abkco)
Through The Past, Darkly (Big Hits Vol. 2) . . . .(Abkco)
2000 Blacks Got To Be Free
Fela Anikulapo Kuti & Roy Ayers; *Music Of Many Colours* . . . .(Celluloid)
2120 South Michigan Avenue
Rolling Stones; *12 X 5.* . . . .(Abkco)
30,000 Pounds Of Bananas
Harry Chapin; *Greatest Stories-Live* . . . . (Elektra)

Harry Chapin-Anthology . . . . (Elektra)
Verities & Balderdash . . . . (Elektra)
50,000 Names
George Jones; *The Rock: Stone Cold Country 2001* . . . .(BNA)
634-5789
Ry Cooder; *Borderline* . . . . (Warner Bros.)
Wilson Pickett; *Wilson Pickett's Greatest Hits* . . . .(Atlantic)
America The Beautiful, 1976
Charlie Rich; *Charlie Rich's Greatest Hits* . . . . (Epic)
Anthem For The Year 2000
Silverchair; *Neon Ballroom.* . . . .(Epic)
April 2031
Warrant; *Dog Eat Dog.* . . . .(Columbia)
April 24, 1981
Rick Springfield; *Success Hasn't Spoiled Me Yet* . . . .(RCA)
August 1967
Holy Modal Rounders; *Last Round* . . . .(Adelphi)
Clean My Wounds (1000)
Corrosion Of Conformity; *Deliverance.* . . . .(Columbia)
December, 1963 (Oh, What A Night)
4 Seasons; *25th Anniversary Collection* . . . . (Rhino)
4 Seasons-Anthology . . . . (Rhino)
Oh What A Night. . . . . (Curb)
For A Thousand Mothers
Jethro Tull; *Stand Up.* . . . . (Chrysalis)
Forty Thousand Headmen
Traffic; *Traffic.* . . . . (Island)
Welcome To The Canteen . . . . (Island)
Happy Birthday 1975
Joni Mitchell; *Mingus* . . . . (Elektra)
Happy Birthday Dear America/In 1776
Ella Jenkins; *We Are All America's Children* . . . . (Smithsonian Folkways)
I Wanna Love You Forever
Jessica Simpson; *Sweet Kisses* . . . . (Columbia)
I Was Born About Ten Thousand Years Ago
Elvis Presley; *Elvis Now* . . . .(RCA)
Odetta; *Odetta-Live.* . . . .(Fantasy)
In The Year 2525 (Exordium & Terminus)
Zager & Evans; *Nipper's Greatest Hits Of The '60s-#2-C* . . . .(RCA)
Land Of 1000 Dances
Cannibal & The Headhunters; *History Of Latino Rock-#1-C* . . . . (Rhino)
Super Oldies Of The '60s-#8-C . . . . (Audio Fidelity)
Toga Rock-C. . . . . (Dunhill Compact Classics)
Wilson Pickett; *Atlantic Rhythm & Blues 1947-1974-#6 (1966-*
1969)-C . . . .(Atlantic)
Best Of Wilson Pickett . . . .(Atlantic)
ST/Forrest Gump . . . . (Epic/Sony Music Soundtrax)
Wilson Pickett's Greatest Hits . . . .(Atlantic)
Land Of A Thousand Autumns
Steve Hackett; *Please Don't Touch* . . . . (Chrysalis)
Miss Texas 1967
Colourfield; *Deception* . . . . (Chrysalis)
My Beach 2000
Surf Punks; *Oh No! Not Them Again!* . . . . (Enigma Capitol)
My Niece From Pittsburgh In 1992
PFS; *Illustrative Problems* . . . . (Cuneiform)
Nashville Cats (1352) (16,021)
Del McCoury Band; *The Family* . . . .(Ceili Music)
Lovin' Spoonful; *Lovin' Spoonful-Anthology* . . . . (Rhino)
Night Has A Thousand Eyes
Anita O'Day; *Night Has A Thousand Eyes* . . . . (Emily)
Bobby Vee; *Best Of Bobby Vee* . . . . (EMI)
Bobby Vee-Legendary Masters. . . . . (EMI)
Golden Years-1962-C. . . . . (Dominion Entert.)
November 22, 1963
Original Cast; *Assassins* . . . .(RCA)
October 17, 1988
Keith Jarrett; *Paris Concert.* . . . .(ECM)
On Saturday Afternoons In 1963
Rickie Lee Jones; *Rickie Lee Jones* . . . . (Warner Bros.)
One Thousand Dollar Wedding
Gram Parsons; *Grievous Angel* . . . . (Reprise)
Painted Perfect
One Way Ride; *Strait Up!* . . . . (Refuge/MCA)
Pennsylvania 6-5000
Glenn Miller; *Glenn Miller-A Legendary Performer-#1 & 2* . . . . (Bluebird)
Memorial-1944-1969 . . . . (Bluebird)
The Glenn Miller Story . . . .(RCA)
Glenn Miller & His Orchestra; *Complete Glenn Miller & His*
Orchestra-#4 . . . . (Bluebird)
Glenn Miller & His Orchestra-Pure Gold . . . . (Bluebird)
Moonlight Serenade . . . . (Ranwood)
The Unforgettable Glenn Miller & His Orchestra . . . .(RCA)
Reasons For Waiting
Jethro Tull; *Stand Up.* . . . . (Chrysalis)
Ten Thousand Angels
Mindy McCready; *Ten Thousand Angels* . . . .(BNA)

Ten Thousand Angels Cried
LeAnn Rimes; *You Light Up My Life-Inspirational Songs* .....(Curb)
Texas In 1880
Foster & Lloyd; *Foster & Lloyd* ....(RCA)
Theme From ''Beverly Hills 90210''
John Davis; *Beverly Hills 90210: Songs From The Peach Pit* ....(Rhino)
ST/*Beverly Hills, 90210-College Years* ....(Giant)
Television's Greatest Hits-#7-Cable Ready-C ....(TVT)
Theme From ''Summer Of '42''
George Benson; *Best Of George Benson* ....(CBS Associated)
White Rabbit ....(CBS Associated)
Peter Nero; *''Summer Of '42'' Theme* ....(Columbia)
Peter Nero's Greatest Hits ....(Columbia)
Thousand Miles From Nowhere
Dwight Yoakam; *This Time* ....(Reprise)
Thousand Stars In The Sky
Kathy Young with The Innocents; *20 Great Love Songs Of The '50s &*
'60s-#2-C ....(Laurie)
Collectables Presents The History Of Rock-#10-C ....(Collectables)
Oldies But Goodies-#5-C ....(Original Sound)
Thousand Times A Day
Patty Loveless; *The Trouble With The Truth* ....(Epic)
Thousand Words, A
Savage Garden; *Savage Garden* ....(Columbia)
Thousands Are Sailing
Pogues; *Essential Pogues* ....(Island)
If I Should Fall From Grace With God ....(Island)
Train No. 1262
Flatt & Scruggs; *Hear The Whistles Blow* ....(International Mktg. Group)
Two Thousand Pound Bee
Ventures; *Radical Guitars* ....(Iloki)
ST/*Wired* ....(Varese Sarabande)
Two Thousand Shoes
Big Audio Dynamite; *Tighten Up-#88* ....(Columbia)
War Is Hell (On The Homefront Too) (1942)
T.G. Sheppard; *Perfect Stranger* ....(Warner Bros.)
T.G. Sheppard's All-Time Greatest Hits ....(Warner Bros.)
T.G. Sheppard's Greatest Hits ....(Warner Bros./Curb)
Warsaw 1943 (I Never Betrayed The Revolution)
Johnny Clegg & Savuka; *Cruel, Crazy, Beautiful World* ....(Capitol)
Will 2K
Will Smith; *Willenium* ....(Columbia)
Year 2003 Minus 25
Waylon Jennings & Willie Nelson; *Waylon & Willie* ....(RCA)

OCEAN, Bay, Beach, Coast, Drifting (on water), Harbor, Lake, Sea, Swamp

See Also: ANIMALS (various), DROWN, FLOOD, LIGHTHOUSES,
PIRATES, RIVERS, SAILING, SHIPS, SPORTS: SURFING,
SPORTS: SWIMMING, WATER

''Take Her To Sea, Mr. Murdoch''
James Horner; *ST/Titanic* ....(Sony Music Classical)
(Sittin' On) The Dock Of The Bay
Michael Bolton; *The Hunger* ....(Columbia)
Otis Redding; *(Sittin' On) The Dock Of The Bay* ....(Atco)
Best Of Otis Redding ....(Atco)
Golden Age Of Black Music-1960-1970-C ....(Atlantic)
Golden Soul-C ....(Atlantic)
Soul Years-C ....(Atlantic)
The Otis Redding Story ....(Atlantic)
Adios
Jimmy Webb; *Suspending Disbelief* ....(Elektra)
Linda Ronstadt; *Cry Like A Rainstorm-Howl Like The Wind* ....(Elektra)
All The Fuckers Live In Newport Beach
Fluf; *The Classic Years* ....(Headhunter)
And The Tide Rushes In
Moody Blues; *A Question Of Balance* ....(Polydor)
This Is The Moody Blues ....(Polydor)
At The Seaside Cafe
Adrian Belew; *Desire Caught By The Tail* ....(Island)
August Tides
Woody Simmons; *Woody Simmons* ....(Deep River)
Autumn Sea
Robyn Hitchcock & The Egyptians; *Queen Elvis* ....(A&M)
Backstreets
Bruce Springsteen; *Born To Run* ....(Columbia)
Backwater
Meat Puppets; *Too High To Die* ....(London)
Bay Of Mexico
Kingston Trio; *Folk Era Sampler-Digitally* ....(Folk Era)
Stereo Concert Plus ....(Folk Era)
Tom Dooley ....(Capitol)
Bayou Girl
Bob Woodruff; *Dreams & Saturday Nights* ....(Asylum)

Beaches Of Cheyenne
Garth Brooks; *Fresh Horses* ....(Capitol)
Limited Series Box ....(Capitol)
Between The Devil And The Deep Blue Sea
Cab Calloway; *Jazz Heritage: Mr. Hi-De-Ho* ....(MCA)
Chris Rea; *Espresso Logic* ....(East West)
Diana Krall; *Stepping Out* ....(Justin Time)
Ella Fitzgerald; *Harold Arlen Songbook-#1* ....(Verve)
Beyond The Sea
Bobby Darin; *The Bobby Darin Story* ....(Atlantic)
Black Diamond Bay
Bob Dylan; *Desire* ....(Columbia)
Blue Bayou
Linda Ronstadt; *Linda Ronstadt's Greatest Hits, Volume Two* ....(Asylum)
Simple Dreams ....(Asylum)
Roy Orbison; *For The Lonely: A Roy Orbison Anthology 1959-1965* ....(Rhino)
In Dreams-Greatest Hits ....(Orbison)
Roy Orbison-More Greatest Hits ....(Monument)
Roy Orbison's All-Time Greatest Hits-#1 & 2 ....(Monument)
Roy Orbison & Friends; *Black & White Night-Live* ....(Virgin)
By The Waters Of Lake Minnetonka
Glenn Miller; *Best Of Glenn Miller-#2* ....(RCA)
Glenn Miller & His Orchestra: Complete ....(Bluebird)
By-U, By-O (The Lou'siana Lullaby)
Woody Herman; *Woody Herman-Best Of The Decca Years* ....(Decca)
California Nights
Lesley Gore; *Summer & Sun-C* ....(Rhino)
Captain Nemo
Michael Schenker Group; *Built To Destroy* ....(Chrysalis)
Rock Will Never Die ....(Chrysalis)
Caribbean Breeze
Rippingtons; *Life In The Tropics* ....(Peak/Concord)
Carmel By The Sea
Kitty Wells; *45-#31123* ....(Decca)
Carolina By The Sea
Super Grit Cowboy Band; *If You Can't Hang-Drag Your*
Country Ass ....(Hoodswamp)
Castles In The Sand
Stevie Wonder; *Stevie Wonder's Greatest Hits* ....(Motown)
Castles In The Sand
David Allan Coe; *Castles In The Sand* ....(Columbia)
Castles In The Sand
Seals & Crofts; *Seals & Crofts' Greatest Hits* ....(Warner Bros.)
Castles Made Of Sand
Jimi Hendrix; *Axis: Bold As Love* ....(Reprise)
Essential Jimi Hendrix ....(Reprise)
Kiss The Sky ....(Reprise)
Tuck & Patti; *Love Warriors* ....(Windham Hill)
Castles Of Steam
Jermaine Jackson; *Motown Superstar Series-#17-Jermaine Jackson* ..(Motown)
Circle In The Sand
Belinda Carlisle; *Heaven On Earth* ....(MCA)
Coast Of Colorado
Skip Ewing; *Coast Of Colorado* ....(MCA)
Coast Of Marseilles
Jimmy Buffett; *Son Of A Son Of A Sailor* ....(MCA)
Cool Change
Little River Band; *First Under The Wire* ....(Capitol)
Little River Band's Greatest Hits ....(Capitol)
Creature From The Black Lagoon
Dave Edmunds; *Best Of Dave Edmunds* ....(Swan Song)
Elvira Presents Haunted Hits-C ....(Rhino)
Repeat When Necessary ....(Swan Song)
Dancin', Shaggin' On The Boulevard
Alabama; *Dancin' On The Boulevard* ....(RCA)
Dark & Rolling Sea
Al Stewart; *Modern Times* ....(Janus)
Daughters Of The Sea
Doobie Brothers; *What Were Once Vices Are Now Habits* ....(Warner Bros.)
Days Of Sand & Shovels
Bobby Vinton; *Bobby Vinton's All-Time Greatest Hits* ....(Epic)
Waylon Jennings; *Best Of Waylon Jennings* ....(RCA)
Dolphins & Whales (Come Home To The Sea)
Mannheim Steamroller; *Saving The Wildlife* ....(American Gramaphone)
Don't Take Your Love From Me
Etta James; *These Foolish Things-The Classic Balladry Of Etta James* ...(MCA)
King Sisters; *Spotlight On The King Sisters* ....(Capitol)
Three Suns; *Very Best Of The Three Suns* ....(Taragon)
Down By The Bay
Eric Heatherly; *Country Goes Raffi-C* ....(Rounder)
Down By The Sea
Strawbs; *Best Of The Strawbs* ....(A&M)
Bursting At The Seams ....(A&M)
Down By The Sea
Men At Work; *Business As Usual* ....(Columbia)
Down By The Seaside
Led Zeppelin; *Physical Graffiti* ....(Swan Song)

Drifting
Jimi Hendrix; *Cry Of Love* . . . . (Reprise)
Essential Jimi Hendrix . . . . (Reprise)

Drowning In The Sea Of Love
Boz Scaggs; *Live At The Beacon-C* . . . . (Giant)
Joe Simon; *Didn't It Blow Your Mind: Soul Hits Of The '70s-#7-C* . . . . (Rhino)
Music In My Bones: The Best Of Joe Simon . . . . (Rhino)
Ringo Starr; *Ringo The 4th* . . . . (Atlantic)

Ebb Tide
Righteous Brothers; *Phil Spector's Greatest Hits-C* . . . . (Spector)
Righteous Brothers' Greatest Hits . . . . (Verve)
Righteous Brothers-Anthology 1962-1974 . . . . (Rhino)

Echo Beach
Martha & The Muffins; *Metro Music* . . . . (Virgin)

Einstein On The Beach
Counting Crows; *August And Everything After* . . . . (David Geffen Co.)

Erie Canal
Burl Ives; *Best Of Burl Ives* . . . . (MCA)
Weavers; *Greatest Folksingers Of The '60s-C* . . . . (Vanguard)
Weavers' Greatest Hits . . . . (Vanguard)
Weavers-Classics . . . . (Vanguard)

February Sea
George Winston; *Winter Into Spring* . . . . (Windham Hill)

Fig Tree Bay
Peter Frampton; *Wind Of Change* . . . . (A&M)

Fire Lake
Bob Seger & The Silver Bullet Band; *Against The Wind* . . . . . (Capitol)
Nine Tonight . . . . (Capitol)

Follow Me
Original Cast; *Camelot* . . . . (Columbia)
ST/Camelot . . . . (Warner Bros.)

For You I Will
Monica; *The Boy Is Mine* . . . . (Arista)

From Silver Lake
Jackson Browne; *Jackson Browne* . . . . (Asylum)

Galveston Bay
Bruce Springsteen; *The Ghost Of Tom Joad* . . . . (Columbia)

Galway Bay
Bing Crosby; *Best Of Bing Crosby* . . . . (MCA)
When Irish Eyes Are Smiling . . . . (MCA)

Girls On The Beach
Beach Boys; *Absolute Best-#1* . . . . (Capitol)
Endless Summer . . . . (Capitol)
Little Deuce Coupe/All Summer Long . . . . (Capitol)

Going Back To Big Sur
Johnny Rivers; *Johnny Rivers-Anthology 1964-1977* . . . . . . (Rhino)
Touch Of Gold . . . . (Imperial)

Going To Malibu
Malibooz; *Malibooz Rule* . . . . (Rhino)

Green Grass & High Tides
Outlaws; *Bring It Back Alive* . . . . (Arista)
Outlaws . . . . (Arista)

Grey Lagoons
Roxy Music; *For Your Pleasure...* . . . . (Reprise)

Gulf And The Shell
Clinton Gregory; *Clinton Gregory* . . . . (Polydor Country)

Harbor Lights
Boz Scaggs; *Silk Degrees* . . . . (Columbia)
Dinah Washington; *Complete Dinah Washington On Mercury-#2-1950-1952* . . . . (Mercury)
Dinah Washington-Golden Hits . . . . (Mercury)
For Lonely Lovers . . . . (Mercury)
This Is My Story . . . . (Mercury)
Platters; *Super Oldies Of The '60s-#9-C* . . . . (Audio Fidelity)

Homeless
Paul Simon; *Graceland* . . . . (Warner Bros.)

How Deep Is The Ocean? (How High Is The Sky?)
Diana Krall; *Love Scenes* . . . . (Impulse!)
Frank Sinatra; *Nice 'N' Easy* . . . . (Capitol)
Liza Minnelli; *Liza Minnelli-At Carnegie Hall* . . . . (Telarc)

Hymn To The Sea
James Horner; *ST/Titanic* . . . . (Sony Music Classical)

I Can't Turn The Tide
Baillie & The Boys; *Turn The Tide* . . . . (RCA)

I Cover The Waterfront
Art Tatum; *Solo Masterpieces-#5* . . . . (Pablo)
Billie Holiday; *Billie's Blues* . . . . (Blue Note)
Songbook . . . . (Verve)
Eddie Jefferson; *Letter From Home* . . . . (Original Jazz Classics)
Erroll Garner; *Long Ago And Far Away* . . . . (Columbia)
Frank Sinatra; *Where Are You?* . . . . (Capitol)
John Lee Hooker; *John Lee Hooker-The Ultimate Collection-1948-1990* . . . . (Rhino)
Woody Herman; *20 Golden Pieces Of Woody Herman* . . . . (Bulldog)

I Live For The Sun
Sunrays; *Beach Classics-All Original Recordings-C* . . . . . . (Dunhill Compact Classics)
Summer And Surf-C . . . . (Rhino)

I Wanna Marry A Lighthouse Keeper
Erika Eigen; *ST/A Clockwork Orange* . . . . (Warner Bros.)

If I Had A Boat
Lyle Lovett; *Pontiac* . . . . (MCA)

In A Restaurant By The Sea
Holly Near & Ronnie Gilbert; *Singing With You* . . . . (Redwood)

Indian Lake
Freddy Weller; *Freddy Weller's Greatest Hits* . . . . (Columbia)

Itsy Bitsy Teenie Weenie Yellow Polkadot Bikini
Brian Hyland; *Brian Hyland's Greatest Hits* . . . . (Rhino)
Dr. Demento Presents The Greatest Novelty Records-#3-1960s-C . . . . (Rhino)
Vintage Music-#5-C . . . . (MCA)

I've Got Sand In My Shoes
Drifters; *1959-1965-All-Time Greatest Hits And More* . . . . . . (Atlantic)
Very Best Of The Drifters . . . . (Rhino)

Jump Up Behind Me
James Taylor; *Hourglass* . . . . (Columbia)
Songs From The Heart-C . . . . (Columbia)

Kern River
Merle Haggard; *For The Record: Merle Haggard-43 Legendary Hits* . . . . (BNA)
Kern River . . . . (Epic)

Lake Of Fire
Nirvana; *MTV Unplugged In New York* . . . . (David Geffen Co.)

Land Ho
Doors; *Doors 13* . . . . (Elektra)
Doors-Classics . . . . (Elektra)
Morrison Hotel/Hard Rock Cafe . . . . (Elektra)

Legend Of Wooly Swamp
Charlie Daniels Band; *A Decade Of Hits* . . . . (Epic)
Full Moon . . . . (Epic)
Me & The Boys . . . . (Epic)

Lights
Journey; *Infinity* . . . . (Columbia)
Journey-Captured . . . . (Columbia)

Like A River To The Sea
Steve Wariner; *I Am Ready* . . . . (Arista)

Love At The Pier
Blondie; *Plastic Letters* . . . . (Chrysalis)

Love Letters In The Sand
Mac Wiseman; *24 Greatest Bluegrass Hits-C* . . . . (C.M.H. Prod.)
Pat Boone; *Best Of Pat Boone* . . . . (MCA)
Pat Boone-16 Great Performances . . . . (MCA)
Vintage Music-#2-C . . . . (MCA)
Ted Black & His Orchestra; *78-#22799* . . . . (Victor)

Malibu
Hole; *Celebrity Skin* . . . . (David Geffen Co.)

Mariner, The (Old Spice Cologne)
Original Soundtrack; *TeeVee Toons-The Commercials-#1-C* . . . . (TVT)

Miami
Will Smith; *Big Willie Style* . . . . (Columbia)

Midnight On The Bay
Stills/Young Band; *Long May You Run* . . . . (Reprise)

Mobile Bay
Hank Crawford; *Night Beat* . . . . (Milestone)
Rex Stewart; *RCA Victor Jazz: First Half-Century-C* . . . . (RCA)

Mobile Bay (Magnolia Blossoms)
Cal Smith; *Stories Of Life By Cal Smith* . . . . (Step One)
Johnny Cash; *Johnny Cash's Biggest Hits* . . . . (Columbia)
Merle Haggard & George Jones; *Taste Of Yesterday's Wine* . . . . (Epic)

Montego Bay
Amazulu; *The Island Story-1962-1987-25th Anniversary-C* . . . . (Island)
Bobby Bloom; *Super Hits Of The '70s-Have A Nice Day-#3-C* . . . . (Rhino)

Moon, Turn The Tides...Gently Gently Away
Jimi Hendrix Experience; *Electric Ladyland* . . . . (Reprise)

Moonlight Bay
Beatles; *The Beatles-Anthology-#1* . . . . (Capitol)
Bing Crosby; *The Radio Years-#4* . . . . (Crescendo)
The Radio Years: 20 Songs . . . . (Crescendo)
Drifters; *Clyde McPhatter & The Drifters-Rockin' & Driftin'* . . . . (Collectables)
Glenn Miller; *Big Bands-#1-C* . . . . (Universal)

My Beach 2000
Surf Punks; *Oh No! Not Them Again!* . . . . (Enigma Capitol)

My Bonnie Lies Over The Ocean
Beatles With Tony Sheridan; *History Of British Rock-#5-C* . . . . (Rhino)
The Beatles featuring Tony Sheridan-In The Beginning (Circa 1960) . . . . (Polydor)
Ed McCurdy; *Best Of Ed McCurdy* . . . . (Tradition)
Mitch Miller; *Favorite Irish Sing-Alongs* . . . . (Legacy)

My Favorite Headache
Geddy Lee; *My Favorite Headache* . . . . (Anthem/Atlantic)

Ocean
Led Zeppelin; *Houses Of The Holy* . . . . (Atlantic)

Ocean
U2; *Boy* . . . . (Island)

Ocean
John Hiatt; *Hangin' Around The Observatory* . . . . (Epic)

Ocean
Velvet Underground; *V.U.* . . . . (Verve)

Ocean
Zebra; *Zebra-Live* . . . . (Atlantic)
Ocean Breakup
Electric Light Orchestra; *On The Third Day* . . . .(Jet)
Ocean Breeze
Pablo Cruise; *Pablo Cruise* . . . . (A&M)
Ocean Front Property
George Strait; *Country Classics-#8-1986-1987-C* . . . . (Universal)
  George Strait's Greatest Hits-#2 . . . . (MCA)
  MCA Records 30 Years Of Hits-1958-1988-C . . . . (MCA)
  Ocean Front Property . . . . (MCA)
Ocean Gypsy
Renaissance; *Renaissance-Live At Carnegie Hall* . . . .(Sire)
  Scheherazade . . . .(Sire)
  Tales Of 1001 Nights-#1 . . . .(Sire)
Ocean I'll Cry
Jackie Wilson; *Soul Time* . . . . (Brunswick)
Ocean Of Life
Gene Cotton; *No Strings Attached* . . . . (Ariola America)
Ocean Of Memories
James Horner; *ST/Titanic* . . . .(Sony Music Classical)
Ocean Of Thoughts & Dreams
Dramatics; *Shake It Well* . . . . (MCA)
Oceans Apart
Judy Garland; *Judy Garland-Collector's Items-1936-1945* . . . . (MCA)
Oceans Away
Phillip Goodhand-Tait; *Oceans Away* . . . . (Chrysalis)
Octopus's Garden
Beatles; *Abbey Road* . . . .(Parlophone)
  Beatles-Box Set . . . . (Capitol)
  The Beatles/1967-1970 . . . . (Capitol)
On A Sunday By The Sea
Original Broadway Cast; *Jerome Robbins' Broadway* . . . .(RCA)
On Danish Shore
Oscar Peterson Four; *If You Could See Me Now* . . . . (Pablo)
On Jersey Shore
Paragon Ragtime Orchestra; *On The Boardwalk* . . . .(Newport Classic)
On Silver Waves
101 Strings Orchestra; *Romantic Songs Of The Sea* . . . . (Alshire)
On The Banks Of The Old Pontchartrain
Hank Williams; *American Legends-#18* . . . .(Laserlight)
  Complete Hank Williams . . . . (Mercury)
On The Beach
Southside Johnny And The Asbury Jukes; *Love Is A Sacrifice* . . . . (Mercury)
On The Beach
Neil Young; *On The Beach* . . . .(Reprise)
On The Beach
Sister Double Happiness; *Sister Double Happiness* . . . . (SST)
On The Old Kentucky Shore
J.D. Crowe & Others; *Bluegrass Album-#5-Sweet Sunny South* . . . . . . (Rounder)
On Your Shore
Enya; *Watermark* . . . .(Reprise)
One Big Love
Emmylou Harris; *Red Dirt Girl* . . . .(Nonesuch)
Patty Griffin; *Flaming Red* . . . . (A&M)
One Day In March I Go Down To The Sea And Listen
Jan Garbarek Group; *It's OK To Listen To The Gray Voice* . . . . (ECM)
Only Love
Wynonna; *Tell Me Why* . . . . (MCA)
Paddy's Green Shamrock Shore
Chieftains; *Another Country* . . . .(RCA)
Possum Kingdom
Toadies; *ESPN Presents X Games-#1-C* . . . .(Tommy Boy)
  Rubberneck . . . . (Interscope)
Prince Of Tides
Jimmy Buffett; *Hot Water* . . . . (MCA)
Puff The Magic Dragon
Peter, Paul & Mary; *10 Years Together/The Best Of Peter, Paul*
  and Mary . . . . (Warner Bros.)
  Moving . . . . (Warner Bros.)
  Peter, Paul & Mommy . . . . (Warner Bros.)
  Peter, Paul and Mary In Concert . . . . (Warner Bros.)
Puget Sound
Gillan; *Mr. Universe* . . . . (Metal Blade)
Push Me, Pull Me
Pearl Jam; *Yield* . . . . (Epic)
Reach The Beach
Fixx; *Reach The Beach* . . . . (MCA)
Reach, The
Dan Fogelberg; *Innocent Age* . . . . (Full Moon)
Red Tide
Rush; *Presto* . . . . (Atlantic)
Redneck Riviera
Tom T. Hall; *Songs From Sopchoppy* . . . . (Mercury)
Redondo Beach
Patti Smith; *Horses* . . . . (Arista)
Remember (Walkin' In The Sand)
Aerosmith; *Aerosmith's Greatest Hits* . . . . (Columbia)

  Night In The Ruts . . . . (Columbia)
Go-Go's; *Return To The Valley Of The Go-Go's* . . . . (I.R.S.)
Shangri-Las; *Girl Groups-Story Of A Sound-C* . . . .(Rhino)
  Oldies But Goodies-#6-C . . . . (Original Sound)
  Original Golden Hits Of The Great Groups-#1-C . . . .(SSS International)
  ST/Goodfellas . . . . (Atlantic)
Remember Pearl Harbor
Sammy Kaye & His Orchestra; *ST/Radio Days* . . . . (Novus)
Ride The Tide
Screamin' Cheetah Wheelies; *Screamin' Cheetah Wheelies* . . . . (Atlantic)
Rock Coast Blues
Country Joe & The Fish; *Collected-1965-1970* . . . .(Vanguard)
  I-Feel-Like-I'm-Fixin'-To-Die . . . .(Vanguard)
Rockaway Beach
Ramones; *Loco Live* . . . . (Sire)
  Ramones Mania . . . . (Sire)
  Rocket To Russia . . . . (Sire)
  Summer & Sun-C . . . .(Rhino)
Safe Harbour
Fleetwood Mac; *Heroes Are Hard To Find* . . . . (Reprise)
Sail Away
Linda Ronstadt; *Don't Cry Now* . . . . (Asylum)
Randy Newman; *Guilty: 30 Years Of Randy Newman* . . . .(Rhino)
  Sail Away . . . . (Reprise)
Sail Away To The Sea
Sandy Denny; *Who Knows Where The Time Goes* . . . . (Hannibal)
Sailing Down The Chesapeake Bay
John Townley & The Press Gang; *Chesapeake Sailor's Companion* . . . (Adelphi)
Sailing, Sailing
Original Soundtrack; *Children's Favorites* . . . . (Kid Rhino/Rhino 4 Kids)
San Francisco Bay Blues
Eric Clapton; *Eric Clapton-Unplugged* . . . . (Reprise)
Janis Joplin; *ST/Janis* . . . .(Columbia)
Jesse Fuller; *Brother Lowdown* . . . . (Fantasy)
  Great Blues Men-C . . . .(Vanguard)
  San Francisco Bay Blues . . . .(Good Time Jazz)
Paul McCartney; *Unplugged (The Official Bootleg)* . . . .(Capitol)
Ramblin' Jack Elliott; *Bread & Roses Festival Of Acoustic*
  Music-#1-C . . . . (Fantasy)
  Essential Ramblin' Jack Elliott . . . .(Vanguard)
  Hard Travelin' . . . . (Fantasy)
  Troubadours Of The Folk Era-#1-C . . . .(Rhino)
Sand & The Sea
Nat "King" Cole; *Ballads Of The Day* . . . .(Capitol)
  The Nat "King" Cole Story . . . .(Capitol)
Sand And Water
Beth Nielsen Chapman; *Sand And Water* . . . . (Reprise)
Sand Castles In The Snow
Public Image Ltd.; *9* . . . . (Virgin)
Santa Monica (Watch The World Die)
Everclear; *Sparkle And Fade* . . . .(Capitol)
Santa Monica Pier
Christine Lavin; *Good Thing He Can't Read My Mind* . . . . (Philo)
Holly Near; *Live Album* . . . . (Redwood)
Nitty Gritty Dirt Band; *Dream* . . . . (United Artists)
Satellite Beach
Peter Case; *Peter Case* . . . . (Geffen)
Saturday Night At Sea
John Townley & The Press Gang; *Chesapeake Sailor's Companion* . . . (Adelphi)
Save Your Heart For Me
Gary Lewis And The Playboys; *Gary Lewis & The Playboys* . . . . . . (Gold Rush)
  Gary Lewis And The Playboys' Greatest Hits . . . .(Curb)
Sea & Sand
Who; *ST/Quadrophenia* . . . . (MCA)
Sea Breezes
Bryan Ferry; *Let's Stick Together* . . . . (Virgin)
Roxy Music; *Roxy Music* . . . . (Reprise)
Siouxsie And The Banshees; *Through The Looking Glass* . . . . (Geffen)
Sea Cruise
Billy "Crash" Craddock; *Billy "Crash" Craddock's Greatest Hits* . . . .(Capitol)
  Changes . . . .(Capitol)
Frankie Ford; *American Hot Wax* . . . . (A&M)
  Best Of New Orleans Rhythm & Blues-#2-C . . . .(Rhino)
  Oldies But Goodies-#3-C . . . . (Original Sound)
  Rock & Roll Show-C . . . . (Gusto)
Glenn Frey; *No Fun Aloud* . . . . (Asylum)
Johnny Rivers; *Johnny Rivers-Anthology 1964-1977* . . . .(Rhino)
Nighthawks; *Best Of The Nighthawks* . . . . (Genes CD Co.)
Robert Gordon & Link Wray; *Fresh Fish Special* . . . .(RCA)
Sea Diver
Mott The Hoople; *All The Young Dudes* . . . .(Columbia)
  The Ballad Of Mott: A Retrospective . . . .(Columbia)
Sea Of Heartbreak
Don Gibson; *Billboard Top Country Hits-1961-C* . . . .(Rhino)
  Don Gibson's All-Time Greatest Hits . . . .(RCA)
Sea Of Joy
Blind Faith; *Blind Faith* . . . . (Polydor)
Eric Clapton; *History Of Eric Clapton* . . . .(Atco)

Sea Of Love
Honeydrippers; *Volume One*..........................(Es Paranza)
Phil Phillips With The Twilights; *Cruisin'-1959-C* ....(Increase)
Remember When-C ....(Garland)
Sea Of Madness
Crosby, Stills, Nash & Young; *ST/Woodstock* ....(Atlantic)
Sea Of Monsters
Beatles; *Beatles-Box Set* ....(Capitol)
Yellow Submarine ....(Capitol)
Sea Of Time & Sea Of Holes
Beatles; *Beatles-Box Set* ....(Capitol)
Yellow Submarine ....(Capitol)
Sea Still Stings
Marc Almond; *Enchanted*......................(Columbia)
Seashores Of Old Mexico
Merle Haggard & Willie Nelson; *Seashores Of Old Mexico*...........(Epic)
Seasick, Yet Still Docked
Morrissey; *Your Arsenal*......................(Sire)
Seaside Bar Song
Bruce Springsteen; *Tracks* ....(Columbia)
Little Bob Story; *One Step Up/Two Steps Back-The Songs Of Bruce*
Springsteen-C ....(Right Stuff)
Second Home By The Sea
Genesis; *Genesis*.........................(Atlantic)
Second Wind
Darryl Worley; *Hard Rain Don't Last* ....(DreamWorks/SKG)
Secret Of The Sea
Billy Bragg & Wilco; *Mermaid Avenue-#2* ....(Elektra)
Seminole Wind
John Anderson; *Seminole Wind* ....(BNA)
Seven Seas
Babyface; *The Day* ....(Epic)
Shining In The Light
Jimmy Page/Robert Plant; *Walking Into Clarksdale*...............(Atlantic)
Ship To Shore
Chris DeBurgh; *The Getaway*....................(A&M)
Sinkin' In The Sea
Barefoot Jerry; *You Can't Get Off With Your Shoes On* ....(Monument)
Sleeping On The Beach
Nitty Gritty Dirt Band; *Dream* ....(United Artists)
Sleepy Lagoon
Boston Pops Orchestra/Arthur Fiedler; *Boston Pops Orchestra/Arthur
Fiedler* ....(RCA)
Greatest Hits Of The '40s.....................(RCA)
Boston Pops Orchestra/John Williams; *Swing Swing Swing*..........(Philips)
Harry James; *Best Of The Big Bands-C* ....(Columbia)
Harry James & His Orchestra; *16 Most Requested Songs Of The
'40s-#2-C* ....(Legacy)
Platters; *More Encore Of Golden Hits* ....(Mercury)
Soft Sands
Chordettes; *Best Of The Chordettes* ....(Rhino)
Golden Classics-Chordettes ....(Collectables)
Sparkling In The Sand
Tower Of Power; *East Bay Grease* ....(Rhino)
Live & In Living Color.................(Warner Bros.)
Standing Together
George Benson; *Standing Together* ....(GRP)
Storm Over Tokyo Bay
Jessie Allen Cooper; *Soft Wave*...................(Sona Gaia)
Storms Are On The Ocean
Carter Family; *Bristol Sessions-#1 & 2-C*.........(Country Music Foundation)
Stranger On The Shore
Acker Bilk; *Best Of Acker Bilk*...................(Crescendo)
Collectables Presents The History Of Rock-#8-C ....(Collectables)
Stranger On The Shore ....(Atco)
Kenny G; *Classics In The Key Of G* ....(Arista)
Roger Whittaker; *Roger Whittaker-Classics Collection-#2* ....(Liberty)
Sullen Girl
Fiona Apple; *Tidal* ....(Clean Slate/Work)
Summer's Comin'
Clint Black; *Clint Black-The Greatest Hits* ....(RCA)
One Emotion ....(RCA)
Swamp
Talking Heads; *Popular Favorites-1984-1992*......................(Sire)
Speaking In Tongues ....(Sire)
ST/Stop Making Sense ....(Sire)
Swamp Fire
Duke Ellington; *Best Of The Swing Bands-C* ....(Hindsight)
Black, Brown & Beige: 1944-1946 Band Recordings ....(Bluebird)
Swamp Gas
Screamin' Jay Hawkins; *Black Music For White People* ....(Rhino)
Swamp Goo
Duke Ellington & His Orchestra; *Yale Concert* ....(Fantasy)
Swamp Music
Lynyrd Skynyrd; *Second Helping*...................(MCA)
Skynyrd's Innards-Their Greatest Hits ....(MCA)
Southern By The Grace Of God-Tribute '87 ....(MCA)

Swamp Sauce
Albert Collins; *Albert Collins-Complete Imperial Recordings* ....(EMI)
Swamp Thing
Malcolm McLaren; *Swamp Thing*....................(Island)
Swampy River
Duke Ellington; *Okeh Ellington* ....(Columbia)
Swimming In The Ocean
David & David; *Boomtown* ....(A&M)
Tahitian Moon
Porno For Pyros; *Good God's Urge* ....(Warner Bros.)
Takin' It Easy
Lacy J. Dalton; *Dream Baby* ....(Columbia)
Lacy J. Dalton's Greatest Hits ....(Columbia)
Talk To Me Like The Sea
Everything But The Girl; *Worldwide* ....(Atlantic)
That Was A River
Collin Raye; *In This Life* ....(Epic)
Theme From "Sea Hunt"
Original Soundtrack; *Television's Greatest Hits-#2-C* ....(TVT)
Theme From "Surfside 6"
Original Soundtrack; *Television's Greatest Hits-#1-C* ....(TVT)
Theme From "Voyage To The Bottom Of The Sea"
Original Soundtrack; *Television's Greatest Hits-#2-C* ....(TVT)
There's A Hole In The Bottom Of The Sea
Original Soundtrack; *School Days-Kids Classics* ....(Benson)
There's A Lovely Lake In London
Gracie Fields; *That Old Feeling* ....(ASV)
Thinking About Your Troubles
Nilsson; *The Point*.........................(RCA)
Thunder Bay
Sawyer Brown; *Buick* ....(Curb)
Tidal Wave
Sugarcubes; *Here Today, Tomorrow Next Week!* ....(Elektra)
Tide Is High
Blondie; *Autoamerican* ....(Chrysalis)
Best Of Blondie ....(Chrysalis)
Billboard Top Hits-1981-C ....(Rhino)
Time & Tide
Basia; *No Boundaries* ....(Columbia)
Time And Tide ....(Epic)
Time (Keeps Flowing Like A River)
Alan Parsons Project; *Best Of The Alan Parsons Project* ....(Arista)
Turn Of A Friendly Card ....(Arista)
Too Many Fish In The Sea
Marvelettes; *Marvelettes' Greatest Hits* ....(Motown)
Marvelettes-Anthology ....(Motown)
Mitch Ryder And The Detroit Wheels; *Mitch Ryder And The Detroit Wheels'
Greatest Hits* ....(Virgo)
Rascals; *Rascals-Anthology 1965-1972* ....(Rhino)
Tremeloes; *Best Of The Tremeloes* ....(Rhino)
Transatlantic Westbound Jet
Hollies; *Hollies* ....(Epic)
True Love Never Dies
Earl Scruggs & Gary Scruggs & Travis Tritt; *Earl Scruggs And
Friends-C* ....(MCA)
Kevin Welch; *Kevin Welch* ....(Reprise)
Truly Madly Deeply
Savage Garden; *Savage Garden* ....(Columbia)
Two Teardrops
Steve Wariner; *Two Teardrops* ....(Capitol)
Under The Boardwalk
Bette Midler; *ST/Beaches* ....(Atlantic)
Bruce Willis; *Return Of Bruno* ....(Motown)
Drifters; *Atlantic Rhythm & Blues 1947-1974-#5 (1962-1966)-C*......(Atlantic)
Drifters-16 Greatest Hits ....(Trip)
Drifters-Golden Hits ....(Atlantic)
Super Oldies Of The '60s-#5-C ....(Audio Fidelity)
John Mellencamp; *Rough Harvest* ....(Mercury)
Lynn Anderson; *What She Does Best* ....(Mercury)
Rickie Lee Jones; *Girl At Her Volcano* ....(Warner Bros.)
Rolling Stones; *12 X 5* ....(Abkco)
Untouchables; *Agent Double O Soul* ....(Restless)
Undertow
Firefall; *Undertow* ....(Atlantic)
Undertow
Genesis; *And Then There Were Three* ....(Atlantic)
Undertow
Suzanne Vega; *Suzanne Vega* ....(A&M)
Up The Beach
Jane's Addiction; *Nothing's Shocking* ....(Warner Bros.)
Waiting For The Tide To Turn
Robert Cray Band; *Bad Influence* ....(Hightone)
Walk On The Ocean
Toad The Wet Sprocket; *Fear* ....(Columbia)
Washed Ashore (On A Lonely Island In The Sea)
Platters; *Platters-16 Greatest Hits*....................(Trip)
Platters-Anthology ....(Rhino)

Waterfront
Simple Minds; *Greenpeace/Rainbow Warriors-C* . . . . (Geffen)
Simple Minds Live: In The City Of Light . . . . (A&M)
Sparkle In The Rain . . . . (A&M)
Wave
Antonio Carlos Jobim; *Wave* . . . . (A&M)
Ella Fitzgerald; *Ella Abraca Jobim* . . . . (Pablo)
Frank Sinatra & Antonio Carlos Jobim; *Sinatra & Company* . . . . (Reprise)
Tony Bennett; *Essence Of Tony Bennett* . . . . (Columbia)
Waves Roll In On Oregon
Jim Post; *Magic-In Concert* . . . . (Flying Fish)
West Coast Sunset
Billy Joe Walker, Jr.; *Life Is Good* . . . . (Liberty)
When The Coast Is Clear
Jimmy Buffett; *Boats Beaches Bars & Ballads* . . . . (Margaritaville)
Floridays . . . . (MCA)
White Silver Sands
Ace Cannon; *Golden Classics-Ace Cannon* . . . . (Gusto)
Ray Anthony; *Great Golden Hits* . . . . (Ranwood)
Sonny James; *45-#4-45706* . . . . (Columbia)
Widow's Walk
Suzanne Vega; *Songs In Red & Gray* . . . . (A&M)
Wish You Were Here
Mark Wills; *Wish You Were Here* . . . . (Mercury)
Wish You Were Here
Incubus; *Morning View* . . . . (Epic)
Wishing You Were Here
Chicago; *Chicago IX-Chicago's Greatest Hits* . . . . (Chicago)
Chicago VII . . . . (Chicago)
Group Portrait . . . . (Chicago)
If You Leave Me Now . . . . (Chicago)
Written In Sand
Santana; *Beyond Appearances* . . . . (Columbia)
Yellow Beach Umbrella
Bette Midler; *Broken Blossom* . . . . (Atlantic)
You're An Ocean
Fastball; *Harsh Light Of Day* . . . . (Hollywood)

OLD

See Also: **AGES (various), AGING, ANNIVERSARY, BIRTHDAY,
LOVE: LONG GONE, REMEMBER, YOUNG**

(Remember The Days Of) The Old Schoolyard
Cat Stevens; *Cat Stevens-Classics-#24* . . . . (A&M)
Izitso . . . . (A&M)
An Old Fashioned Wedding
Ethel Merman/Bruce Yarnell/Original Cast; *Annie Get
Your Gun* . . . . (RCA Victor)
Another Old Soldier
Mark Collie; *Hardin County Line* . . . . (MCA)
As Long As I'm Rockin' With You
John Conlee; *Best Of John Conlee* . . . . (Curb)
In My Eyes . . . . (MCA)
John Conlee-20 Greatest Hits . . . . (MCA)
John Conlee-Legends . . . . (MCA)
Auld Lang Syne
Beach Boys; *Beach Boys Christmas Album* . . . . (Capitol)
Duke Ellington & His Orchestra; *Take The Holiday Train* . . (Special Music Co.)
Guy Lombardo & His Royal Canadians; *All Occasions Album* . . . . . (Gateway)
Best Of Guy Lombardo . . . . (Curb)
Merry Christmas Baby-Romance & Reindeer-C . . . . (Capitol)
Patti LaBelle & The Blue Belles; *A Soulful Christmas-C* . . . . (Collectables)
Stylistics; *Stylistics-Christmas* . . . . (Amherst)
Believe Me If All Those Endearing Young Charms
Bronn Journey; *Celtic Journey* . . . . (Phileo)
Mitch Miller; *Favorite Irish Sing-Alongs* . . . . (Legacy)
Roger Whittaker; *Danny Boy & Other Irish Favorites* . . . . . (RCA Victor)
Best Old Friend
Bonnie Raitt; *The Glow* . . . . (Warner Bros.)
Between An Old Memory And Me
Keith Whitley; *I Wonder Do You Think Of Me* . . . . (RCA)
Travis Tritt; *Ten Feet Tall And Bulletproof* . . . . (Warner Bros.)
Big Ole Brew
Mel McDaniel; *Mel McDaniel's Greatest Hits* . . . . (Capitol)
Take Me To The Country . . . . (Capitol)
Blue Turning Grey Over You
Billie Holiday; *Billie's Blues* . . . . (Blue Note)
Louis Armstrong & Luis Russell & Orchestra; *Satchmo Style*. . . (Disques Swing)
Ringo Starr; *Sentimental Journey* . . . . (Capitol)
Bummin' An Old Freight Train
Lester Flatt & The Nashville Grass; *Great American Train
Songs-C* . . . . (C.M.H. Prod.)
Burnin' Old Memories With A Brand New Flame
Kathy Mattea; *Country Hits 4: Sweet Country-C* . . . . (Priority)
Willow In The Wind . . . . (Mercury)

Carry Me Back To Old Virginny
Jerry Lee Lewis; *Doin' Just Fine* . . . . (Accord)
Ole Tyme Country Music . . . . (Sun)
Sunday Down South . . . . (Sun)
Clack Clack/Oldest Living Son
John Stewart; *Last Campaign* . . . . (Laserlight)
Come & Grow Old With Me In Colorado
Tom Paxton; *One Million Lawyers & Other Disasters* . . . . (Flying Fish)
Come To The Supermarket (In Old Peking)
Barbra Streisand; *The Barbra Streisand Album* . . . . (Columbia)
Daddy Was An Old Time Preacher Man
Porter Wagoner & Dolly Parton; *Best Of Porter Wagoner & Dolly
Parton.* . . . . (RCA)
Damned Old Dog
k.d. lang; *Tame Yourself-C* . . . . (Rhino)
Roches; *Roches* . . . . (Warner Bros.)
Dear Old Nebraska U.
University Of Michigan Band; *Greatest College Football Marches* . .(Vanguard)
Dear Old Stockholm
Miles Davis; *Best Of Miles Davis: The Capitol And Blue Note
Years.* . . . . (Blue Note)
Miles Davis Quintet; *Round About Midnight* . . . . (Columbia)
Terence Blanchard; *Simply Stated* . . . . (Columbia)
Toots Thielemans; *East Coast West Coast* . . . . (Private Music)
Dear Old Syracuse
Original New York Cast; *Boys From Syracuse* . . . . (Angel)
Dirty Old Egg-Sucking Dog
Johnny Cash; *Essential Johnny Cash* . . . . (Columbia)
Johnny Cash At Folsom Prison & San Quentin . . . . (Columbia)
Down At The Old Corral
Randy Travis; *Wind In The Wire* . . . . (Warner Bros.)
Down By The Old Mill Stream
Mitch Miller; *Sing Along With Mitch* . . . . (Columbia)
Sammy Kaye & His Orchestra; *Best Of Sammy Kaye & His Orchestra*. . . (MCA)
Dublin In The Rare Old Times
Garrison Brothers; *Songs & Stories* . . . . (Boot)
Dust On The Bottle
David Lee Murphy; *Out With A Bang* . . . . (MCA)
Elderly Woman Behind The Counter In A Small Town
Pearl Jam; *Vs.* . . . . (Epic Portrait Assoc.)
Few More Memories
Dolly Parton; *The Grass Is Blue* . . . . (Sugar Hill)
Fire Of Two Old Flames
Roy Head; *In Our Room* . . . . (Elektra)
Fourteen Minutes Old
Doug Stone; *Doug Stone* . . . . (Epic)
Goin' Back To Old Kentucky
New Grass Revival; *Festival Tapes* . . . . (Flying Fish)
Golden Olden Days Of Rock & Roll
Johnny Winter; *J.D. Winter III* . . . . (Blue Sky)
Good Old American Guest
Merle Haggard; *Big City* . . . . (Epic)
Good Old Cabbage Greens
Washboard Sam; *Rockin' My Blues Away* . . . . (RCA)
Good Old Desk
Nilsson; *Aerial Ballet* . . . . (RCA)
Good Ole Boys From Louisiana
Jimmy C. Newman & Cajun Country; *Jimmy C. Newman & Cajun
Country.* . . . . (Dot)
Goodbye Old Buddies
Seals & Crofts; *Get Closer* . . . . (Warner Bros.)
Grandpa (Tell Me 'Bout The Good Old Days)
Judds; *Judds' Greatest Hits* . . . . (MCA)
Rockin' With The Rhythm . . . . (MCA)
Super 10-#2-C . . . . (RCA)
Grow Old With Me
John Lennon; *The John Lennon Anthology* . . . . (Capitol)
Wonsaponatime . . . . (Capitol)
Mary Chapin Carpenter; *Party Doll And Other Favorites* . . . . . (Columbia)
Heart Of Gold
Neil Young; *Decade* . . . . (Reprise)
Harvest . . . . (Reprise)
Hello In There
Bette Midler; *Live At Last* . . . . (Atlantic)
John Prine; *John Prine* . . . . (Atlantic)
John Prine-Souvenirs . . . . (Oh Boy)
Hello Old Friend
Eric Clapton; *Eric Clapton-Crossroads-C* . . . . (Polydor)
No Reason To Cry . . . . (RSO)
He's A Good Ole Boy
Chely Wright; *Woman In The Moon* . . . . (Polydor Country)
Hi De Ho (That Old Sweet Roll)
Bobby Darin; *Live At The Desert Inn* . . . . (Motown)
Highlands
Bob Dylan; *Time Out Of Mind* . . . . (Columbia)
Hills Of Old Wyomin'
Sons Of The Pioneers; *The Country Music Hall Of Fame-Sons Of The
Pioneers* . . . . (MCA)

Tex Ritter; *The Country Music Hall Of Fame-Tex Ritter* . . . . (MCA)

Hold An Old Friend's Hand
Rita Coolidge; *Fall Into Spring* . . . . (A&M)
Tiffany; *Hold An Old Friend's Hand* . . . . (MCA)

I Don't Need Your Rockin' Chair
George Jones; *Platinum Country-C* . . . . (MCA)
Walls Can Fall . . . . (MCA)

I Found My Girl In The Good Old U.S.A.
Jimmie Skinner; *45-#2095* . . . . (Gusto)

I Know An Old Lady Who Swallowed A Fly
Original Soundtrack; *More Silly Songs* . . . . (Disney)
Peter, Paul & Mary; *Peter, Paul & Mommy, Too* . . . . (Warner Bros.)

I Ride An Old Paint/Whoopee Ti-Yi-Yo/Git Along Little Doggies
Michael Martin Murphey; *Cowboy Songs* . . . . (Warner Western)

I Wonder How The Old Folks Are At Home
Doc & Merle Watson; *Home Sweet Home* . . . . (Sugar Hill)

I'd Rather Be Dead
Nilsson; *Son Of Schmilsson* . . . . (RCA)

If These Old Walls Could Speak
Nanci Griffith with Jimmy Webb; *Red Hot + Country-C* . . . . . (Mercury)

I'm An Old Cowhand
Bing Crosby; *Best Of Bing Crosby* . . . . (MCA)
Sons Of The Pioneers; *Empty Saddles* . . . . (MCA)

I'm Going Back To Old Kentucky
Bill Monroe; *Best Of Bill Monroe & His Blue Grass Boys* . . . . (MCA)
Bill Monroe And Flatt & Scruggs . . . . (Rounder)
Columbia Historic Edition-Bill Monroe . . . . (Columbia)
Bill Monroe & The Stars Of The Bluegrass Hall Of Fame; *Bill Monroe &*
The Stars Of The Bluegrass Hall Of Fame . . . . (MCA)
Osborne Brothers; *Red, White & Bluegrass-C* . . . . (C.M.H. Prod.)

I'm Going Back To The Old Home
Doc Watson; *Legacy-A Tribute To The First Generation Of*
Bluegrass-C . . . . (Sugar Hill)

I'm Just An Old Chunk Of Coal (But I'm Gonna Be A Diamond Someday)
Billy Joe Shaver; *Restless Wind-The Legendary Billy Joe Shaver-1973-1987* . . . . (Razor & Tie)
John Anderson; *John Anderson's Greatest Hits* . . . . (Warner Bros.)

In The Good Old Summertime
Andrews Sisters; *45-#65016* . . . . (MCA)
Mom & Dads; *In The Good Old Summertime* . . . . (Crescendo)

It's A Lonesome Old Town (When You're Not Around)
Ben Bernie & His Orchestra featuring Donald Saxon; *78-#4943* . . . . (Brunswick)
Frank Sinatra; *Sings For Only The Lonely* . . . . . (EMI-Capitol Entert. Properties)
Lena Horne; *Love Is The Thing* . . . . (RCA)
Les Paul; *Les Paul's Greatest Hits* . . . . (Pair)
Sting; *ST/Leaving Las Vegas* . . . . (Pangaea)

It's Raining, It's Pouring
Original Soundtrack; *Children's Favorites* . . . . (Kid Rhino/Rhino 4 Kids)

It's The Same Old Song
Four Tops; *Billboard Top R&B Hits-1965-C* . . . . (Rhino)
Compact Command Performances-Four Tops . . . . (Motown)
Four Tops' Greatest Hits . . . . (Motown)
Four Tops-Anthology . . . . (Motown)

Just Good Ol' Boys
Moe Bandy & Joe Stampley; *Just Good Ol' Boys* . . . . (Columbia)
Moe Bandy & Joe Stampley's Greatest Hits . . . . (Columbia)
Trucker's Jukebox-#2-C . . . . (Legacy)

Lack Of Water
Why Store; *The Why Store* . . . . (MCA)

Lees Of Old Virginia
William Daniels/Original Cast; *1776* . . . . (Sony Music Classical)

Little Old Church In England
Glenn Miller & His Orchestra; *Complete Glenn Miller & His*
Orchestra . . . . (Bluebird)

Little Old Fashioned Karma
Willie Nelson; *Tougher Than Leather* . . . . (Columbia)

Little Old Lady (From Pasadena)
Beach Boys; *Concert/'69-Live In London* . . . . (Capitol)
Jan & Dean; *Best Of Jan & Dean* . . . . (EMI)
Billboard Top Rock 'N' Roll Hits-1964-C . . . . (Rhino)
Dead Man's Curve . . . . (EMI)
Surf City-Best Of Jan & Dean . . . . (EMI)

Little Old Wine Drinker Me
Dean Martin; *Dean Martin's Greatest Hits-#2* . . . . (Reprise)
Welcome To My World . . . . (Reprise)
Mel Tillis; *Best Of Mel Tillis* . . . . (MCA)

Lonely Ol' Night
John Cougar Mellencamp; *Scarecrow* . . . . (Riva)

Love Letters From Old Mexico
Leslie Satcher; *Love Letters* . . . . (Warner Bros.)

Love Story
Randy Newman; *Randy Newman* . . . . (Warner Archives)

Mean Mr. Mustard
Beatles; *Abbey Road* . . . . (Parlophone)

Mean Old Frisco
Eric Clapton; *Slowhand* . . . . (Polydor)
Jimmy Witherspoon; *Best Of Jimmy Witherspoon* . . . . (Prestige)

Mean Old Frisco . . . . (Prestige)

Mean Old World
Bobby Bland & B.B. King; *Together Again Live* . . . . (MCA)
Climax Blues Band; *Climax Chicago Blues Band* . . . . (Sire)
Duane Allman & Eric Clapton; *Duane Allman-An Anthology* . . . . . (Capricorn)
Eric Clapton-Crossroads-C . . . . (Polydor)
Robert Palmer; *Secrets* . . . . (Island)

Meet Me Tonight By My Old Kentucky Home
Joe Val & The New England Bluegrass Boys; *Joe Val & The New England*
Bluegrass Boys-Vol. 2 . . . . (Rounder)

Midnight In Old Amarillo
Buddy Emmons & Ray Pennington; *Swing & Other Things* . . . . (Step One)

Much Too Young (To Feel This Damn Old)
Garth Brooks; *Garth Brooks-Double Live* . . . . (Capitol)

My Back Pages
Bob Dylan; *Another Side Of Bob Dylan* . . . . (Columbia)
Bob Dylan's Greatest Hits-#2 . . . . (Columbia)
Byrds; *20 Essential Tracks From The Box Set.* . . . . (Columbia)
Byrds Play Dylan . . . . (Columbia)
The Byrds' Greatest Hits . . . . (Columbia)
Younger Than Yesterday . . . . (Columbia)

My Cowboy's Getting Old
Tanya Tucker; *Lovin' & Learnin'* . . . . (MCA)

My Dear Old Arizona Home
Rex Allen; *Back In The Saddle Again: American Cowboy*
Songs-C . . . . (New World)

My Ol' Kentucky Rock & Roll Home
Original New York Cast; *Oil City Symphony* . . . . (DRG)

My Old Flame
Duke Ellington; *Nipper's Greatest Hits Of The '30s-#1-C* . . . . . . (RCA)
Guy Lombardo & His Royal Canadians; *Guy Lombardo-16 Most Requested*
Songs . . . . (Legacy)
J.J. Johnson; *Trombone Master* . . . . (Columbia)
Linda Ronstadt; *Lush Life* . . . . (Asylum)
Rosemary Clooney; *Great Girl Singers Sing 22 Original*
Recordings-C . . . . (Hindsight)
Stan Kenton & His Orchestra; *Road Show* . . . . (Capitol)
Tommy Smith; *Standards* . . . . (Blue Note)

My Old Friend
John Hiatt; *Tiki Bar Is Open* . . . . (Vanguard)

My Old Kentucky Home
Al Jolson; *The Al Jolson Story-#5* . . . . (MCA)
Ry Cooder; *Ry Cooder* . . . . (Reprise)
Salli Terri; *Songs Of The American Land* . . . . (Angel)

My Old Man
Jerry Jeff Walker; *Gypsy Songman* . . . . (Rykodisc)
Mr. Bojangles . . . . (Bainbridge)
Walker's Collectibles . . . . (MCA)
John Denver; *Rhymes & Reasons* . . . . (RCA)
Steve Goodman; *Say It In Private* . . . . (Asylum)

My Old Piano
Diana Ross; *Diana* . . . . (Motown)
Diana Ross-All The Great Hits . . . . (Motown)
Diana Ross-Anthology . . . . (Motown)

My Old School
Steely Dan; *Countdown To Ecstasy* . . . . (MCA)
Decade Of Steely Dan. . . . . (MCA)
Steely Dan's Greatest Hits . . . . (MCA)

My Old Yellow Car
Dan Seals; *Best Of Dan Seals* . . . . (Capitol)
Dan Seals-Classics Collection-#1 . . . . (Capitol)
Early Dan Seals . . . . (Capitol)
San Antone . . . . (EMI)
Lacy J. Dalton; *Blue Eyed Blues* . . . . (Columbia)
Dream Baby . . . . (Columbia)

My Rose Of Old Kentucky
Bill Monroe; *Bill Monroe & Friends* . . . . (MCA)
Bill Monroe & Flatt & Scruggs; *Bill Monroe And Flatt & Scruggs* . . . . (Rounder)

Never Never Land
Original Cast/Mary Martin; *Peter Pan-The 1954 Broadway*
Production . . . . (RCA Victor)

New Fool At An Old Game
Reba McEntire; *Country's Greatest Hits-#4-Sweet Country-C* . . . . (Priority)
Reba . . . . (MCA)
Reba McEntire-Live . . . . (MCA)

Oh My Old Train
Lonesome Strangers; *Lonesome Strangers* . . . . (Hightone)

Ol' '55
Eagles; *On The Border* . . . . (Elektra)
Tom Waits; *Tom Waits-Anthology* . . . . (Asylum)

Ol' Country
Mark Chesnutt; *Longnecks & Short Stories* . . . . (MCA)

Ol' Man River
Al Jolson; *Best Of Al Jolson* . . . . (MCA)
The Al Jolson Story-#6 . . . . (MCA)
Frank Sinatra; *The Concert Sinatra* . . . . (Reprise)
Voice: The Columbia Years-1943-1952 . . . . (Columbia)
Paul Robeson; *A Lonesome Road* . . . . (Living Era)
American Balladeer-Golden Classics-#1-C . . . . (Collectables)

William Warfield; *ST/All Those Glorious MGM Musicals* . . . . (MGM)
William Warfield/Original Cast; *Show Boat* . . . . (Columbia)

Old
Paul Simon; *You're The One* . . . . (Warner Bros.)

Old Black Choo Choo
Rose Maddox; *Rose Of The West Coast Country* . . . . (Arhoolie)

Old Blue
Byrds; *The Byrds* . . . . (Columbia)
Furry Lewis; *Back On My Feet Again* . . . . (Prestige)
  Shake 'Em On Down . . . . (Fantasy)
Joan Baez; *Joan Baez, Vol. 2* . . . . (Vanguard)
  The Joan Baez Ballad Book . . . . (Vanguard)

Old Blue Car
Peter Case; *Peter Case* . . . . (Geffen)

Old Brown Shoe
Beatles; *Beatles-Box Set* . . . . (Capitol)
  Hey Jude . . . . (Capitol)
  Past Masters-Volume Two . . . . (Parlophone)

Old Cape Cod
Patti Page; *Patti Page-16 Most Requested Songs* . . . . (Legacy)
  Patti Page-Golden Hits . . . . (Mercury)
  Patti Page's Greatest Hits . . . . (Columbia)

Old Chisholm Trail
Michael Martin Murphey; *Cowboy Songs* . . . . (Warner Western)
Randy Travis; *Wind In The Wire* . . . . (Warner Bros.)

Old Count Basie Is Gone (Old Piney Brown Is Gone)
Tony Bennett; *Playin' With My Friends-Bennett Sings The
  Blues-C* . . . . (Columbia)

Old Country Church
Hank Williams; *I Ain't Got Nothin' But Time-1946-1947* . . . . (Polydor)

Old Coyote Town
Don Williams; *Traces* . . . . (Capitol)

Old Dan Tucker
Original Soundtrack; *Children's Favorites* . . . . (Kid Rhino/Rhino 4 Kids)

Old Days/Old Ways
Ronnie Laws; *Dream A Little* . . . . (HDH)

Old Deuteronomy
Original Broadway Cast; *Cats* . . . . (Geffen)
Original London Cast; *Cats* . . . . (Geffen)

Old Devil Moon
Anita O'Day; *Anita Sings The Most* . . . . (Verve)
Frank Sinatra & Nelson Riddle Orchestra; *songs for Swingin'
  Lovers!* . . . . (Capitol)
John Raitt; *Highlights Of Broadway-Under Open Skies* . . . . (Capitol)
Lena Horne; *The Lady* . . . . (Dunhill Compact Classics)
Michael Feinstein; *Michael Feinstein Sings The Burton Lane
  Songbook-#1* . . . . (Nonesuch)
Miles Davis; *Blue Haze* . . . . (Prestige)
Original Cast; *Finian's Rainbow* . . . . (Columbia)
Tony Bennett; *Forty Years-The Artistry Of Tony Bennett* . . . . (Columbia)

Old Dirt Road
John Lennon; *Lennon* . . . . (Capitol)
  Menlove Ave. . . . . (Capitol)
  Walls And Bridges . . . . (Capitol)

Old Dogs, Children & Watermelon Wine
Tom T. Hall; *Essential Tom T. Hall-20th Anniversary Collection* . . . (Mercury)
  Tom T. Hall's Greatest Hits-#2 . . . . (Mercury)

Old Dope Peddler
Tom Lehrer; *Songs By Tom Lehrer* . . . . (Reprise)

Old England
Waterboys; *This Is The Sea* . . . . (Chrysalis)

Old Enough To Know Better
Wade Hayes; *Country Dance Hits-C* . . . . (Columbia)
  Old Enough To Know Better . . . . (Columbia)
  Steppin' Country-#2-C . . . . (Columbia)
  Super Hits Of 1994-C . . . . (Columbia)

Old Farm 1939
Randy Newman; *ST/The Natural* . . . . (Warner Bros.)

Old Fashioned Love
Asleep At The Wheel featuring Suzy Bogguss; *Tribute To The Music Of Bob
  Wills And The Texas Playboys-C* . . . . (Liberty)

Old Flame
Alabama; *60 Years Of Country Music-C* . . . . (RCA)
  Alabama's Greatest Hits . . . . (RCA)
  Feels So Right . . . . (RCA)

Old Flame
Church; *Priest-Aura* . . . . (Arista)

Old Flame
Juice Newton; *Old Flame* . . . . (RCA)

Old Flames Can't Hold A Candle To You
Dolly Parton; *Dolly Dolly Dolly* . . . . (RCA)
  Dolly Parton's Greatest Hits . . . . (RCA)
Joe Sun; *Old Flames Can't Hold A Candle To You* . . . . (Ovation)
Merle Haggard; *Kern River* . . . . (Epic)

Old Flames Have New Names
Mark Chesnutt; *Longnecks & Short Stories* . . . . (MCA)

Old Folks At Home
Mormon Tabernacle Choir; *Songs Of The Civil War And Stephen Foster
  Favorites* . . . . (Sony Music Classical)

Paul Robeson; *A Man & His Beliefs-Golden Classics-#2* . . . . (Collectables)

Old Folks Boogie
Little Feat; *Time Loves A Hero* . . . . (Warner Bros.)
  Waiting For Columbus . . . . (Warner Bros.)

Old Friends
Barry Manilow; *Showstoppers* . . . . (Arista)
Liza Minnelli; *Liza Minnelli-At Carnegie Hall* . . . . (Telarc)
Original Cast; *Merrily We Roll Along* . . . . (RCA)
Stephen Sondheim & Angela Lansbury & Co.; *Collector's Sondheim-C* . (RCA)

Old Friends
Simon & Garfunkel; *Bookends* . . . . (Columbia)
  Collected Works . . . . (Columbia)
  The Concert In Central Park . . . . (Warner Bros.)

Old Friends
Willie Nelson & Roger Miller; *Old Friends* . . . . (Columbia)
Willie Nelson & Waylon Jennings; *Take It To The Limit* . . . . (Columbia)

Old Friends
Everything But The Girl; *Worldwide* . . . . (Atlantic)

Old Gray Mare, The
Original Soundtrack; *School Days-Kids Classics* . . . . (Benson)

Old Gumbie Cat
Original Broadway Cast; *Cats* . . . . (Geffen)

Old Home Filler Up & Keep On A Truckin'
C.W. McCall; *C.W. McCall's Greatest Hits* . . . . (Polydor)
  Wolf Creek Pass . . . . (MGM)

Old Joe Clark
Dillards; *Bluegrass Breakdown* . . . . (Vanguard)
Eric Weissberg; *ST/Deliverance* . . . . (Warner Bros.)

Old Judge Jones
Les Dudek; *Say No More* . . . . (Columbia)

Old Kentucky Fiddle
Hoot Hester; *45-#114* . . . . (Nationwide Sound Distrib.)

Old Kentucky Home
Randy Newman; *12 Songs* . . . . (Reprise)
  Randy Newman/Live . . . . (Warner Archives)

Old Kentucky Land
Kingston Trio; *Rediscovering The Kingston Trio* . . . . (Folk Era)
  Tune Up! . . . . (Folk Era)

Old Kentucky Song
Oak Ridge Boys; *Bobbie Sue* . . . . (MCA)

Old Kidney Stew Is Fine
Eddie "Cleanhead" Vinson; *Old Kidney Stew Is Fine* . . . . (Delmark)

Old King Cole
Original Soundtrack; *Children's Favorites* . . . . (Kid Rhino/Rhino 4 Kids)

Old Lamplighter, The
Bing Crosby; *The Radio Years-#2* . . . . (Crescendo)
Browns; *45-#7700* . . . . (RCA)
  Nipper's Greatest Hits Of The '60s-#2-C . . . . (RCA)
Kay Kyser & His Orchestra; *Best Of The Big Bands-Kay Kyser & His
  Orchestra* . . . . (Legacy)
Sammy Kaye & His Orchestra; *Nipper's Greatest Hits Of The
  '40s-#2-C* . . . . (RCA)

Old Love
Eric Clapton; *Eric Clapton-Unplugged* . . . . (Reprise)

Old MacDonald Had A Farm
Original Soundtrack; *Toddler Favorites* . . . . (Kid Rhino/Rhino 4 Kids)

Old Maid Boogie
Eddie "Cleanhead" Vinson; *Late Show* . . . . (Fantasy)

Old Man
Neil Young; *Decade* . . . . (Reprise)
  Harvest . . . . (Reprise)

Old Man
Alabama; *Just Us* . . . . (RCA)

Old Man
Randy Newman; *Sail Away* . . . . (Reprise)

Old Man
ZZ Top; *Six Pack* . . . . (Warner Bros.)
  ZZ Top . . . . (Warner Bros.)

Old Man & Me
J.J. Cale; *Okie* . . . . (MCA)

Old Man And Me
Hootie & The Blowfish; *Fairweather Johnson* . . . . (Atlantic)

Old Man Down The Road
John Fogerty; *Centerfield* . . . . (Warner Bros.)

Old Man From The Mountain
Merle Haggard & The Strangers; *For The Record: Merle Haggard-43
  Legendary Hits* . . . . (BNA)

Old Man On The Farm
Randy Newman; *Little Criminals* . . . . (Warner Bros.)

Old Mexico
Orion; *Fresh* . . . . (Sun)

Old Mexico
Bad Company; *Rough Diamonds* . . . . (Swan Song)

Old Nashville Cowboys
Hank Williams, Jr.; *Whiskey Bent & Hell Bound* . . . . (WB/Curb)

Old Oaken Bucket, The
Old Homestead Double Quartet; *Music From The New York Stage (1890-
  1920)-#1-1890-1908-C* . . . . (Pearl)

Old Paint
Chris LeDoux; *Old Cowboy Classics* . . . . (Capitol)
Western Tunesmith . . . . (Liberty)
Linda Ronstadt; *Simple Dreams* . . . . (Asylum)
Old Pair Of Shoes
Randy Travis; *Randy Travis' Greatest Hits-#1* . . . .(Warner Bros.)
Old Photographs
Carlene Carter; *Two Sides To Every Woman* . . . .(Warner Bros.)
Old Photographs
Charley Pride; *Amazing Love* . . . . (RCA)
Old Photographs
Sawyer Brown; *Somewhere In The Night* . . . . (Liberty)
Old Playground
Bruce Hornsby & The Range; *Scenes From The Southside* . . . . (RCA)
Old Rockin' Horse
Slim Dusty; *Australia Is His Name* . . . . (Philo)
Old Rose Motel
Great White; *Psycho City* . . . . (Capitol)
Old San Juan
Spyro Gyra; *Access All Areas* . . . .(MCA)
Incognito . . . .(MCA)
Spyro Gyra-Collection. . . . . (GRP)
Old School, The
John Conlee; *Country Classics-#6-1985-1986-C* . . . . (Universal)
John Conlee-20 Greatest Hits . . . .(MCA)
The Old School. . . . .(MCA Special Prod.)
Old Shoes
Tom Waits; *Tom Waits-Early Years-Volume Two* . . . . (Rhino)
Old Shoes
Eddie Jefferson; *Bebop Singers* . . . .(Prestige)
Old Songs
Barry Manilow; *Barry Manilow's Greatest Hits-#3* . . . . (Arista)
If I Should Love Again . . . . (Arista)
Old Tennessee
Dan Fogelberg; *Captured Angel* . . . . (Full Moon)
Live-Greetings From The West . . . . (Full Moon)
Old Time Rock & Roll
Bob Seger & The Silver Bullet Band; *Nine Tonight* . . . . (Capitol)
Stranger In Town . . . . (Capitol)
Old Toy Trains
Billy Strange; *Railroad Man*. . . . .(Crescendo)
Glen Campbell; *All-Star Country Christmas-C* . . . . (Capitol)
That Christmas Feeling . . . . (Capitol)
Statler Brothers; *Statler Brothers Christmas Present* . . . . (Mercury)
Old Tucson
Youssou N'Dour; *The Lion*. . . . . (Virgin)
Old Virginia Lowlands
John Townley & The Press Gang; *Chesapeake Sailor's Companion* . . .(Adelphi)
Old Virginia March
Sam McNeil/Dent Wimmer/Others; *Old Originals-#2*. . . . . (Rounder)
Oldest Baby In The World
John Prine; *Aimless Love* . . . . (Oh Boy)
Great Days-Anthology . . . . (Rhino)
John Prine-Live . . . . (Oh Boy)
Oldest Established (Permanent Floating Crap Game In New York)
Original Cast; *ST/Guys & Dolls* . . . .(MCA)
Ole Buttermilk Sky
Hoagy Carmichael; *Ole Buttermilk Sky* . . . . (Collector's Choice)
Kay Kyser & His Orchestra; *Best Of Kay Kyser & His
Orchestra* . . . . (Collector's Choice)
Mello-Larks; *The Hoagy Carmichael Songbook-C* . . . . (Bluebird)
Willie Nelson; *What A Wonderful World* . . . . (Columbia)
On The Banks Of The Old Tennessee
Doc Watson; *Old Timey Concert* . . . . (Vanguard)
On The Old Kentucky Shore
J.D. Crowe & Others; *Bluegrass Album-#5-Sweet Sunny South* . . . . . . (Rounder)
On Top Of Old Smokey
Bing Crosby; *The Radio Years-#3* . . . .(Crescendo)
Weavers; *Best Of The Weavers* . . . .(MCA)
Reunion-At Carnegie Hall-1963-#2. . . . . (Vanguard)
Weavers' Greatest Hits . . . . (Vanguard)
Pack Up Your Troubles In Your Old Kit Bag (And Smile, Smile, Smile)
James F. Harrison & Knickerbocker Quartet; *78-#2181*. . . . . (Columbia)
Pair Of Old Sneakers
George Jones; *George Jones & Tammy Wynette-16
Biggest Hits*. . . . . (Epic/Legacy)
Put On Your Old Grey Bonnet
Jimmy Dean; *Jimmy Dean's Greatest Hits* . . . . (Columbia)
Pete Fountain; *Best Of Pete Fountain* . . . .(MCA)
Mr. New Orleans . . . .(MCA)
Question Everything
8Stops7; *In Moderation* . . . . (Reprise)
Ragged Old Flag
Johnny Cash; *Patriot* . . . . (Columbia)
We The People-C . . . . (Folk Era)
Rock And Roll Waltz
Kay Starr; *Capitol Collectors Series-Kay Starr* . . . . (Capitol)

Rock Me Tonight (For Old Time's Sake)
Freddie Jackson; *Rock Me Tonight (For Old Time's Sake)* . . . . (Capitol)
Rockin' In The Same Old Boat
Bobby Bland; *Spotlighting The Man*. . . . . (MCA)
Rose Of Old Monterey
Happy Polkateers; *Happy Polkateers* . . . .(Crescendo)
Sad Old Red
Simply Red; *Picture Book* . . . . (Elektra)
Sam, The Old Accordion Man
Doris Day & James Cagney; *ST/Love Me Or
Leave Me* . . . . (Sony Music Special Prod.)
Same Ol' Fishing Hole
Blues Boy Willie; *Be-Who* . . . . (Ichiban Int'l)
Same Ol' Love
Ricky Skaggs; *My Father's Son* . . . . (Epic)
Same Old Fashioned Girl
Gene Autry; *Columbia Historic Edition-Gene Autry* . . . . (Columbia)
Same Old Lang Syne
Dan Fogelberg; *Dan Fogelberg/Greatest Hits* . . . .(Full Moon)
Innocent Age. . . . .(Full Moon)
Live-Greetings From The West. (Full Moon)
Same Old Rain
Kevin Welch & The Overtones; *Western Beat* . . . . (Reprise)
Same Old Saturday Night
Frank Sinatra; *Capitol Collectors Series-Frank Sinatra* . . . . (Capitol)
Same Old Song & Dance
Aerosmith; *Aerosmith-Classics Live 2* . . . . (Columbia)
Aerosmith's Greatest Hits . . . . (Columbia)
Get Your Wings . . . . (Columbia)
Pandora's Box . . . . (Columbia)
Same Old Story
Billie Holiday; *Fine & Mellow* . . . . (Collectables)
Quintessential-#8-1939-1940. . . . . (Legacy)
Same Old Story
Stevie Wonder; *Journey Through The Secret Life Of Plants* . . . . (Motown)
Same Old Story
Garth Brooks; *No Fences* . . . . (Capitol)
Same Old Story
Ronna Reeves; *Only The Heart* . . . . (Mercury)
Same Old Wine
Loggins & Messina; *Sittin' In* . . . . (Columbia)
Same Ole Love
Billy Cobham; *Billy's Best Hits*. . . . . (GRP)
Same Ole Love
Anita Baker; *Rapture* . . . . (Elektra)
Seashores Of Old Mexico
Merle Haggard & Willie Nelson; *Seashores Of Old Mexico* . . . . (Epic)
Second Hand Heart
Gary Morris; *Faded Blue*. . . . . (Warner Bros.)
Second Hand News
Fleetwood Mac; *25 Years-The Chain* . . . . (Warner Bros.)
Rumours . . . . (Warner Bros.)
Tonic; *Legacy-A Tribute To Fleetwood Mac's Rumours-C* . . . . (Lava)
Second Hand Rose
Barbra Streisand; *A Happening In Central Park* . . . . (Columbia)
Barbra Streisand...and other musical instruments. . . . . (Columbia)
Barbra Streisand's Greatest Hits . . . . (Columbia)
Just For The Record . . . . (Columbia)
My Name Is Barbra, Two . . . . (Columbia)
She Misses Him
Tim Rushlow; *Tim Rushlow* . . . .(Atlantic)
Spirits Of Ancient Egypt
Wings; *Venus And Mars* . . . . (Capitol)
Wings Over America . . . . (Capitol)
Stories Of Old
Depeche Mode; *Some Great Reward* . . . .(Sire)
Streets Of Old Chicago
Carl Martin/Ted Bogan/Howard Armstrong; *That Old Gang
Of Mine* . . . . (Flying Fish)
Take Me Back To My Old Carolina Home
Uncle Dave Macon; *Laugh Your Blues Away* . . . . (Rounder)
Take Me Back To Old Wyoming
Chris LeDoux; *Thirty-Dollar Cowboy* . . . . (Liberty)
Tattoos & Scars
Montgomery Gentry; *Tattoos & Scars* . . . . (Columbia)
That Lucky Old Sun
Asleep At The Wheel; *Western Standard Time* . . . . (Epic)
Bing Crosby; *The Radio Years: 25 Songs* . . . .(Crescendo)
Frankie Laine; *Frankie Laine-16 Most Requested Songs* . . . . (Legacy)
Frankie Laine-Golden Hits . . . . (Mercury)
Frankie Laine's Greatest Hits . . . . (Columbia)
Jerry Garcia Band; *Jerry Garcia Band* . . . . (Arista)
Louis Armstrong; *Louis Armstrong's Greatest Hits* . . . . (Curb)
Ray Charles; *Ray Charles-Anthology* . . . . (Rhino)
Willie Nelson; *Sound In Your Mind* . . . . (Columbia)
That Ol' Wind
Garth Brooks; *Fresh Horses* . . . . (Capitol)
Limited Series Box . . . . (Capitol)

That Old Beat Up Guitar
Jerry Jeff Walker; *Jerry Jeff Walker* . . . . (MCA)

That Old Black Magic
Ella Fitzgerald; *Best Of Ella Fitzgerald* . . . . (MCA)
   Big Bands Of The Swinging Years-C . . . . (Everest)
   In Rome-Birthday Concert . . . . (Verve)
Frank Sinatra; *Come Swing With Me!* . . . . (Capitol)
Glenn Miller & His Orchestra; *Chattanooga Choo Choo-#1 Hits* . . . . . (Bluebird)
Judy Garland; *Best Of Judy Garland* . . . . (MCA)
Louis Prima & Keely Smith; *Memories Are Made Of This-C* . . . . . (Capitol)
Marcels; *Best Of The Marcels* . . . . (Rhino)
Sammy Davis, Jr.; *Hey There-At His Dynamite Greatest* . . . . (MCA)
Spike Jones; *Best Of Spike Jones-#2* . . . . (RCA)

That Old Devil Called Love
Chet Baker; *Baker's Holiday* . . . . (Verve)
   Compact Jazz-Chet Baker . . . . (Verve)
Ella Fitzgerald; *All That Jazz* . . . . (Pablo)

That Old Gang Of Mine
Mitch Miller; *Sing Along With Mitch* . . . . (Columbia)

That Old Song
Ray Parker Jr.; *Ray Parker Jr.'s Greatest Hits* . . . . (Arista)
Ray Parker Jr./Raydio; *A Woman Needs Love* . . . . (Arista)

That Same Old Train
Blind Snooks Eaglin; *Legacy Of The Blues-#2* . . . . (Crescendo)

Theme From "Golden Girls"
Original Soundtrack; *Television's Greatest Hits-#6-Remote Control-C* . . . (TVT)

There Goes That Old Steel Guitar
Tammy Wynette; *Tammy Wynette's Greatest Hits-#3* . . . . (Epic)

There'll Be A Hot Time In The Old Town Tonight
Bessie Smith; *Bessie Smith-The Complete Recordings-#3* . . . . . (Legacy)
Louis Armstrong; *Best Of Louis Armstrong* . . . . (Audio Fidelity)
Turk Murphy's San Francisco Jazz Band; *Turk Murphy's San Francisco Jazz Band* . . . . (Good Time Jazz)
Woody Herman; *The Uncollected Woody Herman & His First Herd* . . . . (Hindsight)

They Wounded Old Ireland
Andy M. Stewart; *By The Hush* . . . . (Green Linnet)

This Ol' Cowboy
Marshall Tucker Band; *Marshall Tucker Band's Greatest Hits* . . . . . (Capricorn)
   Where We All Belong . . . . (AJK Music)

This Old Guitar
John Denver; *Back Home Again* . . . . (RCA)
   Evening With John Denver . . . . (RCA)
   John Denver's Greatest Hits-#2 . . . . (RCA)

This Old Heart Of Mine
Isley Brothers; *25 Hard-To-Find Motown Classics-#3-C* . . . (Motown)
   Good Feeling Music Of The Big Chill Generation-#1-C . . . . (Motown)
   Greatest By Holland/Dozier/Holland-C . . . . (Motown)
   Motown Story-First 25 Years-C . . . . (Motown)
   Motown Superstar Series-#6-Isley Brothers . . . . (Motown)
   This Old Heart Of Mine . . . . (Motown)
Rod Stewart; *Atlantic Crossing* . . . . (Warner Bros.)
Rod Stewart & Ronald Isley; *Downtown Train-Selections From The Storyteller Anthology* . . . . (Warner Bros.)
   Storyteller/The Complete Anthology: 1964-1990 . . . . (Warner Bros.)

This Old Man
Dana; *Dana's Best Sing & Play-Along Tunes!* . . . . (Real Music For Kidz)
Original Soundtrack; *Children's Favorites* . . . . (Kid Rhino/Rhino 4 Kids)

This Old Piano
Mike Gray; *This Old Piano* . . . . (Twin-Tone)

This Ole House
Rosemary Clooney; *Rosemary Clooney-16 Most Requested Songs* . . . . (Legacy)
Statler Brothers; *The World Of The Statler Brothers* . . . . (Columbia)
Stuart Hamblen; *Stuart Hamblen-A Man & His Music* . . . . (Lamb & Lion)

Those Good Old Dreams
Carpenters; *Carpenters-Classics-#2* . . . . (A&M)
   Yesterday Once More . . . . (A&M)

Those Good Old Sun Records
Sun Rhythm Section; *Old Time Rock 'N Roll* . . . . (Flying Fish)

Tie A Yellow Ribbon Round The Ole Oak Tree
Dawn Featuring Tony Orlando; *'70s Party Killers-C* . . . . (Rhino)
   Fantastic-#1-C . . . . (K-Tel)
Frank Sinatra; *Some Nice Things I've Missed* . . . . (Reprise)
Lawrence Welk; *Best Of Lawrence Welk-20 Great Hits* . . . . (Ranwood)
Sonny James & Karla Taylor; *Classic Country Duets-C* . . . . (Curb)

Till I'm Too Old To Die Young
Moe Bandy; *Great Records Of The Decade-'80s Hits-Country-C* . . . . . (Curb)
   Moe Bandy's Greatest Hits . . . . (Curb)

Times They Are A-Changin'
Billy Joel; *KOHUEPT* . . . . (Columbia)
Bob Dylan; *Biograph* . . . . (Columbia)
   Bob Dylan At Budokan . . . . (Columbia)
   Bob Dylan's Greatest Hits . . . . (Columbia)
   The Bootleg Series-Volumes 1-3 [Rare & Unreleased] . . . (Columbia)
   The Times They Are A-Changin' . . . . (Columbia)
Byrds; *The Byrds* . . . . (Columbia)
   Turn! Turn! Turn! . . . . (Legacy)
Peter, Paul & Mary; *Peter, Paul and Mary In Concert* . . . . (Warner Bros.)
Simon & Garfunkel; *Collected Works* . . . . (Columbia)

Wednesday Morning 3 A.M. . . . . (Columbia)

Too Old To Cut The Mustard
Carlisles; *45-#6348* . . . . (Mercury)
Ernest Tubb; *Ernest Tubb-Retrospective-#2* . . . . (MCA Special Prod.)

Too Old To Rock 'N' Roll: Too Young To Die
Jethro Tull; *Bursting Out* . . . . (Chrysalis)
   Classic Case with the London Symphony Orchestra . . . . . . (RCA)
   Original Masters . . . . (Chrysalis)
   Repeat-The Best Of Jethro Tull, Vol. II . . . . (Chrysalis)

Touch Of Grey
Grateful Dead; *Heart Of Rock-C* . . . . (Columbia)
   In The Dark . . . . (Arista)

Tuck Me To Sleep In My Old Kentucky Home
Firehouse Five Plus Two; *Goes South* . . . . (Good Time Jazz)

Two Old Cats Like Us
Hank Williams, Jr. & Ray Charles; *Hank Williams, Jr.'s Greatest Hits-#2* . . . . (WB/Curb)
Ray Charles & Hank Williams, Jr.; *Friendship-C* . . . . (Columbia)
   Seven Spanish Angels & Other Hits . . . . (Columbia)

Two Sparrows In A Hurricane
Tanya Tucker; *Can't Run From Yourself* . . . . (Liberty)
   Tanya Tucker's Greatest Hits-1990-1992 . . . . (Capitol)

Visiting An Old Friend
Nitty Gritty Dirt Band; *Dirt, Silver & Gold* . . . . (One Way)

Voices Of Old People
Simon & Garfunkel; *Bookends* . . . . (Columbia)
   Collected Works . . . . (Columbia)

W.O.L.D.
Harry Chapin; *Gold Medal Collection* . . . . (Elektra)
   Greatest Stories-Live . . . . (Elektra)
   Harry Chapin-Anthology . . . . (Elektra)
   Short Stories . . . . (Elektra)

Wedding Bells (Are Breaking Up That Old Gang Of Mine)
Four Aces; *Best Of The Four Aces* . . . . (MCA)

When I Grow Too Old To Dream
Benny Goodman & His Orchestra; *Best Of Benny Goodman & His Orchestra* . . . . (Curb)
Linda Ronstadt; *Living In The USA* . . . . (Asylum)
Louis Armstrong; *Essential Louis Armstrong* . . . . (Vanguard)

When I'm Sixty-Four
Beatles; *Beatles-Box Set* . . . . (Capitol)
   Sgt. Pepper's Lonely Hearts Club Band . . . . (Capitol)

When They're Old Enough To Know Better
Eddie Cantor; *Music From The New York Stage (1890-1920)-#4-1917-1920-C* . . . . (Pearl)

When You Are Old
Gretchen Peters; *The Secret Of Life* . . . . (Purple Crayon Prod.)

Where've You Been
Kathy Mattea; *Collection Of Hits* . . . . (Mercury)
   Willow In The Wind . . . . (Mercury)

Who's Gonna Play This Old Piano
Jerry Lee Lewis; *Best Of Jerry Lee Lewis-#2* . . . . (Mercury)
   Milestones . . . . (Rhino)

Wreck Of The Old '97
Johnny Cash; *Johnny Cash At Folsom Prison & San Quentin* . . . . (Columbia)
   Johnny Cash-Original Golden Hits-#3 . . . . (Sun)
   Story Songs Of The Trains & Rivers . . . . (Sun)
   Superbilly . . . . (Sun)
   The Man-The World-His Music . . . . (Sun)

Young Man, Older Woman
Millie Jackson; *Very Best Of Millie Jackson* . . . . (Jive)

Your Old Love Letters
Ricky Skaggs; *Favorite Country Songs* . . . . (Epic)
   Waitin' For The Sun To Shine . . . . (Epic)

You're A Grand Old Flag
Marilyn Horne; *Beautiful Dreamer-Great American Songbook* . . . . . (London)
Mormon Tabernacle Choir; *God Bless America* . . . . (Sony Music Classical)
Original Soundtrack; *School Days-Kids Classics* . . . . (Benson)
Robert Merrill & Mormon Tabernacle Choir; *Yankee Doodle Dandies* . . . . (Columbia)

You're The Best Break This Old Heart Ever Had
Ed Bruce; *Ed Bruce's Greatest Hits* . . . . (MCA)
   One To One . . . . (MCA)

OPEN & CLOSED

See Also: BEGINNINGS, DOORS, ENDINGS, INSIDE/ OUTSIDE, WINDOWS

All My Loving
Beatles; *Meet The Beatles!* . . . . (Capitol)
   The Beatles At The Hollywood Bowl . . . . (Capitol)
   The Beatles/1962-1966 . . . . (Capitol)
   With The Beatles . . . . (Parlophone)

Analyse
Cranberries; *Wake Up And Smell The Coffee* . . . . (MCA)

Ana's Song (Open Fire)
Silverchair; *Neon Ballroom* . . . .(Epic)
Behind Closed Doors
Charlie Rich; *American Originals-Charlie Rich.* . . . . (Columbia)
   Behind Closed Doors. . . . .(Epic)
   Charlie Rich's Greatest Hits . . . .(Epic)
   Columbia Country Classics-#4-Nashville Sound-C. . . . . (Columbia)
Black Jesus
Everlast; *Eat At Whitey's* . . . . (Tommy Boy)
Close Your Eyes
Peaches & Herb; *Love Is Strange-The Best Of Peaches & Herb* . . . . (Legacy)
Closing Time
Semisonic; *Feeling Strangely Fine.* . . . .(MCA)
   Now That's What I Call Music!-#2-C . . . . (Virgin)
Don't The Girls All Get Prettier At Closing Time
Mickey Gilley; *Make It Like The First Time* . . . . (ISD/Intersound)
Door, The
Keb' Mo'; *The Door.* . . . .(550/Epic/Okeh)
Frozen
Madonna; *GHV2.* . . . .(Warner Bros.)
   Ray Of Light. . . . .(Maverick)
I'm So Open
Cowboy Junkies; *Open.* . . . . (Latent/Zoe/Rounder)
Let My Love Open The Door
Pete Townshend; *Empty Glass* . . . . (Atco)
My Arms Stay Open All Night
Tanya Tucker; *Tanya Tucker's Greatest Hits* . . . . (Liberty)
Open All Night
Bruce Springsteen; *Nebraska* . . . . (Columbia)
Open All Night
Daryl Hall & John Oates; *H2O* . . . . (RCA)
Open Arms
Journey; *Escape* . . . . (Columbia)
   Journey's Greatest Hits . . . . (Columbia)
   Seems Like Yesterday-#4-Early '80s-C . . . . (K-Tel)
   ST/Heavy Metal . . . . (Asylum)
Open Casket
Death; *Best Of Death* . . . . (Relativity)
Open Letter (To A Landlord)
Living Colour; *Vivid.* . . . .(Epic)
Open Letter To George Bush
Wayne Horvitz/The President; *Miracle Mile* . . . . (Elektra)
Open My Heart
Yolanda Adams; *Mountain High Valley Low* . . . . (Elektra)
Open Our Eyes
Earth, Wind & Fire; *Open Our Eyes* . . . . (Columbia)
Open Pit Mine
Nashville Bluegrass Band; *Waitin' For The Hard Times To Go* . . . . . (Sugar Hill)
Open Sesame
Kool & The Gang; *Everything's Kool & The Gang-Greatest Hits*
   & More . . . . (Mercury)
   Kool & The Gang Spin Their Top Hits . . . . (De-Lite)
   ST/Saturday Night Fever . . . . (Polydor)
Open Sesame
Freddie Hubbard; *Best Of Freddie Hubbard* . . . . (Blue Note)
   Open Sesame . . . . (Blue Note)
Open The Door
Royal Teens; *Short Shorts* . . . . (Collectables)
Open The Door
Michael McDonald; *Blue Obsession* . . . . (Ramp)
Open The Door
Otis Redding; *Dock Of The Bay* . . . . (Atco)
   Remember Me . . . . (Stax)
Open The Door
Betty Carter; *Now It's My Turn.* . . . . (Roulette)
Open The Door To Your Heart
Little Milton; *Stax Blues Masters-Blue Monday-C.* . . . .(Stax)
   Walking The Back Streets . . . .(Stax)
Open The Door, Homer
Bob Dylan And The Band; *Basement Tapes.* . . . . (Columbia)
Thunderclap Newman; *Hollywood Dream.* . . . .(MCA)
Open The Door, Richard
Louis Jordan; *Jazz Heritage-Greatest Hits-#2-1941-1947.* . . . .(MCA)
Open Up A New Door
John Mayall's Bluesbreakers; *Bare Wires* . . . . (London)
Open Up My Window
Christopher Cross; *Window.* . . . .(Rhythm Safari)
Open Up The Doghouse (Two Cats Are Comin' In)
Nat ''King'' Cole; *Nat ''King'' Cole (Box Set)* . . . . (Capitol)
Open Up Your Door
Romantics; *In Heat* . . . . (Epic Portrait Assoc.)
   What I Like About You (And Other Romantic Hits) . . . . (Nemperor)
Open Up Your Door
Steve Earle & The Dukes; *Early Tracks* . . . .(Epic)
Open Up Your Eyes
Tonic; *Lemon Parade* . . . . (Polydor)
Open Up Your Heart
Buck Owens; *Buck Owens Collection-1959-1990* . . . . (Rhino)

Open Your Eyes
Black Box; *Dreamland* . . . .(RCA)
Open Your Eyes
Yes; *Open Your Eyes.* . . . .(Beyond)
Open Your Eyes
Asia; *Alpha* . . . . (Geffen)
   Live In Moscow . . . . (Rhino)
Open Your Eyes
Chiffons; *22 Leaders Of The Pack-#2-C* . . . .(Laurie)
   Best Of The Chiffons. . . . .(Laurie)
   Chiffons-Golden Classics . . . . (Collectables)
Open Your Eyes
Doobie Brothers; *Minute By Minute* . . . . (Warner Bros.)
Open Your Eyes
Organized Konfusion; *Basic Beats Sampler-C* . . . . (Hollywood Basic)
   Organized Konfusion . . . . (Hollywood Basic)
Open Your Eyes
Bobby Caldwell; *Cat In The Hat* . . . . (Sin-Drome)
Open Your Eyes
Julian Lennon; *Mr. Jordan* . . . .(Atlantic)
Open Your Eyes
Lords Of The New Church; *Lords Of The New Church.* . . . . (I.R.S.)
Open Your Heart
Madonna; *Immaculate Collection* . . . .(Sire)
   Royal Box . . . .(Sire)
   True Blue . . . .(Sire)
Open Your Heart
Europe; *Out Of This World* . . . . (Epic)
   Wings Of Tomorrow . . . . (Epic)
Open Your Heart
Human League; *Dare* . . . . (A&M)
   Human League's Greatest Hits . . . . (A&M)
Opened The Door
Journey; *Infinity.* . . . . (Columbia)
Shut Out The Light
Bruce Springsteen; *Tracks* . . . . (Columbia)
Shut Up And Dance
Pointer Sisters; *Serious Slammin'* . . . .(RCA)
Shut Up And Kiss Me
Mary Chapin Carpenter; *Stones In The Road* . . . . (Columbia)
Thing, The
Phil Harris; *The Thing About Phil Harris* . . . . (Living Era)
Warmth, The
Incubus; *Make Yourself.* . . . . (Immortal/Epic)
We're All Alone
Boz Scaggs; *Boz Scaggs-Hits!.* . . . . (Columbia)
   Slow Dancer. . . . . (Columbia)
Rita Coolidge; *Rita Coolidge's Greatest Hits* . . . . (A&M)
When I Close My Eyes
Kenny Chesney; *Kenny Chesney's Greatest Hits* . . . . (BNA)
   Me And You . . . . (BNA)
When I Close My Eyes
Shanice; *Shanice.* . . . . (LaFace)
Wide Open Spaces
Dixie Chicks; *Big Country Hits '99-C* . . . . (K-Tel)
   Wide Open Spaces . . . . (Monument)
With Arms Wide Open
Creed; *Human Clay.* . . . .(Wind-up)
   Now That's What I Call Music!-#6-C. . . . .(Virgin)
With My Eyes Wide Open I'm Dreaming
Mandy Barnett; *I've Got A Right To Cry.* . . . .(Sire)
Patti Page; *Patti Page-Golden Hits* . . . . (Mercury)
   Patti Page's Greatest Hits . . . . (Columbia)
You Can Close Your Eyes
James Taylor; *Mud Slide Slim And The Blue Horizon* . . . . (Warner Bros.)
Linda Ronstadt; *Heart Like A Wheel* . . . . (Capitol)

OPPOSITES, Contradictions
See Also: EXTREMES

(Just Like) Romeo & Juliet
Reflections; *'60s Dance Party-C.* . . . . (Dominion Entert.)
   Sensational '60s-#1-C . . . . (Dominion Entert.)
(You're The) Devil In Disguise
Elvis Presley; *Elvis' Gold Records, Volume 4* . . . . (RCA)
   The Top Ten Hits . . . . (RCA)
Aeroplane
Red Hot Chili Peppers; *One Hot Minute* . . . . (Warner Bros.)
All Or Nothin' At All
Bruce Springsteen; *Human Touch.* . . . . (Columbia)
All Or Nothing
Original Broadway Cast; *Oklahoma!* . . . . (RCA)
Original Cast; *Oklahoma!* . . . . (MCA)
Shirley Jones; *ST/Oklahoma!* . . . . (Capitol)
All Or Nothing
X; *Ain't Love Grand* . . . . (Elektra)

All Or Nothing
Milli Vanilli; *Girl You Know It's True*.....................(Arista)
All Or Nothing At All
Al Jarreau; *Heart's Horizon* ....(Reprise)
Diana Krall; *Love Scenes*.......................(Impulse!)
Frank Sinatra; *Sinatra Reprise-The Very Good Years* ....(Reprise)
 Sinatra: A Man And His Music ....(Reprise)
 Strangers In The Night ....(Reprise)
 The Frank Sinatra Story ....(Sony Music Special Prod.)
 The Reprise Collection ....(Reprise)
Am I Getting Through (Part I & II)
Sheryl Crow; *The Globe Sessions* ....(A&M)
Anything But Strong
Eurythmics; *Peace*.............................(Arista)
Anything Goes
Count Basie & Tony Bennett; *Anything Goes-Capitol Sings Cole
 Porter-C*...............................(Capitol)
 Basie Swings Bennett Sings ....(Roulette)
Dionne Warwick; *Dionne Warwick Sings Cole Porter* ....(Arista)
Ella Fitzgerald; *Night & Day-Cole Porter Songbook-C* ......(Verve)
Frank Sinatra; *Frank Sinatra Sings The Select Cole Porter*.........(Capitol)
Mary Martin; *Mary Martin-16 Most Requested Songs* .....(Columbia)
Original Cast; *Anything Goes* ....(Epic)
Paul Whiteman & His Orchestra; *78-#24770* ....(Victor)
Yo-Yo Ma; *Anything Goes-The Music Of Cole Porter* .....(Columbia)
Anyway You Want Me
Elvis Presley; *Elvis' Golden Records* ....(RCA)
Awake
Letters To Cleo; *Wholesale Meats & Fish*...............(Giant)
Back & Forth
Aaliyah; *Age Ain't Nothing But A Number* ....(Jive)
Bad Goodbye, A
Clint Black with Wynonna; *Clint Black-The Greatest Hits*....(RCA)
 Grammy's Greatest Country Moments-#1-C ......(Atlantic)
 No Time To Kill............................(RCA)
Bad Religion
Godsmack; *Godsmack*...............(Republic/Universal)
Beauty And The Beast
Celine Dion & Peabo Bryson; *All The Way...A Decade Of Song*.... (550 Music)
 Celine Dion............................(Epic)
 ST/Beauty And The Beast ....(Disney)
Better Class Of Losers
Randy Travis; *High Lonesome* ....(Warner Bros.)
Better Days (And The Bottom Drops Out)
Citizen King; *Mobile Estates*...............(Warner Bros.)
Better Than You
Metallica; *Reload* ....(Elektra)
Big Bad Bill Is Sweet William Now
Ry Cooder; *Jazz*.......................(Warner Bros.)
Big Fish, Little Fish
Original Broadway Cast; *Purlie* ....(RCA)
Binge & Purge
Clutch; *Transnational Speedway League* ....(East West)
Bitch
Meredith Brooks; *Blurring The Edges*..............(Capitol)
Bittersweet
Big Head Todd & The Monsters; *Midnight Radio* ....(Giant)
 Sister Sweetly ....(Giant)
Bittersweet
Crosby, Stills & Nash; *CSN*.................. (Atlantic)
Bittersweet
Fuel; *Sunburn* ....(550 Music)
Bittersweet
Verve; *Urban Hymns*......................(Hut/Virgin)
Bittersweet Me
R.E.M.; *New Adventures In Hi-Fi* ....(Warner Bros.)
Black Chick, White Guy
Kid Rock; *Devil Without A Cause* ....(Top Dog/Lava/Atlantic)
Bosnia
Cranberries; *To The Faithful Departed* ....(Island)
Both Sides Now
Joni Mitchell; *Clouds*..........................(Reprise)
Judy Collins; *Colors Of The Day-The Best Of Judy Collins* ......(Elektra)
 So Early In The Spring, The First 15 Years........(Elektra)
 Wildflowers............................(Elektra)
Neil Diamond; *Neil Diamond-Gold*.................. (MCA)
 Neil Diamond-Love Songs ....(MCA)
 Rainbow ....(MCA)
 Touching You Touching Me ....(MCA)
Both Sides Now
Sammy Hagar; *Marching To Mars* .... (MCA)
Both Sides Of The Story
Phil Collins; *Both Sides* ....(Atlantic)
Brian Wilson
Barenaked Ladies; *Gordon* ....(Reprise)
 Rock Spectacle ....(Reprise)
Brother, Can You Spare A Dime
Bing Crosby; *Bing Crosby-16 Most Requested Songs*..............(Legacy)

Odetta/Dr. John/John Campbell/Rufus Reid; *Strike A Deep Chord-Blues For
 The Homeless-C* ....(Justice)
Peter, Paul & Mary; *See What Tomorrow Brings*............(Warner Bros.)
Weavers; *Weavers' Greatest Hits* ....(Vanguard)
Bubba Hyde
Diamond Rio; *Diamond Rio's Greatest Hits* ....(Arista)
 Love A Little Stronger ....(Arista)
Burnin' Old Memories With A Brand New Flame
Kathy Mattea; *Country Hits 4: Sweet Country-C*............ (Priority)
 Willow In The Wind ....(Mercury)
But Anyway
Blues Traveler; *Blues Traveler*...................(A&M)
 Live From The Fall ....(A&M)
California Girls
Beach Boys; *Beach Boys '69 (The Beach Boys Live In London)* ......(Capitol)
 Best Of The Beach Boys-#2 ....(Capitol)
 Endless Summer ....(Capitol)
 Good Vibrations-Thirty Years Of The Beach Boys ......(Capitol)
 The Beach Boys In Concert ....(Brother)
David Lee Roth; *Crazy From The Heat* ....(Warner Bros.)
 ST/Down & Out In Beverly Hills ....(Warner Bros.)
Check Yes Or No
George Strait; *Strait Out Of The Box* ....(MCA)
Chocolate Mood
Marc Nelson; *chocolate mood* ....(Columbia)
Cold Day In July
Dixie Chicks; *Fly* ....(Monument)
Joy White; *Between Midnight & Hindsight* ....(Columbia)
Ray Price; *For The Good Times/I Won't Mention It Again* ....(Columbia)
Suzy Bogguss; *Voices In The Wind* ....(Liberty)
Come Rain Or Come Shine
Ella Fitzgerald; *Harold Arlen Songbook-#2*...........(Verve)
Frank Sinatra; *Very Best Of Frank Sinatra*................. (Reprise)
Frank Sinatra & Gloria Estefan; *Frank Sinatra-Duets-C*........(Capitol)
Judy Garland; *America's Treasure*.........(Dunhill Compact Classics)
 Hits Of Judy Garland ....(Capitol)
 Judy ....(Capitol)
 Judy Garland-At Carnegie Hall ....(Capitol)
Michael Crawford; *With Love* .... (Atlantic)
Complicated
Carolyn Dawn Johnson; *Room With A View*............(Arista)
Cowboy & The Hippie
Chris LeDoux; *Gold Buckle Dreams* ....(Liberty)
 He Rides The Wild Horses ....(Liberty)
Cowboy Love
John Michael Montgomery; *John Michael Montgomery* .... (Atlantic)
 John Michael Montgomery's Greatest Hits ....(Atlantic)
Cowgirl & The Dandy
Brenda Lee; *Brenda Lee-Greatest Country Hits* .... (MCA)
 Even Better .... (MCA)
Dolly Parton; *Here You Come Again* ....(Dunhill Compact Classics)
Cruel To Be Kind
Nick Lowe; *Basher: Best Of*.....................(Columbia)
 Labour Of Lust ....(Columbia)
Crying Shame
Kate Wolf; *Evening In Austin*...................(Kaleidoscope)
 Poet's Heart ....(Kaleidoscope)
Cure Me...Or Kill Me
Gilby Clarke; *Pawnshop Guitars* .... (Virgin)
Cuts Both Ways
Gloria Estefan; *Cuts Both Ways* ....(Epic)
Darling Lorraine
Paul Simon; *You're The One* .... (Warner Bros.)
Darned If I Don't (Danged If I Do)
Shenandoah; *In The Vicinity Of The Heart*................(Capitol)
Daysleeper
R.E.M.; *Up*..........................(Warner Bros.)
Dead & Alive
Dead Boys; *We Have Come For Your Children*...............(Sire)
Dead Or Alive
Oingo Boingo; *Boingo Alive* .... (MCA)
 Good For Your Soul ....(A&M)
Dead Or Alive
Journey; *Escape* ....(Columbia)
Dead Or Alive
Deep Purple; *Nobody's Perfect* ....(Mercury)
Dead Or Alive
Too $hort; *Short Dog's In The House*................. (Jive)
Death or Glory
Clash; *London Calling* ....(Epic)
Devil In Disguise
J.J. Cale; *Grasshopper*.......................(Mercury)
 Special Edition ....(Mercury)
Devil Or Angel
Bobby Vee; *Best Of Bobby Vee* ....(EMI)
 Bobby Vee-Golden Greats ....(Liberty)
 Bobby Vee-Legendary Masters ....(EMI)
Clovers; *Atlantic Rhythm & Blues 1947-1974-#3 (1955-1958)-C* .....(Atlantic)

Oldies But Goodies-#2-C. . . . . (Original Sound)
Very Best Of The Clovers . . . . (Rhino)

Diana
Paul Anka; *21 Legendary Superstars-C* . . . . (Original Sound)
  Billboard Top Rock 'N' Roll Hits-1957-C . . . . (Rhino)
  Paul Anka's 21 Golden Hits . . . . (RCA)

Difference, The
Wallflowers; *Bringing Down The Horse*. . . . . (Interscope)

Different Drum
Linda Ronstadt; *Different Drum* . . . . (Capitol)
  Linda Ronstadt-Retrospective . . . . (Capitol)
  Linda Ronstadt's Greatest Hits . . . . (Asylum)
Stone Poneys Featuring Linda Ronstadt; *Baby Boomer Classics-Mellow
  '60s-C* . . . . (JCI Assoc. Labels)
  On The Road Again-Rock's New Frontiers-C . . . . (Capitol)
  The Stone Poneys Featuring Linda Ronstadt . . . . (EMI)
Victoria Shaw; *Victoria Shaw* . . . . (Reprise)

Down In The Boondocks
Billy Joe Royal; *Billy Joe Royal's Greatest Hits*. . . . . (Columbia)
  Rock Classics Of The '60s-C . . . . (Columbia)

Drowning On Dry Land
Albert King; *Hard Bargain*. . . . . (Stax)
  The Stax Blues Brothers-C . . . . (Stax)
  Years Gone By . . . . (Stax)
Roy Buchanan; *Dancing On The Edge* . . . . (Alligator)

Easy Come Easy Go
George Strait; *Easy Come Easy Go*. . . . . (MCA)

Easy Tonight
Five For Fighting; *America Town*. . . . .(Aware/C2/Columbia)

Ebony And Ivory
Paul McCartney & Stevie Wonder; *All The Best!* . . . . (Capitol)
  Tug Of War . . . .(Gold Rush)

Every Other Time
LFO; *Life Is Good*. . . . . (J)

Every Rose Has Its Thorn
Poison; *Open Up And Say...Ahh!* . . . . (Capitol)
  Rock The First-#5-C . . . .(Sandstone Music)
  Swallow This Live . . . . (Capitol)

Everybody's Got Something To Hide Except Me And My Monkey
Beatles; *The Beatles (White Album)* . . . . (Capitol)

Exactly Like You
Andy Williams; *Moon River-Days Of Wine And Roses* . . . . (Columbia)
Sarah Vaughan; *Complete Sarah Vaughan On Mercury-#1-Great Jazz Years-
  1954-1956* . . . . (Mercury)
Willie Nelson; *Somewhere Over The Rainbow*. . . . . (Columbia)

Ex-Factor
Lauryn Hill; *The Miseducation Of Lauryn Hill*. . . . . . . (Ruffhouse/Columbia)

Falling For The First Time
Barenaked Ladies; *Maroon*. . . . . (Reprise)

Father Of Day, Father Of Night
Manfred Mann's Earth Band; *Solar Fire* . . . . (Polydor)

Feelin' Good About Feelin' Bad
Patty Loveless; *When Fallen Angels Fly*. . . . . (Epic)

Feels Like Home
Bonnie Raitt; *ST/Michael* . . . . (Revolution)
Chantal Kreviazuk; *Songs From Dawson's Creek* . . . . . (Sony Music Soundtrax)
Linda Ronstadt; *Feels Like Home*. . . . . (Elektra)
Randy Newman; *Guilty: 30 Years Of Randy Newman* . . . . (Rhino)
  Randy Newman's Faust . . . . (Reprise)

Finders Keepers, Losers Weepers
Soul Children; *Lost Soul-#1-C* . . . . (Epic)

Finders Keepers, Losers Weepers
Elvis Presley; *Elvis For Everyone!* . . . . (RCA)

Fire
Bruce Springsteen & The E Street Band; *Bruce Springsteen & The E Street
  Band/1975-85* . . . . (Legacy)
Pointer Sisters; *Cover Me (Bruce Springsteen Tribute)-C* . . . . (Rhino)
  Energy . . . . (Planet)
  I Am Woman-C. . . . . (Nick At Nite)

Fire And Ice
Pat Benatar; *Best Shots* . . . .(Chrysalis)
  Live From Earth. . . . .(Chrysalis)
  Precious Time . . . .(Chrysalis)

Fire And Rain
James Taylor; *James Taylor's Greatest Hits* . . . .(Warner Bros.)
  Sweet Baby James. . . . .(Warner Bros.)
  The Concert For New York City-C. . . . . (Columbia)
Sammy Kershaw; *Red Hot + Country-C* . . . . (Mercury)

Fire And Water
Free; *Best Of Free* . . . . (A&M)
  Fire And Water . . . . (A&M)
  Free-Live . . . . (A&M)

Fire And Water
Wilson Pickett; *Very Best Of Wilson Pickett*. . . . . (Rhino)

Follow You, Follow Me
Genesis; *And Then There Were Three*. . . . . (Atlantic)
  Three Sides Live . . . . (Atlantic)

Freak On A Leash
Korn; *Follow The Leader* . . . . (Immortal/Epic)

Friday Night Blues
John Conlee; *John Conlee-Live At Billy Bob's* . . . . (Razor & Tie)
  John Conlee's Greatest Hits. . . . . (MCA)
Sonny Throckmorton; *45-#57018* . . . . (Mercury)

From Cotton To Satin
Gene Watson; *This Dream's On Me* . . . . (MCA)
Johnny Paycheck; *Take This Job And Shove It* . . . . (Epic)

From Hell To Paradise
Mavericks; *From Hell To Paradise* . . . . (MCA)

Ginger Bread
Frankie Avalon; *Gold For The Road-Carburetor Classics-C* . . . . . . (Compose)
  Venus: The Very Best Of Frankie Avalon . . . . (Collectables)

Glad To Be Unhappy
Mamas & The Papas; *Mamas & The Papas-16 Of Their Greatest Hits*. . . (MCA)

Glycerine
Bush; *Sixteen Stone* . . . . (Trauma)

Good News, Bad News
Eddy Raven; *Eddy Raven-Greatest Country Hits* . . . . (Curb)

Good Times Bad Times
Led Zeppelin; *Led Zeppelin* . . . .(Atlantic)

Good Times, Bad Times
Rolling Stones; *12 X 5* . . . .(Abkco)
  Big Hits (High Tide & Green Grass) . . . . (Abkco)
  More Hot Rocks (big hits & fazed cookies) . . . . (Abkco)
  Singles Collection-The London Years . . . . (Abkco)

Gotham City
R. Kelly; *ST/Batman & Robin-Music From And Inspired By The Motion
  Picture* . . . . (Jive)

Half The World
Rush; *Test For Echo* . . . .(Atlantic)

Half Way Up
Clint Black; *Clint Black-The Greatest Hits* . . . . (RCA)

Hand In My Pocket
Alanis Morissette; *Jagged Little Pill* . . . . (Maverick)

Happy
Sister Hazel; *...Somewhere More Familiar*. . . . . (Universal)

Hard Times Come Easy
Richie Sambora; *Undiscovered Soul* . . . . (Mercury)

Head To Toe
Lisa Lisa & Cult Jam; *Spanish Fly* . . . . (Columbia)

Heads Carolina, Tails California
Jo Dee Messina; *Greatest Hits Of Country Dance-C* . . . . (Curb)
  Jo Dee Messina . . . . (Curb)

Hello Goodbye
Beatles; *Beatles 1* . . . . (Capitol)
  Beatles-20 Greatest Hits . . . . (Capitol)
  Beatles-Box Set. . . . . (Capitol)
  Magical Mystery Tour . . . . (Capitol)
  The Beatles/1967-1970. . . . . (Capitol)

Hello Hello
Talk Show; *Talk Show* . . . .(Atlantic)

Heroes & Villains
Beach Boys; *Concert/'69-Live In London* . . . . (Capitol)
  Endless Harmony. . . . . (Capitol)
  Good Vibrations-Thirty Years Of The Beach Boys . . . . (Capitol)
  Made In The U.S.A. . . . . (Capitol)
  Smiley Smile/Wild Honey . . . . (Capitol)
  Sunshine Dream . . . . (Capitol)

High Head Blues
Black Crowes; *Amorica* . . . . (American)

Honey Don't
Beatles; *For Sale* . . . . (Capitol)

Hot Corn, Cold Corn
Flatt & Scruggs; *Flatt & Scruggs At Carnegie Hall!* . . . . . . (Koch International)

Hot Love Cold World
Bob Welch; *French Kiss* . . . . (Capitol)

Hunter Gets Captured By The Game
Marvelettes; *Compact Command Performances-Marvelettes*. . . . . . (Motown)
  Marvelettes-Anthology. . . . . (Motown)
Smokey Robinson & The Miracles; *Motown Legends-Smokey Robinson &
  The Miracles* . . . . (Motown)

I Cried For You (Now It's Your Turn To Cry)
Billie Holiday; *First Verve Sessions* . . . . Verve)
  Quintessential-#2-1936 . . . . (Columbia)
  Songbook . . . . (Verve)
Sarah Vaughan; *Complete Sarah Vaughan On Mercury-#2* . . . . . . (Mercury)
  Divine Sarah Vaughan-Columbia Years-1949-1953 . . . . . . (Columbia)
  Roulette Years . . . . (Roulette)

I Go To Extremes
Billy Joel; *Storm Front* . . . . (Columbia)

I Hate You Then I Love You
Celine Dion with Luciano Pavarotti; *Let's Talk About Love-C* . . . . . .(550 Music)

I Lost It
Kenny Chesney; *Kenny Chesney's Greatest Hits* . . . . (BNA)

I Started A Joke
Bee Gees; *Best Of Bee Gees-#1* . . . . (Polydor)
  Here At Last...Bee Gees...Live . . . . (Polydor)
  One Night Only. . . . . (Polydor)

Wallflowers; *ST/Zoolander* .... (Hollywood)

I Want You Bad (And That Ain't Good)
Collin Raye; *In This Life* .... (Epic)

I'd Lie For You (And That's The Truth)
Meat Loaf; *Welcome To The Neighborhood* .... (MCA)

If I Never Stop Loving You
David Kersh; *If I Never Stop Loving You* .... (Curb)

If It Makes You Happy
Sheryl Crow; *Sheryl Crow* .... (A&M)

I'm Just An Old Chunk Of Coal (But I'm Gonna Be A Diamond Someday)
Billy Joe Shaver; *Restless Wind-The Legendary Billy Joe Shaver-1973-1987* .... (Razor & Tie)
John Anderson; *John Anderson's Greatest Hits* .... (Warner Bros.)

I'm So Happy I Can't Stop Crying
Sting; *Mercury Falling* .... (A&M)
Toby Keith with Sting; *Dream Walkin'* .... (Mercury)
Toby Keith's Greatest Hits, Volume One .... (Mercury)

Inside Out
Eve 6; *Eve 6* .... (RCA)

Ironic
Alanis Morissette; *Jagged Little Pill* .... (Maverick)

It Must Be Love
Alan Jackson; *Under The Influence* .... (Arista)

It Was
Chely Wright; *Single White Female* .... (MCA)

It's A Little Too Late
Mark Chesnutt; *Mark Chesnutt's Greatest Hits* .... (Decca)

It's All Coming Back To Me Now
Celine Dion; *All The Way...A Decade Of Song* .... (550 Music)
Falling Into You .... (550 Music)

Jenny Says
Cowboy Mouth; *Are You With Me?* .... (MCA)
Word Of Mouth .... (Monkey Hill)

Joy And Pain
Maze & Kurtis Blow; *Lifelines-#1* .... (Capitol)
Maze featuring Frankie Beverly; *Live In Los Angeles* .... (Capitol)
Live In New Orleans .... (Capitol)

Joy And Pain
Donna Allen; *Heaven On Earth* .... (Oceana)

Joy And Pain
Rob Base & D.J. EZ-Rock; *It Takes Two* .... (Profile)

Just Like A Woman
Bob Dylan; *Before The Flood* .... (Columbia)
Biograph .... (Columbia)
Blonde On Blonde .... (Columbia)
Bob Dylan At Budokan .... (Columbia)
Bob Dylan's Greatest Hits .... (Columbia)
Byrds; *The Byrds* .... (Columbia)

Kill For Peace
Fugs; *Best Of Broadside 1962-1968: Anthems Of The American Underground From The Pages Of Broadside Magazine-C* .... (Smithsonian Folkways)
Fugs .... (ESP Disk)
Fugs 4 Rounders Score .... (ESP Disk)

King Of The Mountain
George Strait; *Blue Clear Sky* .... (MCA)
Latest Greatest Straitest Hits .... (MCA)

Leather & Lace
Stevie Nicks & Don Henley; *Bella Donna* .... (Modern)

Leave Virginia Alone
Rod Stewart; *A Spanner In The Works* .... (Warner Bros.)

Let Me Fall
Wood; *Songs From Stamford Hill* .... (Columbia)

Let's Call The Whole Thing Off
Fred Astaire; *Steppin' Out-Astaire Sings* .... (Verve)

Life Has Its Little Ups & Downs
Charlie Rich; *Best Of Charlie Rich* .... (Epic)
Charlie Rich's Greatest Hits .... (Epic)

Life's Little Ups And Downs
Ricky Van Shelton; *RVS III* .... (Columbia)

Like A Rolling Stone
Bob Dylan; *Biograph* .... (Columbia)
Bob Dylan At Budokan .... (Columbia)
Bob Dylan's Greatest Hits .... (Columbia)
Highway 61 Revisited .... (Columbia)
More American Graffiti-#4-C .... (MCA)
Self Portrait .... (Columbia)
Bob Dylan And The Band; *Before The Flood* .... (Columbia)
Jimi Hendrix; *ST/Jimi Plays Monterey* .... (Reprise)
Jimi Hendrix Experience; *Jimi Hendrix Experience* .... (Reprise)
Rolling Stones; *Stripped* .... (Virgin)

Lipstick And Bruises
Lit; *Atomic* .... (RCA)

Little Things
Bush; *Sixteen Stone* .... (Trauma)

Live And Let Die
Paul McCartney; *13 Original James Bond Themes-C* .... (EMI)
All The Best! .... (Capitol)

Wings; *ST/Live And Let Die* .... (EMI)
Wings Greatest .... (Capitol)
Wings Over America .... (Capitol)

London Rain (Nothing Heals Like You Do)
Heather Nova; *Siren* .... (Big Cat)
Songs From Dawson's Creek .... (Sony Music Soundtrax)

Lookin' Good But Feelin' Bad
Original Cast; *Ain't Misbehavin'* .... (RCA)

Lookin' In The Same Direction
Ken Mellons; *Ken Mellons* .... (Epic)

Lost & Found
Sparks; *Profile-The Ultimate Sparks Collection* .... (Rhino)

Lost & Found
Brooks & Dunn; *Brand New Man* .... (Arista)

Lost & Found
Original Broadway Cast; *City Of Angels* .... (Columbia)

Lost & Found
Echo & The Bunnymen; *Echo & The Bunnymen* .... (Sire)

Louisiana Woman, Mississippi Man
Loretta Lynn & Conway Twitty; *Louisiana Woman Mississippi Man* .... (MCA)
Very Best Of Loretta Lynn & Conway Twitty .... (MCA)

Love Hurt Me Love Healed Me
Lenny Williams; *Love Current* .... (MCA)

Love Hurts Love Heals
Daryl Hall & John Oates; *Beauty On A Back Street* .... (RCA)

Magnet And Steel
Walter Egan; *Rock Artifacts-From The Vaults-#2-C* .... (Legacy)

Mansion In The Slums
Crowded House; *Temple Of Low Men* .... (Capitol)

Meanwhile Back At The Ranch
Clark Family Experience; *Meanwhile Back At The Ranch* ..... (Curb)

Midnight Girl/Sunset Town
Sweethearts Of The Rodeo; *Sweethearts Of The Rodeo* ..... (Columbia)

Mimi
Maurice Chevalier; *Early Movie Hits* .... (DRG)
Nipper's Greatest Hits Of The '30s-#1-C .... (RCA)
ST/Pepe .... (DRG)

Minority
Green Day; *Warning* .... (Reprise)

Missing You
Case; *Open Letter* .... (Def Soul/IDJMG)

More Today Than Yesterday
Spiral Staircase; *CBS Classics-Pop Classics Of The '60s-C* .... (Columbia)
Rock Artifacts-From The Vaults-#1-C .... (Columbia)
Super Hits Of The '70s-Have A Nice Day-#1-C .... (Rhino)

Most Likely You'll Go Your Way & I'll Go Mine
Bob Dylan; *Biograph* .... (Columbia)
Blonde On Blonde .... (Columbia)
Bob Dylan And The Band; *Before The Flood* .... (Columbia)

Move It On Over
Hank Williams; *Complete Hank Williams* .... (Mercury)

Much Too Young (To Feel This Damn Old)
Garth Brooks; *Garth Brooks-Double Live* .... (Capitol)

My Kind Of Girl
Collin Raye; *Best Of Collin Raye-Direct Hits* .... (Epic)
Extremes .... (Epic)

My Kind Of Woman, My Kind Of Man
Patty Loveless; *Patty Loveless-Classics* .... (Epic)
Vince Gill with Patty Loveless; *The Key* .... (MCA)

My Up And Down
Adina Howard; *Do You Wanna Ride?* .... (East West)

My World Begins & Ends With You
Dave & Sugar; *Stay With Me/Golden Tears* .... (RCA)
Eddy Arnold; *Collector's Series-Eddy Arnold* .... (RCA)

Night And Day
Bette Midler; *Some People's Lives* .... (Atlantic)
Billie Holiday; *Legacy Box-1933-1958* .... (Columbia)
Ella Fitzgerald; *Cole Porter Songbook* .... (Verve)
Frank Sinatra; *Nipper's Greatest Hits Of The '40s-#1-C* .... (RCA)
Sinatra & Strings .... (Reprise)
Sinatra Reprise-The Very Good Years .... (Reprise)
Sinatra: A Man And His Music .... (Reprise)
The Capitol Years .... (Capitol)
The Reprise Collection .... (Reprise)
Fred Astaire; *Cheek To Cheek* .... (Pro-Arte)
Steppin' Out-Astaire Sings .... (Verve)
Tony Bennett; *Perfectly Frank* .... (Columbia)
U2; *Red Hot + Blue-Tribute To Cole Porter-C* .... (Chrysalis)

Nite And Day
Al B. Sure!; *In Effect Mode* .... (Warner Bros.)

No Not Much
Four Lads; *Four Lads-16 Most Requested Songs* .... (Legacy)

No, No, No
Destiny's Child; *Destiny's Child* .... (Grass Roots/Columbia)

Nobody In His Right Mind Would've Left Her
George Strait; *Country Classics-#6-1985-1986-C* .... (Universal)
George Strait-Number 7 .... (MCA)
George Strait's Greatest Hits-#2 .... (MCA)

Northbound-Southbound
Wynton Marsalis; *Big Train* .... (Columbia)
Not Counting You
Garth Brooks; *Garth Brooks*............................. (Liberty)
Not That Different
Collin Raye; *I Think About You* ....(Epic)
Nothin' To Somethin'
Gerald Levert; *G* .... (East West)
Old Enough To Know Better
Wade Hayes; *Country Dance Hits-C* .... (Columbia)
   Old Enough To Know Better .... (Columbia)
   Steppin' Country-#2-C .... (Columbia)
   Super Hits Of 1994-C .... (Columbia)
On Again Off Again
Nashville Bluegrass Band; *Waitin' For The Hard Times To Go* ..... (Sugar Hill)
One I Gave My Heart To
Aaliyah; *One In A Million*............... (BlackGround Enterp./Atlantic)
One On The Right Is On The Left, The
Johnny Cash; *Johnny Cash-16 Biggest Hits-#2* .... (Legacy)
Only Happy When It Rains
Garbage; *Garbage* .... (Almo Sounds)
Only One You
T.G. Sheppard; *Best Of T.G. Sheppard* .... (Curb)
   T.G. Sheppard's All-Time Greatest Hits ....(Warner Bros.)
Opposites
Eric Clapton; *There's One In Every Crowd* .... (Polydor)
Opposites Attract
Paula Abdul; *Forever Your Girl* .... (Virgin)
   Rock The First-#3-C .... (Priority)
   Shut Up And Dance (The Dance Mixes). .... (Virgin)
Opposites Attract
Natalie Cole; *Dangerous* .... (Modern)
Other Side
Kevin Welch & The Overtones; *Western Beat* .... (Reprise)
Other Side
Aerosmith; *Pump* ....(Geffen)
Other Side
Sweet Honey In The Rock; *Other Side* .... (Flying Fish)
Other Side Of Life
Moody Blues; *Other Side Of Life* .... (Polydor)
Other Side Of This Life
Fred Neil; *Little Bit Of Rain* .... (Elektra)
   Troubadours Of The Folk Era-#2-C .... (Rhino)
Jefferson Airplane; *Bless Its Pointed Little Head* .... (RCA)
   Loves You. .... (RCA)
Peter, Paul & Mary; *Peter, Paul and Mary Album* ....(Warner Bros.)
Otherside
Red Hot Chili Peppers; *Californication* ....(Warner Bros.)
Part Of Me, Part Of You
Glenn Frey; *ST/Thelma & Louise* .... (MCA)
   Strange Weather .... (MCA)
Picture From Life's Other Side
George Jones; *Hallelujah Weekend* ....(Epic)
Goebel Reeves; *Texas Drifter* .... (Glendale)
Hank Williams; *Beyond The Sunset* .... (Polydor)
   Hey Good Lookin' (December 1950-July 1951) .... (Polydor)
Please Don't Tell Her
Big Head Todd & The Monsters; *Beautiful World* .... (Revolution)
   Live Monsters .... (Revolution)
Poles Apart
Pink Floyd; *The Division Bell*. .... (Columbia)
Police And Thieves
Clash; *On Broadway*. ....(Epic)
   The Clash. ....(Epic)
   The Story Of The Clash, Volume 1 ....(Epic)
Junior Murvin; *Jammin'* ....(Mango)
   Police And Thieves. .... (Mango)
   ST/Rockers. .... (Mango)
   This Is Reggae Music #3-C .... (Island)
Poor Man's Roses (Or A Rich Man's Gold)
Patsy Cline; *Best Of Patsy Cline*...................... (Curb)
   Forever & Always ....(Epic)
   Stop, Look & Listen ....(MCA)
   The Patsy Cline Story. ....(MCA)
Reba McEntire; *Feel The Fire* .... (Mercury)
Poor People Of Paris
Les Baxter & His Orchestra; *Memories Are Made Of This-C* .... (Capitol)
Quiche Woman In A Barbecue Town
Tarwater Band; *Walking Across Egypt* .... (Flying Fish)
Rags To Riches
Kool & The Gang; *Everything Is-Greatest Hits* .... (Mercury)
Rags To Riches
Tony Bennett; *Tony Bennett-16 Most Requested Songs* .... (Legacy)
   Tony Bennett's All-Time Greatest Hits .... (Columbia)
Tony Bennett & Percy Faith & His Orchestra; *Radio Classics Of The '50s-C* .... (Columbia)
Rags To Riches
Electric Boys; *Funk-O-Metal Carpet Ride* .... (Atco)

Rags To Riches
John Scofield; *Shinola*. .... (Enja)
Raining In My Heart
Anne Murray; *New Kind Of Feeling* .... (Capitol)
Buddy Holly; *Buddy Holly-20 Golden Greats*. .... (MCA)
   The Buddy Holly Collection .... (MCA)
   Vintage Music-#6-C ....(MCA)
Jo-el Sonnier; *Come On Joe* ....(RCA)
Leo Sayer; *Leo Sayer*. .... (Warner Bros.)
Rascal King
Mighty Mighty Bosstones; *Let's Face It* .... (Big Rig/Mercury)
   Live From The Middle East .... (Big Rig/Mercury)
Rich & Poor
Randy Crawford; *Rich & Poor* .... (Warner Bros.)
Rich Man Poor Man
Peter, Paul & Mary; *Late Again*. .... (Warner Bros.)
Rich Man, Poor Boy
Joe Ely; *Dig All Night* ....(Hightone)
Right And Wrong
Joe Jackson; *Big World* .... (A&M)
Right Left Hand
George Jones; *Greatest Country Hits Of The '80s-1987-C* .... (Columbia)
   More Hot Country Requests-#2-C .... (Epic)
   Wine-Colored Glasses .... (Epic)
Right Or Wrong
George Strait; *George Strait's Greatest Hits*. .... (MCA)
   Right Or Wrong .... (MCA)
   Strait Out Of The Box .... (MCA)
Reba McEntire & Asleep At The Wheel; *Ride With Bob-C* .... (DreamWorks/SKG)
River And The Highway
Pam Tillis; *All Of This Love* .... (Arista)
   Pam Tillis' Greatest Hits .... (Arista)
River Deep, Mountain High
Celine Dion; *Falling Into You* ....(550 Music)
Erasure; *Innocents*. ....(Sire)
Four Tops; *Four Tops-Anthology* .... (Motown)
Ike & Tina Turner; *Best Of Ike & Tina Turner* .... (EMI)
   Phil Spector's Greatest Hits-C ....(Spector)
   Proud Mary-Best Of Ike & Tina Turner .... (EMI)
Tina Turner; *Simply The Best* .... (Capitol)
Rock And Roll Waltz
Kay Starr; *Capitol Collectors Series-Kay Starr* .... (Capitol)
San Diego Serenade
Nanci Griffith; *Late Night Grande Hotel*. .... (MCA)
Tom Waits; *The Heart Of Saturday Night* ....(Asylum)
   Tom Waits-Anthology. ....(Asylum)
Say You, Say Me
Lionel Richie; *Back To Front* .... (Motown)
   Dancing On The Ceiling. .... (Motown)
See Saw
Moonglows; *Moonglows-Their Greatest Hits*. .... (Chess)
Shacks & Chalets
Critton Hollow; *Great Dreams* .... (Flying Fish)
Shadows & Light
Joni Mitchell; *Hissing Of Summer Lawns* .... (Asylum)
   Shadows & Light .... (Asylum)
She Got The Goldmine (I Got The Shaft)
Jerry Reed; *14 #1 Country Hits-C* .... (RCA)
   Jerry Reed's Greatest Hits. .... (RCA)
   Solid Country Gold-C. .... (RCA)
Sheep Go To Heaven
Cake; *Prolonging The Magic* .... (Capricorn)
She's All I Got
Jimmy Cozier; *Jimmy Cozier* .... (J)
She's Every Woman
Garth Brooks; *Fresh Horses* .... (Capitol)
She's Got The Rhythm (And I Got The Blues)
Alan Jackson; *A Lot About Livin' (And A Little 'Bout Love)* .... (Arista)
She's Playing Hell Trying To Get Me To Heaven
George Strait; *Strait Country*. .... (MCA)
She's Sure Taking It Well
Kevin Sharp; *Measure Of A Man*. .... (143/Asylum)
Shoe Was On The Other Foot
Patti LaBelle; *Flame* .... (MCA)
Short Skirt/Long Jacket
Cake; *Comfort Eagle*. .... (Columbia)
Sick & Beautiful
Artificial Joy Club; *Melt* ....(Interscope)
Sick Of Myself
Matthew Sweet; *100% Fun* .... (Zoo)
Silver & Gold
Dolly Parton; *Eagle When She Flies* .... (Columbia)
Silver & Gold
U2; *Rattle And Hum* .... (Island)
Silver & Gold (Our Love Is Like)
Sweethearts Of The Rodeo; *Sisters* .... (Columbia)

Simple Twist Of Fate
Bob Dylan; *Blood On The Tracks* . . . . (Columbia)
  Bob Dylan At Budokan . . . . (Columbia)
Jerry Garcia Band; *Jerry Garcia Band* . . . . (Arista)
Joan Baez; *Best Of Joan Baez* . . . . (A&M)
  Diamonds & Rust . . . . (A&M)

Simple Twist Of Fate
Tim Curry; *Best Of Tim Curry* . . . . (A&M)

Smells Like Teen Spirit
Nirvana; *Nevermind* . . . . (David Geffen Co.)

Smiling Up The Frown
Agents Of Good Roots; *One By One* . . . . (RCA)
  Where'd You Get That Vibe? . . . . (RCA)

So Emotional
Christina Aguilera; *Christina Aguilera* . . . . (RCA)

Soft Lights And Hard Country Music
Moe Bandy; *Honky Tonk Amnesia-The Hard Country Sound Of Moe*
  Bandy . . . . (Razor & Tie)

Soft Lips And Hard Liquor
Charlie Walker; *45-#0870* . . . . (RCA)

Sooner Or Later
Eddy Raven; *Best Of Eddy Raven* . . . . (Liberty)
  Temporary Sanity . . . . (Capitol)

Sooner Or Later
Grass Roots; *Grass Roots-All-Time Greatest Hits* . . . . (MCA)
  Grass Roots-Anthology (1966-1975) . . . . (Rhino)
  Super Hits-#2-C . . . . (Gusto)

Sooner Or Later
Barbara Cook; *Disney Album* . . . . (Disney)

Sooner Or Later
Madonna; *I'm Breathless-Music From Dick Tracy* . . . .(Sire)

Sooner Or Later
Gary Morris; *Stones* . . . . (Liberty)

Spider & The Fly
Rolling Stones; *Out Of Our Heads* . . . . (Abkco)
  Singles Collection-The London Years . . . . (Abkco)

Spirit Of A Boy, Wisdom Of A Man
Randy Travis; *Big Country Hits '99-C* . . . . (K-Tel)
  You And You Alone . . . . (DreamWorks/SKG)

Standing Knee Deep In A River (Dying Of Thirst)
Kathy Mattea; *Lonesome Standard Time* . . . . (Mercury)

Stay (Faraway, So Close!)
U2; *Zooropa* . . . . (Island)

Still In Love
Brian McKnight; *I Remember You* . . . . (Mercury)

Stupid Einstein
Three O'Clock; *Sixteen Tambourines* . . . . (Frontier)

Success Has Made A Failure Of Our Home
Sinead O'Connor; *Am I Not Your Girl?* . . . . (Ensign)
  So Far...The Best Of Sinead O'Connor . . . . (EMI)

Summer Kisses, Winter Tears
Elvis Presley; *Collector's Gold* . . . .(RCA)

Summer Me, Winter Me
Barbra Streisand; *The Way We Were* . . . . (Columbia)

Summer Snow
Lou Christie; *Enlightnin'ment-Best Of Lou Christie* . . . . (Rhino)

Summer Snow
Blue Magic; *Magic Of The Blue-Greatest Hits* . . . . (Collectables)

Sun & The Rainfall
Depeche Mode; *Broken Frame* . . . .(Sire)

Sunny Side To Every Situation
Original Broadway Cast; *42nd Street* . . . . (RCA Victor)

Sunrise, Sunset
Original Cast; *Fiddler On The Roof* . . . . (RCA Victor)

Survivor
Destiny's Child; *Now That's What I Call Music!-#7-C* . . . .(Virgin)
  Survivor . . . . (Columbia)

Swallowed
Bush; *Razorblade Suitcase* . . . .(Trauma)

Sweet 'N' Sour Jesus
Supersuckers; *Smoke Of Hell* . . . . (Sub Pop)

Sweetest Kittens (Have The Sharpest Claws)
Meatmen; *Rock 'N' Roll Juggernaut* . . . . (Caroline)

Sweetest Thing
U2; *Best Of 1980-1990* . . . . (Island)
  Now That's What I Call Music!-#2-C . . . .(Virgin)

Taste Of Honey
Barbra Streisand; *The Barbra Streisand Album* . . . . (Columbia)
Beatles; *Beatles-Box Set* . . . . (Capitol)
  Please Please Me . . . . (Parlophone)
  The Early Beatles . . . . (Capitol)
Herb Alpert; *Midnight Sun* . . . . (A&M)
Herb Alpert & The Tijuana Brass; *Herb Alpert & The Tijuana Brass'*
  Greatest Hits . . . . (A&M)
  Herb Alpert & The Tijuana Brass-Classics-#1 . . . . (A&M)
Tony Bennett; *Forty Years-The Artistry Of Tony Bennett* . . . . . . (Columbia)

Teenager In Love
Dion And The Belmonts; *Classic Old & Gold-C* . . . . (Laurie)
  Collectables Presents The History Of Rock-#6-C . . . .(Collectables)
  Dion And The Belmonts-Their Best . . . . (Laurie)
  Oldies But Goodies-#6-C . . . . (Original Sound)
  Party Time Fifties-C . . . . (JCI Assoc. Labels)

Texas Size Heartache
Joe Diffie; *Joe Diffie's Greatest Hits* . . . .(Epic)

That's Cool, That's Trash
Kingsmen; *Best Of The Kingsmen* . . . .(Rhino)

Theme From "Green Acres"
Eddie Albert & Eva Gabor; *ST/Son In Law* . . . .(Hollywood)
Original Soundtrack; *CBS: The First 50 Years* . . . . (TVT)
  Television's Greatest Hits-#1-C . . . . (TVT)

Theme From "The Odd Couple"
Original Soundtrack; *Television's Greatest Hits-#7-Cable Ready-C* . . . . . (TVT)

Theme From "The Patty Duke Show"
Original Soundtrack; *Just Patty: The Best Of Patty Duke* . . . . (EMI)
  Television's Greatest Hits-#1-C . . . . (TVT)

There's A Red-Neck In The Soul Band
Latimore; *Straighten It Out: The Best Of Latimore* . . . . (Rhino)

There's No Place Like Home For The Holidays
Perry Como; *Now That's What I Call Christmas!-C* . . . . (UTV)
  Perry Como's Greatest Hits . . . . (RCA)

This Door Swings Both Ways
Herman's Hermits; *Herman's Hermits-Their Greatest Hits* . . . . (Abkco)

This Is Me
Dream; *It Was All A Dream* . . . . (Bad Boy/Arista)
  Totally Hits 2001-C . . . . (Arista)

Till I'm Too Old To Die Young
Moe Bandy; *Great Records Of The Decade-'80s Hits-Country-C* . . . . . .(Curb)
  Moe Bandy's Greatest Hits . . . . (Curb)

Times They Are A-Changin'
Billy Joel; *KOHUEPT* . . . . (Columbia)
Bob Dylan; *Biograph* . . . . (Columbia)
  Bob Dylan At Budokan . . . . (Columbia)
  Bob Dylan's Greatest Hits . . . . (Columbia)
  The Bootleg Series-Volumes 1-3 [Rare & Unreleased] . . . . (Columbia)
  The Times They Are A-Changin' . . . . (Columbia)
Byrds; *The Byrds* . . . . (Columbia)
  Turn! Turn! Turn! . . . . (Legacy)
Peter, Paul & Mary; *Peter, Paul and Mary In Concert* . . . . . . (Warner Bros.)
Simon & Garfunkel; *Collected Works* . . . . (Columbia)
  Wednesday Morning 3 A.M. . . . . (Columbia)

To Have And Not To Hold
Madonna; *Ray Of Light* . . . . (Maverick)

To Live Is To Die
Metallica; *...And Justice For All* . . . . (Elektra)

Too Late, Too Soon
Jon Secada; *Secada* . . . . (Capitol)

Too Old To Cut The Mustard
Carlisles; *45-#6348* . . . . (Mercury)
Ernest Tubb; *Ernest Tubb-Retrospective-#2* . . . . (MCA Special Prod.)

Toy Or Treasure
Kay Starr; *Capitol Collectors Series-Kay Starr* . . . .(Capitol)

Treat You Like A Queen
Rahsaan Patterson; *Love In Stereo* . . . . (MCA)

Turn It Up Or Turn It Off
Drivin' N' Cryin'; *Smoke* . . . .(Island)

Turn You Inside-Out
R.E.M.; *Green* . . . . (Warner Bros.)

Two Lovers
Mary Wells; *Hitsville USA-The Motown Singles Collection-1959-*
  1971-C . . . . (Motown)
  Mary Wells' Greatest Hits . . . . (Motown)

Two Teardrops
Steve Wariner; *Two Teardrops* . . . . (Capitol)

Unable To Stay, Unwilling To Leave
James Horner; *ST/Titanic* . . . . (Sony Music Classical)

Ups & Downs
Paul Revere And The Raiders; *Legend Of Paul Revere And The*
  Raiders . . . . (Columbia)
  Paul Revere And The Raiders' Greatest Hits . . . . (Columbia)

Violet
Hole; *Ask For It* . . . . (Caroline)
  Live Through This . . . . (David Geffen Co.)

Waking & Dreaming
Orleans; *Waking & Dreaming* . . . . (Asylum)

Walk A Mile In My Shoes
Bryan Ferry; *Another Time Another Place* . . . . (Reprise)
Elvis Presley; *On Stage-February, 1970* . . . . (RCA)
Joe South; *Best Of Joe South* . . . . (Rhino)

Walk Like I Do
William Topley; *Spanish Wells* . . . . (Mercury)

Wanted Dead Or Alive
Bon Jovi; *Slippery When Wet* . . . . (Jambco)

The Concert For New York City-C . . . . (Columbia)
Warm Beer & Cold Women
Tom Waits; *Nighthawks At The Diner* . . . . (Asylum)
Way You Do The Things You Do
Rita Coolidge; *Rita Coolidge's Greatest Hits* . . . . (A&M)
Temptations; *Temptations' Greatest Hits-#1* . . . . (Motown)
Temptations-Anthology-The Best Of The Temptations . . . . (Motown)
Temptations-The Ultimate Collection . . . . (Motown)
UB40; *Labour Of Love II* . . . . (Virgin)
We Live In Two Different Worlds
Auldridge/Bennett/Gaudreau; *This Old Town* . . . . (Rebel)
Welfare Cadillac
Gary B.B. Coleman; *Too Much Weekend* . . . . (Ichiban Int'l)
Well Fed Slave/Hungry Free Man
Lucky Dube; *Taxman* . . . . (Shanachie)
What Is And What Should Never Be
Jimmy Page & Black Crowes; *Live At The Greek* . . . . (TVT)
Led Zeppelin; *BBC Sessions* . . . . (Atlantic)
Led Zeppelin II . . . . (Atlantic)
Led Zeppelin-Box Set . . . . (Atlantic)
Led Zeppelin-The Complete Studio Recordings . . . . (Atlantic)
What It's Like
Everlast; *Whitey Ford Sings The Blues* . . . . (Tommy Boy)
What Kind Of Love Are You On
Aerosmith; *ST/Armageddon-The Album* . . . . (Columbia)
When Doves Cry
Ginuwine; *The Bachelor* . . . . (550 Music)
Prince and the Revolution; *ST/Purple Rain* . . . . (Warner Bros.)
When He Shines
Sheena Easton; *Sheena Easton's Greatest Hits* . . . . (EMI Special Markets)
The World Of Sheena Easton: The Singles Collection-C . . . . (EMI)
When It Hurts So Bad
Lauryn Hill; *The Miseducation Of Lauryn Hill* . . . . (Ruffhouse/Columbia)
When Two Worlds Collide
Rex Allen, Jr.; *20 Golden Souvenirs Of Music City U.S.A.-C* . . . . . . (Plantation)
Roger Miller; *Best Of Roger Miller-His Greatest Songs* . . . . (Curb)
Wherever You Go
Clint Black; *Clint Black-The Greatest Hits* . . . . (RCA)
One Emotion . . . . (RCA)
Which Bridge To Cross (Which Bridge To Burn)
Vince Gill; *When Love Finds You* . . . . (MCA)
Which Side Of The Glass
George Strait; *George Strait* . . . . (MCA)
White Man/Black Man
James Gang; *James Gang-16 Greatest Hits* . . . . (MCA)
Thirds . . . . (One Way)
Win Or Lose
Earth, Wind & Fire; *Faces* . . . . (Columbia)
Win Or Lose
Nitty Gritty Dirt Band; *Dirt, Silver & Gold* . . . . (One Way)
Win Some, Lose Some
Scandal; *Scandal* . . . . (Columbia)
Win Some, Lose Some
Bryan Adams; *Bryan Adams* . . . . (A&M)
Winner/Loser
Stomu Yamashta & Go; *Live From Paris* . . . . (Island)
Stomu Yamashta & Go . . . . (Island)
Winners & Losers
Rossington-Collins Band; *Anytime, Anyplace, Anywhere* . . . . (MCA)
Winter & The Summer
Strawbs; *Bursting At The Seams* . . . . (A&M)
Wish You Were Here
Limp Bizkit & John Rzeznik; *America: A Tribute To Heroes-C* . . . . . (Interscope)
Pink Floyd; *Collection Of Great Dance Songs* . . . . (Columbia)
Delicate Sound Of Thunder . . . . (Columbia)
Wish You Were Here . . . . (Columbia)
With My Eyes Wide Open I'm Dreaming
Mandy Barnett; *I've Got A Right To Cry* . . . . (Sire)
Patti Page; *Patti Page-Golden Hits* . . . . (Mercury)
Patti Page's Greatest Hits . . . . (Columbia)
Worlds Apart
Vince Gill; *High Lonesome Sound* . . . . (MCA)
Worst That Could Happen
Brooklyn Bridge; *Billboard Top Pop Hits-1969-C* . . . . (Rhino)
Brooklyn Bridge-Greatest Hits . . . . (Collectables)
Yesterday's Winner Is A Loser Today
Ernest Tubb; *Ernest Tubb Collection-C* . . . . (Step One)
You
Queensryche; *Hear In The Now Frontier* . . . . (Virgin)
You Blew Me Off
Bare Jr.; *Boo-Tay* . . . . (Immortal/Epic)
ST/Cruel Intentions . . . . (Virgin)
You Can Feel Bad
Patty Loveless; *Patty Loveless-Classics* . . . . (Epic)
Super Hits Of 1996-C . . . . (Epic)
The Trouble With The Truth . . . . (Epic)

You Gotta Love That
Neal McCoy; *Neal McCoy's Greatest Hits* . . . . (Atlantic)
Today's Country Love-C . . . . (K-Tel)
You Gotta Love That! . . . . (Atlantic)
You Make Me Sick
Pink; *Can't Take Me Home* . . . . (LaFace)
You Make Your Own Heaven & Hell Right Here On Earth
Temptations; *Psychedelic Shack* . . . . (Motown)
You Turned The Tables On Me
Anita O'Day; *Anita Sings The Most* . . . . (Verve)
Benny Goodman; *Benny Goodman's Greatest Hits* . . . . (RCA Victor)
Birth Of Swing . . . . (Bluebird)
Billie Holiday; *Solitude* . . . . (Verve)
Louis Armstrong; *Compact Jazz-Louis Armstrong* . . . . (Verve)
You'd Be Surprised
Eddie Cantor; *Music From The New York Stage (1890-1920)-#4-1917-1920-C* . . . . (Pearl)
Johnnie Ray; *45-#40154* . . . . (Columbia)
Marilyn Monroe; *Never Before & Never Again-1953-1954* . . . . . . (DRG)
Orrin Tucker & His Orchestra; *Best Of Orrin Tucker & His Orchestra* . . . (DRG)
Young Man, Older Woman
Millie Jackson; *Very Best Of Millie Jackson* . . . . (Jive)
Younger Than Springtime
Original Cast; *South Pacific* . . . . (CBS Masterworks)
Your Good Girl's Gonna Go Bad
Billie Jo Spears; *Best Of Billie Jo Spears* . . . . (CEMA Special Prod.)
Best Of Billie Jo Spears . . . . (Razor & Tie)
K.T. Oslin; *Tammy Wynette-Remembered-C* . . . . (Asylum)
Tammy Wynette; *Tammy Wynette-Anniversary-20 Years Of Hits* . . . . (Epic)
Tammy Wynette's Greatest Hits . . . . (Epic)
Your Good Girl's Gonna Go Bad . . . . (Legacy)

OPTIMISM, Positive Attitude

> *See Also:* **ADVICE, BACK ON MY FEET, BEGINNINGS,**
> **CAREFREE, FAITH, FRIENDS, GOD, HAPPINESS, HELP, LOVE**
> **(various), MORNING, MOTIVATION, RELAX, SMILE,**
> **SUN, WINNING**

Ac-Cent-Tchu-Ate The Positive
Andrews Sisters; *Andrews Sisters Greatest Hits* . . . . (Curb)
Bing Crosby; *Bing Crosby's Greatest Hits* . . . . (MCA)
Original Soundtrack; *ST/Bugsy* . . . . (Epic)
All Things Must Pass
George Harrison; *All Things Must Pass* . . . . (Parlophone)
Alone Together
Judy Garland; *Judy Garland-At Carnegie Hall* . . . . (Capitol)
April Showers
Al Jolson; *Best Of Al Jolson* . . . . (MCA)
The Al Jolson Story-#2 . . . . (MCA)
Judy Garland; *Hits Of Judy Garland* . . . . (Capitol)
Judy . . . . (Capitol)
Beautiful Day
U2; *All That You Can't Leave Behind* . . . . (Interscope)
Now That's What I Call Music!-#6-C . . . . (Virgin)
Best Is Yet To Come
Frank Sinatra; *It Might As Well Be Swing* . . . . (Reprise)
Sinatra Reprise-The Very Good Years . . . . (Reprise)
Johnny Mathis; *I'll Buy You A Star* . . . . (Legacy)
Rosemary Clooney; *Girl Singer* . . . . (Concord Jazz)
Tony Bennett; *I Left My Heart In San Francisco* . . . . (Columbia)
The Ultimate Tony Bennett . . . . (Legacy)
Best Things In Life Are Free
June Allyson; *ST/Good News* . . . . (Sony Music Special Prod.)
Luther Vandross & Janet Jackson; *ST/Mo' Money* . . . . (Bluebird)
Mel Torme; *Easy To Remember* . . . . (Glendale)
Sam Cooke; *Sam Cooke-At The Copa* . . . . (RCA)
Better Man, Better Off
Tracy Lawrence; *The Coast Is Clear* . . . . (Atlantic)
Beyond The Blue Horizon
Jeanette MacDonald; *Hollywood Sings-C* . . . . (Living Era)
Lou Christie; *ST/Rain Man* . . . . (Capitol)
Blue Skies
Benny Goodman; *Benny Goodman Today* . . . . (London)
Carnegie Hall Jazz Concert . . . . (Columbia)
The Birth Of Swing (1935-1936) . . . . (Bluebird)
This Is Benny Goodman . . . . (RCA)
Bing Crosby; *Bing Crosby's Greatest Hits* . . . . (MCA)
Duke Ellington; *Carnegie Hall Concert* . . . . (Prestige)
Golden Duke . . . . (Prestige)
Willie Nelson; *Stardust* . . . . (Legacy)
Bye Bye Blues
Bert Lown; *Fabulous Thirties-C* . . . . (Pro Jazz)
Cockeyed Optimist
Mitzi Gaynor; *ST/South Pacific* . . . . (RCA)
Original Cast; *South Pacific* . . . . (CBS Masterworks)

Coming Up
Paul McCartney; *All The Best!* . . . . (Capitol)
Tripping The Live Fantastic-Highlights! . . . . (Capitol)
Don't Let It Bother You
Fats Waller; *Have A Little Dream On Me* . . . . (Eclipse)
Don't Stop
Elton John; *Legacy-A Tribute To Fleetwood Mac's Rumours-C* . . . . (Lava)
Fleetwood Mac; *25 Years-The Chain* . . . . (Warner Bros.)
Fleetwood Mac Live . . . . (Warner Bros.)
Fleetwood Mac's Greatest Hits . . . . (Warner Bros.)
Rumours . . . . (Warner Bros.)
Don't Worry, Be Happy
Bobby McFerrin; *Simple Pleasures* . . . . (EMI)
ST/Cocktail . . . . (Elektra)
Everything's Coming Up Roses
Ethel Merman; *Broadway Magic-The 1960s-C* . . . . (Columbia)
Original Cast; *Gypsy* . . . . (Columbia)
Original London Cast; *Gypsy* . . . . (RCA)
Get Happy
Benny Goodman; *Benny Goodman's Greatest Hits* . . . . (RCA Victor)
Ella Fitzgerald; *Harold Arlen Songbook-#2* . . . . (Verve)
Judy Garland; *Best Of Judy Garland In Hollywood* . . . . . (Turner Classic Movies)
Nat Shilkret & The Victor Orchestra; *78-#22444* . . . . (Victor)
Getting Better
Beatles; *Sgt. Pepper's Lonely Hearts Club Band.* . . . . (Capitol)
Got A Lot O' Livin' To Do!
Elvis Presley; *Loving You* . . . . (RCA)
The Great Performances . . . . (RCA)
The Other Sides-Worldwide Gold Award Hits, Vol. 2. . . . . . . (RCA)
Hand In My Pocket
Alanis Morissette; *Jagged Little Pill* . . . . (Maverick)
Handcuffed To A Fence In Mississippi
Jim White; *No Such Place* . . . . (Luaka Bop)
Happy Days Are Here Again
Barbra Streisand; *A Happening In Central Park* . . . . (Columbia)
Barbra Streisand's Greatest Hits . . . . (Columbia)
One Voice . . . . (Columbia)
The Barbra Streisand Album . . . . (Columbia)
Leo Reisman & His Orchestra; *Nipper's Greatest Hits Of The '30s-#1-C* . . . . (RCA)
Happy Talk
Original Cast; *South Pacific.* . . . . (CBS Masterworks)
Happy Trails
Michael Martin Murphey; *Cowboy Songs* . . . . (Warner Western)
Original Soundtrack; *Television's Greatest Hits-#1-C* . . . . (TVT)
Quicksilver Messenger Service; *Sons Of Mercury* . . . . (Rhino)
Randy Travis & Roy Rogers; *Heroes And Friends* . . . . . (Warner Bros.)
Riders In The Sky; *Cowboy Way* . . . . (MCA)
Roy Rogers/Dale Evans/Dusty Rogers; *Roy Rogers Tribute-C* . . . . (RCA)
Van Halen; *Diver Down* . . . . (Warner Bros.)
Here Comes The Sun
Beatles; *Abbey Road* . . . . (Parlophone)
The Beatles/1967-1970. . . . . (Capitol)
George Benson; *Best Of George Benson* . . . . (A&M)
George Benson-Collection . . . . (Warner Bros.)
George Harrison; *Bangladesh* . . . . (Capitol)
Best Of George Harrison . . . . (Capitol)
Hold On (Change Is Comin')
Sounds Of Blackness; *Time For Healing.* . . . . (Perspective/A&M)
I Believe
Elvis Presley; *Amazing Grace-His Greatest Sacred Performances* . . . . (RCA)
Frankie Laine; *Frankie Laine-16 Most Requested Songs* . . . . (Legacy)
Frankie Laine's Greatest Hits . . . . (Columbia)
Jo Stafford; *You'll Never Walk Alone* . . . . (CEMA Special Prod.)
I Believe
Robert Plant; *Fate Of Nations* . . . . (Es Paranza)
I Believe I Can Fly
R. Kelly; *1998 Grammy Nominees-C* . . . . (MCA)
R. . . . . (Jive)
ST/Space Jam . . . . (Warner Sunset)
I Can See Clearly Now
Gladys Knight & The Pips; *Gladys Knight & The Pips' Greatest Hits* . . . . (Buddah)
Imagination . . . . (Right Stuff)
On & On . . . . (Fifty One West)
Johnny Nash; *Billboard Top Rock 'N' Roll Hits-1972-C* . . . . . (Rhino)
Rock Artifacts-From The Vaults-#2-C . . . . (Legacy)
I Got Dreams
Steve Wariner; *I Got Dreams* . . . . (MCA)
I Got The Sun In The Morning
Ethel Merman/Bruce Yarnell/Original Cast; *Annie Get Your Gun* . . . . (RCA Victor)
Ethel Merman/Ray Middleton/Original Cast; *Annie Get Your Gun.* . . . . . (MCA)
Original Broadway Cast; *Annie Get Your Gun* . . . . (Angel)
I Hope You Dance
Lee Ann Womack; *I Hope You Dance* . . . . (MCA)
I'll Be All Right
Jorma Kaukonen & Tom Hobson; *Quah* . . . . (Relix)

I'm Into Something Good
Herman's Hermits; *Herman's Hermits-Their Greatest Hits* . . . . (Abkco)
I'm Just An Old Chunk Of Coal (But I'm Gonna Be A Diamond Someday)
Billy Joe Shaver; *Restless Wind-The Legendary Billy Joe Shaver-1973-1987* . . . . (Razor & Tie)
John Anderson; *John Anderson's Greatest Hits.* . . . . (Warner Bros.)
I've Got This Feeling
Mavericks; *Trampoline* . . . . (MCA)
Keep On The Sunny Side
Randy Scruggs with Earl Scruggs & Doc Watson; *Red Hot + Country-C* . . . . (Mercury)
Whites; *ST/O Brother, Where Art Thou?* . . . . (Mercury)
Let A Smile Be Your Umbrella
Sammy Kaye & His Orchestra; *Best Of Sammy Kaye & His Orchestra* . . . (MCA)
Let's Have Another Cup Of Coffee
Glenn Miller; *Complete Glenn Miller & His Orchestra-#8* . . . . (Bluebird)
Michael Feinstein; *Remember-Michael Feinstein Sings Irving Berlin.* . . . (Elektra)
Life Is Beautiful
Amy Correia; *Carnival Love* . . . . (Capitol)
Little More Love
Vince Gill; *High Lonesome Sound* . . . . (MCA)
Look For The Silver Lining
Alberta Hunter; *Look For The Silver Lining.* . . . . (Columbia)
Chet Baker; *Let's Get Lost-Best Of Chet Baker Sings* . . . . (Blue Note)
Dave Brubeck Quartet; *Stardust.* . . . . (Fantasy)
Judy Garland; *Best Of Judy Garland In Hollywood* . . . . . (Turner Classic Movies)
Marion Harris; *78-#3367* . . . . (Columbia)
Love's Gonna Live Here
Buck Owens; *Billboard Top Country Hits-1963-C* . . . . (Rhino)
Buck Owens' All-Time Greatest Hits-#2 . . . . (Curb)
Buck Owens & The Buckaroos; *Buck Owens & The Buckaroos-Live At Carnegie Hall.* . . . . (Country Music Foundation)
Memory
Original Broadway Cast; *Cats* . . . . (Geffen)
On The Road Again
Willie Nelson; *Greatest Country Hits Of The '80s-1980-C* . . . . (Columbia)
Greatest Hits (& Some That Will Be). . . . . (Columbia)
Hot Country Rock-#1-C . . . . (Epic)
ST/Forrest Gump. . . . . (Epic/Sony Music Soundtrax)
ST/Honeysuckle Rose . . . . (Columbia)
On The Sunny Side Of The Street
Diana Krall; *Stepping Out* . . . . (Justin Time)
Frank Sinatra; *Come Swing With Me!* . . . . (Capitol)
One More For The Road . . . . (Capitol)
Sentimental Journey . . . . (Capitol)
The Capitol Years . . . . (Capitol)
Judy Garland; *Best Of Judy Garland* . . . . (MCA)
Louis Armstrong; *Best Of Louis Armstrong.* . . . . (MCA)
Chicago Concert 1956 . . . . (Columbia)
Jazz Club-Vocal . . . . (Verve)
Music Autobiography . . . . (MCA)
Ted Lewis & His Orchestra; *Charming Gents Of Stage & Screen-C* . . . . (Legacy)
Those Wonderful Years: Puttin' On The Ritz-C . . . . (JCI Assoc. Labels)
One Headlight
Wallflowers; *Bringing Down The Horse* . . . . (Interscope)
O-o-h Child
Five Stairsteps; *Didn't It Blow Your Mind: Soul Hits Of The '70s-#2-C* . . . . (Rhino)
Five Stairsteps' Greatest Hits . . . . (Collectables)
Radio Active Hits-#2-C . . . . (Accord)
Spinners; *Best Of The Spinners* . . . . (Motown)
Valerie Carter; *Just A Stone's Throw Away* . . . . (Columbia)
ST/Over The Edge . . . . (Warner Bros.)
Optimistic
Radiohead; *Kid A* . . . . (Capitol)
Pack Up Your Sorrows
Joan Baez; *Best Of Joan Baez* . . . . (Vanguard)
Judy Collins; *Judy Collins' Fifth Album* . . . . (Elektra)
Mimi & Richard Farina; *Best Of Mimi & Richard Farina* . . . . (Vanguard)
Greatest Folksingers Of The '60s-C . . . . (Vanguard)
Mimi Farina; *Celebrations For A Grey Day.* . . . . (Vanguard)
Peter, Paul & Mary; *Peter, Paul and Mary Album* . . . . (Warner Bros.)
Pack Up Your Troubles In Your Old Kit Bag (And Smile, Smile, Smile)
James F. Harrison & Knickerbocker Quartet; *78-#2181* . . . . . . (Columbia)
Pennies From Heaven
Billie Holiday; *Billie Holiday-16 Most Requested Songs.* . . . . (Legacy)
Bing Crosby; *Pennies From Heaven* . . . . (Pro-Arte)
Frank Sinatra & Nelson Riddle Orchestra; *songs for Swingin' Lovers!* . . . . (Capitol)
Lester Young; *Birdland All-Stars At Carnegie Hall.* . . . . (Roulette)
Louis Armstrong; *RCA Victor Jazz: First Half-Century-C* . . . . (RCA)
Mandy Patinkin; *Mandy Patinkin.* . . . . (Columbia)
Skyliners; *Skyliners' Greatest Hits* . . . . (Original Sound)
Stan Getz; *Essential Stan Getz Songbook.* . . . . (Verve)
Stephane Grappelli; *Satin Doll-#1-Best Of Stephane Grappelli.* . . . . (Vanguard)
Perfect Day
Collective Soul; *Blender* . . . . (Atlantic)

Revolution 1
Beatles; *Beatles-Box Set* (Capitol)
The Beatles (White Album) (Capitol)
Shine
Ry Cooder; *Jazz* (Warner Bros.)
Shine
Amel Larrieux; *Infinite Possibilities* (Epic)
Steppin' Out With My Baby
Fred Astaire; *Cheek To Cheek: The Irving Berlin Songbook-C* (Verve)
Fred Astaire At MGM (Rhino)
ST/Easter Parade (Rhino)
Steppin' Out-Astaire Sings (Verve)
Tony Bennett; *MTV Unplugged-Tony Bennett* (Columbia)
Steppin' Out (Columbia)
Stepping Stone
Lari White; *Stepping Stone* (Lyric Street)
Sunny Side To Every Situation
Original Broadway Cast; *42nd Street* (RCA Victor)
There Are No Cats In America
Nehemiah Persoff/John Guarnieri/Warren Hays; *ST/An American Tail* (MCA)
This Night Won't Last Forever
Bill LaBounty; *The Right Direction* (Noteworthy)
This Night Won't Last Forever (Warner Bros.)
Michael Johnson; *Dialogue* (EMI)
Have A Nice Night-Romantic Hits Of The '70s-C (Rhino)
Radio Daze-Pop Hits Of The '80s-#1-C (Rhino)
Then & Now (ISD/Intersound)
Moe Bandy; *Many Mansions* (Curb)
Sawyer Brown; *Six Days On The Road* (Curb)
To Ev'ry Girl-To Ev'ry Boy (The Meaning Of Love)
Johnnie Ray; *45-#40252* (Columbia)
Tomorrow
Barbra Streisand; *Songbird* (Columbia)
Original Broadway Cast; *Annie* (Columbia)
Original Cast; *ST/Annie* (Columbia)
Walking On Sunshine
Katrina And The Waves; *Katrina And The Waves* (Capitol)
Spring Break-#2-Cold Kegs & Tan Legs (Capitol)
Walking On Sunshine
Eddy Grant; *Let's Dance-DJ's Collection* (Columbia)
Walking On Sunshine (Epic)
We Can Work It Out
Beatles; *"Yesterday"...And Today* (Capitol)
Beatles 1 (Capitol)
Beatles-20 Greatest Hits (Capitol)
Beatles-Box Set (Capitol)
Past Masters-Volume Two (Parlophone)
The Beatles/1962-1966 (Capitol)
Paul McCartney; *Unplugged (The Official Bootleg)* (Capitol)
Stevie Wonder; *Beatles Songs By Greatest Stars* (Motown)
Signed Sealed & Delivered (Motown)
Stevie Wonder's Greatest Hits-#2 (Motown)
Top 10 With A Bullet-Motown Solo Stars-C (Motown)
We're In The Money
Fred Astaire; *Nipper's Greatest Hits Of The '30s-#2-C* (RCA)
Original Broadway Cast; *42nd Street* (RCA Victor)
What A Wonderful World
Louis Armstrong; *ST/Good Morning, Vietnam* (A&M)
Vocalists-Jazz Masters-C (Bluebird)
What A Wonderful World (Decca Jazz)
Mormon Tabernacle Choir; *Songs From America's Heartland* (London)
Willie Nelson; *What A Wonderful World* (Columbia)
When You're Smiling (The Whole World Smiles With You)
Frank Sinatra; *Sinatra's Swingin' Session!!!* (Capitol)
Judy Garland; *Judy Garland-At Carnegie Hall* (Capitol)
Judy Garland's Greatest Hits (Curb)
One & Only (Capitol)
Louis Armstrong; *Best Of Louis Armstrong* (MCA)
Louis Armstrong-Vol. 4-In New York (Columbia)
Musical Autobiography-#2 (MCA)
White Cliffs Of Dover
Kay Kyser & His Orchestra; *16 Most Requested Songs Of The '40s-#1-C* (Legacy)
Lee Andrews And The Hearts; *Lee Andrews And The Hearts' Biggest Hits* (Collectables)
Mystics; *Mystics-16 Golden Classics* (Collectables)
Righteous Brothers; *Righteous Brothers' Greatest Hits* (Verve)
Righteous Brothers-Anthology 1962-1974 (Rhino)
Rosemary Clooney; *For The Duration* (Concord Jazz)
You Can Get It If You Really Want
Jimmy Cliff; *In Concert-Best Of Jimmy Cliff* (Reprise)
ST/The Harder They Come (Mango)
You Can Make It If You Try
Sly & The Family Stone; *Sly & The Family Stone-Anthology* (Epic)
Sly & The Family Stone's Greatest Hits (Epic)
Stand! (Epic)
You're Never Fully Dressed Without A Smile
Original Broadway Cast; *Annie* (Columbia)

ORPHANS

See Also: ***CHILDREN, FAMILY (various), LONELY, LOSING & LOSS, PARENTS (various)***

Artificial Flowers
Bobby Darin; *The Bobby Darin Story* (Atlantic)
Boy For Sale
Original Broadway Cast; *Oliver!* (RCA Victor)
Original London Cast; *Oliver!* (EMI-Angel)
Motherless Child
Steve Miller Band; *Steve Miller Band-Anthology* (Capitol)
Your Saving Grace (Capitol)
Motherless Children
Eric Clapton; *461 Ocean Boulevard* (Polydor)
Eric Clapton-Crossroads-C (Polydor)
From The Cradle (Duck/Reprise)
Nobody's Child
Beatles With Tony Sheridan; *The Beatles featuring Tony Sheridan-In The Beginning (Circa 1960)* (Polydor)
Electric Light Orchestra; *Eldorado* (Jet)
Hank Williams, Jr.; *Best Of Hank Williams, Jr.-#1-Roots & Branches* (Mercury)
Maria McKee; *Maria McKee* (Geffen)
Traveling Wilburys; *Nobody's Child-Romanian Angel Appeal-C* (Warner Bros.)
Orphan Girl
Emmylou Harris; *Wrecking Ball* (Asylum)
Gillian Welch; *Revival* (Almo Sounds)
Tim O'Brien; *Away Out On The Mountain* (Sugar Hill)
Poor Little Orphaned Boy
Carter Family; *Their Complete Victor Recordings-Gold Watch And Chain-1933-1934* (Rounder)
Sometimes I Feel Like A Motherless Child
Dave Van Ronk; *Folksinger* (Prestige)
Inside Dave Van Ronk (Fantasy)
Grant Green; *Feelin' The Spirit* (Blue Note)
Iron City (Muse)
Jerry Butler; *Jerry Butler-Gold* (Vee-Jay)
Mormon Tabernacle Choir; *Songs Of The Civil War And Stephen Foster Favorites* (Sony Music Classical)
O.V. Wright; *O.V. Wright* (MCA)
Odetta; *Essential Odetta* (Vanguard)
Peter, Paul & Mary; *The Song Will Rise* (Warner Bros.)
Van Morrison; *Poetic Champions Compose* (Mercury)
Theme From "Diff'rent Strokes"
Original Soundtrack; *Television's Greatest Hits-#6-Remote Control-C* (TVT)
Theme From "Webster" (Then Came You)
Original Soundtrack; *Television's Greatest Hits-#6-Remote Control-C* (TVT)
You Won't Be An Orphan For Long
Original Broadway Cast; *Annie* (Columbia)

PAIN & HEALING, Dentists, Diseases, Doctors, Feeling Better, Heartache, Hospitals, Hurting, Sickness, Suffering

See Also: ***AIDS, ALCOHOL: RECOVERING ALCOHOLIC, BACK ON MY FEET, BLOOD, BREAK, CRAZY, DEATH, DESPAIR, DIVORCE, DOMESTIC ABUSE, DRUGS (various), GUILT, HEART, IDENTITY CRISIS, LONELY, LOSING & LOSS, LOVE (various), LOW SELF-ESTEEM, MISTREATMENT, SADNESS***

98.6
Keith; *'60s Pop-#1-Those Were The Days-C* (Dominion Entert.)
Achy Breaky Heart
Billy Ray Cyrus; *Some Gave All* (Mercury)
Adelaide's Lament
Original Cast; *Guys & Dolls* (MCA)
Guys & Dolls (Motown)
Adrian
Jewel; *Pieces Of You* (Atlantic)
Aeroplane
Red Hot Chili Peppers; *One Hot Minute* (Warner Bros.)
Again
Alice In Chains; *Alice In Chains* (Columbia)
Amnesia
Pousette-Dart Band; *Amnesia* (Capitol)
Ana's Song (Open Fire)
Silverchair; *Neon Ballroom* (Epic)
And The Healing Has Begun
Van Morrison; *Into The Music* (Warner Bros.)
Angels In Waiting
Tammy Cochran; *Tammy Cochran* (Epic)
Angel's Son
Strait Up featuring Lajon of Sevendust; *Strait Up-C* (Immortal/Virgin)
Annalee The Healer
Beach Boys; *Friends-20/20* (Capitol)

Appointment At The Fat Clinic
Digable Planets; *Reachin'-New Refutation Of Time & Space* . . . . (Pendulum)
Arthritis Blues
Ramblin' Jack Elliott; *Country Style* . . . . (Prestige)
Awake
Godsmack; *Awake* . . . . (Republic/Universal)
Back On My Feet Again
Babys; *Babys-Anthology* . . . . (Chrysalis)
Union Jacks . . . . (Chrysalis)
Bad Case Of Love
B.B. King; *Blues On The Bayou* . . . . (MCA)
Bad Case Of Lovin' You
Robert Palmer; *Addictions-#1* . . . . (Island)
Secrets . . . . (Island)
Bad Habits & Infections
Daryl Hall & John Oates; *Beauty On A Back Street* . . . . (RCA)
Bad Liver & A Broken Heart
Tom Waits; *Small Change* . . . . (Asylum)
Bad Medicine
Bon Jovi; *New Jersey.* . . . . (Jambco)
Beast In Me
Johnny Cash; *American Recordings* . . . . (American)
Nick Lowe; *The Impossible Bird* . . . . (Upstart)
The Sopranos-Music From The HBO Original Series . . . . (Sony Music Soundtrax)
Biggest Hurt, The
Barbara Fairchild; *The Biggest Hurt* . . . . (Audiograph)
Bingo Fever
Da Yoopers; *Camp Fever* . . . . (You Guys)
Bitter Pill
Motley Crue; *Motley Crue's Greatest Hits* . . . . (Beyond)
Blister
Our Lady Peace; *Happiness...Is Not A Fish That You Can Catch* . . . . (Columbia)
Blister In The Sun
Violent Femmes; *ST/Gross Pointe Blank* . . . . (Mercury)
Blistered
Johnny Cash; *Johnny Cash-16 Biggest Hits-#2* . . . . (Legacy)
Blistering
Machine Head; *The More Things Change...* . . . . (Roadrunner)
Blue Moon With Heartache
Rosanne Cash; *19 Hot Country Requests-#2-C* . . . . (Epic)
Rosanne Cash-Hits-1979-1989 . . . . (Columbia)
Seven Year Ache . . . . (Columbia)
Breakout
Foo Fighters; *There Is Nothing Left To Lose* . . . . (Roswell/RCA)
Bumble Bee
LaVern Baker; *Live In Hollywood '91* . . . . (Rhino)
Searchers; *Searchers' Greatest Hits* . . . . (Rhino)
Bush Doctor
Peter Tosh; *Bush Doctor* . . . . (Rolling Stones)
Captured Live . . . . (EMI)
The Toughest . . . . (Capitol)
Call The Doctor
J.J. Cale; *Naturally* . . . . (MCA)
Calling Dr. Love
Kiss; *Alive II* . . . . (Casablanca)
Double Platinum. . . . . (Mercury)
Rock & Roll Over . . . . (Casablanca)
Smashes, Thrashes & Hits . . . . (Mercury)
Cancer
Filter; *Title Of Record* . . . . (Reprise)
Cat Fever
Little Feat; *Sailin' Shoes* . . . . (Warner Bros.)
Cat Scratch Fever
Ted Nugent; *Cat Scratch Fever* . . . . (Epic)
Double Live Gonzo . . . . (Epic)
Caught A Lite Sneeze
Tori Amos; *Boys For Pele* . . . . (Atlantic)
Chanel No. Fever
De La Soul; *ST/Men In Black.* . . . . (Columbia)
Chest Fever
Band; *Music From Big Pink* . . . . (Capitol)
Rock Of Ages. . . . . (Capitol)
The Band-Anthology-#1 . . . . (Capitol)
To Kingdom Come-The Definitive Collection . . . . (Capitol)
Chest Pains
Greg ''Fingers'' Taylor; *Chest Pains* . . . . (MCA)
Christmas Shoes
Newsong; *Sheltering Tree* . . . . (Benson/Jive)
Cigarette
Ben Folds Five; *Whatever And Ever Amen* . . . . (Caroline/550)
Clean My Wounds
Corrosion Of Conformity; *Deliverance* . . . . (Columbia)
Coconut
Nilsson; *Nilsson Schmilsson* . . . . (RCA)
Nilsson's Greatest Hits . . . . (RCA)
Songwriter . . . . (RCA)

Cold Contagious
Bush; *Razorblade Suitcase.* . . . . (Trauma)
Cold Fever
Models; *Out Of Mind Out Of Sight.* . . . . (Geffen)
Come In Out Of The Pain
Doug Stone; *I Thought It Was You* . . . . (Epic)
Connection
Montrose; *Paper Money.* . . . . (Warner Bros.)
Constipated Duck
Jeff Beck; *Blow By Blow* . . . . (Epic)
Constipated Monkey
Kain; *The Blue Guerilla* . . . . (Collectables)
Constipation Blues
Screamin' Jay Hawkins; *Voodoo Jive: Best Of Screamin' Jay Hawkins* . . . . (Rhino)
Contagious
Whispers; *So Good.* . . . . (Solar)
Contagious
Y & T; *Contagious.* . . . . (Geffen)
Convulsion
Skinny Puppy; *Too Dark Park* . . . . (Capitol)
Cosmetic Surgery
Dixie Carter; *Dixie Carter Sings John Wallowitch Live At The Carlyle* . . . (DRG)
John Wallowitch; *My Manhattan* . . . . (DRG)
Crash Course In Brain Surgery
Metallica; *Garage Days Re-Revisited* . . . . (Elektra)
Crippled Inside
John Lennon/Plastic Ono Band; *Imagine* . . . . (Capitol)
Cry Baby
Enchanters; *Billboard Top R&B Hits-1963-C* . . . . (Rhino)
Soul Shots-#5-La-La Means I Love You-C . . . . (Rhino)
Garnet Mimms; *18 Soulful Ballads-C* . . . . (Rhino)
Beg, Scream & Shout! The Big Ol' Box Of '60s Soul-C . . . (Rhino)
Janis Joplin; *Janis Joplin's Greatest Hits.* . . . . (Columbia)
Pearl . . . . (Legacy)
ST/Janis. . . . . (Columbia)
Cure Me...Or Kill Me
Gilby Clarke; *Pawnshop Guitars* . . . . (Virgin)
Cure, The
Nitty Gritty Dirt Band; *Dirt, Silver & Gold* . . . . (One Way)
Uncle Charlie And His Dog Teddy . . . . (Liberty)
D.O.C. & The Doctor
D.O.C.; *No One Can Do It Better.* . . . . (Ruthless)
Daysleeper
R.E.M.; *Up.* . . . . (Warner Bros.)
Daytime Nightime Suffering
Wings; *Back To The Egg* . . . . (Capitol)
Dear Doctor
Rolling Stones; *Beggars Banquet.* . . . . (Abkco)
Dear Uncle Sam
Loretta Lynn; *Honky Tonk Girl: The Loretta Lynn Collection* . . . . (MCA)
Loretta Lynn's Greatest Hits . . . . (MCA)
Desperately Wanting
Better Than Ezra; *Friction, Baby* . . . . (Swell/Elektra)
Disco Doctor
Robert Parker; *Golden Classics-Barefootin'* . . . . (Collectables)
Dizzy
Tommy Roe; *Original Classic Oldies Of The '60s-#10-C* . . . . (MCA)
Super Hits-#1-C . . . . (Gusto)
Tommy Roe's Greatest Hits. . . . . (MCA)
Dizzy Spells
Benny Goodman; *Carnegie Hall Jazz Concert* . . . . (Columbia)
Do You Really Want To Hurt Me
Culture Club; *Billboard Top Hits-1983-C* . . . . (Rhino)
Kissing To Be Clever. . . . . (Virgin)
Doc's Guitar
Doc Watson; *Doc Watson* . . . . (Vanguard)
On Stage (Featuring Merle Watson) . . . . (Vanguard)
Out In The Country . . . . (Intermedia)
Doc's Tune
Pure Prairie League; *Pure Prairie League* . . . . (RCA)
Doctor
Cheap Trick; *Doctor* . . . . (Epic)
Doctor
Doobie Brothers; *Cycles* . . . . (Warner Bros.)
Doctor
INXS; *INXS* . . . . (Atco)
Doctor
Wishbone Ash; *Wishbone Four* . . . . (MCA)
Doctor Boogie
Don Downing; *Doctor Boogie* . . . . (Roadshow)
Doctor Brown
Buster Brown; *Collectables Blues Collection-#2-C.* . . . . (Collectables)
New King Of The Blues . . . . (Collectables)
Fleetwood Mac; *Vintage Years* . . . . (Sire)
Doctor Do It Good
Vernon Burch; *Get Up* . . . . (Chocolate City)

Doctor Doctor
UFO; *Phenomenon* . . . .(Chrysalis)
  Strangers In The Night . . . .(Chrysalis)
Doctor Doctor
Who; *Magic Bus-The Who On Tour* . . . .(MCA)
Doctor Feelgood
Aretha Franklin; *Aretha Franklin-30 Greatest Hits* . . . . . . (Rhino)
  Aretha's Gold . . . .(Atlantic)
  Best Of Aretha Franklin . . . .(Atlantic)
  I Never Loved A Man The Way I Love You . . . .(Atlantic)
  Live At Fillmore West . . . .(Atlantic)
Doctor Hip
Country Joe McDonald; *Country Joe* . . . . (Vanguard)
  Essential Country Joe McDonald . . . . (Vanguard)
Doctor My Eyes
Jackson Browne; *Jackson Browne* . . . .(Asylum)
Doctor Time
Rick Trevino; *Rick Trevino* . . . .(Columbia)
Doctor Wu
Steely Dan; *Katy Lied* . . . .(MCA)
  Steely Dan's Greatest Hits . . . .(MCA)
Doctor! Doctor!
Thompson Twins; *Greatest Mixes-Best Of The Thompson Twins* . . . . . (Arista)
  Into The Gap . . . .(Arista)
Doctor's Orders
Joe Stampley; *Memory Lane* . . . .(Epic)
Oak Ridge Boys; *Bobby Sue* . . . .(MCA)
Don't Call Me No Doctor
Pyramid; *Pyramid* . . . .(Bang)
Don't Pick It Up
Offspring; *Ixnay On The Hombre* . . . . (Columbia)
Don't Speak
No Doubt; *Tragic Kingdom* . . . . (Trauma)
Don't Tear Me Up
Mick Jagger; *Wandering Spirit* . . . .(Atlantic)
Don't You Care
Buckinghams; *Buckinghams' Greatest Hits* . . . . (Columbia)
Don't You Ever Get Tired Of Hurtin' Me
Ray Price; *Ray Price's Greatest Hits-#2* . . . . (Step One)
Ronnie Milsap; *Stranger Things Have Happened* . . . . (RCA)
Dose Of You
Nick Lowe; *Labour Of Lust* . . . . (Columbia)
Down With Disease
Phish; *Hoist* . . . . (Elektra)
Down With The Sickness
Disturbed; *The Sickness* . . . .(Giant)
Dr. Funkenstein
Parliament; *Parliament Live/P. Funk Earth Tour* . . . .(Casablanca)
  The Clones Of Dr. Funkenstein . . . .(Casablanca)
Dr. Heckyll & Mr. Jive
Men At Work; *Cargo* . . . . (Columbia)
Dr. Jimmy
Who; *ST/Quadrophenia* . . . .(MCA)
Dr. Love
Whispers; *Excellence* . . . .(Allegiance)
  Shhhh . . . .(Dore)
Dr. Love
Bananarama; *Deep Sea Skiving* . . . . (London)
Dr. Music
Blue Oyster Cult; *Extraterrestrial Live* . . . . (Columbia)
  Mirrors . . . .(Columbia)
Dr. Robert
Beatles; *''Yesterday''...And Today* . . . . (Capitol)
  Revolver . . . .(Capitol)
Drive The Pain
Soup Dragons; *Lovegod* . . . .(Big Life)
Dyslexic Heart
Paul Westerberg; *ST/Singles* . . . .(Epic)
Earache My Eye featuring Alice Bowie
Cheech & Chong; *Dr. Demento: 20th Anniversary Collection-C* . . . . . (Rhino)
  Greatest Hit . . . .(Warner Bros.)
  Wedding Album . . . .(Warner Bros.)
Easy On The Pain
Michael Martin Murphey; *Cowboy Songs Four* . . . . (Valley Entert.)
Epistle To Dippy
Donovan; *Donovan's Greatest Hits* . . . .(Epic)
Every Little Bit Hurts
Brenda Holloway; *Motown Love Songs-C* . . . . (Motown)
  Motown Memories-#2-C . . . .(Motown)
  Motown Story-First 25 Years-C . . . .(Motown)
Gladys Knight & The Pips; *Gladys Knight & The Pips-Anthology* . . . . (Motown)
  Motown Legends-Gladys Knight & The Pips . . . . (Motown)
Spencer Davis Group; *Best Of The Spencer Davis Group* . . . .(EMI)
  Best Of The Spencer Davis Group . . . .(Rhino)
Every Morning
Sugar Ray; *14:59* . . . . (Lava)
Everybody Hurts
R.E.M.; *Automatic For The People* . . . .(Warner Bros.)

Diana, Princess Of Wales-Tribute-C . . . . (Columbia)
Everybody's Free (To Wear Sunscreen)
Baz Luhrmann; *Now That's What I Call Music!-#2-C* . . . .(Virgin)
  Something For Everybody . . . .(Capitol)
Everything For Free
K's Choice; *Cocoon Choice* . . . .(550 Music)
Ex-Factor
Lauryn Hill; *The Miseducation Of Lauryn Hill* . . . . (Ruffhouse/Columbia)
Fake Plastic Trees
Radiohead; *Bends* . . . .(Capitol)
  ST/Clueless . . . .(Capitol)
Feel A Whole Lot Better
Flamin' Groovies; *Flamin' Groovies Now* . . . .(Sire)
Gene Clark; *Firebyrd* . . . . (Takoma)
Feel The Pain
Dinosaur Jr.; *Without A Sound* . . . .(Sire)
Feelin' Alright?
Dave Mason; *Best Of Dave Mason* . . . . (Columbia)
  Certified Live . . . .(Columbia)
  Dave Mason's Greatest Hits . . . .(Columbia)
  Skatetown U.S.A.-C . . . .(Columbia)
  U.S.A. . . . .(MCA)
Joe Cocker; *Joe Cocker's Greatest Hits* . . . . (A&M)
  Mad Dogs & Englishmen . . . .(A&M)
  Rockin' '60s-C . . . .(Priority)
  With A Little Help From My Friends . . . .(A&M)
Feelin' Stronger Every Day
Chicago; *Chicago IX-Chicago's Greatest Hits* . . . . (Chicago)
  Chicago VI . . . .(Chicago)
  Group Portrait . . . .(Chicago)
  If You Leave Me Now . . . .(Chicago)
Fever
Buddy Guy; *This Is Buddy Guy* . . . . (Vanguard)
Elvis Presley; *A Valentine Gift For You* . . . .(RCA)
  Aloha from Hawaii via Satellite . . . .(RCA)
  Elvis Presley-Pure Gold . . . .(RCA)
Little Willie John; *Best Of Little Willie John-Fever* . . . . (Rhino)
Peggy Lee; *Memories Are Made Of This-C* . . . .(Capitol)
Rita Coolidge; *Rita Coolidge-Classics-#5* . . . .(A&M)
  Rita Coolidge's Greatest Hits . . . .(A&M)
Fever
Aerosmith; *Get A Grip* . . . .(Geffen)
Fever
Garth Brooks; *Fresh Horses* . . . . (Capitol)
  Garth Brooks-Double Live . . . . (Capitol)
Fever
Bruce Springsteen; *18 Tracks* . . . . (Columbia)
Southside Johnny And The Asbury Jukes; *Cover Me (Bruce Springsteen Tribute)-C* . . . . (Rhino)
  Havin' A Party With Southside Johnny And The Asbury Jukes . . . . . (Epic)
  I Don't Want To Go Home . . . .(Epic)
Flagpole Sitta
Harvey Danger; *Now That's What I Call Music!-#1-C* . . . . (Virgin)
  Where Have All The Merrymakers Gone . . . .(Slash)
Fool In Love
Michael Smotherman; *ST/Always* . . . .(MCA)
For You
Bruce Springsteen; *Greetings From Asbury Park, N.J.* . . . . . (Columbia)
Greg Kihn; *Kihnsolidation-Best Of Greg Kihn* . . . . (Rhino)
  Unkihntrollable-Live . . . . (Rhino)
Manfred Mann's Earth Band; *Chance* . . . . (Warner Bros.)
Forty Six & 2
Tool; *Aenima* . . . . (Freeworld/Capitol)
Found A Peanut
Wonder Kids; *Really Silly Songs* . . . .(Madacy)
Freak
Silverchair; *Freak Show* . . . .(Epic)
Girl, I've Been Hurt
Snow; *12 Inches Of Snow* . . . . (East West)
Good Bye
Martina McBride; *Emotion* . . . .(RCA)
Good Lovin'
Grateful Dead; *Shakedown Street* . . . . (Arista)
Rascals; *Hit Singles-1958-1977-C* . . . .(Atlantic)
  Rascals' Greatest Hits . . . .(Atlantic)
  Rascals-Super Hits . . . .(Atlantic)
  ST/Big Chill . . . .(Motown)
Goodbye To You
Scandal; *I Am Woman-C* . . . . (Nick At Nite)
  Patty Smyth's Greatest Hits Featuring Scandal . . . .(Legacy)
Groundzero (In Our Hearts You Remain)
Cash & Computa; *Groundzero (In Our Hearts You Remain)-CD Single* . . . .(Select)
Hand Song, The
Nickel Creek; *Nickel Creek* . . . . (Sugar Hill)
Happy Birthday Dear Heartache
Barbara Mandrell; *Barbara Mandrell's Greatest Hits* . . . .(MCA)
  Country Classics-#1-C . . . . (Universal)
  Today's Country Classics-C . . . . (MCA Special Prod.)

Hard Times Come Easy
Richie Sambora; *Undiscovered Soul* . . . .(Mercury)
Have You Ever Loved A Woman
Derek And The Dominos; *Layla* . . . . (Polydor)
Haven't Got Time For The Pain
Carly Simon; *Best Of Carly Simon* . . . . (Elektra)
Hotcakes . . . . (Elektra)
Hay Fever
Kinks; *Misfits* . . . .(Arista)
Headache Tomorrow (Or A Heartache Tonight)
Mickey Gilley; *Mickey Gilley's Biggest Hits* . . . . (Epic)
Ten Years Of Hits . . . . (Epic)
That's All That Matters To Me . . . . (Epic)
Healing
Wynonna & Michael English; *ST/Silent Fall.* . . . .(Curb)
Healing Game
Van Morrison; *The Healing Game* . . . .(A&M)
Healing Hands
Elton John; *Sleeping With The Past* . . . . (MCA)
Healing Hands Of Time
Willie Nelson; *Healing Hands Of Time* . . . . (Liberty)
Heart Attack
Olivia Newton-John; *Olivia Newton-John's Greatest Hits-#2* . . (MCA)
Physical . . . . (MCA)
Heart Trouble
Steve Wariner; *Country Classics-#3-1984-1985-C* . . . .(Universal)
One Good Night Deserves Another. . . . . (MCA)
Steve Wariner's Greatest Hits . . . . (MCA)
Heart Trouble
Martina McBride; *The Way That I Am* . . . .(RCA)
Heartaches
Marcels; *The Doo Wop Box II* . . . . (Rhino)
Patsy Cline; *The Patsy Cline Story* . . . . (MCA)
Ted Weems & His Orchestra; *Billboard Pop Memories-1945-1949-C* . . .(Rhino)
Nipper's Greatest Hits Of The '40s-#2-C . . . (RCA)
Heartaches By The Number
Guy Mitchell; *Sentimental Journey-C* . . . .(Dominion Entert.)
Sunshine Guitar . . . . (Collectables)
Unforgettable-Love Songs-Fabulous '50s-C . . . .(Dominion Entert.)
Ray Price; *Columbia Country Classics-#2-Honky Tonk Heroes-C* . . . (Columbia)
Ray Price's Greatest Hits . . . .(Columbia)
Ray Price's Greatest Hits-#1-3. . . . .(Step One)
Heartbreak Town
Dixie Chicks; *Fly.* . . . . (Monument)
Heirloom
Bjork; *Vespertine.* . . . . (Elektra)
Hello Mr. Heartache
Dixie Chicks; *Fly.* . . . . (Monument)
Here Comes The Rain
Mavericks; *Music For All Occasions* . . . . (MCA)
He's A Heartache (Looking For A Place To Happen)
Janie Fricke; *19 Hot Country Requests-C* . . . . (Epic)
It Ain't Easy . . . . (Columbia)
Janie Fricke-17 Greatest Hits. . . . . (Columbia)
Very Best Of Janie Fricke . . . .(Columbia)
High Blood Pressure
Huey "Piano" Smith And The Clowns; *Serious Clownin'-History Of Huey "Piano" Smith And The Clowns* . . . . (Rhino)
High Blood Pressure
Paula Lockheart & Peter Ecklund; *Paula Lockheart & Peter Ecklund* . . . .(Flying Fish)
Hole In My Soul
Aerosmith; *Nine Lives* . . . . (Columbia)
Hope You're Feeling Better
Santana; *Abraxas.* . . . . (Columbia)
Rock Classics-#2-C . . . . (K-Tel)
Santana's Greatest Hits . . . .(Columbia)
Hospital Lady
Loudon Wainwright III; *Loudon Wainwright III* . . . . (Atlantic)
Hospital Song
Ben Folds Five; *The Unauthorized Biography Of Reinhold Messner* . . . . (550 Music)
Hot Blooded
Foreigner; *Double Vision.* . . . . (Atlantic)
Records. . . . . (Atlantic)
ST/Vision Quest . . . . (Geffen)
Hotel Illness
Black Crowes; *Southern Harmony & Musical Companion* . . . . . .(Def American)
House Of Pain
Van Halen; *1984* . . . . (Warner Bros.)
House Of Pain
Faster Pussycat; *Wake Me When It's Over.* . . . . (Elektra)
How Can I Ease The Pain
Lisa Fischer; *So Intense.* . . . . (Elektra)
How Can I Help You Say Goodbye
Patty Loveless; *Only What I Feel.* . . . . (Epic)
Patty Loveless-Classics. . . . . (Epic)

How Could An Angel Break My Heart
Kenny G with Toni Braxton; *Kenny G's Greatest Hits* . . . .(Arista)
Toni Braxton with Kenny G; *Diana, Princess Of Wales-Tribute-C* . . .(Columbia)
Secrets. . . . .(LaFace)
Hurt
Carly Simon; *Torch* . . . .(Warner Bros.)
Elvis Presley; *Always On My Mind* . . . . (RCA)
From Elvis Presley Boulevard, Memphis, Tennessee . . . . (RCA)
Juice Newton; *Old Flame* . . . . (RCA)
Little Anthony And The Imperials; *Best Of Little Anthony And The Imperials* . . . . (EMI)
Manhattans; *Manhattans Greatest Hits* . . . .(Columbia)
Hurt
Nine Inch Nails; *The Downward Spiral* . . . . (Interscope)
Hurt
Tom Petty And The Heartbreakers; *You're Gonna Get It!* . . . . (Gone Gator)
Hurt By Love
BoDeans; *Blend* . . . . (Reprise)
Hurt Her Once For Me
Wilburn Brothers; *Only Country-1965-1969-C* . . . . (JCI Assoc. Labels)
Hurt Me Bad (In A Real Good Way)
Patty Loveless; *Patty Loveless' Greatest Hits* . . . . (MCA)
Up Against My Heart. . . . . (MCA)
Hurt So Bad
Lettermen; *The Lettermen's All-Time Greatest Hits* . . . .(Capitol)
Linda Ronstadt; *Linda Ronstadt's Greatest Hits, Volume Two* . . . . (Asylum)
Mad Love. . . . .(Elektra)
Little Anthony And The Imperials; *Best Of Little Anthony And The Imperials* . . . .(Rhino)
Best Of Little Anthony And The Imperials . . . . (EMI)
Hurtin' Inside
Brook Benton; *Brook Benton-Golden Hits.* . . . .(Mercury)
Hurting Kind (I've Got My Eyes On You)
Robert Plant; *Manic Nirvana* . . . . (Es Paranza)
Hurts So Good
John Cougar; *American Fool* . . . .(Riva)
Hurts To Be In Love
Gino Vannelli; *Black Cars* . . . .(CBS Associated)
Hush Hush Hush
Paula Cole; *This Fire* . . . . (Imago)
I Ain't Got The Fever No More
Southside Johnny And The Asbury Jukes; *This Time It's For Real* . . . . (Epic)
I Disappear
Metallica; *ST/Mission: Impossible 2* . . . .(Hollywood)
I Don't Hurt Anymore
Hank Snow; *Stars Of The Grand Ole Opry-1926-1974-C* . . . . (RCA)
I Don't Need No Doctor
Humble Pie; *Best Of Humble Pie* . . . .(A&M)
Humble Pie-Classics-#14 . . . . (A&M)
Performance-Rockin' The Fillmore . . . . (A&M)
New Riders Of The Purple Sage; *Best Of New Riders Of The Purple Sage* . . . .(Columbia)
Ray Charles; *Ray Charles' Greatest Hits* . . . .(Rhino)
Ray Charles-Anthology. . . . .(Rhino)
I Feel Like Homemade Shit
Fugs; *Fugs' Greatest Hits* . . . .(PVC)
I Feel So Bad
Elvis Presley; *Elvis' Golden Records, Volume 3* . . . . (RCA)
Reconsider Baby . . . . (RCA)
The Top Ten Hits . . . . (RCA)
Worldwide 50 Gold Award Hits, Vol. 1, Parts 1 & 2 . . . . (RCA)
I Get The Fever
Bill Anderson; *Bill Anderson's Greatest Hits* . . . . (Varese Sarabande)
I Get Weak
Belinda Carlisle; *Heaven On Earth* . . . . (MCA)
I Go Wild
Rolling Stones; *Voodoo Lounge.* . . . . (Virgin)
I Got It Bad & That Ain't Good
Duke Ellington; *All Star Road Band* . . . .(Doctor Jazz)
Intimate . . . . (Pablo)
This Is Duke Ellington. . . . . (RCA)
Johnny Mathis; *In A Sentimental Mood-Johnny Mathis Sings Ellington.* . . . .(Columbia)
I Guess It Never Hurts To Hurt Sometimes
Oak Ridge Boys; *Deliver* . . . . (MCA)
Oak Ridge Boys' Greatest Hits 2 . . . . (MCA)
I Hurt For You
Conway Twitty; *Final Touches* . . . . (MCA)
Deborah Allen; *45-#13776.* . . . . (RCA)
I Just Cut Myself
Ronnie McDowell; *Love To Burn* . . . . (Epic)
I Think I Got It (V.D.)
Legs Diamond; *Diamond Is A Hard Rock* . . . .(Mercury)
I Will Take You There
Nilsson; *ST/Skidoo* . . . . (RCA)
If I Didn't Have A Goiter
Johnny Socko; *Oh I Do Hope It's Roast Beef.* . . . .(Bib)
If I Fell
Beatles; *Beatles-Love Songs* . . . . (Capitol)

Something New . . . . (Capitol)
ST/A Hard Day's Night . . . . (Capitol)
I'll Be Here Awhile
311; *From Chaos* . . . .(Volcano Entertainment)
I'll Never Break Your Heart
Backstreet Boys; *Backstreet Boys* . . . . (Jive)
Now That's What I Call Music!-#2-C . . . . (Virgin)
I'm Not A Well Man
Original Cast; *I Can Get It For You Wholesale* . . . . (Columbia)
I'm Tore Down
Eric Clapton; *From The Cradle* . . . . (Duck/Reprise)
Infekshun
Ron Wood; *Gimme Some Neck* . . . . (Columbia)
Influenza
Todd Rundgren; *Ever Popular Tortured Artist Effect* . . . . (Rhino)
It Doesn't Have To Hurt Everytime
Johnny Mathis; *First 25 Years-Silver Anniversary Album* . . . . (Columbia)
It Don't Hurt
Sheryl Crow; *The Globe Sessions* . . . . (A&M)
It Hurt Me Too
Marvin Gaye; *Marvin Gaye's Greatest Hits* . . . . (Motown)
That Stubborn Kinda Fellow . . . . (Motown)
It Hurts As Much In Texas (As It Did In Tennessee)
George Jones & Ricky Van Shelton; *Friends In High Places-C* . . . .(Epic)
It Hurts Me Too
Bob Dylan; *Self Portrait* . . . . (Columbia)
Elmore James; *Golden Classics-Elmore James* . . . . (Collectables)
Eric Clapton; *From The Cradle* . . . . (Duck/Reprise)
It Hurts Me Too
Keb' Mo'; *The Door* . . . . (550/Epic/Okeh)
It Hurts To Be In Love
Betty Everett; *Very Best Of Betty Everett* . . . .(Vee-Jay)
Gene Pitney; *Gene Pitney-Anthology 1961-1968* . . . . (Rhino)
Gene Pitney's Greatest Hits . . . .(Evergreen Music)
It Might As Well Be Spring
Bing Crosby; *The Radio Years: 25 Songs* . . . .(Crescendo)
Frank Sinatra; *Days Of Wine And Roses, Moon River, And Other Academy
Award Winners* . . . . (Reprise)
Sinatra & Strings . . . . (Reprise)
Sarah Vaughan; *Divine Sarah Vaughan-Columbia Years-1949-
1953* . . . . (Columbia)
It Only Hurts When I Cry
Dwight Yoakam; *If There Was A Way* . . . . (Reprise)
It's Going To Take Some Time
Carole King; *A Natural Woman: The Ode Collection-1968-1976* . . . . . (Legacy)
Music . . . . (Epic)
Carpenters; *A Song For You* . . . . (A&M)
Carpenters-The Singles 1969-1973 . . . . (A&M)
Yesterday Once More . . . . (A&M)
I've Been Hurt
Bill Deal & The Rhondels; *Best Of Bill Deal & The Rhondels* . . . . . . (Rhino)
Oldies But Goodies-#7-C . . . . (Original Sound)
Soul Shots-#2-The "In" Crowd-Sweet Soul-C . . . . (Rhino)
Soul Shots-#6-Blue-Eyed Soul-C . . . . (Rhino)
I've Had Enough
Regina Belle; *Believe In Me* . . . .(MCA)
Jack, The (V.D.)
AC/DC; *High Voltage* . . . . (Atco)
If You Want Blood You've Got It . . . .(Atlantic)
Joy And Pain
Maze & Kurtis Blow; *Lifelines-#1* . . . . (Capitol)
Maze featuring Frankie Beverly; *Live In Los Angeles* . . . . (Capitol)
Live In New Orleans . . . . (Capitol)
Joy And Pain
Donna Allen; *Heaven On Earth* . . . . (Oceana)
Joy And Pain
Rob Base & D.J. EZ-Rock; *It Takes Two* . . . . (Profile)
Jumper
Third Eye Blind; *Third Eye Blind* . . . . (Elektra)
Totally Hits-#1-C . . . . (Arista)
Jungle Fever
Stevie Wonder; *ST/Jungle Fever* . . . . (Motown)
Just Can't Last
Natalie Merchant; *Motherland* . . . . (Elektra)
Just Dropped In (To See What Condition My Condition Was In)
First Edition; *Even More Nuggets-C* . . . . (Rhino)
Kenny Rogers; *Kenny Rogers' Greatest Hits* . . . .(MCA)
Ten Years Of Gold . . . .(EMI)
Just Like You
Keb' Mo'; *Just Like You* . . . . (Okeh)
Just What The Doctor Ordered
Ted Nugent; *Double Live Gonzo* . . . . (Epic)
Ted Nugent . . . .(Epic)
Kevorkian
Public Enemy; *There's A Poison Goin On* . . . .(Atomic Pop)
King Of Pain
Police; *Every Breath You Take-The Classics* . . . . (A&M)
MTV's Rock 'N' Roll To Go-C . . . . (Elektra)

Synchronicity . . . . (A&M)
Kiss Away The Pain
Patti LaBelle; *Winner In You* . . . . (MCA)
Lady Doctor
Graham Parker; *Howlin' Wind* . . . . (Mercury)
Graham Parker And The Rumour; *The Parkerilla* . . . . (Mercury)
Lean On Me
Kirk Franklin; *The Nu Nation Project* . . . .(Gospo Centric/Interscope)
Like A Surgeon
"Weird Al" Yankovic; *"Weird Al" Yankovic's Greatest Hits* . . . .(Scotti Bros.)
Dare To Be Stupid . . . .(Scotti Bros.)
Lipstick And Bruises
Lit; *Atomic* . . . . (RCA)
Little Arrows
Leapy Lee; *Bubble Gum Classics-C* . . . . (MCA Special Prod.)
Country Music Classics-#3-1965-1970-C . . . . (K-Tel)
Little Bit Of You
Lee Roy Parnell; *We All Get Lucky Sometimes* . . . .(Career)
Little Town Flirt
Del Shannon; *Del Shannon's Greatest Hits* . . . . (Rhino)
Del Shannon's Greatest Hits . . . . (Curb)
Living With A Hernia
"Weird Al" Yankovic; *"Weird Al" Yankovic's Greatest Hits* . . . .(Scotti Bros.)
Polka Party . . . .(Scotti Bros.)
Living With AIDS
Romanovsky & Phillips; *Brave Boys-Best & More Of Romanovsky &
Phillips* . . . . (Fresh Fruit)
Emotional Rollercoaster . . . . (Fresh Fruit)
London Homesick Blues
David Allan Coe; *David Allan Coe's Biggest Hits* . . . . (Legacy)
Jerry Jeff Walker; *Great Gonzos* . . . . (MCA)
Viva Terlingua . . . . (MCA)
London Rain (Nothing Heals Like You Do)
Heather Nova; *Siren* . . . . (Big Cat)
Songs From Dawson's Creek . . . . (Sony Music Soundtrax)
Lookin' Good But Feelin' Bad
Original Cast; *Ain't Misbehavin'* . . . .(RCA)
Love All The Hurt Away
George Benson; *George Benson-Collection* . . . . (Warner Bros.)
Love Disease
Butterfield Blues Band; *The Butterfield Blues Band/Live* . . . . (Elektra)
Love Hangover
Diana Ross; *20 Greatest Songs In Motown History-C* . . . . (Motown)
20/20-C . . . . (Motown)
Diana Ross-All The Great Hits . . . . (Motown)
Diana Ross-Anthology . . . . (Motown)
Diana Ross-The Ultimate Collection . . . . (Motown)
Love Hurt Me Love Healed Me
Lenny Williams; *Love Current* . . . . (MCA)
Love Hurts
Cher; *Love Hurts* . . . . (Geffen)
Emmylou Harris & Gram Parsons; *Duets-C* . . . . (Reprise)
Gram Parsons; *Grievous Angel* . . . . (Reprise)
Jim Capaldi; *The Island Story-1962-1987-25th Anniversary-C* . . . . (Island)
Judy Collins; *Bread & Roses* . . . . (Elektra)
Nazareth; *Hair Of The Dog* . . . . (A&M)
Hot Tracks . . . . (A&M)
Nazareth-Classics-#16 . . . . (A&M)
'Snaz . . . . (A&M)
Roy Orbison; *Legendary Roy Orbison* . . . . (Sony Music Special Prod.)
Roy Orbison's All-Time Greatest Hits-#1 & 2 . . . . (Monument)
Love Hurts
Ralph Tresvant; *Ralph Tresvant* . . . . (MCA)
Love Hurts
Jon B.; *Cool Relax* . . . .(Yab Yum/550)
Love Hurts Love Heals
Daryl Hall & John Oates; *Beauty On A Back Street* . . . . (RCA)
Love Is A Hurtin' Thing
Lou Rawls; *Best Of Lou Rawls* . . . . (Capitol)
Lou Rawls-Live (Right Stuff) . . . . (Right Stuff)
Soul Shots-#5-La-La Means I Love You-C . . . . (Rhino)
Love Is Like An Itching In My Heart
Diana Ross & The Supremes; *Beg, Scream & Shout! The Big Ol' Box Of
'60s Soul-C* . . . . (Rhino)
Love Is The Healing
Roberta Flack & Donny Hathaway; *Blue Lights In The Basement* . . . . .(Atlantic)
Love Letters In The Sand
Mac Wiseman; *24 Greatest Bluegrass Hits-C* . . . . (C.M.H. Prod.)
Pat Boone; *Best Of Pat Boone* . . . . (MCA)
Pat Boone-16 Great Performances . . . . (MCA)
Vintage Music-#2-C . . . . (MCA)
Ted Black & His Orchestra; *78-#22799* . . . . (Victor)
Love Shouldn't Hurt
All Star Group; *Love Shouldn't Hurt-C* . . . .(Qwest)
Love Sick
Bob Dylan; *Time Out Of Mind* . . . . (Columbia)
Love-itis
J. Geils Band; *Blow Your Face Out* . . . . (Rhino)

Hotline .... (Atlantic)
Love's Got A Hold On You
Alan Jackson; *Don't Rock The Jukebox* .... (Arista)
Love's The Only House
Martina McBride; *Emotion* .... (RCA)
Lovesick Blues
Gary Morris; *Plain Brown Wrapper* .... (Warner Bros.)
Hank Williams With His Drifting Cowboys; *24 Of Hank Williams'*
    Greatest Hits .... (Polydor)
    Lovesick Blues .... (Polydor)
Linda Ronstadt; *Linda Ronstadt-Retrospective* .... (Capitol)
    Silk Purse .... (Capitol)
Patsy Cline; *Live At The Opry* .... (MCA)
Ryan Adams; *Timeless: Hank Williams Tribute-C* ..... (Lost Highway/IDJMG)
Make Me Bad
Korn; *Issues* .... (Immortal/Epic)
Mammas Don't Let Your Babies Grow Up To Be Cowboys
Gibson/Miller Band; *Cowboy Super Hits-C* .... (Columbia)
    ST/The Cowboy Way .... (Epic)
Waylon Jennings & Willie Nelson; *Waylon & Willie* .... (RCA)
    Waylon Jennings & Willie Nelson's Greatest Hits .... (RCA)
Willie Nelson; *Greatest Hits (& Some That Will Be)* .... (Columbia)
    ST/The Electric Horseman .... (Columbia)
    Willie & Family Live .... (Columbia)
Medicated Goo
Traffic; *Best Of Traffic* .... (Island)
    Last Exit .... (Island)
    Welcome To The Canteen .... (Island)
Medicine Jar
Wings; *Venus And Mars* .... (Capitol)
    Wings Over America .... (Capitol)
Medicine Man
George Benson; *Absolute Benson* .... (GRP/VMG)
Medicine Song
Stephanie Mills; *Greatest Hits In My Life* .... (Casablanca)
    I've Got The Cure .... (Casablanca)
Medicine Woman
Paul Davis; *Southern Tracks & Fantasies* .... (Bang)
Minnesota Massage
Mount Shasta; *Who's The Hottie* .... (Skin Graft)
Miracle Cure
Who; *Join Together* .... (MCA)
    ST/Tommy .... (Polydor)
    Tommy .... (MCA)
Murder (Or A Heart Attack)
Old 97's; *Fight Songs* .... (Elektra)
My Asthma Problem
John Trubee & The Ugly Janitors Of America; *Communists Are Coming To*
    Kill Us .... (Enigma)
My Gift To You
Korn; *Follow The Leader* .... (Immortal/Epic)
My Head Hurts, My Feet Stink And I Don't Love Jesus
Jimmy Buffett; *Havana Daydreamin'* .... (MCA)
My Heart Is Failing Me
Riff; *Riff* .... (SBK)
Narcolepsy
Ben Folds Five; *The Unauthorized Biography Of Reinhold*
    Messner .... (550 Music)
Needles And Pins
Jackie DeShannon; *Very Best Of Jackie DeShannon* .... (EMI)
Searchers; *History Of British Rock-#1-C* .... (Rhino)
    Searchers' Greatest Hits .... (Rhino)
Tom Petty And The Heartbreakers; *Pack Up The Plantation-Live!* ..... (MCA)
Never Let You Go
Third Eye Blind; *Blue* .... (Elektra)
    Totally Hits-#2-C .... (Elektra)
Night Fever
Bee Gees; *Bee Gees' Greatest* .... (Polydor)
    ST/Saturday Night Fever .... (Polydor)
No More Drama
Mary J. Blige; *No More Drama* .... (MCA)
Nothin' But A Heartache
Doobie Brothers; *Livin' On The Fault Line* .... (Warner Bros.)
Nothing But A Heartache
Flirtations; *Soul Shots-#2-The "In" Crowd-Sweet Soul-C* .... (Rhino)
Nothing But Heartaches
Diana Ross & The Supremes; *Diana Ross & The Supremes'*
    Greatest Hits .... (Motown)
    Diana Ross & The Supremes-Anthology (1962-1969) .... (Motown)
    Motown Story-First 25 Years-C .... (Motown)
    Motown Superstar Series-#1-Diana Ross & The Supremes .... (Motown)
Novocaine For The Soul
Eels; *Beautiful Freak* .... (DreamWorks/SKG)
One Angry Dwarf And 200 Solemn Faces
Ben Folds Five; *Whatever And Ever Amen* .... (Caroline/550)
Only Love Is Worth This Pain
Country Joe McDonald; *Hold On It's Coming* .... (Vanguard)
Ooh! My Feet!
Original Broadway Cast; *Most Happy Fella* .... (Sony Music Classical)

Ordinary Pain
Stevie Wonder; *Songs In The Key Of Life* .... (Motown)
Out Of My Bones
Randy Travis; *You And You Alone* .... (DreamWorks/SKG)
Outside
Staind; *Break The Cycle* .... (Flip/Elektra)
P.M.S. Blues
Dolly Parton; *Heart Songs* .... (Columbia)
Pac-Man Fever
Buckner & Garcia; *Pac Man Fever* .... (Columbia)
Pain
Stereomud; *Perfect Self* .... (Loud)
Pain In My Heart
Otis Redding; *Best Of Otis Redding* .... (Atco)
    History Of Otis Redding .... (Atco)
    In Person At The Whisky A Go Go .... (Rhino)
    Pain In My Heart .... (Atco)
    The Otis Redding Story .... (Atlantic)
Rolling Stones; *The Rolling Stones, Now!* .... (Abkco)
Pain In My Heart
David Johansen; *David Johansen* .... (Blue Sky)
Paralysed
Gang Of Four; *Brief History Of The Twentieth Century* ..... (Warner Bros.)
Paralyzed
Elvis Presley; *Elvis* .... (RCA)
    Million-Dollar Quartet .... (RCA)
Paralyzed
Dave Mason; *Best Of Dave Mason* .... (Columbia)
Paralyzed
Dave Edmunds Band; *I Hear You Rockin'* .... (Columbia)
Paralyzed
Black Flag; *In My Head* .... (SST)
Paralyzed
Rosanne Cash; *Interiors* .... (Columbia)
Paralyzed
Kiss; *Revenge* .... (Mercury)
Paralyzed
Ted Nugent; *State Of Shock* .... (Epic)
Paralyzed
Fabulous Thunderbirds; *Walk That Walk Talk That Talk* ...(Epic Portrait Assoc.)
Party Doll
Buddy Knox; *Best Of Buddy Knox* .... (Rhino)
    Billboard Top Rock 'N' Roll Hits-1957-C .... (Rhino)
    ST/American Graffiti .... (MCA)
Pearl, The
Emmylou Harris; *Red Dirt Girl* .... (Nonesuch)
Penny Lane
Beatles; *Beatles 1* .... (Capitol)
    Magical Mystery Tour .... (Capitol)
    The Beatles/1967-1970 .... (Capitol)
    The Beatles-Anthology-#2 .... (Capitol)
People That We Love, The
Bush; *Golden State* .... (Atlantic)
Pervert Nurse
D.I.; *Horse Bites Dog Cries* .... (Triple X Entert.)
Pins And Needles
Whites; *Forever You* .... (Curb/MCA)
    Whites' Greatest Hits .... (Curb)
Plastic Surgery
Adam & The Ants; *Fun Filth & Fury* .... (Blue Plate)
Plop, Plop, Fizz, Fizz (Alka-Seltzer)
Original Soundtrack; *TeeVee Toons-The Commercials-#1-C* .... (TVT)
PMS
Mary J. Blige; *No More Drama* .... (MCA)
Pneumonia Blues
Lightnin' Hopkins; *How Many More Years I Got* .... (Fantasy)
Poison Ivy
Coasters; *Atlantic Rhythm & Blues 1947-1974-#4 (1958-1962)-C* .... (Atlantic)
    Billboard Top R&B Hits-1959-C .... (Rhino)
    Coasters' Greatest Hits .... (Atco)
    Coasters-Their Greatest Recordings-Early Years .... (Atco)
    More American Graffiti-C .... (MCA)
Nylons; *Rockapella* .... (Windham Hill)
    ST/Stealing Home .... (Atlantic)
Rolling Stones; *More Hot Rocks (big hits & fazed cookies)* .... (Abkco)
Poison Was The Cure
Megadeth; *Rust In Peace* .... (Capitol)
Postpone The Pain
Mark Chesnutt; *Longnecks & Short Stories* .... (MCA)
Price Of Love
Bryan Ferry; *Let's Stick Together* .... (Virgin)
Cactus Brothers; *Cactus Brothers* .... (Liberty)
Everly Brothers; *The Reunion Concert-Live At Albert Hall 1983* ..... (Mercury)
    Walk Right Back: The Everly Brothers On Warner Bros.-1960-
    1969 .... (Warner Archives)
Poco; *Crazy Loving-Best Of Poco-1975-1982* .... (MCA)
Promised Land
Bruce Springsteen; *Darkness On The Edge Of Town* .... (Columbia)

Bruce Springsteen & The E Street Band; *Bruce Springsteen & The E Street Band Live/1975-85* . . . . (Legacy)

Puke & Cry
Dinosaur Jr.; *Green Mind* . . . . (Sire)
Just Say Anything-#5 Of Just Say Yes-C. . . . . (Sire)

Purple People Eater Meets The Witch Doctor
Big Bopper; *Hellooo Baby! Best Of The Big Bopper-1954-1959* . . . . (Rhino)

Ramblin' Fever
Merle Haggard; *Merle Haggard's Greatest Hits* . . . .(MCA)
More Of The Best . . . .(Rhino)
Ramblin' Fever . . . .(MCA)
Merle Haggard & Alabama; *For The Record: Merle Haggard-43 Legendary Hits* . . . . (BNA)

Remedy
Black Crowes; *Southern Harmony & Musical Companion* . . . . . (Def American)

Return Of Dr. X
UB40; *Present Arms* . . . . (Virgin)

Return Of The Mack
Mark Morrison; *Return Of The Mack* . . . .(Atlantic)

Ring Of Fire
Country Joe McDonald; *Best Of Country Joe McDonald-The Vanguard Years-1969-1975* . . . . (Vanguard)
Tonight I'm Singing Just For You . . . . (Vanguard)
Dwight Yoakam; *Guitars, Cadillacs, Etc., Etc.* . . . . (Reprise)
Earl Scruggs & Billy Bob Thornton; *Earl Scruggs And Friends-C* . . . . . .(MCA)
Johnny Cash; *All Time Legends Of Country Music-C.* . . . . (Legacy)
Billboard Top Country Hits-1963-C . . . . (Rhino)
Classic Cash-Hall Of Fame Series. . . . . (Mercury)
Johnny Cash's Greatest Hits . . . . (Columbia)
The Man In Black-His Greatest Hits . . . . (Legacy)
Stan Ridgway & Wall Of Voodoo; *Best Of Stan Ridgway & Wall Of Voodoo* . . . .(I.R.S.)
Wall Of Voodoo; *Ugly Americans In Australia* . . . .(I.R.S.)

River Of Deceit
Mad Season; *Above.* . . . . (Columbia)

Road Fever
Foghat; *Foghat* . . . . (Rhino)
Foghat-Live . . . . (Rhino)

Road Fever
Blackfoot; *Strikes* . . . . (Atco)

Road To Dead
Paula Cole; *This Fire* . . . . (Imago)

Rock & Roll Doctor
Little Feat; *Feats Don't Fail Me Now* . . . .(Warner Bros.)
Hoy-Hoy! . . . .(Warner Bros.)

Rock & Roll Doctor
Travesty Ltd.; *Dr. Demento Presents The Greatest Novelty Records-#5-1980s-C.* . . . . (Rhino)

Rock & Roll Doctor
Black Sabbath; *Technical Ecstasy* . . . .(Warner Bros.)

Rock N Roll Disease
Green On Red; *Here Come The Snakes* . . . .(Restless)

Rockin' Pneumonia And The Boogie Woogie Flu
Aerosmith; *ST/Less Than Zero* . . . .(Def Jam)
Huey ''Piano'' Smith; *All-Star Chartbusters* . . . . (Intermedia)
Huey ''Piano'' Smith And The Clowns; *Jimpin' Jive '50s-C.* . . . . (Priority)
Johnny Rivers; *Best Of Johnny Rivers* . . . . (EMI)
Johnny Rivers-Anthology 1964-1977. . . . . (Rhino)
Professor Longhair; *Rock 'N' Roll Gumbo* . . . . (Dancing Cat)
Rodney Lay & Wild West; *Rockabilly Nuggets-C* . . . . (Sun)

Ross Memorial Hospital
Phil Cunningham; *Palomino Waltz.* . . . .(Green Linnet)

Ruby, Don't Take Your Love To Town
Kenny Rogers; *Kenny Rogers-20 Great Years* . . . . (Reprise)
Kenny Rogers-Twenty Greatest Hits . . . .(EMI)
Ten Years Of Gold . . . .(EMI)
Kenny Rogers And The First Edition; *Hits & Pieces* . . . . (MCA)
Kenny Rogers And The First Edition's Greatest Hits. . . . . (K-Tel)
Mel Tillis; *Best Of Mel Tillis.* . . . . (MCA)
Mel Tillis & The Statesiders; *Mel Tillis & The Statesiders-24 Great Hits* . . . . (MGM)
M-M-Mel Live . . . .(MCA)

Saturday Morning Fever
Loudon Wainwright III; *Fame & Wealth* . . . .(Rounder)

Scarlet Fever
Kenny Rogers; *We've Got Tonight* . . . . (Razor & Tie)

Seasick, Yet Still Docked
Morrissey; *Your Arsenal.* . . . . (Sire)

Seven Year Ache
Rosanne Cash; *Columbia Country Classics-#5-A New Tradition-C.* . . (Columbia)
Greatest Country Hits Of The '80s-1981-C . . . . (Columbia)
Hits-1979-1989 . . . . (Columbia)
Seven Year Ache . . . . (Columbia)

Sexual Healing
Marvin Gaye; *Last Concert Tour* . . . . (Giant)
Midnight Love . . . . (Columbia)
Seems Like Yesterday-#4-Early '80s-C . . . . (K-Tel)
Tribute To Black Entertainers-C . . . . (Columbia)
Max-A-Million; *Take Your Time* . . . . (S.O.S./Zoo)

Shadowboxer
Fiona Apple; *Tidal* . . . .(Clean Slate/Work)

Shake The Disease
Depeche Mode; *101* . . . .(Sire)
Catching Up With Depeche Mode . . . .(Sire)

Shape I'm In, The
Band; *Best Of The Band* . . . . (Capitol)
Rock Of Ages . . . . (Capitol)
Stage Fright . . . . (Capitol)
The Band-Anthology-#1 . . . . (Capitol)
The Last Waltz . . . . (Warner Bros.)
To Kingdom Come-The Definitive Collection. . . . . (Capitol)
Bob Dylan And The Band; *Before The Flood* . . . . (Columbia)

Shape I'm In, The
Marty Stuart; *Marty Stuart* . . . . (Columbia)

She Thinks His Name Was John
Reba McEntire; *Read My Mind* . . . . (MCA)
Reba McEntire's Greatest Hits-#3: I'm A Survivor . . . . (MCA)

She's Gonna Fly
Collin Raye; *Tracks.* . . . . (Epic)

Shotgun Blues
Blues Brothers; *Briefcase Full Of Blues* . . . .(Atlantic)

Shut Out The Light
Bruce Springsteen; *Tracks* . . . . (Columbia)

Sick & Beautiful
Artificial Joy Club; *Melt* . . . .(Interscope)

Sick Again
Led Zeppelin; *Physical Graffiti* . . . . (Swan Song)

Sick As A Dog
Aerosmith; *Live! Bootleg* . . . . (Columbia)
Rocks . . . . (Columbia)

Sick Of Myself
Matthew Sweet; *100% Fun* . . . .(Zoo)

Silver Threads And Golden Needles
Honky Tonk Angels; *Honky Tonk Angels* . . . . (Columbia)
Linda Ronstadt; *Don't Cry Now* . . . .(Asylum)
Hand Sown Home Grown . . . . (Capitol)
Linda Ronstadt-Retrospective . . . . (Capitol)
Linda Ronstadt's Greatest Hits . . . . (Asylum)
Springfields; *Troubadours Of The Folk Era-#3-C* . . . . (Rhino)

Sister Morphine
Marianne Faithull; *Blazing Away.* . . . . (Island)
Marianne Faithull's Greatest Hits . . . .(Abkco)
Rolling Stones; *Sticky Fingers* . . . . (Virgin)

Sister Of Pain
Vince Neil; *Exposed* . . . . (Warner Bros.)

Smiling Up The Frown
Agents Of Good Roots; *One By One* . . . . (RCA)
Where'd You Get That Vibe? . . . . (RCA)

So Hip It Hurts
ABC; *How To Be A Zillionaire* . . . . (Mercury)

Social Disease
Bon Jovi; *Slippery When Wet* . . . . (Jambco)

Social Disease
Elton John; *Goodbye Yellow Brick Road.* . . . . (Polydor)

Solitude
Edwin McCain; *Honor Among Thieves.* . . . . (Lava)
Edwin McCain & Darius Rucker; *VH-1 Crossroads-C.* . . . .(Atlantic)

Some Broken Hearts Never Mend
Don Williams; *Best Of Don Williams-#2* . . . . (MCA)
Don Williams-20 Greatest Hits . . . . (MCA)
Some Broken Hearts Never Mend. . . . . (MCA Special Prod.)

Somebody Get Me A Doctor
Van Halen; *Van Halen II* . . . . (Warner Bros.)

Sometimes It Hurts
Stabbing Westward; *Darkest Days* . . . . (Columbia)

Soul Doctor
Foreigner; *Very Best Of Foreigner...And Beyond* . . . .(Atlantic)

Soul Vaccination
Tower Of Power; *Tower Of Power* . . . . (Warner Bros.)

Souvenir Of London (V.D.)
Procol Harum; *Grand Hotel* . . . . (Chrysalis)

Spring Fever
Loretta Lynn; *Out Of My Head And Back In My Bed.* . . . . (MCA)

Spring Fever
Nantucket; *Nantucket* . . . . (Epic)

Spring Fever
Elvis Presley; *ST/Girl Happy* . . . . (RCA)

Standing In The Shadows Of Love
Barry White; *Barry White's Greatest Hits* . . . .(20th Century Fox)
I've Got So Much To Give. . . . .(20th Century Fox)
Four Tops; *Four Tops' Greatest Hits* . . . . (Motown)
Four Tops Reach Out . . . . (Motown)
Four Tops-Anthology . . . . (Motown)
Motown Story-First 25 Years-C . . . . (Motown)
Motown Superstar Series-#14-Four Tops . . . . (Motown)
Rod Stewart; *Blondes Have More Fun* . . . . (Warner Bros.)

Stone Cold Fever
Humble Pie; *Best Of Humble Pie.* . . . . (A&M)

Humble Pie-Classics-#14 . . . . (A&M)
Performance-Rockin' The Fillmore . . . . (A&M)
Rock On . . . . (A&M)
Streets Of Pain
Richard Marx; Rush Street. . . . . (Capitol)
Streets Of Philadelphia
Bruce Springsteen; Bruce Springsteen's Greatest Hits . . . . (Columbia)
Diana, Princess Of Wales-Tribute-C . . . . (Columbia)
ST/Philadelphia . . . . (Epic/Sony Music Soundtrax)
Subterranean Homesick Blues
Bob Dylan; Biograph. . . . . (Columbia)
Bob Dylan's Greatest Hits . . . . (Columbia)
Bringing It All Back Home . . . . (Columbia)
The Bootleg Series-Volumes 1-3 [Rare & Unreleased] . . . . (Columbia)
Red Hot Chili Peppers; Uplift Mofo Party Plan. . . . . (EMI)
Suffer To Sing The Blues
David Bromberg; Out Of The Blues-Best Of David Bromberg . . . . . . (Columbia)
Summer Rain
Carl Thomas; Emotional . . . . (Bad Boy/Arista)
Summertime Blues
Alan Jackson; Who I Am . . . . (Arista)
Blue Cheer; Good Times Are So Hard To Find-History Of Blue
Cheer . . . . (Mercury)
Louder Than God-Best Of Blue Cheer . . . . (Rhino)
San Francisco Nights-C . . . . (Rhino)
Brian Setzer; ST/La Bamba . . . . (Slash)
Eddie Cochran; Eddie Cochran-Legendary Masters . . . . (EMI)
Eddie Cochran's Greatest Hits . . . . (Curb)
EMI Legends Of Rock & Roll-24 Greatest Hits-C . . . . (EMI)
Joan Jett & The Blackhearts; I Love Rock 'n' Roll . . . . (Blackheart)
Who; Hooligans . . . . (MCA)
Live At Leeds. . . . . (MCA)
Who's Last . . . . (MCA)
Sunshower
Chris Cornell; ST/Great Expectations . . . . (Atlantic)
T.B. Is Whipping Me
Wilco & Syd Straw; Red Hot + Country-C . . . . (Mercury)
Take Me Down To The Hospital
Replacements; Hootenanny . . . . (Chameleon)
Take Your Pain Away
Eurythmics; Revenge . . . . (RCA)
Talk About Suffering
Doc Watson; Doc Watson . . . . (Vanguard)
Ricky Skaggs; Family & Friends . . . . (Rounder)
Live In London . . . . (Epic)
Teenage Brain Surgeon
Spike Jones; In Stereo . . . . (Warner Bros.)
Tennessee Homesick Blues
Dolly Parton; Best Of Dolly Parton-#3 . . . . (RCA)
RCA Years-1967-1986 . . . . (RCA)
ST/Rhinestone . . . . (RCA)
Star Spangled Country-C . . . . (RCA)
Theme From "Ben Casey"
Original Soundtrack; Television's Greatest Hits-#2-C . . . . (TVT)
Theme From "Chicago Hope"
Original Soundtrack; CBS: The First 50 Years. . . . . (TVT)
Theme From "Daktari"
Original Soundtrack; Television's Greatest Hits-#2-C . . . . (TVT)
Theme From "Doctor Zhivago"
101 Strings Orchestra; Music From Doctor Zhivago & Others . . . . (Alshire)
Theme From "Doogie Howser, M.D."
Original Soundtrack; Television's Greatest Hits-#7-Cable Ready-C . . . . . (TVT)
Theme From "Dr. Kildare" (Three Stars Will Shine Tonight)
Betty Carter; 'Round Midnight . . . . (Atlantic)
Original Soundtrack; Television's Greatest Hits-#4-Black & White
Classics-C . . . . (TVT)
Theme From "Empty Nest"
Original Soundtrack; Television's Greatest Hits-#7-Cable Ready-C . . . . . (TVT)
Theme From "General Hospital"
Original Soundtrack; Television's Greatest Hits-#5-In Living Color-C . . . (TVT)
Theme From "M*A*S*H" (Suicide Is Painless)
Ahmad Jamal; Digital Works. . . . . (Atlantic)
ST/M*A*S*H . . . . (Columbia)
Original Soundtrack; CBS: The First 50 Years . . . . (TVT)
Television's Greatest Hits-#3-1970s & 1980s-C . . . . (TVT)
Percy Faith & His Orchestra; Percy Faith & His Orchestra's All-Time
Greatest Hits . . . . (Columbia)
Theme From "Marcus Welby, M.D."
Original Soundtrack; Television's Greatest Hits-#3-1970s & 1980s-C. . . . (TVT)
Theme From "Medic"
Original Soundtrack; Television's Greatest Hits-#4-Black & White
Classics-C . . . . (TVT)
Theme From "Medical Center"
Original Soundtrack; Television's Greatest Hits-#2-C . . . . (TVT)
Theme From "Northern Exposure"
David Schwartz; ST/Music From "Northern Exposure" . . . . (MCA)
Original Soundtrack; CBS: The First 50 Years . . . . (TVT)
Theme From "Quincy, M.E."
Original Soundtrack; Television's Greatest Hits-#3-1970s & 1980s-C . . . . (TVT)

Theme From "St. Elsewhere"
Dave Grusin; Night-Lines . . . . (GRP)
Original Soundtrack; Television's Greatest Hits-#3-1970s & 1980s-C . . . . (TVT)
Theme From "The Bob Newhart Show"
Original Soundtrack; CBS: The First 50 Years. . . . . (TVT)
Television's Greatest Hits-#3-1970s & 1980s-C. . . . . (TVT)
Theme From "Trapper John, M.D."
Original Soundtrack; Television's Greatest Hits-#6-Remote Control-C . . . (TVT)
There's A Doctor I've Found
Who; Join Together . . . . (MCA)
ST/Tommy . . . . (Polydor)
Tommy . . . . (MCA)
These Eyes
Guess Who; Best Of The Guess Who . . . . (RCA)
Greatest Of The Guess Who . . . . (RCA)
Nipper's Greatest Hits Of The '60s-#1-C . . . . (RCA)
Track Record-Collection . . . . (RCA)
Thinkin' Problem
David Ball; Thinkin' Problem . . . . (Warner Bros.)
This Heartache Never Sleeps
Mark Chesnutt; I Don't Want To Miss A Thing . . . . (MCA)
This One's Gonna Hurt You (For A Long, Long Time)
Marty Stuart & Travis Tritt; Marty Stuart-This One's Gonna Hurt You . . (MCA)
Thorn In My Side
Eurythmics; Eurythmics' Greatest Hits . . . . (Arista)
Live-1983-1989. . . . . (Arista)
Revenge . . . . (RCA)
Thursday Night Fever
Legendary Pink Dots; Legendary Pink Dots . . . . . . (Play It Again Sam)
Tie You Up (The Pain Of Love)
Rolling Stones; Undercover. . . . . (Rolling Stones)
Till I Can't Take it Anymore
Billy Joe Royal; Billy Joe Royal's Greatest Hits . . . . (Atlantic)
Tell It Like It Is . . . . (Atlantic)
Charlie Rich; Behind Closed Doors . . . . (Epic)
Don Williams; Traces . . . . (Capitol)
Time Heals
Todd Rundgren; Healing . . . . (Rhino)
Todd Rundgren-Anthology 1968-1985 . . . . (Rhino)
Time Heals Everything
Barbara Cook; Barbara Cook-Live At Carnegie Hall . . . (Sony Music Classical)
Bernadette Peters; Bernadette Peters-Live At Carnegie Hall . . . . . . (EMI-Angel)
Original Cast; Mack & Mabel . . . . (MCA)
Tonight The Heartache's On Me
Dixie Chicks; Wide Open Spaces . . . . (Monument)
Torn
Natalie Imbruglia; Left Of The Middle . . . . (RCA)
Transfusion
Nervous Norvus; Dr. Demento Presents The Greatest Novelty Records-#2-
1950s-C . . . . (Rhino)
Dr. Demento: 20th Anniversary Collection-C . . . . (Rhino)
Vintage Music-#3-C . . . . (MCA)
Wacky Weirdos-C . . . . (K-Tel)
Try Not To Look So Pretty
Dwight Yoakam; This Time . . . . (Reprise)
U.M.M.G. (Upper Manhattan Medical Group)
Art Farmer Quartet; Warm Valley . . . . (Concord Jazz)
Branford Marsalis; Trio Jeepy . . . . (Columbia)
Duke Ellington & Dizzy Gillespie; Jazz Party . . . . (Legacy)
Ulcer
Michael Schenker Group; Assault Attack. . . . . (Chrysalis)
Un-Break My Heart
Toni Braxton; Secrets. . . . . (LaFace)
Universal Heart-Beat
Juliana Hatfield; Box Presents Big Ones Of Alternative
Rock-#1-C . . . . (Box Tunes)
Only Everything . . . . (Mammoth)
Vasectomy
Limeliters; Singing For The Fun . . . . (Crescendo)
Virus Called The Blues
Charles Brown & Dr. John; All My Life . . . . (Bullseye Blues)
Voodoo Medicine Man
Aerosmith; Pump . . . . (Geffen)
W.S. Walcott Medicine Show
Band; Rock Of Ages . . . . (Capitol)
Stage Fright. . . . . (Capitol)
To Kingdom Come-The Definitive Collection . . . . (Capitol)
Walk On
U2; America: A Tribute To Heroes-C . . . . (Interscope)
Now That's What I Call Music!-#8-C . . . . (Virgin)
Washington, D.C. Hospital Center Blues
Skip James; Greatest Of The Delta Blues Singers . . . . (Biograph)
Skip James Today . . . . (Vanguard)
We Need A Resolution
Aaliyah; Aaliyah . . . . (BlackGround Enterp./Atlantic)
Weak
SWV; It's About Time . . . . (RCA)
Weapon And The Wound
Days Of The New; Days Of The New 2 . . . . (Outpost/Interscope)

Welcome To The Fold
Filter; *Title Of Record* . . . . (Reprise)
Whatever
En Vogue; *Bass In Your Face: Essential Drum And Bass-C* . . . . (Elektra)
What's The New Mary Jane
Beatles; *The Beatles-Anthology-#3* . . . . (Capitol)
When It Hurts So Bad
Lauryn Hill; *The Miseducation Of Lauryn Hill* . . . . (Ruffhouse/Columbia)
Where Did Our Love Go
Diana Ross; *Diana Ross-The Ultimate Collection* . . . . (Motown)
Diana Ross & The Supremes; *Every Great Motown Song-First 25 Years-C* . . . . (Motown)
Where've You Been
Kathy Mattea; *Collection Of Hits* . . . . (Mercury)
Willow In The Wind . . . . (Mercury)
White Line Fever
Flying Burrito Brothers; *Close Encounters To The West Coast* . . . . (Relix)
Merle Haggard; *More Of The Best* . . . . (Rhino)
Merle Haggard & The Strangers; *Okie From Muskogee* . . . . (Capitol)
Who Needs You Baby
Clay Walker; *Hypnotize The Moon* . . . . (Giant)
Why Does It Hurt So Bad
Whitney Houston; *ST/Waiting To Exhale* . . . . (Arista)
Wink
Neal McCoy; *No Doubt About It* . . . . (Atlantic)
Witch Doctor
Chipmunks; *Rockin' Through The Decades* . . . . (EMI)
David Seville; *Dr. Demento: 20th Anniversary Collection-C* . . . . (Rhino)
Wacky Weirdos-C . . . . (K-Tel)
With My Eyes Wide Open I'm Dreaming
Mandy Barnett; *I've Got A Right To Cry* . . . . (Sire)
Patti Page; *Patti Page-Golden Hits* . . . . (Mercury)
Patti Page's Greatest Hits . . . . (Columbia)
World Is A Little Bit Under The Weather
Meters; *Trick Bag* . . . . (Reprise)
World Of Pain
Cream; *Disraeli Gears* . . . . (Polydor)
X-Ray Hip
Bona Fide; *Royal Function* . . . . (N-Coded)
You Always Hurt The One You Love
Brenda Lee; *The Brenda Lee Story-Her Greatest Hits* . . . . (MCA)
Clarence Henry; *Rich Roots* . . . . (Allegiance)
Mills Brothers; *Best Of The Mills Brothers* . . . . (MCA)
Mills Brothers' Greatest Hits . . . . (MCA)
Mills Brothers-16 Great Performances . . . . (MCA)
Spike Jones & His City Slickers; *Best Of Spike Jones & His City Slickers* . . . . (RCA)
You Can't Hurry Love
Diana Ross; *Diana Ross-The Ultimate Collection* . . . . (Motown)
Diana Ross & The Supremes; *16 #1 Hits From The Early '60s-C* . . . . (Motown)
Phil Collins; *Hello, I Must Be Going* . . . . (Atlantic)
You Don't Have To Hurt No More
Mint Condition; *Definition Of A Band* . . . . (Perspective/A&M)
Mint Condition-Collection (1991-1998) . . . . (Perspective/A&M)
You Learn
Alanis Morissette; *Jagged Little Pill* . . . . (Maverick)
You Make Me Sick
Pink; *Can't Take Me Home* . . . . (LaFace)
You Were On My Mind
We Five; *Baby Boomer Classics-Folk Sixties-C* . . . . (JCI Assoc. Labels)
Billboard Top Pop Hits-1965-C . . . . (Rhino)
Your Disease
Saliva; *Every Six Seconds* . . . . (Island/IDJMG)
You've Got A Cold
10 CC; *Deceptive Bends* . . . . (Mercury)
Live & Let Live . . . . (Mercury)
You've Got It Bad Girl
Quincy Jones; *Best Of Quincy Jones-#2* . . . . (A&M)
Quincy Jones-Classics-#3 . . . . (A&M)
Stevie Wonder; *Talking Book* . . . . (Motown)

PAPER

See Also: **BOOKS, COMMUNICATION (various), MAIL, NEWS**

Coffee In A Cardboard Cup
Original Broadway Cast; *70 Girls 70* . . . . (Sony Music Classical)
Original Cast; *And The World Goes 'Round: Songs Of Kander & Ebb* . . . . (RCA Victor)
It's Only A Paper Moon
Art Blakey & His Jazz Messengers; *Big Beat* . . . . (Blue Note)
Bing Crosby; *The Radio Years-#2* . . . . (Crescendo)
David Rose & His Orchestra; *Music Of The 1930s-C* . . . . (MCA)
Ella Fitzgerald; *Harold Arlen Songbook-#2* . . . . (Verve)
Frank Sinatra; *Round #1* . . . . (Capitol)
Mystics; *Mystics-16 Golden Classics* . . . . (Collectables)

Nat "King" Cole; *Capitol Sings Harold Arlen: Over The Rainbow-C* . . . . (Gold Rush)
The Nat "King" Cole Story . . . . (Capitol)
Sammy Kaye & His Orchestra; *Sammy Kaye & His Orchestra Play 22 Original Big Band Recordings* . . . . (Hindsight)
Paper
Queen Latifah; *Order In The Court* . . . . (Motown)
Paper
Talking Heads; *Fear Of Music* . . . . (Sire)
Paper Airplane
Willy Porter; *Falling Forward* . . . . (Six Degrees)
Paper Airplanes
Seals & Crofts; *Year Of Sunday* . . . . (Warner Bros.)
Paper And Ink
Tracy Chapman; *Telling Stories* . . . . (Elektra)
Paper And Iron
XTC; *Black Sea* . . . . (Geffen)
Paper Bag
Fiona Apple; *When The Pawn Hits The Conflicts* . . . . (Epic)
Paper Blood
Emerson, Lake & Palmer; *Black Moon* . . . . (Rhino)
Greg Lake; *From The Beginning-The Greg Lake Retrospective* . . . . . . (Rhino)
Paper Boy
Louis Jordan; *1944-1945* . . . . (Circle)
Paper Boy
Roy Orbison; *Rare Orbison* . . . . (Monument)
Paper Boy Blues
Bill Haley; *From The Original Master Tapes-Bill Haley* . . . . (MCA)
Paper Castles
Frankie Lymon and The Teenagers; *Best Of Frankie Lymon and The Teenagers* . . . . (Rhino)
Very Best Of Frankie Lymon & The Teenagers . . . . (Rhino)
Paper Chase
Original Soundtrack; *Television's Greatest Hits-#6-Remote Control-C* . . . (TVT)
Paper Chase
Jay-Z; *Vol. 2-Hard Knock Life* . . . . (Def Jam)
Paper Chase
Art Garfunkel; *Watermark* . . . . (Legacy)
Paper Cup
5th Dimension; *Up-Up And Away-The Definitive Collection* . . . . (Arista)
Paper Cuts
Nirvana; *Bleach* . . . . (Sub Pop)
Paper Doll
Bar-Kays; *Banging The Wall* . . . . (Mercury)
Mills Brothers; *Best Of The Mills Brothers* . . . . (MCA)
Billboard Pop Memories-1940-1944-C . . . . (Rhino)
Mills Brothers' All Time Greatest Hits . . . . (MCA)
Mills Brothers' Greatest Hits . . . . (MCA)
Mills Brothers-22 Great Hits . . . . (Ranwood)
Paper Doll . . . . (MCA)
Sentimental Journey: Pop Vocal Classics-#1-1942-1946-C . . . . . (Rhino)
The Mills Brothers-Best Of The Decca Years . . . . (Decca)
Paper Doll
Fleetwood Mac; *25 Years-The Chain* . . . . (Warner Bros.)
Paper Doll
Gatlin Brothers; *Moments To Remember* . . . . (ISD/Intersound)
Paper Dress
Toadies; *ST/The Crow-City Of Angels* . . . . (Hollywood)
Paper Heart
Jane Wiedlin; *Very Best Of Jane Wiedlin* . . . . (EMI)
Paper In Fire
John Cougar Mellencamp; *The Lonesome Jubilee* . . . . (Mercury)
John Mellencamp; *Best That I Could Do-1978-1988* . . . . (Mercury)
Paper In My Shoe
Boozoo Chavis & The Majic Sounds; *Alligator Stomp-#1-C* . . . . . . (Rhino)
Lake Charles Atomic Bomb-Original Goldband Recordings . . . . . . (Rounder)
Clifton Chenier; *Sings The Blues* . . . . (Arhoolie)
Paper Is White
Mandy Patinkin; *Mamaloshen* . . . . (Nonesuch)
Paper Lanterns
Green Day; *1039-Smoothed Out Slappy Hours* . . . . (Lookout)
Paper Mache
Dionne Warwick; *The Look Of Love-The Burt Bacharach Collection* . . . (Rhino)
Paper Mache, Cabbages And Kings
Bee Gees; *To Whom It May Concern* . . . . (Polydor)
Paper Mansions
Dottie West; *Essential Dottie West* . . . . (RCA)
Paper Money
Montrose; *Paper Money* . . . . (Warner Bros.)
Paper Of Pins
Oscar Brand & Jean Ritchie; *Greatest Folksingers Of The '60s-C* . . . (Vanguard)
Paper Paradise
Little River Band; *No Reins* . . . . (One Way)
Paper Roses
Kitty Wells; *Kitty Wells' Greatest Hits-#2* . . . . (Step One)
Marie Osmond; *All Time Greatest Hits Of Country-C* . . . . (Curb)
Marie Osmond-25 Hits-Special Collection . . . . (Curb)

Paper Rosie
Don Walser; *Here's To Country Music* .... (Sire)
Gene Watson; *Gene Watson's Greatest Hits* .... (Curb)
Osborne Brothers; *Hillbilly Fever* .... (C.M.H. Prod.)

Paper Scratcher
Blind Melon; *Blind Melon* .... (Capitol)

Paper Shoes
Yoko Ono Band; *Yoko Ono & Plastic Ono Band* .... (Rykodisc)

Paper Sun
Def Leppard; *Euphoria* .... (Mercury)

Paper Sun
Traffic; *20th Century Masters-The Millennium Collection-The Best Of Steve Winwood-Traffic* .... (Island)
Best Of Traffic .... (Island)
Feelin' Alright-Very Best Of Traffic .... (Island)
Island Story 1962-1987-C .... (Island)
Smiling Phases .... (Island)

Paper Thin
John Hiatt; *Hiatt Comes Alive At Budokan* .... (A&M)
John Hiatt's Greatest Hits-The A&M Years '87-'94 .... (A&M)
Slow Turning .... (A&M)
M.C. Lyte; *Lyte As A Rock* .... (First Priority)

Paper Thin Hotel
Leonard Cohen; *Death Of A Ladies' Man* .... (Columbia)

Paper Tiger
Sue Thompson; *Collectables Presents The History Of Rock-#4-C* .... (Collectables)
Golden Classics-Sue Thompson .... (Collectables)
Sue Thompson's Greatest Hits .... (Curb)

Paper Tiger
Painted Willie; *Relics Of The Incredible String Band* .... (Elektra)

Paper Toilet
Henry Threadgill; *Too Much Sugar For A Dime* .... (Axiom)

Paper Walls
Marc Cohn; *Rainy Season* .... (Atlantic)

Paper Wings
Gillian Welch; *Revival* .... (Almo Sounds)
ST/Hope Floats .... (Capitol)

Paperback Writer
Beatles; *Beatles 1* .... (Capitol)
Beatles-20 Greatest Hits .... (Capitol)
Beatles-Box Set .... (Capitol)
Hey Jude .... (Capitol)
Past Masters-Volume Two .... (Parlophone)
The Beatles/1962-1966 .... (Capitol)
Paul McCartney; *Paul Is Live* .... (Capitol)

Paperdoll
Kittie; *Spit* .... (Artemis)

Papermaker
Kittie; *Anything Goes!* .... (Columbia)

Papers And Pens
Ernest Tubb; *Walking The Floor Over You* .... (Laserlight)

Pretty Paper
Asleep At The Wheel; *Merry Texas Christmas, Y'all* .... (High Street)
Don McLean; *Christmas Country Classics-#1-C* .... (Curb)
Don McLean-Christmas .... (Curb)
Freddy Fender; *Country Christmas To Remember-C* ..... (MCA Special Prod.)
Glen Campbell; *Merry Christmas* .... (Liberty)
Randy Travis; *Old Time Christmas* .... (Warner Bros.)
Roy Orbison; *Legendary Roy Orbison* .... (Sony Music Special Prod.)
Roy Orbison's All-Time Greatest Hits-#1 & 2 .... (Monument)
Willie Nelson; *Best Of Christmas-C* .... (RCA)
Country Christmas-#1-C .... (RCA)
Hillbilly Holiday-C .... (Rhino)
Nashville's Greatest Christmas Hits-#2-C .... (Columbia)
What A Wonderful World .... (Columbia)

Trippin' On A Hole In A Paper Heart
Stone Temple Pilots; *Tiny Music...Songs From The Vatican Gift Shop* .... (Atlantic)

Yesterday's Paper
Tish Hinojosa; *Destiny's Gate* .... (Warner Bros.)

Yesterday's Papers
Rolling Stones; *Between The Buttons* .... (Abkco)

You Never Give Me Your Money
Beatles; *Abbey Road* .... (Parlophone)
Beatles-Box Set .... (Capitol)
George Benson; *The Best* .... (Rebound)

PARADISE, Utopia
See Also: *HAPPINESS, HEAVEN, ISLANDS, PLACES*

Afternoons In Utopia
Alphaville; *Afternoons In Utopia* .... (Atlantic)
Alice You've Made Dallas (Paradise)
Lee Ferrell; *Hard Times* .... (TMS)

Almost Paradise
Eric Carmen & Merry Clayton; *Dirty Dancing Live In Concert-C* ...... (RCA)
Mike Reno & Ann Wilson; *ST/Footloose* .... (Columbia)
Almost Paradise
Roger Williams; *Best Of Roger Williams* .... (MCA)
Roger Williams-Golden Hits-#2 .... (MCA)
Another Day In Paradise
Phil Collins; *...But Seriously* .... (Atlantic)
Serious Hits...Live! .... (Atlantic)
Anyplace In Paradise
Elvis Presley; *Elvis* .... (RCA)
Bali Ha'i
Original Cast; *South Pacific* .... (CBS Masterworks)
Big Rock Candy Mountain
Burl Ives; *Burl Ives' Greatest Hits* .... (MCA)
Poor Wayfaring Stranger .... (Flapper)
Harry McClintock; *ST/O Brother, Where Art Thou?* .... (Mercury)
John Hartford; *ST/Down From The Mountain* ...... (Lost Highway/IDJMG)
Pete Seeger; *20 Golden Pieces Of Pete Seeger* .... (Bulldog)
Tex Ritter; *Capitol Collectors Series-Tex Ritter* .... (Capitol)
Big Yellow Taxi
Amy Grant; *House Of Love* .... (A&M)
Joni Mitchell; *Ladies Of The Canyon* .... (Reprise)
Joni Mitchell with Tom Scott & The L.A. Express; *Miles Of Aisles*.... (Asylum)
Birds Of Paradise
Ed Bruce; *Tell 'Em I've Gone Crazy* .... (MCA)
Birds Of Paradise
Pretenders; *Pretenders II* .... (Sire)
California Paradise
Runaways; *Queens Of Noise* .... (Mercury)
Camelot
Original 1982 London Cast; *Camelot* .... (Varese Sarabande)
Original Cast; *Camelot* .... (Columbia)
Richard Burton; *Broadway Magic-The 1960s-C* .... (Columbia)
Richard Harris; *ST/Camelot* .... (Warner Bros.)
Cheeseburger In Paradise
Jimmy Buffett; *Son Of A Son Of A Sailor* .... (MCA)
Songs You Know By Heart-Jimmy Buffett's Greatest Hit(s) .... (MCA)
Faith In Me
Crosby, Stills, Nash & Young; *Looking Forward* .... (Reprise)
Fall From Paradise
Little River Band; *Sleeper Catcher* .... (Capitol)
From Hell To Paradise
Mavericks; *From Hell To Paradise* .... (MCA)
Halfway To Paradise
Bobby Vinton; *Bobby Vinton's All-Time Greatest Hits* ...... (Epic)
Bobby Vinton's Greatest Hits/Greatest Hits Of Love .... (Columbia)
Heaven On Earth
Platters; *Encore Of Golden Hits-Platters* .... (Mercury)
Platters-16 Greatest Hits .... (Trip)
Platters-Anthology .... (Rhino)
Red Sails In The Sunset .... (Allegiance)
Highlands
Bob Dylan; *Time Out Of Mind* .... (Columbia)
Hole In Paradise
Prism; *Small Change* .... (Capitol)
Hotel California
Eagles; *Eagles Greatest Hits, Volume 2* .... (Asylum)
Eagles Live .... (Asylum)
Hell Freezes Over .... (Geffen)
Hotel California .... (Asylum)
I'll Build A Stairway To Paradise
George Gershwin; *Manhattan* .... (Klavier)
Issy Van Randwyck; *Glory Of Gershwin Featuring Larry Adler-C* ... (Mercury)
Liza Minnelli; *Fascinatin' Rhythm-Capitol Sings Gershwin-C* ...... (Capitol)
In Paradise
Cookies; *Atlantic Rhythm & Blues 1947-1974-#3 (1955-1958)-C* ..... (Atlantic)
I've Committed Murder
Macy Gray; *On How Life Is* .... (Epic)
Just Another Day In Paradise
Bertie Higgins; *Just Another Day In Paradise* .... (Kat Family)
Just Another Day In Paradise
Phil Vassar; *Phil Vassar* .... (Arista)
Just Like Paradise
David Lee Roth; *Skyscraper* .... (Warner Bros.)
Kentucky Means Paradise
Barbara Mandrell; *Vintage Barbara Mandrell* .... (Audiograph)
Roger Bellow & The Drifting Troubadours; *On The Road To Prosperity* .... (Flying Fish)
Kokomo
Beach Boys; *ST/Cocktail* .... (Elektra)
Still Cruisin' .... (Capitol)
Little Paradise
Pat Benatar; *Crimes Of Passion* .... (Chrysalis)
Living In Paradise
Elvis Costello; *This Year's Model* .... (Rykodisc)
March Winds And April Showers
Wingy Manone; *Wingy Manone Collection-#3-1934-1935* .... (Collector's Classics)

May The Bird Of Paradise Fly Up Your Nose
"Little" Jimmy Dickens; *Columbia Country Classics-#3-*
Americana-C. . . . . (Columbia)
Super Hits Of The '60s-C. . . . . (Epic)
Harlow Wilcox and the Oakies; *Cripple Cricket* . . . . (Plantation)
Monday Morning In Paradise
Tom Paxton; *One Million Lawyers & Other Disasters* . . . . (Flying Fish)
Paradise
Tesla; *Five Man Acoustical Jam* . . . .(Geffen)
Great Radio Controversy. . . . .(Geffen)
Paradise
Styx; *Return To Paradise* . . . . (CMC Int'l)
Paradise
Nat "King" Cole; *Nat "King" Cole-Gift Set* . . . . (Capitol)
The Nat "King" Cole Story. . . . . (Capitol)
Ray Conniff; *'S Awful Nice*. . . . . (Columbia)
Russ Colombo; *Nipper's Greatest Hits Of The '30s-#2-C* . . . . . . (RCA)
Paradise
Everly Brothers; *Home Again*. . . . . (RCA)
Paradise
Roger Whittaker; *Special Kind Of Man* . . . . (RCA)
Paradise
BoDeans; *Black & White* . . . . (Slash)
Paradise
Eugene Wilde; *How About Tonight* . . . .(MCA)
Paradise
Meat Puppets; *Huevos* . . . .(SST)
Paradise
John Prine; *John Prine* . . . . (Atlantic)
Paradise
Temptations; *Meet The Temptations*. . . . . (Motown)
Paradise
Michael Bolton; *Michael Bolton*. . . . . (Columbia)
Paradise
John Denver; *Rocky Mountain High* . . . . (RCA)
Paradise
Bette Midler; *ST/Divine Madness* . . . . (Atlantic)
Paradise
Grandmaster Flash; *They Said It Couldn't Be Done* . . . . (Elektra)
Paradise
Change; *Very Best Of Change*. . . . . (Rhino)
Paradise By The Dashboard Light
Meat Loaf; *Bat Out Of Hell*. . . . .(Epic)
Paradise Cafe
Barry Manilow; *2:00 Paradise Cafe*. (Arista)
Paradise Cafe
Arc Angels; *Arc Angels* . . . . (David Geffen Co.)
Paradise City
Guns N' Roses; *Appetite For Destruction* . . . . (Geffen)
Paradise Knife & Gun Club
Jerry Lansdowne; *Travel Light* . . . . (Step One)
Roy Clark; *Live From Austin City Limits* . . . .(Churchill)
Paradise Place
Siouxsie And The Banshees; *Kaleidoscope* . . . . (Geffen)
Nocturne . . . . (Geffen)
Paradise Tonight
Charly McClain & Mickey Gilley; *19 Hot Country Requests-C*. . . . . . .(Epic)
Charly McClain's Biggest Hits . . . .(Epic)
It Takes Believers. . . . .(Epic)
Paradise. . . . .(Epic)
Ten Year Anniversary . . . .(Epic)
Price Of Paradise
Minutemen; *3-Way Tie (For Last)* . . . .(SST)
Ballot Result . . . .(SST)
Promised Land
Bruce Springsteen; *Darkness On The Edge Of Town* . . . . (Columbia)
Bruce Springsteen & The E Street Band; *Bruce Springsteen & The E Street*
Band Live/1975-85 . . . . (Legacy)
P'tit Fille O' Paradis
Queen Ida; *On Tour* . . . .(Crescendo)
Race To Paradise
Jeff Paris; *Race To Paradise*. . . . . (Mercury)
Rainbow Stew
Merle Haggard; *For The Record: Merle Haggard-43 Legendary Hits* . . . . (BNA)
Merle Haggard's Greatest Hits . . . .(MCA)
More Of The Best . . . .(Rhino)
Rainbow Stew-Live At Anaheim Stadium. . . . .(MCA)
Return To Paradise
Martin Denny; *From Maui With Love*. . . . . (First Warning)
Return To Paradise
Elton John; *A Single Man*. . . . .(MCA)
Rockin' The Paradise
Styx; *Caught In The Act* . . . .(A&M)
Paradise Theater . . . . (A&M)
Rose In Paradise
Waylon Jennings; *Country Classics-#8-1986-1987-C* . . . . (Universal)
MCA #1 Hits Of The '80s-#3-C . . . .(MCA Special Prod.)
New Classic Waylon . . . .(MCA)

Sailin' To Paradise
Pablo Cruise; *Worlds Away*. . . . . (A&M)
Sailing
Christopher Cross; *Christopher Cross* . . . . (Warner Bros.)
Santa Lucia
Elvis Presley; *Elvis For Everyone!* . . . .(RCA)
Mario Lanza; *Legendary Tenor*. . . . .(RCA)
See You In Paradise
Saints; *All Fools Day*. . . . .(TVT)
Shangri La
Four Coins; *'50s Vocal Groups-C*. . . . .(K-Tel)
Lettermen; *Capitol Collectors Series-The Lettermen* . . . . (Capitol)
The Lettermen's All-Time Greatest Hits. . . . . (Capitol)
Shangri La
Electric Light Orchestra; *Box Of Their Best* . . . . (Jet)
New World Record . . . . (Jet)
Shangri La
Kinks; *Kink Kronikles*. . . . . (Reprise)
Shangri La
Don Henley; *End Of The Innocence* . . . . (Geffen)
Shangri La
Steve Miller Band; *Italian X-Rays*. (Capitol)
Shangri La
Kim Wilde; *Teases & Dares* . . . . (MCA)
Sh-Boom
Chords; *Atlantic Rhythm & Blues 1947-1974-#2 (1952-1955)-C* . . . . .(Atlantic)
Crew-Cuts; *Partytime '50s-C*. . . . . (Priority)
Stan Freberg; *Capitol Collectors Series-Stan Freberg* . . . . (Capitol)
Small Paradise
John Cougar; *John Cougar* . . . . (Riva)
Straight To Paradise
Koinonia; *Koinonia*. . . . . (Blue Moon)
Stranger In Paradise
Arthur Lyman; *Pearly Shells*. . . . . (Crescendo)
Bing Crosby; *The Radio Years: 20 Songs* . . . .(Crescendo)
Original Cast; *Kismet* . . . . (Columbia)
Tony Bennett; *Tony Bennett-16 Most Requested Songs* . . . . (Legacy)
Tony Bennett's All-Time Greatest Hits. . . . . (Columbia)
Streets Of Paradise
Richard & Linda Thompson; *Pour Down Like Silver* . . . .(Hannibal)
Streets Of Paradise
Poco; *Blue & Gray* . . . . (One Way)
Surrender Paradise
Miami Sound Machine; *Primitive Love*. . . . . (Epic)
Sweet Little Miss Blue Eyes
Jim & Jesse/The Virginia Boys; *Appalachian Stomp: More Bluegrass*
Classics-C . . . . (Rhino)
Takin' It Easy
Lacy J. Dalton; *Dream Baby*. . . . . (Columbia)
Lacy J. Dalton's Greatest Hits . . . . (Columbia)
Thanks For The Trip To Paradise
Jim & Jesse; *Music Among Friends*. . . . . (Rounder)
Theme From "Cinema Paradiso"
Original Soundtrack; *Ennio Morricone With Love* . . . .(DRG)
There Are No Cats In America
Nehemiah Persoff/John Guarnieri/Warren Hays; *ST/An American Tail* . . (MCA)
To One In Paradise
Alan Parsons Project; *Tales Of Mystery & Imagination* . . . . (Mercury)
Town Called Paradise
Van Morrison; *No Guru No Method No Teacher* . . . . (Mercury)
Travelin' Light
Eric Clapton; *Reptile*. . . . . (Duck/Reprise)
Trouble In Paradise
Huey Lewis and the News; *Huey Lewis and the News*. . . . . (Chrysalis)
We Are The World-C. . . . . (Columbia)
Trouble In Paradise
Loretta Lynn; *Best Of Loretta Lynn-#2* . . . . (MCA Special Prod.)
Trouble In Paradise
Crests; *Crests Greatest Hits* . . . . (Collectables)
Trouble In Paradise
Al Jarreau; *Jarreau* . . . . (Warner Bros.)
Trouble In Paradise
Princess Pang; *Princess Pang* . . . . (Metal Blade)
Trouble In Paradise
Greg Kihn; *Rockihn'* . . . . (Beserkley)
Trouble In Paradise
J.D. Souther; *You're Only Lonely* . . . . (Legacy)
Two Tickets To Paradise
Eddie Money; *Eddie Money* . . . . (Columbia)
Eddie Money's Greatest Hits-Sound Of Money . . . . (Columbia)
Unplug It In . . . . (Columbia)
Visions Of Paradise
Moody Blues; *In Search Of The Lost Chord* . . . .(Polydor)
Way Over Yonder
Carole King; *Tapestry*. . . . . (Epic)
Welcome To Paradise
Green Day; *Dookie* . . . . (Reprise)

Who But A Fool (Thief In Paradise)
Bonnie Raitt; *Nine Lives* .... (Warner Bros.)
You'd Be So Nice To Come Home To
Dinah Shore; *Songs That Got Us Through WWII-#2-C* .... (Rhino)

PARENTS: CONCERNED ABOUT TEEN LOVE

*See Also: ADVICE, AGES (various), AGING, FAMILY (various),
FAMILY PLANNING, LOVE (various), SEX, SEX: RESISTING
TEMPTATION, TEACHING VALUES, TEENAGERS, YOUNG*

Blues In The Night
Benny Goodman; *Small Groups-1941-1945* .... (Columbia)
Bobby Bland; *Introspective Of The Early Years* .... (MCA)
Dinah Shore; *Nipper's Greatest Hits Of The '40s-#1-C* .... (RCA)
Doc Severinsen; *Best Of Doc Severinsen* .... (MCA)
Frank Sinatra; *Frank Sinatra sings for Only The Lonely* .... (Capitol)
Jimmie Lunceford & His Orchestra; *Warner Bros.' 75 Years Entertaining
   The World-Film Music-C* .... (Rhino)
Mel Torme; *Torme* .... (Verve)
Robins; *Best Of The Robins* .... (Crescendo)
Rosemary Clooney; *Rosemary Clooney-16 Most Requested Songs* .... (Legacy)
Tony Bennett; *Playin' With My Friends-Bennett Sings The
   Blues-C* .... (Columbia)
Woody Herman; *Blues On Parade* .... (GRP)
   Woody Herman-Best Of The Decca Years .... (Decca)
Woody Herman & His Orchestra; *Big Bands Greatest
   Hits-#3-C* .... (MCA Special Prod.)
Dawn (Go Away)
4 Seasons; *25th Anniversary Collection* .... (Rhino)
   4 Seasons-Anthology .... (Rhino)
Drop Down Mama, Let Your Papa See
John Hammond; *Best Of John Hammond* .... (Vanguard)
Sleepy John Estes; *Legend Of Sleepy John Estes* .... (Delmark)
Tom Rush; *Best Of Tom Rush: No Regrets* .... (Legacy)
   Tom Rush .... (Columbia)
Fill Me In
Craig David; *Born To Do It* .... (Wildside/Atlantic)
   Totally Hits 2001-C .... (Arista)
Fun, Fun, Fun
Beach Boys; *Beach Boys-Gift Set* .... (Capitol)
   Best Of The Beach Boys .... (Capitol)
   Endless Summer .... (Capitol)
   Made In The U.S.A. .... (Capitol)
   The Beach Boys In Concert .... (Brother)
Ginger Bread
Frankie Avalon; *Gold For The Road-Carburetor Classics-C* ...... (Compose)
   Venus: The Very Best Of Frankie Avalon .... (Collectables)
Is Zat You, Myrtle
Carlisles; *45-#70174* .... (Mercury)
Louvin Brothers; *Live At New River Ranch* .... (Copper Creek)
It's Late
Ricky Nelson; *Lonesome Town* .... (CEMA Special Prod.)
   Ricky Nelson Volume 1 .... (Gold Rush)
Jacob's Ladder
Mark Wills; *Mark Wills* .... (Mercury)
Leader Of The Pack
Bette Midler; *Divine Miss M* .... (Atlantic)
   ST/Divine Madness .... (Atlantic)
Original Cast; *Leader Of The Pack* .... (Elektra)
Shangri-Las; *21 Number One Hits-C* .... (Original Sound)
   Billboard Top Rock 'N' Roll Hits-1964-C .... (Rhino)
   Girl Groups-Story Of A Sound-C .... (Rhino)
   Golden Hits Of The Shangri-Las .... (Mercury)
   Oldies But Goodies-#15-C .... (Original Sound)
   Radio Active Hits-#2-C .... (Accord)
   Remember The Shangri-Las At Their Best .... (Collectables)
Lend Me Your Comb
Beatles; *The Beatles-Anthology-#1* .... (Capitol)
Carl Perkins; *Carl Perkins-Original Sun Greatest Hits* .... (Rhino)
Mama Said
Shirelles; *Original Rock 'N' Roll Hits Of The '60s-C* .... (Roulette)
   Shirelles' Greatest Hits .... (Everest)
   Shirelles-Anthology 1959-1964 .... (Rhino)
   Shirelles-Classics .... (Bac-Trac)
   Super Oldies Of The '60s-#3-C .... (Audio Fidelity)
Mommy Can I Come Home
Keb' Mo'; *The Door* .... (550/Epic/Okeh)
Ms. Jackson
Outkast; *Stankonia* .... (LaFace/Arista)
On A Night Like This
Trick Pony; *Trick Pony* .... (H2E/Warner Bros.)
She's In Love With The Boy
Trisha Yearwood; *Trisha Yearwood* .... (MCA)
Shop Around
Captain & Tennille; *Captain & Tennille's Greatest Hits* .... (A&M)
Miracles; *Greatest Hits From The Beginning* .... (Motown)

   Hi-We're The Miracles .... (Motown)
Smokey Robinson & The Miracles; *16 #1 Hits From The Early
   '60s-C* .... (Motown)
   Every Great Motown Song-First 25 Years-C .... (Motown)
   Smokey Robinson & The Miracles' Anthology .... (Motown)
Someday Soon
Chris LeDoux; *Rodeo Songs Old & New* .... (Liberty)
Ian & Sylvia; *Ian & Sylvia's Greatest Hits* .... (Vanguard)
   Northern Journey .... (Vanguard)
Judy Collins; *Colors Of The Day-The Best Of Judy Collins* ...... (Elektra)
   Who Knows Where The Time Goes .... (Elektra)
Moe Bandy; *Moe Bandy's Greatest Hits* .... (Columbia)
   Rodeo Romeo .... (Columbia)
Suzy Bogguss; *Aces* .... (Liberty)
   Suzy Bogguss' Greatest Hits .... (Liberty)
Take Time To Know Her
Percy Sledge; *Best Of Percy Sledge* .... (Atlantic)
   It Tears Me Up-Best Of Percy Sledge .... (Rhino)
Tennessee Border
Hank Williams; *Alone With His Guitar* .... (Mercury)
   I Ain't Got Nothin' But Time-1946-1947 .... (Polydor)
Red Foley; *Red Foley: The Country Music Hall
   Of Fame* .... (MCA Special Prod.)
Sonny Burgess & Dave Alvin; *Tennessee Border* .... (Hightone)
Tennessee Ernie Ford; *Best Of Tennessee Ernie Ford-16 Tons Of
   Boogie* .... (Rhino)
   Capitol Collectors Series-Tennessee Ernie Ford .... (Capitol)
That's All Right (Mama)
Arthur "Big Boy" Crudup; *Best Of The Blues* .... (Pair)
   That's All Right (Mama) .... (Bluebird)
Carl Perkins; *Restless-Columbia Recordings* .... (Columbia)
Elvis Presley; *For LP Fans Only* .... (RCA)
   Sun Story-C .... (Rhino)
   Sun's Greatest Hits-C .... (RCA)
   The Sun Sessions .... (RCA)
Marty Robbins; *Essential Marty Robbins-1951-1982* .... (Columbia)
Merl Saunders/Jerry Garcia/Bill Vitt/John Kahn; *Live At Keystone* .... (Fantasy)
Paul McCartney; *CHOBA B CCCP-The Russian Album* .... (Capitol)
Rick Nelson; *Stay Young-Epic Recordings* .... (Epic)
Rod Stewart; *Every Picture Tells A Story* .... (Mercury)
   Vintage Rod Stewart .... (Mercury)
Vince Gill; *ST/Honeymoon In Vegas* .... (Epic/Sony Music Soundtrax)
Theme From "A Summer Place"
Andy Williams; *Moon River & Other Great Movie Themes* .... (Columbia)
Percy Faith & His Orchestra; *Best Love Songs-C* ...... (Original Sound)
   Billboard Top Pop Hits-1960-C .... (Rhino)
   Percy Faith & His Orchestra-16 Most Requested Songs ...... (Columbia)
   Percy Faith & His Orchestra's All-Time Greatest Hits ...... (Columbia)
   Percy Faith & His Orchestra's Greatest Hits .... (Columbia)
Wake Up Little Susie
Everly Brothers; *All They Had To Do Was Dream* .... (Rhino)
   American Graffiti-#3-C .... (MCA)
   Everly Brothers .... (Rhino)
   Everly Brothers' All-Time Greatest Hits .... (Curb)
   Oldies But Goodies-#7-C .... (Original Sound)
   Very Best Of The Everly Brothers .... (Warner Bros.)
Grateful Dead; *History Of The Grateful Dead-Vol. 1 (Bear's
   Choice)* .... (Warner Bros.)
Simon & Garfunkel; *The Concert In Central Park* .... (Warner Bros.)
Walkaway Joe
Trisha Yearwood; *Hearts In Armor* .... (MCA)
   Songbook-A Collection Of Hits .... (MCA)
Young Blood
Bad Company; *Run With The Pack* .... (Swan Song)
Coasters; *Coasters' Greatest Hits* .... (Atco)
   Coasters-Their Greatest Recordings-Early Years .... (Atco)
   The Ultimate Coasters .... (Warner Special Prod.)

PARENTS: GENERAL

*See Also: AGES (various), BABY, CHILDREN, CHILDREN
LEAVING HOME, FAMILY (various), MARRIAGE, PARENTS:
CONCERNED ABOUT TEEN LOVE, PARENTS: SINGLE, STEP,
ABSENT, TEENAGERS, YOUNG*

Alone Again (Naturally)
Gilbert O'Sullivan; *Best Of Gilbert O'Sullivan* .... (Rhino)
   Billboard Top Rock 'N' Roll Hits-1972-C .... (Rhino)
Charlie Brown's Parents
Dishwalla; *Pet Your Friends* .... (A&M)
Children Of The Korn
Korn with Ice Cube; *Follow The Leader* .... (Immortal/Epic)
Child's Song
Tom Rush; *Best Of Tom Rush: No Regrets* .... (Legacy)
   Tom Rush .... (Columbia)
Fields Have Turned Brown
Stanley Brothers & The Clinch Mountain Boys; *Bluegrass Super
   Hits-C* .... (Columbia)

Fight For Your Right (To Party)
Beastie Boys; *Def Jam Classics-#1-C*.........................(Def Jam)
  Heart Of Soul-C...........................(Columbia)
  Licensed To Ill..........................(Def Jam)
I Don't Wanna Play House
Sara Evans; *Tammy Wynette...Remembered-C*................(Asylum)
Tammy Wynette; *Tammy Wynette-Anniversary-20 Years Of Hits*.......(Epic)
  Tammy Wynette's Greatest Hits.......................(Epic)
  Tammy Wynette-Super Hits............................(Epic)
I Wish I Could Have Been There
John Anderson; *Solid Ground*......................(BNA)
I Wonder How The Old Folks Are At Home
Doc & Merle Watson; *Home Sweet Home*...............(Sugar Hill)
If I Could
Barbra Streisand; *Higher Ground*.....................(Columbia)
It Works
Alabama; *In Pictures*.........................(RCA)
Life Is Sweet
Natalie Merchant; *Ophelia*.........................(Elektra)
Little Girl, The
John Michael Montgomery; *Brand New Me*.................(Atlantic)
  Totally Hits-#3-C................................(Atlantic)
Me
Staind; *Dysfunction*........................(Flip/Elektra)
Me And Julio Down By The Schoolyard
Paul Simon; *Greatest Hits, Etc.*......................(Columbia)
  Negotiations And Love Songs, 1971-1986..............(Warner Bros.)
  Paul Simon....................................(Columbia)
  Paul Simon In Concert/Live Rhymin'................(Columbia)
Simon & Garfunkel; *The Concert In Central Park*...........(Warner Bros.)
Mockingbird
Carly Simon & James Taylor; *Best Of Carly Simon & James Taylor*...(Elektra)
  Hotcakes.......................................(Elektra)
Inez Foxx with Charlie Foxx; *Billboard Top R&B Hits-1963-C*.......(Rhino)
  Oldies But Goodies-#8-C.......................(Original Sound)
  Super Oldies Of The '60s-#4-C...................(Audio Fidelity)
Peter, Paul & Mary; *Peter, Paul & Mommy*...............(Warner Bros.)
Other Generation, The
Original Cast; *Flower Drum Song*....................(Angel)
  Flower Drum Song........................(Sony Music Classical)
Papa Loved Mama
Garth Brooks; *Garth Brooks-Double Live*................(Capitol)
  Ropin' The Wind................................(Liberty)
Parents Just Don't Understand
D.J. Jazzy Jeff & The Fresh Prince; *He's The D.J. I'm The Rapper*.......(Jive)
Rock And Roll Waltz
Kay Starr; *Capitol Collectors Series-Kay Starr*..................(Capitol)
Rock Show, The
Blink-182; *Now That's What I Call Music!-#8-C*.............(Virgin)
  Take Off Your Pants And Jacket.........................(MCA)
She's Leaving Home
Al Jarreau; *All Fly Home*...........................(Warner Bros.)
Beatles; *Beatles-Box Set*...........................(Capitol)
  Beatles-Love Songs..............................(Capitol)
  Sgt. Pepper's Lonely Hearts Club Band.............(Capitol)
Slide
Goo Goo Dolls; *Dizzy Up The Girl*...........(Warner Sunset/Reprise)
Somebody Should Leave
Reba McEntire; *Grand Ole Opry-75 Years-#2-C*.............(MCA)
  MCA #1 Hits Of The '80s-#2-C..............(MCA Special Prod.)
  My Kind Of Country..............................(MCA)
  Reba McEntire's Greatest Hits.....................(MCA)
Soul Of My Soul
Michael Bolton; *Love Shouldn't Hurt-C*..................(Qwest)
Squeezebox
Who; *By Numbers*.................................(MCA)
  Hooligans......................................(MCA)
  Who Greatest Hits...............................(MCA)
Teach Your Children
Crosby, Stills & Nash; *CSN*.......................(Atlantic)
Crosby, Stills, Nash & Young; *4 Way Street*..............(Atlantic)
  Deja Vu......................................(Atlantic)
  So Far.......................................(Atlantic)
  ST/The Wonder Years-Music From The Show & Era.......(Atlantic)
Suzy Bogguss/Alison Krauss/Kathy Mattea/Crosby, Stills & Nash; *Red Hot + Country-C*...........................(Mercury)
Thank God For You
Sawyer Brown; *Outskirts Of Town*....................(Curb)
  Sawyer Brown's Greatest Hits 1990-1995..............(Curb)
Way Down The Line
Offspring; *Ixnay On The Hombre*.....................(Columbia)
When Doves Cry
Ginuwine; *The Bachelor*.......................(550 Music)
Prince and the Revolution; *ST/Purple Rain*............(Warner Bros.)
Wonderful
Everclear; *Now That's What I Call Music!-#5-C*.............(Virgin)
  Songs From An American Movie-#1-Learning How To Smile.......(Capitol)
XXX's And OOO's
Trisha Yearwood; *Thinkin' About You*..................(MCA)

Yakety Yak
2 Live Crew; *ST/Twins*..........................(WTG)
Coasters; *Atlantic Rhythm & Blues 1947-1974-#3 (1955-1958)-C*.....(Atlantic)
  Billboard Top Rock 'N' Roll Hits-1958-C..............(Rhino)
  Coasters' Greatest Hits...........................(Atco)
  Cruisin'-1958-C................................(Increase)
  ST/Stand By Me................................(Atlantic)
Your Mama Don't Dance
Loggins & Messina; *Loggins & Messina-On Stage*..............(Columbia)
  Loggins And Messina............................(Columbia)
  Pop Classics Of The '70s-C........................(Columbia)
  The Best Of Friends............................(Columbia)
Poison; *Open Up And Say...Ahh!*....................(Capitol)
  Swallow This Live...............................(Capitol)
You're The Reason Our Kids Are Ugly
Loretta Lynn & Conway Twitty; *Conway Twittty-20 Greatest Hits*.....(MCA)
  Very Best Of Loretta Lynn & Conway Twitty.............(MCA)

PARENTS: SINGLE, STEP, ABSENT, Child Visitation

See Also: BABY, CHILDREN, DEATH, DIVORCE, FAMILY (various), FAMILY PLANNING, LOVE (various), PARENTS: GENERAL, PARENTS: CONCERNED ABOUT TEEN LOVE, TEENAGERS

Another Night
Ricky Skaggs and Kentucky Thunder; *Bluegrass Rules!*..........(Rounder)
Ashes To Ashes
Wallflowers; *The Wallflowers*.........................(Virgin)
Billie Jean
Michael Jackson; *Thriller*............................(Epic)
Black Chick, White Guy
Kid Rock; *Devil Without A Cause*............(Top Dog/Lava/Atlantic)
Boy Named Sue
Johnny Cash; *Columbia Country Classics-#3-Americana-C*.......(Columbia)
  Johnny Cash's Biggest Hits........................(Columbia)
  Johnny Cash's Greatest Hits-#2.....................(Columbia)
  The Man In Black-His Greatest Hits...................(Legacy)
Brand New Mister Me
Mel Tillis & The Statesiders; *The Ultimate Mel Tillis*...........(Bransounds)
Bridge
Queensryche; *Promised Land*.........................(EMI)
Broken Home
Papa Roach; *Infest*........................(DreamWorks/SKG)
Broken Pieces
Strato Vocalz; *Love Shouldn't Hurt-C*....................(Qwest)
Can't Stay
Dave Hollister; *Ghetto Hymns*................(Def Squad/DreamWorks)
Car Wash
Bruce Springsteen; *Tracks*.........................(Columbia)
Cat's In The Cradle
Harry Chapin; *Greatest Stories-Live*....................(Elektra)
  Harry Chapin-Anthology..........................(Elektra)
  Verities & Balderdash............................(Elektra)
Father Of Mine
Everclear; *Now That's What I Call Music!-#2-C*.............(Virgin)
  So Much For The Afterglow.........................(Capitol)
Free To Go
Folk Implosion; *One Part Lullaby*.....................(Interscope)
Good Man Is Hard To Find (Pittsburgh)
Bruce Springsteen; *Tracks*.........................(Columbia)
Have You Seen Mary
Sponge; *Wax Ecstatic*............................(Columbia)
He Didn't Have To Be
Brad Paisley; *Who Needs Pictures*.....................(Arista)
Hungry Heart
Bruce Springsteen; *Bruce Springsteen's Greatest Hits*............(Columbia)
  The River....................................(Columbia)
Bruce Springsteen & The E Street Band; *Bruce Springsteen & The E Street Band Live/1975-85*.........................(Legacy)
I Ain't Ever Satisfied
Gretchen Peters; *The Secret Of Life*................(Purple Crayon Prod.)
Steve Earle & The Dukes; *Ain't Ever Satisfied: The Steve Earle Collection*..................................(Hip-O)
  Exit 0.......................................(MCA)
  Shut Up And Die Like An Aviator....................(MCA)
I Could Never Take The Place Of Your Man
Jordan Knight; *Jordan Knight*.......................(Interscope)
I Don't Call Him Daddy
Doug Supernaw; *Pure Country-Best Of The '90s-C*..............(Priority)
  Red And Rio Grande............................(BNA)
I Take A Lot Of Pride In What I Am
Clint Black; *Mama's Hungry Eyes-Merle Haggard Tribute-C*......(Arista)
Merle Haggard; *Capitol Collectors Series-Merle Haggard*..........(Capitol)
  Merle Haggard's Greatest Hits.....................(Curb)
I Wish I Could Have Been There
John Anderson; *Solid Ground*......................(BNA)

I Wonder If Heaven Got A Ghetto
2Pac; *R U Still Down (Remember Me)* . . . . (Amaru/Jive)
I'm A Survivor
Reba McEntire; *Reba McEntire's Greatest Hits-#3: I'm A Survivor* . . . . . (MCA)
In Pictures
Alabama; *Alabama-Super Hits* . . . .(RCA)
  In Pictures . . . . (RCA)
It Wasn't His Child
Skip Ewing; *Following Yonder Star* . . . . (MCA Special Prod.)
Trisha Yearwood; *The Sweetest Gift* . . . . (MCA)
It's All In Your Head
Diamond Rio; *Diamond Rio IV* . . . . (Arista)
  Diamond Rio's Greatest Hits . . . . (Arista)
Just The Two Of Us
Will Smith; *Big Willie Style* . . . . (Columbia)
Lady Madonna
Beatles; *Beatles 1* . . . . (Capitol)
  Hey Jude . . . . (Capitol)
  Past Masters-Volume Two . . . .(Parlophone)
  The Beatles/1967-1970 . . . . (Capitol)
Wings; *Wings Over America* . . . . (Capitol)
Little Girl, The
John Michael Montgomery; *Brand New Me* . . . . (Atlantic)
  Totally Hits-#3-C . . . . (Atlantic)
Little Green
Joni Mitchell; *Blue.* . . . . (Reprise)
Little Joe The Wrangler's Sister Nell
Skip Gorman; *A Cowboy's Wild Song To His Herd* . . . . (Rounder)
Love Child
Diana Ross & The Supremes; *Billboard Top Rock 'N' Roll Hits-*
  1968-C . . . . (Rhino)
  Diana Ross & The Supremes' Greatest Hits-#3 . . . . (Motown)
  Diana Ross & The Supremes-Anthology (1962-1969) . . . . (Motown)
  Every Great #1 Hit . . . . (Motown)
  Motown Story-First 25 Years-C . . . . (Motown)
  Motown's Biggest Pop Hits-C . . . . (Motown)
Sweet Sensation; *Love Child* . . . . (Atco)
Love Keep Us Together
Martin Sexton; *Black Sheep.* . . . . (Eastern Front)
  The American . . . . (Atlantic)
Memphis
Chuck Berry; *Chuck Berry* . . . . (Audio Fidelity)
  Chuck Berry-Golden Hits . . . . (Mercury)
  Chuck Berry's Greatest Hits . . . . (Everest)
  St. Louis To Liverpool . . . . (Chess)
  ST/Hail! Hail! Rock 'N' Roll. . . . . (MCA)
  The Chess Box-Chuck Berry . . . . (Chess)
  Toronto Rock 'N' Roll Revival-#2-C. . . . . (Accord)
John Cale; *IRS Greatest Hits-#2 & #3-C* . . . . (I.R.S.)
Johnny Rivers; *Best Of Johnny Rivers.* . . . . (EMI)
  Johnny Rivers 1964-1977 . . . . (Rhino)
Lonnie Mack; *Rock Instrumental Classics-#2-'60s-C.* . . . . (Rhino)
  Teen Beat-Instrumental Rock-1957-1965-C . . . . (Capitol)
Momma, Where's My Daddy
Keb' Mo'; *Just Like You* . . . . (Okeh)
Ms. Jackson
Outkast; *Stankonia* . . . . (LaFace/Arista)
My Daddy Was A Milkman
Kentucky HeadHunters; *Pickin' On Nashville* . . . . (Mercury)
My Son Calls Another Man Daddy
Hank Williams With His Drifting Cowboys; *Hank Williams-16*
  Great Hits . . . . (Everest)
  Hank Williams-40 Greatest Hits . . . . (Polydor)
  Rare Takes & Radio Cuts . . . . (Polydor)
New Timer
Bruce Springsteen; *The Ghost Of Tom Joad* . . . . (Columbia)
No Man's Land
John Michael Montgomery; *John Michael Montgomery.* . . . . (Atlantic)
Papa Was A Rollin' Stone
Temptations; *20/20-C* . . . . (Motown)
  25 #1 Hits From 25 Years-C . . . . (Motown)
  All The Million-Sellers . . . . (Motown)
  Billboard Top Rock 'N' Roll Hits-1972-C . . . . (Rhino)
  Compact Command Performances-Temptations . . . . (Motown)
  Temptations-Anthology-The Best Of The Temptations . . . . (Motown)
Serve The Servants
Nirvana; *In Utero.* . . . . (David Geffen Co.)
Son Of Hickory Holler's Tramp
O.C. Smith; *Me And You* . . . . (Columbia Special Prod.)
  Story Songs-C . . . . (K-Tel)
Teddy Boy
Beatles; *The Beatles-Anthology-#3* . . . . (Capitol)
Paul McCartney; *McCartney.* . . . . (Capitol)
Theme From "Alice"
Original Soundtrack; *Television's Greatest Hits-#6-Remote Control-C* . . . (TVT)
Theme From "Augie Doggie"
Original Soundtrack; *Hanna-Barbera Classics-#1-Original Recordings Of*
  The World's Most Famous Cartoon Themes &
  Scores . . . . (Kid Rhino/Rhino 4 Kids)

Hanna-Barbera Pic-A-Nic Basket Of Cartoon
  Classics . . . . (Kid Rhino/Rhino 4 Kids)
Theme From "Blossom"
Original Soundtrack; *Television's Greatest Hits-#7-Cable Ready-C* . . . . .(TVT)
Theme From "Bonanza"
Al Caiola & His Orchestra; *Songs Of The West-#4-Movie & Television*
  Themes-C . . . .(Rhino)
Cincinnati Pops Orchestra/Erich Kunzel; *Round-Up* . . . . (Telarc)
Original Soundtrack; *Television's Greatest Hits-#1-C* . . . . (TVT)
  TV Classic Themes: 25th Anniversary Edition-C . . . . (Breakable)
Theme From "Daktari"
Original Soundtrack; *Television's Greatest Hits-#2-C* . . . . (TVT)
Theme From "Davis Rules"
Original Soundtrack; *Television's Greatest Hits-#7-Cable Ready-C* . . . . .(TVT)
Theme From "Diff'rent Strokes"
Original Soundtrack; *Television's Greatest Hits-#6-Remote Control-C* . . .(TVT)
Theme From "Eight Is Enough"
Original Soundtrack; *Television's Greatest Hits-#6-Remote Control-C* . . .(TVT)
Theme From "Empty Nest"
Original Soundtrack; *Television's Greatest Hits-#7-Cable Ready-C* . . . . .(TVT)
Theme From "Family Affair"
Original Soundtrack; *Television's Greatest Hits-#5-In Living Color-C* . . . .(TVT)
Theme From "Full House"
Original Soundtrack; *Television's Greatest Hits-#7-Cable Ready-C* . . . . .(TVT)
Theme From "I'll Fly Away"
Original Soundtrack; *Television's Greatest Hits-#7-Cable Ready-C* . . . . .(TVT)
Theme From "Johnny Quest"
Original Soundtrack; *Hanna-Barbera Pic-A-Nic Basket Of Cartoon*
  Classics . . . . (Kid Rhino/Rhino 4 Kids)
  Television's Greatest Hits-#2-C . . . . (TVT)
Theme From "Major Dad"
Original Soundtrack; *Television's Greatest Hits-#7-Cable Ready-C* . . . . .(TVT)
Theme From "Murphy Brown"
Original Soundtrack; *CBS: The First 50 Years.* . . . .(TVT)
Theme From "My Little Margie"
Original Soundtrack; *Television's Greatest Hits-#4-Black & White*
  Classics-C . . . . (TVT)
Theme From "My Three Sons"
Original Soundtrack; *CBS: The First 50 Years.* . . . .(TVT)
  Television's Greatest Hits-#1-C . . . . (TVT)
Theme From "My Two Dads"
Original Soundtrack; *Television's Greatest Hits-#7-Cable Ready-C* . . . . .(TVT)
Theme From "Nanny And The Professor"
Original Soundtrack; *Television's Greatest Hits-#5-In Living Color-C* . . . .(TVT)
Theme From "One Day At A Time"
Original Soundtrack; *CBS: The First 50 Years.* . . . .(TVT)
Theme From "The Andy Griffith Show"
Original Soundtrack; *CBS: The First 50 Years.* . . . .(TVT)
  Television's Greatest Hits-#1-C . . . . (TVT)
Theme From "The Beverly Hillbillies"
Original Soundtrack; *CBS: The First 50 Years.* . . . .(TVT)
  Television's Greatest Hits-#1-C . . . . (TVT)
Theme From "The Brady Bunch"
Brady Bunch Kids; *It's A Sunshine Day-Best Of The Brady*
  Bunch Kids. . . . . (MCA)
  Television's Greatest Hits-#2-C . . . . (TVT)
Theme From "The Courtship Of Eddie's Father" (Best Friend)
Nilsson; *Television's Greatest Hits-#2-C.* . . . . (TVT)
Theme From "The Nanny"
Original Soundtrack; *Television's Greatest Hits-#7-Cable Ready-C* . . . . .(TVT)
Theme From "Webster" (Then Came You)
Original Soundtrack; *Television's Greatest Hits-#6-Remote Control-C* . . .(TVT)
Theme From "What's Happening?"
Original Soundtrack; *Television's Greatest Hits-#6-Remote Control-C* . . .(TVT)
Theme From "Who's The Boss"
Original Soundtrack; *Television's Greatest Hits-#6-Remote Control-C* . . .(TVT)
Way Down The Line
Offspring; *Ixnay On The Hombre.* . . . .(Columbia)
What About Us
Total; *Kima, Keisha & Pam* . . . . (Bad Boy/Arista)
  LaFace Records Presents The Platinum Collection-C . . . .(LaFace)
  ST/Soul Food. . . . . (LaFace)
You And Me Against The World
Helen Reddy; *Helen Reddy's Greatest Hits* . . . . (Capitol)
You Better Sit Down Kids
Cher; *Bang, Bang The Early Years.* . . . .(Capitol)

PARTY, Celebrate, Going Out On The Town

See Also: **ALCOHOL, ANNIVERSARY, BARS, BIRTHDAY,
CARNIVALS, DANCE, DRUGS (various), FUN, HAPPINESS,
MUSIC, MUSICAL INSTRUMENTS (various), NIGHT,
SMILE, WEEKEND**

(We're Gonna) Rock Around The Clock
Bill Haley & His Comets; *Bill Haley & His Comets' Greatest Hits* . . . . . . (MCA)

Bill Haley & His Comets' Greatest Hits . . . . (Everest)
Bill Haley & His Comets-Golden Hits . . . . (MCA)
Billboard Top Rock 'N' Roll Hits-1955-C . . . . (Rhino)
ST/American Graffiti . . . . (MCA)

1,2,3,4 (Sumpin' New)
Coolio; ESPN Presents Jock Jams-#2-C. . . . . (Tommy Boy)
MTV Party To Go-#9-C . . . . (Tommy Boy)
Tommy Boy's Greatest Beats-#2-C . . . . (Tommy Boy)

1999
Prince; 1999 . . . .(Warner Bros.)

1st Of Tha Month
Bone Thugs-N-Harmony; E. 1999 Eternal . . . .(Ruthless/Relativity)

After Party
Koffee Brown; Mars/Venus . . . . (Arista)

Ain't Going Down (Til The Sun Comes Up)
Garth Brooks; In Pieces . . . . (Liberty)

All My Rowdy Friends Are Coming Over Tonight
Hank Williams, Jr.; Great Divorce Songs For Him-C . . . .(Warner Bros.)
Hank Williams, Jr.'s Greatest Hits-#2 . . . . (WB/Curb)
Major Moves . . . . (WB/Curb)

All Night Long
Faith Evans featuring Puff Daddy; Keep The Faith . . . .(Bad Boy/Arista)

All Night Long
Montgomery Gentry; Tattoos & Scars . . . . (Columbia)

All Night Long
Asleep At The Wheel featuring Leon Rausch; Tribute To The Music Of Bob
Wills And The Texas Playboys-C . . . . (Liberty)

All Night Long (All Night)
Lionel Richie; Can't Slow Down . . . . (Motown)
Motown Story-First 25 Years-C . . . . (Motown)

Animal House
Stephen Bishop; ST/Animal House . . . .(MCA)

At An Arabian House Party
Raymond Scott; Reckless Nights & Turkish Twilights . . . . (Columbia)

At The Christmas Ball
Bessie Smith; Bessie Smith-The Complete Recordings-#2 . . . . (Legacy)
Jingle Blues-C . . . .(House Of Blues)
Nobody's Blues But Mine . . . . (Columbia)

At The President's Birthday Ball
Glenn Miller & His Orchestra; Complete Glenn Miller & His
Orchestra . . . . (Bluebird)

Bad Boy/Having A Party
Luther Vandross; Best Of Luther Vandross...The Best Of Love . . . . .(Epic)
Forever For Always For Love . . . .(Epic)

Barbie Girl
Aqua; Aquarium . . . .(MCA)
Now That's What I Call Music!-#1-C . . . . (Virgin)

Beer Barrel Polka
Andrews Sisters; Andrews Sisters-16 Great Performances . . . .(MCA)
Best Of The Andrews Sisters . . . .(MCA)
Frankie Yankovic & His Yanks; Frankie Yankovic & His Yanks'
Greatest Hits . . . . (Columbia)
Will Glahe; This Is Will Glahe-Decade Of The '30s . . . . (RCA)

Birthday
Beatles; The Beatles (White Album) . . . . (Capitol)
Daffy Duck; Bugs & Friends Sing The Beatles . . . .(Kid Rhino/Rhino 4 Kids)
Paul McCartney; Tripping The Live Fantastic-Highlights! . . . . (Capitol)
Texas Chainsaw Orchestra; The Texas Chainsaw Orchestra . . . . (Rhino)

Birthday Party
Grandmaster Flash & The Furious Five; Message From Beat Street-The
Best Of-C . . . . (Rhino)

Birthday Party
Pixies Three; Growin' Up Too Fast-The Girl Group Anthology-C . . . . (Mercury)

Bossanovanight
Judson Spence; I Guess I Love It. . . . .(Pioneer)

Boys & Me
Sawyer Brown; Outskirts Of Town . . . . (Curb)

California Love
2Pac featuring Dr. Dre; All Eyez On Me . . . . (Death Row)
MTV Party To Go-#10-C . . . . (Tommy Boy)

Can't Get Enough
Patty Loveless; Patty Loveless-Classics . . . .(Epic)

Celebrate Me Home
Kenny Loggins; Celebrate Me Home . . . . (Columbia)
Kenny Loggins Alive . . . . (Columbia)

Celebration
Kool & The Gang; Celebrate . . . . (De-Lite)
Everything Is-Greatest Hits . . . . (Mercury)

Celebration
Kevin Toney; Pastel Mood . . . . (Ichiban Int'l)

Celebration Day
Led Zeppelin; Led Zeppelin III . . . . (Atlantic)
Led Zeppelin-Box Set . . . . (Atlantic)
ST/The Song Remains The Same . . . . (Swan Song)

Celebration For A Grey Day
Mimi & Richard Farina; Best Of Mimi & Richard Farina . . . . (Vanguard)
Celebrations For A Grey Day . . . . (Vanguard)
Memories . . . . (Vanguard)

Celebration Of The Lizard
Doors; Absolutely Live . . . . (Elektra)

Celebration Song
Steve Miller Band; Brave New World . . . . (Capitol)
Steve Miller Band-Anthology . . . . (Capitol)

Clock Strikes Ten
Cheap Trick; Cheap Trick At Budokan . . . . (Epic)
In Color . . . . (Epic)

Cold Rock A Party
MC Lyte; Bad As I Wanna B . . . . (East West)

Come On Over (All I Want Is You)
Christina Aguilera; Christina Aguilera . . . . (RCA)

Company's Comin'
Porter Wagoner; Essential Porter Wagoner . . . . (RCA)

Cowboys & Playboys
Moe Bandy; Best Of Moe Bandy-Vol. 1 . . . . (Columbia)

Cup Of Life
Ricky Martin; Ricky Martin. . . . . (Columbia)

Dance Little Sister
Rolling Stones; It's Only Rock 'N Roll . . . . (Rolling Stones)
Made In The Shade . . . . (Rolling Stones)

Dance Tonight
Lucy Pearl; Lucy Pearl . . . . (Overbrook/Pookie/Beyond)

Dance With Me
112; Part III . . . .(Bad Boy/Arista)

Dancing On The Ceiling
Lionel Richie; Dancing On The Ceiling . . . . (Motown)

Dig A Pony
Beatles; Let It Be . . . . (Capitol)
The Beatles-Anthology-#3 . . . . (Capitol)

Dim, Dim The Lights (I Want Some Atmosphere)
Bill Haley; From The Original Master Tapes-Bill Haley . . . . (MCA)

Down At The Twist And Shout
Mary Chapin Carpenter; Greatest Country Hits Of The '90s-
1992-C . . . . (Columbia)
Hitchhiker Examplar 2-C . . . . (Columbia)
Shooting Straight In The Dark . . . . (Columbia)
Today's Hot Country-C . . . . (K-Tel)

Enema Party
Buck Naked & The Bare Bottom Boys; Buck Naked & The Bare
Bottom Boys. . . . . (Heyday)

Enjoy Yourself
Guy Lombardo & His Royal Canadians; Best Of Guy Lombardo . . . . . . (MCA)

Enjoy Yourself
Jacksons; Jacksons . . . . (Epic)

Escapade
Janet Jackson; Design Of A Decade-1986/1996 . . . . (A&M)
Janet Jackson's Rhythm Nation 1814 . . . . (A&M)

Everybody's Everything
Santana; Santana . . . . (Columbia)
Santana's Greatest Hits . . . . (Columbia)
Viva Santana! . . . . (Columbia)

Feel So Good
Mase; Harlem World . . . .(Bad Boy/Arista)

Feelin' Single, Seein' Double
Emmylou Harris; Elite Hotel. . . . . (Reprise)

Fiesta
R. Kelly; TP-2.com . . . . (Jive)
R. Kelly featuring Jay-Z; Now That's What I Call Music!-#7-C . . . . .(Virgin)

Fiesta In Rio
Bette Midler; Live At Last . . . .(Atlantic)

Fight For Your Right (To Party)
Beastie Boys; Def Jam Classics-#1-C . . . . (Def Jam)
Heart Of Soul-C . . . . (Columbia)
Licensed To Ill . . . . (Def Jam)

Get On Up
Jodeci; The Show, The After-Party, The Hotel. . . . . (Uptown/MCA)

Get The Party Started
Pink; Missundaztood . . . . (Arista)

Give It Up, Turn It Loose
En Vogue; Funky Divas. . . . . (East West)

Give Myself A Party
Mandy Barnett; I've Got A Right To Cry . . . . (Sire)

Go To The Mardi Gras
Professor Longhair; New Orleans Party Classics-C . . . . (Rhino)

Going Away Party
Manhattan Transfer & Willie Nelson & Asleep At The Wheel; Ride With
Bob-C . . . .(DreamWorks/SKG)

Going Out With The Boys
Jimmie Mack; Jimmie Mack . . . . (Big Tree)

Going To A Go-Go
Miracles; Billboard Top R&B Hits-1966-C. . . . . (Rhino)
Rolling Stones; ''Still Life'' (American Concert 1981). . . . . (Virgin)
Smokey Robinson & The Miracles; Compact Command Performances-
Smokey Robinson & The Miracles . . . . (Motown)
Smokey Robinson & The Miracles' Anthology . . . . (Motown)
Smokey Robinson & The Miracles' Greatest Hits-#2 . . . . (Motown)

Good Time Boy
Buffalo Springfield; *Buffalo Springfield Again* . . . . (Atco)
Good Time Charlie's Got The Blues
Danny O'Keefe; *Breezy Stories*. . . . . (Atlantic)
Seattle Tapes. . . . . (First Warning)
Willie Nelson; *City Of New Orleans* . . . . (Columbia)
Good Time Girl
Lee Ferrell; *Hard Times*. . . . .(TMS)
Good Times
Willie Nelson; *Best Of Willie*. . . . . (RCA)
Minstrel Man . . . . (RCA)
Music From ''Songwriter''. . . . . (Columbia)
Good Times
Rita Coolidge; *Anytime...Anywhere* . . . . (A&M)
Good Times
Hoodoo Gurus; *Blow Your Cool* . . . . (Elektra)
Good Times
Dan Seals; *Dan Seals' Greatest Hits* . . . . (Liberty)
On Arrival. . . . . (Capitol)
Good Times
Jimi Hendrix; *Jimi Hendrix* . . . . (Audio Fidelity)
Good Times
Rolling Stones; *Out Of Our Heads* . . . . (Abkco)
Good Times
Chic; *Plus Grands Succes De Chic* . . . . (Atlantic)
Risque. . . . . (Atlantic)
Good Times
Nat ''King'' Cole; *Ramblin' Rose* . . . . (Capitol)
Good Times
Persuasions; *Street Corner Symphony* . . . . (Capitol)
Green Door
Jim Lowe; *Billboard Top Rock 'N' Roll Hits-1956-C* . . . . . . (Rhino)
Super Hits-#4-C . . . . (Gusto)
Gypsies In The Palace
Jimmy Buffett; *Feeding Frenzy*. . . . . (MCA)
Last Mango In Paris . . . . (MCA)
Have A Good Time
Paul Simon; *Greatest Hits, Etc.*. . . . . (Columbia)
Negotiations And Love Songs, 1971-1986 . . . . (Warner Bros.)
Still Crazy After All These Years. . . . . (Columbia)
Have A Good Time
Elvin Bishop; *Struttin' My Stuff*. . . . . (Capricorn)
Have A Good Time
Rufus Featuring Chaka Khan; *Rufus featuring Chaka Khan* . . . . . . (MCA)
Having A Party
Norma Jean; *Norma Jean*. . . . . (Bearsville)
Pointer Sisters; *Having A Party* . . . . (MCA)
Rod Stewart & Ronnie Wood; *Unplugged...And Seated* . . . . (Warner Bros.)
Sam Cooke; *Best Of Sam Cooke* . . . . (RCA)
Feel It . . . . (RCA)
Live At The Harlem Square Club . . . . (RCA)
This Is Sam Cooke. . . . . (RCA)
Southside Johnny And The Asbury Jukes; *Havin' A Party With Southside
Johnny And The Asbury Jukes* . . . . (Epic)
Hellzapoppin'
Louis Armstrong; *What A Wonderful World* . . . . (Decca Jazz)
Home Alone
R. Kelly featuring Keith Murray; *R. Kelly*. . . . .(Jive)
Honky Tonk Attitude
Joe Diffie; *Honky Tonk Attitude*. (Epic)
Honky Tonk Man
Dwight Yoakam; *Guitars, Cadillacs, Etc., Etc.*. . . . .(Reprise)
Just Lookin' For A Hit . . . . (Reprise)
Johnny Horton; *All Time Legends Of Country Music-C* . . . . (Legacy)
Columbia Country Classics-#2-Honky Tonk Heroes-C . . . . . . (Columbia)
Marty Robbins; *Greatest Country Hits From The Movies-C* . . . . . (Epic)
Horse & Carriage
Cam'ron featuring Mase; *Confessions Of Fire* . . . . (Untertainment/Epic)
House Arrest
Bryan Adams; *Waking Up The Neighbours*. . . . . (A&M)
House Party
J. Geils Band; *Best Of The J. Geils Band* . . . . (Atlantic)
Bloodshot . . . . (Atlantic)
Blow Your Face Out . . . . (Rhino)
I Don't Want To Spoil The Party
Beatles; *Beatles VI*. . . . . (Capitol)
For Sale . . . . (Capitol)
Rosanne Cash; *Greatest Country Hits Of The '80s-1989-C*. . . . . . (Columbia)
Rosanne Cash-Hits-1979-1989 . . . . (Columbia)
I Just Want To Celebrate
Rare Earth; *20 Hard-To-Find Motown Classics-#2-C* . . . . . (Motown)
Motown Superstar Series-#16-Rare Earth . . . . (Motown)
Rare Earth In Concert . . . . (Rare Earth)
I Love The Night Life
Alicia Bridges; *Alicia Bridges* . . . . (Polydor)
Night At Studio 54-C . . . .(Casablanca)
Oldies But Goodies-#14-C . . . . (Original Sound)
Polydor Dance Classics-C . . . . (Polydor)

I Need A Joint
Basehead; *Not In Kansas Anymore* . . . . (Imago)
If You've Got The Money I've Got The Time
Lefty Frizzell; *American Originals-Lefty Frizzell* . . . .(Columbia)
Columbia Country Classics-#2-Honky Tonk Heroes-C . . . . . .(Columbia)
Lefty Frizzell's Greatest Hits. . . . . (Columbia)
Willie Nelson; *Greatest Hits (& Some That Will Be)* . . . .(Columbia)
Sound In Your Mind. . . . . (Columbia)
Willie & Family Live . . . . (Columbia)
In The Cool, Cool, Cool Of The Evening
Bing Crosby; *Best Of Bing Crosby*. . . . . (MCA)
Frank Sinatra; *Days Of Wine And Roses, Moon River, And Other Academy
Award Winners*. . . . . (Reprise)
Rosemary Clooney; *Rosemary Clooney-16 Most Requested Songs* . . . . .(Legacy)
It Sure Is Monday
Mark Chesnutt; *Almost Goodbye* . . . . (MCA)
It's Been A Great Afternoon
Merle Haggard; *For The Record: Merle Haggard-43 Legendary Hits* . . . . (BNA)
I'm Always On A Mountain When I Fall . . . . (MCA)
Merle Haggard's Greatest Hits. . . . . (MCA)
More Of The Best. . . . . (Rhino)
It's My Party
Lesley Gore; *Billboard Top Rock 'N' Roll Hits-1963-C* . . . .(Rhino)
Golden Hits Of Lesley Gore . . . . (Mercury)
Good Time Rock 'N' Roll-C . . . . (MCA)
Lesley Gore-Anthology . . . . (Mercury)
Oldies But Goodies-#3-C . . . . (Original Sound)
Jailhouse Rock
Blues Brothers; *ST/The Blues Brothers* . . . . (Atlantic)
Elvis Presley; *Billboard Top Rock 'N' Roll Hits-1957-C* . . . . . .(Rhino)
Elvis Recorded Live On Stage In Memphis . . . . (RCA)
Elvis-A Legendary Performer, Volume 2. . . . . (RCA)
Number One Hits. . . . . (RCA)
Rocker. . . . . (RCA)
Worldwide 50 Gold Award Hits, Vol. 1, Parts 1 & 2 . . . . . . (RCA)
Jeff Beck Group; *Beck-Ola* . . . . (Epic)
Jamboree
Naughty By Nature Featuring Zhane'; *19 Naughty Nine:
Nature's Fury* . . . .(Arista)
Josie
Steely Dan; *Aja* . . . . (MCA)
Steely Dan's Greatest Hits . . . . (MCA)
Jump Jive An' Wail
Brian Setzer Orchestra; *Dirty Boogie*. . . . . (Interscope)
Now That's What I Call Music!-#1-C . . . . (Virgin)
Louis Prima; *Capitol Collectors Series-Louis Prima*. . . . . . . (Capitol)
Ultra-Lounge-#5-Wild, Cool & Swingin'-C . . . .(Capitol)
Just Got Paid
'N Sync; *No Strings Attached*. . . . . (Jive)
Let The Good Times Roll
Barbra Streisand; *Butterfly* . . . .(Columbia)
Betty Everett & Jerry Butler; *Delicious Together* . . . . (Vee-Jay)
Starring Betty Everett . . . . (Tradition)
Bobby Bland & B.B. King; *Together Again Live* . . . . (MCA)
Jerry Lee Lewis; *Golden Rock & Roll* . . . . (Sun)
Louis Jordan; *Best Of Louis Jordan* . . . . (MCA)
Molly Hatchet; *Flirtin' With Disaster* . . . . (Epic)
Nilsson; *Nilsson Schmilsson* . . . . (RCA)
Phoebe Snow; *Phoebe Snow* . . . . (MCA)
Ray Charles; *Genius Of Ray Charles* . . . . (Atlantic)
Shirley & Lee; *Billboard Top R&B Hits-1956-C* . . . .(Rhino)
History Of New Orleans R&B-#1-1950-1958-C . . . . (Rhino)
ST/Stand By Me . . . . (Atlantic)
Super Oldies Of The '50s-#4-C . . . . (Audio Fidelity)
Tony Bennett with B.B. King; *Playin' With My Friends-Bennett Sings The
Blues-C*. . . . .(Columbia)
Let's Celebrate
Stranglers; *Stranglers-10* . . . . (Epic)
Let's Celebrate
Skyy; *Best Of Skyy* . . . . (ZYX)
Let's Celebrate
Midnight Star; *Planetary Invasion*. . . . . (Solar)
Let's Get Down
Tony Toni Tone; *House Of Music* . . . .(Mercury)
Tony Toni Tone-Hits . . . .(Mercury)
Ultimate Hip Hop Party-1998-C . . . .(Arista)
Let's Get Rocked
Def Leppard; *Adrenalize* . . . . (Mercury)
Life In The Fast Lane
Eagles; *Eagles Live* . . . . (Asylum)
Hotel California . . . . (Asylum)
ST/FM . . . . (MCA)
Lipstick On Your Collar
Connie Francis; *Very Best Of Connie Francis* . . . . (Polydor)
Listen To A Country Song
Loggins & Messina; *Loggins & Messina-On Stage* . . . .(Columbia)
Sittin' In . . . .(Columbia)
Lynn Anderson; *Country Chartbusters-#2*. . . . . (Columbia)
Lynn Anderson's Greatest Hits . . . . (Columbia)

Live It Up
Isley Brothers; *Forever Gold* . . . .(T-Neck/Columbia)
   Isley Brothers' Greatest Hits . . . .(T-Neck/Columbia)
   Live It Up . . . .(T-Neck/Columbia)
Live It Up
Ted Nugent; *Cat Scratch Fever* . . . .(Epic)
Live It Up
Crosby, Stills & Nash; *Live It Up* . . . . (Atlantic)
Lively Up Yourself
Bob Marley & The Wailers; *Babylon By Bus* . . . . (Tuff Gong)
   Bob Marley & The Wailers-Live . . . . (Tuff Gong)
   Natty Dread . . . . (Tuff Gong)
Livin' It Up (Friday Night)
Bell & James; *Bell & James* . . . .(A&M)
Loosen Up My Strings
Clint Black; *Nothin' But The Taillights* . . . .(RCA)
Louisiana Saturday Night
Don Williams; *Best Of Cajun Country-C* . . . . (Era)
   Best Of Don Williams-#4 . . . .(MCA)
   Don Williams-Country Boy . . . .(MCA)
Jimmy C. Newman; *From The Vaults: Decca Country Classics-1934-*
   1973-C . . . . (Decca)
   Grand Ole Opry-75 Years-#2-C . . . . (MCA)
   Progressive CC . . . . (Plantation)
Mel McDaniel; *Mel McDaniel's Greatest Hits* . . . . (Capitol)
Mama Don't Get Dressed Up For Nothing
Brooks & Dunn; *Borderline* . . . . (Arista)
Mama Told Me Not To Come
Randy Newman; *12 Songs* . . . . (Reprise)
   Randy Newman/Live . . . .(Warner Archives)
Three Dog Night; *Best Of Three Dog Night* . . . . (MCA)
   Billboard Top Rock 'N' Roll Hits-1970-C . . . . (Rhino)
Wilson Pickett; *Wilson Pickett's Greatest Hits* . . . . (Atlantic)
Man! I Feel Like A Woman
Shania Twain; *Come On Over* . . . . (Mercury)
   VH-1 Divas Live-C . . . .(Epic)
Miami
Will Smith; *Big Willie Style* . . . . (Columbia)
Midnight Girl/Sunset Town
Sweethearts Of The Rodeo; *Sweethearts Of The Rodeo* . . . . (Columbia)
Million Dollar Bash
Bob Dylan; *Biograph* . . . . (Columbia)
Bob Dylan And The Band; *Basement Tapes* . . . . (Columbia)
Motel Party Baby
Dinosaurs; *Dinosaurs* . . . .(Relix)
New Orleans Ceremony
Dukes Of Dixieland; *Best Of Dukes Of Dixieland* . . . . (Columbia)
Night (Feel Like Getting Down)
Billy Ocean; *Night (Feel Like Getting Down)* . . . .(Epic)
Night Fever
Bee Gees; *Bee Gees' Greatest* . . . . (Polydor)
   ST/Saturday Night Fever . . . . (Polydor)
Nothin' But A Good Time
Poison; *Open Up And Say...Ahh!* . . . . (Capitol)
   Swallow This Live . . . . (Capitol)
Off The Wall
Jacksons; *Jacksons Live* . . . .(Epic)
Michael Jackson; *Off The Wall* . . . .(Epic)
Old Enough To Know Better
Wade Hayes; *Country Dance Hits-C* . . . . (Columbia)
   Old Enough To Know Better . . . . (Columbia)
   Steppin' Country-#2-C . . . . (Columbia)
   Super Hits Of 1994-C . . . . (Columbia)
Omaha Celebration
Pat Metheny; *Bright Size Life* . . . . (ECM)
Once-A-Year Day!
Original Cast; *ST/Pajama Game* . . . . (Collectables)
One More Last Chance
Vince Gill; *I Still Believe In You* . . . . (MCA)
   The Ultimate Country Party-C . . . . (Arista)
   Vince Gill-Souvenirs . . . . (MCA)
One O'clock Jump
Count Basie & His Orchestra; *Swingingest Sounds Ever Heard-C* . . . . . (Hip-O)
One Of Those Nights Tonight
Lorrie Morgan; *Shakin' Things Up* . . . . (BNA)
   To Get To You-Greatest Hits Collection . . . . (BNA)
Out With A Bang
David Lee Murphy; *Out With A Bang* . . . . (MCA)
Ozark Mountain Jubilee
Oak Ridge Boys; *Deliver* . . . . (MCA)
   Oak Ridge Boys' Greatest Hits 2 . . . . (MCA)
   Ozark Mountain Jubilee . . . .(MCA Special Prod.)
P.A.R.T.Y.
Denise LaSalle; *Under The Influence* . . . . (MCA)
Party
Elvis Presley; *Essential Elvis-The First Movies* . . . . (RCA)
   ST/Loving You . . . . (RCA)
Party
En Vogue; *Born To Sing* . . . . (Atlantic)

Party
Boston; *Don't Look Back* . . . . (Epic)
Party
Marillion; *Holidays In Eden* . . . . (I.R.S.)
Party
Big Audio Dynamite; *This Is Big Audio Dynamite* . . . . (Columbia)
Party
Kris Kross; *Totally Krossed Out* . . . .(Ruffhouse)
Party Ain't A Party
Queen Pen with Lost Boyz & Crew; *My Melody* . . . . . . (Lil' Man/Interscope)
   The Source Presents Hip Hop Hits-#2-C . . . .(PolyGram TV)
Party All Night
Quiet Riot; *Condition Critical* . . . . (Epic Portrait Assoc.)
   Winners Take All . . . . (Sony Music Special Prod.)
Party All The Time
Eddie Murphy; *How Could It Be* . . . . (Columbia)
Party At Ground Zero
Fishbone; *Fishbone* . . . . (Columbia)
   Richard Blade's Flashback Favorites-C . . . . (Oglio)
Party At The Berlin Wall
Root Boy Slim & The Sex Change Band; *Root 6* . . . . (Naked Language)
Party At The Prune Farm
Lou & Peter Berryman; *Cupid's Trash Truck* . . . . (Cornbelt)
Party Continues
Jermaine Dupri; *Presents Life In 1472-Original*
   Soundtrack . . . . (So So Def/Columbia)
Party Crowd
David Lee Murphy; *Out With A Bang* . . . . (MCA)
Party Doll
Buddy Knox; *Best Of Buddy Knox* . . . . (Rhino)
   Billboard Top Rock 'N' Roll Hits-1957-C . . . . (Rhino)
   ST/American Graffiti . . . . (MCA)
Party Down
Willie Hutch; *Very Best Of Willie Hutch* . . . . (Motown)
Party Freak
Cashflow; *45-#884454* . . . . (Atlanta Int'l)
Party Girl
Elvis Costello; *Girls Girls Girls* . . . . (Columbia)
Elvis Costello & The Attractions; *Armed Forces* . . . . (Rykodisc)
Linda Ronstadt; *Mad Love* . . . . (Elektra)
Party Girl
Bernadette Carroll; *20 Million-Dollar Memories-#2-C* . . . . (Laurie)
   22 Leaders Of The Pack-#1-C . . . . (Laurie)
Party Girl
T-Bone Walker; *T-Bone Walker* . . . . (Blue Note)
   T-Bone Walker-Complete Imperial Recordings-1950-1954 . . . . (EMI)
Party Girl
U2; *Under A Blood Red Sky* . . . . (Island)
Party Girls
Rick James Presents The Stone City Band; *In 'n' Out* . . . . (Gordy)
Party Girls
Mink De Ville; *Mink De Ville* . . . . (Capitol)
Party In Senegal
Wallets; *Take It* . . . . (Twin-Tone)
Party In The Graveyard
Haunted Garage; *Possession Park* . . . . (Metal Blade)
Party In The Parking Lot
Johnny Van Zant; *Brickyard Road* . . . .(Atlantic)
Party Lights
Claudine Clark; *Collectables Presents The History Of*
   Rock-#4-C . . . .(Collectables)
   Wonder Women-History Of Girl Group Sound-C . . . . (Rhino)
Party Lights
Natalie Cole; *Natalie Cole-Collection* . . . . (Capitol)
   Natalie Cole-Live . . . . (Capitol)
   Unpredictable . . . . (Capitol)
Party Lights
Gap Band; *The Gap Band II* . . . . (Mercury)
Party Night
Curtis Mayfield; *Do It All Night* . . . . (Curtom)
   Give, Get, Take And Have . . . . (Curtom)
Party Night
Isley Brothers; *Grand Slam* . . . . (T-Neck/Columbia)
Party People
Solomon Burke; *Home In Your Heart-Best Of Solomon Burke* . . . . . . (Rhino)
Party People
Joe South; *Best Of Joe South* . . . . (Rhino)
Party People
Parliament; *Gloryhallastoopid* . . . . (Casablanca)
Party Till The Cows Come Home
Elvin Bishop Group; *Bill Graham Presents The Last Days Of The*
   Fillmore-C . . . . (Epic Portrait Assoc.)
Party 'Till The Money Runs Out
Radiators; *Total Evaporation* . . . . (Epic)
Party Time
T.G. Sheppard; *Great Divorce Songs For Him-C* . . . . (Warner Bros.)
   T.G. Sheppard's All-Time Greatest Hits . . . . (Warner Bros.)
   T.G. Sheppard's Greatest Hits . . . . (Warner Bros./Curb)

Party Time U.S.A.
Oscar Peterson; *Silent Partner* . . . (Pablo)
Party Train
Gap Band; *Train Trax-C* . . . (Sony Music Special Prod.)
Partyin' Gal
Charlie Daniels Band; *Windows* . . . (Epic)
Party's Over
Judy Garland; *One & Only* . . . (Capitol)
Judy Holliday; *Broadway Magic-The 1960s-C* . . . (Columbia)
Judy Holliday/Original Cast; *Bells Are Ringing* . . . (Columbia)
Mel Torme; *Live At The Maisonette* . . . (Atlantic)
Shirley Bassey; *Shirley Bassey-Live At Carnegie Hall* . . . (United Artists)
Party's Over
Journey; *Journey-Captured* . . . (Columbia)
Party's Over
Tesla; *Great Radio Controversy* . . . (Geffen)
Party's Over
Raspberries; *Capitol Collectors Series-The Raspberries* . . . (Capitol)
Party's Over
Willie Nelson; *Always On My Mind* . . . (Columbia)
Party's Over
Marvin Gaye; *Hello Broadway* . . . (Motown)
Partytown
Glenn Frey; *No Fun Aloud* . . . (Asylum)
Praise You
Fatboy Slim; *Now That's What I Call Music!-#2-C* . . . (Virgin)
You've Come A Long Way, Baby . . . (Skint)
Prince Is Giving A Ball
Television Cast; *Cinderella-The CBS Television Network Production* . . . (Columbia)
Put Your Hands Where My Eyes Could See
Busta Rhymes; *When Disaster Strikes* . . . (Elektra)
Raisin' Cane In Texas
Gene Watson; *All-Time Country Classics-#1-C* . . . (Capitol)
Texas State Of Mind-C . . . (Capitol)
Raisin' Hell
Elvin Bishop; *Live! Raisin' Hell* . . . (Capricorn)
Raising Hell
Run-D.M.C.; *Raising Hell* . . . (Profile)
Really Good Time
Roxy Music; *Country Life* . . . (Atco)
Rip It Up
Elvis Presley; *Elvis* . . . (RCA)
Rocker . . . (RCA)
Little Richard; *Big Hits* . . . (Crescendo)
Grooviest 17 Original Hits . . . (Specialty)
Little Richard-18 Greatest Hits . . . (Rhino)
Little Richard's Greatest Hits . . . (Everest)
Rip This Joint
Rolling Stones; *Exile On Main Street* . . . (Virgin)
Made In The Shade . . . (Rolling Stones)
Road Goes On Forever, The
Joe Ely; *Love & Danger* . . . (MCA)
Rock And Roll All Nite
Kiss; *Alive!* . . . (Mercury)
Double Platinum . . . (Mercury)
Dressed To Kill . . . (Mercury)
Heavy Metal Memories-C . . . (Rhino)
Smashes, Thrashes & Hits . . . (Mercury)
The Originals . . . (Casablanca)
Route 66
Asleep At The Wheel; *Served Live* . . . (Capitol)
Very Best Of Asleep At The Wheel Since 1970 . . . (Relentless/Madacy)
Wheelin' & Dealin' . . . (Capitol)
Depeche Mode; *ST/Earth Girls Are Easy* . . . (Sire)
George Maharis; *45-#15-2227* . . . (Epic)
Manhattan Transfer; *Bop doo-wopp* . . . (Atlantic)
Nat "King" Cole; *Capitol Collectors Series-Nat "King" Cole* . . . (Capitol)
The Nat "King" Cole Story . . . (Capitol)
Natalie Cole; *Unforgettable With Love* . . . (Elektra)
Rolling Stones; *December's Children (and everybody's)* . . . (Abkco)
England's Newest Hit Makers/The Rolling Stones . . . (Abkco)
Sam's Place
Buck Owens & The Buckaroos; *Billboard Top Country Hits-1967-C* . . . (Rhino)
Shit You Hear At Parties
Minutemen; *Ballot Result* . . . (SST)
Shoot Your Shot
J. Geils Band; *Blow Your Face Out* . . . (Rhino)
Junior Walker & The All Stars; *Junior Walker & The All Stars' Greatest Hits* . . . (Motown)
Junior Walker & The All Stars-Anthology . . . (Motown)
Shotgun . . . (Motown)
Slow Bus Movin' (Howard's Beach Party)
Fishbone; *Truth & Soul* . . . (Columbia)
Somethin' 4 Da Honeyz
Montell Jordan; *This Is How We Do It* . . . (PMP/RAL)
Splish Splash
Barbra Streisand; *Wet* . . . (Columbia)
Bobby Darin; *Bobby Darin's Greatest Hits* . . . (Curb)
Oldies But Goodies-#8-C . . . (Original Sound)
Splish Splash-Best Of Bobby Darin-#1 . . . (Atlantic)
The Bobby Darin Story . . . (Atlantic)
Sha Na Na; *Having An Oldies Party With Sha Na Na* . . . (K-Tel)
Start The Commotion
Wiseguys; *Now That's What I Call Music!-#8-C* . . . (Virgin)
The Antidote . . . (Mammoth)
Stay All Night (Stay A Little Longer)
Backwoods Banjo; *Jes' Fine* . . . (Rounder)
Mark Chesnutt & Asleep At The Wheel; *Ride With Bob-C* . . . (DreamWorks/SKG)
Willie Nelson; *Willie & Family Live* . . . (Columbia)
Steppin' Out With My Baby
Fred Astaire; *Cheek To Cheek: The Irving Berlin Songbook-C* . . . (Verve)
Fred Astaire At MGM . . . (Rhino)
ST/Easter Parade . . . (Rhino)
Steppin' Out-Astaire Sings . . . (Verve)
Tony Bennett; *MTV Unplugged-Tony Bennett* . . . (Columbia)
Steppin' Out . . . (Columbia)
Stoned Soul Picnic
5th Dimension; *Greatest Hits On Earth* . . . (Arista)
Laura Nyro; *Eli And The Thirteenth Confession* . . . (Columbia)
Live At The Bottom Line . . . (Cypress)
Swingin'
John Anderson; *John Anderson's Greatest Hits* . . . (Warner Bros.)
Swingin' Country Favorites-C . . . (Warner Bros.)
Wild & Blue . . . (Warner Bros.)
Swiss Celebration
David Friedman; *Of The Wind's Eye* . . . (Enja)
Tearin' It Up (And Burnin' It Down)
Garth Brooks; *Garth Brooks-Double Live* . . . (Capitol)
Telephone Road
Steve Earle; *Alt. Country-C* . . . (Simitar)
El Corazon . . . (E Squared)
Texas Party
Johnny Copeland; *Boom Boom* . . . (Rounder)
Texas Tea Party
Benny Goodman; *Benny Goodman-Early Years* . . . (Biograph)
That Party
Harry Connick, Jr.; *She* . . . (Columbia)
Theme From "Monday Night Football"
Original Soundtrack; *Television's Greatest Hits-#6-Remote Control-C* . . . (TVT)
Theme From "Wayne's World"
Mike Myers & Dana Carvey; *ST/Wayne's World* . . . (Reprise)
There Goes The Neighborhood
Sheryl Crow; *The Globe Sessions* . . . (A&M)
There'll Be A Hot Time In The Old Town Tonight
Bessie Smith; *Bessie Smith-The Complete Recordings-#3* . . . (Legacy)
Louis Armstrong; *Best Of Louis Armstrong* . . . (Audio Fidelity)
Turk Murphy's San Francisco Jazz Band; *Turk Murphy's San Francisco Jazz Band* . . . (Good Time Jazz)
Woody Herman; *The Uncollected Woody Herman & His First Herd* . . . (Hindsight)
There's Going To Be A Party
Bob Wills; *Stay A Little Longer-The Original Columbia Recordings* . . . (Roswell/RCA)
They're All Out Of Liquor, Let's Find Another Party
Waitresses; *Best Of The Waitresses* . . . (Polydor)
This Is How We Do It
Montell Jordan; *ABC Monday Night Football Jamz-C* . . . (Hollywood)
This Is How We Do It . . . (PMP/RAL)
Tonight, I Celebrate My Love
Peabo Bryson; *Tonight I Celebrate My Love* . . . (Capitol)
Peabo Bryson & Roberta Flack; *Born To Love* . . . (Capitol)
Quiet Storms 2-C . . . (MCA)
The Peabo Bryson Collection . . . (Capitol)
Roberta Flack; *Softly With These Songs-The Best Of Roberta Flack* . . . (Atlantic)
Tonight's Tha Night
Kris Kross; *Ruffhouse Records Greatest Hits-C* . . . (Ruffhouse)
Young Rich & Dangerous . . . (Ruffhouse)
Too Much Fun
Commander Cody & His Lost Planet Airmen; *Live From Deep In The Heart Of Texas* . . . (MCA)
Too Much Fun-Best Of Commander Cody & His Lost Planet Airmen . . . (MCA)
Too Pooped To Pop
Chuck Berry; *Rockin' At The Hops* . . . (Chess)
The Chess Box-Chuck Berry . . . (Chess)
Top Hat, White Tie And Tails
Fred Astaire; *Irving Berlin Songbook* . . . (Verve)
Tupperware Party
Doughboys; *Happy Accidents* . . . (Restless)
Turn It Up
Busta Rhymes; *When Disaster Strikes* . . . (Elektra)
TV Party
Black Flag; *7-Inch Wonders Of The World-C* . . . (SST)
Damaged . . . (SST)
ST/Repo Man . . . (MCA)

Two Step
Dave Matthews Band; *Crash* (RCA)
Up Around The Bend
Creedence Clearwater Revival; *1970* (Fantasy)
Cosmo's Factory (Fantasy)
Creedence Clearwater Revival-Chronicle (Fantasy)
More Creedence Gold (Fantasy)
Hanoi Rocks; *Two Steps From The Move* (Epic)
Virtual Party (See_You@Party.net)
Peter, Paul & Mary; *Lifelines Live* (Warner Bros.)
Wait A Minute
Ray-J; *This Ain't A Game* (Atlantic)
Waltz For A Ball
Television Cast; *Cinderella-The CBS Television Network Production* (Columbia)
Wasn't That A Party
Rovers; *Wasn't That A Party* (Epic)
We Just Wanna Party With You
Snoop Doggy Dogg; *ST/Men In Black* (Columbia)
We Thuggin'
Fat Joe; *Jealous Ones Still Envy (J.O.S.E.)* (Terror Squad/Atlantic)
Welcome To The Fold
Filter; *Title Of Record* (Reprise)
What's The New Mary Jane
Beatles; *The Beatles-Anthology-#3* (Capitol)
Where Have All The Good Times Gone
Kinks; *Kinks' Greatest Hits* (Rhino)
One For The Road (Arista)
Where Have All The Good Times Gone
David Bowie; *Bowie Pin Ups* (Rykodisc)
Where Have All The Good Times Gone
Van Halen; *Diver Down* (Warner Bros.)
Where Have All The Good Times Gone
Elton John; *Jump Up!* (MCA)
Where The Party At
Jagged Edge; *Jagged Little Thrill* (So So Def/Columbia)
Wildwood Days
Bobby Rydell; *Bobby Rydell* (Big Top)
Will 2K
Will Smith; *Willenium* (Columbia)
Your Good Girl's Gonna Go Bad
Billie Jo Spears; *Best Of Billie Jo Spears* (CEMA Special Prod.)
Best Of Billie Jo Spears (Razor & Tie)
K.T. Oslin; *Tammy Wynette...Remembered-C* (Asylum)
Tammy Wynette; *Tammy Wynette-Anniversary-20 Years Of Hits* (Epic)
Tammy Wynette's Greatest Hits (Epic)
Your Good Girl's Gonna Go Bad (Legacy)
Your Mama Don't Dance
Loggins & Messina; *Loggins & Messina-On Stage* (Columbia)
Loggins And Messina (Columbia)
Pop Classics Of The '70s-C (Columbia)
The Best Of Friends (Columbia)
Poison; *Open Up And Say...Ahh!* (Capitol)
Swallow This Live (Capitol)

PATRIOTISM, National Pride

See Also: **COUNTRIES: A-Z, COUNTRIES: AMERICA, DRAFT, FREEDOM, HEROISM, MONTHS & DATES: JULY, POLITICS (various), PRESIDENTS, PROTEST, WAR**

America
Neil Diamond; *12 Greatest Hits-#2* (Columbia)
Hot August Night II (Columbia)
ST/The Jazz Singer (Capitol)
America
Waylon Jennings; *Waylon Jennings' Greatest Hits-#2* (RCA)
America (My Country 'Tis Of Thee)
Mormon Tabernacle Choir; *God Bless America* (Sony Music Classical)
Original Soundtrack; *School Days-Kids Classics* (Benson)
Pat Boone; *Star Spangled Banner* (Word)
Spirit Of Freedom Singers with Roland Shaw & His Orchestra; *Stars And Stripes Forever-#2-C* (Volcano Entertainment)
America The Beautiful
American Philharmonic Orchestra Orchestra & Chorus; *Stars And Stripes Forever-#2-C* (Volcano Entertainment)
Elvis Presley; *Elvis Aron Presley* (RCA)
Frank Sinatra; *God Bless America-C* (Columbia)
Keb' Mo'; *Big Wide Grin* (Sony Wonder)
Lee Greenwood; *American Patriot* (Capitol)
Mormon Tabernacle Choir; *God Bless America* (Sony Music Classical)
This Is My Country (Columbia)
Original Soundtrack; *School Days-Kids Classics* (Benson)
Ray Charles; *Ray Charles' Greatest Hits-#2* (Rhino)
Ray Charles-His Greatest Hits-#2 (Dunhill Compact Classics)
Star Spangled Band; *Red, White & Bluegrass-C* (C.M.H. Prod.)
Willie Nelson; *America: A Tribute To Heroes-C* (Interscope)
American Patrol
Glenn Miller & His Orchestra; *Glenn Miller & His Orchestra-Pure Gold* (Bluebird)
Moonlight Serenade (Ranwood)
Stars And Stripes Forever-#2-C (Volcano Entertainment)
The Unforgettable Glenn Miller & His Orchestra (RCA)
An American Trilogy
Elvis Presley; *Aloha from Hawaii via Satellite* (RCA)
Elvis Aron Presley (RCA)
Elvis Recorded Live On Stage In Memphis (RCA)
Madison Square Garden (RCA)
ST/This Is Elvis (RCA)
Mickey Newbury; *Frisco Mabel Joy* (Mountain Retreat)
Stars And Stripes Forever-#2-C (Volcano Entertainment)
Anchors Aweigh
Firehouse Five Plus Two; *Goes To Sea* (Good Time Jazz)
Original Soundtrack; *Top Ten College Fight Songs* (K-Tel)
Pat Boone; *Star Spangled Banner* (Word)
Angels Of Mercy
Glenn Miller & His Orchestra; *Complete Glenn Miller & His Orchestra* (Bluebird)
Any Bonds Today?
Andrews Sisters; *Swing Out To Victory: Songs Of World War II-C* (ISD/Intersound)
Barry Wood; *78-#27478* (Victor)
Bing Crosby; *Original Soundtrack Sessions* (Vintage Jazz Classics)
Are The Good Times Really Over (I Wish A Buck Was Still Silver)
Merle Haggard; *Big City* (Epic)
For The Record: Merle Haggard-43 Legendary Hits (BNA)
Greatest Country Hits Of The '80s-1982-C (Columbia)
His Epic Hits-First 11 To Be Continued-C (Epic)
Army Air Corps
Fred Waring's Pennsylvanians; *Very Best Of Fred Waring & The Pennsylvanians* (Reader's Digest Music)
Glenn Miller; *Best Of The Lost Recordings And The Secret Broadcasts* (RCA Victor)
V-Disc Recordings-Glenn Miller (Collector's Choice)
Ballad Of The Green Berets
Barry Sadler; *Cruisin'-1966-C* (Increase)
Hits Of The Sixties-C (Intercom Music)
More American Graffiti-#4-C (MCA)
Nipper's Greatest Hits Of The '60s-#2-C (RCA)
Super Hits-#3-C (Gusto)
Bang The Drum Slowly
Emmylou Harris; *Red Dirt Girl* (Nonesuch)
Fightin' Side Of Me
Merle Haggard; *All American* (Capitol)
Best Of Merle Haggard (Capitol)
Capitol Collectors Series-Merle Haggard (Capitol)
The Fightin' Side Of Me (Capitol)
Merle Haggard & The Strangers; *Songs I'll Always Sing* (Capitol)
For Your Country And My Country
Frances Alda; *78-#64689* (Victor)
Peerless Quartet; *78-#2273* (Columbia)
Freedom
Paul McCartney; *Driving Rain* (Columbia)
The Concert For New York City-C (Columbia)
Freedom Train, The
Bing Crosby; *Bing Crosby-Complete Recordings* (MCA)
Peggy Lee; *Peggy Lee-Complete Recordings-1941-1947* (Legacy)
Give Me Your Tired, Your Poor
Mormon Tabernacle Choir; *Around The World: A Musical Journey Of Best-Loved Favorites* (Sony Music Classical)
God Bless America
Anita Bryant; *Golden Classics-Anita Bryant* (Collectables)
Bill & Gloria Gaither; *Kennedy Center Homecoming: A Celebration Of Our Faith And Heritage* (Springhouse Music Grp./Chordant)
Celine Dion; *America: A Tribute To Heroes-C* (Interscope)
God Bless America-C (Columbia)
Drew Carey; *ST/The Drew Carey Show* (Rhino)
Frank Zappa; *Uncle Meat* (Barking Pumpkin)
Kate Smith; *Best Of Kate Smith* (RCA)
God Bless America (Pickwick)
Kate Smith-Legendary Performer (RCA)
Nipper's Greatest Hits Of The '30s-#1-C (RCA)
Stars And Stripes Forever-#2-C (Volcano Entertainment)
LeAnn Rimes; *You Light Up My Life-Inspirational Songs* (Curb)
Lee Greenwood; *American Patriot* (Capitol)
Mormon Tabernacle Choir; *God Bless America* (Sony Music Classical)
Original Soundtrack; *ST/The Deer Hunter* (Capitol)
Peter Pan Kids; *I Love America Sing Along* (Compose)
Robert Shaw Chorale; *Battle Cry Of Freedom* (RCA)
God Bless America Again
Bobby Bare; *Best Of Bobby Bare* (Razor & Tie)
Country Shots: God Bless America-C (Rhino)
Loretta Lynn & Conway Twitty; *From Seven Till Ten* (MCA Special Prod.)
United Talent (MCA)
Very Best Of Loretta Lynn & Conway Twitty (MCA)

God Bless The USA
Lee Greenwood; *American Patriot* .... (Capitol)
God Bless America-C .... (Columbia)
God Bless The USA .... (MCA Special Prod.)
Inside Out/You've Got A Good Love Comin' .... (MCA)
Lee Greenwood's Greatest Hits .... (MCA)
Lee Greenwood's Greatest Hits-#2 .... (MCA)
Today's Country Classics-C .... (MCA Special Prod.)
Happy Birthday Dear America/In 1776
Ella Jenkins; *We Are All America's Children* .... (Smithsonian Folkways)
I Am A Patriot
Jackson Browne; *World In Motion* .... (Elektra)
Little Steven; *Voice Of America* .... (Razor & Tie)
I Want To Hear A Yankee Doodle Tune
George M. Cohan; *Music From The New York Stage (1890-1920)-#1-1890-1908-C* .... (Pearl)
I'm Getting Tired So I Can Sleep
Dinah Shore; *The Eddie Cantor Radio Show-1942-1943* .... (Original Cast)
In America
Charlie Daniels Band; *A Decade Of Hits* .... (Epic)
Full Moon .... (Epic)
Me & The Boys .... (Epic)
Let's Roll
Neil Young; *Let's Roll-CD Single* .... (Reprise)
Living In America
James Brown; *Gravity* .... (Scotti Bros.)
Rocky Story-C .... (Scotti Bros.)
ST/Rocky IV .... (Scotti Bros.)
Mr. Lincoln
Hank Williams, Jr.; *America (The Way I See It)* .... (WB/Curb)
Major Moves .... (WB/Curb)
My Own United States
William H. Thompson; *Music From The New York Stage (1890-1920)-#1-1890-1908-C* .... (Pearl)
Oh! How I Hate To Get Up In The Morning
Irving Berlin; *American Songbook Series-Irving Berlin* .... (Smithsonian Collection)
War Years-C .... (ISD/Intersound)
Soundtrack; *American Musical Theater-#2* .... (Smithsonian Collection)
Okie From Muskogee
Merle Haggard; *Friend In California* .... (Epic)
Merle Haggard & The Strangers; *Best Of Merle Haggard & The Strangers* .... (Capitol)
Capitol Collectors Series-Merle Haggard & The Strangers .... (Capitol)
Country Music Classics-#3-1965-1970-C .... (K-Tel)
For The Record: Merle Haggard-43 Legendary Hits .... (BNA)
Songs I'll Always Sing .... (Capitol)
ST/Platoon .... (Atlantic)
Orange Crush
R.E.M.; *Best Of MTV's 120 Minutes-#2-C* .... (Rhino)
Green .... (Warner Bros.)
Osama, Yo' Mama
Ray Stevens; *Osama-Yo' Mama* .... (Curb)
Patriot Game
Clancy Brothers; *Clancy Brothers-Super Hits* .... (Legacy)
Clancy Brothers & Tommy Makem; *Folk, Gospel & Blues: Will The Circle Be Unbroken-C* .... (Legacy)
Judy Collins; *Whales & Nightingales* .... (Elektra)
Kingston Trio; *Capitol Collectors Series-The Kingston Trio* .... (Capitol)
Patriotic Fantasy
Original New York Cast; *Oil City Symphony* .... (DRG)
Patriotic Finale
Original Cast; *When Pigs Fly* .... (RCA Victor)
Patriotic Rag
Tom Hazleton; *Ragtime's Greatest Hits* .... (Pro-Arte)
Patriotic Rally
George Gershwin; *Strike Up The Band* .... (Nonesuch)
Patriot's Dream
Arlo Guthrie; *Amigo* .... (Koch International)
Gordon Lightfoot; *Don Quixote* .... (Warner Archives)
Ragged Old Flag
Johnny Cash; *Patriot* .... (Columbia)
We The People-C .... (Folk Era)
Rednecks, White Socks And Blue Ribbon Beer
Johnny Russell; *Beer Redneck Mothers* .... (RCA)
Country Legends-C .... (Madacy)
Country's Greatest Drinking Songs-C .... (All-Star Music)
Rednecks, White Socks & Blue Ribbon Beer .... (RCA)
Semper Fidelis
Killer Cadet Band; *Stars And Stripes Forever-#2-C* ... (Volcano Entertainment)
Song Of Freedom
Bing Crosby; *Original Soundtrack Sessions* .... (Vintage Jazz Classics)
Star Spangled Banner
American Brass Band; *National Anthems* .... (Laserlight)
Banda Sinfonica De Madrid; *National Anthems* .... (International Music)
Duke Ellington; *Carnegie Hall Concert-January 23, 1943* .... (Prestige)
Houston Symphony Orchestra; *Celebrate America* .... (Pro-Arte)
Jimi Hendrix; *Essential Jimi Hendrix, Volume 2* .... (Reprise)
Lifelines/Jimi Hendrix Story .... (Reprise)
ST/Jimi Hendrix .... (Reprise)
ST/Woodstock .... (Atlantic)
Lee Greenwood; *American Patriot* .... (Capitol)
Marvin Gaye; *Musical Testament 1964-1984* .... (Motown)
Mormon Tabernacle Choir; *God Bless America* .... (Sony Music Classical)
God Bless America-C .... (Columbia)
This Is My Country .... (Columbia)
Original Soundtrack; *The Greatest College Fight Songs* .... (Laserlight)
Sandi Patty; *Stars And Stripes Forever-#2-C* .... (Volcano Entertainment)
Vienna State Opera Orchestra; *National Anthems Of The World* ... (Bescol, Ltd.)
Vinnie Vincent Invasion; *Head Banging Metal-C* .... (Priority)
Whitney Houston; *Whitney Houston's Greatest Hits* .... (Arista)
Stars And Stripes Forever
Boston Pops Orchestra/Arthur Fiedler; *Boston Pops Orchestra/Arthur Fiedler-Legendary Performer* .... (RCA)
Boston Pops Orchestra/Arthur Fiedler's Greatest Hits .... (Polydor)
Forever Fiedler .... (RCA)
Mister Music U.S.A. .... (Deutsche Grammophon)
Yankee Doodle Dandy .... (RCA)
Killer Cadet Band; *Stars And Stripes Forever-#2-C* ... (Volcano Entertainment)
Mormon Tabernacle Choir; *God Bless America* .... (Sony Music Classical)
Stars And Stripes Forever .... (Columbia)
Star Spangled Band; *Red, White & Bluegrass-C* .... (C.M.H. Prod.)
This Ain't No Rag, It's A Flag
Charlie Daniels Band; *This Ain't No Rag, It's A Flag-CD Single* .... (Blue Hat)
This Is A Great Country
Original Cast; *Mr. President* .... (Sony Broadway)
This Land Is Your Land
Bruce Springsteen & The E Street Band; *Bruce Springsteen & The E Street Band Live/1975-85* .... (Legacy)
Glen Campbell; *All American* .... (Liberty)
Lee Greenwood; *American Patriot* .... (Capitol)
Odetta, Arlo Guthrie & Company; *Tribute To Woody Guthrie-C* .... (Warner Bros.)
Pete Seeger; *God Bless America-C* .... (Columbia)
Pete Seeger Sings Woody Guthrie .... (Smithsonian Folkways)
Pete Seeger-Complete Carnegie Hall Concert-1963 .... (Columbia)
Weavers; *Weavers' Greatest Hits* .... (Vanguard)
Woody Guthrie; *Greatest Songs Of Woody Guthrie-C* .... (Vanguard)
Troubadours Of The Folk Era-#1-C .... (Rhino)
Woody Guthrie .... (Vanguard)
U.S.A. Today
George Jones; *Too WIld Too Long* .... (Epic)
Hank Williams, Jr.; *America (The Way I See It)* .... (WB/Curb)
Lone Wolf .... (WB/Curb)
Where Stars And Stripes And The Eagle Fly
Aaron Tippin; *CD Single-#164059* .... (Lyric Street)
Yankee Doodle
Boston Pops Orchestra/Arthur Fiedler; *Fiedler's Favorite Marches* .... (RCA)
Music For All Occasions .... (RCA)
Yankee Doodle Dandy
"C" Company & Terry Nelson; *Wake Up America* .... (Plantation)
Houston Symphony Orchestra; *Top Of The Pops* .... (Pro-Arte)
You're A Grand Old Flag
Marilyn Horne; *Beautiful Dreamer-Great American Songbook* .... (London)
Mormon Tabernacle Choir; *God Bless America* .... (Sony Music Classical)
Original Soundtrack; *School Days-Kids Classics* .... (Benson)
Robert Merrill & Mormon Tabernacle Choir; *Yankee Doodle Dandies* .... (Columbia)

PEACE, Calm, Serenity, Tranquility

See Also: ***BROTHERHOOD, FAITH, FIGHT, FRIENDS, HAPPINESS, POLITICS (various), PROTEST, SILENCE, WAR, WORLD***

Air That I Breathe
Hollies; *Best Of The Hollies-#2* .... (EMI)
Hollies .... (Epic)
Hollies-Epic Anthology From The Original Master Tapes .... (Epic)
Alive
P.O.D.; *Satellite* .... (Atlantic)
All Quiet Along The Potomac Tonight
Hermes Nye; *Ballads Of The Civil War-#1 & 2* .... (Smithsonian Folkways)
All Through The Night
Judy Collins; *Baby's Bedtime* .... (Lightyear)
Angel
Sarah McLachlan; *Mirrorball* .... (Arista)
ST/City Of Angels .... (Warner Sunset/Reprise)
Surfacing .... (Arista)
Totally Hits-#1-C .... (Arista)
Believe
Elton John; *Elton John-Love Songs* .... (MCA)
Made In England .... (Rocket)
Caravan Of Love
Isley, Jasper, Isley; *Caravan Of Love* .... (CBS Associated)
Clasp
Jethro Tull; *20 Years Of Jethro Tull* .... (Chrysalis)
The Broadsword And The Beast .... (Chrysalis)

Computer Incantations For World Peace
Jean-Luc Ponty; *Individual Choice*............................ (Rhino)
Le Voyage: The Jean-Luc Ponty Anthology.................... (Rhino)
Crystal Blue Persuasion
Tommy James And The Shondells; *Best Of Tommy James And The Shondells*.. (Roulette)
Tommy James And The Shondells-Anthology................... (Rhino)
Ebony And Ivory
Paul McCartney & Stevie Wonder; *All The Best!*.......... (Capitol)
Tug Of War.. (Gold Rush)
Everyday People
Sly & The Family Stone; *Sly & The Family Stone-Anthology*........... (Epic)
Sly & The Family Stone's Greatest Hits.....................(Epic)
Stand!...(Epic)
From A Distance
Bette Midler; *Some People's Lives*..................... (Atlantic)
Byrds; *20 Essential Tracks From The Box Set*.......... (Columbia)
The Byrds.. (Columbia)
Judy Collins; *Fires Of Eden*.......................... (Columbia)
Kathy Mattea; *Time Passes By*.......................... (Mercury)
Nanci Griffith; *Lone Star State Of Mind*..................(MCA)
One Fair Summer Evening..................................(MCA)
Get Together
Big Mountain; *Resistance*................................ (Giant)
Youngbloods; *Best Of The Youngbloods*...................... (RCA)
Billboard Top Rock 'N' Roll Hits-1969-C.................. (Rhino)
Chicken Soup For The Soul: I'll Be There For You-Songs Of Friendship, Brotherhood And Sisterhood-C....................... (Rhino)
ST/Forrest Gump................... (Epic/Sony Music Soundtrax)
Summer Of Love-#1-C.................................... (Rhino)
Give Me Love (Give Me Peace On Earth)
George Harrison; *Best Of George Harrison*............... (Capitol)
Living In The Material World.......................... (Capitol)
Give Peace A Chance
John Lennon; *Lennon*.................................... (Capitol)
Live In New York City................................. (Capitol)
ST/Imagine: John Lennon............................... (Capitol)
The John Lennon Collection............................ (Capitol)
John Lennon/Plastic Ono Band; *Shaved Fish*............. (Capitol)
Plastic Ono Band; *Plastic Ono Band-Live Peace In Toronto 1969*..... (Capitol)
Go Rest High On That Mountain
Vince Gill; *When Love Finds You*..........................(MCA)
Guns Of Love
Pamela Rose; *Morpheus*.................................. (Grace)
Harmony
John Conlee; *45-#13-08398*............................ (Columbia)
Harmony
Bar-Kays; *Coldblooded*....................................(Stax)
Harmony
Elton John; *Goodbye Yellow Brick Road*.................. (Polydor)
Harmony
Take 6 (featuring Queen Latifah); *Join The Band-C*.............. (Reprise)
Harmony
Limeliters; *Live In Concert*...........................(Crescendo)
Harmony
Happy Mondays; *Pills 'N' Thrills & Bellyaches*................. (Elektra)
Hurricane Eye
Paul Simon; *You're The One*.......................(Warner Bros.)
I Wish You Peace
Eagles; *One Of These Nights*........................... (Asylum)
I'd Like To Buy The World A Coke (Coca-Cola)
Original Soundtrack; *TeeVee Toons-The Commercials-#1-C*........... (TVT)
I'd Like To Teach The World To Sing (In Perfect Harmony)
New Seekers; *Chicken Soup For The Soul-Celebrating Life-C*........ (Rhino)
If The World Had A Front Porch
Tracy Lawrence; *Best Of Tracy Lawrence*............... (Atlantic)
I See It Now... (Atlantic)
Imagine
Diana Ross; *Best Of The Beatles Songs-C*.............. (Motown)
Diana Ross-Anthology................................. (Motown)
Touch Me In The Morning.............................. (Motown)
Joan Baez; *Best Of Joan Baez*............................ (A&M)
Come From The Shadows................................... (A&M)
John Lennon; *Lennon*................................... (Capitol)
Live In New York City................................ (Capitol)
ST/Imagine: John Lennon.............................. (Capitol)
John Lennon & Yoko Ono; *The John Lennon Collection*........... (Capitol)
John Lennon/Plastic Ono Band; *Imagine*................ (Capitol)
Shaved Fish.. (Capitol)
Neil Young; *America: A Tribute To Heroes-C*......... (Interscope)
Jesus Is The Missing Peace
Whites; *A Lifetime In The Making*.................. (Ceili Music)
Kill For Peace
Fugs; *Best Of Broadside 1962-1968: Anthems Of The American Underground From The Pages Of Broadside Magazine-C*....... (Smithsonian Folkways)
Fugs...(ESP Disk)
Fugs 4 Rounders Score...............................(ESP Disk)
Let The Rest Of The World Go By
Mitch Miller; *Sing Along With Mitch*.................. (Columbia)

Mom & Dads; *Down The River Of Golden Dreams*.............(Crescendo)
Live In Peace
Country Joe McDonald; *Peace On Earth*................. (Rag Baby)
Live In Peace
Firm; *Mean Business*..................................(Atlantic)
Love Can Build A Bridge
Judds; *Love Can Build A Bridge*.......................... (MCA)
Make Me A Channel Of Your Peace
Sinead O'Connor; *Diana, Princess Of Wales-Tribute-C*.......... (Columbia)
Mind Games
John Lennon; *Mind Games*.............................. (Capitol)
John Lennon/Plastic Ono Band; *Shaved Fish*............ (Capitol)
Most High
Jimmy Page/Robert Plant; *Walking Into Clarksdale*..........(Atlantic)
One Big Love
Emmylou Harris; *Red Dirt Girl*...................... (Nonesuch)
Patty Griffin; *Flaming Red*.............................. (A&M)
Peace
Greater Than One; *Funky Alternatives-18 Techno Remixes-C*.......... (Roir)
London.. (Wax Trax)
Peace
Bobby McFerrin; *Bobby McFerrin*....................... (Elektra)
Peace
Los Lobos; *Kiko*..(Slash)
Peace
Barry McGuire; *Seeds*................................... (Myrrh)
Peace
Branford Marsalis; *Trio Jeepy*....................... (Columbia)
Peace
Michael McDonald; *In The Spirit-A Christmas Album*.............. (MCA)
Peace & Understanding Is Hard To Find
Junior Walker & The All Stars; *Junior Walker & The All Stars-Anthology*.. (Motown)
Motown Superstar Series-#5-Junior Walker & The All Stars...... (Motown)
Peace Brother Peace
Bill Medley; *Best Of The Righteous Brothers-#2*..........(Curb)
Peace Dog
Cult; *Electric*..(Sire)
Peace For South Africa
Oscar Peterson Trio; *Live At The Blue Note*............ (Telarc)
Peace Frog
Doors; *Doors-Classics*................................ (Elektra)
Morrison Hotel/Hard Rock Cafe........................ (Elektra)
Weird Scenes Inside The Gold Mine.................... (Elektra)
Peace In Liberia
Alpha Blondy; *Masada*............................ (World Pacific)
Peace In Mind
Joan Armatrading; *Show Some Emotion*..................... (A&M)
Peace In Mississippi
Jimi Hendrix; *Crash Landing*........................... (Reprise)
Peace In My Heart
Carole Bayer Sager; *Too*............................. (Elektra)
Peace In Our Time
Eddie Money; *Eddie Money's Greatest Hits-Sound Of Money*...... (Columbia)
Peace In Our Time
Elvis Costello & The Attractions; *Goodbye Cruel World*...... (Columbia)
Peace In The Valley
Elvis Presley; *A Golden Celebration*..................... (RCA)
Elvis-A Legendary Performer, Volume 1................... (RCA)
Million-Dollar Quartet................................. (RCA)
Johnny Cash; *At San Quentin*......................... (Columbia)
Classic Cash-Hall Of Fame Series.................... (Mercury)
J.L. Lewis/Carl Perkins-The Survivors............... (Columbia)
Red Foley; *Grand Ole Opry-75 Years-#1-C*................. (MCA)
Peace In The Valley
Carole King; *Rhymes & Reasons*....................... (Legacy)
Peace Is Just A Word
Eurythmics; *Peace*..................................... (Arista)
Peace Like A River
Paul Simon; *Paul Simon*.............................. (Columbia)
Peace Of Mind
Loggins & Messina; *Loggins & Messina-On Stage*....... (Columbia)
Sittin' In.. (Columbia)
The Best Of Friends................................. (Columbia)
Peace Of Mind
Boston; *Boston*... (Epic)
Peace Of Mind
Bad Company; *Burnin' Sky*.......................... (Swan Song)
Peace Of Mind
Neil Young; *Comes A Time*............................. (Reprise)
Peace Of Mind
Eddy Raven; *Eddy Raven's Greatest Hits*........... (Warner Bros.)
Peace Of Mind
Blue Cheer; *Good Times Are So Hard To Find-History Of Blue Cheer*... (Mercury)
Louder Than God-Best Of Blue Cheer.................... (Rhino)
Peace Of Mind
Engelbert Humperdinck; *Miracles*......................... (Epic)

Peace Officer
Jimmy Cliff; *Rhythm Come Forward: Volume III-C* . . . . (Columbia)
Special . . . . (Columbia)
Peace On You
Charlie Rich; *Behind Closed Doors* . . . . (Epic)
Peace Pipe
Cry Of Love; *Brother* . . . . (Columbia)
Peace Pipe
Edgar Winter; *Entrance* . . . . (Epic)
Peace Sign
Night Ranger; *Seven* . . . . (CMC Int'l)
Peace Sign
War; *War-Anthology (1970-1994)* . . . . (Avenue)
Peace To New York
Doug E. Fresh & The Get Fresh Crew; *Doin' What I Gotta Do* . . . .(Bust It)
Peace Tonight
Indigo Girls; *Come On Now Social* . . . . (Epic)
Peace Train
Cat Stevens; *Cat Stevens Greatest Hits* . . . . (A&M)
Cat Stevens-Classics-#24 . . . . (A&M)
Teaser And The Firecat . . . . (A&M)
Peace Will Come
Melanie; *Beautiful* . . . . (Fifty One West)
Best Of Melanie . . . . (Rhino)
Peace, Love & Understanding (What's So Funny About)
Curtis Stigers; *ST/The Bodyguard* . . . . (Arista)
Elvis Costello & The Attractions; *Armed Forces* . . . . (Rykodisc)
Best Of Elvis Costello & The Attractions . . . . (Columbia)
Peaceful
Helen Reddy; *Helen Reddy's Greatest Hits* . . . . (Capitol)
Kenny Rankin; *Like A Seed* . . . . (Little David)
Peaceful Easy Feeling
Eagles; *Eagles* . . . . (Asylum)
Eagles/Their Greatest Hits 1971-1975 . . . . (Asylum)
Little Texas; *Common Thread-Songs Of The Eagles-C* . . . . (Giant)
Peaceful Journey
Fat Larry's Band; *Sweet Soul Music-Stax Groups-C* . . . . (Stax)
Peaceful Journey
Heavy D & The Boyz; *Peaceful Journey* . . . . (Uptown)
Peaceful Waters
Gordon Lightfoot; *Lightfoot* . . . . (EMI)
Peaceful World
Rascals; *Peaceful World* . . . . (Columbia)
Peaceful World
John Mellencamp; *Cuttin' Heads* . . . . (Columbia)
God Bless America-C . . . . (Columbia)
The Concert For New York City-C . . . . (Columbia)
Peacemaker
Kool & The Gang; *Everything's Kool & The Gang-Greatest Hits*
& More . . . . (Mercury)
Peacemaker
Loggins & Messina; *Native Sons* . . . . (Columbia)
People Got To Be Free
Rascals; *Atlantic's Hit Singles-1958-1977-C* . . . . (Atlantic)
Billboard Top Rock 'N' Roll Hits-1968-C . . . . (Rhino)
Hit Singles-1958-1977-C . . . . (Atlantic)
Rascals-Anthology 1965-1972 . . . . (Rhino)
Songs Of Protest-C . . . . (Rhino)
Very Best Of The Rascals . . . . (Rhino)
Quartet (A Model Of Decorum And Tranquility)
Original Cast; *Chess* . . . . (Polydor)
Quiet
Paul Simon; *You're The One* . . . . (Warner Bros.)
Reach Out And Touch
Diana Ross; *Diana Ross-All The Great Hits* . . . . (Motown)
Diana Ross-Anthology . . . . (Motown)
Live At Caesar's Palace . . . . (Motown)
Most Played Songs On America's Jukeboxes . . . . (Motown)
Motown Story-First 25 Years-C . . . . (Motown)
Remembrance Day
Bryan Adams; *Into The Fire* . . . . (A&M)
Rest In Peace
Extreme; *III Sides To Every Story* . . . . (A&M)
Ripple
Grateful Dead; *American Beauty* . . . . (Warner Bros.)
Reckoning . . . . (Arista)
What A Long Strange Trip It's Been: The Best Of The
Grateful Dead . . . . (Warner Bros.)
Jane's Addiction; *Deadicated-C* . . . . (Arista)
Sailing
Christopher Cross; *Christopher Cross* . . . . (Warner Bros.)
Santa Lucia
Elvis Presley; *Elvis For Everyone!* . . . . (RCA)
Mario Lanza; *Legendary Tenor* . . . . (RCA)
Savannah The Serene
Billy Cobham; *Crosswinds* . . . . (Atlantic)
Shalom
Original Cast; *Milk & Honey* . . . . (RCA Victor)

Shhh/Peaceful
Miles Davis; *In A Silent Way* . . . . (Columbia)
Still Water Runs The Deepest
Asleep At The Wheel featuring Willie Nelson; *Tribute To The Music Of Bob*
Wills And The Texas Playboys-C . . . . (Liberty)
Stomp Dance (Unity)
Robbie Robertson featuring The Six Nations Women Singers; *Contact From*
The Underworld of Redboy . . . . (Capitol)
Sunday In The South
Shenandoah; *30 Years Of #1 Hits-#19-C* . . . . (Columbia)
Road Not Taken . . . . (Columbia)
Shenandoah's Greatest Hits . . . . (Columbia)
Sweet Afton
Nickel Creek; *Nickel Creek* . . . . (Sugar Hill)
There Will Never Be Any Peace (Until God Is Seated At The
Conference Table)
Chi-Lites; *Chi-Lites' Greatest Hits* . . . . (Rhino)
Thicker Than Blood
Garth Brooks; *Scarecrow* . . . . (Capitol)
Waitress, The
Tori Amos; *Under The Pink* . . . . (Atlantic)
War Is Over
Phil Ochs; *Chords Of Fame* . . . . (A&M)
Tape From California . . . . (A&M)
The War Is Over-Best Of Phil Ochs . . . . (A&M)
We're All In The Same Gang
West Coast Rap All-Stars; *We're All In The Same Gang-C* . . . . . . (Warner Bros.)
What If
Reba McEntire; *CD Single-#72026* . . . . (MCA)
What's Going On
Cyndi Lauper; *True Colors* . . . . (Portrait)
Marvin Gaye; *20/20-C* . . . . (Motown)
Marvin Gaye Live At The London Palladium . . . . (Motown)
Marvin Gaye-Anthology . . . . (Motown)
Marvin Gaye's Greatest Hits/ . . . . (Motown)
More Songs From "The Big Chill" Soundtrack-C . . . . (Motown)
What's Going On . . . . (Motown)
Quincy Jones; *Quincy Jones-The Best* . . . . (A&M)
White Cliffs Of Dover
Kay Kyser & His Orchestra; *16 Most Requested Songs Of The*
'40s-#1-C . . . . (Legacy)
Lee Andrews And The Hearts; *Lee Andrews And The Hearts'*
Biggest Hits . . . . (Collectables)
Mystics; *Mystics-16 Golden Classics.* . . . . (Collectables)
Righteous Brothers; *Righteous Brothers' Greatest Hits* . . . . (Verve)
Righteous Brothers-Anthology 1962-1974 . . . . (Rhino)
Rosemary Clooney; *For The Duration.* . . . . (Concord Jazz)
Woodstock
Crosby, Stills & Nash; *CSN* . . . . (Atlantic)
Crosby, Stills, Nash & Young; *Deja Vu* . . . . (Atlantic)
So Far . . . . (Atlantic)
Joni Mitchell; *Ladies Of The Canyon* . . . . (Reprise)
Shadows & Light . . . . (Asylum)
Joni Mitchell with Tom Scott & The L.A. Express; *Miles Of Aisles.* . . . . (Asylum)
You Gave Me Peace Of Mind
Spaniels; *16 Soulful Serenades-C* . . . . (Solid Smoke)
Goodnight, Well It's Time To Go. . . . . (Vee-Jay)

PEOPLE, Adults, Crowd, Human Beings, Human Nature

See Also: **BABY, BROTHERHOOD, CELEBRITIES: SPECIFIC,**
CHILDREN, FAMILY (various), LIFE, MEN: GENERAL, MEN'S
NAMES: A-Z, SOCIAL CLASS: GENERAL, SOCIAL CLASS:
RURAL, TEENAGERS, WOMEN: GENERAL, WOMEN'S
NAMES: A-Z

"In" Crowd, The
Dobie Gray; *Beg, Scream & Shout! The Big Ol' Box Of '60s Soul-C* . . . . .(Rhino)
Dobie Gray Sings For In Crowders That Go "Go Go" . . . .(Collectables)
Ramsey Lewis; *Greatest Hits Of Ramsey Lewis.* . . . . (Chess)
Party Super Hits-C . . . . (Columbia)
Ramsey Lewis' Greatest Hits. . . . . (Columbia)
"They Just Can't Stop It" (The Games People Play)
Spinners; *Best Of The Spinners* . . . . (Atlantic)
Golden Age Of Black Music-1970-1975-C . . . . (Atlantic)
Adia
Sarah McLachlan; *Mirrorball* . . . . (Arista)
Surfacing. . . . . (Arista)
Are You That Somebody?
Aaliyah; *ST/Dr. Dolittle* . . . . (Atlantic)
A-sleepin' At The Foot Of The Bed
"Little" Jimmy Dickens; *Bluegrass Super Hits-C* . . . . (Columbia)
Baby You're A Rich Man
Beatles; *Beatles-Box Set.* . . . . (Capitol)
Magical Mystery Tour. . . . . (Capitol)
Back 2 Good
Matchbox Twenty; *Yourself Or Someone Like You* . . . . (Lava)

Banditos
  Refreshments; *Fizzy Fuzzy Big & Buzzy* . . . . (Mercury)
Beautiful Day
  U2; *All That You Can't Leave Behind* . . . . (Interscope)
    Now That's What I Call Music!-#6-C . . . . (Virgin)
Beautiful People
  Marilyn Manson; *Antichrist Superstar* . . . . (Interscope)
Beautiful People
  Bobby Vee; *Very Best Of Bobby Vee* . . . . (Collectables)
Beautiful People Of Denver
  Original Cast; *The Unsinkable Molly Brown* . . . . (EMI-Angel)
Birds Of A Feather
  Phish; *The Story Of The Ghost* . . . . (Elektra)
Bitter Sweet Symphony
  Verve; *Urban Hymns* . . . . (Hut/Virgin)
Blue Monday People
  Curtis Mayfield; *America Today* . . . . (Curtom)
Born Again Human
  B.B. King; *There Must Be A Better World Somewhere* . . . . (MCA)
Cat People (Putting Out Fire)
  David Bowie; *Let's Dance* . . . . (EMI)
    ST/Cat People . . . . (MCA)
    The Singles-1969-1993 . . . . (Rykodisc)
Closer To Free
  BoDeans; *Chicago Bulls Greatest Hits-#3-C* . . . . (Atlantic)
    Go Slow Down . . . . (Slash)
    Joe Dirt Car . . . . (Reprise)
    ST/Party Of Five . . . . (Reprise)
Company's Comin'
  Porter Wagoner; *Essential Porter Wagoner* . . . . (RCA)
Do The Evolution
  Pearl Jam; *Yield* . . . . (Epic)
Don't Wanna Be A Player
  Joe; *All That I Am* . . . . (Jive)
Easy To Be Hard
  Original Broadway Cast; *Hair* . . . . (RCA)
  Original Cast; *ST/Hair* . . . . (RCA)
  Three Dog Night; *Best Of Three Dog Night* . . . . (MCA)
    Captured Live At The Forum . . . . (MCA)
    Celebrate-The Three Dog Night Story . . . . (MCA)
Eleanor Rigby
  Beatles; *Beatles 1* . . . . (Capitol)
    Revolver . . . . (Capitol)
    The Beatles/1962-1966 . . . . (Capitol)
  Ray Charles; *Ray Charles' Greatest Hits-#2* . . . . (Rhino)
    Ray Charles-Anthology . . . . (Rhino)
Every Kinda People
  Robert Palmer; *Addictions-#1* . . . . (Island)
    Double Fun . . . . (Island)
    Maybe It's Live . . . . (Island)
Everybody (Backstreet's Back)
  Backstreet Boys; *Backstreet Boys* . . . . (Jive)
Everybody Everybody
  Black Box; *Dreamland* . . . . (RCA)
Everybody Loves Somebody
  Dean Martin; *Dean Martin's Greatest Hits* . . . . (EMI)
Everybody's Had The Blues
  Merle Haggard & The Strangers; *For The Record: Merle Haggard-43
    Legendary Hits* . . . . (BNA)
Everyday People
  Sly & The Family Stone; *Sly & The Family Stone-Anthology* . . . . (Epic)
    Sly & The Family Stone's Greatest Hits . . . . (Epic)
    Stand! . . . . (Epic)
Everything's Got 'Em
  Nilsson; *The Point* . . . . (RCA)
Expressway To Your Heart
  Blues Brothers; *Best Of The Blues Brothers* . . . . (Atlantic)
  Soul Survivors; *Dick Bartley's One-Hit Wonders Of The '60s-#2-C* . . . . (Rhino)
    Oldies But Goodies-#11-C . . . . (Original Sound)
    Super Oldies Of The '60s-#6-C . . . . (Audio Fidelity)
    When The Whistle Blows Anything Goes . . . . (Collectables)
Face In The Crowd
  Michael Martin Murphey & Holly Dunn; *Americana* . . . . (Warner Bros.)
    Favorite Country Duets-C . . . . (Warner Bros.)
    Milestones-Greatest Hits . . . . (Warner Bros.)
Face In The Crowd
  Tom Petty; *Full Moon Fever* . . . . (MCA)
Face In The Crowd
  Kinks; *Soap Opera* . . . . (Rhino)
Face In The Crowd
  Lisa Lisa & Cult Jam; *Spanish Fly* . . . . (Columbia)
Fair
  Ben Folds Five; *Whatever And Ever Amen* . . . . (Caroline/550)
Folks Who Live On The Hill
  Diana Krall; *Only Trust Your Heart* . . . . (GRP)
Free The People
  Barbra Streisand; *Stoney End* . . . . (Columbia)
  Delaney & Bonnie; *Best Of Delaney & Bonnie* . . . . (Rhino)

Games People Play
  Joe South; *On The Road Again-Rock's New Frontiers-C* . . . . (Capitol)
Games People Play
  Alan Parsons Project; *Best Of The Alan Parsons Project* . . . . (Arista)
    Turn Of A Friendly Card . . . . (Arista)
Gang That Sang "Heart Of My Heart"
  Four Aces; *Best Of The Four Aces* . . . . (MCA)
Give More Power To The People
  Chi-Lites; *Chi-Lites' Greatest Hits* . . . . (Epic)
God's Gonna Get'cha (For That)
  George Jones & Tammy Wynette; *George Jones & Tammy Wynette-16
    Biggest Hits* . . . . (Epic/Legacy)
  George Jones & Tammy Wynette's Greatest Hits . . . . (Epic)
Graveyard People
  Traffic; *When The Eagle Flies* . . . . (Asylum)
Groovy People
  Lou Rawls; *All Things In Time* . . . . (Right Stuff)
    Lou Rawls-Live (Right Stuff) . . . . (Right Stuff)
Guy Is A Guy, A
  Doris Day; *Doris Day's Greatest Hits* . . . . (Columbia)
Handful Of Dust
  Patty Loveless; *When Fallen Angels Fly* . . . . (Epic)
Hello Brother
  Louis Armstrong; *What A Wonderful World* . . . . (Decca Jazz)
Honky Tonk Crowd
  Rick Trevino; *Rick Trevino* . . . . (Columbia)
Human
  Pretenders; *Viva El Amor!* . . . . (Warner Bros.)
Human Beings
  Seal; *Human Being* . . . . (Warner Bros.)
Human Hands
  Elvis Costello & The Attractions; *Imperial Bedroom* . . . . (Columbia)
Human Highway
  Neil Young; *Comes A Time* . . . . (Reprise)
Human Jukebox
  Scientists; *Absolute* . . . . (Sub Pop)
Human Nature
  Michael Jackson; *Thriller* . . . . (Epic)
  Miles Davis; *You're Under Arrest* . . . . (Columbia)
Human Nature
  Madonna; *Bedtime Stories* . . . . (Maverick/Sire)
    GHV2 . . . . (Warner Bros.)
Human Touch
  Rick Springfield; *Living In Oz* . . . . (RCA)
    Rick Springfield's Greatest Hits . . . . (RCA)
Human Touch
  Bruce Springsteen; *Bruce Springsteen's Greatest Hits* . . . . (Columbia)
    Human Touch . . . . (Columbia)
Human Touch
  Elvis Costello & The Attractions; *Get Happy!* . . . . (Rykodisc)
Human Touch
  Joe Jackson; *Blaze Of Glory* . . . . (A&M)
Human Toy
  Ready For The World; *Ready For The World* . . . . (MCA)
Human Wheels
  John Mellencamp; *Human Wheels* . . . . (Mercury)
Humans Being
  Van Halen; *Best Of Van Halen-#1* . . . . (Warner Bros.)
Hungry Heart
  Bruce Springsteen; *Bruce Springsteen's Greatest Hits* . . . . (Columbia)
    The River . . . . (Columbia)
  Bruce Springsteen & The E Street Band; *Bruce Springsteen & The E Street
    Band Live/1975-85* . . . . (Legacy)
I Do
  Lisa Loeb; *Firecracker* . . . . (Geffen)
I'm A Man
  Spencer Davis Group; *Baby Boomer Classics-Rockin'
    Sixties-C* . . . . (JCI Assoc. Labels)
    Best Of The Spencer Davis Group . . . . (EMI)
Inside
  Patti Rothberg; *Between The 1 And The 9* . . . . (EMI)
I've Seen All The Good People
  Yes; *Classic Rock 1966-1988-C* . . . . (Atlantic)
    The Yes Album . . . . (Atlantic)
    Yessongs . . . . (Atlantic)
Jesus Is My Kind Of People
  Ray Price; *You're The Best Thing That Ever Happened To Me* . . . . . . (Columbia)
Just Like Anyone
  Soul Asylum; *Let Your Dim Light Shine* . . . . (Columbia)
Law Is For The Protection Of The People
  Kris Kristofferson; *Me & Bobby McGee* . . . . (Columbia)
Let's Talk About Love
  Celine Dion with The Bee Gees; *Let's Talk About Love-C* . . . . (550 Music)
Life (Everybody Needs Somebody)
  Haddaway; *Haddaway* . . . . (Arista)
Like Humans Do
  David Byrne; *Look Into The Eyeball* . . . . (Luaka Bop)

Listen People
Herman's Hermits; *Herman's Hermits-Their Greatest Hits* . . . . (Abkco)
Lotus
R.E.M.; *Up* . . . . (Warner Bros.)
Miles From Our Home
Cowboy Junkies; *Miles From Our Home* . . . . (Geffen)
More Human Than Human
White Zombie; *Astro-Creep: 2000 Songs Of Love* . . . . (Geffen)
My People
Bill Miller; *The Red Road* . . . . (Warner Western)
Night Of The Thumpasorus Peoples
Parliament; *Mothership Connection* . . . . (Casablanca)
  Parliament Live/P. Funk Earth Tour . . . . (Casablanca)
Old
Paul Simon; *You're The One* . . . . (Warner Bros.)
Old Folks Boogie
Little Feat; *Time Loves A Hero* . . . . (Warner Bros.)
  Waiting For Columbus . . . . (Warner Bros.)
Only Human
Rosanne Cash; *Seven Year Ache* . . . . (Columbia)
Only Human
Jeffrey Osborne; *Only Human* . . . . (Arista)
Ordinary Average Guy
Joe Walsh; *Ordinary Average Guy* . . . . (Epic Portrait Assoc.)
Part Man, Part Monkey
Bruce Springsteen; *Tracks* . . . . (Columbia)
Party People
Solomon Burke; *Home In Your Heart-Best Of Solomon Burke* . . . . (Rhino)
Party People
Joe South; *Best Of Joe South* . . . . (Rhino)
Party People
Parliament; *Gloryhallastoopid* . . . . (Casablanca)
People Are Still Having Sex
LaTour; *LaTour* . . . . (Smash)
People Are Strange
Doors; *Best Of The Doors* . . . . (Elektra)
People Asking Why
Seal; *Seal 2* . . . . (Sire)
People Get Ready
Aretha Franklin; *Aretha-Lady Soul* . . . . (Atlantic)
Impressions; *Impressions' Greatest Hits* . . . . (MCA)
  Soul Shots-#5-La-La Means I Love You-C . . . . (Rhino)
  Train Trax-C . . . . (Sony Music Special Prod.)
Jeff Beck; *Flash* . . . . (Epic)
Rod Stewart; *Storyteller/The Complete Anthology: 1964-1990* . . (Warner Bros.)
People Got To Be Free
Rascals; *Atlantic's Hit Singles-1958-1977-C* . . . . (Atlantic)
  Billboard Top Rock 'N' Roll Hits-1968-C . . . . (Rhino)
  Hit Singles-1958-1977-C . . . . (Atlantic)
  Rascals-Anthology 1965-1972 . . . . (Rhino)
  Songs Of Protest-C . . . . (Rhino)
  Very Best Of The Rascals . . . . (Rhino)
People Like Us
Aaron Tippin; *People Like Us* . . . . (Lyric Street)
People Of The Southwind
Kansas; *Monolith* . . . . (Kirshner)
People Say
Dixie Cups; *Girl Groups-Story Of A Sound-C* . . . . (Rhino)
  Original Golden Hits Of The Great Groups-#1-C . . . . (SSS International)
  Wonder Women-History Of Girl Group Sound-C . . . . (Rhino)
People Take Pictures Of Each Other
Kinks; *Are The Village Green Preservation Society* . . . . (Reprise)
People That We Love, The
Bush; *Golden State* . . . . (Atlantic)
People Tree
Sammy Davis, Jr.; *Best Of Sammy Davis, Jr.* . . . . (Curb)
People Up In Texas
Waylon Jennings; *Never Could Toe The Mark* . . . . (RCA)
People Who Died
Jim Carroll Band; *Catholic Boy* . . . . (Atco)
  ST/Tuff Turf . . . . (Rhino)
People Will Say We're In Love
Frank Sinatra; *A Lovely Way To Spend An Evening* . . . . (ASV)
Original Broadway Cast; *Oklahoma!* . . . . (RCA)
Spaniels; *Spaniels' Golden Hits* . . . . (Juke Box Treasures)
  The Acapella Collection . . . . (Juke Box Treasures)
Pigs, Sheep & Wolves
Paul Simon; *You're The One* . . . . (Warner Bros.)
Plastic People
Mothers Of Invention; *Absolutely Free* . . . . (Rykodisc)
Po' Folks
Bill Anderson; *Bill Anderson's Greatest Hits* . . . . (Varese Sarabande)
Poem For The People
Chicago; *Chicago II* . . . . (Chicago)
Poor People
Alan Price; *ST/O Lucky Man* . . . . (Warner Bros.)
Poor People Of Paris
Les Baxter & His Orchestra; *Memories Are Made Of This-C* . . . . (Capitol)

Powerful People
Gino Vannelli; *Best Of Gino Vannelli* . . . . (A&M)
  Gino Vannelli-Classics-#7 . . . . (A&M)
  Powerful People . . . . (A&M)
Primitive People
Country Joe McDonald; *Goodbye Blues* . . . . (Fantasy)
Private Conversation
Lyle Lovett; *The Road To Ensenada* . . . . (MCA)
Purple People Eater
Sheb Wooley; *45s On CD-#1-1956-1959-C* . . . . (Mercury)
  Dr. Demento: 20th Anniversary Collection-C . . . . (Rhino)
  Halloween Hits-C . . . . (Rhino)
  Horror Rock Classics-#2-C . . . . (Rhino)
  Super Hits-#4-C . . . . (Gusto)
Radio People
Zapp; *The New Zapp IV U* . . . . (Warner Bros.)
Rainy Day People
Gordon Lightfoot; *Cold On The Shoulder* . . . . (Reprise)
  Gord's Gold . . . . (Reprise)
Revival
Allman Brothers Band; *An Evening With The Allman Brothers Band-*
  First Set . . . . (Epic)
  Beginnings . . . . (Polydor)
  Decade Of Hits-1969-1979 . . . . (Polydor)
  Dreams . . . . (Polydor)
  Idlewild South . . . . (Polydor)
Rock & Roll People
John Lennon; *Menlove Ave.* . . . . (Capitol)
Rock & Roll People
Johnny Winter; *Captured Live* . . . . (Blue Sky)
Rock The People
Stryper; *Against The Law* . . . . (Hollywood)
Salt Of The Earth
Mick Jagger & Keith Richards; *The Concert For New York City-C* . . (Columbia)
Rolling Stones; *Beggars Banquet* . . . . (Abkco)
Save The People
Original Cast; *Godspell* . . . . (Arista)
Senorita With A Necklace Of Tears
Paul Simon; *You're The One* . . . . (Warner Bros.)
Shiny Happy People
R.E.M.; *Out Of Time* . . . . (Warner Bros.)
Short People
Randy Newman; *Dr. Demento Presents The Greatest Novelty Records-#4-*
  1970s-C . . . . (Rhino)
  Little Criminals . . . . (Warner Bros.)
Shower The People
James Taylor; *In The Pocket* . . . . (Warner Bros.)
  James Taylor's Greatest Hits . . . . (Warner Bros.)
Some Enchanted Evening
Jay & The Americans; *Come A Little Bit Closer-Best Of Jay & The*
  Americans . . . . (Gold Rush)
  Jay & The Americans' All-Time Greatest Hits . . . . (Rhino)
Original Cast; *South Pacific* . . . . (CBS Masterworks)
Perry Como; *Perry Como's All-Time Greatest Hits-#1* . . . . (RCA)
Rosanno Brazzi; *ST/South Pacific* . . . . (RCA)
Willie Nelson; *What A Wonderful World* . . . . (Columbia)
Some People
Original Cast; *ST/Gypsy* . . . . (Columbia)
Some People Can Do What They Like
Robert Palmer; *Some People Can Do What They Like* . . . . (Island)
Somebody
Aerosmith; *Aerosmith* . . . . (Columbia)
Somebody
J. Geils Band; *Monkey Island* . . . . (Atlantic)
Somebody's Somebody
"AFKAP"; *Emancipation* . . . . (NPG)
Somebody's Somebody
Christina Aguilera; *Christina Aguilera* . . . . (RCA)
Someday
All-4-One; *ST/The Hunchback Of Notre Dame* . . . . (Disney)
Stop Hurting People
Pete Townshend; *All The Best Cowboys Have Chinese Eyes* . . . . . . (Atco)
  Pete Townshend's Deep End Live! . . . . (Atco)
Sunset People
Donna Summer; *Bad Girls* . . . . (Casablanca)
  Donna Summer's Greatest Hits . . . . (Casablanca)
  On The Radio-Greatest Hits-Volumes I & II . . . . (Casablanca)
  Walk Away-Best Of Donna Summer-1977-1980 . . . . (Casablanca)
Swallowed
Bush; *Razorblade Suitcase* . . . . (Trauma)
Tattva
Kula Shaker; *K* . . . . (Columbia)
Television People
Psychefunkapus; *Skin* . . . . (Atlantic)
Tell All The People
Doors; *Soft Parade* . . . . (Elektra)
Thank U
Alanis Morissette; *Supposed Former Infatuation Junkie* . . . . (Maverick)

That's Where The Happy People Go
Trammps; *Disco Hits-#1-C* . . . . (Rhino)
That's Where The Happy People Go . . . . (Out Of Print)
Theme From ''The People's Court''
Original Soundtrack; *Television's Greatest Hits-#6-Remote Control-C* . . (TVT)
This Time
Curtis Stigers; *Time Was* . . . . (Arista)
Toytown People
Fabulous Poodles; *Mirror Stars* . . . .(Epic)
Tripping Billies
Dave Matthews Band; *Crash* . . . . (RCA)
True Friends
Shannon Curfman; *Loud Guitars Big Suspicions* . . . . (Arista)
Two Less Lonely People In The World
Air Supply; *Now & Forever* . . . . (Arista)
Two People Fell In Love
Brad Paisley; *Brad Paisley-Part II* . . . . (Arista)
Two Sleepy People
Art Garfunkel; *Up 'Til Now* . . . . (Columbia)
Fats Waller; *Fats Waller-Masterpieces-#3* . . . . (EPM)
Jo Sullivan Loesser & Others; *Loesser By Loesser* . . . . (DRG)
Kay Kyser & His Orchestra; *Best Of The Big Bands-C* . . . . . . (Columbia)
Victims Of Comfort
Keb' Mo'; *Keb' Mo'* . . . .(Okeh)
Voices Of Old People
Simon & Garfunkel; *Bookends* . . . . (Columbia)
Collected Works . . . . (Columbia)
We Are The Other People
Mothers Of Invention; *We're Only In It For The Money* . . . .(Rykodisc)
What It's Like
Everlast; *Whitey Ford Sings The Blues* . . . . (Tommy Boy)
Wonderful World, Beautiful People
Jimmy Cliff; *In Concert-Best Of Jimmy Cliff* . . . . (Reprise)
Reggae Spectacular-C . . . . (A&M)
Wonderful World, Beautiful People . . . . (A&M)

PIRATES, Buccaneers

See Also: CRIME, OCEAN, REBELS, SAILING, SHIPS

Buccaneers
Erich Wolfgang Korngold; *The Warner Bros. Years-Motion Picture Soundtrack Anthology* . . . . (Turner Classic Movies)
Buccaneers' Cove
Mad Professor; *Caribbean Taste Of Technology* . . . . (Ariwa)
Captain Hook's Waltz
Original Cast/Cyril Ritchard; *Peter Pan-The 1954 Broadway Production* . . . .(RCA Victor)
Lincoln Park Pirates
Steve Goodman; *No Big Surprise: The Steve Goodman Anthology* . . . .(Red Pajama)
Somebody Else's Troubles . . . .(Buddah)
Now For The Pirates' Liar
Original Broadway Cast; *Pirates Of Penzance* . . . . (Elektra)
Pirate Dance
New Broadway Cast; *How To Succeed In Business Without Really Trying* . . . .(RCA Victor)
Pirate Jenny
Judy Collins; *Forever-Judy Collin's Anthology* . . . . (Elektra)
In My Life . . . . (Elektra)
Nina Simone; *Best Of Nina Simone* . . . . (Verve)
Pirate Looks At Forty, A
Jimmy Buffett; *A1A* . . . .(MCA)
Boats Beaches Bars & Ballads . . . . (Margaritaville)
Songs You Know By Heart-Jimmy Buffett's Greatest Hit(s) . . . .(MCA)
You Had To Be There . . . .(MCA)
Pirate Love
Johnny Thunders; *Live At Max's Kansas City '79* . . . .(Roir)
Pirate Of Penance, The
Joni Mitchell; *Song To A Seagull* . . . . (Reprise)
Pirate Radio
John Hiatt; *Little Head* . . . . (Capitol)
Pirate Ships
Judy Collins; *Judith* . . . . (Elektra)
Wendy Waldman; *Love Is The Only Goal-Best Of Wendy Waldman* . . . .(Warner Archives)
Pirate Song
Original Cast; *Peter Pan-The 1954 Broadway Production* . . . .(RCA Victor)
Pirate Song, The (I Want To Sing And Dance)
Ray Stevens; *I Have Returned* . . . .(MCA)
Pirate Story
Ted Jacobs; *A Child's Garden Of Songs* . . . . (Kid Rhino/Rhino 4 Kids)
Pirates
Original Soundtrack; *ST/Six Days Seven Nights* . . . . (Hollywood)
Pirates
Emerson, Lake & Palmer; *Works, Volume 1* . . . . (Rhino)

Pirates
String Cheese Incident; *A String Cheese Incident* . . . . (Scifidel)
Pirates (Black Plastic)
Lee ''Scratch'' Perry; *Mystic Warrior* . . . . (Ariwa)
Pirates (So Long Lonely Avenue)
Rickie Lee Jones; *Pirates* . . . . (Warner Bros.)
Pirates Anthem
Shabba Ranks; *Shabba & Friends* . . . . (Epic)
Pirates Cove
David Lee Murphy; *Gettin' Out The Good Stuff* . . . . (MCA)
Pirate's Life, A
Original Soundtrack; *ST/Peter Pan* . . . . (Disney)
Pirates Of Stone Canyon Road
John Stewart; *Last Campaign* . . . . (Laserlight)
Phoenix Concerts . . . . (One Way)
Pour, O Pour The Pirate Sherry
Original Broadway Cast; *Pirates Of Penzance* . . . . (Elektra)
Rollicking Band Of Pirates We
Broadway Cast; *Pirates Of Penzance* . . . . (Elektra)
Roving Kind, The
Guy Mitchell; *Guy Mitchell-16 Most Requested Songs* . . . . (Legacy)
Shiver Me Timbers
Bette Midler; *Live At Last* . . . .(Atlantic)
Songs For The New Depression . . . .(Atlantic)
ST/Divine Madness . . . .(Atlantic)
Tom Waits; *The Heart Of Saturday Night* . . . .(Asylum)
When You Had Left Our Pirate Fold
Original Broadway Cast; *Pirates Of Penzance* . . . . (Elektra)
Yo Ho (A Pirate's Life For Me)
Pointer Sisters; *Disney's Music From The Park-C* . . . . (Disney)
Various Artists; *Disneyland-Official Album-C* . . . . (Disney)
Yo Ho Ho And A Bottle Of Rum
Original Cast; *Rugrats Sing-Along* . . . .(Interscope)

PLACES, Locations

See Also: AMERICAN WEST, CITIES: A-Z, COUNTRIES: A-Z, COUNTRY, DIRECTIONS (various), HARD CITY LIFE, HEAVEN, HELL, HOLLYWOOD, MOUNTAINS, NATURE, OCEAN, PARADISE, POVERTY (ghetto), PRISON, SMALL TOWN LIFE, SPACE, STATES: A-Z, STREETS: GENERAL, STREETS: SPECIFIC

53 Miles West Of Venus
B-52's; *Wild Planet* . . . . (Warner Bros.)
Across The Alley From The Alamo
Asleep At The Wheel featuring Johnny Rodriguez; *Tribute To The Music Of Bob Wills And The Texas Playboys-C* . . . . (Liberty)
Bob Wills & His Texas Playboys; *Best Of Bob Wills & His Texas Playboys* . . . . (MCA)
Tiffany Transcriptions-#4-You're From Texas . . . . (Rhino)
Alice In Wonderland
Neil Sedaka; *Neil Sedaka's All-Time Greatest Hits* . . . .(RCA)
All The Places (I Will Kiss You)
Aaron Hall; *Inside Of You* . . . . (MCA)
Any Time, Any Place
Janet Jackson; *janet.* . . . .(Virgin)
Anyplace In Paradise
Elvis Presley; *Elvis* . . . .(RCA)
Anywhere
112; *Room 112* . . . .(Bad Boy/Arista)
Anywhere But Here
Sammy Kershaw; *Haunted Heart* . . . . (Mercury)
Anywhere Like Heaven
James Taylor; *Sweet Baby James* . . . . (Warner Bros.)
Baba O'Reilly (Teenage Wasteland)
Who; *Hooligans* . . . . (MCA)
ST/The Kids Are Alright . . . . (MCA)
The Concert For New York City-C . . . . (Columbia)
Who's Last . . . . (MCA)
Who's next . . . . (MCA)
Badlands
Bruce Springsteen; *Bruce Springsteen's Greatest Hits* . . . . (Columbia)
Darkness On The Edge Of Town . . . . (Columbia)
Bruce Springsteen & The E Street Band; *Bruce Springsteen & The E Street Band Live/1975-85* . . . . (Legacy)
Been There
Clint Black with Steve Wariner; *D'lectrified* . . . .(RCA)
Bermuda Triangle
Fleetwood Mac; *Heroes Are Hard To Find* . . . . (Reprise)
Bermuda Triangle Blues (Flight 45)
Blondie; *Plastic Letters* . . . . (Chrysalis)
Between The Devil And The Deep Blue Sea
Cab Calloway; *Jazz Heritage: Mr. Hi-De-Ho* . . . . (MCA)
Chris Rea; *Espresso Logic* . . . . (East West)
Diana Krall; *Stepping Out* . . . .(Justin Time)
Ella Fitzgerald; *Harold Arlen Songbook-#1* . . . . (Verve)

Beyond The Wall Of Sleep
Ozzy Osbourne; *The Ozzman Cometh* . . . . (Epic)
Big Ball's In Cowtown
Asleep At The Wheel; *Very Best Of Asleep At The Wheel*
  Since 1970 . . . . (Relentless/Madacy)
Asleep At The Wheel featuring George Strait; *Tribute To The Music Of Bob*
  Wills And The Texas Playboys-C . . . . (Liberty)
Bob Wills & His Texas Playboys; *Best Of Bob Wills & His Texas*
  Playboys . . . . (MCA)
  For The Last Time . . . . (Capitol)
Big Rock Candy Mountain
Burl Ives; *Burl Ives' Greatest Hits* . . . . (MCA)
  Poor Wayfaring Stranger . . . . (Flapper)
Harry McClintock; *ST/O Brother, Where Art Thou?* . . . . (Mercury)
John Hartford; *ST/Down From The Mountain* . . . . . (Lost Highway/IDJMG)
Pete Seeger; *20 Golden Pieces Of Pete Seeger* . . . . (Bulldog)
Tex Ritter; *Capitol Collectors Series-Tex Ritter* . . . . (Capitol)
Birdland
Manhattan Transfer; *Atlantic Jazz Vocal Classics-C* . . . . (Rhino)
  Best Of The Manhattan Transfer . . . . (Atlantic)
  Billboard Top Contemporary Jazz Vocals-C . . . . (Rhino)
  Extensions . . . . (Rhino)
Quincy Jones; *Back On The Block* . . . . (Qwest)
Weather Report; *8:30* . . . . (Legacy)
  Heavy Weather . . . . (Legacy)
Birdman Of Alkatrash
Strawberry Alarm Clock; *Strawberry Alarm Clock-Anthology* . . . . . . (One Way)
Blue Eden
Neil Young & Crazy Horse; *Sleeps With Angels* . . . . (Reprise)
Blueberry Hill
Elvis Presley; *Elvis Recorded Live On Stage In Memphis* . . . . (RCA)
  Loving You . . . . (RCA)
Fats Domino; *Fats Domino's Greatest Hits* . . . . (Everest)
  Fats Domino's Greatest Hits . . . . (MCA)
  My Blue Heaven-Best Of Fats Domino-#1 . . . . (EMI)
Little Richard; *Big Hits* . . . . (Crescendo)
Louis Armstrong; *Best Of Louis Armstrong* . . . . (MCA)
  Essential Louis Armstrong . . . . (Vanguard)
  I Like Jazz-Essence Of Louis Armstrong . . . . (Columbia)
Boogie Wonderland
Earth, Wind & Fire; *Best Of Earth, Wind & Fire-#2* . . . . (Columbia)
  I Am . . . . (Columbia)
  Roller Boogie-C . . . . (Casablanca)
  Skatetown U.S.A.-C . . . . (Columbia)
Brain Damage
Pink Floyd; *Dark Side Of The Moon* . . . . (Capitol)
  Pink Floyd-Gift Set . . . . (Capitol)
  Works . . . . (Capitol)
Breakdown
Queensryche; *Q2k* . . . . (Atlantic)
Breakfast At Tiffany's
Deep Blue Something; *Home* . . . . (RainMaker/Interscope)
Breakfast At Tiffany's
Henry Mancini; *Days Of Wine And Roses* . . . . (RCA)
Breakfast In Mayfair
Fairport Convention; *Babbacombe Lee* . . . . (A&M)
  Fairport Convention-Chronicles . . . . (A&M)
Broken Promise Land
Mark Chesnutt; *Too Cold At Home* . . . . (MCA)
Camelot
Original 1982 London Cast; *Camelot* . . . . (Varese Sarabande)
Original Cast; *Camelot* . . . . (Columbia)
Richard Burton; *Broadway Magic-The 1960s-C* . . . . (Columbia)
Richard Harris; *ST/Camelot* . . . . (Warner Bros.)
Can I Touch You...There?
Michael Bolton; *Michael Bolton's Greatest Hits-1985-1995* . . . . . . (Columbia)
Carroll County Accident
Porter Wagoner; *Essential Porter Wagoner* . . . . (RCA)
  Porter Wagoner-Greatest Songs . . . . (Curb)
Cherry Hill Park
Billy Joe Royal; *Billy Joe Royal's Greatest Hits* . . . . (Columbia)
  Super Hits Of The '70s-Have A Nice Day-#1-C . . . . (Rhino)
Child Of The Wild Blue Yonder
John Hiatt; *Stolen Moments* . . . . (A&M)
Come Over To My Place
Davina; *Best Of Both Worlds* . . . . (Loud/RCA)
Come With Me
Keith Sweat featuring Ronald Isley; *Keith Sweat* . . . . (Elektra)
Copacabana (At The Copa)
Barry Manilow; *Barry Manilow's Greatest Hits-#2* . . . . (Arista)
  Even Now . . . . (Arista)
  ST/Foul Play . . . . (Arista)
  The Manilow Collection-Twenty Classic Hits . . . . (Arista)
Columbia Ballroom Orchestra; *Let's Dance-#6* . . . . (Denon)
Cowboy Love Song (Red River Valley)
Skip Gorman; *A Cowboy's Wild Song To His Herd* . . . . (Rounder)
Cuyahoga
R.E.M.; *Life's Rich Pageant* . . . . (EMI-Capitol Entert. Properties)

Danger Zone
Ramones; *Too Tough To Die* . . . . (Sire)
Danger Zone
Kenny Loggins; *ST/Top Gun* . . . . (Columbia)
Danger Zone
Klymaxx; *Klymaxx* . . . . (Constellation)
Danger Zone
Crystal Gayle; *Miss The Mississippi* . . . . (Capitol)
Danger Zone
Planet Patrol; *Planet Patrol* . . . . (Tommy Boy)
  Tommy Boy's Greatest Beats-#2-C . . . . (Tommy Boy)
Danger Zone
Shirley Murdock; *Shirley Murdock* . . . . (Elektra)
Danger Zone
L.A. Posse; *They Come In All Colors* . . . . (Atlantic)
Dark End Of The Street
Commitments; *ST/The Commitments* . . . . (MCA)
James Carr; *Essential James Carr* . . . . (Razor & Tie)
Linda Ronstadt; *Heart Like A Wheel* . . . . (Capitol)
Percy Sledge; *Best Of Percy Sledge* . . . . (Atlantic)
Darkness On The Edge Of Town
Bruce Springsteen; *Darkness On The Edge Of Town* . . . . (Columbia)
Bruce Springsteen & The E Street Band; *Bruce Springsteen & The E Street*
  Band Live/1975-85 . . . . (Legacy)
Darlington County
Bruce Springsteen; *Born In The U.S.A.* . . . . (Columbia)
Dead Man's Curve
Jan & Dean; *21 Legendary Superstars-C* . . . . (Original Sound)
  Best Of Jan & Dean . . . . (EMI)
  Dead Man's Curve . . . . (EMI)
Dead Man's Hill
Indigo Girls; *Swamp Ophelia* . . . . (Epic)
Dear Brother
Hank Williams; *I Saw The Light* . . . . (Polydor)
Don't Wanna Be Here
Cool For August; *Grand World* . . . . (Warner Bros.)
Down In The Boondocks
Billy Joe Royal; *Billy Joe Royal's Greatest Hits* . . . . (Columbia)
  Rock Classics Of The '60s-C . . . . (Columbia)
Down Town, The
Days Of The New; *Days Of The New* . . . . (Outpost/Interscope)
Drag City
Jan & Dean; *Beach Party Blasts* . . . . (EMI)
  Best Of Jan & Dean . . . . (EMI)
  Dead Man's Curve . . . . (EMI)
  One Summer Night-Live . . . . (Rhino)
Dreams Of Wounded Knee
Bill Miller; *The Red Road* . . . . (Warner Western)
Dreamsville
Henry Mancini; *Brass On Ivory* . . . . (RCA)
  Henry Mancini With Doc Severinsen . . . . (RCA)
  Peter Gunn . . . . (RCA)
  This Is Henry Mancini . . . . (RCA)
East Of The Sun & West Of The Moon
Al Cohn & Zoot Sims; *RCA Victor Jazz: First Half-Century-C* . . . . . . (RCA)
Billie Holiday; *Billie's Best* . . . . (Verve)
Diana Krall; *When I Look In Your Eyes* . . . . (GRP)
Tommy Dorsey & Frank Sinatra; *Stardust* . . . . (Bluebird)
El Rancho Grande
Tune Wranglers; *Doughboys, Playboys And Cowboys: The Golden Years Of*
  Western Swing-C . . . . (Proper)
Electric Land
Bad Company; *10 From 6* . . . . (Atlantic)
  Rough Diamonds . . . . (Swan Song)
Erotik City
Emoja; *ST/Men In Black* . . . . (Columbia)
Every Ghetto, Every City
Lauryn Hill; *The Miseducation Of Lauryn Hill* . . . . (Ruffhouse/Columbia)
Everywhere
Fleetwood Mac; *25 Years-The Chain* . . . . (Warner Bros.)
  Fleetwood Mac's Greatest Hits . . . . (Warner Bros.)
  Tango In The Night . . . . (Warner Bros.)
Everywhere
Tim McGraw; *Everywhere* . . . . (Curb)
Everywhere
Michelle Branch; *The Spirit Room* . . . . (Maverick)
Ferry Cross The Mersey
Gerry And The Pacemakers; *Ferry Across The Mersey-Best Of Gerry And*
  The Pacemakers . . . . (EMI)
  History Of British Rock-#4-C . . . . (Rhino)
Fist City
Loretta Lynn; *Loretta Lynn-20 Greatest Hits* . . . . (MCA)
  Loretta Lynn-Greatest Hits Live . . . . (K-Tel)
  Loretta Lynn's Greatest Hits-#2 . . . . (MCA)
  The Country Music Hall Of Fame-Loretta Lynn . . . . (MCA)
Fogtown
Michelle Shocked; *Texas Campfire Tapes* . . . . (Mercury)
Gentle Place, A
Clannad; *Banba* . . . . (Atlantic)

Lisa Lynne; *Daughters Of The Celtic Moon* . . . . (Windham Hill)

Georgia Pineywoods
Osborne Brothers; *Best Of The Osborne Brothers* . . . . (MCA)
  Country Bluegrass . . . . (MCA Special Prod.)
  Red, White & Bluegrass-C . . . . (C.M.H. Prod.)

Gotham City
R. Kelly; *ST/Batman & Robin-Music From And Inspired By The Motion*
  Picture . . . . (Jive)

Graceland
Paul Simon; *Graceland* . . . . (Warner Bros.)

Grantchester Meadows
Pink Floyd; *Ummagumma* . . . . (Capitol)

Green, Green
New Christy Minstrels; *New Christy Minstrels' Greatest Hits* . . . . . . (Columbia)

Hanginaround
Counting Crows; *This Desert Life* . . . . (David Geffen Co.)

Happiness Street
Georgia Gibbs; *Best Of Georgia Gibbs-The Mercury Years* . . . . (Chronicles)

Hardin County Line
Mark Collie; *Even The Man In The Moon Is Cryin'* . . . . (MCA)

Hate This Place
Goo Goo Dolls; *Dizzy Up The Girl* . . . . (Warner Sunset/Reprise)

Have You Ever Been (To Electric Ladyland)
Jimi Hendrix Experience; *Electric Ladyland* . . . . (Reprise)

Healing Game
Van Morrison; *The Healing Game* . . . . (A&M)

Heartbreak U.S.A.
Kitty Wells; *I Love Country-Hits Of The '60s-#1-C* . . . . (Priority)
  Kitty Wells' Greatest Hits . . . . (Curb)
  The Country Music Hall Of Fame-Kitty Wells . . . . (MCA Special Prod.)

Heaven Right Here
Jeb Loy Nichols; *Just What Time It Is* . . . . (Rykodisc)

Hello, Central, Give Me No Man's Land
Al Jolson; *Music From The New York Stage (1890-1920)-#4-1917-*
  1920-C . . . . (Pearl)

Here
Tony Martin; *Best Of Tony Martin On RCA* . . . . (Collector's Choice)

Here In Your Bedroom
Goldfinger; *Richter* . . . . (Mojo Music/Universal)

Here To Stay
Pat Metheny; *We Live Here* . . . . (Geffen)

Here, There & Everywhere
Beatles; *Beatles-Box Set* . . . . (Capitol)
  Beatles-Love Songs . . . . (Capitol)
  Revolver . . . . (Capitol)
Kenny Loggins; *Kenny Loggins Alive* . . . . (Columbia)

Hernando's Hideaway
Original Cast; *Pajama Game* . . . . (Columbia)
  ST/Pajama Game . . . . (Collectables)

Hidden Place
Bjork; *Vespertine* . . . . (Elektra)

Hidin' Places
Shylo; *45-#811097-7* . . . . (Mercury)

Higher Ground
Barbra Streisand; *Higher Ground* . . . . (Columbia)

Higher Place
Tom Petty; *Wildflowers* . . . . (Warner Bros.)

Hippie Crash Pad
Jump With Joey; *Ska-Ba* . . . . (Rykodisc)

Hold My Hand
Hootie & The Blowfish; *Cracked Rear View* . . . . (Atlantic)

Hyde Park ("Ah, Ooh" Song)
Jeff Kashiwa; *Another Door Opens* . . . . (Native Language)

I Am Going To Like It Here
Original Cast; *ST/Flower Drum Song* . . . . (Sony Music Classical)

I Got A Woman
Ray Charles; *Ray Charles' Greatest Hits* . . . . (Rhino)
  Ray Charles-Anthology . . . . (Rhino)

I Know A Place
Petula Clark; *History Of British Rock-#7-C* . . . . (Rhino)
  Petula Clark's Greatest Hits . . . . (Crescendo)

I Like It Like That, Part 1
Chris Kenner; *Billboard Top Rock 'N' Roll Hits-1961-C* . . . . (Rhino)
  ST/Full Metal Jacket . . . . (Warner Bros.)

I Will Get There
Boyz II Men; *ST/The Prince Of Egypt-Inspirational* . . . . . . (DreamWorks/SKG)

I Will Take You There
Nilsson; *ST/Skidoo* . . . . (RCA)

Ignoreland
R.E.M.; *Automatic For The People* . . . . (Warner Bros.)

I'll Always Be Right There
Bryan Adams; *18 Til I Die* . . . . (A&M)
  MTV Unplugged-Bryan Adams . . . . (A&M)

I'll Be Here Awhile
311; *From Chaos* . . . . (Volcano Entertainment)

I'll Take You There
Staple Singers; *15 Original Big Hits-#1-C* . . . . (Stax)
  I Am Woman-C . . . . (Nick At Nite)

  Staple Singers' Greatest Hits . . . . (Fantasy)
  Staple Singers-Chronicle . . . . (Stax)

I'll Take You There
General Public; *ST/Threesome* . . . . (Epic/Sony Music Soundtrax)

In Another World
Joe Diffie; *In Another World* . . . . (Monument)

In My Life
Beatles; *Beatles-Love Songs* . . . . (Capitol)
  Rubber Soul . . . . (Capitol)
  ST/Imagine: John Lennon . . . . (Capitol)
  The Beatles/1962-1966 . . . . (Capitol)
Crosby, Stills & Nash; *After The Storm* . . . . (Atlantic)
Judy Collins; *Colors Of The Day-The Best Of Judy Collins* . . . . (Elektra)
  In My Life . . . . (Elektra)

In My Own Little Corner
Julie Andrews; *A Little Bit Of Broadway* . . . . (Columbia)
  Cinderella-The CBS Television Production . . . . (Columbia)
Lesley Ann Warren; *Cinderella-The CBS Television Network*
  Production . . . . (Columbia)

In My Room
Tammy Wynette & Brian Wilson; *Tammy Wynette...Remembered-C* . . (Asylum)

In The Closet
Michael Jackson; *Dangerous* . . . . (Epic)

In The Cool, Cool, Cool Of The Evening
Bing Crosby; *Best Of Bing Crosby* . . . . (MCA)
Frank Sinatra; *Days Of Wine And Roses, Moon River, And Other Academy*
  Award Winners . . . . (Reprise)
Rosemary Clooney; *Rosemary Clooney-16 Most Requested Songs* . . . . (Legacy)

In The House Of Stone And Light
Martin Page; *In The House Of Stone And Light* . . . . (Mercury)

In The Valley
Marty Robbins; *Gunfighter Ballads & Trail Songs* . . . . (Legacy)

Itchycoo Park
Small Faces; *Baby Boomer Classics-British Sixties-C* . . . . . . (JCI Assoc. Labels)

Land Of Confusion
Genesis; *Invisible Touch* . . . . (Atlantic)

Land Of Make Believe
Chuck Mangione; *Best Of Chuck Mangione* . . . . (Mercury)
  Chuck Mangione-Classics-#6 . . . . (A&M)
  Encore-Chuck Mangione . . . . (Mercury)
  Evening Of Magic . . . . (A&M)
  Land Of Make Believe . . . . (Mercury)

Land Of Make Believe
Moody Blues; *Seventh Sojourn* . . . . (Polydor)

Land Of The Living
Pam Tillis; *Pam Tillis' Greatest Hits* . . . . (Arista)

Let The Rest Of The World Go By
Mitch Miller; *Sing Along With Mitch* . . . . (Columbia)
Mom & Dads; *Down The River Of Golden Dreams* . . . . (Crescendo)

Letters From The Wasteland
Wallflowers; *Breach* . . . . (Interscope)

Little Green Valley
Marty Robbins; *Gunfighter Ballads & Trail Songs* . . . . (Legacy)

Living In The Promiseland
Willie Nelson; *30 Years Of #1 Hits-#18-C* . . . . (Columbia)
  Greatest Country Hits Of The '80s-1986-C . . . . (Columbia)
  More Hot Country Requests-C . . . . (Epic)
  The Promiseland . . . . (Columbia)

Living On The Edge Of The World
Bruce Springsteen; *Tracks* . . . . (Columbia)

Lollipop Guild
Original Cast; *The Wizard Of Oz-Selections From The Original Motion*
  Picture Soundtrack . . . . (Turner Classic Movies)

Lonesome Town
Ricky Nelson; *Best Of Ricky Nelson* . . . . (Curb)

Lost In The Ozone
Commander Cody; *We've Got A Live One Here!* . . . . (Warner Bros.)

Love Is The Right Place
Bryan White; *The Right Place* . . . . (Asylum)

Lullaby Of Birdland
Ella Fitzgerald; *Best Of Ella Fitzgerald-#2* . . . . (MCA)
  Ella Fitzgerald With Billie Holiday . . . . (MCA)
Four Freshmen; *Greatest Hits-Four Freshman* . . . . (Curb)
Mel Torme; *Songs Of New York* . . . . (Rhino)
Sarah Vaughan; *Sarah Vaughan-Golden Hits* . . . . (Mercury)
Tito Puente & His Latin Ensemble; *Mambo Diablo* . . . . (Concord Jazz)

Make Me Believe
Martina McBride; *Emotion* . . . . (RCA)

Mama's Opry
Iris DeMent; *Infamous Angel* . . . . (Warner Bros.)

Man From Music Mountain
Gene Autry; *The Singing Cowboy-Chapter Two* . . . . (Varese Sarabande)

Man From Out Of Town
Bill Morrissey; *Inside* . . . . (Rounder)

Mann's Chinese
Naked; *Naked* . . . . (Red Ant)

Margaritaville
Jimmy Buffett; *Changes In Latitudes, Changes In Attitudes* . . . . (MCA)

Songs You Know By Heart-Jimmy Buffett's Greatest Hit(s) . . . . (MCA)
You Had To Be There . . . . (MCA)
Meet In The Middle
Diamond Rio; *Diamond Rio* . . . . (Arista)
Diamond Rio's Greatest Hits . . . . (Arista)
Meet On The Ledge
Fairport Convention; *Fairport Convention* . . . . (A&M)
Fairport Convention-Chronicles . . . . (A&M)
In Real Time-Live '87 . . . . (Island)
Midnight Mary
Joey Powers; *Dick Bartley's One-Hit Wonders Of The '60s-#1-C* . . . . . . (Rhino)
Mocking Bird Hill
Patti Page; *Patti Page-16 Most Requested Songs* . . . . (Legacy)
Patti Page-Golden Hits . . . . (Mercury)
Patti Page's Greatest Hits . . . . (Columbia)
Russ Morgan; *Best Of Russ Morgan* . . . . (MCA)
More Than Seven Dwarfs In Penis-Land
Ron Geesin; *ST/The Body* . . . . (Restless)
Mrs. Clara Sullivan's Letter (Perry County)
Pete Seeger; *Best Of Broadside 1962-1968: Anthems Of The American Underground From The Pages Of Broadside Magazine-C* . . . . (Smithsonian Folkways)
Near You
Francis Craig & His Orchestra; *Cigar Classics-#1-The Standards-C* . . . . (Hip-O)
George Jones & Tammy Wynette; *George Jones & Tammy Wynette-16 Biggest Hits* . . . . (Epic/Legacy)
Neighborhood
Vonda Shepard; *ST/Songs From "Ally McBeal" Featuring Vonda Shepard* . . . . (550/Epic)
Never Never Land
Original Cast/Mary Martin; *Peter Pan-The 1954 Broadway Production* . . . . (RCA Victor)
Never There
Cake; *Now That's What I Call Music!-#1-2-C* . . . . (Virgin)
Prolonging The Magic . . . . (Capricorn)
Nightingale Sang In Berkeley Square
Harry Connick, Jr.; *We Are In Love* . . . . (Columbia)
Manhattan Transfer; *Best Of The Manhattan Transfer* . . . . (Atlantic)
Mecca For Moderns . . . . (Atlantic)
Tony Bennett; *Perfectly Frank* . . . . (Columbia)
No Man's Land
Billy Joel; *River Of Dreams* . . . . (Columbia)
No Man's Land
John Michael Montgomery; *John Michael Montgomery* . . . . (Atlantic)
No Place But Texas
Willie Nelson; *Texas Super Hits-C* . . . . (Columbia)
The Promiseland . . . . (Columbia)
No Place That Far
Sara Evans; *No Place That Far* . . . . (RCA)
Nobody's Supposed To Be Here
Deborah Cox; *One Wish* . . . . (Arista)
Totally Hits-#1-C . . . . (Arista)
Norwegian Wood (This Bird Has Flown)
Beatles; *Beatles-Box Set* . . . . (Capitol)
Beatles-Love Songs . . . . (Capitol)
Rubber Soul . . . . (Capitol)
The Beatles/1962-1966 . . . . (Capitol)
Nowhere Man
Beatles; *"Yesterday"...And Today* . . . . (Capitol)
Beatles-Box Set . . . . (Capitol)
Compact Disc Singles Collection . . . . (Capitol)
The Beatles/1962-1966 . . . . (Capitol)
O Bury Me Not On The Lone Prairie
Michael Martin Murphey; *Cowboy Songs* . . . . (Warner Western)
Sons Of The Pioneers; *Sunset On The Range* . . . . (Pair)
Ode To Billy Joe
Bobbi Gentry; *All-Time Country Classics-#1-C* . . . . (Capitol)
Old Cape Cod
Patti Page; *Patti Page-16 Most Requested Songs* . . . . (Legacy)
Patti Page-Golden Hits . . . . (Mercury)
Patti Page's Greatest Hits . . . . (Columbia)
On Holy Ground
Barbra Streisand; *Higher Ground* . . . . (Columbia)
On The Dark Side
John Cafferty And The Beaver Brown Band; *ST/Eddie & The Cruisers* . . . . (Scotti Bros.)
On The Street Where You Live
Andy Williams; *Andy Williams-16 Most Requested Songs-Encore!* . . . . (Legacy)
Bobby Darin; *Unreleased Capitol Sides* . . . . (Collector's Choice)
Eddie Fisher; *Very Best Of Eddie Fisher* . . . . (Taragon)
Four Tops; *Lost & Found: Breaking Through* . . . . (Motown)
Harry Connick, Jr.; *25* . . . . (Columbia)
Mel Torme; *Swings Shubert Alley* . . . . (Verve)
Original Cast; *My Fair Lady* . . . . (Columbia)
Ray Conniff; *'S Awful Nice* . . . . (Columbia)
Once In A While
Dishwalla; *And You Think You Know What Life's About* . . . . (A&M)
Otherside
Red Hot Chili Peppers; *Californication* . . . . (Warner Bros.)

Out Behind The Barn
"Little" Jimmy Dickens; *Columbia Historic Edition-"Little" Jimmy Dickens* . . . . (Columbia)
Over The Rainbow
Barbra Streisand; *Just For The Record* . . . . (Columbia)
Dave Brubeck; *Greatest Hits From The Fantasy Years* . . . . (Fantasy)
Ella Fitzgerald; *Silver Collection-Songbooks* . . . . (Verve)
Judy Garland; *Best Of The Capitol Masters-One & Only Box* . . . . . . (Capitol)
Judy Garland-At Carnegie Hall . . . . (Capitol)
Judy Garland's Greatest Hits . . . . (Curb)
Miss Show Business . . . . (Capitol)
One & Only . . . . (Capitol)
ST/The Wizard Of Oz . . . . (Sony Music Special Prod.)
Over There
Glenn Miller; *Original Recordings-#3-Army/Air Force Band* . . . . (Pair)
Glenn Miller & His Army/Air Force Band; *Glenn Miller-A Legendary Performer-#3* . . . . (Bluebird)
Mormon Tabernacle Choir; *God Bless America* . . . . . . (Sony Music Classical)
Penny Lane
Beatles; *Beatles 1* . . . . (Capitol)
Magical Mystery Tour . . . . (Capitol)
The Beatles/1967-1970 . . . . (Capitol)
The Beatles-Anthology-#2 . . . . (Capitol)
Place In France
Death Squad; *Split You At The Seams* . . . . (Ever Rat)
Place In The Country
Adam Ant; *Antics In The Forbidden Zone* . . . . (Epic)
Friend Or Foe . . . . (Epic)
Place In The Country
George Jones; *One Woman Man* . . . . (Epic)
Place In The Sun
Stevie Wonder; *Looking Back* . . . . (Motown)
Stevie Wonder's Greatest Hits . . . . (Motown)
Place In The Sun
Pablo Cruise; *A Place In The Sun* . . . . (A&M)
Place In This World
Michael W. Smith; *Go West Young Man* . . . . (Reunion)
Place To Fall Apart
Merle Haggard & Janie Fricke; *For The Record: Merle Haggard-43 Legendary Hits* . . . . (BNA)
Place Where You Belong
Shai; *ST/Beverly Hills Cop 3* . . . . (MCA)
Places I've Never Been
Mark Wills; *Mark Wills* . . . . (Mercury)
Pleasant Valley Sunday
Monkees; *Listen To The Band* . . . . (Rhino)
Monkees' Greatest Hits . . . . (Rhino)
Nuggets-Classic Collection From The Psychedelic '60s-C . . . . (Rhino)
Pride Of Franklin County
Tanya Tucker; *Lovin' & Learnin'* . . . . (MCA)
Tanya Tucker's Greatest Hits . . . . (MCA)
Promised Land
Band; *Moondog Matinee* . . . . (Capitol)
Chuck Berry; *Rock 'N' Roll Rarities-20 Magic Tracks* . . . . (Chess)
The Chess Box-Chuck Berry . . . . (Chess)
Elvis Presley; *Promised Land* . . . . (RCA)
ST/This Is Elvis . . . . (RCA)
Freddy Weller; *Country Music Classics-#11-Early '70s-C* . . . . . . (K-Tel)
Freddy Weller's Greatest Hits . . . . (Columbia)
Gary Morris; *Full Moon Empty Heart* . . . . (Liberty)
Grateful Dead; *Steal Your Face* . . . . (Grateful Dead)
James Taylor; *Walking Man* . . . . (Warner Bros.)
Kingfish; *Kingfish/Alive In Eighty Five-Double Dose* . . . . (Relix)
Promised Land
Bruce Springsteen; *Darkness On The Edge Of Town* . . . . (Columbia)
Bruce Springsteen & The E Street Band; *Bruce Springsteen & The E Street Band Live/1975-85* . . . . (Legacy)
Promised Land
Bobby Caldwell; *Stuck On You* . . . . (Sin-Drome)
Promised Land
Julian Cope; *Peggy Suicide* . . . . (Island)
Promised Land
Hollies; *Distant Light* . . . . (Epic)
Radio Land
Michael Martin Murphey; *Best Of Michael Martin Murphey* . . . . . . (Liberty)
Heart Never Lies . . . . (Liberty)
Radioland
Nicolette Larson; *Radioland* . . . . (MCA)
Redneck Riviera
Tom T. Hall; *Songs From Sopchoppy* . . . . (Mercury)
Redneck Wonderland
Midnight Oil; *Redneck Wonderland* . . . . (Columbia)
Remember Pearl Harbor
Sammy Kaye & His Orchestra; *ST/Radio Days* . . . . (Novus)
Right Here Right Now
Charlie Major & Joy Lynn White; *444* . . . . (Dead Reckoning)
Right Where I Need To Be
Gary Allan; *Smoke Rings In The Dark* . . . . (MCA)

River And The Highway
Pam Tillis; *All Of This Love* .... (Arista)
Pam Tillis' Greatest Hits .... (Arista)
Road To Nowhere
Ozzy Osbourne; *No More Tears* .... (Epic Portrait Assoc.)
Road To Utopia
Utopia; *Adventures In Utopia* .... (Rhino)
Rock & Roll Babylon
Love And Rockets; *Love And Rockets* .... (Beggar's Banquet)
Rockaway Beach
Ramones; *Loco Live* .... (Sire)
Ramones Mania .... (Sire)
Rocket To Russia .... (Sire)
Summer & Sun-C .... (Rhino)
Round Here
Counting Crows; *August And Everything After* .... (David Geffen Co.)
Sad Eyed Lady Of The Lowlands
Bob Dylan; *Blonde On Blonde* .... (Columbia)
Joan Baez; *Any Day Now: Songs Of Bob Dylan* .... (Vanguard)
Lovesong Album .... (Vanguard)
Safe Place From The Storm
Michael Bolton; *All That Matters* .... (Columbia)
Sahara
Esther Walker; *Music From The New York Stage (1890-1920)-#4-1917-
1920-C* .... (Pearl)
Sailing To Philadelphia
Mark Knopfler; *Sailing To Philadelphia*. .... (Warner Bros.)
Sam's Place
Buck Owens & The Buckaroos; *Billboard Top Country Hits-1967-C* ... (Rhino)
Satan Place
Jeannie C. Riley; *Harper Valley P.T.A.* .... (Plantation)
Secret Place
Megadeth; *Cryptic Writings* .... (Capitol)
Shoot Out At The Fantasy Factory
Traffic; *On The Road* .... (Island)
Shoot Out At The Fantasy Factory. .... (Island)
Silicon Valley
Peter Seiler; *Flying Frames* .... (Innovative Comm.)
Sittin' Up In My Room
Brandy; *ST/Waiting To Exhale* .... (Arista)
Slim Jenkins' Place
Booker T. & The M.G.s; *Best Of Booker T. & The M.G.s* .... (Atlantic)
Hip Hug-Her .... (Rhino)
Smokey Places
Billy Walker; *Billy Walker's Greatest Hits.* .... (Monument)
Corsairs; *Best Of Chess Rhythm & Blues-#1-C.* .... (Chess)
Collectables Presents The History Of Rock-#5-C .... (Collectables)
Soft Place To Fall
Allison Moorer; *Alabama Song* .... (MCA)
ST/The Horse Whisperer .... (MCA)
Softest Place On Earth
Xscape; *Traces Of My Lipstick* .... (So So Def/Columbia)
Solsbury Hill
Peter Gabriel; *Peter Gabriel* .... (Atco)
Peter Gabriel/Plays Live .... (Geffen)
Shaking The Tree-Sixteen Golden Greats .... (Geffen)
Somehow, Somewhere, Someway
Kenny Wayne Shepherd; *Trouble Is...* .... (Revolution)
Somewhere
Aretha Franklin; *Aretha's Jazz* .... (Rhino)
Barbra Streisand; *The Broadway Album* .... (Columbia)
Dave Brubeck; *Music From West Side Story* .... (Columbia)
Jose Carreras; *Amigos Para Siempre-Friends For Life* .... (Atlantic)
Original Cast; *ST/West Side Story.* .... (Sony Broadway)
Tom Waits; *Tom Waits-Anthology* .... (Asylum)
Somewhere Down The Road
Barry Manilow; *If I Should Love Again* .... (Arista)
Somewhere Down The Road
Kathy Mattea; *Kathy Mattea.* .... (Mercury)
Somewhere In Kentucky
Charlie Bandy; *45-#4611* .... (Soundwaves)
Somewhere In My Broken Heart
Billy Dean; *Billy Dean's Greatest Hits.* .... (Liberty)
Heart Beats-Country Lovin': Songs From The Heart-C .... (Rhino)
Young Man .... (SBK)
Randy Travis; *No Holdin' Back* .... (Warner Bros.)
Somewhere In Texas
Ray Price; *Ray Price's Greatest Hits-#4-By Request* .... (Step One)
Willie Nelson; *Tougher Than Leather* .... (Columbia)
Somewhere In The Night
Barry Manilow; *Barry Manilow's Greatest Hits-#2* .... (Arista)
Even Now .... (Arista)
Somewhere In The Vicinity Of The Heart
Shenandoah; *In The Vicinity Of The Heart* .... (Capitol)
Now And Then .... (Capitol)
Pure Country-Best Of The '90s-#2-C. .... (Priority)
Somewhere Out There
James Ingram & Linda Ronstadt; *The Power Of Great Music* .... (Warner Bros.)

Linda Ronstadt & James Ingram; *ST/An American Tail* .... (MCA)
Somewhere South Of Macon
Marshall Chapman; *Me I'm Feeling Free* .... (Epic)
Somewhere There's A Rainbow Over Texas
Ruby Falls; *45-#39* .... (Fifty States)
Somewhere They Can't Find Me
Simon & Garfunkel; *Collected Works.* .... (Columbia)
Sounds Of Silence .... (Columbia)
Somewhere Tonight
Highway 101; *Featuring Paulette Carlson* .... (Warner Bros.)
Highway 101's Greatest Hits .... (Warner Bros.)
Somewhere Tonight
Toto; *Fahrenheit* .... (Columbia)
Somewhere Tonight
Bob Seger & The Silver Bullet Band; *Like A Rock* .... (Capitol)
St. James Infirmary Blues
Benny Goodman; *Yale Recordings-#5-Private Collection* ...... (Musicmasters)
Cab Calloway; *Cab Calloway* .... (Glendale)
Jack Teagarden; *Hundred Years From Today* .... (Grudge)
Joe Cocker; *Joe Cocker.* .... (A&M)
Lou Rawls; *Best From Lou Rawls* .... (Capitol)
Louis Armstrong; *Best Of Louis Armstrong-Story-#3* .... (Audio Fidelity)
Essential Louis Armstrong .... (Vanguard)
Pops: 1940s Small Band Sides .... (Bluebird)
Volume IV-Louis Armstrong And Earl Hines .... (Columbia)
Louis Armstrong & Earl Hines; *Louis Armstrong-Vol. 4-In
New York* .... (Columbia)
Preservation Hall Jazz Band; *New Orleans-#4* .... (Columbia)
Standing Outside A Broken Phone Booth With Money In My Hand
Primitive Radio Gods; *MTV Best Of The Buzz Bin-#2-C.* .... (Mammoth)
Rocket. .... (Ergo)
Steppin' In A Slide Zone
Moody Blues; *Octave* .... (Polydor)
Stompin' At The Savoy
Benny Goodman; *Benny Goodman-Pure Gold.* .... (RCA)
Benny Goodman's All-Time Greatest Hits .... (Columbia)
Carnegie Hall Jazz Concert .... (Columbia)
Stompin' At The Savoy .... (Bluebird)
Doc Severinsen; *Facets* .... (Amherst)
Ella Fitzgerald & Louis Armstrong; *Ella & Louis* .... (Verve)
Louis Armstrong; *Essential Louis Armstrong* .... (Vanguard)
Stoney End
Barbra Streisand; *Barbra Streisand's Greatest Hits, Volume 2* ...... (Columbia)
Stoney End .... (Columbia)
Laura Nyro; *First Songs* .... (Columbia)
Strawberry Fields Forever
Beatles; *Beatles-Box Set* .... (Capitol)
Magical Mystery Tour .... (Capitol)
ST/Imagine: John Lennon .... (Capitol)
The Beatles/1967-1970. .... (Capitol)
Sugar Mountain
Neil Young; *Decade* .... (Reprise)
Neil Young & Crazy Horse; *Live Rust.* .... (Reprise)
Summer, Highland Falls
Billy Joel; *Songs In The Attic* .... (Columbia)
Turnstiles .... (Columbia)
Summerland
Everclear; *Sparkle And Fade.* .... (Capitol)
Sunnyland
Elmore James; *Golden Classics-Elmore James* .... (Collectables)
Take Me There
Blackstreet & Mya featuring Mase & Blinky Blink;
Finally .... (Lil' Man/Interscope)
Now That's What I Call Music!-#2-C. .... (Virgin)
ST/Rugrats .... (Interscope)
Telling Stories
Tracy Chapman; *Telling Stories* .... (Elektra)
Tha Crossroads
Bone Thugs-N-Harmony; *Club Mix '97* .... (Cold Front)
MTV Party To Go-#10-C. .... (Tommy Boy)
That's Where I Belong
Paul Simon; *You're The One* .... (Warner Bros.)
Theme From "A Summer Place"
Andy Williams; *Moon River & Other Great Movie Themes* .... (Columbia)
Percy Faith & His Orchestra; *Best Love Songs-C* .... (Original Sound)
Billboard Top Pop Hits-1960-C. .... (Rhino)
Percy Faith & His Orchestra-16 Most Requested Songs .... (Columbia)
Percy Faith & His Orchestra's All-Time Greatest Hits .... (Columbia)
Percy Faith & His Orchestra's Greatest Hits. .... (Columbia)
Theme From "Fantasy Island"
Original Soundtrack; *Television's Greatest Hits-#6-Remote Control-C.* ... (TVT)
Theme From "Gilligan's Island"
Original Soundtrack; *CBS: The First 50 Years* .... (TVT)
Television's Greatest Hits-#1-C. .... (TVT)
Theme From "Jurassic Park"
John Williams; *ST/Jurassic Park* .... (MCA)
Theme From "Knots Landing"
Original Soundtrack; *CBS: The First 50 Years* .... (TVT)
Television's Greatest Hits-#3-1970s & 1980s-C .... (TVT)

Theme From "Mr. Rogers' Neighborhood"
Original Soundtrack; *Television's Greatest Hits-#2-C* . . . . (TVT)
Theme From "Petticoat Junction"
Flatt & Scruggs; *20 All-Time Great Recordings* . . . . (Columbia)
Original Soundtrack; *Television's Greatest Hits-#1-C* . . . . (TVT)
TV Theme Sing-Along Album . . . . (Rhino)
Theme From "Promised Land"
Original Soundtrack; *CBS: The First 50 Years* . . . . (TVT)
Theme From "The Flintstones"
Original Soundtrack; *Hanna-Barbera Classics-#1-Original Recordings Of*
The World's Most Famous Cartoon Themes &
Scores . . . . (Kid Rhino/Rhino 4 Kids)
Hanna-Barbera Pic-A-Nic Basket Of Cartoon
Classics . . . . (Kid Rhino/Rhino 4 Kids)
Television's Greatest Hits-#1-C . . . . (TVT)
Steve Hobbs; *Escape* . . . . (Cexton)
Theme From "The Twilight Zone"
Original Soundtrack; *CBS: The First 50 Years* . . . . (TVT)
Television's Greatest Hits-#1-C . . . . (TVT)
There You Are
Martina McBride; *Emotion* . . . . (RCA)
There You'll Be
Faith Hill; *ST/Pearl Harbor* . . . . (Warner Bros.)
There's A Place
Beatles; *Introducing...The Beatles* . . . . (Vee-Jay)
Rarities . . . . (Capitol)
There's A Place In Hell For Me And My Friends
Morrissey; *Kill Uncle* . . . . (Sire)
There's A Place In The World For A Gambler
Dan Fogelberg; *Dan Fogelberg-Souvenirs* . . . . (Full Moon)
Live-Greetings From The West . . . . (Full Moon)
ST/FM . . . . (MCA)
There's No Place Like Home For The Holidays
Perry Como; *Now That's What I Call Christmas!-C* . . . . (UTV)
Perry Como's Greatest Hits . . . . (RCA)
This Hard Land
Bruce Springsteen; *Bruce Springsteen's Greatest Hits* . . . . (Columbia)
Tracks . . . . (Columbia)
This Lonely Place
Goldfinger; *Hang-Ups* . . . . (Mojo Music/Universal)
This Part Of Town
Widespread Panic; *Don't Tell The Band* . . . . (Widespread/SRG)
Thousand Miles From Nowhere
Dwight Yoakam; *This Time* . . . . (Reprise)
Tickets To A Better Place
7 Seconds; *Soulforce Revolution* . . . . (Restless)
Tiki Tiki Tiki Room
Original Music; *Disney Collection-#1-C* . . . . (Disney)
Train To Nowhere
Rare Earth; *Get Ready* . . . . (Motown)
Tucker's Town
Hootie & The Blowfish; *Fairweather Johnson* . . . . (Atlantic)
Tuxedo Junction
Boston Pops Orchestra/Arthur Fiedler; *Greatest Hits Of The '40s-#2* . . . . . (RCA)
Ella Fitzgerald; *Things Ain't What They Used To Be* . . . . (Bainbridge)
Glenn Miller; *Best Of Glenn Miller* . . . . (RCA)
Glenn Miller-A Legendary Performer-#1 & 2 . . . . (Bluebird)
Memorial-1944-1969 . . . . (Bluebird)
ST/The Glenn Miller Story . . . . (MCA)
Glenn Miller & His Orchestra; *Glenn Miller & His Orchestra-*
Pure Gold . . . . (Bluebird)
The Unforgettable Glenn Miller & His Orchestra . . . . (RCA)
Harry James Sextet; *1940s-Small Groups-C* . . . . (Columbia)
Joe Jackson; *Jumpin' Jive* . . . . (A&M)
Manhattan Transfer; *Best Of The Manhattan Transfer* . . . . (Atlantic)
Manhattan Transfer-Anthology-Down In Birdland . . . . (Rhino)
The Manhattan Transfer . . . . (Rhino)
New York City Gay Men's Chorus; *Love Lives On* . . . . (Virgin)
Up Around The Bend
Creedence Clearwater Revival; *1970* . . . . (Fantasy)
Cosmo's Factory . . . . (Fantasy)
Creedence Clearwater Revival-Chronicle . . . . (Fantasy)
More Creedence Gold . . . . (Fantasy)
Hanoi Rocks; *Two Steps From The Move* . . . . (Epic)
Up On The Roof
Cryan' Shames; *Scratch In The Sky* . . . . (Columbia)
Drifters; *Cruisin'-1962-C* . . . . (Increase)
Drifters' Greatest Hits . . . . (Gusto)
Drifters-16 Greatest Hits . . . . (Trip)
Drifters-Golden Hits . . . . (Atlantic)
James Taylor; *Flag* . . . . (Columbia)
The Concert For New York City-C . . . . (Columbia)
Nylons; *Four On The Floor* . . . . (Scotti Bros.)
Walk In The Sun
Bruce Hornsby; *Hot House* . . . . (RCA)
Washington Square
Village Stompers; *Havin' A '60s Hootenanny-C* . . . . (K-Tel)
Washington Square . . . . (Epic)

Way Over Yonder
Carole King; *Tapestry* . . . . (Epic)
Wedding In Cherokee County
Randy Newman; *Good Old Boys* . . . . (Reprise)
Weekend In New England
Barry Manilow; *Barry Manilow/Live* . . . . (Arista)
Barry Manilow's Greatest Hits-#2 . . . . (Arista)
This One's For You . . . . (Arista)
Welcome To The Boomtown
David & David; *Boomtown* . . . . (A&M)
We're Off To See The Wizard
Jewel/Jackson Browne/Ry Cooder; *The Wizard Of Oz In Concert: Dreams*
Come True-C . . . . (Rhino)
Judy Garland; *A&E Biography: A Musical Anthology* . . . . (Capitol)
Original Cast; *The Wizard Of Oz* . . . . (TVT)
Original Soundtrack; *The Wizard Of Oz-Selections From The Original Motion*
Picture Soundtrack . . . . (Turner Classic Movies)
Westside
TQ; *They Never Saw Me Coming* . . . . (ClockWork/Epic)
When I Reach The Place I'm Going
Patty Loveless; *Red Hot + Country-C* . . . . (Mercury)
Whenever Wherever
Shakira; *Laundry Service* . . . . (Epic)
Whenever Wherever Whatever
Maxwell; *Maxwell's Urban Hang Suite* . . . . (Columbia)
Where Are You Now
Blue Rodeo; *Lost Together* . . . . (Atlantic)
Where Are You Now
Clint Black; *Put Yourself In My Shoes* . . . . (RCA)
Where Did You Go?
Full Devil Jacket; *Full Devil Jacket* . . . . (Island/IDJMG)
Where Do We Go From Here
Vanessa Williams; *Vanessa Williams' Greatest Hits-The First Ten*
Years . . . . (Mercury)
Where Do You Go
No Mercy; *No Mercy* . . . . (Arista)
Where I Come From
Alan Jackson; *When Somebody Loves You* . . . . (Arista)
Where It's At
Beck; *Odelay* . . . . (David Geffen Co.)
Where Or When
Barbra Streisand; *Color Me Barbra* . . . . (Columbia)
Benny Goodman; *Small Groups-1941-1945* . . . . (Columbia)
Bryan Ferry; *As Time Goes By* . . . . (Virgin)
Dion And The Belmonts; *Best Of Doo Wop Ballads-C* . . . . (Rhino)
Complete Dion And The Belmonts . . . . (Collector's Choice)
Ella Fitzgerald; *Ella Fitzgerald Sings The Rodgers & Hart Songbook* . . . . (Verve)
Frank Sinatra; *Sinatra At The Sands* . . . . (Reprise)
Johnny Mathis; *You Light Up My Life* . . . . (Columbia)
Peggy Lee; *Peggy Lee-Complete Recordings-1941-1947* . . . . (Legacy)
Wynton Marsalis; *Standard Time-#3-The Resolution Of Romance* . . . (Columbia)
Where Time Stands Still
Mary Chapin Carpenter; *Stones In The Road* . . . . (Columbia)
Where You Are
Rahsaan Patterson; *Rahsaan Patterson* . . . . (MCA)
Where You Get Love
Matthew Sweet; *Blue Sky On Mars* . . . . (Freeworld/Capitol)
Wherever You Go
Clint Black; *Clint Black-The Greatest Hits* . . . . (RCA)
One Emotion . . . . (RCA)
Wherever You Will Go
Calling; *Camino Palmero* . . . . (RCA)
White Man In Hammersmith Palais
Clash; *On Broadway* . . . . (Epic)
The Clash . . . . (Epic)
The Story Of The Clash, Volume 1 . . . . (Epic)
White Silver Sands
Ace Cannon; *Golden Classics-Ace Cannon* . . . . (Gusto)
Ray Anthony; *Great Golden Hits* . . . . (Ranwood)
Sonny James; *45-#4-45706* . . . . (Columbia)
Why I'm Here
Oleander; *February Son* . . . . (Republic/Universal)
Now That's What I Call Music!-#3-C . . . . (Virgin)
Oleander Live At The Fillmore . . . . (Republic/Universal)
Wide Awake In Dreamland
Pat Benatar; *Wide Awake In Dreamland* . . . . (Chrysalis)
Wild Eyed Boy From Freecloud
David Bowie; *Sound + Vision* . . . . (Rykodisc)
Space Oddity . . . . (Rykodisc)
ST/Ziggy Stardust-The Motion Picture . . . . (Rykodisc)
Wild Places
Dan Fogelberg; *Live-Greetings From The West* . . . . (Full Moon)
Wish You Were Here
Fleetwood Mac; *Mirage* . . . . (Warner Bros.)
Wish You Were Here
Limp Bizkit & John Rzeznik; *America: A Tribute To Heroes-C* . . . . (Interscope)
Pink Floyd; *Collection Of Great Dance Songs* . . . . (Columbia)
Delicate Sound Of Thunder . . . . (Columbia)

Wish You Were Here . . . . (Columbia)
Wish You Were Here
  Mark Wills; *Wish You Were Here* . . . . (Mercury)
Wish You Were Here
  Bing Crosby; *The Radio Years: 20 Songs* . . . . (Crescendo)
  Eddie Fisher; *Best Of Eddie Fisher* . . . . (MCA)
Wish You Were Here
  Nick Lowe; *Abominable Showman* . . . . (Columbia)
Wish You Were Here
  Barbara Mandrell; *Barbara Mandrell Live* . . . . (MCA)
  Barbara Mandrell's Greatest Hits . . . . (MCA)
Wish You Were Here
  Bee Gees; *Diana, Princess Of Wales-Tribute-C* . . . . (Columbia)
Wish You Were Here
  Alice Cooper; *Goes To Hell* . . . . (Warner Bros.)
  The Alice Cooper Show . . . . (Warner Bros.)
Wish You Were Here
  Dead Or Alive; *Sophisticated Boom Boom* . . . . (Epic)
Wolverton Mountain
  Claude King; *American Originals-Claude King* . . . . (Columbia)
  Best Of Claude King . . . . (Gusto)
  Billboard Top Country Hits-1962-C . . . . (Rhino)
  Super Hits Of The '60s-C . . . . (Epic)
Wrecking Ball
  Emmylou Harris; *Wrecking Ball* . . . . (Asylum)
Xanadu
  Olivia Newton-John; *ST/Xanadu* . . . . (MCA)
  Olivia Newton-John & Electric Light Orchestra; *Olivia Newton-John's*
   Greatest Hits-#2 . . . . (MCA)
You Belong To Me
  Dean Martin; *Dean Martin's All Time Greatest Hits* . . . . (Curb)
  Duprees; *13 Of The Best Doo Wop Love Songs-#2-C* . . . . (Original Sound)
  Baby Boomer's Best-Mellow '60s-C . . . . (Priority)
  Best Of The Duprees . . . . (Rhino)
  Jo Stafford; *Billboard Pop Memories-1950-1954-C* . . . . (Rhino)
  Jo Stafford's Greatest Hits . . . . (Curb)
  Johnny Mathis; *In The Still Of The Night* . . . . (Columbia)
  Patsy Cline; *Patsy Cline Sings Songs Of Love* . . . . (MCA Special Prod.)
  Sentimentally Yours . . . . (MCA)
  Vonda Shepard; *ST/Songs From ''Ally McBeal'' Featuring Vonda*
   Shepard . . . . (550/Epic)
You'll Never Leave Harlan Alive
  Patty Loveless; *Mountain Soul* . . . . (Epic)
You're Not In Kansas Anymore
  Jo Dee Messina; *Jo Dee Messina* . . . . (Curb)

POISON

See Also: **CRIME, DEATH, KILL, PAIN & HEALING, SUICIDE**

Gave It A Name
  Bruce Springsteen; *Tracks* . . . . (Columbia)
Goodbye Earl
  Dixie Chicks; *Fly* . . . . (Monument)
I Don't Wanna Talk About It Now
  Emmylou Harris; *Red Dirt Girl* . . . . (Nonesuch)
Kryptonite
  3 Doors Down; *Better Life* . . . . (Republic/Universal)
  Now That's What I Call Music!-#5-C . . . . (Virgin)
Pennyroyal Tea
  Nirvana; *In Utero* . . . . (David Geffen Co.)
  MTV Unplugged In New York . . . . (David Geffen Co.)
Poison
  Bell Biv Devoe; *Poison* . . . . (MCA)
Poison
  Lisa Stansfield; *Affection* . . . . (Arista)
Poison
  Motorhead; *Bomber* . . . . (Roadracer)
Poison
  Wonder Stuff; *Eight-Legged Groove Machine* . . . . (Polydor)
Poison
  MC5; *High Times* . . . . (Rhino)
Poison
  Generation X; *Kiss Me Deadly* . . . . (Chrysalis)
Poison
  Alice Cooper; *Trash* . . . . (Epic)
Poison Angel
  Winger; *Winger* . . . . (Atlantic)
Poison Arrow
  ABC; *Absolutely ABC* . . . . (Mercury)
  Lexicon Of Love . . . . (Mercury)
Poison Arrow
  Flesheaters; *Prehistoric Fits-#2* . . . . (SST)
Poison Heart
  Ramones; *Mondo Bizarro* . . . . (Radioactive/MCA)
Poison In The Well
  10,000 Maniacs; *Blind Man's Zoo* . . . . (Elektra)

Poison Ivy
  Coasters; *Atlantic Rhythm & Blues 1947-1974-#4 (1958-1962)-C* . . . . . (Atlantic)
  Billboard Top R&B Hits-1959-C . . . . (Rhino)
  Coasters' Greatest Hits . . . . (Atco)
  Coasters-Their Greatest Recordings-Early Years . . . . (Atco)
  More American Graffiti-C . . . . (MCA)
  Nylons; *Rockapella* . . . . (Windham Hill)
  ST/Stealing Home . . . . (Atlantic)
  Rolling Stones; *More Hot Rocks (big hits & fazed cookies)* . . . . (Abkco)
Poison Love
  Blood On The Saddle; *Poison Love* . . . . (Charisma)
Poison Love
  T Bone Burnett; *T Bone Burnett* . . . . (Dot)
Poison Pen
  Hoodoo Gurus; *Mars Needs Guitars* . . . . (Elektra)
Poison Pen
  Molly Hatchet; *Beatin' The Odds* . . . . (Epic)
Poison Sugar
  Reba McEntire; *Just A Little Love* . . . . (MCA)
Poison To The Mind
  Pop Will Eat Itself; *This Is The Day...This Is The Hour* . . . . (RCA)
Poison Was The Cure
  Megadeth; *Rust In Peace* . . . . (Capitol)
Poison Whiskey
  Lynyrd Skynyrd; *Pronounced Leh-nerd Skin-nerd* . . . . (MCA)
Poisoned Heart & A Twisted Memory
  Richard Thompson; *Hand Of Kindness* . . . . (Hannibal)
Poisoned Rose
  Costello Show (Featuring Elvis Costello); *King Of America* . . . . . . (Columbia)
  Elvis Costello; *Girls Girls Girls* . . . . (Columbia)
Poisoning Pigeons In The Park
  Tom Lehrer; *Dr. Demento Presents The Greatest Novelty Records-C* . . . (Rhino)
  Dr. Demento: 20th Anniversary Collection-C . . . . (Rhino)
  Evening Wasted With Tom Lehrer . . . . (Reprise)
Venom Wearin' Denim
  Junior Brown; *Semi Crazy* . . . . (Curb)

POLICE, Detectives, Secret Agents, Spies

See Also: **CAPITAL PUNISHMENT, CRIME, GUNS, HELP, LAW &
ORDER, POWER & CONTROL, PRISON, REBELS, WAR**

10-4 (Calling All Cars)
  Benny Spellman; *Fortune Teller-Golden Classics* . . . . (Collectables)
911
  Wyclef Jean featuring Mary J. Blige; *The Ecleftic-2 Sides II*
   A Book . . . . (Ruffhouse/Columbia)
Alice's Restaurant Massacree
  Arlo Guthrie; *Alice's Restaurant* . . . . (Reprise)
  Best Of Arlo Guthrie . . . . (Warner Bros.)
And The Mouse Police Never Sleeps
  Jethro Tull; *Heavy Horses* . . . . (Chrysalis)
Arrest The President
  Intelligent Hoodlum; *Intelligent Hoodlum* . . . . (A&M)
Battle Flag
  Lo Fidelity Allstars; *How To Operate With A Blown Mind* . . . . (Skint)
Bette Davis Eyes
  Kim Carnes; *Best Of Kim Carnes* . . . . (EMI Special Markets)
  Billboard Top Hits-1981-C . . . . (Rhino)
  Mistaken Identity . . . . (EMI)
Big Brother
  David Bowie; *David Live* . . . . (Rykodisc)
  Diamond Dogs . . . . (Rykodisc)
  Sound + Vision . . . . (Rykodisc)
  ST/Breaking Glass . . . . (A&M)
Big Iron
  Marty Robbins; *Columbia Country Classics-#3-Americana-C* . . . . . . (Columbia)
  Gunfighter Ballads & Trail Songs . . . . (Legacy)
  Marty Robbins' All-Time Greatest Hits . . . . (Columbia)
  Marty Robbins-More Greatest Hits . . . . (Columbia)
Body Count
  Ice-T; *Body Count* . . . . (Warner Bros.)
Bridge Of Spies
  T'Pau; *Bridge Of Spies* . . . . (Virgin)
Call The Police
  Hot Chocolate; *Hot Chocolate* . . . . (Big Tree)
  Nat ''King'' Cole; *From The Very Beginning* . . . . (MCA)
Cop Killer
  Ice-T; *Body Count* . . . . (Warner Bros.)
Cops
  John Stewart; *Phoenix Concerts* . . . . (One Way)
Cops Of The World
  Phil Ochs; *Phil Ochs In Concert* . . . . (Elektra)
  There But For Fortune . . . . (Elektra)
Detective Man
  Detective; *Detective* . . . . (Swan Song)

Don't Let Nobody Turn You Around
Steve Miller Band; *Steve Miller Band-Anthology* . . . . (Capitol)
Your Saving Grace . . . . (Capitol)
Dream Police
Cheap Trick; *Dream Police* . . . . (Epic)
Every Breath You Take
Police; *Every Breath You Take-The Classics* . . . . (A&M)
Synchronicity . . . . (A&M)
Tammy Wynette & Sting; *Without Walls-C* . . . . (Epic)
Fingerprint File
Rolling Stones; *It's Only Rock 'N Roll* . . . . (Rolling Stones)
Love You Live . . . . (Virgin)
Friendly Neighborhood Narco Agent
Jef Jaisun; *Dr. Demento's Delights-C* . . . . (Warner Bros.)
Fuck Tha Police
N.W.A.; *Straight Outta Compton* . . . . (Ruthless/Priority)
Gee, Officer Krupke!
Original Cast; *ST/West Side Story* . . . . (Sony Broadway)
Goldfinger
Shirley Bassey; *13 Original James Bond Themes-C* . . . . (EMI)
Best Of Shirley Bassey . . . . (EMI)
Great Performances . . . . (Liberty)
Shirley Bassey-Live At Carnegie Hall . . . . (United Artists)
Shirley Bassey's Greatest Hits . . . . (EMI)
ST/Goldfinger . . . . (United Artists)
Harder Cards
Collin Raye; *Tracks* . . . . (Epic)
Harder They Come
Jimmy Cliff; *In Concert-Best Of Jimmy Cliff* . . . . (Reprise)
ST/The Harder They Come . . . . (Mango)
The Island Story-1962-1987-25th Anniversary-C . . . . (Island)
Highway Patrol
Reggie Knighton Band; *Reggie Knighton Band* . . . . (Columbia)
Highway Patrolman
Bruce Springsteen; *Nebraska* . . . . (Columbia)
Hot Cop
Village People; *Cruisin'* . . . . (Casablanca)
Live & Sleazy . . . . (Casablanca)
Village People's Greatest Hits . . . . (Rhino)
Hot Rod Lincoln
Asleep At The Wheel; *Western Standard Time* . . . . (Epic)
Commander Cody & His Lost Planet Airmen; *Lost In The Ozone* . . . . . . (MCA)
Super Hits Of The '70s-Have A Nice Day-#8-C . . . . (Rhino)
Johnny Bond; *Best Of Johnny Bond* . . . . (Starday)
I Ain't Livin' Long Like This
Emmylou Harris; *Quarter Moon In A Ten Cent Town* . . . . (Warner Bros.)
Rodney Crowell; *I Ain't Livin' Long Like This* . . . . (Warner Bros.)
Rodney Crowell-Collection . . . . (Warner Bros.)
Waylon Jennings; *Waylon Jennings' Greatest Hits-#2* . . . . (RCA)
What Goes Around Comes Around . . . . (RCA)
I Did It
Dave Matthews Band; *Everyday* . . . . (RCA)
I Shot The Sheriff
Bob Marley & The Wailers; *Bob Marley & The Wailers-Live* . . . . . (Tuff Gong)
Legend: The Best Of Bob Marley & The Wailers . . . . (Island)
This Is Reggae Music-#1-C . . . . (Island)
Eric Clapton; *461 Ocean Boulevard* . . . . (Polydor)
Eric Clapton-Crossroads-C . . . . (Polydor)
Time Pieces-#1-The Best Of Eric Clapton . . . . (Polydor)
Wailers; *Burnin'* . . . . (Tuff Gong)
I'll Tell A Policeman On You
Jerry Lewis; *Capitol Collectors Series-Jerry Lewis* . . . . (Capitol)
I'm A Rocker
Bruce Springsteen; *The River* . . . . (Columbia)
Indiana Wants Me
R. Dean Taylor; *Hard-To-Find Motown Classics-#2-C* . . . . . . (Motown)
Super Hits Of The '70s-Have A Nice Day-#3-C . . . . (Rhino)
Super Hits-#5-C . . . . (Gusto)
Informer
Snow; *12 Inches Of Snow* . . . . (East West)
Jeannie Needs A Shooter
Warren Zevon; *Bad Luck Streak In Dancing School* . . . . (Asylum)
Stand In The Fire . . . . (Asylum)
Jolly Coppers On Parade
Randy Newman; *Little Criminals* . . . . (Warner Bros.)
Jungleland
Bruce Springsteen; *Born To Run* . . . . (Columbia)
Just Like Tom Thumb's Blues
Bob Dylan; *Highway 61 Revisited* . . . . (Columbia)
Grateful Dead; *Terrapin Station* . . . . (Arista)
Judy Collins; *In My Life* . . . . (Elektra)
Linda Ronstadt; *We Ran* . . . . (Elektra)
Lawyers, Guns & Money
Warren Zevon; *Excitable Boy* . . . . (Asylum)
Quiet Normal Life-Best Of Warren Zevon . . . . (Asylum)
Stand In The Fire . . . . (Asylum)
Line, The
Bruce Springsteen; *The Ghost Of Tom Joad* . . . . (Columbia)

Lovely Rita
Beatles; *Sgt. Pepper's Lonely Hearts Club Band* . . . . (Capitol)
Men In Black
Will Smith; *Big Willie Style* . . . . (Columbia)
ST/Men In Black . . . . (Columbia)
Mr. Policeman
Rick James; *Street Songs* . . . . (Motown)
New York State Police
UK Subs; *Left For Dead (Alive In Holland '86)* . . . . (Roir)
UK Subs-The Singles 1978-1982 . . . . (Progressive Int'l)
Night The Lights Went Out In Georgia
Lynn Anderson; *Top Of The World* . . . . (Columbia)
Reba McEntire; *For My Broken Heart* . . . . (MCA)
Reba McEntire's Greatest Hits-#3: I'm A Survivor . . . . . . (MCA)
Vicki Lawrence; *Super Hits Of The '70s-Have A Nice Day-#10-C* . . . . . (Rhino)
Nightwatchman
Tom Petty And The Heartbreakers; *Hard Promises* . . . . (MCA)
Ninety Nine
Toto; *Hydra* . . . . (Columbia)
Nobody Does It Better
Carly Simon; *13 Original James Bond Themes-C* . . . . (EMI)
Carly Simon-Greatest Hits Live . . . . (Arista)
ST/The Spy Who Loved Me . . . . (EMI)
Nutbush City Limits
Bob Seger; *Beautiful Loser* . . . . (Capitol)
Live Bullet . . . . (Capitol)
Ike & Tina Turner; *Best Of Ike & Tina Turner* . . . . (EMI)
Proud Mary-Best Of Ike & Tina Turner . . . . (EMI)
Tina Turner; *Live In Europe* . . . . (Capitol)
Simply The Best . . . . (Capitol)
One Way Mirror
Venus Beads; *Black Aspirin* . . . . (Roadrunner)
Pancho And Lefty
Merle Haggard; *For The Record: Merle Haggard-43 Legendary Hits* . . . . (BNA)
Merle Haggard & Willie Nelson; *19 Hot Country Requests-C* . . . . . . (Epic)
All Time Legends Of Country Music-C . . . . (Legacy)
Columbia Country Classics-#3-Americana-C . . . . (Columbia)
His Epic Hits-First 11 To Be Continued-C . . . . (Epic)
Pancho And Lefty . . . . (Epic)
Townes Van Zandt; *Live & Obscure* . . . . (Sugar Hill)
Passing Policeman
Johnson Brothers; *Bristol Sessions-#1 & 2-C* . . . . . (Country Music Foundation)
Peace Officer
Jimmy Cliff; *Rhythm Come Forward: Volume III-C* . . . . (Columbia)
Special . . . . (Columbia)
Police And Thieves
Clash; *On Broadway* . . . . (Epic)
The Clash . . . . (Epic)
The Story Of The Clash, Volume 1 . . . . (Epic)
Junior Murvin; *Jammin'* . . . . (Mango)
Police And Thieves . . . . (Mango)
ST/Rockers . . . . (Mango)
This Is Reggae Music #3-C . . . . (Island)
Police Dog Blues
Blind Blake; *Georgia Blues-1927-1930* . . . . (Yazoo)
Hot Tuna; *Splashdown* . . . . (Relix)
Jorma Kaukonen & Tom Hobson; *Quah* . . . . (Relix)
Ry Cooder; *Ry Cooder* . . . . (Reprise)
Police On My Back
Clash; *On Broadway* . . . . (Epic)
Sandinista . . . . (Epic)
Police Story
Black Flag; *Damaged* . . . . (SST)
Police Woman
Henry Mancini; *Cop Show Themes* . . . . (RCA)
Police, Police
Atlanta Rhythm Section; *Red Tape* . . . . (Polydor)
Policeman
Chicago; *Chicago XI* . . . . (Chicago)
Private Eyes
Daryl Hall & John Oates; *Private Eyes* . . . . (RCA)
Rock 'N Soul, Part 1 . . . . (RCA)
Pull Over
Trina; *Da Baddest B***h* . . . . (Slip 'N Slide)
Radar Blues
Dave Dudley & Charlie Doublas; *Diesel Duets* . . . . (Sun)
Radar Gun
Bottle Rockets; *The Brooklyn Side* . . . . (East Side Digital)
Raid
Graham Parker And The Rumour; *Stick To Me* . . . . (Mercury)
Robot Police
Baby Buddha; *Music For Teenage Sex* . . . . (Posh Boy)
Searchin'
Beatles; *The Beatles-Anthology-#1* . . . . (Capitol)
Secret Agent Man
Devo; *Duty Now For The Future* . . . . (Warner Bros.)
Johnny Rivers; *Best Of Johnny Rivers* . . . . (EMI)
Johnny Rivers-Anthology 1964-1977 . . . . (Rhino)
Television's Greatest Hits-#1-C . . . . (TVT)

Very Best Of Johnny Rivers . . . .(EMI)
Secret Service
Original Cast; *Mr. President*. . . . .(Sony Broadway)
Shakedown
Bob Seger; *ST/Beverly Hills Cop II* . . . . (MCA)
Sheriff
Emerson, Lake & Palmer; *Trilogy* . . . .(Atlantic)
Sheriff O.E. & Me
Big Mama Thornton; *Jail* . . . . (Vanguard)
Sheriff Of Hong Kong
Captain Beefheart; *Doc At The Radar Station* . . . . (Blue Plate)
Shoot Low Sheriff
Murry Kellum; *Country Comedy-20 Country Comedy Hits* . . . . (Plantation)
Shoot Your Shot
J. Geils Band; *Blow Your Face Out*. . . . . (Rhino)
Junior Walker & The All Stars; *Junior Walker & The All Stars'*
Greatest Hits. . . . . (Motown)
Junior Walker & The All Stars-Anthology . . . . (Motown)
Shotgun . . . . (Motown)
Somebody's Watching Me
Rockwell; *Somebody's Watching Me* . . . . (Motown)
Space Patrol
Country Joe McDonald; *Country Joe McDonald-Classics* . . . . . . (Fantasy)
Rock & Roll Music From The Planet Earth . . . . (Fantasy)
Spies
Randy Newman; *Born Again* . . . .(Warner Bros.)
Spy
Doors; *Morrison Hotel/Hard Rock Cafe*. . . . . (Elektra)
Weird Scenes Inside The Gold Mine . . . . (Elektra)
Spy
Carly Simon; *Spy* . . . . (Elektra)
St. George & The Dragonet
Stan Freberg; *Greatest Hits-Stan Freberg* . . . . (Curb)
Tip Of The Freberg: The Stan Freberg Collection-1951-1998 . . . . (Rhino)
State Trooper
Bruce Springsteen; *Nebraska* . . . . (Columbia)
The Sopranos-Music From The HBO Original
Series . . . . (Sony Music Soundtrax)
Texas Lawman
Regulators; *Regulators* . . . .(Polydor)
Texas Rangers
Ian & Sylvia; *Ian & Sylvia's Greatest Hits* . . . . (Vanguard)
Northern Journey. . . . . (Vanguard)
Michael Martin Murphey; *Cowboy Songs* . . . . (Warner Western)
That Girl's Been Spyin' On Me
Billy Dean; *It's What I Do* . . . . (Capitol)
Theme From "21 Jump Street"
Original Soundtrack; *Television's Greatest Hits-#7-Cable Ready-C* . . . . . (TVT)
Theme From "77 Sunset Strip"
Original Soundtrack; *Television's Greatest Hits-#1-C* . . . . (TVT)
TV Classic Themes: 25th Anniversary Edition-C. . . . . (Breakable)
Theme From "Adam-12"
Original Soundtrack; *Television's Greatest Hits-#1-C* . . . . (TVT)
Theme From "America's Most Wanted"
Original Soundtrack; *Television's Greatest Hits-#7-Cable Ready-C* . . . . . (TVT)
Theme From "Baretta"
Original Soundtrack; *Television's Greatest Hits-#3-1970s & 1980s-C* . . . . (TVT)
Theme From "Barnaby Jones"
Original Soundtrack; *CBS: The First 50 Years* . . . . (TVT)
Television's Greatest Hits-#3-1970s & 1980s-C. . . . . (TVT)
Theme From "Barney Miller"
Original Soundtrack; *Television's Greatest Hits-#3-1970s & 1980s-C* . . . (TVT)
Theme From "Bat Masterson"
Original Soundtrack; *Television's Greatest Hits-#2-C* . . . . (TVT)
Theme From "Blade Runner"
Original Soundtrack; *Sci-Fi's Greatest Hits-#1-Final Frontiers* . . . . (TVT)
Theme From "Bourbon Street Beat"
Original Soundtrack; *Television's Greatest Hits-#4-Black & White*
Classics-C. . . . . (TVT)
Theme From "Burke's Law"
Original Soundtrack; *Television's Greatest Hits-#4-Black & White*
Classics-C. . . . . (TVT)
Theme From "Cagney & Lacey"
Original Soundtrack; *CBS: The First 50 Years* . . . . (TVT)
Television's Greatest Hits-#6-Remote Control-C . . . . (TVT)
Theme From "Car 54, Where Are You?"
Original Soundtrack; *Television's Greatest Hits-#2-C*. . . . . (TVT)
Theme From "Charlie's Angels"
Original Soundtrack; *Television's Greatest Hits-#3-1970s & 1980s-C* . . . (TVT)
TV Classic Themes: 25th Anniversary Edition-C. . . . . (Breakable)
Theme From "CHiPs"
Original Soundtrack; *Television's Greatest Hits-#6-Remote Control-C* . . (TVT)
Theme From "Dragnet"
Original Soundtrack; *Television's Greatest Hits-#1-C* . . . . (TVT)
Theme From "Dudley-Do-Right"
Original Soundtrack; *Television's Greatest Hits-#3-1970s & 1980s-C* . . . (TVT)
Theme From "Fish"
Original Soundtrack; *Television's Greatest Hits-#6-Remote Control-C* . . (TVT)

Theme From "Get Smart"
Original Soundtrack; *Television's Greatest Hits-#1-C* . . . . (TVT)
Theme From "Hart To Hart"
Original Soundtrack; *Television's Greatest Hits-#3-1970s & 1980s-C* . . . (TVT)
Theme From "Hawaii Five-O"
Original Soundtrack; *CBS: The First 50 Years* . . . . (TVT)
Television's Greatest Hits-#1-C . . . . (TVT)
Ventures; *Billboard Top Pop Hits-1969-C* . . . . (Rhino)
Drew's Famous Luau Party Music-C . . . . (Turn Up The Music)
Theme From "Highway Patrol"
Original Soundtrack; *Television's Greatest Hits-#4-Black & White*
Classics-C . . . . (TVT)
Theme From "Hill Street Blues"
Original Soundtrack; *Television's Greatest Hits-#3-1970s & 1980s-C* . . . (TVT)
Theme From "Huckleberry Hound"
Original Soundtrack; *Hanna-Barbera Classics-#1-Original Recordings Of*
The World's Most Famous Cartoon Themes &
Scores . . . .(Kid Rhino/Rhino 4 Kids)
Hanna-Barbera Pic-A-Nic Basket Of Cartoon
Classics . . . .(Kid Rhino/Rhino 4 Kids)
Television's Greatest Hits-#2-C . . . . (TVT)
Theme From "Hunter"
Original Soundtrack; *Television's Greatest Hits-#6-Remote Control-C* . . . (TVT)
Theme From "I Spy"
Original Soundtrack; *Television's Greatest Hits-#2-C* . . . . (TVT)
Theme From "In The Heat Of The Night"
Original Soundtrack; *Television's Greatest Hits-#7-Cable Ready-C* . . . . . (TVT)
Theme From "Inspector Gadget"
Original Soundtrack; *Television's Greatest Hits-#3-1970s & 1980s-C* . . . (TVT)
Theme From "It Takes A Thief"
Original Soundtrack; *Television's Greatest Hits-#5-In Living Color-C* . . . (TVT)
Theme From "James Bond"
John Barry Orchestra; *Best Of James Bond-30th Anniversary-C* . . . . (EMI)
London Symphony Orchestra; *From London With Love-Music Of*
James Bond . . . .(Pro-Arte)
Theme From "Kojak"
Henry Mancini; *Cop Show Themes* . . . .(RCA)
John Gregory; *TV's Greatest Detective Hits* . . . . (Mercury)
Original Soundtrack; *Television's Greatest Hits-#3-1970s & 1980s-C* . . . (TVT)
Theme From "Law And Order"
Original Soundtrack; *Television's Greatest Hits-#7-Cable Ready-C* . . . . . (TVT)
Theme From "MacGyver"
Original Soundtrack; *Television's Greatest Hits-#6-Remote Control-C* . . . (TVT)
Theme From "Magnum P.I."
Original Soundtrack; *Television's Greatest Hits-#3-1970s & 1980s-C* . . . (TVT)
Theme From "Mannix"
Original Soundtrack; *CBS: The First 50 Years* . . . . (TVT)
Television's Greatest Hits-#1-C . . . . (TVT)
San Diego Symphony & Lalo Schifrin; *Hitchcock-Master Of*
Mayhem . . . .(Pro-Arte)
Theme From "Matt Houston"
Original Soundtrack; *Television's Greatest Hits-#6-Remote Control-C* . . . (TVT)
Theme From "Miami Vice"
Jan Hammer; *Escape From Television* . . . . (MCA)
Soundtrack Smashes-'80s & More-C . . . . (MCA)
ST/Miami Vice . . . . (MCA)
Original Soundtrack; *Television's Greatest Hits-#3-1970s & 1980s-C* . . . (TVT)
Theme From "Mike Hammer"
Original Soundtrack; *TV Classic Themes: 25th Anniversary*
Edition-C . . . . (Breakable)
Theme From "Mission: Impossible"
Adam Clayton & Larry Mullen; *ST/Mission: Impossible* . . . .(Mother/Island)
Lalo Schifrin; *The Reel Lalo Schifrin* . . . . (Hip-O)
Original Soundtrack; *CBS: The First 50 Years* . . . . (TVT)
Television's Greatest Hits-#1-C. . . . . (TVT)
San Diego Symphony & Lalo Schifrin; *Hitchcock-Master Of*
Mayhem . . . .(Pro-Arte)
Theme From "Mod Squad"
Original Soundtrack; *Television's Greatest Hits-#1-C* . . . . (TVT)
Theme From "Moonlighting"
Al Jarreau; *ST/Moonlighting* . . . . (MCA)
Television's Greatest Hits-#6-Remote Control-C . . . . (TVT)
Theme From "Moonraker"
John Barry & Shirley Bassey; *ST/Moonraker* . . . . (EMI)
Shirley Bassey; *Best Of James Bond-30th Anniversary-C* . . . . (EMI)
Theme From "M-Squad"
Original Soundtrack; *Television's Greatest Hits-#4-Black & White*
Classics-C . . . . (TVT)
Theme From "Murder, She Wrote"
Original Soundtrack; *CBS: The First 50 Years* . . . . (TVT)
Theme From "N.Y.P.D. Blue"
Original Soundtrack; *Television's Greatest Hits-#7-Cable Ready-C* . . . . . (TVT)
Theme From "Police Story"
Original Soundtrack; *Television's Greatest Hits-#5-In Living Color-C* . . . (TVT)
Ventures; *TV Themes* . . . .(United Artists)
Theme From "Police Woman"
Original Soundtrack; *Television's Greatest Hits-#5-In Living Color-C* . . . (TVT)
Theme From "Quincy, M.E."
Original Soundtrack; *Television's Greatest Hits-#3-1970s & 1980s-C* . . . (TVT)

Theme From "Rockford Files"
Original Soundtrack; *Television's Greatest Hits-#3-1970s & 1980s-C*.... (TVT)
Theme From "S.W.A.T."
Original Soundtrack; *Television's Greatest Hits-#3-1970s & 1980s-C*.... (TVT)
Rhythm Heritage; *Billboard Top Rock 'N' Roll Hits-1976-C* .... (Rhino)
Theme From "Shaft"
Isaac Hayes; *Isaac Hayes' Greatest Hit Singles* .... (Stax)
Pimps, Players & Private Eyes-C.................................(Sire)
Top Of The Stax-Twenty Greatest Hits-C .... (Stax)
Theme From "Simon And Simon"
Original Soundtrack; *Television's Greatest Hits-#3-1970s & 1980s-C*.... (TVT)
Theme From "Sledge Hammer"
Original Soundtrack; *Television's Greatest Hits-#7-Cable Ready-C* ..... (TVT)
Theme From "Starsky & Hutch"
Original Soundtrack; *Television's Greatest Hits-#3-1970s & 1980s-C*.... (TVT)
Theme From "Surfside 6"
Original Soundtrack; *Television's Greatest Hits-#1-C* .... (TVT)
Theme From "T.J. Hooker"
Original Soundtrack; *Television's Greatest Hits-#6-Remote Control-C* .... (TVT)
Theme From "The Andy Griffith Show"
Original Soundtrack; *CBS: The First 50 Years* .... (TVT)
Television's Greatest Hits-#1-C .... (TVT)
Theme From "The Avengers"
Original Soundtrack; *Television's Greatest Hits-#2-C* .... (TVT)
Theme From "The Bodyguard"
Original Soundtrack; *ST/The Bodyguard*........................(Arista)
Theme From "The Equalizer"
Original Soundtrack; *Television's Greatest Hits-#7-Cable Ready-C* ..... (TVT)
Theme From "The F.B.I."
101 Strings Orchestra; *TV Themes*.............................(Alshire)
Original Soundtrack; *Television's Greatest Hits-#1-C* .... (TVT)
Theme From "The Felony Squad"
Original Soundtrack; *Television's Greatest Hits-#5-In Living Color-C* ... (TVT)
Theme From "The Girl From U.N.C.L.E."
Original Soundtrack; *Television's Greatest Hits-#5-In Living Color-C* ... (TVT)
Theme From "The Green Hornet"
Original Soundtrack; *Television's Greatest Hits-#2-C* .... (TVT)
Theme From "The Lawman"
Original Soundtrack; *Television's Greatest Hits-#4-Black & White Classics-C* .... (TVT)
Theme From "The Life And Legend Of Wyatt Earp"
Original Soundtrack; *Television's Greatest Hits-#4-Black & White Classics-C* .... (TVT)
Theme From "The Lone Ranger" (William Tell Overture)
Boston Pops Orchestra; *TV Classics-C* ....(RCA)
Boston Pops Orchestra/Arthur Fiedler; *Fiedler-Greatest Hits* ....(RCA)
Original Soundtrack; *Television's Greatest Hits-#7-Cable Ready-C* ..... (TVT)
Spike Jones & His City Slickers; *Best Of Spike Jones & His City Slickers* ....(RCA)
Theme From "The Man From U.N.C.L.E."
Challengers; *25 Greatest Instrumental Hits-C* .... (Crescendo)
Original Soundtrack; *Television's Greatest Hits-#1-C* .... (TVT)
The Man From U.N.C.L.E.: The Music From U.N.C.L.E. ...... (Razor & Tie)
TV Classic Themes: 25th Anniversary Edition-C ....(Breakable)
Theme From "The Rookies"
Original Soundtrack; *Television's Greatest Hits-#3-1970s & 1980s-C*.... (TVT)
Theme From "The Streets Of San Francisco"
Original Soundtrack; *Television's Greatest Hits-#3-1970s & 1980s-C*.... (TVT)
TV Cop Show Theme Songs.................................(Laserlight)
Theme From "The Untouchables"
Original Soundtrack; *Television's Greatest Hits-#4-Black & White Classics-C* .... (TVT)
Theme From "Twin Peaks"
Original Soundtrack; *Television's Greatest Hits-#7-Cable Ready-C* ..... (TVT)
Theme From "Walker, Texas Ranger"
Original Soundtrack; *CBS: The First 50 Years* .... (TVT)
Too Much Fun
Daryle Singletary; *Daryle Singletary* .... (Giant)
Today's Country Love-C.....................................(K-Tel)
TV Private Eye
Now; *Now* .... (Maison De Soul)
Undercover Of The Night
Rolling Stones; *Rewind (1971-1984)*..................... (Rolling Stones)
Undercover.. (Rolling Stones)
Watching The Detectives
Elvis Costello; *Girls Girls Girls* .... (Columbia)
My Aim Is True .... (Columbia)
Elvis Costello & The Attractions; *Best Of Elvis Costello & The Attractions* .... (Columbia)
Who Are The Brain Police
Frank Zappa; *Disconnected Synapses* .... (Rhino)
Mothers Of Invention; *Freak Out* .... (Barking Pumpkin)
Whodunit
Tavares; *Love Storm* .... (Capitol)
Window Up Above
George Jones; *Cup Of Loneliness-Classic Mercury Years* .... (Mercury)
George Jones' All-Time Greatest Hits .... (Epic)
George Jones-Super Hits .... (Epic)

George Jones-Super Hits .... (Epic)
Hank Wilson; *Hank Wilson's Back, Vol. 1* .... (Right Stuff)
Hot Rize; *Red Knuckle-Hot Rize Live* .... (Flying Fish)
Johnny Cash; *Back To Back* ....(K-Tel)
Mickey Gilley; *Mickey Gilley's Greatest Hits-#1* .... (Epic)
Ten Years Of Hits .... (Epic)
Ralph Stanley; *Clinch Mountain Country* .... (Rebel)
Ricky Skaggs; *Ricky Skaggs-Country Boy*...................... (Epic)
Wanda Jackson; *Wanda Jackson-Vintage Collection* ....(Capitol)
Your Mama Don't Dance
Loggins & Messina; *Loggins & Messina-On Stage* .... (Columbia)
Loggins And Messina ....(Columbia)
Pop Classics Of The '70s-C .... (Columbia)
The Best Of Friends.....................................(Columbia)
Poison; *Open Up And Say...Ahh!* .... (Capitol)
Swallow This Live .... (Capitol)
Zero And Blind Terry
Bruce Springsteen; *Tracks* ....(Columbia)

POLITICS: POLITICAL CLASSICS

See Also: ***BROTHERHOOD, COUNTRIES: AMERICA, FREEDOM, HIPPIES, HISTORY, LAW & ORDER, NATURE, NUCLEAR ENERGY, PATRIOTISM, PEACE, POLICE, POLITICS (various), POVERTY, POWER & CONTROL, PREJUDICE, PRESIDENTS, PROTEST, SLAVERY, WAR, WORK, WORLD***

Abraham, Martin And John
Dion; *Collectables Presents The History Of Rock-#3-C* ....(Collectables)
Dion-24 Original Classics ....(Arista)
Songs Of Protest-C ....(Rhino)
WCBS FM 101 History Of Rock-'60s-#2-C.............(Collectables)
Harry Belafonte; *Harry Belafonte's All Time Greatest Hits-#1* .... (RCA)
Smokey Robinson & The Miracles; *Smokey Robinson & The Miracles' Anthology*...(Motown)
Time Out For Smokey Robinson & The Miracles/Special Occasion. ....(Motown)
Alabama
Neil Young; *Harvest* .... (Reprise)
ST/Journey Through The Past ....(Warner Bros.)
Alice's Restaurant Massacree
Arlo Guthrie; *Alice's Restaurant* .... (Reprise)
Best Of Arlo Guthrie ....(Warner Bros.)
Almost Cut My Hair
Crosby, Stills, Nash & Young; *Deja Vu* .... (Atlantic)
Ball Of Confusion (That's What The World Is Today)
Temptations; *All The Million-Sellers* .... (Motown)
Compact Command Performances-Temptations ....(Motown)
Songs Of Protest-C ....(Rhino)
Temptations' Greatest Hits-#2 ....(Motown)
Temptations-Anthology-The Best Of The Temptations ....(Motown)
Top 10 With A Bullet-Motown Male Groups-C ....(Motown)
Big Yellow Taxi
Amy Grant; *House Of Love* ....(A&M)
Joni Mitchell; *Ladies Of The Canyon* .... (Reprise)
Joni Mitchell with Tom Scott & The L.A. Express; *Miles Of Aisles*.... (Asylum)
Blowin' In The Wind
Bob Dylan; *Before The Flood* ....(Columbia)
Biograph ....(Columbia)
Bob Dylan At Budokan ....(Columbia)
Bob Dylan's Greatest Hits...............................(Columbia)
Freewheelin' ....(Columbia)
God Bless America-C ....(Columbia)
Greatest Folksingers Of The '60s-C ....(Vanguard)
Joan Baez; *ST/Forrest Gump* .... (Epic/Sony Music Soundtrax)
Peter, Paul & Mary; *10 Years Together/The Best Of Peter, Paul and Mary* ....(Warner Bros.)
Holiday Celebration ....(Warner Bros.)
In The Wind ....(Warner Bros.)
Peter, Paul and Mary In Concert ....(Warner Bros.)
Stevie Wonder; *Motown Year By Year-The Sound Of Young America-1966-C* ....(Motown)
Born In The U.S.A.
Bruce Springsteen; *Born In The U.S.A.* ....(Columbia)
Bruce Springsteen's Greatest Hits ....(Columbia)
Tracks ....(Columbia)
Bruce Springsteen & The E Street Band; *Bruce Springsteen & The E Street Band Live/1975-85* ....(Legacy)
Brother, Can You Spare A Dime
Bing Crosby; *Bing Crosby-16 Most Requested Songs* ....(Legacy)
Odetta/Dr. John/John Campbell/Rufus Reid; *Strike A Deep Chord-Blues For The Homeless-C* ....(Justice)
Peter, Paul & Mary; *See What Tomorrow Brings* .... (Warner Bros.)
Weavers; *Weavers' Greatest Hits* ....(Vanguard)
Caravan Of Love
Isley, Jasper, Isley; *Caravan Of Love* ....(CBS Associated)
Chimes Of Freedom
Bob Dylan; *Another Side Of Bob Dylan*....................(Columbia)

Bruce Springsteen; *Chimes Of Freedom* (Columbia)
Byrds; *The Byrds* (Columbia)
The Byrds' Greatest Hits (Columbia)

Come Together
Aerosmith; *ST/Armageddon-The Album* (Columbia)
Beatles; *Abbey Road* (Parlophone)
Beatles 1 (Capitol)
Beatles-20 Greatest Hits (Capitol)
The Beatles/1967-1970 (Capitol)
Ike & Tina Turner; *Proud Mary-Best Of Ike & Tina Turner* (EMI)
Workin' Together (EMI)
John Lennon; *Live In New York City* (Capitol)

Country's In The Best Of Hands
Original Cast; *Li'l Abner* (Columbia)

Eve Of Destruction
Barry McGuire; *Billboard Top Rock 'N' Roll Hits-1965-C* (Rhino)
Cruisin'-1965-C (Increase)
Good Feeling Music Of The Big Chill Generation-#3-C (Motown)
Songs Of Protest-C (Rhino)
Vintage Music-#9 & 10-C (MCA)
Dickies; *Great Dictations (Definitive Collection)* (A&M)
Incredible Shrinking Dickies (A&M)
Turtles; *Turtle Wax-Best Of The Turtles-#2* (Rhino)
Turtlesized (Rhino)

Everyday People
Sly & The Family Stone; *Sly & The Family Stone-Anthology* (Epic)
Sly & The Family Stone's Greatest Hits (Epic)
Stand! (Epic)

Fight The Power
Isley Brothers; *Forever Gold* (T-Neck/Columbia)
Heat Is On (T-Neck/Columbia)
Isley Brothers' Greatest Hits (T-Neck/Columbia)
The Isley Brothers Story-#2-The T-Neck Years-1969-1985 (Rhino)

For What It's Worth
Buffalo Springfield; *Buffalo Springfield* (Atco)
Buffalo Springfield-Retrospective (Atco)
Double History (Atco)
Hit Singles-1958-1977-C (Atlantic)
ST/Forrest Gump (Epic/Sony Music Soundtrax)

Freedom
Jimi Hendrix; *Cry Of Love* (Reprise)
Essential Jimi Hendrix (Reprise)
Voodoo Soup (MCA)
Richie Havens; *ST/Woodstock* (Atlantic)
The Best Of Woodstock-C (Atlantic)

Get Together
Big Mountain; *Resistance* (Giant)
Youngbloods; *Best Of The Youngbloods* (RCA)
Billboard Top Rock 'N' Roll Hits-1969-C (Rhino)
Chicken Soup For The Soul: I'll Be There For You-Songs Of Friendship, Brotherhood And Sisterhood-C (Rhino)
ST/Forrest Gump (Epic/Sony Music Soundtrax)
Summer Of Love-#1-C (Rhino)

Give Me Love (Give Me Peace On Earth)
George Harrison; *Best Of George Harrison* (Capitol)
Living In The Material World (Capitol)

Give More Power To The People
Chi-Lites; *Chi-Lites' Greatest Hits* (Epic)

Give Peace A Chance
John Lennon; *Lennon* (Capitol)
Live In New York City (Capitol)
ST/Imagine: John Lennon (Capitol)
The John Lennon Collection (Capitol)
John Lennon/Plastic Ono Band; *Shaved Fish* (Capitol)
Plastic Ono Band; *Plastic Ono Band-Live Peace In Toronto 1969* (Capitol)

He Ain't Heavy, He's My Brother
Hollies; *Best Of The Hollies* (EMI)
Best Of The Hollies-#2 (EMI)
Chicken Soup For The Soul: I'll Be There For You-Songs Of Friendship, Brotherhood And Sisterhood-C (Rhino)
Hollies-Epic Anthology From The Original Master Tapes (Epic)
The Hollies' Greatest Hits (Epic)
Neil Diamond; *Glory Road-1968-1972* (MCA)
Tap Root Manuscript (MCA)

I Shall Be Released
Band; *Music From Big Pink* (Capitol)
The Band-Anthology-#1 (Capitol)
The Last Waltz (Warner Bros.)
To Kingdom Come-The Definitive Collection (Capitol)
Bette Midler; *Bette Midler* (Atlantic)
ST/Divine Madness (Atlantic)
Bob Dylan; *Biograph* (Columbia)
Bob Dylan At Budokan (Columbia)
Bob Dylan's Greatest Hits-#2 (Columbia)
The Bootleg Series-Volumes 1-3 [Rare & Unreleased] (Columbia)
Bob Dylan And The Band; *Before The Flood* (Columbia)
Box Tops; *Box Tops' Greatest Hits* (Rhino)
Flying Burrito Brothers; *Farther Along-Best Of The Flying Burrito Brothers* (A&M)
Joan Baez; *Any Day Now: Songs Of Bob Dylan* (Vanguard)
Carry It On (Vanguard)
From Every Stage (A&M)
Joe Cocker; *With A Little Help From My Friends* (A&M)
Nina Simone; *Best Of Nina Simone* (Verve)
Rick Nelson; *Rick Nelson In Concert-Troubadour 1969* (MCA)

I'd Love To Change The World
Ten Years After; *A Space In Time* (Columbia)
Classic Performances Of Ten Years After (Columbia)
Universal (Chrysalis)

If I Had A Hammer (The Hammer Song)
Pete Seeger; *Sing-A-Long-Live At Sanders Theatre 1980* (Smithsonian Folkways)
Peter, Paul & Mary; *10 Years Together/The Best Of Peter, Paul and Mary* (Warner Bros.)
Peter, Paul and Mary (Warner Bros.)
Peter, Paul and Mary In Concert (Warner Bros.)
Trini Lopez; *Best Of Trini Lopez* (Exact)
Weavers; *Weavers' Greatest Hits* (Vanguard)

I-Feel-Like-I'm-Fixin'-To-Die Rag
Country Joe & The Fish; *Country Joe & The Fish-Greatest Hits* (Vanguard)
Greatest '60s Folksingers-C (Vanguard)
I-Feel-Like-I'm-Fixin'-To-Die (Vanguard)
Life & Times Of Country Joe & The Fish (Vanguard)
More American Graffiti-#4-C (MCA)
Songs Of Protest-C (Rhino)
ST/Woodstock (Atlantic)

Imagine
Diana Ross; *Best Of The Beatles Songs-C* (Motown)
Diana Ross-Anthology (Motown)
Touch Me In The Morning (Motown)
Joan Baez; *Best Of Joan Baez* (A&M)
Come From The Shadows (A&M)
John Lennon; *Lennon* (Capitol)
Live In New York City (Capitol)
ST/Imagine: John Lennon (Capitol)
John Lennon & Yoko Ono; *The John Lennon Collection* (Capitol)
John Lennon/Plastic Ono Band; *Imagine* (Capitol)
Shaved Fish (Capitol)
Neil Young; *America: A Tribute To Heroes-C* (Interscope)

In The Ghetto
Elvis Presley; *Elvis Presley-Pure Gold* (RCA)
From Elvis In Memphis (RCA)
From Memphis To Vegas/From Vegas To Memphis (RCA)
The Top Ten Hits (RCA)
Worldwide 50 Gold Award Hits, Vol. 1, Parts 1 & 2 (RCA)
Mac Davis; *Mac Davis' Greatest Hits* (Columbia)

Joe Hill
Arlo Guthrie & Pete Seeger; *Together In Concert* (Reprise)
Joan Baez; *Carry It On* (Vanguard)
From Every Stage (A&M)
One Day At A Time (Vanguard)
ST/Woodstock (Atlantic)

Joy To The World
Three Dog Night; *Best Of Three Dog Night* (MCA)
Good Feeling Music Of The Big Chill Generation-#2-C (Motown)
Good Feeling Music Of The Big Chill Generation-#3-C (Motown)
Joy To The World-Greatest Hits (MCA)
ST/Big Chill (Motown)
ST/Forrest Gump (Epic/Sony Music Soundtrax)

Living For The City
Stevie Wonder; *Innervisions* (Motown)
Original Musiquarium (Motown)

M.T.A.
Kingston Trio; *25 Years Non-Stop* (Xeres)
Best Of The Kingston Trio (Capitol)
Capitol Collectors Series-The Kingston Trio (Capitol)
Scarlet Ribbons (Capitol)
Very Best Of The Kingston Trio (Capitol)

Ohio
Crosby, Stills & Nash; *CSN* (Atlantic)
Crosby, Stills, Nash & Young; *4 Way Street* (Atlantic)
So Far (Atlantic)
Neil Young; *Decade* (Reprise)
ST/Journey Through The Past (Warner Bros.)

One Tin Soldier
Coven; *Super Hits Of The '70s-Have A Nice Day-#7-C* (Rhino)

Peace Train
Cat Stevens; *Cat Stevens Greatest Hits* (A&M)
Cat Stevens-Classics-#24 (A&M)
Teaser And The Firecat (A&M)

People Got To Be Free
Rascals; *Atlantic's Hit Singles-1958-1977-C* (Atlantic)
Billboard Top Rock 'N' Roll Hits-1968-C (Rhino)
Hit Singles-1958-1977-C (Atlantic)
Rascals-Anthology 1965-1972 (Rhino)
Songs Of Protest-C (Rhino)
Very Best Of The Rascals (Rhino)

Power To The People
John Lennon; *Lennon* (Capitol)
John Lennon/Plastic Ono Band; *Shaved Fish* (Capitol)

Reach Out And Touch
Diana Ross; *Diana Ross-All The Great Hits* . . . . (Motown)
  Diana Ross-Anthology . . . . (Motown)
  Live At Caesar's Palace . . . . (Motown)
  Most Played Songs On America's Jukeboxes . . . . (Motown)
  Motown Story-First 25 Years-C . . . . (Motown)
Reach Out Of The Darkness
Friend And Lover; *Chicken Soup For The Soul: I'll Be There For You-Songs
  Of Friendship, Brotherhood And Sisterhood-C* . . . . (Rhino)
  Flower Power-Psychedelic Rock Classics-C . . . . (K-Tel)
Revolution
Beatles; *Beatles-Box Set* . . . . (Capitol)
  Hey Jude . . . . (Capitol)
  Past Masters-Volume Two . . . . (Parlophone)
  Rock 'N' Roll Music . . . . (Capitol)
  ST/Imagine: John Lennon . . . . (Capitol)
  The Beatles/1967-1970 . . . . (Capitol)
Revolution 1
Beatles; *Beatles-Box Set* . . . . (Capitol)
  The Beatles (White Album) . . . . (Capitol)
Save The People
Original Cast; *Godspell* . . . . (Arista)
Share The Land
Guess Who; *American Woman, These Eyes & Other Hits* . . . . (RCA)
  Best Of The Guess Who . . . . (RCA)
  Track Record-Collection . . . . (RCA)
Society's Child (Baby I've Been Thinking)
Janis Ian; *Songs Of Protest-C* . . . . (Rhino)
  The Bottom Line Encore Collection . . . . (Bottom Line)
Lou Gramm; *A Foreigner In His Own Land: Best Of Early
  Years* . . . . (Collectables)
  Past Times Behind Rock & Roll-C . . . . (Intermedia)
Something In The Air
Thunderclap Newman; *History Of British Rock-#9-C* . . . . (Rhino)
  Hollywood Dream . . . . (MCA)
  ST/The Strawberry Statement . . . . (MCA)
Sound Of Silence, The
Paul Simon; *Paul Simon In Concert/Live Rhymin'* . . . . (Columbia)
Simon & Garfunkel; *Collected Works* . . . . (Columbia)
  More American Graffiti-#4-C . . . . (MCA)
  Simon & Garfunkel's Greatest Hits . . . . (Columbia)
  Sounds Of Silence . . . . (Columbia)
  ST/The Graduate . . . . (Columbia)
  The Concert In Central Park . . . . (Warner Bros.)
Stand
Sly & The Family Stone; *10 Years Too Soon* . . . . (Epic)
  Sly & The Family Stone-Anthology . . . . (Epic)
  Sly & The Family Stone's Greatest Hits . . . . (Epic)
Sun City
Artists United Against Apartheid; *Sun City-C* . . . . (Manhattan)
Teach Your Children
Crosby, Stills & Nash; *CSN* . . . . (Atlantic)
Crosby, Stills, Nash & Young; *4 Way Street* . . . . (Atlantic)
  Deja Vu . . . . (Atlantic)
  So Far . . . . (Atlantic)
  ST/The Wonder Years-Music From The Show & Era . . . . (Atlantic)
Suzy Bogguss/Alison Krauss/Kathy Mattea/Crosby, Stills & Nash; *Red Hot +
  Country-C* . . . . (Mercury)
This Land Is Your Land
Bruce Springsteen & The E Street Band; *Bruce Springsteen & The E Street
  Band Live/1975-85* . . . . (Legacy)
Glen Campbell; *All American* . . . . (Liberty)
Lee Greenwood; *American Patriot* . . . . (Capitol)
Odetta, Arlo Guthrie & Company; *Tribute To Woody
  Guthrie-C* . . . . (Warner Bros.)
Pete Seeger; *God Bless America-C* . . . . (Columbia)
  Pete Seeger Sings Woody Guthrie . . . . (Smithsonian Folkways)
  Pete Seeger-Complete Carnegie Hall Concert-1963 . . . . (Columbia)
Weavers; *Weavers' Greatest Hits* . . . . (Vanguard)
Woody Guthrie; *Greatest Songs Of Woody Guthrie-C* . . . . (Vanguard)
  Troubadours Of The Folk Era-#1-C . . . . (Rhino)
  Woody Guthrie . . . . (Vanguard)
Times They Are A-Changin'
Billy Joel; *KOHUEPT* . . . . (Columbia)
Bob Dylan; *Biograph* . . . . (Columbia)
  Bob Dylan At Budokan . . . . (Columbia)
  Bob Dylan's Greatest Hits . . . . (Columbia)
  The Bootleg Series-Volumes 1-3 [Rare & Unreleased] . . . . (Columbia)
  The Times They Are A-Changin' . . . . (Columbia)
Byrds; *The Byrds* . . . . (Columbia)
  Turn! Turn! Turn! . . . . (Legacy)
Peter, Paul & Mary; *Peter, Paul and Mary In Concert* . . . . . . (Warner Bros.)
Simon & Garfunkel; *Collected Works* . . . . (Columbia)
  Wednesday Morning 3 A.M. . . . . (Columbia)
Turn! Turn! Turn! (To Everything There Is A Season)
Byrds; *Billboard Top Rock 'N' Roll Hits-1965-C* . . . . (Rhino)
  Original Singles-#1-1965-1967 . . . . (Columbia)
  ST/Forrest Gump . . . . (Epic/Sony Music Soundtrax)
  The Byrds . . . . (Columbia)
  The Byrds' Greatest Hits . . . . (Columbia)

  Turn! Turn! Turn! . . . . (Legacy)
Pete Seeger; *Pete Seeger's Greatest Hits* . . . . (Columbia)
  Troubadours Of The Folk Era-#2-C . . . . (Rhino)
United We Stand
Brotherhood Of Man; *Chicken Soup For The Soul: I'll Be There For You-
  Songs Of Friendship, Brotherhood And Sisterhood-C* . . . . (Rhino)
  Super Hits Of The '70s-Have A Nice Day-#2-C . . . . (Rhino)
Mike Curb Congregation; *Mike Curb Congregation's Greatest Hits* . . . . . (Curb)
Universal Soldier
Buffy Sainte-Marie; *Best Of Buffy Sainte-Marie* . . . . (Vanguard)
  Festival Of Acoustic Music-#1 . . . . (Fantasy)
  Troubadours Of The Folk Era-#1-C . . . . (Rhino)
Donovan; *Catch The Wind* . . . . (Garland)
  History Of British Rock-#4-C . . . . (Rhino)
  Songs Of Protest-C . . . . (Rhino)
  The Secret Policeman's Other Ball/The Music . . . . (Rhino)
Volunteers
Jefferson Airplane; *"White Rabbit" & Other Hits* . . . . (RCA)
  2400 Fulton Street-An Anthology . . . . (RCA)
  Flight Log (1966-1976) . . . . (Grunt)
  ST/Forrest Gump . . . . (Epic/Sony Music Soundtrax)
  ST/Woodstock . . . . (Atlantic)
  The Worst Of Jefferson Airplane . . . . (RCA)
  Volunteers . . . . (RCA)
War
Bruce Springsteen & The E Street Band; *Bruce Springsteen & The E Street
  Band Live/1975-85* . . . . (Legacy)
Edwin Starr; *Billboard Top Rock 'N' Roll Hits-1970-C* . . . . (Rhino)
  Didn't It Blow Your Mind: Soul Hits Of The '70s-#3-C . . . . (Rhino)
  Motown Superstar Series-#3-Edwin Starr . . . . (Motown)
  Songs Of Protest-C . . . . (Rhino)
  War & Peace . . . . (Motown)
We Are The World
USA For Africa; *We Are The World-C* . . . . (Columbia)
We Didn't Start The Fire
Billy Joel; *Storm Front* . . . . (Columbia)
We Shall Overcome
Bruce Springsteen; *Where Have All The Flowers Gone: The Songs Of Pete
  Seeger* . . . . (Appleseed)
James Cleveland & The Troubadors; *James Cleveland & The
  Troubadors* . . . . (Savoy)
Joan Baez; *Carry It On* . . . . (Vanguard)
  Joan Baez In Concert, Part 2 . . . . (Vanguard)
Mahalia Jackson; *God Bless America-C* . . . . (Columbia)
Pete Seeger; *Bitter & The Sweet* . . . . (Mobile Fidelity Sound Lab)
  Pete Seeger's Greatest Hits . . . . (Columbia)
What The World Needs Now Is Love
Burt Bacharach; *Burt Bacharach's Greatest Hits* . . . . (A&M)
Jackie DeShannon; *Flower Power-Psychedelic Rock Classics-C* . . . . . . (K-Tel)
  Good Vibrations (Sounds Of Top 40 Radio: 1964-1967)-C . . . . . . (Capitol)
  Oldies But Goodies-#14-C . . . . (Original Sound)
  ST/Forrest Gump . . . . (Epic/Sony Music Soundtrax)
  ST/My Best Friend's Wedding . . . . (Work/Epic)
  Very Best Of Jackie DeShannon . . . . (EMI)
Luther Vandross; *Songs* . . . . (Epic)
Tom Clay; *20 Hard-To-Find Motown Classics-#2-C* . . . . (Motown)
What's Going On
Cyndi Lauper; *True Colors* . . . . (Portrait)
Marvin Gaye; *20/20-C* . . . . (Motown)
  Marvin Gaye Live At The London Palladium . . . . (Motown)
  Marvin Gaye-Anthology . . . . (Motown)
  Marvin Gaye's Greatest Hits . . . . (Motown)
  More Songs From "The Big Chill" Soundtrack-C . . . . (Motown)
  What's Going On . . . . (Motown)
Quincy Jones; *Quincy Jones-The Best* . . . . (A&M)
Where Have All The Flowers Gone
Johnny Rivers; *Best Of Johnny Rivers* . . . . (EMI)
  Johnny Rivers-Anthology 1964-1977 . . . . (Rhino)
Kingston Trio; *Capitol Collectors Series-The Kingston Trio* . . . . (Capitol)
  Songs Of Protest-C . . . . (Rhino)
Pete Seeger; *Essential Pete Seeger* . . . . (Vanguard)
  Pete Seeger's Greatest Hits . . . . (Columbia)
Peter, Paul & Mary; *Peter, Paul and Mary* . . . . (Warner Bros.)
Wes Montgomery; *Wes Montgomery-Classics#22* . . . . (A&M)
Woman Is The Nigger Of The World
John Lennon; *Live In New York City* . . . . (Capitol)
John Lennon/Plastic Ono Band; *Lennon* . . . . (Capitol)
  Shaved Fish . . . . (Capitol)
  Some Time In New York City . . . . (Capitol)
Won't Get Fooled Again
Van Halen; *LIVE: Right here, right now.* . . . . (Warner Bros.)
Who; *ST/The Kids Are Alright* . . . . (MCA)
  The Concert For New York City-C . . . . (Columbia)
  Who Greatest Hits . . . . (MCA)
  Who's Last . . . . (MCA)
  Who's next. . . . . (MCA)
Woodstock
Crosby, Stills & Nash; *CSN* . . . . (Atlantic)
Crosby, Stills, Nash & Young; *Deja Vu* . . . . (Atlantic)
  So Far . . . . (Atlantic)

Joni Mitchell; *Ladies Of The Canyon* . . . . (Reprise)
   Shadows & Light . . . . (Asylum)
Joni Mitchell with Tom Scott & The L.A. Express; *Miles Of Aisles* . . . . (Asylum)
World Is A Ghetto
George Benson; *In Flight* . . . .(Warner Bros.)
War; *Best Of War...And More-#2* . . . . (Avenue)
   The Music Band . . . . (MCA)
   The Music Band 2 . . . . (MCA)
   The World Is A Ghetto . . . . (Avenue)
   War-Anthology (1970-1994) . . . . (Avenue)

POLITICS: POLITICS & GOVERNMENT, Political
Systems, Politicians

See Also: **COUNTRIES: A-Z, COUNTRIES: AMERICA, HISTORY, KINGS, LAW & ORDER, MONEY (taxes), PATRIOTISM, POLICE, POLITICS (various), POWER & CONTROL, PREJUDICE, PRESIDENTS, PROTEST, QUEENS, ROYALTY, SLAVERY, WAR, WORK, WORLD**

Back In The U.S.S.R.
Beatles; *Beatles-Box Set* . . . . (Capitol)
   Rock 'N' Roll Music . . . . (Capitol)
   The Beatles (White Album) . . . . (Capitol)
   The Beatles/1967-1970 . . . . (Capitol)
Billy Joel; *KOHUEPT* . . . . (Columbia)
Ballad Of Davy Crockett
Bill Hayes; *Songs Of The West-#4-Movie & Television Themes-C* . . . . . . (Rhino)
Fess Parker; *16 Most Requested Songs Of The '50s-#1-C* . . . . (Legacy)
   Columbia Country Classics-#3-Americana-C . . . . (Columbia)
   Hollywood Magic-1950s-C . . . . (Columbia)
Kentucky HeadHunters; *Electric Barnyard* . . . . (Mercury)
Mac Wiseman; *45-#1240* . . . . (Dot)
Original Soundtrack; *Television's Greatest Hits-#4-Black & White Classics-C* . . . . (TVT)
Tennessee Ernie Ford; *Capitol Collectors Series-Tennessee Ernie Ford* . . . . (Capitol)
Ballad Of William Worthy
Phil Ochs; *Best Of Broadside 1962-1968: Anthems Of The American Underground From The Pages Of Broadside Magazine-C* . . . . (Smithsonian Folkways)
Big Brother
Stevie Wonder; *Talking Book* . . . . (Motown)
Der Kommisar
After The Fire; *Club Epic-#5-C* . . . .(Epic)
Don't Cry For Me Argentina
Madonna; *GHV2* . . . .(Warner Bros.)
ST/*Evita-Music From The Motion Picture* . . . .(Warner Bros.)
Original Cast; *Evita* . . . .(MCA)
Don't Worry About The Government
Talking Heads; *'77* . . . . (Sire)
   Name Of This Band Is Talking Heads . . . . (Sire)
   Popular Favorites-1984-1992 . . . . (Sire)
Exhuming McCarthy
R.E.M.; *Document* . . . .(EMI-Capitol Entert. Properties)
Gingrich The Newt
Austin Lounge Lizards; *Small Minds* . . . . (Sugar Hill)
Give Peace A Chance
John Lennon; *Lennon* . . . . (Capitol)
   Live In New York City . . . . (Capitol)
   ST/*Imagine: John Lennon* . . . . (Capitol)
   The John Lennon Collection . . . . (Capitol)
John Lennon/Plastic Ono Band; *Shaved Fish* . . . . (Capitol)
Plastic Ono Band; *Plastic Ono Band-Live Peace In Toronto 1969* . . . . . (Capitol)
Hay Una Mujer Desaparecida
Holly Near; *Imagine My Surprise* . . . .(Redwood)
Holly Near & Ronnie Gilbert; *Lifeline* . . . .(Redwood)
Highwire
Rolling Stones; *Flashpoint* . . . . (Virgin)
House Un-American Blues Activity Dream
Mimi & Richard Farina; *Best Of Mimi & Richard Farina* . . . . (Vanguard)
   Memories . . . . (Vanguard)
   Reflections In A Crystal Wind . . . . (Vanguard)
I Am A Patriot
Jackson Browne; *World In Motion* . . . . (Elektra)
Little Steven; *Voice Of America* . . . . (Razor & Tie)
I Wanna Grow Up To Be A Politician
Byrds; *20 Essential Tracks From The Box Set* . . . . (Columbia)
   Best Of The Byrds-Greatest Hits-#2 . . . . (Columbia)
   Byrdmaniax . . . . (Columbia)
   The Byrds . . . . (Columbia)
If You Love That Politician
Tom Paxton; *One Million Lawyers & Other Disasters* . . . . (Flying Fish)
Internationale, The
Ani DiFranco & Utah Phillips; *Fellow Workers* . . . .(Righteous Babe)
Juneteenth
Anthony Rivers & Others; *I've Known Rivers* . . . . (Gramavision)

Lie On Lie
Chalk Farm; *Notwithstanding* . . . . (Columbia)
One On The Right Is On The Left, The
Johnny Cash; *Johnny Cash-16 Biggest Hits-#2* . . . . (Legacy)
Politics & Poker
Tom Bosley/Original Cast; ST/*Fiorello!* . . . .(EMI-Angel)
Revolution
Beatles; *Beatles-Box Set* . . . . (Capitol)
   Hey Jude . . . . (Capitol)
   Past Masters-Volume Two . . . . (Parlophone)
   Rock 'N' Roll Music . . . . (Capitol)
   ST/*Imagine: John Lennon* . . . . (Capitol)
   The Beatles/1967-1970 . . . . (Capitol)
Revolution
Bob Marley & The Wailers; *Natty Dread* . . . .(Tuff Gong)
Revolution 1
Beatles; *Beatles-Box Set* . . . . (Capitol)
   The Beatles (White Album) . . . . (Capitol)
Rudiger
Mark Knopfler; *Golden Heart* . . . . (Warner Bros.)
Russians
Sting; *Dream Of The Blue Turtles* . . . . (A&M)
   Fields Of Gold-The Best Of Sting 1984-1994 . . . . (A&M)
Serious Juju
Sammy Hagar; *Ten 13* . . . .(Cabo Wabo/Beyond)
Sign Of The Times
Queensryche; *Hear In The Now Frontier* . . . .(Virgin)
Simple Desultory Phillipic, A (Or How I Was Robert McNamara'd Into Submission)
Simon & Garfunkel; *Parsley Sage Rosemary & Thyme* . . . . (Columbia)
State Of The World
Janet Jackson; *Janet Jackson's Rhythm Nation 1814* . . . . (A&M)
Subway Ride
Sheryl Crow; *The Globe Sessions* . . . . (A&M)
Theme From "Benson"
Original Soundtrack; *Television's Greatest Hits-#6-Remote Control-C* . . . (TVT)
Times They Are A-Changin'
Billy Joel; *KOHUEPT* . . . . (Columbia)
Bob Dylan; *Biograph* . . . . (Columbia)
   Bob Dylan At Budokan . . . . (Columbia)
   Bob Dylan's Greatest Hits . . . . (Columbia)
   The Bootleg Series-Volumes 1-3 [Rare & Unreleased] . . . . (Columbia)
   The Times They Are A-Changin' . . . . (Columbia)
Byrds; *The Byrds* . . . . (Columbia)
   Turn! Turn! Turn! . . . . (Legacy)
Peter, Paul & Mary; *Peter, Paul and Mary In Concert* . . . . (Warner Bros.)
Simon & Garfunkel; *Collected Works* . . . . (Columbia)
   Wednesday Morning 3 A.M. . . . . (Columbia)
Voices That Care
Voices That Care; *Voices That Care* . . . .(Giant)
Welcome To The Occupation
R.E.M.; *Document* . . . . (EMI-Capitol Entert. Properties)
Where Were You (When The World Stopped Turning)
Alan Jackson; *Alan Jackson-Drive* . . . . (Arista)
White, Discussion
Live; ST/*Virtuosity* . . . . (Radioactive/MCA)
   Throwing Copper . . . . (Radioactive/MCA)
Won't Get Fooled Again
Van Halen; *LIVE: Right here, right now.* . . . . (Warner Bros.)
Who; ST/*The Kids Are Alright.* . . . . (MCA)
   The Concert For New York City-C . . . . (Columbia)
   Who Greatest Hits . . . . (MCA)
   Who's Last . . . . (MCA)
   Who's next . . . . (MCA)

POLITICS: SOCIAL INJUSTICE, Oppression

See Also: **BROTHEROOD, COUNTRIES: A-Z, COUNTRIES: AMERICA, FIGHT, FREEDOM, HARD CITY LIFE, HISTORY, LAW & ORDER, PATRIOTISM, POLICE, POLITICS (various), POVERTY, POWER & CONTROL, PREJUDICE, PRESIDENTS, PROTEST, SLAVERY, SOCIAL CLASS: GENERAL, WAR, WORK, WORLD**

1040 Blues
Robert Cray Band; *Shame + Sin* . . . . (Mercury)
1913 Massacre
Arlo Guthrie; *Hobo's Lullaby* . . . .(Reprise)
Jack Elliot; *Tribute To Woody Guthrie-C* . . . . (Warner Bros.)
Ramblin' Jack Elliott; *Greatest Songs Of Woody Guthrie-C* . . . . (Vanguard)
Woody Guthrie; *Struggle* . . . . (Smithsonian Folkways)
9 To 5
Dolly Parton; *9 To 5 And Odd Jobs* . . . .(RCA)
   Best There Is . . . . (RCA)
   Dolly Parton's Greatest Hits . . . . (RCA)
   I Am Woman-C . . . . (Nick At Nite)
   Nipper's Greatest Hits Of The '80s-C . . . . (RCA)

American Skin (41 Shots)
Bruce Springsteen & The E Street Band; *Live In New York City* . . . . . (Columbia)
Amerikka's Most Wanted
Ice Cube; *AmeriKKKa's Most Wanted* . . . . (Priority)
Balboa Park
Bruce Springsteen; *The Ghost Of Tom Joad* . . . . (Columbia)
Ballad Of Ira Hayes, The
Johnny Cash; *The Man In Black-His Greatest Hits* . . . . (Legacy)
Peter La Farge; *Best Of Broadside 1962-1968: Anthems Of The American*
  Underground From The Pages Of Broadside
  Magazine-C . . . .(Smithsonian Folkways)
Big Brother
Stevie Wonder; *Talking Book* . . . . (Motown)
Blowin' In The Wind
Bob Dylan; *Before The Flood* . . . . (Columbia)
  Biograph . . . .(Columbia)
  Bob Dylan At Budokan . . . .(Columbia)
  Bob Dylan's Greatest Hits . . . .(Columbia)
  Freewheelin'. . . . .(Columbia)
  God Bless America-C . . . .(Columbia)
  Greatest Folksingers Of The '60s-C . . . .(Vanguard)
Joan Baez; *ST/Forrest Gump* . . . . (Epic/Sony Music Soundtrax)
Peter, Paul & Mary; *10 Years Together/The Best Of Peter, Paul*
  and Mary . . . . (Warner Bros.)
  Holiday Celebration . . . . (Warner Bros.)
  In The Wind. . . . . (Warner Bros.)
  Peter, Paul and Mary In Concert . . . . (Warner Bros.)
Stevie Wonder; *Motown Year By Year-The Sound Of Young America-*
  1966-C . . . . (Motown)
Born In The U.S.A.
Bruce Springsteen; *Born In The U.S.A.* . . . .(Columbia)
  Bruce Springsteen's Greatest Hits . . . .(Columbia)
  Tracks . . . .(Columbia)
Bruce Springsteen & The E Street Band; *Bruce Springsteen & The E Street*
  Band Live/1975-85 . . . . (Legacy)
Brenda's Got A Baby
Tupac; *2Pacalypse Now* . . . .(Priority)
Brother, Can You Spare A Dime
Bing Crosby; *Bing Crosby-16 Most Requested Songs* . . . . (Legacy)
Odetta/Dr. John/John Campbell/Rufus Reid; *Strike A Deep Chord-Blues For*
  The Homeless-C . . . . (Justice)
Peter, Paul & Mary; *See What Tomorrow Brings* . . . . (Warner Bros.)
Weavers; *Weavers' Greatest Hits* . . . .(Vanguard)
Change
Keb' Mo'; *The Door* . . . .(550/Epic/Okeh)
Changes
2Pac; *2Pac Greatest Hits* . . . . (Amaru/Death Row/Interscope)
Dear God
XTC; *Best Of MTV's 120 Minutes-#1-C* . . . . (Rhino)
  Skylarking. . . . . (Geffen)
  Upsy Daisy Assortment . . . . (Geffen)
Dear Mrs. Roosevelt
Bob Dylan; *Tribute To Woody Guthrie-C* . . . . (Warner Bros.)
Deportee (Plane Wreck At Los Gatos)
Arlo Guthrie & Pete Seeger; *Together In Concert* . . . .(Reprise)
Byrds; *The Byrds* . . . .(Columbia)
Cisco Houston; *Greatest Songs Of Woody Guthrie-C* . . . .(Vanguard)
Gene Clark & Carla Olson; *So Rebellious A Lover* . . . . (Rhino)
Judy Collins; *Tribute To Woody Guthrie-C* . . . . (Warner Bros.)
Waylon Jennings, Willie Nelson, Johnny Cash, Kris Kristofferson;
  Highwayman . . . . (Columbia)
Desaperecidos (Central America)
Little Steven; *Voice Of America* . . . . (Razor & Tie)
Do Re Mi
Arlo Guthrie; *Tribute To Woody Guthrie-C.* . . . . (Warner Bros.)
John Cougar Mellencamp; *Folkways: A Vision Shared-C.* . . . .(Columbia)
Ry Cooder; *Ry Cooder.* . . . .(Reprise)
  Show Time . . . . (Warner Bros.)
Woody Guthrie; *Dust Bowl Ballads* . . . .(Rounder)
Doing The Reactionary
Barbra Streisand; *Pins And Needles* . . . . (Columbia)
Don't Drink The Water
Dave Matthews Band; *Before These Crowded Streets.* . . . .(RCA)
Dreamer
Ozzy Osbourne; *Down To Earth* . . . . (Epic)
Easy To Be Hard
Original Broadway Cast; *Hair.* . . . .(RCA)
Original Cast; *ST/Hair.* . . . . (RCA)
Three Dog Night; *Best Of Three Dog Night.* . . . . (MCA)
  Captured Live At The Forum . . . . (MCA)
  Celebrate-The Three Dog Night Story . . . .(MCA)
Failed Christian
Nick Lowe; *Dig My Mood.* . . . . (Upstart)
Faith In Me, Faith In You
Doug Stone; *Country Lovin'-Songs From The Heart-C* . . . . (Rhino)
  Faith In Me Faith In You. . . . .(Columbia)
  Super Hits Of 1995-C . . . . (Epic)
Final Hour
Lauryn Hill; *The Miseducation Of Lauryn Hill* . . . . (Ruffhouse/Columbia)

From A Distance
Bette Midler; *Some People's Lives.* . . . .(Atlantic)
Byrds; *20 Essential Tracks From The Box Set* . . . .(Columbia)
  The Byrds . . . .(Columbia)
Judy Collins; *Fires Of Eden* . . . .(Columbia)
Kathy Mattea; *Time Passes By* . . . . (Mercury)
Nanci Griffith; *Lone Star State Of Mind.* . . . .(MCA)
  One Fair Summer Evening . . . .(MCA)
Gangsta's Paradise
Coolio; *1996 Grammy Nominees-C* . . . . (Columbia)
  Gangsta's Paradise. . . . . (Tommy Boy)
  ST/Dangerous Minds. . . . .(MCA)
Ghost Of Tom Joad
Bruce Springsteen; *The Ghost Of Tom Joad.* . . . .(Columbia)
Gotham City
R. Kelly; *ST/Batman & Robin-Music From And Inspired By The Motion*
  Picture . . . . (Jive)
He Was My Brother
Simon & Garfunkel; *Wednesday Morning 3 A.M.* . . . .(Columbia)
House Burning Down
Jimi Hendrix; *Essential Jimi Hendrix* . . . .(Reprise)
Jimi Hendrix Experience; *Electric Ladyland* . . . .(Reprise)
I Ain't Got No Home
Bob Dylan; *Tribute To Woody Guthrie-C* . . . . (Warner Bros.)
I Am Woman
Helen Reddy; *Helen Reddy's Greatest Hits* . . . .(Capitol)
  I Am Woman . . . . (Capitol)
  I Am Woman-C . . . . (Nick At Nite)
  I Don't Know How To Love Him . . . . (Capitol)
I Believe
Blessid Union Of Souls; *Home.* . . . .(EMI)
I Think About You
Collin Raye; *Best Of Collin Raye-Direct Hits* . . . . (Epic)
  I Think About You . . . . (Epic)
I Wonder If Heaven Got A Ghetto
2Pac; *R U Still Down (Remember Me)* . . . .(Amaru/Jive)
If I Had A Rocket Launcher (Central America)
Bruce Cockburn; *Stealing Fire.* . . . .(Columbia)
  Waiting For A Miracle-Singles 1970-1987 . . . .(Gold Castle)
I'll Be Around
Rappin' 4-Tay; *Don't Fight The Feelin'* . . . . (Rag Top/EMI)
Imelda
Mark Knopfler; *Golden Heart* . . . . (Warner Bros.)
Indian Reservation (The Lament Of The Cherokee Reservation Indian)
Don Fardon; *45-#408* . . . .(GNP/Crescendo)
Raiders; *Billboard Top Rock 'N' Roll Hits-1971-C* . . . .(Rhino)
  Legend Of Paul Revere And The Raiders . . . .(Columbia)
  Pop Classics Of The '70s-C . . . .(Columbia)
  Super Hits Of The '70s-Have A Nice Day-#5-C . . . . (Rhino)
Inner City Blues (Make Me Wanna Holler)
Marvin Gaye; *What's Going On.* . . . .(Motown)
Internationale, The
Ani DiFranco & Utah Phillips; *Fellow Workers.* . . . .(Righteous Babe)
Kevorkian
Public Enemy; *There's A Poison Goin On* . . . . (Atomic Pop)
Links On The Chain
Broadside Singers & Phil Ochs; *Best Of Broadside 1962-1968: Anthems*
  Of The American Underground From The Pages Of Broadside
  Magazine-C . . . . (Smithsonian Folkways)
Little Man
Alan Jackson; *High Mileage* . . . .(Arista)
Looking East
Jackson Browne; *Looking East* . . . . (Elektra)
Love's The Only House
Martina McBride; *Emotion* . . . . (RCA)
Mrs. Clara Sullivan's Letter
Pete Seeger; *Best Of Broadside 1962-1968: Anthems Of The American*
  Underground From The Pages Of Broadside
  Magazine-C . . . . (Smithsonian Folkways)
New Beginning
Tracy Chapman; *New Beginning* . . . .(Elektra)
No Can Do
Mark Knopfler; *Golden Heart* . . . . (Warner Bros.)
Old Man And Me
Hootie & The Blowfish; *Fairweather Johnson* . . . . (Atlantic)
One
Creed; *My Own Prison.* . . . .(Wind-up)
One Voice
Billy Gilman; *One Voice* . . . . (Epic)
Pink Houses
John Cougar Mellencamp; *Rock For Amnesty-C* . . . .(Mercury)
  Uh-Huh. . . . . (Riva)
John Mellencamp featuring Kid Rock; *The Concert For New York*
  City-C . . . . (Columbia)
Pure Massacre
Silverchair; *Frogstomp* . . . . (Epic)
Redemption Day
Sheryl Crow; *Sheryl Crow* . . . . (A&M)

Right On
Marvin Gaye; *What's Going On* . . . . (Motown)
Rosa Parks
Outkast; *Aquemini* . . . . (LaFace/Arista)
Scream
Michael Jackson with Janet Jackson; *HIStory: Past, Present And Future-Book 1-C* . . . .(Epic)
Searchin' For My Soul
Amel Larrieux; *Infinite Possibilities* . . . .(Epic)
Shoes You're Wearing
Clint Black; *Nothin' But The Taillights* . . . . (RCA)
Sinaloa Cowboys
Bruce Springsteen; *The Ghost Of Tom Joad* . . . . (Columbia)
Sing Me A Song With Social Significance
Barbra Streisand; *Pins And Needles* . . . . (Columbia)
Some Bridges
Jackson Browne; *Looking East* . . . . (Elektra)
Stones In The Road
Mary Chapin Carpenter; *Stones In The Road* . . . . (Columbia)
Strange Fruit
Billie Holiday; *History Of The Real Billie Holiday* . . . . (Verve)
Lady Sings The Blues . . . . (Verve)
Songbook . . . . (Verve)
Nina Simone; *Compact Jazz-Nina Simone* . . . . (Verve)
Siouxsie And The Banshees; *Through The Looking Glass* . . . .(Geffen)
They Dance Alone (Cueca Solo)
Sting; *...Nothing Like The Sun* . . . . (A&M)
Fields Of Gold-The Best Of Sting 1984-1994 . . . . (A&M)
Union Maid
Judy Collins; *Tribute To Woody Guthrie-C* . . . .(Warner Bros.)
Us & Them
Pink Floyd; *Dark Side Of The Moon* . . . . (Capitol)
Delicate Sound Of Thunder . . . . (Columbia)
Pink Floyd-Gift Set . . . . (Capitol)
Shine On . . . . (Columbia)
Vic And Ray
Mark Knopfler; *Golden Heart* . . . .(Warner Bros.)
Walkin' On The Sun
Smash Mouth; *Fush Yu Mang* . . . . (Interscope)
We Shall Be Free
Garth Brooks; *The Chase* . . . . (Liberty)
Welcome, Welcome Emigrante
Broadside Singers & Buffy Sainte-Marie; *Best Of Broadside 1962-1968: Anthems Of The American Underground From The Pages Of Broadside Magazine-C* . . . . (Smithsonian Folkways)
Westside
TQ; *They Never Saw Me Coming* . . . .(ClockWork/Epic)
What It's Like
Everlast; *Whitey Ford Sings The Blues* . . . . (Tommy Boy)
What Would You Do?
City High; *City High* . . . . (Interscope)
Now That's What I Call Music!-#7-C . . . . (Virgin)
ST/Life . . . .(Rock Land/Interscope)
What's Going On
Cyndi Lauper; *True Colors* . . . . (Portrait)
Marvin Gaye; *20/20-C* . . . . (Motown)
Marvin Gaye Live At The London Palladium . . . . (Motown)
Marvin Gaye-Anthology . . . . (Motown)
Marvin Gaye's Greatest Hits/ . . . . (Motown)
More Songs From "The Big Chill" Soundtrack-C . . . . (Motown)
What's Going On . . . . (Motown)
Quincy Jones; *Quincy Jones-The Best* . . . . (A&M)
What's Happening, Brother
Marvin Gaye; *What's Going On* . . . . (Motown)
Workin' It
Don Henley; *Inside Job* . . . .(Warner Bros.)
You Haven't Done Nothin'
Stevie Wonder; *Fulfillingness' First Finale* . . . . (Motown)

POVERTY, Broke, Ghetto, Hard Times, Homeless, Poor

See Also: DIFFICULT, GAMBLING, HARD CITY LIFE, LOVE: LOVE & MONEY, LUCK, MONEY, POLITICS (various), ROYALTY, SLAVERY, SOCIAL CLASS: GENERAL, SOCIAL CLASS: RURAL, TRAINS, TROUBLE, WORK

1st Of Tha Month
Bone Thugs-N-Harmony; *E. 1999 Eternal* . . . .(Ruthless/Relativity)
Ain't Got No Money
Bob Seger & The Silver Bullet Band; *Stranger In Town* . . . . (Capitol)
All I Have To Give
Backstreet Boys; *Backstreet Boys* . . . . (Jive)
Now That's What I Call Music!-#3-C . . . . (Virgin)
All I Have To Offer You Is Me
Aaron Tippin; *Essential Aaron Tippin* . . . . (RCA)

Charley Pride; *Charley Pride-Super Hits* . . . . (RCA)
Essential Charley Pride . . . .(RCA)
Ricky Van Shelton; *Fried Green Tomatoes* . . . . (Audium)
All I Want Is A Life
Tim McGraw; *All I Want* . . . .(Curb)
Amarillo By Morning
George Strait; *George Strait's Greatest Hits* . . . . (MCA)
Strait From The Heart . . . . (MCA)
Angel From Montgomery
Bonnie Raitt; *Streetlights* . . . . (Warner Bros.)
Bonnie Raitt & John Prine; *Bonnie Raitt-Collection* . . . . (Warner Bros.)
John Prine; *John Prine* . . . .(Atlantic)
John Prine-Souvenirs . . . . (Oh Boy)
Another Day
Bryan Adams; *Into The Fire* . . . . (A&M)
Another Day In Paradise
Phil Collins; *...But Seriously* . . . .(Atlantic)
Serious Hits...Live! . . . .(Atlantic)
Anyway
Keb' Mo'; *The Door* . . . . (550/Epic/Okeh)
Aqualung
Jethro Tull; *20 Years Of Jethro Tull* . . . . (Chrysalis)
Bursting Out . . . . (Chrysalis)
M.U.-The Best Of Jethro Tull . . . . (Chrysalis)
Too Old To Rock 'N' Roll: Too Young To Die! . . . . (Chrysalis)
Artificial Flowers
Bobby Darin; *The Bobby Darin Story* . . . .(Atlantic)
Back When He Was Hungry
Bill Anderson; *A Lot Of Things Different* . . . .(Varese Sarabande)
Bag Lady
Todd Rundgren; *Hermit Of Mink Hollow* . . . . (Rhino)
Bag Lady
Erykah Badu; *Mama's Gun* . . . . (Motown)
Bag Lady
Robby Krieger; *Versions/Robby Krieger* . . . . (One Way)
Bag Lady Song, The
Accused; *Martha Splatterhead's Maddest Stories Ever Told* . . . . (Relativity)
Ballad Of Jed Clampett
Flatt & Scruggs; *Columbia Country Classics-#3-Americana-C* . . . . . (Columbia)
On Foggy Mountain . . . . (Fifty One West)
Bangladesh
George Harrison; *Best Of George Harrison* . . . . (Capitol)
Concert For Bangladesh-C . . . . (Capitol)
Banquet
Joni Mitchell; *For The Roses* . . . .(Asylum)
Be Like That
3 Doors Down; *Better Life* . . . . (Republic/Universal)
Now That's What I Call Music!-#8-C . . . .(Virgin)
Be Thankful For What You Got
William DeVaughn; *Didn't It Blow Your Mind: Soul Hits Of The '70s-#12-C* . . . . (Rhino)
Oldies But Goodies-#11-C . . . .(Original Sound)
Beggar In Blue Jeans
Rowans; *Rowans* . . . .(Asylum)
Beggar's Day
Nils Lofgren; *Nils Lofgren-Classics-#13* . . . . (A&M)
Nils Lofgren & Grin; *Best Of Nils Lofgren* . . . . (A&M)
Gone Crazy . . . . (A&M)
Beggar's Day
Nazareth; *Hair Of The Dog* . . . . (A&M)
'Snaz . . . . (A&M)
Beggar's Day
Skid Row; *Slave To The Grind* . . . .(Atlantic)
Beggar's Game
Dan Fogelberg; *Phoenix* . . . .(Full Moon)
Better Days (And The Bottom Drops Out)
Citizen King; *Mobile Estates* . . . . (Warner Bros.)
Big Brother
Stevie Wonder; *Talking Book* . . . . (Motown)
Bizzness Ain't Dead
New World Singers; *Best Of Broadside 1962-1968: Anthems Of The American Underground From The Pages Of Broadside Magazine-C* . . . .(Smithsonian Folkways)
Bohemian Rhapsody
Braids; *Here We Come* . . . . (Big Beat)
ST/High School High . . . . (Big Beat)
Queen; *A Night At The Opera* . . . . (Hollywood)
Classic Queen . . . . (Hollywood)
Live At Wembley '86 . . . . (Hollywood)
ST/Wayne's World . . . . (Reprise)
Both Sides Of The Story
Phil Collins; *Both Sides* . . . .(Atlantic)
Boxcars
Butch Hancock; *Eats Away The Night* . . . . (Sugar Hill)
Joe Ely; *Best Of Joe Ely* . . . . (MCA)
Freight Train Blues-Classic Railroad Songs-#4-C . . . . (Rounder)
Honky Tonk Masquerade . . . . (MCA)
Rosie Flores; *Rockabilly Filly* . . . .(Hightone)

Breadline Blues
New Lost City Ramblers; *Depression Songs* . . . .(Smithsonian Folkways)
Broke Again
Little River Band; *Diamantina Cocktail* . . . . (Capitol)
Brother, Can You Spare A Dime
Bing Crosby; *Bing Crosby-16 Most Requested Songs* . . . . (Legacy)
Odetta/Dr. John/John Campbell/Rufus Reid; *Strike A Deep Chord-Blues For The Homeless-C* . . . . (Justice)
Peter, Paul & Mary; *See What Tomorrow Brings* . . . . (Warner Bros.)
Weavers; *Weavers' Greatest Hits* . . . . (Vanguard)
Bumming Around
''T'' Texas Tyler; *Only Country-1950-1954-C* . . . .(JCI Assoc. Labels)
Busted
Harlan Howard; *All-Time Favorite Country Songwriter* . . . . (Koch International)
John Conlee; *John Conlee's Greatest Hits* . . . . (MCA)
Songs For The Working Man . . . . (MCA)
Johnny Cash; *Johnny Cash-16 Biggest Hits-#2* . . . . (Legacy)
Ray Charles; *Ray Charles' Greatest Hits* . . . . (Rhino)
Ray Charles-His Greatest Hits-#2 . . . . (Dunhill Compact Classics)
Cadillac Style
Sammy Kershaw; *Don't Go Near The Water* . . . . (Mercury)
Cafe On The Corner
Sawyer Brown; *Cafe On The Corner* . . . . (Curb)
Calling Mr. Welfare
Big Daddy Kane; *It's A Big Daddy Thing* . . . . (Cold Chillin')
Can't Afford No Shoes
Frank Zappa/Mothers Of Invention; *One Size Fits All* . . . . (Rykodisc)
Change
Keb' Mo'; *The Door* . . . .(550/Epic/Okeh)
Changes
2Pac; *2Pac Greatest Hits* . . . .(Amaru/Death Row/Interscope)
Chantilly Lace
Big Bopper; *45s On CD-#1-1956-1959-C* . . . . (Mercury)
Cruisin'-1958-C . . . . (Increase)
Oldies But Goodies-#4-C . . . .(Original Sound)
ST/American Graffiti . . . . (MCA)
Jerry Lee Lewis; ''Killer'' Rocks On . . . . (Mercury)
Best Of Jerry Lee Lewis-#2 . . . . (Mercury)
Child Of Poverty
Paul Martin; *Country Gold-Paul Martin* . . . .(Plantation)
Great Country Gold . . . .(Plantation)
Children Of The Ghetto
Courtney Pine; *Journey To The Urge Within* . . . . (Antilles)
Children Of The Ghetto
Philip Bailey; *Chinese Wall* . . . . (Columbia)
Children Of The Night
Richard Marx; *Repeat Offender* . . . . (EMI)
Christmas Shoes
Newsong; *Sheltering Tree* . . . . (Benson/Jive)
Cloud Nine
Temptations; *25 Years Of Grammy Greats-C* . . . . (Motown)
Cloud Nine . . . . (Motown)
Motown Grammy R&B Performances Of The '60s & '70s-C . . . . . . (Motown)
Motown Story-First 25 Years-C . . . . (Motown)
Temptations' Greatest Hits-#2 . . . . (Motown)
Coal Miner's Daughter
Loretta Lynn; *Coal Miner's Daughter* . . . . (MCA)
Coal Miner's Daughter . . . . (MCA)
Loretta Lynn-20 Greatest Hits . . . . (MCA)
Loretta Lynn-Greatest Hits Live . . . . (K-Tel)
Loretta Lynn's Greatest Hits-#2 . . . . (MCA)
The Country Music Hall Of Fame-Loretta Lynn . . . . (MCA)
Coat Of Many Colors
Dolly Parton; *Best Of Dolly Parton* . . . . (RCA)
Dolly Parton-Super Hits . . . . (Columbia)
Essential Dolly Parton-#2 . . . . (RCA)
Emmylou Harris; *Pieces Of The Sky* . . . . (Reprise)
Creeque Alley
Mamas & The Papas; *Best Of The Mamas & The Papas* . . . . (MCA)
Mamas & The Papas' Greatest Hits . . . . (MCA)
Mamas & The Papas-16 Of Their Greatest Hits . . . . (MCA)
Daddy Sang Bass
Johnny Cash; *Columbia Country Classics-#5-A New Tradition-C* . . . (Columbia)
Johnny Cash's Greatest Hits-#2 . . . . (Columbia)
The Man In Black-His Greatest Hits . . . . (Legacy)
Date With Poverty
Metal Church; *Human Factor* . . . . (Epic)
Dawn (Go Away)
4 Seasons; *25th Anniversary Collection* . . . . (Rhino)
4 Seasons-Anthology . . . . (Rhino)
Daydream Believer
Anne Murray; *Anne Murray's Greatest Hits* . . . . (Capitol)
I'll Always Love You . . . . (Capitol)
Monkees; *Billboard Top Rock 'N' Roll Hits-1967-C* . . . . (Rhino)
Mellow '60s-C . . . . (Priority)
Monkees' Greatest Hits . . . . (Rhino)
Dead End Street
Lou Rawls; *Best From Lou Rawls* . . . . (Capitol)
Lou Rawls-Live (Right Stuff) . . . . (Right Stuff)

Do For Love
2Pac featuring Eric Williams; *R U Still Down (Remember Me)* . . . . (Amaru/Jive)
Do You Want My Job
Little Village; *Little Village* . . . . (Reprise)
Domestic Life
John Conlee; *American Faces* . . . . (Columbia)
Greatest Country Hits Of The '80s-1987-C . . . . (Columbia)
More Hot Country Requests-#2-C . . . . (Epic)
Double Trouble
Eric Clapton; *Eric Clapton-Crossroads-C* . . . . (Polydor)
Just One Night . . . . (Polydor)
No Reason To Cry . . . .(RSO)
Down In The Boondocks
Billy Joe Royal; *Billy Joe Royal's Greatest Hits* . . . . (Columbia)
Rock Classics Of The '60s-C . . . . (Columbia)
Drifter
Sylvia; *Drifter* . . . . (RCA)
Sylvia's Greatest Hits . . . . (RCA)
Drifter
Deep Purple; *Come Taste The Band* . . . .(Metal Blade)
Drifter
John Lee Hooker & Canned Heat; *Infinite Boogie* . . . .(Rhino)
Drifter
Iron Maiden; *Killers* . . . .(Capitol)
Drifter
Neil Young; *Landing On Water* . . . . (Geffen)
Drifter
Neil Diamond; *On The Way To The Sky* . . . .(Columbia)
Drifter
Textones; *Through The Canyon* . . . . (Rhino)
Drifter's Escape
Bob Dylan; *John Wesley Harding* . . . .(Columbia)
Jimi Hendrix; *Lifelines/Jimi Hendrix Story* . . . . (Reprise)
Drifting Blues
Albert King; *Thursday Night In San Francisco* . . . . (Stax)
Charles Brown; *Blues Masters-#3-Texas Blues-C* . . . .(Rhino)
John Hammond; *Solo* . . . . (Vanguard)
Pete Townshend; *Another Scoop* . . . . (Atco)
Electric Avenue
Eddy Grant; *Killer On The Rampage* . . . . (Portrait)
Every Ghetto, Every City
Lauryn Hill; *The Miseducation Of Lauryn Hill* . . . .(Ruffhouse/Columbia)
Fallen On Hard Times
Jethro Tull; *20 Years Of Jethro Tull* . . . .(Chrysalis)
The Broadsword And The Beast . . . .(Chrysalis)
Fancy
Bobbi Gentry; *All-Time Country Classics-#1-C* . . . .(Capitol)
Reba McEntire; *Rumor Has It* . . . . (MCA)
Follow The Drinking Gourd
Richie Havens; *Songs Of The Civil War-C* . . . .(Columbia)
Weavers; *Weavers' Greatest Hits* . . . . (Vanguard)
Gangsta's Paradise
Coolio; *1996 Grammy Nominees-C* . . . . (Tommy Boy)
Gangsta's Paradise . . . . (Tommy Boy)
ST/Dangerous Minds . . . . (MCA)
Getto Jam
Domino; *Domino* . . . . (OutBurst)
Ghetto
Donny Hathaway; *Atlantic Rhythm & Blues 1947-1974-#7 (1969-1974)-C* . . . . (Atlantic)
Best Of Donny Hathaway . . . . (Atco)
Donny Hathaway-Live . . . . (Atco)
Everything Is Everything . . . . (Atco)
Ghetto
Joan Baez; *One Day At A Time* . . . . (Vanguard)
The First 10 Years . . . .(Vanguard)
Ghetto
Too $hort; *Short Dog's In The House* . . . . (Jive)
Ghetto Child
Spinners; *Best Of The Spinners* . . . . (Atlantic)
Ghetto Heaven
Family Stand; *Chain* . . . . (Atlantic)
Ghetto Supastar (That Is What You Are)
Pras Michel featuring Old Dirty Bastard & Mya; *ST/Bulworth* . . . . . (Interscope)
Ghost Of Tom Joad
Bruce Springsteen; *The Ghost Of Tom Joad* . . . .(Columbia)
Give Me Your Tired, Your Poor
Mormon Tabernacle Choir; *Around The World: A Musical Journey Of Best-Loved Favorites* . . . . (Sony Music Classical)
God Bless The Child
Billie Holiday; *Billie Holiday's Greatest Hits* . . . .(Decca Jazz)
Billie Holiday's Greatest Hits . . . .(Legacy)
From The Original Decca Masters . . . . (MCA)
Songbook . . . . (Verve)
The Billie Holiday Story-#2 . . . .(Columbia)
Blood, Sweat & Tears; *Blood, Sweat & Tears* . . . .(Columbia)
Blood, Sweat & Tears Greatest Hits . . . .(Columbia)
Diana Ross; *ST/Lady Sings The Blues* . . . . (Motown)

Liza Minnelli; *4-Sider*. . . . . (Cypress)
ST/Liza With A "Z". . . . . (Columbia)
Lou Rawls; *Best From Lou Rawls*. . . . . (Capitol)
Gonna Make It Somehow
Albert King; *Truckload Of Lovin'*. . . . . (Tomato)
Grapes Of Wrath
Charlie Daniels Band; *Midnight Wind* . . . .(Epic)
Green, Green
New Christy Minstrels; *New Christy Minstrels' Greatest Hits* . . . . . . (Columbia)
Gypsy Woman (She's Homeless)
Crystal Waters; *Red Hot + Dance-C*. . . . . (Columbia)
Surprise . . . . (Mercury)
Hallelujah, I'm A Bum
Al Jolson; *You Ain't Heard Nothin' Yet* . . . . (Legacy)
Bobby Short; *Bobby Short Celebrates Rodgers & Hart* . . . .(Atlantic)
Hang On Sloopy
McCoys; *21 Oldies But Goodies-C*. . . . . (Original Sound)
Billboard Top Rock 'N' Roll Hits-1965-C . . . . (Rhino)
Frat Rock!-C . . . . (Rhino)
Oldies But Goodies-#14-C . . . . (Original Sound)
Ramsey Lewis; *Greatest Hits Of Ramsey Lewis* . . . . (Chess)
Vintage Music-#20-C. . . . .(MCA)
Hard Candy Christmas
Dolly Parton; *Best Of Christmas-C*. . . . . (RCA)
Country Christmas-#2-C . . . . (RCA)
Dolly Parton's Greatest Hits . . . . (RCA)
Season's Greetings-C . . . . (RCA)
ST/Best Little Whorehouse In Texas. . . . . (MCA)
Original Cast; *Best Little Whorehouse In Texas* . . . . (MCA)
RuPaul; *Ho Ho Ho* . . . . (Rhino)
Hard Knock Life
Original Broadway Cast; *Annie* . . . . (Columbia)
Hard Knock Life (Ghetto Anthem)
Jay-Z; *Now That's What I Call Music!-#2-C* . . . . (Virgin)
Vol. 2-Hard Knock Life . . . .(Def Jam)
Hard Time Killing Floor Blues
Chris Thomas King; *ST/O Brother, Where Art Thou?* . . . . (Mercury)
Hard Times
Boz Scaggs; *Down Two Then Left* . . . . (Columbia)
Hits! . . . . (Columbia)
Hard Times
Emmylou Harris & The Nash Ramblers; *At The Ryman* . . . . (Reprise)
Hard Times
Eric Clapton; *24 Nights*. . . . . (Duck/Reprise)
Journeyman . . . . (Duck/Reprise)
Hard Times
Ray Charles; *Best Of Ray Charles* . . . . (Atlantic)
Hard Times
Crusaders; *Best Of The Crusaders* . . . .(MCA)
Scratch. . . . .(MCA)
Hard Times
James Taylor; *Dad Loves His Work* . . . . (Columbia)
Hard Times
Desert Rose Band; *Desert Rose Band* . . . .(MCA)
Hard Times
Houston Person; *Goodness* . . . .(Prestige)
Hard Times
Skip James; *Great Bluesmen At Newport-C* . . . . (Vanguard)
Hard Times
Red Clay Ramblers; *Hard Times* . . . . (Flying Fish)
Hard Times
Lacy J. Dalton; *Lacy J. Dalton's Greatest Hits* . . . . (Columbia)
Hard Times
Run-D.M.C.; *Run-D.M.C.* . . . . (Profile)
Hard Times Come Again No More
Jennifer Warnes; *Shot Through The Heart* . . . . (Arista)
Mustard's Retreat; *Home By The Morning* . . . .(Red House)
Nanci Griffith; *Other Voices, Too (A Trip Back To Bountiful)* . . . . . . (Elektra)
High Hopes And Empty Pockets
McBride & The Ride; *McBride & The Ride* . . . . (MCA)
Hit The Road Jack
Ray Charles; *Ray Charles' Greatest Hits* . . . . (Rhino)
Ray Charles-Anthology . . . . (Rhino)
Ray Charles-His Greatest Hits-#2 . . . .(Dunhill Compact Classics)
Hole In My Pocket
Ricky Van Shelton; *Loving Proof*. . . . . (Columbia)
Ricky Van Shelton-16 Biggest Hits. . . . . (Legacy)
Ricky Van Shelton-Super Hits-#2. . . . . (Columbia)
Home Sweet Home
Carl Jackson; *Songs Of The South*. . . . . (Sugar Hill)
Doc & Merle Watson; *Home Sweet Home* . . . . (Sugar Hill)
Lawrence Welk; *200 Years Of American Music* . . . .(Ranwood)
Homeless
Paul Simon; *Graceland*. . . . .(Warner Bros.)
How Can A Poor Man Stand Such Times And Live?
Blind Alfred Reed; *How Can A Poor Man Stand Such Times And
Live?* . . . . (Rounder)
Ry Cooder; *Ry Cooder* . . . . (Reprise)

Show Time . . . . (Warner Bros.)
Hubbin' It
Asleep At The Wheel featuring Huey Lewis; *Tribute To The Music Of Bob
Wills And The Texas Playboys-C* . . . . (Liberty)
Hungry Eyes
Emmylou Harris; *Mama's Hungry Eyes-Merle Haggard Tribute-C* . . . . . (Arista)
Merle Haggard; *For The Record: Merle Haggard-43 Legendary Hits* . . . .(BNA)
I Ain't Got No Home
Bob Dylan; *Tribute To Woody Guthrie-C* . . . . (Warner Bros.)
I Got Plenty O'Nuttin'
Barbra Streisand; *My Name Is Barbra, Two* . . . . (Columbia)
Cleo Laine & Ray Charles; *Porgy & Bess*. . . . . (RCA)
Ella Fitzgerald & Louis Armstrong; *Porgy & Bess* . . . . (Verve)
Original Cast; *Porgy & Bess* . . . . (MCA)
I Got You Babe
Cher with Beavis & Butt-head; *The Beavis & Butt-head
Experience-C*. . . . . (Geffen)
Sonny & Cher; *I Got You Babe* . . . . (Rhino)
The Beat Goes On-Best Of Sonny & Cher . . . . (Rhino)
UB40 & Chrissie Hynde; *Chicken Soup For The Couples Soul-C* . . . . . (Rhino)
I Miss My Homies
Master P; *Ghetto D* . . . .(No Limit/Priority)
I Wanna Get Next To You
Rose Royce; *Mellow Classics-C* . . . . (MCA Special Prod.)
Rose Royce's Greatest Hits . . . . (Whitfield)
ST/Car Wash . . . . (MCA)
I Will Buy You A New Life
Everclear; *Now That's What I Call Music!-#1-C* . . . .(Virgin)
So Much For The Afterglow . . . . (Capitol)
I Wonder If Heaven Got A Ghetto
2Pac; *R U Still Down (Remember Me)*. . . . .(Amaru/Jive)
I.O.U.
Lee Greenwood; *Lee Greenwood's Greatest Hits* . . . . (MCA)
MCA Records 30 Years Of Hits-1958-1988-C . . . . (MCA)
Somebody's Gonna Love You . . . . (MCA)
If I Didn't Have A Dime (To Play The Jukebox)
Gene Pitney; *Gene Pitney-Anthology 1961-1968* . . . . (Rhino)
Gene Pitney's Greatest Hits . . . . (Evergreen Music)
If I Didn't Have You
Randy Travis; *Randy Travis' Greatest Hits-#1* . . . . (Warner Bros.)
If I Had No Loot
Tony Toni Tone; *Sons Of Soul* . . . .(Wing)
If I Were A Rich Man
Original Cast; *Fiddler On The Roof* . . . . (RCA Victor)
If The Devil Danced (In Empty Pockets)
Joe Diffie; *A Thousand Winding Roads* . . . . (Epic)
If We Make It Through December
Merle Haggard; *A Christmas Present* . . . . (Curb)
Eleven Winners . . . .(Capitol)
Goin' Home For Christmas . . . . (Sony Music Special Prod.)
Merle Haggard-Christmas Gift . . . . (Curb)
Very Best Of Merle Haggard . . . . (Capitol)
Ike's Rap
Isaac Hayes; *The Ultimate Collection-Isaac Hayes*. . . . .(Hip-O)
Imelda
Mark Knopfler; *Golden Heart* . . . . (Warner Bros.)
In A Shanty In Old Shanty Town
Ink Spots; *Java Jive*. . . . .(Laserlight)
In The Ghetto
Elvis Presley; *Elvis Presley-Pure Gold*. . . . .(RCA)
From Elvis In Memphis . . . .(RCA)
From Memphis To Vegas/From Vegas To Memphis . . . .(RCA)
The Top Ten Hits . . . .(RCA)
Worldwide 50 Gold Award Hits, Vol. 1, Parts 1 & 2 . . . . . .(RCA)
Mac Davis; *Mac Davis' Greatest Hits*. . . . . (Columbia)
In Times Like These
Barbara Mandrell; *Barbara Mandrell's Greatest Hits* . . . . . . (MCA)
Spun Gold . . . . (MCA)
Inner City Blues (Make Me Wanna Holler)
Marvin Gaye; *What's Going On* . . . . (Motown)
Invitation To The Blues
Holly Cole; *Temptation*. . . . . (Metro Blue)
Tom Waits; *Small Change*. . . . .(Asylum)
It's The Hard-Knock Life
Original Broadway Cast; *Annie* . . . . (Columbia)
Original Cast; *ST/Annie* . . . . (Columbia)
Jesus Christ
Arlo Guthrie; *Tribute To Woody Guthrie-C* . . . . (Warner Bros.)
Cisco Houston; *Greatest Songs Of Woody Guthrie-C* . . . . . . (Vanguard)
U2; *Folkways: A Vision Shared-C*. . . . . (Columbia)
Woody Guthrie; *Woody Guthrie* . . . . (Warner Bros.)
Johnny 99
Bruce Springsteen; *Nebraska* . . . . (Columbia)
Bruce Springsteen & The E Street Band; *Bruce Springsteen & The E Street
Band Live/1975-85* . . . . (Legacy)
Johnny Cash; *Cover Me (Bruce Springsteen Tribute)-C* . . . . (Rhino)
Just Like Tom Thumb's Blues
Bob Dylan; *Highway 61 Revisited*. . . . . (Columbia)

Grateful Dead; *Terrapin Station* . . . . (Arista)
Judy Collins; *In My Life* . . . . (Elektra)
Linda Ronstadt; *We Ran* . . . . (Elektra)

King Of The Road
R.E.M.; *Dead Letter Office* . . . . (I.R.S.)
Roger Miller; *Billboard Top Country Hits-1965-C* . . . . (Rhino)
Cruisin'-1965-C . . . . (Increase)
Roger Miller-Golden Hits . . . . (Smash)

Lady Came From Baltimore
Joan Baez; *Contemporary Ballad Book* . . . . (Vanguard)
Joan . . . . (Vanguard)
John Stewart; *Neon Beach* . . . . (Homecoming)
Johnny Cash; *Johnny Cash-16 Biggest Hits-#2* . . . . (Legacy)
Tim Hardin; *Hang On To A Dream-Verve Recordings* . . . . (Polydor)

Lady Madonna
Beatles; *Beatles 1* . . . . (Capitol)
Hey Jude . . . . (Capitol)
Past Masters-Volume Two . . . . (Parlophone)
The Beatles/1967-1970 . . . . (Capitol)
Wings; *Wings Over America* . . . . (Capitol)

Lean On Me
Kirk Franklin; *The Nu Nation Project* . . . . (Gospo Centric/Interscope)

Let's Have Another Cup Of Coffee
Glenn Miller; *Complete Glenn Miller & His Orchestra-#8* . . . . (Bluebird)
Michael Feinstein; *Remember-Michael Feinstein Sings Irving Berlin* . . (Elektra)

Life Ain't Easy
Dr. Hook & The Medicine Show; *Dr. Hook At His Best* . . . . (Queen)

Life So Cruel
Charlie; *Lines* . . . . (Janus)

Like A Rolling Stone
Bob Dylan; *Biograph* . . . . (Columbia)
Bob Dylan At Budokan . . . . (Columbia)
Bob Dylan's Greatest Hits . . . . (Columbia)
Highway 61 Revisited . . . . (Columbia)
More American Graffiti-#4-C . . . . (MCA)
Self Portrait . . . . (Columbia)
Bob Dylan And The Band; *Before The Flood* . . . . (Columbia)
Jimi Hendrix; *ST/Jimi Plays Monterey* . . . . (Reprise)
Jimi Hendrix Experience; *Jimi Hendrix Experience* . . . . (Reprise)
Rolling Stones; *Stripped* . . . . (Virgin)

Little Beggar Man
Ian & Sylvia; *Ian & Sylvia's Greatest Hits* . . . . (Vanguard)
Northern Journey . . . . (Vanguard)

Little Man
Alan Jackson; *High Mileage* . . . . (Arista)

Livin' In These Troubled Times
Crystal Gayle; *Crystal Gayle Greatest Hits* . . . . (Columbia)
Hollywood, Tennessee . . . . (Columbia)

Livin' On A Prayer
Bon Jovi; *America: A Tribute To Heroes-C* . . . . (Interscope)
Cross Road-14 Classic Grooves . . . . (Mercury)
Slippery When Wet . . . . (Jambco)
The Concert For New York City-C . . . . (Columbia)

Livin' On Borrowed Time
Travis Tritt; *Down The Road I Go* . . . . (Columbia)

Living For The City
Stevie Wonder; *Innervisions* . . . . (Motown)
Original Musiquarium . . . . (Motown)

Living In The Ghetto
Toots & The Maytals; *Reggae Got Soul* . . . . (Island)

Loan Me A Dime
Boz Scaggs; *Boz Scaggs* . . . . (Atlantic)
Duane Allman-An Anthology . . . . (Capricorn)

Long Hard Road (Sharecropper's Dream)
Nitty Gritty Dirt Band; *Live Two Five* . . . . (Capitol)
Plain Dirt Fashion . . . . (Warner Bros.)
Twenty Years Of Dirt-Best Of The Nitty Gritty Dirt Band . . . . . (Warner Bros.)

Lookin' At Tomorrow
Beach Boys; *Surf's Up* . . . . (Caribou)

Lookin' In The Same Direction
Ken Mellons; *Ken Mellons* . . . . (Epic)

Love Child
Diana Ross & The Supremes; *Billboard Top Rock 'N' Roll Hits-1968-C* . . . . (Rhino)
Diana Ross & The Supremes' Greatest Hits-#3 . . . . (Motown)
Diana Ross & The Supremes-Anthology (1962-1969) . . . . (Motown)
Every Great #1 Hit . . . . (Motown)
Motown Story-First 25 Years-C . . . . (Motown)
Motown's Biggest Pop Hits-C . . . . (Motown)
Sweet Sensation; *Love Child* . . . . (Atco)

Maggie's Farm
Bob Dylan; *Bob Dylan At Budokan* . . . . (Columbia)
Bob Dylan's Greatest Hits-#2 . . . . (Columbia)
Bringing It All Back Home . . . . (Columbia)
Hard Rain . . . . (Columbia)
Real Live . . . . (Columbia)

Mama Sang A Song
Bill Anderson; *Bill Anderson's Greatest Hits* . . . . (Varese Sarabande)
Country Music Classics-#17-C . . . . (K-Tel)

Mansion In The Slums
Crowded House; *Temple Of Low Men* . . . . (Capitol)

Maria Maria
Santana; *Supernatural* . . . . (Arista)
Totally Hits-#2-C . . . . (Elektra)

Matchbox
Beatles; *Past Masters-Volume Two* . . . . (Parlophone)
Rock 'N' Roll Music . . . . (Capitol)
Something New . . . . (Capitol)

Mean Mr. Mustard
Beatles; *Abbey Road* . . . . (Parlophone)

Midnight Mary
Joey Powers; *Dick Bartley's One-Hit Wonders Of The '60s-#1-C* . . . . . . (Rhino)

Mr. Bojangles
David Bromberg; *Out Of The Blues-Best Of David Bromberg* . . . . . . (Columbia)
Jerry Jeff Walker; *A Man Must Carry On* . . . . (MCA)
Best Of Jerry Jeff Walker . . . . (MCA)
Gypsy Songman . . . . (Rykodisc)
Mr. Bojangles . . . . (Bainbridge)
Nitty Gritty Dirt Band; *Best Of The Nitty Gritty Dirt Band* . . . . . . (Liberty)
On The Road Again . . . . (Capitol)
Super Hits Of The '70s-Have A Nice Day-#4-C . . . . (Rhino)
Twenty Years Of Dirt-Best Of The Nitty Gritty Dirt Band . . . . . (Warner Bros.)
Uncle Charlie And His Dog Teddy . . . . (Liberty)

Mrs. Clara Sullivan's Letter
Pete Seeger; *Best Of Broadside 1962-1968: Anthems Of The American Underground From The Pages Of Broadside Magazine-C* . . . . (Smithsonian Folkways)

My Oklahoma Home (It Blowed Away)
Sis Cunningham; *Best Of Broadside 1962-1968: Anthems Of The American Underground From The Pages Of Broadside Magazine-C* . . . . (Smithsonian Folkways)

Nigga Out The Projects
1-5ive Posse; *Lifestyles Of The Young & Crazy* . . . . (World Export)

Nights In Harlem
Luther Vandross; *I Know* . . . . (LV/Virgin)

No Depression
Johnson Mountain Boys; *Goin' Up Copper Creek-C* . . . . (Copper Creek)
Uncle Tupelo; *No Depression* . . . . (Rockville)

No Guarantee
Chico DeBarge; *Long Time No See* . . . . (Kedar Entert./Universal)
MTV Jams-C . . . . (Kedar Entert./Universal)
ST/Hoodlum . . . . (Interscope)

No Job Blues
Ramblin' Thomas; *Ramblin' Mind Blues* . . . . (Biograph)

Nobody Knows You When You're Down And Out
Bessie Smith; *Bessie Smith-The Collection* . . . . (Legacy)
Bessie Smith-The Complete Recordings-#4 . . . . (Legacy)
Derek And The Dominos; *Layla* . . . . (Polydor)
Eric Clapton; *Eric Clapton-Unplugged* . . . . (Reprise)
Otis Redding; *Soul Album* . . . . (Atco)
Rod Stewart; *Out Of Order* . . . . (Warner Bros.)

Old Man And Me
Hootie & The Blowfish; *Fairweather Johnson* . . . . (Atlantic)

On Broadway
Drifters; *Drifters-16 Greatest Hits* . . . . (Trip)
Drifters-Golden Hits . . . . (Atlantic)
George Benson; *George Benson-Collection* . . . . (Warner Bros.)
ST/All That Jazz . . . . (Casablanca)
Weekend In L.A. . . . . (Warner Bros.)

Once Upon A Time In The Projects
Ice Cube; *AmeriKKKa's Most Wanted* . . . . (Priority)

One Room Country Shack
Buddy Guy; *Man & The Blues* . . . . (Vanguard)
My Time After Awhile . . . . (Vanguard)
Mercy Dee Walton; *Mercy's Troubles* . . . . (Arhoolie)
One Room Country Shack . . . . (Specialty)
Pity & A Shame . . . . (Prestige)
Mose Allison; *Mose Allison's Greatest Hits* . . . . (Prestige)

Only In America
Jay & The Americans; *Come A Little Bit Closer-Best Of Jay & The Americans* . . . . (Gold Rush)
Jay & The Americans' All-Time Greatest Hits . . . . (Rhino)

Outlaw's Prayer
Johnny Paycheck; *Armed & Crazy* . . . . (Epic)
Johnny Paycheck's Biggest Hits . . . . (Epic)

Papa Was A Rollin' Stone
Temptations; *20/20-C* . . . . (Motown)
25 #1 Hits From 25 Years-C . . . . (Motown)
All The Million-Sellers . . . . (Motown)
Billboard Top Rock 'N' Roll Hits-1972-C . . . . (Rhino)
Compact Command Performances-Temptations . . . . (Motown)
Temptations-Anthology-The Best Of The Temptations . . . . . (Motown)

Pits, The
Sammy Hagar; *Sammy Hagar* . . . . (Capitol)

Pittsburgh, Pennsylvania
101 Strings Orchestra; *Million-Seller Hits From Mexico* . . . . (Alshire)
Guy Mitchell; *Guy Mitchell-16 Most Requested Songs* . . . . (Legacy)

Po' Folks
Bill Anderson; *Bill Anderson's Greatest Hits*. . . . . (Varese Sarabande)
Po' White Trash
White Trash; *White Trash*. . . . . (Elektra)
Poor Boy
Howlin' Wolf; *Real Folk Blues-C*. . . . . (Chess)
Poor Boy
Royaltones; *Rock Instrumental Classics-#1-'50s-C*. . . . . (Rhino)
Poor Boy
Elvis Presley; *Essential Elvis-The First Movies* . . . . (RCA)
For LP Fans Only . . . . (RCA)
Poor Boy
Woody Guthrie; *Legendary Woody Guthrie*. . . . . (Tradition)
Woody Guthrie. . . . . (Everest)
Worried Man Blues-Golden Classics-#1 . . . . (Collectables)
Poor Boy
Split Enz; *History Never Repeats-Best Of Split Enz* . . . . (A&M)
True Colours . . . . (A&M)
Poor Boy
Nick Drake; *Bryter Layter* . . . . (Hannibal)
Fruit Tree . . . . (Hannibal)
Poor Boy
Champion Jack Dupree; *Forever & Ever* . . . . (Bullseye Blues)
Poor Boy
Supertramp; *Crisis? What Crisis?* . . . . (A&M)
Poor Boy
Fabulous Thunderbirds; *T-Bird Rhythm* . . . .(Chrysalis)
Poor Boy Blues
Chet Atkins & Mark Knopfler; *Neck And Neck*. . . . . (Columbia)
Poor Boy Shuffle
Creedence Clearwater Revival; *1969* . . . . (Fantasy)
Willy & The Poor Boys. . . . . (Fantasy)
Poor Howard
Leadbelly; *Gwine Dig A Hole To Put The Devil In* . . . . (Rounder)
Leadbelly. . . . . (Everest)
Leadbelly. . . . . (Fantasy)
Memorial-#4 . . . . (Stinson)
Poor Immigrant
Judy Collins; *Who Knows Where The Time Goes* . . . . (Elektra)
Poor Jenny
Everly Brothers; *All They Had To Do Was Dream* . . . . (Rhino)
Everly Brothers . . . . (Rhino)
Fabulous Style Of The Everly Brothers . . . . (Rhino)
Poor Little Jimmie
Burl Ives; *Best Of Burl Ives-#2*. . . . .(MCA)
Poor Little Rich Girl
Count Basie & Tony Bennett; *Basie Swings Bennett Sings*. . . . (Roulette)
Judy Garland; *Best Of Judy Garland* . . . . (MCA)
Poor Little Rich Girl
Uriah Heep; *Equator*. . . . . (Columbia)
Poor Little Rich Girl
Romantics; *National Breakout* . . . . (Nemperor)
Poor Man
Tom Rush; *Tom Rush* . . . . (Elektra)
Poor Man's Roses (Or A Rich Man's Gold)
Patsy Cline; *Best Of Patsy Cline*. . . . . (Curb)
Forever & Always . . . .(Epic)
Stop, Look & Listen . . . . (MCA)
The Patsy Cline Story. . . . . (MCA)
Reba McEntire; *Feel The Fire* . . . . (Mercury)
Poor Man's Son
Rockin' Berries; *History Of British Rock-#2-C* . . . . (Rhino)
Poor People
Alan Price; *ST/O Lucky Man*. . . . .(Warner Bros.)
Poor People Of Paris
Les Baxter & His Orchestra; *Memories Are Made Of This-C* . . . . (Capitol)
Poor Red Georgia Dirt
Robin & Linda Williams; *Close As We Can Get* . . . . (Flying Fish)
Poor Side Of Town
Johnny Rivers; *Best Of Johnny Rivers* . . . .(EMI)
Changes/Rewind . . . .(EMI)
Johnny Rivers-Anthology 1964-1977. . . . . (Rhino)
Very Best Of Johnny Rivers . . . .(EMI)
Poor Wayfaring Stranger
Jim Hendricks; *Appalachian Memories-Front Porch Favorites*. . . . . . . (Benson)
Jo Stafford; *American Folk Songs*. . . . .(Corinthian)
Poverty
Bobby Bland; *Best Of Bobby Bland* . . . . (MCA)
Poverty Train
Laura Nyro; *Eli And The Thirteenth Confession*. . . . . (Columbia)
Rag Doll
4 Seasons; *25th Anniversary Collection* . . . . (Rhino)
4 Seasons' Greatest Hits-#2. . . . . (Rhino)
4 Seasons-Anthology . . . . (Rhino)
Billboard Top Rock 'N' Roll Hits-1964-C . . . . (Rhino)
Rags To Riches
Kool & The Gang; *Everything Is-Greatest Hits* . . . . (Mercury)

Rags To Riches
Tony Bennett; *Tony Bennett-16 Most Requested Songs* . . . . (Legacy)
Tony Bennett's All-Time Greatest Hits. . . . . (Columbia)
Tony Bennett & Percy Faith & His Orchestra; *Radio Classics Of The
'50s-C* . . . . (Columbia)
Rags To Riches
Electric Boys; *Funk-O-Metal Carpet Ride* . . . . (Atco)
Rags To Riches
John Scofield; *Shinola*. . . . . (Enja)
Raised In The Alley Blues
Freddy Brown; *Barrelhouse Mamas: Born In The Alley, Raised In The
Slums-C* . . . .(Yazoo)
Ramblin' Hobo
Doc Watson; *Don Watson & Family-Treasures Untold* . . . . (Vanguard)
Essential Doc Watson. . . . . (Vanguard)
Old Time Music At Newport . . . . (Vanguard)
Watson Family; *Watson Family* . . . .(Smithsonian Folkways)
Ramshackle Shack
Doc Watson; *Riding That Midnight Train*. . . . .(Sugar Hill)
Rich & Poor
Randy Crawford; *Rich & Poor* . . . . (Warner Bros.)
Rich Kind Of Poverty
Sam & Dave; *Soul Men* . . . . (Rhino)
Rich Man Poor Man
Peter, Paul & Mary; *Late Again*. . . . . (Warner Bros.)
Rich Man, Poor Boy
Joe Ely; *Dig All Night* . . . .(Hightone)
Royal Scam
Steely Dan; *The Royal Scam* . . . . (MCA)
Saginaw, Michigan
Lefty Frizzell; *American Originals-Lefty Frizzell*. . . . . (Columbia)
Billboard Top Country Hits-1964-C . . . . (Rhino)
Columbia Country Classics-#3-Americana-C . . . . (Columbia)
Lefty Frizzell's Greatest Hits . . . . (Columbia)
Sail Away
Linda Ronstadt; *Don't Cry Now* . . . .(Asylum)
Randy Newman; *Guilty: 30 Years Of Randy Newman* . . . . . . (Rhino)
Sail Away . . . . (Reprise)
Santa I'm Right Here
Toby Keith; *Christmas To Christmas* . . . .(Polydor Country)
Second Hand Rose
Barbra Streisand; *A Happening In Central Park* . . . . (Columbia)
Barbra Streisand...and other musical instruments. . . . . (Columbia)
Barbra Streisand's Greatest Hits . . . . (Columbia)
Just For The Record . . . . (Columbia)
My Name Is Barbra, Two . . . . (Columbia)
She's Just A Drifter
Marty Robbins; *El Paso City*. . . . . (Columbia)
Marty Robbins' Biggest Hits . . . . (Columbia)
Simple Days
Babyface; *The Day* . . . . (Epic)
Six Pack To Go, A
Hank Thompson and His Brazos Valley Boys; *Best Of The Best Of Hank
Thompson* . . . . (Gusto)
Capitol Collectors Series-Hank Thompson . . . . (Capitol)
Country Comes To Carnegie Hall-C . . . . (MCA)
Hank Thompson . . . . (Dot)
Hank Thompson's Greatest Hits-#2 . . . .(Step One)
Sixteen Tons
Cactus Brothers; *Cactus Brothers* . . . . (Liberty)
Tennessee Ernie Ford; *Best Of Tennessee Ernie Ford-16 Tons Of
Boogie* . . . . (Rhino)
Capitol Collectors Series-Tennessee Ernie Ford . . . . (Capitol)
When AM Was King-C . . . . (Capitol)
Weavers; *Weavers' Greatest Hits* . . . . (Vanguard)
Skid Row
Original Cast; *Little Shop Of Horrors* . . . . (Geffen)
Skid Row
Herman Brood; *Herman Brood & His Wild Romance*. . . . . . .(Ariola America)
Skid Row Joe
Porter Wagoner; *Best Of Porter Wagoner-#1* . . . . (RCA)
Porter Wagoner's Greatest . . . . (Tudor)
Some Bridges
Jackson Browne; *Looking East* . . . . (Elektra)
Son Of A Poor Man
REO Speedwagon; *A Decade Of Rock And Roll 1970 To 1980* . . . . (Epic)
REO Speedwagon Live/You Get What You Play For . . . . (Epic)
Ridin' The Storm Out . . . . (Epic)
Son Of Hickory Holler's Tramp
O.C. Smith; *Me And You* . . . . (Columbia Special Prod.)
Story Songs-C . . . . (K-Tel)
Spanish Harlem
Aretha Franklin; *Aretha Franklin-30 Greatest Hits* . . . . (Rhino)
Best Of Aretha Franklin . . . .(Atlantic)
Ten Years Of Gold . . . .(Atlantic)
Ben E. King; *Ben E. King's Greatest Hits* . . . . (Atco)
Phil Spector-Back To Mono 1958-1969-C . . . .(Abkco)
Crusaders; *Crusaders-At Their Best* . . . . (Motown)
Drifters; *Drifters' Greatest Hits* . . . . (Gusto)

Standing On The Corner
Broadway Cast; *Most Happy Fella* . . . . (RCA)
Dean Martin; *Best Of Dean Martin* . . . . (CEMA Special Prod.)
Four Lads; *Four Lads-16 Most Requested Songs* . . . . (Legacy)
Original Broadway Cast; *Most Happy Fella* . . . . (Sony Music Classical)

Stray Cat Strut
Stray Cats; *Best Of Stray Cats-Rock This Town* . . . . (EMI)
Built For Speed . . . . (EMI)
Rock The First-#4-C . . . . (Sandstone Music)

Street Fighting Man
Rod Stewart; *Best Of Rod Stewart* . . . . (Mercury)
Sing It Again, Rod . . . . (Mercury)
Storyteller/The Complete Anthology: 1964-1990 . . . . . . (Warner Bros.)
Rolling Stones; *Beggars Banquet* . . . . (Abkco)
Get Yer Ya-Ya's Out! . . . . (Abkco)
Hot Rocks 1964-1971 . . . . (Abkco)
Singles Collection-The London Years . . . . (Abkco)
Through The Past, Darkly (Big Hits Vol. 2) . . . . (Abkco)

Street Man Named Desire
Pirates Of The Mississippi; *Street Man Named Desire* . . . . (Liberty)

Struggling Man
Jimmy Cliff; *In Concert-Best Of Jimmy Cliff* . . . . (Reprise)
Struggling Man . . . . (Island)

Teenage Immigrant Welfare Mothers On Drugs
Austin Lounge Lizards; *Live Bait* . . . . (Sugar Hill)

Theme From "Good Times"
Original Soundtrack; *CBS: The First 50 Years* . . . . (TVT)
Television's Greatest Hits-#3-1970s & 1980s-C . . . . (TVT)

Theme From "The Waltons"
Original Soundtrack; *CBS: The First 50 Years* . . . . (TVT)
Television's Greatest Hits-#3-1970s & 1980s-C . . . . (TVT)

Third World Child
Johnny Clegg & Savuka; *Sounds Of Soweto* . . . . (Capitol)
Third World Child . . . . (Capitol)

This Part Of Town
Widespread Panic; *Don't Tell The Band* . . . . (Widespread/SRG)

This Uncivil War
Martina McBride; *Emotion* . . . . (RCA)

To Hell With Poverty!
Gang Of Four; *Brief History Of The Twentieth Century* . . . . (Warner Bros.)

Too Broke To Spend The Night
Buddy Guy; *Damn Right, I've Got The Blues* . . . . (Silvertone)

Too Much Month At The End Of The Money
Billy Hill; *I Am Just A Rebel* . . . . (Reprise)

Top Of The World
Brandy featuring Mase; *Never Say Never* . . . . (Atlantic)

Town Without Pity
Gene Pitney; *Gene Pitney-Anthology 1961-1968* . . . . (Rhino)
ST/*Hairspray* . . . . (MCA Special Prod.)
WCBS FM 101 History Of Rock-'60s-#3-C . . . . (Collectables)

Tramp
Otis Redding; *Best Of Otis Redding* . . . . (Atco)
The Otis Redding Story . . . . (Atlantic)

Tramp
Salt-N-Pepa; *Blitz Of Salt-N-Pepa Hits* . . . . (London)
Hot Cool & Vicious . . . . (London)

Tramp
Cisco Houston; *Don't Mourn-Organize-Songs Of Joe Hill-C* . . . . (Smithsonian Folkways)

Tramp
Lowell Fulsom; *Soul Shots-#4-Urban Blues-C* . . . . (Rhino)

Tropicalia
Beck; *Mutations* . . . . (David Geffen Co.)

Twentieth Century Drifter
Marty Robbins; *Best Of Marty Robbins* . . . . (Curb)

Two Sparrows In A Hurricane
Tanya Tucker; *Can't Run From Yourself* . . . . (Liberty)
Tanya Tucker's Greatest Hits-1990-1992 . . . . (Capitol)

UFO Has Landed In The Ghetto
Ry Cooder; *The Slide Area* . . . . (Warner Bros.)

Uptight (Everything's Alright)
Stevie Wonder; *16 #1 Hits From The Early '60s-C* . . . . (Motown)
Looking Back . . . . (Motown)
Motown Dance Party-#1-C . . . . (Motown)
Motown Legends-Stevie Wonder . . . . (Motown)
Stevie Wonder's Greatest Hits . . . . (Motown)
Uptight (Everything's Alright) . . . . (Motown)

Us & Them
Pink Floyd; *Dark Side Of The Moon* . . . . (Capitol)
Delicate Sound Of Thunder . . . . (Columbia)
Pink Floyd-Gift Set . . . . (Capitol)
Shine On . . . . (Columbia)

Used Cars
Bruce Springsteen; *Nebraska* . . . . (Columbia)

Vagabond Virgin
Traffic; *Traffic* . . . . (Island)

Victim Of The Ghetto
College Boyz; *Radio Fusion Radio* . . . . (Virgin)

Village Ghetto Land
Stevie Wonder; *Songs In The Key Of Life* . . . . (Motown)

Waitin' In Your Welfare Line
Buck Owens & The Buckaroos; *Billboard Top Country Hits-1966-C* . . . . (Rhino)
Buck Owens & The Buckaroos-Live At Carnegie Hall . . . . (Country Music Foundation)
Buck Owens Collection-1959-1990 . . . . (Rhino)

Walking To New Orleans
Fats Domino; *Fats Domino's All Time Greatest Hits* . . . . (Curb)
Fats Domino's Greatest Hits . . . . (CEMA Special Prod.)
Fats Domino's Greatest Hits . . . . (MCA)
My Blue Heaven-Best Of Fats Domino-#1 . . . . (EMI)
They Call Me The Fat Man . . . . (EMI)

Wanderer
Dion; *20 Million-Dollar Memories-#1-C* . . . . (Laurie)
Billboard Top Rock 'N' Roll Hits-1962-C . . . . (Rhino)
Cruisin'-1962-C . . . . (Increase)
Oldies But Goodies-#5-C . . . . (Original Sound)
ST/*The Wanderers* . . . . (Warner Bros.)
The Wanderer . . . . (Laurie)

Wandering
James Taylor; *Gorilla* . . . . (Warner Bros.)

Welfare Cadillac
Gary B.B. Coleman; *Too Much Weekend* . . . . (Ichiban Int'l)

What It's Like
Everlast; *Whitey Ford Sings The Blues* . . . . (Tommy Boy)

What Would You Do?
City High; *City High* . . . . (Interscope)
Now That's What I Call Music!-#7-C . . . . (Virgin)
ST/*Life* . . . . (Rock Land/Interscope)

What You Want
Mase Featuring Total; *Harlem World* . . . . (Bad Boy/Arista)

Working Man Can't Get Nowhere Today
Merle Haggard; *18 Rare Classics* . . . . (Curb)
Merle Haggard & The Strangers; *Working Man Can't Get Nowhere Today* . . . . (Capitol)

World Is A Ghetto
George Benson; *In Flight* . . . . (Warner Bros.)
War; *Best Of War...And More-#2* . . . . (Avenue)
The Music Band . . . . (MCA)
The Music Band 2 . . . . (MCA)
The World Is A Ghetto . . . . (Avenue)
War-Anthology (1970-1994) . . . . (Avenue)

You Got What It Takes
Dave Clark Five; *History Of The Dave Clark Five* . . . . (Hollywood)
Marv Johnson; *All-Time Greatest Hits Of Rock 'N' Roll-C* . . . . (Curb)

POWER & CONTROL, Authority, Force

See Also: **BOSSES, BUSINESS & INDUSTRY, EGO, ENERGY, KINGS, LAW & ORDER, MACHINES, MONEY, MOTIVATION, POLICE, POLITICS (various), QUEENS, ROYALTY, SOCIAL CLASS: GENERAL, STRONG, STUCK**

All I Want
Offspring; *Ixnay On The Hombre* . . . . (Columbia)

An Acceptable Level Of Ecstasy (The Wedding Song)
Lyle Lovett; *Lyle Lovett* . . . . (MCA)

Another Brick In The Wall, Part 2
Class Of '99; ST/*The Faculty* . . . . (Columbia)
Pink Floyd; *Collection Of Great Dance Songs* . . . . (Columbia)
Delicate Sound Of Thunder . . . . (Columbia)
The Wall . . . . (Columbia)
Roger Waters; *The Wall-Live In Berlin* . . . . (Mercury)

Badlands
Bruce Springsteen; *Bruce Springsteen's Greatest Hits* . . . . (Columbia)
Darkness On The Edge Of Town . . . . (Columbia)
Bruce Springsteen & The E Street Band; *Bruce Springsteen & The E Street Band Live/1975-85* . . . . (Legacy)

Barbie Girl
Aqua; *Aquarium* . . . . (MCA)
Now That's What I Call Music!-#1-C . . . . (Virgin)

Bend Me, Shape Me
American Breed; *The Ultimate History Of Rock 'N' Roll-#7-C* . . . . (K-Tel)

Birth Control
Lloyd Charmers; *Reggae Chartbusters-#2-C* . . . . (Metronome)
Wonderful World, Beautiful People-C . . . . (Recall)

Birth Control
Crass; *Christ: The Album/Well Forked But Not Dead* . . . . (Crass)

Bitch
Rolling Stones; *Made In The Shade* . . . . (Rolling Stones)
Sticky Fingers . . . . (Virgin)

Boys
Britney Spears; *Britney* . . . . (Jive)

Breakdown
Mariah Carey featuring Bone Thugs-N-Harmony; *Butterfly* . . . . (Columbia)

Breakdown
Tantric; *Tantric*. . . . .(Maverick)
Butterflyz
Alicia Keys; *Songs In A Minor* . . . . (J)
Can't Tame The Lion
Journey; *Trial By Fire*. . . . . (Columbia)
Casual Affair
Tonic; *Lemon Parade* . . . . (Polydor)
Chains
Tina Arena; *Don't Ask* . . . .(Epic)
Complete Control
Clash; *The Clash* . . . . (Legacy)
The Story Of The Clash, Volume 1 . . . .(Epic)
Computer Power
Jamie Jupitor; *Electro Funk-#2-C*. . . . . (Priority)
Street Jams-Electric Funk-#4-C . . . . (Rhino)
Control
Janet Jackson; *Control* . . . . (A&M)
Control
Stabbing Westward; *Ungod* . . . . (Columbia)
Control
Puddle Of Mudd; *Come Clean* . . . . (Flawless/Geffen/Interscope)
Controlled By Hatred
Suicidal Tendencies; *Controlled By Hatred/Feel Like Shit...Deja Vu* . . . . .(Epic)
Controller
Oingo Boingo; *Only A Lad* . . . . (A&M)
Crawling
Linkin Park; *Hybrid Theory* . . . .(Warner Bros.)
Cruise Control
Bruce Hornsby; *Hot House* . . . . (RCA)
Day After Day
Def Leppard; *Euphoria*. . . . . (Mercury)
Dead Bodies Everywhere
Korn; *Follow The Leader* . . . .(Immortal/Epic)
Don't Let Go (Love)
En Vogue; *Best Of En Vogue* . . . . (Elektra)
EV3 . . . . (East West)
Drive
Incubus; *Make Yourself* . . . . (Immortal/Epic)
Now That's What I Call Music!-#6-C . . . . (Virgin)
Everything To Everyone
Everclear; *Ka-Boom!-C* . . . . (Beast)
So Much For The Afterglow . . . . (Capitol)
Fast As You
Dwight Yoakam; *This Time* . . . . (Reprise)
Fiction (Dreams In Digital)
Orgy; *Vapor Transmission* . . . . (Elementree/Reprise)
Fight The Power
Isley Brothers; *Forever Gold* . . . . (T-Neck/Columbia)
Heat Is On . . . . (T-Neck/Columbia)
Isley Brothers' Greatest Hits . . . . (T-Neck/Columbia)
The Isley Brothers Story-#2-The T-Neck Years-1969-1985 . . . . (Rhino)
Fight The Power
Public Enemy; *Def Jam Classics-#2-C*. . . . .(Def Jam)
Fear Of A Black Planet . . . . (Def Jam)
ST/Do The Right Thing . . . . (Motown)
Final Hour
Lauryn Hill; *The Miseducation Of Lauryn Hill*. . . . . (Ruffhouse/Columbia)
Free
Vast; *Music For People* . . . . (Elektra)
Giving In
Adema; *Adema*. . . . . (Arista)
Go Deep
Janet Jackson; *Velvet Rope* . . . . (Virgin)
Got You (Where I Want You)
Flys; *Holiday Man* . . . .(Delicious Vinyl)
ST/Disturbing Behavior . . . . (Trauma)
Greed
Godsmack; *Awake* . . . .(Republic/Universal)
High And The Mighty
Les Baxter & His Orchestra; *Instrumental Gems Of The
'50s-C* . . . . (Collector's Choice)
Roger Williams; *Roger Williams' Greatest Hits*. . . . . (Curb)
Victor Young & His Orchestra; *Hard To Find Orchestral
Instrumentals-C* . . . . (Eric)
Victor Young & His Singing Strings; *Billboard Top Movie Hits-1950-
1954-C* . . . . (Rhino)
High Powered Love
Emmylou Harris; *Cowgirl's Prayer* . . . . (Asylum)
I Cain't Say No
Original Broadway Cast; *Oklahoma!* . . . . (RCA)
Original Cast; *Oklahoma!* . . . .(MCA)
I Can't Control Myself
Troggs; *Archeology-1967-1977* . . . . (Polydor)
I Got Id
Pearl Jam; *Merkinball*. . . . .(Epic)
I Have Learned To Respect The Power Of Love
Angela Winbush; *Real Thing* . . . . (Mercury)

Stephanie Mills; *Stephanie Mills*. (MCA)
I Used To Love Him
Lauryn Hill featuring Mary J. Blige; *The Miseducation Of
Lauryn Hill* . . . . (Ruffhouse/Columbia)
I Wanna Grow Up To Be A Politician
Byrds; *20 Essential Tracks From The Box Set*. . . . . (Columbia)
Best Of The Byrds-Greatest Hits-#2 . . . . (Columbia)
Byrdmaniax . . . . (Columbia)
The Byrds . . . . (Columbia)
If I Wanted To
Melissa Etheridge; *Yes I Am* . . . . (Island)
I'm A Slave 4 U
Britney Spears; *Britney* . . . .(Jive)
I'm Gonna Wash That Man Right Outta My Hair
Mitzi Gaynor; *ST/South Pacific* . . . .(RCA)
Original Cast; *South Pacific* . . . . (CBS Masterworks)
Weather Girls; *Success* . . . . (Columbia)
I'm Your Puppet
James & Bobby Purify; *Oldies But Goodies-#12-C* . . . .(Original Sound)
Soul Shots-#5-La-La Means I Love You-C . . . . (Rhino)
Sweet & Soulful '60s-C . . . . (K-Tel)
It's Not Up To You
Bjork; *Vespertine* . . . . (Elektra)
Keep A Lid On Things
Crash Test Dummies; *Give Yourself A Hand*. . . . . (Arista)
Let The Beat Control Your Body
2 Unlimited; *No Limits* . . . . (Critique)
Life Gets Away
Clint Black; *Clint Black-The Greatest Hits* . . . . (RCA)
One Emotion. . . . . (RCA)
Like There Ain't No Yesterday
BlackHawk; *Strong Enough* . . . . (Arista)
The Hits-Love & Gravity . . . . (Arista)
Links On The Chain
Broadside Singers & Phil Ochs; *Best Of Broadside 1962-1968: Anthems
Of The American Underground From The Pages Of Broadside
Magazine-C* . . . . (Smithsonian Folkways)
Lock And Load
Bob Seger; *It's A Mystery* . . . . (Capitol)
Looking East
Jackson Browne; *Looking East* . . . . (Elektra)
Love Is In Control (Finger On The Trigger)
Donna Summer; *Donna Summer* . . . . (Geffen)
Love Is The Power
Michael Bolton; *This Is The Time-The Christmas Album* . . . . (Columbia)
Love Power
Sand Pebbles; *Dick Bartley Presents On The Radio-#4-C* . . . . . .(VSI)
Love T.K.O.
Bette Midler; *Bette* . . . . (Warner Bros.)
Magic Power
Triumph; *Allied Forces* . . . . (RCA)
Stages . . . . (MCA)
Triumph-Classics . . . . (MCA)
Make Me Lose Control
Eric Carmen; *Best Of Eric Carmen* . . . . (Arista)
Dirty Dancing Live In Concert-C . . . . (RCA)
Man At The Top
Bruce Springsteen; *Tracks* . . . . (Columbia)
Man Who Sold The World
David Bowie; *Man Who Sold The World*. . . . . (Rykodisc)
Sound + Vision . . . . (Rykodisc)
Nirvana; *MTV Unplugged In New York*. . . . . (David Geffen Co.)
Mind Control
Slayer; *Divine Intervention* . . . . (American)
N.I.B.
Primus with Ozzy; *Nativity In Black II: Tribute To Black
Sabbath-C* . . . . (Divine/Priority)
New Attitude
Patti LaBelle; *Classic Soul-C* . . . . (MCA)
I Am Woman-C. . . . . (Nick At Nite)
Soundtrack Smashes-'80s & More-C . . . . (MCA)
ST/Beverly Hills Cop . . . . (MCA)
No Control
Eddie Money; *Eddie Money's Greatest Hits-Sound Of Money* . . . . . . (Columbia)
No Control . . . . (Columbia)
No Control
311; *Transistor* . . . . (Capricorn)
No Control
Bad Religion; *All Ages* . . . . (Epitaph)
No Control . . . . (Epitaph)
No Man's Woman
Sinead O'Connor; *Faith & Courage* . . . .(Atlantic)
No Self-Control
Peter Gabriel; *Peter Gabriel* . . . . (Geffen)
Out Of Control
Jefferson Starship; *Winds Of Change* . . . . (Grunt)
Out Of Control
Rolling Stones; *Bridges To Babylon* . . . .(Virgin)

Out Of Control
Oingo Boingo; *Best O' Boingo* . . . . (MCA)
Out Of Control
U2; *Boy* . . . . (Island)
Out Of Control
Judy Collins; *Bread & Roses* . . . . (Elektra)
Out Of Control
Ted Nugent; *Cat Scratch Fever* . . . . (Epic)
Out Of Control
Saxon; *Denim & Leather* . . . . (Capitol)
Out Of Control
Eagles; *Desperado* . . . . (Asylum)
Out Of Control
Todd Rundgren; *Hermit Of Mink Hollow* . . . . (Rhino)
Out Of Control
Tribe After Tribe; *Tribe After Tribe* . . . . (Megaforce)
Out Of Control
Squeeze; *U.K. Squeeze* . . . . (A&M)
Out Of Control
George Jones; *Very Best Of George Jones* . . . . (Epic)
P Control
Prince; *The Gold Experience* . . . . (NPG)
Power
Temptations; *Temptations-25th Anniversary* . . . . (Motown)
Temptations-Anthology-The Best Of The Temptations . . . . (Motown)
Power
Almighty; *Blood Fire & Love* . . . . (Polydor)
Power
Earth, Wind & Fire; *Eternal Dance* . . . . (Columbia)
Last Days & Time . . . . (Columbia)
Power
Rainbow; *Finyl Vinyl* . . . . (Mercury)
Straight Between The Eyes . . . . (Mercury)
Power
Ice-T; *Power* . . . . (Sire)
Power
Holly Near; *Speed Of Light* . . . . (Redwood)
Power & The Glory
Phil Ochs; *Chords Of Fame* . . . . (A&M)
There But For Fortune . . . . (Elektra)
Power & The Glory
Wee Papa Girls; *Be Aware* . . . . (Jive)
Power & The Glory
Limeliters; *Harmony!* . . . . (Folk Era)
We The People-C . . . . (Folk Era)
Power & The Glory
Jimmy Cliff; *Power & The Glory* . . . . (Columbia)
Power & The Glory
Twisted Sister; *You Can't Stop Rock 'N' Roll* . . . . (Atlantic)
Power & The Passion
Midnight Oil; *10-9-8-7-6-5-4-3-2-1* . . . . (Columbia)
Power Age
Triumph; *Allied Forces* . . . . (RCA)
Power In The Blood
Weary Hearts; *By Heart* . . . . (Flying Fish)
Power In The Darkness
Tom Robinson Band; *Power In The Darkness* . . . . (Harvest)
Power Inside Of Me
Richard Marx; *ST/The Mirror Has Two Faces* . . . . (Columbia)
Power Of God
L.L. Cool J; *Mama Said Knock You Out* . . . . (Def Jam)
Power Of Gold
Dan Fogelberg; *Live-Greetings From The West* . . . . (Full Moon)
Dan Fogelberg & Tim Weisberg; *Dan Fogelberg/Greatest Hits* . . . . (Full Moon)
Twin Sons Of Different Mothers . . . . (Full Moon)
Power Of Good-Bye
Madonna; *GHV2* . . . . (Warner Bros.)
Ray Of Light . . . . (Maverick)
Power Of Love
Charley Pride; *Charley Pride's Greatest Hits-#2* . . . . (RCA)
Power Of Love . . . . (RCA)
Power Of Love
Celine Dion; *All The Way...A Decade Of Song* . . . . (550 Music)
The Colour Of My Love . . . . (550 Music)
Power Of Love
Air Supply; *Air Supply* . . . . (Arista)
Power Of Love
T. Graham Brown; *Brilliant Conversationalist* . . . . (Capitol)
Power Of Love
Trixter; *Hear!* . . . . (MCA)
Power Of Love
Jennifer Rush; *Jennifer Rush* . . . . (Epic)
Power Of Love
Nana Mouskouri; *Nana* . . . . (Philips)
Only Love-Very Best Of Nana Mouskouri . . . . (Rhino)
Power Of Love
Lee Roy Parnell; *On The Road* . . . . (Arista)

Power Of Love
Luther Vandross; *Power Of Love* . . . . (Epic)
Power Of Love
Huey Lewis and the News; *ST/Back To The Future* . . . . (MCA)
Power Of Love
Laura Branigan; *Touch* . . . . (Atlantic)
Power Of Love
T Bone Burnett; *Truth Decay* . . . . (Takoma)
Power Of Love
Deee-Lite; *World Clique* . . . . (Elektra)
Power Of My Love
Elvis Presley; *From Elvis In Memphis* . . . . (RCA)
Memphis Record . . . . (RCA)
Power Of Positive Drinkin'
Mickey Gilley; *Mickey Gilley's Biggest Hits* . . . . (Epic)
Ten Years Of Hits . . . . (Epic)
Power Of The Press
Angelic Upstarts; *Brighton Bomb* . . . . (Charisma)
Power Of Two
Indigo Girls; *Swamp Ophelia* . . . . (Epic)
Power To The People
John Lennon; *Lennon* . . . . (Capitol)
John Lennon/Plastic Ono Band; *Shaved Fish* . . . . (Capitol)
Power Trip
Defiance; *Beyond Recognition* . . . . (Roadrunner)
Power, The
Snap!; *ST/Hangin' With The Homeboys* . . . . (Luke)
World Power . . . . (Arista)
Power, The
Alias; *Alias* . . . . (EMI)
Power, The
Chill Rob G; *Rap Attack-C* . . . . (K-Tel)
Power Jam featuring Chill Rob G; *Best Of '90s Dance Music-#1-Hip
House-C* . . . . (PWL America)
Power, The
Jeffrey Osborne; *Don't Stop* . . . . (A&M)
Power, The
Amy Grant; *House Of Love* . . . . (A&M)
Power, The
Warrant; *ST/Gladiator* . . . . (Columbia)
Powerful People
Gino Vannelli; *Best Of Gino Vannelli* . . . . (A&M)
Gino Vannelli-Classics-#7 . . . . (A&M)
Powerful People . . . . (A&M)
Powerful Thing
Trisha Yearwood; *Where Your Road Leads* . . . . (MCA)
Powerman
Kinks; *Lola Versus Powerman And The Moneygoround, Part One* . . . . (Reprise)
Push Me, Pull Me
Pearl Jam; *Yield* . . . . (Epic)
Radio Control
Mick Jagger; *Primitive Cool* . . . . (Columbia)
Real World
Matchbox Twenty; *Yourself Or Someone Like You* . . . . (Lava)
Remote Control
Beastie Boys; *Hello Nasty* . . . . (Grand Royal)
Remote Control
Clash; *The Clash* . . . . (Legacy)
Rose Is Still A Rose
Aretha Franklin; *A Rose Is Still A Rose* . . . . (Arista)
Run Away
Real McCoy; *Another Night* . . . . (Arista)
Self Control
Laura Branigan; *Hit Singles-1980-1988-C* . . . . (Atlantic)
Self Control . . . . (Atlantic)
Set The Controls For The Heart Of The Sun
Pink Floyd; *Nice Pair* . . . . (Capitol)
Saucerful Of Secrets . . . . (Capitol)
Ummagumma . . . . (Capitol)
Works . . . . (Capitol)
She
Green Day; *Dookie* . . . . (Reprise)
She's Lost Control
Joy Division; *Substance* . . . . (Qwest)
Sign Of The Times
Queensryche; *Hear In The Now Frontier* . . . . (Virgin)
Strength Of A Woman
Carpenters; *Made In America* . . . . (A&M)
Stupify
Disturbed; *The Sickness* . . . . (Giant)
Superman
R.E.M.; *Life's Rich Pageant* . . . . (EMI-Capitol Entert. Properties)
Sway
Rolling Stones; *Sticky Fingers* . . . . (Virgin)
Take Control
Culture Club; *Kissing To Be Clever* . . . . (Virgin)
Tap Into The Power
Suicidal Tendencies; *Art Of Rebellion* . . . . (Epic)

Thing Called Love
Johnny Cash; *Johnny Cash-16 Biggest Hits-#2* . . . . (Legacy)
The Man In Black-His Greatest Hits . . . . (Legacy)
This Lil' Game We Play
Subway; *Good Times* . . . . (Biv 10/Motown)
This Time Around
Michael Jackson; *HIStory: Past, Present And Future-Book 1-C* . . . .(Epic)
'Til I Gain Control Again
Crystal Gayle; *Best Of Crystal Gayle* . . . .(Warner Bros.)
True Love . . . . (Elektra)
Emmylou Harris; *Elite Hotel* . . . . (Reprise)
Rodney Crowell; *Rodney Crowell* . . . .(Warner Bros.)
Rodney Crowell-Collection . . . .(Warner Bros.)
Willie Nelson; *Greatest Hits (& Some That Will Be)* . . . . (Columbia)
Willie Nelson & Waylon Jennings; *Take It To The Limit* . . . . (Columbia)
Willie & Family Live . . . . (Columbia)
Willie Nelson & Waylon Jennings' Greatest Hits . . . . (Columbia)
Torn
Creed; *My Own Prison* . . . . (Wind-up)
Touch Me Tease Me
Case Featuring Foxy Brown; *Case* . . . .(Def Jam/RAL/Mercury)
Def Jam Greatest Hits-C . . . . (Def Jam)
ST/The Nutty Professor . . . . (Def Jam)
Ultimate Hip Hop Party-1998-C . . . . (Arista)
Uncontrollable Urge
Devo; *Live-The Mongoloid Years* . . . .(Rykodisc)
Understanding
Candlebox; *Lucy* . . . .(Maverick)
Use The Force
Jamiroquai; *Traveling Without Moving* . . . . (Work/Epic)
Wag The Dog
Mark Knopfler; *ST/Wag The Dog* . . . . (Mercury)
We R In Control
Neil Young; *Trans* . . . .(Geffen)
When It Hurts So Bad
Lauryn Hill; *The Miseducation Of Lauryn Hill* . . . . (Ruffhouse/Columbia)
Woman (Sensuous Woman)
Don Gibson; *Don Gibson-18 Greatest Hits* . . . . (Curb)
Mark Chesnutt; *Almost Goodbye* . . . .(MCA)
World Leader Pretend
R.E.M.; *Green* . . . .(Warner Bros.)
Wrapped Around
Brad Paisley; *Brad Paisley-Part II* . . . . (Arista)
Wrapped Around Your Finger
Police; *Every Breath You Take-The Classics* . . . . (A&M)
Message In A Box-Complete Recordings . . . . (A&M)
Police-Live . . . . (A&M)
Synchronicity . . . . (A&M)
Wrapped Around Your Finger
Dan Hill; *I'm Doing Fine* . . . . (Spontaneous)
You Don't Own Me
Joan Jett; *Bad Reputation* . . . .(Blackheart)
Lesley Gore; *Billboard Top Pop Hits-1964-C* . . . . (Rhino)
You Got The Power
Esquires; *Chi-Town Show Down* . . . . (Solid Smoke)
You Got To Me
Neil Diamond; *Neil Diamond's Greatest Hits-1966-1992* . . . . (Columbia)
You Gotta Move
Rolling Stones; *Love You Live* . . . . (Virgin)
Sticky Fingers . . . . (Virgin)
You Make Me Sick
Pink; *Can't Take Me Home* . . . . (LaFace)
You're The Power
Kathy Mattea; *New Faces Of Country-C* . . . . (K-Tel)
Walk The Way The Wind Blows . . . . (Mercury)

PREJUDICE, Bigotry, Segregation

See Also: **BROTHERHOOD, GENDER CONFLICT, GENDER
STEREOTYPES, HARD CITY LIFE, HATE, HISTORY, LOVE:
FORBIDDEN LOVE, MISTREATMENT, POLITICS (various),
PROTEST, SLAVERY, SOCIAL CLASS: GENERAL, SOCIAL
CLASS: RURAL**

Abraham, Martin And John
Dion; *Collectables Presents The History Of Rock-#3-C* . . . . (Collectables)
Dion-24 Original Classics . . . . (Arista)
Songs Of Protest-C . . . . (Rhino)
WCBS FM 101 History Of Rock-'60s-#2-C . . . . (Collectables)
Harry Belafonte; *Harry Belafonte's All Time Greatest Hits-#1* . . . . (RCA)
Smokey Robinson & The Miracles; *Smokey Robinson & The Miracles'
Anthology* . . . . (Motown)
*Time Out For Smokey Robinson & The Miracles/Special
Occasion* . . . . (Motown)
America
Original Cast; *ST/West Side Story* . . . .(Sony Broadway)

American Skin (41 Shots)
Bruce Springsteen & The E Street Band; *Live In New York City* . . . . . (Columbia)
An Acceptable Level Of Ecstasy (The Wedding Song)
Lyle Lovett; *Lyle Lovett* . . . . (MCA)
Apartheid
C. Chris & Rich E. Rich/Rudy Pardee; *Apartheid-12"* . . . . (MCA)
Apartheid
Peter Tosh; *Equal Rights* . . . . (Columbia)
Apartheid
K-9 Posse; *On A Different Tip* . . . . (Arista)
Aryanisms
Napalm Death; *Utopia Banished* . . . .(Earache)
Avinu Malkeinu
Barbra Streisand; *Higher Ground* . . . . (Columbia)
Ballad Of Ira Hayes, The
Johnny Cash; *The Man In Black-His Greatest Hits* . . . . (Legacy)
Peter La Farge; *Best Of Broadside 1962-1968: Anthems Of The American
Underground From The Pages Of Broadside
Magazine-C* . . . .(Smithsonian Folkways)
Ballad Of Martin Luther King
Mike Millius; *Best Of Broadside 1962-1968: Anthems Of The American
Underground From The Pages Of Broadside
Magazine-C* . . . .(Smithsonian Folkways)
Baloney Again
Mark Knopfler; *Sailing To Philadelphia* . . . . (Warner Bros.)
Biko
Peter Gabriel; *Peter Gabriel* . . . . (Geffen)
Peter Gabriel/Plays Live . . . . (Geffen)
Shaking The Tree-Sixteen Golden Greats . . . . (Geffen)
Birmingham Sunday
Joan Baez; *Contemporary Ballad Book* . . . . (Vanguard)
Joan Baez/5 . . . .(Vanguard)
Richard Farina; *Best Of Broadside 1962-1968: Anthems Of The American
Underground From The Pages Of Broadside
Magazine-C* . . . .(Smithsonian Folkways)
Black Man Can't Get A Cab
U.T.F.O.; *Bag It & Bone It* . . . . (Jive)
Black Or White
Michael Jackson; *Dangerous* . . . . (Epic)
Blacks Are Giving Me The Blues
Martin Mull; *No Hits Four Errors* . . . . (Capricorn)
Normal . . . .(Capricorn)
Boom Bye Bye
Buju Banton; *Voice Of Jamaica* . . . . (Mercury)
Brother Louie
Stories; *Billboard Top Rock 'N' Roll Hits-1973-C* . . . . (Rhino)
Changes
2Pac; *2Pac Greatest Hits* . . . . (Amaru/Death Row/Interscope)
Company Time
Linda Davis; *Shoot For The Moon* . . . . (Arista)
Cop Killer
Ice-T; *Body Count* . . . . (Warner Bros.)
Cuttin' Heads
John Mellencamp; *Cuttin' Heads* . . . . (Columbia)
Die Nigger Die
Schoolly D; *How A Black Man Feels* . . . . (Capitol)
Don't Call Me Nigger, Whitey
Sly & The Family Stone; *Sly & The Family Stone-Anthology* . . . . (Epic)
Stand! . . . . (Epic)
Don't Laugh At Me
Mark Wills; *Wish You Were Here* . . . . (Mercury)
Drug Store Truck Drivin' Man
Byrds; *Best Of The Byrds-Greatest Hits-#2* . . . . (Columbia)
Dr. Byrds & Mr. Hyde . . . . (Legacy)
The Byrds . . . . (Columbia)
Gram Parsons & Fallen Angels; *Live 1973* . . . . (Sierra)
Joan Baez & Jeffrey Shurtleff; *ST/Woodstock* . . . . (Atlantic)
Ebony And Ivory
Paul McCartney & Stevie Wonder; *All The Best!* . . . . (Capitol)
Tug Of War . . . . (Gold Rush)
Equal Rights
Peter Tosh; *Equal Rights* . . . . (Columbia)
Every Kinda People
Robert Palmer; *Addictions-#1* . . . . (Island)
Double Fun . . . . (Island)
Maybe It's Live . . . . (Island)
Everyday People
Sly & The Family Stone; *Sly & The Family Stone-Anthology* . . . . (Epic)
Sly & The Family Stone's Greatest Hits . . . . (Epic)
Stand! . . . . (Epic)
Fear Of A Black Planet
Public Enemy; *Fear Of A Black Planet* . . . . (Def Jam)
Fight Apartheid
Peter Tosh; *No Nuclear War* . . . . (EMI)
Fight The Power
Isley Brothers; *Forever Gold* . . . . (T-Neck/Columbia)
Heat Is On . . . . (T-Neck/Columbia)
Isley Brothers' Greatest Hits . . . . (T-Neck/Columbia)

The Isley Brothers Story-#2-The T-Neck Years-1969-1985 . . . . (Rhino)

Follow The Drinking Gourd
Richie Havens; *Songs Of The Civil War-C* . . . . (Columbia)
Weavers; *Weavers' Greatest Hits* . . . . (Vanguard)

Forgive Them Father
Lauryn Hill featuring Shelly Thunder; *The Miseducation Of*
Lauryn Hill . . . . (Ruffhouse/Columbia)

Free Your Mind
En Vogue; *Funky Divas* . . . . (East West)

Freedom Riders
Phil Ochs; *Best Of Broadside 1962-1968: Anthems Of The American*
Underground From The Pages Of Broadside
Magazine-C . . . . (Smithsonian Folkways)

Gangsta's Paradise
Coolio; *1996 Grammy Nominees-C* . . . . (Columbia)
Gangsta's Paradise . . . . (Tommy Boy)
ST/Dangerous Minds . . . . (MCA)

He Thinks He'll Keep Her
Mary Chapin Carpenter; *Come On Come On* . . . . (Columbia)

He Was My Brother
Simon & Garfunkel; *Wednesday Morning 3 A.M.* . . . . (Columbia)

Heartspark Dollarsign
Everclear; *Sparkle And Fade* . . . . (Capitol)

Here's To The State Of Mississippi
Phil Ochs; *I Ain't Marching Anymore* . . . . (Carthage)
There But For Fortune . . . . (Elektra)

Hey Porter
Johnny Cash; *First Years* . . . . (Allegiance)
Johnny Cash-Legend . . . . (Sun)
Johnny Cash-Original Golden Hits-#1 . . . . (Sun)
Johnny Cash's Greatest Hits-#2 . . . . (Columbia)
Johnny Cash-Sun Years . . . . (Rhino)
Vintage Years-1955-1963 . . . . (Rhino)

Hurricane
Bob Dylan; *Desire* . . . . (Columbia)

I Believe
Blessid Union Of Souls; *Home* . . . . (EMI)

I Wonder If Heaven Got A Ghetto
2Pac; *R U Still Down (Remember Me)* . . . . (Amaru/Jive)

If I Ruled The World
NaS; *It Was Written* . . . . (Columbia)

I'm Not That Man
10,000 Maniacs; *MTV Unplugged-10,000 Maniacs* . . . . (Elektra)
Our Time In Eden . . . . (Elektra)

I'm Proud To Be A Redneck
Barefoot Jerry; *Barefoot Jerry's Grocery* . . . . (Monument)

John Brown's Body
Pete Seeger; *American Favorite Ballads-#3* . . . . . (Smithsonian Folkways)
Sonny Terry & Brownie McGhee; *Every Tone A*
Testimony-C . . . . (Smithsonian Folkways)

Ku Klux Klan
Steel Pulse; *ST/Urgh! A Music War* . . . . (A&M)

Lady Is A Tramp
Ella Fitzgerald; *Rodgers & Hart Songbook* . . . . (Verve)
Frank Sinatra; *Sinatra Reprise-The Very Good Years* . . . . (Reprise)
The Capitol Years . . . . (Capitol)
Frank Sinatra & Luther Vandross; *Frank Sinatra-Duets-C* . . . . . (Capitol)

Links On The Chain
Broadside Singers & Phil Ochs; *Best Of Broadside 1962-1968: Anthems*
Of The American Underground From The Pages Of Broadside
Magazine-C . . . . (Smithsonian Folkways)

Little Plastic Castle
Ani DiFranco; *Little Plastic Castle* . . . . (Righteous Babe)

Living For The City
Stevie Wonder; *Innervisions* . . . . (Motown)
Original Musiquarium . . . . (Motown)

Longhaired Redneck
David Allan Coe; *David Allan Coe-17 Greatest Hits* . . . . (Columbia)
For The Record-The First 10 Years . . . . (Columbia)
Longhaired Redneck . . . . (Columbia)

Miami Beach
Garland Jeffreys; *Escape Artist* . . . . (Epic)

My Hometown
Bruce Springsteen; *Born In The U.S.A.* . . . . (Columbia)
Bruce Springsteen's Greatest Hits . . . . (Columbia)

Nigga Ya Love To Hate
Ice Cube; *AmeriKKKa's Most Wanted* . . . . (Priority)

Niggas Come In All Colors
L.A. Posse; *They Come In All Colors* . . . . (Atlantic)

Niggaz 4 Life
N.W.A.; *Efil4zaggin* . . . . (Ruthless/Priority)

Nigger Whitie
Sly Dunbar; *Sly Wicked & Slick* . . . . (Front Line)

One
Creed; *My Own Prison* . . . . (Wind-up)

Political Science
Randy Newman; *Sail Away* . . . . (Reprise)

Power In The Darkness
Tom Robinson Band; *Power In The Darkness* . . . . (Harvest)

Proud To Be Black
Young Black Teenagers; *Young Black Teenagers* . . . . (S.O.U.L.)

Proud To Be Black
Run-D.M.C.; *Raising Hell* . . . . (Profile)

Racist
Boogie Down Productions; *Edutainment (Education + Entertainment)* . . . (Jive)

Racist Friend
Special AKA; *In The Studio* . . . . (Chrysalis)

Rednecks
Randy Newman; *Good Old Boys* . . . . (Reprise)
Guilty: 30 Years Of Randy Newman . . . . (Rhino)

Rosa Parks
Outkast; *Aquemini* . . . . (LaFace/Arista)

Royal Scam
Steely Dan; *The Royal Scam* . . . . (MCA)

Sail Away
Linda Ronstadt; *Don't Cry Now* . . . . (Asylum)
Randy Newman; *Guilty: 30 Years Of Randy Newman* . . . . (Rhino)
Sail Away . . . . (Reprise)

Scream
Michael Jackson with Janet Jackson; *HIStory: Past, Present And Future-*
Book 1-C . . . . (Epic)

Second Class Wait Here
Slim Dusty; *Australia Is His Name* . . . . (Philo)

Shame On You
Indigo Girls; *Shaming Of The Sun* . . . . (Epic)

Shine
Ry Cooder; *Jazz* . . . . (Warner Bros.)

Short People
Randy Newman; *Dr. Demento Presents The Greatest Novelty Records-#4-*
1970s-C . . . . (Rhino)
Little Criminals . . . . (Warner Bros.)

Sister Rosa
Neville Brothers; *Yellow Moon* . . . . (A&M)

Society's Child (Baby I've Been Thinking)
Janis Ian; *Songs Of Protest-C* . . . . (Rhino)
The Bottom Line Encore Collection . . . . (Bottom Line)
Lou Gramm; *A Foreigner In His Own Land: Best Of Early*
Years. . . . . (Collectables)
Past Times Behind Rock & Roll-C . . . . (Intermedia)

Somewhere
Aretha Franklin; *Aretha's Jazz* . . . . (Rhino)
Barbra Streisand; *The Broadway Album* . . . . (Columbia)
Dave Brubeck; *Music From West Side Story* . . . . (Columbia)
Jose Carreras; *Amigos Para Siempre-Friends For Life* . . . . (Atlantic)
Original Cast; *ST/West Side Story* . . . . (Sony Broadway)
Tom Waits; *Tom Waits-Anthology* . . . . (Asylum)

Strange Fruit
Billie Holiday; *History Of The Real Billie Holiday* . . . . (Verve)
Lady Sings The Blues. . . . . (Verve)
Songbook. . . . . (Verve)
Nina Simone; *Compact Jazz-Nina Simone* . . . . (Verve)
Siouxsie And The Banshees; *Through The Looking Glass.* . . . . . (Geffen)

Struggle (Free South Africa)
Rochester/Easley Band; *One Minute Of Love* . . . . (Gramavision)

Sun City
Artists United Against Apartheid; *Sun City-C* . . . . (Manhattan)

Sweet Black Angel
Rolling Stones; *Exile On Main Street.* . . . . (Virgin)

Theme From "I'll Fly Away"
Original Soundtrack; *Television's Greatest Hits-#7-Cable Ready-C* . . . . . (TVT)

They Don't Care About Us
Michael Jackson; *HIStory: Past, Present And Future-Book 1-C* . . . . (Epic)

Tomorrow We'll See
Sting; *Brand New Day* . . . . (A&M)

Train For Auschwitz
Tom Paxton; *Best Of Broadside 1962-1968: Anthems Of The American*
Underground From The Pages Of Broadside
Magazine-C . . . . (Smithsonian Folkways)

Two Tribes
Frankie Goes To Hollywood; *Welcome To The Pleasuredome* . . . . (Island)

Uneasy Rider
Charlie Daniels Band; *A Decade Of Hits* . . . . (Epic)
Homesick Heroes . . . . (Epic)
Super Hits Of The '70s-Have A Nice Day-#11-C . . . . (Rhino)
Uneasy Rider. . . . . (Epic)

We Shall Be Free
Garth Brooks; *The Chase* . . . . (Liberty)

We Shall Overcome
Bruce Springsteen; *Where Have All The Flowers Gone: The Songs Of Pete*
Seeger. . . . . (Appleseed)
James Cleveland & The Troubadors; *James Cleveland & The*
Troubadors. . . . . (Savoy)
Joan Baez; *Carry It On.* . . . . (Vanguard)
Joan Baez In Concert, Part 2. . . . . (Vanguard)
Mahalia Jackson; *God Bless America-C* . . . . (Columbia)

Pete Seeger; *Bitter & The Sweet* . . . . (Mobile Fidelity Sound Lab)
  Pete Seeger's Greatest Hits . . . . (Columbia)
We're All In The Same Gang
  West Coast Rap All-Stars; *We're All In The Same Gang-C* . . . . . .(Warner Bros.)
White Minority
  Black Flag; *First Four Years* . . . .(SST)
  ST/Decline Of Western Civilization . . . . (Slash)
White Trash
  Orchestral Manoeuvres In The Dark; *Junk Culture* . . . . (A&M)
White Trash
  Redd Kross; *Born Innocent*. . . . .(Frontier)
White Trash
  Bellamy Brothers; *Crazy From The Heart* . . . . (MCA)
White Trash
  Bad Religion; *How Could Hell Be Any Worse* . . . . (Epitaph)
White Trash
  Steve Cash; *White Mansions*. . . . . (A&M)
White Trash Song
  Steve Young; *Honky-Tonk Man* . . . . (Rounder)
  Solo/Live . . . . (Watermelon)
Whitey On The Moon
  Gil Scott-Heron; *Whitey On The Moon*. . . . . (Bluebird)
Woman Is The Nigger Of The World
  John Lennon; *Live In New York City*. . . . . (Capitol)
  John Lennon/Plastic Ono Band; *Lennon*. . . . . (Capitol)
  Shaved Fish . . . . (Capitol)
  Some Time In New York City . . . . (Capitol)
You Haven't Done Nothin'
  Stevie Wonder; *Fulfillingness' First Finale* . . . . (Motown)
Your Friendly, Liberal, Neighborhood Ku-Klux-Klan
  Chad Mitchell Trio; *Best Of The Chad Mitchell Trio-The Mercury
    Years* . . . .(Chronicles)
Your Racist Friend
  They Might Be Giants; *Flood* . . . . (Elektra)
You've Got To Be Carefully Taught
  Original Cast; *South Pacific* . . . .(CBS Masterworks)

PRESIDENTS

*See Also: **CELEBRITIES: SPECIFIC, COUNTRIES: A-Z,
COUNTRIES: AMERICA, HISTORY, KINGS, MEN'S NAMES: A-
Z, PATRIOTISM, POLITICS (various), POWER & CONTROL,
QUEENS, ROYALTY, WOMEN'S NAMES: A-Z***

Abraham, Martin And John
  Dion; *Collectables Presents The History Of Rock-#3-C* . . . . (Collectables)
  Dion-24 Original Classics . . . . (Arista)
  Songs Of Protest-C . . . . (Rhino)
  WCBS FM 101 History Of Rock-'60s-#2-C . . . . (Collectables)
  Harry Belafonte; *Harry Belafonte's All Time Greatest Hits-#1* . . . . (RCA)
  Smokey Robinson & The Miracles; *Smokey Robinson & The Miracles'
    Anthology* . . . . (Motown)
  *Time Out For Smokey Robinson & The Miracles/Special
    Occasion* . . . . (Motown)
Alvin For President
  Alvin & The Chipmunks; *Greatest Hits: Still Squeaky After All These
    Years* . . . . (Capitol)
Arrest The President
  Intelligent Hoodlum; *Intelligent Hoodlum* . . . . (A&M)
At The President's Birthday Ball
  Glenn Miller & His Orchestra; *Complete Glenn Miller & His
    Orchestra* . . . . (Bluebird)
Ballad Of Richard Nixon
  John Denver; *Rhymes & Reasons* . . . . (RCA)
Ballad Of Spiro Agnew
  John Denver; *Rhymes & Reasons* . . . . (RCA)
Big Brother
  Stevie Wonder; *Talking Book*. . . . . (Motown)
Bizzness Ain't Dead
  New World Singers; *Best Of Broadside 1962-1968: Anthems Of The
    American Underground From The Pages Of Broadside
    Magazine-C* . . . . (Smithsonian Folkways)
Dear Mr. President
  4 Non Blondes; *Bigger, Better, Faster, More!* . . . . (Interscope)
Dear Mr. President
  Next Issue; *Next Issue*. . . . . (Epic)
Dear Mrs. Roosevelt
  Bob Dylan; *Tribute To Woody Guthrie-C* . . . .(Warner Bros.)
Eisenhower
  John Scofield; *Meant To Be* . . . . (Blue Note)
Eisenhower Blues
  J.B. Lenoir; *Best Of Chess Blues-C*. (Chess)
  Natural Man . . . . (Chess)
Eisenhower Blues
  Costello Show (Featuring Elvis Costello); *King Of America* . . . . (Columbia)

El Presidente
  Swimming Pool Q's; *Firing Squad For God*. . . . . (DB)
Franklin D. Roosevelt's Back Again
  New Lost City Ramblers; *New Lost City Ramblers-Early Years-1958-
    1962*. . . . .(Smithsonian Folkways)
Good Evening Mr. Waldheim
  Lou Reed; *New York* . . . . (Sire)
Happy Birthday Mr. President
  Marilyn Monroe; *20 Golden Greatest Hits* . . . . (Stardance)
  Marilyn Monroe-The Essential Recordings . . . .(Music Club)
Happy Birthday Mr. President
  John Southworth; *Mars Pennsylvania*. . . . . (Bar/None)
Here Comes President Kill Again
  XTC; *Oranges & Lemons* . . . . (Geffen)
Here's To The State Of Nixon
  Phil Ochs; *Chords Of Fame*. . . . . (A&M)
I Wanna Grow Up To Be A Politician
  Byrds; *20 Essential Tracks From The Box Set*. . . . . (Columbia)
  Best Of The Byrds-Greatest Hits-#2. . . . . (Columbia)
  Byrdmaniax . . . . (Columbia)
  The Byrds . . . . (Columbia)
In Memoriam-John F. & Robert F. Kennedy
  Clare Fischer; *'Twas Only Yesterday* . . . . (Discovery)
Lee Harvey Oswald
  Skatalites; *Stretching Out* . . . . (Roir)
Letters To The President
  Sly & Robbie; *Silent Assassin* . . . . (Island)
Mr. Lincoln
  Hank Williams, Jr.; *America (The Way I See It)* . . . . (WB/Curb)
  Major Moves . . . . (WB/Curb)
Mr. President
  Big Boy Henry; *Work's Many Voices-#1 & 2-C* . . . . (Arhoolie)
Mr. President
  Meat Beat Manifesto; *Armed Audio Warfare* . . . . (Wax Trax)
Mr. President
  Crack The Sky; *Dog City*. . . . . (Grudge)
Mr. President
  George Fox; *With All My Might*. . . . . (Warner Bros.)
Mr. President
  Elliot Lawrence Band; *Elliot Lawrence Band Plays Gerry Mulligan
    Arrangements* . . . .(Fantasy)
Mr. President (Have Pity On The Working Man)
  Randy Newman; *Good Old Boys*. . . . . (Reprise)
  ST/Forrest Gump . . . .(Epic/Sony Music Soundtrax)
November 22, 1963
  Original Cast; *Assassins* . . . . (RCA)
Open Letter To George Bush
  Wayne Horvitz/The President; *Miracle Mile* . . . . (Elektra)
President Garfield
  Jerry Holland; *Jerry Holland*. . . . . (Rounder)
President Gas
  Psychedelic Furs; *All Of This & Nothing*. . . . . (Columbia)
  Forever Now. . . . . (Columbia)
President Hayes
  Sonny Rollins; *Don't Stop The Carnival* . . . . (Milestone)
President Kennedy
  Son House; *Father Of The Delta Blues-1965 Sessions* . . . . (Columbia)
President Kennedy
  Ry Cooder; *Boomer's Story*. . . . . (Reprise)
President Kennedy March
  Lawrence Welk; *10th Anniversary Television Show* . . . . (Ranwood)
President Kennedy Stayed Away Too Long
  Sleepy John Estes; *Electric Sleep* . . . . (Delmark)
  Kings Of Country Blues-#1. . . . . (Arhoolie)
President Kennedy's Mile
  Screaming Blue Messiahs; *Gun-Shy* . . . . (Elektra)
President Roosevelt
  Big Joe Williams; *Shake Your Boogie*. . . . . (Arhoolie)
  Tough Times. . . . . (Arhoolie)
Presidente
  Tijuana Brass; *South Of The Border* . . . . (A&M)
Presidential Rag
  Arlo Guthrie & Pete Seeger; *Together In Concert*. . . . .(Reprise)
President's Nap
  Power Tools; *Strange Meeting* . . . .(Antilles)
President's Share Of The Promised Land
  Doves; *Affinity*. . . . . (Elektra)
Reagan Der Fuhrer
  D.I.; *Team Goon* . . . . (Triple X Entert.)
Reagonomics
  D.R.I.; *Dealing With It* . . . . (Metal Blade)
  Johnnie Taylor; *Just Ain't Good Enough*. . . . . (Beverly Glen)
Richard Nixon
  Christmas; *Ultraprophets Of Thee Psykick Revolution*. . . . . (I.R.S.)
Ronnie, Talk To Russia
  Prince; *Controversy*. . . . . (Warner Bros.)
Secret Service
  Original Cast; *Mr. President* . . . . (Sony Broadway)

Song Of The South (Roosevelt)
Alabama; *Alabama's Greatest Hits-#2* . . . .(RCA)
Southern Star . . . .(RCA)

Still A G Thang
Snoop Dogg; *Da Game Is To Be Sold, Not To Be Told* . . . . . .(No Limit/Priority)

Subway Ride (Bill Clinton/Monica Lewinsky)
Sheryl Crow; *The Globe Sessions* . . . .(A&M)

Talking Watergate
Tom Paxton; *New Songs From The Briarpatch* . . . .(Vanguard)

Tweedledee For President
Michael Tilson Thomas; *Of Thee I Sing/Let 'Em Eat Cake* . . . .(Columbia)

Warren Harding
Al Stewart; *Past, Present & Future* . . . .(Rhino)

Washington's Birthday
Bob Hope; *Thanks For The Memories* . . . .(Collectables)

We'd Like To Thank You Herbert Hoover
Original Broadway Cast; *Annie* . . . .(Columbia)

What The President Meant To Say
Leaving Trains; *Fuck.* . . . . (SST)

When The Flintstones Meet The President
Dirty Dozen Brass Band; *Louisiana Scrapbook-C* . . . .(Rykodisc)

White House Blues
Doc Watson; *Essential Doc Watson* . . . .(Vanguard)
Doc Watson & Family; *Treasures Untold-C* . . . .(Vanguard)
Stanley Brothers; *Shadows Of The Past.* . . . .(Copper Creek)

Wintergreen For President
Michael Tilson Thomas; *Of Thee I Sing/Let 'Em Eat Cake* . . . .(Columbia)

PRETEND, Disguise, Fantasy, Imagine, Virtual, Wish, Wonder

See Also: **CHARACTER & INTEGRITY, CHEATING & LIES, DESIRE, DREAMS, FAKE, HIDING, QUESTIONS & ANSWERS, SECRETS, STRANGE, TRUTH**

(You're The) Devil In Disguise
Elvis Presley; *Elvis' Gold Records, Volume 4* . . . .(RCA)
The Top Ten Hits. . . . .(RCA)

16 Candles
Crests; *Alan Freed's Memory Lane-C* . . . . (MCA)
Billboard Top Rock 'N' Roll Hits-1959-C . . . .(Rhino)
Crests Greatest Hits . . . .(Collectables)
Cruisin'-1959-C . . . . (Increase)
Oldies But Goodies-#14-C . . . .(Original Sound)
Rock & Roll U.S.A.-21 Rock & Roll Favorites-#2-C . . . .(Laurie)
ST/American Graffiti . . . . (MCA)

1983… (A Merman I Should Turn To Be)
Jimi Hendrix Experience; *Electric Ladyland.* . . . .(Reprise)

3am
Matchbox Twenty; *Yourself Or Someone Like You* . . . .(Lava)

5 Miles To Empty
Brownstone; *Still Climbing* . . . .(MJJ Music/Work)

Again
Lenny Kravitz; *Lenny Kravitz's Greatest Hits.* . . . .(Virgin)
Now That's What I Call Music!-#6-C . . . .(Virgin)

Alice In Wonderland
Neil Sedaka; *Neil Sedaka's All-Time Greatest Hits* . . . .(RCA)

All In My Mind
Maxine Brown; *Golden Classics-Maxine Brown* . . . .(Collectables)
Sultry Soul Sisters-Wonder Women-#3-C . . . .(Rhino)
Super Oldies Of The '60s-#3-C. . . . . (Audio Fidelity)

Almost Like Being In Love
Frank Sinatra; *Hello Young Lovers* . . . .(Columbia)
The Capitol Years . . . .(Capitol)
Original Cast; *Brigadoon.* . . . .(RCA)

Am I Dreaming
Ol Skool featuring Keith Sweat & Xscape; *Ol Skool* . . . .(Keia/Universal)

Angel
Madonna; *Like A Virgin.* . . . .(Sire)

Angel In Disguise
Earl Thomas Conley; *Don't Make It Easy For Me.* . . . .(RCA)
Earl Thomas Conley's Greatest Hits . . . .(RCA)

Any Lucky Penny
Nikki Hassman; *Songs From Dawson's Creek* . . . .(Sony Music Soundtrax)

Anymore
Travis Tritt; *It's All About To Change* . . . .(Warner Bros.)
Travis Tritt's Greatest Hits-From The Beginning. . . . .(Warner Bros.)

Anything And Everything
Martina McBride; *Emotion* . . . .(RCA)

Artificial Flowers
Bobby Darin; *The Bobby Darin Story* . . . . (Atlantic)

Artificial Rose
Jimmy C. Newman; *Jimmy C. Newman's Greatest Hits* . . . .(Plantation)

Ascension (Don't Ever Wonder)
Maxwell; *Maxwell's Urban Hang Suite* . . . .(Columbia)

At The Ballet
Original Cast; *A Chorus Line* . . . .(Columbia)

Barbie Girl
Aqua; *Aquarium.* . . . . (MCA)
Now That's What I Call Music!-#1-C . . . . (Virgin)

Be Like That
3 Doors Down; *Better Life* . . . .(Republic/Universal)
Now That's What I Call Music!-#8-C . . . . (Virgin)

Be True
Bruce Springsteen; *Tracks* . . . .(Columbia)

Big Rock Candy Mountain
Burl Ives; *Burl Ives' Greatest Hits* . . . . (MCA)
Poor Wayfaring Stranger . . . . (Flapper)
Harry McClintock; *ST/O Brother, Where Art Thou?* . . . .(Mercury)
John Hartford; *ST/Down From The Mountain* . . . .(Lost Highway/IDJMG)
Pete Seeger; *20 Golden Pieces Of Pete Seeger.* . . . .(Bulldog)
Tex Ritter; *Capitol Collectors Series-Tex Ritter* . . . .(Capitol)

Billy The Kid (I Miss…)
Billy Dean; *Billy Dean* . . . .(Liberty)

Black & Tan Fantasy
Duke Ellington; *Beginning.* . . . . (MCA)
Carnegie Hall Concert . . . .(Prestige)
Carnegie Hall Concert -December 11, 1943. . . . . (Everest)
Continuum. . . . . (Fantasy)
Duke Ellington-Pure Gold . . . . (RCA)
Duke Ellington's Greatest Hits . . . . (Reprise)
Echoes Of An Era-Duke Ellington & Louis Armstrong . . . .(Roulette)
Duke Ellington & Mercer Ellington; *Duke Ellington & Mercer
Ellington.* . . . . (Fantasy)

Blessed
Elton John; *Elton John-Love Songs* . . . . (MCA)
Made In England. . . . .(Rocket)

Blow Up The Outside World
Soundgarden; *A-Sides.* . . . .(A&M)
Down On The Upside . . . .(A&M)

Book Of Love
Monotones; *Bedrock-Late '50s/'60s Rock 'N' Roll* . . . .(Allegiance)
Best Of Chess Rock 'N' Roll-#1-C. . . . . (Chess)
Original Golden Rock Oldies-#1-C. . . . .(Specialty)
ST/American Graffiti . . . . (MCA)
Super Oldies Of The '50s-#2-C . . . .(Audio Fidelity)

Brian Wilson
Barenaked Ladies; *Gordon* . . . .(Reprise)
Rock Spectacle . . . .(Reprise)

Brilliant Disguise
Bruce Springsteen; *Bruce Springsteen's Greatest Hits* . . . .(Columbia)
Tunnel Of Love . . . .(Columbia)

Button Off My Shirt
Ronnie Milsap; *Heart & Soul.* . . . .(RCA)
Ronnie Milsap's Greatest Hits-#3 . . . .(RCA)

California Girls
Beach Boys; *Beach Boys '69 (The Beach Boys Live In London)* . . . .(Capitol)
Best Of The Beach Boys-#2 . . . .(Capitol)
Endless Summer . . . .(Capitol)
Good Vibrations-Thirty Years Of The Beach Boys . . . .(Capitol)
The Beach Boys In Concert . . . .(Brother)
David Lee Roth; *Crazy From The Heat* . . . .(Warner Bros.)
ST/Down & Out In Beverly Hills . . . .(Warner Bros.)

Can't Cry Anymore
Sheryl Crow; *MTV Party To Go-#8-C* . . . . (Tommy Boy)
Tuesday Night Music Club . . . .(A&M)

Car Wash
Bruce Springsteen; *Tracks* . . . .(Columbia)

Cherish
Association; *Association Greatest Hits* . . . .(Warner Bros.)
Billboard Top Pop Hits-1966-C . . . .(Rhino)

Cleopatra, Queen Of Denial
Pam Tillis; *Homeward Looking Angel* . . . .(Arista)

Could've Been
Tiffany; *Tiffany* . . . . (MCA)
Tiffany's Greatest Hits . . . .(Hip-O)

Cry Wolf
Laura Branigan; *Touch.* . . . .(Atlantic)
Stevie Nicks; *Other Side Of The Mirror.* . . . .(Modern)

Cuban Fantasy
Cal Tjader; *Good Vibes* . . . .(Concord Picante Jazz)

Dallas
Alan Jackson; *Don't Rock The Jukebox* . . . .(Arista)

Damn I Wish I Was Your Lover
Sophie B. Hawkins; *Tongues & Tales* . . . .(Columbia)

Dear Mr. Fantasy
Traffic; *Best Of Traffic* . . . .(Island)
Dear Mr. Fantasy . . . .(Island)
Welcome To The Canteen . . . .(Island)

Denial
Sevendust; *Home.* . . . . (TVT)

Devil In Disguise
J.J. Cale; *Grasshopper* . . . .(Mercury)
Special Edition . . . .(Mercury)

Ditty Wa Ditty
Ry Cooder; *Paradise And Lunch* . . . . (Reprise)
Do I Love You Because You're Beautiful
Julie Andrews & Jon Cypher; *Cinderella-The CBS Television*
Production . . . . (Columbia)
Rodgers & Hammerstein Songbook . . . . (Sony Music Classical)
Mel Torme; *Mel Torme-16 Most Requested Songs* . . . . (Columbia)
Stuart Damon & Lesley Ann Warren; *Cinderella-The CBS Television*
Network Production . . . . (Columbia)
Do Something
Macy Gray; *On How Life Is* . . . .(Epic)
ST/Music Of The Heart . . . . (Epic/Sony Music Soundtrax)
Does That Blue Moon Ever Shine On You
Toby Keith; *Blue Moon* . . . . (Polydor Country)
Toby Keith's Greatest Hits, Volume One . . . . (Mercury)
Don't Close Your Eyes
Keith Whitley; *Don't Close Your Eyes* . . . . (RCA)
Keith Whitley's Greatest Hits . . . . (RCA)
Down At The Old Corral
Randy Travis; *Wind In The Wire* . . . .(Warner Bros.)
Down Incognito
Winger; *Pull* . . . .(Atlantic)
Dream Is A Wish Your Heart Makes
Barbara Cook; *Disney Album* . . . .(Disney)
Linda Ronstadt; *Disney's Music From The Park-C* . . . .(Disney)
Music Of Disney's Cinderella-C . . . . (Disney)
Michael Bolton; *Simply Mad About The Mouse-C* . . . . (Columbia)
Original Soundtrack; *ST/Cinderella* . . . .(Disney)
El Condor Pasa (If I Could)
Paul Simon; *Paul Simon In Concert/Live Rhymin'* . . . . (Columbia)
Simon & Garfunkel; *Bridge Over Troubled Water* . . . . (Columbia)
Collected Works . . . . (Columbia)
Simon & Garfunkel's Greatest Hits . . . . (Columbia)
Escape (Pina Colada Song)
Rupert Holmes; *Billboard Top Hits-1979-C* . . . . (Rhino)
Partners In Crime . . . .(MCA)
Even If
Amel Larrieux; *Infinite Possibilities* . . . .(Epic)
Everlong
Foo Fighters; *The Colour And The Shape* . . . . (Roswell/RCA)
Everything That Glitters (Is Not Gold)
Dan Seals; *Best Of Dan Seals* . . . . (Capitol)
Dan Seals' Greatest Hits . . . . (Liberty)
Dan Seals-Classics Collection-#2 . . . . (Liberty)
Won't Be Blue Anymore . . . .(EMI)
Fantasy
Earth, Wind & Fire; *All 'N All* . . . . (Columbia)
Best Of Earth, Wind & Fire-#1 . . . . (Legacy)
Best Of Earth, Wind & Fire-#2 . . . . (Columbia)
ST/Private Lessons . . . .(MCA)
Fantasy
Aldo Nova; *Aldo Nova* . . . . (Portrait)
Fantasy
Mariah Carey; *Daydream* . . . . (Columbia)
Fantasy
Alabama; *Feels So Right* . . . . (RCA)
Fantasy
Black Box; *Decoded & Danced Up* . . . . (RCA)
Dreamland . . . . (RCA)
Fantasy Girl
38 Special; *Flashback-Best Of 38 Special* . . . . (A&M)
Wild-Eyed Southern Boys . . . . (A&M)
Fantasy Serenade
Triumph; *Just A Game* . . . . (RCA)
First Taste
Fiona Apple; *Tidal* . . . . (Clean Slate/Work)
Fixing A Hole
Beatles; *Sgt. Pepper's Lonely Hearts Club Band* . . . . (Capitol)
Flesh For Fantasy
Billy Idol; *Rebel Yell* . . . .(Chrysalis)
Vital Idol . . . .(Chrysalis)
Flood, The (Wish I Was In Nashville)
Don Williams; *I've Got A Winner In You* . . . . (Universal)
Fly Away
Lenny Kravitz; *5* . . . . (Virgin)
Now That's What I Call Music!-#1-C . . . . (Virgin)
Fool's Gold
Stone Roses; *The Stone Roses* . . . . (Silvertone)
Footlights
Merle Haggard; *For The Record: Merle Haggard-43 Legendary Hits* . . . . (BNA)
Four Percent Pantomime
Band; *Cahoots* . . . . (Capitol)
To Kingdom Come-The Definitive Collection . . . . (Capitol)
Get Born Again
Alice In Chains; *Nothing Safe* . . . . (Columbia)
Gold Digger
EPMD; *Business As Usual* . . . .(Def Jam)
Good Bye
Martina McBride; *Emotion* . . . . (RCA)

Good Life
Bruce Robison; *Long Way Home From Anywhere* . . . . (Lucky Dog)
Goodnight My Someone
Shirley Jones; *ST/The Music Man* . . . . (Warner Bros.)
Grand Illusion
Styx; *Grand Illusion* . . . . (A&M)
Styx-Classics-#15 . . . . (A&M)
Grand Illusion
Eric Clapton; *August* . . . . (Duck/Reprise)
Great Pretender
Band; *Moondog Matinee* . . . . (Capitol)
Platters; *Billboard Top R&B Hits-1956-C* . . . . (Rhino)
Cruisin'-1956-C . . . . (Increase)
Encore Of Golden Hits-Platters . . . . (Mercury)
Platters-Anthology . . . . (Rhino)
ST/American Graffiti . . . . (MCA)
Super Oldies Of The '50s-#3-C . . . . (Audio Fidelity)
Roy Orbison; *Best Of Roy Orbison-Loved Standards* . . . . (Monument)
Stan Freberg; *Capitol Collectors Series-Stan Freberg* . . . . (Capitol)
Happy Talk
Original Cast; *South Pacific* . . . . (CBS Masterworks)
He Would Be Sixteen
Michelle Wright; *Now & Then* . . . . (Arista)
Heart Won't Lie, The
Reba McEntire & Vince Gill; *It's Your Call* . . . . (MCA)
Reba McEntire's Greatest Hits-#3: I'm A Survivor . . . . (MCA)
Hello
Lionel Richie; *Back To Front* . . . . (Motown)
Can't Slow Down . . . . (Motown)
Truly-The Love Songs . . . . (Motown)
Luther Vandross; *Songs* . . . . (Epic)
He's So Fine
Chiffons; *Best Of The Girl Groups-#1-C* . . . . (Rhino)
Billboard Top Rock 'N' Roll Hits-1963-C . . . . (Rhino)
Chiffons Greatest Hits . . . . (Right Stuff)
Jody Miller; *Jody Miller's Greatest Hits* . . . . (Epic)
Hey Lover
L.L. Cool J; *All World* . . . . (Def Jam)
Mr. Smith . . . . (Def Jam)
MTV Party To Go-#9-C . . . . (Tommy Boy)
Hey, Cinderella
Suzy Bogguss; *Something Up My Sleeve* . . . . (Liberty)
High Hopes And Empty Pockets
McBride & The Ride; *McBride & The Ride* . . . . (MCA)
Highlands
Bob Dylan; *Time Out Of Mind* . . . . (Columbia)
Holding Her & Loving You
Earl Thomas Conley; *Don't Make It Easy For Me* . . . . (RCA)
Earl Thomas Conley's Greatest Hits . . . . (RCA)
Homeward Bound
Paul Simon; *Paul Simon In Concert/Live Rhymin'* . . . . (Columbia)
Paul Simon & George Harrison; *Nobody's Child-Romanian Angel*
Appeal-C . . . . (Warner Bros.)
Simon & Garfunkel; *Collected Works* . . . . (Columbia)
Parsley Sage Rosemary & Thyme . . . . (Columbia)
Simon & Garfunkel's Greatest Hits . . . . (Columbia)
The Concert In Central Park . . . . (Warner Bros.)
Willie Nelson & Waylon Jennings; *Take It To The Limit* . . . . (Columbia)
House Of Cards
Mary Chapin Carpenter; *Stones In The Road* . . . . (Columbia)
How Could An Angel Break My Heart
Kenny G with Toni Braxton; *Kenny G's Greatest Hits* . . . . (Arista)
Toni Braxton with Kenny G; *Diana, Princess Of Wales-Tribute-C* . . (Columbia)
Secrets . . . . (LaFace)
I Can Dream, Can't I?
Andrews Sisters; *Best Of The Andrews Sisters* . . . . (MCA)
I Can't Do That Anymore
Faith Hill; *It Matters To Me* . . . . (Warner Bros.)
I Do
Toya; *Totally Hits 2001-C* . . . . (Arista)
Toya . . . . (Arista)
I Pretend
Kim Carnes; *Cafe Racers* . . . . (EMI)
I Really Don't Want To Know
Charlie McCoy; *Greatest Hits Of Charlie McCoy* . . . . (Columbia)
Eddy Arnold; *Best Of Eddy Arnold* . . . . (RCA)
Essential Eddy Arnold . . . . (RCA)
Elvis Presley; *Elvis Country ("I'm 10,000 Years Old")* . . . . (RCA)
Great Country Songs . . . . (RCA)
Les Paul; *Best Of The Capitol Masters* . . . . (Gold Rush)
Les Paul & Mary Ford; *Les Paul's Greatest Hits* . . . . (Pair)
Ronnie Dove; *Ronnie Dove-His Best* . . . . (Laurie)
Tommy Edwards; *It's All In The Game-The Complete Hits Of Tommy*
Edwards . . . .(Eric)
I Still Miss Someone
Johnny Cash; *The Man In Black-His Greatest Hits* . . . . (Legacy)
I Wish
Skee-Lo; *I Wish* . . . . (Sunshine/Scotti Bros.)
Stevie Wonder; *Original Musiquarium* . . . . (Motown)

Songs In The Key Of Life . . . . (Motown)
I Wish
Gabrielle; *Find Your Way* . . . . (Go! Discs)
I Wish
Carl Thomas; *Emotional* . . . . (Bad Boy/Arista)
I Wish
R. Kelly; *Now That's What I Call Music!-#6-C* . . . . (Virgin)
TP-2.com . . . . (Jive)
I Wish He Didn't Trust Me So Much
Bobby Womack; *So Many Rivers* . . . . (MCA)
I Wish I Could Have Been There
John Anderson; *Solid Ground* . . . . (BNA)
I Wish I Felt Nothing
Wallflowers; *Bringing Down The Horse* . . . . (Interscope)
I Wish I Had A Girl
Henry Lee Summer; *Henry Lee Summer* . . . . (CBS Associated)
I Wish I Knew
Carmen McRae; *Monterey Jazz Festival: 40 Legendary*
Years-C . . . . (Warner Bros.)
Chet Baker; *Grey December* . . . . (Blue Note)
Jimmy Scott; *Lost And Found* . . . . (Rhino)
John Coltrane; *ST/The Fisher King* . . . . (MCA)
I Wish I Was A Painter
Greg Brown; *One More Goodnight Kiss* . . . . (Red House)
I Wish I Was In Chicago
Original Cast; *Charlie Sent Me* . . . . (Glendale)
I Wish I Was In Nashville
Mel McDaniel; *Take Me To The Country* . . . . (Capitol)
I Wish I Was In New Orleans
Tom Waits; *Small Change* . . . . (Asylum)
I Wish I Was In Peoria
Max Morath; *Max Morath & His Ragtime Stompers* . . . . (Vanguard)
I Wish I Was In Texas Tonight
Patti Ford; *45-#25* . . . .(Nationwide Sound Distrib.)
I Wish I Was Still In Your Dreams
Conway Twitty; *Still In Your Dreams* . . . . (MCA)
I Wish I Were Blind
Bruce Springsteen; *Human Touch* . . . . (Columbia)
I Wish It Would Rain
Temptations; *16 #1 Hits From The Late '60s-C* . . . . (Motown)
All The Million-Sellers . . . . (Motown)
Billboard Top R&B Hits-1968-C . . . . (Rhino)
Compact Command Performances-Temptations . . . . (Motown)
Motown Story-First 25 Years-C . . . . (Motown)
Temptations-Anthology-The Best Of The Temptations . . . . . . (Motown)
I Wish It Would Rain Down
Phil Collins; *...But Seriously* . . . . (Atlantic)
I Wish That We Were Married
Ronnie and The Hi-Lites; *Rockin' & Rollin' Wedding Songs-#2-C* . . . . . (Rhino)
I Wish You Could Have Turned My Head
Oak Ridge Boys; *Bobbie Sue* . . . . (MCA)
I Wish You Were Here Tonight
Ray Charles; *Greatest Hits Of Country Blues-C* . . . . (Columbia)
I Wish You Were Here Tonight . . . . (Columbia)
I Wished On The Moon
Billie Holiday; *Billie Holiday-Live* . . . . (Verve)
Stormy Blues . . . . (Verve)
Ella Fitzgerald; *Best Of Ella Fitzgerald* . . . . (MCA)
I Wonder
Abba; *Abba's Greatest Hits-#2* . . . . (Atlantic)
I Love Abba . . . . (Atlantic)
The Album . . . . (Atlantic)
I Wonder
Jimmy Witherspoon; *Best Of Jimmy Witherspoon* . . . . (Prestige)
Blue Spoon . . . . (Prestige)
I Wonder
Rosanne Cash; *Hits-1979-1989* . . . . (Columbia)
Somewhere In The Stars . . . . (Columbia)
I Wonder As I Wander
Barbra Streisand; *Barbra Streisand Christmas Album* . . . . (Columbia)
Gary Morris; *Every Christmas* . . . . (Liberty)
Grover Washington, Jr.; *Breath Of Heaven-A Holiday Collection* . . . (Columbia)
Joan Baez; *Noel* . . . . (Vanguard)
Julie Andrews; *Christmas With Julie Andrews* . . . . (Columbia)
Mormon Tabernacle Choir; *This Land Is Your Land* . . . . (Columbia)
Peter, Paul & Mary; *Holiday Celebration* . . . . (Warner Bros.)
Philadelphia Orchestra & Eugene Ormandy; *Sleigh Ride!-Classic Christmas*
Favorites-C . . . . (RCA)
Sandi Patty; *Gift Goes On* . . . . (Word)
Vanessa Williams; *Star Bright* . . . . (Mercury)
I Wonder Do You Think Of Me
Keith Whitley; *I Wonder Do You Think Of Me* . . . . (RCA)
I Wonder How It Is In Colorado
Gene Watson; *Reflections* . . . . (Capitol)
I Wonder How The Old Folks Are At Home
Doc & Merle Watson; *Home Sweet Home* . . . . (Sugar Hill)
I Wonder If Heaven Got A Ghetto
2Pac; *R U Still Down (Remember Me)* . . . . (Amaru/Jive)

I Wonder If I Care As Much
Everly Brothers; *All They Had To Do Was Dream* . . . . (Rhino)
Everly Brothers . . . . (Rhino)
Everly Brothers-Cadence Classics-Their 20 Greatest Hits . . . . . (Rhino)
Ricky Skaggs; *Love's Gonna Get Ya* . . . . (Epic)
I Wonder If I Take You Home
Lisa Lisa & Cult Jam With Full Force; *Breakdancing* . . . . (Columbia)
Lisa Lisa & Cult Jam With Full Force . . . . (Columbia)
I Wonder If You Feel The Way I Do
Asleep At The Wheel featuring Merle Haggard; *Tribute To The Music Of*
Bob Wills And The Texas Playboys-C . . . . (Liberty)
Bob Wills & His Texas Playboys; *For The Last Time* . . . . (Capitol)
I Wonder What She's Doing Tonite
Tommy Boyce & Bobby Hart; *More Nuggets-C* . . . . (Rhino)
I Wonder What The King Is Doing Tonight
Original Cast; *Camelot* . . . . (Columbia)
Richard Harris; *ST/Camelot* . . . . (Warner Bros.)
I Wonder Where You Are Tonight
Bill Monroe; *Bean Blossom* . . . . (MCA)
Jerry Lee Lewis; *Country Music Hall Of Fame Hits* . . . . (Smash)
Keith Whitley; *L.A. To Miami* . . . . (RCA)
I Wonder Who's Holding My Baby
Whites; *Whites' Greatest Hits* . . . . (Curb)
I Wonder Who's Kissing Her Now
Bobby Darin; *Capitol Collectors Series-Bobby Darin* . . . . (Capitol)
Ted Weems & His Orchestra; *Sweetest Sounds Ever Heard-C* . . . (Hip-O)
I Wonder Why
Dion And The Belmonts; *Doo-Wop Uptempo-#2-C* . . . . (Rhino)
Everything You Always Wanted . . . . (Laurie)
Million-Dollar Memories #1-C . . . . (RCA)
Oldies But Goodies-#12-C . . . . (Original Sound)
Super Oldies Of The '50s-#7-C . . . . (Audio Fidelity)
You Found The Vocal Group Sound-#1-C . . . . (Solid Smoke)
I Wonder Why
Curtis Stigers; *Curtis Stigers* . . . . (Arista)
I Wonder Why She Kept On Saying "Si-Si-Si-Si Senor"
Al Jolson; *Music From The New York Stage (1890-1920)-#4-1917-*
1920-C . . . . (Pearl)
I'd Like To Be A Cowboy
Cathy Fink; *Grandma Slid Down The Mountain* . . . . (Rounder)
Mary-Kate & Ashley Olsen; *Give Us A Mystery* . . . . (Zoom Express)
I'd Like To Teach The World To Sing (In Perfect Harmony)
New Seekers; *Chicken Soup For The Soul-Celebrating Life-C* . . . . (Rhino)
If
Bread; *Best Of Bread* . . . . (Elektra)
Bread-Anthology . . . . (Elektra)
Bread-Retrospective . . . . (Rhino)
Manna . . . . (Rhino)
If
Janet Jackson; *janet.* . . . . (Virgin)
If
Perry Como; *Perry Como's All-Time Greatest Hits-#1* . . . . (RCA)
If 6 Was 9
Jimi Hendrix; *Axis: Bold As Love* . . . . (Reprise)
Essential Jimi Hendrix . . . . (Reprise)
If He Walked Into My Life
Original Cast; *Mame* . . . . (Columbia)
If I Could
Barbra Streisand; *Higher Ground* . . . . (Columbia)
If I Could Be With You
Helen Humes; *Ladies Sing The Blues-#2-C* . . . . (Savoy)
Louis Armstrong; *Best Of Louis Armstrong* . . . . (MCA)
Satchmo-Musical Autobiography-#2 . . . . (MCA)
The Louis Armstrong Story-#4 . . . . (Columbia)
If I Could Build My Whole World Around You
Marvin Gaye & Tammi Terrell; *Every Great Motown Hit Of*
Marvin Gaye . . . . (Motown)
Marvin Gaye & Tammi Terrell's Greatest Hits . . . . (Motown)
Marvin Gaye-Anthology . . . . (Motown)
Motown Superstar Series-#2-Marvin Gaye . . . . (Motown)
United . . . . (Motown)
If I Could Have Her Tonight
Neil Young; *Neil Young* . . . . (Reprise)
If I Could Only Dance With You
Jim Glaser; *Man In The Mirror* . . . . (Noble Vision)
If I Could Only Win Your Love
Emmylou Harris; *Pieces Of The Sky* . . . . (Reprise)
Profile/Best Of Emmylou Harris . . . . (Warner Bros.)
If I Could Turn Back The Hands Of Time
R. Kelly; *Now That's What I Call Music!-#3-C* . . . . (Virgin)
R. . . . . (Jive)
If I Could Turn Back Time
Cher; *Heart Of Stone* . . . . (Geffen)
If I Fell
Beatles; *Beatles-Love Songs* . . . . (Capitol)
Something New . . . . (Capitol)
ST/A Hard Day's Night . . . . (Capitol)
If I Had A $1,000,000
Barenaked Ladies; *Disc One 1991-2001-All Their Greatest Hits* . . . . (Reprise)

If I Had A Boat
Lyle Lovett; *Pontiac* . . . . (MCA)
If I Had You
Frank Sinatra; *Round #1* . . . . (Capitol)
  Voice: The Columbia Years-1943-1952 . . . . (Columbia)
Judy Garland; *Judy Garland-Collector's Items-1936-1945* . . . . (MCA)
Platters; *Platters Greatest Hits* . . . . (Everest)
If I Had You
Alabama; *Southern Star* . . . . (RCA)
If I Loved You
Barbra Streisand; *The Broadway Album* . . . . (Columbia)
Original Cast; *Carousel* . . . . (MCA)
If I Needed You
Don Williams; *Especially For You* . . . . (MCA)
Emmylou Harris; *Cimarron* . . . . (Warner Bros.)
Emmylou Harris & Don Williams; *Classic Country Duets-C* . . . . (Reprise)
  Duets-C . . . . (Reprise)
If I Only Had A Brain
Harry Connick, Jr.; *20* . . . . (Columbia)
Kay Kyser & His Orchestra; *Best Of The Big Bands-C* . . . . (Columbia)
Original Soundtrack; *The Wizard Of Oz-The Deluxe Edition* . . . . (Rhino)
  The Wizard Of Oz-The Story And Songs . . . . (Rhino)
If I Only Had A Heart
Jack Haley; *ST/The Wizard Of Oz* . . . . (Sony Music Special Prod.)
Original Soundtrack; *The Wizard Of Oz-The Deluxe Edition* . . . . (Rhino)
  The Wizard Of Oz-The Story And Songs . . . . (Rhino)
If I Ruled The World
NaS; *It Was Written* . . . . (Columbia)
If I Wanted To
Melissa Etheridge; *Yes I Am* . . . . (Island)
If I Was Your Girlfriend
Prince; *The Hits 2* . . . . (Paisley Park)
  The Hits/The B-Sides . . . . (Paisley Park)
If I Were A Bell
Original Cast; *Guys & Dolls* . . . . (MCA)
If I Were A Bell
Teena Marie; *Ivory* . . . . (Epic)
If I Were A Carpenter
Bobby Darin; *Live At The Desert Inn* . . . . (Motown)
Four Tops; *Compact Command Performances-Four Tops* . . . . . . (Motown)
  Four Tops Reach Out . . . . (Motown)
  Four Tops-Anthology . . . . (Motown)
Johnny Cash & June Carter; *The Man In Black-His Greatest Hits* . . . . . (Legacy)
Tim Hardin; *Memorial Album* . . . . (Polydor)
If I Were A Rich Man
Original Cast; *Fiddler On The Roof* . . . . (RCA Victor)
If I Were King Of The Forest
Bert Lahr; *ST/The Wizard Of Oz* . . . . (Sony Music Special Prod.)
If I Were Your Woman
Gladys Knight; *At Last* . . . . (MCA)
Gladys Knight & The Pips; *Compact Command Performances-Gladys Knight
  & The Pips* . . . . (Motown)
  Every Great Motown Song-First 25 Years-C . . . . (Motown)
  Gladys Knight & The Pips-All The Great Hits . . . . . . (Motown)
  Gladys Knight & The Pips-Anthology . . . . (Motown)
  If I Were Your Woman . . . . (Motown)
  Motown Superstar Series-#13-Gladys Knight & The Pips . (Motown)
If I'd Been The One
38 Special; *Flashback-Best Of 38 Special* . . . . (A&M)
  Tour De Force . . . . (A&M)
If Momma Was Married
Cynthia Gibb & Jennifer Beck; *ST/Gypsy* . . . . (Atlantic)
Original Cast; *Gypsy* . . . . (Columbia)
If My Friends Could See Me Now
Original Cast/Gwen Verdon; *Sweet Charity* . . . . (Columbia)
If The South Woulda Won
Hank Williams, Jr.; *Wild Streak* . . . . (WB/Curb)
If There Hadn't Been You
Billy Dean; *Billy Dean* . . . . (Liberty)
If This World Were Mine
Cheryl Lynn; *Instant Love* . . . . (Columbia)
Luther Vandross & Cheryl Lynn; *Best Of Luther Vandross...The Best
  Of Love* . . . . (Epic)
Marvin Gaye & Tammi Terrell; *All The Great Motown Love Song
  Duets-C* . . . . (Motown)
  Classic Duets-Marvin Gaye & His Women-C . . . . (Motown)
  Marvin Gaye & Tammi Terrell's Greatest Hits . . . . . . (Motown)
  Marvin Gaye-Anthology . . . . (Motown)
  Motown Superstar Series-#2-Marvin Gaye . . . . (Motown)
  United . . . . (Motown)
If Tomorrow Never Comes
Garth Brooks; *Garth Brooks* . . . . (Liberty)
  Limited Series-Box . . . . (Capitol)
Joose; *Joose* . . . . (Flavor Unit)
If Walls Could Talk
Celine Dion; *All The Way...A Decade Of Song* . . . . (550 Music)
If Wishes Came True
Sweet Sensation; *Love Child* . . . . (Atco)

If You Asked Me To
Celine Dion; *All The Way...A Decade Of Song* . . . . (550 Music)
  Celine Dion . . . . (Epic)
Patti LaBelle; *Be Yourself* . . . . (MCA)
  Soundtrack Smashes-'80s & More-C . . . . (MCA)
  ST/License To Kill . . . . (MCA)
If You Could Only See
Tonic; *Lemon Parade* . . . . (Polydor)
  Now That's What I Call Music!-#1-C . . . . (Virgin)
If You Could Read My Mind
Gordon Lightfoot; *Gord's Gold* . . . . (Reprise)
  If You Could Read My Mind . . . . (Reprise)
  Sit Down Young Stranger . . . . (Reprise)
If You Could See Me Now
Sarah Vaughan & Count Basie; *Pablo Today-Send In The Clowns* . . . . (Pablo)
If You Ever Change Your Mind
Crystal Gayle; *Crystal Gayle Greatest Hits* . . . . (Columbia)
  These Days . . . . (Columbia)
If You Go Away
Neil Diamond; *Neil Diamond-Love Songs* . . . . (MCA)
  Rainbow . . . . (MCA)
  Stones . . . . (MCA)
If You Were The Only Boy (In The World)
Barbra Streisand; *My Name Is Barbra* . . . . (Columbia)
If You Were Wondering
Peter Allen; *I Could Have Been A Sailor* . . . . (A&M)
I'll Be Back
Beatles; *Beatles '65* . . . . (Capitol)
  Beatles-Love Songs . . . . (Capitol)
I'll Get You
Beatles; *Past Masters-Volume One* . . . . (Parlophone)
  The Beatles' Second Album . . . . (Capitol)
I'm A Loser
Beatles; *Beatles '65* . . . . (Capitol)
I'm Gonna Sit Right Down And Write Myself A Letter
Billy Williams; *Stardust: The Classic Decca Hits & Standards
  Collection-C* . . . . (Decca)
Fats Waller; *Fats Waller* . . . . (RCA Special Prod.)
Frank Sinatra; *Sinatra-Basie* . . . . (Reprise)
  Songs For Young Lovers & Swing Easy . . . . (Capitol)
Nat "King" Cole; *Just One Of Those Things (& More)* . . . . . . (Capitol)
  Nat "King" Cole-Gift Set . . . . (Capitol)
Original Cast; *Ain't Misbehavin'* . . . . (RCA)
I'm So Happy I Can't Stop Crying
Sting; *Mercury Falling* . . . . (A&M)
Toby Keith with Sting; *Dream Walkin'* . . . . (Mercury)
  Toby Keith's Greatest Hits, Volume One . . . . (Mercury)
I'm Wondering
Stevie Wonder; *Stevie Wonder's Greatest Hits-#1* . . . . . . (Motown)
Imaginary Lover
Atlanta Rhythm Section; *Champagne Jam* . . . . (Polydor)
Imagination
Cleo Laine; *That Old Feeling* . . . . (Columbia)
Frank Sinatra; *I Remember Tommy* . . . . (Reprise)
Glenn Miller & His Orchestra; *Complete Glenn Miller & His
  Orchestra-#4* . . . . (Bluebird)
Harry Connick, Jr.; *Twenty* . . . . (Columbia)
Tommy Dorsey & Frank Sinatra; *Dorsey/Sinatra Sessions-#1* . . . . . (Bluebird)
Imagination
Tamia; *Tamia* . . . . (Qwest)
Imagination
B.B. & Q. Band; *B.B. & Q. Band* . . . . (Capitol)
Imagine
Diana Ross; *Best Of The Beatles Songs-C* . . . . (Motown)
  Diana Ross-Anthology . . . . (Motown)
  Touch Me In The Morning . . . . (Motown)
Joan Baez; *Best Of Joan Baez* . . . . (A&M)
  Come From The Shadows . . . . (A&M)
John Lennon; *Lennon* . . . . (Capitol)
  Live In New York City . . . . (Capitol)
  ST/Imagine: John Lennon . . . . (Capitol)
John Lennon & Yoko Ono; *The John Lennon Collection* . . . . (Capitol)
John Lennon/Plastic Ono Band; *Imagine* . . . . (Capitol)
  Shaved Fish . . . . (Capitol)
Neil Young; *America: A Tribute To Heroes-C* . . . . (Interscope)
Imagine That
Diamond Rio; *Diamond Rio's Greatest Hits* . . . . (Arista)
Impossible!; It's Possible!
Celeste Holm & Lesley Ann Warren; *Cinderella-The CBS Television Network
  Production* . . . . (Columbia)
In A Perfect World
Lorrie Morgan; *Shakin' Things Up* . . . . (BNA)
In My Own Little Corner
Julie Andrews; *A Little Bit Of Broadway* . . . . (Columbia)
Cinderella-The CBS Television Production . . . . (Columbia)
Lesley Ann Warren; *Cinderella-The CBS Television Network
  Production* . . . . (Columbia)
Incomplete
Sisqo; *Now That's What I Call Music!-#5-C* . . . . (Virgin)

Unleash The Dragon. . . . .(Dragon/Def Soul/IDJMG)

Invisible Man
98 Degrees; *98 Degrees*. . . . . (Motown)

Is There Life Out There
Reba McEntire; *For My Broken Heart* . . . . (MCA)
Reba McEntire's Greatest Hits Volume Two . . . . (MCA)

It Should Have Been Me
Gladys Knight & The Pips; *Compact Command Performances-Gladys Knight & The Pips*. . . . . (Motown)
Gladys Knight & The Pips-Anthology. . . . . (Motown)
Motown Superstar Series-#13-Gladys Knight & The Pips . . . . (Motown)

It Should Have Been Me
Ray Charles; *Birth Of Soul-Complete Atlantic R&B 1952-1959-C* . . . . (Atlantic)

It Should Have Been Me
Carly Simon; *Coming Around Again*. (Arista)

It Should Have Been Me
Neil Diamond; *Headed For The Future*. . . . . (Columbia)

It Should've Been Me
Commander Cody & His Lost Planet Airmen; *Hot Licks, Cold Steel & Trucker's Favorites* . . . . (MCA)

It's Good To Be King
Tom Petty; *Wildflowers*. . . . . (Warner Bros.)

It's Only A Paper Moon
Art Blakey & His Jazz Messengers; *Big Beat* . . . .(Blue Note)
Bing Crosby; *The Radio Years-#2* . . . . (Crescendo)
David Rose & His Orchestra; *Music Of The 1930s-C* . . . . (MCA)
Ella Fitzgerald; *Harold Arlen Songbook-#2* . . . . (Verve)
Frank Sinatra; *Round #1* . . . . (Capitol)
Mystics; *Mystics-16 Golden Classics* . . . . (Collectables)
Nat ''King'' Cole; *Capitol Sings Harold Arlen: Over The Rainbow-C*. . . . . (Gold Rush)
The Nat ''King'' Cole Story . . . . (Capitol)
Sammy Kaye & His Orchestra; *Sammy Kaye & His Orchestra Play 22 Original Big Band Recordings*. . . . .(Hindsight)

It's Only Make Believe
Conway Twitty; *Conway Twitty-Number Ones-#1* . . . .(Liberty)
Conway Twitty's Greatest Hits-#2 . . . . (MCA)
Conway's #1 Classics-#2 . . . . (Warner Bros.)
Very Best Of Conway Twitty . . . . (MCA)
Glen Campbell; *Very Best Of Glen Campbell* . . . . (Capitol)

I've Got To Use My Imagination
Gladys Knight & The Pips; *Best Of Gladys Knight & The Pips*. . . . .(Pair)
Gladys Knight & The Pips' Greatest Hits. . . . . (Curb)
Soul Survivors-Best Of Gladys Knight & The Pips-1973-1988. . . . . . . (Rhino)
ST/Forrest Gump . . . . (Epic/Sony Music Soundtrax)
Joe Cocker; *One Night Of Sin* . . . . (Capitol)

January Friend
Goo Goo Dolls; *Dizzy Up The Girl* . . . . (Warner Sunset/Reprise)

Johnny Angel
Shelley Fabares; *Billboard Top Rock 'N' Roll Hits-1962-C* . . . .(Rhino)
ST/Mermaids . . . . (Geffen)

Joining You
Alanis Morissette; *Supposed Former Infatuation Junkie*. . . . . (Maverick)

Judy In Disguise (With Glasses)
John Fred & His Playboy Band; *Billboard Top Rock 'N' Roll Hits-1968-C* . . . . (Rhino)
Cruisin'-1967-C . . . . (Increase)
ST/Drugstore Cowboy . . . . (Novus)
Super Oldies Of The '60s-#7-C . . . . (Audio Fidelity)

Just Like Anyone
Soul Asylum; *Let Your Dim Light Shine* . . . . (Columbia)

Just My Imagination (Running Away With Me)
Rolling Stones; *''Still Life'' (American Concert 1981)*. . . . .(Virgin)
Some Girls . . . . (Virgin)
Temptations; *12 #1 Hits From The '70s-C* . . . . (Motown)
20 Greatest Songs In Motown History-C . . . . (Motown)
25 #1 Hits From 25 Years-C . . . . (Motown)
All The Million-Sellers . . . . (Motown)
Compact Command Performances-Temptations . . . . (Motown)
Temptations-25th Anniversary . . . . (Motown)
Temptations-Anthology-The Best Of The Temptations . . . . (Motown)

Just One Night
McBride & The Ride; *Sacred Ground*. . . . . (MCA)

Just You Wait
Julie Andrews/Original Cast; *My Fair Lady* . . . . (Columbia)

King Nothing
Metallica; *Load* . . . . (Elektra)

King Of Wishful Thinking
Go West; *ST/Pretty Woman* . . . . (EMI)

Land Of Make Believe
Chuck Mangione; *Best Of Chuck Mangione* . . . . (Mercury)
Chuck Mangione-Classics-#6. . . . . (A&M)
Encore-Chuck Mangione . . . . (Mercury)
Evening Of Magic . . . . (A&M)
Land Of Make Believe . . . . (Mercury)

Land Of Make Believe
Moody Blues; *Seventh Sojourn* . . . . (Polydor)

Last Day, The
Marilyn Scott; *Avenues Of Love* . . . . (Warner Bros.)

Last Resort
Papa Roach; *Infest* . . . . (DreamWorks/SKG)

Lately
Tyrese; *Tyrese* . . . . (RCA)

Let's Pretend
Al Jarreau; *Al Jarreau In London* . . . .(Warner Bros.)
High Crime . . . .(Warner Bros.)

Let's Pretend
Raspberries; *Best Of The Raspberries* . . . .(Capitol)
Capitol Collectors Series-The Raspberries . . . .(Capitol)

Let's Pretend
Willie Nelson; *Broken Promises* . . . . (Intermedia)
Diamonds In The Rough . . . .(Delmark)

Let's Pretend We're Married
Prince; *1999* . . . .(Warner Bros.)
Tina Turner; *Collected Recordings: Sixties To Nineties*. . . . .(Capitol)

Lie To Me
Jonny Lang; *Lie To Me*. . . . .(A&M)

Life Of Illusion
Joe Walsh; *There Goes The Neighborhood* . . . . (Asylum)

Little Bitty Tear
Burl Ives; *Best Of Burl Ives-#2*. (MCA)
Burl Ives Live . . . . (MCA)
MCA Records 30 Years Of Hits-1958-1988-C. . . . . (MCA)
Hank Cochran; *45-#47062* . . . . (Elektra)

Little Star
Elegants; *Billboard Top Rock 'N' Roll Hits-1958-C* . . . .(Rhino)
Oldies But Goodies-#5-C . . . . (Original Sound)
Super Oldies Of The '50s-#7-C . . . . (Audio Fidelity)

Living In A Fantasy
Leo Sayer; *All The Best* . . . . (Chrysalis)

Longing In Their Hearts
Bonnie Raitt; *Longing In Their Hearts*. . . . .(Capitol)

Love Scene
Joe; *All That I Am* . . . . (Jive)

Lovely Night, A
Julie Andrews; *A Little Bit Of Broadway* . . . . (Columbia)
Julie Andrews/Original Cast; *Cinderella-The CBS Television Production* . . . . (Columbia)

Lucy In The Sky With Diamonds
Beatles; *Sgt. Pepper's Lonely Hearts Club Band* . . . . (Capitol)
The Beatles/1967-1970 . . . .(Capitol)
Yellow Submarine . . . .(Capitol)
Elton John; *All This & World War 2*. . . . .(20th Century Fox)
Elton John's Greatest Hits-#2 . . . . (Polydor)
John Lennon; *Lennon*. . . . .(Capitol)

Lyin' Eyes
Eagles; *Eagles/Their Greatest Hits 1971-1975* . . . . (Asylum)
One Of These Nights . . . . (Asylum)
ST/Urban Cowboy. . . . . (Asylum)

Make Believe
Barbara Cook & John Raitt/Original Cast; *Show Boat*. . . . .(Columbia)
Barbra Streisand; *Third Album*. . . . . (Columbia)

Make Believe
Kenny Rankin; *The Kenny Rankin Album* . . . . (Little David)

Make Believe
Toto; *Toto IV* . . . .(Columbia)

Make Believe Ballroom Time
Glenn Miller; *Glenn Miller-A Legendary Performer-#1 & 2* . . . .(Bluebird)
Glenn Miller & His Orchestra; *Complete Glenn Miller & His Orchestra-#5* . . . .(Bluebird)

Make Believe It's Your First Time
Carpenters; *Carpenters-Classics-#2* . . . .(A&M)
Voice Of The Heart . . . .(A&M)
Yesterday Once More . . . .(A&M)

Make Believe It's Your First Time
Bobby Vinton; *Encore-Bobby Vinton* . . . .(Tapestry)

Make Me A Mask
Fleetwood Mac; *25 Years-The Chain*. . . . . (Warner Bros.)

Marriage On Paper Only
Dramatics; *Anytime Anyplace* . . . . (MCA)

Mary Lou
Bruce Springsteen; *Tracks* . . . .(Columbia)

Masquerade
Original London Cast; *Phantom Of The Opera* . . . . (Polydor)

Masquerade
Howard Hewett; *Allegiance* . . . .(Elektra)

Masquerade
Frames; *Another Love Song* . . . .(Island)

Masquerade
Berlin; *Best Of Berlin 1979-1988*. . . . .(Geffen)
Pleasure Victim . . . . (Geffen)

Masquerade
Evelyn Thomas; *Best Of Evelyn Thomas* . . . . (Hot Prod.)

Masquerade
Basia; *Brave New Hope* . . . . (Epic)

Masquerade
Dave Valentin; *Dave Valentin-Legends*. . . . .(GRP)

Masquerade
First Call; *Human Song*. . . . .(Epic)
Masquerade
Swing Out Sister; *Kaleidoscope World*. . . . .(Fontana)
Masquerade
Yes; *Union* . . . . (Arista)
Masquerade Is Over (I'm Afraid)
Al Jarreau; *1965* . . . . (Bainbridge)
Carmen McRae; *Jazzy Ladies-C*. . . . .(Dunhill Compact Classics)
Ms. Magic. . . . .(Dunhill Compact Classics)
Five Satins; *Five Satins Sing Their Greatest Hits* . . . . (Collectables)
Lodi Carr; *Lady Bird*. . . . . (Laurie)
Nancy Wilson & Cannonball Adderley; *Blue Series-Female*
Vocals-C . . . . (Blue Note)
Misery And Gin
Merle Haggard; *Back To The Barrooms* . . . .(MCA)
Merle Haggard's Greatest Hits . . . .(MCA)
Rainbow Stew-Live At Anaheim Stadium . . . .(MCA)
Modern Age, The
Strokes; *Is This It* . . . . (RCA)
Money Burns A Hole In My Pocket
Dean Martin; *Capitol Collectors Series-Dean Martin* . . . . (Capitol)
Mrs. Steven Rudy
Mark McGuinn; *Mark McGuinn*. . . . . (VFR)
My All
Mariah Carey; *Butterfly* . . . . (Columbia)
Mariah Carey-#1's . . . . (Columbia)
VH-1 Divas Live-C. . . . . (Epic)
My Baby Thinks He's A Train
Rosanne Cash; *Rosanne Cash-Hits-1979-1989* . . . . (Columbia)
Seven Year Ache. . . . . (Columbia)
My Baby Thinks She's A Train
Asleep At The Wheel; *Freight Train Blues-Classic Railroad*
Songs-#4-C . . . . (Rounder)
Very Best Of Asleep At The Wheel Since 1970 . . . . (Relentless/Madacy)
My Cherie Amour
Stevie Wonder; *My Cherie Amour* . . . . (Motown)
Natural Wonder . . . . (Motown)
Song Review-A Greatest Hits Collection . . . . (Motown)
Stevie Wonder's Greatest Hits-#2 . . . . (Motown)
My Silent Love
Bing Crosby; *Where The Blue Of The Night Meets The Gold Of*
The Day. . . . . (Biograph)
Peggy Lee; *Mink Jazz* . . . . (Blue Note)
Never Had A Dream Come True
S Club 7; *Now That's What I Call Music!-#7-C* . . . . (Virgin)
S Club 7 . . . . (A&M)
Never Never Land
Original Cast/Mary Martin; *Peter Pan-The 1954 Broadway*
Production . . . .(RCA Victor)
Nickel In The Well
Shenandoah; *Under The Kudzu* . . . . (RCA)
Nietzche's Eyes
Paula Cole; *This Fire* . . . . (Imago)
No Imagination
Blondie; *Plastic Letters* . . . .(Chrysalis)
No Myth
Michael Penn; *March* . . . . (RCA)
Nobody Knows
Kevin Sharp; *Measure Of A Man* . . . . (143/Asylum)
Tony Rich Project; *Words*. . . . . (LaFace)
Nobody Knows You When You're Down And Out
Bessie Smith; *Bessie Smith-The Collection* . . . . (Legacy)
Bessie Smith-The Complete Recordings-#4 . . . . (Legacy)
Derek And The Dominos; *Layla*. . . . . (Polydor)
Eric Clapton; *Eric Clapton-Unplugged* . . . . (Reprise)
Otis Redding; *Soul Album*. . . . . (Atco)
Rod Stewart; *Out Of Order*. . . . .(Warner Bros.)
Old Man And Me
Hootie & The Blowfish; *Fairweather Johnson* . . . . (Atlantic)
On A Bus To St. Cloud
Gretchen Peters; *The Secret Of Life* . . . . (Purple Crayon Prod.)
Trisha Yearwood; *Thinkin' About You* . . . . (MCA)
One More Day
Diamond Rio; *One More Day*. . . . . (Arista)
One Wish
Hiroshima; *Another Place* . . . . (Epic)
Only In America
Brooks & Dunn; *Steers & Stripes* . . . . (Arista)
Ooh La La
Rod Stewart; *When We Were The New Boys* . . . .(Warner Bros.)
Open Your Eyes
Yes; *Open Your Eyes* . . . . (Beyond)
Out Of The Woods
Nickel Creek; *Nickel Creek* . . . . (Sugar Hill)
Over The Rainbow
Barbra Streisand; *Just For The Record* . . . . (Columbia)
Dave Brubeck; *Greatest Hits From The Fantasy Years* . . . . (Fantasy)

Ella Fitzgerald; *Silver Collection-Songbooks* . . . . (Verve)
Judy Garland; *Best Of The Capitol Masters-One & Only Box*. . . . . (Capitol)
Judy Garland-At Carnegie Hall . . . . (Capitol)
Judy Garland's Greatest Hits . . . . (Curb)
Miss Show Business . . . . (Capitol)
One & Only . . . . (Capitol)
ST/The Wizard Of Oz . . . .(Sony Music Special Prod.)
Patriotic Fantasy
Original New York Cast; *Oil City Symphony* . . . .(DRG)
Picture Postcards From L.A.
Joshua Kadison; *Painted Desert Serenade* . . . . (SBK)
Picture This
Jim Brickman; *Picture This*. . . . .(Windham Hill)
Plastic People
Mothers Of Invention; *Absolutely Free*. . . . . (Rykodisc)
Pore Jud Is Daid
Original Cast; *Oklahoma!* . . . . (MCA)
Prayin' For Daylight
Rascal Flatts; *Rascal Flatts* . . . .(Lyric Street)
Pretend
Nat ''King'' Cole; *Capitol Collectors Series-Nat ''King'' Cole* . . . . . . (Capitol)
The Nat ''King'' Cole Story . . . . (Capitol)
Unforgettable . . . . (Capitol)
Pretend I Never Happened
Willie Nelson; *Me & Paul* . . . . (Columbia)
Phases & Stages . . . . (Atlantic)
Pretend You Don't See Her
Jerry Vale; *Jerry Vale-17 Most Requested Songs* . . . . (Legacy)
Jerry Vale's All-Time Greatest Hits . . . . (Columbia)
Jerry Vale's Greatest Hits . . . . (Columbia)
Pretender
Hanoi Rocks; *Bangkok Shocks Saigon Shakes Hanoi Rocks* . . . . (Geffen)
Pretender
Madonna; *Like A Virgin* . . . . (Sire)
Pretender
Jackson Browne; *The Pretender* . . . .(Asylum)
Pretending
Eric Clapton; *24 Nights* . . . . (Duck/Reprise)
Journeyman . . . . (Duck/Reprise)
Pretending
Karen Brooks & Randy Sharp; *That's Another Story* . . . . (Mercury)
Pretending Love
Little Johnny & Ted Taylor; *Super Taylors* . . . .(Ronn)
Pretending She's You
Jimmie Davis; *Jimmie Davis-Golden Hits-#2* . . . . (Plantation)
Pretending To Be Drunk
Sparks; *Pulling Rabbits Out Of A Hat* . . . .(Atlantic)
Pretending To Care
Jennifer Warnes; *The Hunter* . . . . (Private Music)
Todd Rundgren; *A Cappella* . . . . (Warner Bros.)
Pretending To Care
Daryl Braithwaite; *Edge* . . . . (Epic Portrait Assoc.)
Pseudo Silk Kimono
Marillion; *Misplaced Childhood* . . . . (Capitol)
Punky's Dilemma
Simon & Garfunkel; *Bookends* . . . . (Columbia)
Collected Works . . . . (Columbia)
Puppy Song
Nilsson; *Harry*. (Dunhill Compact Classics)
ST/You've Got Mail . . . .(Atlantic)
Put Yourself In My Place
Pam Tillis; *Put Yourself In My Place*. (Arista)
Quittin' Time
Mary Chapin Carpenter; *Greatest Country Hits Of The '90s-*
1990-C . . . . (Columbia)
State Of The Heart . . . . (Columbia)
Rainbow Stew
Merle Haggard; *For The Record: Merle Haggard-43 Legendary Hits* . . . .(BNA)
Merle Haggard's Greatest Hits . . . . (MCA)
More Of The Best . . . . (Rhino)
Rainbow Stew-Live At Anaheim Stadium . . . . (MCA)
Razor Love
Neil Young; *Silver & Gold* . . . . (Reprise)
Real World
Matchbox Twenty; *Yourself Or Someone Like You*. . . . . (Lava)
Re-Arranged
Limp Bizkit; *Significant Other* . . . .(Flip/Interscope)
Reflection
Christina Aguilera; *Christina Aguilera*. (RCA)
ST/Mulan . . . . (Walt Disney)
Remember Me This Way
Jordan Hill; *Jordan Hill*. . . . .(Atlantic)
ST/Casper. . . . . (MCA)
River
Betty Buckley; *With One Look* . . . .(Sterling)
Joni Mitchell; *Blue* . . . . (Reprise)
Rock & Roll Fantasy
Kinks; *15-Year History Of Rock* . . . . (Arista)

'70s Greatest Rock Hits-#14-King Of Rock-C . . . (Priority)
Come Dancing With The Kinks-Best Of The Kinks 1977-1986 . . . (Arista)
Misfits . . . (Arista)

Rock & Roll Fantasy
Bad Company; *10 From 6* . . . (Atlantic)
Desolation Angels . . . (Swan Song)

Runaway
Bonnie Raitt; *Bonnie Raitt-Collection* . . . (Warner Bros.)
Sweet Forgiveness . . . (Warner Bros.)
Del Shannon; *Billboard Top Rock 'N' Roll Hits-1961-C* . . . (Rhino)
Cruisin'-1961-C . . . (Increase)
Del Shannon's Greatest Hits . . . (Rhino)
Heart & Soul Of Rock 'N' Roll-#1-C . . . (Rhino)
Little Town Flirt . . . (Rhino)
ST/American Graffiti . . . (MCA)
Elvis Presley; *Collector's Gold* . . . (RCA)

She Dreams
Mark Chesnutt; *What A Way To Live* . . . (Decca)

She Said
Collective Soul; *Dosage* . . . (Atlantic)
ST/Scream 2 . . . (Dimension/Capitol)

Should've Been A Cowboy
Toby Keith; *Toby Keith* . . . (Mercury)

Simple Days
Babyface; *The Day* . . . (Epic)

Smile
Lonestar; *Lonely Grill* . . . (BNA)

So Much For Pretending
Bryan White; *Between Now And Forever* . . . (Asylum)

Somebody's Baby
Jackson Browne; *ST/Fast Times At Ridgemont High* . . . (Elektra)
The Next Voice You Hear-Best Of Jackson Browne . . . (Elektra)

Someday
Sugar Ray; *14:59* . . . (Lava)
Totally Hits-#1-C . . . (Arista)

Someone Else's Star
Bryan White; *Bryan White* . . . (Asylum)
Real Luv: Ultimate Country Love Songs-C . . . (EMI)

Sometimes A Fantasy
Billy Joel; *Glass Houses* . . . (Columbia)
KOHUEPT . . . (Columbia)

Spanish Guitar
Toni Braxton; *The Heat* . . . (LaFace)

Standing On The Corner
Broadway Cast; *Most Happy Fella* . . . (RCA)
Dean Martin; *Best Of Dean Martin* . . . (CEMA Special Prod.)
Four Lads; *Four Lads-16 Most Requested Songs* . . . (Legacy)
Original Broadway Cast; *Most Happy Fella* . . . (Sony Music Classical)

Starlight, Starbright
Linda Scott; *45-#133* . . . (Eric)

Stranger
Johnny Duncan; *Country Music Classics-#12-C* . . . (K-Tel)
Johnny Duncan-Classic Country . . . (Simitar)

Strut
Sheena Easton; *Best Of Sheena Easton* . . . (EMI)
Dance Mix . . . (EMI)
Private Heaven . . . (EMI)
The World Of Sheena Easton: The Singles Collection-C . . . (EMI)

Substitute
Great White; *Great White* . . . (EMI)
Sex Pistols; *Live At Chelmsford Top Security Prison* . . . (Restless)
Who; *Live At Leeds* . . . (MCA)
Meaty Beaty Big & Bouncy . . . (MCA)
Who Greatest Hits . . . (MCA)
Who's Last . . . (MCA)

Summertime
Sundays; *Static & Silence* . . . (David Geffen Co.)

Superman (I Wish I Could Fly Like)
Kinks; *Come Dancing With The Kinks-Best Of The Kinks 1977-1986* . . . (Arista)
Low Budget . . . (Arista)

Surrey With The Fringe On Top
Ellis Marsalis; *Heart Of Gold* . . . (Columbia)
Original Broadway Cast; *Oklahoma!* . . . (RCA)
Original Cast; *Oklahoma!* . . . (MCA)

Swinging On A Star
Bing Crosby; *All-Time Best* . . . (Curb)
Best Of Bing Crosby . . . (MCA)
Dion And The Belmonts; *Dion And The Belmonts-Their Best* . . . (Laurie)
Frank Sinatra; *Frank Sinatra Sings The Songs Of Van Heusen & Cahn* . . . (Reprise)

Take Me There
Blackstreet & Mya featuring Mase & Blinky Blink; *Finally* . . . (Lil' Man/Interscope)
Now That's What I Call Music!-#2-C . . . (Virgin)
ST/Rugrats . . . (Interscope)

Talking In Your Sleep
Crystal Gayle; *Classic Crystal* . . . (EMI)
Country Gold-C . . . (Priority)
Crystal Gayle's All-Time Greatest Hits . . . (Curb)
When I Dream . . . (Liberty)
Reba McEntire; *Starting Over* . . . (MCA)

Tears Of A Clown
English Beat; *I Just Can't Stop It* . . . (I.R.S.)
What Is Beat . . . (I.R.S.)
Smokey Robinson & The Miracles; *25 #1 Hits From 25 Years-C* . . . (Motown)
Billboard Top Rock 'N' Roll Hits-1970-C . . . (Rhino)
Compact Command Performances-Smokey Robinson & The Miracles . . . (Motown)
Endless Love-Motown's Greatest Love Songs-C . . . (Motown)
Smokey Robinson & The Miracles' Anthology . . . (Motown)
Tears Of A Clown . . . (Motown)

Teenage Dirtbag
Wheatus; *Wheatus* . . . (Columbia)

Tell Me I Was Dreaming
Travis Tritt; *Ten Feet Tall And Bulletproof* . . . (Warner Bros.)
Travis Tritt's Greatest Hits-From The Beginning . . . (Warner Bros.)

Ten Feet Tall And Bulletproof
Travis Tritt; *Ten Feet Tall And Bulletproof* . . . (Warner Bros.)

That's As Close As I'll Get To Loving You
Aaron Tippin; *Aaron Tippin-Super Hits* . . . (RCA)
Essential Aaron Tippin . . . (RCA)
Greatest Hits And Then Some . . . (RCA)
Tool Box . . . (RCA)

Theme From "Fantasy Island"
Original Soundtrack; *Television's Greatest Hits-#6-Remote Control-C* . . . (TVT)

This Masquerade
Carpenters; *Carpenters-Classics-#2* . . . (A&M)
Now & Then . . . (A&M)
Yesterday Once More . . . (A&M)
David Sanborn; *Pearls* . . . (Elektra)
George Benson; *Breezin'* . . . (Warner Bros.)
George Benson-Collection . . . (Warner Bros.)
Leon Russell; *Best Of Leon Russell* . . . (MCA)
Carney . . . (Right Stuff)
Gimme Shelter! The Best Of Leon Russell . . . (Capitol)

This Nearly Was Mine
Original Cast; *South Pacific* . . . (CBS Masterworks)

Those Lazy Hazy Crazy Days Of Summer
Nat "King" Cole; *Best Of Nat "King" Cole-Vol. 1* . . . (Capitol)
Capitol Collectors Series-Nat "King" Cole . . . (Capitol)

Three Coins In The Fountain
Andy Williams; *Moon River & Other Great Movie Themes* . . . (Columbia)
Doris Day & Frank De Vol Orchestra; *Hooray For Hollywood-#2-C* . . . (Columbia)
Four Aces; *Billboard Top Movie Hits-1950-1954-C* . . . (Rhino)
Four Aces' Greatest Hits . . . (MCA)
Frank Sinatra; *At The Movies* . . . (Capitol)
Capitol Collectors Series-Frank Sinatra . . . (Capitol)
Harry James; *Harry James Plays The Songs That Sold A Million* . . . (Columbia)
Julius LaRosa; *The Envelope Please-Academy Award Winning Songs-#2 (1946-1957)-C* . . . (Rhino)

Three Marlenas
Wallflowers; *Bringing Down The Horse* . . . (Interscope)

Till You Love Me
Reba McEntire; *Read My Mind* . . . (MCA)

To The Moon And Back
Savage Garden; *Savage Garden* . . . (Columbia)

Tonight You Belong To Me
Patience & Prudence; *Great Jukebox Hits Of The '50s-#2-C* . . . (CEMA Special Prod.)

Tracks Of My Tears, The
Bryan Ferry; *These Foolish Things* . . . (Reprise)
Gladys Knight & The Pips; *Gladys Knight & The Pips-Anthology* . . . (Motown)
Johnny Rivers; *Best Of Johnny Rivers* . . . (EMI)
Linda Ronstadt; *Linda Ronstadt's Greatest Hits* . . . (Asylum)
Prisoner In Disguise . . . (Asylum)
Smokey Robinson & The Miracles; *Billboard Top R&B Hits-1965-1969-C* . . . (Rhino)
Smokey Robinson & The Miracles' Anthology . . . (Motown)
Smokey Robinson & The Miracles' Greatest Hits-#2 . . . (Motown)
ST/Big Chill . . . (Motown)
ST/Sound Of "Murphy Brown" . . . (MCA)

Truly Madly Deeply
Savage Garden; *Savage Garden* . . . (Columbia)

Turn Back Time
Aqua; *Aquarium* . . . (MCA)
ST/Sliding Doors . . . (MCA)

Twinkle, Twinkle Lucky Star
Merle Haggard; *Chill Factor* . . . (Epic)
Greatest Country Hits Of The '80s-1988-C . . . (Columbia)

Two Faces Have I
Lou Christie; *Back To The '60s-#4-C* . . . (Dominion Entert.)
Enlightnin'ment-Best Of Lou Christie . . . (Rhino)

U Don't Love Me
Kumbia Kings; *Amor Familia Respeto* . . . (EMI Latin)

Um, Um, Um, Um, Um, Um (Curious Mind)
Major Lance; *Seems Like Yesterday-#5-Mid '60s-C* . . . (K-Tel)

Unbelievable
Bob Dylan; *Under The Red Sky* .... (Columbia)
EMF; *Schubert Dip* .... (Capitol)
Uninvited
Ruth Wallis; *Laughing Gallery* .... (American)
Until My Dreams Come True
Jack Greene; *Until My Dreams Come True* .... (Decca)
Up, Up & Away
5th Dimension; *5th Dimension-Anthology 1967-1973* .... (Rhino)
  Greatest Hits On Earth .... (Arista)
Virtual Insanity
Jamiroquai; *Traveling Without Moving* .... (Work/Epic)
Was It Just The Moonlight
Timothy B. Schmit; *Tell Me The Truth* ....(MCA)
Was It Just The Wine
Vern Gosdin; *10 Years Of Greatest Hits Newly Recorded* .... (Columbia)
Way You Love Me, The
Faith Hill; *Breathe* ....(Warner Bros.)
  Totally Hits-#3-C .... (Atlantic)
We Tell Ourselves
Clint Black; *The Hard Way* .... (RCA)
West Virginia Fantasies
Chicago; *Chicago At Carnegie Hall* ....(Chicago)
  Chicago II ....(Chicago)
  Group Portrait ....(Chicago)
What If
Reba McEntire; *CD Single-#72026* ....(MCA)
What If
Creed; *Human Clay* .... (Wind-up)
What If
Babyface; *Face 2 Face* .... (Arista)
What If God Smoked Cannabis
Bob Rivers; *Best Of Twisted Tunes-#2* ....(Atlantic)
What If I Said
Anita Cochran & Steve Wariner; *Back To You* ....(Warner Bros.)
Steve Wariner & Anita Cochran; *Burnin' The Roadhouse Down* ...... (Capitol)
What Might Have Been
Little Texas; *Big Time* ....(Warner Bros.)
What She's Doing Now
Garth Brooks; *Ropin' The Wind* .... (Liberty)
What's Your Fantasy
Ludacris; *Back For The First Time* ....(Def Jam South/IDJMG)
  Totally Hits 2001-C .... (Arista)
When I Dream At Night
Marc Anthony; *Marc Anthony* .... (Columbia)
When You Wish Upon A Star
Barbara Cook; *Disney Album* ....(Disney)
Billy Joel; *Simply Mad About The Mouse-C* .... (Columbia)
Cliff Edwards; *ST/Pinocchio* .... (Laurie)
Dion; *The Wanderer* .... (Laurie)
Glenn Miller & Ray Eberle; *Chattanooga Choo Choo-#1 Hits* .... (Bluebird)
Linda Ronstadt; *For Sentimental Reasons* .... (Asylum)
Little Anthony And The Imperials; *We Are The Imperials* .... (Roulette)
Rosemary Clooney; *Rosemary Clooney-16 Most Requested Songs* .... (Legacy)
Stevie Wonder; *With A Song In My Heart* .... (Motown)
Wynton Marsalis; *Hot House Flowers* .... (Columbia)
Where The Blue Of The Night Meets The Gold Of The Day
Bing Crosby; *All-Time Best Of* .... (Curb)
  Best Of Bing Crosby ....(MCA)
  Where The Blue Of The Night Meets The Gold Of The Day .... (Biograph)
Who's Holding Donna Now
DeBarge; *DeBarge's Greatest Hits* .... (Motown)
  Rhythm Of The Night .... (Motown)
Wish
Nine Inch Nails; *Broken* .... (Interscope)
Wish
Fixx; *Phantoms* ....(MCA)
Wish I Had My Baby
Five Satins; *Five Satins Sing Their Greatest Hits* .... (Collectables)
Wish I Were You
Patty Smyth; *ST/Armageddon-The Album* .... (Columbia)
Wish Upon A Star
Steve Miller Band; *Book Of Dreams* .... (Capitol)
  Steve Miller Band-Gift Set .... (Capitol)
Wish We Were Back In Missouri
Emmylou Harris; *Legend Of Jesse James-C* .... (A&M)
Wish You Were Here
Fleetwood Mac; *Mirage* ....(Warner Bros.)
Wish You Were Here
Limp Bizkit & John Rzeznik; *America: A Tribute To Heroes-C* ..... (Interscope)
Pink Floyd; *Collection Of Great Dance Songs* .... (Columbia)
  Delicate Sound Of Thunder .... (Columbia)
  Wish You Were Here .... (Columbia)
Wish You Were Here
Mark Wills; *Wish You Were Here* .... (Mercury)
Wish You Were Here
Bing Crosby; *The Radio Years: 20 Songs* .... (Crescendo)
Eddie Fisher; *Best Of Eddie Fisher* ....(MCA)

Wish You Were Here
Nick Lowe; *Abominable Showman* .... (Columbia)
Wish You Were Here
Barbara Mandrell; *Barbara Mandrell Live* .... (MCA)
  Barbara Mandrell's Greatest Hits .... (MCA)
Wish You Were Here
Bee Gees; *Diana, Princess Of Wales-Tribute-C* .... (Columbia)
Wish You Were Here
Alice Cooper; *Goes To Hell* .... (Warner Bros.)
  The Alice Cooper Show .... (Warner Bros.)
Wish You Were Here
Dead Or Alive; *Sophisticated Boom Boom* .... (Epic)
Wish You Were Here
Incubus; *Morning View* .... (Epic)
Wish You Were Mine Again
Mickey Gilley; *Fool For Your Love* .... (Epic)
Wish You Were There
REO Speedwagon; *Hi Infidelity* .... (Epic)
Wish, The
Eddie Money; *Playing For Keeps* .... (Columbia)
Wishful Thinking
Dan Hill & Celine Dion; *Real Love* .... (Columbia)
Wishful Thinking
Wynn Stewart; *Heroes Of Country Music-#4-Legends Of The West*
  Coast-C .... (Rhino)
Wishful Thinking
Little Anthony And The Imperials; *Best Of Little Anthony And The*
  Imperials .... (Rhino)
Wishful Thinking
Dolly Parton & Donna Fargo; *Queens Of Country* .... (Intermedia)
Wishful Thinking
China Crisis; *Working With Fire & Steel* .... (Warner Bros.)
Wishin' & Hopin'
Ani DiFranco; *ST/My Best Friend's Wedding* .... (Work/Epic)
Dusty Springfield; *Dusty Springfield-Golden Hits* .... (Mercury)
  History Of British Rock-#6-C .... (Rhino)
Wishing
Electric Light Orchestra; *Box Of Their Best* .... (Jet)
  Discovery ....(Jet)
Wishing
Asia; *Astra* .... (Geffen)
Wishing
Buddy Holly/The Crickets; *Buddy Holly-20 Golden Greats* .... (MCA)
Wishing
Joan Armatrading; *To The Limit* .... (A&M)
Wishing (If I Had A Photograph Of You)
A Flock Of Seagulls; *Best Of A Flock Of Seagulls* .... (Jive)
  Listen .... (Jive)
Wishing I Was There
Natalie Imbruglia; *Left Of The Middle* ....(RCA)
Wishing On A Star
Cover Girls; *Here It Is* .... (Epic)
Rose Royce; *Rose Royce's Greatest Hits* .... (Whitfield)
Wishing On The Moon
Dan Fogelberg; *Phoenix* ....(Full Moon)
Wishing Well
INXS; *Welcome To Wherever You Are* ....(Atlantic)
Wishing Well
Terence Trent D'Arby; *Introducing The Hardline According To Terence*
  Trent D'Arby .... (Columbia)
Wishing Well
Bobby Bland; *Call On Me* .... (MCA)
Wishing Well
Mission U.K.; *First Chapeter* .... (Mercury)
Wishing Well
Gary Moore; *Gary Moore-Early Years* .... (WTG)
Wishing Well
Black Sabbath; *Heaven And Hell* .... (Warner Bros.)
Wishing Well
Jackie Wilson; *Mr. Excitement* .... (Rhino)
Wishing Well
Nitty Gritty Dirt Band; *Rest Of The Dream* .... (MCA)
Wishing Well
Tyrone Davis; *Something's Mighty Wrong* .... (Ichiban Int'l)
Wishing You Were Here
Chicago; *Chicago IX-Chicago's Greatest Hits* .... (Chicago)
  Chicago VII .... (Chicago)
  Group Portrait .... (Chicago)
  If You Leave Me Now .... (Chicago)
Wishlist
Pearl Jam; *Yield* .... (Epic)
With Every Wish
Bruce Springsteen; *Human Touch* .... (Columbia)
With My Eyes Wide Open I'm Dreaming
Mandy Barnett; *I've Got A Right To Cry* ....(Sire)
Patti Page; *Patti Page-Golden Hits* .... (Mercury)
  Patti Page's Greatest Hits .... (Columbia)

Wonder
Natalie Merchant; *Tigerlily* . . . . (Elektra)
Wonder
Freddy Jones Band; *A Mile High Live* . . . . (Capricorn)
  Lucid . . . . (Capricorn)
Wonderful World
Art Garfunkel; *Watermark* . . . . (Legacy)
Herman's Hermits; *Herman's Hermits-Their Greatest Hits* . . . . (Abkco)
Sam Cooke; *Best Of Sam Cooke* . . . . (RCA)
  ST/Animal House . . . . (MCA)
  This Is Sam Cooke . . . . (RCA)
Wond'ring Aloud
Jethro Tull; *20 Years Of Jethro Tull* . . . . (Chrysalis)
  Aqualung . . . . (Chrysalis)
World Leader Pretend
R.E.M.; *Green* . . . . (Warner Bros.)
World's A Masquerade
Earth, Wind & Fire; *Head To The Sky* . . . . (Columbia)
Wouldn't It Be Loverly
Original Cast; *My Fair Lady* . . . . (Columbia)
  My Fair Lady . . . . (London)
Wouldn't It Be Nice
Beach Boys; *Absolutely Best-#2* . . . . (Capitol)
  Made In The U.S.A. . . . . (Capitol)
  Pet Sounds . . . . (Capitol)
  Still Cruisin' . . . . (Capitol)
You Belong To Me
Carly Simon; *Boys In The Trees* . . . . (Elektra)
  Carly Simon-Greatest Hits Live . . . . (Arista)
  Chicken Soup For The Woman's Soul-C . . . . (Rhino)
Doobie Brothers; *Best Of The Doobies, Volume II* . . . . . (Warner Bros.)
  Livin' On The Fault Line . . . . (Warner Bros.)
You Could Be Mine
Guns N' Roses; *Use Your Illusion II* . . . . (Geffen)
You Cried Wolf
Todd Rundgren; *Hermit Of Mink Hollow* . . . . (Rhino)
  Todd Rundgren-Anthology 1968-1985 . . . . (Rhino)
You Look So Good In Love
George Strait; *George Strait's Greatest Hits* . . . . (MCA)
  Right Or Wrong . . . . (MCA)
  Strait Out Of The Box . . . . (MCA)
You Were Meant For Me
Jewel; *Pieces Of You* . . . . (Atlantic)
Your Imagination
Daryl Hall & John Oates; *Private Eyes* . . . . (RCA)
Your Imagination
Brian Wilson; *Imagination* . . . . (Giant)

PRISON, Chains, Doing Time

See Also: CAPITAL PUNISHMENT, CRIME, ESCAPE, FREEDOM, LAW & ORDER, POLICE, POLITICS (various), PROTEST, REBELS, STRINGS & ROPE, STUCK, WALLS

21 Days In Jail
Magic Sam; *Chicago Boss Guitar* . . . . (Paula)
Alcatraz
Leon Russell; *Leon Russell & The Shelter People* . . . . (MCA)
Nazareth; *Razamanaz* . . . . (A&M)
Allentown Jail
Jo Stafford; *International Hits* . . . . (Corinthian)
Kingston Trio; *Rediscovering The Kingston Trio* . . . . (Folk Era)
Another Brick In The Wall, Part 2
Class Of '99; *ST/The Faculty* . . . . (Columbia)
Pink Floyd; *Collection Of Great Dance Songs* . . . . (Columbia)
  Delicate Sound Of Thunder . . . . (Columbia)
  The Wall . . . . (Columbia)
Roger Waters; *The Wall-Live In Berlin* . . . . (Mercury)
Attica State
John Lennon/Plastic Ono Band; *Sometime In New York City* . . (Capitol)
Back On The Chain Gang
Pretenders; *Learning To Crawl* . . . . (Sire)
  Pretenders-The Singles . . . . (Sire)
  ST/King Of Comedy . . . . (Warner Bros.)
Back On The Street
Todd Rundgren's Utopia; *Jail* . . . . (Vanguard)
Utopia; *Oops! Wrong Planet* . . . . (Rhino)
Ball & Chain
Big Brother & The Holding Company; *Cheap Thrills* . . . . (Columbia)
  Legends Of Rock Guitar-'60s-#1-C . . . . (Rhino)
  ST/Janis . . . . (Columbia)
Ball & Chain
Dan Seals; *Dan Seals' Greatest Hits* . . . . (Liberty)
Ball & Chain
Janis Joplin; *Janis Joplin's Greatest Hits* . . . . (Columbia)
Ball & Chain
Elton John; *Jump Up!* . . . . (MCA)

Ball & Chain
Big Mama Thornton; *Ball & Chain* . . . . (Arhoolie)
  Jail . . . . (Vanguard)
Ball And Chain
Paul Overstreet; *Heroes* . . . . (RCA)
Beast In Me
Johnny Cash; *American Recordings* . . . . (American)
Nick Lowe; *The Impossible Bird* . . . . (Upstart)
  *The Sopranos-Music From The HBO Original
    Series* . . . . (Sony Music Soundtrax)
Behind These Prison Walls Of Love
Blue Sky Boys; *Blue Sky Boys In Concert-1964* . . . . (Rounder)
Country Gentlemen; *Folk Songs & Bluegrass* . . . . . . (Smithsonian Folkways)
Peter Rowan; *All On A Rising Day* . . . . (Sugar Hill)
Birmingham Jail
Leadbelly; *Last Sessions* . . . . (Smithsonian Folkways)
Michael Martin Murphey; *Cowboy Songs-#3-Rhymes Of The
  Renegades* . . . . (Warner Western)
Birmingham Jail
Peggy Lee; *Peggy Lee Sings The Blues* . . . . (Musicmasters)
Black Jack County Chain
Henson Cargill; *Jailhouse Rock (Hits From The Big
  House)-C* . . . . (Sony Music Special Prod.)
Bleed Together
Soundgarden; *A-Sides* . . . . (A&M)
Born In A Prison
John Lennon/Plastic Ono Band; *Sometime In New York City* . . (Capitol)
Branded Man
Merle Haggard & The Strangers; *For The Record: Merle Haggard-43
  Legendary Hits* . . . . (BNA)
Break These Chains
Deborah Allen; *All That I Am* . . . . (Giant)
Broken Barricades
Procol Harum; *Broken Barricades* . . . . (A&M)
Cage Of Freedom
Jon Anderson; *ST/Metropolis* . . . . (Columbia)
Cage The Songbird
Elton John; *Blue Moves* . . . . (MCA)
  Elton John . . . . (Polydor)
Caged Bird
Alicia Keys; *Songs In A Minor* . . . . (J)
Chain Gang
Nylons; *Happy Together* . . . . (Open Air)
Otis Redding; *Best Of Otis Redding* . . . . (Atco)
  The Otis Redding Story . . . . (Atlantic)
Persuasions; *We Came To Play* . . . . (Capitol)
Sam Cooke; *Best Of Sam Cooke* . . . . (RCA)
  Nipper's Greatest Hits Of The '60s-#1-C . . . . (RCA)
  The Man And His Music . . . . (RCA)
Chained
Marvin Gaye; *I Heard It Through The Grapevine/I Want You* . . . . . (Motown)
  Marvin Gaye-Anthology . . . . (Motown)
  Marvin Gaye-Super Hits . . . . (Motown)
Chained
Giant; *Time To Burn* . . . . (Epic)
Chains
Patty Loveless; *Honky Tonk Angel* . . . . (MCA)
  Patty Loveless' Greatest Hits . . . . (MCA)
Chains
Tina Arena; *Don't Ask* . . . . (Epic)
Chains Around My Heart
Richard Marx; *Rush Street* . . . . (Capitol)
Chains Of Gold
Sweethearts Of The Rodeo; *More Hot Country Requests-#2-C* . . . . (Epic)
  Sweethearts Of The Rodeo . . . . (Columbia)
Chains Of Love
Erasure; *Innocents* . . . . (Sire)
  Just Say Yo-#2 Of Just Say Yes-C . . . . (Sire)
Chains Of Love
Big Joe Turner; *Big Joe Turner's Greatest Hits* . . . . (Atlantic)
  In The Evening . . . . (Pablo)
  Turns On The Blues . . . . (Kent)
Bobby Bland; *Introspective Of The Early Years* . . . . (MCA)
  Spotlighting The Man . . . . (MCA)
Mickey Gilley; *First Class* . . . . (Playboy)
  Mickey Gilley's Biggest Hits . . . . (Epic)
Christmas In Prison
John Prine; *John Prine Christmas* . . . . (Oh Boy)
  John Prine-Souvenirs . . . . (Oh Boy)
  Sweet Revenge . . . . (Atlantic)
Cincinnati Jail
Lonnie Mack; *Attack Of The Killer V* . . . . (Alligator)
  Second Sight . . . . (Alligator)
Cold Hard Facts Of Life, The
Porter Wagoner; *Essential Porter Wagoner* . . . . (RCA)
  Porter Wagoner's Greatest Hits . . . . (Pair)
Columbus Stockade Blues
Doc Watson; *Memories* . . . . (Sugar Hill)

Lenny Dee; *Best Of Lenny Dee* . . . . (MCA)
Pete Fountain; *Best Of Pete Fountain* . . . . (MCA)

Come On Down To My Boat
Every Mother's Son; *Battle Of The Bands-#3-C* . . . . (K-Tel)

Convict's Prayer
Li'l Wally; *One Man Band* . . . . (Jay Jay)

Country Jail
Volumes; *I Love You-Golden Classics* . . . . (Collectables)

Country Jail Blues
Eric Clapton; *No Reason To Cry* . . . . (RSO)
John T. Smith; *Original Howling Wolf* . . . . (Yazoo)

Crumblin' Down
John Cougar Mellencamp; *Uh-Huh* . . . . (Riva)

Dark As A Dungeon
Johnny Cash; *Essential Johnny Cash* . . . . (Columbia)
 Johnny Cash At Folsom Prison & San Quentin . . . . (Columbia)
Maddox Brothers & Rose; *1946-1951-#1 & 2* . . . . (Arhoolie)
Merle Travis; *Best Of Merle Travis* . . . . (Rhino)
Nitty Gritty Dirt Band; *Will The Circle Be Unbroken* . . . . (EMI)
Rose Maddox; *Rose Of The West Coast Country* . . . . (Arhoolie)
Wall Of Voodoo; *Seven Days In Sammystown* . . . . (I.R.S.)

Death Row #172
Pacific Gas & Electric; *Jailhouse Rock (Hits From The Big
 House)-C* . . . . (Sony Music Special Prod.)

Doin' Time
Spooner; *Every Corner Dance* . . . . (Mountain Railroad)
 Wildest Dreams/Every Corner Dance . . . . (Dali)

Doin' Time
Meg Christian & Cris Williamson; *Meg-Cris At
 Carnegie Hall* . . . . (Second Wave)

Doin' Time
Justin Hayward; *Songwriter* . . . . (Deram)

Drifter's Escape
Bob Dylan; *John Wesley Harding* . . . . (Columbia)
Jimi Hendrix; *Lifelines/Jimi Hendrix Story* . . . . (Reprise)

Duck, The
Jackie Lee; *Only Dance 1965-1969-C* . . . . (JCI Assoc. Labels)
 Sock Hop-C . . . . (Dunhill Compact Classics)
 Super Oldies Of The '60s-#6-C . . . . (Audio Fidelity)
Olympics; *Best Of The Olympics* . . . . (Vee-Jay)

Ellis Unit One
Steve Earle; *Johnny Too Bad* . . . . (E Squared)
 ST/Dead Man Walking . . . . (Columbia)

Empty Cages
Dan Fogelberg; *Innocent Age* . . . . (Full Moon)

Escape From The Island Of Living Puke
Zoogz Rift; *Island Of Living Puke* . . . . (SST)

**Eyes Of Laura Mars (Prisoner), Love Theme From "Eyes Of
 Laura Mars"**
Barbra Streisand; *Barbra Streisand's Greatest Hits, Volume 2* . . . . . (Columbia)
 Lazy Afternoon . . . . (Columbia)

Folsom Prison Blues
Brooks & Dunn with Johnny Cash; *Red Hot + Country-C* . . . . (Mercury)
Johnny Cash; *Billboard Top Country Hits-1968-C* . . . . (Rhino)
 Classic Cash-Hall Of Fame Series . . . . (Mercury)
 Hot Tracks-Train Super Hits-C . . . . (Epic)
 Jailhouse Rock (Hits From The Big House)-C . . . . . (Sony Music Special Prod.)
 Johnny Cash At Folsom Prison & San Quentin . . . . (Columbia)
 Johnny Cash-Original Golden Hits-#1 . . . . (Sun)
 Johnny Cash's Greatest Hits-#2 . . . . (Columbia)
 Superbilly . . . . (Sun)
 The Man In Black-His Greatest Hits . . . . (Legacy)

Fort Worth Jail
Tex Ritter; *Hillbilly Music-Thank God!-#1-C* . . . . (Bug)

Free Nelson Mandela
Special AKA; *In The Studio* . . . . (Chrysalis)

Gimme Some Slack
Cars; *Panorama* . . . . (Elektra)

Give My Love To Rose
George Jones; *George Jones Sings The Hits Of His Country
 Cousins* . . . . (Razor & Tie)
Johnny Cash; *Johnny Cash-Sun Years* . . . . (Rhino)

Green Green Grass Of Home
Burl Ives; *Best Of Burl Ives-#2* . . . . (MCA)
Elvis Presley; *Elvis Presley Today* . . . . (RCA)
 Our Memories Of Elvis, Volume 2 . . . . (RCA)
George Jones; *20 Golden Pieces Of George Jones* . . . . (Bulldog)
Johnny Cash; *Johnny Cash-16 Biggest Hits-#2* . . . . (Legacy)
Tom Jones; *Country Side Of Tom Jones* . . . . (London)
 Things That Matter Most To Me . . . . (Mercury)
 Tom Jones-London Collector-Greatest Hits . . . . (London)

Handcuffed To A Fence In Mississippi
Jim White; *No Such Place* . . . . (Luaka Bop)

Hard Knock Life (Ghetto Anthem)
Jay-Z; *Now That's What I Call Music!-#2-C* . . . . (Virgin)
 Vol. 2-Hard Knock Life . . . . (Def Jam)

Have Mercy Judge
Chuck Berry; *Jailhouse Rock (Hits From The Big
 House)-C* . . . . (Sony Music Special Prod.)

House Of The Rising Sun
Animals; *Animals Greatest Hits* . . . . (Allegiance)
 Best Of The Animals . . . . (Abkco)
 Greatest Hits Live!-Rip It To Shreds . . . . (I.R.S.)
Hank Williams, Jr.; *Hank Williams, Jr. "Live"* . . . . (WB/Curb)
Ronnie Milsap; *Ronnie Milsap-16 Greatest Hits-#2* . . . . (Trip)

Hurricane
Bob Dylan; *Desire* . . . . (Columbia)

I Ain't Livin' Long Like This
Emmylou Harris; *Quarter Moon In A Ten Cent Town* . . . . (Warner Bros.)
Rodney Crowell; *I Ain't Livin' Long Like This* . . . . (Warner Bros.)
 Rodney Crowell-Collection . . . . (Warner Bros.)
Waylon Jennings; *Waylon Jennings' Greatest Hits-#2* . . . . (RCA)
 What Goes Around Comes Around . . . . (RCA)

I Got Stripes
Johnny Cash; *Johnny Cash-16 Biggest Hits-#2* . . . . (Legacy)

I Hope You've Learned
Ricky Skaggs and Kentucky Thunder; *Bluegrass Rules!* . . . . (Rounder)

I'd Be Better Off (In A Pine Box)
Doug Stone; *Doug Stone* . . . . (Epic)
 Greatest Country Hits Of The '90s-1990-C . . . . (Columbia)

I'll Kiss The World Goodbye
J.J. Cale; *Really* . . . . (Mercury)

In The Jailhouse Now
Jimmie Rodgers; *First Sessions-1927-1928-#1* . . . . (Rounder)
 Short But Brilliant Life . . . . (RCA)
 This Is Jimmie Rodgers . . . . (RCA)
Soggy Bottom Boys featuring Jim Blake Nelson; *ST/O Brother, Where Art
 Thou?* . . . . (Mercury)
Webb Pierce; *Best Of Webb Pierce* . . . . (MCA)
 Webb Pierce-Golden Hits-#2 . . . . (Plantation)

In The Jailhouse Now-#2
Jimmie Rodgers; *Jimmie Rodgers-Legendary Performer* . . . . (RCA)
 My Rough & Rowdy Ways . . . . (RCA)

Israelites (The)
Desmond Dekker & The Aces; *ST/Drugstore Cowboy* . . . . (Novus)
 The Island Story-1962-1987-25th Anniversary-C . . . . (Island)

Jackson Cage
Bruce Springsteen; *The River* . . . . (Columbia)

Jailbait
Aerosmith; *Gems* . . . . (Columbia)
 Rock In A Hard Place . . . . (Columbia)

Jailbait
Nils Lofgren; *Cry Tough* . . . . (A&M)

Jailbait
Ted Nugent; *Intensities In 10 Cities* . . . . (Epic)

Jailbreak
Thin Lizzy; *Jailbreak* . . . . (Mercury)
 Jailhouse Rock (Hits From The Big House)-C . . . . (Sony Music Special Prod.)
 Live And Dangerous . . . . (Warner Bros.)
 Lizzy Lives! (1976-1984) . . . . (Gland Slamm)

Jailhouse Blues
Dinah Washington; *Bessie Smith Songbook* . . . . (Emarcy)
Doc & Merle Watson; *Pickin' The Blues* . . . . (Flying Fish)
Sam Collins; *Jailhouse Blues* . . . . (Yazoo)

Jailhouse Rock
Blues Brothers; *ST/The Blues Brothers* . . . . (Atlantic)
Elvis Presley; *Billboard Top Rock 'N' Roll Hits-1957-C* . . . . (Rhino)
 Elvis Recorded Live On Stage In Memphis . . . . (RCA)
 Elvis-A Legendary Performer, Volume 2 . . . . (RCA)
 Number One Hits . . . . (RCA)
 Rocker . . . . (RCA)
 Worldwide 50 Gold Award Hits, Vol. 1, Parts 1 & 2 . . . . (RCA)
Jeff Beck Group; *Beck-Ola* . . . . (Epic)

Johnny 99
Bruce Springsteen; *Nebraska* . . . . (Columbia)
Bruce Springsteen & The E Street Band; *Bruce Springsteen & The E Street
 Band Live/1975-85* . . . . (Legacy)
Johnny Cash; *Cover Me (Bruce Springsteen Tribute)-C* . . . . (Rhino)

Last Meal
Asleep At The Wheel; *Very Best Of Asleep At The Wheel
 Since 1970* . . . . (Relentless/Madacy)

Laws Must Change
John Mayall; *Best Of John Mayall* . . . . (Polydor)
 The Turning Point . . . . (Polydor)
John Mayall's Bluesbreakers; *Behind The Iron Curtain* . . . . (Crescendo)

Life
K-Ci & JoJo; *It's Real* . . . . (Rock Land/Interscope)

Life In Prison
Byrds; *Jailhouse Rock (Hits From The Big
 House)-C* . . . . (Sony Music Special Prod.)
 Sweetheart Of The Rodeo . . . . (Columbia)

Life On A Chain
Pete Yorn; *Musicforthemorningafter* . . . . (Columbia)

Lilies Of The Field
Gretchen Peters; *Gretchen Peters* . . . . (Purple Crayon Prod.)

Lonesome Jailhouse Blues
Aunt Molly Jackson; *Library Of Congress Recordings* . . . . (Rounder)

Lonesome Whistle
Hank Williams With His Drifting Cowboys; *Between The Rails: America's Train Songs-C* . . . . (Crescendo)
   Hank Williams-24 Greatest Hits-#2 . . . . (Polydor)
   Hank Williams-40 Greatest Hits . . . . (Polydor)
Johnny Cash; *Story Songs Of The Trains & Rivers* . . . . (Sun)
Little Feat; *Hoy-Hoy!*. . . . . (Warner Bros.)

Mama Tried
Grateful Dead; *Grateful Dead (Skull & Roses)* . . . . (Warner Bros.)
John Anderson & Marty Stuart; *Mama's Hungry Eyes-Merle Haggard Tribute-C* . . . . (Arista)
Merle Haggard; *Jailhouse Rock (Hits From The Big House)-C* . . . . (Sony Music Special Prod.)
Merle Haggard & The Strangers; *Best Of Merle Haggard & The Strangers* . . . . (Capitol)
   For The Record: Merle Haggard-43 Legendary Hits . . . .(BNA)
   Okie From Muskogee . . . . (Capitol)
   Songs I'll Always Sing . . . . (Capitol)
   Very Best Of Merle Haggard . . . . (Capitol)

Midnight Special
Creedence Clearwater Revival; *1969* . . . .(Fantasy)
   Creedence Clearwater Revival-Chronicle-#2 . . . .(Fantasy)
   Creedence Clearwater Revival-Gold . . . .(Fantasy)
   Movie Album . . . .(Fantasy)
   Willy & The Poor Boys . . . .(Fantasy)
Johnny Rivers; *Johnny Rivers-Anthology 1964-1977* . . . . (Rhino)
   Very Best Of Johnny Rivers. . . . . (EMI)

Monkey Wrench
Foo Fighters; *The Colour And The Shape* . . . .(Roswell/RCA)

Monterrey Pen
Marc Benno; *Lost In Austin* . . . . (A&M)

My Love Is Your Love
Whitney Houston; *My Love Is Your Love* . . . . (Arista)
   Totally Hits-#2-C . . . . (Elektra)

My Own Prison
Clarence "Gatemouth" Brown; *No Looking Back* . . . .(Alligator)

My Own Prison
Creed; *My Own Prison* . . . . (Wind-up)

My Son Calls Another Man Daddy
Hank Williams With His Drifting Cowboys; *Hank Williams-16 Great Hits* . . . . (Everest)
   Hank Williams-40 Greatest Hits. . . . . (Polydor)
   Rare Takes & Radio Cuts . . . . (Polydor)

My Song Bird
Emmylou Harris; *Quarter Moon In A Ten Cent Town* . . . . (Warner Bros.)
McCarters; *The Gift* . . . . (Warner Bros.)

New Huntsville Jail
Joe Evans & John Dilleshaw; *Early Country Music* . . . . (Historical)

Nine Pound Steel
Joe Simon; *Jailhouse Rock (Hits From The Big House)-C* . . . . (Sony Music Special Prod.)

Ninety Nine Years (Dead Or Alive)
Guy Mitchell; *Definitive Guy Mitchell* . . . . (Collector's Choice)

Ninety-Nine
Bill Anderson; *45-#30914* . . . . (Decca)

No Easy Way Out
Robert Tepper; *Rocky Story-C* . . . . (Scotti Bros.)
   ST/Rocky IV . . . . (Scotti Bros.)

Ol' Red
Blake Shelton; *Blake Shelton*. . . . . (Giant)

On Parole
Motorhead; *Motorhead* . . . .(Roadracer)

On The Banks Of The Old Pontchartrain
Hank Williams; *American Legends-#18* . . . .(Laserlight)
   Complete Hank Williams . . . . (Mercury)

One Chain
Santana; *Inner Secrets* . . . . (Columbia)

One Chain
Doobie Brothers; *Cycles* . . . . (Warner Bros.)

Padlock
Gwen Guthrie; *Portrait* . . . . (Island)
   The Island Story-1962-1987-25th Anniversary-C . . . . (Island)

Papa Loved Mama
Garth Brooks; *Garth Brooks-Double Live* . . . . (Capitol)
   Ropin' The Wind. . . . . (Liberty)

Parchman Farm
John Mayall's Bluesbreakers; *Behind The Iron Curtain* . . . . (Crescendo)
   John Mayall's Bluesbreakers-London Collector . . . .(London)
   Last Of The British Blues . . . . (MCA)
John Mayall's Bluesbreakers with Eric Clapton; *John Mayall's Bluesbreakers with Eric Clapton* . . . . (Deram)
Johnny Winter; *About Blues* . . . . (Janus)
   Before The Storm . . . . (Janus)
Mose Allison; *Mose Allison* . . . . (Prestige)
   Mose Allison's Greatest Hits . . . . (Prestige)

Percy's Song
Arlo Guthrie; *Washington County* . . . .(Reprise)
Bob Dylan; *Biograph*. . . . . (Columbia)

Phone Call From Leavenworth
Chris Whitley; *Living With The Law* . . . .(Columbia)

Please Mr. Jailer
Wynona Carr; *Jump Jack Jump!* . . . . (Specialty)

Please Take Me Out Of Jail
Fats Waller; *Fats Waller & His Buddies-1927-1929* . . . .(Bluebird)

Prison Blues Come Down On Me
Lightnin' Hopkins; *Best Of Lightnin' Hopkins* . . . . (Tradition)
   Prison Blues-Golden Classics-#2 . . . .(Collectables)

Prison Farm Blues
Lightnin' Hopkins; *Best Of Lightnin' Hopkins* . . . . (Prestige)
   How Many More Years I Got . . . . (Fantasy)
   Lightnin' Hopkins-Complete Prestige/Bluesville Recordings . . . . . (Bluesville)

Prison Sex
Tool; *Undertow* . . . . (Zoo/Volcano)

Prison Song
Crosby, Stills & Nash; *CSN* . . . . (Atlantic)
Graham Nash; *Wild Tales*. . . . . (Atlantic)

Prison Trilogy
Joan Baez; *Best Of Joan Baez* . . . . (A&M)
   Come From The Shadows . . . . (A&M)
   Joan Baez-Classics-#8 . . . . (A&M)

Prison Women
REO Speedwagon; *Jailhouse Rock (Hits From The Big House)-C* . . . . (Sony Music Special Prod.)

Prisoner
Outlaws; *Bring It Back Alive* . . . .(Arista)
   Lady In Waiting. . . . .(Arista)

Prisoner
Dokken; *Back For The Attack* . . . .(Elektra)

Prisoner
Howard Jones; *Cross That Line* . . . .(Elektra)

Prisoner
Accept; *Eat The Heat* . . . . (Epic)

Prisoner
Suicidal Tendencies; *Join The Army* . . . .(Caroline)

Prisoner
Mariah Carey; *Mariah Carey* . . . .(Columbia)

Prisoner
Roger Daltrey; *One Of The Boys* . . . . (MCA)

Prisoner
Squeeze; *Squeeze-Classics-#25* . . . .(A&M)

Prisoner For Life
Skip Gorman; *A Cowboy's Wild Song To His Herd* . . . .(Rounder)

Prisoner In Disguise
Linda Ronstadt; *Different Drum*. (Capitol)

Prisoner Of Hope
Johnny Lee; *Johnny Lee's Greatest Hits* . . . . (Full Moon/Asylum)

Prisoner Of Love
Foreigner; *Very Best Of Foreigner...And Beyond* . . . . (Atlantic)

Prisoner Of Love
Art Tatum; *Solo Masterpieces-#3* . . . . (Pablo)
Frank Sinatra; *Sinatra & Strings* . . . . (Reprise)
Perry Como; *Como's Golden Records* . . . . (RCA)
   Nipper's Greatest Hits Of The '40s-#2-C . . . . (RCA)
   Perry Como-Pure Gold . . . . (RCA)
   This Is Perry Como . . . . (RCA)

Prisoner Of Love
Bloodstone; *Bloodstone's Greatest Hits* . . . . (T-Neck/Columbia)

Prisoner Of Love
Pat Benatar; *Crimes Of Passion* . . . .(Chrysalis)

Prisoner Of Love
Miami Sound Machine; *Eyes Of Innocence* . . . . (Epic)

Prisoner Of Love
Kiss; *Hot In The Shade* . . . .(Mercury)

Prisoner Of Love
Truth; *Jump* . . . . (I.R.S.)

Prisoner Of Love
James Brown; *Live At The Apollo-Vol. 2-Part 2*. . . . .(Rhino)

Prisoner Of The Highway
Ronnie Milsap; *One More Try For Love* . . . . (RCA)
   Ronnie Milsap's Greatest Hits-#3. . . . . (RCA)

Prisoner Of Your Love
Player; *Danger Zone* . . . .(RSO)

Prisoner's Song
Burl Ives; *Best Of Burl Ives* . . . . (MCA)
Vernon Dalhart; *Nipper's Greatest Hits Of The '20s-C* . . . . (RCA)

Put Me In That Dungeon
Charles Mingus; *Mingus Dynasty* . . . .(Columbia)

Rage In The Cage
J. Geils Band; *Freeze-Frame* . . . .(EMI)

Ragin' Cajun
Charlie Daniels Band; *Windows*. (Epic)

Rascal King
Mighty Mighty Bosstones; *Let's Face It* . . . . (Big Rig/Mercury)
   Live From The Middle East. . . . . (Big Rig/Mercury)

Rex Bob Lowenstein
Mark Germino; *Rank & File* . . . . (Winter Harvest Entert.)

Riot In Cell Block #9
Blues Brothers; *Made In America*............................(Atlantic)
Coasters; *Very Best Of The Coasters* .... (Rhino)
Commander Cody & His Lost Planet Airmen; *Live From Deep In The Heart*
Of Texas ....(MCA)
Robins; *50 Coastin' Classics-C* ....(Rhino)
There's A Riot Goin' On! Rock Classics-C ....(Rhino)
Wanda Jackson; *Rockin' In The Country-Best Of Wanda Jackson* ......(Rhino)

Rivers Of Babylon
Boney M; *Nightflight To Venus*...............................(Sire)
Linda Ronstadt; *Hasten Down The Wind* ....(Asylum)
Melodians; *Groveyard-C* ....(Mango)
ST/The Harder They Come ....(Mango)

San Quentin
Johnny Cash; *At San Quentin* ....(Columbia)
Columbia Records-1958-1986............................(Columbia)
Johnny Cash At Folsom Prison & San Quentin ....(Columbia)

Set Me Free (Rosa Lee)
Los Lobos; *By The Light Of The Moon* ....(Slash)

Shackles
R.J.'s Latest Arrival; *Jointz From Back In Da Dayz-#2-C* ....(Quality)

Shackles & Chains
Arlo Guthrie; *Hobo's Lullaby*................................(Reprise)
Jimmie Davis; *Jimmie Davis-Golden Hits* ....(Plantation)
Souvenirs Of Yesterday ....(Plantation)

Shackles (Praise You)
Mary Mary; *Thankful*...................................(C2/Columbia)

Shakin' The Cage
Zoo; *Shakin' The Cage* ....(Capricorn)

Sing Me Back Home
Alabama; *Mama's Hungry Eyes-Merle Haggard Tribute-C* ....(Arista)
Flying Burrito Brothers; *Farther Along-Best Of The Flying Burrito*
Brothers ....(A&M)
Merle Haggard & The Strangers; *Best Of Merle Haggard & The*
Strangers..(Capitol)
Capitol Collectors Series-Merle Haggard & The Strangers ....(Capitol)
For The Record: Merle Haggard-43 Legendary Hits ....(BNA)
Okie From Muskogee...................................(Capitol)
Songs I'll Always Sing ....(Capitol)

Snowbound
Genesis; *And Then There Were Three*.....................(Atlantic)

Solitude
Edwin McCain; *Honor Among Thieves* ....(Lava)
Edwin McCain & Darius Rucker; *VH-1 Crossroads-C* ....(Atlantic)

Some Days You Gotta Dance
Dixie Chicks; *Fly* ....(Monument)

Soul Cages
Sting; *Soul Cages* ....(A&M)

Spiderwebs
No Doubt; *1997 Grammy Nominees-C* ....(Chronicles)
Tragic Kingdom ....(Trauma)

Starkville City Jail
Johnny Cash; *Johnny Cash At Folsom Prison & San Quentin* ......(Columbia)

Still Doin' Time
George Jones; *By Request*..................................(Epic)
George Jones-Anniversary-Ten Years Of Hits ....(Epic)
Greatest Country Hits Of The '80s-1981-C ....(Columbia)

Straight Time
Bruce Springsteen; *The Ghost Of Tom Joad* ....(Columbia)

Take A Message To Mary
Bob Dylan; *Self Portrait* ....(Columbia)
Everly Brothers; *Everly Brothers-All-Time Original Hits* ....(Rhino)
Everly Brothers-Cadence Classics-Their 20 Greatest Hits ....(Rhino)
Rockpile; *Seconds Of Pleasure*.............................(Columbia)

Take These Chains
Lee Roy Parnell; *On The Road* ....(Arista)

Take These Chains From My Heart
Hank Williams With His Drifting Cowboys; *24 Of Hank Williams'*
Greatest Hits..(Polydor)
Hank Williams-40 Greatest Hits ....(Polydor)
Ray Charles; *Ray Charles-His Greatest Hits-#2*.....(Dunhill Compact Classics)

Teenage Jail
Eagles; *Long Run* ....(Asylum)

Texas
Merle Haggard; *Friend In California* ....(Epic)
Merle Haggard & Freddy Powers; *Texas Super Hits-C* ....(Columbia)

Theme From ''The Prisoner''
Neil Norman; *Greatest Science Fiction Hits*..................(Crescendo)

There Ain't No Good Chain Gang
Johnny Cash & Waylon Jennings; *Country's Greatest Hits-#15-Outlaw*
Country-C ....(Priority)
Hot Country Rock-#1-C ....(Priority)
Johnny Cash-16 Biggest Hits-#2 ....(Legacy)
The Man In Black-His Greatest Hits ....(Legacy)

Thirteen Years In Prison
Big Leon Brooks' Blues Harp Band; *Living Chicago Blues-#4* ......(Alligator)

Thirty Days In The Hole
Gov't Mule; *Live With A Little Help From Our Friends-Collector's*
Edition ....(Capricorn)

Humble Pie; *Best Of Humble Pie*.........................(A&M)
Humble Pie-Classics-#14................................(A&M)
Rock This Way Live-#1-C ....(BMG Special Prod.)
Smokin' ....(A&M)
Mr. Big; *Mr. Big*.......................................(Atlantic)

This Body Is A Prison
Spencer Bohren; *Live In New Orleans*...................(Great Southern)

Tie A Yellow Ribbon Round The Ole Oak Tree
Dawn Featuring Tony Orlando; *'70s Party Killers-C* ....(Rhino)
Fantastic-#1-C ....(K-Tel)
Frank Sinatra; *Some Nice Things I've Missed* ....(Reprise)
Lawrence Welk; *Best Of Lawrence Welk-20 Great Hits* ....(Ranwood)
Sonny James & Karla Taylor; *Classic Country Duets-C*..........(Curb)

Ties That Bind
Bruce Springsteen; *The River* ....(Columbia)

Tijuana Jail
Gilby Clarke; *Pawnshop Guitars* ....(Virgin)
Kingston Trio; *25 Years Non-Stop* ....(Xeres)
Best Of The Kingston Trio ....(Capitol)
Capitol Collectors Series-The Kingston Trio ....(Capitol)
Kingston Trio's Greatest Hits............................(Curb)

Too Many Walls
Cathy Dennis; *Move To This* ....(Polydor)

Tower Of London
ABC; *How To Be A Zillionaire* ....(Mercury)

Tupelo County Jail
Mel Tillis; *American Originals-Mel Tillis*....................(Columbia)
Webb Pierce; *Webb Pierce-Golden Hits* ....(Plantation)

Unchain My Heart
Joe Cocker; *Joe Cocker Live* ....(Capitol)
Unchain My Heart ....(Capitol)
Ray Charles; *Ray Charles' Greatest Hits* ....(Rhino)
Ray Charles-Anthology ....(Rhino)
Ray Charles-His Greatest Hits-#1 ....(Dunhill Compact Classics)

Unchained
Van Halen; *Fair Warning* ....(Warner Bros.)

Various Tracks
Various Artists; *Wake Up Dead Man: Black Convict Worksongs From Texas*
Prisons...(Rounder)

Velvet Chains
Gary Morris; *Gary Morris-Hits*........................(Warner Bros.)
Swingin' Country Favorites-C ....(Warner Bros.)
Why Lady Why ....(Warner Bros.)

Wall
Kansas; *Best Of Kansas* ....(CBS Associated)
Leftoverture ....(Kirshner)
Two For The Show ....(Kirshner)

Walls Came Down
Call; *Modern Romans* ....(Mercury)
The Walls Came Down-Best Of Mercury Years ....(Mercury)

Week In A County Jail, A
Tom T. Hall; *Storyteller, Poet, Philospher* ....(Mercury)
Tom T. Hall's Greatest Hits-#1 ....(Mercury)

Whiskey In The Jar
Metallica; *Garage Inc.* ....(Elektra)

White Bird
It's A Beautiful Day; *Bill Graham Presents The Last Days Of The*
Fillmore-C......................................(Epic Portrait Assoc.)
It's A Beautiful Day ....(Columbia)

Wichita Jail
Charlie Daniels Band; *Banded Together-C*...................(Epic)
Saddle Tramp ....(Epic)

Willie Jones
Charlie Daniels Band; *Night Rider* ....(Epic)
Renegade ....(Epic)

Woman On The Tier (I'll See You Through)
Suzanne Vega; *ST/Dead Man Walking* ....(Columbia)

Working For The Clampdown
Clash; *London Calling* ....(Epic)

Zoomin'
Lionel Richie; *Time*....................................(Mercury)

PRODUCTS & BRANDS: SPECIFIC

*See Also: **BUSINESS & INDUSTRY, CARS: CADILLAC, CARS:***
SPECIFIC MAKES & MODELS, FOOD & BEVERAGES (various),
SHOPPING, TELEVISION (theme songs)

#1 (Motorola, Sprint)
Nelly; *Soundtrack Single*.................................(Priority)

Add A Ring (Ballantine Premium Beer)
Original Soundtrack; *TeeVee Toons-The Commercials-#1-C* ....(TVT)

America (Mrs. Wagner's Pies)
Paul Simon; *Paul Simon In Concert/Live Rhymin'* ....(Columbia)
Simon & Bard Group; *The Concert In Central Park* ....(Warner Bros.)
Simon & Garfunkel; *Bookends* ....(Columbia)

Collected Works . . . . (Columbia)
   Simon & Garfunkel's Greatest Hits . . . . (Columbia)
American Made (Sony, Nikon)
  Oak Ridge Boys; *American Made* . . . . (MCA)
   Oak Ridge Boys' Greatest Hits 2 . . . . (MCA)
Back When He Was Hungry (KFC)
  Bill Anderson; *A Lot Of Things Different* . . . . (Varese Sarabande)
Bad Touch, The (Waffle House, FedEx, Coca-Cola, Mister Coffee)
  Bloodhound Gang; *Hooray For Boobies* . . . . (Republic/Geffen)
Ballad Of John And Yoko (Hilton)
  Beatles; *Beatles 1* . . . . (Capitol)
   Beatles-Box Set . . . . (Capitol)
   Hey Jude . . . . (Capitol)
   Past Masters-Volume Two . . . . (Parlophone)
   ST/Imagine: John Lennon . . . . (Capitol)
   The Beatles/1967-1970 . . . . (Capitol)
Be A Pepper (Dr. Pepper)
  Original Soundtrack; *TeeVee Toons-The Commercials-#1-C* . . . . (TVT)
Best Day (Coke)
  George Strait; *Latest Greatest Straitest Hits* . . . . (MCA)
Big Spender (Muriel Cigars)
  Original Soundtrack; *TeeVee Toons-The Commercials-#1-C* . . . . (TVT)
Bob Away My Blues (Maxwell House)
  Clint Black; *D'lectrified* . . . . (RCA)
Boyz-N-The-Hood (Bacardi)
  Dynamite Hack; *Superfast* . . . . (Farm Club/Universal)
Brown Eyed Handsome Man (TWA)
  Buddy Holly; *Buddy Holly-20 Golden Greats* . . . . (MCA)
   For The First Time Anywhere . . . . (MCA)
   Rock & Roll Collection . . . . (MCA)
  Chuck Berry; *Best Of The Best Of Chuck Berry* . . . . . (International Mktg. Group)
   Roll Over Beethoven . . . . (Allegiance)
   The Chess Box-Chuck Berry . . . . (Chess)
  Waylon Jennings; *Essential Waylon Jennings* . . . . (RCA)
   Waylon Jennings-Super Hits . . . . (RCA)
Brunswick Bowling Spot
  4 Seasons; *Rarities-#1* . . . . (Rhino)
Bubba Hyde (AMC, K-Mart, Hai Karate, A&P)
  Diamond Rio; *Diamond Rio's Greatest Hits* . . . . (Arista)
   Love A Little Stronger . . . . (Arista)
Bug A Boo (MCI)
  Destiny's Child; *The Writing's On The Wall* . . . . (Columbia)
Caligula (Jacuzzi)
  Macy Gray; *On How Life Is* . . . . (Epic)
Candy-Coated Popcorn, Peanuts And A Prize (Cracker Jack)
  Original Soundtrack; *TeeVee Toons-The Commercials-#1-C* . . . . (TVT)
Cannibals (G.I. Joe)
  Mark Knopfler; *Golden Heart* . . . . (Warner Bros.)
Carlene (Vogue)
  Phil Vassar; *Phil Vassar* . . . . (Arista)
Chock Full O'Nuts Is That Heavenly Coffee
  Original Sins; *TeeVee Toons-The Commercials-#1-C* . . . . (TVT)
Choo Choo Charlie (Good & Plenty)
  Original Soundtrack; *TeeVee Toons-The Commercials-#1-C* . . . . (TVT)
Coca Cola Cowboy
  Mel Tillis; *Mel Tillis' Greatest Hits* . . . . (Curb)
   Very Best Of Mel Tillis . . . . (MCA)
Come Alive (Pepsi)
  Original Soundtrack; *TeeVee Toons-The Commercials-#1-C* . . . . (TVT)
Completely Unique Experience, A (Colt 45 Malt Liquor)
  Original Soundtrack; *TeeVee Toons-The Commercials-#1-C* . . . . (TVT)
Coors In Colorado
  Ray Price; *Master Of The Art* . . . . (Warner Bros.)
Cover Of Rolling Stone
  Dr. Hook & The Medicine Show; *Dr. Hook & The Medicine Show's*
   Greatest Hits . . . . (Capitol)
   Revisited . . . . (Columbia)
Day Job (Frisbee)
  Gin Blossoms; *Congratulations I'm Sorry* . . . . (A&M)
   Outside Looking In: The Best Of The Gin Blossoms . . . . . . (A&M)
Diggin' On You (Kool-Aid)
  TLC; *CrazySexyCool* . . . . (LaFace)
Dippity-Do, Dippity-Do (Styling Gel)
  Original Soundtrack; *TeeVee Toons-The Commercials-#1-C* . . . . (TVT)
Do You Know Exactly How (Oreo Cookies)
  Original Soundtrack; *TeeVee Toons-The Commercials-#1-C* . . . . (TVT)
Dogs Kids Love To Bite, The (Armour Hot Dogs)
  Original Soundtrack; *TeeVee Toons-The Commercials-#1-C* . . . . (TVT)
Don't Happen Twice (Dixie cups)
  Kenny Chesney; *Kenny Chesney's Greatest Hits* . . . . (BNA)
Down Home (Dairy Queen)
  Alabama; *Pass It On Down* . . . . (BMG Special Prod.)
Eddie's First Wife (Betty Crocker)
  Gretchen Peters; *Gretchen Peters* . . . . (Purple Crayon Prod.)
Electric Aunt Jemima
  Frank Zappa; *Uncle Meat* . . . . (Barking Pumpkin)
Emma Jean's Guitar (Gibson)
  Chely Wright; *Let Me In* . . . . (MCA)

Everything I Love (Jack Daniels)
  Alan Jackson; *Everything I Love* . . . . (Arista)
Everything's Changed (Wal-Mart)
  Lonestar; *Country Cares For Kids II-C* . . . . (BNA)
   Crazy Nights . . . . (BNA)
   Lonely Grill . . . . (BNA)
Exhuming McCarthy (Bank Of America)
  R.E.M.; *Document* . . . . (EMI-Capitol Entert. Properties)
Flavor Of The Weak (Nintendo)
  American Hi-Fi; *American Hi-Fi* . . . . (Island)
Fruit Juicy (Hawaiian Punch)
  Original Soundtrack; *TeeVee Toons-The Commercials-#1-C* . . . . (TVT)
Here's To Good Friends (Lowenbrau Beer)
  Original Soundtrack; *TeeVee Toons-The Commercials-#1-C* . . . . (TVT)
Hey Get Your Cold Beer (Ballantine Premium Beer)
  Original Soundtrack; *TeeVee Toons-The Commercials-#1-C* . . . . (TVT)
Hit 'Em Up Style (Oops!) (Neiman-Marcus)
  Blu Cantrell; *So Blu* . . . . (Arista)
   Totally Hits 2001-C . . . . (Arista)
Hot Boyz (Visa)
  Missy ''Misdemeanor'' Elliot; *Da Real World* . . . . (East West)
   Totally Hits-#2-C . . . . (Elektra)
How A Cowgirl Says Goodbye (Texaco)
  Tracy Lawrence; *The Coast Is Clear* . . . . (Atlantic)
How're You Fixed For Blades (Gillette)
  Original Soundtrack; *TeeVee Toons-The Commercials-#1-C* . . . . (TVT)
I Can Do That (Victoria's Secret)
  Montell Jordan; *Let's Ride* . . . . (Def Jam/RAL/Mercury)
I Got 5 On It (Nyquil)
  Luniz; *Operation Stackola* . . . . (Noo Trybe)
I Got Mexico (Coke)
  Eddy Raven; *14 #1 Country Hits-C* . . . . (RCA)
   Best Of Eddy Raven . . . . (RCA)
   I Could Use Another You . . . . (RCA)
I Just Wanna Love U (Give It 2 Me) (Prada, Gucci, Fifth Mart, Cristal)
  Jay-Z; *Dynasty-Roc La Familia 2000* . . . . (Roc-A-Fella/DJMG)
I Like Them Girls (Cartier, Gucci)
  Tyrese; *2000 Watts* . . . . (RCA)
I Love Bosco
  Original Soundtrack; *TeeVee Toons-The Commercials-#1-C* . . . . (TVT)
I Want You (Coca-Cola)
  Savage Garden; *Best Of Savage Garden* . . . . (Columbia)
   Savage Garden . . . . (Columbia)
I'd Like To Buy The World A Coke (Coca-Cola)
  Original Soundtrack; *TeeVee Toons-The Commercials-#1-C* . . . . (TVT)
If You Like Fluff, Fluff, Fluff (Marshallow Fluff)
  Original Soundtrack; *TeeVee Toons-The Commercials-#1-C* . . . . (TVT)
If You've Got The Time (Miller High Life Beer)
  Original Soundtrack; *TeeVee Toons-The Commercials-#1-C* . . . . (TVT)
I'm A Chiquita Banana
  Original Soundtrack; *TeeVee Toons-The Commercials-#1-C* . . . . (TVT)
I'm My Own Walkman
  Bobby McFerrin; *The Voice* . . . . (Elektra)
It Ain't My Fault (Billboard)
  Silkk The Shocker; *Charge It 2 Da Game* . . . . (No Limit/Priority)
It's All About You (Not About Me) (Samsonite)
  Tracie Spencer; *Tracie* . . . . (Capitol)
It's Slinky
  Original Soundtrack; *TeeVee Toons-The Commercials-#1-C* . . . . (TVT)
It's The Real Thing (Coca-Cola)
  Original Cast; *TeeVee Toons-The Commercials-#1-C* . . . . (TVT)
Jack Daniel And Mr. Jim Beam
  Philip Claypool; *Perfect World* . . . . (Curb)
Jack Daniel's If You Please
  David Allan Coe; *David Allan Coe-Super Hits* . . . . (Columbia)
   For The Record-The First 10 Years . . . . (Columbia)
Jack Daniel's Kind Of Day
  Johnny Winter; *Lone Star Kind Of Day* . . . . (Relix)
Jack Daniel's Old No. 7
  Jerry Lee Lewis; *Killer Country* . . . . (Mercury)
Jack Daniels, You Lied To Me Again
  Ray Stevens; *20 Comedy Hits Special Collection* . . . . (Curb)
Jesus At McDonald's
  Mojo Nixon; *Get Out Of My Way* . . . . (Restless)
John Deere Green
  Joe Diffie; *Honky Tonk Attitude* . . . . (Epic)
   Joe Diffie's Greatest Hits . . . . (Epic)
John Deere Tractor
  Judds; *Judds' Greatest Hits-#2* . . . . (MCA)
   Love Can Build A Bridge . . . . (MCA)
John Deere Tractor Song
  Don Walser; *Uprooted: Best Of Roots Country-C* . . . . (Shanachie)
Jose Cuervo
  Shelly West; *West By West* . . . . (Viva)
Jungleland (Exxon)
  Bruce Springsteen; *Born To Run* . . . . (Columbia)
Just Another Day In Paradise (Domino's Pizza)
  Phil Vassar; *Phil Vassar* . . . . (Arista)

Just Be Straight With Me (Billboard) (Cristal champagne)
Silkk The Shocker; *Charge It 2 Da Game* . . . . (No Limit/Priority)

Kodachrome
Paul Simon; *Greatest Hits, Etc.* . . . . (Columbia)
  Negotiations And Love Songs, 1971-1986 . . . .(Warner Bros.)
  There Goes Rhymin' Simon . . . . (Columbia)
Simon & Garfunkel; *The Concert In Central Park* . . . .(Warner Bros.)

Last Chance Texaco
Rickie Lee Jones; *Naked Songs Live And Acoustic* . . . . (Reprise)
  Rickie Lee Jones . . . .(Warner Bros.)

Letter, The (That Johnny Walker Read)
Asleep At The Wheel; *Very Best Of Asleep At The Wheel*
  Since 1970. . . . . (Relentless/Madacy)

Little Dab'll Do Ya (Brylcreem)
Original Soundtrack; *TeeVee Toons-The Commercials-#1-C.* . . . . (TVT)

Look Sharp March (Gillette)
Original Sins; *TeeVee Toons-The Commercials-#1-C* . . . . (TVT)

Love And Texaco
Gretchen Peters; *Gretchen Peters* . . . . (Purple Crayon Prod.)

Love At The Five & Dime (Woolworth's)
Kathy Mattea; *Collection Of Hits* . . . . (Mercury)
  Fourteen Country Favorites-C . . . . (Mercury)
  Walk The Way The Wind Blows . . . . (Mercury)
Nanci Griffith; *Last Of The True Believers* . . . . (Philo)
  One Fair Summer Evening . . . .(MCA)

Love Is A Good Thing (Wal-Mart)
Sheryl Crow; *Sheryl Crow* . . . . (A&M)

M.T.A.
Kingston Trio; *25 Years Non-Stop* . . . . (Xeres)
  Best Of The Kingston Trio . . . . (Capitol)
  Capitol Collectors Series-The Kingston Trio . . . . (Capitol)
  Scarlet Ribbons . . . . (Capitol)
  Very Best Of The Kingston Trio . . . . (Capitol)

Mariner, The (Old Spice Cologne)
Original Soundtrack; *TeeVee Toons-The Commercials-#1-C.* . . . . (TVT)

Marlboro Song, The (Theme From "Magnificent 7")
Original Soundtrack; *TeeVee Toons-The Commercials-#1-C.* . . . . (TVT)

Meet The Swinger (Polaroid Swinger)
Original Soundtrack; *TeeVee Toons-The Commercials-#1-C.* . . . . (TVT)

Members Only (Members Only, J. Crew)
Sheryl Crow; *The Globe Sessions* . . . . (A&M)

Meow Meow Meow Meow (Meow Mix Cat Food)
Original Soundtrack; *TeeVee Toons-The Commercials-#1-C.* . . . . (TVT)

Mercury Poisoning
Graham Parker And The Rumour; *Live Sparks* . . . . (Arista)

Miss America
Styx; *Caught In The Act* . . . . (A&M)
  Grand Illusion . . . . (A&M)
  Styx-Classics-#15 . . . . (A&M)

Miss America
Mark Lindsey; *Mark Lindsey: Golden Classics* . . . . (Collectables)

Miss America
Big Dish; *Satellites* . . . . (East West)

Mr. Clean, Mr. Clean
Original Soundtrack; *TeeVee Toons-The Commercials-#1-C.* . . . . (TVT)

My Beer Is Rheingold, The Dry Beer
Original Soundtrack; *TeeVee Toons-The Commercials-#1-C.* . . . . (TVT)

My Dog's Better Than Your Dog (Ken-L Ration Dog & Puppy Food)
Original Soundtrack; *TeeVee Toons-The Commercials-#1-C.* . . . . (TVT)

N-E-S-T-L-E-S (Nestle's Quik Chocolate Flavor)
Original Soundtrack; *TeeVee Toons-The Commercials-#1-C.* . . . . (TVT)

New York State Of Mind (Greyhound)
Barbra Streisand; *Memories* . . . . (Columbia)
  Streisand Superman . . . . (Columbia)
Billy Joel; *Billy Joel-Greatest Hits, Volume I & Volume II.* . . . . (Columbia)
  Turnstiles . . . . (Columbia)
Carmen McRae; *Ms. Magic* . . . .(Dunhill Compact Classics)

Nobody Doesn't Like Sara Lee
Original Soundtrack; *TeeVee Toons-The Commercials-#1-C.* . . . . (TVT)

Oh Fab, I'm Glad (Fab Laundry Detergent)
Original Soundtrack; *TeeVee Toons-The Commercials-#1-C.* . . . . (TVT)

One I Loved Back Then (Corvette Song) (Kwik Sak)
George Jones; *19 Hot Country Requests-#3-C* . . . .(Epic)
  George Jones-Super Hits . . . .(Epic)
  Greatest Country Hits Of The '80s-1986-C . . . . (Columbia)
  Who's Gonna Fill Their Shoes . . . .(Epic)

One More Last Chance (John Deere)
Vince Gill; *I Still Believe In You* . . . .(MCA)
  The Ultimate Country Party-C . . . . (Arista)
  Vince Gill-Souvenirs . . . .(MCA)

Pack Of Pall Malls
Joe LoCascio; *Marionette* . . . . (Chase Music Group)

Pack Of Winstons
Green & Checkers; *Green & Checkers* . . . .(Trip)

Pick One Up And Smoke It Sometime (Muriel Cigars)
Original Soundtrack; *TeeVee Toons-The Commercials-#1-C.* . . . . (TVT)

Plop, Plop, Fizz, Fizz (Alka-Seltzer)
Original Soundtrack; *TeeVee Toons-The Commercials-#1-C.* . . . . (TVT)

Polaroids
Shawn Colvin; *Best Of The Columbia Records Radio Hour-#1-C* . . . (Columbia)
  Fat City. . . . . (Columbia)

Popsicle
Jan & Dean; *Jan & Dean-Legendary Masters.* . . . . (EMI)
  Surf City-Best Of Jan & Dean. . . . . (EMI)

Popsicle
New Kids On The Block; *New Kids On The Block* . . . . (Columbia)

Popsicle
Talking Heads; *Popular Favorites-1984-1992* . . . .(Sire)

Popsicle Toes
Diana Krall; *When I Look In Your Eyes* . . . . (GRP)
Manhattan Transfer; *Coming Out* . . . .(Atlantic)
Michael Franks; *Art Of Tea* . . . . (Reprise)

Popsicles & Icicles
Murmaids; *Golden Girl Groups-C* . . . . (K-Tel)
  Oldies But Goodies-#2-C . . . .(Original Sound)

Prozac Baby
Broken Toys; *Shreds-#2: American Underground 1994-C.* . . . .(Shredder)

Pure Love (Captain Crunch)
Ronnie Milsap; *Ronnie Milsap's Greatest Hits* . . . .(RCA)
  Ronnie Milsap-Super Hits . . . .(RCA)

Rainbow Stew (Bubble Up)
Merle Haggard; *For The Record: Merle Haggard-43 Legendary Hits* . . . .(BNA)
  Merle Haggard's Greatest Hits . . . .(MCA)
  More Of The Best . . . . (Rhino)
  Rainbow Stew-Live At Anaheim Stadium . . . .(MCA)

Rednecks, White Socks And Blue Ribbon Beer
Johnny Russell; *Beer Redneck Mothers* . . . .(RCA)
  Country Legends-C . . . .(Madacy)
  Country's Greatest Drinking Songs-C . . . . (All-Star Music)
  Rednecks, White Socks & Blue Ribbon Beer. . . . .(RCA)

Rexall
Dave Navarro; *Trust No One* . . . . (Capitol)

Rose And A Baby Ruth, A
George Hamilton IV; *At The Hop* . . . . (MCA)
  Vintage Music-#12-C. . . . . (MCA)

Rum & Coca-Cola
Andrews Sisters; *Andrews Sisters-16 Great Performances.* . . . . (MCA)
  Best Of The Andrews Sisters . . . . (MCA)
  Boogie Woogie Bugle Girls . . . . (MCA)
  Capitol Collectors Series-The Andrews Sisters . . . . (Capitol)
Professor Longhair; *Last Mardi Gras* . . . .(Atlantic)
  Mardi Gras In Baton Rouge . . . . (Rhino)

Safeway Cart
Neil Young & Crazy Horse; *Sleeps With Angels* . . . .(Reprise)

San Francisco Treat, The (Rice-A-Roni)
Original Soundtrack; *TeeVee Toons-The Commercials-#1-C.* . . . . (TVT)

Schaefer Is The One Beer To Have
Original Soundtrack; *TeeVee Toons-The Commercials-#1-C.* . . . . (TVT)

Sears-Roebuck Routine
Doc Watson; *Old Timey Concert.* . . . . (Vanguard)

Shape Your Stomach's In (Alka-Seltzer)
Original Soundtrack; *TeeVee Toons-The Commercials-#1-C.* . . . . (TVT)

She Thinks My Tractor's Sexy (John Deere)
Kenny Chesney; *Everywhere We Go.* . . . .(BNA)

Shut Up (Bugle Boy, Polo)
Trick Daddy; *Book Of Thugs-Chapter AK Verse 47* . . . .(Slip 'N Slide)

Sick & Beautiful (Marlboro, Penthouse, Milky Way)
Artificial Joy Club; *Melt* . . . .(Interscope)

Singing In My Sleep (Sony)
Semisonic; *Feeling Strangely Fine* . . . . (MCA)

Smells Like Teen Spirit
Nirvana; *Nevermind* . . . .(David Geffen Co.)

Snap Crackle Pop (Kellogg's Rice Krispies)
Original Soundtrack; *TeeVee Toons-The Commercials-#1-C.* . . . . (TVT)

Something Like That (Coke)
Tim McGraw; *A Place In The Sun.* . . . . (Curb)
  Tim McGraw's Greatest Hits. . . . . (Curb)

Sometimes You Feel Like A Nut (Mounds & Almond Joy Candy Bars)
Original Soundtrack; *TeeVee Toons-The Commercials-#1-C.* . . . . (TVT)

Strawberries (Hennessey)
Smooth; *Reality.* . . . . (Perspective/A&M)

Stripper (Take It Off), The (Noxema Shave Cream)
Original Soundtrack; *TeeVee Toons-The Commercials-#1-C.* . . . . (TVT)

Stronger Than Dirt (Ajax)
Original Soundtrack; *TeeVee Toons-The Commercials-#1-C.* . . . . (TVT)

Take Me Out To The Ball Game (Cracker Jack)
Bruce Springstone; *Baseball's Greatest Hits-C* . . . . (Rhino)
Doc & Merle Watson; *Baseball's Greatest Hits-C* . . . . (Rhino)
Frank Zappa; *You Can't Do That On Stage Anymore-#4.* . . . . (Rykodisc)

Tanqueray
Vern Gosdin; *Alone* . . . . (Columbia)
  Vern Gosdin's Greatest Hits . . . . (Columbia)
  Vern Gosdin-Super Hits . . . . (Columbia)

Texaco Star Theme
Original Soundtrack; *TeeVee Toons-The Commercials-#1-C.* . . . . (TVT)

Thank God & Greyhound
Roy Clark; *Best Of Roy Clark* . . . . (MCA)
 Great Picks And New Tricks . . . . (ISD/Intersound)
 Roy Clark-Live . . . . (MCA)
 Roy Clark's Greatest Hits . . . . (MCA)
Theme From "Colt .45"
Original Soundtrack; *Television's Greatest Hits-#4-Black & White*
 Classics-C . . . . (TVT)
Theme From "The Miss America Pageant" (There She Is, Miss America)
Bert Parks; *Television's Greatest Hits-#4-Black & White Classics-C* . . . . (TVT)
Things Go Better With Coke
Original Soundtrack; *TeeVee Toons-The Commercials-#1-C* . . . . (TVT)
To A Smoker It's A Kent
Original Soundtrack; *TeeVee Toons-The Commercials-#1-C* . . . . (TVT)
Tupperware Party
Doughboys; *Happy Accidents* . . . . (Restless)
Twentieth Century Fox
Doors; *Doors* . . . . (Elektra)
Two Sleepy People (Frigidaire)
Art Garfunkel; *Up 'Til Now* . . . . (Columbia)
Fats Waller; *Fats Waller-Masterpieces-#3* . . . . (EPM)
Jo Sullivan Loesser & Others; *Loesser By Loesser* . . . . (DRG)
Kay Kyser & His Orchestra; *Best Of The Big Bands-C* . . . . (Columbia)
Use Ajax The Foaming Cleanser
Original Soundtrack; *TeeVee Toons-The Commercials-#1-C* . . . . (TVT)
Vibrant Thing (Ben & Jerry)
Q-Tip; *Amplified* . . . . (Def Jam/IDJMG)
Vogue
Madonna; *I'm Breathless-Music From Dick Tracy* . . . . (Sire)
 Immaculate Collection . . . . (Sire)
 Royal Box . . . . (Sire)
Walkaway Joe (Texaco)
Trisha Yearwood; *Hearts In Armor* . . . . (MCA)
 Songbook-A Collection Of Hits . . . . (MCA)
Wells Fargo Wagon
Original Broadway Cast; *The Music Man* . . . . (Angel)
Original Cast; *The Music Man* . . . . (Gold Rush)
Western Union
Five Americans; *Back To The '60s-Rock 'N' Roll-C* . . . . (Dominion Entert.)
 Nuggets-#1-The Hits-C . . . . (Rhino)
Western Union
Elvis Presley; *From Nashville To Memphis-The Essential '60s Masters* . . . (RCA)
When It All Goes South (Moon Pie, RC Cola, John Deere, Jack Daniel's)
Alabama; *When It All Goes South* . . . . (RCA)
When You Say Bud (Budweiser Beer)
Original Soundtrack; *TeeVee Toons-The Commercials-#1-C* . . . . (TVT)
When You're Out Of Schlitz (Schlitz Beer)
Original Soundtrack; *TeeVee Toons-The Commercials-#1-C* . . . . (TVT)
Where Have All The Cowboys Gone? (Marlboro)
Paula Cole; *This Fire* . . . . (Imago)
Who Needs Pictures (Kodak)
Brad Paisley; *Who Needs Pictures* . . . . (Arista)
Winston Tastes Good (Winston Cigarettes)
Original Soundtrack; *TeeVee Toons-The Commercials-#1-C* . . . . (TVT)
Wood And Wire (Sears & Roebuck)
George Jones; *The Rock: Stone Cold Country 2001* . . . . (BNA)
Wurlitzer Prize (I Don't Want To Get Over You)
Waylon Jennings; *Waylon & Willie* . . . . (RCA)
Y.M.C.A.
Village People; *Billboard Top Dance Hits-1978-C* . . . . (Rhino)
 Billboard Top Rock 'N' Roll Hits-1979-C . . . . (Rhino)
 Cruisin' . . . . (Casablanca)
 Live & Sleazy . . . . (Casablanca)
 Night At Studio 54-C . . . . (Casablanca)
 Village People's Greatest Hits . . . . (Rhino)
You Can Take Salem Out Of The Country
Original Soundtrack; *TeeVee Toons-The Commercials-#1-C* . . . . (TVT)
Zip-Lock
Lit; *A Place In The Sun* . . . . (RCA)

PROMISE, Pledge, Swear

See Also: CHARACTER & INTEGRITY, CHEATING & LIES,
DECISIONS, FAITH, GOD, HELP, LOVE: DEVOTION, MARRIAGE,
MOTIVATION, SEX: RESISTING TEMPTATION,
TOGETHERNESS, TRUTH

Ain't No Mountain High Enough
Diana Ross; *20/20-C* . . . . (Motown)
 25 #1 Hits From 25 Years-C . . . . (Motown)
 Diana Ross . . . . (Motown)
 Diana Ross-The Ultimate Collection . . . . (Motown)
 Every Great Motown Song-First 25 Years-C . . . . (Motown)
 Greatest Songs By Ashford & Simpson . . . . (Motown)
 Motown Legends-Diana Ross . . . . (Motown)

Motown Story-First 25 Years-C . . . . (Motown)
 Motown's Biggest Pop Hits-C . . . . (Motown)
 TV ST/Diana-C . . . . (Motown)
Marvin Gaye & Tammi Terrell; *20 Greatest Songs In Motown*
 History-C . . . . (Motown)
 Classic Duets-Marvin Gaye & His Women-C . . . . (Motown)
 Marvin Gaye & Tammi Terrell's Greatest Hits . . . . (Motown)
 Marvin Gaye Live At The London Palladium . . . . (Motown)
 Motown Grammy R&B Performances Of The '60s & '70s-C . . . (Motown)
 Performances Of The '60s & '70s-C . . . . (Motown)
 United . . . . (Motown)
American Girl
Goo Goo Dolls; *The Concert For New York City-C* . . . . (Columbia)
Tom Petty And The Heartbreakers; *Pack Up The Plantation-Live!* . . . . (MCA)
 Tom Petty & The Heartbreakers . . . . (Gone Gator)
 You're Gonna Get It! . . . . (Gone Gator)
Best Of Intentions
Travis Tritt; *Down The Road I Go* . . . . (Columbia)
Blessed
Elton John; *Elton John-Love Songs* . . . . (MCA)
 Made In England . . . . (Rocket)
Can't Stop My Heart From Loving You
Aaron Neville; *The Tattooed Heart* . . . . (A&M)
O'Kanes; *Greatest Country Hits Of The '80s-1987-C* . . . . . . (Columbia)
 More Hot Country Requests-#2-C . . . . (Epic)
 O'Kanes . . . . (Columbia)
Caught In Your Web (Swear To Your Heart)
Russell Hitchcock; *ST/Arachnophobia* . . . . (Hollywood)
Ceremony, The
George Jones & Tammy Wynette; *George Jones & Tammy Wynette-16*
 Biggest Hits . . . . (Epic/Legacy)
 George Jones & Tammy Wynette's Greatest Hits . . . . (Epic)
Chain, The
Fleetwood Mac; *25 Years-The Chain* . . . . (Warner Bros.)
 Rumours . . . . (Warner Bros.)
Shawn Colvin; *Legacy-A Tribute To Fleetwood Mac's Rumours-C* . . . . (Lava)
Commitment
LeAnn Rimes; *Big Country Hits '99-C* . . . . (K-Tel)
 Sittin' On Top Of The World . . . . (Curb)
Cross My Heart & Hope To Die
Elvis Presley; *ST/Girl Happy* . . . . (RCA)
Everlong
Foo Fighters; *The Colour And The Shape* . . . . (Roswell/RCA)
For You I Will
Monica; *The Boy Is Mine* . . . . (Arista)
Forever's As Far As I'll Go
Alabama; *Alabama's Greatest Hits-#3* . . . . (RCA)
 Alabama-Super Hits . . . . (RCA)
 For The Record: 41 Number One Hits . . . . (RCA)
 Pass It On Down . . . . (BMG Special Prod.)
From Here To Eternity
Michael Peterson; *Michael Peterson* . . . . (Reprise)
 Wedding Day Music-C . . . . (Reprise)
From This Moment On
Shania Twain & Bryan White; *Come On Over* . . . . (Mercury)
High Noon
Frankie Laine; *Billboard Top Movie Hits-1950-1954-C* . . . . . . (Rhino)
Tex Ritter; *Heroes Of Country Music-#4-Legends Of The West*
 Coast-C . . . . (Rhino)
 The Envelope Please-Academy Award Winning Songs (1946-
 1957)-C . . . . (Rhino)
How Do You Tell The One
After 7; *Reflections* . . . . (Virgin)
I Am That Man
Brooks & Dunn; *Borderline* . . . . (Arista)
I Can Love You Like That
All-4-One; *1996 Grammy Nominees-C* . . . . (Columbia)
 And The Music Speaks . . . . (Blitzz)
John Michael Montgomery; *John Michael Montgomery* . . . . . . (Atlantic)
I Can Make It Better
Luther Vandross; *Your Secret Love* . . . . (LV/Epic)
I Cross My Heart
George Strait; *ST/Pure Country* . . . . (MCA)
I Do
Paul Brandt; *Calm Before The Storm* . . . . (Reprise)
I Don't Make Promises (I Can't Break)
Shannon Curfman; *Loud Guitars Big Suspicions* . . . . (Arista)
I Swear
All-4-One; *All-4-One* . . . . (Blitzz)
John Michael Montgomery; *John Michael Montgomery's*
 Greatest Hits . . . . (Atlantic)
 Kickin' It Up . . . . (Atlantic)
I Will Buy You A New Life
Everclear; *Now That's What I Call Music!-#1-C* . . . . (Virgin)
 So Much For The Afterglow . . . . (Capitol)
I Will, If You Will
John Berry; *Faces* . . . . (Capitol)
I Will...But
SHeDAISY; *The Whole Shebang* . . . . (Lyric Street)

I'd Do Anything For Love
Meat Loaf; *Bat Out Of Hell II: Back Into Hell* ....(MCA)
I'll Always Be Right There
Bryan Adams; *18 Til I Die* .... (A&M)
MTV Unplugged-Bryan Adams ....(A&M)
I'll Be
Edwin McCain; *Misguided Roses*.....................(Lava)
I'll Be Around
Rappin' 4-Tay; *Don't Fight The Feelin'*...................(Rag Top/EMI)
I'll Be Home
Barbra Streisand; *Stoney End* ....(Columbia)
Randy Newman; *Little Criminals*.....................(Warner Bros.)
Randy Newman/Live ....(Warner Archives)
I'll Be There For You
Bon Jovi; *New Jersey* ....(Jambco)
I'll Keep You Satisfied
Billy J. Kramer With The Dakotas; *History Of British Rock-#2-C* ......(Rhino)
I'll Never Be Jealous Again
Original Cast; *ST/Pajama Game* ....(Collectables)
I'll Never Break Your Heart
Backstreet Boys; *Backstreet Boys* ....(Jive)
Now That's What I Call Music!-#2-C ....(Virgin)
I'll Take Care Of You
Dixie Chicks; *Wide Open Spaces* ....(Monument)
Just The Two Of Us
Will Smith; *Big Willie Style* ....(Columbia)
Lean On Me
Kirk Franklin; *The Nu Nation Project*............(Gospo Centric/Interscope)
Long As I Live
John Michael Montgomery; *John Michael Montgomery* ....(Atlantic)
Love Travels
Kathy Mattea; *Love Travels* ....(Mercury)
Love Will Be Waiting
Kevon Edmonds; *24/7* ....(RCA)
My Love Will Not Let You Down
Bruce Springsteen; *Tracks* ....(Columbia)
Never Is A Promise
Fiona Apple; *Tidal* ....(Clean Slate/Work)
Never Let You Go
Third Eye Blind; *Blue* ....(Elektra)
Totally Hits-#2-C ....(Elektra)
Never Make A Promise
Dru Hill; *Dru Hill* ....(Island)
No Guarantee
Chico DeBarge; *Long Time No See*.......(Kedar Entert./Universal)
MTV Jams-C ....(Kedar Entert./Universal)
ST/Hoodlum.....................(Interscope)
O Promise Me
Jessie Bartlett Davis; *Music From The New York Stage (1890-1920)-#1-1890-1908-C* ....(Pearl)
Oh Promise Me
Liberace; *Piano Magic* ....(Sony Music Special Prod.)
Tommy Dorsey; *Tommy Dorsey-1937-1938* ....(Classics)
On My Word Of Honor
Platters; *Enchanted-The Best Of The Platters*.....................(Rhino)
One Promise Too Late
Reba McEntire; *Country Classics-#10-1987-C* ....(Universal)
Reba McEntire's Greatest Hits ....(MCA)
What Am I Gonna Do About You ....(MCA)
Over The Rise
Bruce Springsteen; *Tracks* ....(Columbia)
Perfect
Smashing Pumpkins; *Adore* ....(Virgin)
Pledge Pin
Robert Plant; *Pictures At Eleven* ....(Swan Song)
Pledge Your Allegiance
Suicidal Tendencies; *How Will I Laugh Tomorrow When I Can't Even Smile Today* ....(Epic)
Prime Cuts ....(Epic)
Pledging My Time
Bob Dylan; *Blonde On Blonde* ....(Columbia)
Luther ''Guitar Jr.'' Johnson; *Tangled Up In Blues-Songs Of Bob Dylan-This Ain't No Tribute-C* ....(House Of Blues)
Prayin' For Daylight
Rascal Flatts; *Rascal Flatts* ....(Lyric Street)
Promise
Eve 6; *Horrorscope* ....(RCA)
Promise
Jagged Edge; *J.E. Heartbreak* ....(So So Def/Columbia)
Promise Ain't Enough
Daryl Hall & John Oates; *Marigold Sky* ....(Push)
Modern Bride Presents The Wedding Album-C ....(Columbia)
Promise Her Anything
Burt Bacharach; *The Look Of Love-The Burt Bacharach Collection* ....(Rhino)
Promise I Make
Dakota Moon; *Dakota Moon* ....(Elektra)
Promise Kept, A
James Horner; *ST/Titanic* ....(Sony Music Classical)

Promise Me You'll Try
Jennifer Lopez; *On The 6* ....(Work)
Promise Of A Fisherman
Paul Winter; *Common Ground* ....(A&M)
Sergio Mendes; *Sergio Mendes-Classics-#18* ....(A&M)
Promise Of A New Day
Paula Abdul; *Spellbound* ....(Captive)
Promise Of Shadows
Peter Gabriel; *Passion: Music For The Last Temptation Of Christ* .....(Geffen)
Promise To Try
Madonna; *Like A Prayer* ....(Sire)
Promise, A
Echo & The Bunnymen; *Heaven Up Here* ....(Sire)
Songs To Learn & Sing-The Hits ....(Sire)
Promise, The
Tracy Chapman; *New Beginning*.....................(Elektra)
Promise, The (The Dolphin Song)
Olivia Newton-John; *Physical* ....(MCA)
Promised Land
Band; *Moondog Matinee*.....................(Capitol)
Chuck Berry; *Rock 'N' Roll Rarities-20 Magic Tracks* ....(Chess)
The Chess Box-Chuck Berry ....(Chess)
Elvis Presley; *Promised Land* ....(RCA)
ST/This Is Elvis ....(RCA)
Freddy Weller; *Country Music Classics-#11-Early '70s-C* ....(K-Tel)
Freddy Weller's Greatest Hits ....(Columbia)
Gary Morris; *Full Moon Empty Heart* ....(Liberty)
Grateful Dead; *Steal Your Face* ....(Grateful Dead)
James Taylor; *Walking Man* ....(Warner Bros.)
Kingfish; *Kingfish/Alive In Eighty Five-Double Dose* ....(Relix)
Promised Land
Bruce Springsteen; *Darkness On The Edge Of Town* ....(Columbia)
Bruce Springsteen & The E Street Band; *Bruce Springsteen & The E Street Band Live/1975-85* ....(Legacy)
Promised Land
Bobby Caldwell; *Stuck On You* ....(Sin-Drome)
Promised Land
Julian Cope; *Peggy Suicide* ....(Island)
Promised Land
Hollies; *Distant Light* ....(Epic)
Promises
Cranberries; *Bury The Hatchet* ....(Island/IDJMG)
Promises
Def Leppard; *Euphoria* ....(Mercury)
Promises
Basia; *Time And Tide* ....(Epic)
Promises
Randy Travis; *Old 8 X 10* ....(Warner Bros.)
Randy Travis' Greatest Hits-#2 ....(Warner Bros.)
Randy Travis-Super Hits-#1 ....(Warner Bros.)
Promises
Eric Clapton; *Backless* ....(Polydor)
Eric Clapton-Crossroads-C ....(Polydor)
Time Pieces-#1-The Best Of Eric Clapton ....(Polydor)
Promises
Lyle Lovett; *ST/Dead Man Walking* ....(Columbia)
The Road To Ensenada ....(MCA)
Promises Broken
Soul Asylum; *Let Your Dim Light Shine* ....(Columbia)
Promises For Spring
Tom Browne; *Browne Sugar* ....(GRP)
Promises In The Dark
Pat Benatar; *Best Shots* ....(Chrysalis)
Live From Earth ....(Chrysalis)
Precious Time ....(Chrysalis)
Promises, Promises
Naked Eyes; *Back To Back Hits* ....(EMI Special Markets)
Best Of Naked Eyes ....(EMI)
Just Can't Get Enough: New Wave Hits Of The '80s-#10-C ....(Rhino)
Promises, Promises
Dionne Warwick; *Dionne Warwick Collection-Her All-Time Greatest Hits* ....(Rhino)
The Look Of Love-The Burt Bacharach Collection ....(Rhino)
Jerry Orbach/Original Cast; *ST/Promises, Promises* ....(Rykodisc)
Rest Of Mine, The
Trace Adkins; *Big Time* ....(Capitol)
Rose Garden
k.d. lang; *Swingin' Country Favorites-C* ....(Warner Bros.)
k.d. lang and The Reclines; *Angel With A Lariat* ....(Sire)
Lynn Anderson; *All Time Legends Of Country Music-C* ....(Legacy)
Country Music Classics-#4-1970-1975-C ....(K-Tel)
Lynn Anderson's Greatest Hits ....(Columbia)
Rose Garden ....(Columbia)
Super Hits Of The '70s-Have A Nice Day-#4-C ....(Rhino)
Very Special Love Song-C ....(Fifty One West)
Satisfy You
Puff Daddy Featuring R. Kelly; *Forever* ....(Bad Boy/Arista)
Say You'll Be There
Spice Girls; *Now That's What I Call Music!-#1-C* ....(Virgin)

Spice . . . .(Virgin)

Sealed With A Kiss
Bobby Vinton; *Bobby Vinton's Greatest Hits* . . . . (Curb)
Brian Hyland; *Cruisin'-1962-C* . . . . (Increase)
  Oldies But Goodies-#2-C . . . .(Original Sound)
  Original Rock 'N' Roll Hits Of The '50s-C . . . . (Roulette)
Lettermen; *Best Of The Lettermen-#2* . . . . (Capitol)
  Capitol Collectors Series-The Lettermen . . . . (Capitol)

So Help Me Girl
Gary Barlow; *Open Road* . . . . (Arista)
Joe Diffie; *Third Rock From The Sun* . . . . (Epic)

So In Love With You
U.N.V.; *Universal Nubian Voices* . . . . (Maverick/Warner Bros.)

Something That We Do
Clint Black; *Country Cares For Kids II-C* . . . .(BNA)
  Nothin' But The Taillights . . . .(RCA)

These Eyes
Guess Who; *Best Of The Guess Who* . . . .(RCA)
  Greatest Of The Guess Who . . . .(RCA)
  Nipper's Greatest Hits Of The '60s-#1-C . . . . (RCA)
  Track Record-Collection . . . .(RCA)

This I Promise You
'N Sync; *No Strings Attached* . . . .(Jive)
  Now That's What I Call Music!-#7-C . . . . (Virgin)

Till I Waltz Again With You
Teresa Brewer; *Best Of Teresa Brewer* . . . . (MCA Jazz)

To Be Loved By You
Wynonna; *Revelations* . . . .(Curb/MCA)
  Wynonna-Collection . . . . (Curb)

Too Little Too Late
Barenaked Ladies; *Maroon* . . . .(Reprise)

Touch Me
Doors; *Best Of The Doors* . . . . (Elektra)
  Doors 13 . . . . (Elektra)
  Doors' Greatest Hits . . . . (Elektra)
  Soft Parade . . . . (Elektra)

Transfusion
Nervous Norvus; *Dr. Demento Presents The Greatest Novelty Records-#2-
  1950s-C* . . . . (Rhino)
  Dr. Demento: 20th Anniversary Collection-C . . . . (Rhino)
  Vintage Music-#3-C . . . . (MCA)
  Wacky Weirdos-C . . . . (K-Tel)

True Friends
Shannon Curfman; *Loud Guitars Big Suspicions* . . . . (Arista)

Used Cars
Bruce Springsteen; *Nebraska* . . . . (Columbia)

We've Only Just Begun
Barbra Streisand; *Just For The Record* . . . . (Columbia)
Carpenters; *Carpenters-Classics-#2* . . . . (A&M)
  Carpenters-The Singles 1969-1973 . . . . (A&M)
  Close To You . . . . (A&M)
  From The Top . . . . (A&M)
  Yesterday Once More . . . . (A&M)

Who Do U Love
Deborah Cox; *Deborah Cox* . . . . (Arista)
  Ultimate Dance Party-1997-C . . . . (Arista)

Wild Horses
Garth Brooks; *No Fences* . . . . (Capitol)

With This Ring
Platters; *Enchanted-The Best Of The Platters* . . . . (Rhino)
  Only Their Best For You . . . .(Pair)
  Rockin' & Rollin' Wedding Songs-#2-C . . . . (Rhino)
  The Musicor Years . . . . (Collectables)
T. Graham Brown; *Best Of T. Graham Brown* . . . .(Liberty)
  T. Graham Brown's All-Time Greatest Hits . . . . (Curb)

Wonderful
Everclear; *Now That's What I Call Music!-#5-C* . . . . (Virgin)
  Songs From An American Movie-#1-Learning How To Smile . . . (Capitol)

You Got It
Bonnie Raitt; *ST/Boys On The Side* . . . . (Arista)
Roy Orbison; *Mystery Girl* . . . . (Virgin)

You Gotta Love That
Neal McCoy; *Neal McCoy's Greatest Hits* . . . . (Atlantic)
  Today's Country Love-C . . . . (K-Tel)
  You Gotta Love That! . . . . (Atlantic)

You Won't Be Lonely Now
Billy Ray Cyrus; *Southern Rain* . . . . (Monument)

You Won't Ever Be Lonely
Andy Griggs; *Andy Griggs* . . . .(RCA)

You'll Be In My Heart
Phil Collins; *ST/Tarzan* . . . . (Hollywood)

PROSTITUTES, Exotic Dancers, Gigolos, Pimps, Strippers
See Also: DANCE, LOVE: COMMITTED OR NOT, SEX

Ain't No Free
NRBQ; *At Yankee Stadium* . . . . (Mercury)

Amsterdam
Van Halen; *Balance* . . . . (Warner Bros.)

Bad Girls
Donna Summer; *Bad Girls* . . . . (Casablanca)
  Dance Collection . . . . (Casablanca)
  On The Radio-Greatest Hits-Volumes I & II . . . . (Casablanca)
  Summer Collection . . . . (Mercury)
  Walk Away-Best Of Donna Summer-1977-1980 . . . . (Casablanca)

Bordello Night
City Boy; *Young Men Gone West* . . . .(Mercury)

Brenda's Got A Baby
Tupac; *2Pacalypse Now* . . . . (Priority)

Charlotte The Harlot
Iron Maiden; *Iron Maiden* . . . .(Capitol)

Christmas Card From A Hooker In Minneapolis
Tom Waits; *Blue Valentine* . . . . (Asylum)

Cowboy
Kid Rock; *Devil Without A Cause* . . . . (Top Dog/Lava/Atlantic)

Devil's Whorehouse
Misfits; *Walk Among Us* . . . . (Ruby)

Down By The Water
PJ Harvey; *ST/Basketball Diaries* . . . .(Island)
  To Bring You My Love . . . .(Island)

Edge
Danny O'Keefe; *Breezy Stories* . . . . (Atlantic)

Ends
Everlast; *Whitey Ford Sings The Blues* . . . . (Tommy Boy)

Fancy Lady
Billy Preston; *Best Of Billy Preston* . . . . (A&M)
  It's My Pleasure . . . . (Out Of Print)

Gigolo
O'Bryan; *Doin' Alright* . . . .(Capitol)

Gigolo
Damned; *Anything* . . . . (MCA)

God Don't Make Lonely Girls
Wallflowers; *Bringing Down The Horse* . . . . (Interscope)

Hell On High Heels
Motley Crue; *New Tattoo* . . . . (Motley/Beyond)

He's A Whore
Cheap Trick; *Cheap Trick* . . . . (Epic)

Hey Negrita
Rolling Stones; *Black And Blue* . . . . (Rolling Stones)

Honky Tonk Women
Elton John; *11-17-70* . . . . (Polydor)
Humble Pie; *Best Of Humble Pie* . . . .(A&M)
  Eat It . . . .(A&M)
  Humble Pie-Classics-#14 . . . . (A&M)
Ike & Tina Turner; *Best Of Ike & Tina Turner* . . . . (EMI)
  Get Back . . . . (Liberty)
Joe Cocker; *Mad Dogs & Englishmen* . . . . (A&M)
Rolling Stones; *Get Yer Ya-Ya's Out!* . . . . (Abkco)
  Hot Rocks 1964-1971 . . . . (Abkco)
  Love You Live . . . . (Virgin)
  Through The Past, Darkly (Big Hits Vol. 2) . . . . (Abkco)
Willie Nelson & Leon Russell; *Half Nelson-C* . . . .(Columbia)

Hooker
Tom Paxton; *Morning After* . . . . (Elektra)

Hotel California
Eagles; *Eagles Greatest Hits, Volume 2* . . . . (Asylum)
  Eagles Live . . . . (Asylum)
  Hell Freezes Over . . . . (Geffen)
  Hotel California . . . . (Asylum)

House Of Flowers
Barbra Streisand; *Just For The Record* . . . . (Columbia)
Harold Arlen & Barbra Streisand; *Harold Sings Arlen (With
  Friend)* . . . . (Sony Music Special Prod.)
Original Cast; *House Of Flowers* . . . . (Sony Music Special Prod.)

I Fell In Love With A Prostitute
James Peterson; *The Kingsnake Collection: Bag O' Blues-C* . . . . . . (Kingsnake)

I'm Watching You
Daryl Hall & John Oates; *War Babies* . . . . (Atlantic)

I'm Your Late Night Evening Prostitute
Tom Waits; *Tom Waits-Early Years-Volume One* . . . . (Planet 3)

Just A Pimp
Angie Stone; *Black Diamond* . . . .(Arista)

Ladies Of The Night
Leon Russell; *Americana* . . . . (Paradise)

Lady Marmalade
Christina Aguilera, Lil' Kim, Mya & Pink; *ST/Moulin Rouge* . . . . . (Interscope)
Labelle; *Nightbirds* . . . .(Epic)
Patti LaBelle; *Best Of Patti LaBelle* . . . . (Epic)
Sheila E.; *Sex Cymbal* . . . . (Warner Bros.)

Lady's Not For Sale
Rita Coolidge; *Lady's Not For Sale* . . . .(A&M)

Let's Ride
Montell Jordan; *Let's Ride* . . . . (Def Jam/RAL/Mercury)
  MTV Jams-C . . . . (Kedar Entert./Universal)
  MTV Party To Go '99-C . . . . (Tommy Boy)

Little Sally, The Super Sex Star
Camille Yarborough; *Iron Pot Cooker* . . . . (Vanguard)
Louise
Bonnie Raitt; *Bonnie Raitt-Collection* . . . .(Warner Bros.)
   Sweet Forgiveness . . . .(Warner Bros.)
Leo Kottke; *Greenhouse* . . . . (Capitol)
   My Feet Are Smiling . . . . (Capitol)
   Very Best Of Leo Kottke . . . . (Capitol)
Linda Ronstadt; *Linda Ronstadt-Retrospective* . . . . (Capitol)
   Silk Purse . . . . (Capitol)
Paul Siebel; *Woodsmoke & Oranges* . . . . (Elektra)
Mommy Can I Come Home
Keb' Mo'; *The Door* . . . . (550/Epic/Okeh)
Naughty Lady Of Shady Lane
Ames Brothers; *Best Of The Ames Brothers* . . . . (Pair)
   Nipper's Greatest Hits Of The '50s-#2-C . . . . (RCA)
No Other Name
Peter, Paul & Mary; *Album 1700* . . . .(Warner Bros.)
Nutbush City Limits
Bob Seger; *Beautiful Loser* . . . . (Capitol)
   Live Bullet . . . . (Capitol)
Ike & Tina Turner; *Best Of Ike & Tina Turner* . . . .(EMI)
   Proud Mary-Best Of Ike & Tina Turner . . . .(EMI)
Tina Turner; *Live In Europe* . . . . (Capitol)
   Simply The Best . . . . (Capitol)
One More Time Around Rosie
Manhattan Transfer; *Jukin'.* . . . . (Capitol)
Painted Ladies
Ian Thomas; *Super Hits Of The '70s-Have A Nice Day-#17-C* . . . . (Rhino)
Pearl Of The Quarter
Steely Dan; *Countdown To Ecstasy* . . . .(MCA)
Penicillin Penny
Dr. Hook; *Dr. Hook & The Medicine Show Revisited* . . . . (Columbia)
Phenomenon
L.L. Cool J; *Phenomenon* . . . . (Def Jam/Mercury)
Pimp
Tubes; *Young And Rich.* . . . . (A&M)
Pimp Behind The Wheels
Ice-T; *Home Invasion* . . . . (Rhyme Syndicate)
Pimp Lane
Penthouse Players Clique; *Paid The Cost* . . . .(Ruthless/Priority)
Pimp Mentality
Who Am I; *Addictive Hip Hop Muzick* . . . . (Ruthless)
Pimp Of The Nation
Kid Rock; *Grits Sandwiches For Breakfast* . . . . (Jive)
Pimp Of The Year
D-Nice; *Call Me D-Nice.* . . . . (Jive)
Pimp Or Die
Father M.C.; *ST/Who's The Man?* . . . . (Uptown)
Pimp Posse
Cargo Cult; *Strange Men Bearing Gifts* . . . . (Touch & Go)
Pimp The Ho
Too $hort; *Life Is...Too Short (Dirty Version)* . . . . (Jive)
Pimpin' Ain't Easy
Big Daddy Kane; *It's A Big Daddy Thing* . . . .(Cold Chillin')
Pimpology
Too $hort; *Short Dog's In The House* . . . . (Jive)
Queer
Garbage; *Garbage* . . . . (Almo Sounds)
Raised On Robbery
Joni Mitchell; *Court & Spark* . . . . (Asylum)
Red Light Mama Red Hot
Humble Pie; *Humble Pie* . . . . (A&M)
Roll 'Em Easy
Linda Ronstadt; *Prisoner In Disguise.* . . . . (Asylum)
Little Feat; *Dixie Chicken.* . . . .(Warner Bros.)
Roxanne
Police; *Every Breath You Take-The Classics* . . . . (A&M)
   Outlandos D'Amour . . . . (A&M)
Sting; *The Secret Policeman's Other Ball/The Music.* . . . . (Rhino)
She Sells
Roxy Music; *Siren* . . . . (Atco)
Son Of Hickory Holler's Tramp
O.C. Smith; *Me And You.* . . . . (Columbia Special Prod.)
   Story Songs-C . . . . (K-Tel)
Spanish Moon
Little Feat; *Feats Don't Fail Me Now* . . . .(Warner Bros.)
   Waiting For Columbus. . . . .(Warner Bros.)
Robert Palmer; *Some People Can Do What They Like* . . . . (Island)
Star Spangled Bummer (Whores Die Hard)
Kris Kristofferson; *Spokey Lady's Sideshow* . . . . (Columbia)
Star Whores
Christ Child; *Hard* . . . . (Buddah)
Street Walker
Band; *Islands* . . . . (Capitol)
Street Walker
Ian Akkerman; *Ian Akkerman.* . . . . (Atlantic)

Sugar Shack
Jimmy Gilmer And The Fireballs; *Billboard Top Rock 'N' Roll Hits-*
   1963-C. . . . . (Rhino)
   Golden Years-1963-C. . . . . (Dominion Entert.)
   Good Old Rock & Roll-C . . . . (International Mktg. Group)
Sweet Painted Lady
Elton John; *Goodbye Yellow Brick Road.* . . . .(Polydor)
Teenage Prostitute
Frank Zappa; *Ship arriving too late to save a drowning witch* . . . . . . (Rykodisc)
Teenage Whore
Hole; *Pretty On The Inside* . . . . (Caroline)
Telephone Girl
Eddie & The Hot Rods; *Life On The Line* . . . . (Island)
Texas Has A Whorehouse In It
Dom Deluise/Dogettes; *ST/Best Little Whorehouse In Texas* . . . . (MCA)
Original Cast; *Best Little Whorehouse In Texas* . . . . (MCA)
Thanks To The Cat House
Johnny Paycheck; *Armed & Crazy* . . . . (Epic)
Theme From "Miami Vice"
Jan Hammer; *Escape From Television* . . . . (MCA)
   Soundtrack Smashes-'80s & More-C . . . . (MCA)
   ST/Miami Vice . . . . (MCA)
Original Soundtrack; *Television's Greatest Hits-#3-1970s & 1980s-C* . . . (TVT)
To Kill A Hooker
N.W.A.; *Efil4zaggin* . . . . (Ruthless/Priority)
Tomorrow We'll See
Sting; *Brand New Day.* . . . . (A&M)
Treat Her Like A Prostitute
Slick Rick; *Great Adventures Of Slick Rick.* . . . .(Def Jam/Columbia)
Walk In The Sun
Bruce Hornsby; *Hot House* . . . .(RCA)
What Would You Do?
City High; *City High* . . . .(Interscope)
   Now That's What I Call Music!-#7-C . . . . (Virgin)
   ST/Life . . . . (Rock Land/Interscope)
Whore
Bay Of Pigs; *Plastic Pig* . . . . (Chameleon)
Whore Said It's Yours
Threat; *Sickinnahead.* . . . . (Mercury)
Whores
Jane's Addiction; *Jane's Addiction* . . . . (Triple X Entert.)
Whore's Lament
Hedy West; *Welcome To Caffe Lena.* . . . .(Biograph)
Whores Of Paris
Bernie Taupin; *He Who Rides The Tiger* . . . .(Asylum)
Wife & The Whore
Kristin Lems; *Born A Woman* . . . . (Flying Fish)
Willie The Pimp
Frank Zappa; *Hot Rats.* . . . . (Rykodisc)
   You Can't Do That On Stage Anymore-#4 . . . . (Rykodisc)
Mothers Of Invention; *Fillmore East-June 1971.* . . . .(Reprise)
Working Class Whore
Pulley; *Pulley* . . . .(Epitaph)
Wrong Way
Sublime; *Sublime* . . . . (Gasoline Alley)
You Make Me Feel Like A Whore
Everclear; *Sparkle And Fade.* . . . . (Capitol)

PROTEST, Political Demonstrations, Revolution

See Also: BROTHERHOOD, COUNTRIES: A-Z, COUNTRIES:
AMERICA, DRAFT, FIGHT, FREEDOM, LAW & ORDER, NATURE,
NUCLEAR ENERGY, PATRIOTISM, POLITICS (various), POWER &
CONTROL, PREJUDICE, WAR, WORK

---

911 Is A Joke
Public Enemy; *Fear Of A Black Planet* . . . . (Def Jam)
   Yo! MTV Raps-C . . . . (Def Jam)
Abraham, Martin And John
Dion; *Collectables Presents The History Of Rock-#3-C* . . . . (Collectables)
   Dion-24 Original Classics . . . . (Arista)
   Songs Of Protest-C . . . . (Rhino)
   WCBS FM 101 History Of Rock-'60s-#2-C . . . . (Collectables)
Harry Belafonte; *Harry Belafonte's All Time Greatest Hits-#1* . . . .(RCA)
Smokey Robinson & The Miracles; *Smokey Robinson & The Miracles'*
   Anthology . . . . (Motown)
   Time Out For Smokey Robinson & The Miracles/Special
   Occasion . . . . (Motown)
Africa Unite
Bob Marley & The Wailers; *Survival* . . . . (Island)
Alice's Restaurant Massacree
Arlo Guthrie; *Alice's Restaurant.* . . . . (Reprise)
   Best Of Arlo Guthrie . . . .(Warner Bros.)
All Around The World
Oasis; *Be Here Now.* . . . . (Epic)
Anarchy In The U.K.
Megadeth; *so far, so good...so what!* . . . . (Capitol)

Sex Pistols; *Never Mind The Bollocks, Here's The Sex Pistols* . . . (Warner Bros.)
Another Brick In The Wall, Part 2
Class Of '99; *ST/The Faculty* . . . (Columbia)
Pink Floyd; *Collection Of Great Dance Songs* . . . (Columbia)
Delicate Sound Of Thunder . . . (Columbia)
The Wall . . . (Columbia)
Roger Waters; *The Wall-Live In Berlin* . . . (Mercury)
Anthem For The Year 2000
Silverchair; *Neon Ballroom* . . . (Epic)
Ball Of Confusion (That's What The World Is Today)
Temptations; *All The Million-Sellers* . . . (Motown)
Compact Command Performances-Temptations . . . (Motown)
Songs Of Protest-C . . . (Rhino)
Temptations' Greatest Hits-#2 . . . (Motown)
Temptations-Anthology-The Best Of The Temptations . . . (Motown)
Top 10 With A Bullet-Motown Male Groups-C . . . (Motown)
Ballad Of Ira Hayes, The
Johnny Cash; *The Man In Black-His Greatest Hits* . . . (Legacy)
Peter La Farge; *Best Of Broadside 1962-1968: Anthems Of The American Underground From The Pages Of Broadside Magazine-C* . . . (Smithsonian Folkways)
Ballad Of William Worthy
Phil Ochs; *Best Of Broadside 1962-1968: Anthems Of The American Underground From The Pages Of Broadside Magazine-C* . . . (Smithsonian Folkways)
Banned In The U.S.A.
Luke Skyywalker; *Banned In The U.S.A.* . . . (Luke)
Battle Flag
Lo Fidelity Allstars; *How To Operate With A Blown Mind* . . . (Skint)
Big Brother
Stevie Wonder; *Talking Book* . . . (Motown)
Biko
Peter Gabriel; *Peter Gabriel* . . . (Geffen)
Peter Gabriel/Plays Live . . . (Geffen)
Shaking The Tree-Sixteen Golden Greats . . . (Geffen)
Birmingham Sunday
Joan Baez; *Contemporary Ballad Book* . . . (Vanguard)
Joan Baez/5 . . . (Vanguard)
Richard Farina; *Best Of Broadside 1962-1968: Anthems Of The American Underground From The Pages Of Broadside Magazine-C* . . . (Smithsonian Folkways)
Bizzness Ain't Dead
New World Singers; *Best Of Broadside 1962-1968: Anthems Of The American Underground From The Pages Of Broadside Magazine-C* . . . (Smithsonian Folkways)
Bleed American
Jimmy Eat World; *Bleed American* . . . (DreamWorks/SKG)
Blowin' In The Wind
Bob Dylan; *Before The Flood* . . . (Columbia)
Biograph . . . (Columbia)
Bob Dylan At Budokan . . . (Columbia)
Bob Dylan's Greatest Hits . . . (Columbia)
Freewheelin' . . . (Columbia)
God Bless America-C . . . (Columbia)
Greatest Folksingers Of The '60s-C . . . (Vanguard)
Joan Baez; *ST/Forrest Gump* . . . (Epic/Sony Music Soundtrax)
Peter, Paul & Mary; *10 Years Together/The Best Of Peter, Paul and Mary* . . . (Warner Bros.)
Holiday Celebration . . . (Warner Bros.)
In The Wind . . . (Warner Bros.)
Peter, Paul and Mary In Concert . . . (Warner Bros.)
Stevie Wonder; *Motown Year By Year-The Sound Of Young America-1966-C* . . . (Motown)
Body Count
Ice-T; *Body Count* . . . (Warner Bros.)
Bosnia
Cranberries; *To The Faithful Departed* . . . (Island)
Bread And Roses
Ani DiFranco & Utah Phillips; *Fellow Workers* . . . (Righteous Babe)
Judy Collins; *So Early In The Spring, The First 15 Years* . . . (Elektra)
Bulls On Parade
Rage Against The Machine; *Evil Empire* . . . (Epic)
Business
Pete Seeger; *Best Of Broadside 1962-1968: Anthems Of The American Underground From The Pages Of Broadside Magazine-C* . . . (Smithsonian Folkways)
God Bless The Grass . . . (Legacy)
Change
Keb' Mo'; *The Door* . . . (550/Epic/Okeh)
Changes
2Pac; *2Pac Greatest Hits* . . . (Amaru/Death Row/Interscope)
Children Of The Revolution
Violent Femmes; *Blind Leading The Naked* . . . (Slash)
Cuttin' Heads
John Mellencamp; *Cuttin' Heads* . . . (Columbia)
Deportee (Plane Wreck At Los Gatos)
Arlo Guthrie & Pete Seeger; *Together In Concert* . . . (Reprise)
Byrds; *The Byrds* . . . (Columbia)
Cisco Houston; *Greatest Songs Of Woody Guthrie-C* . . . (Vanguard)
Gene Clark & Carla Olson; *So Rebellious A Lover* . . . (Rhino)
Judy Collins; *Tribute To Woody Guthrie-C* . . . (Warner Bros.)
Waylon Jennings, Willie Nelson, Johnny Cash, Kris Kristofferson; *Highwayman* . . . (Columbia)
Dirty Business
New Riders Of The Purple Sage; *New Riders Of The Purple Sage* . . . (Columbia)
Dissident
Pearl Jam; *Vs.* . . . (Epic Portrait Assoc.)
Doing The Reactionary
Barbra Streisand; *Pins And Needles* . . . (Columbia)
Done With Bonaparte
Mark Knopfler; *Golden Heart* . . . (Warner Bros.)
Don't Give Up
Peter Gabriel; *Shaking The Tree-Sixteen Golden Greats* . . . (Geffen)
So . . . (Geffen)
Don't Take No For An Answer
Tom Robinson Band; *Power In The Darkness* . . . (Harvest)
Download (I Will)
Expanding Man; *Head To The Ground* . . . (Columbia)
ST/The Cable Guy . . . (Work)
Dreams Of Wounded Knee
Bill Miller; *The Red Road* . . . (Warner Western)
El Picket Sign
Dr. Loco's Rockin' Jalepeno Band; *Movimento Music* . . . (Flying Fish)
El Teatro Campesino; *Best Of Broadside 1962-1968: Anthems Of The American Underground From The Pages Of Broadside Magazine-C* . . . (Smithsonian Folkways)
Equal Rights
Peter Tosh; *Equal Rights* . . . (Columbia)
Eve Of Destruction
Barry McGuire; *Billboard Top Rock 'N' Roll Hits-1965-C* . . . (Rhino)
Cruisin'-1965-C . . . (Increase)
Good Feeling Music Of The Big Chill Generation-#3-C . . . (Motown)
Songs Of Protest-C . . . (Rhino)
Vintage Music-#9 & 10-C . . . (MCA)
Dickies; *Great Dictations (Definitive Collection)* . . . (A&M)
Incredible Shrinking Dickies . . . (A&M)
Turtles; *Turtle Wax-Best Of The Turtles-#2* . . . (Rhino)
Turtlesized . . . (Rhino)
Exhuming McCarthy
R.E.M.; *Document* . . . (EMI-Capitol Entert. Properties)
Fight The Power
Isley Brothers; *Forever Gold* . . . (T-Neck/Columbia)
Heat Is On . . . (T-Neck/Columbia)
Isley Brothers' Greatest Hits . . . (T-Neck/Columbia)
The Isley Brothers Story-#2-The T-Neck Years-1969-1985 . . . (Rhino)
Fight The Power
Public Enemy; *Def Jam Classics-#2-C* . . . (Def Jam)
Fear Of A Black Planet . . . (Def Jam)
ST/Do The Right Thing . . . (Motown)
For What It's Worth
Buffalo Springfield; *Buffalo Springfield* . . . (Atco)
Buffalo Springfield-Retrospective . . . (Atco)
Double History . . . (Atco)
Hit Singles-1958-1977-C . . . (Atlantic)
ST/Forrest Gump . . . (Epic/Sony Music Soundtrax)
Free Nelson Mandela
Special AKA; *In The Studio* . . . (Chrysalis)
Free South Africa
Kinsey Report; *Midnight Drive* . . . (Alligator)
Tackhead; *Friendly As A Hand Grenade* . . . (TVT)
Freedom Riders
Phil Ochs; *Best Of Broadside 1962-1968: Anthems Of The American Underground From The Pages Of Broadside Magazine-C* . . . (Smithsonian Folkways)
Freedom Train, The
Bing Crosby; *Bing Crosby-Complete Recordings* . . . (MCA)
Peggy Lee; *Peggy Lee-Complete Recordings-1941-1947* . . . (Legacy)
From Hell To Paradise
Mavericks; *From Hell To Paradise* . . . (MCA)
Get Up
Kinks; *Misfits* . . . (Arista)
Get Up, Stand Up
Bob Marley & The Wailers; *Bob Marley & The Wailers-Live* . . . (Tuff Gong)
Legend: The Best Of Bob Marley & The Wailers . . . (Island)
Rebel Music . . . (Tuff Gong)
Songs Of Freedom . . . (Tuff Gong)
Peter Tosh; *Captured Live* . . . (EMI)
Equal Rights . . . (Columbia)
Rhythm Come Forward: Volume II-C . . . (Columbia)
Wailers; *Burnin'* . . . (Tuff Gong)
Ghost Of Tom Joad
Bruce Springsteen; *The Ghost Of Tom Joad* . . . (Columbia)
Give Peace A Chance
John Lennon; *Lennon* . . . (Capitol)
Live In New York City . . . (Capitol)
ST/Imagine: John Lennon . . . (Capitol)
The John Lennon Collection . . . (Capitol)
John Lennon/Plastic Ono Band; *Shaved Fish* . . . (Capitol)

Plastic Ono Band; *Plastic Ono Band-Live Peace In Toronto 1969* . . . . . (Capitol)
Go Limp
Matt McGinn; *Best Of Broadside 1962-1968: Anthems Of The American Underground From The Pages Of Broadside Magazine-C* . . . . (Smithsonian Folkways)
Grown Up Wrong
Rolling Stones; *12 X 5.* . . . .(Abkco)
Guerrilla Radio
Rage Against The Machine; *The Battle Of Los Angeles* . . . .(Epic)
Hard To Make A Stand
Sheryl Crow; *Sheryl Crow* . . . . (A&M)
Harder They Come
Jimmy Cliff; *In Concert-Best Of Jimmy Cliff* . . . . (Reprise)
ST/The Harder They Come . . . . (Mango)
The Island Story-1962-1987-25th Anniversary-C . . . . (Island)
Hell No, I Ain't Gonna Go
Matt Jones & Elaine Laron; *Best Of Broadside 1962-1968: Anthems Of The American Underground From The Pages Of Broadside Magazine-C* . . . . (Smithsonian Folkways)
Hey Joe
Jimi Hendrix; *Essential Jimi Hendrix, Volume 2* . . . . (Reprise)
Live At Winterland . . . .(Rykodisc)
Jimi Hendrix Experience; *Are You Experienced?* . . . . (Reprise)
Smash Hits . . . . (Reprise)
Love; *Best Of Love* . . . . (Rhino)
Hiroshima, Nagasaki Russian Roulette
Jim Page; *Best Of Broadside 1962-1968: Anthems Of The American Underground From The Pages Of Broadside Magazine-C* . . . . (Smithsonian Folkways)
Hollywood
Wallflowers; *The Wallflowers.* . . . . (Virgin)
I Ain't Goin' Down
Nashville Bluegrass Band; *Waitin' For The Hard Times To Go* . . . . . (Sugar Hill)
I Ain't Gonna Stand For It
Stevie Wonder; *Hotter Than July* . . . . (Motown)
I Ain't Marchin' Anymore
Phil Ochs; *Chords Of Fame* . . . . (A&M)
Songs Of Protest-C . . . . (Rhino)
The War Is Over-Best Of Phil Ochs . . . . (A&M)
I Did It
Dave Matthews Band; *Everyday.* . . . . (RCA)
I Miss My Homies
Master P; *Ghetto D* . . . . (No Limit/Priority)
I'd Love To Change The World
Ten Years After; *A Space In Time* . . . . (Columbia)
Classic Performances Of Ten Years After . . . . (Columbia)
Universal . . . .(Chrysalis)
If I Had A Hammer (The Hammer Song)
Pete Seeger; *Sing-A-Long-Live At Sanders Theatre 1980* . . . . (Smithsonian Folkways)
Peter, Paul & Mary; *10 Years Together/The Best Of Peter, Paul and Mary.* . . . .(Warner Bros.)
Peter, Paul and Mary. . . . .(Warner Bros.)
Peter, Paul and Mary In Concert . . . .(Warner Bros.)
Trini Lopez; *Best Of Trini Lopez* . . . . (Exact)
Weavers; *Weavers' Greatest Hits* . . . . (Vanguard)
If I Had A Rocket Launcher (Central America)
Bruce Cockburn; *Stealing Fire* . . . . (Columbia)
Waiting For A Miracle-Singles 1970-1987 . . . .(Gold Castle)
I-Feel-Like-I'm-Fixin'-To-Die Rag
Country Joe & The Fish; *Country Joe & The Fish-Greatest Hits* . . . . (Vanguard)
Greatest '60s Folksingers-C . . . . (Vanguard)
I-Feel-Like-I'm-Fixin'-To-Die . . . . (Vanguard)
Life & Times Of Country Joe & The Fish . . . . (Vanguard)
More American Graffiti-#4-C . . . .(MCA)
Songs Of Protest-C . . . . (Rhino)
ST/Woodstock . . . .(Atlantic)
I'll Be Around
Rappin' 4-Tay; *Don't Fight The Feelin'.* . . . . (Rag Top/EMI)
In The Year 2525 (Exordium & Terminus)
Zager & Evans; *Nipper's Greatest Hits Of The '60s-#2-C* . . . . (RCA)
Indian Reservation (The Lament Of The Cherokee Reservation Indian)
Don Fardon; *45-#408* . . . . (GNP/Crescendo)
Raiders; *Billboard Top Rock 'N' Roll Hits-1971-C* . . . . (Rhino)
Legend Of Paul Revere And The Raiders . . . . (Columbia)
Pop Classics Of The '70s-C . . . . (Columbia)
Super Hits Of The '70s-Have A Nice Day-#5-C . . . . (Rhino)
Internationale, The
Ani DiFranco & Utah Phillips; *Fellow Workers* . . . .(Righteous Babe)
It's Good News Week
Hedgehoppers Anonymous; *Songs Of Protest-C* . . . . (Rhino)
Jesus Christ
Arlo Guthrie; *Tribute To Woody Guthrie-C* . . . .(Warner Bros.)
Cisco Houston; *Greatest Songs Of Woody Guthrie-C* . . . . (Vanguard)
U2; *Folkways: A Vision Shared-C* . . . . (Columbia)
Woody Guthrie; *Woody Guthrie.* . . . .(Warner Bros.)
Johnny Too Bad
Slickers; *ST/The Harder They Come.* . . . . (Mango)
Taj Mahal; *Best Of Taj Mahal.* . . . . (Columbia)

Mo' Roots . . . . (Legacy)
UB40; *Labour Of Love* . . . . (A&M)
Live In Moscow . . . . (A&M)
Kevorkian
Public Enemy; *There's A Poison Goin On* . . . . (Atomic Pop)
Kill For Peace
Fugs; *Best Of Broadside 1962-1968: Anthems Of The American Underground From The Pages Of Broadside Magazine-C* . . . .(Smithsonian Folkways)
Fugs . . . . (ESP Disk)
Fugs 4 Rounders Score . . . . (ESP Disk)
La Marseillaise
Mormon Tabernacle Choir; *This Is My Country* . . . . (Columbia)
Laugh At Me
Sonny Bono; *Songs Of Protest-C* . . . . (Rhino)
Let Me Be
Turtles; *Songs Of Protest-C.* . . . . (Rhino)
Little Man
Alan Jackson; *High Mileage* . . . . (Arista)
Long Time Gone
Crosby, Stills & Nash; *Crosby, Stills & Nash* . . . .(Atlantic)
CSN . . . .(Atlantic)
Crosby, Stills, Nash & Young; *4 Way Street.* . . . .(Atlantic)
Love Is A Good Thing
Sheryl Crow; *Sheryl Crow.* . . . . (A&M)
Love Shouldn't Hurt
All Star Group; *Love Shouldn't Hurt-C* . . . .(Qwest)
Love's The Only House
Martina McBride; *Emotion* . . . . (RCA)
M.T.A.
Kingston Trio; *25 Years Non-Stop* . . . . (Xeres)
Best Of The Kingston Trio . . . . (Capitol)
Capitol Collectors Series-The Kingston Trio . . . . (Capitol)
Scarlet Ribbons . . . . (Capitol)
Very Best Of The Kingston Trio . . . . (Capitol)
Man In Black
Johnny Cash; *Essential Johnny Cash* . . . . (Columbia)
Patriot . . . . (Columbia)
The Man In Black-His Greatest Hits. . . . . (Legacy)
Murder On Music Row
George Strait & Alan Jackson; *Latest Greatest Straitest Hits* . . . . (MCA)
My Back Pages
Bob Dylan; *Another Side Of Bob Dylan* . . . . (Columbia)
Bob Dylan's Greatest Hits-#2 . . . . (Columbia)
Byrds; *20 Essential Tracks From The Box Set.* . . . . (Columbia)
Byrds Play Dylan . . . . (Columbia)
The Byrds' Greatest Hits . . . . (Columbia)
Younger Than Yesterday . . . . (Columbia)
My Generation
Who; *Live At Leeds* . . . . (MCA)
Meaty Beaty Big & Bouncy. . . . . (MCA)
ST/The Kids Are Alright . . . . (MCA)
The Who Sings "My Generation" . . . . (MCA)
Who Greatest Hits . . . . (MCA)
No More Genocide
Holly Near; *Lifeline* . . . . (Redwood)
No No No To Draft & War
Minutemen; *Ballot Result* . . . .(SST)
No Tears Left
Crosby, Stills, Nash & Young; *Looking Forward* . . . . (Reprise)
Ohio
Crosby, Stills & Nash; *CSN.* . . . .(Atlantic)
Crosby, Stills, Nash & Young; *4 Way Street.* . . . .(Atlantic)
So Far. . . . .(Atlantic)
Neil Young; *Decade* . . . . (Reprise)
ST/Journey Through The Past . . . . (Warner Bros.)
One
Creed; *My Own Prison* . . . .(Wind-up)
Orange Crush
R.E.M.; *Best Of MTV's 120 Minutes-#2-C* . . . . (Rhino)
Green . . . . (Warner Bros.)
Pardon Me
Incubus; *Make Yourself.* . . . . (Immortal/Epic)
Peace For South Africa
Oscar Peterson Trio; *Live At The Blue Note* . . . . (Telarc)
Peaceful World
John Mellencamp; *Cuttin' Heads* . . . . (Columbia)
God Bless America-C . . . . (Columbia)
The Concert For New York City-C . . . . (Columbia)
People Got To Be Free
Rascals; *Atlantic's Hit Singles-1958-1977-C* . . . .(Atlantic)
Billboard Top Rock 'N' Roll Hits-1968-C . . . . (Rhino)
Hit Singles-1958-1977-C . . . .(Atlantic)
Rascals-Anthology 1965-1972 . . . . (Rhino)
Songs Of Protest-C . . . . (Rhino)
Very Best Of The Rascals . . . . (Rhino)
Power In The Darkness
Tom Robinson Band; *Power In The Darkness* . . . .(Harvest)
Power To The People
John Lennon; *Lennon* . . . . (Capitol)

John Lennon/Plastic Ono Band; *Shaved Fish* . . . . (Capitol)

Pure Massacre
Silverchair; *Frogstomp* . . . . (Epic)

Question
Moody Blues; *A Night At Red Rocks With The Colorado Symphony*
   Orchestra . . . . (Polydor)
A Question Of Balance . . . . (Polydor)
This Is The Moody Blues . . . . (Polydor)

Reggae Revolution
Ziggy Marley & The Melody Makers; *Hey World!* . . . . (EMI)
Time Has Come...Best Of Ziggy Marley & The Melody Makers . . . . . . (EMI)

Revolution
Beatles; *Beatles-Box Set* . . . . (Capitol)
Hey Jude . . . . (Capitol)
Past Masters-Volume Two . . . . (Parlophone)
Rock 'N' Roll Music . . . . (Capitol)
ST/Imagine: John Lennon . . . . (Capitol)
The Beatles/1967-1970 . . . . (Capitol)

Revolution
Pretenders; *Last Of The Independents* . . . . (Sire)

Revolution
Cult; *Love* . . . . (Sire)

Revolution
Bob Marley & The Wailers; *Natty Dread* . . . . (Tuff Gong)

Revolution 1
Beatles; *Beatles-Box Set* . . . . (Capitol)
The Beatles (White Album) . . . . (Capitol)

Revolution Blues
Neil Young; *On The Beach* . . . . (Reprise)

Revolution Calling
Queensryche; *Operation: Mindcrime* . . . . (EMI)

Revolution Rock
Clash; *London Calling* . . . . (Epic)

Revolution Will Not Be Televised
Gil Scott-Heron; *Gil Scott-Heron* . . . . (Bluebird)
Pieces Of A Man . . . . (Flying Dutchman)
Revolution Will Not Be Televised . . . . (Flying Dutchman)

Revolutionary Generation
Public Enemy; *Fear Of A Black Planet* . . . . (Def Jam)

Revolutionary Words
Mutabaruka; *Mystery Unfolds* . . . . (Shanachie)

Ringing Of Revolution
Phil Ochs; *There But For Fortune* . . . . (Elektra)

Riot Act
Elvis Costello; *Girls Girls Girls* . . . . (Columbia)
Elvis Costello & The Attractions; *Get Happy!* . . . . (Rykodisc)

Riot Act
Skid Row; *Slave To The Grind* . . . . (Atlantic)

Riot In Cell Block #9
Blues Brothers; *Made In America* . . . . (Atlantic)
Coasters; *Very Best Of The Coasters* . . . . (Rhino)
Commander Cody & His Lost Planet Airmen; *Live From Deep In The Heart*
   Of Texas . . . . (MCA)
Robins; *50 Coastin' Classics-C* . . . . (Rhino)
There's A Riot Goin' On! Rock Classics-C . . . . (Rhino)
Wanda Jackson; *Rockin' In The Country-Best Of Wanda Jackson* . . . . . (Rhino)

Roulette
Bruce Springsteen; *Tracks* . . . . (Columbia)

Russians
Sting; *Dream Of The Blue Turtles* . . . . (A&M)
Fields Of Gold-The Best Of Sting 1984-1994 . . . . (A&M)

Saturday Night Special
Lynyrd Skynyrd; *Gold & Platinum* . . . . (MCA)
Nuthin' Fancy . . . . (MCA)
One More From The Road . . . . (MCA)
Skynyrd's Innards-Their Greatest Hits . . . . (MCA)
McBride & The Ride; *Skynyrd Frynds-C* . . . . (MCA)

Say It Loud I'm Black & I'm Proud
Afrika Bambaataa; *Decade Of Darkness* . . . . (EMI)
James Brown; *Billboard Top R&B Hits-1965-1969-C* . . . . (Rhino)

Seen Enough
Crosby, Stills, Nash & Young; *Looking Forward* . . . . (Reprise)

Sign Of The Times
Queensryche; *Hear In The Now Frontier* . . . . (Virgin)

Signs
Five Man Electrical Band; *Songs Of Protest-C* . . . . (Rhino)

Sky Pilot
Eric Burdon & The Animals; *Eric Burdon & The Animals'*
   Greatest Hits . . . . (MGM)
History Of British Rock-#9-C . . . . (Rhino)
Songs Of Protest-C . . . . (Rhino)

Sleep Now In The Fire
Rage Against The Machine; *The Battle Of Los Angeles* . . . . (Epic)

Something In The Air
Thunderclap Newman; *History Of British Rock-#9-C* . . . . (Rhino)
Hollywood Dream . . . . (MCA)
ST/The Strawberry Statement . . . . (MCA)

Stand
Sly & The Family Stone; *10 Years Too Soon* . . . . (Epic)

Sly & The Family Stone-Anthology . . . . (Epic)
Sly & The Family Stone's Greatest Hits . . . . (Epic)

Stand And Be Counted
Crosby, Stills, Nash & Young; *Looking Forward* . . . . (Reprise)

Stand Up
Keb' Mo'; *The Door* . . . . (550/Epic/Okeh)

Stand Up & Fight Back
Jimmy Cliff; *Give Thanx* . . . . (Warner Bros.)

Street Fighting Man
Rod Stewart; *Best Of Rod Stewart* . . . . (Mercury)
Sing It Again, Rod . . . . (Mercury)
Storyteller/The Complete Anthology: 1964-1990 . . . . (Warner Bros.)
Rolling Stones; *Beggars Banquet* . . . . (Abkco)
Get Yer Ya-Ya's Out! . . . . (Abkco)
Hot Rocks 1964-1971 . . . . (Abkco)
Singles Collection-The London Years . . . . (Abkco)
Through The Past, Darkly (Big Hits Vol. 2) . . . . (Abkco)

Student Demonstration Time
Beach Boys; *Surf's Up* . . . . (Caribou)

Stupid, Stupid War
D.R.I.; *Dealing With It* . . . . (Metal Blade)

They Dance Alone (Cueca Solo)
Sting; *...Nothing Like The Sun* . . . . (A&M)
Fields Of Gold-The Best Of Sting 1984-1994 . . . . (A&M)

They're Moving Father's Grave To Build A Sewer
Clancy Brothers & Tommy Makem; *Luck Of The Irish* . . . . (Columbia)

This Land Is Your Land
Bruce Springsteen & The E Street Band; *Bruce Springsteen & The E Street*
   Band Live/1975-85 . . . . (Legacy)
Glen Campbell; *All American* . . . . (Liberty)
Lee Greenwood; *American Patriot* . . . . (Capitol)
Odetta, Arlo Guthrie & Company; *Tribute To Woody*
   Guthrie-C . . . . (Warner Bros.)
Pete Seeger; *God Bless America-C* . . . . (Columbia)
Pete Seeger Sings Woody Guthrie . . . . (Smithsonian Folkways)
Pete Seeger-Complete Carnegie Hall Concert-1963 . . . . (Columbia)
Weavers; *Weavers' Greatest Hits* . . . . (Vanguard)
Woody Guthrie; *Greatest Songs Of Woody Guthrie-C* . . . . (Vanguard)
Troubadours Of The Folk Era-#1-C . . . . (Rhino)
Woody Guthrie . . . . (Vanguard)

Tiananmen Square
Blazing Redheads; *Crazed Women* . . . . (Reference)

United We Stand
Brotherhood Of Man; *Chicken Soup For The Soul: I'll Be There For You-*
   Songs Of Friendship, Brotherhood And Sisterhood-C . . . . (Rhino)
Super Hits Of The '70s-Have A Nice Day-#2-C . . . . (Rhino)
Mike Curb Congregation; *Mike Curb Congregation's Greatest Hits* . . . . (Curb)

Universal Soldier
Buffy Sainte-Marie; *Best Of Buffy Sainte-Marie* . . . . (Vanguard)
Festival Of Acoustic Music-#1 . . . . (Fantasy)
Troubadours Of The Folk Era-#1-C . . . . (Rhino)
Donovan; *Catch The Wind* . . . . (Garland)
History Of British Rock-#4-C . . . . (Rhino)
Songs Of Protest-C . . . . (Rhino)
The Secret Policeman's Other Ball/The Music . . . . (Rhino)

Untitled Protest
Country Joe & The Fish; *Life & Times Of Country Joe &*
   The Fish . . . . (Vanguard)
Together . . . . (Vanguard)

Victims Of Comfort
Keb' Mo'; *Keb' Mo'* . . . . (Okeh)

Vietnam
Paul Kaplan; *Best Of Broadside 1962-1968: Anthems Of The American*
   Underground From The Pages Of Broadside
   Magazine-C . . . . (Smithsonian Folkways)

Volunteers
Jefferson Airplane; *"White Rabbit" & Other Hits* . . . . (RCA)
2400 Fulton Street-An Anthology . . . . (RCA)
Flight Log (1966-1976) . . . . (Grunt)
ST/Forrest Gump . . . . (Epic/Sony Music Soundtrax)
ST/Woodstock . . . . (Atlantic)
The Worst Of Jefferson Airplane . . . . (RCA)
Volunteers . . . . (RCA)

Waist Deep In The Big Muddy
Pete Seeger; *Best Of Broadside 1962-1968: Anthems Of The American*
   Underground From The Pages Of Broadside
   Magazine-C . . . . (Smithsonian Folkways)

Walkin' On The Sun
Smash Mouth; *Fush Yu Mang* . . . . (Interscope)

War
Bruce Springsteen & The E Street Band; *Bruce Springsteen & The E Street*
   Band Live/1975-85 . . . . (Legacy)
Edwin Starr; *Billboard Top Rock 'N' Roll Hits-1970-C* . . . . (Rhino)
Didn't It Blow Your Mind: Soul Hits Of The '70s-#3-C . . . . (Rhino)
Motown Superstar Series-#3-Edwin Starr . . . . (Motown)
Songs Of Protest-C . . . . (Rhino)
War & Peace . . . . (Motown)

Warning
Green Day; *Warning* . . . . (Reprise)

Warsaw 1943 (I Never Betrayed The Revolution)
Johnny Clegg & Savuka; *Cruel, Crazy, Beautiful World* . . . . (Capitol)
Wat About Di Workin' Class?
Linton Kwesi Johnson; *Linton Kwesi Johnson In Concert With The
Dub Band* . . . . (Shanachie)
We Seek No Wider War
Phil Ochs; *Best Of Broadside 1962-1968: Anthems Of The American
Underground From The Pages Of Broadside
Magazine-C* . . . . (Smithsonian Folkways)
We Shall Be Free
Garth Brooks; *The Chase* . . . . (Liberty)
We Shall Overcome
Bruce Springsteen; *Where Have All The Flowers Gone: The Songs Of Pete
Seeger* . . . . (Appleseed)
James Cleveland & The Troubadors; *James Cleveland & The
Troubadors* . . . . (Savoy)
Joan Baez; *Carry It On* . . . . (Vanguard)
Joan Baez In Concert, Part 2 . . . . (Vanguard)
Mahalia Jackson; *God Bless America-C* . . . . (Columbia)
Pete Seeger; *Bitter & The Sweet* . . . . (Mobile Fidelity Sound Lab)
Pete Seeger's Greatest Hits . . . . (Columbia)
Welcome To The Occupation
R.E.M.; *Document* . . . . (EMI-Capitol Entert. Properties)
We'll Never Turn Back
Freedom Singers; *Best Of Broadside 1962-1968: Anthems Of The
American Underground From The Pages Of Broadside
Magazine-C* . . . . (Smithsonian Folkways)
We're Not Gonna Take It
Who; *Join Together* . . . . (MCA)
ST/Woodstock . . . . (Atlantic)
Tommy . . . . (MCA)
We're Not Gonna Take It
Twisted Sister; *Big Hits & Nasty Cuts* . . . . (Atlantic)
Stay Hungry . . . . (Atlantic)
What Did You Learn In School Today?
Tom Paxton; *Best Of Broadside 1962-1968: Anthems Of The American
Underground From The Pages Of Broadside
Magazine-C* . . . . (Smithsonian Folkways)
What Have They Done To The Rain
Malvina Reynolds; *Best Of Broadside 1962-1968: Anthems Of The
American Underground From The Pages Of Broadside
Magazine-C* . . . . (Smithsonian Folkways)
ST/Dogfight . . . . (Nouveau)
Searchers; *Searchers' Greatest Hits* . . . . (Rhino)
What It's Like
Everlast; *Whitey Ford Sings The Blues* . . . . (Tommy Boy)
What's Going On
Cyndi Lauper; *True Colors* . . . . (Portrait)
Marvin Gaye; *20/20-C* . . . . (Motown)
Marvin Gaye Live At The London Palladium . . . . (Motown)
Marvin Gaye-Anthology . . . . (Motown)
Marvin Gaye's Greatest Hits/ . . . . (Motown)
More Songs From "The Big Chill" Soundtrack-C . . . . (Motown)
What's Going On . . . . (Motown)
Quincy Jones; *Quincy Jones-The Best* . . . . (A&M)
Where Have All The Flowers Gone
Johnny Rivers; *Best Of Johnny Rivers* . . . . (EMI)
Johnny Rivers-Anthology 1964-1977 . . . . (Rhino)
Kingston Trio; *Capitol Collectors Series-The Kingston Trio* . . . . (Capitol)
Songs Of Protest-C . . . . (Rhino)
Pete Seeger; *Essential Pete Seeger* . . . . (Vanguard)
Pete Seeger's Greatest Hits . . . . (Columbia)
Peter, Paul & Mary; *Peter, Paul and Mary* . . . . (Warner Bros.)
Wes Montgomery; *Wes Montgomery-Classics-#22* . . . . (A&M)
Whitey On The Moon
Gil Scott-Heron; *Whitey On The Moon* . . . . (Bluebird)
Windows Of The World
Burt Bacharach; *One Amazing Night* . . . . (N2K)
Dionne Warwick; *Dionne Warwick Collection-Her All-Time
Greatest Hits* . . . . (Rhino)
Dionne Warwick-Definitive Collection . . . . (Arista)
Isaac Hayes; *Live At The Sahara Tahoe* . . . . (Stax)
Mormon Tabernacle Choir; *Voices In Harmony* . . . . (CBS Masterworks)
Pretenders; *ST/1969* . . . . (Polydor)
With God On Our Side
Bob Dylan; *The Times They Are A-Changin'* . . . . (Columbia)
Joan Baez; *The First 10 Years* . . . . (Vanguard)
Manfred Mann; *Songs Of Protest-C* . . . . (Rhino)
Neville Brothers; *Uptown Rulin': The Best Of The Neville Brothers* . . . . (A&M)
Yellow Moon . . . . (A&M)
Wire Train; *Best Of 415 Records-C* . . . . (Legacy)
Won't Get Fooled Again
Van Halen; *LIVE: Right here, right now.* . . . . (Warner Bros.)
Who; *ST/The Kids Are Alright* . . . . (MCA)
The Concert For New York City-C . . . . (Columbia)
Who Greatest Hits . . . . (MCA)
Who's Last . . . . (MCA)
Who's next . . . . (MCA)

Wooden Ships
Crosby, Stills & Nash; *Crosby, Stills & Nash* . . . . (Atlantic)
CSN . . . . (Atlantic)
Crosby, Stills, Nash & Young; *So Far* . . . . (Atlantic)
ST/Woodstock . . . . (Atlantic)
Jefferson Airplane; *2400 Fulton Street-An Anthology* . . . . (RCA)
Flight Log (1966-1976) . . . . (Grunt)
Loves You . . . . (RCA)
Volunteers . . . . (RCA)
Workin' It
Don Henley; *Inside Job* . . . . (Warner Bros.)
You Don't Have To Be In The Army To Fight In The War
Mungo Jerry; *In The Summertime-Best Of Mungo Jerry* . . . . (Rhino)
You Haven't Done Nothin'
Stevie Wonder; *Fulfillingness' First Finale* . . . . (Motown)
Your Flag Decal Won't Get You Into Heaven Anymore
John Prine; *John Prine* . . . . (Atlantic)
Your Generation
Generation X; *Generation X* . . . . (Chrysalis)
Perfect Hits-1975-1981 . . . . (Chrysalis)

QUEENS, Princesses

See Also: **BOSSES, CELEBRITIES: SPECIFIC, COUNTRIES: A-Z,
KINGS, POLITICS (various), POWER & CONTROL, PRESIDENTS,
PROTEST, ROYALTY, SOCIAL CLASS: GENERAL, WOMEN'S
NAMES: A-Z**

Acid Queen
Ike & Tina Turner; *Best Of Ike & Tina Turner* . . . . (EMI)
Proud Mary-Best Of Ike & Tina Turner . . . . (EMI)
Who; *Join Together* . . . . (MCA)
Tommy . . . . (MCA)
African Queen
Ali Thompson; *Take A Little Rhythm* . . . . (A&M)
After The Rain Has Fallen
Sting; *Brand New Day* . . . . (A&M)
Alaskan Queen
Joe Hackney; *Heavy Hitter* . . . . (Happy Hour Music)
Arcade Queen
Rubinoos; *Back To The Drawing Board* . . . . (Beserkley)
Backstage Queen
Scorpions; *Best Of The Scorpions* . . . . (RCA)
Tokyo Tapes . . . . (RCA)
Virgin Killer . . . . (RCA)
Ballad Of A Teenage Queen
Johnny Cash; *Johnny Cash* . . . . (Sun)
Johnny Cash-Original Golden Hits-#2 . . . . (Sun)
Johnny Cash-Sun Years . . . . (Rhino)
ST/Harper Valley PTA . . . . (Sun)
The Legend . . . . (Plantation)
The Man In Black-His Greatest Hits . . . . (Legacy)
Beauty Queen
Roxy Music; *For Your Pleasure...* . . . . (Reprise)
Black Queen
Crosby, Stills & Nash; *CSN* . . . . (Atlantic)
Stephen Stills; *Stephen Stills* . . . . (Atlantic)
Black Queen
Jimmy Cliff; *Unlimited* . . . . (Reprise)
Candle In The Wind 1997
Elton John; *Candle In The Wind 1997 (Diana, Princess Of Wales)
(Single)* . . . . (Rocket)
Caribbean Queen
Billy Ocean; *Billy Ocean's Greatest Hits* . . . . (Jive)
Suddenly . . . . (Jive)
Celestial The Queen
Blue Oyster Cult; *Spectres* . . . . (Columbia)
Cleopatra, Queen Of Denial
Pam Tillis; *Homeward Looking Angel* . . . . (Arista)
Cleopatra's Cat
Spin Doctors; *Turn It Upside Down* . . . . (Epic)
Colorado Queenie
Little David Wilkins; *20 Great Hits-C* . . . . (Plantation)
Cry Baby Cry
Beatles; *The Beatles (White Album)* . . . . (Capitol)
Dancing Queen
Abba; *Abba Live* . . . . (Atlantic)
Abba's Greatest Hits-#2 . . . . (Atlantic)
Arrival . . . . (Polydor)
Gold-Greatest Hits . . . . (Polydor)
The Singles-First 10 Years . . . . (Atlantic)
Daydream Believer
Anne Murray; *Anne Murray's Greatest Hits* . . . . (Capitol)
I'll Always Love You . . . . (Capitol)
Monkees; *Billboard Top Rock 'N' Roll Hits-1967-C* . . . . (Rhino)
Mellow '60s-C . . . . (Priority)

Monkees' Greatest Hits . . . . (Rhino)

Dead Flowers
Rolling Stones; *Sticky Fingers* . . . .(Virgin)
Steve Earle & The Dukes; *Shut Up And Die Like An Aviator* . . . . (MCA)

Death Of Queen Jane
Joan Baez; *Joan Baez/5* . . . . (Vanguard)
Love Song Album . . . . (Vanguard)

Dime Queen Of Nevada
Tom Jones; *Darlin'* . . . . (Mercury)

Ethelene (The Truckstop Queen)
Ray Stevens; *I Never Made A Record I Didn't Like* . . . . (MCA)

God Save The Queen
Queen; *A Night At The Opera* . . . . (Hollywood)
Live Killers . . . . (Hollywood)

God Save The Queen
Anthrax; *Armed & Dangerous* . . . . (Megaforce)

God Save The Queen
Sex Pistols; *Never Mind The Bollocks, Here's The Sex Pistols* . . . (Warner Bros.)

Guenevere
Original Cast; *Camelot* . . . . (Columbia)
Original Soundtrack; *ST/Camelot* . . . . (Warner Bros.)

Gypsy Queen
Santana; *Abraxas* . . . . (Columbia)
Lotus . . . . (Columbia)
Moonflower . . . . (Columbia)

Gypsy Queen
Van Morrison; *His Band And The Street Choir* . . . . (Warner Bros.)

Her Majesty
Beatles; *Abbey Road* . . . . (Parlophone)

Her Royal Majesty
James Darren; *Best Of James Darren* . . . . (Rhino)

Heroes
Wallflowers; *ST/Godzilla-The Album* . . . . (Epic/Sony Music Soundtrax)

High Fashion Queen
Flying Burrito Brothers; *Last Of The Red Hot Burritos* . . . . (A&M)

Homecoming Queen's Got A Gun
Julie Brown; *Dr. Demento Presents The Greatest Novelty Records-#5-
1980s-C* . . . . (Rhino)
Teenage Tragedies-C . . . . (Rhino)
Trapped In The Body Of A White Girl . . . . (Sire)

Honolulu Lulu
Jan & Dean; *Dead Man's Curve* . . . . (EMI)
Jan & Dean-Legendary Masters . . . . (EMI)
One Summer Night-Live . . . . (Rhino)
Surf City-Best Of Jan & Dean . . . . (EMI)

In A Shanty In Old Shanty Town
Ink Spots; *Java Jive* . . . . (Laserlight)

J.A.P. Rap
2 Live Jews; *As Kosher As They Wanna Be* . . . . (Kosher)

Killer Queen
Queen; *Live Killers* . . . . (Hollywood)
Queen's Greatest Hits I & II . . . . (Hollywood)
Sheer Heart Attack . . . . (Hollywood)

King & Queen
Moody Blues; *Caught Live Plus Five* . . . . (Polydor)

King & Queen Of America
Eurythmics; *Eurythmics' Greatest Hits* . . . . (Arista)
We Too Are One . . . . (Arista)

King & Queen Of England
Sandy Denny; *Circle Dance-Hokey Pokey Charity-C* . . . . (Green Linnet)

Kings & Queens
Aerosmith; *Aerosmith-Classics Live* . . . . (Columbia)
Aerosmith's Greatest Hits . . . . (Columbia)
Draw The Line . . . . (Columbia)

Little Queen
Heart; *Little Queen* . . . . (Portrait)

Little Queenie
Chuck Berry; *Rock & Roll Rarities* . . . . (Chess)
The Chess Box-Chuck Berry . . . . (Chess)
Jerry Lee Lewis; *Jerry Lee Lewis-Original Golden Hits-#1* . . . . (Sun)
Rockin' R&B-C . . . . (Sun)
REO Speedwagon; *REO Speedwagon Live/You Get What You Play For* . . (Epic)
Rolling Stones; *Get Yer Ya-Ya's Out!* . . . . (Abkco)

Lost Queen
Shok Paris; *Steel & Starlight* . . . . (I.R.S.)

Love Spreads
Stone Roses; *Second Coming* . . . . (Geffen)

Mary Queen Of Arkansas
Bruce Springsteen; *Greetings From Asbury Park, N.J.* . . . . (Columbia)
Tracks . . . . (Columbia)

Memphis Queen
Southern Pacific; *County Line* . . . . (Warner Bros.)

Mississippi Queen
Mountain; *Best Of Mountain* . . . . (Columbia)
Heavy Metal Memories-C . . . . (Rhino)
Twin Peaks . . . . (Columbia)

Mother The Queen Of My Heart
Pete Seeger & Arlo Guthrie; *Together In Concert* . . . . (Reprise)

Movie Queen
Bill Anderson; *Scorpio* . . . . (MCA)

No Matter What They Say
Lil' Kim; *Notorious K.I.M.* . . . . (Queen Bee/Undeas/Atlantic)

Pearly Queen
Dave Mason; *Certified Live* . . . . (Columbia)
Very Best Of Dave Mason . . . . (MCA)
Traffic; *Traffic* . . . . (Island)

Pineapple Princess
Annette Funicello; *Frankie Avalon/Annette Funicello* . . . . (K-Tel)

Planet Queen
T. Rex; *Electric Warrior* . . . . (Reprise)

Powder Blue Mercedes Queen
Paul Revere And The Raiders; *Legend Of Paul Revere And The
Raiders* . . . . (Columbia)

Precious Time
Van Morrison; *Back On Top* . . . . (Point Blank/Virgin)

Pretty Princess
Loggins & Messina; *Native Sons* . . . . (Columbia)

Princess
Elton John; *Jump Up!* . . . . (MCA)

Princess Leia's Theme
John Williams; *ST/Star Wars* . . . . (Polydor)

Princess Of The Dawn
Accept; *Compilation* . . . . (Portrait)
Restless & Wild . . . . (Portrait)
Staying A Life . . . . (Epic)

Queen & Country
Jethro Tull; *War Child* . . . . (Chrysalis)

Queen Bee
Taj Mahal; *Evolution* . . . . (Warner Bros.)

Queen Bee
Barbra Streisand; *ST/A Star Is Born* . . . . (Columbia)

Queen Bee
John Lee Hooker; *Greatest Hits Of John Lee Hooker* . . . . (Kent)

Queen Bee
Koko Taylor; *Queen Of The Blues* . . . . (Alligator)

Queen Bee
Grand Funk Railroad; *ST/Heavy Metal* . . . . (Asylum)

Queen Bitch
David Bowie; *Hunky Dory* . . . . (Rykodisc)

Queen For A Day
Bobby Bland; *Best Of Bobby Bland-#2* . . . . (MCA)
Call On Me . . . . (MCA)
Tell Mr. Bland . . . . (MCA)

Queen For A Day
Donna Summer; *Once Upon A Time* . . . . (Casablanca)

Queen Jane Approximately
4 Seasons; *The 4 Seasons Sing Big Hits By Bacharach/David/Dylan* . . . .(Rhino)
Bob Dylan; *Highway 61 Revisited* . . . . (Columbia)
Bob Dylan & The Grateful Dead; *Dylan & The Dead* . . . . (Columbia)

Queen Lucy
Original Cast; *You're A Good Man, Charlie Brown* . . . . (Polydor)

Queen Of Hearts
Dave Edmunds; *Best Of Dave Edmunds* . . . . (Swan Song)
Repeat When Necessary . . . . (Swan Song)
Juice Newton; *All-Time Country Classics-#2-C* . . . . (Capitol)
Juice . . . . (Capitol)
Juice Newton-Greatest Hits & More . . . . (Capitol)
Juice Newton's Greatest Hits . . . . (Gold Rush)
Rodney Crowell; *Rodney Crowell-Collection* . . . . (Warner Bros.)

Queen Of Hearts
Joan Baez; *Joan Baez In Concert, Part 2* . . . . (Vanguard)
The Joan Baez Ballad Book . . . . (Vanguard)

Queen Of Hearts
Whitesnake; *Snakebite* . . . . (Geffen)

Queen Of Hearts
Gregg Allman; *Laid Back* . . . . (Polydor)

Queen Of Hollywood High
John Stewart; *Blondes* . . . . (Allegiance)

Queen Of Las Vegas
B-52's; *Whammy* . . . . (Warner Bros.)

Queen Of Memphis
Confederate Railroad; *Confederate Railroad* . . . . (Atlantic)

Queen Of My Double Wide Trailer
Sammy Kershaw; *Haunted Heart* . . . . (Mercury)

Queen Of My Heart
Hank Williams, Jr.; *Hank Williams, Jr.'s Greatest Hits-#2* . . . . (WB/Curb)
Man Of Steel . . . . (WB/Curb)

Queen Of My Heart
DeBarge; *In A Special Way* . . . . (Motown)

Queen Of My Heart
Rene & Ray; *History Of Latino Rock-#1-C* . . . . (Rhino)

Queen Of Siam
Holy Moses; *Queen Of Siam* . . . . (GWR)

Queen Of Spades
Styx; *Pieces Of Eight* . . . . (A&M)

Queen Of Sydney
Oregon; *Crossing* . . . . (ECM)
Queen Of Tears
Gladys Knight & The Pips; *Every Beat Of My Heart-*
Greatest Hits . . . . (Chameleon)
Queen Of The Broken Hearts
Loverboy; *Keep It Up* . . . . (Columbia)
Queen Of The Cowboy Cafe
Si Kahn; *Home* . . . . (Flying Fish)
Queen Of The Forest
Ted Nugent; *Ted Nugent* . . . .(Epic)
Queen Of The Highway
Doors; *Morrison Hotel/Hard Rock Cafe* . . . . (Elektra)
Queen Of The Hop
Bobby Darin; *The Bobby Darin Story* . . . .(Atlantic)
Dave Edmunds; *ST/Porky's Revenge!* . . . . (Columbia)
Dion; *Dion Sings The Hits Of The '50s & '60s* . . . . (Laurie)
Queen Of The Hours
Electric Light Orchestra; *No Answer* . . . . (Jet)
Queen Of The House
Jody Miller; *20th Century Country-#1-Honky Tonk*
Angels-C . . . . (Dominion Entert.)
Queen Of The House
Diana Ross & The Supremes; *Diana Ross & The Supremes-At*
The Copa . . . . (Motown)
Queen Of The Jungle
Zarkons; *Riders In The Long Black Parade* . . . . (Enigma)
Queen Of The Night
Whitney Houston; *ST/The Bodyguard* . . . . (Arista)
Queen Of The Nile
Dangerous Toys; *Dangerous Toys* . . . . (Columbia)
Queen Of The Reich
Queensryche; *Queensryche* . . . .(EMI)
Queen Of The Senior Prom
Mills Brothers; *Best Of The Mills Brothers* . . . .(MCA)
Queen Of The Silver Dollar
Dave & Sugar; *Dave & Sugar's Greatest Hits* . . . . (RCA)
Dr. Hook; *Dr. Hook & The Medicine Show Revisited* . . . . (Columbia)
Emmylou Harris; *Pieces Of The Sky* . . . . (Reprise)
Queen Of The U.S.A.
Thompson Twins; *Big Trash* . . . .(Red Eye)
Queen Of The Underground
Michael Franks; *Skin Dive* . . . .(Warner Bros.)
Queens Of Noise
Runaways; *Queens Of Noise* . . . . (Mercury)
Queen's Suite
Duke Ellington; *Best Of Duke Ellington* . . . .(Pablo)
Ellington Suites . . . .(Pablo)
Queen's Tattoos
Aztec Camera; *High Land Hard Rain* . . . . (Sire)
Rock & Roll Queen
Mott The Hoople; *Mott The Hoople* . . . .(Atlantic)
The Ballad Of Mott: A Retrospective . . . . (Columbia)
Roller Derby Queen
Jim Croce; *Life & Times* . . . . (Lifesong)
Photographs & Memories/His Greatest Hits . . . .(Atlantic)
Space Lord
Monster Magnet; *Powertrip* . . . . (A&M)
Teenage Queen
Rick Derringer; *All American Boy* . . . . (Blue Sky)
Then You May Take Me To The Fair
Original Cast; *Camelot* . . . . (Columbia)
Vanessa Redgrave; *ST/Camelot* . . . .(Warner Bros.)
Treat You Like A Queen
Rahsaan Patterson; *Love In Stereo* . . . .(MCA)
Truck Driver's Queen
Moore And Napier; *Truckin' On-C* . . . . (Hollywood)
Willis Brothers; *45-#2043* . . . . (Gusto)
Tulsa Queen
Emmylou Harris; *Luxury Liner* . . . .(Warner Bros.)
Victoria
Kinks; *Arthur Or The Decline And Fall Of The British Empire* . . . . (Reprise)
Kink Kronikles . . . . (Reprise)
Video
India.Arie; *Acoustic Soul* . . . . (Motown)
White Queen (As It Began)
Queen; *Queen II* . . . . (Hollywood)

QUESTIONS & ANSWERS
See Also: **COMMUNICATION (various), DECISIONS, DESIRE,**
PRETEND, REASONS, STRANGE, THINKING & KNOWING

(Best Part Of) Breakin' Up
Ronettes; *Best Of The Ronettes* . . . . (Abkco)
Phil Spector-Back To Mono 1958-1969-C . . . . (Abkco)

(Hey Won't You Play) Another Somebody Done Somebody Wrong Song
B.J. Thomas; *Class Of Country-1975-1979-C* . . . . (Hip-O)
(Who Says) You Can't Have It All
Alan Jackson; *A Lot About Livin' (And A Little 'Bout Love)* . . . . (Arista)
(Without You) What Do I Do With Me
Tanya Tucker; *What Do I Do With Me* . . . . (Capitol)
6, 8, 12
Brian McKnight; *Back At One* . . . . (Motown)
Abraham, Martin And John
Dion; *Collectables Presents The History Of Rock-#3-C* . . . . (Collectables)
Dion-24 Original Classics . . . . (Arista)
Songs Of Protest-C . . . . (Rhino)
WCBS FM 101 History Of Rock-'60s-#2-C . . . . (Collectables)
Harry Belafonte; *Harry Belafonte's All Time Greatest Hits-#1* . . . . . . (RCA)
Smokey Robinson & The Miracles; *Smokey Robinson & The Miracles'*
Anthology . . . . (Motown)
Time Out For Smokey Robinson & The Miracles/Special
Occasion . . . . (Motown)
Absolutely Sweet Marie
Bob Dylan; *Blonde On Blonde* . . . . (Columbia)
Again
Lenny Kravitz; *Lenny Kravitz's Greatest Hits* . . . .(Virgin)
Now That's What I Call Music!-#6-C . . . .(Virgin)
Ain't It Crazy
Lightnin' Hopkins; *Hootin' The Blues* . . . .(Prestige)
Lightnin' . . . .(Arhoolie)
Ain't It Great To Be Crazy
Wonder Kids; *Really Silly Songs* . . . .(Madacy)
Ain't It Heavy
Melissa Etheridge; *Never Enough* . . . . (Island)
Ain't It Strange
Patti Smith Group; *Radio Ethiopia* . . . . (Arista)
Ain't Life Hell
Hank Cochran; *Hank Cochran* . . . . (Capitol)
Ain't She Sweet?
Beatles; *History Of British Rock-#5-C* . . . . (Rhino)
The Beatles-Anthology-#3 . . . . (Capitol)
Erroll Garner; *Body And Soul* . . . . (Legacy)
Frank Sinatra; *Sinatra and Swingin' Brass* . . . . (Reprise)
Pearl Bailey; *Pearl Bailey-16 Most Requested Songs* . . . . (Legacy)
Ain't That Good News
David ''Fathead'' Newman; *Bigger & Better-Many Facets Of David*
''Fathead'' Newman . . . . (Rhino)
Ain't That News?
Broadside Singers & Tom Paxton; *Best Of Broadside 1962-1968: Anthems*
Of The American Underground From The Pages Of Broadside
Magazine-C . . . .(Smithsonian Folkways)
Ain't That Peculiar
Marvin Gaye; *Marvin Gaye-Anthology* . . . . (Motown)
Ain't Your Memory Got No Pride?
Merle Haggard; *Ramblin' Fever* . . . .(MCA)
Alfie
Barbra Streisand; *What About Today* . . . . (Columbia)
Dionne Warwick; *Dionne Warwick Greatest Hits* . . . . (Everest)
Dionne Warwick-Anthology 1962-1971 . . . . (Rhino)
All About Me Intro
Xscape; *Traces Of My Lipstick* . . . . (So So Def/Columbia)
All Er Nothin'
Original Broadway Cast; *Oklahoma!* . . . . (RCA)
Original Cast; *Oklahoma!* . . . . (MCA)
All N My Grill
Missy ''Misdemeanor'' Elliot; *Da Real World* . . . . (East West)
Am I Blue
George Strait; *Country Classics-#11-1987-1988-C* . . . . (Universal)
George Strait's Greatest Hits-#2 . . . . (MCA)
MCA #1 Hits Of The '80s-#3-C . . . . (MCA Special Prod.)
Ocean Front Property . . . . (MCA)
Am I Blue
Barbra Streisand; *ST/Funny Lady* . . . . (Arista)
Billie Holiday; *God Bless The Child* . . . . (Columbia)
Ray Charles; *Genius Of Ray Charles* . . . . (Atlantic)
Am I Dreaming
Ol Skool featuring Keith Sweat & Xscape; *Ol Skool* . . . . (Keia/Universal)
Am I Ever Going To Change
Extreme; *III Sides To Every Story* . . . . (A&M)
Am I Getting Through (Part I & II)
Sheryl Crow; *The Globe Sessions* . . . . (A&M)
Am I Going Crazy
Korn; *Issues* . . . . (Immortal/Epic)
Am I High
Asleep At The Wheel; *Served Live* . . . . (Capitol)
Am I Losing You
Jim Reeves; *Best Of Jim Reeves* . . . . (RCA)
Essential Jim Reeves . . . . (RCA)
Jim Reeves' Greatest Hits . . . . (RCA)
Ronnie Milsap; *Ronnie Milsap's Greatest Hits-#2* . . . . (RCA)
Am I That Easy To Forget
Carl Belew; *24 Hits: Best Of Country Stars On LP-C* . . . . (Tee Vee)
Debbie Reynolds; *Debbie Reynolds' Greatest Hits* . . . . (Curb)

Engelbert Humperdinck; *Engelbert Humperdinck-16 Most Requested
   Songs* .... (Epic)

Am I The Only One
Marc Anthony; *Marc Anthony*............................... (Columbia)

Am I The Only One (Who's Ever Felt This Way)
Dixie Chicks; *Wide Open Spaces* .... (Monument)

Am I The Same Girl
Swing Out Sister; *Get In Touch With Yourself*.................... (Mercury)

Am I Wrong
Keb' Mo'; *Keb' Mo'* .... (Okeh)

Amigone
Goo Goo Dolls; *Dizzy Up The Girl* .... (Warner Sunset/Reprise)

Angel
Lionel Richie; *Renaissance* .... (Island/IDJMG)

Angry All The Time
Bruce Robison with Kelly Willis; *Wrapped* .... (Lucky Dog)
Tim McGraw with Faith Hill; *Set This Circus Down*................. (Curb)

Answer Me, My Love
Nat "King" Cole; *Best Of Nat "King" Cole-Vol. 1* ....(Capitol)
   The Nat "King" Cole Story-#2.............................(Capitol)
   Unforgettable ....(Capitol)

Any Bonds Today?
Andrews Sisters; *Swing Out To Victory: Songs Of World
   War II-C*.................................... (ISD/Intersound)
Barry Wood; *78-#27478* ....(Victor)
Bing Crosby; *Original Soundtrack Sessions* .... (Vintage Jazz Classics)

Anybody Listening?
Queensryche; *Empire* .... (EMI)

Anybody Seen My Baby?
Rolling Stones; *1998 Grammy Nominees-C* .... (MCA)
   Bridges To Babylon ....(Virgin)

Anyone For Tennis
Cream; *Eric Clapton-Crossroads-C* .... (Polydor)
   Strange Brew-Very Best Of Cream...................... (Polydor)

Are The Good Times Really Over (I Wish A Buck Was Still Silver)
Merle Haggard; *Big City* .... (Epic)
   For The Record: Merle Haggard-43 Legendary Hits................(BNA)
   Greatest Country Hits Of The '80s-1982-C ....(Columbia)
   His Epic Hits-First 11 To Be Continued-C.................... (Epic)

Are The Roses Not Blooming
Judds; *Love Can Build A Bridge* .... (MCA)

Are There Any Cowboys Left (In The Good Ol' U.S.A.?)
Lacy J. Dalton; *Lacy J. Dalton*........................ (Columbia)

Are There Any More Real Cowboys
Willie Nelson & Neil Young; *Half Nelson-C* .... (Columbia)

Are U Still Down?
Jon B.; *Cool Relax* ....(Yab Yum/550)

Are We In Trouble Now
Mark Knopfler; *Golden Heart* .... (Warner Bros.)

Are We Making Love Or Making Friends
Moe Bandy; *Soft Lights And Hard Country Music* .... (Columbia)

Are We Ourselves
Fixx; *One Thing Leads To Another-Greatest Hits*.................. (MCA)
   React... (MCA)

Are You Building A Temple In Heaven
Hank Williams; *I'm So Lonesome I Could Cry-1949*............. (Polydor)

Are You Crazy
Freddie McGregor; *Come On Over* .... (Real Authentic Sound)

Are You Experienced?
Jimi Hendrix; *Kiss The Sky* ....(Reprise)
Jimi Hendrix Experience; *Are You Experienced?* ....(Reprise)
   Essential Jimi Hendrix ....(Reprise)

Are You Gonna Go My Way
Lenny Kravitz; *Are You Gonna Go My Way* ....(Virgin)

Are You Happy Baby?
Dottie West; *Dottie West's Greatest Hits* .... (Curb)

Are You Hung Up
Mothers Of Invention; *We're Only In It For The Money* .... (Rykodisc)

Are You Jimmy Ray?
Jimmy Ray; *Jimmy Ray*..................................... (Epic)

Are You Lonely For Me
Rude Boys; *Rude Awakening*........................... (Atlantic)

Are You Lonesome To-night?
Elvis Presley; *A Valentine Gift For You*....................(RCA)
   Elvis' Golden Records, Volume 3 ....(RCA)
   From Memphis To Vegas/From Memphis To Memphis.............(RCA)
   Worldwide 50 Gold Award Hits, Vol. 1, Parts 1 & 2.................(RCA)

Are You Lovin' Me Like I'm Lovin' You
Ronnie Milsap; *Back To The Grindstone*.....................(RCA)

Are You On The Road To Lovin' Me Again
Debby Boone; *Best Of Debby Boone*..................... (Curb)

Are You Ready For The Sex Girls
Gleaming Spires; *Best Of Rodney On The 'ROQ*................ (Posh Boy)

Are You Ready To Rock
Michael Schenker Group; *One Night At Budokan*.............. (Chrysalis)
   Rock Will Never Die .... (Chrysalis)

Are You Ready?
Creed; *Human Clay*.....................................(Wind-up)

Are You Satisfied?
Rusty Draper; *Rusty Draper's Greatest Hits* ....(Collector's Choice)

Are You Sitting Comfortably/The Dream
Moody Blues; *Caught Live Plus Five* .... (Polydor)
   On The Threshold Of A Dream .... (Polydor)
   This Is The Moody Blues .... (Polydor)

Are You Sleeping?
Nilsson; *The Point* .... (RCA)

Are You Sure Hank Done It This Way
Hank Williams, Jr.; *Rowdy*..............................(WB/Curb)
Waylon Jennings; *Waylon Jennings' Greatest Hits* .... (RCA)

Are You Teasing Me
Carl Smith; *Carl Smith's Greatest Hits* ....(Gusto)
   Essential Carl Smith-1950-1956........................(Legacy)

Are You That Somebody?
Aaliyah; *ST/Dr. Dolittle* .... (Atlantic)

Are You There?
Oleander; *Unwind* .... (Republic/Universal)

Are You Weepin'
Gary Wright; *Light Of Smiles* .... (Warner Bros.)

Aren't You Glad?
Beach Boys; *Beach Boys '69 (The Beach Boys Live In London)* ....(Capitol)
   Smiley Smile/Wild Honey ....(Capitol)
   Sunshine Dream ....(Capitol)

Aren't You Glad?
Original Broadway Cast; *The Most Happy Fella* .... (Sony Music Classical)

Ask Any Girl
Diana Ross & The Supremes; *Diana Ross & The Supremes'
   Greatest Hits*...(Motown)
Supremes; *Where Did Our Love Go*........................(Motown)

Ask Me Why
Beatles; *Please Please Me* .... (Parlophone)

Ask The Lonely
Vonda Shepard; *ST/Songs From "Ally McBeal" Featuring Vonda
   Shepard* .... (550/Epic)

At This Moment
Billy Vera & The Beaters; *Billboard Top Hits-1987-C* ....(Rhino)
   By Request: Best Of Billy Vera & The Beaters ....(Rhino)

B.B.D. (I Thought It Was Me)?
Bell Biv Devoe; *Poison* .... (MCA)

Baa Baa Black Sheep
Original Soundtrack; *Toddler Favorites* .... (Kid Rhino/Rhino 4 Kids)

Baby Did A Bad Thing
Chris Isaak; *Forever Blue*.............................. (Reprise)
   ST/Eyes Wide Shut.................................... (Reprise)

Baby Won't You Let Me Rock & Roll You
Ten Years After; *A Space In Time* ....(Columbia)

Baby Won't You Please Come Home
Billie Holiday; *Last Recordings*.........................(Verve)
Dinah Washington; *Echoes Of An Era-Dinah Washington* .... (Roulette)
Frank Sinatra; *Night We Called It A Day* ....(Capitol)
Louis Armstrong; *Most Blues*...........................(Olympic)
Louis Armstrong & Friends; *20 Golden Pieces Of Louis Armstrong &
   Friends* .... (Bulldog)
Ray Charles; *20 Golden Pieces Of Ray Charles*.............(Bulldog)

Baby Won't You Tell Me
Johnny Hammond; *Big City Blues* ....(Vanguard)

Baby You're A Rich Man
Beatles; *Beatles-Box Set* ....(Capitol)
   Magical Mystery Tour...................................(Capitol)

Baby's In Black
Beatles; *Beatles '65* ....(Capitol)
   Beatles-Box Set ....(Capitol)
   For Sale ....(Capitol)

Bad Boyz
Shyne featuring Levy, Barrington; *Shyne* .... (Bad Boy/Arista)

Battle Flag
Lo Fidelity Allstars; *How To Operate With A Blown Mind* .... (Skint)

Be My Baby Tonight
John Michael Montgomery; *John Michael Montgomery's
   Greatest Hits* .... (Atlantic)
   Kickin' It Up .... (Atlantic)

Been Around The World
Puff Daddy & The Family; *No Way Out* .... (Bad Boy/Arista)

Been There
Clint Black with Steve Wariner; *D'lectrified* .... (RCA)

Believe
Cher; *Believe* .... (Warner Bros.)
   Totally Hits-#1-C ....(Arista)

Bicycle Built For Two
Kidsongs; *Cars, Boats, Trains, Planes*.....................(Sony Wonder)
Original Soundtrack; *School Days-Kids Classics* ....(Benson)

Big Boss Man
B.B. King; *Six Silver Strings* .... (MCA)
Elvis Presley; *ST/Clambake* ....(RCA)
Grateful Dead; *Grateful Dead (Skull & Roses)* .... (Warner Bros.)
Jimmy Reed; *Best Of Jimmy Reed* .... (Crescendo)
   Oldies But Goodies-#1-C .... (Original Sound)

John Hammond; *Best Of John Hammond* . . . . (Vanguard)
So Many Roads . . . . (Vanguard)
Bill Bailey
Louis Armstrong; *Essential Louis Armstrong* . . . . (Vanguard)
Louis Armstrong . . . . (Audio Fidelity)
Pearl Bailey; *Echoes Of An Era-Pearl Bailey* . . . . (Roulette)
Preservation Hall Jazz Band; *New Orleans-#1* . . . . (Columbia)
Blowin' In The Wind
Bob Dylan; *Before The Flood* . . . . (Columbia)
Biograph . . . . (Columbia)
Bob Dylan At Budokan . . . . (Columbia)
Bob Dylan's Greatest Hits . . . . (Columbia)
Freewheelin' . . . . (Columbia)
God Bless America-C . . . . (Columbia)
Greatest Folksingers Of The '60s-C . . . . (Vanguard)
Joan Baez; *ST/Forrest Gump* . . . . (Epic/Sony Music Soundtrax)
Peter, Paul & Mary; *10 Years Together/The Best Of Peter, Paul*
and Mary . . . . (Warner Bros.)
Holiday Celebration . . . . (Warner Bros.)
In The Wind . . . . (Warner Bros.)
Peter, Paul and Mary In Concert . . . . (Warner Bros.)
Stevie Wonder; *Motown Year By Year-The Sound Of Young America-*
1966-C . . . . (Motown)
Blue
LeAnn Rimes; *Blue* . . . . (MCG/Curb)
Blue Monday
Orgy; *Candyass* . . . . (Elementree/Reprise)
Book Of Love
Monotones; *Bedrock-Late '50s/'60s Rock 'N' Roll* . . . . (Allegiance)
Best Of Chess Rock 'N' Roll-#1-C . . . . (Chess)
Original Golden Rock Oldies-#1-C . . . . (Specialty)
ST/American Graffiti . . . . (MCA)
Super Oldies Of The '50s-#2-C . . . . (Audio Fidelity)
Born To Fly
Sara Evans; *Born To Fly* . . . . (RCA)
Boy From Tupelo
Emmylou Harris; *Red Dirt Girl* . . . . (Nonesuch)
Brand New Mister Me
Mel Tillis & The Statesiders; *The Ultimate Mel Tillis* . . . . (Bransounds)
Brilliant Disguise
Bruce Springsteen; *Bruce Springsteen's Greatest Hits* . . . . (Columbia)
Tunnel Of Love . . . . (Columbia)
Broken Pieces
Strato Vocalz; *Love Shouldn't Hurt-C* . . . . (Qwest)
Brother, Can You Spare A Dime
Bing Crosby; *Bing Crosby-16 Most Requested Songs* . . . . (Legacy)
Odetta/Dr. John/John Campbell/Rufus Reid; *Strike A Deep Chord-Blues For*
The Homeless-C . . . . (Justice)
Peter, Paul & Mary; *See What Tomorrow Brings* . . . . (Warner Bros.)
Weavers; *Weavers' Greatest Hits* . . . . (Vanguard)
Build Me Up Buttercup
Foundations; *Billboard Top Rock 'N' Roll Hits-1969-C* . . . . (Rhino)
History Of British Rock-#9-C . . . . (Rhino)
ST/There's Something About Mary . . . . (Capitol)
Burn
Jo Dee Messina; *Burn* . . . . (Curb)
Caldonia (What Makes Your Big Head So Hard?)
Louis Jordan; *No Moe! Louis Jordan's Greatest Hits* . . . . (Verve)
Original Cast; *Five Guys Named Moe* . . . . (Columbia)
Woody Herman & His Orchestra; *Verve Jazz Masters 54* . . . . (Verve)
Can Heaven Wait
Luther Vandross; *Luther Vandross* . . . . (J)
Can I Change My Mind
Tyrone Davis; *Soul Shots-#2-The "In" Crowd-Sweet Soul-C* . . . . . . (Rhino)
Tyrone Davis' Greatest Hits . . . . (Rhino)
Can I Count On You
McBride & The Ride; *Burnin' Up The Road* . . . . (MCA)
Can I Get A Witness
Marvin Gaye; *Marvin Gaye-Anthology* . . . . (Motown)
Marvin Gaye's Greatest Hits . . . . (Motown)
Marvin Gaye-Super Hits . . . . (Motown)
Rod Stewart; *Storyteller/The Complete Anthology: 1964-1990* . . . (Warner Bros.)
Rolling Stones; *England's Newest Hit Makers/The Rolling Stones* . . . . . (Abkco)
Can I Get A…
Jay-Z featuring Amil & Ja Rule; *Vol. 2-Hard Knock Life* . . . . (Def Jam)
Can I Get To Know You Better
Turtles; *Best Of The Turtles-Golden Archive Series* . . . . (Rhino)
Turtles-20 Greatest Hits . . . . (Rhino)
Can I Have A Smoke, Dude?
Mary's Danish; *Edge Of Rock-C* . . . . (Era)
There Goes The Wondertruck . . . . (Chameleon)
Can I Have My Money Back
Gerry Rafferty; *Can I Have My Money Back* . . . . (MCA)
Can I Run
L7; *Hungry For Stink* . . . . (Slash)
Can I See You In The Morning
Jackson 5; *Third Album* . . . . (Motown)
Can I See You Tonight
Tanya Tucker; *Best Of Tanya Tucker* . . . . (MCA)

Tanya Tucker Live . . . . (MCA Special Prod.)
Can I Stay With You
Karyn White; *Make Him Do Right* . . . . (Warner Bros.)
Can I Touch You…There?
Michael Bolton; *Michael Bolton's Greatest Hits-1985-1995* . . . . (Columbia)
Can I Trust You With My Heart
Travis Tritt; *T-R-O-U-B-L-E* . . . . (Warner Bros.)
Can We
SWV; *Release Some Tension* . . . . (RCA)
Can We Spend Some Time
Surface; *2nd Wave* . . . . (Columbia)
Can We Still Be Friends?
Robert Palmer; *Secrets* . . . . (Island)
Rod Stewart; *Camouflage* . . . . (Warner Bros.)
Todd Rundgren; *Hermit Of Mink Hollow* . . . . (Rhino)
Todd Rundgren-Anthology 1968-1985 . . . . (Rhino)
Can We Talk
Tevin Campbell; *I'm Ready* . . . . (Qwest)
Can You Dance (Baby Tell Me)
Shanice Wilson; *Discovery* . . . . (A&M)
Can You Feel The Love Tonight
Elton John; *ST/The Lion King* . . . . (Walt Disney)
John Tesh; *Sax On The Beach* . . . . (GTS)
Can You Hear Me?
David Bowie; *Young Americans* . . . . (Rykodisc)
Can You Hear The Music?
Rolling Stones; *Goats Head Soup* . . . . (Rolling Stones)
Can You Help Me
Jesse Johnson's Revue; *Jesse Johnson's Revue* . . . . (A&M)
Can You Read My Mind
Maureen McGovern; *Maureen McGovern* . . . . (Warner Bros.)
Can You See Me
Jimi Hendrix; *ST/Jimi Plays Monterey* . . . . (Reprise)
Jimi Hendrix Experience; *Are You Experienced?* . . . . (Reprise)
Smash Hits . . . . (Reprise)
Can You Stand The Rain
New Edition; *Heart Break* . . . . (MCA)
Can You Stop The Rain
Grover Washington, Jr.; *Soulful Strut* . . . . (Columbia)
Peabo Bryson; *Can You Stop The Rain* . . . . (Columbia)
Cannibals
Mark Knopfler; *Golden Heart* . . . . (Warner Bros.)
Can't We Be Friends
Art Tatum; *Standards* . . . . (Black Lion)
Buck Clayton & Buddy Tate; *Buck & Buddy* . . . . (Prestige)
Ella Fitzgerald & Louis Armstrong; *Ella & Louis* . . . . (Verve)
Frank Sinatra; *In The Wee Small Hours* . . . . (Capitol)
Linda Ronstadt; *Lush Life* . . . . (Asylum)
Can't We Talk It Over?
Bing Crosby; *Bing Crosby-16 Most Requested Songs* . . . . (Legacy)
Helen O'Connell; *Great Girl Singers Sing 22 Original*
Recordings-C . . . . (Hindsight)
Can't You Hear Me Callin'?
Ricky Skaggs; *Bluegrass Super Hits-C* . . . . (Columbia)
Favorite Country Songs . . . . (Epic)
Highway & Heartaches . . . . (Epic)
Can't You Hear Me Knockin'
Rolling Stones; *Sticky Fingers* . . . . (Virgin)
Can't You Hear My Heartbeat
Herman's Hermits; *Herman's Hermits-Their Greatest Hits* . . . . (Abkco)
Can't You See
Alabama; *Alabama-Live* . . . . (RCA)
Charlie Daniels Band; *Volunteer Jam VII-C* . . . . (Epic)
Hank Williams, Jr.; *Hank Williams, Jr. & Friends* . . . . (Polydor)
Rebels, Renegades & Ramblers-C . . . . (Polydor)
Standing In The Shadows . . . . (Polydor)
Marshall Tucker Band; *Marshall Tucker Band* . . . . (AJK Music)
Searchin' For A Rainbow . . . . (AJK Music)
Can't You See
Total; *Total* . . . . (Bad Boy/Arista)
Total featuring Notorious B.I.G.; *Bad Boy Greatest*
Hits-#1-C . . . . (Bad Boy/Arista)
ST/New Jersey Drive-#1-C . . . . (Tommy Boy)
Can't You See
Peter Tosh; *Mystic Man* . . . . (Rolling Stones)
Can't You See (You Doin' Me Wrong)
Tower Of Power; *Back To Oakland* . . . . (Warner Bros.)
Can't You See Darling
Ray Charles; *20 Golden Pieces Of Ray Charles* . . . . (Bulldog)
Can't You See What You're Doing To Me
Albert King & Little Milton; *Albert King & Little Milton-Chronicle* . . . . . (Stax)
Cara Mia
Jay & The Americans; *I Got Rhythm-C* . . . . (K-Tel)
Jay & The Americans' Greatest Hits . . . . (CEMA Special Prod.)
Jay & The Americans' Greatest Hits . . . . (Curb)
Carnival
Natalie Merchant; *Tigerlily* . . . . (Elektra)
Carry On
Crosby, Stills, Nash & Young; *Deja Vu* . . . . (Atlantic)

Case Of The Ex (Whatcha Gonna Do)
Mya; *Fear Of Flying* . . . . (University/Interscope)
Now That's What I Call Music!-#5-C . . . .(Virgin)
Chasing Forever
Will Smith; *Big Willie Style* . . . .(Columbia)
Check Yes Or No
George Strait; *Strait Out Of The Box* . . . . (MCA)
Chop Suey!
System Of A Down; *Toxicity* . . . . (American/Columbia)
Cold Cold Heart
Hank Williams; *Complete Hank Williams* . . . . (Mercury)
Hank Williams With His Drifting Cowboys; *24 Of Hank Williams'*
Greatest Hits . . . . (Polydor)
Hank Williams . . . . (MGM)
Hank Williams-40 Greatest Hits . . . . (Polydor)
Live At Opry . . . . (MGM)
Long Gone Lonesome Blues . . . . (Polydor)
Jerry Lee Lewis; *Duets* . . . .(Sun)
Golden Cream Of Jerry Lee Lewis . . . .(Sun)
Jerry Lee Lewis & Friends-Duets . . . .(Sun)
Lucinda Williams; *Timeless: Hank Williams*
Tribute-C . . . . (Lost Highway/IDJMG)
Tony Bennett; *Tony Bennett-16 Most Requested Songs* . . . .(Legacy)
Colors Of The Wind
Judy Kuhn; *Princess Collection* . . . . (Disney)
Vanessa Williams; *ST/Pocahontas* . . . . (Hollywood)
Vanessa Williams' Greatest Hits-The First Ten Years . . . . (Mercury)
Come With Me
Shai; *Blackface* . . . . (Gasoline Alley)
Compared To What
Les McCann; *Atlantic Jazz-Soul-C* . . . . (Atlantic)
Les McCann & Eddie Harris; *Great Moments In Jazz-C* . . . . (Atlantic)
Jazz Years . . . . (Atlantic)
Swiss Movement . . . . (Atlantic)
Continuing Story Of Bungalow Bill, The
Beatles; *The Beatles (White Album)* . . . . (Capitol)
Could I Be
Wood; *Songs From Stamford Hill* . . . . (Columbia)
Could I Be Your Girl
Jann Arden; *Living Under June* . . . . (A&M)
Could I Have This Dance?
Anne Murray; *Anne Murray's Greatest Hits* . . . . (Capitol)
ST/Urban Cowboy . . . . (Asylum)
Could I Have Your Autograph
Dolly Parton; *Rainbow* . . . . (Columbia)
Could It Be
Jaheim; *Ghetto Love* . . . . (Divine Mill/Warner Bros.)
Could It Be I'm Falling In Love
Spinners; *One Of A Kind Love Affair-Anthology* . . . .(Rhino)
Spinners . . . . (Rhino)
Very Best Of The Spinners . . . . (Rhino)
Could It Be Magic
Barry Manilow; *Barry Manilow/Live* . . . . (Arista)
Barry Manilow's Greatest Hits-#2 . . . . (Arista)
The Manilow Collection-Twenty Classic Hits . . . . (Arista)
Donna Summer; *Love Trilogy* . . . .(Casablanca)
Could This Be Love
Jennifer Lopez; *On The 6* . . . . (Work)
Could This Be Magic
Dubs; *Doo Wop Memories-#1-C* . . . . (Rhino)
Cup Of Life
Ricky Martin; *Ricky Martin* . . . . (Columbia)
Curious
LSG featuring L.L. Cool J, Busta Rhymes & MC Lyte; *Levert-Sweat-*
Gill . . . . (East West)
Daddy What If
Bobby Bare; *Bobby Bare* . . . .(RCA)
Great Moments At The Grand Ole Opry-C . . . .(RCA)
Daddy, What's A Train?
Utah Phillips; *Steel Rails-Classic Railroad Songs-#1-C* . . . . . . (Rounder)
Darling Are You Ever Coming Home
Jeannie Seely; *Jeannie Seely's Greatest Hits* . . . . (Monument)
Dat Dere
Rickie Lee Jones; *Pop Pop* . . . . (Geffen)
Tony Bennett; *The Playground* . . . . (Sony Wonder)
David Duchovny
Bree Sharp; *Cheap & Evil Girl* . . . .(Trauma)
Desperately Wanting
Better Than Ezra; *Friction, Baby* . . . .(Swell/Elektra)
Did Beethoven Do The Dishes
Reilly & Maloney; *Profiles* . . . . (Freckle)
Did I Do That?
Mariah Carey; *Rainbow* . . . . (Columbia)
Did You Ever Have To Make Up Your Mind?
Lovin' Spoonful; *Best Of The Lovin' Spoonful* . . . . (Rhino)
Lovin' Spoonful-Anthology . . . . (Rhino)
Did You Ever Love Somebody
Jessica Simpson; *Songs From Dawson's Creek* . . . . (Sony Music Soundtrax)

Did You Ever See A Dream Walking
Bing Crosby; *Crosby Classics* . . . .(Columbia)
Hal Kemp & Skinnay Ennis; *The Uncollected Hal Kemp-#2 & #3* . . .(Hindsight)
Did You Ever Think
R. Kelly; *R.* . . . . (Jive)
Did You Get That Letter
Arthur "Big Boy" Crudup; *Crudup's Mood* . . . .(Delmark)
Did You See His Name
Kinks; *Kink Kronikles* . . . . (Reprise)
Did You See Jackie Robinson Hit That Ball?
Count Basie; *RCA Victor Blues & Rhythm Revue-C* . . . . (RCA)
Count Basie & His Orchestra; *Baseball's Greatest Hits-C* . . . . (Rhino)
Did You Steal My Money
Who; *Face Dances* . . . . (MCA)
Did Your Mother Come From Ireland
Bing Crosby; *Shillelaghs & Shamrocks* . . . . (MCA)
Didn't Cha Know
Erykah Badu; *Mama's Gun* . . . .(Motown)
Didn't We Almost Have It All
Whitney Houston; *Whitney* . . . .(Arista)
Whitney Houston's Greatest Hits . . . .(Arista)
Dites-Moi
Original Cast; *South Pacific* . . . . (CBS Masterworks)
Do I Have To Come Right Out & Say It
Buffalo Springfield; *Buffalo Springfield* . . . .(Atco)
Do I Have To Say The Words?
Bryan Adams; *Waking Up The Neighbours* . . . .(A&M)
Do I Hear A Waltz?
Elizabeth Allen; *Broadway Magic-The 1960s-C* . . . .(Columbia)
Original Broadway Cast; *Do I Hear A Waltz?* . . . . (Sony Music Classical)
Do I Love You Because You're Beautiful
Julie Andrews & Jon Cypher; *Cinderella-The CBS Television*
Production . . . .(Columbia)
Rodgers & Hammerstein Songbook . . . . (Sony Music Classical)
Mel Torme; *Mel Torme-16 Most Requested Songs* . . . .(Columbia)
Stuart Damon & Lesley Ann Warren; *Cinderella-The CBS Television*
Network Production . . . .(Columbia)
Do Right
Jimmie's Chicken Shack; *Bring Your Own Stereo* . . . .(Rocket)
Do Ya Think I'm Sexy?
Rod Stewart; *Absolutely Live* . . . . (Warner Bros.)
Blondes Have More Fun . . . . (Warner Bros.)
Rod Stewart's Greatest Hits . . . . (Warner Bros.)
Do You Believe In Magic
Lovin' Spoonful; *Lovin' Spoonful-Anthology* . . . .(Rhino)
Do You Believe In Us?
Jon Secada; *Jon Secada* . . . .(SBK)
Do You Ever Dream Of Vienna
Original Cast; *Little Mary Sunshine* . . . .(Out Of Print)
Do You Feel What I'm Feeling
Warren Hill; *Truth* . . . . (RCA)
Do You Hear Wedding Bells
Jive Five; *Jive Five-Their Greatest Hits* . . . .(Collectables)
Do You Know
Xscape; *Traces Of My Lipstick* . . . . (So So Def/Columbia)
Do You Know (What It Takes)
Robyn; *Robyn Is Here* . . . . (RCA)
Do You Know The Way To San Jose
Dionne Warwick; *Dionne Warwick Greatest Hits* . . . .(Everest)
Dionne Warwick-Anthology 1962-1971 . . . .(Rhino)
Hot! Live & Otherwise . . . .(Arista)
Do You Know What It Means To Miss New Orleans
Billie Holiday; *Sing 2* . . . .(Kent)
Harry Connick, Jr.; *Twenty* . . . .(Columbia)
Louis Armstrong; *Chicago Concert 1956* . . . .(Columbia)
Mostly Blues . . . .(Olympic)
Pops . . . .(Bluebird)
Pete Fountain; *Best Of Pete Fountain* . . . . (MCA)
Do You Know Where Your Man Is
Pam Tillis; *Homeward Looking Angel* . . . .(Arista)
Do You Know You Are My Sunshine
Statler Brothers; *Statler Brothers-30th Anniversary Celebration* . . . . .(Mercury)
Do You Like This
Rome; *Rome* . . . . (RCA)
Do You Love Me (Now That I Can Dance?)
Contours; *Frat Rock!-C* . . . .(Rhino)
Greatest Movie Rock Hits-C . . . .(Rhino)
Oldies But Goodies-#12-C . . . . (Original Sound)
ST/More Dirty Dancing . . . .(RCA)
ST/The Wanderers . . . . (Warner Bros.)
Dave Clark Five; *History Of The Dave Clark Five* . . . .(Hollywood)
Do You Love Me That Much?
Peter Cetera; *You're The Inspiration-A Collection* . . . . (River North)
Do You Love Me?
Jonathan Butler; *Do You Love Me?* . . . .(N2K)
Do You Love Me?
Original Cast; *Fiddler On The Roof* . . . .(RCA Victor)

Do You Really Love Me
Brian Culbertson; *Somethin' 'Bout Love* . . . .(Atlantic)
Do You Really Want Me
Robyn; *Robyn Is Here* . . . . (RCA)
Do You Really Want To Hurt Me
Culture Club; *Billboard Top Hits-1983-C* . . . . (Rhino)
Kissing To Be Clever . . . . (Virgin)
Do You Remember Rock 'N' Roll Radio
Ramones; *End Of The Century* . . . . (Sire)
Mania . . . . (Sire)
Do You Remember?
Bob Marley & The Wailers; *Birth Of A Legend 1963-*
1966 . . . . (Epic Portrait Assoc.)
Early Music . . . . (Calla)
Do You Remember?
Phil Collins; *...But Seriously* . . . .(Atlantic)
Serious Hits...Live! . . . .(Atlantic)
Do You Remember?
Five Satins; *Five Satins Sing Their Greatest Hits* . . . . (Collectables)
Do You Remember?
Beach Boys; *Little Deuce Coupe/All Summer Long* . . . . (Capitol)
Spirit Of America . . . . (Capitol)
Do You Sleep?
Lisa Loeb & Nine Stories; *Tails* . . . .(Geffen)
Do You Wanna Dance?
Beach Boys; *Absolute Best-#1* . . . . (Capitol)
Spirit Of America . . . . (Capitol)
Bette Midler; *Divine Miss M.* . . . .(Atlantic)
Live At Last . . . .(Atlantic)
Bobby Freeman; *ST/American Graffiti* . . . .(MCA)
Do You Wanna Get Away
Shannon; *Do You Wanna Get Away* . . . . (Mirage)
Do You Wanna Go To Heaven
Original Broadway Cast; *Big River-The Adventures Of*
Huckleberry Finn . . . .(MCA)
T.G. Sheppard; *Smooth Sailin'* . . . .(Warner Bros.)
T.G. Sheppard's All-Time Greatest Hits . . . . (Warner Bros.)
T.G. Sheppard's Greatest Hits . . . . (Warner Bros./Curb)
Do You Wanna Make Love
Peter McCann; *Peter McCann* . . . . (20th Century Fox)
Do You Want Me
Salt-N-Pepa; *Blacks' Magic* . . . .(Next Plateau/London/Island)
Do You Want My Job
Little Village; *Little Village* . . . . (Reprise)
Do You Want To
Xscape; *Off The Hook* . . . .(So So Def/Columbia)
Do You Want To Know A Secret
Beatles; *Introducing...The Beatles* . . . .(Vee-Jay)
Please Please Me . . . . (Parlophone)
The Early Beatles . . . . (Capitol)
Does Anybody Really Know What Time It Is?
Chicago; *Chicago At Carnegie Hall* . . . .(Chicago)
Chicago IX-Chicago's Greatest Hits . . . .(Chicago)
Chicago Transit Authority . . . .(Chicago)
If You Leave Me Now . . . .(Chicago)
Does Fort Worth Ever Cross Your Mind
George Strait; *Country Classics-#3-1984-1985-C* . . . . (Universal)
Does Fort Worth Ever Cross Your Mind . . . .(MCA)
George Strait's Greatest Hits-#2 . . . .(MCA)
MCA #1 Hits Of The '80s-#1-C . . . .(MCA Special Prod.)
Does He Love You
Reba McEntire & Linda Davis; *Reba McEntire's Greatest Hits*
Volume Two . . . .(MCA)
Does My Ring Hurt Your Finger
Charley Pride; *Charley Pride-24 Greatest Hits* . . . .(Tee Vee)
Essential Charley Pride . . . . (RCA)
Does She Love That Man?
Breathe; *Peace Of Mind* . . . . (A&M)
Does That Blue Moon Ever Shine On You
Toby Keith; *Blue Moon* . . . . (Polydor Country)
Toby Keith's Greatest Hits, Volume One . . . . (Mercury)
Does This Bus Stop At 82nd Street?
Bruce Springsteen; *Greetings From Asbury Park, N.J.* . . . . (Columbia)
Tracks . . . . (Columbia)
Does Your Chewing Gum Lose Its Flavor (On The Bedpost Overnight)
Lonnie Donegan; *Dr. Demento Presents The Greatest Novelty Records-#3-*
1960s-C . . . .(Rhino)
Dr. Demento Presents The Greatest Novelty Records-C . . . . (Rhino)
Does Your Heart Beat For Me
Blue Barron; *Big Band Treasures-#2-C* . . . .(Dunhill Compact Classics)
Patsy Cline; *Always* . . . .(MCA)
Portrait Of Patsy Cline . . . .(MCA)
Russ Morgan; *Best Of Russ Morgan* . . . .(MCA)
Russ Morgan & His Orchestra; *Russ Morgan & His Orchestra Play 22*
Original Big Band Recordings . . . . (Hindsight)
Does Your Mother Know?
Abba; *Abba Live* . . . .(Atlantic)
Abba's Greatest Hits-#2 . . . .(Atlantic)

The Singles-First 10 Years . . . .(Atlantic)
Voulez-Vous . . . .(Atlantic)
Doggie In The Window
Patti Page; *Patti Page-16 Most Requested Songs* . . . . (Legacy)
Patti Page-Golden Hits . . . . (Mercury)
Patti Page's Greatest Hits . . . . (Columbia)
Donna
Los Lobos; *ST/La Bamba* . . . .(Slash)
Ritchie Valens; *American Graffiti-#3-C* . . . .(MCA)
Best Of Ritchie Valens . . . . (Rhino)
Heart & Soul Of Rock 'N' Roll-#1-C . . . . (Rhino)
History Of Latino Rock-#1-C . . . . (Rhino)
History Of Ritchie Valens . . . . (Rhino)
Don't Take Your Love From Me
Etta James; *These Foolish Things-The Classic Balladry Of Etta James* . . (MCA)
King Sisters; *Spotlight On The King Sisters* . . . .(Capitol)
Three Suns; *Very Best Of The Three Suns* . . . . (Taragon)
Don't The Girls All Get Prettier At Closing Time
Mickey Gilley; *Make It Like The First Time* . . . .(ISD/Intersound)
Don't You Care
Buckinghams; *Buckinghams' Greatest Hits* . . . . (Columbia)
Don't You Ever Get Tired Of Hurtin' Me
Ray Price; *Ray Price's Greatest Hits-#2* . . . . (Step One)
Ronnie Milsap; *Stranger Things Have Happened* . . . . (RCA)
Don't You Get It
Mark Knopfler; *Golden Heart* . . . . (Warner Bros.)
Don't You Know I Care
Cleo Laine; *Solitude* . . . . (RCA Victor)
Duke Ellington; *Black, Brown & Beige: 1944-1946 Band*
Recordings . . . . (Bluebird)
Joe Williams; *Every Day: The Best Of The Verve Years* . . . . (Verve)
Don't You Know What The Night Can Do?
Steve Winwood; *Roll With It* . . . . (Virgin)
Don't You See That Train
Laurie Lewis & Kathy Kallick; *Freight Train Blues-Classic Railroad*
Songs-#4-C . . . . (Rounder)
Don't You Want Me
Jody Watley; *Jody Watley* . . . .(MCA)
Jody Watley's Greatest Hits . . . .(MCA)
You Wanna Dance With Me? . . . .(MCA)
Don't Your Mem'ry Ever Sleep At Night
Ronnie Milsap; *Keyed Up* . . . . (RCA)
Steve Wariner; *Best Of Steve Wariner.* . . . . (RCA)
Don't Your Peaches Look Mellow
Luke & The Locomotives; *Luke & The Locomotives* . . . .(Audioquest)
Down In The Valley
Elvis Presley; *Reconsider Baby* . . . . (RCA)
Leadbelly; *Defense Blues-Golden Classics-#2* . . . . (Collectables)
Pete Seeger; *American Favorite Ballads-#1* . . . .(Smithsonian Folkways)
Dream Baby (How Long Must I Dream)
Lacy J. Dalton; *Dream Baby* . . . . (Columbia)
Greatest Country Hits Of The '80s-1983-C . . . . (Columbia)
Lacy J. Dalton's Greatest Hits . . . . (Columbia)
Roy Orbison; *For The Lonely: 18 Greatest Hits* . . . . (Rhino)
For The Lonely: A Roy Orbison Anthology 1959-1965 . . . . (Rhino)
In Dreams-Greatest Hits . . . . (Orbison)
Roy Orbison's All-Time Greatest Hits-#1 & 2 . . . . (Monument)
Drive
Cars; *Heartbeat City* . . . . (Elektra)
MTV's Rock 'N' Roll To Go-C . . . . (Elektra)
The Cars' Greatest Hits . . . . (Elektra)
Drops Of Jupiter (Tell Me)
Train; *Drops Of Jupiter* . . . . (Aware/C2/Columbia)
D'You Know What I Mean
Oasis; *Be Here Now* . . . . (Epic)
Earth Angel
Elvis Presley; *A Golden Celebration* . . . . (RCA)
New Edition; *ST/Under The Blue Moon* . . . .(MCA)
Penguins; *Billboard Top Rock 'N' Roll Hits-1955-C* . . . . (Rhino)
Golden Classics-Penguins . . . . (Collectables)
Oldies But Goodies-#1-C . . . .(Original Sound)
ST/American Graffiti . . . .(MCA)
Eleanor Rigby
Beatles; *Beatles 1* . . . . (Capitol)
Revolver . . . . (Capitol)
The Beatles/1962-1966. . . . . (Capitol)
Ray Charles; *Ray Charles' Greatest Hits-#2.* . . . . (Rhino)
Ray Charles-Anthology . . . . (Rhino)
End Of The World
Skeeter Davis; *Best Of Skeeter Davis* . . . . (Gusto)
Billboard Top Country Hits-1963-C. . . . . (Rhino)
Nipper's Greatest Hits Of The '60s-#1-C. . . . . (RCA)
Stars Of The Grand Ole Opry-1926-1974-C . . . . (RCA)
Super Country Hits Of The '60s-C . . . . (Gusto)
Enough Of Me
Melissa Etheridge; *Breakdown* . . . . (Island)
Eternal Flame
Bangles; *Bangles' Greatest Hits* . . . . (Columbia)
Everything . . . . (Columbia)

Everything For Free
K's Choice; *Cocoon Choice* . . . . (550 Music)
Faded
soulDecision; *No One Does It Better* . . . . (MCA)
Now That's What I Call Music!-#5-C . . . . (Virgin)
Fall In Love
Kenny Chesney; *All I Need To Know* . . . . (BNA)
Kenny Chesney's Greatest Hits . . . . (BNA)
Feelin' Alright?
Dave Mason; *Best Of Dave Mason* . . . . (Columbia)
Certified Live . . . . (Columbia)
Dave Mason's Greatest Hits . . . . (Columbia)
Skatetown U.S.A.-C . . . . (Columbia)
U.S.A. . . . . (MCA)
Joe Cocker; *Joe Cocker's Greatest Hits* . . . . (A&M)
Mad Dogs & Englishmen . . . . (A&M)
Rockin' '60s-C . . . . (Priority)
With A Little Help From My Friends . . . . (A&M)
Fire Escape
Fastball; *All The Pain Money Can Buy* . . . . (Hollywood)
Five Foot Two, Eyes Of Blue
Mom & Dads; *Very Best Of The Mom & Dads* . . . . (Crescendo)
Freaks
Live; *Secret Samadhi* . . . . (Radioactive/MCA)
Frere Jacques
Original Soundtrack; *Toddler Favorites* . . . . (Kid Rhino/Rhino 4 Kids)
Friend Of Mine
Kelly Price; *Soul Of A Woman* . . . . (T-Neck/Island)
From Here To Eternity
Michael Peterson; *Michael Peterson* . . . . (Reprise)
Wedding Day Music-C . . . . (Reprise)
Funny How Time Slips Away
Al Green & Lyle Lovett; *Rhythm Country And Blues-C* . . . . (MCA)
Jimmy Elledge; *Nipper's Greatest Hits Of The '60s-#2-C* . . . . (RCA)
RCA's Greatest One-Hit Wonders-C . . . . (RCA)
Willie Nelson; *Best Of Willie Nelson* . . . . (Capitol)
Collector's Series-Willie Nelson . . . . (RCA)
Healing Hands Of Time . . . . (Liberty)
My Own Way . . . . (RCA)
San Antonio Rose . . . . (Columbia)
Willie & Family Live . . . . (Columbia)
Willie Nelson & Faron Young; *Funny How Time Slips Away* . . . . . . (Columbia)
Gee Baby, Ain't I Good To You
Diana Krall; *All For You (A Dedication To The Nat "King" Cole*
Trio) . . . . (Impulse!)
Girl Inside My Head
Blues Traveler; *Bridge* . . . . (A&M)
Gold Dust Woman
Fleetwood Mac; *25 Years-The Chain* . . . . (Warner Bros.)
Rumours . . . . (Warner Bros.)
Sister Hazel; *Legacy-A Tribute To Fleetwood Mac's Rumours-C* . . . . . . (Lava)
Good Girls
Joe; *All That I Am* . . . . (Jive)
Goodnight My Love (Pleasant Dreams)
Fleetwoods; *Best Of The Fleetwoods* . . . . (Rhino)
Fleetwoods' Greatest Hits . . . . (CEMA Special Prod.)
Jesse Belvin; *Collectables Presents The History Of Rock-#9-C* . . . (Collectables)
Oldies But Goodies-#2-C . . . . (Original Sound)
Graduate
Third Eye Blind; *Third Eye Blind* . . . . (Elektra)
Groove Is In The Heart/What Is Love
Deee-Lite; *World Clique* . . . . (Elektra)
Guess Things Happen That Way
Johnny Cash; *The Man In Black-His Greatest Hits* . . . . (Legacy)
Has Anybody Seen Amy
John & Audrey Wiggins; *John & Audrey* . . . . (Mercury)
Hate This Place
Goo Goo Dolls; *Dizzy Up The Girl* . . . . (Warner Sunset/Reprise)
Have I The Right?
Honeycombs; *Watch Your Step: The Beat Era-#1-C* . . . . (Collectables)
Have I Told You Lately?
Rod Stewart; *Unplugged...And Seated* . . . . (Warner Bros.)
Vagabond Heart . . . . (Warner Bros.)
Van Morrison; *Best Of Van Morrison* . . . . (Polydor)
Have You Ever Been (To Electric Ladyland)
Jimi Hendrix Experience; *Electric Ladyland* . . . . (Reprise)
Have You Ever Been Lonely (Have You Ever Been Blue)
Ernest Tubb; *Best Of Ernest Tubb* . . . . (Curb)
The Country Music Hall Of Fame-Ernest Tubb . . . . (MCA)
Jim Reeves & Patsy Cline; *Jim Reeves' Greatest Hits* . . . . (RCA)
Patsy Cline; *Showcase-With The Jordanaires* . . . . (MCA)
Have You Ever Loved A Woman
Derek And The Dominos; *Layla* . . . . (Polydor)
Have You Ever Needed Someone So Bad
Def Leppard; *Adrenalize* . . . . (Mercury)
Have You Ever Really Loved A Woman?
Bryan Adams; *18 Til I Die* . . . . (A&M)
Number One Movie Hits-C . . . . (ESX Entert.)

ST/Don Juan De Marco . . . . (A&M)
Have You Ever Seen The Rain
Creedence Clearwater Revival; *1970* . . . . (Fantasy)
Creedence Clearwater Revival-Chronicle . . . . (Fantasy)
Pendulum . . . . (Fantasy)
Have You Ever?
Brandy; *Never Say Never* . . . . (Atlantic)
Have You Heard
Duprees; *Best Of The Duprees* . . . . (Collectables)
Best Of The Duprees . . . . (Rhino)
WCBS FM 101 History Of Rock-'60s-#3-C . . . . (Collectables)
Have You Heard
Moody Blues; *Caught Live Plus Five* . . . . (Polydor)
On The Threshold Of A Dream . . . . (Polydor)
This Is The Moody Blues . . . . (Polydor)
Have You Heard The News
Ben Sidran; *Puttin' In Time On Planet Earth* . . . . (MCA)
Vikki Carr; *Live At The Greek Theatre* . . . . (Columbia)
Have You Met Miss Jones
Art Tatum; *Best Of Art Tatum* . . . . (Pablo)
Coleman Hawkins; *April In Paris* . . . . (Bluebird)
Ella Fitzgerald; *Silver Collection-Songbooks* . . . . (Verve)
Frank Sinatra; *Swing Along With Me* . . . . (Reprise)
Louis Armstrong; *American Songbook* . . . . (Verve)
Tony Bennett; *Jazz* . . . . (Columbia)
Rodgers & Hart Songbook . . . . (DRG)
Have You Seen Her
Chi-Lites; *Chi-Lites' Greatest Hits* . . . . (Rhino)
Hammer; *Please Hammer Don't Hurt 'Em* . . . . (Capitol)
Have You Seen Mary
Sponge; *Wax Ecstatic* . . . . (Columbia)
Have You Seen The Saucers
Jefferson Airplane; *2400 Fulton Street-An Anthology* . . . . (RCA)
30 Seconds Over Winterland . . . . (RCA)
Have You Seen The Stars Tonight
Jefferson Airplane; *Flight Log (1966-1976)* . . . . (Grunt)
Paul Kantner/Jefferson Starship; *Blows Against The Empire* . . . . (RCA)
Have You Seen Your Mother, Baby, Standing In The Shadow?
Rolling Stones; *Flowers* . . . . (Abkco)
got Live if you want it! . . . . (Abkco)
More Hot Rocks (big hits & fazed cookies) . . . . (Abkco)
Through The Past, Darkly (Big Hits Vol. 2) . . . . (Abkco)
Haven't You Heard
Patrice Rushen; *Patrice Rushen-Anthology* . . . . (Elektra)
Pizzazz . . . . (Elektra)
Haven't You Heard
George Strait; *Something Special* . . . . (MCA)
Heartbreaker
Bee Gees; *One Night Only* . . . . (Polydor)
Heartbroke Every Day
Lonestar; *Lonestar* . . . . (BNA)
Hello
Lionel Richie; *Back To Front* . . . . (Motown)
Can't Slow Down . . . . (Motown)
Truly-The Love Songs . . . . (Motown)
Luther Vandross; *Songs* . . . . (Epic)
Hello, I Love You
Doors; *Best Of The Doors* . . . . (Elektra)
Doors' Greatest Hits . . . . (Elektra)
Doors-Box Set . . . . (Elektra)
Waiting For The Sun . . . . (Elektra)
Hero
Enrique Iglesias; *America: A Tribute To Heroes-C* . . . . (Interscope)
Escape . . . . (Interscope)
Hey Hey What Can I Do
Hootie & The Blowfish; *Encomium: Tribute To Led Zeppelin-C* . . . . . (Atlantic)
Led Zeppelin; *Led Zeppelin-Box Set* . . . . (Atlantic)
Led Zeppelin-The Complete Studio Recordings . . . . (Atlantic)
Hey Pretty
Poe; *Haunted* . . . . (FEI/Atlantic)
Hey, Good Lookin'
Hank Williams With His Drifting Cowboys; *24 Of Hank Williams'*
Greatest Hits . . . . (Polydor)
Hank Williams-40 Greatest Hits . . . . (Polydor)
Hey, Good Lookin'-December 1950-July 1951 . . . . (Polydor)
Loretta Lynn & Conway Twitty; *Hey, Good Lookin'* . . . . . (MCA Special Prod.)
High
Jimmie's Chicken Shack; *Pushing The Salmanilla Envelope* . . . . (Rocket)
High Enough
Damn Yankees; *Damn Yankees* . . . . (Warner Bros.)
Him
Rupert Holmes; *Partners In Crime* . . . . (MCA)
Him Or Me, What's It Going To Be
Paul Revere And The Raiders; *Essential Ride-'63-'67* . . . . (Legacy)
Hold Me
Brian McKnight; *Anytime* . . . . (Motown)
Hold On
Xscape; *Traces Of My Lipstick* . . . . (So So Def/Columbia)

Honey Can I Put On Your Clothes
Barbra Streisand; *Songbird* . . . . (Columbia)
Honey, Do You Love Me, Huh
Hank Williams; *Complete Hank Williams* . . . . (Mercury)
Hooch
Everything; *Super Natural* . . . .(Blackbird/Sire)
How About That
Bad Company; *Here Comes Trouble* . . . . (Atco)
How Am I Supposed To Live Without You
Laura Branigan; *Branigan 2* . . . .(Atlantic)
Michael Bolton; *Soul Provider* . . . . (Columbia)
How Are Things In Glocca Mora
Julie Andrews; *A Little Bit Of Broadway* . . . . (Columbia)
Original Cast; *Finian's Rainbow* . . . . (RCA)
Rosemary Clooney; *Show Tunes* . . . .(Concord Jazz)
How Blue
Reba McEntire; *MCA #1 Hits Of The '80s-#1-C* . . (MCA Special Prod.)
My Kind Of Country . . . .(MCA)
Reba McEntire's Greatest Hits . . . .(MCA)
How Blue Can You Get
B.B. King; *Best Of B.B. King* . . . .(MCA)
Live At The Regal . . . .(MCA)
Live In Cook County Jail . . . .(MCA)
How Can A Poor Man Stand Such Times And Live?
Blind Alfred Reed; *How Can A Poor Man Stand Such Times And
Live?* . . . . (Rounder)
Ry Cooder; *Ry Cooder* . . . . (Reprise)
Show Time . . . .(Warner Bros.)
How Can I Be Sure
Rascals; *Groovin'* . . . . (Warner Special Prod.)
Rascals-Anthology 1965-1972 . . . . (Rhino)
The Ultimate Rascals . . . . (Warner Special Prod.)
Very Best Of The Rascals . . . . (Rhino)
How Can I Ease The Pain
Lisa Fischer; *So Intense* . . . . (Elektra)
How Can I Fall
Breathe; *All That Jazz* . . . . (A&M)
How Can I Help You Say Goodbye
Patty Loveless; *Only What I Feel* . . . .(Epic)
Patty Loveless-Classics . . . .(Epic)
How Can We Be Lovers
Michael Bolton; *Soul Provider* . . . . (Columbia)
How Can We Hang Onto A Dream
Tim Hardin; *Memorial Album* . . . . (Polydor)
How Can You Mend A Broken Heart
Al Green; *Al Green's Greatest Hits-#1* . . . . (Motown)
Compact Command Performances-Al Green . . . . (Motown)
Let's Stay Together . . . . (Right Stuff)
Bee Gees; *Bee Gees-Gold* . . . . (Polydor)
Here At Last...Bee Gees...Live . . . . (Polydor)
Nobody's Child-Romanian Angel Appeal-C . . . .(Warner Bros.)
How Come U Don't Call Me Anymore
Stephanie Mills; *Merciless* . . . . (Casablanca)
How Come You Don't Call Me
Alicia Keys; *Songs In A Minor* . . . . (J)
How Come, How Long
Babyface & Stevie Wonder; *The Day* . . . .(Epic)
How Could An Angel Break My Heart
Kenny G with Toni Braxton; *Kenny G's Greatest Hits* . . . . (Arista)
Toni Braxton with Kenny G; *Diana, Princess Of Wales-Tribute-C* . . (Columbia)
Secrets . . . . (LaFace)
How Could I
Marc Anthony; *Marc Anthony* . . . . (Columbia)
How Could You
K-Ci & JoJo; *Love Always* . . . .(MCA)
How Deep Is The Ocean? (How High Is The Sky?)
Diana Krall; *Love Scenes* . . . . (Impulse!)
Frank Sinatra; *Nice 'N' Easy* . . . . (Capitol)
Liza Minnelli; *Liza Minnelli-At Carnegie Hall* . . . . (Telarc)
How Deep Is Your Love
Bee Gees; *Bee Gees' Greatest* . . . . (Polydor)
ST/Saturday Night Fever . . . . (Polydor)
How Deep Is Your Love
Dru Hill featuring Redman; *Enter The Dru* . . . . (Def Jam/RAL/Mercury/Island)
ST/Rush Hour . . . . (Def Jam)
How Did I Get By Without You
John Waite; *Complete John Waite-#1-Falling Backwards* . . . .(EMI)
Temple Bar . . . . (Coyote/Imago)
How Do I Get There
Deana Carter; *Did I Shave My Legs For This?* . . . . (Capitol)
How Do I Live
LeAnn Rimes; *Absolute Dance Hits-C* . . . . (Curb)
You Light Up My Life-Inspirational Songs . . . . (Curb)
Trisha Yearwood; *Songbook-A Collection Of Hits* . . . .(MCA)
How Do I Make You
Linda Ronstadt; *Linda Ronstadt's Greatest Hits, Volume Two* . . . .(Asylum)
Mad Love . . . . (Elektra)
How Do I Say I'm Sorry
Tami Davis; *Only You* . . . .(Red Ant)

How Do The Fools Survive
Doobie Brothers; *Minute By Minute* . . . . (Warner Bros.)
How Do You Do It
Beatles; *The Beatles-Anthology-#1* . . . . (Capitol)
How Do You Fall In Love
Alabama; *For The Record: 41 Number One Hits* . . . .(RCA)
How Do You Keep The Music Playing
James Ingram & Patti Austin; *It's Your Night-C* . . . .(Qwest)
ST/Listen Up-The Lives Of Quincy Jones . . . .(Qwest)
How Do You Like Me Now?!
Toby Keith; *How Do You Like Me Now?!* . . . .(DreamWorks/SKG)
How Do You Like Your Eggs In The Morning?
Jane Powell/Vic Damone/Four Freshmen; *ST/Romantic Duets From MGM
Classics-C* . . . . (Turner Classic Movies)
How Do You Raise A Barn?
Original Cast; *Plain And Fancy* . . . .(EMI-Angel)
How Do You Say Auf Wiedersehen
George Shearing & Mel Torme; *Top Drawer* . . . . (Concord Jazz)
How Do You Sleep At Night
Wade Hayes; *When The Wrong One Loves You Right* . . . . (Columbia/DKC)
How Do You Speak To An Angel?
Etta James; *These Foolish Things-The Classic Balladry Of Etta James* . . (MCA)
How Do You Talk To An Angel
Heights; *ST/Heights* . . . . (Capitol)
How Do You Talk To Girls
Rick Springfield; *Success Hasn't Spoiled Me Yet* . . . .(RCA)
How Do You Tell The One
After 7; *Reflections* . . . . (Virgin)
How Does It Feel
Ian Moore; *Ian Moore* . . . . (Capricorn)
How Does That Grab You, Darlin'?
Nancy Sinatra; *How Does That Grab You?* . . . .(Sundazed Music)
The Hit Years . . . . (Rhino)
How Far Is Heaven
Kitty Wells; *Kitty Wells-20 Greatest Hits* . . . . (Tee Vee)
How Far To Little Rock
Stanley Brothers; *Stanley Series-Vol. 1-#2* . . . . (Copper Creek)
How It's Going To Be
Third Eye Blind; *Third Eye Blind* . . . . (Elektra)
How Long
Ace; *Lava Love-C* . . . . (K-Tel)
Super Hits Of The '70s-Have A Nice Day-#14-C . . . .(Rhino)
How Long Blues
Eric Clapton; *From The Cradle* . . . .(Duck/Reprise)
How Long Gone
Brooks & Dunn; *If You See Her* . . . . (Arista)
How Long Has This Been Going On?
Bon Jovi featuring Richie Sambora; *Glory Of Gershwin Featuring Larry
Adler-C* . . . . (Mercury)
Ella Fitzgerald & Oscar Peterson; *Ella & Oscar* . . . . (Pablo)
Judy Garland; *Judy Garland-At Carnegie Hall* . . . . (Capitol)
Louis Armstrong & Oscar Peterson; *Louis Armstrong Meets Oscar
Peterson* . . . . (Verve)
Original Cast; *My One And Only* . . . .(Atlantic)
Patti Austin; *Real Me* . . . .(Qwest)
Sarah Vaughan; *How Long Has This Been Going On?* . . . . (Pablo)
How Long Must I Wait For You
Joe Jackson; *Jumpin' Jive* . . . . (A&M)
How Many Friends
Who; *By Numbers* . . . .(MCA)
How Many Licks
Lil' Kim featuring Sisqo; *Notorious K.I.M.* . . . .(Queen Bee/Undeas/Atlantic)
How Many Moons
Whites; *A Lifetime In The Making* . . . .(Ceili Music)
How Many More Times
Led Zeppelin; *Led Zeppelin* . . . .(Atlantic)
How Many Tears
Bobby Vee; *Bobby Vee-Legendary Masters* . . . . (EMI)
How Many Ways
Toni Braxton; *Toni Braxton* . . . . (LaFace)
How Much Is Enough
Fixx; *Ink* . . . . (Impact)
How Was I To Know
Reba McEntire; *Forever Reba* . . . . (Universal)
What If It's You . . . .(MCA)
How Was I To Know
John Michael Montgomery; *What I Do The Best* . . . .(Atlantic)
How Will I Know
Whitney Houston; *Soul Train 25th Anniv. Hall Of Fame-Box* . . . . (MCA)
Whitney Houston . . . . (Arista)
Whitney Houston's Greatest Hits . . . . (Arista)
How You Gonna See Me Now
Alice Cooper; *From The Inside* . . . . (Warner Bros.)
How'd You Like To Be My Daddy?
Farber Sisters; *Music From The New York Stage (1890-1920)-#4-1917-
1920-C* . . . .(Pearl)
How're You Fixed For Blades (Gillette)
Original Soundtrack; *TeeVee Toons-The Commercials-#1-C* . . . . (TVT)

Hymn To Him
Audrey Hepburn; *ST/My Fair Lady* . . . . (Columbia)
Julie Andrews/Original Cast; *My Fair Lady* . . . . (Columbia)
I Can Dream, Can't I?
Andrews Sisters; *Best Of The Andrews Sisters* . . . . (MCA)
I Can't Tell You Why
Brownstone; *From The Bottom Up* . . . . (MJJ/Epic)
Eagles; *Eagles Greatest Hits, Volume 2* . . . . (Asylum)
   Eagles Live . . . . (Asylum)
   The Long Run . . . . (Asylum)
Vince Gill; *Common Thread-Songs Of The Eagles-C* . . . . (Giant)
I Care 'Bout You
Milestone; *ST/Soul Food* . . . . (LaFace)
I Do
Toya; *Totally Hits 2001-C* . . . . (Arista)
   Toya . . . . (Arista)
I Do (Cherish You)
98 Degrees; *98 Degrees And Rising* . . . . (Universal)
Mark Wills; *Wish You Were Here* . . . . (Mercury)
I Do (Whatcha Say Boo)
Jon B.; *Cool Relax* . . . . (Yab Yum/550)
I Don't Know Why
Frank Sinatra; *The Golden Days Of Radio* . . . . (K-Tel)
I Don't Live Today
Jimi Hendrix; *Concerts* . . . . (Reprise)
   Essential Jimi Hendrix, Volume 2 . . . . (Reprise)
   Kiss The Sky . . . . (Reprise)
Jimi Hendrix Experience; *Are You Experienced?* . . . . (Reprise)
I Don't Want To Wait
Paula Cole; *Live On Letterman-From The Late Show* . . . . (Reprise)
   Songs From Dawson's Creek . . . . (Sony Music Soundtrax)
   This Fire . . . . (Imago)
I Got Rhythm
Ella Fitzgerald; *George & Ira Gershwin Songbook* . . . . (Verve)
Ethel Waters; *I Got Rhythm: The Smithsonian George Gershwin
   Collection-C* . . . . (Smithsonian Collection)
Happenings; *'60s Rock Classics-#1-C* . . . . (Rhino)
Judy Garland; *Judy Garland-Collector's Items-1936-1945* . . . . . . (MCA)
Louis Armstrong; *Essential Louis Armstrong* . . . . (Verve)
Original Cast; *Girl Crazy* . . . . (Nonesuch)
Original London Cast; *Crazy For You* . . . . (RCA)
Robert Palmer; *Glory Of Gershwin Featuring Larry Adler-C* . . . . . . (Mercury)
I Hope You've Learned
Ricky Skaggs and Kentucky Thunder; *Bluegrass Rules!* . . . . . . (Rounder)
I Know An Old Lady Who Swallowed A Fly
Original Soundtrack; *More Silly Songs* . . . . (Disney)
Peter, Paul & Mary; *Peter, Paul & Mommy, Too* . . . . (Warner Bros.)
I Know There's An Answer
Beach Boys; *Pet Sounds* . . . . (Capitol)
   The Pet Sounds Sessions: A 30th Anniversary Collection . . . . (Capitol)
I Really Don't Want To Know
Charlie McCoy; *Greatest Hits Of Charlie McCoy* . . . . (Columbia)
Eddy Arnold; *Best Of Eddy Arnold* . . . . (RCA)
   Essential Eddy Arnold . . . . (RCA)
Elvis Presley; *Elvis Country ("I'm 10,000 Years Old")* . . . . (RCA)
   Great Country Songs . . . . (RCA)
Les Paul; *Best Of The Capitol Masters* . . . . (Gold Rush)
Les Paul & Mary Ford; *Les Paul's Greatest Hits* . . . . (Pair)
Ronnie Dove; *Ronnie Dove-His Best* . . . . (Laurie)
Tommy Edwards; *It's All In The Game-The Complete Hits Of Tommy
   Edwards* . . . . (Eric)
I Want It That Way
Backstreet Boys; *Millennium* . . . . (Jive)
I Will Remember You
Sarah McLachlan; *Mirrorball* . . . . (Arista)
   ST/Brothers McMullen . . . . (Arista)
   Surfacing . . . . (Arista)
   Totally Hits-#2-C . . . . (Elektra)
I Wonder Why
Dion And The Belmonts; *Doo-Wop Uptempo-#2-C* . . . . (Rhino)
   Everything You Always Wanted . . . . (Laurie)
   Million-Dollar Memories #1-C . . . . (RCA)
   Oldies But Goodies-#12-C . . . . (Original Sound)
   Super Oldies Of The '50s-#7-C . . . . (Audio Fidelity)
   You Found The Vocal Group Sound-#1-C . . . . (Solid Smoke)
I Wonder Why
Curtis Stigers; *Curtis Stigers* . . . . (Arista)
I Wonder Why She Kept On Saying "Si-Si-Si-Si Senor"
Al Jolson; *Music From The New York Stage (1890-1920)-#4-1917-
   1920-C* . . . . (Pearl)
If I Didn't Care
Connie Francis; *Very Best Of Connie Francis* . . . . (Polydor)
Hilltoppers; *45-#15220* . . . . (Dot)
Ink Spots; *Best Of The Ink Spots* . . . . (Pro-Arte)
   If I Didn't Care . . . . (Pro-Arte)
Ink Spots' Greatest Hits-Original Recordings-1939-1946 . . . . (MCA)
   ST/The Shawshank Redemption . . . . (Epic)
Moments; *Best Of The Moments: Love On A Two-Way Street* . . . . . (Rhino)
Platters; *Magic Touch-An Anthology* . . . . (Mercury)

   Very Best Of The Platters . . . . (Mercury)
If I Give My Heart To You
Nat "King" Cole; *Nat "King" Cole (Box Set)* . . . . (Capitol)
If It Makes You Happy
Sheryl Crow; *Sheryl Crow* . . . . (A&M)
If There's A God On My Side
Rosanne Cash; *The Wheel* . . . . (Columbia)
If Tomorrow Never Comes
Garth Brooks; *Garth Brooks* . . . . (Liberty)
   Limited Series-Box . . . . (Capitol)
Joose; *Joose* . . . . (Flavor Unit)
If You Wanna Leave Me (Can I Come Too?)
Bryan Adams; *Waking Up The Neighbours* . . . . (A&M)
I'll Never Fall In Love Again
Dionne Warwick; *Billboard Top Soft Rock Hits-1970-C* . . . . (Rhino)
   Her Classic Songs-#1 . . . . (Curb)
Elvis Presley; *From Elvis Presley Boulevard, Memphis, Tennessee* . . . . (RCA)
Mary Chapin Carpenter; *ST/My Best Friend's Wedding* . . . . . (Work/Epic)
I'm Good At Being Bad
TLC; *Fanmail* . . . . (LaFace)
I'm Payin' Taxes, What Am I Buyin'
JB's; *Funky Good Time-The Anthology* . . . . (Polydor)
I'm Wondering
Stevie Wonder; *Stevie Wonder's Greatest Hits-#1* . . . . (Motown)
In The Blood
Better Than Ezra; *Deluxe* . . . . (Swell/Elektra)
Ironic
Alanis Morissette; *Jagged Little Pill* . . . . (Maverick)
Is A Bluebird Blue
Conway Twitty; *Rockin' Conway-MGM Years* . . . . (Mercury)
Is It A Crime
Sade; *Promise* . . . . (Portrait)
Is It A Crime
Judy Holliday/Original Cast; *Bells Are Ringing* . . . . (Columbia)
Is It A Star
Daryl Hall & John Oates; *War Babies* . . . . (Atlantic)
Is It Cold In Here
Joe Diffie; *Regular Joe* . . . . (Epic)
Is It Over Yet
Wynonna; *Tell Me Why* . . . . (MCA)
Is It Raining At Your House
Vern Gosdin; *10 Years Of Greatest Hits Newly Recorded* . . . . . (Columbia)
   Chiseled In Stone . . . . (Columbia)
   Greatest Country Hits Of The '90s-1991-C . . . . (Columbia)
Is It Really Over?
Jim Reeves; *Essential Jim Reeves* . . . . (RCA)
Is It Still Over
Randy Travis; *Old 8 X 10* . . . . (Warner Bros.)
Is It What You Wanted
Greta; *No Biting* . . . . (Stardog)
Is She Really Going Out With Him
Joe Jackson; *Live 1980/86* . . . . (A&M)
   Look Sharp! . . . . (A&M)
Is That A Tear
Tracy Lawrence; *Best Of Tracy Lawrence* . . . . (Atlantic)
   Time Marches On . . . . (Atlantic)
Is There Life Out There
Reba McEntire; *For My Broken Heart* . . . . (MCA)
   Reba McEntire's Greatest Hits Volume Two . . . . (MCA)
Is This Love
Bob Marley & The Wailers; *Babylon By Bus* . . . . (Tuff Gong)
   Kaya . . . . (Tuff Gong)
   Legend: The Best Of Bob Marley & The Wailers . . . . (Island)
Is This Love
Carly Simon; *Hello Big Man* . . . . (Warner Bros.)
Is This Love
Alison Moyet; *Raindancing* . . . . (Columbia)
Is This Love
Whitesnake; *Whitesnake* . . . . (Geffen)
Is You Is Or Is You Ain't My Baby
Diana Krall; *Only Trust Your Heart* . . . . (GRP)
Louis Jordan; *Five Guys Named Moe-Original Decca Recordings-#2* . . . (MCA)
   Rock 'N Roll . . . . (Mercury)
Is Your Mama Gonna Miss Ya?
Bryan Adams; *Waking Up The Neighbours* . . . . (A&M)
Is Zat You, Myrtle
Carlisles; *45-#70174* . . . . (Mercury)
Louvin Brothers; *Live At New River Ranch* . . . . (Copper Creek)
Isn't It A Pity?
Mel Torme; *That's All* . . . . (Sony Music Special Prod.)
Michael Feinstein; *Pure Gershwin* . . . . (Elektra)
Isn't It A Pity?
George Harrison; *All Things Must Pass* . . . . (Parlophone)
Isn't It Midnight
Fleetwood Mac; *25 Years-The Chain* . . . . (Warner Bros.)
   Tango In The Night . . . . (Warner Bros.)
Isn't It Romantic
Michael Feinstein; *Isn't It Romantic* . . . . (Elektra)

Tony Bennett; *Rodgers & Hart Songbook* (DRG)
Isn't It Time
Babys; *Babys-Anthology* (Chrysalis)
Broken Heart (Chrysalis)
Isn't Life Strange
Moody Blues; *A Night At Red Rocks With The Colorado Symphony Orchestra* (Polydor)
Seventh Sojourn (Polydor)
This Is The Moody Blues (Polydor)
Voices In The Sky-The Best Of The Moody Blues (Threshold)
Isn't She Lovely
Keb' Mo'; *Big Wide Grin* (Sony Wonder)
Lee Ritenour; *Best Of Lee Ritenour* (Epic)
Stevie Wonder; *Original Musiquarium* (Motown)
Songs In The Key Of Life (Motown)
Isn't This A Lovely Day
Ella Fitzgerald; *The Irving Berlin Songbook-#2* (Verve)
Fred Astaire; *Fred Astaire Sings* (MCA)
Irving Berlin Songbook (Verve)
Starring Fred Astaire (Columbia)
Istanbul (Not Constantinople)
Four Lads; *Four Lads-16 Most Requested Songs* (Legacy)
It's Bad You Know
R.L. Burnside; *The Sopranos-Music From The HBO Original Series* (Sony Music Soundtrax)
It's In His Kiss (Shoop Shoop Song)
Betty Everett; *Billboard Top R&B Hits-1964-C* (Rhino)
Hits Of The Sixties-C (Intercom Music)
More American Graffiti-C (MCA)
Oldies But Goodies-#3-C (Original Sound)
Very Best Of Betty Everett (Vee-Jay)
Wonder Women-History Of Girl Group Sound-C (Rhino)
Cher; *ST/Mermaids* (Geffen)
Vonda Shepard; *ST/Songs From "Ally McBeal" Featuring Vonda Shepard* (550/Epic)
Jealousy
Natalie Merchant; *Tigerlily* (Elektra)
Jim, What's Wrong With Him
Dramatics; *Dramatic Experience* (Stax)
Jimmy Mack
Martha & The Vandellas; *Billboard Top R&B Hits-1967-C* (Rhino)
Compact Command Performances-Martha Reeves & The Vandellas (Motown)
Martha Reeves & The Vandellas-Anthology (Motown)
Motown Story-First 25 Years-C (Motown)
Motown Superstar Series-#11-Martha Reeves & The Vandellas (Motown)
Top 10 With A Bullet-Motown Girl Groups-C (Motown)
Jocko Homo
Devo; *Best Of Devo-Greatest Hits* (Warner Bros.)
Q: Are We Not Men? A: We Are Devo! (Warner Bros.)
Rest Of Devo-Greatest Misses (Warner Bros.)
John 3:16
Wyclef; *Muggs Presents...The Soul Assassins-C* (Columbia)
Johnny Have You Seen Her?
Rembrandts; *United* (Atco)
Julie, Do Ya Love Me
Bobby Sherman; *Rock & Roll Is Here To Stay-C* (Gusto)
Super Hits Of The '70s-Have A Nice Day-#3-C (Rhino)
Kids
Original Broadway Cast; *Bye Bye Birdie* (Columbia)
Paul Lynde; *ST/Bye Bye Birdie* (RCA)
Kryptonite
3 Doors Down; *Better Life* (Republic/Universal)
Now That's What I Call Music!-#5-C (Virgin)
Lady Marmalade
Christina Aguilera, Lil' Kim, Mya & Pink; *ST/Moulin Rouge* (Interscope)
Labelle; *Nightbirds* (Epic)
Patti LaBelle; *Best Of Patti LaBelle* (Epic)
Sheila E.; *Sex Cymbal* (Warner Bros.)
Last Day, The
Marilyn Scott; *Avenues Of Love* (Warner Bros.)
Last Kiss
J. Frank Wilson and The Cavaliers; *Billboard Top Rock 'N' Roll Hits-1964-C* (Rhino)
Collectables Presents The History Of Rock-#2-C (Collectables)
Oldies But Goodies-#9-C (Original Sound)
Teenage Tragedies-C (Rhino)
Pearl Jam; *No Boundaries-Benefit For The Kosovar Refugees-C* (Epic)
Last Night Of The World
Bruce Cockburn; *Breakfast In New Orleans, Dinner In Timbuktu* (Rykodisc)
Last Nite
Strokes; *Is This It* (RCA)
Lately
Tyrese; *Tyrese* (RCA)
Lazybones
Don Redman & His Orchestra; *Don Redman-1933-1936* (Classics)
Harry Connick, Jr.; *25* (Columbia)
Kay Starr; *The Hoagy Carmichael Songbook-C* (Bluebird)
Mildred Bailey; *Mildred Bailey-1932-1936* (Classics)
Leave It Behind
Offspring; *Ixnay On The Hombre* (Columbia)
Let It Be
Aretha Franklin; *Aretha Franklin's Greatest Hits* (Atlantic)
Beatles; *Beatles 1* (Capitol)
Beatles-20 Greatest Hits (Capitol)
Past Masters-Volume Two (Parlophone)
Reel Music (Capitol)
The Beatles/1967-1970 (Capitol)
Paul McCartney; *The Concert For New York City-C* (Columbia)
Tripping The Live Fantastic-Highlights! (Capitol)
Rockestra; *Kampuchea-C* (Atlantic)
Let Me Be There
Olivia Newton-John; *Let Me Be There* (MCA)
Olivia Newton-John's Greatest Hits (MCA)
Let's Build A World Together
George Jones & Tammy Wynette; *George Jones & Tammy Wynette-16 Biggest Hits* (Epic/Legacy)
Life On Mars?
David Bowie; *Hunky Dory* (Rykodisc)
The Singles-1969-1993 (Rykodisc)
Light In Your Eyes
Blessid Union Of Souls; *Blessid Union Of Souls* (Capitol)
Like A Rolling Stone
Bob Dylan; *Biograph* (Columbia)
Bob Dylan At Budokan (Columbia)
Bob Dylan's Greatest Hits (Columbia)
Highway 61 Revisited (Columbia)
More American Graffiti-#4-C (MCA)
Self Portrait (Columbia)
Bob Dylan And The Band; *Before The Flood* (Columbia)
Jimi Hendrix; *ST/Jimi Plays Monterey* (Reprise)
Jimi Hendrix Experience; *Jimi Hendrix Experience* (Reprise)
Rolling Stones; *Stripped* (Virgin)
Little Bird
Sherrie Austin; *Love In The Real World* (Arista)
Locked & Loaded
Jackyl; *Cut The Crap-C* (Epic)
Love Can Build A Bridge
Judds; *Love Can Build A Bridge* (MCA)
Love Or Confusion
Jimi Hendrix Experience; *Are You Experienced?* (Reprise)
Lover Man (Oh, Where Can You Be?)
Barbra Streisand; *Simply Streisand* (Columbia)
Billie Holiday; *Fine & Mellow* (Collectables)
History Of The Real Billie Holiday (Verve)
Blossom Dearie; *Blossom Dearie* (Verve)
Lena Horne; *Goes Latin & Sings Your Requests* (DRG)
Sarah Vaughan; *Compact Jazz-Sarah Vaughan* (Verve)
Jazz 'Round Midnight-Sarah Vaughan (Verve)
Sonny Stitt; *Soul Classics* (Prestige)
Lucky
Britney Spears; *Now That's What I Call Music!-#5-C* (Virgin)
Oops!...I Did It Again (Jive)
Lucky Me
Anne Murray; *Anne Murray-Country Hits* (Capitol)
Somebody's Waiting (Capitol)
Mahogany (Do You Know Where You're Going To), Theme From "Mahogany"
Diana Ross; *20/20-C* (Motown)
Diana Ross (Motown)
Diana Ross-Anthology (Motown)
Diana Ross-The Ultimate Collection (Motown)
Evening With Diana Ross (Motown)
Man On The Moon
R.E.M.; *Automatic For The People* (Warner Bros.)
Maybelline
Chuck Berry; *Chuck Berry-Golden Hits* (Mercury)
Chuck Berry's Greatest Hits (Everest)
Cruisin'-1955-C (Increase)
Oldies But Goodies-#11-C (Original Sound)
Super Oldies Of The '50s-#5-C (Audio Fidelity)
Johnny Rivers; *Johnny Rivers-Anthology 1964-1977* (Rhino)
Very Best Of Johnny Rivers (EMI)
Meaning Of Love, The
Michael McDonald; *Blue Obsession* (Ramp)
MFC
Pearl Jam; *Yield* (Epic)
Mirror Mirror
Diamond Rio; *Diamond Rio* (Arista)
Diamond Rio's Greatest Hits (Arista)
Momma, Where's My Daddy
Keb' Mo'; *Just Like You* (Okeh)
Mommy Can I Come Home
Keb' Mo'; *The Door* (550/Epic/Okeh)
Mommy Where's Daddy
Red Hot Chili Peppers; *Red Hot Chili Peppers* (EMI)
Mommy, Can I Go Out & Kill Tonight
Misfits; *Walk Among Us* (Ruby)

Mona Lisa
Carl Mann; *Original Memphis Rock & Roll* . . . . (Sun)
Sun Story-C . . . . (Rhino)
Elvis Presley; *Elvis-A Legendary Performer, Volume 4* . . . . (RCA)
Jim Reeves; *Jim Reeves-Pure Gold* . . . . (RCA)
Nat ''King'' Cole; *Best Of Nat ''King'' Cole-Vol. 1* . . . . (Capitol)
Capitol Collectors Series-Nat ''King'' Cole . . . . (Capitol)
The Nat ''King'' Cole Story . . . . (Capitol)
Unforgettable . . . . (Capitol)
Neville Brothers; *Fiyo On The Bayou* . . . . (A&M)
Moon Love
Frank Sinatra; *Moonlight Sinatra* . . . . (Reprise)
Glenn Miller; *Essential Glenn Miller* . . . . (Bluebird)
Glenn Miller's Greatest Hits . . . . (RCA Victor)
Morning Glory
Oasis; *(What's The Story) Morning Glory* . . . . (Epic)
Most Beautiful Girl
Charlie Rich; *Behind Closed Doors* . . . . (Epic)
Charlie Rich's Greatest Hits . . . . (Epic)
Columbia Country Classics-#4-Nashville Sound-C . . . . (Columbia)
Most High
Jimmy Page/Robert Plant; *Walking Into Clarksdale* . . . . (Atlantic)
Mr. Big Stuff
Jean Knight; *'70s Hit(s) Back Again-C* . . . . (Hip-O)
Have A Nice Decade-The '70s Pop Culture Box-C . . . . (Rhino)
Mr. Goldstone
Original Cast; *ST/Gypsy* . . . . (Columbia)
Mr. Wonderful
Peggy Lee; *Best Of Peggy Lee* . . . . (MCA)
Must You Throw Dirt In My Face
Elvis Costello; *Kojak Variety* . . . . (Warner Bros.)
Louvin Brothers; *45-#4822* . . . . (Capitol)
My Love Is For Real
Paula Abdul; *Head Over Heels* . . . . (Captive/Virgin)
My Own Worst Enemy
Lit; *A Place In The Sun* . . . . (RCA)
Never Can Say Goodbye
Jackson 5; *Jackson 5's Greatest Hits* . . . . (Motown)
Jackson 5-The Ultimate Collection . . . . (Motown)
Never My Love
Association; *Association Greatest Hits* . . . . (Warner Bros.)
Songs That Made Them Famous . . . . (Pair)
There Is Still Love-Anniversary Songs-C . . . . (Scotti Bros.)
New York Mining Disaster 1941 (Mr. Jones)
Bee Gees; *Bee Gees-Gold* . . . . (Polydor)
Here At Last...Bee Gees...Live . . . . (Polydor)
History Of British Rock-#8-C . . . . (Rhino)
Nobody's Supposed To Be Here
Deborah Cox; *One Wish* . . . . (Arista)
Totally Hits-#1-C . . . . (Arista)
Not Too Much To Ask
Mary Chapin Carpenter & Joe Diffie; *Come On Come On* . . . . (Columbia)
Obvious
Christina Aguilera; *Christina Aguilera* . . . . (RCA)
Oh Baby Doll
Chuck Berry; *The Chess Box-Chuck Berry* . . . . (Chess)
Oh Well - Pt. I
Fleetwood Mac; *Then Play On* . . . . (Reprise)
On Bended Knee
Boyz II Men; *Boyz II Men II* . . . . (Motown)
Once In A Lifetime
Talking Heads; *Remain In Light* . . . . (Sire)
ST/Stop Making Sense . . . . (Sire)
One I Gave My Heart To
Aaliyah; *One In A Million* . . . . (BlackGround Enterp./Atlantic)
One Less Bell To Answer
5th Dimension; *5th Dimension-Anthology 1967-1973* . . . . (Rhino)
Greatest Hits On Earth . . . . (Arista)
Barbra Streisand; *Barbra Joan Streisand* . . . . (Columbia)
Gladys Knight & The Pips; *Gladys Knight & The Pips-Anthology* . . . . (Motown)
If I Were Your Woman . . . . (Motown)
One Of Us
Joan Osborne; *Relish* . . . . (Blue Gorilla/Mercury)
One Promise Too Late
Reba McEntire; *Country Classics-#10-1987-C* . . . . (Universal)
Reba McEntire's Greatest Hits . . . . (MCA)
What Am I Gonna Do About You . . . . (MCA)
Only Time
Enya; *A Day Without Rain* . . . . (Reprise)
Other Generation, The
Original Cast; *Flower Drum Song* . . . . (Angel)
Flower Drum Song . . . . (Sony Music Classical)
Otherside
Red Hot Chili Peppers; *Californication* . . . . (Warner Bros.)
Oye Como Va
Santana; *Abraxas* . . . . (Columbia)
Lotus . . . . (Columbia)
Santana's Greatest Hits . . . . (Columbia)
Viva Santana! . . . . (Columbia)
Tito Puente; *El Rey* . . . . (Concord Picante Jazz)
ST/Salsa . . . . (MCA)
Paddy Won't You Drink Some Cider
Red Clay Ramblers; *Chuckin' The Frizz* . . . . (Flying Fish)
Papa Can You Hear Me?
Barbra Streisand; *One Voice* . . . . (Columbia)
ST/Yentl . . . . (Columbia)
Past The Point Of Rescue
Hal Ketchum; *Past The Point Of Rescue* . . . . (Curb)
People Asking Why
Seal; *Seal 2* . . . . (Sire)
Please
Chris Isaak; *Speak Of The Devil* . . . . (Reprise)
Prairie Wedding
Mark Knopfler; *Sailing To Philadelphia* . . . . (Warner Bros.)
Pretty Penny
Stone Temple Pilots; *Purple* . . . . (Atlantic)
Put It On Me
Ja Rule featuring Li'l Mo And Vita; *Rule 3:36* . . . (Murder Inc./Def Jam/IDJMG)
Que Sera, Sera
Doris Day; *Doris Day-16 Most Requested Songs-Encore!* . . . . (Columbia)
Doris Day's Greatest Hits . . . . (Columbia)
Radio Classics Of The '50s-C . . . . (Columbia)
Sly & The Family Stone; *Fresh* . . . . (Legacy)
Sly & The Family Stone-Anthology . . . . (Epic)
Question
Moody Blues; *A Night At Red Rocks With The Colorado Symphony Orchestra* . . . . (Polydor)
A Question Of Balance . . . . (Polydor)
This Is The Moody Blues . . . . (Polydor)
Question Everything
8Stops7; *In Moderation* . . . . (Reprise)
Question Of Time
Depeche Mode; *101* . . . . (Sire)
Black Celebration . . . . (Sire)
Question Of Time
Jack Bruce; *Question Of Time* . . . . (Epic)
Question This
Charlie Sexton; *Charlie Sexton* . . . . (MCA)
Questions
INXS; *Welcome To Wherever You Are* . . . . (Atlantic)
Questions
Buffalo Springfield; *Last Time Around* . . . . (Atco)
Questions 67 & 68
Chicago; *Chicago At Carnegie Hall* . . . . (Chicago)
Chicago Transit Authority . . . . (Chicago)
Chicago's Greatest Hits-#2 (1974-81) . . . . (Chicago)
Group Portrait . . . . (Chicago)
R U Ready
Salt-N-Pepa; *Brand New* . . . . (Island)
R. U. Ready To Rock
Blue Oyster Cult; *On Flame With Rock & Roll* . . . . . (Sony Music Special Prod.)
Some Enchanted Evening . . . . (Columbia)
Spectres . . . . (Columbia)
Razorblades
Chris Stills; *100 Year Thing* . . . . (Atlantic)
Ready To Run
Dixie Chicks; *Fly* . . . . (Monument)
ST/Runaway Bride . . . . (Sony Music Soundtrax)
Rebecca
Pat McGhee Band; *Shine* . . . . (Giant/Warner Bros.)
Reflection
Christina Aguilera; *Christina Aguilera* . . . . (RCA)
ST/Mulan . . . . (Walt Disney)
Rhiannon (Will You Ever Win)
Fleetwood Mac; *25 Years-The Chain* . . . . (Warner Bros.)
Fleetwood Mac . . . . (Reprise)
Fleetwood Mac Live . . . . (Warner Bros.)
Fleetwood Mac's Greatest Hits . . . . (Warner Bros.)
Riddle Song
Doc Watson; *Southbound* . . . . (Vanguard)
Joan Baez & Pete Seeger; *Very Early Joan Baez* . . . . (Vanguard)
Riding With The King
B.B. King & Eric Clapton; *Riding With The King* . . . . (Duck/Reprise)
RU Ready
Pieces Of A Dream; *Acquainted With The Night* . . . . . . (Heads Up Records Int'l)
Ruby Baby
Beatles; *The Beatles featuring Tony Sheridan-In The Beginning (Circa 1960)* . . . . (Polydor)
Dion; *Bronx Blues-Columbia Recordings 1962-1965* . . . . (Columbia)
Dion-24 Original Classics . . . . (Arista)
Donald Fagen; *The Nightfly* . . . . (Warner Bros.)
Drifters; *Atlantic Rhythm & Blues 1947-1974-#3 (1955-1958)-C* . . . . . (Atlantic)
Drifters-Their Greatest Recordings . . . . (Atco)
Let The Boogie Woogie Roll-Greatest Hits . . . . (Atlantic)
Save The Children
Diana Ross; *Diana Ross-Anthology* . . . . (Motown)

Touch Me In The Morning . . . . (Motown)
Gil Scott-Heron; *Gil Scott-Heron* . . . . (Bluebird)
Revolution Will Not Be Televised . . . . (Flying Dutchman)
Marvin Gaye; *Marvin Gaye Live At The London Palladium* . . . (Motown)
Marvin Gaye-Anthology . . . . (Motown)
Musical Testament 1964-1984 . . . . (Motown)
What's Going On . . . . (Motown)

Scarborough Fair/Canticle
Simon & Garfunkel; *Collected Works* . . . . (Columbia)
Parsley Sage Rosemary & Thyme . . . . (Columbia)
Simon & Garfunkel's Greatest Hits . . . . (Columbia)
ST/The Graduate . . . . (Columbia)
The Concert In Central Park . . . .(Warner Bros.)

Sense Of Purpose
Pretenders; *Isle Of View* . . . .(Warner Bros.)
Packed . . . . (Sire)

Shall We Dance
Original Broadway Cast; *The King And I* . . . .(RCA Victor)
Original Cast; *The King And I* . . . .(MCA)

Shall We Dance
Ella Fitzgerald; *George & Ira Gershwin Songbook* . . . . (Verve)

Shall We Gather At The River?
Chuck Wagon Gang; *16 Country-Gospel Favorites* . . . .(MCA)
Tennessee Ernie Ford; *All-Time Greatest Hymns* . . . . (Curb)
Tennessee Ernie Ford Sings 22 Favorite Hymns . . . .(Ranwood)

Shoe Was On The Other Foot
Patti LaBelle; *Flame* . . . .(MCA)

Should've Asked Her Faster
Ty England; *Ty England* . . . . (RCA)

Simple Joys Of Maidenhood
Julie Andrews; *Camelot* . . . . (Columbia)
Various Artists; *ST/Camelot* . . . .(Warner Bros.)

Sincere
Original Cast; *ST/The Music Man* . . . .(Warner Bros.)

Sixteen Reasons
Connie Stevens; *Only Rock 'N Roll-1960-1964-#1 Radio Hits-C* . . . . . . (Rhino)

Smooth Criminal
Alien Ant Farm; *Alien Ant Farm-Anthology* . . . .(DreamWorks/SKG)
Michael Jackson; *Bad* . . . .(Epic)

So How Come (No One Loves Me)
Everly Brothers; *Heartaches 'N' Harmonies* . . . . (Rhino)

Some Cow Fonque (More Tea, Vicar?)
Buckshot LeFonque; *ST/Men In Black* . . . . (Columbia)

Somebody To Love
Jefferson Airplane; *2400 Fulton Street-An Anthology* . . . . (RCA)
Loves You . . . . (RCA)
Nipper's Greatest Hits Of The '60s-#1-C . . . . (RCA)
Surrealistic Pillow . . . . (RCA)
The Worst Of Jefferson Airplane . . . . (RCA)

Somebody's Knockin'
Terri Gibbs; *Best Of Terri Gibbs* . . . .(MCA)
Country Gold-C . . . . (Priority)
Country Music Classics-#6-1980-1985-C . . . . (K-Tel)

Someday We'll Know
New Radicals; *Maybe You've Been Brainwashed Too* . . . .(MCA)

Someone Else's Star
Bryan White; *Bryan White* . . . . (Asylum)
Real Luv: Ultimate Country Love Songs-C . . . .(EMI)

Song From Moulin Rouge (Where Is Your Heart)
Percy Faith & His Orchestra; *Percy Faith & His Orchestra's All-Time
Greatest Hits* . . . . (Columbia)

Sour Girl
Stone Temple Pilots; *No. 4* . . . .(Atlantic)

Sparrow
Simon & Garfunkel; *Wednesday Morning 3 A.M.* . . . . (Columbia)

Special
Garbage; *Now That's What I Call Music!-#3-C* . . . . (Virgin)
Version 2.0 . . . . (Almo Sounds)

Spend My Life With You
Eric Benet; *A Day In The Life* . . . .(Warner Bros.)

Squeeze Me In
Garth Brooks; *Scarecrow* . . . . (Capitol)

Star Spangled Banner
American Brass Band; *National Anthems* . . . . (Laserlight)
Banda Sinfonica De Madrid; *National Anthems* . . . .(International Music)
Duke Ellington; *Carnegie Hall Concert-January 23, 1943* . . . . (Prestige)
Houston Symphony Orchestra; *Celebrate America* . . . . (Pro-Arte)
Jimi Hendrix; *Essential Jimi Hendrix, Volume 2* . . . . (Reprise)
Lifelines/Jimi Hendrix Story . . . . (Reprise)
ST/Jimi Hendrix . . . . (Reprise)
ST/Woodstock . . . . (Atlantic)
Lee Greenwood; *American Patriot* . . . . (Capitol)
Marvin Gaye; *Musical Testament 1964-1984* . . . . (Motown)
Mormon Tabernacle Choir; *God Bless America* . . . . (Sony Music Classical)
God Bless America-C . . . . (Columbia)
This Is My Country . . . . (Columbia)
Original Soundtrack; *The Greatest College Fight Songs* . . . .(Laserlight)
Sandi Patty; *Stars And Stripes Forever-#2-C* . . . .(Volcano Entertainment)
Vienna State Opera Orchestra; *National Anthems Of The World* . . .(Bescol, Ltd.)

Vinnie Vincent Invasion; *Head Banging Metal-C* . . . .(Priority)
Whitney Houston; *Whitney Houston's Greatest Hits* . . . . (Arista)

Stay Or Let It Go
Brian McKnight; *Back At One* . . . . (Motown)

Stellar
Incubus; *Make Yourself* . . . . (Immortal/Epic)

Still On Your Side
BBMak; *Sooner Or Later* . . . . (Hollywood)

Strong Enough
Sheryl Crow; *Tuesday Night Music Club* . . . . (A&M)

Sucked Out
Superdrag; *Regretfully Yours* . . . . (Elektra)

Suitelady
Maxwell; *Maxwell's Urban Hang Suite* . . . . (Columbia)

Superstar
Lauryn Hill; *The Miseducation Of Lauryn Hill* . . . . (Ruffhouse/Columbia)

Sweet Daze
Pete.; *Pete.* . . . . (Warner Bros.)

Sweet Old Fashioned Girl, A
Teresa Brewer; *Music! Music! Music!-Best Of Teresa
Brewer* . . . .(Varese Vintage)

Sweet Sixteen
Destiny's Child; *The Writing's On The Wall* . . . . (Columbia)

Sweet Soul Music
Arthur Conley; *Atlantic Soul Classics-C* . . . . (Warner Special Prod.)
Golden Age Of Black Music-1960-1970-C . . . .(Atlantic)

Take You Out
Luther Vandross; *Luther Vandross* . . . . (J)

Teen Angel
Dion And The Belmonts; *Everything You Always Wanted* . . . . .(Laurie)
Rock & Roll U.S.A.-21 Rock & Roll Favorites-#2-C . . . . . .(Laurie)
Mark Dinning; *Golden Years-1959-C* . . . . (Dominion Entert.)
Oldies But Goodies-#7-C . . . . (Original Sound)
ST/American Graffiti . . . . (MCA)
Teenage Tragedies-C . . . . (Rhino)

Teenager In Love
Dion And The Belmonts; *Classic Old & Gold-C* . . . .(Laurie)
Collectables Presents The History Of Rock-#6-C . . . . . . (Collectables)
Dion And The Belmonts-Their Best . . . .(Laurie)
Oldies But Goodies-#6-C . . . . (Original Sound)
Party Time Fifties-C . . . .(JCI Assoc. Labels)

Tell Me (I'll Be Around)
Shades; *110% Love Jams-C* . . . . (Simitar)
Shades . . . . (Motown)

Tell Me Do U Wanna
Ginuwine; *Ginuwine...The Bachelor* . . . .(550 Music)

Tell Me When
Human League; *Octopus* . . . . (East West)

Tell Me Why
Belmonts; *Classic Old & Gold-C* . . . .(Laurie)
I Got Rhythm-C . . . . (K-Tel)

Tennis Anyone
Today; *New Formula* . . . . (Motown)

Thank U
Alanis Morissette; *Supposed Former Infatuation Junkie* . . . . (Maverick)

That Don't Impress Me Much
Shania Twain; *Come On Over* . . . . (Mercury)

That Lady
Isley Brothers; *Isley Brothers' Greatest Hits* . . . . (T-Neck/Columbia)
Rock Artifacts-From The Vaults-#1-C . . . . (Columbia)
The Isley Brothers Story-#2-The T-Neck Years-1969-1985 . . . . (Rhino)

Theme From "Car 54, Where Are You?"
Original Soundtrack; *Television's Greatest Hits-#2-C* . . . . (TVT)

Theme From "Mr. Rogers' Neighborhood"
Original Soundtrack; *Television's Greatest Hits-#2-C* . . . . (TVT)

Theme From "What's Happening?"
Original Soundtrack; *Television's Greatest Hits-#6-Remote Control-C* . . . (TVT)

Theme From "Where In The World Is Carmen Sandiego?"
Original Soundtrack; *Television's Greatest Hits-#7-Cable Ready-C* . . . . . (TVT)

Theme From "Who's The Boss"
Original Soundtrack; *Television's Greatest Hits-#6-Remote Control-C* . . . (TVT)

Then What
Clay Walker; *Clay Walker's Greatest Hits* . . . .(Giant)

Thing Called Love
Bonnie Raitt; *Nick Of Time* . . . . (Capitol)

Think Of What You've Done
Ricky Skaggs and Kentucky Thunder; *Bluegrass Rules!* . . . . (Rounder)

This Door Swings Both Ways
Herman's Hermits; *Herman's Hermits-Their Greatest Hits* . . . .(Abkco)

Through Your Hands
Don Henley; *ST/Michael* . . . . (Revolution)

To Beat The Devil
Johnny Cash; *Johnny Cash-16 Biggest Hits-#2* . . . . (Legacy)

To Make You Love Me (What Can I Say)
Alexander O'Neal; *All Mixed Up* . . . . (Tabu)
Hearsay . . . . (Tabu)

Tommy Can You Hear Me
Who; *Join Together* . . . . (MCA)

ST/The Kids Are Alright . . . . (MCA)
ST/Tommy. . . . . (Polydor)
Tommy . . . . (MCA)
Tripping Billies
Dave Matthews Band; Crash. . . . .(RCA)
U Know What's Up
Donell Jones; Totally Hits-#2-C . . . . (Elektra)
Where I Wanna Be . . . . (LaFace)
Until I Find You Again
Richard Marx; Flesh And Bone . . . . (Capitol)
Richard Marx's Greatest Hits. . . . . (Capitol)
Untitled (How Does It Feel)
D'Angelo; Voodoo . . . .(Cheeba Sound/Virgin)
Voice Of The Heart
Diana Ross; Take Me Higher . . . . (Motown)
Wag The Dog
Mark Knopfler; ST/Wag The Dog . . . . (Mercury)
Waiting For The Light To Turn Green
Gretchen Peters; The Secret Of Life . . . .(Purple Crayon Prod.)
Was It Just The Moonlight
Timothy B. Schmit; Tell Me The Truth . . . . (MCA)
Was It Just The Wine
Vern Gosdin; 10 Years Of Greatest Hits Newly Recorded . . . . (Columbia)
Was My Brother In The Battle
Kate & Anna McGarrigle; Songs Of The Civil War-C . . . . (Columbia)
Wasn't That A Mighty Storm
Eric Von Schmidt; Troubadours Of The Folk Era-#1-C . . . . (Rhino)
Wasn't That A Party
Rovers; Wasn't That A Party . . . . (Epic)
Wat About Di Workin' Class?
Linton Kwesi Johnson; Linton Kwesi Johnson In Concert With The
Dub Band. . . . .(Shanachie)
Way, The
Fastball; All The Pain Money Can Buy . . . .(Hollywood)
Now That's What I Call Music!-#1-C . . . .(Virgin)
We Need A Resolution
Aaliyah; Aaliyah . . . . (BlackGround Enterp./Atlantic)
Were You There (When They Crucified My Lord?)
Johnny Cash with The Carter Family; The Man In Black-His
Greatest Hits . . . . (Legacy)
What About Me
Anne Murray; Anne Murray-Country . . . . (Capitol)
Kenny Rogers with Kim Carnes & James Ingram; What About Me?. . . . . .(RCA)
Quicksilver Messenger Service; Quicksilver Messenger Service-
Anthology. . . . . (Capitol)
Sons Of Mercury . . . . (Rhino)
What About Now
Lonestar; Lonely Grill . . . .(BNA)
What About Us
Total; Kima, Keisha & Pam . . . . (Bad Boy/Arista)
LaFace Records Presents The Platinum Collection-C . . . . (LaFace)
ST/Soul Food . . . . (LaFace)
What About Your Friends
TLC; Oooooooohhh...On The TLC Tip . . . .(LaFace)
What Are We Doin' Lonesome
Larry Gatlin & The Gatlin Brothers Band; Best Of The Gatlins-All The Gold
In California . . . . (Legacy)
Larry Gatlin & The Gatlin Brothers' Greatest Hits-#2. . . . . (Columbia)
Larry Gatlin & The Gatlin Brothers-17 Greatest Hits . . . . (Columbia)
What Are You Doing In My Life
Tom Petty And The Heartbreakers; Damn The Torpedoes . . . . (MCA)
What Are You Doing The Rest Of Your Life?
Barbra Streisand; Just For The Record . . . . (Columbia)
The Way We Were . . . . (Columbia)
Carmen McRae; Great American Songbook . . . . (Atlantic)
Joe Pass; Best Of Joe Pass . . . . (Pablo)
What Becomes Of The Brokenhearted
Jimmy & David Ruffin; Motown Superstar Series-#8-Jimmy & David
Ruffin . . . .(Motown)
Jimmy Ruffin; Motown Story-First 25 Years-C . . . .(Motown)
Paul Young; ST/Fried Green Tomatoes . . . . (MCA)
What Can I Tell My Heart
Vanessa Williams; The Comfort Zone . . . . (Wing)
What Did You Learn In School Today?
Tom Paxton; Best Of Broadside 1962-1968: Anthems Of The American
Underground From The Pages Of Broadside
Magazine-C . . . .(Smithsonian Folkways)
What Do I Have To Do?
Stabbing Westward; Wither Blister Burn & Peel . . . . (Columbia)
What Do I Know
Ricochet; Pure Country-Best Of The '90s-#2-C . . . .(Priority)
Ricochet . . . . (Columbia)
What Do The Simple Folk Do?
Julie Andrews; Best Of Julie Andrews . . . . (Rhino)
Julie Andrews & Richard Burton; Camelot . . . . (Columbia)
Original Soundtrack; Camelot . . . . (Warner Bros.)
What Do They Know
Tammy Wynette; Without Walls-C . . . . (Epic)

What Do You Say
Reba McEntire; So Good Together . . . . (MCA)
What Do You Say To That
George Strait; Always Never The Same . . . . (MCA)
What Do You Want From Life
Tubes; T.R.A.S.H. (Tubes Rarities And Smash Hits) . . . .(A&M)
Tubes . . . .(A&M)
What Do You Want From Live . . . .(A&M)
What Do You Want From Me
Pink Floyd; The Division Bell . . . .(Columbia)
What Does A Woman See In A Man
Jimmy Webb; Suspending Disbelief. . . . .(Elektra)
What Does It Take (To Win Your Love)
Junior Walker & The All Stars; Billboard Top R&B Hits-1965-
1969-C . . . .(Rhino)
Junior Walker & The All Stars' Greatest Hits . . . .(Motown)
Junior Walker & The All Stars-Anthology. . . . .(Motown)
Oldies But Goodies-#13-C . . . . (Original Sound)
What Goes On
Beatles; "Yesterday"...And Today . . . .(Capitol)
What Have I Done To Deserve This
Pet Shop Boys & Dusty Springfield; Actually . . . . (EMI)
Discography-Complete Singles Collection . . . . (EMI)
What Have They Done To The Rain
Malvina Reynolds; Best Of Broadside 1962-1968: Anthems Of The
American Underground From The Pages Of Broadside
Magazine-C . . . . (Smithsonian Folkways)
ST/Dogfight . . . . (Nouveau)
Searchers; Searchers' Greatest Hits. . . . .(Rhino)
What Have You Done For Me Lately
Janet Jackson; Control . . . .(A&M)
What If
Creed; Human Clay . . . . (Wind-up)
What If
Babyface; Face 2 Face . . . .(Arista)
What If God Smoked Cannabis
Bob Rivers; Best Of Twisted Tunes-#2 . . . . (Atlantic)
What If I Came Knocking
John Mellencamp; Human Wheels . . . .(Mercury)
What If I Said
Anita Cochran & Steve Wariner; Back To You. . . . . (Warner Bros.)
Steve Wariner & Anita Cochran; Burnin' The Roadhouse Down. . . . . .(Capitol)
What If It's You
Reba McEntire; What If It's You . . . . (MCA)
What Is Hip
Tower Of Power; In Yo' Face!-History Of Funk-#2-C . . . .(Rhino)
Tower Of Power . . . . (Warner Bros.)
What Is Life
George Harrison; All Things Must Pass . . . . (Parlophone)
Best Of George Harrison. . . . . (Capitol)
Live In Japan . . . . (Dark Horse)
What Is Love
Deee-Lite; World Clique . . . .(Elektra)
What Is Love
Howard Jones; Best Of Howard Jones 1983-1993 . . . .(Elektra)
Human's Lib . . . .(Elektra)
What Is Love
En Vogue; Funky Divas . . . .(East West)
What Is Love
Haddaway; House Of Groove. . . . .(Arista)
What Is Love
Shangri-Las; Remember The Shangri-Las At Their Best . . . .(Collectables)
What Is Love
Shirelles; Shirelles-16 Greatest Hits . . . . (Trip)
What Is Love
Marc Almond; Tenement Symphony . . . . (Sire)
What Is This Thing Called Love
Alexander O'Neal; All True Man . . . . (Tabu)
Greatest Hits Of Alexander O'Neal. . . . . (Epic)
Artie Shaw; Begin The Beguine . . . . (Bluebird)
Charlie Parker; Cole Porter Songbook . . . .(Verve)
Ella Fitzgerald; Cole Porter Songbook. . . . .(Verve)
Frank Sinatra; Frank Sinatra Sings The Select Cole Porter . . . .(Capitol)
Julie London; Julie London Sings Cole Porter. . . . . (EMI)
Kay Starr; Back To The Roots . . . . (Crescendo)
Mel Torme; Night & Day-Cole Porter Songbook-C . . . .(Verve)
What Is Truth
Johnny Cash; The Man In Black-His Greatest Hits . . . .(Legacy)
What It Feels Like For A Girl
Madonna; GHV2 . . . . (Warner Bros.)
Music. . . . . (Maverick)
What Kind Of Fool
Barbra Streisand; Collection-Greatest Hits...And More . . . . (Columbia)
One Voice . . . . (Columbia)
Barbra Streisand & Barry Gibb; Guilty . . . . (Columbia)
What Kind Of Fool
Lionel Cartwright; Chasin' The Sun. . . . . (MCA)
What Kind Of Fool Am I
Bill Evans; Solo Sessions-#1 . . . .(Milestone)

Marvin Gaye; *Hello Broadway* . . . . (Motown)
Original Broadway Cast; *Stop The World I Want To Get Off* . . . . (Polydor)
Robert Goulet; *Robert Goulet-16 Most Requested Songs* . . . . (Columbia)
Robert Goulet's Greatest Hits . . . . (Columbia)
Sammy Davis, Jr.; *Sammy Davis, Jr.'s Greatest Songs* . . . . (Curb)

What Kind Of Fool Am I
Rick Springfield; *Rick Springfield's Greatest Hits* . . . . (RCA)
Success Hasn't Spoiled Me Yet . . . . (RCA)

What Kind Of Fool Do You Think I Am
Bill Deal & The Rhondels; *Frat Rock!-#2-C* . . . . (Rhino)
Oldies But Goodies-#15-C . . . . (Original Sound)

What Kind Of Fool Do You Think I Am
Lee Roy Parnell; *Love Without Mercy* . . . . (Arista)

What Kind Of Love
Rodney Crowell; *Life Is Messy* . . . . (Columbia)

What Kind Of Love Are You On
Aerosmith; *ST/Armageddon-The Album* . . . . (Columbia)

What Kind Of Man Would I Be
Mint Condition; *Definition Of A Band* . . . . (Perspective/A&M)

What Kind Of Man Would I Be?
Chicago; *Chicago 19* . . . . (Reprise)
Chicago's Greatest Hits-1982-1989 . . . . (Full Moon)

What Makes You Think You're The One
Fleetwood Mac; *25 Years-The Chain* . . . . (Warner Bros.)

What Now My Love
Barbra Streisand; *Je m'appelle Barbra* . . . . (Columbia)
Elvis Presley; *Alternate Aloha* . . . . (RCA)
Frank Sinatra; *That's Life* . . . . (Reprise)
Frank Sinatra & Aretha Franklin; *Frank Sinatra-Duets-C* . . . . (Capitol)
Herb Alpert & The Tijuana Brass; *Herb Alpert & The Tijuana Brass-
Classics-#1* . . . . (A&M)
Herb Alpert & The Tijuana Brass-Greatest Hits-#2 . . . . (A&M)
Robert Goulet; *Robert Goulet-16 Most Requested Songs* . . . . (Columbia)
Temptations; *In A Mellow Mood* . . . . (Motown)

What Part Of No
Lorrie Morgan; *Lorrie Morgan's Greatest Hits* . . . . (BNA)
Watch Me . . . . (BNA)

What Time Is It?
Ken Nordine; *Best Of Word Jazz-#1* . . . . (Rhino)

What Time Is It?
Spin Doctors; *Pocket Full Of Kryptonite* . . . . (Epic Portrait Assoc.)

What Were You Thinkin'
Little Texas; *First Time For Everything* . . . . (Warner Bros.)

What Will My Mary Say
Jay & The Americans; *Come A Little Bit Closer-Best Of Jay & The
Americans* . . . . (Gold Rush)
Johnny Mathis; *Johnny Mathis' All-Time Greatest Hits* . . . . (Columbia)
Johnny Mathis-16 Most Requested Songs . . . . (Columbia)

What Would Happen
Meredith Brooks; *Blurring The Edges* . . . . (Capitol)

What Would You Do?
City High; *City High* . . . . (Interscope)
Now That's What I Call Music!-#7-C . . . . (Virgin)
ST/Life . . . . (Rock Land/Interscope)

What Would You Say
Dave Matthews Band; *MTV Buzz Bin-C* . . . . (Mammoth)
Under The Table And Dreaming . . . . (RCA)

What Ya Want
Ruff Ryders Featuring Eve & Nokio; *Ruff Ryders: Ride Or
Die-#1* . . . . (Ruff Ryders/IDJMG)

What You Want
DMX; *...And Then There Was X* . . . . (Ruff Ryders/IDJMG)

What You're Doing
Beatles; *For Sale* . . . . (Capitol)

Whatcha Gonna Do With A Cowboy
Chris LeDoux & Garth Brooks; *Whatcha Gonna Do With A Cowboy* . . (Liberty)

Whatcha Gonna Do?
New Riders Of The Purple Sage; *New Riders Of The Purple Sage* . . . (Columbia)
Vintage NRPS . . . . (Relix)
Tyler Collins; *Girls Nite Out* . . . . (RCA)

What'd I Say
Elvis Presley; *Collector's Gold* . . . . (RCA)
Elvis' Gold Records, Volume 4 . . . . (RCA)
Elvis In Concert . . . . (RCA)
Elvis-Greatest Hits, Volume One . . . . (RCA)
Jerry Lee Lewis; *Jerry Lee Lewis-Original Golden Hits-#2* . . . . (Sun)
Jerry Lee Lewis-Original Golden Hits-#2 . . . . (Sun)
Milestones . . . . (Rhino)
Rocket 88 . . . . (Tomato)
Rockin' My Life Away . . . . (Tomato)
John Mayall's Bluesbreakers with Eric Clapton; *John Mayall's Bluesbreakers
with Eric Clapton* . . . . (Deram)
Ray Charles; *Atlantic Rhythm & Blues 1947-1974-#4 (1958-1962)-C* . . (Atlantic)
Atlantic Soul Classics-C . . . . (Warner Special Prod.)
Frat Rock!-#3-Grandson Of Frat Rock!-C . . . . (Rhino)
Life In Music . . . . (Atlantic)
Ray Charles-Anthology . . . . (Rhino)

What'd You Come Here For?
Trina & Tamara; *Trina & Tamara* . . . . (C2/Columbia)

Whatever Happened To Saturday Night
Tim Curry; *ST/Rocky Horror Picture Show* . . . . (Rhino)
Tim Curry & Original Roxy Cast; *Rocky Horror Show* . . . . (Rhino)

What'll I Do
Nat "King" Cole; *The Vocal Classics-1947-1950* . . . . (Capitol)
Rosemary Clooney; *Rosemary Clooney Sings The Music Of Irving
Berlin* . . . . (Concord Jazz)

What's A Telephone Bill
Bootsy's Rubber Band; *The Name Is Bootsy Baby* . . . . (Warner Bros.)

What's Forever For
Michael Martin Murphey; *Best Of Michael Martin Murphey* . . . . (Liberty)
What's Forever For . . . . (EMI Special Markets)

What's Going On In Your World
George Strait; *Beyond The Blue Neon* . . . . (MCA)
Ten Strait Hits . . . . (MCA)

What's Happening, Brother
Marvin Gaye; *What's Going On* . . . . (Motown)

What's In It For Me
John Berry; *John Berry* . . . . (Liberty)

What's It Gonna Be
Busta Rhymes Featuring Janet Jackson; *E.L.E.* . . . . (Elektra)

What's It Gonna Be
Dusty Springfield; *Dusty Springfield-Anthology* . . . . (Mercury)

What's It To You
Clay Walker; *Clay Walker* . . . . (Giant)

What's Love Got To Do With It
Tina Turner; *Live In Europe* . . . . (Capitol)
Private Dancer . . . . (Capitol)
Simply The Best . . . . (Capitol)

What's My Age Again?
Blink-182; *Enema Of The State* . . . . (MCA)
Now That's What I Call Music!-#3-C . . . . (Virgin)

What's My Name?
Snoop Doggy Dogg; *Doggystyle* . . . . (Death Row)

What's New In Baltimore?
Frank Zappa; *Meets The Mothers Of Prevention* . . . . (Rykodisc)
You Can't Do That On Stage Anymore-#5 . . . . (Rykodisc)

What's New Pussycat
Tom Jones; *Tom Jones-London Collector-Greatest Hits* . . . . (London)

What's On Your Mind (Pure Energy)
Information Society; *Information Society* . . . . (Tommy Boy)

What's Stopping You
O'Jays; *Love You To Tears* . . . . (Volcano Entertainment)

What's The 411?
Mary J. Blige; *What's The 411?* . . . . (Uptown)

What's The Frequency, Kenneth?
R.E.M.; *Monster* . . . . (Warner Bros.)

What's The Ugliest Part Of Your Body
Mothers Of Invention; *We're Only In It For The Money* . . . . (Rykodisc)

What's This Life For
Creed; *My Own Prison* . . . . (Wind-up)

What's This Shit Called Love
Meatmen; *We're The Meatmen...& You Still Suck!* . . . . (Caroline)

What's Up
4 Non Blondes; *Bigger, Better, Faster, More!* . . . . (Interscope)
DJ Miko; *ESPN Presents Jock Jams-#2-C* . . . . (Tommy Boy)

What's Up
Bob James; *Joy Ride* . . . . (Warner Bros.)

What's Up With That
ZZ Top; *Rhythmeen* . . . . (RCA)

What's Your Name
Lynyrd Skynyrd; *Gold & Platinum* . . . . (MCA)
Skynyrd's Innards-Their Greatest Hits . . . . (MCA)
Street Survivors . . . . (MCA)
What's Your Name . . . . (MCA Special Prod.)

What's Your Name
Don & Juan; *WCBS FM 101 History Of Rock-For Lovers-#2-C* . . . (Collectables)

When Can I See You
Babyface; *For The Cool In You* . . . . (Epic)

When Can I See You Again
Babyface; *For The Cool In You* . . . . (Epic)

When Did We Have Sauerkraut?
Lou & Peter Berryman; *So Comfortable* . . . . (Cornbelt)

When Did You Leave Heaven?
Bob Dylan; *Down In The Groove* . . . . (Columbia)

When Did You Leave Heaven?
Hank Crawford; *After Hours* . . . . (Atlantic)

When Did You Stop Loving Me
George Strait; *ST/Pure Country* . . . . (MCA)

When I'm Sixty-Four
Beatles; *Beatles-Box Set* . . . . (Capitol)
Sgt. Pepper's Lonely Hearts Club Band . . . . (Capitol)

When It Hurts So Bad
Lauryn Hill; *The Miseducation Of Lauryn Hill* . . . . (Ruffhouse/Columbia)

When Will I Be Loved
Everly Brothers; *Everly Brothers' All-Time Greatest Hits* . . . . (Curb)
Fabulous Style Of The Everly Brothers . . . . (Rhino)
Oldies But Goodies-#11-C . . . . (Original Sound)

Linda Ronstadt; *Heart Like A Wheel* . . . . (Capitol)
Linda Ronstadt's Greatest Hits . . . . (Asylum)
When Will I See You Again
Three Degrees; *Didn't It Blow Your Mind: Soul Hits Of The*
'70s-#14-C . . . . (Rhino)
Mega Hits Dance Classics-#2-C . . . . (Priority)
When Will I See You Smile Again?
Bell Biv Devoe; *Poison* . . . . (MCA)
WBBD-Bootcity-Remix Album . . . . (MCA)
When Will It Rain
Jackyl; *Jackyl* . . . . (Geffen)
When You Ask About Love
Crickets; *45-#9-55153* . . . . (Brunswick)
Where Am I Going?
Original Cast/Gwen Verdon; *Sweet Charity* . . . . (Columbia)
Where Are You Now
Blue Rodeo; *Lost Together* . . . . (Atlantic)
Where Are You Now
Trisha Yearwood; *Real Live Woman* . . . . (MCA)
Where Are You Now
Clint Black; *Put Yourself In My Shoes* . . . . (RCA)
Where Can I Go Without You?
Nat ''King'' Cole; *Love Is The Thing* . . . . (Capitol)
Natalie Cole; *Stardust* . . . . (Elektra)
Peggy Lee; *Best Of The Decca Years-Peggy Lee* . . . . (MCA)
Where Did I Go Wrong
Steve Wariner; *Country's Greatest Hits-#3-C* . . . . (Priority)
I Got Dreams . . . . (MCA)
Steve Wariner's Greatest Hits-#2 . . . . (MCA)
Where Did I Go Wrong
UB40; *UB40* . . . . (A&M)
Where Did Our Love Go
Diana Ross; *Diana Ross-The Ultimate Collection* . . . . (Motown)
Diana Ross & The Supremes; *Every Great Motown Song-First 25*
Years-C . . . . (Motown)
Where Did Robinson Crusoe Go With Friday On Saturday Night
Ian Whitcomb; *You Turn Me On-The Very Best Of Ian*
Whitcomb . . . . (Varese Sarabande)
Where Did That Little Dog Go
Original Cast; *Snoopy* . . . . (DRG)
Where Did You Go?
Full Devil Jacket; *Full Devil Jacket* . . . . (Island/IDJMG)
Where Do Broken Hearts Go
Whitney Houston; *Whitney* . . . . (Arista)
Whitney Houston's Greatest Hits . . . . (Arista)
Where Do I Fit In
Clay Walker; *Clay Walker* . . . . (Giant)
Where Do I Go From You
Jon Secada; *Heart, Soul & A Voice* . . . . (SBK)
Where Do My Socks Go?
Ray Stevens; *Lend Me Your Ears* . . . . (Curb)
Where Do The Children Play
Cat Stevens; *Cat Stevens-Classics-#24* . . . . (A&M)
Footsteps In The Dark-Greatest Hits-#2 . . . . (A&M)
Tea For The Tillerman . . . . (A&M)
Where Do The Nights Go
Ronnie Milsap; *Heart & Soul* . . . . (RCA)
Ronnie Milsap's Greatest Hits-#3 . . . . (RCA)
Where Do We Go From Here
Chicago; *Chicago At Carnegie Hall* . . . . (Chicago)
Chicago II . . . . (Chicago)
Group Portrait . . . . (Chicago)
Where Do We Go From Here
Vanessa Williams; *Vanessa Williams' Greatest Hits-The First Ten*
Years . . . . (Mercury)
Where Do We Go From Here
Charles & Eddie; *Duophonic* . . . . (Capitol)
Where Do We Go From Here
Waylon Jennings; *Man Called Hoss* . . . . (MCA)
Where Do We Go From Here
Stacy Lattisaw & Johnny Gill; *What You Need* . . . . (Motown)
Where Do You Go
Strawbs; *Best Of The Strawbs* . . . . (A&M)
Ghosts . . . . (A&M)
Where Do You Go
No Mercy; *No Mercy* . . . . (Arista)
Where Do You Go
Frank Sinatra; *No One Cares* . . . . (Capitol)
Where Do You Keep Your Heart
Tommy Dorsey & Frank Sinatra; *Dorsey/Sinatra Sessions-#1* . . . . . . (Bluebird)
Tommy Dorsey & Frank Sinatra's All-Time Greatest Hits-#4 . . . . . . (Bluebird)
Where Does My Heart Beat Now?
Celine Dion; *Unison* . . . . (Epic)
Where Has My Little Dog Gone
Horace Heidt & His Musical Knights; *The Uncollected Horace Heidt & His*
Musical Knights-1939 . . . . (Hindsight)
Where Have All The Cowboys Gone?
Paula Cole; *This Fire* . . . . (Imago)

Where Have All The Flowers Gone
Johnny Rivers; *Best Of Johnny Rivers* . . . . (EMI)
Johnny Rivers-Anthology 1964-1977 . . . . (Rhino)
Kingston Trio; *Capitol Collectors Series-The Kingston Trio* . . . . (Capitol)
Songs Of Protest-C . . . . (Rhino)
Pete Seeger; *Essential Pete Seeger* . . . . (Vanguard)
Pete Seeger's Greatest Hits . . . . (Columbia)
Peter, Paul & Mary; *Peter, Paul and Mary* . . . . (Warner Bros.)
Wes Montgomery; *Wes Montgomery-Classics-#22* . . . . (A&M)
Where Have All The Good Times Gone
Kinks; *Kinks' Greatest Hits* . . . . (Rhino)
One For The Road . . . . (Arista)
Where Have All The Good Times Gone
David Bowie; *Bowie Pin Ups* . . . . (Rykodisc)
Where Have All The Good Times Gone
Van Halen; *Diver Down* . . . . (Warner Bros.)
Where Have All The Good Times Gone
Elton John; *Jump Up!* . . . . (MCA)
Where Is My Love?
El DeBarge; *Heart Mind & Soul* . . . . (Reprise)
Where Is The Love
Celine Dion; *Let's Talk About Love-C* . . . . (550 Music)
Jesse & Trina; *ST/Dead Presidents* . . . . (Capitol)
Roberta Flack; *Softly With These Songs-The Best Of Roberta Flack* . . . (Atlantic)
Roberta Flack & Donny Hathaway; *Roberta Flack & Donny*
Hathaway . . . . (Atlantic)
Where The Party At
Jagged Edge; *Jagged Little Thrill* . . . . (So So Def/Columbia)
Where Was I
Ricky Van Shelton; *Bridge I Didn't Burn* . . . . (Columbia)
Where Were You (When The World Stopped Turning)
Alan Jackson; *Alan Jackson-Drive* . . . . (Arista)
Where Were You When I Needed You
Bangles; *Bangles' Greatest Hits* . . . . (Columbia)
Grass Roots; *Grass Roots-All-Time Greatest Hits* . . . . (MCA)
Grass Roots-Anthology (1966-1975) . . . . (Rhino)
Where Were You When I Was Falling In Love
Lobo; *Lobo's Greatest Hits* . . . . (Curb)
Your Favorite Songs-C . . . . (Curb)
Where You Get Love
Matthew Sweet; *Blue Sky On Mars* . . . . (Freeworld/Capitol)
Where You Goin' Now
Damn Yankees; *Don't Tread* . . . . (Warner Bros.)
Where'm I Gonna Live?
Billy Ray Cyrus; *Some Gave All* . . . . (Mercury)
Where's The Love
Hanson; *Middle Of Nowhere* . . . . (Mercury)
Where's The Playground Susie
Glen Campbell; *Best Of Glen Campbell* . . . . (Capitol)
Where've You Been
Kathy Mattea; *Collection Of Hits* . . . . (Mercury)
Willow In The Wind . . . . (Mercury)
Which Side Of The Glass
George Strait; *George Strait* . . . . (MCA)
Which Way To America
Living Colour; *Vivid* . . . . (Epic)
Which Way You Goin' Billy
Poppy Family; *Super Hits Of The '70s-Have A Nice Day-#2-C* . . . . . . (Rhino)
Who
Mandy Barnett; *I've Got A Right To Cry* . . . . (Sire)
Who Am I (What's My Name)?
Snoop Doggy Dogg; *Doggystyle* . . . . (Death Row)
Who Am I?
Original Broadway Cast; *Les Miserables* . . . . (Geffen)
Who Am I?
Elvis Presley; *Memphis Record* . . . . (RCA)
Who Am I?
Petula Clark; *Greatest Hits Of Petula Clark* . . . . (Crescendo)
Who Are The Brain Police
Frank Zappa; *Disconnected Synapses* . . . . (Rhino)
Mothers Of Invention; *Freak Out* . . . . (Barking Pumpkin)
Who Are You
Who; *Hooligans* . . . . (MCA)
The Concert For New York City-C . . . . (Columbia)
Who Are You . . . . (MCA)
Who Greatest Hits . . . . (MCA)
Who's Last . . . . (MCA)
Who Are Your Heroes
Bill Blue; *Givin' Good Boys A Bad Name* . . . . (Adelphi)
Who But A Fool (Thief In Paradise)
Bonnie Raitt; *Nine Lives* . . . . (Warner Bros.)
Who Can I Count On
Patsy Cline; *Portrait Of Patsy Cline* . . . . (MCA)
Who Can I Run To
Xscape; *Off The Hook* . . . . (So So Def/Columbia)
Smooth Love: Ultimate R&B Love Songs-C . . . . (EMI)

Who Can I Turn To (When Nobody Needs Me)
Tony Bennett; *Tony Bennett Sings His All-Time Hall Of Fame Hits* .... (Columbia)

Who Can It Be Now
Men At Work; *Billboard Top Hits-1982-C* .... (Rhino)
Business As Usual .... (Columbia)

Who Dat
JT Money; *Pimpin' On Wax* .... (Tony Mercedes/Freeworld/Priority)

Who Do U Love
Deborah Cox; *Deborah Cox* .... (Arista)
Ultimate Dance Party-1997-C .... (Arista)

Who Do You Love, I Hope
Original Broadway Cast; *Annie Get Your Gun* .... (Angel)

Who Do You Think You Are
Spice Girls; *Spice* .... (Virgin)

Who Found Who
Jellybean with Elisa Fiorillo; *Jellybean-Just Visiting This Planet* .... (Chrysalis)

Who Is Egen?
Thomas Q. Seabrooke; *Music From The New York Stage (1890-1920)-#1-1890-1908-C* .... (Pearl)

Who Is He And What Is He To You
Me'Shell Ndegeocello; *Peace Beyond Passion* .... (Maverick)

Who Is It
Michael Jackson; *Dangerous* .... (Epic)

Who Knows Where The Time Goes
Fairport Convention; *Circle Dance-Hokey Pokey Charity-C* ..... (Green Linnet)
Fairport Convention-Chronicles .... (A&M)
Judy Collins; *Colors Of The Day-The Best Of Judy Collins* .... (Elektra)
Who Knows Where The Time Goes .... (Elektra)
Sandy Denny; *Best Of Sandy Denny* .... (Hannibal)
Who Knows Where The Time Goes .... (Hannibal)

Who Let The Dogs Out
Baha Men; *Who Let The Dogs Out* .... (S-Curve)

Who Needs Pictures
Brad Paisley; *Who Needs Pictures* .... (Arista)

Who Needs You
Lisa Brokop; *Every Little Girl's Dream* .... (Patriot)

Who Needs You Baby
Clay Walker; *Hypnotize The Moon* .... (Giant)

Who Played Poker With Pocahontas?
Fannie Watson; *Music From The New York Stage (1890-1920)-#4-1917-1920-C* .... (Pearl)

Who Put The Benzedrine In Mrs. Murphy's Ovaltine?
Harry Gibson; *Dr. Demento's Delights-C* .... (Warner Bros.)

Who Put The Bomp (In The Bomp, Bomp, Bomp)
Barry Mann; *Goofy Greats-C* .... (K-Tel)
Sixties Rule! Chapter Two-C .... (One Way)

Who Scared You
Doors; *Weird Scenes Inside The Gold Mine* .... (Elektra)

Who Stole The Jukebox (From Lucy's Perfume Parlor)
Johnny Bond; *Johnny Gimble's Texas Honky-Tonk Hits-C* .... (C.M.H. Prod.)

Who Threw The Overalls In Mrs. Murphy's Chowder
Bing Crosby; *Shillelaghs & Shamrocks* .... (MCA)

Who Walks In When I Walk Out
Bob Wills; *Stay A Little Longer-The Original Columbia Recordings* .... (Roswell/RCA)

Who Wants To Live Forever
Queen; *A Kind Of Magic* .... (Hollywood)
Classic Queen .... (Hollywood)
Diana, Princess Of Wales-Tribute-C .... (Columbia)

Who Wears These Shoes
Elton John; *Breaking Hearts* .... (MCA)

Who Will Buy?
Barbra Streisand; *The Second Barbra Streisand Album* .... (Columbia)
Original Broadway Cast; *Oliver!* .... (RCA Victor)
Original London Cast; *Oliver!* .... (EMI-Angel)

Who Will Call You Sweetheart
Stanley Brothers & The Clinch Mountain Boys; *Best Of Bluegrass-#1-Standards-C* .... (Mercury)

Who Will Save Your Soul
Jewel; *Pieces Of You* .... (Atlantic)

Who Will The Next Fool Be
Charlie Rich; *Charlie Rich-The Ultimate Collection* .... (Hip-O)
Lonely Weekends-The Very Best Of Charlie Rich .... (Collectables)
Jerry Lee Lewis; *The Mercury & Smash Years Recordings* ...... (Collectables)

Who?
Richard Elliot; *Best Of Richard Elliot* .... (Blue Note)

Who'll Be The Next In Line
Kinks; *Kinks' Greatest Hits* .... (Rhino)
Kinks-Size Kinkdom .... (Rhino)

Who'll Stop The Rain
Creedence Clearwater Revival; *1970* .... (Fantasy)
Cosmo's Factory .... (Fantasy)
Creedence Clearwater Revival-Chronicle .... (Fantasy)
More Creedence Gold .... (Fantasy)
Royal Albert Hall Concert .... (Fantasy)

Who's Afraid Of The Big Bad Wolf
Barbra Streisand; *Just For The Record* .... (Columbia)

The Barbra Streisand Album .... (Columbia)
L.L. Cool J; *Simply Mad About The Mouse-C* .... (Columbia)
Mormon Tabernacle Choir & Columbia Symphony Orchestra; *When You Wish Upon A Star-A Tribute To Walt Disney* .... (CBS Masterworks)

Who's Been Sleeping Here
Rolling Stones; *Between The Buttons* .... (Abkco)

Who's Been Sleeping In My Bed
Melanie; *Am I Real Or What* .... (Amherst)

Who's Behind The Door
Zebra; *Zebra* .... (Atlantic)
Zebra-Live .... (Atlantic)

Who's Cheatin' Who
Charly McClain; *Charly McClain's Greatest Hits* .... (Epic)
Encore-Charly McClain .... (Epic)
Greatest Country Hits Of The '80s-1980-C .... (Columbia)
Greatest Hits From The Jukebox-C .... (Epic)
Ten Year Anniversary .... (Epic)

Who's Cheatin' Who
Alan Jackson; *Everything I Love* .... (Arista)

Who's Crying Now
Journey; *Escape* .... (Columbia)
Journey-Greatest Hits Live .... (Columbia)
Journey's Greatest Hits .... (Columbia)
Time Cubed (Box) .... (Columbia)

Who's Driving Your Plane?
Rolling Stones; *Singles Collection-The London Years* .... (Abkco)

Who's Gonna Fill Their Shoes
George Jones; *George Jones-Super Hits* .... (Epic)
Greatest Country Hits Of The '80s-1985-C .... (Columbia)
Who's Gonna Fill Their Shoes .... (Epic)

Who's Gonna Mow Your Grass
Buck Owens; *Buck Owens' All-Time Greatest Hits-#1* .... (Curb)
Buck Owens Collection-1959-1990 .... (Rhino)

Who's Gonna Play This Old Piano
Jerry Lee Lewis; *Best Of Jerry Lee Lewis-#2* .... (Mercury)
Milestones .... (Rhino)

Who's Gonna Ride Your Wild Horses
U2; *Achtung Baby* .... (Island)

Who's Gonna Take The Garbage Out
Ernest Tubb & Loretta Lynn; *Ernest Tubb & Loretta Lynn* .... (MCA)
More Great Country Duets-C .... (MCA Special Prod.)
The Ernest Tubb/Loretta Lynn Story .... (MCA)

Who's Got The Herb?
311; *Hempilation-C* .... (Capricorn)

Who's Johnny
El DeBarge; *El DeBarge* .... (Motown)

Who's Lonely Now
Highway 101; *Country's Greatest Hits-#8-Lonely Hearts-C* .... (Priority)
Highway 101's Greatest Hits .... (Warner Bros.)
Paint The Town .... (Warner Bros.)

Who's Sorry Now
Benny Goodman; *Stompin'* .... (Drive)
Big Bill Broonzy; *Black, Brown & White* .... (Evidence Music)
Bob Crosby; *Bob Crosby & His Orchestra* .... (EPM)
Connie Francis; *Dick Clark's 21 All-Time Hits-#1-C* ....(Original Sound)
Very Best Of Connie Francis .... (Polydor)
Ella Fitzgerald; *The Intimate Ella* .... (Verve)
Esquivel; *Space-Age Bachelor Pad Music* .... (Bar/None)
Glen Gray; *Moonglow: 1930-1936* .... (Aero Space)
Nat "King" Cole; *The Billy May Sessions* .... (Capitol)
Ray Anthony; *Swing Back To The '40s* .... (Aero Space)

Who's Sucking On Grandpa's Balls Since Grandma Ain't Home Tonight?
Frogs; *My Daughter The Broad* .... (Matador)

Who's That Girl
Madonna; *ST/Who's That Girl* .... (Sire)

Who's That Girl
Eve; *Scorpion* .... (Ruff Ryders/IDJMG)

Who's That Knockin'
Genies; *WOGL Oldies 98-History Of Rock-#2-C* .... (Collectables)

Who's The Man
Toby Keith; *Boomtown* .... (Polydor Country)

Who's The Thief?
Original Cast; *Joseph & The Amazing Technicolor Dreamcoat* ....(Polydor)
Joseph & The Amazing Technicolor Dreamcoat .... (MCA)

Who's Your Baby Now
Mark Knopfler; *Sailing To Philadelphia* .... (Warner Bros.)

Who's Zoomin' Who
Aretha Franklin; *Who's Zoomin' Who?* .... (Arista)

Whose Bed Have Your Boots Been Under?
Shania Twain; *The Woman In Me* .... (Mercury)

Whose Shoulder Will You Cry On
Kitty Wells; *Kitty Wells' Greatest Hits* .... (Step One)

Why
Byrds; *Original Singles-#1-1965-1967* .... (Columbia)
The Byrds .... (Columbia)
Younger Than Yesterday .... (Columbia)

Why
Beatles; *The Beatles featuring Tony Sheridan-In The Beginning (Circa 1960)* . . . . (Polydor)
Why
Annie Lennox; *Diva* . . . . (Arista)
Why
Fleetwood Mac; *25 Years-The Chain* . . . . (Warner Bros.)
Why
Donny Osmond; *Donny Osmond's Greatest Hits* . . . . (Curb)
Why
Cathy Dennis; *Into The Skyline* . . . . (Polydor)
Why
Robert Plant; *Now And Zen* . . . . (Es Paranza)
Why Ain't I Running
Garth Brooks; *Scarecrow* . . . . (Capitol)
Why Am I A Fool For You
Jarmels; *Jarmels-Golden Classics* . . . . (Collectables)
Why Am I Drinkin'
Merle Haggard; *Going Where The Lonely Go* . . . . (Epic)
Merle Haggard-Super Hits . . . . (Epic)
Why Am I So Shy
Chiffons; *Chiffons-Golden Classics* . . . . (Collectables)
Everything You Always Wanted To Hear By . . . .(Laurie)
Why Baby Why
Charley Pride; *Charley Pride's Greatest Hits-#2* . . . .(RCA)
George Jones; *George Jones' All-Time Greatest Hits* . . . . (Epic)
George Jones-Super Hits . . . . (Epic)
Red Sovine & Webb Pierce; *Greatest Country Duets Of All Time-C* . . . . (MCA Special Prod.)
Webb Pierce; *Webb Pierce-Golden Hits-#2* . . . . (Plantation)
Willie Nelson & Waylon Jennings; *Take It To The Limit* . . . . .(Columbia)
Why Can't The English
Rex Harrison; *ST/My Fair Lady* . . . . (Columbia)
Rex Harrison/Original Cast; *My Fair Lady* . . . . (Columbia)
Why Can't We Be Friends
War; *Best Of War...And More* . . . .(Avenue)
Why Can't We Be Friends . . . .(Avenue)
Why Can't You Bring Me Home
Jay & The Americans; *Come A Little Bit Closer-Best Of Jay & The Americans* . . . . (Gold Rush)
Jay & The Americans' All-Time Greatest Hits . . . . (Rhino)
Why Can't You Come Home
Ex-Girlfriend; *X Marks The Spot* . . . .(Reprise)
Why Did I Choose You
Barbra Streisand; *Barbra Streisand's Greatest Hits* . . . .(Columbia)
My Name Is Barbra . . . . (Columbia)
Marvin Gaye; *Romantically Yours* . . . . (Columbia)
Michael Crawford; *Michael Crawford With Love* . . . . (Atlantic)
Why Did You Waste My Time?
Screamin' Jay Hawkins; *Collectables Blues Collection-#1-C* . . . . . (Collectables)
Why Didn't I Think Of That
Doug Stone; *From The Heart* . . . . (Epic)
Why Didn't You Call Me
Macy Gray; *On How Life Is* . . . . (Epic)
Why Do Fools Fall In Love
Beach Boys; *Spirit Of America* . . . .(Capitol)
Diamonds; *Best Of The Diamonds-The Mercury Years* . . . .(Mercury)
Diana Ross; *Why Do Fools Fall In Love* . . . .(RCA)
Frankie Lymon and The Teenagers; *Best Of Frankie Lymon and The Teenagers* . . . . (Rhino)
Billboard Top Rock 'N' Roll Hits-1956-C . . . . (Rhino)
ST/American Graffiti . . . . (MCA)
Joni Mitchell; *Shadows & Light* . . . . (Asylum)
Why Do Hawaiians Sing Aloha?
Fats Waller; *The Middle Years-#1-1936-1938* . . . . (Bluebird)
Why Do I Feel So Sad
Alicia Keys; *Songs In A Minor* . . . . (J)
Why Do I LoveYou?
Barbara Cook; *Oscar Winners: The Lyrics Of Oscar Hammerstein II* . . . . .(DRG)
Charlie Parker; *Yesterdays: The Jerome Kern Songbook-C* . . . .(Verve)
Margaret Whiting; *The Jerome Kern Songbook: A Fine Romance-C* . . . .(Verve)
Original Cast; *Show Boat* . . . . (RCA Victor)
ST/Show Boat . . . . (Rhino)
Stephane Grappelli; *Stephane Grappelli Plays Berlin, Kern, Porter And Rodgers & Hart* . . . .(EMI-Angel)
Why Does It Hurt So Bad
Whitney Houston; *ST/Waiting To Exhale* . . . . (Arista)
Why Does Love Got To Be So Sad?
Derek And The Dominos; *Layla* . . . . (Polydor)
Why Don't That Telephone Ring
Tracy Byrd; *Tracy Byrd* . . . . (MCA)
Why Don't We Do It In The Road
Beatles; *Beatles-Box Set* . . . . (Capitol)
The Beatles (White Album) . . . . (Capitol)
Why Don't We Get Drunk
Jimmy Buffett; *Boats Beaches Bars & Ballads* . . . . (Margaritaville)
Songs You Know By Heart-Jimmy Buffett's Greatest Hit(s) . . . .(MCA)
White Sport Coat & A Pink Crustacean . . . . (MCA)

You Had To Be There . . . . (MCA)
Why Don't You Believe Me?
Duprees; *Best Of The Duprees* . . . .(Rhino)
Best Of The Duprees . . . .(Collectables)
Joni James; *Platinum & Gold Hits* . . . . (Taragon)
Patti Page; *Patti Page-Golden Celebration* . . . .(Mercury)
Why Don't You Do Right
Benny Goodman; *Benny Goodman-16 Most Requested Songs* . . . . .(Columbia)
Ella Fitzgerald & Joe Pass; *Easy Living* . . . . (Pablo)
Peggy Lee; *Capitol Collectors Series-Peggy Lee-#1-Early Years* . . . . . (Capitol)
Peggy Lee's All-Time Greatest Hits . . . .(Curb)
Why Don't You Fall In Love With Me?
Les Elgart; *Best Of The Big Bands: Sophisticated Swing* . . . .(Columbia)
Why Don't You Get A Job?
Offspring; *Americana* . . . . (Columbia)
Why Don't You Spend The Night
Ronnie Milsap; *Milsap Magic* . . . . (RCA)
Why Don't You Write Me
Simon & Garfunkel; *Bridge Over Troubled Water* . . . .(Columbia)
Why Haven't I Heard From You
Reba McEntire; *Read My Mind* . . . . (MCA)
Reba McEntire's Greatest Hits-#3: I'm A Survivor . . . . (MCA)
Why Me Lord
Johnny Cash; *American Recordings* . . . .(American)
Why Not
Chris Botti; *Slowing Down The World* . . . . (GRP/VMG)
Why Oh Why
Celine Dion; *Let's Talk About Love-C* . . . . (550 Music)
Why Should I Cry For You?
Sting; *Fields Of Gold-The Best Of Sting 1984-1994* . . . . (A&M)
Soul Cages . . . . (A&M)
Why Walk When You Can Fly
Mary Chapin Carpenter; *Stones In The Road* . . . .(Columbia)
Why Was I Born
Billie Holiday; *Quintessential-#3-1936-1937* . . . .(Columbia)
Elisabeth Welch; *Elisabeth Welch Sings Jerome Kern* . . . . (RCA)
Frank Sinatra; *Voice: The Columbia Years-1943-1952* . . . .(Columbia)
Lena Horne; *20 Golden Pieces Of Lena Horne* . . . . (Bulldog)
The Lady . . . . (Dunhill Compact Classics)
Why Would I Say Goodbye
Brooks & Dunn; *Borderline* . . . .(Arista)
Why You Get Funky On Me?
Today; *New Formula* . . . . (Motown)
ST/House Party . . . .(Motown)
Why'd You Come In Here Lookin' Like That
Dolly Parton; *White Limozeen* . . . .(Columbia)
Will He Wait A Little Longer
Stanley Brothers; *Stanley Series-Vol. 1-#3* . . . . (Copper Creek)
Will I Ever Understand You
Berlin; *Best Of Berlin 1979-1988* . . . . (Geffen)
Count Three & Pray . . . . (Geffen)
Will I Start To Bleed
Marty Willson-Piper; *Spirit Level* . . . . (Rykodisc)
Will It Be Love By Morning
Michael Martin Murphey; *Best Of Michael Martin Murphey* . . . .(Liberty)
Heart Never Lies . . . . (Liberty)
Will It Go Round In Circles
Billy Preston; *Best Of Billy Preston* . . . . (A&M)
Billboard Top Rock 'N' Roll Hits-1973-C . . . . (Rhino)
Didn't It Blow Your Mind: Soul Hits Of The '70s-#11-C . . . .(Rhino)
Will The Circle Be Unbroken
Charlie Daniels Band & Friends; *Volunteer Jam 3 & 4* . . . . (Epic)
Joan Baez; *Country Music Album* . . . .(Vanguard)
The First 10 Years . . . .(Vanguard)
Nitty Gritty Dirt Band; *Will The Circle Be Unbroken* . . . .(EMI)
Roy Acuff; *Best Of Roy Acuff* . . . .(Liberty)
Willie Nelson; *Willie & Family Live* . . . .(Columbia)
Will The Wolf Survive
Los Lobos; *How Will The Wolf Survive* . . . . (Slash)
Waylon Jennings; *Country Classics-#6-1985-1986-C* . . . .(Universal)
New Classic Waylon . . . . (MCA)
Will The Wolf Survive . . . . (MCA)
Will There Be A Shopping Mall In Heaven?
Reverend Billy C. Wirtz; *Deep Fried & Sanctified* . . . . (Hightone)
Will You Be Loving Another Man
Bill Monroe & His Blue Grass Boys; *Essential Bill Monroe & His Blue Grass Boys* . . . .(Legacy)
Essential Bill Monroe-1945-1949 . . . .(Columbia)
Will You Be Staying After Sunday
Peppermint Rainbow; *Bubble Gum Classics-C* . . . . (MCA Special Prod.)
Will You Be There
Michael Jackson; *Dangerous* . . . . (Epic)
ST/Free Willy . . . .(MJJ Music/Work)
Will You Be There (In The Morning)
Heart; *Desire Walks On* . . . . (Capitol)
Will You Ever Save
Lisette Melendez; *True To Life* . . . . (Fever)
Will You Love Me Tomorrow
4 Seasons; *4 Seasons' Greatest Hits-#2* . . . .(Rhino)

Carole King; *Tapestry*. . . . .(Epic)
Linda Ronstadt; *Linda Ronstadt-Retrospective* . . . . (Capitol)
Lorrie Morgan; *Chicken Soup For The Woman's Soul-C* . . . . (Rhino)
Roberta Flack; *Best Of Roberta Flack* . . . . (Atlantic)
   Quiet Fire . . . . (Atlantic)
Shirelles; *Girl Groups-Story Of A Sound-C* . . . . (Rhino)
   More Dirty Dancing-C. . . . . (RCA)
   Oldies But Goodies-#14-C . . . . (Original Sound)
   Shirelles-16 Greatest Hits . . . .(Trip)
   Shirelles-Anthology 1959-1964 . . . . (Rhino)
   Wonder Women-#2-History Of Girl Group-C . . . . (Rhino)

Will You Marry Me?
Vonda Shepard; *ST/Songs From "Ally McBeal" Featuring Vonda
   Shepard*. . . . . (550/Epic)

Will You Marry Me?
Original Cast; *Pipe Dream* . . . . (RCA)
Paula Abdul; *Spellbound* . . . . (Captive)

Will You Remember?
John Charles Thomas; *Music From The New York Stage (1890-1920)-#4-
   1917-1920-C*. . . . . (Pearl)

Will You Still Be Mine
Morgana King; *Simply Eloquent*. . . . . (Muse)
Mundell Lowe; *Mundell Lowe Quartet*. . . . . (Riverside)
Red Garland Trio; *Groovy* . . . . (Prestige)
Rosemary Clooney; *Rosemary Clooney With Love* . . . .(Concord Jazz)

Wind Beneath My Wings
Bette Midler; *ST/Beaches* . . . .(Atlantic)
Gary Morris; *Chicken Soup For The Soul: I'll Be There For You-Songs Of
   Friendship, Brotherhood And Sisterhood-C* . . . . (Rhino)
   Country Love Songs-C . . . .(Warner Bros.)
   Gary Morris-Hits . . . .(Warner Bros.)
   Why Lady Why . . . .(Warner Bros.)
James Galway; *Wind Beneath My Wings* . . . . (RCA)
Lee Greenwood; *Somebody's Gonna Love You* . . . . (MCA)
Lou Rawls; *When The Night Comes* . . . .(Epic)
Roger Whittaker; *Roger Whittaker Greatest Hits* . . . . (RCA)
   Wind Beneath My Wings . . . . (RCA)
Willie Nelson; *City Of New Orleans*. . . . . (Columbia)

Windy
Association; *Association Greatest Hits* . . . .(Warner Bros.)
   Billboard Top Rock 'N' Roll Hits-1967-C . . . . (Rhino)
   Summer Of Love-#1-C . . . . (Rhino)
   Vintage Association . . . . (Fifty One West)
Wes Montgomery; *A Day In The Life* . . . . (A&M)
   Wes Montgomery-Classics-#22 . . . . (A&M)
   Wes Montgomery's Greatest Hits . . . . (A&M)

Woman
Peter And Gordon; *Best Of Peter And Gordon* . . . . (Rhino)
   History Of British Rock-#4-C . . . . (Rhino)

Woman, Woman
Union Gap Featuring Gary Puckett; *Best Of Gary
   Puckett* . . . .(Hollywood/DNA-Rounder)
   Gary Puckett And The Union Gap's Greatest Hits . . . . (Columbia)

Won'tcha Come Out Tonight
Beach Boys; *M.I.U. Album*. . . . . (Brother)

Word Up
Cameo; *Word Up* . . . . (Casablanca)

Would I Lie To You
Charles & Eddie; *Duophonic* . . . . (Capitol)

Would I Lie To You
Eurythmics; *Be Yourself Tonight* . . . . (RCA)
   Eurythmics' Greatest Hits . . . . (Arista)

Would I Lie To You
Whitesnake; *Come An' Get It* . . . .(Geffen)

Would Jesus Wear A Rolex
Ray Stevens; *Ray Stevens' Greatest Hits-#2*. . . . . (MCA)
   Ray Stevens-All-Time Greatest Comic Hits . . . . (Curb)
   Ray Stevens-Collection . . . .(MCA)

Would They Love Him Down In Shreveport
George Jones; *Hallelujah Weekend* . . . .(Epic)
Oak Ridge Boys; *Bobbie Sue* . . . .(MCA)

Would You Catch A Falling Star
John Anderson; *I Just Came Home To Count The Memories* . . . . .(Warner Bros.)
   John Anderson's Greatest Hits . . . . (Warner Bros.)

Would You Like To Take A Walk?
Ella Fitzgerald; *Ella & Friends*. . . . . (Decca Jazz)
Julia Sanderson/Frank Crumit/Leonard Joy; *The Song Is...Harry
   Warren-C* . . . . (Living Era)
Rudy Vallee & His Connecticut Yankees; *78-#22611* . . . . (Victor)

Would?
Alice In Chains; *Dirt*. . . . . (Columbia)
   ST/Singles . . . .(Epic)

Wouldn't It Be Loverly
Original Cast; *My Fair Lady*. . . . . (Columbia)
   My Fair Lady . . . . (London)

Wouldn't It Be Nice
Beach Boys; *Absolutely Best-#2*. (Capitol)
   Made In The U.S.A. . . . .(Capitol)
   Pet Sounds . . . . (Capitol)

   Still Cruisin' . . . . (Capitol)

Written In The Stars
Elton John & LeAnn Rimes; *ST/Aida* . . . . (Island)

Yes!
Chad Brock; *Yes!*. . . . . (Warner Bros.)

Yester-Me, Yester-You, Yesterday
Stevie Wonder; *My Cherie Amour* . . . . (Motown)
   Stevie Wonder's Greatest Hits-#2 . . . . (Motown)

You Beat Me To The Punch
Mary Wells; *Hitsville USA-The Motown Singles Collection-1959-
   1971-C* . . . . (Motown)
   Mary Wells' Greatest Hits . . . . (Motown)

You Can Always Explain Things Away
DeWolf Hopper; *Music From The New York Stage (1890-1920)-#1-1890-
   1908-C* . . . . (Pearl)

You're Driving Me Crazy
Art Pepper; *Return Of Art Pepper-Complete Aladdin
   Recordings-#1* . . . . (Blue Note)
Big Joe Turner; *Boss Of The Blues* . . . .(Atlantic)
Dinah Shore; *Love & Kisses Dinah* . . . . (RCA)
Frank Sinatra; *Strangers In The Night* . . . . (Reprise)
Louis Armstrong; *Louis Armstrong-Vol. 7-You're Driving Me
   Crazy* . . . . (Columbia)

RADIO, DJs, Radio Stations

   See Also: **CARS (various), FUN, HEAR, JUKEBOX, MUSIC,
   PARTY, RECORD BUSINESS, ROCK & ROCKING, SHOW BIZ,
   TELEVISION**

(Radio Station) EXP
Jimi Hendrix; *Axis: Bold As Love* . . . .(Reprise)

7 Dee Jays
Boogie Down Productions; *Edutainment (Education + Entertainment)* . . . .(Jive)

Airwaves
Thomas Dolby; *Blinded By Science* . . . . (Capitol)
   Golden Age Of Wireless . . . . (Capitol)

All The Love Is On The Radio
Tom Jones; *45-#880173* . . . . (Mercury)

AM Radio
Everclear; *Now That's What I Call Music!-#6-C*. . . . .(Virgin)
   Songs From An American Movie-#1-Learning How To Smile . . . . . . (Capitol)

Around The Dial
Kinks; *Give The People What They Want* . . . . (Arista)
   The Road . . . . (MCA)

As The Radio Plays
Rick Hearst; *Rick Hearst With Love From The Soaps* . . . . (Quality)

Atmospherics: Listen To The Radio
Tom Robinson; *Hope & Glory* . . . . (Geffen)

Baby Won't You Let Me Rock & Roll You
Ten Years After; *A Space In Time* . . . . (Columbia)

Backroads
Ricky Van Shelton; *Backroads* . . . . (Columbia)

Bad Boy/Having A Party
Luther Vandross; *Best Of Luther Vandross...The Best Of Love* . . . . (Epic)
   Forever For Always For Love . . . .(Epic)

Beat Box
Art Of Noise; *Art Of Noise* . . . . (Island)
   Best Of Art Of Noise . . . . (China)

Beau's All Night Radio Love Line
Joshua Kadison; *Painted Desert Serenade* . . . . (SBK)

Bedside Radio
Krokus; *Alive & Screamin'* . . . . (Arista)
   Metal Rendez-vous . . . . (Arista)

Canned Music
Dan Hicks & His Hot Licks; *Striking It Rich!* . . . . (MCA)

Capital Radio One
Clash; *The Story Of The Clash, Volume 1* . . . .(Epic)

Caravan
Van Morrison; *Moondance* . . . . (Warner Bros.)
Van Morrison & The Band; *The Last Waltz* . . . . (Warner Bros.)

Clap For The Wolfman
Guess Who; *Only Dance 1970-1974-C* . . . . (Rhino)

D.J.
David Bowie; *Changestwobowie* . . . . (RCA)
   Lodger . . . . (Rykodisc)
   The Singles-1969-1993. . . . . (Rykodisc)

Dance Dance Dance
Beach Boys; *Absolute Best-#1*. . . . . (Capitol)
   Beach Boys' Greatest Hits . . . . (Bovema)
   Good Vibrations-Thirty Years Of The Beach Boys . . . . (Capitol)
   Made In The U.S.A. . . . . (Capitol)
   Spirit Of America . . . . (Capitol)

Devil's Radio
George Harrison; *Cloud Nine* . . . . (Dark Horse)
   Live In Japan . . . . (Dark Horse)

Disc Jockey Jump
Gene Krupa; *Be Bop Era* . . . . (Columbia)
Do You Remember Rock 'N' Roll Radio
Ramones; *End Of The Century* . . . .(Sire)
Mania . . . .(Sire)
Don't Touch That Dial
Engelbert Humperdinck; *Live In Concert/All Of Me* . . . . (Epic)
Love's Only Love . . . . (Epic)
Every Little Thing
Beatles; *Beatles VI.* . . . . (Capitol)
Beatles-Love Songs . . . . (Capitol)
For Sale . . . . (Capitol)
Fadin' In, Fadin' Out
Tommy Overstreet; *Audiograph Alive-C.* . . . . (Audiograph)
FM
Steely Dan; *ST/FM* . . . . (MCA)
Steely Dan-Gold . . . . (MCA)
Guerrilla Radio
Rage Against The Machine; *The Battle Of Los Angeles* . . . . (Epic)
H.A.P.P.Y. Radio
Edwin Starr; *The Disco Years-#5-Must Be The Music-C.* . . . . (Rhino)
Having A Party
Norma Jean; *Norma Jean* . . . .(Bearsville)
Pointer Sisters; *Having A Party* . . . . (MCA)
Rod Stewart & Ronnie Wood; *Unplugged...And Seated* . . . . (Warner Bros.)
Sam Cooke; *Best Of Sam Cooke* . . . . (RCA)
Feel It . . . . (RCA)
Live At The Harlem Square Club . . . .(RCA)
This Is Sam Cooke . . . . (RCA)
Southside Johnny And The Asbury Jukes; *Havin' A Party With Southside Johnny And The Asbury Jukes* . . . . (Epic)
Hey D.J.
Lighter Shade Of Brown; *ST/Mi Vida Loca* . . . .(Mercury)
Hey D.J.
Bingoboys; *Best Of Bingoboys* . . . . (Atlantic)
Hey D.J.
World's Famous Supreme Team; *Jointz From Back In Da Day-C* . . . . . (Quality)
Hey Mr. D.J.
Zhane'; *Pronounced Jah-Nay* . . . .(Motown)
Hey Mr. D.J.
Army Of Lovers; *Army Of Lovers* . . . . (Giant)
How Do You Like Me Now?!
Toby Keith; *How Do You Like Me Now?!* . . . . (DreamWorks/SKG)
How To Kill A Radio Consultant
Public Enemy; *Apocalypse 91...The Enemy Strikes Black* . .(Def Jam/Columbia)
Greatest Misses . . . . (Chaos)
I Can't Say It On The Radio
Susie Allanson; *45-#75001* . . . .(Enigma)
I Can't Say It On The Radio
Girls Next Door; *Girls Next Door* . . . . (MTM)
I Love The Radio
Joey Welz; *Return Of Haley's Comet* . . . .(Caprice Int'l)
I Watched It All (On My Radio)
Lionel Cartwright; *I Watched It All On The Radio* . . . . (MCA)
I've Got A Radio
Coyote Sisters; *Coyote Sisters* . . . .(Morocco)
Jesus On The Radio
Tom T. Hall; *Ol' T's In Town* . . . .(RCA)
Just Push Play
Aerosmith; *Just Push Play* . . . .(Columbia)
King Of Sorrow
Sade; *Lovers Rock* . . . . (Epic)
KSOS
Emmylou Harris; *Ballad Of Sally Rose* . . . . (Warner Bros.)
Last Night A D.J. Saved My Life
Indeep; *Last Night A D.J. Saved My Life* . . . .(Sound Of New York)
The Disco Years-#2-On The Beat-1978-1982-C. . . . . (Rhino)
Late Night Radio
John Denver; *Windsong* . . . .(RCA)
Life Is A Rock (But The Radio Rolled Me)
Reunion; *Super Hits Of The '70s-Have A Nice Day-#13-C* . . (Rhino)
Lipstick On The Radio
Neal McCoy; *Life Of The Party* . . . . (Atlantic)
Listen To The Radio
Don Williams; *Best Of Don Williams-#3.* . . . . (MCA)
Listen To The Radio . . . . (MCA)
Kathy Mattea; *Lonesome Standard Time.* . . . .(Mercury)
Nanci Griffith; *Storms* . . . . (MCA)
Living On The Edge Of The World
Bruce Springsteen; *Tracks.* . . . .(Columbia)
Mexican Radio
Wall Of Voodoo; *Call Of The West.* . . . . (I.R.S.)
Ugly Americans In Australia . . . . (I.R.S.)
Wall Of Voodoo . . . . (I.R.S.)
Midnight On The Radio
Mike Bloomfield; *Try It Before You Buy It* . . . . (One Way)
Mohammed's Radio
Linda Ronstadt; *Living In The USA* . . . .(Asylum)

Warren Zevon; *Quiet Normal Life-Best Of Warren Zevon* . . . . (Asylum)
Stand In The Fire . . . . (Asylum)
Warren Zevon . . . . (Asylum)
Morning Man
Joy; *Joy* . . . . (Fantasy)
Mr. D.J.
Manhattans; *45-#38-07010* . . . .(Columbia)
Mr. D.J.
Joyce "Fenderella" Irby; *Maximum Thrust.* . . . .(Motown)
Mr. D.J.
Charlie Daniels Band; *Simple Man* . . . . (Epic)
Mr. D.J.
Times Two; *X2* . . . . (Reprise)
Mr. Midnight
Garth Brooks; *Scarecrow.* . . . .(Capitol)
Mr. Radio
Electric Light Orchestra; *Afterglow* . . . . (Epic)
No Answer . . . . (Jet)
Music
Madonna; *GHV2* . . . .(Warner Bros.)
Music. . . . .(Maverick)
Totally Hits-#3-C . . . . (Atlantic)
My Radio Sure Sounds Good To Me
Larry Graham; *My Radio Sure Sounds Good To Me* . . . . .(Warner Bros.)
My Radio Sure Sounds Good To Me
Oak Ridge Boys; *Oak Ridge Boys Have Arrived* . . . . (MCA)
Nightfly, The
Donald Fagen; *The Nightfly* . . . .(Warner Bros.)
Nothing But The Radio On
Dave Koz & Joey Diggs; *Dave Koz* . . . .(Capitol)
Oh Yeah
Roxy Music; *Flesh + Blood* . . . .(Atco)
Street Life-20 Great Hits . . . . (Reprise)
On My Radio
Selecter; *Selected Selections* . . . . (Chrysalis)
Too Much Pressure . . . . (Chrysalis)
On The Radio
Donna Summer; *Donna Summer's Greatest Hits.* . . . . (Casablanca)
On The Radio-Greatest Hits-Volumes I & II . . . . (Casablanca)
Summer Collection . . . .(Mercury)
Walk Away-Best Of Donna Summer-1977-1980 . . . . (Casablanca)
On The Radio
Cheap Trick; *Heaven Tonight* . . . . (Epic)
On The Radio
Emmylou Harris; *White Shoes* . . . .(Warner Bros.)
On Your Radio
Joe Jackson; *I'm The Man* . . . .(A&M)
Live 1980/86 . . . . (A&M)
Overnight Sensation (Hit Record)
Eric Carmen; *Eric Carmen-The Definitive Collection* . . . . .(Arista)
Raspberries; *Raspberries' Best Featuring Eric Carmen* . . . .(Capitol)
Pilot Of The Airwaves
Charlie Dore; *Where To Now* . . . . (Island)
Play
Jennifer Lopez; *J. Lo* . . . . (Epic)
Now That's What I Call Music!-#7-C . . . . (Virgin)
Play Those Oldies Mr. DJ
Anthony And The Sophomores; *WCBS FM 101 History Of Rock-Doo-Wop-#2-C.* . . . .(Collectables)
Potato Radio
King & Moore; *Potato Radio* . . . . (Justice)
Radio
Nick Drake; *Fruit Tree* . . . . (Hannibal)
Pink Moon . . . . (Hannibal)
Radio
Accelerators; *Accelerators* . . . . (Profile)
Radio
Vince Gill; *Best Of Vince Gill* . . . . (RCA)
Radio
Dr. Hook; *Dr. Hook-Greatest Hits & More* . . . .(Capitol)
Little Bit More . . . . (Capitol)
Radio
Eazy-E; *Eazy Duz It* . . . .(Ruthless/Priority)
Radio
Steve Miller Band; *Italian X-Rays* . . . .(Capitol)
Radio
Steve Hillage; *Motivation Radio* . . . . (Blue Plate)
Radio
Roderick Falconer; *New Nation* . . . . (United Artists)
Radio 4
Public Image Ltd.; *Second Edition* . . . .(Island)
Radio Active
Bryan Austin; *Bryan Austin* . . . . (Patriot)
Radio Control
Mick Jagger; *Primitive Cool* . . . .(Columbia)
Radio Dream Girl
Roger Voudouris; *Radio Dream Girl* . . . .(Warner Bros.)

Radio Ethiopia
Patti Smith Group; *Radio Ethiopia* . . . . (Arista)
Radio Free Europe
R.E.M.; *Eponymous* . . . .(I.R.S.)
Murmur . . . . (I.R.S.)
Radio Free Moscow
Jethro Tull; *Under Wraps* . . . .(Chrysalis)
Radio Ga Ga
Queen; *Classic Queen*. . . . . (Hollywood)
Queen-The Works . . . . (Hollywood)
Radio Girl
John Hiatt; *Slug Line*. . . . .(MCA)
Y'All Caught? Ones That Got Away, 1979-85 . . . .(Geffen)
Radio Girl
Marshall Crenshaw; *Good Evening* . . . .(Warner Bros.)
Radio Head
Talking Heads; *True Stories* . . . . (Sire)
Radio Heart
Charly McClain; *19 Hot Country Requests-#3-C* . . . .(Epic)
Charly McClain's Biggest Hits . . . .(Epic)
Greatest Country Hits Of The '80s-1985-C . . . . (Columbia)
Radio Heart . . . .(Epic)
Radio Is Broken
Frank Zappa; *Man From Utopia*. . . . . (Barking Pumpkin)
Radio Kingdom
Beach Boys; *Holland* . . . . (Brother)
Radio Land
Michael Martin Murphey; *Best Of Michael Martin Murphey*. . . . . . . (Liberty)
Heart Never Lies . . . . (Liberty)
Radio Lover
George Jones; *By Request*. . . . .(Epic)
Jones Country . . . .(Epic)
One Woman Man . . . .(Epic)
Radio M.U.S.I.C. Man
Womack & Womack; *Radio M.U.S.I.C. Man*. . . . . (Elektra)
Radio Man
World's Famous Supreme Team; *45-#99683* . . . . (Island)
Radio People
Zapp; *The New Zapp IV U.*. . . . .(Warner Bros.)
Radio Radio
Elvis Costello; *This Year's Model*. . . . .(Rykodisc)
Elvis Costello & The Attractions; *Best Of Elvis Costello & The*
Attractions . . . . (Columbia)
Radio Romance
Tiffany; *Hold An Old Friend's Hand* . . . .(MCA)
Tommy Roe; *45-#52778.*. . . . .(MCA)
Radio Silence
Boris Grebenshikov; *Radio Silence* . . . . (Columbia)
Radio Silence
Thomas Dolby; *Golden Age Of Wireless* . . . . (Capitol)
Radio Song
Dillard & Clark; *Fantastic Expedition/Through The*
Morning . . . .(Mobile Fidelity Sound Lab)
Radio Song
Joe Walsh; *Got Any Gum* . . . . (Full Moon)
Radio Song
R.E.M.; *Out Of Time.*. . . . .(Warner Bros.)
Radio Spot/Nervous Breakdown
Bobby Fuller Four; *Tapes-#1* . . . . (Rhino)
Radio Station
Run-D.M.C.; *Tougher Than Leather* . . . . (Profile)
Radio Suckers
Ice-T; *Power*. . . . . (Sire)
Radio Sweetheart
Elvis Costello; *Taking Liberties* . . . . (Columbia)
Radio Waves
Roger Waters; *Radio K.A.O.S.* . . . . (Columbia)
Radioland
Nicolette Larson; *Radioland*. . . . .(MCA)
Radios In Motion
XTC; *White Music* . . . .(Geffen)
Raised On Radio
Journey; *Raised On Radio* . . . . (Columbia)
Redneck Radio
Brother Russell; *Radio Jihad (Phone Pranks)* . . . . (Vinyl Comm.)
Reggae Radio Station
Third World; *Hold On To Love*. . . . . (Columbia)
Rex Bob Lowenstein
Mark Germino; *Rank & File* . . . . (Winter Harvest Entert.)
Roadrunner
Greg Kihn Band; *With The Naked Eye* . . . . (Beserkley)
Joan Jett; *The Hit List* . . . .(Epic)
Joan Jett & The Blackhearts; *Good Music* . . . . . . (Epic Portrait Assoc.)
Jonathan Richman & The Modern Lovers; *Beserkley Years-Best Of* . . . . (Rhino)
Modern Lovers; *Modern Lovers* . . . . (Rhino)
Rock & Roll Radio
Ramones; *End Of The Century* . . . . (Sire)

Rock 'N' Roll
Lou Reed; *Rock N Roll Animal* . . . . (RCA)
Velvet Underground; *1969: Velvet Underground Live* . . . . (Mercury)
Another View . . . . (Verve)
Live MCMXCIII . . . . (Sire)
Loaded . . . . (Warner Special Prod.)
Rock On The Radio
Firehouse; *Firehouse.* . . . . (Epic)
Rock Radio Into The Nineties & Beyond
KLF; *Chill Out* . . . . (Wax Trax)
Rockabilly On The Radio
Jack Smith & The Rockabilly Planet; *Jack Smith & The Rockabilly*
Planet . . . . (Flying Fish)
Rockin' Radio
Tom Browne; *45-#9088* . . . . (Arista)
Rodney On The ROQ
Target 13; *Rodney On The ROQ-#2-C.* . . . . (Posh Boy)
Roll Over Beethoven
Beatles; *Beatles-Box Set* . . . . (Capitol)
Rock 'N' Roll Music . . . . (Capitol)
The Beatles At The Hollywood Bowl. . . . . (Capitol)
The Beatles' Second Album . . . . (Capitol)
With The Beatles. . . . . (Parlophone)
Byrds; *The Byrds* . . . . (Columbia)
Chuck Berry; *Chuck Berry-Golden Hits* . . . . (Mercury)
Chuck Berry's Greatest Hits. . . . . (Everest)
Cruisin'-1956-C. . . . . (Increase)
Oldies But Goodies-#10-C . . . . (Original Sound)
The Chess Box-Chuck Berry. . . . . (Chess)
Electric Light Orchestra; *Afterglow.* . . . . (Epic)
Ole ELO . . . . (Jet)
Russian Radio
Red Flag; *Naive Art.* . . . . (Enigma Capitol)
Sell Out
Reel Big Fish; *Turn The Radio Off* . . . . (Mojo Music/Universal)
She Got The Radio
Cory Hart; *First Offense* . . . . (EMI)
Shut Up And Drive
Chely Wright; *Woman In The Moon* . . . .(Polydor Country)
Sleepin' With The Radio On
Charly McClain; *Charly McClain's Greatest Hits* . . . . (Epic)
Surround Me With Love . . . . (Epic)
Ten Year Anniversary . . . . (Epic)
Song On The Radio
Al Stewart; *Best Of Al Stewart* . . . . (Arista)
Time Passages . . . . (Arista)
Jane Gillman; *Jane Gillman* . . . . (Green Linnet)
Spirit Of Radio
Rush; *Exit...Stage Left* . . . . (Mercury)
Permanent Waves . . . . (Mercury)
Rush-Chronicles . . . . (Mercury)
State Trooper
Bruce Springsteen; *Nebraska* . . . . (Columbia)
The Sopranos-Music From The HBO Original
Series . . . . (Sony Music Soundtrax)
Stone Cold Country
Gibson/Miller Band; *Where There's Smoke* . . . . (Epic)
Sunday Morning Radio
Sha Na Na; *Sh-Boom* . . . . (Accord)
Surfin' U.S.A.
Beach Boys; *Absolute Best-#1.* . . . . (Capitol)
Best Of The Beach Boys . . . . (Capitol)
Billboard Top Rock 'N' Roll Hits-1963-C . . . . (Rhino)
Endless Summer . . . . (Capitol)
Made In The U.S.A. . . . . (Capitol)
Texas Radio Horror
Strip Mind; *What's In Your Mouth* . . . .(Sire)
Thank God For The Radio
Kendalls; *Kendalls-20 Favorites.* . . . . (Epic)
Movin' Train . . . . (Mercury)
Theme From "Midnight Caller"
Original Soundtrack; *Television's Greatest Hits-#7-Cable Ready-C* . . . . (TVT)
Theme From "WKRP In Cincinnati"
Original Soundtrack; *CBS: The First 50 Years* . . . . (TVT)
Television's Greatest Hits-#3-1970s & 1980s-C . . . . (TVT)
Steve Carlisle; *Steve Carlisle Sings WKRP* . . . . (MCA)
There Ain't Nothin' Wrong With The Radio
Aaron Tippin; *Read Between The Lines* . . . . (RCA)
Today's Hit Country-C. . . . . (K-Tel)
They're Playin' Our Song
Neal McCoy; *Neal McCoy's Greatest Hits* . . . .(Atlantic)
You Gotta Love That! . . . .(Atlantic)
This D.J.
Warren G.; *Regulate...G Funk Era* . . . . (Violator)
This Is Radio Clash
Clash; *On Broadway* . . . . (Epic)
The Story Of The Clash, Volume 1 . . . . (Epic)
This Is Radio Etienne
Saint Etienne; *Foxbase Alpha* . . . . (Warner Bros.)

This Is Something For The Radio
Biz Markie; *Goin' Off* . . . . (Cold Chillin')
Top 40 Radio (The History Of Rock)
Joey Welz; *Return Of Haley's Comet* . . . .(Caprice Int'l)
Turn On The Radio
Tommy Page; *Paintings In My Mind* . . . .(Sire)
Turn On The Radio
Rollers; *Elevator* . . . . (Arista)
Turn On Your Radio
Nilsson; *Son Of Schmilsson* . . . .(RCA)
Turn That Radio On
Ronnie Milsap; *Back To The Grindstone* . . . .(RCA)
  Club . . . .(RCA)
Turn Up The Music
Sammy Hagar; *All Night Long* . . . . (One Way)
  Best Of Sammy Hagar . . . .(Capitol)
  Musical Chairs . . . . (Capitol)
Turn Up The Radio
Autograph; *Sign in Please* . . . .(RCA)
Turn Up The Radio
Rockets; *Live Rockets* . . . . (Capitol)
Turn Yo' Radio On
Leadbelly; *Gwine Dig A Hole To Put The Devil In* . . . . (Rounder)
Turn Your Radio On
Chris Hillman; *Desert Rose* . . . .(Sugar Hill)
John Hartford; *Aereo-Plain* . . . . (Warner Bros.)
Ray Stevens; *Country Music Classics-#4-1970-1975-C* . . . . (K-Tel)
  Ray Stevens' Greatest Hits . . . . (MCA)
Roy Acuff; *Best Of Roy Acuff* . . . . (Liberty)
  Roy Acuff's Greatest Hits . . . .(Elektra)
Turn Your Radio On, Kentucky
Blue Sky Boys; *Sunny Side Of Life* . . . . (Rounder)
Video Killed The Radio Star
Bruce Woolley & The Camera Club; *Bruce Woolley & The*
  Camera Club . . . . (Columbia)
Buggles; *Age Of Plastic* . . . .(Island)
  Rock Of The '80s-#2-C . . . . (Priority)
  The Island Story-1962-1987-25th Anniversary-C . . . . (Island)
Voice On The Radio
Andre Cymone; *Livin' In The New Wave* . . . . (Columbia)
Voice On The Radio
Sheena Easton; *Sheena Easton* . . . . (EMI)
W.O.L.D.
Harry Chapin; *Gold Medal Collection* . . . . (Elektra)
  Greatest Stories-Live . . . . (Elektra)
  Harry Chapin-Anthology . . . . (Elektra)
  Short Stories . . . . (Elektra)
Wasp (Texas Radio & The Big Beat)
Doors; *Alive She Cried* . . . . (Elektra)
  Doors-Classics . . . . (Elektra)
  L.A. Woman . . . . (Elektra)
  Weird Scenes Inside The Gold Mine . . . . (Elektra)
We Want The Airwaves
Ramones; *Pleasant Dreams* . . . .(Sire)
  Ramones Mania . . . .(Sire)
Where It's At
Beck; *Odelay* . . . .(David Geffen Co.)
Yesterday Once More
Carpenters; *Carpenters-Classics-#2* . . . . (A&M)
  Carpenters-The Singles 1969-1973 . . . . (A&M)
  Now & Then . . . .(A&M)
  Yesterday Once More . . . . (A&M)
You Turn Me On I'm A Radio
Gail Davies; *Gail Davies' Greatest Hits* . . . .(Little Chickadee)
Joni Mitchell; *For The Roses* . . . . (Asylum)
Joni Mitchell with Tom Scott & The L.A. Express; *Miles Of Aisles* . . . (Asylum)
You Turn Me On I'm A Radio
Ed Bruce; *Homecoming* . . . .(RCA)

RAIN, Fog, Hurricanes, Lightning, Storms, Thunder, Tornado

See Also: CRYING, DANGER & DISASTER, DROWN, FLOOD,
LIGHTHOUSES, NATURE, OCEAN, RAINBOWS, RIVERS,
SADNESS, SAILING, SHIPS, SKY, SUN, TROUBLE, WARNINGS,
WATER, WIND

100% Chance Of Rain
Gary Morris; *Anything Goes* . . . . (Warner Bros.)
  Gary Morris-Hits . . . . (Warner Bros.)
3am
Matchbox Twenty; *Yourself Or Someone Like You* . . . . (Lava)
Acid Rain
John Martyn; *Sapphire* . . . .(Island)
Acid Rain
Saigon Kick; *Saigon Kick* . . . . (Third Stone)

After The Rain
John Coltrane; *Best Of John Coltrane-His Greatest Years* . . . . (MCA)
  Impressions . . . .(MCA/Impulse)
  The Gentle Side Of John Coltrane . . . .(GRP)
After The Rain
Nelson; *After The Rain* . . . . (David Geffen Co.)
After The Rain
Bruce Cockburn; *Dancing In The Dragon's Jaws* . . . . (Columbia)
After The Rain Has Fallen
Sting; *Brand New Day* . . . .(A&M)
After The Storm
Crosby, Stills & Nash; *After The Storm* . . . . (Atlantic)
Ain't No Sunshine When She's Gone
Bill Withers; *Bill Withers' Greatest Hits* . . . .(Columbia)
  Bill Withers Live At Carnegie Hall . . . .(Columbia)
Michael Jackson; *Original Soul Of Michael Jackson* . . . .(Motown)
Alabama Rain
Jim Croce; *Down The Highway* . . . . (Atlantic)
  Time In A Bottle/Jim Croce's Greatest Love Songs . . . . (Atlantic)
American Storm
Bob Seger & The Silver Bullet Band; *Like A Rock* . . . .(Capitol)
And It Stoned Me
Van Morrison; *Best Of Van Morrison* . . . . (Polydor)
  Moondance . . . . (Warner Bros.)
And The Heavens Cried
Anthony Newley; *Genuis Of Anthony Newley* . . . . (London)
Another Rainy Day In New York City
Chicago; *Chicago X* . . . .(Chicago)
  If You Leave Me Now . . . . (Chicago)
Another Rainy Night
Queensryche; *Empire* . . . . (EMI)
April In Portugal
Eartha Kitt; *Best Of Eartha Kitt* . . . . (MCA)
April Mist
Tom Harrell; *Visions* . . . . (Contemporary)
April Showers
Al Jolson; *Best Of Al Jolson* . . . . (MCA)
  The Al Jolson Story-#2 . . . . (MCA)
Judy Garland; *Hits Of Judy Garland* . . . . (Capitol)
  Judy . . . .(Capitol)
Arkansas Traveler
Albert Lee; *Speechless* . . . . (MCA)
Fiddlin' Red Herron; *Red, White & Bluegrass-C* . . . .(C.M.H. Prod.)
Floyd Cramer; *Country Gold-Floyd Cramer* . . . . (Step One)
Mark O'Connor; *Championship Years* . . . . (Country Music Foundation)
Michelle Shocked; *Arkansas Traveler* . . . .(Mercury)
Sam Hinton; *Newport Broadside: Newport Folk Festival-1963-C* . . .(Vanguard)
Ashes The Rain And I
James Gang; *Best Of The James Gang* . . . . (MCA)
  James Gang Rides Again . . . . (MCA)
  James Gang-16 Greatest Hits . . . . (MCA)
August Rain
Murray Attaway; *In Thrall* . . . . (David Geffen Co.)
Baby The Rain Must Fall
Glenn Yarbrough; *Best Of Glenn Yarbrough* . . . . (RCA)
  Nipper's Greatest Hits Of The '60s-#1-C . . . . (RCA)
Bangkok Rain
Cult; *Ceremony* . . . . (Sire)
Before The Deluge
Jackson Browne; *Late For The Sky* . . . . (Asylum)
Joan Baez; *Honest Lullaby* . . . .(Portrait)
Black Summer Rain
Eric Clapton; *No Reason To Cry* . . . .(RSO)
Blame It On The Rain
Milli Vanilli; *Girl You Know It's True* . . . .(Arista)
Blue Eyes Crying In The Rain
Roy Acuff; *Roy Acuff's Greatest Hits* . . . .(Elektra)
Roy Acuff and his Smoky Mountain Boys; *Columbia Country Classics-#1-*
  Golden Age-C . . . .(Columbia)
Willie Nelson; *Columbia Country Classics-#5-A New Tradition-C* . . .(Columbia)
  Greatest Hits (& Some That Will Be) . . . .(Columbia)
  Red Headed Stranger . . . . (Columbia)
  ST/Honeysuckle Rose . . . . (Columbia)
Blue Umbrella
John Prine; *Sweet Revenge* . . . . (Atlantic)
Blue Umbrella
Ed Bruce; *Ed Bruce* . . . . (MCA)
Box Of Rain
Grateful Dead; *American Beauty* . . . . (Warner Bros.)
Bride Of Rain Dog
Tom Waits; *Rain Dogs* . . . .(Island)
Bridge Washed Out
Warner Mack; *Country's Greatest Hits-#3-C* . . . . (MCA)
  MCA Records 30 Years Of Hits-1958-1988-C. . . . . (MCA)
Bring On The Rain
Jo Dee Messina with Tim McGraw; *Burn* . . . .(Curb)
Buckets Of Rain
Bob Dylan; *Blood On The Tracks* . . . . (Columbia)

Bus Stop
Hollies; *Best Of The Hollies* . . . . (EMI)
   History Of British Rock-#3-C . . . . (Rhino)
   The Hollies' Greatest Hits . . . .(Epic)

But I Do Love You
LeAnn Rimes; *I Need You* . . . . (Curb)

Can You Stand The Rain
New Edition; *Heart Break* . . . . (MCA)

Can You Stop The Rain
Grover Washington, Jr.; *Soulful Strut* . . . . (Columbia)
Peabo Bryson; *Can You Stop The Rain* . . . . (Columbia)

Candy Rain
Soul For Real; *Candy Rain* . . . . (Uptown/MCA)

Cannibals
Mark Knopfler; *Golden Heart* . . . . (Warner Bros.)

Can't Stop My Heart From Loving You
Aaron Neville; *The Tattooed Heart* . . . . (A&M)
O'Kanes; *Greatest Country Hits Of The '80s-1987-C* . . . . (Columbia)
   More Hot Country Requests-#2-C . . . .(Epic)
   O'Kanes . . . . (Columbia)

Can't Stop The Rain
Subdudes; *Colossal Head* . . . . (Warner Bros.)

Catch A Falling Star
Perry Como; *Como's Golden Records* . . . . (RCA)
   Nipper's Greatest Hits Of The '50s-#1-C . . . . (RCA)
   Perry Como-Pure Gold . . . . (RCA)
   Perry Como's All-Time Greatest Hits-#1 . . . . (RCA)
   This Is Perry Como . . . . (RCA)

Chain Lightning
Steely Dan; *Katy Lied* . . . .(MCA)
   Steely Dan-Gold . . . .(MCA)

Chain Lightning
Rush; *Presto* . . . .(Atlantic)

Chain Lightning
38 Special; *Special Forces* . . . . (A&M)

Cloudburst
Jon Hendricks; *Jon Hendricks* . . . .(Enja)
Lambert, Hendricks & Bavan; *Swingin' Till The Girls Come Home* . . (Bluebird)
Lambert, Hendricks & Ross; *Best Of Lambert, Hendricks & Ross* . . . (Columbia)
   Lambert, Hendricks & Ross & Ike Isaacs Trio: Everybody's Boppin' . . . . (Columbia)
Pointer Sisters; *Retrospect* . . . .(MCA)

Cold Rain
Crosby, Stills & Nash; *CSN* . . . .(Atlantic)

Cold Rain And Snow
Grateful Dead; *Grateful Dead (Skull & Roses)* . . .(Warner Bros.)
   Steal Your Face . . . . (Grateful Dead)

Cold Rain In Kansas
Don Lange; *Natural Born Heathen* . . . . (Flying Fish)

Coloured Rain
Traffic; *Best Of Traffic* . . . . (Island)
   Mr. Fantasy . . . . (Island)

Come In From The Rain
Captain & Tennille; *Captain & Tennille's Greatest Hits* . . . . (A&M)
Melissa Manchester; *Melissa Manchester's Greatest Hits* . . . . (Arista)

Come Rain Or Come Shine
Ella Fitzgerald; *Harold Arlen Songbook-#2* . . . . (Verve)
Frank Sinatra; *Very Best Of Frank Sinatra* . . . . (Reprise)
Frank Sinatra & Gloria Estefan; *Frank Sinatra-Duets-C* . . (Capitol)
Judy Garland; *America's Treasure* . . . .(Dunhill Compact Classics)
   Hits Of Judy Garland . . . . (Capitol)
   Judy . . . . (Capitol)
   Judy Garland-At Carnegie Hall . . . . (Capitol)
Michael Crawford; *With Love* . . . .(Atlantic)

Come Some Rainy Day
Wynonna; *The Other Side* . . . . (Curb/MCA)

Cry Like A Rainstorm
Bonnie Raitt; *Takin' My Time* . . . . (Warner Bros.)
Linda Ronstadt; *Cry Like A Rainstorm-Howl Like The Wind* . . . . (Elektra)

Crying In The Rain
Art Garfunkel & James Taylor; *Up 'Til Now* . . . . . . (Columbia)
Dave Edmunds & Nick Lowe; *Dave Edmunds-Anthology-1968-1990* . . . (Rhino)
Everly Brothers; *Everly Brothers' All-Time Greatest Hits* . . . . (Curb)
   Golden Hits Of The Everly Brothers . . . . (Warner Bros.)
   Very Best Of The Everly Brothers . . . .(Warner Bros.)
Londonbeat; *In The Blood* . . . . (Radioactive/MCA)
Rockpile; *Seconds Of Pleasure* . . . . (Columbia)
Tammy Wynette; *Tammy Wynette's Biggest Hits* . . . .(Epic)
   Tears Of Fire-25th Anniversary Collection . . . .(Epic)

Crying In The Rain
A-Ha; *East Of The Sun-West Of The Moon* . . . . . .(Warner Bros.)
   Moments In Love-C . . . .(EMI)

Crying In The Rain
Whitesnake; *Saints & Sinners* . . . .(Geffen)
   Whitesnake . . . .(Geffen)

Day That She Left Tulsa (In A Chevy)
Wade Hayes; *When The Wrong One Loves You Right* . . . . . . (Columbia/DKC)

December African Rain
Juluka; *Best Of Juluka* . . . . (Rhythm Safari)

Stand Your Ground . . . . (Warner Bros.)

Desert Rose
Sting; *Brand New Day* . . . . (A&M)

Diamonds On My Windshield
Tom Waits; *The Heart Of Saturday Night* . . . .(Asylum)
   Tom Waits-Anthology . . . .(Asylum)

Don't Count The Rainy Days
John Conlee; *In My Eyes* . . . . (MCA)
Michael Martin Murphey; *Best Of Michael Martin Murphey* . . . . . . (Liberty)
   Heart Never Lies . . . . (Liberty)

Don't Feel Like Cryin'
Abra Moore; *Strangest Places* . . . . (Arista Austin)

Don't Rain On My Parade
Barbra Streisand; *Barbra Streisand...and other musical instruments* . . . . (Columbia)
   Barbra Streisand's Greatest Hits . . . . (Columbia)
   Live Concert At The Forum . . . . (Columbia)
   Original Cast-Funny Girl . . . . (Capitol)
   ST/Funny Girl . . . . (Columbia)

Don't Sleep In The Subway
Frank Sinatra; *Frank Sinatra* . . . . (Reprise)
Petula Clark; *Petula Clark's Greatest Hits* . . . .(Crescendo)
   Summer Of Love-#1-C . . . . (Rhino)

Down In The Flood
Bob Dylan; *Bob Dylan's Greatest Hits-#2* . . . . (Columbia)
Chris Smither; *Another Way To Find You* . . . .(Hightone)
Jimmy LaFave; *Trail* . . . .(Bohemia Beat)
Sandy Denny; *North Star Grassman And The Ravens* . . . . . .(Hannibal)

Down Under
Men At Work; *Business As Usual* . . . . (Columbia)

Downbound Train
Chuck Berry; *Chuck Berry-The Anthology* . . . . (MCA)

Dreams
Corrs; *Legacy-A Tribute To Fleetwood Mac's Rumours-C* . . . . (Lava)
Fleetwood Mac; *25 Years-The Chain* . . . .(Warner Bros.)
   Fleetwood Mac Live . . . .(Warner Bros.)
   Fleetwood Mac's Greatest Hits . . . .(Warner Bros.)
   Rumours . . . .(Warner Bros.)

Driving Rain
Paul McCartney; *Driving Rain* . . . . (Columbia)

Dry Lightning
Bruce Springsteen; *The Ghost Of Tom Joad* . . . . (Columbia)

Earth, The Sun, The Rain
Color Me Badd; *Now & Forever* . . . .(Giant)

Earthquake & Hurricane
Tina Turner; *Rough* . . . .(United Artists)
Willie Dixon; *Mighty Earthquake & Hurricane* . . . . (Pausa)

Elegantly Wasted
INXS; *Elegantly Wasted* . . . . (Mercury)

Everybody's Talkin'
Nilsson; *Everybody's Talkin': The Encore Collection* . . . (BMG Special Prod.)
   ST/Forrest Gump . . . .(Epic/Sony Music Soundtrax)
   ST/Midnight Cowboy . . . . (EMI)
Willie Nelson; *Best Of Willie* . . . . (RCA)
   Sweet Memories . . . . (RCA)

Faith In You
Steve Wariner; *Faith In You* . . . . (Capitol)

Feels Like Love
Vince Gill; *Let's Make Sure We Kiss Goodbye* . . . . (MCA)

Fire And Rain
James Taylor; *James Taylor's Greatest Hits* . . . .(Warner Bros.)
   Sweet Baby James . . . .(Warner Bros.)
   The Concert For New York City-C . . . . (Columbia)
Sammy Kershaw; *Red Hot + Country-C* . . . . (Mercury)

Fire Escape
Fastball; *All The Pain Money Can Buy* . . . . (Hollywood)

Fixing A Hole
Beatles; *Sgt. Pepper's Lonely Hearts Club Band* . . . . . . (Capitol)

Flood And The Storm
Woody Guthrie; *Ballads Of Sacco & Vanzetti* . . . (Smithsonian Collection)

Flowers Never Bend With The Rainfall
Simon & Garfunkel; *Collected Works* . . . . (Columbia)
   Parsley Sage Rosemary & Thyme . . . . (Columbia)

Fog In Monterey
Mary Black; *No Frontiers* . . . .(Gift Horse)

Fog, The
Kate Bush; *Sensual World* . . . . (Columbia)

Foggy Day
Billie Holiday; *All Or Nothing At All* . . . . (Verve)
Dick Hyman; *Music Of 1937-Maybeck Recital Hall-#3* . . . . . . (Concord Jazz)
Ella Fitzgerald; *Ella In Rome-Birthday Concert* . . . . . . (Verve)
   George & Ira Gershwin Songbook . . . . (Verve)
Ella Fitzgerald & Joe Pass; *Take Love Easy* . . . . (Pablo)
Ella Fitzgerald & Louis Armstrong; *Ella & Louis* . . . . . . (Verve)
Frank Sinatra; *Songs For Young Lovers & Swing Easy* . . . . (Capitol)
Fred Astaire; *Fred Astaire Sings* . . . . (MCA)
   Starring Fred Astaire . . . . (Columbia)
Judy Garland; *Judy Garland-At Carnegie Hall* . . . . (Capitol)

Wynton Marsalis; *Marsalis Standard Time-#1* . . . . (Columbia)

Foggy Mountain Breakdown
Earl Scruggs & Friends; *Earl Scruggs And Friends-C.* . . . . (MCA)
Flatt & Scruggs; *20 All-Time Great Recordings* . . . . (Columbia)
  Truckers' Jukebox-10 All-Time Radio Requests-C . . . . (Legacy)
Lester Flatt; *Foggy Mountain Breakdown* . . . . (RCA)
  Live Bluegrass Festival . . . . (RCA)
Tony Trischka; *Banjoland* . . . . (Rounder)

Foggy Streets Of London
Special EFX; *Special EFX* . . . . (GRP)

Foggy Waterfall
Left Banke; *History Of The Left Banke* . . . . (Rhino)

Foggy, Foggy Dew
Burl Ives; *Best Of Burl Ives* . . . . (MCA)

Fogtown
Michelle Shocked; *Texas Campfire Tapes* . . . . (Mercury)

Fool In The Rain
Led Zeppelin; *In Through The Out Door* . . . . (Swan Song)
  Led Zeppelin-Box Set . . . . (Atlantic)

For A Change
Neal McCoy; *You Gotta Love That!* . . . . (Atlantic)

Fragile
Sting; *...Nothing Like The Sun* . . . . (A&M)
  America: A Tribute To Heroes-C . . . . (Interscope)
  Fields Of Gold-The Best Of Sting 1984-1994 . . . . (A&M)

Garden In The Rain
Four Aces; *Best Of The Four Aces* . . . . (MCA)
  Four Aces' 20 Greatest Hits . . . . (Everest)
  Precious Memories . . . . (Accord)

Gentle Rain
Astrud Gilberto; *Compact Jazz-Best Of Bossa Nova Compact Jazz-C* . . . (Verve)
  The Silver Collection: The Astrud Gilberto Album . . . . (Verve)
Tony Bennett; *The Movie Song Album* . . . . (Columbia)

Gentle Rains Of Home
George Morgan; *45-#32886* . . . . (Decca)

God Of Thunder
Kiss; *Alive II* . . . . (Casablanca)
  Destroyer . . . . (Casablanca)
  Double Platinum . . . . (Mercury)

Grease Megamix
Grease Megamix; *Pure Disco* . . . . (A&M)

Hard Rain's Gonna Fall
Bob Dylan; *Bob Dylan's Greatest Hits-#2* . . . . (Columbia)
  Concert For Bangladesh-C . . . . (Capitol)
  Freewheelin' . . . . (Columbia)
Bryan Ferry; *Street Life-20 Great Hits* . . . . (Reprise)
  These Foolish Things . . . . (Reprise)
Edie Brickell & New Bohemians; *ST/Born On The Fourth Of July* . . . . . (MCA)
Joan Baez; *Farewell Angelina* . . . . (Vanguard)
  The First 10 Years . . . . (Vanguard)

Have You Ever Seen The Rain
Creedence Clearwater Revival; *1970* . . . . (Fantasy)
  Creedence Clearwater Revival-Chronicle . . . . (Fantasy)
  Pendulum . . . . (Fantasy)

Heart Like A Hurricane
Larry Stewart; *Heart Like A Hurricane* . . . . (Columbia)

Here Comes The Rain
Mavericks; *Music For All Occasions* . . . . (MCA)

Here Comes The Rain Again
Eurythmics; *Eurythmics' Greatest Hits* . . . . (Arista)
  Eurythmics' Greatest Hits . . . . (Arista)

Here's That Rainy Day
Frank Sinatra; *The Capitol Years* . . . . (Capitol)
Gene Ammons; *The Boss Is Back* . . . . (Prestige)
Kenny Rankin; *Kenny Rankin Album* . . . . (Little David)
Rosemary Clooney; *Rosemary Clooney Sings Ballads* . . . . (Concord Jazz)
Tony Bennett; *Perfectly Frank* . . . . (Columbia)

Hi-Lili, Hi-Lo
Anne Murray; *There's A Hippo In My Tub* . . . . (Capitol)
Ray Conniff; *Encore! 16 Most Requested Songs* . . . . (Legacy)

Holes In The Floor Of Heaven
Steve Wariner; *Burnin' The Roadhouse Down* . . . . (Capitol)

Homeless
Paul Simon; *Graceland* . . . . (Warner Bros.)

Horse With No Name
America; *America* . . . . (Warner Bros.)
  America Live . . . . (Warner Bros.)
  Billboard Top Rock 'N' Roll Hits-1972-C . . . . (Rhino)
  History-Greatest Hits . . . . (Warner Bros.)

Hurricane
Joe Memphis & Larry Collins; *Rockabilly Stars-#3-C* . . . . (Epic)

Hurricane
Bob Dylan; *Desire* . . . . (Columbia)

Hurricane
Leon Everette; *Classic Country-#1-C* . . . . (Renaissance)

Hurricane
Neil Diamond; *Heartlight* . . . . (Columbia)

Hurricane Eye
Paul Simon; *You're The One* . . . . (Warner Bros.)

I Love A Rainy Night
Eddie Rabbitt; *Eddie Rabbitt's All-Time Greatest Hits* . . . . (Warner Bros.)
  Eddie Rabbitt's Greatest Hits-#2 . . . . (Warner Bros.)
  Horizon . . . . (Elektra)
  Number 1's . . . . (Warner Bros.)
  Ten Years Of Greatest Hits . . . . (Capitol)

I Made It Through The Rain
Barry Manilow; *Barry* . . . . (Arista)
  Barry Manilow's Greatest Hits-#3 . . . . (Arista)

I Need You
LeAnn Rimes; *ST/Jesus-The Epic Mini-Series* . . . . (Sparrow/Curb/Capitol)

I Sure Can Smell The Rain
BlackHawk; *BlackHawk* . . . . (Arista)

I Think It's Gonna Rain Today
Bette Midler; *ST/Beaches* . . . . (Atlantic)
Judy Collins; *In My Life* . . . . (Elektra)
Neil Diamond; *Rainbow* . . . . (MCA)
  Stones . . . . (MCA)
Randy Newman; *12 Songs* . . . . (Reprise)
  Randy Newman . . . . (Warner Archives)

I Wish It Would Rain
Temptations; *16 #1 Hits From The Late '60s-C* . . . . (Motown)
  All The Million-Sellers . . . . (Motown)
  Billboard Top R&B Hits-1968-C . . . . (Rhino)
  Compact Command Performances-Temptations . . . . (Motown)
  Motown Story-First 25 Years-C . . . . (Motown)
  Temptations-Anthology-The Best Of The Temptations . . . . . (Motown)

I Wish It Would Rain
Nanci Griffith; *Little Love Affairs* . . . . (MCA)

I Wish It Would Rain Down
Phil Collins; *...But Seriously* . . . . (Atlantic)

I'll Follow The Sun
Beatles; *Beatles '65* . . . . (Capitol)
  Beatles-Box Set . . . . (Capitol)
  Beatles-Love Songs . . . . (Capitol)
  For Sale . . . . (Capitol)

I'm No Stranger To The Rain
Keith Whitley; *Don't Close Your Eyes* . . . . (RCA)
  Keith Whitley's Greatest Hits . . . . (RCA)

In The Rain
Xscape; *ST/Love Jones* . . . . (Columbia)

Into Each Life Some Rain Must Fall
Ella Fitzgerald; *Ella & Friends* . . . . (Decca Jazz)
Ink Spots; *Encore Of Golden Hits-Ink Spots* . . . . (Juke Box Treasures)

Ironic
Alanis Morissette; *Jagged Little Pill* . . . . (Maverick)

Is It Raining At Your House
Vern Gosdin; *10 Years Of Greatest Hits Newly Recorded* . . . . (Columbia)
  Chiseled In Stone . . . . (Columbia)
  Greatest Country Hits Of The '90s-1991-C . . . . (Columbia)

It Always Rains On Saturday
Reba McEntire; *Sweet Sixteen* . . . . (MCA)

It Always Rains On Sundays
Box; *Pleasure & The Pain* . . . . (Capitol)

It Might As Well Rain Until September
Carole King; *More American Graffiti-C* . . . . (MCA)

It Never Rains In Southern California
Albert Hammond; *Rock Artifacts-From The Vaults-#2-C* . . . . (Legacy)
  Super Hits Of The '70s-Have A Nice Day-#10-C . . . . (Rhino)
Tony Toni Tone; *Revival* . . . . (Wing)

It's Gonna Rain
Take 6; *Join The Band-C* . . . . (Reprise)

It's Just The Rain
Journey; *Trial By Fire* . . . . (Columbia)

It's Raining Again
Supertramp; *Famous Last Words* . . . . (A&M)
  Supertramp-Classics-#9 . . . . (A&M)

It's Raining, It's Pouring
Original Soundtrack; *Children's Favorites* . . . . (Kid Rhino/Rhino 4 Kids)

Itsy Bitsy Spider, The
Original Soundtrack; *Mother Goose Songs* . . . . (Madacy)

January Rain
Hunters & Collectors; *Living Daylight* . . . . (I.R.S.)

Jig Saw Puzzle
Rolling Stones; *Beggars Banquet* . . . . (Abkco)

Just A Little Bit Of Rain
Fred Neil; *Just A Little Bit Of Rain* . . . . (Elektra)
Linda Ronstadt; *Linda Ronstadt-Retrospective* . . . . (Capitol)

Just Like The Weather
Suzy Bogguss; *Something Up My Sleeve* . . . . (Liberty)

Just Walking In The Rain
Johnnie Ray; *16 Most Requested Songs Of The '50s-#1-C* . . . . (Legacy)
  Best Of Johnnie Ray . . . . (Columbia)
  Johnnie Ray-16 Most Requested Songs . . . . (Legacy)
  Johnnie Ray's Greatest Hits . . . . (Sony Music Special Prod.)

Kathy's Song
Simon & Garfunkel; *Collected Works* . . . . (Columbia)
  Simon & Garfunkel's Greatest Hits . . . . (Columbia)

Sounds Of Silence . . . . (Columbia)
Kentucky Rain
Elvis Presley; *Elvis Presley-Pure Gold*. . . . . (RCA)
   Memphis Record. . . . . (RCA)
   Worldwide 50 Gold Award Hits, Vol. 1, Parts 1 & 2 . . . . . (RCA)
Kiss Me In The Rain
Barbra Streisand; *Wet* . . . . (Columbia)
Kiss The Rain
Billie Myers; *A Taste Of '98-C* . . . . (Universal)
   Growing Pains. . . . . (Universal)
Kisses In The Rain
Rick Braun; *Kisses In The Rain* . . . .(Warner Bros.)
Knock On Wood
Amii Stewart; *Double Smash Hits-C* . . . . (Volcano Entertainment)
Buddy Guy; *This Is Buddy Guy*. . . . . (Vanguard)
Eddie Floyd; *15 Original Big Hits-#3-C*. . . . . (Stax)
   Atlantic Rhythm & Blues 1947-1974-#6 (1966-1969)-C . .(Atlantic)
   Best Of Wattstax-C. . . . .(Stax)
   Super Oldies Of The '60s-#11-C . . . . (Audio Fidelity)
Eric Clapton; *Behind The Sun*. . . . . (Duck/Reprise)
Ike & Tina Turner; *Ike & Tina Turner's Greatest Hits-#3* . . . . (Saja)
Laughter In The Rain
Johnny Mathis; *When Will Is See You Again*. . . . . (Columbia)
Neil Sedaka; *My Friend*. . . . . (Polydor)
Let A Smile Be Your Umbrella
Sammy Kaye & His Orchestra; *Best Of Sammy Kaye & His Orchestra* . . .(MCA)
Let It Rain
Eric Clapton; *Derek & The Dominos In Concert* . . . . (RSO)
   Eric Clapton . . . . (Polydor)
   Eric Clapton-Crossroads-C. . . . . (Polydor)
Let It Rain
Mark Chesnutt; *Mark Chesnutt's Greatest Hits* . . . . (Decca)
Let It Rain
UFO; *Best Of The Rest Of UFO* . . . .(Chrysalis)
Lightnin' Strikes
Lou Christie; *Oldies But Goodies-#14-C* . . . . (Original Sound)
Lightning Crashes
Live; *Throwing Copper* . . . .(Radioactive/MCA)
Lightning Does The Work
Chad Brock; *Chad Brock* . . . .(Warner Bros.)
Like A Hurricane
Neil Young; *Decade* . . . . (Reprise)
Neil Young & Crazy Horse; *Live Rust* . . . . (Reprise)
Neil Young, Crazy Horse & The Bullets; *American Stars 'N Bars* . . . . (Reprise)
Like The Rain
Evan And Jaron; *We've Never Heard Of You Either*. . . . . (Island)
Like The Rain
Clint Black; *Clint Black-The Greatest Hits*. . . . . (RCA)
Like The Rain
Zippers; *Zippers* . . . .(MCA Special Prod.)
Little White Cloud That Cried
Johnny Ray; *Best Of Johnnie Ray* . . . . (Columbia)
   Best Of Johnnie Ray. . . . .(Exact)
   Johnnie Ray's Greatest Hits . . . . (Sony Music Special Prod.)
London Rain (Nothing Heals Like You Do)
Heather Nova; *Siren* . . . . (Big Cat)
   Songs From Dawson's Creek. . . . . (Sony Music Soundtrax)
Louisiana Rain
Tom Petty; *Playback*. . . . .(MCA)
Tom Petty And The Heartbreakers; *Damn The Torpedoes* . . . .(MCA)
MacArthur Park
Andy Williams; *Andy Williams' Greatest Hits-#2* . . . . (Columbia)
Donna Summer; *Live & More*. . . . . (Casablanca)
   On The Radio-Greatest Hits-Volumes I & II . . . . (Casablanca)
   Summer Collection . . . . (Mercury)
   Walk Away-Best Of Donna Summer-1977-1980 . . . . . (Casablanca)
Richard Harris; *Love Album* . . . .(MCA)
   Richard Harris-His Greatest Performances . . . . (MCA)
   Tramp Shining . . . . (MCA)
   Vintage Music-#13-C. . . . . (MCA)
Waylon Jennings; *Are You Ready For The Country* . . . . (RCA)
   Best Of Waylon Jennings . . . . (RCA)
Mandolin Rain
Bruce Hornsby & The Range; *The Way It Is* . . . . (RCA)
March Winds And April Showers
Wingy Manone; *Wingy Manone Collection-#3-1934-1935* . . . . (Collector's Classics)
Master's Call
Marty Robbins; *Gunfighter Ballads & Trail Songs*. . . . . (Legacy)
Mexico Rain
Johnny Rodriguez; *Johnny Rodriguez's Biggest Hits* . . . .(Epic)
Michigan Rain
Gregg Alexander; *Intoxifornication* . . . . (Epic Portrait Assoc.)
Missing
Everything But The Girl; *Amplified Heart* . . . .(Atlantic)
   MTV Party To Go-#9-C . . . . (Tommy Boy)
   The Absolute Hits-C. . . . .(Atlantic)
   The Ultimate Dance Party-1997-C . . . . (Arista)

Monterey Mist
Modern Jazz Quartet; *Blues At Carnegie Hall*. . . . .(Atlantic)
Montgomery In The Rain
Hank Williams, Jr.; *Hank Williams, Jr.-Early Years*. . . . . (WB/Curb)
Steve Young; *No Place To Fall*. . . . . (RCA)
   Seven Bridges Road . . . . (Rounder)
Naked In The Rain
David Crosby & Graham Nash; *Wind On The Water* . . . . (MCA)
Naked In The Rain
Loretta Lynn; *Best Of Loretta Lynn-#2* . . . . (MCA Special Prod.)
Naked In The Rain
Red Hot Chili Peppers; *Blood Sugar Sex Magik* . . . . (Warner Bros.)
Naked In The Rain
Dio; *Dream Evil* . . . . (Warner Bros.)
Naked In The Rain
Hank Ballard And The Midnighters; *Naked In The Rain*. . . . . . . (After Hours)
Nashville In The Rain
Ginger Boatwright; *Fertile Ground*. . . . . (Flying Fish)
No More Rain (In This Cloud)
Angie Stone; *Black Diamond* . . . . (Arista)
No Rain
Blind Melon; *Blind Melon*. (Capitol)
Nobody's Gonna Rain On Our Parade
Kathy Mattea; *Walking Away A Winner* . . . . (Mercury)
November Rain
Guns N' Roses; *Use Your Illusion I*. . . . . (Geffen)
On Rainy Afternoons
Barbra Streisand; *Wet* . . . . (Columbia)
On The Banks Of The Old Pontchartrain
Hank Williams; *American Legends-#18* . . . . (Laserlight)
   Complete Hank Williams . . . . (Mercury)
One Way Ticket (Because I Can)
LeAnn Rimes; *Blue* . . . . (MCG/Curb)
Only Happy When It Rains
Garbage; *Garbage*. . . . . (Almo Sounds)
Only Love
Wynonna; *Tell Me Why*. . . . . (MCA)
Oregon Rain Song
George Roessler; *Still Life & Old Dreams* . . . .(Eagle Int'l)
Pennies From Heaven
Billie Holiday; *Billie Holiday-16 Most Requested Songs* . . . . (Legacy)
Bing Crosby; *Pennies From Heaven* . . . . (Pro-Arte)
Frank Sinatra & Nelson Riddle Orchestra; *songs for Swingin' Lovers!*. . . . . (Capitol)
Lester Young; *Birdland All-Stars At Carnegie Hall* . . . . (Roulette)
Louis Armstrong; *RCA Victor Jazz: First Half-Century-C* . . . .(RCA)
Mandy Patinkin; *Mandy Patinkin* . . . . (Columbia)
Skyliners; *Skyliners' Greatest Hits* . . . .(Original Sound)
Stan Getz; *Essential Stan Getz Songbook* . . . . (Verve)
Stephane Grappelli; *Satin Doll-#1-Best Of Stephane Grappelli* . . . . . (Vanguard)
People Are Strange
Doors; *Best Of The Doors* . . . . (Elektra)
Please Forgive Me
David Gray; *White Ladder* . . . . (ATO/RCA)
Please Mr. Sun
Johnnie Ray; *Back To The Early '50s* . . . . (Dominion Entert.)
   Johnnie Ray-16 Most Requested Songs . . . . (Legacy)
Vogues; *Vogues' Greatest Hits* . . . . (Rhino)
Promised Land
Bruce Springsteen; *Darkness On The Edge Of Town* . . . . (Columbia)
Bruce Springsteen & The E Street Band; *Bruce Springsteen & The E Street Band Live/1975-85* . . . . (Legacy)
Purple Rain
Prince and the Revolution; *ST/Purple Rain* . . . . (Warner Bros.)
Quicksilver Lightning
Roger Daltrey; *ST/Quicksilver* . . . .(Atlantic)
Quiet Storm
Smokey Robinson; *Compact Command Performances-Smokey Robinson* . . . . (Motown)
   Motown Superstar Series-#18-Smokey Robinson. . . . . (Motown)
   Quiet Storm . . . . (Motown)
   Smokin'. . . . . (Motown)
Radium Rain
Bruce Cockburn; *Big Circumstance* . . . . (Columbia)
Rain
Beatles; *Beatles-Box Set* . . . . (Capitol)
   Hey Jude. . . . . (Capitol)
   Past Masters-Volume Two . . . .(Parlophone)
Rain
Norman Brown featuring Vesta; *Celebration* . . . . (Warner Bros.)
Rain
Little Charlie & The Nightcats; *Alligator Records 20th Anniversary Collection-C* . . . .(Alligator)
Rain
Candlebox; *Candlebox* . . . . (Maverick)
Rain
Jerry Garcia; *Cats Under The Stars*. . . . . (Arista)

Rain
Wally Badarou; *Echoes* . . . . (Island)
Rain
Madonna; *Erotica* . . . . (Maverick/Sire)
   Something To Remember . . . . (Maverick/Sire)
Rain
Todd Rundgren; *Faithful* . . . . (Rhino)
Rain
Ella Fitzgerald & Joe Pass; *Fitzgerald & Pass...Again* . . . . (Pablo)
Rain
Marquees; *For Collectors Only-#1-The Rarities-C* . . . . (Collectables)
Rain
Terence Trent D'Arby; *Introducing The Hardline According To Terence*
   Trent D'Arby . . . . (Columbia)
Rain
Jive Five; *Jive Five-Their Greatest Hits* . . . . (Collectables)
Rain
Jose Feliciano; *Jose Feliciano's All-Time Greatest Hits* . . . . (RCA)
Rain
Cult; *Love* . . . . (Sire)
Rain
Uriah Heep; *Magician's Birthday* . . . . (Mercury)
Rain
Larry Gatlin & The Gatlin Brothers Band; *Pure N' Simple* . . . . (Capitol)
Rain
Skinny Puppy; *Rabies* . . . . (Capitol)
Rain
Levert; *Rope A Dope Style* . . . . (Atlantic)
Rain
21 Guns; *Salute* . . . . (RCA)
Rain
Bette Midler; *Thighs And Whispers* . . . . (Atlantic)
Rain
Lee Greenwood; *When You're In Love* . . . . (Capitol)
Rain
Johnny Winter; *Winter Of '88* . . . . (Voyager)
Rain (Falling From The Skies)
Frank Sinatra; *Where Are You?* . . . . (Capitol)
Rain Check
Duke Ellington; *Complete Standard Transcriptions* . . . . (DRG)
Rain Dogs
Tom Waits; *Big Time* . . . . (Island)
   Rain Dogs . . . . (Island)
Rain Fallin'
Reba McEntire; *Out Of A Dream* . . . . (Mercury)
Rain Forest
Paul Hardcastle; *Dance 2-C* . . . . (Profile)
   Paul Hardcastle . . . . (Chrysalis)
   Rain Forest . . . . (Profile)
Rain Forest
Cut To The Chase; *Cut To The Chase* . . . . (Art & Commerce)
Rain Forest
David Lanz & Paul Speer; *Narada Equinox Sampler One-C* . . . . (Narada)
   Natural States . . . . (Narada)
Rain Forest
Nelson Rangell; *Nelson Rangell* . . . . (GRP)
Rain Forest
Jeremy Steig & Eddie Gomez; *Rain Forest* . . . . (Creative Music Prod.)
Rain Forest
Jessica Williams; *Rivers Of Memory* . . . . (Clean Cuts)
Rain In My Heart
Frank Sinatra; *Cycles* . . . . (Reprise)
Rain In Spain
Original Cast; *Forbidden Broadway-#2* . . . . (DRG)
   My Fair Lady . . . . (Columbia)
Rex Harrison & Audrey Hepburn; *ST/My Fair Lady* . . . . (Columbia)
Rain In The Summertime
Alarm; *Eye Of The Hurricane* . . . . (I.R.S.)
Rain King
Counting Crows; *August And Everything After* . . . . . . (David Geffen Co.)
Rain On The Roof
Lovin' Spoonful; *Best Of The Lovin' Spoonful* . . . . (Radio Active Gold)
   Lovin' Spoonful-Anthology . . . . (Rhino)
Rain On The Roof
Original Cast; *ST/Follies-In Concert* . . . . (RCA Victor)
Rain On The Scarecrow
John Cougar Mellencamp; *Scarecrow* . . . . (Riva)
Rain Rain Go Away
Gerry Mulligan; *Happy Anniversary Charlie Brown!-C* . . . . (GRP)
Rain Rain Go Away
Bobby Vinton; *Bobby Vinton's All-Time Greatest Hits* . . . . (Epic)
Rain Song
Led Zeppelin; *Houses Of The Holy* . . . . (Atlantic)
   Led Zeppelin-Box Set . . . . (Atlantic)
   Remasters . . . . (Atlantic)
   ST/The Song Remains The Same . . . . (Swan Song)
Rain, Rain, Rain
Frankie Laine; *Frankie Laine-16 Most Requested Songs* . . . . (Legacy)

Rain, The
Oran "Juice" Jones; *Rap's Greatest Hits-#3-C* . . . . (Priority)
Rain, The (Supa Dupa Fly)
Missy "Misdemeanor" Elliot; *Supa Dupa Fly* . . . . (East West)
Rain, The Park And Other Things
Cowsills; *Cowsills* . . . . (Razor & Tie)
Raindrops
Dee Clark; *Best Of Dee Clark* . . . . (Vee-Jay)
   Collectables Presents The History Of Rock-#7-C . . . . (Collectables)
   Hits From The Legendary Vee-Jay Records-C . . . . (Motown)
   Oldies But Goodies-#6-C . . . . (Original Sound)
Del Shannon; *Liberty Years (Runaway)* . . . . (EMI)
Honeys; *Capitol Collectors Series-The Honeys* . . . . (Capitol)
Raindrops Keep Fallin' On My Head
B.J. Thomas; *'70s Greatest Rock Hits-#9-#1 Hits-C* . . . . (Priority)
   B.J. Thomas' Greatest Hits . . . . (Rhino)
   B.J. Thomas-16 Greatest Hits . . . . (Trip)
   Best Of B.J. Thomas . . . . (Dominion Entert.)
   ST/Butch Cassidy & The Sundance Kid . . . . (A&M)
   ST/Forrest Gump . . . . (Epic/Sony Music Soundtrax)
Raining In Baltimore
Counting Crows; *August And Everything After* . . . . . . (David Geffen Co.)
Raining In Dallas
Kelly Schoppa; *Amarillo By Morning* . . . . (Bellaire)
Raining In My Heart
Anne Murray; *New Kind Of Feeling* . . . . (Capitol)
Buddy Holly; *Buddy Holly-20 Golden Greats* . . . . (MCA)
   The Buddy Holly Collection . . . . (MCA)
   Vintage Music-#6-C . . . . (MCA)
Jo-el Sonnier; *Come On Joe* . . . . (RCA)
Leo Sayer; *Leo Sayer* . . . . (Warner Bros.)
Rainmaker
Dillards; *There Is A Time-1963-1970* . . . . (Vanguard)
Rainmaker
Traffic; *The Low Spark Of High Heeled Boys* . . . . (Island)
Rainmaker
Nilsson; *Harry* . . . . (Dunhill Compact Classics)
Rains Came
Freddy Fender; *Best Of Freddy Fender* . . . . (MCA)
Rainy Afternoon
Lee Konitz; *In Rio* . . . . (M-A Music Int'l)
Rainy Day
America; *America* . . . . (Warner Bros.)
Rainy Day
Tony Bennett; *Art Of Excellence* . . . . (Columbia)
Rainy Day Blues
Lightnin' Hopkins; *Prison Blues-Golden Classics-#2* . . . . (Collectables)
Willie Nelson; *Nite Life-Greatest Hits & Rare Tracks* . . . . (Rhino)
Rainy Day In London
Boulevard; *Into The Street* . . . . (MCA)
Rainy Day In Monterey
Joe Sample; *Carmel* . . . . (MCA)
   Joe Sample-Collection . . . . (GRP)
Rainy Day Man
Bonnie Raitt; *Streetlights* . . . . (Warner Bros.)
James Taylor; *Flag* . . . . (Columbia)
   James Taylor . . . . (Capitol)
Tom Rush; *Tom Rush* . . . . (Columbia)
Rainy Day People
Gordon Lightfoot; *Cold On The Shoulder* . . . . (Reprise)
   Gord's Gold . . . . (Reprise)
Rainy Day Woman
Waylon Jennings; *Ramblin' Man* . . . . (RCA)
   Waylon Live . . . . (RCA)
Rainy Day Women #12 & 35
Bob Dylan; *Blonde On Blonde* . . . . (Columbia)
   Bob Dylan's Greatest Hits . . . . (Columbia)
   Rock Classics Of The '60s-C . . . . (Columbia)
   ST/Forrest Gump . . . . (Epic/Sony Music Soundtrax)
Bob Dylan And The Band; *Before The Flood* . . . . (Columbia)
Rainy Day, Dream Away
Jimi Hendrix Experience; *Electric Ladyland* . . . . (Reprise)
Rainy Days & Mondays
Carpenters; *Carpenters* . . . . (A&M)
   Carpenters-Classics-#2 . . . . (A&M)
   Carpenters-The Singles 1969-1973 . . . . (A&M)
   Yesterday Once More . . . . (A&M)
Paul Williams; *Classics-Here Comes Inspiration* . . . . (A&M)
Rainy Night House
Joni Mitchell; *Ladies Of The Canyon* . . . . (Reprise)
Joni Mitchell with Tom Scott & The L.A. Express; *Miles Of Aisles* . . . . (Asylum)
Rainy Night In Georgia
Brook Benton; *Atlantic Rhythm & Blues 1947-1974-#6 (1966-*
   1969)-C . . . . (Atlantic)
   Brook Benton Today . . . . (Cotillion)
   Brook Benton-Anthology . . . . (Rhino)
   Golden Age Of Black Music-1960-1970-C . . . . (Atlantic)
   Pick Of Brook Benton . . . . (Fifty One West)
   Soul Years-C . . . . (Atlantic)

Hank Williams, Jr.; *Hank Williams, Jr.-14 Greatest Hits* . . . . (Polydor)
Sam Moore & Conway Twitty; *Rhythm Country And Blues-C* . . . .(MCA)
Rainy Night In Rio
Susannah McCorkle; *Thanks For The Memory* . . . .(Pausa)
Rainy Night In Tokyo
Michael Franks; *Passionfruit* . . . .(Warner Bros.)
Red Rain
Peter Gabriel; *Greenpeace/Rainbow Warriors-C* . . . .(Geffen)
Secret World Live . . . .(Geffen)
Shaking The Tree-Sixteen Golden Greats . . . .(Geffen)
So . . . .(Geffen)
Rhythm Of The Rain
Cascades; *Collectables Presents The History Of Rock-#7-C* . . . . . (Collectables)
Golden Years-1963-C . . . . (Dominion Entert.)
Rider In The Rain
Randy Newman; *Little Criminals* . . . .(Warner Bros.)
Riders On The Storm
Doors; *Best Of The Doors* . . . . (Elektra)
Doors' Greatest Hits . . . . (Elektra)
L.A. Woman . . . . (Elektra)
ST/The Doors . . . . (Elektra)
Weird Scenes Inside The Gold Mine . . . . (Elektra)
Ridin' Around In The Rain
Bing Crosby; *The Crooner-Columbia Years-1928-1934* . . . . (Columbia)
River In The Rain
Original Broadway Cast; *Big River-The Adventures Of*
Huckleberry Finn . . . .(MCA)
Rock Me Like A Hurricane
Scorpions; *Love At First Sting* . . . . (Mercury)
Rock You Like A Hurricane
Scorpions; *Best Of Rockers 'N' Ballads* . . . . (Mercury)
Love At First Sting . . . . (Mercury)
Worldwide Live . . . . (Mercury)
Rockin' With The Rhythm Of The Rain
Judds; *Judds' Greatest Hits* . . . .(MCA)
Rockin' With The Rhythm . . . .(MCA)
Rollin' Thunder
Bellamy Brothers; *Rollin' Thunder* . . . .(Atlantic)
Rollin' Thunder
A-Ha; *East Of The Sun-West Of The Moon* . . . .(Warner Bros.)
Roof Is Leaking
Phil Collins; *Face Value* . . . .(Atlantic)
Saddle In The Rain
John Prine; *Common Sense* . . . .(Atlantic)
Prime Prine-The Best Of John Prine . . . .(Atlantic)
Safe Place From The Storm
Michael Bolton; *All That Matters* . . . . (Columbia)
Sailing, Sailing
Original Soundtrack; *Children's Favorites* . . . . (Kid Rhino/Rhino 4 Kids)
Same Old Rain
Kevin Welch & The Overtones; *Western Beat* . . . . (Reprise)
Scottish Rain
Silencers; *Blues For Buddha* . . . .(RCA)
Greenpeace/Rainbow Warriors-C . . . .(Geffen)
See The Sky About to Rain
Neil Young; *On The Beach* . . . . (Reprise)
September In The Rain
Chad & Jeremy; *Capitol Gold-Best Of Chad & Jeremy* . . . . (Capitol)
The Soft Sound Of Chad & Jeremy . . . . (K-Tel)
Dinah Washington; *Dinah Washington-Golden Hits* . . . . (Mercury)
This Is My Story . . . . (Mercury)
Doris Day; *Doris Day Sings 22 Great Songs-Original Big Band* . . . . (Hindsight)
Duprees; *Best Of The Duprees* . . . . (Rhino)
Frank Sinatra; *Round #1* . . . . (Capitol)
Sinatra's Swingin' Session!!!. . . . . (Capitol)
Joe Williams; *Swingin'...At Birdland* . . . . (Roulette)
Marty Robbins; *Essential Marty Robbins-1951-1982* . . . . (Columbia)
Peggy Lee; *You Can Depend On Me* . . . . (Glendale)
September Rain
Full Swing; *Full Swing* . . . . (Cypress)
George Howard; *Love Will Follow* . . . .(GRP)
Shadows In The Rain
Police; *Zenyatta Mondatta* . . . . (A&M)
Sting; *Dream Of The Blue Turtles* . . . . (A&M)
Shame, Shame
Magic Lanterns; *Shame, Shame* . . . . (Collectables)
Shelter From The Storm
Bob Dylan; *Blood On The Tracks* . . . . (Columbia)
Bob Dylan At Budokan . . . . (Columbia)
Hard Rain . . . . (Columbia)
She's Coming Back Some Cold Rainy Day
Georgia Cotton Pickers; *The Greatest In Country Blues (1929-*
1956)-#3-C . . . .(Sony Broadway)
Sign Of The Storm
Eric Gales Band; *Eric Gales Band* . . . . (Elektra)
Silvery Rain
Olivia Newton-John; *Physical* . . . .(MCA)
Singin' In The Rain
Gene Kelly; *ST/A Clockwork Orange* . . . .(Warner Bros.)

ST/Singin' In The Rain . . . . (Sony Music Special Prod.)
ST/Those Glorious MGM Musicals . . . . (MGM)
Sky Is Crying
Albert King; *I'm In A Phone Booth Baby* . . . . (Stax)
Years Gone By . . . . (Stax)
Elmore James; *Elmore James-Complete Fire & Enjoy*
Sessions-#1 . . . . (Collectables)
Red Hot Blues . . . . (Intermedia)
Eric Clapton; *Eric Clapton-Crossroads-C* . . . . (Polydor)
George Thorogood & The Destroyers; *George Thorogood & The Destroyers-*
Live . . . .(EMI)
Move It On Over . . . . (Rounder)
Stevie Ray Vaughan and Double Trouble; *The Sky Is Crying* . . . . (Epic)
Smokestack Lightning
George Thorogood & The Destroyers; *Born To Be Bad* . . . . (Gold Rush)
Grateful Dead; *History Of The Grateful Dead-Vol. 1 (Bear's*
Choice) . . . .(Warner Bros.)
Howlin' Wolf; *Best Of Chess Blues-C.* . . . . (Chess)
Between The Rails: America's Train Songs-C . . . .(Crescendo)
Blues-#1-C . . . . (Chess)
Moanin' In The Moonlight . . . . (Chess)
Lynyrd Skynyrd; *1991* . . . . (Atlantic)
Muddy Waters; *The Chess Box-Muddy Waters* . . . . (Chess)
Soundgarden; *Ultramega OK* . . . .(SST)
Yardbirds; *Five Live Yardbirds* . . . . (Rhino)
For Your Love . . . . (Accord)
Yardbirds' Greatest Hits-#1 (1964-1966) . . . . (Rhino)
Smokey Mountain Rain
Ronnie Milsap; *Ronnie Milsap's Greatest Hits* . . . . (RCA)
Soft Rain
Ray Price; *Ray Price's Greatest Hits-#1-3* . . . . (Step One)
Soldier In The Rain
England Dan & John Ford Coley; *Best Of England Dan & John Ford*
Coley . . . . (Big Tree)
Dowdy Ferry Road . . . . (Big Tree)
Soon It's Gonna Rain
Barbra Streisand; *The Barbra Streisand Album.* . . . . (Columbia)
Original Cast; *Fantasticks* . . . . (Polydor)
Southern Rains
Mel Tillis; *Mel Tillis' Greatest Hits* . . . . (Curb)
Southside
Moby featuring Gwen Stefani; *12'' Maxi Single* . . . .(V2)
Play . . . .(V2)
Stand A Little Rain
Nitty Gritty Dirt Band; *Live Two Five* . . . . (Capitol)
Twenty Years Of Dirt-Best Of The Nitty Gritty Dirt Band . . . . (Warner Bros.)
State Trooper
Bruce Springsteen; *Nebraska* . . . . (Columbia)
The Sopranos-Music From The HBO Original
Series . . . . (Sony Music Soundtrax)
Still Rainin'
Jonny Lang; *Wander This World* . . . . (A&M)
Stop The Rain
Shenandoah; *Shenandoah* . . . . (Columbia)
Storm
Soul II Soul; *Soul II Soul-Vol. 3-Just Right* . . . . (Virgin)
Storm
Bonham; *Mad Hatter* . . . . (WTG)
Storm
Original London Cast; *Moby Dick.* . . . . (RCA)
Storm
Ray Simpson; *Ray Simpson.* . . . . (Virgin)
Storm
Pirates Of The Mississippi; *Walk The Plank* . . . . (Liberty)
Storm
Ray Kennedy; *What A Way To Go.* . . . .(Atlantic)
Storm Front
Billy Joel; *Storm Front* . . . . (Columbia)
Storm In The Heartland
Billy Ray Cyrus; *Storm In The Heartland* . . . . (Mercury)
Storm Of Love
Buck Owens; *Together Again/My Heart Skips A Beat* . . . . . . (Sundazed Music)
Storm Of Love
Highway 101; *Bing Bang Boom* . . . . (Warner Bros.)
Storm Over Tokyo Bay
Jessie Allen Cooper; *Soft Wave* . . . . (Sona Gaia)
Storm Warning
Bonnie Raitt; *Longing In Their Hearts* . . . . (Capitol)
Storm, The
Garth Brooks; *Scarecrow* . . . . (Capitol)
Stormbringer
Deep Purple; *Deepest Purple/The Very Best Of Deep Purple* . . . . (Warner Bros.)
Made In Europe . . . . (Warner Bros.)
Stormbringer . . . . (Warner Bros.)
Storms
Fleetwood Mac; *25 Years-The Chain* . . . . (Warner Bros.)
Tusk . . . . (Warner Bros.)
Storms
Nanci Griffith; *Storms* . . . . (MCA)

Storms Are On The Ocean
Carter Family; *Bristol Sessions-#1 & 2-C* . . . . (Country Music Foundation)

Storms In Africa
Enya; *Watermark* . . . . (Reprise)

Storms Never Last
Hank Williams, Jr.; *Hank Williams, Jr.-Early Years* . . . . (WB/Curb)

Storms Of Life
Randy Travis; *Storms Of Life* . . . . (Warner Bros.)

Stormy
Classics IV; *Back To The '60s-#4-C* . . . . (Dominion Entert.)
Spring Break-#2-Cold Kegs & Tan Legs . . . . (Capitol)
Very Best Of The Classics IV . . . . (EMI)
Santana; *Inner Secrets* . . . . (Columbia)

Stormy Blues
Billie Holiday; *Lady Sings The Blues* . . . . (Verve)
Songbook . . . . (Verve)
Stormy Blues . . . . (Verve)

Stormy Monday (They Call It)
Allman Brothers Band; *At Fillmore East* . . . . (Capricorn)
*The Road Goes On Forever, A Collection Of Their Greatest
Recordings* . . . . (Polydor)
Big Joe Turner; *Stormy Monday* . . . . (Pablo)
Bobby Bland; *Best Of Bobby Bland* . . . . (MCA)
Here's The Man . . . . (MCA)
Legends Of Electric Blues Guitar-#1-C . . . . (Rhino)
Tuesday's Just As Bad . . . . (MCA)
Buddy Guy; *My Time After Awhile* . . . . (Vanguard)
Little Milton; *Best Of Chess Blues-C* . . . . (Chess)
Lou Rawls; *Legendary Lou Rawls* . . . . (Blue Note)
T-Bone Walker; *Best Of Blues-#2-C* . . . . (MCA Special Prod.)
Jazz Heritage-Dirty Mistreater . . . . (MCA)

Stormy Weather
Billie Holiday; *Fine & Mellow* . . . . (Collectables)
Jazz Club-Vocal . . . . (Verve)
Ethel Waters; *Fabulous Thirties-C* . . . . (Pro Jazz)
Frank Sinatra; *No One Cares* . . . . (Capitol)
Jackie Wilson; *Mr. Excitement* . . . . (Rhino)
Judy Garland; *Judy Garland-At Carnegie Hall* . . . . (Capitol)
Lena Horne; *20 Golden Pieces Of Lena Horne* . . . . (Bulldog)
Goes Latin & Sings Your Requests . . . . (DRG)
Live On Broadway . . . . (Qwest)
Nipper's Greatest Hits Of The '40s-#1-C . . . . (RCA)
Pixies; *Bossanova* . . . . (Elektra)
Tony Bennett with Natalie Cole; *Playin' With My Friends-Bennett Sings The
Blues-C* . . . . (Columbia)
Willie Nelson & Leon Russell; *One For The Road* . . . . (Columbia)

Such Sweet Thunder
Duke Ellington; *Duke Ellington-Vol. 6-Dance Dates-California-1958* . . . (Saja)
Duke Ellington & His Orchestra; *Such Sweet
Thunder* . . . . (Sony Music Special Prod.)

Summer Rain
Johnny Rivers; *Best Of Johnny Rivers* . . . . (EMI)
Johnny Rivers-Anthology 1964-1977 . . . . (Rhino)

Summer Rain
Andreas Vollenweider; *The Trilogy* . . . . (Columbia)

Summer Rain
Carl Thomas; *Emotional* . . . . (Bad Boy/Arista)

Summer Rain
Belinda Carlisle; *Belinda Carlisle-Her Greatest Hits* . . . . (MCA)
Runaway Horses . . . . (MCA)

Summer Rain
Alphaville; *Breathtaking Blue* . . . . (Atlantic)

Summer Song
Chad & Jeremy; *Best Of Chad & Jeremy* . . . . (K-Tel)
Capitol Gold-Best Of Chad & Jeremy . . . . (Capitol)
History Of British Rock-#2-C . . . . (Rhino)

Sun & The Rainfall
Depeche Mode; *Broken Frame* . . . . (Sire)

Sunshower
Kenny Barron & John Hicks Quartet; *Rhythm-A-Ning* . . . . (Candid)

Sunshower
Chris Cornell; *ST/Great Expectations* . . . . (Atlantic)

Sunshower
Chuck Mangione; *Best Of Chuck Mangione* . . . . (Mercury)

Sunshower
Jeanie Bryson; *I Love Being Here With You* . . . . (Telarc)

Sunshowers
Billie Holiday; *Golden Years-#2* . . . . (Columbia)
The Billie Holiday Story-#3 . . . . (Columbia)

Sure Got Cold After The Rain
ZZ Top; *Rio Grande Mud* . . . . (Warner Bros.)
Six Pack . . . . (Warner Bros.)

Sweet Rain
Stan Getz; *Artistry Of-Stan Getz-Best Of Verve Years-#1* . . . . (Verve)
Stan Getz Quartet; *Sweet Rain* . . . . (Verve)

Sweetest Thing
U2; *Best Of 1980-1990* . . . . (Island)
Now That's What I Call Music!-#2-C . . . . (Virgin)

Tears In The Rain
Triumph; *Sport Of Kings* . . . . (MCA)
Triumph-Classics . . . . (MCA)

Tell It To The Rain
4 Seasons; *4 Seasons' Greatest Hits-#2* . . . . (Rhino)
4 Seasons-Anthology . . . . (Rhino)

Tell Me Why
Wynonna; *Tell Me Why* . . . . (MCA)

Texas Flood
Fenton Robinson; *Somebody Loan Me A Dime* . . . . (Alligator)
Larry Davis; *Best Of Duke-Peacock Blues-C* . . . . (MCA Special Prod.)
Stevie Ray Vaughan and Double Trouble; *Live Alive* . . . . (Epic)
Stevie Ray Vaughan and Double Trouble . . . . (Epic)
Taste Of Texas-Songs 'Bout Texas By Texans-C . . . . (Columbia)

Texas Tornado
Doug Sahm; *Best Of Doug Sahm & Friends-Atlantic Sessions* . . . . . . (Rhino)
Best Of Doug Sahm & Sir Douglas Quintet . . . . (Mercury)

Texas Tornado
Tracy Lawrence; *Best Of Tracy Lawrence* . . . . (Atlantic)
I See It Now . . . . (Atlantic)

Texas Twister
Little Feat; *Representing The Mambo* . . . . (Warner Bros.)

That's How You Know (When You're In Love)
Lari White; *Best Of Lari White* . . . . (RCA)
Wishes . . . . (RCA)

This Is Me Missing You
James House; *Days Gone By* . . . . (Epic)
Super Hits Of 1995-C . . . . (Epic)

Through The Storm
Aretha Franklin & Elton John; *Through The Storm* . . . . (Arista)

Thunder
Prince And The New Power Generation; *Diamonds And Pearls* . . . (Paisley Park)

Thunder & Lightnin'
Holly Dunn; *Blue Rose Of Texas* . . . . (Warner Bros.)

Thunder & Lightning
Chi Coltrane; *Rock Artifacts-From The Vaults-#1-C* . . . . (Columbia)
Super Hits Of The '70s-Have A Nice Day-#9-C . . . . (Rhino)

Thunder & Lightning
Argent; *Argent-Anthology-Collection Of Greatest Hits* . . . . (Epic)

Thunder & Lightning
Chicago; *Chicago XIV* . . . . (Chicago)
Group Portrait . . . . (Chicago)
Take Me Back To Chicago . . . . (Columbia)

Thunder & Lightning
Phil Collins; *Face Value* . . . . (Atlantic)

Thunder & Rain
Graham Parker And The Rumour; *Stick To Me* . . . . (Mercury)

Thunder Bay
Sawyer Brown; *Buick* . . . . (Curb)

Thunder Island
Jay Ferguson; *Jay Ferguson* . . . . (Asylum)

Thunder Rising
Gary Moore; *Wild Frontier* . . . . (Virgin)

Thunder Rolls, The
Garth Brooks; *Garth Brooks-Double Live* . . . . (Capitol)
No Fences . . . . (Capitol)

Thundercrack
Bruce Springsteen; *Tracks* . . . . (Columbia)

Thunderer
Michigan University Band; *Hail Sousa* . . . . (Vanguard)

Tiger In The Rain
Michael Franks; *Tiger In The Rain* . . . . (Warner Bros.)

Tokyo Storm Warning
Elvis Costello; *Girls Girls Girls* . . . . (Columbia)
Elvis Costello & The Attractions; *Blood & Chocolate* . . . . (Columbia)

Tom's Diner
D.N.A. Featuring Suzanne Vega; *Solitude Standing* . . . . (A&M)
Tom's Album . . . . (A&M)

Tryin' To Reason With Hurricane Season
Jimmy Buffett; *A1A* . . . . (MCA)
Boats Beaches Bars & Ballads . . . . (Margaritaville)

Two Sparrows In A Hurricane
Tanya Tucker; *Can't Run From Yourself* . . . . (Liberty)
Tanya Tucker's Greatest Hits-1990-1992 . . . . (Capitol)

Umbrella Man
Kay Kyser & His Orchestra; *Sentimental Favorites* . . . . (Columbia)

Voices In The Rain
Joe Sample; *Voices In The Rain* . . . . (MCA)

Waiting For The Rain To Fall
Chris Isaak; *Chris Isaak* . . . . (Warner Bros.)

Walk Away Renee
Four Tops; *Compact Command Performances-Four Tops* . . . . . . (Motown)
Four Tops Reach Out . . . . (Motown)
Four Tops-Anthology . . . . (Motown)
Left Banke; *Cruisin'-1966-C* . . . . (Increase)
History Of The Left Banke . . . . (Rhino)
Vonda Shepard; *ST/Songs From "Ally McBeal" Featuring Vonda
Shepard* . . . . (550/Epic)

Walk Out In The Rain
Eric Clapton; *Backless* . . . . (Polydor)
I Shall Be Unreleased-Songs Of Bob Dylan . . . . (Rhino)
Walkin' In The Rain
Grace Jones; *Island Life* . . . . (Island)
Nightclubbing . . . . (Island)
Walkin' In The Rain With The One I Love
Love Unlimited; *Didn't It Blow Your Mind: Soul Hits Of The*
'70s-#11-C . . . . (Rhino)
Walking In A Hurricane
John Fogerty; *Blue Moon Swamp* . . . . (Warner Bros.)
Walking In The Rain
Jay & The Americans; *Come A Little Bit Closer-Best Of Jay & The*
Americans . . . . (Gold Rush)
Jay & The Americans' All-Time Greatest Hits . . . . (Rhino)
Jay & The Americans' Greatest Hits . . . . (Curb)
Rhythm Of The Rain-C . . . . (Varese Vintage)
Ronettes; *Best Of The Ronettes* . . . . (Abkco)
Phil Spector-Back To Mono 1958-1969-C . . . . (Abkco)
Walking In The Rain
Marvin Gaye; *Romantically Yours* . . . . (Columbia)
Wasn't That A Mighty Storm
Eric Von Schmidt; *Troubadours Of The Folk Era-#1-C* . . . . (Rhino)
What Have They Done To The Rain
Malvina Reynolds; *Best Of Broadside 1962-1968: Anthems Of The*
American Underground From The Pages Of Broadside
Magazine-C . . . . (Smithsonian Folkways)
ST/Dogfight . . . . (Nouveau)
Searchers; *Searchers' Greatest Hits* . . . . (Rhino)
When I Think About Angels
Jamie O'Neal; *Shiver* . . . . (Mercury)
When It Rains
Steve Wariner; *It's A Crazy World* . . . . (MCA)
When It Rains In America
Sarah Brightman; *Dive* . . . . (A&M)
When It Rains, It Really Pours
Elvis Presley; *Reconsider Baby* . . . . (RCA)
The Sun Sessions . . . . (RCA)
When The Rain Turns To Snow
Lee Greenwood; *Lee Greenwood-Christmas To*
Christmas . . . . (MCA Special Prod.)
When Will It Rain
Jackyl; *Jackyl* . . . . (Geffen)
Wherever You Will Go
Calling; *Camino Palmero* . . . . (RCA)
White Lightning
Angel; *Live Without A Net* . . . . (Casablanca)
On Earth As It Is In Heaven . . . . (Casablanca)
White Lightning
Big Bopper; *Helloo Baby! Best Of The Big Bopper-1954-1959* . . . . (Rhino)
George Jones; *Best Of George Jones-1955-1967* . . . . (Rhino)
Billboard Top Country Hits-1959-C . . . . (Rhino)
George Jones' All-Time Greatest Hits . . . . (Epic)
The Bradley Barn Sessions . . . . (MCA)
Hank Williams, Jr.; *Whiskey Bent & Hell Bound* . . . . (WB/Curb)
White Lightning
Def Leppard; *Adrenalize* . . . . (Mercury)
White Lightning
Furry Lewis; *Back On My Feet Again* . . . . (Prestige)
Shake 'Em On Down . . . . (Fantasy)
White Lightning
Babys; *Head First* . . . . (Chrysalis)
White Lightning & Wine
Heart; *Dreamboat Annie* . . . . (Capitol)
White Tornado
R.E.M.; *Dead Letter Office* . . . . (I.R.S.)
Who'll Stop The Rain
Creedence Clearwater Revival; *1970* . . . . (Fantasy)
Cosmo's Factory . . . . (Fantasy)
Creedence Clearwater Revival-Chronicle . . . . (Fantasy)
More Creedence Gold . . . . (Fantasy)
Royal Albert Hall Concert . . . . (Fantasy)
Wicked Rain
Los Lobos; *Just Another Band From East L.A.* . . . . (Slash)
Kiko . . . . (Slash)
Windows Of The World
Burt Bacharach; *One Amazing Night* . . . . (N2K)
Dionne Warwick; *Dionne Warwick Collection-Her All-Time*
Greatest Hits . . . . (Rhino)
Dionne Warwick-Definitive Collection . . . . (Arista)
Isaac Hayes; *Live At The Sahara Tahoe* . . . . (Stax)
Mormon Tabernacle Choir; *Voices In Harmony* . . . . (CBS Masterworks)
Pretenders; *ST/1969* . . . . (Polydor)
Windy
Association; *Association Greatest Hits* . . . . (Warner Bros.)
Billboard Top Rock 'N' Roll Hits-1967-C . . . . (Rhino)
Summer Of Love-#1-C . . . . (Rhino)
Vintage Association . . . . (Fifty One West)
Wes Montgomery; *A Day In The Life* . . . . (A&M)

Wes Montgomery-Classics-#22 . . . . (A&M)
Wes Montgomery's Greatest Hits . . . . (A&M)
Yesterday, I Heard The Rain
Bill Evans; *Tokyo Concert* . . . . (Fantasy)
Tony Bennett; *Essence Of Tony Bennett* . . . . (Columbia)
Yesterday's Rain
Spanky & Our Gang; *Spanky & Our Gang's Greatest Hits* . . . . (Mercury)
You Love The Thunder
Hank Williams, Jr.; *Hank Williams, Jr.-Early Years* . . . . (WB/Curb)
Jackson Browne; *Running On Empty* . . . . (Asylum)
You're An Ocean
Fastball; *Harsh Light Of Day* . . . . (Hollywood)

RAINBOWS

See Also: **COLORS (various), HAPPINESS, NATURE, RAIN**

Above The Rainbow
Flora Purim; *Encounter* . . . . (Milestone)
April Showers
Al Jolson; *Best Of Al Jolson* . . . . (MCA)
The Al Jolson Story-#2 . . . . (MCA)
Judy Garland; *Hits Of Judy Garland* . . . . (Capitol)
Judy . . . . (Capitol)
At The End Of A Rainbow
Earl Grant; *Best Of Earl Grant-Singin' And Swingin'* . . . . (MCA)
Jerry Wallace; *45-#006* . . . . (BMA)
Blinded By Rainbows
Rolling Stones; *Voodoo Lounge* . . . . (Virgin)
Catch The Rainbow
Blackmore's Rainbow; *Ritchie Blackmore's R-A-I-N-B-O-W* . . . . . . (Polydor)
Rainbow; *Rainbow-On Stage* . . . . (Oyster)
Chasin' That Neon Rainbow
Alan Jackson; *Here In The Real World* . . . . (Arista)
End Of The Rainbow
Judy Garland; *Judy Garland-Collector's Items-1936-1945* . . . . (MCA)
Evening Rainbow
Sylvia St. James; *Echoes & Images* . . . . (Elektra)
God Gave Noah The Rainbow Sign
Carter Family; *My Clinch Mountain Home-Their Complete Victor*
Recordings-1928-1929 . . . . (Rounder)
God's Coloring Book
Dolly Parton; *Here You Come Again* . . . . (Dunhill Compact Classics)
Gold At The End Of My Rainbow
Be Bop Deluxe; *Modern Music* . . . . (Capitol)
Golden Rainbow
Looking Glass; *45-#15-2330* . . . . (Epic)
Seals & Crofts; *I'll Play For You* . . . . (Warner Bros.)
Golden Rainbow
Seals & Crofts; *I'll Play For You* . . . . (Warner Bros.)
Gone The Rainbow
Peter, Paul & Mary; *(Moving)* . . . . (Warner Bros.)
Moving . . . . (Warner Bros.)
Here Comes The Rainbow
Crystal Gayle; *In Harmony 2-C* . . . . (Columbia)
I'm Always Chasing Rainbows
Harry Fox; *Music From The New York Stage (1890-1920)-#4-1917-*
1920-C . . . . (Pearl)
Judy Garland; *Best Of Judy Garland* . . . . (MCA)
Judy Garland . . . . (Audio Fidelity)
Pick Of Judy Garland . . . . (Fifty One West)
I've Got The World On A String
Count Basie; *Standards* . . . . (Verve)
Diana Krall; *Only Trust Your Heart* . . . . (GRP)
Ella Fitzgerald; *Harold Arlen Songbook-#1* . . . . (Verve)
Frank Sinatra; *Capitol Collectors Series-Frank Sinatra* . . . . (Capitol)
Frank Sinatra & Liza Minnelli; *Frank Sinatra-Duets-C* . . . . (Capitol)
Sarah Vaughan; *Best Of Sarah Vaughan* . . . . (Pablo)
Stephane Grappelli & Martin Taylor; *We've Got The World On A*
String . . . . (Angel)
Livin' At The End Of The Rainbow
Dave & Sugar; *That's The Way Love Should Be* . . . . (RCA)
Look To The Rainbow
Al Jarreau; *Look To The Rainbow-Live In Europe* . . . . (Warner Bros.)
Look To The Rainbow
Aretha Franklin; *Aretha* . . . . (Arista)
Look To The Rainbow
Original Cast; *Finian's Rainbow* . . . . (Columbia)
Make Me Rainbows
Ella Fitzgerald & Count Basie; *Perfect Match* . . . . (Pablo)
Sue Raney & Bob Florence; *Flight Of Fancy* . . . . (Discovery)
Neon Rainbow
Box Tops; *Box Tops' Greatest Hits* . . . . (Rhino)
Old Rainbow Jukebox & You
John Schneider; *Memory Like You* . . . . (MCA)
Over The Rainbow
Barbra Streisand; *Just For The Record* . . . . (Columbia)

Dave Brubeck; *Greatest Hits From The Fantasy Years* . . . .(Fantasy)
Ella Fitzgerald; *Silver Collection-Songbooks* . . . . (Verve)
Judy Garland; *Best Of The Capitol Masters-One & Only Box* . . . . (Capitol)
  Judy Garland-At Carnegie Hall . . . . (Capitol)
  Judy Garland's Greatest Hits . . . . (Curb)
  Miss Show Business . . . . (Capitol)
  One & Only . . . . (Capitol)
  ST/The Wizard Of Oz . . . . (Sony Music Special Prod.)

Please Mr. Sun
Johnnie Ray; *Back To The Early '50s* . . . . (Dominion Entert.)
  Johnnie Ray-16 Most Requested Songs . . . . (Legacy)
Vogues; *Vogues' Greatest Hits* . . . . (Rhino)

Quick As Rainbows
Kitchens Of Distinction; *Strange Free World* . . . . (One Little Indian)

Rainbow
O'Jays; *Serious* . . . . (EMI)

Rainbow
Candyland; *Suck It & See* . . . . (East West)

Rainbow
Marmalade; *45-#20059* . . . . (London)

Rainbow
Sandy Owen; *Soliloquy* . . . . (Ivory)

Rainbow
Gene Chandler; *Beg, Scream & Shout! The Big Ol' Box Of '60s*
  Soul-C . . . . (Rhino)
  Gene Chandler's Greatest Hits . . . . (Varese Vintage)
  Soul Hits-#1-C . . . . (MCA Special Prod.)

Rainbow
Russ Hamilton; *45-#184* . . . . (Kapp)

Rainbow (Interlude)
Mariah Carey; *Rainbow* . . . . (Columbia)

Rainbow '65
Gene Chandler; *Hits From The Legendary Vee-Jay Records-C* . . . . . . (Motown)

Rainbow '80
Gene Chandler; *Ear Candy-#2-C* . . . . (20th Century Fox)
  Gene Chandler '80 . . . . (20th Century Fox)

Rainbow At Midnight
Carlisle Brothers; *45-#535.* . . . . (King)
Ernest Tubb; *Ernest Tubb Collection-C* . . . .(Step One)
  Ernest Tubb-Retrospective-#1 . . . . (MCA Special Prod.)
  The Ernest Tubb Story . . . . (MCA)

Rainbow Blues
Jethro Tull; *''M.U.''-Best Of* . . . . (Chrysalis)

Rainbow Connection
Muppets with Kermit The Frog; *45-#3610* . . . . (Atlantic)

Rainbow Demon
Uriah Heep; *Demons And Wizards* . . . . (Mercury)

Rainbow Doll
Jimmy Dell; *Get Hot Or Go Home-Vintage*
  Rockabilly-C . . . . (Country Music Foundation)

Rainbow Eyes
Rainbow; *Long Live Rock 'n' Roll* . . . . (Polydor)

Rainbow High
Original Cast; *Evita* . . . . (MCA)

Rainbow In Your Eyes
Al Jarreau; *Glow* . . . .(Reprise)
  Look To The Rainbow-Live In Europe . . . . (Warner Bros.)
Leon Russell; *Wedding Album.* . . . . (Paradise)

Rainbow Ride
Charlie Daniels Band; *Million Mile Reflections.* . . . . (Epic)
Jerry Reed; *East Bound & Down* . . . .(RCA)

Rainbow Song
America; *Hat Trick* . . . . (Warner Bros.)

Rainbow Stew
Merle Haggard; *For The Record: Merle Haggard-43 Legendary Hits* . . . .(BNA)
  Merle Haggard's Greatest Hits . . . . (MCA)
  More Of The Best . . . . (Rhino)
  Rainbow Stew-Live At Anaheim Stadium . . . . (MCA)

Rainbow Trout
Gordon Lightfoot; *Cold On The Shoulder* . . . .(Reprise)

Rainbows All Over Your Blues
John Sebastian; *John B. Sebastian.* . . . .(Reprise)
  ST/Woodstock . . . . (Atlantic)

Rainbows Are Back In Style
Slim Whitman; *Best Of Slim Whitman 1952-1972.* . . . . (Rhino)
  Paloma Blanca-Best Of Slim Whitman-Legendary Masters . . . . (EMI)

Rainbow's Cadillac
Bruce Hornsby; *Harbor Lights* . . . .(RCA)

Rainbow's End
Sergio Mendes; *Sergio Mendes* . . . . (A&M)

Ride On A Rainbow
Johnny Mathis; *Heavenly* . . . . (Columbia)

Searchin' For A Rainbow
Marshall Tucker Band; *Searchin' For A Rainbow.* . . . .(AJK Music)

Searching For A Rainbow
Chris LeDoux; *Chris LeDoux & The Saddle Boogie Band* . . . . (Liberty)

Seven Wonders
Fleetwood Mac; *Tango In The Night* . . . . (Warner Bros.)

She Brakes For Rainbows
B-52's; *Bouncing Off The Satellites* . . . . (Warner Bros.)

She's A Rainbow
Rolling Stones; *Get Yer Ya-Ya's Out!* . . . . (Abkco)
  More Hot Rocks (big hits & fazed cookies) . . . . (Abkco)
  Singles Collection-The London Years . . . . (Abkco)
  Their Satanic Majesties Request . . . . (Abkco)
  Through The Past, Darkly (Big Hits Vol. 2) . . . . (Abkco)

Sign Of The Rainbow
Robbie Robertson; *Storyville* . . . . (Geffen)

Silver Rainbow
Genesis; *Genesis* . . . . (Atlantic)

Somewhere There's A Rainbow Over Texas
Ruby Falls; *45-#39.* . . . . (Fifty States)

Stairway To Heaven
Neil Sedaka; *Neil Sedaka Sings His Greatest Hits* . . . . (RCA)
  Neil Sedaka's All-Time Greatest Hits . . . . (RCA)

Sunshine, Lollipops & Rainbows
Lesley Gore; *Golden Hits Of Lesley Gore* . . . . (Mercury)
  Lesley Gore-Anthology . . . .(Rhino)

Swinging On A Rainbow
Frankie Avalon; *Best Of Frankie Avalon* . . . . (MCA)

That Terrific Rainbow
Original Broadway Cast; *Pal Joey* . . . .(Angel)
Original Cast; *Pal Joey.* . . . . (Columbia)

There's A Rainbow 'Round My Shoulder
Al Jolson; *Jolson Sang 'Em* . . . . (Biograph)
  Mammy . . . .(Pro-Arte)

True Colors
Cyndi Lauper; *She's So Unusual/True Colors/Hat Full of Stars (Box)* . . . .(Epic)
  True Colors . . . . (Portrait)
  Twelve Deadly Cyns...And Then Some . . . . (Epic)
Phil Collins; *Phil Collins-Hits* . . . . (Atlantic)

Under The Rainbow
Raindogs; *Lost Souls* . . . .(Atco)
Tommy Page; *From The Heart* . . . . (Sire)

Vintage Eyes
Second Coming; *Second Coming* . . . . (Capitol)

When The Rainbow Comes
Shawn Colvin; *ST/Armageddon-The Album* . . . .(Columbia)

When The Rainbow Comes
World Party; *Goodbye Jumbo* . . . . (Ensign)

Wrong End Of The Rainbow
Anne Murray; *Yes I Do.* . . . .(Liberty)
  You Will. . . . .(Liberty)

Wrong End Of The Rainbow
Tom Rush; *Wrong End Of The Rainbow* . . . .(Columbia)

Wrong Side Of The Rainbow
Jim Chestnut; *Show Me A Sign* . . . . (MCA)

REASONS, Excuses, Explanations
See Also: GUILT, PRETEND, QUESTIONS & ANSWERS, STRANGE, THINKING & KNOWING

49 Bye-Byes
Crosby, Stills & Nash; *Crosby, Stills & Nash.* . . . . (Atlantic)

Back To You
Bryan Adams; *MTV Unplugged-Bryan Adams* . . . .(A&M)

Because
Beatles; *Abbey Road* . . . . (Parlophone)
  Beatles-Box Set . . . .(Capitol)

Because
Dave Clark Five; *History Of The Dave Clark Five* . . . .(Hollywood)

Because I Got High
Afroman; *Good Times* . . . . (Universal)

Because Of You
Bobby Vinton; *Bobby Vinton's Greatest Hits* . . . .(Curb)
Tony Bennett; *Tony Bennett Sings His All-Time Hall Of*
  Fame Hits . . . . (Columbia)
  Tony Bennett-16 Most Requested Songs . . . . (Legacy)
Willie Nelson; *One For The Road* . . . . (Columbia)

Because You Love Me
Jo Dee Messina; *I'm Alright.* . . . .(Curb)

Because You Loved Me
Celine Dion; *All The Way...A Decade Of Song* . . . . (550 Music)
  Diana, Princess Of Wales-Tribute-C . . . . (Columbia)
  Falling Into You . . . . (550 Music)

Big Me
Foo Fighters; *Foo Fighters.* . . . . (Roswell/RCA)

Bitch
Meredith Brooks; *Blurring The Edges* . . . . (Capitol)

Blurry
Puddle Of Mudd; *Come Clean* . . . .(Flawless/Geffen/Interscope)

Breakdown
Tantric; *Tantric* . . . . (Maverick)

Can't Find My Way Home
Blind Faith; *Blind Faith* . . . . (Polydor)
  Eric Clapton-Crossroads-C. . . . .(Polydor)
  ST/1969 . . . . (Polydor)
Captain Bligh
Filter; *Title Of Record* . . . . (Reprise)
Case Of The Ex (Whatcha Gonna Do)
Mya; *Fear Of Flying* . . . . (University/Interscope)
  Now That's What I Call Music!-#5-C . . . . (Virgin)
Could It Be
Jaheim; *Ghetto Love* . . . .(Divine Mill/Warner Bros.)
Crawling In The Dark
Hoobastank; *Hoobastank* . . . .(Island/IDJMG)
Day Tripper
Beatles; *''Yesterday''...And Today* . . . . (Capitol)
  Beatles 1 . . . . (Capitol)
  Beatles-Box Set . . . . (Capitol)
  Past Masters-Volume Two . . . . (Parlophone)
  The Beatles/1962-1966 . . . . (Capitol)
Jimi Hendrix Experience; *Radio One* . . . .(Rykodisc)
Otis Redding; *Dictionary Of Soul* . . . . (Atco)
  The Otis Redding Story . . . . (Atlantic)
Sergio Mendes & Brasil '66; *Sergio Mendes & Brasil '66's*
  Greatest Hits . . . . (A&M)
Don't Speak
No Doubt; *Tragic Kingdom* . . . . (Trauma)
Don't Take It Personal (Just One Of Dem Days)
Monica; *Miss Thang* . . . . (Rowdy/Arista)
Everything You Want
Vertical Horizon; *Everything You Want* . . . . (RCA)
  Totally Hits-#3-C . . . . (Atlantic)
Extra Pale
Goo Goo Dolls; *Dizzy Up The Girl* . . . . (Warner Sunset/Reprise)
Give Me One Reason
Tracy Chapman; *New Beginning* . . . . (Elektra)
Got Me Wrong
Alice In Chains; *Alice In Chains-MTV Unplugged* . . . . (Columbia)
  ST/Clerks . . . . (Chaos)
Heard It All Before
Sunshine Anderson; *Your Woman* . . . . (Soullife/Atlantic)
Hello Goodbye
Beatles; *Beatles 1* . . . . (Capitol)
  Beatles-20 Greatest Hits . . . . (Capitol)
  Beatles-Box Set . . . . (Capitol)
  Magical Mystery Tour . . . . (Capitol)
  The Beatles/1967-1970 . . . . (Capitol)
High
Jimmie's Chicken Shack; *Pushing The Salmanilla Envelope* . . . . .(Rocket)
How Come You Don't Call Me
Alicia Keys; *Songs In A Minor* . . . . (J)
Hungry Eyes
Emmylou Harris; *Mama's Hungry Eyes-Merle Haggard Tribute-C* . . . . (Arista)
Merle Haggard; *For The Record: Merle Haggard-43 Legendary Hits* . . . . (BNA)
Husbands And Wives
Brooks & Dunn; *Big Country Hits '99-C* . . . . (K-Tel)
  If You See Her . . . . (Arista)
Neil Diamond; *Neil Diamond-Love Songs* . . . . (MCA)
  Rainbow . . . . (MCA)
  Stones . . . . (MCA)
Roger Miller; *Best Of Roger Miller* . . . . (Mercury)
  Best Of Roger Miller-His Greatest Songs . . . . (Curb)
  Roger Miller-Super Hits . . . . (Epic)
  Roger Miller-The Hits . . . . (Mercury)
I Ain't Going Out
Jon B.; *Cool Relax* . . . . (Yab Yum/550)
I Believe
Elvis Presley; *Amazing Grace-His Greatest Sacred Performances* . . . . . . (RCA)
Frankie Laine; *Frankie Laine-16 Most Requested Songs* . . . . (Legacy)
  Frankie Laine's Greatest Hits . . . . (Columbia)
Jo Stafford; *You'll Never Walk Alone* . . . . (CEMA Special Prod.)
I Can't Explain
Who; *Hooligans* . . . . (MCA)
  Meaty Beaty Big & Bouncy . . . . (MCA)
  ST/The Kids Are Alright . . . . (MCA)
  Who's Last . . . . (MCA)
I Can't Explain
Scorpions; *Crazy World* . . . . (Mercury)
I Can't Tell You Why
Brownstone; *From The Bottom Up* . . . .(MJJ/Epic)
Eagles; *Eagles Greatest Hits, Volume 2* . . . . (Asylum)
  Eagles Live . . . . (Asylum)
  The Long Run . . . . (Asylum)
Vince Gill; *Common Thread-Songs Of The Eagles-C* . . . .(Giant)
I Don't Know Why
Frank Sinatra; *The Golden Days Of Radio* . . . . (K-Tel)
I Don't Want To Know
Fleetwood Mac; *Rumours* . . . .(Warner Bros.)
Goo Goo Dolls; *Legacy-A Tribute To Fleetwood Mac's Rumours-C* . . . . . (Lava)

I Guess That's Why They Call It The Blues
Elton John; *Elton John's Greatest Hits-1976-1986*. . . . . (MCA)
  Too Low For Zero. . . . . (MCA)
I Think God Can Explain
Splender; *ST/Dawson's Creek-#2* . . . . (C2/Columbia)
I Want It That Way
Backstreet Boys; *Millennium* . . . .(Jive)
I Was Wrong
Social Distortion; *White Light White Heat White Trash* . . . .(550 Music)
I Wish You Didn't Love Me So Much
''Little'' Jimmy Dickens; *All Time Legends Of Country Music-C* . . . . . (Legacy)
I Wonder Why
Dion And The Belmonts; *Doo-Wop Uptempo-#2-C* . . . . (Rhino)
  Everything You Always Wanted . . . .(Laurie)
  Million-Dollar Memories #1-C . . . .(RCA)
  Oldies But Goodies-#12-C . . . .(Original Sound)
  Super Oldies Of The '50s-#7-C . . . . (Audio Fidelity)
  You Found The Vocal Group Sound-#1-C . . . .(Solid Smoke)
If I Didn't Care
Connie Francis; *Very Best Of Connie Francis*. . . . .(Polydor)
Hilltoppers; *45-#15220* . . . . (Dot)
Ink Spots; *Best Of The Ink Spots* . . . . (MCA)
  If I Didn't Care . . . . (Pro-Arte)
  Ink Spots' Greatest Hits-Original Recordings-1939-1946. . . . . (MCA)
  ST/The Shawshank Redemption . . . . (Epic)
Moments; *Best Of The Moments: Love On A Two-Way Street* . . . . (Rhino)
Platters; *Magic Touch-An Anthology*. . . . . (Mercury)
  Very Best Of The Platters . . . . (Mercury)
If You Could Only See
Tonic; *Lemon Parade* . . . .(Polydor)
  Now That's What I Call Music!-#1-C . . . .(Virgin)
I'll Cry Instead
Beatles; *Beatles-Box Set* . . . . (Capitol)
  Something New . . . . (Capitol)
  ST/A Hard Day's Night . . . . (Capitol)
In The Blood
Better Than Ezra; *Deluxe* . . . . (Swell/Elektra)
Istanbul (Not Constantinople)
Four Lads; *Four Lads-16 Most Requested Songs* . . . . (Legacy)
It Wasn't Me
Shaggy; *Hotshot* . . . . (MCA)
  Now That's What I Call Music!-#6-C . . . .(Virgin)
It's Bad You Know
R.L. Burnside; *The Sopranos-Music From The HBO Original*
  Series . . . .(Sony Music Soundtrax)
It's Your Body
Johnny Gill; *Let's Get The Mood Right* . . . . (Motown)
Just Because
Shelton Brothers; *Classic Country Music-#1-C* . . . . . . (Smithsonian Collection)
Lessons To Be Learned
Barbra Streisand; *Higher Ground* . . . . (Columbia)
Love Power
Sand Pebbles; *Dick Bartley Presents On The Radio-#4-C* . . . .(VSI)
Make Me Bad
Korn; *Issues*. . . . . (Immortal/Epic)
Man In Black
Johnny Cash; *Essential Johnny Cash* . . . . (Columbia)
  Patriot . . . . (Columbia)
  The Man In Black-His Greatest Hits. . . . . (Legacy)
Maybe
Nilsson; *Harry*. . . . . (Dunhill Compact Classics)
My Baby You
Marc Anthony; *Marc Anthony*. . . . . (Columbia)
Never Ever
All Saints; *All Saints* . . . .(London)
  Now That's What I Call Music!-#1-C . . . .(Virgin)
New York State Of Mind
Barbra Streisand; *Memories* . . . . (Columbia)
  Streisand Superman . . . . (Columbia)
Billy Joel; *America: A Tribute To Heroes-C* . . . .(Interscope)
  Billy Joel-Greatest Hits, Volume I & Volume II . . . . (Columbia)
  The Concert For New York City-C . . . . (Columbia)
  Turnstiles . . . . (Columbia)
Carmen McRae; *Ms. Magic*. . . . . (Dunhill Compact Classics)
Tony Bennett with Billy Joel; *Playin' With My Friends-Bennett Sings The*
  Blues-C . . . . (Columbia)
Nothing To Prove
Caroline's Spine; *Attention Please* . . . . (Hollywood)
Only God Knows Why
Kid Rock; *Devil Without A Cause* . . . . (Top Dog/Lava/Atlantic)
Papa Can You Hear Me?
Barbra Streisand; *One Voice* . . . . (Columbia)
  ST/Yentl . . . . (Columbia)
Pinch Me
Barenaked Ladies; *Maroon* . . . . (Reprise)
  Totally Hits-#3-C . . . .(Atlantic)
Please
Chris Isaak; *Speak Of The Devil* . . . . (Reprise)

Re-Arranged
Limp Bizkit; *Significant Other* . . . .(Flip/Interscope)
Reason For Breathing
Babyface; *Collection Of His Greatest Hits* . . . .(Arista/Epic)
Reason To Believe
Rod Stewart; *Best Of Rod Stewart-#2* . . . .(Mercury)
   Every Picture Tells A Story . . . .(Mercury)
   Sing It Again, Rod . . . .(Mercury)
   Storyteller/The Complete Anthology: 1964-1990 . . . .(Warner Bros.)
   Unplugged...And Seated . . . .(Warner Bros.)
Reason To Believe
Bruce Springsteen; *Nebraska* . . . .(Columbia)
Bruce Springsteen & The E Street Band; *Bruce Springsteen & The E Street
   Band Live/1975-85* . . . .(Legacy)
Reason To Cry
Lucinda Williams; *Essence* . . . .(Lost Highway/IDJMG)
Reason, The
Celine Dion with Carole King; *Let's Talk About Love-C* . . . .(550 Music)
Reasons
Earth, Wind & Fire; *Best Of Earth, Wind & Fire-#1* . . . .(Legacy)
   Gratitude . . . .(Legacy)
   That's The Way Of The World . . . .(Legacy)
Reasons For Living
Duncan Sheik; *Duncan Sheik* . . . .(Atlantic)
   ST/E.R.-Original Television Theme Music And Score . . . . . .(Atlantic)
Reasons For Waiting
Jethro Tull; *Stand Up* . . . .(Chrysalis)
Reasons Why
Nickel Creek; *Nickel Creek* . . . .(Sugar Hill)
Running Out Of Reasons To Run
Rick Trevino; *Learning As You Go* . . . .(Columbia)
Sawyer Brown; *Wide Open* . . . .(Curb)
So How Come (No One Loves Me)
Everly Brothers; *Heartaches 'N' Harmonies* . . . .(Rhino)
Someone Else's Star
Bryan White; *Bryan White* . . . .(Asylum)
   Real Luv: Ultimate Country Love Songs-C . . . .(EMI)
Sweet Summer
Diamond Rio; *One More Day* . . . .(Arista)
Teenager In Love
Dion And The Belmonts; *Classic Old & Gold-C* . . . .(Laurie)
   Collectables Presents The History Of Rock-#6-C . . . . .(Collectables)
   Dion And The Belmonts-Their Best . . . .(Laurie)
   Oldies But Goodies-#6-C . . . .(Original Sound)
   Party Time Fifties-C . . . .(JCI Assoc. Labels)
Tell Me Why
Beatles; *Beatles-Box Set* . . . .(Capitol)
   Something New . . . .(Capitol)
   ST/A Hard Day's Night . . . .(Capitol)
Tell Me Why
Sunbeams; *Harlem Holiday-New York Rhythm & Blues-#5-C* . . . .(Collectables)
Tell Me Why
Belmonts; *Classic Old & Gold-C* . . . .(Laurie)
   I Got Rhythm-C . . . .(K-Tel)
Tell Me Why
Mavericks; *Trampoline* . . . .(MCA)
Tell Me Why
Elvis Presley; *A Valentine Gift For You* . . . .(RCA)
   The King Of Rock 'N' Roll-The Complete 50's Masters . . . .(RCA)
   The Other Sides-Worldwide Gold Award Hits, Vol. 2 . . . .(RCA)
Tell Me Why
Bobby Vinton; *Bobby Vinton-16 Most Requested Songs* . . . .(Legacy)
   Bobby Vinton's Greatest Hits/Greatest Hits Of Love . . . .(Columbia)
Four Aces; *Four Aces' Greatest Hits* . . . .(MCA)
Tell Me Why
Wynonna; *Tell Me Why* . . . . (MCA)
Tell Me Why
Neil Young; *After The Gold Rush* . . . .(Reprise)
Tell Me Why
Berlin; *Pleasure Victim* . . . .(Geffen)
Tell Me Why
Jann Browne; *'Til A Tear Becomes A Rose* . . . .(Curb)
Tell Me Why
Genesis; *We Can't Dance* . . . .(Atlantic)
That's My Story
Collin Raye; *Extremes* . . . .(Epic)
There's No Reason In The World
Original Cast; *Milk & Honey* . . . .(RCA Victor)
To Go To California Anymore (I Don't Have A Reason)
Willie Nelson; *Born For Trouble* . . . .(Columbia)
To The Moon And Back
Savage Garden; *Savage Garden* . . . .(Columbia)
Tumble In The Rough
Stone Temple Pilots; *Tiny Music...Songs From The Vatican
   Gift Shop* . . . .(Atlantic)
Two People Fell In Love
Brad Paisley; *Brad Paisley-Part II* . . . .(Arista)

Walk Away
Cool For August; *Grand World* . . . .(Warner Bros.)
Was
Kenny Wayne Shepherd Band; *Live On* . . . . (Giant)
We're Off To See The Wizard
Jewel/Jackson Browne/Ry Cooder; *The Wizard Of Oz In Concert: Dreams
   Come True-C* . . . .(Rhino)
Judy Garland; *A&E Biography: A Musical Anthology* . . . .(Capitol)
Original Cast; *The Wizard Of Oz* . . . .(TVT)
Original Soundtrack; *The Wizard Of Oz-Selections From The Original Motion
   Picture Soundtrack* . . . .(Turner Classic Movies)
Why
Annie Lennox; *Diva* . . . .(Arista)
Why Do Fools Fall In Love
Beach Boys; *Spirit Of America* . . . .(Capitol)
Diamonds; *Best Of The Diamonds-The Mercury Years* . . . .(Mercury)
Diana Ross; *Why Do Fools Fall In Love* . . . . (RCA)
Frankie Lymon and The Teenagers; *Best Of Frankie Lymon and The
   Teenagers* . . . .(Rhino)
   Billboard Top Rock 'N' Roll Hits-1956-C . . . .(Rhino)
   ST/American Graffiti . . . .(MCA)
Joni Mitchell; *Shadows & Light* . . . .(Asylum)
Why Do I LoveYou?
Barbara Cook; *Oscar Winners: The Lyrics Of Oscar Hammerstein II* . . . .(DRG)
Charlie Parker; *Yesterdays: The Jerome Kern Songbook-C* . . . .(Verve)
Margaret Whiting; *The Jerome Kern Songbook: A Fine Romance-C* . . . . .(Verve)
Original Cast; *Show Boat* . . . .(RCA Victor)
   ST/Show Boat . . . .(Rhino)
Stephane Grappelli; *Stephane Grappelli Plays Berlin, Kern, Porter And
   Rodgers & Hart* . . . .(EMI-Angel)
Why I Love You So Much
Monica; *Miss Thang* . . . . (Rowdy/Arista)
Why I'm Here
Oleander; *February Son* . . . .(Republic/Universal)
   Now That's What I Call Music!-#3-C . . . . (Virgin)
   Oleander Live At The Fillmore . . . .(Republic/Universal)
Why Pt. 2
Collective Soul; *Blender* . . . . (Atlantic)
Wonder
Natalie Merchant; *Tigerlily* . . . .(Elektra)
Yer Blues
Beatles; *The Beatles (White Album)* . . . .(Capitol)
Yesterday
Beatles; *"Yesterday"...And Today* . . . .(Capitol)
   Beatles 1 . . . .(Capitol)
   Beatles-20 Greatest Hits . . . .(Capitol)
   Beatles-Box Set . . . .(Capitol)
   Beatles-Love Songs . . . .(Capitol)
   Compact Disc Singles Collection . . . .(Capitol)
   The Beatles/1962-1966 . . . .(Capitol)
Elvis Presley; *On Stage-February, 1970* . . . . (RCA)
En Vogue; *Funky Divas* . . . .(East West)
Frank Sinatra; *My Way* . . . .(Reprise)
Paul McCartney; *The Concert For New York City-C* . . . .(Columbia)
Placido Domingo; *Domingo Songbook* . . . .(Sony Music Classical)
Ray Charles; *Ray Charles-His Greatest Hits-#1* . . . .(Dunhill Compact Classics)
Supremes; *I Hear A Symphony* . . . .(Motown)
Wings; *Wings Over America* . . . .(Capitol)
You
Jesse Powell; *'Bout It* . . . .(Silas)
You're A God
Vertical Horizon; *Everything You Want* . . . . (RCA)

REBELS, Outlaws, Rowdy, Runaways

   See Also: **CAPITAL PUNISHMENT, COWBOYS, CRIME, GUNS,
   LAW & ORDER, PIRATES, POLICE, PRISON, PROTEST, SOCIAL
   OUTCASTS, TEENAGERS, TRAVELING, WILD**

(Man Who Shot) Liberty Valance
Gene Pitney; *Gene Pitney-Anthology 1961-1968* . . . .(Rhino)
   Gene Pitney's Greatest Hits . . . .(Evergreen Music)
   Super Oldies Of The '60s-#9-C . . . . (Audio Fidelity)
Greg Kihn; *Glass House Rock* . . . .(Beserkley)
1952 Vincent Black Lightning
Richard Thompson; *Richard Thompson-Best Of Capitol Years* . . . .(Capitol)
Against The Grain
Golden Earring; *Grab It For A Second* . . . . (MCA)
Against The Law
Warrant; *Dirty Rotten Filthy Stinking Rich* . . . .(Columbia)
All I Want
Offspring; *Ixnay On The Hombre* . . . .(Columbia)
American Bad Ass
Kid Rock; *History Of Rock* . . . .(Top Dog/Lava/Atlantic)
Are You Ready?
Creed; *Human Clay* . . . . (Wind-up)

Awful
Hole; *Celebrity Skin* . . . . (David Geffen Co.)
Bad Boy For Life
P. Diddy & The Bad Boy Family; *The Saga Continues* . . . . (Bad Boy/Arista)
Totally Hits 2001-C . . . . (Arista)
Bad Boys Running Wild
Scorpions; *Love At First Sting* . . . . (Mercury)
Wold Wide Live . . . . (Mercury)
Bad Boyz
Shyne featuring Levy, Barrington; *Shyne* . . . . (Bad Boy/Arista)
Ballad Of Billy The Kid
Billy Joel; *Piano Man* . . . . (Columbia)
Songs In The Attic . . . . (Columbia)
Ballad Of Bonnie And Clyde
Georgie Fame; *History Of British Rock-#8-C* . . . . (Rhino)
Been Caught Stealing
Jane's Addiction; *Kettle Whistle* . . . .(Warner Bros.)
Big Iron
Marty Robbins; *Columbia Country Classics-#3-Americana-C* . . . . . (Columbia)
Gunfighter Ballads & Trail Songs . . . . (Legacy)
Marty Robbins' All-Time Greatest Hits . . . . (Columbia)
Marty Robbins-More Greatest Hits . . . . (Columbia)
Billy 1, 2 & 7
Bob Dylan; *ST/Pat Garrett & Billy The Kid* . . . . (Columbia)
Billy The Kid
Charlie Daniels Band; *High Lonesome* . . . .(Epic)
Billy The Kid
Marty Robbins; *Gunfighter Ballads & Trail Songs* . . . . (Legacy)
Billy The Kid
Ry Cooder; *Into The Purple Valley* . . . . (Reprise)
Billy The Kid (I Miss…)
Billy Dean; *Billy Dean* . . . . (Liberty)
Black Sheep
John Anderson; *All The People Are Talkin'* . . . .(Warner Bros.)
John Anderson's Greatest Hits . . . .(Warner Bros.)
Black Sheep
Sam The Sham and The Pharaohs; *Pharaohization! (Best Of)* . . . . (Rhino)
Black Sheep Boy
Tim Hardin; *Memorial Album* . . . . (Polydor)
Black Sheep Of The Family
Blackmore's Rainbow; *Ritchie Blackmore's R-A-I-N-B-O-W* . . . . . . (Polydor)
Bohemian Like You
Dandy Warhols; *Thirteen Tales From Urban Bohemia* . . . . . . (Capitol)
Born To Be Wild
Steppenwolf; *Billboard Top Rock 'N' Roll Hits-1968-C* . . . . (Rhino)
Live Steppenwolf . . . .(MCA)
Steppenwolf . . . .(MCA)
Steppenwolf-16 Greatest Hits . . . .(MCA)
Vintage Music-#9 & 10-C . . . .(MCA)
Born To Run
Bruce Springsteen; *Born To Run* . . . . (Columbia)
Chimes Of Freedom . . . . (Columbia)
Bruce Springsteen & The E Street Band; *Bruce Springsteen & The E Street
Band Live/1975-85* . . . . (Legacy)
Melissa Etheridge; *The Concert For New York City-C* . . . . . . (Columbia)
Breaking All The Rules
Peter Frampton; *Breaking All The Rules* . . . . (A&M)
Shine On-Collection . . . . (A&M)
Breaking All The Rules
She Moves; *Boom! 17 Explosive Hits-C* . . . . (Simitar)
Breaking All The Rules . . . . (Geffen)
Breaking All The Rules
Ozzy Osbourne; *No Rest For The Wicked* . . . .(Epic)
Buckaroo
Lee Ann Womack; *Lee Ann Womack* . . . . (Decca)
Children Of The Korn
Korn with Ice Cube; *Follow The Leader* . . . .(Immortal/Epic)
Come Back To Us Barbara Lewis Hare Krisha Beauregard
John Prine; *Common Sense* . . . . (Atlantic)
Great Days-Anthology . . . . (Rhino)
Prime Prine-The Best Of John Prine . . . . (Atlantic)
Cowboy In Me, The
Tim McGraw; *Set This Circus Down* . . . . (Curb)
Cry For The Bad Man
Lynyrd Skynyrd; *Best Of Lynyrd Skynyrd* . . . .(MCA Special Prod.)
Gimme Back My Bullets . . . .(MCA)
Cup Of Tea
Verve Pipe; *Villains* . . . . (RCA)
Damn Good Cowboy
Charlie Daniels Band; *Cowboy Super Hits-C* . . . . (Columbia)
Night Rider . . . .(Epic)
Defy You
Offspring; *Defy You-CD Single* . . . . (Columbia)
Desperado
Clint Black; *Common Thread-Songs Of The Eagles-C* . . . . . . (Giant)
Eagles; *Desperado* . . . . (Asylum)
Eagles Live . . . . (Asylum)
Eagles/Their Greatest Hits 1971-1975 . . . . (Asylum)

Hell Freezes Over . . . . (Geffen)
Linda Ronstadt; *Don't Cry Now* . . . .(Asylum)
Linda Ronstadt's Greatest Hits . . . . (Asylum)
Desperado
Alice Cooper; *Alice Cooper's Greatest Hits* . . . . (Warner Bros.)
Killer . . . . (Warner Bros.)
Desperado Love
Conway Twitty; *Fallin' For You For Years* . . . . (Warner Bros.)
Number One's: The Warner Bros. Years . . . . (Warner Bros.)
Desperados Waiting For A Train
Guy Clark; *Old No. 1* . . . . (Sugar Hill)
Jerry Jeff Walker; *Best Of Jerry Jeff Walker* . . . . (MCA)
Great Gonzos . . . . (MCA)
Viva Terlingua . . . . (MCA)
Waylon Jennings, Willie Nelson, Johnny Cash, Kris Kristofferson;
Highwayman . . . . (Columbia)
Hot Tracks-Train Super Hits-C . . . . (Epic)
Don't Take Me Alive
Steely Dan; *The Royal Scam* . . . . (MCA)
Don't You Get It
Mark Knopfler; *Golden Heart* . . . . (Warner Bros.)
El Paso
Grateful Dead; *Steal Your Face* . . . .(Grateful Dead)
Marty Robbins; *Billboard Top Country Hits-1960-C* . . . . (Rhino)
Gunfighter Ballads & Trail Songs . . . . (Legacy)
Marty Robbins' Biggest Hits . . . . (Columbia)
Radio Classics Of The '50s-C . . . . (Columbia)
Texas Super Hits-C . . . . (Columbia)
Ends
Everlast; *Whitey Ford Sings The Blues* . . . . (Tommy Boy)
Even Cowgirls Get The Blues
Emmylou Harris; *Blue Kentucky Girl* . . . . (Warner Bros.)
Johnny Cash & Waylon Jennings; *Cowboy Super Hits-C* . . . . (Columbia)
Heroes . . . . (Columbia)
Fat Lip
Sum 41; *All Killer No Filler* . . . . (Island/IDJMG)
Now That's What I Call Music!-#8-C . . . .(Virgin)
Father Christmas
Kinks; *Billboard Rock 'N Roll Christmas-C* . . . . Rhino)
Come Dancing With The Kinks-Best Of The Kinks 1977-1986 . . . . (Arista)
Friend Of The Devil
Grateful Dead; *American Beauty* . . . . (Warner Bros.)
Best Of The Grateful Dead-Skeletons From The Closet . . . . (Warner Bros.)
Dead Set . . . . (Arista)
Lyle Lovett; *Deadicated-C* . . . . (Arista)
Fugitive
Indigo Girls; *Swamp Ophelia* . . . . (Epic)
Fun, Fun, Fun
Beach Boys; *Beach Boys-Gift Set* . . . . (Capitol)
Best Of The Beach Boys . . . . (Capitol)
Endless Summer . . . . (Capitol)
Made In The U.S.A. . . . . (Capitol)
The Beach Boys In Concert . . . . (Brother)
Gee, Officer Krupke!
Original Cast; *ST/West Side Story* . . . . (Sony Broadway)
Glendale Train
New Riders Of The Purple Sage; *Best Of New Riders Of The
Purple Sage* . . . . (Columbia)
New Riders Of The Purple Sage . . . . (Columbia)
Gorilla, You're A Desperado
Warren Zevon; *Bad Luck Streak In Dancing School* . . . .(Asylum)
Growin' Up
Bruce Springsteen; *Greetings From Asbury Park, N.J.* . . . . . . (Columbia)
Live 1975-1985 . . . . (Legacy)
Tracks . . . . (Columbia)
Bruce Springsteen & The E Street Band; *Bruce Springsteen & The E Street
Band Live/1975-85* . . . . (Legacy)
Hard To Handle
Black Crowes; *Shake Your Money Maker* . . . .(Def American)
Grateful Dead; *History Of The Grateful Dead-Vol. 1 (Bear's
Choice)* . . . . (Warner Bros.)
Otis Redding; *Best Of Otis Redding* . . . .(Atlantic)
The Otis Redding Story . . . .(Atlantic)
Very Best Of Otis Redding-#2 . . . . (Rhino)
Heroes & Villains
Beach Boys; *Concert/'69-Live In London* . . . . (Capitol)
Endless Harmony . . . . (Capitol)
Good Vibrations-Thirty Years Of The Beach Boys . . . . (Capitol)
Made In The U.S.A. . . . . (Capitol)
Smiley Smile/Wild Honey . . . . (Capitol)
Sunshine Dream . . . . (Capitol)
He's A Rebel
Crystals; *Good Time Rock 'N' Roll-C* . . . . (MCA)
Phil Spector's Greatest Hits-C . . . . (Spector)
Human Nature
Madonna; *Bedtime Stories* . . . .(Maverick/Sire)
GHV2 . . . . (Warner Bros.)
I Ain't Gonna Stand For It
Stevie Wonder; *Hotter Than July* . . . . (Motown)

I Ain't Livin' Long Like This
Emmylou Harris; *Quarter Moon In A Ten Cent Town* . . . . (Warner Bros.)
Rodney Crowell; *I Ain't Livin' Long Like This* . . . . (Warner Bros.)
Rodney Crowell-Collection . . . . (Warner Bros.)
Waylon Jennings; *Waylon Jennings' Greatest Hits-#2* . . . . (RCA)
What Goes Around Comes Around . . . . (RCA)
I Fought The Law
Bobby Fuller Four; *Best Of The Bobby Fuller Four* . . . . (Rhino)
Heart & Soul Of Rock 'N' Roll-#1-C . . . . (Rhino)
Jailhouse Rock (Hits From The Big House)-C . . . . (Sony Music Special Prod.)
Oldies But Goodies-#9-C . . . . (Original Sound)
Super Oldies Of The '60s-#7-C . . . . (Audio Fidelity)
Clash; *The Clash* . . . . (Epic)
The Story Of The Clash, Volume 1 . . . . (Epic)
I Will Not Go Quietly
Don Henley; *End Of The Innocence* . . . . (Geffen)
I Won't Grow Up
Original Cast/Mary Martin; *Peter Pan-The 1954 Broadway
Production* . . . . (RCA Victor)
Iceman
Bruce Springsteen; *Tracks* . . . . (Columbia)
If The Good Die Young
Tracy Lawrence; *Alibis* . . . . (Atlantic)
I'm A Lonesome Fugitive
Merle Haggard; *Merle Haggard-16 Biggest Hits* . . . . (Legacy)
Merle Haggard & The Strangers; *Best Of Merle Haggard & The
Strangers* . . . . (Capitol)
Capitol Collectors Series-Merle Haggard & The Strangers . . . . (Capitol)
Songs I'll Always Sing . . . . (Capitol)
Roy Buchanan; *Roy Buchanan* . . . . (Polydor)
I'm Not A Juvenile Delinquent
Frankie Lymon and The Teenagers; *Best Of Frankie Lymon and The
Teenagers* . . . . (Rhino)
Original Rock 'N' Roll Hits Of The '50s-C . . . . (Roulette)
Independence Day
Bruce Springsteen; *The River* . . . . (Columbia)
Bruce Springsteen & The E Street Band; *Bruce Springsteen & The E Street
Band Live/1975-85* . . . . (Legacy)
Indian Outlaw
Tim McGraw; *Not A Moment Too Soon* . . . . (Curb)
Tim McGraw's Greatest Hits . . . . (Curb)
Indiana Wants Me
R. Dean Taylor; *Hard-To-Find Motown Classics-#2-C* . . . . (Motown)
Super Hits Of The '70s-Have A Nice Day-#3-C . . . . (Rhino)
Super Hits-#5-C . . . . (Gusto)
Infamous Angel
Iris DeMent; *Infamous Angel* . . . . (Warner Bros.)
James Dean
Eagles; *On The Border* . . . . (Elektra)
Jesse James
Country Joe McDonald; *Country Joe* . . . . (Vanguard)
Essential Country Joe McDonald . . . . (Vanguard)
Jesse James
Sam McGee; *Granddad Of The Country Guitar Pickers* . . . . (Arhoolie)
Jesse James
Bob Seger; *Smokin' O.P.'s* . . . . (Capitol)
Johnny Too Bad
Slickers; *ST/The Harder They Come* . . . . (Mango)
Taj Mahal; *Best Of Taj Mahal* . . . . (Columbia)
Mo' Roots . . . . (Legacy)
UB40; *Labour Of Love* . . . . (A&M)
Live In Moscow . . . . (A&M)
Just Like Jesse James
Cher; *Heart Of Stone* . . . . (Geffen)
Kid Charlemagne
Steely Dan; *Steely Dan's Greatest Hits* . . . . (MCA)
The Royal Scam . . . . (MCA)
Kids
Original Broadway Cast; *Bye Bye Birdie* . . . . (Columbia)
Paul Lynde; *ST/Bye Bye Birdie* . . . . (RCA)
Legend Of Bonnie And Clyde
Merle Haggard & The Strangers; *For The Record: Merle Haggard-43
Legendary Hits* . . . . (BNA)
Linda Let Me Be The One
Bruce Springsteen; *Tracks* . . . . (Columbia)
Lookin' After #1
Boomtown Rats; *Boomtown Rats* . . . . (Mercury)
Love Child
Diana Ross & The Supremes; *Billboard Top Rock 'N' Roll Hits-
1968-C* . . . . (Rhino)
Diana Ross & The Supremes' Greatest Hits-#3 . . . . (Motown)
Diana Ross & The Supremes-Anthology (1962-1969) . . . . (Motown)
Every Great #1 Hit . . . . (Motown)
Motown Story-First 25 Years-C . . . . (Motown)
Motown's Biggest Pop Hits-C . . . . (Motown)
Sweet Sensation; *Love Child* . . . . (Atco)
Maggie's Farm
Bob Dylan; *Bob Dylan At Budokan* . . . . (Columbia)
Bob Dylan's Greatest Hits-#2 . . . . (Columbia)

Bringing It All Back Home . . . . (Columbia)
Hard Rain . . . . (Columbia)
Real Live . . . . (Columbia)
Mama Tried
Grateful Dead; *Grateful Dead (Skull & Roses)* . . . . (Warner Bros.)
John Anderson & Marty Stuart; *Mama's Hungry Eyes-Merle Haggard
Tribute-C* . . . . (Arista)
Merle Haggard; *Jailhouse Rock (Hits From The Big
House)-C* . . . . (Sony Music Special Prod.)
Merle Haggard & The Strangers; *Best Of Merle Haggard & The
Strangers* . . . . (Capitol)
For The Record: Merle Haggard-43 Legendary Hits . . . . (BNA)
Okie From Muskogee . . . . (Capitol)
Songs I'll Always Sing . . . . (Capitol)
Very Best Of Merle Haggard . . . . (Capitol)
Mammas Don't Let Your Babies Grow Up To Be Cowboys
Gibson/Miller Band; *Cowboy Super Hits-C* . . . . (Columbia)
ST/The Cowboy Way . . . . (Epic)
Waylon Jennings & Willie Nelson; *Waylon & Willie* . . . . (RCA)
Waylon Jennings & Willie Nelson's Greatest Hits . . . . (RCA)
Willie Nelson; *Greatest Hits (& Some That Will Be)* . . . . (Columbia)
ST/The Electric Horseman . . . . (Columbia)
Willie & Family Live . . . . (Columbia)
Midnight Rider
Allman Brothers Band; *Beginnings* . . . . (Polydor)
Best Of The Allman Brothers Band . . . . (Polydor)
Decade Of Hits-1969-1979 . . . . (Polydor)
Idlewild South . . . . (Polydor)
*The Road Goes On Forever, A Collection Of Their Greatest
Recordings* . . . . (Polydor)
Duane Allman; *Duane Allman-An Anthology-Vol. II* . . . . (Capricorn)
Gregg Allman; *Laid Back* . . . . (Polydor)
South's Greatest Hits-C . . . . (Capricorn)
Willie Nelson; *ST/The Electric Horseman* . . . . (Columbia)
Minority
Green Day; *Warning* . . . . (Reprise)
Music
Madonna; *GHV2* . . . . (Warner Bros.)
Music . . . . (Maverick)
Totally Hits-#3-C . . . . (Atlantic)
My Generation
Who; *Live At Leeds* . . . . (MCA)
Meaty Beaty Big & Bouncy . . . . (MCA)
ST/The Kids Are Alright . . . . (MCA)
The Who Sings "My Generation" . . . . (MCA)
Who Greatest Hits . . . . (MCA)
My Kind Of Girl
Collin Raye; *Best Of Collin Raye-Direct Hits* . . . . (Epic)
Extremes . . . . (Epic)
My Life
Billy Joel; *52nd Street* . . . . (Columbia)
Billy Joel-Greatest Hits, Volume I & Volume II . . . . (Columbia)
My Way
Elvis Presley; *Aloha from Hawaii via Satellite* . . . . (RCA)
Canadian Tribute . . . . (RCA)
Elvis In Concert . . . . (RCA)
Frank Sinatra; *Frank Sinatra's Greatest Hits-#2* . . . . (Reprise)
My Way . . . . (Reprise)
Sinatra Reprise-The Very Good Years . . . . (Reprise)
Sinatra-The Main Event Live . . . . (Reprise)
The Reprise Collection . . . . (Reprise)
Paul Anka; *Very Best Of Paul Anka* . . . . (Ranwood)
Natural One
Folk Implosion; *MTV Best Of The Buzz Bin-#2-C* . . . . (Mammoth)
ST/Kids . . . . (London)
Never Could Toe The Mark
Waylon Jennings; *Never Could Toe The Mark* . . . . (RCA)
New Delhi Freight Train
Little Feat; *Time Loves A Hero* . . . . (Warner Bros.)
No Son Of Mine
Genesis; *We Can't Dance* . . . . (Atlantic)
No Such Thing
John Mayer; *Room For Squares* . . . . (Aware/C2/Columbia)
Northfield, The Disaster
Charlie Daniels Band; *Legend Of Jesse James-C* . . . . (A&M)
Northfield, The Plan
Levon Helm; *Legend Of Jesse James-C* . . . . (A&M)
Nowhere Man
Beatles; *"Yesterday"...And Today* . . . . (Capitol)
Beatles-Box Set . . . . (Capitol)
Compact Disc Singles Collection . . . . (Capitol)
The Beatles/1962-1966 . . . . (Capitol)
Oaf, The
Big Wreck; *In Loving Memory Of...* . . . . (Atlantic)
On The Banks Of The Old Pontchartrain
Hank Williams; *American Legends-#18* . . . . (Laserlight)
Complete Hank Williams . . . . (Mercury)
One Man Army
Our Lady Peace; *Happiness...Is Not A Fish That You Can Catch* . . . .(Columbia)

Original Prankster
Offspring; *Conspiracy Of One* . . . . (Columbia)
Outlaw
Joan Jett & The Blackhearts; *Good Music* . . . . (Epic Portrait Assoc.)
Outlaw
War; *Best Of War...And More-#2* . . . . (Avenue)
Outlaw
Dangerous Toys; *Dangerous Toys* . . . . (Columbia)
Outlaw
Cult; *Electric* . . . . (Sire)
Outlaw
Tom Johnston; *Everything You've Heard Is True* . . . . (Warner Bros.)
Outlaw
Dan Fogelberg; *High Country Snows* . . . . (Full Moon)
Outlaw
Scream; *Let It Scream* . . . . (Hollywood)
Outlaw
Whitesnake; *Love Hunter* . . . . (Geffen)
Outlaw & The Stranger
Ed Bruce; *Ed Bruce* . . . . (MCA)
Outlaw Blues
Pat Benatar; *Best Shots* . . . . (Chrysalis)
Tropico . . . . (Chrysalis)
Outlaw Blues
Bob Dylan; *Bringing It All Back Home* . . . . (Columbia)
Outlaw Man
Eagles; *Desperado* . . . . (Asylum)
Outlaw Women
Hank Williams, Jr.; *Bocephus Box-Collection-1979-1992* . . . . (Capricorn)
Whiskey Bent & Hell Bound . . . . (WB/Curb)
Outlaws & Lone Star Beer
C.W. McCall; *C.W. McCall & Company* . . . . (Polydor)
Outlaw's Prayer
Johnny Paycheck; *Armed & Crazy* . . . . (Epic)
Johnny Paycheck's Biggest Hits . . . . (Epic)
Outside The Law
Rundle Chowning Band; *Heart On Fire* . . . . (A&M)
Pancho And Lefty
Merle Haggard; *For The Record: Merle Haggard-43 Legendary Hits* . . . . (BNA)
Merle Haggard & Willie Nelson; *19 Hot Country Requests-C* . . . . (Epic)
All Time Legends Of Country Music-C . . . . (Legacy)
Columbia Country Classics-#3-Americana-C . . . . (Columbia)
His Epic Hits-First 11 To Be Continued-C . . . . (Epic)
Pancho And Lefty . . . . (Epic)
Townes Van Zandt; *Live & Obscure* . . . . (Sugar Hill)
Pepper
Butthole Surfers; *Electriclarryland* . . . . (Capitol)
Prince Of The Punks
Kinks; *One For The Road* . . . . (Arista)
Problem Child
AC/DC; *Dirty Deeds Done Dirt Cheap* . . . . (Atlantic)
If You Want Blood You've Got It . . . . (Atlantic)
Let There Be Rock . . . . (Atco)
Problem Child
Royal Tramps; *Dangerous & Extremely Unhealthy* . . . . (Red Light)
Problem Child
3rd Bass; *Derelicts Of Dialect* . . . . (Def Jam)
Problem Child
Damned; *Light At The End Of The Tunnel* . . . . (MCA)
Problem Child
Mitch Malloy; *Mitch Malloy* . . . . (RCA)
Problem Child
Hanoi Rocks; *Self-Destruction Blues* . . . . (Geffen)
Problem Child
Graham Parker And The Rumour; *Stick To Me* . . . . (Mercury)
Punks Not Dead
Exploited; *Apocalypse '77* . . . . (Relativity)
Put Up Or Shut Up
Ted Nugent; *Intensities In 10 Cities* . . . . (Epic)
Question Everything
8Stops7; *In Moderation* . . . . (Reprise)
Rascal King
Mighty Mighty Bosstones; *Let's Face It* . . . . (Big Rig/Mercury)
Live From The Middle East . . . . (Big Rig/Mercury)
Rebel
Roger Daltrey; *Under A Raging Moon* . . . . (Atlantic)
Rebel
Bryan Adams; *Into The Fire* . . . . (A&M)
Rebel
Black Oak Arkansas; *Live Mutha* . . . . (Atco)
Rebel
Quicksilver Messenger Service; *Quicksilver* . . . . (Capitol)
Rebel
Sly & Robbie; *Silent Assassin* . . . . (Island)
Rebel Girl
Joe Glazer; *Songs Of Joe Hill* . . . . (Smithsonian Folkways)
Rebel Girl
Outlaws; *Los Hombres Malo* . . . . (Arista)

Rebel Heart
Rod Stewart; *Vagabond Heart* . . . . (Warner Bros.)
Rebel Music
Bob Marley & The Wailers; *Babylon By Bus* . . . .(Tuff Gong)
Natty Dread . . . .(Tuff Gong)
Rebel Music . . . .(Tuff Gong)
Rebel Rebel
David Bowie; *Changesbowie* . . . . (Rykodisc)
David Live . . . . (Rykodisc)
Diamond Dogs . . . . (Rykodisc)
Sound + Vision . . . . (Rykodisc)
The Singles-1969-1993 . . . . (Rykodisc)
Rebel Rock Me
Pretenders; *Last Of The Independents* . . . .(Sire)
Rebel Rouser
Bob Welch; *Another One* . . . . (Capitol)
Duane Eddy; *Cruisin'-1958-C* . . . . (Increase)
Duane Eddy-16 Greatest Hits . . . . (Jamie)
Duane Eddy-Pure Gold . . . . (RCA)
Legends Of Rock Guitar-'50s-#1-C . . . . (Rhino)
Old 'N Golden . . . . (Jamie)
ST/Forrest Gump . . . .(Epic/Sony Music Soundtrax)
Ventures; *Best Of The Ventures* . . . . (EMI)
Rebel With A Cause
Silent Rage; *Shattered Hearts* . . . . (Chameleon)
Rebel With A Cause
Indecent Obsession; *Indio* . . . . (MCA)
Rebel Without A Clue
Bonnie Tyler; *Secret Dreams And Forbidden Fire* . . . . (Columbia)
Rebel Without A Pause
Public Enemy; *Def Jam Classics-#1-C* . . . . (Def Jam)
It Takes A Nation Of Millions To Hold Us Back . . . . (Def Jam)
Rap's Biggest Hits-C . . . . (K-Tel)
Rebel Yell
Billy Idol; *MTV's Rock 'N' Roll To Go-C* . . . . (Elektra)
Rebel Yell . . . . (Chrysalis)
Rebel-Johnny Yuma
Johnny Cash; *The Man In Black-His Greatest Hits* . . . . (Legacy)
Rebels
Tom Petty And The Heartbreakers; *Pack Up The Plantation-Live!* . . . . . (MCA)
Southern Accents . . . . (MCA)
Rebels Are We
Chic; *Real People* . . . .(Atlantic)
Rebels Without A Clue
Bellamy Brothers; *Bellamy Brothers' Greatest Hits-#3* . . . . (MCA)
Rebels Without A Clue . . . . (MCA)
Renegade
Styx; *Pieces Of Eight* . . . . (A&M)
Styx-Classics-#15 . . . . (A&M)
Renegade, The
Ian & Sylvia; *Ian & Sylvia's Greatest Hits* . . . . (Vanguard)
Nashville . . . . (Vanguard)
Renegades Of Funk
Rage Against The Machine; *Renegades* . . . . (Epic)
Renegades, Rebels And Rogues
Tracy Lawrence; *ST/Maverick* . . . .(Atlantic)
Ride Like The Wind
Christopher Cross; *Christopher Cross* . . . . (Warner Bros.)
Rock & Roll Outlaw
Foghat; *Rock & Roll Outlaws* . . . . (Rhino)
Rock 'N' Roll Outlaw
Peter Wells; *Everything You Like Tries To Kill You* . . . .(Zoo)
Rock 'N' Roll Rebel
Ozzy Osbourne; *Bark At The Moon* . . . . (CBS Associated)
Rollin' Stoned
Great White; *Can't Get There From Here* . . . . (Portrait)
Rough Boy
ZZ Top; *Afterburner* . . . . (Warner Bros.)
ZZ Top's Greatest Hits . . . . (Warner Bros.)
Rough Boys
Pete Townshend; *Classic Rock 1966-1988-C* . . . .(Atlantic)
Empty Glass . . . . (Atco)
Who; *Join Together* . . . . (MCA)
Run Away
Slade; *Keep Your Hands Off My Power Supply* . . . . (CBS Associated)
Run Away Child, Running Wild
Temptations; *All The Million-Sellers* . . . . (Motown)
Cloud Nine . . . . (Motown)
Compact Command Performances-Temptations . . . . (Motown)
Temptations' Greatest Hits-#2 . . . . (Motown)
Temptations-Anthology-The Best Of The Temptations . . . . (Motown)
Runaway
Bonnie Raitt; *Bonnie Raitt-Collection* . . . . (Warner Bros.)
Sweet Forgiveness . . . . (Warner Bros.)
Del Shannon; *Billboard Top Rock 'N' Roll Hits-1961-C* . . . . (Rhino)
Cruisin'-1961-C . . . . (Increase)
Del Shannon's Greatest Hits . . . . (Rhino)
Heart & Soul Of Rock 'N' Roll-#1-C . . . . (Rhino)

Little Town Flirt . . . . (Rhino)
ST/American Graffiti . . . . (MCA)
Elvis Presley; *Collector's Gold* . . . . (RCA)

Runaway Girl
Dion; *Runaround Sue* . . . . (Collectables)
Dion And The Belmonts; *Dion And The Belmonts-20 Golden
Classics* . . . . (Collectables)
Everything You Always Wanted To Hear . . . .(Laurie)

Runaway Train
Soul Asylum; *Grave Dancers Union* . . . . (Columbia)

Sad Punk
Pixies; *Trompe Le Monde* . . . . (Elektra)

She's Leaving Home
Al Jarreau; *All Fly Home* . . . . (Warner Bros.)
Beatles; *Beatles-Box Set* . . . . (Capitol)
Beatles-Love Songs . . . . (Capitol)
Sgt. Pepper's Lonely Hearts Club Band . . . . (Capitol)

Shy Of The Moon
Wallflowers; *The Wallflowers* . . . .(Virgin)

Sitting In Limbo
Jimmy Cliff; *ST/The Harder They Come* . . . . (Mango)
ST/The Harder They Come . . . . (Mango)

Stop Running Away
Brenda Russell; *Brenda Russell's Greatest Hits* . . . . (A&M)

Street Fighting Man
Rod Stewart; *Best Of Rod Stewart* . . . . (Mercury)
Sing It Again, Rod . . . . (Mercury)
Storyteller/The Complete Anthology: 1964-1990 . . . . (Warner Bros.)
Rolling Stones; *Beggars Banquet* . . . . (Abkco)
Get Yer Ya-Ya's Out! . . . . (Abkco)
Hot Rocks 1964-1971 . . . . (Abkco)
Singles Collection-The London Years . . . . (Abkco)
Through The Past, Darkly (Big Hits Vol. 2) . . . . (Abkco)

Streets Of Fire
Bruce Springsteen; *Darkness On The Edge Of Town* . . . . . . (Columbia)

Swingin'
Tom Petty And The Heartbreakers; *Echo* . . . . (Warner Bros.)

Take The Skinheads Bowling
Camper Van Beethoven; *Telephone Free Landslide Victory* . . . . (I.R.S.)

Theme From "The Fugitive"
Original Soundtrack; *Television's Greatest Hits-#4-Black & White
Classics-C* . . . . (TVT)

Theme From "The Legend Of Jesse James"
Original Soundtrack; *Television's Greatest Hits-#4-Black & White
Classics-C* . . . . (TVT)

Theme From "The Magnificent Seven"
BBC Concert Orchestra; *Golden Cinema Classics-#1-The
Adventure Film* . . . . (Bainbridge)

Theme From "The Rebel"
Original Soundtrack; *Television's Greatest Hits-#2-C* . . . . . . (TVT)

Ties That Bind
Bruce Springsteen; *The River* . . . . (Columbia)

Trouble Child
Joni Mitchell; *Court & Spark* . . . . (Asylum)

Walk Unafraid
R.E.M.; *Up* . . . . (Warner Bros.)

Walkaway Joe
Trisha Yearwood; *Hearts In Armor* . . . . (MCA)
Songbook-A Collection Of Hits . . . . (MCA)

Wanderer
Dion; *20 Million-Dollar Memories-#1-C* . . . . (Laurie)
Billboard Top Rock 'N' Roll Hits-1962-C . . . . (Rhino)
Cruisin'-1962-C . . . . (Increase)
Oldies But Goodies-#5-C . . . . (Original Sound)
ST/The Wanderers . . . . (Warner Bros.)
The Wanderer . . . . (Laurie)

Wanted
Alan Jackson; *Alan Jackson-The Greatest Hits Collection* . . . . (Arista)
Country's Greatest Hits-#8-Lonely Hearts-C . . . .(Priority)
Here In The Real World . . . . (Arista)

Wanted Man
Johnny Cash; *Essential Johnny Cash* . . . . (Columbia)
Johnny Cash At Folsom Prison & San Quentin . . . . (Columbia)

Wanted Man
George Thorogood & The Destroyers; *Bad To The Bone* . . . . (EMI)

Wanted Man
Ratt; *Out Of The Cellar* . . . . (Atlantic)
Ratt & Roll 8191 . . . . (Atlantic)

Warning
Green Day; *Warning* . . . .(Reprise)

Way I Am
Eminem; *The Marshall Mathers LP* . . . .(Aftermath/Interscope)

We're All In The Same Gang
West Coast Rap All-Stars; *We're All In The Same Gang-C* . . . . . . (Warner Bros.)

We're Not Gonna Take It
Who; *Join Together* . . . . (MCA)
ST/Woodstock . . . . (Atlantic)
Tommy . . . . (MCA)

We're Not Gonna Take It
Twisted Sister; *Big Hits & Nasty Cuts* . . . . (Atlantic)
Stay Hungry . . . . (Atlantic)

White Punks On Dope
Tubes; *T.R.A.S.H. (Tubes Rarities And Smash Hits)* . . . . (A&M)
Tubes . . . .(A&M)
What Do You Want From Live . . . .(A&M)

You Can't Run From Love
Eddie Rabbitt; *Best Of Eddie Rabbitt/Greatest Hits-II* . . . . (Warner Bros.)
Eddie Rabbitt-#1's . . . . (Warner Bros.)
Radio Romance . . . . (Elektra)

You Keep Runnin' Away
38 Special; *Special Forces* . . . . (A&M)

Your Body Is An Outlaw
Mel Tillis; *Your Body Is An Outlaw* . . . . (Elektra)

RECORD BUSINESS, Music Business

**See Also: BUSINESS & INDUSTRY, CITIES: A-Z, COUNTRY,
ELVIS, HOLLYWOOD, JUKEBOX, MONEY, MUSIC, MUSICAL
INSTRUMENTS (various), RADIO, ROCK & ROCKING, SHOW BIZ,
TELEVISION**

16th Avenue
Lacy J. Dalton; *19 Hot Country Requests-#2-C* . . . . (Epic)
Greatest Country Hits Of The '80s-1982-C . . . .(Columbia)
Lacy J. Dalton's Greatest Hits . . . .(Columbia)

2120 South Michigan Avenue
Rolling Stones; *12 X 5* . . . . (Abkco)

Aluminum Record Award
Nitty Gritty Dirt Band; *Stars And Stripes Forever* . . . .(Capitol)

American Bad Ass
Kid Rock; *History Of Rock* . . . . (Top Dog/Lava/Atlantic)

Are You Sure Hank Done It This Way
Hank Williams, Jr.; *Rowdy* . . . .(WB/Curb)
Waylon Jennings; *Waylon Jennings' Greatest Hits* . . . . (RCA)

Back When He Was Hungry
Bill Anderson; *A Lot Of Things Different* . . . . (Varese Sarabande)

Been Around The World
Puff Daddy & The Family; *No Way Out* . . . . (Bad Boy/Arista)

Can't Nobody Hold Me Down
Puff Daddy; *No Way Out* . . . . (Bad Boy/Arista)

Creeque Alley
Mamas & The Papas; *Best Of The Mamas & The Papas* . . . . (MCA)
Mamas & The Papas' Greatest Hits . . . . (MCA)
Mamas & The Papas-16 Of Their Greatest Hits . . . . (MCA)

Fake Your Way To The Top
Original Cast; *Dreamgirls* . . . . (Geffen)

Feel So Good
Mase; *Harlem World* . . . . (Bad Boy/Arista)

Forgot About Dre
Dr. Dre featuring Eminem; *Dr. Dre 2001* . . . . (Aftermath/Interscope)

Free Man In Paris
Joni Mitchell; *Court & Spark* . . . . (Asylum)
Shadows & Light . . . . (Asylum)

Gimme Back My Bullets
Lynyrd Skynyrd; *Gimme Back My Bullets* . . . . (MCA)
Gold & Platinum . . . . (MCA)
Southern By The Grace Of God-Tribute '87 . . . . (MCA)

Have A Cigar
Pink Floyd; *Wish You Were Here* . . . .(Columbia)

How To Kill A Radio Consultant
Public Enemy; *Apocalypse 91...The Enemy Strikes Black* . . (Def Jam/Columbia)
Greatest Misses . . . .(Chaos)

I Wonder What It Takes To Make A Record Good
Kent Smith & Renda; *45-#103* . . . . (Fountain)

It Ain't My Fault
Silkk The Shocker; *Charge It 2 Da Game* . . . .(No Limit/Priority)

It's A Long Way To The Top
AC/DC; *High Voltage* . . . .(Atco)

Just Be Straight With Me
Silkk The Shocker; *Charge It 2 Da Game* . . . .(No Limit/Priority)

Just Push Play
Aerosmith; *Just Push Play* . . . .(Columbia)

Look Into My Eyes
Bone Thugs-N-Harmony; *Art Of War* . . . . (Ruthless/Relativity)

Love Me
112 Featuring Mase; *Room 112* . . . . (Bad Boy/Arista)

Mercury Poisoning
Graham Parker And The Rumour; *Live Sparks* . . . .(Arista)

Motown Song
Larry John McNally; *Fade To Black* . . . . (Atco)
Rod Stewart; *Vagabond Heart* . . . . (Warner Bros.)

Mr. Record Man
Willie Nelson; *Best Of Willie Nelson* . . . .(Capitol)

Horse Called Music . . . . (Columbia)
Willie & Family Live . . . . (Columbia)
Murder On Music Row
George Strait & Alan Jackson; *Latest Greatest Straitest Hits* . . . .(MCA)
One Hit Wonder
Everclear; *So Much For The Afterglow* . . . . (Capitol)
Overnight Sensation (Hit Record)
Eric Carmen; *Eric Carmen-The Definitive Collection* . . . . (Arista)
Raspberries; *Raspberries' Best Featuring Eric Carmen*. . . . . (Capitol)
Put Your Hands Where My Eyes Could See
Busta Rhymes; *When Disaster Strikes* . . . . (Elektra)
Record Executive Blues
Catfish Hodge Band; *Eyewitness Blues*. . . . . (Adelphi)
Rex Bob Lowenstein
Mark Germino; *Rank & File* . . . . (Winter Harvest Entert.)
Rosalita
Bruce Springsteen; *The Wild, The Innocent & The E Street Shuffle* . . (Columbia)
Bruce Springsteen & The E Street Band; *Bruce Springsteen & The E Street Band Live/1975-85* . . . . (Legacy)
Sell Out
Reel Big Fish; *Turn The Radio Off* . . . . (Mojo Music/Universal)
Show Business
AC/DC; *High Voltage*. . . . . (Atco)
Singing In My Sleep
Semisonic; *Feeling Strangely Fine* . . . .(MCA)
So You Want To Be A Rock 'N' Roll Star
Byrds; *Original Singles-#1-1965-1967* . . . . (Columbia)
Rock Classics Of The '60s-C . . . . (Columbia)
The Byrds (Untitled) . . . . (Columbia)
The Byrds (Untitled) . . . . (Legacy)
The Byrds' Greatest Hits . . . . (Columbia)
Patti Smith Group; *Wave* . . . . (Arista)
Tom Petty And The Heartbreakers; *Pack Up The Plantation-Live!* . . . . . .(MCA)
The Ultimate Rock Album-C . . . . (Foundation)
Still A G Thang
Snoop Dogg; *Da Game Is To Be Sold, Not To Be Told* . . . . . (No Limit/Priority)
Suzi Wants To Be A Rock Star
Professor Griff & His Last Asiatic Disciples; *Pawns In The Game* . . . . . . (Luke)
Take 54
Nilsson; *Son Of Schmilsson* . . . . (RCA)
Tenth Avenue Freeze-Out
Bruce Springsteen; *Born To Run*. . . . . (Columbia)
Bruce Springsteen & The E Street Band; *Bruce Springsteen & The E Street Band Live/1975-85* . . . . (Legacy)
They Call It Rock
Nick Lowe; *Pure Pop For Now People* . . . . (Columbia)
Transistor
311; *Transistor* . . . . (Capricorn)
Under Assistant West Coast Promotion Man
Rolling Stones; *Out Of Our Heads* . . . . (Abkco)
Singles Collection-The London Years . . . . (Abkco)
Voice Of Harold
R.E.M.; *Dead Letter Office* . . . .(I.R.S.)
Workin' It
Don Henley; *Inside Job* . . . .(Warner Bros.)
Working For MCA
Hank Williams, Jr.; *Hank Williams, Jr. "Live"* . . . . (WB/Curb)
Lynyrd Skynyrd; *Best Of The Rest Of Lynyrd Skynyrd* . . . .(MCA)
One More From The Road . . . .(MCA)
Second Helping . . . .(MCA)
Write Your Own Songs (Mr. Record Executive)
Asleep At The Wheel; *Asleep At The Wheel* . . . . (MCA Special Prod.)
Waylon Jennings & Willie Nelson; *WWII* . . . . (RCA)
Willie Nelson; *Revolutions In Time-The Journey-1975-1993* . . . . (Legacy)
Willie Nelson & Kris Kristofferson; *Music From "Songwriter"*. . . . (Columbia)
Wrong Side Of Memphis
Matraca Berg; *Bittersweet Surrender* . . . . (RCA)
Trisha Yearwood; *Grand Ole Opry-75 Years-#1-C* . . . .(MCA)
Hearts In Armor. . . . .(MCA)

REFLECTIONS, Mirrors

See Also: **ECHOES, REMEMBER, SHADOWS**

Go To The Mirror Boy
Who; *Tommy* . . . .(MCA)
I Never Go Around Mirrors
Lefty Frizzell; *Grand Ole Opry-75 Years-#1-C* . . . .(MCA)
Landslide
Fleetwood Mac; *25 Years-The Chain* . . . .(Warner Bros.)
Fleetwood Mac . . . . (Reprise)
Fleetwood Mac Live . . . .(Warner Bros.)
The Dance . . . . (Reprise)
Smashing Pumpkins; *Pisces Iscariot* . . . . (Virgin)
Look Into The Mirror
Juluka; *Stand Your Ground*. . . . .(Warner Bros.)

Magic Mirror
Whirlers; *Harlem Holiday-New York Rhythm & Blues-#1-C* . . . . . (Collectables)
Magic Mirror
Leon Russell; *Carney* . . . . (Right Stuff)
Man In The Mirror
Michael Jackson; *Bad* . . . . (Epic)
Man In The Mirror
Jim Glaser; *Man In The Mirror* . . . . (Noble Vision)
Mirror
Graham Central Station; *Mirror* . . . . (Warner Bros.)
Mirror
King Swamp; *King Swamp* . . . .(Virgin)
Mirror
Spooky Tooth; *Mirror*. . . . . (Island)
Mirror Freak
Steve Harley & Cockney Rebel; *Closer Look* . . . .(Harvest)
Mirror Image
Cher; *Prisoner*. . . . . (Casablanca)
Mirror Image
Rosanne Cash; *Interiors* . . . . (Columbia)
Mirror In The Bathroom
English Beat; *I Just Can't Stop It*. (I.R.S.)
ST/Dance Craze . . . . (Chrysalis)
What Is Beat . . . . (I.R.S.)
Mirror Man
Captain Beefheart & His Magic Band; *Mirror Man* . . . . (One Way)
Mirror Man
Prism; *Armageddon*. . . . . (Capitol)
Mirror Man
Human League; *Human League's Greatest Hits* . . . . (A&M)
Mirror Man
Talk Talk; *Party's Over*. . . . . (EMI)
Mirror Man
Pere Ubu; *Worlds In Collision* . . . .(Fontana)
Mirror Mirror
Diamond Rio; *Diamond Rio* . . . . (Arista)
Diamond Rio's Greatest Hits . . . . (Arista)
Mirror Mirror
Barbara Mandrell; *I'll Be Your Jukebox Tonight* . . . . (Capitol)
The Barbara Mandrell Collection . . . . (EMI Special Markets)
Mirror Star
Fabulous Poodles; *Mirror Stars* . . . . (Epic)
Mirror, The
Marvin Hamlisch; *ST/The Mirror Has Two Faces* . . . . (Columbia)
Mirrors
King Crimson; *In The Court Of The Crimson King-An Observation By King Crimson* . . . . (Editions E.G.)
Mirrors
Blue Oyster Cult; *Mirrors* . . . . (Columbia)
Objects In The Rear View Mirror May Appear Closer Than They Are
Meat Loaf; *Bat Out Of Hell II: Back Into Hell*. . . . . (MCA)
Piggy In the Mirror
Cure; *Top*. . . . .(Sire)
Rearviewmirror
Pearl Jam; *Vs*. . . . . (Epic Portrait Assoc.)
Reflection
Tony Bennett; *Life Is Beautiful* . . . . (Improv)
Reflection
Christina Aguilera; *Christina Aguilera*. . . . .(RCA)
ST/Mulan . . . . (Walt Disney)
Reflection
Cure; *Seventeen Seconds* . . . . (Elektra)
Reflections
Diana Ross & The Supremes; *Diana Ross & The Supremes' Greatest Hits-#3*. . . . . (Motown)
Diana Ross & The Supremes-25th Anniversary . . . . (Motown)
Diana Ross & The Supremes-Anthology (1962-1969) . . . . (Motown)
Motown Story-First 25 Years-C . . . . (Motown)
Four Tops; *Four Tops-Anthology* . . . . (Motown)
Still Waters Run Deep. . . . . (Motown)
Until You Love Someone: More Of The Best (1965-1970) . . . . (Rhino)
Luther Vandross; *Songs* . . . . (Epic)
Reflections
Thelonius Monk; *Alone In San Francisco* . . . . (Riverside)
Thelonius Monk-Composer . . . . (Columbia)
Reflections
Steppenwolf; *The Second* . . . . (MCA)
Reflections
Charlie Daniels Band; *Million Mile Reflections* . . . . (Epic)
Reflections In A Crystal Wind
Mimi & Richard Farina; *Best Of Mimi & Richard Farina*. . . . . (Vanguard)
Reflections In A Crystal Wind. . . . . (Vanguard)
Reflections Of My Life
Marmalade; *History Of British Rock-#1-C* . . . . (Rhino)
London Collector-Rock Invasion-C . . . . (London)
Super Hits Of The '70s-Have A Nice Day-#2-C . . . . (Rhino)
Room Full Of Mirrors
Jimi Hendrix; *Essential Jimi Hendrix* . . . . (Reprise)

Lifelines/Jimi Hendrix Story . . . .(Reprise)
Pretenders; *Get Close* . . . .(Sire)
Silver Future
Monster Magnet; *ST/Heavy Metal 2000* . . . . (Restless)
Smash The Mirror
Who; *Join Together* . . . . (MCA)
Tommy . . . . (MCA)
Wherever You Go
Clint Black; *Clint Black-The Greatest Hits* . . . .(RCA)
One Emotion . . . .(RCA)

RELAX, At Ease, Comfortable, Laid Back, Lazy

See Also: **BUSY, CAREFREE, EASY, FUN, HAPPINESS, PARTY,**
PEACE, SLOW, TIME: GENERAL

(Sittin' On) The Dock Of The Bay
Michael Bolton; *The Hunger* . . . . (Columbia)
Otis Redding; *(Sittin' On) The Dock Of The Bay* . . . . (Atco)
Best Of Otis Redding . . . . (Atco)
Golden Age Of Black Music-1960-1970-C . . . . (Atlantic)
Golden Soul-C . . . . (Atlantic)
Soul Years-C . . . . (Atlantic)
The Otis Redding Story . . . . (Atlantic)
59th Street Bridge Song (Feelin' Groovy)
Harper's Bizarre; *Baby Boomer Classics-More Mellow*
Sixties-C . . . .(JCI Assoc. Labels)
Better Days-C . . . . (Rhino)
Simon & Garfunkel; *Collected Works* . . . . (Columbia)
Parsley Sage Rosemary & Thyme . . . . (Columbia)
Simon & Garfunkel's Greatest Hits . . . . (Columbia)
The Concert In Central Park . . . . (Warner Bros.)
All Night Long
Faith Evans featuring Puff Daddy; *Keep The Faith* . . . . (Bad Boy/Arista)
Boy Who Wouldn't Hoe Corn
Alison Krauss & Union Station; *New Favorite* . . . . (Rounder)
Come On Over
Shania Twain; *Come On Over* . . . . (Mercury)
Cool Relax
Jon B.; *Cool Relax* . . . .(Yab Yum/550)
Country State Of Mind
Hank Williams, Jr.; *Hank Williams, Jr.'s Greatest Hits III* . . . .(Curb)
Montana Cafe . . . . (WB/Curb)
Crazy Little Thing Called Love
Dwight Yoakam; *Last Chance For A Thousand Years-Greatest Hits From*
The '90s . . . .(Reprise)
Queen; *Queen's Greatest Hits I & II* . . . . (Hollywood)
The Game . . . . (Hollywood)
Cuddle Up A Little Closer
Jimmy Roselli; *When Your Old Wedding Ring Was* . . . . (M&R)
Everybody's Got Something To Hide Except Me And My Monkey
Beatles; *The Beatles (White Album)* . . . . (Capitol)
Flowers On The Wall
Eric Heatherly; *Swimming In Champagne* . . . . (Mercury)
Statler Brothers; *All Time Legends Of Country Music-C* . . . . (Legacy)
Best Of The Statler Brothers . . . . (Mercury)
Billboard Top Country Hits-1966-C . . . . (Rhino)
Columbia Country Classics-#3-Americana-C . . . . (Columbia)
Pop Classics Of The '60s-C . . . . (Columbia)
Gimme Some Lovin'
Spencer Davis Group; *Best Of The Spencer Davis Group* . . . . (EMI)
Grazing In The Grass
Boney James & Rick Braun; *Shake It Up* . . . . (Warner Bros.)
Hugh Masekela; *Promise Of A Future* . . . . (Uni)
Sixties Rule! Chapter 1-C . . . . (One Way)
Groovin'
Aretha Franklin; *Lady Soul* . . . . (Atlantic)
Booker T. & The M.G.s; *Best Of Booker T. & The M.G.s* . . . . (Atlantic)
Soul Shots-#3-Soul Twist-C . . . . (Rhino)
Rascals; *Groovin'* . . . . (Warner Special Prod.)
Hit Singles-1958-1977-C . . . . (Atlantic)
Rascals' Greatest Hits . . . . (Atlantic)
ST/Platoon . . . . (Atlantic)
Heaven Right Here
Jeb Loy Nichols; *Just What Time It Is* . . . . (Rykodisc)
Honey, I'm Home
Shania Twain; *Come On Over* . . . . (Mercury)
Honeysuckle Honey
Commander Cody & His Lost Planet Airmen; *Country Casanova* . . . . . . (MCA)
I Think God Can Explain
Splender; *ST/Dawson's Creek-#2* . . . . (C2/Columbia)
I'm The Laziest Gal In Town
Julie Wilson; *Cole Porter Songbook* . . . .(DRG)
In The Summertime
Mungo Jerry; *In The Summertime-Best Of Mungo Jerry* . . . .(Rhino)
Super Hits Of The '70s-Have A Nice Day-#3-C . . . .(Rhino)

Just Cruisin'
Will Smith; *ST/Men In Black* . . . . (Columbia)
Keep It Gay
Original Cast; *Me & Juliet* . . . . (RCA Victor)
Kicking Back In Amsterdam
Kevin Welch; *Life Down Here On Earth* . . . . (Dead Reckoning)
Kokomo
Beach Boys; *ST/Cocktail* . . . .(Elektra)
Still Cruisin' . . . . (Capitol)
Lazy Afternoon
Barbra Streisand; *Lazy Afternoon* . . . . (Columbia)
Marlene Dietrich; *At The Cafe De Paris* . . . . (Columbia)
Patti Austin; *Real Me* . . . . (Qwest)
Tony Bennett; *Forty Years-The Artistry Of Tony Bennett* . . . . (Columbia)
Tony Bennett At Carnegie Hall . . . . (Sony Music Special Prod.)
Lazy Day
Moody Blues; *On The Threshold Of A Dream* . . . . (Polydor)
Lazy Day
Spanky & Our Gang; *Best Of Spanky & Our Gang* . . . .(Rhino)
Lazy Days
Enya; *A Day Without Rain* . . . . (Reprise)
Lazy Eye
Goo Goo Dolls; *ST/Batman & Robin-Music From And Inspired By The*
Motion Picture . . . . (Jive)
Lazy River
Bing Crosby; *All-Time Best Of* . . . .(Curb)
Bobby Darin; *Mack The Knife-Best Of Bobby Darin-#2* . . . . (Atlantic)
Chet Atkins & Les Paul; *Masters Of The Guitar-Together* . . . . (Pair)
Harry Connick, Jr.; *Eleven* . . . .(Columbia)
Kay Starr; *Kay Starr's Greatest Hits* . . . .(Curb)
Leon Redbone; *Up A Lazy River* . . . . (Private Music)
Louis Armstrong; *Louis Armstrong-Best Of The Decca Years-#1-The*
Singer-C . . . . (Decca)
Mills Brothers; *Mills Brothers' Greatest Hits* . . . . (MCA)
The Mills Brothers-Best Of The Decca Years . . . .(Decca)
Lazy Sunday
Small Faces; *Immediate Singles Collection-#2-C* . . . (Sony Music Special Prod.)
Ogdens' Nut Gone Flake . . . . (Abkco)
Lazybones
Don Redman & His Orchestra; *Don Redman-1933-1936* . . . . (Classics)
Harry Connick, Jr.; *25* . . . . (Columbia)
Kay Starr; *The Hoagy Carmichael Songbook-C* . . . .(Bluebird)
Mildred Bailey; *Mildred Bailey-1932-1936* . . . . (Classics)
Let It All Out (Let It All Hang Out)
Hombres; *Dick Bartley's One-Hit Wonders Of The '60s-#2-C* . . . .(Rhino)
Let It Out (Let It All Hang Out) . . . . (Verve/Forecast)
Summer Of Love-#2-Turn On-Mind Expansion & Signs Of The
Times-C . . . .(Rhino)
Let's Get Rocked
Def Leppard; *Adrenalize* . . . .(Mercury)
Listen To A Country Song
Loggins & Messina; *Loggins & Messina-On Stage* . . . .(Columbia)
Sittin' In. . . . . (Columbia)
Lynn Anderson; *Country Chartbusters-#2.* . . . . (Columbia)
Lynn Anderson's Greatest Hits . . . . (Columbia)
Lookin' Out My Back Door
Creedence Clearwater Revival; *1970.* . . . . (Fantasy)
Cosmo's Factory. . . . . (Fantasy)
Creedence Clearwater Revival-Chronicle . . . . (Fantasy)
Creedence Country . . . . (Fantasy)
More Creedence Gold. . . . . (Fantasy)
Loungin
L.L. Cool J; *All World* . . . . (Def Jam)
Hip Hop Coast 2 Coast-C . . . . (Priority)
Yo! MTV Raps-C . . . . (Def Jam)
Margaritaville
Jimmy Buffett; *Changes In Latitudes, Changes In Attitudes* . . . . (MCA)
Songs You Know By Heart-Jimmy Buffett's Greatest Hit(s) . . . . (MCA)
You Had To Be There . . . . (MCA)
Meanwhile Back At The Ranch
Clark Family Experience; *Meanwhile Back At The Ranch* . . . .(Curb)
Mercedes Benz
Janis Joplin; *Pearl* . . . .(Legacy)
ST/Janis. . . . .(Columbia)
Nice & Slow
Usher; *My Way* . . . .(LaFace)
Rainy Day, Dream Away
Jimi Hendrix Experience; *Electric Ladyland* . . . . (Reprise)
Recover Your Soul
Elton John; *The Big Picture* . . . . (Rocket)
Restless
Carl Perkins; *Jive After Five-Best Of Carl Perkins-1959-1978* . . . .(Rhino)
Mark O'Connor; *Great Divorce Songs For Him-C* . . . . (Warner Bros.)
The New Nashville Cats. . . . . (Warner Bros.)
Rockin' Chair Money
Hank Williams; *Alone With His Guitar* . . . . (Mercury)
Rollin' In My Sweet Baby's Arms
Bill Monroe; *Bean Blossom* . . . . (MCA)
Del McCoury Band; *Appalachian Stomp: Bluegrass Classics-C* . . . .(Rhino)

Dillard & Clark; *Fantastic Expedition/Through The
   Morning* . . . . (Mobile Fidelity Sound Lab)
Flatt & Scruggs; *Flatt & Scruggs At Carnegie Hall!* . . . . . . (Koch International)
   Flatt & Scruggs-20 Greatest Hits . . . . (Deluxe)
Flying Burrito Brothers; *Close Encounters To The West Coast* . . . . (Relix)
Leon Russell; *Hank Wilson's Back, Vol. 1* . . . . (Right Stuff)
New Lost City Ramblers; *Greatest Folksingers Of The '60s-C* . . . . . (Vanguard)
Ramblin' Jack Elliott; *Hard Travelin'* . . . . (Fantasy)
Ricky Skaggs and Kentucky Thunder; *History Of The Future* . . (Skaggs Family)
Tony Trischka; *Heartlands* . . . . (Rounder)
Willie Nelson; *Willie & Family Live* . . . . (Columbia)

Set Adrift On Memory Bliss
PM Dawn; *MTV Party To Go-#2-C* . . . . (Tommy Boy)
   Red Hot + Dance-C . . . . (Columbia)

Six-Pack Summer
Phil Vassar; *Phil Vassar* . . . . (Arista)

Smells Like Teen Spirit
Nirvana; *Nevermind* . . . . (David Geffen Co.)

Some Days You Gotta Dance
Dixie Chicks; *Fly* . . . . (Monument)

Stay (Wasting Time)
Dave Matthews Band; *Before These Crowded Streets* . . . . (RCA)

Stinkfist
Tool; *Aenima* . . . .(Freeworld/Capitol)

Sunny Afternoon
Kinks; *Compleat Collection-20th Anniversary* . . . . (Compleat)
   Kink Kronikles . . . . (Reprise)
   Kinks' Greatest Hits . . . . (Rhino)
   Kinks-Live . . . . (Reprise)

Take It Easy
Eagles; *Eagles* . . . . (Asylum)
   Eagles Live . . . . (Asylum)
   Eagles/Their Greatest Hits 1971-1975 . . . . (Asylum)
   Hell Freezes Over . . . .(Geffen)
Jackson Browne; *For Everyman* . . . . (Asylum)
Travis Tritt; *Common Thread-Songs Of The Eagles-C* . . . .(Giant)

Takin' It Easy
Lacy J. Dalton; *Dream Baby* . . . . (Columbia)
   Lacy J. Dalton's Greatest Hits . . . . (Columbia)

Thank The Lord For The Night Time
Neil Diamond; *Glory Road-1968-1972* . . . .(MCA)
   Hot August Night II . . . . (Columbia)
   Neil Diamond-Classics (Early Years) . . . . (Columbia)
   Neil Diamond-Gold . . . .(MCA)
   Neil Diamond's Greatest Hits-1966-1992 . . . . (Columbia)

Those Lazy Hazy Crazy Days Of Summer
Nat "King" Cole; *Best Of Nat "King" Cole-Vol. 1* . . . . (Capitol)
   Capitol Collectors Series-Nat "King" Cole . . . . (Capitol)

Too Lazy To Work, Too Nervous To Steal
BR549; *This Is BR549* . . . . (Lucky Dog)

Undo
Bjork; *Vespertine* . . . . (Elektra)

Waiting For Love
3T; *ST/Men In Black* . . . . (Columbia)

Why Don't You Get A Job?
Offspring; *Americana* . . . . (Columbia)

REMEMBER, Forget, Nostalgia, Sentimental

*See Also: AGING, ANNIVERSARY, HISTORY, LOVE (various),
THINKING & KNOWING, TIME: GENERAL, TIME: SPECIFIC,
YEARS: SPECIFIC, YESTERDAY*

(Remember The Days Of) The Old Schoolyard
Cat Stevens; *Cat Stevens-Classics-#24* . . . . (A&M)
   Izitso . . . . (A&M)

4 Seasons Of Loneliness
Boyz II Men; *Evolution* . . . . (Motown)

80's Ladies
K.T. Oslin; *80's Ladies* . . . . (RCA)
   K.T. Oslin's Greatest Hits: Songs From An Aging Sex Bomb . . . . (RCA)
   Nipper's Greatest Hits Of The '80s-C . . . . (RCA)

Ain't Your Memory Got No Pride?
Merle Haggard; *Ramblin' Fever* . . . .(MCA)

Alcohol
Kinks; *Everybody's In Show-Biz* . . . . (Rhino)
   Muswell Hillbillies . . . . (VelVel)
   The Kinks' Greatest-Celluloid Heroes . . . . (RCA)

Almost A Memory Now
BlackHawk; *Strong Enough* . . . . (Arista)
   The Hits-Love & Gravity . . . . (Arista)

Alright Already
Larry Stewart; *Down The Road* . . . . (RCA)

Always On My Mind
Willie Nelson; *Always On My Mind* . . . . (Columbia)
   Super Hits Of The '80s-C . . . .(Epic)

Willie Nelson-Super Hits . . . . (Columbia)
Always Something There To Remind Me
Naked Eyes; *Best Of Naked Eyes* . . . . (Gold Rush)
Sandie Shaw; *Burt Bacharach Songbook-C* . . . .(Varese Sarabande)

Am I That Easy To Forget
Carl Belew; *24 Hits: Best Of Country Stars On LP-C* . . . . (Tee Vee)
Debbie Reynolds; *Debbie Reynolds' Greatest Hits* . . . . (Curb)
Engelbert Humperdinck; *Engelbert Humperdinck-16 Most Requested
   Songs* . . . . (Epic)

Among My Souvenirs
Connie Francis; *Connie Francis' Greatest Hits* . . . .(Polydor)
Frank Sinatra; *Columbia Years-1943-1952-Complete Recordings* . . . . . (Legacy)
Marty Robbins; *Marty Robbins-Super Hits* . . . . (Columbia)
Sons Of The Pioneers; *Country & Western Memories* . . . .(Pair)

An Affair To Remember
Original Soundtrack; *ST/An Affair To Remember* . . . . (Epic)

Anniversary Song
Al Jolson; *Al Jolson-Best Of The Decca Years* . . . . (MCA)
   Cocktail Hour . . . . (Columbia River Entert. Group)
Dinah Shore; *Buttons & Bows* . . . . (ASV)
   Dinah Shore-16 Most Requested Songs-Encore! . . . . (Legacy)
Django Reinhardt; *Verve Jazz Masters 38* . . . . (Verve)
Eva Cassidy; *Time After Time* . . . . (Blix Street)
Guy Lombardo & His Royal Canadians; *Enjoy Yourself, The Hits Of Guy
   Lombardo* . . . . (MCA)

Another Motel Memory
Shelly West; *David Frizzell & Shelly West-Greatest Hits-Alone &
   Together* . . . . (K-Tel)

Another You
David Kersh; *Goodnight Sweetheart* . . . . (Curb)

Ashes To Ashes
Wallflowers; *The Wallflowers* . . . .(Virgin)

Attics Of My Life
Grateful Dead; *American Beauty* . . . . (Warner Bros.)

Auld Lang Syne
Beach Boys; *Beach Boys Christmas Album* . . . . (Capitol)
Duke Ellington & His Orchestra; *Take The Holiday Train* . . (Special Music Co.)
Guy Lombardo & His Royal Canadians; *All Occasions Album* . . . . . . (Gateway)
   Best Of Guy Lombardo . . . . (Curb)
   Merry Christmas Baby-Romance & Reindeer-C . . . . (Capitol)
Patti LaBelle & The Blue Belles; *A Soulful Christmas-C* . . . . . . (Collectables)
Stylistics; *Stylistics-Christmas* . . . . (Amherst)

Baby Don't Forget My Number
Milli Vanilli; *All Or Nothing* . . . . (Arista)

Back In The Day
Ahmad; *Ahmad* . . . .(Giant)

Back In The Day
Brian Culbertson; *Somethin' 'Bout Love* . . . .(Atlantic)

Back In The Day
Blues Traveler; *Bridge* . . . . (A&M)

Back On The Street Again
Sunshine Company; *Even More Nuggets-C* . . . . (Rhino)

Back When Gas Was Thirty Cents A Gallon
Tom T. Hall; *Soldier Of Fortune* . . . . (RCA)

Begin The Beguine
Art Tatum; *Solos-1940* . . . . (MCA)
Ella Fitzgerald; *Cole Porter Songbook* . . . . (Verve)
Johnny Mathis; *Best Days Of My Life* . . . . (Columbia)
   First 25 Years-Silver Anniversary Album . . . . (Columbia)
   Johnny Mathis-Live . . . . (Columbia)
Tony Bennett; *Forty Years-The Artistry Of Tony Bennett* . . . . (Columbia)

Between An Old Memory And Me
Keith Whitley; *I Wonder Do You Think Of Me* . . . . (RCA)
Travis Tritt; *Ten Feet Tall And Bulletproof* . . . . (Warner Bros.)

Billy The Kid (I Miss...)
Billy Dean; *Billy Dean* . . . . (Liberty)

Blue Memories
Patty Loveless; *On Down The Line* . . . . (MCA)

Bobbie Ann Mason
Rick Trevino; *Looking For The Light* . . . . (Columbia)

Book, The
Sheryl Crow; *Sheryl Crow* . . . . (A&M)

Bookends
Simon & Garfunkel; *Bookends* . . . . (Columbia)
   Collected Works . . . . (Columbia)
   Simon & Garfunkel's Greatest Hits . . . . (Columbia)

Box, The
Randy Travis; *This Is Me* . . . . (Warner Bros.)

Boys & Me
Sawyer Brown; *Outskirts Of Town* . . . . (Curb)

Boys Of Summer
Don Henley; *Building The Perfect Beast* . . . . (Geffen)

Brazilian Memories
Grover Washington, Jr.; *Best Is Yet To Come* . . . . (Elektra)

Break These Chains
Deborah Allen; *All That I Am* . . . .(Giant)

Brothers Under The Bridge
Bruce Springsteen; *Tracks* . . . . (Columbia)

Brown Eyed Girl
Isley Brothers; *Live It Up* . . . . (T-Neck/Columbia)
Jimmy Buffett; *One Particular Harbour* . . . . (MCA)
Van Morrison; *Bang Masters* . . . . (Epic)
  Best Of Van Morrison . . . . (Polydor)
  ST/Born On The Fourth Of July . . . . (MCA)
  ST/Sleeping With The Enemy . . . . (Columbia)
  Wonder Years-Music From Emmy Shows/Era-C . . . . (Atlantic)
Burnin' Old Memories With A Brand New Flame
Kathy Mattea; *Country Hits 4: Sweet Country-C* . . . .(Priority)
  Willow In The Wind . . . . (Mercury)
Burning Memories
Mel Tillis; *Best Of Mel Tillis* . . . . (MCA)
  Heart Healer . . . . (MCA)
  Very Best Of Mel Tillis . . . . (MCA)
Ray Price; *Ray Price's Greatest Hits-#1-3* . . . .(Step One)
By Heart
Jim Brickman; *By Heart* . . . . (Windham Hill)
Can't Forget You
Gloria Estefan; *Into The Light* . . . . (Epic)
Car Wheels On A Gravel Road
Lucinda Williams; *Car Wheels On A Gravel Road* . . . . (Mercury)
Carolina In My Mind
James Taylor; *James Taylor's Greatest Hits* . . . . (Warner Bros.)
Carolina On My Mind
Melanie; *What Have They Done To My Song Ma* . . . . (Accord)
Chemicals Between Us, The
Bush; *The Science Of Things* . . . .(Trauma)
Christmas Memories
Alabama; *Alabama-Christmas* . . . . (RCA)
Steve Wariner; *Steve Wariner Christmas Memories* . . . . . . (MCA Special Prod.)
Cold Cold Heart
Hank Williams; *Complete Hank Williams* . . . . (Mercury)
Hank Williams With His Drifting Cowboys; *24 Of Hank Williams'*
  Greatest Hits . . . . (Polydor)
  Hank Williams . . . . (MGM)
  Hank Williams-40 Greatest Hits . . . . (Polydor)
  Live At Opry . . . . (MGM)
  Long Gone Lonesome Blues . . . . (Polydor)
Jerry Lee Lewis; *Duets* . . . .(Sun)
  Golden Cream Of Jerry Lee Lewis . . . .(Sun)
  Jerry Lee Lewis & Friends-Duets . . . .(Sun)
Lucinda Williams; *Timeless: Hank Williams*
  Tribute-C . . . . (Lost Highway/IDJMG)
Tony Bennett; *Tony Bennett-16 Most Requested Songs* . . . . (Legacy)
Come Some Rainy Day
Wynonna; *The Other Side* . . . .(Curb/MCA)
Crocodile Rock
Elton John; *Billboard Top Rock 'N' Roll Hits-1973-C* . . . . (Rhino)
  Don't Shoot Me I'm Only The Piano Player . . . . (Polydor)
  Elton John's Greatest Hits . . . . (Polydor)
  Here And There . . . . (Rocket)
Daddy You've Been On My Mind
Joan Baez; *Farewell Angelina* . . . . (Vanguard)
Judy Collins; *Judy Collins' Fifth Album* . . . . (Elektra)
  Recollections . . . . (Elektra)
Dancing Your Memory Away
Charly McClain; *Charly McClain's Biggest Hits* . . . . (Epic)
  Ten Year Anniversary . . . . (Epic)
  Too Good To Hurry . . . . (Epic)
Danke Schoen
Wayne Newton; *Best Of Wayne Newton-Now* . . . . (Curb)
  Capitol Collectors Series-Wayne Newton . . . . (Capitol)
  Jackpot! The Las Vegas Story-C . . . . (Rhino)
  Wayne Newton's Greatest Hits . . . . (Curb)
Deep Purple
Art Tatum; *Group Masterpieces-#2* . . . . (Pablo)
  Masterpieces . . . . (MCA)
  Solo Masterpieces-#3 . . . . (Pablo)
Johnny Mathis; *First 25 Years-Silver Anniversary Album* . . . . . (Columbia)
Nino Tempo & April Stevens; *Hit Singles-1958-1977-C* . . . . . . (Atlantic)
Sarah Vaughan; *After Hours* . . . . (Sony Music Special Prod.)
  Divine Sarah Vaughan-Columbia Years-1949-1953 . . . . (Columbia)
Diary Of My Mind
George Jones; *Alone Again* . . . . (Epic)
Diggin' Up Bones
Randy Travis; *Storms Of Life* . . . . (Warner Bros.)
Distant Melody
Original Cast/Mary Martin; *Peter Pan-The 1954 Broadway*
  Production . . . . (RCA Victor)
Distant Memories
James Horner; *ST/Titanic* . . . .(Sony Music Classical)
Dixie Road
Lee Greenwood; *Country Classics-#3-1984-1985-C* . . . . (Universal)
  Lee Greenwood's Greatest Hits . . . . (MCA)
  MCA #1 Hits Of The '80s-#2-C . . . . (MCA Special Prod.)
Do It Again
Beach Boys; *Best Of The Beach Boys* . . . . (Capitol)
  Friends-20/20 . . . . (Capitol)

  Made In The U.S.A. . . . .(Capitol)
Do You Know What It Means To Miss New Orleans
Billie Holiday; *Sing 2* . . . .(Kent)
Harry Connick, Jr.; *Twenty* . . . .(Columbia)
Louis Armstrong; *Chicago Concert 1956* . . . .(Columbia)
  Mostly Blues . . . .(Olympic)
  Pops . . . .(Bluebird)
Pete Fountain; *Best Of Pete Fountain* . . . . (MCA)
Do You Remember Rock 'N' Roll Radio
Ramones; *End Of The Century* . . . . (Sire)
  Mania . . . . (Sire)
Do You Remember?
Bob Marley & The Wailers; *Birth Of A Legend 1963-*
  1966 . . . .(Epic Portrait Assoc.)
  Early Music . . . . (Calla)
Do You Remember?
Phil Collins; *...But Seriously* . . . . (Atlantic)
  Serious Hits...Live! . . . . (Atlantic)
Do You Remember?
Five Satins; *Five Satins Sing Their Greatest Hits* . . . .(Collectables)
Do You Remember?
Beach Boys; *Little Deuce Coupe/All Summer Long* . . . .(Capitol)
  Spirit Of America . . . . (Capitol)
Doctor Time
Rick Trevino; *Rick Trevino* . . . .(Columbia)
Does Fort Worth Ever Cross Your Mind
George Strait; *Country Classics-#3-1984-1985-C* . . . . (Universal)
  Does Fort Worth Ever Cross Your Mind . . . . (MCA)
  George Strait's Greatest Hits-#2 . . . . (MCA)
  MCA #1 Hits Of The '80s-#1-C . . . . (MCA Special Prod.)
Don't Forget The Coffee Billy Joe
Tom T. Hall; *Essential Tom T. Hall-20th Anniversary Collection* . . . . .(Mercury)
Don't Forget The Trains
Asleep At The Wheel; *Route 66* . . . .(Liberty)
Don't Forget To Cry
Mandy Barnett; *I've Got A Right To Cry* . . . . (Sire)
Don't Your Mem'ry Ever Sleep At Night
Ronnie Milsap; *Keyed Up* . . . . (RCA)
Steve Wariner; *Best Of Steve Wariner* . . . . (RCA)
Dream Walkin'
Toby Keith; *Dream Walkin'* . . . .(Mercury)
  Toby Keith's Greatest Hits, Volume One . . . .(Mercury)
Drinkin' My Baby (Off My Mind)
Eddie Rabbitt; *Best Of Eddie Rabbitt/Greatest Hits-II* . . . . (Warner Bros.)
  Great Divorce Songs For Him-C . . . . (Warner Bros.)
  Number 1's . . . . (Warner Bros.)
  Rocky Mountain Music . . . . (Elektra)
Drowning In Memories
T.G. Sheppard; *T.G. Sheppard's All-Time Greatest Hits* . . . .(Curb)
Easy On The Pain
Michael Martin Murphey; *Cowboy Songs Four* . . . . (Valley Entert.)
Ecuadorean Memories
Butch Thompson; *New Orleans Joys* . . . . (Daring)
Elderly Woman Behind The Counter In A Small Town
Pearl Jam; *Vs.* . . . .(Epic Portrait Assoc.)
Every Ghetto, Every City
Lauryn Hill; *The Miseducation Of Lauryn Hill* . . . .(Ruffhouse/Columbia)
Faded Love
Bob Wills & His Texas Playboys; *Bob Wills & His Texas Playboys-24*
  Great Hits . . . . (Polydor)
  For The Last Time . . . .(Capitol)
  Tiffany Transcriptions-#2-Best Of The Tiffanys . . . . (Rhino)
Mickey Gilley; *Mickey Gilley's Greatest Hits-#1* . . . . (Epic)
Patsy Cline; *12 Greatest Hits* . . . . (MCA)
Shawn Colvin & Lyle Lovett & Asleep At The Wheel; *Ride With*
  Bob-C . . . . (DreamWorks/SKG)
Willie Nelson; *Greatest Hits (& Some That Will Be)* . . . . (Columbia)
Few More Memories
Dolly Parton; *The Grass Is Blue* . . . . (Sugar Hill)
Fire I Can't Put Out
George Strait; *George Strait's Greatest Hits* . . . . (MCA)
  Strait From The Heart . . . . (MCA)
First Time Ever I Saw Your Face
Celine Dion; *All The Way...A Decade Of Song* . . . . (550 Music)
Roberta Flack; *Atlantic Rhythm & Blues 1947-1974-#6 (1966-*
  1969)-C . . . . (Atlantic)
  Best Of Roberta Flack . . . . (Atlantic)
  First Take . . . . (Atlantic)
Fool Hearted Memory
George Strait; *George Strait's Greatest Hits* . . . . (MCA)
  Night Game . . . . (MCA)
  Strait From The Heart . . . . (MCA)
For A Little While
Tim McGraw; *Everywhere* . . . .(Curb)
  Tim McGraw's Greatest Hits . . . .(Curb)
Forget Me Nots
Patrice Rushen; *Patrice Rushen-Anthology* . . . .(Elektra)
  Straight From The Heart . . . . (Elektra)
  The Disco Years-#2-On The Beat-1978-1982-C . . . . (Rhino)

Forgot About Dre
Dr. Dre featuring Eminem; *Dr. Dre 2001* . . . . (Aftermath/Interscope)
Forgotten Years
Midnight Oil; *Blue Sky Mining* . . . . (Columbia)
Forty Again
John Berry; *Faces* . . . . (Capitol)
Fourth Of July
Mariah Carey; *Butterfly* . . . . (Columbia)
Free Bird
Lynyrd Skynyrd; *Gold & Platinum*. . . . .(MCA)
  One More From The Road . . . .(MCA)
  Pronounced Leh-nerd Skin-nerd . . . .(MCA)
  Southern By The Grace Of God-Tribute '87 . . . .(MCA)
Wynonna; *Skynyrd Frynds-C* . . . .(MCA)
From The Vine Came The Grape
Gaylords; *X-tra Cheese-Originals By The Originals-C* . . . .(Compose)
Funny Familiar Forgotten Feelings
Don Gibson; *Best Of Don Gibson-#1* . . . . (Curb)
Mandy Barnett; *I've Got A Right To Cry*. . . . . (Sire)
Tom Jones; *Back To Back-Greatest Hits* . . . . (Rebound)
  Country Side Of Tom Jones . . . . (London)
  Tom Jones-London Collector-Greatest Hits . . . . (London)
Funny How Time Slips Away
Al Green & Lyle Lovett; *Rhythm Country And Blues-C* . . . .(MCA)
Jimmy Elledge; *Nipper's Greatest Hits Of The '60s-#2-C* . . . . (RCA)
  RCA's Greatest One-Hit Wonders-C . . . . (RCA)
Willie Nelson; *Best Of Willie Nelson* . . . . (Capitol)
  Collector's Series-Willie Nelson . . . . (RCA)
  Healing Hands Of Time . . . . (Liberty)
  My Own Way . . . . (RCA)
  San Antonio Rose . . . . (Columbia)
  Willie & Family Live . . . . (Columbia)
Willie Nelson & Faron Young; *Funny How Time Slips Away*. . . . . . (Columbia)
Gang That Sang "Heart Of My Heart"
Four Aces; *Best Of The Four Aces* . . . .(MCA)
Gentle On My Mind
Elvis Presley; *From Elvis In Memphis* . . . . (RCA)
  Great Country Songs . . . . (RCA)
Glen Campbell; *Best Of Austin City Limits-Legends Of Country
  Music-C* . . . . (Legacy)
  Best Of Glen Campbell . . . . (Capitol)
  Glen Campbell-Best Of The Early Years . . . . (Curb)
John Hartford; *Me Oh My-How The Time Does Fly-Anthology* . . . . (Flying Fish)
Patti Page; *Patti Page-16 Most Requested Songs* . . . . . . (Legacy)
Georgia On My Mind
Billie Holiday; *God Bless The Child* . . . . (Columbia)
  The Billie Holiday Story-#2 . . . . (Columbia)
Hoagy Carmichael; *Hoagy Carmichael-Legendary Performer* . . . . (RCA)
  Hoagy Sings Carmichael . . . . (EMI)
Mildred Bailey; *Harlem Lullaby*. . . . . (ASV)
Preservation Hall Jazz Band; *Best Of The Preservation Hall
  Jazz Band* . . . . (Columbia)
Ray Charles; *Ray Charles' Greatest Hits-#2* . . . . (Rhino)
  Ray Charles-Anthology . . . . (Rhino)
Willie Nelson; *Greatest Hits (& Some That Will Be)* . . . . (Columbia)
  Stardust . . . . (Legacy)
  Willie & Family Live . . . . (Columbia)
Getting Sentimental Over You
Ella Fitzgerald; *Best Of Ella Fitzgerald* . . . .(Pablo)
Frank Sinatra; *I Remember Tommy* . . . . (Reprise)
Helen O'Connell; *Sentimental Journey: Capitol's Great Ladies Of
  Song-C* . . . . (Gold Rush)
Shirley Scott; *For Members Only/Great Scott* . . . .(MCA Special Prod.)
Tommy Dorsey & His Orchestra; *Best Of Tommy Dorsey* . . . . (Bluebird)
  Best Of Tommy Dorsey & His Orchestra . . . . (Curb)
Girl From The North Country
Bob Dylan; *Freewheelin'* . . . . (Columbia)
  Nashville Skyline . . . . (Columbia)
  Real Live . . . . (Columbia)
Joe Cocker; *Mad Dogs & Englishmen* . . . . (A&M)
Johnny Cash with Bob Dylan; *The Man In Black-His Greatest Hits*. . . . (Legacy)
Give Myself A Party
Mandy Barnett; *I've Got A Right To Cry*. . . . . (Sire)
Gliding Through My Memoree
Original Cast; *ST/Flower Drum Song*. . . . . (Sony Music Classical)
Glory Days
Bruce Springsteen; *Born In The U.S.A.* . . . . (Columbia)
  Bruce Springsteen's Greatest Hits . . . . (Columbia)
Golden Memories And Silver Tears
Jim Reeves; *Best Of Jim Reeves* . . . . (RCA)
  Great Moments With Jim Reeves . . . . (RCA)
  Jim Reeves' Greatest Hits . . . . (RCA)
Good Man Is Hard To Find (Pittsburgh)
Bruce Springsteen; *Tracks* . . . . (Columbia)
Graduation (Friends Forever)
Vitamin C; *Totally Hits-#3-C* . . . . (Atlantic)
  Vitamin C . . . . (Elektra)
Graduation Day
Beach Boys; *Beach Boys-Gift Set* . . . . (Capitol)

  Spirit Of America . . . . (Capitol)
Rover Boys; *Choice Voices! Pop Vocal Group Gems Of The
  '50s-C* . . . . (Collector's Choice)
Greatest Man I Never Knew
Reba McEntire; *For My Broken Heart* . . . . (MCA)
  Reba McEntire's Greatest Hits Volume Two . . . . (MCA)
Groundzero (In Our Hearts You Remain)
Cash & Computa; *Groundzero (In Our Hearts You Remain)-CD
  Single* . . . . (Select)
Guinnevere
Crosby, Stills & Nash; *Crosby, Stills & Nash* . . . .(Atlantic)
  CSN . . . . (Atlantic)
Crosby, Stills, Nash & Young; *So Far* . . . .(Atlantic)
  Woodstock Two . . . . (Atlantic)
Hanging Tree
Marty Robbins; *Gunfighter Ballads & Trail Songs* . . . . . . (Legacy)
  Hollywood Magic-1950s-C . . . . (Columbia)
  Lifetime Of Song-1951-1982 . . . . (Columbia)
  Marty Robbins' All-Time Greatest Hits . . . . (Columbia)
Harlem On My Mind
Ethel Waters; *Irving Berlin 100th Anniversary Collection-C* . . . . (MCA)
Harlem On My Mind
Tim Curry; *Read By Lips* . . . . (A&M)
Has Anybody Seen Amy
John & Audrey Wiggins; *John & Audrey* . . . . (Mercury)
Heart Of Saturday Night, The (Looking For)
Shawn Colvin; *Cover Girl* . . . . (Columbia)
Tom Waits; *The Heart Of Saturday Night* . . . .(Asylum)
  Tom Waits-Anthology . . . .(Asylum)
Hearts Of Stone
Bruce Springsteen; *Tracks* . . . . (Columbia)
Southside Johnny And The Asbury Jukes; *Best Of Southside Johnny And The
  Asbury Jukes* . . . . (Legacy)
  Cover Me (Bruce Springsteen Tribute)-C . . . . (Rhino)
  Hearts Of Stone . . . . (Epic)
Heaven On Their Minds
Original Cast; *ST/Jesus Christ Superstar* . . . . (MCA)
Hello, Young Lovers
Frank Sinatra; *Frank Sinatra Sings Rodgers & Hammerstein* . . . . . (Columbia)
Mel Torme; *Jazz 'Round Midnight-Mel Torme* . . . . (Verve)
Original Broadway Cast; *The King And I* . . . . (RCA Victor)
Original Cast; *ST/The King And I* . . . . (Angel)
Here I Am (Just When I Thought I Was Over You)
Air Supply; *Air Supply-The Definitive Collection* . . . . (Arista)
Hey Jude
Beatles; *Beatles 1* . . . . (Capitol)
  Beatles-20 Greatest Hits . . . . (Capitol)
  Past Masters-Volume Two . . . . (Parlophone)
  The Beatles/1967-1970. . . . . (Capitol)
Paul McCartney; *Knebworth-The Album-C* . . . . (Polydor)
Wilson Pickett; *Wilson Pickett's Greatest Hits* . . . .(Atlantic)
Hey Nineteen
Steely Dan; *Gaucho* . . . . (MCA)
  Steely Dan-Gold . . . . (MCA)
High Cotton
Alabama; *Southern Star* . . . .(RCA)
Hold On To The Nights
Richard Marx; *Richard Marx* . . . . (Capitol)
House Of Memories
Merle Haggard & The Strangers; *Best Of Merle Haggard & The
  Strangers* . . . . (Capitol)
How You Remind Me
Nickelback; *Silver Side Up* . . . .(Roadrunner)
I Can Still Feel You
Collin Raye; *The Walls Came Down* . . . . (Epic)
I Can't See Your Face In My Mind
Doors; *Doors-Classics* . . . . (Elektra)
  Strange Days . . . . (Elektra)
I Can't Stop Loving You
Don Gibson; *60 Years Of Country Music-C* . . . . (RCA)
  Collector's Series-Don Gibson . . . . (RCA)
  Stars Of The Grand Ole Opry-1926-1974-C . . . . (RCA)
Elvis Presley; *Aloha from Hawaii via Satellite* . . . . (RCA)
  Elvis As Recorded At Madison Square Garden . . . . (RCA)
  Elvis Recorded Live On Stage In Memphis. . . . . (RCA)
  From Memphis To Vegas/From Vegas To Memphis. . . . . . (RCA)
Ray Charles; *Ray Charles' Greatest Hits-#2*. . . . . (Rhino)
  Ray Charles-Anthology . . . . (Rhino)
Roy Orbison; *Best Of Roy Orbison-Loved Standards* . . . . (Monument)
  Legendary Roy Orbison . . . . (Sony Music Special Prod.)
I Do
Mila Mason; *That's Enough Of That*. . . . .(Atlantic)
I Forgot To Remember To Forget
Elvis Presley; *A Date With Elvis* . . . .(RCA)
Johnny Cash; *Survivors, The* . . . . (Razor & Tie)
I Got A Mind To Give Up Living
Paul Butterfield Blues Band; *East-West* . . . . (Elektra)
I Hear Your Voice
Lionel Richie; *Time* . . . . (Mercury)

I Just Came Home To Count The Memories
John Anderson; *Honky-Tonk Country-Tender Lovin' Country* . . . . (Priority)
I Just Came Home To Count The Memories . . . . (Warner Bros.)
John Anderson's Greatest Hits . . . . (Warner Bros.)
I Knew You When
Billy Joe Royal; *Billy Joe Royal's Greatest Hits* . . . . (Columbia)
I Left My Heart In San Francisco
Tony Bennett; *I Left My Heart In San Francisco* . . . . (Columbia)
Pop Classics Of The '60s-C . . . . (Columbia)
Tony Bennett's All-Time Greatest Hits . . . . (Columbia)
I Miss My Homies
Master P; *Ghetto D* . . . . (No Limit/Priority)
I Remember
Barbra Streisand; *Christmas Memories* . . . . (Columbia)
I Remember California
R.E.M.; *Green* . . . . (Warner Bros.)
I Remember Clifford
Lee Morgan; *Best Of Lee Morgan* . . . . (Blue Note)
Pieces Of A Dream & Manhattan Transfer; *In Performance At The Playboy
Jazz Festival* . . . . (Elektra)
I Remember Coney Island
Lounge Lizards; *Lounge Lizards* . . . . (Editions E.G.)
I Remember Harlem
Roy Eldridge; *Roy Eldridge* . . . . (Crescendo)
I Remember Holding You
Boys Club; *'80s Greatest Rock Hits-Teen Idols-C* . . . . (Priority)
Boys Club . . . . (MCA)
Retro Lunchbox-Gooey Love Songs-C . . . . (ISD/Intersound)
I Remember It Well
Original Cast; *Gigi* . . . . (RCA Victor)
I Remember You
Diana Krall; *The Look Of Love* . . . . (Impulse!)
Rosemary Clooney; *Rosemary Clooney Sings The Lyrics Of Johnny
Mercer* . . . . (Concord Jazz)
I Remember You
Ramones; *All The Stuff & More-#1* . . . . (Sire)
Leave Home . . . . (Sire)
I Remember You
Pretenders; *Get Close* . . . . (Sire)
I Remember You
Lou Reed; *Mistrial* . . . . (RCA)
I Remember You
Eurythmics; *Revenge* . . . . (RCA)
I Remember You
Skid Row; *Skid Row* . . . . (Atlantic)
I Remember You
Glen Campbell; *Still Within The Sound Of My Voice* . . . . (MCA)
I Tell It Like It Used To Be
T. Graham Brown; *45-#5524* . . . . (Capitol)
I Used To Love Him
Lauryn Hill featuring Mary J. Blige; *The Miseducation Of
Lauryn Hill* . . . . (Ruffhouse/Columbia)
I Walk The Line (Revisited)
Rodney Crowell; *The Houston Kid* . . . . (Sugar Hill)
I Wanna Remember This
Linda Davis; *I'm Yours* . . . . (DreamWorks/SKG)
ST/Black Dog . . . . (Decca)
I Will Remember You
Amy Grant; *Heart In Motion* . . . . (A&M)
I Will Remember You
Sarah McLachlan; *Mirrorball* . . . . (Arista)
ST/Brothers McMullen . . . . (Arista)
Surfacing . . . . (Arista)
Totally Hits-#2-C . . . . (Elektra)
I Wish
R. Kelly; *Now That's What I Call Music!-#6-C* . . . . (Virgin)
TP-2.com . . . . (Jive)
I Wish I Could Have Been There
John Anderson; *Solid Ground* . . . . (BNA)
If Drinkin' Don't Kill Me (Her Memory Will)
George Jones; *10 Years Of Hits* . . . . (Epic)
I Am What I Am . . . . (Epic)
I'll Always Remember That Song
Charlie Daniels Band; *Whiskey* . . . . (Epic)
I'll Be Missing You
Puff Daddy & Family & Faith Evans & 112; *No Way Out* . . . . . (Bad Boy/Arista)
I'll Be Seeing You
Billie Holiday; *Billie Holiday At Carnegie Hall-Billie Holiday
Story-#6* . . . . (Verve)
Essential Billie Holiday-Carnegie Hall Concert . . . . (Verve)
Jackie Gleason; *Best Of Jackie Gleason & His Orchestra* . . . . (Curb)
Judy Collins; *Judith* . . . . (Elektra)
Skyliners; *Skyliners' Greatest Hits* . . . . (Original Sound)
Tommy Dorsey & Frank Sinatra; *Those Wonderful Years (WWII Love
Songs)-C* . . . . (JCI Assoc. Labels)
Tommy Dorsey & His Orchestra; *Kiss The Boys Goodbye-Classic Songs Of
WWII-#1* . . . . (RCA)
I'll Go On Loving You
Alan Jackson; *High Mileage* . . . . (Arista)

I'll Never Fall In Love Again
Dionne Warwick; *Billboard Top Soft Rock Hits-1970-C* . . . . (Rhino)
Her Classic Songs-#1 . . . . (Curb)
Elvis Presley; *From Elvis Presley Boulevard, Memphis, Tennessee* . . . . (RCA)
Mary Chapin Carpenter; *ST/My Best Friend's Wedding* . . . . . . (Work/Epic)
I'll Remember
Madonna; *ST/With Honors* . . . . (Maverick)
I'll Remember April
Cal Tjader; *Mambo With Cal Tjader* . . . . (Fantasy)
Charlie Parker; *Charlie Parker With Strings* . . . . (Verve)
Chet Baker; *Chet Baker* . . . . (Emarcy)
Cleo Laine; *Cleo's Choice* . . . . (Crescendo)
Doris Day & The Frank DeVol Orchestra; *Hooray For
Hollywood-#1-C* . . . . (Columbia)
Erroll Garner; *Erroll Garner-Concert By The Sea* . . . . (Columbia)
Frank Sinatra; *Point Of No Return* . . . . (Capitol)
June Christy; *June Christy-#2-1957* . . . . (Hindsight)
Modern Jazz Quartet; *Concorde* . . . . (Prestige)
Modern Jazz Quartet . . . . (Prestige)
Stephane Grappelli & Martin Taylor; *Just One Of Those Things* . . . . . (Angel)
Wynton Marsalis; *Standard Time-#2-Intimacy Calling* . . . . (Columbia)
I'll Remember You
Atlantic Starr; *Time* . . . . (Arista)
I'll See You Again
Frank Sinatra; *Point Of No Return* . . . . (Capitol)
I'm Gonna Change Everything
Mandy Barnett; *I've Got A Right To Cry* . . . . (Sire)
Immortality
Celine Dion with The Bee Gees; *Let's Talk About Love-C* . . . . . (550 Music)
In A Sentimental Mood
Duke Ellington & John Coltrane; *ST/Love Jones* . . . . (Columbia)
Marvin Hamlisch; *ST/The Mirror Has Two Faces* . . . . (Columbia)
In Memory Of Elizabeth Reid
Allman Brothers Band; *At Fillmore East* . . . . (Capricorn)
Beginnings . . . . (Polydor)
Decade Of Hits-1969-1979 . . . . (Polydor)
In My Life
Beatles; *Beatles-Love Songs* . . . . (Capitol)
Rubber Soul . . . . (Capitol)
ST/Imagine: John Lennon . . . . (Capitol)
The Beatles/1962-1966 . . . . (Capitol)
Crosby, Stills & Nash; *After The Storm* . . . . (Atlantic)
Judy Collins; *Colors Of The Day-The Best Of Judy Collins* . . . . . (Elektra)
In My Life . . . . (Elektra)
It Happened In Monterey
Frank Sinatra & Nelson Riddle Orchestra; *songs for Swingin'
Lovers!* . . . . (Capitol)
Mel Torme & The Mel-Tones; *Back In Town* . . . . (Verve)
It Was A Very Good Year
Frank Sinatra; *Frank Sinatra-The Very Good Years* . . . . (Reprise)
September Of My Years . . . . (Reprise)
The Reprise Collection . . . . (Reprise)
*The Sopranos-Music From The HBO Original
Series* . . . . (Sony Music Soundtrax)
Frank Sinatra with Count Basie & The Orchestra; *Sinatra At The
Sands* . . . . (Reprise)
It's All Coming Back To Me Now
Celine Dion; *All The Way...A Decade Of Song* . . . . (550 Music)
Falling Into You . . . . (550 Music)
It's The Same Old Song
Four Tops; *Billboard Top R&B Hits-1965-C* . . . . (Rhino)
Compact Command Performances-Four Tops . . . . (Motown)
Four Tops' Greatest Hits . . . . (Motown)
Four Tops-Anthology . . . . (Motown)
I've Got Dreams To Remember
Delbert McClinton; *Live From Austin* . . . . (Alligator)
Etta James; *Sticking To My Guns* . . . . (Island)
Otis Redding; *The Otis Redding Story* . . . . (Atlantic)
I've Got Sand In My Shoes
Drifters; *1959-1965-All-Time Greatest Hits And More* . . . . (Atlantic)
Very Best Of The Drifters . . . . (Rhino)
Jamaica In My Mind
McGuffey Lane; *Day By Day* . . . . (Atlantic America)
Jukebox In My Mind
Alabama; *Pass It On Down* . . . . (BMG Special Prod.)
Just Remember I Love You
Firefall; *Firefall's Greatest Hits* . . . . (Rhino)
Luna Sea . . . . (Rhino)
Just Walking In The Rain
Johnnie Ray; *16 Most Requested Songs Of The '50s-#1-C* . . . . (Legacy)
Best Of Johnnie Ray . . . . (Columbia)
Johnnie Ray-16 Most Requested Songs . . . . (Legacy)
Johnnie Ray's Greatest Hits . . . . (Sony Music Special Prod.)
Keep This Heart In Mind
Bonnie Raitt; *Green Light* . . . . (Warner Bros.)
Killin' Time
Clint Black; *Killin' Time* . . . . (RCA)
RCA Award Winners-C . . . . (RCA)

King Of The Mountain
George Strait; *Blue Clear Sky* . . . . (MCA)
Latest Greatest Straitest Hits . . . . (MCA)
Laredo
Chris Cagle; *Play It Loud* . . . . (Capitol)
Leaving October
Sons Of The Desert; *Whatever Comes First* . . . .(Epic)
Let's Make A Night To Remember
Bryan Adams; *18 Til I Die* . . . . (A&M)
Life As We Knew It
Kathy Mattea; *Class Of Country-C* . . . . (K-Tel)
Collection Of Hits . . . . (Mercury)
Untasted Honey . . . . (Polydor Country)
Linda On My Mind
Conway Twitty; *Conway Twitty's Greatest Hits-#2* . . . . (MCA)
Conway's #1 Classics-#2 . . . .(Warner Bros.)
Songwriter . . . . (MCA)
Very Best Of Conway Twitty . . . . (MCA)
Little White Cloud That Cried
Johnnie Ray; *Best Of Johnnie Ray* . . . . (Columbia)
Best Of Johnnie Ray . . . . (Exact)
Johnnie Ray's Greatest Hits . . . .(Sony Music Special Prod.)
Living Years, The
Mike & The Mechanics; *Living Years* . . . . (Atlantic)
Lone Star State Of Mind
Don Williams; *Currents* . . . . (RCA)
Nanci Griffith; *Country Classics-#8-1986-1987-C* . . . . (Universal)
Lone Star State Of Mind . . . .(MCA)
Pat Alger/Nanci Griffith/Trisha Yearwood; *True Love & Other Short
Stories-C* . . . . (Sugar Hill)
Lonely And Gone
Montgomery Gentry; *Tattoos & Scars* . . . . (Columbia)
Long Ago And Far Away
Erroll Garner; *Long Ago And Far Away* . . . .(Columbia)
Glenn Miller; *Glenn Miller-A Legendary Performer-#1 & 2* . . . . (Bluebird)
Helen Forrest & Dick Haymes; *American Songbook Series-
Jerome Kern* . . . .(Smithsonian Collection)
Jo Stafford; *Capitol Collectors Series-Jo Stafford* . . . . (Capitol)
International Hits . . . . (Corinthian)
Jukebox Saturday Night-Great Vocal Hits-C . . . . (Capitol)
Songs That Got Us Through WWII-C . . . .(Rhino)
ST/Bugsy . . . .(Epic)
Johnny Mathis; *Hollywood Musicals* . . . . (Columbia)
Mantovani; *More Golden Hits* . . . . (London)
Perry Como; *Always In My Heart-Classic Songs Of World War II-#2* . . . . (RCA)
Rosemary Clooney; *Rosemary Clooney Sings The Lyrics Of Ira
Gershwin* . . . .(Concord Jazz)
Look What Followed Me Home
David Ball; *Thinkin' Problem* . . . .(Warner Bros.)
Love Scene
Joe; *All That I Am* . . . . (Jive)
Love So Beautiful, A
Michael Bolton; *Michael Bolton's Greatest Hits-1985-1995* . . . . . . (Columbia)
Roy Orbison; *Mystery Girl* . . . . (Virgin)
ST/Indecent Proposal . . . . (MCA)
Loving Arms
Dixie Chicks; *Wide Open Spaces* . . . . (Monument)
Lullaby Of The Leaves
Various Artists; *Birdlanders-#1-C* . . . .(Original Jazz Classics)
Making Memories
Frankie Laine; *Very Best Of The ABC Years* . . . .(Taragon)
Mama From The Train
Patti Page; *Patti Page-Golden Celebration* . . . . (Mercury)
Mama Sang A Song
Bill Anderson; *Bill Anderson's Greatest Hits* . . . . (Varese Sarabande)
Country Music Classics-#17-C . . . . (K-Tel)
Man Of My Word
Collin Raye; *Extremes* . . . .(Epic)
Marie
Tommy Dorsey & His Orchestra; *Seventeen Number Ones* . . . . (RCA)
Maybe It Was Memphis
Pam Tillis; *Pam Tillis' Greatest Hits* . . . . (Arista)
Pam Tillis-Collection . . . .(Warner Bros.)
Put Yourself In My Place . . . . (Arista)
Meanwhile
George Strait; *Always Never The Same* . . . . (MCA)
Memories Are Made Of This
Dean Martin; *Billboard Pop Memories-1955-1959-C* . . . . (Rhino)
Dean Martin-Love Songs . . . .(Ranwood)
Dean Martin's All Time Greatest Hits . . . . (Curb)
Memories Of East Texas
Michelle Shocked; *Short Sharp Shocked* . . . . (Mercury)
Memories Of Ireland
Paddy Noonan; *Memories Of Ireland* . . . . (Rego Irish)
Memories Of Madrid
Herb Alpert & The Tijuana Brass; *Herb Alpert & The Tijuana Brass-
Classics-#1* . . . . (A&M)
Memories Of Old Santa Fe
Randy Travis; *Wind In The Wire* . . . .(Warner Bros.)

Memories Of Paris
Michel Petrucciani; *Music* . . . . (Blue Note)
Memories To Burn
Gene Watson; *Country Heartbreakers-C* . . . . (K-Tel)
Memory
Original Broadway Cast; *Cats* . . . . (Geffen)
Memory Motel
Rolling Stones; *Black And Blue* . . . . (Rolling Stones)
No Security . . . . (Virgin)
Memory Remains
Metallica; *Reload* . . . . (Elektra)
Men In Black
Will Smith; *Big Willie Style* . . . . (Columbia)
ST/Men In Black . . . . (Columbia)
Mental Picture
Jon Secada; *Heart, Soul & A Voice* . . . . (SBK)
ST/The Specialist . . . .(Epic/Sony Music Soundtrax)
Miami 2017
Billy Joel; *Songs In The Attic* . . . . (Columbia)
The Concert For New York City-C . . . . (Columbia)
Turnstiles . . . . (Columbia)
Minutes To Memories
John Cougar Mellencamp; *Scarecrow* . . . . (Riva)
Miseducation Of Lauryn Hill
Lauryn Hill; *The Miseducation Of Lauryn Hill* . . . . (Ruffhouse/Columbia)
Mississippi, You're On My Mind
Jerry Jeff Walker; *Ridin' High* . . . . (MCA)
Jesse Winchester; *Best Of Jesse Winchester* . . . . (Rhino)
Moments To Remember
Four Lads; *'50s Vocal Groups-C* . . . . (K-Tel)
Four Lads-16 Most Requested Songs . . . . (Legacy)
Radio Classics Of The '50s-C . . . . (Columbia)
Original Cast; *Forever Plaid* . . . . (RCA)
Ray Conniff & His Orchestra; *Memories Are Made Of This* . . . . (Columbia)
Vogues; *Vogues' Greatest Hits* . . . . (Rhino)
Moonlight On The Colorado
Sons Of The Pioneers; *Songs Of The Trail* . . . .(Pair)
Motels And Memories
T.G. Sheppard; *Motels And Memories* . . . . (Melodyland)
Mrs. Potter's Lullaby
Counting Crows; *This Desert Life* . . . . (David Geffen Co.)
My Antonia
Emmylou Harris; *Red Dirt Girl* . . . . (Nonesuch)
My Back Pages
Bob Dylan; *Another Side Of Bob Dylan* . . . . (Columbia)
Bob Dylan's Greatest Hits-#2 . . . . (Columbia)
Byrds; *20 Essential Tracks From The Box Set* . . . . (Columbia)
Byrds Play Dylan . . . . (Columbia)
The Byrds' Greatest Hits . . . . (Columbia)
Younger Than Yesterday . . . . (Columbia)
My Favorite Memory
Merle Haggard; *For The Record: Merle Haggard-43 Legendary Hits* . . . .(BNA)
My Girl Josephine
Fats Domino; *Fats Domino's Greatest Hits* . . . . (MCA)
They Call Me The Fat Man . . . . (EMI)
My Lips Remember Your Kisses
Nat "King" Cole; *1941-1943* . . . . (Classics)
Neighborhood
Vonda Shepard; *ST/Songs From "Ally McBeal" Featuring Vonda
Shepard* . . . . (550/Epic)
Never Ending
Wood; *Songs From Stamford Hill* . . . . (Columbia)
Never Too Far
Mariah Carey; *Glitter* . . . . (Virgin)
New San Antonio Rose
Bob Wills & His Texas Playboys; *Bob Wills & His Texas Playboys-
Greatest Hits* . . . . (Curb)
Columbia Country Classics-#1-Golden Age-C . . . . (Columbia)
Essential Bob Wills & His Texas Playboys-1935-1973 . . . . (Legacy)
Dwight Yoakam & Asleep At The Wheel; *Ride With
Bob-C* . . . . (DreamWorks/SKG)
New York On My Mind
John McLaughlin; *Electric Guitarist* . . . . (Columbia)
Night To Remember
Shalamar; *Friends* . . . . (Solar)
Mega Hits Dance Classics-#5-C . . . . (Priority)
Shalamar's Greatest Hits . . . .(Solar)
Night To Remember
Joe Diffie; *A Night To Remember* . . . .(Epic)
Night To Remember
Jody Watley; *Beginnings* . . . .(Solar)
Night To Remember
Foreigner; *Inside Information* . . . .(Atlantic)
Night To Remember
Cyndi Lauper; *Night To Remember* . . . . (Epic)
Nights
Ed Bruce; *Night Things* . . . . (RCA)

Nights In Harlem
Luther Vandross; *I Know*. . . . . (LV/Virgin)
Ocean Of Memories
James Horner; *ST/Titanic* . . . .(Sony Music Classical)
Ochone! When I Used To Be Young
Joseph O'Mara; *Music From The New York Stage (1890-1920)-#1-1890-
1908-C* . . . .(Pearl)
Oh! My Papa
Eddie Fisher; *Eddie Fisher's All-Time Greatest Hits-#1* . . . .(RCA)
Hebrew National Kosher Classics-C . . . .(RCA)
Nipper's Greatest Hits Of The '50s-#2-C . . . .(RCA)
On My Own
Peach Union; *Audiopeach* . . . .(Epic)
ST/Sliding Doors . . . .(MCA)
On Your Shore
Enya; *Watermark*. . . . .(Reprise)
Once In A While
Tommy Dorsey; *Boogie Woogie* . . . .(Pro-Arte)
Once Upon A Time
Frank Sinatra; *September Of My Years* . . . .(Reprise)
Tony Bennett; *I Left My Heart In San Francisco*. . . . .(Columbia)
One I Loved Back Then (Corvette Song)
George Jones; *19 Hot Country Requests-#3-C* . . . .(Epic)
George Jones-Super Hits . . . .(Epic)
Greatest Country Hits Of The '80s-1986-C . . . .(Columbia)
Who's Gonna Fill Their Shoes . . . .(Epic)
One Man Army
Our Lady Peace; *Happiness...Is Not A Fish That You Can Catch* . . . .(Columbia)
Ooh La La
Rod Stewart; *When We Were The New Boys* . . . . (Warner Bros.)
Out Of Sight, Out Of Mind
Five Keys; *Golden Classics-Five Keys* . . . .(Collectables)
Over Your Shoulder
Seven Mary Three; *Orange Ave.* . . . . (Atlantic)
P.S. I Love You
Beatles; *Beatles-Box Set* . . . .(Capitol)
Beatles-Love Songs . . . .(Capitol)
Introducing...The Beatles . . . .(Vee-Jay)
Please Please Me . . . .(Parlophone)
The Early Beatles . . . .(Capitol)
Pages Of My Mind
Ray Charles; *From The Pages Of My Mind* . . . .(Columbia)
Penny Lane
Beatles; *Beatles 1*. . . . .(Capitol)
Magical Mystery Tour . . . .(Capitol)
The Beatles/1967-1970. . . . .(Capitol)
The Beatles-Anthology-#2 . . . .(Capitol)
Photographs & Memories
Jim Croce; *Photographs & Memories/His Greatest Hits*. . . . . . (Atlantic)
Time In A Bottle/Jim Croce's Greatest Love Songs . . . . (Atlantic)
You Don't Mess Around With Jim. . . . .(Lifesong)
Picnic
McGuire Sisters; *Songs Of Steve Allen-C* . . . .(Varese Sarabande)
Pinch Me
Barenaked Ladies; *Maroon* . . . .(Reprise)
Totally Hits-#3-C . . . .(Atlantic)
Please Remember Me
Tim McGraw; *A Place In The Sun* . . . .(Curb)
Tim McGraw's Greatest Hits . . . .(Curb)
Poisoned Heart & A Twisted Memory
Richard Thompson; *Hand Of Kindness* . . . .(Hannibal)
Polish Memories Waltz
New Yorkers; *Polka Smile*. . . . .(Jay Jay)
Red Wine & Blue Memories
Joe Stampley; *Joe Stampley's Biggest Hits* . . . .(Epic)
Reflections
Diana Ross & The Supremes; *Diana Ross & The Supremes' Greatest
Hits-#3*. . . . .(Motown)
Diana Ross & The Supremes-25th Anniversary . . . .(Motown)
Diana Ross & The Supremes-Anthology (1962-1969) . . . . . .(Motown)
Motown Story-First 25 Years-C . . . .(Motown)
Four Tops; *Four Tops-Anthology* . . . .(Motown)
Still Waters Run Deep . . . .(Motown)
Until You Love Someone: More Of The Best (1965-1970) . . . .(Rhino)
Luther Vandross; *Songs*. . . . .(Epic)
Reflections Of My Life
Marmalade; *History Of British Rock-#1-C* . . . .(Rhino)
London Collector-Rock Invasion-C . . . .(London)
Super Hits Of The '70s-Have A Nice Day-#2-C . . . .(Rhino)
Remember
Jimi Hendrix Experience; *Are You Experienced?* . . . .(Reprise)
Remember (Christmas)
Nilsson; *Son Of Schmilsson*. . . . .(RCA)
Remember (Walkin' In The Sand)
Aerosmith; *Aerosmith's Greatest Hits*. . . . .(Columbia)
Night In The Ruts . . . .(Columbia)
Go-Go's; *Return To The Valley Of The Go-Go's*. . . . .(I.R.S.)
Shangri-Las; *Girl Groups-Story Of A Sound-C* . . . .(Rhino)

Oldies But Goodies-#6-C . . . .(Original Sound)
Original Golden Hits Of The Great Groups-#1-C . . . . . .(SSS International)
ST/Goodfellas . . . .(Atlantic)
Remember Me
Journey; *ST/Armageddon-The Album* . . . .(Columbia)
Remember Me
Marc Anthony; *Marc Anthony* . . . .(Columbia)
Remember Me This Way
Jordan Hill; *Jordan Hill* . . . . (Atlantic)
ST/Casper . . . .(MCA)
Remember Mother's Day
Al Jolson; *The Al Jolson Story-#5* . . . .(MCA)
Remember Pat Boone
David Steinberg; *Booga! Booga!* . . . .(Columbia)
Remember Pearl Harbor
Sammy Kaye & His Orchestra; *ST/Radio Days* . . . . (Novus)
Remember The Alamo
Johnny Cash; *We The People-C* . . . .(Folk Era)
Kingston Trio; *At Large/Here We Go Again!* . . . .(Capitol)
Remember The Children
Earth, Wind & Fire; *Last Days & Time* . . . .(Columbia)
Remember The Heroes
Sammy Hagar; *Three Lock Box* . . . .(Geffen)
Remember The Night
Johnny Law; *Johnny Law*. . . . .(Metal Blade)
ST/Freddy's Dead-The Final Nightmare . . . .(Metal Blade)
Remember The Night
Loungers; *Harlem Holiday-New York Rhythm & Blues-#6-C* . . . . .(Collectables)
Remember The Nights
Motels; *Best Of The Motels-No Vacancy* . . . .(Capitol)
Little Robbers . . . .(Capitol)
Remember The Time
Michael Jackson; *Dangerous*. . . . . (Epic)
Remembrance Day
Bryan Adams; *Into The Fire*. . . . .(A&M)
Reminiscing
Little River Band; *'70's Super Groups-C* . . . .(Rhino)
Reminiscing: The Twentieth Anniversary Collection . . . .(Rhino)
Restless Nights
Bruce Springsteen; *Tracks* . . . .(Columbia)
Rocking Chairs; *One Step Up/Two Steps Back-The Songs Of Bruce
Springsteen-C*. . . . .(Right Stuff)
River, The
Bruce Springsteen; *Bruce Springsteen's Greatest Hits* . . . .(Columbia)
The River. . . . .(Columbia)
Bruce Springsteen & The E Street Band; *Bruce Springsteen & The E Street
Band Live/1975-85* . . . .(Legacy)
Rock & Roll Never Forgets
Bob Seger; *Night Moves* . . . .(Capitol)
Bob Seger & The Silver Bullet Band; *Nine Tonight*. . . . .(Capitol)
Rock For The Forgotten
David & David; *Boomtown* . . . .(A&M)
Rock Me Tonight (For Old Time's Sake)
Freddie Jackson; *Rock Me Tonight (For Old Time's Sake)* . . . .(Capitol)
Roll On Mississippi
Charley Pride; *Charley Pride's Greatest Hits* . . . . (RCA)
Rollin' Stoned
Great White; *Can't Get There From Here* . . . .(Portrait)
Roof, The
Mariah Carey; *Butterfly* . . . .(Columbia)
Rose Bouquet
Phil Vassar; *Phil Vassar*. . . . .(Arista)
Scarborough Fair/Canticle
Simon & Garfunkel; *Collected Works* . . . .(Columbia)
Parsley Sage Rosemary & Thyme . . . .(Columbia)
Simon & Garfunkel's Greatest Hits. . . . .(Columbia)
ST/The Graduate . . . .(Columbia)
The Concert In Central Park . . . .(Warner Bros.)
Send Me The Pillow You Dream On
Browns; *45-#7804* . . . . (RCA)
Dwight Yoakam; *Buenas Noches From A Lonely Room* . . . .(Reprise)
Hank Locklin; *Hank Locklin-20 Golden Souvenirs* . . . . (RCA)
Nipper's Greatest Hits Of The '50s-#1-C . . . .(RCA)
Please Help Me I'm Falling . . . .(Collectables)
Stars Of The Grand Ole Opry-1926-1974-C . . . .(RCA)
Johnny Tillotson; *Golden Classics-Johnny Tillotson* . . . .(Collectables)
Willie Nelson & Hank Snow; *Brand On My Heart* . . . .(Columbia)
Sentimental
Kenny G; *Breathless* . . . .(Arista)
Sentimental
Deborah Cox; *Deborah Cox*. . . . .(Arista)
Sentimental Journey
Dinah Shore; *Sentimental Journey: Capitol's Great Ladies Of
Song-C* . . . .(Gold Rush)
Doris Day; *Doris Day Sings 22 Great Songs-Original Big Band* . . . . .(Hindsight)
Hal McIntyre & His Orchestra; *Nipper's Greatest Hits Of The
'40s-#2-C* . . . . (RCA)
Les Brown & His Orchestra; *Best Of The Big Bands-C* . . . .(Columbia)

Sentimental Lady
Fleetwood Mac; *25 Years-The Chain* (Warner Bros.)
Bare Trees (Reprise)
Sentimental Street
Night Ranger; *7 Wishes* (MCA)
Night Ranger's Greatest Hits (Camel)
September
Earth, Wind & Fire; *Best Of Earth, Wind & Fire-#1* (Legacy)
Eternal Dance (Columbia)
Mega Hits Dance Classics-#7-C (Priority)
September In The Rain
Chad & Jeremy; *Capitol Gold-Best Of Chad & Jeremy* (Capitol)
The Soft Sound Of Chad & Jeremy (K-Tel)
Dinah Washington; *Dinah Washington-Golden Hits* (Mercury)
This Is My Story (Mercury)
Doris Day; *Doris Day Sings 22 Great Songs-Original Big Band* (Hindsight)
Duprees; *Best Of The Duprees* (Rhino)
Frank Sinatra; *Round #1* (Capitol)
Sinatra's Swingin' Session!!! (Capitol)
Joe Williams; *Swingin'...At Birdland* (Roulette)
Marty Robbins; *Essential Marty Robbins-1951-1982* (Columbia)
Peggy Lee; *You Can Depend On Me* (Glendale)
September Song
Boston Pops Orchestra/Arthur Fiedler; *Greatest Hits Of The '30s* (RCA)
Mister Music U.S.A. (Deutsche Grammophon)
Music For Every Mood-Yesterday (RCA)
Eddy Duchin & Stanley Worth; *Best Of The Big Bands-C* (Columbia)
Eydie Gorme; *Best Of Eydie Gorme* (Curb)
Flamingos & Moonglows; *On The Dusty Road Of Hits* (Vee-Jay)
Frank Sinatra; *A Lovely Way To Spend An Evening* (ASV)
Point Of No Return (Capitol)
September Of My Years (Reprise)
Kate Wolf; *Safe At Anchor* (Kaleidoscope)
Lindsey Buckingham; *Law And Order* (Asylum)
Lou Reed; *Lost In The Stars-Music Of Kurt Weill-C* (A&M)
Roger Williams; *Roger Williams' Greatest Hits* (MCA)
Roy Clark; *Best Of Roy Clark* (MCA)
Sarah Vaughan & Clifford Brown; *Sarah Vaughan & Clifford Brown* (Emarcy)
Stan Kenton; *Comprehensive Stan Kenton* (Capitol)
Retrospective-Capitol Years (Blue Note)
Tony Bennett; *Forty Years-The Artistry Of Tony Bennett* (Columbia)
Willie Nelson; *Stardust* (Legacy)
Set Adrift On Memory Bliss
PM Dawn; *MTV Party To Go-#2-C* (Tommy Boy)
Red Hot + Dance-C (Columbia)
Shades Of '45
Gary O'; *Strange Behavior* (RCA)
She Has No Memory Of Me
Moe Bandy; *Moe Bandy's Greatest Hits* (Curb)
She Misses Him On Sunday The Most
Diamond Rio; *Diamond Rio IV* (Arista)
Diamond Rio's Greatest Hits (Arista)
She Thinks His Name Was John
Reba McEntire; *Read My Mind* (MCA)
Reba McEntire's Greatest Hits-#3: I'm A Survivor (MCA)
She's Got You
Patsy Cline; *12 Greatest Hits* (MCA)
Billboard Top Country Hits-1962-C (Rhino)
The Patsy Cline Story (MCA)
She's Playing Hard To Forget
Eddy Raven; *Eddy Raven-Greatest Country Hits* (Curb)
Eddy Raven's Greatest Hits (Warner Bros.)
Silver Medals & Sweet Memories
Statler Brothers; *Best Of The Statler Brothers-Rides Again-#2* (Mercury)
Short Stories (Mercury)
Simple Days
Babyface; *The Day* (Epic)
Sing Me Back Home
Alabama; *Mama's Hungry Eyes-Merle Haggard Tribute-C* (Arista)
Flying Burrito Brothers; *Farther Along-Best Of The Flying Burrito Brothers* (A&M)
Merle Haggard & The Strangers; *Best Of Merle Haggard & The Strangers* (Capitol)
Capitol Collectors Series-Merle Haggard & The Strangers (Capitol)
For The Record: Merle Haggard-43 Legendary Hits (BNA)
Okie From Muskogee (Capitol)
Songs I'll Always Sing (Capitol)
Sinner
Neil Finn; *Try Whistling This* (Work)
Skellig
Loreena McKennitt; *The Book Of Secrets* (Quinlan Rd./Warner Bros.)
Slow Burning Memory
Vern Gosdin; *10 Years Of Greatest Hits Newly Recorded* (Columbia)
There Is A Season (Compleat)
Some Memories Just Won't Die
Marty Robbins; *American Originals-Marty Robbins* (Columbia)
Come Back To Me (Columbia)
Lifetime Of Song-1951-1982 (Columbia)
Some Memories Just Won't Die (Columbia)
Something Like That
Tim McGraw; *A Place In The Sun* (Curb)
Tim McGraw's Greatest Hits (Curb)
Something To Remember You By
Dinah Shore; *Blues In The Night* (ASV)
Judy Garland & Bing Crosby; *Mail Call! Armed Forces Radio Broadcasts* (Laserlight)
Libby Holman; *78-#4910* (Brunswick)
Sometimes I Get Lucky And Forget
Gene Watson; *Gene Watson's Greatest Hits* (MCA)
Sometimes I Get Lucky (MCA)
Sometimes She Forgets
Steve Earle; *Train A Comin'* (Warner Bros.)
Travis Tritt; *Greatest Hits-From The Beginning* (Warner Bros.)
Song Remembers When
Trisha Yearwood; *The Song Remembers When* (MCA)
Stardust
Artie Shaw; *Begin The Beguine* (Bluebird)
Artie Shaw & His Orchestra; *22 Original Big Band Recordings-C* (Hindsight)
Nipper's Greatest Hits Of The '40s-#1-C (RCA)
Benny Goodman; *Benny Goodman Sextet featuring Charlie Christian-1939-1941* (Columbia)
Benny Goodman-Live At Carnegie Hall (London)
Carly Simon; *Come Upstairs* (Warner Bros.)
Coleman Hawkins; *Hollywood Stampede* (Capitol)
Dave Brubeck; *Art Of Dave Brubeck* (Atlantic)
Greatest Hits From The Fantasy Years (Fantasy)
Dave Brubeck Quartet; *Jazz At Oberlin* (Fantasy)
Stardust (Fantasy)
Frank Sinatra; *Sinatra & Strings* (Reprise)
Harry Connick, Jr.; *25* (Columbia)
Hoagy Carmichael; *Nipper's Greatest Hits Of The '30s-#1-C* (RCA)
Stardust Road (MCA)
Johnny Mathis; *Feelings* (Columbia)
First 25 Years-Silver Anniversary Album (Columbia)
Nat "King" Cole; *The Nat "King" Cole Story* (Capitol)
Rob Wasserman & Aaron Neville; *Duets-C* (MCA)
Roger Williams; *Best Of Roger Williams* (MCA)
Tommy Dorsey; *Best Of Tommy Dorsey* (Bluebird)
This Is Tommy Dorsey (RCA)
Tommy Dorsey & Frank Sinatra; *Stardust* (Bluebird)
Wayne King & His Orchestra; *78-#22656* (Victor)
State Of Mind
Clint Black; *No Time To Kill* (RCA)
Still
Bill Anderson; *Best Of Bill Anderson* (Curb)
Bill Anderson's Greatest Hits (Varese Sarabande)
Billboard Top Country Hits-1963-C (Rhino)
From The Vaults: Decca Country Classics-1934-1973-C (Decca)
Grand Ole Opry-75 Years-#2-C (MCA)
Strawberry Wine
Deana Carter; *Did I Shave My Legs For This?* (Capitol)
Such A Night
Elvis Presley; *From Nashville To Memphis-The Essential '60s Masters* (RCA)
Sugar Shack
Jimmy Gilmer And The Fireballs; *Billboard Top Rock 'N' Roll Hits-1963-C* (Rhino)
Golden Years-1963-C (Dominion Entert.)
Good Old Rock & Roll-C (International Mktg. Group)
Sullivan
Caroline's Spine; *Monsoon* (Hollywood)
Summer Of '69
Bryan Adams; *Reckless* (A&M)
Summer Song
Chad & Jeremy; *Best Of Chad & Jeremy* (K-Tel)
Capitol Gold-Best Of Chad & Jeremy (Capitol)
History Of British Rock-#2-C (Rhino)
Sunday Will Never Be The Same
Spanky & Our Gang; *Flower Power-Psychedelic Rock Classics-C* (K-Tel)
Superstar (Remember How You Got Where You Are)
Temptations; *Temptations-Anthology-The Best Of The Temptations* (Motown)
Sweet Child O' Mine
Guns N' Roses; *Appetite For Destruction* (Geffen)
Sweet Summer
Diamond Rio; *One More Day* (Arista)
Take A Picture
Filter; *Title Of Record* (Reprise)
Totally Hits-#2-C (Elektra)
Take Your Memory With You
Vince Gill; *Platinum Country-C* (JCI Assoc. Labels)
Pocket Full Of Gold (MCA)
Vince Gill-Souvenirs (MCA)
Tenderly
Billie Holiday; *Verve Jazz Masters 47-Billie Holiday Sings Standards* (Verve)
Ella Fitzgerald; *Verve Jazz Masters 24* (Verve)
Oscar Peterson; *Essential Oscar Peterson-The Swinger* (Verve)
Rosemary Clooney; *Essence Of Rosemary Clooney* (Legacy)
Rosemary Clooney-16 Most Requested Songs (Legacy)

Sarah Vaughan; *Compact Jazz-Sarah Vaughan* ....(Verve)
Verve Jazz Masters 42-The Jazz Sides ....(Verve)
Tony Bennett; *Here's To The Ladies*....................(Columbia)

Tennessee Waltz
Cowboy Copas; *45-#696*....................(King)
Emmylou Harris; *Cimarron*....................(Warner Bros.)
Country's Greatest Hits-#5-C....................(Warner Bros.)
New Tradition Sings The Old Tradition-C ....(Warner Bros.)
Guy Lombardo & His Royal Canadians; *Best Of Guy Lombardo* ....(Curb)
Hank Williams, Jr.; *Living Proof-MGM Recordings 1963-1975*......(Mercury)
Lacy J. Dalton; *Lacy J. Dalton's Greatest Hits* ....(Columbia)
Les Paul & Mary Ford; *Les Paul-Selections From Legend & Legacy* ...(Capitol)
Patti Page; *Patti Page-Golden Hits* ....(Mercury)
Patti Page's Greatest Hits ....(Columbia)
Roy Acuff; *Essential Roy Acuff-1936-1949* ....(Legacy)
Roy Acuff's Greatest Hits ....(Columbia)
Roy Rogers; *Best Of Roy Rogers*....................(Curb)
Sammy Kaye & His Orchestra; *Best Of The Big Bands-C*..........(Columbia)
Spike Jones & His City Slickers; *Best Of Spike Jones & His City Slickers* ....(RCA)

Texas State Of Mind
David Frizzell & Shelly West; *Carryin' On The Family Names* ....(Warner Bros.)
Golden Duets ....(Viva)

Thank The Lord For The Night Time
Neil Diamond; *Glory Road-1968-1972*....................(MCA)
Hot August Night II....................(Columbia)
Neil Diamond-Classics (Early Years)....................(Columbia)
Neil Diamond-Gold ....(MCA)
Neil Diamond's Greatest Hits-1966-1992 ....(Columbia)

Thanks For The Memories
Benny Goodman; *Benny Goodman-More Greatest Hits*...............(RCA)
Bob Hope; *Thanks For The Memories*....................(MCA)
Bob Hope & Shirley Ross; *The Envelope Please-Academy Award Winning Songs-#1 (1934-1945)-C*....................(Rhino)

That Summer
Garth Brooks; *The Chase*....................(Liberty)

Theme From "All In The Family"
Original Soundtrack; *CBS: The First 50 Years* ....(TVT)
Television's Greatest Hits-#3-1970s & 1980s-C ....(TVT)

Theme From "The Bob Hope Show" (Thanks For The Memories)
Original Soundtrack; *Television's Greatest Hits-#4-Black & White Classics-C*....................(TVT)

Theme From "The Sandpiper" (Shadow Of Your Smile)
Astrud Gilberto; *ST/Sandpiper* ....(Verve)
The Envelope Please-Academy Award Winning Songs-#3 (1958-1969)-C....................(Rhino)
Barbra Streisand; *My Name Is Barbra, Two* ....(Columbia)
Boston Pops Orchestra/Arthur Fiedler; *Greatest Hits Of The '60s-#2*.....(RCA)
Motion Picture Classics-#1 ....(RCA Victor)
Music For Every Mood-Yesterday ....(RCA)
Carmen McRae; *Carmen McRae-Alive*....................(Mainstream)
I Want You ....(Mainstream)
Frank Sinatra; *At The Sands*....................(Reprise)
The Reprise Collection ....(Reprise)
Henry Mancini; *Days Of Wine And Roses*....................(RCA)
James Morrison; *Snappy Doo* ....(Atlantic)
Jose Carreras; *Hollywood Golden Classics* ....(Atlantic)
Marvin Gaye; *Romantically Yours* ....(Columbia)
Tony Bennett; *Academy Award Winners: 16 Most Requested*........(LeGrand)
The Movie Song Album....................(Columbia)
Tony Bennett-16 Most Requested Songs....................(Legacy)
Tony Bennett's All-Time Greatest Hits....................(Columbia)

These Foolish Things (Remind Me Of You)
Aaron Neville; *The Grand Tour* ....(A&M)
Art Pepper; *Art Pepper Today*....................(Galaxy)
Benny Goodman; *Stompin' At The Savoy* ....(Bluebird)
Billie Holiday; *Billie Holiday-16 Most Requested Songs* ....(Legacy)
Bobby Watson; *This Little Light Of Mine* ....(Red)
Boston Pops Orchestra/Arthur Fiedler; *Popular Favorites By The Boston Pops Orchestra* ....(Pair)
Bryan Ferry; *Street Life-20 Great Hits* ....(Reprise)
These Foolish Things ....(Reprise)
Chet Baker; *Baker's Holiday*....................(Verve)
Somewhere Over The Rainbow....................(Bluebird)
Count Basie Jam; *Montreux '77-C* ....(Pablo)
Dave Brubeck; *Greatest Hits From The Fantasy Years*..............(Fantasy)
Dinah Washington; *In Love*....................(Roulette)
Frank Sinatra; *Point Of No Return*....................(Capitol)
Nat "King" Cole; *Just One Of Those Things (& More)* ....(Capitol)
Ronnie Milsap; *True Believer*....................(Liberty)
Ruby Braff; *Jazz Club-Mainstream-Trumpet* ....(Verve)
Stan Getz; *Essential Stan Getz Songbook* ....(Verve)

They Can't Take That Away From Me
Billie Holiday; *God Bless The Child* ....(Pro-Arte)
I Like Jazz-Essence Of Billie Holiday....................(Columbia)
Diana Krall; *Love Scenes*....................(Impulse!)
Ella Fitzgerald; *Ella & Louis Again*....................(Verve)
Frank Sinatra; *My Kind Of Broadway* ....(Reprise)
Frank Sinatra & Natalie Cole; *Duets* ....(Capitol)
Fred Astaire; *Starring Fred Astaire* ....(Columbia)
Kate Smith; *Best Of Kate Smith* ....(Curb)
Lisa Stansfield; *Glory Of Gershwin Featuring Larry Adler-C*........(Mercury)
Mary Lou Williams; *Mary Lou Williams In London* ....(Crescendo)
Original Broadway Cast; *Crazy For You* ....(Angel)
Original London Cast; *Crazy For You* ....(RCA)
Patti Austin; *The Real Me*....................(Qwest)
Sarah Vaughan; *Sarah Vaughan Sings George Gershwin Songbook, Vol. 1* ....(Emarcy)
Stanley Turrentine; *Blue Gershwin* ....(Blue Note)

Things We Said Today
Beatles; *Beatles-Box Set*....................(Capitol)
Something New ....(Capitol)
The Beatles At The Hollywood Bowl....................(Capitol)
Paul McCartney; *Tripping The Live Fantastic-Highlights!* ....(Capitol)

Think Of Laura
Christopher Cross; *Another Page*....................(Warner Bros.)
Soap Opera's Greatest Love Themes ....(Scotti Bros.)

Think Of Me
Buck Owens & The Buckaroos; *Buck Owens Collection-1959-1990* ....(Rhino)
Very Best Of Buck Owens-#2....................(Rhino)

Thinkin' Problem
David Ball; *Thinkin' Problem* ....(Warner Bros.)

Third Man Theme (Harry Lime Theme)
Band; *Moondog Matinee* ....(Capitol)
Dukes Of Dixieland; *Dukes Of Dixieland's Greatest Hits*.............(MCA)
Guy Lombardo & His Royal Canadians; *Best Of Guy Lombardo* ....(Curb)

This Ain't The Denver I Remember
Pirates Of The Mississippi; *Walk The Plank* ....(Liberty)

This Heartache Never Sleeps
Mark Chesnutt; *I Don't Want To Miss A Thing* ....(MCA)

Those Oldies But Goodies (Remind Me Of You)
John Cafferty And The Beaver Brown Band; *ST/Eddie & The Cruisers* ....(Scotti Bros.)
Little Caesar and The Romans; *Best Love Songs-C* .... (Original Sound)
Collectables Presents The History Of Rock-#2-C.............(Collectables)
Cruisin'-1961-C ....(Increase)
Oldies But Goodies-#6-C .... (Original Sound)

Thousand Times A Day
Patty Loveless; *The Trouble With The Truth* ....(Epic)

Time After Time
Cyndi Lauper; *Chicken Soup For The Woman's Soul-C* ....(Rhino)
She's So Unusual....................(Portrait)
Twelve Deadly Cyns...And Then Some ....(Epic)
Everything But The Girl; *Acoustic*....................(Atlantic)
INOJ & So So Def Bass All-Stars; *Time After Time (Maxi Single)* .... (So So Def/Columbia)
Miles Davis; *Live Around The World*....................(Warner Bros.)
You're Under Arrest ....(Columbia)

Time Remembered
Bill Evans; *Loose Blues* ....(Milestone)
Time Remembered....................(Milestone)

Tokyo Road
Bon Jovi; *7800 Degrees Fahrenheit*....................(Mercury)

Too Old To Cut The Mustard
Carlisles; *45-#6348* ....(Mercury)
Ernest Tubb; *Ernest Tubb-Retrospective-#2* .... (MCA Special Prod.)

Traces/Memories
Lettermen; *Capitol Collectors Series-The Lettermen*...............(Capitol)
The Lettermen's All-Time Greatest Hits ....(Capitol)

Train Of Memories
Kathy Mattea; *14 Country Favorites-C* ....(Mercury)
Collection Of Hits ....(Mercury)
Walk The Way The Wind Blows....................(Mercury)

Travelin' Man
Bob Seger; *Beautiful Loser* ....(Capitol)
Live Bullet....................(Capitol)

Tripping Billies
Dave Matthews Band; *Crash* ....(RCA)

Try To Remember
Original Cast; *Fantasticks* ....(Polydor)

Tubthumping
Chumbawamba; *Tubthumper*....................(Universal)

Turn Back Time
Aqua; *Aquarium*....................(MCA)
ST/Sliding Doors....................(MCA)

Turn The Page
Metallica; *Garage Inc.*....................(Elektra)

Two Of Us
Beatles; *Beatles-Box Set*....................(Capitol)
Let It Be....................(Capitol)

U Remind Me
Usher; *8701* ....(LaFace)
Totally Hits 2001-C....................(Arista)

Under African Skies
Paul Simon; *Graceland* ....(Warner Bros.)

Unforgettable
Nat "King" Cole; *Capitol Collectors Series-Nat "King" Cole* ......(Capitol)
The Nat "King" Cole Story ....(Capitol)

Unforgettable. . . . . (Capitol)
Natalie Cole with Nat ''King'' Cole; *Unforgettable With Love* . . . . (Elektra)
Unforgettable Fire
U2; *Unforgettable Fire*. . . . . (Island)
Unsent
Alanis Morissette; *Supposed Former Infatuation Junkie* . . . .(Maverick)
Used Cars
Bruce Springsteen; *Nebraska* . . . . (Columbia)
Viking
Los Lobos; *The Sopranos-Music From The HBO Original
Series* . . . . (Sony Music Soundtrax)
Walk In My Mind
Siegel-Schwall Band; *'70*. . . . . (Vanguard)
Best Of The Siegel-Schwall Band. . . . . (Vanguard)
Walk On Out Of My Mind
Waylon Jennings; *Best Of Waylon Jennings*. . . . . (RCA)
Walk Right In
Rooftop Singers; *Best Of The Rooftop Singers*. . . . . (Vanguard)
Cruisin'-1963-C . . . .(Increase)
Greatest Folksingers Of The '60s-C . . . . (Vanguard)
ST/Forrest Gump . . . . (Epic/Sony Music Soundtrax)
Troubadours Of The Folk Era-#3-C . . . . (Rhino)
Walk Softly
Billy ''Crash'' Craddock; *Billy ''Crash'' Craddock Live* . . . .(MCA)
Billy ''Crash'' Craddock Sings His Greatest Hits . . . .(MCA)
Easy As Pie . . . .(MCA)
Waltz You Saved For Me
Bob Wills; *Bob Wills-Anthology*. . . . . (Sony Music Special Prod.)
Lawrence Welk; *22 All-Time Big Band Favorites* . . . .(Ranwood)
Mom & Dads; *Mom & Dads-20 Favorite Waltzes* . . . . (Crescendo)
Wayne King & His Orchestra; *Best Of Wayne King* . . . .(MCA)
Way We Were, The
Barbra Streisand; *Just For The Record* . . . . (Columbia)
ST/The Way We Were . . . . (Columbia)
Way You Look Tonight, The
Billie Holiday; *Quintessential-#2-1936* . . . . (Columbia)
Erroll Garner; *Body And Soul* . . . . (Legacy)
Frank Sinatra; *Days Of Wine And Roses, Moon River, And Other Academy
Award Winners* . . . . (Reprise)
Sinatra Reprise-The Very Good Years . . . . (Reprise)
The Reprise Collection . . . . (Reprise)
Fred Astaire; *Steppin' Out-Astaire Sings* . . . . (Verve)
Lettermen; *Best Of The Lettermen-All Original Recordings* . . . . (Curb)
Capitol Collectors Series-The Lettermen. . . . . (Capitol)
The Lettermen's All-Time Greatest Hits . . . . (Capitol)
Tony Bennett; *ST/My Best Friend's Wedding*. . . . . (Work/Epic)
We Danced Anyway
Deana Carter; *Did I Shave My Legs For This?* . . . . (Capitol)
We Were In Love
Toby Keith; *Dream Walkin'* . . . . (Mercury)
Toby Keith's Greatest Hits, Volume One . . . . (Mercury)
Westside
TQ; *They Never Saw Me Coming* . . . .(ClockWork/Epic)
What Might Have Been
Little Texas; *Big Time*. . . . . (Warner Bros.)
When I Was Young
Animals; *Best Of The Animals* . . . . (Abkco)
Greatest Hits Live!-Rip It To Shreds . . . .(I.R.S.)
History Of British Rock-#8-C . . . . (Rhino)
When My Blue Moon Turns To Gold Again
Elvis Presley; *A Golden Celebration* . . . . (RCA)
Elvis . . . . (RCA)
The Other Sides-Worldwide Gold Award Hits, Vol. 2 . . . . (RCA)
Merle Haggard; *Merle Haggard-His Best*. . . . .(MCA)
Ramblin' Fever . . . .(MCA)
Where Or When
Barbra Streisand; *Color Me Barbra* . . . . (Columbia)
Benny Goodman; *Small Groups-1941-1945* . . . . (Columbia)
Bryan Ferry; *As Time Goes By* . . . . (Virgin)
Dion And The Belmonts; *Best Of Doo Wop Ballads-C*. . . . . (Rhino)
Complete Dion And The Belmonts. . . . . (Collector's Choice)
Ella Fitzgerald; *Ella Fitzgerald Sings The Rodgers & Hart Songbook* . . . (Verve)
Frank Sinatra; *Sinatra At The Sands* . . . . (Reprise)
Johnny Mathis; *You Light Up My Life* . . . . (Columbia)
Peggy Lee; *Peggy Lee-Complete Recordings-1941-1947* . . . . (Legacy)
Wynton Marsalis; *Standard Time-#3-The Resolution Of Romance* . . (Columbia)
Where Was I
Ricky Van Shelton; *Bridge I Didn't Burn* . . . . (Columbia)
White Silver Sands
Ace Cannon; *Golden Classics-Ace Cannon* . . . . (Gusto)
Ray Anthony; *Great Golden Hits* . . . .(Ranwood)
Sonny James; *45-#4-45706*. . . . . (Columbia)
Who Needs Pictures
Brad Paisley; *Who Needs Pictures* . . . . (Arista)
Why I'm Walkin'
Stonewall Jackson; *Columbia Country Classics-#2-Honky Tonk
Heroes-C* . . . . (Columbia)
Waterloo . . . . (Laserlight)

Will You Remember?
John Charles Thomas; *Music From The New York Stage (1890-1920)-#4-
1917-1920-C* . . . .(Pearl)
Wish, The
Bruce Springsteen; *Tracks* . . . . (Columbia)
Words By Heart
Billy Ray Cyrus; *It Won't Be The Last* . . . . (Mercury)
World I Used To Know
Glenn Yarbrough; *Best Of Glenn Yarbrough* . . . .(RCA)
World We Knew (Over And Over)
Frank Sinatra; *Frank Sinatra's Greatest Hits!*. . . . . (Reprise)
The World We Knew . . . . (Reprise)
Write This Down
George Strait; *Always Never The Same* . . . . (MCA)
www.Memory
Alan Jackson; *Under The Influence* . . . . (Arista)
You Belong To Me
Dean Martin; *Dean Martin's All Time Greatest Hits*. . . . . (Curb)
Duprees; *13 Of The Best Doo Wop Love Songs-#2-C* . . . .(Original Sound)
Baby Boomer's Best-Mellow '60s-C . . . . (Priority)
Best Of The Duprees. . . . . (Rhino)
Jo Stafford; *Billboard Pop Memories-1950-1954-C* . . . . (Rhino)
Jo Stafford's Greatest Hits . . . . (Curb)
Johnny Mathis; *In The Still Of The Night* . . . . (Columbia)
Patsy Cline; *Patsy Cline Sings Songs Of Love* . . . . (MCA Special Prod.)
Sentimentally Yours . . . .(MCA)
Vonda Shepard; *ST/Songs From ''Ally McBeal'' Featuring Vonda
Shepard* . . . .(550/Epic)
You Don't Have To Remind Me
Sass Jordan; *Racine*. . . . . (Impact)
You Remind Me Of Something
R. Kelly; *R. Kelly*. . . . .(Jive)
You Stay With Me
Ricky Martin; *Ricky Martin*. . . . . (Columbia)
You Used To Love Me
Faith Evans; *Faith Evans*. . . . .(Bad Boy/Arista)
ST/All That . . . . (Loud/RCA)
The Ultimate Hip Hop Party-1998-C . . . . (Arista)
You Were Mine
Dixie Chicks; *Big Country Hits '99-C*. . . . . (K-Tel)
Wide Open Spaces . . . . (Monument)

RESTAURANTS, Cafes, Diners

**See Also: ALCOHOL, BARS, FOOD & BEVERAGES (various),
WAITRESSES**

Abandoned Luncheonette
Daryl Hall & John Oates; *Abandoned Luncheonette* . . . .(Atlantic)
Livetime . . . . (RCA)
Alice's Restaurant Massacree
Arlo Guthrie; *Alice's Restaurant*. . . . . (Reprise)
Best Of Arlo Guthrie. . . . . (Warner Bros.)
Amy's Back In Austin
Little Texas; *Kick A Little* . . . . (Warner Bros.)
Little Texas' Greatest Hits . . . . (Warner Bros.)
Annie Mae's Cafe
Little Milton; *Annie Mae's Cafe* . . . . (Malaco)
At A Dixie Roadside Diner
Duke Ellington; *Duke Ellington & The Blanton-Webster Band* . . . . . . (Bluebird)
At The Banjo Cafe
Pat Cloud; *Higher Power* . . . . (Flying Fish)
At The Grand Hotel/Table With A View
Broadway Cast; *Grand Hotel* . . . . (RCA)
At The Seaside Cafe
Adrian Belew; *Desire Caught By The Tail* . . . . (Island)
Atomic Cafe
Motels; *Motels*. . . . . (Capitol)
Bigger Than The Beatles
Joe Diffie; *Life's So Funny* . . . . (Epic)
Cafe Carnival
Craig Chaquico; *Panorama: The Best Of Craig Chaquico* . . . . . (Higher Octave)
Cafe On The Corner
Sawyer Brown; *Cafe On The Corner*. (Curb)
Cafe On The Left Bank
Wings; *London Town* . . . . (Capitol)
Carey
Joni Mitchell; *Blue* . . . . (Reprise)
Joni Mitchell with Tom Scott & The L.A. Express; *Miles Of Aisles* . . . .(Asylum)
Chinese Cafe
Joni Mitchell; *Wild Things Run Fast* . . . . (Geffen)
Coffee Shoppe
Margaret Whiting; *Then & Now* . . . .(DRG)
Danny's All-Star Joint
Rickie Lee Jones; *Rickie Lee Jones* . . . . (Warner Bros.)
Days Of Pup & Taco
Lawndale; *Beyond Barbecue*. . . . .(SST)

No Age-Compilation Of SST Instrumentals-C . . . . (SST)
Detroit Snackbar Dreamer
  Edgar Froese; *Stuntman* . . . .(Blue Plate)
Diesel Cafe
  Bellamy Brothers; *Restless* . . . . (MCA Special Prod.)
Dinner At The Ritz
  City Boy; *Dinner At The Ritz* . . . . (Mercury)
Dinner For One Please James
  Nat ''King'' Cole; *Blossom Fell* . . . .(Capitol)
  Nat ''King'' Cole-Gift Set . . . .(Capitol)
Dixie Diner
  Jimmy Buffett; *You Had To Be There* . . . . (MCA)
Do Fries Go With That Shake
  George Clinton; *Best Of George Clinton* . . . .(Capitol)
Drive-In
  Beach Boys; *All Summer Long* . . . .(Capitol)
  Spirit Of America . . . .(Capitol)
Easy On The Pain
  Michael Martin Murphey; *Cowboy Songs Four* . . . .(Valley Entert.)
Empty Chairs At Empty Tables
  Original Broadway Cast; *Les Miserables* . . . . (Geffen)
Fast Food
  Stevens & Grdnic; *Dr. Demento Presents The Greatest Novelty Records-#5-*
    1980s-C . . . .(Rhino)
Fast Food
  Pete Townshend; *The Iron Man* . . . . (Atlantic)
Gimme A Pigfoot (And A Bottle Of Beer)
  Billie Holiday; *Complete Decca Recordings* . . . . (Decca Jazz)
  From The Original Decca Masters . . . . (MCA)
Good As I Was To You
  Lorrie Morgan; *Greater Need* . . . .(BNA)
  Lorrie Morgan-Super Hits . . . .(RCA)
  To Get To You-Greatest Hits Collection . . . .(BNA)
Halfway Home Cafe
  Ricky Skaggs and Kentucky Thunder; *History Of The Future* . . (Skaggs Family)
Hard Rock Cafe
  Carole King; *Simple Things* . . . .(Capitol)
I Guess You Had To Be There
  Lorrie Morgan; *To Get To You-Greatest Hits Collection* . . . .(BNA)
  Watch Me . . . .(BNA)
In A Restaurant By The Sea
  Holly Near & Ronnie Gilbert; *Singing With You* . . . . (Redwood)
Invitation To The Blues
  Holly Cole; *Temptation* . . . .(Metro Blue)
  Tom Waits; *Small Change* . . . . (Asylum)
Ladies Who Lunch
  Original Cast; *Company* . . . . (Columbia)
Learning To Live Again
  Garth Brooks; *The Chase* . . . . (Liberty)
Little Plastic Castle
  Ani DiFranco; *Little Plastic Castle* . . . . (Righteous Babe)
Montana Cafe
  Hank Williams, Jr.; *Montana Cafe* . . . . (WB/Curb)
More Wine Waiter Please
  Poor; *Who Cares* . . . . (550 Music)
My Girlfriend Is A Waitress
  Iguanas; *Nuevo Boogaloo* . . . . (Margaritaville)
Nobody Eats At Linebaugh's Anymore
  John Hartford; *Me Oh My-How The Time Does Fly-Anthology* . . . . .(Flying Fish)
Not In A Chinese Restaurant
  Country Joe McDonald; *Child's Play* . . . . (Rag Baby)
Ooh! My Feet!
  Original Broadway Cast; *Most Happy Fella* . . . .(Sony Music Classical)
Overnight Cafe
  Chicago; *Chicago XIV* . . . . (Chicago)
Paper Rosie
  Don Walser; *Here's To Country Music* . . . . (Sire)
  Gene Watson; *Gene Watson's Greatest Hits* . . . . (Curb)
  Osborne Brothers; *Hillbilly Fever* . . . . (C.M.H. Prod.)
Paradise Cafe
  Barry Manilow; *2:00 Paradise Cafe* . . . . (Arista)
Paradise Cafe
  Arc Angels; *Arc Angels* . . . .(David Geffen Co.)
Picture Postcards From L.A.
  Joshua Kadison; *Painted Desert Serenade* . . . . (SBK)
Pretty Women/Ladies Who Lunch
  Barbra Streisand; *The Broadway Album* . . . . (Columbia)
Queen Of The Cowboy Cafe
  Si Kahn; *Home* . . . . (Flying Fish)
River Diner
  Jack Smith & The Rockabilly Planet; *Jack Smith & The Rockabilly*
    Planet . . . . (Flying Fish)
Sad Cafe
  Eagles; *Eagles Greatest Hits, Volume 2* . . . . (Asylum)
  The Long Run . . . . (Asylum)
  Lorrie Morgan; *Common Thread-Songs Of The Eagles-C* . . . . (Giant)
Scenes From An Italian Restaurant
  Billy Joel; *The Stranger* . . . . (Columbia)

She's Not On The Menu
  SNFU; *Last Of The Big Time Suspenders* . . . .(Cargo)
She's Taken A Shine
  John Berry; *Faces* . . . .(Capitol)
Showdown At The Big Boy
  Nazareth; *Malice In Wonderland* . . . .(A&M)
Smokey Joe's Cafe
  Coasters; *Coasters-Their Greatest Recordings-Early Years* . . . .(Atco)
  Young Blood . . . . (Atlantic)
  Loudon Wainwright III; *Album III* . . . .(Columbia)
Street Cafe
  Icehouse; *Fresco* . . . . (Chrysalis)
  Great Southern Land . . . . (Chrysalis)
  Primitive Man . . . . (Chrysalis)
Sunset Grill
  Don Henley; *Building The Perfect Beast* . . . . (Geffen)
Sweet Little Cafe In A Square
  Lena Spencer & Others; *Welcome To Caffe Lena* . . . . (Biograph)
Sweetheart
  Dan Hicks & His Hot Licks; *Last Train To Hicksville* . . . . (MCA)
  Maria Muldaur; *Waitress In The Donut Shop* . . . .(Warner Archives)
Taco Stand
  Normaltown Flyers; *Normaltown Flyers* . . . .(Mercury)
Taco Wagon
  Dick Dale And The Del-Tones; *King Of The Surf Guitar-Best Of Dick Dale*
    And The Del-Tones . . . .(Rhino)
  Young Fresh Fellows; *This One's For The Ladies* . . . . (Frontier)
Texas Rose Cafe
  Little Feat; *Sailin' Shoes* . . . . (Warner Bros.)
Tomb Of The Unknown Love
  Cassell Webb; *Songs Of A Stranger* . . . . (Venture)
  Kenny Rogers; *The Heart Of The Matter* . . . . (RCA)
Tom's Diner
  D.N.A. Featuring Suzanne Vega; *Solitude Standing* . . . . (A&M)
  Tom's Album . . . . (A&M)
Truck Drivers Coffee Shop
  Dick Reinhart & His Lone Star Boys; *Truck Driver Boogie Big Rig Hits-*
    1939-1969-C . . . . (Audium)
Two Triple Cheese, Side Order Of Fries
  Commander Cody & His Lost Planet Airmen; *Aces High* . . . . (Relix)
Waitress In The Sky
  Replacements; *Tim* . . . . (Sire)
Waitress, The
  Tori Amos; *Under The Pink* . . . . (Atlantic)
We Reserve The Right To Refuse Service To You
  Kinky Friedman; *Sold American* . . . . (Vanguard)

RETURNING, Coming Back, Going Back
   See Also: **CIRCLES, HELLO, HOME, LEAVING, LOVE (various),**
    SEPARATION, TRAVELING

Across The Border
  Bruce Springsteen; *The Ghost Of Tom Joad* . . . .(Columbia)
Adam Raised A Cain
  Bruce Springsteen; *Darkness On The Edge Of Town* . . . .(Columbia)
Adrian
  Jewel; *Pieces Of You* . . . . (Atlantic)
Already Home
  Marc Cohn; *Burning The Daze* . . . . (Atlantic)
Angeline Is Coming Home
  Badlees; *River Songs* . . . . (Atlas)
Are You On The Road To Lovin' Me Again
  Debby Boone; *Best Of Debby Boone* . . . .(Curb)
Austin
  Blake Shelton; *Blake Shelton* . . . . (Giant)
Back At One
  Brian McKnight; *Back At One* . . . . (Motown)
  Mark Wills; *Permanently* . . . .(Mercury)
Back For Good
  Take That; *Nobody Else* . . . .(Arista)
Back In The Day
  Blues Traveler; *Bridge* . . . .(A&M)
Back In The High Life Again
  Steve Winwood; *Back In The High Life* . . . .(Island)
Back In The U.S.A.
  Chuck Berry; *Chuck Berry-Golden Hits* . . . .(Mercury)
  Chuck Berry's Greatest Hits . . . . (Everest)
  Roll Over Beethoven . . . . (Allegiance)
  The Chess Box-Chuck Berry . . . . (Chess)
  Linda Ronstadt; *Linda Ronstadt's Greatest Hits, Volume Two* . . . . . . (Asylum)
  Living In The USA . . . . (Asylum)
Back In The U.S.S.R.
  Beatles; *Beatles-Box Set* . . . .(Capitol)
  Rock 'N' Roll Music . . . .(Capitol)
  The Beatles (White Album) . . . .(Capitol)
  The Beatles/1967-1970 . . . .(Capitol)

Billy Joel; *KOHUEPT* .... (Columbia)
Back In Your Arms
Bruce Springsteen; *Tracks* .... (Columbia)
Back On Earth
Ozzy Osbourne; *The Ozzman Cometh* .... (Epic)
Back On The Street Again
Sunshine Company; *Even More Nuggets-C* .... (Rhino)
Bitch Is Back
Elton John; *Caribou* .... (Rocket)
   Elton John's Greatest Hits-#2 .... (Polydor)
   Here And There .... (Rocket)
Tina Turner; *Two Rooms-Celebrating The Songs Of Elton John & Bernie
   Taupin-C* .... (Polydor)
Blue Bayou
Linda Ronstadt; *Linda Ronstadt's Greatest Hits, Volume Two* .... (Asylum)
   Simple Dreams .... (Asylum)
Roy Orbison; *For The Lonely: A Roy Orbison Anthology 1959-1965* ... (Rhino)
   In Dreams-Greatest Hits .... (Orbison)
   Roy Orbison-More Greatest Hits .... (Monument)
   Roy Orbison's All-Time Greatest Hits-#1 & 2 ... (Monument)
Roy Orbison & Friends; *Black & White Night-Live* ..... (Virgin)
Blue Ridge Mountain Blues
Blue Ridge Rangers; *Blue Ridge Rangers* .... (Fantasy)
Doc Watson; *Essential Doc Watson* .... (Vanguard)
Earl Scruggs & John Fogerty; *Earl Scruggs And Friends-C* .... (MCA)
Norman Blake; *Directions* .... (Takoma)
Boogie Back To Texas
Asleep At The Wheel; *Asleep At The Wheel-10* .... (Epic)
   Swinging Best Of Asleep At The Wheel .... (Epic)
   Texas Super Hits-C .... (Columbia)
   Very Best Of Asleep At The Wheel Since 1970 .... (Relentless/Madacy)
Boxer, The
Simon & Garfunkel; *Bridge Over Troubled Water* .... (Columbia)
   Collected Works .... (Columbia)
   Simon & Garfunkel's Greatest Hits .... (Columbia)
   The Concert In Central Park .... (Warner Bros.)
Cabin On The Hill
Flatt & Scruggs; *Columbia Historic Edition-Flatt & Scruggs* ... (Columbia)
Lester Flatt & Earl Scruggs; *Bluegrass Super Hits-C* ...... (Columbia)
California
Joni Mitchell; *Blue* .... (Reprise)
Choo Choo Ch'Boogie (Jack)
Asleep At The Wheel; *All Time Legends Of Country Music-C* ... (Legacy)
   Asleep At The Wheel .... (Epic)
   Hot Tracks-Train Super Hits-C .... (Capitol)
   Served Live .... (Capitol)
   Very Best Of Asleep At The Wheel Since 1970 ...... (Relentless/Madacy)
Beach Boys; *Ten Years Of Harmony* .... (Caribou)
Clifton Chenier; *Alligator Stomp-#2-C* .... (Rhino)
Louis Jordan; *Best Of Louis Jordan* .... (MCA)
Quincy Jones; *Birth Of A Band-#2* .... (Mercury)
Come Back To Me
Janet Jackson; *Janet Jackson's Rhythm Nation 1814* .... (A&M)
Come Back To Me
Barbra Streisand; *Barbra Streisand...and other musical
   instruments* .... (Columbia)
Come Back To Me
Rosemary Clooney; *Show Tunes* .... (Concord Jazz)
Come Back To Me
Yves Montand; *ST/On A Clear Day You Can See
   Forever* .... (Columbia Special Prod.)
Come Back To Me
Big Country; *Steeltown* .... (Mercury)
Come Back To Me
X; *Under The Big Black Sun* .... (Elektra)
Come Back When You Grow Up
Bobby Vee; *Best Of Bobby Vee* .... (EMI)
   Bobby Vee-Legendary Masters .... (EMI)
   Good Vibrations (Sounds Of Top 40 Radio: 1964-1967)-C ... (Capitol)
Come On Back
Keb' Mo'; *The Door* .... (550/Epic/Okeh)
Come To My Window
Melissa Etheridge; *The Concert For New York City-C* .... (Columbia)
   Yes I Am .... (Island)
Comin' In On A Wing & A Prayer
Anita Ellis; *Songs That Won The War-C* ...... (Columbia River Entert. Group)
Anne Shelton; *V-E Day 50th Anniversary-The Musical
   Memories-C* .... (Living Era)
Four Vagabonds; *The Victory Collection: The Smithsonian Remembers When
   America Went To War-C* .... (RCA)
Ry Cooder; *Boomer's Story* .... (Reprise)
Coming Back Home
Bebe Winans featuring Brian McKnight & Joe; *Love & Freedom* .... (Motown)
Detroit City
Ace Cannon; *Golden Favorites* .... (Ranwood)
Bill Anderson; *Best Of Bill Anderson* .... (Curb)
Bobby Bare; *Nipper's Greatest Hits Of The '60s-#2-C* ...... (RCA)
   This Is Bobby Bare .... (RCA)
Chet Atkins; *Country Gems* .... (Pair)

Flatt & Scruggs; *20 All-Time Great Recordings* .... (Columbia)
Hank Williams, Jr.; *Live At Cobo Hall Detroit* .... (Polydor)
   Standing In The Shadows .... (Polydor)
Mel Tillis; *Best Of Mel Tillis* .... (MCA)
   Live At The Sam Houston Coliseum .... (MGM)
Solomon Burke; *Home In Your Heart-Best Of Solomon Burke* .... (Rhino)
Do You Know The Way To San Jose
Dionne Warwick; *Dionne Warwick Greatest Hits* .... (Everest)
   Dionne Warwick-Anthology 1962-1971 .... (Rhino)
   Hot! Live & Otherwise .... (Arista)
Don't Cry, I'll Be Back Before You Know It Baby
Ted Nugent; *Scream Dream* .... (Epic)
Drops Of Jupiter (Tell Me)
Train; *Drops Of Jupiter* .... (Aware/C2/Columbia)
El Paso
Grateful Dead; *Steal Your Face* .... (Grateful Dead)
Marty Robbins; *Billboard Top Country Hits-1960-C* ... (Rhino)
   Gunfighter Ballads & Trail Songs .... (Legacy)
   Marty Robbins' Biggest Hits .... (Columbia)
   Radio Classics Of The '50s-C .... (Columbia)
   Texas Super Hits-C .... (Columbia)
Everybody (Backstreet's Back)
Backstreet Boys; *Backstreet Boys* .... (Jive)
Exile
Enya; *Watermark* .... (Reprise)
Feels Like Home
Bonnie Raitt; *ST/Michael* .... (Revolution)
Chantal Kreviazuk; *Songs From Dawson's Creek* ..... (Sony Music Soundtrax)
Linda Ronstadt; *Feels Like Home* .... (Elektra)
Randy Newman; *Guilty: 30 Years Of Randy Newman* ... (Rhino)
   Randy Newman's Faust .... (Reprise)
Forever
Kid Rock; *Cocky* .... (Top Dog/Lava/Atlantic)
Get Back
Beatles; *Beatles 1* .... (Capitol)
   Beatles-20 Greatest Hits .... (Capitol)
   Beatles-Box Set .... (Capitol)
   Let It Be .... (Capitol)
   Past Masters-Volume Two .... (Parlophone)
   Reel Music .... (Capitol)
   Rock 'N' Roll Music .... (Capitol)
   The Beatles/1967-1970 .... (Capitol)
Girl I Love
Led Zeppelin; *BBC Sessions* .... (Atlantic)
Goin' Back To Texas
Bobby Bare; *Bobby Bare's Biggest Hits* .... (Columbia)
Don Edwards; *Best Of Don Edwards* .... (Warner Western)
   Goin' Back To Texas .... (Warner Western)
Going Back To Texas
R.C. Smith; *I Have To Paint My Face: Mississippi Blues-1960* ...... (Arhoolie)
Going Back To Texas
Wayne Hancock; *Wild, Free & Reckless* .... (Ark 21)
Golden Slumbers
Beatles; *Abbey Road* .... (Parlophone)
   Beatles-Box Set .... (Capitol)
Good To See You
Neil Young; *Silver & Gold* .... (Reprise)
Goodbye Yellow Brick Road
Elton John; *Billboard Top Rock 'N' Roll Hits-1973-C* .... (Rhino)
   Elton John's Greatest Hits .... (Polydor)
   Goodbye Yellow Brick Road .... (Polydor)
Halfway Home Cafe
Ricky Skaggs and Kentucky Thunder; *History Of The Future* .. (Skaggs Family)
Healing Game
Van Morrison; *The Healing Game* .... (A&M)
Home
Staind; *Dysfunction* .... (Flip/Elektra)
Homeward Bound
Paul Simon; *Paul Simon In Concert/Live Rhymin'* .... (Columbia)
Paul Simon & George Harrison; *Nobody's Child-Romanian Angel
   Appeal-C* .... (Warner Bros.)
Simon & Garfunkel; *Collected Works* .... (Columbia)
   Parsley Sage Rosemary & Thyme .... (Columbia)
   Simon & Garfunkel's Greatest Hits .... (Columbia)
   The Concert In Central Park .... (Warner Bros.)
Willie Nelson & Waylon Jennings; *Take It To The Limit* .... (Columbia)
Hook
Blues Traveler; *Four* .... (A&M)
I Left My Heart In San Francisco
Tony Bennett; *I Left My Heart In San Francisco* ..... (Columbia)
   Pop Classics Of The '60s-C .... (Columbia)
   Tony Bennett's All-Time Greatest Hits .... (Columbia)
If You're Gone
Matchbox Twenty; *Mad Season By Matchbox Twenty* .... (Lava)
I'll Be Back
Beatles; *Beatles '65* .... (Capitol)
   Beatles-Love Songs .... (Capitol)
I'll Be Home
Barbra Streisand; *Stoney End* .... (Columbia)

Randy Newman; *Little Criminals* . . . . . (Warner Bros.)
Randy Newman/Live . . . . . (Warner Archives)

I'm Going Back
Judy Holliday/Original Cast; *Bells Are Ringing* . . . . . (Columbia)

I'm Going Back To Old Kentucky
Bill Monroe; *Best Of Bill Monroe & His Blue Grass Boys* . . . . . (MCA)
Bill Monroe And Flatt & Scruggs . . . . . (Rounder)
Columbia Historic Edition-Bill Monroe . . . . . (Columbia)
Bill Monroe & The Stars Of The Bluegrass Hall Of Fame; *Bill Monroe & The Stars Of The Bluegrass Hall Of Fame* . . . . . (MCA)
Osborne Brothers; *Red, White & Bluegrass-C* . . . . . (C.M.H. Prod.)

I'm Going Back To The Old Home
Doc Watson; *Legacy-A Tribute To The First Generation Of Bluegrass-C* . . . . . (Sugar Hill)

Indian Reservation (The Lament Of The Cherokee Reservation Indian)
Don Fardon; *45-#408* . . . . . (GNP/Crescendo)
Raiders; *Billboard Top Rock 'N' Roll Hits-1971-C* . . . . . (Rhino)
Legend Of Paul Revere And The Raiders . . . . . (Columbia)
Pop Classics Of The '70s-C . . . . . (Columbia)
Super Hits Of The '70s-Have A Nice Day-#5-C . . . . . (Rhino)

It Won't Be Long
Beatles; *Meet The Beatles!* . . . . . (Capitol)
With The Beatles . . . . . (Parlophone)

It's All Coming Back To Me Now
Celine Dion; *All The Way...A Decade Of Song* . . . . . (550 Music)
Falling Into You . . . . . (550 Music)

Jimmy Mack
Martha & The Vandellas; *Billboard Top R&B Hits-1967-C* . . . . . (Rhino)
Compact Command Performances-Martha Reeves & The Vandellas . . . . . (Motown)
Martha Reeves & The Vandellas-Anthology . . . . . (Motown)
Motown Story-First 25 Years-C . . . . . (Motown)
Motown Superstar Series-#11-Martha Reeves & The Vandellas . . . . . (Motown)
Top 10 With A Bullet-Motown Girl Groups-C . . . . . (Motown)

Josie
Steely Dan; *Aja* . . . . . (MCA)
Steely Dan's Greatest Hits . . . . . (MCA)

Judy's Turn To Cry
Lesley Gore; *'60s Dance Party-#2-C* . . . . . (Dominion Entert.)
Golden Hits Of Lesley Gore . . . . . (Mercury)
Lesley Gore-Anthology . . . . . (Rhino)

L.A. Song
Beth Hart; *Screamin' For My Supper* . . . . . (143/Lava/Atlantic)

Letter, The
Box Tops; *Billboard Top Rock 'N' Roll Hits-1967-C* . . . . . (Rhino)
Box Tops' Greatest Hits . . . . . (Rhino)
Cruisin'-1967-C . . . . . (Increase)
Oldies But Goodies-#12-C . . . . . (Original Sound)
Rockin' '60s-C . . . . . (Priority)
Joe Cocker; *Joe Cocker Live* . . . . . (Capitol)
Joe Cocker-Classics-#4 . . . . . (A&M)
Joe Cocker's Greatest Hits . . . . . (A&M)
Mad Dogs & Englishmen . . . . . (A&M)
Vernon Green & The Medallions; *Oldies But Goodies-#1-C* . . . (Original Sound)
Vernon Green & The Medallions-Golden Classics . . . . . (Collectables)

Little Green Valley
Marty Robbins; *Gunfighter Ballads & Trail Songs* . . . . . (Legacy)

London Rain (Nothing Heals Like You Do)
Heather Nova; *Siren* . . . . . (Big Cat)
Songs From Dawson's Creek . . . . . (Sony Music Soundtrax)

M.T.A.
Kingston Trio; *25 Years Non-Stop* . . . . . (Xeres)
Best Of The Kingston Trio . . . . . (Capitol)
Capitol Collectors Series-The Kingston Trio . . . . . (Capitol)
Scarlet Ribbons . . . . . (Capitol)
Very Best Of The Kingston Trio . . . . . (Capitol)

Mack The Knife
Bobby Darin; *Bobby Darin-At The Copa* . . . . . (Bainbridge)
Hit Singles-1958-1977-C . . . . . (Atlantic)
The Bobby Darin Story . . . . . (Atlantic)
Frank Sinatra; *The Reprise Collection* . . . . . (Reprise)
Louis Armstrong; *Best Of Louis Armstrong* . . . . . (Vanguard)

Mama I'm Coming Home
Ozzy Osbourne; *The Ozzman Cometh* . . . . . (Epic)

Maryland
Vonda Shepard; *ST/Songs From "Ally McBeal" Featuring Vonda Shepard* . . . . . (550/Epic)

Massachusetts
Bee Gees; *Bee Gees-Gold* . . . . . (Polydor)
Here At Last...Bee Gees...Live . . . . . (Polydor)

Mommy Can I Come Home
Keb' Mo'; *The Door* . . . . . (550/Epic/Okeh)

Murder (Or A Heart Attack)
Old 97's; *Fight Songs* . . . . . (Elektra)

My Heart Cries For You
Charlie Rich; *Charlie Rich-20 Golden Hits* . . . . . (Sun)
Time For Tears-C . . . . . (Sun)
Dinah Shore; *Nipper's Greatest Hits Of The '50s-#1-C* . . . . . (RCA)
Guy Mitchell; *Guy Mitchell-16 Most Requested Songs* . . . . . (Legacy)

My Lover Man
Bruce Springsteen; *Tracks* . . . . . (Columbia)

Never Going Back Again
Fleetwood Mac; *25 Years-The Chain* . . . . . (Warner Bros.)
Fleetwood Mac Live . . . . . (Warner Bros.)
Rumours . . . . . (Warner Bros.)
Matchbox Twenty; *Legacy-A Tribute To Fleetwood Mac's Rumours-C* . . . (Lava)

New York State Of Mind
Barbra Streisand; *Memories* . . . . . (Columbia)
Streisand Superman . . . . . (Columbia)
Billy Joel; *America: A Tribute To Heroes-C* . . . . . (Interscope)
Billy Joel-Greatest Hits, Volume I & Volume II . . . . . (Columbia)
The Concert For New York City-C . . . . . (Columbia)
Turnstiles . . . . . (Columbia)
Carmen McRae; *Ms. Magic* . . . . . (Dunhill Compact Classics)
Tony Bennett with Billy Joel; *Playin' With My Friends-Bennett Sings The Blues-C* . . . . . (Columbia)

Next Year
Foo Fighters; *There Is Nothing Left To Lose* . . . . . (Roswell/RCA)

No Other Love
Perry Como; *Easy Listening* . . . . . (Pair)

Old Man From The Mountain
Merle Haggard & The Strangers; *For The Record: Merle Haggard-43 Legendary Hits* . . . . . (BNA)

Prodigal Son
Rolling Stones; *Beggars Banquet* . . . . . (Abkco)

Put Me On A Train Back To Texas
Waylon Jennings & Willie Nelson; *Clean Shirt* . . . . . (Epic)
Hot Tracks-Train Super Hits-C . . . . . (Epic)

Ready To Go
Republica; *Republica* . . . . . (RCA)

Return Of The Mack
Mark Morrison; *Return Of The Mack* . . . . . (Atlantic)

Return Of The Red Baron
Royal Guardsmen; *Royal Guardsmen-Anthology* . . . . . (One Way)

Return To Sender
Elvis Presley; *Girls Girls Girls* . . . . . (RCA)
The Great Performances . . . . . (RCA)
The Top Ten Hits . . . . . (RCA)
Worldwide 50 Gold Award Hits, Vol. 1, Parts 1 & 2 . . . . . (RCA)

Return To Sender
Residents; *The King & Eye* . . . . . (Restless)

Right Back Where We Started From
Maxine Nightingale; *Mega Hits Dance Classics-#10-C* . . . . . (Priority)

Rollin' In My Sweet Baby's Arms
Bill Monroe; *Bean Blossom* . . . . . (MCA)
Del McCoury Band; *Appalachian Stomp: Bluegrass Classics-C* . . . . . (Rhino)
Dillard & Clark; *Fantastic Expedition/Through The Morning* . . . . . (Mobile Fidelity Sound Lab)
Flatt & Scruggs; *Flatt & Scruggs At Carnegie Hall!* . . . . . (Koch International)
Flatt & Scruggs-20 Greatest Hits . . . . . (Deluxe)
Flying Burrito Brothers; *Close Encounters To The West Coast* . . . . . (Relix)
Leon Russell; *Hank Wilson's Back, Vol. 1* . . . . . (Right Stuff)
New Lost City Ramblers; *Greatest Folksingers Of The '60s-C* . . . . . (Vanguard)
Ramblin' Jack Elliott; *Hard Travelin'* . . . . . (Fantasy)
Ricky Skaggs and Kentucky Thunder; *History Of The Future* . . . (Skaggs Family)
Tony Trischka; *Heartlands* . . . . . (Rounder)
Willie Nelson; *Willie & Family Live* . . . . . (Columbia)

Sentimental Journey
Dinah Shore; *Sentimental Journey: Capitol's Great Ladies Of Song-C* . . . . . (Gold Rush)
Doris Day; *Doris Day Sings 22 Great Songs-Original Big Band* . . . . . (Hindsight)
Hal McIntyre & His Orchestra; *Nipper's Greatest Hits Of The '40s-#2-C* . . . . . (RCA)
Les Brown & His Orchestra; *Best Of The Big Bands-C* . . . . . (Columbia)

Stupify
Disturbed; *The Sickness* . . . . . (Giant)

Sunny Came Home
Shawn Colvin; *1998 Grammy Nominees-C* . . . . . (MCA)
A Few Small Repairs . . . . . (Columbia)

Swanee
Al Jolson; *Al Jolson-Best Of The Decca Years* . . . . . (MCA)
Best Of Al Jolson . . . . . (MCA)
Jolson Sang 'Em . . . . . (Biograph)
Music From The New York Stage (1890-1920)-#4-1917-1920-C . . . . . (Pearl)
George Gershwin; *Rhapsody In Blue* . . . . . (Biograph)
Judy Garland; *Judy Garland-At Carnegie Hall* . . . . . (Capitol)
Judy Garland's All-Time Greatest Hits . . . . . (Curb)

Taste Of Honey
Barbra Streisand; *The Barbra Streisand Album* . . . . . (Columbia)
Beatles; *Beatles-Box Set* . . . . . (Capitol)
Please Please Me . . . . . (Parlophone)
The Early Beatles . . . . . (Capitol)
Herb Alpert; *Midnight Sun* . . . . . (A&M)
Herb Alpert & The Tijuana Brass; *Herb Alpert & The Tijuana Brass' Greatest Hits* . . . . . (A&M)
Herb Alpert & The Tijuana Brass-Classics-#1 . . . . . (A&M)
Tony Bennett; *Forty Years-The Artistry Of Tony Bennett* . . . . . (Columbia)

That's Not Me
Beach Boys; *Pet Sounds* . . . . (Capitol)
The Pet Sounds Sessions: A 30th Anniversary Collection . . . . (Capitol)

Theme From "Welcome Back, Kotter"
John Sebastian; *Best Of John Sebastian* . . . . (Rhino)
Original Soundtrack; *Television's Greatest Hits-#3-1970s & 1980s-C* . . . (TVT)

They Were Doin' The Mambo
Vaughn Monroe; *Very Best Of Vaughn Monroe* . . . .(Taragon)

Think Of Tomorrow
Chris Isaak; *Baja Sessions* . . . . (Reprise)

Thundercrack
Bruce Springsteen; *Tracks* . . . . (Columbia)

To The Moon And Back
Savage Garden; *Savage Garden* . . . . (Columbia)

Too Late, Too Soon
Jon Secada; *Secada* . . . . (Capitol)

Train Of Love
Johnny Cash; *Johnny Cash-Legend* . . . . (Sun)
Johnny Cash-Original Golden Hits-#1 . . . . (Sun)
Johnny Cash-Sun Years . . . . (Rhino)
Superbilly . . . . (Sun)
Trucks,Trains & Airplanes-C . . . . (International Mktg. Group)

Tulsa Time
Don Williams; *Best Of Don Williams-#2* . . . . (MCA)
Country's Greatest Hits-#6-Superstars-C . . . . (Priority)
Don Williams-Legends . . . .(MCA)
Expressions . . . . (MCA)
Eric Clapton; *Backless* . . . . (Polydor)
Just One Night . . . . (Polydor)

Two Of Us
Beatles; *Beatles-Box Set* . . . . (Capitol)
Let It Be . . . . (Capitol)

Until You Come Back To Me
Aretha Franklin; *Aretha Franklin-30 Greatest Hits* . . . . (Rhino)
Best Of Aretha Franklin . . . . (Atlantic)
Golden Age Of Black Music-1970-1975-C . . . . (Atlantic)
Basia; *Brave New Hope* . . . .(Epic)
London Warsaw New York . . . .(Epic)
Hil St. Soul; *Soul Organic* . . . .(Dome/Select-O-Hits)
Miki Howard; *Miki Howard* . . . . (Atlantic)
Stevie Wonder; *Stevie Wonder-Love Songs-20 Classic Hits* . . . (Motown)

Voodoo
Godsmack; *Godsmack* . . . .(Republic/Universal)

Wait
Beatles; *Beatles-Box Set* . . . . (Capitol)
Rubber Soul . . . . (Capitol)

What I Need To Do
Kenny Chesney; *Everywhere We Go* . . . . (BNA)
Kenny Chesney's Greatest Hits . . . . (BNA)

What You Won't Do For Love
Bobby Caldwell; *Love Shouldn't Hurt-C* . . . . (Qwest)
Go West; *Chicken Soup For The Woman's Soul-C* . . . . (Rhino)

What's Happening, Brother
Marvin Gaye; *What's Going On* . . . . (Motown)

When My Dreamboat Comes Home
Fats Domino; *My Blue Heaven* . . . . (Gold Rush)
Kay Starr; *Capitol Collectors Series-Kay Starr* . . . . (Capitol)

When You Come Back To Me Again
Garth Brooks; *Scarecrow* . . . . (Capitol)

Where The Blacktop Ends
keith urban; *keith urban* . . . . (Capitol)

Will You Be Loving Another Man
Bill Monroe & His Blue Grass Boys; *Essential Bill Monroe & His Blue
Grass Boys* . . . . (Legacy)
Essential Bill Monroe-1945-1949 . . . . (Columbia)

REVENGE, Getting Even

See Also: **ANGER, FIGHT, INSULTS, JEALOUSY, LAW &
ORDER, LOVE: SOMEBODY DONE SOMEBODY WRONG,
MISTREATMENT, WAR, WARNINGS**

96 Tears
? & The Mysterians; *? & The Mysterians* . . . .(Collectables)
Ten Long Years . . . .(Roir)

Blame It On Your Heart
Patty Loveless; *Only What I Feel* . . . .(Epic)
Patty Loveless-Classics . . . .(Epic)

Blistering
Machine Head; *The More Things Change...* . . . .(Roadrunner)

But It's Alright
J.J. Jackson; *Didn't It Blow Your Mind: Soul Hits Of The '70s-#3-C* . . . . (Rhino)
Soul Shots-C . . . . (Rhino)

Common Disaster
Cowboy Junkies; *Lay It Down* . . . .(Geffen)

Complicated Shadows
Elvis Costello & The Attractions; *The Sopranos-Music From The HBO
Original Series* . . . .(Sony Music Soundtrax)

Coward Of The County
Kenny Rogers; *Kenny* . . . .(Liberty)
Kenny Rogers' Greatest Hits . . . . (EMI)
Kenny Rogers-Twenty Greatest Hits . . . . (EMI)

Fast As You
Dwight Yoakam; *This Time* . . . .(Reprise)

Forgot About Dre
Dr. Dre featuring Eminem; *Dr. Dre 2001* . . . .(Aftermath/Interscope)

Frances Farmer Will Have Her Revenge On Seattle
Nirvana; *In Utero* . . . .(David Geffen Co.)

Groundzero (In Our Hearts You Remain)
Cash & Computa; *Groundzero (In Our Hearts You Remain)-CD
Single* . . . . (Select)

Hats Off To Larry
Del Shannon; *Runaway Hits!* . . . . (Rhino)
Super Oldies Of The '60s-#2-C . . . . (Audio Fidelity)
WCBS FM 101 History Of Rock-'60s-#3-C . . . .(Collectables)

Hero Takes A Fall
Bangles; *All Over The Place* . . . . (Columbia)
Bangles' Greatest Hits . . . . (Columbia)
Bangles-Super Hits . . . . (Legacy)

Hey Joe
Jimi Hendrix; *Essential Jimi Hendrix, Volume 2* . . . .(Reprise)
Live At Winterland . . . . (Rykodisc)
Jimi Hendrix Experience; *Are You Experienced?* . . . .(Reprise)
Smash Hits . . . . (Reprise)
Love; *Best Of Love* . . . . (Rhino)

Hit 'Em Up Style (Oops!)
Blu Cantrell; *So Blu* . . . .(Arista)
Totally Hits 2001-C . . . . (Arista)

How Do You Like Me Now?!
Toby Keith; *How Do You Like Me Now?!* . . . .(DreamWorks/SKG)

Hurt Her Once For Me
Wilburn Brothers; *Only Country-1965-1969-C* . . . .(JCI Assoc. Labels)

I Can See For Miles
Who; *Hooligans* . . . . (MCA)
Join Together . . . . (MCA)
Meaty Beaty Big & Bouncy . . . . (MCA)
ST/The Kids Are Alright . . . . (MCA)
The Who Sell Out . . . . (MCA)

I Cried For You (Now It's Your Turn To Cry)
Billie Holiday; *First Verve Sessions* . . . . (Verve)
Quintessential-#2-1936 . . . . (Columbia)
Songbook . . . . (Verve)
Sarah Vaughan; *Complete Sarah Vaughan On Mercury-#2* . . . . . . (Mercury)
Divine Sarah Vaughan-Columbia Years-1949-1953 . . . . (Columbia)
Roulette Years . . . . (Roulette)

I Wanna Be Free
Loretta Lynn; *Loretta Lynn's Greatest Hits-#2* . . . . (MCA)

If I Fell
Beatles; *Beatles-Love Songs* . . . . (Capitol)
Something New . . . . (Capitol)
ST/A Hard Day's Night . . . . (Capitol)

If I Had A Rocket Launcher (Central America)
Bruce Cockburn; *Stealing Fire* . . . . (Columbia)
Waiting For A Miracle-Singles 1970-1987 . . . .(Gold Castle)

I'll Cry Instead
Beatles; *Beatles-Box Set* . . . . (Capitol)
Something New . . . . (Capitol)
ST/A Hard Day's Night . . . . (Capitol)

It's All Over Now
Bobby Womack; *Lookin' For A Love-Best Of Bobby Womack-1968-
1975* . . . .(Razor & Tie)
John Anderson; *Great Divorce Songs For Him-C* . . . .(Warner Bros.)
John Anderson's Greatest Hits-#2 . . . . (Warner Bros.)
Rod Stewart; *Best Of Rod Stewart* . . . .(Mercury)
Gasoline Alley . . . . (Mercury)
Vintage Rod Stewart . . . . (Mercury)
Rolling Stones; *12 X 5* . . . .(Abkco)
Big Hits (High Tide & Green Grass) . . . .(Abkco)
More Hot Rocks (big hits & fazed cookies) . . . .(Abkco)
Singles Collection-The London Years . . . . (Abkco)
Ry Cooder; *Paradise And Lunch* . . . . (Reprise)

I've Committed Murder
Macy Gray; *On How Life Is* . . . . (Epic)

Judy's Turn To Cry
Lesley Gore; *'60s Dance Party-#2-C* . . . . (Dominion Entert.)
Golden Hits Of Lesley Gore . . . . (Mercury)
Lesley Gore-Anthology . . . . (Rhino)

Just You Wait
Julie Andrews/Original Cast; *My Fair Lady* . . . . (Columbia)

Kasparov's Revenge
Lo Fidelity Allstars; *How To Operate With A Blown Mind* . . . .(Skint)

Laugh Laugh
Beau Brummels; *Best Of The Beau Brummels* . . . . (Rhino)
Heart & Soul Of Rock 'N' Roll-#1-C . . . . (Rhino)

Introducing The Beau Brummels . . . . (Rhino)
Nuggets-#7-Early San Francisco-C . . . . (Rhino)

Lesson In Leavin'
Dottie West; *Special Delivery* . . . . (EMI)
Jo Dee Messina; *I'm Alright* . . . . (Curb)

Love Is Blind
Eve; *First Lady Of Ruff Ryders* . . . . (Ruff Ryders/IDJMG)

Maybe
Chantels; *Back To The '50s-C* . . . . (Dominion Entert.)
Fabulous '50s-#3-C . . . . (Dominion Entert.)
Ink Spots; *Ink Spots' Greatest Hits-Original Recordings-1939-1946* . . . . (MCA)
Ink Spots-The Anthology . . . . (MCA)

My Boyfriend's Back
Angels; *Billboard Top Rock 'N' Roll Hits-1963-C* . . . . (Rhino)
Girl Groups/Story Of A Sound-C . . . . (Rhino)
My Boyfriend's Back . . . . (Collectables)
Oldies But Goodies-#11-C . . . . (Original Sound)
ST/The Wanderers . . . . (Warner Bros.)
Wonder Women-#2-History Of Girl Group-C . . . . (Rhino)

Needles And Pins
Jackie DeShannon; *Very Best Of Jackie DeShannon* . . . . (EMI)
Searchers; *History Of British Rock-#1-C* . . . . (Rhino)
Searchers' Greatest Hits . . . . (Rhino)
Tom Petty And The Heartbreakers; *Pack Up The Plantation-Live!* . . . . . . (MCA)

Nothin' But The Taillights
Clint Black; *Nothin' But The Taillights* . . . . (RCA)

One Of These Days
Pink Floyd; *Collection Of Great Dance Songs* . . . . (Columbia)
Delicate Sound Of Thunder . . . . (Columbia)
Meddle . . . . (Capitol)
Pink Floyd-Gift Set . . . . (Capitol)
Works . . . . (Capitol)

Oney
Johnny Cash; *Johnny Cash-16 Biggest Hits-#2* . . . . (Legacy)

Popstar
Pretenders; *Viva El Amor!* . . . . (Warner Bros.)

Run For Your Life
Beatles; *Beatles-Box Set* . . . . (Capitol)
Rubber Soul . . . . (Capitol)

See You Later, Alligator
Bill Haley & His Comets; *Bill Haley & His Comets* . . . . . . (Everest)
Bill Haley & His Comets' Greatest Hits . . . . (MCA)
Bill Haley & His Comets-Golden Hits . . . . (MCA)
Billboard Top Rock 'N' Roll Hits-1956-C . . . . (Rhino)
Mr. Rock 'N' Roll . . . . (Accord)
Rock & Roll Is Here To Stay-C . . . . (Gusto)
Rockin' & Rollin' . . . . (Accord)

So Good
Destiny's Child; *The Writing's On The Wall* . . . . (Columbia)

Tell It To The Rain
4 Seasons; *4 Seasons' Greatest Hits-#2* . . . . (Rhino)
4 Seasons-Anthology . . . . (Rhino)

That'll Be The Day
Buddy Holly; *ST/American Graffiti* . . . . (MCA)
Buddy Holly/The Crickets; *Buddy Holly-20 Golden Greats* . . . . . . (MCA)
Chirping Crickets . . . . (MCA)
Crickets; *Billboard Top Rock 'N' Roll Hits-1957-C* . . . . (Rhino)
Foghat; *Best Of Foghat-#2* . . . . (Rhino)
Energized . . . . (Rhino)
Linda Ronstadt; *Hasten Down The Wind* . . . . (Asylum)
Linda Ronstadt's Greatest Hits . . . . (Asylum)

These Boots Are Made For Walkin'
Billy Ray Cyrus; *Some Gave All* . . . . (Mercury)
Nancy Sinatra; *Billboard Top Rock 'N' Roll Hits-1966-C* . . . . (Rhino)
Boots-Nancy Sinatra's Greatest Hits . . . . (Rhino)

They All Laughed
Carmen McRae; *Setting Standards* . . . . (Pair)
Ella Fitzgerald & Louis Armstrong & Oscar Peterson Trio; *Great American
    Songwriters-#1George & Ira Gershwin-C* . . . . (Rhino)
Fred Astaire; *Starring Fred Astaire* . . . . (Columbia)
Sarah Vaughan; *Sarah Vaughan Sings George Gershwin Songbook,
    Vol. 1* . . . . (Emarcy)
Tony Bennett; *Steppin' Out* . . . . (Columbia)

This Ain't No Rag, It's A Flag
Charlie Daniels Band; *This Ain't No Rag, It's A Flag-CD Single* . . . . . (Blue Hat)

Thunder Rolls, The
Garth Brooks; *Garth Brooks-Double Live* . . . . (Capitol)
No Fences . . . . (Capitol)

Under My Thumb
Rolling Stones; *"Still Life" (American Concert 1981)* . . . . (Virgin)
12 X 5 . . . . (Abkco)
Aftermath . . . . (Abkco)
got Live if you want it! . . . . (Abkco)
Hot Rocks 1964-1971 . . . . (Abkco)
Who; *Odds & Sods* . . . . (MCA)
Who's Missing . . . . (MCA)

Unpretty
TLC; *Fanmail* . . . . (LaFace)

What If
Creed; *Human Clay* . . . . (Wind-up)

When You Need My Love
Darryl Worley; *Hard Rain Don't Last* . . . . (DreamWorks/SKG)

When You Think Of Me
Eric Benet; *A Day In The Life* . . . . (Warner Bros.)

Who's Sorry Now
Benny Goodman; *Stompin'* . . . . (Drive)
Big Bill Broonzy; *Black, Brown & White* . . . . (Evidence Music)
Bob Crosby; *Bob Crosby & His Orchestra* . . . . (EPM)
Connie Francis; *Dick Clark's 21 All-Time Hits-#1-C* . . . . . . (Original Sound)
Very Best Of Connie Francis . . . . (Polydor)
Ella Fitzgerald; *The Intimate Ella* . . . . (Verve)
Esquivel; *Space-Age Bachelor Pad Music* . . . . (Bar/None)
Glen Gray; *Moonglow: 1930-1936* . . . . (Aero Space)
Nat "King" Cole; *The Billy May Sessions* . . . . (Capitol)
Ray Anthony; *Swing Back To The '40s* . . . . (Aero Space)

With Me Part 1
Destiny's Child featuring JD; *Destiny's Child* . . . . (Grass Roots/Columbia)

You Will Have To Pay
Tex Ritter; *Tex Ritter's Greatest Hits* . . . . (Curb)

Your Cheatin' Heart
Beck; *Timeless: Hank Williams Tribute-C* . . . . . (Lost Highway/IDJMG)
Elvis Presley; *Elvis For Everyone!* . . . . (RCA)
Welcome To My World . . . . (RCA)
Frankie Laine; *Frankie Laine's 16 Greatest Hits* . . . . (Trip)
Frankie Laine's Greatest Hits . . . . (Columbia)
Hank Williams With His Drifting Cowboys; *24 Of Hank Williams'
    Greatest Hits* . . . . (Polydor)
Hank Williams-16 Great Hits . . . . (Everest)
Hank Williams-40 Greatest Hits . . . . (Polydor)
Hank Williams, Jr.; *Very Best Of Hank Williams, Jr.* . . . . . (Polydor)
Jerry Lee Lewis; *Live At The Star Club-Hamburg 1964* . . . . . . (Rhino)
The Golden Hits Of Jerry Lee Lewis . . . . (Smash)
Patsy Cline; *ST/Sweet Dreams* . . . . (MCA)
The Patsy Cline Story . . . . (MCA)
Ray Charles; *Ray Charles' Greatest Hits-#2* . . . . (Rhino)

You're Going To Lose That Girl
Beatles; *ST/Help!* . . . . (Capitol)

You're Gonna Get It
Tom Petty; *You're Gonna Get It!* . . . . (Gone Gator)

You're Gonna Get What's Coming
Bonnie Raitt; *The Glow* . . . . (Warner Bros.)
Robert Palmer; *Addictions-#2* . . . . (Island)
Double Fun . . . . (Island)

RHYTHM, Beat

See Also: **DANCE, MUSIC, MUSICAL INSTRUMENTS (various)**

42nd Street
Diana Krall; *Stepping Out* . . . . (Justin Time)
Hal Kemp; *Best Of The Big Bands-C* . . . . (Columbia)
Mel Torme; *Cocktail Mix-#3-Swingin' Singles-C* . . . . (Rhino)
Original Broadway Cast; *42nd Street* . . . . (RCA Victor)

All God's Chillun Got Rhythm
Judy Garland; *Judy Garland-Collector's Items-1936-1945* . . . . . . (MCA)

And The Beat Goes On
Whispers; *Club Epic-#1-C* . . . . (Legacy)

Artistry In Rhythm
Stan Kenton; *Comprehensive Stan Kenton* . . . . (Capitol)
Live In Europe . . . . (Mercury)
Stan Kenton's Greatest Hits . . . . (Capitol)
Summer Of '51 . . . . (Garland)
Stan Kenton & His Orchestra; *Road Show* . . . . (Capitol)

Beat
Elvis Costello; *This Year's Model* . . . . (Rykodisc)

Beat Goes On, The
Sonny & Cher; *Best Of Sonny & Cher* . . . . (Atco)
Hit Singles-1958-1977-C . . . . (Atlantic)
Sonny & Cher-Live . . . . (MCA)
The Beat Goes On-Best Of Sonny & Cher . . . . (Rhino)
Two Of Us . . . . (Atco)

Beat Me Daddy Eight To The Bar
Andrews Sisters; *Andrews Sisters-16 Great Performances* . . . . . (MCA)
Best Of The Andrews Sisters . . . . (MCA)
Boogie Woogie Bugle Girls . . . . (MCA)
Capitol Collectors Series-The Andrews Sisters . . . . (Capitol)
Commander Cody & His Lost Planet Airmen; *Lost In The Ozone* . . . . . (MCA)

Beat Street
Melle Mel; *Rap Hall Of Fame-C* . . . . (K-Tel)
ST/Beat Street . . . . (Atlantic)

Boogie Back To Texas
Asleep At The Wheel; *Asleep At The Wheel-10* . . . . (Epic)
Swinging Best Of Asleep At The Wheel . . . . (Epic)
Texas Super Hits-C . . . . (Columbia)
Very Best Of Asleep At The Wheel Since 1970 . . . . (Relentless/Madacy)

Drift Away
Dobie Gray; *Classic Rock-#1-C* (MCA)
Oldies But Goodies-#10-C (Original Sound)
Oldies But Goodies-#3-C (Original Sound)
Super Hits Of The '70s-Have A Nice Day-#10-C (Rhino)
Michael Bolton; *Timeless-Classics* (Columbia)
Rod Stewart; *Atlantic Crossing* (Warner Bros.)
Eat To The Beat
Blondie; *Eat To The Beat* (Chrysalis)
Fascinating Rhythm
Fred Astaire; *Crazy Feet!* (ASV Living Era)
Fire Of The Newly Alive
Rosanne Cash; *The Wheel* (Columbia)
Foolish Beat
Debbie Gibson; *Hit Singles-1980-1988-C* (Atlantic)
Out Of The Blue (Atlantic)
Georgia Rhythm
Atlanta Rhythm Section; *Rock & Roll Alternative* (Polydor)
Good Beat
Deee-Lite; *World Clique* (Elektra)
Hit Me With Your Rhythm Stick
Ian Dury/Blockheads; *Best Of Ian Dury And The Blockheads-Sex&Drugs&Rock'n'Roll* (Rhino)
I Got Rhythm
Ella Fitzgerald; *George & Ira Gershwin Songbook* (Verve)
Ethel Waters; *I Got Rhythm: The Smithsonian George Gershwin Collection-C* (Smithsonian Collection)
Happenings; *'60s Rock Classics-#1-C* (Rhino)
Judy Garland; *Judy Garland-Collector's Items-1936-1945* (MCA)
Louis Armstrong; *Essential Louis Armstrong* (Verve)
Original Cast; *Girl Crazy* (Nonesuch)
Original London Cast; *Crazy For You* (RCA)
Robert Palmer; *Glory Of Gershwin Featuring Larry Adler-C* (Mercury)
I'm An Errand Girl For Rhythm
Diana Krall; *All For You (A Dedication To The Nat ''King'' Cole Trio)* (Impulse!)
Let The Beat Hit 'Em
Lisa Lisa & Cult Jam; *Clivilles & Cole's Greatest Remixes-#1* (Columbia)
Straight Outta Hell's Kitchen (Columbia)
Let The Rhythm Hit 'Em
Erik B. & Rakim; *Let The Rhythm Hit 'Em* (MCA)
Let The Rhythm Pump
Doug Lazy; *Gettin' Crazy* (Atlantic)
Mystic Rhythms
Rush; *Power Windows* (Mercury)
Rush-Chronicles (Mercury)
Show Of Hands (Mercury)
On The Beat
B.B. & Q. Band; *B.B. & Q. Band* (Capitol)
The Disco Years-#2-On The Beat-1978-1982-C (Rhino)
Painted Rhythm
Stan Kenton; *Comprehensive Stan Kenton* (Capitol)
Kenton In Hi-Fi (Blue Note)
Stan Kenton's Greatest Hits (Capitol)
Play In Time
Jethro Tull; *Benefit* (Chrysalis)
Puerto Rican Rhythms
Last Poets; *Right On!* (Collectables)
R&B Skeletons (In The Closet)
George Clinton; *R&B Skeletons (In The Closet)* (Capitol)
Redneck Rhythm & Blues
Brooks & Dunn; *Borderline* (Arista)
Rhythm (Devoted To Art Of Moving Butts)
Tribe Called Quest; *People's Instinctive Travels And The Paths Of Rhythm* (Jive)
Rhythm Divine
Enrique Iglesias; *Enrique* (Overbrook/Interscope)
Rhythm From A Red Car
Hardline; *Double Eclipse* (MCA)
Rhythm In Gold
Jethro Tull; *20 Years Of Jethro Tull* (Chrysalis)
Rhythm In My Nursery Rhymes
Tommy Dorsey & His Clambake Seven; *Music Goes Round & Round* (Bluebird)
Rhythm In The Barnyard
Joe Liggins & The Honeydrippers; *Joe Liggins & The Honeydrippers* (Specialty)
Rhythm Is Gonna Get Ya
Gloria Estefan and Miami Sound Machine; *Heart Of Soul-C* (Columbia)
Let It Loose (Epic)
Rhythm Machine
Bad Company; *Desolation Angels* (Swan Song)
Rhythm Nation
Janet Jackson; *Janet Jackson's Rhythm Nation 1814* (A&M)
Rhythm Of Life
Original Cast; *Sweet Charity* (Columbia)
Rhythm Of Life
Oleta Adams; *Circle Of One* (Fontana)
Rhythm Of Life
Richard Marx; *Richard Marx* (Capitol)
Rhythm Of Love
Scorpions; *Best Of Rockers 'N' Ballads* (Mercury)
Savage Amusement (Mercury)
Rhythm Of Love
Yes; *Big Generator* (Atco)
Yesyears (Atco)
Rhythm Of Love
Screaming Iguanas Of Love; *Screaming Iguanas Of Love* (Long Song)
Rhythm Of My Heart
Rod Stewart; *Vagabond Heart* (Warner Bros.)
Rhythm Of The Heat
Peter Gabriel; *Peter Gabriel/Plays Live* (Geffen)
Security (Geffen)
Rhythm Of The Night
Corona; *Hot Luv-Ultimate Dance Songs Collection-C* (EMI)
Rhythm Of The Night (East West)
DeBarge; *DeBarge's Greatest Hits* (Motown)
Motown Story-First 25 Years-C (Motown)
Rhythm Of The Night (Motown)
Rhythm Of The Rain
Cascades; *Collectables Presents The History Of Rock-#7-C* (Collectables)
Golden Years-1963-C (Dominion Entert.)
Rhythm Of The Road
George Strait; *George Strait-Number 7* (MCA)
Rhythm Of The Saints
Paul Simon; *Rhythm Of The Saints* (Warner Bros.)
Rhythm Of Time
Front 242; *Tyranny For You* (Epic)
Rhythm Saved The World
Bunny Berigan & His Boys; *Take It Bunny* (Sony Music Special Prod.)
Rhythm-A-Ning
Art Blakey & His Jazz Messengers; *Art Blakey & His Jazz Messengers With Thelonius Monk* (Atlantic)
Milt Jackson & The Gold Medal Winners; *Brother Jim* (Pablo)
Thelonius Monk; *In Italy* (Riverside)
Thelonius Monk & Gerry Mulligan; *Mullligan Meets Monk* (Riverside)
Ride On The Rhythm
Little Louie & Marc Anthony; *When The Night Is Over* (Atlantic)
Rock And Roll Music
Beach Boys; *15 Big Ones* (Brother)
Beach Boys-Gift Set (Capitol)
Made In The U.S.A. (Capitol)
Ten Years Of Harmony (Caribou)
Beatles; *Beatles '65* (Capitol)
Beatles-Box Set (Capitol)
For Sale (Capitol)
Rock 'N' Roll Music (Capitol)
Chuck Berry; *Chuck Berry-Golden Hits* (Mercury)
Chuck Berry's Greatest Hits (Everest)
Cruisin'-1958-C (Increase)
The Chess Box-Chuck Berry (Chess)
REO Speedwagon; *Nine Lives* (Epic)
Rock Me In The Rhythm Of Your Love
Eddy Raven; *Best Of Eddy Raven* (Liberty)
Right For The Flight (Liberty)
Rockabilly Blues (Texas 1955)
Johnny Cash; *Texas Super Hits-C* (Columbia)
Rockin' In Rhythm
Duke Ellington; *Great Paris Concert* (Atlantic)
Duke Ellington/Ella Fitzgerald/Oscar Peterson; *Greatest Jazz Concert In The World* (Pablo)
Hank Jones/Ray Brown/Jimmie Smith; *Rockin' In Rhythm* (Concord Jazz)
Modern Jazz Quartet; *For Ellington* (East West)
Rockin' Over The Beat
Technotronic; *Pump Up The Jam-The Album* (SBK)
Rockin' With The Rhythm Of The Rain
Judds; *Judds' Greatest Hits* (MCA)
Rockin' With The Rhythm (MCA)
Roll Over Beethoven
Beatles; *Beatles-Box Set* (Capitol)
Rock 'N' Roll Music (Capitol)
The Beatles At The Hollywood Bowl (Capitol)
The Beatles' Second Album (Capitol)
With The Beatles (Parlophone)
Byrds; *The Byrds* (Columbia)
Chuck Berry; *Chuck Berry-Golden Hits* (Mercury)
Chuck Berry's Greatest Hits (Everest)
Cruisin'-1956-C (Increase)
Oldies But Goodies-#10-C (Original Sound)
The Chess Box-Chuck Berry (Chess)
Electric Light Orchestra; *Afterglow* (Epic)
Ole ELO (Jet)
She's Got Rhythm
Beach Boys; *M.I.U. Album* (Brother)
She's Got The Rhythm (And I Got The Blues)
Alan Jackson; *A Lot About Livin' (And A Little 'Bout Love)* (Arista)

Skate To The Rhythm
High Inergy; *Frenzie* ....(Gordy)
Surf Beat
Dick Dale And The Del-Tones; *Dick Dale And The Del-Tones'*
Greatest Hits .... (Crescendo)
King Of The Surf Guitar-Best Of Dick Dale And The Del-Tones ...... (Rhino)
Take A Little Rhythm
Ali Thompson; *Take A Little Rhythm*...........................(A&M)
Teen Beat
Fleetwood Mac; *25 Years-The Chain* .... (Warner Bros.)
Texas Rhythm Club
Joe McBride; *Texas Rhythm Club* .... (Heads Up Records Int'l)
That Rhythm Man
Louis Armstrong & His Orchestra; *Louis Armstrong & The Big*
Bands ....(Disques Swing)
That's The Beat Of A Heart
Warren Brothers with Sara Evans; *King Of Nothing* ....(BNA)
ST/Where The Heart Is ....(RCA)
This Beat Is Hot
B.G. The Prince Of Rap; *Power Of Rhythm*.....................(Epic)
This Beat Is Hot-C .... (Epic)
Thong Song
Sisqo; *Unleash The Dragon*..................(Dragon/Def Soul/IDJMG)
Throw That Beat In The Garbage Can
B-52's; *Mesopotamia* .... (Warner Bros.)
Turn On (The Beat Box)
Earth, Wind & Fire; *Best Of Earth, Wind & Fire-#2* .... (Columbia)
Turn The Beat Around
Gloria Estefan; *Hold Me, Thrill Me, Kiss Me*...................... (Epic)
ST/The Specialist .... (Epic/Sony Music Soundtrax)
Vicki Sue Robinson; *Dance Floor Divas-The '70s-C* ....(Rhino)
Never Gonna Let You Go ....(RCA)
Nipper's Greatest Hits Of The '70s-C.......................(RCA)
Under African Skies
Paul Simon; *Graceland* .... (Warner Bros.)
Wasp (Texas Radio & The Big Beat)
Doors; *Alive She Cried* ....(Elektra)
Doors-Classics.................................(Elektra)
L.A. Woman ....(Elektra)
Weird Scenes Inside The Gold Mine ....(Elektra)
We Got The Beat
Go-Go's; *Beauty & The Beat*.........................(I.R.S.)
Go-Go's Greatest ....(I.R.S.)
ST/Brimstone & Treacle ....(A&M)
ST/Urgh! A Music War ....(A&M)

RIBBONS, Adornments
See Also: **ANATOMY: HAIR, CLOTHES, COSMETICS,**
FABRICS, HATS

Baubles, Bangles And Beads
Frank Sinatra & Antonio Carlos Jobim; *Francis Albert Sinatra & Antonio*
Carlos Jobim ....(Reprise)
Marlene Dietrich; *Marlene Dietrich-Live* ....(Columbia)
Original Cast; *Kismet*.............................(Columbia)
Peggy Lee; *Best Of Peggy Lee*........................(MCA)
Percy Faith & His Orchestra; *Percy Faith & His Orchestra's All-Time*
Greatest Hits ....(Columbia)
Buttons And Bows
Dinah Shore; *16 Most Requested Songs Of The '40s-#1-C* .... (Legacy)
Golden Hits Of The '40s-C .... (Columbia Special Prod.)
Gene Autry; *Ridin' West-#2-C* ....(Crescendo)
Songs Of The West-#3-Gene Autry & Roy Rogers-C ....(Rhino)
Heart Of Innocence
Jessica Simpson; *Sweet Kisses*.......................(Columbia)
Kohoutek
R.E.M.; *Fables Of The Reconstruction* ....(I.R.S.)
Prove It All Night
Bruce Springsteen; *Darkness On The Edge Of Town*.............(Columbia)
Ribbons Down My Back
Carol Channing/Original Cast; *Hello Dolly!* ....(RCA)
Scarlet Ribbons (For Her Hair)
Harry Belafonte; *Harry Belafonte-Legendary Performer* ....(RCA)
Harry Belafonte's All Time Greatest Hits-#1 ....(RCA)
This Is Harry Belafonte.............................(RCA)
Jim Ed Brown & Maxine Brown; *Essential Jim Ed Brown* ....(RCA)
Kingston Trio; *At Large/Here We Go Again!* ....(Capitol)
Capitol Collectors Series-The Kingston Trio .... (Capitol)
Lennon Sisters; *Best Of The Lennon Sisters* ....(Ranwood)
Les Paul; *Legend & The Legacy-#1-4* ....(Capitol)
NRBQ; *Diggin' Uncle Q* ....(Rounder)
Patti Page; *Patti Page-16 Most Requested Songs* ....(Legacy)
Roger Whittaker; *Roger Whittaker-Classics Collection-#2* ....(Liberty)
She Wears Red Feathers
Guy Mitchell; *Guy Mitchell-16 Most Requested Songs*...........(Legacy)

She Wore A Yellow Ribbon
Mitch Miller; *Sing Along With Mitch*.......................(Columbia)
Tie A Yellow Ribbon Round The Ole Oak Tree
Dawn Featuring Tony Orlando; *'70s Party Killers-C*...........(Rhino)
Fantastic-#1-C ....(K-Tel)
Frank Sinatra; *Some Nice Things I've Missed* .... (Reprise)
Lawrence Welk; *Best Of Lawrence Welk-20 Great Hits* ....(Ranwood)
Sonny James & Karla Taylor; *Classic Country Duets-C* ....(Curb)
XXX's And OOO's
Trisha Yearwood; *Thinkin' About You*.........................(MCA)

RIGHT
See Also: **WRONG**

All The Kids Are Right
Local H; *Pack Up The Cats* ....(Island)
Beat It
Michael Jackson; *Thriller* ....(Epic)
Bloody Well Right
Supertramp; *Crime Of The Century* ....(A&M)
Cuts Like A Knife
Bryan Adams; *Cuts Like A Knife* ....(A&M)
Live! Live! Live! ....(A&M)
MTV Unplugged-Bryan Adams ....(A&M)
So Far So Good ....(A&M)
Damn Right, I've Got The Blues
Buddy Guy; *Best Blues Album In The World...Ever!-C* .... (Virgin)
Buddy's Baddest: The Best Of Buddy Guy ....(Silvertone)
Damn Right, I've Got The Blues ....(Silvertone)
Do Right
Paul Davis; *Best Of Paul Davis* .... (Bang)
Paul Davis...................................(Bang)
Do Right
Jimmie's Chicken Shack; *Bring Your Own Stereo* ....(Rocket)
Do Right Woman, Do Right Man
Aretha Franklin; *Aretha Franklin-30 Greatest Hits* ....(Rhino)
ST/Dead Presidents ....(Capitol)
Commitments; *ST/The Commitments*.....................(MCA)
Doggone Right
Smokey Robinson & The Miracles; *Compact Command Performances-*
Smokey Robinson & The Miracles ....(Motown)
Smokey Robinson & The Miracles' Anthology ....(Motown)
Don't Seem Right
Steve James; *Two Track Mind* .... (Antone's)
Drown
Son Volt; *Trace* .... (Warner Bros.)
Easy Tonight
Five For Fighting; *America Town* .... (Aware/C2/Columbia)
Elegantly Wasted
INXS; *Elegantly Wasted* ....(Mercury)
Everything You Want
Vertical Horizon; *Everything You Want*...................... (RCA)
Totally Hits-#3-C ....(Atlantic)
Feels So Right
Alabama; *Alabama's Greatest Hits* .... (RCA)
Feels So Right ....(RCA)
Fixing A Hole
Beatles; *Sgt. Pepper's Lonely Hearts Club Band* ....(Capitol)
Good Lovin' (Makes It Right)
Tammy Wynette; *Tammy Wynette-16 Biggest Hits* ....(Legacy)
Tammy Wynette-Anniversary-20 Years Of Hits.............(Epic)
Tears Of Fire-25th Anniversary Collection................(Epic)
Got Me Wrong
Alice In Chains; *Alice In Chains-MTV Unplugged* ....(Columbia)
ST/Clerks...................................(Chaos)
Gotta Tell You
Samantha Mumba; *Gotta Tell You* .... (Wildcard/Polydor/Interscope)
Now That's What I Call Music!-#6-C ....(Virgin)
How Come, How Long
Babyface & Stevie Wonder; *The Day* ....(Epic)
I Did It
Dave Matthews Band; *Everyday* .... (RCA)
I May Be Wrong (But I Think You're Wonderful)
Doris Day; *Doris Day-16 Most Requested Songs-Encore!*.........(Columbia)
Harry James; *Harry James-22 Original Big Band Recordings* ......(Hindsight)
I'll Be On My Way
Beatles; *Live At The BBC* ....(Apple)
I'm A Honky Tonk Girl
Loretta Lynn; *The Country Music Hall Of Fame-Loretta Lynn* ......(MCA)
It's Not Right But It's Okay
Whitney Houston; *My Love Is Your Love* ....(Arista)
Kid's Last Fight
Frankie Laine; *Frankie Laine-16 Most Requested Songs* ....(Legacy)
Last Resort
Papa Roach; *Infest* .... (DreamWorks/SKG)

Lessons To Be Learned
Barbra Streisand; *Higher Ground* . . . . (Columbia)
Little Bit Me, A Little Bit You
Monkees; *Monkees' Greatest Hits* . . . . (Rhino)
Love Is The Right Place
Bryan White; *The Right Place* . . . . (Asylum)
Love You Down
INOJ; *So So Def Bass All-Stars-#2-C* . . . . (So So Def/Columbia)
Total Dance Explosion-C . . . . (Columbia)
Make It Right
Econoline Crush; *Brand New History* . . . . (Restless)
Maker Said Take Her
Alabama; *In Pictures* . . . . (RCA)
Nevertheless
Frank Sinatra; *Best Of The Columbia Years-1943-1952* . . . . (Columbia)
McGuire Sisters; *McGuire Sisters-Anthology* . . . . (MCA)
No More (Baby I'ma Do Right)
3LW; *3LW* . . . . (Epic)
Now That's What I Call Music!-#6-C . . . . (Virgin)
One On The Right Is On The Left, The
Johnny Cash; *Johnny Cash-16 Biggest Hits-#2* . . . . (Legacy)
Right Here Waiting
Richard Marx; *Chicken Soup For The Woman's Soul-C* . . . . (Rhino)
Repeat Offender . . . . (EMI)
Right In Time
Lucinda Williams; *Car Wheels On A Gravel Road* . . . . (Mercury)
Right On
Marvin Gaye; *What's Going On* . . . . (Motown)
Right Or Wrong
George Strait; *George Strait's Greatest Hits* . . . . (MCA)
Right Or Wrong . . . . (MCA)
Strait Out Of The Box . . . . (MCA)
Reba McEntire & Asleep At The Wheel; *Ride With*
Bob-C . . . . (DreamWorks/SKG)
Right Thing To Do
Carly Simon; *Best Of Carly Simon* . . . . (Elektra)
Carly Simon-Greatest Hits Live . . . . (Arista)
No Secrets . . . . (Elektra)
Right Time Of The Night
Jennifer Warnes; *Best Of Jennifer Warnes* . . . . (Arista)
Jennifer Warnes . . . . (Arista)
Rock Island Line
Johnny Cash; *Johnny Cash-Sun Years* . . . . (Rhino)
Story Songs Of The Trains & Rivers . . . . (Sun)
Vintage Years-1955-1963 . . . . (Rhino)
Sonny Terry & Brownie McGhee; *Hootin'* . . . . (Muse)
Jazz Heritage . . . . (MCA)
Weavers; *Best Of The Weavers* . . . . (MCA)
Weavers At Carnegie Hall . . . . (Vanguard)
Weavers' Greatest Hits . . . . (Vanguard)
She's Always Right
Clay Walker; *Live, Laugh, Love* . . . . (Giant)
Somebody's Doin' Me Right
Glen Campbell; *Unconditional Love* . . . . (Liberty)
Keith Whitley; *Kentucky Bluebird* . . . . (RCA)
S-K-O; *S-K-O* . . . . (MTM)
Something So Right
Annie Lennox; *Medusa* . . . . (Arista)
Barbra Streisand; *The Way We Were* . . . . (Columbia)
Paul Simon; *1964-1993-Box Set* . . . . (Warner Bros.)
There Goes Rhymin' Simon . . . . (Columbia)
Sometimes
Brand New Heavies; *Shelter* . . . . (Delicious Vinyl)
Stand Up
Keb' Mo'; *The Door* . . . . (550/Epic/Okeh)
Still On Your Side
BBMak; *Sooner Or Later* . . . . (Hollywood)
Straighten Up And Fly Right
Andrews Sisters; *Best Of The Andrews Sisters-#2* . . . . (MCA)
Diana Krall; *Stepping Out* . . . . (Justin Time)
Linda Ronstadt; *For Sentimental Reasons* . . . . (Asylum)
Nat "King" Cole; *Best Of Nat "King" Cole-Vol. 2* . . . . (Capitol)
Take Your Time (Do It Right) Part 1
Max-A-Million; *Club Hitz Of The '90s-#2-C* . . . . (Beast)
Take Your Time . . . . (S.O.S./Zoo)
S.O.S. Band; *Best Of The S.O.S. Band* . . . . (Tabu)
Billboard Top Hits-1980-C . . . . (Rhino)
Club Epic-#1-C . . . . (Legacy)
S.O.S. Band . . . . (Rhino)
That's Just About Right
BlackHawk; *BlackHawk* . . . . (Arista)
The Hits-Love & Gravity . . . . (Arista)
That's Right (You're Not From Texas)
Lyle Lovett; *Live In Texas* . . . . (MCA)
The Road To Ensenada . . . . (MCA)
Theme From "Dudley-Do-Right"
Original Soundtrack; *Television's Greatest Hits-#3-1970s & 1980s-C* . . . (TVT)
Theme From "The Price Is Right"
Original Soundtrack; *Television's Greatest Hits-#6-Remote Control-C* . . (TVT)

'Til I Get It Right
Tammy Wynette; *Tammy Wynette's Biggest Hits* . . . . (Epic)
Tammy Wynette's Greatest Hits-#3 . . . . (Epic)
Tears Of Fire-25th Anniversary Collection . . . . (Epic)
Trisha Yearwood; *Tammy Wynette...Remembered-C* . . . . (Asylum)
'Til You Do Me Right
After 7; *Rock On 1995-C* . . . . (Madacy)
Very Best Of After 7 . . . . (Virgin)
We Can Work It Out
Beatles; *"Yesterday"...And Today* . . . . (Capitol)
Beatles 1 . . . . (Capitol)
Beatles-20 Greatest Hits . . . . (Capitol)
Beatles-Box Set . . . . (Capitol)
Past Masters-Volume Two . . . . (Parlophone)
The Beatles/1962-1966 . . . . (Capitol)
Paul McCartney; *Unplugged (The Official Bootleg)* . . . . (Capitol)
Stevie Wonder; *Beatles Songs By Greatest Stars* . . . . (Motown)
Signed Sealed & Delivered . . . . (Motown)
Stevie Wonder's Greatest Hits-#2 . . . . (Motown)
Top 10 With A Bullet-Motown Solo Stars-C . . . . (Motown)
Well...All Right
Buddy Holly; *Buddy Holly-20 Golden Greats* . . . . (MCA)
Nanci Griffith; *Not Fade Away-Remembering Buddy Holly-C* . . . . (Decca)
Why Don't You Do Right
Benny Goodman; *Benny Goodman-16 Most Requested Songs* . . . . . (Columbia)
Ella Fitzgerald & Joe Pass; *Easy Living* . . . . (Pablo)
Peggy Lee; *Capitol Collectors Series-Peggy Lee-#1-Early Years* . . . . (Capitol)
Peggy Lee's All-Time Greatest Hits . . . . (Curb)
Without You
Van Halen; *Van Halen 3* . . . . (Warner Bros.)
You May Be Right
Billy Joel; *Billy Joel-Greatest Hits, Volume I & Volume II* . . . . (Columbia)
Glass Houses . . . . (Columbia)

RIVERS, Bayou, Creeks, Delta, Streams

See Also: DANGER & DISASTER, DROWN, FLOOD, OCEAN, RAIN, SAILING, SHIPS, SPORTS: SWIMMING, WATER

Across The Great Divide
Band; *Rock Of Ages* . . . . (Capitol)
The Band . . . . (Capitol)
Across The River
Bruce Hornsby & The Range; *Night On The Town* . . . . (RCA)
Ain't No Mountain High Enough
Diana Ross; *20/20-C* . . . . (Motown)
25 #1 Hits From 25 Years-C . . . . (Motown)
Diana Ross . . . . (Motown)
Diana Ross-The Ultimate Collection . . . . (Motown)
Every Great Motown Song-First 25 Years-C . . . . (Motown)
Greatest Songs By Ashford & Simpson . . . . (Motown)
Motown Legends-Diana Ross . . . . (Motown)
Motown Story-First 25 Years-C . . . . (Motown)
Motown's Biggest Pop Hits-C . . . . (Motown)
TV ST/Diana-C . . . . (Motown)
Marvin Gaye & Tammi Terrell; *20 Greatest Songs In Motown*
History-C . . . . (Motown)
Classic Duets-Marvin Gaye & His Women-C . . . . (Motown)
Marvin Gaye & Tammi Terrell's Greatest Hits . . . . (Motown)
Marvin Gaye Live At The London Palladium . . . . (Motown)
Motown Grammy R&B Performances Of The '60s & '70s-C . . . . . . (Motown)
Performances Of The '60s & '70s-C . . . . (Motown)
United . . . . (Motown)
All Quiet Along The Potomac Tonight
Hermes Nye; *Ballads Of The Civil War-#1 & 2* . . . . . . (Smithsonian Folkways)
American Pie
Don McLean; *American Pie* . . . . (EMI)
Best Of Don McLean . . . . (EMI)
Greatest Hits Then & Now . . . . (EMI)
ST/Born On The Fourth Of July . . . . (MCA)
Madonna; *ST/The Next Big Thing* . . . . (Maverick)
At The Beginning
Richard Marx & Donna Lewis; *ST/Anastasia-Music From The Motion*
Picture . . . . (Atlantic)
Banks Of The Ohio
Doc Watson; *On Stage (Featuring Merle Watson)* . . . . (Vanguard)
Joan Baez; *Best Of Joan Baez* . . . . (A&M)
Joan Baez, Vol. 2 . . . . (Vanguard)
Battle Of New Orleans
Chet Atkins & The Boston Pops; *Best Of Chet Atkins & The*
Boston Pops . . . . (RCA)
Johnny Horton; *American Originals-Johnny Horton* . . . . (Columbia)
Johnny Horton's Greatest Hits . . . . (Columbia)
Radio Classics Of The '50s-C . . . . (Columbia)
Nitty Gritty Dirt Band; *Dirt, Silver & Gold* . . . . (One Way)
Dream . . . . (United Artists)
Stars And Stripes Forever . . . . (Capitol)

Bayou Jubilee
Nitty Gritty Dirt Band; *Dirt, Silver & Gold* . . . . (One Way)
Dream . . . . (United Artists)
Will The Circle Be Unbroken-#2-C . . . . (Uni)
Bayou Lullaby
Penny De Haven; *ST/Bronco Billy* . . . . (Elektra)
Big River
Grateful Dead; *One From The Vault* . . . . (Grateful Dead)
Steal Your Face . . . . (Grateful Dead)
Johnny Cash; *Johnny Cash-Legend* . . . . (Sun)
Johnny Cash's Greatest Hits-#2 . . . . (Columbia)
Johnny Cash-Sun Years . . . . (Rhino)
Superbilly . . . . (Sun)
The Man In Black-His Greatest Hits . . . . (Legacy)
Rosanne Cash; *Right Or Wrong* . . . . (Columbia)
Big River
Bob Seger System; *Mongrel* . . . . (Capitol)
Big River
Beat Farmers; *The Pursuit Of Happiness* . . . . (Curb)
Big River, Big Man
Claude King; *American Originals-Claude King* . . . . (Columbia)
Best Of Claude King . . . . (Gusto)
Bitter Creek
Eagles; *Desperado* . . . . (Asylum)
Black Bayou
Charlie Daniels Band; *Midnight Wind* . . . . (Epic)
Black Water
Doobie Brothers; *Best Of The Doobies* . . . . (Warner Bros.)
What Were Once Vices Are Now Habits . . . . (Warner Bros.)
Blue On Black
Kenny Wayne Shepherd; *Trouble Is...* . . . . (Revolution)
Blue River
Elvis Presley; *Lost Album* . . . . (RCA)
ST/Double Trouble . . . . (RCA)
Boat On The River
Styx; *Cornerstone* . . . . (A&M)
Born On The Bayou
Creedence Clearwater Revival; *Bayou Country* . . . . (Fantasy)
Chooglin' . . . . (Fantasy)
Creedence Clearwater Revival-Gold . . . . (Fantasy)
Creedence Gold . . . . (Fantasy)
Live In Europe . . . . (Fantasy)
The Concert . . . . (Fantasy)
Bridge On The River Kwai
Magic Organ; *The Magic Organ Plays Movie Themes* . . . . (Ranwood)
Bridge Washed Out
Warner Mack; *Country's Greatest Hits-#3-C* . . . . (MCA)
MCA Records 30 Years Of Hits-1958-1988-C . . . . (MCA)
Brokedown Palace
Grateful Dead; *American Beauty* . . . . (Warner Bros.)
Persuasions; *Might As Well...The Persuasions Sing
Grateful Dead* . . . . (Grateful Dead)
Buffalo River Home
John Hiatt; *Perfectly Good Guitar* . . . . (A&M)
Burn On
Randy Newman; *Sail Away* . . . . (Reprise)
By A Waterfall
Ruby Keeler & Dick Powell; *Lullaby Of Broadway-The Best Of Busby
Berkeley At Warner Brothers* . . . . (Rhino)
Sammy Fain; *Sammy Sings Fain* . . . . (Living Era)
Can't Stop My Heart From Loving You
Aaron Neville; *The Tattooed Heart* . . . . (A&M)
O'Kanes; *Greatest Country Hits Of The '80s-1987-C* . . . . . . (Columbia)
More Hot Country Requests-#2-C . . . . (Epic)
O'Kanes . . . . (Columbia)
Catfish John
Johnny Russell; *Johnny Russell's Greatest Hits* . . . . . (Dominion Entert.)
Chattahoochee
Alan Jackson; *A Lot About Livin' (And A Little 'Bout Love)* . . . . (Arista)
Chocolate River
Seeds; *Travel With Your Mind* . . . . (Crescendo)
Climb Ev'ry Mountain
Mormon Tabernacle Choir; *Climb Ev'ry Mountain* . . . . (Columbia)
Original Cast/Mary Martin; *The Sound Of Music* . . . . (Sony Broadway)
Trapp Family Singers; *The Sound Of Music* . . . . (Warner Bros.)
Cowboy Love Song (Red River Valley)
Skip Gorman; *A Cowboy's Wild Song To His Herd* . . . . (Rounder)
Cripple Creek
Leo Kottke; *Best Of Leo Kottke* . . . . (Capitol)
Did You Hear Me . . . . (Capitol)
Mudlark . . . . (Capitol)
Peter Lang/John Fahey . . . . (Takoma)
Very Best Of Leo Kottke . . . . (Capitol)
Cripple Creek Ferry
Neil Young; *After The Gold Rush* . . . . (Reprise)
Cross The Brazos At Waco
Billy Walker; *Columbia Country Classics-#3-Americana-C* . . . . . . (Columbia)
Super Country Hits Of The '60s-C . . . . (Gusto)

Crossing Muddy Waters
John Hiatt; *Crossing Muddy Waters* . . . . (Vanguard)
Cry Me A River
Aerosmith; *Rock In A Hard Place* . . . . (Columbia)
Barbra Streisand; *A Happening In Central Park* . . . . (Columbia)
The Barbra Streisand Album . . . . (Columbia)
Diana Krall; *The Look Of Love* . . . . (Impulse!)
Joe Cocker; *Joe Cocker-Classics-#4* . . . . (A&M)
Joe Cocker's Greatest Hits . . . . (A&M)
Mad Dogs & Englishmen . . . . (A&M)
Cry Me A River
Crystal Gayle; *When I Dream* . . . . (Liberty)
Cumberland Blues
Grateful Dead; *Europe '72* . . . . (Warner Bros.)
*What A Long Strange Trip It's Been: The Best Of The
Grateful Dead* . . . . (Warner Bros.)
Workingman's Dead . . . . (Warner Bros.)
Cuyahoga
R.E.M.; *Life's Rich Pageant* . . . . (EMI-Capitol Entert. Properties)
Deep Creek
Butch Thompson; *New Orleans Joys* . . . . (Daring)
Jelly Roll Morton; *Jelly Roll Morton* . . . . (Bluebird)
Deep River
Fats Waller; *Fats Waller In London* . . . . (Disques Swing)
Mormon Tabernacle Choir; *Songs From America's Heartland* . . . . . . (London)
Paul Robeson; *Historic Paul Robeson-Golden Classics-#3* . . . . . . (Collectables)
Deep River Blues
Doc Watson; *Doc Watson* . . . . (Vanguard)
Deep River Woman
Lionel Richie; *Dancing On The Ceiling* . . . . (Motown)
Delta Lady
Joe Cocker; *Joe Cocker!* . . . . (A&M)
Joe Cocker-Classics-#4 . . . . (A&M)
Joe Cocker's Greatest Hits . . . . (A&M)
Mad Dogs & Englishmen . . . . (A&M)
Leon Russell; *Best Of Leon Russell* . . . . (MCA)
Leon Russell . . . . (MCA)
Dirty Water
Standells; *Best Of The Standells* . . . . (Rhino)
Nuggets-Classic Collection From The Psychedelic '60s-C . . . . . . (Rhino)
Super Oldies Of The '60s-#10-C . . . . (Audio Fidelity)
Don't Change Horses
Tower Of Power; *Back To Oakland* . . . . (Warner Bros.)
Don't Cross The River
America; *History-Greatest Hits* . . . . (Warner Bros.)
Homecoming . . . . (Warner Bros.)
Don't Cross The River
Garth Brooks; *Scarecrow* . . . . (Capitol)
Down By The Ohio
Andrews Sisters; *Best Of The Andrews Sisters-#2* . . . . (MCA)
Down By The Old Mill Stream
Mitch Miller; *Sing Along With Mitch* . . . . (Columbia)
Sammy Kaye & His Orchestra; *Best Of Sammy Kaye & His Orchestra* . . . (MCA)
Down By The River
Neil Young; *Decade* . . . . (Reprise)
Neil Young & Crazy Horse; *Everybody Knows This Is Nowhere* . . . . . . (Reprise)
Down By The Riverside
Elvis Presley; *Million-Dollar Quartet* . . . . (RCA)
Mormon Tabernacle Choir; *Songs From America's Heartland* . . . . . . (London)
Original Soundtrack; *School Days-Kids Classics* . . . . (Benson)
Sonny Terry & Brownie McGhee; *Blowin' The Fuses-Golden
Classics* . . . . (Collectables)
Coffeehouse Blues . . . . (Vee-Jay)
Giants Of The Blues . . . . (Bescol, Ltd.)
Down In The Flood
Bob Dylan; *Bob Dylan's Greatest Hits-#2* . . . . (Columbia)
Chris Smither; *Another Way To Find You* . . . . (Hightone)
Jimmy LaFave; *Trail* . . . . (Bohemia Beat)
Sandy Denny; *North Star Grassman And The Ravens* . . . . (Hannibal)
Down On Deep River
Leon Russell; *Will O' The Wisp* . . . . (MCA)
Down On The Rio Grande
Brian Sharp; *Rio Grande Valley* . . . . (Westwind)
Johnny Rodriguez; *Rodriguez* . . . . (Epic)
Down The River Of Golden Dreams
Mom & Dads; *Down The River Of Golden Dreams* . . . . (Crescendo)
Slim Whitman; *Home On The Range* . . . . (United Artists)
Down To The River To Pray
Alison Krauss; *ST/O Brother, Where Art Thou?* . . . . (Mercury)
Downstream
Rainmakers; *Rainmakers* . . . . (Mercury)
Downstream
Supertramp; *Even In The Quietest Moments* . . . . (A&M)
Dream River
Mavericks; *Trampoline* . . . . (MCA)
Every River
Kim Richey; *Bitter Sweet* . . . . (Mercury)

Ferry Cross The Mersey
Gerry And The Pacemakers; *Ferry Across The Mersey-Best Of Gerry And The Pacemakers* ....(EMI)
History Of British Rock-#4-C ....(Rhino)

Fishin' In The Dark
Nitty Gritty Dirt Band; *Billboard Top Country Hits-1987-C* .... (Rhino)
Hold On ....(Warner Bros.)
More Great Dirt-Best Of Nitty Gritty Dirt Band ....(Warner Bros.)

Five Feet High And Rising
Johnny Cash; *The Man In Black-His Greatest Hits*..............(Legacy)

Flow Gently, Sweet Afton
Mormon Tabernacle Choir; *Old Beloved Songs* ....(Columbia)

Gentle On My Mind
Elvis Presley; *From Elvis In Memphis* ....(RCA)
Great Country Songs ....(RCA)
Glen Campbell; *Best Of Austin City Limits-Legends Of Country Music-C* ....(Legacy)
Best Of Glen Campbell ....(Capitol)
Glen Campbell-Best Of The Early Years ....(Curb)
John Hartford; *Me Oh My-How The Time Does Fly-Anthology* .... (Flying Fish)
Patti Page; *Patti Page-16 Most Requested Songs* ....(Legacy)

God Must Have Spent A Little More Time On You
Alabama Featuring 'N Sync; *Twentieth Century* ....(RCA)
'N Sync; *'N Sync*.......................................(RCA)
Totally Hits-#1-C ....(Arista)

Grand Coulee Dam
Bob Dylan; *Tribute To Woody Guthrie-C* ....(Warner Bros.)

Green River
Alabama; *Mountain Music* ....(RCA)
Creedence Clearwater Revival; *1969* ....(Fantasy)
Creedence Clearwater Revival-Chronicle..................(Fantasy)
Green River ....(Fantasy)
Live In Europe ....(Fantasy)
Royal Albert Hall Concert ....(Fantasy)
ST/1969 ....(Polydor)

Green River Ramble
Skip Gorman; *A Cowboy's Wild Song To His Herd* ....(Rounder)

Greenwood Creek
Doobie Brothers; *Doobie Brothers* ....(Warner Bros.)

Hazard (The River)
Richard Marx; *Rush Street* ....(Capitol)

High And Dry
Marty Brown; *High And Dry* ....(MCA)

Higher Place
Tom Petty; *Wildflowers* ....(Warner Bros.)

Holy River
''AFKAP''; *Emancipation* ....(NPG)

I Am A Patriot
Jackson Browne; *World In Motion* ....(Elektra)
Little Steven; *Voice Of America* ....(Razor & Tie)

I Will Get There
Boyz II Men; *ST/The Prince Of Egypt-Inspirational* ......(DreamWorks/SKG)

If The River Was Whiskey
Mississippi Fred McDowell; *Great Bluesmen At Newport-C* ....(Vanguard)

Islands In The Stream
Kenny Rogers & Dolly Parton; *Eyes That See In The Dark* ...... (RCA)
Kenny Rogers' Greatest Hits ....(RCA)

It Happened In Monterey
Frank Sinatra & Nelson Riddle Orchestra; *songs for Swingin' Lovers!* ....(Capitol)
Mel Torme & The Mel-Tones; *Back In Town* ....(Verve)

Jambalaya (On The Bayou)
Blue Ridge Rangers; *Blue Ridge Rangers*................(Fantasy)
Fats Domino; *Fats Domino's Greatest Hits* ....(MCA)
Hank Williams With His Drifting Cowboys; *24 Of Hank Williams' Greatest Hits* ....(Polydor)
Hank Williams-16 Great Hits ....(Everest)
Hank Williams-40 Greatest Hits ....(Polydor)
Hank Williams, Jr.; *ST/Your Cheatin' Heart* ....(Sony Music Special Prod.)
Jerry Lee Lewis; *Twenty Classic Hits* ....(Sun)
Nitty Gritty Dirt Band; *All The Good Times* ....(United Artists)
Stars And Stripes Forever ....(Capitol)

Just Across The River
Original Cast; *Starting Here Starting Now* ....(RCA)

Keep Me Turning
Pete Townshend & Ronnie Lane; *Rough Mix*.............(Atlantic)

Kern River
Merle Haggard; *For The Record: Merle Haggard-43 Legendary Hits* .... (BNA)
Kern River ....(Epic)

Lazy River
Bing Crosby; *All-Time Best Of* ....(Curb)
Bobby Darin; *Mack The Knife-Best Of Bobby Darin-#2*............(Atlantic)
Chet Atkins & Les Paul; *Masters Of The Guitar-Together* ....(Pair)
Harry Connick, Jr.; *Eleven* ....(Columbia)
Kay Starr; *Kay Starr's Greatest Hits* ....(Capitol)
Leon Redbone; *Up A Lazy River* ....(Private Music)
Louis Armstrong; *Louis Armstrong-Best Of The Decca Years-#1-The Singer-C* ....(Decca)
Mills Brothers; *Mills Brothers' Greatest Hits*...........(MCA)

The Mills Brothers-Best Of The Decca Years .... (Decca)

Let The River Run
Carly Simon; *Coming Around Again*.......................(Arista)
ST/Working Girl ....(Arista)

Let's All Go Down To The River
Jody Miller & Johnny Paycheck; *Johnny Paycheck's Greatest Hits* ...... (Epic)

Like A River To The Sea
Steve Wariner; *I Am Ready* ....(Arista)

Many Rivers To Cross
Jimmy Cliff; *In Concert-Best Of Jimmy Cliff* ....(Reprise)
Reggae Spectacular-C ....(A&M)
ST/The Harder They Come ....(Mango)
Wonderful World, Beautiful People ....(A&M)
Linda Ronstadt; *Prisoner In Disguise* ....(Asylum)
UB40; *Labour Of Love* ....(A&M)

Meeting Across The River
Bruce Springsteen; *Born To Run* ....(Columbia)

Mississippi
Paula Cole; *This Fire*................................(Imago)

Mississippi Delta Blues
Bob Wills; *Bob Wills-Anthology* ....(Sony Music Special Prod.)
Jimmie Rodgers; *Train Whistle Blues* ....(RCA)
Leon Redbone; *Double Time* ....(Warner Bros.)

Mississippi Delta City Blues
Chicago; *Chicago XI* ....(Chicago)
Group Portrait ....(Chicago)

Mississippi Mud
Bob Crosby & His Orchestra; *1952-1953* ....(Hindsight)
Bob Crosby & His Orchestra Play 22 Original Big Band Hits .....(Hindsight)

Mississippi River
J.J. Cale; *Grasshopper* ....(Mercury)
Paul Davis; *Little Bit Of Paul Davis* ....(Bang)

Mississippi River Blues
Leon Redbone; *Double Time*............................(Warner Bros.)

Moon River
Andy Williams; *Andy Williams' Greatest Hits* ....(Columbia)
Andy Williams-16 Most Requested Songs ....(Legacy)
More American Graffiti-#4-C ....(MCA)
Henry Mancini; *Henry Mancini-Pure Gold* ....(RCA)
Peter Gunn ....(RCA)
Jerry Butler; *Best Of Jerry Butler* ....(Rhino)

Moonlight On The Colorado
Sons Of The Pioneers; *Songs Of The Trail* ....(Pair)

Moonlight On The Ganges
Frank Sinatra; *Sinatra Swings* ....(Reprise)
Glenn Miller; *Best Of The Big Bands-C* ....(Columbia)

Muddy Water
Original Broadway Cast; *Big River-The Adventures Of Huckleberry Finn* ....(MCA)

Muddy Water
Keb' Mo'; *Slow Down*.................................(550/Epic/Okeh)

My Home Is In The Delta
Muddy Waters; *Folk Singer* ....(Chess)
The Chess Box-Muddy Waters ....(Chess)

New River Train
Doc & Merle Watson; *Remembering Merle* ....(Sugar Hill)
White Brothers & New Kentucky Colonels; *Live In Sweden*.........(Rounder)

Ode To Billy Joe
Bobbi Gentry; *All-Time Country Classics-#1-C* ....(Capitol)

Ol' Man River
Al Jolson; *Best Of Al Jolson* ....(MCA)
The Al Jolson Story-#6 ....(MCA)
Frank Sinatra; *The Concert Sinatra* ....(Reprise)
Voice: The Columbia Years-1943-1952 ....(Columbia)
Paul Robeson; *A Lonesome Road* ....(Living Era)
American Balladeer-Golden Classics-#1-C ....(Collectables)
William Warfield; *ST/All Those Glorious MGM Musicals* ...... (MGM)
William Warfield/Original Cast; *Show Boat* ....(Columbia)

Old Folks At Home
Mormon Tabernacle Choir; *Songs Of The Civil War And Stephen Foster Favorites* ....(Sony Music Classical)
Paul Robeson; *A Man & His Beliefs-Golden Classics-#2* .... (Collectables)

On London Bridge
Jo Stafford; *International Hits*.......................(Corinthian)

On The Amazon
Mabel Mercer & Bobby Short; *At Town Hall* ....(Atlantic)

On The Banks Of The Ohio
Carter Family & Johnny Cash; *Folk Classics: Roots Of American Folk Music-C* ....(Columbia)
Hodges Brothers; *Watermelon Hangin' On The Vine* ......(Arhoolie)
Joan Baez; *Country Music Album* ....(Vanguard)

On The Banks Of The Old Tennessee
Doc Watson; *Old Timey Concert*.........................(Vanguard)

On The Banks Of The Wabash
Mills Brothers; *Mills Brothers-22 Great Hits* ....(Ranwood)
The Mills Brothers Story.............................(Ranwood)

On The Mississippi
Claude Bolling; *Original Ragtime*.....................(Columbia)

One More River
Soul Stirrers featuring Sam Cooke; *The Specialty Story* . . . . (Specialty)
One More River
Alan Parsons Project; *Pyramid* . . . . (Arista)
One More River
Max Carl And Big Dance; *One Planet, One Groove* . . . . (Mission)
Peace Like A River
Paul Simon; *Paul Simon* . . . . (Columbia)
Pissing In A River
Patti Smith Group; *Radio Ethiopia* . . . . (Arista)
Please Mr. Sun
Johnnie Ray; *Back To The Early '50s* . . . . (Dominion Entert.)
Johnnie Ray-16 Most Requested Songs . . . . (Legacy)
Vogues; *Vogues' Greatest Hits* . . . . (Rhino)
Pond & The Stream
Sandy Denny; *Best Of Sandy Denny* . . . . (Hannibal)
Who Knows Where The Time Goes . . . . (Hannibal)
Powder River/Carrie's Gone To Kansas City
Bill Shute & Lisa Null; *American Primitive* . . . . (Green Linnet)
Proud Mary
Creedence Clearwater Revival; *1968-1969* . . . . (Fantasy)
Bayou Country . . . . (Fantasy)
Creedence Clearwater Revival-Chronicle . . . . (Fantasy)
Creedence Clearwater Revival-Gold . . . . (Fantasy)
Live In Europe . . . . (Fantasy)
George Jones & Johnny Paycheck; *My Very Special Guests* . . . . (Epic)
Ike & Tina Turner; *Best Of Ike & Tina Turner* . . . . (EMI)
Didn't It Blow Your Mind: Soul Hits Of The '70s-#4-C . . . . (Rhino)
EMI Legends Of Rock & Roll-24 Greatest Hits-C . . . . (EMI)
Ike & Tina Turner's Greatest Hits . . . . (Curb)
Purple Rivers
Swimming Pool Q's; *Swimming Pool Q's* . . . . (A&M)
Queen Of The Nile
Dangerous Toys; *Dangerous Toys* . . . . (Columbia)
Red And Rio Grande
Doug Supernaw; *Red And Rio Grande* . . . . (BNA)
Red River
Alabama; *Alabama-Live* . . . . (RCA)
Closer You Get . . . . (RCA)
Red River
BoDeans; *Home* . . . . (Slash)
Red River
Leadbelly; *Leadbelly* . . . . (Columbia)
Midnight Special . . . . (Rounder)
Red River Blues
Jesse Fuller; *Jesse Fuller's Favorites* . . . . (Prestige)
Sonny Terry; *Sonny Terry* . . . . (Everest)
Sonny Terry With Brownie McGhee-Midnight Special . . . . (Fantasy)
Red River Rock
Johnny And The Hurricanes; *Echoes Of A Rock Era-Middle*
Years-C . . . . (Roulette)
History Of Rock Instrumentals-#1-C . . . . (Rhino)
Red River Valley
Gene Autry; *Cowboy Hall Of Fame* . . . . (Republic/Universal)
The Country Music Hall Of Fame-Gene Autry-15 Of His All-Time
Greatest Hits . . . . (Columbia)
Western Classics . . . . (Columbia)
Pete Seeger; *American Favorite Ballads-#5* . . . . (Smithsonian Folkways)
Ride Across The River
Dire Straits; *Brothers In Arms* . . . . (Warner Bros.)
Rio Grande
Floyd Tillman; *The Country Music Hall Of Fame-Floyd Tillman* . . . . (MCA)
Sam Eskin; *Shanty Men-Songs Of Sailormen And*
Lumbermen . . . . (Smithsonian Folkways)
River
Betty Buckley; *With One Look* . . . . (Sterling)
Joni Mitchell; *Blue* . . . . (Reprise)
River And The Highway
Pam Tillis; *All Of This Love* . . . . (Arista)
Pam Tillis' Greatest Hits . . . . (Arista)
River Blood
Walkabouts; *Scavenger* . . . . (Sub Pop)
River Boy
Willie Nelson; *There'll Be No Teardrops Tonight* . . . . (United Artists)
River Deep, Mountain High
Celine Dion; *Falling Into You* . . . . (550 Music)
Erasure; *Innocents* . . . . (Sire)
Four Tops; *Four Tops-Anthology* . . . . (Motown)
Ike & Tina Turner; *Best Of Ike & Tina Turner* . . . . (EMI)
Phil Spector's Greatest Hits-C . . . . (Spector)
Proud Mary-Best Of Ike & Tina Turner . . . . (EMI)
Tina Turner; *Simply The Best* . . . . (Capitol)
River Diner
Jack Smith & The Rockabilly Planet; *Jack Smith & The Rockabilly*
Planet . . . . (Flying Fish)
River Hymn
Band; *Cahoots* . . . . (Capitol)
To Kingdom Come-The Definitive Collection . . . . (Capitol)

River In The Pines
Joan Baez; *Farewell Angelina* . . . . (Vanguard)
Love Song Album . . . . (Vanguard)
River In The Rain
Original Broadway Cast; *Big River-The Adventures Of*
Huckleberry Finn . . . . (MCA)
River Is Wide
Grass Roots; *Grass Roots-All-Time Greatest Hits* . . . . (MCA)
Grass Roots-Anthology (1966-1975) . . . . (Rhino)
River Jordan
Clancy Eddle & Others; *Ska Bonanza-Studio One Ska Years-C* . . . . . . (Heartbeat)
River Must Flow
Gino Vannelli; *Brother To Brother* . . . . (A&M)
Gino Vannelli's Greatest Hits . . . . (A&M)
River Of Deceit
Mad Season; *Above* . . . . (Columbia)
River Of Dreams
Billy Joel; *River Of Dreams* . . . . (Columbia)
River Of Endless Love
Moody Blues; *Sur La Mer* . . . . (Polydor)
River Of Jordan
Ricky Skaggs; *Family & Friends* . . . . (Rounder)
Stained Glass Hour . . . . (Rounder)
River Of Life
REO Speedwagon; *This Time We Mean It* . . . . (Epic)
River Of Life
Neville Brothers; *Brother's Keeper* . . . . (A&M)
River Of Love
Lynch Mob; *Wicked Sensation* . . . . (Elektra)
River Of Love
John Denver; *Farewell Andromeda* . . . . (RCA)
River Of Love
Angels; *My Boyfriend's Back* . . . . (Collectables)
River Of Love
David Foster; *River Of Love* . . . . (Atlantic)
River Of Love
Richie Sambora; *Stranger In This Town* . . . . (Mercury)
River Of Love
T Bone Burnett; *T Bone Burnett* . . . . (Dot)
River Of No Return
Marilyn Monroe; *I Wanna Be Loved By You* . . . . (Eclipse)
River Of Stone
Restless Heart; *Fast Moving Train* . . . . (RCA)
River Of Tears
York Brothers; *Super Country Hits Of The '40s-C* . . . . (Gusto)
River Of Tears
Highway 101; *Bing Bang Boom* . . . . (Warner Bros.)
River Of Tears
Bonnie Raitt; *Green Light* . . . . (Warner Bros.)
River Path
Little Anthony And The Imperials; *Forever Yours* . . . . (Roulette)
River Road
Crystal Gayle; *Favorites-Crystal Gayle* . . . . (Liberty)
We Must Believe In Magic . . . . (United Artists)
River Roll On
Judds; *Rockin' With The Rhythm* . . . . (MCA)
River Runs Deep
J.J. Cale; *Naturally* . . . . (MCA)
River Runs Low
Bruce Hornsby & The Range; *The Way It Is* . . . . (RCA)
River Runs Red
Midnight Oil; *Blue Sky Mining* . . . . (Columbia)
River Song
Beach Boys; *10 Years Of Harmony* . . . . (Caribou)
River, Stay 'Way From My Door
Guy Lombardo & His Royal Canadians; *Auld Lang Syne* . . . . (Pro-Arte)
River, The
Santana; *Festival* . . . . (Columbia)
River, The
Bruce Springsteen; *Bruce Springsteen's Greatest Hits* . . . . (Columbia)
The River . . . . (Columbia)
Bruce Springsteen & The E Street Band; *Bruce Springsteen & The E Street*
Band Live/1975-85 . . . . (Legacy)
River, The
Garth Brooks; *Ropin' The Wind* . . . . (Liberty)
The Limited Series . . . . (Capitol)
River, The
Dan Fogelberg; *Home Free* . . . . (Columbia)
River, The
Roberta Flack; *Killing Me Softly* . . . . (Atlantic)
River, The
Enya; *Watermark* . . . . (Reprise)
Riverboat
Robert Palmer; *Pressure Drop* . . . . (Island)
Riverboat Gambler
Chris LeDoux; *Songs Of Rodeo Life* . . . . (Capitol)
Riverboat Shuffle
Hoagy Carmichael; *Stardust Road* . . . . (MCA)

River's Invitation
Freddie Robinson; *Stax Blues Masters-Blue Monday-C* . . . (Stax)
Percy Mayfield; *Best Of Percy Mayfield* . . . (Specialty)
Stanley Turrentine; *Best Of Stanley Turrentine* . . . (Blue Note)
Joyride . . . (Blue Note)
Ted Taylor; *Atlantic Blues-Vocalists-C* . . . (Atlantic)
Rivers Of Babylon
Boney M; *Nightflight To Venus* . . . (Sire)
Linda Ronstadt; *Hasten Down The Wind* . . . (Asylum)
Melodians; *Grooveyard-C* . . . (Mango)
ST/The Harder They Come . . . (Mango)
Riverwide
Sheryl Crow; *The Globe Sessions* . . . (A&M)
Rock A Bye Your Baby With A Dixie Melody
Al Jolson; *Best Of Al Jolson* . . . (MCA)
Jolson Sang 'Em . . . (Biograph)
Music From The New York Stage (1890-1920)-#4-1917-1920-C . . . (Pearl)
The Al Jolson Story-#1 . . . (MCA)
Jerry Lewis; *Just Sings* . . . (Razor & Tie)
Judy Garland; *Judy Garland-At Carnegie Hall* . . . (Capitol)
Miss Show Business . . . (Capitol)
One & Only . . . (Capitol)
Rockin' On The River
Jerry Jeff Walker; *Navajo Rug* . . . (Rykodisc)
Roll On Columbia
Judy Collins; *Tribute To Woody Guthrie-C* . . . (Warner Bros.)
Roll On Mississippi
Charley Pride; *Charley Pride's Greatest Hits* . . . (RCA)
Roll Tennessee River
Oak Ridge Boys; *Step On Out* . . . (MCA)
Rose Of The Rio Grande
Bob Crosby & His Orchestra; *Bob Crosby & His Orchestra Play 22 Original Big Band Hits* . . . (Hindsight)
Duke Ellington; *Great Paris Concert* . . . (Atlantic)
Ella Fitzgerald & Duke Ellington; *At The Cote D'Azur* . . . (Verve)
Row, Row, Row Your Boat
Bobby Darin/Johnny Mercer/Billy May Orchestra; *Two Of A Kind* . . . (Atlantic)
Original Soundtrack; *Children's Favorites* . . . (Kid Rhino/Rhino 4 Kids)
Spike Jones & His City Slickers; *King Of Corn* . . . (Glendale)
Running Bear
Johnny Preston; *45s On CD-#1-1956-1959-C* . . . (Mercury)
Billboard Top Rock 'N' Roll Hits-1960-C . . . (Rhino)
Cruisin'-1960-C . . . (Increase)
Sonny James; *All-Time Country Classics-#1-C* . . . (Capitol)
Sailing Down This Golden River
Pete Seeger; *Bread & Roses Festival Of Acoustic Music-#1-C* . . . (Fantasy)
Circles & Seasons . . . (Warner Bros.)
Shady River Gal/Alabama Gals
Beverly Cotton; *Clogging Lessons* . . . (Flying Fish)
Shall We Gather At The River?
Chuck Wagon Gang; *16 Country-Gospel Favorites* . . . (MCA)
Tennessee Ernie Ford; *All-Time Greatest Hymns* . . . (Curb)
Tennessee Ernie Ford Sings 22 Favorite Hymns . . . (Ranwood)
Shenandoah
Bob Dylan; *Down In The Groove* . . . (Columbia)
Harry Belafonte; *Harry Belafonte-Legendary Performer* . . . (RCA)
James Galway; *James Galway's Greatest Hits* . . . (RCA)
Leontyne Price; *God Bless America* . . . (RCA)
Van Morrison & The Chieftains; *ST/Long Journey Home: The Irish In America* . . . (RCA Victor)
Vienna Boys Choir; *International Folk Songs: Around The World With The Vienna Boys' Choir* . . . (Philips)
She's A River
Simple Minds; *Good News From The Next World* . . . (Virgin)
Sittin' On Top Of The World
Bob Dylan; *Good As I Been To You* . . . (Columbia)
Bob Wills & His Texas Playboys; *Bob Wills & His Texas Playboys-24 Great Hits* . . . (Polydor)
Bob Wills-Anthology . . . (Sony Music Special Prod.)
Tiffany Transcriptions-#8-More Of The Best . . . (Rhino)
Cream; *Wheels Of Fire* . . . (Polydor)
Doc Watson; *Doc Watson* . . . (Vanguard)
Greatest Folksingers Of The '60s-C . . . (Vanguard)
Old Timey Concert . . . (Vanguard)
Grateful Dead; *Grateful Dead (Skull & Roses)* . . . (Warner Bros.)
Jerry Jeff Walker; *Will The Circle Be Unbroken-#2-C* . . . (Uni)
Ray Charles; *20 Golden Pieces Of Ray Charles* . . . (Bulldog)
Sweet Honey In The Rock; *Believe I'll Run On, See What The End's Gonna Be* . . . (Redwood)
Sitting By The Riverside
Kinks; *Are The Village Green Preservation Society* . . . (Reprise)
Skunk Creek
Poco; *Forgotten Trail-1969-1974* . . . (Epic)
Song Of The Volga Boatmen
Glenn Miller; *Best Of Glenn Miller* . . . (RCA)
Chattanooga Choo Choo-#1 Hits . . . (Bluebird)
Glenn Miller-A Legendary Performer-#1 & 2 . . . (Bluebird)
Memorial-1944-1969 . . . (Bluebird)
This Is Glenn Miller . . . (RCA)
Tuxedo Junction; *Tuxedo Junction* . . . (Butterfly)
Squaws Along The Yukon
Hank Thompson; *Capitol Collectors Series-Hank Thompson* . . . (Capitol)
Hank Thompson's Greatest Hits-#2 . . . (Step One)
Standing By A River
Climax Blues Band; *FM/Live* . . . (Sire)
Standing Knee Deep In A River (Dying Of Thirst)
Kathy Mattea; *Lonesome Standard Time* . . . (Mercury)
Strawberry Wine
Deana Carter; *Did I Shave My Legs For This?* . . . (Capitol)
Sunflower River Blues
John Fahey; *John Fahey With Peter Lang & Leo Kottke* . . . (Takoma)
Surfin' Down The Swanee River
Honeys; *Capitol Collectors Series-The Honeys* . . . (Capitol)
Suwanee River
William H. Thompson; *Music From The New York Stage (1890-1920)-#1-1890-1908-C* . . . (Pearl)
Swampy River
Duke Ellington; *Okeh Ellington* . . . (Columbia)
Swanee
Al Jolson; *Al Jolson-Best Of The Decca Years* . . . (MCA)
Best Of Al Jolson . . . (MCA)
Jolson Sang 'Em . . . (Biograph)
Music From The New York Stage (1890-1920)-#4-1917-1920-C . . . (Pearl)
George Gershwin; *Rhapsody In Blue* . . . (Biograph)
Judy Garland; *Judy Garland-At Carnegie Hall* . . . (Capitol)
Judy Garland's All-Time Greatest Hits . . . (Curb)
Swanee River
Dave Brubeck Quartet; *Gone With The Wind* . . . (Columbia)
Firehouse Five Plus Two; *Goes South* . . . (Good Time Jazz)
Swanee River Rock
Ray Charles; *Birth Of Soul-Complete Atlantic R&B 1952-1959-C* . . . (Atlantic)
Sweet Afton
Nickel Creek; *Nickel Creek* . . . (Sugar Hill)
Sweet Thames Flow Softly
Alison Brown; *Twilight Motel* . . . (Vanguard)
Swimming In The Delaware
Sam Hinton; *Wandering Folk Song* . . . (Smithsonian Folkways)
Swimming Upstream
Ricky Van Shelton; *Loving Proof* . . . (Columbia)
Swimming Upstream
Glen Campbell; *Somebody Like That* . . . (Liberty)
Take A Ride On A Riverboat
Louisiana's Le Roux; *Louisiana's Le Roux* . . . (Capitol)
Take Me To The River
Al Green; *Al Green Explores Your Mind* . . . (Motown)
Al Green's Greatest Hits-#2 . . . (Hi)
Bryan Ferry; *Bride Stripped Bare* . . . (Reprise)
Commitments; *ST/The Commitments* . . . (MCA)
Foghat; *Best Of Foghat-#2* . . . (Rhino)
Night Shift . . . (Rhino)
Talking Heads; *More Songs About Buildings & Food* . . . (Sire)
Popular Favorites-1984-1992 . . . (Sire)
Take Me To The River
Exile; *Exile* . . . (Epic)
Exile-Super Hits . . . (Epic)
Tennessee River
Alabama; *Alabama-Live* . . . (RCA)
Alabama's Greatest Hits . . . (RCA)
Best Of The '80s...So Far-C . . . (RCA)
My Home's In Alabama . . . (RCA)
Hank Williams, Jr.; *Rowdy* . . . (WB/Curb)
Thanks For The Beautiful Land On The Delta
Duke Ellington; *New Orleans Suite* . . . (Atlantic)
That Song About The River
Don Williams; *Currents* . . . (RCA)
That Was A River
Collin Raye; *In This Life* . . . (Epic)
Till The Rivers All Run Dry
Don Williams; *Best Of Don Williams-#2* . . . (MCA)
Country Comes To Carnegie Hall-C . . . (MCA)
Don Williams' Greatest Country Hits . . . (Curb)
Harmony-C . . . (MCA Special Prod.)
Till The Rivers All Run Dry . . . (MCA Special Prod.)
Pete Townshend & Ronnie Lane; *Rough Mix* . . . (Atlantic)
Time (Keeps Flowing Like A River)
Alan Parsons Project; *Best Of The Alan Parsons Project* . . . (Arista)
Turn Of A Friendly Card . . . (Arista)
Too Many Rivers
Brenda Lee; *The Brenda Lee Story-Her Greatest Hits* . . . (MCA)
Eddy Arnold; *Country Gold-Eddy Arnold* . . . (RCA)
Forester Sisters; *New Tradition Sings The Old Tradition-C* . . . (Warner Bros.)
Train & The River
Jimmy Giuffre; *Jimmy Giuffre Three* . . . (Atlantic)

Traveling Riverside Blues
Hindu Love Gods; *Hindu Love Gods* . . . . (Giant)
John Hammond; *Best Of John Hammond* . . . . (Vanguard)
Led Zeppelin; *Led Zeppelin-Box Set* . . . . (Atlantic)
Robert Johnson; *King Of The Delta Blues Singers* . . . . (Columbia)
The Slide Guitar-Bottles Knives & Steel-C . . . . (Legacy)
Two Rivers In Montana
Gove Scrivenor; *Coconut Gove* . . . .(Flying Fish)
Two Teardrops
Steve Wariner; *Two Teardrops* . . . . (Capitol)
Up On Cripple Creek
Band; *Best Of The Band* . . . . (Capitol)
The Band . . . . (Capitol)
The Band-Gift Set . . . . (Capitol)
The Last Waltz . . . . (Warner Bros.)
Bob Dylan And The Band; *Before The Flood* . . . . (Columbia)
Wabash Cannonball
Billy Strange; *Between The Rails: America's Train Songs-C* . . . . (Crescendo)
Nitty Gritty Dirt Band; *Will The Circle Be Unbroken* . . . . (EMI)
Roy Acuff; *All Time Legends Of Country Music-C* . . . . (Legacy)
Backstage At The Grand Ole Opry-C . . . . (RCA)
Best Of Roy Acuff . . . . (Liberty)
Columbia Historic Edition-Roy Acuff . . . . (Columbia)
Essential Roy Acuff-1936-1949 . . . . (Legacy)
Hot Tracks-Train Super Hits-C . . . . (Epic)
Roy Acuff's Greatest Hits . . . . (Columbia)
Steel Rails-Classic Railroad Songs-#1-C . . . . (Rounder)
Waist Deep In The Big Muddy
Pete Seeger; *Best Of Broadside 1962-1968: Anthems Of The American
Underground From The Pages Of Broadside
Magazine-C* . . . .(Smithsonian Folkways)
Walkin' By The River
Ella Fitzgerald; *Best Of Ella Fitzgerald* . . . . (MCA)
Watching The River Flow
Bob Dylan; *Bob Dylan's Greatest Hits-#2* . . . . (Columbia)
Joe Cocker; *Luxury You Can Afford* . . . . (Asylum)
Watching The River Run
Loggins & Messina; *Full Sail* . . . . (Columbia)
The Best Of Friends . . . . (Columbia)
Water Is Wide
Joan Baez; *Very Early Joan Baez* . . . . (Vanguard)
Karla Bonoff; *ST/Thirtysomething* . . . . (Geffen)
Roger McGuinn; *Born To Rock & Roll* . . . . (Columbia)
Waterfall
Electric Light Orchestra; *Afterglow* . . . . (Epic)
Face The Music . . . .(Jet)
Waterfall
10 CC; *Live & Let Live* . . . . (Mercury)
Waterfall
Carly Simon; *Playing Possum* . . . . (Elektra)
Waterfall
Peter Frampton; *Somethin's Happening* . . . . (A&M)
Waterfall
Stone Roses; *The Stone Roses* . . . . (Silvertone)
Waterfalls
TLC; *1996 Grammy Nominees-C* . . . . (Columbia)
CrazySexyCool . . . . (LaFace)
Water's Edge
Seven Mary Three; *American Standard* . . . . (Mammoth)
Where The River Flows
Collective Soul; *Collective Soul* . . . . (Atlantic)
Whiskey River
Willie Nelson; *Greatest Hits (& Some That Will Be)* . . . . (Columbia)
Shotgun Willie . . . . (Atlantic)
ST/Honeysuckle Rose . . . . (Columbia)
Willie & Family Live . . . . (Columbia)
Wide River
Steve Miller Band; *Wide River* . . . . (Sailor)
Wild River
Golden Palominos; *Dead Horse* . . . . (Celluloid)
Our World Of Music . . . . (Celluloid)
Yellow River
Christie; *Rock Artifacts-From The Vaults-#1-C* . . . . (Columbia)
Super Hits Of The '70s-Have A Nice Day-#4-C . . . . (Rhino)
Yes The River Knows
Doors; *Waiting For The Sun* . . . . (Elektra)
You Belong To Me
Dean Martin; *Dean Martin's All Time Greatest Hits* . . . . (Curb)
Duprees; *13 Of The Best Doo Wop Love Songs-#2-C* . . . . (Original Sound)
Baby Boomer's Best-Mellow '60s-C . . . . (Priority)
Best Of The Duprees . . . . (Rhino)
Jo Stafford; *Billboard Pop Memories-1950-1954-C* . . . . (Rhino)
Jo Stafford's Greatest Hits . . . . (Curb)
Johnny Mathis; *In The Still Of The Night* . . . . (Columbia)
Patsy Cline; *Patsy Cline Sings Songs Of Love* . . . . (MCA Special Prod.)
Sentimentally Yours . . . . (MCA)
Vonda Shepard; *ST/Songs From ''Ally McBeal'' Featuring Vonda
Shepard* . . . . (550/Epic)

ROAD, Highway, Trail

See Also: **BUS, CARS (various), DIRECTIONS (various),
DISTANCE, HITCHHIKING, LEAVING, MOTORCYCLES, REBELS,
RETURNING, ROAD ACCIDENTS, SPORTS: CAR RACING, SIGNS,
STREETS: GENERAL, STREETS: SPECIFIC, TAXI,
TRAVELING, TRUCKS**

10 Miles To Go On A 9 Mile Road
Jim White; *No Such Place* . . . .(Luaka Bop)
Alabama Highway
Steve Young; *Honky-Tonk Man* . . . .(Rounder)
Alaska Highway
Neon Judgement; *The Insult* . . . . (Play It Again Sam)
All Roads Lead To Rome
Stranglers; *Feline* . . . . (Epic)
All Roads Lead To You
Steve Wariner; *14 #1 Country Hits-C* . . . . (RCA)
Best Of The '80s...So Far-C . . . . (RCA)
Steve Wariner . . . . (RCA)
Steve Wariner's Greatest Hits . . . . (RCA)
All Roads Lead To You
Chicago; *The Heart Of Chicago-1967-1988-#2* . . . . (Reprise)
Along The Navajo Trail
Riders In The Sky; *Riders Go Commercial* . . . . (MCA)
Roy Rogers; *Hooray For Hollywood* . . . . (RCA)
Along The Road
Dan Fogelberg; *Phoenix* . . . . (Full Moon)
Along The Santa Fe Trail
Glenn Miller; *Original Live Recordings* . . . . (Pair)
Sons Of The Pioneers; *Sunset On The Range* . . . . (Pair)
Are You On The Road To Lovin' Me Again
Debby Boone; *Best Of Debby Boone* . . . .(Curb)
Arizona Highway
Tim Rex & Oklahoma; *45-#103* . . . . (Dee-Jay)
Asphalt Cowboy
Sleepy LaBeef; *Bull's Night Out* . . . . (Sun)
At A Dixie Roadside Diner
Duke Ellington; *Duke Ellington & The Blanton-Webster Band* . . . . . .(Bluebird)
At The Beginning
Richard Marx & Donna Lewis; *ST/Anastasia-Music From The Motion
Picture* . . . . (Atlantic)
Backroads
Ricky Van Shelton; *Backroads* . . . .(Columbia)
Big Log
Robert Plant; *Principle Of Moments* . . . . (Es Paranza)
Black Bear Road
C.W. McCall; *C.W. McCall's Greatest Hits* . . . . (Polydor)
Black Denim Trousers & Motorcycle Boots
Cheers; *Monster Summer Hits-Drag City-C* . . . .(Capitol)
Born Ready
Jesse Hunter; *A Man Like Me* . . . . (BNA)
Born To Be Wild
Steppenwolf; *Billboard Top Rock 'N' Roll Hits-1968-C* . . . .(Rhino)
Live Steppenwolf . . . . (MCA)
Steppenwolf . . . . (MCA)
Steppenwolf-16 Greatest Hits . . . . (MCA)
Vintage Music-#9 & 10-C . . . . (MCA)
Brickyard Road
Johnny Van Zant; *Brickyard Road* . . . . (Atlantic)
Bright Side Of The Road
Van Morrison; *Best Of Van Morrison* . . . . (Polydor)
Into The Music . . . .(Warner Bros.)
Brooklyn Roads
Neil Diamond; *And The Singer Sings His Song* . . . . (MCA)
Neil Diamond-His 12 Greatest Hits . . . . (MCA)
Velvet Gloves & Spit . . . . (MCA Special Prod.)
Brownsville Road
Peter Lang; *Prime Cuts* . . . . (Waterhouse)
California Road
Mel Tillis; *45-#14175* . . . . (RCA)
Car Wheels On A Gravel Road
Lucinda Williams; *Car Wheels On A Gravel Road* . . . .(Mercury)
Church On Cumberland Road
Shenandoah; *Greatest Country Hits Of The '80s-1989-C* . . . .(Columbia)
Road Not Taken . . . .(Columbia)
Company's Comin'
Porter Wagoner; *Essential Porter Wagoner* . . . . (RCA)
Country Road
James Taylor; *James Taylor's Greatest Hits* . . . .(Warner Bros.)
Sweet Baby James . . . .(Warner Bros.)
Country Road
Dolly Parton; *Eagle When She Flies* . . . . (Columbia)
Crossroads
Cream; *Eric Clapton-Crossroads-C* . . . . (Polydor)
Strange Brew-Very Best Of Cream . . . . (Polydor)
Wheels Of Fire . . . . (Polydor)

Eric Clapton; *Eric Clapton & Jeff Beck* . . . . (Island)
 History Of Eric Clapton . . . . (Atco)
Crossroads
Jeff Beck & Seal; *The Secret Policeman's Other Ball/The Music* . . (Rhino)
Crossroads
Cowboy Junkies; *Whites Off Earth Now!!* . . . . (RCA)
Crossroads
Ry Cooder; *ST/Crossroads* . . . .(Warner Bros.)
Crossroads
Lynyrd Skynyrd; *One More From The Road* . . . .(MCA)
Darlington County
Bruce Springsteen; *Born In The U.S.A.* . . . . (Columbia)
Dead Man's Curve
Jan & Dean; *21 Legendary Superstars-C* . . . . (Original Sound)
 Best Of Jan & Dean . . . . (EMI)
 Dead Man's Curve . . . . (EMI)
Detour (Devil Took A)
Patti Page; *Patti Page-Golden Hits* . . . . (Mercury)
Dirt Road Blues
Bob Dylan; *Time Out Of Mind* . . . . (Columbia)
Dirt Road, The
Sawyer Brown; *Dirt Road* . . . . (Curb)
Divided Highway
Doobie Brothers; *Brotherhood* . . . . (Capitol)
Dixie Road
Lee Greenwood; *Country Classics-#3-1984-1985-C* . . . . . (Universal)
 Lee Greenwood's Greatest Hits . . . . (MCA)
 MCA #1 Hits Of The '80s-#2-C . . . .(MCA Special Prod.)
Down That Road Tonight
Nitty Gritty Dirt Band; *More Great Dirt-Best Of Nitty Gritty
 Dirt Band* . . . .(Warner Bros.)
 Workin' Band . . . .(Warner Bros.)
Down The Road
Kansas; *Song For America* . . . . (Kirshner)
Down The Road
Cadillacs; *Best Of The Cadillacs* . . . . (Rhino)
Down The Road
Stephen Stills; *Down The Road* . . . . (Atlantic)
Down The Road
Little Feat; *Feats Don't Fail Me Now* . . . .(Warner Bros.)
Down The Road
Steve Earle & The Dukes; *Guitar Town* . . . .(MCA)
Down The Road
Dan Fogelberg; *High Country Snows* . . . . (Full Moon)
Down The Road
Doucette; *Mama Let Him Play* . . . . (Mushroom)
Down The Road A Piece
Chuck Berry; *More Rock 'N' Roll Rarities-Golden Era* . . . . . (Chess)
 Rockin' At The Hops . . . . (Chess)
 The Chess Box-Chuck Berry . . . . (Chess)
 The Rolling Stones, Now! . . . . (Abkco)
Down The Road I Go
Albert King; *Lost Session* . . . .(Stax)
Down The Road I Go
Don Williams; *Don Williams-Vol. 2* . . . .(MCA)
Down The Road Tonight
Bruce Hornsby & The Range; *The Way It Is* . . . . (RCA)
Driven
Rush; *Test For Echo* . . . . (Atlantic)
Ease On Down The Road
Grateful Dead; *Go To Heaven* . . . . (Arista)
Ease On Down The Road
Original Cast; *ST/The Wiz* . . . .(MCA)
Eight Days On The Road
Foghat; *Best Of Foghat* . . . . (Rhino)
 Rock & Roll Outlaws . . . . (Rhino)
End Of Our Road
Gladys Knight & The Pips; *Compact Command Performances-Gladys Knight
 & The Pips* . . . . (Motown)
 Gladys Knight & The Pips-All The Great Hits . . . . (Motown)
 Gladys Knight & The Pips-Anthology . . . . (Motown)
Jerry Lee Lewis; *Jerry Lee Lewis-Original Golden Hits-#1* . . . (Sun)
 Jerry Lee Lewis-Original Golden Hits-#1 . . . . (Sun)
Marvin Gaye; *Marvin Gaye-Anthology* . . . . (Motown)
 Marvin Gaye-Super Hits . . . . (Motown)
 Musical Testament 1964-1984 . . . . (Motown)
End Of The Road
Boyz II Men; *Cooleyhighharmony* . . . . (Motown)
Endless Black Ribbon
Red Simpson; *Trucks,Trains & Airplanes-C* . . . . . . (International Mktg. Group)
Red Sovine/Willis Bros./Reno & Smiley; *Heavy Haulers* . . . .(Power Pak)
Endless Highway
Band; *To Kingdom Come-The Definitive Collection* . . . . (Capitol)
Bob Dylan And The Band; *Before The Flood* . . . . (Columbia)
Eternity Road
Moody Blues; *To Our Children's Children's Children* . . . .(Polydor)
Everyday Is A Winding Road
Sheryl Crow; *1998 Grammy Nominees-C* . . . .(MCA)

Sheryl Crow . . . . (A&M)
Expressway To Your Heart
Blues Brothers; *Best Of The Blues Brothers* . . . .(Atlantic)
Soul Survivors; *Dick Bartley's One-Hit Wonders Of The '60s-#2-C* . . . . (Rhino)
 Oldies But Goodies-#11-C . . . . (Original Sound)
 Super Oldies Of The '60s-#6-C . . . . (Audio Fidelity)
 When The Whistle Blows Anything Goes . . . . (Collectables)
Fast Lanes & Country Roads
Barbara Mandrell; *Country Classics-#2-Today's Country
 Classics-C* . . . . (Universal)
 Country Classics-#6-1985-1986-C . . . . (Universal)
 Get To The Heart . . . . (MCA)
Fort Worth Blues
Guy Clark; *Cold Dog Soup* . . . .(Sugar Hill)
Forty Miles Of Bad Road
Duane Eddy; *Compact Command Performances-Duane Eddy* . . . . . . (Motown)
 Duane Eddy-16 Greatest Hits . . . . (Jamie)
Roy Clark; *Hookin' It* . . . . (MCA)
 My Music & Me . . . . (MCA)
Freeway Of Love
Aretha Franklin; *Who's Zoomin' Who?* . . . . (Arista)
Further Up The Road
Band; *The Last Waltz* . . . . (Warner Bros.)
Eric Clapton; *Eric Clapton-Crossroads-C* . . . .(Polydor)
Gabriel's Mother's Hiway Ballad 16 Blues
Arlo Guthrie; *Best Of Arlo Guthrie* . . . . (Warner Bros.)
Galilee Road
Marcus Hummon; *Looking For The Child* . . . . (Velvet Armadillo)
Ghost Of Tom Joad
Bruce Springsteen; *The Ghost Of Tom Joad* . . . . (Columbia)
Girl On The Billboard
Boxcar Willie; *Truck Driving Favorites* . . . .(Madacy)
Del Reeves; *101 Greatest Country Hits-#10-C* . . . . (K-Tel)
 Truck Driver Boogie Big Rig Hits-1939-1969-C . . . . . . (Audium)
 Truckin' On-C . . . . (Hollywood)
Glory Road
Neil Diamond; *Love At The Greek* . . . . (Columbia)
 Sweet Caroline . . . . (MCA)
Go The Distance
Michael Bolton; *All That Matters* . . . . (Columbia)
Goin' Down The Road Feeling Bad
Delaney & Bonnie; *Best Of Delaney & Bonnie* . . . . (Rhino)
Doc Watson; *Elementary Doctor Watson* . . . .(Poppy)
 Essential Doc Watson . . . . (Vanguard)
Grateful Dead; *Grateful Dead (Skull & Roses)* . . . . (Warner Bros.)
 One From The Vault . . . .(Grateful Dead)
Going Down The China Road
Peter Lang; *Back To The Wall* . . . . (Waterhouse)
Golden Road
Grateful Dead; *Best Of The Grateful Dead-Skeletons From The
 Closet* . . . . (Warner Bros.)
 Grateful Dead (Skull & Roses) . . . . (Warner Bros.)
Good Day To Run
Darryl Worley; *Hard Rain Don't Last* . . . .(DreamWorks/SKG)
Goodbye Yellow Brick Road
Elton John; *Billboard Top Rock 'N' Roll Hits-1973-C* . . . . (Rhino)
 Elton John's Greatest Hits . . . .(Polydor)
 Goodbye Yellow Brick Road . . . .(Polydor)
Green Rocky Road
Dave Van Ronk; *In The Tradition* . . . .(Prestige)
Tim Hardin; *Memorial Album* . . . .(Polydor)
Ground Beneath Her Feet, The
U2; *ST/The Million Dollar Hotel* . . . .(Interscope)
Hard Nose The Highway
Van Morrison; *Hard Nose The Highway* . . . .(Polydor)
Hard Road
Deep Purple; *Purple Passages* . . . . (Warner Bros.)
 When We Rock We Rock & When We Roll We Roll . . . . (Warner Bros.)
Hard Road
Rod Stewart; *Best Of Rod Stewart-#2* . . . . (Mercury)
Hard Road
Joneses; *Hard* . . . .(Atlantic)
Hard Road
John Mayall's Bluesbreakers; *Hard Road* . . . .(London)
Hard Road
Black Sabbath; *Never Say Die* . . . . (Warner Bros.)
Hard Road
Triumph; *Progressions Of Power* . . . . (MCA)
Hard Road To Travel
Jimmy Cliff; *Wonderful World, Beautiful People* . . . . (A&M)
Heading Down The Highway
Judas Priest; *Point Of Entry* . . . . (Columbia)
High Road Easy
Sass Jordan; *Rats* . . . . (Impact)
Highway 28
Paul Butterfield's Better Days; *Better Days* . . . . (Rhino)
Highway 29
Bruce Springsteen; *The Ghost Of Tom Joad* . . . . (Columbia)

Highway 40 Blues
Ricky Skaggs; *19 Hot Country Requests-C* . . . . (Epic)
Greatest Country Hits Of The '80s-1983-C . . . . (Columbia)
Highways & Heartaches . . . . (Epic)
Live In London . . . . (Epic)
Highway 61 Revisited
Bob Dylan; *Highway 61 Revisited* . . . . (Columbia)
Real Live . . . . (Columbia)
Bob Dylan And The Band; *Before The Flood* . . . . (Columbia)
James Taylor; *Mud Slide Slim And The Blue Horizon* . . . . (Warner Bros.)
Johnny Winter; *Johnny Winter-Anthology* . . . . (Bac-Trac)
Second Winter . . . . (Columbia)
Highway Blues
Champion Jack Dupree; *Collectables Blues Collection-#2-C* . . . . . (Collectables)
Harlem Rock 'N' Blues-#3-C . . . . (Collectables)
Roy Harper; *Flashes From The Archives Of Oblivion* . . . . (Chrysalis)
Lifemask . . . . (Chrysalis)
Highway Child
Bob Seger System; *Mongrel* . . . . (Capitol)
Highway Chile
Jimi Hendrix Experience; *Are You Experienced?* . . . . (Reprise)
Highway Headin' South
Porter Wagoner; *Great Moments At The Grand Ole Opry-C* . . . . . (RCA)
Highway Lady
UFO; *No Heavy Petting* . . . . (Chrysalis)
Highway Man
Curtis Leach; *Truck Driver Boogie Big Rig Hits-1939-1969-C* . . . . (Audium)
Highway Of Sorrow
Bill Monroe; *Best Of Bill Monroe & His Blue Grass Boys* . . . . . . (MCA)
Highway One
B.W. Stevenson; *B.W. Stevenson* . . . . (RCA)
Highway Patrol
Reggie Knighton Band; *Reggie Knighton Band* . . . . (Columbia)
Highway Patrolman
Bruce Springsteen; *Nebraska* . . . . (Columbia)
Highway Robbery
Tanya Tucker; *Strong Enough To Bend* . . . . (Liberty)
Highway Song
Free; *Best Of Free* . . . . (A&M)
Highway . . . . (A&M)
Highway Song
James Taylor; *Mud Slide Slim And The Blue Horizon* . . . . (Warner Bros.)
Highway Song
Blackfoot; *Strikes* . . . . (Atco)
Highway Star
Deep Purple; *Deepest Purple/The Very Best Of Deep Purple* . . . . (Warner Bros.)
Machine Head . . . . (Warner Bros.)
Made In Japan . . . . (Warner Bros.)
When We Rock We Rock & When We Roll We Roll . . . . (Warner Bros.)
Highway To Hell
AC/DC; *AC/DC Live* . . . . (Atco)
Atlantic Rock & Roll-C . . . . (Atlantic)
Back In Black . . . . (Atco)
Highway To Hell . . . . (Atco)
Highwayman
Glen Campbell; *Highwayman* . . . . (Capitol)
Johnny Cash with Waylon Jennings, Kris Kristofferson, Willie Nelson; *The*
Man In Black-His Greatest Hits . . . . (Legacy)
Waylon Jennings, Willie Nelson, Johnny Cash, Kris Kristofferson; *Columbia*
Country Classics-#3-Americana-C . . . . (Columbia)
Johnny Cash-16 Biggest Hits-#2 . . . . (Legacy)
Willie Nelson; *Greatest Country Hits Of The '80s-1985-C* . . . . . . (Columbia)
Highways
Jeff Beck Group; *Jeff Beck Group* . . . . (Epic)
Hit The Road Jack
Ray Charles; *Ray Charles' Greatest Hits* . . . . (Rhino)
Ray Charles-Anthology . . . . (Rhino)
Ray Charles-His Greatest Hits-#2 . . . . (Dunhill Compact Classics)
Hot Dusty Roads
Buffalo Springfield; *Buffalo Springfield* . . . . (Atco)
How A Cowgirl Says Goodbye
Tracy Lawrence; *The Coast Is Clear* . . . . (Atlantic)
Hubbin' It
Asleep At The Wheel featuring Huey Lewis; *Tribute To The Music Of Bob*
Wills And The Texas Playboys-C . . . . (Liberty)
Human Highway
Neil Young; *Comes A Time* . . . . (Reprise)
I'd Rather Ride Around With You
Reba McEntire; *What If It's You* . . . . (MCA)
I'm A Cadillac/El Camino Dolo Roso
Mott The Hoople; *Mott* . . . . (Columbia)
I'm A Lonesome Fugitive
Merle Haggard; *Merle Haggard-16 Biggest Hits* . . . . (Legacy)
Merle Haggard & The Strangers; *Best Of Merle Haggard & The*
Strangers . . . . (Capitol)
Capitol Collectors Series-Merle Haggard & The Strangers . . . . (Capitol)
Songs I'll Always Sing . . . . (Capitol)
Roy Buchanan; *Roy Buchanan* . . . . (Polydor)

In The Highways
Sarah, Hannah And Leah Peasall; *ST/O Brother, Where Art Thou?* . . . . (Mercury)
Interstate Love Song
Stone Temple Pilots; *Purple*. . . . . (Atlantic)
I've Been Down That Road Before
Hank Williams; *Alone And Forsaken* . . . . (Mercury)
Beyond The Sunset . . . . (Polydor)
Jump Up Behind Me
James Taylor; *Hourglass* . . . . (Columbia)
Songs From The Heart-C . . . . (Columbia)
Keep It In The Middle Of The Road
Exile; *Country's Greatest Hits-#1-C* . . . . (Priority)
Still Standing . . . . (Arista)
Key To The Highway
David Bromberg; *You Should See The Rest Of The Band* . . . . . . (Fantasy)
Derek And The Dominos; *Eric Clapton-Crossroads-C* . . . . (Polydor)
Layla . . . . (Polydor)
John Hammond; *Best Of John Hammond* . . . . (Vanguard)
Little Walter; *Best Of Little Walter-#2* . . . . (Chess)
Blues-#2-C . . . . (Chess)
Sonny Terry & Brownie McGhee; *Great Blues Men-C* . . . . (Vanguard)
King Of The Road
R.E.M.; *Dead Letter Office* . . . . (I.R.S.)
Roger Miller; *Billboard Top Country Hits-1965-C* . . . . (Rhino)
Cruisin'-1965-C . . . . (Increase)
Roger Miller-Golden Hits . . . . (Smash)
King's Highway
Tom Petty And The Heartbreakers; *Into The Great Wide Open* . . . . . . (MCA)
Kings Road
Tom Petty And The Heartbreakers; *Hard Promises* . . . . (MCA)
L.A. Freeway
Guy Clark; *Old No. 1* . . . . (Sugar Hill)
Jerry Jeff Walker; *Best Of Jerry Jeff Walker* . . . . (MCA)
Great Gonzos . . . . (MCA)
Life In The Fast Lane
Eagles; *Eagles Live* . . . . (Asylum)
Hotel California . . . . (Asylum)
ST/FM . . . . (MCA)
Life Is A Highway
Tom Cochrane; *Mad Mad World* . . . . (Capitol)
Life On The Road
Kinks; *Sleepwalker* . . . . (Arista)
Life's Highway
Steve Wariner; *Country Classics-#2-Today's Country Classics-C* . . (Universal)
Grand Ole Opry-75 Years-#2-C . . . . (MCA)
Life's Highway . . . . (MCA)
Little Gasoline, A
Terri Clark; *Fearless* . . . . (Mercury)
Living On The Edge Of The World
Bruce Springsteen; *Tracks* . . . . (Columbia)
Living On The Highway
Freddie King; *Best Of Freddie King* . . . . (MCA)
Living On The Open Road
Delaney & Bonnie; *Duane Allman-An Anthology* . . . . (Capricorn)
Lonesome Road
4 Seasons; *25th Anniversary Collection* . . . . (Rhino)
Anita O'Day; *Rules Of The Road* . . . . (Pablo)
Frank Sinatra; *The Capitol Years* . . . . (Capitol)
Preservation Hall Jazz Band; *New Orleans-#4* . . . . (Columbia)
Tommy Dorsey; *Sentimental Memories* . . . . (Pair)
Lonesome Road
Van Morrison; *Too Long In Exile* . . . . (Polydor)
Lonesome Road Blues
Big Bill Broonzy; *Feelin' Low Down* . . . . (Crescendo)
Lonesome Road Blues . . . . (Crescendo)
Kentucky Colonels/Clarence White/Doc Watson; *Long Journey Home-*
Newport Folk Festival-1964 . . . . (Vanguard)
Muddy Waters; *Muddy Waters Sings Big Bill Broonzy* . . . . (Chess)
Lonesome Roads
Dwight Yoakam; *This Time* . . . . (Reprise)
Long And Winding Road, The
Beatles; *Beatles 1* . . . . (Capitol)
Beatles-20 Greatest Hits . . . . (Capitol)
Beatles-Love Songs . . . . (Capitol)
Let It Be . . . . (Capitol)
Reel Music . . . . (Capitol)
The Beatles/1967-1970 . . . . (Capitol)
Paul McCartney; *Tripping The Live Fantastic-Highlights!* . . . . . (Capitol)
Wings; *Wings Over America* . . . . (Capitol)
Long Dark Road
Hollies; *Best Of The Hollies-#2* . . . . (EMI)
Hollies-Epic Anthology From The Original Master Tapes . . . . . (Epic)
The Hollies' Greatest Hits . . . . (Epic)
Long Hard Road (Sharecropper's Dream)
Nitty Gritty Dirt Band; *Live Two Five* . . . . (Capitol)
Plain Dirt Fashion . . . . (Warner Bros.)
Twenty Years Of Dirt-Best Of The Nitty Gritty Dirt Band . . . . . (Warner Bros.)
Long Lonely Highway
Elvis Presley; *ST/Kissin' Cousins* . . . . (RCA)

Long Long Texas Road
Roy Drusky; *Roy Drusky-Golden Hits* . . . . (Plantation)
Long Promised Road
Beach Boys; *10 Years Of Harmony* . . . .(Caribou)
Surf's Up . . . .(Caribou)
Long Road To Texas
Bill Wray; *ST/Tilt* . . . .(MCA)
Long Road, The
Eddie Vedder; *America: A Tribute To Heroes-C* . . . . (Interscope)
Lord Of The Highway
Joe Ely; *Lord Of The Highway* . . . .(Hightone)
Lost Highway
Hank Williams With His Drifting Cowboys; *Hank Williams-24 Greatest Hits-#2* . . . . (Polydor)
Hank Williams-40 Greatest Hits . . . . (Polydor)
Nitty Gritty Dirt Band; *Will The Circle Be Unbroken* . . . .(EMI)
Louisiana Road Song
Tish Hinojosa; *Culture Swing* . . . . (Rounder)
Mama Knows The Highway
Hal Ketchum; *Sure Love* . . . . (Curb)
Many A Long & Lonesome Highway
Rodney Crowell; *Keys To The Highway* . . . . (Columbia)
Taste Of Texas-Songs 'Bout Texas By Texans-C . . . . (Columbia)
Meet In The Middle
Diamond Rio; *Diamond Rio* . . . . (Arista)
Diamond Rio's Greatest Hits . . . . (Arista)
Middle Of The Road
Pretenders; *Greenpeace/Rainbow Warriors-C* . . . . (Geffen)
Learning To Crawl . . . . (Sire)
Pretenders-The Singles . . . . (Sire)
Miles And Miles Of Texas
Asleep At The Wheel; *Texas State Of Mind-C* . . . . (Capitol)
Very Best Of Asleep At The Wheel Since 1970 . . . . (Relentless/Macady)
Moonlight Mile
Rolling Stones; *Sticky Fingers* . . . . (Virgin)
Moonshadow Road
T. Graham Brown; *Best Of T. Graham Brown* . . . . (Liberty)
More Than One Way Home
Keb' Mo'; *Just Like You* . . . . (Okeh)
Navajo Trail
Michael Nesmith; *From A Radio Engine To The Photon Wing* . . . . . (Pacific Arts)
New Cut Road
Bobby Bare; *Bare Tracks* . . . . (Koch International)
New Jersey Roadbase
Johnboy; *Pistolswing* . . . . (Trance Syndicate)
New Jersey Turnpike
Laurie Anderson; *United States Live* . . . .(Warner Bros.)
New Lee Highway Blues
David Bromberg; *Out Of The Blues-Best Of David Bromberg* . . . . . (Columbia)
Wanted Dead Or Alive . . . . (Columbia)
Nothin' But The Taillights
Clint Black; *Nothin' But The Taillights* . . . . (RCA)
Nothin' But The Wheel
Patty Loveless; *Only What I Feel* . . . .(Epic)
Patty Loveless-Classics . . . .(Epic)
Old Dirt Road
John Lennon; *Lennon* . . . . (Capitol)
Menlove Ave. . . . . (Capitol)
Walls And Bridges . . . . (Capitol)
Old Man Down The Road
John Fogerty; *Centerfield* . . . .(Warner Bros.)
On Down The Line
Patty Loveless; *On Down The Line* . . . .(MCA)
Patty Loveless' Greatest Hits . . . .(MCA)
On The Road
Lee Roy Parnell; *On The Road* . . . . (Arista)
On The Road Again
Willie Nelson; *Greatest Country Hits Of The '80s-1980-C* . . . . (Columbia)
Greatest Hits (& Some That Will Be) . . . . (Columbia)
Hot Country Rock-#1-C . . . .(Epic)
ST/Forrest Gump . . . . (Epic/Sony Music Soundtrax)
ST/Honeysuckle Rose . . . . (Columbia)
On The Road Again
Bob Dylan; *Bringing It All Back Home* . . . . (Columbia)
On The Road Again
Tom Rush; *Classic Rush* . . . . (Elektra)
Tom Rush . . . . (Elektra)
On The Road Again
Aerosmith; *Pandora's Box* . . . . (Columbia)
On The Road Again
Grateful Dead; *Reckoning* . . . . (Arista)
So Many Roads (1965-1995) . . . . (Arista)
On The Road To Calais
Al Jolson; *Music From The New York Stage (1890-1920)-#4-1917-1920-C* . . . . (Pearl)
On The Road To Find Out
Cat Stevens; *Cat Stevens-Classics-#24* . . . . (A&M)
Footsteps In The Dark-Greatest Hits-#2 . . . . (A&M)

Tea For The Tillerman . . . . (A&M)
On The Road To Mandalay
Count Basie; *Compact Jazz-The Standards* . . . . (Verve)
Frank Sinatra; *Come Fly With Me* . . . . (Capitol)
Only One Road
Celine Dion; *The Colour Of My Love* . . . .(550 Music)
Pacific Coast Highway
Mamas & The Papas; *People Like Us* . . . . (MCA Special Prod.)
Pacific Coast Highway
Bryan Savage; *Bryan Savage* . . . . (Elation)
Passing Lane
Charlie Daniels Band; *Million Mile Reflections* . . . . (Epic)
Pathway To Glory
Loggins & Messina; *Full Sail* . . . . (Columbia)
Patty On The Turnpike
Don Stover; *Things In Life* . . . . (Rounder)
Pirates Of Stone Canyon Road
John Stewart; *Last Campaign* . . . .(Laserlight)
Phoenix Concerts . . . . (One Way)
Prisoner Of The Highway
Ronnie Milsap; *One More Try For Love* . . . . (RCA)
Ronnie Milsap's Greatest Hits-#3 . . . . (RCA)
Queen Of The Highway
Doors; *Morrison Hotel/Hard Rock Cafe* . . . . (Elektra)
Reservation Road
Bill Miller; *The Red Road* . . . .(Warner Western)
Rhythm Of The Road
George Strait; *George Strait-Number 7.* . . . . (MCA)
Ribbon Of Darkness
Marty Robbins; *Marty Robbins' All-Time Greatest Hits* . . . . (Columbia)
Marty Robbins' Greatest Hits. . . . . (Columbia)
Trucker's Jukebox-#2-C. . . . . (Legacy)
River And The Highway
Pam Tillis; *All Of This Love* . . . . (Arista)
Pam Tillis' Greatest Hits . . . . (Arista)
River Road
Crystal Gayle; *Favorites-Crystal Gayle* . . . . (Liberty)
We Must Believe In Magic . . . .(United Artists)
Road And The Sky
Jackson Browne; *Late For The Sky* . . . . (Asylum)
Road Angel
Doobie Brothers; *What Were Once Vices Are Now Habits* . . . . . . (Warner Bros.)
Road Beneath My Wheels
Dan Fogelberg; *Live-Greetings From The West* . . . .(Full Moon)
Road Fever
Foghat; *Foghat* . . . . (Rhino)
Foghat-Live . . . . (Rhino)
Road Fever
Blackfoot; *Strikes* . . . . (Atco)
Road Goes On Forever, The
Joe Ely; *Love & Danger* . . . . (MCA)
Road Less Traveled, The
George Strait; *The Road Less Traveled* . . . . (MCA)
Road Less Travelled
Preston Reed; *Road Less Travelled* . . . . (Flying Fish)
Road Movie To Berlin
They Might Be Giants; *Flood* . . . . (Elektra)
Road Mutants
Death Angel; *Frolic Through The Park* . . . . (Enigma Capitol)
Speed Metal-C . . . . (Priority)
Road Of Broken Hearted Men
Bobby Bland; *Introspective Of The Early Years* . . . . (MCA)
Touch Of The Blues . . . . (MCA)
Road Rats
Alice Cooper; *Lace And Whiskey* . . . . (Warner Bros.)
Road Runner
Pretty Things; *History Of British Rock-#5-C* . . . . (Rhino)
Road Runner (I'm A)
Fleetwood Mac; *Penguin* . . . . (Reprise)
Humble Pie; *Eat It* . . . . (A&M)
Smokin'. . . . . (A&M)
Junior Walker & The All Stars; *Junior Walker & The All Stars' Greatest Hits* . . . . (Motown)
Junior Walker & The All Stars-Anthology . . . . (Motown)
Motown Superstar Series-#5-Junior Walker & The All Stars . . . . (Motown)
Shotgun. . . . . (Motown)
Road To Bangor
Northeast Winds; *Songs Of Ireland & The Sea* . . . . (Folk Era)
Road To Columbus
Sally Van Meter; *All In Good Time* . . . .(Sugar Hill)
Road To Dead
Paula Cole; *This Fire* . . . . (Imago)
Road To Hong Kong
Billy May; *I Believe In You* . . . . (Bainbridge)
Road To Jakarta
Steve Hunter; *The Deacon* . . . . (I.R.S./No Speak)
Road To My Riches
Vanilla Ice; *Extremely Live* . . . . (SBK)

Road To Nowhere
Ozzy Osbourne; *No More Tears* . . . . (Epic Portrait Assoc.)
Road To Poland
Mike Figgis; *ST/Stormy Monday* . . . .(Virgin Movie Music)
Road To Rome
PFS; *279* . . . . (Cuneiform)
Road To Santa Rosa
Frank Chacksfield; *Mirrors* . . . . (Starborn)
Road To Spencer
Ricky Skaggs and Kentucky Thunder; *History Of The Future* . . (Skaggs Family)
Road To Utopia
Utopia; *Adventures In Utopia* . . . . (Rhino)
Road To Your Heart
Barbara Mandrell; *Key's In The Mailbox* . . . . (Capitol)
Road To Your Heart
Highway 101; *101 2* . . . . (Warner Bros.)
Road You Didn't Take
Original Broadway Cast; *Follies* . . . . (Capitol)
Original Cast; *ST/Follies-In Concert* . . . . (RCA Victor)
Road You Leave Behind
David Lee Murphy; *Gettin' Out The Good Stuff* . . . . (MCA)
Road, The
Kinks; *The Road* . . . . (MCA)
Road, The
Jackson Browne; *Running On Empty* . . . . (Asylum)
Road, The
Chicago; *Chicago II* . . . . (Chicago)
Road, The
Doors; *Doors 13* . . . . (Elektra)
Road, The
Everything But The Girl; *Language Of Life* . . . . (Atlantic)
Roadhouse Blues
Doors; *Best Of The Doors* . . . . (Elektra)
Doors 13 . . . . (Elektra)
Doors' Greatest Hits . . . . (Elektra)
Doors-Classics . . . . (Elektra)
Morrison Hotel/Hard Rock Cafe . . . . (Elektra)
ST/The Doors . . . . (Elektra)
Roadrunner
Greg Kihn Band; *With The Naked Eye* . . . . (Beserkley)
Joan Jett; *The Hit List* . . . . (Epic)
Joan Jett & The Blackhearts; *Good Music* . . . . (Epic Portrait Assoc.)
Jonathan Richman & The Modern Lovers; *Beserkley Years-Best Of.* . . . . (Rhino)
Modern Lovers; *Modern Lovers* . . . . (Rhino)
Roads Girdle The Globe
XTC; *Drums & Wires* . . . . (Geffen)
Road's My Middle Name
Bonnie Raitt; *Nick Of Time* . . . . (Capitol)
Roads Of Life
Bobby Womack; *Roads Of Life* . . . . (Arista)
Roads To Freedom
Robin Trower; *Victims Of The Fury* . . . . (Chrysalis)
Roads To Madness
Queensryche; *The Warning* . . . . (EMI)
Roads To Moscow
Al Stewart; *Past, Present & Future* . . . . (Rhino)
Rockin' Down The Highway
Doobie Brothers; *Best Of The Doobies* . . . . (Warner Bros.)
Toulouse Street . . . . (Warner Bros.)
Rocky Road Blues
Bill Monroe & His Blue Grass Boys; *All Time Legends Of Country Music-C* . . . . (Legacy)
Rocky Road To Dublin
Dubliners; *Dublin Songs-C* . . . . (AJK Music)
Skip Gorman; *A Cowboy's Wild Song To His Herd* . . . . (Rounder)
Rocky Road To Kansas
Tony Ellis; *Dixie Banner* . . . . (Flying Fish)
Rodeo Road
Roy Rogers & Willie Nelson; *Roy Rogers Tribute-C* . . . . (RCA)
Roll On Down The Highway
Bachman-Turner Overdrive; *Best Of B.T.O.-So Far* . . . . (Mercury)
Not Fragile . . . . (Mercury)
Rock Of The '70s-C . . . . (MCA Special Prod.)
Route 66
Asleep At The Wheel; *Served Live* . . . . (Capitol)
Very Best Of Asleep At The Wheel Since 1970 . . . .(Relentless/Madacy)
Wheelin' & Dealin' . . . . (Capitol)
Depeche Mode; *ST/Earth Girls Are Easy* . . . . (Sire)
George Maharis; *45-#15-2227.* . . . . (Capitol)
Manhattan Transfer; *Bop doo-wopp* . . . . (Atlantic)
Nat "King" Cole; *Capitol Collectors Series-Nat "King" Cole* . . . . (Capitol)
The Nat "King" Cole Story . . . . (Capitol)
Natalie Cole; *Unforgettable With Love* . . . . (Elektra)
Rolling Stones; *December's Children (and everybody's)* . . . . (Abkco)
England's Newest Hit Makers/The Rolling Stones . . . . (Abkco)
Serengeti Trail
Starr Parodi; *Change* . . . . (Gift Horse)

Seven Bridges Road
Eagles; *Eagles Greatest Hits, Volume 2* . . . . (Asylum)
Eagles Live . . . . (Asylum)
Steve Young; *Seven Bridges Road* . . . . (Rounder)
Shoulder Of The Road
Johnny & The Distractions; *Let It Rock* . . . . (A&M)
My Desire . . . . (Burnside)
Show Me The Road
Bill Staines; *Going To The West* . . . . (Red House)
Sittin' On Go
Bryan White; *Between Now And Forever* . . . . (Asylum)
Six Days On The Road
Boxcar Willie; *Truck Driving Favorites* . . . . (Madacy)
Dave Dudley; *Billboard Top Country Hits-1963-C* . . . .(Rhino)
Country Music Classics-#2-1960-1965-C . . . . (K-Tel)
Legends Of Country Guitar-#2-C . . . . (Rhino)
Truck Driver Boogie Big Rig Hits-1939-1969-C . . . . (Audium)
Flying Burrito Brothers; *Cabin Fever* . . . . (Relix)
Farther Along-Best Of The Flying Burrito Brothers . . . . . . (A&M)
Last Of The Red Hot Burritos . . . . (A&M)
Sawyer Brown; *Six Days On The Road* . . . .(Curb)
Taj Mahal; *Giant Step/De Ole Folks At Home* . . . .(Columbia)
Legends Of Rock Guitar-'60s-#2-C . . . . (Rhino)
Somewhere Down The Road
Barry Manilow; *If I Should Love Again* . . . .(Arista)
Somewhere Down The Road
Kathy Mattea; *Kathy Mattea* . . . .(Mercury)
State Trooper
Bruce Springsteen; *Nebraska* . . . .(Columbia)
The Sopranos-Music From The HBO Original Series . . . . (Sony Music Soundtrax)
Stones In The Road
Mary Chapin Carpenter; *Stones In The Road* . . . .(Columbia)
Take It To The Limit
Eagles; *Eagles Live* . . . . (Asylum)
Eagles/Their Greatest Hits 1971-1975 . . . . (Asylum)
One Of These Nights . . . . (Asylum)
Take Me Home, Country Roads
John Denver; *Evening With John Denver* . . . . (RCA)
John Denver's Greatest Hits . . . . (RCA)
Poems, Prayers & Promises . . . . (RCA)
Take Me Home, Country Roads & Other Hits . . . . (RCA)
Toots & The Maytals; *Brand New Second-Hand* . . . . (Rykodisc)
Take The Highway
Marshall Tucker Band; *Best Of The Marshall Tucker Band-The Capricorn Years* . . . . (Era)
Marshall Tucker Band . . . . (AJK Music)
Where We All Belong . . . . (AJK Music)
Telephone Road
Steve Earle; *Alt. Country-C* . . . .(Simitar)
El Corazon . . . . (E Squared)
Tennessee Road
Anne Hills; *Woman Of A Calm Heart* . . . . (Flying Fish)
That Road Still Looks Real Good To Me
Lacy J. Dalton; *Lacy J.* . . . .(Capitol)
Theme From "Highway Patrol"
Original Soundtrack; *Television's Greatest Hits-#4-Black & White Classics-C* . . . .(TVT)
Theme From "Highway To Heaven"
Original Soundtrack; *Television's Greatest Hits-#6-Remote Control-C* . . .(TVT)
Theme From "Road Runner"
Original Soundtrack; *Television's Greatest Hits-#2-C* . . . . (TVT)
Theme From "Route 66"
Nelson Riddle & His Orchestra; *Beat Generation* . . . .(Rhino)
Television's Greatest Hits-#2-C . . . . (TVT)
Original Soundtrack; *CBS: The First 50 Years* . . . . (TVT)
There's A Rugged Road
Shawn Colvin; *Cover Girl* . . . .(Columbia)
Thunder Road
Bruce Springsteen; *Born To Run* . . . .(Columbia)
Bruce Springsteen's Greatest Hits . . . .(Columbia)
Bruce Springsteen & The E Street Band; *Bruce Springsteen & The E Street Band Live/1975-85* . . . .(Legacy)
Tie Dye On The Highway
Robert Plant; *Manic Nirvana* . . . . (Es Paranza)
Tobacco Road
Dan Seals; *Won't Be Blue Anymore* . . . . (EMI)
David Lee Roth; *Eat 'Em & Smile* . . . . (Warner Bros.)
Edgar Winter; *Edgar Winter Group-Collection* . . . .(Rhino)
Entrance . . . .(Epic)
Edgar Winter's White Trash; *Roadwork* . . . . (Epic)
Eric Burdon; *Eric Burdon Sings The Animals' Greatest Hits* . . . . . (Rhino)
Jefferson Airplane; *Loves You* . . . . (RCA)
Takes Off . . . . (RCA)
John D. Loudermilk; *Rockabilly Stars-#3-C* . . . . (Epic)
Junior Wells; *Best Of The Chicago Blues-C* . . . . (Vanguard)
Comin' At You . . . . (Vanguard)
Lou Rawls; *Best From Lou Rawls* . . . .(Capitol)
Legendary Lou Rawls . . . . (Blue Note)

Lou Rawls' Greatest Hits . . . . (Curb)
Lou Rawls-Live . . . . (Capitol)
Nashville Teens; *London Collector-Rock Invasion-C* . . . . (London)
Rare Earth; *Get Ready* . . . . (Motown)
Steve Young; *Redneck Mothers-C* . . . . (RCA)
Solo/Live . . . . (Watermelon)

Tokyo Road
Bon Jovi; *7800 Degrees Fahrenheit* . . . . (Mercury)

Tombstone Every Mile
Dave Dudley; *Interstate Gold* . . . . (Sun)
Dick Curless; *Truck Driver Boogie Big Rig Hits-1939-1969-C* . . . . (Audium)

Trail Of Freedom
Bill Miller; *The Red Road* . . . . (Warner Western)

Trail To Mexico
Peter La Farge; *Cowboy Songs On Folkways-C* . . . . (Smithsonian Folkways)

True Love Travels On A Gravel Road
Elvis Presley; *From Elvis In Memphis* . . . . (RCA)
Memphis Record . . . . (RCA)
Percy Sledge; *It Tears Me Up-Best Of Percy Sledge* . . . . (Rhino)

Turn The Page
Metallica; *Garage Inc.* . . . . (Elektra)

Twenty-Five Miles
Edwin Starr; *Motown Superstar Series-#3-Edwin Starr* . . . . (Motown)
Michael Jackson; *Original Soul Of Michael Jackson* . . . . (Motown)

Two For The Road
Henry Mancini; *Henry Mancini-Legendary Performer* . . . . (RCA)
Peter Gunn . . . . (RCA)
James Galway; *James Galway's Greatest Hits-#2* . . . . (RCA)

Two Lane Highway
Pure Prairie League; *Two Lane Highway* . . . . (RCA)

Up Around The Bend
Creedence Clearwater Revival; *1970* . . . . (Fantasy)
Cosmo's Factory . . . . (Fantasy)
Creedence Clearwater Revival-Chronicle . . . . (Fantasy)
More Creedence Gold . . . . (Fantasy)
Hanoi Rocks; *Two Steps From The Move* . . . . (Epic)

Valley Road
Bruce Hornsby & The Nitty Gritty Dirt Band; *Will The Circle Be
Unbroken-#2-C* . . . . (Uni)
Bruce Hornsby & The Range; *Scenes From The Southside* . . . . (RCA)

Ventura Highway
America; *'70s Greatest Rock Hits-#6-FM Hits-C* . . . . (Priority)
America Live . . . . (Warner Bros.)
History-Greatest Hits . . . . (Warner Bros.)
Homecoming . . . . (Warner Bros.)

Walkin' Down The Road
Ozark Mountain Daredevils; *Best Of The Ozark Mountain Daredevils* . . (A&M)
It'll Shine When It Shines . . . . (A&M)
It's Alive . . . . (A&M)

West Texas Highway & Me
Gary Morris; *Faded Blue* . . . . (Warner Bros.)

Western Highway
Maura O'Connell; *Helpless Heart* . . . . (Warner Bros.)

What About Now
Lonestar; *Lonely Grill* . . . . (BNA)

Where The Blacktop Ends
keith urban; *keith urban* . . . . (Capitol)

Where Your Road Leads
Trisha Yearwood & Garth Brooks; *Where Your Road Leads* . . . . (MCA)

White Line Fever
Flying Burrito Brothers; *Close Encounters To The West Coast* . . . . . . (Relix)
Merle Haggard; *More Of The Best* . . . . (Rhino)
Merle Haggard & The Strangers; *Okie From Muskogee* . . . . (Capitol)

Why Don't We Do It In The Road
Beatles; *Beatles-Box Set* . . . . (Capitol)
The Beatles (White Album) . . . . (Capitol)

Wicked Path
Bill Monroe & His Blue Grass Boys; *Essential Bill Monroe-1945-
1949* . . . . (Columbia)
Jim & Jesse; *Music Among Friends* . . . . (Rounder)
New Grass Revival; *Commonwealth* . . . . (Flying Fish)

Working On The Highway
Bruce Springsteen; *Born In The U.S.A.* . . . . (Columbia)
Bruce Springsteen & The E Street Band; *Bruce Springsteen & The E Street
Band Live/1975-85* . . . . (Legacy)

Working On The Road
Ten Years After; *Cricklewood Green* . . . . (Chrysalis)

You Don't Know How It Feels
Tom Petty; *Wildflowers* . . . . (Warner Bros.)

ROAD ACCIDENTS, Wrecks

*See Also: CARS (various), DANGER & DISASTER, DEATH,
MOTORCYCLES, ROAD, TRUCKS*

Accidents
Thunderclap Newman; *Hollywood Dream* . . . . (MCA)

Always Crashing In The Same Car
David Bowie; *Low* . . . . (Rykodisc)

Auto Wreck
All; *Allroy Sez* . . . . (Cruz)

Barbie & Ken Ferrari
John Hiatt; *Perfectly Good Guitar* . . . . (A&M)

Big Joe & Phantom 309
Tom Waits; *Double Live* . . . . (Asylum)
Nighthawks At The Diner . . . . (Asylum)

Black Denim Trousers & Motorcycle Boots
Cheers; *Monster Summer Hits-Drag City-C* . . . . (Capitol)

Carroll County Accident
Porter Wagoner; *Essential Porter Wagoner* . . . . (RCA)
Porter Wagoner-Greatest Songs . . . . (Curb)

Crawling From The Wreckage
Dave Edmunds; *Best Of Dave Edmunds* . . . . (Swan Song)
Repeat When Necessary . . . . (Swan Song)
Rockpile; *Kampuchea-C* . . . . (Atlantic)

Dead Man's Curve
Jan & Dean; *21 Legendary Superstars-C* . . . . (Original Sound)
Best Of Jan & Dean . . . . (EMI)
Dead Man's Curve . . . . (EMI)

Don't Crash The Car Tonight
Mary's Danish; *Experience (Live + Foxey Lady)* . . . . (Chameleon)
There Goes The Wondertruck . . . . (Chameleon)

Drunken Driver
Ricky Skaggs and Kentucky Thunder; *Bluegrass Rules!* . . . . (Rounder)

Grandma Got Run Over By A Reindeer
Elmo & Patsy; *Billboard's Greatest Christmas Hits-C* . . . . (Rhino)
*Dr. Demento Presents The Greatest Novelty Records-#6-
Christmas-C* . . . . (Rhino)
Dr. Demento Presents The Greatest Novelty Records-C . . . . (Rhino)
Grandma Got Run Over By A Reindeer . . . . (Epic)
Greatest Children's Christmas Hits-C . . . . (Columbia)
Now That's What I Call Christmas!-C . . . . (UTV)

Last Kiss
J. Frank Wilson and The Cavaliers; *Billboard Top Rock 'N' Roll Hits-
1964-C* . . . . (Rhino)
Collectables Presents The History Of Rock-#2-C . . . . (Collectables)
Oldies But Goodies-#9-C . . . . (Original Sound)
Teenage Tragedies-C . . . . (Rhino)
Pearl Jam; *No Boundaries-Benefit For The Kosovar Refugees-C* . . . . (Epic)

Leader Of The Pack
Bette Midler; *Divine Miss M* . . . . (Atlantic)
ST/Divine Madness . . . . (Atlantic)
Original Cast; *Leader Of The Pack* . . . . (Elektra)
Shangri-Las; *21 Number One Hits-C* . . . . (Original Sound)
Billboard Top Rock 'N' Roll Hits-1964-C . . . . (Rhino)
Girl Groups-Story Of A Sound-C . . . . (Rhino)
Golden Hits Of The Shangri-Las . . . . (Mercury)
Oldies But Goodies-#15-C . . . . (Original Sound)
Radio Active Hits-#2-C . . . . (Accord)
Remember The Shangri-Las At Their Best . . . . (Collectables)

Mach 5
Presidents Of The United States Of America; *Presidents Of The United States
Of America II* . . . . (Columbia)

Radar Love
Golden Earring; *'70s Greatest Rock Hits-#1-Hard N' Heavy-C* . . . . . (Priority)
Classic Rock-#1-C . . . . (MCA)
Golden Earring-Live . . . . (MCA)
Moontan . . . . (MCA)
Super Hits Of The '70s-Have A Nice Day-#13-C . . . . (Rhino)

Riding With Private Malone
David Ball; *Amigo* . . . . (Razor & Tie)

Rockaway The Days
Bruce Springsteen; *Tracks* . . . . (Columbia)

Teen Angel
Dion And The Belmonts; *Everything You Always Wanted* . . . . (Laurie)
Rock & Roll U.S.A.-21 Rock & Roll Favorites-#2-C . . . . (Laurie)
Mark Dinning; *Golden Years-1959-C* . . . . (Dominion Entert.)
Oldies But Goodies-#7-C . . . . (Original Sound)
ST/American Graffiti . . . . (MCA)
Teenage Tragedies-C . . . . (Rhino)

Teenage Queen
Rick Derringer; *All American Boy* . . . . (Blue Sky)

Tell Laura I Love Her
Ray Peterson; *Nipper's Greatest Hits Of The '60s-#1-C* . . . . (RCA)
Teenage Tragedies-C . . . . (Rhino)

Tonight Is The Night I Fell Asleep At The Wheel
Barenaked Ladies; *Maroon* . . . . (Reprise)

Transfusion
Nervous Norvus; *Dr. Demento Presents The Greatest Novelty Records-#2-
1950s-C* . . . . (Rhino)
Dr. Demento 20th Anniversary Collection-C . . . . (Rhino)
Vintage Music-#3-C . . . . (MCA)
Wacky Weirdos-C . . . . (K-Tel)

Wreck On The Highway
Nitty Gritty Dirt Band; *Will The Circle Be Unbroken* . . . . (EMI)
Roy Acuff; *Best Of Roy Acuff* . . . . (Liberty)

Essential Roy Acuff-1936-1949 . . . . (Legacy)
Roy Acuff's Greatest Hits . . . . (Columbia)
Wreck On The Highway
Bruce Springsteen; The River . . . . (Columbia)
You Wreck Me
Tom Petty; Wildflowers . . . . (Warner Bros.)

ROCK & ROCKING, Rock & Roll, Rock 'n' Roll

See Also: **BABY, DANCE, ELVIS, FUN, MOUNTAINS, MUSIC, MUSICAL INSTRUMENTS (various), PARTY, RADIO, RECORD BUSINESS, RHYTHM, SEX, SHOW BIZ, STONES**

(We're Gonna) Rock Around The Clock
Bill Haley & His Comets; Bill Haley & His Comets' Greatest Hits . . . . . . (MCA)
Bill Haley & His Comets' Greatest Hits . . . . (Everest)
Bill Haley & His Comets-Golden Hits . . . . (MCA)
Billboard Top Rock 'N' Roll Hits-1955-C . . . . (Rhino)
ST/American Graffiti . . . . (MCA)
(You Can Still) Rock In America
Night Ranger; Midnight Madness . . . . (MCA)
And The Cradle Will Rock
Van Halen; Women & Children First . . . . (Warner Bros.)
Anything That's Rock 'N' Roll
Tom Petty And The Heartbreakers; ST/Voices . . . . (Planet)
Tom Petty & The Heartbreakers . . . . (Gone Gator)
Are You Ready To Rock
Michael Schenker Group; One Night At Budokan . . . . (Chrysalis)
Rock Will Never Die . . . . (Chrysalis)
Around & Around
38 Special; 38 Special . . . . (A&M)
Animals; Best Of The Animals . . . . (Abkco)
Chuck Berry; Berry Is On Top . . . . (Chess)
ST/Hail! Hail! Rock 'N' Roll . . . . (MCA)
The Chess Box-Chuck Berry . . . . (Chess)
Grateful Dead; One From The Vault . . . . (Grateful Dead)
Steal Your Face . . . . (Grateful Dead)
Rolling Stones; 12 X 5 . . . . (Abkco)
Love You Live . . . . (Virgin)
As Long As I'm Rockin' With You
John Conlee; Best Of John Conlee . . . . (Curb)
In My Eyes . . . . (MCA)
John Conlee-20 Greatest Hits . . . . (MCA)
John Conlee-Legends . . . . (MCA)
Baby Likes To Rock It
Tractors; Tractors . . . . (Arista)
Baby Won't You Let Me Rock & Roll You
Ten Years After; A Space In Time . . . . (Columbia)
Baby's A Rock 'N' Roller
Tom Petty And The Heartbreakers; You're Gonna Get It! . . . . . . (Gone Gator)
Bad Boy
Beatles; Beatles VI. . . . . (Capitol)
Beatles-Box Set . . . . (Capitol)
Past Masters-Volume One . . . . (Parlophone)
Rock 'N' Roll Music . . . . (Capitol)
Bad Boy
Ringo Starr; Bad Boy . . . . (Epic)
Barbara Ann
Beach Boys; Beach Boys '69 (The Beach Boys Live In London) . . . . . . (Capitol)
Beach Boys-Gift Set . . . . (Capitol)
Best Of The Beach Boys-#2 . . . . (Capitol)
Frat Rock!-C . . . . (Rhino)
Spirit Of America . . . . (Capitol)
Regents; Cruisin'-1961-C . . . . (Increase)
Original Rock 'N' Roll Hits Of The '60s-C . . . . (Roulette)
ST/American Graffiti . . . . (MCA)
Who; Who's Missing . . . . (MCA)
Black Country Rock
David Bowie; Man Who Sold The World . . . . (Rykodisc)
Sound + Vision . . . . (Rykodisc)
Blue Rock Montana/Red Headed Stranger
Willie Nelson; Red Headed Stranger . . . . (Columbia)
Born To Rock
Quiet Riot; Condition Critical . . . . (Epic Portrait Assoc.)
Call It Rock N' Roll
Great White; Hooked . . . . (Capitol)
Candy Store Rock
Led Zeppelin; Led Zeppelin-Box Set . . . . (Atlantic)
Presence . . . . (Swan Song)
Can't Stop Rockin'
ZZ Top; Afterburner . . . . (Warner Bros.)
Champagne & Rock & Roll
Climax Blues Band; Shine On . . . . (Sire)
Cherub Rock
Smashing Pumpkins; Siamese Dream . . . . (Virgin)
Cities On Flame With Rock & Roll
Blue Oyster Cult; Blue Oyster Cult . . . . (Columbia)

Career Of Evil . . . . (Columbia)
Extraterrestrial Live . . . . (Columbia)
On Your Feet Or On Your Knees . . . . (Columbia)
Clash City Rockers
Clash; The Clash . . . . (Epic)
The Story Of The Clash, Volume 1 . . . . (Epic)
Cleveland Rocks
Ian Hunter; ST/Light Of Day . . . . (CBS Associated)
You're Never Alone With A Schizophrenic . . . . (Razor & Tie)
Cold Rock A Party
MC Lyte; Bad As I Wanna B . . . . (East West)
Crocodile Rock
Elton John; Billboard Top Rock 'N' Roll Hits-1973-C . . . . (Rhino)
Don't Shoot Me I'm Only The Piano Player . . . . (Polydor)
Elton John's Greatest Hits . . . . (Polydor)
Here And There . . . . (Rocket)
Detroit Rock City
Kiss; Alive II. . . . . (Casablanca)
Destroyer. . . . . (Casablanca)
Double Platinum . . . . (Mercury)
Smashes, Thrashes & Hits. (Mercury)
Dixieland Rock
Elvis Presley; ST/King Creole . . . . (RCA)
The Other Sides-Worldwide Gold Award Hits, Vol. 2 . . . . . . (RCA)
Dizzy Miss Lizzy
Beatles; Beatles VI . . . . (Capitol)
Rock 'N' Roll Music . . . . (Capitol)
The Beatles At The Hollywood Bowl . . . . (Capitol)
Ronnie Hawkins and The Hawks; Best Of Ronnie Hawkins and The
Hawks. . . . . (Rhino)
Do You Remember Rock 'N' Roll Radio
Ramones; End Of The Century . . . . (Sire)
Mania . . . . (Sire)
Don't Rock The Jukebox
Alan Jackson; Alan Jackson-The Greatest Hits Collection . . . . (Arista)
Don't Rock The Jukebox . . . . (Arista)
Drift Away
Dobie Gray; Classic Rock-#1-C . . . . (MCA)
Oldies But Goodies-#10-C . . . . (Original Sound)
Oldies But Goodies-#3-C . . . . (Original Sound)
Super Hits Of The '70s-Have A Nice Day-#10-C . . . . (Rhino)
Michael Bolton; Timeless-Classics . . . . (Columbia)
Rod Stewart; Atlantic Crossing . . . . (Warner Bros.)
England Rocks
Ian Hunter & Mott The Hoople; Shades Of Ian Hunter . . . . . . (Chrysalis)
Everybody (Backstreet's Back)
Backstreet Boys; Backstreet Boys . . . . (Jive)
Flying Saucers Rock 'N' Roll
Billy Lee Riley & His Little Green Men; Legends Of Rock Guitar-
'50s-#2-C . . . . (Rhino)
Sun Story-C . . . . (Rhino)
For A Rocker
Jackson Browne; Lawyers In Love . . . . (Asylum)
For Those About To Rock
AC/DC; For Those About To Rock. . . . . (Atlantic)
Who Made Who . . . . (Atlantic)
Forever
Kid Rock; Cocky . . . . (Top Dog/Lava/Atlantic)
God Gave Rock & Roll To You
Argent; Argent-Anthology-Collection Of Greatest Hits. . . . . (Epic)
Encore-Argent. . . . . (Epic)
Truth; Jump . . . . (I.R.S.)
Golden Age Of Rock & Roll
Mott The Hoople; Mott The Hoople's Greatest Hits . . . . (Columbia)
The Ballad Of Mott: A Retrospective. . . . . (Columbia)
Golden Olden Days Of Rock & Roll
Johnny Winter; J.D. Winter III . . . . (Blue Sky)
Good Golly, Miss Molly
Creedence Clearwater Revival; 1968-1969 . . . . (Fantasy)
Bayou Country . . . . (Fantasy)
Creedence Clearwater Revival-Chronicle-#2 . . . . (Fantasy)
Little Richard; Big Hits . . . . (Crescendo)
Cruisin'-1958-C . . . . (Increase)
Greatest Hits Recorded Live . . . . (Epic)
Little Richard-18 Greatest Hits . . . . (Rhino)
Little Richard-His Greatest Hits . . . . (Vee-Jay)
ST/The Flamingo Kid . . . . (Motown)
Super Oldies Of The '50s-#2-C . . . . (Audio Fidelity)
Good Rockin' Tonight
Elvis Presley; A Date With Elvis . . . . (RCA)
Sun Story-C . . . . (Rhino)
The Sun Sessions . . . . (RCA)
Jerry Lee Lewis; 20 Classic Jerry Lee Lewis Hits . . . . (Original Sound)
Trio Plus . . . . (Sun)
Jimmy Witherspoon; Best Of Jimmy Witherspoon . . . . (Prestige)
'Spoon Concerts . . . . (Fantasy)
Hang Up My Rock & Roll Shoes
Band; Rock Of Ages . . . . (Capitol)

Chuck Willis; *Atlantic Rhythm & Blues 1947-1974-#3 (1955-1958)-C* .... (Atlantic)

Hannukah Rocks
Gefilte Joe & The Fish; *Tales From The Rhino-Rhino Records Story-C* .... (Rhino)

Hard Rock Bottom Of Your Heart
Randy Travis; *No Holdin' Back* .... (Warner Bros.)

Hard Rock Cafe
Carole King; *Simple Things* .... (Capitol)

Heart Of Rock & Roll
Huey Lewis and the News; *Sports* .... (Chrysalis)

Here We Go, Let's Rock And Roll
C & C Music Factory; *Gonna Make You Sweat* .... (Columbia)

Hillbilly Rock
Marty Stuart; *Hillbilly Rock* .... (MCA)
Marty Party Hit Pack .... (MCA)

Hot Rockin'
Judas Priest; *Point Of Entry* .... (Columbia)

House Is Rockin'
Stevie Ray Vaughan and Double Trouble; *In Step* .... (Epic)

House Is Rockin'
Cheap Trick; *Dream Police* .... (Epic)

House Of Rock
James Brown; *45-#38-ZS4-06568* .... (Scotti Bros.)

I Dig Rock & Roll Music
Peter, Paul & Mary; *10 Years Together/The Best Of Peter, Paul and Mary* .... (Warner Bros.)
1700 .... (Warner Bros.)

I Don't Need Your Rockin' Chair
George Jones; *Platinum Country-C* .... (MCA)
Walls Can Fall .... (MCA)

I Knew The Bride
Dave Edmunds; *Best Of Dave Edmunds* .... (Swan Song)
Get It .... (Swan Song)
Nick Lowe; *Basher: Best Of* .... (Columbia)

I Like To Rock
April Wine; *Harder...Faster* .... (Capitol)

I Love Rock 'N Roll
Britney Spears; *Britney* .... (Jive)
Joan Jett & The Blackhearts; *I Love Rock 'n' Roll* .... (Blackheart)
ST/Wayne's World 2 .... (Reprise)

I Want To Sing That Rock And Roll
Gillian Welch; *Time (The Revelator)* .... (Acony)

If You Can't Rock Me
Rolling Stones; *It's Only Rock 'N Roll* .... (Rolling Stones)
Love You Live .... (Virgin)

If You Can't Rock Me
Rick Nelson; *Legends Of Rock & Roll Series-Best Of Rick Nelson-#2* ..... (EMI)

If You Don't Like Rock 'N' Roll
Blackmore's Rainbow; *Ritchie Blackmore's R-A-I-N-B-O-W* .... (Polydor)

I'm A Rocker
Bruce Springsteen; *The River* .... (Columbia)

I'm Just A Singer In A Rock & Roll Band
Moody Blues; *Seventh Sojourn* .... (Polydor)
This Is The Moody Blues .... (Polydor)
Voices In The Sky-The Best Of The Moody Blues ...... (Threshold)

It's A Long Way To The Top
AC/DC; *High Voltage* .... (Atco)

It's Only Rock 'N Roll (But I Like It)
Rolling Stones; *It's Only Rock 'N Roll* .... (Rolling Stones)
Love You Live .... (Virgin)
Made In The Shade .... (Rolling Stones)
Rewind (1971-1984) .... (Rolling Stones)

It's Still Rock & Roll To Me
Billy Joel; *Billy Joel-Greatest Hits, Volume I & Volume II* .... (Columbia)
Glass Houses .... (Columbia)

I've Got A Rock 'N' Roll Heart
Eric Clapton; *Money And Cigarettes* .... (Duck/Reprise)

Jailhouse Rock
Blues Brothers; *ST/The Blues Brothers* .... (Atlantic)
Elvis Presley; *Billboard Top Rock 'N' Roll Hits-1957-C* .... (Rhino)
Elvis Recorded Live On Stage In Memphis .... (RCA)
Elvis-A Legendary Performer, Volume 2 .... (RCA)
Number One Hits .... (RCA)
Rocker .... (RCA)
Worldwide 50 Gold Award Hits, Vol. 1, Parts 1 & 2 ... (RCA)
Jeff Beck Group; *Beck-Ola* .... (Epic)

Just A-Sittin' & A-Rockin'
Cleo Laine; *Jazz* .... (RCA)
Duke Ellington; *Intimacy Of The Blues* .... (Fantasy)
Mel Torme; *Duke Ellington & Count Basie Songbook* ...... (Verve)

Justice Tonight/Rock It Over
Clash; *Black Market Clash* .... (Epic)

King Of Rock
Run-D.M.C.; *King Of Rock* .... (Profile)
Mr. Magic's Rap Attack-C .... (Profile)

Let It Rock
Chuck Berry; *Rockin' At The Hops* .... (Chess)
The Chess Box-Chuck Berry .... (Chess)

Let It Rock
Bob Seger; *Live Bullet* .... (Capitol)
Smokin' O.P.'s .... (Capitol)
Bob Seger & The Silver Bullet Band; *Nine Tonight* ..... (Capitol)

Let It Rock
Bon Jovi; *Slippery When Wet* .... (Jambco)

Let It Roll (Let It Rock)
Mel McDaniel; *Let It Roll (Let It Rock)* .... (Capitol)
Mel McDaniel's Greatest Hits .... (Capitol)

Let There Be Rock
AC/DC; *If You Want Blood You've Got It* .... (Atlantic)
Let There Be Rock .... (Atco)

Let's Get Rocked
Def Leppard; *Adrenalize* .... (Mercury)

Life Is A Rock (But The Radio Rolled Me)
Reunion; *Super Hits Of The '70s-Have A Nice Day-#13-C* ..... (Rhino)

Limbo Rock
Chubby Checker; *Chubby Checker's Greatest Hits* ...... (Everest)
Moonlighting .... (MCA)
Rock-O-Rama-#2-C .... (Abkco)

Long Live Rock
Who; *Odds & Sods* .... (MCA)
ST/The Kids Are Alright .... (MCA)
Who's Last .... (MCA)

Long Live Rock 'N' Roll
Rainbow; *Finyl Vinyl* .... (Mercury)
Long Live Rock 'n' Roll .... (Polydor)

Long Live Rock 'N' Roll
Elvis Presley; *Elvis Aron Presley* .... (RCA)

Louisiana Cajun Rock Band
Carol Channing & Jimmy C. Newman; *Carol Channing & Her Country Friends* .... (Plantation)

Love Is Like A Rock
Donnie Iris; *King Cool* .... (MCA)

Lullaby
Shawn Mullins; *Soul's Core* .... (Columbia)

Memphis, Tennessee Hot Rock
Gordon Terry; *Tennessee Hot Rock* .... (Plantation)

Midnight Rocks
Al Stewart; *24 Carrots* .... (Arista)

Modern Times Rock & Roll
Queen; *Queen* .... (Hollywood)

Monday Morning Rock
Marshall Crenshaw; *Field Day* .... (Warner Bros.)

My Daddy Rocks Me
Benny Goodman Sextet; *Slipped Disc-1945-1946* ...... (Columbia)
Mae West; *Fabulous Mae West* .... (MCA)

My Ol' Kentucky Rock & Roll Home
Original New York Cast; *Oil City Symphony* .... (DRG)

My Rock & Roll Man
Rita Coolidge; *It's Only Love* .... (A&M)

New Rock & Roll
Frank Marino & Mahogany Rush; *Frank Marino & Mahogany Rush-Live* .... (Columbia)

Old Time Rock & Roll
Bob Seger & The Silver Bullet Band; *Nine Tonight* ..... (Capitol)
Stranger In Town .... (Capitol)

One Of The Survivors
Kinks; *Preservation Act 1* .... (Rhino)
The Kinks' Greatest-Celluloid Heroes .... (RCA)

One Rock & Roll Too Many
Marc Cohn; *ST/Starlight Express* .... (MCA)

Only One Way To Rock
Sammy Hagar; *Standing Hampton* .... (Geffen)

Only You Can Rock Me
UFO; *Obsession* .... (Chrysalis)
Strangers In The Night .... (Chrysalis)

Osaka Rocka
Jeff Watson; *Lone Ranger* .... (Shrapnel)

Planet Rock
Afrika Bambaataa & Soulsonic Force; *Street Jams-Electric Funk-#1-C* ... (Rhino)
Tommy Boy's Greatest Beats-C .... (Tommy Boy)

Purple People Eater
Sheb Wooley; *45s On CD-#1-1956-1959-C* .... (Mercury)
Dr. Demento: 20th Anniversary Collection-C .... (Rhino)
Halloween Hits-C .... (Rhino)
Horror Rock Classics-#2-C .... (Rhino)
Super Hits-#4-C .... (Gusto)

R. U. Ready To Rock
Blue Oyster Cult; *On Flame With Rock & Roll* .... (Sony Music Special Prod.)
Some Enchanted Evening .... (Columbia)
Spectres .... (Columbia)

R.O.C.K. In The U.S.A.
John Cougar Mellencamp; *Scarecrow* .... (Riva)

Raging Rock & Roll
Zeros; *4-3-2-1...The Zeroes* .... (Restless)

Rattlesnake Rock 'N' Roller
Blackfoot; *Marauder* .... (Atco)

Ready Teddy
Buddy Holly; *Buddy Holly* . . . . (MCA)
   Rock & Roll Collection . . . . (MCA)
Elvis Presley; *Elvis* . . . .(RCA)
   Rocker. . . . .(RCA)
   The Great Performances. . . . .(RCA)
Little Richard; *Georgia Peach.* . . . . (Specialty)
   Grooviest 17 Original Hits . . . . (Specialty)
   More American Graffiti-C . . . . (MCA)

Rebel Rock Me
Pretenders; *Last Of The Independents* . . . .(Sire)

Redneck In A Rock & Roll Bar
Jerry Reed; *Redneck Mothers-C* . . . .(RCA)

Redneck Rock N' Roll
Pirates Of The Mississippi; *Pirates Of The Mississippi* . . . .(Liberty)

Reeling And Rocking
Chuck Berry; *Best Of The Best Of Chuck Berry* . . . . . (International Mktg. Group)
   Chuck Berry's Greatest Hits . . . . (Everest)
   Frat Rock!-C. . . . . (Rhino)
   Rock & Roll Show-C . . . . (Gusto)
   The Chess Box-Chuck Berry . . . . (Chess)

Revolution Rock
Clash; *London Calling.* . . . . (Epic)

Rich Don't Rock
Vamp; *Rich Don't Rock.* . . . . (Atlantic)

Rip It Up
Elvis Presley; *Elvis* . . . .(RCA)
   Rocker. . . . .(RCA)
Little Richard; *Big Hits* . . . . (Crescendo)
   Grooviest 17 Original Hits . . . . (Specialty)
   Little Richard-18 Greatest Hits . . . . (Rhino)
   Little Richard's Greatest Hits. . . . .(Everest)

Rock
Frankie Miller; *Rock.* . . . . (Chrysalis)
Garland Jeffreys; *Escape Artist* . . . . (Epic)
Otis Rush; *Chicago Blues Today-C* . . . . (Vanguard)
Who; *ST/Quadrophenia* . . . . (MCA)

R-O-C-K
Bill Haley & His Comets; *Bill Haley & His Comets-Golden Hits* . . . . (MCA)
   R-O-C-K. . . . .(Sun)

Rock & Roll
Led Zeppelin; *Led Zeppelin IV* . . . . (Atlantic)
   Led Zeppelin-Box Set . . . . (Atlantic)
   Remasters. . . . . (Atlantic)
   ST/The Song Remains The Same. . . . . (Swan Song)

Rock & Roll
Velvet Underground; *Another View* . . . . (Verve)

Rock & Roll
Zapp; *The New Zapp IV U* . . . . (Warner Bros.)

Rock & Roll
Dwight Twilley Band; *Twilley Don't Mind* . . . . (Arista)

Rock & Roll
Jimmy Rushing; *Essential Jimmy Rushing* . . . . (Vanguard)

Rock & Roll
Mitch Ryder And The Detroit Wheels; *Detroit With Mitch Ryder And The*
   Detroit Wheels. . . . . (MCA)
   Rev Up-Best Of Mitch Ryder. . . . . (Rhino)

Rock & Roll
Gary Glitter; *Gary Glitter's Greatest Hits.* . . . . (Rhino)
   Super Hits Of The '70s-Have A Nice Day-#9-C . . . . (Rhino)

Rock & Roll
Heart; *Heart's Greatest Hits/Live* . . . . (Epic)

Rock & Roll
Jane's Addiction; *Jane's Addiction* . . . . (Triple X Entert.)

Rock & Roll
R.B. Greaves; *Rock & Roll* . . . . (Intermedia)

Rock & Roll
Johnny Winter; *Still Alive & Well* . . . . (Columbia)

Rock & Roll All Nite
Poison; *ST/Less Than Zero* . . . . (Def Jam)

Rock & Roll Babylon
Love And Rockets; *Love And Rockets* . . . . (Beggar's Banquet)

Rock & Roll Band
Wet Willie; *Wet Willie.* . . . . (Capricorn)

Rock & Roll Band
Boston; *Boston.* . . . . (Epic)

Rock & Roll Band
Mano Negra; *Puta's Fever* . . . . (Virgin)

Rock & Roll Boogie Woogie Blues
Edgar Winter Group; *They Only Come Out At Night* . . . . (Epic)

Rock & Roll Crazies
Stephen Stills; *Manassas.* . . . . (Atlantic)
   Still Stills. . . . . (Atlantic)

Rock & Roll Creation
Spinal Tap; *ST/Spinal Tap* . . . . (Polydor)

Rock & Roll Doctor
Little Feat; *Feats Don't Fail Me Now* . . . . (Warner Bros.)
   Hoy-Hoy! . . . . (Warner Bros.)

Rock & Roll Doctor
Travesty Ltd.; *Dr. Demento Presents The Greatest Novelty Records-#5-*
   1980s-C . . . .(Rhino)

Rock & Roll Doctor
Black Sabbath; *Technical Ecstasy* . . . . (Warner Bros.)

Rock & Roll Fantasy
Kinks; *15-Year History Of Rock.* . . . .(Arista)
   '70s Greatest Rock Hits-#14-King Of Rock-C. . . . . (Priority)
   Come Dancing With The Kinks-Best Of The Kinks 1977-1986 . . . .(Arista)
   Misfits . . . .(Arista)

Rock & Roll Fantasy
Bad Company; *10 From 6* . . . . (Atlantic)
   Desolation Angels . . . . (Swan Song)

Rock & Roll Feeling
Styx; *Miracles-Best Of Styx* . . . . (RCA)

Rock & Roll Gas Station
Adrenalin O.D.; *Wacky Hi-Jinks Of Adrenalin O.D.* . . . . (Buy Our Records)

Rock & Roll Heaven
Righteous Brothers; *Righteous Brothers-Anthology 1962-1974* . . . .(Rhino)

Rock & Roll Is Back Again
Village People; *Live & Sleazy* . . . . (Casablanca)

Rock & Roll Is Here To Stay
Danny & The Juniors; *'50s Dance Party-#2-C* . . . .(Dominion Entert.)
   Rock & Roll Is Here To Stay-C . . . . (Gusto)
   Rockin' With Danny & The Juniors. . . . . (MCA Special Prod.)
Sha Na Na; *Sha Na Na Is Here To Stay* . . . . (Buddah)
   ST/Grease . . . . (Polydor)

Rock & Roll Is Music
James Taylor; *Walking Man.* . . . . (Warner Bros.)

Rock & Roll Junkie
Herman Brood; *Herman Brood & His Wild Romance* . . . . (Ariola America)

Rock & Roll Junkie
Back Street Crawler; *Band Plays On* . . . .(Atco)

Rock & Roll Lawyer
Austin Lounge Lizards; *Lizard Vision* . . . . (Flying Fish)

Rock & Roll Love Letter
Bay City Rollers; *Bay City Rollers' Greatest Hits* . . . .(Arista)
   Rock & Roll Love Letters . . . .(Arista)

Rock & Roll Machine
Triumph; *Rock & Roll Machine* . . . . (MCA)
   Stages . . . . (MCA)
   Triumph-Classics . . . . (MCA)

Rock & Roll Man
Kenny Rogers; *Daytime Friends* . . . . (EMI)

Rock & Roll Man
Savoy Brown; *Savage Return.* . . . . (London)

Rock & Roll Mood
Loggins & Messina; *Sittin' In* . . . .(Columbia)

Rock & Roll Music To The World
Ten Years After; *Classic Performances Of Ten Years After.* . . . .(Columbia)

Rock & Roll Never Forgets
Bob Seger; *Night Moves.* . . . .(Capitol)
Bob Seger & The Silver Bullet Band; *Nine Tonight* . . . .(Capitol)

Rock & Roll Outlaw
Foghat; *Rock & Roll Outlaws* . . . .(Rhino)

Rock & Roll Over
Mr. Big; *Mr. Big.* . . . . (Atlantic)

Rock & Roll Part 2 (The Sports Anthem ["The Hey Song"])
Gary Glitter; *Gary Glitter's Greatest Hits* . . . .(Rhino)

Rock & Roll People
John Lennon; *Menlove Ave.* . . . .(Capitol)

Rock & Roll People
Johnny Winter; *Captured Live* . . . . (Blue Sky)

Rock & Roll Pussy
Todd Rundgren; *A Wizard A True Star.* . . . . (Rhino)

Rock & Roll Queen
Mott The Hoople; *Mott The Hoople.* . . . . (Atlantic)
   The Ballad Of Mott: A Retrospective. . . . .(Columbia)

Rock & Roll Radio
Ramones; *End Of The Century.* . . . . (Sire)

Rock & Roll Records
J.J. Cale; *Okie.* . . . . (MCA)

Rock & Roll Ruby
Warren Smith; *Memphis Country-C.* . . . . (Sun)
   Original Memphis Rock & Roll. . . . . (Sun)

Rock & Roll Shoes
Ray Charles & B.J. Thomas; *Friendship-C* . . . .(Columbia)
   Seven Spanish Angels & Other Hits. . . . .(Columbia)

Rock & Roll Shoes
Amos Garrett; *Go Cat Go.* . . . . (Flying Fish)

Rock & Roll Stew
Traffic; *The Low Spark Of High Heeled Boys* . . . .(Island)

Rock & Roll Strategy
38 Special; *Rock & Roll Strategy* . . . . (A&M)

Rock & Roll Suicide
David Bowie; *David Live* . . . .(Rykodisc)
   Rise & Fall Of Ziggy Stardust And The Spiders From Mars . . . .(Rykodisc)
   Sound + Vision . . . .(Rykodisc)

ST/Ziggy Stardust-The Motion Picture . . . . (Rykodisc)
Rock & Roll The Place
   Eddie Money; *Life For The Taking*. (Columbia)
Rock & Roll Time
   Roger McGuinn; *Cardiff Rose* . . . . (Columbia)
Rock & Roll Tonight
   Grim Reaper; *Fear No Evil*. . . . . (RCA)
Rock & Roll Waltz
   Kay Starr; *Capitol Collectors Series-Kay Starr* . . . . (Capitol)
   Nipper's Greatest Hits Of The '50s-#1-C . . . . (RCA)
Rock & Roll Widow
   Wishbone Ash; *Live Dates* . . . .(MCA)
   Wishbone Four . . . . (MCA)
Rock & Roll With Me
   David Bowie; *Diamond Dogs*. . . . . (Rykodisc)
Rock & Roll Woman
   Buffalo Springfield; *Buffalo Springfield* . . . . (Atco)
   Buffalo Springfield Again . . . . (Atco)
   Buffalo Springfield-Retrospective . . . . (Atco)
Rock & Roll Women
   Whitesnake; *Love Hunter* . . . .(Geffen)
Rock & Roll Women
   Brinsley Schwarz; *Brinsley Schwarz* . . . . (Capitol)
Rock & Roller
   Pablo Cruise; *Pablo Cruise* . . . . (A&M)
Rock & Soul Music
   Country Joe & The Fish; *ST/Woodstock* . . . . (Atlantic)
Rock A Beatin' Boogie
   Bill Haley & His Comets; *Bill Haley & His Comets' Greatest Hits* . . . . (Everest)
   Bill Haley & His Comets-Golden Hits . . . . (MCA)
   Legends Of Rock Guitar-'50s-#2-C . . . . (Rhino)
Rock A Bye Your Baby With A Dixie Melody
   Al Jolson; *Best Of Al Jolson* . . . . (MCA)
   Jolson Sang 'Em . . . . (Biograph)
   Music From The New York Stage (1890-1920)-#4-1917-1920-C . . . . . (Pearl)
   The Al Jolson Story-#1 . . . . (MCA)
   Jerry Lewis; *Just Sings* . . . . (Razor & Tie)
   Judy Garland; *Judy Garland-At Carnegie Hall* . . . . (Capitol)
   Miss Show Business . . . . (Capitol)
   One & Only . . . . (Capitol)
Rock America
   Afrika & Family Bambaataa; *Beware (The Funk Is*
    Everywhere) . . . . (Tommy Boy)
Rock America
   Danger Danger; *Danger Danger* . . . . (Imagine)
Rock An' Roll Angels
   Whitesnake; *Saints & Sinners* . . . .(Geffen)
Rock And Roll All Nite
   Kiss; *Alive!* . . . . (Mercury)
   Double Platinum . . . . (Mercury)
   Dressed To Kill . . . . (Mercury)
   Heavy Metal Memories-C . . . . (Rhino)
   Smashes, Thrashes & Hits . . . . (Mercury)
   The Originals . . . . (Casablanca)
Rock And Roll Crook
   Nils Lofgren; *Best Of Nils Lofgren* . . . . (A&M)
   Night After Night . . . . (A&M)
   Nils Lofgren . . . . (Rykodisc)
   Nils Lofgren-Classics-#13 . . . . (A&M)
Rock And Roll Dreams Come Through
   Meat Loaf; *Bat Out Of Hell II: Back Into Hell* . . . .(MCA)
Rock And Roll Heart
   Lou Reed; *Between Thought & Expression-Anthology*. . . . . (RCA)
   Rock And Roll Heart . . . . (Arista)
Rock And Roll Is Dead
   Lenny Kravitz; *Circus* . . . . (Virgin)
Rock And Roll Music
   Beach Boys; *15 Big Ones* . . . . (Brother)
   Beach Boys-Gift Set . . . . (Capitol)
   Made In The U.S.A. . . . . (Capitol)
   Ten Years Of Harmony . . . . (Caribou)
   Beatles; *Beatles '65* . . . . (Capitol)
   Beatles-Box Set . . . . (Capitol)
   For Sale . . . . (Capitol)
   Rock 'N' Roll Music . . . . (Capitol)
   Chuck Berry; *Chuck Berry-Golden Hits* . . . . (Mercury)
   Chuck Berry's Greatest Hits . . . . (Everest)
   Cruisin'-1958-C . . . . (Increase)
   The Chess Box-Chuck Berry . . . . (Chess)
   REO Speedwagon; *Nine Lives* . . . .(Epic)
Rock And Roll Waltz
   Kay Starr; *Capitol Collectors Series-Kay Starr* . . . . (Capitol)
Rock And Roll, Hoochie Koo
   Edgar Winter's White Trash; *Roadwork*. . . . .(Epic)
   Johnny Winter; *Johnny Winter And* . . . . (Columbia)
   Rock Classics-C . . . . (K-Tel)
   Johnny Winter & Rick Derringer; *Metal Age-Roots Of Metal-C* . . . . . (Rhino)
   Rick Derringer; *All American Boy* . . . . (Blue Sky)
   Legends Of Rock Guitar-'70s-C . . . . (Rhino)

Super Hits Of The '70s-Have A Nice Day-#12-C . . . . (Rhino)
Rock And Soul Music
   Country Joe & The Fish; *Collected-1965-1970*. . . . . (Vanguard)
   Life & Times Of Country Joe & The Fish . . . . (Vanguard)
   Together . . . . (Vanguard)
Rock Around With Ollie Vee
   Buddy Holly; *Legend-From The Original Master Tapes* . . . . (MCA)
Rock Billy Boogie
   Robert Gordon; *Rock Billy Boogie* . . . .(RCA)
Rock Box
   Run-D.M.C.; *Rapmasters 3-Best Of The Cut-C* . . . . (Priority)
   Run-D.M.C. . . . . (Profile)
Rock City
   Damn Yankees; *Damn Yankees*. . . . . (Warner Bros.)
Rock Coast Blues
   Country Joe & The Fish; *Collected-1965-1970*. . . . . (Vanguard)
   I-Feel-Like-I'm-Fixin'-To-Die . . . . (Vanguard)
Rock Dis Funky Joint
   Poor Righteous Teachers; *Holy Intellect* . . . .(Profile)
Rock For The Forgotten
   David & David; *Boomtown* . . . . (A&M)
Rock Forever
   Judas Priest; *Hell Bent For Leather* . . . . (Columbia)
Rock In America
   Night Ranger; *Midnight Madness* . . . . (MCA)
   Night Ranger's Greatest Hits . . . . (Camel)
Rock Is Hot
   Crown Heights Affair; *Dance Lady Dance* . . . .(De-Lite)
Rock Is In My Blood
   Sammy Hagar; *VOA* . . . . (Geffen)
Rock Is My Life And This Is My Song
   Bachman-Turner Overdrive; *Not Fragile* . . . . (Mercury)
Rock It
   Queen; *The Game* . . . . (Hollywood)
   Steve Miller Band; *Steve Miller Band-Gift Set* . . . . (Capitol)
Rock It Baby
   Bob Marley & The Wailers; *Catch A Fire* . . . .(Tuff Gong)
Rock Lobster
   B-52's; *B-52's* . . . . (Warner Bros.)
Rock Love
   Steve Miller Band; *Rock Love* . . . . (Capitol)
   Utopia; *Adventures In Utopia* . . . . (Rhino)
Rock Me
   Muddy Waters; *I'm Ready*. . . . . (Blue Sky)
   The Chess Box-Muddy Waters . . . . (Chess)
Rock Me
   Abba; *Abba* . . . . (Atlantic)
   Abba's Greatest Hits-#2 . . . . (Atlantic)
Rock Me
   Steppenwolf; *Steppenwolf Gold/Their Great Hits* . . . . (MCA)
   Steppenwolf-16 Greatest Hits . . . . (MCA)
Rock Me
   Deborah Allen; *Delta Dreamland* . . . .(Giant)
Rock Me
   Nick Gilder; *Frequency* . . . . (Chrysalis)
Rock Me
   Nutmegs; *Nutmegs' Greatest Hits* . . . . (Collectables)
Rock Me
   Great White; *Once Bitten* . . . . (Capitol)
Rock Me
   Fresh Force Crew; *Rapmasters 2-Best Of The Rhyme-C* . . . . (Priority)
Rock Me Amadeus
   Falco; *Falco 3* . . . . (A&M)
   Remix Hit Collection . . . .(Sire)
Rock Me Baby
   B.B. King; *B.B. King Greatest Hits* . . . . (Kent)
   Now Appearing Live At Ole Miss . . . . (MCA)
   Rock Me Baby . . . . (Kent)
   Etta James; *Red Hot 'N' Live* . . . . (Intermedia)
   Hot Tuna; *Historic Hot Tuna* . . . .(Relix)
   Jefferson Airplane; *Bless Its Pointed Little Head* . . . . (RCA)
   Jimi Hendrix; *ST/Jimi Hendrix* . . . . (Reprise)
   ST/Jimi Plays Monterey . . . . (Reprise)
   Otis Redding; *Best Of Otis Redding* . . . . (Atco)
   Robin Trower; *Robin Trower-Live* . . . . (Chrysalis)
   Twice Removed From Yesterday . . . . (Chrysalis)
Rock Me Baby
   Slim Harpo; *Best Of Slim Harpo* . . . . (Rhino)
Rock Me In The Rhythm Of Your Love
   Eddy Raven; *Best Of Eddy Raven* . . . . (Liberty)
   Right For The Flight . . . . (Liberty)
Rock Me Like A Hurricane
   Scorpions; *Love At First Sting*. (Mercury)
Rock Me Mama
   Blind Snooks Eaglin; *Country Boy In New Orleans* . . . . (Arhoolie)
   Buddy Guy/Junior Mance/Junior Wells; *Buddy & The Juniors* . . . . (MCA)
   Sonny Terry; *Chain Gang Blues* . . . . (Collectables)

Rock Me On The Water
Jackson Browne; *Jackson Browne*. . . . . (Asylum)
Kathy Mattea with Jackson Browne; *Red Hot + Country-C* . . . . . . (Mercury)
Linda Ronstadt; *Different Drum* . . . . (Capitol)
   Linda Ronstadt . . . . (Capitol)
   Linda Ronstadt-Retrospective . . . . (Capitol)

Rock Me Roll Me
Jerry Jeff Walker; *Collectibles* . . . . (MCA)

Rock Me 'Till I Die
Grim Reaper; *Rock You To Hell*. . . . . (RCA)

Rock Me Tonight (For Old Time's Sake)
Freddie Jackson; *Rock Me Tonight (For Old Time's Sake)* . . . . (Capitol)

Rock Me Tonite
Billy Squier; *Signs Of Life* . . . . (Capitol)

Rock Music
Jefferson Starship; *Freedom At Point Zero* . . . . (Grunt)

Rock My Baby
Shenandoah; *Best Of Shenandoah* . . . . (RCA)

Rock My Plimsoul
Jeff Beck Group; *Beckology-C* . . . . (Epic)
   Truth . . . . (Epic)

Rock My Soul
Elvin Bishop; *Best Of Elvin Bishop* . . . . (Epic)
   Live! Raisin' Hell . . . . (Capricorn)

Rock My World (Little Country Girl)
Brooks & Dunn; *Hard Workin' Man* . . . . (Arista)

Rock 'N' Roll
Lou Reed; *Rock N Roll Animal* . . . . (RCA)
Velvet Underground; *1969: Velvet Underground Live* . . . . (Mercury)
   Another View . . . . (Verve)
   Live MCMXCIII . . . . (Sire)
   Loaded . . . . (Warner Special Prod.)

Rock 'N' Roll
Atlantic Starr; *Straight To The Point* . . . . (A&M)

Rock 'N' Roll
Mac Davis; *All The Love In The World* . . . . (Columbia)

Rock 'N' Roll Angel
Kentucky HeadHunters; *Pickin' On Nashville* . . . . (Mercury)

Rock 'N' Roll Children
Dio; *Intermission* . . . . (Warner Bros.)
   Sacred Heart . . . . (Warner Bros.)

Rock 'N' Roll Damnation
AC/DC; *If You Want Blood You've Got It* . . . . (Atlantic)
   Powerage . . . . (Atlantic)

Rock N Roll Disease
Green On Red; *Here Come The Snakes* . . . . (Restless)

Rock 'N' Roll Ghost
Replacements; *Don't Tell A Soul* . . . . (Sire)

Rock 'N' Roll Hall Of Fame
Frank Marino & Mahogany Rush; *What's Next* . . . . (Columbia)

Rock 'N' Roll High School
Ramones; *End Of The Century* . . . . (Sire)
   Loco Live . . . . (Sire)
   Ramones Mania . . . . (Sire)
   ST/Rock 'N' Roll High School . . . . (Sire)

Rock 'N' Roll Is A Vicious Game
April Wine; *First Glance* . . . . (Capitol)

Rock 'N' Roll Is King
Electric Light Orchestra; *Afterglow* . . . . (Epic)
   Secret Messages . . . . (Jet)

Rock 'N' Roll Juggernaut
Meatmen; *Rock 'N' Roll Juggernaut* . . . . (Caroline)

Rock 'N' Roll Junkie
Motley Crue; *Decade Of Decadence* . . . . (Elektra)

Rock 'N' Roll Juvenile
Cliff Richard; *We Don't Talk Anymore* . . . . (EMI)

Rock 'N' Roll Lullaby
B.J. Thomas; *B.J. Thomas' Greatest Hits* . . . . (Rhino)
   B.J. Thomas-16 Greatest Hits . . . . (Trip)
   Back To The '70s-#2-C . . . . (Dominion Entert.)
   Super Hits-#2-C . . . . (Gusto)

Rock 'N' Roll Lullaby
10 CC; *How Dare You!* . . . . (Mercury)

Rock 'N' Roll Murder
Leaving Trains; *Loser Illusion-Pt. 0* . . . . (SST)

Rock N Roll Nigger
Patti Smith Group; *Easter* . . . . (Arista)

Rock 'N' Roll Outlaw
Peter Wells; *Everything You Like Tries To Kill You* . . . . (Zoo)

Rock 'N' Roll Over You
Moody Blues; *Other Side Of Life* . . . . (Polydor)

Rock 'N' Roll Rebel
Ozzy Osbourne; *Bark At The Moon* . . . . (CBS Associated)

Rock 'N' Roll Susie
Pat Travers; *Makin' Magic* . . . . (Polydor)

Rock 'N' Roll The Weekend
Sammy Hagar; *All Night Long* . . . . (One Way)
   Sammy Hagar . . . . (Capitol)

Rock 'N' Roll To The Rescue
Beach Boys; *Beach Boys-Gift Set* . . . . (Capitol)
   Made In The U.S.A. . . . . (Capitol)

Rock 'N' Roll Tonight
Cheap Trick; *Busted* . . . . (Epic)

Rock 'N' Rollers
Angel; *Angel* . . . . (Casablanca)
   Live Without A Net . . . . (Casablanca)

Rock 'N' Soul
Grand Funk Railroad; *Caught In The Act* . . . . (Capitol)
   Phoenix . . . . (Capitol)

Rock 'N' Soul
Oaktown's 3.5.7.; *Wild & Loose* . . . . (Capitol)

Rock Of Ages
Bryan Ferry; *In Your Mind* . . . . (Reprise)
Def Leppard; *Pyromania* . . . . (Mercury)

Rock Of America
Bad Company; *Dangerous Age* . . . . (Atlantic)

Rock Ola Jive
Hank Burnette; *Don't Mess With My Ducktail* . . . . (Sun)

Rock On
David Essex; *Billboard Top Rock 'N' Roll Hits-1974-C* . . . . (Rhino)
   Pop Classics Of The '70s-C . . . . (Columbia)
   Super Hits Of The '70s-Have A Nice Day-#12-C . . . . (Rhino)

Rock On
Michael Damian; *Greatest Movie Rock Hits-C* . . . . (Rhino)
   ST/Dream A Little Dream . . . . (Cypress)

Rock On
Vandenberg; *Best Of Vandenberg* . . . . (Atco)

Rock On
Gary Glitter; *Gary Glitter's Greatest Hits* . . . . (Rhino)

Rock On
Fastway; *Waiting For The Roar* . . . . (Columbia)

Rock On The Moon
Cramps; *Songs The Lord Taught Us* . . . . (I.R.S.)

Rock On The Radio
Firehouse; *Firehouse* . . . . (Epic)

Rock Radio Into The Nineties & Beyond
KLF; *Chill Out* . . . . (Wax Trax)

Rock Show, The
Blink-182; *Now That's What I Call Music!-#8-C* . . . . (Virgin)
   Take Off Your Pants And Jacket . . . . (MCA)

Rock Soldiers
Ace Frehley; *Frehley's Comet* . . . . (Megaforce)
   Metal Mania-C . . . . (Priority)

Rock Steady
Aretha Franklin; *Aretha Franklin-30 Greatest Hits* . . . . (Rhino)
   Best Of Aretha Franklin . . . . (Atlantic)
   Ten Years Of Gold . . . . (Atlantic)
   Young, Gifted And Black . . . . (Atlantic & Atco Remasters)

Rock Steady
Whispers; *Just Gets Better With Time* . . . . (Solar)

Rock That
Earth, Wind & Fire; *I Am* . . . . (Columbia)

Rock That Boogie
Commander Cody & His Lost Planet Airmen; *Country Casanova* . . . . . . (MCA)
   Too Much Fun-Best Of Commander Cody & His Lost Planet Airmen. . . (MCA)

Rock That Makes Me Roll
Stryper; *Head Banging Metal-C* . . . . (Priority)
   Soldiers Under Command . . . . (Hollywood)

Rock The Boat
Aaliyah; *Aaliyah* . . . . (BlackGround Enterp./Atlantic)

Rock The Casbah
Clash; *Combat Rock* . . . . (Epic)
   On Broadway . . . . (Epic)
   Seems Like Yesterday-#4-Early '80s-C . . . . (K-Tel)
   The Story Of The Clash, Volume 1 . . . . (Epic)

Rock The House
D.J. Jazzy Jeff & The Fresh Prince; *Rock The House* . . . . (Jive)

Rock The Joint
Bill Haley & His Comets; *Bill Haley & His Comets' Greatest Hits* . . . (Everest)
Bill Haley & The Saddlemen; *Rock This Town-Rockabilly Hits-#1-C* . . . (Rhino)

Rock The Nation
Montrose; *Montrose* . . . . (Warner Bros.)

Rock The Night
Europe; *Final Countdown* . . . . (Epic)

Rock The People
Stryper; *Against The Law* . . . . (Hollywood)

Rock The World
Third World; *Rock The World* . . . . (Columbia)

Rock This Boat
Thompson Twins; *Big Trash* . . . . (Red Eye)

Rock This Joint
Alannah Myles; *Alannah Myles* . . . . (Atlantic)

Rock This Town
Stray Cats; *Best Of Stray Cats-Rock This Town* . . . . (EMI)
   Built For Speed . . . . (EMI)
   Reelin' In The Years-#1-C . . . . (Sandstone Music)

Rock This Town-Rockabilly Hits-#2-C . . . . (Rhino)

Rock Will Never Die
Michael Schenker Group; *Built To Destroy* . . . .(Chrysalis)
Rock Will Never Die . . . .(Chrysalis)

Rock Wit U
Alicia Keys; *Songs In A Minor* . . . . (J)

Rock Wit'cha
Bobby Brown; *Dance!...Ya Know It!* . . . .(MCA)
Don't Be Cruel . . . .(MCA)

Rock With You
Jacksons; *Jacksons Live* . . . .(Epic)
Michael Jackson; *Off The Wall* . . . .(Epic)

Rock You
Kool Moe Dee; *How Ya Like Me Now* . . . . (Jive)

Rock You All Around The World
Judas Priest; *Priest...Live!* . . . . (Columbia)
Turbo . . . . (Columbia)

Rock You Like A Hurricane
Scorpions; *Best Of Rockers 'N' Ballads* . . . . (Mercury)
Love At First Sting . . . . (Mercury)
Worldwide Live . . . . (Mercury)

Rock You To Hell
Grim Reaper; *Rock You To Hell* . . . . (RCA)

Rock You Up
Romantics; *What I Like About You (And Other Romantic Hits)* . . . . . (Nemperor)

Rock Your Baby
George McCrae; *Didn't It Blow Your Mind: Soul Hits Of The
'70s-#13-C* . . . . (Rhino)
Get Down Tonight! Best Of T.K. Records-C . . . . (Rhino)
Mega Hits Dance Classics-#2-C . . . . (Priority)
Rock Your Baby . . . .(TK)

Rock Your Mama
Ten Years After; *Alvin Lee & Company* . . . . (Deram)
Ten Years After-London Collector . . . . (London)

Rock, The
George Jones; *The Rock: Stone Cold Country 2001* . . . . (BNA)

Rocka Rolla
Judas Priest; *Best Of Judas Priest* . . . . (RCA)
Hero Hero . . . . (RCA)
Rocka-Rolla . . . . (RCA)

Rockabilly On The Radio
Jack Smith & The Rockabilly Planet; *Jack Smith & The Rockabilly
Planet* . . . . (Flying Fish)

Rock-A-Hula Baby
Elvis Presley; *ST/Blue Hawaii* . . . . (RCA)
Worldwide 50 Gold Award Hits, Vol. 1, Parts 1 & 2 . . . . (RCA)

Rockaria
Electric Light Orchestra; *Afterglow* . . . .(Epic)
E.L.O. Classics . . . . (Sony Music Special Prod.)
Electric Light Orchestra's Greatest Hits . . . . (Jet)
New World Record . . . . (Jet)

Rockaway The Days
Bruce Springsteen; *Tracks* . . . . (Columbia)

Rocker
Thin Lizzy; *Live And Dangerous* . . . .(Warner Bros.)
Thin Lizzy-London Collector . . . . (London)

Rocker
Charlie Parker; *Bebop & Bird-#2* . . . . (Rhino)
Verve Years-1950-1951 . . . . (Verve)

Rocker
AC/DC; *Dirty Deeds Done Dirt Cheap* . . . . (Atlantic)
If You Want Blood You've Got It . . . . (Atlantic)

Rockers 'N' Rollers
Brownsville Station; *Brownsville Station* . . . .(Private Stock)

Rockestra Theme
Wings; *Back To The Egg* . . . . (Capitol)

Rockhouse
Roy Orbison; *Original Sound Of Roy Orbison* . . . . (Sun)
Roy Orbison-The Sun Years . . . . (Rhino)

Rockhouse
Ray Charles; *Best Of Ray Charles* . . . . (Atlantic)

Rockin' After Midnight
Marvin Gaye; *Midnight Love* . . . . (Columbia)

Rockin' Around (With You)
Tom Petty And The Heartbreakers; *Pack Up The Plantation-Live!* . . . . . .(MCA)
Tom Petty & The Heartbreakers . . . . (Gone Gator)

Rockin' Around In N.Y.C.
Marshall Crenshaw; *Marshall Crenshaw* . . . . (Rhino)

Rockin' At Midnight
Honeydrippers; *Little By Little-Collector's Edition* . . . .(Es Paranza)
Volume One . . . .(Es Paranza)

Rockin' Blues
Johnny Otis; *Original Johnny Otis Show* . . . .(Savoy)

Rockin' Boogie
Fleetwood Mac; *In Chicago* . . . . (Sire)

Rockin' Chair
Band; *The Band* . . . . (Capitol)
The Band-Gift Set . . . . (Capitol)

Rockin' Chair
Jerry Jeff Walker; *A Man Must Carry On* . . . . (MCA)

Rockin' Chair On The Moon
Bill Haley & His Comets; *King Of Rock & Roll* . . . . (Alshire)

Rockin' Chair Stomp
Gwen McCrae; *Didn't It Blow Your Mind: Soul Hits Of The
'70s-#15-C* . . . . (Rhino)
Get Down Tonight! Best Of T.K. Records-C . . . . (Rhino)
Hi-Lo's; *Swing-Best Of The Big Bands-C* . . . . (MCA)
Hoagy Carmichael; *Stardust Road* . . . . (MCA)
Jerry Garcia & David Grisman; *Jerry Garcia & David
Grisman* . . . . (Grateful Dead)
John Lee Hooker; *The Healer* . . . . (Chameleon)
Louis Armstrong & Jack Teagarden; *Evening With Louis Armstrong & Jack
Teagarden-#2* . . . .(Crescendo)
Mildred Bailey; *Jazz Singers* . . . .(Prestige)
Nipper's Greatest Hits Of The '30s-#2-C . . . . (RCA)
Tom Waits; *Tom Waits-Early Years-Volume One* . . . .(Planet 3)

Rockin' Daddy
Howlin' Wolf; *The Chess Box-Howlin' Wolf* . . . . (Chess)

Rockin' Down The Highway
Doobie Brothers; *Best Of The Doobies* . . . .(Warner Bros.)
Toulouse Street . . . .(Warner Bros.)

Rockin' Every Night
Gary Moore; *Gary Moore-Early Years* . . . . (WTG)

Rockin' Good Way (To Mess Around And Fall In Love)
Arthur Prysock; *Rockin' Good Way* . . . .(Milestone)
Brook Benton & Dinah Washington; *Brook Benton-Anthology* . . . . (Rhino)

Rockin' Goose
Johnny And The Hurricanes; *45-#1289.* . . . . (Collectables)

Rockin' Heaven Down
Heart; *Bebe Le Strange* . . . . (Epic)

Rockin' Horse
Bad English; *Bad English* . . . . (Epic)

Rockin' In Rhythm
Duke Ellington; *Great Paris Concert* . . . .(Atlantic)
Duke Ellington/Ella Fitzgerald/Oscar Peterson; *Greatest Jazz Concert In The
World.* . . . . (Pablo)
Hank Jones/Ray Brown/Jimmie Smith; *Rockin' In Rhythm* . . . . . (Concord Jazz)
Modern Jazz Quartet; *For Ellington* . . . . (East West)

Rockin' In The Congo
Hank Thompson; *Capitol Collectors Series-Hank Thompson* . . . . (Capitol)

Rockin' In The Free World
Bon Jovi; *One Wild Night: Live 1985-2001.* . . . . (Island)
Neil Young; *Freedom* . . . . (Reprise)
Neil Young & Crazy Horse; *WELD.* . . . . (Reprise)
Pearl Jam; *8/17/00: Tampa, Florida* . . . . (Epic)

Rockin' In The Jungle
Eternals; *WCBS FM 101 History Of Rock-Doo-Wop-#2-C* . . . . (Collectables)

Rockin' In The Parkin' Lot
Razzy Bailey; *Country Classics-#6-1985-1986-C* . . . . (Universal)

Rockin' In The U.S.A.
Kiss; *Alive II* . . . . (Casablanca)

Rockin' Into The Night
38 Special; *Flashback-Best Of 38 Special* . . . . (A&M)
Rockin' Into The Night . . . . (A&M)

Rockin' It
Fearless Four; *Hip Hop Heritage-#1-C* . . . . (Jive)

Rockin' Little Tune
Bill Haley & His Comets; *Bill Haley & His Comets-Golden Hits* . . . . . . (MCA)

Rockin' My Boogie
Big Walter Horton; *Chicago Blues Today-C* . . . . (Vanguard)
Memphis Charlie; *Best Of The Chicago Blues-C* . . . . (Vanguard)

Rockin' My Life Away
Jerry Lee Lewis; *Rockin' My Life Away* . . . .(Tomato)
Survivors . . . . (Columbia)
Swingin' Country Favorites-C . . . . (Warner Bros.)

Rockin' On A Saturday Night
Jason D. Williams; *Tore Up* . . . . (RCA)

Rockin' On The River
Jerry Jeff Walker; *Navajo Rug* . . . . (Rykodisc)

Rockin' Over China
Commander Cody; *Let's Rock.* . . . . (Blind Pig)

Rockin' Over The Beat
Technotronic; *Pump Up The Jam-The Album* . . . . (SBK)

Rockin' Pneumonia And The Boogie Woogie Flu
Aerosmith; *ST/Less Than Zero* . . . . (Def Jam)
Huey "Piano" Smith; *All-Star Chartbusters* . . . . (Intermedia)
Huey "Piano" Smith And The Clowns; *Jimpin' Jive '50s-C* . . . . (Priority)
Johnny Rivers; *Best Of Johnny Rivers* . . . . (EMI)
Johnny Rivers-Anthology 1964-1977 . . . . (Rhino)
Professor Longhair; *Rock 'N' Roll Gumbo* . . . . (Dancing Cat)
Rodney Lay & Wild West; *Rockabilly Nuggets-C* . . . . (Sun)

Rockin' Radio
Tom Browne; *45-#9088* . . . . (Arista)

Rockin' Robin
Bobby Day; *Cruisin'-1958-C* . . . . (Increase)
Oldies But Goodies-#5-C . . . . (Original Sound)
Rockin' Robin . . . . (Collectables)

Super Oldies Of The '50s-#2-C. .... (Audio Fidelity)
Michael Jackson; *Best Of Michael Jackson* .... (Motown)
Got To Be There .... (Motown)
Michael Jackson-Anthology .... (Motown)
Original Soul Of Michael Jackson .... (Motown)

Rockin' Rockin' Leprechauns
Jonathan Richman & The Modern Lovers; *Rock 'N' Roll With Jonathan Richman & The Modern Lovers* .... (Rhino)

Rockin' Roll Baby
Stylistics; *Best Of The Stylistics* .... (Amherst)
Rockin' Roll Baby .... (H&L)

Rockin' Rollin' Rover
Bill Haley & His Comets; *Bill Haley & His Comets-Golden Hits* .... (MCA)

Rockin' Shopping Center
Jonathan Richman & The Modern Lovers; *Jonathan Richman & The Modern Lovers* .... (Rhino)

Rockin' The Boat
Ricky Skaggs; *Live In London* .... (Epic)
Wayland Patton; *Gulf Stream Dreamin'* .... (Capitol)

Rockin' The Boat Of Love
Jerry Lee Lewis; *Golden Rock & Roll* .... (Sun)

Rockin' The Dog
Hellecasters; *Town South Of Bakersfield-#3* .... (Restless)

Rockin' The Mule
Barrence Whitfield & The Savages; *Ow Ow Ow Ow* .... (Rounder)

Rockin' The Paradise
Styx; *Caught In The Act* .... (A&M)
Paradise Theater .... (A&M)

Rockin' The Rock
Larry Stewart; *Heart Like A Hurricane* .... (Columbia)

Rockin' Time
Bunny Wailer; *Roots Radics Rockers Reggae* .... (Shanachie)

Rockin' Train
Joe Perry Project; *Let The Music Do The Talking* .... (Columbia)

Rockin' With Fes
Professor Longhair; *Mardi Gras In New Orleans-1949-1957* ... (Nighthawk)

Rockin' With Fire
Isley Brothers; *Showdown* .... (T-Neck/Columbia)

Rockin' With The Rhythm Of The Rain
Judds; *Judds' Greatest Hits* .... (MCA)
Rockin' With The Rhythm .... (MCA)

Rockin' Years
Dolly Parton & Ricky Van Shelton; *Eagle When She Flies* .... (Columbia)
Ricky Van Shelton & Dolly Parton; *Backroads* .... (Columbia)

Rocking Chair Blues
Bessie Smith; *Bessie Smith-The Complete Recordings-#1* .... (Legacy)
Ray Charles; *20 Golden Pieces Of Ray Charles* .... (Bulldog)

Rocking Over Russia
Elvis Hitler; *Disgraceland* .... (Restless)

Rocking Steady
Bob Marley & The Wailers; *One Love* .... (Heartbeat)

Rocking Surfer
Beach Boys; *Surfer Girl* .... (Capitol)

Rockit
Herbie Hancock; *Best Of Herbie Hancock* .... (Legacy)
Future Shock .... (Legacy)
ST/Zoolander .... (Hollywood)

Rock'n Me
Steve Miller Band; *Fly Like An Eagle* .... (Capitol)
Steve Miller Band-Gift Set .... (Capitol)
Steve Miller Band's Greatest Hits-1974-78 .... (Capitol)

Rock-N-Roll Lady
Rick Nelson; *Best Of Rick Nelson 1963-1975* .... (MCA)

Rock-N-Roll Weasel
Dead Serios; *Ralph Rules* .... (Long Song)

Rocks
Primal Scream; *Give Out But Don't Give Up* .... (Sire)

Roll Over Beethoven
Beatles; *Beatles-Box Set* .... (Capitol)
Rock 'N' Roll Music .... (Capitol)
The Beatles At The Hollywood Bowl .... (Capitol)
The Beatles' Second Album .... (Capitol)
With The Beatles .... (Parlophone)
Byrds; *The Byrds* .... (Columbia)
Chuck Berry; *Chuck Berry-Golden Hits* .... (Mercury)
Chuck Berry's Greatest Hits .... (Everest)
Cruisin'-1956-C .... (Increase)
Oldies But Goodies-#10-C .... (Original Sound)
The Chess Box-Chuck Berry .... (Chess)
Electric Light Orchestra; *Afterglow* .... (Epic)
Ole ELO .... (Jet)

Roots, Rock, Reggae
Bob Marley & The Wailers; *Rastaman Vibration* .... (Tuff Gong)

Saints Rock 'n Roll, The
Bill Haley & His Comets; *Twentieth Century Masters-Millenium Collection-Bill Haley & His Comets* .... (MCA)

School Days
Chuck Berry; *Best Of Chuck Berry* .... (Gusto)
Billboard Top Rock 'N' Roll Hits-1957-C .... (Rhino)

Chuck Berry-Golden Hits .... (Mercury)
ST/Rock 'N' Roll High School .... (Sire)

Sex, Drugs & Rock & Roll
Ian Dury; *New Boots & Panties* .... (Stiff)
Mantronix; *This Should Move Ya* .... (Capitol)

Shake, Rattle And Roll
Big Joe Turner; *Big Joe Turner's Greatest Hits* .... (Atlantic)
Every Day I Have The Blues .... (Pablo)
Oldies But Goodies-#2-C .... (Original Sound)
Soul Years-C .... (Atlantic)
Bill Haley & His Comets; *Bill Haley & His Comets' Greatest Hits* ...... (MCA)
Bill Haley & His Comets-Golden Hits .... (MCA)
Elvis Presley; *For LP Fans Only* .... (RCA)
Rocker .... (RCA)
ST/This Is Elvis .... (RCA)
Fats Domino; *Fats Domino's Greatest Hits* .... (MCA)
Huey Lewis and the News; *Four Chords & Several Years Ago* .... (Elektra)
NRBQ; *At Yankee Stadium* .... (Mercury)
Vern Gosdin; *Best Of Vern Gosdin* .... (Warner Bros.)

Sheena Is A Punk Rocker
Ramones; *Leave Home* .... (Sire)
Loco Live .... (Sire)
Mania .... (Sire)
Rocket To Russia .... (Sire)

Show Business
AC/DC; *High Voltage* .... (Atco)

Sixty Minute Man
Billy Ward & His Dominoes; *Rock & Roll Show-C* .... (Gusto)
Dominos; *Oldies But Goodies-#5-C* .... (Original Sound)
Rufus Thomas & Carla Thomas; *Rufus Thomas & Carla Thomas-Chronicle* .... (Stax)

Smack Dab In The Middle
Ry Cooder; *Chicken Skin Music* .... (Reprise)
Show Time .... (Warner Bros.)

So High
Dave Mason; *Best Of Dave Mason* .... (Columbia)
Let It Flow .... (Columbia)

So You Want To Be A Rock 'N' Roll Star
Byrds; *Original Singles-#1-1965-1967* .... (Columbia)
Rock Classics Of The '60s-C .... (Columbia)
The Byrds .... (Columbia)
The Byrds (Untitled) .... (Legacy)
The Byrds' Greatest Hits .... (Columbia)
Patti Smith Group; *Wave* .... (Arista)
Tom Petty And The Heartbreakers; *Pack Up The Plantation-Live!* ...... (MCA)
The Ultimate Rock Album-C .... (Foundation)

Stay
Temptations; *Phoenix Rising* .... (Motown)

Stick Around For Rock & Roll
Outlaws; *Bring It Back Alive* .... (Arista)
Lady In Waiting .... (Arista)
Outlaws' Greatest Hits .... (Arista)

Story Of Rock & Roll
Turtles; *Best Of The Turtles-Golden Archive Series* .... (Rhino)
Chalon Road .... (Rhino)
Turtles-20 Greatest Hits .... (Rhino)

Susy Is A Headbanger
Ramones; *All The Stuff & More-#1* .... (Sire)
Leave Home .... (Sire)

Suzi Wants To Be A Rock Star
Professor Griff & His Last Asiatic Disciples; *Pawns In The Game* ...... (Luke)

Swanee River Rock
Ray Charles; *Birth Of Soul-Complete Atlantic R&B 1952-1959-C* .... (Atlantic)

Sweet Feelin'
Doobie Brothers; *Minute By Minute* .... (Warner Bros.)

Sweet Little Rock & Roller
Chuck Berry; *Chuck Berry Is On Top* .... (Chess)
The Chess Box-Chuck Berry .... (Chess)
Richard Thompson; *Guitar/Vocal* .... (Hannibal)
Rod Stewart; *Absolutely Live* .... (Warner Bros.)
Best Of Rod Stewart .... (Mercury)
Storyteller/The Complete Anthology: 1964-1990 .... (Warner Bros.)

Sweet Little Sixteen
Beatles; *45-#1502* .... (Collectables)
Chuck Berry; *Best Of The Best Of Chuck Berry* ..... (International Mktg. Group)
Chuck Berry-Golden Hits .... (Mercury)
Chuck Berry-Greatest Hits Live .... (Quicksilver)
Cruisin'-1965-C .... (Increase)
Oldies But Goodies-#12-C .... (Original Sound)
Jerry Lee Lewis; *Jerry Lee Lewis-Original Golden Hits-#3* .... (Sun)
Jerry Lee Lewis & Friends; *Jerry Lee Lewis & Friends-Duets* .... (Sun)
John Lennon; *Lennon* .... (Capitol)
Rock 'N' Roll .... (Capitol)

Sweet Old Fashioned Girl, A
Teresa Brewer; *Music! Music! Music!-Best Of Teresa Brewer* .... (Varese Vintage)

Take Me In Your Arms
Doobie Brothers; *Best Of The Doobies* .... (Warner Bros.)
Stampede .... (Warner Bros.)

Isley Brothers; *Motown Superstar Series-#6-Isley Brothers* . . . . (Motown)
  The Isley Brothers Story-#1-Rockin' Soul-1959-1968 . . . . (Rhino)
Kim Weston; *25 Hard-To-Find Motown Classics-#3-C* . . . . (Motown)
  Every Great Motown Song-First 25 Years-C . . . . (Motown)
  Greatest By Holland/Dozier/Holland-C . . . . (Motown)
  Motown Dance Party-#1-C . . . . (Motown)

That Is Rock & Roll
Chesterfields; *ST/American Hot Wax* . . . . (A&M)
Coasters; *50 Coastin' Classics-C* . . . . (Rhino)
  Coasters' Greatest Hits . . . . (Atco)

That Rock Won't Roll
Restless Heart; *Best Of Restless Heart* . . . . (RCA)
  Country Music Classics-#22-1985-1990-C . . . . (K-Tel)
  Wheels . . . . (RCA)

That's Rock 'N' Roll
Eric Carmen; *Best Of Eric Carmen* . . . . (Arista)
  Eric Carmen . . . . (Rhino)
Shaun Cassidy; *Shaun Cassidy's Greatest Hits* . . . . (Curb)
  Yesterday's Heroes-'70s Teen Idols-C . . . . (Rhino)

That's The Way I Wanna Rock N Roll
AC/DC; *Blow Up Your Video* . . . . (Atco)
  Live (Special Collector's Edition) . . . . (Atco)

There Won't Be No Country Music (There Won't Be No Rock 'N' Roll)
C.W. McCall; *C.W. McCall's Greatest Hits* . . . . (Polydor)

There's Only One Way To Rock
Sammy Hagar; *Standing Hampton* . . . . (Geffen)
  The Ultimate Rock Album-C . . . . (Foundation)
Van Halen; *LIVE: Right here, right now.* . . . . (Warner Bros.)

They Call It Rock
Nick Lowe; *Pure Pop For Now People* . . . . (Columbia)

This Boy Needs To Rock
Night Ranger; *7 Wishes* . . . . (MCA)
  ST/Explorers . . . . (Varese Sarabande)

This Is The Rock
Fleetwood Mac; *Kiln House* . . . . (Reprise)

Too Old To Rock 'N' Roll: Too Young To Die
Jethro Tull; *Bursting Out* . . . . (Chrysalis)
  Classic Case with the London Symphony Orchestra . . . . (RCA)
  Original Masters . . . . (Chrysalis)
  Repeat-The Best Of Jethro Tull, Vol. II . . . . (Chrysalis)

Top 40 Radio (The History Of Rock)
Joey Welz; *Return Of Haley's Comet* . . . . (Caprice Int'l)

Trenchtown Rock
Bob Marley & The Wailers; *Bob Marley & The Wailers-Live* . . . . . . (Tuff Gong)
  Confrontation . . . . (Tuff Gong)
  More Of The Mighty . . . . (Tuff Gong)
  Songs Of Freedom . . . . (Tuff Gong)

Truck Stop Rock
Commander Cody & His Lost Planet Airmen; *Hot Licks, Cold Steel &*
  Trucker's Favorites. . . . . (MCA)

Turtle Rock
Bela Fleck & The Flecktones; *Flight Of The Cosmic Hippo* . . . . . (Warner Bros.)

Twenty Flight Rock
Commander Cody & His Lost Planet Airmen; *Lost In The Ozone* . . . . . (MCA)
  Too Much Fun-Best Of Commander Cody & His Lost Planet Airmen . . (MCA)
Eddie Cochran; *Eddie Cochran-Legendary Masters* . . . . (EMI)
  Eddie Cochran's Greatest Hits . . . . (Curb)
  On The Air . . . . (EMI)
Montrose; *Montrose* . . . . (Warner Bros.)
Paul McCartney; *CHOBA B CCCP-The Russian Album* . . . . (Capitol)
Rolling Stones; *''Still Life'' (American Concert 1981)* . . . . (Virgin)

Uranium Rock
Cramps; *Bad Music For Bad People* . . . . (I.R.S.)

Wanna Be A Rock 'N' Roll Star
Eddie Money; *Eddie Money* . . . . (Columbia)

We Built This City
Starship; *Greatest Hits-Ten Years & Change-1979-1991* . . . . (RCA)
  Knee Deep In The Hoopla . . . . (Grunt)
  Nipper's Greatest Hits Of The '80s-C . . . . (RCA)

We Need A Lot More Of Jesus (& A Lot Less Of Rock & Roll)
Linda Ronstadt; *Hand Sown Home Grown* . . . . (Capitol)

We Will Rock You
Queen; *Live At Wembley '86* . . . . (Hollywood)
  Live Killers . . . . (Hollywood)
  News Of The World . . . . (Hollywood)
  Queen's Greatest Hits I & II . . . . (Hollywood)
  ST/FM . . . . (MCA)

When The Machines Rock
Gary Numan & Tubeway Army; *Replicas* . . . . (Atco)

When You Rock 'N' Roll With Me
David Bowie; *David Live* . . . . (Rykodisc)

Whiskey Rock A Roller
Lynyrd Skynyrd; *Gold & Platinum.* . . . . (MCA)
  Nuthin' Fancy . . . . (MCA)
  One More From The Road . . . . (MCA)

White Noise
Jay Ferguson; *White Noise* . . . . (Capitol)

You Can't Kill Rock & Roll
Ozzy Osbourne; *Diary Of A Madman* . . . . (Jet)

You Got Me Rocking
Rolling Stones; *Voodoo Lounge* . . . . (Virgin)

You Rock My World
Michael Jackson; *Invincible* . . . . (Epic)

Young Thing, Wild Dreams (Rock Me)
Red Rider; *Breaking Curfew* . . . . (Capitol)

Your Mama Don't Dance
Loggins & Messina; *Loggins & Messina-On Stage.* . . . . (Columbia)
  Loggins And Messina . . . . (Columbia)
  Pop Classics Of The '70s-C . . . . (Columbia)
  The Best Of Friends . . . . (Columbia)
Poison; *Open Up And Say...Ahh!* . . . . (Capitol)
  Swallow This Live. . . . . (Capitol)

RODEO

See Also: **AMERICAN WEST, ANIMALS: COWS, ANIMALS: HORSES, COWBOYS**

Amarillo By Morning
George Strait; *George Strait's Greatest Hits* . . . . (MCA)
  Strait From The Heart . . . . (MCA)

Beaches Of Cheyenne
Garth Brooks; *Fresh Horses* . . . . (Capitol)
  Limited Series Box . . . . (Capitol)

Blame It On Texas
Mark Chesnutt; *Mark Chesnutt's Greatest Hits* . . . . (Decca)
  Too Cold At Home . . . . (MCA)

I Can Still Make Cheyenne
George Strait; *Blue Clear Sky* . . . . (MCA)
  Latest Greatest Straitest Hits . . . . (MCA)

Lonesome Rodeo Cowboy
George Strait; *Livin' It Up* . . . . (MCA)

Midnight Rodeo
Leon Everette; *45-#12355* . . . . (RCA)

Montana Rodeo
Chris LeDoux; *Thirty-Dollar Cowboy* . . . . (Liberty)

Much Too Young (To Feel This Damn Old)
Garth Brooks; *Garth Brooks-Double Live* . . . . (Capitol)

One More For The Rodeo
UFO; *Obsession* . . . . (Chrysalis)

Ride 'Em Cowboy
Roy Rogers & Sons Of The Pioneers; *Roy Rogers & Sons Of The*
  Pioneers. . . . . (Varese Sarabande)

Ride 'Em Cowboy
Paul Davis; *Ride 'Em Cowboy.* . . . . (Bang)

Riding The Rodeo
Vince Gill; *When I Call Your Name* . . . . (MCA)

Ro Deo Deo Cowboy
Jerry Jeff Walker; *A Man Must Carry On* . . . . (MCA)

Rodeo
Garth Brooks; *Ropin' The Wind* . . . . (Liberty)
Red Steagall & The Coleman County Cowboys; *For All Our Cowboy*
  Friends . . . . (MCA)

Rodeo Cowboys
Lynn Anderson; *Lynn Anderson's Greatest Hits-#2* . . . . (Columbia)

Rodeo Girl
Rickie Lee Jones; *Flying Cowboys* . . . . (Geffen)

Rodeo Girls
Tanya Tucker; *Best Of Tanya Tucker* . . . . (MCA)

Rodeo Or Mexico
Garth Brooks; *Scarecrow* . . . . (Capitol)

Rodeo Road
Roy Rogers & Willie Nelson; *Roy Rogers Tribute-C* . . . . (RCA)

Rodeo Romeo
Moe Bandy; *Moe Bandy's Greatest Hits* . . . . (Columbia)

Rodeo Song
Moe Bandy; *You Haven't Heard The Last Of Me* . . . . (MCA)

Rodeo Trails
Chris LeDoux; *Rodeo Songs Old & New* . . . . (Liberty)

She's In Love With A Rodeo Man
Chris LeDoux; *Songs Of Rodeo & Country* . . . . (Liberty)
Don Williams; *Don Williams' Greatest Hits* . . . . (MCA)

Silence On The Line
Chris LeDoux; *Cowboy* . . . . (Capitol)

Someday Soon
Chris LeDoux; *Rodeo Songs Old & New* . . . . (Liberty)
Ian & Sylvia; *Ian & Sylvia's Greatest Hits* . . . . (Vanguard)
  Northern Journey . . . . (Vanguard)
Judy Collins; *Colors Of The Day-The Best Of Judy Collins* . . . . . . (Elektra)
  Who Knows Where The Time Goes . . . . (Elektra)
Moe Bandy; *Moe Bandy's Greatest Hits* . . . . (Columbia)
  Rodeo Romeo . . . . (Columbia)
Suzy Bogguss; *Aces* . . . . (Liberty)
  Suzy Bogguss' Greatest Hits. . . . . (Liberty)

Sweetheart Of The Rodeo
Emmylou Harris; *Ballad Of Sally Rose* . . . . (Warner Bros.)

This Ain't My First Rodeo
Vern Gosdin; *10 Years Of Greatest Hits Newly Recorded*. . . . . (Columbia)
   Vern Gosdin's Greatest Hits. . . . . (Columbia)
   Vern Gosdin-Super Hits. . . . . (Columbia)
When The Rodeo Comes To Town
Chris LeDoux; *He Rides The Wild Horses*. (Liberty)
Wild Horses
Garth Brooks; *No Fences*. . . . . (Capitol)

ROYALTY, Castles, Nobility

See Also: **BOSSES, KINGS, MONEY, POLITICS (various), POWER
& CONTROL, PREJUDICE, PRESIDENTS, PROTEST, QUEENS,
SOCIAL CLASS: GENERAL**

All Along The Watchtower
Bob Dylan; *Before The Flood* . . . . (Columbia)
   Biograph. . . . . (Columbia)
   Bob Dylan At Budokan . . . . (Columbia)
   Bob Dylan's Greatest Hits-#2. . . . . (Columbia)
   John Wesley Harding. . . . . (Columbia)
Jimi Hendrix; *Kiss The Sky* . . . . (Reprise)
   Lifelines/Jimi Hendrix Story . . . . (Reprise)
Jimi Hendrix Experience; *Electric Ladyland*. . . . . (Reprise)
   Essential Jimi Hendrix . . . . (Reprise)
   Smash Hits . . . . (Reprise)
U2; *Rattle And Hum*. . . . . (Island)
All The King's Castles
Shawn Phillips; *Bright White*. . . . . (A&M)
Arabian Knights
Siouxsie And The Banshees; *Juju* . . . . (Geffen)
   Once Upon A Time-The Singles . . . . (Geffen)
Brokedown Palace
Grateful Dead; *American Beauty*. . . . . (Warner Bros.)
Persuasions; *Might As Well...The Persuasions Sing
   Grateful Dead* . . . .(Grateful Dead)
Camelot
Original 1982 London Cast; *Camelot* . . . .(Varese Sarabande)
Original Cast; *Camelot* . . . . (Columbia)
Richard Burton; *Broadway Magic-The 1960s-C* . . . . (Columbia)
Richard Harris; *ST/Camelot*. . . . . (Warner Bros.)
Candle In The Wind 1997 (Diana, Princess Of Wales)
Elton John; *Candle In The Wind 1997 (Diana, Princess Of Wales)
   (Single)* . . . . (Rocket)
Castle Of Dreams
Dave Koz; *Dave Koz* . . . . (Capitol)
Castle Walls
Styx; *Grand Illusion* . . . . (A&M)
Castles Burning
Journey; *Trial By Fire* . . . . (Columbia)
Castles In The Air
Don McLean; *Best Of Don McLean*. . . . . (EMI)
   Greatest Hits-Then & Now . . . . (EMI)
   Tapestry . . . . (Liberty)
Castles In The Sand
Stevie Wonder; *Stevie Wonder's Greatest Hits* . . . . (Motown)
Castles In The Sand
David Allan Coe; *Castles In The Sand*. . . . . (Columbia)
Castles In The Sand
Seals & Crofts; *Seals & Crofts' Greatest Hits* . . . . (Warner Bros.)
Castles Made Of Sand
Jimi Hendrix; *Axis: Bold As Love* . . . . (Reprise)
   Essential Jimi Hendrix . . . . (Reprise)
   Kiss The Sky . . . . (Reprise)
Tuck & Patti; *Love Warriors* . . . . (Windham Hill)
Castles Of Sand
Jermaine Jackson; *Motown Superstar Series-#17-Jermaine Jackson* . . (Motown)
C'est Moi
Original Cast; *ST/Camelot*. . . . . (Warner Bros.)
Robert Goulet; *Camelot*. . . . . (Columbia)
Cry Baby Cry
Beatles; *The Beatles (White Album)* . . . . (Capitol)
Don't Let It Bring You Down
Crosby, Stills, Nash & Young; *4 Way Street*. . . . . (Atlantic)
Neil Young; *After The Gold Rush* . . . . (Reprise)
Don't Rob Another Man's Castle
Ernest Tubb; *The Ernest Tubb Story* . . . . (MCA)
Duchess
Stranglers; *Stranglers' Greatest Hits-1977-1990* . . . . (Epic)
   Stranglers IV. . . . . (I.R.S.)
Duchess
Genesis; *Duke* . . . . (Atlantic)
   Three Sides Live . . . . (Atlantic)
Duke Of Dubuque
Manhattan Transfer; *Bop doo-wopp* . . . . (Atlantic)
   Manhattan Transfer-Live . . . . (Atlantic)

Duke Of Earl
Gene Chandler; *21 Oldies But Goodies-C* . . . . (Original Sound)
   Billboard Top Rock 'N' Roll Hits-1962-C. . . . . (Rhino)
   Cruisin'-1962-C . . . . (Increase)
   Oldies But Goodies-#6-C . . . . (Original Sound)
New Edition; *Under The Blue Moon* . . . . (MCA)
Guenevere
Original Cast; *Camelot*. . . . .(Columbia)
Original Soundtrack; *ST/Camelot* . . . . (Warner Bros.)
Gypsies In The Palace
Jimmy Buffett; *Feeding Frenzy* . . . . (MCA)
   Last Mango In Paris . . . . (MCA)
Ice Cream Castles
Time; *Ice Cream Castle* . . . . (Warner Bros.)
In A Shanty In Old Shanty Town
Ink Spots; *Java Jive* . . . . (Laserlight)
Ivory Tower
Cathy Carr; *Jukebox Classics-#2-C* . . . . (Rhino)
Ivory Tower
Long Ryders; *Native Sons* . . . . (Frontier)
Ivory Tower
Van Morrison; *No Guru No Method No Teacher* . . . . (Mercury)
Joker James
Brian Hyland; *Brian Hyland's Greatest Hits* . . . .(Rhino)
Joker, The
Steve Miller Band; *Best Of Steve Miller 1968-1973*. . . . .(Capitol)
   Steve Miller Band-Gift Set. . . . .(Capitol)
   Steve Miller Band-Live. . . . .(Capitol)
   Steve Miller Band's Greatest Hits-1974-78 . . . .(Capitol)
   The Joker. . . . .(Capitol)
King Of The Castle
Soup Dragons; *This Is Our Art* . . . . (Sire)
Little Plastic Castle
Ani DiFranco; *Little Plastic Castle* . . . . (Righteous Babe)
Loosen Up My Strings
Clint Black; *Nothin' But The Taillights* . . . . (RCA)
Mighty Fortress Is Our God, A
Leontyne Price; *God Bless America*. . . . . (RCA)
My White Knight
Original Broadway Cast; *The Music Man* . . . .(Angel)
Original Cast; *The Music Man* . . . . (Gold Rush)
Night In Summer Long Ago
Mark Knopfler; *Golden Heart* . . . . (Warner Bros.)
November In The Snow/Lord Buckley
Mark Murphy; *Kerouac Then & Now* . . . . (Muse)
Osaka Castle
Peter Erskine; *Transition* . . . . (Denon)
Paper Castles
Frankie Lymon and The Teenagers; *Best Of Frankie Lymon and The
   Teenagers* . . . .(Rhino)
   Very Best Of Frankie Lymon & The Teenagers . . . .(Rhino)
Return Of The Red Baron
Royal Guardsmen; *Royal Guardsmen-Anthology* . . . . (One Way)
Rock The Casbah
Clash; *Combat Rock* . . . . (Epic)
   On Broadway . . . . (Epic)
   Seems Like Yesterday-#4-Early '80s-C . . . . (K-Tel)
   The Story Of The Clash, Volume 1. (Epic)
Royal Canal
Ian & Sylvia; *Four Strong Winds* . . . . (Vanguard)
   Ian & Sylvia's Greatest Hits . . . . (Vanguard)
Royal Garden Blues
Bix Beiderbecke; *At The Jazz Band Ball-#2*. . . . .(Columbia)
Bix Beiderbecke & His Wolverines; *History Of Classic Jazz-C* . . . . (Riverside)
Original Broadway Cast; *Black & Blue* . . . . (DRG)
Tommy Dorsey; *Best Of Tommy Dorsey* . . . .(Bluebird)
   Complete Tommy Dorsey-#2. . . . . (RCA)
Royal Nonesuch
Original Broadway Cast; *Big River-The Adventures Of
   Huckleberry Finn* . . . . (MCA)
Royal Orleans
Led Zeppelin; *Presence* . . . .(Swan Song)
Royal Scam
Steely Dan; *The Royal Scam* . . . . (MCA)
Royal Telephone
Burl Ives; *Best Of Burl Ives-#2*. . . . . (MCA)
George Lewis & Eclipse Alley Five; *George Lewis Of New
   Orleans*. . . . . (Riverside)
Sheik Of Araby
Beatles; *The Beatles-Anthology-#1* . . . .(Capitol)
Benny Goodman; *Benny Goodman Sextet featuring Charlie Christian-1939-
   1941* . . . .(Columbia)
Django Reinhardt; *Djangologie USA-#1* . . . .(Disques Swing)
Fred Astaire; *Three Evenings With Fred Astaire* . . . . (DRG)
Leon Redbone; *Double Time* . . . . (Warner Bros.)
Sheik Of Chicago
Joe Stampley; *Joe Stampley's Greatest Hits* . . . . (Epic)
Sir Duke
Stevie Wonder; *Original Musiquarium* . . . .(Motown)

Songs In The Key Of Life . . . . (Motown)
Skye Boat Song
King's Singers; *American Balladeer-Golden Classics-#1-C* . . . . . (Collectables)
Annie Laurie-Folk Songs Of British Isles. . . . . (Angel)
Roger Whittaker; *Live In Concert*. . . . . (RCA)
Spanish Castle Magic
Jimi Hendrix; *Axis: Bold As Love* . . . . (Reprise)
Lifelines/Jimi Hendrix Story . . . . (Reprise)
Live At Winterland. . . . . (Rykodisc)
Jimi Hendrix Experience; *Radio One* . . . . (Rykodisc)
Steal Away
Jackson Southernaires; *Presenting Joy, Peace, Happiness*
& Love. . . . . (MCA Special Prod.)
Reverend James Cleveland; *Reverend James Cleveland Sings With The*
World's Greatest Gospel Stars . . . . (Savoy)
Street Fighting Man
Rod Stewart; *Best Of Rod Stewart* . . . . (Mercury)
Sing It Again, Rod . . . . (Mercury)
Storyteller/The Complete Anthology: 1964-1990 . . . .(Warner Bros.)
Rolling Stones; *Beggars Banquet* . . . . (Abkco)
Get Yer Ya-Ya's Out! . . . . (Abkco)
Hot Rocks 1964-1971. . . . . (Abkco)
Singles Collection-The London Years . . . . (Abkco)
Through The Past, Darkly (Big Hits Vol. 2) . . . . (Abkco)
Sultan Of Sex
Neon Judgement; *Horny As Hell*. . . . . (Play It Again Sam)
Sultans Of Swing
Dire Straits; *Dire Straits* . . . .(Warner Bros.)
Live-Alchemy . . . .(Warner Bros.)
Money For Nothing . . . .(Warner Bros.)
Then You May Take Me To The Fair
Original Cast; *Camelot* . . . . (Columbia)
Vanessa Redgrave; *ST/Camelot* . . . .(Warner Bros.)
Tower Of London
ABC; *How To Be A Zillionaire* . . . . (Mercury)
Trader
Beach Boys; *10 Years Of Harmony* . . . . (Caribou)
Holland . . . . (Brother)
What Do The Simple Folk Do?
Julie Andrews; *Best Of Julie Andrews* . . . . (Rhino)
Julie Andrews & Richard Burton; *Camelot* . . . . (Columbia)
Original Soundtrack; *Camelot* . . . .(Warner Bros.)
White Palace
Clay Walker; *Clay Walker* . . . . (Giant)

SADNESS, Depression, Discouragement, Disillusionment, Melancholy

*See Also: **BREAK, CRYING, DEATH, DESPAIR, DIVORCE, ENDINGS, FEELINGS, GUILT, HEART, LONELY, LOSING & LOSS, LOVE (various), LOW SELF-ESTEEM, PAIN & HEALING, RAIN, SEPARATION, SUICIDE, TROUBLE***

1979
Smashing Pumpkins; *Mellon Collie And The Infinite Sadness* . . . . (Virgin)
The Aeroplane Flies High . . . . (Virgin)
2,000 Light Years From Home
Rolling Stones; *More Hot Rocks (big hits & fazed cookies)* . . . . (Abkco)
Singles Collection-The London Years . . . . (Abkco)
Their Satanic Majesties Request . . . . (Abkco)
Through The Past, Darkly (Big Hits Vol. 2) . . . . (Abkco)
3am
Matchbox Twenty; *Yourself Or Someone Like You* . . . . (Lava)
Absolutely (Story Of A Girl)
Nine Days; *Maddening Crowd* . . . . (550 Music)
Now That's What I Call Music!-#5-C . . . . (Virgin)
Act Naturally
Beatles; *''Yesterday''...And Today* . . . . (Capitol)
Buck Owens; *Beatles Originals* . . . . (Rhino)
Buck Owens & Ringo Starr; *Act Naturally* . . . . (Capitol)
Buck Owens & The Buckaroos; *Buck Owens & The Buckaroos-Live At*
Carnegie Hall . . . .(Country Music Foundation)
Charley Pride; *Country Pride* . . . . (RCA)
Johnny Russell; *20 Great Country Hits-C* . . . . (RCA)
Adam's Song
Blink-182; *Enema Of The State* . . . . (MCA)
Adelaide's Lament
Original Cast; *Guys & Dolls* . . . .(MCA)
Guys & Dolls . . . . (Motown)
Adrian
Jewel; *Pieces Of You*. . . . .(Atlantic)
Ain't No Fun (Waiting Round To Be A Millionaire)
AC/DC; *Dirty Deeds Done Dirt Cheap* . . . .(Atlantic)
Ain't No Fun To Be Alone In San Antone
Gene Watson; *Mack In The Fire* . . . .(Warner Bros.)
Ain't No Sunshine When She's Gone
Bill Withers; *Bill Withers' Greatest Hits* . . . . (Columbia)

Bill Withers Live At Carnegie Hall. . . . . (Columbia)
Michael Jackson; *Original Soul Of Michael Jackson* . . . . (Motown)
All The Good Ones Are Gone
Pam Tillis; *Pam Tillis' Greatest Hits* . . . . (Arista)
All You Ever Do Is Bring Me Down
Mavericks; *Best Of The Mavericks-Super Colossal Smash Hits Of*
The '90s . . . . (Mercury)
Country Superstar Hits-C. . . . .(Hip-O)
Honky Tonk Boogie-C . . . .(Hip-O)
Music For All Occasions . . . . (MCA)
Alone And Forsaken
Emmylou Harris & Mark Knopfler; *Timeless: Hank Williams*
Tribute-C. . . . . (Lost Highway/IDJMG)
Hank Williams; *Alone And Forsaken* . . . . (Mercury)
Alone With His Guitar . . . . (Mercury)
Hank Williams-The Original Singles Collection . . . .(Polydor)
America
David Bowie; *The Concert For New York City-C* . . . . (Columbia)
Paul Simon; *Paul Simon In Concert/Live Rhymin'* . . . . (Columbia)
Simon & Garfunkel; *Bookends* . . . . (Columbia)
Collected Works . . . . (Columbia)
Simon & Garfunkel's Greatest Hits . . . . (Columbia)
The Concert In Central Park . . . .(Warner Bros.)
American Tune
Paul Simon; *Paul Simon In Concert/Live Rhymin'* . . . . (Columbia)
There Goes Rhymin' Simon . . . . (Columbia)
Simon & Garfunkel; *The Concert In Central Park* . . . . (Warner Bros.)
Amigone
Goo Goo Dolls; *Dizzy Up The Girl* . . . .(Warner Sunset/Reprise)
Among My Souvenirs
Connie Francis; *Connie Francis' Greatest Hits* . . . .(Polydor)
Frank Sinatra; *Columbia Years-1943-1952-Complete Recordings* . . . . . (Legacy)
Marty Robbins; *Marty Robbins-Super Hits*. . . . . (Columbia)
Sons Of The Pioneers; *Country & Western Memories* . . . .(Pair)
Angel
Sarah McLachlan; *Mirrorball* . . . . (Arista)
ST/City Of Angels . . . .(Warner Sunset/Reprise)
Surfacing . . . . (Arista)
Totally Hits-#1-C . . . . (Arista)
Angels Of The Silences
Counting Crows; *Recovering The Satellites* . . . .(David Geffen Co.)
Angel's Son
Strait Up featuring Lajon of Sevendust; *Strait Up-C*. . . . . (Immortal/Virgin)
Another Day
Bryan Adams; *Into The Fire* . . . . (A&M)
Another Night
Ricky Skaggs and Kentucky Thunder; *Bluegrass Rules!* . . . . (Rounder)
Another Sad Love Song
Toni Braxton; *Toni Braxton* . . . . (LaFace)
Anything's Better Than Feelin' The Blues
Martina McBride; *Emotion* . . . . (RCA)
Are U Still Down?
Jon B.; *Cool Relax* . . . .(Yab Yum/550)
As Tears Go By
Marianne Faithfull; *Marianne Faithfull's Greatest Hits* . . . .(Abkco)
Strange Weather . . . . (Island)
Rolling Stones; *Big Hits (High Tide & Green Grass)* . . . .(Abkco)
December's Children (and everybody's) . . . .(Abkco)
Hot Rocks 1964-1971 . . . .(Abkco)
Singles Collection-The London Years . . . . (Abkco)
Ask The Lonely
Vonda Shepard; *ST/Songs From ''Ally McBeal'' Featuring Vonda*
Shepard . . . .(550/Epic)
Baby's In Black
Beatles; *Beatles '65* . . . . (Capitol)
Beatles-Box Set. . . . . (Capitol)
For Sale . . . . (Capitol)
Back 2 Good
Matchbox Twenty; *Yourself Or Someone Like You*. . . . . (Lava)
Back On The Street Again
Sunshine Company; *Even More Nuggets-C* . . . . (Rhino)
Backstreets
Bruce Springsteen; *Born To Run* . . . . (Columbia)
Bad Day
Fuel; *Now That's What I Call Music!-#8-C* . . . .(Virgin)
Something Like Human . . . . (Epic)
Bad Girls
Donna Summer; *Bad Girls* . . . . (Casablanca)
Dance Collection . . . . (Casablanca)
On The Radio-Greatest Hits-Volumes I & II . . . . (Casablanca)
Summer Collection . . . . (Mercury)
Walk Away-Best Of Donna Summer-1977-1980 . . . . (Casablanca)
Bad Magik
Godsmack; *Awake*. (Republic/Universal)
Bad To Me
Billy J. Kramer With The Dakotas; *History Of British Rock-#1-C* . . . . . (Rhino)
Rock Is Dead But It Won't Lie Down-C . . . . (Gold Rush)
Bang The Drum Slowly
Emmylou Harris; *Red Dirt Girl*. . . . .(Nonesuch)

Be True
Bruce Springsteen; *Tracks*.....................................(Columbia)
Beautiful Day
U2; *All That You Can't Leave Behind* ....(Interscope)
  Now That's What I Call Music!-#6-C ....(Virgin)
Before The Blues
Colin Linden; *Raised By Wolves* ....(Compass)
Best Of Intentions
Travis Tritt; *Down The Road I Go* ....(Columbia)
Best Things
Filter; *Title Of Record* ....(Reprise)
Better Days (And The Bottom Drops Out)
Citizen King; *Mobile Estates*........................(Warner Bros.)
Better Your Heart Than Mine
Trisha Yearwood; *The Song Remembers When*....................(MCA)
Big Man
Four Preps; *Best Of The Four Preps* ....(Curb)
  Capitol Collectors Series-Four Preps ....(Collectables)
Billy Dale
Asleep At The Wheel featuring Dolly Parton; *Tribute To The Music Of Bob
  Wills And The Texas Playboys-C* ....(Liberty)
Bits And Pieces
Dave Clark Five; *History Of The Dave Clark Five* ....(Hollywood)
Bitter Sweet Symphony
Verve; *Urban Hymns* ....(Hut/Virgin)
Black Balloon
Goo Goo Dolls; *Dizzy Up The Girl* ....(Warner Sunset/Reprise)
Black Is Black
Los Bravos; *History Of British Rock-#7-C* ....(Rhino)
  London Collector-Rock Invasion-C ....(London)
Bleeders
Wallflowers; *Bringing Down The Horse* ....(Interscope)
Blue
LeAnn Rimes; *Blue* ....(MCG/Curb)
Blue Angel
Roy Orbison; *For The Lonely: 18 Greatest Hits* ....(Rhino)
  In Dreams-Greatest Hits.............................(Orbison)
  Roy Orbison Greatest Hits ....(Monument)
  Roy Orbison's All-Time Greatest Hits-#1 & 2 ....(Monument)
  Very Best Of Roy Orbison ....(Monument)
Blue Monday
Orgy; *Candyass* ....(Elementree/Reprise)
Blue Moon Of Kentucky
Bill Monroe; *American Originals-Bill Monroe* ....(Columbia)
  Bean Blossom ....(MCA)
  Best Of Bill Monroe & His Blue Grass Boys...............(MCA)
Bill Monroe & His Blue Grass Boys; *Bluegrass Super Hits-C* ....(Columbia)
Elvis Presley; *A Date With Elvis* ....(RCA)
  A Golden Celebration................................(RCA)
  The Sun Sessions ....(RCA)
Blue Moon With Heartache
Rosanne Cash; *19 Hot Country Requests-#2-C* ....(Epic)
  Rosanne Cash-Hits-1979-1989 ....(Columbia)
  Seven Year Ache ....(Columbia)
Blue Train, The
Linda Ronstadt; *Feels Like Home* ....(Elektra)
Maura O'Connell; *Blue Is The Colour Of Hope* ....(Warner Bros.)
Bluer Than Blue
Michael Johnson; *The Michael Johnson Album*.............(EMI)
  Then & Now ....(ISD/Intersound)
Blues For Dixie
Asleep At The Wheel featuring Lyle Lovett; *Tribute To The Music Of Bob
  Wills And The Texas Playboys-C* ....(Liberty)
Barry & Holly Tashian; *Harmony*.......................(Rounder)
Bob Wills & His Texas Playboys; *Bob Wills & His Texas Playboys-
  Anthology 1935-1973* ....(Rhino)
  Tiffany Transcriptions-#8-More Of The Best ....(Rhino)
Merle Haggard & The Strangers; *Best Of Country Blues*.............(Curb)
  Train Whistle Blues ....(Rounder)
Blues In The Night
Benny Goodman; *Small Groups-1941-1945* ....(Columbia)
Bobby Bland; *Introspective Of The Early Years* ....(MCA)
Dinah Shore; *Nipper's Greatest Hits Of The '40s-#1-C* ....(RCA)
Doc Severinsen; *Best Of Doc Severinsen*.................(MCA)
Frank Sinatra; *Frank Sinatra sings for Only The Lonely* ....(Capitol)
Jimmie Lunceford & His Orchestra; *Warner Bros.' 75 Years Entertaining
  The World-Film Music-C* ....(Rhino)
Mel Torme; *Torme*...................................(Verve)
Robins; *Best Of The Robins*..........................(Crescendo)
Rosemary Clooney; *Rosemary Clooney-16 Most Requested Songs* ....(Legacy)
Tony Bennett; *Playin' With My Friends-Bennett Sings The
  Blues-C* ....(Columbia)
Woody Herman; *Blues On Parade* ....(GRP)
  Woody Herman-Best Of The Decca Years ....(Decca)
Woody Herman & His Orchestra; *Big Bands Greatest
  Hits-#3-C* ....(MCA Special Prod.)
Bob Away My Blues
Clint Black; *D'lectrified*...............................(RCA)

Born To Be Blue
George Shearing & Mel Torme; *Evening With George Shearing & Mel
  Torme*......................................(Concord Jazz)
Judds; *Judds' Greatest Hits-#2* ....(MCA)
  Love Can Build A Bridge ....(MCA)
Mel Torme; *Mel Torme-Compact Jazz*....................(Verve)
Steve Miller; *Born 2 B Blue* ....(Gold Rush)
Born With A Broken Heart
Kenny Wayne Shepherd; *Ledbetter Heights* ....(Giant)
Bound For The Floor
Local H; *As Good As Dead*..............................(Island)
Breakdown
Mariah Carey featuring Bone Thugs-N-Harmony; *Butterfly* ....(Columbia)
Bridge Over Troubled Water
Aretha Franklin; *Aretha Franklin-30 Greatest Hits* ....(Rhino)
  Aretha Franklin's Greatest Hits ....(Atlantic)
  Live At Fillmore West ....(Atlantic)
Paul Simon; *America: A Tribute To Heroes-C* ....(Interscope)
  Concert In The Park-August 15 1991 ....(Warner Bros.)
  Paul Simon In Concert/Live Rhymin' ....(Columbia)
Simon & Garfunkel; *Bridge Over Troubled Water* ....(Columbia)
  Collected Works ....(Columbia)
  God Bless America-C ....(Columbia)
  Simon & Garfunkel's Greatest Hits...................(Columbia)
  The Concert In Central Park......................(Warner Bros.)
Broadway
Goo Goo Dolls; *Dizzy Up The Girl*................(Warner Sunset/Reprise)
Broken Hearted Savior
Big Head Todd & The Monsters; *Sister Sweetly* ....(Giant)
Broken Home
Papa Roach; *Infest* ....(DreamWorks/SKG)
Brokenhearted
Brandy featuring Wanya Morris; *Brandy*.....................(Atlantic)
Brokenhearted Me
Anne Murray; *15 Of The Best*..........................(Liberty)
  Anne Murray's Greatest Hits ....(Capitol)
Brother, Brother
Carole King; *Music* ....(Epic)
Brother, Can You Spare A Dime
Bing Crosby; *Bing Crosby-16 Most Requested Songs* ....(Legacy)
Odetta/Dr. John/John Campbell/Rufus Reid; *Strike A Deep Chord-Blues For
  The Homeless-C* ....(Justice)
Peter, Paul & Mary; *See What Tomorrow Brings* ....(Warner Bros.)
Weavers; *Weavers' Greatest Hits* ....(Vanguard)
Burn To Shine
Ben Harper; *Burn To Shine* ....(Virgin)
Caged Bird
Alicia Keys; *Songs In A Minor*...............................(J)
Candy's Room
Bruce Springsteen; *Darkness On The Edge Of Town*...........(Columbia)
Bruce Springsteen & The E Street Band; *Bruce Springsteen & The E Street
  Band Live/1975-85*................................(Legacy)
Captain Bligh
Filter; *Title Of Record* ....(Reprise)
Carolina Blues
Blues Traveler; *Straight On Till Morning* ....(A&M)
Chance, A
Kenny Chesney; *I Will Stand* ....(BNA)
Cherchez La Femme
Dr. Buzzard's Original "Savannah" Band; *Nipper's Greatest Hits Of The
  '70s-C* ....(RCA)
Gloria Estefan; *Hold Me, Thrill Me, Kiss Me* ....(Epic)
Child Is Gone
Fiona Apple; *Tidal* ....(Clean Slate/Work)
Close My Eyes
Mariah Carey; *Butterfly*..............................(Columbia)
Cool To Hate
Offspring; *Ixnay On The Hombre*.......................(Columbia)
Corvair
Jim White; *No Such Place* ....(Luaka Bop)
Count On Me
Whitney Houston and CeCe Winans; *ST/Waiting To Exhale*..........(Arista)
Crawling In The Dark
Hoobastank; *Hoobastank*.......................(Island/IDJMG)
Cruel Summer
Ace Of Base; *Cruel Summer* ....(Arista)
Bananarama; *Bananarama*..............................(London)
Cry
Crystal Gayle; *Best Of Crystal Gayle*.................(Warner Bros.)
Janie Fricke; *Celebration* ....(Columbia)
  I'll Need To Hold Someone When I Cry.................(Columbia)
Johnnie Ray; *Best Of Johnnie Ray* ....(Exact)
  Johnnie Ray-16 Most Requested Songs ....(Legacy)
  Radio Classics Of The '50s-C ....(Columbia)
Lynn Anderson; *Lynn Anderson's Greatest Hits* ....(Columbia)
Ray Charles; *Ray Charles' Greatest Hits-#2* ....(Rhino)
  Ray Charles-Anthology.............................(Rhino)
Cry
Roxette; *Look Sharp!* ....(EMI)

Cry Ophelia
Adam Cohen; *Songs From Dawson's Creek* . . . . (Sony Music Soundtrax)
Cumbersome
Seven Mary Three; *American Standard* . . . . (Mammoth)
Dammit (Growing Up)
Blink-182; *Dude Ranch* . . . . (Cargo)
Damn Right, I've Got The Blues
Buddy Guy; *Best Blues Album In The World...Ever!-C* . . . . (Virgin)
Buddy's Baddest: The Best Of Buddy Guy . . . . (Silvertone)
Damn Right, I've Got The Blues . . . . (Silvertone)
Dance, The
Garth Brooks; *Garth Brooks* . . . . (Liberty)
Garth Brooks-Double Live . . . . (Capitol)
Dear Me
Lorrie Morgan; *Lorrie Morgan's Greatest Hits* . . . . (BNA)
Desperately Wanting
Better Than Ezra; *Friction, Baby* . . . . (Swell/Elektra)
Diamonds On The Soles Of Her Shoes
Paul Simon; *Concert In The Park-August 15 1991* . . . . (Warner Bros.)
Graceland . . . . (Warner Bros.)
Negotiations And Love Songs, 1971-1986 . . . . (Warner Bros.)
Diary
Bread; *Baby I'm-A Want You* . . . . (Elektra)
Best Of Bread . . . . (Elektra)
Bread-Anthology . . . . (Elektra)
Difficult Kind, The
Sheryl Crow; *The Globe Sessions* . . . . (A&M)
Dis-Satisfied
Bill Anderson & Jan Howard; *More Great Country
Duets-C* . . . . (MCA Special Prod.)
Don't It Make My Brown Eyes Blue
Crystal Gayle; *Classic Crystal* . . . . (EMI)
Heartbreak Hotel-C . . . . (EMI)
ST/Convoy . . . . (Polydor)
We Must Believe In Magic . . . . (United Artists)
Don't Let It Bring You Down
Crosby, Stills, Nash & Young; *4 Way Street* . . . . (Atlantic)
Neil Young; *After The Gold Rush* . . . . (Reprise)
Don't Rock The Jukebox
Alan Jackson; *Alan Jackson-The Greatest Hits Collection* . . . . (Arista)
Don't Rock The Jukebox . . . . (Arista)
Down
Amel Larrieux; *Infinite Possibilities* . . . .(Epic)
Down And Out In Birmingham
Pirates Of The Mississippi; *Pirates Of The Mississippi* . . . . (Liberty)
Down In A Hole
Alice In Chains; *Dirt* . . . . (Columbia)
Down So Long
Jewel; *Spirit* . . . . (Atlantic)
Drift Away
Dobie Gray; *Classic Rock-#1-C* . . . . (MCA)
Oldies But Goodies-#10-C . . . . (Original Sound)
Oldies But Goodies-#3-C . . . . (Original Sound)
Super Hits Of The '70s-Have A Nice Day-#10-C . . . . (Rhino)
Michael Bolton; *Timeless-Classics* . . . . (Columbia)
Rod Stewart; *Atlantic Crossing* . . . . (Warner Bros.)
Easier Said Than Done
Essex; *Best Of The Girl Groups-#2-C* . . . . (Rhino)
Billboard Top Rock 'N' Roll Hits-1963-C . . . . (Rhino)
Original Rock 'N' Roll Hits Of The '60s-C . . . . (Roulette)
Eddie My Love
Fontane Sisters; *History Of Dot-#1-Young Love-C* . . . . (Varese Sarabande)
El Condor Pasa (If I Could)
Paul Simon; *Paul Simon In Concert/Live Rhymin'* . . . . (Columbia)
Simon & Garfunkel; *Bridge Over Troubled Water* . . . . (Columbia)
Collected Works . . . . (Columbia)
Simon & Garfunkel's Greatest Hits . . . . (Columbia)
Elegantly Wasted
INXS; *Elegantly Wasted* . . . . (Mercury)
Elvis Presley Blues
Gillian Welch; *Time (The Revelator)* . . . . (Acony)
Emotion
Destiny's Child; *Survivor* . . . . (Columbia)
The Concert For New York City-C . . . . (Columbia)
End Of The Innocence
Don Henley; *The End Of The Innocence* . . . .(Geffen)
Even Cowgirls Get The Blues
Emmylou Harris; *Blue Kentucky Girl* . . . . (Warner Bros.)
Johnny Cash & Waylon Jennings; *Cowboy Super Hits-C* . . . . (Columbia)
Heroes . . . . (Columbia)
Everybody Knows
Trisha Yearwood; *Everybody Knows* . . . .(MCA)
Everybody's Had The Blues
Merle Haggard & The Strangers; *For The Record: Merle Haggard-43
Legendary Hits* . . . . (BNA)
Everyone's Gone To The Moon
Jonathan King; *British Rock-#3-C* . . . . (Original Sound)
History Of British Rock-#7-C . . . . (Rhino)

Everything Falls Apart
Dog's Eye View; *Happy Nowhere* . . . . (Columbia)
Everything Is Broken
Kenny Wayne Shepherd; *Trouble Is...* . . . . (Revolution)
Fa Fa Fa Fa Fa
Otis Redding; *Best Of Otis Redding* . . . .(Atlantic)
Live In Europe . . . . (Atco)
Otis Redding-History . . . . (Atco)
The Otis Redding Story . . . .(Atlantic)
Fall From Grace
Amanda Marshall; *Amanda Marshall* . . . . (Epic)
Falls Apart
Sugar Ray; *14:59* . . . . (Lava)
Totally Hits-#2-C . . . . (Elektra)
Fear Of Falling
Badlees; *River Songs* . . . .(Atlas)
Feelin' Good About Feelin' Bad
Patty Loveless; *When Fallen Angels Fly* . . . . (Epic)
Fell On Black Days
Soundgarden; *Superunknown* . . . . (A&M)
Fire And Rain
James Taylor; *James Taylor's Greatest Hits* . . . . (Warner Bros.)
Sweet Baby James . . . . (Warner Bros.)
The Concert For New York City-C . . . . (Columbia)
Sammy Kershaw; *Red Hot + Country-C* . . . . (Mercury)
First Taste
Fiona Apple; *Tidal* . . . .(Clean Slate/Work)
Folsom Prison Blues
Brooks & Dunn with Johnny Cash; *Red Hot + Country-C* . . . . (Mercury)
Johnny Cash; *Billboard Top Country Hits-1968-C* . . . . (Rhino)
Classic Cash-Hall Of Fame Series . . . . (Mercury)
Hot Tracks-Train Super Hits-C . . . . (Epic)
Jailhouse Rock (Hits From The Big House)-C . . . . (Sony Music Special Prod.)
Johnny Cash At Folsom Prison & San Quentin . . . . (Columbia)
Johnny Cash-Original Golden Hits-#1 . . . . (Sun)
Johnny Cash's Greatest Hits-#2 . . . . (Columbia)
Superbilly . . . . (Sun)
The Man In Black-His Greatest Hits . . . . (Legacy)
Foolish Games
Jewel; *Pieces Of You* . . . .(Atlantic)
ST/Batman & Robin-Music From And Inspired By The Motion Picture . .(Jive)
VH-1 Crossroads-C . . . .(Atlantic)
For My Broken Heart
Reba McEntire; *For My Broken Heart* . . . . (MCA)
Reba McEntire's Greatest Hits Volume Two . . . . (MCA)
Friday Night Blues
John Conlee; *John Conlee-Live At Billy Bob's* . . . . (Razor & Tie)
John Conlee's Greatest Hits . . . . (MCA)
Sonny Throckmorton; *45-#57018* . . . . (Mercury)
Full Forever
Goo Goo Dolls; *Dizzy Up The Girl* . . . .(Warner Sunset/Reprise)
Georgy Girl
Seekers; *History Of British Rock-#4-C* . . . . (Rhino)
Get Born Again
Alice In Chains; *Nothing Safe* . . . . (Columbia)
Get Rhythm
Johnny Cash; *Johnny Cash-Sun Years* . . . . (Rhino)
Ry Cooder; *Get Rhythm* . . . . (Warner Bros.)
Get Up
Amel Larrieux; *Infinite Possibilities* . . . . (Epic)
Give Myself A Party
Mandy Barnett; *I've Got A Right To Cry* . . . . (Sire)
Glad To Be Unhappy
Mamas & The Papas; *Mamas & The Papas-16 Of Their Greatest Hits* . . . (MCA)
Gloomy December
Jean Redpath; *Songs Of Robert Burns-#6* . . . .(Philo)
Gloomy Monday
Jimi Hendrix & Curtis Knight; *Get That Feeling* . . . . (Fifty One West)
Gloomy Sunday
Billie Holiday; *Billie Holiday's Greatest Hits* . . . . (Legacy)
Legacy Box-1933-1958 . . . . (Columbia)
Gloria: The Enchantment Medley
Jesse Powell; *Jesse Powell* . . . . (Silas)
Go Walking Down There
Chris Isaak; *Forever Blue* . . . . (Reprise)
Goin' Down The Road Feeling Bad
Delaney & Bonnie; *Best Of Delaney & Bonnie* . . . . (Rhino)
Doc Watson; *Elementary Doctor Watson* . . . .(Poppy)
Essential Doc Watson . . . . (Vanguard)
Grateful Dead; *Grateful Dead (Skull & Roses)* . . . . (Warner Bros.)
One From The Vault . . . .(Grateful Dead)
Going Away Party
Manhattan Transfer & Willie Nelson & Asleep At The Wheel; *Ride With
Bob-C* . . . .(DreamWorks/SKG)
Gone
Ferlin Husky; *Ferlin Husky's Greatest Hits* . . . . (Curb)
Heroes Of Country Music-#4-Legends Of The West Coast-C . . . . . . (Rhino)
Gone Away
Offspring; *Ixnay On The Hombre* . . . . (Columbia)

Good Man Is Hard To Find (Pittsburgh)
Bruce Springsteen; *Tracks* . . . . (Columbia)
Good Morning Heartache
Billie Holiday; *All Or Nothing At All* . . . . (Verve)
Billie Holiday's Greatest Hits . . . . (Decca Jazz)
From The Original Decca Masters . . . . (MCA)
History Of Billie Holiday . . . . (Verve)
Diana Ross; *Diana Ross-Anthology* . . . . (Motown)
ST/Lady Sings The Blues . . . . (Motown)
Tony Bennett with Sheryl Crow; *Playin' With My Friends-Bennett Sings The Blues-C* . . . . (Columbia)
Good Time Man Like Me Got No Business (Singin' The Blues), A
Jim Croce; *Life & Times* . . . . (Lifesong)
Words And Music . . . . (Dunhill Compact Classics)
Good Times Bad Times
Led Zeppelin; *Led Zeppelin* . . . . (Atlantic)
Good Times, Bad Times
Rolling Stones; *12 X 5* . . . . (Abkco)
Big Hits (High Tide & Green Grass) . . . . (Abkco)
More Hot Rocks (big hits & fazed cookies) . . . . (Abkco)
Singles Collection-The London Years . . . . (Abkco)
Goodbye Lament
Iommi; *Iommi* . . . . (Divine/Priority)
Goodbye To Love
Carpenters; *Carpenters-Classics-#2* . . . . (A&M)
Carpenters-Love Songs . . . . (A&M)
Graduation Day
Beach Boys; *Beach Boys-Gift Set* . . . . (Capitol)
Spirit Of America . . . . (Capitol)
Rover Boys; *Choice Voices! Pop Vocal Group Gems Of The '50s-C* . . . . (Collector's Choice)
Great Pretender
Band; *Moondog Matinee* . . . . (Capitol)
Platters; *Billboard Top R&B Hits-1956-C* . . . . (Rhino)
Cruisin'-1956-C . . . . (Increase)
Encore Of Golden Hits-Platters . . . . (Mercury)
Platters-Anthology . . . . (Rhino)
ST/American Graffiti . . . . (MCA)
Super Oldies Of The '50s-#3-C . . . . (Audio Fidelity)
Roy Orbison; *Best Of Roy Orbison-Loved Standards* . . . . (Monument)
Stan Freberg; *Capitol Collectors Series-Stan Freberg* . . . . (Capitol)
Guys & Dolls
Original Cast; *ST/Guys & Dolls* . . . . (MCA)
Happening, The
Diana Ross; *Diana Ross-Anthology* . . . . (Motown)
Diana Ross & The Supremes; *Diana Ross & The Supremes-Superstar Series-#1* . . . . (Motown)
Happy Girl
Beth Nielsen Chapman; *Sand And Water* . . . . (Reprise)
Martina McBride; *Evolution* . . . . (RCA)
Hard Candy Christmas
Dolly Parton; *Best Of Christmas-C* . . . . (RCA)
Country Christmas-#2-C . . . . (RCA)
Dolly Parton's Greatest Hits . . . . (RCA)
Season's Greetings-C . . . . (RCA)
ST/Best Little Whorehouse In Texas . . . . (MCA)
Original Cast; *Best Little Whorehouse In Texas* . . . . (MCA)
RuPaul; *Ho Ho Ho* . . . . (Rhino)
Have You Ever Been Lonely (Have You Ever Been Blue)
Ernest Tubb; *Best Of Ernest Tubb* . . . . (Curb)
The Country Music Hall Of Fame-Ernest Tubb . . . . (MCA)
Jim Reeves & Patsy Cline; *Jim Reeves' Greatest Hits* . . . . (RCA)
Patsy Cline; *Showcase-With The Jordanaires* . . . . (MCA)
Heartaches By The Number
Guy Mitchell; *Sentimental Journey-C* . . . . (Dominion Entert.)
Sunshine Guitar . . . . (Collectables)
Unforgettable-Love Songs-Fabulous '50s-C . . . . (Dominion Entert.)
Ray Price; *Columbia Country Classics-#2-Honky Tonk Heroes-C* . . . (Columbia)
Ray Price's Greatest Hits . . . . (Columbia)
Ray Price's Greatest Hits-#1-3 . . . . (Step One)
Heartbreak Hotel
Albert King; *Blues For Elvis* . . . . (Stax)
Elvis Presley; *Elvis As Recorded At Madison Square Garden* . . . . (RCA)
Elvis' Golden Records . . . . (RCA)
Elvis-A Legendary Performer, Volume 1 . . . . (RCA)
Nipper's Greatest Hits Of The '50s-#1-C . . . . (RCA)
Worldwide 50 Gold Award Hits, Vol. 1, Parts 1 & 2 . . . . (RCA)
Stan Freberg; *Capitol Collectors Series-Stan Freberg* . . . . (Capitol)
Willie Nelson; *Greatest Hits (& Some That Will Be)* . . . . (Columbia)
Willie Nelson & Leon Russell: One For The Road . . . . (Columbia)
Heartbreak Hotel
Whitney Houston Featuring Faith Evans & Kelly Price; *My Love Is Your Love* . . . . (Arista)
Totally Hits-#1-C . . . . (Arista)
Whitney Houston's Greatest Hits . . . . (Arista)
Heartbreaker
Grand Funk Railroad; *Capitol Collectors Series-Grand Funk Railroad* . . . . (Capitol)
Heartbroke Every Day
Lonestar; *Lonestar* . . . . (BNA)
Heavy
Collective Soul; *Dosage* . . . . (Atlantic)
Help!
Beatles; *Beatles 1* . . . . (Capitol)
Beatles-20 Greatest Hits . . . . (Capitol)
Rarities . . . . (Capitol)
Reel Music . . . . (Capitol)
ST/Help! . . . . (Capitol)
The Beatles At The Hollywood Bowl . . . . (Capitol)
The Beatles/1962-1966 . . . . (Capitol)
Hemorrhage (In My Hands)
Fuel; *Now That's What I Call Music!-#6-C* . . . . (Virgin)
Something Like Human . . . . (Epic)
Here Today
Beach Boys; *Pet Sounds* . . . . (Capitol)
The Pet Sounds Sessions: A 30th Anniversary Collection . . . . (Capitol)
Here's That Rainy Day
Frank Sinatra; *The Capitol Years* . . . . (Capitol)
Gene Ammons; *The Boss Is Back* . . . . (Prestige)
Kenny Rankin; *Kenny Rankin Album* . . . . (Little David)
Rosemary Clooney; *Rosemary Clooney Sings Ballads* . . . . (Concord Jazz)
Tony Bennett; *Perfectly Frank* . . . . (Columbia)
Hey Jude
Beatles; *Beatles 1* . . . . (Capitol)
Beatles-20 Greatest Hits . . . . (Capitol)
Past Masters-Volume Two . . . . (Parlophone)
The Beatles/1967-1970 . . . . (Capitol)
Paul McCartney; *Knebworth-The Album-C* . . . . (Polydor)
Wilson Pickett; *Wilson Pickett's Greatest Hits* . . . . (Atlantic)
High Head Blues
Black Crowes; *Amorica* . . . . (American)
High Lonesome Sound
Vince Gill; *Bluegrass Essentials-C* . . . . (Hip-O)
High Lonesome Sound . . . . (MCA)
Vince Gill with Alison Krauss & Union Station; *Grand Ole Opry-75 Years-#1-C* . . . . (MCA)
Highway Of Sorrow
Bill Monroe; *Best Of Bill Monroe & His Blue Grass Boys* . . . . (MCA)
Hi-Lili, Hi-Lo
Anne Murray; *There's A Hippo In My Tub* . . . . (Capitol)
Ray Conniff; *Encore! 16 Most Requested Songs* . . . . (Legacy)
Hole Hearted
Extreme; *Pornograffitti* . . . . (A&M)
Hollywood
Wallflowers; *The Wallflowers* . . . . (Virgin)
Home
Sheryl Crow; *Sheryl Crow* . . . . (A&M)
How Can You Mend A Broken Heart
Al Green; *Al Green's Greatest Hits-#1* . . . . (Motown)
Compact Command Performances-Al Green . . . . (Motown)
Let's Stay Together . . . . (Right Stuff)
Bee Gees; *Bee Gees-Gold* . . . . (Polydor)
Here At Last...Bee Gees...Live . . . . (Polydor)
Nobody's Child-Romanian Angel Appeal-C . . . . (Warner Bros.)
How The West Was Won And Where It Got Us
R.E.M.; *New Adventures In Hi-Fi* . . . . (Warner Bros.)
Hungry Eyes
Emmylou Harris; *Mama's Hungry Eyes-Merle Haggard Tribute-C* . . . . (Arista)
Merle Haggard; *For The Record: Merle Haggard-43 Legendary Hits* . . . . (BNA)
Hurt By Love
BoDeans; *Blend* . . . . (Reprise)
Hurt So Bad
Lettermen; *The Lettermen's All-Time Greatest Hits* . . . . (Capitol)
Linda Ronstadt; *Linda Ronstadt's Greatest Hits, Volume Two* . . . . (Asylum)
Mad Love . . . . (Elektra)
Little Anthony And The Imperials; *Best Of Little Anthony And The Imperials* . . . . (Rhino)
Best Of Little Anthony And The Imperials . . . . (EMI)
I Ain't Ever Satisfied
Gretchen Peters; *The Secret Of Life* . . . . (Purple Crayon Prod.)
Steve Earle & The Dukes; *Ain't Ever Satisfied: The Steve Earle Collection* . . . . (Hip-O)
Exit 0 . . . . (MCA)
Shut Up And Die Like An Aviator . . . . (MCA)
I Ain't Got Nobody
Bob Wills; *Stay A Little Longer-The Original Columbia Recordings* . . . . (Roswell/RCA)
Preservation Hall Jazz Band; *Best Of The Preservation Hall Jazz Band* . . . . (Columbia)
I Almost Lost My Mind
Eddy Arnold; *World Of Hits* . . . . (MGM)
Fats Domino; *Fats Domino's Greatest Hits* . . . . (MCA)
Ivory Joe Hunter; *Since I Met You Baby* . . . . (Mercury)
Pat Boone; *Pat Boone's Greatest Hits* . . . . (Curb)
I Am A Man Of Constant Sorrow
Ralph Stanley; *Rebel Records: 35 Years Of The Best In Bluegrass-1960-1995-C* . . . . (Rebel)

Soggy Bottom Boys featuring Dan Tyminski; *ST/O Brother, Where Art Thou?* .... (Mercury)
Stanley Brothers; *All Time Legends Of Country Music-C* .... (Legacy)

I Can Dream, Can't I?
Andrews Sisters; *Best Of The Andrews Sisters* .... (MCA)

I Disappear
Metallica; *ST/Mission: Impossible 2* .... (Hollywood)

I Don't Want To
Toni Braxton; *Secrets* .... (LaFace)

I Don't Want To Spoil The Party
Beatles; *Beatles VI* .... (Capitol)
For Sale .... (Capitol)
Rosanne Cash; *Greatest Country Hits Of The '80s-1989-C* .... (Columbia)
Rosanne Cash-Hits-1979-1989 .... (Columbia)

I Don't Want To Wait
Paula Cole; *Live On Letterman-From The Late Show* .... (Reprise)
Songs From Dawson's Creek .... (Sony Music Soundtrax)
This Fire .... (Imago)

I Fall To Pieces
Aaron Neville & Trisha Yearwood; *Rhythm Country And Blues-C* .....(MCA)
Patsy Cline; *12 Greatest Hits* .... (MCA)
Always .... (MCA)
ST/Sweet Dreams .... (MCA)
The Patsy Cline Story .... (MCA)

I Fell In The Water
John Anderson; *On Solid Ground* .... (BNA)

I Got The Blues
Rolling Stones; *Sticky Fingers* .... (Virgin)

I Guess The Lord Must Be In New York City
Nilsson; *Harry* .... (Dunhill Compact Classics)
Nilsson's Greatest Hits .... (RCA)

I Have Nothing
Whitney Houston; *ST/The Bodyguard* .... (Arista)

I Just Shot John Lennon
Cranberries; *To The Faithful Departed* .... (Island)

I Just Want To See His Face
Rolling Stones; *Exile On Main Street* .... (Virgin)

I Just Wasn't Made For These Times
Beach Boys; *Pet Sounds* .... (Capitol)
The Pet Sounds Sessions: A 30th Anniversary Collection ...... (Capitol)

I Loved You Once In Silence
Original Cast; *Camelot* .... (Columbia)
Original Soundtrack; *ST/Camelot* .... (Warner Bros.)

I Miss My Homies
Master P; *Ghetto D* .... (No Limit/Priority)

I Need You Now
Eddie Fisher; *Very Best Of Eddie Fisher* .... (MCA)

I Saw The Light
Hank Williams; *Hank Williams-24 Greatest Hits-#2* .... (Polydor)
Hank Williams-40 Greatest Hits .... (Polydor)
I Ain't Got Nothin' But Time-1946-1947 .... (Polydor)
Legend In Song-With Hank Williams, Jr. .... (Polydor)
Rare Takes & Radio Cuts .... (Polydor)

I Think It's Gonna Rain Today
Bette Midler; *ST/Beaches* .... (Atlantic)
Judy Collins; *In My Life* .... (Elektra)
Neil Diamond; *Rainbow* .... (MCA)
Stones .... (MCA)
Randy Newman; *12 Songs* .... (Reprise)
Randy Newman .... (Warner Archives)

I Went To Your Wedding
Patti Page; *Patti Page-Golden Hits* .... (Mercury)

I Wish
R. Kelly; *Now That's What I Call Music!-#6-C* .... (Virgin)
TP-2.com .... (Jive)

I Wish I Could Have Been There
John Anderson; *Solid Ground* .... (BNA)

I Wish I Felt Nothing
Wallflowers; *Bringing Down The Horse* .... (Interscope)

I Wish It Would Rain
Temptations; *16 #1 Hits From The Late '60s-C* .... (Motown)
All The Million-Sellers .... (Motown)
Billboard Top R&B Hits-1968-C .... (Rhino)
Compact Command Performances-Temptations .... (Motown)
Motown Story-First 25 Years-C .... (Motown)
Temptations-Anthology-The Best Of The Temptations .... (Motown)

I Wish It Would Rain Down
Phil Collins; *...But Seriously* .... (Atlantic)

I Wonder If Heaven Got A Ghetto
2Pac; *R U Still Down (Remember Me)* .... (Amaru/Jive)

If It Makes You Happy
Sheryl Crow; *Sheryl Crow* .... (A&M)

If She Don't Love You
Buffalo Club; *Buffalo Club* .... (Rising Tide)

I'll Be Here Awhile
311; *From Chaos* .... (Volcano Entertainment)

I'll Be Missing You
Puff Daddy & Family & Faith Evans & 112; *No Way Out* ..... (Bad Boy/Arista)

I'll Never Fall In Love Again
Dionne Warwick; *Billboard Top Soft Rock Hits-1970-C* .... (Rhino)
Her Classic Songs-#1 .... (Curb)
Elvis Presley; *From Elvis Presley Boulevard, Memphis, Tennessee* ...... (RCA)
Mary Chapin Carpenter; *ST/My Best Friend's Wedding* ...... (Work/Epic)

I'm A Loser
Beatles; *Beatles '65* .... (Capitol)

I'm Always On A Mountain When I Fall
Merle Haggard; *For The Record: Merle Haggard-43 Legendary Hits* ....(BNA)

I'm Blue (The Gong-Gong Song)
Ikettes; *Great R&B Female Groups-Hits Of The '60s-C* .... (K-Tel)

I'm Down
Beatles; *The Beatles-Anthology-#2* .... (Capitol)
Paul McCartney; *The Concert For New York City-C* .... (Columbia)

I'm Goin' Down
Mary J. Blige; *My Life* .... (Uptown/MCA)

I'm Not In Love
10 CC; *10 CC's Greatest Hits-1972-1978.* ....(Polydor)
Super Hits Of The '70s-Have A Nice Day-#14-C .... (Rhino)
Will To Power; *Journey Home* .... (Epic)

I'm Over You
Keith Whitley; *I Wonder Do You Think Of Me* .... (RCA)
Keith Whitley's Greatest Hits .... (RCA)

I'm So Lonesome I Could Cry
B.J. Thomas; *B.J. Thomas' Greatest Hits* .... (Rhino)
Cowboy Junkies; *Trinity Session.* .... (RCA)
Hank Williams; *24 Of Hank Williams' Greatest Hits* .... (Polydor)
Hank Williams-40 Greatest Hits. .... (Polydor)
I'm So Lonesome I Could Cry-1949 .... (Polydor)
Hank Williams, Jr.; *Very Best Of Hank Williams, Jr.* ....(Polydor)
Jim Rooney; *One Day At A Time* .... (Rounder)
Johnny Cash; *Hank Williams Songbook-C* .... (Columbia)
Keb' Mo'; *Timeless: Hank Williams Tribute-C* .... (Lost Highway/IDJMG)

I'm Tore Down
Eric Clapton; *From The Cradle* .... (Duck/Reprise)

In Dreams
Roy Orbison; *For The Lonely: A Roy Orbison Anthology 1959-1965* .... (Rhino)
In Dreams-Greatest Hits .... (Orbison)

In The Valley
Marty Robbins; *Gunfighter Ballads & Trail Songs* .... (Legacy)

Inner City Blues (Make Me Wanna Holler)
Marvin Gaye; *What's Going On* .... (Motown)

Inside
Patti Rothberg; *Between The 1 And The 9* .... (EMI)

Into Each Life Some Rain Must Fall
Ella Fitzgerald; *Ella & Friends* .... (Decca Jazz)
Ink Spots; *Encore Of Golden Hits-Ink Spots* .... (Juke Box Treasures)

Invisible City
Wallflowers; *Bringing Down The Horse* ....(Interscope)

Is A Bluebird Blue
Conway Twitty; *Rockin' Conway-MGM Years.* .... (Mercury)

I've Got A Right To Cry
Mandy Barnett; *I've Got A Right To Cry* .... (Sire)

I've Got A Right To Sing The Blues
Tony Bennett with Bonnie Raitt; *Playin' With My Friends-Bennett Sings The Blues-C* .... (Columbia)

I've Had It
Danielle Brisebois; *Portable Life* .... (RCA)

Jamaica Farewell
Harry Belafonte; *Calypso* .... (RCA)
Harry Belafonte-Legendary Performer .... (RCA)
Harry Belafonte-Pure Gold .... (RCA)
Harry Belafonte's All Time Greatest Hits-#1 .... (RCA)
This Is Harry Belafonte .... (RCA)

Janey Don't You Lose Heart
Bruce Springsteen; *Tracks* .... (Columbia)

Je Suis Desole
Mark Knopfler; *Golden Heart* .... (Warner Bros.)

Jenny Says
Cowboy Mouth; *Are You With Me?* .... (MCA)
Word Of Mouth .... (Monkey Hill)

Jesus To A Child
George Michael; *Ladies & Gentlemen: The Best Of George Michael* ..... (Epic)
Older ....(DreamWorks/SKG)

Joy
Nilsson; *Son Of Schmilsson* .... (RCA)

Just Can't Last
Natalie Merchant; *Motherland* .... (Elektra)

Kind Of A Drag
Buckinghams; *Kind Of A Drag* .... (Sundazed Music)
Mercy, Mercy, Mercy .... (Legacy Rock Artifacts Series)

Kindly Keep It Country
Vince Gill; *The Key* .... (MCA)

King Of Sorrow
Sade; *Lovers Rock* .... (Epic)

Last Cowboy Song
Ed Bruce; *16 Top Country Hits-#2-C* .... (MCA)
Ed Bruce's Greatest Hits .... (MCA)

Waylon Jennings, Willie Nelson, Johnny Cash, Kris Kristofferson; *Cowboy Super Hits-C* .... (Columbia)
Highwayman... (Columbia)

Last Cup Of Sorrow
Faith No More; *Album Of The Year* ....(Reprise)

Last Train To Clarksville
Monkees; *Monkees* .... (Arista)
Monkees' Greatest Hits .... (Rhino)
Monkees-Live-1967 .... (Rhino)
Then & Now...The Best Of The Monkees .... (Arista)

Learning As You Go
Rick Trevino; *Learning As You Go* .... (Columbia)
Super Hits Of 1996-C .... (Epic)

Learning The Game
Buddy Holly; *Complete Buddy Holly* .... (MCA)
The Buddy Holly Collection .... (MCA)

Leaving October
Sons Of The Desert; *Whatever Comes First* .... (Epic)

Let's Think About Living
Bob Luman; *Bob Luman-Classic Country*........................... (Simitar)

Letter, The
Macy Gray; *On How Life Is* .... (Epic)

Life
K-Ci & JoJo; *It's Real* .... (Rock Land/Interscope)

Life Line
Nilsson; *The Point* ....(RCA)

Lilly Dale
Bob Wills & His Texas Playboys; *The Country Music Hall Of Fame-Bob Wills* .... (Universal)

Little Bit Of Soul
Music Explosion; *Best Of Ohio Express & Other Bubblegum Smashes-#1-C* .... (Rhino)
Cruisin'-1967-C .... (Increase)
Million-Dollar Memories #1-C.................................... (RCA)

Little Boy Sad
Johnny Burnette; *Best Of Johnny Burnette-You're Sixteen* .... (Gold Rush)

Little Child
Beatles; *Meet The Beatles!* .... (Capitol)

Little Girl, The
John Michael Montgomery; *Brand New Me* .... (Atlantic)
Totally Hits-#3-C .... (Atlantic)

Lodi
Creedence Clearwater Revival; *1969* ....(Fantasy)
Creedence Clearwater Revival-Chronicle ....(Fantasy)
Creedence Country ....(Fantasy)
Green River ....(Fantasy)
Live In Europe ....(Fantasy)
More Creedence Gold...(Fantasy)
Travelin' Band ....(Fantasy)

Lonely
Tracy Lawrence; *Lessons Learned* .... (Atlantic)

Lonely And Gone
Montgomery Gentry; *Tattoos & Scars* .... (Columbia)

Lonesome Road
4 Seasons; *25th Anniversary Collection* .... (Rhino)
Anita O'Day; *Rules Of The Road*.................................. (Pablo)
Frank Sinatra; *The Capitol Years*................................. (Capitol)
Preservation Hall Jazz Band; *New Orleans-#4* .... (Columbia)
Tommy Dorsey; *Sentimental Memories* ....(Pair)

Long Day
Matchbox Twenty; *Yourself Or Someone Like You* .... (Lava)

Lord I Hope This Day Is Good
Don Williams; *Best Of Don Williams-#3*.......................... (MCA)
Especially For You .... (MCA)
Lee Ann Womack; *Grand Ole Opry-75 Years-#1-C* .... (MCA)

Losing My Religion
R.E.M.; *Out Of Time* .... (Warner Bros.)

Lost Without Your Love
Bread; *Bread-Anthology* .... (Elektra)
Bread-Retrospective .... (Rhino)

Love Blues
Keb' Mo'; *Keb' Mo'* .... (Okeh)

Love Is Here And Now You're Gone
Diana Ross; *Diana Ross-Anthology*.............................. (Motown)

Lovesick Blues
Gary Morris; *Plain Brown Wrapper* .... (Warner Bros.)
Hank Williams With His Drifting Cowboys; *24 Of Hank Williams' Greatest Hits* .... (Polydor)
Lovesick Blues .... (Polydor)
Linda Ronstadt; *Linda Ronstadt-Retrospective* .... (Capitol)
Silk Purse .... (Capitol)
Patsy Cline; *Live At The Opry* .... (MCA)
Ryan Adams; *Timeless: Hank Williams Tribute-C* ..... (Lost Highway/IDJMG)

Lullaby
Shawn Mullins; *Soul's Core* .... (Columbia)

Lying To The Moon
Matraca Berg; *Lying To The Moon And Other Stories*............ (RCA)

Mailman, Bring Me No More Blues
Beatles; *The Beatles-Anthology-#3* .... (Capitol)

Buddy Holly; *Buddy Holly*... (MCA)

Mama Don't Forget To Pray For Me
Diamond Rio; *Diamond Rio*..(Arista)
Diamond Rio's Greatest Hits ....(Arista)

Man This Lonely, A
Brooks & Dunn; *Borderline*.......................................(Arista)

Mandy
Barry Manilow; *Barry Manilow II* ....(Arista)
Barry Manilow's Greatest Hits-#1 ....(Arista)
Live On Broadway...(Arista)

Manic Depression
Jeff Beck & Seal; *Stone Free: A Tribute To Jimi Hendrix-C* .... (Reprise)

March Winds Gonna Blow My Blues All Away
Carter Family; *Longing For Old Virginia: Their Complete Victor Recordings-1934* ....(Rounder)

Mary Lou
Bruce Springsteen; *Tracks* ....(Columbia)

Maryland
Vonda Shepard; *ST/Songs From ''Ally McBeal'' Featuring Vonda Shepard* .... (550/Epic)

Maybe Someday
Cure; *Bloodflowers*...(Fiction/Elektra)

Me
Staind; *Dysfunction* ....(Flip/Elektra)

Mean Mama Blues
Bob Wills; *Stay A Little Longer-The Original Columbia Recordings* ....(Roswell/RCA)

Meet Virginia
Train; *Now That's What I Call Music!-#4-C* .... (Virgin)
Train ....(Aware/C2/Columbia)

Melancholy Blue
Trisha Yearwood; *Inside Out* .... (MCA)

Members Only
Sheryl Crow; *The Globe Sessions* ....(A&M)

Mercy Mercy Me (The Ecology)
Marvin Gaye; *Every Great Motown Hit Of Marvin Gaye*........... (Motown)
Marvin Gaye-Anthology.. (Motown)
Marvin Gaye's Greatest Hits.................................... (Motown)
What's Going On... (Motown)
Robert Palmer; *Don't Explain* .... (EMI)

Michelangelo
Emmylou Harris; *Red Dirt Girl* ....(Nonesuch)

Million Miles
Bob Dylan; *Time Out Of Mind* ....(Columbia)

Miserable
Lit; *Place In The Sun* .... (RCA)

Misery
Soul Asylum; *Let Your Dim Light Shine* ....(Columbia)

Misery
Beatles; *Introducing...The Beatles*.............................. (Vee-Jay)
Rarities ....(Capitol)

Misery
Asleep At The Wheel featuring Marty Stuart; *Tribute To The Music Of Bob Wills And The Texas Playboys-C* ....(Liberty)

Misery And Gin
Merle Haggard; *Back To The Barrooms*......................... (MCA)
Merle Haggard's Greatest Hits .... (MCA)
Rainbow Stew-Live At Anaheim Stadium .... (MCA)

Miss Blue
Filter; *Title Of Record* .... (Reprise)

Misty Blue
Dorothy Moore; *Blues Is Alright* ....(Malaco)
Misty Blue ....(Malaco)
Sexy Soul-C ....(K-Tel)
Eddy Arnold; *Best Of Eddy Arnold-#2*.............(Dunhill Compact Classics)
Country Gold-Eddy Arnold .... (RCA)
This Is Eddy Arnold... (RCA)
Wilma Burgess; *From The Vaults: Decca Country Classics-1934-1973-C* ....(Decca)

Mood Indigo
Duke Ellington; *1954 Los Angeles Concert* .... (Crescendo)
Black, Brown & Beige: 1944-1946 Band Recordings .... (Bluebird)
Carnegie Hall Concert-January 23, 1943 .... (Prestige)
Ellington Indigos... (Columbia)
Sophisticated Ellington .... (RCA)
Ella Fitzgerald; *Ella A Nice* .... (Pablo)
Ella Fitzgerald Sings-#2 .... (Verve)
Four Freshmen; *Capitol Collectors Series-Four Freshman* .... (Capitol)
Frank Sinatra; *In The Wee Small Hours* .... (Capitol)
Jimmie Lunceford & His Orchestra; *Stomp It Off-#1-1934-1935* .... (GRP)
Preservation Hall Jazz Band; *Best Of The Preservation Hall Jazz Band* ....(Columbia)
New Orleans-#4 ....(Columbia)

Mournin' Glory Story
Nilsson; *Harry* ....(Dunhill Compact Classics)

Mourning
Tantric; *Tantric* .... (Maverick)

Mrs. Brown You've Got A Lovely Daughter
Herman's Hermits; *Herman's Hermits-Their Greatest Hits* .... (Abkco)

Something Good Again . . . . (Abkco)

My Dark Hour
Steve Miller Band; *Best Of Steve Miller 1968-1973* . . . . (Capitol)
Steve Miller Band-Anthology . . . . (Capitol)

My Man's Gone Now
Ella Fitzgerald & Louis Armstrong; *Porgy & Bess* . . . . (Verve)
Nina Simone; *Vocalists-Jazz Masters-C* . . . . (Bluebird)
Original Cast; *Porgy & Bess* . . . . (MCA)
Sarah Vaughan & L.A. Philharmonic; *Gershwin Live* . . . . (Columbia)
Sinead O'Connor; *Glory Of Gershwin Featuring Larry Adler-C* . . . . . (Mercury)

My Melancholy Baby
Barbra Streisand; *Third Album* . . . . (Columbia)
Bing Crosby; *Hits Of 1939-C* . . . . (Living Era)
Coleman Hawkins; *Genius Of Coleman Hawkins* . . . . (Verve)
Dorothy Loudon; *Saloon* . . . . (DRG)
Frank Sinatra; *Voice: The Columbia Years-1943-1952* . . . . (Columbia)
Gene Austin; *78-#21015* . . . . (Victor)
Jan Garber & His Orchestra; *Jan Garber & His Orchestra Play 22 Original Big Band Favorites* . . . . (Hindsight)
Kate Smith; *Kate Smith-16 Most Requested Songs* . . . . (Columbia)
Leon Redbone; *Double Time* . . . . (Warner Bros.)
Marcels; *Best Of The Marcels* . . . . (Rhino)

My World Is Empty Without You
Diana Ross; *Diana Ross-Anthology* . . . . (Motown)
Evening With Diana Ross . . . . (Motown)
Stevie Wonder; *Down To Earth* . . . . (Motown)

Navy Blue
Diane Renay; *Growin' Up Too Fast-The Girl Group Anthology-C* . . . (Mercury)

Neon Moon
Brooks & Dunn; *Brand New Man* . . . . (Arista)

Never Bit A Bullet Like This
George Jones; *High-Tech Redneck* . . . . (MCA)

Never Ever
All Saints; *All Saints* . . . . (London)
Now That's What I Call Music!-#1-C . . . . (Virgin)

Night Rider's Lament
Chris LeDoux; *Chris LeDoux & The Saddle Boogie Band* . . . . . (Liberty)
Old Cowboy Classics . . . . (Capitol)
Paint Me Back Home In Wyoming . . . . (Liberty)
Garth Brooks; *The Chase* . . . . (Liberty)
Jerry Jeff Walker; *Ridin' High* . . . . (MCA)
Nanci Griffith; *Other Voices Other Rooms* . . . . (Elektra)
Suzy Bogguss; *Somewhere Between* . . . . (Capitol)

Night To Remember
Joe Diffie; *A Night To Remember* . . . . (Epic)

No More Drama
Mary J. Blige; *No More Drama* . . . . (MCA)

No More, No Less
Collective Soul; *Dosage* . . . . (Atlantic)

Nobody Knows
Kevin Sharp; *Measure Of A Man* . . . . (143/Asylum)
Tony Rich Project; *Words* . . . . (LaFace)

Nothing As It Seems
Pearl Jam; *Binaural* . . . . (Epic)

Ol' Man River
Al Jolson; *Best Of Al Jolson* . . . . (MCA)
The Al Jolson Story-#6 . . . . (MCA)
Frank Sinatra; *The Concert Sinatra* . . . . (Reprise)
Voice: The Columbia Years-1943-1952 . . . . (Columbia)
Paul Robeson; *A Lonesome Road* . . . . (Living Era)
American Balladeer-Golden Classics-#1-C . . . . (Collectables)
William Warfield; *ST/All Those Glorious MGM Musicals* . . . . . . (MGM)
William Warfield/Original Cast; *Show Boat* . . . . (Columbia)

Old Folks At Home
Mormon Tabernacle Choir; *Songs Of The Civil War And Stephen Foster Favorites* . . . . (Sony Music Classical)
Paul Robeson; *A Man & His Beliefs-Golden Classics-#2* . . . . (Collectables)

One
Nilsson; *Aerial Ballet* . . . . (RCA)
Everybody's Talkin': The Encore Collection . . . . (BMG Special Prod.)
Nilsson-All-Time Greatest Hits . . . . (RCA)
Three Dog Night; *Best Of Three Dog Night* . . . . (MCA)
Captured Live At The Forum . . . . (MCA)
Joy To The World-Greatest Hits . . . . (MCA)

One Headlight
Wallflowers; *Bringing Down The Horse* . . . . (Interscope)

One Less Bell To Answer
5th Dimension; *5th Dimension-Anthology 1967-1973* . . . . (Rhino)
Greatest Hits On Earth . . . . (Arista)
Barbra Streisand; *Barbra Joan Streisand* . . . . (Columbia)
Gladys Knight & The Pips; *Gladys Knight & The Pips-Anthology* . . . . (Motown)
If I Were Your Woman . . . . (Motown)

One Sad Night In Kerrville
Tom Kell; *Sad Night* . . . . (Warner Bros.)

One, The
Backstreet Boys; *Millennium* . . . . (Jive)

Only Happy When It Rains
Garbage; *Garbage* . . . . (Almo Sounds)

Open My Heart
Yolanda Adams; *Mountain High Valley Low* . . . . (Elektra)

Over And Over
Dave Clark Five; *History Of The Dave Clark Five* . . . . (Hollywood)
The Dave Clark Five's Greatest Hits . . . . (Epic)

P.M.S. Blues
Dolly Parton; *Heart Songs* . . . . (Columbia)

Pack Up Your Sorrows
Joan Baez; *Best Of Joan Baez* . . . . (Vanguard)
Judy Collins; *Judy Collins' Fifth Album* . . . . (Elektra)
Mimi & Richard Farina; *Best Of Mimi & Richard Farina* . . . . (Vanguard)
Greatest Folksingers Of The '60s-C . . . . (Vanguard)
Mimi Farina; *Celebrations For A Grey Day* . . . . (Vanguard)
Peter, Paul & Mary; *Peter, Paul and Mary Album* . . . . (Warner Bros.)

Pain
Stereomud; *Perfect Self* . . . . (Loud)

Paint It, Black
Eric Burdon; *Eric Burdon Sings The Animals' Greatest Hits* . . . . . . (Rhino)
Rolling Stones; *Aftermath* . . . . (Abkco)
Flashpoint . . . . (Virgin)
Hot Rocks 1964-1971 . . . . (Abkco)
Singles Collection-The London Years . . . . (Abkco)
Through The Past, Darkly (Big Hits Vol. 2) . . . . (Abkco)

Peggy Sue
Buddy Holly; *Billboard Top Rock 'N' Roll Hits-1957-C* . . . . (Rhino)
Buddy Holly . . . . (MCA)
Buddy Holly-20 Golden Greats . . . . (MCA)
Buddy Holly's Greatest Hits . . . . (MCA)
More American Graffiti-C . . . . (MCA)
Oldies But Goodies-#4-C . . . . (Original Sound)
Rock & Roll Collection . . . . (MCA)

Perpetual Blues Machine
Keb' Mo'; *Just Like You* . . . . (Okeh)

Petals
Mariah Carey; *Rainbow* . . . . (Columbia)

Piece Of My Heart
Big Brother & The Holding Company; *Cheap Thrills* . . . . (Columbia)
Rock Classics Of The '60s-C . . . . (Columbia)
Seems Like Yesterday-#6-Late '60s-C . . . . (K-Tel)
Bryan Ferry; *These Foolish Things* . . . . (Reprise)
Delaney & Bonnie; *Best Of Delaney & Bonnie* . . . . (Rhino)
Faith Hill; *Take Me As I Am* . . . . (Warner Bros.)
Janis Joplin; *Janis Joplin In Concert* . . . . (Columbia)
Janis Joplin's Greatest Hits . . . . (Columbia)
ST/Janis . . . . (Columbia)
Sammy Hagar; *Standing Hampton* . . . . (Geffen)

Place To Fall Apart
Merle Haggard & Janie Fricke; *For The Record: Merle Haggard-43 Legendary Hits* . . . . (BNA)

Play The Saddest Song On The Jukebox
Carmol Taylor; *Songwriter* . . . . (Elektra)

Please
Bing Crosby; *Bing Crosby-16 Most Requested Songs* . . . . (Legacy)

PMS
Mary J. Blige; *No More Drama* . . . . (MCA)

Poor Boy
Champion Jack Dupree; *Forever & Ever* . . . . (Bullseye Blues)

Poor Me
Joe Diffie; *Joe Diffie's Greatest Hits* . . . . (Epic)

Poor People Of Paris
Les Baxter & His Orchestra; *Memories Are Made Of This-C* . . . . . . (Capitol)

Poor Poor Pitiful Me
Linda Ronstadt; *Linda Ronstadt's Greatest Hits, Volume Two* . . . . . (Asylum)
Simple Dreams . . . . (Asylum)
Terri Clark; *Just The Same* . . . . (Mercury)
Warren Zevon; *A Quiet Normal Life-Best Of* . . . . (Asylum)
Stand In The Fire . . . . (Asylum)

Pretty
Korn; *Follow The Leader* . . . . (Immortal/Epic)

Private Emotion
Ricky Martin & Meja; *Ricky Martin* . . . . (Columbia)

Prohibition Blues
Nora Bayes; *Music From The New York Stage (1890-1920)-#4-1917-1920-C* . . . . (Pearl)

Promises
Cranberries; *Bury The Hatchet* . . . . (Island/IDJMG)

Prozac Baby
Broken Toys; *Shreds-#2: American Underground 1994-C* . . . . (Shredder)

Purple Rain
Prince and the Revolution; *ST/Purple Rain* . . . . (Warner Bros.)

R U Still Down
2Pac; *R U Still Down (Remember Me)* . . . . (Amaru/Jive)

Racing In The Street
Bruce Springsteen; *Darkness On The Edge Of Town* . . . . (Columbia)
Bruce Springsteen & The E Street Band; *Bruce Springsteen & The E Street Band Live/1975-85* . . . . (Legacy)

Rain, The (Supa Dupa Fly)
Missy "Misdemeanor" Elliot; *Supa Dupa Fly* . . . . (East West)

Raining In My Heart
Anne Murray; *New Kind Of Feeling* . . . . (Capitol)
Buddy Holly; *Buddy Holly-20 Golden Greats* . . . . (MCA)
   The Buddy Holly Collection . . . . (MCA)
   Vintage Music-#6-C . . . . (MCA)
Jo-el Sonnier; *Come On Joe* . . . . (RCA)
Leo Sayer; *Leo Sayer* . . . . (Warner Bros.)

Rainy Days & Mondays
Carpenters; *Carpenters* . . . . (A&M)
   Carpenters-Classics-#2 . . . . (A&M)
   Carpenters-The Singles 1969-1973 . . . . (A&M)
   Yesterday Once More . . . . (A&M)
Paul Williams; *Classics-Here Comes Inspiration* . . . . (A&M)

Ray Of Light
Madonna; *GHV2* . . . . (Warner Bros.)
   Ray Of Light . . . . (Maverick)
   Totally Hits-1-C . . . . (Arista)

Red Roses For A Blue Lady
Al Martino; *Best Of Al Martino* . . . . (Capitol)
   Capitol Collectors Series-Al Martino . . . . (Capitol)
Andy Williams; *Andy Williams-16 Most Requested Songs* . . . . (Legacy)
Mom & Dads; *Best Of The Mom & Dads* . . . . (Crescendo)
Roger Whittaker; *All-Time Heart-Touching Favorites* . . . . (Capitol)
   Roger Whittaker-Classics Collection-#1 . . . . (Capitol)
Vaughn Monroe; *Best Of Vaughn Monroe* . . . . (RCA)

Regretful Blues
Nora Bayes; *Music From The New York Stage (1890-1920)-#4-1917-1920-C* . . . . (Pearl)

Remember Me
Marc Anthony; *Marc Anthony* . . . . (Columbia)

Resignation Superman
Big Head Todd & The Monsters; *Beautiful World* . . . . (Revolution)
   Live Monsters . . . . (Revolution)

Restless Nights
Bruce Springsteen; *Tracks* . . . . (Columbia)
Rocking Chairs; *One Step Up/Two Steps Back-The Songs Of Bruce Springsteen-C* . . . . (Right Stuff)

Rexall
Dave Navarro; *Trust No One* . . . . (Capitol)

Rhythm Of The Rain
Cascades; *Collectables Presents The History Of Rock-#7-C* . . . . . . (Collectables)
   Golden Years-1963-C . . . . (Dominion Entert.)

Ridin' That Midnight Train
Ricky Skaggs and Kentucky Thunder; *Bluegrass Rules!* . . . . . (Rounder)

Riverwide
Sheryl Crow; *The Globe Sessions* . . . . (A&M)

Roll To Me
Del Amitri; *ST/Crossroads-VH1 Television Program* . . . . (Atlantic)
   Twisted . . . . (A&M)

Roof, The
Mariah Carey; *Butterfly* . . . . (Columbia)

Run
Collective Soul; *Dosage* . . . . (Atlantic)

Sad Banjo
Shrimp Boat; *Duende* . . . . (Bar/None)

Sad Cafe
Eagles; *Eagles Greatest Hits, Volume 2* . . . . (Asylum)
   The Long Run . . . . (Asylum)
Lorrie Morgan; *Common Thread-Songs Of The Eagles-C* . . . . (Giant)

Sad Eyed Lady Of The Lowlands
Bob Dylan; *Blonde On Blonde* . . . . (Columbia)
Joan Baez; *Any Day Now: Songs Of Bob Dylan* . . . . (Vanguard)
   Lovesong Album . . . . (Vanguard)

Sad Eyes
Robert John; *Billboard Top Rock 'N' Roll Hits-1979-C* . . . . (Rhino)
   Robert John . . . . (EMI)

Sad Eyes
Bruce Springsteen; *Tracks* . . . . (Columbia)
Trisha Yearwood; *Real Live Woman* . . . . (MCA)

Sad Eyes
Robin Lee; *Black Velvet* . . . . (Atlantic)

Sad Eyes
Gary Wright; *Critics Choice-#2-C* . . . . (Cypress)
   Who I Am . . . . (Cypress)

Sad Letter
Muddy Waters; *Can't Get No Grindin'* . . . . (Chess)
   More Real Folk Blues-Muddy Waters . . . . (Chess)

Sad Lookin' Moon
Alabama; *Dancin' On The Boulevard* . . . . (RCA)
   For The Record: 41 Number One Hits . . . . (RCA)

Sad Movies (Make Me Cry)
Sue Thompson; *Collectables Presents The History Of Rock-#10-C* . . . . (Collectables)
   Sue Thompson's Greatest Hits . . . . (Curb)

Sad News From Korea
Lightnin' Hopkins; *Houston's King of the Blues-1952-1953* . . . (Blues Classics)

Sad Old Red
Simply Red; *Picture Book* . . . . (Elektra)

Sad Pig Dance
Chris Proctor; *Delicate Dance* . . . . (Flying Fish)

Sad Punk
Pixies; *Trompe Le Monde* . . . . (Elektra)

Sad Rush on Sunday
Dylans; *Dylans* . . . . (Beggar's Banquet)

Sad Song
Lou Reed; *Between Thought & Expression-Anthology* . . . . (RCA)
   Lou Reed Live . . . . (RCA)

Sad Song
Rachel Sweet; *Fool Around* . . . . (Rhino)

Sad Song
Joe Williams; *Joe Williams-Live* . . . . (Fantasy)

Sad Songs
Olivia Newton-John; *Making A Good Thing Better* . . . . (MCA)

Sad Songs (Say So Much)
Elton John; *Breaking Hearts* . . . . (MCA)
   Elton John's Greatest Hits-1976-1986 . . . . (MCA)
   Knebworth-The Album-C . . . . (Polydor)

Sad Story
Jack Scott; *Capitol Collectors Series-Jack Scott* . . . . (Capitol)

Sad Theresa
Warrant; *Dog Eat Dog* . . . . (Columbia)

Sad Wedding
Marvin Gaye & Tammi Terrell; *United* . . . . (Motown)

Sadder & Wiser Beaver
Original Broadway Cast; *Beyond The Fringe* . . . . (Capitol)

Sadder-But-Wiser Girl For Me
Original Cast; *The Music Man* . . . . (Gold Rush)
Robert Preston; *ST/The Music Man* . . . . (Warner Bros.)

Santa Monica (Watch The World Die)
Everclear; *Sparkle And Fade* . . . . (Capitol)

Satellite Blues
AC/DC; *Stiff Upper Lip* . . . . (East West)

Satin Sheets
Jeannie Pruett; *16 Top Country Hits-#1-C* . . . . (MCA)
   Country Chart-Toppers . . . . (Dominion Entert.)
   Grand Ole Opry-75 Years-#2-C . . . . (MCA)
   MCA Records 30 Years Of Hits-1958-1988-C . . . . (MCA)
Shawn Colvin; *Cover Girl* . . . . (Columbia)

Save The Children
Diana Ross; *Diana Ross-Anthology* . . . . (Motown)
   Touch Me In The Morning . . . . (Motown)
Gil Scott-Heron; *Gil Scott-Heron* . . . . (Bluebird)
   Revolution Will Not Be Televised . . . . (Flying Dutchman)
Marvin Gaye; *Marvin Gaye Live At The London Palladium* . . . . . (Motown)
   Marvin Gaye-Anthology . . . . (Motown)
   Musical Testament 1964-1984 . . . . (Motown)
   What's Going On . . . . (Motown)

Save Tonight
Eagle-Eye Cherry; *Desireless* . . . . (Work)

Scar Tissue
Red Hot Chili Peppers; *Californication* . . . . (Warner Bros.)

Searchin' For My Soul
Amel Larrieux; *Infinite Possibilities* . . . . (Epic)

Secret Smile
Semisonic; *Feeling Strangely Fine* . . . . (MCA)

Seven Rooms Of Gloom
Four Tops; *Four Tops' Greatest Hits* . . . . (Motown)
   Four Tops Reach Out . . . . (Motown)
   Four Tops-Anthology . . . . (Motown)

She Misses Him
Tim Rushlow; *Tim Rushlow* . . . . (Atlantic)

She Put The Sad In All His Songs
Alabama; *Closer You Get* . . . . (RCA)

She Said She Said
Beatles; *Beatles-Box Set* . . . . (Capitol)
   Revolver . . . . (Capitol)

She's Gone
Daryl Hall & John Oates; *Abandoned Luncheonette* . . . . (Atlantic)
   Rock 'N Soul, Part 1 . . . . (RCA)

She's Got The Rhythm (And I Got The Blues)
Alan Jackson; *A Lot About Livin' (And A Little 'Bout Love)* . . . . (Arista)

Shimmer
Fuel; *Sunburn* . . . . (550 Music)

Shut Out The Light
Bruce Springsteen; *Tracks* . . . . (Columbia)

Silver Threads And Golden Needles
Honky Tonk Angels; *Honky Tonk Angels* . . . . (Columbia)
Linda Ronstadt; *Don't Cry Now* . . . . (Asylum)
   Hand Sown Home Grown . . . . (Capitol)
   Linda Ronstadt-Retrospective . . . . (Capitol)
   Linda Ronstadt's Greatest Hits . . . . (Asylum)
Springfields; *Troubadours Of The Folk Era-#3-C* . . . . (Rhino)

Silver Wings
Merle Haggard; *More Of The Best* . . . . (Rhino)
   The Seashores Of Old Mexico . . . . (Epic)
Merle Haggard & Jewel; *For The Record: Merle Haggard-43 Legendary Hits* . . . . (BNA)

Merle Haggard & The Strangers; *Okie From Muskogee* .... (Capitol)
Songs I'll Always Sing .... (Capitol)
Pam Tillis; *Mama's Hungry Eyes-Merle Haggard Tribute-C* .... (Arista)

Silvertown Blues
Mark Knopfler; *Sailing To Philadelphia* .... (Warner Bros.)

Since I Lost My Baby
Temptations; *Temptations' Greatest Hits-#1* .... (Motown)
Temptations-Anthology-The Best Of The Temptations .... (Motown)
Temptations-The Ultimate Collection .... (Motown)

Sing A Sad Song
Merle Haggard; *Epic Collection-Recorded Live* .... (Epic)
For The Record: Merle Haggard-43 Legendary Hits .... (BNA)
More Of The Best .... (Rhino)
Sing A Sad Song .... (Capitol)
Merle Haggard & The Strangers; *Songs I'll Always Sing* .... (Capitol)

Singing The Blues
Guy Mitchell; *CBS Classics-Radio Classics Of The '50s-C* .... (Columbia)
Guy Mitchell-16 Most Requested Songs .... (Legacy)

Sky Is Crying
Albert King; *I'm In A Phone Booth Baby* .... (Stax)
Years Gone By .... (Stax)
Elmore James; *Elmore James-Complete Fire & Enjoy Sessions-#1* .... (Collectables)
Red Hot Blues .... (Intermedia)
Eric Clapton; *Eric Clapton-Crossroads-C* .... (Polydor)
George Thorogood & The Destroyers; *George Thorogood & The Destroyers-Live* .... (EMI)
Move It On Over .... (Rounder)
Stevie Ray Vaughan and Double Trouble; *The Sky Is Crying* .... (Epic)

Smile
Dexter Gordon; *Best Of Dexter Gordon* .... (Blue Note)
Lyle Lovett; *ST/Hope Floats* .... (Capitol)
Nat "King" Cole; *The Nat "King" Cole Story* .... (Capitol)
Natalie Cole; *Unforgettable With Love* .... (Elektra)
Tony Bennett; *The Movie Song Album* .... (Columbia)
Tony Bennett's All-Time Greatest Hits .... (Columbia)

Smiling Up The Frown
Agents Of Good Roots; *One By One* .... (RCA)
Where'd You Get That Vibe? .... (RCA)

Smoke Rings In The Dark
Gary Allan; *Smoke Rings In The Dark* .... (MCA)

So Far Away
Carole King; *A Natural Worman: The Ode Collection-1968-1976* ..... (Legacy)
Tapestry .... (Epic)
Rod Stewart; *If We Fall In Love Tonight* .... (Warner Bros.)
Tapestry Revisited: Tribute To Carole King-C .... (Lava)

So Sad (To Watch Good Love Go Bad)
Everly Brothers; *The Reunion Concert-Live At Albert Hall 1983* ..... (Mercury)
Walk Right Back: The Everly Brothers On Warner Bros.-1960-1969 .... (Warner Archives)
Frank Ifield; *Best Of Frank Ifield* .... (Curb)
Sweethearts Of The Rodeo; *Columbia Country Classics-#5-A New Tradition-C* .... (Columbia)

So Sad To Say
Mighty Mighty Bosstones; *Pay Attention* .... (Big Rig/DJMG)

So Very Hard To Go
Tower Of Power; *Didn't It Blow Your Mind: Soul Hits Of The '70s-#17-C* .... (Rhino)
Tower Of Power .... (Warner Bros.)

Somehow Tonight
Ricky Skaggs and Kentucky Thunder; *Bluegrass Rules!* .... (Rounder)

Someone Else's Star
Bryan White; *Bryan White* .... (Asylum)
Real Luv: Ultimate Country Love Songs-C .... (EMI)

Something So Right
Annie Lennox; *Medusa* .... (Arista)
Barbra Streisand; *The Way We Were* .... (Columbia)
Paul Simon; *1964-1993-Box Set* .... (Warner Bros.)
There Goes Rhymin' Simon .... (Columbia)

Sometimes I Feel Like A Motherless Child
Dave Van Ronk; *Folksinger* .... (Prestige)
Inside Dave Van Ronk .... (Fantasy)
Grant Green; *Feelin' The Spirit* .... (Blue Note)
Iron City .... (Muse)
Jerry Butler; *Jerry Butler-Gold* .... (Vee-Jay)
Mormon Tabernacle Choir; *Songs Of The Civil War And Stephen Foster Favorites* .... (Sony Music Classical)
O.V. Wright; *O.V. Wright* .... (MCA)
Odetta; *Essential Odetta* .... (Vanguard)
Peter, Paul & Mary; *The Song Will Rise* .... (Warner Bros.)
Van Morrison; *Poetic Champions Compose* .... (Mercury)

Sometimes She Forgets
Steve Earle; *Train A Comin'* .... (Warner Bros.)
Travis Tritt; *Greatest Hits-From The Beginning* .... (Warner Bros.)

Somewhere In My Broken Heart
Billy Dean; *Billy Dean's Greatest Hits* .... (Liberty)
Heart Beats-Country Lovin': Songs From The Heart-C .... (Rhino)
Young Man .... (SBK)
Randy Travis; *No Holdin' Back* .... (Warner Bros.)

Sorcerer
Stevie Nicks; *Trouble In Shangri-La* .... (Reprise)

Spending Christmas With The Blues
Floyd Miles; *Mountain To Climb* .... (Kingsnake)

Spilled Perfume
Pam Tillis; *Sweetheart's Dance* .... (Arista)

St. Louis Blues
Bessie Smith; *Beauty Of The Blues* .... (Columbia)
Bessie Smith-The Collection .... (Legacy)
Big Joe Turner; *Boss Of The Blues* .... (Atlantic)
Billie Holiday; *Quintessential-#9-1940-1942* .... (Columbia)
The Billie Holiday Story-#3 .... (Columbia)
Bob Wills & His Texas Playboys; *Bob Wills & His Texas Playboys-24 Great Hits* .... (Polydor)
Cleo Laine; *Jazz* .... (RCA)
Dave Brubeck Quartet; *25th Anniversary Reunion* .... (A&M)
Dave Brubeck Quartet-At Carnegie Hall .... (Columbia)
Paper Moon .... (Concord Jazz)
Duke Ellington; *1953 Pasadena Concert* .... (Crescendo)
Ella Fitzgerald; *These Are The Blues* .... (Verve)
Louis Armstrong; *At The Crescendo* .... (MCA)
Louis Armstrong-Legendary Performer .... (RCA)
Louis Armstrong-Vol. 6-St. Louis Blues .... (Columbia)
Nipper's Greatest Hits Of The '30s-#2-C .... (RCA)
Merle Haggard & Asleep At The Wheel; *Ride With Bob-C* .... (DreamWorks/SKG)
Original Broadway Cast; *Black & Blue* .... (DRG)
Pete Fountain; *Best Of Pete Fountain* .... (MCA)
Preservation Hall Jazz Band; *Best Of The Preservation Hall Jazz Band* .... (Columbia)
New Orleans-#2 .... (Columbia)

Standing Outside A Broken Phone Booth With Money In My Hand
Primitive Radio Gods; *MTV Best Of The Buzz Bin-#2-C* .... (Mammoth)
Rocket .... (Ergo)

Stay Together For The Kids
Blink-182; *Take Off Your Pants And Jacket* .... (MCA)

Steal My Sunshine
Len; *You Can't Stop The Bum Rush* .... (Work)

Still Got The Blues
Gary Moore; *Ballads & Blues-1982-1994* .... (Charisma)
Out In The Fields-The Very Best Of Gary Moore .... (Virgin)
Still Got The Blues .... (Charisma)
Stanley Jordan; *Best Of Stanley Jordan* .... (Blue Note)

Stormy Weather
Billie Holiday; *Fine & Mellow* .... (Collectables)
Jazz Club-Vocal .... (Verve)
Ethel Waters; *Fabulous Thirties-C* .... (Pro Jazz)
Frank Sinatra; *No One Cares* .... (Capitol)
Jackie Wilson; *Mr. Excitement* .... (Rhino)
Judy Garland; *Judy Garland-At Carnegie Hall* .... (Capitol)
Lena Horne; *20 Golden Pieces Of Lena Horne* .... (Bulldog)
Goes Latin & Sings Your Requests .... (DRG)
Live On Broadway .... (Qwest)
Nipper's Greatest Hits Of The '40s-#1-C .... (RCA)
Pixies; *Bossanova* .... (Elektra)
Tony Bennett with Natalie Cole; *Playin' With My Friends-Bennett Sings The Blues-C* .... (Columbia)
Willie Nelson & Leon Russell; *One For The Road* .... (Columbia)

Stuck Inside Of Mobile With The Memphis Blues Again
Bob Dylan; *Blonde On Blonde* .... (Columbia)
Bob Dylan's Greatest Hits-#2 .... (Columbia)
Hard Rain .... (Columbia)

Sukiyaki
4 P.M.; *Now's The Time* .... (Next Plateau/London/Island)
Kyu Sakamoto; *When AM Was King-C* .... (Capitol)
Taste Of Honey; *Golden Honey* .... (Capitol)
Twice As Sweet .... (Capitol)

Sullen Girl
Fiona Apple; *Tidal* .... (Clean Slate/Work)

Sullivan
Caroline's Spine; *Monsoon* .... (Hollywood)

Summertime Blues
Alan Jackson; *Who I Am* .... (Arista)
Blue Cheer; *Good Times Are So Hard To Find-History Of Blue Cheer* .... (Mercury)
Louder Than God-Best Of Blue Cheer .... (Rhino)
San Francisco Nights-C .... (Rhino)
Brian Setzer; *ST/La Bamba* .... (Slash)
Eddie Cochran; *Eddie Cochran-Legendary Masters* .... (EMI)
Eddie Cochran's Greatest Hits .... (Curb)
EMI Legends Of Rock & Roll-24 Greatest Hits-C .... (EMI)
Joan Jett & The Blackhearts; *I Love Rock 'n' Roll* .... (Blackheart)
Who; *Hooligans* .... (MCA)
Live At Leeds .... (MCA)
Who's Last .... (MCA)

Sun Ain't Gonna Shine Anymore
Walker Brothers; *History Of British Rock-#7-C* .... (Rhino)
Love Sixties-C .... (JCI Assoc. Labels)

Sunday Morning Coming Down
Johnny Cash; *Classic Cash-Hall Of Fame Series* .... (Mercury)

Johnny Cash's Greatest Hits-#2 ....(Columbia)
The Man In Black-His Greatest Hits ....(Legacy)
Kris Kristofferson; *Me & Bobby McGee* ....(Columbia)
Songs Of Kris Kristofferson ....(Columbia)
Vikki Carr; *Best Of Vikki Carr* .... (EMI)
Willie Nelson; *Willie* ....(RCA)
Willie Nelson Sings Kristofferson ....(Columbia)

Sunshower
Chris Cornell; *ST/Great Expectations* .... (Atlantic)

Swallowed
Bush; *Razorblade Suitcase* ....(Trauma)

Sweet Misery
Amel Larrieux; *Infinite Possibilities* .... (Epic)

Take 'Em As They Come
Bruce Springsteen; *Tracks* ....(Columbia)

Takes A Little Time
Amy Grant; *Behind The Eyes* .... (A&M)

Tears Of A Clown
English Beat; *I Just Can't Stop It* .... (I.R.S.)
What Is Beat .... (I.R.S.)
Smokey Robinson & The Miracles; *25 #1 Hits From 25 Years-C* ..... (Motown)
Billboard Top Rock 'N' Roll Hits-1970-C .... (Rhino)
Compact Command Performances-Smokey Robinson & The Miracles .... (Motown)
Endless Love-Motown's Greatest Love Songs-C ...... (Motown)
Smokey Robinson & The Miracles' Anthology .... (Motown)
Tears Of A Clown .... (Motown)

Teenage Depression
Eddie & The Hot Rods; *D.I.Y.-#1-UK Punk-Anarchy In UK-1976-1977-C* .... (Rhino)
ST/Rock 'N' Roll High School .... (Sire)
Teenage Depression .... (Island)

Tell Me Why
Wynonna; *Tell Me Why* .... (MCA)

That Ain't My Truck
Rhett Akins; *A Thousand Memories* .... (Decca)
Cryin' Lyin' Lovin' & Leavin'-C .... (Universal)

That Don't Satisfy Me
Brother Cane; *Brother Cane* ....(Virgin)

That Joke Isn't Funny Anymore
Smiths; *Best...2* .... (Sire)
Meat Is Murder .... (Sire)

That's Not Love
Keb' Mo'; *Just Like You* .... (Okeh)

That's What I Get (For Losin' You)
Hal Ketchum; *Every Little Word* .... (Curb)

There Goes My Baby
Trisha Yearwood; *Where Your Road Leads* .... (MCA)

There'll Be Sad Songs (To Make You Cry)
Billy Ocean; *Billy Ocean's Greatest Hits* ....(Jive)
Love Zone ....(Jive)

There's A Place
Beatles; *Introducing...The Beatles* .... (Vee-Jay)
Rarities .... (Capitol)

Thinking About Your Troubles
Nilsson; *The Point* .... (RCA)

This Is Me Missing You
James House; *Days Gone By* .... (Epic)
Super Hits Of 1995-C .... (Epic)

This Night Won't Last Forever
Bill LaBounty; *The Right Direction* .... (Noteworthy)
This Night Won't Last Forever .... (Warner Bros.)
Michael Johnson; *Dialogue* .... (EMI)
Have A Nice Night-Romantic Hits Of The '70s-C ...... (Rhino)
Radio Daze-Pop Hits Of The '80s-#1-C .... (Rhino)
Then & Now .... (ISD/Intersound)
Moe Bandy; *Many Mansions* .... (Curb)
Sawyer Brown; *Six Days On The Road* ....(Curb)

This Woman And This Man
Clay Walker; *If I Could Make A Living* .... (Giant)

Ticket To Ride
Beatles; *Beatles 1* .... (Capitol)
Beatles-20 Greatest Hits .... (Capitol)
Beatles-Box Set .... (Capitol)
Reel Music .... (Capitol)
ST/Help! .... (Capitol)
The Beatles At The Hollywood Bowl .... (Capitol)
The Beatles/1962-1966 .... (Capitol)
Carpenters; *Carpenters-Classics-#2* .... (A&M)
Carpenters-The Singles 1969-1973 .... (A&M)
From The Top .... (A&M)
Ticket To Ride .... (A&M)
Yesterday Once More .... (A&M)
Vanilla Fudge; *Best Of Vanilla Fudge* .... (Atco)
Vanilla Fudge .... (Atco)

'Til I Fell In Love With You
Bob Dylan; *Time Out Of Mind* .... (Columbia)

Time
Hootie & The Blowfish; *Cracked Rear View* .... (Atlantic)

To Be Loved
Curtis Stigers; *Songs From Dawson's Creek* .... (Sony Music Soundtrax)

Torn
Natalie Imbruglia; *Left Of The Middle* .... (RCA)

Touch Me
Willie Nelson; *Best Of Willie Nelson* .... (Capitol)

Traces
Classics IV; *Very Best Of The Classics IV* .... (EMI)
Classics IV Featuring Dennis Yost; *Oldies But Goodies-#11-C* .... (Original Sound)
Ronnie Milsap; *Ronnie Milsap-16 Greatest Hits-#2* .... (Trip)

Tragedy
Emmylou Harris; *Red Dirt Girl* .... (Nonesuch)

Transcendental Blues
Steve Earle; *Transcendental Blues* .... (Artemis)

Tropicalia
Beck; *Mutations* .... (David Geffen Co.)

Trouble In Paradise
Bruce Springsteen; *Tracks* ....(Columbia)

Troubles
Alicia Keys; *Songs In A Minor* ....(J)

Two Story House
George Jones & Tammy Wynette; *George Jones & Tammy Wynette-16 Biggest Hits* .... (Epic/Legacy)

Two Teardrops
Steve Wariner; *Two Teardrops* .... (Capitol)

Un-Break My Heart
Toni Braxton; *Secrets* ....(LaFace)

Unbreakable Heart
Carlene Carter; *Little Love Letters* .... (Giant)
Jessica Andrews; *Heart Shaped World* .... (DreamWorks/SKG)

Uncle Dave's Travels-Misery In Arkansas
Uncle Dave Macon; *The Country Music Hall Of Fame-Uncle Dave Macon* .... (MCA)

Understanding
Candlebox; *Lucy* .... (Maverick)

Unforgiven II
Metallica; *Reload* .... (Elektra)

Unfortunate Miss Bailey
Kingston Trio; *At Large/Here We Go Again!* .... (Capitol)

Uninvited
Ruth Wallis; *Laughing Gallery* .... (American)

Universal Heart-Beat
Juliana Hatfield; *Box Presents Big Ones Of Alternative Rock-#1-C* .... (Box Tunes)
Only Everything .... (Mammoth)

Utah Carol
Harry K. McClintock; *Cowboy Songs On Folkways-C* .... (Smithsonian Folkways)
Marty Robbins; *Gunfighter Ballads & Trail Songs* .... (Legacy)

Vintage Eyes
Second Coming; *Second Coming* ....(Capitol)

Walk In The Sun
Bruce Hornsby; *Hot House* .... (RCA)

Walk Softly
Billy "Crash" Craddock; *Billy "Crash" Craddock Live* .... (MCA)
Billy "Crash" Craddock Sings His Greatest Hits .... (MCA)
Easy As Pie .... (MCA)

Walkin', Talkin'...Beatin' Broken Heart
Highway 101; *Country's Greatest Hits-#4-Sweet Country-C* .... (Priority)
Paint The Town .... (Warner Bros.)

Wander This World
Jonny Lang; *Wander This World* ....(A&M)

Warm Beer & Cold Women
Tom Waits; *Nighthawks At The Diner* .... (Asylum)

Warning Labels
Doug Stone; *From The Heart* .... (Epic)

Wasted Days And Wasted Nights
Freddy Fender; *Before The Next Teardrop Falls* .... (Universal)
Best Of Freddy Fender .... (MCA)
Country Comes To Carnegie Hall-C .... (MCA)
Happy Trails .... (United Artists)
Texas Country .... (United Artists)
The Freddy Fender Collection .... (MCA)

Waydown
Catherine Wheel; *Happy Days* .... (Fontana)

Weather
Amel Larrieux; *Infinite Possibilities* .... (Epic)

What A Dream
Conway Twitty; *Conway Twitty's Greatest Hits* .... (Curb)
Patti Page; *45-#70416* .... (Mercury)
Slim Harpo; *Raining In My Heart* .... (Hip-O)

What Becomes Of The Brokenhearted
Jimmy & David Ruffin; *Motown Superstar Series-#8-Jimmy & David Ruffin* .... (Motown)
Jimmy Ruffin; *Motown Story-First 25 Years-C* .... (Motown)
Paul Young; *ST/Fried Green Tomatoes* .... (MCA)

What Do The Simple Folk Do?
Julie Andrews; *Best Of Julie Andrews* . . . . (Rhino)
Julie Andrews & Richard Burton; *Camelot* . . . . (Columbia)
Original Soundtrack; *Camelot* . . . .(Warner Bros.)
What Mattered Most
Ty Herndon; *Super Hits Of 1995-C* . . . .(Epic)
   What Mattered Most . . . .(Epic)
What'll I Do
Nat "King" Cole; *The Vocal Classics-1947-1950*. . . . . (Capitol)
Rosemary Clooney; *Rosemary Clooney Sings The Music Of Irving Berlin* . . . .(Concord Jazz)
When God Fearin' Women Get The Blues
Martina McBride; *Martina McBride's Greatest Hits* . . . . (RCA)
Where Do I Go From You
Jon Secada; *Heart, Soul & A Voice* . . . . (SBK)
Where Do You Go
No Mercy; *No Mercy* . . . . (Arista)
Where Have All The Cowboys Gone?
Paula Cole; *This Fire* . . . . (Imago)
Whiskey Ain't Workin'
Travis Tritt & Marty Stuart; *It's All About To Change* . . . .(Warner Bros.)
White Sport Coat (And A Pink Carnation)
Marty Robbins; *16 Most Requested Songs Of The '50s-#2-C* . . . . (Legacy)
   Lifetime Of Song-1951-1982 . . . . (Columbia)
   Marty Robbins' Greatest Hits . . . . (Columbia)
Who Needs You Baby
Clay Walker; *Hypnotize The Moon*. . . . . (Giant)
Who's Sorry Now
Benny Goodman; *Stompin'*. . . . .(Drive)
Big Bill Broonzy; *Black, Brown & White* . . . . (Evidence Music)
Bob Crosby; *Bob Crosby & His Orchestra*. . . . . (EPM)
Connie Francis; *Dick Clark's 21 All-Time Hits-#1-C* . . . . . . (Original Sound)
   Very Best Of Connie Francis . . . . (Polydor)
Ella Fitzgerald; *The Intimate Ella* . . . . (Verve)
Esquivel; *Space-Age Bachelor Pad Music* . . . . (Bar/None)
Glen Gray; *Moonglow: 1930-1936*. . . . . (Aero Space)
Nat "King" Cole; *The Billy May Sessions* . . . . (Capitol)
Ray Anthony; *Swing Back To The '40s*. . . . . (Aero Space)
Why Didn't You Call Me
Macy Gray; *On How Life Is* . . . .(Epic)
Why Do I Feel So Sad
Alicia Keys; *Songs In A Minor* . . . . (J)
Why Does It Hurt So Bad
Whitney Houston; *ST/Waiting To Exhale* . . . . (Arista)
Why Does Love Got To Be So Sad?
Derek And The Dominos; *Layla*. . . . . (Polydor)
Why Pt. 2
Collective Soul; *Blender*. . . . .(Atlantic)
Winchester Cathedral
New Vaudeville Band; *History Of British Rock-#7-C* . . . . (Rhino)
Wind Cries Mary
Jimi Hendrix; *Essential Jimi Hendrix, Volume 2* . . . . (Reprise)
Jimi Hendrix Experience; *Are You Experienced?*. . . . . (Reprise)
   Smash Hits . . . . (Reprise)
Without Her
Nilsson; *Pandemonium Shadow Show* . . . . (RCA)
Without You
Dixie Chicks; *Fly* . . . . (Monument)
Without You
Nilsson; *Nilsson Schmilsson* . . . . (RCA)
   Nilsson's Greatest Hits . . . . (RCA)
   Nipper's Greatest Hits Of The '70s-C . . . . (RCA)
Woke Up This Morning
A3; *Exile On Coldharbour Lane*. . . . . (C2/Columbia)
   The Sopranos-Music From The HBO Original Series . . . . (Sony Music Soundtrax)
Wonderful
Everclear; *Now That's What I Call Music!-#5-C* . . . . (Virgin)
   Songs From An American Movie-#1-Learning How To Smile . . . . . . (Capitol)
World I Know, The
Collective Soul; *Collective Soul* . . . .(Atlantic)
World Without Love, A
Peter And Gordon; *Billboard Top Pop Hits-1964-C*. . . . . (Rhino)
   History Of British Rock-#1-C . . . . (Rhino)
   Peter & Gordon's Greatest Hits . . . . (CEMA Special Prod.)
Written In The Stars
Elton John & LeAnn Rimes; *ST/Aida* . . . . (Island)
Yesterday
Beatles; *"Yesterday"...And Today* . . . . (Capitol)
   Beatles 1 . . . . (Capitol)
   Beatles-20 Greatest Hits . . . . (Capitol)
   Beatles-Box Set . . . . (Capitol)
   Beatles-Love Songs . . . . (Capitol)
   Compact Disc Singles Collection. (Capitol)
   The Beatles/1962-1966 . . . . (Capitol)
Elvis Presley; *On Stage-February, 1970* . . . . (RCA)
En Vogue; *Funky Divas* . . . . (East West)
Frank Sinatra; *My Way* . . . . (Reprise)

Paul McCartney; *The Concert For New York City-C* . . . . (Columbia)
Placido Domingo; *Domingo Songbook* . . . . (Sony Music Classical)
Ray Charles; *Ray Charles-His Greatest Hits-#1* . . . . (Dunhill Compact Classics)
Supremes; *I Hear A Symphony* . . . . (Motown)
Wings; *Wings Over America*. . . . . (Capitol)
You Can Feel Bad
Patty Loveless; *Patty Loveless-Classics* . . . . (Epic)
   Super Hits Of 1996-C . . . . (Epic)
   The Trouble With The Truth . . . . (Epic)
You Get What You Give
New Radicals; *Maybe You've Been Brainwashed Too* . . . . (MCA)
   Now That's What I Call Music!-#2-C. . . . .(Virgin)
You Keep Me Hangin' On
Diana Ross; *Evening With Diana Ross* . . . . (Motown)
Diana Ross & The Supremes; *Diana Ross & The Supremes-Anthology (1962-1969)* . . . . (Motown)
   Motown Story-First 25 Years-C . . . . (Motown)
Kim Wilde; *Another Step* . . . . (MCA)
Reba McEntire; *Starting Over*. . . . . (MCA)
Supremes; *Billboard Top R&B Hits-1965-C*. . . . . (Rhino)
   Diana Ross & The Supremes' Greatest Hits-#2 . . . . (Motown)
Vanilla Fudge; *Best Of Vanilla Fudge*. (Atco)
   Vanilla Fudge . . . . (Atco)
Wilson Pickett; *A Man & A Half-Best Of Wilson Pickett*. . . . . (Rhino)
   Wilson Pickett's Greatest Hits . . . .(Atlantic)
Youngstown
Bruce Springsteen; *The Ghost Of Tom Joad* . . . . (Columbia)
You're Only Lonely
J.D. Souther; *Radio Daze-Pop Hits Of The '80s-#1-C* . . . . (Rhino)
   You're Only Lonely . . . . (Legacy)
You're Still On My Mind
Byrds; *Sweetheart Of The Rodeo*. . . . . (Columbia)
You've Lost That Lovin' Feelin'
Daryl Hall & John Oates; *Voices*. . . . . (RCA)
Righteous Brothers; *Best Of The Righteous Brothers* . . . . (Curb)
   Billboard Top Rock 'N' Roll Hits-1965-C . . . . (Rhino)
   Cruisin'-1965-C. . . . . (Increase)
   Unchained Melody-Very Best Of The Righteous Brothers . . . .(Polydor)

SAILING, Sailors

See Also: DANGER & DISASTER, DROWN, FLOOD, LIGHTHOUSES, OCEAN, PIRATES, RIVERS, SHIPS, WAR, WATER, WIND

Anchors Aweigh
Firehouse Five Plus Two; *Goes To Sea* . . . . (Good Time Jazz)
Original Soundtrack; *Top Ten College Fight Songs* . . . . (K-Tel)
Pat Boone; *Star Spangled Banner* . . . . (Word)
Angels And Sailors
Doors; *An American Prayer-Jim Morrison* . . . . (Elektra)
Beyond The Sea
Bobby Darin; *The Bobby Darin Story* . . . .(Atlantic)
Blow The Man Down
Paul Clayton; *Bay State Ballads* . . . .(Smithsonian Folkways)
Brandy
Looking Glass; *Billboard Top Rock 'N' Roll Hits-1972-C* . . . . (Rhino)
   Rock Artifacts-From The Vaults-#2-C . . . . (Legacy)
Clear Sailin'
Ian Thomas Band; *Still Here* . . . .(Atlantic)
Clear Sailin'
Chris Hillman; *Clear Sailin'* . . . .(Asylum)
Clear Sailin'
Barbra Streisand; *Emotion* . . . . (Columbia)
Come On Down To My Boat
Every Mother's Son; *Battle Of The Bands-#3-C* . . . . (K-Tel)
Come Sail Away
Styx; *Caught In The Act* . . . . (A&M)
   Grand Illusion . . . . (A&M)
   Styx-Classics-#15. . . . . (A&M)
Commodore Song, The
Edward M. Favor; *Music From The New York Stage (1890-1920)-#1-1890-1908-C*. . . . .(Pearl)
Cool Change
Little River Band; *First Under The Wire* . . . . (Capitol)
   Little River Band's Greatest Hits . . . . (Capitol)
Davy's Dinghy
Ruth Wallis; *Dr. Demento Presents The Greatest Novelty Records-#2-1950s-C* . . . . (Rhino)
   Dr. Demento's Dementia Royale-C . . . . (Rhino)
Day We Lost The America's Cup
Tom Paxton; *One Million Lawyers & Other Disasters* . . . . (Flying Fish)
Heartbreak U.S.A.
Kitty Wells; *I Love Country-Hits Of The '60s-#1-C* . . . .(Priority)
   Kitty Wells' Greatest Hits . . . . (Curb)
   The Country Music Hall Of Fame-Kitty Wells . . . . (MCA Special Prod.)

I Can Sail To China
  John Conlee; *American Faces* . . . . (Columbia)
I Go Sailing
  Stevie Wonder; *ST/Jungle Fever* . . . . (Motown)
I Used To Be A Sailor
  Tracy Chapman; *Matters Of The Heart* . . . . (Elektra)
I'll Sail My Ship Alone
  George Jones; *20 Golden Pieces Of George Jones* . . . . (Bulldog)
  Mickey Gilley; *Mickey Gilley's Greatest Hits-#1* . . . . (Epic)
  Patsy Cline; *Always* . . . . (MCA)
    Portrait Of Patsy Cline . . . . (MCA)
  Ray Price; *Ray Price's Greatest Hits-#1-3* . . . . (Step One)
I'm Popeye The Sailor Man
  Billy Costello; *Dr. Demento Presents The Greatest Novelty Records-#1-1940s*
    & Before-C . . . . (Rhino)
Islands In The Stream
  Kenny Rogers & Dolly Parton; *Eyes That See In The Dark* . . . . (RCA)
    Kenny Rogers' Greatest Hits . . . . (RCA)
Je Suis Desole
  Mark Knopfler; *Golden Heart* . . . . (Warner Bros.)
Lee Shore
  Crosby, Stills, Nash & Young; *4 Way Street* . . . . (Atlantic)
  David Crosby; *Bread & Roses Festival Of Acoustic Music-#2-C* . . . . . . (Fantasy)
Mariner, The (Old Spice Cologne)
  Original Soundtrack; *TeeVee Toons-The Commercials-#1-C* . . . . (TVT)
Moonlight Bay
  Beatles; *The Beatles-Anthology-#1* . . . . (Capitol)
  Bing Crosby; *The Radio Years-#4* . . . . (Crescendo)
    The Radio Years: 20 Songs . . . . (Crescendo)
  Drifters; *Clyde McPhatter & The Drifters-Rockin' & Driftin'* . . . . (Collectables)
  Glenn Miller; *Big Bands-#1-C* . . . . (Universal)
Morrisey & The Russian Sailor
  Tom Dahill; *Irish Music From St. Paul To Donegal* . . . . (Flying Fish)
Nautical Wheelers
  Jimmy Buffett; *A1A* . . . . (MCA)
    Boats Beaches Bars & Ballads . . . . (Margaritaville)
New York, New York/Sailors On The Town
  Original Broadway Cast; *Jerome Robbins' Broadway* . . . . (RCA)
Only Love
  Wynonna; *Tell Me Why* . . . . (MCA)
Orinoco Flow (Sail Away)
  Enya; *Watermark* . . . . (Reprise)
Red Sails
  David Bowie; *Lodger* . . . . (Rykodisc)
    Sound + Vision . . . . (Rykodisc)
Red Sails In The Sunset
  Big Joe Turner; *Nobody In Mind* . . . . (Pablo)
  Dinah Washington; *Echoes Of An Era-Dinah Washington* . . . . (Roulette)
  Jarmels; *Jarmels-Golden Classics* . . . . (Collectables)
  Nat "King" Cole; *Unforgettable* . . . . (Capitol)
  Platters; *Platters Greatest Hits* . . . . (Everest)
Ride Captain Ride
  Blues Image; *Back To The '70s-#3-C* . . . . (Dominion Entert.)
    Hit Singles-1958-1977-C . . . . (Atlantic)
Rime Of The Ancient Mariner
  Iron Maiden; *Live After Death-World Slavery Tour* . . . . (Capitol)
    Powerslave . . . . (Capitol)
Rio Grande
  Floyd Tillman; *The Country Music Hall Of Fame-Floyd Tillman* . . . . (MCA)
  Sam Eskin; *Shanty Men-Songs Of Sailormen And*
    Lumbermen . . . . (Smithsonian Folkways)
River, The
  Garth Brooks; *Ropin' The Wind* . . . . (Liberty)
    The Limited Series . . . . (Capitol)
Roving Kind, The
  Guy Mitchell; *Guy Mitchell-16 Most Requested Songs* . . . . (Legacy)
Sail Along, Silv'ry Moon
  Andy Williams; *Unchained Melody-Greatest Songs* . . . . (Curb)
  Billy Vaughn; *Best Of Billy Vaughn* . . . . (MCA)
    Billy Vaughn's Greatest Hits . . . . (Curb)
  Billy Vaughn & His Orchestra; *Billy Vaughn & His Orchestra Play 22 Of*
    His Greatest Hits . . . . (Ranwood)
Sail Around The World
  David Gates; *First* . . . . (Elektra)
Sail Away
  Oak Ridge Boys; *Have Arrived* . . . . (MCA)
    Oak Ridge Boys' Greatest Hits . . . . (MCA)
Sail Away
  Linda Ronstadt; *Don't Cry Now* . . . . (Asylum)
  Randy Newman; *Guilty: 30 Years Of Randy Newman* . . . . (Rhino)
    Sail Away . . . . (Reprise)
Sail Away
  Bobby Darin; *Darin 1963-1973* . . . . (Motown)
Sail Away
  Allman Brothers Band; *Enlightened Rogues* . . . . (Polydor)
Sail Away
  Stylistics; *In Fashion* . . . . (Mercury)
Sail Away
  Judy Garland; *Judy Garland-Live* . . . . (Capitol)

Sail Away
  Noel Coward; *Live From Las Vegas & New York* . . . . (Columbia)
Sail Away
  Creedence Clearwater Revival; *Mardi Gras* . . . . (Fantasy)
Sail Away
  Neil Young & Crazy Horse; *Rust Never Sleeps* . . . . (Reprise)
Sail Away
  Great White; *Sail Away* . . . . (Zoo)
Sail Away
  Peter Frampton; *Somethin's Happening* . . . . (A&M)
Sail Away
  Temptations; *Temptations-Anthology-The Best Of The Temptations* . . . (Motown)
Sail Away
  Roger Whittaker; *Voyager* . . . . (RCA)
Sail Away
  David Gray; *White Ladder* . . . . (ATO/RCA)
Sail Away Ladies
  Kingston Trio; *Hidden Treasures* . . . . (Folk Era)
  Odetta; *At The Gate Of Horn* . . . . (Vanguard)
    Movin' It On . . . . (Rose Quartz)
    One Grain Of Sand . . . . (Vanguard)
Sail Away Sweet Sister
  Queen; *The Game* . . . . (Hollywood)
Sail Away To The Sea
  Sandy Denny; *Who Knows Where The Time Goes* . . . . (Hannibal)
Sail On
  Commodores; *All The Great Love Songs-Commodores* . . . . (Motown)
    Commodores-All The Great Hits . . . . (Motown)
    Lionel Richie-Composer Series . . . . (Motown)
    Midnight Magic . . . . (Motown)
Sail On
  Robin Trower; *Caravan To Midnight* . . . . (Chrysalis)
Sail On Flying Dutchman
  Nick Seeger; *Sail On Flying Dutchman* . . . . (Biograph)
Sail On Sailor
  Beach Boys; *10 Years Of Harmony* . . . . (Caribou)
    Best Of The Beach Boys-Good Vibrations . . . . (Reprise)
    Holland . . . . (Brother)
    The Beach Boys In Concert . . . . (Brother)
Sail On White Moon
  Boz Scaggs; *Slow Dancer* . . . . (Columbia)
Sail To Australia
  New Grass Revival; *When The Storm Is Over* . . . . (Flying Fish)
Sailboat In The Moonlight
  Billie Holiday; *Billie Holiday's Greatest Hits* . . . . (Legacy)
    Lady Day . . . . (Columbia)
    Legacy Box-1933-1958 . . . . (Columbia)
    Quintessential-#4-1937 . . . . (Columbia)
Sailin'
  New Riders Of The Purple Sage; *Gypsy Cowboy* . . . . (Columbia)
Sailin'
  Cecilio & Kapono; *Night Music* . . . . (Columbia)
Sailin' On
  Bad Brains; *Rock For Light* . . . . (Caroline)
    The Youth Are Getting Restless-Paradiso-1987 . . . . (Caroline)
Sailin' On The Hawaii
  Nitty Gritty Dirt Band; *Will The Circle Be Unbroken* . . . . (EMI)
Sailin' Shoes
  Little Feat; *Sailin' Shoes* . . . . (Warner Bros.)
    Waiting For Columbus . . . . (Warner Bros.)
Sailin' To Paradise
  Pablo Cruise; *Worlds Away* . . . . (A&M)
Sailing
  Rod Stewart; *Absolutely Live* . . . . (Warner Bros.)
    Atlantic Crossing . . . . (Warner Bros.)
    Rod Stewart's Greatest Hits . . . . (Warner Bros.)
    Storyteller/The Complete Anthology: 1964-1990 . . . . (Warner Bros.)
Sailing
  Christopher Cross; *Christopher Cross* . . . . (Warner Bros.)
Sailing Blues
  John Lee Hooker; *Alone* . . . . (Specialty)
Sailing Down The Chesapeake Bay
  John Townley & The Press Gang; *Chesapeake Sailor's Companion* . . . (Adelphi)
Sailing Down The Tears
  Hanoi Rocks; *Back To Mystery City* . . . . (Geffen)
Sailing Down This Golden River
  Pete Seeger; *Bread & Roses Festival Of Acoustic Music-#1-C* . . . . . (Fantasy)
    Circles & Seasons . . . . (Warner Bros.)
Sailing Home For Christmas
  Doug Stone; *First Christmas* . . . . (Epic)
Sailing Nights
  Bob Seger; *Beautiful Loser* . . . . (Capitol)
Sailing Ships
  Whitesnake; *Slip Of The Tongue* . . . . (Geffen)
Sailing The Wind
  Loggins & Messina; *Full Sail* . . . . (Columbia)
Sailing To America
  Saxon; *Crusader* . . . . (Carrere)

Sailing To Philadelphia
  Mark Knopfler; *Sailing To Philadelphia* . . . .(Warner Bros.)
Sailing Toward Home
  Oak Ridge Boys; *All Our Favorite Songs* . . . . (Columbia)
Sailing Without A Sail
  Michael Johnson; *Michael Johnson* . . . . (A&M)
Sailing, Sailing
  Original Soundtrack; *Children's Favorites* . . . . (Kid Rhino/Rhino 4 Kids)
Sailor
  Rick Derringer; *Derringer* . . . . (Blue Sky)
    Derringer Live . . . . (Blue Sky)
Sailor
  Molly Hatchet; *Beatin' The Odds* . . . .(Epic)
Sailor & The Mermaid
  Libby Titus & Dr. John; *In Harmony-Sesame Street-C* . . . . (Columbia)
Sailor Boy
  Chiffons; *Best Of The Chiffons* . . . . (Laurie)
Sailor Song
  Sister Double Happiness; *Heart & Soul* . . . . (Reprise)
Sailor's Lament
  Creedence Clearwater Revival; *1970* . . . . (Fantasy)
    Pendulum . . . . (Fantasy)
Sailor's Life
  Fairport Convention; *Fairport Convention-Chronicles* . . . . (A&M)
    Unhalfbricking . . . . (A&M)
  Judy Collins; *Maid Of Constant Sorrow* . . . . (Elektra)
Sailor's Misfortune
  Dave Loggins; *Personal Belongings* . . . . (Vanguard)
Sails
  Chet Atkins; *Sails* . . . . (Columbia)
  Elton John; *Empty Sky* . . . . (Polydor)
Salty Dog, A
  Procol Harum; *A Salty Dog* . . . . (A&M)
    Best Of Procol Harum . . . . (A&M)
    Procol Harum Live In Concert with the Edmonton Symphony . . . . (A&M)
    Procol Harum-Classics-#17 . . . . (A&M)
Saturday Sailing
  James Morrison; *Postcards From Down Under* . . . .(Atlantic)
Sea Cruise
  Billy "Crash" Craddock; *Billy "Crash" Craddock's Greatest Hits* . . . (Capitol)
    Changes . . . . (Capitol)
  Frankie Ford; *American Hot Wax* . . . . (A&M)
    Best Of New Orleans Rhythm & Blues-#2-C . . . . (Rhino)
    Oldies But Goodies-#3-C . . . . (Original Sound)
    Rock & Roll Show-C . . . . (Gusto)
  Glenn Frey; *No Fun Aloud* . . . . (Asylum)
  Johnny Rivers; *Johnny Rivers-Anthology 1964-1977* . . . . (Rhino)
  Nighthawks; *Best Of The Nighthawks* . . . . (Genes CD Co.)
  Robert Gordon & Link Wray; *Fresh Fish Special* . . . . (RCA)
Shadow Captain
  Crosby, Stills & Nash; *Allies* . . . .(Atlantic)
    CSN . . . .(Atlantic)
    Replay . . . .(Atlantic)
Shakedown Cruise
  Jay Ferguson; *Real Life Ain't This Way* . . . . (Asylum)
Ship Without A Sail
  Dave Frishberg; *Let's Eat Home* . . . .(Concord Jazz)
  Ella Fitzgerald; *Rodgers & Hart Songbook* . . . . (Verve)
  Sarah Vaughan; *Rodgers & Hart Songbook* . . . . (Emarcy)
Shiver Me Timbers
  Bette Midler; *Live At Last* . . . .(Atlantic)
    Songs For The New Depression . . . .(Atlantic)
    ST/Divine Madness . . . .(Atlantic)
  Tom Waits; *The Heart Of Saturday Night* . . . . (Asylum)
Skye Boat Song
  King's Singers; *American Balladeer-Golden Classics-#1-C* . . . . . (Collectables)
    Annie Laurie-Folk Songs Of British Isles . . . . (Angel)
  Roger Whittaker; *Live In Concert* . . . . (RCA)
Sloop John B
  Beach Boys; *Absolute Best-#2* . . . . (Capitol)
    Beach Boys '69 (The Beach Boys Live In London) . . . . (Capitol)
    Beach Boys-Gift Set . . . . (Capitol)
    Best Of (Good Vibrations) . . . . (Reprise)
    Made In The U.S.A. . . . . (Capitol)
    Pet Sounds . . . . (Capitol)
    ST/Forrest Gump . . . .(Epic/Sony Music Soundtrax)
    The Pet Sounds Sessions: A 30th Anniversary Collection . . . . (Capitol)
Smooth Sailin'
  T.G. Sheppard; *T.G. Sheppard's All-Time Greatest Hits* . . . . . . (Warner Bros.)
Smooth Sailing
  Arnett Cobb; *Giants Of The Blues-Tenor Sax* . . . . (Prestige)
    Smooth Sailing . . . . (Prestige)
  Ella Fitzgerald; *Best Of Ella Fitzgerald* . . . . (MCA)
    Live In Tokyo . . . . (Pablo)
    Newport Jazz Festival . . . . (Columbia)
Son Of A Son Of A Sailor
  Jimmy Buffett; *Boats Beaches Bars & Ballads* . . . .(Margaritaville)
    Son Of A Son Of A Sailor . . . . (MCA)
    Songs You Know By Heart-Jimmy Buffett's Greatest Hit(s) . . . .(MCA)

  You Had To Be There . . . . (MCA)
Sullen Girl
  Fiona Apple; *Tidal* . . . .(Clean Slate/Work)
Theme From "Popeye"
  Original Soundtrack; *Television's Greatest Hits-#1-C* . . . . (TVT)
Theme From "The Ghost And Mrs. Muir"
  Original Soundtrack; *Television's Greatest Hits-#5-In Living Color-C* . . . (TVT)
Thousands Are Sailing
  Pogues; *Essential Pogues* . . . . (Island)
    If I Should Fall From Grace With God . . . . (Island)
Through My Sails
  Neil Young & Crazy Horse; *Zuma* . . . . (Reprise)
Times Have Changed
  Supertramp; *Indelibly Stamped* . . . . (A&M)
True Love Never Dies
  Earl Scruggs & Gary Scruggs & Travis Tritt; *Earl Scruggs And
    Friends-C* . . . . (MCA)
  Kevin Welch; *Kevin Welch* . . . . (Reprise)
Uncle Albert/Admiral Halsey
  Paul And Linda McCartney; *RAM* . . . . (Capitol)
  Paul McCartney; *All The Best!* . . . . (Capitol)
    Paul McCartney-Gift Set . . . . (Capitol)
  Wings; *Wings Greatest* . . . . (Capitol)
Vahevala
  Loggins & Messina; *Loggins & Messina-On Stage* . . . . (Columbia)
    Sittin' In . . . . (Columbia)
    The Best Of Friends . . . . (Columbia)
Various Tracks
  Paul Clayton; *Whaling And Sailing Songs* . . . .(Tradition)
When My Ship Comes In
  Clint Black; *The Hard Way* . . . . (RCA)

SCHOOL, Classrooms, Graduation, Guidance, Instruction, Learning, Teachers

  See Also: *ADVICE, AGING, BOOKS, CHILDREN, FAMILY
  (various), PARENTS (various), SPORTS: FOOTBALL (fight songs),
  TEACHING VALUES, TEENAGERS, THINKING & KNOWING,
  WARNINGS*

(Remember The Days Of) The Old Schoolyard
  Cat Stevens; *Cat Stevens-Classics-#24* . . . . (A&M)
    Izitso . . . . (A&M)
26 Cents
  Wilkinsons; *Nothing But Love* . . . .(Giant)
3 O'Clock...School's Out!
  Full Force; *Guess Who's Comin' To The Crib?* . . . . (Columbia)
ABC
  Jackson 5; *ABC* . . . . (Motown)
    Jackson 5-Anthology . . . . (Motown)
    Jackson 5's Greatest Hits . . . . (Motown)
Abigail Beecher
  Freddy Cannon; *14 Booming Hits* . . . . (Rhino)
    *Big Blast From Boston: The Best Of Freddy "Boom Boom"
    Cannon* . . . . (Rhino)
Across The Field
  Ohio State University Marching Band; *Pride Of The
    Buckeyes* . . . . (Fidelity Sound)
  Original Soundtrack; *College Fight Songs: The Big Ten-C* . . . . (K-Tel)
    The Greatest College Fight Songs . . . . (Laserlight)
    Top Ten College Fight Songs . . . . (K-Tel)
Adult Education
  Daryl Hall & John Oates; *Live At The Apollo* . . . . (RCA)
    Rock 'N Soul, Part 1 . . . . (RCA)
After School
  Randy Starr; *Teenage Crush #3-C* . . . .(Ace)
After School
  Linda Allen; *Women's Work* . . . . (Flying Fish)
After School
  Young M.C.; *Brainstorm* . . . . (Capitol)
Aggie War Hymn
  Original Soundtrack; *The Greatest College Fight Songs* . . . . . . (Laserlight)
All Hail Blue & Gold
  University Of California Marching Band; *University Of California
    Marching Band* . . . . (Fidelity Sound)
All You Need Is Love
  Beatles; *Beatles 1* . . . . (Capitol)
    Compact Disc Singles Collection . . . . (Capitol)
    Magical Mystery Tour . . . . (Capitol)
    The Beatles/1967-1970 . . . . (Capitol)
    Yellow Submarine . . . . (Capitol)
Alma Mater
  Original Broadway Cast; *Grease* . . . . (Polydor)
Alma Mater
  Alice Cooper; *School's Out* . . . . (Warner Bros.)

Alma Mater
Chicago; *Chicago V* .... (Chicago)
Animal House
Stephen Bishop; *ST/Animal House* .... (MCA)
Another Brick In The Wall, Part 2
Class Of '99; *ST/The Faculty* .... (Columbia)
Pink Floyd; *Collection Of Great Dance Songs* .... (Columbia)
Delicate Sound Of Thunder .... (Columbia)
The Wall .... (Columbia)
Roger Waters; *The Wall-Live In Berlin* .... (Mercury)
Auctioneer, The
Leroy Van Dyke; *Deep In The Heart Of Country-C* .... (Drive)
Back On Top
Van Morrison; *Back On Top* .... (Point Blank/Virgin)
Back To Schooldays
Graham Parker; *Howlin' Wind* .... (Mercury)
Live! Alone In America .... (RCA)
Graham Parker And The Rumour; *The Parkerilla* .... (Mercury)
Bad Luck Streak In Dancing School
Warren Zevon; *Bad Luck Streak In Dancing School* .... (Asylum)
Bar Exam
Derailers; *Here Come The Derailers* .... (Lucky Dog)
Be True To Your School
Beach Boys; *Absolute Best-#1* .... (Capitol)
Beach Boys-Gift Set .... (Capitol)
Endless Summer .... (Capitol)
Little Deuce Coupe/All Summer Long .... (Capitol)
Made In The U.S.A. .... (Capitol)
Bear Down Arizona
Original Soundtrack; *College Fight Songs: The Pac Ten-C* .... (K-Tel)
Beauty School Dropout
Original Broadway Cast; *Grease* .... (Polydor)
Birds And The Bees
Jewel Akens; *American Graffiti-#3-C* .... (MCA)
Collectables Presents The History Of Rock-#4-C .... (Collectables)
Cruisin'-1965-C .... (Increase)
Oldies But Goodies-#9-C .... (Original Sound)
Super Hits-#3-C .... (Gusto)
Bobbie Ann Mason
Rick Trevino; *Looking For The Light* .... (Columbia)
Both Sides Now
Sammy Hagar; *Marching To Mars* .... (MCA)
Bow Down To Washington
Original Soundtrack; *College Fight Songs: The Pac Ten-C* .... (K-Tel)
The Greatest College Fight Songs .... (Laserlight)
Bust The High School Students
Austin Lounge Lizards; *Lizard Vision* .... (Flying Fish)
Carlene
Phil Vassar; *Phil Vassar* .... (Arista)
Carol
Chuck Berry; *Berry Is On Top* .... (Chess)
Chuck Berry-Golden Hits .... (Mercury)
Chuck Berry's Greatest Hits .... (Everest)
Roll Over Beethoven .... (Allegiance)
Rolling Stones; *England's Newest Hit Makers/The Rolling Stones* .... (Abkco)
Get Yer Ya-Ya's Out! .... (Abkco)
Carrie-Anne
Hollies; *Best Of The Hollies* .... (EMI)
Evolution .... (Epic)
Hollies-Epic Anthology From The Original Master Tapes .... (Epic)
The Hollies' Greatest Hits .... (Epic)
Catholic School Girls Rule
Red Hot Chili Peppers; *Abbey Road E.P.* .... (EMI)
Freaky Styley .... (EMI)
What Hits!? .... (EMI)
Centerfold
J. Geils Band; *Flashback-Best Of The J. Geils Band* .... (EMI)
Freeze-Frame .... (EMI)
Showtime .... (EMI)
Charlie Brown
Coasters; *Billboard Top Rock 'N' Roll Hits-1957-C* .... (Rhino)
Coasters' Greatest Hits .... (Atco)
Coasters-Their Greatest Recordings-Early Years .... (Atco)
Cruisin'-1959-C .... (Increase)
Super Oldies Of The '50s-#7-C .... (Audio Fidelity)
Young Blood .... (Atlantic)
Chattahoochee
Alan Jackson; *A Lot About Livin' (And A Little 'Bout Love)* .... (Arista)
Cheatin' In School
Corey Hart; *First Offense* .... (EMI)
Check Yes Or No
George Strait; *Strait Out Of The Box* .... (MCA)
Chemistry
Semisonic; *All About Chemistry* .... (MCA)
Chinese Arithmetic
Faith No More; *Introduce Yourself* .... (Slash)
Class Of '57
Statler Brothers; *Best Of The Statler Brothers* .... (Mercury)
Come Join The Band
Original Soundtrack; *College Fight Songs: The Pac Ten-C* .... (K-Tel)
Cowboy Love
John Michael Montgomery; *John Michael Montgomery* .... (Atlantic)
John Michael Montgomery's Greatest Hits .... (Atlantic)
Crash Course In Brain Surgery
Metallica; *Garage Days Re-Revisited* .... (Elektra)
Cuban Love Song
George Shearing; *Best Of George Shearing* .... (Capitol)
Cup Of Tea
Verve Pipe; *Villains* .... (RCA)
Daddy Should Have Stayed In High School
Cheap Trick; *Cheap Trick* .... (Epic)
Day Job
Gin Blossoms; *Congratulations I'm Sorry* .... (A&M)
Outside Looking In: The Best Of The Gin Blossoms .... (A&M)
Dear Old Nebraska U.
University Of Michigan Band; *Greatest College Football Marches* .... (Vanguard)
Doin' What Comes Natur'lly
Dinah Shore; *16 Most Requested Songs Of The '40s-#1-C* .... (Legacy)
Dinah Shore-16 Most Requested Songs .... (Legacy)
Ethel Merman/Ray Middleton/Original Cast; *Annie Get Your Gun* .... (MCA)
Down, Down The Field
Original Soundtrack; *The Greatest College Fight Songs* .... (Laserlight)
Duke Blue & White
University Of Michigan Band; *Greatest College Football Marches* .... (Vanguard)
Education
Kinks; *Schoolboys In Disgrace* .... (Rhino)
Education
Untouchables; *Agent Double O Soul* .... (Restless)
Everybody's Free (To Wear Sunscreen)
Baz Luhrmann; *Now That's What I Call Music!-#2-C* .... (Virgin)
Something For Everybody .... (Capitol)
Everybody's Got To Learn Sometime
Korgis; *Dumb Waiters* .... (Asylum)
Fight For California
Original Soundtrack; *The Greatest College Fight Songs* .... (Laserlight)
University Of California Marching Band; *University Of California Marching Band* .... (Fidelity Sound)
Fight On State
Original Soundtrack; *College Fight Songs: The Big Ten-C* .... (K-Tel)
The Greatest College Fight Songs .... (Laserlight)
Fight On, Pennsylvania
All-Star Inter-Conference Band; *College Marches At Halftime* .... (Alshire)
University Of Michigan Band; *Greatest College Football Marches* .... (Vanguard)
Fight On, U.S.C.
Michigan University Band; *Kick Off, U.S.A.* .... (Vanguard)
Original Soundtrack; *College Fight Songs: The Pac Ten-C* .... (K-Tel)
The Greatest College Fight Songs .... (Laserlight)
Top Ten College Fight Songs .... (K-Tel)
Fight Song, The
Original Soundtrack; *College Fight Songs: The Pac Ten-C* .... (K-Tel)
Fight The Team Across The Field
Ohio State University Marching Band; *Across The Field* .... (Fidelity Sound)
Found Out About You
Gin Blossoms; *New Miserable Experience* .... (A&M)
Freshmen, The
Verve Pipe; *Villains* .... (RCA)
Getting Better
Beatles; *Sgt. Pepper's Lonely Hearts Club Band* .... (Capitol)
Girls' School
Wings; *London Town* .... (Capitol)
Glory Days
Bruce Springsteen; *Born In The U.S.A.* .... (Columbia)
Bruce Springsteen's Greatest Hits .... (Columbia)
Go U Northwestern
Northwestern University Marching Band; *Go U Northwestern* .... (Fidelity Sound)
Original Soundtrack; *College Fight Songs: The Big Ten-C* .... (K-Tel)
The Greatest College Fight Songs .... (Laserlight)
Good Morning Little School Girl
Grateful Dead; *Grateful Dead (Skull & Roses)* .... (Warner Bros.)
Huey Lewis and the News; *Four Chords & Several Years Ago* .... (Elektra)
Johnny Winter; *Johnny Winter* .... (Columbia)
Live/Johnny Winter And .... (Columbia)
Ten Years After; *Classic Performances Of Ten Years After* .... (Columbia)
Recorded Live .... (Columbia)
SSSSH .... (Chrysalis)
Universal .... (Chrysalis)
Yardbirds; *Eric Clapton-Crossroads-C* .... (Polydor)
Five Live Yardbirds .... (Rhino)
Gotta Learn To Love Without You
Michael Johnson; *Best Of Michael Johnson* .... (RCA)
Wings .... (RCA)
Graduate
Third Eye Blind; *Third Eye Blind* .... (Elektra)
Graduation (Friends Forever)
Vitamin C; *Totally Hits-#3-C* .... (Atlantic)
Vitamin C .... (Elektra)

Graduation Day
Beach Boys; *Beach Boys-Gift Set* . . . . (Capitol)
  Spirit Of America . . . . (Capitol)
Rover Boys; *Choice Voices! Pop Vocal Group Gems Of The*
  '50s-C . . . . (Collector's Choice)

Graduation's Here
Fleetwoods; *Best Of The Fleetwoods* . . . . (Rhino)

Great Joe Bob (A Regional Tragedy)
Country Gazette; *Hello Operator...This Is Country Gazette* . . . . . . (Flying Fish)

Hail New Mexico
Original Soundtrack; *The Greatest College Fight Songs* . . . . (Laserlight)

Hail Purdue
Original Soundtrack; *College Fight Songs: The Big Ten-C* . . . . (K-Tel)
  The Greatest College Fight Songs . . . . (Laserlight)
University Of Michigan Band; *Greatest College Football Marches* . (Vanguard)

Hail To California
University Of California Marching Band; *Hail To California* . . .(Fidelity Sound)

Hail To Old O.S.U.
Original Soundtrack; *College Fight Songs: The Pac Ten-C* . . . . (K-Tel)
  The Greatest College Fight Songs . . . . (Laserlight)

Hail Varsity
Original Soundtrack; *The Greatest College Fight Songs* . . . . (Laserlight)

Hail Wichita
Wichita State University Marching Band; *Wichita State University*
  Marching Band . . . .(Fidelity Sound)

Harper Valley P.T.A.
Jeannie C. Riley; *Harper Valley P.T.A.* . . . . (Plantation)
  Jeannie C. Riley's Greatest Hits . . . . (Plantation)
  Oldies But Goodies-#4-C . . . . (Original Sound)
  Souvenirs Of Music City U.S.A.-C . . . . (Plantation)

Heartbreaker
Bee Gees; *One Night Only* . . . . (Polydor)

Here Comes Carolina
Ohio State University Marching Band; *Saturday Afternoon At*
  Columbus . . . .(Fidelity Sound)

High School Cadets
Band Of H.M. Royal Marines; *Stars And Stripes Forever* . . . . (Angel)

High School Confidential
Jerry Lee Lewis; *20 Classic Jerry Lee Lewis Hits* . . . . (Original Sound)
  Jerry Lee Lewis-Original Golden Hits-#2 . . . . (Sun)
  ST/Harper Valley PTA . . . . (Sun)
  Sun Story-C . . . . (Rhino)

High School Nights
Dave Edmunds; *Dave Edmunds-Anthology-1968-1990* . . . . (Rhino)
  ST/Porky's Revenge! . . . . (Columbia)

High School U.S.A.
Tommy Facenda; *45-#51 to #78* . . . . (Atlantic)

Homecoming Queen's Got A Gun
Julie Brown; *Dr. Demento Presents The Greatest Novelty Records-#5-*
  1980s-C. . . . . (Rhino)
  Teenage Tragedies-C. . . . . (Rhino)
  Trapped In The Body Of A White Girl . . . . (Sire)

Hot For Teacher
Van Halen; *1984* . . . .(Warner Bros.)

How Do You Like Me Now?!
Toby Keith; *How Do You Like Me Now?!* . . . .(DreamWorks/SKG)

How To Dance
Bingoboys; *Best Of Bingoboys* . . . .(Atlantic)

I Am Made Of You
Ricky Martin; *Ricky Martin* . . . . (Columbia)

I Deal With Mathematics
Movement Ex; *Movement Ex* . . . . (Columbia)

I Disappear
Metallica; *ST/Mission: Impossible 2* . . . . (Hollywood)

I Hope You've Learned
Ricky Skaggs and Kentucky Thunder; *Bluegrass Rules!* . . . . (Rounder)

I Learned From The Best
Whitney Houston; *My Love Is Your Love* . . . . (Arista)

I Taught Her Everything She Knows
Billy Walker; *Billy Walker's Greatest Hits* . . . . (Monument)

I Was The One
Elvis Presley; *Elvis' Golden Records* . . . . (RCA)

I Won't Grow Up
Original Cast/Mary Martin; *Peter Pan-The 1954 Broadway*
  Production . . . .(RCA Victor)

I'd Like To Teach The World To Sing (In Perfect Harmony)
New Seekers; *Chicken Soup For The Soul-Celebrating Life-C* . . . . (Rhino)

Illinois Loyalty
Original Soundtrack; *College Fight Songs: The Big Ten-C* . . . . (K-Tel)
University Of Michigan Band; *Greatest College Football Marches* . (Vanguard)

I'm Already Taken
Steve Wariner; *Country Cares For Kids II-C* . . . . (BNA)
  Two Teardrops . . . . (Capitol)

I'm Flying
Original Cast/Mary Martin; *Peter Pan-The 1954 Broadway*
  Production . . . .(RCA Victor)

Immortality
Pearl Jam; *Vitalogy* . . . .(Epic)

Indiana, Our Indiana
Indiana University Marching 100; *Indiana Our Indiana* . . . . (Fidelity Sound)
  Indiana University Marching 100 . . . . (Fidelity Sound)
Original Soundtrack; *College Fight Songs: The Big Ten-C* . . . . (K-Tel)

Iowa Fight Song
Original Soundtrack; *College Fight Songs: The Big Ten-C* . . . . (K-Tel)
University Of Iowa Band; *Go Hawkeyes Go* . . . . (Fidelity Sound)
University Of Michigan Band; *Greatest College Football Marches* . . (Vanguard)

I've Got A Lot To Learn About Love
Storm; *Storm* . . . .(Interscope)

Jeremy
Pearl Jam; *Ten* . . . . (Epic Portrait Assoc.)

Johnny B. Goode
Chuck Berry; *Chuck Berry's Greatest Hits* . . . . (Everest)
  Classic Rock-#2-C . . . . (MCA)
  Roll Over Beethoven . . . . (Allegiance)
  ST/American Graffiti . . . . (MCA)
  The Chess Box-Chuck Berry. . . . . (Chess)
Elvis Presley; *Elvis In Concert* . . . . (RCA)
  From Memphis To Vegas/From Vegas To Memphis. . . . .(RCA)
Grateful Dead; *Bill Graham Presents The Last Days Of The*
  Fillmore-C . . . . (Epic Portrait Assoc.)
Johnny Winter; *Live/Johnny Winter And.* . . . . (Columbia)
  Second Winter . . . . (Columbia)

Josephine
Wallflowers; *Bringing Down The Horse* . . . .(Interscope)

Juke Box Baby
Perry Como; *Perry Como's Greatest Hits.* . . . .(RCA)

Just The Two Of Us
Will Smith; *Big Willie Style.* . . . . (Columbia)

K.S.U. Fight Song
Kent State University Marching Band; *Kent State University*
  Marching Band . . . . (Fidelity Sound)

Laugh Laugh
Beau Brummels; *Best Of The Beau Brummels* . . . . (Rhino)
  Heart & Soul Of Rock 'N' Roll-#1-C . . . . (Rhino)
  Introducing The Beau Brummels . . . . (Rhino)
  Nuggets-#7-Early San Francisco-C . . . . (Rhino)

Learn How To Live
Billy Squier; *Emotions In Motion* . . . . (Capitol)

Learn To Be Still
Eagles; *Hell Freezes Over* . . . . (Geffen)

Learn To Fly
Foo Fighters; *There Is Nothing Left To Lose* . . . .(Roswell/RCA)

Learnin' The Blues
Frank Sinatra; *Capitol Collectors Series-Frank Sinatra* . . . . (Capitol)
  Sinatra-Basie . . . . (Reprise)
  The Capitol Years . . . . (Capitol)

Learning As You Go
Rick Trevino; *Learning As You Go* . . . . (Columbia)
  Super Hits Of 1996-C . . . . (Epic)

Learning How To Love You
John Hiatt; *Bring The Family* . . . . (A&M)

Learning How To Love You
George Harrison; *33 1/3* . . . .(Dark Horse)

Learning The Game
Andrew Gold; *What's Wrong With This Picture?* . . . .(Asylum)

Learning The Game
Buddy Holly; *Complete Buddy Holly* . . . . (MCA)
  The Buddy Holly Collection . . . . (MCA)

Learning The Game
Santa Esmeralda; *Beauty.* . . . .(Casablanca)

Learning To Fly
Pink Floyd; *Delicate Sound Of Thunder* . . . . (Columbia)
  Momentary Lapse Of Reason . . . . (Columbia)

Learning To Fly
Tom Petty And The Heartbreakers; *Into The Great Wide Open* . . . . (MCA)

Learning To Live Again
Garth Brooks; *The Chase* . . . . (Liberty)

Leech
Eve 6; *Eve 6.* . . . . (RCA)

Lesson In Leavin'
Dottie West; *Special Delivery* . . . . (EMI)
Jo Dee Messina; *I'm Alright* . . . . (Curb)

Lesson In Survival
Joni Mitchell; *For The Roses.* . . . .(Asylum)

Lessons To Be Learned
Barbra Streisand; *Higher Ground* . . . . (Columbia)

Letting Go
Suzy Bogguss; *Aces* . . . . (Liberty)
  Voices In The Wind. . . . . (Liberty)

Life Gets Away
Clint Black; *Clint Black-The Greatest Hits* . . . .(RCA)
  One Emotion. . . . . (RCA)

Life's A Dance
John Michael Montgomery; *Life's A Dance* . . . .(Atlantic)

Live & Learn
Joe Public; *Joe Public* . . . . (Columbia)

Living & Learning
Mel Tillis & The Statesiders; *Mel Tillis & The Statesiders-24*
  Great Hits .... (MGM)
Lonely Boy
Andrew Gold; *Listen To The Music-'70s California-C* .... (Rhino)
  Super Hits Of The '70s-Have A Nice Day-#19-C .... (Rhino)
  What's Wrong With This Picture? .... (Asylum)
Look At That
Paul Simon; *You're The One* .... (Warner Bros.)
Love Hurts
Cher; *Love Hurts* .... (Geffen)
Emmylou Harris & Gram Parsons; *Duets-C* .... (Reprise)
Gram Parsons; *Grievous Angel* .... (Reprise)
Jim Capaldi; *The Island Story-1962-1987-25th Anniversary-C* .... (Island)
Judy Collins; *Bread & Roses* .... (Elektra)
Nazareth; *Hair Of The Dog* .... (A&M)
  Hot Tracks .... (A&M)
  Nazareth-Classics-#16 .... (A&M)
  'Snaz .... (A&M)
Roy Orbison; *Legendary Roy Orbison* ...... (Sony Music Special Prod.)
  Roy Orbison's All-Time Greatest Hits-#1 & 2 .... (Monument)
Love Lessons
Tracy Byrd; *Love Lessons* .... (MCA)
Love School
Divinyls; *Divinyls* ....(Virgin)
M.S.U. Fight Song
Michigan State University Band; *Michigan State*
  University Band .... (Fidelity Sound)
Original Soundtrack; *College Fight Songs: The Big Ten-C* .... (K-Tel)
Maggie Mae
Beatles; *Let It Be* .... (Capitol)
Maggie May
Rod Stewart; *Absolutely Live* .... (Warner Bros.)
  Best Of Rod Stewart .... (Mercury)
  Billboard Top Rock 'N' Roll Hits-1971-C .... (Rhino)
  Every Picture Tells A Story .... (Mercury)
  Rod Stewart's Greatest Hits .... (Warner Bros.)
  Sing It Again, Rod .... (Mercury)
  Storyteller/The Complete Anthology: 1964-1990 .... (Warner Bros.)
Maroon And Gold
Original Soundtrack; *College Fight Songs: The Pac Ten-C* .... (K-Tel)
Marquette University
Band Of H.M. Royal Marines; *Solid Men To The Front-Sousa*
  Marches-#3 .... (Angel)
Mary Had A Little Lamb
Garth Brooks; *The Magic Of Christmas: Songs From Call Me Claus* ... (Capitol)
Original Soundtrack; *Sesame Street: Kids' Favorite Songs-#2* ... (Sony Wonder)
Stevie Ray Vaughan and Double Trouble; *Live Alive* .... (Epic)
  Texas Flood .... (Epic)
Wings; *Wild Life* .... (Capitol)
Maxwell's Silver Hammer
Beatles; *Abbey Road* ....(Parlophone)
Me And Julio Down By The Schoolyard
Paul Simon; *Greatest Hits, Etc.* .... (Columbia)
  Negotiations And Love Songs, 1971-1986 .... (Warner Bros.)
  Paul Simon .... (Columbia)
  Paul Simon In Concert/Live Rhymin' ....(Columbia)
Simon & Garfunkel; *The Concert In Central Park* .... (Warner Bros.)
Men Of Ohio
Ohio State University Marching Band; *Foot Tappers* .... (Fidelity Sound)
Mighty Bears Of Baylor
Southern Methodist Mustang Band; *Southwest*
  Conference Jazz.................................. (Fidelity Sound)
Mighty Oregon
Original Soundtrack; *College Fight Songs: The Pac Ten-C* .... (K-Tel)
  The Greatest College Fight Songs ....(Laserlight)
Minnesota Rouser
Ohio State University Marching Band; *Stadium Favorites In*
  Brass .... (Fidelity Sound)
Original Soundtrack; *College Fight Songs: The Big Ten-C* .... (K-Tel)
  Top Ten College Fight Songs .... (K-Tel)
Miseducation Of Lauryn Hill
Lauryn Hill; *The Miseducation Of Lauryn Hill* .... (Ruffhouse/Columbia)
Moments To Remember
Four Lads; *'50s Vocal Groups-C* .... (K-Tel)
  Four Lads-16 Most Requested Songs .... (Legacy)
  Radio Classics Of The '50s-C .... (Columbia)
Original Cast; *Forever Plaid* ....(RCA)
Ray Conniff & His Orchestra; *Memories Are Made Of This* ...... (Columbia)
Vogues; *Vogues' Greatest Hits* .... (Rhino)
My Back Pages
Bob Dylan; *Another Side Of Bob Dylan* .... (Columbia)
  Bob Dylan's Greatest Hits-#2. .... (Columbia)
Byrds; *20 Essential Tracks From The Box Set* .... (Columbia)
  Byrds Play Dylan .... (Columbia)
  The Byrds' Greatest Hits .... (Columbia)
  Younger Than Yesterday .... (Columbia)
My Old School
Steely Dan; *Countdown To Ecstasy*.......................... (MCA)

  Decade Of Steely Dan .... (MCA)
  Steely Dan's Greatest Hits .... (MCA)
National Education Week
10,000 Maniacs; *Hope Chest-Fredonia Recordings-1982-1983* ...... (Elektra)
Never Ending
Wood; *Songs From Stamford Hill* .... (Columbia)
New Girl In School
Jan & Dean; *Jan & Dean-Legendary Masters* .... (EMI)
  Surf City-Best Of Jan & Dean .... (EMI)
New Math
Tom Lehrer; *That Was The Year That Was* .... (Reprise)
No More Homework
Gary U.S. Bonds; *School Of Rock 'N' Roll-Best Of Gary U.S. Bonds* ....(Rhino)
No Such Thing
John Mayer; *Room For Squares* .... (Aware/C2/Columbia)
Notre Dame Our Mother
University Of Notre Dame Band; *Songs Of The Fighting*
  Irish .... (Fidelity Sound)
Notre Dame Victory March
Original Soundtrack; *The Greatest College Fight Songs* .... (Laserlight)
  Top Ten College Fight Songs ....(K-Tel)
University Of Notre Dame Band; *Songs Of The Fighting*
  Irish .... (Fidelity Sound)
Ode To A Gym Teacher
Meg Christian; *I Know You Know* ....(Olivia)
  Scrapbook ....(Olivia)
Oh Baby Doll
Chuck Berry; *The Chess Box-Chuck Berry* .... (Chess)
Ohio
Crosby, Stills & Nash; *CSN* .... (Atlantic)
Crosby, Stills, Nash & Young; *4 Way Street* .... (Atlantic)
  So Far .... (Atlantic)
Neil Young; *Decade*....................................... (Reprise)
  ST/Journey Through The Past .... (Warner Bros.)
Old School, The
John Conlee; *Country Classics-#6-1985-1986-C.* ....(Universal)
  John Conlee-20 Greatest Hits .... (MCA)
  The Old School .... (MCA Special Prod.)
On Iowa
Original Soundtrack; *The Greatest College Fight Songs* ..... (Laserlight)
University Of Iowa Marching Band; *Go Hawkeyes Go* .... (Fidelity Sound)
On, Brave Old Army Team
All-Star Inter-Conference Band; *College Marches At Halftime*....... (Alshire)
Glenn Miller; *Pennsylvania 6-5000-Sustaining*
  Remotes .... (Vintage Jazz Classics)
Original Soundtrack; *Top Ten College Fight Songs* ....(K-Tel)
On, Wisconsin
Magic Organ; *22 Great Organ Favorites* .... (Ranwood)
  Traveling With The Magic Organ .... (Ranwood)
Original Soundtrack; *College Fight Songs: The Big Ten-C* .... (K-Tel)
  The Greatest College Fight Songs .... (Laserlight)
One More Try
George Michael; *Faith* ....(Columbia)
One More Try
Divine; *Fairy Tales* .... (Pendulum)
Open My Heart
Yolanda Adams; *Mountain High Valley Low*....................(Elektra)
Orange And Blue
Original Soundtrack; *The Greatest College Fight Songs* .... (Laserlight)
Passin' Thru
Earl Scruggs & Don Henley & Johnny Cash; *Earl Scruggs And*
  Friends-C .... (MCA)
Randy Scruggs; *Crown Of Jewels* .... (Reprise)
Randy Scruggs & Joan Osborne; *ST/Happy Texas*...............(Arista)
Pomp & Circumstance March #1 In D Op. 39
Boston Pops Orchestra/Arthur Fiedler; *Fiedler-Greatest Hits* .... (RCA)
  Fiedler's Favorite Marches .... (RCA)
Sir Edward Elgar; *ST/A Clockwork Orange* .... (Warner Bros.)
Popular
Nada Surf; *High/Low* .... (Elektra)
Power Of Good-Bye
Madonna; *GHV2* .... (Warner Bros.)
  Ray Of Light .... (Maverick)
Practice What You Preach
Barry White; *The Icon Is Love* ....(A&M)
Prayer For The Dying
Seal; *Diana, Princess Of Wales-Tribute-C* ....(Columbia)
  Seal 2 .... (Sire)
Pride Of The Illini
University Of Michigan Band; *Greatest College Football Marches* ..(Vanguard)
Pride Of The Wolverines
University Of Michigan Band; *Stars And Stripes Forever-Sousa*
  Marches ....(Vanguard)
Princeton Cannon Song
University Of Michigan Band; *Greatest College Football Marches* ..(Vanguard)
Principal's Office
Young M.C.; *Stone Cold Rhymin'* .... (Delicious Vinyl)
Problems
Everly Brothers; *Everly Brothers' All-Time Greatest Hits*..............(Curb)

Everly Brothers-Cadence Classics-Their 20 Greatest Hits . . . . (Rhino)
Fabulous Style Of The Everly Brothers . . . . (Rhino)
Queen Of Hollywood High
John Stewart; *Blondes.* . . . .(Allegiance)
Queen Of The Senior Prom
Mills Brothers; *Best Of The Mills Brothers.* . . . .(MCA)
Rambling Wreck From Georgia Tech
Original Soundtrack; *The Greatest College Fight Songs* . . . . (Laserlight)
Top Ten College Fight Songs. . . . . (K-Tel)
Rebecca Lynn
Bryan White; *Bryan White* . . . . (Asylum)
Red Raider Fanfare & Fight Song
Texas Tech University Band; *Grandioso* . . . .(Fidelity Sound)
Redneck School Of Technology
Flaming Lips; *Telepathic Surgery* . . . . (Restless)
Rice University Fight Song
Original Soundtrack; *The Greatest College Fight Songs* . . . . (Laserlight)
Rock 'N' Roll High School
Ramones; *End Of The Century* . . . . (Sire)
Loco Live . . . . (Sire)
Ramones Mania . . . . (Sire)
ST/Rock 'N' Roll High School . . . . (Sire)
Roll On, Tulane
Michigan University Band; *Kick Off, U.S.A.* . . . . (Vanguard)
Rose Goes To Yale
Jefferson Starship; *Nuclear Furniture* . . . .(Grunt)
Roses Are Red
Bobby Vinton; *Bobby Vinton-16 Most Requested Songs* . . . . (Legacy)
Bobby Vinton's All-Time Greatest Hits . . . .(Epic)
Spring Sensations . . . .(Epic)
School
Supertramp; *Crime Of The Century* . . . . (A&M)
Live In Paris . . . . (A&M)
School
Nirvana; *Bleach* . . . .(Sub Pop)
School
Lou & Peter Berryman; *Cupid's Trash Truck* . . . . (Cornbelt)
School Boy Crush
Average White Band; *Cut The Cake* . . . .(Atlantic)
Person To Person. . . . .(Atlantic)
School Boy Romance
Danny & The Juniors; *Rockin' With Danny & The
Juniors* . . . .(MCA Special Prod.)
School Days
Chuck Berry; *Best Of Chuck Berry* . . . . (Gusto)
Billboard Top Rock 'N' Roll Hits-1957-C . . . . (Rhino)
Chuck Berry-Golden Hits . . . . (Mercury)
ST/Rock 'N' Roll High School . . . . (Sire)
School Days
Louis Jordan; *Best Of Louis Jordan* . . . .(MCA)
School Days
Original Soundtrack; *School Days-Kids Classics* . . . . (Benson)
School Is In
Gary U.S. Bonds; *School Of Rock 'N' Roll-Best Of Gary U.S. Bonds* . . . (Rhino)
School Is Out
Gary U.S. Bonds; *School Of Rock 'N' Roll-Best Of Gary U.S. Bonds* . . . (Rhino)
School's Out
Alice Cooper; *Alice Cooper's Greatest Hits* . . . .(Warner Bros.)
School's Out . . . .(Warner Bros.)
ST/Rock 'N' Roll High School . . . . (Sire)
The Alice Cooper Show . . . .(Warner Bros.)
Krokus; *First Degree Metal* . . . . (Priority)
Stayed Awake All Night-Best Of Krokus . . . . (Arista)
Secret
Madonna; *Bedtime Stories* . . . .(Maverick/Sire)
GHV2 . . . .(Warner Bros.)
See You In September
Chiffons; *Best Of The Chiffons* . . . . (Laurie)
Happenings; *ST/Purple People Eater* . . . . (AJK Music)
Tempos; *Cruisin'-1960-C* . . . . (Increase)
ST/American Graffiti . . . .(MCA)
Sexy + 17
Stray Cats; *Best Of Stray Cats-Rock This Town* . . . .(EMI)
Rant 'N' Rave With The Stray Cats . . . .(EMI)
Shimmer
Shawn Mullins; *Songs From Dawson's Creek* . . . . (Sony Music Soundtrax)
Soul's Core . . . . (Columbia)
Show Her
Ronnie Milsap; *Collector's Series-Ronnie Milsap* . . . . (RCA)
Keyed Up . . . . (RCA)
Ronnie Milsap's Greatest Hits-#2 . . . . (RCA)
Show Me
Percy Faith & His Orchestra; *Percy Faith & His Orchestra-16 Most
Requested Songs* . . . . (Columbia)
Percy Faith & His Orchestra's All-Time Greatest Hits . . . . (Columbia)
Show Me
Joe Tex; *Best Of Joe Tex.* . . . .(Atlantic)
Commitments-Original Artist Recordings . . . . (Atco)

Show Me
Cover Girls; *Dance Club Beat.* . . . . (K-Tel)
Show Me
Del Shannon; *Del Shannon's Greatest Hits.* . . . . (Rhino)
Liberty Years (Runaway) . . . . (EMI)
Show Me
Howard Hewett; *Howard Hewett* . . . . (Elektra)
Show Me
Howard Jones; *In The Running* . . . . (Elektra)
Show Me
Pretenders; *Learning To Crawl* . . . .(Sire)
Pretenders-The Singles . . . . (Sire)
Show Me
Seal; *Seal.* . . . . (Sire)
Show Me
Stacy Earl; *Stadium Favorites In Brass* . . . .(Fidelity Sound)
Show Me
Dells; *There Is* . . . . (Chess)
Show Me Love
Robyn; *Robyn Is Here* . . . . (RCA)
Show Me The Way
Peter Frampton; *'70s Greatest Rock Hits-#8-Super Songs-C* . . . . (Priority)
Frampton Comes Alive . . . . (A&M)
Peter Frampton-Classics-#12 . . . . (A&M)
Show Me The Way
Regina Belle; *All By Myself* . . . . (Columbia)
Show Me The Way
Styx; *Edge Of The Century.* . . . . (A&M)
Show Me The Way
Storm; *Storm* . . . .(Interscope)
Simple Lessons
Candlebox; *Lucy* . . . . (Maverick)
Sing U.C.L.A.
University Of Michigan Band; *Greatest College Football Marches* . . (Vanguard)
Some Fools Never Learn
Steve Wariner; *One Good Night Deserves Another.* . . . . (MCA)
Steve Wariner's Greatest Hits . . . . (MCA)
Sons Of California
Original Soundtrack; *College Fight Songs: The Pac Ten-C* . . . . (K-Tel)
University Of California Marching Band; *University Of California
Marching Band* . . . .(Fidelity Sound)
Sons Of Westwood
Original Soundtrack; *College Fight Songs: The Pac Ten-C* . . . . (K-Tel)
The Greatest College Fight Songs . . . .(Laserlight)
Stein Song (University Of Maine)
Rudy Vallee & His Connecticut Yankees; *Billboard Pop Memories-The
1930s-C* . . . . (Rhino)
Heigh-Ho Everybody: This Is Rudy Vallee. . . . . (Living Era)
Those Wonderful Years: Puttin' On The Ritz-C . . . .(JCI Assoc. Labels)
University Of Michigan Band; *Greatest College Football Marches* . . (Vanguard)
Straight A's In Love
Johnny Cash; *Johnny Cash-Original Golden Hits-#3* . . . . (Sun)
King Of Country Music. . . . . (Sun)
Sun Story-C . . . . (Rhino)
Student Demonstration Time
Beach Boys; *Surf's Up* . . . .(Caribou)
Summertime, Summertime
Jamies; *Summer & Sun-C* . . . . (Rhino)
Sunday School To Broadway
Sammi Smith; *45-#45334* . . . . (Elektra)
Sweetheart Of Sigma Chi
Fred Waring's Pennsylvanians; *Very Best Of Fred Waring & The
Pennsylvanians* . . . .(Reader's Digest Music)
Gene Austin; *The Voice Of The Southland* . . . . (Living Era)
Swingin' On The Campus
Duke Ellington And Johnny Hodges & His Orchestra; *Duke's Men-Small
Groups-#2-C* . . . . (Columbia)
T.C.U. Fight Song
Southern Methodist Mustang Band; *Southwest
Conference Jazz.* . . . .(Fidelity Sound)
Take Care Of Your Homework
Johnnie Taylor; *Johnnie Taylor-Super Hits* . . . . (Stax)
Teach Me (The "Philly" Dog)
Manhattans; *Dedicated To You-Golden Classics-#1* . . . . (Collectables)
Teach Me How To Shimmy
Calamities; *Calamities* . . . . (Posh Boy)
Teach Me Tonight
Al Jarreau; *Al Jarreau In London* . . . .(Warner Bros.)
Breakin' Away . . . .(Warner Bros.)
Diane Schuur; *Diane Schuur-Collection* . . . . (GRP)
Ella Fitzgerald; *Montreux '75* . . . . (Pablo)
Phoebe Snow; *Best Of Phoebe Snow.* . . . . (Columbia)
It Looks Like Snow . . . . (Columbia)
Sarah Vaughan; *How Long Has This Been Going On?* . . . . (Pablo)
Teach The Gifted Children
Lou Reed; *Between Thought & Expression-Anthology* . . . . (RCA)

Teach Them To Pray
Junior Walker & The All Stars; *Motown Superstar Series-#5-Junior Walker & The All Stars* . . . . (Motown)
Teach Your Children
Crosby, Stills & Nash; *CSN* . . . . (Atlantic)
Crosby, Stills, Nash & Young; *4 Way Street* . . . . (Atlantic)
  Deja Vu . . . . (Atlantic)
  So Far . . . . (Atlantic)
  ST/The Wonder Years-Music From The Show & Era . . . . (Atlantic)
Suzy Bogguss/Alison Krauss/Kathy Mattea/Crosby, Stills & Nash; *Red Hot + Country-C* . . . . (Mercury)
Teacher
Jethro Tull; *"M.U."-Best Of* . . . . (Chrysalis)
  20 Years Of Jethro Tull . . . . (Chrysalis)
  Benefit . . . . (Chrysalis)
  Living In The Past . . . . (Chrysalis)
Teacher (African Teacher)
Burning Spear; *Living Dub-#2* . . . . (Heartbeat)
Teacher I Need You
Elton John; *Don't Shoot Me I'm Only The Piano Player* . . . . (Polydor)
Teacher Teacher
38 Special; *Flashback-Best Of 38 Special* . . . . (A&M)
  ST/Teachers . . . . (Capitol)
Teacher Teacher
Johnny Mathis; *Johnny Mathis-More Greatest Hits* . . . . (Columbia)
Teacher Teacher
Rockpile; *Seconds Of Pleasure* . . . . (Columbia)
Teacher, The
Paul Simon; *You're The One* . . . . (Warner Bros.)
Teacher's Pet
Doris Day; *Doris Day's Greatest Hits* . . . . (Columbia)
Teacher's Pet
Extreme; *Extreme* . . . . (A&M)
Teachin' The Blues
John Lee Hooker; *John Lee Hooker-The Ultimate Collection-1948-1990* . . . . (Rhino)
  That's Where It's At . . . . (Stax)
Ten Little Numbers
Hank Williams; *Complete Hank Williams* . . . . (Mercury)
Theme From "A Different World"
Original Soundtrack; *Television's Greatest Hits-#7-Cable Ready-C* . . . . . (TVT)
Theme From "Davis Rules"
Original Soundtrack; *Television's Greatest Hits-#7-Cable Ready-C* . . . . . (TVT)
Theme From "Facts Of Life"
Original Soundtrack; *Television's Greatest Hits-#3-1970s & 1980s-C* . . . . (TVT)
Theme From "Fame"
Original Soundtrack; *Television's Greatest Hits-#5-In Living Color-C* . . . (TVT)
Theme From "Nanny And The Professor"
Original Soundtrack; *Television's Greatest Hits-#5-In Living Color-C* . . . (TVT)
Theme From "Our Miss Brooks"
Original Soundtrack; *Television's Greatest Hits-#4-Black & White Classics-C* . . . . (TVT)
Theme From "Paper Chase"
Original Soundtrack; *Television's Greatest Hits-#6-Remote Control-C* . . . (TVT)
Theme From "Room 222"
Original Soundtrack; *Television's Greatest Hits-#3-1970s & 1980s-C* . . . . (TVT)
Theme From "Saved By The Bell"
Original Soundtrack; *Television's Greatest Hits-#7-Cable Ready-C* . . . . . (TVT)
Theme From "Welcome Back, Kotter"
John Sebastian; *Best Of John Sebastian* . . . . (Rhino)
Original Soundtrack; *Television's Greatest Hits-#3-1970s & 1980s-C* . . . . (TVT)
There Ain't No Good Chain Gang
Johnny Cash & Waylon Jennings; *Country's Greatest Hits-#15-Outlaw Country-C* . . . . (Priority)
  Hot Country Rock-#1-C . . . . (Epic)
  Johnny Cash-16 Biggest Hits-#2 . . . . (Legacy)
  The Man In Black-His Greatest Hits . . . . (Legacy)
Tippin' Home From Sunday School
Oliver Jones; *Class Act* . . . . (Justin Time)
To Sir With Love
Lulu; *History Of British Rock-#6-C* . . . . (Rhino)
  Hollywood Magic-1960s-C . . . . (Columbia)
  Rock Artifacts-From The Vaults-#3-C . . . . (Columbia)
Too Little Too Late
Barenaked Ladies; *Maroon* . . . . (Reprise)
Train Wreck On Prom Night
Pajama Slave Dancers; *Blood Sweat & Beers* . . . . (Restless)
Trials
Jackopierce; *Finest Hour* . . . . (A&M)
True Friends
Shannon Curfman; *Loud Guitars Big Suspicions* . . . . (Arista)
U.N.M. Fight Song
University Of New Mexico Lobos Pep Band; *University Of New Mexico Lobos Pep Band* . . . . (Fidelity Sound)
Vacation Bible School
Ray Stevens; *Everything Is Beautiful* . . . . (MCA Special Prod.)
  I Have Returned . . . . (MCA)

Varsity Drag
Jonathan & Darlene Edwards; *Songs For Shieks & Flappers* . . . . (Corinthian)
Les Elgart; *Best Of The Big Bands-#2* . . . . (Columbia)
Victors, The
Ohio State University Marching Band; *Music For Cheerleaders & Song Girls* . . . . (Fidelity Sound)
  Saturday Afternoon At Columbus . . . . (Fidelity Sound)
Original Soundtrack; *College Fight Songs: The Big Ten-C* . . . . (K-Tel)
  The Greatest College Fight Songs . . . . (Laserlight)
  Top Ten College Fight Songs . . . . (K-Tel)
University Of Michigan Band; *41 Great College Victory Songs* . . . . . (Vanguard)
Waitin' In School
Rick Nelson; *Legends Of Rock Guitar-'50s-#2-C* . . . . (Rhino)
Ricky Nelson; *Ricky Nelson-Legendary Masters* . . . . (EMI)
What Did You Learn In School Today?
Tom Paxton; *Best Of Broadside 1962-1968: Anthems Of The American Underground From The Pages Of Broadside Magazine-C* . . . . (Smithsonian Folkways)
Whiffenpoof Song
Bing Crosby & Fred Waring & His Glee Club; *Bing Crosby's Greatest Hits* . . . . (MCA)
Count Basie & Mills Brothers; *Count Basie & Mills Brothers-16 Great Performances* . . . . (MCA)
Louis Armstrong; *Best Of Louis Armstrong* . . . . (MCA)
Mitch Miller; *34 All-Time Great Sing-Along Selections-C* . . . . (Columbia)
Statler Brothers; *The World Of The Statler Brothers* . . . . (Columbia)
Wonderful World
Art Garfunkel; *Watermark* . . . . (Legacy)
Herman's Hermits; *Herman's Hermits-Their Greatest Hits* . . . . (Abkco)
Sam Cooke; *Best Of Sam Cooke* . . . . (RCA)
  ST/Animal House . . . . (MCA)
  This Is Sam Cooke . . . . (RCA)
Words By Heart
Billy Ray Cyrus; *It Won't Be The Last* . . . . (Mercury)
Working Man's Ph.D.
Aaron Tippin; *Call Of The Wild* . . . . (RCA)
Yale Boola
All-Star Inter-Conference Band; *College Marches At Halftime* . . . . . . (Alshire)
Yea Alabama
Original Soundtrack; *The Greatest College Fight Songs* . . . . (Laserlight)
Yes, I'm Ready
Barbara Mason; *Cruisin'-1965-C* . . . . (Increase)
Teri DeSario; *Casablanca Records Greatest Hits-C* . . . . (Casablanca)
You Learn
Alanis Morissette; *Jagged Little Pill* . . . . (Maverick)
You Must Have Been A Beautiful Baby
Bobby Darin; *Splish Splash-Best Of Bobby Darin-#1* . . . . (Atlantic)
Johnny Mercer; *Johnny Mercer Sings Johnny Mercer* . . . . (Everest)
Russ Morgan & His Orchestra; *Russ Morgan & His Orchestra Play 22 Original Big Band Recordings* . . . . (Hindsight)
You Showed Me
Turtles; *Turtles-20 Greatest Hits* . . . . (Rhino)
Youth Of The Nation
P.O.D.; *Satellite* . . . . (Atlantic)
You've Got To Be Carefully Taught
Original Cast; *South Pacific* . . . . (CBS Masterworks)

SEARCH, Looking For

*See Also: **DESIRE, EYES, FINDING, LOSING & LOSS, LOST & MISPLACED, LOVE: SEARCHING FOR LOVE, MOTIVATION, SEEING, TRAVELING***

10 Miles To Go On A 9 Mile Road
Jim White; *No Such Place* . . . . (Luaka Bop)
59th Street Bridge Song (Feelin' Groovy)
Harper's Bizarre; *Baby Boomer Classics-More Mellow Sixties-C* . . . . (JCI Assoc. Labels)
  Better Days-C . . . . (Rhino)
Simon & Garfunkel; *Collected Works* . . . . (Columbia)
  Parsley Sage Rosemary & Thyme . . . . (Columbia)
  Simon & Garfunkel's Greatest Hits . . . . (Columbia)
  The Concert In Central Park . . . . (Warner Bros.)
All I Really Want
Alanis Morissette; *Jagged Little Pill* . . . . (Maverick)
All I Want
Joni Mitchell; *Blue* . . . . (Reprise)
Joni Mitchell with Tom Scott & The L.A. Express; *Miles Of Aisles* . . . . (Asylum)
America
Neil Diamond; *12 Greatest Hits-#2* . . . . (Columbia)
  Hot August Night II . . . . (Columbia)
  ST/The Jazz Singer . . . . (Capitol)
America
David Bowie; *The Concert For New York City-C* . . . . (Columbia)
Paul Simon; *Paul Simon In Concert/Live Rhymin'.* . . . . (Columbia)
Simon & Garfunkel; *Bookends* . . . . (Columbia)
  Collected Works . . . . (Columbia)

Simon & Garfunkel's Greatest Hits . . . . (Columbia)
The Concert In Central Park . . . . (Warner Bros.)

Anybody Seen My Baby?
Rolling Stones; *1998 Grammy Nominees-C* . . . . (MCA)
Bridges To Babylon . . . . (Virgin)

Apples Peaches Pumpkin Pie
Jay And The Techniques; *Cruisin'-1967-C* . . . . (Increase)

April Showers
Al Jolson; *Best Of Al Jolson* . . . . (MCA)
The Al Jolson Story-#2 . . . . (MCA)
Judy Garland; *Hits Of Judy Garland* . . . . (Capitol)
Judy . . . . (Capitol)

Are You Ready?
Creed; *Human Clay* . . . . (Wind-up)

Around The World In Eighty Days
Boston Pops Orchestra/Arthur Fiedler; *Greatest Hits Of The '50s-#2* . . . . (RCA)
Frank Sinatra; *Come Fly With Me* . . . . (Capitol)
Roger Williams; *Roger Williams' Greatest Hits* . . . . (MCA)
Victor Young & His Singing Strings; *Hollywood's Greatest Hits-#2* . . . . (Telarc)

Aurora
Bjork; *Vespertine* . . . . (Elektra)

Badlands
Bruce Springsteen; *Bruce Springsteen's Greatest Hits* . . . . (Columbia)
Darkness On The Edge Of Town . . . . (Columbia)
Bruce Springsteen & The E Street Band; *Bruce Springsteen & The E Street Band Live/1975-85* . . . . (Legacy)

Big River
Grateful Dead; *One From The Vault* . . . . (Grateful Dead)
Steal Your Face . . . . (Grateful Dead)
Johnny Cash; *Johnny Cash-Legend* . . . . (Sun)
Johnny Cash's Greatest Hits-#2 . . . . (Columbia)
Johnny Cash-Sun Years . . . . (Rhino)
Superbilly . . . . (Sun)
The Man In Black-His Greatest Hits . . . . (Legacy)
Rosanne Cash; *Right Or Wrong* . . . . (Columbia)

Blue Sky Mine
Midnight Oil; *Blue Sky Mining* . . . . (Columbia)

Boy Named Sue
Johnny Cash; *Columbia Country Classics-#3-Americana-C* . . . . (Columbia)
Johnny Cash's Biggest Hits . . . . (Columbia)
Johnny Cash's Greatest Hits-#2 . . . . (Columbia)
The Man In Black-His Greatest Hits . . . . (Legacy)

Chasing Forever
Will Smith; *Big Willie Style* . . . . (Columbia)

Closer To Free
BoDeans; *Chicago Bulls Greatest Hits-#3-C* . . . . (Atlantic)
Go Slow Down . . . . (Slash)
Joe Dirt Car . . . . (Reprise)
ST/Party Of Five . . . . (Reprise)

Commitment
LeAnn Rimes; *Big Country Hits '99-C* . . . . (K-Tel)
Sittin' On Top Of The World . . . . (Curb)

Cool Water
Bob Nolan; *Sound Of A Pioneer* . . . . (Elektra)
Frankie Laine; *Frankie Laine-16 Most Requested Songs* . . . . (Legacy)
Jack Scott; *Capitol Collectors Series-Jack Scott* . . . . (Capitol)
Joni Mitchell; *Chalk Mark In A Rain Storm* . . . . (Geffen)
Marty Robbins; *Gunfighter Ballads & Trail Songs* . . . . (Legacy)
Sons Of The Pioneers; *60 Years Of Country Music-C* . . . . (RCA)
Best Of The Sons Of The Pioneers . . . . (RCA)
Cool Water . . . . (RCA)
Western Country . . . . (Granite)

Crawling In The Dark
Hoobastank; *Hoobastank* . . . . (Island/IDJMG)

Crazy
Alana Davis; *Blame It On Me* . . . . (Elektra)

Crying In The Chapel
Elvis Presley; *Elvis-A Legendary Performer, Volume 3* . . . . (RCA)
How Great Thou Art . . . . (RCA)
The Top Ten Hits . . . . (RCA)
Worldwide 50 Gold Award Hits, Vol. 1, Parts 1 & 2 . . . . (RCA)
June Valli; *Nipper's Greatest Hits Of The '50s-#2-C* . . . . (RCA)
Little Richard; *Shut Up-Collection Of Rare Tracks-1951-1964* . . . . . . (Rhino)
Orioles; *Super Oldies Of The '50s-#1-C* . . . . (Audio Fidelity)
Rex Allen; *Only Country-1950-1954-C* . . . . (JCI Assoc. Labels)
Sonny Til & The Orioles; *Echoes Of A Rock Era-Early Years-C* . . . . . (Roulette)
Sonny Til & The Orioles' Greatest Hits . . . . (Collectables)
ST/American Graffiti . . . . (MCA)

Dirt Road Blues
Bob Dylan; *Time Out Of Mind* . . . . (Columbia)

Don't Look Any Further
Dennis Edwards & Siedah Garrett; *Don't Look Any Further* . . . . . . (Motown)

Drops Of Jupiter (Tell Me)
Train; *Drops Of Jupiter* . . . . (Aware/C2/Columbia)

Fastlove
George Michael; *Ladies & Gentlemen: The Best Of George Michael* . . . . (Epic)
Older . . . . (DreamWorks/SKG)

Five Foot Two, Eyes Of Blue
Mom & Dads; *Very Best Of The Mom & Dads* . . . . (Crescendo)

Followin' A Feelin'
Sherrie Austin; *Followin' A Feelin'* . . . . (We/Madacy)

Frankie
Bruce Springsteen; *Tracks* . . . . (Columbia)

Ghost Of Tom Joad
Bruce Springsteen; *The Ghost Of Tom Joad* . . . . (Columbia)

Go The Distance
Michael Bolton; *All That Matters* . . . . (Columbia)

Go Walking Down There
Chris Isaak; *Forever Blue* . . . . (Reprise)

Goin' Cali
Bruce Springsteen; *Tracks* . . . . (Columbia)

Good
Better Than Ezra; *Deluxe* . . . . (Swell/Elektra)

Good Lovin's Hard To Find
Lynyrd Skynyrd; *Last Rebel* . . . . (Atlantic)

Good Woman Blues
Mel Tillis; *Mel Tillis' Greatest Hits* . . . . (Curb)

Got To Get You Into My Life
Beatles; *Beatles-Box Set* . . . . (Capitol)
Revolver . . . . (Capitol)
Rock 'N' Roll Music . . . . (Capitol)
The Beatles-Anthology-#2 . . . . (Capitol)
Earth, Wind & Fire; *Best Of Earth, Wind & Fire-#1* . . . . (Legacy)
ST/Sgt. Pepper's Lonely Hearts Club Band . . . . (RSO)
Paul McCartney & Wings; *Kampuchea-C* . . . . (Atlantic)

Graceland
Paul Simon; *Graceland* . . . . (Warner Bros.)

Great Beyond, The
R.E.M.; *Man On The Moon* . . . . (Warner Bros.)
Totally Hits-#2-C . . . . (Elektra)

Green, Green
New Christy Minstrels; *New Christy Minstrels' Greatest Hits* . . . . . . (Columbia)

Gypsy Eyes
Jimi Hendrix Experience; *Electric Ladyland* . . . . (Reprise)

Hanging Tree
Marty Robbins; *Gunfighter Ballads & Trail Songs* . . . . (Legacy)
Hollywood Magic-1950s-C . . . . (Columbia)
Lifetime Of Song-1951-1982 . . . . (Columbia)
Marty Robbins' All-Time Greatest Hits . . . . (Columbia)

Have You Seen Mary
Sponge; *Wax Ecstatic* . . . . (Columbia)

Heart Of Gold
Neil Young; *Decade* . . . . (Reprise)
Harvest . . . . (Reprise)

Heart Of Saturday Night, The (Looking For)
Shawn Colvin; *Cover Girl* . . . . (Columbia)
Tom Waits; *The Heart Of Saturday Night* . . . . (Asylum)
Tom Waits-Anthology . . . . (Asylum)

Hello
Lionel Richie; *Back To Front* . . . . (Motown)
Can't Slow Down . . . . (Motown)
Truly-The Love Songs . . . . (Motown)
Luther Vandross; *Songs* . . . . (Epic)

Hello
Poe; *Hello* . . . . (Modern)

He's A Heartache (Looking For A Place To Happen)
Janie Fricke; *19 Hot Country Requests-C* . . . . (Epic)
It Ain't Easy . . . . (Columbia)
Janie Fricke-17 Greatest Hits . . . . (Columbia)
Very Best Of Janie Fricke . . . . (Columbia)

Hey, Look Me Over
Jo Basile; *Hit Broadway Musicals* . . . . (Audio Fidelity)
Judy Garland; *Judy Garland-Live* . . . . (Capitol)

Hide & Go Seek
Big Joe Turner; *Rock This Joint* . . . . (Intermedia)

Hide & Seek
Chuck Mangione; *Evening Of Magic* . . . . (A&M)
Feels So Good . . . . (A&M)

Hide & Seek
Howard Jones; *Action Replay* . . . . (Elektra)
Human's Lib . . . . (Elektra)

Hide & Seek
Bill Haley & His Comets; *Bill Haley & His Comets-Golden Hits* . . . . . (MCA)

Hide & Seek
Spencer Davis Group; *Greatest & Latest* . . . . (Priority)

I Don't Want To Spoil The Party
Beatles; *Beatles VI* . . . . (Capitol)
For Sale . . . . (Capitol)
Rosanne Cash; *Greatest Country Hits Of The '80s-1989-C* . . . . (Columbia)
Rosanne Cash-Hits-1979-1989 . . . . (Columbia)

I Got To Find My Baby
Animals; *In The Beginning* . . . . (Sundazed Music)

I Know There's An Answer
Beach Boys; *Pet Sounds* . . . . (Capitol)
The Pet Sounds Sessions: A 30th Anniversary Collection . . . . (Capitol)

I Need A Lover
John Cougar; *John Cougar* . . . . (Riva)

Pat Benatar; *In The Heat Of The Night*. . . . . (Chrysalis)
I Still Haven't Found What I'm Looking For
U2; *Joshua Tree*. . . . . (Island)
Rattle And Hum. . . . . (Island)
I Will Take You There
Nilsson; *ST/Skidoo* . . . . (RCA)
Iceman
Bruce Springsteen; *Tracks*. . . . . (Columbia)
If I Had My Way
Nancy Wilson; *If I Had My Way* . . . . (Columbia)
I'm Looking High And Low For My Baby
Ernest Tubb; *Ernest Tubb's Greatest Hits* . . . . (MCA)
I'm That Kind Of Girl
Patty Loveless; *On Down The Line* . . . . (MCA)
Patty Loveless' Greatest Hits . . . . (MCA)
In The Heat Of The Night
Pat Benatar; *In The Heat Of The Night*. . . . . (Chrysalis)
It Ain't Me Babe
Bob Dylan; *Another Side Of Bob Dylan* . . . . (Columbia)
Before The Flood . . . . (Columbia)
Biograph. . . . . (Columbia)
Bob Dylan's Greatest Hits . . . . (Columbia)
Real Live . . . . (Columbia)
Johnny Cash; *Johnny Cash's Greatest Hits* . . . . (Columbia)
Turtles; *Best Of The Turtles-Golden Archive Series* . . . . (Rhino)
Cruisin'-1965-C . . . . (Increase)
Oldies But Goodies-#4-C . . . . (Original Sound)
Super Oldies Of The '60s-#4-C . . . . (Audio Fidelity)
Turtles-20 Greatest Hits . . . . (Rhino)
Just One Look
Doris Troy; *Atlantic Soul Classics-C*. . . . . (Warner Special Prod.)
Soul Sixties . . . . (JCI Assoc. Labels)
ST/Mermaids . . . . (Geffen)
Hollies; *Best Of The Hollies* . . . . (EMI)
Hollies' Greatest Hits . . . . (Epic)
The Hollies' Greatest Hits . . . . (Epic)
Linda Ronstadt; *Linda Ronstadt's Greatest Hits, Volume Two* . . . . . . (Asylum)
Living In The USA . . . . (Asylum)
Keep Searchin' (We'll Follow The Sun)
Del Shannon; *Del Shannon's Greatest Hits* . . . . (Rhino)
Del Shannon's Greatest Hits . . . . (Curb)
Kentucky Rain
Elvis Presley; *Elvis Presley-Pure Gold* . . . . (RCA)
Memphis Record . . . . (RCA)
Worldwide 50 Gold Award Hits, Vol. 1, Parts 1 & 2 . . . . (RCA)
Learn To Fly
Foo Fighters; *There Is Nothing Left To Lose* . . . . (Roswell/RCA)
Leaving Town
Dexter Freebish; *Life Of Saturdays* . . . . (Capitol)
Little Joe The Wrangler's Sister Nell
Skip Gorman; *A Cowboy's Wild Song To His Herd* . . . . (Rounder)
Look At Us
Vince Gill; *Pocket Full Of Gold* . . . . (MCA)
Look For The Silver Lining
Alberta Hunter; *Look For The Silver Lining* . . . . (Columbia)
Chet Baker; *Let's Get Lost-Best Of Chet Baker Sings* . . . . (Blue Note)
Dave Brubeck Quartet; *Stardust* . . . . (Fantasy)
Judy Garland; *Best Of Judy Garland In Hollywood*. . . . . (Turner Classic Movies)
Marion Harris; *78-#3367* . . . . (Columbia)
Look Into My Eyes
Bone Thugs-N-Harmony; *Art Of War* . . . . (Ruthless/Relativity)
Look Into The Sun
Jethro Tull; *Stand Up*. . . . . (Chrysalis)
Look To The Rainbow
Al Jarreau; *Look To The Rainbow-Live In Europe*. . . . . (Warner Bros.)
Look To The Rainbow
Aretha Franklin; *Aretha*. . . . . (Arista)
Look To The Rainbow
Original Cast; *Finian's Rainbow* . . . . (Columbia)
Looking At The Front Door
Main Source; *Breaking Atoms* . . . . (EMI)
Nasty Wax-C . . . . (K-Tel)
Looking For
Stir; *Stir* . . . . (Aware/C2/Columbia)
Looking For A Boy
Eileen Farrell; *I Gotta Right To Sing The Blues* . . . . (Sony Music Classical)
Sarah Vaughan; *Sarah Vaughan Sings George Gershwin Songbook,*
Vol. 1 . . . . (Emarcy)
Looking For A Corner
Rosanne Cash; *Somewhere In The Stars* . . . . (Columbia)
Looking For A Feeling
Waylon Jennings & Willie Nelson; *Waylon & Willie* . . . . (RCA)
Looking For A Good Sign
Daryl Hall & John Oates; *Private Eyes* . . . . (RCA)
Looking For A Love
J. Geils Band; *Best Of The J. Geils Band* . . . . (Atlantic)
Full House . . . . (Atlantic)
Morning After . . . . (Atlantic)

Looking For A Love
Bobby Womack; *Bobby Womack Greatest Hits*. . . . . (Liberty)
Soul Survivor . . . . (EMI)
Looking For A New Love
Jody Watley; *Do You Wanna Dance With Me?* . . . . (MCA)
Jody Watley . . . . (MCA)
Looking For A Reason
Creedence Clearwater Revival; *Creedence Clearwater Revival-*
Chronicle-#2 . . . . (Fantasy)
Creedence Country . . . . (Fantasy)
Mardi Gras . . . . (Fantasy)
Looking For A Stranger
Pat Benatar; *Get Nervous* . . . . (Chrysalis)
Live From Earth . . . . (Chrysalis)
Looking For A U.F.O.
Adrian Belew; *Young Lions* . . . . (Atlantic)
Looking For Another Pure Love
Stevie Wonder; *Talking Book*. . . . . (Motown)
Looking For Mary Jane
Charlie Daniels Band; *Whiskey* . . . . (Epic)
Looking For My Baby
Little Milton; *Between The Rails: America's Train Songs-C* . . . . . . (Crescendo)
Looking For Space
John Denver; *John Denver's Greatest Hits-#2*. . . . . (RCA)
Windsong. . . . . (RCA)
Looking For Suzanne
Waylon Jennings; *Waylon Jennings' Greatest Hits-#2* . . . . (RCA)
Looking For The Right One
Stephen Bishop; *Best Of Bish*. . . . . (Rhino)
Bish . . . . (MCA)
Looking For The Right One
Art Garfunkel; *Breakaway* . . . . (Columbia)
Looking Through Patient Eyes
PM Dawn; *Bliss Album...?* . . . . (Gee Street)
Love Is A Battlefield
Pat Benatar; *Best Shots* . . . . (Chrysalis)
I Am Woman-C . . . . (Nick At Nite)
Live From Earth . . . . (Chrysalis)
Love That Never Fails
Jim White; *No Such Place* . . . . (Luaka Bop)
Lover Man (Oh, Where Can You Be?)
Barbra Streisand; *Simply Streisand* . . . . (Columbia)
Billie Holiday; *Fine & Mellow* . . . . (Collectables)
History Of The Real Billie Holiday . . . . (Verve)
Blossom Dearie; *Blossom Dearie*. . . . . (Verve)
Lena Horne; *Goes Latin & Sings Your Requests* . . . . (DRG)
Sarah Vaughan; *Compact Jazz-Sarah Vaughan* . . . . (Verve)
Jazz 'Round Midnight-Sarah Vaughan . . . . (Verve)
Sonny Stitt; *Soul Classics* . . . . (Prestige)
**Mahogany (Do You Know Where You're Going To), Theme From
"Mahogany"**
Diana Ross; *20/20-C* . . . . (Motown)
Diana Ross . . . . (Motown)
Diana Ross-Anthology . . . . (Motown)
Diana Ross-The Ultimate Collection. . . . . (Motown)
Evening With Diana Ross . . . . (Motown)
Make Me Believe
Martina McBride; *Emotion* . . . . (RCA)
Marching To Mars
Sammy Hagar; *Marching To Mars*. . . . . (MCA)
Meaning Of Life
Offspring; *Ixnay On The Hombre*. . . . . (Columbia)
Mer Girl
Madonna; *Ray Of Light*. . . . . (Maverick)
Miles From Our Home
Cowboy Junkies; *Miles From Our Home*. . . . . (Geffen)
More Than One Way Home
Keb' Mo'; *Just Like You*. . . . . (Okeh)
My Bucket's Got A Hole In It
Hank Williams; *Complete Hank Williams* . . . . (Mercury)
My Heroes Have Always Been Cowboys
Willie Nelson; *All Time Legends Of Country Music-C* . . . . (Legacy)
Cowboy Super Hits-C . . . . (Columbia)
Greatest Country Hits Of The '80s-1980-C. . . . . (Columbia)
Greatest Hits (& Some That Will Be). . . . . (Columbia)
ST/My Heroes Have Always Been Cowboys . . . . (RCA)
ST/The Electric Horseman . . . . (Columbia)
Nadine (Is It You?)
Chuck Berry; *Rock & Roll Rarities* . . . . (Chess)
No More Looking Back
Kinks; *Schoolboys In Disgrace* . . . . (Rhino)
Second Time Around . . . . (RCA)
Oh Marie
Sheryl Crow; *Sheryl Crow* . . . . (A&M)
One Good Man
Michelle Wright; *The Reasons Why* . . . . (Arista)
One Of These Nights
Eagles; *Eagles/Their Greatest Hits 1971-1975* . . . . (Asylum)
One Of These Nights . . . . (Asylum)

Only God Knows Why
Kid Rock; *Devil Without A Cause*. . . . .(Top Dog/Lava/Atlantic)
Other Man's Grass Is Always Greener
Petula Clark; *Petula Clark's Greatest Hits* . . . . (Crescendo)
Over The Rainbow
Barbra Streisand; *Just For The Record*. . . . . (Columbia)
Dave Brubeck; *Greatest Hits From The Fantasy Years* . . . . (Fantasy)
Ella Fitzgerald; *Silver Collection-Songbooks*. . . . . (Verve)
Judy Garland; *Best Of The Capitol Masters-One & Only Box* . . . . (Capitol)
Judy Garland-At Carnegie Hall. . . . . (Capitol)
Judy Garland's Greatest Hits. . . . . (Curb)
Miss Show Business . . . . (Capitol)
One & Only . . . . (Capitol)
ST/The Wizard Of Oz . . . . (Sony Music Special Prod.)
Party Crowd
David Lee Murphy; *Out With A Bang*. . . . .(MCA)
Peace & Understanding Is Hard To Find
Junior Walker & The All Stars; *Junior Walker & The All Stars-Anthology* . . . . (Motown)
Motown Superstar Series-#5-Junior Walker & The All Stars . . . . . . (Motown)
Place To Fall Apart
Merle Haggard & Janie Fricke; *For The Record: Merle Haggard-43 Legendary Hits* . . . . (BNA)
Pleasure Seekers
System; *System* . . . . (Mirage)
Prodigal Son
Rolling Stones; *Beggars Banquet*. . . . . (Abkco)
Question
Moody Blues; *A Night At Red Rocks With The Colorado Symphony Orchestra* . . . . (Polydor)
A Question Of Balance. . . . . (Polydor)
This Is The Moody Blues . . . . (Polydor)
Ramble On
Led Zeppelin; *Led Zeppelin II*. . . . . (Atlantic)
Led Zeppelin-Box Set. . . . . (Atlantic)
Remasters . . . . (Atlantic)
Razor Love
Neil Young; *Silver & Gold* . . . . (Reprise)
River Of Dreams
Billy Joel; *River Of Dreams* . . . . (Columbia)
Roll Me Away
Bob Seger & The Silver Bullet Band; *ST/Armageddon-The Album* . . (Columbia)
Run To The Water
Live; *The Distance To Here* . . . .(Radioactive/MCA)
Santa I'm Right Here
Toby Keith; *Christmas To Christmas* . . . . (Polydor Country)
Scarlet Ribbons (For Her Hair)
Harry Belafonte; *Harry Belafonte-Legendary Performer*. . . . . (RCA)
Harry Belafonte's All Time Greatest Hits-#1. . . . . (RCA)
This Is Harry Belafonte . . . . (RCA)
Jim Ed Brown & Maxine Brown; *Essential Jim Ed Brown*. . . . . (RCA)
Kingston Trio; *At Large/Here We Go Again!* . . . . (Capitol)
Capitol Collectors Series-The Kingston Trio . . . . (Capitol)
Lennon Sisters; *Best Of The Lennon Sisters* . . . .(Ranwood)
Les Paul; *Legend & The Legacy-#1-4*. . . . . (Capitol)
NRBQ; *Diggin' Uncle Q* . . . . (Rounder)
Patti Page; *Patti Page-16 Most Requested Songs* . . . . (Legacy)
Roger Whittaker; *Roger Whittaker-Classics Collection-#2* . . . . . . (Liberty)
Search & Destroy
Dictators; *10 Roir Years-Anthology-C* . . . .(Roir)
Live-F..k 'Em If They Can't Take A Joke . . . . 'Roir)
Manifest Destiny . . . . (Asylum)
Search & Destroy
Deadly Blessing; *Ascend From The Cauldron* . . . . (New Renaissance)
Search & Destroy
Overlords; *Organic?*. . . . . (Antler Subway)
Search & Destroy
Iggy & The Stooges; *Raw Power* . . . . (Columbia)
Search Find
Bee Gees; *Spirits Having Flown*. . . . . (Polydor)
Search Is Over
Survivor; *Survivor's Greatest Hits* . . . . (Scotti Bros.)
Vital Signs . . . . (Scotti Bros.)
Search On
Aretha Franklin; *Love All The Hurt Away*. . . . . (Arista)
Searchin'
Coasters; *50 Coastin' Classics-C* . . . . (Rhino)
All-Star Chartbusters. . . . .(Intermedia)
Coasters' Greatest Hits . . . . (Atco)
Golden Years-1957-C . . . . (Dominion Entert.)
Oldies But Goodies #8-C . . . . (Original Sound)
The Ultimate Coasters . . . . (Warner Special Prod.)
Very Best Of The Coasters . . . . (Rhino)
Spencer Davis Group; *Best Of The Spencer Davis Group* . . . .(EMI)
Best Of The Spencer Davis Group . . . . (Rhino)
Searchin'
Blackfoot; *Marauder* . . . . (Atco)
Searchin'
Santana; *Zebop!* . . . . (Columbia)

Searchin' For A Rainbow
Marshall Tucker Band; *Searchin' For A Rainbow* . . . . (AJK Music)
Searchin' For Celine
Blue Oyster Cult; *Spectres* . . . . (Columbia)
Searchin' For My Soul
Amel Larrieux; *Infinite Possibilities* . . . . (Epic)
Searchin' My Soul
Vonda Shepard; *ST/Songs From "Ally McBeal" Featuring Vonda Shepard* . . . .(550/Epic)
The Radical Light . . . . (Vesperally)
Searching
Change featuring Luther Vandross; *Glow Of Love* . . . . (Warner Bros.)
Luther Vandross; *Best Of Luther Vandross...The Best Of Love* . . . . (Epic)
Searching
Lynyrd Skynyrd; *Gimme Back My Bullets* . . . . (MCA)
One More From The Road . . . . (MCA)
Searching
Neil Sedaka; *Come See About Me* . . . . (MCA)
Searching For A Rainbow
Chris LeDoux; *Chris LeDoux & The Saddle Boogie Band* . . . . (Liberty)
Searching For Lambs
June Tabor; *Aqaba* . . . .(Shanachie)
Peter Bellamy; *Peter Bellamy* . . . . (Green Linnet)
Searching For Love
Bobby Porter; *Capricorn Records Presents-Fire/Fury Story-C* . . . . . (Capricorn)
Searching For Madge
Fleetwood Mac; *Then Play On* . . . .(Reprise)
Searching For My Love
Bobby Moore & The Rhythm Aces; *Best Of Chess Rhythm & Blues-#1-C* . . . . (Chess)
Soul Shots-#10-More Sweet Soul-C . . . . (Rhino)
Soul Shots-#2-The "In" Crowd-Sweet Soul-C . . . . (Rhino)
Huey Lewis and the News; *Four Chords & Several Years Ago* . . . . (Elektra)
Searching For Someone Like You
Kitty Wells; *Kitty Wells' Greatest Hits* . . . . (MCA)
The Kitty Wells Story . . . . (MCA)
Searching For You
Jamies; *45-#9281* . . . . (Epic)
Searching For You
Rhythm Tribe; *Sol Moderno* . . . .(Zoo)
Searching So Long
Chicago; *Chicago IX-Chicago's Greatest Hits* . . . . (Chicago)
Chicago VII . . . . (Chicago)
Group Portrait . . . . (Chicago)
If You Leave Me Now . . . . (Chicago)
Searching With My Good Eye Closed
Soundgarden; *Badmotorfinger* . . . . (A&M)
Searchlight
John Fogerty; *Centerfield* . . . . (Warner Bros.)
She Came From Fort Worth
Kathy Mattea; *Willow In The Wind* . . . . (Mercury)
Pat Alger & Kathy Mattea; *True Love & Other Short Stories-C* . . . . . (Sugar Hill)
She Don't Look Back
Dan Fogelberg; *Exiles* . . . .(Full Moon)
She Said
Collective Soul; *Dosage* . . . . (Atlantic)
ST/Scream 2 . . . .(Dimension/Capitol)
Since I Lost My Baby
Temptations; *Temptations' Greatest Hits-#1* . . . . (Motown)
Temptations-Anthology-The Best Of The Temptations . . . . . . (Motown)
Temptations-The Ultimate Collection . . . . (Motown)
Single White Female
Chely Wright; *Single White Female* . . . . (MCA)
Sky Is Crying
Albert King; *I'm In A Phone Booth Baby* . . . . (Stax)
Years Gone By . . . . (Stax)
Elmore James; *Elmore James-Complete Fire & Enjoy Sessions-#1* . . . . (Collectables)
Red Hot Blues. . . . . (Intermedia)
Eric Clapton; *Eric Clapton-Crossroads-C* . . . . (Polydor)
George Thorogood & The Destroyers; *George Thorogood & The Destroyers-Live* . . . . (EMI)
Move It On Over . . . . (Rounder)
Stevie Ray Vaughan and Double Trouble; *The Sky Is Crying* . . . . (Epic)
Soft Place To Fall
Allison Moorer; *Alabama Song* . . . . (MCA)
ST/The Horse Whisperer . . . . (MCA)
Someday I'll Find You
Bobby Short; *Mad About Noel Coward*. . . . .(Atlantic)
Mary Martin & Noel Coward; *Together With Music* . . . .(DRG)
Something In Red
Lorrie Morgan; *Lorrie Morgan's Greatest Hits* . . . .(BNA)
Something In Red . . . .(RCA)
To Get To You-Greatest Hits Collection. . . . .(BNA)
Something In The Night
Bruce Springsteen; *Darkness On The Edge Of Town* . . . . (Columbia)
Somewhere Out There
James Ingram & Linda Ronstadt; *The Power Of Great Music* . . . . (Warner Bros.)

Linda Ronstadt & James Ingram; *ST/An American Tail* . . . . (MCA)
Soul Searcher
Joe Lynn Turner; *Rescue You* . . . . (Elektra)
Soul Searchin'
Leon Everette; *45-#13282* . . . . (RCA)
Soul Searchin'
Glenn Frey; *Soul Searchin'* . . . . (MCA)
Southern California
George Jones & Tammy Wynette; *George Jones & Tammy Wynette-16*
Biggest Hits . . . .(Epic/Legacy)
Tammy Wynette & George Jones; *Encore-Tammy Wynette & George*
Jones . . . . (Epic)
Tammy Wynette & George Jones' Greatest Hits . . . . (Epic)
Spanish Eyes
Ricky Martin; *Ricky Martin* . . . . (Columbia)
Starseed
Our Lady Peace; *ST/Armageddon-The Album* . . . . (Columbia)
Starseed
Our Lady Peace; *Naveed* . . . . (Relativity)
Stop, Look & Listen
Patsy Cline; *Loved & Lost Again* . . . .(Fifty One West)
Rockin' Side-Her First Recordings-#3 . . . . (Rhino)
Stop, Look & Listen . . . . (MCA)
Try Again . . . . (Quicksilver)
Stop, Look & Listen
Dorsey Brothers; *1934-1935 Decca Sessions* . . . . (MCA)
Complete Tommy Dorsey-#4 . . . . (RCA)
Stop, Look & Listen
Chiffons; *Best Of The Chiffons* . . . .(Laurie)
Stop, Look & Listen
Elvis Presley; *Collector's Gold* . . . .(RCA)
Stop, Look & Listen
Donna Summer; *She Works Hard For The Money* . . . . (Mercury)
Summer Collection . . . . (Mercury)
Stop, Look & Listen To Your Heart
Johnny Mathis; *I'm Coming Home* . . . . (Columbia)
Johnny Mathis-Love Songs . . . . (Columbia)
Marvin Gaye & Diana Ross; *Diana & Marvin* . . . . (Motown)
Patti Austin; *Every Home Should Have One* . . . . (Qwest)
Stylistics; *Stylistics-1st Album* . . . . (Amherst)
Superman (It's Not Easy)
Five For Fighting; *America Town* . . . . (Aware/C2/Columbia)
The Concert For New York City-C . . . . (Columbia)
Sweet Dreams (Are Made Of This)
Eurythmics; *Eurythmics' Greatest Hits* . . . . (Arista)
Sweet Dreams (Are Made Of This) . . . . (RCA)
Marilyn Manson; *Smells Like Children* . . . . (Interscope)
Tahitian Moon
Porno For Pyros; *Good God's Urge* . . . . (Warner Bros.)
Take Me As I Am
Faith Hill; *Take Me As I Am* . . . . (Warner Bros.)
Theme From "The Brothers Grunt"
Original Soundtrack; *Television's Greatest Hits-#7-Cable Ready-C* . . . . . (TVT)
Theme From "The Fall Guy"
Original Soundtrack; *Television's Greatest Hits-#6-Remote Control-C* . . . (TVT)
There You Are
Martina McBride; *Emotion* . . . . (RCA)
There's Gotta Be Something Better Than This
Original Cast/Gwen Verdon; *Sweet Charity* . . . . (Columbia)
They're All Out Of Liquor, Let's Find Another Party
Waitresses; *Best Of The Waitresses* . . . . (Polydor)
Things That I Used To Do
Guitar Slim; *Blues Classics-C* . . . . (K-Tel)
Tumble In The Rough
Stone Temple Pilots; *Tiny Music...Songs From The Vatican*
Gift Shop . . . . (Atlantic)
Walkin' After Midnight
Garth Brooks; *The Chase* . . . . (Liberty)
Loretta Lynn; *I Remember Patsy* . . . . (MCA)
Oak Ridge Boys; *Unstoppable* . . . .(RCA)
Patsy Cline; *20 Golden Pieces Of Patsy Cline* . . . . (Bulldog)
Let The Teardrops Fall . . . . (Accord)
Live At The Opry . . . . (MCA)
Patsy Cline . . . . (MCA)
Patsy Cline's Greatest Hits . . . . (MCA)
The Patsy Cline Story . . . . (MCA)
Want Ads
Honey Cone; *Honey Cone's Greatest Hits* . . . . (HDH)
We Hide & Seek
Jerry Douglas; *Slide Rule* . . . .(Sugar Hill)
We're Off To See The Wizard
Jewel/Jackson Browne/Ry Cooder; *The Wizard Of Oz In Concert: Dreams*
Come True-C . . . . (Rhino)
Judy Garland; *A&E Biography: A Musical Anthology* . . . . (Capitol)
Original Cast; *The Wizard Of Oz* . . . . (TVT)
Original Soundtrack; *The Wizard Of Oz-Selections From The Original Motion*
Picture Soundtrack . . . . (Turner Classic Movies)
When I Find My Life
Marianne Faithfull; *Blazing Away* . . . . (Island)

Where Am I Going?
Original Cast/Gwen Verdon; *Sweet Charity* . . . .(Columbia)
Where The River Flows
Collective Soul; *Collective Soul* . . . .(Atlantic)
You Stay With Me
Ricky Martin; *Ricky Martin* . . . .(Columbia)
Young Blood
Rickie Lee Jones; *Naked Songs Live And Acoustic* . . . . (Reprise)
Rickie Lee Jones . . . .(Warner Bros.)

SEASONS: AUTUMN

See Also: **ENDINGS, MONTHS & DATES: SEPTEMBER,**
OCTOBER, NOVEMBER, SCHOOL, TREES

And Then Comes September
Doris Day; *Duet* . . . . (DRG)
Sacha Distel; *Amour Tout Court* . . . . (DRG)
April Come She Will
Simon & Garfunkel; *Collected Works* . . . . (Columbia)
Sounds Of Silence . . . . (Columbia)
ST/The Graduate . . . . (Columbia)
The Concert In Central Park . . . . (Warner Bros.)
August & September
The The; *Mind Bomb* . . . . (Epic)
Autumn
Edgar Winter Group; *They Only Come Out At Night* . . . . (Epic)
Autumn
Strawbs; *Hero & Heroine* . . . . (A&M)
Autumn
Barbra Streisand; *People* . . . . (Columbia)
Autumn Almanac
Kinks; *Kink Kronikles* . . . . (Reprise)
Autumn Changes
Donna Summer; *Four Seasons Of Love* . . . . (Casablanca)
Autumn In London Town
Norrie Paramor; *Autumn* . . . .(Angel)
Autumn In New York
Frank Sinatra; *Come Fly With Me* . . . .(Capitol)
Round #1 . . . .(Capitol)
Sinatra-The Main Event Live . . . . (Reprise)
The Capitol Years . . . .(Capitol)
Mel Torme; *Songs Of New York* . . . . (Rhino)
Sarah Vaughan; *Complete Sarah Vaughan On Mercury-#2* . . . . .(Mercury)
Sarah Vaughan-Golden Hits . . . .(Mercury)
Autumn Leaves
Barbra Streisand; *Je m'appelle Barbra* . . . . (Columbia)
Frank Sinatra; *Night We Called It A Day* . . . .(Capitol)
Nat "King" Cole; *Blossom Fell* . . . . (Capitol)
Roger Miller; *Music Of The 1950s-C* . . . . (MCA)
Roger Williams; *Best Of Roger Williams* . . . . (MCA)
Roger Williams-Golden Hits-#2 . . . . (MCA)
Autumn Leaves
Grace Jones; *Fame* . . . .(Island)
Autumn Nocturne
Sonny Rollins; *Don't Stop The Carnival* . . . .(Milestone)
Autumn Of My Life
Bobby Goldsboro; *10th Anniversary Album-#1* . . . . (EMI)
Bobby Goldsboro's Greatest Hits . . . . (Liberty)
Autumn Sea
Robyn Hitchcock & The Egyptians; *Queen Elvis* . . . .(A&M)
Autumn Serenade
Harry James & His Orchestra; *70 Ounces Of Big Band-*
Instrumentals-C . . . . (Compose)
John Coltrane & Johnny Hartman; *John Coltrane & Johnny Hartman* . . . .(GRP)
Mel Torme; *Velvet & Brass* . . . .(Concord Jazz)
Autumn Song
Mose Allison; *Ol' Devil Mose* . . . .(Prestige)
Autumn Song
Van Morrison; *Hard Nose The Highway* . . . . (Polydor)
Autumn Suite
Strawbs; *Best Of The Strawbs* . . . .(A&M)
Autumn To May
Peter, Paul & Mary; *Peter, Paul and Mary* . . . .(Warner Bros.)
Autumn's Not That Cold
Lorrie Morgan; *Something In Red* . . . . (RCA)
Skip Ewing; *Coast Of Colorado* . . . . (MCA)
Black Autumn
Roy Buchanan; *Sweet Dreams-The Anthology* . . . . (Polydor)
Blue Autumn
Bobby Goldsboro; *10th Anniversary Album-#1* . . . . (EMI)
Bobby Goldsboro's Greatest Hits . . . . (Liberty)
Honey-Best Of Bobby Goldsboro . . . . (EMI)
Bluegrass Autumn
Bottle Hill; *Light Our Way Along The Highway-#2* . . . . (Biograph)
Cheyenne Autumn
Kansas; *Leftoverture* . . . .(Kirshner)

Chill Of An Early Fall
George Strait; *The Chill Of An Early Fall* . . . . (MCA)
Cold November
John O'Connor; *Songs For Our Times* . . . . (Flying Fish)
Danny Boy
Bill Evans; *Bill Evans-Complete Riverside Recordings* . . . . (Riverside)
Bing Crosby; *When Irish Eyes Are Smiling* . . . . (MCA)
Conway Twitty; *Conway Twitty-Classics-#1* . . . .(Warner Bros.)
Very Best Of Conway Twitty . . . . (MCA)
Tony Bennett; *Jazz* . . . . (Columbia)
Days Of Autumn Gold
Hank Locklin; *There Never Was A Time* . . . . (Plantation)
Death In The Autumn Air
Michael McDermott; *620 W. Surf* . . . . (Giant)
Early Autumn
Cleo Laine & John Dankworth Orchestra; *Jazz Master* . . . . (DRG)
Mel Torme; *Night At The Concord Pavilion* . . . .(Concord Jazz)
Stan Getz; *Essential Stan Getz Songbook* . . . . (Verve)
Woody Herman & His Orchestra; *Best Of Woody Herman & His*
Orchestra . . . . (Curb)
Woody Herman & Stan Getz; *Early Autumn* . . . . (Bluebird)
Evidence Of Autumn
Genesis; *Three Sides Live* . . . . (Atlantic)
Fall Breaks & Back To Winter
Beach Boys; *Smiley Smile/Wild Honey* . . . . (Capitol)
Fall In Philadelphia
Daryl Hall & John Oates; *Whole Oats* . . . . (Atlantic)
Forever Autumn
Justin Hayward; *War Of The Worlds* . . . . (Columbia)
Grey October Clouds
Tommy Makem & Liam Clancy; *Two For The Early Dew* . . . . (Shanachie)
I Cried
Patti Page; *Patti Page's Greatest Hits-Finest Performances* . . . . (Sun)
In The Autumn
Bob Marsh; *The Forest* . . . . (Dali)
Indian Summer
Ella Fitzgerald; *Newport Jazz Festival* . . . . (Columbia)
Frank Sinatra; *The Reprise Collection* . . . . (Reprise)
Glenn Miller; *Memorial-1944-1969* . . . . (Bluebird)
Stan Getz; *Stan Getz's Greatest Hits* . . . . (Prestige)
Indian Summer
Joe Walsh; *But Seriously Folks* . . . . (Asylum)
Indian Summer
Poco; *Indian Summer* . . . . (MCA)
Indian Summer
Roy Orbison & The Gatlin Brothers; *Legendary Roy*
Orbison . . . . (Sony Music Special Prod.)
Indian Summer
Doors; *Morrison Hotel/Hard Rock Cafe* . . . . (Elektra)
Indian Summer Love
Con Funk Shun; *Secrets* . . . . (Mercury)
It Might As Well Rain Until September
Carole King; *More American Graffiti-C* . . . . (MCA)
It Was A Very Good Year
Frank Sinatra; *Frank Sinatra-The Very Good Years* . . . . (Reprise)
September Of My Years . . . . (Reprise)
The Reprise Collection . . . . (Reprise)
The Sopranos-Music From The HBO Original
Series . . . . (Sony Music Soundtrax)
Frank Sinatra with Count Basie & The Orchestra; *Sinatra At The*
Sands. . . . . (Reprise)
Land Of A Thousand Autumns
Steve Hackett; *Please Don't Touch* . . . .(Chrysalis)
Leaving October
Sons Of The Desert; *Whatever Comes First* . . . .(Epic)
Maybe September
Tony Bennett; *Forty Years-The Artistry Of Tony Bennett.* . . . . (Columbia)
The Movie Song Album . . . . (Columbia)
Moondance
Van Morrison; *Best Of Van Morrison.* . . . . (Polydor)
Moondance . . . .(Warner Bros.)
Moonlight On The Colorado
Sons Of The Pioneers; *Songs Of The Trail* . . . . (Pair)
My Autumn Love
Frank Chacksfield; *Unmistakable.* . . . . (Rim)
November
Paul Greaver; *Joy* . . . . (Global Pacific)
November
Chyld; *Chyld.* . . . . (New Renaissance)
November
Duncan Sheik; *Duncan Sheik* . . . . (Atlantic)
November
Anthony Phillips; *Private Parts & Pieces V-Twelve* . . . . (PVC)
November 22, 1963
Original Cast; *Assassins* . . . . (RCA)
November 68th
Chick Corea; *CTI Masters Of The Keyboard* . . . . (CBS Associated)
Joe Farrell; *Outback* . . . . (CTI)

November Afternoon
Dizzy Gillespie; *Composer's Concepts* . . . . (Emarcy)
James Moody; *Moving Forward* . . . .(Novus)
Paul Christopher; *Lavender* . . . . (Arylis)
November Cotillion
Country Cooking; *Barrel Of Fun* . . . . (Rounder)
November Day
Rob Mullins; *Nite Street* . . . . (RMC)
November Days
Origin; *Origin* . . . . (Virgin)
November Girl
Carmen McRae; *November Girl* . . . . (Jazz Man)
November In The Snow/Lord Buckley
Mark Murphy; *Kerouac Then & Now* . . . .(Muse)
November Nights
Flim & The BB's; *Tunnel* . . . . (Digital Music Prod.)
November Rain
Guns N' Roses; *Use Your Illusion I.* . . . . (Geffen)
November Song
Norrie Paramor; *Autumn* . . . . (Angel)
November Song
Didier Lockwood; *Out Of The Blue.* . . . . (Gramavision)
November Spawned A Monster
Morrissey; *Bona Drag.* . . . . (Sire)
Just Say Da-#4 Of Just Say Yes-C. . . . . (Sire)
November Winds
Friedemann; *Indian Summer.* . . . . (Narada)
Narada Equinox Sampler One-C. . . . . (Narada)
Novembering
Claudia Schmidt; *Big Earful* . . . . (Red House)
November's Eve
Tim Story; *Untitled* . . . . (Lost Lake Arts)
October
Borghesia; *Resistance* . . . .(Play It Again Sam)
October
Terry Garland; *Edge Of The Valley* . . . . (First Warning)
October
Paul Desmond; *From The Hot Afternoon* . . . . (A&M)
October
Warren Bernhardt; *Hands On* . . . . (Digital Music Prod.)
October
U2; *October.* . . . . (Island)
October
Danny Wright; *Phantasys* . . . . (Moulin D'Or)
October
Larry McNeely; *Power Play* . . . . (Flying Fish)
October
Anthony Phillips; *Private Parts & Pieces V-Twelve* . . . . (PVC)
October
A-Ha; *Scoundrel Days* . . . . (Warner Bros.)
October
Leif Strand; *The Year* . . . . (Innovative Comm.)
October & The Frost Is Early
Dusing Singers; *Cool Of The Day-Music Of Jean Ritchie* . . . .(Green Hays)
October 17, 1988
Keith Jarrett; *Paris Concert.* . . . .(ECM)
October 7
Mitch Watkins; *Strings With Wings* . . . . (Enja)
October Anywhere
Giant Sand; *Valley Of Rain* . . . . (Enigma)
October Ballad
Chick Corea; *Griffith Park-#2: The Concert* . . . . (Elektra)
October Country
October Country; *Nuggets-#3-Pop-C* . . . . (Rhino)
October Fool
Charlie Shoemaker & Bill Holman; *Collaboration* . . . . (Pausa)
October Impressions (No. 38)
Mark O'Connor; *Elysian Forest* . . . . (Warner Bros.)
October In September
John Nilsen; *October In September* . . . . (Magic Wind)
October Morning
Fourplay; *Fourplay.* . . . . (Warner Bros.)
October Night
Cliff Sarde; *Every Bit Better/Waiting* . . . . (MCA)
Waiting. . . . . (MCA)
October Nights
Stone Soup; *October Nights* . . . .(Windchime)
October Sigh
Phil Sheeran; *Breaking Through* . . . . (Sonic Atmospheres)
October Song
Pat Kilbride; *Rock & More Roses* . . . . (Temple)
October Sunshine
First Brass; *First Brass* . . . . (M-A Music Int'l)
Jazz Horizons-Best Of M-A Music-#1-C . . . . (M-A Music Int'l)
October Thorns
Flotsam & Jetsam; *When The Storm Comes Down* . . . . (MCA)
October Wedding
Montreux; *Let Them Say* . . . . (Windham Hill)

Montreux-Windham Hill Retrospective . . . . (Windham Hill)

October Winds
Bela Fleck; *Natural Bridge* . . . . (Rounder)

October-Love Song
Chris & Cosey; *Funky Alternatives-18 Techno Remixes-C* . . . . (Roir)

October's Child
Elvin Jones; *Brother John* . . . . (Palo Alto Jazz)

Pale September
Fiona Apple; *Tidal* . . . .(Clean Slate/Work)

Pumpkin Season
Dave Maloney; *Harvest Is In* . . . . (Folk Era)

Reach, The
Dan Fogelberg; *Innocent Age* . . . . (Full Moon)

See You In September
Chiffons; *Best Of The Chiffons* . . . .(Laurie)
Happenings; *ST/Purple People Eater* . . . . (AJK Music)
Tempos; *Cruisin'-1960-C* . . . . (Increase)
ST/American Graffiti . . . . (MCA)

September
Michael Urbaniak; *Folk Songs, Children's Melodies, Jazz Tunes & Others* . . . . (Antilles)

September
Earth, Wind & Fire; *Best Of Earth, Wind & Fire-#1* . . . .(Legacy)
Eternal Dance . . . . (Columbia)
Mega Hits Dance Classics-#7-C . . . .(Priority)

September
Nashville Rhythm Section; *Keep On Dancing* . . . . (Koala)

September
Vladislav Sendecki; *Men From Wilnau* . . . . (Antilles)

September
Anthony Phillips; *Private Parts & Pieces V-Twelve* . . . .(PVC)

September
David Sylvian; *Secrets Of The Beehive* . . . .(Virgin)

September 13
Deodato; *Live At The Felt Forum-2001 Concert* . . . .(CBS Associated)
Prelude . . . .(CBS Associated)

September 1979
Bill Barron; *Variations In Blue* . . . . (Muse)

September Blue
Chris Rea; *Dancing With The Strangers* . . . . (Motown)

September Fifteenth
Mark Murphy; *September Ballads* . . . .(Milestone)
Pat Metheny & Lyle Mays; *As Falls Wichita, So Falls Wichita Falls* . . . . (ECM)

September Girls
Bangles; *Different Light* . . . .(Columbia)

September Girls
Big Star; *Big Star Live* . . . .(Rykodisc)

September In The Rain
Chad & Jeremy; *Capitol Gold-Best Of Chad & Jeremy* . . . .(Capitol)
The Soft Sound Of Chad & Jeremy . . . . (K-Tel)
Dinah Washington; *Dinah Washington-Golden Hits* . . . . (Mercury)
This Is My Story . . . .(Mercury)
Doris Day; *Doris Day Sings 22 Great Songs-Original Big Band* . . . . (Hindsight)
Duprees; *Best Of The Duprees* . . . .(Rhino)
Frank Sinatra; *Round #1* . . . .(Capitol)
Sinatra's Swingin' Session!!! . . . .(Capitol)
Joe Williams; *Swingin'...At Birdland* . . . .(Roulette)
Marty Robbins; *Essential Marty Robbins-1951-1982* . . . .(Columbia)
Peggy Lee; *You Can Depend On Me* . . . .(Glendale)

September Love
Kool & The Gang; *In The Heart* . . . .(De-Lite)

September Morn
Mark Masters Jazz Composer Orchestra; *Early Start* . . . . (Sea Breeze)
Neil Diamond; *12 Greatest Hits-#2* . . . .(Columbia)
Hot August Night II . . . .(Columbia)
September Morn . . . .(Columbia)

September Night
Van Morrison; *Inarticulate Speech Of The Heart* . . . . (Warner Bros.)

September Of My Years
Frank Sinatra; *At The Sands* . . . .(Reprise)
Frank Sinatra Sings The Songs Of Van Heusen & Cahn . . . . . .(Reprise)
Frank Sinatra's Greatest Hits-#2 . . . . (Reprise)
September Of My Years . . . . (Reprise)
Sinatra: A Man And His Music . . . . (Reprise)

September Rain
Full Swing; *Full Swing* . . . . (Cypress)
George Howard; *Love Will Follow* . . . .(GRP)

September Song
Boston Pops Orchestra/Arthur Fiedler; *Greatest Hits Of The '30s* . . . . . .(RCA)
Mister Music U.S.A. . . . . (Deutsche Grammophon)
Music For Every Mood-Yesterday . . . .(RCA)
Eddy Duchin & Stanley Worth; *Best Of The Big Bands-C* . . . .(Columbia)
Eydie Gorme; *Best Of Eydie Gorme* . . . .(Curb)
Flamingos & Moonglows; *On The Dusty Road Of Hits* . . . .(Vee-Jay)
Frank Sinatra; *A Lovely Way To Spend An Evening* . . . . (ASV)
Point Of No Return . . . .(Capitol)
September Of My Years . . . . (Reprise)
Kate Wolf; *Safe At Anchor* . . . . (Kaleidoscope)

Lindsey Buckingham; *Law And Order* . . . . (Asylum)
Lou Reed; *Lost In The Stars-Music Of Kurt Weill-C* . . . .(A&M)
Roger Williams; *Roger Williams' Greatest Hits* . . . . (MCA)
Roy Clark; *Best Of Roy Clark* . . . . (MCA)
Sarah Vaughan & Clifford Brown; *Sarah Vaughan & Clifford Brown* . . . . (Emarcy)
Stan Kenton; *Comprehensive Stan Kenton* . . . . (Capitol)
Retrospective-Capitol Years . . . . (Blue Note)
Tony Bennett; *Forty Years-The Artistry Of Tony Bennett* . . . .(Columbia)
Willie Nelson; *Stardust* . . . . (Legacy)

Shine On Harvest Moon
Dorsey Brothers; *I'm Getting Sentimental Over You* . . . .(Pro-Arte)
Jimmy Dorsey & His Orchestra; *Then & Now-Fabulous New Jimmy Dorsey & His Orchestra* . . . . (Atlantic)
Leon Redbone; *Double Time* . . . . (Warner Bros.)
Mitch Miller; *Mitch Miller-16 Most Requested Songs* . . . .(Columbia)

Summer Song
Chad & Jeremy; *Best Of Chad & Jeremy* . . . .(K-Tel)
Capitol Gold-Best Of Chad & Jeremy . . . .(Capitol)
History Of British Rock-#2-C . . . .(Rhino)

Summer Song (In The Autumn)
Peter Hammill; *Fools Mate* . . . . (Blue Plate)

Time Passed Autumn
Claus Ogerman Orchestra; *Gate Of Dreams* . . . . (Warner Bros.)

'Tis Autumn
Ella Fitzgerald & Joe Pass; *Ella Fitzgerald & Joe Pass-Again* . . . . (Pablo)

Two Shades Of Autumn
Stan Kenton; *Rendezvous With Stan Kenton* . . . . (Creative World)

Vermont Is Afire In The Autumn
Lui Collins; *Made In New England* . . . . (Green Linnet)

What She's Doing Now
Garth Brooks; *Ropin' The Wind* . . . .(Liberty)

When Autumn Comes
Bill Evans; *Tokyo Concert* . . . . (Fantasy)

When October Goes
Barry Manilow; *2 AM Paradise Cafe* . . . .(Arista)
Rosemary Clooney; *Rosemary Clooney Sings The Lyrics Of Johnny Mercer* . . . .(Concord Jazz)

When The Golden Leaves Begin To Fall
Joe Val & The New England Bluegrass Boys; *Diamond Joe* . . . .(Rounder)
Joe Val & The New England Bluegrass Boys-Vol. 2 . . . .(Rounder)

When The Work's All Done This Fall
Doc Watson; *On Stage (Featuring Merle Watson)* . . . .(Vanguard)
Michael Martin Murphey; *Cowboy Songs* . . . . (Warner Western)

Wreck Of The Edmund Fitzgerald
Gordon Lightfoot; *Gord's Gold-#2* . . . .(Warner Bros.)
Summertime Dream . . . . (Reprise)

SEASONS: GENERAL

See Also: **CHANGES, MONTHS & DATES (various), SEASONS (various), YEARS: GENERAL**

4 Seasons Of Loneliness
Boyz II Men; *Evolution* . . . .(Motown)

All Season
Levert; *Rope A Dope Style* . . . . (Atlantic)

As The Seasons Grey
Testament; *The Ritual* . . . . (Atlantic)

Danny Boy
Bill Evans; *Bill Evans-Complete Riverside Recordings* . . . . (Riverside)
Bing Crosby; *When Irish Eyes Are Smiling* . . . . (MCA)
Conway Twitty; *Conway Twitty-Classics-#1* . . . . (Warner Bros.)
Very Best Of Conway Twitty . . . . (MCA)
Tony Bennett; *Jazz* . . . .(Columbia)

Eloise
David Frishberg; *Live At Vine Street* . . . . (Original Jazz Classics)

End Of The Seasons
Kinks; *Something Else* . . . . (Reprise)

If Ever I Would Leave You
Richard Harris; *ST/Camelot* . . . . (Warner Bros.)
Robert Goulet; *Robert Goulet's Greatest Hits* . . . .(Columbia)
Robert Goulet/Original Cast; *Camelot* . . . .(Columbia)

Longer
Dan Fogelberg; *Dan Fogelberg/Greatest Hits* . . . . (Full Moon)
Phoenix . . . . (Full Moon)

Love For All Seasons
Christina Aguilera; *Christina Aguilera* . . . . (RCA)

Mad Season
Matchbox Twenty; *Mad Season By Matchbox Twenty* . . . .(Lava)

Man For All Seasons
Billy Idol; *Whiplash Smile* . . . . (Chrysalis)

Man For All Seasons
Al Stewart; *Time Passages* . . . .(Arista)

Rain Song
Led Zeppelin; *Houses Of The Holy* . . . . (Atlantic)

Led Zeppelin-Box Set . . . . (Atlantic)
Remasters . . . . (Atlantic)
ST/The Song Remains The Same . . . . (Swan Song)

Season In Hell (Fire Suite)
John Cafferty And The Beaver Brown Band; *ST/Eddie & The Cruisers* . . . . (Scotti Bros.)

Season Of Hollow Soul
k.d. lang; *Ingenue* . . . . (Sire)

Season Of The Witch
Donovan; *American Graffiti-#4-C* . . . . (MCA)
Donovan's Greatest Hits . . . . (Epic)
Sunshine Superman . . . . (Epic)
Troubadour-Definitive Collection . . . . (Epic)
Vanilla Fudge; *Best Of Vanilla Fudge* . . . . (Atco)

Season Suite
John Denver; *Rocky Mountain High* . . . . (RCA)

Seasons
Steve Miller Band; *Best Of Steve Miller 1968-1973* . . . . (Capitol)
Brave New World . . . . (Capitol)
Steve Miller Band-Anthology . . . . (Capitol)

Seasons
Sarah Vaughan; *Crazy & Mixed Up* . . . . (Pablo)

Seasons
Lynyrd Skynyrd; *First & Last* . . . . (MCA)

Seasons
UB40; *Geffery Morgan* . . . . (A&M)

Seasons
America; *Hearts* . . . . (Warner Bros.)

Seasons
Stevie Wonder; *Journey Through The Secret Life Of Plants* . . . . (Motown)

Seasons
Dave Mason; *Let It Flow* . . . . (Columbia)

Seasons
Oak Ridge Boys; *Seasons* . . . . (MCA)

Seasons Change
Expose; *Exposure* . . . . (Arista)
Making Love-C . . . . (Priority)
Romantic Hits Of The '80s-C . . . . (K-Tel)

Seasons Change
Michael Murphey; *Swans Against The Sun* . . . . (Epic)

Seasons End
Marillion; *Seasons End* . . . . (Capitol)

Seasons For Girls
Trammps; *Trammps III* . . . . (Atlantic)

Seasons In The Abyss
Slayer; *Live-Decade Of Aggression* . . . . (Def American)

Seasons In The Sun
Kingston Trio; *Capitol Collectors Series-The Kingston Trio* . . . . (Capitol)
Terry Jacks; *'70s Greatest Rock Hits-#9-#1 Hits-C* . . . . (Priority)
Super Hits Of The '70s-Have A Nice Day-#12-C . . . . . (Rhino)

Season's No Reason To Change
Gap Band; *Gap Band IV* . . . . (Mercury)
Gap Gold/Best Of The Gap Band . . . . (Mercury)

Seasons Of My Heart
George Jones; *20 Golden Pieces Of George Jones* . . . . . . (Bulldog)
Jerry Lee Lewis; *Golden Cream Of Jerry Lee Lewis* . . . . . . (Sun)
Johnny Cash; *Columbia Records-1958-1986* . . . . (Columbia)
Now, There Was A Song! Memories From The Past-C . . . . . (Legacy)

Seasons Of The Heart
John Denver; *John Denver's Greatest Hits-#3* . . . . (RCA)
Seasons Of The Heart . . . . (RCA)

Seasons Of Wither
Aerosmith; *Get Your Wings* . . . . (Columbia)
Pandora's Box . . . . (Columbia)

Song For All Seasons
Jefferson Airplane; *Volunteers* . . . . (RCA)

Time Of The Season
Argent; *Argent-Anthology-Collection Of Greatest Hits* . . . . . . (Epic)
Encore-Argent . . . . (Epic)
ST/Awakenings . . . . (Reprise)
Zombies; *Billboard Top Rock 'N' Roll Hits-1969-C* . . . . . . (Rhino)
Odyssey & Oracle . . . . (Rhino)
Rock Classics-#3-C . . . . (K-Tel)
ST/1969 . . . . (Polydor)

To The Morning
Dan Fogelberg; *Home Free* . . . . (Columbia)

Turn! Turn! Turn! (To Everything There Is A Season)
Byrds; *Billboard Top Rock 'N' Roll Hits-1965-C* . . . . (Rhino)
Original Singles-#1-1965-1967 . . . . (Columbia)
ST/Forrest Gump . . . . (Epic/Sony Music Soundtrax)
The Byrds . . . . (Columbia)
The Byrds' Greatest Hits . . . . (Columbia)
Turn! Turn! Turn! . . . . (Legacy)
Pete Seeger; *Pete Seeger's Greatest Hits* . . . . (Columbia)
Troubadours Of The Folk Era-#2-C . . . . (Rhino)

Weather
Amel Larrieux; *Infinite Possibilities* . . . . (Epic)

You've Got A Friend
Barbra Streisand; *Barbra Joan Streisand* . . . . (Columbia)

Carole King; *Tapestry* . . . . (Epic)
Donny Hathaway & Roberta Flack; *Best Of Donny Hathaway* . . . . (Atco)
Jamaica Boys; *J Boys* . . . . (Reprise)
James Taylor; *James Taylor's Greatest Hits* . . . . . . (Warner Bros.)
Mud Slide Slim And The Blue Horizon . . . . (Warner Bros.)
Michael Jackson; *Got To Be There* . . . . (Motown)
Original Soul Of Michael Jackson . . . . (Motown)
Roberta Flack & Donny Hathaway; *Best Of Roberta Flack* . . . . . . (Atlantic)
Roberta Flack & Donny Hathaway . . . . (Atlantic)

SEASONS: SPRING

See Also: FLOWERS: GENERAL, FLOWERS: ROSES, MONTHS & DATES: MARCH, APRIL, MAY

23rd Of March
Gene Pitney; *Many Sides Of Gene Pitney* . . . . (Out Of Print)

After All It's Spring
Original Cast; *Seventeen* . . . . (RCA)

April
Dave Mallett; *Vital Signs* . . . . (Flying Fish)

April
Brand X; *Project* . . . . (Passport)

April
Sarah Vaughan; *Singles Sessions* . . . . (Roulette)

April 2031
Warrant; *Dog Eat Dog* . . . . (Columbia)

April 24, 1981
Rick Springfield; *Success Hasn't Spoiled Me Yet* . . . . (RCA)

April 5th
Talk Talk; *Colour Of Spring* . . . . (EMI)

April Afternoon
Joan Amalbert Latin Jazz Quintet; *Hot Sauce* . . . . (Prestige)

April Come She Will
Simon & Garfunkel; *Collected Works* . . . . (Columbia)
Sounds Of Silence . . . . (Columbia)
ST/The Graduate . . . . (Columbia)
The Concert In Central Park . . . . (Warner Bros.)

April Fool
Pete Townshend & Ronnie Lane; *Rough Mix* . . . . (Atlantic)

April Fool
Soul Asylum; *Grave Dancers Union* . . . . (Columbia)

April Fool
Eric Dolphy; *Here & There* . . . . (Prestige)

April Fools
Dionne Warwick; *Dionne Warwick-Anthology 1962-1971* . . . . (Rhino)

April Fools
Earl Klugh; *Living Inside Your Love* . . . . (EMI)

April Fools
Aretha Franklin; *Young, Gifted And Black* . . . . (Atlantic & Atco Remasters)

April Fool's Day Morn
Loudon Wainwright III; *Career Moves* . . . . (Virgin)
Fame & Wealth . . . . (Rounder)

April Give Me One More Day
Sarah Vaughan; *Complete Sarah Vaughan On Mercury-#2* . . . . . . (Mercury)

April In Cambridge
Peter Walker; *Rainy Day Raga* . . . . (Vanguard)

April In My Heart
Billie Holiday; *Quintessential-#6-1938* . . . . (Columbia)

April In Paris
Charlie Parker; *Charlie Parker With Strings* . . . . (Verve)
Verve Years-1950-1951 . . . . (Verve)
Ella Fitzgerald & Oscar Peterson; *Ella & Oscar* . . . . . . (Pablo)
Frank Sinatra; *Come Fly With Me* . . . . (Capitol)
Mel Torme; *Mel Torme* . . . . (Glendale)
Sarah Vaughan; *Complete Sarah Vaughan On Mercury-#1-Great Jazz Years-1954-1956* . . . . (Mercury)
Sarah Vaughan . . . . (Emarcy)
Wynton Marsalis; *Marsalis Standard Time-#1* . . . . . . (Columbia)
Perspectives: Columbia Jazz Sampler . . . . (Columbia)

April In Portugal
Eartha Kitt; *Best Of Eartha Kitt* . . . . (MCA)

April Joy
Pat Metheny Group; *Pat Metheny Group* . . . . (ECM)

April Love
Pat Boone; *Best Of Pat Boone* . . . . (MCA)
Pat Boone's Greatest Hits . . . . (Curb)

April Love
L.T.D.; *L.T.D.-Classics-#27 (Featuring Jeffrey Osborne)* . . . . . (A&M)

April Mist
Tom Harrell; *Visions* . . . . (Contemporary)

April Seventh
Larry Coryell & John Scofield & Joe Beck; *Tributaries* . . . . . . (Novus)

April Showers
Al Jolson; *Best Of Al Jolson* . . . . (MCA)
The Al Jolson Story-#2 . . . . (MCA)

Judy Garland; *Hits Of Judy Garland* . . . . (Capitol)
   Judy . . . . (Capitol)
April Skies
Wardell Gray; *Memorial-#2* . . . . (Prestige)
April Skies
Jesus & Mary Chain; *Darklands* . . . . (Warner Bros.)
April Sky
Vinnie Moore; *Time Odyssey* . . . . (Mercury)
April Snow
Northern Lights; *Take You To The Sky* . . . . (Flying Fish)
April Snow
Hi-Lo's; *Cherries & Other Delights* . . . . (Hindsight)
April Song
John Tesh; *Monterey Nights* . . . . (GTS)
   The Games . . . . (GTS)
April The 14th, Part 1
Gillian Welch; *Time (The Revelator)* . . . . (Acony)
April Waltz
Critton Hollow; *Great Dreams* . . . . (Flying Fish)
April Was The Month
Chris Farlowe; *Chris Farlowe-Collection* . . . . (Sony Music Special Prod.)
Aprilling
Lee Konitz & Gil Evans; *Heroes* . . . . (Verve)
April's Fool
Ray Price; *Ray Price's Greatest Hits-#4-By Request* . . . . (Step One)
April's Fool
Mark Chesnutt; *Almost Goodbye* . . . . (MCA)
April's Fool
Tracy Lawrence; *Sticks & Stones* . . . . (Atlantic)
Autumn Of My Life
Bobby Goldsboro; *10th Anniversary Album-#1* . . . . (EMI)
   Bobby Goldsboro's Greatest Hits . . . . (Liberty)
Blue Ridge Mountains Turnin' Green
Charley Pride; *Amazing Love* . . . . (RCA)
Blues For The Month Of May
Stan Getz & Others; *Tenors Anyone?* . . . . (Biograph)
Echoes Of Spring
Willie ''The Lion'' Smith; *Echoes Of Spring* . . . . (Milan)
Eight More Miles
Kieran Kane/Kevin Welch; *11/12/13: Live In Melbourne,*
   Australia . . . . (Dead Reckoning)
Fine Spring Morning
Blossom Dearie; *Blossom Dearie* . . . . (Verve)
First Day Of May
James Taylor; *Never Die Young* . . . . (Columbia)
First Of May
Bee Gees; *Odessa* . . . . (RSO)
First Of May
So; *Horseshoe In The Glove* . . . . (EMI)
Fishin' In The Dark
Nitty Gritty Dirt Band; *Billboard Top Country Hits-1987-C* . . . . (Rhino)
   Hold On . . . . (Warner Bros.)
   More Great Dirt-Best Of Nitty Gritty Dirt Band . . . . (Warner Bros.)
Green Grass
Gary Lewis And The Playboys; *Gary Lewis & The Playboys* . . . . . . (Gold Rush)
   Gary Lewis And The Playboys' Greatest Hits . . . . (Curb)
Here Comes The Sun
Beatles; *Abbey Road* . . . . (Parlophone)
   The Beatles/1967-1970 . . . . (Capitol)
George Benson; *Best Of George Benson* . . . . (A&M)
   George Benson-Collection . . . . (Warner Bros.)
George Harrison; *Bangladesh* . . . . (Capitol)
   Best Of George Harrison . . . . (Capitol)
I Cried
Patti Page; *Patti Page's Greatest Hits-Finest Performances* . . . . (Sun)
I'll Remember April
Cal Tjader; *Mambo With Cal Tjader* . . . . (Fantasy)
Charlie Parker; *Charlie Parker With Strings* . . . . (Verve)
Chet Baker; *Chet Baker* . . . . (Emarcy)
Cleo Laine; *Cleo's Choice* . . . . (Crescendo)
Doris Day & The Frank DeVol Orchestra; *Hooray For*
   Hollywood-#1-C . . . . (Columbia)
Erroll Garner; *Erroll Garner-Concert By The Sea* . . . . (Columbia)
Frank Sinatra; *Point Of No Return* . . . . (Capitol)
June Christy; *June Christy-#2-1957* . . . . (Hindsight)
Modern Jazz Quartet; *Concorde* . . . . (Prestige)
   Modern Jazz Quartet . . . . (Prestige)
Stephane Grappelli & Martin Taylor; *Just One Of Those Things* . . . . . . (Angel)
Wynton Marsalis; *Standard Time-#2-Intimacy Calling* . . . . (Columbia)
I'll See You Again
Frank Sinatra; *Point Of No Return* . . . . (Capitol)
In The Still Of The Nite
Dion; *Dion Sings The 15 Million Sellers* . . . . (Laurie)
   Dion's Greatest Hits . . . . (Laurie)
Dion And The Belmonts; *Wish Upon A Star With Dion And The*
   Belmonts . . . . (Collectables)
Five Satins; *Billboard Top R&B Hits-1956-C* . . . . (Rhino)
   Cruisin'-1956-C . . . . (Increase)

Five Satins Sing Their Greatest Hits . . . . (Collectables)
In The Still Of The Night . . . . (Capitol)
ST/Dirty Dancing . . . . (RCA)
Johnny Mathis; *In The Still Of The Night* . . . . (Columbia)
Irish Spring
Country Gentlemen; *Country Gentlemen With Ricky Skaggs* . . . . . . (Vanguard)
It Might As Well Be Spring
Bing Crosby; *The Radio Years: 25 Songs* . . . . (Crescendo)
Frank Sinatra; *Days Of Wine And Roses, Moon River, And Other Academy*
   Award Winners . . . . (Reprise)
   Sinatra & Strings . . . . (Reprise)
Sarah Vaughan; *Divine Sarah Vaughan-Columbia Years-1949-*
   1953 . . . . (Columbia)
Late Winter, Early Spring
John Denver; *Rocky Mountain High* . . . . (RCA)
Lazy Day
Spanky & Our Gang; *Best Of Spanky & Our Gang* . . . . (Rhino)
Lusty Month Of May
Julie Andrews; *A Little Bit Of Broadway* . . . . (Columbia)
Original 1982 London Cast; *Camelot* . . . . (Varese Sarabande)
Original Cast; *Camelot* . . . . (Columbia)
Various Artists; *ST/Camelot* . . . . (Warner Bros.)
March 7th
Leaving Trains; *Well Down Blue Highway* . . . . (Enigma)
March Sky
Alex DeGrassi; *Slow Circle* . . . . (Windham Hill)
March Winds And April Showers
Wingy Manone; *Wingy Manone Collection-#3-1934-*
   1935 . . . . (Collector's Classics)
March Winds Gonna Blow My Blues All Away
Carter Family; *Longing For Old Virginia: Their Complete Victor Recordings-*
   1934 . . . . (Rounder)
Mummer's Dance
Loreena McKennitt; *The Book Of Secrets* . . . . (Quinlan Rd./Warner Bros.)
My Favorite Spring
Tom Paxton; *Live For The Record* . . . . (Sugar Hill)
Night On The 4th Of May
Al Stewart; *Al Stewart-Early Years* . . . . (Janus)
One Day In March I Go Down To The Sea And Listen
Jan Garbarek Group; *It's OK To Listen To The Gray Voice* . . . . (ECM)
One Morning In May
Charlie Byrd Trio; *Isn't It Romantic?* . . . . (Concord Jazz)
Jean Ritchie; *Love Is Teasin'* . . . . (Elektra)
Paris In The Spring
Michel Legrand; *Legrand Piano* . . . . (Columbia)
Peach Blossom Spring
Yutaka; *Yutaka* . . . . (GRP)
Prague Spring
Legendary Pink Dots; *Shadow Weaver* . . . . (Play It Again Sam)
Promises For Spring
Tom Browne; *Browne Sugar* . . . . (GRP)
Rambles Of Spring
Tommy Makem & Liam Clancy; *Tommy Makem & Liam Clancy*
   Concert . . . . (Shanachie)
Rite Of Spring
Hubert Laws; *Best Of Hubert Laws* . . . . (CBS Associated)
   Rite Of Spring . . . . (CBS Associated)
Rite Of Spring
Willie Nile; *Places I Have Never Been* . . . . (Columbia)
Santa Claus Came In The Spring
Benny Goodman; *Birth Of Swing* . . . . (Bluebird)
September In The Rain
Chad & Jeremy; *Capitol Gold-Best Of Chad & Jeremy* . . . . (Capitol)
   The Soft Sound Of Chad & Jeremy . . . . (K-Tel)
Dinah Washington; *Dinah Washington-Golden Hits* . . . . (Mercury)
   This Is My Story . . . . (Mercury)
Doris Day; *Doris Day Sings 22 Great Songs-Original Big Band* . . . . (Hindsight)
Duprees; *Best Of The Duprees* . . . . (Rhino)
Frank Sinatra; *Round #1* . . . . (Capitol)
   Sinatra's Swingin' Session!!! . . . . (Capitol)
Joe Williams; *Swingin'...At Birdland* . . . . (Roulette)
Marty Robbins; *Essential Marty Robbins-1951-1982* . . . . (Columbia)
Peggy Lee; *You Can Depend On Me* . . . . (Glendale)
So Early, Early In The Spring
Judy Collins; *Judy Collins' Fifth Album* . . . . (Elektra)
   So Early In The Spring, The First 15 Years . . . . (Elektra)
Some Other Spring
Billie Holiday; *All Or Nothing At All* . . . . (Verve)
   Billie Holiday's Greatest Hits . . . . (Legacy)
   Lady Sings The Blues . . . . (Verve)
Ella Fitzgerald & Count Basie; *Perfect Match* . . . . (Pablo)
Spring
Tanya Tucker; *You Are So Beautiful* . . . . (Columbia)
Spring
Peter Walker; *Rainy Day Raga* . . . . (Vanguard)
Spring
John Denver; *Rocky Mountain High* . . . . (RCA)
Spring
James Brown; *Take A Look At Those Cakes* . . . . (Polydor)

Spring Affair
Donna Summer; *Billboard Top Dance Hits-1976-C* . . . . (Rhino)
Four Seasons Of Love . . . . (Casablanca)
Live & More . . . . (Casablanca)
Spring Again
Lou Rawls; *Unmistakably Lou* . . . . (Philadelphia Int'l)
Spring Can Really Hang You Up The Most
Barbra Streisand; *Just For The Record* . . . . (Columbia)
Bette Midler; *Some People's Lives* . . . .(Atlantic)
Betty Carter; *Compact Jazz-Betty Carter* . . . . (Verve)
Carmen McRae; *Carmen McRae* . . . .(Mainstream)
Ellis Marsalis; *Heart Of Gold* . . . . (Columbia)
Rickie Lee Jones; *Pop Pop* . . . .(Geffen)
Toots Thielemans; *East Coast West Coast* . . . . (Private Music)
Spring Fever
Loretta Lynn; *Out Of My Head And Back In My Bed* . . . .(MCA)
Spring Fever
Nantucket; *Nantucket* . . . .(Epic)
Spring Fever
Elvis Presley; *ST/Girl Happy* . . . . (RCA)
Spring Is Here
Carly Simon; *Torch* . . . .(Warner Bros.)
Ella Fitzgerald; *Rodgers & Hart Songbook* . . . . (Verve)
Frank Sinatra; *Frank Sinatra sings for Only The Lonely* . . . . (Capitol)
John Coltrane; *Standard Coltrane* . . . .(Prestige)
Shirley Bassey; *Shirley Bassey* . . . . (United Artists)
Tony Bennett; *Rodgers & Hart Songbook* . . . . (DRG)
Tony Bennett Sings 10 Rodgers & Hart Songs . . . . (Improv)
Spring Manifestations
Santana; *Borboletta* . . . . (Columbia)
Spring Will Be A Little Late This Year
Sarah Vaughan; *Divine Sarah Vaughan-Columbia Years-1949-*
1953 . . . . (Columbia)
In Hi-Fi . . . . (Sony Music Special Prod.)
Spring Wind
Shawn Phillips; *Collaboration* . . . . (A&M)
Spring, Spring, Spring
Bing Crosby & Fred Astaire; *Couple Of Song & Dance Men* . . . . (United Artists)
Michael Feinstein; *M.G.M. Album* . . . . (Elektra)
Springtime For Hitler
Mel Brooks; *ST/High Anxiety* . . . .(Asylum)
Original Broadway Cast; *The Producers* . . . . (Sony Music Classical)
Springtime Magic
Lonnie Liston Smith; *Loveland* . . . . (Columbia)
Suddenly It's Spring
Frank Sinatra; *Now Is The Hour* . . . .(Intermedia)
Phil Woods; *Altology* . . . .(Prestige)
Their Hearts Were Full Of Spring
Beach Boys; *Concert/'69-Live In London* . . . . (Capitol)
Good Vibrations-Thirty Years Of The Beach Boys . . . . (Capitol)
Smiley Smile/Wild Honey . . . . (Capitol)
Then Came The Last Days Of May
Blue Oyster Cult; *Blue Oyster Cult* . . . . (Columbia)
On Your Feet Or On Your Knees . . . . (Columbia)
There'll Be Another Spring
Peggy Lee & George Shearing; *Beauty & The Beat!* . . . . (Blue Note)
They Say It's Spring
Bobby Short; *Swing That Music* . . . . (Telarc)
When It's Springtime In Alaska
Johnny Horton; *American Originals-Johnny Horton* . . . . (Columbia)
Johnny Horton's Greatest Hits . . . . (Columbia)
Winds Of March
Journey; *Infinity* . . . . (Columbia)
Younger Than Springtime
Original Cast; *South Pacific* . . . .(CBS Masterworks)

SEASONS: SUMMER

See Also: **HOT, MONTHS & DATES: JUNE, JULY, AUGUST,**
SCHOOL, SUN

(Only A) Summer Love
REO Speedwagon; *R.E.O.* . . . .(Epic)
REO Speedwagon Live/You Get What You Play For . . . .(Epic)
4th Of July
U2; *Unforgettable Fire* . . . . (Island)
4th Of July, Asbury Park (Sandy)
Bruce Springsteen; *The Wild, The Innocent & The E Street Shuffle* . . (Columbia)
Bruce Springsteen & The E Street Band; *Bruce Springsteen & The E Street*
Band Live/1975-85 . . . . (Legacy)
Adios
Jimmy Webb; *Suspending Disbelief* . . . . (Elektra)
Linda Ronstadt; *Cry Like A Rainstorm-Howl Like The Wind* . . . . (Elektra)
African Summer
Herb Alpert & Hugh Masekela; *Herb Alpert & Hugh Masekela* . . . . . . (A&M)
All Summer Long
Beach Boys; *Absolute Best-#1* . . . . (Capitol)

Endless Summer . . . . (Capitol)
Good Vibrations-Thirty Years Of The Beach Boys . . . . (Capitol)
ST/American Graffiti . . . . (MCA)
Summer & Sun-C . . . . (Rhino)
Almost Summer
Celebration featuring Mike Love; *ST/Celebration* . . . . (MCA)
April Come She Will
Simon & Garfunkel; *Collected Works* . . . . (Columbia)
Sounds Of Silence . . . . (Columbia)
ST/The Graduate . . . . (Columbia)
The Concert In Central Park . . . . (Warner Bros.)
August
Lyle Mays; *Street Dreams* . . . . (Geffen)
August
Anthony Phillips; *Private Parts & Pieces V-Twelve* . . . . (PVC)
August & September
The The; *Mind Bomb* . . . . (Epic)
August 19
Ralph Simon; *Time Being* . . . .(Gramavision)
August 1967
Holy Modal Rounders; *Last Round* . . . .(Adelphi)
August Afternoon
Mulgrew Miller; *The Countdown* . . . .(Landmark)
August Blues
Dexter Gordon; *Tangerine* . . . .(Prestige)
August Day
Daryl Hall & John Oates; *Along The Red Ledge* . . . . (RCA)
August Freeze
Grace Pool; *Where We Live* . . . . (Reprise)
August In Forest City
Carol Montag; *Song For Carrie* . . . .(Salek)
August Moon
Ottmar Liebert & Luna Negra; *Borrasca.* . . . . (Higher Octave)
August Rain
Murray Attaway; *In Thrall* . . . . (David Geffen Co.)
August Tides
Woody Simmons; *Woody Simmons.* . . . . (Deep River)
August Was A Heavy Month
Bob Geldof; *Deep In The Heart Of Nowhere* . . . .(Atlantic)
Autumn Leaves
Barbra Streisand; *Je m'appelle Barbra* . . . . (Columbia)
Frank Sinatra; *Night We Called It A Day* . . . . (Capitol)
Nat "King" Cole; *Blossom Fell* . . . . (Capitol)
Roger Miller; *Music Of The 1950s-C* . . . . (MCA)
Roger Williams; *Best Of Roger Williams* . . . . (MCA)
Roger Williams-Golden Hits-#2 . . . . (MCA)
Autumn Of My Life
Bobby Goldsboro; *10th Anniversary Album-#1* . . . . (EMI)
Bobby Goldsboro's Greatest Hits . . . . (Liberty)
Backstreets
Bruce Springsteen; *Born To Run* . . . . (Columbia)
Black Day In July
Gordon Lightfoot; *Best Of Gordon Lightfoot* . . . . (EMI)
Did She Mention My Name . . . .(United Artists)
Lightfoot . . . . (EMI)
Black Summer Rain
Eric Clapton; *No Reason To Cry* . . . . (RSO)
Boys Of Summer
Don Henley; *Building The Perfect Beast* . . . . (Geffen)
British Summertime
Everything But The Girl; *Worldwide* . . . .(Atlantic)
Bus Stop
Hollies; *Best Of The Hollies* . . . . (EMI)
History Of British Rock-#3-C . . . . (Rhino)
The Hollies' Greatest Hits . . . . (Epic)
California Girls
Beach Boys; *Beach Boys '69 (The Beach Boys Live In London)* . . . . . . (Capitol)
Best Of The Beach Boys-#2 . . . . (Capitol)
Endless Summer . . . . (Capitol)
Good Vibrations-Thirty Years Of The Beach Boys . . . . (Capitol)
The Beach Boys In Concert . . . .(Brother)
David Lee Roth; *Crazy From The Heat* . . . . (Warner Bros.)
ST/Down & Out In Beverly Hills . . . . (Warner Bros.)
Canned Goods
Greg Brown; *One More Goodnight Kiss* . . . . (Red House)
Cold Day In July
Dixie Chicks; *Fly* . . . . (Monument)
Joy White; *Between Midnight & Hindsight* . . . . (Columbia)
Ray Price; *For The Good Times/I Won't Mention It Again* . . . . (Columbia)
Suzy Bogguss; *Voices In The Wind* . . . . (Liberty)
Cold Summer Day In Georgia
Gene Watson; *Memories To Burn* . . . . (Epic)
Cold Wind In August
Van Morrison; *Period Of Transition* . . . . (Warner Bros.)
Cruel Summer
Ace Of Base; *Cruel Summer* . . . . (Arista)
Bananarama; *Bananarama* . . . .(London)
Dancing Days
Led Zeppelin; *Houses Of The Holy* . . . .(Atlantic)

Stone Temple Pilots; *Encomium: Tribute To Led Zeppelin-C* . . . . (Atlantic)
Dancing In The Street
David Bowie & Mick Jagger; *Bowie-The Singles-1969-1993* . . . . . . (Rykodisc)
Grateful Dead; *Terrapin Station* . . . . (Arista)
Martha & The Vandellas; *20 Greatest Songs In Motown History-C* . . . (Motown)
  Compact Command Performances-Martha Reeves & The
   Vandellas . . . . (Motown)
  Motown Story-First 25 Years-C . . . . (Motown)
  Oldies But Goodies-#14-C . . . . (Original Sound)
Van Halen; *Diver Down* . . . . (Warner Bros.)
Dream In June
Tom Harrell; *Sail Away* . . . . (Contemporary)
El Verano
Pablo Cruise; *A Place In The Sun* . . . . (A&M)
Endless Summer Nights
Richard Marx; *Richard Marx* . . . . (Capitol)
  Richard Marx's Greatest Hits . . . . (Capitol)
English Summer
Eurythmics; *In The Garden* . . . . (RCA)
First Day In August
Carole King; *Rhymes & Reasons* . . . . (Legacy)
First Day Of Summer
Tony Carey; *Some Tough City* . . . . (MCA)
  ST/Secret Admirer . . . . (MCA)
For A Little While
Tim McGraw; *Everywhere* . . . . (Curb)
  Tim McGraw's Greatest Hits . . . . (Curb)
Fourth Of July
X; *See How We Are* . . . . (Elektra)
Fourth Of July
Linda Waterfall; *Body English* . . . . (Flying Fish)
Fourth Of July
Rosalie Sorrels; *Lonesome Roving Wolves-Songs & Ballads Of*
  The West . . . . (Green Linnet)
Fourth Of July
Dave Alvin; *Romeo's Escape* . . . . (Epic)
Girls Of Summer
Original Cast; *Marry Me A Little* . . . . (RCA)
Gotta Travel On
Bill Monroe & His Blue Grass Boys; *20th Century Masters-The Millennium*
  Collection-The Best Of Bill Monroe . . . . (MCA)
  Country's Greatest Hits-#1-C . . . . (MCA Special Prod.)
Grease Megamix
Grease Megamix; *Pure Disco* . . . . (A&M)
Green Grass
Gary Lewis And The Playboys; *Gary Lewis & The Playboys* . . . . . . (Gold Rush)
  Gary Lewis And The Playboys' Greatest Hits . . . . (Curb)
Green Leaves Of Summer
Brothers Four; *Brothers Four-Greatest Hits* . . . . (Columbia)
  Greenfields & Other Gold . . . . (First Warning)
  Hollywood Magic-1950s-C . . . . (Columbia)
Has Anybody Seen Amy
John & Audrey Wiggins; *John & Audrey* . . . . (Mercury)
Hello Muddah, Hello Fadduh
Allan Sherman; *Dr. Demento Presents The Greatest Novelty Records-#3-*
  1960s-C . . . . (Rhino)
  Dr. Demento Presents The Greatest Novelty Records-C . . . . (Rhino)
Here Comes Summer
Jerry Keller; *Vintage Music-#14-C* . . . . (MCA)
Here Comes The Summer
Undertones; *All Wraped Up* . . . . (Capitol)
Hissing Of Summer Lawns
Joni Mitchell; *Hissing Of Summer Lawns* . . . . (Asylum)
Honeysuckle Honey
Commander Cody & His Lost Planet Airmen; *Country Casanova* . . . . . (MCA)
Hot Fun In The Summertime
Sly & The Family Stone; *Billboard Top R&B Hits-1969-C* . . . . (Rhino)
  Sly & The Family Stone-Anthology . . . . (Epic)
  Sly & The Family Stone's Greatest Hits . . . . (Epic)
  Summer & Sun-C . . . . (Rhino)
Hot Pants In The Summertime
Dramatics; *Whatcha See Is Whatcha Get* . . . . (Stax)
Hot Summer Day
David LaFlamme; *White Bird* . . . . (Amherst)
It's A Beautiful Day; *It's A Beautiful Day* . . . . (Columbia)
Hot Summer Nights
Rick James; *Wonderful* . . . . (Reprise)
Hot Summer Nights
Walter Egan; *Not Shy* . . . . (Columbia)
Hot Summer Nights
Miami Sound Machine; *ST/Top Gun* . . . . (Columbia)
I Cried
Patti Page; *Patti Page's Greatest Hits-Finest Performances* . . . . (Sun)
In The Good Old Summertime
Andrews Sisters; *45-#65016* . . . . (MCA)
Mom & Dads; *In The Good Old Summertime* . . . . (Crescendo)
In The Summertime
Mungo Jerry; *In The Summertime-Best Of Mungo Jerry* . . . . (Rhino)

Super Hits Of The '70s-Have A Nice Day-#3-C . . . . (Rhino)
In The Summertime
Bob Dylan; *Shot Of Love* . . . . (Columbia)
In The Summertime (You Don't Want My Love)
Roger Miller; *Roger Miller's Greatest Hits* . . . . (Smash)
Independence Day
Martina McBride; *The Way That I Am* . . . . (RCA)
Indian Summer
Ella Fitzgerald; *Newport Jazz Festival* . . . . (Columbia)
Frank Sinatra; *The Reprise Collection* . . . . (Reprise)
Glenn Miller; *Memorial-1944-1969* . . . . (Bluebird)
Stan Getz; *Stan Getz's Greatest Hits* . . . . (Prestige)
Indian Summer
Joe Walsh; *But Seriously Folks* . . . . (Asylum)
Indian Summer
Poco; *Indian Summer* . . . . (MCA)
Indian Summer
Roy Orbison & The Gatlin Brothers; *Legendary Roy*
  Orbison . . . . (Sony Music Special Prod.)
Indian Summer
Doors; *Morrison Hotel/Hard Rock Cafe* . . . . (Elektra)
Indian Summer Love
Con Funk Shun; *Secrets* . . . . (Mercury)
It Might As Well Rain Until September
Carole King; *More American Graffiti-C* . . . . (MCA)
It Was A Very Good Year
Frank Sinatra; *Frank Sinatra-The Very Good Years* . . . . (Reprise)
  September Of My Years . . . . (Reprise)
  The Reprise Collection . . . . (Reprise)
  The Sopranos-Music From The HBO Original
   Series . . . . (Sony Music Soundtrax)
Frank Sinatra with Count Basie & The Orchestra; *Sinatra At The*
  Sands . . . . (Reprise)
It's OK
Beach Boys; *10 Years Of Harmony* . . . . (Caribou)
  15 Big Ones . . . . (Brother)
  ST/Almost Summer . . . . (MCA)
It's Summer
Gladys Knight & The Pips; *Motown Legends-Gladys Knight &*
  The Pips . . . . (Motown)
John Deere Green
Joe Diffie; *Honky Tonk Attitude* . . . . (Epic)
  Joe Diffie's Greatest Hits . . . . (Epic)
July
Al DiMeola; *Soaring Through A Dream* . . . . (Manhattan)
July
Vienna; *Guess What* . . . . (Warner Bros.)
July
Anthony Phillips; *Private Parts & Pieces V-Twelve* . . . . (PVC)
July Morning
Uriah Heep; *Best Of Uriah Heep* . . . . (Mercury)
  Uriah Heep-Live . . . . (Mercury)
June Bug
Leo Kottke; *Best Of Leo Kottke* . . . . (Capitol)
  Did You Hear Me . . . . (Capitol)
  Mudlark . . . . (Capitol)
  My Feet Are Smiling . . . . (Capitol)
June Bug
Lester Young; *Lester Young-Complete Savoy Recordings* . . . . (Savoy)
  Master Takes . . . . (Savoy)
June Is Bustin' Out All Over
Original Cast; *Carousel* . . . . (MCA)
June Night
Betty Everett; *Very Best Of Betty Everett* . . . . (Vee-Jay)
June The 15, 1967
Gary Burton; *Artist's Choice* . . . . (Bluebird)
June's Blues
Commandos; *Instrumentals (1959-1967)-Beat Is On* . . . . (EMI)
June's Blues
June Christy; *The Uncollected June Christy with The Kentones-*
  1946 . . . . (Hindsight)
Kid Who Hates Summer
John McCutcheon; *John McCutcheon's Four Seasons:*
  Summersongs . . . . (Rounder)
Last Rose Of Summer
Boston Pops Orchestra/Arthur Fiedler; *Irish Album* . . . . (RCA)
James Galway & The Chieftains; *Over The Sea To Skye-Celtic*
  Connection . . . . (RCA)
Kiri Te Kanawa; *Come To The Fair* . . . . (Angel)
Phil Coulter; *Sea Of Tranquility* . . . . (Shanachie)
Last Rose Of Summer
Judas Priest; *Sin After Sin* . . . . (Columbia)
Last Summer
Rod Stewart; *Blondes Have More Fun* . . . . (Warner Bros.)
Lick Summer Love
Hanoi Rocks; *Back To Mystery City* . . . . (Geffen)
Like A Summer Thursday
Townes Van Zandt; *Our Mother The Mountain* . . . . (Tomato)

Long Hot Summer
Aldo Nova; *Twitch* . . . . (Portrait)
Long Hot Summer
Jimmie Rodgers; *Best Of Jimmie Rodgers* . . . . (Rhino)
Long Hot Summer
Style Council; *Introducing The Style Council.* . . . . (Mercury)
Long Hot Summer Night
Jimi Hendrix Experience; *Electric Ladyland* . . . . (Reprise)
Look Into The Sun
Jethro Tull; *Stand Up* . . . .(Chrysalis)
Love Letters In The Sand
Mac Wiseman; *24 Greatest Bluegrass Hits-C* . . . .(C.M.H. Prod.)
Pat Boone; *Best Of Pat Boone.* . . . .(MCA)
Pat Boone-16 Great Performances . . . .(MCA)
Vintage Music-#2-C. . . . .(MCA)
Ted Black & His Orchestra; *78-#22799* . . . . (Victor)
Magic
Cars; *Heartbeat City* . . . . (Elektra)
The Cars' Greatest Hits . . . . (Elektra)
Mary Jane's Last Dance
Tom Petty And The Heartbreakers; *Playback.* . . . . (MCA)
Tom Petty And The Heartbreakers' Greatest Hits . . . . (MCA)
Maybe It Was Memphis
Pam Tillis; *Pam Tillis' Greatest Hits* . . . . (Arista)
Pam Tillis-Collection . . . . (Warner Bros.)
Put Yourself In My Place . . . . (Arista)
Memphis In June
Eddie Miller & His Orchestra; *The Uncollected Eddie Miller & His
Orchestra-1944-1945* . . . . (Hindsight)
Hoagy Carmichael; *Hoagy Sings Carmichael* . . . .(Pausa)
Hoagy Sings Carmichael . . . .(EMI)
Mississippi Summer
Si Kahn; *Doing My Job.* . . . . (Flying Fish)
My Summer Love
Malta; *High Pressure* . . . .(JVC Musical Industries)
My Summer Vacation
Ice Cube; *Death Certificate* . . . . (Priority)
My Summertime Thang
Time; *Pandemonium* . . . . (Paisley Park)
Never Dreamed You'd Leave In Summer
Joan Baez; *Best Of Joan Baez.* . . . . (A&M)
Diamonds & Rust. . . . . (A&M)
Joan Baez-Classics-#8. . . . . (A&M)
Stevie Wonder; *Looking Back* . . . . (Motown)
Stevie Wonder-20 Classic Hits. . . . . (Motown)
Stevie Wonder's Greatest Hits-#2 . . . . (Motown)
Where I'm Coming From. . . . . (Motown)
Night In Summer Long Ago
Mark Knopfler; *Golden Heart* . . . .(Warner Bros.)
Night Moves
Bob Seger; *Night Moves* . . . . (Capitol)
ST/FM. . . . .(MCA)
Bob Seger & The Silver Bullet Band; *Nine Tonight* . . . . (Capitol)
Of A Summer Morn
Nightnoise; *At The End Of The Evening* . . . .(Windham Hill)
Oh Baby Doll
Chuck Berry; *The Chess Box-Chuck Berry.* . . . . (Chess)
Oh, The Last Rose Of Summer
Eddie Cantor; *Music From The New York Stage (1890-1920)-#4-1917-
1920-C* . . . . (Pearl)
Once Upon A Summertime
Barbra Streisand; *Je m'appelle Barbra.* . . . . (Columbia)
Dinah Shore; *Once Upon A Summertime* . . . . (Bainbridge)
Miles Davis; *Jazz Sampler-#5-C* . . . . (Columbia)
One Summer Dream
Electric Light Orchestra; *Afterglow* . . . . (Epic)
Face The Music . . . . (Jet)
One Summer Night
Danleers; *Mercury Vocal Group Collection-C* . . . . (Mercury)
More American Graffiti-C . . . .(MCA)
Remember When-C . . . . (Garland)
Super Oldies Of The '50s-#1-C . . . .(Audio Fidelity)
WCBS FM 101 History Of Rock-'50s-#1-C . . . . (Collectables)
One Summer Night In Brazil
Rippingtons; *Tourist In Paradise* . . . . (GRP)
Other Side Of Summer
Elvis Costello; *Mighty Like A Rose.* . . . .(Warner Bros.)
Our Summer Love
Joey Welz; *Best Of Joey Welz-Decades* . . . . (Caprice Int'l)
Blue Memories. . . . . (Caprice Int'l)
Over The Summer
Sparks; *Profile-The Ultimate Sparks Collection.* . . . . (Rhino)
Palisades Park
Beach Boys; *15 Big Ones* . . . . (Brother)
Freddy Cannon; *14 Booming Hits.* . . . . (Rhino)
Billboard Top Rock 'N' Roll Hits-1962-C . . . . (Rhino)
Freddy Cannon-His Latest & Greatest . . . . (Critique)
Memories Of The Cow Palace . . . . (Rhino)

Oldies But Goodies-#11-C . . . .(Original Sound)
Ramones; *Brain Drain* . . . .(Sire)
Paris Summer
Nancy Sinatra & Lee Hazlewood; *Fairy Tales & Fantasies-Best Of.* . . . . . (Rhino)
Poem Of Summer
J.D. Robb; *Triptyque/Other Electronic Compositions* . .(Smithsonian Folkways)
Portraits Of Summer
Jim Bajor; *Gentle Images* . . . . (JBX)
Racing In The Street
Bruce Springsteen; *Darkness On The Edge Of Town* . . . . (Columbia)
Bruce Springsteen & The E Street Band; *Bruce Springsteen & The E Street
Band Live/1975-85* . . . . (Legacy)
Rain In The Summertime
Alarm; *Eye Of The Hurricane* . . . . (I.R.S.)
San Francisco (Be Sure To Wear Some Flowers In Your Hair)
Scott McKenzie; *Nuggets-#10-Folk Rock-C* . . . . (Rhino)
Rock Artifacts-From The Vaults-#3-C . . . . (Columbia)
ST/Forrest Gump . . . .(Epic/Sony Music Soundtrax)
Summer Of Love-#1-C . . . . (Rhino)
Sausalito Summernight
Diesel; *Watts In A Tank* . . . .(Regency/Atco)
Save Your Heart For Me
Gary Lewis And The Playboys; *Gary Lewis & The Playboys* . . . . . (Gold Rush)
Gary Lewis And The Playboys' Greatest Hits . . . . (Curb)
School's Out
Alice Cooper; *Alice Cooper's Greatest Hits* . . . . (Warner Bros.)
School's Out . . . . (Warner Bros.)
ST/Rock 'N' Roll High School . . . . (Sire)
The Alice Cooper Show . . . . (Warner Bros.)
Krokus; *First Degree Metal* . . . . (Priority)
Stayed Awake All Night-Best Of Krokus . . . . (Arista)
Sealed With A Kiss
Bobby Vinton; *Bobby Vinton's Greatest Hits* . . . . (Curb)
Brian Hyland; *Cruisin'-1962-C* . . . . (Increase)
Oldies But Goodies-#2-C . . . .(Original Sound)
Original Rock 'N' Roll Hits Of The '50s-C. . . . . (Roulette)
Lettermen; *Best Of The Lettermen-#2* . . . . (Capitol)
Capitol Collectors Series-The Lettermen . . . . (Capitol)
See You In September
Chiffons; *Best Of The Chiffons* . . . .(Laurie)
Happenings; *ST/Purple People Eater* . . . .(AJK Music)
Tempos; *Cruisin'-1960-C.* . . . . (Increase)
ST/American Graffiti . . . . (MCA)
She's My Summer Girl
Jan & Dean; *Surf City-Best Of Jan & Dean.* . . . . (EMI)
Six-Pack Summer
Phil Vassar; *Phil Vassar* . . . . (Arista)
Soft Summer Breeze
Diamonds; *45-#70934.* . . . . (Mercury)
Eddie Heywood; *Chart Toppers-Romantic Hits Of The '50s-C* . . . . (Priority)
Great Instrumental Hits Of The '50s-'80s-C . . . . (Rebound)
Someday, August 29, 1968
Chicago; *Chicago Transit Authority* . . . . (Chicago)
Song Of A Summer Night
Original Broadway Cast; *The Most Happy Fella.* . . . .(Sony Music Classical)
Strawberry Wine
Deana Carter; *Did I Shave My Legs For This?* . . . . (Capitol)
Street Fighting Man
Rod Stewart; *Best Of Rod Stewart.* . . . . (Mercury)
Sing It Again, Rod. . . . . (Mercury)
Storyteller/The Complete Anthology: 1964-1990. . . . . (Warner Bros.)
Rolling Stones; *Beggars Banquet* . . . . (Abkco)
Get Yer Ya-Ya's Out! . . . . (Abkco)
Hot Rocks 1964-1971 . . . . (Abkco)
Singles Collection-The London Years . . . . (Abkco)
Through The Past, Darkly (Big Hits Vol. 2) . . . . (Abkco)
Suddenly Last Summer
Motels; *Best Of The Motels-No Vacancy.* . . . . (Capitol)
Little Robbers. . . . . (Capitol)
Rock The First-#5-C. . . . . (Sandstone Music)
Summer
John Denver; *Evening With John Denver* . . . . (RCA)
Rocky Mountain High. . . . . (RCA)
Summer
War; *Best Of War...And More.* . . . .(Avenue)
Summer & Sun-C . . . . (Rhino)
Summer
Nuclear Valdez; *I Am I* . . . . (Epic)
Summer
David Sanborn; *Change Of Heart.* . . . . (Warner Bros.)
Summer (Estate)
Shirley Horn; *Here's To Life* . . . . (Verve)
Summer (The First Time)
Bobby Goldsboro; *Honey-Best Of Bobby Goldsboro* . . . . (EMI)
Summer (The First Time)
Bette Midler; *ST/Divine Madness* . . . .(Atlantic)
Summer Afternoon
Vogues; *Vogues' Greatest Hits* . . . . (Rhino)

Summer And Sandy
Lesley Gore; *Best Of Lesley Gore-Sunshine, Lollipops And Rainbows* . . . (Rhino)
Summer Boy
Buffy Sainte-Marie; *Best Of Buffy Sainte-Marie* . . . . (Vanguard)
Summer Breeze
Isley Brothers; *3+3* . . . . (T-Neck/Columbia)
Forever Gold . . . . (T-Neck/Columbia)
The Isley Brothers Story-#2-The T-Neck Years-1969-1985 . . . . (Rhino)
Seals & Crofts; *Seals & Crofts' Greatest Hits* . . . . (Warner Bros.)
Summer Breeze . . . . (Warner Bros.)
Summer Bunnies
R. Kelly; *12 Play* . . . . (Jive)
Summer Chill
Grover Washington, Jr.; *Next Exit* . . . . (Columbia)
Summer Days
Roger Whittaker; *Best Of Roger Whittaker* . . . . (RCA)
Reflections Of Love . . . . (RCA)
Summer Days
Partridge Family; *Partridge Family's Greatest Hits* . . . . (Arista)
Summer Days
Bob Dylan; *''Love And Theft''* . . . . (Columbia)
Summer Days Alone
Brothers Four; *Brothers Four-Greatest Hits* . . . . (Columbia)
Summer Girls
LFO; *Summer Girls-CD Single* . . . . (Logic)
Totally Hits-#1-C . . . . (Arista)
Summer I Read Collette, The
Rosanne Cash; *10 Song Demo* . . . . (Capitol)
Summer In Berlin
Alphaville; *Forever Young* . . . . (Atlantic)
Summer In Dixie
Confederate Railroad; *Notorious* . . . . (Atlantic)
Summer In Hell
Fred Schneider; *Fred Schneider* . . . . (Qwest)
Summer In San Francisco
Hendrik Meurkens; *Sambahia* . . . . (Concord Picante Jazz)
Summer In Siam
Pogues; *Essential Pogues* . . . . (Island)
Hell's Ditch . . . . (Island)
Summer In The City
Lovin' Spoonful; *Billboard Top Rock 'N' Roll Hits-1966-C* . . . . (Rhino)
Lovin' Spoonful-Anthology . . . . (Rhino)
Rockin' '60s-C . . . . (Priority)
Summer Kisses, Winter Tears
Elvis Presley; *Collector's Gold* . . . . (RCA)
Summer Knows
Barbra Streisand; *Barbra Joan Streisand* . . . . (Columbia)
Frank Sinatra; *Some Nice Things I've Missed* . . . . (Reprise)
Freddie Hubbard; *Best Of Freddie Hubbard* . . . . (Pablo)
Live At The North Sea Jazz Festival . . . . (Pablo)
Johnny Mathis; *First Time Ever I Saw Your Face* . . . . (Columbia)
Summer Love
Chris Rea; *Espresso Logic* . . . . (East West)
Summer Me, Winter Me
Barbra Streisand; *The Way We Were* . . . . (Columbia)
Summer Means New Love
Beach Boys; *Today/Summer Days (& Summer Nights!)* . . . . (Capitol)
Summer Nights
Olivia Newton-John & John Travolta; *Back To Basics-Essential Collection 1971-1992* . . . . (Geffen)
ST/Grease . . . . (Polydor)
Original Broadway Cast; *Grease* . . . . (Polydor)
Summer Nights
Marianne Faithfull; *Marianne Faithfull's Greatest Hits* . . . . (Abkco)
Summer Nights
Van Halen; *5150* . . . . (Warner Bros.)
Summer Nights
Earl Klugh; *Whispers & Promises* . . . . (Warner Bros.)
Summer Of '69
Bryan Adams; *Reckless* . . . . (A&M)
Summer Of Love
Jefferson Airplane; *Jefferson Airplane* . . . . (Epic)
Summer Of Love
B-52's; *Bouncing Off The Satellites* . . . . (Warner Bros.)
Summer Of Roses
Willie Nelson; *Tougher Than Leather* . . . . (Columbia)
Summer Of The Silver Comet
Tracy Nelson; *Homemade Songs* . . . . (Flying Fish)
Summer Rain
Johnny Rivers; *Best Of Johnny Rivers* . . . . (EMI)
Johnny Rivers-Anthology 1964-1977 . . . . (Rhino)
Summer Rain
Andreas Vollenweider; *The Trilogy* . . . . (Columbia)
Summer Rain
Carl Thomas; *Emotional* . . . . (Bad Boy/Arista)
Summer Rain
Belinda Carlisle; *Belinda Carlisle-Her Greatest Hits* . . . . (MCA)
Runaway Horses . . . . (MCA)

Summer Rain
Alphaville; *Breathtaking Blue* . . . . (Atlantic)
Summer Romance
Rolling Stones; *Emotional Rescue* . . . . (Rolling Stones)
Summer Samba
Astrud Gilberto; *Compact Jazz-Astrud Gilberto* . . . . (Verve)
Summer Sequence
Woody Herman; *Woody Herman's Greatest Hits* . . . . (Columbia)
Summer Side Of Life
Gordon Lightfoot; *Gord's Gold* . . . . (Reprise)
Summer Side Of Life . . . . (Reprise)
Summer Snow
Lou Christie; *Enlightnin'ment-Best Of Lou Christie* . . . . (Rhino)
Summer Snow
Blue Magic; *Magic Of The Blue-Greatest Hits* . . . . (Collectables)
Summer Soft
Stevie Wonder; *Songs In The Key Of Life* . . . . (Motown)
Summer Song
Joe Satriani; *The Extremist* . . . . (Relativity)
Summer Song
Chad & Jeremy; *Best Of Chad & Jeremy* . . . . (K-Tel)
Capitol Gold-Best Of Chad & Jeremy . . . . (Capitol)
History Of British Rock-#2-C . . . . (Rhino)
Summer Song
Dave Brubeck; *For Iola* . . . . (Concord Jazz)
Summer Song
Grover Washington, Jr.; *Grover Washington, Jr.-Anthology* . . . . (Motown)
Summer Song
Tom Chapin; *Let Me Back Into Your Life* . . . . (Flying Fish)
Summer Song
Matt Bianco; *Matt Bianco* . . . . (Atlantic)
Summer Song
Kenny G; *Silhouette* . . . . (Arista)
Summer Song (In The Autumn)
Peter Hammill; *Fools Mate* . . . . (Blue Plate)
Summer Sounds
Robert Goulet; *Robert Goulet's Greatest Hits* . . . . (Columbia)
Summer Wind
Frank Sinatra; *Frank Sinatra's Greatest Hits!* . . . . (Reprise)
Sinatra Reprise-The Very Good Years . . . . (Reprise)
Strangers In The Night . . . . (Reprise)
Frank Sinatra & Julio Iglesias; *Frank Sinatra-Duets-C* . . . . (Capitol)
Summer Wind
Desert Rose Band; *Running* . . . . (MCA)
Summer, Highland Falls
Billy Joel; *Songs In The Attic* . . . . (Columbia)
Turnstiles . . . . (Columbia)
Summerland
Everclear; *Sparkle And Fade* . . . . (Capitol)
Summerlove
Neil Diamond; *ST/The Jazz Singer* . . . . (Capitol)
Summer's Almost Gone
Doors; *Waiting For The Sun* . . . . (Elektra)
Summer's Cauldron
XTC; *Skylarking* . . . . (Geffen)
Summer's Comin'
Clint Black; *Clint Black-The Greatest Hits* . . . . (RCA)
One Emotion . . . . (RCA)
Summer's Coming Around Again
Carly Simon; *Anticipation* . . . . (Elektra)
Summer's Day Song
Paul McCartney; *McCartney II* . . . . (Gold Rush)
Paul McCartney-Gift Set . . . . (Capitol)
Summer's Gone
Paul Anka; *Paul Anka-30th Anniversary Anthology* . . . . (Rhino)
Paul Anka's 21 Golden Hits . . . . (RCA)
Summer's Here
James Taylor; *Dad Loves His Work* . . . . (Columbia)
Summersong
Roy Orbison; *Legendary Roy Orbison* . . . . (Sony Music Special Prod.)
Summertime
Billy Stewart; *Best Of Chess Rhythm & Blues-#1-C* . . . . (Chess)
Summer & Sun-C . . . . (Rhino)
Booker T. & The M.G.s; *Best Of Booker T. & The M.G.s* . . . . (Atlantic)
Carmen McRae; *Greatest Of Carmen McRae* . . . . (MCA)
Chet Baker; *My Favourite Songs-#1-Last Great Concert* . . . . (Enja)
Courtney Pine; *Glory Of Gershwin Featuring Larry Adler-C* . . . . . . (Mercury)
Ella Fitzgerald & Louis Armstrong; *Porgy & Bess* . . . . (Verve)
George Benson; *Best Of George Benson* . . . . (CBS Associated)
Janis Joplin; *Janis Joplin's Greatest Hits* . . . . (Columbia)
ST/Janis . . . . (Columbia)
Lambert, Hendricks & Ross; *Best Of Lambert, Hendricks & Ross* . . . . (Columbia)
Miles Davis & His Orchestra; *Porgy & Bess* . . . . (Columbia)
Original Cast; *Porgy & Bess* . . . . (MCA)
Peter Gabriel; *Glory Of Gershwin Featuring Larry Adler-C* . . . . (Mercury)
Rick Nelson; *Best Of Rick Nelson-#2* . . . . (EMI)
Sam Cooke; *Best Of Sam Cooke* . . . . (RCA)
Sarah Vaughan; *1940s-The Singers-C* . . . . (Columbia)

Divine Sarah Vaughan-Columbia Years-1949-1953 . . . . (Columbia)
Stan Getz; *Compact Jazz-Stan Getz* . . . . (Verve)
Willie Nelson & Leon Russell; *One For The Road* . . . . (Columbia)

Summertime
Sundays; *Static & Silence* . . . . (David Geffen Co.)

Summertime
D.J. Jazzy Jeff & The Fresh Prince; *Homebase* . . . . (Jive)

Summertime Blues
Alan Jackson; *Who I Am* . . . . (Arista)
Blue Cheer; *Good Times Are So Hard To Find-History Of Blue
  Cheer* . . . . (Mercury)
  Louder Than God-Best Of Blue Cheer . . . . (Rhino)
  San Francisco Nights-C . . . . (Rhino)
Brian Setzer; *ST/La Bamba* . . . . (Slash)
Eddie Cochran; *Eddie Cochran-Legendary Masters* . . . . (EMI)
  Eddie Cochran's Greatest Hits . . . . (Curb)
  EMI Legends Of Rock & Roll-24 Greatest Hits-C . . . . (EMI)
Joan Jett & The Blackhearts; *I Love Rock 'n' Roll* . . . . (Blackheart)
Who; *Hooligans* . . . . (MCA)
  Live At Leeds . . . . (MCA)
  Who's Last . . . . (MCA)

Summertime Dream
Gordon Lightfoot; *Summertime Dream* . . . . (Reprise)

Summertime In England
Van Morrison; *Common One* . . . . (Warner Bros.)

Summertime In The City
Manhattans; *45-#13-33330* . . . . (Columbia)

Summertime Is Past & Gone
Bill Monroe & His Blue Grass Boys; *Essential Bill Monroe-1945-
  1949* . . . . (Columbia)
Elvis Presley; *Million-Dollar Quartet* . . . . (RCA)

Summertime Love
Ta Mara & The Seen; *Ta Mara & The Seen* . . . . (A&M)

Summertime Rolls
Jane's Addiction; *Nothing's Shocking* . . . . (Warner Bros.)

Summertime, Summertime
Jamies; *Summer & Sun-C* . . . . (Rhino)

Swedish Rhapsody (Midsummer Vigil)
Chet Atkins; *RCA Years* . . . . (RCA)
Percy Faith & His Orchestra; *Percy Faith & His Orchestra's
  Greatest Hits* . . . . (Columbia)

Sweet Summer
Diamond Rio; *One More Day* . . . . (Arista)

Sweet Summer Blue And Gold
Stone Poneys Featuring Linda Ronstadt; *The Stone Poneys Featuring Linda
  Ronstadt* . . . . (EMI)

Sweet Summer Day
Freddy Fender; *Before The Next Teardrop Falls* . . . . (Universal)

Sweet Summer Lovin'
Dolly Parton; *Essential Dolly Parton* . . . . (RCA)

That Summer
Garth Brooks; *The Chase* . . . . (Liberty)

That Sunday, That Summer
Betty Carter; *Compact Jazz-Best Of The Compact Jazz Vocalists-C* . . . . (Verve)
Nat "King" Cole; *Nat "King" Cole (Box Set)* . . . . (Capitol)
  Unforgettable . . . . (Capitol)
Natalie Cole; *Unforgettable With Love* . . . . (Elektra)

Theme From "A Summer Place"
Andy Williams; *Moon River & Other Great Movie Themes* . . . . (Columbia)
Percy Faith & His Orchestra; *Best Love Songs-C* . . . . (Original Sound)
  Billboard Top Pop Hits-1960-C . . . . (Rhino)
  Percy Faith & His Orchestra-16 Most Requested Songs . . . . (Columbia)
  Percy Faith & His Orchestra's All-Time Greatest Hits . . . . (Columbia)
  Percy Faith & His Orchestra's Greatest Hits . . . . (Columbia)

Theme From "Endless Summer"
Sandals; *Monster Summer Hits-Wild Surf-C* . . . . (Capitol)

Theme From "Summer Of '42"
George Benson; *Best Of George Benson* . . . . (CBS Associated)
  White Rabbit . . . . (CBS Associated)
Peter Nero; *"Summer Of '42" Theme* . . . . (Columbia)
  Peter Nero's Greatest Hits . . . . (Columbia)

Things We Did Last Summer
Beach Boys; *Good Vibrations-Thirty Years Of The Beach Boys* . . . . . (Capitol)
Frank Sinatra; *Sinatra Rarities-Columbia Years* . . . . (Columbia)
Michael Feinstein; *Michael Feinstein Sings The Jule Styne
  Songbook* . . . . (Nonesuch)

This Ain't The Summer Of Love
Blue Oyster Cult; *Agents Of Fortune* . . . . (Columbia)

Those Lazy Hazy Crazy Days Of Summer
Nat "King" Cole; *Best Of Nat "King" Cole-Vol. 1* . . . . (Capitol)
  Capitol Collectors Series-Nat "King" Cole . . . . (Capitol)

'Tis The Last Rose Of Summer
Lucy Shelton & Others; *Moore's Irish Melodies* . . . . (Nonesuch)

To The Summer In Our Hearts
Curlew; *Bee* . . . . (Cuneiform)
  Live In Berlin . . . . (Cuneiform)

Two Hot Girls (On A Hot Summer Night)
Carly Simon; *Carly Simon-Greatest Hits Live* . . . . (Arista)

Coming Around Again . . . . (Arista)

Two Weeks Last Summer
Sandy Denny; *Who Knows Where The Time Goes* . . . . (Hannibal)
Sandy Denny & The Strawbs; *Sandy Denny & The Strawbs* . . . . (Hannibal)

Under The Boardwalk
Bette Midler; *ST/Beaches* . . . . (Atlantic)
Bruce Willis; *Return Of Bruno* . . . . (Motown)
Drifters; *Atlantic Rhythm & Blues 1947-1974-#5 (1962-1966)-C* . . . . (Atlantic)
  Drifters-16 Greatest Hits . . . . (Trip)
  Drifters-Golden Hits . . . . (Atlantic)
  Super Oldies Of The '60s-#5-C . . . . (Audio Fidelity)
John Mellencamp; *Rough Harvest* . . . . (Mercury)
Lynn Anderson; *What She Does Best* . . . . (Mercury)
Rickie Lee Jones; *Girl At Her Volcano* . . . . (Warner Bros.)
Rolling Stones; *12 X 5* . . . . (Abkco)
Untouchables; *Agent Double O Soul* . . . . (Restless)

Unimaginable Zero Summer
Young Fresh Fellows; *The Men Who Loved Music* . . . . (Frontier)

Up On The Roof
Cryan' Shames; *Scratch In The Sky* . . . . (Columbia)
Drifters; *Cruisin'-1962-C* . . . . (Increase)
  Drifters' Greatest Hits . . . . (Gusto)
  Drifters-16 Greatest Hits . . . . (Trip)
  Drifters-Golden Hits . . . . (Atlantic)
James Taylor; *Flag* . . . . (Columbia)
  The Concert For New York City-C . . . . (Columbia)
Nylons; *Four On The Floor* . . . . (Scotti Bros.)

Warm Summer Daze
Vybe; *Vybe* . . . . (Island)

Watermelon Weather
Perry Como; *Yesterday And Today-A Celebration In Song* . . . . (RCA)

We Danced Anyway
Deana Carter; *Did I Shave My Legs For This?* . . . . (Capitol)

We Were In Love
Toby Keith; *Dream Walkin'* . . . . (Mercury)
  Toby Keith's Greatest Hits, Volume One . . . . (Mercury)

Winter & The Summer
Strawbs; *Bursting At The Seams* . . . . (A&M)

Wonderful Summer
Robin Ward; *Sixties Rule! Chapter Two-C* . . . . (One Way)

You Took The Words Right Out Of My Mouth
Meat Loaf; *Bat Out Of Hell* . . . . (Epic)

Your Summer Dream
Beach Boys; *Surfer Girl* . . . . (Capitol)

SEASONS: WINTER

**See Also: CHRISTMAS, COLD, MONTHS & DATES: DECEMBER,
JANUARY, FEBRUARY, SNOW**

Anos Dourados (Looks Like December)
Antonio Carlos Jobim & His New Band; *Passarim* . . . . (Verve)
Joanne Brackeen; *Breath Of Brazil* . . . . (Concord Picante Jazz)

Apples In Winter
Kim Robertson; *Angels In Disguise* . . . . (Invincible)

April Come She Will
Simon & Garfunkel; *Collected Works* . . . . (Columbia)
  Sounds Of Silence . . . . (Columbia)
  ST/The Graduate . . . . (Columbia)
  The Concert In Central Park . . . . (Warner Bros.)

Autumn Leaves
Barbra Streisand; *Je m'appelle Barbra* . . . . (Columbia)
Frank Sinatra; *Night We Called It A Day* . . . . (Capitol)
Nat "King" Cole; *Blossom Fell* . . . . (Capitol)
Roger Miller; *Music Of The 1950s-C* . . . . (MCA)
Roger Williams; *Best Of Roger Williams* . . . . (MCA)
  Roger Williams-Golden Hits-#2 . . . . (MCA)

Back In January
Angst; *Mystery Spot* . . . . (SST)

Birds Of Winter
Zamfir; *Return To Romance* . . . . (Philips)

California Dreamin'
Beach Boys; *Made In The U.S.A.* . . . . (Capitol)
Mamas & The Papas; *At The Hop* . . . . (MCA)
  Good Feeling Music Of The Big Chill Generation-#1-C . . . . (Motown)
  Mamas & The Papas-20 Golden Hits . . . . (MCA)
  ST/Air America . . . . (MCA)
  ST/American Pop . . . . (MCA)
  ST/Forrest Gump . . . . (Epic/Sony Music Soundtrax)

Cold Winter Day
Blind Willie McTell; *Doing That Atlanta Strut-1927-1935* . . . . (Yazoo)

Cold Winter's Day
BoDeans; *Go Slow Down* . . . . (Slash)

Colder Than Winter
Vince Gill; *Things That Matter* . . . . (RCA)

Cover You In Kisses
John Michael Montgomery; *Leave A Mark* . . . . (Atlantic)

December
Robert Vaughan & The Shadows; *Love & War* . . . . (Exit)
December
Collective Soul; *Collective Soul* . . . . (Atlantic)
December
Expose; *Exposure* . . . . (Arista)
December
Anthony Phillips; *Private Parts & Pieces V-Twelve* . . . . (PVC)
December
Waterboys; *Waterboys* . . . . (Ensign)
December Days
Willie Nelson; *Love & Pain* . . . . (Aura)
Sweet Memories . . . . (RCA)
December Will Be Magic Again
Kate Bush; *December Will Be Magic Again-12''* . . . . (EMI)
December, 1963 (Oh, What A Night)
4 Seasons; *25th Anniversary Collection* . . . . (Rhino)
4 Seasons-Anthology . . . . (Rhino)
Oh What A Night . . . . (Curb)
December's Boudoir
Laura Nyro; *Eli And The Thirteenth Confession* . . . . (Columbia)
Don't Cut The Tree Down In Winter
Penny Little; *In A Light Garden* . . . . (Global Pacific)
Fall Breaks & Back To Winter
Beach Boys; *Smiley Smile/Wild Honey* . . . . (Capitol)
February
Anthony Phillips; *Private Parts & Pieces V-Twelve* . . . . (PVC)
Jennifer Hall; *Fortune & Men's Eyes* . . . . (Warner Bros.)
February In My Heart
Osborne Brothers; *Some Things I Want To Sing About* . . . . (Sugar Hill)
February Ingenue
Don Dixon; *Romeo At Juilliard* . . . . (Enigma)
February March
Lou & Peter Berryman; *February March* . . . . (Cornbelt)
February Moment
Herbie Hancock & Chick Corea; *Evening With Herbie Hancock & Chick Corea* . . . . (Columbia)
February Sea
George Winston; *Winter Into Spring* . . . . (Windham Hill)
February Song
Barbi Benton & Jamii Szmadzinski; *Kinetic Voyage* . . . . (Takoma)
February Song
Blazing Redheads & Patricia Thumas; *Blazing Redheads* . . . . (Reference)
Gotta Travel On
Bill Monroe & His Blue Grass Boys; *20th Century Masters-The Millennium Collection-The Best Of Bill Monroe* . . . . (MCA)
Country's Greatest Hits-#1-C. . . . . (MCA Special Prod.)
Hard, Hard Winter
Strawbs; *Deep Cuts* . . . . (Oyster)
Hazy Shade Of Winter
Bangles; *Bangles' Greatest Hits* . . . . (Columbia)
ST/Less Than Zero . . . . (Def Jam)
Simon & Garfunkel; *Bookends* . . . . (Columbia)
Collected Works . . . . (Columbia)
Here Comes The Sun
Beatles; *Abbey Road* . . . . (Parlophone)
The Beatles/1967-1970. . . . . (Capitol)
George Benson; *Best Of George Benson* . . . . (A&M)
George Benson-Collection . . . . (Warner Bros.)
George Harrison; *Bangladesh* . . . . (Capitol)
Best Of George Harrison . . . . (Capitol)
I Am A Rock
Simon & Garfunkel; *Collected Works* . . . . (Columbia)
Simon & Garfunkel's Greatest Hits . . . . (Columbia)
Sounds Of Silence . . . . (Columbia)
I Cried
Patti Page; *Patti Page's Greatest Hits-Finest Performances.* . . . . . . (Sun)
I Love The Winter Weather
Tony Bennett; *Snowfall: The Tony Bennett Christmas Album.* . . . . . (Columbia)
In The Winter
Janis Ian; *Between The Lines* . . . . (Columbia)
January
Anthony Phillips; *Private Parts & Pieces V-Twelve* . . . . (PVC)
January
Mose Allison; *Back Country Suite* . . . . (Prestige)
January
Painted Willie; *Mind Bowling* . . . . (SST)
June In January
Bing Crosby; *Best Of Bing Crosby* . . . . (MCA)
Dean Martin; *Best Of Dean Martin* . . . . (CEMA Special Prod.)
Late Winter, Early Spring
John Denver; *Rocky Mountain High* . . . . (RCA)
Life In A Northern Town
Dream Academy; *Dream Academy* . . . . (Warner Bros.)
Lion In The Winter
Hoyt Axton; *Road Songs* . . . . (A&M)
Southbound. . . . . (A&M)

Long Cold Winter
Pure Prairie League; *If The Shoe Fits* . . . . (RCA)
Long December
Counting Crows; *Recovering The Satellites* . . . . (David Geffen Co.)
Magic In December
Tom Barabas; *Incredible Invincible Sampler* . . . . (Invincible)
Monkey In Winter
Colourfield; *Deception* . . . . (Chrysalis)
New England Winter
Shep Cooke; *Concert Tour Of Mars* . . . . (Sierra)
Our Winter Love
Lettermen; *Capitol Collectors Series-The Lettermen.* . . . . (Capitol)
Pale September
Fiona Apple; *Tidal* . . . . (Clean Slate/Work)
Roses In The Winter
Merle Haggard; *Merle Haggard-His Best* . . . . (MCA)
Serving 190 Proof . . . . (MCA)
Russian Winter
Krokus; *Headhunter.* . . . . (Arista)
Santa Monica
Savage Garden; *Savage Garden.* . . . . (Columbia)
Sometimes In Winter
Blood, Sweat & Tears; *Blood, Sweat & Tears* . . . . (Columbia)
Blood, Sweat & Tears Greatest Hits . . . . (Columbia)
Song For A Winter's Night
Gordon Lightfoot; *Gord's Gold* . . . . (Reprise)
The Way I Feel . . . . (United Artists)
Summer Kisses, Winter Tears
Elvis Presley; *Collector's Gold* . . . . (RCA)
Summer Me, Winter Me
Barbra Streisand; *The Way We Were* . . . . (Columbia)
Superwoman
Karyn White; *Karyn White.* . . . . (Warner Bros.)
Stevie Wonder; *Music Of My Mind* . . . . (Motown)
Original Musiquarium . . . . (Motown)
Three Seasons Of Winter
Joel Mabus; *Fairies & Fools* . . . . (Flying Fish)
Too Cold In The Winter
Cry Of Love; *Brother.* . . . . (Columbia)
Whispering Pines
Johnny Horton; *Johnny Horton's Greatest Hits* . . . . (Columbia)
Winter
Tori Amos; *Crucify* . . . . (Atlantic)
Little Earthquakes. . . . . (Atlantic)
Winter
Rolling Stones; *Goats Head Soup* . . . . (Rolling Stones)
Winter
John Denver; *Rocky Mountain High* . . . . (RCA)
Winter & The Summer
Strawbs; *Bursting At The Seams.* . . . . (A&M)
Winter And My Soul
Grand Funk Railroad; *Grand Funk* . . . . (Capitol)
Winter Boy
Buffy Sainte-Marie; *Best Of Buffy Sainte-Marie* . . . . (Vanguard)
Little Wheel Spin & Spin . . . . (Vanguard)
Winter In America
Gil Scott-Heron; *Best Of Gil Scott-Heron* . . . . (Arista)
First Minute Of a New Day . . . . (Arista)
Winter In America
Margaret Roadknight; *Living In The Land Of Oz* . . . . (Redwood)
Winter In Austria
L. Subramaniam; *Spanish Wave.* . . . . (Milestone)
Winter In Madrid
Stan Kenton & Ann Richards; *By Request-#5-1953-1960* . . . . . (Creative World)
Winter In Maine
Bruce Fowler; *Ants Can Count.* . . . . (Terra Nova)
Winter In Winnipeg
Rob McConnell & His Boss Brass; *Brass Is Back* . . . . (Concord Jazz)
Winter Long
Neil Young; *Decade.* . . . . (Reprise)
Winter Of My Life
Freddy Fender; *Are You Ready For Freddy* . . . . (MCA)
Winter Paradise
Destiny's Child; *8 Days Of Christmas* . . . . (Columbia)
Winter Plume
Adventure Babies; *Laugh.* . . . . (London)
Winter Rose Love Awake
Wings; *Back To The Egg* . . . . (Capitol)
Winter Sky
Judy Collins; *Judy Collins Concert* . . . . (Elektra)
Recollections . . . . (Elektra)
Winter Song
Harry Chapin; *Gold Medal Collection* . . . . (Elektra)
Sniper & Other Love Songs . . . . (Elektra)
Winter Song
Screaming Trees; *Sweet Oblivion.* . . . . (Epic)
Winter Song
Angel; *White Hot* . . . . (Casablanca)

Winter Song
Crash Test Dummies; *Ghosts That Haunt Me* . . . . (Arista)
Winter Time
Steve Miller Band; *Book Of Dreams* . . . . (Capitol)
  Steve Miller Band-Gift Set . . . . (Capitol)
  Steve Miller Band's Greatest Hits-1974-78 . . . . (Capitol)
Winter Wonderland
Air Supply; *Air Supply Christmas Album* . . . . (Arista)
  White Christmas . . . . (Word)
Alexander O'Neal; *My Gift To You* . . . . (Tabu)
Amy Grant; *Home For Christmas* . . . . (A&M)
Andrews Sisters; *Andrews Sisters-Christmas* . . . . (MCA Special Prod.)
Anne Murray; *Best Of The Season* . . . . (EMI America)
Aretha Franklin; *Rock 'N' Roll Christmas*
  Classics-C . . . . (Music For Little People)
Barbara Mandrell; *Christmas At Our House* . . . . (MCA Special Prod.)
  Tennessee Christmas-C . . . . (MCA)
Bing Crosby; *Bing Crosby Christmas Classics* . . . . (Capitol)
Blue Notes; *Rhythm & Blues Christmas-#1-C* . . . . (Collectables)
Brenda Lee; *Jingle Bell Rock* . . . . (MCA Special Prod.)
Carnie & Wendy Wilson; *Hey Santa!* . . . . (SBK)
Darlene Love; *Christmas Gift For You From Phil Spector-C* . . . (Rhino)
  Phil Spector-Back To Mono 1958-1969-C . . . . (Abkco)
  Phil Spector's Christmas Album-C . . . . (Passport)
Eddy Arnold; *Christmas With Eddy Arnold* . . . . (RCA)
Elvis Presley; *If Every Day Was Like Christmas* . . . . (RCA)
Eurythmics; *Very Special Christmas-C* . . . . (A&M)
Faron Young; *Country Christmas* . . . . (Step One)
Frank Sinatra; *Christmas Songs By Sinatra* . . . . (Legacy)
George Strait; *Merry Christmas Strait To You* . . . . (MCA Special Prod.)
Hank Crawford; *We Got A Good Thing Going* . . . . (Kudo)
Johnny Mercer & The Pied Pipers; *Merry Christmas Baby-Romance &*
  Reindeer-C . . . . (Capitol)
Kathie Lee Gifford; *It's Christmas Time* . . . . (Warner Bros.)
Kenny Rogers; *Christmas In America* . . . . (Reprise)
London Symphony Orchestra; *Christmas Traditions* . . . (Special Music Co.)
Merle Haggard; *Merle Haggard-Christmas Gift* . . . . (Curb)
Patti LaBelle & The Blue Belles; *A Soulful Christmas-C* . . . . (Collectables)
Randy Travis; *An Old Time Christmas* . . . . (Warner Bros.)
Robert Goulet; *Essence Of Christmas* . . . . (A&M)
Rosie O'Donnell & Macy Gray; *Another Rosie Christmas-C* . . . . . . (Columbia)
Tanya Tucker; *Christmas For The '90s-#1-C* . . . . (Liberty)
Tony Bennett; *Now That's What I Call Christmas!-C* . . . . (UTV)
Travis Tritt; *Christmas-Loving Time Of The Year* . . . . (Warner Bros.)
Winter World Of Love
Engelbert Humperdinck; *Engelbert Humperdinck* . . . . (Parrot)
  Engelbert Humperdinck-His Greatest Hits . . . . (Parrot)
Winterlude
Bob Dylan; *New Morning* . . . . (Columbia)
Winterness
Pousette-Dart Band; *Amnesia* . . . . (Capitol)
Wintertime Love
Doors; *Waiting For The Sun* . . . . (Elektra)
Winterwhite
Nitty Gritty Dirt Band; *Dream* . . . . (United Artists)
Wintry Feeling
Anne Murray; *Country Collection* . . . . (Capitol)
  I'll Always Love You . . . . (Capitol)
Jesse Winchester; *Touch On The Rainy Side* . . . . (Rhino)
Your Love Is Forever
George Harrison; *George Harrison* . . . . (Dark Horse)

SECRETS, Personal Business, Private

See Also: **CHEATING & LIES, COMMUNICATION (various),**
DOORS, GOSSIP, HIDING, LOVE: FORBIDDEN LOVE,
PRETEND, STRANGE

Ace In The Hole
George Strait; *Beyond The Blue Neon* . . . . (MCA)
Achy Breaky Heart
Billy Ray Cyrus; *Some Gave All* . . . . (Mercury)
Ain't Nobody's Business
Billie Holiday; *From The Original Decca Masters* . . . . (MCA)
Bobby Bland; *Soul Of The Man* . . . . (MCA)
Jimmy Witherspoon; *Jazz Legacy* . . . . (Inner City)
  Monterey Jazz Festival . . . . (Everest)
  'Spoon Concerts . . . . (Fantasy)
Ain't She Sweet?
Beatles; *History Of British Rock-#5-C* . . . . (Rhino)
  The Beatles-Anthology-#3 . . . . (Capitol)
Erroll Garner; *Body And Soul* . . . . (Legacy)
Frank Sinatra; *Sinatra and Swingin' Brass* . . . . (Reprise)
Pearl Bailey; *Pearl Bailey-16 Most Requested Songs* . . . . (Legacy)
Angels Would Fall
Melissa Etheridge; *Breakdown* . . . . (Island)
Anonymous Love
Ray Charles; *True To Life* . . . . (Atlantic)

Are You That Somebody?
Aaliyah; *ST/Dr. Dolittle* . . . . (Atlantic)
Baby Come Back To Me (The Morse Code Of Love)
Manhattan Transfer; *Bop doo-wopp* . . . . (Atlantic)
Baby Won't You Tell Me
Johnny Hammond; *Big City Blues* . . . . (Vanguard)
Beauty Secrets
Be Bop Deluxe; *Sunburst Finish* . . . . (Capitol)
Behind Closed Doors
Charlie Rich; *American Originals-Charlie Rich* . . . . (Columbia)
  Behind Closed Doors . . . . (Epic)
  Charlie Rich's Greatest Hits . . . . (Epic)
  Columbia Country Classics-#4-Nashville Sound-C . . . . (Columbia)
Behind That Locked Door
George Harrison; *All Things Must Pass* . . . . (Parlophone)
Between An Old Memory And Me
Keith Whitley; *I Wonder Do You Think Of Me* . . . . (RCA)
Travis Tritt; *Ten Feet Tall And Bulletproof* . . . . (Warner Bros.)
Between Me And You
Ja Rule featuring Christina Milian; *Rule 3:36* . . . . (Murder Inc./Def Jam/IDJMG)
Buried Treasure
Kenny Rogers; *Eyes That See In The Dark* . . . . (RCA)
  Kenny Rogers' Greatest Hits . . . . (RCA)
Buried Treasure
Flesheaters; *Prehistoric Fits-#2* . . . . (SST)
Can't Break It To My Heart
Tracy Lawrence; *Alibis* . . . . (Atlantic)
Certain Girl, A
Warren Zevon; *Bad Luck Streak In Dancing School* . . . . (Asylum)
Yardbirds; *Yardbirds' Greatest Hits-#1 (1964-1966)* . . . . (Rhino)
Complicated
Carolyn Dawn Johnson; *Room With A View* . . . . (Arista)
Confessin' Midnight
Robin Trower; *For Earth Below* . . . . (Chrysalis)
Confessing The Blues
B.B. King; *Completely Well* . . . . (MCA)
Jay McShann; *Atlantic Jazz-Kansas City-C* . . . . (Atlantic)
  Atlantic Jazz-Singers-C . . . . (Atlantic)
  Confessing The Blues . . . . (Classic Jazz)
Confessing The Blues
Rolling Stones; *12 X 5* . . . . (Abkco)
Confession
Mabel Mercer & Bobby Short; *At Town Hall* . . . . (Atlantic)
Confession
Maureen McGovern; *Another Woman In Love* . . . . (Columbia)
Confession
Laura Nyro; *Eli And The Thirteenth Confession* . . . . (Columbia)
Confession
Sammy Hagar; *Nine On A Ten Scale* . . . . (Capitol)
Confessions
Destiny's Child; *The Writing's On The Wall* . . . . (Columbia)
Confessor, The
Joe Walsh; *The Confessor* . . . . (Full Moon/Asylum)
Confidential
Fleetwoods; *Best Of The Fleetwoods* . . . . (Rhino)
Radiators; *Zig-Zaggin' Through Ghostland* . . . . (Epic)
Sonny Knight; *Oldies But Goodies-#1-C* . . . . (Original Sound)
Creep
TLC; *CrazySexyCool* . . . . (LaFace)
Darkness On The Edge Of Town
Bruce Springsteen; *Darkness On The Edge Of Town* . . . . (Columbia)
Bruce Springsteen & The E Street Band; *Bruce Springsteen & The E Street*
  Band Live/1975-85 . . . . (Legacy)
Daytime Friends
Kenny Rogers; *Daytime Friends* . . . . (EMI)
  Kenny Rogers-Twenty Greatest Hits . . . . (EMI)
  Ten Years Of Gold . . . . (EMI)
Diary
Bread; *Baby I'm-A Want You* . . . . (Elektra)
  Best Of Bread . . . . (Elektra)
  Bread-Anthology . . . . (Elektra)
Did You Ever Love Somebody
Jessica Simpson; *Songs From Dawson's Creek* . . . . (Sony Music Soundtrax)
Do I Have To Come Right Out & Say It
Buffalo Springfield; *Buffalo Springfield* . . . . (Atco)
Do You Want To Know A Secret
Beatles; *Introducing...The Beatles* . . . . (Vee-Jay)
  Please Please Me . . . . (Parlophone)
  The Early Beatles . . . . (Capitol)
Don't Tell Your Mama
Eddie Floyd; *Eddie Floyd-Chronicle* . . . . (Stax)
Don'tcha Tell Henry
Bob Dylan And The Band; *Basement Tapes* . . . . (Columbia)
Eddie's First Wife
Gretchen Peters; *Gretchen Peters* . . . . (Purple Crayon Prod.)
Everybody's Got Something To Hide Except Me And My Monkey
Beatles; *The Beatles (White Album)* . . . . (Capitol)

Flora's Secret
Enya; *A Day Without Rain*. . . . .(Reprise)
For Your Eyes Only
Sheena Easton; *13 Original James Bond Themes-C* . . . . (EMI)
ST/*For Your Eyes Only*. . . . .(Liberty)
Found Out About You
Gin Blossoms; *New Miserable Experience* . . . .(A&M)
Freak Like Me
Adina Howard; *Do You Wanna Ride?* . . . .(East West)
MTV *Party To Go-#7-C* . . . .(Tommy Boy)
Freaks
Live; *Secret Samadhi*. . . . . (Radioactive/MCA)
God Must Have Spent A Little More Time On You
Alabama Featuring 'N Sync; *Twentieth Century* . . . .(RCA)
'N Sync; *'N Sync* . . . .(RCA)
Totally Hits-#1-C . . . .(Arista)
Green Door
Jim Lowe; *Billboard Top Rock 'N' Roll Hits-1956-C* . . . .(Rhino)
Super Hits-#4-C . . . .(Gusto)
Hernando's Hideaway
Original Cast; *Pajama Game*. . . . .(Columbia)
ST/*Pajama Game* . . . .(Collectables)
Hidden Treasure
Traffic; *The Low Spark Of High Heeled Boys* . . . .(Island)
High School Confidential
Jerry Lee Lewis; *20 Classic Jerry Lee Lewis Hits* . . . .(Original Sound)
Jerry Lee Lewis-Original Golden Hits-#2 . . . .(Sun)
ST/*Harper Valley PTA* . . . .(Sun)
Sun Story-C. . . . .(Rhino)
How Deep Is Your Love
Dru Hill featuring Redman; *Enter The Dru* . . . . .(Def Jam/RAL/Mercury/Island)
ST/*Rush Hour* . . . .(Def Jam)
I Heard It Through The Grapevine
Creedence Clearwater Revival; *Chooglin'* . . . .(Fantasy)
Cosmo's Factory . . . .(Fantasy)
Creedence Clearwater Revival-Chronicle . . . .(Fantasy)
Creedence Clearwater Revival-Gold . . . .(Fantasy)
Movie Album . . . .(Fantasy)
Gladys Knight & The Pips; *16 #1 Hits From The Late '60s-C* . . . .(Motown)
Compact Command Performances-Gladys Knight & The Pips . . . . .(Motown)
Every Great Motown Song-First 25 Years-C . . . .(Motown)
Motown Grammy R&B Performances Of The '60s & '70s-C . . . .(Motown)
Motown Superstar Series-#13-Gladys Knight & The Pips . . . .(Motown)
Top 10 With A Bullet-Motown Girl Groups-C . . . .(Motown)
Marvin Gaye; *25 #1 Hits From 25 Years-C* . . . .(Motown)
Every Great Motown Hit Of Marvin Gaye . . . .(Motown)
Marvin Gaye Live At The London Palladium . . . .(Motown)
Marvin Gaye-Anthology . . . .(Motown)
Most Played Songs On America's Jukeboxes . . . .(Motown)
Motown Story-First 25 Years-C . . . .(Motown)
I Know There's Something Going On
Frida; *Something's Going On* . . . . (Atlantic)
I Really Don't Want To Know
Charlie McCoy; *Greatest Hits Of Charlie McCoy*. . . . .(Columbia)
Eddy Arnold; *Best Of Eddy Arnold* . . . .(RCA)
Essential Eddy Arnold . . . .(RCA)
Elvis Presley; *Elvis Country ("I'm 10,000 Years Old")* . . . .(RCA)
Great Country Songs . . . .(RCA)
Les Paul; *Best Of The Capitol Masters* . . . .(Gold Rush)
Les Paul & Mary Ford; *Les Paul's Greatest Hits*. . . . .(Pair)
Ronnie Dove; *Ronnie Dove-His Best*. . . . .(Laurie)
Tommy Edwards; *It's All In The Game-The Complete Hits Of Tommy Edwards* . . . .(Eric)
I Think We're Alone Now
Tiffany; *Tiffany* . . . . (MCA)
Tiffany's Greatest Hits . . . .(Hip-O)
Tommy James And The Shondells; *Best Of Tommy James And The Shondells* . . . .(Roulette)
Billboard Top Rock 'N' Roll Hits-1967-C . . . .(Rhino)
Tommy James And The Shondells-Anthology. . . . .(Rhino)
I Wonder What The King Is Doing Tonight
Original Cast; *Camelot* . . . .(Columbia)
Richard Harris; ST/*Camelot* . . . .(Warner Bros.)
If Walls Could Talk
Little Milton; *If Walls Could Talk* . . . .(Chess)
Little Milton's Greatest Hits. . . . .(Chess)
Ry Cooder; *Paradise And Lunch* . . . .(Reprise)
If Walls Could Talk
Celine Dion; *All The Way...A Decade Of Song* . . . . (550 Music)
I'll Follow My Secret Heart
Mary Martin & Noel Coward; *Together With Music* . . . .(DRG)
I'm Confessin' (That I Love You)
Ella Fitzgerald; *Ella Sings/Chick Swings*. . . . .(Olympic)
Lady Time . . . .(Pablo)
In My Room
Tammy Wynette & Brian Wilson; *Tammy Wynette...Remembered-C* . (Asylum)
In The Closet
Michael Jackson; *Dangerous*. . . . .(Epic)

It Ain't Nobody's Business
Billie Holiday; *History Of The Real Billie Holiday* . . . .(Verve)
Mississippi John Hurt; *Best Of Mississippi John Hurt* . . . .(Vanguard)
It Is No Secret
Mark Collie; *Unleashed* . . . .(MCA)
It's Nobody's Business But My Own
Bert Williams; *Music From The New York Stage (1890-1920)-#4-1917-1920-C* . . . .(Pearl)
I've Got A Secret Miniature Camera
Peter Murphy; ST/*Pump Up The Volume* . . . .(MCA)
Just Between You And Me
DC Talk; *First Generation: 25 Years Of Virgin Records-C* . . . . (Virgin)
Jesus Freak . . . .(Virgin)
Keep It Confidential
Nona Hendryx; *Best Of Nona Hendryx-Transformation* . . . .(Razor & Tie)
Leavin' Train
Bruce Springsteen; *Tracks* . . . .(Columbia)
Live To Tell
Madonna; *Immaculate Collection* . . . . (Sire)
Royal Box . . . .(Sire)
Something To Remember. . . . .(Maverick/Sire)
True Blue . . . .(Sire)
Love Letters From Old Mexico
Leslie Satcher; *Love Letters* . . . .(Warner Bros.)
Midnight Confessions
Grass Roots; *Grass Roots-Anthology (1966-1975)* . . . .(Rhino)
Original Rock 'N' Roll Hits Of The '60s-C . . . .(Roulette)
Vintage Music-#9-C . . . .(MCA)
Midnight Mary
Joey Powers; *Dick Bartley's One-Hit Wonders Of The '60s-#1-C* . . . . . .(Rhino)
Midnight Prowl
John David Souther; *Black Rose* . . . .(Asylum)
More Than You Know
Barbra Streisand; ST/*Funny Lady*. . . . .(Arista)
Mrs. Robinson
Simon & Garfunkel; *Bookends*. . . . .(Columbia)
Collected Works . . . .(Columbia)
Hollywood Magic-1960s-C . . . .(Columbia)
Simon & Garfunkel's Greatest Hits . . . .(Columbia)
ST/*Forrest Gump*. . . . .(Epic/Sony Music Soundtrax)
ST/*The Graduate*. . . . .(Columbia)
The Concert In Central Park . . . .(Warner Bros.)
My Little Secret
Xscape; *Traces Of My Lipstick*. . . . . (So So Def/Columbia)
Name
Goo Goo Dolls; *Boy Named Goo* . . . .(Metal Blade)
Goo Goo Dolls . . . .(Metal Blade)
Never Keeping Secrets
Babyface; *For The Cool In You* . . . . (Epic)
No One Needs To Know
Shania Twain; *The Woman In Me* . . . .(Mercury)
No Secrets
Van Stephenson; ST/*Secret Admirer* . . . .(MCA)
Suspicious Heart . . . .(MCA)
No Secrets
Carly Simon; *Best Of Carly Simon*. . . . .(Elektra)
No Secrets . . . .(Elektra)
No Secrets
Missing Persons; *Best Of Missing Persons* . . . .(Capitol)
No Tell Lover
Chicago; *Chicago's Greatest Hits-#2 (1974-81)* . . . .(Chicago)
Group Portrait . . . .(Chicago)
Hot Streets . . . .(Columbia)
If You Leave Me Now. . . . .(Chicago)
No Tell Motel
David Houston; *Best Of David Houston*. . . . .(Gusto)
Nobody Knows
Kevin Sharp; *Measure Of A Man* . . . .(143/Asylum)
Tony Rich Project; *Words* . . . .(LaFace)
Nobody Knows But Me
Jimmie Rodgers; *Riding High-1929-1930* . . . .(Rounder)
Merle Haggard & The Strangers; *Same Train Different Time* . . . .(Capitol)
Nobody's Business
Frank Stokes; *Creator Of The Memphis Blues* . . . . (Yazoo)
Oswald Brothers & Charlie Collins; *That's Country* . . . .(Rounder)
Stanley Brothers; *Together For The Last Time* . . . .(Rebel)
Nobody's Business
Don Henley; *I Can't Stand Still* . . . .(Asylum)
Nobody's Business
Billy Idol; *Billy Idol* . . . .(Chrysalis)
None Of Ur Friends Business
Ginuwine; *100 Percent Ginuwine* . . . . (550 Music)
Oh, My Mysterious Lady
Original Cast; *Peter Pan-The 1954 Broadway Production* . . . .(RCA Victor)
On The Down Low
Brian McKnight; *I Remember You*. . . . .(Mercury)
Password
Kitty Wells; *Kitty Wells' Greatest Hits* . . . . (Step One)

Kitty Wells' Greatest Hits . . . .(MCA)
MCA Records 30 Years Of Hits-1958-1988-C . . . .(MCA)
The Country Music Hall Of Fame-Kitty Wells . . . .(MCA Special Prod.)

Please Don't Tell Her
Big Head Todd & The Monsters; *Beautiful World* . . . . (Revolution)
Live Monsters . . . . (Revolution)

Private Conversation
Lyle Lovett; *The Road To Ensenada* . . . .(MCA)

Private Dancer
Tina Turner; *Live In Europe* . . . . (Capitol)
Private Dancer. . . . . (Capitol)
Simply The Best . . . . (Capitol)

Private Emotion
Ricky Martin & Meja; *Ricky Martin* . . . . (Columbia)

Private Eyes
Daryl Hall & John Oates; *Private Eyes* . . . . (RCA)
Rock 'N Soul, Part 1 . . . . (RCA)

Private Number
Judy Clay & William Bell; *15 Original Big Hits-#2-C* . . . . (Stax)
Private Numbers . . . . (Stax)
Top Of The Stax-Twenty Greatest Hits-#2-C . . . .(Stax)

Reflection
Christina Aguilera; *Christina Aguilera* . . . . (RCA)
ST/Mulan . . . . (Walt Disney)

Rumor Has It
Clay Walker; *Clay Walker's Greatest Hits* . . . . (Giant)
Rumor Has It . . . . (Giant)

Runaround, The
Xscape; *Traces Of My Lipstick* . . . . (So So Def/Columbia)

Satellite
Dave Matthews Band; *Under The Table And Dreaming* . . . . (RCA)

Saucerful Of Secrets
Pink Floyd; *Nice Pair* . . . . (Capitol)
Saucerful Of Secrets . . . . (Capitol)
Ummagumma . . . . (Capitol)

Secret
Orchestral Manoeuvres In The Dark; *Crush* . . . . (A&M)
in the dark/the best of OMD . . . . (A&M)

Secret
Madonna; *Bedtime Stories* . . . . (Maverick/Sire)
GHV2. . . . . (Warner Bros.)

Secret
Heart; *Brigade* . . . . (Capitol)

Secret
Lynch Mob; *Lynch Mob* . . . . (Elektra)

Secret Agent Man
Devo; *Duty Now For The Future* . . . . (Warner Bros.)
Johnny Rivers; *Best Of Johnny Rivers* . . . .(EMI)
Johnny Rivers-Anthology 1964-1977 . . . . (Rhino)
Television's Greatest Hits-#1-C . . . . (TVT)
Very Best Of Johnny Rivers . . . . (EMI)

Secret Combination
Randy Crawford; *Secret Combination* . . . . (Warner Bros.)

Secret Friend
Paul McCartney; *McCartney II*. . . . . (Gold Rush)
Paul McCartney-Gift Set . . . . (Capitol)

Secret Garden
Alan Parsons Project; *Eve* . . . . (Arista)

Secret Garden
Bruce Springsteen; *Bruce Springsteen's Greatest Hits* . . . . (Columbia)
ST/Jerry Maguire . . . . (Epic/Sony Music Soundtrax)

Secret Garden
Quincy Jones; *Back On The Block* . . . . (Qwest)

Secret Garden
Johnny Rivers; *Johnny Rivers-Golden Hits* . . . . (Imperial)

Secret Gardens
Judy Collins; *So Early In The Spring, The First 15 Years* . . . . (Elektra)
True Stories & Other Dreams . . . . (Elektra)

Secret Journey
Police; *Ghost In The Machine*. . . . . (A&M)

Secret Life Of Arabia
David Bowie; *Heroes* . . . . (Rykodisc)

Secret Love
Doris Day; *Doris Day's Greatest Hits* . . . . (Columbia)
Hollywood Magic-1950s-C . . . . (Columbia)
Frank Sinatra; *Days Of Wine And Roses, Moon River, And Other Academy*
Award Winners . . . . (Reprise)
Freddy Fender; *Freddy Fender-Collection*. . . . . (Reprise)
Guy Lombardo & His Royal Canadians; *Golden Medleys* . . . .(MCA)
Moonglows; *Doo-Wop's Greatest Hits-C* . . . . (Vee-Jay)
Nancy Wilson; *Capitol Sings The Best Movie Songs-C* . . . . (Capitol)
Slim Whitman; *Best Of Slim Whitman 1952-1972* . . . . (Rhino)
Slim Whitman's Greatest Hits . . . . (Curb)

Secret Lovers
Atlantic Starr; *As The Band Turns* . . . . (A&M)
Atlantic Starr-Classics-#10 . . . . (A&M)
Secret Lovers: Best Of Atlantic Starr . . . . (A&M)

Secret Marriage
Sting; *...Nothing Like The Sun* . . . . (A&M)

Secret Meetings
Greg Kihn; *Next Of Kihn* . . . . (Beserkley)

Secret Messages
Electric Light Orchestra; *Secret Messages* . . . . (Jet)

Secret Mountain Hideout
Michael Martin Murphey; *Blue Sky-Night Thunder* . . . . (Epic)

Secret O' Life
James Taylor; *JT* . . . . (Columbia)

Secret Of Life
Faith Hill; *Faith*. . . . . (Warner Bros.)
Gretchen Peters; *The Secret Of Life* . . . .(Purple Crayon Prod.)

Secret Of The Andes
Victor Feldman; *Secret Of The Andes* . . . .(Palo Alto Jazz)
Victor Feldman/Generation Band; *Best Of Victor Feldman/*
Generation Band . . . .(Nova)

Secret Of The Sea
Billy Bragg & Wilco; *Mermaid Avenue-#2* . . . . (Elektra)

Secret Place
Megadeth; *Cryptic Writings* . . . . (Capitol)

Secret Rendezvous
Karyn White; *Karyn White* . . . . (Warner Bros.)

Secret Secrets
Joan Armatrading; *Secret Secrets* . . . . (A&M)

Secret Separation
Fixx; *One Thing Leads To Another-Greatest Hits* . . . . (MCA)
Walkabout . . . . (MCA)

Secret Smile
Semisonic; *Feeling Strangely Fine* . . . . (MCA)

Secret To A Long Life
Michelle Shocked; *Arkansas Traveler* . . . . (Mercury)
Texas Campfire Tapes . . . . (Mercury)

Secretly
Jimmie Rodgers; *Best Of Jimmie Rodgers*. . . . . (Rhino)
Original Rock 'N' Roll Hits Of The '50s-C . . . . (Roulette)
Yours Truly . . . . (Roulette)
Lettermen; *And I Love Her* . . . . (Capitol)
Best Of The Lettermen . . . . (Capitol)
Capitol Collectors Series-The Lettermen . . . . (Capitol)

Secrets
Bobby Womack; *The Poet*. . . . . (Razor & Tie)

Secrets
Golden Earring; *Cut* . . . . (21)

Secrets
Natalie Cole; *Dangerous*. . . . . (Modern)

Secrets
Van Halen; *Diver Down* . . . . (Warner Bros.)

Secrets
Kidd Glove; *Kidd Glove* . . . . (Morocco)

Secrets
Mac Davis; *Mac Davis-Very Best & More* . . . . (Casablanca)

Secrets
Bonham; *Mad Hatter* . . . . (WTG)

Secrets
Cure; *Seventeen Seconds* . . . . (Elektra)

Secrets
Mick Jagger; *She's The Boss* . . . . (Columbia)

Secrets Told
Kim Waters; *One Special Moment* . . . . (Shanachie)

Shhh, It's A Military Secret
Glenn Miller & His Orchestra; *Complete Glenn Miller & His*
Orchestra. . . . . (Bluebird)

Silence Is Golden
4 Seasons; *25th Anniversary Collection* . . . . (Rhino)
4 Seasons-Anthology . . . . (Rhino)
Tremeloes; *Best Of The Tremeloes* . . . . (Rhino)
History Of British Rock-#7-C . . . . (Rhino)
Rock Artifacts-From The Vaults-#4-C . . . . (Columbia)

Six O'Clock News
John Prine; *John Prine* . . . . (Atlantic)
John Prine-Souvenirs . . . . (Oh Boy)

Slipping Around
Ernest Tubb; *45-#46173* . . . . (Decca)
Margaret Whiting & Jimmy Wakely; *45-#40224* . . . . (Capitol)

Slow Like Honey
Fiona Apple; *Tidal* . . . . (Clean Slate/Work)

Smoky Places
Corsairs; *Best Of Chess Rhythm & Blues-#1-C* . . . . (Chess)
Hard To Find Hits Of Rock 'N Roll-#1-C . . . . (Curb)

Stairs, The
Reba McEntire; *The Last One To Know* . . . . (MCA)

Suspicion
Elvis Presley; *ST/Pot Luck* . . . . (RCA)
Terry Stafford; *Billboard Top Rock 'N' Roll Hits-1964-C* . . . . (Rhino)
Cruisin'-1964-C . . . . (Increase)
Oldies But Goodies-#8-C . . . . (Original Sound)

Suspicions
Eddie Rabbitt; *Country's Greatest Hits-#6-Superstars-C*. . . . . (Priority)
Eddie Rabbitt's All-Time Greatest Hits . . . . (Warner Bros.)

Number 1's . . . . (Warner Bros.)
Ten Years Of Greatest Hits . . . . (Capitol)
'Tain't Nobody's Bus'ness If I Do
Bessie Smith; *Bessie Smith-The Collection* . . . . (Legacy)
Billie Holiday; *Billie Holiday's Greatest Hits* . . . . (Decca Jazz)
Diana Ross; *ST/Lady Sings The Blues* . . . . (Motown)
Miki Howard; *Miki Sings Billie-Tribute To Billie Holiday* . . . . (Giant)
Original Broadway Cast; *Black & Blue* . . . . (DRG)
Take A Message To Mary
Bob Dylan; *Self Portrait* . . . . (Columbia)
Everly Brothers; *Everly Brothers-All-Time Original Hits* . . . . (Rhino)
Everly Brothers-Cadence Classics-Their 20 Greatest Hits . . . . (Rhino)
Rockpile; *Seconds Of Pleasure* . . . . (Columbia)
Take Me There
Blackstreet & Mya featuring Mase & Blinky Blink;
Finally . . . . (Lil' Man/Interscope)
Now That's What I Call Music!-#2-C . . . . (Virgin)
ST/Rugrats . . . . (Interscope)
Talk Back Trembling Lips
Ernest Ashworth; *Best Of Ernest Ashworth* . . . . (Curb)
Johnny Tillotson; *Cruisin'-1964-C* . . . . (Increase)
Talk Show Shhh!
Shae Jones; *Talk Show* . . . . (Universal)
Talking In Your Sleep
Romantics; *Billboard Top Hits-1984-C* . . . . (Rhino)
In Heat . . . . (Epic Portrait Assoc.)
Rock Of The '80s-#3-C . . . . (Priority)
Theme From "Greatest American Hero"
Joey Scarbury; *Television's Greatest Hits-#3-1970s & 1980s-C* . . . . (TVT)
Tube Tunes-#3-The '70s & '80s-C . . . . (Rhino)
Theme From "Secret Squirrel"
Original Soundtrack; *Hanna-Barbera Pic-A-Nic Basket Of Cartoon
Classics* . . . . (Kid Rhino/Rhino 4 Kids)
Television's Greatest Hits-#5-In Living Color-C . . . . (TVT)
They Don't Know
Tracey Ullman; *Best Of Tracey Ullman* . . . . (Rhino)
You Broke My Heart In 17 Places . . . . (MCA)
Third Rate Romance
Amazing Rhythm Aces; *Stacked Deck* . . . . (MCA)
Rosanne Cash; *Somewhere In The Stars* . . . . (Columbia)
Sammy Kershaw; *Cryin' Lyin' Lovin' & Leavin'-C* . . . . (Universal)
Feelin' Good Train . . . . (Mercury)
The Hits-Chapter 1 . . . . (Mercury)
Time Will Reveal
DeBarge; *In A Special Way* . . . . (Motown)
Too Many Secrets
Patsy Cline; *20 Golden Pieces Of Patsy Cline* . . . . (Bulldog)
Patsy Cline . . . . (MCA)
Under Suspicion
Robert Palmer; *Secrets* . . . . (Island)
Under Suspicion
Roy Orbison; *Legendary Roy Orbison* . . . . (Sony Music Special Prod.)
Under Suspicion
Vanilla Fudge; *Mystery* . . . . (Atco)
Undercover Lover
38 Special; *Tour De Force* . . . . (A&M)
Undercover Lover
Dazz Band; *Jukebox* . . . . (Motown)
Undercover Man
Edgar Winter Group; *They Only Come Out At Night* . . . . (Epic)
Undercover Of The Night
Rolling Stones; *Rewind (1971-1984)* . . . . (Rolling Stones)
Undercover . . . . (Rolling Stones)
Walk On By
Leroy Van Dyke; *Billboard Top Country Hits-1961-C* . . . . (Rhino)
Country Classics-C . . . . (Sun)
Country Music Classics-#2-1960-1965-C . . . . (K-Tel)
Souvenirs Of Music City U.S.A.-C . . . . (Plantation)
What She Don't Know Won't Hurt Her
Gene Watson; *Gene Watson's Greatest Hits* . . . . (MCA)
When She Cries
Restless Heart; *Big Iron Horses* . . . . (RCA)
Restless Heart's Greatest Hits . . . . (RCA)
Today's Number One Country-C . . . . (K-Tel)
When The Lights Go Out
Bruce Springsteen; *Tracks* . . . . (Columbia)
Where Do You Go
No Mercy; *No Mercy* . . . . (Arista)
Who's Behind The Door
Zebra; *Zebra* . . . . (Atlantic)
Zebra-Live . . . . (Atlantic)
Wild Week-End
Bill Anderson; *Bill Anderson-Legend* . . . . (Masters)
MCA Records 30 Years Of Hits-1958-1988-C . . . . (MCA)
Still . . . . (MCA Special Prod.)
You Have The Right To Remain Silent
Perfect Stranger; *From Nashville With Love-C* . . . . (Curb)
You'll Never Never Know
Platters; *Magic Touch-An Anthology* . . . . (Mercury)

Very Best Of The Platters . . . . (Mercury)
Your Eyes
Xscape; *Traces Of My Lipstick* . . . . (So So Def/Columbia)
Your Little Secret
Melissa Etheridge; *Your Little Secret* . . . . (Island)
Your Secret's Safe With Me
Robert Cray Band; *Don't Be Afraid Of The Dark* . . . . (Mercury)
Your Secret's Safe With Me
Michael Franks; *Skin Dive* . . . . (Warner Bros.)
You're The One
SWV; *MTV Party To Go-#10-C* . . . . (Tommy Boy)
New Beginning . . . . (RCA)
SWV's Greatest Hits . . . . (Beast)

SEEING, Blind, Looking At, Watching

See Also: **EYES, FINDING, INVISIBLE, LOVE: SEARCHING FOR
LOVE, POLICE (spies), SEARCH**

(Now You See Me) Now You Don't
Lee Ann Womack; *Some Things I Know* . . . . (Decca)
3 Libras
A Perfect Circle; *Mer De Noms* . . . . (Virgin)
32 Flavors
Alana Davis; *Blame It On Me* . . . . (Elektra)
Ani DiFranco; *Living In Clip* . . . . (Righteous Babe)
Not A Pretty Girl . . . . (Righteous Babe)
Abraham, Martin And John
Dion; *Collectables Presents The History Of Rock-#3-C* . . . . . (Collectables)
Dion-24 Original Classics . . . . (Arista)
Songs Of Protest-C . . . . (Rhino)
WCBS FM 101 History Of Rock-'60s-#2-C . . . . (Collectables)
Harry Belafonte; *Harry Belafonte's All Time Greatest Hits-#1* . . . . (RCA)
Smokey Robinson & The Miracles; *Smokey Robinson & The Miracles'
Anthology* . . . . (Motown)
*Time Out For Smokey Robinson & The Miracles/Special
Occasion* . . . . (Motown)
Again
Lenny Kravitz; *Lenny Kravitz's Greatest Hits* . . . . (Virgin)
Now That's What I Call Music!-#6-C . . . . (Virgin)
Against All Odds (Take A Look At Me Now)
Mariah Carey; *Rainbow* . . . . (Columbia)
Phil Collins; *Hit Singles-1980-1988-C* . . . . (Atlantic)
Serious Hits...Live! . . . . (Atlantic)
ST/Against All Odds . . . . (Atlantic)
Ain't Seen Love Like That
Mr. Big; *Bump Ahead* . . . . (Atlantic)
Anybody Seen My Baby?
Rolling Stones; *1998 Grammy Nominees-C* . . . . (MCA)
Bridges To Babylon . . . . (Virgin)
Anything
Third Eye Blind; *Blue* . . . . (Elektra)
Arrested For Driving While Blind
ZZ Top; *Six Pack* . . . . (Warner Bros.)
Tejas . . . . (Warner Bros.)
As Any Fool Can See
Tracy Lawrence; *I See It Now* . . . . (Atlantic)
Live & Unplugged . . . . (Atlantic)
As Tears Go By
Marianne Faithfull; *Marianne Faithfull's Greatest Hits* . . . . (Abkco)
Strange Weather . . . . (Island)
Rolling Stones; *Big Hits (High Tide & Green Grass)* . . . . (Abkco)
December's Children (and everybody's) . . . . (Abkco)
Hot Rocks 1964-1971 . . . . (Abkco)
Singles Collection-The London Years . . . . (Abkco)
Bear Went Over The Mountain, The
Original Soundtrack; *Children's Favorites* . . . . (Kid Rhino/Rhino 4 Kids)
Beautiful Day
U2; *All That You Can't Leave Behind* . . . . (Interscope)
Now That's What I Call Music!-#6-C . . . . (Virgin)
Believe Me If All Those Endearing Young Charms
Bronn Journey; *Celtic Journey* . . . . (Phileo)
Mitch Miller; *Favorite Irish Sing-Alongs* . . . . (Legacy)
Roger Whittaker; *Danny Boy & Other Irish Favorites* . . . . (RCA Victor)
Between The Devil And Me
Alan Jackson; *Everything I Love* . . . . (Arista)
Big Man
Four Preps; *Best Of The Four Preps* . . . . (Curb)
Capitol Collectors Series-Four Preps . . . . (Collectables)
Blind In Texas
W.A.S.P.; *Last Command* . . . . (Capitol)
Blind Love & Whiskey
Little Mike & The Tornadoes; *Heart Attack* . . . . (Blind Pig)
Blind Man
Bobby Bland; *Best Of Bobby Bland* . . . . (MCA)
Introspective Of The Early Years . . . . (MCA)

Blind Man
Champion Jack Dupree; *Back Home In New Orleans* . . . . (Bullseye Blues)
Blind Man
Aerosmith; *Big Ones*. . . . .(Geffen)
Blinded By Rainbows
Rolling Stones; *Voodoo Lounge* . . . . (Virgin)
Blinded By The Light
Bruce Springsteen; *Greetings From Asbury Park, N.J.* . . . . . (Columbia)
Manfred Mann's Earth Band; *Roaring Silence* . . . .(Warner Bros.)
Both Sides Now
Sammy Hagar; *Marching To Mars* . . . .(MCA)
Can I See You In The Morning
Jackson 5; *Third Album* . . . . (Motown)
Can I See You Tonight
Tanya Tucker; *Best Of Tanya Tucker* . . . .(MCA)
Tanya Tucker Live . . . .(MCA Special Prod.)
Can You See Me
Jimi Hendrix; *ST/Jimi Plays Monterey* . . . . (Reprise)
Jimi Hendrix Experience; *Are You Experienced?* . . . . (Reprise)
Smash Hits . . . . (Reprise)
Can't Take My Eyes Off You
Frankie Valli; *25th Anniversary Collection* . . . . (Rhino)
Frankie Valli-Anthology . . . . (Rhino)
Very Best Of Frankie Valli . . . .(MCA)
Lauryn Hill; *The Miseducation Of Lauryn Hill* . . . . (Ruffhouse/Columbia)
Can't You See
Alabama; *Alabama-Live* . . . . (RCA)
Charlie Daniels Band; *Volunteer Jam VII-C* . . . .(Epic)
Hank Williams, Jr.; *Hank Williams, Jr. & Friends* . . . . (Polydor)
Rebels, Renegades & Ramblers-C . . . . (Polydor)
Standing In The Shadows . . . . (Polydor)
Marshall Tucker Band; *Marshall Tucker Band*. . . . . (AJK Music)
Searchin' For A Rainbow . . . . (AJK Music)
Can't You See
Total; *Total* . . . .(Bad Boy/Arista)
Total featuring Notorious B.I.G.; *Bad Boy Greatest*
Hits-#1-C . . . .(Bad Boy/Arista)
ST/New Jersey Drive-#1-C . . . . (Tommy Boy)
Can't You See
Peter Tosh; *Mystic Man* . . . .(Rolling Stones)
Can't You See (You Doin' Me Wrong)
Tower Of Power; *Back To Oakland* . . . .(Warner Bros.)
Can't You See Darling
Ray Charles; *20 Golden Pieces Of Ray Charles* . . . .(Bulldog)
Can't You See That She's Mine
Dave Clark Five; *History Of The Dave Clark Five* . . . . (Hollywood)
Can't You See What You're Doing To Me
Albert King & Little Milton; *Albert King & Little Milton-Chronicle* . . . . . .(Stax)
Change (In The House Of Flies)
Deftones; *White Pony* . . . .(Maverick)
Child Of Vision
Supertramp; *Breakfast In America* . . . . (A&M)
Come See About Me
Diana Ross & The Supremes; *16 #1 Hits From The Early '60s-C* . . . . (Motown)
Diana Ross & The Supremes' Greatest Hits . . . . (Motown)
Diana Ross & The Supremes-Anthology (1962-1969) . . . . (Motown)
Diana Ross & The Supremes-At The Copa . . . . (Motown)
Every Great #1 Hit . . . . (Motown)
Girl Groups-Story Of A Sound-C . . . . (Rhino)
Motown Story-First 25 Years-C . . . . (Motown)
Motown Superstar Series-#1-Diana Ross & The Supremes . . . . (Motown)
Come See Me
112; *112* . . . .(Bad Boy/Arista)
Coming Home To See You
Supertramp; *Indelibly Stamped*. . . . . (A&M)
Crazy For This Girl
Evan And Jaron; *Evan And Jaron* . . . . (Columbia)
Now That's What I Call Music!-#6-C . . . . (Virgin)
Daddy Frank (The Guitar Man)
Merle Haggard; *Best Of Merle Haggard*. . . . . (Capitol)
Capitol Collectors Series-Merle Haggard. . . . . (Capitol)
Merle Haggard & The Strangers; *For The Record: Merle Haggard-43*
Legendary Hits . . . . (BNA)
Songs I'll Always Sing . . . . (Capitol)
Did You Ever See A Dream Walking
Bing Crosby; *Crosby Classics* . . . . (Columbia)
Hal Kemp & Skinnay Ennis; *The Uncollected Hal Kemp-#2 & #3* . . . (Hindsight)
Did You See His Name
Kinks; *Kink Kronikles*. . . . . (Reprise)
Did You See Jackie Robinson Hit That Ball?
Count Basie; *RCA Victor Blues & Rhythm Revue-C*. . . . . (RCA)
Count Basie & His Orchestra; *Baseball's Greatest Hits-C*. . . . . (Rhino)
Doesn't Really Matter
Janet Jackson; *Now That's What I Call Music!-#5-C* . . . . (Virgin)
ST/Nutty Professor 2: The Klumps. . . . .(Def Soul/IDJMG)
Don't Look Back
Bruce Springsteen; *Tracks* . . . . (Columbia)
Knack; *One Step Up/Two Steps Back-The Songs Of Bruce*
Springsteen-C . . . . (Right Stuff)

Retrospective-Best Of The Knack. . . . . (Gold Rush)
Don't Look Back
Boston; *Boston's Greatest Hits* . . . . (Epic)
Don't Look Back. . . . . (Epic)
Don't Look Back In Anger
Oasis; *What's The Story Morning Glory?* . . . . (Epic)
Don't Turn Around
Ace Of Base; *The Sign*. . . . . (Arista)
Don't You Know
Keb' Mo'; *The Door* . . . .(550/Epic/Okeh)
Dreams (I'll Never See)
Allman Brothers Band; *Allman Brothers Band* . . . .(Polydor)
An Evening With The Allman Brothers Band-First Set. . . . . (Epic)
Beginnings . . . .(Polydor)
Best Of The Allman Brothers Band. (Polydor)
Decade Of Hits-1969-1979 . . . . (Polydor)
Gregg Allman Tour . . . . (Capricorn)
The Road Goes On Forever, A Collection Of Their Greatest
Recordings. . . . .(Polydor)
Molly Hatchet; *Molly Hatchet*. . . . . (Epic)
Drop Down Mama, Let Your Papa See
John Hammond; *Best Of John Hammond* . . . . (Vanguard)
Sleepy John Estes; *Legend Of Sleepy John Estes* . . . . (Delmark)
Tom Rush; *Best Of Tom Rush: No Regrets* . . . . (Legacy)
Tom Rush . . . . (Columbia)
Every Breath You Take
Police; *Every Breath You Take-The Classics* . . . . (A&M)
Synchronicity . . . . (A&M)
Tammy Wynette & Sting; *Without Walls-C* . . . . (Epic)
Everywhere
Tim McGraw; *Everywhere* . . . . (Curb)
Everywhere
Michelle Branch; *The Spirit Room* . . . . (Maverick)
Feelin' Single, Seein' Double
Emmylou Harris; *Elite Hotel*. . . . . (Reprise)
Fire And Rain
James Taylor; *James Taylor's Greatest Hits* . . . . (Warner Bros.)
Sweet Baby James . . . . (Warner Bros.)
The Concert For New York City-C . . . . (Columbia)
Sammy Kershaw; *Red Hot + Country-C* . . . . (Mercury)
First Time Ever I Saw Your Face
Celine Dion; *All The Way...A Decade Of Song* . . . .(550 Music)
Roberta Flack; *Atlantic Rhythm & Blues 1947-1974-#6 (1966-*
1969)-C . . . .(Atlantic)
Best Of Roberta Flack . . . . (Atlantic)
First Take . . . . (Atlantic)
For The First Time
Kenny Loggins; *ST/One Fine Day* . . . . (Columbia)
For Your Eyes Only
Sheena Easton; *13 Original James Bond Themes-C* . . . . (EMI)
ST/For Your Eyes Only. . . . . (Liberty)
From A Distance
Bette Midler; *Some People's Lives* . . . .(Atlantic)
Byrds; *20 Essential Tracks From The Box Set*. . . . . (Columbia)
The Byrds . . . . (Columbia)
Judy Collins; *Fires Of Eden* . . . . (Columbia)
Kathy Mattea; *Time Passes By* . . . . (Mercury)
Nanci Griffith; *Lone Star State Of Mind* . . . . (MCA)
One Fair Summer Evening . . . . (MCA)
Frozen
Madonna; *GHV2* . . . . (Warner Bros.)
Ray Of Light . . . . (Maverick)
Gee Whiz (Look At His Eyes)
Carla Thomas; *Gee Whiz: The Best Of Carla Thomas* . . . . (Rhino)
Glass Onion
Beatles; *Beatles-Box Set* . . . . (Capitol)
The Beatles (White Album) . . . . (Capitol)
Gloria: The Enchantment Medley
Jesse Powell; *Jesse Powell* . . . . (Silas)
Good To See You
Neil Young; *Silver & Gold* . . . . (Reprise)
Has Anybody Seen Amy
John & Audrey Wiggins; *John & Audrey* . . . . (Mercury)
Have You Ever Seen The Rain
Creedence Clearwater Revival; *1970* . . . .(Fantasy)
Creedence Clearwater Revival-Chronicle . . . . (Fantasy)
Pendulum . . . .(Fantasy)
Have You Seen Her
Chi-Lites; *Chi-Lites' Greatest Hits* . . . . (Rhino)
Hammer; *Please Hammer Don't Hurt 'Em* . . . . (Capitol)
Have You Seen Mary
Sponge; *Wax Ecstatic* . . . . (Columbia)
Have You Seen The Saucers
Jefferson Airplane; *2400 Fulton Street-An Anthology*. . . . . (RCA)
30 Seconds Over Winterland . . . . (RCA)
Have You Seen The Stars Tonight
Jefferson Airplane; *Flight Log (1966-1976)* . . . . (Grunt)
Paul Kantner/Jefferson Starship; *Blows Against The Empire* . . . .(RCA)

Have You Seen Your Mother, Baby, Standing In The Shadow?
Rolling Stones; *Flowers* .... (Abkco)
  got Live if you want it! .... (Abkco)
  More Hot Rocks (big hits & fazed cookies) .... (Abkco)
  Through The Past, Darkly (Big Hits Vol. 2) .... (Abkco)
How Bizarre
OMC; *How Bizarre* .... (Huh!/Mercury)
How You Gonna See Me Now
Alice Cooper; *From The Inside* .... (Warner Bros.)
I Am Looking At Music
Nia Long; *ST/Love Jones* .... (Columbia)
I Belong To You (Every Time I See Your Face)
Rome; *Rome* .... (RCA)
I Can See An Angel
Patsy Cline; *20 Golden Pieces Of Patsy Cline* .... (Bulldog)
  Hungry For Love-Her First Recordings-#2 .... (Rhino)
  Today Tomorrow & Forever .... (MCA)
I Can See Arkansas
Anne Murray; *Fifteen Of The Best* .... (Liberty)
I Can See Clearly Now
Gladys Knight & The Pips; *Gladys Knight & The Pips'*
  Greatest Hits .... (Buddah)
  Imagination .... (Right Stuff)
  On & On .... (Fifty One West)
Johnny Nash; *Billboard Top Rock 'N' Roll Hits-1972-C* .... (Rhino)
  Rock Artifacts-From The Vaults-#2-C .... (Legacy)
I Can See For Miles
Who; *Hooligans* .... (MCA)
  Join Together .... (MCA)
  Meaty Beaty Big & Bouncy .... (MCA)
  ST/The Kids Are Alright .... (MCA)
  The Who Sell Out .... (MCA)
I Can See Forever In Your Eyes
Reba McEntire; *Feel The Fire* .... (Mercury)
I Can See It
Barbra Streisand; *A Happening In Central Park* .... (Columbia)
  My Name Is Barbra .... (Columbia)
I Can't See Nobody
Bee Gees; *Bee Gees-Gold* .... (Polydor)
  Here At Last...Bee Gees...Live .... (Polydor)
I Can't See Texas From Here
George Strait; *Strait From The Heart* .... (MCA)
I Can't See You
Tim Buckley; *Best Of Tim Buckley* .... (Rhino)
  Elektrock-Sixties-C .... (Elektra)
I Can't See You
Dokken; *Breaking The Chains* .... (Elektra)
I Can't See Your Face In My Mind
Doors; *Doors-Classics* .... (Elektra)
  Strange Days .... (Elektra)
I Couldn't See You Leavin'
Conway Twitty; *Crazy In Love* .... (MCA)
I Don't Ever Want To See You Again
Uncle Sam; *Uncle Sam* .... (Stone Creek/Epic)
I Don't Want To See You Again
Peter And Gordon; *Peter & Gordon's Greatest Hits* ..... (CEMA Special Prod.)
I Go Blind
Hootie & The Blowfish; *ST/Friends-Music From The TV Series* ...(Reprise)
I Just Want To See His Face
Rolling Stones; *Exile On Main Street* .... (Virgin)
I Know A Heartache When I See One
Jennifer Warnes; *Best Of Jennifer Warnes* .... (Arista)
  Shot Through The Heart .... (Arista)
I Looked Away
Derek And The Dominos; *Layla* .... (Polydor)
I Never Go Around Mirrors
Lefty Frizzell; *Grand Ole Opry-75 Years-#1-C* .... (MCA)
I Really Don't Need No Light
Jeffrey Osborne; *Jeffrey Osborne* .... (A&M)
I Saw Her Again
Mamas & The Papas; *Best Of The Mamas & The Papas* ..... (MCA)
  Farewell To The First Golden Era .... (MCA)
  Mamas & The Papas .... (MCA)
I Saw Her Standing There
Beatles; *Introducing...The Beatles* .... (Vee-Jay)
  Meet The Beatles! .... (Capitol)
  Please Please Me .... (Parlophone)
  Rock 'N' Roll Music .... (Capitol)
  The Beatles-Anthology-#1 .... (Capitol)
Paul McCartney; *Tripping The Live Fantastic-Highlights!* ... (Capitol)
I Saw Him Standing There
Tiffany; *Tiffany* .... (MCA)
  Tiffany's Greatest Hits .... (Hip-O)
I Saw It On TV
John Fogerty; *Centerfield* .... (Warner Bros.)
I Saw Linda Yesterday
Dickey Lee; *45s On CD-#2-1960-1966-C* .... (Mercury)
I Saw The Light
Hank Williams; *Hank Williams-24 Greatest Hits-#2* .... (Polydor)

  Hank Williams-40 Greatest Hits .... (Polydor)
  I Ain't Got Nothin' But Time-1946-1947 .... (Polydor)
  Legend In Song-With Hank Williams, Jr. .... (Polydor)
  Rare Takes & Radio Cuts .... (Polydor)
I Saw The Light
Wynonna; *Wynonna* .... (MCA)
I Saw You Dancing
Yaki-Da; *Pride* .... (London)
I See It Now
Tracy Lawrence; *I See It Now* .... (Atlantic)
I See The Lovelight In Your Eyes
Conway Twitty; *Number Ones* .... (MCA)
I See The Want In Your Eyes
Conway Twitty; *I'm Not Through Loving You Yet* .... (MCA)
  Night With Conway Twitty .... (MCA)
  Number Ones .... (MCA)
I See Your Face Before Me
Frank Sinatra; *In The Wee Small Hours* .... (Capitol)
Miles Davis; *Green Haze* .... (Prestige)
  Miles Davis-Chronicle-Complete Prestige Recordings ..... (Prestige)
I Used To Be Color Blind
Anita O'Day; *Blue Skies: The Irving Berlin Songbook-C* .... (Verve)
Fred Astaire; *The Irving Berlin Songbook* .... (Verve)
I Wish I Were Blind
Bruce Springsteen; *Human Touch* .... (Columbia)
I'd Love Just Once To See You
Beach Boys; *Smiley Smile/Wild Honey* .... (Capitol)
I'd Rather Go Blind
Etta James; *Best Blues Album In The World...Ever!-C* ...... (Virgin)
  Best Blues Album In The World...Ever!-C .... (Virgin)
I'd Really Love To See You Tonight
England Dan & John Ford Coley; *Best Of England Dan & John Ford*
  Coley .... (Big Tree)
  Hit Singles-1958-1977-C .... (Atlantic)
  Nights Are Forever Without You .... (Big Tree)
If Ever I See You Again
Roberta Flack; *Best Of Roberta Flack* .... (Atlantic)
If My Friends Could See Me Now
Original Cast/Gwen Verdon; *Sweet Charity* .... (Columbia)
If You Could Only See
Tonic; *Lemon Parade* .... (Polydor)
  Now That's What I Call Music!-#1-C .... (Virgin)
If You Could Only See Me Now
T. Graham Brown; *Bumper To Bumper* .... (Capitol)
If You Could See Me Now
Sarah Vaughan & Count Basie; *Pablo Today-Send In The Clowns* ...... (Pablo)
If You See Him/If You See Her
Brooks & Dunn & Reba McEntire; *If You See Her.* .... (Arista)
Reba McEntire & Brooks & Dunn; *If You See Her.* .... (MCA)
  Reba McEntire's Greatest Hits-#3: I'm A Survivor. .... (MCA)
If You See Kay
Memphis Slim/Tampa Red/Lonnie Johnson; *Bawdy Blues* .... (Bluesville)
I'll Be Seeing You
Billie Holiday; *Billie Holiday At Carnegie Hall-Billie Holiday*
  Story-#6 .... (Verve)
  Essential Billie Holiday-Carnegie Hall Concert .... (Verve)
Jackie Gleason; *Best Of Jackie Gleason & His Orchestra* .... (Curb)
Judy Collins; *Judith* .... (Elektra)
Skyliners; *Skyliners' Greatest Hits* .... (Original Sound)
Tommy Dorsey & Frank Sinatra; *Those Wonderful Years (WWII Love*
  Songs)-C .... (JCI Assoc. Labels)
Tommy Dorsey & His Orchestra; *Kiss The Boys Goodbye-Classic Songs Of*
  WWII-#1 .... (RCA)
I'll See You In My Dreams
Doris Day; *At The Movies* .... (Columbia)
Doris Day & Danny Thomas; *Calamity Jane/I'll See You In My*
  Dreams .... (Sony Music Special Prod.)
I'm Looking Through You
Beatles; *The Beatles-Anthology-#2* .... (Capitol)
In A Different Light
Doug Stone; *Doug Stone* .... (Epic)
In Another's Eyes
Trisha Yearwood & Garth Brooks; *Songbook-A Collection Of Hits* ..... (MCA)
Infinite Eyes
Keb' Mo'; *Big Wide Grin* .... (Sony Wonder)
Invisible Man
98 Degrees; *98 Degrees* .... (Motown)
I've Just Seen A Face
Beatles; *Rubber Soul* .... (Capitol)
Paul McCartney; *Unplugged (The Official Bootleg)* .... (Capitol)
Wings; *Wings Over America* .... (Capitol)
I've Never Seen The Likes Of You
Conway Twitty; *Heart & Soul* .... (MCA)
  Number Ones .... (MCA)
I've Seen All The Good People
Yes; *Classic Rock 1966-1988-C* .... (Atlantic)
  The Yes Album .... (Atlantic)
  Yessongs .... (Atlantic)

I've Seen Better Days
Tammy Wynette & George Jones; *Golden Ring* . . . .(Epic)
I've Seen Better Days
Reba McEntire; *Whoever's In New England* . . . .(MCA)
I've Seen That Face Before
Grace Jones; *Island Life* . . . . (Island)
Nightclubbing . . . . (Island)
I've Seen That Look On Me
George Strait; *Something Special* . . . .(MCA)
Willie Nelson; *Don't You Ever Get Tired Of Hurting Me* . . . .(RCA)
Willie . . . .(RCA)
I've Seen That Movie Too
Elton John; *Goodbye Yellow Brick Road* . . . . (Polydor)
I've Seen The Saucers
Elton John; *Caribou* . . . .(Rocket)
Johnny Have You Seen Her?
Rembrandts; *United* . . . . Atco)
Just To See Her
Smokey Robinson; *One Heartbeat* . . . . (Motown)
Just To See You Smile
Tim McGraw; *Everywhere* . . . . (Curb)
Tim McGraw's Greatest Hits . . . . (Curb)
Key West Intermezzo (I Saw You First)
John Mellencamp; *Mr. Happy Go Lucky* . . . . (Mercury)
Lady
D'Angelo; *Brown Sugar* . . . .(EMI)
Last Time I Saw Paris
Dinah Shore; *That's Entertainment-The Ultimate Anthology Of MGM
    Musicals-C* . . . . (Turner Classic Movies)
Jonathan & Darlene Edwards; *In Paris* . . . .(Corinthian)
Jonathan & Darlene Edwards' Greatest Hits . . . .(Corinthian)
Long As I Can See The Light
Creedence Clearwater Revival; *1970* . . . . (Fantasy)
Cosmo's Factory . . . . (Fantasy)
Creedence Clearwater Revival-Chronicle . . . . (Fantasy)
Long Time No See
Chicago; *Chicago VIII* . . . .(Chicago)
Long Time No See, Baby
Glenn Miller & His Orchestra; *Complete Glenn Miller & His
    Orchestra-#5* . . . . (Bluebird)
Complete Glenn Miller & His Orchestra-#9 . . . . (Bluebird)
Look At All Those Idiots
Simpsons; *Simpsons Sing The Blues* . . . .(Geffen)
Look At California
Maze featuring Frankie Beverly; *Live In New Orleans* . . . . (Capitol)
Maze featuring Frankie Beverly . . . . (Capitol)
Look At That
Paul Simon; *You're The One* . . . .(Warner Bros.)
Look At That Cadillac
Stray Cats; *Best Of Stray Cats-Rock This Town* . . . .(EMI)
Look Away
Chicago; *Chicago 19* . . . . (Reprise)
Chicago's Greatest Hits-1982-1989 . . . .(Full Moon)
The Heart Of Chicago-1967-1997 . . . . (Reprise)
Look Through Any Window
Hollies; *History Of British Rock-#6-C* . . . . (Rhino)
The Hollies' Greatest Hits . . . . (Epic)
Look What Love Has Done
Patty Smyth; *ST/Junior* . . . .(MCA)
Lookin' In The Same Direction
Ken Mellons; *Ken Mellons* . . . .(Epic)
Looking Back To See
Goldie Hill & Justin Tubb; *Justin Tubb-Star Of The Grand
    Ole Opry* . . . . (Starday)
Jim Ed Brown & Maxine Brown; *Essential Jim Ed Brown* . . . .(RCA)
Looking East
Jackson Browne; *Looking East* . . . . (Elektra)
Looking Through Your Eyes
LeAnn Rimes; *Sittin' On Top Of The World* . . . . (Curb)
ST/Quest For Camelot . . . . (Curb/Atlantic)
Love At First Sight
Outlaws; *Playin' To Win* . . . . (Arista)
Love At First Sight
Styx; *End Of The Century* . . . .(A&M)
Love At First Sight
Kylie Minogue; *Kylie* . . . . (Geffen)
Love At First Sight
Mello-Kings; *Mello-Kings' Greatest Hits* . . . . (Collectables)
Love Is Blind
Eve; *First Lady Of Ruff Ryders* . . . .(Ruff Ryders/IDJMG)
Love Saw It
Karyn White; *Karyn White* . . . .(Warner Bros.)
Loving Blind
Clint Black; *Put Yourself In My Shoes* . . . . (RCA)
Mama's Never Seen Those Eyes
Forester Sisters; *Forester Sisters* . . . . (Warner Bros.)
Matchbox
Beatles; *Past Masters-Volume Two* . . . . (Parlophone)

Rock 'N' Roll Music . . . . (Capitol)
Something New . . . . (Capitol)
Mental Picture
Jon Secada; *Heart, Soul & A Voice* . . . . (SBK)
ST/The Specialist . . . . (Epic/Sony Music Soundtrax)
Mirage
Tommy James And The Shondells; *Tommy James And The Shondells-
    Anthology* . . . . (Rhino)
Miss Me Blind
Culture Club; *Colour By Numbers* . . . . (Virgin)
More I See You
Boston Pops Orchestra/Arthur Fiedler; *Music For Every Mood-
    Yesterday* . . . .(RCA)
Chet Baker; *Chet Baker Sings It Could Happen
    To You* . . . . (Original Jazz Classics)
Chris Montez; *Bachelor Pad Pleasures-C* . . . . (Chronicles)
Dick Haymes; *Best Of Dick Haymes* . . . . (Curb)
Nat "King" Cole; *Very Thought Of You* . . . . (Capitol)
Most Beautiful Girl
Charlie Rich; *Behind Closed Doors* . . . . (Epic)
Charlie Rich's Greatest Hits . . . . (Epic)
Columbia Country Classics-#4-Nashville Sound-C . . . . (Columbia)
Music To Watch Girls By
Andy Williams; *Andy Williams' Greatest Hits-#2* . . . . (Columbia)
Mustang Burn
Jack Ingram; *Hey You* . . . .(Lucky Dog)
My Favorite Headache
Geddy Lee; *My Favorite Headache* . . . .(Anthem/Atlantic)
My Heart Stood Still
Bud Powell; *Genius Of Bud Powell-#2* . . . . (Verve)
Frank Sinatra; *The Concert Sinatra* . . . . (Reprise)
Tony Bennett; *Rodgers & Hart Songbook* . . . . (DRG)
My Hero
Foo Fighters; *The Colour And The Shape* . . . .(Roswell/RCA)
Never Saw A Miracle
Curtis Stigers; *Curtis Stigers* . . . . (Arista)
New York Mining Disaster 1941 (Mr. Jones)
Bee Gees; *Bee Gees-Gold* . . . .(Polydor)
Here At Last...Bee Gees...Live . . . . (Polydor)
History Of British Rock-#8-C . . . . (Rhino)
Next Time You See Her
Eric Clapton; *Slowhand* . . . .(Polydor)
Next Time You See Me
Little Junior Parker; *Best Of Little Junior Parker* . . . . (MCA)
Superblues-#2-All-Time Classic Blues-C . . . . (Stax)
Nobody Knows The Trouble I've Seen
Mahalia Jackson; *Gospels, Spirituals & Hymns* . . . . (Columbia)
Mahalia Jackson's Greatest Hits . . . . (Columbia)
Nat "King" Cole; *Every Time I Feel The Spirit* . . . . (Capitol)
Oh, Look At Me Now
Frank Sinatra; *a Swingin' Affair!* . . . . (Capitol)
Nancy Wilson; *But Beautiful* . . . . (Blue Note)
Sammy Kaye & His Orchestra; *Sammy Kaye & His Orchestra Play 22
    Original Big Band Recordings* . . . . (Hindsight)
Tommy Dorsey; *Boogie Woogie* . . . . (Pro-Arte)
Tommy Dorsey & Frank Sinatra; *Tommy Dorsey & Frank Sinatra's All-Time
    Greatest Hits-#1* . . . . (Bluebird)
Old Man And Me
Hootie & The Blowfish; *Fairweather Johnson* . . . .(Atlantic)
On A Clear Day (You Can See Forever)
Barbra Streisand; *Just For The Record* . . . . (Columbia)
Live Concert At The Forum . . . . (Columbia)
ST/On A Clear Day You Can See Forever . . . . . . (Columbia Special Prod.)
The Concert . . . . (Columbia)
Roger Williams; *Best Of Roger Williams* . . . . (MCA)
Somewhere In Time . . . . (Bainbridge)
One Vision
Queen; *A Kind Of Magic* . . . . (Hollywood)
Classic Queen . . . . (Hollywood)
Live At Wembley '86 . . . . (Hollywood)
Only A Lonely Heart Sees
Felix Cavaliere; *Castles In The Air* . . . . (Out Of Print)
Out Of Sight, Out Of Mind
Five Keys; *Golden Classics-Five Keys* . . . . (Collectables)
Outside
Staind; *Break The Cycle* . . . . (Flip/Elektra)
Outside Looking In
Mary Chapin Carpenter; *Stones In The Road* . . . . (Columbia)
Over Now
Alice In Chains; *Alice In Chains* . . . . (Columbia)
Pinball Wizard
Elton John; *Elton John's Greatest Hits-#2* . . . .(Polydor)
Pete Townshend; *Another Scoop* . . . . (Atco)
Pete Townshend's Deep End Live! . . . . (Atco)
Rod Stewart; *Best Of Rod Stewart* . . . . (Mercury)
Sing It Again, Rod . . . . (Mercury)
Storyteller/The Complete Anthology: 1964-1990 . . . . (Warner Bros.)
Who; *Meaty Beaty Big & Bouncy* . . . . (MCA)
ST/The Kids Are Alright . . . . (MCA)

ST/Tommy. . . . . (Polydor)
Tommy . . . . (MCA)
Who Greatest Hits. . . . . (MCA)
Who's Last . . . . (MCA)

Please Forgive Me
David Gray; White Ladder. . . . . (ATO/RCA)

Pretend You Don't See Her
Jerry Vale; Jerry Vale-17 Most Requested Songs . . . . (Legacy)
Jerry Vale's All-Time Greatest Hits . . . . (Columbia)
Jerry Vale's Greatest Hits . . . . (Columbia)

Pretty Fuck Look
Pussy Galore; Corpse Love-The First Year . . . . (Caroline)

Put Your Hands Where My Eyes Could See
Busta Rhymes; When Disaster Strikes. . . . . (Elektra)

Que Sera, Sera
Doris Day; Doris Day-16 Most Requested Songs-Encore! . . . . (Columbia)
Doris Day's Greatest Hits . . . . (Columbia)
Radio Classics Of The '50s-C . . . . (Columbia)
Sly & The Family Stone; Fresh . . . . (Legacy)
Sly & The Family Stone-Anthology . . . . (Epic)

Run, Come See Jerusalem
Arlo Guthrie & Pete Seeger; Precious Friend . . . . (Warner Bros.)

Santa Monica (Watch The World Die)
Everclear; Sparkle And Fade . . . . (Capitol)

See Emily Play
David Bowie; Bowie Pin Ups . . . . (Rykodisc)
Pink Floyd; Relics . . . . (Capitol)
Works . . . . (Capitol)

See Me In Your Eyes
38 Special; Tour De Force . . . . (A&M)

See Me, Feel Me
Who; ST/The Kids Are Alright . . . . (MCA)
Tommy . . . . (MCA)
Who's Last . . . . (MCA)

See My Way
Blodwyn Pig; Ahead Rings Out . . . . (A&M)

See My Way
Who; Happy Jack . . . . (MCA)

See Ruby Fall
Johnny Cash; Essential Johnny Cash . . . . (Columbia)

See The Changes
Crosby, Stills & Nash; CSN . . . . (Atlantic)
CSN. . . . . (Atlantic)

See The Funny Little Clown
Bobby Goldsboro; 10th Anniversary Album-#1 . . . . (EMI)
Bobby Goldsboro's Greatest Hits . . . . (Liberty)
Honey-Best Of Bobby Goldsboro . . . . (EMI)

See The Light
Aldo Nova; Aldo Nova. . . . . (Portrait)
Portrait Of Aldo Nova. . . . . (Epic)

See The Light
Marty Balin; Better Generation. . . . . (GWE)

See The Light
Five Americans; Nuggets-Classic Collection From The Psychedelic
'60s-C . . . . (Rhino)

See The Light
Jeff Healey Band; See The Light . . . . (Arista)

See The Light
Earth, Wind & Fire; That's The Way Of The World . . . . (Legacy)

See The Lights
Simple Minds; Real Life . . . . (A&M)

See The Sign Of Judgement
Birmingham Jubilee Singers; Complete Recorded Works-1926-
1927 . . . . (Document)

See The Sky About to Rain
Neil Young; On The Beach . . . . (Reprise)

See You
Depeche Mode; Broken Frame . . . . (Sire)
Catching Up With Depeche Mode. . . . . (Sire)

See You In Hell
Grim Reaper; See You In Hell . . . . (RCA)

See You In Hell (Don't Be Late)
Yngwie Malmsteen; Eclipse . . . . (Polydor)

See You In Hell, Blind Boy
Ry Cooder; ST/Crossroads . . . . (Warner Bros.)

See You In Paradise
Saints; All Fools Day. . . . . (TVT)

See You In Rio
Joyce; Music Inside . . . . (Verve/Forecast)

See You In September
Chiffons; Best Of The Chiffons . . . . (Laurie)
Happenings; ST/Purple People Eater . . . . (AJK Music)
Tempos; Cruisin'-1960-C . . . . (Increase)
ST/American Graffiti . . . . (MCA)

See You Later, Alligator
Bill Haley & His Comets; Bill Haley & His Comets . . . . (Everest)
Bill Haley & His Comets' Greatest Hits . . . . (MCA)
Bill Haley & His Comets-Golden Hits . . . . (MCA)
Billboard Top Rock 'N' Roll Hits-1956-C . . . . (Rhino)

Mr. Rock 'N' Roll . . . . (Accord)
Rock & Roll Is Here To Stay-C . . . . (Gusto)
Rockin' & Rollin' . . . . (Accord)

See You Next Year
Cleftones; Best Of The Cleftones . . . . (Rhino)

See You On The Other Side
Ozzy Osbourne; Ozzmosis . . . . (Epic)

See You Sometime
Joni Mitchell; For The Roses . . . . (Asylum)

See You When I Git There
Lou Rawls; Lou Rawls-Classics. . . . . (Philadelphia Int'l)
Lou Rawls-Live (Right Stuff) . . . . (Right Stuff)
Unmistakably Lou . . . . (Philadelphia Int'l)

Seein' My Father In Me
Paul Overstreet; Sowin' Love . . . . (RCA)

Seeing Is Believing
Three O'Clock; Sixteen Tambourines . . . . (Frontier)

Seeing Is Believing
Bobby King & Terry Evans; Live & Let Live . . . . (Rounder)

Seeing Is Believing
Mike & The Mechanics; Living Years . . . . (Atlantic)

Seeing The Elephant
Debby McClatchy & The Red Clay Ramblers; Debby McClatchy & The Red
Clay Ramblers . . . . (Green Linnet)

Seeing Things
Black Crowes; Shake Your Money Maker . . . . (Def American)

Seen Enough
Crosby, Stills, Nash & Young; Looking Forward . . . . (Reprise)

Seven Wonders
Fleetwood Mac; Tango In The Night . . . . (Warner Bros.)

She Blinded Me With Science
Thomas Dolby; Golden Age Of Wireless . . . . (Capitol)

She's Got That Look In Her Eyes
Alabama; Dancin' On The Boulevard . . . . (RCA)

Smile Like Yours
Natalie Cole; ST/A Smile Like Yours . . . . (Elektra)

Smoke Gets In Your Eyes
Bryan Ferry; Another Time Another Place. . . . . (Reprise)
Street Life-20 Great Hits . . . . (Reprise)
Dinah Washington; Golden Classics-Dinah Washington . . . . (Collectables)
Lawrence Welk; Musical Memories With Lawrence Welk. . . . . (Ranwood)
Patti Austin; Real Me . . . . (Qwest)
Platters; Encore Of Golden Hits-Platters . . . . (Mercury)
Oldies But Goodies-#14-C . . . . (Original Sound)
Platters Greatest Hits . . . . (Everest)
ST/Always . . . . (MCA)
ST/American Graffiti . . . . (MCA)
Super Oldies Of The '50s-#5-C . . . . (Audio Fidelity)

Snowblind
Black Sabbath; Black Sabbath-Vol. 4. . . . . (Warner Bros.)
We Sold Our Soul For Rock 'N' Roll . . . . (Warner Bros.)
Ozzy Osbourne; Speak Of The Devil . . . . (Jet)

Snowblind
Styx; Caught In The Act . . . . (A&M)
Paradise Theater. . . . . (A&M)

Snowblind Friend
David Allan Coe; Unchained . . . . (Columbia)
Hoyt Axton; Snowblind Friend . . . . (MCA)
Steppenwolf; Steppenwolf 7. . . . . (MCA)
Steppenwolf-16 Greatest Hits . . . . (MCA)

So Sad (To Watch Good Love Go Bad)
Everly Brothers; The Reunion Concert-Live At Albert Hall 1983 . . . . (Mercury)
Walk Right Back: The Everly Brothers On Warner Bros.-1960-
1969 . . . . (Warner Archives)
Frank Ifield; Best Of Frank Ifield . . . . (Curb)
Sweethearts Of The Rodeo; Columbia Country Classics-#5-A New
Tradition-C. . . . . (Columbia)

So You Like What You See
Samuelle; Living In Black Paradise . . . . (Atlantic)

Somebody's Out There Watching
Kinleys; Kinleys II . . . . (Epic)

Sound & Vision
David Bowie; Changestwobowie . . . . (RCA)
Low . . . . (Rykodisc)
Sound + Vision . . . . (Rykodisc)
The Singles-1969-1993 . . . . (Rykodisc)

Sour Girl
Stone Temple Pilots; No. 4. . . . . (Atlantic)

Standing On The Corner
Broadway Cast; Most Happy Fella . . . . (RCA)
Dean Martin; Best Of Dean Martin . . . . (CEMA Special Prod.)
Four Lads; Four Lads-16 Most Requested Songs. . . . . (Legacy)
Original Broadway Cast; Most Happy Fella . . . . (Sony Music Classical)

Staring At The Sun
U2; Pop . . . . (Island)

Stealin' Each Other Blind
Chip Taylor; 45-#4840. . . . . (Capitol)

Surrounded
Chantal Kreviazuk; Under These Rocks And Stones . . . . (Columbia)

Take A Look At My Face
Michael Bolton; *The Hunger* .... (Columbia)
Tell Me What You See
Beatles; *Beatles VI* .... (Capitol)
   Beatles-Box Set .... (Capitol)
   Beatles-Love Songs .... (Capitol)
Tell Me When
Human League; *Octopus* .... (East West)
Tennes-See Me
Jeannie C. Riley; *Here's Jeannie C. Riley* .... (Playback)
Theme From "Mr. Magoo"
Original Soundtrack; *Television's Greatest Hits-#3-1970s & 1980s-C* ... (TVT)
Then You Look At Me
Celine Dion; *All The Way...A Decade Of Song* .... (550 Music)
This Part Of Town
Widespread Panic; *Don't Tell The Band* .... (Widespread/SRG)
Three Blind Mice
Van Alexander; *Small Fry-Capitol Sings Kids Songs For Grownups-C* .... (Capitol)
To See My Angel Cry
Conway Twitty; *Conway Twitty-Number Ones-#1* .... (Liberty)
   Conway Twitty's Greatest Hits-#1 .... (MCA)
To See My Angel In Virginia
Livewire; *Wired* .... (Rounder)
Tomorrow We'll See
Sting; *Brand New Day* .... (A&M)
Tucker's Town
Hootie & The Blowfish; *Fairweather Johnson* .... (Atlantic)
Turn A Blind Eye
Call; *Modern Romans* .... (Mercury)
   Walls Came Down-Best Of The Mercury Years .... (Mercury)
Turn Around, Look At Me
Vogues; *Vogues' Greatest Hits* .... (Rhino)
Up Above My Head/Blind Bartimus
Marty Stuart with Jerry & Tammy Sullivan; *Red Hot + Country-C* ... (Mercury)
Veni-Vidi-Vici (I Came, I Saw, I Conquered)
Gaylords; *Best Of The Gaylords* .... (Chronicles)
Vision Of A Child
Steve Young; *Honky Tonk Man* .... (Rounder)
Vision Of A Kiss
B-52's; *Good Stuff* .... (Reprise)
Vision Of Mother
Ricky Skaggs; *Don't Cheat In Our Hometown* .... (Epic)
Stanley Brothers; *Complete Columbia Stanley Brothers* .... (Legacy)
Vision Of The Future
Roachford; *Get Ready!* .... (Epic)
Vision Of You
Belinda Carlisle; *Belinda Carlisle-Her Greatest Hits* .... (MCA)
   Runaway Horses .... (MCA)
Visions
Commodores; *Natural High* .... (Motown)
Visions
Stevie Wonder; *Innervisions* .... (Motown)
Visions
Eagles; *One Of These Nights* .... (Asylum)
Visions In Blue
Ultravox; *Ultravox-Collection* .... (Chrysalis)
Visions Of Angels
Genesis; *Trespass* .... (MCA)
Visions Of China
Japan; *Oil On Canvas* .... (Blue Plate)
   Tin Drum .... (Blue Plate)
Visions Of Johanna
Bob Dylan; *Biograph* .... (Columbia)
   Blonde On Blonde .... (Columbia)
Visions Of Paradise
Moody Blues; *In Search Of The Lost Chord* .... (Polydor)
Watch Me Bleed
Tears For Fears; *The Hurting* .... (Mercury)
Watch Me Do My Thing
Immature; *ST/All That* .... (Loud/RCA)
Watch My .38
Commander Cody & His Lost Planet Airmen; *Hot Licks, Cold Steel & Trucker's Favorites* .... (MCA)
Watch The Moon Come Down
Graham Parker And The Rumour; *Stick To Me* .... (Mercury)
   The Parkerilla .... (Mercury)
Watch The Sun Go Down
X; *Ain't Love Grand* .... (Elektra)
Watch This
Clay Walker; *Rumor Has It* .... (Giant)
Watch What Happens (Lola's Theme)
Frank Sinatra; *My Way* .... (Reprise)
Henry Mancini; *Mancini Magic* .... (Pair)
Sergio Mendes; *Foursider* .... (A&M)
Watcher Of The Skies
Genesis; *Foxtrot* .... (Atlantic)
   Genesis-Live .... (Atlantic)

Watching Me Watching You
Jethro Tull; *The Broadsword And The Beast* .... (Chrysalis)
Watching Out For Jesus
Rave-Ups; *Chance* .... (Epic)
Watching Scotty Grow
Bobby Goldsboro; *Bobby Goldsboro's All-Time Greatest Hits* .... (Curb)
   Honey-Best Of Bobby Goldsboro .... (EMI)
Mac Davis; *Mac Davis' Greatest Hits* .... (Columbia)
Watching The Clothes
Pretenders; *Learning To Crawl* .... (Sire)
Watching The Detectives
Elvis Costello; *Girls Girls Girls* .... (Columbia)
   My Aim Is True .... (Columbia)
Elvis Costello & The Attractions; *Best Of Elvis Costello & The Attractions* .... (Columbia)
Watching The River Flow
Bob Dylan; *Bob Dylan's Greatest Hits-#2* .... (Columbia)
Joe Cocker; *Luxury You Can Afford* .... (Asylum)
Watching The River Run
Loggins & Messina; *Full Sail* .... (Columbia)
   The Best Of Friends .... (Columbia)
Watching The World Go By
Gun; *Gallus* .... (A&M)
Way You Love Me, The
Faith Hill; *Breathe* .... (Warner Bros.)
   Totally Hits-#3-C .... (Atlantic)
We Can Work It Out
Beatles; *"Yesterday"...And Today* .... (Capitol)
   Beatles 1 .... (Capitol)
   Beatles-20 Greatest Hits .... (Capitol)
   Beatles-Box Set .... (Capitol)
   Past Masters-Volume Two .... (Parlophone)
   The Beatles/1962-1966 .... (Capitol)
Paul McCartney; *Unplugged (The Official Bootleg)* .... (Capitol)
Stevie Wonder; *Beatles Songs By Greatest Stars* .... (Motown)
   Signed Sealed & Delivered .... (Motown)
   Stevie Wonder's Greatest Hits-#2 .... (Motown)
   Top 10 With A Bullet-Motown Solo Stars-C .... (Motown)
We Didn't See A Thing
Ray Charles/George Jones/Chet Atkins; *Friendship-C* .... (Columbia)
We're Off To See The Wizard
Jewel/Jackson Browne/Ry Cooder; *The Wizard Of Oz In Concert: Dreams Come True-C* .... (Rhino)
Judy Garland; *A&E Biography: A Musical Anthology* .... (Capitol)
Original Cast; *The Wizard Of Oz* .... (TVT)
Original Soundtrack; *The Wizard Of Oz-Selections From The Original Motion Picture Soundtrack* .... (Turner Classic Movies)
What Does A Woman See In A Man
Jimmy Webb; *Suspending Disbelief* .... (Elektra)
When Can I See You
Babyface; *For The Cool In You* .... (Epic)
When Can I See You Again
Babyface; *For The Cool In You* .... (Epic)
When I See You Smile
Bad English; *Bad English* .... (Epic)
   Keep On Loving You-C .... (Columbia Special Prod.)
   Read The Hits-Best Of The '80s-C .... (Sony Music Special Prod.)
When Will I See You Again
Three Degrees; *Didn't It Blow Your Mind: Soul Hits Of The '70s-#14-C* .... (Rhino)
   Mega Hits Dance Classics-#2-C .... (Priority)
When Will I See You Smile Again?
Bell Biv Devoe; *Poison* .... (MCA)
   WBBD-Bootcity-Remix Album .... (MCA)
While You See A Chance
Steve Winwood; *Arc Of A Diver* .... (Island)
   Steve Winwood-Chronicles .... (Island)
Why Didn't You Call Me
Macy Gray; *On How Life Is* .... (Epic)
Why Don't We Do It In The Road
Beatles; *Beatles-Box Set* .... (Capitol)
   The Beatles (White Album) .... (Capitol)
Window Up Above
George Jones; *Cup Of Loneliness-Classic Mercury Years* ..... (Mercury)
   George Jones' All-Time Greatest Hits .... (Epic)
   George Jones-Super Hits .... (Epic)
   George Jones-Super Hits .... (Epic)
Hank Wilson; *Hank Wilson's Back, Vol. 1* .... (Right Stuff)
Hot Rize; *Red Knuckle-Hot Rize Live* .... (Flying Fish)
Johnny Cash; *Back To Back* .... (K-Tel)
Mickey Gilley; *Mickey Gilley's Greatest Hits-#1* .... (Epic)
   Ten Years Of Hits .... (Epic)
Ralph Stanley; *Clinch Mountain Country* .... (Rebel)
Ricky Skaggs; *Ricky Skaggs-Country Boy* .... (Epic)
Wanda Jackson; *Wanda Jackson-Vintage Collection* .... (Capitol)
Woman In Me
Jessica Simpson featuring Destiny's Child; *Sweet Kisses* ...... (Columbia)
Yellow
Coldplay; *Now That's What I Call Music!-#6-C* .... (Virgin)

    Parachutes . . . . (Nettwerk/Capitol)
You Ain't Seen Nothing Yet
    Bachman-Turner Overdrive; *Best Of B.T.O.-So Far* . . . . (Mercury)
      Metal Age-Roots Of Metal-C . . . . (Rhino)
      Not Fragile . . . . (Mercury)
You Just Watch Me
    Tanya Tucker; *Soon* . . . . (Liberty)
You Sang To Me
    Marc Anthony; *Marc Anthony* . . . . (Columbia)
You Won't See Me
    Anne Murray; *Anne Murray's Greatest Hits* . . . . (Capitol)
      Love Song . . . . (Capitol)
    Beatles; *Beatles-Box Set* . . . . (Capitol)
      Rubber Soul . . . . (Capitol)
    Bryan Ferry; *These Foolish Things* . . . . (Reprise)
You Won't See Me Cry
    Wilson Phillips; *Shadows & Light* . . . . (SBK)
You'll See
    Madonna; *Something To Remember* . . . . (Maverick/Sire)
Zero And Blind Terry
    Bruce Springsteen; *Tracks* . . . . (Columbia)

SEPARATION, Being Apart

    See Also: DISTANCE, DIVORCE, LEAVING, LOVE (various),
      LONELY, RETURNING, SADNESS, SOLITUDE,
      TRAVELING, WAITING

Ain't No Mountain High Enough
    Diana Ross; *20/20-C* . . . . (Motown)
      25 #1 Hits From 25 Years-C . . . . (Motown)
      Diana Ross . . . . (Motown)
      Diana Ross-The Ultimate Collection . . . . (Motown)
      Every Great Motown Song-First 25 Years-C . . . . (Motown)
      Greatest Songs By Ashford & Simpson . . . . (Motown)
      Motown Legends-Diana Ross . . . . (Motown)
      Motown Story-First 25 Years-C . . . . (Motown)
      Motown's Biggest Pop Hits-C . . . . (Motown)
      TV ST/Diana-C . . . . (Motown)
    Marvin Gaye & Tammi Terrell; *20 Greatest Songs In Motown*
      History-C . . . . (Motown)
      Classic Duets-Marvin Gaye & His Women-C . . . . (Motown)
      Marvin Gaye & Tammi Terrell's Greatest Hits . . . . (Motown)
      Marvin Gaye Live At The London Palladium . . . . (Motown)
      Motown Grammy R&B Performances Of The '60s & '70s-C . (Motown)
      Performances Of The '60s & '70s-C. . . . . (Motown)
      United . . . . (Motown)
All My Loving
    Beatles; *Meet The Beatles!* . . . . (Capitol)
      The Beatles At The Hollywood Bowl. . . . . (Capitol)
      The Beatles/1962-1966. . . . . (Capitol)
      With The Beatles . . . . (Parlophone)
Amukiriki
    Les Paul; *Legend And The Legacy* . . . . (Gold Rush)
As I Lay Me Down
    Sophie B. Hawkins; *Whaler.* . . . . (Columbia)
Auf Wiederseh'n, My Dear
    Greta Keller; *These Foolish Things* . . . . (ASV)
Auf Wiedersehn-Sweetheart
    Vera Lynn; *Those Wonderful Years: Tenderly-C* . . . . (JCI Assoc. Labels)
Austin
    Blake Shelton; *Blake Shelton.* . . . . (Giant)
By The Time I Get To Phoenix
    Glen Campbell; *All-Time Country Classics-#1-C* . . . . (Capitol)
      Glen Campbell-Classics Collection . . . . (Capitol)
      Glen Campbell-Live . . . . (Capitol)
      Glen Campbell's Greatest Hits . . . . (Capitol)
      Very Best Of Glen Campbell . . . . (Capitol)
    Reba McEntire; *Starting Over.* . . . . (MCA)
Cara Mia
    Jay & The Americans; *I Got Rhythm-C* . . . . (K-Tel)
      Jay & The Americans' Greatest Hits . . . . (CEMA Special Prod.)
      Jay & The Americans' Greatest Hits . . . . (Curb)
Carrying Your Love With Me
    George Strait; *Carrying Your Love With Me* . . . . (MCA)
      Latest Greatest Straitest Hits . . . . (MCA)
Cherokee Maiden
    Asleep At The Wheel; *Ride With Bob-C* . . . . (DreamWorks/SKG)
    Merle Haggard; *All Time Greatest Hits Of Country-C.* . . . . (Curb)
      Capitol Collectors Series-Merle Haggard . . . . (Capitol)
Corrina, Corrina
    Asleep At The Wheel featuring Brooks & Dunn; *Tribute To The Music Of*
      Bob Wills And The Texas Playboys-C . . . . (Liberty)
    Big Joe Turner; *Best Of Big Joe Turner.* . . . . (Pablo)
      Big Joe Turner's Greatest Hits . . . . (Atlantic)
    Bob Dylan; *Freewheelin'* . . . . (Columbia)
    Ray Peterson; *Good Old Rock & Roll-C* . . . . . (International Mktg. Group)
      Super Hits-#1-C . . . . (Gusto)

    Steppenwolf; *Live Steppenwolf* . . . . (MCA)
Cover You In Kisses
    John Michael Montgomery; *Leave A Mark* . . . . (Atlantic)
Dedicated To The One I Love
    Mamas & The Papas; *Best Of The Mamas & The Papas* . . . . . . (MCA)
      Farewell To The First Golden Era . . . . (MCA)
      Original Classic Oldies Of The '50s & '60s-#13-C. . . . . . . (MCA)
    Shirelles; *Oldies But Goodies-#10-C* . . . . (Original Sound)
      Shirelles' Greatest Hits . . . . (Everest)
      Shirelles-Anthology 1959-1964. . . . . (Rhino)
      Super Oldies Of The '50s-#4-C . . . . (Audio Fidelity)
Don't Be Cruel
    Cheap Trick; *Cheap Trick's Greatest Hits* . . . . (Epic)
      Lap Of Luxury . . . . (Epic)
    Elvis Presley; *Billboard Top Rock 'N' Roll Hits-1956-C* . . . . . . (Rhino)
      Nipper's Greatest Hits Of The '50s-#2-C . . . . (RCA)
      Number One Hits. . . . . (RCA)
      The Great Performances . . . . (RCA)
      The Top Ten Hits . . . . (RCA)
    Judds; *Heartland* . . . . (MCA)
Don't Let The Stars Get In Your Eyes
    Perry Como; *Como's Golden Records* . . . . (RCA)
      Perry Como-Pure Gold . . . . (RCA)
      Perry Como's All-Time Greatest Hits-#1 . . . . (RCA)
      This Is Perry Como . . . . (RCA)
Everytime You Go Away
    Daryl Hall & John Oates; *Best Of Daryl Hall & John Oates* . . . . . (RCA)
      Voices . . . . (RCA)
    Paul Young; *From Time To Time-The Singles Collection* . . . . . (Columbia)
      Secret Of Association . . . . (Columbia)
      T.J. Martell-Music For The Miracle-C . . . . . . (Epic Portrait Assoc.)
Exile
    Enya; *Watermark.* . . . . (Reprise)
Fare Thee Well Love
    Rankin Family; *North Country.* . . . . (Guardian/Angel)
      The Rankins-Collection. . . . . (Rounder)
Forever Love
    Reba McEntire; *If You See Him* . . . . (MCA)
      Reba McEntire's Greatest Hits-#3: I'm A Survivor. . . . . (MCA)
From A Distance
    Bette Midler; *Some People's Lives.* . . . . (Atlantic)
    Byrds; *20 Essential Tracks From The Box Set* . . . . (Columbia)
      The Byrds . . . . (Columbia)
    Judy Collins; *Fires Of Eden* . . . . (Columbia)
    Kathy Mattea; *Time Passes By.* . . . . (Mercury)
    Nanci Griffith; *Lone Star State Of Mind.* . . . . (MCA)
      One Fair Summer Evening . . . . (MCA)
Golden Heart
    Mark Knopfler; *Golden Heart* . . . . (Warner Bros.)
Got A Letter From My Kid Today
    Asleep At The Wheel; *Tribute To The Music Of Bob Wills And The Texas*
      Playboys-C. . . . . (Liberty)
    Merle Haggard & The Strangers; *18 Rare Classics* . . . . (Curb)
      Working Man Can't Get Nowhere Today . . . . (Capitol)
Harbor Lights
    Boz Scaggs; *Silk Degrees.* . . . . (Columbia)
    Dinah Washington; *Complete Dinah Washington On Mercury-#2-1950-*
      1952 . . . . (Mercury)
      Dinah Washington-Golden Hits . . . . (Mercury)
      For Lonely Lovers . . . . (Mercury)
      This Is My Story . . . . (Mercury)
    Platters; *Super Oldies Of The '60s-#9-C* . . . . (Audio Fidelity)
Hard To Say I'm Sorry
    Az Yet; *Az Yet* . . . . (LaFace)
    Chicago; *Chicago 16* . . . . (Full Moon/Warner Bros.)
High Country Snows
    Dan Fogelberg; *High Country Snows.* . . . . (Full Moon)
Home Again
    Carole King; *Tapestry* . . . . (Epic)
Homeward Bound
    Paul Simon; *Paul Simon In Concert/Live Rhymin'.* . . . . (Columbia)
    Paul Simon & George Harrison; *Nobody's Child-Romanian Angel*
      Appeal-C . . . . (Warner Bros.)
    Simon & Garfunkel; *Collected Works* . . . . (Columbia)
      Parsley Sage Rosemary & Thyme . . . . (Columbia)
      Simon & Garfunkel's Greatest Hits . . . . (Columbia)
      The Concert In Central Park . . . . (Warner Bros.)
    Willie Nelson & Waylon Jennings; *Take It To The Limit* . . . . . (Columbia)
Honey Pie
    Beatles; *The Beatles (White Album)* . . . . (Capitol)
      The Beatles-Anthology-#3. . . . . (Capitol)
How Do I Live
    LeAnn Rimes; *Absolute Dance Hits-C.* . . . . (Curb)
      You Light Up My Life-Inspirational Songs . . . . (Curb)
    Trisha Yearwood; *Songbook-A Collection Of Hits* . . . . (MCA)
I Am Yours
    Derek And The Dominos; *Layla* . . . . (Polydor)
I Can Dream, Can't I?
    Andrews Sisters; *Best Of The Andrews Sisters?* . . . . (MCA)

I Don't Know You Anymore
Savage Garden; *Affirmation* .... (Columbia)
I Guess That's Why They Call It The Blues
Elton John; *Elton John's Greatest Hits-1976-1986* ...(MCA)
  Too Low For Zero ....(MCA)
I Love You Drops
Bill Anderson; *Bill Anderson's Greatest Hits* ....(Varese Sarabande)
I Will
Beatles; *The Beatles (White Album)* .... (Capitol)
  The Beatles-Anthology-#3 .... (Capitol)
Ben Taylor; *ST/Bye Bye, Love* .... (Giant)
Dean Martin; *Dean Martin's Greatest Hits* ....(EMI)
If My Heart Had Wings
Faith Hill; *Breathe* ....(Warner Bros.)
I'll Be Seeing You
Billie Holiday; *Billie Holiday At Carnegie Hall-Billie Holiday*
  Story-#6 .... (Verve)
  Essential Billie Holiday-Carnegie Hall Concert ...... (Verve)
Jackie Gleason; *Best Of Jackie Gleason & His Orchestra* ....(Curb)
Judy Collins; *Judith* ....(Elektra)
Skyliners; *Skyliners' Greatest Hits* .... (Original Sound)
Tommy Dorsey & Frank Sinatra; *Those Wonderful Years (WWII Love*
  Songs)-C .... (JCI Assoc. Labels)
Tommy Dorsey & His Orchestra; *Kiss The Boys Goodbye-Classic Songs Of*
  WWII-#1 .... (RCA)
I'll Hold You In My Heart (Till I Can Hold You In My Arms)
Eddy Arnold; *Best Of Eddy Arnold* .... (RCA)
  Eddy Arnold-The Hits .... (Mercury)
  Memories Are Made Of This .... (Mercury)
I'll Walk Alone
Dinah Shore; *Dinah Shore's Greatest Hits* .... (Curtom)
I'm Already There
Lonestar; *I'm Already There* .... (BNA)
I'm Thinking Tonight Of My Blue Eyes
Gene Autry; *All Time Legends Of Country Music-C* .... (Legacy)
In A Perfect World
Lorrie Morgan; *Shakin' Things Up* .... (BNA)
It Might As Well Rain Until September
Carole King; *More American Graffiti-C* ....(MCA)
It Won't Be Long
Beatles; *Meet The Beatles!* .... (Capitol)
  With The Beatles .... (Parlophone)
It's Been A Long, Long Time
Bing Crosby; *Best Of Bing Crosby* ....(MCA)
Harry James & His Orchestra; *Words & Music Of World*
  War II-C .... (Columbia)
Harry James & Kitty Kallen; *Best Of The Big Bands-C* ..... (Columbia)
Jan Garber & His Orchestra; *Best Of Jan Garber* ....(MCA)
Louis Armstrong; *Hello Dolly! & Other Hits* ....(MCA)
Jimmy Mack
Martha & The Vandellas; *Billboard Top R&B Hits-1967-C* ..... (Rhino)
  Compact Command Performances-Martha Reeves & The
  Vandellas .... (Motown)
  Martha Reeves & The Vandellas-Anthology .... (Motown)
  Motown Story-First 25 Years-C .... (Motown)
  Motown Superstar Series-#11-Martha Reeves & The Vandellas .... (Motown)
  Top 10 With A Bullet-Motown Girl Groups-C .... (Motown)
Kansas City Song
Buck Owens; *Buck Owens Collection-1959-1990* .... (Rhino)
Kathy's Song
Simon & Garfunkel; *Collected Works* .... (Columbia)
  Simon & Garfunkel's Greatest Hits .... (Columbia)
  Sounds Of Silence .... (Columbia)
Kiss The Rain
Billie Myers; *A Taste Of '98-C* .... (Universal)
  Growing Pains .... (Universal)
Lara's Theme
Maurice Jarre Orchestra; *Hollywood's Great*
  Composers-C .... (Columbia Special Prod.)
MGM Studio Orchestra; *ST/Dr. Zhivago* ....(MCA)
Last Train To Clarksville
Monkees; *Monkees* .... (Arista)
  Monkees' Greatest Hits .... (Rhino)
  Monkees-Live-1967 .... (Rhino)
  Then & Now...The Best Of The Monkees .... (Arista)
Lay Down Your Arms
Chordettes; *Best Of The Chordettes* .... (Rhino)
Leaving On A Jet Plane
Chantal Kreviazuk; *ST/Armageddon-The Album* .... (Columbia)
John Denver; *John Denver's Greatest Hits* .... (RCA)
  Rhymes & Reasons .... (RCA)
Kendalls; *Super Country Hits Of The '70s-C* .... (Gusto)
Peter, Paul & Mary; *10 Years Together/The Best Of Peter, Paul*
  and Mary ....(Warner Bros.)
  Album 1700 ....(Warner Bros.)
Letter, The
Box Tops; *Billboard Top Rock 'N' Roll Hits-1967-C* ..... (Rhino)
  Box Tops' Greatest Hits .... (Rhino)
  Cruisin'-1967-C .... (Increase)

Oldies But Goodies-#12-C ....(Original Sound)
  Rockin' '60s-C .... (Priority)
Joe Cocker; *Joe Cocker Live* .... (Capitol)
  Joe Cocker-Classics-#4 .... (A&M)
  Joe Cocker's Greatest Hits .... (A&M)
  Mad Dogs & Englishmen .... (A&M)
Vernon Green & The Medallions; *Oldies But Goodies-#1-C* ...(Original Sound)
  Vernon Green & The Medallions-Golden Classics .... (Collectables)
Lili Marlene
Marlene Dietrich; *Best Of Marlene Dietrich* .... (Columbia)
  Essential Marlene Dietrich .... (Capitol)
  Live At The Cafe De Paris .... (Columbia)
  This Is Art Deco-C .... (Columbia)
Long Ago And Far Away
Erroll Garner; *Long Ago And Far Away* .... (Columbia)
Glenn Miller; *Glenn Miller-A Legendary Performer-#1 & 2* .... (Bluebird)
Helen Forrest & Dick Haymes; *American Songbook Series-*
  Jerome Kern .... (Smithsonian Collection)
Jo Stafford; *Capitol Collectors Series-Jo Stafford* .... (Capitol)
  International Hits .... (Corinthian)
  Jukebox Saturday Night-Great Vocal Hits-C .... (Capitol)
  Songs That Got Us Through WWII-C .... (Rhino)
  ST/Bugsy .... (Epic)
Johnny Mathis; *Hollywood Musicals* .... (Columbia)
Mantovani; *More Golden Hits* .... (London)
Perry Como; *Always In My Heart-Classic Songs Of World War II-#2* .... (RCA)
Rosemary Clooney; *Rosemary Clooney Sings The Lyrics Of Ira*
  Gershwin .... (Concord Jazz)
Long Live Our Love
Shangri-Las; *Best Of The Shangri-Las* .... (Mercury)
Love Travels
Kathy Mattea; *Love Travels* .... (Mercury)
Message To Michael
Dionne Warwick; *Dionne Warwick* .... (Everest)
  Dionne Warwick Greatest Hits .... (Everest)
  Dionne Warwick-Anthology 1962-1971 .... (Rhino)
  Hot! Live & Otherwise .... (Arista)
  Original Rock 'N' Roll Hits Of The '60s-C ...... (Roulette)
Miss You
Mick Jagger & Keith Richards; *The Concert For New York City-C* .. (Columbia)
Rolling Stones; *Rewind (1971-1984)* .... (Rolling Stones)
  Some Girls .... (Virgin)
  Flashpoint .... (Virgin)
Missing My Baby
Selena; *Dreaming Of You* ....(EMI Latin)
Missing You
Mary J. Blige; *Share My World* .... (MCA)
  The Tour .... (MCA)
Moonlight Mile
Rolling Stones; *Sticky Fingers* .... (Virgin)
Morning Side Of The Mountain, The
Tommy Edwards; *It's All In The Game-The Complete Hits Of Tommy*
  Edwards ....(Eric)
My Antonia
Emmylou Harris; *Red Dirt Girl* .... (Nonesuch)
My Bonnie Lies Over The Ocean
Beatles With Tony Sheridan; *History Of British Rock-#5-C* .... (Rhino)
  The Beatles featuring Tony Sheridan-In The Beginning (Circa
  1960) ....(Polydor)
Ed McCurdy; *Best Of Ed McCurdy* ....(Tradition)
Mitch Miller; *Favorite Irish Sing-Alongs* .... (Legacy)
My Boyfriend's Back
Angels; *Billboard Top Rock 'N' Roll Hits-1963-C* ..... (Rhino)
  Girl Groups-Story Of A Sound-C .... (Rhino)
  My Boyfriend's Back .... (Collectables)
  Oldies But Goodies-#11-C ....(Original Sound)
  ST/The Wanderers .... (Warner Bros.)
  Wonder Women-#2-History Of Girl Group-C .... (Rhino)
Navy Blue
Diane Renay; *Growin' Up Too Fast-The Girl Group Anthology-C* .... (Mercury)
Never There
Cake; *Now That's What I Call Music!-#2-C* ....(Virgin)
  Prolonging The Magic .... (Capricorn)
No Other Love
Perry Como; *Easy Listening* ....(Pair)
On My Own
Original Broadway Cast; *Les Miserables* .... (Geffen)
Open Up My Window
Christopher Cross; *Window* .... (Rhythm Safari)
P.S. I Love You
Bette Midler; *ST/For The Boys* ....(Atlantic)
Billie Holiday; *Lady Sings The Blues* .... (Verve)
Bing Crosby; *Thanks For The Memories Mr. Crosby* .... (J-Bird)
Dion; *Dion-His Best* ....(Laurie)
Kay Starr; *Too Marvelous For Words-Capitol Sings Jonny Mercer-C* .. (Capitol)
Mel Torme; *That's All* .... (Sony Music Special Prod.)
Rosemary Clooney; *Rosemary Clooney Sings The Lyrics Of Johnny*
  Mercer .... (Concord Jazz)
Tom T. Hall; *Natural Dreams* .... (Mercury)

Woody Herman; *Best Of The Big Bands-C* . . . (Columbia)

P.S. I Love You
Beatles; *Beatles-Box Set* . . . (Capitol)
Beatles-Love Songs . . . (Capitol)
Introducing...The Beatles . . . (Vee-Jay)
Please Please Me . . . (Parlophone)
The Early Beatles . . . (Capitol)

Please Mister Postman
Beatles; *Beatles-Box Set* . . . (Capitol)
The Beatles' Second Album . . . (Capitol)
With The Beatles . . . (Parlophone)
Carpenters; *Carpenters-Classics-#2* . . . (A&M)
Horizon . . . (A&M)
Yesterday Once More . . . (A&M)
Marvelettes; *Billboard Top Rock 'N' Roll Hits-1961-C* . . . (Rhino)
Marvelettes' Greatest Hits . . . (Motown)
Marvelettes-Anthology . . . (Motown)
Motown Story-First 25 Years-C . . . (Motown)

Poor Butterfly
Sarah Vaughan; *Compact Jazz-Sarah Vaughan* . . . (Verve)
Live In Japan . . . (Mainstream)
Sarah Vaughan-Golden Hits . . . (Mercury)
Sonny Rollins; *Best Of Sonny Rollins-The Blue Note Years* . . . (Blue Note)
Sonny Rollins-Vol. 2 . . . (Blue Note)

Pretty Little Dogies
Skip Gorman; *A Cowboy's Wild Song To His Herd* . . . (Rounder)

Save Your Heart For Me
Gary Lewis And The Playboys; *Gary Lewis & The Playboys* . . . (Gold Rush)
Gary Lewis And The Playboys' Greatest Hits . . . (Curb)

Sealed With A Kiss
Bobby Vinton; *Bobby Vinton's Greatest Hits* . . . (Curb)
Brian Hyland; *Cruisin'-1962-C* . . . (Increase)
Oldies But Goodies-#2-C . . . (Original Sound)
Original Rock 'N' Roll Hits Of The '50s-C . . . (Roulette)
Lettermen; *Best Of The Lettermen-#2* . . . (Capitol)
Capitol Collectors Series-The Lettermen . . . (Capitol)

Separate Lives
Phil Collins; *Serious Hits...Live!* . . . (Atlantic)
Phil Collins & Marilyn Martin; *ST/White Nights* . . . (Atlantic)

Silver Wings
Merle Haggard; *More Of The Best* . . . (Rhino)
The Seashores Of Old Mexico . . . (Epic)
Merle Haggard & Jewel; *For The Record: Merle Haggard-43 Legendary Hits* . . . (BNA)
Merle Haggard & The Strangers; *Okie From Muskogee* . . . (Capitol)
Songs I'll Always Sing . . . (Capitol)
Pam Tillis; *Mama's Hungry Eyes-Merle Haggard Tribute-C* . . . (Arista)

So Far Away
Carole King; *A Natural Worman: The Ode Collection-1968-1976* . . . (Legacy)
Tapestry . . . (Epic)
Rod Stewart; *If We Fall In Love Tonight* . . . (Warner Bros.)
Tapestry Revisited: Tribute To Carole King-C . . . (Lava)

Soldier Boy
Shirelles; *Billboard Top Rock 'N' Roll Hits-1962-C* . . . (Rhino)
Oldies But Goodies-#4-C . . . (Original Sound)
Shirelles-Anthology 1959-1964 . . . (Rhino)
ST/The Wanderers . . . (Warner Bros.)

Someday We'll Be Together
Diana Ross & The Supremes; *20/20-C* . . . (Motown)
Diana Ross & The Supremes' Greatest Hits-#3 . . . (Motown)
Diana Ross & The Supremes-Anthology (1962-1969) . . . (Motown)
Evening With Diana Ross . . . (Motown)
Motown Story-First 25 Years-C . . . (Motown)
Motown Superstar Series-#1-Diana Ross & The Supremes . . . (Motown)

Something To Remember You By
Dinah Shore; *Blues In The Night* . . . (ASV)
Judy Garland & Bing Crosby; *Mail Call! Armed Forces Radio Broadcasts* . . . (Laserlight)
Libby Holman; *78-#4910* . . . (Brunswick)

Somewhere Out There
James Ingram & Linda Ronstadt; *The Power Of Great Music* . . . (Warner Bros.)
Linda Ronstadt & James Ingram; *ST/An American Tail* . . . (MCA)

Standing Outside A Broken Phone Booth With Money In My Hand
Primitive Radio Gods; *MTV Best Of The Buzz Bin-#2-C* . . . (Mammoth)
Rocket . . . (Ergo)

Summer Rain
Carl Thomas; *Emotional* . . . (Bad Boy/Arista)

Summer Song
Chad & Jeremy; *Best Of Chad & Jeremy* . . . (K-Tel)
Capitol Gold-Best Of Chad & Jeremy . . . (Capitol)
History Of British Rock-#2-C . . . (Rhino)

Sweet Dreams
Air Supply; *Air Supply's Greatest Hits* . . . (Arista)
The One That You Love . . . (Arista)

Take The Highway
Marshall Tucker Band; *Best Of The Marshall Tucker Band-The Capricorn Years* . . . (Era)
Marshall Tucker Band . . . (AJK Music)
Where We All Belong . . . (AJK Music)

Taste Of Honey
Barbra Streisand; *The Barbra Streisand Album* . . . (Columbia)
Beatles; *Beatles-Box Set* . . . (Capitol)
Please Please Me . . . (Parlophone)
The Early Beatles . . . (Capitol)
Herb Alpert; *Midnight Sun* . . . (A&M)
Herb Alpert & The Tijuana Brass; *Herb Alpert & The Tijuana Brass' Greatest Hits* . . . (A&M)
Herb Alpert & The Tijuana Brass-Classics-#1 . . . (A&M)
Tony Bennett; *Forty Years-The Artistry Of Tony Bennett* . . . (Columbia)

Telefone (Long Distance Love Affair)
Sheena Easton; *Best Kept Secret* . . . (EMI)
Sheena Easton's Greatest Hits . . . (EMI Special Markets)
The World Of Sheena Easton: The Singles Collection-C . . . (EMI)

Things We Said Today
Beatles; *Beatles-Box Set* . . . (Capitol)
Something New . . . (Capitol)
The Beatles At The Hollywood Bowl . . . (Capitol)
Paul McCartney; *Tripping The Live Fantastic-Highlights!* . . . (Capitol)

This Is Me Missing You
James House; *Days Gone By* . . . (Epic)
Super Hits Of 1995-C . . . (Epic)

Till I Waltz Again With You
Teresa Brewer; *Best Of Teresa Brewer* . . . (MCA Jazz)

Till Then
Mills Brothers; *Best Of The Mills Brothers* . . . (MCA)
Cab Driver . . . (Ranwood)
Lazy River . . . (MCA Special Prod.)
Mills Brothers . . . (Everest)
Mills Brothers' Greatest Hits . . . (MCA)

To Be Loved By You
Wynonna; *Revelations* . . . (Curb/MCA)
Wynonna-Collection . . . (Curb)

Tonight You Belong To Me
Patience & Prudence; *Great Jukebox Hits Of The '50s-#2-C* . . . (CEMA Special Prod.)

Travelin' Soldier
Bruce Robison; *Bruce Robison* . . . (Vireo)

Unchained Melody
Elvis Presley; *Always On My Mind* . . . (RCA)
Moody Blue . . . (RCA)
The Great Performances . . . (RCA)
George Benson; *Livin' Inside Your Love* . . . (Warner Bros.)
LeAnn Rimes; *LeAnn Rimes-Early Years-Unchained Melody* . . . (MCG/Curb)
Platters; *Platters Greatest Hits* . . . (Everest)
Red Sails In The Sunset . . . (Allegiance)
Richard Clayderman; *Richard Clayderman Plays Love Songs Of The World* . . . (Columbia)
Righteous Brothers; *Righteous Brothers' Greatest Hits* . . . (Verve)
ST/Ghost . . . (Varese Sarabande)
Willie Nelson; *Stardust* . . . (Legacy)

Vaya Con Dios
Bing Crosby; *The Radio Years-#2* . . . (Crescendo)
Freddy Fender; *Freddy Fender-Collection* . . . (Reprise)
Les Paul & Mary Ford; *Memories Are Made Of This-C* . . . (Capitol)
Roger Whittaker; *All-Time Heart-Touching Favorites* . . . (Capitol)

Wait
Beatles; *Beatles-Box Set* . . . (Capitol)
Rubber Soul . . . (Capitol)

We Live In Two Different Worlds
Auldridge/Bennett/Gaudreau; *This Old Town* . . . (Rebel)

We'll Be Together Again
Barbara Cook; *All I Ask Of You* . . . (DRG)
Billie Holiday; *Verve Jazz Masters 47-Billie Holiday Sings Standards* . . . (Verve)
Frankie Laine; *The Frankie Laine Collection* . . . (Mercury)
Lena Horne; *We'll Be Together Again* . . . (Blue Note)
Louis Armstrong; *Essential Louis Armstrong* . . . (Verve)
McCoy Tyner; *Priceless Jazz Collection* . . . (GRP)
Rosemary Clooney; *Do You Miss New York?* . . . (Concord Jazz)
Sammy Davis, Jr.; *Sammy Davis, Jr.'s Greatest Hits-#2* . . . (Dunhill Compact Classics)

What'll I Do
Nat "King" Cole; *The Vocal Classics-1947-1950* . . . (Capitol)
Rosemary Clooney; *Rosemary Clooney Sings The Music Of Irving Berlin* . . . (Concord Jazz)

When I Need You
Celine Dion; *Let's Talk About Love-C* . . . (550 Music)
Leo Sayer; *'70s Greatest Rock Hits-#5-Kickin' Back-C* . . . (Priority)
Show Must Go On-Anthology . . . (Rhino)

When The Golden Leaves Begin To Fall
Joe Val & The New England Bluegrass Boys; *Diamond Joe* . . . (Rounder)
Joe Val & The New England Bluegrass Boys-Vol. 2 . . . (Rounder)

When You Come Back To Me Again
Garth Brooks; *Scarecrow* . . . (Capitol)

Whenever Wherever
Shakira; *Laundry Service* . . . (Epic)

Where You Are
Jessica Simpson featuring Nick Lachey; *Sweet Kisses* . . . (Columbia)

Without You
Charlie Wilson; *Bridging The Gap* . . . .(Major Hits)
Worlds Apart
Vince Gill; *High Lonesome Sound* . . . .(MCA)
Written In The Stars
Elton John & LeAnn Rimes; *ST/Aida* . . . . (Island)
You Are Not Alone
Michael Jackson; *1996 Grammy Nominees-C* . . . . (Columbia)
  HIStory: Past, Present And Future-Book 1-C . . . .(Epic)
You Belong To Me
Dean Martin; *Dean Martin's All Time Greatest Hits* . . . . (Curb)
Duprees; *13 Of The Best Doo Wop Love Songs-#2-C* . . . . (Original Sound)
  Baby Boomer's Best-Mellow '60s-C . . . . (Priority)
  Best Of The Duprees . . . . (Rhino)
Jo Stafford; *Billboard Pop Memories-1950-1954-C* . . . . (Rhino)
  Jo Stafford's Greatest Hits . . . . (Curb)
Johnny Mathis; *In The Still Of The Night* . . . . (Columbia)
Patsy Cline; *Patsy Cline Sings Songs Of Love* . . . . . .(MCA Special Prod.)
  Sentimentally Yours . . . .(MCA)
Vonda Shepard; *ST/Songs From "Ally McBeal" Featuring Vonda
  Shepard* . . . . (550/Epic)
You'll Never Know
Dick Haymes; *Best Of Dick Haymes* . . . . (Curb)
  You'll Never Know . . . .(MCA Special Prod.)
Dick Haymes & His Song Spinners; *Billboard Pop Memories-1940-
  1944-C* . . . .(Rhino)
  Billboard Top Movie Hits-1940s-C . . . . (Rhino)

SEX, Having Sex, Impotence, Lust, Sex Appeal, Sexy
*See Also: AIDS, ANATOMY (various), DESIRE, FAMILY
PLANNING, KISSING, LOVE (various), PROSTITUTES, SEX:
RESISTING TEMPTATION*

(You're My) Aphrodisiac
Dennis Edwards; *Don't Look Any Further* . . . . (Motown)
15 Minutes
Marc Nelson; *chocolate mood* . . . . (Columbia)
36-22-36
Bobby Bland; *Best Of Bobby Bland-#2.* . . . .(MCA)
  Bobby Bland . . . .(MCA)
  Here's The Man . . . .(MCA)
Adultress
Pretenders; *Pretenders II* . . . . (Sire)
After Party
Koffee Brown; *Mars/Venus* . . . . (Arista)
After Sex
Curtis Mayfield; *ST/Let's Do It Again* . . . . (Curtom)
After The Lovin'
Engelbert Humperdinck; *All Of Me-In Concert* . . . .(Epic)
  Engelbert Humperdinck-16 Most Requested Songs . . . .(Epic)
  Engelbert Humperdinck-Super Hits . . . .(Epic)
Afternoon Delight
Starland Vocal Band; *Starland Vocal Band* . . . . (Windsong)
All I Wanna Do Is Make Love To You
Heart; *Brigade* . . . . (Capitol)
All I Want To Do Is Make Love To You
Impressions; *Come To My Party* . . . . (20th Century Fox)
All Of This Making Love
Bee Gees; *Main Course* . . . . (RSO)
All The Places (I Will Kiss You)
Aaron Hall; *Inside Of You.* . . . .(MCA)
All The Things (Your Man Won't Do)
Joe; *ST/Don't Be A Menace To South Central* . . . . (Island)
All The Way
Whispers; *Headlights* . . . . (Solar)
All The Way Lover
Millie Jackson; *Feelin' Bitchy* . . . . (Spring)
  Live & Uncensored . . . . (Spring)
Always Makin' Love
Kentucky HeadHunters; *Electric Barnyard* . . . . (Mercury)
Amsterdam
Van Halen; *Balance* . . . .(Warner Bros.)
Another Way
Tevin Campbell; *Tevin Campbell* . . . . (Qwest)
Anti-Sex Backlash Of The '80s
Roches; *Speak.* . . . .(MCA)
Anytime You Wanna Make Love To Me
Trini Lopez; *Transformed By Time.* . . . . (Roulette)
Anywhere
112; *Room 112* . . . .(Bad Boy/Arista)
Arabian Lover
Duke Ellington; *Jungle Nights In Harlem.* . . . . (Bluebird)
Are U Still Down?
Jon B.; *Cool Relax* . . . .(Yab Yum/550)
Are We Making Love Or Making Friends
Moe Bandy; *Soft Lights And Hard Country Music* . . . . (Columbia)

Are You Ready For The Sex Girls
Gleaming Spires; *Best Of Rodney On The 'ROQ.* . . . . (Posh Boy)
Area Codes
Ludacris; *Word Of Mouf* . . . .(Murder Inc./Def Jam/IDJMG)
Ask Of You
Raphael Saadiq; *ST/Higher Learning* . . . .(550 Music)
Baby Baby Please (Just A Little More Head)
2 Live Crew; *Sports Weekend (As Nasty As They Wanna Be Part II)* . . . . .(Luke)
Baby Got Back
Sir Mix-A-Lot; *Mack Daddy* . . . .(Def American)
Baby Talks Dirty
Knack; *But The Little Girls Understand* . . . . (Capitol)
Baby Workout
Jackie Wilson; *Billboard Top R&B Hits-1963-C* . . . . (Rhino)
  Reet Petite-Best Of Jackie Wilson . . . . (Columbia)
  The Jackie Wilson Story . . . . (Epic)
Baby, Let Me Kiss You
King Floyd; *Didn't It Blow Your Mind: Soul Hits Of The '70s-#5-C.* . . . . (Rhino)
Back Seat Of My Car
Paul And Linda McCartney; *RAM.* . . . . (Capitol)
Paul McCartney; *Paul McCartney-Gift Set.* . . . . (Capitol)
Back That Azz Up
Juvenile; *Back That Azz Up (single)* . . . .(Cash Money/Universal)
Bad Touch, The
Bloodhound Gang; *Hooray For Boobies.* . . . .(Republic/Geffen)
Bang And Blame
R.E.M.; *Monster* . . . . (Warner Bros.)
Bang Bang
Stevie Wonder; *Down To Earth* . . . . (Motown)
Barbie Girl
Aqua; *Aquarium* . . . .(MCA)
  Now That's What I Call Music!-#1-C. . . . .(Virgin)
Bedroom
Jim Ed Brown & Helen Cornelius; *One Man-One Woman* . . . . (RCA)
Bedroom Eyes
Evelyn "Champagne" King; *Sweet Delight* . . . . (RCA)
Bedroom Eyes
Eddie Rabbitt; *Radio Romance* . . . . (Elektra)
Bedroom Reunion
Barbara Mandrell; *Lovers, Friends & Strangers* . . . . (MCA)
Bedroom Thang
ZZ Top; *Six Pack.* . . . . (Warner Bros.)
  ZZ Top . . . . (Warner Bros.)
Bed's Too Big Without You
Police; *Regatta De Blanc.* . . . .(A&M)
Been Around The World
Puff Daddy & The Family; *No Way Out* . . . .(Bad Boy/Arista)
Behind Closed Doors
Charlie Rich; *American Originals-Charlie Rich* . . . . (Columbia)
  Behind Closed Doors . . . . (Epic)
  Charlie Rich's Greatest Hits . . . . (Epic)
  Columbia Country Classics-#4-Nashville Sound-C . . . . (Columbia)
Between Me And You
Ja Rule featuring Christina Milian; *Rule 3:36* . . . .(Murder Inc./Def Jam/IDJMG)
Big Balls
AC/DC; *Dirty Deeds Done Dirt Cheap* . . . .(Atlantic)
Big Daddy
Heavy D; *Waterbed Hev* . . . . (Universal)
Birds And The Bees
Jewel Akens; *American Graffiti-#3-C* . . . . (MCA)
  Collectables Presents The History Of Rock-#4-C. . . . . (Collectables)
  Cruisin'-1965-C. . . . . (Increase)
  Oldies But Goodies-#9-C. . . . .(Original Sound)
  Super Hits-#3-C . . . . (Gusto)
Birthday Suit
Johnny Kemp; *ST/Sing* . . . . (Columbia)
Bling Bling
B.G.; *Chopper City In The Ghetto.* . . . .(Cash Money/Universal)
Blood On The Dance Floor
Michael Jackson; *Blood On The Dance Floor-HIStory.* . . . . . (MJJ Music/Work)
Blueberry Hill
Elvis Presley; *Elvis Recorded Live On Stage In Memphis* . . . .(RCA)
  Loving You . . . .(RCA)
Fats Domino; *Fats Domino's Greatest Hits* . . . .(Everest)
  Fats Domino's Greatest Hits . . . .(MCA)
  My Blue Heaven-Best Of Fats Domino-#1 . . . .(EMI)
Little Richard; *Big Hits* . . . .(Crescendo)
Louis Armstrong; *Best Of Louis Armstrong* . . . .(MCA)
  Essential Louis Armstrong . . . . (Vanguard)
  I Like Jazz-Essence Of Louis Armstrong . . . . (Columbia)
Body Bumpin'
Mytown; *Mytown* . . . .(Cherry/Universal)
Body Bumpin'-Yippie-Yi-Yo
Public Announcement; *All Work, No Play* . . . .(A&M)
Body Talk
Ratt; *Dancing Undercover* . . . .(Atlantic)
  Ratt & Roll 8191. . . . .(Atlantic)
  ST/The Golden Child . . . . (Capitol)

Body Talk
Deele; *Body Talk* . . . .(Solar)
Street Beat . . . .(Solar)
Body Talk
Wallets; *Body Talk*. . . . .(Twin-Tone)
Body Talk
Kix; *Cool Kids* . . . . (Atlantic)
Boobs A Lot
Fugs; *Fugs 4 Rounders Score* . . . . (ESP Disk)
Fugs' Greatest Hits. . . . .(PVC)
The Fugs First Album . . . . (ESP Disk)
Holy Modal Rounders; *Dr. Demento's Delights-C* . . . . (Warner Bros.)
Boombastic
Shaggy; *Boombastic* . . . .(Virgin)
Bop Gun
Ice Cube & George Clinton; *Featuring...Ice Cube* . . . .(Priority)
Bring It On
Keith Washington; *KW* . . . . (Silas)
Brown Sugar
D'Angelo; *Brown Sugar* . . . . (EMI)
Butt Fuck
Human Sexual Response; *Fig. 15* . . . . (Eat)
Butta Love
Next; *Rated Next* . . . . (Divine Mill/Arista)
Butterfly
Crazy Town; *Gift Of Game* . . . . (Columbia)
Californicatin'
J. Geils Band; *You're Gettin' Even While I'm Gettin' Odd* . . . . (EMI)
Californication
Red Hot Chili Peppers; *Californication*. . . . . (Warner Bros.)
Can I Get A...
Jay-Z featuring Amil & Ja Rule; *Vol. 2-Hard Knock Life* . . . . (Def Jam)
Can We
SWV; *Release Some Tension*. . . . .(RCA)
Can't Get Enough Of Your Love
Taylor Dayne; *Soul Dancing* . . . . (Arista)
Can't Get Enough Of Your Love
Bad Company; *Bad Company* . . . . (Swan Song)
Careless Love
Dinah Washington; *Bessie Smith Songbook* . . . .(Emarcy)
Pete Fountain; *Mr. New Orleans* . . . . (MCA)
Preservation Hall Jazz Band; *Best Of The Preservation Hall
Jazz Band*. . . . .(Columbia)
New Orleans-#3-When The Saints Go Marchin' In . . . .(Columbia)
Casanova
Levert; *Big Throwdown*. . . . . (Atlantic)
Golden Age Of Black Music-1977-1988-C. . . . . (Atlantic)
ST/Fatal Beauty . . . . (Atlantic)
Casanova
Bryan Ferry; *Let's Stick Together* . . . .(Virgin)
Roxy Music; *Country Life* . . . . (Atco)
Centerfold
J. Geils Band; *Flashback-Best Of The J. Geils Band* . . . . (EMI)
Freeze-Frame . . . . (EMI)
Showtime . . . . (EMI)
Cherry Hill Park
Billy Joe Royal; *Billy Joe Royal's Greatest Hits* . . . . (Columbia)
Super Hits Of The '70s-Have A Nice Day-#1-C . . . . (Rhino)
Children Of The Korn
Korn with Ice Cube; *Follow The Leader* . . . .(Immortal/Epic)
Chocolate Mood
Marc Nelson; *chocolate mood* . . . . (Columbia)
Closer
Nine Inch Nails; *The Downward Spiral*. . . . . (Interscope)
C'mon 'N Ride It (The Train)
Quad City DJ's; *110% Hits-C* . . . . (Simitar)
ESPN Presents Jock Jams-#3-C . . . .(Tommy Boy)
Get On Up And Dance . . . . (Big Beat)
The Ultimate Dance Party-1997-C. (Arista)
Come And Get With Me
Keith Sweat featuring Snoop Dogg; *Still In The Game* . . . . (Elektra)
Come See Me
112; *112*. . . . . (Bad Boy/Arista)
Company Time
Linda Davis; *Shoot For The Moon*. . . . . (Arista)
Computer Sex And Self Help
Carl Reiner; *The 2000-Year-Old Man In The Year 2000* . . . .(Rhino)
Cover You In Oil
AC/DC; *Ballbreaker* . . . . (East West)
Crash Into Me
Dave Matthews Band; *Crash*. . . . .(RCA)
Dah Dee Dah (Sexy Thing)
Alicia Keys; *ST/Men In Black* . . . . (Columbia)
Dancing In The Sheets
Shalamar; *Shalamar's Greatest Hits*. (Solar)
ST/Footloose. . . . . (Columbia)
Danger (Been So Long)
Mystikal; *Now That's What I Call Music!-#7-C* . . . .(Virgin)

Mystikal featuring Nivea; *Let's Get Ready* . . . . (Jive)
Date Rape
Tribe Called Quest; *Low End Theory* . . . . (Jive)
Davy's Dinghy
Ruth Wallis; *Dr. Demento Presents The Greatest Novelty Records-#2-
1950s-C* . . . .(Rhino)
Dr. Demento's Dementia Royale-C. . . . .(Rhino)
Daytime Friends
Kenny Rogers; *Daytime Friends* . . . .(EMI)
Kenny Rogers-Twenty Greatest Hits . . . . (EMI)
Ten Years Of Gold . . . . (EMI)
Delta Lady
Joe Cocker; *Joe Cocker!*. . . . .(A&M)
Joe Cocker-Classics-#4. . . . .(A&M)
Joe Cocker's Greatest Hits . . . .(A&M)
Mad Dogs & Englishmen . . . .(A&M)
Leon Russell; *Best Of Leon Russell* . . . . (MCA)
Leon Russell . . . . (MCA)
Differences
Ginuwine; *Life* . . . . (Epic)
Digital Display
Ready For The World; *Ready For The World* . . . . (MCA)
Digital Get Down
'N Sync; *No Strings Attached*. . . . . (Jive)
Dim All The Lights
Donna Summer; *Bad Girls* . . . . (Casablanca)
Dance Collection. . . . . (Casablanca)
Donna Summer's Greatest Hits. . . . . (Casablanca)
On The Radio-Greatest Hits-Volumes I & II . . . . (Casablanca)
Dirty Eyes
AC/DC; *Bonfire* . . . .(East West)
Dirty Movies
Van Halen; *Fair Warning*. . . . . (Warner Bros.)
Dirty White Boy
Foreigner; *Head Games* . . . . (Atlantic)
Records . . . . (Atlantic)
Do Me Again
Freddie Jackson; *Do Me Again*. . . . .(Capitol)
Do Me Baby
Meli'sa Morgan; *Do Me Baby* . . . .(Capitol)
Prince; *Controversy* . . . . (Warner Bros.)
Do Me!
Bell Biv Devoe; *Poison* . . . . (MCA)
Do That To Me One More Time
Captain & Tennille; *Make Your Move* . . . . (Casablanca)
Do Ya Think I'm Sexy?
Rod Stewart; *Absolutely Live* . . . . (Warner Bros.)
Blondes Have More Fun . . . . (Warner Bros.)
Rod Stewart's Greatest Hits . . . . (Warner Bros.)
Do You Wanna Make Love
Peter McCann; *Peter McCann* . . . .(20th Century Fox)
Doin' What Comes Natur'lly
Dinah Shore; *16 Most Requested Songs Of The '40s-#1-C* . . . .(Legacy)
Dinah Shore-16 Most Requested Songs. . . . .(Legacy)
Ethel Merman/Ray Middleton/Original Cast; *Annie Get Your Gun* . . . . . . (MCA)
Don't Come Home A'Drinkin' (With Lovin' On Your Mind)
Loretta Lynn; *Loretta Lynn-Greatest Hits Live* . . . . (K-Tel)
Loretta Lynn's Greatest Hits. . . . . (MCA)
MCA Records 30 Years Of Hits-1958-1988-C. . . . . (MCA)
Don't Go Home With Your Hard On
Leonard Cohen; *Death Of A Ladies' Man* . . . .(Columbia)
Don't Make Love To Mary
Merle Travis; *Johnny Gimble's Texas Honky-Tonk Hits-C* . . . . . .(C.M.H. Prod.)
Don't Pick It Up
Offspring; *Ixnay On The Hombre*. . . . .(Columbia)
Don't Stop Till You Get Enough
Jacksons; *Jacksons Live* . . . . (Epic)
Michael Jackson; *Off The Wall*. . . . .(Epic)
Don't Touch Me There
Tubes; *T.R.A.S.H. (Tubes Rarities And Smash Hits)* . . . .(A&M)
What Do You Want From Live. . . . .(A&M)
Young And Rich. . . . .(A&M)
Doo Wop (That Thing)
Lauryn Hill; *The Miseducation Of Lauryn Hill* . . . . (Ruffhouse/Columbia)
Dreamlover
Mariah Carey; *Music Box*. . . . .(Columbia)
Dress You Up
Madonna; *Like A Virgin* . . . . (Sire)
Dynamo Humm
Mothers; *Over-nite Sensation* . . . . (Rykodisc)
E.I.
Nelly; *Country Grammar*. (Fo' Reel/Universal)
Earth Girls Are Easy
Julie Brown; *Goddess In Progress* . . . .(Rhino)
Easy Lover
Phil Collins; *Phil Collins-Hits* . . . . (Atlantic)
Serious Hits...Live! . . . . (Atlantic)
Philip Bailey & Phil Collins; *Chinese Wall* . . . .(Columbia)

Empty Bed Blues
Bessie Smith; *Bessie Smith-The Collection* . . . . (Legacy)
 Empty Bed Blues . . . . (Columbia)
Bette Midler; *Broken Blossom* . . . . (Atlantic)
LaVern Baker; *Atlantic Jazz-Singers-C* . . . . (Atlantic)
 LaVern Baker Sings Bessie Smith . . . . (Atlantic)

Erotica
Madonna; *Erotica* . . . . (Maverick/Sire)
 GHV2 . . . . (Warner Bros.)

Erotik City
Emoja; *ST/Men In Black* . . . . (Columbia)

Every Morning
Sugar Ray; *14:59* . . . . (Lava)

Everybody's Doin' It
Commander Cody & His Lost Planet Airmen; *Country Casanova* . . . . . . (MCA)

Falling In Love (Is Hard On The Knees)
Aerosmith; *A Little South Of Sanity* . . . . (Geffen)
 Nine Lives . . . . (Columbia)

Fastlove
George Michael; *Ladies & Gentlemen: The Best Of George Michael* . . . . . (Epic)
 Older . . . . (DreamWorks/SKG)

Feel Like Makin' Love
Roberta Flack; *Atlantic Rhythm & Blues 1947-1974-#6 (1966-*
 1969)-C . . . . (Atlantic)
 Best Of Roberta Flack . . . . (Atlantic)
 Feel Like Makin' Love . . . . (Atlantic)
 Golden Age Of Black Music-1970-1975-C . . . . (Atlantic)
 Golden Soul-C . . . . (Atlantic)

Feel Like Makin' Love
Bad Company; *10 From 6* . . . . (Atlantic)
 Straight Shooter . . . . (Swan Song)

Feel So Good
Mase; *Harlem World* . . . . (Bad Boy/Arista)

Feelin' On Yo Booty
R. Kelly; *TP-2.com* . . . . (Jive)

Feels Like The First Time
Foreigner; *Classic Rock 1966-1988-C* . . . . (Atlantic)
 Foreigner . . . . (Atlantic)
 Records . . . . (Atlantic)

Fez
Steely Dan; *Steely Dan's Greatest Hits* . . . . (MCA)
 The Royal Scam . . . . (MCA)

Fire
Jimi Hendrix; *Concerts* . . . . (Reprise)
 Essential Jimi Hendrix, Volume 2 . . . . (Reprise)
Jimi Hendrix Experience; *Are You Experienced?* . . . . (Reprise)
 Smash Hits . . . . (Reprise)

Fired Up!
Funky Green Dogs; *Get Fired Up!* . . . . (MCA)

First Night
Monica; *The Boy Is Mine* . . . . (Arista)

Fix
Blackstreet; *Another Level* . . . . (Interscope)

Flirt
Cameo; *Alligator Woman* . . . . (Chocolate City)

Forever Tonight
Peter Cetera & Crystal Bernard; *One Clear Voice* . . . . (River North)

Foxey Lady
Jimi Hendrix; *Essential Jimi Hendrix, Volume 2* . . . . (Reprise)
 ST/Jimi Plays Monterey . . . . (Reprise)
 ST/Wayne's World . . . . (Reprise)
Jimi Hendrix Experience; *Are You Experienced?* . . . . (Reprise)
 Smash Hits . . . . (Reprise)
Mary's Danish; *Circa* . . . . (Morgan Creek)

Freak Like Me
Adina Howard; *Do You Wanna Ride?* . . . . (East West)
 MTV Party To Go-#7-C . . . . (Tommy Boy)

Free
Mya; *ST/Bait* . . . . (Warner Bros.)

Freek'n You
Jodeci; *MTV Party To Go-#7-C* . . . . (Tommy Boy)
 The Show, The After-Party, The Hotel . . . . (Uptown/MCA)

Friends & Lovers
Bread; *Best Of Bread-#2* . . . . (Elektra)
 Bread . . . . (Elektra)

Friends And Lovers
Gloria Loring & Carl Anderson; *Chicken Soup For The Couples*
 Soul-C . . . . (Rhino)
 Chicken Soup For The Soul: I'll Be There For You-Songs Of Friendship,
 Brotherhood And Sisterhood-C . . . . (Rhino)
 Gloria Loring . . . . (Atlantic)

Funky Cold Medina
Tone Loc; *Loc-ed After Dark* . . . . (Delicious Vinyl)

Get Down
War; *All Day Music* . . . . (MCA)
 War Live! . . . . (Avenue)

Get Down Make Love
Queen; *Live Killers* . . . . (Hollywood)

News Of The World . . . . (Hollywood)

Get Down Tonight
KC And The Sunshine Band; *Best Of KC And The Sunshine Band* . . . . . (Rhino)
 Billboard Top Hits-1975-C . . . . (Rhino)
 Get Down Tonight! Best Of T.K. Records-C . . . . (Rhino)

Get It On (Bang A Gong)
Power Station; *Power Station* . . . . (Capitol)
T. Rex; *Electric Warrior* . . . . (Reprise)

Get Me Home
Foxy Brown; *Ill Na Na* . . . . (Violator)

Get My Rocks Off
Dr. Hook & The Medicine Show; *Revisited* . . . . (Columbia)
 Sloppy Seconds . . . . (Columbia)

Get Off
Foxy; *Get Down Tonight! Best Of T.K. Records-C* . . . . (Rhino)
 Get Off . . . . (Dash)

Gettin' Jiggy Wit It
Will Smith; *Big Willie Style* . . . . (Columbia)

Gigolo
O'Bryan; *Doin' Alright* . . . . (Capitol)

Gigolo
Damned; *Anything* . . . . (MCA)

Girl With The Hungry Eyes
Jefferson Starship; *At Point Zero* . . . . (Grunt)

Girlfriend/Boyfriend
Blackstreet featuring Janet; *Finally* . . . . (Lil' Man/Interscope)

Girls Of Porn
Mr. Bungle; *Mr. Bungle* . . . . (Warner Bros.)

Give It To Me Baby
Rick James; *25 #1 Hits From 25 Years-C* . . . . (Motown)
 Rick James' Greatest Hits . . . . (Motown)
 Street Songs . . . . (Motown)

Give Me A Ring Sometime
Lisa Brokop; *Every Little Girl's Dream* . . . . (Patriot)

Give You What You Want
Chico DeBarge; *Game* . . . . (Motown)

Giving Him Something He Can Feel
En Vogue; *Funky Divas* . . . . (East West)

Go All The Way
Raspberries; *Best Of The Raspberries* . . . . (Capitol)
 Capitol Collectors Series-The Raspberries . . . . (Capitol)

Good Girls Don't
Knack; *Get The Knack* . . . . (Capitol)

Good Girls Go To Heaven
Charlie Floyd; *Charlie Floyd* . . . . (Liberty)

Got To Get It
Sisqo; *Got To Get It (single)* . . . . (Dragon/Def Soul/IDJMG)

Got You (Where I Want You)
Flys; *Holiday Man* . . . . (Delicious Vinyl)
 ST/Disturbing Behavior . . . . (Trauma)

Got Your Money
Ol' Dirty Bastard; *Nigga Please* . . . . (Elektra)

Hanky Panky
Tommy James And The Shondells; *Billboard Top Rock 'N' Roll Hits-*
 1966-C . . . . (Rhino)
 Tommy James And The Shondells-Anthology . . . . (Rhino)

Hard As A Rock
AC/DC; *Ballbreaker* . . . . (East West)

Harry
Macy Gray; *The Id* . . . . (Epic)

He Wants My Body
Starpoint; *Sensational* . . . . (Elektra)

Heaven In The Back Seat
Eddie Money; *Right Here* . . . . (Columbia)

Help Me Make It Through The Night
Bryan Ferry; *Another Time Another Place* . . . . (Reprise)
Gladys Knight & The Pips; *Compact Command Performances-Gladys Knight*
 & The Pips . . . . (Motown)
 Gladys Knight & The Pips-Anthology . . . . (Motown)
Joan Baez; *Blessed Are* . . . . (Vanguard)
 Hits/Greatest & Others . . . . (Vanguard)
Sammi Smith; *Super Hits Of The '70s-Have A Nice Day-#4-C* . . . . . . (Rhino)
Willie Nelson; *Greatest Hits (& Some That Will Be)* . . . . (Columbia)
 Sweet Memories . . . . (RCA)
 Willie Nelson Sings Kristofferson . . . . (Columbia)

Her Strut
Bob Seger & The Silver Bullet Band; *Against The Wind* . . . . (Capitol)
 Nine Tonight . . . . (Capitol)

Hey Baby
No Doubt; *Rock Steady* . . . . (Interscope)

Hey Hey What Can I Do
Hootie & The Blowfish; *Encomium: Tribute To Led Zeppelin-C* . . . . . (Atlantic)
Led Zeppelin; *Led Zeppelin-Box Set* . . . . (Atlantic)
 Led Zeppelin-The Complete Studio Recordings . . . . (Atlantic)

Hit Me Off
New Edition; *Home Again* . . . . (MCA)

Hit Me With Your Best Shot
Pat Benatar; *Crimes Of Passion* . . . . (Chrysalis)

Live From Earth . . . . (Chrysalis)
Hold Me
Brian McKnight; *Anytime* . . . . (Motown)
Hold On
Xscape; *Traces Of My Lipstick* . . . . (So So Def/Columbia)
Holla Holla
Ja Rule; *Venni Vetti Vecci* . . . .(Murder Inc./Def Jam/IDJMG)
Hollow, The
A Perfect Circle; *Mer De Noms* . . . .(Virgin)
Hooch
Everything; *Super Natural.* . . . . (Blackbird/Sire)
Horse & Carriage
Cam'ron featuring Mase; *Confessions Of Fire* . . . . (Untertainment/Epic)
Hot Blooded
Foreigner; *Double Vision.* . . . . (Atlantic)
Records . . . . (Atlantic)
ST/Vision Quest . . . . (Geffen)
Hot For Teacher
Van Halen; *1984* . . . . (Warner Bros.)
Hot Legs
Rod Stewart; *Absolutely Live.* . . . . (Warner Bros.)
Footloose & Fancy Free . . . . (Warner Bros.)
Rod Stewart's Greatest Hits . . . . (Warner Bros.)
Storyteller/The Complete Anthology: 1964-1990 . . . . (Warner Bros.)
Hot Stuff
Donna Summer; *Bad Girls* . . . .(Casablanca)
Dance Collection . . . .(Casablanca)
On The Radio-Greatest Hits-Volumes I & II. . . . .(Casablanca)
Walk Away-Best Of Donna Summer-1977-1980. . . . .(Casablanca)
Hot Stuff
Whitesnake; *Come An' Get It* . . . . (Geffen)
Hot Stuff
Rolling Stones; *Black And Blue.* . . . . (Rolling Stones)
Love You Live . . . .(Virgin)
Sucking In The Seventies. . . . . (Rolling Stones)
Hot, Wet & Sticky
Galaxy; *Hot, Wet & Sticky* . . . . (Arista)
House Of Blue Lights
Andrews Sisters; *Best Of The Andrews Sisters-#2.* . . . . (MCA)
Asleep At The Wheel; *Asleep At The Wheel-10.* . . . . (Epic)
Greatest Country Hits Of The '80s-1987-C . . . . (Columbia)
More Hot Country Requests-#2-C . . . . (Epic)
Trucker's Jukebox-#2-C . . . . (Legacy)
Very Best Of Asleep At The Wheel Since 1970 . . . .(Relentless/Madacy)
Canned Heat; *Canned Heat & John Lee Hooker: Live At The Fox*
Venice . . . . (Rhino)
Human Conditions . . . . (Takoma)
Chuck Berry; *More Rock 'N' Roll Rarities-Golden Era* . . . . (Chess)
The Chess Box-Chuck Berry. . . . . (Chess)
Chuck Miller; *Hard To Find 45s On CD-#1-1955-1960-C* . . . . (Eric)
How Can We Be Lovers
Michael Bolton; *Soul Provider* . . . . (Columbia)
How Deep Is Your Love
Dru Hill featuring Redman; *Enter The Dru* . . . . .(Def Jam/RAL/Mercury/Island)
ST/Rush Hour . . . . (Def Jam)
How Many Licks
Lil' Kim featuring Sisqo; *Notorious K.I.M.* . . . .(Queen Bee/Undeas/Atlantic)
How's It Goin' Down
DMX; *It's Dark And Hell Is Hot* . . . . (Def Jam)
Human Nature
Madonna; *Bedtime Stories.* . . . . (Maverick/Sire)
GHV2 . . . . (Warner Bros.)
Humming Song
Martin Mull; *I'm Everyone I Ever Loved.* . . . . (MCA)
Hungry Eyes
Eric Carmen; *Best Of Eric Carmen* . . . . (Arista)
Dirty Dancing Live In Concert-C . . . .(RCA)
ST/Dirty Dancing . . . .(RCA)
Hungry For Love
Todd Rundgren; *A Wizard A True Star* . . . . (Rhino)
Hungry For Your Love
Van Morrison; *ST/An Officer And A Gentleman* . . . . (Island)
Wavelength . . . . (Warner Bros.)
I Cain't Say No
Original Broadway Cast; *Oklahoma!* . . . .(RCA)
Original Cast; *Oklahoma!* . . . . (MCA)
I Didn't Mean To Turn You On
Cherrelle; *Fragile* . . . . (Tabu)
Robert Palmer; *Heart Of Rock-C* . . . . (Columbia)
MTV-VH1 Powerplayers-C . . . . (EMI)
Riptide . . . . (Island)
I Don't Know
Blues Brothers; *Best Of The Blues Brothers* . . . . (Atlantic)
Briefcase Full Of Blues. . . . . (Atlantic)
I Don't Know If It's Right
Evelyn "Champagne" King; *Dance! Dance! Dance!-#2-C* . . . . (RCA)
Smooth Talk . . . .(RCA)

I Don't Want To Have To Marry You
Jim Ed Brown & Helen Cornelius; *Jim Ed Brown & Helen Cornelius'*
Greatest Hits . . . .(RCA)
I Drove All Night
Cyndi Lauper; *Night To Remember* . . . .(Epic)
I Just Wanna Love U (Give It 2 Me)
Jay-Z; *Dynasty-Roc La Familia 2000* . . . .(Roc-A-Fella/DJMG)
I Just Want To Make Love To You
Bill Medley; *Best Of Bill Medley* . . . . (MCA)
Cold Blood; *Bill Graham Presents The Last Days Of The*
Fillmore-C . . . . (Epic Portrait Assoc.)
Etta James; *Etta James-At Last* . . . . (Chess)
Foghat; *Best Of Foghat* . . . . (Rhino)
Foghat. . . . . (Rhino)
Muddy Waters; *Best Of Muddy Waters* . . . . (Chess)
The Chess Box-Muddy Waters. . . . . (Chess)
Righteous Brothers; *Righteous Brothers-Anthology 1962-1974* . . . . . . (Rhino)
Rolling Stones; *England's Newest Hit Makers/The Rolling Stones* . . . . (Abkco)
Singles Collection-The London Years . . . . (Abkco)
Van Morrison; *It's Too Late To Stop Now* . . . . (Warner Bros.)
I Know What Boys Like
Waitresses; *Best Of The Waitresses* . . . . (Polydor)
Just Can't Get Enough: New Wave Hits Of The '80s-#5-C . . . . (Rhino)
I Left Something Turned On At Home
Trace Adkins; *Dreamin' Out Loud.* . . . .(Capitol)
I Like The Way (The Kissing Game)
Hi-Five; *Hi-Five.* . . . . (Jive)
I Like Them Girls
Tyrese; *2000 Watts.* . . . . (RCA)
I Need A Hot Girl
Hot Boys; *Guerrilla Warfare* . . . . (Cash Money/Universal)
I Touch Myself
Divinyls; *Divinyls* . . . . (Virgin)
I Wanna Be Bad
Willa Ford; *Totally Hits 2001-C.* . . . .(Arista)
Willa Was Here. . . . .(Lava)
I Wanna Be Your Lover
Prince; *Prince.* . . . . (Warner Bros.)
I Wanna Be Your Lover
Bob Dylan; *Biograph.* . . . .(Columbia)
I Wanna Sex You Up
Color Me Badd; *C.M.B.* . . . . (Giant)
ST/New Jack City . . . . (Giant)
I Want It Now
Cameo; *Real Men Wear Black* . . . . (Atlanta Artists)
I Want To Come Over
Melissa Etheridge; *Your Little Secret.* . . . .(Island)
I Want To Know You Before We Make Love
Conway Twitty; *Borderline* . . . . (MCA)
I Want Your Sex
George Michael; *Faith* . . . .(Columbia)
ST/Beverly Hills Cop II . . . . (MCA)
I Wonder If I Take You Home
Lisa Lisa & Cult Jam With Full Force; *Breakdancing* . . . .(Columbia)
Lisa Lisa & Cult Jam With Full Force. . . . .(Columbia)
I'd Love To Lay You Down
Conway Twitty; *Conway Twittty-20 Greatest Hits* . . . . (MCA)
If I Ruled The World
NaS; *It Was Written* . . . .(Columbia)
If You Don't Wanna Get Pregnant
U.T.F.O.; *Bag It & Bone It* . . . . (Jive)
If You See Kay
Memphis Slim/Tampa Red/Lonnie Johnson; *Bawdy Blues* . . . . (Bluesville)
I'll Go On Loving You
Alan Jackson; *High Mileage* . . . .(Arista)
I'll Make Love To You Anytime
Eric Clapton; *Backless* . . . . (Polydor)
I'm A Bad, Bad Man
Ethel Merman/Bruce Yarnell/Original Cast; *Annie Get*
Your Gun . . . . (RCA Victor)
I'm Good At Being Bad
TLC; *Fanmail* . . . .(LaFace)
I'm In You
Peter Frampton; *Breaking All The Rules* . . . .(A&M)
Peter Frampton-Classics-#12 . . . . (A&M)
I'm Not Ready
Keith Sweat; *Still In The Game* . . . .(Elektra)
I'm The One
Roberta Flack; *I'm The One* . . . . (Atlantic)
I'm Too Sexy
Right Said Fred; *Up* . . . . (Charisma)
In Your Room
Bangles; *Bangles' Greatest Hits* . . . .(Columbia)
Everything. . . . .(Columbia)
Insatiable Woman
Isley, Jasper, Isley; *Caravan Of Love* . . . .(CBS Associated)
It Ain't The Meat
Swallows; *Risque Blues: It Ain't The Meat-C* . . . .(King)

Risque Rhythms: Nasty '50s R&B-C . . . . (Rhino)
It's All About Me
  Mya featuring Sisqo of Dru Hill; *Mya* . . . . (University/Interscope)
It's Ecstasy When You Lay Down Next To Me
  Barry White; *Barry White Sings For Someone You Love* . . . . (20th Century Fox)
   Barry White's All-Time Greatest Hits . . . . (Mercury)
Jack, The
  AC/DC; *High Voltage*. . . . . (Atco)
   If You Want Blood You've Got It . . . .(Atlantic)
Joker, The
  Steve Miller Band; *Best Of Steve Miller 1968-1973* . . . . (Capitol)
   Steve Miller Band-Gift Set . . . . (Capitol)
   Steve Miller Band-Live . . . . (Capitol)
   Steve Miller Band's Greatest Hits-1974-78 . . . . (Capitol)
   The Joker . . . . (Capitol)
Josie
  Steely Dan; *Aja* . . . .(MCA)
   Steely Dan's Greatest Hits . . . .(MCA)
Joyride
  Roxette; *Joyride* . . . .(EMI)
Joystick
  Dazz Band; *Dazz Band's Greatest Hits* . . . . (Motown)
   Joystick . . . . (Motown)
Just A Gigolo/I Ain't Got Nobody
  David Lee Roth; *Crazy From The Heat* . . . .(Warner Bros.)
  Louis Prima; *Capitol Collectors Series-Louis Prima* . . . . (Capitol)
  Thelonius Monk Quartet; *Monk's Dream* . . . . (Columbia)
Just The Way You Like It
  S.O.S. Band; *Just The Way You Like It* . . . . (Tabu)
Justify My Love
  Madonna; *Immaculate Collection*. . . . . (Sire)
   Royal Box . . . . (Sire)
Keep On Keepin' On
  MC Lyte Featuring Xscape; *Bad As I Wanna B* . . . . (East West)
   ST/Sunset Park . . . . (East West)
Keepin' My Lover Satisfied
  Melba Moore; *Never Say Never* . . . . (Capitol)
King Of Sleaze
  Beat Farmers; *Loud & Plowed &...Live!* . . . . (Curb)
   Poor & Famous . . . . (Curb)
Last Time I Made Love
  Joyce Kennedy & Jeffrey Osborne; *Looking For Trouble* . . . . . (A&M)
Lay Lady Lay
  Bob Dylan; *Biograph* . . . . (Columbia)
   Bob Dylan's Greatest Hits-#2 . . . . (Columbia)
   Hard Rain . . . . (Columbia)
   Nashville Skyline . . . . (Columbia)
  Bob Dylan And The Band; *Before The Flood* . . . . (Columbia)
  Byrds; *The Byrds* . . . . (Columbia)
Lay Low
  Snoop Dogg; *The Last Meal* . . . . (No Limit/Priority)
Lemon Song
  Led Zeppelin; *Led Zeppelin II*. . . . .(Atlantic)
Lemon Squeezing Daddy
  Sultans; *Risque Rhythms: Nasty '50s R&B-C*. . . . . (Rhino)
Let Me Bang Your Box
  Toppers; *Risque Rhythms: Nasty '50s R&B-C* . . . . (Rhino)
Let Me Make Love To You
  O'Jays; *O'Jays-Collector's Item* . . . . (Philadelphia Int'l)
   Survival . . . . (Philadelphia Int'l)
Let Me Make Love To You
  Charlie Gonzales; *Charlie Gonzales*. . . . . (Collectables)
Let's Get Down
  Tony Toni Tone; *House Of Music*. . . . . (Mercury)
   Tony Toni Tone-Hits . . . . (Mercury)
   Ultimate Hip Hop Party-1998-C . . . . (Arista)
Let's Get It On
  Marvin Gaye; *Billboard Top Rock 'N' Roll Hits-1973-C* . . . . . . (Rhino)
   Let's Get It On . . . . (Motown)
   Marvin Gaye's Greatest Hits . . . . (Motown)
Let's Get It On
  By All Means; *Beyond A Dream* . . . . (Island)
Let's Go All The Way
  Sly Fox; *Hot Dance Hits Of The '80s-C* . . . . (E Squared)
Let's Go Crazy
  Prince and the Revolution; *ST/Purple Rain* . . . .(Warner Bros.)
Let's Go To Bed
  Cure; *Japanese Whispers-The Singles* . . . . (Sire)
   Standing On A Beach-The Singles . . . . (Elektra)
   The Walk . . . . (Sire)
Let's Just Get Naked
  Joan Osborne; *Relish* . . . . (Blue Gorilla/Mercury)
Let's Put The X In Sex
  Kiss; *Smashes, Thrashes & Hits* . . . . (Mercury)
Let's Ride
  Montell Jordan; *Let's Ride* . . . .(Def Jam/RAL/Mercury)
   MTV Jams-C . . . . (Kedar Entert./Universal)
   MTV Party To Go '99-C . . . . (Tommy Boy)

Let's Spend The Night Together
  David Bowie; *Aladdin Sane* . . . . (Rykodisc)
   ST/Ziggy Stardust-The Motion Picture. . . . . (Rykodisc)
  Rolling Stones; *"Still Life" (American Concert 1981)* . . . .(Virgin)
   Between The Buttons . . . .(Abkco)
   Flowers. . . . .(Abkco)
   Hot Rocks 1964-1971 . . . .(Abkco)
   Through The Past, Darkly (Big Hits Vol. 2) . . . .(Abkco)
Let's Take All Night (To Say Goodbye)
  Barry Manilow; *If I Should Love Again*. . . . . (Arista)
Let's Talk About Sex
  Salt-N-Pepa; *Blacks' Magic* . . . .(Next Plateau/London/Island)
   Blitz Of Salt-N-Pepa Hits . . . . (London)
   MTV Party To Go-#2-C . . . . (Tommy Boy)
Lick It Up
  Kiss; *Lick It Up* . . . . (Mercury)
   MTV's Rock 'N' Roll To Go-C . . . . (Elektra)
   Smashes, Thrashes & Hits . . . . (Mercury)
Light My Fire
  Doors; *Best Of The Doors* . . . . (Elektra)
   Doors . . . . (Elektra)
   Doors 13 . . . . (Elektra)
   Doors' Greatest Hits . . . . (Elektra)
   ST/The Doors . . . . (Elektra)
  Jose Feliciano; *Encore-Jose Feliciano* . . . . (RCA)
   Jose Feliciano's All-Time Greatest Hits . . . . (RCA)
Like A Virgin
  Madonna; *Immaculate Collection* . . . . (Sire)
   Like A Virgin . . . . (Sire)
   Royal Box . . . . (Sire)
Lipstick On My Dick
  Luke; *Luke's Greatest Hits* . . . . (Lil' Joe)
Little Less Talk And A Lot More Action
  Toby Keith; *Toby Keith* . . . . (Mercury)
Little Miss Lover
  Jimi Hendrix; *Axis: Bold As Love* . . . . (Reprise)
   Essential Jimi Hendrix . . . . (Reprise)
Little T & A
  Rolling Stones; *Tattoo You* . . . . (Virgin)
Live With Me
  Rolling Stones; *Get Yer Ya-Ya's Out!* . . . .(Abkco)
   Let It Bleed . . . .(Abkco)
Livin' It Up
  Ja Rule; *Pain Is Love* . . . .(Murder Inc./Def Jam/IDJMG)
Longview
  Green Day; *Dookie* . . . . (Reprise)
Lookin' At Me
  Mase Featuring Puff Daddy; *Harlem World* . . . .(Bad Boy/Arista)
Loungin
  L.L. Cool J; *All World* . . . . (Def Jam)
   Hip Hop Coast 2 Coast-C . . . . (Priority)
   Yo! MTV Raps-C . . . . (Def Jam)
Love Child
  Diana Ross & The Supremes; *Billboard Top Rock 'N' Roll Hits-*
   1968-C . . . . (Rhino)
   Diana Ross & The Supremes' Greatest Hits-#3 . . . . (Motown)
   Diana Ross & The Supremes-Anthology (1962-1969) . . . . . . (Motown)
   Every Great #1 Hit . . . . (Motown)
   Motown Story-First 25 Years-C . . . . (Motown)
   Motown's Biggest Pop Hits-C . . . . (Motown)
  Sweet Sensation; *Love Child* . . . . (Atco)
Love Come Down
  Evelyn "Champagne" King; *Best Of Evelyn "Champagne" King-Love*
   Come Down . . . . (RCA)
  James Ingram; *It's Real* . . . .(Warner Bros.)
Love In An Elevator
  Aerosmith; *Pump* . . . . (Geffen)
Love Machine
  Miracles; *12 #1 Hits From The '70s-C* . . . . (Motown)
   20/20-C . . . . (Motown)
   Billboard Top Hits-1976-C . . . . (Rhino)
   Motown Story-First 25 Years-C . . . . (Motown)
   Top 10 With A Bullet-Motown Dance Songs-C . . . . (Motown)
Love Machine
  Country Joe & The Fish; *C.J. Fish* . . . . (Vanguard)
   Life & Times Of Country Joe & The Fish . . . . (Vanguard)
Love Machine
  Wham! Featuring George Michael; *Fantastic*. . . . . (Columbia)
Love Machine
  Paul Butterfield Blues Band; *Keep On Movin'* . . . . (Elektra)
Love Machine
  Uriah Heep; *Look At Yourself* . . . . (Mercury)
   Uriah Heep-Live . . . . (Mercury)
Love Machine
  W.A.S.P.; *W.A.S.P.* . . . . (Capitol)
Love On Top Of Love-Killer Kiss
  Grace Jones; *Bulletproof Heart* . . . . (Capitol)
Love Potion Number 9
  Clovers; *ST/American Graffiti*. (MCA)

Super Oldies Of The '50s-#7-C . . . . (Audio Fidelity)
Herb Alpert & The Tijuana Brass; *Herb Alpert & The Tijuana Brass'*
Greatest Hits . . . . (A&M)
Herb Alpert & The Tijuana Brass-Classics-#1 . . . . (A&M)
Searchers; *History Of British Rock-#3-C* . . . . (Rhino)
Searchers' Greatest Hits . . . . (Rhino)

Love To Love You Baby
Donna Summer; *Donna Summer's Greatest Hits* . . . . (Casablanca)
Live & More . . . . (Casablanca)
Love To Love You Baby . . . . (Casablanca)
On The Radio-Greatest Hits-Volumes I & II . . . . (Casablanca)
No Doubt; *ST/Zoolander* . . . . (Hollywood)

Love Won't Let Me Wait
Luther Vandross; *Any Love* . . . . (Epic)
Best Of Luther Vandross...The Best Of Love . . . . (Epic)
Major Harris; *Atlantic Rhythm & Blues 1947-1974-#6 (1966-*
1969)-C . . . . (Atlantic)
Major Harris-Live . . . . (WMOT)
My Way . . . . (Atlantic)

Love You To
Beatles; *Revolver* . . . . (Capitol)

Lover
Ella Fitzgerald; *Rodgers & Hart Songbook* . . . . (Verve)
John Coltrane; *Last Trane* . . . . (Prestige)
Tony Bennett; *Rodgers & Hart Songbook* . . . . (DRG)

Lover Boy
Billy Ocean; *Billy Ocean's Greatest Hits* . . . . (Jive)
Suddenly . . . . (Jive)

Lover Boy
Supertramp; *Even In The Quietest Moments* . . . . (A&M)

Lover Who Rocks You (All Night)
India; *Breaking Out* . . . . (Jellybean Prod.)

Lovergirl
Teena Marie; *Club Epic-#1-C* . . . . (Legacy)
Starchild . . . . (Epic)

Lovin', Touchin', Squeezin'
Journey; *Evolution* . . . . (Columbia)
Journey-Captured . . . . (Columbia)
Journey's Greatest Hits . . . . (Columbia)

Lusty Month Of May
Julie Andrews; *A Little Bit Of Broadway* . . . . (Columbia)
Original 1982 London Cast; *Camelot* . . . . (Varese Sarabande)
Original Cast; *Camelot* . . . . (Columbia)
Various Artists; *ST/Camelot* . . . . (Warner Bros.)

Luv 2 Luv You
Timbaland & Magoo; *Welcome To Our World* . . (BlackGround Enterp./Atlantic)

Make A Move On Me
Olivia Newton-John; *Olivia Newton-John's Greatest Hits-#2* . . . . (MCA)
Physical . . . . (MCA)

Make It With You
Bread; *Best Of Bread* . . . . (Elektra)
Bread-Anthology . . . . (Elektra)
On The Waters . . . . (Elektra)

Make Love Like A Man
Def Leppard; *Adrenalize* . . . . (Mercury)

Make Love To Me
Anne Murray; *Croonin'* . . . . (SBK)

Make Your Move On Me Baby
Charlie Singleton; *Modern Man* . . . . (Arista)

Makin' Love
Kiss; *Alive II* . . . . (Casablanca)
Double Platinum . . . . (Mercury)
Rock & Roll Over . . . . (Casablanca)

Makin' Love
Floyd Robinson; *Nipper's Greatest Hits Of The '50s-#1-C* . . . . (RCA)

Makin' Love
Climax Blues Band; *Shine On* . . . . (Sire)

Makin' Whoopie
Art Tatum; *Solo Masterpieces-#5* . . . . (Pablo)
Eddie Cantor; *Nipper's Greatest Hits Of The '20s-C* . . . . (RCA)
Nilsson; *A Little Touch Of Schmilsson In The Night* . . . . (RCA)
Ray Charles; *Ray Charles-His Greatest Hits-#2* . . . . (Dunhill Compact Classics)

Making Love
Roberta Flack; *I'm The One* . . . . (Atlantic)

Making Love In A Subaru
Damaskas; *Dr. Demento's Dementia Royale-C* . . . . (Rhino)

Me & My Old Lady
Offspring; *Ixnay On The Hombre* . . . . (Columbia)

Me So Horny
2 Live Crew; *As Clean As They Wanna Be* . . . . (Luke)
As Nasty As They Wanna Be . . . . (Luke)
Bass Waves-#3-C . . . . (Luke)

Meeting In My Bedroom
Silk; *Tonight* . . . . (Elektra)

Melt In Your Mouth
Candyman; *Ain't No Shame In My Game* . . . . (Epic)

Meltdown
AC/DC; *Stiff Upper Lip* . . . . (East West)

Motel Lover
Marvin Sease; *Real Deal* . . . . (London)

Mud Shark, The
Mothers Of Invention; *Fillmore East-June 1971* . . . . (Reprise)

Muscle Of Love
Alice Cooper; *Alice Cooper's Greatest Hits* . . . . (Warner Bros.)
Muscle Of Love . . . . (Warner Bros.)

My Baby Gives It Away
Pete Townshend & Ronnie Lane; *Rough Mix* . . . . (Atlantic)

My Body
LSG; *Levert-Sweat-Gill* . . . . (East West)

My Sexual Life
Everclear; *Sparkle And Fade* . . . . (Capitol)

Naked
Spice Girls; *Spice* . . . . (Virgin)

Need Your Love
Cheap Trick; *Cheap Trick At Budokan* . . . . (Epic)
Dream Police . . . . (Epic)

Need Your Loving Tonight
Queen; *The Game* . . . . (Hollywood)

Nice & Slow
Usher; *My Way* . . . . (LaFace)

Night Moves
Bob Seger; *Night Moves* . . . . (Capitol)
ST/FM . . . . (MCA)
Bob Seger & The Silver Bullet Band; *Nine Tonight* . . . . (Capitol)

No Condom, No Sex
Cruise Control; *No Condom, No Sex-12"* . . . . (Sire)

No Diggity
Blackstreet; *Another Level* . . . . (Interscope)

Nobody
Keith Sweat; *Keith Sweat* . . . . (Elektra)

None Of Ur Friends Business
Ginuwine; *100 Percent Ginuwine* . . . . (550 Music)

Nookie
Limp Bizkit; *Now That's What I Call Music!-#3-C* . . . . (Virgin)
Significant Other . . . . (Flip/Interscope)

Not Tonight
Lil' Kim; *Hard Core* . . . . (Atlantic)

Nothing But The Radio On
Dave Koz & Joey Diggs; *Dave Koz* . . . . (Capitol)

Nothing Sure Looked Good On You
Gene Watson; *All-Time Country Classics-#2-C* . . . . (Capitol)
Country's Greatest Hits-#7-C . . . . (Priority)
Should I Come Home . . . . (Capitol)

November Rain
Guns N' Roses; *Use Your Illusion I* . . . . (Geffen)

Now You're Talkin'
Dixiana; *Now You're Talkin'* . . . . (Epic)

Nubian Nut
George Clinton; *You Shouldn't-Nuf Bit Fish* . . . . (Capitol)

O.P.P.
Naughty By Nature; *MTV Party To Go-#2-C* . . . . (Tommy Boy)

Obscene Phone Caller
Rockwell; *Somebody's Watching Me* . . . . (Motown)

One Minute Man
Missy "Misdemeanor" Elliot; *Miss E...So*
Addictive . . . . (Gold Mind/East West/EEG)

One More Chance
Notorious B.I.G.; *Ready To Die* . . . . (Bad Boy/Arista)

One Night Love Affair
Bryan Adams; *Reckless* . . . . (A&M)

One Night Stands
Hank Williams, Jr.; *Hank Williams, Jr.-Early Years* . . . . (WB/Curb)
One Night Stands . . . . (Warner Bros.)

Oochie Wally
QB's Finest featuring Nas; *QB Finest* . . . . (Columbia)

Orgasm
Prince; *Come* . . . . (Warner Bros.)

Out Of Your Shoes
Lorrie Morgan; *Essential Lorrie Morgan* . . . . (RCA)
Leave The Light On . . . . (RCA)
Lorrie Morgan-Super Hits . . . . (RCA)

P.A.S.S.I.O.N.
Rythm Syndicate; *Rythm Syndicate* . . . . (Impact)

Paradise By The Dashboard Light
Meat Loaf; *Bat Out Of Hell* . . . . (Epic)

Part Man, Part Monkey
Bruce Springsteen; *Tracks* . . . . (Columbia)

Part-Time Lover
Stevie Wonder; *In Square Circle* . . . . (Motown)

Peaches And Cream
112; *Part III* . . . . (Bad Boy/Arista)
Totally Hits 2001-C . . . . (Arista)

People Are Still Having Sex
LaTour; *LaTour* . . . . (Smash)

Perfume And Pink Chiffon
Sonny Lester & His Orchestra; *Take It Off: Striptease Classics-C* . . . . . . (Rhino)

Personally
Karla Bonoff; *Wild Heart Of The Young* . . . . (Columbia)
Pervert Nurse
D.I.; *Horse Bites Dog Cries* . . . . (Triple X Entert.)
Phenomenon
L.L. Cool J; *Phenomenon* . . . . (Def Jam/Mercury)
Phone Sexxx
Jimmy Z; *Muzical Madness* . . . . (Ruthless)
Physical
Olivia Newton-John; *Back To Basics-Essential Collection 1971-1992* . . (Geffen)
Olivia Newton-John's Greatest Hits-#2 . . . . (MCA)
Physical . . . . (MCA)
Pill, The
Loretta Lynn; *Loretta Lynn-20 Greatest Hits* . . . . (MCA)
The Country Music Hall Of Fame-Loretta Lynn . . . . (MCA)
Pillow Talk
Sylvia; *All Platinum Gold* . . . . (All Platinum)
Super Bad Is Back-Soul Love-C . . . . (K-Tel)
Pink
Aerosmith; *Nine Lives* . . . . (Columbia)
Playboy Channel
Negativeland; *Escape From Noise* . . . . (SST)
Pocket Porn
Renegade Soundwave; *In Dub* . . . . (Elektra)
Pony
Ginuwine; *Ginuwine...The Bachelor* . . . . (550 Music)
Pop My Dick Song
Sloppy Seconds; *First Seven Inches... & Then Some!* . . . . (Taang!)
Pop That Pussy
2 Live Crew; *Sports Weekend (As Nasty As They Wanna Be Part II)* . . . . . (Luke)
Porn Wars
Frank Zappa; *Meets The Mothers Of Prevention* . . . . (Rykodisc)
Porno For Pyros
Porno For Pyros; *Porno For Pyros* . . . . (Warner Bros.)
Porno Freak
Blowfly; *Twisted World Of Blowfly* . . . . (Oops)
Pornograffitti
Extreme; *Pornograffitti* . . . . (A&M)
Pornography
Cure; *Cure* . . . . (Elektra)
Pour Some Sugar On Me
Def Leppard; *Hysteria* . . . . (Mercury)
Pretty Fuck Look
Pussy Galore; *Corpse Love-The First Year* . . . . (Caroline)
Prison Sex
Tool; *Undertow* . . . . (Zoo/Volcano)
Project Chick/Project Bitch
Cash Money Millionaires; *12'' Maxi Single* . . . . (Cash Money/Universal)
Psychedelic Sex Reaction
Babylon A.D.; *Nothing Sacred* . . . . (Arista)
Pull Over
Trina; *Da Baddest B***h* . . . . (Slip 'N Slide)
Push It
Garbage; *Version 2.0* . . . . (Almo Sounds)
Queen Of Memphis
Confederate Railroad; *Confederate Railroad* . . . . (Atlantic)
Question Of Lust
Depeche Mode; *101* . . . . (Sire)
Black Celebration . . . . (Sire)
Rated ''X''
Loretta Lynn; *Best Of Loretta Lynn* . . . . (MCA Special Prod.)
Rated X
Pat Benatar; *In The Heat Of The Night* . . . . (Chrysalis)
Raunchy
Bill Justice; *Golden Years-1957-C* . . . . (Dominion Entert.)
Raunchy . . . . (Smash)
Sun Story-C . . . . (Rhino)
Bill Justice & His Orchestra; *History Of Rock Instrumentals-#2-C* . . . (Rhino)
Ernie Freeman; *Oldies But Goodies-#8-C* . . . . (Original Sound)
Really Suck
Pussy Galore; *Right Now!* . . . . (Caroline)
Red Light Special
TLC; *CrazySexyCool* . . . . (LaFace)
Red Neckin' Love Makin' Night
Conway Twitty; *Classic Conway* . . . . (MCA)
Conway Twitty-Legends . . . . (MCA)
Mr. T . . . . (MCA)
Night With Conway Twitty . . . . (MCA)
Red Sex Dress
Alfonia Tims & The Flying Tigers; *Future Funk/Uncut!* . . . . (Roir)
Reeling And Rocking
Chuck Berry; *Best Of The Best Of Chuck Berry* . . . . (International Mktg. Group)
Chuck Berry's Greatest Hits . . . . (Everest)
Frat Rock!-C . . . . (Rhino)
Rock & Roll Show-C . . . . (Gusto)
The Chess Box-Chuck Berry . . . . (Chess)
Ridin'
Buckcherry; *Time Bomb* . . . . (DreamWorks/SKG)

Right Time Of The Night
Jennifer Warnes; *Best Of Jennifer Warnes* . . . . (Arista)
Jennifer Warnes . . . . (Arista)
Ring My Bell
Anita Ward; *Billboard Top Dance Hits-1979-C* . . . . (Rhino)
Billboard Top Rock 'N' Roll Hits-1979-C . . . . (Rhino)
Get Down Tonight! Best Of T.K. Records-C . . . . (Rhino)
Mega Hits Dance Classics-#1-C . . . . (Priority)
Songs Of Love . . . . (Juana)
Sweet Surrender . . . . (Juana)
Rock & Roll Pussy
Todd Rundgren; *A Wizard A True Star* . . . . (Rhino)
Rock Me Baby
B.B. King; *B.B. King Greatest Hits* . . . . (Kent)
Now Appearing Live At Ole Miss . . . . (MCA)
Rock Me Baby . . . . (Kent)
Etta James; *Red Hot 'N' Live* . . . . (Intermedia)
Hot Tuna; *Historic Hot Tuna* . . . . (Relix)
Jefferson Airplane; *Bless Its Pointed Little Head* . . . . (RCA)
Jimi Hendrix; *ST/Jimi Hendrix* . . . . (Reprise)
ST/Jimi Plays Monterey . . . . (Reprise)
Otis Redding; *Best Of Otis Redding* . . . . (Atco)
Robin Trower; *Robin Trower-Live* . . . . (Chrysalis)
Twice Removed From Yesterday . . . . (Chrysalis)
Rock The Boat
Aaliyah; *Aaliyah* . . . . (BlackGround Enterp./Atlantic)
Rocks Off
Rolling Stones; *Exile On Main Street* . . . . (Virgin)
Let There Be Drums!-#3-The '70s-C . . . . (Rhino)
Rocks Off
Def Leppard; *On Through The Night* . . . . (Mercury)
Rump Shaker
Wreckx-N-Effect; *Hard Or Smooth* . . . . (MCA)
Run Away
Real McCoy; *Another Night* . . . . (Arista)
Sadder-But-Wiser Girl For Me
Original Cast; *The Music Man* . . . . (Gold Rush)
Robert Preston; *ST/The Music Man* . . . . (Warner Bros.)
Safe Sex
Erick Sermon; *No Pressure* . . . . (Def Jam/IDJMG)
Saving All My Love For You
Whitney Houston; *Whitney Houston* . . . . (Arista)
Whitney Houston's Greatest Hits . . . . (Arista)
Set Adrift On Memory Bliss
PM Dawn; *MTV Party To Go-#2-C* . . . . (Tommy Boy)
Red Hot + Dance-C . . . . (Columbia)
Sex
Lee ''Scratch'' Perry; *The Upsetter & The Beat* . . . . (Heartbeat)
Sex
Kix; *Midnite Dynamite* . . . . (Atlantic)
Sex
Paul Young; *No Parlez* . . . . (Columbia)
Sex
Ice-T; *Rhyme Pays* . . . . (Sire)
Sex (I'm A...)
Berlin; *Best Of Berlin 1979-1988* . . . . (Geffen)
Pleasure Victim . . . . (Geffen)
Sex And Candy
Marcy Playground; *Marcy Playground* . . . . (Capitol)
Now That's What I Call Music!-#1-C . . . . (Virgin)
Sex And Dying In High Society
X; *Los Angeles/Wild Gift* . . . . (Slash)
Sex As A Weapon
Pat Benatar; *Seven The Hard Way* . . . . (Chrysalis)
Sex Beat
Gun Club; *Fire Of Love* . . . . (Slash)
Sex Bomb
Flipper; *Generic* . . . . (Def American)
Sex By Mail
Free Hot Lunch; *Penguin Love* . . . . (Flying Fish)
Sex Crime
Eurythmics; *Eurythmics' Greatest Hits* . . . . (Arista)
Sex Cymbal
Sheila E.; *Sex Cymbal* . . . . (Warner Bros.)
Sex Drive
Rolling Stones; *Flashpoint* . . . . (Virgin)
Sex Farm
Spinal Tap; *ST/Spinal Tap* . . . . (Polydor)
Sex Fiend
Awesome Dre & The Hardcore Committee; *Explicit Rap-C* . . . . (Priority)
You Can't Hold Me Back . . . . (Priority)
Sex In A Pan
Bela Fleck & The Flecktones; *UFO Tofu* . . . . (Warner Bros.)
Sex In The '90s
Gloria Estefan; *Into The Light* . . . . (Epic)
Sex Machine
James Brown; *Revolution Of The Mind* . . . . (Polydor)
John Wagner Coalition; *Shades Of Brown-James Brown's Greatest* . . . . (Koala)

Sex Maniac
Bobby Nunn; *Private Party* . . . . (Motown)
Sex Me, Talk Me
Berlin; *Count Three & Pray* . . . . (Geffen)
Sex On Wheelz
My Life With The Thrill Kill Kult; *Sexplosion!* . . . . (Rykodisc)
Sex Symbols
Ray Stevens; *Crackin' Up* . . . . (MCA)
Sex Wanderer
Freewheelers; *Freewheelers* . . . . (David Geffen Co.)
Sex, Drugs & Rock & Roll
Ian Dury; *New Boots & Panties* . . . . (Stiff)
Mantronix; *This Should Move Ya* . . . . (Capitol)
Sex-O-Matic Venus Freak
Macy Gray; *On How Life Is* . . . . (Epic)
Sexual Harassment In The Workplace
Frank Zappa; *Guitar* . . . . (Rykodisc)
Sexual Healing
Marvin Gaye; *Last Concert Tour* . . . . (Giant)
Midnight Love . . . . (Columbia)
Seems Like Yesterday-#4-Early '80s-C . . . . (K-Tel)
Tribute To Black Entertainers-C . . . . (Columbia)
Max-A-Million; *Take Your Time* . . . . (S.O.S./Zoo)
Sexual Revolution
Macy Gray; *The Id* . . . . (Epic)
Sexuality
Jamie Principle; *Midnite Hour* . . . . (Smash)
Sexuality
Erasure; *Chorus* . . . . (Sire)
Sexuality
Prince; *Controversy* . . . . (Warner Bros.)
Sexuality
Billy Bragg; *Don't Try This At Home* . . . . (Elektra)
Sexy + 17
Stray Cats; *Best Of Stray Cats-Rock This Town* . . . . (EMI)
Rant 'N' Rave With The Stray Cats . . . . (EMI)
Sexy Dancer
Prince; *Prince* . . . . (Warner Bros.)
Sexy Eyes
Dr. Hook; *Dr. Hook-Greatest Hits & More* . . . . (Capitol)
Sometimes You Win . . . . (Capitol)
Sexy Girl
Lillo Thomas; *Lillo Thomas* . . . . (Capitol)
Sexy Girl
Glenn Frey; *Allnighter* . . . . (MCA)
Sexy Ida
Ike & Tina Turner; *Proud Mary-Best Of Ike & Tina Turner* . . . . (EMI)
Sexy Lady
Carl Carlton; *Carl Carlton* . . . . (20th Century Fox)
Ear Candy-#2-C . . . . (20th Century Fox)
Sexy Lady
Rick James; *Come Get It!* . . . . (Motown)
Sexy Lady
Commodores; *Midnight Magic* . . . . (Motown)
Sexy M.F.
Prince And The New Power Generation; *Love Symbol Album* . . . . (Paisley Park)
Sexy Mexican Maid
Red Hot Chili Peppers; *Mother's Milk* . . . . (EMI)
Sexy Music
Meat Puppets; *Huevos* . . . . (SST)
Sexy Rhino
Adrian Belew; *Desire Of The Rhino King* . . . . (Island)
Sexy Sadie
Beatles; *Beatles-Box Set* . . . . (Capitol)
The Beatles (White Album) . . . . (Capitol)
Shake Ya Ass
Mystikal; *Let's Get Ready* . . . . (Jive)
Shake Your Bon-Bon
Ricky Martin; *Ricky Martin* . . . . (Columbia)
Shaking Your Tree (Somebody Else Been)
ZZ Top; *Six Pack* . . . . (Warner Bros.)
ZZ Top . . . . (Warner Bros.)
Sharin' The Night Together
Dr. Hook; *Dr. Hook-Greatest Hits & More* . . . . (Capitol)
Pleasure & Pain . . . . (Capitol)
Shaving Cream
Benny Bell & Paul Wynn; *Dr. Demento Presents The Greatest Novelty*
Records-#1-1940s & Before-C . . . . (Rhino)
Dr. Demento's Dementia Royale-C . . . . (Rhino)
She Bangs
Ricky Martin; *Sound Loaded* . . . . (Columbia)
She Bop
Cyndi Lauper; *Music For The Miracle-C* . . . . (Epic Portrait Assoc.)
She's So Unusual . . . . (Portrait)
She Thinks His Name Was John
Reba McEntire; *Read My Mind* . . . . (MCA)
Reba McEntire's Greatest Hits-#3: I'm A Survivor . . . . (MCA)

She Thinks My Tractor's Sexy
Kenny Chesney; *Everywhere We Go* . . . . (BNA)
She Was Hot
Rolling Stones; *Undercover* . . . . (Rolling Stones)
She's Vibrator Dependent
Mojo Nixon & Skid Roper; *Root Hog Or Die* . . . . (I.R.S.)
Silverfuck
Smashing Pumpkins; *Siamese Dream* . . . . (Virgin)
Sin Wagon
Dixie Chicks; *Fly* . . . . (Monument)
Sixty Minute Man
Billy Ward & His Dominoes; *Rock & Roll Show-C* . . . . (Gusto)
Dominos; *Oldies But Goodies-#5-C* . . . . (Original Sound)
Rufus Thomas & Carla Thomas; *Rufus Thomas & Carla Thomas-*
Chronicle . . . . (Stax)
Slide
Goo Goo Dolls; *Dizzy Up The Girl* . . . . (Warner Sunset/Reprise)
Slow Ride
Foghat; *Best Of Foghat* . . . . (Rhino)
Best Of King Biscuit Live-#1-C . . . . (Sandstone Music)
Foghat-Live . . . . (Rhino)
Fool For The City . . . . (Rhino)
So Anxious
Ginuwine; *100 Percent Ginuwine* . . . . (550 Music)
Sock It 2 Me
Missy "Misdemeanor" Elliot; *Supa Dupa Fly* . . . . (East West)
Softest Place On Earth
Xscape; *Traces Of My Lipstick* . . . . (So So Def/Columbia)
Some Girls
Rolling Stones; *Some Girls* . . . . (Virgin)
Son Of A Preacher Man
Dusty Springfield; *Dusty Springfield* . . . . (Rhino)
Dusty Springfield-Anthology . . . . (Mercury)
Southern Hospitality
Ludacris; *Back For The First Time* . . . . (Def Jam South/IDJMG)
Souvenir Of London (V.D.)
Procol Harum; *Grand Hotel* . . . . (Chrysalis)
Spanish Fly
Van Halen; *Van Halen II* . . . . (Warner Bros.)
Splackavellie
Pressha; *Don't Get It Twisted* . . . . (Tony Mercedes/LaFace/Arista)
Squeezebox
Who; *By Numbers* . . . . (MCA)
Hooligans . . . . (MCA)
Who Greatest Hits . . . . (MCA)
Steam
Ty Herndon; *Steam* . . . . (Epic)
Still A G Thang
Snoop Dogg; *Da Game Is To Be Sold, Not To Be Told* . . . . . . (No Limit/Priority)
Still Not A Player
Big Punisher Featuring Joe; *Capital Punishment* . . . . (Loud/RCA)
Strawberries
Smooth; *Reality* . . . . (Perspective/A&M)
Strawberry Wine
Deana Carter; *Did I Shave My Legs For This?* . . . . (Capitol)
Stripper
David Rose; *Dick Bartley's One-Hit Wonders Of The '60s-#1-C* . . . . . . (Rhino)
Strut
Sheena Easton; *Best Of Sheena Easton* . . . . (EMI)
Dance Mix . . . . (EMI)
Private Heaven . . . . (EMI)
The World Of Sheena Easton: The Singles Collection-C . . . . . . (EMI)
Stuck In A Closet With Vanna White
"Weird Al" Yankovic; *Even Worse* . . . . (Scotti Bros.)
Stutter
Elastica; *Elastica* . . . . (David Geffen Co.)
Sugar Walls
Sheena Easton; *Dance Mix* . . . . (EMI)
Private Heaven . . . . (EMI)
Sultan Of Sex
Neon Judgement; *Horny As Hell* . . . . (Play It Again Sam)
Surfin' Sex Machine
Pajama Slave Dancers; *Blood Sweat & Beers* . . . . (Restless)
Sweet & Sexy Thing
Rick James; *Flag* . . . . (Motown)
Sweet Lover Man
Pointer Sisters; *Best Of The Pointer Sisters 1978-1981* . . . . (RCA)
Sweet & Soulful . . . . (RCA)
Sweet Sexy Eyes
Cristy Lane; *Country Classics* . . . . (Arrival)
Cristy Lane-At Her Best . . . . (EMI)
Sweet Sexy Thing
Nu Flavor; *Nu Flavor* . . . . (Reprise)
Swimsuit Issue
Sonic Youth; *Dirty* . . . . (David Geffen Co.)
Swing My Way
K.P. & Envyi; *ST/Can't Hardly Wait* . . . . (Elektra)

Take A Little Trip
Alabama; *American Pride* . . . . (RCA)
Take It To Da House
Trick Daddy; *Thugs Are Us* . . . . (Slip 'N Slide/Atlantic)
Take Me Down
Alabama; *Alabama-Live* . . . . (RCA)
   Alabama's Greatest Hits-#2 . . . . (RCA)
   Mountain Music . . . . (RCA)
Talk Dirty To Me
Poison; *Look What The Cat Dragged In* . . . . (Capitol)
   Swallow This Live . . . . (Capitol)
Taste Of India
Aerosmith; *Nine Lives* . . . . (Columbia)
Teach Me Tonight
Al Jarreau; *Al Jarreau In London* . . . . (Warner Bros.)
   Breakin' Away . . . . (Warner Bros.)
Diane Schuur; *Diane Schuur-Collection* . . . . (GRP)
Ella Fitzgerald; *Montreux '75* . . . . (Pablo)
Phoebe Snow; *Best Of Phoebe Snow* . . . . (Columbia)
   It Looks Like Snow . . . . (Columbia)
Sarah Vaughan; *How Long Has This Been Going On?* . . . . (Pablo)
Teenage Lust
Jesus & Mary Chain; *Honey's Dead* . . . . (Def American)
Tell Me
Dru Hill; *ST/Eddie* . . . . (Island)
Tender Lover
Babyface; *Tender Lover* . . . . (Solar)
Tennessee Stud
Chris LeDoux; *Old Cowboy Classics* . . . . (Capitol)
Eddy Arnold; *Best Of Eddy Arnold-#2* . . . . (Dunhill Compact Classics)
   Eddy Arnold-Legendary Performer . . . . (RCA)
Hank Williams, Jr.; *The Pressure Is On-Original Classics*
   Collection-#7 . . . . (Curb)
Johnny Cash; *American Recordings* . . . . (American)
Nitty Gritty Dirt Band; *Will The Circle Be Unbroken* . . . . (EMI)
That Summer
Garth Brooks; *The Chase* . . . . (Liberty)
That's The Way (I Like It)
KC And The Sunshine Band; *Best Of KC And The Sunshine Band* . . . . . (Rhino)
   Disco Hits-#1-C . . . . (Rhino)
   Mega Hits Dance Classics-#3-C . . . . (Priority)
Theme From "Shaft"
Isaac Hayes; *Isaac Hayes' Greatest Hit Singles* . . . . (Stax)
   Pimps, Players & Private Eyes-C . . . . (Sire)
   Top Of The Stax-Twenty Greatest Hits-C . . . . (Stax)
Theme From "Soap"
Original Soundtrack; *Television's Greatest Hits-#6-Remote Control-C* . . (TVT)
Theme From "Summer Of '42"
George Benson; *Best Of George Benson* . . . . (CBS Associated)
   White Rabbit . . . . (CBS Associated)
Peter Nero; *"Summer Of '42" Theme* . . . . (Columbia)
   Peter Nero's Greatest Hits . . . . (Columbia)
There Is Nothin' Like A Dame
Original Cast; *South Pacific* . . . . (CBS Masterworks)
They Call It Making Love
Tammy Wynette; *Tears Of Fire-25th Anniversary Collection* . . . . (Epic)
Tammy Wynette & George Jones; *Encore-Tammy Wynette & George
   Jones* . . . . (Epic)
They Like It Slow
H-Town; *Ladies Edition* . . . . (Relativity)
Thinkin' 'Bout It
Gerald Levert; *Love & Consequences* . . . . (East West)
Thinking About Sex Again
Waitresses; *Best Of The Waitresses* . . . . (Polydor)
Third Rate Romance
Amazing Rhythm Aces; *Stacked Deck* . . . . (MCA)
Rosanne Cash; *Somewhere In The Stars* . . . . (Columbia)
Sammy Kershaw; *Cryin' Lyin' Lovin' & Leavin'-C* . . . . (Universal)
   Feelin' Good Train . . . . (Mercury)
   The Hits-Chapter 1 . . . . (Mercury)
Thong Song
Sisqo; *Unleash The Dragon* . . . . (Dragon/Def Soul/IDJMG)
To Be A Lover
Billy Idol; *Vital Idol* . . . . (Chrysalis)
   Whiplash Smile . . . . (Chrysalis)
Tonight's The Night (Gonna Be All Right)
Rod Stewart; *Absolutely Live* . . . . (Warner Bros.)
   Downtown Train-Selections From The Storyteller Anthology . . (Warner Bros.)
   Night On The Town . . . . (Warner Bros.)
   Rod Stewart's Greatest Hits . . . . (Warner Bros.)
Too Close
Next; *Rated Next* . . . . (Divine Mill/Arista)
Too Fat To Fuck
Blowfly; *Fresh Juice* . . . . (Oops)
Too Many Lovers
Crystal Gayle; *Crystal Gayle Greatest Hits* . . . . (Capitol)
   Greatest Country Hits Of The '80s-1981-C . . . . (Columbia)
   These Days . . . . (Columbia)

Touch It
Monifah; *Mo'hogany* . . . . (Uptown)
Touch Me (All Night Long)
Cathy Dennis; *Move To This* . . . . (Polydor)
Touch Me (I Want Your Body)
Samantha Fox; *Samantha Fox's Greatest Hits* . . . . (Jive)
   Touch Me (I Want Your Body) . . . . (Jive)
Trash
Korn; *Issues* . . . . (Immortal/Epic)
Tumbling Dice
Linda Ronstadt; *Linda Ronstadt's Greatest Hits, Volume Two* . . . . . (Asylum)
   Simple Dreams . . . . (Asylum)
   ST/FM . . . . (MCA)
Rolling Stones; *Exile On Main Street* . . . . (Virgin)
   Love You Live . . . . (Virgin)
   Made In The Shade . . . . (Rolling Stones)
   Rewind (1971-1984) . . . . (Rolling Stones)
Turn It Up
Busta Rhymes; *When Disaster Strikes* . . . . (Elektra)
Tush
ZZ Top; *Best Of ZZ Top* . . . . (Warner Bros.)
   Fandango . . . . (Warner Bros.)
   Six Pack . . . . (Warner Bros.)
   ST/An Officer And A Gentleman . . . . (Island)
   ZZ Top's Greatest Hits . . . . (Warner Bros.)
Two Headed Sex Change
Cramps; *Look Mom No Head!* . . . . (Restless)
Two Lovers
Mary Wells; *Hitsville USA-The Motown Singles Collection-1959-
   1971-C* . . . . (Motown)
   Mary Wells' Greatest Hits . . . . (Motown)
U Can't Touch This
Hammer; *Please Hammer Don't Hurt 'Em* . . . . (Capitol)
U Know What's Up
Donell Jones; *Totally Hits-#2-C* . . . . (Elektra)
   Where I Wanna Be . . . . (LaFace)
Up Jumps Da' Boogie
Timbaland & Magoo; *Welcome To Our World* . . (BlackGround Enterp./Atlantic)
Vagabond Virgin
Traffic; *Traffic* . . . . (Island)
Voodoo Sex Doll
Crisis Party; *Rude Awakening* . . . . (Metal Blade)
Wake Up & Make Love To Me
Ian Dury; *New Boots & Panties* . . . . (Stiff)
   Stiff Live . . . . (Stiff)
Wanna Be A Baller
Lil' Troy; *Sittin' Fat Down South* . . . . (Short Stop/Republic/Universal)
War Is Hell (On The Homefront Too)
T.G. Sheppard; *Perfect Stranger* . . . . (Warner Bros.)
   T.G. Sheppard's All-Time Greatest Hits . . . . (Warner Bros.)
   T.G. Sheppard's Greatest Hits . . . . (Warner Bros./Curb)
We Be Clubbin'
Ice Cube; *ST/The Player's Club* . . . . (Heavyweight/A&M)
We Don't Have To Take Our Clothes Off
Jermaine Stewart; *Frantic Romantic* . . . . (Arista)
We Don't Make Love Anymore
Anne Murray; *Country Collection* . . . . (Capitol)
   Let's Keep It That Way . . . . (Liberty)
We Should Be Making Love
Huey Lewis and the News; *Hard At Play* . . . . (EMI)
Wet My Whistle
Midnight Star; *Midnight Star's Greatest Hits* . . . . (Solar)
   No Parking On The Dance Floor . . . . (Solar)
What Would Happen
Meredith Brooks; *Blurring The Edges* . . . . (Capitol)
What Ya Want
Ruff Ryders Featuring Eve & Nokio; *Ruff Ryders: Ride Or
   Die-#1* . . . . (Ruff Ryders/IDJMG)
What You Want
DMX; *...And Then There Was X* . . . . (Ruff Ryders/IDJMG)
Whatcha Gone Do?
Link; *Sex Down* . . . . (Relativity)
What'chu Like
Da Brat; *Unrestricted* . . . . (So So Def/Columbia)
What's It Gonna Be
Busta Rhymes Featuring Janet Jackson; *E.L.E.* . . . . (Elektra)
What's Your Fantasy
Ludacris; *Back For The First Time* . . . . (Def Jam South/IDJMG)
   Totally Hits 2001-C . . . . (Arista)
When We Make Love
Alabama; *Roll On* . . . . (RCA)
Whoa
Black Rob; *Life Story* . . . . (Bad Boy/Arista)
Whole Lotta Love
Led Zeppelin; *Led Zeppelin II* . . . . (Atlantic)
   Led Zeppelin-Box Set . . . . (Atlantic)
   Remasters . . . . (Atlantic)
   ST/The Song Remains The Same . . . . (Swan Song)

Who's Makin' Love
Blues Brothers; *Blues Brothers-The Definitive Collection* . . . . (Atlantic)
  Made In America . . . . (Atlantic)
Johnnie Taylor; *Billboard Top R&B Hits-1965-1969-C* . . . . (Rhino)
  Johnnie Taylor-Super Hits . . . . (Stax)
  Oldies But Goodies-#5-C . . . .(Original Sound)
  Top Of The Stax-Twenty Greatest Hits-C . . . . (Stax)
Who's Sucking On Grandpa's Balls Since Grandma Ain't Home Tonight?
Frogs; *My Daughter The Broad* . . . . (Matador)
Who's Zoomin' Who
Aretha Franklin; *Who's Zoomin' Who?* . . . . (Arista)
Whose Bed Have Your Boots Been Under?
Shania Twain; *The Woman In Me* . . . . (Mercury)
Why Don't We Do It In The Road
Beatles; *Beatles-Box Set* . . . . (Capitol)
  The Beatles (White Album) . . . . (Capitol)
Why Don't We Get Drunk
Jimmy Buffett; *Boats Beaches Bars & Ballads* . . . . (Margaritaville)
  Songs You Know By Heart-Jimmy Buffett's Greatest Hit(s) . . . . (MCA)
  White Sport Coat & A Pink Crustacean . . . . (MCA)
  You Had To Be There . . . . (MCA)
Wild Sex (In The Working Class)
Oingo Boingo; *Best O' Boingo* . . . . (MCA)
  Boingo Alive . . . . (MCA)
  Nothing To Fear . . . . (A&M)
With Me Part 1
Destiny's Child featuring JD; *Destiny's Child* . . . .(Grass Roots/Columbia)
Wobble Wobble
504 Boyz; *Goodfellas* . . . . (No Limit/Priority)
Woman, A Lover, A Friend
Jackie Wilson; *Jackie Wilson's Greatest Hits-#2* . . . . (Brunswick)
  Mr. Excitement . . . . (Rhino)
Otis Redding; *The Otis Redding Story* . . . . (Atlantic)
Work With Me Annie
Hank Ballard And The Midnighters; *Best Of Hank Ballard And The Midnighters-Sexy Ways* . . . . (Rhino)
Royals; *Risque Rhythms: Nasty '50s R&B-C* . . . . (Rhino)
World's Greatest Lover
Bellamy Brothers; *Bellamy Brothers' Greatest Hits-#2* . . . . (MCA)
  Bellamy Brothers' Greatest Hits-#2 . . . . (Curb)
Written In Sand
Santana; *Beyond Appearances* . . . . (Columbia)
Yank Me Crank Me
Ted Nugent; *Double Live Gonzo* . . . . (Epic)
  Twisted Metal . . . . (K-Tel)
You Can Leave Your Hat On
Joe Cocker; *Cocker* . . . . (Capitol)
  Joe Cocker Live . . . . (Capitol)
  ST/9 1/2 Weeks . . . . (Capitol)
Randy Newman; *Sail Away* . . . . (Reprise)
You Can't Play With My Yo-Yo
Yo-Yo & Ice Cube; *Make Way For The Motherlode* . . . . (East West)
You Don't Have To Go Home Tonight
Triplets; *...Thicker Than Water* . . . . (Mercury)
You Make Me Sick
Pink; *Can't Take Me Home* . . . . (LaFace)
You Need A Woman Tonight
Captain & Tennille; *Dreams* . . . . (A&M)
You Never Done It Like That
Captain & Tennille; *Dreams* . . . . (A&M)
You Owe Me
NaS featuring Ginuwine; *NaStradamus* . . . . (Columbia)
You Remind Me Of Something
R. Kelly; *R. Kelly* . . . .(Jive)
You Sexy Thing
Hot Chocolate; *Hot Chocolate* . . . . (Big Tree)
  Mega Hits Dance Classics-#8-C . . . .(Priority)
  Super Hits Of The '70s-Have A Nice Day-#15-C . . . . (Rhino)
You Shook Me
Jeff Beck Group; *Truth* . . . . (Epic)
Led Zeppelin; *Led Zeppelin* . . . . (Atlantic)
Muddy Waters; *The Chess Box-Muddy Waters* . . . . (Chess)
Willie Dixon; *I Am The Blues* . . . . (Columbia)
You Shook Me All Night Long
AC/DC; *Back In Black* . . . . (Atco)
  Who Made Who . . . . (Atlantic)
You Sure Love To Ball
Marvin Gaye; *Let's Get It On* . . . . (Motown)
Your Body's Callin'
R. Kelly; *12 Play* . . . .(Jive)
Your Friend In The Cowboy Hat (The Viagra Song)
Croatan; *Violent Passion Surrogate* . . . . (Man's Ruin)
You're Makin' Me High
Toni Braxton; *Secrets* . . . . (LaFace)
You're Out Doing What I'm Here Doing Without
Gene Watson; *Gene Watson's Greatest Hits* . . . . (MCA)
  Sometimes I Get Lucky . . . . (MCA)

SEX: RESISTING TEMPTATION

See Also: **AIDS, CHARACTER & INTEGRITY, FAMILY PLANNING, LOVE (various), PARENTS: CONCERNED ABOUT TEEN LOVE, SEX**

All Good
Mo Thugs Family Scriptures; *Chapter II: Family Reunion* . . . .(Relativity)
Best Of Me
Mya featuring Jadakiss; *Fear Of Flying* . . . . (University/Interscope)
Don't Rush (Take Love Slowly)
K-Ci & JoJo; *Love Always* . . . . (MCA)
Don't You Feel My Leg
Maria Muldaur; *Maria Muldaur* . . . . (Reprise)
Faded
soulDecision; *No One Does It Better* . . . . (MCA)
  Now That's What I Call Music!-#5-C . . . . (Virgin)
First Night
Monica; *The Boy Is Mine* . . . .(Arista)
Genie In A Bottle
Christina Aguilera; *Christina Aguilera* . . . . (RCA)
  Totally Hits-#2-C . . . . (Elektra)
Heart Is A Lonely Hunter
Reba McEntire; *Read My Mind* . . . . (MCA)
  Reba McEntire's Greatest Hits-#3: I'm A Survivor . . . . (MCA)
Heart Of Innocence
Jessica Simpson; *Sweet Kisses* . . . .(Columbia)
Heartbreak U.S.A.
Kitty Wells; *I Love Country-Hits Of The '60s-#1-C* . . . . (Priority)
  Kitty Wells' Greatest Songs . . . .(Curb)
  The Country Music Hall Of Fame-Kitty Wells . . . . (MCA Special Prod.)
If It Ain't Love (Let's Leave It Alone)
Connie Smith; *Essential Connie Smith* . . . . (RCA)
Whites; *Whites' Greatest Hits* . . . .(Curb)
Let's Wait Awhile
Janet Jackson; *Control* . . . .(A&M)
Paradise By The Dashboard Light
Meat Loaf; *Bat Out Of Hell* . . . . (Epic)
Pretty Polly
Judy Collins; *Who Knows Where The Time Goes* . . . .(Elektra)
Stanley Brothers; *Complete Columbia Stanley Brothers* . . . .(Legacy)
  Folk Classics: Roots Of American Folk Music-C . . . .(Columbia)
  Long Journey Home . . . . (Rebel)
She's Been Good To Me
Marc Anthony; *Marc Anthony* . . . .(Columbia)
Sometimes
Britney Spears; *...Baby One More Time* . . . . (Jive)
  Now That's What I Call Music!-#3-C . . . . (Virgin)
Spirit Of A Boy, Wisdom Of A Man
Randy Travis; *Big Country Hits '99-C* . . . .(K-Tel)
  You And You Alone . . . . (DreamWorks/SKG)
Stay
Destiny's Child; *The Writing's On The Wall* . . . .(Columbia)
Ten Thousand Angels
Mindy McCready; *Ten Thousand Angels* . . . . (BNA)
These Are The Times
Dru Hill; *Enter The Dru* . . . . (Def Jam/RAL/Mercury/Island)
Too Close For Comfort
Eydie Gorme; *Eydie Gorme* . . . .(Taragon)
Try Again
Aaliyah; *Now That's What I Call Music!-#4-C* . . . . (Virgin)
  ST/Romeo Must Die . . . .(BlackGround Enterp./Atlantic)
We Don't Have To Take Our Clothes Off
Jermaine Stewart; *Frantic Romantic* . . . .(Arista)

SHADOWS, Eclipse

See Also: **ECHOES, LIGHT, REFLECTIONS**

African Shadow Man
Johnny Clegg & Savuka; *Shadow Man* . . . .(Capitol)
And I Love You So
Perry Como; *Perry Como's Greatest Hits* . . . . (RCA)
Blue Shadows
B.B. King; *B.B. King Greatest Hits* . . . .(Kent)
  From The Beginning . . . .(Kent)
  The Jungle . . . .(Kent)
Blue Shadows
Blasters; *ST/Streets Of Fire* . . . . (MCA)
Blue Shadows On The Trail
Sons Of The Pioneers; *Cool Water* . . . . (RCA)
Chain, The
Fleetwood Mac; *25 Years-The Chain* . . . .(Warner Bros.)
  Rumours . . . . (Warner Bros.)
Shawn Colvin; *Legacy-A Tribute To Fleetwood Mac's Rumours-C* . . . . .(Lava)

Chasing Shadows
Kansas; *Vinyl Confessions* .... (Kirshner)
Chasing Shadows
Deep Purple; *Purple Passages* .... (Warner Bros.)
Complicated Shadows
Elvis Costello & The Attractions; *The Sopranos-Music From The HBO Original Series* .... (Sony Music Soundtrax)
Cry For A Shadow
Beatles; *Beatles* .... (Audio Fidelity)
The Beatles featuring Tony Sheridan-In The Beginning (Circa 1960) .... (Polydor)
Crying In The Shadows
Gary Moore; *Wild Frontier* .... (Virgin)
Eclipse
Pink Floyd; *Dark Side Of The Moon* .... (Capitol)
Works .... (Capitol)
Forty Six & 2
Tool; *Aenima* .... (Freeworld/Capitol)
Got No Shadow
Little Feat; *Sailin' Shoes* .... (Warner Bros.)
Have You Seen Your Mother, Baby, Standing In The Shadow?
Rolling Stones; *Flowers* .... (Abkco)
got Live if you want it! .... (Abkco)
More Hot Rocks (big hits & fazed cookies) .... (Abkco)
Through The Past, Darkly (Big Hits Vol. 2) .... (Abkco)
Heartache, A Shadow, A Lifetime
Dave Mason; *Best Of Dave Mason* .... (MCA)
Dave Mason-At His Very Best .... (MCA)
In The Shadows
Stranglers; *Black & White* .... (A&M)
Love Walked In
Chet Baker; *Chet Baker With Strings* .... (Columbia)
Frank Sinatra; *Sinatra Swings* .... (Reprise)
The Reprise Collection .... (Reprise)
Sarah Vaughan; *Complete Sarah Vaughan On Mercury-#2* .... (Mercury)
Moon Shadow
Cat Stevens; *Cat Stevens Greatest Hits* .... (A&M)
Cat Stevens-Classics-#24 .... (A&M)
Teaser And The Firecat .... (A&M)
Moonshadow Road
T. Graham Brown; *Best Of T. Graham Brown* .... (Liberty)
Promise Of Shadows
Peter Gabriel; *Passion: Music For The Last Temptation Of Christ* .... (Geffen)
Razor Love
Neil Young; *Silver & Gold* .... (Reprise)
Shadow & Me
Leon Russell; *Americana* .... (Paradise)
Shadow Boxer
Angel City; *Face To Face* .... (Epic)
Shadow Boxing
Giles Reaves & Jon Goin; *Letting Go* .... (MCA)
Shadow Boxing
Teena Marie; *Robbery* .... (Epic)
Shadow Captain
Crosby, Stills & Nash; *Allies* .... (Atlantic)
CSN .... (Atlantic)
Replay .... (Atlantic)
Shadow Dancing
Andy Gibb; *Andy Gibb's Greatest Hits* .... (RSO)
Collection Of His Greatest Hits .... (Polydor)
Shadow Dancing .... (RSO)
Shadow Dream Song
Tom Rush; *Classic Rush* .... (Elektra)
The Circle Game .... (Elektra)
Shadow In The Street
Allan Clarke; *I Wasn't Born Yesterday* .... (Atlantic)
Shadow Knows
Coasters; *Coasters' Greatest Hits* .... (Atco)
Shadow Of A Doubt
Earl Thomas Conley; *Yours Truly* .... (RCA)
Shadow Of A Doubt
Tom Petty And The Heartbreakers; *Damn The Torpedoes* .... (MCA)
Shadow Of A Doubt
Sonic Youth; *Evol* .... (SST)
Shadow Of A Doubt
Roxette; *Look Sharp!* .... (EMI)
Shadow Of A Lonely Man
Alan Parsons Project; *Pyramid* .... (Arista)
Shadow Of California
Blue Oyster Cult; *Revolution By Night* .... (Columbia)
Shadow Of Doubt
Bonnie Raitt; *Longing In Their Hearts* .... (Capitol)
Shadow Of Love
Damned; *Light At The End Of The Tunnel* .... (MCA)
Phantasmagoria .... (MCA)
Shadow Of Love
Laura Branigan; *Touch* .... (Atlantic)
Shadow Of Your Love
Temptations; *Power* .... (Motown)
Shadow On A Harvest Moon
Everything But The Girl; *Idlewild* .... (Sire)
Shadow Puppets
Tor Dietrichson; *Global Village* .... (Global Pacific)
Shadow Song
Supertramp; *Supertramp* .... (A&M)
Shadow Waltz
Bing Crosby; *Crooner-Columbia Years-1928-1934* .... (Columbia)
Original Broadway Cast; *42nd Street* .... (RCA Victor)
Wayne King & His Orchestra; *Best Of Wayne King* .... (MCA)
Shadowboxer
Fiona Apple; *Tidal* .... (Clean Slate/Work)
Shadows & Light
Joni Mitchell; *Hissing Of Summer Lawns* .... (Asylum)
Shadows & Light .... (Asylum)
Shadows & The Wind
Uriah Heep; *Wonderworld* .... (Sequel)
Shadows Break
Jules & The Polar Bears; *Got No Breeding* .... (Columbia)
Shadows In The Moonlight
Anne Murray; *15 Of The Best* .... (Liberty)
Anne Murray's Greatest Hits .... (Capitol)
New Kind Of Feeling .... (Capitol)
Shadows In The Rain
Police; *Zenyatta Mondatta* .... (A&M)
Sting; *Dream Of The Blue Turtles* .... (A&M)
Shadows Of Love
Bing Crosby; *Crooner-Columbia Years-1928-1934* .... (Columbia)
Glen Gray; *Best Of The Big Bands-C* .... (Columbia)
Rayburn Anthony; *45-#55053* .... (Mercury)
Shadows Of The Night
Pat Benatar; *Best Shots* .... (Chrysalis)
Get Nervous .... (Chrysalis)
Shadows On The Wall
Moody Blues; *Keys Of The Kingdom* .... (Polydor)
Shadows On The Wall
Gene Watson; *Best Of Gene Watson* .... (Capitol)
Silhouettes
Diamonds; *Good Time Rock 'N' Roll-C* .... (MCA)
Herman's Hermits; *Herman's Hermits-Their Greatest Hits* .... (Abkco)
Nylons; *One Size Fits All* .... (Open Air)
Rays; *Oldies But Goodies-#4-C* .... (Original Sound)
Rock-O-Rama-#1-C .... (Abkco)
Silhouettes In Disguise
Kansas; *Power* .... (MCA)
Silver Shadow
Atlantic Starr; *As The Band Turns* .... (A&M)
Atlantic Starr-Classics-#10 .... (A&M)
Secret Lovers: Best Of Atlantic Starr .... (A&M)
Standing In The Shadows Of Love
Barry White; *Barry White's Greatest Hits* .... (20th Century Fox)
I've Got So Much To Give .... (20th Century Fox)
Four Tops; *Four Tops' Greatest Hits* .... (Motown)
Four Tops Reach Out .... (Motown)
Four Tops-Anthology .... (Motown)
Motown Story-First 25 Years-C .... (Motown)
Motown Superstar Series-#14-Four Tops .... (Motown)
Rod Stewart; *Blondes Have More Fun* .... (Warner Bros.)
Theme From "Dark Shadows"
Original Soundtrack; *Television's Greatest Hits-#2-C* .... (TVT)
Theme From "Evening Shade"
Original Soundtrack; *Television's Greatest Hits-#7-Cable Ready-C* .... (TVT)
Theme From "The Sandpiper" (Shadow Of Your Smile)
Astrud Gilberto; *ST/Sandpiper* .... (Verve)
The Envelope Please-Academy Award Winning Songs-#3 (1958-1969)-C .... (Rhino)
Barbra Streisand; *My Name Is Barbra, Two* .... (Columbia)
Boston Pops Orchestra/Arthur Fiedler; *Greatest Hits Of The '60s-#2* .... (RCA)
Motion Picture Classics-#1 .... (RCA Victor)
Music For Every Mood-Yesterday .... (RCA)
Carmen McRae; *Carmen McRae-Alive* .... (Mainstream)
I Want You .... (Mainstream)
Frank Sinatra; *At The Sands* .... (Reprise)
The Reprise Collection .... (Reprise)
Henry Mancini; *Days Of Wine And Roses* .... (RCA)
James Morrison; *Snappy Doo* .... (Atlantic)
Jose Carreras; *Hollywood Golden Classics* .... (Atlantic)
Marvin Gaye; *Romantically Yours* .... (Columbia)
Tony Bennett; *Academy Award Winners: 16 Most Requested* .... (LeGrand)
The Movie Song Album .... (Columbia)
Tony Bennett-16 Most Requested Songs .... (Legacy)
Tony Bennett's All-Time Greatest Hits .... (Columbia)
Tombstone Shadow
Creedence Clearwater Revival; *1969* .... (Fantasy)
Creedence Clearwater Revival-Chronicle-#2 .... (Fantasy)
Green River .... (Fantasy)
The Concert .... (Fantasy)

Total Eclipse
Alan Parsons Project; *I Robot* . . . . (Arista)
Total Eclipse Of The Heart
Bonnie Tyler; *Billboard Top Hits-1983-C* . . . . (Rhino)
Faster Than The Speed Of Night . . . . (Columbia)
Seems Like Yesterday-#4-Early '80s-C . . . . (K-Tel)
Nicki French; *Dance Hits '96 Supermix-C* . . . . (Critique)
Secrets . . . . (Critique)
Two Purple Shadows
Jerry Vale; *Jerry Vale-17 Most Requested Songs* . . . . (Legacy)
Jerry Vale's All-Time Greatest Hits . . . . (Columbia)
Two Silhouettes
Dinah Shore; *Dinah Shore-16 Most Requested Songs* . . . . (Legacy)
Two Silhouettes
Sha Na Na; *Best Of Sha Na Na* . . . . (Pair)
Walking In The Shadow Of The Blues
Whitesnake; *Live In The Heart Of The City* . . . . (Geffen)
Love Hunter . . . . (Geffen)
We Kiss In A Shadow
Barbra Streisand; *The Broadway Album* . . . . (Columbia)
Original Broadway Cast; *The King And I* . . . . (RCA Victor)
Original Cast; *The King And I* . . . . (MCA)
White Shadow
Peter Gabriel; *Peter Gabriel* . . . . (Atlantic)

SHIPS, Boats, Shipwrecks, Submarines

See Also: **ANIMALS (various), DROWNING, LIGHTHOUSES, OCEAN, PIRATES, RIVERS, SAILING, TRAVELING, WAR, WATER**

"Hard To Starboard"
James Horner; *ST/Titanic* . . . . (Sony Music Classical)
"Take Her To Sea, Mr. Murdoch"
James Horner; *ST/Titanic* . . . . (Sony Music Classical)
Adrian
Jewel; *Pieces Of You* . . . . (Atlantic)
Attack Ships On Fire
Revolting Cocks; *Big Sexy Land* . . . . (Wax Trax)
Banana Boat (Day-O)
Harry Belafonte; *Belafonte '89* . . . . (EMI)
Nipper's Greatest Hits Of The '50s-#1-C . . . . (RCA)
Kinks; *Everybody's In Show-Biz* . . . . (Rhino)
Blue Bayou
Linda Ronstadt; *Linda Ronstadt's Greatest Hits, Volume Two* . . . . (Asylum)
Simple Dreams . . . . (Asylum)
Roy Orbison; *For The Lonely: A Roy Orbison Anthology 1959-1965* . . . . (Rhino)
In Dreams-Greatest Hits . . . . (Orbison)
Roy Orbison-More Greatest Hits . . . . (Monument)
Roy Orbison's All-Time Greatest Hits-#1 & 2 . . . . (Monument)
Roy Orbison & Friends; *Black & White Night-Live* . . . . (Virgin)
Boat Drinks
Jimmy Buffett; *Songs You Know By Heart-Jimmy Buffett's Greatest Hit(s)* . . . . (MCA)
Volcano . . . . (MCA)
Boat On The River
Styx; *Cornerstone* . . . . (A&M)
Boat That I Row
Neil Diamond; *Do It* . . . . (Bang)
Double Gold-Neil Diamond . . . . (Bang)
Just For You . . . . (Bang)
Neil Diamond-Classics (Early Years) . . . . (Columbia)
Neil Diamond's Greatest Hits . . . . (Bang)
Boats Against The Current
Eric Carmen; *Best Of Eric Carmen* . . . . (Arista)
Boats Against The Current . . . . (Arista)
Olivia Newton-John; *Totally Hot* . . . . (MCA)
Burning My Rowboat
Maura O'Connell; *Real Life Story* . . . . (Warner Bros.)
Captain Nemo
Michael Schenker Group; *Built To Destroy* . . . . (Chrysalis)
Rock Will Never Die . . . . (Chrysalis)
Captain Of Her Heart
Double; *Blue* . . . . (A&M)
Romantic Hits Of The '80s-C . . . . (K-Tel)
Carried Away
Television; *Adventure* . . . . (Elektra)
Come On Down To My Boat
Every Mother's Son; *Battle Of The Bands-#3-C* . . . . (K-Tel)
Commodore Song, The
Edward M. Favor; *Music From The New York Stage (1890-1920)-#1-1890-1908-C* . . . . (Pearl)
Cripple Creek Ferry
Neil Young; *After The Gold Rush* . . . . (Reprise)
Crystal Ship
Doors; *Best Of The Doors* . . . . (Elektra)
Doors . . . . (Elektra)

Doors 13 . . . . (Elektra)
Doors-Classics . . . . (Elektra)
Dark Ship
Country Joe McDonald; *Rock & Roll Music From The Planet Earth* . . . (Fantasy)
Davy's Dinghy
Ruth Wallis; *Dr. Demento Presents The Greatest Novelty Records-#2-1950s-C* . . . . (Rhino)
Dr. Demento's Dementia Royale-C . . . . (Rhino)
Death Of Titanic
James Horner; *ST/Titanic* . . . . (Sony Music Classical)
Do You Want My Job
Little Village; *Little Village* . . . . (Reprise)
Don't Pay The Ferryman
Chris DeBurgh; *Getaway* . . . . (A&M)
Erie Canal
Burl Ives; *Best Of Burl Ives* . . . . (MCA)
Weavers; *Greatest Folksingers Of The '60s-C* . . . . (Vanguard)
Weavers' Greatest Hits . . . . (Vanguard)
Weavers-Classics . . . . (Vanguard)
Ferry Cross The Mersey
Gerry And The Pacemakers; *Ferry Across The Mersey-Best Of Gerry And The Pacemakers* . . . . (EMI)
History Of British Rock-#4-C . . . . (Rhino)
Goin' Gone
Kathy Mattea; *Collection Of Hits* . . . . (Mercury)
Untasted Honey . . . . (Polydor Country)
Golden Vanity
Pete Seeger & Arlo Guthrie; *Together In Concert* . . . . (Reprise)
Harbor Lights
Boz Scaggs; *Silk Degrees* . . . . (Columbia)
Dinah Washington; *Complete Dinah Washington On Mercury-#2-1950-1952* . . . . (Mercury)
Dinah Washington-Golden Hits . . . . (Mercury)
For Lonely Lovers . . . . (Mercury)
This Is My Story . . . . (Mercury)
Platters; *Super Oldies Of The '60s-#9-C* . . . . (Audio Fidelity)
If I Had A Boat
Lyle Lovett; *Pontiac* . . . . (MCA)
I'll Sail My Ship Alone
George Jones; *20 Golden Pieces Of George Jones* . . . . (Bulldog)
Mickey Gilley; *Mickey Gilley's Greatest Hits-#1* . . . . (Epic)
Patsy Cline; *Always* . . . . (MCA)
Portrait Of Patsy Cline . . . . (MCA)
Ray Price; *Ray Price's Greatest Hits-#1-3* . . . . (Step One)
Jamaica Farewell
Harry Belafonte; *Calypso* . . . . (RCA)
Harry Belafonte-Legendary Performer . . . . (RCA)
Harry Belafonte-Pure Gold . . . . (RCA)
Harry Belafonte's All Time Greatest Hits-#1 . . . . (RCA)
This Is Harry Belafonte . . . . (RCA)
Leaving Port
James Horner; *ST/Titanic* . . . . (Sony Music Classical)
Lighthouse's Tale
Nickel Creek; *Nickel Creek* . . . . (Sugar Hill)
Longer Boats
Cat Stevens; *Tea For The Tillerman* . . . . (A&M)
Love Overboard
Gladys Knight & The Pips; *All Our Love* . . . . (MCA)
Soul Survivors-Best Of Gladys Knight & The Pips-1973-1988 . . . . . (Rhino)
Man Overboard
Blondie; *Blondie* . . . . (Chrysalis)
Man Overboard
Blink-182; *The Mark, Tom & Travis Show-The Enema Strikes Back* . . . . (MCA)
Man Overboard
Eric Clapton; *Money And Cigarettes* . . . . (Duck/Reprise)
Michael
Highwaymen; *Billboard Top Pop Hits-1961-C* . . . . (Rhino)
Michael Row The Boat Ashore
Joe & Eddie; *Best Of Joe & Eddie* . . . . (Crescendo)
Gospel Truth . . . . (Crescendo)
Weavers; *Weavers' Greatest Hits* . . . . (Vanguard)
Mighty Quinn (Quinn The Eskimo)
Bob Dylan; *Biograph* . . . . (Columbia)
Bob Dylan's Greatest Hits-#2 . . . . (Columbia)
Self Portrait . . . . (Columbia)
Ian & Sylvia; *Ian & Sylvia's Greatest Hits* . . . . (Vanguard)
Manfred Mann; *Chapter Two-The Best Of The Fontana Years* . . . . . (Fontana)
Motorboat To Mars
Chicago; *Chicago At Carnegie Hall* . . . . (Chicago)
Chicago III . . . . (Chicago)
My Heart Will Go On (Love Theme from "Titanic")
Celine Dion; *All The Way...A Decade Of Song* . . . . (550 Music)
ST/Titanic . . . . (Sony Music Classical)
Celine Dion with The Bee Gees; *Let's Talk About Love-C* . . . . . (550 Music)
Kenny G; *Kenny G's Greatest Hits* . . . . (Arista)
My Ship
Lena Horne; *A New Album* . . . . (RCA)
Lena Horne & Phil Woods; *I Have Dreamed* . . . . (Novus)

Navy Blue
Diane Renay; *Growin' Up Too Fast-The Girl Group Anthology-C* . . . (Mercury)
Night Boat To Cairo
Madness; *One Step Beyond*. . . . . (Sire)
ST/Dance Craze . . . .(Chrysalis)
Norfolk Ferry
Panama Francis; *Panama Francis & The Savoy Sultans*. . . . .(Classic Jazz)
On A Slow Boat To China
Jimmy Buffett; *Somewhere Over China* . . . .(MCA)
Kay Kyser & His Orchestra; *16 Most Requested Songs Of The*
'40s-#2-C . . . . (Legacy)
Sentimental Favorites . . . . (Columbia)
Sonny Rollins; *First Recordings*. . . . .(Prestige)
Vintage Sonny Rollins . . . .(Prestige)
On The Good Ship Lollipop
4 Seasons; *Rarities-#1* . . . . (Rhino)
Firehouse Five Plus Two; *Goes To Sea*. . . . . (Good Time Jazz)
One Of Our Submarines
Thomas Dolby; *Golden Age Of Wireless* . . . . (Capitol)
One Small Boat
Altered State; *Altered State*. . . . .(Warner Bros.)
Only Love
Wynonna; *Tell Me Why* . . . .(MCA)
Proud Mary
Creedence Clearwater Revival; *1968-1969* . . . . (Fantasy)
Bayou Country. . . . . (Fantasy)
Creedence Clearwater Revival-Chronicle. . . . . (Fantasy)
Creedence Clearwater Revival-Gold. . . . . (Fantasy)
Live In Europe . . . . (Fantasy)
George Jones & Johnny Paycheck; *My Very Special Guests* . . . .(Epic)
Ike & Tina Turner; *Best Of Ike & Tina Turner* . . . .(EMI)
Didn't It Blow Your Mind: Soul Hits Of The '70s-#4-C . . . . . . (Rhino)
EMI Legends Of Rock & Roll-24 Greatest Hits-C . . . .(EMI)
Ike & Tina Turner's Greatest Hits . . . . (Curb)
Rain, Rain, Rain
Frankie Laine; *Frankie Laine-16 Most Requested Songs* . . . . . . (Legacy)
Ride Captain Ride
Blues Image; *Back To The '70s-#3-C* . . . . (Dominion Entert.)
Hit Singles-1958-1977-C . . . .(Atlantic)
Rio Grande
Floyd Tillman; *The Country Music Hall Of Fame-Floyd Tillman* . . . .(MCA)
Sam Eskin; *Shanty Men-Songs Of Sailormen And*
Lumbermen. . . . . (Smithsonian Folkways)
River, The
Garth Brooks; *Ropin' The Wind* . . . . (Liberty)
The Limited Series . . . . (Capitol)
Riverboat
Robert Palmer; *Pressure Drop* . . . . (Island)
Riverboat Gambler
Chris LeDoux; *Songs Of Rodeo Life* . . . . (Capitol)
Riverboat Shuffle
Hoagy Carmichael; *Stardust Road* . . . .(MCA)
Rock The Boat
Hues Corporation; *Dance! Dance! Dance! Greatest Dance-C*. . . . . . . (RCA)
Didn't It Blow Your Mind: Soul Hits Of The '70s-#13-C . . . . . . (Rhino)
Nipper's Greatest Hits Of The '70s-C . . . . (RCA)
Rock The Boat
Aaliyah; *Aaliyah*. . . . . (BlackGround Enterp./Atlantic)
Rock This Boat
Thompson Twins; *Big Trash* . . . .(Red Eye)
Rockin' In The Same Old Boat
Bobby Bland; *Spotlighting The Man*. . . . .(MCA)
Rockin' The Boat
Ricky Skaggs; *Live In London* . . . .(Epic)
Wayland Patton; *Gulf Stream Dreamin'* . . . . (Capitol)
Rockin' The Boat Of Love
Jerry Lee Lewis; *Golden Rock & Roll*. . . . . (Sun)
Roving Kind, The
Guy Mitchell; *Guy Mitchell-16 Most Requested Songs* . . . . (Legacy)
Row Jimmy
Grateful Dead; *Wake Of The Flood*. . . . .(Grateful Dead)
Row, Row, Row Your Boat
Bobby Darin/Johnny Mercer/Billy May Orchestra; *Two Of A Kind* . . . .(Atlantic)
Original Soundtrack; *Children's Favorites* . . . . (Kid Rhino/Rhino 4 Kids)
Spike Jones & His City Slickers; *King Of Corn* . . . . (Glendale)
Sail On Flying Dutchman
Nick Seeger; *Sail On Flying Dutchman* . . . .(Biograph)
Sailboat
Jonathan Edwards; *Sailboat*. . . . .(Warner Bros.)
Sailboat In The Moonlight
Billie Holiday; *Billie Holiday's Greatest Hits* . . . . (Legacy)
Lady Day . . . . (Columbia)
Legacy Box-1933-1958 . . . . (Columbia)
Quintessential-#4-1937 . . . . (Columbia)
Sailing Ships
Whitesnake; *Slip Of The Tongue*. . . . . (Geffen)
Sailing To Philadelphia
Mark Knopfler; *Sailing To Philadelphia*. . . . .(Warner Bros.)

Salty Dog, A
Procol Harum; *A Salty Dog* . . . . (A&M)
Best Of Procol Harum . . . . (A&M)
Procol Harum Live In Concert with the Edmonton Symphony . . . .(A&M)
Procol Harum-Classics-#17. . . . . (A&M)
Santa Lucia
Elvis Presley; *Elvis For Everyone!* . . . .(RCA)
Mario Lanza; *Legendary Tenor* . . . .(RCA)
Sea Cruise
Billy "Crash" Craddock; *Billy "Crash" Craddock's Greatest Hits* . . . (Capitol)
Changes . . . . (Capitol)
Frankie Ford; *American Hot Wax* . . . . (A&M)
Best Of New Orleans Rhythm & Blues-#2-C . . . . (Rhino)
Oldies But Goodies-#3-C . . . .(Original Sound)
Rock & Roll Show-C . . . . (Gusto)
Glenn Frey; *No Fun Aloud* . . . . (Asylum)
Johnny Rivers; *Johnny Rivers-Anthology 1964-1977* . . . . (Rhino)
Nighthawks; *Best Of The Nighthawks* . . . .(Genes CD Co.)
Robert Gordon & Link Wray; *Fresh Fish Special* . . . .(RCA)
Shining In The Light
Jimmy Page/Robert Plant; *Walking Into Clarksdale*. . . . .(Atlantic)
Ship Ahoy
O'Jays; *Ship Ahoy* . . . . (Philadelphia Int'l)
Ship In A Bottle
Dave Loggins; *One Way Ticket To Paradise* . . . . (Epic)
Ship Of Dreams
Nazareth; *Malice In Wonderland* . . . . (A&M)
Ship Of Fools
Elvis Costello; *Deadicated-C* . . . . (Arista)
Grateful Dead; *From The Mars Hotel* . . . .(Grateful Dead)
Steal Your Face . . . .(Grateful Dead)
Ship Of Fools
Garland Jeffreys; *American Boy & Girl* . . . . (A&M)
Ship Of Fools
World Party; *Greenpeace/Rainbow Warriors-C*. . . . . (Geffen)
Private Revolution . . . . (Ensign)
Ship Of Fools
Doors; *Morrison Hotel/Hard Rock Cafe* . . . . (Elektra)
Weird Scenes Inside The Gold Mine . . . . (Elektra)
Ship Of Fools
Bob Seger; *Night Moves* . . . . (Capitol)
Ship Of Fools
Robert Plant; *Now And Zen* . . . . (Es Paranza)
Ship Of Love
Nutmegs; *Echoes Down The Hall-16 Original Doo-Wop Hits-C* . . . . . . (Arista)
Nutmegs' Greatest Hits . . . . (Collectables)
Ship Titanic
Pink Anderson; *Gospel Blues & Street Songs* . . . . (Riverside)
Ship To Shore
Chris DeBurgh; *The Getaway* . . . . (A&M)
Ship Without A Sail
Dave Frishberg; *Let's Eat Home* . . . . (Concord Jazz)
Ella Fitzgerald; *Rodgers & Hart Songbook*. . . . . (Verve)
Sarah Vaughan; *Rodgers & Hart Songbook* . . . . (Emarcy)
Shipbuilding
Elvis Costello; *Girls Girls Girls* . . . . (Columbia)
Elvis Costello & The Attractions; *Punch The Clock* . . . . (Rykodisc)
Shipmates In Cheyenne
Bobby Darin; *1936-1973*. . . . . (Motown)
Ships
Ian Hunter; *You're Never Alone With A Schizophrenic* . . . . (Razor & Tie)
Ships
Barry Manilow; *Barry Manilow's Greatest Hits-#3* . . . . (Arista)
One Voice . . . . (Arista)
Ships
Red Rider; *As Far As Siam* . . . . (Capitol)
Ships
Patty Loveless; *When Fallen Angels Fly* . . . . (Epic)
Ships Don't Disappear In The Night
10 CC; *Live & Let Live* . . . . (Mercury)
Ships In The Night
Be Bop Deluxe; *Best Of Be Bop Deluxe-Raiding The Divine Archive*. . . (Capitol)
Live! In The Air Age . . . . (Harvest)
Sunburst Finish . . . . (Capitol)
Ships That Don't Come In
Joe Diffie; *Regular Joe* . . . . (Epic)
Shipyards Of New Zealand
Midnight Oil; *Red Sails In The Sunset*. . . . . (Columbia)
Sink The Bismarck
Johnny Horton; *American Originals-Johnny Horton* . . . . (Columbia)
Billboard Top Country Hits-1960-C . . . . (Rhino)
Johnny Horton's Greatest Hits. . . . . (Columbia)
Sinkin' In The Sea
Barefoot Jerry; *You Can't Get Off With Your Shoes On* . . . . (Monument)
Sinking, The
James Horner; *ST/Titanic* . . . .(Sony Music Classical)
Sit Down, You're Rockin' The Boat
Don Henley; *ST/Leap Of Faith* . . . .(MCA)

Original Cast; *Guys & Dolls* . . . . (MCA)
Skye Boat Song
King's Singers; *American Balladeer-Golden Classics-#1-C* . . . . . (Collectables)
Annie Laurie-Folk Songs Of British Isles . . . . (Angel)
Roger Whittaker; *Live In Concert* . . . . (RCA)
Slave Ships
Original Cast; *Bring In 'Da Noise, Bring In 'Da Funk* . . . . (RCA Victor)
Sloop John B
Beach Boys; *Absolute Best-#2* . . . . (Capitol)
Beach Boys '69 (The Beach Boys Live In London) . . . . (Capitol)
Beach Boys-Gift Set . . . . (Capitol)
Best Of (Good Vibrations) . . . . (Reprise)
Made In The U.S.A. . . . . (Capitol)
Pet Sounds . . . . (Capitol)
ST/Forrest Gump . . . . (Epic/Sony Music Soundtrax)
The Pet Sounds Sessions: A 30th Anniversary Collection . . . . (Capitol)
Slow Boat To China
Spike Robinson & Harry ''Sweets'' Edison; *Jusa Bit O' Blues-#1* . . (Capri Ltd.)
Song Of The Volga Boatmen
Glenn Miller; *Best Of Glenn Miller* . . . . (RCA)
Chattanooga Choo Choo-#1 Hits . . . . (Bluebird)
Glenn Miller-A Legendary Performer-#1 & 2 . . . . (Bluebird)
Memorial-1944-1969 . . . . (Bluebird)
This Is Glenn Miller . . . . (RCA)
Tuxedo Junction; *Tuxedo Junction* . . . . (Butterfly)
Soul Survivor
Rolling Stones; *Exile On Main Street* . . . . (Virgin)
Steamboat
Drifters; *Drifters-Their Greatest Recordings* . . . . (Atco)
Let The Boogie Woogie Roll-Greatest Hits . . . . (Atlantic)
Steamboat
Beach Boys; *Carl & The Passions/Holland* . . . . (Capitol)
Holland . . . . (Brother)
Steamboat Whistle Blues
John Hartford; *Aereo-Plain* . . . . (Warner Bros.)
Submarine Bells
Chills; *Submarine Bells* . . . . (Slash)
Submarine Song
Candy Skins; *Space I'm In* . . . . (David Geffen Co.)
Submarine Soul
Barbie Bones; *Brake For Nobody* . . . . (Restless)
Take A Ride On A Riverboat
Louisiana's Le Roux; *Louisiana's Le Roux* . . . . (Capitol)
Tarantella
Original Cast/Cyril Ritchard; *Peter Pan-The 1954 Broadway
Production* . . . . (RCA Victor)
Theme From ''Gilligan's Island''
Original Soundtrack; *CBS: The First 50 Years* . . . . (TVT)
Television's Greatest Hits-#1-C . . . . (TVT)
Theme From ''Mr. Lucky''
Original Soundtrack; *Television's Greatest Hits-#4-Black & White
Classics-C* . . . . (TVT)
Theme From ''Surfside 6''
Original Soundtrack; *Television's Greatest Hits-#1-C* . . . . (TVT)
Theme From ''The Love Boat''
Original Soundtrack; *Television's Greatest Hits-#3-1970s & 1980s-C* . . . (TVT)
Theme From ''Voyage To The Bottom Of The Sea''
Original Soundtrack; *Television's Greatest Hits-#2-C* . . . . (TVT)
There Is A Ship
Peter, Paul & Mary; *Peter, Paul and Mary In Concert* . . . . (Warner Bros.)
There's A Boat Dat's Leavin' Soon For New York
Ella Fitzgerald & Louis Armstrong; *Porgy & Bess* . . . . (Verve)
Original Cast; *Porgy & Bess* . . . . (MCA)
Titanic, The
John Townley & The Press Gang; *Chesapeake Sailor's Companion* . . (Adelphi)
Trains & Boats & Planes
Billy J. Kramer With The Dakotas; *Billy J. Kramer With The Dakotas-The
Definitive Collection* . . . . (EMI)
History Of British Rock-#4-C . . . . (Rhino)
Dionne Warwick; *Dionne Warwick* . . . . (Everest)
Dionne Warwick Greatest Hits . . . . (Everest)
Dionne Warwick-Anthology 1962-1971 . . . . (Rhino)
Hot! Live & Otherwise . . . . (Arista)
Turn That Boat Around
Rankin Family; *North Country* . . . . (Guardian/Angel)
Turn The Boat Around
Larry Kaplan; *Worth All The Telling* . . . . (Folk Legacy)
Uncle Albert/Admiral Halsey
Paul And Linda McCartney; *RAM* . . . . (Capitol)
Paul McCartney; *All The Best!* . . . . (Capitol)
Paul McCartney-Gift Set . . . . (Capitol)
Wings; *Wings Greatest* . . . . (Capitol)
Volga Boatman
Les Elgart; *Greatest Dance Band In The Land* . . . . . (Sony Music Special Prod.)
Waiting For The Robert E. Lee
Al Jolson; *My Mammy* . . . . (MCA Special Prod.)
Eddie Cantor; *Centennial Celebration* . . . . (RCA)
When My Ship Comes In
Clint Black; *The Hard Way* . . . . (RCA)

When The Ship Comes In
Bob Dylan; *The Bootleg Series-Volumes 1-3 [Rare & Unreleased]* . . (Columbia)
The Times They Are A-Changin' . . . . (Columbia)
Peter, Paul & Mary; *A Song Will Rise* . . . . (Warner Bros.)
White Mountain Singers; *Best Of The White Mountain Singers* . . . . . (Folk Era)
White Ship
H.P. Lovecraft; *H.P. Lovecraft* . . . . (Out Of Print)
Wooden Ships
Crosby, Stills & Nash; *Crosby, Stills & Nash* . . . . (Atlantic)
CSN . . . . (Atlantic)
Crosby, Stills, Nash & Young; *So Far* . . . . (Atlantic)
ST/Woodstock . . . . (Atlantic)
Jefferson Airplane; *2400 Fulton Street-An Anthology* . . . . (RCA)
Flight Log (1966-1976) . . . . (Grunt)
Loves You . . . . (RCA)
Volunteers . . . . (RCA)
Wreck Of The Edmund Fitzgerald
Gordon Lightfoot; *Gord's Gold-#2* . . . . (Warner Bros.)
Summertime Dream . . . . (Reprise)
Yellow Submarine
Beatles; *Beatles 1* . . . . (Capitol)
Beatles-Box Set . . . . (Capitol)
Reel Music . . . . (Capitol)
Revolver . . . . (Capitol)
The Beatles/1962-1966 . . . . (Capitol)
Yo Ho Ho And A Bottle Of Rum
Original Cast; *Rugrats Sing-Along* . . . . (Interscope)

SHOES, Boots

See Also: *ANATOMY: FEET, CLOTHES, HATS, SHOPPING,
TRAVELING*

(Only Angels Wanna Wear My) Red Shoes
Elvis Costello; *Girls Girls Girls* . . . . (Columbia)
My Aim Is True . . . . (Columbia)
Elvis Costello & The Attractions; *Best Of Elvis Costello & The
Attractions* . . . . (Columbia)
1, 2, Buckle My Shoe
Bob McGrath; *The Baby Record* . . . . (Golden Boy Jazz/Optimism)
Baby Needs New Shoes
Restless Heart; *Matters Of The Heart* . . . . (RCA)
Bad Sneakers
Steely Dan; *Katy Lied* . . . . (MCA)
Steely Dan's Greatest Hits . . . . (MCA)
Be Like That
3 Doors Down; *Better Life* . . . . (Republic/Universal)
Now That's What I Call Music!-#8-C . . . . (Virgin)
Black Denim Trousers & Motorcycle Boots
Cheers; *Monster Summer Hits-Drag City-C* . . . . (Capitol)
Blue Suede Shoes
Carl Perkins; *Blue Suede Shoes* . . . . (Sun)
Carl Perkins-Original Sun Greatest Hits . . . . (Rhino)
Cruisin'-1956-1957-C . . . . (Dunhill Compact Classics)
Oldies But Goodies-#4-C . . . . (Original Sound)
Elvis Presley; *Aloha from Hawaii via Satellite* . . . . (RCA)
Elvis Presley . . . . (RCA)
Elvis-A Legendary Performer, Volume 2 . . . . (RCA)
From Memphis To Vegas/From Vegas To Memphis . . . . (RCA)
ST/G.I. Blues . . . . (RCA)
Boot Scootin' Boogie
Brooks & Dunn; *Brand New Man* . . . . (Arista)
Boots Of Spanish Leather
Bob Dylan; *The Times They Are A-Changin'* . . . . (Columbia)
Can't Afford No Shoes
Frank Zappa/Mothers Of Invention; *One Size Fits All* . . . . (Rykodisc)
Charlie's Shoes
Billy Walker; *Best Of Billy Walker* . . . . (Deluxe)
Columbia Country Classics-#4-Nashville Sound-C . . . . (Columbia)
Chattanoogie Shoe Shine Boy
Freddy Cannon; *14 Booming Hits* . . . . (Rhino)
Red Foley; *Red Foley: The Country Music Hall
Of Fame* . . . . (MCA Special Prod.)
The Nashville Sound: Owen Bradley-C . . . . (Decca)
Christmas Shoes
Newsong; *Sheltering Tree* . . . . (Benson/Jive)
Cowboy Boots
Dave Dudley; *Red Simpson/Red Sovine/Dave Dudley-C* . . . . (Gusto)
Dancing Shoes
Bob Marley & The Wailers; *Birth Of A Legend 1963-
1966* . . . . (Epic Portrait Assoc.)
Early Music . . . . (Calla)
Dancing Shoes
Dan Fogelberg; *Nether Lands* . . . . (Full Moon)
Dancing Shoes
Side Effect; *Side Effect's Greatest Hits* . . . . (Fantasy)

Diamonds On The Soles Of Her Shoes
Paul Simon; *Concert In The Park-August 15 1991* . . . .(Warner Bros.)
  Graceland . . . .(Warner Bros.)
  Negotiations And Love Songs, 1971-1986 . . . .(Warner Bros.)
Die With Your Boots On
Iron Maiden; *Live After Death-World Slavery Tour* . . . . (Capitol)
  Piece Of Mind . . . . (Capitol)
Fairies Wear Boots
Ozzy Osbourne; *The Ozzman Cometh* . . . .(Epic)
Gold-Tipped Boots, Black Jacket And Tie
Jethro Tull; *Catfish Rising* . . . .(Chrysalis)
Goody Two Shoes
Adam Ant; *Antics In The Forbidden Zone* . . . .(Epic)
  Friend Or Foe . . . .(Epic)
Hand Me Down My Jogging Shoes
Shaw Brothers; *Best Of The Shaw Brothers* . . . . (Folk Era)
  Shaw Brothers-Collection . . . . (Folk Era)
Hang Up My Rock & Roll Shoes
Band; *Rock Of Ages* . . . . (Capitol)
Chuck Willis; *Atlantic Rhythm & Blues 1947-1974-#3 (1955-
  1958)-C* . . . .(Atlantic)
Hell On High Heels
Motley Crue; *New Tattoo* . . . .(Motley/Beyond)
High Heel Shoes
Melky Sedeck; *Sister & Brother* . . . .(MCA)
Hi-Heel Sneakers
Tommy Tucker; *Soul Shots-#4-Urban Blues-C* . . . . (Rhino)
  The Chess Blues-Rock Songbook-C . . . .(MCA)
  Vintage Music-#7-C . . . .(MCA)
Hillbilly Shoes
Montgomery Gentry; *Tattoos & Scars* . . . . (Columbia)
Imelda
Mark Knopfler; *Golden Heart* . . . .(Warner Bros.)
Is It Really Over?
Jim Reeves; *Essential Jim Reeves* . . . . (RCA)
Italian Shoes
Dynatones; *Shameless* . . . .(Warner Bros.)
I've Got Sand In My Shoes
Drifters; *1959-1965-All-Time Greatest Hits And More* . . . .(Atlantic)
  Very Best Of The Drifters . . . . (Rhino)
Jack-Ass
Beck; *Odelay* . . . . (David Geffen Co.)
Just Walk In My Shoes
Gladys Knight & The Pips; *Gladys Knight & The Pips-Anthology*. . . . (Motown)
  Motown Legends-Gladys Knight & The Pips . . . . (Motown)
Knockin' Boots
Candyman; *Ain't No Shame In My Game* . . . .(Epic)
Knockin' Da Boots
H-Town; *Fever For Da Flavor* . . . . (Luke)
Leather Boots
Alice Cooper; *Flush The Fashion*. . . . .(Warner Bros.)
Let's See How Far You Get
BR549; *This Is BR549* . . . . (Lucky Dog)
Little Shoe Maker
Eddie Fisher; *Very Best Of Eddie Fisher* . . . .(Taragon)
Gaylords; *Choice Voices! Pop Vocal Group Gems Of The
  '50s-C* . . . . (Collector's Choice)
London Blues (Shoe Shiner's Drag)
Jelly Roll Morton; *1923-1924* . . . . (Milestone)
Murder In High Heels
Kiss; *Animalize* . . . . (Mercury)
My Adidas
Run-D.M.C.; *Raising Hell* . . . . (Profile)
  Rap Hall Of Fame-C . . . . (K-Tel)
  Rapmasters 4-Best Of Hip Hop-C . . . . (Priority)
  Rap's Greatest Hits-#3-C . . . . (Priority)
My Father's Shoes
Level 42; *Guaranteed* . . . . (RCA)
My Father's Shoes
Leon Russell; *Will O' The Wisp* . . . .(MCA)
My Shoes Keep Walking Back To You
Ray Price; *All Time Legends Of Country Music-C* . . . . (Legacy)
  Essential Ray Price-1951-1962 . . . . (Columbia)
  Ray Price's Greatest Hits . . . . (Columbia)
Old Brown Shoe
Beatles; *Beatles-Box Set* . . . . (Capitol)
  Hey Jude . . . . (Capitol)
  Past Masters-Volume Two . . . . (Parlophone)
Old Pair Of Shoes
Randy Travis; *Randy Travis' Greatest Hits-#1*. . . . . (Warner Bros.)
Old Shoes
Tom Waits; *Tom Waits-Early Years-Volume Two* . . . . (Rhino)
Old Shoes
Eddie Jefferson; *Bebop Singers* . . . .(Prestige)
One Shirt, Soulless Shoes
Latimore; *I'll Do Anything For You* . . . . (Malaco)
One, Two, Button Your Shoe
Artie Shaw & Tony Pastor; *Best Of The Big Bands-C*. . . . . (Columbia)

Billie Holiday; *Quintessential-#2-1936* . . . . (Columbia)
Out Of Your Shoes
Lorrie Morgan; *Essential Lorrie Morgan* . . . .(RCA)
  Leave The Light On . . . .(RCA)
  Lorrie Morgan-Super Hits . . . .(RCA)
Paddy Doyle's Boots
Clancy Brothers & Tommy Makem; *Best Of Clancy Brothers & Tommy
  Makem* . . . .(Tradition)
Pair Of Old Sneakers
George Jones; *George Jones & Tammy Wynette-16
  Biggest Hits* . . . . (Epic/Legacy)
Penny Loafers & Bobby Socks
Joe Bennett and The Sparkletones; *Rock This Town-Rockabilly
  Hits-#2-C* . . . . (Rhino)
Pink Shoe Laces
Dodie Stevens; *Original Classic Oldies Of The '50s & '60s-#18-C* . . . . . (MCA)
Put My Little Shoes Away
Everly Brothers; *Songs Our Daddy Taught Us* . . . . (Rhino)
Put Yourself In My Shoes
Clint Black; *Put Yourself In My Shoes*. (RCA)
Ramblin' In My Shoes
Hank Williams, Jr.; *The Pressure Is On-Original Classics
  Collection-#7*. . . . . (Curb)
Red Shoes
Tom Waits; *Big Time*. . . . . (Island)
Red Shoes
Chris Rea; *Auberge*. . . . . (Atco)
Red Shoes By The Drugstore
Tom Waits; *Blue Valentine* . . . .(Asylum)
Rock & Roll Shoes
Ray Charles & B.J. Thomas; *Friendship-C* . . . . (Columbia)
  Seven Spanish Angels & Other Hits . . . . (Columbia)
Rock & Roll Shoes
Amos Garrett; *Go Cat Go* . . . . (Flying Fish)
Sailin' Shoes
Little Feat; *Sailin' Shoes* . . . . (Warner Bros.)
  Waiting For Columbus . . . . (Warner Bros.)
Sensible Shoes
David Lee Roth; *A Little Ain't Enough* . . . . (Warner Bros.)
She Can Put Her Shoes Under My Bed (Anytime)
Johnny Duncan; *Classic Country* . . . . (Simitar)
She's Got Another Pair Of Shoes
Little Richard; *Grooviest 17 Original Hits* . . . .(Specialty)
Shine On Your Shoes
Mel Torme; *Fujitsu-Concord Jazz Festival In Japan* . . . . (Concord Jazz)
Shoe Goes On The Other Foot Tonight
George Jones; *20 Golden Pieces Of George Jones* . . . .(Bulldog)
Shoe Salesman
Alice Cooper; *Easy Action* . . . . (Bizarre/Straight)
Shoe Shoe Shine
Dynamic Superiors; *Baddest Love Jams-Volume 1-Quite Storm-C* . . . (Motown)
Shoe Soul
Smokey Robinson; *Love Breeze* . . . . (Motown)
  Smokin'. . . . . (Motown)
Shoe Was On The Other Foot
Patti LaBelle; *Flame* . . . . (MCA)
Shoeless Joe From Hannibal, Mo.
Original Broadway Cast; *Damn Yankees* . . . . (RCA)
Shoes
Bobby Bland; *Touch Of The Blues* . . . . (MCA)
Brook Benton; *Brook Benton-Anthology*. . . . . (Rhino)
Shoes You're Wearing
Clint Black; *Nothin' But The Taillights* . . . . (RCA)
Shoeshine Boy
Count Basie & His Kansas City 7; *Count Basie & His Kansas
  City 7* . . . . (MCA/Impulse)
Eddie Kendricks; *Eddie Kendricks-At His Best*. . . . . (Motown)
  Motown Superstar Series-#19-Eddie Kendricks. . . . . (Motown)
Shoeshine Man
Tom T. Hall; *Tom T. Hall's Greatest Hits-#1* . . . . (Mercury)
Silver Heels
Fleetwood Mac; *Heroes Are Hard To Find*. . . . .(Reprise)
Soft Shoe
Gerry Mulligan; *Gerry Mulligan's Greatest Hits* . . . . (RCA Victor)
Spanish Boots
Jeff Beck Group; *Beck-Ola* . . . . (Epic)
Sweet Virginia
Rolling Stones; *Exile On Main Street* . . . .(Virgin)
Take Off Them Shoes
Gene Watson; *Reflections* . . . . (Capitol)
Take Your Shoes Off Baby
Artie Shaw & His Orchestra; *Blues In The Night* . . . . (Bluebird)
Dinah Washington; *Echoes Of An Era-Dinah Washington* . . . . (Roulette)
Tennis Shoes
Jimmy C. Newman; *Alligator Man* . . . . (Rounder)
These Boots Are Made For Walkin'
Billy Ray Cyrus; *Some Gave All* . . . . (Mercury)
Nancy Sinatra; *Billboard Top Rock 'N' Roll Hits-1966-C* . . . . (Rhino)

Boots-Nancy Sinatra's Greatest Hits . . . . (Rhino)

Those Shoes
Eagles; *Long Run*. . . . . (Asylum)

Turtle Shoes
Bobby McFerrin; *Spontaneous Inventions* . . . . (Blue Note)
Bobby McFerrin & Herbie Hancock; *ST/Twins*. . . . . (WTG)

Two Thousand Shoes
Big Audio Dynamite; *Tighten Up-#88* . . . . (Columbia)

Two-Tone Shoes
Homer & Jethro; *Get Hot Or Go Home-Vintage*
Rockabilly-C . . . . (Country Music Foundation)

Walk A Mile In My Shoes
Bryan Ferry; *Another Time Another Place* . . . . (Reprise)
Elvis Presley; *On Stage-February, 1970* . . . . (RCA)
Joe South; *Best Of Joe South*. . . . . (Rhino)

Walking Shoes
Tanya Tucker; *Tennessee Woman* . . . . (Capitol)

Where The Blacktop Ends
keith urban; *keith urban*. . . . . (Capitol)

Who Wears These Shoes
Elton John; *Breaking Hearts* . . . . (MCA)

Who's Gonna Fill Their Shoes
George Jones; *George Jones-Super Hits* . . . . (Epic)
Greatest Country Hits Of The '80s-1985-C . . . . (Columbia)
Who's Gonna Fill Their Shoes . . . . (Epic)

Whose Bed Have Your Boots Been Under?
Shania Twain; *The Woman In Me* . . . . (Mercury)

Wrong Side Of Memphis
Matraca Berg; *Bittersweet Surrender* . . . . (RCA)
Trisha Yearwood; *Grand Ole Opry-75 Years-#1-C*. . . . . (MCA)
Hearts In Armor . . . . (MCA)

SHOPPING, Buying, Selling, Stores

See Also: BUSINESS & INDUSTRY, LOVE: LOVE & MONEY,
MONEY, NEWS, PRODUCTS & BRANDS: SPECIFIC, RADIO,
TELEVISION

(I Can't Get No) Satisfaction
Devo; *Best Of Devo-Greatest Hits*. . . . . (Warner Bros.)
Q: Are We Not Men? A: We Are Devo! . . . . (Warner Bros.)
Otis Redding; *Best Of Otis Redding*. . . . . (Atlantic)
History Of Otis Redding . . . . (Atco)
Otis Redding. . . . . (Atlantic)
The Otis Redding Story. . . . . (Atlantic)
Rolling Stones; *Big Hits (High Tide & Green Grass)* . . . . (Abkco)
Flashpoint. . . . . (Virgin)
got Live if you want it!. . . . . (Abkco)
Hot Rocks 1964-1971 . . . . (Abkco)
Out Of Our Heads. . . . . (Abkco)
Singles Collection-The London Years . . . . (Abkco)

(Just Like) Romeo & Juliet
Reflections; *'60s Dance Party-C*. . . . . (Dominion Entert.)
Sensational '60s-#1-C . . . . (Dominion Entert.)

90 Days (Same As Cash)
Midnight Star; *Midnight Star*. . . . . (Solar)

Any Bonds Today?
Andrews Sisters; *Swing Out To Victory: Songs Of World*
War II-C. . . . . (ISD/Intersound)
Barry Wood; *78-#27478* . . . . (Victor)
Bing Crosby; *Original Soundtrack Sessions* . . . . (Vintage Jazz Classics)

At The Mall
Patty Larkin; *Live In The Square* . . . . (Philo)

Ballad Of A Teenage Queen
Johnny Cash; *Johnny Cash* . . . . (Sun)
Johnny Cash-Original Golden Hits-#2 . . . . (Sun)
Johnny Cash-Sun Years . . . . (Rhino)
ST/Harper Valley PTA . . . . (Sun)
The Legend . . . . (Plantation)
The Man In Black-His Greatest Hits. . . . . (Legacy)

Bargain
Who; *Who's next* . . . . (MCA)

Best Things In Life Are Free
June Allyson; *ST/Good News* . . . . (Sony Music Special Prod.)
Luther Vandross & Janet Jackson; *ST/Mo' Money* . . . . (Bluebird)
Mel Torme; *Easy To Remember* . . . . (Glendale)
Sam Cooke; *Sam Cooke-At The Copa* . . . . (RCA)

Big Bright Green Pleasure Machine
Simon & Garfunkel; *Collected Works*. . . . . (Columbia)
Parsley Sage Rosemary & Thyme . . . . (Columbia)
ST/The Graduate . . . . (Columbia)

Bills, Bills, Bills
Destiny's Child; *The Writing's On The Wall* . . . . (Columbia)

Boy For Sale
Original Broadway Cast; *Oliver!* . . . . (RCA Victor)
Original London Cast; *Oliver!*. . . . . (EMI-Angel)

Burn Down The Malls
Mojo Nixon & Skid Roper; *Enigma Variations-#2-C* . . . . (Enigma Capitol)

Bus Stop
Hollies; *Best Of The Hollies*. . . . . (EMI)
History Of British Rock-#3-C . . . . (Rhino)
The Hollies' Greatest Hits. . . . . (Epic)

Buy American
Tex Payer; *Work's Many Voices-#1 & 2-C* . . . . (Arhoolie)

Buy Me A Rose
Kenny Rogers; *She Rides Wild Horses*. . . . . (Dreamcatcher)

Buy The Bitch A Cadillac
Annie Moscow; *Wolves At My Door* . . . . (Melonball)

Buy, Buy This American Car
Charlie King; *Food Phone Gas Lodging* . . . . (Flying Fish)

Buying My Way Into Heaven
Sammy Hagar; *Unboxed* . . . . (Geffen)

Buying Time
Clint Black; *The Hard Way* . . . . (RCA)

Candy (Sugar Shoppe)
Brady Bunch Kids; *It's A Sunshine Day-Best Of The Brady*
Bunch Kids . . . . (MCA)

Candy Store Blues
Maria Muldaur; *Big Blues-C*. . . . . (Music For Little People)

Candy Store Love
Valchords; *Legends Of Doo-Wop-#1-C* . . . . (Juke Box Treasures)

Candy Store Rock
Led Zeppelin; *Led Zeppelin-Box Set* . . . . (Atlantic)
Presence . . . . (Swan Song)

Can't Buy Me Love
Beatles; *Beatles 1* . . . . (Capitol)
Hey Jude . . . . (Capitol)
Reel Music. . . . . (Capitol)
ST/A Hard Day's Night . . . . (Capitol)
The Beatles At The Hollywood Bowl . . . . (Capitol)
The Beatles/1962-1966 . . . . (Capitol)

Checking Out The Checkout Girl
Wazmo Nariz; *10th Anniversary-These People Are Nuts-C*. . . . . (I.R.S.)

Christmas Shoes
Newsong; *Sheltering Tree* . . . . (Benson/Jive)

Cockles & Mussels
Emily Mitchell; *The Irish Album* . . . . (RCA)

Come & Buy My Toys
David Bowie; *Starting Point* . . . . (Deram)

Come To The Supermarket (In Old Peking)
Barbra Streisand; *The Barbra Streisand Album* . . . . (Columbia)

Crazy Things I Do
Sammie; *From The Bottom To The Top* . . . . (Freeworld/Capitol)

Daddy Won't Sell The Farm
Montgomery Gentry; *Tattoos & Scars*. . . . . (Columbia)

Dillon's Store
Lightnin' Hopkins; *Prison Blues-Golden Classics-#2* . . . . (Collectables)

Dime Store Mystery
Lou Reed; *New York*. . . . . (Sire)

Discount Dogs
Joe Perry Project; *Let The Music Do The Talking*. . . . . (Columbia)

Doggie In The Window
Patti Page; *Patti Page-16 Most Requested Songs* . . . . (Legacy)
Patti Page-Golden Hits . . . . (Mercury)
Patti Page's Greatest Hits. . . . . (Columbia)

Don't Buy Me No Beer
Rockin' Louie; *It Will Stand*. . . . . (Ripete)

Don't Let Your Eyes Go Shopping
Mark Murphy; *Mark Murphy Sings Nat's Choice-Nat ''King'' Cole*
Songbook-#2. . . . . (Muse)

Don't Sell Daddy Any More Whiskey
Joe Val & The New England Bluegrass Boys; *Not A Word*
From Home . . . . (Rounder)

Don't Sell This Diamond Ring
Gary Lewis And The Playboys; *Good Old Rock &*
Roll-C. . . . . (International Mktg. Group)

Don't You Get It
Mark Knopfler; *Golden Heart* . . . . (Warner Bros.)

Down In The Mall
Warren Zevon; *Transverse City* . . . . (Virgin)

Dream Merchant
New Birth; *Smooth Grooves-A Sensual Collection-#5-C*. . . . . (Rhino)

Elderly Woman Behind The Counter In A Small Town
Pearl Jam; *Vs.*. . . . . (Epic Portrait Assoc.)

Emma Jean's Guitar
Chely Wright; *Let Me In*. . . . . (MCA)

Excuse Me Mr.
No Doubt; *Tragic Kingdom* . . . . (Trauma)

Fear Of The Marketplace
Neil Diamond; *On The Way To The Sky* . . . . (Columbia)

Funk Boutique
Cover Girls; *This Beat Is Hot-C* . . . . (Epic)

Girl On The Billboard
Boxcar Willie; *Truck Driving Favorites* . . . . (Madacy)

Del Reeves; *101 Greatest Country Hits-#10-C*. . . . . (K-Tel)
   Truck Driver Boogie Big Rig Hits-1939-1969-C . . . . (Audium)
   Truckin' On-C . . . . (Hollywood)
Go To The Mall
Dead Serios; *Ralph Rules* . . . .(Long Song)
Golden Ring
Emmylou Harris/Linda Ronstadt/Anna & Kate McGarrigle; *Tammy*
   Wynette...Remembered-C. . . . . (Asylum)
George Jones & Tammy Wynette; *George Jones & Tammy Wynette-16*
   Biggest Hits. . . . . (Epic/Legacy)
Tammy Wynette & George Jones; *Encore-Tammy Wynette & George*
   Jones . . . .(Epic)
   Tammy Wynette & George Jones' Greatest Hits . . . .(Epic)
   Tammy Wynette-Anniversary-20 Years Of Hits . . . .(Epic)
Green Christmas
Stan Freberg; *Capitol Collectors Series-Stan Freberg* . . . . (Capitol)
   Christmas Comedy Classics-C. . . . . (Priority)
   Dr. Demento Presents The Greatest Novelty Records-#6-
   Christmas-C . . . . (Rhino)
   Dr. Demento's Greatest Christmas CD-C . . . . (Rhino)
Hey Get Your Cold Beer (Ballantine Premium Beer)
Original Soundtrack; *TeeVee Toons-The Commercials-#1-C*. . . . . (TVT)
Hit 'Em Up Style (Oops!) (Neiman-Marcus)
Blu Cantrell; *So Blu* . . . . (Arista)
   Totally Hits 2001-C . . . . (Arista)
I Don't Go Shopping
Peter Allen; *Best Of Peter Allen* . . . . (A&M)
I Found A Million-Dollar Baby (In A Five-And-Ten-Cent Store)
Barbra Streisand; *ST/Funny Girl* . . . . (Columbia)
Bing Crosby; *Pennies From Heaven*. . . . . (Pro-Arte)
Fred Waring's Pennsylvanians; *78-#22707* . . . . (Victor)
Nat "King" Cole; *Nat "King" Cole-Gift Set* . . . . (Capitol)
I Will Buy You A New Life
Everclear; *Now That's What I Call Music!-#1-C* . . . . (Virgin)
   So Much For The Afterglow . . . . (Capitol)
I'd Like To Buy The World A Coke (Coca-Cola)
Original Soundtrack; *TeeVee Toons-The Commercials-#1-C*. . . . . (TVT)
I'm A Pleasure To Shop For
Ogden Nash; *Christmas With Ogden Nash* . . . .(Caedmon)
I'm Payin' Taxes, What Am I Buyin'
JB's; *Funky Good Time-The Anthology* . . . . (Polydor)
Imelda
Mark Knopfler; *Golden Heart* . . . .(Warner Bros.)
In A Persian Market
Wilbur DeParis; *ST/New York Stories*. . . . . (Elektra)
In The Market Place
Earth, Wind & Fire; *All 'N All*. . . . . (Columbia)
Independent Women Pt.1
Destiny's Child; *Now That's What I Call Music!-#6-C* . . . . (Virgin)
   ST/Charlie's Angels . . . . (Columbia)
Junk
Paul McCartney; *McCartney* . . . . (Capitol)
   Paul McCartney-Gift Set . . . . (Capitol)
Keep The Customer Satisfied
Simon & Garfunkel; *Bridge Over Troubled Water* . . . . (Columbia)
   Collected Works. . . . . (Columbia)
Let's Go Spend Your Money Honey
Evangeline; *French Quarter Moon*. . . . .(Margaritaville)
Life Is A Lemon And I Want My Money Back
Meat Loaf; *Bat Out Of Hell II: Back Into Hell* . . . .(MCA)
Little Man
Alan Jackson; *High Mileage*. . . . . (Arista)
Lost In The Supermarket
Clash; *London Calling* . . . .(Epic)
   On Broadway. . . . .(Epic)
   The Story Of The Clash, Volume 1 . . . .(Epic)
Love Ain't Like That
Faith Hill; *Faith* . . . .(Warner Bros.)
Love At The Five & Dime
Kathy Mattea; *Collection Of Hits* . . . . (Mercury)
   Fourteen Country Favorites-C . . . . (Mercury)
   Walk The Way The Wind Blows . . . . (Mercury)
Nanci Griffith; *Last Of The True Believers* . . . . (Philo)
   One Fair Summer Evening. . . . .(MCA)
Love Don't Cost A Thing
Jennifer Lopez; *J. Lo*. . . . .(Epic)
   Now That's What I Call Music!-#6-C . . . . (Virgin)
Love For Sale
Charlie Parker; *Cole Porter Songbook* . . . . (Verve)
Dexter Gordon; *Blue Porter* . . . . (Blue Note)
Dr. John; *In A Sentimental Mood* . . . .(Warner Bros.)
Ella Fitzgerald; *Cole Porter Songbook* . . . . (Verve)
Fine Young Cannibals; *Red Hot + Blue-Tribute To Cole Porter-C* . . .(Chrysalis)
Tony Bennett; *I Left My Heart In San Francisco* . . . . (Columbia)
Love Under New Management
Miki Howard; *Miki Howard*. . . . .(Atlantic)
Love's The Only House
Martina McBride; *Emotion*. . . . .(RCA)

Magic Fingers (25 Cents)
Birdsongs Of The Mesozoic; *Faultline* . . . . (Cuneiform)
Mama Can't Buy You Love
Elton John; *Complete Thom Bell Sessions*. . . . . (MCA)
   Elton John's Greatest Hits-1976-1986. (MCA)
Man In The Corner Shop
Jam; *Snap!*. . . . .(Polydor)
Mockingbird
Carly Simon & James Taylor; *Best Of Carly Simon & James Taylor* . . . (Elektra)
   Hotcakes. . . . . (Elektra)
Inez Foxx with Charlie Foxx; *Billboard Top R&B Hits-1963-C* . . . . (Rhino)
   Oldies But Goodies-#8-C. . . . .(Original Sound)
   Super Oldies Of The '60s-#4-C . . . . (Audio Fidelity)
Peter, Paul & Mary; *Peter, Paul & Mommy* . . . . (Warner Bros.)
Money Burns A Hole In My Pocket
Dean Martin; *Capitol Collectors Series-Dean Martin*. . . . . (Capitol)
Money Can't Buy It
Annie Lennox; *Diva* . . . . (Arista)
Money For Nothing
Dire Straits; *Brothers In Arms* . . . . (Warner Bros.)
   Money For Nothing . . . . (Warner Bros.)
Mr. Dream Merchant
Jerry Butler; *Best Of Jerry Butler* . . . . (Rhino)
   Soul Shots-#2-The "In" Crowd-Sweet Soul-C. . . . . (Rhino)
My Arms Stay Open All Night
Tanya Tucker; *Tanya Tucker's Greatest Hits* . . . . (Liberty)
My One And Only Heart
Perry Como; *Sing Just For You* . . . .(RCA)
Nigerian Marketplace
Oscar Peterson Trio; *Nigerian Marketplace* . . . . (Pablo)
No More
Ruff Endz; *Love Crimes* . . . . (Epic)
Paper Doll
Bar-Kays; *Banging The Wall*. . . . . (Mercury)
Mills Brothers; *Best Of The Mills Brothers* . . . . (MCA)
   Billboard Pop Memories-1940-1944-C . . . . (Rhino)
   Mills Brothers' All Time Greatest Hits . . . . (MCA)
   Mills Brothers' Greatest Hits . . . . (MCA)
   Mills Brothers-22 Great Hits . . . . (Ranwood)
   Paper Doll . . . . (MCA)
   Sentimental Journey: Pop Vocal Classics-#1-1942-1946-C . . . . (Rhino)
   The Mills Brothers-Best Of The Decca Years . . . . (Decca)
Paper Rosie
Don Walser; *Here's To Country Music* . . . . (Sire)
Gene Watson; *Gene Watson's Greatest Hits* . . . . (Curb)
Osborne Brothers; *Hillbilly Fever* . . . . (C.M.H. Prod.)
Peanut Vendor
Judy Garland; *Star Is Born* . . . . (Columbia)
Stan Kenton; *Comprehensive Stan Kenton* . . . . (Capitol)
   Retrospective-Capitol Years. . . . . (Blue Note)
   Stan Kenton's Greatest Hits . . . . (Capitol)
   The Uncollected Stan Kenton & His Orchestra-#6-1962 . . . . (Hindsight)
Pick One Up And Smoke It Sometime (Muriel Cigars)
Original Soundtrack; *TeeVee Toons-The Commercials-#1-C* . . . . (TVT)
Price Of Love
Bryan Ferry; *Let's Stick Together* . . . .(Virgin)
Cactus Brothers; *Cactus Brothers* . . . . (Liberty)
Everly Brothers; *The Reunion Concert-Live At Albert Hall 1983* . . . (Mercury)
   Walk Right Back: The Everly Brothers On Warner Bros.-1960-
   1969. . . . . (Warner Archives)
Poco; *Crazy Loving-Best Of Poco-1975-1982* . . . . (MCA)
Price Of Love
Bon Jovi; *7800 Degrees Fahrenheit* . . . . (Mercury)
Price Of Love
Roger Daltrey; *ST/Secret Of My Success* . . . . (MCA)
Price Of Love
Bad English; *Bad English* . . . . (Epic)
   Legends Of Pop In The '90s-C . . . .(Madacy)
Rainbow
Russ Hamilton; *45-#184* . . . .(Kapp)
Red Roses For A Blue Lady
Al Martino; *Best Of Al Martino* . . . . (Capitol)
   Capitol Collectors Series-Al Martino. . . . . (Capitol)
Andy Williams; *Andy Williams-16 Most Requested Songs* . . . . (Legacy)
Mom & Dads; *Best Of The Mom & Dads* . . . .(Crescendo)
Roger Whittaker; *All-Time Heart-Touching Favorites* . . . . (Capitol)
   Roger Whittaker-Classics Collection-#1 . . . . (Capitol)
Vaughn Monroe; *Best Of Vaughn Monroe* . . . . (RCA)
Riding With Private Malone
David Ball; *Amigo*. . . . . (Razor & Tie)
Rockin' Shopping Center
Jonathan Richman & The Modern Lovers; *Jonathan Richman & The Modern*
   Lovers . . . . (Rhino)
Safeway Cart
Neil Young & Crazy Horse; *Sleeps With Angels* . . . . (Reprise)
Sales Tax On The Woman
New Lost City Ramblers; *New Lost City Ramblers-Early Years-1958-*
   1962. . . . .(Smithsonian Folkways)

Salesgirl Blues
Rick Parker; *Wicked World* . . . . (Geffen)
Saturday Night At The General Store
Margo Smith; *Happiness* . . . . (Warner Bros.)
Scarborough Fair/Canticle
Simon & Garfunkel; *Collected Works* . . . . (Columbia)
Parsley Sage Rosemary & Thyme . . . . (Columbia)
Simon & Garfunkel's Greatest Hits . . . . (Columbia)
ST/The Graduate . . . . (Columbia)
The Concert In Central Park . . . . (Warner Bros.)
Sears-Roebuck Routine
Doc Watson; *Old Timey Concert* . . . . (Vanguard)
Second Hand Rose
Barbra Streisand; *A Happening In Central Park* . . . . (Columbia)
Barbra Streisand...and other musical instruments . . . . (Columbia)
Barbra Streisand's Greatest Hits . . . . (Columbia)
Just For The Record . . . . (Columbia)
My Name Is Barbra, Two . . . . (Columbia)
Second Hand Store
Joe Walsh; *But Seriously Folks* . . . . (Asylum)
Sell My Monkey
B.B. King; *Blues 'N' Jazz/Electric B.B. King* . . . . (MCA)
Blues 'N' Jazz/Electric B.B. King . . . . (MCA)
Selling The Drama
Live; *Throwing Copper* . . . . (Radioactive/MCA)
Senegal Market Place
Sly Dunbar; *Sly Wicked & Slick* . . . . (Front Line)
Shop Around
Captain & Tennille; *Captain & Tennille's Greatest Hits* . . . . (A&M)
Miracles; *Greatest Hits From The Beginning* . . . . (Motown)
Hi-We're The Miracles . . . . (Motown)
Smokey Robinson & The Miracles; *16 #1 Hits From The Early '60s-C* . . . . (Motown)
Every Great Motown Song-First 25 Years-C . . . . (Motown)
Smokey Robinson & The Miracles' Anthology . . . . (Motown)
Shopping For Clothes
Coasters; *Coasters-Their Greatest Recordings-Early Years* . . . . (Atco)
Sixteen Tons
Cactus Brothers; *Cactus Brothers* . . . . (Liberty)
Tennessee Ernie Ford; *Best Of Tennessee Ernie Ford-16 Tons Of Boogie* . . . . (Rhino)
Capitol Collectors Series-Tennessee Ernie Ford . . . . (Capitol)
When AM Was King-C . . . . (Capitol)
Weavers; *Weavers' Greatest Hits* . . . . (Vanguard)
Sold (The Grundy County Auction Incident)
John Michael Montgomery; *Drew's Famous Country Party Music-C* . . . . (Turn Up The Music)
John Michael Montgomery . . . . (Atlantic)
John Michael Montgomery's Greatest Hits . . . . (Atlantic)
Sold My Fortune
Sugartooth; *Sugartooth* . . . . (Geffen)
Somebody Else's Money
Wallflowers; *The Wallflowers* . . . . (Virgin)
Something In Red
Lorrie Morgan; *Lorrie Morgan's Greatest Hits* . . . . (BNA)
Something In Red . . . . (RCA)
To Get To You-Greatest Hits Collection . . . . (BNA)
Souvenirs
Gretchen Peters; *Gretchen Peters* . . . . (Purple Crayon Prod.)
Stairway To Heaven
Led Zeppelin; *Led Zeppelin IV* . . . . (Atlantic)
Led Zeppelin-Box Set . . . . (Atlantic)
Remasters . . . . (Atlantic)
ST/The Song Remains The Same . . . . (Swan Song)
Stanley Jordan; *Best Of Stanley Jordan* . . . . (Blue Note)
Flying Home . . . . (EMI)
Stone Cold Dead In The Market
Ella Fitzgerald; *Best Of Ella Fitzgerald-#2* . . . . (MCA)
Streak, The
Ray Stevens; *Ray Stevens' Greatest Hits* . . . . (RCA)
Ray Stevens' Greatest Hits . . . . (MCA)
Ray Stevens-All-Time Greatest Comic Hits . . . . (Curb)
Super Hits Of The '70s-Have A Nice Day-#12-C . . . . (Rhino)
Swap Meet
Nirvana; *Bleach* . . . . (Sub Pop)
Swap Meet Louie
Sir Mix-A-Lot; *Mack Daddy* . . . . (Def American)
That Ain't In Any Catalog
Mustard & Gravy; *Long Gone Daddy-C* . . . . (Collectables)
That's Where My Money Goes
101 Strings Orchestra; *Beer Drinkin' Sing Alongs!!* . . . . (Alshire)
Theme From "The Price Is Right"
Original Soundtrack; *Television's Greatest Hits-#6-Remote Control-C* . . . (TVT)
Then God Made Malls
Uncle Bonsai; *Myn Ynd Wymyn* . . . . (Yellow Tail)
Too High A Price
Doobie Brothers; *Cycles* . . . . (Warner Bros.)
Try It Before You Buy It
Mike Bloomfield; *Try It Before You Buy It* . . . . (One Way)

Tupperware Party
Doughboys; *Happy Accidents* . . . . (Restless)
Unbelievable
Diamond Rio; *Unbelievable* . . . . (Arista)
Video Shop
Kinks; *Lost & Found-1986-1989* . . . . (MCA)
Think Visual . . . . (MCA Special Prod.)
Waldo's Discount Donuts
Red Knuckles & The Trailblazers; *Hot Rize Presents* . . . . (Flying Fish)
Walkin' On The Sun
Smash Mouth; *Fush Yu Mang* . . . . (Interscope)
Want Ads
Honey Cone; *Honey Cone's Greatest Hits* . . . . (HDH)
War Is Hell (On The Homefront Too)
T.G. Sheppard; *Perfect Stranger* . . . . (Warner Bros.)
T.G. Sheppard's All-Time Greatest Hits . . . . (Warner Bros.)
T.G. Sheppard's Greatest Hits . . . . (Warner Bros./Curb)
What You Want
Mase Featuring Total; *Harlem World* . . . . (Bad Boy/Arista)
Who Will Buy?
Barbra Streisand; *The Second Barbra Streisand Album* . . . . (Columbia)
Original Broadway Cast; *Oliver!* . . . . (RCA Victor)
Original London Cast; *Oliver!* . . . . (EMI-Angel)
Will There Be A Shopping Mall In Heaven?
Reverend Billy C. Wirtz; *Deep Fried & Sanctified* . . . . (Hightone)
Window Shoppin'
Hiram Bullock; *From All Sides* . . . . (Atlantic)
Window Shopping
Hank Williams; *24 Of Hank Williams' Greatest Hits* . . . . (Polydor)
Hank Williams-40 Greatest Hits . . . . (Polydor)
Live At The Grand Ole Opry . . . . (Mercury)
X-Mas Shopping Blues
Christmas Jug Band; *Mistletoe Jam* . . . . (Relix)
Yard Sale
Sammy Kershaw; *Don't Go Near The Water* . . . . (Mercury)
The Hits-Chapter 1 . . . . (Mercury)
Yes We Have No Bananas
Authentic Band Organ; *Catch The Brass Ring-Merry-Go-Round* . . . . . (Klavier)
Spike Jones; *Best Of Spike Jones-#2* . . . . (RCA)

SHOW BIZ, Fame, Stardom

See Also: **BUSINESS & INDUSTRY, CITIES: A-Z, CITIES: NEW YORK (Broadway), COUNTRY, ELVIS, HOLLYWOOD, MONEY, MOVIES, MUSIC, RADIO, RECORD BUSINESS, ROCK & ROCKING, STREETS: SPECIFIC, TELEVISION**

"Star Is Born" (Evergreen), Love Theme From "A Star Is Born"
Barbra Streisand; *Barbra Streisand's Greatest Hits* . . . . (Columbia)
Barbra Streisand's Greatest Hits, Volume 2 . . . . (Columbia)
Diana, Princess Of Wales-Tribute-C . . . . (Columbia)
Memories . . . . (Columbia)
ST/A Star Is Born . . . . (Columbia)
Luther Vandross; *Songs* . . . . (Epic)
Paul Williams; *Paul Williams-Classics* . . . . (A&M)
(I'd Be) A Legend In My Time
Don Gibson; *Best Of Don Gibson-#1* . . . . (Curb)
Leon Russell; *Legend In My Time: Hank Wilson-#3* . . . . (Ark 21)
Ronnie Milsap; *Ronnie Milsap's Greatest Hits* . . . . (RCA)
42nd Street
Diana Krall; *Stepping Out* . . . . (Justin Time)
Hal Kemp; *Best Of The Big Bands-C* . . . . (Columbia)
Mel Torme; *Cocktail Mix-#3-Swingin' Singles-C* . . . . (Rhino)
Original Broadway Cast; *42nd Street* . . . . (RCA Victor)
Academy Award
Jo Jo Gunne; *Jo Jo Gunne* . . . . (Asylum)
Academy Award Performance
Sparks; *No. 1 In Heaven* . . . . (Elektra)
Act Naturally
Beatles; *"Yesterday"...And Today* . . . . (Capitol)
Buck Owens; *Beatles Originals* . . . . (Rhino)
Buck Owens & Ringo Starr; *Act Naturally* . . . . (Capitol)
Buck Owens & The Buckaroos; *Buck Owens & The Buckaroos-Live At Carnegie Hall* . . . . (Country Music Foundation)
Charley Pride; *Country Pride* . . . . (RCA)
Johnny Russell; *20 Great Country Hits-C* . . . . (RCA)
Actor
Moody Blues; *In Search Of The Lost Chord* . . . . (Polydor)
This Is The Moody Blues . . . . (Polydor)
Adam's Song
Blink-182; *Enema Of The State* . . . . (MCA)
All For You
Janet; *All For You* . . . . (Virgin)
Now That's What I Call Music!-#7-C . . . . (Virgin)
All Mixed Up
311; *311* . . . . (Capricorn)

All Star
Smash Mouth; *Astro Lounge* . . . . (Interscope)
Now That's What I Call Music!-#3-C . . . . (Virgin)
All The Rage In Paris
Derailers; *Here Come The Derailers* . . . . (Lucky Dog)
All The Way To Reno (You're Gonna Be A Star)
R.E.M.; *Reveal* . . . . (Warner Bros.)
Amanda
Don Williams; *Don Williams' Greatest Hits* . . . . (MCA)
Volume One . . . . (MCA)
Waylon Jennings; *Waylon Jennings' Greatest Hits* . . . . (RCA)
Another Op'nin', Another Show
Original Cast; *Kiss Me Kate* . . . . (Sony Music Classical)
Kiss Me Kate . . . . (MCA)
Kiss Me Kate . . . . (EMI-Angel)
*There's No Business Like Show Business: Broadway
Showstoppers-C* . . . . (Sony Broadway)
Are You Sure Hank Done It This Way
Hank Williams, Jr.; *Rowdy* . . . . (WB/Curb)
Waylon Jennings; *Waylon Jennings' Greatest Hits* . . . . (RCA)
Artist Relations
Martin Mull; *I'm Everyone I Ever Loved* . . . . (MCA)
Baby I'm A Star
Prince and the Revolution; *ST/Purple Rain* . . . . (Warner Bros.)
Baby I'm A Star
Helen Reddy; *Ear Candy* . . . . (Capitol)
Back When He Was Hungry
Bill Anderson; *A Lot Of Things Different* . . . . (Varese Sarabande)
Backstage Queen
Scorpions; *Best Of The Scorpions* . . . . (RCA)
Tokyo Tapes . . . . (RCA)
Virgin Killer . . . . (RCA)
Ballad Of A Teenage Queen
Johnny Cash; *Johnny Cash* . . . . (Sun)
Johnny Cash-Original Golden Hits-#2 . . . . (Sun)
Johnny Cash-Sun Years . . . . (Rhino)
ST/Harper Valley PTA . . . . (Sun)
The Legend . . . . (Plantation)
The Man In Black-His Greatest Hits . . . . (Legacy)
Ballad Of John And Yoko
Beatles; *Beatles 1* . . . . (Capitol)
Beatles-Box Set . . . . (Capitol)
Hey Jude . . . . (Capitol)
Past Masters-Volume Two . . . . (Parlophone)
ST/Imagine: John Lennon . . . . (Capitol)
The Beatles/1967-1970 . . . . (Capitol)
Ballroom Blitz
Sweet; *Desolation Boulevard* . . . . (Capitol)
Be Like That
3 Doors Down; *Better Life* . . . . (Republic/Universal)
Now That's What I Call Music!-#8-C . . . . (Virgin)
Big Willie Style
Will Smith featuring Left Eye; *Big Willie Style* . . . . (Columbia)
Bigger Than The Beatles
Joe Diffie; *Life's So Funny* . . . . (Epic)
Black Velvet
Alannah Myles; *Alannah Myles* . . . . (Atlantic)
Robin Lee; *Black Velvet* . . . . (Atlantic)
Blaze Of Glory
Jon Bon Jovi; *Blaze Of Glory-ST/Young Guns II* . . . . (Mercury)
Brand New Country Star
Jimmy Buffett; *Living & Dying In 3/4 Time* . . . . (MCA)
Broadway
Count Basie; *Essential Count Basie-#3* . . . . (Columbia)
Count Basie & His Orchestra; *Best Of Count Basie & His Orchestra-The
Roulette Years* . . . . (Roulette)
Broadway
Jack McDuff & Friends; *Color Me Blue* . . . . (Concord Jazz)
Broadway
Mel Torme; *Songs Of New York* . . . . (Rhino)
Broadway
Clash; *On Broadway* . . . . (Epic)
Sandinista . . . . (Epic)
Broadway Baby
Julia McKenzie; *Collector's Sondheim-C* . . . . (RCA)
Original Broadway Cast; *Follies* . . . . (Capitol)
Broadway Ballet
Gene Kelly/Chorus; *ST/Singin' In The Rain* . . . . (Sony Music Special Prod.)
Broadway Fools
Branford Marsalis; *Random Abstract* . . . . (Columbia)
Broadway My Street
Original Broadway Cast; *70 Girls 70* . . . . (Sony Music Classical)
Californication
Red Hot Chili Peppers; *Californication* . . . . (Warner Bros.)
Camera One
Josh Joplin Group; *Useful Music* . . . . (Artemis)
Candle In The Wind
Elton John; *Goodbye Yellow Brick Road* . . . . (Polydor)

Live In Australia With The Melbourne Symphony Orchestra . . . . (MCA)
Your Songs . . . . (Polydor)
Celebrity Skin
Hole; *Celebrity Skin* . . . . (David Geffen Co.)
Celluloid Heroes
Joan Jett; *The Hit List* . . . . (Epic)
Kinks; *Come Dancing With The Kinks-Best Of The Kinks 1977-1986* . . . (Arista)
Everybody's In Show-Biz . . . . (Rhino)
The Kinks' Greatest-Celluloid Heroes . . . . (RCA)
Child Star
Joan Armatrading; *Whatever's For Us* . . . . (A&M)
Chords Of Fame
Phil Ochs; *Chords Of Fame* . . . . (A&M)
Phil Ochs' Greatest Hits . . . . (A&M)
The War Is Over-Best Of Phil Ochs . . . . (A&M)
Circus Girl
Gretchen Peters; *The Secret Of Life* . . . . (Purple Crayon Prod.)
Come Original
311; *Soundsystem* . . . . (Capricorn)
Comedians
Elvis Costello & The Attractions; *Goodbye Cruel World* . . . . (Columbia)
Roy Orbison; *Mystery Girl* . . . . (Virgin)
Roy Orbison & Friends: Black & White Night-Live . . . . (Virgin)
Could I Have Your Autograph
Dolly Parton; *Rainbow* . . . . (Columbia)
Cover Of Rolling Stone
Dr. Hook & The Medicine Show; *Dr. Hook & The Medicine Show's
Greatest Hits* . . . . (Capitol)
Revisited . . . . (Columbia)
Cowboy Heaven
Roy Rogers; *Peace In The Valley* . . . . (Pair)
Cracked Actor
David Bowie; *Aladdin Sane* . . . . (Rykodisc)
David Live . . . . (Rykodisc)
Sound + Vision . . . . (Rykodisc)
ST/Ziggy Stardust-The Motion Picture . . . . (Rykodisc)
Creeque Alley
Mamas & The Papas; *Best Of The Mamas & The Papas* . . . . (MCA)
Mamas & The Papas' Greatest Hits . . . . (MCA)
Mamas & The Papas-16 Of Their Greatest Hits . . . . (MCA)
Danger (Been So Long)
Mystikal; *Now That's What I Call Music!-#7-C* . . . . (Virgin)
Mystikal featuring Nivea; *Let's Get Ready* . . . . (Jive)
Day After Day
Alan Parsons Project; *I Robot* . . . . (Arista)
Deep Inside
Mary J. Blige; *Mary* . . . . (MCA)
Did You Ever Think
R. Kelly; *R.* . . . . (Jive)
Dirty Laundry
Don Henley; *I Can't Stand Still* . . . . (Asylum)
Dixie Road
Lee Greenwood; *Country Classics-#3-1984-1985-C* . . . . (Universal)
Lee Greenwood's Greatest Hits . . . . (MCA)
MCA #1 Hits Of The '80s-#2-C . . . . (MCA Special Prod.)
Do America
Mark Knopfler; *Sailing To Philadelphia* . . . . (Warner Bros.)
Do You Know The Way To San Jose
Dionne Warwick; *Dionne Warwick Greatest Hits* . . . . (Everest)
Dionne Warwick-Anthology 1962-1971 . . . . (Rhino)
Hot! Live & Otherwise . . . . (Arista)
Dope Show
Marilyn Manson; *Mechanical Animals* . . . . (Nothing)
Drive My Car
Beatles; *"Yesterday"...And Today* . . . . (Capitol)
Rock 'N' Roll Music . . . . (Capitol)
The Beatles/1962-1966 . . . . (Capitol)
Drowned World (My Substitute For Love)
Madonna; *GHV2* . . . . (Warner Bros.)
Ray Of Light . . . . (Maverick)
E-Bow The Letter
R.E.M.; *New Adventures In Hi-Fi* . . . . (Warner Bros.)
El Macho
Mark Knopfler; *Sailing To Philadelphia* . . . . (Warner Bros.)
Eminence Front
Who; *It's Hard* . . . . (MCA)
Join Together . . . . (MCA)
Entertainer, The
Marvin Hamlisch; *Super Hits Of The '70s-Have A Nice Day-#12-C* . . . . (Rhino)
Scott Joplin; *The Entertainer-#4* . . . . (Biograph)
Entertainer, The
Larry Graham & Graham Central Station; *Star Walk* . . . . (Warner Bros.)
Entertainer, The
Tony Clarke; *Best Of Chess Rhythm & Blues-#1-C* . . . . (Chess)
Soul Shots #10-More Sweet Soul-C . . . . (Rhino)
Entertainer, The
Billy Joel; *Billy Joel-Greatest Hits, Volume I & Volume II* . . . . (Columbia)
Streetlife Serenade . . . . (Columbia)

Everybody Is A Star
Gladys Knight & The Pips; *Everybody Needs Love/If I Were Your Woman* .... (Motown)
Sly & The Family Stone; *Sly & The Family Stone-Anthology* .... (Epic)
   Sly & The Family Stone's Greatest Hits .... (Epic)

Everybody's A Star
Kinks; *Soap Opera* .... (Rhino)

Everybody's In Shobizz
Shobizz; *Shobizz* .... (Capitol)

Everybody's Making It Big But Me
Dr. Hook; *Bankrupt* .... (Capitol)

Everything's Coming Up Roses
Ethel Merman; *Broadway Magic-The 1960s-C* .... (Columbia)
Original Cast; *Gypsy* .... (Columbia)
Original London Cast; *Gypsy* .... (RCA)

Fake Your Way To The Top
Original Cast; *Dreamgirls* .... (Geffen)

Fame
David Bowie; *Changesonebowie* .... (RCA)
   ST/Pretty Woman .... (EMI)
   The Singles-1969-1993 .... (Rykodisc)
   Young Americans .... (Rykodisc)
Irene Cara; *ST/Fame* .... (RSO)

Fame And Fortune
Bad Company; *Fame & Fortune* .... (Atlantic)

Fame And Fortune
Elvis Presley; *A Valentine Gift For You* .... (RCA)
   Elvis' Golden Records, Volume 3 .... (RCA)
   Elvis-A Legendary Performer, Volume 3 .... (RCA)

Famous Groupies
Wings; *London Town* .... (Capitol)

Fan Mail
Dickies; *Dawn Of* .... (A&M)
   Great Dictations (Definitive Collection) .... (A&M)

Fan Mail
Blondie; *Plastic Letters* .... (Chrysalis)

Fool's Hall Of Fame
Johnny Cash; *Rough Cut King Of Country Music* .... (Sun)
   The Man-The World-His Music .... (Sun)
Roy Orbison; *Roy Orbison-The Sun Years* .... (Rhino)

Footlights
Merle Haggard; *For The Record: Merle Haggard-43 Legendary Hits* .... (BNA)

Future Legend
David Bowie; *Diamond Dogs* .... (Rykodisc)

Ghetto Supastar (That Is What You Are)
Pras Michel featuring Old Dirty Bastard & Mya; *ST/Bulworth* ..... (Interscope)

Give My Regards To Broadway
Barry Manilow; *Showstoppers* .... (Arista)
Joel Grey; *Broadway Magic-The 1960s-C* .... (Columbia)
Original Cast; *George M.* .... (Columbia)

Glamorous Life
Sheila E.; *The Glamorous Life* .... (Warner Bros.)

Glamorous Life
Original London Cast; *A Little Night Music* .... (RCA)

Glory
Television; *Adventure* .... (Elektra)

Glory Road
Neil Diamond; *Love At The Greek* .... (Columbia)
   Sweet Caroline .... (MCA)

Greatest Show On Earth
Michael Jackson; *2 Classic Albums: Got To Be There/Ben* .... (Motown)
   Ben .... (Motown)

Hard Act To Follow
Brother Cane; *Brother Cane* .... (Virgin)

Hard To Be A Husband, Hard To Be A Wife
Chely Wright & Brad Paisley; *Grand Ole Opry-75 Years-#2-C* .... (MCA)

Have A Cigar
Pink Floyd; *Wish You Were Here* .... (Columbia)

Heartbreak Town
Dixie Chicks; *Fly* .... (Monument)

Hello There
Cheap Trick; *Cheap Trick At Budokan* .... (Epic)
   In Color .... (Epic)
   ST/Over The Edge .... (Warner Bros.)

Hey Mister, That's Me Up On The Jukebox
Linda Ronstadt; *Prisoner In Disguise* .... (Asylum)

Homeward Bound
Paul Simon; *Paul Simon In Concert/Live Rhymin'* .... (Columbia)
Paul Simon & George Harrison; *Nobody's Child-Romanian Angel Appeal-C* .... (Warner Bros.)
Simon & Garfunkel; *Collected Works* .... (Columbia)
   Parsley Sage Rosemary & Thyme .... (Columbia)
   Simon & Garfunkel's Greatest Hits .... (Columbia)
   The Concert In Central Park .... (Warner Bros.)
Willie Nelson & Waylon Jennings; *Take It To The Limit* .... (Columbia)

Hot Blooded
Foreigner; *Double Vision* .... (Atlantic)
   Records .... (Atlantic)
   ST/Vision Quest .... (Geffen)

How Do You Like Me Now?!
Toby Keith; *How Do You Like Me Now?!* .... (DreamWorks/SKG)

How To Be A Country Star
Statler Brothers; *Best Of The Statler Brothers-Rides Again-#2* .... (Mercury)

I Knew Jesus (Before He Was A Star)
Glen Campbell; *Best Of Glen Campbell* .... (Capitol)

I Left My Heart At The Stage Door Canteen
Jo Stafford; *G.I. Jo* .... (Corinthian)

I Wish
R. Kelly; *Now That's What I Call Music!-#6-C* .... (Virgin)
   TP-2.com .... (Jive)

If Momma Was Married
Cynthia Gibb & Jennifer Beck; *ST/Gypsy* .... (Atlantic)
Original Cast; *Gypsy* .... (Columbia)

I'll Be Your Audience
Shirley Bassey; *Good Bad But Beautiful* .... (EMI)
   Great Performances .... (Liberty)
   Live In London .... (Capitol)
   Shirley Bassey's Greatest Hits .... (EMI)

I'll Trade (A Million Bucks)
Keith Sweat featuring Lil' Mo; *Didn't See Me Coming* .... (Elektra)

I'm Going To Be A Teenage Idol
Elton John; *Don't Shoot Me I'm Only The Piano Player* .... (Polydor)

I'm Gonna Be Somebody
Travis Tritt; *Country Club* .... (Warner Bros.)

I'm Playing For You
Ronnie Milsap; *True Believer* .... (Liberty)

I'm The Greatest Star
Barbra Streisand; *ST/Funny Girl* .... (Columbia)
Diana Ross & The Supremes; *Diana Ross & The Supremes-Anthology (1962-1969)* .... (Motown)

Incomplete
Sisqo; *Now That's What I Call Music!-#5-C* .... (Virgin)
   Unleash The Dragon .... (Dragon/Def Soul/IDJMG)

It Never Rains In Southern California
Albert Hammond; *Rock Artifacts-From The Vaults-#2-C* .... (Legacy)
   Super Hits Of The '70s-Have A Nice Day-#10-C .... (Rhino)
Tony Toni Tone; *Revival* .... (Wing)

Johnny B. Goode
Chuck Berry; *Chuck Berry's Greatest Hits* .... (Everest)
   Classic Rock-#2-C .... (MCA)
   Roll Over Beethoven .... (Allegiance)
   ST/American Graffiti .... (MCA)
   The Chess Box-Chuck Berry .... (Chess)
Elvis Presley; *Elvis In Concert* .... (RCA)
   From Memphis To Vegas/From Vegas To Memphis .... (RCA)
Grateful Dead; *Bill Graham Presents The Last Days Of The Fillmore-C* .... (Epic Portrait Assoc.)
Johnny Winter; *Live/Johnny Winter And* .... (Columbia)
   Second Winter .... (Columbia)

Just Be Straight With Me
Silkk The Shocker; *Charge It 2 Da Game* .... (No Limit/Priority)

Key To Life, The
Vince Gill; *The Key* .... (MCA)

King Of Hollywood
Eagles; *The Long Run* .... (Asylum)

Larger Than Life
Backstreet Boys; *Millennium* .... (Jive)
   Now That's What I Call Music!-#4-C .... (Virgin)

Legend In My Time
Don Gibson; *Don Gibson's All-Time Greatest Hits* .... (RCA)
Ronnie Milsap; *Lost In The Fifties Tonight* .... (RCA)
   Ronnie Milsap-Live .... (RCA)
   Ronnie Milsap's Greatest Hits .... (RCA)

Legend In Your Own Time
Carly Simon; *Anticipation* .... (Elektra)
   Best Of Carly Simon .... (Elektra)

Let Me Blow Ya Mind
Eve featuring Gwen Stefani; *Now That's What I Call Music!-#7-C* ..... (Virgin)
   Scorpion .... (Ruff Ryders/IDJMG)

Let Me Entertain You
Original Cast; *Gypsy* .... (Columbia)
Original London Cast; *Gypsy* .... (RCA)
Pearl Bailey; *Back On Broadway* .... (Roulette)
   Echoes Of An Era-Pearl Bailey .... (Roulette)

Let Me Entertain You
Queen; *Jazz* .... (Hollywood)
   Live Killers .... (Hollywood)

Life's Been Good
Eagles; *Eagles Live* .... (Asylum)
Joe Walsh; *But Seriously Folks* .... (Asylum)
   ST/FM .... (MCA)

Lifestyles Of The Not-So-Rich & Famous
Tracy Byrd; *No Ordinary Man* .... (MCA)

Little Sally, The Super Sex Star
Camille Yarborough; *Iron Pot Cooker* .... (Vanguard)

Lodi
Creedence Clearwater Revival; *1969* .... (Fantasy)
   Creedence Clearwater Revival-Chronicle .... (Fantasy)

Creedence Country . . . . (Fantasy)
Green River . . . . (Fantasy)
Live In Europe . . . . (Fantasy)
More Creedence Gold . . . . (Fantasy)
Travelin' Band . . . . (Fantasy)
Lonely At The Top
Randy Newman; *Randy Newman/Live* . . . .(Warner Archives)
Sail Away . . . . (Reprise)
Lost In The Lights Of Broadway
Bernie Shanahan; *Bernie Shanahan* . . . . (Atlantic)
Love Me
112 Featuring Mase; *Room 112* . . . . (Bad Boy/Arista)
Lucky
Britney Spears; *Now That's What I Call Music!-#5-C* . . . . (Virgin)
Oops!...I Did It Again . . . . (Jive)
Lullaby
Shawn Mullins; *Soul's Core* . . . . (Columbia)
Lullaby Of Broadway
Andrews Sisters; *Best Of The Andrews Sisters-#2* . . . .(MCA)
Bette Midler; *Bette Midler* . . . .(Atlantic)
Live At Last . . . .(Atlantic)
Original Broadway Cast; *42nd Street* . . . .(RCA Victor)
Tony Bennett; *Jazz* . . . . (Columbia)
Mama's Always On Stage
Arrested Development; *3 Years 5 Months 2 Days In The Life Of* . . . . .(Chrysalis)
Arrested Development-Unplugged . . . .(Chrysalis)
Man At The Top
Bruce Springsteen; *Tracks* . . . . (Columbia)
Maria Maria
Santana; *Supernatural* . . . . (Arista)
Totally Hits-#2-C . . . . (Elektra)
Memory Remains
Metallica; *Reload* . . . . (Elektra)
Message To Michael
Dionne Warwick; *Dionne Warwick* . . . . (Everest)
Dionne Warwick Greatest Hits . . . . (Everest)
Dionne Warwick-Anthology 1962-1971 . . . . (Rhino)
Hot! Live & Otherwise . . . . (Arista)
Original Rock 'N' Roll Hits Of The '60s-C . . . . (Roulette)
Midnight Train To Georgia
Gladys Knight & The Pips; *Billboard Top Rock 'N' Roll Hits-1973-C*. . .(Buddah)
Gladys Knight & The Pips' Greatest Hits . . . . (Buddah)
Imagination . . . . (Right Stuff)
On & On . . . . (Fifty One West)
Radio Active Hits-C . . . . (Accord)
Train Trax-C . . . .(Sony Music Special Prod.)
Very Best Of Gladys Knight & The Pips. . . . . (Buddah)
Mirror Star
Fabulous Poodles; *Mirror Stars* . . . .(Epic)
Mister Big Time
Jon Bon Jovi; *ST/Armageddon-The Album.* . . . . (Columbia)
Money For Nothing
Dire Straits; *Brothers In Arms.* . . . .(Warner Bros.)
Money For Nothing . . . .(Warner Bros.)
Mr. Bojangles
David Bromberg; *Out Of The Blues-Best Of David Bromberg* . . . . . . (Columbia)
Jerry Jeff Walker; *A Man Must Carry On* . . . .(MCA)
Best Of Jerry Jeff Walker . . . .(MCA)
Gypsy Songman . . . .(Rykodisc)
Mr. Bojangles . . . . (Bainbridge)
Nitty Gritty Dirt Band; *Best Of The Nitty Gritty Dirt Band.* . . . .(Liberty)
On The Road Again . . . . (Capitol)
Super Hits Of The '70s-Have A Nice Day-#4-C. . . . . . . (Rhino)
Twenty Years Of Dirt-Best Of The Nitty Gritty Dirt Band . . . . . .(Warner Bros.)
Uncle Charlie And His Dog Teddy. . . . . (Liberty)
Mud Shark, The
Mothers Of Invention; *Fillmore East-June 1971* . . . . (Reprise)
Mummer's Dance
Loreena McKennitt; *The Book Of Secrets.* . . . . (Quinlan Rd./Warner Bros.)
My Home Ain't In The Hall Of Fame
J.D. Crowe and the New South; *My Home Ain't In The Hall
Of Fame* . . . . (Rounder)
Jonathan Edwards; *Lucky Day* . . . . (Atco)
Next Plane To London
Rose Garden; *Only Love-1965-1969-C* . . . . (JCI Assoc. Labels)
On Broadway
Drifters; *Drifters-16 Greatest Hits* . . . .(Trip)
Drifters-Golden Hits . . . . (Atlantic)
George Benson; *George Benson-Collection* . . . .(Warner Bros.)
ST/All That Jazz. . . . . (Casablanca)
Weekend In L.A. . . . .(Warner Bros.)
On With The Show
Rolling Stones; *Their Satanic Majesties Request* . . . . (Abkco)
One Hit Wonder
Everclear; *So Much For The Afterglow.* . . . . (Capitol)
One Monkey Don't Stop No Show
Big Maybelle; *Okeh R&B Story-1949-1957* . . . .(Epic)
Honey Cone; *Honey Cone's Greatest Hits* . . . . (HDH)
Joe Tex; *I Believe I'm Gonna Make It!-Best Of Joe Tex* . . . . (Rhino)

Joe Tex's Greatest Hits. . . . . (Curb)
One On The Right Is On The Left, The
Johnny Cash; *Johnny Cash-16 Biggest Hits-#2* . . . . (Legacy)
One's On The Way (Here In Topeka)
Loretta Lynn; *Loretta Lynn-20 Greatest Hits* . . . . (MCA)
Loretta Lynn-Greatest Hits Live. . . . . (K-Tel)
Loretta Lynn's Greatest Hits-#2. . . . . (MCA)
The Country Music Hall Of Fame-Loretta Lynn. . . . . . (MCA)
Only God Knows Why
Kid Rock; *Devil Without A Cause* . . . . (Top Dog/Lava/Atlantic)
Overnight Sensation
Tina Turner; *Break Every Rule* . . . . (Capitol)
Overnight Sensation
Mickey Gilley; *Mickey Gilley's Greatest Hits-#2* . . . . (Epic)
Overnight Sensation (Hit Record)
Eric Carmen; *Eric Carmen-The Definitive Collection.* . . . . (Arista)
Raspberries; *Raspberries' Best Featuring Eric Carmen* . . . . . . (Capitol)
Overnight Success
George Strait; *Beyond The Blue Neon* . . . . (MCA)
Ten Strait Hits . . . . (MCA)
Paradise
Styx; *Return To Paradise* . . . .(CMC Int'l)
Pathway To Glory
Loggins & Messina; *Full Sail* . . . . (Columbia)
Pay You Back With Interest
Hollies; *Best Of The Hollies* . . . . (EMI)
History Of British Rock-#4-C . . . . (Rhino)
The Hollies' Greatest Hits . . . . (Epic)
Performance
Neville Brothers; *Treacherous: A History Of The Neville Brothers* . . . . . (Rhino)
Performance
Esther Phillips; *Best Of Esther Phillips* . . . . (CBS Associated)
Performance
Joe Cocker; *I Can Stand A Little Rain* . . . . (A&M)
Performer
Marty Robbins; *The Performer* . . . . (Columbia)
Picture Postcards From L.A.
Joshua Kadison; *Painted Desert Serenade* . . . . (SBK)
Poor Little Hollywood Star
Virginia Martin; *Little Me* . . . . (RCA)
Popstar
Pretenders; *Viva El Amor!* . . . . (Warner Bros.)
Pre-Road Downs
Crosby, Stills & Nash; *Crosby, Stills & Nash* . . . .(Atlantic)
Privacy
Michael Jackson; *Invincible* . . . . (Epic)
Private Audition
Heart; *Private Audition* . . . . (Epic)
Psycho Circus
Kiss; *Psycho Circus* . . . . (Mercury)
Ride Wit Me
Nelly; *Country Grammar* . . . .(Fo' Reel/Universal)
Now That's What I Call Music!-#7-C . . . .(Virgin)
Riding With A Movie Star
L7; *Hungry For Stink* . . . .(Slash)
Rock And Roll Is Dead
Lenny Kravitz; *Circus* . . . .(Virgin)
Rock 'N' Roll Hall Of Fame
Frank Marino & Mahogany Rush; *What's Next* . . . . . . (Columbia)
Rudiger
Mark Knopfler; *Golden Heart.* . . . . (Warner Bros.)
Same Ol' G
Ginuwine; *ST/Dr. Dolittle* . . . .(Atlantic)
Sensation
Who; *Join Together.* . . . . (MCA)
Tommy . . . . (MCA)
Sgt. Pepper's Lonely Hearts Club Band
Beatles; *Beatles-Box Set* . . . . (Capitol)
The Beatles/1967-1970. . . . . (Capitol)
Jimi Hendrix; *Stages-Stockholm/Paris/San Diego/Atlanta* . . . . . .(Reprise)
Show
Doug E. Fresh & The Get Fresh Crew; *Rapmasters 3-Best Of The
Cut-C* . . . .(Priority)
Show Biz
Dudley Moore; *Songs Without Words* . . . . (GRP)
Show Biz
2 Deep; *Honey That's Show Biz.* . . . . (Cold Chillin')
Show Biz
Helen Reddy; *Free & Easy* . . . . (Capitol)
Show Biz Blues
Fleetwood Mac; *Then Play On* . . . . (Reprise)
Show Biz Kids
Steely Dan; *Countdown To Ecstasy.* . . . . (MCA)
Steely Dan's Greatest Hits. . . . . (MCA)
Show Bizness
Gil Scott-Heron & Brian Jackson; *Secrets.* . . . . (Arista)
Show Bizness
Fred Koller; *Songs From The Night Before* . . . .(Alcazar)

Show Business
AC/DC; *High Voltage* . . . . (Atco)
Show Must Go On
Queen; *Classic Queen* . . . . (Hollywood)
Innuendo . . . . (Hollywood)
Show Must Go On
Four Tops; *45-#12315* . . . . (ABC)
Show Must Go On
Three Dog Night; *Best Of Three Dog Night* . . . . (MCA)
Joy To The World-Greatest Hits . . . . (MCA)
Show Must Go On
Dinah Washington; *Dinah '63* . . . . (Roulette)
Show Must Go On
Carly Simon; *ST/This Is My Life* . . . . (Qwest)
Show Must Go On
Grim Reaper; *See You In Hell* . . . . (RCA)
Show Must Go On
Shenandoah; *Shenandoah* . . . . (Columbia)
Show Must Go On
Leo Sayer; *Silverbird* . . . . (Warner Bros.)
Show Must Go On
Pink Floyd; *The Wall* . . . . (Columbia)
Show Time
Sammy Davis, Jr.; *Live Performance* . . . . (Warner Bros.)
Show Time
Undisputed Truth; *Smokin'* . . . . (Whitfield)
Showman's Life
Jesse Winchester; *Best Of Jesse Winchester* . . . . (Rhino)
Touch On The Rainy Side . . . . (Rhino)
Showtime
Gary's Gang; *Keep On Dancin'* . . . . (Columbia)
Simon Smith & His Amazing Dancing Bear
Randy Newman; *Sail Away* . . . . (Reprise)
So You Are A Star
Hudson Brothers; *Super Hits Of The '70s-Have A Nice Day-#14-C* . . . . . (Rhino)
Yesterday's Heroes-'70s Teen Idols-C . . . . (Rhino)
So You Want To Be A Rock 'N' Roll Star
Byrds; *Original Singles-#1-1965-1967* . . . . (Columbia)
Rock Classics Of The '60s-C . . . . (Columbia)
The Byrds . . . . (Columbia)
The Byrds (Untitled) . . . . (Legacy)
The Byrds' Greatest Hits . . . . (Columbia)
Patti Smith Group; *Wave* . . . . (Arista)
Tom Petty And The Heartbreakers; *Pack Up The Plantation-Live!* . . . . . (MCA)
The Ultimate Rock Album-C . . . . (Foundation)
Stacked Actors
Foo Fighters; *There Is Nothing Left To Lose* . . . . (Roswell/RCA)
Stage Door
Justin Hayward; *Songwriter* . . . . (Deram)
Stage Fright
Band; *Best Of The Band* . . . . (Capitol)
Rock Of Ages . . . . (Capitol)
Stage Fright . . . . (Capitol)
The Last Waltz . . . . (Warner Bros.)
To Kingdom Come-The Definitive Collection . . . . (Capitol)
Bob Dylan And The Band; *Before The Flood* . . . . (Columbia)
Stan
Eminem; *The Marshall Mathers LP* . . . . (Aftermath/Interscope)
Star Star
Rolling Stones; *Goats Head Soup* . . . . (Rolling Stones)
Love You Live . . . . (Virgin)
Star Struck
Blackmore's Rainbow; *Rainbow Rising* . . . . (Polydor)
Star Struck
Kinks; *Are The Village Green Preservation Society* . . . . (Reprise)
Stardom In Action
Pete Townshend; *All The Best Cowboys Have Chinese Eyes* . . . . (Atco)
Starmaker
Kinks; *Celluloid Heroes* . . . . (RCA)
Sucked Out
Superdrag; *Regretfully Yours* . . . . (Elektra)
Superstar
Bette Midler; *Divine Miss M* . . . . (Atlantic)
Carpenters; *Carpenters* . . . . (A&M)
Carpenters-The Singles 1969-1973 . . . . (A&M)
Yesterday Once More . . . . (A&M)
Murray Head; *Premiere Collection-Best Of Andrew Lloyd Webber-C* . . . (MCA)
Super Hits Of The '70s-Have A Nice Day-#5-C . . . . (Rhino)
Superstar
Lauryn Hill; *The Miseducation Of Lauryn Hill* . . . . (Ruffhouse/Columbia)
Superstar
Joe Cocker; *Mad Dogs & Englishmen* . . . . (A&M)
Superstar
Paul Davis; *Southern Tracks & Fantasies* . . . . (Bang)
Superstar
Richard Marx; *Rush Street* . . . . (Capitol)
Superstar (Remember How You Got Where You Are)
Temptations; *Temptations-Anthology-The Best Of The Temptations* . . (Motown)

Superstars
Styx; *Grand Illusion* . . . . (A&M)
Suzi Wants To Be A Rock Star
Professor Griff & His Last Asiatic Disciples; *Pawns In The Game* . . . . . . (Luke)
Take A Bow
Madonna; *Bedtime Stories* . . . . (Maverick/Sire)
GHV2 . . . . (Warner Bros.)
Something To Remember . . . . (Maverick/Sire)
Teen Age Idol
Rick Nelson; *Rick Nelson's Greatest Hits* . . . . (Rhino)
Ricky Nelson; *Best Of Ricky Nelson* . . . . (EMI)
Ricky Nelson-Legendary Masters . . . . (EMI)
Teen Age Idol
Blackfoot; *Blackfoot* . . . . (Atco)
That Ol' Wind
Garth Brooks; *Fresh Horses* . . . . (Capitol)
Limited Series Box . . . . (Capitol)
Theme From "Entertainment Tonight"
Original Soundtrack; *Television's Greatest Hits-#3-1970s & 1980s-C* . . . . (TVT)
Theme From "Fame"
Original Soundtrack; *Television's Greatest Hits-#5-In Living Color-C* . . . . (TVT)
Theme From "It's Garry Shandling's Show"
Original Soundtrack; *Television's Greatest Hits-#7-Cable Ready-C* . . . . . (TVT)
Theme From "Lifestyles Of The Rich And Famous"
Original Soundtrack; *Television's Greatest Hits-#6-Remote Control-C* . . . (TVT)
Theme From "Masterpiece Theatre"
Original Soundtrack; *Television's Greatest Hits-#5-In Living Color-C* . . . . (TVT)
Theme From "Ted Mack's Original Amateur Hour"
Original Soundtrack; *Television's Greatest Hits-#4-Black & White Classics-C* . . . . (TVT)
Theme From "The Dick Van Dyke Show"
Original Soundtrack; *CBS: The First 50 Years* . . . . (TVT)
Television's Greatest Hits-#1-C . . . . (TVT)
Theme From "The Partridge Family"
Original Soundtrack; *Television's Greatest Hits-#2-C* . . . . (TVT)
Then The Morning Comes
Smash Mouth; *Astro Lounge* . . . . (Interscope)
Now That's What I Call Music!-#4-C . . . . (Virgin)
There's No Business Like Show Business
Ethel Merman; *Irving Berlin 100th Anniversary Collection-C* . . . . (MCA)
Merman Sings Merman . . . . (London)
Original Cast; *Annie Get Your Gun* . . . . (MCA)
Top Of The World
Brandy featuring Mase; *Never Say Never* . . . . (Atlantic)
Tulsa Time
Don Williams; *Best Of Don Williams-#2* . . . . (MCA)
Country's Greatest Hits-#6-Superstars-C . . . . (Priority)
Don Williams-Legends . . . . (MCA)
Expressions . . . . (MCA)
Eric Clapton; *Backless* . . . . (Polydor)
Just One Night . . . . (Polydor)
Turn Me On "Mr. Deadman"
Union Underground; *...An Education In Rebellion* . . . . (Portrait)
Turn The Page
Metallica; *Garage Inc.* . . . . (Elektra)
Video Killed The Radio Star
Bruce Woolley & The Camera Club; *Bruce Woolley & The Camera Club* . . . . (Columbia)
Buggles; *Age Of Plastic* . . . . (Island)
Rock Of The '80s-#2-C . . . . (Priority)
The Island Story-1962-1987-25th Anniversary-C . . . . (Island)
Wanna Be A Rock 'N' Roll Star
Eddie Money; *Eddie Money* . . . . (Columbia)
Wanted Dead Or Alive
Bon Jovi; *Slippery When Wet* . . . . (Jambco)
The Concert For New York City-C . . . . (Columbia)
Watching The Wheels
John Lennon; *Lennon* . . . . (Capitol)
John Lennon & Yoko Ono; *Double Fantasy* . . . . (Capitol)
Way I Am
Eminem; *The Marshall Mathers LP* . . . . (Aftermath/Interscope)
We Be Clubbin'
Ice Cube; *ST/The Player's Club* . . . . (Heavyweight/A&M)
Who Do You Think You Are
Spice Girls; *Spice* . . . . (Virgin)
Wild West Show/Dog Act
Original Broadway Cast; *Will Rogers Follies* . . . . (Columbia)
Workin' It
Don Henley; *Inside Job* . . . . (Warner Bros.)
Yes, Yes Y'all
Will Smith; *Big Willie Style* . . . . (Columbia)
You Are The Show
Outlaws; *Playin' To Win* . . . . (Arista)
You Are The Star Of My Show
Eugene Record; *Trying To Get To You* . . . . (Warner Bros.)
You Don't Have To Be A Star
Marilyn McCoo & Billy Davis, Jr.; *Soft Rockin' '70s #2* . . . . (Madacy)

You Got Me
Roots featuring Erykah Badu; *Things Fall Apart* . . . .(MCA)
You Oughta Be In Pictures
Doris Day; *Sentimental Journey* . . . . (Hindsight)
Jackie Gleason; *The Romantic Moods Of Jackie Gleason* . . . . (Capitol)
Rudy Vallee & His Connecticut Yankees; 78-#24580 . . . . (Victor)
You Walked In
Lonestar; *Crazy Nights* . . . . (BNA)
Zap Zap
Frankie Miller; *Standing On The Edge* . . . . (Capitol)

SIGNS

See Also: ASTROLOGY, TRAVELING

...Baby One More Time
Britney Spears; *...Baby One More Time* . . . . (Jive)
Now That's What I Call Music!-#2-C . . . . (Virgin)
7 Sign (Bizzy)
Bone Thugs-N-Harmony; *Art Of War* . . . . (Ruthless/Relativity)
Bad Bad Sign
Joe Cocker; *One Night Of Sin* . . . . (Capitol)
Born Under A Bad Sign
Albert King; *Atlantic Blues-Guitar-C* . . . . (Atlantic)
Best Blues Album In The World...Ever!-C . . . . (Virgin)
Masterworks . . . . (Atlantic)
Stax Blues Masters-Blue Monday-C . . . .(Stax)
Booker T. & The M.G.s; *Best Of Booker T. & The M.G.s* . . . .(Atlantic)
Cream; *Strange Brew-Very Best Of Cream* . . . . (Polydor)
Wheels Of Fire . . . . (Polydor)
Jimi Hendrix; *Blues* . . . . (MCA)
Koko Taylor & Buddy Guy; *Force Of Nature* . . . . (Alligator)
Paul Butterfield Blues Band; *Paul Butterfield Blues Band-Live* . . . . . . (Elektra)
Rita Coolidge; *Rita Coolidge* . . . . (A&M)
Rita Coolidge's Greatest Hits . . . . (A&M)
Simpsons; *Simpsons Sing The Blues* . . . .(Geffen)
Born Under The Wrong Sign
Nazareth; *Close Enough For Rock 'N' Roll* . . . . (A&M)
Civil Defense Sign, The
Mark Spoelstra; *Best Of Broadside 1962-1968: Anthems Of The American
Underground From The Pages Of Broadside
Magazine-C* . . . . (Smithsonian Folkways)
Daylight Fading
Counting Crows; *Recovering The Satellites* . . . . (David Geffen Co.)
Detour (Devil Took A)
Patti Page; *Patti Page-Golden Hits* . . . . (Mercury)
El Picket Sign
Dr. Loco's Rockin' Jalepeno Band; *Movimento Music* . . . . (Flying Fish)
El Teatro Campesino; *Best Of Broadside 1962-1968: Anthems Of
The American Underground From The Pages Of Broadside
Magazine-C* . . . . (Smithsonian Folkways)
Everyday Is A Winding Road
Sheryl Crow; *1998 Grammy Nominees-C* . . . .(MCA)
Sheryl Crow . . . . (A&M)
Exhuming McCarthy
R.E.M.; *Document* . . . .(EMI-Capitol Entert. Properties)
Exile
Enya; *Watermark* . . . . (Reprise)
Gimme Little Sign
Brenton Wood; *18 Best-Brenton Wood* . . . . (Original Sound)
Collectables Presents The History Of Rock-#7-C . . . . (Collectables)
Cruisin'-1957-C . . . . (Increase)
Soul Shots-#3-Soul Twist-C . . . . (Rhino)
Girl On The Billboard
Boxcar Willie; *Truck Driving Favorites* . . . . (Madacy)
Del Reeves; *101 Greatest Country Hits-#10-C* . . . . (K-Tel)
Truck Driver Boogie Big Rig Hits-1939-1969-C . . . . (Audium)
Truckin' On-C . . . . (Hollywood)
Give Me A Little Sign
Rick Nelson; *Stay Young-Epic Recordings* . . . .(Epic)
God Gave Noah The Rainbow Sign
Carter Family; *My Clinch Mountain Home-Their Complete Victor
Recordings-1928-1929* . . . . (Rounder)
Heart Is A Lonely Hunter
Reba McEntire; *Read My Mind* . . . . (MCA)
Reba McEntire's Greatest Hits-#3: I'm A Survivor . . . . (MCA)
High Sign
Diamonds; *Best Of The Diamonds-The Mercury Years* . . . . (Mercury)
I'm Not Strong Enough To Say No
BlackHawk; *Strong Enough* . . . . (Arista)
Jungleland
Bruce Springsteen; *Born To Run* . . . . (Columbia)
Lazy Eye
Goo Goo Dolls; *ST/Batman & Robin-Music From And Inspired By The
Motion Picture* . . . . (Jive)
Looking For A Good Sign
Daryl Hall & John Oates; *Private Eyes* . . . . (RCA)

No Disturb Sign
Beres Hammond; *In Control* . . . . (Elektra)
No Matter What Sign You Are
Diana Ross; *Diana Ross-Anthology* . . . . (Motown)
Diana Ross-The Ultimate Collection . . . . (Motown)
No Sign Of Yesterday
Men At Work; *Brazil* . . . . (Columbia)
Cargo . . . . (Columbia)
Peace Sign
Night Ranger; *Seven* . . . . (CMC Int'l)
Peace Sign
War; *War-Anthology (1970-1994)* . . . . (Avenue)
See The Sign Of Judgement
Birmingham Jubilee Singers; *Complete Recorded Works-1926-
1927* . . . . (Document)
Show Me A Sign
Chicago; *The Heart Of Chicago-1967-1988-#2* . . . . (Reprise)
Sign Language
Eric Clapton; *No Reason To Cry* . . . . (RSO)
Sign O' the times
Prince; *Sign "O" The Times* . . . . (Paisley Park)
Sign Of Judgement
Marianne Faithfull; *Strange Weather* . . . . (Island)
Sign Of The Judgement
Mahalia Jackson; *Gospels, Spirituals & Hymns-#2* . . . . (Legacy)
Sign Of The Rainbow
Robbie Robertson; *Storyville* . . . . (Geffen)
Sign Of The Times
Queensryche; *Hear In The Now Frontier* . . . . (Virgin)
Sign Of The Times
Travis Tritt; *Country Club* . . . . (Warner Bros.)
Sign Of The Times
Petula Clark; *Greatest Hits Of Petula Clark* . . . . (Crescendo)
Sign Of The Times
Bryan Ferry; *Bride Stripped Bare* . . . . (Reprise)
Sign On The Window
Bob Dylan; *New Morning* . . . . (Columbia)
Sign, The
Ace Of Base; *The Sign* . . . . (Arista)
Signed, Sealed, Delivered I'm Yours
Stevie Wonder; *20/20-C* . . . . (Motown)
Motown Grammy R&B Performances Of The '60s & '70s-C . . . . . . (Motown)
Stevie Wonder's Greatest Hits-#2 . . . . (Motown)
Uptight (Everything's Alright) . . . . (Motown)
Signs
Five Man Electrical Band; *Songs Of Protest-C* . . . . (Rhino)
Signs Of Life
Steven Curtis Chapman; *Signs Of Life* . . . . (Sparrow)
Signs That We Never Change
Hollies; *Evolution* . . . . (Epic)
Smooth Criminal
Alien Ant Farm; *Alien Ant Farm-Anthology* . . . .(DreamWorks/SKG)
Michael Jackson; *Bad* . . . . (Epic)
Sound Of Silence, The
Paul Simon; *Paul Simon In Concert/Live Rhymin'* . . . . (Columbia)
Simon & Garfunkel; *Collected Works* . . . . (Columbia)
More American Graffiti-#4-C . . . . (MCA)
Simon & Garfunkel's Greatest Hits . . . . (Columbia)
Sounds Of Silence . . . . (Columbia)
ST/The Graduate . . . . (Columbia)
The Concert In Central Park . . . . (Warner Bros.)
That's The Kind Of Mood I'm In
Patty Loveless; *Strong Heart* . . . . (Epic)
Tie A Yellow Ribbon Round The Ole Oak Tree
Dawn Featuring Tony Orlando; *'70s Party Killers-C* . . . . (Rhino)
Fantastic-#1-C . . . . (K-Tel)
Frank Sinatra; *Some Nice Things I've Missed* . . . . (Reprise)
Lawrence Welk; *Best Of Lawrence Welk-20 Great Hits* . . . . (Ranwood)
Sonny James & Karla Taylor; *Classic Country Duets-C* . . . . (Curb)
Warning Sign
Talking Heads; *More Songs About Buildings & Food* . . . . (Sire)
Water Sign
Gary Wright; *Light Of Smiles* . . . . (Warner Bros.)
Westbound Sign
Green Day; *Insomniac* . . . . (Reprise)

SILENCE, Quiet, Silent, Stillness

*See Also: ANATOMY: HEAD, COMMUNICATION (various),
HEAR, PEACE, SECRETS*

Angels Of The Silences
Counting Crows; *Recovering The Satellites* . . . . (David Geffen Co.)
Be Still My Beating Heart
Sting; *...Nothing Like The Sun* . . . . (A&M)
Fields Of Gold-The Best Of Sting 1984-1994 . . . . (A&M)

Enjoy The Silence
Depeche Mode; *Violator* . . . .(Sire)
Even In The Quietest Moments
Supertramp; *Even In The Quietest Moments* . . . . (A&M)
Hush
Deep Purple; *Nobody's Perfect* . . . . (Mercury)
Purple Passages . . . . (Warner Bros.)
Super Oldies Of The '60s-#10-C . . . .(Audio Fidelity)
When We Rock We Rock & When We Roll We Roll . . . . (Warner Bros.)
Hush Hush Hush
Paula Cole; *This Fire* . . . . (Imago)
I Loved You Once In Silence
Original Cast; *Camelot* . . . . (Columbia)
Original Soundtrack; *ST/Camelot* . . . . (Warner Bros.)
In A Silent Way
Joe Zawinul; *Joe Zawinul* . . . . (Atlantic)
Miles Davis; *In A Silent Way* . . . . (Columbia)
In My Own Quiet Way
Pablo Cruise; *Pablo Cruise* . . . . (A&M)
In The Still Of The Nite
Dion; *Dion Sings The 15 Million Sellers* . . . .(Laurie)
Dion's Greatest Hits . . . .(Laurie)
Dion And The Belmonts; *Wish Upon A Star With Dion And The
Belmonts* . . . . (Collectables)
Five Satins; *Billboard Top R&B Hits-1956-C* . . . . (Rhino)
Cruisin'-1956-C . . . . (Increase)
Five Satins Sing Their Greatest Hits . . . . (Collectables)
In The Still Of The Night . . . . (Capitol)
ST/Dirty Dancing . . . . (RCA)
Johnny Mathis; *In The Still Of The Night* . . . . (Columbia)
Learn To Be Still
Eagles; *Hell Freezes Over* . . . . (Geffen)
My Silent Love
Bing Crosby; *Where The Blue Of The Night Meets The Gold Of
The Day* . . . . (Biograph)
Peggy Lee; *Mink Jazz* . . . . (Blue Note)
No News
Lonestar; *Lonestar* . . . . (BNA)
Quiet
Smashing Pumpkins; *Siamese Dream* . . . .(Virgin)
Quiet
Paul Simon; *You're The One* . . . . (Warner Bros.)
Quiet Afternoon
Stanley Clarke; *Live 1976-1977* . . . . (Epic)
School Days . . . . (Epic)
Quiet Afternoon
Paul Rebhan; *Colors* . . . . (Carmel)
Quiet Friday
Stan Kenton & His Orchestra; *Fire, Fury And Fun* . . . .(Creative World)
Quiet Nights Of Quiet Stars
Antonio Carlos Jobim; *Terra Brasilis* . . . . (Warner Bros.)
Shirley Horn; *I Thought About You-Live At Vine Street* . . . . (Verve)
Radio Silence
Boris Grebenshikov; *Radio Silence* . . . . (Columbia)
Radio Silence
Thomas Dolby; *Golden Age Of Wireless* . . . .(Capitol)
Right To Remain Silent
Doug Stone; *I Thought It Was You* . . . . (Epic)
Shine Silently
Nils Lofgren; *Nils* . . . . (A&M)
Nils Lofgren-Classics-#13 . . . . (A&M)
Silence Is Broken
Damn Yankees; *Don't Tread* . . . . (Warner Bros.)
Silence Is Golden
4 Seasons; *25th Anniversary Collection* . . . .(Rhino)
4 Seasons-Anthology . . . .(Rhino)
Tremeloes; *Best Of The Tremeloes* . . . .(Rhino)
History Of British Rock-#7-C . . . . (Rhino)
Rock Artifacts-From The Vaults-#4-C . . . . (Columbia)
Silence Of A Candle
Oregon; *Essential Oregon* . . . . (Vanguard)
Paul Winter Consort; *Icarus* . . . . (Epic)
Silence On The Line
Chris LeDoux; *Cowboy* . . . . (Capitol)
Silent Eyes
Paul Simon; *Still Crazy After All These Years* . . . . (Columbia)
Silent Fury
Gary Wright; *Light Of Smiles* . . . . (Warner Bros.)
Silent Lucidity
Queensryche; *Empire* . . . . (EMI)
Silent Movies
Neil Sedaka; *Singer- Songwriter-Melody Maker* . . . .(Accord)
Solitaire . . . .(Fifty One West)
Superbird . . . . (Intermedia)
Silent Partners
David Frizzell & Shelly West; *Golden Duets* . . . . (Viva)
In Session . . . . (Viva)
Silent Partners
Laura Branigan; *Self Control* . . . . (Atlantic)

Silent Partners
Waylon Jennings; *Too Dumb For New York City, Too Ugly For L.A.* . . . . .(Epic)
Silent Running
Klaus Schulze; *Trancefer* . . . . (Gramavision)
Silent Running
Mike & The Mechanics; *Mike & The Mechanics* . . . . (Atlantic)
Silent Treatment
Earl Thomas Conley; *Earl Thomas Conley's Greatest Hits* . . . . (RCA)
Fire & Smoke . . . . (RCA)
Sleep's Dark & Silent Gate
Bonnie Raitt; *The Glow* . . . . (Warner Bros.)
Jackson Browne; *The Pretender* . . . . (Asylum)
Sound Of Silence, The
Paul Simon; *Paul Simon In Concert/Live Rhymin'* . . . .(Columbia)
Simon & Garfunkel; *Collected Works* . . . .(Columbia)
More American Graffiti-#4-C . . . . (MCA)
Simon & Garfunkel's Greatest Hits . . . . (Columbia)
Sounds Of Silence . . . . (Columbia)
ST/The Graduate . . . . (Columbia)
The Concert In Central Park . . . . (Warner Bros.)
Stillness Of The Night
REO Speedwagon; *Good Trouble* . . . . (Epic)
There's A Kind Of Hush (All Over The World)
Carpenters; *A Kind Of Hush* . . . . (A&M)
Carpenters-Classics-#2 . . . . (A&M)
Yesterday Once More . . . . (A&M)
Herman's Hermits; *Herman's Hermits-Their Greatest Hits* . . . . (Abkco)
When You Say Nothing At All
Alison Krauss & Union Station; *Kieth Whitley-A Tribute Album* . . . . (BNA)
Now That I've Found You: A Collection . . . .(Rounder)
ST/Switchback . . . . (RCA)
Keith Whitley; *Billboard Top Country Hits-1988-C* . . . . (Rhino)
Country Wedding Album-C . . . . (Scotti Bros.)
Don't Close Your Eyes . . . . (RCA)
Essential Keith Whitley . . . . (RCA)
Keith Whitley's Greatest Hits . . . . (RCA)
You Have The Right To Remain Silent
Perfect Stranger; *From Nashville With Love-C* . . . .(Curb)

SILVER

See Also: *GOLD, JEWELRY, MINING, MONEY*

Are The Good Times Really Over (I Wish A Buck Was Still Silver)
Merle Haggard; *Big City* . . . .(Epic)
For The Record: Merle Haggard-43 Legendary Hits . . . . (BNA)
Greatest Country Hits Of The '80s-1982-C . . . .(Columbia)
His Epic Hits-First 11 To Be Continued-C . . . .(Epic)
Be My Life's Companion
Mills Brothers; *Best Of The Mills Brothers* . . . . (MCA)
The Mills Brothers-Best Of The Decca Years . . . .(Decca)
Rosemary Clooney; *Rosemary Clooney-16 Most Requested Songs* . . . . .(Legacy)
By The Light Of The Silvery Moon
Al Jolson; *The Al Jolson Story-#1* . . . . (MCA)
Doris Day; *Day At The Movies* . . . .(Columbia)
Julie Andrews; *A Little Bit Of Broadway* . . . .(Columbia)
Mitch Miller; *34 All-Time Great Sing-Along Selections-C* . . . . (Columbia)
Sing Along With Mitch . . . .(Columbia)
Carey
Joni Mitchell; *Blue* . . . . (Reprise)
Joni Mitchell with Tom Scott & The L.A. Express; *Miles Of Aisles* . . . . . (Asylum)
Eyes Of Silver
Doobie Brothers; *What Were Once Vices Are Now Habits* . . . . (Warner Bros.)
From Silver Lake
Jackson Browne; *Jackson Browne* . . . . (Asylum)
Gold And Silver
Quicksilver Messenger Service; *Legends Of Rock Guitar-'60s-#1-C* . . . .(Rhino)
Quicksilver Messenger Service . . . .(Capitol)
Sons Of Mercury . . . .(Rhino)
Gold Dust Woman
Fleetwood Mac; *25 Years-The Chain* . . . . (Warner Bros.)
Rumours . . . . (Warner Bros.)
Sister Hazel; *Legacy-A Tribute To Fleetwood Mac's Rumours-C* . . . .(Lava)
Golden Memories And Silver Tears
Jim Reeves; *Best Of Jim Reeves* . . . . (RCA)
Great Moments With Jim Reeves . . . . (RCA)
Jim Reeves' Greatest Hits . . . . (RCA)
Hi Ho Silver
Fleetwood Mac; *Kiln House* . . . . (Reprise)
Jet Silver & The Dolls Of Venus
Be Bop Deluxe; *Axe Victim* . . . .(Capitol)
Best Of Be Bop Deluxe-Raiding The Divine Archive . . . .(Capitol)
King Of The Silver Screen
Alice Cooper; *Lace And Whiskey* . . . . (Warner Bros.)
Look For The Silver Lining
Alberta Hunter; *Look For The Silver Lining* . . . .(Columbia)
Chet Baker; *Let's Get Lost-Best Of Chet Baker Sings* . . . . (Blue Note)

Dave Brubeck Quartet; *Stardust* . . . . (Fantasy)
Judy Garland; *Best Of Judy Garland In Hollywood* . . . . (Turner Classic Movies)
Marion Harris; 78-#3367 . . . . (Columbia)
Man On The Silver Mountain
Blackmore's Rainbow; *Ritchie Blackmore's R-A-I-N-B-O-W* . . . . (Polydor)
Rainbow; *Finyl Vinyl* . . . . (Mercury)
Maxwell's Silver Hammer
Beatles; *Abbey Road* . . . . (Parlophone)
Midnight Rider
Allman Brothers Band; *Beginnings* . . . . (Polydor)
Best Of The Allman Brothers Band . . . . (Polydor)
Decade Of Hits-1969-1979 . . . . (Polydor)
Idlewild South . . . . (Polydor)
*The Road Goes On Forever, A Collection Of Their Greatest
Recordings* . . . . (Polydor)
Duane Allman; *Duane Allman-An Anthology-Vol. II* . . . . (Capricorn)
Gregg Allman; *Laid Back* . . . . (Polydor)
South's Greatest Hits-C . . . . (Capricorn)
Willie Nelson; *ST/The Electric Horseman* . . . . (Columbia)
On Silver Waves
101 Strings Orchestra; *Romantic Songs Of The Sea* . . . . (Alshire)
Queen Of The Silver Dollar
Dave & Sugar; *Dave & Sugar's Greatest Hits* . . . . (RCA)
Dr. Hook; *Dr. Hook & The Medicine Show Revisited* . . . . (Columbia)
Emmylou Harris; *Pieces Of The Sky* . . . . (Reprise)
Quicksilver
Pink Floyd; *ST/More* . . . . (Capitol)
Quicksilver
Horace Silver; *Horace Silver Trio* . . . . (Blue Note)
Quicksilver Girl
Steve Miller Band; *Best Of Steve Miller 1968-1973* . . . . (Capitol)
More Songs From "The Big Chill" Soundtrack-C . . . . (Motown)
Sailor . . . . (Capitol)
Quicksilver Lightning
Roger Daltrey; *ST/Quicksilver* . . . . (Atlantic)
Sail Along, Silv'ry Moon
Andy Williams; *Unchained Melody-Greatest Songs* . . . . (Curb)
Billy Vaughn; *Best Of Billy Vaughn* . . . . (MCA)
Billy Vaughn's Greatest Hits . . . . (Curb)
Billy Vaughn & His Orchestra; *Billy Vaughn & His Orchestra Play 22 Of
His Greatest Hits* . . . . (Ranwood)
Silver
Echo & The Bunnymen; *Ocean Rain* . . . . (Sire)
Songs To Learn & Sing-The Hits . . . . (Sire)
Silver
Textones; *Through The Canyon* . . . . (Rhino)
Silver & Gold
Dolly Parton; *Eagle When She Flies* . . . . (Columbia)
Silver & Gold
U2; *Rattle And Hum* . . . . (Island)
Silver & Gold (Our Love Is Like)
Sweethearts Of The Rodeo; *Sisters* . . . . (Columbia)
Silver Bells
Atlantic Starr; *ST/Home Alone 2-Lost In New York* . . . . (Fox/Arista)
Bob Wills; *Fiddle* . . . . (Country Music Foundation)
Booker T. & The M.G.s; *Soul Christmas-C* . . . . (Atlantic)
Brady Bunch Kids; *Christmas With The Brady Bunch* . . . . . (MCA Special Prod.)
Brenda Lee; *Brenda Lee-Christmas* . . . . (Warner Bros.)
Diana Ross & The Supremes; *Merry Christmas* . . . . (Motown)
Dwight Yoakam; *Come On Christmas* . . . . (Reprise)
Earl Grant; *Winter Wonderland* . . . . (MCA Special Prod.)
Elvis Presley; *If Every Day Was Like Christmas* . . . . (RCA)
Memories Of Christmas . . . . (RCA)
Fats Domino; *Christmas Is A Special Day* . . . . (Right Stuff)
Gary Morris; *Every Christmas* . . . . (Liberty)
John Denver; *Rocky Mountain Christmas* . . . . (RCA)
Johnny Mathis & Percy Faith and his Orchestra; *Merry Christmas* . . (Columbia)
Judds; *Christmas Time With The Judds* . . . . (RCA)
Kenny Rogers; *Christmas In America* . . . . (Reprise)
Kevin Eubanks; *GRP Christmas Collection-C* . . . . (GRP)
Lacy J. Dalton; *Christmas For The '90s-#1-C* . . . . (Liberty)
Liberace; *That Old Christmas Feeling* . . . . (MCA Special Prod.)
Loretta Lynn; *Christmas Without Daddy* . . . . (MCA Special Prod.)
Margaret Whiting & Jimmy Wakely; *Christmas On The Range-Cowboy
Classics-C* . . . . (Capitol)
Merle Haggard; *Merle Haggard-Christmas Gift* . . . . (Curb)
Miracles; *Christmas With The Miracles* . . . . (Motown)
Mormon Tabernacle Choir; *White Christmas* . . . . (Columbia)
Oak Ridge Boys; *Oak Ridge Boys-Christmas* . . . . (MCA Special Prod.)
Perry Como; *I Wish It Could Be Christmas Forever* . . . . (RCA)
Ray Price; *Christmas Gift For You From Ray Price* . . . . (Step One)
Roches; *We Three Kings* . . . . (Rykodisc)
Ronnie Milsap; *Christmas With Ronnie Milsap* . . . . (RCA)
Rosie O'Donnell & Sugar Ray; *Another Rosie Christmas-C* . . . . . . (Columbia)
Stevie Wonder; *Someday At Christmas* . . . . (Motown)
Travis Tritt; *Christmas-Loving Time Of The Year* . . . . (Warner Bros.)
Silver Bells (That Ring In The Night)
Bob Wills; *Best Of Bob Wills & His Texas Playboys* . . . . (MCA)
Best Of Bob Wills-#2 . . . . (MCA)
Bob Wills-Anthology . . . . (Sony Music Special Prod.)

Silver Bird
Mark Lindsay; *Super Hits Of The '70s-Have A Nice Day-#4-C* . . . . . . (Rhino)
Silver Blue
Linda Ronstadt; *Prisoner In Disguise* . . . . (Asylum)
Silver Bullet
Flo & Eddie; *History Of Flo & Eddie And The Turtles* . . . . (Rhino)
Silver City
Joe Ely; *Lord Of The Highway* . . . . (Hightone)
Mance Lipscomb; *Texas Songwriter-#2* . . . . (Arhoolie)
Silver Dagger
Dave Van Ronk; *Dave Van Ronk* . . . . (Fantasy)
Inside Dave Van Ronk . . . . (Fantasy)
Joan Baez; *Ballad Book-#2* . . . . (Vanguard)
Joan Baez . . . . (Vanguard)
The Joan Baez Ballad Book . . . . (Vanguard)
Very Early Joan Baez . . . . (Vanguard)
Silver Dew On The Bluegrass Tonight
Johnnie Lee Wills; *Tulsa Swing* . . . . (Rounder)
Silver Dollar
Lee Greenwood; *If There's Any Justice* . . . . (Panorama)
Silver Dollar
April Wine; *First Glance* . . . . (Capitol)
Silver Dreams
Babys; *Broken Heart* . . . . (Chrysalis)
Silver Eagle
Merle Haggard & George Jones; *Taste Of Yesterday's Wine* . . . . (Epic)
Reba McEntire; *Just A Little Love* . . . . (MCA)
Silver Future
Monster Magnet; *ST/Heavy Metal 2000* . . . . (Restless)
Silver Ghost, The
Merle Haggard & The Strangers; *Train Whistle Blues* . . . . (Rounder)
Silver Girl
Survivor; *Eye Of The Tiger* . . . . (Scotti Bros.)
Silver Gun
Robert Palmer; *Addictions-#2* . . . . (Island)
Pride . . . . (Island)
Silver Haired Daddy Of Mine
Frankie Yankovic & His Yanks; *I Wish I Was 18 Again* . . . . (Smash)
Silver Heels
Fleetwood Mac; *Heroes Are Hard To Find* . . . . (Reprise)
Silver Inches
Enya; *A Day Without Rain* . . . . (Reprise)
Silver Lights
Sammy Hagar; *Nine On A Ten Scale* . . . . (Capitol)
Silver Lining
Nils Lofgren & Levon Helm; *Silver Lining* . . . . (Rykodisc)
Silver Lining
Player; *Danger Zone* . . . . (RSO)
Silver Medals & Sweet Memories
Statler Brothers; *Best Of The Statler Brothers-Rides Again-#2* . . . . . (Mercury)
Short Stories . . . . (Mercury)
Silver Moon
Lawrence Welk; *22 Great Waltzes* . . . . (Ranwood)
Mom & Dads; *Mom & Dads-20 Favorite Waltzes* . . . . (Crescendo)
Silver Moon
David Sylvian; *Gone To Earth* . . . . (Virgin)
Silver Moon
Kitaro; *In Person* . . . . (Gramavision)
My Best . . . . (Gramavision)
Silk Road II . . . . (Gramavision)
Silver Moon
Michael Nesmith; *Older Stuff* . . . . (Rhino)
Silver Morning
Kenny Rankin; *Silver Morning* . . . . (Little David)
Silver Paper
Mountain; *Mountain Climbing!* . . . . (Columbia)
Twin Peaks . . . . (Columbia)
Silver Rainbow
Genesis; *Genesis* . . . . (Atlantic)
Silver Screen
Little Feat; *Representing The Mambo* . . . . (Warner Bros.)
Silver Shadow
Atlantic Starr; *As The Band Turns* . . . . (A&M)
Atlantic Starr-Classics-#10 . . . . (A&M)
Secret Lovers: Best Of Atlantic Starr . . . . (A&M)
Silver Springs
Fleetwood Mac; *1998 Grammy Nominees-C* . . . . (MCA)
25 Years-The Chain . . . . (Warner Bros.)
The Dance . . . . (Reprise)
Silver Stallion
Waylon Jennings, Willie Nelson, Johnny Cash, Kris Kristofferson; *Greatest
Country Hits Of The '90s-1990-C* . . . . (Columbia)
Highwayman 2 . . . . (Columbia)
Silver Stars, Purple Sage, Eyes Of Blue
Roy Rogers & Sons Of The Pioneers; *Roy Rogers & Sons Of The
Pioneers* . . . . (Varese Sarabande)
Silver Swan Rag
Scott Joplin; *Elite Syncopations* . . . . (Biograph)

Ragtime-#3-Early 1900s .... (Biograph)
Silver Sword
Flora Purim; *Stories To Tell* .... (Milestone)
Silver Threads Among The Gold
Mike Auldridge; *Dobro/Blues & Bluegrass* .... (Takoma)
Silver Threads And Golden Needles
Honky Tonk Angels; *Honky Tonk Angels* .... (Columbia)
Linda Ronstadt; *Don't Cry Now* .... (Asylum)
Hand Sown Home Grown .... (Capitol)
Linda Ronstadt-Retrospective .... (Capitol)
Linda Ronstadt's Greatest Hits .... (Asylum)
Springfields; *Troubadours Of The Folk Era-#3-C* ...... (Rhino)
Silver Thunderbird
Jo Dee Messina; *I'm Alright* .... (Curb)
Marc Cohn; *Marc Cohn* .... (Atlantic)
Silver Tongue & Gold Plated Lies
Hotmud Family; *Meat & Potatoes (& Stuff Like That)* .... (Flying Fish)
Silver Train
Johnny Winter; *Still Alive & Well* .... (Columbia)
Rolling Stones; *Goats Head Soup* .... (Rolling Stones)
Silver Waters
Ken Stover; *Cruisers 1.0* .... (Hearts Of Space)
Sir Dancelot's Dream .... (Hearts Of Space)
Silver Wheels
Heart; *Bebe Le Strange* .... (Epic)
Heart's Greatest Hits/Live .... (Epic)
Silver Wheels
Bruce Cockburn; *Waiting For A Miracle-Singles 1970-1987* ..... (Gold Castle)
Silver Wings
Merle Haggard; *More Of The Best* .... (Rhino)
The Seashores Of Old Mexico .... (Epic)
Merle Haggard & Jewel; *For The Record: Merle Haggard-43 Legendary Hits* .... (BNA)
Merle Haggard & The Strangers; *Okie From Muskogee* .... (Capitol)
Songs I'll Always Sing .... (Capitol)
Pam Tillis; *Mama's Hungry Eyes-Merle Haggard Tribute-C* .... (Arista)
Silver, Blue & Gold
Bad Company; *Run With The Pack* .... (Swan Song)
Silverfuck
Smashing Pumpkins; *Siamese Dream* .... (Virgin)
Silverthorn Mountain
Merle Haggard; *Friend In California* .... (Epic)
Silverton
C.W. McCall; *C.W. McCall's Greatest Hits* .... (Polydor)
Silvertown Blues
Mark Knopfler; *Sailing To Philadelphia* .... (Warner Bros.)
Silvery Rain
Olivia Newton-John; *Physical* .... (MCA)
Summer Of The Silver Comet
Tracy Nelson; *Homemade Songs* .... (Flying Fish)
That Silver Haired Daddy Of Mine
Doc Watson; *My Dear Old Southern Home* .... (Sugar Hill)
Gene Autry; *The Country Music Hall Of Fame-Gene Autry-15 Of His All-Time Greatest Hits* .... (Columbia)
Theme From "Silver Spoons"
Original Soundtrack; *Television's Greatest Hits-#6-Remote Control-C* ... (TVT)
Theme From "The Lone Ranger" (William Tell Overture)
Boston Pops Orchestra; *TV Classics-C* .... (RCA)
Boston Pops Orchestra/Arthur Fiedler; *Fiedler-Greatest Hits* .... (RCA)
Original Soundtrack; *Television's Greatest Hits-#7-Cable Ready-C* ..... (TVT)
Spike Jones & His City Slickers; *Best Of Spike Jones & His City Slickers* .... (RCA)
White Silver Sands
Ace Cannon; *Golden Classics-Ace Cannon* .... (Gusto)
Ray Anthony; *Great Golden Hits* .... (Ranwood)
Sonny James; *45-#4-45706* .... (Columbia)
Wurlitzer Prize (I Don't Want To Get Over You)
Waylon Jennings; *Waylon & Willie* .... (RCA)

SITTING

See Also: **FURNITURE, RELAX, SLEEP**

(Sittin' On) The Dock Of The Bay
Michael Bolton; *The Hunger* .... (Columbia)
Otis Redding; *(Sittin' On) The Dock Of The Bay* .... (Atco)
Best Of Otis Redding .... (Atco)
Golden Age Of Black Music-1960-1970-C .... (Atlantic)
Golden Soul-C .... (Atlantic)
Soul Years-C .... (Atlantic)
The Otis Redding Story .... (Atlantic)
Are You Sitting Comfortably/The Dream
Moody Blues; *Caught Live Plus Five* .... (Polydor)
On The Threshold Of A Dream .... (Polydor)
This Is The Moody Blues .... (Polydor)
As Tears Go By
Marianne Faithfull; *Marianne Faithfull's Greatest Hits* .... (Abkco)

Strange Weather .... (Island)
Rolling Stones; *Big Hits (High Tide & Green Grass)* .... (Abkco)
December's Children (and everybody's) .... (Abkco)
Hot Rocks 1964-1971 .... (Abkco)
Singles Collection-The London Years .... (Abkco)
Broadway
Goo Goo Dolls; *Dizzy Up The Girl* .... (Warner Sunset/Reprise)
Cowboy Love Song
Skip Gorman; *A Cowboy's Wild Song To His Herd* .... (Rounder)
Don't Sit Under The Apple Tree
Andrews Sisters; *Andrews Sisters Greatest Hits* .... (Curb)
Andrews Sisters-16 Great Performances .... (MCA)
Capitol Collectors Series-The Andrews Sisters ...... (Capitol)
Glenn Miller; *Memorial-1944-1969* .... (Bluebird)
Glenn Miller & His Orchestra; *The Unforgettable Glenn Miller & His Orchestra* .... (RCA)
Hi-Lili, Hi-Lo
Anne Murray; *There's A Hippo In My Tub* .... (Capitol)
Ray Conniff; *Encore! 16 Most Requested Songs* ...... (Legacy)
I Got The Train Sittin' Waitin'
Waylon Jennings; *Between The Rails: America's Train Songs-C* ... (Crescendo)
I'm Going To Sit Right Down And Cry Over You
Elvis Presley; *Elvis Presley* .... (RCA)
I'm Gonna Sit Right Down And Write Myself A Letter
Billy Williams; *Stardust: The Classic Decca Hits & Standards Collection-C* .... (Decca)
Fats Waller; *Fats Waller* .... (RCA Special Prod.)
Frank Sinatra; *Sinatra-Basie* .... (Reprise)
Songs For Young Lovers & Swing Easy .... (Capitol)
Nat "King" Cole; *Just One Of Those Things (& More)* .... (Capitol)
Nat "King" Cole-Gift Set .... (Capitol)
Original Cast; *Ain't Misbehavin'* .... (RCA)
I'm Sitting On Top Of The World
Al Jolson; *Jolson Sang 'Em* .... (Biograph)
The Al Jolson Story-#3 .... (MCA)
In Between Dances
Pam Tillis; *Pam Tillis' Greatest Hits* .... (Arista)
Sweetheart's Dance .... (Arista)
I've Got The World On A String
Count Basie; *Standards* .... (Verve)
Diana Krall; *Only Trust Your Heart* .... (GRP)
Ella Fitzgerald; *Harold Arlen Songbook-#1* .... (Verve)
Frank Sinatra; *Capitol Collectors Series-Frank Sinatra* .... (Capitol)
Frank Sinatra & Liza Minnelli; *Frank Sinatra-Duets-C* .... (Capitol)
Sarah Vaughan; *Best Of Sarah Vaughan* .... (Pablo)
Stephane Grappelli & Martin Taylor; *We've Got The World On A String* .... (Angel)
Lately
Divine; *Fairy Tales* .... (Pendulum)
Pennyroyal Tea
Nirvana; *In Utero* .... (David Geffen Co.)
MTV Unplugged In New York .... (David Geffen Co.)
Sit Down I Think I Love You
Buffalo Springfield; *Buffalo Springfield-Retrospective* .... (Atco)
Sittin' In The Balcony
Eddie Cochran; *Eddie Cochran's Greatest Hits* ...... (Curb)
Singin' To My Baby/Never To Be Forgotten .... (EMI)
Somethin' Else: The Fine Lookin' Hits Of Eddie Cochran ...... (Razor & Tie)
Sittin' On Go
Bryan White; *Between Now And Forever* .... (Asylum)
Sittin' On Top Of The World
Bob Dylan; *Good As I Been To You* .... (Columbia)
Bob Wills & His Texas Playboys; *Bob Wills & His Texas Playboys-24 Great Hits* .... (Polydor)
Bob Wills-Anthology .... (Sony Music Special Prod.)
Tiffany Transcriptions-#8-More Of The Best .... (Rhino)
Cream; *Wheels Of Fire* .... (Polydor)
Doc Watson; *Doc Watson* .... (Vanguard)
Greatest Folksingers Of The '60s-C .... (Vanguard)
Old Timey Concert .... (Vanguard)
Grateful Dead; *Grateful Dead (Skull & Roses)* .... (Warner Bros.)
Jerry Jeff Walker; *Will The Circle Be Unbroken-#2-C* .... (Uni)
Ray Charles; *20 Golden Pieces Of Ray Charles* ...... (Bulldog)
Sweet Honey In The Rock; *Believe I'll Run On, See What The End's Gonna Be* .... (Redwood)
Sittin' Up In My Room
Brandy; *ST/Waiting To Exhale* .... (Arista)
Sitting By The Riverside
Kinks; *Are The Village Green Preservation Society* .... (Reprise)
Sitting Home
Total; *Kima, Keisha & Pam* .... (Bad Boy/Arista)
Sitting In Limbo
Jimmy Cliff; *ST/The Harder They Come* .... (Mango)
ST/The Harder They Come .... (Mango)
Sitting On Top Of The World
Cream; *Goodbye* .... (Polydor)
Very Best Of Cream .... (Polydor)
Wheels Of Fire .... (Polydor)
Howlin' Wolf; *Real Folk Blues-C* .... (Chess)

The Chess Box-Howlin' Wolf. . . . . (Chess)
There Will Never Be Any Peace (Until God Is Seated At The Conference Table)
Chi-Lites; *Chi-Lites' Greatest Hits*. . . . . (Rhino)
Walk Right In
Rooftop Singers; *Best Of The Rooftop Singers* . . . . (Vanguard)
Cruisin'-1963-C . . . . (Increase)
Greatest Folksingers Of The '60s-C . . . . (Vanguard)
ST/Forrest Gump . . . . (Epic/Sony Music Soundtrax)
Troubadours Of The Folk Era-#3-C . . . . (Rhino)
You Better Sit Down Kids
Cher; *Bang, Bang The Early Years* . . . . (Capitol)

SKY, Clouds, Horizon

See Also: **AIR, AIRPLANES, FLYING, LIGHT, MOON, NIGHT, RAIN, SPACE, STARS, SUN, WIND**

(Ghost) Riders In The Sky
Gene Autry; *50th Anniversary* . . . . (Republic/Universal)
Cowboy Hall Of Fame . . . . (Republic/Universal)
Johnny Cash; *The Man In Black-His Greatest Hits*. . . . . (Legacy)
Outlaws; *Ghost Riders* . . . . (Arista)
Roy Clark; *Roy Clark In Concert* . . . . (MCA)
Roy Clark's Greatest Hits . . . . (MCA)
Superpicker . . . . (MCA)
Vaughn Monroe; *Best Of Vaughn Monroe* . . . . (RCA)
This Is Vaughn Monroe/Decade Of The '40s . . . . (RCA)
4:37 AM (Arabs With Knives & West German Skies)
Roger Waters; *Pros & Cons Of Hitchhiking* . . . . (Columbia)
Above The Clouds
Electric Light Orchestra; *New World Record* . . . . (Jet)
Alabama Sky
Alabama; *Closer You Get* . . . . (RCA)
Alaskan Suite: Northern Lights
Lyle Mays; *Lyle Mays*. . . . . (Geffen)
Angel In The Sky
Rose Royce; *Rose Royce III/Strikes Again!* . . . . (Whitfield)
Angels In The Sky
Crew-Cuts; *Best Of The Crew-Cuts-The Mercury Years* . . . . (Mercury)
April Skies
Wardell Gray; *Memorial-#2* . . . . (Prestige)
April Skies
Jesus & Mary Chain; *Darklands* . . . . (Warner Bros.)
April Sky
Vinnie Moore; *Time Odyssey* . . . . (Mercury)
Arizona Skies
Los Lobos; *Kiko* . . . . (Slash)
Arizona Sky
China Crisis; *What Price Paradise* . . . . (A&M)
Armenia City In The Sky
Who; *The Who Sell Out*. . . . . (MCA)
Army Air Corps
Fred Waring's Pennsylvanians; *Very Best Of Fred Waring & The Pennsylvanians* . . . . (Reader's Digest Music)
Glenn Miller; *Best Of The Lost Recordings And The Secret Broadcasts* . . . . (RCA Victor)
V-Disc Recordings-Glenn Miller . . . . (Collector's Choice)
Aurora Borealis
Meat Puppets; *Meat Puppets II* . . . . (SST)
Aurora Borealis
C.W. McCall; *C.W. McCall's Greatest Hits* . . . . (Polydor)
Away From The Sky
Rickie Lee Jones; *Flying Cowboys* . . . . (Geffen)
Beautiful Day
U2; *All That You Can't Leave Behind* . . . . (Interscope)
Now That's What I Call Music!-#6-C . . . . (Virgin)
Because
Beatles; *Abbey Road*. . . . . (Parlophone)
Beatles-Box Set . . . . (Capitol)
Best I Ever Had (Grey Sky Morning)
Vertical Horizon; *Everything You Want* . . . . (RCA)
Beyond The Blue Horizon
Jeanette MacDonald; *Hollywood Sings-C* . . . . (Living Era)
Lou Christie; *ST/Rain Man* . . . . (Capitol)
Big Sky
Kate Bush; *Hounds Of Love* . . . . (EMI)
Big White Cloud
John Cale; *Vintage Violence* . . . . (Columbia)
Black Skies
Rex Allen, Jr.; *Today's Generation* . . . . (SSS International)
Black Sky
Ozark Mountain Daredevils; *It's Alive* . . . . (A&M)
Ozark Mountain Daredevils. . . . . (A&M)
Blue Clear Sky
George Strait; *Blue Clear Sky* . . . . (MCA)

Latest Greatest Straitest Hits . . . . (MCA)
Blue Ridge Mountain Sky
Marshall Tucker Band; *New Life*. . . . . (AJK Music)
Blue Skies
Benny Goodman; *Benny Goodman Today* . . . . (London)
Carnegie Hall Jazz Concert . . . . (Columbia)
The Birth Of Swing (1935-1936) . . . . (Bluebird)
This Is Benny Goodman . . . . (RCA)
Bing Crosby; *Bing Crosby's Greatest Hits* . . . . (MCA)
Duke Ellington; *Carnegie Hall Concert* . . . . (Prestige)
Golden Duke . . . . (Prestige)
Willie Nelson; *Stardust* . . . . (Legacy)
Blue Sky
Allman Brothers Band; *An Evening With The Allman Brothers Band-First Set* . . . . (Epic)
Best Of The Allman Brothers Band . . . . (Polydor)
Decade Of Hits-1969-1979 . . . . (Polydor)
Dreams . . . . (Polydor)
Eat A Peach . . . . (Polydor)
The Road Goes On Forever, A Collection Of Their Greatest Recordings . . . . (Polydor)
Blue Sky
Sweethearts Of The Rodeo; *Buffalo Zone* . . . . (Columbia)
Blue Sky
Patty Griffin; *Flaming Red* . . . . (A&M)
Blue Sky Mine
Midnight Oil; *Blue Sky Mining* . . . . (Columbia)
Blue Sky Shinin'
Marie Osmond; *There's No Stopping Your Heart* . . . . (Curb)
Mickey Newbury; *Sailor* . . . . (MCA)
Both Sides Now
Joni Mitchell; *Clouds* . . . . (Reprise)
Judy Collins; *Colors Of The Day-The Best Of Judy Collins* . . . . (Elektra)
So Early In The Spring, The First 15 Years . . . . (Elektra)
Wildflowers. . . . . (Elektra)
Neil Diamond; *Neil Diamond-Gold* . . . . (MCA)
Neil Diamond-Love Songs . . . . (MCA)
Rainbow . . . . (MCA)
Touching You Touching Me . . . . (MCA)
Bullet The Blue Sky
U2; *Joshua Tree* . . . . (Island)
Rattle And Hum . . . . (Island)
Burnin' Sky
Bad Company; *Burnin' Sky* . . . . (Swan Song)
But Not For Me
Billie Holiday; *Silver Collection* . . . . (Verve)
Chet Baker; *Let's Get Lost-Best Of Chet Baker Sings* . . . . (Blue Note)
Ella Fitzgerald; *Ella Sings Jazz* . . . . (MCA Jazz)
Elvis Costello; *Glory Of Gershwin Featuring Larry Adler-C* . . . . (Mercury)
Harry Connick, Jr.; *ST/When Harry Met Sally* . . . . (Columbia)
Judy Garland; *Best Of Judy Garland* . . . . (MCA)
Original London Cast; *Crazy For You*. . . . . (RCA)
Original Soundtrack; *Manhattan* . . . . (CBS Masterworks)
Sarah Vaughan; *Sarah Vaughan Sings George Gershwin Songbook, Vol. 2* . . . . (Emarcy)
Cabin In The Sky
Andre Previn; *Andre Previn Plays Songs By Vernon Duke* . . . . . (Contemporary)
Mose Allison; *Creek Bank*. (Prestige)
Cadillac Of The Skies
American Boy Choir; *Spielberg/Williams Collaboration* . . . . (Columbia)
California Dreamin'
Beach Boys; *Made In The U.S.A.* . . . . (Capitol)
Mamas & The Papas; *At The Hop* . . . . (MCA)
Good Feeling Music Of The Big Chill Generation-#1-C . . . . . (Motown)
Mamas & The Papas-20 Golden Hits . . . . (MCA)
ST/Air America . . . . (MCA)
ST/American Pop . . . . (MCA)
ST/Forrest Gump . . . . (Epic/Sony Music Soundtrax)
Clear Blue Skies
Crosby, Stills, Nash & Young; *American Dream* . . . . (Atlantic)
Cloud 9
George Harrison; *Best Of Dark Horse 1976-1989*. . . . . (Dark Horse)
Cloud Nine . . . . (Dark Horse)
Cloud Busting
Kate Bush; *Hounds Of Love* . . . . (EMI)
Whole Story . . . . (EMI)
Cloud Dancing
Roches; *Speak* . . . . (MCA)
Cloud Nine
Temptations; *25 Years Of Grammy Greats-C* . . . . (Motown)
Cloud Nine . . . . (Motown)
Motown Grammy R&B Performances Of The '60s & '70s-C . . . . . . (Motown)
Motown Story-First 25 Years-C . . . . (Motown)
Temptations' Greatest Hits-#2 . . . . (Motown)
Cloud On My Tongue
Tori Amos; *Under The Pink* . . . . (Atlantic)
Cloudburst
Jon Hendricks; *Jon Hendricks*. . . . . (Enja)
Lambert, Hendricks & Bavan; *Swingin' Till The Girls Come Home* . . . (Bluebird)

Lambert, Hendricks & Ross; *Best Of Lambert, Hendricks & Ross* . . . (Columbia)
  Lambert, Hendricks & Ross & Ike Isaacs Trio: Everybody's
    Boppin' . . . . (Columbia)
Pointer Sisters; *Retrospect*. . . . . (MCA)

Clouds
Go-Betweens; *16 Lovers Lane*. . . . . (Capitol)

Clouds In My Heart
Muddy Waters; *Blues Deluxe* . . . . (Allegiance)

Cloudscape
Philip Glass; *Life Out Of Balance* . . . . (Antilles)
  ST/Koyaanisqatsi-Life Out Of Balance. . . . . (Antilles)

Cloudy
Simon & Garfunkel; *Collected Works* . . . . (Columbia)
  Parsley Sage Rosemary & Thyme. . . . . (Columbia)

Cloudy
Average White Band; *Cut The Cake* . . . . (Atlantic)

Cloudy Morning
Carmen McRae & George Shearing; *Two For The Road*. . . . . . . (Concord Jazz)

Cloudy Skies
Benny Carter; *Chocolate Dandies (1928-1933)* . . . . (Disques Swing)

Cloudy, With A Chance Of Tears
Manhattans; *After Midnight* . . . . (Columbia)

Cold Sky
Cyndi Lauper; *Music Speaks Louder Than Words-C* . . . . (Epic)

Comedown
Bush; *Sixteen Stone* . . . .(Trauma)

Daddy Sang Bass
Johnny Cash; *Columbia Country Classics-#5-A New Tradition-C* . . . (Columbia)
  Johnny Cash's Greatest Hits-#2 . . . . (Columbia)
  The Man In Black-His Greatest Hits . . . . (Legacy)

Divided Sky
Phish; *Junta* . . . . (Elektra)

Dusty Skies
Asleep At The Wheel featuring Riders In The Sky; *Tribute To The Music Of*
  Bob Wills And The Texas Playboys-C . . . . (Liberty)
Bob Wills & His Texas Playboys; *Bob Wills & His Texas Playboys-Historic*
  Edition . . . . (Columbia)
  Don't Fence Me In-Western Music's Early Golden Era-C . . . . (Rounder)

Eye In The Sky
Alan Parsons Project; *Eye In The Sky* . . . . (Arista)
  Turn Of A Friendly Card . . . . (Arista)

Feel So High
Des'ree; *I Ain't Movin'* . . . . (550 Music)
  Mind Adventures . . . . (550 Music)
  Siren Song:Celebration Of Women In Music-C . . . . (550 Music)

Fire In The Sky
Nitty Gritty Dirt Band; *Twenty Years Of Dirt-Best Of The Nitty Gritty*
  Dirt Band . . . . (Warner Bros.)

Fire In The Sky
Saxon; *Denim & Leather* . . . . (Capitol)

Fire In The Sky
Ozzy Osbourne; *No Rest For The Wicked* . . . . (Epic)

Flyin' High In The Friendly Sky
Marvin Gaye; *What's Going On* . . . . (Motown)

Flying Cloud
Doobie Brothers; *What Were Once Vices Are Now Habits* . . . . . . (Warner Bros.)

Foggy Waterfall
Left Banke; *History Of The Left Banke* . . . . (Rhino)

Get Off Of My Cloud
Rolling Stones; *Big Hits (High Tide & Green Grass)* . . . . (Abkco)
  December's Children (and everybody's) . . . . (Abkco)
  got Live if you want it! . . . . (Abkco)
  Hot Rocks 1964-1971 . . . . (Abkco)
  Singles Collection-The London Years. . . . . (Abkco)

Girls Dem Sugar
Beenie Man; *Art And Life* . . . .(Virgin)

Goodbye Blue Sky
Pink Floyd; *The Wall* . . . . (Columbia)
Roger Waters; *The Wall-Live In Berlin* . . . . (Mercury)

Goodbye Blue Sky
Daryl Braithwaite; *Higher Than Hope* . . . . (Epic Portrait Assoc.)
  Rise . . . . (Epic Portrait Assoc.)

Great Gig In The Sky
Pink Floyd; *Dark Side Of The Moon* . . . . (Capitol)
  Pink Floyd-Gift Set . . . . (Capitol)

Grey Cloud Over New York
Philip Glass; *1000 Airplanes On The Roof* . . . . (Virgin)

Grey Cloudy Lies
George Harrison; *Extra Texture* . . . . (Capitol)

Grey October Clouds
Tommy Makem & Liam Clancy; *Two For The Early Dew* . . . .(Shanachie)

Hazy Shade Of Winter
Bangles; *Bangles' Greatest Hits* . . . . (Columbia)
  ST/Less Than Zero . . . . (Def Jam)
Simon & Garfunkel; *Bookends* . . . . (Columbia)
  Collected Works . . . . (Columbia)

Home On The Range
Bing Crosby; *Crooner-Columbia Years-1928-1934* . . . . (Columbia)

Boston Pops Orchestra/Arthur Fiedler; *Yankee Doodle Dandy* . . . . (RCA)
Gene Autry; *50th Anniversary* . . . . (Republic/Universal)
  The Country Music Hall Of Fame-Gene Autry-15 Of His All-Time
    Greatest Hits . . . .(Columbia)
Neil Young; *ST/Where The Buffalo Roam* . . . . (Backstreet)

How Deep Is The Ocean? (How High Is The Sky?)
Diana Krall; *Love Scenes* . . . . (Impulse!)
Frank Sinatra; *Nice 'N' Easy* . . . . (Capitol)
Liza Minnelli; *Liza Minnelli-At Carnegie Hall* . . . . (Telarc)

I Believe In The Man In The Sky
Elvis Presley; *The Other Sides-Worldwide Gold Award Hits, Vol. 2* . . . . . (RCA)

I Sure Can Smell The Rain
BlackHawk; *BlackHawk* . . . .(Arista)

It Came Out Of The Sky
Creedence Clearwater Revival; *1969* . . . . (Fantasy)
  Creedence Clearwater Revival-Chronicle-#2 . . . . (Fantasy)
  Live In Europe . . . . (Fantasy)
  Willie & The Poor Boys . . . . (Fantasy)

Keep Your Head To The Sky
Earth, Wind & Fire; *Best Of Earth, Wind & Fire-#2* . . . .(Columbia)
  Elements Of Love: The Ballads . . . . (Legacy)
  Head To The Sky . . . . (Columbia)

Light The Sky On Fire
Jefferson Starship; *Jefferson Starship-Gold*. . . . . (RCA)

Little White Cloud That Cried
Johnnie Ray; *Best Of Johnnie Ray* . . . . (Columbia)
  Best Of Johnnie Ray . . . . (Exact)
  Johnnie Ray's Greatest Hits . . . . (Sony Music Special Prod.)

Log Cabin Home In The Sky
Michael Martin Murphey; *Cowboy Christmas* . . . .(Warner Bros.)

London Skyline
Acoustic Alchemy; *New Edge* . . . .(GRP)

Lonely Looking Sky
Neil Diamond; *Love At The Greek* . . . .(Columbia)
  ST/Jonathan Livingston Seagull . . . .(Columbia)

Lucy In The Sky With Diamonds
Beatles; *Sgt. Pepper's Lonely Hearts Club Band* . . . .(Capitol)
  The Beatles/1967-1970 . . . .(Capitol)
  Yellow Submarine . . . .(Capitol)
Elton John; *All This & World War 2* . . . .(20th Century Fox)
  Elton John's Greatest Hits-#2 . . . . (Polydor)
John Lennon; *Lennon* . . . .(Capitol)

Manhattan Skyline
David Shire; *ST/Saturday Night Fever* . . . . (Polydor)

Manhattan Skyline
Julia Fordham; *New York Songs-C* . . . .(Rhino)
  Porcelain. . . . . (Virgin)
  The Julia Fordham Collection . . . . (Virgin)

March Sky
Alex DeGrassi; *Slow Circle* . . . . (Windham Hill)

Midnight Sky
Isley Brothers; *Live It Up* . . . . (T-Neck/Columbia)
  The Isley Brothers Story-#2-The T-Neck Years-1969-1985. . . . .(Rhino)

Mona Lisas And Mad Hatters
Elton John; *Honky Chateau* . . . . (Rocket)
  Reg Strikes Back . . . . (MCA)
  The Concert For New York City-C . . . .(Columbia)

Montana Skies
James Galway; *Wayward Wind* . . . . (RCA)

Morning Sky
Dan Fogelberg; *Dan Fogelberg-Souvenirs* . . . . (Full Moon)

Mr. Blue Sky
Electric Light Orchestra; *Afterglow* . . . . (Epic)
  Electric Light Orchestra's Greatest Hits. . . . . (Jet)
  Out Of The Blue. . . . . (Jet)

Murder In The Skies
Gary Moore; *Gary Moore-Early Years* . . . . (WTG)
  We Want Moore. . . . . (Virgin)

Natural High
Bloodstone; *Bloodstone's Greatest Hits* . . . . (T-Neck/Columbia)
  Didn't It Blow Your Mind: Soul Hits Of The '70s-#11-C. . . . .(Rhino)

Navajo Sky
James Asher; *Globalarium*. . . . .(Silver Wave)

Next Year
Foo Fighters; *There Is Nothing Left To Lose* . . . . (Roswell/RCA)

No More Rain (In This Cloud)
Angie Stone; *Black Diamond* . . . .(Arista)

Northern White Clouds
Bill Monroe; *Live From Mountain Stage* . . . . (Blue Plate)

Ole Buttermilk Sky
Hoagy Carmichael; *Ole Buttermilk Sky* . . . .(Collector's Choice)
Kay Kyser & His Orchestra; *Best Of Kay Kyser & His*
  Orchestra . . . .(Collector's Choice)
Mello-Larks; *The Hoagy Carmichael Songbook-C* . . . .(Bluebird)
Willie Nelson; *What A Wonderful World* . . . .(Columbia)

Orange Colored Sky
Johnny Mathis; *Johnny Mathis-Live* . . . .(Columbia)
Nat "King" Cole; *The Nat "King" Cole Story*. . . . .(Capitol)

Natalie Cole; *Unforgettable With Love* . . . . (Elektra)
Orange Skies
    Love; *Best Of Love* . . . . (Rhino)
Orion In The Sky
    Shawn Colvin; *Fat City* . . . . (Columbia)
Piece Of Sky
    Barbra Streisand; *Just For The Record* . . . . (Columbia)
    ST/Yentl . . . . (Columbia)
Porcelain Sky
    Don Harriss; *Abacus Moon* . . . . (Sonic Atmospheres)
Purple Haze
    Cure; *Stone Free: A Tribute To Jimi Hendrix-C* . . . . (Reprise)
    Jimi Hendrix; *Kiss The Sky* . . . . (Reprise)
    ST/Jimi Hendrix . . . . (Reprise)
    Jimi Hendrix Experience; *Are You Experienced?* . . . . (Reprise)
    Essential Jimi Hendrix . . . . (Reprise)
    Radio One . . . . (Rykodisc)
    Smash Hits . . . . (Reprise)
    Winger; *Winger* . . . . (Atlantic)
Purple Sky
    Gillan; *Magic* . . . . (Metal Blade)
Rain (Falling From The Skies)
    Frank Sinatra; *Where Are You?* . . . . (Capitol)
Reach For The Sky
    No Man; *How The West Was Won* . . . . (SST)
Reaching For The Sky
    Peabo Bryson; *Reaching For The Sky-Towering Soul From The
      '70s-C* . . . . (Capitol)
    The Peabo Bryson Collection . . . . (Capitol)
Red Skies
    Fixx; *One Thing Leads To Another-Greatest Hits* . . . . (MCA)
    React . . . . (MCA)
    Shuttered Room . . . . (MCA)
Red Skies Over Georgia
    Charlie Walker; *45-#172* . . . . (Plantation)
Red Sky
    Michael Schenker Group; *Built To Destroy* . . . . (Chrysalis)
Red Sky
    Status Quo; *Status Quo* . . . . (Mercury)
Ribbon In The Sky
    Stevie Wonder; *Original Musiquarium* . . . . (Motown)
Road And The Sky
    Jackson Browne; *Late For The Sky* . . . . (Asylum)
Rolling Sky
    Speedy West & Jimmy Bryant; *For The Last Time* . . . . (Step One)
Scandinavian Skies
    Billy Joel; *Nylon Curtain* . . . . (Columbia)
See The Sky About to Rain
    Neil Young; *On The Beach* . . . . (Reprise)
She's My Girl
    Turtles; *'60s Sound Explosion-C* . . . . (K-Tel)
    Nuggets-#9-Acid Rock-C . . . . (Rhino)
    Turtles-20 Greatest Hits . . . . (Rhino)
Sky Blues
    REO Speedwagon; *Lost In A Dream* . . . . (Epic)
Sky Fell
    Judy Collins; *Wildflowers* . . . . (Elektra)
Sky Fell Down
    Glenn Miller & His Orchestra; *Complete Glenn Miller & His
      Orchestra-#3* . . . . (Bluebird)
    Tommy Dorsey & Frank Sinatra; *Sessions-#1-February 1, 1940-July
      17, 1940* . . . . (RCA)
    Tommy Dorsey & Frank Sinatra's All-Time Greatest Hits-#1 . . . . (Bluebird)
Sky Fits Heaven
    Madonna; *Ray Of Light* . . . . (Maverick)
Sky High
    Jigsaw; *Billboard Top Hits-1975-C* . . . . (Rhino)
    Super Hits Of The '70s-Have A Nice Day-#15-C . . . . (Rhino)
Sky Is A Poisonous Garden
    Concrete Blonde; *Bloodletting* . . . . (I.R.S.)
Sky Is Crying
    Albert King; *I'm In A Phone Booth Baby* . . . . (Stax)
    Years Gone By . . . . (Stax)
    Elmore James; *Elmore James-Complete Fire & Enjoy
      Sessions-#1* . . . . (Collectables)
    Red Hot Blues . . . . (Intermedia)
    Eric Clapton; *Eric Clapton-Crossroads-C* . . . . (Polydor)
    George Thorogood & The Destroyers; *George Thorogood & The Destroyers-
      Live* . . . . (EMI)
    Move It On Over . . . . (Rounder)
    Stevie Ray Vaughan and Double Trouble; *The Sky Is Crying* . . . . (Epic)
Sky Is Falling
    Daryl Hall & John Oates; *Marigold Sky* . . . . (Push)
Sky Over Michigan
    Harmony Sisters; *Harmony Pie* . . . . (Flying Fish)
Sky Pilot
    Eric Burdon & The Animals; *Eric Burdon & The Animals'
      Greatest Hits* . . . . (MGM)

History Of British Rock-#9-C . . . . (Rhino)
    Songs Of Protest-C . . . . (Rhino)
Sky Takes The Soul
    Proclaimers; *This Is The Story* . . . . (Chrysalis)
Skybird
    Neil Diamond; *Love At The Greek* . . . . (Columbia)
    ST/Jonathan Livingston Seagull . . . . (Columbia)
Skylark
    Anita O'Day; *1940s-The Singers-C* . . . . (Columbia)
    Bette Midler; *Bette Midler* . . . . (Atlantic)
    Erroll Garner Trio; *Greatest Garner* . . . . (Atlantic)
    Glenn Miller; *Best Of Glenn Miller-#3* . . . . (RCA)
    Hoagy Carmichael; *Hoagy Sings Carmichael* . . . . (EMI)
    Too Marvelous For Words-Capitol Sings Jonny Mercer-C . . . . . (Capitol)
    Linda Ronstadt; *Lush Life* . . . . (Asylum)
    Tony Bennett; *Forty Years-The Artistry Of Tony Bennett* . . . . (Columbia)
Skyline Pigeon
    Elton John; *Empty Sky* . . . . (Polydor)
    Here And There . . . . (Rocket)
Sky's Got The Blues
    Aaron Tippin; *You've Got To Stand For Something* . . . . (RCA)
Sky's The Limit
    Tony Toni Tone; *Revival* . . . . (Wing)
Skyscraper
    David Lee Roth; *Skyscraper* . . . . (Warner Bros.)
Skyway
    Replacements; *Pleased To Meet Me* . . . . (Sire)
Skywriter
    Jackson 5; *Jackson 5-Anthology* . . . . (Motown)
Spirit In The Sky
    Kentucky HeadHunters; *Electric Barnyard* . . . . (Mercury)
    Norman Greenbaum; *Billboard Top Rock 'N' Roll Hits-1970-C* . . . (Rhino)
    Super Hits Of The '70s-Have A Nice Day-#2-C . . . . (Rhino)
Starry Sky In Oregon
    Andrew White; *Conversations* . . . . (Sona Gaia)
Sunny Skies
    James Taylor; *In Harmony 2-C* . . . . (Columbia)
    Sweet Baby James . . . . (Warner Bros.)
    Jerry Douglas; *Fluxedo* . . . . (Rounder)
Sunny Skies
    Teena Marie; *Emerald City* . . . . (Epic)
Tahitian Skies
    Chet Atkins & Mark Knopfler; *Neck And Neck* . . . . (Columbia)
There's A Blue Sky Way Out Yonder
    Riders In The Sky; *Riders Go Commercial* . . . . (MCA)
    Saturday Morning With Riders In The Sky . . . . (MCA)
There's A Gold Mine In The Sky
    Jimmy C. Newman; *Cajun Cowboy* . . . . (Plantation)
    Pat Boone; *Love Letters In The Sand* . . . . (MCA Special Prod.)
Thousand Stars In The Sky
    Kathy Young with The Innocents; *20 Great Love Songs Of The '50s &
      '60s-#2-C* . . . . (Laurie)
    Collectables Presents The History Of Rock-#10-C . . . . (Collectables)
    Oldies But Goodies-#5-C . . . . (Original Sound)
Till The Clouds Roll By
    Anna Wheaton & James Harrod; *Music From The New York Stage (1890-
      1920)-#4-1917-1920-C* . . . . (Pearl)
    Tom Powers & Beatrice Lillie; *Music From The New York Stage (1890-
      1920)-#4-1917-1920-C* . . . . (Pearl)
Truly Madly Deeply
    Savage Garden; *Savage Garden* . . . . (Columbia)
Uncloudy Day
    Willie Nelson; *Greatest Hits (& Some That Will Be)* . . . . . . (Columbia)
    Willie Nelson & Dyan Cannon; *ST/Honeysuckle Rose* . . . . . . (Columbia)
Uncloudy Day
    Don Henley; *I Can't Stand Still* . . . . (Asylum)
Under African Skies
    Paul Simon; *Graceland* . . . . (Warner Bros.)
Under Blue Canadian Skies
    Glenn Miller & His Orchestra; *Complete Glenn Miller & His
      Orchestra* . . . . (Bluebird)
Under Paris Skies
    Arthur Murray & His Orchestra; *Music For Dancing-Waltz* . . . . (RCA)
    Gordon Jenkins; *France* . . . . (Bainbridge)
Under The Falling Sky
    Bonnie Raitt; *Bonnie Raitt-Collection* . . . . (Warner Bros.)
    Give It Up . . . . (Warner Bros.)
    Jackson Browne; *Jackson Browne* . . . . (Asylum)
Under The Red Sky
    Bob Dylan; *Under The Red Sky* . . . . (Columbia)
Under The Sky
    Heart; *Brigade* . . . . (Capitol)
    Rock The House "Live" . . . . (Capitol)
Voices In The Sky
    Moody Blues; *In Search Of The Lost Chord* . . . . (Polydor)
Waitress In The Sky
    Replacements; *Tim* . . . . (Sire)
Walk In The Sun
    Bruce Hornsby; *Hot House* . . . . (RCA)

War Clouds
New Orleans Ragtime Orchestra; *New Orleans Jazz-C* . . . .(Arhoolie)
Watcher Of The Skies
Genesis; *Foxtrot* . . . . (Atlantic)
Genesis-Live . . . . (Atlantic)
We Almost Had Texas Skies Today
Hank Thompson; *Here's To Country Music* . . . .(Step One)
Wheel In The Sky
Journey; *Infinity* . . . .(Columbia)
Journey-Captured . . . .(Columbia)
Journey's Greatest Hits . . . .(Columbia)
When The Night Comes Falling From The Sky
Bob Dylan; *Empire Burlesque* . . . .(Columbia)
The Bootleg Series-Volumes 1-3 [Rare & Unreleased] . . . .(Columbia)
Jeff Healey Band; *ST/Road House* . . . . (Arista)
Wild Kentucky Skies
Marty Brown; *Wild Kentucky Skies* . . . . (MCA)
Wild Montana Skies
John Denver; *It's About Time* . . . . (RCA)
John Denver's Greatest Hits-#3 . . . . (RCA)
John Denver & Emmylou Harris; *Collector's Series-Duets-C* . . . .(RCA)
Will It Go Round In Circles
Billy Preston; *Best Of Billy Preston* . . . .(A&M)
Billboard Top Rock 'N' Roll Hits-1973-C . . . .(Rhino)
Didn't It Blow Your Mind: Soul Hits Of The '70s-#11-C . . . .(Rhino)
Will The Circle Be Unbroken
Charlie Daniels Band & Friends; *Volunteer Jam 3 & 4* . . . . (Epic)
Joan Baez; *Country Music Album* . . . .(Vanguard)
The First 10 Years . . . .(Vanguard)
Nitty Gritty Dirt Band; *Will The Circle Be Unbroken* . . . . (EMI)
Roy Acuff; *Best Of Roy Acuff* . . . .(Liberty)
Willie Nelson; *Willie & Family Live* . . . .(Columbia)
Winter Sky
Judy Collins; *Judy Collins Concert* . . . . (Elektra)
Recollections . . . . (Elektra)
You Sang To Me
Marc Anthony; *Marc Anthony* . . . .(Columbia)

SLAVERY

See Also: **BOSSES, COUNTRIES: AMERICA, FREEDOM, KINGS, POLITICS (various), PREJUDICE, PRISON, PROTEST, QUEENS, ROYALTY, STUCK, WAR, WORK**

Abolitionist Hymn
Hermes Nye; *Ballads Of The Civil War-#1 & 2* . . . .(Smithsonian Folkways)
Brown Sugar
Rolling Stones; *Classic Rock 1966-1988-C* . . . . (Atlantic)
Hot Rocks 1964-1971 . . . . (Abkco)
Made In The Shade . . . . (Rolling Stones)
Sticky Fingers . . . .(Virgin)
Free At Last
Dock Read & Vera Hall Ward; *Every Tone A Testimony-C* . . . .(Smithsonian Folkways)
Go Down Moses
Arlo Guthrie; *Arlo Guthrie* . . . .(Rising Son)
Fats Waller; *Ain't Misbehavin'* . . . .(Laserlight)
Paul Robeson; *Ballad For Americans* . . . .(Vanguard)
The Power & The Glory . . . .(Columbia)
Simon Estes; *Spirituals* . . . .(Philips)
John Brown's Body
Pete Seeger; *American Favorite Ballads-#3* . . . .(Smithsonian Folkways)
Sonny Terry & Brownie McGhee; *Every Tone A Testimony-C* . . . .(Smithsonian Folkways)
Juneteenth
Anthony Rivers & Others; *I've Known Rivers* . . . . (Gramavision)
No More Auction Block
Paul Robeson; *Every Tone A Testimony-C* . . . .(Smithsonian Folkways)
Nobody Knows The Trouble I've Seen
Mahalia Jackson; *Gospels, Spirituals & Hymns* . . . .(Columbia)
Mahalia Jackson's Greatest Hits . . . .(Columbia)
Nat "King" Cole; *Every Time I Feel The Spirit* . . . .(Capitol)
Pharaoh's Host Got Lost
Lawrence McKiver; *Every Tone A Testimony-C* . . . . . .(Smithsonian Folkways)
Redemption Song
Bob Marley & The Wailers; *Legend: The Best Of Bob Marley & The Wailers* . . . . (Island)
Uprising . . . . (Island)
Wyclef Jean; *America: A Tribute To Heroes-C* . . . . (Interscope)
Sail Away
Linda Ronstadt; *Don't Cry Now* . . . . (Asylum)
Randy Newman; *Guilty: 30 Years Of Randy Newman.* . . . .(Rhino)
Sail Away . . . .(Reprise)
Screaming Slave
Nine Inch Nails; *Fixed* . . . . (Nothing)
Slave
Rolling Stones; *Tattoo You* . . . .(Virgin)

Slave
Germs; *Germs* . . . . (Slash)
Slave
Elton John; *Honky Chateau* . . . .(Rocket)
Slave
Carly Simon; *Playing Possum* . . . .(Elektra)
Slave Driver
Bob Marley & The Wailers; *Catch A Fire* . . . . (Tuff Gong)
Rebel Music. . . . . (Tuff Gong)
Slave Driver
Taj Mahal; *Mo' Roots.* . . . .(Legacy)
Slave Girl
Goo Goo Dolls; *A Boy Named Goo* . . . .(Metal Blade)
Slave Master
Gregory Isaacs; *Mr. Isaacs.* . . . . (Shanachie)
Revolutionary Sounds: Essential Rockers Reggae Classics-1973-1981-C . . . . (Shanachie)
Slave Ships
Original Cast; *Bring In 'Da Noise, Bring In 'Da Funk* . . . .(RCA Victor)
Slave Song
Sade; *Lovers Rock* . . . . (Epic)
Slave To Love
Bryan Ferry; *Boys And Girls* . . . .(Reprise)
Roxy Music; *Street Life-20 Great Hits* . . . . (Reprise)
Slavery Days
Burning Spear; *Burning Spear-24 Great Hits* . . . .(MGM)
Burning Spear-Live . . . .(Columbia)
Marcus Garvey/Garvey's Ghost . . . .(Mango)
Revolutionary Sounds: Essential Rockers Reggae Classics-1973-1981-C . . . . (Shanachie)
Third World; *Third World* . . . . (Island)
Slavery, Deliverance And Faith
Clint Black; *ST/The Prince Of Egypt-Nashville* . . . . (DreamWorks/SKG)
Slaves
Temptations; *Puzzle People* . . . .(Motown)
Slaves
Dionne Warwick; *Hidden Gems-Best Of Dionne Warwick-#2.* . . . .(Rhino)
Slaves
Bad Religion; *80-85.* . . . . (Epitaph)
Slaves And Bulldozers
Soundgarden; *Badmotorfinger.* . . . .(A&M)
Slave's Lament, The
Jean Redpath; *Songs Of Robert Burns-#3 & 4* . . . . (Philo)
Sun City
Artists United Against Apartheid; *Sun City-C* . . . .(Manhattan)
Theme From "Roots"
Original Soundtrack; *Television's Greatest Hits-#6-Remote Control-C* . . .(TVT)
Unfaithful Servant
Band; *Rock Of Ages* . . . .(Capitol)
The Band . . . .(Capitol)
The Band-Gift Set . . . . (Capitol)
To Kingdom Come-The Definitive Collection . . . . (Capitol)
Well Fed Slave/Hungry Free Man
Lucky Dube; *Taxman.* . . . . (Shanachie)
What It Is
Mark Knopfler; *Sailing To Philadelphia* . . . .(Warner Bros.)
When I Lay My Burden Down
Fred McDowell & Furry Lewis; *When I Lay My Burden Down* . . . . . . (Biograph)
Roy Acuff; *Columbia Historic Edition-Roy Acuff* . . . . (Columbia)

SLEAZY, Scum Of The Earth, Seamy, Seedy, Underbelly Of Life

See Also: **DIRT, INSULTS, LOW SELF-ESTEEM, SOCIAL CLASS: GENERAL, SOCIAL OUTCASTS**

Aqualung
Jethro Tull; *20 Years Of Jethro Tull* . . . .(Chrysalis)
Bursting Out . . . . (Chrysalis)
M.U.-The Best Of Jethro Tull . . . . (Chrysalis)
Too Old To Rock 'N' Roll: Too Young To Die! . . . .(Chrysalis)
Bawitdaba
Kid Rock; *Devil Without A Cause* . . . .(Top Dog/Lava/Atlantic)
Totally Hits-#1-C . . . .(Arista)
Ends
Everlast; *Whitey Ford Sings The Blues* . . . . (Tommy Boy)
Hands In The Air
Bob Seger; *It's A Mystery.* . . . .(Capitol)
He's Misstra Know-It-All
Stevie Wonder; *Innervisions* . . . .(Motown)
Immortality
Pearl Jam; *Vitalogy* . . . . (Epic)
Jerry Springer
"Weird Al" Yankovic; *Running With Scissors* . . . .(Volcano Entertainment)
King Of Hollywood
Eagles; *The Long Run.* . . . .(Asylum)

King Of New Orleans
Better Than Ezra; *Friction, Baby* . . . . (Swell/Elektra)
Papa Was A Rollin' Stone
Temptations; *20/20-C* . . . . (Motown)
25 #1 Hits From 25 Years-C . . . . (Motown)
All The Million-Sellers . . . . (Motown)
Billboard Top Rock 'N' Roll Hits-1972-C . . . . (Rhino)
Compact Command Performances-Temptations . . . . (Motown)
Temptations-Anthology-The Best Of The Temptations . . . . (Motown)
Post-modern Sleaze
Sneaker Pimps; *Becoming X* . . . . (Virgin)
She's Single Again
Janie Fricke; *19 Hot Country Requests-#3-C* . . . .(Epic)
Greatest Country Hits Of The '80s-1985-C . . . . (Columbia)
Janie Fricke-17 Greatest Hits . . . . (Columbia)
Very Best Of Janie Fricke . . . . (Columbia)
Reba McEntire; *Have I Got A Deal For You* . . . .(MCA)
Sleazy Come Easy Go
L.A. Guns; *Cocked And Loaded* . . . . (Polydor)
Swing Street
Bruce Hornsby; *Hot House* . . . . (RCA)
Taker, The
Kris Kristofferson; *The Silver Tongued Devil And I* . . . . (Columbia)
Waylon Jennings; *Essential Waylon Jennings* . . . . (RCA)
Only Daddy That'll Walk The Line-The RCA Years . . . . (RCA)
Teenage Dirtbag
Wheatus; *Wheatus* . . . . (Columbia)
Walk In The Sun
Bruce Hornsby; *Hot House* . . . . (RCA)
Walkaway Joe
Trisha Yearwood; *Hearts In Armor* . . . .(MCA)
Songbook-A Collection Of Hits . . . .(MCA)
You're So Vain
Carly Simon; *'70s Greatest Rock Hits-#3-High Times-C* . . . . (Priority)
Best Of Carly Simon . . . . (Elektra)
Carly Simon-Greatest Hits Live . . . . (Arista)
No Secrets . . . . (Elektra)

SLEEP, Awake, Insomnia, Tired
See Also: *BORED, DREAMS, NIGHT, RELAX, SEX, STUCK, WAITING*

(Lay Your Head On My) Pillow
Tony Toni Tone; *Sons Of Soul* . . . . (Wing)
(You Drive Me) Crazy
Britney Spears; *...Baby One More Time* . . . . (Jive)
Now That's What I Call Music!-#4-C . . . . (Virgin)
1st Of Tha Month
Bone Thugs-N-Harmony; *E. 1999 Eternal* . . . . (Ruthless/Relativity)
500 Miles Away From Home
Bobby Bare; *500 Miles Away From Home* . . . . (RCA)
Foy Willing; *Cowboy/The New Sound Of American Folk* . . . . (DRG)
Reba McEntire; *Starting Over* . . . .(MCA)
Ain't Nobody Here But Us Chickens
Asleep At The Wheel; *Very Best Of Asleep At The Wheel
Since 1970* . . . . (Relentless/Madacy)
Louis Jordan; *Best Of Louis Jordan* . . . .(MCA)
All Through The Night
Judy Collins; *Baby's Bedtime* . . . . (Lightyear)
And The Mouse Police Never Sleeps
Jethro Tull; *Heavy Horses* . . . .(Chrysalis)
Animal Crackers
Steven Tyler featuring Liv Tyler and Ben Affleck; *ST/Armageddon-The
Album* . . . . (Columbia)
Another Sleepless Night
Anne Murray; *Anne Murray-Country Hits* . . . . (Capitol)
Anne Murray's Greatest Hits . . . . (Capitol)
Where Do You Go When You Dream . . . . (Capitol)
Another Sleepless Night
Shawn Christopher; *Divas Of Dance-#2-C* . . . .(Dunhill Compact Classics)
Are You Sleeping?
Nilsson; *The Point* . . . . (RCA)
As I Lay Me Down
Sophie B. Hawkins; *Whaler* . . . . (Columbia)
As We Lay
Kelly Price; *Mirror Mirror* . . . .(Def Soul/IDJMG)
Asleep In The Desert
ZZ Top; *Six Pack* . . . .(Warner Bros.)
Tejas . . . .(Warner Bros.)
A-sleepin' At The Foot Of The Bed
''Little'' Jimmy Dickens; *Bluegrass Super Hits-C* . . . . (Columbia)
At Night She Sleeps
Night Ranger; *Dawn Patrol* . . . . (Camel)
Awake
Letters To Cleo; *Wholesale Meats & Fish* . . . . (Giant)

Awake
Godsmack; *Awake* . . . . (Republic/Universal)
Awake Ye Drowsy Sleepers
Ian & Sylvia; *Ian & Sylvia* . . . . (Vanguard)
Ian & Sylvia's Greatest Hits . . . . (Vanguard)
Awakening
John Mahavishnu McLaughlin; *Inner Mounting Flame* . . . . (Columbia)
Awakening
Alice Cooper; *Welcome To My Nightmare* . . . .(Atlantic)
Babydoll
Mariah Carey; *Butterfly* . . . . (Columbia)
Banana Boat (Day-O)
Harry Belafonte; *Belafonte '89* . . . . (EMI)
Nipper's Greatest Hits Of The '50s-#1-C . . . .(RCA)
Kinks; *Everybody's In Show-Biz* . . . . (Rhino)
Be Bop/Drop
Daryl Hall & John Oates; *X-Static* . . . . (RCA)
Bedside Radio
Krokus; *Alive & Screamin'* . . . . (Arista)
Metal Rendez-vous . . . . (Arista)
Bedtime Story
Tammy Wynette; *First Lady Of Country Music* . . . . (Epic)
Tammy Wynette's Biggest Hits . . . . (Epic)
Tammy Wynette's Greatest Hits-#3 . . . . (Epic)
Bedtime Story
Madonna; *Bedtime Stories* . . . .(Maverick/Sire)
GHV2 . . . .(Warner Bros.)
Been There
Clint Black with Steve Wariner; *D'lectrified* . . . .(RCA)
Behind The Wall Of Sleep
Smithereens; *Especially For You* . . . .(Enigma)
Behind The Wall Of Sleep
Black Sabbath; *Black Sabbath* . . . . (Warner Bros.)
Better Get Back In Bed
Beach Boys; *Holland* . . . . (Brother)
Bewitched
Anita O'Day; *Anita Sings The Most* . . . . (Verve)
Barbra Streisand; *Third Album* . . . . (Columbia)
Doris Day; *Doris Day's Greatest Hits* . . . . (Columbia)
Original Cast; *Pal Joey* . . . . (Columbia)
Beyond The Wall Of Sleep
Ozzy Osbourne; *The Ozzman Cometh* . . . . (Epic)
Big Sleep
Simple Minds; *New Gold Dream* . . . . (A&M)
Simple Minds Live: In The City Of Light . . . . (A&M)
Bittersweet Me
R.E.M.; *New Adventures In Hi-Fi* . . . . (Warner Bros.)
Black Coffee In Bed
Squeeze; *Sweets From A Stranger* . . . . (A&M)
Blue Jay Way
Beatles; *Beatles-Box Set* . . . . (Capitol)
Magical Mystery Tour . . . . (Capitol)
Blue Love
O'Kanes; *Tired Of The Runnin'* . . . . (Columbia)
Brian Wilson
Barenaked Ladies; *Gordon* . . . . (Reprise)
Rock Spectacle . . . . (Reprise)
Can't Sleep
Rockets; *Rockets* . . . . (RSO)
Rockets-Live . . . . (Capitol)
Chemicals Between Us, The
Bush; *The Science Of Things* . . . . (Trauma)
Cigarette
Ben Folds Five; *Whatever And Ever Amen* . . . .(Caroline/550)
Count Your Blessings (Instead Of Sheep)
Bing Crosby; *45-#29251* . . . . (Decca)
Eddie Fisher; *Best Of Eddie Fisher* . . . . (MCA)
Rosemary Clooney; *Essence Of Rosemary Clooney* . . . . (Legacy)
Cry Myself To Sleep
Judds; *Collector's Series-The Judds* . . . . (RCA)
Hits Of '87-C . . . . (RCA)
Judds' Greatest Hits . . . . (MCA)
Rockin' With The Rhythm . . . . (MCA)
Cry Myself To Sleep
Del Shannon; *Runaway Hits!* . . . . (Rhino)
Cry Myself To Sleep
4 Seasons; *Rarities-#1* . . . . (Rhino)
Daydream Believer
Anne Murray; *Anne Murray's Greatest Hits* . . . . (Capitol)
I'll Always Love You . . . . (Capitol)
Monkees; *Billboard Top Rock 'N' Roll Hits-1967-C* . . . . (Rhino)
Mellow '60s-C . . . . (Priority)
Monkees' Greatest Hits . . . . (Rhino)
Daysleeper
R.E.M.; *Up* . . . . (Warner Bros.)
Didn't Leave Nobody But The Baby
Emmylou Harris/Alison Krauss/Gillian Welch; *ST/O Brother, Where Art
Thou?* . . . . (Mercury)

Distant Melody
Original Cast/Mary Martin; *Peter Pan-The 1954 Broadway
Production* . . . . (RCA Victor)
Do You Sleep?
Lisa Loeb & Nine Stories; *Tails*. . . . . (Geffen)
Don't Sleep In The Subway
Frank Sinatra; *Frank Sinatra* . . . . (Reprise)
Petula Clark; *Petula Clark's Greatest Hits* . . . . (Crescendo)
Summer Of Love-#1-C . . . . (Rhino)
Don't Smoke In Bed
Nina Simone; *Finest Of* . . . . (Bethlehem)
Nina Simone In Concert/I Put A Spell On You . . . . (Mercury)
Peggy Lee; *Capitol Collectors Series-Peggy Lee-#1-Early Years* . . . (Capitol)
Peggy Lee's Greatest Hits . . . . (Capitol)
Don't You Ever Get Tired Of Hurtin' Me
Ray Price; *Ray Price's Greatest Hits-#2* . . . . (Step One)
Ronnie Milsap; *Stranger Things Have Happened* . . . . (RCA)
Don't Your Mem'ry Ever Sleep At Night
Ronnie Milsap; *Keyed Up* . . . . (RCA)
Steve Wariner; *Best Of Steve Wariner* . . . . (RCA)
Dream Walkin'
Toby Keith; *Dream Walkin'* . . . . (Mercury)
Toby Keith's Greatest Hits, Volume One . . . . (Mercury)
Dreaming While You Sleep
Genesis; *We Can't Dance* . . . . (Atlantic)
Early To Bed
Morphine; *Like Swimming*. . . . . (DreamWorks/Rykodisc)
Endless Sleep
Jody Reynolds; *American Graffiti-#3-C* . . . . (MCA)
Teenage Tragedies-C . . . . (Rhino)
Endless Sleep
Babys; *Babys* . . . . (Chrysalis)
Enter Sandman
Metallica; *Metallica* . . . . (Elektra)
Every Time I Close My Eyes
Babyface; *The Day* . . . . (Epic)
Everywhere
Michelle Branch; *The Spirit Room* . . . . (Maverick)
Flow Gently, Sweet Afton
Mormon Tabernacle Choir; *Old Beloved Songs* . . . . (Columbia)
Frere Jacques
Original Soundtrack; *Toddler Favorites* . . . . (Kid Rhino/Rhino 4 Kids)
Ft. Worth Featherbed
Donnie Rohrs; *Country Music USA* . . . . (Pacific Challenger)
Get Up
Amel Larrieux; *Infinite Possibilities* . . . . (Epic)
Ghost Of You And Me
BBMak; *Sooner Or Later* . . . . (Hollywood)
Give Me Your Tired, Your Poor
Mormon Tabernacle Choir; *Around The World: A Musical Journey Of Best-
Loved Favorites* . . . . (Sony Music Classical)
Golden Slumbers
Beatles; *Abbey Road* . . . . (Parlophone)
Beatles-Box Set . . . . (Capitol)
Goodnight
Beatles; *The Beatles (White Album)* . . . . (Capitol)
Green Door
Jim Lowe; *Billboard Top Rock 'N' Roll Hits-1956-C* . . . . (Rhino)
Super Hits-#4-C . . . . (Gusto)
Had A Dream (Sleeping With The Enemy)
Roger Hodgson; *In The Eye Of The Storm* . . . . (A&M)
Hard Day's Night, A
Beatles; *Beatles 1* . . . . (Capitol)
Beatles-20 Greatest Hits . . . . (Capitol)
ST/A Hard Day's Night . . . . (Capitol)
The Beatles At The Hollywood Bowl . . . . (Capitol)
The Beatles/1962-1966 . . . . (Capitol)
Hobo's Lullaby
Arlo Guthrie; *Hobo's Lullaby* . . . . (Reprise)
Goebel Reeves; *Texas Drifter* . . . . (Glendale)
Joan Baez; *Tribute To Woody Guthrie-C* . . . . (Warner Bros.)
Homeless
Paul Simon; *Graceland* . . . . (Warner Bros.)
How Do You Sleep At Night
Wade Hayes; *When The Wrong One Loves You Right* . . . . . . (Columbia/DKC)
Hushabye
Mystics; *Doo-Wop Uptempo-#2-C* . . . . (Rhino)
Million-Dollar Memories #1-C. . . . . (RCA)
Mystics-16 Golden Classics . . . . (Collectables)
I Am Weary (Let Me Rest)
Cox Family; *ST/O Brother, Where Art Thou?* . . . . (Mercury)
I Call Your Name
Beatles; *Past Masters-Volume One* . . . . (Parlophone)
Rock 'N' Roll Music . . . . (Capitol)
The Beatles' Second Album . . . . (Capitol)
I Can't Sleep Baby (If I)
R. Kelly; *R. Kelly*. . . . . (Jive)

I Couldn't Sleep A Wink Last Night
Frank Sinatra; *A Lovely Way To Spend An Evening* . . . .(ASV)
Voice: The Columbia Years-1943-1952 . . . . (Columbia)
Mello Moods; *Great Groups Of The '50s-#3-C* . . . .(Collectables)
I Don't Sleep, I Dream
R.E.M.; *Monster* . . . . (Warner Bros.)
I Don't Want To Miss A Thing
Aerosmith; *ST/Armageddon-The Album* . . . . (Columbia)
Mark Chesnutt; *I Don't Want To Miss A Thing* . . . . (MCA)
I Go To Sleep
Pretenders; *Pretenders II* . . . . (Sire)
Pretenders-The Singles . . . . (Sire)
If You Were To Wake Up
Tammy Wynette & Lyle Lovett; *Without Walls-C* . . . . (Epic)
I'll Lie Myself To Sleep
Shelby Lynne; *Greatest Country Hits Of The '90s-1990-C* . . . . . (Columbia)
Tough All Over . . . . (Epic)
I'm Getting Tired So I Can Sleep
Dinah Shore; *The Eddie Cantor Radio Show-1942-1943* . . . . . (Original Cast)
I'm Only Sleeping
Beatles; *"Yesterday"...And Today* . . . . (Capitol)
Rarities . . . . (Capitol)
I'm So Tired
Beatles; *The Beatles (White Album)* . . . . (Capitol)
I'm Tired
Mel Tillis; *American Originals-Mel Tillis* . . . . (Columbia)
Ricky Skaggs; *Comin' Home To Stay* . . . . (Epic)
Webb Pierce; *Best Of Webb Pierce* . . . . (MCA)
Webb Pierce-Golden Hits . . . . (Plantation)
I'm Tired
Savoy Brown; *Savoy Brown-London Collector* . . . . (London)
Step Further . . . . (Parrot)
I'm Tired
Phil Ochs; *Toast To Those Who Are Gone* . . . . (Rhino)
I'm Tired
Mel Brooks; *ST/High Anxiety*. . . . . (Asylum)
Image Of A Girl
Safaris; *Brown Eyed Soul...East L.A.-#3-C* . . . . (Rhino)
In Dreams
Roy Orbison; *For The Lonely: A Roy Orbison Anthology 1959-1965* . . . .(Rhino)
In Dreams-Greatest Hits . . . . (Orbison)
In My Bed
Dru Hill; *Dru Hill*. . . . . (Island)
It Sure Is Monday
Mark Chesnutt; *Almost Goodbye* . . . . (MCA)
It's Raining, It's Pouring
Original Soundtrack; *Children's Favorites* . . . . (Kid Rhino/Rhino 4 Kids)
Jet Lag
Nazareth; *Rampant*. . . . . (A&M)
Just Can't Go To Sleep
Kinks; *Kinks*. . . . . (Reprise)
You Really Got Me. . . . . (Rhino)
Last Night I Didn't Get To Sleep At All
5th Dimension; *Greatest Hits On Earth* . . . . (Arista)
Last Nite
Strokes; *Is This It* . . . . (RCA)
Lay Down Your Weary Tune
Ashley Hutchings; *The Guv'nor*. . . . . (Wildcat)
Bob Dylan; *Biograph*. . . . . (Columbia)
Byrds; *The Byrds* . . . . (Columbia)
Turn! Turn! Turn! . . . . (Legacy)
Tim O'Brien; *Red On Blonde*. . . . . (Sugar Hill)
Lazybones
Don Redman & His Orchestra; *Don Redman-1933-1936* . . . . (Classics)
Harry Connick, Jr.; *25* . . . . (Columbia)
Kay Starr; *The Hoagy Carmichael Songbook-C* . . . . (Bluebird)
Mildred Bailey; *Mildred Bailey-1932-1936*. . . . . (Classics)
Let's Put Out The Lights And Go To Sleep
Rudy Vallee; *American Legend Series-Vagabond Lover*. . . . .(Pro-Arte)
Letting The Cables Sleep
Bush; *Science Of Things*. . . . . (Trauma)
Long Day
Matchbox Twenty; *Yourself Or Someone Like You* . . . . (Lava)
Lullaby
Cure; *Disintegration* . . . . (Elektra)
Mixed Up. . . . . (Elektra)
Lullaby
Shawn Mullins; *Soul's Core*. (Columbia)
Lullaby
Take 6; *Join The Band-C* . . . . (Reprise)
Love Shouldn't Hurt-C . . . . (Qwest)
Lullaby
Book Of Love; *Lullaby*. . . . . (Sire)
Lullaby
Tom Rush; *Tom Rush*. . . . . (Columbia)
Lullaby For Myself
Barbra Streisand; *Streisand Superman*. . . . . (Columbia)

Lullaby For Nancy Carol
Chuck Mangione; *Best Of Chuck Mangione* . . . . (Mercury)
   Land Of Make Believe . . . . (Mercury)
   Together . . . . (Mercury)
Lullaby Of Birdland
Ella Fitzgerald; *Best Of Ella Fitzgerald-#2* . . . .(MCA)
   Ella Fitzgerald With Billie Holiday . . . .(MCA)
Four Freshmen; *Greatest Hits-Four Freshman* . . . . (Curb)
Mel Torme; *Songs Of New York* . . . . (Rhino)
Sarah Vaughan; *Sarah Vaughan-Golden Hits* . . . . (Mercury)
Tito Puente & His Latin Ensemble; *Mambo Diablo* . . . .(Concord Jazz)
Lullaby Of Broadway
Andrews Sisters; *Best Of The Andrews Sisters-#2* . . . . (MCA)
Bette Midler; *Bette Midler* . . . .(Atlantic)
   Live At Last . . . . (Atlantic)
Original Broadway Cast; *42nd Street* . . . .(RCA Victor)
Tony Bennett; *Jazz* . . . . (Columbia)
Lullaby Of The Leaves
Various Artists; *Birdlanders-#1-C* . . . .(Original Jazz Classics)
Magic Fingers (25 Cents)
Birdsongs Of The Mesozoic; *Faultline* . . . .(Cuneiform)
Maybe We Should Just Sleep On It
Tim McGraw; *All I Want* . . . . (Curb)
   Tim McGraw's Greatest Hits . . . . (Curb)
Miles To Go (Before I Sleep)
Celine Dion; *Let's Talk About Love-C* . . . .(550 Music)
Missing The War
Ben Folds Five; *Whatever And Ever Amen* . . . .(Caroline/550)
Mister Sandman
Chordettes; *Best Of The Chordettes* . . . . (Rhino)
Emmylou Harris; *Evangeline* . . . .(Warner Bros.)
   Profile II-The Best Of Emmylou Harris . . . .(Warner Bros.)
Morning Glory
Oasis; *(What's The Story) Morning Glory* . . . .(Epic)
Mother's Only Sleeping
Ricky Skaggs and Kentucky Thunder; *History Of The Future* . . (Skaggs Family)
Mrs. Potter's Lullaby
Counting Crows; *This Desert Life* . . . . (David Geffen Co.)
My Clone Sleeps Alone
Pat Benatar; *In The Heat Of The Night* . . . .(Chrysalis)
Narcolepsy
Ben Folds Five; *The Unauthorized Biography Of Reinhold
   Messner* . . . .(550 Music)
No Sleep Till Brooklyn
Beastie Boys; *Licensed To Ill* . . . .(Def Jam)
Oh! How I Hate To Get Up In The Morning
Irving Berlin; *American Songbook Series-Irving
   Berlin* . . . .(Smithsonian Collection)
   War Years-C . . . .(ISD/Intersound)
Soundtrack; *American Musical Theater-#2* . . . .(Smithsonian Collection)
Oh, Baby Mine (I Get So Lonely)
Chet Atkins; *Tennessee Guitar Man* . . . . (Pair)
Four Knights; *Those Wonderful Years: Mr. Sandman-C* . . . . (JCI Assoc. Labels)
Oh, How I Hate To Get Up In The Afternoon
Harry "Sweets" Edison; *Swing Trumpet Kings-C* . . . . (Verve)
Pinch Me
Barenaked Ladies; *Maroon* . . . .(Reprise)
   Totally Hits-#3-C . . . .(Atlantic)
Prayin' For Daylight
Rascal Flatts; *Rascal Flatts* . . . .(Lyric Street)
President's Nap
Power Tools; *Strange Meeting* . . . .(Antilles)
Rest My Mind On Jesus
Charles Ford Band; *Charles Ford Band* . . . . (Arhoolie)
River Of Dreams
Billy Joel; *River Of Dreams* . . . . (Columbia)
Rock A Bye Your Baby With A Dixie Melody
Al Jolson; *Best Of Al Jolson* . . . .(MCA)
   Jolson Sang 'Em . . . .(Biograph)
   Music From The New York Stage (1890-1920)-#4-1917-1920-C . . . . . . (Pearl)
   The Al Jolson Story-#1 . . . .(MCA)
Jerry Lewis; *Just Sings* . . . . (Razor & Tie)
Judy Garland; *Judy Garland-At Carnegie Hall* . . . . (Capitol)
   Miss Show Business . . . . (Capitol)
   One & Only . . . . (Capitol)
Rock 'N' Roll Lullaby
B.J. Thomas; *B.J. Thomas' Greatest Hits* . . . . (Rhino)
   B.J. Thomas-16 Greatest Hits . . . . (Trip)
   Back To The '70s-#2-C . . . . (Dominion Entert.)
   Super Hits-#2-C . . . . (Gusto)
Rock 'N' Roll Lullaby
10 CC; *How Dare You!* . . . . (Mercury)
Rocks Off
Rolling Stones; *Exile On Main Street* . . . . (Virgin)
   Let There Be Drums!-#3-The '70s-C . . . . (Rhino)
Rude Awakening No. 2
Creedence Clearwater Revival; *1970* . . . . (Fantasy)
   Pendulum . . . . (Fantasy)

Satin Sheets
Jeannie Pruett; *16 Top Country Hits-#1-C* . . . . (MCA)
   Country Chart-Toppers . . . .(Dominion Entert.)
   Grand Ole Opry-75 Years-#2-C . . . .(MCA)
   MCA Records 30 Years Of Hits-1958-1988-C . . . . (MCA)
Shawn Colvin; *Cover Girl* . . . . (Columbia)
Savannah Awakes
Barbra Streisand; *ST/Prince Of Tides* . . . . (Columbia)
Send Me Your Pillow
John Lee Hooker; *Big Soul Of John Lee Hooker* . . . . (Vee-Jay)
John Lee Hooker & Canned Heat; *Hooker 'N Heat* . . . . (EMI)
Set Adrift On Memory Bliss
PM Dawn; *MTV Party To Go-#2-C* . . . . (Tommy Boy)
   Red Hot + Dance-C . . . . (Columbia)
Shake Me Wake Me
Barbra Streisand; *Lazy Afternoon* . . . . (Columbia)
Four Tops; *Four Tops' Greatest Hits* . . . . (Motown)
   Four Tops-Anthology . . . . (Motown)
   Motown Superstar Series-#14-Four Tops . . . . (Motown)
She Even Woke Me Up To Say Goodbye
Jerry Lee Lewis; *Best Of Jerry Lee Lewis* . . . .(Smash)
   Heartbreak . . . .(Tomato)
Kenny Rogers And The First Edition; *Kenny Rogers And The First Edition-
   Love Songs* . . . . (MCA Special Prod.)
Show Me The Way To Go Home
Artie Shaw; *Best Of Artie Shaw* . . . . (MCA)
Randy Erwin; *Back Home* . . . . (Really Outstanding Music)
Singing In My Sleep
Semisonic; *Feeling Strangely Fine* . . . . (MCA)
Sleep
Les Paul; *Legend & The Legacy-#1-4* . . . . (Capitol)
   Les Paul Now . . . . (London)
   Les Paul-London Collector . . . . (London)
Sleep
Little Willie John; *Best Of Little Willie John-Fever* . . . . (Rhino)
Sleep
Midnight Oil; *Red Sails In The Sunset* . . . . (Columbia)
Sleep
'Til Tuesday; *Voices Carry* . . . . (Epic)
Sleep
Benny Goodman; *Yale Recordings-#5-Private Collection* . . . . . . (Musicmasters)
Sleep Come Free Me
James Taylor; *Flag* . . . . (Columbia)
Sleep My Baby Sleep
Judy Garland; *Judy Garland-Collector's Items-1936-1945* . . . . (MCA)
Sleep Now In The Fire
Rage Against The Machine; *The Battle Of Los Angeles* . . . . (Epic)
Sleep On It
Chaka Khan; *Chaka* . . . . (Warner Bros.)
Sleep Song
Glenn Miller & His Orchestra; *Complete Glenn Miller & His
   Orchestra* . . . .(Bluebird)
Sleep Song
Hot Tuna; *America's Choice* . . . . (RCA)
Sleep Song
Graham Nash; *Songs For Beginners* . . . .(Atlantic)
Sleep Talk
Alyson Williams; *Raw* . . . . (Def Jam)
Sleep That Burns
Be Bop Deluxe; *Best Of And The Rest Of Be Bop Deluxe* . . . . . (Capitol)
   Best Of Be Bop Deluxe-Raiding The Divine Archive . . . . (Capitol)
   Sunburst Finish . . . . (Capitol)
Sleep Tight, Good Night Man
Kenny Rogers; *The Gambler* . . . . (EMI)
Sleep To Dream
Fiona Apple; *Tidal* . . . .(Clean Slate/Work)
Sleep Walk
Santo & Johnny; *Billboard Top Rock 'N' Roll Hits-1959-C* . . . . . . (Rhino)
   Oldies But Goodies-#1-C . . . .(Original Sound)
Sleepin'
Diana Ross; *Diana Ross-Anthology* . . . . (Motown)
Sleepin' Bee
Al Jarreau; *1965* . . . . (Bainbridge)
Barbra Streisand; *Highlights From "Just For The Record"* . . . . . . (Columbia)
   Just For The Record . . . . (Columbia)
   The Barbra Streisand Album . . . . (Columbia)
Bill Evans; *Compact Jazz-Bill Evans* . . . . (Verve)
Carmen McRae; *Setting Standards* . . . . (Pair)
Harold Arlen & Barbra Streisand; *Harold Sings Arlen (With
   Friend)* . . . . (Sony Music Special Prod.)
Kiri Te Kanawa & Andre Previn; *Kiri Side Tracks-Jazz Album* . . . . . . (Philips)
Mel Torme; *Swings Shubert Alley* . . . . (Verve)
Original Cast; *House Of Flowers* . . . . (Sony Music Special Prod.)
Tony Bennett; *Consummate Collection-Classics Songs* . . . . (Columbia)
   Forty Years-The Artistry Of Tony Bennett . . . . (Columbia)
Sleepin' With The Radio On
Charly McClain; *Charly McClain's Greatest Hits* . . . . (Epic)
   Surround Me With Love . . . . (Epic)

Ten Year Anniversary . . . . (Epic)
Sleeping
Dwight Twilley Band; *Twilley Don't Mind* . . . . (Arista)
Sleeping
Band; *Stage Fright*. . . . . (Capitol)
Sleeping Bag
ZZ Top; *Afterburner* . . . . (Warner Bros.)
ZZ Top's Greatest Hits . . . . (Warner Bros.)
Sleeping Beauty Waltz
101 Strings Orchestra; *Million-Seller Themes From Tchaikovsky*. . . . . . (Alshire)
Sleeping Heart
Judds; *Talk About Love* . . . . (RCA)
Why Not Me . . . . (MCA)
Sleeping In My Car
Roxette; *Crash! Boom! Bang!* . . . . (EMI)
Sleeping In Paris
Rosanne Cash; *The Wheel* . . . . (Columbia)
Sleeping Late
Dr. Hook; *Makin' Love & Music* . . . . (Capitol)
Sleeping On The Beach
Nitty Gritty Dirt Band; *Dream*. . . . .(United Artists)
Sleeping On The Sidewalk
Hank Crawford; *Night Beat* . . . . (Milestone)
Sleeping On The Sidewalk
Queen; *News Of The World* . . . . (Hollywood)
Sleeping Satellite
Tasmin Archer; *Great Expectations* . . . . (SBK)
Sleeping Single In A Double Bed
Barbara Mandrell; *Barbara Mandrell Live* . . . . (MCA)
Best Of Barbara Mandrell . . . . (MCA)
Moods . . . . (MCA)
Sleeping With The Television On
Billy Joel; *Glass Houses* . . . . (Columbia)
Sleeping With The TV On
Dictators; *Manifest Destiny* . . . . (Asylum)
Sleepless Night
Dokken; *Back For The Attack* . . . . (Elektra)
Beast From The East. . . . . (Elektra)
Sleepless Night
John Lennon & Yoko Ono; *Milk & Honey*. . . . . (Polydor)
Sleepless Night
Kinks; *Sleepwalker* . . . . (Arista)
Sleepless Nights
Emmylou Harris; *Pieces Of The Sky* . . . . (Reprise)
Gram Parsons & The Flying Burrito Brothers; *Sleepless Nights* . . . . (A&M)
Judds; *Collector's Series-The Judds* . . . . (RCA)
River Of Time . . . . (RCA)
Sleep's Dark & Silent Gate
Bonnie Raitt; *The Glow* . . . . (Warner Bros.)
Jackson Browne; *The Pretender* . . . . (Asylum)
Sleeps With Angels
Neil Young & Crazy Horse; *Sleeps With Angels* . . . .(Reprise)
Sleepwalker
Kinks; *Come Dancing With The Kinks-Best Of The Kinks 1977-1986* . . . (Arista)
Sleepwalker . . . . (Arista)
Sleepwalker
Wallflowers; *Breach* . . . . (Interscope)
Sleepwalker
Shawn Phillips; *Second Contribution* . . . . (A&M)
Sleepwalking
Daniel Cage; *Loud On Earth* . . . . (MCA)
Sleepy Lagoon
Boston Pops Orchestra/Arthur Fiedler; *Boston Pops Orchestra/Arthur
Fiedler* . . . . (RCA)
Greatest Hits Of The '40s . . . . (RCA)
Boston Pops Orchestra/John Williams; *Swing Swing Swing* . . . . (Philips)
Harry James; *Best Of The Big Bands-C* . . . . (Columbia)
Harry James & His Orchestra; *16 Most Requested Songs Of The
'40s-#2-C* . . . . (Legacy)
Platters; *More Encore Of Golden Hits* . . . . (Mercury)
Sleepy Maggie
Ashley MacIsaac; *Hi How Are You Today?*. . . . . (A&M)
Sleepy Serenade
Wayne King & His Orchestra; *Best Of Wayne King-#2* . . . . (MCA)
Sleepy Time Gal
Glenn Miller; *Best Of The Big Bands-C*. . . . . (Columbia)
Harry James; *All-Time Favorites By Harry James* . . (Sony Music Special Prod.)
Liberace; *Encore-Liberace*. . . . .(American Variety)
Liberace . . . .(American Variety)
Piano Memories . . . .(American Variety)
Mose Allison; *Creek Bank*. . . . . (Prestige)
Sleepy Time Time
Cream; *Cream-Live-#1* . . . . (Polydor)
Fresh Cream . . . . (Polydor)
Summer Rain
Carl Thomas; *Emotional* . . . . (Bad Boy/Arista)
Sweet Afton
Nickel Creek; *Nickel Creek* . . . . (Sugar Hill)

Sweet Baby James
James Taylor; *James Taylor's Greatest Hits* . . . .(Warner Bros.)
Sweet Baby James . . . .(Warner Bros.)
Take A Picture
Filter; *Title Of Record* . . . . (Reprise)
Totally Hits-#2-C . . . . (Elektra)
Talking In Your Sleep
Crystal Gayle; *Classic Crystal* . . . . (EMI)
Country Gold-C . . . . (Priority)
Crystal Gayle's All-Time Greatest Hits. . . . . (EMI)
When I Dream . . . .(Liberty)
Reba McEntire; *Starting Over* . . . . (MCA)
Talking In Your Sleep
Romantics; *Billboard Top Hits-1984-C* . . . .(Rhino)
In Heat. . . . .(Epic Portrait Assoc.)
Rock Of The '80s-#3-C . . . . (Priority)
Tears Before Bedtime
Elvis Costello & The Attractions; *Imperial Bedroom* . . . .(Columbia)
Tears On My Pillow
Chimes; *Golden Groups-C* . . . . (Specialty)
Original Rock Oldies-Golden Hits-#2-C . . . . (Specialty)
Kylie Minogue; *Enjoy Yourself* . . . . (Geffen)
Little Anthony And The Imperials; *Best Of Little Anthony And The
Imperials* . . . . (EMI)
Best Of Little Anthony And The Imperials . . . .(Rhino)
Billboard Top R&B Hits-1958-C. . . . . (Rhino)
Good Time Rock 'N' Roll-C . . . . (MCA)
Lorrie Morgan; *Something In Red* . . . . (RCA)
New Edition & Little Anthony; *Under The Blue Moon* . . . . (MCA)
Reba McEntire; *Feel The Fire* . . . . (Mercury)
Sha Na Na; *ST/Grease* . . . . (Polydor)
Tell Me A Bedtime Story
Norman Connors; *Remember Who You Are* . . . .(Mojazz)
Quincy Jones; *Sounds... And Stuff Like That!!* . . . . (A&M)
Tender Shepherd
Original Cast; *Peter Pan-The 1954 Broadway Production* . . . . (RCA Victor)
Texas Lullaby
David Allan Coe; *Cowboys* . . . .(Columbia)
Longhaired Redneck . . . .(Columbia)
Taste Of Texas-Songs 'Bout Texas By Texans-C . . . .(Columbia)
Texas Lullaby
Doobie Brothers; *Stampede* . . . . (Warner Bros.)
This Heartache Never Sleeps
Mark Chesnutt; *I Don't Want To Miss A Thing* . . . . (MCA)
Tired Wings
Four Horsemen; *Nobody Said It Was Easy*. . . . . (Def American)
Tonight I Shall Sleep With A Smile On My Face
Duke Ellington; *Black, Brown & Beige: 1944-1946 Band
Recordings* . . . .(Bluebird)
Sarah Vaughan; *Duke Ellington Songbook Two*. . . . . (Pablo)
Tonight Is The Night I Fell Asleep At The Wheel
Barenaked Ladies; *Maroon* . . . . (Reprise)
Too Hot To Sleep
Louise Mandrell; *Too Hot To Sleep* . . . . (RCA)
Too Old To Cut The Mustard
Carlisles; *45-#6348* . . . .(Mercury)
Ernest Tubb; *Ernest Tubb-Retrospective-#2* . . . . (MCA Special Prod.)
Too Pooped To Pop
Chuck Berry; *Rockin' At The Hops* . . . .(Chess)
The Chess Box-Chuck Berry . . . .(Chess)
Too Tired
Gary Moore; *Still Got The Blues* . . . .(Charisma)
Too Tired
Mary Chapin Carpenter; *State Of The Heart* . . . .(Columbia)
Tossin' & Turnin'
Bobby Lewis; *21 Oldies But Goodies-C* . . . . (Original Sound)
Billboard Top Rock 'N' Roll Hits-1961-C . . . .(Rhino)
Collectables Presents The History Of Rock-#6-C . . . .(Collectables)
Cruisin'-1961-C . . . .(Increase)
Tranquillo (Melt My Heart)
Carly Simon; *Boys In The Trees* . . . . (Elektra)
Travelin' Man
Lynyrd Skynyrd; *Live From Steel Town* . . . . (CMC Int'l)
One More From The Road. . . . . (MCA)
Try Counting Sheep
Black Sheep; *A Wolf In Sheep's Clothing*. . . . . (Mercury)
Trying To Sleep Tonight
Clarence Carter; *Hooked On Love* . . . .(Ichiban Int'l)
The Dr.'s Greatest Prescriptions-Best Of Clarence Carter . . . . . (Ichiban Int'l)
Tuck Me In
Kimberly Scott; *Kimberly Scott* . . . . (Columbia)
Tuck Me To Sleep In My Old Kentucky Home
Firehouse Five Plus Two; *Goes South* . . . . (Good Time Jazz)
TV Snooze
Nina Hagen; *Fearless*. . . . .(Columbia)
Two Sleepy People
Art Garfunkel; *Up 'Til Now* . . . .(Columbia)
Fats Waller; *Fats Waller-Masterpieces-#3* . . . . (EPM)
Jo Sullivan Loesser & Others; *Loesser By Loesser* . . . . (DRG)

Kay Kyser & His Orchestra; *Best Of The Big Bands-C* . . . . (Columbia)
Until It Sleeps
Metallica; *Load*. . . . . (Elektra)
Wake Me Up Before You Go Go
Wham! Featuring George Michael; *Billboard Top Hits-1984-C* . . . . . . (Rhino)
Make It Big. . . . . (Columbia)
ST/Zoolander. . . . . (Hollywood)
Wake Me When It's Over
Willie Nelson; *Best Of Willie Nelson* . . . . (Capitol)
Island In The Sea . . . . (Columbia)
Sweet Memories . . . . (RCA)
Sweet Memories . . . . (RCA)
Wake The World
Beach Boys; *Concert/'69-Live In London* . . . . (Capitol)
Friends-20/20 . . . . (Capitol)
Wake Up & Live
Bob Marley & The Wailers; *Survival* . . . . (Tuff Gong)
Wake Up & Live
Cab Calloway; *Best Of The Big Bands-C* . . . . (Columbia)
Wake Up & Make Love To Me
Ian Dury; *New Boots & Panties* . . . . (Stiff)
Stiff Live . . . . (Stiff)
Wake Up & Smell The Coffee
Killbilly; *Stranger In This Place* . . . . (Flying Fish)
Wake Up Dreaming
Little Feat; *Down On The Farm* . . . . (Warner Bros.)
Wake Up Everybody
Harold Melvin And The Blue Notes; *Harold Melvin And The Blue Notes-
Collector's Item* . . . . (Philadelphia Int'l)
Wake Up Everybody. . . . . (Philadelphia Int'l)
Wake Up Little Susie
Everly Brothers; *All They Had To Do Was Dream* . . . . (Rhino)
American Graffiti-#3-C . . . . (MCA)
Everly Brothers . . . . (Rhino)
Everly Brothers' All-Time Greatest Hits . . . . (Curb)
Oldies But Goodies-#7-C . . . . (Original Sound)
Very Best Of The Everly Brothers . . . . (Warner Bros.)
Grateful Dead; *History Of The Grateful Dead-Vol. 1 (Bear's
Choice)* . . . . (Warner Bros.)
Simon & Garfunkel; *The Concert In Central Park* . . . . (Warner Bros.)
Wake Up Morning
Rex Allen, Jr.; *Country Comfort* . . . . (Plantation)
Today's Generation . . . . (SSS International)
Wake Up Sunshine
Chicago; *Chicago II* . . . . (Chicago)
Wake Up Susan
Spinners; *Happiness Is Being With The Detroit Spinners* . . . . (Atlantic)
One Of A Kind Love Affair-Anthology . . . . (Rhino)
Walk Softly
Billy "Crash" Craddock; *Billy "Crash" Craddock Live* . . . . (MCA)
Billy "Crash" Craddock Sings His Greatest Hits . . . . (MCA)
Easy As Pie . . . . (MCA)
Walkin' The Floor Over You
Asleep At The Wheel; *Western Standard Time* . . . . (Epic)
Ernest Tubb; *Legend & The Legacy* . . . . (First Generation)
The Ernest Tubb Story . . . . (MCA)
Ernest Tubb/Merle Haggard/Charlie Daniels; *Ernest Tubb
Collection-C* . . . . (Step One)
Sandy Denny; *Who Knows Where The Time Goes* . . . . (Hannibal)
Webb Pierce; *Webb Pierce-Golden Hits*. . . . . (Plantation)
We All Sleep Alone
Cher; *Cher* . . . . (Geffen)
We Should Be Sleeping
Eddie Money; *Can't Hold Back* . . . . (Columbia)
Eddie Money's Greatest Hits-Sound Of Money . . . . (Columbia)
When It's Sleepy Time Down South
Billie Holiday; *Last Recordings* . . . . (Verve)
Dizzy Gillespie; *20 Golden Pieces Of Dizzy Gillespie* . . . . (Bulldog)
Louis Armstrong; *At The Crescendo*. . . . . (MCA)
Best Of Louis Armstrong . . . . (MCA)
Best Of The Decca Years-#1-Hits!-C. . . . . (Decca)
Essential Louis Armstrong . . . . (Vanguard)
I Like Jazz-Essence Of Louis Armstrong . . . . (Columbia)
Louis Armstrong's Greatest Hits . . . . (Legacy)
Satchmo-Musical Autobiography . . . . (MCA)
Mel Torme; *Mel Torme*. . . . . (Glendale)
Wynton Marsalis; *Standard Time-#2-Intimacy Calling* . . . . (Columbia)
When The Children Are Asleep
Original Broadway Cast; *Carousel* . . . . (Angel)
Original Cast; *Carousel* . . . . (MCA)
When You Awake
Band; *The Band* . . . . (Capitol)
Bob Dylan And The Band; *Before The Flood* . . . . (Columbia)
Who's Been Sleeping Here
Rolling Stones; *Between The Buttons* . . . . (Abkco)
Who's Been Sleeping In My Bed
Melanie; *Am I Real Or What*. . . . . (Amherst)
Wimoweh (Mbube)-The Lion Sleeps Tonight
Chet Atkins; *RCA Years* . . . . (RCA)

Kingston Trio; *Kingston Trio/From The Hungry i* . . . . (Capitol)
Nylons; *Seamless* . . . . (Open Air)
Pete Seeger; *Pete Seeger's Greatest Hits* . . . . (Columbia)
Tokens; *Billboard Top Rock 'N' Roll Hits-1961-C* . . . . (Rhino)
Nipper's Greatest Hits Of The '60s-#1-C. . . . . (RCA)
Weavers; *Weavers' Greatest Hits* . . . . (Vanguard)
Woke Up In Love
Exile; *Exile* . . . . (Epic)
Exile's Greatest Hits . . . . (Epic)
Woke Up This Morning
A3; *Exile On Coldharbour Lane* . . . . (C2/Columbia)
*The Sopranos-Music From The HBO Original
Series*. . . . . (Sony Music Soundtrax)
Woke Up With A Monster
Cheap Trick; *Woke Up With A Monster*. . . . . (Warner Bros.)
You Can Close Your Eyes
James Taylor; *Mud Slide Slim And The Blue Horizon* . . . . (Warner Bros.)
Linda Ronstadt; *Heart Like A Wheel*. . . . . (Capitol)

SMALL, Things Of Small Size

See Also: BIG, BITS & PIECES, LITTLE (little in amount)

36 Inches High
Nick Lowe; *Pure Pop For Now People* . . . . (Columbia)
All The Small Things
Blink-182; *Enema Of The State* . . . . (MCA)
Now That's What I Call Music!-#4-C . . . . (Virgin)
Any Little Fish
Bobby Short; *Bobby Noel & Cole* . . . . (Atlantic)
Be My Baby
Linda Ronstadt; *Dedicated To The One I Love* . . . . (Elektra)
Melissa Etheridge; *Concert For The Rock & Roll Hall Of Fame-C*. . . (Columbia)
Ronettes; *Best Of The Ronettes* . . . . (Abkco)
Phil Spector-Back To Mono 1958-1969-C . . . . (Abkco)
ST/Dirty Dancing . . . . (RCA)
Be My Little Bumble Bee
Jonathan & Darlene Edwards; *Jonathan & Darlene Edwards'
Greatest Hits* . . . . (Corinthian)
Big Dreams In A Small Town
Restless Heart; *Big Dreams In A Small Town* . . . . (RCA)
Big Fish, Little Fish
Original Broadway Cast; *Purlie* . . . . (RCA)
Bonnie Jean (Little Sister)
David Lynn Jones; *Best Of Country Rock-C* . . . . (K-Tel)
Hard Times On Easy Street . . . . (Mercury)
Circle Is Small
Gordon Lightfoot; *Back Here On Earth* . . . . (United Artists)
Endless Wire . . . . (Warner Bros.)
Claudette
Dwight Yoakam; *Under The Covers* . . . . (Reprise)
Everly Brothers; *Everly Brothers' Greatest Hits*. . . . . (Delta)
Everly Brothers-Cadence Classics-Their 20 Greatest Hits . . . . (Rhino)
Roy Orbison; *Roy Orbison-The Sun Years* . . . . (Rhino)
Very Best Of Roy Orbison. . . . . (Virgin)
Crazy Little Mama
Eldorados; *Greatest Groups Of The '50s-#2-C* . . . . (Collectables)
Sock Hop-C . . . . (Dunhill Compact Classics)
Crazy Little Thing Called Love
Dwight Yoakam; *Last Chance For A Thousand Years-Greatest Hits From
The '90s*. . . . . (Reprise)
Queen; *Queen's Greatest Hits I & II* . . . . (Hollywood)
The Game . . . . (Hollywood)
Cruel Little Number
Jeff Healey Band; *Feel This* . . . . (Arista)
Cut Across Shorty
Eddie Cochran; *Eddie Cochran-Legendary Masters*. . . . . (EMI)
Rod Stewart; *Best Of Rod Stewart* . . . . (Mercury)
Faces Live . . . . (Mercury)
Gasoline Alley . . . . (Mercury)
Storyteller/The Complete Anthology: 1964-1990. . . . . (Warner Bros.)
Unplugged...And Seated . . . . (Warner Bros.)
Vintage Rod Stewart . . . . (Mercury)
Daddy's Little Boy
Mills Brothers; *45-#60098* . . . . (MCA)
Daddy's Little Girl
Al Martino; *Best Of Al Martino* . . . . (Capitol)
Mills Brothers; *50th Anniversary* . . . . (Ranwood)
All Occasions Album . . . . (Gateway)
Best Of The Mills Brothers . . . . (MCA)
The Mills Brothers Story. . . . . (Ranwood)
Daddy's Little Girl
Nikki D; *1st Ladies Of Rap-C* . . . . (K-Tel)
Dance Little Jean
Nitty Gritty Dirt Band; *Let's Go* . . . . (Warner Bros.)
Twenty Years Of Dirt-Best Of The Nitty Gritty Dirt Band . . . . . (Warner Bros.)
Dance Little Sister
Rolling Stones; *It's Only Rock 'N Roll* . . . . (Rolling Stones)

Made In The Shade . . . . (Rolling Stones)

Dance Little Sister
Terence Trent D'Arby; *Introducing The Hardline According To Terence Trent D'Arby* . . . . (Columbia)

Dance On Little Girl
Paul Anka; *Best Of Paul Anka* . . . . (Rhino)
Paul Anka Sings His Big 15, Vol. 2 . . . . (RCA)
Paul Anka-30th Anniversary Anthology . . . . (Rhino)
Paul Anka's 21 Golden Hits . . . . (RCA)
She's A Lady . . . . (RCA)

Davy's Dinghy
Ruth Wallis; *Dr. Demento Presents The Greatest Novelty Records-#2-1950s-C* . . . . (Rhino)
Dr. Demento's Dementia Royale-C . . . . (Rhino)

Dirty Little Girl
Elton John; *Goodbye Yellow Brick Road* . . . . (Polydor)

Dream A Little Dream Of Me
Ella Fitzgerald; *All That Jazz* . . . . (Pablo)
Mama Cass; *Mama's Big Ones-Her Greatest Hits* . . . . (MCA)
Mama Cass With The Mamas & The Papas; *Best Of The Mamas & The Papas* . . . . (MCA)
Mamas & The Papas-20 Golden Hits . . . . (MCA)
Wayne King & His Orchestra; *78-#22643* . . . . (Victor)

Every Little Girl's Dream
Lisa Brokop; *Every Little Girl's Dream* . . . . (Patriot)

Every Little Kiss
Bruce Hornsby & The Range; *The Way It Is* . . . . (RCA)

Every Little Step
Bobby Brown; *Dance!...Ya Know It!* . . . . (MCA)
Don't Be Cruel . . . . (MCA)

Every Little Thing
Beatles; *Beatles VI.* . . . . (Capitol)
Beatles-Love Songs . . . . (Capitol)
For Sale . . . . (Capitol)

Every Little Thing
Carlene Carter; *Little Love Letters* . . . . (Giant)

Every Little Thing
Yes; *Yes* . . . . (Atlantic)
Yesyears . . . . (Atco)

Every Little Thing He Does Is Magic
Shawn Colvin; *Cover Girl* . . . . (Columbia)

Every Little Thing I Do
Soul For Real; *100% Party-Hits Of The '90s-#2-C* . . . . (Priority)
Candy Rain . . . . (Uptown/MCA)

Every Little Thing She Does Is Magic
Police; *Every Breath You Take-The Classics* . . . . (A&M)
Ghost In The Machine . . . . (A&M)

Everytime You Go Away
Daryl Hall & John Oates; *Best Of Daryl Hall & John Oates* . . . . . (RCA)
Voices . . . . (RCA)
Paul Young; *From Time To Time-The Singles Collection* . . . (Columbia)
Secret Of Association . . . . (Columbia)
T.J. Martell-Music For The Miracle-C . . . . (Epic Portrait Assoc.)

Foolish Little Girl
Shirelles; *Shirelles' Greatest Hits* . . . . (Everest)
Shirelles-16 Greatest Hits. . . . . (Trip)
Shirelles-Anthology 1959-1964 . . . . (Rhino)

Frogs With Dirty Little Lips
Frank Zappa; *Them Or Us* . . . . (Rykodisc)

Get A Little Closer
Ricky Lynn Gregg; *Get A Little Closer* . . . . (Liberty)

Get Along Little Dogies
Riders In The Sky; *Saddle Pals* . . . . (Rounder)
Tex Ritter; *Tex Ritter: Country Music Hall Of Fame* . . . . . . (MCA Special Prod.)

Gimme Little Sign
Brenton Wood; *18 Best-Brenton Wood* . . . . (Original Sound)
Collectables Presents The History Of Rock-#7-C . . . . . (Collectables)
Cruisin'-1957-C . . . . (Increase)
Soul Shots-#3-Soul Twist-C . . . . (Rhino)

Go Away Little Girl
Happenings; *The Ultimate History Of Rock 'N' Roll-#6-C* . . . (K-Tel)
Steve Lawrence; *Steve Lawrence's Greatest Hits* . . . . (Columbia)

Good Morning Little School Girl
Grateful Dead; *Grateful Dead (Skull & Roses)* . . . . . (Warner Bros.)
Huey Lewis and the News; *Four Chords & Several Years Ago* . . . . . . (Elektra)
Johnny Winter; *Johnny Winter* . . . . (Columbia)
Live/Johnny Winter And . . . . (Columbia)
Ten Years After; *Classic Performances Of Ten Years After* . . . (Columbia)
Recorded Live . . . . (Columbia)
SSSSH . . . . (Chrysalis)
Universal . . . . (Chrysalis)
Yardbirds; *Eric Clapton-Crossroads-C* . . . . (Polydor)
Five Live Yardbirds . . . . (Rhino)

Hands
Jewel; *Spirit* . . . . (Atlantic)

Happy Birthday To Little Sally Spingel Spungel Sporn
Dr. Seuss; *The Cat In The Hat Songbook* . . . . (RCA Special Prod.)

Hello Little Friend
Joe Cocker; *Joe Cocker!* . . . . (A&M)

Hello Little Girl
Beatles; *The Beatles-Anthology-#1* . . . . (Capitol)

Hey Little Bird
Buffy Sainte-Marie; *Best Of Buffy Sainte-Marie-#2* . . . . (Vanguard)
Fire & Fleet & Candlelight . . . . (Vanguard)

Hey Little Cobra
Rip Chords; *Beach Classics-All Original Recordings-C* . . . . (Dunhill Compact Classics)
Rock Classics Of The '60s-C . . . . (Columbia)

Hey Little Girl
Professor Longhair; *Atlantic Rhythm & Blues 1947-1974-#1 (1947-1952)-C* . . . . (Atlantic)
New Orleans Piano-Blues Originals-#2 . . . . (Atlantic)

Hey Little Girl
Icehouse; *Primitive Man* . . . . (Chrysalis)

Hey Little Girl
Dee Clark; *Jukebox Classics-#1-C* . . . . (Rhino)
Super Oldies Of The '50s-#2-C . . . . (Audio Fidelity)

Hey Little Minivan
Austin Lounge Lizards; *Employee Of The Month* . . . . (Sugar Hill)

Hey Little One
Dorsey Burnette; *American Graffiti-#3-C* . . . . (MCA)
Glen Campbell; *Glen Campbell-Classics Collection* . . . . (Capitol)
Very Best Of Glen Campbell . . . . (Capitol)

Honey Bun
Original Cast; *South Pacific* . . . . (CBS Masterworks)

I Buyed Me A Little Dog
Dave Van Ronk; *Van Ronk* . . . . (Fantasy)

I Say A Little Prayer
Aretha Franklin; *Aretha Franklin's Greatest Hits* . . . . (Atlantic)
Aretha's Gold . . . . (Atlantic)
Best Of Aretha Franklin . . . . (Atlantic)
Burt Bacharach; *Burt Bacharach-Classics-#23* . . . . (A&M)
Burt Bacharach's Greatest Hits . . . . (A&M)
Reach Out . . . . (A&M)
Diana King; *ST/My Best Friend's Wedding* . . . . (Work/Epic)
Dionne Warwick; *Dionne Warwick* . . . . (Everest)
Dionne Warwick Greatest Hits . . . . (Everest)
Dionne Warwick-Anthology 1962-1971 . . . . (Rhino)
Original Rock 'N' Roll Hits Of The '60s-C . . . . (Roulette)

I Wanna Marry You
Bruce Springsteen; *The River* . . . . (Columbia)

I Want A Little Girl
Big Joe Turner; *Atlantic Jazz-Singers-C* . . . . (Atlantic)
Ray Charles; *Life In Music* . . . . (Atlantic)

I'm A Little Dinosaur
Jonathan Richman & The Modern Lovers; *Beserkley Years-Best Of* . . . . (Rhino)

I'm A Little Liar
Kings; *45-#1019.* . . . . (Collectables)

I'm In Love With My Little Red Tricycle
Napoleon XIV; *The Second Coming* . . . . (Rhino)

In A Little Spanish Town
Ray Charles; *Ray Charles-Live* . . . . (Atlantic)

In A Small Moment
Carly Simon; *Boys In The Trees* . . . . (Elektra)

In The Wee Small Hours Of The Morning
Frank Sinatra; *In The Wee Small Hours* . . . . (Capitol)
Sinatra: A Man And His Music . . . . (Reprise)
Sinatra's Sinatra . . . . (Reprise)
The Capitol Years . . . . (Capitol)

It's A Small World
Various Artists; *Disney's Theme Park Sing-Along* . . . . (Disney)

It's Such A Small World
Rodney Crowell & Rosanne Cash; *Dynamic Duets-Super Hits-C* . . . (Columbia)
Rodney Crowell-Super Hits. . . . . (Columbia)

Itsy Bitsy Spider, The
Original Soundtrack; *Mother Goose Songs* . . . . (Madacy)

Itsy Bitsy Teenie Weenie Yellow Polkadot Bikini
Brian Hyland; *Brian Hyland's Greatest Hits* . . . . (Rhino)
Dr. Demento Presents The Greatest Novelty Records-#3-1960s-C. . . . (Rhino)
Vintage Music-#5-C . . . . (MCA)

I've Got A Secret Miniature Camera
Peter Murphy; *ST/Pump Up The Volume* . . . . (MCA)

I've Told Ev'ry Little Star
David Allyn; *David Allyn Sings Jerome Kern* . . . . (Discovery)
Linda Scott; *Billboard Top Pop Hits-1961-C* . . . . (Rhino)

Just A Little Talk With Jesus
Elvis Presley; *Million-Dollar Quartet* . . . . (RCA)

Li'l Red Riding Hood
Sam The Sham and The Pharaohs; *Best Of Sam The Sham and The Pharaohs* . . . . (Polydor)
Cruisin'-1966-C . . . . (Increase)
Pharaohization! (Best Of) . . . . (Rhino)

Little America
R.E.M.; *Reckoning.* . . . . (I.R.S.)

Little Arrows
Leapy Lee; *Bubble Gum Classics-C.* . . . . (MCA Special Prod.)
Country Music Classics-#3-1965-1970-C. . . . . (K-Tel)

Little Band Of Gold
Sonny James; *American Originals-Sonny James* . . . . (Columbia)
   Little Bit South Of Saskatoon . . . . (Columbia)
   Sonny James' Greatest Hits . . . . (Columbia)
Little Beggar Man
Ian & Sylvia; *Ian & Sylvia's Greatest Hits* . . . . (Vanguard)
   Northern Journey. . . . . (Vanguard)
Little Bird
Jerry Jeff Walker; *Mr. Bojangles* . . . . (Bainbridge)
   Viva Terlingua. . . . . (MCA)
Little Bird
Sherrie Austin; *Love In The Real World* . . . . (Arista)
Little Bird
Beach Boys; *Friends-20/20* . . . . (Capitol)
Little Bird, Little Bird
Original London Cast; *Man Of La Mancha* . . . . (MCA)
Little Birdie
Stanley Brothers; *Stanley Brothers* . . . . (Melodian)
   Stanley Series-Vol. 2-#1. . . . . (Copper Creek)
Little Birdie
Joe Williams; *Happy Anniversary Charlie Brown!-C* . . . . (GRP)
Little Bits & Pieces
Jim Stafford; *45-#04339.* . . . . (Columbia)
Little Bitty
Alan Jackson; *Everything I Love.* . . . . (Arista)
Tom T. Hall; *Songs From Sopchoppy* . . . . (Mercury)
   Tom T. Hall-The Hits . . . . (Mercury)
Little Bitty Pretty One
Huey Lewis and the News; *Four Chords & Several Years Ago* . . . . (Elektra)
Jackson 5; *Jackson 5-16 Greatest Hits* . . . . (Motown)
   Jackson 5-Anthology . . . . (Motown)
   Lookin' Through The Windows . . . . (Motown)
   Motown Legends-Jackson 5 . . . . (Motown)
   Top 10 With A Bullet-Motown Male Groups-C . . . . (Motown)
Thurston Harris; *Billboard Top R&B Hits-1957-C* . . . . (Rhino)
   Collectables Presents The History Of Rock-#2-C . . . . (Collectables)
Little Bitty Tear
Burl Ives; *Best Of Burl Ives-#2* . . . . (MCA)
   Burl Ives Live. . . . . (MCA)
   MCA Records 30 Years Of Hits-1958-1988-C . . . . (MCA)
Hank Cochran; *45-#47062* . . . . (Elektra)
Little Black Backpack
Stroke9; *Nasty Little Thoughts* . . . . (Cherry/Universal)
Little Black Book
Jimmy Dean; *American Originals-Jimmy Dean* . . . . (Columbia)
   Jimmy Dean's Greatest Hits . . . . (Columbia)
Little Blue Man
Betty Johnson; *45-#13146* . . . . (Atlantic)
Little Blue Whale
Country Joe McDonald; *Goodbye Blues.* . . . . (Fantasy)
Little Boxes
Malvina Reynolds; *Best Of Broadside 1962-1968: Anthems Of The*
   American Underground From The Pages Of Broadside
   Magazine-C . . . . (Smithsonian Folkways)
   Folk Classics: Roots Of American Folk Music-C. . . . . (Columbia)
Pete Seeger; *Pete Seeger's Greatest Hits* . . . . (Columbia)
Little Boy Blue
Elegants; *Best Of The Elegants.* . . . . (Collectables)
Little Boy Sad
Johnny Burnette; *Best Of Johnny Burnette-You're Sixteen.* . . . . . . (Gold Rush)
Little Brown Bird
Elvin Bishop; *Live! Raisin' Hell.* . . . . (Capricorn)
Little Brown Dog
Judy Collins; *Golden Apples Of The Sun* . . . . (Elektra)
Little Brown Jug
Glenn Miller; *Best Of Glenn Miller* . . . . (RCA)
   Glenn Miller-A Legendary Performer-#1 & 2 . . . . (Bluebird)
   The Glenn Miller Story. . . . . (RCA)
Glenn Miller & His Orchestra; *Glenn Miller & His Orchestra-*
   Pure Gold . . . . (Bluebird)
   The Unforgettable Glenn Miller & His Orchestra . . . . (RCA)
Little Chicago Fire
Count Basie & His Orchestra; *Live At El Morocco* . . . . (Telarc)
Little Child
Beatles; *Meet The Beatles!* . . . . (Capitol)
Little Children
Billy J. Kramer With The Dakotas; *History Of British Rock-#1-C* . . . . . (Rhino)
Little Criminals
Randy Newman; *Little Criminals* . . . . (Warner Bros.)
Little Darlin'
Diamonds; *Best Of The Diamonds* . . . . (Rhino)
   Billboard Top Rock 'N' Roll Hits-1957-C . . . . (Rhino)
   Cruisin'-1957-C . . . . (Increase)
   Good Time Rock 'N' Roll-C. . . . . (Rhino)
   Oldies But Goodies-#11-C. . . . . (Original Sound)
   ST/American Graffiti . . . . (MCA)
Little Darlin' (I Need You)
Doobie Brothers; *Livin' On The Fault Line* . . . . (Warner Bros.)

Marvin Gaye; *Marvin Gaye Live At The London Palladium* . . . . (Motown)
   Marvin Gaye-Anthology. . . . . (Motown)
   Motown Legends-Marvin Gaye . . . . (Motown)
   Musical Testament 1964-1984 . . . . (Motown)
Little Deuce Coupe
Beach Boys; *Best Of The Beach Boys* . . . . (Capitol)
   Concert/'69-Live In London . . . . (Capitol)
   Endless Summer . . . . (Capitol)
   Good Vibrations-Thirty Years Of The Beach Boys . . . . (Capitol)
   Summer Means Fun-California Surf Music-C . . . . (Capitol)
Little Diane
Dion; *Dion-24 Original Classics.* . . . . (Arista)
Dion And The Belmonts; *Everything You Always Wanted To Hear By.* . .(Laurie)
   Reunion-Live At Madison Square Garden 1972 . . . . (Rhino)
Little Dreamer
Van Halen; *Van Halen.* . . . . (Warner Bros.)
Little Dutch Girl
George Morgan; *American Originals-George Morgan.* . . . . (Columbia)
Little Dutch Mill
Bing Crosby; *Crooner-Columbia Years-1928-1934* . . . . (Columbia)
Little Dutch Town
Mac Davis; *Mac Davis With Love.* . . . . (Accord)
   Volume XC . . . . (Allegiance)
Little Earthquakes
Tori Amos; *Little Earthquakes* . . . . (Atlantic)
Little Egypt
Coasters; *Atlantic Rhythm & Blues 1947-1974-#4 (1958-1962)-C* . . . .(Atlantic)
   Coasters-Their Greatest Recordings-Early Years . . . . (Atco)
Elvis Presley; *Elvis Presley Sings Leiber & Stoller* . . . . (RCA)
Little Fighter
White Lion; *Big Game.* . . . . (Atlantic)
Little Girl
Monkees; *Monkee Flips* . . . . (Rhino)
   Present . . . . (Rhino)
Little Girl
Ritchie Valens; *Best Of Ritchie Valens* . . . . (Rhino)
   History Of Ritchie Valens. . . . . (Rhino)
Little Girl
Steve Miller Band; *Steve Miller Band-Anthology* . . . . (Capitol)
   Your Saving Grace . . . . (Capitol)
Little Girl
Reba McEntire; *Sweet Sixteen.* . . . . (MCA)
Little Girl Blue
Ella Fitzgerald; *Rodgers & Hart Songbook.* . . . . (Verve)
Little Girl From Little Rock
Original Cast; *Gentlemen Prefer Blondes* . . . . (Sony Music Special Prod.)
Little Girl Of Mine
Cleftones; *Original Rock 'N' Roll Hits Of The '50s-C* . . . . (Roulette)
Dion; *Bronx Blues-Columbia Recordings 1962-1965* . . . . (Columbia)
Little Girl, The
John Michael Montgomery; *Brand New Me* . . . .(Atlantic)
   Totally Hits-#3-C . . . .(Atlantic)
Little Girls
Original Broadway Cast; *Annie* . . . . (Columbia)
Little Girls
Patti LaBelle; *Best Of Patti LaBelle* . . . . (Epic)
Little Girls, Goodbye
John Charles Thomas; *Music From The New York Stage (1890-1920)-#4-*
   1917-1920-C. . . . . (Pearl)
Little Good-byes
SHeDAISY; *The Whole Shebang* . . . .(Lyric Street)
Little Green
Joni Mitchell; *Blue* . . . . (Reprise)
Little Green Apples
O.C. Smith; *Pop Classics Of The '60s-C* . . . . (Columbia)
Little Green Valley
Marty Robbins; *Gunfighter Ballads & Trail Songs* . . . . (Legacy)
Little Ground In Texas
Capitals; *45-#01080* . . . .(Ridgetop)
Little Guitars
Van Halen; *Diver Down* . . . . (Warner Bros.)
Little Hitler
Nick Lowe; *Pure Pop For Now People* . . . . (Columbia)
Little Hollywood Girl
Crickets; *Liberty Years* . . . . (EMI)
Little Home In Tennessee
Bill Harrell & The Virginians; *Ballads & Bluegrass* . . . .(Adelphi)
Mac Wiseman; *Classic Bluegrass-Mac Wiseman* . . . . (Rebel)
Little Home In West Virginia
Josh Graves; *King Of The Dobro.* . . . . (C.M.H. Prod.)
Little Honda
Beach Boys; *Absolute Best-#1.* . . . . (Capitol)
   All Summer Long . . . . (Capitol)
   Best Of The Beach Boys . . . . (Capitol)
   Spirit Of America . . . . (Capitol)
Hondells; *Beach Classics-All Original*
   Recordings-C. . . . . (Dunhill Compact Classics)
   Cruisin'-1964-C. . . . . (Increase)

Little Hotel Room
Merle Haggard; *Friendship*-C . . . .(Columbia)
It's All In The Game . . . . (Epic)
Little Houses
Doug Stone; *Doug Stone G.H.* . . . . (Epic)
Little Jeannie
Elton John; *21 At 33* . . . . (Polydor)
Elton John's Greatest Hits-1976-1986 . . . . (MCA)
Little Joe From Chicago
Mary Lou Williams; *Best Of Mary Lou Williams* . . . . (Pablo)
Nat "King" Cole; *Straighten Up And Fly Right* . . . .(Pro-Arte)
Little Joe The Wrangler
Goebel Reeves; *Songs Of Old West* . . . .(Glendale)
Texas Drifter . . . .(Glendale)
Little Joe The Wrangler's Sister Nell
Skip Gorman; *A Cowboy's Wild Song To His Herd* . . . . (Rounder)
Little John Of God
Los Lobos; *The Neighborhood* . . . . (Slash)
Little Lady Preacher
Tom T. Hall; *Tom T. Hall's Greatest Hits-#2* . . . . (Mercury)
Little Lamb
Original Cast; *Gypsy* . . . . (Columbia)
Little Latin Lupe Lu
Mitch Ryder And The Detroit Wheels; *Mitch Ryder And The Detroit Wheels'*
Greatest Hits . . . . (Roulette)
Rev Up-Best Of Mitch Ryder . . . . (Rhino)
Righteous Brothers; *Righteous Brothers-Anthology 1962-1974* . . . (Rhino)
Little Lies
Fleetwood Mac; *Fleetwood Mac's Greatest Hits* . . . . (Warner Bros.)
Tango In The Night . . . . (Warner Bros.)
Little London Boys
Johnny Thunders; *Stations Of The Cross* . . . . (Roir)
Little Maggie
Kingston Trio; *Tom Dooley* . . . . (Capitol)
Ricky Skaggs and Kentucky Thunder; *Bluegrass Rules!* . . . .(Rounder)
Little Mama
Clovers; *Down In The Alley* . . . . (Rhino)
Little Man
Alan Jackson; *High Mileage* . . . . (Arista)
Little Marie
Chuck Berry; *Rock 'N' Roll Rarities-20 Magic Tracks* . . . . (Chess)
St. Louis To Liverpool . . . . (Chess)
The Chess Box-Chuck Berry . . . . (Chess)
Little Martha
Allman Brothers Band; *Best Of The Allman Brothers Band* . . . . (Polydor)
Decade Of Hits-1969-1979 . . . . (Polydor)
Eat A Peach . . . . (Polydor)
Little Miss Can't Be Wrong
Spin Doctors; *Homebelly Groove* . . . . (Epic Portrait Assoc.)
Pocket Full Of Kryptonite . . . . (Epic Portrait Assoc.)
Up For Grabs...Live . . . . (Epic Portrait Assoc.)
Little Miss Honky Tonk
Brooks & Dunn; *Waitin' On Sundown* . . . . (Arista)
Little Miss Love
Eldorados; *45-#1451* . . . . (Collectables)
Little Miss Lover
Jimi Hendrix; *Axis: Bold As Love* . . . . (Reprise)
Essential Jimi Hendrix . . . . (Reprise)
Little Miss Magic
Jimmy Buffett; *Boats Beaches Bars & Ballads* . . . . (Margaritaville)
Coconut Telegraph . . . . (MCA)
Little Miss Strange
Jimi Hendrix Experience; *Electric Ladyland* . . . . (Reprise)
Little Old Church In England
Glenn Miller & His Orchestra; *Complete Glenn Miller & His*
Orchestra . . . . (Bluebird)
Little Old Lady (From Pasadena)
Beach Boys; *Concert/'69-Live In London* . . . . (Capitol)
Jan & Dean; *Best Of Jan & Dean* . . . . (EMI)
Billboard Top Rock 'N' Roll Hits-1964-C . . . . (Rhino)
Dead Man's Curve . . . . (EMI)
Surf City-Best Of Jan & Dean . . . . (EMI)
Little Old Wine Drinker Me
Dean Martin; *Dean Martin's Greatest Hits-#2* . . . . (Reprise)
Welcome To My World . . . . (Reprise)
Mel Tillis; *Best Of Mel Tillis* . . . . (MCA)
Little One
Chicago; *Chicago XI* . . . . (Chicago)
Take Me Back To Chicago . . . . (Columbia)
Little Pad
Beach Boys; *Smiley Smile/Wild Honey* . . . . (Capitol)
Little Pal
Jimmy Roselli; *Daddy's Little Girl* . . . . (M&R)
Rock-A-Bye Your Baby . . . . (M&R)
Sold Out-Carnegie Hall Concert . . . . (M&R)
Little Paper Boy
Hank Williams; *Rare Takes & Radio Cuts* . . . . (Polydor)
Little Paradise
Pat Benatar; *Crimes Of Passion* . . . . (Chrysalis)

Little Plastic Castle
Ani DiFranco; *Little Plastic Castle* . . . . (Righteous Babe)
Little Priest
Original Cast; *Sweeney Todd* . . . . (RCA)
Little Queen
Heart; *Little Queen* . . . .(Portrait)
Little Queenie
Chuck Berry; *Rock & Roll Rarities* . . . .(Chess)
The Chess Box-Chuck Berry . . . .(Chess)
Jerry Lee Lewis; *Jerry Lee Lewis-Original Golden Hits-#1* . . . . (Sun)
Rockin' R&B-C . . . . (Sun)
REO Speedwagon; *REO Speedwagon Live/You Get What You Play For*. . .(Epic)
Rolling Stones; *Get Yer Ya-Ya's Out!* . . . . (Abkco)
Little Rachel
Eric Clapton; *There's One In Every Crowd* . . . . (Polydor)
Little Red Corvette
Prince; *1999* . . . . (Warner Bros.)
Little Red Hen
Johnny Otis; *Original Johnny Otis Show* . . . .(Savoy)
Little Red Lights
Todd Rundgren; *Something/Anything?* . . . . (Rhino)
Little Red Rodeo
Collin Raye; *Best Of Collin Raye-Direct Hits* . . . . (Epic)
Little Red Rooster
B.B. King/Muddy Waters/Big Mama Thornton; *Live At Newport* . . . (Intermedia)
Big Mama Thornton; *Jail*. . . . .(Vanguard)
Rolling Stones; *Love You Live* . . . . (Virgin)
The Rolling Stones, Now! . . . . (Abkco)
Sam Cooke; *Having A Party* . . . . (RCA)
This Is Sam Cooke . . . . (RCA)
Little Rock
Reba McEntire; *Whoever's In New England* . . . . (MCA)
Woman To Woman-#2-C . . . . (MCA)
Little Sadie
Bob Dylan; *Self Portrait*. . . . .(Columbia)
Little Sally Tease
Standells; *Best Of The Standells*. . . . .(Rhino)
Little Sally, The Super Sex Star
Camille Yarborough; *Iron Pot Cooker*. . . . .(Vanguard)
Little Shoe Maker
Eddie Fisher; *Very Best Of Eddie Fisher* . . . .(Taragon)
Gaylords; *Choice Voices! Pop Vocal Group Gems Of The*
'50s-C . . . .(Collector's Choice)
Little Sister
Elvis Presley; *Elvis' Golden Records, Volume 3* . . . . (RCA)
Elvis In Concert. . . . . (RCA)
I Was The One . . . . (RCA)
The Top Ten Hits . . . . (RCA)
Worldwide 50 Gold Award Hits, Vol. 1, Parts 1 & 2 . . . . (RCA)
Little Spain
Lee Morgan Quintet; *Take Twelve* . . . .(Jazz Land)
Little Star
Elegants; *Billboard Top Rock 'N' Roll Hits-1958*-C . . . .(Rhino)
Oldies But Goodies-#5-C . . . . (Original Sound)
Super Oldies Of The '50s-#7-C . . . . (Audio Fidelity)
Little Street Where Old Friends Meet, A
Tony Bennett; *I Left My Heart In San Francisco* . . . .(Columbia)
Little Superstar
Sheryl Crow; *Sheryl Crow* . . . . (A&M)
Little Things
Bobby Goldsboro; *Bobby Goldsboro's All-Time Greatest Hits* . . . .(Curb)
Honey-Best Of Bobby Goldsboro . . . . (EMI)
ST/Drugstore Cowboy . . . . (Novus)
Little Things
Bush; *Sixteen Stone* . . . . (Trauma)
Little Things
Boyz II Men; *Cooleyhighharmony*. . . . .(Motown)
Little Things
Willie Nelson; *Best Of Willie* . . . . (RCA)
Little Things
Oak Ridge Boys; *Oak Ridge Boys' Greatest Hits 3* . . . . (MCA)
Step On Out . . . . (MCA)
Little Things Mean A Lot
Kitty Kallen; *Hard To Find 45s On CD-#3-The Mid '50s*-C . . . . (Eric)
McGuire Sisters; *Best Of The McGuire Sisters* . . . . (MCA)
Little Things You Do Together
Original Cast; *Company*. . . . .(Columbia)
Little Tin God
Don Henley; *End Of The Innocence* . . . . (Geffen)
Little Triggers
Elvis Costello; *This Year's Model* . . . .(Rykodisc)
Little Turtle Dove
Bobby Day; *Best Of Bobby Day*. . . . .(Rhino)
Little Victories
Bob Seger & The Silver Bullet Band; *The Distance*. . . . .(Capitol)
Little Wheel
John Lee Hooker; *Best Of John Lee Hooker* . . . .(Crescendo)
Best Of John Lee Hooker. . . . .(Vee-Jay)

John Lee Hooker . . . . (Everest)

Little Wheel Spin & Spin
Buffy Sainte-Marie; *Best Of Buffy Sainte-Marie* . . . . (Vanguard)
Little Wheel Spin & Spin . . . . (Vanguard)
Native North American Child . . . . (Vanguard)

Little White Lie
Sammy Hagar; *Marching To Mars* . . . .(MCA)

Little White Lies
Dick Haymes with Gordon Jenkins & His Orchestra; *Sentimental Journey:*
Pop Vocal Classics-#2-1947-1950-C . . . . (Rhino)
Dinah Shore; *Dinah Shore-16 Most Requested Songs-Encore!* . . . . (Legacy)
Fred Waring's Pennsylvanians featuring Clare Hanlon; *Very Best Of Fred*
Waring & The Pennsylvanians . . . . (Reader's Digest Music)
Tommy Dorsey; *Best Of Tommy Dorsey* . . . . (Bluebird)
Complete Tommy Dorsey-#6 . . . . (RCA)

Little White Lies
Romantics; *The Romantics* . . . . (Columbia)

Little Willie
Sweet; *Best Of The 1910 Fruitgum Company-#2-C* . . . . (Rhino)

Little Willow
Paul McCartney; *Diana, Princess Of Wales-Tribute-C* . . . . (Columbia)

Little Wing
Derek And The Dominos; *Layla* . . . . (Polydor)
Jimi Hendrix; *Axis: Bold As Love* . . . . (Reprise)
Concerts . . . . (Reprise)
Essential Jimi Hendrix . . . . (Reprise)
Lifelines/Jimi Hendrix Story . . . . (Reprise)
Sting; *...Nothing Like The Sun* . . . . (A&M)

Little Woman
Bobby Sherman; *Bobby Sherman's Greatest Hits* . . . . (K-Tel)
Bubblegum Classics-#3-C . . . . (Varese Vintage)

Littlest Cowboy Rides Again
Chris LeDoux; *Songbook Of The American West* . . . . (Liberty)
Sounds Of The Western Country . . . . (Liberty)

Mary Had A Little Lamb
Garth Brooks; *The Magic Of Christmas: Songs From Call Me Claus* . . (Capitol)
Original Soundtrack; *Sesame Street: Kids' Favorite Songs-#2* . . (Sony Wonder)
Stevie Ray Vaughan and Double Trouble; *Live Alive* . . . .(Epic)
Texas Flood . . . .(Epic)
Wings; *Wild Life* . . . . (Capitol)

Me & Little Andy
Dolly Parton; *Collector's Series-Dolly Parton* . . . . (RCA)
Dolly Parton's Greatest Hits . . . . (RCA)
Here You Come Again . . . .(Dunhill Compact Classics)

Mother's Little Helper
Rolling Stones; *Flowers* . . . . (Abkco)
Hot Rocks 1964-1971 . . . . (Abkco)
Through The Past, Darkly (Big Hits Vol. 2) . . . . (Abkco)
Tesla; *Five Man Acoustical Jam* . . . .(Geffen)

Mr. Shorty
Marty Robbins; *The Drifter* . . . . (Koch International)

My Little Ballerina
Brent Mason; *Hot Wired* . . . . (Mercury)

My Little Bimbo
Clancy Hayes & The Salt Dogs; *Oh By Jingo* . . . . (Delmark)

My Little Brown Book
Duke Ellington; *Duke Ellington & John Coltrane* . . . .(MCA/Impulse)
John Coltrane; *The Gentle Side Of John Coltrane* . . . . (GRP)

My Little Friend
Elvis Presley; *Suspicious Minds* . . . . (RCA)

My Little Georgia Rose
David Grisman; *Home Is Where The Heart Is* . . . . (Rounder)
Herb Pederson; *Son Of Rounder Banjo* . . . . (Rounder)

My Little Girl
Crickets; *EMI Legends Of Rock & Roll-24 Greatest Hits-C* . . . . (EMI)
Liberty Years . . . .(EMI)

My Little Girl
Crescendos; *Excello Vocal Groups-C* . . . . (Excello)

My Little Girl
Spike Jones & His City Slickers; *King Of Corn* . . . . (Glendale)

My Little Girl
Roxy Music; *Manifesto* . . . . (Atco)

My Little Girl In Tennessee
Lester Flatt, Earl Scruggs & The Foggy Mountain Boys; *Lester Flatt,*
Earl Scruggs & The Foggy Mountain Boys-Complete Mercury
Sessions . . . . (Mercury)

My Little Grass Shack In Kealakekua, Hawaii
Mom & Dads; *Blue Hawaii* . . . .(Crescendo)

My Little Home Down In New Orleans
Jimmie Rodgers; *Jimmie Rodgers-Early Years-1928-1929* . . . . (Rounder)

My Little Lady
Jimmie Rodgers; *Jimmie Rodgers-Early Years-1928-1929* . . . . (Rounder)
Roy Rogers; *Columbia Historic Edition-Roy Rogers* . . . . (Columbia)

My Little Marine
Jamie Horton; *45-#118* . . . . (Eric)

My Little Miss America
Gary U.S. Bonds; *45-#1034* . . . . (LeGrand)

My Little Red Book
Love; *Best Of Love* . . . . (Rhino)

Elektrock-Sixties-C. . . . . (Elektra)
Nuggets-#2-Punk-C. . . . . (Rhino)

My Little Secret
Xscape; *Traces Of My Lipstick* . . . . (So So Def/Columbia)

My Little Town
Paul Simon; *Still Crazy After All These Years* . . . . (Columbia)

On A Little Street In Singapore
Glenn Miller; *Original Recordings-#4* . . . .(Pair)
Harry James; *Two O'Clock Jump* . . . . (Pro-Arte)
Manhattan Transfer; *Manhattan Transfer-Anthology-Down In*
Birdland. . . . . (Rhino)

One Angry Dwarf And 200 Solemn Faces
Ben Folds Five; *Whatever And Ever Amen* . . . .(Caroline/550)

One Little Coyote
Riders In The Sky; *Harmony Ranch* . . . . (Columbia)

One Small Boat
Altered State; *Altered State* . . . . (Warner Bros.)

One Small Miracle
Bryan White; *The Right Place* . . . .(Asylum)

Piggies
Beatles; *Beatles-Box Set* . . . . (Capitol)
The Beatles (White Album) . . . . (Capitol)
George Harrison; *Live In Japan* . . . .(Dark Horse)

Pink Houses
John Cougar Mellencamp; *Rock For Amnesty-C.* . . . . (Mercury)
Uh-Huh. . . . . (Riva)
John Mellencamp featuring Kid Rock; *The Concert For New York*
City-C . . . . (Columbia)

Poor Little Fool
Rick Nelson; *Live In '85* . . . . (Rhino)
Ricky Nelson; *Best Of Ricky Nelson* . . . . (EMI)
EMI Legends Of Rock & Roll-24 Greatest Hits-C . . . . (EMI)
Ricky Nelson-Legendary Masters . . . . (EMI)

Poor Little Hollywood Star
Virginia Martin; *Little Me* . . . . (RCA)

Poor Little Jesus
Weavers; *On Tour* . . . . (Vanguard)

Poor Little Jimmie
Burl Ives; *Best Of Burl Ives-#2* . . . . (MCA)

Poor Little Rich Girl
Count Basie & Tony Bennett; *Basie Swings Bennett Sings* . . . . (Roulette)
Judy Garland; *Best Of Judy Garland* . . . . (MCA)

Poor Little Rich Girl
Uriah Heep; *Equator* . . . . (Columbia)

Poor Little Rich Girl
Romantics; *National Breakout* . . . .(Nemperor)

Pretty Little Lady From Beaumont, Texas
George Jones; *One Woman Man* . . . . (Epic)
Texas Super Hits-C. . . . . (Columbia)

Pretty Little Adriana
Vince Gill; *High Lonesome Sound* . . . . (MCA)

Pretty Little Angel
Stevie Wonder; *Uptight (Everything's Alright)* . . . . (Motown)

Pretty Little Angel
Crests; *Crests Greatest Hits* . . . . (Collectables)

Pretty Little Angel Eyes
Curtis Lee; *Million-Dollar Memories-#2-C* . . . . (RCA)
Oldies But Goodies-#2-C . . . .(Original Sound)
Phil Spector-Back To Mono 1958-1969-C . . . .(Abkco)
Phil Spector-The Early Years-1958-1961-C . . . . (Rhino)
Rock & Roll U.S.A.-21 Rock & Roll Favorites-#2-C . . . .(Laurie)

Pretty Little Dogies
Skip Gorman; *A Cowboy's Wild Song To His Herd.* . . . . (Rounder)

Pretty Little Indian
Dan Crary; *Lady's Fancy* . . . . (Rounder)

Pretty Little Miss
Patty Loveless; *Mountain Soul* . . . . (Epic)

Pretty Little Picture
Original Cast; *A Funny Thing Happened On The Way To The Forum.* . . . (Angel)
Stephen Sondheim; *Collector's Sondheim-C* . . . . (RCA)

Pretty Little Pink
Doc Watson; *Old Timey Concert.* . . . . (Vanguard)

Put My Little Shoes Away
Everly Brothers; *Songs Our Daddy Taught Us* . . . . (Rhino)

Put Your Little Foot Right Out
Myron Floren; *22 Great Accordion Classics* . . . . (Ranwood)
Russ Morgan; *Best Of Russ Morgan* . . . . (MCA)

Re-Doo-Wopp-Little Star
Tokens; *Re-Doo-Wopp-Little Star* . . . . (RCA)

Rich Little Bitch
Dash Rip Rock; *Boiled Alive!* . . . .(Mammoth)
Not Of This World. . . . .(Mammoth)

Rock My World (Little Country Girl)
Brooks & Dunn; *Hard Workin' Man* . . . . (Arista)

Rockin' Little Tune
Bill Haley & His Comets; *Bill Haley & His Comets-Golden Hits* . . . . . . (MCA)

Run For Your Life
Beatles; *Beatles-Box Set* . . . . (Capitol)

Rubber Soul . . . . (Capitol)
Run Little Rabbit
  John & Jamie Hartford; *Hartford & Hartford* . . . . (Flying Fish)
See The Funny Little Clown
  Bobby Goldsboro; *10th Anniversary Album-#1* . . . . (EMI)
   Bobby Goldsboro's Greatest Hits . . . . (Liberty)
   Honey-Best Of Bobby Goldsboro . . . . (EMI)
Seven Little Girls Sitting In The Back Seat
  Paul Evans; *Music To Remember-C* . . . . (Dominion Entert.)
Sex And Candy
  Marcy Playground; *Marcy Playground* . . . . (Capitol)
   Now That's What I Call Music!-#1-C . . . . (Virgin)
Short Fat Fannie
  Larry Williams; *Original Rock Oldies-Golden Hits-#1-C* . . . . (Specialty)
   The Ultimate '50s Party-C . . . . (Era)
   This Is How It All Began-#2-C . . . . (Specialty)
Short People
  Randy Newman; *Dr. Demento Presents The Greatest Novelty Records-#4-*
   1970s-C . . . . (Rhino)
   Little Criminals . . . . (Warner Bros.)
Short Shorts
  Royal Teens; *Cruisin'-1958-C* . . . . (Increase)
   Goofy Greats-C . . . . (K-Tel)
   Short Shorts . . . . (MCA)
Shorty Falls In Love
  Dan Hicks & His Hot Licks; *Where's The Money?* . . . . (MCA)
Shorty George
  Count Basie; *Best Of Count Basie* . . . . (MCA)
   Command Performances . . . . (Accord)
   Country Party . . . . (Accord)
   Sing Along With Count Basie . . . . (Roulette)
  Leadbelly; *King Of The 12-String Guitar* . . . . (Legacy)
   Take This Hammer . . . . (Smithsonian Folkways)
Simple Little Words
  Cristy Lane; *Cristy Lane-At Her Best* . . . . (EMI)
Small Axe
  Gladiators; *Calling Rastafari* . . . . (Nighthawk)
   Symbol Of Reality . . . . (Nighthawk)
  Wailers; *Burnin'* . . . . (Tuff Gong)
Small Fry
  Georgie Fame/Annie Ross/Hoagy Carmichael; *In Hoagland* . . . . (DRG)
  June Christy; *Small Fry-Capitol Sings Kids Songs For Grownups-C* . . . (Capitol)
Small Hills Of Offaly
  Irish Tradition; *Times We've Had* . . . . (Green Linnet)
Small Paradise
  John Cougar; *John Cougar* . . . . (Riva)
Small Talk
  Doris Day & John Raitt; *ST/Pajama Game* . . . . (Collectables)
  Original Cast; *Pajama Game* . . . . (Columbia)
Small Town
  John Cougar Mellencamp; *Scarecrow* . . . . (Riva)
Small Town Saturday Night
  Hal Ketchum; *Past The Point Of Rescue* . . . . (Curb)
Small Victory
  Faith No More; *Angel Dust* . . . . (Slash)
Small World
  Johnny Mathis; *Johnny Mathis' All-Time Greatest Hits* . . . . (Columbia)
   Johnny Mathis-16 Most Requested Songs . . . . (Columbia)
  Original Cast; *Gypsy* . . . . (Columbia)
  Original London Cast; *Gypsy* . . . . (RCA)
Small World
  Huey Lewis and the News; *Greenpeace/Rainbow Warriors-C* . . . . (Geffen)
   Small World . . . . (Chrysalis)
Small World
  Adrian Belew; *Young Lions* . . . . (Atlantic)
Sweet Little '66
  Steve Earle & The Dukes; *Exit 0* . . . . (MCA)
Sweet Little Angel
  B.B. King; *B.B. King-16 Original Big Hits* . . . . (Fantasy)
   Back In The Alley . . . . (MCA)
   Live & Well . . . . (MCA)
   Live At The Regal . . . . (MCA)
  Buddy Guy; *Best Of Chicago Blues-C* . . . . (Vanguard)
   Man & The Blues . . . . (Vanguard)
  Etta James; *Late Show* . . . . (Fantasy)
   Rocks The House . . . . (Chess)
Sweet Little Bullet From A Pretty Blue Gun
  Tom Waits; *Blue Valentine* . . . . (Asylum)
Sweet Little Cafe In A Square
  Lena Spencer & Others; *Welcome To Caffe Lena* . . . . (Biograph)
Sweet Little Country Girl
  Charlie Daniels; *America, I Believe In You* . . . . (Liberty)
Sweet Little Flower
  Sleepy John Estes; *Electric Sleep* . . . . (Delmark)
Sweet Little Girl
  Stevie Wonder; *Music Of My Mind* . . . . (Motown)
Sweet Little Miss Blue Eyes
  Jim & Jesse/The Virginia Boys; *Appalachian Stomp: More Bluegrass*
   Classics-C . . . . (Rhino)

Sweet Little Missy
  Lynyrd Skynyrd; *Lynyrd Skynyrd-Legend* . . . . (MCA)
Sweet Little Papa
  Louis Armstrong; *Hot Fives & Hot Sevens-#2* . . . . (Columbia)
Sweet Little Rock & Roller
  Chuck Berry; *Chuck Berry Is On Top* . . . . (Chess)
   The Chess Box-Chuck Berry . . . . (Chess)
  Richard Thompson; *Guitar/Vocal* . . . . (Hannibal)
  Rod Stewart; *Absolutely Live* . . . . (Warner Bros.)
   Best Of Rod Stewart . . . . (Mercury)
   Storyteller/The Complete Anthology: 1964-1990 . . . . (Warner Bros.)
Sweet Little Sixteen
  Beatles; *45-#1502* . . . . (Collectables)
  Chuck Berry; *Best Of The Best Of Chuck Berry* . . . . . (International Mktg. Group)
   Chuck Berry-Golden Hits . . . . (Mercury)
   Chuck Berry-Greatest Hits Live . . . . (Quicksilver)
   Cruisin'-1965-C . . . . (Increase)
   Oldies But Goodies-#12-C . . . . (Original Sound)
  Jerry Lee Lewis; *Jerry Lee Lewis-Original Golden Hits-#3* . . . . (Sun)
  Jerry Lee Lewis & Friends; *Jerry Lee Lewis & Friends-Duets* . . . . (Sun)
  John Lennon; *Lennon* . . . . (Capitol)
   Rock 'N' Roll . . . . (Capitol)
Ten Little Indians
  Beach Boys; *Surfin' Safari* . . . . (Capitol)
Ten Little Indians
  Nilsson; *Pandemonium Shadow Show* . . . . (RCA)
Ten Little Numbers
  Hank Williams; *Complete Hank Williams* . . . . (Mercury)
Texas Size Heartache
  Joe Diffie; *Joe Diffie's Greatest Hits* . . . . (Epic)
Thank Heaven For Little Girls
  Maurice Chevalier; *ST/Gigi* . . . . (Sony Music Special Prod.)
  Merle Haggard & Janie Fricke; *It's All In The Game* . . . . (Epic)
That's My Little Suzie
  Ritchie Valens; *Best Of Ritchie Valens* . . . . (Rhino)
Theme From "Little House On The Prairie"
  Original Soundtrack; *Television's Greatest Hits-#3-1970s & 1980s-C* . . . . (TVT)
Theme From "Little Rascals"
  Original Soundtrack; *Television's Greatest Hits-#1-C* . . . . (TVT)
Theme From "My Little Margie"
  Original Soundtrack; *Television's Greatest Hits-#4-Black & White*
   Classics-C . . . . (TVT)
There's A Small Hotel
  Benny Goodman; *Birth Of Swing* . . . . (Bluebird)
   The Birth Of Swing (1935-1936) . . . . (Bluebird)
  Bobby Short; *Bobby Short Celebrates Rodgers & Hart* . . . . (Atlantic)
  Ella Fitzgerald; *Rodgers & Hart Songbook* . . . . (Verve)
  Tony Bennett; *Rodgers & Hart Songbook* . . . . (DRG)
This Little Girl
  Dion; *Bronx Blues-Columbia Recordings 1962-1965* . . . . (Columbia)
   Dion-24 Original Classics . . . . (Arista)
  Gary U.S. Bonds; *Cover Me (Bruce Springsteen Tribute)-C* . . . . (Rhino)
  Gary U.S. Bonds & Bruce Springsteen; *Dedication* . . . . (Razor & Tie)
This Little Girl Of Mine
  Everly Brothers; *Everly Brothers-Cadence Classics-Their 20*
   Greatest Hits . . . . (Rhino)
  Herbie Mann; *Best Of Herbie Mann* . . . . (Atlantic)
  Ray Charles; *Atlantic Rhythm & Blues 1947-1974-#2 (1952-1955)-C* . (Atlantic)
   Birth Of Soul-Complete Atlantic R&B 1952-1959-C . . . . (Atlantic)
   Life In Music . . . . (Atlantic)
This Little Girl Of Mine
  Faron Young; *Faron Young's Greatest Hits-#3* . . . . (Step One)
This Little Pig
  Living Colour; *Stain* . . . . (Epic)
This Town Ain't Big Enough For The Both Of Us
  Siouxsie And The Banshees; *Through The Looking Glass* . . . . (Geffen)
  Sparks; *Profile-The Ultimate Sparks Collection* . . . . (Rhino)
   The Island Story-1962-1987-25th Anniversary-C . . . . (Island)
Three Little Birds
  Bob Marley & The Wailers; *Exodus* . . . . (Tuff Gong)
   Legend: The Best Of Bob Marley & The Wailers . . . . (Island)
   Songs Of Freedom . . . . (Tuff Gong)
Three Little Fishes
  Andrews Sisters; *Boogie Woogie Bugle Girls* . . . . (MCA)
  Kay Kyser & His Orchestra; *Dr. Demento Presents The Greatest Novelty*
   Records-#1-1940s & Before-C . . . . (Rhino)
   Sentimental Favorites . . . . (Columbia)
Three Little Pigs
  Lloyd Price; *Lloyd Price's Greatest Hits* . . . . (MCA)
Three Little Words
  Carmen McRae; *Great American Songbook* . . . . (Atlantic)
  Duke Ellington & His Orchestra; *Nipper's Greatest Hits Of The*
   '30s-#2-C . . . . (RCA)
  Nat "King" Cole; *L-O-V-E* . . . . (Capitol)
Throw Back The Little Ones
  Steely Dan; *Katy Lied* . . . . (MCA)
Tiny Bubbles (Hua Li'l)
  Don Ho; *Don Ho's Greatest Hits* . . . . (Reprise)
  Lawrence Welk; *Lawrence Welk In Concert* . . . . (Ranwood)

Tiny Dancer
Elton John; *Live In Australia With The Melbourne Symphony
  Orchestra* ....(MCA)
  Madman Across The Water ....(Polydor)
Tiny Sparrow
Peter, Paul & Mary; *Moving* ....(Warner Bros.)
Tiny Steps
Elvis Costello; *Girls Girls Girls* ....(Columbia)
Toys Are Made For Children
Joe Stampley/The Uniques; *Joe Stampley-Golden Hits* ....(Paula)
Truckin' Little Baby
John Hammond; *Solo* ....(Vanguard)
Twinkle Twinkle Little Star
Bob Wills & His Texas Playboys; *Tiffany Transcriptions-#8-More Of
  The Best.* ....(Rhino)
Willie Nelson; *Somewhere Over The Rainbow*.................(Columbia)
Two Little Bees
Hollywood Flames; *Hollywood Flames* ....(Specialty)
Wake Up Little Susie
Everly Brothers; *All They Had To Do Was Dream* ....(Rhino)
  American Graffiti-#3-C ....(MCA)
  Everly Brothers ....(Rhino)
  Everly Brothers' All-Time Greatest Hits ....(Curb)
  Oldies But Goodies-#7-C ....(Original Sound)
  Very Best Of The Everly Brothers ....(Warner Bros.)
Grateful Dead; *History Of The Grateful Dead-Vol. 1 (Bear's
  Choice)* ....(Warner Bros.)
Simon & Garfunkel; *The Concert In Central Park*............(Warner Bros.)
What's Your Name
Lynyrd Skynyrd; *Gold & Platinum.* ....(MCA)
  Skynyrd's Innards-Their Greatest Hits ....(MCA)
  Street Survivors ....(MCA)
  What's Your Name ....(MCA Special Prod.)
Where Did That Little Dog Go
Original Cast; *Snoopy*.....................................(DRG)
Where Has My Little Dog Gone
Horace Heidt & His Musical Knights; *The Uncollected Horace Heidt & His
  Musical Knights-1939.* ....(Hindsight)
White Rabbit
Damned; *Best Of The Damned* ....(Roadracer)
  Machine Gun Etiquette ....(Roadracer)
George Benson; *George Benson-Collection.* ....(Warner Bros.)
  White Rabbit ....(CBS Associated)
Jefferson Airplane; *2400 Fulton Street-An Anthology* ....(RCA)
  Flight Log (1966-1976) ....(Grunt)
  Loves You. ....(RCA)
  ST/Platoon ....(Atlantic)
  Surrealistic Pillow ....(RCA)
  The Worst Of Jefferson Airplane ....(RCA)
Wild Little Willy
Ronnie Hawkins and The Hawks; *Best Of Ronnie Hawkins and The
  Hawks* ....(Rhino)
With A Little Help From My Friends
Beatles; *Beatles-Box Set* ....(Capitol)
  Rarities ....(Capitol)
  Sgt. Pepper's Lonely Hearts Club Band. ....(Capitol)
  The Beatles/1967-1970 ....(Capitol)
Joe Cocker; *History Of British Rock-#9-C* ....(Rhino)
  Joe Cocker-Classics-#4 ....(A&M)
  Joe Cocker's Greatest Hits ....(A&M)
  ST/Woodstock ....(Atlantic)
  With A Little Help From My Friends ....(A&M)
Ringo Starr & His All-Star Band; *Nobody's Child-Romanian Angel
  Appeal-C*..(Warner Bros.)
Words
Bee Gees; *Bee Gees-Gold.* ....(Polydor)
  Here At Last...Bee Gees...Live ....(Polydor)
  History Of British Rock-#9-C ....(Rhino)
Elvis Presley; *From Memphis To Vegas/From Vegas To Memphis* ......(RCA)
  That's The Way It Is. ....(RCA)
Joan Armatrading; *Shouting Stage* ....(A&M)
Rita Coolidge; *Anytime...Anywhere* ....(A&M)
  Rita Coolidge-Classics-#5 ....(A&M)
  Rita Coolidge's Greatest Hits ....(A&M)
You're Lost, Little Girl
Doors; *Doors 13* ....(Elektra)
  Strange Days ....(Elektra)

SMALL TOWN LIFE, Rural Living

**See Also: CITIES A-Z, COUNTRY, FARMS, GAS STATIONS,
HOME, LIFE, POVERTY, ROAD, SOCIAL CLASS: RURAL,
TRAVELING**

(We're Not) The Jet Set
George Jones & Tammy Wynette; *George Jones & Tammy Wynette-16
  Biggest Hits.* ....(Epic/Legacy)

Ballad Of A Teenage Queen
Johnny Cash; *Johnny Cash* ....(Sun)
  Johnny Cash-Original Golden Hits-#2. ....(Sun)
  Johnny Cash-Sun Years ....(Rhino)
  ST/Harper Valley PTA ....(Sun)
  The Legend ....(Plantation)
  The Man In Black-His Greatest Hits. ....(Legacy)
Baloney Again
Mark Knopfler; *Sailing To Philadelphia* ....(Warner Bros.)
Blue Kentucky Girl
Emmylou Harris; *Blue Kentucky Girl* ....(Warner Bros.)
  Profile II-The Best Of Emmylou Harris ....(Warner Bros.)
Loretta Lynn; *Loretta Lynn's Greatest Hits* ....(MCA)
Buttons And Bows
Dinah Shore; *16 Most Requested Songs Of The '40s-#1-C* ...(Legacy)
  Golden Hits Of The '40s-C ....(Columbia Special Prod.)
Gene Autry; *Ridin' West-#2-C* ....(Crescendo)
  Songs Of The West-#3-Gene Autry & Roy Rogers-C ....(Rhino)
Carroll County Accident
Porter Wagoner; *Essential Porter Wagoner* ....(RCA)
  Porter Wagoner-Greatest Songs ....(Curb)
Coal Miner's Daughter
Loretta Lynn; *Coal Miner's Daughter* ....(MCA)
  Coal Miner's Daughter ....(MCA)
  Loretta Lynn-20 Greatest Hits ....(MCA)
  Loretta Lynn-Greatest Hits Live ....(K-Tel)
  Loretta Lynn's Greatest Hits-#2. ....(MCA)
  The Country Music Hall Of Fame-Loretta Lynn. ....(MCA)
Cotton Mill Man
Jim & Jesse; *Old Dominion Masters* ....(Pinecastle)
Cryin' For The Carolines
Fred Waring's Pennsylvanians; *Fred Waring's
  Greatest Hits* ....(Collector's Choice)
Daddy Won't Sell The Farm
Montgomery Gentry; *Tattoos & Scars* ....(Columbia)
Dayton Ohio 1903
Randy Newman; *Sail Away.* ....(Reprise)
Domestic Life
John Conlee; *American Faces* ....(Columbia)
  Greatest Country Hits Of The '80s-1987-C ....(Columbia)
  More Hot Country Requests-#2-C ....(Epic)
Down Home
Alabama; *Pass It On Down* ....(BMG Special Prod.)
Dust On The Bottle
David Lee Murphy; *Out With A Bang* ....(MCA)
Elderly Woman Behind The Counter In A Small Town
Pearl Jam; *Vs.* ....(Epic Portrait Assoc.)
Elvis And Andy
Confederate Railroad; *Confederate Railroad's Greatest Hits*........(Atlantic)
  Notorious ....(Atlantic)
Everything's Changed
Lonestar; *Country Cares For Kids II-C* ....(BNA)
  Crazy Nights ....(BNA)
  Lonely Grill ....(BNA)
Everywhere
Tim McGraw; *Everywhere* ....(Curb)
Frankie
Bruce Springsteen; *Tracks* ....(Columbia)
Friends In Low Places
Garth Brooks; *Garth Brooks-Double Live.* ....(Capitol)
  No Fences ....(Capitol)
Hands Of A Working Man
Ty Herndon; *Big Hopes.* ....(Epic)
He Will, She Knows
Kenny Rogers; *There You Go Again* ....(Dreamcatcher)
Home
Alan Jackson; *Alan Jackson-The Greatest Hits Collection* ....(Arista)
  Here In The Real World ....(Arista)
I Let Her Lie
Daryle Singletary; *Daryle Singletary* ....(Giant)
In My Own Backyard
Joe Diffie; *A Thousand Winding Roads* ....(Epic)
It Gets Lonely In A Small Town
Greg Brown; *One More Goodnight Kiss* ....(Red House)
John Deere Green
Joe Diffie; *Honky Tonk Attitude* ....(Epic)
  Joe Diffie's Greatest Hits ....(Epic)
Lead On
George Strait; *Latest Greatest Straitest Hits* ....(MCA)
  Lead On ....(MCA)
Lifestyles Of The Not-So-Rich & Famous
Tracy Byrd; *No Ordinary Man* ....(MCA)
Little Bitty
Alan Jackson; *Everything I Love* ....(Arista)
Tom T. Hall; *Songs From Sopchoppy* ....(Mercury)
  Tom T. Hall-The Hits ....(Mercury)
Little Man
Alan Jackson; *High Mileage* ....(Arista)

Little Street Where Old Friends Meet, A
Tony Bennett; *I Left My Heart In San Francisco* . . . . (Columbia)
Little Town Flirt
Del Shannon; *Del Shannon's Greatest Hits* . . . . (Rhino)
Del Shannon's Greatest Hits . . . . (Curb)
Livin' On Borrowed Time
Travis Tritt; *Down The Road I Go* . . . . (Columbia)
Love At The Five & Dime
Kathy Mattea; *Collection Of Hits* . . . . (Mercury)
Fourteen Country Favorites-C . . . . (Mercury)
Walk The Way The Wind Blows . . . . (Mercury)
Nanci Griffith; *Last Of The True Believers* . . . . (Philo)
One Fair Summer Evening . . . . (MCA)
Luckenbach Texas (Back To The Basics Of Love)
Waylon Jennings; *Ol' Waylon* . . . . (RCA)
Stars Are Out In Texas-C . . . . (RCA)
Waylon Jennings' Greatest Hits . . . . (RCA)
Mary Jane's Last Dance
Tom Petty And The Heartbreakers; *Playback* . . . . (MCA)
Tom Petty And The Heartbreakers' Greatest Hits . . . . (MCA)
Meet In The Middle
Diamond Rio; *Diamond Rio* . . . . (Arista)
Diamond Rio's Greatest Hits . . . . (Arista)
Midnight Girl/Sunset Town
Sweethearts Of The Rodeo; *Sweethearts Of The Rodeo* . . . . (Columbia)
My Hometown
Bruce Springsteen; *Born In The U.S.A.* . . . . (Columbia)
Bruce Springsteen's Greatest Hits . . . . (Columbia)
Night The Lights Went Out In Georgia
Lynn Anderson; *Top Of The World* . . . . (Columbia)
Reba McEntire; *For My Broken Heart* . . . . (MCA)
Reba McEntire's Greatest Hits-#3: I'm A Survivor . . . . (MCA)
Vicki Lawrence; *Super Hits Of The '70s-Have A Nice Day-#10-C* . . . . . . (Rhino)
Okie From Muskogee
Merle Haggard; *Friend In California* . . . . (Epic)
Merle Haggard & The Strangers; *Best Of Merle Haggard & The Strangers* . . . . (Capitol)
Capitol Collectors Series-Merle Haggard & The Strangers . . . . . (Capitol)
Country Music Classics-#3-1965-1970-C . . . . (K-Tel)
For The Record: Merle Haggard-43 Legendary Hits . . . . (BNA)
Songs I'll Always Sing . . . . (Capitol)
ST/Platoon . . . . (Atlantic)
Old Coyote Town
Don Williams; *Traces* . . . . (Capitol)
One Headlight
Wallflowers; *Bringing Down The Horse* . . . . (Interscope)
One Horse Town
Bobby Bland; *Introspective Of The Early Years* . . . . (MCA)
Touch Of The Blues . . . . (MCA)
One Horse Town
Elton John; *Blue Moves* . . . . (MCA)
One Horse Town
David Frishberg; *Live At Vine Street* . . . . (Original Jazz Classics)
One Horse Town
Rembrandts; *Untitled* . . . . (Atco)
One's On The Way (Here In Topeka)
Loretta Lynn; *Loretta Lynn-20 Greatest Hits* . . . . (MCA)
Loretta Lynn-Greatest Hits Live . . . . (K-Tel)
Loretta Lynn's Greatest Hits-#2 . . . . (MCA)
The Country Music Hall Of Fame-Loretta Lynn . . . . (MCA)
Outskirts Of Town
Sawyer Brown; *Outskirts Of Town* . . . . (Curb)
Paris, Tennessee
Dennis Robbins; *Man With A Plan* . . . . (Giant)
Kenny Chesney; *All I Need To Know* . . . . (BNA)
Tracy Lawrence; *Sticks & Stones* . . . . (Atlantic)
Pink Houses
John Cougar Mellencamp; *Rock For Amnesty-C* . . . . (Mercury)
Uh-Huh . . . . (Riva)
John Mellencamp featuring Kid Rock; *The Concert For New York City-C* . . . . (Columbia)
Queen Of My Double Wide Trailer
Sammy Kershaw; *Haunted Heart* . . . . (Mercury)
Red Dirt Girl
Emmylou Harris; *Red Dirt Girl* . . . . (Nonesuch)
River, The
Bruce Springsteen; *Bruce Springsteen's Greatest Hits* . . . . (Columbia)
The River . . . . (Columbia)
Bruce Springsteen & The E Street Band; *Bruce Springsteen & The E Street Band Live/1975-85* . . . . (Legacy)
Santa Ana
Bruce Springsteen; *Tracks* . . . . (Columbia)
Small Town
John Cougar Mellencamp; *Scarecrow* . . . . (Riva)
Small Town Girl
Steve Wariner; *It's A Crazy World* . . . . (MCA)
Steve Wariner's Greatest Hits . . . . (MCA)
Small Town Girl
Larry Carlton; *Larry Carlton-Collection* . . . . (GRP)

Small Town Girl
John Cafferty And The Beaver Brown Band; *Tough All Over* . . . . . (Scotti Bros.)
Small Town Saturday Night
Hal Ketchum; *Past The Point Of Rescue* . . . . (Curb)
Someday
Steve Earle & The Dukes; *Guitar Town* . . . . (MCA)
Shut Up And Die Like An Aviator . . . . (MCA)
Son Of Hickory Holler's Tramp
O.C. Smith; *Me And You* . . . . (Columbia Special Prod.)
Story Songs-C . . . . (K-Tel)
Starting Over Again
Dolly Parton; *Dolly Dolly Dolly* . . . . (RCA)
Dolly Parton-Super Hits-#2 . . . . (RCA)
Essential Dolly Parton . . . . (RCA)
Reba McEntire; *Starting Over* . . . . (MCA)
Theme From "Evening Shade"
Original Soundtrack; *Television's Greatest Hits-#7-Cable Ready-C* . . . . . (TVT)
Theme From "Peyton Place"
Original Soundtrack; *Television's Greatest Hits-#5-In Living Color-C* . . . . (TVT)
Theme From "The Andy Griffith Show"
Original Soundtrack; *CBS: The First 50 Years* . . . . (TVT)
Television's Greatest Hits-#1-C . . . . (TVT)
Theme From "Twin Peaks"
Original Soundtrack; *Television's Greatest Hits-#7-Cable Ready-C* . . . . . (TVT)
Third Rate Romance
Amazing Rhythm Aces; *Stacked Deck* . . . . (MCA)
Rosanne Cash; *Somewhere In The Stars* . . . . (Columbia)
Sammy Kershaw; *Cryin' Lyin' Lovin' & Leavin'-C* . . . . (Universal)
Feelin' Good Train . . . . (Mercury)
The Hits-Chapter 1 . . . . (Mercury)
Third Rock From The Sun
Joe Diffie; *A Thousand Winding Roads* . . . . (Epic)
Three Bells, The
Browns; *Billboard Top Country Hits-1959-C* . . . . (Rhino)
Nipper's Greatest Hits Of The '50s-#1-C . . . . (RCA)
Two Pump Texaco
Diamond Rio; *Unbelievable* . . . . (Arista)
Watermelon Crawl
Tracy Byrd; *No Ordinary Man* . . . . (MCA)
Week In A County Jail, A
Tom T. Hall; *Storyteller, Poet, Philospher.* . . . . (Mercury)
Tom T. Hall's Greatest Hits-#1 . . . . (Mercury)
Where The Green Grass Grows
Tim McGraw; *Big Country Hits '99-C* . . . . (K-Tel)
Everywhere . . . . (Curb)
Tim McGraw's Greatest Hits . . . . (Curb)
You're Not In Kansas Anymore
Jo Dee Messina; *Jo Dee Messina* . . . . (Curb)

SMILE, Funny, Joke, Laugh, Silly

See Also: *ANATOMY: FACE, ANATOMY: MOUTH, FUN, HAPPINESS, OPTIMISM, PARTY*

Absolutely (Story Of A Girl)
Nine Days; *Maddening Crowd* . . . . (550 Music)
Now That's What I Call Music!-#5-C . . . . (Virgin)
After My Laughter Came Tears
Big Joe Turner; *Midnight Special* . . . . (Pablo)
Anyday
Derek And The Dominos; *Layla* . . . . (Polydor)
Baby's Smile Woman's Kiss
Johnny Duncan; *Best Of Johnny Duncan* . . . . (Columbia)
Beautiful
Carole King; *Tapestry* . . . . (Epic)
Behind A Painted Smile
Isley Brothers; *The Isley Brothers Story-#1-Rockin' Soul-1959-1968* . . . . (Rhino)
Blue Skies
Benny Goodman; *Benny Goodman Today* . . . . (London)
Carnegie Hall Jazz Concert . . . . (Columbia)
The Birth Of Swing (1935-1936) . . . . (Bluebird)
This Is Benny Goodman. . . . . (RCA)
Bing Crosby; *Bing Crosby's Greatest Hits* . . . . (MCA)
Duke Ellington; *Carnegie Hall Concert.* . . . . (Prestige)
Golden Duke . . . . (Prestige)
Willie Nelson; *Stardust* . . . . (Legacy)
Can't Smile Without You
Barry Manilow; *Barry Manilow's Greatest Hits-#1* . . . . (Arista)
Even Now . . . . (Arista)
Certain Smile, A
Johnny Mathis; *Johnny Mathis' All-Time Greatest Hits* . . . . (Columbia)
Johnny Mathis-16 Most Requested Songs . . . . (Columbia)
Johnny Mathis-Live . . . . (Columbia)
Chemical Smile
Everclear; *Sparkle And Fade* . . . . (Capitol)
Christmas Shoes
Newsong; *Sheltering Tree* . . . . (Benson/Jive)

Comedians
Elvis Costello & The Attractions; *Goodbye Cruel World* . . . . (Columbia)
Roy Orbison; *Mystery Girl* . . . . (Virgin)
   Roy Orbison & Friends: Black & White Night-Live. . . . . (Virgin)
Cracklin' Rosie
Neil Diamond; *Hot August Night* . . . . (MCA)
   Hot August Night II . . . . (Columbia)
   Neil Diamond-His 12 Greatest Hits . . . . (MCA)
   Tap Root Manuscript . . . . (MCA)
Crash And Burn
Sheryl Crow; *The Globe Sessions* . . . . (A&M)
Crying & Laughing
Chris DeBurgh; *The Getaway* . . . . (A&M)
Dandelion
Rolling Stones; *More Hot Rocks (big hits & fazed cookies)* . . . . . . (Abkco)
   Through The Past, Darkly (Big Hits Vol. 2) . . . . (Abkco)
Dear Brother
Hank Williams; *I Saw The Light* . . . . (Polydor)
Dear Prudence
Beatles; *The Beatles (White Album)* . . . . (Capitol)
Siouxsie And The Banshees; *Hyaena* . . . . (Geffen)
   Nocturne . . . . (Geffen)
Diamond Smiles
Boomtown Rats; *Fine Art Of Surfacing* . . . . (Columbia)
Disarm
Smashing Pumpkins; *Siamese Dream* . . . . (Virgin)
Dolphin's Smile
Byrds; *Notorious Byrd Brothers* . . . . (Columbia)
   The Byrds . . . . (Columbia)
Don't Laugh At Me
Mark Wills; *Wish You Were Here* . . . . (Mercury)
Don't Let It Bother You
Fats Waller; *Have A Little Dream On Me* . . . . (Eclipse)
Don't Stop
Elton John; *Legacy-A Tribute To Fleetwood Mac's Rumours-C* . . . . . . (Lava)
Fleetwood Mac; *25 Years-The Chain* . . . . (Warner Bros.)
   Fleetwood Mac Live . . . . (Warner Bros.)
   Fleetwood Mac's Greatest Hits . . . . (Warner Bros.)
   Rumours . . . . (Warner Bros.)
Feet Up (Pat Him On The Po-Po)
Guy Mitchell; *Definitive Guy Mitchell* . . . . (Collector's Choice)
For Your Love
Stevie Wonder; *Conversation Peace* . . . . (Motown)
   Natural Wonder . . . . (Motown)
   Song Review-A Greatest Hits Collection . . . . (Motown)
Funny
Boz Scaggs; *Other Roads* . . . . (Columbia)
Maxine Brown; *Golden Classics-Maxine Brown* . . . . (Collectables)
Nat "King" Cole; *Blossom Fell* . . . . (Capitol)
Ray Charles; *Life In Music* . . . . (Atlantic)
Funny Face
Donna Fargo; *Super Hits Of The '70s-Have A Nice Day-#11-C* . . . . . . (Rhino)
Funny Face
Original Cast; *My One And Only* . . . . (Atlantic)
Funny Familiar Forgotten Feelings
Don Gibson; *Best Of Don Gibson-#1* . . . . (Curb)
Mandy Barnett; *I've Got A Right To Cry*. . . . . (Sire)
Tom Jones; *Back To Back-Greatest Hits* . . . . (Rebound)
   Country Side Of Tom Jones . . . . (London)
   Tom Jones-London Collector-Greatest Hits . . . . (London)
Funny Girl
Barbra Streisand; *ST/Funny Girl* . . . . (Columbia)
Funny How Time Slips Away
Al Green & Lyle Lovett; *Rhythm Country And Blues-C* . . . . (MCA)
Jimmy Elledge; *Nipper's Greatest Hits Of The '60s-#2-C* . . . . (RCA)
   RCA's Greatest One-Hit Wonders-C . . . . (RCA)
Willie Nelson; *Best Of Willie Nelson* . . . . (Capitol)
   Collector's Series-Willie Nelson . . . . (RCA)
   Healing Hands Of Time . . . . (Liberty)
   My Own Way . . . . (RCA)
   San Antonio Rose . . . . (Columbia)
   Willie & Family Live . . . . (Columbia)
Willie Nelson & Faron Young; *Funny How Time Slips Away*. . . . . (Columbia)
Funny Way Of Laughin'
Burl Ives; *Best Of Burl Ives-#2* . . . . (MCA)
   Burl Ives Live . . . . (Everest)
Golden Slumbers
Beatles; *Abbey Road*. . . . . (Parlophone)
   Beatles-Box Set . . . . (Capitol)
Great Beyond, The
R.E.M.; *Man On The Moon* . . . . (Warner Bros.)
   Totally Hits-#2-C . . . . (Elektra)
Guys & Dolls
Original Cast; *ST/Guys & Dolls* . . . . (MCA)
Ha!
Juvenile; *400 Degreez*. (Cash Money/Universal)
Happy
Sister Hazel; *...Somewhere More Familiar* . . . . (Universal)

Heaven And Hot Rods
Stone Temple Pilots; *No. 4* . . . .(Atlantic)
I Go To Rio
Pablo Cruise; *Worlds Away* . . . . (A&M)
Peter Allen; *At His Best*. . . . . (A&M)
   It Is Time For Peter Allen . . . . (A&M)
   Taught By Experts . . . . (A&M)
I Love Your Smile
Shanice; *Inner Child* . . . . (Motown)
I Started A Joke
Bee Gees; *Best Of The Bee Gees-#1* . . . . (Polydor)
   Here At Last...Bee Gees...Live . . . . (Polydor)
   One Night Only . . . . (Polydor)
Wallflowers; *ST/Zoolander* . . . . (Hollywood)
I Will Still Be Laughing
Soul Asylum; *Candy From A Stranger* . . . . (Columbia)
   ST/Baseketball . . . . (Mojo Music/Universal)
I'd Like That
XTC; *Homespun* . . . . (Idea/TVT)
I'll Never Smile Again
Billie Holiday; *Last Recordings* . . . . (Verve)
Frank Sinatra; *Sinatra: A Man And His Music* . . . . (Reprise)
Ink Spots; *Ink Spots' Greatest Hits-Original Recordings-1939-1946*. . . . (MCA)
Keely Smith; *Capitol's Great Ladies Of Song-C*. . . . . (Capitol)
Sarah Vaughan; *In The Land Of Hi-Fi*. . . . . (Emarcy)
Tommy Dorsey & Frank Sinatra; *Masters Of The Big Bands* . . . . . . (Bluebird)
   Tommy Dorsey & Frank Sinatra's All-Time Greatest Hits-#1 . . . . . (Bluebird)
I'll Remember April
Cal Tjader; *Mambo With Cal Tjader* . . . . (Fantasy)
Charlie Parker; *Charlie Parker With Strings* . . . . (Verve)
Chet Baker; *Chet Baker*. . . . . (Emarcy)
Cleo Laine; *Cleo's Choice*. . . . . (Crescendo)
Doris Day & The Frank DeVol Orchestra; *Hooray For*
   Hollywood-#1-C . . . . (Columbia)
Erroll Garner; *Erroll Garner-Concert By The Sea* . . . . (Columbia)
Frank Sinatra; *Point Of No Return* . . . . (Capitol)
June Christy; *June Christy-#2-1957* . . . . (Hindsight)
Modern Jazz Quartet; *Concorde* . . . . (Prestige)
   Modern Jazz Quartet . . . . (Prestige)
Stephane Grappelli & Martin Taylor; *Just One Of Those Things* . . . . . (Angel)
Wynton Marsalis; *Standard Time-#2-Intimacy Calling* . . . . (Columbia)
Illegal Smile
John Prine; *John Prine* . . . . (Atlantic)
   Prime Prine-The Best Of John Prine . . . . (Atlantic)
I'm Down
Beatles; *The Beatles-Anthology-#2* . . . . (Capitol)
Paul McCartney; *The Concert For New York City-C* . . . . (Columbia)
I'm So Happy I Can't Stop Crying
Sting; *Mercury Falling* . . . . (A&M)
Toby Keith with Sting; *Dream Walkin'*. . . . . (Mercury)
   Toby Keith's Greatest Hits, Volume One . . . . (Mercury)
It Takes A Lot To Laugh, It Takes A Train To Cry
Bob Dylan; *Highway 61 Revisited*. (Columbia)
   The Bootleg Series-Volumes 1-3 [Rare & Unreleased] . . . . (Columbia)
Mike Bloomfield/Al Kooper/Stephen Stills; *Super Session* . . . . . . (Columbia)
Jackie Wilson Said (I'm In Heaven When You Smile)
Van Morrison; *Best Of Van Morrison* . . . . (Polydor)
   St. Dominic's Preview . . . . (Warner Bros.)
   ST/Queen's Logic . . . . (Epic)
Joker James
Brian Hyland; *Brian Hyland's Greatest Hits*. . . . . (Rhino)
Joker, The
Steve Miller Band; *Best Of Steve Miller 1968-1973* . . . . (Capitol)
   Steve Miller Band-Gift Set . . . . (Capitol)
   Steve Miller Band-Live . . . . (Capitol)
   Steve Miller Band's Greatest Hits-1974-78 . . . . (Capitol)
   The Joker . . . . (Capitol)
Just To See You Smile
Tim McGraw; *Everywhere* . . . . (Curb)
   Tim McGraw's Greatest Hits . . . . (Curb)
Keep On Smilin'
Wet Willie; *Super Hits Of The '70s-Have A Nice Day-#13-C* . . . . . . (Rhino)
   Wet Willie's Greatest Hits . . . . (Polydor)
Keep On Smilin'
Alfie; *45-#1827* . . . . (Motown)
Keep Smiling At Trouble
Al Jolson; *Rainbow 'Round My Shoulder* . . . . (MCA Special Prod.)
Tony Bennett; *Forty Years-The Artistry Of Tony Bennett* . . . . . . (Columbia)
Lady Grinning Soul
David Bowie; *Aladdin Sane* . . . . (Rykodisc)
Last Laugh
Mark Knopfler; *Sailing To Philadelphia* . . . . (Warner Bros.)
Laugh
Adventure Babies; *Laugh* . . . . (London)
Laugh At Me
Sonny Bono; *Songs Of Protest-C* . . . . (Rhino)
Laugh Laugh
Beau Brummels; *Best Of The Beau Brummels* . . . . (Rhino)
   Heart & Soul Of Rock 'N' Roll-#1-C . . . . (Rhino)

Introducing The Beau Brummels .... (Rhino)
Nuggets-#7-Early San Francisco-C .... (Rhino)
Laughing
Guess Who; *Best Of The Guess Who* .... (RCA)
Greatest Of The Guess Who .... (RCA)
Laughing
Stranglers; *Aural Sculpture* .... (Epic)
Laughing
Church; *Gold Afternoon Fix* .... (Arista)
Laughing
R.E.M.; *Murmur* .... (I.R.S.)
Laughing At Life
Billie Holiday; *Billie Holiday* .... (Columbia)
Quintessential-#8-1939-1940........................ (Legacy)
The Billie Holiday Story-#2 .... (Columbia)
Laughing At The Blues
Jimmy Reed; *Best Of Jimmy Reed* .... (Crescendo)
Now Appearing.................................. (Vee-Jay)
Laughing Blues
Bonzo Dog Band; *Tadpoles*...................... (Liberty)
Leon Redbone; *Sugar* .... (Private Music)
Laughing Boy
Mary Wells; *Compact Command Performances-Mary Wells* .... (Motown)
Mary Wells' Greatest Hits .... (Motown)
Laughing Gnome
David Bowie; *David Bowie-London Collector-Starting Point* .... (London)
Love You Till Tuesday.......................... (London)
Laughing On The Outside
Aretha Franklin; *Aretha Franklin Sings The Blues* ...... (Columbia)
Laughing Out Loud
Wallflowers; *Bringing Down The Horse* .... (Interscope)
Laughing Song
Dan Hicks & His Hot Licks; *Striking It Rich!* .... (MCA)
Laughing Song
Residents; *Duck Stab/Buster & Glenn/Goosebump*........ (East Side Digital)
Laughing Song
Maurice Farkoa; *Music From The New York Stage (1890-1920)-#1-1890-1908-C*.......................... (Pearl)
Laughing Stock
Love; *Best Of Love* .... (Rhino)
Laughter In The Rain
Johnny Mathis; *When Will Is See You Again* .... (Columbia)
Neil Sedaka; *My Friend*.......................... (Polydor)
Let A Smile Be Your Umbrella
Sammy Kaye & His Orchestra; *Best Of Sammy Kaye & His Orchestra* .. (MCA)
Let Me Touch You For Awhile
Alison Krauss & Union Station; *New Favorite* .... (Rounder)
Light Of Smiles
Gary Wright; *The Light Of Smiles* .... (Warner Bros.)
Little Bitty
Alan Jackson; *Everything I Love* .... (Arista)
Tom T. Hall; *Songs From Sopchoppy* .... (Mercury)
Tom T. Hall-The Hits .... (Mercury)
Live, Laugh, Love
Clay Walker; *Live, Laugh, Love* .... (Giant)
Living A Little, Laughing A Little
John Hiatt; *Warming Up To The Ice Age* .... (Geffen)
Spinners; *New & Improved* .... (Atlantic)
Spinners-Live .... (Atlantic)
Losing My Religion
R.E.M.; *Out Of Time* .... (Warner Bros.)
Make Me Smile
Chicago; *Chicago At Carnegie Hall* .... (Chicago)
Chicago II..................................... (Chicago)
Chicago IX-Chicago's Greatest Hits .... (Chicago)
Mona Lisa
Carl Mann; *Original Memphis Rock & Roll* .... (Sun)
Sun Story-C.................................... (Rhino)
Elvis Presley; *Elvis-A Legendary Performer, Volume 4* ..... (RCA)
Jim Reeves; *Jim Reeves-Pure Gold*................... (RCA)
Nat ''King'' Cole; *Best Of Nat ''King'' Cole-Vol. 1* .... (Capitol)
Capitol Collectors Series-Nat ''King'' Cole.......... (Capitol)
The Nat ''King'' Cole Story .... (Capitol)
Unforgettable .... (Capitol)
Neville Brothers; *Fiyo On The Bayou* .... (A&M)
Mona Lisa's Lost Her Smile
David Allan Coe; *19 Hot Country Requests-#2-C* .... (Epic)
David Allan Coe-17 Greatest Hits .... (Columbia)
For The Record-The First 10 Years .... (Columbia)
Greatest Country Hits Of The '80s-1984-C .... (Columbia)
Just Divorced .... (Columbia)
Mr. Too Damn Good
Gerald Levert; *G* .... (East West)
My Funny Valentine
Anita Baker; *Rhythm Of Love* .... (Atlantic)
Anita O'Day; *Anita O'Day* .... (Glendale)
Anita O'Day Sings The Winners .... (Verve)
Live At The City .... (Emily)

Carly Simon; *My Romance*........................ (Arista)
Ella Fitzgerald; *Rodgers & Hart Songbook* .... (Verve)
Mel Torme; *Easy To Remember* .... (Glendale)
Miles Davis; *Columbia Years-1955-1985* .... (Columbia)
Cookin' With The Miles Davis Quintet .... (Prestige)
Miles Davis' Greatest Hits .... (Columbia)
My Funny Valentine .... (Columbia)
Original Cast/Mary Martin; *Babes In Arms* .... (Sony Music Special Prod.)
Stan Getz; *Artistry-Of-Stan Getz-Best Of Verve Years-#1* .... (Verve)
My Mammy
Al Jolson; *Best Of Al Jolson* .... (MCA)
Let Me Sing And I'm Happy................. (Turner Classic Movies)
The '20s-From Broadway To Hollywood-#3-C........ (Flapper)
Happenings; *Happenings-Golden Hits!* .... (B.T. Puppy)
Nancy (With The Laughing Face)
Frank Sinatra; *Sinatra Reprise-The Very Good Years* ..... (Reprise)
Sinatra's Sinatra .... (Reprise)
John Coltrane; *The Gentle Side Of John Coltrane* .... (GRP)
Tony Bennett; *Perfectly Frank*.................... (Columbia)
Oh How The Years Go By
Vanessa Williams; *NBA At 50-A Musical Celebration-C* .... (Mercury)
Pack Up Your Troubles In Your Old Kit Bag (And Smile, Smile, Smile)
James F. Harrison & Knickerbocker Quartet; *78-#2181* .... (Columbia)
Party Crowd
David Lee Murphy; *Out With A Bang* .... (MCA)
Powder Your Face With Sunshine (Smile!)
Guy Lombardo & His Royal Canadians; *Best Of Guy Lombardo* .... (Curb)
Sammy Kaye & His Orchestra; *Sammy Kaye & His Orchestra Play 22 Original Big Band Recordings* .... (Hindsight)
Ravishing Ruby (Smilin' Jack)
Tom T. Hall; *Essential Tom T. Hall-20th Anniversary Collection* ..... (Mercury)
Tom T. Hall's Greatest Hits-#2 .... (Mercury)
Sara Smile
After 7; *Very Best Of After 7*...................... (Virgin)
Daryl Hall & John Oates; *Best Of Daryl Hall & John Oates* ..... (RCA)
Daryl Hall & John Oates......................... (RCA)
Livetime....................................... (RCA)
Rock 'N Soul, Part 1 .... (RCA)
Soulful Sounds .... (RCA)
Secret Smile
Semisonic; *Feeling Strangely Fine* .... (MCA)
She Smiled Sweetly
Rolling Stones; *Between The Buttons* .... (Abkco)
She's Funny That Way (I Got A Woman Crazy For Me)
Art Tatum; *Solo Masterpieces-#8* .... (Pablo)
Count Basie Jam; *Montreux '77-C*.................. (Pablo)
Frank Sinatra; *At The Movies* .... (Capitol)
Nice 'N' Easy .... (Capitol)
Jackie Gleason; *Lush Moods* .... (Pair)
Nat ''King'' Cole; *Big Band Cole* .... (Blue Note)
Shine
Ry Cooder; *Jazz* .... (Warner Bros.)
Ships
Barry Manilow; *Barry Manilow's Greatest Hits-#3* ...... (Arista)
One Voice..................................... (Arista)
Show Me A Smile
Fleetwood Mac; *Future Games* .... (Reprise)
Silly Love Songs
Paul McCartney; *All The Best!* .... (Capitol)
ST/Give my regards to Broad Street .... (Columbia)
Wings; *Wings At The Speed Of Sound* .... (Capitol)
Wings Greatest .... (Capitol)
Wings Over America .... (Capitol)
Smashing Young Man
Collective Soul; *Collective Soul*.................. (Atlantic)
Smile
Diana Ross; *Diana Ross*......................... (Motown)
Evening With Diana Ross .... (Motown)
Smile
Dexter Gordon; *Best Of Dexter Gordon* .... (Blue Note)
Lyle Lovett; *ST/Hope Floats* .... (Capitol)
Nat ''King'' Cole; *The Nat ''King'' Cole Story* ...... (Capitol)
Natalie Cole; *Unforgettable With Love* .... (Elektra)
Tony Bennett; *The Movie Song Album* .... (Columbia)
Tony Bennett's All-Time Greatest Hits .... (Columbia)
Smile
Scarface; *The Untouchable* .... (Rap-A-Lot/Noo Trybe)
Smile
Lonestar; *Lonely Grill* .... (BNA)
Smile
Was (Not Was); *Born To Laugh At Tornadoes* .... (Geffen)
Smile
One Way; *Lady* .... (MCA)
Smile
Laura Nyro; *Smile* .... (Columbia)
Smile
Betty Everett & Jerry Butler; *Very Best Of Betty Everett* .... (Vee-Jay)
Smile
Stevie Wonder; *With A Song In My Heart* .... (Motown)

Smile Away
Paul And Linda McCartney; *RAM* . . . . (Capitol)
Paul McCartney; *Paul McCartney-Gift Set* . . . . (Capitol)
Smile Has Left Your Eyes
Asia; *Alpha* . . . . (Geffen)
Live In Moscow . . . . (Rhino)
Then & Now . . . . (Geffen)
Smile Like Yours
Natalie Cole; *ST/A Smile Like Yours* . . . . (Elektra)
Smile Please
Stevie Wonder; *Fulfillingness' First Finale* . . . . (Motown)
Smilin'
Sly & The Family Stone; *Sly & The Family Stone-Anthology* . . . . (Epic)
Smilin'
Levert; *Just Coolin'* . . . . (Atlantic)
Smilin' Through
Judy Garland; *Judy Garland-Collector's Items-1936-1945* . . . . (MCA)
Judy Garland & Lyn Murray & His Orchestra; *Changing My Tune-Best Of
Decca Years-#2* . . . . (Decca)
Smiling
Kitchens Of Distinction; *Death of Cool* . . . . (A&M)
Smiling Faces Sometimes
Undisputed Truth; *Didn't It Blow Your Mind: Soul Hits Of The
'70s-#5-C* . . . . (Rhino)
Hard-To-Find Motown Classics-#2-C . . . . (Motown)
Smiling Islands
Robbie Patton; *Orders From Headquarters* . . . . (Atlantic)
Smiling Islands
Chris Proctor; *Delicate Dance* . . . . (Flying Fish)
Smiling Phases
Blood, Sweat & Tears; *Blood, Sweat & Tears* . . . . (Columbia)
Smiling Phases
Traffic; *Best Of Traffic* . . . . (Island)
Smiling Up The Frown
Agents Of Good Roots; *One By One* . . . . (RCA)
Where'd You Get That Vibe? . . . . (RCA)
Some Bridges
Jackson Browne; *Looking East* . . . . (Elektra)
Something
Beatles; *Abbey Road* . . . . (Parlophone)
Beatles 1 . . . . (Capitol)
The Beatles/1967-1970 . . . . (Capitol)
The Beatles-Anthology-#3 . . . . (Capitol)
Something Kinda Funny
Spice Girls; *Spice* . . . . (Virgin)
Sunshine Of Your Smile
Tommy Dorsey & Frank Sinatra; *Tommy Dorsey & Frank Sinatra's All-Time
Greatest Hits-#4* . . . . (Bluebird)
Sweet, Sweet Smile
Carpenters; *Carpenters-Classics-#2* . . . . (A&M)
Passage . . . . (A&M)
Yesterday Once More . . . . (A&M)
Tears Of A Clown
English Beat; *I Just Can't Stop It* . . . . (I.R.S.)
What Is Beat . . . . (I.R.S.)
Smokey Robinson & The Miracles; *25 #1 Hits From 25 Years-C* . . . . (Motown)
Billboard Top Rock 'N' Roll Hits-1970-C . . . . (Rhino)
*Compact Command Performances-Smokey Robinson & The
Miracles* . . . . (Motown)
Endless Love-Motown's Greatest Love Songs-C . . . . (Motown)
Smokey Robinson & The Miracles' Anthology . . . . (Motown)
Tears Of A Clown . . . . (Motown)
That Joke Isn't Funny Anymore
Smiths; *Best...2* . . . . (Sire)
Meat Is Murder . . . . (Sire)
That's What Friends Are For
Dionne Warwick/Elton John/Gladys Knight/Stevie Wonder; *Dionne
Warwick's Greatest Hits-1979-1990* . . . . (Arista)
Friends . . . . (Arista)
That's Where I Belong
Paul Simon; *You're The One* . . . . (Warner Bros.)
Theme From "Candid Camera"
Original Soundtrack; *Television's Greatest Hits-#4-Black & White
Classics-C* . . . . (TVT)
Theme From "Rowan And Martin's Laugh-In"
Original Soundtrack; *Television's Greatest Hits-#5-In Living Color-C* . . . (TVT)
Theme From "The Sandpiper" (Shadow Of Your Smile)
Astrud Gilberto; *ST/Sandpiper* . . . . (Verve)
*The Envelope Please-Academy Award Winning Songs-#3 (1958-
1969)-C* . . . . (Rhino)
Barbra Streisand; *My Name Is Barbra, Two* . . . . (Columbia)
Boston Pops Orchestra/Arthur Fiedler; *Greatest Hits Of The '60s-#2* . . . (RCA)
Motion Picture Classics-#1 . . . . (RCA Victor)
Music For Every Mood-Yesterday . . . . (RCA)
Carmen McRae; *Carmen McRae-Alive* . . . . (Mainstream)
I Want You . . . . (Mainstream)
Frank Sinatra; *At The Sands* . . . . (Reprise)
The Reprise Collection . . . . (Reprise)
Henry Mancini; *Days Of Wine And Roses* . . . . (RCA)

James Morrison; *Snappy Doo* . . . . (Atlantic)
Jose Carreras; *Hollywood Golden Classics* . . . . (Atlantic)
Marvin Gaye; *Romantically Yours* . . . . (Columbia)
Tony Bennett; *Academy Award Winners: 16 Most Requested* . . . . . . (LeGrand)
The Movie Song Album . . . . (Columbia)
Tony Bennett-16 Most Requested Songs . . . . (Legacy)
Tony Bennett's All-Time Greatest Hits . . . . (Columbia)
They All Laughed
Carmen McRae; *Setting Standards* . . . . (Pair)
Ella Fitzgerald & Louis Armstrong & Oscar Peterson Trio; *Great American
Songwriters-#1George & Ira Gershwin-C* . . . . (Rhino)
Fred Astaire; *Starring Fred Astaire* . . . . (Columbia)
Sarah Vaughan; *Sarah Vaughan Sings George Gershwin Songbook,
Vol. 1* . . . . (Emarcy)
Tony Bennett; *Steppin' Out* . . . . (Columbia)
Things Aren't Funny Anymore
Merle Haggard; *Capitol Collectors Series-Merle Haggard* . . . . (Capitol)
Epic Collection-Recorded Live . . . . (Epic)
Merle Haggard-Country Boy . . . . (Pair)
This Funny World
Tony Bennett; *Rodgers & Hart Songbook* . . . . (DRG)
This Is No Laughing Matter
Sammy Kaye & His Orchestra; *Sammy Kaye & His Orchestra Play 22
Original Big Band Recordings* . . . . (Hindsight)
This Will Make You Laugh
Natalie Cole; *Take A Look* . . . . (Elektra)
Three Mile Smile
Aerosmith; *Night In The Ruts* . . . . (Columbia)
Pandora's Box . . . . (Columbia)
Together Again
Janet Jackson; *Now That's What I Call Music!-#1-C* . . . . (Virgin)
Velvet Rope . . . . (Virgin)
Tonight I Shall Sleep With A Smile On My Face
Duke Ellington; *Black, Brown & Beige: 1944-1946 Band
Recordings* . . . . (Bluebird)
Sarah Vaughan; *Duke Ellington Songbook Two* . . . . (Pablo)
Tracks Of My Tears, The
Bryan Ferry; *These Foolish Things* . . . . (Reprise)
Gladys Knight & The Pips; *Gladys Knight & The Pips-Anthology* . . . . (Motown)
Johnny Rivers; *Best Of Johnny Rivers* . . . . (EMI)
Linda Ronstadt; *Linda Ronstadt's Greatest Hits* . . . . (Asylum)
Prisoner In Disguise . . . . (Asylum)
Smokey Robinson & The Miracles; *Billboard Top R&B Hits-1965-
1969-C* . . . . (Rhino)
Smokey Robinson & The Miracles' Anthology . . . . (Motown)
Smokey Robinson & The Miracles' Greatest Hits-#2 . . . . (Motown)
ST/Big Chill . . . . (Motown)
ST/Sound Of "Murphy Brown" . . . . (MCA)
Two Faces Have I
Lou Christie; *Back To The '60s-#4-C* . . . . (Dominion Entert.)
Enlightnin'ment-Best Of Lou Christie . . . . (Rhino)
We Danced Anyway
Deana Carter; *Did I Shave My Legs For This?* . . . . (Capitol)
We'll Sing In The Sunshine
Gale Garnett; *21 Country Rock & Love Songs Of The '50s &
'60s-#1-C* . . . . (Laurie)
Nipper's Greatest Hits Of The '60s-#1-C . . . . (RCA)
When I See You Smile
Bad English; *Bad English* . . . . (Epic)
Keep On Loving You-C . . . . (Columbia Special Prod.)
Read The Hits-Best Of The '80s-C . . . . . . (Sony Music Special Prod.)
When Irish Eyes Are Smiling
Billy Shepherd Singers; *Irish Sing-Along* . . . . (MCA)
Bing Crosby; *When Irish Eyes Are Smiling* . . . . (MCA)
Dennis Day; *Irish Album* . . . . (RCA)
When My Baby Smiles At Me
Pete Fountain; *Best Of Pete Fountain* . . . . (MCA)
Ted Lewis & His Orchestra; *Music From The New York Stage (1890-1920)-
#4-1917-1920-C* . . . . (Pearl)
When Will I See You Smile Again?
Bell Biv Devoe; *Poison* . . . . (MCA)
WBBD-Bootcity-Remix Album . . . . (MCA)
When You Need A Laugh
Patsy Cline; *Portrait Of Patsy Cline* . . . . (MCA)
Songwriter's Tribute . . . . (MCA)
When You're Smiling (The Whole World Smiles With You)
Frank Sinatra; *Sinatra's Swingin' Session!!!* . . . . (Capitol)
Judy Garland; *Judy Garland-At Carnegie Hall* . . . . (Capitol)
Judy Garland's Greatest Hits . . . . (Curb)
One & Only . . . . (Capitol)
Louis Armstrong; *Best Of Louis Armstrong* . . . . (MCA)
Louis Armstrong-Vol. 4-In New York . . . . (Columbia)
Musical Autobiography-#2 . . . . (MCA)
Where You Are
Jessica Simpson featuring Nick Lachey; *Sweet Kisses* . . . . . . (Columbia)
Woke Up In Love
Exile; *Exile* . . . . (Epic)
Exile's Greatest Hits . . . . (Epic)

Wooden Ships
Crosby, Stills & Nash; *Crosby, Stills & Nash* . . . . (Atlantic)
CSN . . . . (Atlantic)
Crosby, Stills, Nash & Young; *So Far* . . . . (Atlantic)
ST/Woodstock . . . . (Atlantic)
Jefferson Airplane; *2400 Fulton Street-An Anthology* . . . . (RCA)
Flight Log (1966-1976) . . . . (Grunt)
Loves You . . . . (RCA)
Volunteers . . . . (RCA)
Wrong Number
Cure; *Galore-The Singles-1987-1997* . . . . (Fiction/Elektra)
You Wouldn't Believe
311; *From Chaos* . . . . (Volcano Entertainment)
Your Smile
Rene & Angela; *Street Called Desire* . . . . (Mercury)
Your Smiling Face
James Taylor; *J.T.* . . . . (Columbia)
ST/FM . . . . (MCA)
You're Never Fully Dressed Without A Smile
Original Broadway Cast; *Annie* . . . . (Columbia)

SNOW

See Also: **CHRISTMAS, COLD, MONTHS & DATES: DECEMBER,
SEASONS: WINTER**

April Snow
Northern Lights; *Take You To The Sky* . . . . (Flying Fish)
April Snow
Hi-Lo's; *Cherries & Other Delights* . . . . (Hindsight)
At The First Fall Of Snow
Hank Williams; *Lovesick Blues* . . . . (Polydor)
Blizzard
Roy Rogers; *Out West-C* . . . . (Capitol)
Blizzard
Jim Reeves; *Best Of Jim Reeves* . . . . (RCA)
Blossoms In The Snow
Skyliners; *Skyliners' Greatest Hits* . . . . (Original Sound)
Clear As The Driven Snow
Doobie Brothers; *Captain & Me* . . . . (Warner Bros.)
Cold Rain And Snow
Grateful Dead; *Grateful Dead (Skull & Roses)* . . . . . . (Warner Bros.)
Steal Your Face . . . . (Grateful Dead)
Cover You In Kisses
John Michael Montgomery; *Leave A Mark* . . . . (Atlantic)
Don't Eat The Yellow Snow
Frank Zappa; *Apostrophe/Overnite Sensation* . . . . (Rykodisc)
Driven Like The Snow
Sisters Of Mercy; *Floodland* . . . . (Elektra)
Footprints In The Snow
Bill Monroe; *Best Of Bill Monroe & His Blue Grass Boys* . . . . (MCA)
Clarence White; *Treasures Untold-C* . . . . (Vanguard)
Kentucky Colonels featuring Clarence White; *Kentucky Colonels featuring
Clarence White* . . . . (Rounder)
Footprints In The Snow
Emerson, Lake & Palmer; *Black Moon* . . . . (Rhino)
Footprints In The Snow
Isley Brothers; *Complete UA Sessions* . . . . (EMI)
I Love The Winter Weather
Tony Bennett; *Snowfall: The Tony Bennett Christmas Album* . . (Columbia)
It Happened In Sun Valley
Glenn Miller & His Orchestra; *Complete Glenn Miller & His
Orchestra* . . . . (Bluebird)
Landslide
Fleetwood Mac; *25 Years-The Chain* . . . . (Warner Bros.)
Fleetwood Mac . . . . (Reprise)
Fleetwood Mac Live . . . . (Warner Bros.)
The Dance . . . . (Reprise)
Smashing Pumpkins; *Pisces Iscariot* . . . . (Virgin)
Last Snow Leopard
Spencer Brewer; *Emerald* . . . . (Narada)
Let It Snow! Let It Snow! Let It Snow!
Asleep At The Wheel; *Merry Texas Christmas, Y'all* . . . . . (High Street)
Bing Crosby; *Bing Crosby Christmas Classics* . . . . (Capitol)
Boys Choir Of Harlem; *Christmas Carols & Sacred Songs* . . . . . (Blue Note)
Carpenters; *Carpenters Christmas Portrait* . . . . (A&M)
Charley Pride; *Country Christmas-#1-C* . . . . (RCA)
Dean Martin; *Now That's What I Call Christmas!-C* . . . . (UTV)
Winter Romance . . . . (Capitol)
Herb Alpert & The Tijuana Brass; *Herb Alpert & The Tijuana Brass
Christmas Album* . . . . (A&M)
Jackie Gleason; *'Tis The Season* . . . . (Capitol)
Joe Williams; *That Holiday Feelin'* . . . . (Verve)
Lee Greenwood; *Christmas In The Country-C* . . . . . . (MCA Special Prod.)
Country Christmas To Remember-C . . . . (MCA Special Prod.)
Lee Greenwood-Christmas To Christmas . . . . (MCA Special Prod.)
Manhattan Transfer; *Manhattan Transfer-The Christmas Album* . . . . (Columbia)

Marcus Roberts; *Merry Jazzmus* . . . . (Novus)
Marie Osmond; *Christmas Country Classics-#1-C* . . . . (Curb)
Miracles; *Christmas With The Miracles* . . . . (Motown)
Mitch Miller; *Yuletide Cheer-C* . . . . (Columbia)
Steve Wariner; *Steve Wariner Christmas Memories* . . . . . (MCA Special Prod.)
Temptations; *Christmas Card/Give Love At Christmas* . . . . (Motown)
Christmas Card/Give Love At Christmas . . . . (Motown)
Trisha Yearwood; *The Sweetest Gift* . . . . (MCA)
Vaughn Monroe; *Billboard's Greatest Christmas Hits-C* . . . . (Rhino)
Wynton Marsalis; *Crescent City Christmas Card* . . . . (Columbia)
Listen, The Snow Is Falling
John Lennon; *Wedding Album* . . . . (Rykodisc)
Little Bit Of Snow
Howard Jones; *One To One* . . . . (Elektra)
New York's A Lonely Town
Tradewinds; *Beach Classics-All Original
Recordings-C* . . . . (Dunhill Compact Classics)
Original Golden Hits Of The Great Groups-#1-C . . . . . (SSS International)
Surfin' Hits-C . . . . (Rhino)
North To Alaska
Dwight Yoakam; *Under The Covers* . . . . (Reprise)
Johnny Horton; *American Originals-Johnny Horton* . . . . (Columbia)
Billboard Top Country Hits-1961-C . . . . (Rhino)
Johnny Horton's Greatest Hits . . . . (Columbia)
Super Hits Of The '60s-C . . . . (Epic)
November In The Snow/Lord Buckley
Mark Murphy; *Kerouac Then & Now* . . . . (Muse)
Old Lamplighter, The
Bing Crosby; *The Radio Years-#2* . . . . (Crescendo)
Browns; *45-#7700* . . . . (RCA)
Nipper's Greatest Hits Of The '60s-#2-C . . . . (RCA)
Kay Kyser & His Orchestra; *Best Of The Big Bands-Kay Kyser & His
Orchestra* . . . . (Legacy)
Sammy Kaye & His Orchestra; *Nipper's Greatest Hits Of The
'40s-#2-C* . . . . (RCA)
On A Snowy Christmas Night
Elvis Presley; *Elvis Sings The Wonderful World Of Christmas* . . . . . (RCA)
If Every Day Was Like Christmas . . . . (RCA)
On Top Of Old Smokey
Bing Crosby; *The Radio Years-#3* . . . . (Crescendo)
Weavers; *Best Of The Weavers* . . . . (MCA)
Reunion-At Carnegie Hall-1963-#2 . . . . (Vanguard)
Weavers' Greatest Hits . . . . (Vanguard)
Out Of The Snow
Amazing Rhythm Aces; *Too Stuffed To Jump* . . . . (MCA)
Pearls In The Snow
Michael Martin Murphey; *Cowboy Christmas* . . . . (Warner Bros.)
Raven In The Snow
Bill Miller; *Raven In The Snow* . . . . (Reprise)
Roses In The Snow
Emmylou Harris; *Roses In The Snow* . . . . (Warner Bros.)
Sand Castles In The Snow
Public Image Ltd.; *9* . . . . (Virgin)
September Snow
Danny Heines; *Aqua Touch* . . . . (Silver Wave)
Six Feet Of Snow
Little Feat; *Down On The Farm* . . . . (Warner Bros.)
Snow In San Anselmo
Van Morrison; *Hard Nose The Highway* . . . . (Polydor)
Snow On The Sahara
Anggun; *Anggun* . . . . (Epic)
Snowbird
Anne Murray; *15 Of The Best* . . . . (Liberty)
Anne Murray-Country . . . . (Capitol)
Anne Murray's Greatest Hits . . . . (Capitol)
Snowbird . . . . (Capitol)
Elvis Presley; *Canadian Tribute* . . . . (RCA)
Elvis Country ("I'm 10,000 Years Old") . . . . (RCA)
Loretta Lynn; *Coal Miner's Daughter* . . . . (MCA)
Snowblind
Black Sabbath; *Black Sabbath-Vol. 4* . . . . (Warner Bros.)
We Sold Our Soul For Rock 'N' Roll . . . . (Warner Bros.)
Ozzy Osbourne; *Speak Of The Devil* . . . . (Jet)
Snowblind
Styx; *Caught In The Act* . . . . (A&M)
Paradise Theater . . . . (A&M)
Snowblind Friend
David Allan Coe; *Unchained* . . . . (Columbia)
Hoyt Axton; *Snowblind Friend* . . . . (MCA)
Steppenwolf; *Steppenwolf 7* . . . . (MCA)
Steppenwolf-16 Greatest Hits . . . . (MCA)
Snowbound
Genesis; *And Then There Were Three* . . . . (Atlantic)
Summer Snow
Lou Christie; *Enlightnin'ment-Best Of Lou Christie* . . . . (Rhino)
Summer Snow
Blue Magic; *Magic Of The Blue-Greatest Hits* . . . . (Collectables)
Till It Snows In Mexico
Reba McEntire; *What Am I Gonna Do About You* . . . . (MCA)

Whales & Snow
Deep Jimi & The Zep Creams; *Funky Dinosaur* . . . . (East West)
When The Rain Turns To Snow
Lee Greenwood; *Lee Greenwood-Christmas To*
Christmas . . . . (MCA Special Prod.)
When The Snow Is On The Roses
Ed Ames; *Best Of Ed Ames* . . . . (RCA)
Ed Ames-Pure Gold . . . . (RCA)
Sonny James; *American Originals-Sonny James* . . . . (Columbia)
Sonny James' Greatest Hits . . . . (Columbia)
Wings Of A Dove
Bob Marley & The Wailers; *Birth Of A Legend 1963-*
1966 . . . . (Epic Portrait Assoc.)
Ferlin Husky; *Billboard Top Country Hits-1960-C* . . . . (Rhino)
Country Music Classics-#2-1960-1965-C . . . . (K-Tel)
Ferlin Husky's Greatest Hits . . . . (Curb)
Winter Wonderland
Air Supply; *Air Supply Christmas Album* . . . . (Arista)
White Christmas . . . . (Word)
Alexander O'Neal; *My Gift To You* . . . . (Tabu)
Amy Grant; *Home For Christmas* . . . . (A&M)
Andrews Sisters; *Andrews Sisters-Christmas* . . . . (MCA Special Prod.)
Anne Murray; *Best Of The Season* . . . . (EMI America)
Aretha Franklin; *Rock 'N' Roll Christmas*
Classics-C . . . . (Music For Little People)
Barbara Mandrell; *Christmas At Our House* . . . . (MCA Special Prod.)
Tennessee Christmas-C . . . . (MCA)
Bing Crosby; *Bing Crosby Christmas Classics* . . . . (Capitol)
Blue Notes; *Rhythm & Blues Christmas-#1-C* . . . . (Collectables)
Brenda Lee; *Jingle Bell Rock* . . . . (MCA Special Prod.)
Carnie & Wendy Wilson; *Hey Santa!* . . . . (SBK)
Darlene Love; *Christmas Gift For You From Phil Spector-C* . . . . (Rhino)
Phil Spector-Back To Mono 1958-1969-C . . . . (Abkco)
Phil Spector's Christmas Album-C . . . . (Passport)
Eddy Arnold; *Christmas With Eddy Arnold* . . . . (RCA)
Elvis Presley; *If Every Day Was Like Christmas* . . . . (RCA)
Eurythmics; *Very Special Christmas-C* . . . . (A&M)
Faron Young; *Country Christmas* . . . . (Step One)
Frank Sinatra; *Christmas Songs By Sinatra* . . . . (Legacy)
George Strait; *Merry Christmas Strait To You* . . . . (MCA Special Prod.)
Hank Crawford; *We Got A Good Thing Going* . . . . (Kudo)
Johnny Mercer & The Pied Pipers; *Merry Christmas Baby-Romance &*
Reindeer-C . . . . (Capitol)
Kathie Lee Gifford; *It's Christmas Time* . . . . (Warner Bros.)
Kenny Rogers; *Christmas In America* . . . . (Reprise)
London Symphony Orchestra; *Christmas Traditions* . . . . . . (Special Music Co.)
Merle Haggard; *Merle Haggard-Christmas Gift* . . . . (Curb)
Patti LaBelle & The Blue Belles; *A Soulful Christmas-C* . . . . . . (Collectables)
Randy Travis; *An Old Time Christmas* . . . . (Warner Bros.)
Robert Goulet; *Essence Of Christmas* . . . . (A&M)
Rosie O'Donnell & Macy Gray; *Another Rosie Christmas-C* . . . . . . (Columbia)
Tanya Tucker; *Christmas For The '90s-#1-C* . . . . (Liberty)
Tony Bennett; *Now That's What I Call Christmas!-C* . . . . (UTV)
Travis Tritt; *Christmas-Loving Time Of The Year* . . . . (Warner Bros.)

SOCIAL CLASS: GENERAL, Class Differences,

Ruling Class

See Also: LIFE, LOVE: FORBIDDEN LOVE, MONEY, POVERTY,
PREJUDICE, ROYALTY, SMALL TOWN LIFE, SOCIAL CLASS:
RURAL, WORK

(I'm Not Your) Steppin' Stone
Monkees; *Monkees' Greatest Hits* . . . . (Rhino)
(We're Not) The Jet Set
George Jones & Tammy Wynette; *George Jones & Tammy Wynette-16*
Biggest Hits . . . . (Epic/Legacy)
Amanda
Don Williams; *Don Williams' Greatest Hits* . . . . (MCA)
Volume One . . . . (MCA)
Waylon Jennings; *Waylon Jennings' Greatest Hits* . . . . (RCA)
An Acceptable Level Of Ecstasy (The Wedding Song)
Lyle Lovett; *Lyle Lovett* . . . . (MCA)
Anyway
Keb' Mo'; *The Door* . . . . (550/Epic/Okeh)
Atlantic City
Bruce Springsteen; *Bruce Springsteen's Greatest Hits* . . . . (Columbia)
Nebraska . . . . (Columbia)
Badlands
Bruce Springsteen; *Bruce Springsteen's Greatest Hits* . . . . (Columbia)
Darkness On The Edge Of Town . . . . (Columbia)
Bruce Springsteen & The E Street Band; *Bruce Springsteen & The E Street*
Band Live/1975-85 . . . . (Legacy)
Beast Of Burden
Bette Midler; *No Frills* . . . . (Atlantic)
Rolling Stones; *Rewind (1971-1984)* . . . . (Rolling Stones)
Some Girls . . . . (Virgin)

Sucking In The Seventies . . . . (Rolling Stones)
Big Spender
Original Cast; *Sweet Charity* . . . . (Columbia)
Born In The U.S.A.
Bruce Springsteen; *Born In The U.S.A.* . . . . (Columbia)
Bruce Springsteen's Greatest Hits . . . . (Columbia)
Tracks . . . . (Columbia)
Bruce Springsteen & The E Street Band; *Bruce Springsteen & The E Street*
Band Live/1975-85 . . . . (Legacy)
Common Man
John Conlee; *Best Of John Conlee* . . . . (Curb)
Busted . . . . (MCA Special Prod.)
John Conlee-20 Greatest Hits . . . . (MCA)
John Conlee's Greatest Hits . . . . (MCA)
Cotton Mill Man
Jim & Jesse; *Old Dominion Masters* . . . . (Pinecastle)
C-O-U-N-T-R-Y
Joe Diffie; *Life's So Funny* . . . . (Epic)
Country Club
Travis Tritt; *Country Club* . . . . (Warner Bros.)
Cowboy Love
John Michael Montgomery; *John Michael Montgomery* . . . . (Atlantic)
John Michael Montgomery's Greatest Hits . . . . (Atlantic)
Cracklin' Rosie
Neil Diamond; *Hot August Night* . . . . (MCA)
Hot August Night II . . . . (Columbia)
Neil Diamond-His 12 Greatest Hits . . . . (MCA)
Tap Root Manuscript . . . . (MCA)
Daddy Never Was The Cadillac Kind
Confederate Railroad; *Notorious* . . . . (Atlantic)
Darkness On The Edge Of Town
Bruce Springsteen; *Darkness On The Edge Of Town* . . . . (Columbia)
Bruce Springsteen & The E Street Band; *Bruce Springsteen & The E Street*
Band Live/1975-85 . . . . (Legacy)
Dawn (Go Away)
4 Seasons; *25th Anniversary Collection* . . . . (Rhino)
4 Seasons-Anthology . . . . (Rhino)
Don't Get Above Your Raising
Lester Flatt, Earl Scruggs & The Foggy Mountain Boys; *Bluegrass Super*
Hits-C . . . . (Columbia)
Down In The Boondocks
Billy Joe Royal; *Billy Joe Royal's Greatest Hits* . . . . (Columbia)
Rock Classics Of The '60s-C . . . . (Columbia)
Factory
Bruce Springsteen; *Darkness On The Edge Of Town* . . . . (Columbia)
Factory Girl
Rolling Stones; *Beggars Banquet* . . . . (Abkco)
Fancy
Bobbi Gentry; *All-Time Country Classics-#1-C* . . . . (Capitol)
Reba McEntire; *Rumor Has It* . . . . (MCA)
Fat Lip
Sum 41; *All Killer No Filler* . . . . (Island/IDJMG)
Now That's What I Call Music!-#8-C . . . . (Virgin)
Fill Her Up
Earl Scruggs & Sting; *Earl Scruggs And Friends-C* . . . . (MCA)
Friends In Low Places
Garth Brooks; *Garth Brooks-Double Live* . . . . (Capitol)
No Fences . . . . (Capitol)
Georgia On A Fast Train
Billy Joe Shaver; *Hot Tracks-Train Super Hits-C* . . . . (Epic)
Girl, You'll Be A Woman Soon
Neil Diamond; *Double Gold-Neil Diamond* . . . . (Bang)
Hot August Night . . . . (MCA)
Neil Diamond-Classics (Early Years) . . . . (Columbia)
Neil Diamond's Greatest Hits . . . . (Bang)
Goodbye Yellow Brick Road
Elton John; *Billboard Top Rock 'N' Roll Hits-1973-C* . . . . (Rhino)
Elton John's Greatest Hits . . . . (Polydor)
Goodbye Yellow Brick Road . . . . (Polydor)
Gotta Serve Somebody
Bob Dylan; *Biograph* . . . . (Columbia)
Slow Train Coming . . . . (Columbia)
The Sopranos-Music From The HBO Original
Series . . . . (Sony Music Soundtrax)
Bob Dylan & The Grateful Dead; *Dylan & The Dead* . . . . (Columbia)
Grand Hotel
Procol Harum; *Grand Hotel* . . . . (Chrysalis)
Gypsies In The Palace
Jimmy Buffett; *Feeding Frenzy* . . . . (MCA)
Last Mango In Paris . . . . (MCA)
Hang On Sloopy
McCoys; *21 Oldies But Goodies-C* . . . . (Original Sound)
Billboard Top Rock 'N' Roll Hits-1965-C . . . . (Rhino)
Frat Rock!-C . . . . (Rhino)
Oldies But Goodies-C . . . . (Original Sound)
Ramsey Lewis; *Greatest Hits Of Ramsey Lewis* . . . . (Chess)
Vintage Music-#20-C . . . . (MCA)
Hard Workin' Man
Brooks & Dunn; *Hard Workin' Man* . . . . (Arista)

High Society
Glen Gray; *The Uncollected Glen Gray & The Casa Loma Orchestra-1939-1940* .... (Hindsight)
Louis Armstrong; *C'Est Si Bon* .... (Rhino)
Pete Fountain; *Best Of Pete Fountain* .... (MCA)
Teddy Buckner; *Salute To Louis Armstrong* .... (Crescendo)

Hungry Eyes
Emmylou Harris; *Mama's Hungry Eyes-Merle Haggard Tribute-C* ..... (Arista)
Merle Haggard; *For The Record: Merle Haggard-43 Legendary Hits* ....(BNA)

I Am A Simple Man
Ricky Van Shelton; *Backroads* .... (Columbia)

If I Were A Carpenter
Bobby Darin; *Live At The Desert Inn* .... (Motown)
Four Tops; *Compact Command Performances-Four Tops* .... (Motown)
  Four Tops Reach Out .... (Motown)
  Four Tops-Anthology .... (Motown)
Johnny Cash & June Carter; *The Man In Black-His Greatest Hits* ...... (Legacy)
Tim Hardin; *Memorial Album* .... (Polydor)

If My Friends Could See Me Now
Original Cast/Gwen Verdon; *Sweet Charity* .... (Columbia)

If You've Got Trouble
Beatles; *The Beatles-Anthology-#2* .... (Capitol)

I've Come To Wive It Wealthily In Padua
Original Soundtrack; *Kiss Me Kate* .... (Rhino)

Jacob's Ladder
Mark Wills; *Mark Wills* .... (Mercury)

Jealousy
Natalie Merchant; *Tigerlily* .... (Elektra)

Lady Came From Baltimore
Joan Baez; *Contemporary Ballad Book* .... (Vanguard)
  Joan .... (Vanguard)
John Stewart; *Neon Beach* .... (Homecoming)
Johnny Cash; *Johnny Cash-16 Biggest Hits-#2* .... (Legacy)
Tim Hardin; *Hang On To A Dream-Verve Recordings* .... (Polydor)

Lady Is A Tramp
Ella Fitzgerald; *Rodgers & Hart Songbook* .... (Verve)
Frank Sinatra; *Sinatra Reprise-The Very Good Years* .... (Reprise)
  The Capitol Years .... (Capitol)
Frank Sinatra & Luther Vandross; *Frank Sinatra-Duets-C* .... (Capitol)

Leader Of The Pack
Bette Midler; *Divine Miss M* .... (Atlantic)
  ST/Divine Madness .... (Atlantic)
Original Cast; *Leader Of The Pack* .... (Elektra)
Shangri-Las; *21 Number One Hits-C* .... (Original Sound)
  Billboard Top Rock 'N' Roll Hits-1964-C .... (Rhino)
  Girl Groups-Story Of A Sound-C .... (Rhino)
  Golden Hits Of The Shangri-Las .... (Mercury)
  Oldies But Goodies-#15-C .... (Original Sound)
  Radio Active Hits-#2-C .... (Accord)
  Remember The Shangri-Las At Their Best .... (Collectables)

Like A Rolling Stone
Bob Dylan; *Biograph.* .... (Columbia)
  Bob Dylan At Budokan .... (Columbia)
  Bob Dylan's Greatest Hits .... (Columbia)
  Highway 61 Revisited .... (Columbia)
  More American Graffiti-#4-C .... (MCA)
  Self Portrait .... (Columbia)
Bob Dylan And The Band; *Before The Flood* .... (Columbia)
Jimi Hendrix; *ST/Jimi Plays Monterey* .... (Reprise)
Jimi Hendrix Experience; *Jimi Hendrix Experience* .... (Reprise)
Rolling Stones; *Stripped* .... (Virgin)

Little Bitty
Alan Jackson; *Everything I Love* .... (Arista)
Tom T. Hall; *Songs From Sopchoppy* .... (Mercury)
  Tom T. Hall-The Hits .... (Mercury)

Losing A Whole Year
Third Eye Blind; *Third Eye Blind* .... (Elektra)

Love Child
Diana Ross & The Supremes; *Billboard Top Rock 'N' Roll Hits-1968-C* .... (Rhino)
  Diana Ross & The Supremes' Greatest Hits-#3 .... (Motown)
  Diana Ross & The Supremes-Anthology (1962-1969) .... (Motown)
  Every Great #1 Hit .... (Motown)
  Motown Story-First 25 Years-C .... (Motown)
  Motown's Biggest Pop Hits-C .... (Motown)
Sweet Sensation; *Love Child* .... (Atco)

Luckenbach Texas (Back To The Basics Of Love)
Waylon Jennings; *Ol' Waylon* .... (RCA)
  Stars Are Out In Texas-C .... (RCA)
  Waylon Jennings' Greatest Hits .... (RCA)

Lyin' Eyes
Eagles; *Eagles/Their Greatest Hits 1971-1975* .... (Asylum)
  One Of These Nights .... (Asylum)
  ST/Urban Cowboy .... (Asylum)

Music
Madonna; *GHV2* .... (Warner Bros.)
  Music .... (Maverick)
  Totally Hits-#3-C .... (Atlantic)

Ordinary Life
Chad Brock; *Chad Brock* .... (Warner Bros.)

Pick Me Up On Your Way Down
Charlie Walker; *Columbia Country Classics-#2-Honky Tonk Heroes-C* .... (Columbia)
  Heroes Of Country Music-#2-Legends Of Honky Tonk-C .... (Rhino)
Harlan Howard; *All-Time Favorite Country Songwriter* ....(Koch International)

Piggies
Beatles; *Beatles-Box Set.* .... (Capitol)
  The Beatles (White Album) .... (Capitol)
George Harrison; *Live In Japan* .... (Dark Horse)

Po' White Trash
White Trash; *White Trash* .... (Elektra)

Poor Side Of Town
Johnny Rivers; *Best Of Johnny Rivers* .... (EMI)
  Changes/Rewind .... (EMI)
  Johnny Rivers-Anthology 1964-1977 .... (Rhino)
  Very Best Of Johnny Rivers .... (EMI)

Puttin' On The Ritz
Ella Fitzgerald; *Silver Collection-Songbooks.* .... (Verve)
Fred Astaire; *Irving Berlin Always-C* .... (Verve)
  Irving Berlin Songbook .... (Verve)
Harry Richman; *Hollywood Sings-C* .... (Living Era)
  Those Wonderful Years: Puttin' On The Ritz-C .... (JCI Assoc. Labels)
Judy Garland; *One & Only* .... (Capitol)
Mandy Patinkin; *Mandy Patinkin.* .... (Columbia)
Taco; *After Eight* .... (RCA)
  Nipper's Greatest Hits Of The '80s-C .... (RCA)

Rag Doll
4 Seasons; *25th Anniversary Collection* .... (Rhino)
  4 Seasons' Greatest Hits-#2 .... (Rhino)
  4 Seasons-Anthology .... (Rhino)
  Billboard Top Rock 'N' Roll Hits-1964-C .... (Rhino)

River, The
Bruce Springsteen; *Bruce Springsteen's Greatest Hits* .... (Columbia)
  The River. .... (Columbia)
Bruce Springsteen & The E Street Band; *Bruce Springsteen & The E Street Band Live/1975-85* .... (Legacy)

Saginaw, Michigan
Lefty Frizzell; *American Originals-Lefty Frizzell* .... (Columbia)
  Billboard Top Country Hits-1964-C .... (Rhino)
  Columbia Country Classics-#3-Americana-C .... (Columbia)
  Lefty Frizzell's Greatest Hits. .... (Columbia)

Salt Of The Earth
Mick Jagger & Keith Richards; *The Concert For New York City-C* ...(Columbia)
Rolling Stones; *Beggars Banquet.* .... (Abkco)

Slumming On Park Avenue
Ella Fitzgerald; *The Irving Berlin Songbook-#2.* .... (Verve)

Society's Child (Baby I've Been Thinking)
Janis Ian; *Songs Of Protest-C* .... (Rhino)
  The Bottom Line Encore Collection .... (Bottom Line)
Lou Gramm; *A Foreigner In His Own Land: Best Of Early Years.* .... (Collectables)
  Past Times Behind Rock & Roll-C .... (Intermedia)

Sophisticated Lady
Diane Schuur; *In Tribute* .... (GRP)
Duke Ellington; *Mood Indigo.* .... (Pro-Arte)
  Reminiscing In Tempo. .... (Columbia)
Linda Ronstadt; *Lush Life* .... (Asylum)
Original Broadway Cast; *Bubbling Brown Sugar* .... (Amherst)
Rosemary Clooney; *Essence Of Rosemary Clooney* .... (Legacy)
Tito Puente & His Latin Ensemble; *On Broadway.* ...... (Concord Picante Jazz)

Substitute
Great White; *Great White.* .... (EMI)
Sex Pistols; *Live At Chelmsford Top Security Prison.* ...... (Restless)
Who; *Live At Leeds* .... (MCA)
  Meaty Beaty Big & Bouncy .... (MCA)
  Who Greatest Hits .... (MCA)
  Who's Last. .... (MCA)

Theme From "Fresh Prince Of Bel-Air"
Original Soundtrack; *Television's Greatest Hits-#7-Cable Ready-C* ..... (TVT)

Theme From "Lifestyles Of The Rich And Famous"
Original Soundtrack; *Television's Greatest Hits-#6-Remote Control-C* ... (TVT)

Theme From "Roseanne"
Original Soundtrack; *Television's Greatest Hits-#7-Cable Ready-C* ..... (TVT)

Theme From "Silver Spoons"
Original Soundtrack; *Television's Greatest Hits-#6-Remote Control-C* ... (TVT)

Theme From "The Jeffersons"
Original Soundtrack; *CBS: The First 50 Years.* .... (TVT)
  Television's Greatest Hits-#3-1970s & 1980s-C. .... (TVT)

Theme From "The Nanny"
Original Soundtrack; *Television's Greatest Hits-#7-Cable Ready-C* ..... (TVT)

There Goes The Neighborhood
Sheryl Crow; *The Globe Sessions* .... (A&M)

Third Rate Romance
Amazing Rhythm Aces; *Stacked Deck* .... (MCA)
Rosanne Cash; *Somewhere In The Stars* .... (Columbia)
Sammy Kershaw; *Cryin' Lyin' Lovin' & Leavin'-C* .... (Universal)
  Feelin' Good Train .... (Mercury)

The Hits-Chapter 1 .... (Mercury)

Top Hat, White Tie And Tails
Fred Astaire; *Irving Berlin Songbook* .... (Verve)

Uptown Girl
Billy Joel; *An Innocent Man* .... (Columbia)
Billy Joel-Greatest Hits, Volume I & Volume II .... (Columbia)
KOHUEPT .... (Columbia)

Wat About Di Workin' Class?
Linton Kwesi Johnson; *Linton Kwesi Johnson In Concert With The Dub Band* .... (Shanachie)

Well Respected Man
Kinks; *History Of British Rock-#4-C* .... (Rhino)
Kinks' Greatest Hits .... (Rhino)
Kinks-Size Kinkdom .... (Rhino)

When Country Comes To Town
Toby Keith; *How Do You Like Me Now?!* .... (DreamWorks/SKG)

When I Take My Sugar To Tea
Boswell Sisters; *78-#6083* .... (Brunswick)
Frank Sinatra; *Ring-A-Ding Ding* .... (Reprise)
Nat "King" Cole; *The Vocal Classics-1947-1950* .... (Capitol)

When Two Worlds Collide
Rex Allen, Jr.; *20 Golden Souvenirs Of Music City U.S.A.-C* ...... (Plantation)
Roger Miller; *Best Of Roger Miller-His Greatest Songs* .... (Curb)

White Trash Wife
Exene Cervenka; *Old Wives' Tales* .... (Rhino)

White Trash With Cash
Southgang; *Group Therapy* .... (Charisma)

Why Can't The English
Rex Harrison; *ST/My Fair Lady* .... (Columbia)
Rex Harrison/Original Cast; *My Fair Lady* .... (Columbia)

Working Man's Ph.D.
Aaron Tippin; *Call Of The Wild* .... (RCA)

You Got What It Takes
Dave Clark Five; *History Of The Dave Clark Five* .... (Hollywood)
Marv Johnson; *All-Time Greatest Hits Of Rock 'N' Roll-C* .... (Curb)

You Know Me Better Than That
George Strait; *Strait Out Of The Box* ....(MCA)
The Chill Of An Early Fall ....(MCA)

Youngstown
Bruce Springsteen; *The Ghost Of Tom Joad* .... (Columbia)

SOCIAL CLASS: RURAL, Hillbillies, Rednecks

See Also: COUNTRY, FARMS, SOCIAL CLASS: GENERAL, SMALL TOWN LIFE, WORK

(What This World Needs Is) A Few More Rednecks
Charlie Daniels; *The Roots Remain* .... (Legacy)

Adalida
George Strait; *Latest Greatest Straitest Hits* ....(MCA)
Lead On ....(MCA)

Bubba Hyde
Diamond Rio; *Diamond Rio's Greatest Hits* .... (Arista)
Love A Little Stronger .... (Arista)

Bubba Shot The Jukebox
Mark Chesnutt; *Longnecks & Short Stories* ....(MCA)

Country In My Jeans
Loretta Lynn; *Still Country* .... (Audium)

Damn Good Cowboy
Charlie Daniels Band; *Cowboy Super Hits-C* .... (Columbia)
Night Rider ....(Epic)

Eat Shit You Fucking Redneck
Pigface; *Eat Shit You F@$king Redneck* .... (Invisible)

Friends In Low Places
Garth Brooks; *Garth Brooks-Double Live* .... (Capitol)
No Fences .... (Capitol)

Hillbillies From Outerspace
Vaughan Brothers; *Family Style* .... (Epic Portrait Assoc.)

Hillbilly Band
Marshall Tucker Band; *Best Of The Marshall Tucker Band-The Capricorn Years* .... (Era)
Country Tucker .... (Era)
Marshall Tucker Band .... (AJK Music)

Hillbilly Blue
Neal McCoy; *At This Moment* .... (Atlantic)

Hillbilly Blues
Eddy Clearwater; *Chicago Ain't Nothin' But A Blues Band-C* ...... (Delmark)

Hillbilly Blues
Lynyrd Skynyrd; *Endangered Species* .... (Capricorn)

Hillbilly Boy With The Rock N' Roll Blues
Mark Collie; *Mark Collie* ....(MCA)

Hillbilly Fever
"Little" Jimmy Dickens; *Heroes Of Country Music-#3-Legends Of Nashville-C* .... (Rhino)
I'm Little, But I'm Loud-The "Little" Jimmy Dickens Collection .... (Razor & Tie)
Osborne Brothers; *Hillbilly Fever* ....(C.M.H. Prod.)

Hillbilly Fever
"Little" Jimmy Dickens; *Sony Music 100 Years-Soundtrack For A Century-C* .... (Sony)

Hillbilly Girl
Greg Brown; *Down In There* .... (Rhyme Syndicate)

Hillbilly Girl In High Heels
Jack Smith & The Rockabilly Planet; *Jack Smith & The Rockabilly Planet* .... (Flying Fish)

Hillbilly Girl With The Blues
Lacy J. Dalton; *Country Shots-Heartbreak-Ups-C* .... (Rhino)

Hillbilly Heaven
Tex Ritter; *Conversation With A Gun* ....(Richmond)

Hillbilly Hell
Bellamy Brothers; *Bellamy Brothers' Greatest Hits-#3* .... (MCA)

Hillbilly Highway
Ricky Skaggs; *Life Is A Journey* ....(Atlantic)
Steve Earle; *Ain't Ever Satisfied: The Steve Earle Collection* .... (Hip-O)
Essential Steve Earle ....(MCA)
Guitar Town ....(MCA)

Hillbilly Hollywood
John Anderson; *Seminole Wind* ....(BNA)

Hillbilly Hula Gal
Junior Brown; *12 Shades Of Brown* ....(Curb)

Hillbilly Jazz
Vassar Clements; *Hillbilly Jazz Rides Again* .... (Flying Fish)

Hillbilly Music
Jerry Lee Lewis; *Jerry Lee's Greatest!* .... (Rhino)

Hillbilly Nation Poem
Goose Creek Symphony; *Goose Is Loose, The* .... (Winter Harvest Entert.)

Hillbilly Rap
Neal McCoy; *Neal McCoy* ....(Atlantic)

Hillbilly Rock
Marty Stuart; *Hillbilly Rock* .... (MCA)
Marty Party Hit Pack ....(MCA)

Hillbilly Serenade
Early Drane; *Blues Hangover-Excello Blues Rarities-C* .... (Excello)

Hillbilly Shoes
Montgomery Gentry; *Tattoos & Scars* .... (Columbia)

Hillbilly Swing
Al & Emily Cantrell; *Under A Southern Moon* .... (Sombrero)

Hillbilly Thang
BR5-49; *Live From Robert's* .... (Arista)

Hillbilly Train
George & The Tennessee Sons; *Nashville-The Other Side Of The Alley-Insurgent Country-#3-C* ....(Bloodshot)

Hillbilly Willie's Blues
Alvin Youngblood Hart; *Big Mama's Door* ....(Okeh)
Blind Willie McTell; *Complete Recorded Works-#3-1933-1935* ....(Document)

Hillbilly With A Heartache
Tracy Lawrence; *I See It Now* ....(Atlantic)

Hillbilly With A Record Deal
Montana Rose; *Highway 191* .... (Cowboy Heaven)

Hillbilly Wolf
Link Wray & The Wraymen; *Hillbilly Wolf-Missing Links-#1* .... (Norton)

Honky Tonk Women Love Redneck Men
Ronnie McDowell; *American Music* ....(Curb)

I'll Think Of A Reason Later
Lee Ann Womack; *Some Things I Know* .... (Decca)

It''s Alright To Be A Redneck
Alan Jackson; *When Somebody Loves You* .... (Arista)

John Deere Green
Joe Diffie; *Honky Tonk Attitude* .... (Epic)
Joe Diffie's Greatest Hits .... (Epic)

No Trash In My Trailer
Gene Watson; *From The Heart* .... (Row Music Group)

Okie From Muskogee
Merle Haggard; *Friend In California* .... (Epic)
Merle Haggard & The Strangers; *Best Of Merle Haggard & The Strangers* .... (Capitol)
Capitol Collectors Series-Merle Haggard & The Strangers .... (Capitol)
Country Music Classics-#3-1965-1970-C .... (K-Tel)
For The Record: Merle Haggard-43 Legendary Hits .... (BNA)
Songs I'll Always Sing .... (Capitol)
ST/Platoon ....(Atlantic)

People Like Us
Aaron Tippin; *People Like Us* ....(Lyric Street)

Queen Of My Double Wide Trailer
Sammy Kershaw; *Haunted Heart* .... (Mercury)

Redneck
Carl Perkins; *Best Of Carl Perkins* .... (Pegasus/Cleopatra)

Redneck 12 Days Of Christmas
Jeff Foxworthy; *Crank It Up: The Music Album* .... (Warner Bros.)
Jeff Foxworthy's Greatest Bits .... (Warner Bros.)

Redneck Eats
Frank Zappa; *200 Motels* .... (Rykodisc)

Redneck Fiddlin' Man
Charlie Daniels Band; *Greatest Fiddlin' Licks* .... (Epic)
Midnight Wind ....(Epic)

Redneck Games
Jeff Foxworthy; *Crank It Up: The Music Album* . . . . (Warner Bros.)
Jeff Foxworthy's Greatest Bits . . . . (Warner Bros.)
Redneck Girl
Bellamy Brothers; *America's Country: Good Time Country-C* . . . . . . (Madacy)
Bellamy Brothers' Greatest Hits . . . . (MCA)
Bellamy Brothers' Greatest Hits-#1 . . . . (Curb)
Bellamy Brothers-At Their Best . . . . (EMI Special Markets)
Redneck Girl
Kentucky HeadHunters; *Best Of The Kentucky HeadHunters-Still
Pickin'* . . . . (Mercury)
Redneck Heaven
Billy Ray Cyrus; *Storm In The Heartland* . . . . (Mercury)
Redneck In A Rock & Roll Bar
Jerry Reed; *Redneck Mothers-C* . . . . (RCA)
Redneck Is The Backbone Of America
John Schneider; *You Ain't Seen The Last Of Me* . . . . (MCA)
Redneck Jazz
Danny Gatton; *Hot Rod Guitar: The Danny Gatton Anthology* . . . . (Rhino)
Redneck Like Me
Little Texas; *Kick A Little* . . . . (Warner Bros.)
Redneck Punk
Jackyl; *Choice Cuts (Greatest Hits)* . . . . (Geffen)
Jackyl . . . . (Geffen)
Redneck Radio
Brother Russell; *Radio Jihad (Phone Pranks)* . . . . (Vinyl Comm.)
Redneck Rampage
Mojo Nixon; *The Real Sock-Ray-Blue* . . . . (Yazoo)
Redneck Rap
Big Ed Johnson; *A Mind Is A Terrible Thing To Waist* . . . . . (Laughing Stock)
Redneck Rhythm & Blues
Brooks & Dunn; *Borderline* . . . . (Arista)
Redneck Riot
Countrypolitans; *Full Tank-#1-C* . . . . (Jackass)
Redneck Riviera
Tom T. Hall; *Songs From Sopchoppy* . . . . (Mercury)
Redneck Rock N' Roll
Pirates Of The Mississippi; *Pirates Of The Mississippi* . . . . (Liberty)
Redneck Romance
Nine Pound Hammer; *Live At The Vera* . . . . (Scooch Pooch)
Redneck Romeo
Confederate Railroad; *Notorious* . . . . (Atlantic)
Redneck Roses
Tracy Byrd; *No Ordinary Man* . . . . (MCA)
Redneck School Of Technology
Flaming Lips; *Telepathic Surgery* . . . . (Restless)
Redneck Society
7 Seconds; *Alt.music.hardcore* . . . . (Headhunter)
Redneck Stomp
Jeff Foxworthy; *America's Country: Good Time Country-C* . . . . (Madacy)
Crank It Up: The Music Album . . . . (Warner Bros.)
Jeff Foxworthy's Greatest Bits . . . . (Warner Bros.)
Redneck U
Keith Perry; *Keith Perry* . . . . (Curb)
Redneck Woman From Planet Mars
Horny Mormons; *Can Of Pork-C* . . . . (Lookout)
Redneck Wonderland
Midnight Oil; *Redneck Wonderland* . . . . (Columbia)
Redneckin'
Daryle Singletary; *All Because Of You* . . . . (Giant)
Rednecks
Randy Newman; *Good Old Boys* . . . . (Reprise)
Guilty: 30 Years Of Randy Newman . . . . (Rhino)
Rednecks Unplugged
Amazing Rhythm Aces; *Chock Full Of Country Goodness* . . . . . . (Valley Entert.)
Rednecks, White Socks And Blue Ribbon Beer
Johnny Russell; *Beer Redneck Mothers* . . . . (RCA)
Country Legends-C . . . . (Madacy)
Country's Greatest Drinking Songs-C . . . . (All-Star Music)
Rednecks, White Socks & Blue Ribbon Beer . . . . (RCA)
Theme From "The Beverly Hillbillies"
Original Soundtrack; *CBS: The First 50 Years* . . . . (TVT)
Television's Greatest Hits-#1-C . . . . (TVT)
Theme From "The Dukes Of Hazzard"
Waylon Jennings; *Only Daddy That'll Walk The Line-The RCA Years* . . . . (RCA)
Television's Greatest Hits-#6-Remote Control-C . . . . (TVT)
Waylon Jennings' Greatest Hits-#2 . . . . (RCA)
There's A Red-Neck In The Soul Band
Latimore; *Straighten It Out: The Best Of Latimore* . . . . (Rhino)
Uneasy Rider
Charlie Daniels Band; *A Decade Of Hits* . . . . (Epic)
Homesick Heroes . . . . (Epic)
Super Hits Of The '70s-Have A Nice Day-#11-C . . . . (Rhino)
Uneasy Rider . . . . (Epic)
When Country Comes To Town
Toby Keith; *How Do You Like Me Now?!* . . . . (DreamWorks/SKG)
When It All Goes South
Alabama; *When It All Goes South* . . . . (RCA)

White Trash
Orchestral Manoeuvres In The Dark; *Junk Culture* . . . . (A&M)
White Trash
Redd Kross; *Born Innocent* . . . . (Frontier)
White Trash
Bellamy Brothers; *Crazy From The Heart* . . . . (MCA)
White Trash
Bad Religion; *How Could Hell Be Any Worse* . . . . (Epitaph)
White Trash
Steve Cash; *White Mansions* . . . . (A&M)
White Trash Song
Steve Young; *Honky-Tonk Man* . . . . (Rounder)
Solo/Live . . . . (Watermelon)

SOCIAL OUTCASTS, Freaks, Social Misfits, Society's Rejects, Throw-away Kids

See Also: CRAZY, LOW SELF-ESTEEM, MISTREATMENT, POLITICS: SOCIAL INJUSTICE, REBELS, SLEAZY

Better Days (And The Bottom Drops Out)
Citizen King; *Mobile Estates* . . . . (Warner Bros.)
Born In The U.S.A.
Bruce Springsteen; *Born In The U.S.A.* . . . . (Columbia)
Bruce Springsteen's Greatest Hits . . . . (Columbia)
Tracks . . . . (Columbia)
Bruce Springsteen & The E Street Band; *Bruce Springsteen & The E Street
Band Live/1975-85* . . . . (Legacy)
Branded Man
Merle Haggard & The Strangers; *For The Record: Merle Haggard-43
Legendary Hits* . . . . (BNA)
Duck And Run
3 Doors Down; *Better Life* . . . . (Republic/Universal)
Eleanor Rigby
Beatles; *Beatles 1* . . . . (Capitol)
Revolver . . . . (Capitol)
The Beatles/1962-1966 . . . . (Capitol)
Ray Charles; *Ray Charles' Greatest Hits-#2* . . . . (Rhino)
Ray Charles-Anthology . . . . (Rhino)
Englishman In New York
Sting; *...Nothing Like The Sun* . . . . (A&M)
Fields Of Gold-The Best Of Sting 1984-1994 . . . . (A&M)
Freak
Silverchair; *Freak Show* . . . . (Epic)
Freak Of The Week
Marvelous 3; *Hey Album* . . . . (HiFi/Elektra)
Freak On A Leash
Korn; *Follow The Leader* . . . . (Immortal/Epic)
Freaks
Live; *Secret Samadhi* . . . . (Radioactive/MCA)
Geek Stink Breath
Green Day; *Insomniac* . . . . (Reprise)
Highway Chile
Jimi Hendrix Experience; *Are You Experienced?* . . . . (Reprise)
Immortality
Pearl Jam; *Vitalogy* . . . . (Epic)
Jeremy
Pearl Jam; *Ten* . . . . (Epic Portrait Assoc.)
Jig Saw Puzzle
Rolling Stones; *Beggars Banquet* . . . . (Abkco)
Jumper
Third Eye Blind; *Third Eye Blind* . . . . (Elektra)
Totally Hits-#1-C . . . . (Arista)
King Of New Orleans
Better Than Ezra; *Friction, Baby* . . . . (Swell/Elektra)
Long Way Down
Goo Goo Dolls; *A Boy Named Goo* . . . . (Metal Blade)
Losing A Whole Year
Third Eye Blind; *Third Eye Blind* . . . . (Elektra)
More Human Than Human
White Zombie; *Astro-Creep: 2000 Songs Of Love* . . . . (Geffen)
My Generation
Who; *Live At Leeds* . . . . (MCA)
Meaty Beaty Big & Bouncy . . . . (MCA)
ST/The Kids Are Alright . . . . (MCA)
The Who Sings "My Generation" . . . . (MCA)
Who Greatest Hits . . . . (MCA)
Nobody's Child
Beatles With Tony Sheridan; *The Beatles featuring Tony Sheridan-In The
Beginning (Circa 1960)* . . . . (Polydor)
Electric Light Orchestra; *Eldorado* . . . . (Jet)
Hank Williams, Jr.; *Best Of Hank Williams, Jr.-#1-Roots &
Branches* . . . . (Mercury)

Maria McKee; *Maria McKee* . . . . (Geffen)
Traveling Wilburys; *Nobody's Child-Romanian Angel Appeal-C* . . . .(Warner Bros.)

Nowhere To Go
Melissa Etheridge; *Your Little Secret* . . . . (Island)

Outside
Mariah Carey; *Butterfly* . . . . (Columbia)

Santa Monica
Savage Garden; *Savage Garden* . . . . (Columbia)

Scum Of The Earth
Rob Zombie; *ST/Mission: Impossible 2* . . . . (Hollywood)

Solitude
Edwin McCain; *Honor Among Thieves* . . . . (Lava)
Edwin McCain & Darius Rucker; *VH-1 Crossroads-C* . . . .(Atlantic)

Stranger Than You
Joe Jackson; *Steppin' Out: The Very Best Of Joe Jackson* . . . . (A&M)

There Goes The Neighborhood
Sheryl Crow; *The Globe Sessions* . . . . (A&M)

Time Bomb
Rancid; *...And Out Come The Wolves* . . . . (Epitaph)

To The Moon And Back
Savage Garden; *Savage Garden* . . . . (Columbia)

Vic And Ray
Mark Knopfler; *Golden Heart* . . . .(Warner Bros.)

What It's Like
Everlast; *Whitey Ford Sings The Blues* . . . . (Tommy Boy)

SOLITUDE, Alone

See Also: **CHILDREN LEAVING HOME, HIDING, LEAVING, LONELY, NUMBERS: 1, SAILING, SECRETS, SILENCE, TRAINS, TRAVELING**

Amazed
Offspring; *Ixnay On The Hombre* . . . . (Columbia)

Between An Old Memory And Me
Keith Whitley; *I Wonder Do You Think Of Me* . . . . (RCA)
Travis Tritt; *Ten Feet Tall And Bulletproof* . . . .(Warner Bros.)

Brick
Ben Folds Five; *Whatever And Ever Amen* . . . .(Caroline/550)

Circus Girl
Gretchen Peters; *The Secret Of Life* . . . . (Purple Crayon Prod.)

Cool Change
Little River Band; *First Under The Wire* . . . . (Capitol)
Little River Band's Greatest Hits . . . . (Capitol)

Cowboy Take Me Away
Dixie Chicks; *Fly* . . . . (Monument)

Cut You In
Jerry Cantrell; *Boggy Depot* . . . . (Columbia)

Don't Bother Me
Beatles; *Meet The Beatles!* . . . . (Capitol)

Don't Fence Me In
Andrews Sisters; *Andrews Sisters' All-Time Greatest Hits* . . . . . (Decca)
Bing Crosby; *Best Of Bing Crosby* . . . .(MCA)
David Byrne; *Red Hot + Blue-Tribute To Cole Porter-C* . . . .(Chrysalis)
Ella Fitzgerald; *Cole Porter Songbook* . . . . (Verve)
Lari White/Shelby Lynne/Trisha Yearwood; *Don't Fence Me In* . . . . . . (RCA)
Willie Nelson & Leon Russell; *Cowboy Super Hits-C* . . . . (Columbia)

Don't Take It Personal (Just One Of Dem Days)
Monica; *Miss Thang* . . . . (Rowdy/Arista)

Guess Things Happen That Way
Johnny Cash; *The Man In Black-His Greatest Hits* . . . . (Legacy)

Home To Myself
Melissa Manchester; *Essence Of Melissa Manchester* . . . . (Arista)

Horse With No Name
America; *America* . . . .(Warner Bros.)
America Live . . . .(Warner Bros.)
Billboard Top Rock 'N' Roll Hits-1972-C . . . . (Rhino)
History-Greatest Hits . . . .(Warner Bros.)

I Alone
Live; *Throwing Copper* . . . .(Radioactive/MCA)

I Am A Man Of Constant Sorrow
Ralph Stanley; *Rebel Records: 35 Years Of The Best In Bluegrass-1960-1995-C* . . . .(Rebel)
Soggy Bottom Boys featuring Dan Tyminski; *ST/O Brother, Where Art Thou?* . . . . (Mercury)
Stanley Brothers; *All Time Legends Of Country Music-C* . . . . (Legacy)

I Am A Rock
Simon & Garfunkel; *Collected Works* . . . . (Columbia)
Simon & Garfunkel's Greatest Hits . . . . (Columbia)
Sounds Of Silence . . . . (Columbia)

I Never Will Marry
Bailey Brothers; *Early Days Of Bluegrass-#6* . . . . (Rounder)
Carter Family; *Wildwood Flower* . . . . (ASV Living Era)

Linda Ronstadt; *Simple Dreams* . . . . (Asylum)

I Stand Alone
Steve Perry; *ST/Quest For Camelot* . . . . (Curb/Atlantic)

I Think We're Alone Now
Tiffany; *Tiffany* . . . . (MCA)
Tiffany's Greatest Hits . . . . (Hip-O)
Tommy James And The Shondells; *Best Of Tommy James And The Shondells* . . . . (Roulette)
Billboard Top Rock 'N' Roll Hits-1967-C . . . . (Rhino)
Tommy James And The Shondells-Anthology . . . . (Rhino)

I Wish I Felt Nothing
Wallflowers; *Bringing Down The Horse* . . . .(Interscope)

In Hiding
Pearl Jam; *Yield* . . . . (Epic)

Leave Me Alone
Jerry Cantrell; *ST/The Cable Guy* . . . . (Work)

Like A Rolling Stone
Bob Dylan; *Biograph* . . . . (Columbia)
Bob Dylan At Budokan . . . . (Columbia)
Bob Dylan's Greatest Hits . . . . (Columbia)
Highway 61 Revisited . . . . (Columbia)
More American Graffiti-#4-C . . . . (MCA)
Self Portrait . . . . (Columbia)
Bob Dylan And The Band; *Before The Flood* . . . . (Columbia)
Jimi Hendrix; *ST/Jimi Plays Monterey* . . . . (Reprise)
Jimi Hendrix Experience; *Jimi Hendrix Experience* . . . . (Reprise)
Rolling Stones; *Stripped* . . . . (Virgin)

Lonely Teenager
Dion; *Collectables Presents The History Of Rock-#4-C* . . . . (Collectables)
Dion-His Best . . . . (Laurie)
Everything You Always Wanted To Hear By . . . . (Laurie)
The Wanderer . . . . (Laurie)

Lucky Man
Bruce Springsteen; *Tracks* . . . . (Columbia)

Lullaby Of The Leaves
Various Artists; *Birdlanders-#1-C* . . . . (Original Jazz Classics)

Moment To Myself
Macy Gray; *On How Life Is* . . . . (Epic)

New Pollution
Beck; *Odelay* . . . .(David Geffen Co.)

Nobody
Ry Cooder; *Jazz* . . . . (Warner Bros.)

On My Own
Peach Union; *Audiopeach* . . . . (Epic)
ST/Sliding Doors . . . . (MCA)

On My Own
Patti LaBelle & Michael McDonald; *Chicken Soup For The Couples Soul-C* . . . . (Rhino)
Patti LaBelle's Greatest Hits . . . . (MCA)
Winner In You . . . . (MCA)

On My Own
Reba McEntire; *Starting Over* . . . . (MCA)

Privacy
Michael Jackson; *Invincible* . . . . (Epic)

Rebel-Johnny Yuma
Johnny Cash; *The Man In Black-His Greatest Hits* . . . . (Legacy)

River And The Highway
Pam Tillis; *All Of This Love* . . . . (Arista)
Pam Tillis' Greatest Hits . . . . (Arista)

Shiver Me Timbers
Bette Midler; *Live At Last* . . . .(Atlantic)
Songs For The New Depression . . . .(Atlantic)
ST/Divine Madness . . . .(Atlantic)
Tom Waits; *The Heart Of Saturday Night* . . . . (Asylum)

Sidewalk Annie
Wallflowers; *The Wallflowers* . . . . (Virgin)

Solitude
Edwin McCain; *Honor Among Thieves* . . . . (Lava)
Edwin McCain & Darius Rucker; *VH-1 Crossroads-C* . . . .(Atlantic)

Stronger
Britney Spears; *Now That's What I Call Music!-#6-C* . . . . (Virgin)
Oops!...I Did It Again . . . . (Jive)

Theme From "The Lone Ranger" (William Tell Overture)
Boston Pops Orchestra; *TV Classics-C* . . . . (RCA)
Boston Pops Orchestra/Arthur Fiedler; *Fiedler-Greatest Hits* . . . . . (RCA)
Original Soundtrack; *Television's Greatest Hits-#7-Cable Ready-C* . . . . . (TVT)
Spike Jones & His City Slickers; *Best Of Spike Jones & His City Slickers* . . . . (RCA)

They Dance Alone (Cueca Solo)
Sting; *...Nothing Like The Sun* . . . . (A&M)
Fields Of Gold-The Best Of Sting 1984-1994 . . . . (A&M)

Unforgiven II
Metallica; *Reload* . . . . (Elektra)

You Are Not Alone
Michael Jackson; *1996 Grammy Nominees-C* . . . . (Columbia)
HIStory: Past, Present And Future-Book 1-C . . . . (Epic)

You'll See
Madonna; *Something To Remember* . . . . (Maverick/Sire)

SOUNDS, Concept Of Sound

See Also: **BELLS, COMMUNICATION (various), HEAR, MUSIC,
MUSICAL INSTRUMENTS (various), NONSENSE WORDS,
SILENCE, WIND**

(I Love The Sound Of) Breaking Glass
Nick Lowe; *Pure Pop For Now People* . . . . (Columbia)
(Sittin' On) The Dock Of The Bay
Michael Bolton; *The Hunger* . . . . (Columbia)
Otis Redding; *(Sittin' On) The Dock Of The Bay* . . . . (Atco)
 Best Of Otis Redding . . . . (Atco)
 Golden Age Of Black Music-1960-1970-C . . . . (Atlantic)
 Golden Soul-C . . . . (Atlantic)
 Soul Years-C . . . . (Atlantic)
 The Otis Redding Story . . . . (Atlantic)
Bang Bang
Cher; *Cher* . . . . (Geffen)
 EMI Legends Of Rock & Roll-24 Greatest Hits-C . . . . (EMI)
Bang Bang
ZZ Top; *Rhythmeen* . . . . (RCA)
Bang Bang
Stevie Wonder; *Down To Earth* . . . . (Motown)
Bang Bang
Bar-Kays; *Too Hot To Stop* . . . . (Mercury)
Bang Bang
Vanilla Fudge; *Vanilla Fudge* . . . . (Atco)
Beep Beep
Playmates; *Dr. Demento: 20th Anniversary Collection-C* . . . . (Rhino)
Blackbird
Beatles; *Beatles-Box Set* . . . . (Capitol)
 The Beatles (White Album) . . . . (Capitol)
Crosby, Stills & Nash; *CSN* . . . . (Atlantic)
Paul McCartney; *Unplugged (The Official Bootleg)* . . . . (Capitol)
Wings; *Wings Over America* . . . . (Capitol)
Boom Boom
John Lee Hooker; *Best Blues Album In The World...Ever!-C* . . . . . (Virgin)
 Blues Masters-#7-Blues Revival-C . . . . (Rhino)
Boom Boom Boom
Iguanas; *Nuevo Boogaloo* . . . . (Margaritaville)
Boom! It Was Over
Robert Ellis Orrall; *Flying Colors* . . . . (RCA)
Boom, Boom, Out Go The Lights
Pat Travers; *Best Of Pat Travers* . . . . (Polydor)
Can't You Hear My Heartbeat
Herman's Hermits; *Herman's Hermits-Their Greatest Hits* . . . . (Abkco)
Chattanooga Choo Choo
Asleep At The Wheel; *Train Trax-C* . . . . (Sony Music Special Prod.)
Billy Strange; *Railroad Man* . . . . (Crescendo)
Boston Pops Orchestra/Arthur Fiedler; *Boston Pops Orchestra/Arthur
 Fiedler* . . . . (RCA)
 Greatest Hits Of The '40s . . . . (RCA)
Glenn Miller; *Best Of Glenn Miller* . . . . (RCA)
 Decade Of The '40s-C . . . . (RCA)
 Glenn Miller-A Legendary Performer-#1 & 2 . . . . (Bluebird)
 Memorial-1944-1969 . . . . (Bluebird)
 Nipper's Greatest Hits Of The '40s-#1-C . . . . (RCA)
Glenn Miller & His Orchestra; *Glenn Miller & His Orchestra-
 Pure Gold* . . . . (Bluebird)
Tuxedo Junction; *Best Of Butterfly Records-C* . . . . (Hot Prod.)
 Tuxedo Junction . . . . (Butterfly)
Click Click Boom
Saliva; *Every Six Seconds* . . . . (Island/IDJMG)
Computer Beeps
Original Soundtrack; *The Outer Limits* . . . . (Crescendo)
Ding Dong The Witch Is Dead
Fifth Estate; *Dick Bartley's One-Hit Wonders Of The '60s-#2-C* . . (Rhino)
Meco; *The Wizard Of Oz* . . . . (Millennium)
MGM Studio Orchestra; *ST/The Wizard Of Oz* . . . . . (Sony Music Special Prod.)
Doggie In The Window
Patti Page; *Patti Page-16 Most Requested Songs* . . . . (Legacy)
 Patti Page-Golden Hits . . . . (Mercury)
 Patti Page's Greatest Hits . . . . (Columbia)
Folsom Prison Blues
Brooks & Dunn with Johnny Cash; *Red Hot + Country-C* . . . . . (Mercury)
Johnny Cash; *Billboard Top Country Hits-1968-C* . . . . (Rhino)
 Classic Cash-Hall Of Fame Series . . . . (Mercury)
 Hot Tracks-Train Super Hits-C . . . . (Epic)
 Jailhouse Rock (Hits From The Big House)-C . . . . (Sony Music Special Prod.)
 Johnny Cash At Folsom Prison & San Quentin . . . . (Columbia)
 Johnny Cash-Original Golden Hits-#1 . . . . (Sun)

Johnny Cash's Greatest Hits-#2 . . . . (Columbia)
 Superbilly . . . . (Sun)
 The Man In Black-His Greatest Hits . . . . (Legacy)
Goes My Mind (Pop, Pop, Pop, Pop)
Levert; *Smooth Grooves-A Sensual Collection-#8-C* . . . . (Rhino)
Gonna Find Me A Bluebird
Frank Ifield; *Best Of Frank Ifield* . . . . (Curb)
Marvin Rainwater; *Greatest Hits-1957-C* . . . . (Deluxe)
 Only Country-1955-1959-C . . . . (JCI Assoc. Labels)
Royal Wade Kimes; *ST/Traveller* . . . . (Asylum)
High Lonesome Sound
Vince Gill; *Bluegrass Essentials-C* . . . . (Hip-O)
 High Lonesome Sound . . . . (MCA)
Vince Gill with Alison Krauss & Union Station; *Grand Ole Opry-75
 Years-#1-C* . . . . (MCA)
I Think We're Alone Now
Tiffany; *Tiffany* . . . . (MCA)
 Tiffany's Greatest Hits . . . . (Hip-O)
Tommy James And The Shondells; *Best Of Tommy James And The
 Shondells* . . . . (Roulette)
 Billboard Top Rock 'N' Roll Hits-1967-C . . . . (Rhino)
 Tommy James And The Shondells-Anthology . . . . (Rhino)
Knock On Wood
Amii Stewart; *Double Smash Hits-C* . . . . (Volcano Entertainment)
Buddy Guy; *This Is Buddy Guy* . . . . (Vanguard)
Eddie Floyd; *15 Original Big Hits-#3-C* . . . . (Stax)
 Atlantic Rhythm & Blues 1947-1974-#6 (1966-1969)-C . . . . . (Atlantic)
 Best Of Wattstax-C . . . . (Stax)
 Super Oldies Of The '60s-#11-C . . . . (Audio Fidelity)
Eric Clapton; *Behind The Sun* . . . . (Duck/Reprise)
Ike & Tina Turner; *Ike & Tina Turner's Greatest Hits-#3* . . . . (Saja)
Knock Three Times
Tony Orlando & Dawn; *Best Of Tony Orlando & Dawn* . . . . (Rhino)
Leader Of The Pack
Bette Midler; *Divine Miss M* . . . . (Atlantic)
 ST/Divine Madness . . . . (Atlantic)
Original Cast; *Leader Of The Pack* . . . . (Elektra)
Shangri-Las; *21 Number One Hits-C* . . . . (Original Sound)
 Billboard Top Rock 'N' Roll Hits-1964-C . . . . (Rhino)
 Girl Groups-Story Of A Sound-C . . . . (Rhino)
 Golden Hits Of The Shangri-Las . . . . (Mercury)
 Oldies But Goodies-#15-C . . . . (Original Sound)
 Radio Active Hits-#2-C . . . . (Accord)
 Remember The Shangri-Las At Their Best . . . . (Collectables)
Li'l Red Riding Hood
Sam The Sham and The Pharaohs; *Best Of Sam The Sham and The
 Pharaohs* . . . . (Polydor)
 Cruisin'-1966-C . . . . (Increase)
 Pharaohization! (Best Of) . . . . (Rhino)
Listen To The Mocking Bird
Lester Flatt; *Lester Raymond Flatt* . . . . (Flying Fish)
Living For The City
Stevie Wonder; *Innervisions* . . . . (Motown)
 Original Musiquarium . . . . (Motown)
Lonely Bull (El Solo Torro)
Herb Alpert & The Tijuana Brass; *Four Sider* . . . . (A&M)
 Herb Alpert & The Tijuana Brass' Greatest Hits . . . . (A&M)
 Herb Alpert & The Tijuana Brass-Classics-#1 . . . . (A&M)
 The Lonely Bull . . . . (A&M)
Money
Pink Floyd; *Collection Of Great Dance Songs* . . . . (Columbia)
 Dark Side Of The Moon . . . . (Capitol)
 Delicate Sound Of Thunder . . . . (Columbia)
 Pink Floyd-Gift Set . . . . (Capitol)
My Love Is The Shhh!
Somethin' For The People; *This Time It's Personal* . . . . (Warner Bros.)
Ninety Nine Years (Dead Or Alive)
Guy Mitchell; *Definitive Guy Mitchell* . . . . (Collector's Choice)
Out With A Bang
David Lee Murphy; *Out With A Bang* . . . . (MCA)
Pop A Top
Alan Jackson; *Under The Influence* . . . . (Arista)
Jim Ed Brown; *Essential Jim Ed Brown* . . . . (RCA)
Rhythm Of The Rain
Cascades; *Collectables Presents The History Of Rock-#7-C* . . . . . (Collectables)
 Golden Years-1963-C . . . . (Dominion Entert.)
Second Chance
38 Special; *Rock & Roll Strategy* . . . . (A&M)
Several Species Of Small Furry Animals
Pink Floyd; *Ummagumma* . . . . (Capitol)
 Works . . . . (Capitol)
Snap Crackle Pop (Kellogg's Rice Krispies)
Original Soundtrack; *TeeVee Toons-The Commercials-#1-C* . . . . . . (TVT)
Snoopy Vs. The Red Baron
Royal Guardsmen; *Best Of The Royal Guardsmen-#1* . . . . (Rhino)
 Collectables Presents The History Of Rock-#9-C . . . . . . (Collectables)
 Cruisin'-1967-C . . . . (Increase)

Million-Dollar Memories #1-C . . . . (RCA)
Super Oldies Of The '60s-#6-C . . . .(Audio Fidelity)

Sound Of Music
Mormon Tabernacle Choir; *Mormon Tabernacle Choir's Greatest Hits-22
Best-Loved Favorites* . . . . (Sony Masterworks)
Original Cast; *The Sound Of Music*. . . . .(Sony Broadway)

Sound Of Silence, The
Paul Simon; *Paul Simon In Concert/Live Rhymin'* . . . . (Columbia)
Simon & Garfunkel; *Collected Works* . . . . (Columbia)
More American Graffiti-#4-C . . . .(MCA)
Simon & Garfunkel's Greatest Hits . . . . (Columbia)
Sounds Of Silence . . . . (Columbia)
ST/The Graduate . . . . (Columbia)
The Concert In Central Park . . . .(Warner Bros.)

Steam Heat
Carol Haney; *ST/Pajama Game* . . . . (Collectables)
Janis Paige/John Raitt/Original Cast; *Pajama Game* . . . . (Columbia)

Summer In The City
Lovin' Spoonful; *Billboard Top Rock 'N' Roll Hits-1966-C* . . . . (Rhino)
Lovin' Spoonful-Anthology . . . . (Rhino)
Rockin' '60s-C . . . . (Priority)

Syncopated Clock
Leroy Anderson; *Best Of Leroy Anderson-Sleigh Ride* . . . . (Decca)

Tears Falling Down
Rosanne Cash; *The Wheel*. . . . . (Columbia)

Theme From ''Rawhide''
Blues Brothers; *Original Soundtrack* . . . .(Atlantic)
Frankie Laine; *CBS: The First 50 Years* . . . . (TVT)
Cowboy Super Hits-C . . . . (Columbia)
Television's Greatest Hits-#2-C . . . . (TVT)
Riders In The Sky; *Cowboy Songs* . . . . (Rounder)

Thing, The
Phil Harris; *The Thing About Phil Harris* . . . .(Living Era)

Thunder
Prince And The New Power Generation; *Diamonds And Pearls* . . (Paisley Park)

Thunder Road
Bruce Springsteen; *Born To Run*. (Columbia)
Bruce Springsteen's Greatest Hits . . . . (Columbia)
Bruce Springsteen & The E Street Band; *Bruce Springsteen & The E Street
Band Live/1975-85* . . . . (Legacy)

Thunder Rolls, The
Garth Brooks; *Garth Brooks-Double Live* . . . . (Capitol)
No Fences . . . . (Capitol)

Thundercrack
Bruce Springsteen; *Tracks* . . . . (Columbia)

Time
Pink Floyd; *Dark Side Of The Moon*. . . . . (Capitol)
Delicate Sound Of Thunder . . . . (Columbia)
Pink Floyd-Gift Set . . . . (Capitol)

Transfusion
Nervous Norvus; *Dr. Demento Presents The Greatest Novelty Records-#2-
1950s-C* . . . . (Rhino)
Dr. Demento: 20th Anniversary Collection-C . . . . (Rhino)
Vintage Music-#3-C . . . .(MCA)
Wacky Weirdos-C . . . . (K-Tel)

Typewriter, The
101 Strings Orchestra; *Strings Have Fun!* . . . . (Alshire)
Rochester Pops Orchestra; *Leroy Anderson's Greatest Hits* . . . . . . (Pro-Arte)
Rochester Pops Orchestra & Erich Kunzel; *Syncopated Clock* . . . . . (Pro-Arte)

Wabash Cannonball
Billy Strange; *Between The Rails: America's Train Songs-C* . . . . . .(Crescendo)
Nitty Gritty Dirt Band; *Will The Circle Be Unbroken* . . . .(EMI)
Roy Acuff; *All Time Legends Of Country Music-C* . . . . (Legacy)
Backstage At The Grand Ole Opry-C . . . . (RCA)
Best Of Roy Acuff . . . . (Liberty)
Columbia Historic Edition-Roy Acuff . . . . (Columbia)
Essential Roy Acuff-1936-1949 . . . . (Legacy)
Hot Tracks-Train Super Hits-C . . . .(Epic)
Roy Acuff's Greatest Hits . . . . (Columbia)
Steel Rails-Classic Railroad Songs-#1-C . . . . (Rounder)

When My Sugar Walks Down The Street
Ella Fitzgerald; *Ella Fitzgerald The Early Years-#2 (1939-1941)* . . . . . . (GRP)
Nat ''King'' Cole; *The Billy May Sessions* . . . . (Capitol)
Peggy Lee; *Capitol Sings Jimmy McHugh: I Feel A Song
Comin' On-C*. . . . . (Capitol)

Whip It
Devo; *Best Of Devo-Greatest Hits* . . . .(Warner Bros.)
EZ Listening Disc. . . . . (Rykodisc)
Freedom Of Choice . . . .(Warner Bros.)
Last American Virgin . . . . (Columbia)

Zing! Went The Strings Of My Heart
Coasters; *Coasters' Greatest Hits* . . . . (Atco)
Rare Soul-Beach Music Classics-#1-C . . . . (Rhino)
Frank Sinatra; *The Reprise Collection* . . . . (Reprise)
Judy Garland; *Best Of Judy Garland* . . . .(MCA)
Best Of The Decca Years-#1-Hits!-C . . . . (Decca)
Judy Garland-At Carnegie Hall . . . . (Capitol)
Judy Garland's All-Time Greatest Hits . . . . (Curb)

SPACE, Astronauts, Cosmos, Rockets, Satellites, Space Travel, Universe

See Also: **ASTROLOGY, EARTH, MOON, STARS, SUN, UFO'S, WORLD**

2,000 Light Years From Home
Rolling Stones; *More Hot Rocks (big hits & fazed cookies)* . . . .(Abkco)
Singles Collection-The London Years . . . .(Abkco)
Their Satanic Majesties Request . . . .(Abkco)
Through The Past, Darkly (Big Hits Vol. 2) . . . .(Abkco)

Across The Universe
Beatles; *Let It Be* . . . . (Capitol)
Past Masters-Volume Two . . . . (Parlophone)
Rarities . . . . (Capitol)
The Beatles/1967-1970. . . . . (Capitol)
David Bowie; *Young Americans* . . . . (Rykodisc)

Alien Nation
Scorpions; *Face The Heat* . . . . (Mercury)

All The Love Of The Universe
Santana; *Caravanserai* . . . . (Columbia)

Another Satellite
XTC; *Rag & Bone Buffet* . . . . (Geffen)
Skylarking. . . . . (Geffen)

Apollo 9
Adam Ant; *Antics In The Forbidden Zone* . . . . (Epic)

Apollo XI
Orchestral Manoeuvres In The Dark; *Sugar Tax* . . . .(Virgin)

Astral Traveller
Yes; *Time And A Word* . . . .(Atlantic)
Yesterdays . . . .(Atlantic)

Astral Weeks
Van Morrison; *Astral Weeks* . . . . (Warner Bros.)

Astronomy
Blue Oyster Cult; *Imaginos*. . . . . (Columbia)
Secret Treaties . . . . (Columbia)
Some Enchanted Evening . . . . (Columbia)

Astronomy Domine
Pink Floyd; *Nice Pair* . . . . (Capitol)
Piper At The Gates Of Dawn . . . . (Capitol)
Ummagumma . . . . (Capitol)

Beyond The Universe
Rick Derringer; *Derringer* . . . .(Blue Sky)
Derringer Live . . . .(Blue Sky)

Blues For Space Travellers
Victor Feldman; *Jazz Club-Vibraphone* . . . . (Verve)

Buck Rogers In The 25th Century
Neil Norman & His Cosmic Orchestra; *Greatest Science Fiction
Hits-#2* . . . .(Crescendo)

Cosmic Charlie
Grateful Dead; *Aoxomoxoa* . . . . (Warner Bros.)
What A Long Strange Trip It's Been: The Best Of The
Grateful Dead . . . . (Warner Bros.)

Cosmic Cowboy
Michael Murphey; *Cosmic Cowboy Souvenir* . . . . (A&M)
Nitty Gritty Dirt Band; *Dirt, Silver & Gold* . . . . (One Way)
Stars And Stripes Forever. . . . . (Capitol)

Defying Gravity
Emmylou Harris; *Quarter Moon In A Ten Cent Town* . . . . (Warner Bros.)
Jesse Winchester; *Best Of Jesse Winchester* . . . . (Rhino)
Jimmy Buffett; *Havana Daydreamin'*. . . . . (MCA)

Drops Of Jupiter (Tell Me)
Train; *Drops Of Jupiter*. . . . . (Aware/C2/Columbia)

Echoes
Gene Clark; *Nuggets-#11-Pop-Part 4-C* . . . . (Rhino)

Echoes
Pink Floyd; *Meddle* . . . . (Capitol)

Echoes
New Riders Of The Purple Sage; *Marin County Line* . . . . (MCA)

Final Countdown
Europe; *Final Countdown* . . . . (Epic)
Heart Of Rock-C . . . . (Columbia)

Golden Rocket
Hank Snow; *All About Trains* . . . .(RCA)
Best Of Hank Snow. . . . . (RCA)
Horse Soldiers; *Between The Rails: America's Train Songs-C* . . . . .(Crescendo)
Willie Nelson & Hank Snow; *Brand On My Heart* . . . . (Columbia)

Major Tom (Coming Home)
Peter Schilling; *Different Story (World Of Lust & Crime)* . . . . . . (Elektra)
Error In The The System . . . . (Elektra)

Man On The Moon
R.E.M.; *Automatic For The People* . . . . (Warner Bros.)

Marching To Mars
Sammy Hagar; *Marching To Mars* . . . . (MCA)

Motel Satellite
Wellsprings Of Hope; *Phonograph*. . . . .(Safety Net)

Mr. Spaceman
Byrds; *Original Singles-#1-1965-1967* . . . . (Columbia)
  The Byrds . . . . (Columbia)
  The Byrds (Untitled) . . . . (Legacy)
  The Byrds' Greatest Hits . . . . (Columbia)

New Satellite Blues
Little Brother Montgomery; *South Side Blues/Chicago-Living*
  Legends . . . . (Riverside)

One More Astronaut
I Mother Earth; *Scenery And Fish* . . . . (Capitol)

Planets Of The Universe
Stevie Nicks; *Trouble In Shangri-La* . . . . (Reprise)

Princes Of The Universe
Queen; *A Kind Of Magic* . . . . (Hollywood)

Ray Of Light
Madonna; *GHV2* . . . . (Warner Bros.)
  Ray Of Light . . . . (Maverick)
  Totally Hits-#1-C . . . . (Arista)

Ride My See Saw
Moody Blues; *Caught Live Plus Five* . . . . (Polydor)
  In Search Of The Lost Chord . . . . (Polydor)
  This Is The Moody Blues . . . . (Polydor)

Rocket
Smashing Pumpkins; *Siamese Dream* . . . .(Virgin)

Rocket
Def Leppard; *Hysteria* . . . . (Mercury)

Rocket 2 U
Jets; *Magic* . . . . (MCA)

Rocket Countdown (Blastoff)
Brothers Johnson; *Blam!* . . . . (A&M)

Rocket Fuel
Alvin Lee; *Rocket Fuel* . . . . (RSO)

Rocket In My Pocket
Little Feat; *Hoy-Hoy!* . . . . (Warner Bros.)
  Time Loves A Hero . . . . (Warner Bros.)
  Waiting For Columbus . . . . (Warner Bros.)

Rocket Man
Elton John; *Elton John's Greatest Hits* . . . . (Polydor)
  Here And There . . . . (Rocket)
  Honky Chateau . . . . (Rocket)
Kate Bush; *Two Rooms-Celebrating The Songs Of Elton John & Bernie*
  Taupin-C . . . . (Polydor)

Rocket O' Love
Knack; *Serious Fun* . . . . (Charisma)

Rocket Ride
Kiss; *Alive II* . . . . (Casablanca)

Rocket To God
Daryl Hall & John Oates; *ooh yeah!* . . . . (Arista)

Rockit Man
J.T.; *Kick The Funk* . . . . (East West)

Santa And The Satellite
Dickie Goodman; *Dr. Demento Presents The Greatest Novelty Records-#6-*
  Christmas-C . . . . (Rhino)

Satellite
War Babies; *War Babies* . . . . (Columbia)

Satellite
Dave Matthews Band; *Under The Table And Dreaming* . . . . (RCA)

Satellite
Depeche Mode; *Broken Frame* . . . .(Sire)

Satellite
John Coltrane; *Coltrane's Sound* . . . . (Atlantic)

Satellite
Echo & The Bunnymen; *Echo & The Bunnymen* . . . .(Sire)

Satellite
Elton John; *Ice On Fire* . . . . (MCA)

Satellite
Sex Pistols; *Live At Chelmsford Top Security Prison* . . . . (Restless)

Satellite
Gang Of Four; *Mall* . . . . (Polydor)

Satellite
Hooters; *One Way Home* . . . . (Columbia)

Satellite
Elvis Costello; *Spike* . . . . (Warner Bros.)

Satellite Beach
Peter Case; *Peter Case* . . . . (Geffen)

Satellite Of Love
Lou Reed; *Between Thought & Expression-Anthology* . . . . (RCA)
  City Lights . . . . (Arista)
  Lou Reed Live . . . . (RCA)
  Transformer . . . . (RCA)
  Walk On The Wild Side-The Best Of Lou Reed . . . . (RCA)

Satellites
Rhythm Corps; *Future's Not What It Used To Be* . . . . (Pasha)

Set The Controls For The Heart Of The Sun
Pink Floyd; *Nice Pair* . . . . (Capitol)
  Saucerful Of Secrets . . . . (Capitol)

  Ummagumma . . . . (Capitol)
  Works . . . . (Capitol)

Sleeping Satellite
Tasmin Archer; *Great Expectations* . . . .(SBK)

Space Baby
Tubes; *Tubes* . . . . (A&M)

Space Captain
Barbra Streisand; *Barbra Joan Streisand* . . . . (Columbia)
Joe Cocker; *Mad Dogs & Englishmen* . . . . (A&M)

Space Child
UFO; *Phenomenon* . . . . (Chrysalis)

Space Child
Spirit; *12 Dreams Of Dr. Sardonicus* . . . . (Epic)

Space Cowboy
Steve Miller Band; *Best Of Steve Miller 1968-1973* . . . . (Capitol)
  Steve Miller Band-Anthology . . . . (Capitol)

Space Cowboy (Yippie-Yi-Yay)
'N Sync featuring Lisa ''Left Eye'' Lopes; *No Strings Attached* . . . (Jive)

Space Dog
Tori Amos; *Under The Pink* . . . . (Atlantic)

Space Invader
Pretenders; *Pretenders* . . . . (Sire)

Space Junk
Devo; *EZ Listening Disc* . . . . (Rykodisc)
  Q: Are We Not Men? A: We Are Devo! . . . . (Warner Bros.)

Space Lord
Monster Magnet; *Powertrip* . . . . (A&M)

Space Monkey
Patti Smith Group; *Easter* . . . . (Arista)

Space Oddity
David Bowie; *Changesbowie* . . . . (Rykodisc)
  Scary Monsters . . . . (Rykodisc)
  Space Oddity . . . . (Rykodisc)
  ST/Ziggy Stardust-The Motion Picture . . . . (Rykodisc)
  The Singles-1969-1993 . . . . (Rykodisc)

Space Patrol
Country Joe McDonald; *Country Joe McDonald-Classics* . . . . (Fantasy)
  Rock & Roll Music From The Planet Earth . . . . (Fantasy)

Space Race
Billy Preston; *Best Of Billy Preston* . . . . (A&M)

Space Safari
Nazareth; *Rampant* . . . . (A&M)

Space Song
Stomu Yamashta & Go; *Live From Paris* . . . .(Island)
  Stomu Yamashta & Go . . . .(Island)

Space Station #5
Montrose; *Montrose* . . . . (Warner Bros.)

Space Truckin'
Deep Purple; *Deepest Purple/The Very Best Of Deep Purple* . . . . (Warner Bros.)
  Machine Head . . . . (Warner Bros.)
  Made In Japan . . . . (Warner Bros.)
  When We Rock We Rock & When We Roll We Roll . . . . . . (Warner Bros.)

Spaceman
Journey; *Journey-In The Beginning* . . . . (Columbia)
  Next . . . . (Columbia)

Spaceman
Nilsson; *Son Of Schmilsson* . . . . (RCA)
  Songwriter . . . . (RCA)

Starship
MC5; *Elektrock-Sixties-C* . . . . (Elektra)

Starship
Paul Kantner/Jefferson Starship; *Blows Against The Empire* . . . . (RCA)

Starship Trooper
Yes; *Classic Yes* . . . . (Atlantic)
  The Yes Album . . . . (Atlantic)
  Yessongs . . . . (Atlantic)

Stellar
Incubus; *Make Yourself* . . . . (Immortal/Epic)

Supersonic Rocket Ship
Kinks; *Everybody's In Show-Biz* . . . .(Rhino)

Theme From ''2001: A Space Odyssey''
Boston Pops Orchestra/John Williams; *Pops Out Of This World* . . . . . . (Philips)
Neil Norman; *Greatest Science Fiction Hits* . . . . (Crescendo)
Original Soundtrack; *2001: A Space Odyssey Theme* . . . . (MGM)

Theme From ''Battlestar Galactica''
Boston Pops Orchestra/John Williams; *Pops Out Of This World* . . . . . . (Philips)
Original Soundtrack; *Science Fiction Move Themes* . . . . (Laserlight)

Theme From ''Flash Gordon''
Neil Norman; *Greatest Science Fiction Hits-#3-C* . . . . (Crescendo)

Theme From ''Lost In Space''
Neil Norman; *Greatest Science Fiction Hits-#3-C* . . . . (Crescendo)
Original Soundtrack; *CBS: The First 50 Years* . . . . (TVT)
  Television's Greatest Hits-#1-C . . . .(TVT)

Theme From ''Space Ghost Coast To Coast''
Original Soundtrack; *Television's Greatest Hits-#7-Cable Ready-C* . . . . . .(TVT)

Theme From ''Star Trek''
Cincinnati Pops Orchestra/Erich Kunzel; *Star Tracks II* . . . . (Telarc)

Theme From "Star Trek: The Next Generation"
Original Soundtrack; *Television's Greatest Hits-#7-Cable Ready-C* . . . . . (TVT)
Theme From "Star Wars"
John Williams; *ST/Star Wars* . . . . (Polydor)
Meco; *Best Of Meco* . . . . (Chronicles)
Neil Norman; *Greatest Science Fiction Hits* . . . . (Crescendo)
Theme From "The Jetsons"
Original Soundtrack; *Hanna-Barbera Pic-A-Nic Basket Of Cartoon*
Classics . . . . (Kid Rhino/Rhino 4 Kids)
Television's Greatest Hits-#1-C . . . . (TVT)
Stunners; *ST/Jetsons-The Movie* . . . . (MCA)
To The Moon And Back
Savage Garden; *Savage Garden* . . . . (Columbia)
Twilight Zone
Manhattan Transfer; *Best Of The Manhattan Transfer* . . . . (Atlantic)
Extensions . . . . (Rhino)
Manhattan Transfer-Anthology-Down In Birdland . . . . (Rhino)
Twilight Zone
Neil Norman & His Cosmic Orchestra; *Elvira Presents Haunted*
Hits-C . . . . (Rhino)
Halloween Hits-C . . . . (Rhino)
Twilight Zone
Golden Earring; *Cut* . . . . (21)
Something Heavy Going Down . . . . (21)
Twilight Zone
Iron Maiden; *Killers* . . . . (Capitol)
Walking In Space
Quincy Jones; *I Heard That!* . . . . (A&M)
ST/Listen Up-The Lives Of Quincy Jones . . . . (Qwest)
Walking In Space . . . . (A&M)
Walking In Space
Original Cast; *ST/Hair* . . . . (RCA)

SPECIAL, Extraordinary, Precious, Unique
See Also: **BEST, COMPLIMENTS, GOOD, LOVE (various)**

All Star
Smash Mouth; *Astro Lounge* . . . . (Interscope)
Now That's What I Call Music!-#3-C . . . . (Virgin)
An Affair To Remember
Original Soundtrack; *ST/An Affair To Remember* . . . . (Epic)
Brass In Pocket (I'm Special)
Pretenders; *Pretenders* . . . . (Sire)
Pretenders-The Singles . . . . (Sire)
Come And Get With Me
Keith Sweat featuring Snoop Dogg; *Still In The Game* . . . . (Elektra)
Come Original
311; *Soundsystem* . . . . (Capricorn)
Completely Unique Experience, A (Colt 45 Malt Liquor)
Original Soundtrack; *TeeVee Toons-The Commercials-#1-C* . . . . (TVT)
Daddy's Little Girl
Al Martino; *Best Of Al Martino* . . . . (Capitol)
Mills Brothers; *50th Anniversary* . . . . (Ranwood)
All Occasions Album . . . . (Gateway)
Best Of The Mills Brothers . . . . (MCA)
The Mills Brothers Story . . . . (Ranwood)
Detroit Special
Big Bill Broonzy; *Unissued Test Pressings* . . . . (Milan)
Dizzy
Goo Goo Dolls; *Dizzy Up The Girl* . . . . (Warner Sunset/Reprise)
Electrolite
Michael Stipe/Mike Mills; *Tibetan Freedom Concert* . . . . (Capitol)
R.E.M.; *New Adventures In Hi-Fi* . . . . (Warner Bros.)
Elegantly Wasted
INXS; *Elegantly Wasted* . . . . (Mercury)
Exclusivity
Damian Dame; *Damian Dame* . . . . (LaFace)
Ex-Girlfriend
No Doubt; *Return Of Saturn* . . . . (Interscope)
Extra Ordinary
Better Than Ezra; *Closer* . . . . (Beyond)
Fabulous Character
Sarah Vaughan; *Complete Sarah Vaughan On Mercury-#1-Great Jazz Years-*
1954-1956 . . . . (Mercury)
Follow Me
Uncle Kracker; *Double Wide* . . . . (Warner Bros.)
Totally Hits 2001-C . . . . (Arista)
German Special
Li'l Wally; *All Around The World* . . . . (Jay Jay)
Here's To Good Friends (Lowenbrau Beer)
Original Soundtrack; *TeeVee Toons-The Commercials-#1-C* . . . . (TVT)
How Your Love Makes Me Feel
Diamond Rio; *Diamond Rio's Greatest Hits* . . . . (Arista)
If You Knew Susie (Like I Know Susie)
Eddie Cantor; *Memories* . . . . (MCA)

In My Life
Beatles; *Beatles-Love Songs* . . . . (Capitol)
Rubber Soul . . . . (Capitol)
ST/Imagine: John Lennon . . . . (Capitol)
The Beatles/1962-1966 . . . . (Capitol)
Crosby, Stills & Nash; *After The Storm* . . . . (Atlantic)
Judy Collins; *Colors Of The Day-The Best Of Judy Collins* . . . . . . (Elektra)
In My Life . . . . (Elektra)
I've Gotta Crow
Original Cast/Mary Martin; *Peter Pan-The 1954 Broadway*
Production . . . . (RCA Victor)
Lily, Rosemary And The Jack Of Hearts
Bob Dylan; *Blood On The Tracks* . . . . (Columbia)
Louisiana Saturday Night
Don Williams; *Best Of Cajun Country-C* . . . . (Era)
Best Of Don Williams-#4 . . . . (MCA)
Don Williams-Country Boy . . . . (MCA)
Jimmy C. Newman; *From The Vaults: Decca Country Classics-1934-*
1973-C . . . . (Decca)
Grand Ole Opry-75 Years-#2-C . . . . (MCA)
Progressive CC . . . . (Plantation)
Mel McDaniel; *Mel McDaniel's Greatest Hits* . . . . (Capitol)
Love Is A Many-Splendored Thing
Andy Williams; *Moon River & Other Great Movie Themes* . . . . . . (Columbia)
Four Aces; *Billboard Pop Memories-1955-1959-C* . . . . (Rhino)
Four Aces' Greatest Hits . . . . (MCA)
Love Story
Tanita Tikaram; *Sweet Keeper* . . . . (Reprise)
Maria
Original Cast; *The Sound Of Music* . . . . (Broadway Angel)
The Sound Of Music . . . . (Sony Broadway)
Mdnite Special
Paul Evans; *Super Oldies Of The '60s-#2-C* . . . . (Audio Fidelity)
Midnight Special
Creedence Clearwater Revival; *1969* . . . . (Fantasy)
Creedence Clearwater Revival-Chronicle-#2 . . . . (Fantasy)
Creedence Clearwater Revival-Gold . . . . (Fantasy)
Movie Album . . . . (Fantasy)
Willy & The Poor Boys . . . . (Fantasy)
Johnny Rivers; *Johnny Rivers-Anthology 1964-1977* . . . . (Rhino)
Very Best Of Johnny Rivers . . . . (EMI)
Midnight Special Train
Big Joe Turner; *Atlantic Rhythm & Blues 1947-1974-#3 (1955-*
1958)-C . . . . (Atlantic)
Joe Turner's Greatest Hits . . . . (Atlantic)
Most Girls
Pink; *Can't Take Me Home* . . . . (LaFace)
Totally Hits-#3-C . . . . (Atlantic)
My Special Angel
Bobby Helms; *American Graffiti-#3-C* . . . . (MCA)
Blue Ribbon Country-#3-C . . . . (Accord)
Oldies But Goodies-#14-C . . . . (Original Sound)
Pop A Billy . . . . (MCA)
Vintage Music-#2-C . . . . (MCA)
Vogues; *Vogues' Greatest Hits* . . . . (Rhino)
Vogues' Greatest Hits/Finest Performances . . . . (Sun)
My Special Prayer
Percy Sledge; *Best Of Percy Sledge* . . . . (Atlantic)
Percy Sledge-The Ultimate Collection-When A Man Loves A
Woman . . . . (Atlantic)
New
No Doubt; *Return Of Saturn* . . . . (Interscope)
ST/Go . . . . (Work/Epic)
No One Else On Earth
Wynonna; *Wynonna* . . . . (MCA)
Nothing Compares 2 U
Sinead O'Connor; *I Do Not Want What I Haven't Got* . . . . (Ensign)
Ohio Special March
Ohio State University Marching Band; *Pride Of The*
Buckeyes . . . . (Fidelity Sound)
Once-A-Year Day!
Original Cast; *ST/Pajama Game* . . . . (Collectables)
One
Original Broadway Cast; *A Chorus Line* . . . . (Columbia)
One And Only
Queensryche; *Empire* . . . . (EMI)
One And Only
Kirsty MacColl; *Electric Landlady* . . . . (Charisma)
One And Only
Chesney Hawkes; *One And Only* . . . . (Chrysalis)
One And Only Man
Steve Winwood; *Refugees Of The Heart* . . . . (Virgin)
One Hit Wonder
Everclear; *So Much For The Afterglow* . . . . (Capitol)
One In A Million
Aaliyah; *One In A Million* . . . . (BlackGround Enterp./Atlantic)
One In A Million You
Larry Graham & Graham Central Station; *The Best Of Larry Graham &*
Graham Central Station-#1 . . . . (Warner Bros.)

One Piece At A Time
Johnny Cash; *The Man In Black-His Greatest Hits* . . . . (Legacy)
Only Daddy That'll Walk The Line
Hank Williams, Jr.; *Family Tradition* . . . . (WB/Curb)
Kentucky HeadHunters; *Electric Barnyard.* . . . . (Mercury)
Ricky Skaggs; *My Father's Son* . . . . (Epic)
Waylon Jennings; *Best Of Waylon Jennings* . . . . (RCA)
  Waylon Jennings' Greatest Hits . . . . (RCA)
  Waylon Jennings-Early Years. . . . . (RCA)
Willie Nelson; *Willie & Family Live* . . . . (Columbia)
Only One You
T.G. Sheppard; *Best Of T.G. Sheppard* . . . . (Curb)
  T.G. Sheppard's All-Time Greatest Hits . . . . (Warner Bros.)
Orange Blossom Special
Bill Monroe; *Bean Blossom.* . . . . (MCA)
  Bill Monroe and His Blue Grass Boys-60 Years Of Country. . . .(RCA)
  Stars Of The Grand Ole Opry-1926-1974-C. . . . . (RCA)
Charlie Daniels Band; *Fire On The Mountain* . . . . (Epic)
  ST/Urban Cowboy 2 . . . . (Epic)
Flatt & Scruggs; *Hear The Whistles Blow* . . . . . . (International Mktg. Group)
Gordon Terry; *Disco Country* . . . . (Plantation)
  Gordon Terry-20 Golden Souvenirs . . . . (Plantation)
Johnny Cash; *Columbia Records-1958-1986* . . . . (Columbia)
  Essential Johnny Cash . . . . (Columbia)
  Johnny Cash-16 Biggest Hits-#2 . . . . (Legacy)
  Johnny Cash's Greatest Hits . . . . (Columbia)
  The Man In Black-His Greatest Hits. . . . . (Legacy)
  Train Trax-C . . . . (Sony Music Special Prod.)
Johnson Mountain Boys; *Steel Rails-Classic Railroad Songs-#1-C* . . . (Rounder)
Nitty Gritty Dirt Band; *Will The Circle Be Unbroken* . . . . (EMI)
Popular
Nada Surf; *High/Low.* . . . . (Elektra)
Precious Time
Journey; *Departure* . . . . (Columbia)
Precious Time
Pat Benatar; *Precious Time* . . . . (Chrysalis)
Precious Time
Van Morrison; *Back On Top* . . . . (Point Blank/Virgin)
Red Light Special
TLC; *CrazySexyCool.* . . . . (LaFace)
Roni
Bobby Brown; *Dance!...Ya Know It!* . . . . (MCA)
  Don't Be Cruel . . . . (MCA)
Secret Smile
Semisonic; *Feeling Strangely Fine* . . . . (MCA)
She Ain't Your Ordinary Girl
Alabama; *Alabama-Super Hits-#2.* . . . . (RCA)
  In Pictures . . . . (RCA)
She's Every Woman
Garth Brooks; *Fresh Horses* . . . . (Capitol)
She's More
Andy Griggs; *You Won't Ever Be Lonely* . . . . (RCA)
She's Not Just Another Woman
Biz Markie; *Diabolical-The Biz Never Sleeps* . . . . (Cold Chillin')
She's Not Just Another Woman
M.C. Peaches; *More Than Just A Pretty Face* . . . . (East West)
She's Not Just Another Woman
8th Day; *Didn't It Blow Your Mind: Soul Hits Of The '70s-#5-C* . . (Rhino)
Simply Irresistible
Robert Palmer; *Super Nova* . . . . (Island)
Smashing Young Man
Collective Soul; *Collective Soul* . . . . (Atlantic)
Something
Beatles; *Abbey Road* . . . . (Parlophone)
  Beatles 1 . . . . (Capitol)
  The Beatles/1967-1970. . . . . (Capitol)
  The Beatles-Anthology-#3 . . . . (Capitol)
Special
Vesta; *Special* . . . . (A&M)
Special
Garbage; *Now That's What I Call Music!-#3-C.* . . . . (Virgin)
  Version 2.0 . . . . (Almo Sounds)
Special
Violent Femmes; *Blind Leading The Naked* . . . . (Slash)
Special
Jimmy Cliff; *Special* . . . . (Columbia)
Stranger In Paradise
Arthur Lyman; *Pearly Shells* . . . . (Crescendo)
Bing Crosby; *The Radio Years: 20 Songs* . . . . (Crescendo)
Original Cast; *Kismet.* . . . . (Columbia)
Tony Bennett; *Tony Bennett-16 Most Requested Songs* . . . . (Legacy)
  Tony Bennett's All-Time Greatest Hits . . . . (Columbia)
Such A Night
Elvis Presley; *From Nashville To Memphis-The Essential '60s Masters.* . .(RCA)
Superman (It's Not Easy)
Five For Fighting; *America Town* . . . . (Aware/C2/Columbia)
  The Concert For New York City-C . . . . (Columbia)
Superman's Dead
Our Lady Peace; *Clumsy* . . . . (Columbia)

Syncopated Clock
Leroy Anderson; *Best Of Leroy Anderson-Sleigh Ride* . . . .(Decca)
That Girl
Maxi Priest featuring Shaggy; *Man With The Fun* . . . . (Virgin)
  Reggae Party 1999-C . . . . (Island)
Theme From "Love Story"
Andy Williams; *Andy Williams' Greatest Hits-#2* . . . . (Columbia)
  Love Story . . . . (Columbia)
Cincinnati Pops Orchestra/Erich Kunzel; *Hollywood's Greatest*
  Hits-#1 . . . . (Telarc)
Francis Lai; *ST/Love Story* . . . . (MCA)
Johnny Mathis; *Johnny Mathis' All-Time Greatest Hits* . . . . . (Columbia)
  Johnny Mathis-16 Most Requested Songs . . . . (Columbia)
Peter Nero; *Peter Nero's Greatest Hits* . . . . (Columbia)
Theme From "The Miss America Pageant" (There She Is, Miss America)
Bert Parks; *Television's Greatest Hits-#4-Black & White Classics-C* . . . . .(TVT)
Theme From "Yogi Bear"
Original Soundtrack; *Hanna-Barbera Classics-#1-Original Recordings Of*
  The World's Most Famous Cartoon Themes &
  Scores . . . . (Kid Rhino/Rhino 4 Kids)
  Hanna-Barbera Pic-A-Nic Basket Of Cartoon
  Classics . . . . (Kid Rhino/Rhino 4 Kids)
  Television's Greatest Hits-#1-C . . . . (TVT)
To Me
South Sixty Five; *South Sixty Five* . . . . (Atlantic)
Unforgettable
Nat "King" Cole; *Capitol Collectors Series-Nat "King" Cole* . . . . . . (Capitol)
  The Nat "King" Cole Story . . . . (Capitol)
  Unforgettable . . . . (Capitol)
Natalie Cole with Nat "King" Cole; *Unforgettable With Love* . . . . (Elektra)
Unique New York
John Scofield; *Grace Under Pressure* . . . . (Blue Note)
Unusually Unusual
Lonestar; *I'm Already There* . . . . (BNA)
Video
India.Arie; *Acoustic Soul* . . . . (Motown)
Way You Love Me, The
Faith Hill; *Breathe* . . . . (Warner Bros.)
  Totally Hits-#3-C . . . . (Atlantic)
Wells Fargo Wagon
Original Broadway Cast; *The Music Man* . . . . (Angel)
Original Cast; *The Music Man* . . . . (Gold Rush)
When He Shines
Sheena Easton; *Sheena Easton's Greatest Hits* . . . . (EMI Special Markets)
  The World Of Sheena Easton: The Singles Collection-C. . . . . (EMI)
When I Close My Eyes
Shanice; *Shanice* . . . . (LaFace)
Where Did You Go?
Full Devil Jacket; *Full Devil Jacket* . . . . (Island/IDJMG)
Winter Wonderland
Air Supply; *Air Supply Christmas Album.* . . . . (Arista)
  White Christmas . . . . (Word)
Alexander O'Neal; *My Gift To You* . . . . (Tabu)
Amy Grant; *Home For Christmas* . . . . (A&M)
Andrews Sisters; *Andrews Sisters-Christmas* . . . . . . (MCA Special Prod.)
Anne Murray; *Best Of The Season* . . . . (EMI America)
Aretha Franklin; *Rock 'N' Roll Christmas*
  Classics-C . . . . (Music For Little People)
Barbara Mandrell; *Christmas At Our House* . . . . (MCA Special Prod.)
  Tennessee Christmas-C. . . . . (MCA)
Bing Crosby; *Bing Crosby Christmas Classics* . . . . (Capitol)
Blue Notes; *Rhythm & Blues Christmas-#1-C* . . . . (Collectables)
Brenda Lee; *Jingle Bell Rock* . . . . (MCA Special Prod.)
Carnie & Wendy Wilson; *Hey Santa!* . . . . (SBK)
Darlene Love; *Christmas Gift For You From Phil Spector-C* . . . . . (Rhino)
  Phil Spector-Back To Mono 1958-1969-C . . . . (Abkco)
  Phil Spector's Christmas Album-C . . . . (Passport)
Eddy Arnold; *Christmas With Eddy Arnold.* . . . . (RCA)
Elvis Presley; *If Every Day Was Like Christmas* . . . . (RCA)
Eurythmics; *Very Special Christmas-C* . . . . (A&M)
Faron Young; *Country Christmas* . . . . (Step One)
Frank Sinatra; *Christmas Songs By Sinatra* . . . . (Legacy)
George Strait; *Merry Christmas Strait To You* . . . . . . (MCA Special Prod.)
Hank Crawford; *We Got A Good Thing Going.* . . . . (Kudo)
Johnny Mercer & The Pied Pipers; *Merry Christmas Baby-Romance &*
  Reindeer-C . . . . (Capitol)
Kathie Lee Gifford; *It's Christmas Time* . . . . (Warner Bros.)
Kenny Rogers; *Christmas In America* . . . . (Reprise)
London Symphony Orchestra; *Christmas Traditions* . . . . . (Special Music Co.)
Merle Haggard; *Merle Haggard-Christmas Gift* . . . . (Curb)
Patti LaBelle & The Blue Belles; *A Soulful Christmas-C* . . . . . .(Collectables)
Randy Travis; *An Old Time Christmas* . . . . (Warner Bros.)
Robert Goulet; *Essence Of Christmas* . . . . (A&M)
Rosie O'Donnell & Macy Gray; *Another Rosie Christmas-C* . . . . . (Columbia)
Tanya Tucker; *Christmas For The '90s-#1-C* . . . . (Liberty)
Tony Bennett; *Now That's What I Call Christmas!-C* . . . . (UTV)
Travis Tritt; *Christmas-Loving Time Of The Year* . . . . (Warner Bros.)
Wonder
Natalie Merchant; *Tigerlily* . . . . (Elektra)

You Brought A New Kind Of Love To Me
Ella Fitzgerald; *Ella Swings Lightly* . . . . (Verve)
You Do Something To Me
Frank Sinatra; *Concepts* . . . . (Capitol)
Ray Conniff; *Ray Conniff -16 Most Requested Songs* . . . . (Legacy)
Your Precious Love
Marvin Gaye; *Last Concert Tour* . . . . (Giant)

SPELLING SONGS

See Also: **COUNTING SONGS, NONSENSE WORDS,
TELEPHONE (telephone numbers)**

ABC
Jackson 5; *ABC* . . . . (Motown)
Jackson 5-Anthology . . . . (Motown)
Jackson 5's Greatest Hits . . . . (Motown)
All Good
Mo Thugs Family Scriptures; *Chapter II: Family Reunion* . . . . (Relativity)
All Together Now
Beatles; *Yellow Submarine* . . . . (Capitol)
Muppets; *Kermit Unpigged* . . . . (Jim Henson)
Alphabet Song
Three Stooges; *ST/Violent Is The Word For Curlee* . . . . (Out Of Print)
Beer Run
Garth Brooks with George Jones; *Scarecrow* . . . . (Capitol)
BFD
Kathy Mattea; *The Innocent Years* . . . . (Mercury)
Big D
Broadway Cast; *Most Happy Fella* . . . . (RCA)
Original Broadway Cast; *Most Happy Fella* . . . . (Sony Music Classical)
B-I-N-G-O
Original Soundtrack; *Mother Goose Songs* . . . . (Madacy)
Christmas Alphabet
McGuire Sisters; *McGuire Sisters' Greatest Hits* . . . . (MCA)
C-O-N-S-T-A-N-T-I-N-O-P-L-E
Paul Whiteman & His Orchestra; *78-#1402* . . . . (Columbia)
C-O-U-N-T-R-Y
Joe Diffie; *Life's So Funny* . . . . (Epic)
Curious
LSG featuring L.L. Cool J, Busta Rhymes & MC Lyte; *Levert-Sweat-
Gill* . . . . (East West)
D-I-V-O-R-C-E
Rosanne Cash; *Tammy Wynette...Remembered-C* . . . . (Asylum)
Tammy Wynette; *Super Hits Of The '60s-C* . . . . (Epic)
Tammy Wynette-Anniversary-20 Years Of Hits . . . . (Epic)
Tammy Wynette's Biggest Hits . . . . (Epic)
Tammy Wynette's Greatest Hits . . . . (Epic)
Do Re Mi
Julie Andrews; *ST/The Sound Of Music* . . . . (RCA)
Original Cast; *The Sound Of Music* . . . . (Sony Broadway)
Harper Valley P.T.A.
Jeannie C. Riley; *Harper Valley P.T.A.* . . . . (Plantation)
Jeannie C. Riley's Greatest Hits . . . . (Plantation)
Oldies But Goodies-#4-C . . . . (Original Sound)
Souvenirs Of Music City U.S.A.-C . . . . (Plantation)
Hell
Squirrel Nut Zippers; *Hot* . . . . (Mammoth)
I'm A Man
Bo Diddley; *Bo Diddley-His Best* . . . . (Chess)
Super Blues . . . . (Chess)
*The Sopranos-Music From The HBO Original
Series* . . . . (Sony Music Soundtrax)
Yardbirds; *Five Live Yardbirds* . . . . (Rhino)
History Of British Rock-#3-C . . . . (Rhino)
Yardbirds' Greatest Hits-#1 (1964-1966) . . . . (Rhino)
I'm A Woman
Maria Muldaur; *Waitress In The Donut Shop* . . . . (Warner Archives)
Peggy Lee; *I Am Woman-C* . . . . (Nick At Nite)
Peggy Lee's All-Time Greatest Hits . . . . (Curb)
Reba McEntire; *Out Of A Dream* . . . . (Mercury)
I've Got A Gal In Kalamazoo
Glenn Miller; *Best Of Glenn Miller* . . . . (RCA)
Decade Of The '40s-C . . . . (RCA)
Glenn Miller-A Legendary Performer-#1 & 2 . . . . (Bluebird)
Memorial-1944-1969 . . . . (Bluebird)
The Glenn Miller Story . . . . (RCA)
Glenn Miller & His Orchestra; *Glenn Miller & His Orchestra-
Pure Gold* . . . . (Bluebird)
The Unforgettable Glenn Miller & His Orchestra . . . . (RCA)
Izzo (H.O.V.A.)
Jay-Z; *Izzo (H.O.V.A.)* . . . . (Roc-A-Fella/DJMG)
The Concert For New York City-C . . . . (Columbia)
Love T.K.O.
Bette Midler; *Bette* . . . . (Warner Bros.)
Mannish Boy
Muddy Waters; *Electric Mud* . . . . (Chess)

King Of The Electric Blues . . . . (Legacy)
The Best Blues Album In The World...Ever!-C . . . . (Virgin)
M-I-S-S-I-S-S-I-P-P-I
Frances White; *Music From The New York Stage (1890-1920)-#4-1917-
1920-C* . . . . (Pearl)
N-E-S-T-L-E-S (Nestle's Quik Chocolate Flavor)
Original Soundtrack; *TeeVee Toons-The Commercials-#1-C* . . . . . (TVT)
Nightfly, The
Donald Fagen; *The Nightfly* . . . . (Warner Bros.)
Oklahoma
Ohio State University Marching Band; *Brass Roots* . . . . (Fidelity Sound)
Original Broadway Cast; *Oklahoma!* . . . . (RCA)
Original Cast; *Broadway Classics-#1* . . . . (MCA)
Oklahoma! . . . . (MCA)
Only On Days That End In "Y"
Clay Walker; *Hypnotize The Moon* . . . . (Giant)
R.O.C.K. In The U.S.A.
John Cougar Mellencamp; *Scarecrow* . . . . (Riva)
R.S.V.P.
Boney James & Rick Braun; *Shake It Up* . . . . (Warner Bros.)
Rag Mop
Ames Brothers; *Best Of The Ames Brothers* . . . . (Pair)
Respect
Aretha Franklin; *Aretha Franklin-30 Greatest Hits* . . . . (Rhino)
Best Of Aretha Franklin . . . . (Atlantic)
I Am Woman-C . . . . (Nick At Nite)
I Never Loved A Man The Way I Love You . . . . (Atlantic)
Live At Fillmore West . . . . (Atlantic)
Soul Years-C . . . . (Atlantic)
ST/Forrest Gump . . . . (Epic/Sony Music Soundtrax)
Otis Redding; *History Of Otis Redding* . . . . (Atco)
Live In Europe . . . . (Atco)
Otis Blue-Sings Soul . . . . (Atco)
The Otis Redding Story . . . . (Atlantic)
Reba McEntire; *Reba* . . . . (MCA)
R-O-C-K
Bill Haley & His Comets; *Bill Haley & His Comets-Golden Hits* . . . . (MCA)
R-O-C-K . . . . (Sun)
T-R-O-U-B-L-E
Elvis Presley; *A Touch Of Platinum-#2* . . . . (RCA)
Travis Tritt; *Travis Tritt's Greatest Hits-From The Beginning* . . . (Warner Bros.)
T-R-O-U-B-L-E . . . . (Warner Bros.)
TV Movie
Bruce Springsteen; *Tracks* . . . . (Columbia)
TVC 15
David Bowie; *Fame & Fashion* . . . . (RCA)
Sound + Vision . . . . (Rykodisc)
ST/Christiane F. . . . . (RCA)
Stage . . . . (Rykodisc)
Station To Station . . . . (Rykodisc)
The Singles-1969-1993 . . . . (Rykodisc)
Y.M.C.A.
Village People; *Billboard Top Dance Hits-1978-C* . . . . (Rhino)
Billboard Top Rock 'N' Roll Hits-1979-C . . . . (Rhino)
Cruisin' . . . . (Casablanca)
Live & Sleazy . . . . (Casablanca)
Night At Studio 54-C . . . . (Casablanca)
Village People's Greatest Hits . . . . (Rhino)

SPIRITS, Ghosts, Goblins, Haunted, Witches

See Also: **ANGELS, ASTROLOGY, DEVILS, MAGIC,
MONSTERS, UFO'S**

(Ghost) Riders In The Sky
Gene Autry; *50th Anniversary* . . . . (Republic/Universal)
Cowboy Hall Of Fame . . . . (Republic/Universal)
Johnny Cash; *The Man In Black-His Greatest Hits* . . . . (Legacy)
Outlaws; *Ghost Riders* . . . . (Arista)
Roy Clark; *Roy Clark In Concert* . . . . (MCA)
Roy Clark's Greatest Hits . . . . (MCA)
Superpicker . . . . (MCA)
Vaughn Monroe; *Best Of Vaughn Monroe* . . . . (RCA)
This Is Vaughn Monroe/Decade Of The '40s . . . . (RCA)
Bewitched
Anita O'Day; *Anita Sings The Most* . . . . (Verve)
Barbra Streisand; *Third Album* . . . . (Columbia)
Doris Day; *Doris Day's Greatest Hits* . . . . (Columbia)
Original Cast; *Pal Joey* . . . . (Columbia)
Big Joe & Phantom 309
Tom Waits; *Double Live* . . . . (Asylum)
Nighthawks At The Diner . . . . (Asylum)
Broomstick Cowboy
Bobby Goldsboro; *10th Anniversary Album-#1* . . . . (EMI)
Honey-Best Of Bobby Goldsboro . . . . (EMI)
Colors Of The Spirit
Journey; *Trial By Fire* . . . . (Columbia)

Ding Dong The Witch Is Dead
Fifth Estate; *Dick Bartley's One-Hit Wonders Of The '60s-#2-C* . . . . (Rhino)
Meco; *The Wizard Of Oz* . . . . (Millennium)
MGM Studio Orchestra; *ST/The Wizard Of Oz* . . . . . (Sony Music Special Prod.)

Drowning Witch
Frank Zappa; *Ship arriving too late to save a drowning witch* . . . . (Rykodisc)

Female Of The Species
Space; *Spiders* . . . . (Gut/Universal)

Ghost
Fleetwood Mac; *Bare Trees* . . . .(Reprise)

Ghost Dance
Patti Smith Group; *Easter* . . . .(Arista)

Ghost In This House
Shenandoah; *Extra Mile* . . . . (Columbia)

Ghost Lover
Ian & Sylvia; *Ian & Sylvia's Greatest Hits* . . . . (Vanguard)
Northern Journey . . . . (Vanguard)

Ghost Of A Chance
Rush; *Roll The Bones* . . . . (Atlantic)

Ghost Of A Chance With You
Billie Holiday; *Billie Holiday-Vol. 2* . . . . (Everest)
Stormy Blues . . . . (Verve)
Mel Torme; *Smooth As Velvet* . . . . (Pickwick)

Ghost Of A Texas Ladies' Man
Concrete Blonde; *Walking In London* . . . . (I.R.S.)

Ghost Of Flight 401
Bob Welch; *Three Hearts* . . . . (Capitol)

Ghost Of Tom Joad
Bruce Springsteen; *The Ghost Of Tom Joad* . . . . (Columbia)

Ghost Of You
Richard Thompson; *Richard Thompson-Best Of Capitol Years* . . . . (Capitol)

Ghost Of You And Me
BBMak; *Sooner Or Later* . . . . (Hollywood)

Ghost Train
Counting Crows; *August And Everything After* . . . .(David Geffen Co.)

Ghost Writer
Garland Jeffreys; *Ghost Writer* . . . . (A&M)

Ghostbusters
Ray Parker Jr.; *Chartbusters* . . . . (Arista)
Elvira Presents Haunted Hits-C . . . . (Rhino)
Greatest Movie Rock Hits-C . . . . (Rhino)
ST/Ghostbusters . . . . (Arista)

Ghosts
Dan Fogelberg; *Innocent Age* . . . . (Full Moon)

Grey Ghost
Henry Paul Band; *Grey Ghost* . . . . (Atlantic)

Highwayman
Glen Campbell; *Highwayman* . . . . (Capitol)
Johnny Cash with Waylon Jennings, Kris Kristofferson, Willie Nelson; *The
Man In Black-His Greatest Hits* . . . . (Legacy)
Waylon Jennings, Willie Nelson, Johnny Cash, Kris Kristofferson; *Columbia
Country Classics-#3-Americana-C* . . . . (Columbia)
Johnny Cash-16 Biggest Hits-#2 . . . . (Legacy)
Willie Nelson; *Greatest Country Hits Of The '80s-1985-C* . . . . (Columbia)

Jean Genie
David Bowie; *Aladdin Sane* . . . . (Rykodisc)
Changesbowie . . . . (Rykodisc)
David Live . . . . (Rykodisc)
The Singles-1969-1993 . . . . (Rykodisc)

Laurie (Strange Things Happen)
Dickey Lee; *Collector's Essentials-#1-1960s-C* . . . .(Varese Sarabande)

Phantom Of The Opera
Iron Maiden; *Iron Maiden* . . . . (Capitol)
Live After Death-World Slavery Tour . . . . (Capitol)

Phantom Of The Opera
Original London Cast; *Phantom Of The Opera* . . . . (Polydor)

Purple People Eater Meets The Witch Doctor
Big Bopper; *Hellooo Baby! Best Of The Big Bopper-1954-1959* . . . . (Rhino)

Rhiannon (Will You Ever Win)
Fleetwood Mac; *25 Years-The Chain* . . . . (Warner Bros.)
Fleetwood Mac . . . .(Reprise)
Fleetwood Mac Live . . . . (Warner Bros.)
Fleetwood Mac's Greatest Hits . . . . (Warner Bros.)

Rock 'N' Roll Ghost
Replacements; *Don't Tell A Soul* . . . .(Sire)

Season Of The Witch
Donovan; *American Graffiti-#4-C* . . . . (MCA)
Donovan's Greatest Hits . . . . (Epic)
Sunshine Superman . . . . (Epic)
Troubadour-Definitive Collection . . . . (Epic)
Vanilla Fudge; *Best Of Vanilla Fudge* . . . . (Atco)

Silver Ghost, The
Merle Haggard & The Strangers; *Train Whistle Blues* . . . . (Rounder)

Spirit
Earth, Wind & Fire; *Eternal Dance* . . . . (Columbia)
Spirit . . . . (Columbia)

Spirit
Sounds Of Blackness; *Time For Healing* . . . . (Perspective/A&M)

Spirit
Van Morrison; *Common One* . . . . (Warner Bros.)

Spirit
Spirit; *Introduce Yourself* . . . . (Slash)

Spirit
Moody Blues; *Other Side Of Life* . . . . (Polydor)

Spirit
Doobie Brothers; *What Were Once Vices Are Now Habits* . . . . (Warner Bros.)

Spirit In The Dark
Aretha Franklin; *Aretha Franklin-30 Greatest Hits* . . . .(Rhino)
Live At Fillmore West . . . . (Atlantic)
Spirit In The Dark . . . . (Atlantic)

Spirit In The Night
Bruce Springsteen; *Greetings From Asbury Park, N.J.* . . . .(Columbia)
Bruce Springsteen & The E Street Band; *Bruce Springsteen & The E Street
Band Live/1975-85* . . . . (Legacy)
Manfred Mann's Earth Band; *Nightingales & Bombers* . . . . (Warner Bros.)
Roaring Silence . . . . (Warner Bros.)

Spirit In The Sky
Kentucky HeadHunters; *Electric Barnyard* . . . .(Mercury)
Norman Greenbaum; *Billboard Top Rock 'N' Roll Hits-1970-C* . . . .(Rhino)
Super Hits Of The '70s-Have A Nice Day-#2-C . . . .(Rhino)

Spirit Of Radio
Rush; *Exit...Stage Left* . . . .(Mercury)
Permanent Waves . . . .(Mercury)
Rush-Chronicles . . . .(Mercury)

Spirit Slips Away
Thin Lizzy; *Fighting* . . . .(Mercury)

Spirits (Having Flown)
Bee Gees; *Bee Gees' Greatest* . . . . (Polydor)
Spirits Having Flown . . . . (Polydor)

Spirits In The Material World
Police; *Every Breath You Take-The Classics* . . . .(A&M)
Ghost In The Machine . . . .(A&M)

Spirits Of Ancient Egypt
Wings; *Venus And Mars* . . . .(Capitol)
Wings Over America . . . .(Capitol)

Spirits Of St. Louis
Johnny Paycheck; *Take This Job And Shove It* . . . . (Epic)

Superman's Ghost
Don McLean; *Greatest Hits Then & Now* . . . . (EMI)

Theme From "Bewitched"
Original Soundtrack; *Television's Greatest Hits-#2-C* . . . .(TVT)

Theme From "Casper The Friendly Ghost"
Original Soundtrack; *Television's Greatest Hits-#1-C* . . . .(TVT)

Theme From "My Mother The Car"
Original Soundtrack; *Television's Greatest Hits-#2-C* . . . .(TVT)

Theme From "Space Ghost Coast To Coast"
Original Soundtrack; *Television's Greatest Hits-#7-Cable Ready-C* . . . . . .(TVT)

Theme From "The Ghost And Mrs. Muir"
Original Soundtrack; *Television's Greatest Hits-#5-In Living Color-C* . . . .(TVT)

Walking The Ghost
James; *Gold Mother* . . . . (Fontana)
James . . . . (Fontana)

Waltzing Matilda
Burl Ives; *Best Of Burl Ives* . . . . (MCA)
Fred Astaire; *Three Evenings With Fred Astaire* . . . . (DRG)
James Galway; *Pachebel Canon & Other Favorites* . . . . (RCA)
Original Soundtrack; *Children's Favorites* . . . . (Kid Rhino/Rhino 4 Kids)

When The Spell Is Broken
Richard Thompson; *Across A Crowded Room* . . . . (Polydor)
Watching The Dark-History Of Richard Thompson . . . . (Rykodisc)

Whiter Shade Of Pale
Annie Lennox; *Medusa* . . . .(Arista)
Procol Harum; *Best Of Procol Harum* . . . . (A&M)
Billboard Top Pop Hits-1967-C . . . . (Rhino)
History Of British Rock-#8-C . . . . (Rhino)
ST/Big Chill . . . . (Motown)

Witch Doctor
Chipmunks; *Rockin' Through The Decades* . . . . (EMI)
David Seville; *Dr. Demento: 20th Anniversary Collection-C* . . . . (Rhino)
Wacky Weirdos-C . . . . (K-Tel)

Witch Wolf
Styx; *Best Of Styx* . . . . (RCA)

Witchcraft
Elvis Presley; *Collector's Gold* . . . . (RCA)
Elvis' Gold Records, Volume 4 . . . . (RCA)
Return Of The Rocker . . . . (RCA)

Witchcraft
Frank Sinatra; *Sinatra: A Man And His Music* . . . . (Reprise)
Sinatra's Sinatra . . . . (Reprise)
The Capitol Years . . . .(Capitol)
Frank Sinatra & Anita Baker; *Frank Sinatra-Duets-C* . . . .(Capitol)

Witches Promise
Jethro Tull; *Original Masters* . . . . (Chrysalis)

Witches' Song
Marianne Faithfull; *Broken English* . . . .(Island)

Witchy Woman
Eagles; *Eagles* . . . . (Asylum)

Eagles/*Their Greatest Hits 1971-1975* . . . . (Asylum)

SPORTS: BASEBALL

See Also: **SPORTS (various), WINNING**

Ball Game, The
Sister Wynona Carr; *Baseball's Greatest Hits-C* . . . . (Rhino)
Baseball
Michael Franks; *One Bad Habit* . . . .(Warner Bros.)
Baseball Card Lover
Rockin' Ritchie Ray; *Baseball's Greatest Hits-C* . . . . (Rhino)
Baseball Dreams
Naturals (with Mel Allen); *Baseball's Greatest Hits-C* . . . . (Rhino)
Baseball Game (Love Is Like A)
Intruders; *Baseball's Greatest Hits-C* . . . . (Rhino)
Boys Of Summer
Don Henley; *Building The Perfect Beast* . . . .(Geffen)
Bug, The
Dire Straits; *On Every Street*. . . . .(Warner Bros.)
Mary Chapin Carpenter; *Come On Come On* . . . . (Columbia)
Centerfield
John Fogerty; *Centerfield* . . . .(Warner Bros.)
ST/Bull Durham . . . . (Capitol)
Cheap Seats, The
Alabama; *Cheap Seats* . . . . (RCA)
Cooperstown
Terry Cashman; *Passin' It On-America's Baseball Heritage In Song* . . (Legacy)
Did You See Jackie Robinson Hit That Ball?
Count Basie; *RCA Victor Blues & Rhythm Revue-C* . . . . (RCA)
Count Basie & His Orchestra; *Baseball's Greatest Hits-C* . . . . (Rhino)
D-O-D-G-E-R-S Song (Oh, Really? No, O'Malley)
Danny Kaye; *Baseball's Greatest Hits-C* . . . . (Rhino)
Dying Cub Fan's Last Request
Steve Goodman; *Baseball's Greatest Hits-C* . . . . (Rhino)
Empty Baseball Park
Whiskeytown; *Faithless Street*. . . . . (Outpost/Interscope)
Glory Days
Bruce Springsteen; *Born In The U.S.A.*. . . . . (Columbia)
Bruce Springsteen's Greatest Hits. (Columbia)
Greatest, The
Kenny Rogers; *She Rides Wild Horses* . . . . (Dreamcatcher)
I Love Mickey
Mickey Mantle & Teresa Brewer; *Baseball's Greatest Hits-C* . . . . (Rhino)
I Wish I Could Have Been There
John Anderson; *Solid Ground.* . . . . (BNA)
Joe DiMaggio Done It Again
Wilco; *Mermaid Avenue-#2* . . . . (Elektra)
Joltin' Joe DiMaggio
Les Brown & His Orchestra; *Baseball's Greatest Hits-C* . . . . (Rhino)
Words & Music Of World War II-C . . . . (Columbia)
Just A Friendly Game Of Baseball
Main Source; *Breaking Atoms* . . . .(EMI)
ST/Boyz N The Hood . . . . (Qwest)
Land Of Wrigley, The
Stormy Weather; *Baseball's Greatest Hits-C* . . . . (Rhino)
Life's Just A Ballgame
Womack & Womack; *Conscience* . . . . (Island)
Love Is Like A Baseball Game
Intruders; *Intruders-Super Hits*. . . . . (Philadelphia Int'l)
Move Over Babe (Here Comes Henry)
Bill Slayback; *Baseball's Greatest Hits-C* . . . . (Rhino)
Mrs. Robinson (Joe DiMaggio)
Simon & Garfunkel; *Bookends* . . . . (Columbia)
Collected Works. . . . . (Columbia)
Hollywood Magic-1960s-C . . . . (Columbia)
Simon & Garfunkel's Greatest Hits . . . . (Columbia)
ST/Forrest Gump . . . .(Epic/Sony Music Soundtrax)
ST/The Graduate . . . . (Columbia)
The Concert In Central Park . . . .(Warner Bros.)
My Favorite Spring
Tom Paxton; *Live For The Record* . . . . (Sugar Hill)
Nolan Ryan (He's A Hero To Us All)
Jerry Jeff Walker; *Navajo Rug* . . . .(Rykodisc)
Operaman
Adam Sandler; *The Concert For New York City-C* . . . . (Columbia)
Out Of Left Field
Hank Williams, Jr.; *Out Of Left Field*. . . . . (Capricorn)
Percy Sledge; *Best Of Percy Sledge* . . . . (Atlantic)
It Tears Me Up-Best Of Percy Sledge. . . . . (Rhino)
*Percy Sledge-The Ultimate Collection-When A Man Loves A
Woman* . . . . (Atlantic)
Red Sox Are Winning
Earth Opera; *Elektrock-Sixties-C* . . . . (Elektra)
Roundin' Third & Heading Home
Fred Koller; *Night Of The Living Fred* . . . . (Alcazar)

Say Hey (The Willie Mays Song)
Treniers; *Baseball's Greatest Hits-C* . . . . (Rhino)
Shoeless Joe From Hannibal, Mo.
Original Broadway Cast; *Damn Yankees* . . . . (RCA)
Strike Zone
Loverboy; *Keep It Up* . . . . (Columbia)
Take Me Out To The Ball Game
Bruce Springstone; *Baseball's Greatest Hits-C* . . . . (Rhino)
Doc & Merle Watson; *Baseball's Greatest Hits-C* . . . . (Rhino)
Frank Zappa; *You Can't Do That On Stage Anymore-#4.* . . . . (Rykodisc)
There Used To Be A Ballpark
Frank Sinatra; *Ol' Blue Eyes Is Back* . . . .(Reprise)
The Reprise Collection . . . . (Reprise)
Three Base Hit
Pat Martino; *Exit* . . . .(Muse)
Van Lingle Mungo
Dave Frishberg; *Baseball's Greatest Hits-C* . . . . (Rhino)
Willie, Mickey & The Duke (Talkin' Baseball)
Terry Cashman; *Baseball's Greatest Hits-C* . . . . (Rhino)

SPORTS: CAR RACING, Drag Racing, Street Racing

See Also: **CARS (various), LOSING & LOSS, ROAD ACCIDENTS,
SPORTS (various), WINNING**

455 Rocket
Kathy Mattea; *Love Travels* . . . . (Mercury)
Beep Beep
Playmates; *Dr. Demento: 20th Anniversary Collection-C* . . . . (Rhino)
Darkness On The Edge Of Town
Bruce Springsteen; *Darkness On The Edge Of Town* . . . . (Columbia)
Bruce Springsteen & The E Street Band; *Bruce Springsteen & The E Street
Band Live/1975-85* . . . . (Legacy)
Dead Man's Curve
Jan & Dean; *21 Legendary Superstars-C* . . . .(Original Sound)
Best Of Jan & Dean . . . . (EMI)
Dead Man's Curve . . . . (EMI)
Don't Worry, Baby
Beach Boys; *Absolute Best-#1.* . . . . (Capitol)
Endless Summer . . . . (Capitol)
Fun Fun Fun. . . . . (Capitol)
Made In The U.S.A. . . . . (Capitol)
Drag City
Jan & Dean; *Beach Party Blasts* . . . . (EMI)
Best Of Jan & Dean . . . . (EMI)
Dead Man's Curve . . . . (EMI)
One Summer Night-Live . . . . (Rhino)
Grease Megamix
Grease Megamix; *Pure Disco* . . . .(A&M)
Hardin County Line
Mark Collie; *Even The Man In The Moon Is Cryin'* . . . . (MCA)
Hot Rod Lincoln
Asleep At The Wheel; *Western Standard Time*. . . . . (Epic)
Commander Cody & His Lost Planet Airmen; *Lost In The Ozone* . . . . . . (MCA)
Super Hits Of The '70s-Have A Nice Day-#8-C . . . . (Rhino)
Johnny Bond; *Best Of Johnny Bond* . . . . (Starday)
Little Old Lady (From Pasadena)
Beach Boys; *Concert/'69-Live In London* . . . . (Capitol)
Jan & Dean; *Best Of Jan & Dean* . . . . (EMI)
Billboard Top Rock 'N' Roll Hits-1964-C . . . . (Rhino)
Dead Man's Curve . . . . (EMI)
Surf City-Best Of Jan & Dean. . . . . (EMI)
Maybelline
Chuck Berry; *Chuck Berry-Golden Hits* . . . . (Mercury)
Chuck Berry's Greatest Hits. . . . . (Everest)
Cruisin'-1955-C . . . . (Increase)
Oldies But Goodies-#11-C . . . .(Original Sound)
Super Oldies Of The '50s-#5-C . . . . (Audio Fidelity)
Johnny Rivers; *Johnny Rivers-Anthology 1964-1977* . . . . (Rhino)
Very Best Of Johnny Rivers . . . . (EMI)
Racing In The Street
Bruce Springsteen; *Darkness On The Edge Of Town* . . . . (Columbia)
Bruce Springsteen & The E Street Band; *Bruce Springsteen & The E Street
Band Live/1975-85* . . . . (Legacy)
Shut Down
Beach Boys; *Absolute Best-#1.* . . . . (Capitol)
Endless Summer . . . . (Capitol)
Little Deuce Coupe/All Summer Long . . . . (Capitol)
Monster Summer Hits-Drag City-C . . . . (Capitol)
Surfin' U.S.A. . . . . (Capitol)
Speedway At Nazareth
Mark Knopfler; *Sailing To Philadelphia* . . . .(Warner Bros.)
Spirit Of America
Beach Boys; *Beach Boys-Gift Set* . . . . (Capitol)
Little Deuce Coupe/All Summer Long . . . . (Capitol)
Spirit Of America . . . . (Capitol)

Street Machine
Super Stocks; *Monster Summer Hits-Drag City-C* . . . . (Capitol)
Theme From "Speed Racer"
Original Soundtrack; *Television's Greatest Hits-#3-1970s & 1980s-C.* . . . (TVT)
You Win My Love
Shania Twain; *The Woman In Me* . . . . (Mercury)

SPORTS: FOOTBALL

See Also: CITIES (various), FIGHT, SCHOOL, SPORTS (various), STATES: A-Z, WINNING

Across The Field
Ohio State University Marching Band; *Pride Of The Buckeyes* . . . . (Fidelity Sound)
Original Soundtrack; *College Fight Songs: The Big Ten-C* . . . . (K-Tel)
The Greatest College Fight Songs . . . . (Laserlight)
Top Ten College Fight Songs . . . . (K-Tel)
Aggie War Hymn
Original Soundtrack; *The Greatest College Fight Songs* . . . . (Laserlight)
All Alone In The End Zone
Jay Ferguson; *All Alone In The End Zone* . . . . (Asylum)
Anchors Aweigh
Firehouse Five Plus Two; *Goes To Sea* . . . . (Good Time Jazz)
Original Soundtrack; *Top Ten College Fight Songs* . . . . (K-Tel)
Pat Boone; *Star Spangled Banner* . . . . (Word)
Another Football Year
Jeannie C. Riley; *45-#14666* . . . . (MGM)
Armchair Quarterback
Ray Stevens; *I Have Returned* . . . . (MCA)
Backfield In Motion
Mel & Tim; *Collectables Presents The History Of Rock-#4-C* . . . . (Collectables)
Oldies But Goodies-#2-C . . . . (Original Sound)
Soul Shots-#2-The "In" Crowd-Sweet Soul-C . . . . (Rhino)
Super Oldies Of The '60s-#10-C . . . . (Audio Fidelity)
Bear Down Arizona
Original Soundtrack; *College Fight Songs: The Pac Ten-C* . . . . (K-Tel)
Bear Down, Chicago Bears
Chicago Symphony Orchestra & Chorus; *Bear Down, Chicago Bears-12"* . . . . (London)
Boomer Sooner
Original Soundtrack; *The Greatest College Fight Songs* . . . . (Laserlight)
Bow Down To Washington
Original Soundtrack; *College Fight Songs: The Pac Ten-C* . . . . (K-Tel)
The Greatest College Fight Songs . . . . (Laserlight)
Come Join The Band
Original Soundtrack; *College Fight Songs: The Pac Ten-C* . . . . (K-Tel)
Dallas Cowboys
Charley Pride; *45-#11736* . . . . (RCA)
Down The Field
Original Soundtrack; *Top Ten College Fight Songs* . . . . (K-Tel)
University Of Michigan Band; *Touchdown, U.S.A.* . . . . (Vanguard)
Down, Down The Field
Original Soundtrack; *The Greatest College Fight Songs* . . . . (Laserlight)
Drop Kick Me Jesus (Through The Goalposts Of Life)
Bobby Bare; *Essential Bobby Bare* . . . . (RCA)
Fight For California
Original Soundtrack; *The Greatest College Fight Songs* . . . . (Laserlight)
University Of California Marching Band; *University Of California Marching Band* . . . . (Fidelity Sound)
Fight On State
Original Soundtrack; *College Fight Songs: The Big Ten-C* . . . . (K-Tel)
The Greatest College Fight Songs . . . . (Laserlight)
Fight On, U.S.C.
Michigan University Band; *Kick Off, U.S.A.* . . . . (Vanguard)
Original Soundtrack; *College Fight Songs: The Pac Ten-C* . . . . (K-Tel)
The Greatest College Fight Songs . . . . (Laserlight)
Top Ten College Fight Songs . . . . (K-Tel)
Fight Song, The
Original Soundtrack; *College Fight Songs: The Pac Ten-C* . . . . (K-Tel)
Fight The Team Across The Field
Ohio State University Marching Band; *Across The Field* . . . . . . (Fidelity Sound)
Football Card
Glenn Sutton; *Close Encounters Of The Sutton Kind.* . . . . (Mercury)
Go U Northwestern
Northwestern University Marching Band; *Go U Northwestern.* . (Fidelity Sound)
Original Soundtrack; *College Fight Songs: The Big Ten-C* . . . . (K-Tel)
The Greatest College Fight Songs . . . . (Laserlight)
God's Footballer
Billy Bragg; *Don't Try This At Home* . . . . (Elektra)
Great Joe Bob (A Regional Tragedy)
Country Gazette; *Hello Operator...This Is Country Gazette* . . . . . (Flying Fish)
Hail New Mexico
Original Soundtrack; *The Greatest College Fight Songs* . . . . (Laserlight)
Hail Purdue
Original Soundtrack; *College Fight Songs: The Big Ten-C* . . . . (K-Tel)

The Greatest College Fight Songs . . . . (Laserlight)
University Of Michigan Band; *Greatest College Football Marches* . .(Vanguard)
Hail To Old O.S.U.
Original Soundtrack; *College Fight Songs: The Pac Ten-C* . . . . (K-Tel)
The Greatest College Fight Songs . . . . (Laserlight)
Hail Varsity
Original Soundtrack; *The Greatest College Fight Songs* . . . . (Laserlight)
Homecoming '63
Keith Whitley; *L.A. To Miami* . . . . (RCA)
Illinois Loyalty
Original Soundtrack; *College Fight Songs: The Big Ten-C* . . . . (K-Tel)
University Of Michigan Band; *Greatest College Football Marches* . .(Vanguard)
Indiana, Our Indiana
Indiana University Marching 100; *Indiana Our Indiana* . . . .(Fidelity Sound)
Indiana University Marching 100 . . . .(Fidelity Sound)
Original Soundtrack; *College Fight Songs: The Big Ten-C* . . . . (K-Tel)
Iowa Fight Song
Original Soundtrack; *College Fight Songs: The Big Ten-C* . . . . (K-Tel)
University Of Iowa Band; *Go Hawkeyes Go* . . . .(Fidelity Sound)
University Of Michigan Band; *Greatest College Football Marches* . .(Vanguard)
Last Game Of The Season (A Blind Man In The Bleachers)
David Geddes; *Super Hits Of The '70s-Have A Nice Day-#20-C* . . . .(Rhino)
M.S.U. Fight Song
Michigan State University Band; *Michigan State University Band* . . . .(Fidelity Sound)
Original Soundtrack; *College Fight Songs: The Big Ten-C* . . . . (K-Tel)
Maroon And Gold
Original Soundtrack; *College Fight Songs: The Pac Ten-C* . . . . (K-Tel)
Mighty Oregon
Original Soundtrack; *College Fight Songs: The Pac Ten-C* . . . . (K-Tel)
The Greatest College Fight Songs . . . . (Laserlight)
Minnesota Rouser
Ohio State University Marching Band; *Stadium Favorites In Brass.* . . . .(Fidelity Sound)
Original Soundtrack; *College Fight Songs: The Big Ten-C* . . . . (K-Tel)
Top Ten College Fight Songs . . . . (K-Tel)
Mister Touchdown U.S.A.
Original Soundtrack; *Top Ten College Fight Songs* . . . . (K-Tel)
University Of Michigan Band; *Greatest College Football Marches* . .(Vanguard)
Monday Morning Quarterback
Frank Sinatra; *She Shot Me Down* . . . . (Reprise)
Moving The Goalposts
Billy Bragg; *Don't Try This At Home* . . . .(Elektra)
Notre Dame Victory March
Original Soundtrack; *The Greatest College Fight Songs* . . . . (Laserlight)
Top Ten College Fight Songs . . . . (K-Tel)
University Of Notre Dame Band; *Songs Of The Fighting Irish* . . . .(Fidelity Sound)
On Iowa
Original Soundtrack; *The Greatest College Fight Songs* . . . . (Laserlight)
University Of Iowa Marching Band; *Go Hawkeyes Go* . . . .(Fidelity Sound)
On, Brave Old Army Team
All-Star Inter-Conference Band; *College Marches At Halftime* . . . .(Alshire)
Glenn Miller; *Pennsylvania 6-5000-Sustaining Remotes* . . . . (Vintage Jazz Classics)
Original Soundtrack; *Top Ten College Fight Songs* . . . .(K-Tel)
On, Wisconsin
Magic Organ; *22 Great Organ Favorites* . . . .(Ranwood)
Traveling With The Magic Organ . . . .(Ranwood)
Original Soundtrack; *College Fight Songs: The Big Ten-C* . . . . (K-Tel)
The Greatest College Fight Songs . . . . (Laserlight)
Orange And Blue
Original Soundtrack; *The Greatest College Fight Songs* . . . . (Laserlight)
Pass The Football
Original Broadway Cast; *Wonderful Town* . . . . (MCA)
Wonderful Town . . . .(Columbia)
Pride Of The Illini
University Of Michigan Band; *Greatest College Football Marches* . .(Vanguard)
Princeton Cannon Song
University Of Michigan Band; *Greatest College Football Marches* . .(Vanguard)
Rambling Wreck From Georgia Tech
Original Soundtrack; *The Greatest College Fight Songs* . . . . (Laserlight)
Top Ten College Fight Songs . . . . (K-Tel)
Rice University Fight Song
Original Soundtrack; *The Greatest College Fight Songs* . . . . (Laserlight)
Roll On, Tulane
Michigan University Band; *Kick Off, U.S.A.* . . . . (Vanguard)
Sing U.C.L.A.
University Of Michigan Band; *Greatest College Football Marches* . .(Vanguard)
Sons Of California
Original Soundtrack; *College Fight Songs: The Pac Ten-C* . . . . (K-Tel)
University Of California Marching Band; *University Of California Marching Band.* . . . .(Fidelity Sound)
Sons Of Westwood
Original Soundtrack; *College Fight Songs: The Pac Ten-C* . . . . (K-Tel)
The Greatest College Fight Songs . . . . (Laserlight)
Super Bowl Shuffle
Chicago Bears Shufflin' Crew; *45-#71012* . . . . (Red Label)

Tall Paul
Annette with the Afterbeats; *Best Of Annette Funicello* . . . . (Rhino)
Sherman Brothers . . . .(Disney)
Too Cute-C . . . .(Dunhill Compact Classics)
Theme From ''Monday Night Football''
Original Soundtrack; *Television's Greatest Hits-#6-Remote Control-C* . . (TVT)
Touchdown Raiders
Santana; *Beyond Appearances* . . . . (Columbia)
Victors, The
Ohio State University Marching Band; *Music For Cheerleaders & Song Girls* . . . . (Fidelity Sound)
Saturday Afternoon At Columbus . . . .(Fidelity Sound)
Original Soundtrack; *College Fight Songs: The Big Ten-C* . . . . (K-Tel)
The Greatest College Fight Songs . . . . (Laserlight)
Top Ten College Fight Songs . . . . (K-Tel)
University Of Michigan Band; *41 Great College Victory Songs* . . . . . (Vanguard)
Wide Receiver
Michael Henderson; *Wide Receiver* . . . . (Right Stuff)
Words By Heart
Billy Ray Cyrus; *It Won't Be The Last* . . . . (Mercury)
Yale Boola
All-Star Inter-Conference Band; *College Marches At Halftime* . . . . (Alshire)
Yea Alabama
Original Soundtrack; *The Greatest College Fight Songs* . . . . (Laserlight)
You've Got To Be A Football Hero
University Of Michigan Band; *Greatest College Football Marches* . (Vanguard)

SPORTS: GENERAL, Basketball, Boxing, Exercise, Golf, Horse Racing, Olympics, Skating

See Also: **COWBOYS, GAMBLING, LOSING & LOSS, RODEO, SAILING, SPORTS (various), TOYS & GAMES, WINNING**

808 (ice skating)
Blaque; *Blaque* . . . . (Track Masters/Columbia)
All Star
Smash Mouth; *Astro Lounge* . . . . (Interscope)
Now That's What I Call Music!-#3-C . . . . (Virgin)
Anyone For Tennis
Cream; *Eric Clapton-Crossroads-C* . . . . (Polydor)
Strange Brew-Very Best Of Cream . . . . (Polydor)
Around The World In Eighty Days
Boston Pops Orchestra/Arthur Fiedler; *Greatest Hits Of The '50s-#2* . . . . (RCA)
Frank Sinatra; *Come Fly With Me* . . . . (Capitol)
Roger Williams; *Roger Williams' Greatest Hits* . . . . (MCA)
Victor Young & His Singing Strings; *Hollywood's Greatest Hits-#2* . . . (Telarc)
Baron, The
Johnny Cash; *Columbia Records-1958-1986* . . . . (Columbia)
Greatest Country Hits Of The '80s-1981-C . . . . (Columbia)
Johnny Cash's Biggest Hits . . . . (Columbia)
Basketball
Greyson & Jasun; *Sweatin' Me Wet* . . . .(Atlantic)
Basketball
Kurtis Blow; *Ego Trip* . . . . (Mercury)
Basketball Jones
Cheech & Chong; *Los Cochinos* . . . .(Warner Bros.)
Bicycle Race
Queen; *Jazz* . . . . (Hollywood)
Live Killers . . . . (Hollywood)
Queen's Greatest Hits I & II . . . . (Hollywood)
Bicyclettes De Belsize
Engelbert Humperdinck; *Engelbert* . . . . (Parrot)
Engelbert Humperdinck-His Greatest Hits . . . . (Parrot)
Live In Concert/All Of Me . . . .(Epic)
Bobby Orr Breakaway
Kirk Elliott; *No Fixed Address* . . . . (Boot)
Bowling Song
Asleep At The Wheel; *Country Goes Raffi-C* . . . . (Rounder)
Boxer, The
Simon & Garfunkel; *Bridge Over Troubled Water* . . . . (Columbia)
Collected Works . . . . (Columbia)
Simon & Garfunkel's Greatest Hits . . . . (Columbia)
The Concert In Central Park . . . .(Warner Bros.)
Brand New Key
Deana Carter; *Everything's Gonna Be Alright* . . . . (Capitol)
Melanie; *Best Of Melanie* . . . . (Rhino)
Super Hits Of The '70s-Have A Nice Day-#7-C . . . . (Rhino)
Brunswick Bowling Spot
4 Seasons; *Rarities-#1* . . . . (Rhino)
Camptown Races
Marilyn Horne; *Beautiful Dreamer-Great American Songbook* . . . . (London)
Mormon Tabernacle Choir; *Songs Of The Civil War And Stephen Foster Favorites* . . . . (Sony Music Classical)
Pete Seeger; *American Favorite Ballads-#3* . . . . (Smithsonian Folkways)
Chariots Of Fire
Vangelis; *ST/Chariots Of Fire* . . . . (Polydor)
Themes . . . . (Polydor)

Country Club (pool)
Travis Tritt; *Country Club* . . . . (Warner Bros.)
Cup Of Life
Ricky Martin; *Ricky Martin* . . . . (Columbia)
Day We Lost The America's Cup
Tom Paxton; *One Million Lawyers & Other Disasters* . . . . (Flying Fish)
Distance, The
Cake; *Fashion Nugget* . . . . (Capricorn)
El Matador
Kingston Trio; *Capitol Collectors Series-The Kingston Trio* . . . . (Capitol)
Sold Out/String Along . . . . (Capitol)
Football Fugue
Pete Townshend; *Another Scoop* . . . . (Atco)
Game Seven
Chuck Brown & The Soul Searchers; *Bustin' Loose* . . . . (Source)
Give It All You Got (1980 W. Olympics)
Chuck Mangione; *Best Of Chuck Mangione* . . . . (A&M)
Chuck Mangione-Classics-#6 . . . . (A&M)
Fun & Games . . . . (A&M)
Goin' To Dallas To See My Pony Run
Lightnin' Hopkins; *Blues In My Bottle* . . . . (Bluesville)
Drinkin' In The Blues-Golden Classics-#1 . . . . (Collectables)
Lightnin' Hopkins . . . . (Everest)
Going To The Racetrack
Etta Baker; *One-Dime Blues* . . . . (Rounder)
Golf Date
Stan Freberg; *Tip Of The Freberg: The Stan Freberg Collection-1951-1998* . . . . (Rhino)
Golf Girl
Caravan; *Best Of Caravan* . . . .(London)
Caravan-London Collector . . . .(London)
In The Land Of Grey & Pink . . . .(London)
Golf Scene, The
G.P. Huntley & George Carroll; *Music From The New York Stage (1890-1920)-#1-1890-1908-C* . . . . (Pearl)
Golfin' Blues
Loudon Wainwright III; *Final Exam* . . . . (Arista)
Hand Me Down My Jogging Shoes
Shaw Brothers; *Best Of The Shaw Brothers* . . . . (Folk Era)
Shaw Brothers-Collection . . . . (Folk Era)
Hit Me With Your Best Shot
Pat Benatar; *Crimes Of Passion* . . . . (Chrysalis)
Live From Earth . . . . (Chrysalis)
Hockey
Jane Siberry; *Bound By The Beauty* . . . . (Warner Bros.)
Hockey Song
Stompin' Tom Connors; *Hockey Song* . . . . (Boot)
Hockey Song, The
Tom Connors; *The Hockey Zone-C* . . . . (Sportsongs)
Hometown Hero
Zamboni Brothers; *The Hockey Zone-C* . . . . (Sportsongs)
Hurricane
Bob Dylan; *Desire* . . . . (Columbia)
I Never Play Basketball Now
Prefab Sprout; *Swoon* . . . . (Epic)
I'll Tumble 4 Ya
Culture Club; *Kissing To Be Clever* . . . .(Virgin)
It Happened In Sun Valley
Glenn Miller & His Orchestra; *Complete Glenn Miller & His Orchestra* . . . . (Bluebird)
I've Got The Horse Right Here
Original Cast; *Guys & Dolls* . . . . (MCA)
Izzo (H.O.V.A.) (basketball)
Jay-Z; *Izzo (H.O.V.A.)* . . . . (Roc-A-Fella/DJMG)
The Concert For New York City-C . . . . (Columbia)
Joggers
Jerry Clower; *Starke Raving* . . . . (MCA)
Joggin'
Patsy; *Patsy* . . . . (Reprise)
Ray Stevens; *He Thinks He's Ray Stevens* . . . . (MCA)
Joggin' Song
Barley Bree; *Castles In The Air* . . . .(Shanachie)
Joystick
Dazz Band; *Dazz Band's Greatest Hits* . . . . (Motown)
Joystick . . . . (Motown)
Kansas Wildcats
Band Of H.M. Royal Marines; *Hands Across The Sea-Sousa Marches* . . (Angel)
Eastman Wind Ensemble; *Sousa On Review* . . . . (Mercury)
Stars And Stripes Forever . . . . (Mercury)
Keepers Of The Flame
Zamboni Brothers; *The Hockey Zone-C* . . . . (Sportsongs)
Kid's Last Fight
Frankie Laine; *Frankie Laine-16 Most Requested Songs* . . . . (Legacy)
Lonely Bull (El Solo Torro)
Herb Alpert & The Tijuana Brass; *Four Sider* . . . . (A&M)
Herb Alpert & The Tijuana Brass' Greatest Hits . . . . (A&M)
Herb Alpert & The Tijuana Brass-Classics-#1 . . . . (A&M)
The Lonely Bull . . . . (A&M)

Lord Stanley's Cup
Zamboni Brothers; *The Hockey Zone-C* . . . . (Sportsongs)

Love Is A Contact Sport
Whitney Houston; *Whitney* . . . . (Arista)

Love T.K.O.
Bette Midler; *Bette*. . . . . (Warner Bros.)

Love TKO
Teddy Pendergrass; *TP* . . . . (Philadelphia Int'l)

Main Event/Fight
Barbra Streisand; *Collection-Greatest Hits...And More* . . . . (Columbia)
   ST/Funny Girl . . . . (Columbia)

Mama Said Knock You Out
L.L. Cool J; *Mama Said Knock You Out* . . . . (Def Jam)

Matador
Sylvia; *Drifter* . . . .(RCA)

Minnesota Man Claims Monkey Bowled Perfect Game
Jad Fair; *Strange But True* . . . . (Matador)

Muscles
Diana Ross; *Endless Love* . . . .(RCA)
   Silk Electric . . . .(RCA)
   Why Do Fools Fall In Love . . . .(RCA)

My Daddy Was A Jockey
John Lee Hooker; *Detroit Blues-1950-1951* . . . . (Collectables)
   Gotham Golden Classics-C . . . . (Collectables)

Ode To A Gym Teacher
Meg Christian; *I Know You Know* . . . . (Olivia)
   Scrapbook . . . . (Olivia)

Olympia
Sergio Mendes; *Olympia* . . . . (A&M)

Olympian-Lighting Of The Torch
Philip Glass; *Official Music Of The XXIIIrd Olympiad* . . . . (Columbia)

Olympic Fanfare & Theme
Felix Slatkin Concert Band; *U.S.A.* . . . . (Angel)
John Williams; *Official Music Of The XXIII Olympiad* . . . . (Columbia)
Original Soundtrack; *Television's Greatest Hits-#5-In Living Color-C* . . . (TVT)

Olympic Joy
Kashif; *1988 Summer Olympics-One Moment In Time-C* . . . . (Arista)

Olympic Spirit
John Williams; *1988 Summer Olympics-One Moment In Time-C* . . . . . . (Arista)

Olympics
Mannheim Steamroller; *Fresh Aire VI* . . . . (American Gramaphone)

One Big Love (boxing)
Emmylou Harris; *Red Dirt Girl* . . . . (Nonesuch)
Patty Griffin; *Flaming Red* . . . . (A&M)

One Hit (To The Body)
Rolling Stones; *Dirty Work* . . . .(Virgin)

One Moment In Time
Whitney Houston; *1984 Olympics Album-C* . . . . (Arista)
   Whitney Houston's Greatest Hits . . . . (Arista)

One On One
Daryl Hall & John Oates; *H2O* . . . .(RCA)
   Live At The Apollo . . . .(RCA)
   Rock 'N Soul, Part 1 . . . .(RCA)
   Soulful Sounds . . . .(RCA)

Physical
Olivia Newton-John; *Back To Basics-Essential Collection 1971-1992*. . (Geffen)
   Olivia Newton-John's Greatest Hits-#2 . . . . (MCA)
   Physical . . . . (MCA)

Poli High
Nilsson; *The Point* . . . .(RCA)

Possessed To Skate
Suicidal Tendencies; *Join The Army* . . . . (Caroline)

Question Of Sport
Martin Carthy & Dave Swarbrick; *Life & Limb*. . . . . (Green Linnet)

Race Is On
Dave Edmunds; *Best Of Dave Edmunds* . . . . (Swan Song)
   Twangin'. . . . . (Swan Song)
George Jones; *Best Of George Jones-1955-1967* . . . . (Rhino)
   Billboard Top Country Hits-1964-C. . . . . (Rhino)
   George Jones' All-Time Greatest Hits . . . . (Epic)
Sawyer Brown; *Boys Are Back* . . . . (Curb)
   Sawyer Brown's Greatest Hits . . . . (Curb)

Race The K-12
Rupert Hine; *ST/Better Off Dead* . . . . (A&M)

Race To Win
Blitzspeer; *Blitzspeer Live* . . . . (Epic)

Race With The Devil
Gene Vincent and His Blue Caps; *Capitol Collectors Series-Gene Vincent
   and His Blue Caps* . . . . (Gold Rush)
   Legends Of Rock Guitar-'50s-#1-C . . . . (Rhino)

Race You To The Top Of The Morning
Original Broadway Cast; *Secret Garden* . . . . (Columbia)

Racehorse
Count Basie & His Kansas City 3; *For The Second Time* . . . . (Pablo)

Racetrack
Bad Company; *Rough Diamonds* . . . . (Swan Song)

Racetrack Blues
Lightnin' Hopkins; *Gold Star Sessions-#1* . . . .(Arhoolie)

Nashville Jug Band . . . .
Nashville Jug Band; *Nashville Jug Band* . . . . (Rounder)

Red Football
Sinead O'Connor; *Universal Mother* . . . . (Ensign)

River (ice skating)
Joni Mitchell; *Blue* . . . . (Reprise)

Rock & Roll Part 2 (The Sports Anthem ["The Hey Song"])
Gary Glitter; *Gary Glitter's Greatest Hits* . . . . (Rhino)

Roller Derby Queen
Jim Croce; *Life & Times* . . . . (Lifesong)
   Photographs & Memories/His Greatest Hits . . . . (Atlantic)

Roller Skatin' Mate
Peaches & Herb; *Twice The Fire* . . . . (Polydor)

Roller Skating Child
Beach Boys; *Love You* . . . . (Caribou)
   Ten Years In Harmony. . . . . (Caribou)

Run For The Roses
Dan Fogelberg; *Dan Fogelberg/Greatest Hits* . . . . (Full Moon)
   Innocent Age . . . . (Full Moon)
   Live-Greetings From The West . . . . (Full Moon)

Runner
Manfred Mann's Earth Band; *Somewhere In Afrika*. . . . . (Arista)

Sagebrush Sports Report
Riders In The Sky; *Riders Radio Theater* . . . . (MCA)

Score, The
Emerson, Lake & Powell; *Emerson, Lake & Powell* . . . . (Polydor)

Shadow Boxer
Angel City; *Face To Face* . . . . (Epic)

Shadow Boxing
Giles Reaves & Jon Goin; *Letting Go*. . . . . (MCA)

Shadow Boxing
Teena Marie; *Robbery* . . . . (Epic)

Shadowboxer
Fiona Apple; *Tidal* . . . . (Clean Slate/Work)

Shake It Up
Zamboni Brothers; *The Hockey Zone-C*. . . . . (Sportsongs)

She Misses Him On Sunday The Most (Bowling)
Diamond Rio; *Diamond Rio IV* . . . . (Arista)
   Diamond Rio's Greatest Hits . . . . (Arista)

Silver Medals & Sweet Memories
Statler Brothers; *Best Of The Statler Brothers-Rides Again-#2* . . . . . (Mercury)
   Short Stories. . . . . (Mercury)

Skate To The Rhythm
High Inergy; *Frenzie* . . . . (Gordy)

Skateaway
Dire Straits; *Making Movies*. . . . . (Warner Bros.)

Skateboard
Jefferson Starship; *Earth* . . . . (Grunt)

Skateboard Surfin' U.S.A.
Jan Berry; *45-#2020*. . . . . (A&M)

Skatetown U.S.A.
Dave Mason; *Skatetown U.S.A.-C* . . . . (Columbia)

Skating Away On The Thin Ice Of A New Day
Jethro Tull; *"M.U."-Best Of* . . . . (Chrysalis)
   Bursting Out . . . . (Chrysalis)
   Original Masters . . . . (Chrysalis)
   War Child . . . . (Chrysalis)

Skating On Thin Ice
Tower Of Power; *Bump City* . . . . (Warner Bros.)

Sports Fans
Tubes; *Best Of The Tubes*. . . . . (Capitol)

Still In The Game
Steve Winwood; *Talking Back To The Night* . . . .(Island)

Streak, The
Ray Stevens; *Ray Stevens' Greatest Hits* . . . . (RCA)
   Ray Stevens' Greatest Hits . . . . (MCA)
   Ray Stevens-All-Time Greatest Comic Hits. . . . . (Curb)
   Super Hits Of The '70s-Have A Nice Day-#12-C . . . . (Rhino)

Sweet Georgia Brown (Harlem Globetrotters Theme)
Ben Bernie & His Orchestra; *78-#15002* . . . . (Vocalion)

T.K.O. (Boxing Day)
Elvis Costello & The Attractions; *Punch The Clock* . . . . (Rykodisc)

Take The Skinheads Bowling
Camper Van Beethoven; *Telephone Free Landslide Victory* . . . . (I.R.S.)

Teen Archer
Blue Oyster Cult; *Tyranny & Mutation* . . . . (Columbia)

Tennis Anyone
Today; *New Formula* . . . . (Motown)

Tennis Shoes
Jimmy C. Newman; *Alligator Man* . . . . (Rounder)

Tennis Song
Original Broadway Cast; *City Of Angels* . . . . (Columbia)
Original London Cast; *City Of Angels* . . . . (RCA)

Theme From "ABC's Wide World Of Sports"
Original Soundtrack; *Television's Greatest Hits-#2-C* . . . . (TVT)

Theme From "Speed Racer"
Original Soundtrack; *Television's Greatest Hits-#3-1970s & 1980s-C* . . . .(TVT)

Theme From Jack Johnson
Miles Davis; *Agharta*. . . . . (Columbia)

Up, Up & Away
5th Dimension; *5th Dimension-Anthology 1967-1973* . . . . (Rhino)
Greatest Hits On Earth . . . . (Arista)
We Are The Champions
Big Blue Wrecking Crew; *Baseball's Greatest Hits-C* . . . . (Rhino)
Queen; *Billboard Top Rock 'N' Roll Hits-1978-C* . . . . (Rhino)
Live At Wembley '86 . . . . (Hollywood)
Live Killers . . . . (Hollywood)
News Of The World . . . . (Hollywood)
Queen's Greatest Hits I & II . . . . (Hollywood)
We Can Have The Olympics...At Our House
Tom Paxton; *One Million Lawyers & Other Disasters* . . . . (Flying Fish)
Wet My Whistle
Midnight Star; *Midnight Star's Greatest Hits* . . . . (Solar)
No Parking On The Dance Floor . . . . (Solar)
Wide World Of Sports
Instant Funk; *Instant Funk* . . . . (Salsoul)
Work That Body
Diana Ross; *Why Do Fools Fall In Love* . . . . (RCA)
Y.M.C.A.
Village People; *Billboard Top Dance Hits-1978-C* . . . . (Rhino)
Billboard Top Rock 'N' Roll Hits-1979-C . . . . (Rhino)
Cruisin' . . . . (Casablanca)
Live & Sleazy . . . . (Casablanca)
Night At Studio 54-C . . . . (Casablanca)
Village People's Greatest Hits . . . . (Rhino)
Ya Got Trouble (pool)
Robert Preston/Original Broadway Cast; *The Music Man* . . . . (Angel)
Robert Preston/Original Cast; *ST/The Music Man* . . . . (Warner Bros.)
The Music Man . . . . (Gold Rush)
You Can't Roller Skate In A Buffalo Herd
Roger Miller; *Best Of Roger Miller-#2-King Of The Road* . . . . (Mercury)
Roger Miller-Golden Hits . . . . (Smash)
Zamboni
Martin Zellar; *The Hockey Zone-C* . . . . (Sportsongs)

SPORTS: SURFING

See Also: *ISLANDS, OCEAN, PARADISE, SPORTS (various),*
STATES: CALIFORNIA

Abigail Beecher
Freddy Cannon; *14 Booming Hits* . . . . (Rhino)
Big Blast From Boston: The Best Of Freddy ''Boom Boom''
Cannon . . . . (Rhino)
Body Surfing
Santana; *Shango* . . . . (Columbia)
California Surfer
Dee D. Hope; *History Of Surf Music-#2-C* . . . . (Rhino)
Catch A Wave
Beach Boys; *Best Of The Beach Boys* . . . . (Capitol)
Endless Summer . . . . (Capitol)
Party!/Stack-O-Tracks . . . . (Capitol)
Charlie Don't Surf
Clash; *Sandinista* . . . . (Epic)
Honolulu Lulu
Jan & Dean; *Dead Man's Curve* . . . . (EMI)
Jan & Dean-Legendary Masters . . . . (EMI)
One Summer Night-Live . . . . (Rhino)
Surf City-Best Of Jan & Dean . . . . (EMI)
Kill Surf City
Jesus & Mary Chain; *Barbed Wire Kisses* . . . . (Warner Bros.)
King Of The Surf Guitar
Dick Dale And The Del-Tones; *Beach Classics-All Original*
Recordings-C . . . . (Dunhill Compact Classics)
Dick Dale And The Del-Tones' Greatest Hits . . . . (Crescendo)
Tigers Loose . . . . (Rhino)
Lonely Surfer
Jack Nitzsche; *Surfin' Hits-C* . . . . (Rhino)
Surfin' Sixties-C . . . . (JCI Assoc. Labels)
Monster Surfing Time
Halibuts; *Halibut Beach* . . . . (Waterhouse)
New York's A Lonely Town
Tradewinds; *Beach Classics-All Original*
Recordings-C . . . . (Dunhill Compact Classics)
Original Golden Hits Of The Great Groups-#1-C . . . . (SSS International)
Surfin' Hits-C . . . . (Rhino)
No Surfin' Today
4 Seasons; *Rarities-#1* . . . . (Rhino)
Pipeline
Chantays; *Surfin' Hits-C* . . . . (Rhino)
Surfin' U.S.A.-C . . . . (Dominion Entert.)
Ride The Wild Surf
Jan & Dean; *Monster Summer Hits-Wild Surf-C* . . . . (Capitol)
Surf City-Best Of Jan & Dean . . . . (EMI)
Surfin' Hits-C . . . . (Rhino)

Rocking Surfer
Beach Boys; *Surfer Girl* . . . . (Capitol)
Skateboard Surfin' U.S.A.
Jan Berry; *45-#2020* . . . . (A&M)
Surf Beat
Dick Dale And The Del-Tones; *Dick Dale And The Del-Tones'*
Greatest Hits . . . . (Crescendo)
King Of The Surf Guitar-Best Of Dick Dale And The Del-Tones . . . . . . (Rhino)
Surf City
Jan & Dean; *Billboard Top Rock 'N' Roll Hits-1963-C* . . . . (Rhino)
Monster Summer Hits-Wild Surf-C . . . . (Capitol)
Surf City-Best Of Jan & Dean . . . . (EMI)
Surf Monkey
Freddie King; *Just Pickin'* . . . . (Modern Blues)
Surf Nicaragua
Sacred Reich; *Mega Metal-C* . . . . (K-Tel)
Surf Rider
Lively Ones; *Bustin' Surfboards* . . . . (Crescendo)
Legends Of Surf Guitar . . . . (Rhino)
Surfer Dan
Turtles; *Turtle Wax-Best Of The Turtles-#2* . . . . (Rhino)
Surfer Girl
Beach Boys; *American Graffiti-#3-C* . . . . (MCA)
Best Of The Beach Boys . . . . (Capitol)
Endless Summer . . . . (Capitol)
Made In The U.S.A. . . . . (Capitol)
Oldies But Goodies-#2-C . . . . (Original Sound)
Surfer Joe
Surfaris; *Surfin' Hits-C* . . . . (Rhino)
Surfin' Sixties-C . . . . (JCI Assoc. Labels)
Surfin'
Beach Boys; *Monster Summer Hits-Wild Surf-C* . . . . (Capitol)
Summer Hits-C . . . . (Rhino)
Surfin' Bird
Pee-Wee Herman; *ST/Back To The Beach* . . . . (Columbia)
Ramones; *All The Stuff & More-#2* . . . . (Sire)
Rocket To Russia . . . . (Sire)
Trashmen; *Collectables Presents The History Of Rock-#1-C* . . . . . (Collectables)
History Of Surf Music-#2-C . . . . (Rhino)
Monster Summer Hits-Wild Surf-C . . . . (Capitol)
ST/Full Metal Jacket . . . . (Warner Bros.)
Super Oldies Of The '60s-#11-C . . . . (Audio Fidelity)
Surfin' Down The Swanee River
Honeys; *Capitol Collectors Series-The Honeys* . . . . (Capitol)
Surfin' In Harlem
Swamp Dogg; *Surfin' In Harlem* . . . . (Volt)
Surfin' On Heroin
Forgotten Rebels; *Surfin' On Heroin* . . . . (Restless)
Surfin' On Jupiter
Psychefunkapus; *Skin* . . . . (Atlantic)
Surfin' Safari
Beach Boys; *Absolute Best-#1* . . . . (Capitol)
Endless Summer . . . . (Capitol)
Made In The U.S.A. . . . . (Capitol)
Monster Summer Hits-Wild Surf-C . . . . (Capitol)
Surfin' Sex Machine
Pajama Slave Dancers; *Blood Sweat & Beers* . . . . (Restless)
Surfin' Tragedy
Bob Vaught & The Renegaids; *Original Surfin' Hits* . . . . (Crescendo)
Breakers; *World's Worst Records-C* . . . . (Rhino)
Surfin' U.S.A.
Beach Boys; *Absolute Best-#1* . . . . (Capitol)
Best Of The Beach Boys . . . . (Capitol)
Billboard Top Rock 'N' Roll Hits-1963-C . . . . (Rhino)
Endless Summer . . . . (Capitol)
Made In The U.S.A. . . . . (Capitol)
Surfin' U.S.A.
Jesus & Mary Chain; *Barbed Wire Kisses* . . . . (Warner Bros.)
Surfin' U.S.S.R.
Ray Stevens; *Everything Is Beautiful* . . . . (MCA Special Prod.)
I Never Made A Record I Didn't Like . . . . (MCA)
Ray Stevens-Collection . . . . (MCA)
Surf's Up
Beach Boys; *Surf's Up* . . . . (Caribou)
Sweet Surf Music
Malibooz; *Malibooz Rule* . . . . (Rhino)
Tell 'Em I'm Surfing
Fantastic Baggies; *Monster Summer Hits-Wild Surf-C* . . . . (Capitol)
Windsurfer
Roy Orbison; *Mystery Girl* . . . . (Virgin)
Wipe Out
Surfaris; *Billboard Top Rock 'N' Roll Hits-1963-C* . . . . (Rhino)
Cruisin'-1966-C . . . . (Increase)
Frat Rock!-C . . . . (Rhino)
Summer Hits-C . . . . (Rhino)
Surfin' Hits-C . . . . (Rhino)

SPORTS: SWIMMING, Diving

See Also: DROWN, OCEAN, RIVERS, SAILING, SHIPS, SPORTS (various), WATER

Adalida
George Strait; *Latest Greatest Straitest Hits* .... (MCA)
Lead On .... (MCA)
Arc Of A Diver
Steve Winwood; *Arc Of A Diver* .... (Island)
Backstrokin'
Fatback Band; *Hot Box* .... (Spring)
Bridge Washed Out
Warner Mack; *Country's Greatest Hits-#3-C* .... (MCA)
MCA Records 30 Years Of Hits-1958-1988-C .... (MCA)
Chattahoochee
Alan Jackson; *A Lot About Livin' (And A Little 'Bout Love)* .... (Arista)
Diving To Be Deeper
Sinead Lohan; *No Mermaid* .... (Grapevine)
I Go Swimming
Peter Gabriel; *Peter Gabriel/Plays Live* .... (Geffen)
Kern River
Merle Haggard; *For The Record: Merle Haggard-43 Legendary Hits* ....(BNA)
Kern River .... (Epic)
Not Swimming Ground
Meat Puppets; *Out My Way* .... (SST)
Swim
Fishbone; *Give A Monkey A Brain And He'll Swear He's The Center Of The
Universe* ....(Columbia)
ST/Last Action Hero ....(Columbia)
Swim
Madonna; *Ray Of Light* .... (Maverick)
Swimmin' Hole
Cactus Brothers; *Cactus Brothers* .... (Liberty)
Swimming Ground
Meat Puppets; *No Strings Attached* .... (SST)
Up On The Sun .... (SST)
Swimming Horses
Siouxsie And The Banshees; *Hyaena* .... (Geffen)
Twice Upon A Time-The Singles .... (Geffen)
Swimming In The Delaware
Sam Hinton; *Wandering Folk Song* ....(Smithsonian Folkways)
Swimming In The Ocean
David & David; *Boomtown* .... (A&M)
Swimming Song
Earl Scruggs Revue; *Live From Austin City Limits* ....(Columbia)
Kate & Anna McGarrigle; *Kate & Anna McGarrigle* .... (Hannibal)
Swimming Upstream
Ricky Van Shelton; *Loving Proof* ....(Columbia)
Swimming Upstream
Glen Campbell; *Somebody Like That* .... (Liberty)
Swimsuit Issue
Sonic Youth; *Dirty*.........................(David Geffen Co.)
Tahitian Moon
Porno For Pyros; *Good God's Urge*. .... (Warner Bros.)

STANDING

See Also: CHARACTER & INTEGRITY, PROTEST, SITTING, WAITING

Anyone Else
Collin Raye; *The Walls Came Down* .... (Epic)
At The Beginning
Richard Marx & Donna Lewis; *ST/Anastasia-Music From The Motion
Picture* .... (Atlantic)
Barrel Of A Gun (4,3,2,1)
Guster; *Lost & Gone Forever* .... (Hybrid/Sire)
Black Chick, White Guy
Kid Rock; *Devil Without A Cause* .... (Top Dog/Lava/Atlantic)
Brand New Day
Sting; *Brand New Day*............................. (A&M)
Breathe
Nickelback; *State*. .... (Roadrunner)
Caravan Of Love
Isley, Jasper, Isley; *Caravan Of Love* .... (CBS Associated)
Don't Sleep In The Subway
Frank Sinatra; *Frank Sinatra*. ....(Reprise)
Petula Clark; *Petula Clark's Greatest Hits* .... (Crescendo)
Summer Of Love-#1-C .... (Rhino)
Fire
Jimi Hendrix; *Concerts* ....(Reprise)
Essential Jimi Hendrix, Volume 2. ....(Reprise)
Jimi Hendrix Experience; *Are You Experienced?* ....(Reprise)
Smash Hits ....(Reprise)

Get Up, Stand Up
Bob Marley & The Wailers; *Bob Marley & The Wailers-Live* ...... (Tuff Gong)
Legend: The Best Of Bob Marley & The Wailers. ....(Island)
Rebel Music. .... (Tuff Gong)
Songs Of Freedom .... (Tuff Gong)
Peter Tosh; *Captured Live* .... (EMI)
Equal Rights ....(Columbia)
Rhythm Come Forward: Volume II-C ....(Columbia)
Wailers; *Burnin'*. .... (Tuff Gong)
God Bless America
Anita Bryant; *Golden Classics-Anita Bryant* ....(Collectables)
Bill & Gloria Gaither; *Kennedy Center Homecoming: A Celebration Of Our
Faith And Heritage*. .... (Springhouse Music Grp./Chordant)
Celine Dion; *America: A Tribute To Heroes-C* .... (Interscope)
God Bless America-C ....(Columbia)
Drew Carey; *ST/The Drew Carey Show* ....(Rhino)
Frank Zappa; *Uncle Meat*. .... (Barking Pumpkin)
Kate Smith; *Best Of Kate Smith* .... (RCA)
God Bless America .... (Pickwick)
Kate Smith-Legendary Performer .... (RCA)
Nipper's Greatest Hits Of The '30s-#1-C .... (RCA)
Stars And Stripes Forever-#2-C .... (Volcano Entertainment)
LeAnn Rimes; *You Light Up My Life-Inspirational Songs*. ....(Curb)
Lee Greenwood; *American Patriot* .... (Capitol)
Mormon Tabernacle Choir; *God Bless America* .... (Sony Music Classical)
Original Soundtrack; *ST/The Deer Hunter*. ....(Capitol)
Peter Pan Kids; *I Love America Sing Along* .... (Compose)
Robert Shaw Chorale; *Battle Cry Of Freedom* .... (RCA)
Hanging By A Moment
Lifehouse; *No Name Face* .... (DreamWorks/SKG)
Now That's What I Call Music!-#7-C .... (Virgin)
Holding On
Steve Winwood; *Roll With It* .... (Virgin)
I Ain't Goin' Nowhere
Martina McBride; *Emotion* .... (RCA)
I Can't Stand Still
Don Henley; *I Can't Stand Still* .... (Asylum)
I Saw Her Standing There
Beatles; *Introducing...The Beatles*. .... (Vee-Jay)
Meet The Beatles! .... (Capitol)
Please Please Me .... (Parlophone)
Rock 'N' Roll Music ....(Capitol)
The Beatles-Anthology-#1. ....(Capitol)
Paul McCartney; *Tripping The Live Fantastic-Highlights!* ....(Capitol)
I Saw Him Standing There
Tiffany; *Tiffany* .... (MCA)
Tiffany's Greatest Hits .... (Hip-O)
I Stand Alone
Steve Perry; *ST/Quest For Camelot* ....(Curb/Atlantic)
I'm Still Standing
Elton John; *Elton John's Greatest Hits-1976-1986* .... (MCA)
Too Low For Zero .... (MCA)
Jamboree
Naughty By Nature Featuring Zhane'; *19 Naughty Nine:
Nature's Fury*. ....(Arista)
Jump
Van Halen; *1984* .... (Warner Bros.)
Best Of Van Halen-#1 .... (Warner Bros.)
LIVE: Right here, right now. .... (Warner Bros.)
Long And Winding Road, The
Beatles; *Beatles 1* .... (Capitol)
Beatles-20 Greatest Hits ....(Capitol)
Beatles-Love Songs ....(Capitol)
Let It Be ....(Capitol)
Reel Music ....(Capitol)
The Beatles/1967-1970 ....(Capitol)
Paul McCartney; *Tripping The Live Fantastic-Highlights!* ....(Capitol)
Wings; *Wings Over America* ....(Capitol)
Maybe It Was Memphis
Pam Tillis; *Pam Tillis' Greatest Hits* ....(Arista)
Pam Tillis-Collection .... (Warner Bros.)
Put Yourself In My Place ....(Arista)
Nobody's Supposed To Be Here
Deborah Cox; *One Wish*. ....(Arista)
Totally Hits-#1-C ....(Arista)
On Holy Ground
Barbra Streisand; *Higher Ground* ....(Columbia)
On The Rock Where Moses Stood
Carter Family; *Worried Man Blues: Their Complete Victor Recordings-
1930* ....(Rounder)
Flatt & Scruggs; *Songs Of The Famous Carter Family* ....(Legacy)
Over Now
Alice In Chains; *Alice In Chains* ....(Columbia)
Real Slim Shady
Eminem; *The Marshall Mathers LP*. .... (Aftermath/Interscope)
So Much To Say
Dave Matthews Band; *Crash* .... (RCA)
Stand
Sly & The Family Stone; *10 Years Too Soon* .... (Epic)

Sly & The Family Stone-*Anthology* . . . .(Epic)
Sly & The Family Stone's *Greatest Hits*. . . . .(Epic)
Stand And Be Counted
Crosby, Stills, Nash & Young; *Looking Forward*. . . . . (Reprise)
Stand Beside Me
Jo Dee Messina; *Big Country Hits '99-C* . . . . (K-Tel)
I'm Alright . . . . (Curb)
Stand By Me
Ben E. King; *Atlantic Soul Classics-C* . . . . (Warner Special Prod.)
Ben E. King's *Greatest Hits* . . . . (Atco)
Golden Age Of Black Music-1960-1970-C . . . . (Atlantic)
ST/Stand By Me . . . . (Atlantic)
Stand By Me-Best Of Ben E. King . . . . (Atlantic)
Drifters; *Drifters' Greatest Hits* . . . . (Gusto)
John Lennon; *Rock 'N' Roll* . . . . (Capitol)
ST/Imagine: John Lennon . . . . (Capitol)
The John Lennon Collection . . . . (Capitol)
Maurice White; *Maurice White* . . . . (Columbia)
Mickey Gilley; *Greatest Country Hits From The Movies-C* . . . .(Epic)
Mickey Gilley's Biggest Hits . . . . (Epic)
ST/Urban Cowboy . . . . (Asylum)
Ten Years Of Hits . . . . (Epic)
Ry Cooder; *Chicken Skin Music* . . . . (Reprise)
Stand Inside Your Love
Smashing Pumpkins; *Machina: The Machines Of God* . . . . (Virgin)
Stand On It
Mel McDaniel; *Hot Rod-Hot Rod Cowboys-C* . . . . (Right Stuff)
Stand On It
Bruce Springsteen; *Tracks* . . . . (Columbia)
Stand Up
Keb' Mo'; *The Door* . . . . (550/Epic/Okeh)
Standin' At The Station
Keb' Mo'; *Just Like You* . . . . (Okeh)
Standing In The Doorway
Bob Dylan; *Time Out Of Mind* . . . . (Columbia)
Standing In The Shadows Of Love
Barry White; *Barry White's Greatest Hits* . . . . (20th Century Fox)
I've Got So Much To Give . . . . (20th Century Fox)
Four Tops; *Four Tops' Greatest Hits* . . . . (Motown)
Four Tops Reach Out . . . . (Motown)
Four Tops-Anthology . . . . (Motown)
Motown Story-First 25 Years-C . . . . (Motown)
Motown Superstar Series-#14-Four Tops . . . . (Motown)
Rod Stewart; *Blondes Have More Fun* . . . .(Warner Bros.)
Standing Knee Deep In A River (Dying Of Thirst)
Kathy Mattea; *Lonesome Standard Time* . . . . (Mercury)
Standing On The Corner
Broadway Cast; *Most Happy Fella* . . . . (RCA)
Dean Martin; *Best Of Dean Martin* . . . . (CEMA Special Prod.)
Four Lads; *Four Lads-16 Most Requested Songs* . . . . (Legacy)
Original Broadway Cast; *Most Happy Fella* . . . . (Sony Music Classical)
Standing On The Edge Of Goodbye
John Berry; *Standing On The Edge* . . . . (Capitol)
Standing On The Top
Temptations featuring Rick James; *Emperors Of Soul* . . . . (Motown)
Standing Outside A Broken Phone Booth With Money In My Hand
Primitive Radio Gods; *MTV Best Of The Buzz Bin-#2-C* . . . . (Mammoth)
Rocket . . . . (Ergo)
Standing Outside The Fire
Garth Brooks; *In Pieces* . . . . (Liberty)
Standing Still
Jewel; *This Way* . . . .(Atlantic)
Standing Tall
Billie Jo Spears; *Best Of Billie Jo Spears* . . . . (CEMA Special Prod.)
Love Ain't Gonna Wait For Us . . . . (United Artists)
Standing Tall . . . . (United Artists)
Brenda Lee; *Brenda Lee* . . . .(Warner Bros.)
Standing Tall
Lorrie Morgan; *Lorrie Morgan's Greatest Hits* . . . . (BNA)
Standing Together
George Benson; *Standing Together* . . . . (GRP)
That Was Your Mother
Paul Simon; *Graceland*. . . . .(Warner Bros.)
There Stands The Glass
Carl Smith; *Best Of Carl Smith* . . . . (Curb)
Webb Pierce; *Webb Pierce-Golden Hits*. . . . . (Plantation)
They Were Doin' The Mambo
Vaughn Monroe; *Very Best Of Vaughn Monroe* . . . .(Taragon)
This Lil' Game We Play
Subway; *Good Times* . . . .(Biv 10/Motown)
This Part Of Town
Widespread Panic; *Don't Tell The Band*. . . . . (Widespread/SRG)
Touch, Peel, And Stand
Days Of The New; *Days Of The New* . . . . (Outpost/Interscope)
X Games-#3-Music From The X Games-C. . . . . (Mammoth)
You're Still Standing There
Steve Earle; *I Feel Alright*. . . . .(Warner Bros.)

STARS, Planets

See Also: **ASTROLOGY, EARTH, MOON, SKY, SPACE, SUN, UFO's, WORLD**

(They Long To Be) Close To You
Carpenters; *Carpenters-Classics-#2* . . . . (A&M)
Carpenters-Love Songs . . . . (A&M)
Carpenters-The Singles 1969-1973 . . . . (A&M)
From The Top . . . . (A&M)
53 Miles West Of Venus
B-52's; *Wild Planet* . . . . (Warner Bros.)
Across The Universe
Beatles; *Let It Be* . . . . (Capitol)
Past Masters-Volume Two . . . . (Parlophone)
Rarities . . . . (Capitol)
The Beatles/1967-1970. . . . . (Capitol)
David Bowie; *Young Americans* . . . . (Rykodisc)
All At Once You Love Her
Perry Como; *Perry Como's Greatest Hits* . . . . (RCA)
All Star
Smash Mouth; *Astro Lounge* . . . .(Interscope)
Now That's What I Call Music!-#3-C . . . .(Virgin)
All The Love Of The Universe
Santana; *Caravanserai* . . . . (Columbia)
Another Planet
Alien Sex Fiend; *Another Planet*. . . . . (Caroline)
Another Star
Stevie Wonder; *Songs In The Key Of Life* . . . . (Motown)
Astronomy
Blue Oyster Cult; *Imaginos* . . . . (Columbia)
Secret Treaties . . . . (Columbia)
Some Enchanted Evening . . . . (Columbia)
Astronomy Domine
Pink Floyd; *Nice Pair* . . . . (Capitol)
Piper At The Gates Of Dawn . . . . (Capitol)
Ummagumma . . . . (Capitol)
At The Stars
Better Than Ezra; *How Does Your Garden Grow?* . . . . (Elektra)
Attack Of The Radioactive Hamsters
"Weird Al" Yankovic; *ST/UHF & Other Stuff* . . . . (Scotti Bros.)
Black Hole Sun
Soundgarden; *Superunknown* . . . . (A&M)
Blow Out The Stars, Turn Off The Moon
Nitty Gritty Dirt Band; *Rest Of The Dream* . . . . (MCA)
Blue Star
Mystics; *Mystics-16 Golden Classics* . . . . (Collectables)
Blue Star
Blue Notes; *Blue Notes-Early Years* . . . . (Collectables)
Blue Star
Charlie Daniels Band; *Million Mile Reflections* . . . . (Epic)
Blue White Planet
Raffi; *Country Goes Raffi-C* . . . . (Rounder)
Born With A Broken Heart
Kenny Wayne Shepherd; *Ledbetter Heights* . . . .(Giant)
Caravan
Duke Ellington; *Best Of Duke Ellington* . . . . (Capitol)
Money Jungle . . . .(Blue Note)
Ella Fitzgerald; *Montreux '75* . . . . (Pablo)
Johnny Mathis; *In A Sentimental Mood-Johnny Mathis Sings
Ellington* . . . . (Columbia)
Wynton Marsalis; *Marsalis Standard Time-#1* . . . . (Columbia)
Carolina Star
Earl Scruggs & Rodney Dillard; *Top Of The World* . . . . (Columbia)
Catch A Falling Star
Perry Como; *Como's Golden Records* . . . . (RCA)
Nipper's Greatest Hits Of The '50s-#1-C . . . . (RCA)
Perry Como-Pure Gold . . . . (RCA)
Perry Como's All-Time Greatest Hits-#1 . . . . (RCA)
This Is Perry Como. . . . . (RCA)
Catch A Star
Men At Work; *Business As Usual* . . . . (Columbia)
Cats Under The Stars
Jerry Garcia; *Cats Under The Stars* . . . . (Arista)
Champagne Supernova
Oasis; *What's The Story Morning Glory?* . . . . (Epic)
Come Down, Ma' Evenin' Star
Lillian Russell; *Music From The New York Stage (1890-1920)-#1-1890-
1908-C*. . . . . (Pearl)
Count Every Star
Grant Green; *Born To Be Blue*. . . . . (Blue Note)
Counting The Stars
Ladders; *Doo-Wop Era-Harlem, New York-40 Hits-C* . . . . (Collectables)
Harlem Holiday-New York Rhythm & Blues-#1-C . . . . (Collectables)
Dark Star
Crosby, Stills & Nash; *Allies* . . . .(Atlantic)
CSN . . . .(Atlantic)

Dark Star
Grateful Dead; *Best Of The Grateful Dead/What A Long Strange Trip*
It's Been. . . . . (Warner Bros.)
Live/Dead . . . . (Warner Bros.)

Dedicated To The One I Love
Mamas & The Papas; *Best Of The Mamas & The Papas* . . . . (MCA)
Farewell To The First Golden Era . . . . (MCA)
Original Classic Oldies Of The '50s & '60s-#13-C . . . . (MCA)
Shirelles; *Oldies But Goodies-#10-C*. . . . . (Original Sound)
Shirelles' Greatest Hits. . . . . (Everest)
Shirelles-Anthology 1959-1964 . . . . (Rhino)
Super Oldies Of The '50s-#4-C. . . . . (Audio Fidelity)

Diamonds In The Stars
Ray Price; *Ray Price's Greatest Hits-#3* . . . .(Step One)

Don't Let The Stars Get In Your Eyes
Perry Como; *Como's Golden Records*. . . . .(RCA)
Perry Como-Pure Gold. . . . .(RCA)
Perry Como's All-Time Greatest Hits-#1 . . . .(RCA)
This Is Perry Como. . . . .(RCA)

Drops Of Jupiter (Tell Me)
Train; *Drops Of Jupiter*. . . . . (Aware/C2/Columbia)

Electrolite
Michael Stipe/Mike Mills; *Tibetan Freedom Concert*. . . . .(Capitol)
R.E.M.; *New Adventures In Hi-Fi* . . . . (Warner Bros.)

Evening Star
Gene Loves Jezebel; *Kiss Of Life*. . . . .(Geffen)

Evening Star
Kenny Rogers; *Eyes That See In The Dark* . . . .(RCA)

Evening Star
Judas Priest; *Hell Bent For Leather*. . . . . (Columbia)

Falling Star
Robin Trower; *In City Dreams* . . . .(Chrysalis)

Falling Star
Karla Bonoff; *Karla Bonoff*. . . . . (Columbia)

Fear Of A Black Planet
Public Enemy; *Fear Of A Black Planet* . . . .(Def Jam)

Fishin' In The Dark
Nitty Gritty Dirt Band; *Billboard Top Country Hits-1987-C*. . . . .(Rhino)
Hold On . . . . (Warner Bros.)
More Great Dirt-Best Of Nitty Gritty Dirt Band . . . . (Warner Bros.)

Five Planets In Leo
Brew Moore Quintet; *Brew Moore Quintet* . . . .(Fantasy)

Girls Dem Sugar
Beenie Man; *Art And Life* . . . .(Virgin)

Going To Mars
Little Ray Rapper; *Get That Future Funk* . . . .(First Warning)

Good Morning Starshine
Oliver; *'60s Rock Classics-#3-C* . . . .(Rhino)
Original Broadway Cast; *Hair* . . . .(RCA)

Have You Seen The Stars Tonight
Jefferson Airplane; *Flight Log (1966-1976)* . . . .(Grunt)
Paul Kantner/Jefferson Starship; *Blows Against The Empire* . . . .(RCA)

Hell Below/Stars Above
Toadies; *Hell Below/Stars Above* . . . . (Interscope)

Hello From Venus
Screamin' Cheetah Wheelies; *Magnolia* . . . .(Mercury)

Highway Star
Deep Purple; *Deepest Purple/The Very Best Of Deep Purple* . . . . (Warner Bros.)
Machine Head . . . . (Warner Bros.)
Made In Japan . . . . (Warner Bros.)
When We Rock We Rock & When We Roll We Roll . . . . (Warner Bros.)

Honeymoon On Mars
Be Bop Deluxe; *Modern Music* . . . . (Capitol)

How Could An Angel Break My Heart
Kenny G with Toni Braxton; *Kenny G's Greatest Hits* . . . . (Arista)
Toni Braxton with Kenny G; *Diana, Princess Of Wales-Tribute-C*. . . (Columbia)
Secrets . . . . (LaFace)

Hypnotize The Moon
Clay Walker; *Hypnotize The Moon* . . . . (Giant)

I'm From Another Planet
Animotion; *Music Speaks Louder Than Words-C* . . . . (Epic)

Impossible Dream
Andy Williams; *Andy Williams' Greatest Hits-#2*. . . . .(Columbia)
Andy Williams-16 Most Requested Songs . . . . (Legacy)
Impossible Dream. . . . . (Columbia)
Ed Ames; *Best Of Ed Ames* . . . .(RCA)
Ed Ames-Pure Gold . . . .(RCA)
Impossible Dream. . . . .(RCA)
This Is Ed Ames. . . . .(RCA)
Jack Jones; *Best Of Jack Jones* . . . .(MCA)
Kate Smith; *Best Of Kate Smith* . . . .(RCA)
Kate Smith-Legendary Performer . . . .(RCA)
Luther Vandross; *Songs*. . . . . (Epic)
Original London Cast; *Man Of La Mancha*. . . . .(MCA)
Robert Goulet; *Robert Goulet's Greatest Hits*. . . . .(Columbia)

Intergalactic
Beastie Boys; *Hello Nasty* . . . .(Grand Royal)

Is It A Star
Daryl Hall & John Oates; *War Babies* . . . . (Atlantic)

It Was Written In The Stars
Ella Fitzgerald; *Harold Arlen Songbook-#2* . . . .(Verve)

I've Told Ev'ry Little Star
David Allyn; *David Allyn Sings Jerome Kern* . . . . (Discovery)
Linda Scott; *Billboard Top Pop Hits-1961-C*. . . . .(Rhino)

January Stars
George Winston; *Winter Into Spring* . . . .(Windham Hill)

Jet Silver & The Dolls Of Venus
Be Bop Deluxe; *Axe Victim* . . . .(Capitol)
Best Of Be Bop Deluxe-Raiding The Divine Archive . . . .(Capitol)

Journey To A Star
Judy Garland; *Judy Garland-Collector's Items-1936-1945* . . . . (MCA)

Judgment Of The Moon & Stars
Joni Mitchell; *For The Roses* . . . . (Asylum)

Jupiter
Earth, Wind & Fire; *All 'N All* . . . . (Columbia)

Jupiter Hollow
Band; *Northern Lights-Southern Cross* . . . .(Capitol)

Jupiter's Child
Steppenwolf; *Steppenwolf-16 Greatest Hits* . . . . (MCA)

Just To Hear You Say That You Love Me
Faith Hill & Tim McGraw; *Faith* . . . . (Warner Bros.)

Keeper Of The Stars
Tracy Byrd; *No Ordinary Man* . . . . (MCA)

Kohoutek
R.E.M.; *Fables Of The Reconstruction* . . . . (I.R.S.)

Lady Stardust
David Bowie; *Rise & Fall Of Ziggy Stardust And The Spiders*
From Mars . . . . (Rykodisc)

Lady Starlight
Scorpions; *Animal Magnetism* . . . .(Mercury)

Life On Mars?
David Bowie; *Hunky Dory* . . . . (Rykodisc)
The Singles-1969-1993 . . . . (Rykodisc)

Light Years
Pearl Jam; *Binaural* . . . . (Epic)

Little Star
Elegants; *Billboard Top Rock 'N' Roll Hits-1958-C* . . . .(Rhino)
Oldies But Goodies-#5-C . . . . (Original Sound)
Super Oldies Of The '50s-#7-C . . . . (Audio Fidelity)

Little Star
Madonna; *Ray Of Light* . . . .(Maverick)

Little Star/Eclipse
Sammy Hagar; *Sammy Hagar* . . . .(Capitol)

Lost In The Stars
Frank Sinatra; *My Kind Of Broadway* . . . . (Reprise)
Mormon Tabernacle Choir; *Climb Ev'ry Mountain* . . . .(Columbia)
Original Cast; *Lost In The Stars* . . . . (MCA)
Sarah Vaughan; *Complete Sarah Vaughan On Mercury-#2* . . . .(Mercury)
Sheila Jordan; *Lost & Found* . . . . (Muse)
Tony Bennett; *Forty Years-The Artistry Of Tony Bennett* . . . . (Columbia)

Lucky Star
Madonna; *Immaculate Collection* . . . . (Sire)
Madonna . . . . (Sire)
MTV's Rock 'N' Roll To Go-C . . . .(Elektra)
Royal Box . . . . (Sire)

Man From Mars
Joni Mitchell; *Taming The Tiger* . . . . (Reprise)

Man From Mars, The
Smokey Wilson; *The Man From Mars* . . . .(Bullseye Blues)

Marching To Mars
Sammy Hagar; *Marching To Mars* . . . . (MCA)

Midnight On Mars
Ashra; *Blackouts* . . . . (Blue Plate)

Might As Well Be On Mars
Alice Cooper; *Hey Stoopid* . . . . (Epic)

Moon-Faced, Starry-Eyed
Benny Goodman; *Jazz Collector Edition* . . . . (Laserlight)

Moons Of Jupiter
Paul Halley; *Pianosong* . . . . (Living Music)

Most High
Jimmy Page/Robert Plant; *Walking Into Clarksdale* . . . . (Atlantic)

Motorboat To Mars
Chicago; *Chicago At Carnegie Hall*. . . . . (Chicago)
Chicago III . . . .(Chicago)

Mr. Too Damn Good
Gerald Levert; *G* . . . . (East West)

North Star Grassman And The Ravens
Sandy Denny; *Gold Dust: Live At The Royalty-The Final Concert* . . . . . .(Island)
North Star Grassman And The Ravens . . . . (Hannibal)

One Way Ticket To Pluto
Dead Kennedys; *ST/Lovedolls To Superstar* . . . . (SST)

Orbit
Fred Schneider/Shake Society; *Fred Schneider* . . . . (Qwest)

Orbit
Meteors; *Teenage Heart*. . . . .(PVC)

Orbit Zero
Little River Band; *Time Exposure* . . . .(Capitol)

Orion In The Sky
Shawn Colvin; *Fat City* . . . . (Columbia)
Pale Green Stars
Everclear; *Sparkle And Fade* . . . . (Capitol)
Passion Planet
Thompson Twins; *Into The Gap* . . . . (Arista)
Planet Caravan
Pantera; *Far Beyond Driven* . . . . (East West)
Planet Claire
B-52's; *B-52's* . . . .(Warner Bros.)
Planet Of My Dreams
Frank Zappa; *Them Or Us* . . . .(Rykodisc)
Planet Of New Orleans
Dire Straits; *On Every Street* . . . .(Warner Bros.)
Planet Of The Clowns
Bruce Cockburn; *Trouble With Normal* . . . . (Columbia)
Planet Of Women
ZZ Top; *Afterburner* . . . .(Warner Bros.)
ZZ Top's Greatest Hits . . . .(Warner Bros.)
Planet Queen
T. Rex; *Electric Warrior* . . . . (Reprise)
Planet Rock
Afrika Bambaataa & Soulsonic Force; *Street Jams-Electric Funk-#1-C* . (Rhino)
Tommy Boy's Greatest Beats-C . . . . (Tommy Boy)
Planet Texas
Kenny Rogers; *Something Inside So Strong* . . . . (Reprise)
Planet Texas
John Andrew Parks; *John Andrew Parks* . . . . (Capitol)
Planetary Invasion
Midnight Star; *Planetary Invasion* . . . . (Solar)
Planets Of Life
Whispers; *I Can Remember* . . . . (Accord)
Vintage Whispers . . . . (Solar)
Planets Of The Universe
Stevie Nicks; *Trouble In Shangri-La* . . . . (Reprise)
Prettiest Star
David Bowie; *Aladdin Sane* . . . .(Rykodisc)
Sound + Vision . . . .(Rykodisc)
Quiet Nights Of Quiet Stars
Antonio Carlos Jobim; *Terra Brasilis* . . . .(Warner Bros.)
Shirley Horn; *I Thought About You-Live At Vine Street* . . . . (Verve)
Ranch On Mars Reprise
Galactic Cowboys; *Galactic Cowboys* . . . . (David Geffen Co.)
Redneck Woman From Planet Mars
Horny Mormons; *Can Of Pork-C* . . . . (Lookout)
Re-Doo-Wopp-Little Star
Tokens; *Re-Doo-Wopp-Little Star* . . . . (RCA)
Right Time Of The Night
Jennifer Warnes; *Best Of Jennifer Warnes* . . . . (Arista)
Jennifer Warnes . . . . (Arista)
Saturn
Stevie Wonder; *Songs In The Key Of Life* . . . . (Motown)
Saturn
Alan Vega; *Saturn Strip* . . . . (Elektra)
Second Star To The Right
Barbara Cook; *Disney Album* . . . .(Disney)
James Taylor; *Stay Awake-Music Of Vintage Disney Films-C* . . . . (A&M)
See The Constellation
They Might Be Giants; *Apollo 18* . . . . (Elektra)
Set U Free
Planet Soul; *Disco Queens-The '90s-C* . . . . (Rhino)
Energy + Harmony . . . .(Strictly Rhythm)
Shake Down These Stars
Benny Goodman; *Best Of The Big Bands-C* . . . . (Columbia)
Shining Star
Earth, Wind & Fire; *Best Of Earth, Wind & Fire-#1* . . . . (Legacy)
Eternal Dance . . . . (Columbia)
Gratitude . . . . (Legacy)
That's The Way Of The World . . . . (Legacy)
Shining Star
Manhattans; *After Midnight* . . . . (Columbia)
Manhattans Greatest Hits . . . . (Columbia)
Seems Like Yesterday-#4-Early '80s-C . . . . (K-Tel)
Shooting Star
Harry Chapin; *Gold Medal Collection* . . . . (Elektra)
Verities & Balderdash . . . . (Elektra)
Shooting Star
Bad Company; *10 From 6* . . . . (Atlantic)
Straight Shooter . . . . (Swan Song)
Shooting Star
Bob Dylan; *Oh Mercy* . . . . (Columbia)
Shooting Star
Elton John; *A Single Man* . . . .(MCA)
Shooting Stars
Billy Idol; *Billy Idol* . . . .(Chrysalis)
Silver Stars, Purple Sage, Eyes Of Blue
Roy Rogers & Sons Of The Pioneers; *Roy Rogers & Sons Of The Pioneers* . . . .(Varese Sarabande)

Somebody Else's Moon
Collin Raye; *In This Life* . . . . (Epic)
Someone Else's Star
Bryan White; *Bryan White* . . . .(Asylum)
Real Luv: Ultimate Country Love Songs-C . . . . (EMI)
South Saturn Delta
Jimi Hendrix; *Lifelines/Jimi Hendrix Story* . . . .(Reprise)
Southern Star
Alabama; *Southern Star* . . . .(RCA)
Stairway To The Stars
Ella Fitzgerald; *Best Of Ella Fitzgerald* . . . . (MCA)
Ella Fitzgerald In Hollywood . . . . (Verve)
Glenn Miller & Ray Eberle; *Chattanooga Choo Choo-#1 Hits* . . . . . (Bluebird)
Memorial-1944-1969 . . . . (Bluebird)
Milt Jackson & Wes Montgomery; *Bags Meets Wes!* . . . . . . (Riverside)
Stairway To The Stars
Blue Oyster Cult; *Blue Oyster Cult* . . . . (Columbia)
Star
Erasure; *Just Say Da-#4 Of Just Say Yes-C* . . . .(Sire)
Wild! . . . .(Sire)
Star
Stealers Wheel; *Super Hits Of The '70s-Have A Nice Day-#12-C* . . . . . (Rhino)
Star
Nazareth; *Nazareth-Classics-#16* . . . .(A&M)
Star
David Bowie; *Rise & Fall Of Ziggy Stardust And The Spiders From Mars* . . . . (Rykodisc)
Stage . . . . (Rykodisc)
Star Eyes
Charlie Parker; *Bebop & Bird-#2* . . . . (Rhino)
Chet Baker; *RCA Victor Jazz: First Half-Century-#5-C* . . . .(RCA)
Sonny Rollins; *Rollins Plays For Bird* . . . . (Prestige)
Saxophone Colossus & More . . . . (Prestige)
Sonny Rollins-Complete Prestige Recordings . . . . (Prestige)
Stephane Grappelli; *Compact Jazz-Stephane Grappelli* . . . . (Verve)
Star Of Africa
Gerry Mulligan & Chet Baker; *Gerry Mulligan & Chet Baker* . . . . .(Crescendo)
Star Of Bethlehem
Emmylou Harris & Neil Young; *Duets-C* . . . .(Reprise)
Neil Young; *Decade* . . . . (Reprise)
Neil Young, Crazy Horse & The Bullets; *American Stars 'N Bars* . . (Reprise)
Star Rider
Foreigner; *Foreigner* . . . .(Atlantic)
Star Spangled Banner
American Brass Band; *National Anthems* . . . .(Laserlight)
Banda Sinfonica De Madrid; *National Anthems* . . . . (International Music)
Duke Ellington; *Carnegie Hall Concert-January 23, 1943* . . . . . .(Prestige)
Houston Symphony Orchestra; *Celebrate America* . . . . (Pro-Arte)
Jimi Hendrix; *Essential Jimi Hendrix, Volume 2* . . . . (Reprise)
Lifelines/Jimi Hendrix Story . . . . (Reprise)
ST/Jimi Hendrix . . . . (Reprise)
ST/Woodstock . . . .(Atlantic)
Lee Greenwood; *American Patriot* . . . . (Capitol)
Marvin Gaye; *Musical Testament 1964-1984* . . . . (Motown)
Mormon Tabernacle Choir; *God Bless America* . . . . (Sony Music Classical)
God Bless America-C . . . . (Columbia)
This Is My Country . . . . (Columbia)
Original Soundtrack; *The Greatest College Fight Songs* . . . .(Laserlight)
Sandi Patty; *Stars And Stripes Forever-#2-C* . . . . (Volcano Entertainment)
Vienna State Opera Orchestra; *National Anthems Of The World* . . (Bescol, Ltd.)
Vinnie Vincent Invasion; *Head Banging Metal-C* . . . .(Priority)
Whitney Houston; *Whitney Houston's Greatest Hits* . . . . (Arista)
Star Track
Jefferson Airplane; *Crown Of Creation* . . . .(RCA)
Star Whores
Christ Child; *Hard* . . . .(Buddah)
Star!
Frank Sinatra; *Frank Sinatra Sings The Songs Of Van Heusen & Cahn* . . . . (Reprise)
Frank Sinatra's Greatest Hits-#2 . . . . (Reprise)
Starchild
Teena Marie; *Starchild* . . . . (Epic)
Stardust
Artie Shaw; *Begin The Beguine* . . . . (Bluebird)
Artie Shaw & His Orchestra; *22 Original Big Band Recordings-C* . . . (Hindsight)
Nipper's Greatest Hits Of The '40s-#1-C . . . . (RCA)
Benny Goodman; *Benny Goodman Sextet featuring Charlie Christian-1939-1941* . . . . (Columbia)
Benny Goodman-Live At Carnegie Hall . . . . (London)
Carly Simon; *Come Upstairs* . . . . (Warner Bros.)
Coleman Hawkins; *Hollywood Stampede* . . . . (Capitol)
Dave Brubeck; *Art Of Dave Brubeck* . . . . (Atlantic)
Greatest Hits From The Fantasy Years . . . . (Fantasy)
Dave Brubeck Quartet; *Jazz At Oberlin* . . . . (Fantasy)
Stardust . . . . (Fantasy)
Frank Sinatra; *Sinatra & Strings* . . . . (Reprise)
Harry Connick, Jr.; *25* . . . . (Columbia)
Hoagy Carmichael; *Nipper's Greatest Hits Of The '30s-#1-C* . . . . (RCA)
Stardust Road . . . . (MCA)

Johnny Mathis; *Feelings* . . . . (Columbia)
  First 25 Years-Silver Anniversary Album . . . . (Columbia)
Nat ''King'' Cole; *The Nat ''King'' Cole Story.* . . . . (Capitol)
Rob Wasserman & Aaron Neville; *Duets-C* . . . . (MCA)
Roger Williams; *Best Of Roger Williams* . . . . (MCA)
Tommy Dorsey; *Best Of Tommy Dorsey* . . . . (Bluebird)
  This Is Tommy Dorsey . . . . (RCA)
Tommy Dorsey & Frank Sinatra; *Stardust* . . . . (Bluebird)
Wayne King & His Orchestra; *78-#22656.* . . . . (Victor)
Stargazer
Neil Diamond; *Beautiful Noise* . . . . (Columbia)
  Love At The Greek . . . . (Columbia)
Stargazer
Mark Knopfler; *Local Hero* . . . . (Warner Bros.)
Starlight
Electric Light Orchestra; *Box Of Their Best* . . . . (Jet)
  Out Of The Blue . . . . (Jet)
Starlight
Tom Rush; *Best Of Tom Rush: No Regrets* . . . . (Legacy)
Starlight, Starbright
Linda Scott; *45-#133* . . . . (Eric)
Starman
David Bowie; *Changestwobowie.* . . . . (RCA)
  Fame & Fashion . . . . (RCA)
  Rise & Fall Of Ziggy Stardust And The Spiders From Mars . . . . . . (Rykodisc)
  The Singles-1969-1993. . . . . (Rykodisc)
Starry Eyes
Motley Crue; *Too Fast For Love* . . . . (Elektra)
Starry Sky In Oregon
Andrew White; *Conversations* . . . . (Sona Gaia)
Stars
Simply Red; *Stars* . . . . (East West)
Stars
Hum; *You'd Prefer An Astronaut* . . . . (RCA)
Stars
Original Broadway Cast; *Les Miserables* . . . . (Geffen)
Stars
Janis Ian; *Stars* . . . . (One Way)
Stars Fell On Alabama
Art Tatum; *Group Masterpieces-#4* . . . . (Pablo)
Frank Sinatra; *The Capitol Years* . . . . (Capitol)
Harry Connick, Jr.; *20* . . . . (Columbia)
Jimmy Buffett; *Boats Beaches Bars & Ballads* . . . . . . (Margaritaville)
  Coconut Telegraph . . . . (MCA)
Stars On The Water
Jimmy Buffett; *Boats Beaches Bars & Ballads* . . . . . . (Margaritaville)
  One Particular Harbour. . . . . (MCA)
Rodney Crowell; *Rodney Crowell.* . . . . (Warner Bros.)
  Rodney Crowell-Collection. . . . . (Warner Bros.)
Stars Over Texas
Tracy Lawrence; *Best Of Tracy Lawrence.* . . . . (Atlantic)
  Time Marches On. . . . . (Atlantic)
Starseed
Our Lady Peace; *ST/Armageddon-The Album.* . . . . (Columbia)
Starseed
Our Lady Peace; *Naveed* . . . . (Relativity)
Stella By Starlight
Bill Evans; *Jazzhouse* . . . . (Milestone)
Frank Sinatra; *Rarities-Columbia Years* . . . . (Columbia)
George Benson; *Tenderly* . . . . (Warner Bros.)
Joe Pass; *Virtuoso* . . . . (Pablo)
Keith Jarrett; *Standards Live* . . . . (ECM)
Miles Davis; *Cookin' At The Plugged Nickel* . . . . (Columbia)
Red Garland; *Red Alert* . . . . (Galaxy)
Stan Getz; *Stan Getz Plays* . . . . (Verve)
Tony Bennett; *Jazz* . . . . (Columbia)
Stellar
Incubus; *Make Yourself.* . . . . (Immortal/Epic)
Subway To Venus
Red Hot Chili Peppers; *Mother's Milk.* . . . . (EMI)
Sullivan
Caroline's Spine; *Monsoon* . . . . (Hollywood)
Summer Of The Silver Comet
Tracy Nelson; *Homemade Songs* . . . . (Flying Fish)
Sun, Moon & Stars
Nanci Griffith; *Late Night Grande Hotel* . . . . (MCA)
Surfin' On Jupiter
Psychefunkapus; *Skin* . . . . (Atlantic)
Swinging On A Star
Bing Crosby; *All-Time Best.* . . . . (Curb)
  Best Of Bing Crosby . . . . (MCA)
Dion And The Belmonts; *Dion And The Belmonts-Their Best.* . . . . . . (Laurie)
Frank Sinatra; *Frank Sinatra Sings The Songs Of Van Heusen*
  & Cahn . . . . (Reprise)
Teacher, The
Paul Simon; *You're The One* . . . . (Warner Bros.)
Telstar
Tornados; *History Of British Rock-#5-C* . . . . (Rhino)

Ventures; *Play Telstar/In Space.* . . . . (EMI)
Texaco Star Theme
Original Soundtrack; *TeeVee Toons-The Commercials-#1-C* . . . . (TVT)
Theme From ''Armageddon''
Trevor Rabin; *ST/Armageddon-The Album* . . . . (Columbia)
Theme From ''Dr. Kildare'' (Three Stars Will Shine Tonight)
Betty Carter; *'Round Midnight.* . . . . (Atlantic)
Original Soundtrack; *Television's Greatest Hits-#4-Black & White*
  Classics-C . . . . (TVT)
Theme From ''Star Trek''
Cincinnati Pops Orchestra/Erich Kunzel; *Star Tracks II* . . . . (Telarc)
Theme From ''Star Trek: The Next Generation''
Original Soundtrack; *Television's Greatest Hits-#7-Cable Ready-C.* . . . . . (TVT)
Theme From ''Star Wars''
John Williams; *ST/Star Wars.* . . . . (Polydor)
Meco; *Best Of Meco.* . . . . (Chronicles)
Neil Norman; *Greatest Science Fiction Hits* . . . . (Crescendo)
They Took The Stars Out Of Heaven
Floyd Tillman; *The Country Music Hall Of Fame-Floyd Tillman* . . . . . . (MCA)
Third Stone From The Sun
Jimi Hendrix; *Essential Jimi Hendrix* . . . . (Reprise)
  Kiss The Sky . . . . (Reprise)
Jimi Hendrix Experience; *Are You Experienced?* . . . . (Reprise)
This Flight Tonight
Joni Mitchell; *Blue* . . . . (Reprise)
Thousand Stars In The Sky
Kathy Young with The Innocents; *20 Great Love Songs Of The '50s &*
  '60s-#2-C . . . . (Laurie)
  Collectables Presents The History Of Rock-#10-C . . . . (Collectables)
  Oldies But Goodies-#5-C . . . . (Original Sound)
To Raise The Morning Star
Bruce Cockburn; *Stealing Fire.* . . . . (Columbia)
Together Again
Janet Jackson; *Now That's What I Call Music!-#1-C* . . . . (Virgin)
  Velvet Rope . . . . (Virgin)
Trash Planet
Stewart & Gaskin; *Spin* . . . . (Rykodisc)
Turn Out The Stars
Bill Evans Trio; *Since We Met* . . . . (Fantasy)
David Benoit; *Waiting For Spring* . . . . (GRP)
Gary Burton & Paul Bley; *Right Time Right Place.* . . . . (Crescendo)
John McLaughlin; *Time Remembered-John McLaughlin Plays Bill*
  Evans . . . . (Verve)
Liz Story; *My Foolish Heart* . . . . (Windham Hill)
Twinkle Twinkle Little Star
Bob Wills & His Texas Playboys; *Tiffany Transcriptions-#8-More Of*
  The Best . . . . (Rhino)
Willie Nelson; *Somewhere Over The Rainbow* . . . . (Columbia)
Twinkle, Twinkle Lucky Star
Merle Haggard; *Chill Factor* . . . . (Epic)
  Greatest Country Hits Of The '80s-1988-C. . . . . (Columbia)
Under The Milky Way
Church; *Best Of MTV's 120 Minutes-#1-C* . . . . (Rhino)
  Starfish . . . . (Arista)
Under The Milky Way
Cinderella; *Long Cold Winter* . . . . (Mercury)
Vampire Planet
Neil Norman & His Cosmic Orchestra; *Greatest Science Fiction*
  Hits-#2 . . . . (Crescendo)
Venus & Mars
Wings; *Venus And Mars.* . . . . (Capitol)
  Wings Over America . . . . (Capitol)
Vincent
Don McLean; *American Pie.* . . . . (EMI)
  Best Of Don McLean . . . . (EMI)
  Greatest Hits Then & Now . . . . (EMI)
Waiting For A Star To Fall
Boy Meets Girl; *Nipper's Greatest Hits Of The '80s-C* . . . . (RCA)
  Reel Life . . . . (RCA)
Wanderin' Star
Original Broadway Cast; *Paint Your Wagon* . . . . (RCA Victor)
We Let The Stars Go
Prefab Sprout; *Jordan-The Comeback.* . . . . (Epic)
  Life Of Surprises-Best Of Prefab Sprout . . . . (Epic)
When I Camped Under The Stars
Roy Rogers; *Songs Of The West-#3-Gene Autry & Roy Rogers-C* . . . . . . (Rhino)
When You Wish Upon A Star
Barbara Cook; *Disney Album* . . . . (Disney)
Billy Joel; *Simply Mad About The Mouse-C* . . . . (Columbia)
Cliff Edwards; *ST/Pinocchio* . . . . (Disney)
Dion; *The Wanderer* . . . . (Laurie)
Glenn Miller & Ray Eberle; *Chattanooga Choo Choo-#1 Hits* . . . . . . (Bluebird)
Linda Ronstadt; *For Sentimental Reasons* . . . . (Asylum)
Little Anthony And The Imperials; *We Are The Imperials.* . . . . . . (Roulette)
Rosemary Clooney; *Rosemary Clooney-16 Most Requested Songs* . . . . . (Legacy)
Stevie Wonder; *With A Song In My Heart* . . . . (Motown)
Wynton Marsalis; *Hot House Flowers* . . . . (Columbia)
Whole New You
Shawn Colvin; *Whole New You* . . . . (Columbia)

Wish Upon A Star
Steve Miller Band; *Book Of Dreams*. . . . . (Capitol)
Steve Miller Band-Gift Set . . . . (Capitol)
Wishing On A Star
Cover Girls; *Here It Is*. . . . .(Epic)
Rose Royce; *Rose Royce's Greatest Hits* . . . .(Whitfield)
Workshop Of The Telescopes
Blue Oyster Cult; *Blue Oyster Cult*. . . . . (Columbia)
World's Greatest, The
R. Kelly; *ST/Ali*. . . . . (Interscope)
Would You Catch A Falling Star
John Anderson; *I Just Came Home To Count The Memories* . . . . .(Warner Bros.)
John Anderson's Greatest Hits . . . .(Warner Bros.)
Written In The Stars
Elton John & LeAnn Rimes; *ST/Aida*. . . . . (Island)
Yellow
Coldplay; *Now That's What I Call Music!-#6-C*. . . . . (Virgin)
Parachutes. . . . . (Nettwerk/Capitol)
Yellow Star
Donovan; *Essence To Essence* . . . .(Epic)
Ziggy Stardust
David Bowie; *Changesbowie* . . . .(Rykodisc)
Rise & Fall Of Ziggy Stardust And The Spiders From Mars . . . .(Rykodisc)
Sound + Vision. . . . .(Rykodisc)
ST/Ziggy Stardust-The Motion Picture . . . .(Rykodisc)
Stage . . . .(Rykodisc)
The Singles-1969-1993 . . . .(Rykodisc)

STATES: ALABAMA

See Also: CITIES: A-Z, CITIES: BIRMINGHAM, CITIES: MOBILE, DIRECTIONS: SOUTH

Alabam
Cowboy Copas; *Only Country-1960-1964-C*. . . . . (JCI Assoc. Labels)
Minnie Pearl; *Trucks,Trains & Airplanes-C*. . . . . . . (International Mktg. Group)
Red Sovine & Minnie Pearl; *Famous Duets* . . . .(Hollywood/DNA-Rounder)
Alabama
Neil Young; *Harvest*. . . . . (Reprise)
ST/Journey Through The Past . . . .(Warner Bros.)
Alabama Bound
Doc & Merle Watson; *Ballads From Deep Gap* . . . . (Vanguard)
Leadbelly/Woody Guthrie/Cisco Houston; *Leadbelly Sings Folk Songs*. . . . . (Smithsonian Folkways)
Alabama Getaway
Grateful Dead; *Go To Heaven*. . . . . (Arista)
Alabama Highway
Steve Young; *Honky-Tonk Man* . . . . (Rounder)
Alabama Jubilee
Boston Pops Orchestra/Arthur Fiedler; *American Salute* . . . . (RCA)
Leon Redbone; *Champagne Charlie* . . . .(Warner Bros.)
Merle Travis & Joe Maphis; *Red, White & Bluegrass-C*. . . . . . .(C.M.H. Prod.)
Alabama Lady
Wright Brothers; *Easy Street* . . . . (Mercury)
Alabama Rain
Jim Croce; *Down The Highway* . . . .(Atlantic)
Time In A Bottle/Jim Croce's Greatest Love Songs . . . .(Atlantic)
Alabama Shine
Ken Pollard; *45-#1183* . . . .(Eagle Int'l)
Alabama Sky
Alabama; *Closer You Get* . . . . (RCA)
Alabama Song
Bette Midler; *Live At Last*. . . . .(Atlantic)
Alabama Song
Doors; *Doors*. . . . . (Elektra)
Alabama Woman Blues
John Hammond; *John Hammond* . . . . (Vanguard)
Alabambama
Willie Nelson & Roger Miller; *Old Friends* . . . . (Columbia)
Alabamy Bound
Tom Rush; *Blues Songs & Ballads* . . . . (Fantasy)
Tom Rush . . . . (Fantasy)
Birmingham Alabama
Harry Belafonte; *Harry Belafonte's All-Time Greatest Hits-#3* . . . . (RCA)
Breeze From Alabama
Max Morath; *Max Morath Plays Ragtime* . . . . (Vanguard)
The World Of Scott Joplin . . . .(Vanguard)
Scott Joplin; *The Entertainer-#4*. . . . . (Biograph)
Dixie Road (Montgomery, Alabama)
Lee Greenwood; *Country Classics-#3-1984-1985-C* . . . .(Universal)
Lee Greenwood's Greatest Hits . . . .(MCA)
MCA #1 Hits Of The '80s-#2-C . . . .(MCA Special Prod.)
Goin' Back To Alabama
Kenny Rogers; *Share Your Love*. (Liberty)
Going Back To Alabam'
Alan Munde & Country Gazette; *Keep On Pushing* . . . . (Flying Fish)

Going Back To Alabama
Asa Martin; *Dr. Ginger Blue* . . . . (Rounder)
Going To Move To Alabama
Charley Patton; *Founder Of The Delta Blues-1929-1934* . . . .(Yazoo)
Hills Of Alabam'
Kathy Mattea; *Willow In The Wind* . . . . (Mercury)
I'm Going Back To Alabama
Jerry Douglas; *Fluxology* . . . . (Rounder)
My Home's In Alabama
Alabama; *Alabama-Live* . . . . (RCA)
Alabama's Greatest Hits . . . . (RCA)
Gonna Have A Party...Live . . . . (RCA)
My Home's In Alabama . . . . (RCA)
My Mammy
Al Jolson; *Best Of Al Jolson* . . . . (MCA)
Let Me Sing And I'm Happy . . . . (Turner Classic Movies)
The '20s-From Broadway To Hollywood-#3-C . . . .(Flapper)
Happenings; *Happenings-Golden Hits!* . . . .(B.T. Puppy)
North Alabama
Cal Smith; *Stories Of Life By Cal Smith* . . . .(Step One)
Oh, Susanna
Disneyland Cast; *Children's Favorite Songs-#1* . . . . (Disney)
James Taylor; *Sweet Baby James* . . . . (Warner Bros.)
Myron Floren; *Best Of The Wurstfest* . . . . (Ranwood)
Myron Floren . . . . (Ranwood)
Red Dirt Girl
Emmylou Harris; *Red Dirt Girl*. (Nonesuch)
Roll Alabama Roll
Northeast Winds; *Ireland By Sail* . . . . (Folk Era)
We The People-C . . . . (Folk Era)
Shady River Gal/Alabama Gals
Beverly Cotton; *Clogging Lessons* . . . . (Flying Fish)
Stars Fell On Alabama
Art Tatum; *Group Masterpieces-#4* . . . . (Pablo)
Frank Sinatra; *The Capitol Years* . . . . (Capitol)
Harry Connick, Jr.; *20* . . . . (Columbia)
Jimmy Buffett; *Boats Beaches Bars & Ballads* . . . .(Margaritaville)
Coconut Telegraph. . . . . (MCA)
Sweet Home Alabama
Alabama; *Skynyrd Frynds-C* . . . . (MCA)
Charlie Daniels Band; *Volunteer Jam VII-C* . . . . (Epic)
Hank Williams, Jr.; *Hank Williams, Jr. "Live"* . . . . (WB/Curb)
Lynyrd Skynyrd; *Billboard Top Rock 'N' Roll Hits-1974-C*. . . . .(Rhino)
Gold & Platinum . . . . (MCA)
One More From The Road . . . . (MCA)
Second Helping . . . . (MCA)
South's Greatest Hits-C . . . . (Capricorn)
ST/Forrest Gump . . . .(Epic/Sony Music Soundtrax)
When The Midnight Choo Choo Leaves For Alabam'
Andrews Sisters; *Best Of The Andrews Sisters-#2*. . . . . (MCA)
Judy Garland & Fred Astaire; *ST/Easter Parade*. . . . . (Rhino)
Yea Alabama
Original Soundtrack; *The Greatest College Fight Songs*. . . . .(Laserlight)

STATES: ALASKA

See Also: CITIES: A-Z

Alaska
Bobby G. Rice; *Audiograph Alive-C*. . . . . (Audiograph)
Silk On Silk . . . . (Audiograph)
Alaska
UK; *Night After Night* . . . . (Editions E.G.)
UK . . . . (Editions E.G.)
Alaska
Danny Gottlieb; *Aquamarine* . . . .(Atlantic)
Alaska Cats
Garrison Keillor & Frederica von Stade; *Songs Of The Cat* . . . .(RCA)
Alaska Highway
Neon Judgement; *The Insult* . . . .(Play It Again Sam)
Alaskan Nights
David Schwartz; *ST/Music From "Northern Exposure"* . . . . (MCA)
Alaskan Queen
Joe Hackney; *Heavy Hitter* . . . .(Happy Hour Music)
Alaskan Suite: Northern Lights
Lyle Mays; *Lyle Mays* . . . . (Geffen)
Alaskan Sunrise
Dick Pinney; *Devil Take My Shiny Coins* . . . . (Mountain Railroad)
North To Alaska
Dwight Yoakam; *Under The Covers*. . . . . (Reprise)
Johnny Horton; *American Originals-Johnny Horton* . . . .(Columbia)
Billboard Top Country Hits-1961-C. . . . . (Rhino)
Johnny Horton's Greatest Hits . . . . (Columbia)
Super Hits Of The '60s-C . . . . (Epic)
Saginaw, Michigan
Lefty Frizzell; *American Originals-Lefty Frizzell*. . . . . (Columbia)

Billboard Top Country Hits-1964-C...........................(Rhino)
Columbia Country Classics-#3-Americana-C................(Columbia)
Lefty Frizzell's Greatest Hits.............................(Columbia)
Theme From "Northern Exposure"
David Schwartz; ST/Music From "Northern Exposure"............(MCA)
Original Soundtrack; CBS: The First 50 Years....................(TVT)
When It's Springtime In Alaska
Johnny Horton; American Originals-Johnny Horton............(Columbia)
Johnny Horton's Greatest Hits............................(Columbia)

STATES: ARIZONA

See Also: **CITIES: A-Z, DESERT**

Arizona
Mark Lindsay; Super Hits Of The '70s-Have A Nice Day-#1-C......(Rhino)
Arizona
Scorpions; Blackout..(Mercury)
Arizona Days
Tex Ritter; Arizona Days.........................(MCA Special Prod.)
Arizona Flash & Cloudy
Rod Hart; 45-#152..(Plantation)
Arizona Highway
Tim Rex & Oklahoma; 45-#103...............................(Dee-Jay)
Arizona Indian Doll
Faster Pussycat; Wake Me When It's Over....................(Elektra)
Arizona Moon
Ranch Romance; Blue Blazes................................(Sugar Hill)
Arizona Moon
Flying Burrito Brothers; Eye Of A Hurricane..................(One Way)
Arizona Rose
Waco Brothers; Do You Think About Me......................(Bloodshot)
Arizona Skies
Los Lobos; Kiko..(Slash)
Arizona Sky
China Crisis; What Price Paradise..............................(A&M)
Arizona State Line
Red Dirt Rangers; Rangers' Command....................(Lazy S.O.B.)
Arizona Waltz
Mom & Dads; Mom & Dads-Souvenirs......................(Crescendo)
Arizona Whiz
George Burns; I Wish I Was 18 Again........................(Mercury)
Arizona-Suite 3
Scott Moulton; Four Corners Suite............................(Revere)
Ballad Of Ira Hayes, The
Johnny Cash; The Man In Black-His Greatest Hits.............(Legacy)
Peter La Farge; Best Of Broadside 1962-1968: Anthems Of The American
Underground From The Pages Of Broadside
Magazine-C.............................(Smithsonian Folkways)
Bear Down Arizona
Original Soundtrack; College Fight Songs: The Pac Ten-C..........(K-Tel)
Everywhere
Tim McGraw; Everywhere......................................(Curb)
Get Back
Beatles; Beatles 1..(Capitol)
Beatles-20 Greatest Hits...................................(Capitol)
Beatles-Box Set...(Capitol)
Let It Be...(Capitol)
Past Masters-Volume Two.................................(Parlophone)
Reel Music...(Capitol)
Rock 'N' Roll Music......................................(Capitol)
The Beatles/1967-1970....................................(Capitol)
It's Still Rock & Roll To Me
Billy Joel; Billy Joel-Greatest Hits, Volume I & Volume II......(Columbia)
Glass Houses..(Columbia)
Maroon And Gold
Original Soundtrack; College Fight Songs: The Pac Ten-C..........(K-Tel)
My Dear Old Arizona Home
Rex Allen; Back In The Saddle Again: American Cowboy
Songs-C..(New World)
My Heart Cries For You
Charlie Rich; Charlie Rich-20 Golden Hits......................(Sun)
Time For Tears-C...(Sun)
Dinah Shore; Nipper's Greatest Hits Of The '50s-#1-C..........(RCA)
Guy Mitchell; Guy Mitchell-16 Most Requested Songs............(Legacy)
Ocean Front Property
George Strait; Country Classics-#8-1986-1987-C.............(Universal)
George Strait's Greatest Hits-#2...........................(MCA)
MCA Records 30 Years Of Hits-1958-1988-C..................(MCA)
Ocean Front Property......................................(MCA)
Rider In The Rain
Randy Newman; Little Criminals.......................(Warner Bros.)
There Is No Arizona
Jamie O'Neal; Shiver.....................................(Mercury)
Tucson, Arizona
Dan Fogelberg; Windows & Walls..........................(Full Moon)

STATES: ARKANSAS

See Also: **CITIES: A-Z**

Arkansas
Glen Campbell; Still Within The Sound Of My Voice..............(MCA)
Arkansas
Whitstein Brothers; Rose Of My Heart.......................(Rounder)
Arkansas
Ron Carter; Spanish Blue............................(CBS Associated)
Arkansas Blues
Eubie Blake; Memories Of You............................(Biograph)
Marcus Roberts; If I Could Be With You......................(Novus)
Arkansas Coal
Nancy Sinatra & Lee Hazlewood; Fairy Tales & Fantasies-Best Of.....(Rhino)
Arkansas Dog
Pinkard & Bowden; Writers In Disguise..................(Warner Bros.)
Arkansas Jane
Kong Cotton; Bo Diddley Beats.............................(Rhino)
Arkansas Road House Blues
Memphis Slim; Traveling With The Blues....................(Storyville)
Arkansas See Saw
Jerry Lee Lewis; Keeps Rockin'.............................(Mercury)
Arkansas Time Traveler
Star-Spangled Washboard Band; Collector's Item.............(Flying Fish)
Arkansas Traveler
Albert Lee; Speechless......................................(MCA)
Fiddlin' Red Herron; Red, White & Bluegrass-C..........(C.M.H. Records)
Floyd Cramer; Country Gold-Floyd Cramer...................(Step One)
Mark O'Connor; Championship Years..........(Country Music Foundation)
Michelle Shocked; Arkansas Traveler.......................(Mercury)
Sam Hinton; Newport Broadside: Newport Folk Festival-1963-C...(Vanguard)
Arkansas/How Blest We Are
Original Broadway Cast; Big River-The Adventures Of
Huckleberry Finn...(MCA)
Hills Of Arkansas
Black Oak Arkansas; Black Oak Arkansas.....................(Atco)
Hot Springs, Arkansas
Bukka White; Three Shades Of Blues-C.....................(Biograph)
I Can See Arkansas
Anne Murray; Fifteen Of The Best............................(Liberty)
Mary Queen Of Arkansas
Bruce Springsteen; Greetings From Asbury Park, N.J............(Columbia)
Tracks..(Columbia)
State Of Arkansas
Rosalie Sorrels; Lonesome Roving Wolves-Songs & Ballads Of
The West...(Green Linnet)
Theme From "Evening Shade"
Original Soundtrack; Television's Greatest Hits-#7-Cable Ready-C......(TVT)
Uncle Dave's Travels-Misery In Arkansas
Uncle Dave Macon; The Country Music Hall Of Fame-Uncle Dave
Macon...(MCA)
What'd I Say
Elvis Presley; Collector's Gold...............................(RCA)
Elvis' Gold Records, Volume 4...............................(RCA)
Elvis In Concert..(RCA)
Elvis-Greatest Hits, Volume One............................(RCA)
Jerry Lee Lewis; Jerry Lee Lewis-Original Golden Hits-#2...........(Sun)
Jerry Lee Lewis-Original Golden Hits-#2.....................(Sun)
Milestones..(Rhino)
Rocket 88...(Tomato)
Rockin' My Life Away......................................(Tomato)
John Mayall's Bluesbreakers with Eric Clapton; John Mayall's Bluesbreakers
with Eric Clapton......................................(Deram)
Ray Charles; Atlantic Rhythm & Blues 1947-1974-#4 (1958-1962)-C.(Atlantic)
Atlantic Soul Classics-C...........................(Warner Special Prod.)
Frat Rock!-#3-Grandson Of Frat Rock!-C....................(Rhino)
Life In Music...(Atlantic)
Ray Charles-Anthology....................................(Rhino)
Wolverton Mountain
Claude King; American Originals-Claude King................(Columbia)
Best Of Claude King..(Gusto)
Billboard Top Country Hits-1962-C..........................(Rhino)
Super Hits Of The '60s-C....................................(Epic)

STATES: CALIFORNIA

See Also: **CITIES: A-Z, CITIES: LOS ANGELES, SAN FRANCISCO,
HOLLYWOOD**

Adios
Jimmy Webb; Suspending Disbelief...........................(Elektra)
Linda Ronstadt; Cry Like A Rainstorm-Howl Like The Wind.........(Elektra)
Ain't No California
Mel Tillis; I Believe In You.................................(MCA)
Very Best Of Mel Tillis....................................(MCA)

Ain't Nobody Home (In California)
John Kay; *All In Good Time* . . . . (Mercury)
Airwaves/Look Out California
Badfinger; *Airwaves* . . . . (Out Of Print)
All Alone In California
Dan Hill; *Hold On* . . . . (20th Century Fox)
All The Gold In California
Larry Gatlin & The Gatlin Brothers Band; *Larry Gatlin & The Gatlin*
    Brothers' Greatest Hits-#2 . . . . (Columbia)
    Larry Gatlin & The Gatlin Brothers' Greatest Hits-Encore . . . . (Capitol)
    Larry Gatlin & The Gatlin Brothers-17 Greatest Hits . . . . (Columbia)
    Live At 8:00 . . . . (Capitol)
    Straight Ahead . . . . (Columbia)
Back To California
Carole King; *Music* . . . . (Epic)
Blue Yodel #4 (California Blues)
Bill Monroe; *Columbia Historic Edition-Bill Monroe* . . . . (Columbia)
Jimmie Rodgers; *Jimmie Rodgers-Early Years-1928-1929* . . . . (Rounder)
    Never No Mo' Blues . . . . (RCA)
    This Is Jimmie Rodgers . . . . (RCA)
Merle Haggard & The Strangers; *Train Whistle Blues* . . . . (Rounder)
Brothers Under The Bridge
Bruce Springsteen; *Tracks* . . . . (Columbia)
California
Kingston Trio; *Aspen Gold* . . . . (Fifty One West)
    Best Of The Best Of The Kingston Trio . . . . (Pro-Arte)
California
Joni Mitchell; *Blue* . . . . (Reprise)
California
Babys; *Head First* . . . . (Chrysalis)
California
Keith Stegall; *Keith Stegall* . . . . (Epic)
California Bloodlines
John Stewart; *American Originals-John Stewart* . . . . (Capitol)
Shaw Brothers; *Shaw Brothers' Greatest Hits* . . . . (Folk Era)
California Blue
Herb Alpert; *Fandango* . . . . (A&M)
California Blue
Roy Orbison; *Mystery Girl* . . . . (Virgin)
California Blues
Josh Graves & Billy Troy; *Red, White & Bluegrass-C* . . . . (C.M.H. Prod.)
Sonny Terry & Brownie McGhee; *California Blues* . . . . (Fantasy)
California Calling
Beach Boys; *Beach Boys* . . . . (Caribou)
California Campground
John Mayall; *Best Of John Mayall* . . . . (Polydor)
California Christmas
Hillary Kanter; *Country Christmas-#4-C* . . . . (RCA)
California Cotton Fields
Gram Parsons & Fallen Angels; *Live 1973* . . . . (Sierra)
California Dreamin'
Beach Boys; *Made In The U.S.A.* . . . . (Capitol)
Mamas & The Papas; *At The Hop* . . . . (MCA)
    Good Feeling Music Of The Big Chill Generation-#1-C . . . . (Motown)
    Mamas & The Papas-20 Golden Hits . . . . (MCA)
    ST/Air America . . . . (MCA)
    ST/American Pop . . . . (MCA)
    ST/Forrest Gump . . . . (Epic/Sony Music Soundtrax)
California Earthquake
John Hartford; *Catalogue* . . . . (Flying Fish)
Rodney Crowell; *Ain't Living Long Like This* . . . . (Warner Bros.)
California Girl
Eddie Floyd; *15 Original Big Hits-#4-C* . . . . (Stax)
    Eddie Floyd-Chronicle . . . . (Stax)
California Girls
Beach Boys; *Beach Boys '69 (The Beach Boys Live In London)* . . . . . . (Capitol)
    Best Of The Beach Boys-#2 . . . . (Capitol)
    Endless Summer . . . . (Capitol)
    Good Vibrations-Thirty Years Of The Beach Boys . . . . (Capitol)
    The Beach Boys In Concert . . . . (Brother)
David Lee Roth; *Crazy From The Heat* . . . . (Warner Bros.)
    ST/Down & Out In Beverly Hills . . . . (Warner Bros.)
California Gold
Rance Allen; *Straight From The Heart* . . . . (Stax)
California Golden West Waltz
Golden West Singers & The Cavaliers; *45-#1378* . . . . (Accent)
California Here I Come
Al Jolson; *Best Of Al Jolson* . . . . (MCA)
California Kid
Beat Farmers; *Tales Of The New West* . . . . (Rhino)
California Love
2Pac featuring Dr. Dre; *All Eyez On Me* . . . . (Death Row)
    MTV Party To Go-#10-C . . . . (Tommy Boy)
California Man
Cheap Trick; *Heaven Tonight* . . . . (Epic)
California Marching Song
UC Marching Band; *UC Marching Band* . . . . (Fidelity Sound)
California Mudslide
Lightnin' Hopkins; *Los Angeles Blues* . . . . (Rhino)

California Nights
Sweet; *Level-Headed* . . . . (Capitol)
California Nights
Lesley Gore; *Summer & Sun-C* . . . . (Rhino)
California Paradise
Runaways; *Queens Of Noise* . . . . (Mercury)
California PM
George Benson; *Weekend In L.A.* . . . . (Warner Bros.)
California Promises
Jimmy Buffett; *One Particular Harbour* . . . . (MCA)
California Road
Mel Tillis; *45-#14175* . . . . (RCA)
California Saga
Beach Boys; *Holland* . . . . (Brother)
    Ten Years Of Harmony . . . . (Caribou)
California Soul
5th Dimension; *5th Dimension-Anthology 1967-1973* . . . . (Rhino)
Marvin Gaye & Tammi Terrell; *Classic Duets-Marvin Gaye & His*
    Women-C . . . . (Motown)
    Motown Superstar Series-#2-Marvin Gaye . . . . (Motown)
California Sun
Ramones; *All The Stuff & More-#1* . . . . (Sire)
    Leave Home . . . . (Sire)
    ST/Rock 'N' Roll High School . . . . (Sire)
Rivieras; *Beach Classics-All Original*
    Recordings-C . . . . (Dunhill Compact Classics)
    Frat Rock!-#4-C . . . . (Rhino)
    Summer & Sun-C . . . . (Rhino)
California Sunset
Neil Young; *Old Ways* . . . . (Geffen)
California Surfer
Dee D. Hope; *History Of Surf Music-#2-C* . . . . (Rhino)
California Turn Arounds
Jack Greene; *Jack Greene's Greatest Hits* . . . . . . (International Mktg. Group)
    Trucks,Trains & Airplanes-C . . . . (International Mktg. Group)
California Wine
Bobby Goldsboro; *10th Anniversary Album-#2* . . . . (United Artists)
Californicatin'
J. Geils Band; *You're Gettin' Even While I'm Gettin' Odd* . . . . (EMI)
Californication
Red Hot Chili Peppers; *Californication* . . . . (Warner Bros.)
Cowboy
Kid Rock; *Devil Without A Cause* . . . . (Top Dog/Lava/Atlantic)
Daylight Fading
Counting Crows; *Recovering The Satellites* . . . . (David Geffen Co.)
Do Re Mi
Arlo Guthrie; *Tribute To Woody Guthrie-C* . . . . (Warner Bros.)
John Cougar Mellencamp; *Folkways: A Vision Shared-C* . . . . (Columbia)
Ry Cooder; *Ry Cooder* . . . . (Reprise)
    Show Time . . . . (Warner Bros.)
Woody Guthrie; *Dust Bowl Ballads* . . . . (Rounder)
Dope Show
Marilyn Manson; *Mechanical Animals* . . . . (Nothing)
Estimated Prophet
Burning Spear; *Deadicated-C* . . . . (Arista)
Grateful Dead; *Terrapin Station* . . . . (Arista)
Everyone I Meet Is From California
America; *Encore-More Greatest Hits* . . . . (Rhino)
Fight For California
Original Soundtrack; *The Greatest College Fight Songs* . . . . (Laserlight)
University Of California Marching Band; *University Of California*
    Marching Band . . . . (Fidelity Sound)
Fight On, U.S.C.
Michigan University Band; *Kick Off, U.S.A.* . . . . (Vanguard)
Original Soundtrack; *College Fight Songs: The Pac Ten-C* . . . . (K-Tel)
    The Greatest College Fight Songs . . . . (Laserlight)
    Top Ten College Fight Songs . . . . (K-Tel)
First Train To California
Cryan' Shames; *Best Of The Cryan' Shames* . . . . (Bac-Trac)
Floodin' In California
Albert King; *Crosscut Saw: Albert King In San Francisco* . . . . (Stax)
Friend In California
Merle Haggard; *Friend In California* . . . . (Epic)
    More Hot Country Requests-C . . . . (Epic)
Goin' Cali
Bruce Springsteen; *Tracks* . . . . (Columbia)
Going To California
Led Zeppelin; *Led Zeppelin IV* . . . . (Atlantic)
    Led Zeppelin-Box Set . . . . (Atlantic)
Going To California
John Lee Hooker; *John Lee Hooker Sings John Lee Hooker* . . . . (Everest)
Good Woman Blues
Mel Tillis; *Mel Tillis' Greatest Hits* . . . . (Curb)
Hail To California
University Of California Marching Band; *Hail To California* . . (Fidelity Sound)
Hanging Out In California
Cruzados; *Cruzados* . . . . (Arista)

Heads Carolina, Tails California
Jo Dee Messina; *Greatest Hits Of Country Dance-C*.................(Curb)
Jo Dee Messina...(Curb)
Here In California
Kate Wolf; *Close To You*..................................(Kaleidoscope)
High School U.S.A.
Tommy Facenda; *45-#51 to #78* ....(Atlantic)
Hotel California
Eagles; *Eagles Greatest Hits, Volume 2* ....(Asylum)
Eagles Live ....(Asylum)
Hell Freezes Over..(Geffen)
Hotel California...(Asylum)
I Got To Get To California
Marvin Gaye; *Trouble Man/M.P.G.* ....(Motown)
I Remember California
R.E.M.; *Green* ....(Warner Bros.)
If We Make It Through December
Merle Haggard; *A Christmas Present* ....(Curb)
Eleven Winners ....(Capitol)
Goin' Home For Christmas ....(Sony Music Special Prod.)
Merle Haggard-Christmas Gift ....(Curb)
Very Best Of Merle Haggard ....(Capitol)
If We'd All Been Living In California
Frank Zappa; *Uncle Meat* ....(Barking Pumpkin)
It Never Rains In Southern California
Albert Hammond; *Rock Artifacts-From The Vaults-#2-C* ....(Legacy)
Super Hits Of The '70s-Have A Nice Day-#10-C ....(Rhino)
Tony Toni Tone; *Revival* ....(Wing)
Lemon Squeezing Daddy
Sultans; *Risque Rhythms: Nasty '50s R&B-C* ....(Rhino)
Line, The
Bruce Springsteen; *The Ghost Of Tom Joad* ....(Columbia)
Look At California
Maze featuring Frankie Beverly; *Live In New Orleans* ....(Capitol)
Maze featuring Frankie Beverly ....(Capitol)
Lord I Want To Go Back To California
Jim Post; *Magic-In Concert*...........................(Flying Fish)
Lost You In The Canyon
Marc Cohn; *Burning The Daze* ....(Atlantic)
Muddy Water
Keb' Mo'; *Slow Down*..............................(550/Epic/Okeh)
My California
Lightnin' Hopkins; *Lightnin' Hopkins-Complete Aladdin Recordings* .... (EMI)
Nevada, California
Jayhawks; *Hollywood Town Hall* ....(Def American)
Off To California
Russell Family; *Of Doolin, County Clare* ....(Green Linnet)
Oklahoma Heartaches & California Dreams
Kris Carpenter; *45-#203* ....(Door Knob)
Prettiest Eyes In California
B.W. Stevenson; *Rainbow Down The Road*. ....(Amazing)
Promised Land
Band; *Moondog Matinee* ....(Capitol)
Chuck Berry; *Rock 'N' Roll Rarities-20 Magic Tracks* ....(Chess)
The Chess Box-Chuck Berry. ....(Chess)
Elvis Presley; *Promised Land* ....(RCA)
ST/This Is Elvis ....(RCA)
Freddy Weller; *Country Music Classics-#11-Early '70s-C*...........(K-Tel)
Freddy Weller's Greatest Hits ....(Columbia)
Gary Morris; *Full Moon Empty Heart* ....(Liberty)
Grateful Dead; *Steal Your Face*. ....(Grateful Dead)
James Taylor; *Walking Man* ....(Warner Bros.)
Kingfish; *Kingfish/Alive In Eighty Five-Double Dose* ....(Relix)
Shadow Of California
Blue Oyster Cult; *Revolution By Night* ....(Columbia)
Sinaloa Cowboys
Bruce Springsteen; *The Ghost Of Tom Joad* ....(Columbia)
Someday Soon
Chris LeDoux; *Rodeo Songs Old & New* ....(Liberty)
Ian & Sylvia; *Ian & Sylvia's Greatest Hits* ....(Vanguard)
Northern Journey ....(Vanguard)
Judy Collins; *Colors Of The Day-The Best Of Judy Collins* ....(Elektra)
Who Knows Where The Time Goes. ....(Elektra)
Moe Bandy; *Moe Bandy's Greatest Hits* ....(Columbia)
Rodeo Romeo ....(Columbia)
Suzy Bogguss; *Aces*. ....(Liberty)
Suzy Bogguss' Greatest Hits. ....(Liberty)
Sons Of California
Original Soundtrack; *College Fight Songs: The Pac Ten-C* ....(K-Tel)
University Of California Marching Band; *University Of California Marching Band* ....(Fidelity Sound)
Sons Of Westwood
Original Soundtrack; *College Fight Songs: The Pac Ten-C* ....(K-Tel)
The Greatest College Fight Songs ....(Laserlight)
Southern California
George Jones & Tammy Wynette; *George Jones & Tammy Wynette-16 Biggest Hits* ....(Epic/Legacy)
Tammy Wynette & George Jones; *Encore-Tammy Wynette & George Jones* ....(Epic)

Tammy Wynette & George Jones' Greatest Hits...................(Epic)
Southern California Purples
Chicago; *Chicago At Carnegie Hall*. ....(Chicago)
Chicago Transit Authority. ....(Chicago)
Sweet Betsy From Pike
Cisco Houston; *Cowboy Ballads* ....(Smithsonian Folkways)
Mormon Tabernacle Choir; *This Land Is Your Land* ....(Columbia)
Tape From California
Phil Ochs; *Gunfight At Carnegie Hall* ....(Mobile Fidelity Sound Lab)
The War Is Over-Best Of Phil Ochs. ....(A&M)
Theme From "CHiPs"
Original Soundtrack; *Television's Greatest Hits-#6-Remote Control-C* ...(TVT)
This Land Is Your Land
Bruce Springsteen & The E Street Band; *Bruce Springsteen & The E Street Band Live/1975-85* ....(Legacy)
Glen Campbell; *All American* ....(Liberty)
Lee Greenwood; *American Patriot* ....(Capitol)
Odetta, Arlo Guthrie & Company; *Tribute To Woody Guthrie-C* ....(Warner Bros.)
Pete Seeger; *God Bless America-C* ....(Columbia)
Pete Seeger Sings Woody Guthrie ....(Smithsonian Folkways)
Pete Seeger-Complete Carnegie Hall Concert-1963 ....(Columbia)
Weavers; *Weavers' Greatest Hits* ....(Vanguard)
Woody Guthrie; *Greatest Songs Of Woody Guthrie-C*. ....(Vanguard)
Troubadours Of The Folk Era-#1-C ....(Rhino)
Woody Guthrie ....(Vanguard)
To Go To California Anymore (I Don't Have A Reason)
Willie Nelson; *Born For Trouble* ....(Columbia)
Tulsa Time
Don Williams; *Best Of Don Williams-#2* ....(MCA)
Country's Greatest Hits-#6-Superstars-C. ....(Priority)
Don Williams-Legends ....(MCA)
Expressions ....(MCA)
Eric Clapton; *Backless* ....(Polydor)
Just One Night ....(Polydor)

STATES: CAROLINAS

See Also: **CITIES: A-Z**

Baby's Got A Hold On Me
Nitty Gritty Dirt Band; *Hold On*. ....(Warner Bros.)
Blue Ridge Mountain Blues
Blue Ridge Rangers; *Blue Ridge Rangers* ....(Fantasy)
Doc Watson; *Essential Doc Watson*. ....(Vanguard)
Earl Scruggs & John Fogerty; *Earl Scruggs And Friends-C* ....(MCA)
Norman Blake; *Directions* ....(Takoma)
Carolina
Charlie Daniels Band; *Full Moon*. ....(Epic)
High Lonesome ....(Epic)
Carolina Blue
Annie McGowan; *Rattlesnakes & Rusty Water* ....(Rattlesnake)
Carolina By The Sea
Super Grit Cowboy Band; *If You Can't Hang-Drag Your Country Ass* ....(Hoodswamp)
Carolina Come On
Lacy J. Dalton; *Lacy J. Dalton*. ....(Columbia)
Carolina Dreams
Ronnie Milsap; *Inside Ronnie Milsap* ....(RCA)
Carolina In My Mind
James Taylor; *James Taylor's Greatest Hits* ....(Warner Bros.)
Carolina In The Morning
Al Jolson; *Best Of Al Jolson*. ....(MCA)
The Al Jolson Story-#2 ....(MCA)
Carolina In The Pines
Michael Martin Murphey; *Best Of Michael Martin Murphey* ....(Liberty)
Blue Sky-Night Thunder ....(Epic)
Carolina Moon
Thelonius Monk; *Genius Of Modern Music-#2* ....(Blue Note)
Carolina Moon
Slim Whitman; *Ghost Riders In The Sky* ....(Liberty)
Carolina Moonshiner
Porter Wagoner; *20 Great Country Hits-C* ....(RCA)
Collector's Porter Wagoner ....(RCA)
Carolina On My Mind
Melanie; *What Have They Done To My Song Ma*. ....(Accord)
Carolina Shout
Fats Waller; *Piano Solos-1929-1941* ....(RCA)
Carolina Star
Earl Scruggs & Rodney Dillard; *Top Of The World* ....(Columbia)
Carolina Sun
Anne Murray; *Keeping In Touch* ....(Capitol)
Carolina Sunshine Girl
Geoff Muldaur & Amos Garrett; *Geoff Muldaur & Amos Garrett* ....(Flying Fish)
Charleston
Paul Whiteman & His Orchestra; *Nipper's Greatest Hits Of The '20s-C*. ....(RCA)

Charlotte's In North Carolina
Ronnie McDowell; *Country Boy's Heart* . . . .(Epic)
Cryin' For The Carolines
Fred Waring's Pennsylvanians; *Fred Waring's
Greatest Hits* . . . . (Collector's Choice)
Dinah
Bing Crosby; *Bing Crosby-16 Most Requested Songs* . . . . (Legacy)
Cab Calloway; *Best Of The Big Bands-C* . . . . (Columbia)
Cliff Edwards; *Singin' In The Rain* . . . . (ASV)
Count Basie & Ethel Waters; *Tribute To Black Entertainers-C* . . . . . (Columbia)
Duke Ellington; *Jubilee Stomp* . . . . (Bluebird)
Ethel Waters; *Am I Blue?* . . . . (ASV)
Fats Waller; *Ain't Misbehavin': 25 Greatest Hits*. . . . .(Living Era)
Lionel Hampton & His Orchestra; *Tempo & Swing* . . . . (Bluebird)
Louis Armstrong; *Louis Armstrong-Vol. 6-St. Louis Blues* . . . . (Columbia)
Mills Brothers; *50th Anniversary* . . . .(Ranwood)
Down A Carolina Lane
Duke Ellington & His Famous Orchestra; *Ridin' In
Rhythm-C* . . . . (Disques Swing)
Everywhere
Tim McGraw; *Everywhere* . . . . (Curb)
Heads Carolina, Tails California
Jo Dee Messina; *Greatest Hits Of Country Dance-C* . . . . (Curb)
Jo Dee Messina . . . . (Curb)
Here Comes Carolina
Ohio State University Marching Band; *Saturday Afternoon At
Columbus* . . . .(Fidelity Sound)
Just A Little Bit South Of North Carolina
Chuck Foster & Jimmy Castle; *The Uncollected Chuck Foster & His
Orchestra-1940*. . . . . (Hindsight)
Dean Martin; *Swingin' Down Yonder*. . . . .(Capitol)
Kinfolks In Carolina
Merle Travis; *Best Of Merle Travis* . . . . (Rhino)
My Cabin In Caroline
Lester Flatt & Earl Scruggs; *Flatt & Scruggs-20 Greatest Hits* . . . . . . (Deluxe)
Lester Flatt & Earl Scruggs & The Foggy Mountain Boys; *Lester Flatt,
Earl Scruggs & The Foggy Mountain Boys-Complete Mercury
Sessions*. . . . . (Mercury)
My Carolina Sunshine Girl
Jimmie Rodgers; *Jimmie Rodgers-Early Years-1928-1929* . . . . (Rounder)
North Carolina
Anne Romaine; *Take A Stand* . . . . (Flying Fish)
North Carolina
Poets Of Rhythm; *More Original Raw Soul-C* . . . . (Instinct)
North Carolina
Les McCann; *Talk To The People/River High, River Low* . . . . (Collectables)
North Carolina (Home In My Heart)
Claudia Church; *Claudia Church* . . . . (Reprise)
North Carolina Blues
Johnie Lewis; *Alabama Slide Guitar* . . . . (Arhoolie)
North Carolina Bound
Connie & Babe & The Backwoods Boys; *Backwoods Bluegrass* . . . . . (Rounder)
North Carolina Breakdown
Sammy Shelor; *Leading Roll* . . . . (Sugar Hill)
North Carolina Tune/Child Of My Heart
Liz Carroll; *Friend Indeed* . . . . (Shanachie)
North Carolina, My Home State
Andy Griffith; *American Originals-Andy Griffith*. . . . . (Capitol)
Oh Carolina
Vince Gill; *Best Of Vince Gill*. . . . . (RCA)
Raise Up
Petey Pablo; *Diary Of A Sinner-1st Entry*. (Jive)
Rebecca Lynn
Bryan White; *Bryan White* . . . . (Asylum)
South Carolina Rag
John Jackson; *Step It Up & Go* . . . . (Rounder)
Steal My Kisses
Ben Harper; *Burn To Shine* . . . . (Virgin)
Now That's What I Call Music!-#4-C . . . . (Virgin)
Take Me Back To My Old Carolina Home
Uncle Dave Macon; *Laugh Your Blues Away*. . . . . (Rounder)
Way Down In North Carolina
Fields Ward & The Buck Mountain Band; *Fields Ward & The Buck
Mountain Band* . . . . (Historical)

STATES: COLORADO

See Also: *CITIES: A-Z, CITIES: DENVER*

Along The Colorado Trail
Weavers; *Best Of The Weavers* . . . .(MCA)
Coast Of Colorado
Skip Ewing; *Coast Of Colorado* . . . .(MCA)
Colorado
Linda Ronstadt; *Don't Cry Now* . . . . (Asylum)
Stephen Stills; *Manassas* . . . . (Atlantic)

Colorado Calling Me
Jim & Jesse; *Red, White & Bluegrass-C* . . . . (C.M.H. Prod.)
Colorado Kool Aid
Johnny Paycheck; *Johnny Paycheck's Biggest Hits* . . . . (Epic)
Johnny Paycheck's Greatest Hits-#2 . . . . (Epic)
Take This Job And Shove It . . . . (Epic)
Colorado Queenie
Little David Wilkins; *20 Great Hits-C* . . . .(Plantation)
Colorado Song
Ozark Mountain Daredevils; *Ozark Mountain Daredevils* . . . . (A&M)
Colorado Trail
Ian Tyson; *Ian Tyson* . . . . (Columbia)
Salli Terri; *Songs Of The American Land* . . . . (Angel)
Come & Grow Old With Me In Colorado
Tom Paxton; *One Million Lawyers & Other Disasters* . . . . (Flying Fish)
Coors In Colorado
Ray Price; *Master Of The Art* . . . . (Warner Bros.)
Don't Blame Me For Colorado
Larry Gatlin & The Gatlin Brothers Band; *Partners* . . . . (Columbia)
I Guess He'd Rather Be In Colorado
John Denver; *Poems, Prayers & Promises* . . . . (RCA)
I Wonder How It Is In Colorado
Gene Watson; *Reflections* . . . . (Capitol)
Long Afternoons
Jerry Jeff Walker; *A Man Must Carry On* . . . . (MCA)
Gypsy Songman . . . . (Rykodisc)
Moonlight On The Colorado
Sons Of The Pioneers; *Songs Of The Trail* . . . .(Pair)
Rocky Mountain High
John Denver; *Evening With John Denver* . . . .(RCA)
John Denver's Greatest Hits . . . .(RCA)
Rocky Mountain High. . . . .(RCA)
Take Me Home, Country Roads & Other Hits . . . .(RCA)
She Came From Fort Worth
Kathy Mattea; *Willow In The Wind* . . . . (Mercury)
Pat Alger & Kathy Mattea; *True Love & Other Short Stories-C* . . . . .(Sugar Hill)
Silence On The Line
Chris LeDoux; *Cowboy*. . . . . (Capitol)
Someday Soon
Chris LeDoux; *Rodeo Songs Old & New*. . . . . (Liberty)
Ian & Sylvia; *Ian & Sylvia's Greatest Hits* . . . . (Vanguard)
Northern Journey . . . . (Vanguard)
Judy Collins; *Colors Of The Day-The Best Of Judy Collins* . . . . (Elektra)
Who Knows Where The Time Goes . . . . (Elektra)
Moe Bandy; *Moe Bandy's Greatest Hits*. . . . . (Columbia)
Rodeo Romeo . . . . (Columbia)
Suzy Bogguss; *Aces* . . . . (Liberty)
Suzy Bogguss' Greatest Hits. . . . . (Liberty)
When My Ship Comes In
Clint Black; *The Hard Way*. . . . .(RCA)

STATES: CONNECTICUT

See Also: *CITIES: A-Z*

Connecticut
Judy Garland & Others; *Changing My Tune-Best Of Decca Years-#2* . . . (Decca)
Too Much Joy; *Son Of Sam I Am*. . . . .(Giant)
Connecticut Yankee In The Court Of King Arthur
Robert Fripp & The League Of Crafty Guitarists; *Show Of
Hands* . . . . (Editions E.G.)
Wives Are In Connecticut
Carly Simon; *Spoiled Girl*. . . . . (Epic)

STATES: DELAWARE

See Also: *CITIES: A-Z*

Delaware
Drop Nineteens; *Delaware* . . . . (Caroline)
Perry Como; *This Is Perry Como* . . . .(RCA)
Delaware Slide
George Thorogood & The Destroyers; *George Thorogood & The
Destroyers* . . . . (Rounder)

STATES: FLORIDA

See Also: *CITIES: A-Z, CITIES: MIAMI*

Deep Down In Florida
Muddy Waters; *Hard Again* . . . .(Blue Sky)
Muddy "Mississippi" Waters Live. . . . .(Blue Sky)
Deep Down In Florida #2
Muddy Waters; *King Bee* . . . .(Blue Sky)

Down In Florida
James Montgomery; *The Oven Is On*. . . . . (Tone Cool)
Down In Florida On A Hog
Darby & Tarlton; *On The Banks Of A Lonely River*. . . . . (County)
Farmer In Florida
Sally Rogers; *Love Will Guide Us* . . . . (Flying Fish)
Florida Blues
Vassar Clements; *Crossing The Catskills* . . . . (Rounder)
Grass Routes. . . . . (Rounder)
Florida Greeting Song
Pat Metheny; *Watercolors*. . . . . (ECM)
Goin' Back To Florida
John Hammond; *Best Of John Hammond* . . . . (Vanguard)
Lightnin' Hopkins; *Lightnin' Hopkins*. . . . . (Smithsonian Folkways)
Roots Of Lightnin' Hopkins. . . . . (Smithsonian Folkways)
Going Back To Florida
Billie & De De Pierce; *New Orleans Jazz-C* . . . . (Arhoolie)
If We're Not Back In Love By Monday
Merle Haggard; *MCA Records 30 Years Of Hits-1958-1988-C*. . . . . (MCA)
Merle Haggard-Legends . . . . (MCA)
Merle Haggard's Greatest Hits . . . . (MCA)
More Of The Best . . . . (MCA)
Ramblin' Fever. . . . . (MCA)
Key Largo
Bertie Higgins; *Just Another Day In Paradise*. . . . . (Kat Family)
Key West Intermezzo (I Saw You First)
John Mellencamp; *Mr. Happy Go Lucky*. . . . . (Mercury)
Love Story
Randy Newman; *Randy Newman* . . . . (Warner Archives)
Mainline Florida
Eric Clapton; *461 Ocean Boulevard* . . . . (Polydor)
Orange And Blue
Original Soundtrack; *The Greatest College Fight Songs*. . . . . (Laserlight)
Orange Blossom Special
Bill Monroe; *Bean Blossom* . . . . (MCA)
Bill Monroe and His Blue Grass Boys-60 Years Of Country. . . . . . (RCA)
Stars Of The Grand Ole Opry-1926-1974-C. . . . . (RCA)
Charlie Daniels Band; *Fire On The Mountain*. . . . . (Epic)
ST/Urban Cowboy 2 . . . . (Epic)
Flatt & Scruggs; *Hear The Whistles Blow* . . . . (International Mktg. Group)
Gordon Terry; *Disco Country* . . . . (Plantation)
Gordon Terry-20 Golden Souvenirs . . . . (Plantation)
Johnny Cash; *Columbia Records-1958-1986* . . . . (Columbia)
Essential Johnny Cash . . . . (Columbia)
Johnny Cash-16 Biggest Hits-#2 . . . . (Legacy)
Johnny Cash's Greatest Hits . . . . (Columbia)
The Man In Black-His Greatest Hits. . . . . (Legacy)
Train Trax-C. . . . . (Sony Music Special Prod.)
Johnson Mountain Boys; *Steel Rails-Classic Railroad Songs-#1-C* . . . (Rounder)
Nitty Gritty Dirt Band; *Will The Circle Be Unbroken* . . . . (EMI)
Seminole Wind
John Anderson; *Seminole Wind*. . . . . (BNA)

STATES: GEORGIA

*See Also: **CITIES: A-Z, CITIES: ATLANTA, SAVANNAH,
DIRECTIONS: SOUTH***

"Way" Cross Georgia
David Sanborn; *Takin' Off*. . . . . (Warner Bros.)
(Sittin' On) The Dock Of The Bay
Michael Bolton; *The Hunger*. . . . . (Columbia)
Otis Redding; *(Sittin' On) The Dock Of The Bay*. . . . . (Atco)
Best Of Otis Redding. . . . . (Atco)
Golden Age Of Black Music-1960-1970-C. . . . . (Atlantic)
Golden Soul-C. . . . . (Atlantic)
Soul Years-C. . . . . (Atlantic)
The Otis Redding Story. . . . . (Atlantic)
Another Dawn Breaking Over Georgia
David Frizzell & Shelly West; *Our Best To You* . . . . (Warner Bros.)
At A Georgia Camp Meeting
Kid Ory's Creole Jazz Band; *1956-The Legendary Kid*. . . . . . . (Good Time Jazz)
Back In Georgia
R.B. Greaves; *Rock & Roll* . . . . (Intermedia)
Back To Georgia
Loggins & Messina; *Loggins & Messina-On Stage*. . . . . (Columbia)
Sittin' In . . . . (Columbia)
Boogie Ala Georgia
Peggy Gilbert; *Dixieland Jazz*. . . . . (Cambria)
Born In Georgia
Tinsley Ellis; *Fanning The Flames* . . . . (Alligator)
Bringin' In The Georgia Mail
Don Reno & Bill Harrell; *Great American Train Songs-C* . . . . . . (C.M.H. Prod.)
Bringing In The Georgia Mail
Norman Blake; *Back Home In Sulphur Springs*. . . . . (Rounder)
Burn Georgia Burn
Alabama; *Feels So Right* . . . . (RCA)

Can't You See
Alabama; *Alabama-Live* . . . . (RCA)
Charlie Daniels Band; *Volunteer Jam VII-C* . . . . (Epic)
Hank Williams, Jr.; *Hank Williams, Jr. & Friends*. . . . . (Polydor)
Rebels, Renegades & Ramblers-C. . . . . (Polydor)
Standing In The Shadows . . . . (Polydor)
Marshall Tucker Band; *Marshall Tucker Band* . . . . (AJK Music)
Searchin' For A Rainbow . . . . (AJK Music)
Caroline's Still In Georgia
Mac Davis; *Soft Talk* . . . . (Casablanca)
Cold Summer Day In Georgia
Gene Watson; *Memories To Burn* . . . . (Epic)
Devil Comes Back To Georgia
Marc O'Connor; *Heroes* . . . . (Warner Bros.)
Devil Loose In Georgia
Orrin Star & Gary Mehalick; *Premium Blend* . . . . (Flying Fish)
Devil Went Down To Georgia
Charlie Daniels Band; *A Decade Of Hits* . . . . (Epic)
Billboard Top Hits-1979-C. . . . . (Rhino)
Me & The Boys . . . . (Epic)
Million Mile Reflections . . . . (Epic)
ST/Urban Cowboy. . . . . (Asylum)
Dreamy Georgiana Moon
Asa Martin; *Dr. Ginger Blue* . . . . (Rounder)
Everywhere
Tim McGraw; *Everywhere*. . . . . (Curb)
Georgia
Carolyn Dawn Johnson; *Room With A View*. . . . . (Arista)
Georgia In A Jug
Johnny Paycheck; *I Don't Need To Know That Right Now* . . . . (Allegiance)
Johnny Paycheck's Greatest Hits-#2. . . . . (Epic)
Take This Job And Shove It . . . . (Epic)
Georgia Keeps Pulling On My Ring
Conway Twitty; *Classic Conway*. . . . . (MCA)
Very Best Of Conway Twitty . . . . (MCA)
Georgia On A Fast Train
Billy Joe Shaver; *Hot Tracks-Train Super Hits-C* . . . . (Epic)
Georgia On My Mind
Billie Holiday; *God Bless The Child* . . . . (Columbia)
The Billie Holiday Story-#2. . . . . (Columbia)
Hoagy Carmichael; *Hoagy Carmichael-Legendary Performer* . . . . (RCA)
Hoagy Sings Carmichael. . . . . (EMI)
Mildred Bailey; *Harlem Lullaby* . . . . (ASV)
Preservation Hall Jazz Band; *Best Of The Preservation Hall
Jazz Band*. . . . . (Columbia)
Ray Charles; *Ray Charles' Greatest Hits-#2* . . . . (Rhino)
Ray Charles-Anthology. . . . . (Rhino)
Willie Nelson; *Greatest Hits (& Some That Will Be)* . . . . (Columbia)
Stardust. . . . . (Legacy)
Willie & Family Live. . . . . (Columbia)
Georgia Pineywoods
Osborne Brothers; *Best Of The Osborne Brothers* . . . . (MCA)
Country Bluegrass. (MCA Special Prod.)
Red, White & Bluegrass-C . . . . (C.M.H. Prod.)
Georgia Rhythm
Atlanta Rhythm Section; *Rock & Roll Alternative* . . . . (Polydor)
Georgia Soul
Carmol Taylor; *I Think They Call It Homesick*. . . . . (Country Int'l)
Georgia Sunshine
Jerry Reed; *Best Of Jerry Reed*. . . . . (RCA)
Going To Georgia
Johnson Mountain Boys; *At The Old Schoolhouse*. . . . . (Rounder)
Stanley Brothers; *Shadows Of The Past* . . . . (Copper Creek)
Hell & Half Of Georgia
Owen Brothers; *Audiograph Alive-C*. . . . . (Audiograph)
Fool Of Fools . . . . (Audiograph)
Home
Alan Jackson; *Alan Jackson-The Greatest Hits Collection* . . . . (Arista)
Here In The Real World. . . . . (Arista)
I Been To Georgia On A Fast Train
Willie Nelson; *Me & Paul* . . . . (Columbia)
I'd Be Better Off (In A Pine Box)
Doug Stone; *Doug Stone* . . . . (Epic)
Greatest Country Hits Of The '90s-1990-C. . . . . (Columbia)
Lonesome Whistle
Hank Williams With His Drifting Cowboys; *Between The Rails: America's
Train Songs-C* . . . . (Crescendo)
Hank Williams-24 Greatest Hits-#2 . . . . (Polydor)
Hank Williams-40 Greatest Hits . . . . (Polydor)
Johnny Cash; *Story Songs Of The Trains & Rivers*. . . . . (Sun)
Little Feat; *Hoy-Hoy!*. . . . . (Warner Bros.)
Long Way Back To Georgia
John McCutcheon; *Gonna Rise Again* . . . . (Rounder)
Macon Georgia Bad Girl
Jeannie C. Riley; *Jeannie C. Riley & Fancy Friends* . . . . (Plantation)
Marching Through Georgia
American Music Consort; *Sentimental Songs Of The Mid-19th
Century* . . . . (Takoma)

Meet In The Middle
Diamond Rio; *Diamond Rio* . . . . (Arista)
Diamond Rio's Greatest Hits . . . . (Arista)
Midnight Train To Georgia
Gladys Knight & The Pips; *Billboard Top Rock 'N' Roll Hits-1973-C*. . . (Rhino)
Gladys Knight & The Pips' Greatest Hits . . . . (Buddah)
Imagination . . . . (Right Stuff)
On & On . . . . (Fifty One West)
Radio Active Hits-C . . . . (Accord)
Train Trax-C . . . . (Sony Music Special Prod.)
Very Best Of Gladys Knight & The Pips. . . . . (Buddah)
Moon Over Georgia
Shenandoah; *Extra Mile* . . . . (Columbia)
Shenandoah's Greatest Hits . . . . (Columbia)
My Little Georgia Rose
David Grisman; *Home Is Where The Heart Is.* . . . . (Rounder)
Herb Pederson; *Son Of Rounder Banjo* . . . . (Rounder)
My Sweet Eyed Georgia Girl
Atlanta; *Atlanta* . . . .(MCA)
Night The Lights Went Out In Georgia
Lynn Anderson; *Top Of The World.* . . . . (Columbia)
Reba McEntire; *For My Broken Heart* . . . . (MCA)
Reba McEntire's Greatest Hits-#3: I'm A Survivor . . . . (MCA)
Vicki Lawrence; *Super Hits Of The '70s-Have A Nice Day-#10-C* . . . . . (Rhino)
Ol' Red
Blake Shelton; *Blake Shelton* . . . .(Giant)
Peach Picking Time Down In Georgia
Jimmie Rodgers; *My Rough & Rowdy Ways.* . . . . (RCA)
This Is Jimmie Rodgers . . . . (RCA)
Merle Travis; *Red, White & Bluegrass-C* . . . . (C.M.H. Prod.)
Superstars Salute Jimmie Rodgers-C. . . . . (Step One)
Poor Red Georgia Dirt
Robin & Linda Williams; *Close As We Can Get* . . . . (Flying Fish)
Rainy Night In Georgia
Brook Benton; *Atlantic Rhythm & Blues 1947-1974-#6 (1966-*
1969)-C . . . .(Atlantic)
Brook Benton Today . . . . (Cotillion)
Brook Benton-Anthology . . . . (Rhino)
Golden Age Of Black Music-1960-1970-C . . . . (Atlantic)
Pick Of Brook Benton . . . . (Fifty One West)
Soul Years-C . . . . (Atlantic)
Hank Williams, Jr.; *Hank Williams, Jr.-14 Greatest Hits* . . . . (Polydor)
Sam Moore & Conway Twitty; *Rhythm Country And Blues-C.* . . . .(MCA)
Rambling Wreck From Georgia Tech
Original Soundtrack; *The Greatest College Fight Songs* . . . . (Laserlight)
Top Ten College Fight Songs . . . . (K-Tel)
Red Skies Over Georgia
Charlie Walker; *45-#172* . . . . (Plantation)
Send Me Back To Georgia
Si Kahn; *Unfinished Portraits.* . . . . (Flying Fish)
Slow Train Through Georgia
Norman Blake; *Whiskey Before Breakfast* . . . . (Rounder)
South Georgia Blues
Sonny Stitt & Sadik Hakim; *Sonny Stitt Meets Sadik Hakim* . . . . . . (Progressive)
Sweet Georgia Brown
Anita O'Day; *Compact Jazz-Best Of The Compact Jazz Vocalists-C* . . . . (Verve)
Beatles; *The Beatles featuring Tony Sheridan-In The Beginning (Circa*
1960). . . . . (Polydor)
Ben Bernie & His Orchestra; *78-#15002* . . . . (Vocalion)
Bing Crosby; *Bing Crosby-16 Most Requested Songs* . . . . (Legacy)
Coasters; *Coasters' Greatest Hits.* . . . . (Atco)
Django Reinhardt; *Djangologie USA-#1* . . . . (Disques Swing)
Quintet Of The Hot Club Of France . . . . (Prestige)
Ella Fitzgerald; *Ella Fitzgerald In London* . . . . (Pablo)
Whisper Not . . . . (Verve)
Ella Fitzgerald & Count Basie; *Perfect Match* . . . . (Pablo)
Original Broadway Cast; *Bubbling Brown Sugar* . . . . (Amherst)
Stephane Grappelli; *Live In London* . . . . (Black Lion)
Tito Puente; *Out Of This World* . . . . (Concord Picante Jazz)
Tall Trees In Georgia
Buffy Sainte-Marie; *Best Of Buffy Sainte-Marie-#2.* . . . . (Vanguard)
I'm Gonna Be A Country Girl Again . . . . (Vanguard)
Theme From "I'll Fly Away"
Original Soundtrack; *Television's Greatest Hits-#7-Cable Ready-C* . . . . (TVT)
Ticket Back To Georgia
Head East; *Flat As A Pancake.* . . . . (A&M)
Walk All Over Georgia
Louisiana Red; *Midnight Rambler* . . . . (Tomato)
Walkin' Back To Georgia
Jim Croce; *50th Anniversary Collection* . . . . (Saja)
Down The Highway . . . . (Atlantic)
War Is Hell (On The Homefront Too)
T.G. Sheppard; *Perfect Stranger* . . . .(Warner Bros.)
T.G. Sheppard's All-Time Greatest Hits . . . .(Warner Bros.)
T.G. Sheppard's Greatest Hits . . . . (Warner Bros./Curb)
Watermelon Crawl
Tracy Byrd; *No Ordinary Man* . . . .(MCA)
Watermelon Time In Georgia
Larry Boone; *Get In Line* . . . . (Columbia)

STATES: GEORGIA—STATES: HAWAII

STATES: HAWAII

See Also: CITIES: A-Z, ISLANDS, PARADISE

Aloha (Also Means Goodbye)
Screamin' Scott Simon; *Transmissions From Space.* . . . . (Rhino)
Aloha I Love You
Martin Denny; *From Maui With Love* . . . . (First Warning)
Aloha Oe
Elvis Presley; *ST/Blue Hawaii.* . . . .(RCA)
Henry Mancini; *Music Of Hawaii* . . . .(RCA)
Marty Robbins; *Marty Robbins' All-Time Greatest Hits.* . . . . (Columbia)
Marty Robbins' Greatest Hits. . . . . (Columbia)
Aloha Waltz
Walter Ostanek; *Little Bird Dance* . . . . (Boot)
Aux Iles Hawaii
Diana Ross; *Evening With Diana Ross* . . . . (Motown)
Beautiful Hawaii
Magic Organ; *Around The World* . . . . (Ranwood)
Blue Hawaii
Billy Vaughn; *Best Of Billy Vaughn* . . . . (MCA)
Billy Vaughn-16 Great Performances . . . . (MCA)
Billy Vaughn-Golden Hits . . . . (MCA)
Billy Vaughn & His Orchestra; *Billy Vaughn & His Orchestra Play 22 Of*
His Greatest Hits . . . . (Ranwood)
Elvis Presley; *Elvis-A Legendary Performer, Volume 2* . . . .(RCA)
ST/Blue Hawaii . . . .(RCA)
Blues For Hawaiians
Chuck Berry; *Chuck Berry Is On Top* . . . . (Chess)
Everybody Does It In Hawaii
Jimmie Rodgers; *On The Way Up-1929* . . . . (Rounder)
Hawaii
Beach Boys; *Concert/'69-Live In London.* . . . . (Capitol)
Spirit Of America . . . . (Capitol)
Surfer Girl . . . . (Capitol)
Hawaii
Kingfish; *Hurricane* . . . . (Accord)
Hawaii
Henry Mancini; *Music Of Hawaii* . . . .(RCA)
Hawaiian Hospitality
Louis Armstrong; *Jazz Heritage-Satchmo's Discoveries* . . . . (MCA)
Hawaiian Lei Song
Les Jansen; *45-#1362* . . . . (Accent)
Hawaiian Nights
Kingston Trio; *Looking For The Sunrise.* . . . . (Xeres)
Hawaiian War Chant
Bette Midler; *Live At Last* . . . .(Atlantic)
Tommy Dorsey; *Complete Tommy Dorsey-#8* . . . . (RCA)
This Is Tommy Dorsey . . . . (RCA)
Hawaiian Wedding Song
Andy Williams; *Andy Williams' Greatest Hits* . . . . (Columbia)
Andy Williams-16 Most Requested Songs. . . . . (Legacy)
Jim Reeves; *Jim Reeves-Pure Gold* . . . . (RCA)
Homeboy Hawaii
Kerosene; *Teenage Secret* . . . .(Caipirinha)
I Like Mountain Music
Roy Acuff; *Grand Ole Opry-75 Years-#1-C* . . . . (MCA)
It Happened In Hawaii
Glenn Miller & His Orchestra; *Complete Glenn Miller & His*
Orchestra-#7 . . . . (Bluebird)
Lovely Hula Hands
101 Strings Orchestra; *Sound Of Magnificence* . . . . (Alshire)
My Hawaii
Rascals; *Once Upon A Dream* . . . . (Rhino)
My Little Grass Shack In Kealakekua, Hawaii
Mom & Dads; *Blue Hawaii* . . . .(Crescendo)
New Hawaiian Boogie
George Thorogood & The Destroyers; *Move It On Over.* . . . . (Rounder)
Pineapple Princess
Annette Funicello; *Frankie Avalon/Annette Funicello* . . . . (K-Tel)
Sailin' On The Hawaii
Nitty Gritty Dirt Band; *Will The Circle Be Unbroken* . . . . (EMI)
Sweet Hawaiian Sunshine
Jorma Kaukonen & Tom Hobson; *Quah* . . . .(Relix)
Sweet Leilani
Bing Crosby; *Best Of Bing Crosby* . . . . (MCA)
King Sisters; *And The Winner Is-Best Movie Songs-C* . . . . (Capitol)
Theme From "Hawaii Five-O"
Original Soundtrack; *CBS: The First 50 Years* . . . . (TVT)
Television's Greatest Hits-#1-C . . . . (TVT)
Ventures; *Billboard Top Pop Hits-1969-C* . . . . (Rhino)
Drew's Famous Luau Party Music-C. . . . . (Turn Up The Music)
Think Of Tomorrow
Chris Isaak; *Baja Sessions* . . . . (Reprise)
Why Do Hawaiians Sing Aloha?
Fats Waller; *The Middle Years-#1-1936-1938* . . . . (Bluebird)

STATES: IDAHO

See Also: **CITIES: A-Z**

Going To Idaho
Grandmothers; *Looking Up Granny's Dress* . . . . (Rhino)
Idaho
Benny Carter; *Gentleman & His Music* . . . . (Concord Jazz)
Count Basie; *Standards* . . . . (Verve)
Idaho
Central Methodist College Band; *Circus Echoes*. . . . . (Fidelity Sound)
Mighty To Save . . . . (Fidelity Sound)
Private Idaho
B-52's; *Party Mix/Mesopotamia* . . . . (Warner Bros.)
Wild Planet . . . . (Warner Bros.)
Private Idaho
Doughboys; *When Up Turns To Down* . . . . (Restless)

STATES: ILLINOIS

See Also: **CITIES: A-Z, CITIES: CHICAGO**

Casey, Illinois
Erica Wheeler; *Three Wishes*. . . . . (Signature)
City Of New Orleans
Arlo Guthrie; *Best Of Arlo Guthrie* . . . . (Warner Bros.)
Hobo's Lullaby . . . . (Reprise)
Together In Concert . . . .(Reprise)
HARP; *HARP* . . . . (Redwood)
Willie Nelson; *19 Hot Country Requests-#2-C* . . . . (Epic)
City Of New Orleans . . . . (Columbia)
Greatest Country Hits Of The '80s-#4-C . . . . (Columbia)
Hot Tracks-Train Super Hits-C . . . . (Epic)
Train Trax-C . . . . (Sony Music Special Prod.)
Fields Of Illinois
Don Lange; *Natural Born Heathen* . . . . (Flying Fish)
Illinois
Dan Fogelberg; *Dan Fogelberg-Souvenirs* . . . . (Full Moon)
Illinois Blues
Skip James; *Devil Got My Woman*. . . . . (Vanguard)
Great Bluesmen At Newport-C . . . . (Vanguard)
Tribute To Skip James-#1-1964 . . . . (Biograph)
Illinois Dawn
Skyline; *Late To Work* . . . .(Flying Fish)
Illinois Loyalty
Original Soundtrack; *College Fight Songs: The Big Ten-C* . . . . (K-Tel)
University Of Michigan Band; *Greatest College Football Marches* . . (Vanguard)
Illinois March
Eastman Wind Ensemble; *Marchtime* . . . . (Mercury)
Johnsburg, Illinois
Tom Waits; *Beautiful Maladies: The Island Years* . . . . (Island)
Swordfishtrombones . . . . (Island)
Lookin' Out My Back Door
Creedence Clearwater Revival; *1970* . . . .(Fantasy)
Cosmo's Factory . . . .(Fantasy)
Creedence Clearwater Revival-Chronicle . . . .(Fantasy)
Creedence Country . . . .(Fantasy)
More Creedence Gold. . . . .(Fantasy)
Pride Of The Illini
University Of Michigan Band; *Greatest College Football Marches* . . (Vanguard)

STATES: INDIANA

See Also: **CITIES: A-Z**

Angels Working Overtime
Deana Carter; *Everything's Gonna Be Alright*. . . . . (Capitol)
Anna In Indiana
Eddie Cantor; *Rare Early Recordings-1919-1921*. . . . . (Biograph)
Back Home Again In Indiana
Les Paul; *Legend & The Legacy-#1-4* . . . . (Capitol)
Back Home In Indiana
Peggy Gilbert & The Dixie Bells; *Dixieland Jazz* . . . . (Cambria)
Gary, Indiana
Original Cast; *ST/The Music Man* . . . . (Gold Rush)
Goin' Back To Indiana
Jackson 5; *Goin' Back To Indiana*. . . . . (Motown)
Jackson 5-Anthology . . . . (Motown)
Jackson 5's Greatest Hits . . . . (Motown)
Third Album . . . . (Motown)
Going Back To Indiana
Sawyer Brown; *Sawyer Brown* . . . .(Curb)
Home In Indiana
Magic Organ; *Traveling With The Magic Organ*. . . . . (Ranwood)

Indiana
Oscar Peterson; *Digital At Montreux* . . . . (Pablo)
Oscar Peterson & Count Basie; *Grandmasters* . . . . (Pablo)
Timekeepers . . . . (Pablo)
Pete Fountain; *Best Of Pete Fountain* . . . . (MCA)
Live In New Orleans . . . . (First Warning)
Indiana Fight
Indiana University Marching 100; *Indiana Our Indiana* . . . . . . (Fidelity Sound)
Indiana University Marching 100 . . . . (Fidelity Sound)
Indiana Loyalty
Indiana University Marching 100; *Indiana Our Indiana* . . . . . . (Fidelity Sound)
Indiana My Indiana
Ohio State University Marching Band; *Saturday Afternoon At
Columbus* . . . . (Fidelity Sound)
Indiana Wants Me
R. Dean Taylor; *Hard-To-Find Motown Classics-#2-C* . . . .(Motown)
Super Hits Of The '70s-Have A Nice Day-#3-C . . . . (Rhino)
Super Hits-#5-C . . . . (Gusto)
Indiana, Our Indiana
Indiana University Marching 100; *Indiana Our Indiana* . . . . . . (Fidelity Sound)
Indiana University Marching 100 . . . . (Fidelity Sound)
Original Soundtrack; *College Fight Songs: The Big Ten-C* . . . . (K-Tel)
Jim Dean Of Indiana
Phil Ochs; *Chords Of Fame* . . . . (A&M)
Phil Ochs' Greatest Hits . . . . (A&M)
The War Is Over-Best Of Phil Ochs . . . . (A&M)
Mary Jane's Last Dance
Tom Petty And The Heartbreakers; *Playback* . . . . (MCA)
Tom Petty And The Heartbreakers' Greatest Hits . . . . (MCA)
Peaceful World
John Mellencamp; *Cuttin' Heads* . . . .(Columbia)
God Bless America-C . . . .(Columbia)
The Concert For New York City-C . . . .(Columbia)
Sweet Indiana Home
Aileen Stanley; *78-#18922*. . . . . (Victor)
Marion Harris; *78-#2310* . . . .(Brunswick)

STATES: IOWA

See Also: **CITIES: A-Z**

Iowa
Stone Soup; *October Nights*. . . . . (Windchime)
Iowa
Phoids; *The Phoids*. . . . .(NG)
Iowa
Spelunkers; *Breakfast Is America* . . . . (Whitehouse)
Iowa
Dar Williams; *Mortal City* . . . .(Razor & Tie)
Iowa Fight Song
Original Soundtrack; *College Fight Songs: The Big Ten-C* . . . .(K-Tel)
University Of Iowa Band; *Go Hawkeyes Go* . . . . (Fidelity Sound)
University Of Michigan Band; *Greatest College Football Marches* . .(Vanguard)
Iowa Lands
Robin Holcomb; *Rockabye* . . . . (Elektra Musician)
Iowa Stubborn
Original Cast; *The Music Man* . . . . (Gold Rush)
Robert Preston; *ST/The Music Man* . . . . (Warner Bros.)
Iowa Waltz
Greg Brown; *Iowa Waltz*. . . . .(Red House)
Jenny (Iowa Sunrise)
Janis Ian; *Night Trains* . . . .(Columbia)
Love Song For Iowa
Bonnie Koloc; *With You On My Side* . . . . (Flying Fish)
On Iowa
Original Soundtrack; *The Greatest College Fight Songs* . . . . (Laserlight)
University Of Iowa Marching Band; *Go Hawkeyes Go* . . . . (Fidelity Sound)
Sullivan
Caroline's Spine; *Monsoon* . . . .(Hollywood)

STATES: KANSAS

See Also: **CITIES: A-Z, CITIES: KANSAS CITY**

Cold Rain In Kansas
Don Lange; *Natural Born Heathen* . . . . (Flying Fish)
Devil Came From Kansas
Procol Harum; *A Salty Dog* . . . . (A&M)
Kansas Polka
Michigan Dutchmen; *New Polka Compositions*. . . . .(Jay Jay)
Kansas Wildcats
Band Of H.M. Royal Marines; *Hands Across The Sea-Sousa Marches* . . .(Angel)
Eastman Wind Ensemble; *Sousa On Review* . . . .(Mercury)
Stars And Stripes Forever . . . .(Mercury)

Kansas You Fooler
Ozark Mountain Daredevils; *It'll Shine When It Shines* . . . . (A&M)
King Of Kansas
Skywalk; *Fall Into Winter Jazz Sampler '88* . . . .(MCA)
No Mountains In The State Of Kansas
Reilly & Maloney; *Everyday* . . . . (Freckle)
Not In Kansas
Basehead; *Not In Kansas Anymore* . . . . (Imago)
Parsons, Kansas Blues
Bob Scobey's Frisco Band & Clancy Hayes; *Bob Scobey's Frisco Band & Clancy Hayes* . . . . (Good Time Jazz)
Rainmaker
Nilsson; *Harry* . . . .(Dunhill Compact Classics)
Rocky Road To Kansas
Tony Ellis; *Dixie Banner* . . . . (Flying Fish)
Way Out West In Kansas
Nimrod Workman; *The Land Of Yahoe: Children's Entertainment From The Days Before Television-C* . . . . (Rounder)
Wonderful Guy, A
Original Cast; *South Pacific* . . . .(CBS Masterworks)
You're Not In Kansas Anymore
Jo Dee Messina; *Jo Dee Messina* . . . . (Curb)

STATES: KENTUCKY

See Also: CITIES: A-Z

Back In Kentucky
Me; *International* . . . . (Priority)
Big Fat Woman
Leadbelly; *Bourgeois Blues-Golden Classics-#1* . . . . (Collectables)
Tom Rush; *Blues Songs & Ballads* . . . . (Fantasy)
Blue Kentucky Girl
Emmylou Harris; *Blue Kentucky Girl* . . . .(Warner Bros.)
Profile II-The Best Of Emmylou Harris . . . .(Warner Bros.)
Loretta Lynn; *Loretta Lynn's Greatest Hits* . . . .(MCA)
Blue Moon Of Kentucky
Bill Monroe; *American Originals-Bill Monroe* . . . . (Columbia)
Bean Blossom . . . .(MCA)
Best Of Bill Monroe & His Blue Grass Boys . . . .(MCA)
Bill Monroe & His Blue Grass Boys; *Bluegrass Super Hits-C* . . . . . . (Columbia)
Elvis Presley; *A Date With Elvis* . . . . (RCA)
A Golden Celebration . . . . (RCA)
The Sun Sessions . . . . (RCA)
Bowling Green
Everly Brothers; *Walk Right Back: The Everly Brothers On Warner Bros.- 1960-1969* . . . .(Warner Archives)
Bus Fare To Kentucky
Skeeter Davis; *Best Of The Best Of Skeeter Davis* . . . . (Gusto)
Cluckin' Hen, Going Back To Kentucky
J.P. Fraley & Annadeene; *Wild Rose Of The Mountain* . . . . (Rounder)
Country In My Jeans
Loretta Lynn; *Still Country* . . . .(Audium)
Down Home In Kentucky
Frankie Jaxon; *Frankie "Half-Pint" Jaxon-1927-1940* . . . . . .(Sony Broadway)
East Kentucky Mountains
Anne Hills; *Don't Panic (Panic Is On/Don't Explain)* . . . . (Hogeye)
Goin' Back To Old Kentucky
New Grass Revival; *Festival Tapes* . . . . (Flying Fish)
Green Kentucky Eyes
Pal Rakes; *Midnight Rain* . . . .(Atlantic America)
Hills Of Kentucky
Debby McClatchy & The Red Clay Ramblers; *Debby McClatchy & The Red Clay Ramblers* . . . .(Green Linnet)
Kendalls; *Kendalls* . . . . (Gusto)
I Am A Man Of Constant Sorrow
Ralph Stanley; *Rebel Records: 35 Years Of The Best In Bluegrass-1960- 1995-C* . . . .(Rebel)
Soggy Bottom Boys featuring Dan Tyminski; *ST/O Brother, Where Art Thou?* . . . . (Mercury)
Stanley Brothers; *All Time Legends Of Country Music-C* . . . . (Legacy)
I Can Hear Kentucky Calling Me
Chet Atkins; *Collector's Chet Atkins* . . . . (RCA)
I Wonder How The Old Folks Are At Home
Doc & Merle Watson; *Home Sweet Home* . . . . (Sugar Hill)
I'm Going Back To Kentucky
Greg Austin Band; *Greg Austin Band* . . . .(Xeres)
I'm Going Back To Old Kentucky
Bill Monroe; *Best Of Bill Monroe & His Blue Grass Boys* . . . .(MCA)
Bill Monroe And Flatt & Scruggs . . . . (Rounder)
Columbia Historic Edition-Bill Monroe . . . . (Columbia)
Bill Monroe & The Stars Of The Bluegrass Hall Of Fame; *Bill Monroe & The Stars Of The Bluegrass Hall Of Fame* . . . .(MCA)
Osborne Brothers; *Red, White & Bluegrass-C* . . . .(C.M.H. Prod.)
Kentuckian Song
Eddy Arnold; *Eddy Arnold-Legendary Performer* . . . . (RCA)

Kentucky
Everly Brothers; *All They Had To Do Was Dream* . . . . (Rhino)
Songs Our Daddy Taught Us . . . . (Rhino)
Gail Davies; *I'll Be There* . . . . (Warner Bros.)
Mac Wiseman; *Red, White & Bluegrass-C* . . . .(C.M.H. Prod.)
Osborne Brothers; *Best Of The Osborne Brothers* . . . . (MCA)
Whitstein Brothers; *Rose Of My Heart* . . . . (Rounder)
Kentucky Avenue
Tom Waits; *Blue Valentine* . . . .(Asylum)
Kentucky Avenue, A.C.
Duke Ellington; *Intimacy Of The Blues* . . . .(Fantasy)
Kentucky Bluebird
Keith Whitley; *Kentucky Bluebird* . . . . (RCA)
Kentucky Blues
Joy Ford; *45-#188* . . . .(Country Int'l)
Roy Bookbinder; *Goin' Back To Tampa* . . . . (Flying Fish)
Kentucky Flower
King Edward IV & The Knights; *45-#4635* . . . .(Soundwaves)
Kentucky Fried Blues
Nazareth; *Expect No Mercy* . . . . (A&M)
Kentucky Gambler
Merle Haggard & The Strangers; *Songs I'll Always Sing* . . . . (Capitol)
Kentucky Hills Of Tennessee
Commander Cody & His Lost Planet Airmen; *Hot Licks, Cold Steel & Trucker's Favorites* . . . . (MCA)
Kentucky Mandolin
Bill Monroe & His Blue Grass Boys; *Best Of Bill Monroe & His Blue Grass Boys* . . . . (MCA)
Kentucky Bluegrass . . . . (MCA)
Kentucky Means Paradise
Barbara Mandrell; *Vintage Barbara Mandrell* . . . . (Audiograph)
Roger Bellow & The Drifting Troubadours; *On The Road To Prosperity* . . . .(Flying Fish)
Kentucky Moonshine
Pure Prairie League; *Takin' The Stage* . . . . (RCA)
Two Lane Highway . . . . (RCA)
Kentucky Moonshiner
Dave Van Ronk; *Inside Dave Van Ronk* . . . .(Fantasy)
George Tucker; *George Tucker* . . . . (Rounder)
Kentucky Pool
John Hartford; *Headin' Down Into The Mystery Below* . . . . . (Flying Fish)
Kentucky Rain
Elvis Presley; *Elvis Presley-Pure Gold* . . . . (RCA)
Memphis Record . . . . (RCA)
Worldwide 50 Gold Award Hits, Vol. 1, Parts 1 & 2 . . . . (RCA)
Kentucky Slop Song
NRBQ; *Best Of NRBQ-Stay With Me* . . . . (Columbia)
Kentucky Song Bird
Roger Whittaker; *Mirrors Of My Mind* . . . . (RCA)
Kentucky Sunrise
Ringling Brothers B & B Band; *Circus Time* . . . . (MCA)
Kentucky Waltz
Bill Monroe; *Columbia Historic Edition-Bill Monroe* . . . . (Columbia)
Bill Monroe & Emmylou Harris; *Bill Monroe & Friends* . . . . (MCA)
Kentucky Woman
Deep Purple; *Purple Passages* . . . . (Warner Bros.)
When We Rock We Rock & When We Roll We Roll . . . . (Warner Bros.)
Gary Puckett And The Union Gap; *Gary Puckett And The Union Gap's Greatest Hits* . . . .(Bac-Trac)
Neil Diamond; *Love At The Greek* . . . . (Columbia)
Neil Diamond-Classics (Early Years) . . . . (Columbia)
Neil Diamond-Gold . . . . (MCA)
Kentucky Woman
Billy Cole Reed; *Audiograph Alive-C* . . . . (Audiograph)
Kentucky Woman
Ronnie Milsap; *Ronnie Milsap-16 Greatest Hits-#2* . . . .(Trip)
Meet Me Tonight By My Old Kentucky Home
Joe Val & The New England Bluegrass Boys; *Joe Val & The New England Bluegrass Boys-Vol. 2* . . . . (Rounder)
Message To Michael
Dionne Warwick; *Dionne Warwick* . . . . (Everest)
Dionne Warwick Greatest Hits . . . . (Everest)
Dionne Warwick-Anthology 1962-1971 . . . . (Rhino)
Hot! Live & Otherwise . . . . (Arista)
Original Rock 'N' Roll Hits Of The '60s-C . . . . (Roulette)
Moon Of Kentucky
Elvis Presley; *A Golden Celebration* . . . . (RCA)
My Ol' Kentucky Rock & Roll Home
Original New York Cast; *Oil City Symphony* . . . .(DRG)
My Old Kentucky Home
Al Jolson; *The Al Jolson Story-#5* . . . . (MCA)
Ry Cooder; *Ry Cooder* . . . . (Reprise)
Salli Terri; *Songs Of The American Land* . . . . (Angel)
My Rose Of Old Kentucky
Bill Monroe; *Bill Monroe & Friends* . . . . (MCA)
Bill Monroe & Flatt & Scruggs; *Bill Monroe And Flatt & Scruggs* . . . . (Rounder)
No Christmas In Kentucky
Phil Ochs; *Toast To Those Who Are Gone* . . . . (Rhino)

Nothin' But The Taillights
Clint Black; *Nothin' But The Taillights* . . . .(RCA)
Old Kentucky Fiddle
Hoot Hester; *45-#114* . . . .(Nationwide Sound Distrib.)
Old Kentucky Home
Randy Newman; *12 Songs* . . . .(Reprise)
Randy Newman/Live . . . . (Warner Archives)
Old Kentucky Land
Kingston Trio; *Rediscovering The Kingston Trio* . . . . (Folk Era)
Tune Up! . . . . (Folk Era)
Old Kentucky Song
Oak Ridge Boys; *Bobbie Sue* . . . . (MCA)
On The Old Kentucky Shore
J.D. Crowe & Others; *Bluegrass Album-#5-Sweet Sunny South* . . . . . . (Rounder)
One Piece At A Time
Johnny Cash; *The Man In Black-His Greatest Hits* . . . . (Legacy)
Roll Along, Kentucky Moon
Jimmie Rodgers; *Down The Old Road-1931-1932* . . . . (Rounder)
Leon Redbone; *Sugar* . . . . (Private Music)
Somewhere In Kentucky
Charlie Bandy; *45-#4611* . . . . (Soundwaves)
Sweet Kentucky Ham
David Frishberg; *Can't Take You Nowhere* . . . .(Fantasy)
David Frishberg-Classics . . . . (Concord Jazz)
Take Me Back To Kentucky
Cross Country Grass; *Tribute To Bluegrass* . . . . (Boot)
Tuck Me To Sleep In My Old Kentucky Home
Firehouse Five Plus Two; *Goes South* . . . .(Good Time Jazz)
Turn Your Radio On, Kentucky
Blue Sky Boys; *Sunny Side Of Life* . . . . (Rounder)
Wild Kentucky Roan
Mike Auldridge; *Mike Auldridge & Old Dog* . . . .(Flying Fish)
Wild Kentucky Skies
Marty Brown; *Wild Kentucky Skies* . . . . (MCA)

STATES: LOUISIANA

See Also: *CITIES: A-Z, CITIES: NEW ORLEANS*

Adalida
George Strait; *Latest Greatest Straitest Hits* . . . . (MCA)
Lead On . . . . (MCA)
Blues From Louisiana
Illinois Jacquet & His Big Band; *Jacquet's Got It* . . . . (Atlantic)
Born In Louisiana
Clarence "Gatemouth" Brown; *Alligator Records 20th Anniversary
Collection-C* . . . .(Alligator)
Standing My Ground . . . .(Alligator)
Born In Louisiana
Troy Turner; *Handful Of Aces* . . . . (Ichiban Int'l)
By-U, By-O (The Lou'siana Lullaby)
Woody Herman; *Woody Herman-Best Of The Decca Years* . . . . (Decca)
Cannibals
Mark Knopfler; *Golden Heart* . . . . (Warner Bros.)
Down At The Twist And Shout
Mary Chapin Carpenter; *Greatest Country Hits Of The '90s-
1992-C* . . . .(Columbia)
Hitchhiker Examplar 2-C . . . .(Columbia)
Shooting Straight In The Dark . . . .(Columbia)
Today's Hot Country-C . . . . (K-Tel)
Down In Louisiana
Whites; *Whole New World* . . . . (MCA)
Give My Love To Rose
George Jones; *George Jones Sings The Hits Of His Country
Cousins* . . . . (Razor & Tie)
Johnny Cash; *Johnny Cash-Sun Years* . . . .(Rhino)
Goin' Down Louisiana
Blues Project; *No Time Like The Right Time-Best Of The Blues
Project* . . . .(Rhino)
Going Back To Louisiana
Delbert McClinton; *Live From Austin* . . . .(Alligator)
Joey Farr; *45-#105* . . . . (Fairview)
Going Home To Louisiana
Chris Thomas; *The Beginning* . . . . (Arhoolie)
Going To Louisiana
John Lee Hooker; *Berkeley Blues Festival* . . . . (Arhoolie)
That's Where It's At . . . . (Stax)
Good Ole Boys From Louisiana
Jimmy C. Newman & Cajun Country; *Jimmy C. Newman & Cajun
Country* . . . . (Dot)
Home In Louisiana
Country Gentlemen; *Home In Louisiana* . . . .(Vanguard)
Remembrances & Forecasts . . . .(Vanguard)
In A State Of Louisiana
Roddie Romero & The Rockin' Cajuns; *Da Big Squeeze* . . . .(Swallow)
It's Christmastime In Louisiana
Johnnie Allan; *Alligator Stomp-#4-Cajun Christmas-C* . . . .(Rhino)

Johnny B. Goode
Chuck Berry; *Chuck Berry's Greatest Hits* . . . .(Everest)
Classic Rock-#2-C . . . . (MCA)
Roll Over Beethoven . . . .(Allegiance)
ST/American Graffiti . . . . (MCA)
The Chess Box-Chuck Berry . . . .(Chess)
Elvis Presley; *Elvis In Concert* . . . . (RCA)
From Memphis To Vegas/From Vegas To Memphis . . . . (RCA)
Grateful Dead; *Bill Graham Presents The Last Days Of The
Fillmore-C* . . . .(Epic Portrait Assoc.)
Johnny Winter; *Live/Johnny Winter And* . . . . (Columbia)
Second Winter . . . .(Columbia)
La Louisianne
Queen Ida; *On Tour* . . . .(Crescendo)
Queen Ida & Her Bon Temps Zydeco Band; *In New Orleans* . . . . . . (Crescendo)
Leaving Louisiana In The Broad Daylight
Emmylou Harris; *Quarter Moon In A Ten Cent Town* . . . .(Warner Bros.)
Oak Ridge Boys; *Have Arrived* . . . . (MCA)
Oak Ridge Boys' Greatest Hits . . . . (MCA)
Rodney Crowell; *Ain't Living Long Like This* . . . .(Warner Bros.)
Rodney Crowell-Collection . . . .(Warner Bros.)
Louisiana
Count Basie; *Essential Count Basie-#2* . . . . (Columbia)
Jimmy C. Newman; *Cajun Country* . . . .(Delmark)
John Wesley Ryles; *Reconsider Me* . . . . (Plantation)
Louisiana 1927
Aaron Neville; *Warm Your Heart* . . . . (A&M)
Jo-el Sonnier; *Come On Joe* . . . . (RCA)
Randy Newman; *Good Old Boys* . . . . (Reprise)
ST/Blaze . . . . (A&M)
Louisiana Anna
Maines Brothers Band; *High Rollin'* . . . .(Mercury)
Louisiana Blues
Clifton Chenier; *Alligator Stomp-Cajun & Zydeco Classics-C* . . . .(Rhino)
Louisiana Blues & Zydeco . . . . (Arhoolie)
Jo-el Sonnier; *Louisiana Scrapbook-C* . . . .(Rykodisc)
Muddy Waters; *Best Of Muddy Waters* . . . .(Chess)
The Chess Box-Muddy Waters . . . .(Chess)
Savoy Brown; *Savoy Brown-London Collector* . . . . (London)
Louisiana Bound
Big Joe Williams; *Shake Your Boogie* . . . . (Arhoolie)
Louisiana Cajun Band
Jimmy C. Newman; *Backstage At The Grand Ole Opry-C* . . . . (RCA)
Cajun Country . . . .(Delmark)
Louisiana Cajun Rock Band
Carol Channing & Jimmy C. Newman; *Carol Channing & Her Country
Friends* . . . . (Plantation)
Louisiana Christmas Day
Aaron Neville; *Soulful Christmas* . . . . (A&M)
Louisiana Fais Dodo
Charlie Daniels Band; *Me & The Boys* . . . . (Epic)
Louisiana Flood
Paul Butterfield's Better Days; *It All Comes Back* . . . .(Rhino)
Louisiana Hannah
Webb Wilder; *Hybrid Vigor* . . . .(Island)
Louisiana Hayride
Boswell Sisters; *That's How Rhythm Was Born* . . . .(Legacy)
Louisiana Joe
Joe Douglas; *45-#1005* . . . . (Bellaire)
Louisiana Lady
New Riders Of The Purple Sage; *Best Of New Riders Of The
Purple Sage* . . . .(Columbia)
New Riders Of The Purple Sage . . . .(Columbia)
Louisiana Lonely
Narvel Felts; *45-#114* . . . . (GMC)
Louisiana Lou & Three-Card Monty John
Allman Brothers Band; *Win, Lose Or Draw* . . . .(Polydor)
Louisiana Man
Doug Kershaw; *Alive & Pickin'* . . . .(Warner Bros.)
Best Of Doug Kershaw . . . .(Warner Bros.)
Louisiana Man . . . .(Warner Bros.)
Louisiana Man
Dave Edmunds; *D.E. 7th* . . . .(Columbia)
Louisiana Rain
Tom Petty; *Playback* . . . . (MCA)
Tom Petty And The Heartbreakers; *Damn The Torpedoes* . . . . (MCA)
Louisiana Road Song
Tish Hinojosa; *Culture Swing* . . . .(Rounder)
Louisiana Saturday Night
Don Williams; *Best Of Cajun Country-C* . . . . (Era)
Best Of Don Williams-#4 . . . . (MCA)
Don Williams-Country Boy . . . . (MCA)
Jimmy C. Newman; *From The Vaults: Decca Country Classics-1934-
1973-C* . . . .(Decca)
Grand Ole Opry-75 Years-#2-C . . . . (MCA)
Progressive CC . . . . (Plantation)
Mel McDaniel; *Mel McDaniel's Greatest Hits* . . . . (Capitol)
Louisiana Stomp
Clifton Chenier; *Zydeco-#1-The Early Years (1961-1962)-C* . . . . (Arhoolie)

Louisiana Sun
Doug Kershaw; *Louisiana Man* . . . .(Warner Bros.)
  Wichita Wildcat . . . . (Fifty One West)
Louisiana Sunday Afternoon
Diane Schuur; *Diane Schuur-Collection* . . . . (GRP)
  Talkin' 'Bout You . . . . (GRP)
Louisiana Two-Step
Clifton Chenier; *King Of Zydeco Live At Montreux* . . . . (Arhoolie)
  Out West . . . . (Arhoolie)
Louisiana Woman
Catfish Hodge; *Bout With The Blues* . . . .(Adelphi)
R.G. & Bayou Zydeco; *Fire On The Bayou* . . . .(Takoma)
Rockin' Tabby Thomas; *King Of Swamp Blues* . . . . (Maison De Soul)
Louisiana Woman, Mississippi Man
Loretta Lynn & Conway Twitty; *Louisiana Woman Mississippi Man* . . . .(MCA)
  Very Best Of Loretta Lynn & Conway Twitty . . . .(MCA)
Louisiana Women
J.J. Cale; *Really* . . . . (Mercury)
Wayne Stewart; *Aspen Skyline* . . . . (Briar)
Louisiana Zydeco
Clarence "Gatemouth" Brown; *Standing My Ground* . . . . (Alligator)
Louisiana, The Key To My Soul
Jimmy C. Newman; *Jimmy C. Newman* . . . . (Dot)
My Louisiana Love
Bill Monroe & Mel Tillis; *Bill Monroe & Friends* . . . .(MCA)
Oh Louisiana
Pete Seeger; *Pete Seeger-Complete Carnegie Hall Concert-1963* . . . (Columbia)
Oh, Susanna
Disneyland Cast; *Children's Favorite Songs-#1* . . . .(Disney)
James Taylor; *Sweet Baby James* . . . .(Warner Bros.)
Myron Floren; *Best Of The Wurstfest* . . . .(Ranwood)
  Myron Floren . . . .(Ranwood)
One More Time
Seals & Crofts; *Takin' It Easy* . . . .(Warner Bros.)
Polly-Wolly-Doodle
Leon Redbone; *Live!* . . . . (Pair)
  On The Track . . . .(Warner Bros.)
Mance Lipscomb; *Mance Lipscomb-Vol. 3-Texas Songster In A Live
  Performance* . . . . (Arhoolie)
Pete Seeger/Woody Guthrie/Cisco Houston; *Lonesome
  Valley* . . . . (Smithsonian Folkways)
Ragin' Cajun
Charlie Daniels Band; *Windows* . . . .(Epic)
Sweet Louisiana
Charlie Daniels Band; *Saddle Tramp* . . . .(Epic)
  Volunteer Jam 3 & 4 . . . .(Epic)
Telephone Road
Steve Earle; *Alt. Country-C* . . . . (Simitar)
  El Corazon . . . . (E Squared)
That Was Your Mother
Paul Simon; *Graceland* . . . .(Warner Bros.)

STATES: MAINE

See Also: CITIES: A-Z

Back In Maine
Neal Davis; *Warm Places* . . . .(Creative Energy Prod.)
Farewell To Maine
Paul Sullivan; *Sketches Of Maine* . . . . (River Music)
From Maine To Mexico
Leon Russell; *Americana* . . . . (Paradise)
Maine
Original Broadway Cast; *No Strings* . . . . (Angel)
Reach, The
Dan Fogelberg; *Innocent Age* . . . . (Full Moon)
Stein Song (University Of Maine)
Rudy Vallee & His Connecticut Yankees; *Billboard Pop Memories-The
  1930s-C* . . . . (Rhino)
  Heigh-Ho Everybody: This Is Rudy Vallee . . . . (Rhino)
  Those Wonderful Years: Puttin' On The Ritz-C . . . . (JCI Assoc. Labels)
University Of Michigan Band; *Greatest College Football Marches* . (Vanguard)
Sweet Woman (From Maine)
Robert Lockwood, Jr.; *Blues Masters-#2-Post-War Chicago Blues-C* . . . (Rhino)
Winter In Maine
Bruce Fowler; *Ants Can Count* . . . . (Terra Nova)

STATES: MARYLAND

See Also: CITIES: A-Z, CITIES: BALTIMORE

Dancing In Rackville, Maryland
Fred Frith; *Gravity* . . . . (Ralph)
Maryland
Vonda Shepard; *ST/Songs From "Ally McBeal" Featuring Vonda
  Shepard* . . . . (550/Epic)

Maryland, My Maryland
Eastman Wind Ensemble; *Music Of The Civil War* . . . . (Mercury)
Tennessee Ernie Ford; *Tennessee Ernie Ford Sings Songs Of The
  Civil War* . . . . (Capitol)

STATES: MASSACHUSETTS

See Also: CITIES: A-Z, CITIES: BOSTON

Massachusetts
Bee Gees; *Bee Gees-Gold* . . . .(Polydor)
  Here At Last...Bee Gees...Live . . . .(Polydor)
Massachusetts
Mystic Moods Orchestra; *English Muffins* . . . . (Bainbridge)
Massachusetts
Stewart Brodian; *Self-Made Man* . . . . (Mountain)
Massachusetts
Ed Ames; *Who Will Answer/My Cup Runneth Over* . . . . (Collectables)
Massachusetts
Ladybug Transistor; *Oh, Merge!-C* . . . .(Merge)
Massachusetts
Anita O'Day; *Let Me Off Uptown* . . . . (Legacy)
Massachusetts
Insect Surfers; *Listen And Learn With Vibro-Phonic* . . . . (Vibro-Phonic)
Massachusetts
Maxine Sullivan; *A Tribute To Andy Razaf* . . . . (Decca Jazz)
Massachusetts
Greg Greenway; *A Road Worth Walking Down* . . . . (Eastern Front)
Massachusetts
Scud Mountain Boys; *Massachusetts* . . . . (Sub Pop)
Massachusetts
Arlo Guthrie; *All Over The World* . . . . (Rising Son)
  Soft Rock Classics-C . . . . (Rhino)
Massachusetts Morning
Peter Gordon; *The Long Way Home* . . . .(Positive)
Old Cape Cod
Patti Page; *Patti Page-16 Most Requested Songs* . . . . (Legacy)
  Patti Page-Golden Hits . . . . (Mercury)
  Patti Page's Greatest Hits . . . . (Columbia)

STATES: MICHIGAN

See Also: CITIES: A-Z, CITIES: DETROIT

America
David Bowie; *The Concert For New York City-C* . . . . (Columbia)
Paul Simon; *Paul Simon In Concert/Live Rhymin'* . . . . (Columbia)
Simon & Garfunkel; *Bookends* . . . . (Columbia)
  Collected Works . . . . (Columbia)
  Simon & Garfunkel's Greatest Hits . . . . (Columbia)
  The Concert In Central Park . . . . (Warner Bros.)
I Want To Go Back To Michigan
Judy Garland; *ST/Easter Parade* . . . . (Rhino)
M.S.U. Fight Song
Michigan State University Band; *Michigan State
  University Band* . . . . (Fidelity Sound)
Original Soundtrack; *College Fight Songs: The Big Ten-C* . . . . (K-Tel)
Man From Michigan
Caustic Resin; *The Medicine Is All Gone* . . . .(Alias)
Michigan Blackhawk
Monkees; *Missing Links-#2* . . . . (Rhino)
Michigan Rain
Gregg Alexander; *Intoxifornication* . . . . (Epic Portrait Assoc.)
Michigan State Fight Song
University Of Michigan Band; *Greatest College Football Marches* . . (Vanguard)
Michigan Stomps
Willie Jones & His Orchestra; *Territory Bands-#2-1927-1931-C* . . . . (Historical)
Michigan Water
Gregory Hines/Original Cast; *Jelly's Last Jam* . . . . (Mercury)
Michigan Water Blues
Little Brother Montgomery & Others; *Chicago Breakdown* . . . . (Takoma)
Michigander Blues
Jabbo Smith; *Jazz Heritage-Ace Of Rhythm* . . . . (MCA)
Panther In Michigan
Michael Smith; *Michael Smith* . . . .(Flying Fish)
Saginaw, Michigan
Lefty Frizzell; *American Originals-Lefty Frizzell* . . . . (Columbia)
  Billboard Top Country Hits-1964-C . . . . (Rhino)
  Columbia Country Classics-#3-Americana-C . . . . (Columbia)
  Lefty Frizzell's Greatest Hits . . . . (Columbia)
Sky Over Michigan
Harmony Sisters; *Harmony Pie* . . . . (Flying Fish)
Victors, The
Ohio State University Marching Band; *Music For Cheerleaders & Song
  Girls* . . . . (Fidelity Sound)

Saturday Afternoon At Columbus . . . . (Fidelity Sound)
Original Soundtrack; *College Fight Songs: The Big Ten-C* . . . . (K-Tel)
The Greatest College Fight Songs . . . . (Laserlight)
Top Ten College Fight Songs . . . . (K-Tel)
University Of Michigan Band; *41 Great College Victory Songs* . . . . . (Vanguard)

STATES: MINNESOTA

See Also: **CITIES: A-Z**

Akapolka, Minnesota
Andy Badale & The Beer Garden Band; *Nashville Beer Garden* . . . . (Ranwood)
Biggest Ball Of Twine In Minnesota
"Weird Al" Yankovic; *ST/UHF & Other Stuff* . . . . (Scotti Bros.)
God Bless The USA
Lee Greenwood; *American Patriot* . . . . (Capitol)
God Bless America-C . . . . (Columbia)
God Bless The USA . . . . (MCA Special Prod.)
Inside Out/You've Got A Good Love Comin' . . . . (MCA)
Lee Greenwood's Greatest Hits . . . . (MCA)
Lee Greenwood's Greatest Hits-#2 . . . . (MCA)
Today's Country Classics-C . . . . (MCA Special Prod.)
Minnesota
Detroit Concert Band; *Sousa American Bicentennial Collection* . . . . (H&L)
George Russell; *Snake River* . . . . (Green Linnet)
Minnesota
Push Stars; *After The Party* . . . . (Capitol)
Minnesota
Mountain Goats; *Full Force Galesburg* . . . . (Emperor Jones)
Minnesota
Converge; *Split CD* . . . . (Relapse)
Minnesota Girl
American Girls; *Welcome To Our Love Sick Porch* . . . . (Manifesto)
Minnesota Man Claims Monkey Bowled Perfect Game
Jad Fair; *Strange But True* . . . . (Matador)
Minnesota Massage
Mount Shasta; *Who's The Hottie* . . . . (Skin Graft)
Minnesota Medley
Los Lobos; *ST/Feeling Minnesota* . . . . (Atlantic)
Minnesota Rouser
Ohio State University Marching Band; *Stadium Favorites In Brass* . . . . (Fidelity Sound)
Original Soundtrack; *College Fight Songs: The Big Ten-C* . . . . (K-Tel)
Top Ten College Fight Songs . . . . (K-Tel)
Minnesota Strip
Dictators; *Live-F..k 'Em If They Can't Take A Joke* . . . . (Roir)
New York Rockers-C . . . . (Roir)
Fallen Angel; *Go For The Ride* . . . . (MCA)
My Heart Cries For You
Charlie Rich; *Charlie Rich-20 Golden Hits* . . . . (Sun)
Time For Tears-C . . . . (Sun)
Dinah Shore; *Nipper's Greatest Hits Of The '50s-#1-C* . . . . (RCA)
Guy Mitchell; *Guy Mitchell-16 Most Requested Songs* . . . . (Legacy)
Senator From Minnesota
Michael Tilson Thomas; *Of Thee I Sing/Let 'Em Eat Cake* . . . . (Columbia)

STATES: MISSISSIPPI

See Also: **CITIES: A-Z, DIRECTIONS: SOUTH**

Back In Mississippi
Elmore James; *King Of The Slide Guitar* . . . . (Capricorn)
Born In Mississippi
Chris LeDoux; *Wild & Wooly* . . . . (Liberty)
Down In Mississippi
Pops Staples; *Peace In The Neighborhood* . . . . (Point Blank/Virgin)
Roy Rogers; *Slidewinder* . . . . (Blind Pig)
Ry Cooder; *ST/Crossroads* . . . . (Warner Bros.)
Far East Mississippi
Ohio Players; *Ohio Players-Gold* . . . . (Mercury)
Freedom Riders
Phil Ochs; *Best Of Broadside 1962-1968: Anthems Of The American Underground From The Pages Of Broadside Magazine-C* . . . . (Smithsonian Folkways)
Going Down To Mississippi
Phil Ochs; *Toast To Those Who Are Gone* . . . . (Rhino)
Handcuffed To A Fence In Mississippi
Jim White; *No Such Place* . . . . (Luaka Bop)
Here's To The State Of Mississippi
Phil Ochs; *I Ain't Marching Anymore* . . . . (Carthage)
There But For Fortune . . . . (Elektra)
I'm From Mississippi
Luther "Guitar Jr." Johnson & His Magic Rockers; *I Want To Groove With You* . . . . (Bullseye Blues)

Living For The City
Stevie Wonder; *Innervisions* . . . . (Motown)
Original Musiquarium . . . . (Motown)
Louisiana Woman, Mississippi Man
Loretta Lynn & Conway Twitty; *Louisiana Woman Mississippi Man* . . . . (MCA)
Very Best Of Loretta Lynn & Conway Twitty . . . . (MCA)
Mississippi
Duke Ellington; *Jubilee Stomp* . . . . (Bluebird)
Kay Starr; *Capitol Collectors Series-Kay Starr* . . . . (Capitol)
Mississippi
Bob Dylan; *"Love And Theft"* . . . . (Columbia)
Sheryl Crow; *The Globe Sessions* . . . . (A&M)
Mississippi
Charlie Daniels Band; *Million Mile Reflections* . . . . (Epic)
M-I-S-S-I-S-S-I-P-P-I
Frances White; *Music From The New York Stage (1890-1920)-#4-1917-1920-C* . . . . (Pearl)
Mississippi Goddam
Nina Simone; *Best Of Broadside 1962-1968: Anthems Of The American Underground From The Pages Of Broadside Magazine-C* . . . . (Smithsonian Folkways)
Mississippi Half-Step Uptown Toodeloo
Grateful Dead; *Steal Your Face* . . . . (Grateful Dead)
Wake Of The Flood . . . . (Grateful Dead)
Without A Net . . . . (Arista)
Mississippi Kid
Lynyrd Skynyrd; *Pronounced Leh-nerd Skin-nerd* . . . . (MCA)
Mississippi Lady
Jim Croce; *Down The Highway* . . . . (Atlantic)
Mississippi Moon
Jimmie Rodgers; *Down The Old Road-1931-1932* . . . . (Rounder)
Jimmie Rodgers-Early Years-1928-1929 . . . . (Rounder)
Mississippi Moon
Jerry Garcia; *Compliments* . . . . (Grateful Dead)
Mississippi Moon
Seatrain; *Marblehead Messenger* . . . . (One Way)
Mississippi Moon
Greg Brown; *One More Goodnight Kiss* . . . . (Red House)
Mississippi Mud
Bob Crosby & His Orchestra; *1952-1953* . . . . (Hindsight)
Bob Crosby & His Orchestra Play 22 Original Big Band Hits . . . . (Hindsight)
Mississippi Queen
Mountain; *Best Of Mountain* . . . . (Columbia)
Heavy Metal Memories-C . . . . (Rhino)
Twin Peaks . . . . (Columbia)
Mississippi Squirrel Revival
Ray Stevens; *Country Classics-#1-C* . . . . (Universal)
He Thinks He's Ray Stevens . . . . (MCA)
Ray Stevens' Greatest Hits . . . . (MCA)
Mississippi Summer
Si Kahn; *Doing My Job* . . . . (Flying Fish)
Mississippi Woman
Willie Nelson; *Longhorn Jamboree* . . . . (Plantation)
Willie Nelson & His Friends . . . . (Plantation)
Mississippi, You're On My Mind
Jerry Jeff Walker; *Ridin' High* . . . . (MCA)
Jesse Winchester; *Best Of Jesse Winchester* . . . . (Rhino)
Mister & Mississippi
Patti Page; *Patti Page's Greatest Hits* . . . . (Columbia)
Muddy Water
Keb' Mo'; *Slow Down* . . . . (550/Epic/Okeh)
My Head's In Mississippi
ZZ Top; *Recycler* . . . . (Warner Bros.)
ZZ Top's Greatest Hits . . . . (Warner Bros.)
Peace In Mississippi
Jimi Hendrix; *Crash Landing* . . . . (Reprise)
Riding With The King
B.B. King & Eric Clapton; *Riding With The King* . . . . (Duck/Reprise)
Skippin' In The Mississippi Dew
John Hartford; *John Hartford-Anthology* . . . . (Flying Fish)
Mark Twang . . . . (Flying Fish)
New Grass Revival; *Fly Through The Country* . . . . (Flying Fish)
There Ain't No Good Chain Gang
Johnny Cash & Waylon Jennings; *Country's Greatest Hits-#15-Outlaw Country-C* . . . . (Priority)
Hot Country Rock-#1-C . . . . (Epic)
Johnny Cash-16 Biggest Hits-#2 . . . . (Legacy)
The Man In Black-His Greatest Hits . . . . (Legacy)
Tupelo Mississippi Flash
Jerry Reed; *Best Of Jerry Reed* . . . . (RCA)

STATES: MISSOURI

See Also: **CITIES: A-Z, CITIES: KANSAS CITY, CITIES: ST. LOUIS**

Missouri
Paul Smith; *Mysterious Barricades* . . . . (Flying Fish)

Missouri
Tirez Tirez; *Against All Flags*..................................(PMRC)
Missouri Loves Company
Art Essery; *Missouri Loves Company-45* ....(AMI)
Missouri Squabble
Alex Jackson Plantation; *Territory Bands-#2-1927-1931-C* .... (Historical)
Missouri Uncompromised
Pat Metheny; *Bright Size Life* ....(ECM)
Missouri Waltz
Mom & Dads; *Mom & Dads-20 Favorite Waltzes* ....(Crescendo)
Mom & Dads-Again.................................(Crescendo)
Wish We Were Back In Missouri
Emmylou Harris; *Legend Of Jesse James-C*....................(A&M)

STATES: MONTANA

See Also: CITIES: A-Z

Big City
Merle Haggard; *For The Record: Merle Haggard-43 Legendary Hits* .... (BNA)
Blue Rock Montana/Red Headed Stranger
Willie Nelson; *Red Headed Stranger* ....(Columbia)
Cut Bank Montana
Hank Williams, Jr.; *Maverick*..............................(Capricorn)
Dynamics For Montana
Joachim Kuhn; *Dynamics*......................... (Creative Music Prod.)
Goodbye Montana
George Winston; *Summer*..............................(Windham Hill)
Long Legged Hannah (From Butte, Montana)
Jesse Hunter; *A Man Like Me* ....(BNA)
Meet Me In Montana
Dan Seals & Marie Osmond; *Best Of Dan Seals*..................(Capitol)
Won't Be Blue Anymore ....(EMI)
Marie Osmond & Dan Seals; *Country Duets Two By Two-C* .... (Capitol)
There's No Stopping Your Heart ....(Curb)
Montana
Frank Zappa; *You Can't Do That On Stage Anymore-#3* ......(Rykodisc)
Mothers Of Invention; *Apostrophe/Overnite Sensation* ....(Rykodisc)
Montana Cafe
Hank Williams, Jr.; *Montana Cafe* .... (WB/Curb)
Montana Cowboy
Emmylou Harris & The Nash Ramblers; *At The Ryman* ....(Reprise)
Hot Rize; *Traditional Ties* ....(Sugar Hill)
Montana Crossing
John Stewart; *Centennial* .... (Homecoming)
Montana Half Light
Philip Aaberg; *High Plains*..............................(Windham Hill)
Windham Hill-First Ten Years-C......................(Windham Hill)
Montana Plains
Moonshine Kate & Others; *Banjo Pickin' Girls* .... (Rounder)
Montana Rodeo
Chris LeDoux; *Thirty-Dollar Cowboy* .... (Liberty)
Montana Skies
James Galway; *Wayward Wind* .... (RCA)
Montana Song
Hank Williams, Jr.; *Hank Williams, Jr. & Friends*................(Polydor)
Living Proof-MGM Recordings 1963-1975..............(Mercury)
Montana Waltz
Ian Tyson; *Old Corrals & Sagebrush* ....(Columbia)
Two Rivers In Montana
Gove Scrivenor; *Coconut Gove* .... (Flying Fish)
Twodot Montana
Hank Williams, Jr.; *Strong Stuff* ....(Warner Bros.)
View From Pony, Montana
Philip Aaberg; *Upright*...............................(Windham Hill)
Wild Montana Skies
John Denver; *It's About Time* .... (RCA)
John Denver's Greatest Hits-#3 .... (RCA)
John Denver & Emmylou Harris; *Collector's Series-Duets-C* .... (RCA)

STATES: NEBRASKA

See Also: CITIES: A-Z

Dear Old Nebraska U.
University Of Michigan Band; *Greatest College Football Marches* . (Vanguard)
Hail Varsity
Original Soundtrack; *The Greatest College Fight Songs* .... (Laserlight)
Hazard (The River)
Richard Marx; *Rush Street* .... (Capitol)
Nebraska
Bruce Springsteen; *Nebraska* ....(Columbia)
Bruce Springsteen & The E Street Band; *Bruce Springsteen & The E Street Band Live/1975-85* ....(Legacy)

Omaha, Nebraska
Doug Mathews; *Legacy II* .... (High Street)
Plains Of Nebrasky-O
Eric Andersen & Phil Ochs; *Best Of Broadside 1962-1968: Anthems Of The American Underground From The Pages Of Broadside Magazine-C*...............................(Smithsonian Folkways)
Wildfire
Michael Martin Murphey; *'70s Greatest Rock Hits-#3-High Times-C* .. (Priority)
Best Of Michael Martin Murphey..........................(Liberty)
Blue Sky-Night Thunder .... (Epic)
Super Hits Of The '70s-Have A Nice Day-#14-C ....(Rhino)

STATES: NEVADA

See Also: CITIES: A-Z, CITIES: LAS VEGAS

Dime Queen Of Nevada
Tom Jones; *Darlin'* ....(Mercury)
Nevada Fighter
Michael Nesmith; *Older Stuff* .... (Rhino)
Nevada Smith
Mystic Moods Orchestra; *Nighttide* .... (Bainbridge)
Nevada, California
Jayhawks; *Hollywood Town Hall* ....(Def American)
Reno, Nevada
Ian Matthews; *Circle Dance-Hokey Pokey Charity-C*......... (Green Linnet)
Mimi & Richard Farina; *Best Of Mimi & Richard Farina*......... (Vanguard)
Celebrations For A Grey Day........................ (Vanguard)
Troubadours Of The Folk Era-#1-C .... (Rhino)
Sands Of Nevada
Mark Knopfler; *Sailing To Philadelphia* .... (Warner Bros.)
Stop In Nevada
Billy Joel; *Piano Man* ....(Columbia)

STATES: NEW HAMPSHIRE

See Also: CITIES: A-Z

Aye, New Hampshire
White Mountain Singers; *We The People-C* .... (Folk Era)
It's Called New Hampshire
White Mountain Singers; *Best Of The White Mountain Singers* ...... (Folk Era)
Sunrise .... (Takoma)
New Hampshire Hornpipe
Erich Kunzel & Cincinnati Pops Orchestra; *Sailing* ....(Telarc)
James Galway; *Beauty & The Beast-Galway At The Movies*...........(RCA)
New Hampshire Naturally
Shaw Brothers; *Shaw Brothers-Collection* .... (Folk Era)
Thing At The End Of New Hampshire Avenue
John Fahey; *Old Girlfriends And Other Horrible Memories*........(Varrick)

STATES: NEW JERSEY

See Also: CITIES: A-Z

Jersey Bounce
Benny Goodman; *Benny Goodman-Live At Carnegie Hall*..........(London)
Hits Of Benny Goodman.................................(Capitol)
Jersey Girl
Bruce Springsteen & The E Street Band; *Bruce Springsteen & The E Street Band Live/1975-85* ....(Legacy)
Tom Waits; *Heartattack & Vine* ....(Asylum)
Tom Waits-Anthology.................................(Asylum)
Living On The Edge Of The World
Bruce Springsteen; *Tracks* ....(Columbia)
New Jersey
Red House Painters; *Red House Painters* ....(4AD)
New Jersey Roadbase
Johnboy; *Pistolswing* .... (Trance Syndicate)
New Jersey Turnpike
Laurie Anderson; *United States Live* .... (Warner Bros.)
On Jersey Shore
Paragon Ragtime Orchestra; *On The Boardwalk*..........(Newport Classic)
Open All Night
Bruce Springsteen; *Nebraska* ....(Columbia)
Rosey From Jersey
Li'l Wally; *I Love To Polka* .... (Jay Jay)
State Trooper
Bruce Springsteen; *Nebraska* ....(Columbia)

The Sopranos-Music From The HBO Original
Series . . . .(Sony Music Soundtrax)

STATES: NEW MEXICO

See Also: **CITIES: A-Z, CITIES: SANTA FE**

Billy The Kid
Marty Robbins; *Gunfighter Ballads & Trail Songs* . . . . (Legacy)
El Paso
Grateful Dead; *Steal Your Face* . . . .(Grateful Dead)
Marty Robbins; *Billboard Top Country Hits-1960-C* . . . . (Rhino)
Gunfighter Ballads & Trail Songs . . . . (Legacy)
Marty Robbins' Biggest Hits . . . . (Columbia)
Radio Classics Of The '50s-C . . . . (Columbia)
Texas Super Hits-C . . . . (Columbia)
Hail New Mexico
Original Soundtrack; *The Greatest College Fight Songs* . . . .(Laserlight)
New Mexican Rose
4 Seasons; *25th Anniversary Collection* . . . . (Rhino)
New Mexican Waltz
Frank Fischer; *Tales Of Mullumbimby* . . . . (Innovative Comm.)
New Mexico
Johnny Cash; *Get Rhythm* . . . .(Sun)
The Man-The World-His Music . . . .(Sun)
New Mexico
Erich Avinger; *Si* . . . .(Heart Music Inc.)
New Mexico March
Eastman Wind Ensemble; *Sousa On Review* . . . . (Mercury)
Stars And Stripes Forever . . . . (Mercury)
New Mexico-Suite 2
Scott Moulton; *Four Corners Suite* . . . . (Revere)
Tomb Of The Unknown Love (Taos, New Mexico)
Cassell Webb; *Songs Of A Stranger* . . . . (Venture)
Kenny Rogers; *The Heart Of The Matter* . . . .(RCA)

STATES: NEW YORK

See Also: **CITIES: A-Z, CITIES: NEW YORK**

New York State Of Mind
Barbra Streisand; *Memories* . . . . (Columbia)
Streisand Superman . . . . (Columbia)
Billy Joel; *America: A Tribute To Heroes-C* . . . . (Interscope)
Billy Joel-Greatest Hits, Volume I & Volume II . . . . (Columbia)
The Concert For New York City-C . . . . (Columbia)
Turnstiles . . . . (Columbia)
Carmen McRae; *Ms. Magic* . . . . (Dunhill Compact Classics)
Tony Bennett with Billy Joel; *Playin' With My Friends-Bennett Sings The
Blues-C* . . . . (Columbia)
New York State Police
UK Subs; *Left For Dead (Alive In Holland '86)* . . . . (Roir)
UK Subs-The Singles 1978-1982 . . . .(Progressive Int'l)
This Land Is Your Land
Bruce Springsteen & The E Street Band; *Bruce Springsteen & The E Street
Band Live/1975-85* . . . . (Legacy)
Glen Campbell; *All American* . . . . (Liberty)
Lee Greenwood; *American Patriot* . . . . (Capitol)
Odetta, Arlo Guthrie & Company; *Tribute To Woody
Guthrie-C* . . . . (Warner Bros.)
Pete Seeger; *God Bless America-C* . . . . (Columbia)
Pete Seeger Sings Woody Guthrie . . . .(Smithsonian Folkways)
Pete Seeger-Complete Carnegie Hall Concert-1963 . . . . (Columbia)
Weavers; *Weavers' Greatest Hits* . . . . (Vanguard)
Woody Guthrie; *Greatest Songs Of Woody Guthrie-C* . . . . (Vanguard)
Troubadours Of The Folk Era-#1-C . . . . (Rhino)
Woody Guthrie . . . . (Vanguard)

STATES: NORTH DAKOTA

See Also: **CITIES: A-Z**

My North Dakota Girl
Dakota Harmony; *My North Dakota Girl-45* . . . . (Accent)
My North Dakota Home
Lawrence Welk; *Reminiscing-#1* . . . . (Ranwood)
North Dakota
Lyle Lovett; *Joshua Judges Ruth* . . . .(Curb/MCA)
Live In Texas . . . . (MCA)
North Dakota
Thrush Hermit; *Sweet Homewrecker* . . . . (Elektra)
North Dakota Sunrise
Metamora; *Metamora* . . . .(Sugar Hill)

STATES: OHIO

See Also: **CITIES: A-Z, CITIES: CINCINNATI**

Across The Field
Ohio State University Marching Band; *Pride Of The
Buckeyes* . . . .(Fidelity Sound)
Original Soundtrack; *College Fight Songs: The Big Ten-C* . . . .(K-Tel)
The Greatest College Fight Songs . . . . (Laserlight)
Top Ten College Fight Songs . . . .(K-Tel)
Boy In Ohio
Phil Ochs; *Phil Ochs' Greatest Hits* . . . .(A&M)
Goodbye Ohio
Too Much Joy; *Cereal Killers* . . . . (Giant)
Men Of Ohio
Ohio State University Marching Band; *Foot Tappers* . . . . (Fidelity Sound)
My City Was Gone
Pretenders; *Learning To Crawl* . . . . (Sire)
Ohio
Crosby, Stills & Nash; *CSN* . . . . (Atlantic)
Crosby, Stills, Nash & Young; *4 Way Street* . . . . (Atlantic)
So Far . . . . (Atlantic)
Neil Young; *Decade* . . . .(Reprise)
ST/Journey Through The Past . . . .(Warner Bros.)
Ohio
Leonard Bernstein; *Bernstein Songbook* . . . .(Columbia)
Original Broadway Cast; *Wonderful Town* . . . . (MCA)
Wonderful Town . . . .(Columbia)
Ohio Afternoon
Original New York Cast; *Oil City Symphony* . . . . (DRG)
Ohio Special March
Ohio State University Marching Band; *Pride Of The
Buckeyes* . . . .(Fidelity Sound)
Ohio Starters' Round
Ohio State University Marching Band; *Buckeye Battle Cry* . . . . .(Fidelity Sound)
Ohio/Machine Gun
Isley Brothers; *Timeless* . . . . (T-Neck/Columbia)
Ohio/Wrong Note Rage
Betty Comden & Adolph Green; *Party With Betty Comden & Adolph
Green* . . . . (DRG)
Polka Ohio
Li'l Wally; *Here Comes Li'l Wally* . . . .(Jay Jay)
That Old Beat Up Guitar
Jerry Jeff Walker; *Jerry Jeff Walker* . . . . (MCA)
Youngstown
Bruce Springsteen; *The Ghost Of Tom Joad* . . . .(Columbia)

STATES: OKLAHOMA

See Also: **CITIES: A-Z, CITIES: TULSA**

Boomer Sooner
Original Soundtrack; *The Greatest College Fight Songs* . . . . (Laserlight)
By The Time I Get To Phoenix
Glen Campbell; *All-Time Country Classics-#1-C* . . . .(Capitol)
Glen Campbell-Classics Collection . . . .(Capitol)
Glen Campbell-Live . . . .(Capitol)
Glen Campbell's Greatest Hits . . . .(Capitol)
Very Best Of Glen Campbell . . . .(Capitol)
Reba McEntire; *Starting Over* . . . . (MCA)
Home, Sweet Oklahoma
Tom Paxton; *It Ain't Easy* . . . . (Flying Fish)
If You're Ever In Oklahoma
J.J. Cale; *Really* . . . .(Mercury)
King Of Oklahoma
Michael Franks; *Previously Unavailable* . . . . (DRG)
My Oklahoma
Riders In The Sky; *Cowboy Way* . . . . (MCA)
Steve Young; *Seven Bridges Road* . . . .(Rounder)
My Oklahoma Home (It Blowed Away)
Sis Cunningham; *Best Of Broadside 1962-1968: Anthems Of The American
Underground From The Pages Of Broadside
Magazine-C* . . . . (Smithsonian Folkways)
Night In Oklahoma
Larry McNeely; *Power Play* . . . . (Flying Fish)
Okie From Muskogee
Merle Haggard; *Friend In California* . . . .(Epic)
Merle Haggard & The Strangers; *Best Of Merle Haggard & The
Strangers* . . . .(Capitol)
Capitol Collectors Series-Merle Haggard & The Strangers . . . .(Capitol)
Country Music Classics-#3-1965-1970-C . . . . (K-Tel)
For The Record: Merle Haggard-43 Legendary Hits . . . . (BNA)
Songs I'll Always Sing . . . .(Capitol)
ST/Platoon . . . .(Atlantic)
Oklahoma
Ohio State University Marching Band; *Brass Roots* . . . .(Fidelity Sound)

Original Broadway Cast; *Oklahoma!* . . . . (RCA)
Original Cast; *Broadway Classics-#1* . . . . (MCA)
   Oklahoma! . . . . (MCA)
Oklahoma
Call; *Reconciled* . . . . (Elektra)
Oklahoma
SWA; *Sex Doctor* . . . . (SST)
Oklahoma Blues
Patti Page; *The Uncollected Patti Page-1949* . . . . (Hindsight)
Oklahoma Borderline
Vince Gill; *Best Of Vince Gill* . . . . (RCA)
Oklahoma Boy
Dewayne Boyd & The Silver Dollar Band;
   45-#162 . . . . (Nationwide Sound Distrib.)
Oklahoma City Times
Limeliters; *Harmony!* . . . . (Folk Era)
Oklahoma Country Girl
Elvin Bishop; *Big Fun* . . . . (Alligator)
Oklahoma Dancer
Monkees; *Monkees Present* . . . . (Rhino)
Oklahoma Going Home
Kate Wolf & Wildwood Flower; *Back Roads* . . . . (Rhino)
Oklahoma Heartaches & California Dreams
Kris Carpenter; *45-#203* . . . . (Door Knob)
Oklahoma Hills
Arlo Guthrie; *Tribute To Woody Guthrie-C* . . . . (Warner Bros.)
Hank Thompson; *Hank Thompson's All-Time Greatest Hits* . . . . (Curb)
Jack Guthrie and his Oklahomans; *Birth Of A Dream-Capitol's Early*
   Hits-C . . . . (Capitol)
   Great Records Of The Decade-'40s-Country-C . . . . (Curb)
Kay Starr; *Kay Starr-Country* . . . . (Crescendo)
Oklahoma Joe
Chris LeDoux; *Songs Of Rodeo & Country* . . . . (Liberty)
Oklahoma Kid
Goebel Reeves; *Texas Drifter* . . . . (Glendale)
Oklahoma Rag
Bob Wills; *Fiddle* . . . . (Country Music Foundation)
Oklahoma Rooster
Backwoods Banjo; *Jes' Fine* . . . . (Rounder)
Oklahoma Stomp
Duke Ellington; *Hot In Harlem* . . . . (MCA)
   Jazz Heritage-Vocalion Rarities-C . . . . (MCA)
Spade Cooley; *Columbia Historic Edition-Spade Cooley* . . . . . (Columbia)
Spade Cooley & His Orchestra; *Legends Of Country Guitar-#1-C* . . . . . (Rhino)
Oklahoma Stroke
Albert Lee; *Gagged But Not Bound* . . . . (MCA)
Oklahoma Sunshine
Mayf Nutter; *Goin' Skinny Dippin'* . . . . (Crescendo)
Oklahoma Sweetheart
George Thorogood & The Destroyers; *Boogie People* . . . . (EMI)
Oklahoma Sweetheart Sally
Maddox Brothers & Rose; *America's Most Colorful Hillbilly Band* . . (Arhoolie)
Oklahoma Swing
Vince Gill & Reba McEntire; *When I Call Your Name* . . . . (MCA)
Oklahoma U.S.A.
Kinks; *Muswell Hillbillies* . . . . (VelVel)
Oklahoma Waltz
Cavaliers; *Have Polka Will Travel* . . . . (Accent)
Take Me Back To Oklahoma
Tim Rex & Oklahoma; *45-#111* . . . . (Dee-Jay)
Tokyo, Oklahoma
John Anderson; *John Anderson's Greatest Hits-#2* . . . . (Warner Bros.)
Tulsa Time
Don Williams; *Best Of Don Williams-#2* . . . . (MCA)
   Country's Greatest Hits-#6-Superstars-C . . . . (Priority)
   Don Williams-Legends . . . . (MCA)
   Expressions . . . . (MCA)
Eric Clapton; *Backless* . . . . (Polydor)
   Just One Night . . . . (Polydor)
What The Cowgirls Do
Vince Gill; *When Love Finds You* . . . . (MCA)
You're The Reason God Made Oklahoma
David Frizzell & Shelly West; *Carryin' On The Family*
   Names . . . . (Warner Bros.)
   Country's Greatest Hits-#9-'80s Duets-C . . . . (Priority)
   Golden Duets . . . . (Viva)

STATES: OREGON

See Also: **CITIES: A-Z**

Don't Take Me Alive
Steely Dan; *The Royal Scam* . . . . (MCA)
Hail To Old O.S.U.
Original Soundtrack; *College Fight Songs: The Pac Ten-C* . . . . (K-Tel)
   The Greatest College Fight Songs . . . . (Laserlight)

Mighty Oregon
Original Soundtrack; *College Fight Songs: The Pac Ten-C* . . . . (K-Tel)
   The Greatest College Fight Songs . . . . (Laserlight)
Oregon
Dan Balmer; *Becoming Became* . . . . (Chase Music Group)
Oregon Hill
Cowboy Junkies; *Black Eyed Man* . . . . (RCA)
Oregon Hills
Martin Oberschelp; *Nightingale Lightdance* . . . . (Higher Octave)
Oregon Mountains
Woody Simmons; *Oregon Mountains* . . . . (Deep River)
Oregon Rain Song
George Roessler; *Still Life & Old Dreams* . . . . (Eagle Int'l)
Oregon Trail
Sons Of The Pioneers; *Sunset On The Range* . . . . (Pair)
Starry Sky In Oregon
Andrew White; *Conversations* . . . . (Sona Gaia)
Waves Roll In On Oregon
Jim Post; *Magic-In Concert* . . . . (Flying Fish)

STATES: PENNSYLVANIA

See Also: **CITIES: A-Z, CITIES: PHILADELPHIA**

Fight On State
Original Soundtrack; *College Fight Songs: The Big Ten-C* . . . . (K-Tel)
   The Greatest College Fight Songs . . . . (Laserlight)
Fight On, Pennsylvania
All-Star Inter-Conference Band; *College Marches At Halftime* . . . . (Alshire)
University Of Michigan Band; *Greatest College Football Marches* . . (Vanguard)
Pennsylvania 6-5000
Glenn Miller; *Glenn Miller-A Legendary Performer-#1 & 2* . . . . (Bluebird)
   Memorial-1944-1969 . . . . (Bluebird)
   The Glenn Miller Story . . . . (RCA)
Glenn Miller & His Orchestra; *Complete Glenn Miller & His*
   Orchestra-#4 . . . . (Bluebird)
   Glenn Miller & His Orchestra-Pure Gold . . . . (Bluebird)
   Moonlight Serenade . . . . (Ranwood)
   The Unforgettable Glenn Miller & His Orchestra . . . . (RCA)
Pennsylvania Polka
Andrews Sisters; *Andrews Sisters-16 Great Performances* . . . . (MCA)
   Best Of The Andrews Sisters . . . . (MCA)
   Boogie Woogie Bugle Girls . . . . (MCA)
Arthur Smith & Don Reno; *Red, White & Bluegrass-C* . . . . (C.M.H. Prod.)
Frankie Yankovic & His Yanks; *Frankie Yankovic & His Yanks'*
   Greatest Hits . . . . (Columbia)
Pittsburgh, Pennsylvania
101 Strings Orchestra; *Million-Seller Hits From Mexico* . . . . (Alshire)
Guy Mitchell; *Guy Mitchell-16 Most Requested Songs* . . . . (Legacy)
There's No Place Like Home For The Holidays
Perry Como; *Now That's What I Call Christmas!-C* . . . . (UTV)
   Perry Como's Greatest Hits . . . . (RCA)

STATES: RHODE ISLAND

See Also: **CITIES: A-Z**

Rhode Island
Lucy Brown; *Lucy Brown* . . . . (Megaforce)
Rhode Island Is Famous For You
Blossom Dearie; *Blossoms On Broadway* . . . . (DRG)
Michael Feinstein; *Live At The Algonquin* . . . . (Elektra)
Rhode Island Red
Brew Moore; *Brew Moore* . . . . (Fantasy)
Sweet Rhode Island Red
Ike & Tina Turner; *Proud Mary-Best Of Ike & Tina Turner* . . . . (EMI)

STATES: SOUTH DAKOTA

See Also: **CITIES: A-Z**

Deadwood, South Dakota
Nanci Griffith; *One Fair Summer Evening* . . . . (MCA)
Floods Of South Dakota
Modern Hicks; *Out Among The Stars* . . . . (Jackalope)
Rocky Raccoon
Beatles; *Beatles-Box Set* . . . . (Capitol)
   The Beatles (White Album) . . . . (Capitol)
South Dakota Lady
Buddy Red Bow; *Buddy Red Bow* . . . . (First Warning)

STATES: TENNESSEE

See Also: **CITIES: A-Z, CITIES: MEMPHIS, CITIES: NASHVILLE**

All My Ex's Live In Texas
George Strait; *Country Classics-#10-1987-C* . . . . (Universal)
 George Strait's Greatest Hits-#2 . . . . (MCA)
 Ocean Front Property. . . . . (MCA)
Back To Tennessee
Commander Cody & His Lost Planet Airmen; *Lost In The Ozone* . . . . . . (MCA)
Ballad Of Davy Crockett
Bill Hayes; *Songs Of The West-#4-Movie & Television Themes-C* . . . . . (Rhino)
Fess Parker; *16 Most Requested Songs Of The '50s-#1-C* . . . . (Legacy)
 Columbia Country Classics-#3-Americana-C . . . . (Columbia)
 Hollywood Magic-1950s-C . . . . (Columbia)
Kentucky HeadHunters; *Electric Barnyard.* . . . . (Mercury)
Mac Wiseman; *45-#1240.* . . . . (Dot)
Original Soundtrack; *Television's Greatest Hits-#4-Black & White*
 Classics-C . . . . (TVT)
Tennessee Ernie Ford; *Capitol Collectors Series-Tennessee*
 Ernie Ford . . . . (Capitol)
Brand New Tennessee Waltz
Jesse Winchester; *Best Of Jesse Winchester* . . . . (Rhino)
 Jesse Winchester. . . . . (Rhino)
Joan Baez; *Country Music Album* . . . . (Vanguard)
C.L.I.T. (Cajuns Living In Tennessee)
Pinkard & Bowden; *Cousins Cattle & Other Love Stories* . . . . . . (Warner Bros.)
Carrying Your Love With Me
George Strait; *Carrying Your Love With Me* . . . . (MCA)
 Latest Greatest Straitest Hits . . . . (MCA)
Cold Day In Tennessee
Rob Crosby; *Another Time & Place* . . . . (Arista)
Cowboy Night Herd Song
Roy Rogers & Sons Of The Pioneers; *Cowboy Super Hits-C* . . . . . . (Columbia)
Curly Headed Baby
Pete Seeger; *Tribute To Woody Guthrie-C* . . . . (Warner Bros.)
Dallas
Alan Jackson; *Don't Rock The Jukebox.* . . . . (Arista)
Damn Good Cowboy
Charlie Daniels Band; *Cowboy Super Hits-C* . . . . (Columbia)
 Night Rider . . . . (Epic)
Davy Crockett
Hermes Nye; *Ballads Of The Civil War-#1 & 2* . . . . . . (Smithsonian Folkways)
Dixie Chicken
Little Feat; *Dixie Chicken* . . . . (Warner Bros.)
 Waiting For Columbus . . . . (Warner Bros.)
Down In Nashville, Tennessee
Reno & Smiley; *1983 Collector's Edition-#2* . . . . (Gusto)
Down In Tennessee
John Anderson; *John Anderson's Greatest Hits-#2* . . . . (Warner Bros.)
 Tokyo Oklahoma. . . . . (Warner Bros.)
Mark Chesnutt; *What A Way To Live.* . . . . (Decca)
Steve Wariner; *Best Of Steve Wariner.* . . . . (RCA)
Drink Muddy Water Leaving Tennessee
Rio Grande Band; *Rio Grande Band* . . . . (Rounder)
Easin' Back To Tennessee
Sleepy John Estes; *Sleepy John Estes In Europe* . . . . (Delmark)
East Tennessee Blues/Goin' Crazy
Stepping Stones; *Fresh Old Time String Band Music* . . . . (Rounder)
Flight 309 To Tennessee
Shelly West; *West By West* . . . . (Viva)
From Tennessee To Texas
Johnny Bush & The Bandoleros; *Live From Texas* . . . . (Delmark)
God Bless The USA
Lee Greenwood; *American Patriot* . . . . (Capitol)
 God Bless America-C . . . . (Columbia)
 God Bless The USA . . . . (MCA Special Prod.)
 Inside Out/You've Got A Good Love Comin' . . . . (MCA)
 Lee Greenwood's Greatest Hits . . . . (MCA)
 Lee Greenwood's Greatest Hits-#2 . . . . (MCA)
 Today's Country Classics-C . . . . (MCA Special Prod.)
God Don't Live In Nashville, Tennessee
Randy Howard; *All-American Redneck* . . . . (Warner Bros.)
Going Back To Tennessee
Tracy Nelson; *Doin' It My Way.* . . . . (Adelphi)
Good Woman Blues
Mel Tillis; *Mel Tillis' Greatest Hits.* . . . . (Curb)
Goodbye To Tennessee
Reilly & Maloney; *Reilly & Maloney-Alive.* . . . . (Freckle)
Graceland
Paul Simon; *Graceland* . . . . (Warner Bros.)
Guitar Town
Steve Earle & The Dukes; *Country Classics-#8-1986-1987-C* . . . . . . (Universal)
 Guitar Town . . . . (MCA)
Heartbreak, Tennessee
Johnny Paycheck; *This Is Country-C.* . . . . (Pegasus/Cleopatra)

Home In Tennessee
Carter Family; *Longing For Old Virginia: Their Complete Victor Recordings-*
 1934 . . . . (Rounder)
I'll Tennessee You In My Dreams
Tanya Tucker; *Love Me Like You Used To* . . . . (Liberty)
It Hurts As Much In Texas (As It Did In Tennessee)
George Jones & Ricky Van Shelton; *Friends In High Places-C* . . . . (Epic)
I've Never Lived In Tennessee
Leon MacAuliffe; *Columbia Historic Edition-Leon MacAuliffe* . . . . . (Columbia)
Just To See You Smile
Tim McGraw; *Everywhere.* . . . . (Curb)
 Tim McGraw's Greatest Hits . . . . (Curb)
Kentucky Hills Of Tennessee
Commander Cody & His Lost Planet Airmen; *Hot Licks, Cold Steel &*
 Trucker's Favorites . . . . (MCA)
Little Home In Tennessee
Bill Harrell & The Virginians; *Ballads & Bluegrass* . . . . (Adelphi)
Mac Wiseman; *Classic Bluegrass-Mac Wiseman* . . . . (Rebel)
Little Old Wine Drinker Me
Dean Martin; *Dean Martin's Greatest Hits-#2* . . . . (Reprise)
 Welcome To My World . . . . (Reprise)
Mel Tillis; *Best Of Mel Tillis* . . . . (MCA)
Maybe It Was Memphis
Pam Tillis; *Pam Tillis' Greatest Hits* . . . . (Arista)
 Pam Tillis-Collection . . . . (Warner Bros.)
 Put Yourself In My Place. . . . . (Arista)
Memphis, Tennessee Hot Rock
Gordon Terry; *Tennessee Hot Rock* . . . . (Plantation)
Midnight Tennessee Woman
Jack Greene; *Jack Greene Sings His Best.* . . . . (Step One)
My Little Girl In Tennessee
Lester Flatt, Earl Scruggs & The Foggy Mountain Boys; *Lester Flatt,*
 Earl Scruggs & The Foggy Mountain Boys-Complete Mercury
 Sessions . . . . (Mercury)
My Sweetheart In Tennessee
Burnett & Rutherford; *Ramblin' Reckless Hobo* . . . . (Rounder)
My Tennessee Baby
Ernest Tubb; *45-#46173.* . . . . (Decca)
My Tennessee Mountain Home
Dolly Parton; *Best Of A Great Year-#3-C* . . . . (RCA)
 Best Of Dolly Parton. . . . . (RCA)
 My Tennessee Mountain Home . . . . (RCA)
Rose Maddox; *Reckless Love & Bold Adventure* . . . . (Takoma)
Nashville, Tenn. Blues
Washboard Sam; *Blues Classics By* . . . . (Blues Classics)
Nashville, Tennessee
Troy Cory; *Real Country* . . . . (Video Record Albums)
Ol' Red
Blake Shelton; *Blake Shelton.* . . . . (Giant)
Old Tennessee
Dan Fogelberg; *Captured Angel.* . . . . (Full Moon)
 Live-Greetings From The West . . . . (Full Moon)
On The Banks Of The Old Tennessee
Doc Watson; *Old Timey Concert* . . . . (Vanguard)
Paris, Tennessee
Dennis Robbins; *Man With A Plan.* . . . . (Giant)
Kenny Chesney; *All I Need To Know* . . . . (BNA)
Tracy Lawrence; *Sticks & Stones* . . . . (Atlantic)
Peaceful World
John Mellencamp; *Cuttin' Heads* . . . . (Columbia)
 God Bless America-C . . . . (Columbia)
 The Concert For New York City-C . . . . (Columbia)
Please Come To Boston
Dave Loggins; *Apprentice (In A Musical Workshop).* . . . . (Epic)
 Rock Artifacts-From The Vaults-#2-C. . . . . (Legacy)
 Super Hits Of The '70s-Have A Nice Day-#13-C . . . . (Rhino)
David Allan Coe; *David Allan Coe-17 Greatest Hits.* . . . . (Columbia)
 For The Record-The First 10 Years . . . . (Columbia)
Joan Baez; *Best Of Joan Baez* . . . . (A&M)
 Joan Baez-Classics-#8 . . . . (A&M)
Reba McEntire; *Starting Over* . . . . (MCA)
Rebecca Lynn
Bryan White; *Bryan White.* . . . . (Asylum)
Red Bird Tennessee Waltz
Clark Kessinger & Gene Meade; *Clark Kessinger & Gene Meade* . . . (Rounder)
Right Now Tennessee Blues
Charlie Daniels Band; *High Lonesome* . . . . (Epic)
Rocky Top
Conway Twitty; *Hello Darlin'.* . . . . (MCA Special Prod.)
Flying Burrito Brothers; *Close Encounters To The West Coast* . . . . . . (Relix)
Osborne Brothers; *Best Of The Osborne Brothers* . . . . (MCA)
 Yesterday, Today & The Osborne Brothers. . . . . (MCA)
Roy Clark; *Roy Clark In Concert.* . . . . (MCA)
White Mountain Singers; *Best Of The White Mountain Singers* . . . . (Folk Era)
Roll Tennessee River
Oak Ridge Boys; *Step On Out* . . . . (MCA)
Singing Bridge Of Memphis Tennessee
John Fahey; *Essential John Fahey* . . . . (Vanguard)

Southern California
George Jones & Tammy Wynette; *George Jones & Tammy Wynette-16*
Biggest Hits . . . . (Epic/Legacy)
Tammy Wynette & George Jones; *Encore-Tammy Wynette & George*
Jones . . . .(Epic)
Tammy Wynette & George Jones' Greatest Hits . . . .(Epic)

Sunday Down In Tennessee
Red Foley; *45-#46197* . . . . (Decca)

Sunny Tennessee
Doc Watson; *Old Timey Concert* . . . . (Vanguard)

Talking To A Tennessee Moon
Candace Anderson; *Talking To A Tennessee Moon* . . . . (Adobe)

Taos To Tennessee
Tish Hinojosa; *Taos To Tennessee* . . . . (Watermelon)

Tennessee Jubilee
Uncle Dave Macon; *The Country Music Hall Of Fame-Uncle Dave*
Macon . . . .(MCA)

Tennessee
Carl Perkins; *Carl Perkins-Original Sun Greatest Hits* . . . . (Rhino)
Legends Of Country Guitar-#1-C . . . . (Rhino)

Tennessee
Arrested Development; *3 Years 5 Months 2 Days In The Life Of* . . . . .(Chrysalis)

Tennessee
Manic Street Preachers; *Generation Terrorists* . . . . (Columbia)

Tennessee
Jan & Dean; *Best Of Jan & Dean* . . . .(EMI)

Tennessee
Carol Channing & Webb Pierce; *C & W* . . . . (Plantation)

Tennessee
Shawn Colvin; *Fat City* . . . . (Columbia)

Tennessee
Hank Williams, Jr.; *Hank Williams, Jr.-Early Years* . . . . (WB/Curb)
New South . . . .(Warner Bros.)

Tennessee
Charlie Daniels Band; *High Lonesome* . . . .(Epic)

Tennessee
Nitty Gritty Dirt Band; *Hold On* . . . .(Warner Bros.)

Tennessee
Crystal Gayle; *Hollywood, Tennessee* . . . . (Columbia)

Tennessee
NRBQ; *Honest Dollar* . . . .(Rykodisc)

Tennessee
Glen Campbell; *Letter To Home* . . . .(Atlantic America)

Tennessee Bird Walk
Blanchard & Morgan; *Super Hits-#2-C* . . . . (Gusto)
Tennessee Guitars; *20 Great Hits-C* . . . . (Plantation)
Golden Guitar Hits . . . . (SSS International)

Tennessee Blues
J.D. Crowe and the New South; *My Home Ain't In The Hall*
Of Fame . . . . (Rounder)
Kris Kristofferson & Rita Coolidge; *Kris & Rita-Full Moon* . . . . (A&M)
Ted, Andy & Ricky Sage/Charlie Smithson;
Sagegrass . . . . (Smithsonian Folkways)

Tennessee Border
Hank Williams; *Alone With His Guitar* . . . . (Mercury)
I Ain't Got Nothin' But Time-1946-1947 . . . . (Polydor)
Red Foley; *Red Foley: The Country Music Hall*
Of Fame . . . .(MCA Special Prod.)
Sonny Burgess & Dave Alvin; *Tennessee Border* . . . .(Hightone)
Tennessee Ernie Ford; *Best Of Tennessee Ernie Ford-16 Tons Of*
Boogie . . . . (Rhino)
Capitol Collectors Series-Tennessee Ernie Ford . . . . (Capitol)

Tennessee Born & Bred
Eddie Rabbitt; *Jersey Boy* . . . . (Capitol)

Tennessee Bottle
Kenny Rogers; *The Gambler* . . . .(EMI)

Tennessee Breakdown
Dillards; *Homecoming & Family Reunion* . . . . (Flying Fish)

Tennessee Choo Choo
Delmore Brothers; *Best Of The Delmore Brothers* . . . . (Starday)

Tennessee Christmas
Alabama; *Alabama-Christmas* . . . . (RCA)
Amy Grant; *Amy Grant Christmas Album* . . . .(Word)
Lee Greenwood; *Lee Greenwood-Christmas To*
Christmas . . . .(MCA Special Prod.)
Steve Wariner; *Country Christmas To Remember-C* . . . . (MCA Special Prod.)
Tennessee Christmas-C . . . . (MCA)

Tennessee Farmer
Stringbean; *Salute To Uncle Dave Macon* . . . . (Starday)

Tennessee Fish Fry
Helen O'Connell; *The Uncollected Helen O'Connell With Irv Orton's*
Orchestra . . . . (Hindsight)

Tennessee Flat Top Box
Johnny Cash; *Classic Cash-Hall Of Fame Series* . . . . (Mercury)
Columbia Country Classics-#3-Americana-C . . . .(Columbia)
Essential Johnny Cash . . . . (Columbia)
The Man In Black-His Greatest Hits . . . . (Legacy)
Rosanne Cash; *30 Years Of #1 Hits-#17-C* . . . . (Columbia)

Hits-1979-1989 . . . . (Columbia)
King's Record Shop . . . . (Columbia)

Tennessee Fluxedo
Jerry Douglas; *Fluxedo* . . . . (Rounder)

Tennessee Girl
Charley Pride; *Charley Pride Live* . . . .(RCA)

Tennessee Homesick Blues
Dolly Parton; *Best Of Dolly Parton-#3* . . . .(RCA)
RCA Years-1967-1986 . . . .(RCA)
ST/Rhinestone . . . .(RCA)
Star Spangled Country-C . . . .(RCA)

Tennessee Hound Dog
Osborne Brothers; *Best Of The Osborne Brothers* . . . . (MCA)

Tennessee Jed
Grateful Dead; *Europe '72* . . . . (Warner Bros.)
What A Long Strange Trip It's Been: The Best Of The
Grateful Dead . . . . (Warner Bros.)

Tennessee Lonesome Blues
Jim & Jesse; *In The Tradition* . . . . (Rounder)

Tennes-See Me
Jeannie C. Riley; *Here's Jeannie C. Riley* . . . .(Playback)

Tennessee Moon
Neil Diamond; *Tennessee Moon* . . . . (Columbia)

Tennessee Moon
Cowboy Copas; *45-#714* . . . . (King)

Tennessee Newsboy (Newsboy Blues)
Frank Sinatra; *Columbia Years-1943-1952-Complete Recordings* . . . . . (Legacy)

Tennessee Nights
Pam Tillis; *Pam Tillis-Collection* . . . . (Warner Bros.)

Tennessee Plates
Charlie Sexton; *ST/Thelma & Louise* . . . . (MCA)
John Hiatt; *Slow Turning* . . . . (A&M)

Tennessee Polka
Mom & Dads; *Gratefully Yours* . . . .(Crescendo)
Red Foley; *45-#46170* . . . . (Decca)

Tennessee Pride
Chet Atkins; *Country Gems* . . . .(Pair)

Tennessee River
Alabama; *Alabama-Live* . . . . (RCA)
Alabama's Greatest Hits . . . .(RCA)
Best Of The '80s...So Far-C . . . .(RCA)
My Home's In Alabama . . . .(RCA)
Hank Williams, Jr.; *Rowdy* . . . . (WB/Curb)

Tennessee Road
Anne Hills; *Woman Of A Calm Heart* . . . . (Flying Fish)

Tennessee Rose
Emmylou Harris; *Cimarron* . . . . (Warner Bros.)

Tennessee Saturday Night
Ella Mae Morse; *Capitol Collectors Series-Ella Mae Morse* . . . . (Capitol)
Red Foley; *Heroes Of Country Music-#2-Legends Of Honky Tonk-C* . . . . (Rhino)
Red Foley: The Country Music Hall Of Fame . . . . (MCA Special Prod.)

Tennessee Saturday Nite
Commander Cody & His Lost Planet Airmen; *Aces High* . . . .(Relix)

Tennessee Stud
Chris LeDoux; *Old Cowboy Classics* . . . . (Capitol)
Eddy Arnold; *Best Of Eddy Arnold-#2* . . . . (Dunhill Compact Classics)
Eddy Arnold-Legendary Performer . . . .(RCA)
Hank Williams, Jr.; *The Pressure Is On-Original Classics*
Collection-#7 . . . .(Curb)
Johnny Cash; *American Recordings* . . . . (American)
Nitty Gritty Dirt Band; *Will The Circle Be Unbroken* . . . . (EMI)

Tennessee Toddy
Marty Robbins; *Essential Marty Robbins-1951-1982* . . . . (Columbia)

Tennessee Traveler
Mike Auldridge; *Mike Auldridge* . . . . (Flying Fish)

Tennessee Two Step
Charlie Daniels; *America, I Believe In You* . . . . (Liberty)

Tennessee Wagoner
New Grass Revival; *When The Storm Is Over* . . . . (Flying Fish)

Tennessee Waltz
Cowboy Copas; *45-#696* . . . . (King)
Emmylou Harris; *Cimarron* . . . . (Warner Bros.)
Country's Greatest Hits-#5-C . . . . (Warner Bros.)
New Tradition Sings The Old Tradition-C . . . . (Warner Bros.)
Guy Lombardo & His Royal Canadians; *Best Of Guy Lombardo* . . . .(Curb)
Hank Williams, Jr.; *Living Proof-MGM Recordings 1963-1975* . . . . . . (Mercury)
Lacy J. Dalton; *Lacy J. Dalton's Greatest Hits* . . . . (Columbia)
Les Paul & Mary Ford; *Les Paul-Selections From Legend & Legacy* . . . (Capitol)
Patti Page; *Patti Page-Golden Hits* . . . . (Mercury)
Patti Page's Greatest Hits . . . . (Columbia)
Roy Acuff; *Essential Roy Acuff-1936-1949* . . . . (Legacy)
Roy Acuff's Greatest Hits . . . . (Columbia)
Roy Rogers; *Best Of Roy Rogers* . . . .(Curb)
Sammy Kaye & His Orchestra; *Best Of The Big Bands-C* . . . . (Columbia)
Spike Jones & His City Slickers; *Best Of Spike Jones & His City*
Slickers . . . . (RCA)

Tennessee Whiskey
David Allan Coe; *David Allan Coe-17 Greatest Hits* . . . . (Columbia)

David Allan Coe's Biggest Hits .... (Legacy)
For The Record-The First 10 Years .... (Columbia)
Tennessee Whiskey .... (Columbia)
George Jones; *By Request* .... (Epic)
First Time Live! .... (Epic)
George Jones-Super Hits .... (Epic)
Greatest Country Hits Of The '80s-1983-C .... (Columbia)
Shine On .... (Epic)
Merle Haggard; *19 Hot Country Requests-#2-C* .... (Epic)

Tennessee Whiskey & Texas Women
Rayburn Anthony; *Audiograph Alive-C* .... (Audiograph)
Dance Floor Crystal Ball .... (Audiograph)

Tennessee Wig Walk
Bonnie Lou; *Super Country Hits Of The '50s-C* .... (Gusto)
Russ Morgan; *Best Of Russ Morgan* .... (MCA)

That's Right (You're Not From Texas)
Lyle Lovett; *Live In Texas* .... (MCA)
The Road To Ensenada .... (MCA)

Theme From "Tennessee Tuxedo"
Original Soundtrack; *Television's Greatest Hits-#4-Black & White
Classics-C* .... (TVT)

There Ain't No Beverly Hills In Tennessee
Shenandoah; *Long Time Comin'* .... (RCA)

There's A Tennessee Woman/Ben's Song
Tanya Tucker; *Tennessee Woman* .... (Capitol)

There's No Love In Tennessee
Barbara Mandrell; *Barbara Mandrell's Greatest Hits* ...... (MCA)
Country Classics-#3-1984-1985-C .... (Universal)

There's No Place Like Home For The Holidays
Perry Como; *Now That's What I Call Christmas!-C* .... (UTV)
Perry Como's Greatest Hits .... (RCA)

This Ain't Tennessee & She Ain't You
Tom Jones; *Don't Let Our Dreams Die Young* .... (Mercury)

Tom Dooley
Doc Watson; *Doc Watson* .... (Vanguard)
Essential Doc Watson .... (Vanguard)
Out In The Country .... (Intermedia)
Kingston Trio; *Capitol Collectors Series-The Kingston Trio* .... (Capitol)
From The Hungry i .... (Capitol)
Kingston Trio's Greatest Hits .... (Curb)
Tom Dooley .... (Capitol)
Troubadours Of The Folk Era-#3-C .... (Rhino)

Trains/Leavin' Tennessee
Tasty Licks; *Tasty Licks* .... (Rounder)

STATES: TEXAS

**See Also: CITIES: A-Z, CITIES: DALLAS, HOUSTON,
SAN ANTONIO**

4 A.M. In Texas
7 Seconds; *Soulforce Revolution* .... (Restless)

Alexis From Texas
Red Steagall; *Lone Star Beer & Bob Wills Music* .... (MCA)

All My Ex's Live In Texas
George Strait; *Country Classics-#10-1987-C* .... (Universal)
George Strait's Greatest Hits-#2 .... (MCA)
Ocean Front Property .... (MCA)

All The Rage In Paris
Derailers; *Here Come The Derailers* .... (Lucky Dog)

Another Texas Song
Eddy Raven; *45-#1011* .... (Dimension/Capitol)

Ballad Of Davy Crockett
Bill Hayes; *Songs Of The West-#4-Movie & Television Themes-C* ...... (Rhino)
Fess Parker; *16 Most Requested Songs Of The '50s-#1-C* .... (Legacy)
Columbia Country Classics-#3-Americana-C .... (Columbia)
Hollywood Magic-1950s-C .... (Columbia)
Kentucky HeadHunters; *Electric Barnyard* .... (Mercury)
Mac Wiseman; *45-#1240* .... (Dot)
Original Soundtrack; *Television's Greatest Hits-#4-Black & White
Classics-C* .... (TVT)
Tennessee Ernie Ford; *Capitol Collectors Series-Tennessee
Ernie Ford* .... (Capitol)

Beautiful Texas
Leon Rausch; *Deep In The Heart Of Texas* .... (Southland)

Big Iron
Marty Robbins; *Columbia Country Classics-#3-Americana-C* ...... (Columbia)
Gunfighter Ballads & Trail Songs .... (Legacy)
Marty Robbins' All-Time Greatest Hits .... (Columbia)
Marty Robbins-More Greatest Hits .... (Columbia)

Big Texas
Jimmy C. Newman; *Happy Cajun* .... (Plantation)

Blame It On Texas
Mark Chesnutt; *Mark Chesnutt's Greatest Hits* .... (Decca)
Too Cold At Home .... (MCA)

Blind In Texas
W.A.S.P.; *Last Command* .... (Capitol)

Blue Rose Of Texas
Holly Dunn; *Blue Rose Of Texas* .... (Warner Bros.)

Blue Texas Waltz
Billy Joe Shaver; *Taste Of Texas-Songs 'Bout Texas By Texans-C* ...(Columbia)

Blue Yodel #1
Bob Wills; *Bob Wills-Anthology* .... (Sony Music Special Prod.)
Lynyrd Skynyrd; *Best Of The Rest Of Lynyrd Skynyrd* .... (MCA)
One More From The Road .... (MCA)

Bluest Eyes In Texas
Restless Heart; *Big Dreams In A Small Town* .... (RCA)

Bob Wills Is Still The King
Clint Black & Asleep At The Wheel; *Ride With Bob-C* .... (DreamWorks/SKG)

Boogie Back To Texas
Asleep At The Wheel; *Asleep At The Wheel-10* .... (Epic)
Swinging Best Of Asleep At The Wheel .... (Epic)
Texas Super Hits-C .... (Columbia)
Very Best Of Asleep At The Wheel Since 1970 .... (Relentless/Madacy)

Brownsville Turnaround On The Tex-Mex Border
KLF; *Chill Out* .... (Wax Trax)

Coca Cola Cowboy
Mel Tillis; *Mel Tillis' Greatest Hits* .... (Curb)
Very Best Of Mel Tillis .... (MCA)

Coming Back To Texas
Kenneth Threadgill; *ST/Honeysuckle Rose* .... (Columbia)

Dallas
Alan Jackson; *Don't Rock The Jukebox* .... (Arista)

Dance Time In Texas
George Strait; *Something Special* .... (MCA)

Daughters Of Texas
Band Of H.M. Royal Marines; *Hands Across The Sea-Sousa Marches* ...(Angel)

David & Me
Jerry Jeff Walker; *Jerry Jeff Walker* .... (MCA)

Deep In The Heart Of Texas
Bing Crosby; *Bing Crosby's Greatest Hits* .... (MCA)
Bob Wills; *Best Of Bob Wills & His Texas Playboys* .... (MCA)
Best Of Bob Wills-#2 .... (MCA)
Gene Autry; *Columbia Historic Edition-Gene Autry* .... (Columbia)
Texas Super Hits-C .... (Columbia)
Moe Bandy; *Taste Of Texas-Songs 'Bout Texas By Texans-C* ...... (Columbia)

Devil Lives In Dallas, The
Rusty Weir Pettit; *Taste Of Texas-Songs 'Bout Texas By Texans-C* ...(Columbia)

Devil Made Texas
Hermes Nye; *Cowboy Songs On Folkways-C* .... (Smithsonian Folkways)
Texas Folk Songs .... (Smithsonian Folkways)

Don't Ask Me Why (I'm Going To Texas)
Asleep At The Wheel; *Asleep At The Wheel* .... (Epic)
Swinging Best Of Asleep At The Wheel .... (Epic)

Don't Sing A Song About Texas
Charlie Walker; *Texas Gold* .... (Plantation)

Down In Texas
Allman Brothers Band; *Dreams* .... (Polydor)

Down In Texas Today
Curtis Potter; *Down In Texas Today* .... (Step One)

Down In Texas Way
John Delafose & The Eunice Playboys; *Pere Et Garcon Zydeco* ...... (Rounder)

Dream On Texas Ladies
John Michael Montgomery; *Life's A Dance* .... (Atlantic)
ST/Maverick .... (Atlantic)

East Texas Red
Arlo Guthrie; *Tribute To Woody Guthrie And Leadbelly-C* .... (Columbia)

Egypt Texas
Shadowy Men On A Shadowy Planet; *Savvy Show Stoppers* .... (Cargo)

El Paso
Grateful Dead; *Steal Your Face* .... (Grateful Dead)
Marty Robbins; *Billboard Top Country Hits-1960-C* .... (Rhino)
Gunfighter Ballads & Trail Songs .... (Legacy)
Marty Robbins' Biggest Hits .... (Columbia)
Radio Classics Of The '50s-C .... (Columbia)
Texas Super Hits-C .... (Columbia)

Ellis Unit One
Steve Earle; *Johnny Too Bad* .... (E Squared)
ST/Dead Man Walking .... (Columbia)

Eyes Of Texas
Michigan University Band; *Kick Off, U.S.A.* .... (Vanguard)
Sharkey & The Kings Of Dixieland; *Sharkey & The Kings Of
Dixieland* .... (Southland)

Eyes Of Texas
Bill Boyd; *Western Swing-#1 & 2* .... (Arhoolie)

Eyes Of Texas
Masters Of Reality; *Masters Of Reality* .... (Delicious Vinyl)

Five Miles To Texas
Stockton & Johnson; *Born By The River* .... (Out Of Print)

Flies Of Texas Are Upon You
Ray Stevens; *Crackin' Up* .... (MCA)

From Tennessee To Texas
Johnny Bush & The Bandoleros; *Live From Texas* .... (Delmark)

Fun In Texas
Britny Fox; *Britny Fox* .... (Columbia)

Ghost Of A Texas Ladies' Man
Concrete Blonde; *Walking In London*. . . . .(I.R.S.)
God Bless The USA
Lee Greenwood; *American Patriot*. . . . . (Capitol)
God Bless America-C. . . . . (Columbia)
God Bless The USA. . . . .(MCA Special Prod.)
Inside Out/You've Got A Good Love Comin'. . . . .(MCA)
Lee Greenwood's Greatest Hits. . . . .(MCA)
Lee Greenwood's Greatest Hits-#2. . . . .(MCA)
Today's Country Classics-C. . . . .(MCA Special Prod.)
God Blessed Texas
Little Texas; *Big Time*. . . . .(Warner Bros.)
Goin' Back To Texas
Bobby Bare; *Bobby Bare's Biggest Hits*. . . . . (Columbia)
Don Edwards; *Best Of Don Edwards*. . . . . (Warner Western)
Goin' Back To Texas. . . . . (Warner Western)
Going Back To Texas
R.C. Smith; *I Have To Paint My Face: Mississippi Blues-1960*. . . . . . (Arhoolie)
Going Back To Texas
Wayne Hancock; *Wild, Free & Reckless*. . . . .(Ark 21)
Going Down To Texas
Shel Silverstein; *Great Conch Train Robbery*. . . . . (Flying Fish)
Good Texan
Vaughan Brothers; *Taste Of Texas-Songs 'Bout Texas By Texans-C*. . . . . (Columbia)
Good Woman Blues
Mel Tillis; *Mel Tillis' Greatest Hits*. (Curb)
Great Joe Bob (A Regional Tragedy)
Country Gazette; *Hello Operator...This Is Country Gazette*. . . . . . (Flying Fish)
Hard Times In The Land Of Plenty
Omar & The Howlers; *Taste Of Texas-Songs 'Bout Texas By Texans-C*. . . . . (Columbia)
Heartache Big As Texas
Ricky Van Shelton; *Texas Super Hits-C*. . . . . (Columbia)
Hello Texas
Jimmy Buffett; *ST/Urban Cowboy*. (Asylum)
Hot Texas Night
Mac Davis; *Texas In My Rear View Mirror*. . . . . (Casablanca)
Hustled Down In Texas
Johnny Winter; *Taste Of Texas-Songs 'Bout Texas By Texans-C*. . . . (Columbia)
I Can't See Texas From Here
George Strait; *Strait From The Heart*. . . . .(MCA)
I Wanna Be Free
Loretta Lynn; *Loretta Lynn's Greatest Hits-#2*. . . . .(MCA)
I Wish I Was In Texas Tonight
Patti Ford; *45-#25*. . . . . (Nationwide Sound Distrib.)
I'd Like To Be In Texas
Don Edwards; *Saddle Songs*. . . . .(Shanachie)
Skip Gorman; *Lonesome Prairie Love*. . . . .(Rounder)
If This Was Texas
Curtis Potter; *Down In Texas Today*. . . . . (Step One)
If You're Gonna Play In Texas
Alabama; *Alabama-Live*. . . . . (RCA)
Roll On. . . . . (RCA)
Stars Are Out In Texas-C. . . . . (RCA)
I'll Take Texas
Clint Black; *Clint Black-Super Hits*. . . . . (RCA)
Country Superstar Hits-C. . . . . (Hip-O)
No Time To Kill. . . . . (RCA)
I'll Take Texas
Vince Gill; *The Key*. . . . .(MCA)
I'm A Texan
Eddie Moore; *Moore Country With*. . . . .(Country Int'l)
I'm Missing Texas Tonight
Kim Grayson; *45-#4800*. . . . . (Soundwaves)
I'm Tired Of Texas
Nancy Walker; *I Can Cook Too*. . . . .(DRG)
Nancy Walker Sings Show Stoppers. (Stet)
It Hurts As Much In Texas (As It Did In Tennessee)
George Jones & Ricky Van Shelton; *Friends In High Places-C*. . . . .(Epic)
Leavin' Texas
Jerry Jeff Walker; *A Man Must Carry On*. . . . .(MCA)
Best Of Jerry Jeff Walker. . . . . (MCA)
Little Ground In Texas
Capitals; *45-#01080*. . . . .(Ridgetop)
Little Red Rodeo
Collin Raye; *Best Of Collin Raye-Direct Hits*. . . . .(Epic)
Little Texas Shaker
Triumph; *Rock & Roll Machine*. . . . .(MCA)
Livingston's Gone To Texas
Jimmy Buffett; *Living & Dying In 3/4 Time*. . . . .(MCA)
Lone Star Beer & Bob Wills Music
Red Steagall; *Lone Star Beer & Bob Wills Music*. . . . . (MCA)
Texas Country. . . . . (MCA)
Lone Star Christmas
Lee Greenwood; *Lee Greenwood-Christmas To Christmas*. . . . .(MCA Special Prod.)

Lone Star Rag
Bob Wills & His Texas Playboys; *Tiffany Transcriptions-#1*. . . . . (Rhino)
Lone Star State Of Mind
Don Williams; *Currents*. . . . . (RCA)
Nanci Griffith; *Country Classics-#8-1986-1987-C*. . . . . (Universal)
Lone Star State Of Mind. . . . . (MCA)
Pat Alger/Nanci Griffith/Trisha Yearwood; *True Love & Other Short Stories-C*. . . . .(Sugar Hill)
Lone Star Trail
Dave Frederickson; *Cowboy Songs On Folkways-C*. . . .(Smithsonian Folkways)
Ken Maynard; *All Time Legends Of Country Music-C*. . . . . (Legacy)
Long Long Texas Road
Roy Drusky; *Roy Drusky-Golden Hits*. . . . .(Plantation)
Long Road To Texas
Bill Wray; *ST/Tilt*. . . . .(MCA)
Long Tall Texan
Beach Boys; *Best Of The Beach Boys-#2*. . . . . (Capitol)
Concert/'69-Live In Concert. . . . . (Capitol)
Murry Kellum; *20 Golden Souvenirs Of Music City U.S.A.-C*. . . . . . (Plantation)
Country Comedy-20 Country Comedy Hits. . . . .(Plantation)
Many A Long & Lonesome Highway
Rodney Crowell; *Keys To The Highway*. . . . . (Columbia)
Taste Of Texas-Songs 'Bout Texas By Texans-C. . . . . (Columbia)
Memories Of East Texas
Michelle Shocked; *Short Sharp Shocked*. . . . . (Mercury)
Merry Texas Christmas You All
Ernest Tubb; *Christmas*. . . . .(MCA Special Prod.)
Michael Martin Murphey; *Cowboy Christmas*. . . . . (Warner Bros.)
Miles And Miles Of Texas
Asleep At The Wheel; *Texas State Of Mind-C*. . . . . (Capitol)
Very Best Of Asleep At The Wheel Since 1970. . . . .(Relentless/Madacy)
Miss Texas 1967
Colourfield; *Deception*. . . . . (Chrysalis)
Mobile/Texas Line
Tom Rush; *Blues Songs & Ballads*. . . . .(Fantasy)
Mind Ramblin'. . . . .(Prestige)
Tom Rush. . . . .(Fantasy)
My Brown Eyed Texas Rose
Tex Ritter; *Arizona Days*. (MCA Special Prod.)
The Country Music Hall Of Fame-Tex Ritter. . . . . (MCA)
My First Taste Of Texas
Ed Bruce; *16 Top Country Hits-#4-C*. . . . . (MCA)
Ed Bruce's Greatest Hits. . . . . (MCA)
I Write It Down. . . . . (MCA)
My Heart's Deep In The Heart Of Texas
Boxcar Willie; *King Of The Freight Train*. . . . . (MCA Special Prod.)
My Train Rolled Up In Texas
Big Joe Turner; *Things That I Used To Do*. . . . . (Pablo)
Never Been To Texas
Power Of Dreams; *Immigrants Emigrants & Me*. . . . . (Polydor)
No Place But Texas
Willie Nelson; *Texas Super Hits-C*. (Columbia)
The Promiseland. . . . . (Columbia)
Northeast Texas Women
David Bromberg; *Bandit In A Bathing Suit*. . . . .(Fantasy)
Jerry Jeff Walker; *Lone Wolf: The Best Of Jerry Jeff Walker Elektra Sessions*. . . . . (Warner Archives)
Willis Alan Ramsey; *Willis Alan Ramsey*. . . . . (Dunhill Compact Classics)
One More Goodtime Band In Texas
Leon Rausch; *Rausch Touch*. . . . . (Southland)
Out On The Texas Plains
Mom & Dads; *Golden Country*. . . . .(Crescendo)
Outlaws & Lone Star Beer
C.W. McCall; *C.W. McCall & Company*. . . . .(Polydor)
Over Yonder (Jonathan's Song)
Steve Earle; *Transcendental Blues*. . . . .(Artemis)
People Up In Texas
Waylon Jennings; *Never Could Toe The Mark*. . . . .(RCA)
Pepper
Butthole Surfers; *Electriclarryland*. (Capitol)
Planet Texas
Kenny Rogers; *Something Inside So Strong*. . . . . (Reprise)
Planet Texas
John Andrew Parks; *John Andrew Parks*. . . . . (Capitol)
Plano Texas Girl
Steve Wariner; *I Got Dreams*. . . . . (MCA)
Pretty Litle Lady From Beaumont, Texas
George Jones; *One Woman Man*. . . . . (Epic)
Texas Super Hits-C. . . . . (Columbia)
Put Me On A Train Back To Texas
Waylon Jennings & Willie Nelson; *Clean Shirt*. . . . .(Epic)
Hot Tracks-Train Super Hits-C. . . . . (Epic)
Quand Je Suit Partis Pour Le Texas
Cleoma Breaux & Others; *Cajun-#1-Abbeville Breakdown*. . . . . . . (Columbia)
Raisin' Cane In Texas
Gene Watson; *All-Time Country Classics-#1-C*. . . . . (Capitol)
Texas State Of Mind-C. . . . . (Capitol)

Raywood Texas
Queen Ida; *Caught In The Act* (Crescendo)
Queen Ida & Her Bon Temps Zydeco Band; *In San Francisco* (Crescendo)
Riding High In Texas
Peter Rowan; *Medicine Trail* (Flying Fish)
Right Man For The Job
Charlie Robison; *Step Right Up* (Lucky Dog)
Rockabilly Blues (Texas 1955)
Johnny Cash; *Texas Super Hits-C* (Columbia)
Somewhere In Texas
Ray Price; *Ray Price's Greatest Hits-#4-By Request* (Step One)
Willie Nelson; *Tougher Than Leather* (Columbia)
Somewhere There's A Rainbow Over Texas
Ruby Falls; *45-#39* (Fifty States)
St. Louis Blues
Bessie Smith; *Beauty Of The Blues* (Columbia)
Bessie Smith-The Collection (Legacy)
Big Joe Turner; *Boss Of The Blues* (Atlantic)
Billie Holiday; *Quintessential-#9-1940-1942* (Columbia)
The Billie Holiday Story-#3 (Columbia)
Bob Wills & His Texas Playboys; *Bob Wills & His Texas Playboys-24 Great Hits* (Polydor)
Cleo Laine; *Jazz* (RCA)
Dave Brubeck Quartet; *25th Anniversary Reunion* (A&M)
Dave Brubeck Quartet-At Carnegie Hall (Columbia)
Paper Moon (Concord Jazz)
Duke Ellington; *1953 Pasadena Concert* (Crescendo)
Ella Fitzgerald; *These Are The Blues* (Verve)
Louis Armstrong; *At The Crescendo* (MCA)
Louis Armstrong-Legendary Performer (RCA)
Louis Armstrong-Vol. 6-St. Louis Blues (Columbia)
Nipper's Greatest Hits Of The '30s-#2-C (RCA)
Merle Haggard & Asleep At The Wheel; *Ride With Bob-C* (DreamWorks/SKG)
Original Broadway Cast; *Black & Blue* (DRG)
Pete Fountain; *Best Of Pete Fountain* (MCA)
Preservation Hall Jazz Band; *Best Of The Preservation Hall Jazz Band* (Columbia)
New Orleans-#2 (Columbia)
Stars Over Texas
Tracy Lawrence; *Best Of Tracy Lawrence* (Atlantic)
Time Marches On (Atlantic)
Stupid Texas Song
Austin Lounge Lizards; *Employee Of The Month* (Sugar Hill)
Sweet Girl In Texas
John Delafose & The Eunice Playboys; *Joe Pete Got Two Women* (Arhoolie)
Sweet Mother Texas
Eddy Raven; *Eddy Raven's Greatest Hits* (Warner Bros.)
Sweetwater, Texas
Charlie Daniels Band; *Saddle Tramp* (Epic)
T For Texas
Lynyrd Skynyrd; *Lynyrd Skynyrd-Box Set* (MCA)
One More From The Road (MCA)
Waylon Jennings; *Only Daddy That'll Walk The Line-The RCA Years* (RCA)
Superstars Salute Jimmie Rodgers-C (Step One)
'Tain't A Cow In Texas
Margaret Whitmire; *Barrelhouse Mamas: Born In The Alley, Raised In The Slums-C* (Yazoo)
Take Care Of Texas
Kris Carpenter; *45-#178* (Door Knob)
Talk To Me Texas
Keith Whitley; *Keith Whitley's Greatest Hits* (RCA)
Tracy Byrd; *Tracy Byrd* (MCA)
Tangled Up In Texas
Billy Burnette; *Coming Home* (Capricorn)
Tennessee Flat Top Box
Johnny Cash; *Classic Cash-Hall Of Fame Series* (Mercury)
Columbia Country Classics-#3-Americana-C (Columbia)
Essential Johnny Cash (Columbia)
The Man In Black-His Greatest Hits (Legacy)
Rosanne Cash; *30 Years Of #1 Hits-#17-C* (Columbia)
Hits-1979-1989 (Columbia)
King's Record Shop (Columbia)
Tennessee Whiskey & Texas Women
Rayburn Anthony; *Audiograph Alive-C* (Audiograph)
Dance Floor Crystal Ball (Audiograph)
Texas
Charlie Daniels Band; *Greatest Fiddlin' Licks* (Epic)
Night Rider (Epic)
ST/Urban Cowboy 2 (Epic)
Texas
Electric Flag; *Legends Of Electric Blues Guitar-#2-C* (Rhino)
Long Time Comin' (Columbia)
Texas
Boiled In Lead; *Boiled In Lead* (Omnium)
Texas
Underworld; *Change The Weather* (Sire)
Texas
Junkyard; *Junkyard* (Geffen)
Texas
Beat Farmers; *Loud & Plowed &...Live!* (Curb)
The Pursuit Of Happiness (Curb)
Texas
Chris Rea; *Road To Hell* (Atlantic)
Texas
Merle Haggard; *Friend In California* (Epic)
Merle Haggard & Freddy Powers; *Texas Super Hits-C* (Columbia)
Texas
Waylon Jennings, Willie Nelson, Johnny Cash, Kris Kristofferson; *Highwayman 2* (Columbia)
Taste Of Texas-Songs 'Bout Texas By Texans-C (Columbia)
Texas & Pacific
Louis Jordan; *Five Guys Named Moe-Original Decca Recordings-#2* (MCA)
Jazz Heritage-Greatest Hits-#2-1941-1947 (MCA)
Texas (When I Die)
Tanya Tucker; *Best Of Tanya Tucker* (MCA)
ST/Hard Country (Epic)
Tanya Tucker Live (MCA Special Prod.)
Tanya Tucker-Greatest Hits Encore (Gold Rush)
The Tanya Tucker Collection (MCA)
Texas Ann
Joe Beck; *Beck & Sanborn* (CBS Associated)
Texas Blues
Marshall Owens; *Alabama Blues-1927-1931-C* (Yazoo)
Roy Willing and His Riders Of The Purple Sage; *Hillbilly Music-Thank God!-#1-C* (Bug)
Texas Playboys & Leon McAuliffe; *San Antonio Rose Story* (Delmark)
Vassar Clements; *Hillbilly Jazz Rides Again* (Flying Fish)
Vassar Clements/David Bromberg/Doug Jernigan; *Hillbilly Jazz* (Flying Fish)
Texas Bound
Gary Morris; *Full Moon Empty Heart* (Liberty)
Texas Bound And Flyin'
Jerry Reed; *ST/Smokey And The Bandit 2* (MCA)
Texas Bound & Flyin' (RCA)
Texas Bound Blues
Margaret Thornton; *Barrelhouse Mamas: Born In The Alley, Raised In The Slums-C* (Yazoo)
Texas Chain Letter Massacre
Pajama Slave Dancers; *Blood Sweat & Beers* (Restless)
Texas Cookin'
Gene Clark/Rodney Crowell/Emmylou Harris/J.J. Walker; *Texas Cookin'* (Sugar Hill)
Guy Clark; *Guy Clark's Greatest Hits* (RCA)
Texas Cowboy
Luther "Guitar Jr." Johnson & His Magic Rockers; *I Want To Groove With You* (Bullseye Blues)
Texas Double Eagle
Bob Wills; *Best Of Bob Wills & His Texas Playboys* (MCA)
Texas Fiddle Man
Asleep At The Wheel; *Keepin' Me Up Nights* (Arista)
Texas Fiddle Song
Merle Haggard; *Big City* (Epic)
Texas Flood
Fenton Robinson; *Somebody Loan Me A Dime* (Alligator)
Larry Davis; *Best Of Duke-Peacock Blues-C* (MCA Special Prod.)
Stevie Ray Vaughan and Double Trouble; *Live Alive* (Epic)
Stevie Ray Vaughan and Double Trouble (Epic)
Taste Of Texas-Songs 'Bout Texas By Texans-C (Columbia)
Texas Gales
Doc & Merle Watson; *Ballads From Deep Gap* (Vanguard)
Texas Girl At The Funeral Of Her Father
Randy Newman; *Little Criminals* (Warner Bros.)
Texas Guitar Stomp
Maddox Brothers & Rose; *1946-1951-#2* (Arhoolie)
Texas Has A Whorehouse In It
Dom Deluise/Dogettes; *ST/Best Little Whorehouse In Texas* (MCA)
Original Cast; *Best Little Whorehouse In Texas* (MCA)
Texas Heartache #1
Mickey Gilley; *Put Your Dreams Away* (Epic)
Texas Hills
Sons Of The Pioneers; *Western Country* (Granite)
Texas Honky Tonk
David Houston; *David Houston Sings Texas Honky Tonk* (Delmark)
Texas Country (Delmark)
Texas Hop
Pee Wee Crayton; *Blues Masters-#3-Texas Blues-C* (Rhino)
Texas I Love You
Marty Robbins; *Lost & Found* (Columbia)
Texas In 1880
Foster & Lloyd; *Foster & Lloyd* (RCA)
Texas In My Rear View Mirror
Mac Davis; *Mac Davis-Very Best & More* (Casablanca)
Texas In My Rear View Mirror (Casablanca)
Texas Is Bigger Than It Used To Be
Mark Chesnutt; *Almost Goodbye* (MCA)
ST/8 Seconds (MCA)
Texas Jalapenos
Texas Rubies; *Working Girl Blues* (Monsterdisc)

Texas Jump
  Ozzie Nelson & His Orchestra; *The Uncollected Ozzie Nelson & His Orchestra-1940-1942* . . . . (Hindsight)
Texas Lawman
  Regulators; *Regulators* . . . . (Polydor)
Texas Lemon Flavor
  Stefan Grossman; *Yazoo Basin Boogie* . . . . (Shanachie)
Texas Love Song
  Elton John; *Don't Shoot Me I'm Only The Piano Player* . . . . (Polydor)
Texas Lullaby
  David Allan Coe; *Cowboys* . . . . (Columbia)
    Longhaired Redneck . . . . (Columbia)
    Taste Of Texas-Songs 'Bout Texas By Texans-C . . . . (Columbia)
Texas Lullaby
  Doobie Brothers; *Stampede* . . . . (Warner Bros.)
Texas Me
  Doug Sahm; *Best Of The Sir Douglas Quintet* . . . . (Takoma)
Texas Me And You
  Asleep At The Wheel; *Very Best Of Asleep At The Wheel Since 1970* . . . . (Relentless/Madacy)
Texas Moaner Blues
  Louis Armstrong & King Oliver; *Louis Armstrong & King Oliver* . . . (Milestone)
Texas Morning
  Michael Nesmith & The First National Band; *Complete Michael Nesmith* . . . . (Pacific Arts)
Texas On A Saturday Night
  Willie Nelson; *Taste Of Texas-Songs 'Bout Texas By Texans-C* . . . . (Columbia)
  Willie Nelson & Mel Tillis; *Half Nelson-C* . . . . (Columbia)
Texas Party
  Johnny Copeland; *Boom Boom* . . . . (Rounder)
Texas Plains
  Riders In The Sky; *Cowboy Way* . . . . (MCA)
    Saturday Morning With Riders In The Sky . . . . (MCA)
  Stuart Hamblen; *Stuart Hamblen-A Man & His Music* . . . . (Lamb & Lion)
Texas Playboy Rag
  Bob Wills & His Texas Playboys; *Essential Bob Wills & His Texas Playboys-1935-1973* . . . . (Legacy)
Texas Radio Horror
  Strip Mind; *What's In Your Mouth* . . . . (Sire)
Texas Rangers
  Ian & Sylvia; *Ian & Sylvia's Greatest Hits* . . . . (Vanguard)
    Northern Journey . . . . (Vanguard)
  Michael Martin Murphey; *Cowboy Songs* . . . . (Warner Western)
Texas Red
  Strength In Numbers; *Telluride Sessions* . . . . (MCA)
Texas Rhythm Club
  Joe McBride; *Texas Rhythm Club* . . . . (Heads Up Records Int'l)
Texas Ride Song
  BoDeans; *Go Slow Down* . . . . (Slash)
Texas Rose Cafe
  Little Feat; *Sailin' Shoes* . . . . (Warner Bros.)
Texas Saturday Night
  Moe Bandy; *Motel Matches* . . . . (Columbia)
Texas Serenade
  Gun Club; *Miami* . . . . (I.R.S.)
Texas Shuffle
  Count Basie; *Basie Reunions* . . . . (Prestige)
    Best Of Count Basie . . . . (MCA)
  Houston Person; *Heavy Juice* . . . . (Muse)
Texas Sidestep
  Deanna Cox; *Country Jukebox Greatest Hits-#2-C* . . . . (Warner Bros.)
Texas Size Heartache
  Joe Diffie; *Joe Diffie's Greatest Hits* . . . . (Epic)
Texas State Of Mind
  David Frizzell & Shelly West; *Carryin' On The Family Names* . . . . (Warner Bros.)
    Golden Duets . . . . (Viva)
Texas Stew
  Louis Jordan & His Tympany Five; *Rock 'N Roll Call* . . . . (Bluebird)
Texas Strut
  Gary Moore; *Still Got The Blues* . . . . (Charisma)
Texas Tattoo
  Gibson/Miller Band; *Steppin' Country-C* . . . . (Columbia)
    Where There's Smoke . . . . (Epic)
Texas Tea
  Dee Mullins; *20 Great Hits-C* . . . . (Plantation)
    Dee Mullins . . . . (Plantation)
Texas Tea Party
  Benny Goodman; *Benny Goodman-Early Years* . . . . (Biograph)
Texas To A "T"
  Whites; *A Lifetime In The Making* . . . . (Ceili Music)
Texas Tornado
  Doug Sahm; *Best Of Doug Sahm & Friends-Atlantic Sessions* . . . . (Rhino)
    Best Of Doug Sahm & Sir Douglas Quintet . . . . (Mercury)
Texas Tornado
  Tracy Lawrence; *Best Of Tracy Lawrence* . . . . (Atlantic)
    I See It Now . . . . (Atlantic)

Texas Twister
  Little Feat; *Representing The Mambo* . . . . (Warner Bros.)
Texas Two Step
  Bob Wills; *The Country Music Hall Of Fame-Bob Wills* . . . . (Universal)
Texas Woman Blues
  Taj Mahal; *Recycling The Blues & Other Related Stuff* . . . . (Columbia)
Texas Women
  Hank Williams, Jr.; *Hank Williams, Jr.'s Greatest Hits* . . . . (WB/Curb)
    Rowdy . . . . (WB/Curb)
Texas Women (Don't Stay Lonely Long)
  Brooks & Dunn; *Hard Workin' Man* . . . . (Arista)
Texas, 1947
  Guy Clark; *Guy Clark's Greatest Hits* . . . . (RCA)
    Old No. 1 . . . . (Sugar Hill)
    Steel Rails-Classic Railroad Songs-#1-C . . . . (Rounder)
Texas, Me & You
  Asleep At The Wheel; *Route 66* . . . . (Liberty)
That Ol' Texas Two-Step
  Charlie Walker; *Charlie Walker* . . . . (Dot)
That's Right (You're Not From Texas)
  Lyle Lovett; *Live In Texas* . . . . (MCA)
    The Road To Ensenada . . . . (MCA)
Theme From "Bronco"
  Original Soundtrack; *Television's Greatest Hits-#4-Black & White Classics-C* . . . . (TVT)
Theme From "The Lone Ranger" (William Tell Overture)
  Boston Pops Orchestra; *TV Classics-C* . . . . (RCA)
  Boston Pops Orchestra/Arthur Fiedler; *Fiedler-Greatest Hits* . . . . (RCA)
  Original Soundtrack; *Television's Greatest Hits-#7-Cable Ready-C* . . . . . (TVT)
  Spike Jones & His City Slickers; *Best Of Spike Jones & His City Slickers* . . . . (RCA)
Theme From "Walker, Texas Ranger"
  Original Soundtrack; *CBS: The First 50 Years* . . . . (TVT)
There Ain't A Cow In Texas
  Merle Travis; *Red, White & Bluegrass-C* . . . . (C.M.H. Prod.)
  Vassar Clements & Buddy Emmons; *Saturday Night Shuffle-Merle Travis Celebration* . . . . (Shanachie)
There'll Always Be Honky Tonks In Texas
  Darrell McCall & Johnny Bush; *Hot Texas Country* . . . . (Step One)
There's A Little Bit Of Everything In Texas
  Ernest Tubb; *The Ernest Tubb Story* . . . . (MCA)
    Walking The Floor Over You . . . . (Laserlight)
  Ernest Tubb & Roy Clark; *Ernest Tubb Collection-C* . . . . (Step One)
Tonight I Feel Like Texas
  Barbara Lamb; *Tonight I Feel Like Texas* . . . . (Sugar Hill)
Waltz Across Texas
  Ernest Tubb; *Ernest Tubb's Greatest Hits* . . . . (MCA)
    The Country Music Hall Of Fame-Ernest Tubb . . . . (MCA)
  Ernest Tubb & Willie Nelson; *Ernest Tubb Collection-C* . . . . (Step One)
Wasp (Texas Radio & The Big Beat)
  Doors; *Alive She Cried* . . . . (Elektra)
    Doors-Classics . . . . (Elektra)
    L.A. Woman . . . . (Elektra)
    Weird Scenes Inside The Gold Mine . . . . (Elektra)
Way Down Texas Way
  Asleep At The Wheel; *Asleep At The Wheel-10* . . . . (Epic)
    Swinging Best Of Asleep At The Wheel . . . . (Epic)
    Taste Of Texas-Songs 'Bout Texas By Texans-C . . . . (Columbia)
Way Out West In Texas
  Don Edwards; *My Hero, Gene Autry: A Tribute* . . . . (Shanachie)
We Almost Had Texas Skies Today
  Hank Thompson; *Here's To Country Music* . . . . (Step One)
West Texas Highway & Me
  Gary Morris; *Faded Blue* . . . . (Warner Bros.)
West Texas Plains
  Rosie Flores; *After The Farm* . . . . (Hightone)
West Texas Waltz
  Butch Hancock; *Own & Own* . . . . (Sugar Hill)
West Texas Wind
  Joe Sun; *45-#1324* . . . . (AMI)
West Texas Women
  Whistlin' Alex Moore; *I'm Wild About My Lovin'-1928-1930* . . . . . . (Historical)
When It's Christmas Time In Texas
  Rick Orozco; *Tejano Country Christmas-C* . . . . (Arista)
Wingin' It Home To Texas
  Jerry Jeff Walker; *Collectibles* . . . . (MCA)
Woman In Texas
  Jerry Jeff Walker; *Live At Gruene Hall* . . . . (Rykodisc)
Yellow Rose Of Texas
  Hoyt Axton; *Songs Of The Civil War-C* . . . . (Columbia)
  Michael Martin Murphey; *Cowboy Songs* . . . . (Warner Western)
  Mitch Miller; *Mitch Miller-16 Most Requested Songs* . . . . (Columbia)
  Roy Rogers; *Great American Singing Cowboys-C* . . . . (Republic/Universal)
You Can't Get The Hell Out Of Texas
  George Jones; *Taste Of Texas-Songs 'Bout Texas By Texans-C* . . . . . (Columbia)
You Don't Have To Be From Texas
  Leon Rausch; *Deep In The Heart Of Texas* . . . . (Southland)

STATES: TEXAS

You're From Texas
Bob Wills & His Texas Playboys; *Tiffany Transcriptions-#4-You're From Texas* . . . . (Rhino)
Tracy Byrd & Asleep At The Wheel; *Ride With Bob-C* . . . . (DreamWorks/SKG)

STATES: UTAH

See Also: **CITIES: A-Z**

Promised Land
Bruce Springsteen; *Darkness On The Edge Of Town* . . . . (Columbia)
Bruce Springsteen & The E Street Band; *Bruce Springsteen & The E Street Band Live/1975-85* . . . . (Legacy)
Utah
Steve Lacy & Michael Smith; *Sidelines* . . . . (Improvising Artists)
X-Tal; *Everything Crash* . . . .(Alias)
Utah Carroll
Skip Gorman; *A Cowboy's Wild Song To His Herd* . . . . (Rounder)
Utah Tribute
Chris LeDoux; *Chris LeDoux & The Saddle Boogie Band* . . . . (Liberty)
Utah-Suite 4
Scott Moulton; *Four Corners Suite* . . . . (Revere)

STATES: VERMONT

See Also: **CITIES: A-Z**

Moonlight In Vermont
Cal Tjader; *Latin Kick* . . . .(Fantasy)
Captain Beefheart & His Magic Band; *Trout Mask Replica* . . . .(Reprise)
Frank Sinatra; *Come Fly With Me* . . . . (Capitol)
Frank Sinatra-Gift Set . . . . (Capitol)
Sarah Vaughan; *Complete Sarah Vaughan On Mercury-#3* . . . . (Mercury)
Sarah Vaughan-Golden Hits . . . . (Mercury)
Vermont Farmer's Song
Margaret MacArthur; *Almanac Of New England Farm Songs* . . . (Green Linnet)
Vermont Is Afire In The Autumn
Lui Collins; *Made In New England* . . . . (Green Linnet)

STATES: VIRGINIA

See Also: **CITIES: A-Z**

Carry Me Back To Old Virginny
Jerry Lee Lewis; *Doin' Just Fine* . . . .(Accord)
Ole Tyme Country Music . . . .(Sun)
Sunday Down South . . . .(Sun)
Down In Virginia
Jimmy Reed; *Best Of Jimmy Reed* . . . . (Crescendo)
East Virginia
Joan Baez; *Greatest Folksingers Of The '60s-C* . . . . (Vanguard)
Joan Baez . . . . (Vanguard)
The Joan Baez Ballad Book . . . . (Vanguard)
Pete Seeger; *Essential Pete Seeger* . . . . (Vanguard)
Folk Classics: Roots Of American Folk Music-C . . . . (Columbia)
Greatest Folksingers Of The '60s-C . . . . (Vanguard)
Going Back To Virginia
Jim & Jesse; *Music Among Friends* . . . . (Rounder)
Going To Virginia
Ralph Willis; *Southern Blues* . . . . (Savoy)
I'm Coming Virginia
Bix Beiderbecke; *Bix Beiderbecke-#1-Singin' The Blues* . . . . (Legacy)
Coleman Hawkins & Benny Carter; *Coleman Hawkins & Benny Carter* . . . . (Disques Swing)
Stephane Grappelli; *Compact Jazz-Stephane Grappelli* . . . . (Verve)
Lees Of Old Virginia
William Daniels/Original Cast; *1776* . . . . (Sony Music Classical)
Missin' You
Little Feat; *Time Loves A Hero* . . . . (Warner Bros.)
Oh Virginia
Blessid Union Of Souls; *Home* . . . . (EMI)
Old Virginia Lowlands
John Townley & The Press Gang; *Chesapeake Sailor's Companion* . . (Adelphi)
Old Virginia March
Sam McNeil/Dent Wimmer/Others; *Old Originals-#2* . . . . (Rounder)
Promised Land
Band; *Moondog Matinee* . . . . (Capitol)
Chuck Berry; *Rock 'N' Roll Rarities-20 Magic Tracks* . . . . (Chess)
The Chess Box-Chuck Berry . . . . (Chess)
Elvis Presley; *Promised Land* . . . . (RCA)
ST/This Is Elvis . . . .(RCA)
Freddy Weller; *Country Music Classics-#11-Early '70s-C* . . . . (K-Tel)
Freddy Weller's Greatest Hits . . . . (Columbia)
Gary Morris; *Full Moon Empty Heart* . . . . (Liberty)

Grateful Dead; *Steal Your Face* . . . . (Grateful Dead)
James Taylor; *Walking Man* . . . . (Warner Bros.)
Kingfish; *Kingfish/Alive In Eighty Five-Double Dose* . . . . (Relix)
Theme From "The Virginian"
101 Strings Orchestra; *Western Themes-#1* . . . .(Alshire)
Original Soundtrack; *Television's Greatest Hits-#2-C* . . . .(TVT)
To See My Angel In Virginia
Livewire; *Wired* . . . .(Rounder)
Virginia
Marshall Tucker Band; *Searchin' For A Rainbow* . . . . (AJK Music)
Virginia
Statler Brothers; *Harold Lew Phil & Don* . . . .(Mercury)
Virginia Boys
Country Gazette; *Hello Operator...This Is Country Gazette* . . . . . . (Flying Fish)
Strictly Instrumental . . . . (Flying Fish)
Virginia Plain
Roxy Music; *Roxy Music* . . . . (Reprise)
Street Life-20 Great Hits . . . . (Reprise)
Virginia's Bloody Soil
Tennessee Ernie Ford; *Tennessee Ernie Ford Sings Songs Of The Civil War* . . . .(Capitol)
Virginia's Heritage
Reno & Smiley; *1983 Collector's Edition-#10* . . . . .(International Mktg. Group)
West Virginia
Maggie & Terre Roche; *Seductive Reasoning* . . . . . . (Sony Music Special Prod.)

STATES: WASHINGTON

See Also: **CITIES: A-Z**

Bow Down To Washington
Original Soundtrack; *College Fight Songs: The Pac Ten-C* . . . .(K-Tel)
The Greatest College Fight Songs . . . . (Laserlight)
Fight Song, The
Original Soundtrack; *College Fight Songs: The Pac Ten-C* . . . .(K-Tel)
My Washington Woman
Kenny Rogers And The First Edition; *Featuring The Songs Of Kenny Rogers And The First Edition* . . . . (MCA Special Prod.)
Kenny Rogers And The First Edition's All Time Greatest Hits-#1 . . . . (MCA Special Prod.)

STATES: WEST VIRGINIA

See Also: **CITIES: A-Z**

Carrying Your Love With Me
George Strait; *Carrying Your Love With Me* . . . . (MCA)
Latest Greatest Straitest Hits . . . . (MCA)
Deeper Than The Holler
Randy Travis; *Randy Travis' Greatest #1 Hits* . . . .(Warner Bros.)
Randy Travis' Greatest Hits-#1 . . . .(Warner Bros.)
Green Rolling Hills (West Virginia)
Bottle Hill; *Rumor In Their Own Time-#1* . . . . (Biograph)
Emmylou Harris; *Quarter Moon In A Ten Cent Town* . . . .(Warner Bros.)
Leaving West Virginia
Kathy Mattea; *Walk The Way The Wind Blows* . . . .(Mercury)
Little Home In West Virginia
Josh Graves; *King Of The Dobro* . . . .(C.M.H. Prod.)
Muswell Hillbilly
Kinks; *Everybody's In Show-Biz* . . . .(Rhino)
Muswell Hillbillies . . . .(VelVel)
Salt Pork, West Virginia
Louis Jordan; *Jazz Heritage-Greatest Hits-#2-1941-1947* . . . .(MCA)
Stony Mountain, West Virginia
Jim & Jesse; *In The Tradition* . . . . (Rounder)
Take Me Home, Country Roads
John Denver; *Evening With John Denver* . . . . (RCA)
John Denver's Greatest Hits . . . . (RCA)
Poems, Prayers & Promises . . . . (RCA)
Take Me Home, Country Roads & Other Hits . . . . (RCA)
Toots & The Maytals; *Brand New Second-Hand* . . . . (Rykodisc)
West Virginia
Tarwater Band; *Walking Across Egypt* . . . . (Flying Fish)
Trapezoid; *Three Forks Of Cheat* . . . .(Rounder)
West Virginia Blues
Edward Thompson; *Alabama Blues-1927-1931-C* . . . . (Yazoo)
West Virginia Fantasies
Chicago; *Chicago At Carnegie Hall* . . . .(Chicago)
Chicago II . . . .(Chicago)
Group Portrait . . . .(Chicago)
West Virginia Friend
Holly Near; *Watch Out* . . . . (Redwood)
West Virginia Man
David Allan Coe; *20 Great Hits-C* . . . . (Plantation)
Willie Nelson; *Longhorn Jamboree* . . . . (Plantation)

Willie Nelson & His Friends . . . . (Plantation)
West Virginia Mine Disaster
Betsy Rutherford; *Betsy Rutherford* . . . .(Biograph)
Cindy Mangsen; *Long Time Traveling* . . . . (Hogeye)
West Virginia My Home
Hazel Dickens & Alice Gerrard; *Hazel Dickens & Alice Gerrard* . . . . (Rounder)

STATES: WISCONSIN
See Also: *CITIES: A-Z*

Back To Wisconsin Waltz
Michigan Dutchmen; *Umpa-Umpa-Umpapa* . . . .(Jay Jay)
On Wisconsin/If You Want To Be A Badger
University Of Wisconsin Marching Band; *Fifth Quarter* . . . . . .(Fidelity Sound)
On, Wisconsin
Magic Organ; *22 Great Organ Favorites* . . . .(Ranwood)
Traveling With The Magic Organ . . . .(Ranwood)
Original Soundtrack; *College Fight Songs: The Big Ten-C* . . . . (K-Tel)
The Greatest College Fight Songs . . . . (Laserlight)
Up In Wisconsin
Peter & Lou Berryman; *No Relation* . . . . (Cornbelt)
Wisconsin Forward Forever
University Of Wisconsin Marching Band; *Fifth Quarter* . . . . . .(Fidelity Sound)
Wisconsin's Pride
University Of Wisconsin Marching Band; *Fifth Quarter* . . . . . .(Fidelity Sound)
Wreck Of The Edmund Fitzgerald
Gordon Lightfoot; *Gord's Gold-#2* . . . .(Warner Bros.)
Summertime Dream . . . . (Reprise)

STATES: WYOMING
See Also: *CITIES: A-Z*

Cowboy From Wyoming
Sammi Smith; *Better Than Ever* . . . . (Step One)
Emperor Of Wyoming
Neil Young; *Neil Young* . . . . (Reprise)
Get Along Little Dogies
Riders In The Sky; *Saddle Pals.* . . . . (Rounder)
Tex Ritter; *Tex Ritter: Country Music Hall Of Fame* . . . . . .(MCA Special Prod.)
Guitar Picker From Rody, Wyoming
Joey Davis; *45-#2248* . . . .(MRC)
Hills Of Old Wyomin'
Sons Of The Pioneers; *The Country Music Hall Of Fame-Sons Of The
Pioneers* . . . .(MCA)
Tex Ritter; *The Country Music Hall Of Fame-Tex Ritter* . . . .(MCA)
Paint Me Back Home In Wyoming
Chris LeDoux; *Paint Me Back Home In Wyoming* . . . . (Liberty)
Sounds Of The Western Country . . . . (Liberty)
Roamin' Wyoming
Randy Travis; *Wind In The Wire.* . . . .(Warner Bros.)
Sweet Wyoming Home
Chris LeDoux; *Chris LeDoux & The Saddle Boogie Band* . . . . (Liberty)
Take Me Back To Old Wyoming
Chris LeDoux; *Thirty-Dollar Cowboy* . . . . (Liberty)
Whoopee Ti Yi Yo
Burl Ives; *Best Of Burl Ives.* . . . .(MCA)
David Bromberg; *How Late'll Ya Play 'Til?* . . . . (Fantasy)
Roy Rogers & Sons Of The Pioneers; *Roy Rogers & Sons Of The
Pioneers* . . . . (Varese Sarabande)
Woody Guthrie & Cisco Houston; *Cowboy Songs On
Folkways-C.* . . . . (Smithsonian Folkways)

STONES, Bricks, Rocks
See Also: *MOUNTAINS, ROCK & ROCKING*

(I'm Not Your) Steppin' Stone
Monkees; *Monkees' Greatest Hits* . . . . (Rhino)
Another Brick In The Wall, Part 2
Class Of '99; *ST/The Faculty* . . . . (Columbia)
Pink Floyd; *Collection Of Great Dance Songs* . . . . (Columbia)
Delicate Sound Of Thunder . . . . (Columbia)
The Wall . . . . (Columbia)
Roger Waters; *The Wall-Live In Berlin.* . . . . (Mercury)
Brick
Ben Folds Five; *Whatever And Ever Amen* . . . . (Caroline/550)
Brick House
Commodores; *Commodores* . . . . (Motown)
Commodores Greatest Hits . . . . (Motown)
Commodores-All The Great Hits . . . . (Motown)
Compact Command Performances-Commodores . . . . (Motown)
Motown Dance Party-#2-C . . . . (Motown)

Daddy Won't Sell The Farm
Montgomery Gentry; *Tattoos & Scars* . . . . (Columbia)
Goin' Gone
Kathy Mattea; *Collection Of Hits* . . . . (Mercury)
Untasted Honey . . . .(Polydor Country)
Hard As A Rock
AC/DC; *Ballbreaker* . . . . (East West)
Hard Rock Bottom Of Your Heart
Randy Travis; *No Holdin' Back* . . . . (Warner Bros.)
Heart Of Stone
Rolling Stones; *Big Hits (High Tide & Green Grass)* . . . .(Abkco)
Hot Rocks 1964-1971 . . . .(Abkco)
Singles Collection-The London Years . . . .(Abkco)
The Rolling Stones, Now! . . . .(Abkco)
Heart Of Stone
Fleetwood Mac; *25 Years-The Chain* . . . . (Warner Bros.)
Hearts Of Stone
Bruce Springsteen; *Tracks* . . . . (Columbia)
Southside Johnny And The Asbury Jukes; *Best Of Southside Johnny And The
Asbury Jukes* . . . . (Legacy)
Cover Me (Bruce Springsteen Tribute)-C . . . . (Rhino)
Hearts Of Stone . . . . (Epic)
Hearts Of Stone
Fontane Sisters; *Hearts Of Stone-The Best Of The Fontane
Sisters* . . . .(Varese Sarabande)
Holiday
Bee Gees; *Bee Gees-Gold* . . . .(Polydor)
Best Of The Bee Gees-#1 . . . .(Polydor)
I Am A Rock
Simon & Garfunkel; *Collected Works* . . . . (Columbia)
Simon & Garfunkel's Greatest Hits . . . . (Columbia)
Sounds Of Silence . . . . (Columbia)
I Threw A Brick Through A Window
U2; *October.* . . . . (Island)
In The House Of Stone And Light
Martin Page; *In The House Of Stone And Light* . . . . (Mercury)
Kryptonite
3 Doors Down; *Better Life.* . . . . (Republic/Universal)
Now That's What I Call Music!-#5-C . . . .(Virgin)
Lift Up Every Stone
John Hiatt; *Crossing Muddy Waters* . . . . (Vanguard)
Like A Rock
Bob Seger & The Silver Bullet Band; *Like A Rock* . . . . (Capitol)
Like A Rolling Stone
Bob Dylan; *Biograph* . . . . (Columbia)
Bob Dylan At Budokan . . . . (Columbia)
Bob Dylan's Greatest Hits . . . . (Columbia)
Highway 61 Revisited . . . . (Columbia)
More American Graffiti-#4-C . . . . (MCA)
Self Portrait . . . . (Columbia)
Bob Dylan And The Band; *Before The Flood* . . . . (Columbia)
Jimi Hendrix; *ST/Jimi Plays Monterey* . . . .(Reprise)
Jimi Hendrix Experience; *Jimi Hendrix Experience* . . . .(Reprise)
Rolling Stones; *Stripped* . . . .(Virgin)
Loves Me Like A Rock
Oak Ridge Boys; *Best Of The Oak Ridge Boys* . . . . (Columbia)
Paul Simon; *Greatest Hits, Etc.* . . . . (Columbia)
Negotiations And Love Songs, 1971-1986 . . . . (Warner Bros.)
Paul Simon In Concert/Live Rhymin' . . . . (Columbia)
There Goes Rhymin' Simon . . . . (Columbia)
On The Rock Where Moses Stood
Carter Family; *Worried Man Blues: Their Complete Victor Recordings-
1930.* . . . . (Rounder)
Flatt & Scruggs; *Songs Of The Famous Carter Family* . . . . (Legacy)
Papa Was A Rollin' Stone
Temptations; *20/20-C* . . . . (Motown)
25 #1 Hits From 25 Years-C . . . . (Motown)
All The Million-Sellers . . . . (Motown)
Billboard Top Rock 'N' Roll Hits-1972-C . . . . (Rhino)
Compact Command Performances-Temptations . . . . (Motown)
Temptations-Anthology-The Best Of The Temptations . . . . (Motown)
River Of Stone
Restless Heart; *Fast Moving Train* . . . . (RCA)
Rock & A Hard Place
Rolling Stones; *Flashpoint* . . . .(Virgin)
Steel Wheels . . . . (Rolling Stones)
Rock, The
George Jones; *The Rock: Stone Cold Country 2001* . . . .(BNA)
Rocks And Gravel
Steve James; *Two Track Mind.* . . . .(Antone's)
Rocks In My Bed
Duke Ellington; *Duke Ellington & The Blanton-Webster Band* . . . . . . (Bluebird)
Jimmy Witherspoon; *Baby Baby Baby* . . . .(Prestige)
Ray Brown All-Stars; *Don't Forget The Blues* . . . . (Concord Jazz)
Sarah Vaughan; *Duke Ellington Songbook Two* . . . . (Pablo)
Rocky Road To Dublin
Dubliners; *Dublin Songs-C* . . . . (AJK Music)
Skip Gorman; *A Cowboy's Wild Song To His Herd.* . . . . (Rounder)

Step By Step
Whitney Houston; *ST/The Preacher's Wife* . . . . (Arista)
Stepping Stone
Lari White; *Stepping Stone* . . . . (Lyric Street)
Sticks & Stones
Tracy Lawrence; *Tracy Lawrence* . . . . (Atlantic)
Stone Cold Sober
Rod Stewart; *Atlantic Crossing* . . . . (Warner Bros.)
Storyteller/The Complete Anthology: 1964-1990 . . . . (Warner Bros.)
Stone Free
Eric Clapton; *Eric Clapton-Unplugged* . . . . (Reprise)
Jimi Hendrix; *Are You Experienced?* . . . . (Reprise)
Stones
Neil Diamond; *Neil Diamond-His 12 Greatest Hits* . . . . (MCA)
Stones . . . . (MCA)
Stones In The Road
Mary Chapin Carpenter; *Stones In The Road.* . . . . (Columbia)
Stoney End
Barbra Streisand; *Barbra Streisand's Greatest Hits, Volume 2* . . . . . (Columbia)
Stoney End . . . . (Columbia)
Laura Nyro; *First Songs* . . . . (Columbia)
That Rock Won't Roll
Restless Heart; *Best Of Restless Heart.* . . . . (RCA)
Country Music Classics-#22-1985-1990-C . . . . (K-Tel)
Wheels . . . . (RCA)
Third Stone From The Sun
Jimi Hendrix; *Essential Jimi Hendrix* . . . . (Reprise)
Kiss The Sky . . . . (Reprise)
Jimi Hendrix Experience; *Are You Experienced?* . . . . (Reprise)
Throwing Stones
Paula Cole; *This Fire* . . . . (Imago)
Who's Your Baby Now
Mark Knopfler; *Sailing To Philadelphia* . . . . (Warner Bros.)
You Made A Rock Of A Rolling Stone
Oak Ridge Boys; *Seasons* . . . . (MCA)

STOP

See Also: **BEGINNINGS, ENDINGS, OPEN & CLOSED**

"They Just Can't Stop It" (The Games People Play)
Spinners; *Best Of The Spinners* . . . . (Atlantic)
Golden Age Of Black Music-1970-1975-C . . . . (Atlantic)
Ain't No Stoppin' Us Now
McFadden & Whitehead; *Ten Years Of #1 Hits-C* . . . . (Philadelphia Int'l)
Ain't No Stoppin' Us Now
Luther Vandross; *Songs* . . . . (Epic)
Baby Stop Crying
Bob Dylan; *Street Legal* . . . . (Columbia)
Bus Stop
Hollies; *Best Of The Hollies* . . . . (EMI)
History Of British Rock-#3-C . . . . (Rhino)
The Hollies' Greatest Hits . . . . (Epic)
Can You Stop The Rain
Grover Washington, Jr.; *Soulful Strut* . . . . (Columbia)
Peabo Bryson; *Can You Stop The Rain* . . . . (Columbia)
Can't Do A Thing (To Stop Me)
Chris Isaak; *San Francisco Days* . . . . (Reprise)
Can't Stop
DeBarge; *All This Love* . . . . (Motown)
Can't Stop
After 7; *After 7* . . . . (Virgin)
Can't Stop
Rick James; *Glow* . . . . (Gordy)
Can't Stop
Madonna; *ST/Who's That Girl.* . . . . (Sire)
Can't Stop Dancin'
Captain & Tennille; *Captain & Tennille's Greatest Hits* . . . . (A&M)
Can't Stop Dancing
Sylvester; *Living Proof* . . . . (Fantasy)
Sylvester's Greatest Hits. . . . . (Fantasy)
Can't Stop Lovin'
George Thorogood & The Destroyers; *George Thorogood & The
Destroyers* . . . . (Rounder)
Can't Stop Lovin' You
Van Halen; *Balance.* . . . . (Warner Bros.)
Can't Stop My Heart From Loving You
Aaron Neville; *The Tattooed Heart* . . . . (A&M)
O'Kanes; *Greatest Country Hits Of The '80s-1987-C* . . . . (Columbia)
More Hot Country Requests-#2-C . . . . (Epic)
O'Kanes . . . . (Columbia)
Can't Stop Rockin'
ZZ Top; *Afterburner* . . . . (Warner Bros.)
Can't Stop The Bum Rush
Kris Kross; *Totally Krossed Out* . . . . (Ruffhouse)
Can't Stop The Music
Daryl Hall & John Oates; *No Goodbyes* . . . . (Atlantic)

War Babies . . . . (Atlantic)
Can't Stop The Music
Village People; *Can't Stop The Music* . . . . (Casablanca)
Village People's Greatest Hits . . . . (Rhino)
Can't Stop The Rain
Subdudes; *Colossal Head* . . . . (Warner Bros.)
Can't Stop The Street (Krush Groove)
Chaka Khan; *45-#7-28923* . . . . (Warner Bros.)
Can't Stop This Thing We Started
Bryan Adams; *Waking Up The Neighbours* . . . . (A&M)
Can't Stop Worrying
Dave Mason; *Alone Together.* . . . . (MCA)
Cool It Now
New Edition; *New Edition* . . . . (MCA)
New Edition's Greatest Hits, Vol. 1. . . . . (MCA)
Crazy Feelin'
Jefferson Starship; *Earth* . . . . (Grunt)
Does This Bus Stop At 82nd Street?
Bruce Springsteen; *Greetings From Asbury Park, N.J.* . . . . (Columbia)
Tracks . . . . (Columbia)
Don't Disturb This Groove
System; *Don't Disturb This Groove* . . . . (Atlantic)
Golden Age Of Black Music-1977-1988-C . . . . (Atlantic)
Don't Stop
Frankie Miller; *Standing On The Edge.* . . . . (Capitol)
Don't Stop
Elton John; *Legacy-A Tribute To Fleetwood Mac's Rumours-C* . . . . . (Lava)
Fleetwood Mac; *25 Years-The Chain* . . . . (Warner Bros.)
Fleetwood Mac Live . . . . (Warner Bros.)
Fleetwood Mac's Greatest Hits. . . . . (Warner Bros.)
Rumours . . . . (Warner Bros.)
Don't Stop
Wade Hayes; *Old Enough To Know Better* . . . . (Columbia)
Steppin' Country-#2-C . . . . (Columbia)
Super Hits Of 1995-C . . . . (Epic)
Don't Stop
Lionel Richie; *Dancing On The Ceiling* . . . . (Motown)
Don't Stop
Jeffrey Osborne; *Don't Stop.* . . . . (A&M)
Don't Stop
Stone Roses; *The Stone Roses* . . . . (Silvertone)
Don't Stop Believin'
Olivia Newton-John; *Olivia Newton-John's Greatest Hits* . . . . (MCA)
Physical. . . . . (MCA)
Don't Stop Believin'
Journey; *Escape* . . . . (Columbia)
Journey's Greatest Hits. . . . . (Columbia)
Don't Stop Dancing
Bar-Kays; *Gotta Groove* . . . . (Stax)
Don't Stop Me Now
Queen; *Jazz* . . . . (Hollywood)
Live Killers . . . . (Hollywood)
Don't Stop The Dance
Bryan Ferry; *Boys & Girls* . . . . (Warner Bros.)
Greenpeace/Rainbow Warriors-C . . . . (Geffen)
Don't Stop The Music
Yarbrough & Peoples; *Two Of Us* . . . . (Mercury)
Don't Stop Till You Get Enough
Jacksons; *Jacksons Live* . . . . (Epic)
Michael Jackson; *Off The Wall.* . . . . (Epic)
Don't Stop To Watch The Wheels
Doobie Brothers; *Minute By Minute.* . . . . (Warner Bros.)
Don't Stop When You're Hot
Larry Graham; *45-#50068* . . . . (Warner Bros.)
Don't Tell Me
Madonna; *GHV2* . . . . (Warner Bros.)
Music. . . . . (Maverick)
For What It's Worth
Buffalo Springfield; *Buffalo Springfield.* . . . . (Atco)
Buffalo Springfield-Retrospective . . . . (Atco)
Double History . . . . (Atco)
Hit Singles-1958-1977-C . . . . (Atlantic)
ST/Forrest Gump. . . . . (Epic/Sony Music Soundtrax)
He Stopped Loving Her Today
George Jones; *All Time Legends Of Country Music-C* . . . . (Legacy)
First Time Live! . . . . (Epic)
George Jones-Anniversary-Ten Years Of Hits . . . . (Epic)
Greatest Country Hits Of The '80s-1980-C . . . . (Columbia)
Greatest Hits From The Jukebox-C . . . . (Epic)
I Am What I Am . . . . (Epic)
Hello Goodbye
Beatles; *Beatles 1* . . . . (Capitol)
Beatles-20 Greatest Hits . . . . (Capitol)
Beatles-Box Set . . . . (Capitol)
Magical Mystery Tour. . . . . (Capitol)
The Beatles/1967-1970 . . . . (Capitol)
How Sweet It Is (To Be Loved By You)
James Taylor; *Gorilla* . . . . (Warner Bros.)

James Taylor-Best Live . . . . (Columbia)
James Taylor's Greatest Hits. . . . .(Warner Bros.)
Junior Walker & The All Stars; *Junior Walker & The All Stars'*
Greatest Hits . . . . (Motown)
Junior Walker & The All Stars-The Ultimate Collection . . . . (Motown)
Marvin Gaye; *20th Century Masters-The Millennium Collection-The Best Of*
Marvin Gaye-#1 (The '60s). . . . . (Motown)
Marvin Gaye-Anthology . . . . (Motown)
Marvin Gaye's Greatest Hits/ . . . . (Motown)

I Can't Stop
Alabama; *Just Us* . . . . (RCA)

I Can't Stop
Honeycombs; *45-#157* . . . . (Eric)

I Can't Stop Crying
Ronnie Milsap; *Ronnie Milsap-16 Greatest Hits-#2*. . . . . (Trip)

I Can't Stop Dancing
Archie Bell; *Greatest Hits 1970-C* . . . . (Deluxe)

I Can't Stop Loving You
Don Gibson; *60 Years Of Country Music-C* . . . . (RCA)
Collector's Series-Don Gibson . . . . (RCA)
Stars Of The Grand Ole Opry-1926-1974-C . . . . (RCA)
Elvis Presley; *Aloha from Hawaii via Satellite* . . . . (RCA)
Elvis As Recorded At Madison Square Garden . . . . (RCA)
Elvis Recorded Live On Stage In Memphis . . . . (RCA)
From Memphis To Vegas/From Vegas To Memphis . . . . (RCA)
Ray Charles; *Ray Charles' Greatest Hits-#2* . . . . (Rhino)
Ray Charles-Anthology . . . . (Rhino)
Roy Orbison; *Best Of Roy Orbison-Loved Standards* . . . . . . (Monument)
Legendary Roy Orbison . . . . (Sony Music Special Prod.)

I Can't Stop Now
Wanda Jackson; *Wanda Jackson's Greatest Hits* . . . . (Gusto)

I Can't Stop The Fire
Eric Martin; *ST/Teachers* . . . . (Capitol)

I Just Can't Stop Loving You
Michael Jackson & Siedah Garrett; *Bad* . . . .(Epic)
HIStory: Past, Present And Future-Book 1-C . . . . (Epic)

I Just Wanna Stop
Gino Vannelli; *Best Of Gino Vannelli*. . . . . (A&M)
Brother To Brother . . . . (A&M)
Gino Vannelli-Classics-#7. . . . . (A&M)

I Might Even Quit Lovin' You
Mark Chesnutt; *Thank God For Believers* . . . . (Decca)

If I Never Stop Loving You
David Kersh; *If I Never Stop Loving You* . . . . (Curb)

I'll Never Stop Loving You
Gary Morris; *Anything Goes*. . . . .(Warner Bros.)
Gary Morris-Hits. . . . .(Warner Bros.)

I'll Never Stop Loving You
Doris Day & James Cagney; *Love Me Or Leave Me* . . . (Columbia Special Prod.)

I'm So Happy I Can't Stop Crying
Sting; *Mercury Falling*. . . . . (A&M)
Toby Keith with Sting; *Dream Walkin'* . . . . (Mercury)
Toby Keith's Greatest Hits, Volume One . . . . (Mercury)

Just Another Whistle Stop
Band; *Stage Fright* . . . . (Capitol)

Just Can't Stop Me
J. Geils Band; *Sanctuary*. . . . . (EMI)
Showtime. . . . .(EMI)

Knock It On The Head
Wood; *Songs From Stamford Hill*. . . . . (Columbia)

Let's Stop Talkin' About It
Janie Fricke; *Janie Fricke-17 Greatest Hits* . . . . (Columbia)
Love Lies . . . . (Columbia)
Very Best Of Janie Fricke . . . . (Columbia)

Love You Save, The
Jackson 5; *14 Greatest Hits*. (Motown)
ABC . . . . (Motown)
Goin' Back To Indiana . . . . (Motown)
Jackson 5-Anthology . . . . (Motown)
Jackson 5's Greatest Hits . . . . (Motown)
Motown Superstar Series-#12-Jackson 5. . . . . (Motown)
TV ST/Diana-C . . . . (Motown)

Machine Stops
Level 42; *Standing In The Light* . . . . (Polydor)

Music Never Stopped
Grateful Dead; *Blues For Allah* . . . . (Grateful Dead)
One From The Vault . . . . (Grateful Dead)

Never Stop
Echo & The Bunnymen; *Songs To Learn & Sing-The Hits* . . . . (Sire)

Never Stop
Brand New Heavies; *Brand New Heavies*. . . . .(Delicious Vinyl)

Never Stop
Front 242; *Front By Front*. . . . .(Epic)

Next Stop Brattleboro
NRBQ; *Freight Train Blues-Classic Railroad Songs-#4-C* . . . . (Rounder)

No More Drama
Mary J. Blige; *No More Drama* . . . .(MCA)

No Stoppin' Us Now
Doobie Brothers; *One Step Closer* . . . .(Warner Bros.)

Other Way Of Stopping
Police; *Zenyatta Mondatta* . . . . (A&M)

Quit Playing Games (With My Heart)
Backstreet Boys; *Backstreet Boys*. . . . .(Jive)
MTV Party To Go '98-C . . . .(Tommy Boy)
The Concert For New York City-C . . . . (Columbia)

Starting Over Again
Steve Wariner; *Best Of Steve Wariner*. . . . . (MCA Special Prod.)
Country Classics-#7-1986-1987-C . . . . (Universal)
Life's Highway . . . .(MCA)
Steve Wariner's Greatest Hits . . . .(MCA)

Stop
James Gang; *Best Of The James Gang* . . . . (MCA)
James Gang-16 Greatest Hits. . . . . (MCA)
Yer Album . . . .(One Way)

Stop
Jane's Addiction; *Ritual De Lo Habitual* . . . . (Warner Bros.)

Stop
Lonnie Mack; *Strike Like Lightning* . . . .(Alligator)

Stop
Pink Floyd; *The Wall*. . . . . (Columbia)

Stop & Smell The Roses
Mac Davis; *Mac Davis' Greatest Hits* . . . . (Columbia)
Stop And Smell The Roses . . . . (Columbia)

Stop And Think It Over
Dale & Grace; *Rockin' '50s & '60s-C* . . . . (Jewel)

Stop Breakin' Down Blues
Robert Johnson; *Legends Of The Blues-#1-C* . . . . (Columbia)
Robert Johnson-Complete Recordings . . . . (Columbia)

Stop Breaking Down
Rolling Stones; *Exile On Main Street* . . . .(Virgin)

Stop By
Rahsaan Patterson; *Rahsaan Patterson* . . . . (MCA)

Stop Dead
Cure; *Standing On A Beach-The Singles* . . . . (Elektra)

Stop Doggin' Me
Johnnie Taylor; *Chronicle: The 20 Greatest Hits* . . . . (Stax)
Little Bluebird . . . . (Stax)

Stop Draggin' My Heart Around
Stevie Nicks with Tom Petty And The Heartbreakers; *Bella Donna* . . . .(Modern)
TimeSpace-The Best Of Stevie Nicks . . . .(Modern)

Stop Hurting People
Pete Townshend; *All The Best Cowboys Have Chinese Eyes* . . . . (Atco)
Pete Townshend's Deep End Live! . . . . (Atco)

Stop In Nevada
Billy Joel; *Piano Man* . . . . (Columbia)

Stop Making Sense
Talking Heads; *Stop Making Sense* . . . .(Sire)

Stop On A Dime
Little Texas; *Big Time* . . . . (Warner Bros.)

Stop Running Away
Brenda Russell; *Brenda Russell's Greatest Hits* . . . . (A&M)

Stop Steppin' On My Heart
Eddie Money; *Eddie Money's Greatest Hits-Sound Of Money* . . . . . (Columbia)

Stop That Train
Bob Marley & The Wailers; *Catch A Fire*. . . . .(Tuff Gong)
Jerry Garcia Band; *Jerry Garcia Band* . . . . (Arista)
Peter Tosh; *Mama Africa*. . . . . (EMI)

Stop The Rain
Shenandoah; *Shenandoah* . . . . (Columbia)

Stop The Violence
Boogie Down Productions; *By All Means Necessary* . . . .(Jive)
Live Hardcore Worldwide-Paris-London-NYC . . . .(Jive)

Stop The War Now
Edwin Starr; *Very Best Of Edwin Starr* . . . . (Motown)

Stop The Wedding
Etta James; *Sweetest Peaches-#1* . . . . (Chess)

Stop The World
Extreme; *III Sides To Every Story* . . . . (A&M)

Stop The World
Clash; *On Broadway* . . . . (Epic)

Stop The World
Teena Marie; *Robbery* . . . . (Epic)

Stop The World (& Let Me Off)
Merle Haggard; *Big City* . . . . (Epic)
Patsy Cline; *20 Golden Pieces Of Patsy Cline*. . . . .(Bulldog)
Forever & Always . . . . (Epic)
Here's Patsy Cline . . . . (MCA)
Waylon Jennings; *Waylon Jennings-Early Years* . . . . (RCA)

Stop The World Right Here
Temptations; *Back To Basics* . . . . (Motown)

Stop Thief
Carla Thomas; *Queen Alone* . . . . (Rhino)

Stop Thief
Fabian; *Best Of Fabian* . . . . (MCA)

Stop This Game
Cheap Trick; *All Shook Up* . . . . (Epic)

Stop To Love
Luther Vandross; *Best Of Luther Vandross...The Best Of Love*. . . . . (Epic)
Give Me The Reason . . . . (Epic)

Stop Your Half Steppin' Mama
Ben Vereen; *Here I Am* . . . . (Accord)
Signed Sealed Delivered . . . . (Fifty One West)

Stop Your Sobbing
Kinks; *Kinks' Greatest Hits* . . . . (Rhino)
One For The Road . . . . (Arista)
You Really Got Me . . . . (Rhino)
Pretenders; *Pretenders* . . . . (Sire)
Pretenders-The Singles . . . . (Sire)

Stop! In The Name Of Love
Diana Ross & The Supremes; *16 #1 Hits From The Early '60s-C* . . . . . (Motown)
Diana Ross & The Supremes' Greatest Hits . . . . (Motown)
Diana Ross & The Supremes-Anthology (1962-1969) . . . . (Motown)
Evening With Diana Ross . . . . (Motown)
Girl Groups-Story Of A Sound-C . . . . (Rhino)
Motown Superstar Series-#1-Diana Ross & The Supremes . . . . (Motown)
Hollies; *45-#89819* . . . . (Atlantic)
Supremes; *Billboard Top Pop Hits-1965-C* . . . . (Rhino)

Stop, Don't Tease Me
DeBarge; *All This Love* . . . . (Motown)
DeBarge's Greatest Hits . . . . (Motown)

Stop, Look & Listen
Patsy Cline; *Loved & Lost Again* . . . . (Fifty One West)
Rockin' Side-Her First Recordings-#3 . . . . (Rhino)
Stop, Look & Listen . . . . (MCA)
Try Again . . . . (Quicksilver)

Stop, Look & Listen
Dorsey Brothers; *1934-1935 Decca Sessions* . . . . (MCA)
Complete Tommy Dorsey-#4 . . . . (RCA)

Stop, Look & Listen
Chiffons; *Best Of The Chiffons* . . . . (Laurie)

Stop, Look & Listen
Elvis Presley; *Collector's Gold* . . . . (RCA)

Stop, Look & Listen
Donna Summer; *She Works Hard For The Money* . . . . (Mercury)
Summer Collection . . . . (Mercury)

Stop, Look & Listen To Your Heart
Johnny Mathis; *I'm Coming Home* . . . . (Columbia)
Johnny Mathis-Love Songs . . . . (Columbia)
Marvin Gaye & Diana Ross; *Diana & Marvin* . . . . (Motown)
Patti Austin; *Every Home Should Have One* . . . . (Qwest)
Stylistics; *Stylistics-1st Album* . . . . (Amherst)

Stop, Stop, Stop
Hollies; *Best Of The Hollies* . . . . (EMI)
Hollies' Greatest Hits . . . . (Epic)
The Hollies' Greatest Hits . . . . (Epic)

Sudden Stop
Percy Sledge; *Best Of Percy Sledge* . . . . (Atlantic)
It Tears Me Up-Best Of Percy Sledge . . . . (Rhino)

Sudden Stop
Colin James; *Sudden Stop* . . . . (Virgin)

That Train Don't Stop Here
Los Lobos; *Kiko* . . . . (Slash)

That Train Don't Stop Here Anymore
Mike Henderson; *Country Music Made Me Do It* . . . . (RCA)

There Are Many Stops Along The Way
Joe Sample; *Joe Sample-Collection* . . . . (GRP)
Rainbow Seeker . . . . (MCA)

There's No Stopping Us Now
Diana Ross & The Supremes; *Diana Ross' Greatest Hits-#2* . . . . (Motown)

There's No Stopping Your Heart
Marie Osmond; *Best Of Branson U.S.A.-#1-C* . . . . (Curb)
Best Of Marie Osmond . . . . (Curb)
There's No Stopping Your Heart . . . . (Curb)

Time Stands Still
Rush; *Hold Your Fire* . . . . (Mercury)
Rush-Chronicles . . . . (Mercury)
Show Of Hands . . . . (Mercury)

Time Stood Still
Vern Gosdin; *10 Years Of Greatest Hits Newly Recorded* . . . . (Columbia)

Too Good To Stop Now
Mickey Gilley; *Too Good To Stop Now* . . . . (Epic)

Train Goin' Nowhere
Steven Beasley; *Between The Rails: America's Train Songs-C* . . . . . (Crescendo)

Truck Stop
Mills Brothers; *Cab Driver* . . . . (Ranwood)

Truck Stop
Lenny Dee; *Best Of Lenny Dee-#2* . . . . (MCA)

Truck Stop Girl
Byrds; *The Byrds* . . . . (Columbia)
The Byrds (Untitled) . . . . (Legacy)
Little Feat; *Little Feat* . . . . (Warner Bros.)

Truck Stop Rock
Commander Cody & His Lost Planet Airmen; *Hot Licks, Cold Steel &*
Trucker's Favorites . . . . (MCA)

What's Stopping You
O'Jays; *Love You To Tears* . . . . (Volcano Entertainment)

When Did You Stop Loving Me
George Strait; *ST/Pure Country* . . . . (MCA)

When I Stop Dreaming
Jim & Jesse; *All Time Legends Of Country Music-C* . . . . (Legacy)
Bluegrass Super Hits-C . . . . (Columbia)

When The Music Stops
Roger Daltrey; *Daltrey* . . . . (MCA)

Where Time Stands Still
Mary Chapin Carpenter; *Stones In The Road* . . . . (Columbia)

Who'll Stop The Rain
Creedence Clearwater Revival; *1970* . . . . (Fantasy)
Cosmo's Factory . . . . (Fantasy)
Creedence Clearwater Revival-Chronicle . . . . (Fantasy)
More Creedence Gold . . . . (Fantasy)
Royal Albert Hall Concert . . . . (Fantasy)

You Can't Stop Love
Schulyer, Knobloch & Overstreet; *S.K.O.* . . . . (MTM)

STORYBOOK CHARACTERS

See Also: BOOKS, CARTOON CHARACTERS

(Just Like) Romeo & Juliet
Reflections; *'60s Dance Party-C* . . . . (Dominion Entert.)
Sensational '60s-#1-C . . . . (Dominion Entert.)

1983... (A Merman I Should Turn To Be)
Jimi Hendrix Experience; *Electric Ladyland* . . . . (Reprise)

After Robinson Crusoe
Ozzie Nelson & His Orchestra; *The Uncollected Ozzie Nelson & His*
Orchestra-#3-1938 . . . . (Hindsight)

Alice In Wonderland
Neil Sedaka; *Neil Sedaka's All-Time Greatest Hits* . . . . (RCA)

Beauty And The Beast
Celine Dion & Peabo Bryson; *All The Way...A Decade Of Song* . . . . (550 Music)
Celine Dion . . . . (Epic)
ST/Beauty And The Beast . . . . (Disney)

Black Orpheus
Roger Williams; *Best Of Roger Williams* . . . . (MCA)
Vince Guaraldi & Bola Sete; *Live At El Matador* . . . . (Fantasy)

Black Uncle Remus
Loudon Wainwright III; *Loudon Wainwright III* . . . . (Atlantic)

Buck Rogers In The 25th Century
Neil Norman & His Cosmic Orchestra; *Greatest Science Fiction*
Hits-#2 . . . . (Crescendo)

Captain Bligh
Filter; *Title Of Record* . . . . (Reprise)

Captain Nemo
Michael Schenker Group; *Built To Destroy* . . . . (Chrysalis)
Rock Will Never Die . . . . (Chrysalis)

Cinderella
Britney Spears; *Britney* . . . . (Jive)

Cry Ophelia
Adam Cohen; *Songs From Dawson's Creek* . . . . (Sony Music Soundtrax)

Cupid
Sam Cooke; *Best Of Sam Cooke* . . . . (RCA)
The Man And His Music . . . . (RCA)
Spinners; *Love Trippin'* . . . . (Atlantic)

Cupid
Graham Parker; *Mona Lisa's Daughter* . . . . (RCA)
ST/True Love . . . . (RCA)

Cupid
112; *112* . . . . (Bad Boy/Arista)

Cupid's Got A Brand New Gun
Michael Penn; *March* . . . . (RCA)

Cupid's Trash Truck
Lou & Peter Berryman; *Cupid's Trash Truck* . . . . (Cornbelt)

Dance Of The Sugar Plum Fairy
Boston Pops Orchestra; *Encores-Boston Pops*
Orchestra . . . . (Deutsche Grammophon)
Sleigh Ride!-Classic Christmas Favorites-C . . . . (RCA)
Carpenters; *Christmas Collection* . . . . (A&M)

Davy Crockett
Hermes Nye; *Ballads Of The Civil War-#1 & 2* . . . . . . (Smithsonian Folkways)

Daybreak (Storybook Children)
Cheryl Lynn; *Cheryl Lynn* . . . . (Columbia)

Ding Dong The Witch Is Dead
Fifth Estate; *Dick Bartley's One-Hit Wonders Of The '60s-#2-C* . . . . . (Rhino)
Meco; *The Wizard Of Oz* . . . . (Millennium)
MGM Studio Orchestra; *ST/The Wizard Of Oz* . . . . . (Sony Music Special Prod.)

Dinner With Drac
Zacherle; *Rock-O-Rama-#2-C* . . . . (Abkco)

Dr. Funkenstein
Parliament; *Parliament Live/P. Funk Earth Tour* . . . . (Casablanca)
The Clones Of Dr. Funkenstein . . . . (Casablanca)

Dr. Jeckyll & Mr. Hyde
Who; *Magic Bus-The Who On Tour* . . . .(MCA)
Dracula Moon
Joan Osborne; *Relish* . . . . (Blue Gorilla/Mercury)
Dracula's Dance
Flip Phillips; *Flipenstein*. . . . . (Progressive)
Electra Made Me Blind
Everclear; *Sparkle And Fade* . . . . (Capitol)
Fairy Tale
Pointer Sisters; *Retrospect* . . . .(MCA)
Fairy Tale
Rita Remington; *Country Girl Gold* . . . . (Plantation)
Fairy Tale
Elvis Presley; *Elvis In Concert* . . . . (RCA)
Fairy Tale High
Donna Summer; *Live & More* . . . . (Casablanca)
Once Upon A Time . . . . (Casablanca)
Fairy Tales
Anita Baker; *Compositions*. . . . . (Elektra)
Fairy Tales
Style Council; *Cost Of Loving* . . . . (Polydor)
Fairy Tales
Rivingtons; *Liberty Years-Legends Of Rock & Roll* . . . .(EMI)
Flight Of Icarus
Iron Maiden; *Live After Death-World Slavery Tour* . . . . (Capitol)
Piece Of Mind . . . . (Capitol)
Frankenstein
Edgar Winter Group; *Billboard Top Rock 'N' Roll Hits-1973-C* . . . . (Rhino)
Edgar Winter Group-Anthology . . . . (Bac-Trac)
Edgar Winter Group-Collection . . . . (Rhino)
They Only Come Out At Night . . . .(Epic)
Frankenstein
New York Dolls; *Lipstick Killers* . . . .(Roir)
New York Dolls . . . . (Mercury)
Genie In A Bottle
Christina Aguilera; *Christina Aguilera*. . . . . (RCA)
Totally Hits-#2-C . . . . (Elektra)
Georgy Porgy
Eric Benet featuring Faith Evans; *A Day In The Life*. . . . .(Warner Bros.)
Toto; *Past To Present 1977-1990* . . . . (Columbia)
Toto . . . . (Columbia)
Ghost Of Tom Joad
Bruce Springsteen; *The Ghost Of Tom Joad* . . . . (Columbia)
Goodbye Yellow Brick Road
Elton John; *Billboard Top Rock 'N' Roll Hits-1973-C* . . . . (Rhino)
Elton John's Greatest Hits . . . . (Polydor)
Goodbye Yellow Brick Road . . . . (Polydor)
Hardest Thing (Dr. Zhivago)
98 Degrees; *98 Degrees And Rising* . . . . (Universal)
Now That's What I Call Music!-#3-C . . . . (Virgin)
Hercules
Aaron Neville; *Classic Aaron Neville*. . . . . (Rounder)
Treacherous: A History Of The Neville Brothers. . . . . (Rhino)
Hercules
Elton John; *Honky Chateau* . . . .(Rocket)
Hercules
Midnight Oil; *Scream In Blue Live* . . . . (Columbia)
Species Deceases. . . . . (Columbia)
Hercules
Boz Scaggs; *Slow Dancer* . . . . (Columbia)
Hey, Cinderella
Suzy Bogguss; *Something Up My Sleeve* . . . . (Liberty)
Hollywood (Robin Hood)
Wallflowers; *The Wallflowers*. (Virgin)
House At Pooh Corner
Loggins & Messina; *Loggins & Messina-On Stage* . . . . . (Columbia)
Sittin' In . . . . (Columbia)
The Best Of Friends . . . . (Columbia)
Nitty Gritty Dirt Band; *Best Of The Nitty Gritty Dirt Band*. . . . . (Liberty)
Best Of The Nitty Gritty Dirt Band . . . . (Curb)
Dirt, Silver & Gold. . . . . (One Way)
Uncle Charlie And His Dog Teddy. . . . . (Liberty)
I Can Love You Like That (Cinderella, Romeo & Juliet)
All-4-One; *1996 Grammy Nominees-C* . . . . (Columbia)
And The Music Speaks. . . . . (Blitzz)
John Michael Montgomery; *John Michael Montgomery* . . . .(Atlantic)
Icarus
Paul Winter; *Common Ground* . . . . (A&M)
Paul Winter Consort; *Earthdance*. . . . . (A&M)
Icarus. . . . .(Epic)
Pioneers Of The New Age . . . . (Columbia)
Road. . . . . (A&M)
If I Had A Boat (Lone Range, Tonto)
Lyle Lovett; *Pontiac*. . . . .(MCA)
It's In The Book (Parts 1 & 2) (Mother Goose)
Johnny Standley; *Dr. Demento Gooses Mother-C* . . . . (Kid Rhino/Rhino 4 Kids)
It's Midnight Cinderella
Garth Brooks; *Fresh Horses* . . . . (Capitol)

Limited Series Box . . . . (Capitol)
Jack And Jill
Ray Parker Jr.; *Chartbusters* . . . . (Arista)
Ray Parker Jr.'s Greatest Hits . . . . (Arista)
Raydio; *Raydio* . . . . (Arista)
Jukebox Cinderella
Johnny Duncan; *Come A Little Bit Closer* . . . . (Columbia)
King Kong
Frank Zappa; *Uncle Meat* . . . . (Barking Pumpkin)
You Can't Do That On Stage Anymore-#3 . . . . (Rykodisc)
King Kong
Kinks; *Kink Kronikles* . . . . (Reprise)
Kiss For Cinderella
Michael Tilson Thomas; *Of Thee I Sing/Let 'Em Eat Cake* . . . . (Columbia)
Li'l Red Riding Hood
Sam The Sham and The Pharaohs; *Best Of Sam The Sham and The Pharaohs* . . . .(Polydor)
Cruisin'-1966-C . . . . (Increase)
Pharaohization! (Best Of) . . . . (Rhino)
Little Arrows (Cupid)
Leapy Lee; *Bubble Gum Classics-C* . . . . (MCA Special Prod.)
Country Music Classics-#3-1965-1970-C . . . . (K-Tel)
Little Green Apples (Dr. Seuss, Disneyland, Mother Goose)
O.C. Smith; *Pop Classics Of The '60s-C* . . . . (Columbia)
Little Left Of Center (Cupid)
Randy Travis; *A Man Ain't Made Of Stone* . . . . (DreamWorks/SKG)
Lonely Goatherd
Julie Andrews; *ST/The Sound Of Music* . . . .(RCA)
Original Cast/Mary Martin; *The Sound Of Music* . . . . (Sony Broadway)
Love Theme From "Romeo & Juliet"
101 Strings Orchestra; *World's Greatest Standards* . . . . (Alshire)
Andre Kostelanetz; *Andre Kostelanetz-16 Most Requested Songs* . . . (Columbia)
Andy Williams & The Royal Philharmonic Orchestra; *Greatest Love Classics* . . . . (Capitol)
Percy Faith & His Orchestra; *Percy Faith & His Orchestra-16 Most Requested Songs* . . . . (Columbia)
Mary Had A Little Lamb
Garth Brooks; *The Magic Of Christmas: Songs From Call Me Claus*. . . (Capitol)
Original Soundtrack; *Sesame Street: Kids' Favorite Songs-#2* . . . (Sony Wonder)
Stevie Ray Vaughan and Double Trouble; *Live Alive* . . . . (Epic)
Texas Flood . . . . (Epic)
Wings; *Wild Life* . . . . (Capitol)
Mona Lisas And Mad Hatters
Elton John; *Honky Chateau* . . . .(Rocket)
Reg Strikes Back . . . . (MCA)
The Concert For New York City-C . . . . (Columbia)
Mother Goose
Jethro Tull; *Aqualung* . . . . (Chrysalis)
Narcissus
City Boy; *Dinner At The Ritz* . . . . (Mercury)
Night Before Christmas Song, The
Gene Autry; *Sing Cowboy Sing: The Gene Autry Collection*. . . . . (Rhino)
No Mermaid
Sinead Lohan; *No Mermaid*. . . . .(Grapevine)
ST/Message In A Bottle . . . .(Grapevine)
One Headlight (Cinderella)
Wallflowers; *Bringing Down The Horse* . . . .(Interscope)
Only Love (The Ballad Of Sleeping Beauty)
Sophie B. Hawkins; *Whaler* . . . . (Columbia)
Over At The Frankenstein Place
Original London Cast; *Rocky Horror Show*. . . . . (Rhino)
Tim Curry & Original Roxy Cast; *Rocky Horror Show*. . . . . (Rhino)
Pegasus
Mahavishnu Orchestra; *Visions Of The Emerald Beyond* . . . . (Columbia)
Pegasus
Allman Brothers Band; *Enlightened Rogues*. . . . .(Polydor)
Pride Of Frankenstein
Too Much Joy; *Cereal Killers* . . . .(Giant)
Puff The Magic Dragon
Peter, Paul & Mary; *10 Years Together/The Best Of Peter, Paul and Mary* . . . . (Warner Bros.)
Moving . . . . (Warner Bros.)
Peter, Paul & Mommy . . . . (Warner Bros.)
Peter, Paul and Mary In Concert . . . . (Warner Bros.)
Ramble On (Lord Of The Rings)
Led Zeppelin; *Led Zeppelin II* . . . .(Atlantic)
Led Zeppelin-Box Set . . . .(Atlantic)
Remasters . . . .(Atlantic)
Redneck Romeo
Confederate Railroad; *Notorious* . . . .(Atlantic)
Rhythm In My Nursery Rhymes
Tommy Dorsey & His Clambake Seven; *Music Goes Round & Round* . . . . (Bluebird)
Rime Of The Ancient Mariner
Iron Maiden; *Live After Death-World Slavery Tour* . . . . (Capitol)
Powerslave . . . . (Capitol)
Robin And Marian
Nickel Creek; *Nickel Creek* . . . .(Sugar Hill)

Robin Hood
38 Special; *Rockin' Into The Night* . . . . (A&M)
Robinson Crusoe
Art Of Noise; *Ambient Collection* . . . . (Polydor)
Below The Waste. . . . . (China)
Robinson Crusoe
Cud; *Cub Band E.P.* . . . . (A&M)
Robinson Crusoe In New York
Silencers; *Dance To The Holy Man* . . . . (RCA)
Rockin' Rockin' Leprechauns
Jonathan Richman & The Modern Lovers; *Rock 'N' Roll With Jonathan Richman & The Modern Lovers* . . . . (Rhino)
Roll On Mississippi (Tom Sawyer, Huck Finn)
Charley Pride; *Charley Pride's Greatest Hits* . . . . (RCA)
Romeo
Dino; *Swingin'.* . . . . (Polydor)
Romeo
Cadillacs; *Best Of The Cadillacs* . . . . (Rhino)
Romeo
Jamaica Boys; *Jamaica Boys.* . . . . (Warner Bros.)
Romeo
Donna Summer; *ST/Flashdance* . . . .(Casablanca)
Romeo
Times Two; *X2* . . . . (Reprise)
Romeo & Juliet
Chambers Brothers; *The Time Has Come* . . . . (Columbia)
Romeo & Juliet
Dire Straits; *Live-Alchemy.* . . . . (Warner Bros.)
Making Movies . . . . (Warner Bros.)
Money For Nothing. . . . . (Warner Bros.)
Indigo Girls; *Rites Of Passage.* . . . . (Epic)
Sailor & The Mermaid
Libby Titus & Dr. John; *In Harmony-Sesame Street-C* . . . . . . (Columbia)
Seven Dwarfs
Airto Moreira; *Struck By Lightning* . . . . (Venture)
Sleeping Beauty Waltz
101 Strings Orchestra; *Million-Seller Themes From Tchaikovsky.* . . . . . (Alshire)
St. George & The Dragonet
Stan Freberg; *Greatest Hits-Stan Freberg* . . . . (Curb)
Tip Of The Freberg: The Stan Freberg Collection-1951-1998. . . . . . . (Rhino)
Storybook Lovers
4 Seasons; *Who Loves You.* . . . . (Warner Bros.)
Stupid Cupid
Connie Francis; *Very Best Of Connie Francis* . . . . (Polydor)
Neil Sedaka; *Neil Sedaka's All-Time Greatest Hits-#2* . . . .(RCA)
Sunshine (Alice In Wonderland)
Aerosmith; *Just Push Play.* . . . . (Columbia)
Super Heroes
Original London Cast; *Rocky Horror Show.* . . . . (Rhino)
Tales Of Brave Ulysses
Cream; *Disraeli Gears.* . . . . (Polydor)
Eric Clapton-Crossroads-C . . . . (Polydor)
Live Cream-#2 . . . . (Polydor)
Tarzan & Jane
Sparks; *Angst In My Pants.* . . . . (Atlantic)
Tarzan Boy
Baltimora; *Living In The Background* . . . . (Manhattan)
Tarzan Was A Bluesman
Timbuk 3; *Eden Alley* . . . . (I.R.S.)
Tarzan's Nuts
Madness; *One Step Beyond* . . . . (Sire)
Temporary Like Achilles
Bob Dylan; *Blonde On Blonde* . . . . (Columbia)
Theme From ''Beauty & The Beast''
Ron Perlman; *Theme From ''Beauty & The Beast''* . . . . (Capitol)
Theme From ''Fractured Fairy Tales''
Original Soundtrack; *Television's Greatest Hits-#3-1970s & 1980s-C* . . . . (TVT)
Theme From ''Sesame Street''
Original Soundtrack; *Television's Greatest Hits-#3-1970s & 1980s-C* . . . . (TVT)
Theme From ''Tarzan''
Original Soundtrack; *Television's Greatest Hits-#2-C* . . . . (TVT)
Theme From ''The Adventures Of Robin Hood''
Original Soundtrack; *Television's Greatest Hits-#2-C* . . . . (TVT)
Theme From ''The Green Hornet''
Original Soundtrack; *Television's Greatest Hits-#2-C* . . . . (TVT)
Theme From ''The Mighty Hercules''
Original Soundtrack; *Television's Greatest Hits-#4-Black & White Classics-C* . . . . (TVT)
Three Little Pigs
Lloyd Price; *Lloyd Price's Greatest Hits.* . . . . (MCA)
Tom Sawyer
Rush; *Exit...Stage Left.* . . . . (Mercury)
Moving Pictures . . . . (Mercury)
Rush-Chronicles. . . . . (Mercury)
Tom Thumb
Wayne Shorter; *Best Of Wayne Shorter-The Blue Note Years* . . . .(Blue Note)
Tweedle Dee & Tweedle Dum
Bob Dylan; *''Love And Theft''* . . . . (Columbia)

Tweedledee For President
Michael Tilson Thomas; *Of Thee I Sing/Let 'Em Eat Cake* . . . .(Columbia)
Venus
Frankie Avalon; *21 Oldies But Goodies-C.* . . . . (Original Sound)
'50s Sock Hop-C . . . .(K-Tel)
Billboard Top Rock 'N' Roll Hits-1959-C. . . . .(Rhino)
Oldies But Goodies-#10-C . . . . (Original Sound)
Venus
Shocking Blue; *'70s Smash Hits-#1-C.* . . . .(Rhino)
Billboard Top Rock 'N' Roll Hits-1970-C. . . . .(Rhino)
Oldies But Goodies-#15-C . . . . (Original Sound)
Super Hits Of The '70s-Have A Nice Day-#1-C . . . . (Rhino)
Venus In Blue Jeans
Jimmy Clanton; *All-Star Chartbusters* . . . . (Intermedia)
Golden Years-1962-C . . . .(Dominion Entert.)
What It Is (Dirty Dick, Little Nell)
Mark Knopfler; *Sailing To Philadelphia* . . . . (Warner Bros.)
Where Did Robinson Crusoe Go With Friday On Saturday Night
Ian Whitcomb; *You Turn Me On-The Very Best Of Ian Whitcomb* . . . . (Varese Sarabande)
White Rabbit
Damned; *Best Of The Damned.* . . . . (Roadracer)
Machine Gun Etiquette . . . . (Roadracer)
George Benson; *George Benson-Collection* . . . . (Warner Bros.)
White Rabbit . . . .(CBS Associated)
Jefferson Airplane; *2400 Fulton Street-An Anthology* . . . . (RCA)
Flight Log (1966-1976). . . . . (Grunt)
Loves You . . . . (RCA)
ST/Platoon . . . . (Atlantic)
Surrealistic Pillow. . . . . (RCA)
The Worst Of Jefferson Airplane . . . . (RCA)
Who's Afraid Of The Big Bad Wolf
Barbra Streisand; *Just For The Record* . . . . (Columbia)
The Barbra Streisand Album. . . . . (Columbia)
L.L. Cool J; *Simply Mad About The Mouse-C* . . . . (Columbia)
Mormon Tabernacle Choir & Columbia Symphony Orchestra; *When You Wish Upon A Star-A Tribute To Walt Disney* . . . . (CBS Masterworks)
You're Not In Kansas Anymore
Jo Dee Messina; *Jo Dee Messina* . . . .(Curb)

STRANGE, Mystery, Strangers, Unknown

See Also: MAGIC, PEOPLE, PRETEND, QUESTIONS & ANSWERS, REASONS, SECRETS, SPIRITS, THINKING & KNOWING, UFO'S

(I Don't Know Why) But I Do
Clarence ''Frogman'' Henry; *ST/Forrest Gump* . . (Epic/Sony Music Soundtrax)
(Man Who Shot) Liberty Valance
Gene Pitney; *Gene Pitney-Anthology 1961-1968.* . . . .(Rhino)
Gene Pitney's Greatest Hits . . . . (Evergreen Music)
Super Oldies Of The '60s-#9-C . . . . (Audio Fidelity)
Greg Kihn; *Glass House Rock* . . . .(Beserkley)
3 Strange Days
School Of Fish; *School Of Fish* . . . .(Capitol)
Ah! Sweet Mystery Of Life
Bing Crosby; *Little Bit Of Irish* . . . . (Atlantic)
Nelson Eddy; *Through The Years* . . . . (Living Era)
Ain't It Strange
Patti Smith Group; *Radio Ethiopia.* . . . .(Arista)
Ain't That Peculiar
Marvin Gaye; *Marvin Gaye-Anthology* . . . .(Motown)
All Over You
Live; *Throwing Copper* . . . .(Radioactive/MCA)
Angry All The Time
Bruce Robison with Kelly Willis; *Wrapped* . . . .(Lucky Dog)
Tim McGraw with Faith Hill; *Set This Circus Down* . . . .(Curb)
Bali Ha'i
Original Cast; *South Pacific.* . . . . (CBS Masterworks)
Ballad Of A Thin Man
Bob Dylan; *Before The Flood* . . . . (Columbia)
Beautiful Stranger
Madonna; *GHV2* . . . . (Warner Bros.)
ST/Austin Powers-The Spy Who Shagged Me . . . . (Maverick)
Totally Hits-#2-C . . . .(Elektra)
Bebe Le Strange
Heart; *Bebe Le Strange.* . . . . (Epic)
Heart's Greatest Hits/Live . . . . (Epic)
Blowin' In The Wind
Bob Dylan; *Before The Flood* . . . . (Columbia)
Biograph . . . . (Columbia)
Bob Dylan At Budokan . . . . (Columbia)
Bob Dylan's Greatest Hits. . . . . (Columbia)
Freewheelin'. . . . . (Columbia)
God Bless America-C . . . . (Columbia)
Greatest Folksingers Of The '60s-C . . . . (Vanguard)

Joan Baez; *ST/Forrest Gump* . . . . (Epic/Sony Music Soundtrax)
Peter, Paul & Mary; *10 Years Together/The Best Of Peter, Paul and Mary* . . . .(Warner Bros.)
  Holiday Celebration . . . .(Warner Bros.)
  In The Wind . . . .(Warner Bros.)
  Peter, Paul and Mary In Concert . . . .(Warner Bros.)
Stevie Wonder; *Motown Year By Year-The Sound Of Young America-1966-C* . . . . (Motown)

Blue Rock Montana/Red Headed Stranger
Willie Nelson; *Red Headed Stranger* . . . . (Columbia)

Book Of Love
Monotones; *Bedrock-Late '50s/'60s Rock 'N' Roll* . . . .(Allegiance)
  Best Of Chess Rock 'N' Roll-#1-C . . . . (Chess)
  Original Golden Rock Oldies-#1-C . . . . (Specialty)
  ST/American Graffiti . . . .(MCA)
  Super Oldies Of The '50s-#2-C . . . .(Audio Fidelity)

Brave Strangers
Bob Seger & The Silver Bullet Band; *Stranger In Town* . . . . (Capitol)

Breakdown
Queensryche; *Q2k* . . . .(Atlantic)

Building A Mystery
Sarah McLachlan; *Lilith Fair-A Celebration Of Women In Music-C* . . . . (Arista)
  Mirrorball . . . . (Arista)
  Surfacing . . . . (Arista)

Camelot
Original 1982 London Cast; *Camelot* . . . .(Varese Sarabande)
Original Cast; *Camelot* . . . . (Columbia)
Richard Burton; *Broadway Magic-The 1960s-C* . . . . (Columbia)
Richard Harris; *ST/Camelot* . . . .(Warner Bros.)

Can't You Hear Me Knockin'
Rolling Stones; *Sticky Fingers* . . . . (Virgin)

Carroll County Accident
Porter Wagoner; *Essential Porter Wagoner* . . . . (RCA)
  Porter Wagoner-Greatest Songs . . . . (Curb)

Chick-A-Boom (Don't Ya Jes' Love It)
Daddy Dewdrop; *'70s Smash Hits-#4-C* . . . . (Rhino)
  Super Hits Of The '70s-Have A Nice Day-#5-C . . . . (Rhino)

Choice In The Matter
Aimee Mann; *I'm With Stupid* . . . .(Geffen)

Danger Stranger
Drivin' N' Cryin'; *Scarred But Smarter* . . . . (Island)

Danger! She's A Stranger
Five Stairsteps; *Five Stairsteps' Greatest Hits* . . . . (Collectables)

Destination Unknown
Electric Light Orchestra; *Afterglow* . . . .(Epic)

Dime Store Mystery
Lou Reed; *New York* . . . . (Sire)

Ditty Wa Ditty
Ry Cooder; *Paradise And Lunch* . . . . (Reprise)

Does Anybody Really Know What Time It Is?
Chicago; *Chicago At Carnegie Hall* . . . .(Chicago)
  Chicago IX-Chicago's Greatest Hits . . . .(Chicago)
  Chicago Transit Authority . . . .(Chicago)
  If You Leave Me Now . . . .(Chicago)

Don't Talk To Strangers
Rick Springfield; *Rick Springfield's Greatest Hits* . . . . (RCA)
  Success Hasn't Spoiled Me Yet . . . . (RCA)

Don't Talk To Strangers
Beau Brummels; *Best Of The Beau Brummels* . . . . (Rhino)
  Just A Little & Other Hits . . . . (Accord)

Don't Talk To Strangers
Dio; *Holy Diver* . . . .(Warner Bros.)

Don't Talk To Strangers
Roger Daltrey; *Under A Raging Moon* . . . .(Atlantic)

Down By The Bay
Eric Heatherly; *Country Goes Raffi-C* . . . . (Rounder)

Drive
Cars; *Heartbeat City* . . . . (Elektra)
  MTV's Rock 'N' Roll To Go-C . . . . (Elektra)
  The Cars' Greatest Hits . . . . (Elektra)

End Is The Beginning Is The End
Smashing Pumpkins; *ST/Batman & Robin-Music From And Inspired By The Motion Picture* . . . . (Jive)

Estranged
Guns N' Roses; *Use Your Illusion II* . . . .(Geffen)

Everything You Want
Vertical Horizon; *Everything You Want* . . . . (RCA)
  Totally Hits-#3-C . . . .(Atlantic)

Fighting For Strangers
Steeleye Span; *Rocket Cottage; Story* . . . .(Chrysalis)

Fire Escape
Fastball; *All The Pain Money Can Buy* . . . . (Hollywood)

Fire Of Unknown Origin
Blue Oyster Cult; *Fire Of Unknown Origin* . . . . (Columbia)

Goodnight My Someone
Shirley Jones; *ST/The Music Man* . . . .(Warner Bros.)

Great Beyond, The
R.E.M.; *Man On The Moon* . . . .(Warner Bros.)
  Totally Hits-#2-C . . . . (Elektra)

Greatest Man I Never Knew
Reba McEntire; *For My Broken Heart* . . . . (MCA)
  Reba McEntire's Greatest Hits Volume Two . . . . (MCA)

Guessing Games
Daryl Hall & John Oates; *H2O* . . . .(RCA)

Hardin County Line
Mark Collie; *Even The Man In The Moon Is Cryin'* . . . . (MCA)

Hello Stranger
Barbara Lewis; *Atlantic Rhythm & Blues 1947-1974-#5 (1962-1966)-C* . . . .(Atlantic)
  Billboard Top R&B Hits-1963-C . . . . (Rhino)
  Collectables Presents The History Of Rock-#5-C . . . .(Collectables)

Hotel California
Eagles; *Eagles Greatest Hits, Volume 2* . . . .(Asylum)
  Eagles Live . . . .(Asylum)
  Hell Freezes Over . . . . (Geffen)
  Hotel California . . . .(Asylum)

How Bizarre
OMC; *How Bizarre* . . . .(Huh!/Mercury)

I Can't Explain
Who; *Hooligans* . . . . (MCA)
  Meaty Beaty Big & Bouncy . . . . (MCA)
  ST/The Kids Are Alright . . . . (MCA)
  Who's Last . . . . (MCA)

I Can't Explain
Scorpions; *Crazy World* . . . . (Mercury)

I Can't Tell You Why
Brownstone; *From The Bottom Up* . . . . (MJJ/Epic)
Eagles; *Eagles Greatest Hits, Volume 2* . . . .(Asylum)
  Eagles Live . . . .(Asylum)
  The Long Run . . . .(Asylum)
Vince Gill; *Common Thread-Songs Of The Eagles-C* . . . .(Giant)

I Don't Even Know Your Name
Alan Jackson; *Alan Jackson-The Greatest Hits Collection* . . . . (Arista)
  Who I Am . . . . (Arista)

I Don't Even Know Your Name
Mavericks; *Trampoline* . . . . (MCA)

I Don't Know Why
Frank Sinatra; *The Golden Days Of Radio* . . . . (K-Tel)

I Don't Know Why You Don't Want Me
Rosanne Cash; *Rosanne Cash-Hits-1979-1989* . . . . (Columbia)
  Rosanne Cash-Super Hits . . . . (Columbia)

I Never Talk To Strangers
Bette Midler; *Broken Blossom* . . . .(Atlantic)
Tom Waits; *Foreign Affairs* . . . .(Asylum)
  Tom Waits-Anthology . . . .(Asylum)

I Wonder Where You Are Tonight
Bill Monroe; *Bean Blossom* . . . . (MCA)
Jerry Lee Lewis; *Country Music Hall Of Fame Hits* . . . .(Smash)
Keith Whitley; *L.A. To Miami* . . . .(RCA)

I'm No Stranger To The Rain
Keith Whitley; *Don't Close Your Eyes* . . . .(RCA)
  Keith Whitley's Greatest Hits . . . .(RCA)

In The Air Tonight
Phil Collins; *Classic Rock 1966-1988-C* . . . .(Atlantic)
  Face Value . . . .(Atlantic)
  Miami Vice-C . . . . (MCA)
  Prince's Trust 10th Anniversary Party-C . . . .(A&M)
  Serious Hits...Live! . . . .(Atlantic)
  The Secret Policeman's Other Ball/The Music . . . . (Rhino)

Is It Really Over?
Jim Reeves; *Essential Jim Reeves* . . . . (RCA)

Isn't Life Strange
Moody Blues; *A Night At Red Rocks With The Colorado Symphony Orchestra* . . . .(Polydor)
  Seventh Sojourn . . . .(Polydor)
  This Is The Moody Blues . . . .(Polydor)
  Voices In The Sky-The Best Of The Moody Blues . . . .(Threshold)

John 3:16
Wyclef; *Muggs Presents...The Soul Assassins-C* . . . . (Columbia)

John Doe No. 24
Mary Chapin Carpenter; *Stones In The Road* . . . . (Columbia)

Last Night I Had The Strangest Dream
Simon & Garfunkel; *Collected Works* . . . . (Columbia)
  Wednesday Morning 3 A.M. . . . . (Columbia)

Laurie (Strange Things Happen)
Dickey Lee; *Collector's Essentials-#1-1960s-C* . . . .(Varese Sarabande)

Let The Mystery Be
10,000 Maniacs; *Few & Far Between* . . . . (Elektra)
Iris DeMent; *Infamous Angel* . . . . (Warner Bros.)

Lie On Lie
Chalk Farm; *Notwithstanding* . . . . (Columbia)

Like A Prayer
Madonna; *Like A Prayer* . . . . (Sire)
  Royal Box . . . . (Sire)

Like Strangers
Everly Brothers; *All They Had To Do Was Dream* . . . . (Rhino)
  Everly Brothers' Greatest Hits . . . .(Delta)
  Everly Brothers-Cadence Classics-Their 20 Greatest Hits . . . . (Rhino)

Little Miss Strange
Jimi Hendrix Experience; *Electric Ladyland*......................(Reprise)
Lonely Stranger
Eric Clapton; *Eric Clapton-Unplugged*...................(Reprise)
Looking For A Stranger
Pat Benatar; *Get Nervous*......................(Chrysalis)
Live From Earth......................(Chrysalis)
Love Bizarre
Sheila E.; *Romance 1600*...................(Paisley Park)
Love Is A Stranger
Eurythmics; *Eurythmics' Greatest Hits*...................(Arista)
Sweet Dreams (Are Made Of This)...................(RCA)
Love Is Strange
Mickey and Sylvia; *Legends Of Guitar-Rock The 50's-#2-C*...(Rhino)
Nipper's Greatest Hits Of The '50s-#2-C...................(RCA)
Oldies But Goodies-#4-C...................(Original Sound)
ST/Dirty Dancing...................(RCA)
Love Moves In Mysterious Ways
Michael English; *Hope*...................(Curb)
Lover Man (Oh, Where Can You Be?)
Barbra Streisand; *Simply Streisand*...................(Columbia)
Billie Holiday; *Fine & Mellow*...................(Collectables)
History Of The Real Billie Holiday...................(Verve)
Blossom Dearie; *Blossom Dearie*...................(Verve)
Lena Horne; *Goes Latin & Sings Your Requests*...................(DRG)
Sarah Vaughan; *Compact Jazz-Sarah Vaughan*...................(Verve)
Jazz 'Round Midnight-Sarah Vaughan...................(Verve)
Sonny Stitt; *Soul Classics*...................(Prestige)
Magical Mystery Tour
Beatles; *Magical Mystery Tour*...................(Capitol)
Reel Music...................(Capitol)
The Beatles/1967-1970...................(Capitol)
Married Strangers
Johnny Russell; *Perspectives*...................(Mercury)
Maybe Angels
Sheryl Crow; *Sheryl Crow*...................(A&M)
Mona Lisa
Carl Mann; *Original Memphis Rock & Roll*...................(Sun)
Sun Story-C...................(Rhino)
Elvis Presley; *Elvis-A Legendary Performer, Volume 4*...................(RCA)
Jim Reeves; *Jim Reeves-Pure Gold*...................(RCA)
Nat "King" Cole; *Best Of Nat "King" Cole-Vol. 1*...................(Capitol)
Capitol Collectors Series-Nat "King" Cole...................(Capitol)
The Nat "King" Cole Story...................(Capitol)
Unforgettable...................(Capitol)
Neville Brothers; *Fiyo On The Bayou*...................(A&M)
More Than This
10,000 Maniacs; *Love Among The Ruins*...................(Geffen)
Roxy Music; *Avalon*...................(Warner Bros.)
Street Life-20 Great Hits...................(Reprise)
Most Peculiar Man
Simon & Garfunkel; *Sounds Of Silence*...................(Columbia)
Murder Mystery
Velvet Underground; *The Velvet Underground*...................(Verve)
Mysterious
Scorpions; *Eye II Eye*...................(Koch International)
Mysterious Ways
U2; *Achtung Baby*...................(Island)
Mystery Dance
Elvis Costello; *Girls Girls Girls*...................(Columbia)
My Aim Is True...................(Columbia)
Mystery Train
Band; *Moondog Matinee*...................(Capitol)
The Band-Anthology-#2...................(Capitol)
The Last Waltz...................(Warner Bros.)
To Kingdom Come-The Definitive Collection...................(Capitol)
Elvis Presley; *For LP Fans Only*...................(RCA)
The Sun Sessions...................(RCA)
Junior Parker; *Between The Rails: America's Train Songs-C*...(Crescendo)
Neil Young; *Neil & The Shocking Pinks*...................(Geffen)
Neville Brothers; *Brother's Keeper*...................(A&M)
Paul Butterfield Blues Band; *Golden Butter*...................(Elektra)
Paul Butterfield Blues Band...................(Elektra)
Sam The Sham and The Pharaohs; *Best Of Sam The Sham and The Pharaohs*...................(Polydor)
Mystic Eyes
Them featuring Van Morrison; *Here Comes The Night*.........(Out Of Print)
History Of British Rock-#6-C...................(Rhino)
The Sopranos-Music From The HBO Original Series...................(Sony Music Soundtrax)
No Love
Kevon Edmonds; *24/7*...................(RCA)
Nowhere Man
Beatles; *"Yesterday"...And Today*...................(Capitol)
Beatles-Box Set...................(Capitol)
Compact Disc Singles Collection...................(Capitol)
The Beatles/1962-1966...................(Capitol)
Oddfellows Local 151
R.E.M.; *Document*...................(EMI-Capitol Entert. Properties)

Ode To Billy Joe
Bobbi Gentry; *All-Time Country Classics-#1-C*...................(Capitol)
Oh, My Mysterious Lady
Original Cast; *Peter Pan-The 1954 Broadway Production*.......(RCA Victor)
On Your Shore
Enya; *Watermark*...................(Reprise)
Once In A Lifetime
Talking Heads; *Remain In Light*...................(Sire)
ST/Stop Making Sense...................(Sire)
Outlaw & The Stranger
Ed Bruce; *Ed Bruce*...................(MCA)
Papa-Oom-Mow-Mow
Rivingtons; *Cruisin'-1962-C*...................(Increase)
EMI Legends Of Rock & Roll-24 Greatest Hits-C...................(EMI)
In The Still Of The Night...................(Capitol)
Kahuna Classics-A Collection Of Surf Music-C...................(K-Tel)
Monster Summer Hits-Wild Surf-C...................(Capitol)
Penny Lane
Beatles; *Beatles 1*...................(Capitol)
Magical Mystery Tour...................(Capitol)
The Beatles/1967-1970...................(Capitol)
The Beatles-Anthology-#2...................(Capitol)
People Are Strange
Doors; *Best Of The Doors*...................(Elektra)
Perfect
Smashing Pumpkins; *Adore*...................(Virgin)
Please Forgive Me
David Gray; *White Ladder*...................(ATO/RCA)
Poor Wayfaring Stranger
Jim Hendricks; *Appalachian Memories-Front Porch Favorites*.......(Benson)
Jo Stafford; *American Folk Songs*...................(Corinthian)
Purple People Eater
Sheb Wooley; *45s On CD-#1-1956-1959-C*...................(Mercury)
Dr. Demento: 20th Anniversary Collection-C...................(Rhino)
Halloween Hits-C...................(Rhino)
Horror Rock Classics-#2-C...................(Rhino)
Super Hits-#4-C...................(Gusto)
Rank Stranger
Ricky Skaggs and Kentucky Thunder; *Bluegrass Rules!*...........(Rounder)
Red Headed Stranger
Willie Nelson; *Red Headed Stranger*...................(Columbia)
What A Wonderful World...................(Columbia)
Riddle Song
Doc Watson; *Southbound*...................(Vanguard)
Joan Baez & Pete Seeger; *Very Early Joan Baez*...................(Vanguard)
Ride Captain Ride
Blues Image; *Back To The '70s-#3-C*...................(Dominion Entert.)
Hit Singles-1958-1977-C...................(Atlantic)
Rudiger
Mark Knopfler; *Golden Heart*...................(Warner Bros.)
Scarlet Ribbons (For Her Hair)
Harry Belafonte; *Harry Belafonte-Legendary Performer*...............(RCA)
Harry Belafonte's All Time Greatest Hits-#1...................(RCA)
This Is Harry Belafonte...................(RCA)
Jim Ed Brown & Maxine Brown; *Essential Jim Ed Brown*...................(RCA)
Kingston Trio; *At Large/Here We Go Again!*...................(Capitol)
Capitol Collectors Series-The Kingston Trio...................(Capitol)
Lennon Sisters; *Best Of The Lennon Sisters*...................(Ranwood)
Les Paul; *Legend & The Legacy-#1-4*...................(Capitol)
NRBQ; *Diggin' Uncle Q*...................(Rounder)
Patti Page; *Patti Page-16 Most Requested Songs*...................(Legacy)
Roger Whittaker; *Roger Whittaker-Classics Collection-#2*...................(Liberty)
Secret Place
Megadeth; *Cryptic Writings*...................(Capitol)
See Saw
Moonglows; *Moonglows-Their Greatest Hits*...................(Chess)
She Is Still A Mystery
Lovin' Spoonful; *Lovin' Spoonful-Anthology*...................(Rhino)
She's A Mystery To Me
Roy Orbison; *Mystery Girl*...................(Virgin)
She's Got A Way
Billy Joel; *Billy Joel-Greatest Hits, Volume I & Volume II*.........(Columbia)
Cold Spring Harbor...................(Columbia)
Songs In The Attic...................(Columbia)
Some Enchanted Evening
Jay & The Americans; *Come A Little Bit Closer-Best Of Jay & The Americans*...................(Gold Rush)
Jay & The Americans' All-Time Greatest Hits...................(Rhino)
Original Cast; *South Pacific*...................(CBS Masterworks)
Perry Como; *Perry Como's All-Time Greatest Hits-#1*...............(RCA)
Rosanno Brazzi; *ST/South Pacific*...................(RCA)
Willie Nelson; *What A Wonderful World*...................(Columbia)
Somebody
J. Geils Band; *Monkey Island*...................(Atlantic)
Somebody For Me
Heavy D & The Boyz; *Big Tyme*...................(Uptown)
Somebody Stole My Gal
Benny Goodman; *B.G. In Hi-Fi*...................(Blue Note)
Best Of The Big Bands-C...................(Columbia)

Somebody's Gonna Love You
Lee Greenwood; *Lee Greenwood's Greatest Hits* (MCA)
Somebody's Gonna Love You (MCA)
Somebody's Knockin'
Terri Gibbs; *Best Of Terri Gibbs* (MCA)
Country Gold-C (Priority)
Country Music Classics-#6-1980-1985-C (K-Tel)
Someone Else's Dream
Faith Hill; *It Matters To Me* (Warner Bros.)
Something's Coming
Barbra Streisand; *One Voice* (Columbia)
The Broadway Album (Columbia)
Original Cast; *ST/West Side Story* (Sony Broadway)
Space Oddity
David Bowie; *Changesbowie* (Rykodisc)
Scary Monsters (Rykodisc)
Space Oddity (Rykodisc)
ST/Ziggy Stardust-The Motion Picture (Rykodisc)
The Singles-1969-1993 (Rykodisc)
Spooky
Atlanta Rhythm Section; *Underdog* (Polydor)
Classics IV; *Ghastly Grooves-C* (K-Tel)
Good Vibrations (Sounds Of Top 40 Radio: 1964-1967)-C (Capitol)
Spooky (Liberty)
Very Best Of The Classics IV (EMI)
Steven's Last Night In Town
Ben Folds Five; *Whatever And Ever Amen* (Caroline/550)
Strange Brew
Cream; *Disraeli Gears* (Polydor)
Eric Clapton-Crossroads-C (Polydor)
Strange Brew-Very Best Of Cream (Polydor)
Strange Currencies
R.E.M.; *Monster* (Warner Bros.)
Strange Days
Doors; *Best Of The Doors* (Elektra)
Doors-Classics (Elektra)
Strange Days (Elektra)
Strange Fruit
Billie Holiday; *History Of The Real Billie Holiday* (Verve)
Lady Sings The Blues (Verve)
Songbook (Verve)
Nina Simone; *Compact Jazz-Nina Simone* (Verve)
Siouxsie And The Banshees; *Through The Looking Glass* (Geffen)
Strange Kind Of Woman
Deep Purple; *Deepest Purple/The Very Best Of Deep Purple* (Warner Bros.)
Fireball (Warner Bros.)
Made In Japan (Warner Bros.)
Nobody's Perfect (Mercury)
Strange Magic
Electric Light Orchestra; *Afterglow* (Epic)
Electric Light Orchestra's Greatest Hits (Jet)
Face The Music (Jet)
Ole ELO (Jet)
Strange Music
John Raitt; *Highlights Of Broadway-Under Open Skies* (Capitol)
Strange Music
Dave Frishberg; *Let's Eat Home* (Concord Jazz)
Strange Night
Heart; *Bebe Le Strange* (Epic)
Stranger
Johnny Duncan; *Country Music Classics-#12-C* (K-Tel)
Johnny Duncan-Classic Country (Simitar)
Stranger In My House
Ronnie Milsap; *Keyed Up* (RCA)
Ronnie Milsap's Greatest Hits-#2 (RCA)
Stranger In My House
Tamia; *Nu Day* (Elektra)
Stranger In My Own House
Foreigner; *Agent Provocateur* (Atlantic)
Stranger In Our House Tonight
Gene Watson; *Memories To Burn* (Epic)
Stranger In Paradise
Arthur Lyman; *Pearly Shells* (Crescendo)
Bing Crosby; *The Radio Years: 20 Songs* (Crescendo)
Original Cast; *Kismet* (Columbia)
Tony Bennett; *Tony Bennett-16 Most Requested Songs* (Legacy)
Tony Bennett's All-Time Greatest Hits (Columbia)
Stranger In The House
George Jones; *The Bradley Barn Sessions* (MCA)
Stranger On The Shore
Acker Bilk; *Best Of Acker Bilk* (Crescendo)
Collectables Presents The History Of Rock-#8-C (Collectables)
Stranger On The Shore (Atco)
Kenny G; *Classics In The Key Of G* (Arista)
Roger Whittaker; *Roger Whittaker-Classics Collection-#2* (Liberty)
Stranger Stranger
Bad Company; *Holy Water* (Atco)
Stranger Than Fiction
Killer Dwarfs; *Method To The Madness* (Epic)
Stranger Than Fiction
Belouis Some; *Belouis Some* (Capitol)
Stranger Than Fiction
Split Enz; *Mental Notes* (Chrysalis)
Stranger Than You
Joe Jackson; *Steppin' Out: The Very Best Of Joe Jackson* (A&M)
Stranger Things Have Happened
George Strait; *No. 7* (MCA)
Larry Boone; *14 Country Favorites-C* (Mercury)
Larry Boone (Mercury)
Ronnie Milsap; *Lost In The Fifties Tonight* (RCA)
Ronnie Milsap's Greatest Hits-#3 (RCA)
Stranger To Himself
Sandy Denny; *Best Of Sandy Denny* (Hannibal)
Who Knows Where The Time Goes (Hannibal)
Stranger To Himself
Traffic; *John Barleycorn Must Die* (Island)
Strangered In The Night
Tom Petty And The Heartbreakers; *Tom Petty & The Heartbreakers* (Gone Gator)
Strangers In A Car
Marc Cohn; *Marc Cohn* (Atlantic)
Strangers In The Night
Frank Sinatra; *Frank Sinatra's Greatest Hits!* (Reprise)
Sinatra Reprise-The Very Good Years (Reprise)
Strangers In The Night (Reprise)
Strangers Of The Heart
Heart; *Bad Animals* (Capitol)
Stray Cat Blues
Rolling Stones; *Beggars Banquet* (Abkco)
Get Yer Ya-Ya's Out! (Abkco)
Streets Of Fire
Bruce Springsteen; *Darkness On The Edge Of Town* (Columbia)
Sympathy For The Devil
Bryan Ferry; *These Foolish Things* (Reprise)
Jane's Addiction; *Jane's Addiction* (Triple X Entert.)
Rolling Stones; *Beggars Banquet* (Abkco)
Flashpoint (Virgin)
Get Yer Ya-Ya's Out! (Abkco)
Hot Rocks 1964-1971 (Abkco)
Love You Live (Virgin)
Syncopated Clock
Leroy Anderson; *Best Of Leroy Anderson-Sleigh Ride* (Decca)
Talking In Your Sleep
Crystal Gayle; *Classic Crystal* (EMI)
Country Gold-C (Priority)
Crystal Gayle's All-Time Greatest Hits (Curb)
When I Dream (Liberty)
Reba McEntire; *Starting Over* (MCA)
Thank You In Advance
Boyz II Men; *Nathan Michael Shawn Wanya* (Universal)
That Girl's Been Spyin' On Me
Billy Dean; *It's What I Do* (Capitol)
That Lady
Isley Brothers; *Isley Brothers' Greatest Hits* (T-Neck/Columbia)
Rock Artifacts-From The Vaults-#1-C (Columbia)
The Isley Brothers Story-#2-The T-Neck Years-1969-1985 (Rhino)
Theme From "Alfred Hitchcock Presents"
Original Soundtrack; *Alfred Hitchcock Presents Signature In Suspense* (Hip-O)
CBS: The First 50 Years (TVT)
Television's Greatest Hits-#1-C (TVT)
Theme From "Midnight Caller"
Original Soundtrack; *Television's Greatest Hits-#7-Cable Ready-C* (TVT)
Theme From "Night Gallery"
Original Soundtrack-Sonny Curtis; *Television's Greatest Hits-#5-In Living Color-C* (TVT)
Theme From "Tales From The Crypt"
Original Soundtrack; *Television's Greatest Hits-#7-Cable Ready-C* (TVT)
Theme From "The Twilight Zone"
Original Soundtrack; *CBS: The First 50 Years* (TVT)
Television's Greatest Hits-#1-C (TVT)
Theme From "Twin Peaks"
Original Soundtrack; *Television's Greatest Hits-#7-Cable Ready-C* (TVT)
Theme From "Unsolved Mysteries"
Original Soundtrack; *Television's Greatest Hits-#7-Cable Ready-C* (TVT)
There Is A Mountain
Donovan; *Donovan's Greatest Hits* (Epic)
Troubadour-Definitive Collection (Epic)
There's A Whole Lot About A Woman (A Man Don't Know)
Jack Greene; *45-#32823* (Decca)
Thing, The
Phil Harris; *The Thing About Phil Harris* (Living Era)
Things Have Changed
Bob Dylan; *Essential Bob Dylan* (Columbia)
ST/Wonder Boys (Columbia)
Third Man Theme (Harry Lime Theme)
Band; *Moondog Matinee* (Capitol)

Dukes Of Dixieland; *Dukes Of Dixieland's Greatest Hits* (MCA)
Guy Lombardo & His Royal Canadians; *Best Of Guy Lombardo* (Curb)

Third Stone From The Sun
Jimi Hendrix; *Essential Jimi Hendrix* (Reprise)
Kiss The Sky (Reprise)
Jimi Hendrix Experience; *Are You Experienced?* (Reprise)

Thorn Tree In The Garden
Derek And The Dominos; *Layla* (Polydor)

Tomb Of The Unknown Love
Cassell Webb; *Songs Of A Stranger* (Venture)
Kenny Rogers; *The Heart Of The Matter* (RCA)

Treat Me Like A Stranger
Baillie & The Boys; *Best Of Baillie & The Boys* (RCA)
Lights Of Home (RCA)

Unknown Soldier
Doors; *Best Of The Doors* (Elektra)
Doors 13 (Elektra)
Doors-Classics (Elektra)
Live At The Hollywood Bowl (Elektra)
Waiting For The Sun (Elektra)

Vanishing Cream
Hunger; *Devil Thumbs A Ride* (Universal)

Walk On By
Leroy Van Dyke; *Billboard Top Country Hits-1961-C* (Rhino)
Country Classics-C (Sun)
Country Music Classics-#2-1960-1965-C (K-Tel)
Souvenirs Of Music City U.S.A.-C (Plantation)

Wandering Stranger
Lionel Richie; *Lionel Richie* (Motown)

Weird-Out
Dandelion; *Dyslexicon* (Ruffhouse/Columbia)

What Is This Thing Called Love
Alexander O'Neal; *All True Man* (Tabu)
Greatest Hits Of Alexander O'Neal (Epic)
Artie Shaw; *Begin The Beguine* (Bluebird)
Charlie Parker; *Cole Porter Songbook* (Verve)
Ella Fitzgerald; *Cole Porter Songbook* (Verve)
Frank Sinatra; *Frank Sinatra Sings The Select Cole Porter* (Capitol)
Julie London; *Julie London Sings Cole Porter* (EMI)
Kay Starr; *Back To The Roots* (Crescendo)
Mel Torme; *Night & Day-Cole Porter Songbook-C* (Verve)

What It Is
Mark Knopfler; *Sailing To Philadelphia* (Warner Bros.)

What's Up With That
ZZ Top; *Rhythmeen* (RCA)

Where Did Robinson Crusoe Go With Friday On Saturday Night
Ian Whitcomb; *You Turn Me On-The Very Best Of Ian Whitcomb* (Varese Sarabande)

Where Do You Go
No Mercy; *No Mercy* (Arista)

Where Do You Keep Your Heart
Tommy Dorsey & Frank Sinatra; *Dorsey/Sinatra Sessions-#1* (Bluebird)
Tommy Dorsey & Frank Sinatra's All-Time Greatest Hits-#4 (Bluebird)

Where Is My Love?
El DeBarge; *Heart Mind & Soul* (Reprise)

Where Or When
Barbra Streisand; *Color Me Barbra* (Columbia)
Benny Goodman; *Small Groups-1941-1945* (Columbia)
Bryan Ferry; *As Time Goes By* (Virgin)
Dion And The Belmonts; *Best Of Doo Wop Ballads-C* (Rhino)
Complete Dion And The Belmonts (Collector's Choice)
Ella Fitzgerald; *Ella Fitzgerald Sings The Rodgers & Hart Songbook* (Verve)
Frank Sinatra; *Sinatra At The Sands* (Reprise)
Johnny Mathis; *You Light Up My Life* (Columbia)
Peggy Lee; *Peggy Lee-Complete Recordings-1941-1947* (Legacy)
Wynton Marsalis; *Standard Time-#3-The Resolution Of Romance* (Columbia)

Where Were You When I Was Falling In Love
Lobo; *Lobo's Greatest Hits* (Curb)
Your Favorite Songs-C (Curb)

White Rabbit
Damned; *Best Of The Damned* (Roadracer)
Machine Gun Etiquette (Roadracer)
George Benson; *George Benson-Collection* (Warner Bros.)
White Rabbit (CBS Associated)
Jefferson Airplane; *2400 Fulton Street-An Anthology* (RCA)
Flight Log (1966-1976) (Grunt)
Loves You (RCA)
ST/Platoon (Atlantic)
Surrealistic Pillow (RCA)
The Worst Of Jefferson Airplane (RCA)

Who Are You
Who; *Hooligans* (MCA)
The Concert For New York City-C (Columbia)
Who Are You (MCA)
Who Greatest Hits (MCA)
Who's Last (MCA)

Who Can It Be Now
Men At Work; *Billboard Top Hits-1982-C* (Rhino)
Business As Usual (Columbia)

Who Do U Love
Deborah Cox; *Deborah Cox* (Arista)
Ultimate Dance Party-1997-C (Arista)

Who Knows What Tomorrow Will Bring
Traffic; *Traffic* (Island)

Who Knows Where The Time Goes
Fairport Convention; *Circle Dance-Hokey Pokey Charity-C* (Green Linnet)
Fairport Convention-Chronicles (A&M)
Judy Collins; *Colors Of The Day-The Best Of Judy Collins* (Elektra)
Who Knows Where The Time Goes (Elektra)
Sandy Denny; *Best Of Sandy Denny* (Hannibal)
Who Knows Where The Time Goes (Hannibal)

Who Stole The Jukebox (From Lucy's Perfume Parlor)
Johnny Bond; *Johnny Gimble's Texas Honky-Tonk Hits-C* (C.M.H. Prod.)

Whodunit
Tavares; *Love Storm* (Capitol)

Whoever You Are
Geggy Tah; *Sacred Cow* (Luaka Bop)

Who's That Knockin'
Genies; *WOGL Oldies 98-History Of Rock-#2-C* (Collectables)

Who's The Thief?
Original Cast; *Joseph & The Amazing Technicolor Dreamcoat* (Polydor)
Joseph & The Amazing Technicolor Dreamcoat (MCA)

Wicker Man
Iron Maiden; *Brave New World* (Portrait)

With My Eyes Wide Open I'm Dreaming
Mandy Barnett; *I've Got A Right To Cry* (Sire)
Patti Page; *Patti Page-Golden Hits* (Mercury)
Patti Page's Greatest Hits (Columbia)

Wonder
Natalie Merchant; *Tigerlily* (Elektra)

Work It Out
Def Leppard; *Slang* (Mercury)

World Full Of Strangers
B.B. King; *Midnight Believer* (MCA)

Yesterday
Beatles; *''Yesterday''...And Today* (Capitol)
Beatles 1 (Capitol)
Beatles-20 Greatest Hits (Capitol)
Beatles-Box Set (Capitol)
Beatles-Love Songs (Capitol)
Compact Disc Singles Collection (Capitol)
The Beatles/1962-1966 (Capitol)
Elvis Presley; *On Stage-February, 1970* (RCA)
En Vogue; *Funky Divas* (East West)
Frank Sinatra; *My Way* (Reprise)
Paul McCartney; *The Concert For New York City-C* (Columbia)
Placido Domingo; *Domingo Songbook* (Sony Music Classical)
Ray Charles; *Ray Charles-His Greatest Hits-#1* (Dunhill Compact Classics)
Supremes; *I Hear A Symphony* (Motown)
Wings; *Wings Over America* (Capitol)

You And The Mona Lisa
Shawn Colvin; *A Few Small Repairs* (Columbia)

You Don't Even Know Who I Am
Patty Loveless; *Patty Loveless-Classics* (Epic)
When Fallen Angels Fly (Epic)

You Don't Know Me
Jerry Vale; *Jerry Vale-17 Most Requested Songs* (Legacy)
Jerry Vale's All-Time Greatest Hits (Columbia)
Jerry Vale's Greatest Hits (Columbia)

Young Lust
Pink Floyd; *1980-1981 Wall Live-Is There Anybody Out There* (Columbia)
The Wall (Columbia)
Roger Waters & Bryan Adams; *The Wall-Live In Berlin* (Mercury)

STREETS: GENERAL, Sidewalks

See Also: ***BUS, CARS (various), CITIES: A-Z, DIRECTIONS (various), HITCHHIKING, MOTORCYCLES, PLACES, ROAD, ROAD ACCIDENTS, STREETS: SPECIFIC, TAXI, TRAVELING, TRUCKS***

Across The Alley From The Alamo
Asleep At The Wheel featuring Johnny Rodriguez; *Tribute To The Music Of Bob Wills And The Texas Playboys-C* (Liberty)
Bob Wills & His Texas Playboys; *Best Of Bob Wills & His Texas Playboys* (MCA)
Tiffany Transcriptions-#4-You're From Texas (Rhino)

Ain't She Sweet?
Beatles; *History Of British Rock-#5-C* (Rhino)
The Beatles-Anthology-#3 (Capitol)
Erroll Garner; *Body And Soul* (Legacy)
Frank Sinatra; *Sinatra and Swingin' Brass* (Reprise)
Pearl Bailey; *Pearl Bailey-16 Most Requested Songs* (Legacy)

Alley Cat
Bent Fabric; *Those Wonderful Instrumentals-#3-C* (K-Tel)
Big Tiny Little; *Piano Memories* (Crescendo)

Alley Katz
Daryl Hall & John Oates; *Along The Red Ledge* . . . . (RCA)
Alleys Of Austin
Michael Murphey; *Cosmic Cowboy Souvenir.* . . . . (A&M)
Asleep At The Wheel
Wallflowers; *The Wallflowers.* . . . . (Virgin)
Avenue
Paul Taylor; *Undercover* . . . . (Peak/Unity/N-Coded)
Back On The Street
Todd Rundgren's Utopia; *Jail* . . . . (Vanguard)
Utopia; *Oops! Wrong Planet* . . . . (Rhino)
Back On The Street Again
Sunshine Company; *Even More Nuggets-C* . . . . (Rhino)
Back On The Streets Again
Tower Of Power; *Bill Graham Presents The Last Days Of The
Fillmore-C* . . . . (Epic Portrait Assoc.)
East Bay Grease. . . . . (Rhino)
Backstreets
Bruce Springsteen; *Born To Run.* . . . . (Columbia)
Bad Man
R. Kelly; *I Wish (import EP).* . . . . (Jive)
Bossanovanight
Judson Spence; *I Guess I Love It.* . . . . (Pioneer)
Boulevard Of Broken Dreams
Diana Krall; *All For You (A Dedication To The Nat ''King'' Cole
Trio)* . . . . (Impulse!)
Tony Bennett; *Forty Years-The Artistry Of Tony Bennett.* . . . . (Columbia)
Tony Bennett-16 Most Requested Songs . . . . (Legacy)
Tony Bennett's All-Time Greatest Hits . . . . (Columbia)
Business On The Street
Stephen Stills; *Down The Road.* . . . . (Atlantic)
Can't Stop The Street (Krush Groove)
Chaka Khan; *45-#7-28923* . . . . (Warner Bros.)
Carnival
Natalie Merchant; *Tigerlily.* . . . . (Elektra)
Club At The End Of The Street
Elton John; *Sleeping With The Past* . . . . (MCA)
Cryin' In The Streets
Lou Christie; *Enlightnin'ment-Best Of Lou Christie* . . . . (Rhino)
Cul De Sac
Van Morrison; *Veedon Fleece* . . . . (Warner Bros.)
Cul De Sac
Genesis; *Duke.* . . . . (Atlantic)
Dancin', Shaggin' On The Boulevard
Alabama; *Dancin' On The Boulevard.* . . . . (RCA)
Dancing In The Streets
David Bowie & Mick Jagger; *Bowie-The Singles-1969-1993* . . . . . . (Rykodisc)
Grateful Dead; *Terrapin Station* . . . . (Arista)
Martha & The Vandellas; *20 Greatest Songs In Motown History-C* . . . (Motown)
*Compact Command Performances-Martha Reeves & The
Vandellas* . . . . (Motown)
Motown Story-First 25 Years-C . . . . (Motown)
Oldies But Goodies-#14-C . . . . (Original Sound)
Van Halen; *Diver Down* . . . . (Warner Bros.)
Dark End Of The Street
Commitments; *ST/The Commitments* . . . . (MCA)
James Carr; *Essential James Carr* . . . . (Razor & Tie)
Linda Ronstadt; *Heart Like A Wheel.* . . . . (Capitol)
Percy Sledge; *Best Of Percy Sledge* . . . . (Atlantic)
Dark Streets Of London
Greater Than One; *Duty & Trust.* . . . . (Roir)
Dead End Street
Lou Rawls; *Best From Lou Rawls.* . . . . (Capitol)
Lou Rawls-Live (Right Stuff) . . . . (Right Stuff)
Do Wah Diddy Diddy
Manfred Mann; *Best Of Manfred Mann* . . . . (EMI Special Markets)
Billboard Top Rock 'N' Roll Hits-1964-C . . . . (Rhino)
History Of British Rock-#2-C . . . . (Rhino)
Does Anybody Really Know What Time It Is?
Chicago; *Chicago At Carnegie Hall* . . . . (Chicago)
Chicago IX-Chicago's Greatest Hits . . . . (Chicago)
Chicago Transit Authority . . . . (Chicago)
If You Leave Me Now . . . . (Chicago)
Ev'ry Street's A Boulevard In Old N.Y.
Norrie Paramor; *Autumn.* . . . . (Angel)
Foggy Streets Of London
Special EFX; *Special EFX* . . . . (GRP)
Gang That Sang ''Heart Of My Heart''
Four Aces; *Best Of The Four Aces* . . . . (MCA)
Gasoline Alley
Rod Stewart; *Absolutely Live* . . . . (Warner Bros.)
Best Of Rod Stewart . . . . (Mercury)
Gasoline Alley . . . . (Mercury)
Sing It Again, Rod . . . . (Mercury)
Storyteller/The Complete Anthology: 1964-1990 . . . . (Warner Bros.)
Guitars, Cadillacs
Dwight Yoakam; *Guitars, Cadillacs, Etc., Etc.* . . . . (Reprise)
Just Lookin' For A Hit . . . . (Reprise)

Hanginaround
Counting Crows; *This Desert Life* . . . . (David Geffen Co.)
Heat In The Street
Pat Travers; *Go For What You Know* . . . . (Polydor)
Heat In The Street. . . . . (Polydor)
Hippies On A Corner
Joe Sample; *Best Of Joe Sample* . . . . (Warner Bros.)
Old Places, Old Faces . . . . (Warner Bros.)
Hot Streets
Chicago; *Hot Streets.* . . . . (Columbia)
Joey's On The Streets Again
Boomtown Rats; *Boomtown Rats' Greatest Hits* . . . . (Columbia)
Ratrospective . . . . (Columbia)
Tonic For The Troops. . . . . (Columbia)
King Of The New York Streets
Dion; *Yo Frankie* . . . . (Arista)
Little Street Where Old Friends Meet, A
Tony Bennett; *I Left My Heart In San Francisco.* . . . . (Columbia)
Lonely Avenue
Crickets; *Liberty Years* . . . . (EMI)
Ramsey Lewis Trio; *Greatest Hits Of Ramsey Lewis* . . . . (Chess)
Ray Charles; *Birth Of Soul-Complete Atlantic R&B 1952-1959-C* . . . (Atlantic)
Lonely Street
Andy Williams; *Andy Williams' Greatest Hits-#2* . . . . (Columbia)
Best Of Andy Williams . . . . (Curb)
Emmylou Harris; *Bluebird* . . . . (Reprise)
George Jones; *20 Golden Pieces Of George Jones* . . . . (Bulldog)
Kitty Wells; *Kitty Wells' Greatest Hits* . . . . (Step One)
Mel Tillis; *American Originals-Mel Tillis.* . . . . (Columbia)
Patsy Cline; *Sentimentally Yours.* . . . . (MCA)
Memphis Streets
Neil Diamond; *Glory Road-1968-1972.* . . . . (MCA)
Sweet Caroline . . . . (MCA)
New Orleans Street Beat
Marlon Jordan; *The Undaunted.* . . . . (Columbia)
News From Up The Street
Dan Hicks & His Hot Licks; *Where's The Money?* . . . . (MCA)
On A Little Street In Singapore
Glenn Miller; *Original Recordings-#4* . . . . (Pair)
Harry James; *Two O'Clock Jump* . . . . (Pro-Arte)
Manhattan Transfer; *Manhattan Transfer-Anthology-Down In
Birdland.* . . . . (Rhino)
On The Street Where You Live
Andy Williams; *Andy Williams-16 Most Requested Songs-Encore!* . . . (Legacy)
Bobby Darin; *Unreleased Capitol Sides* . . . . (Collector's Choice)
Eddie Fisher; *Very Best Of Eddie Fisher* . . . . (Taragon)
Four Tops; *Lost & Found: Breaking Through.* . . . . (Motown)
Harry Connick, Jr.; *25* . . . . (Columbia)
Mel Torme; *Swings Shubert Alley* . . . . (Verve)
Original Cast; *My Fair Lady* . . . . (Columbia)
Ray Conniff; *'S Awful Nice* . . . . (Columbia)
On The Sunny Side Of The Street
Diana Krall; *Stepping Out.* . . . . (Justin Time)
Frank Sinatra; *Come Swing With Me!* . . . . (Capitol)
One More For The Road. . . . . (Capitol)
Sentimental Journey. . . . . (Capitol)
The Capitol Years. . . . . (Capitol)
Judy Garland; *Best Of Judy Garland* . . . . (MCA)
Louis Armstrong; *Best Of Louis Armstrong* . . . . (MCA)
Chicago Concert 1956 . . . . (Columbia)
Jazz Club-Vocal . . . . (Verve)
Music Autobiography . . . . (MCA)
Ted Lewis & His Orchestra; *Charming Gents Of Stage & Screen-C* . . . (Legacy)
Those Wonderful Years: Puttin' On The Ritz-C . . . . . (JCI Assoc. Labels)
Parisian Thoroughfare
Bud Powell; *Amazing-#2.* . . . . (Blue Note)
Genius Of Bud Powell . . . . (Verve)
Clifford Brown/Max Roach/Harold Land; *Compact Jazz-Clifford
Brown* . . . . (Verve)
Stephane Grappelli; *Parisian Thoroughfare* . . . . (Black Lion)
Racing In The Street
Bruce Springsteen; *Darkness On The Edge Of Town* . . . . (Columbia)
Bruce Springsteen & The E Street Band; *Bruce Springsteen & The E Street
Band Live/1975-85* . . . . (Legacy)
Raised In The Alley Blues
Freddy Brown; *Barrelhouse Mamas: Born In The Alley, Raised In The
Slums-C* . . . . (Yazoo)
Shadow In The Street
Allan Clarke; *I Wasn't Born Yesterday* . . . . (Atlantic)
Sidewalk Talk
Jellybean; *Dance Mix* . . . . (EMI)
Wotupski . . . . (EMI)
Sidewalks Of New York
Cannonball Adderley & Milt Jackson; *Things Are Getting Better.* . . . (Riverside)
Mel Torme; *Songs Of New York* . . . . (Rhino)
Sleeping On The Sidewalk
Hank Crawford; *Night Beat.* . . . . (Milestone)
Sleeping On The Sidewalk
Queen; *News Of The World.* . . . . (Hollywood)

Sneakin' Sally Through The Alley
Robert Palmer; *Addictions-#2* . . . . (Island)
Sneakin' Sally Through The Alley . . . . (Island)
Standing On The Corner
Broadway Cast; *Most Happy Fella* . . . . (RCA)
Dean Martin; *Best Of Dean Martin* . . . . (CEMA Special Prod.)
Four Lads; *Four Lads-16 Most Requested Songs* . . . . (Legacy)
Original Broadway Cast; *Most Happy Fella* . . . . (Sony Music Classical)
Street Corner Talking
Savoy Brown; *Savoy Brown-London Collector* . . . . (London)
Street Corner Talking . . . . (Deram)
Street Fighting Man
Rod Stewart; *Best Of Rod Stewart* . . . . (Mercury)
Sing It Again, Rod . . . . (Mercury)
Storyteller/The Complete Anthology: 1964-1990 . . . . (Warner Bros.)
Rolling Stones; *Beggars Banquet* . . . . (Abkco)
Get Yer Ya-Ya's Out! . . . . (Abkco)
Hot Rocks 1964-1971 . . . . (Abkco)
Singles Collection-The London Years . . . . (Abkco)
Through The Past, Darkly (Big Hits Vol. 2) . . . . (Abkco)
Street Kids
Elton John; *Rock Of The Westies* . . . . (Polydor)
Street Life
Crusaders; *Mega Hits Dance Classics-#7-C* . . . . (Priority)
Street Life . . . . (MCA)
Street Life
Neil Diamond; *Beautiful Noise* . . . . (Columbia)
Love At The Greek . . . . (Columbia)
Street Life
Herb Alpert; *Herb Alpert-Classics-#20* . . . . (A&M)
Rise . . . . (A&M)
Street Life
Roxy Music; *Stranded* . . . . (Reprise)
Street Life-20 Great Hits . . . . (Reprise)
Street Machine
Super Stocks; *Monster Summer Hits-Drag City-C* . . . . (Capitol)
Street Man Named Desire
Pirates Of The Mississippi; *Street Man Named Desire* . . . . (Liberty)
Street Of Dreams
Ella Fitzgerald; *Best Of Ella Fitzgerald* . . . . (Pablo)
Frank Sinatra; *The Reprise Collection* . . . . (Reprise)
Frank Sinatra with Count Basie & The Orchestra; *Sinatra At The
Sands* . . . . (Reprise)
Ink Spots; *Best Of The Ink Spots* . . . . (MCA)
Ink Spots' Greatest Hits-Original Recordings-1939-1946 . . . . (MCA)
Nia Peeples; *Nia Peeples* . . . . (Charisma)
Ray Brown Trio; *Red Hot Ray Brown Trio* . . . . (Concord Jazz)
Tommy Dorsey & Frank Sinatra; *Tommy Dorsey & Frank Sinatra's All-Time
Greatest Hits-#1* . . . . (Bluebird)
Tony Bennett; *Jazz* . . . . (Columbia)
Street Of Dreams
Rainbow; *Bent Out Of Shape* . . . . (Mercury)
Finyl Vinyl . . . . (Mercury)
Street Rats
Ted Nugent; *Free-For-All* . . . . (Epic)
Out Of Control . . . . (Epic)
Street Soldiers
Hammer; *Too Legit To Quit* . . . . (Capitol)
Street To Lean On
Crosby, Stills & Nash; *After The Storm* . . . . (Atlantic)
Streets Of Bakersfield
Buck Owens; *Buck Owens' All-Time Greatest Hits-#1* . . . . (Curb)
Buck Owens Collection-1959-1990 . . . . (Rhino)
Dwight Yoakam; *Buenas Noches From A Lonely Room* . . . . (Reprise)
Just Lookin' For A Hit . . . . (Reprise)
Dwight Yoakam & Buck Owens; *Country's Greatest Hits-#9-'80s
Duets-C* . . . . (Priority)
Streets Of Baltimore, The
Bobby Bare; *This Is Bobby Bare* . . . . (RCA)
Flying Burrito Brothers; *Live From Europe* . . . . (Relix)
Gram Parsons; *GP/Grievous Angel* . . . . (Reprise)
Gram Parsons/Fallen Angels Live-1973 . . . . (Sierra)
Streets Of Belfast
Celtic Thunder; *Light Of Other Days* . . . . (Green Linnet)
Streets Of Calgary
Kate Wolf; *Wind Blows Wild* . . . . (Kaleidoscope)
Streets Of Derry
Andy Irvine & Paul Brady; *Andy Irvine & Paul Brady* . . . . (Green Linnet)
Streets Of Fire
Duncan Browne; *Streets Of Fire* . . . . (Sire)
Streets Of Fire
Bruce Springsteen; *Darkness On The Edge Of Town* . . . . (Columbia)
Streets Of Gold
Ronnie Milsap; *Pure Love* . . . . (RCA)
Streets Of Gold
Fabulous Thunderbirds; *Hot Number* . . . . (Epic Portrait Assoc.)
Streets Of Laredo
Buck Owens & The Buckaroos; *Buck Owens & The Buckaroos-Live At
Carnegie Hall* . . . . (Country Music Foundation)

Marty Robbins; *Cowboy Super Hits-C* . . . . (Columbia)
Marty Robbins' All-Time Greatest Hits . . . . (Columbia)
Marty Robbins-More Greatest Hits . . . . (Columbia)
More Gunfighter Ballads & Trail Songs . . . . (Columbia)
Rex Allen; *Great American Singing Cowboys-C* . . . . (Republic/Universal)
Streets Of London
Mary Hopkin; *Earth Song/Ocean Song* . . . . (Capitol)
Streets Of New York
Kool G Rap & D.J. Polo; *Wanted: Dead Or Alive* . . . . (Cold Chillin')
Streets Of New York
Carmel Quinn/Anna McGoldrick/Paddy Noonan/Others; *Let's Have An Irish
Party* . . . . (Rego Irish)
Streets Of Old Chicago
Carl Martin/Ted Bogan/Howard Armstrong; *That Old Gang
Of Mine* . . . . (Flying Fish)
Streets Of Pain
Richard Marx; *Rush Street* . . . . (Capitol)
Streets Of Paradise
Richard & Linda Thompson; *Pour Down Like Silver* . . . . (Hannibal)
Streets Of Paradise
Poco; *Blue & Gray* . . . . (One Way)
Streets Of Philadelphia
Bruce Springsteen; *Bruce Springsteen's Greatest Hits* . . . . (Columbia)
Diana, Princess Of Wales-Tribute-C . . . . (Columbia)
ST/Philadelphia . . . . (Epic/Sony Music Soundtrax)
Streets Of San Francisco
Statler Brothers; *Carry Me Back* . . . . (Mercury)
Streets On Fire
U.K. Subs; *Japan Today* . . . . (Restless)
Streets On Fire
Rhythm Corps; *Common Ground* . . . . (Epic Portrait Assoc.)
Sunny Side Of The Street
Pogues; *Essential Pogues* . . . . (Island)
Hell's Ditch . . . . (Island)
Theme From "The Streets Of San Francisco"
Original Soundtrack; *Television's Greatest Hits-#3-1970s & 1980s-C* . . . . (TVT)
TV Cop Show Theme Songs . . . . (Laserlight)
Tombstone Blues
Bob Dylan; *Biograph* . . . . (Columbia)
Highway 61 Revisited . . . . (Columbia)
Real Live . . . . (Columbia)
Truckin' Down The Avenue
Sonny Burgess; *Sun Rockabillies-#1-C* . . . . (Sun)
Walk Away Renee
Four Tops; *Compact Command Performances-Four Tops* . . . . (Motown)
Four Tops Reach Out . . . . (Motown)
Four Tops-Anthology . . . . (Motown)
Left Banke; *Cruisin'-1966-C* . . . . (Increase)
History Of The Left Banke . . . . (Rhino)
Vonda Shepard; *ST/Songs From "Ally McBeal" Featuring Vonda
Shepard* . . . . (550/Epic)
When My Sugar Walks Down The Street
Ella Fitzgerald; *Ella Fitzgerald-The Early Years-#2 (1939-1941)* . . . . . . (GRP)
Nat "King" Cole; *The Billy May Sessions* . . . . (Capitol)
Peggy Lee; *Capitol Sings Jimmy McHugh: I Feel A Song
Comin' On-C* . . . . (Capitol)
Where The Streets Have No Name
Pet Shop Boys; *Discography-Complete Singles Collection* . . . . (EMI)
U2; *Joshua Tree* . . . . (Island)
Wild In The Streets
Circle Jerks; *Best Of Rodney On The 'ROQ* . . . . (Posh Boy)
Group Sex/Wild In The Streets . . . . (Frontier)
Wild In The Streets
Bon Jovi; *Slippery When Wet* . . . . (Jambco)
You Can Call Me Al
Paul Simon; *Concert In The Park-August 15 1991* . . . . (Warner Bros.)
Graceland . . . . (Warner Bros.)
Negotiations And Love Songs, 1971-1986 . . . . (Warner Bros.)

STREETS: SPECIFIC, Addresses

See Also: **CITIES: A-Z, CITIES: NEW YORK (Broadway), PLACES,
STREETS: GENERAL**

"E" Street Shuffle
Bruce Springsteen; *The Wild, The Innocent & The E Street Shuffle* . . . (Columbia)
16th Avenue
Lacy J. Dalton; *19 Hot Country Requests-#2-C* . . . . (Epic)
Greatest Country Hits Of The '80s-1982-C . . . . (Columbia)
Lacy J. Dalton's Greatest Hits . . . . (Columbia)
2120 South Michigan Avenue
Rolling Stones; *12 X 5* . . . . (Abkco)
317 East 32nd
Lennie Tristano; *Continuity* . . . . (Jazz)
Live In Toronto 1952 . . . . (Jazz)
42nd Street
Diana Krall; *Stepping Out* . . . . (Justin Time)

Hal Kemp; *Best Of The Big Bands-C* . . . . . (Columbia)
Mel Torme; *Cocktail Mix-#3-Swingin' Singles-C* . . . . . (Rhino)
Original Broadway Cast; *42nd Street* . . . . . (RCA Victor)
59th Street Bridge Song (Feelin' Groovy)
Harper's Bizarre; *Baby Boomer Classics-More Mellow Sixties-C* . . . . . (JCI Assoc. Labels)
Better Days-C . . . . . (Rhino)
Simon & Garfunkel; *Collected Works* . . . . . (Columbia)
Parsley Sage Rosemary & Thyme . . . . . (Columbia)
Simon & Garfunkel's Greatest Hits . . . . . (Columbia)
The Concert In Central Park . . . . . (Warner Bros.)
6th Avenue Heartache
Wallflowers; *Best Of Rockline-C* . . . . . (Priority)
Bringing It All Back Home . . . . . (Columbia)
All I Wanna Do (Santa Monica Blvd.)
Sheryl Crow; *Tuesday Night Music Club* . . . . . (A&M)
Allison Road
Gin Blossoms; *New Miserable Experience* . . . . . (A&M)
Another Honky Tonk Night On Broadway
David Frizzell & Shelly West; *Golden Duets* . . . . . (Viva)
The David Frizzell & Shelly West Album . . . . . (Warner Bros.)
April Avenue
Crickets; *Liberty Years* . . . . . (EMI)
Basin Street Blues
Louis Armstrong; *Best Of Louis Armstrong* . . . . . (MCA)
Jazz Heritage-Old Favorites-C . . . . . (MCA)
Satchmo-Musical Autobiography-#2 . . . . . (MCA)
Young Louis Armstrong . . . . . (RCA)
Beat Street
Melle Mel; *Rap Hall Of Fame-C* . . . . . (K-Tel)
ST/Beat Street . . . . . (Atlantic)
Blue Avenue
Elton John; *Sleeping With The Past* . . . . . (MCA)
Blue Jay Way
Beatles; *Beatles-Box Set* . . . . . (Capitol)
Magical Mystery Tour . . . . . (Capitol)
Boogaloo Down Broadway
Fantastic Johnny C; *Dick Bartley Presents On The Radio-#7-C* . . . . . (VSI)
Bourbon Street
Elvin Bishop; *Let It Flow* . . . . . (Capricorn)
Bourbon Street Parade
Al Hirt; *Best Of Al Hirt* . . . . . (RCA)
Dukes Of Dixieland; *Digital Dixieland* . . . . . (Pro Jazz)
Pete Fountain; *Best Of Pete Fountain-#2* . . . . . (MCA)
Preservation Hall Jazz Band; *New Orleans-#4* . . . . . (Columbia)
Wynton Marsalis; *Standard Time-#2-Intimacy Calling* . . . . . (Columbia)
Broadway
Count Basie; *Essential Count Basie-#3* . . . . . (Columbia)
Count Basie & His Orchestra; *Best Of Count Basie & His Orchestra-The Roulette Years* . . . . . (Roulette)
Broadway
Goo Goo Dolls; *Dizzy Up The Girl* . . . . . (Warner Sunset/Reprise)
Broadway
Jack McDuff & Friends; *Color Me Blue* . . . . . (Concord Jazz)
Broadway
Mel Torme; *Songs Of New York* . . . . . (Rhino)
Broadway
Clash; *On Broadway* . . . . . (Epic)
Sandinista . . . . . (Epic)
Broadway Baby
Julia McKenzie; *Collector's Sondheim-C* . . . . . (RCA)
Original Broadway Cast; *Follies* . . . . . (Capitol)
Broadway Ballet
Gene Kelly/Chorus; *ST/Singin' In The Rain* . . . . . (Sony Music Special Prod.)
Broadway Fools
Branford Marsalis; *Random Abstract* . . . . . (Columbia)
Broadway Hotel
Al Stewart; *Year Of The Cat* . . . . . (Arista)
Broadway My Street
Original Broadway Cast; *70 Girls 70* . . . . . (Sony Music Classical)
Central Park West
John Coltrane; *Art Of John Coltrane* . . . . . (Atlantic)
Best Of John Coltrane . . . . . (Atlantic)
Coltrane's Sound . . . . . (Atlantic)
Creeque Alley
Mamas & The Papas; *Best Of The Mamas & The Papas* . . . . . (MCA)
Mamas & The Papas' Greatest Hits . . . . . (MCA)
Mamas & The Papas-16 Of Their Greatest Hits . . . . . (MCA)
Crescent City Crawl
Wynton Marsalis; *ST/Tune In Tomorrow...* . . . . . (Columbia)
Cypress Avenue
Van Morrison; *Astral Weeks* . . . . . (Warner Bros.)
It's Too Late To Stop Now . . . . . (Warner Bros.)
Dead Cat Alley
Dirty White Boy; *Bad Reputation* . . . . . (Polydor)
Death Alley Driver
Rainbow; *Straight Between The Eyes* . . . . . (Mercury)
Denmark Street
Kinks; *Lola Versus Powerman And The Moneygoround, Part One* . . . . (Reprise)
Desolation Row
Bob Dylan; *Highway 61 Revisited* . . . . . (Columbia)
Does This Bus Stop At 82nd Street?
Bruce Springsteen; *Greetings From Asbury Park, N.J.* . . . . . (Columbia)
Tracks . . . . . (Columbia)
Down Dallas Alley
Buckwheat Zydeco; *Taking It Home* . . . . . (Island)
Easter Parade (Fifth Avenue)
Andy Russell; *Puttin' On The Ritz-Capitol Sings Berlin-C* . . . . . (Capitol)
Bing Crosby; *All Time Best Of Bing Crosby* . . . . . (Curb)
Judy Garland & Fred Astaire; *ST/Easter Parade* . . . . . (Rhino)
Sarah Vaughan; *Complete Sarah Vaughan On Mercury-#2* . . . . . (Mercury)
Eighth Avenue Shuffle
Doobie Brothers; *Takin' It To The Streets* . . . . . (Warner Bros.)
Electric Avenue
Eddy Grant; *Killer On The Rampage* . . . . . (Portrait)
Electrolite (Mulholland Drive)
Michael Stipe/Mike Mills; *Tibetan Freedom Concert* . . . . . (Capitol)
R.E.M.; *New Adventures In Hi-Fi* . . . . . (Warner Bros.)
Forty-Five Minutes From Broadway
Mickey Finn; *Caught In The Act* . . . . . (Crescendo)
Funky Broadway
Dyke & The Blasers; *Dyke & The Blasers' Greatest Hits* . . . . . (Original Sound)
Soul Shots-C . . . . . (Rhino)
Wilson Pickett; *Atlantic Rhythm & Blues 1947-1974-#6 (1966-1969)-C* . . . . . (Atlantic)
Best Of Wilson Pickett . . . . . (Atlantic)
Oldies But Goodies-#14-C . . . . . (Original Sound)
Wilson Pickett's Greatest Hits . . . . . (Atlantic)
Galilee Road
Marcus Hummon; *Looking For The Child* . . . . . (Velvet Armadillo)
Give My Regards To Broadway
Barry Manilow; *Showstoppers* . . . . . (Arista)
Joel Grey; *Broadway Magic-The 1960s-C* . . . . . (Columbia)
Original Cast; *George M.* . . . . . (Columbia)
Grant Avenue
Original Cast; *Flower Drum Song* . . . . . (Sony Music Classical)
Happiness Street
Georgia Gibbs; *Best Of Georgia Gibbs-The Mercury Years* . . . . . (Chronicles)
Has Anybody Seen Amy
John & Audrey Wiggins; *John & Audrey* . . . . . (Mercury)
Heartbreak Hotel
Albert King; *Blues For Elvis* . . . . . (Stax)
Elvis Presley; *Elvis As Recorded At Madison Square Garden* . . . . . (RCA)
Elvis' Golden Records . . . . . (RCA)
Elvis-A Legendary Performer, Volume 1 . . . . . (RCA)
Nipper's Greatest Hits Of The '50s-#1-C . . . . . (RCA)
Worldwide 50 Gold Award Hits, Vol. 1, Parts 1 & 2 . . . . . (RCA)
Stan Freberg; *Capitol Collectors Series-Stan Freberg* . . . . . (Capitol)
Willie Nelson; *Greatest Hits (& Some That Will Be)* . . . . . (Columbia)
Willie Nelson & Leon Russell: One For The Road . . . . . (Columbia)
I'm Going Down To Bourbon Street
Waylon Thibodeaux; *Jimmy Buffett's Margaritaville Cafe: New Orleans-C* . . . . . (Margaritaville)
In France They Kiss On Main Street
Joni Mitchell; *Hissing Of Summer Lawns* . . . . . (Asylum)
Shadows & Light . . . . . (Asylum)
Incident On 57th Street
Bruce Springsteen; *The Wild, The Innocent & The E Street Shuffle* . . . (Columbia)
Kansas City (12th St. & Vine)
Beatles; *Beatles VI* . . . . . (Capitol)
Beatles-Box Set . . . . . (Capitol)
Rock 'N' Roll Music . . . . . (Capitol)
Super Oldies Of The '60s-#10-C . . . . . (Audio Fidelity)
Bill Haley & His Comets; *Bill Haley & His Comets' Greatest Hits* . . . . (Everest)
Fats Domino; *Fats Domino's Greatest Hits* . . . . . (Everest)
Wilbert Harrison; *American Graffiti-#3-C* . . . . . (MCA)
Billboard Top Rock 'N' Roll Hits-1959-C . . . . . (Rhino)
Cruisin'-1959-C . . . . . (Increase)
Echoes Of A Rock Era-Middle Years-C . . . . . (Roulette)
Super Oldies Of The '50s-#2-C . . . . . (Audio Fidelity)
Kentucky Avenue
Tom Waits; *Blue Valentine* . . . . . (Asylum)
Kentucky Avenue, A.C.
Duke Ellington; *Intimacy Of The Blues* . . . . . (Fantasy)
King Of Oak Street
Kenny Rogers; *The Gambler* . . . . . (EMI)
Kenny Rogers And The First Edition; *Country Songs* . . . . . (MCA Special Prod.)
Lamb Lies Down On Broadway
Genesis; *Lamb Lies Down On Broadway* . . . . . (Atco)
Seconds Out . . . . . (Atlantic)
Little Old Lady (From Pasadena) (Colorado Blvd.)
Beach Boys; *Concert/'69-Live In London* . . . . . (Capitol)
Jan & Dean; *Best Of Jan & Dean* . . . . . (EMI)
Billboard Top Rock 'N' Roll Hits-1964-C . . . . . (Rhino)
Dead Man's Curve . . . . . (EMI)
Surf City-Best Of Jan & Dean . . . . . (EMI)
Lonely And Gone
Montgomery Gentry; *Tattoos & Scars* . . . . . (Columbia)

Lost In The Lights Of Broadway
Bernie Shanahan; *Bernie Shanahan* . . . . (Atlantic)
Love Potion Number 9
Clovers; *ST/American Graffiti* . . . . (MCA)
   Super Oldies Of The '50s-#7-C . . . . (Audio Fidelity)
Herb Alpert & The Tijuana Brass; *Herb Alpert & The Tijuana Brass'*
   Greatest Hits . . . . (A&M)
   Herb Alpert & The Tijuana Brass-Classics-#1 . . . . (A&M)
Searchers; *History Of British Rock-#3-C* . . . . (Rhino)
   Searchers' Greatest Hits . . . . (Rhino)
Moon Over Bourbon Street
Sting; *Bring On The Night* . . . . (A&M)
   Dream Of The Blue Turtles . . . . (A&M)
Murder On Music Row
George Strait & Alan Jackson; *Latest Greatest Straitest Hits* . . . . (MCA)
Nature Avenue
John Lodge; *Nature Avenue* . . . . (London)
Naughty Lady Of Shady Lane
Ames Brothers; *Best Of The Ames Brothers* . . . . (Pair)
   Nipper's Greatest Hits Of The '50s-#2-C . . . . (RCA)
Nights On Broadway
Bee Gees; *Bee Gees' Greatest* . . . . (Polydor)
   Here At Last...Bee Gees...Live . . . . (Polydor)
   Main Course . . . . (RSO)
On Broadway
Drifters; *Drifters-16 Greatest Hits* . . . . (Trip)
   Drifters-Golden Hits . . . . (Atlantic)
George Benson; *George Benson-Collection* . . . . (Warner Bros.)
   ST/All That Jazz . . . . (Casablanca)
   Weekend In L.A. . . . . (Warner Bros.)
On Dark Street
Elton John; *The One* . . . . (MCA)
On Green Dolphin Street
Anita O'Day; *Anita O'Day* . . . . (Glendale)
Carmen McRae; *At The Great American Music Hall* . . . . (Blue Note)
Miles Davis; *Basic Miles* . . . . (Columbia)
Red Garland; *Saying Something* . . . . (Prestige)
Only One You (Fifth Avenue)
T.G. Sheppard; *Best Of T.G. Sheppard* . . . . (Curb)
   T.G. Sheppard's All-Time Greatest Hits . . . . (Warner Bros.)
Orange Blossom Lane
Glenn Miller & His Orchestra; *Complete Glenn Miller & His*
   Orchestra . . . . (Bluebird)
   Complete Glenn Miller & His Orchestra-#7 . . . . (Bluebird)
Penny Lane
Beatles; *Beatles 1* . . . . (Capitol)
   Magical Mystery Tour . . . . (Capitol)
   The Beatles/1967-1970 . . . . (Capitol)
   The Beatles-Anthology-#2 . . . . (Capitol)
Pimp Lane
Penthouse Players Clique; *Paid The Cost* . . . . (Ruthless/Priority)
Positively 4th Street
Bob Dylan; *Biograph* . . . . (Columbia)
   Bob Dylan's Greatest Hits . . . . (Columbia)
Byrds; *The Byrds* . . . . (Columbia)
   The Byrds (Untitled) . . . . (Legacy)
Posse On Broadway
Sir Mix-A-Lot; *Rap Straight Outta The Ghetto-C* . . . . (K-Tel)
   Swass . . . . (Nastymix)
Promised Land (Main Street)
Bruce Springsteen; *Darkness On The Edge Of Town* . . . . (Columbia)
Bruce Springsteen & The E Street Band; *Bruce Springsteen & The E Street*
   Band Live/1975-85 . . . . (Legacy)
Purple Avenue
Holly Cole Trio; *Blame It On My Youth* . . . . (Blue Note)
Puttin' On The Ritz (Park Avenue)
Ella Fitzgerald; *Silver Collection-Songbooks* . . . . (Verve)
Fred Astaire; *Irving Berlin Always-C* . . . . (Verve)
   Irving Berlin Songbook . . . . (Verve)
Harry Richman; *Hollywood Sings-C* . . . . (Living Era)
   Those Wonderful Years: Puttin' On The Ritz-C . . . . (JCI Assoc. Labels)
Judy Garland; *One & Only* . . . . (Capitol)
Mandy Patinkin; *Mandy Patinkin* . . . . (Columbia)
Taco; *After Eight* . . . . (RCA)
   Nipper's Greatest Hits Of The '80s-C . . . . (RCA)
Sentimental Street
Night Ranger; *7 Wishes* . . . . (MCA)
   Night Ranger's Greatest Hits . . . . (Camel)
Seventh Avenue
Rosanne Cash; *The Wheel* . . . . (Columbia)
Sheep Go To Heaven (Sunset Strip)
Cake; *Prolonging The Magic* . . . . (Capricorn)
Skid Row
Original Cast; *Little Shop Of Horrors* . . . . (Geffen)
Skid Row
Herman Brood; *Herman Brood & His Wild Romance* . . . . (Ariola America)
Skid Row Joe
Porter Wagoner; *Best Of Porter Wagoner-#1* . . . . (RCA)
   Porter Wagoner's Greatest . . . . (Tudor)

South Street
Orlons; *South Street* . . . . (Cameo)
Strollin' Beale No. 1
Rufus Thomas; *Can't Get Away From This Dog* . . . . (Stax)
Suicide On Downing St.
Tim Finn; *Tim Finn* . . . . (Capitol)
Sullivan Street
Counting Crows; *August And Everything After* . . . . (David Geffen Co.)
Sunday School To Broadway
Sammi Smith; *45-#45334* . . . . (Elektra)
Sunny Goodge Street
Donovan; *Catch The Wind* . . . . (Garland)
Judy Collins; *Colors Of The Day-The Best Of Judy Collins* . . . . (Elektra)
Swing Street
Bruce Hornsby; *Hot House* . . . . (RCA)
Tenth Avenue Freeze-Out
Bruce Springsteen; *Born To Run* . . . . (Columbia)
Bruce Springsteen & The E Street Band; *Bruce Springsteen & The E Street*
   Band Live/1975-85 . . . . (Legacy)
That Was Your Mother (Lafayette)
Paul Simon; *Graceland* . . . . (Warner Bros.)
Theme From "21 Jump Street"
Original Soundtrack; *Television's Greatest Hits-#7-Cable Ready-C* . . . . (TVT)
Theme From "77 Sunset Strip"
Original Soundtrack; *Television's Greatest Hits-#1-C* . . . . (TVT)
   TV Classic Themes: 25th Anniversary Edition-C . . . . (Breakable)
Theme From "Bourbon Street Beat"
Original Soundtrack; *Television's Greatest Hits-#4-Black & White*
   Classics-C . . . . (TVT)
Theme From "Hill Street Blues"
Original Soundtrack; *Television's Greatest Hits-#3-1970s & 1980s-C* . . . . (TVT)
Theme From "Hudson Street"
Original Soundtrack; *Television's Greatest Hits-#7-Cable Ready-C* . . . . (TVT)
Theme From "Melrose Place"
Original Soundtrack; *Television's Greatest Hits-#7-Cable Ready-C* . . . . (TVT)
Theme From "Sesame Street"
Original Soundtrack; *Television's Greatest Hits-#3-1970s & 1980s-C* . . . . (TVT)
There's A Broken Heart For Every Light On Broadway
Mel Torme; *Songs Of New York* . . . . (Rhino)
Thing At The End Of New Hampshire Avenue
John Fahey; *Old Girlfriends And Other Horrible Memories* . . . . (Varrick)
Thunder Road
Bruce Springsteen; *Born To Run* . . . . (Columbia)
   Bruce Springsteen's Greatest Hits . . . . (Columbia)
Bruce Springsteen & The E Street Band; *Bruce Springsteen & The E Street*
   Band Live/1975-85 . . . . (Legacy)
Times Square
Marianne Faithfull; *Blazing Away* . . . . (Island)
Under The Boardwalk
Bette Midler; *ST/Beaches* . . . . (Atlantic)
Bruce Willis; *Return Of Bruno* . . . . (Motown)
Drifters; *Atlantic Rhythm & Blues 1947-1974-#5 (1962-1966)-C* . . . . . (Atlantic)
   Drifters-16 Greatest Hits . . . . (Trip)
   Drifters-Golden Hits . . . . (Atlantic)
   Super Oldies Of The '60s-#5-C . . . . (Audio Fidelity)
John Mellencamp; *Rough Harvest* . . . . (Mercury)
Lynn Anderson; *What She Does Best* . . . . (Mercury)
Rickie Lee Jones; *Girl At Her Volcano* . . . . (Warner Bros.)
Rolling Stones; *12 X 5* . . . . (Abkco)
Untouchables; *Agent Double O Soul* . . . . (Restless)
Walking Down Madison
Kirsty MacColl; *Electric Landlady* . . . . (Charisma)
Wall Street Shuffle
10 CC; *10 CC's Greatest Hits-1972-1978* . . . . (Polydor)
   Live & Let Live . . . . (Mercury)
Washington Square
Village Stompers; *Havin' A '60s Hootenanny-C* . . . . (K-Tel)
   Washington Square . . . . (Epic)

STRINGS & ROPE

See Also: CAPITAL PUNISHMENT, HOLDING ON, LOVE: CAN'T
GET OVER YOU, PRISON, STUCK

All Tangled Up In Love
Gus Hardin & Earl Thomas Conley; *Collector's Series-Duets-C* . . . . . . (RCA)
   Wall Of Tears . . . . (RCA)
All Tied Up
Ronnie McDowell; *All Tied Up In Love* . . . . (Curb/MCA)
   Country Classics-#9-1984-1987-C . . . . (Universal)
Angels Would Fall
Melissa Etheridge; *Breakdown* . . . . (Island)
Diving To Be Deeper
Sinead Lohan; *No Mermaid* . . . . (Grapevine)
Hey There
Original Cast; *ST/Pajama Game* . . . . (Collectables)

Rosemary Clooney; *Essence Of Rosemary Clooney* . . . . (Legacy)

I'll String Along With You
Diana Krall; *When I Look In Your Eyes* . . . . (GRP)

I've Got The World On A String
Count Basie; *Standards* . . . . (Verve)
Diana Krall; *Only Trust Your Heart* . . . . (GRP)
Ella Fitzgerald; *Harold Arlen Songbook-#1* . . . . (Verve)
Frank Sinatra; *Capitol Collectors Series-Frank Sinatra* . . . . (Capitol)
Frank Sinatra & Liza Minnelli; *Frank Sinatra-Duets-C* . . . . (Capitol)
Sarah Vaughan; *Best Of Sarah Vaughan* . . . . (Pablo)
Stephane Grappelli & Martin Taylor; *We've Got The World On A
    String* . . . . (Angel)

Loosen Up My Strings
Clint Black; *Nothin' But The Taillights* . . . . (RCA)

Loser
3 Doors Down; *Better Life* . . . . (Republic/Universal)

No Strings
Original Broadway Cast; *No Strings* . . . . (Angel)

No Strings Attached
'N Sync; *No Strings Attached* . . . . (Jive)

Pretty Noose
Soundgarden; *Down On The Upside* . . . . (A&M)

Rope Burn
Janet Jackson; *Velvet Rope* . . . . (Virgin)

Rope Song, The
Devo; *Hardcore-#2 (1974-1977)* . . . . (Rykodisc)

Rope The Moon
John Michael Montgomery; *Kickin' It Up* . . . . (Atlantic)

String
Monty Python's Flying Circus; *Contractual Obligation* . . . . (Arista)
    The Final Rip Off . . . . (Virgin)

String Along
Rick Nelson; *Best Of Rick Nelson 1963-1975* . . . . (MCA)

String Around My Heart
Cleftones; *Best Of The Cleftones* . . . . (Rhino)

String Man
Mamas & The Papas; *Deliver* . . . . (MCA)

String Of Lies
Goo Goo Dolls; *Superstar Car Wash* . . . . (Metal Blade)

String Of Pearls
Boston Pops Orchestra/Arthur Fiedler; *Greatest Hits Of The '40s-#2* . . . . (RCA)
Glenn Miller; *Best Of Glenn Miller* . . . . (RCA)
    Glenn Miller-A Legendary Performer-#1 & 2 . . . . (Bluebird)
    Memorial-1944-1969 . . . . (Bluebird)
    Moonlight Serenade . . . . (Bluebird)
    The Glenn Miller Story . . . . (RCA)
Glenn Miller & His Orchestra; *Glenn Miller & His Orchestra-
    Pure Gold* . . . . (Bluebird)
Lawrence Welk; *22 All-Time Big Band Favorites* . . . . (Ranwood)
Les & Larry Elgart; *Best Of The Big Bands-C* . . . . (Columbia)

String Pull Job
John Hiatt; *Two Bit Monsters* . . . . (MCA)

Stringman
Neil Young; *Neil Young-Unplugged* . . . . (Reprise)

Strings
Kenny Rankin; *After The Roses* . . . . (Atlantic)

Strings
Blink-182; *Cheshire Cat* . . . . (Cargo)

Strings Of Love
Edie Brickell; *Ghost Of A Dog* . . . . (Geffen)

Strings Of My Heart, The
Gaylords; *Best Of The Gaylords-Mercury Years* . . . . (Chronicles)

Strings On Your Heart
Meat Puppets; *Monsters* . . . . (Rykodisc)

Strings That Tie You Down
Vince Gill; *Pocket Full Of Gold* . . . . (MCA)

Tangled Up In Blue
Bob Dylan; *Biograph* . . . . (Columbia)
    Blood On The Tracks . . . . (Columbia)
    Real Live . . . . (Columbia)
    The Bootleg Series-Volumes 1-3 [Rare & Unreleased] . . . . . . (Columbia)

Tangled Up In Texas
Billy Burnette; *Coming Home* . . . . (Capricorn)

Tangled Up Puppet
Harry Chapin; *Gold Medal Collection* . . . . (Elektra)
    Legends Of The Lost & Found . . . . (Elektra)
    Portrait Gallery . . . . (Elektra)

Tie Me Kangaroo Down, Sport
Rolf Harris; *45-#213* . . . . (Eric)
    Tie Me Kangaroo Down, Sport & Sun Arise . . . . (Epic)

World On A String
Neil Young; *Neil Young-Unplugged* . . . . (Reprise)
    Tonight's The Night . . . . (Reprise)

Zing! Went The Strings Of My Heart
Coasters; *Coasters' Greatest Hits* . . . . (Atco)
    Rare Soul-Beach Music Classics-#1-C . . . . (Rhino)
Frank Sinatra; *The Reprise Collection* . . . . (Reprise)
Judy Garland; *Best Of Judy Garland* . . . . (MCA)

Best Of The Decca Years-#1-Hits!-C . . . . (Decca)
Judy Garland-At Carnegie Hall . . . . (Capitol)
Judy Garland's All-Time Greatest Hits . . . . (Curb)

STRONG, Tough

See Also: **CHARACTER & INTEGRITY, EGO, FAITH, FEAR
& COURAGE, FEMINISM, HEROISM, MOTIVATION, POWER
& CONTROL**

Anything But Strong
Eurythmics; *Peace* . . . . (Arista)

Baby I Need Your Loving
Four Tops; *Four Tops' Greatest Hits* . . . . (Motown)
    Four Tops-Anthology . . . . (Motown)
    The Ultimate Collection-Four Tops . . . . (Motown)
Johnny Rivers; *Johnny Rivers' Greatest Hits* . . . . (Capitol)
    Johnny Rivers-Anthology 1964-1977 . . . . (Rhino)

Believe
Cher; *Believe* . . . . (Warner Bros.)
    Totally Hits-#1-C . . . . (Arista)

Big Bad John
Jimmy Dean; *American Originals-Jimmy Dean* . . . . (Columbia)
    Billboard Top Country Hits-1961-C . . . . (Rhino)
    Columbia Country Classics-#3-Americana-C . . . . (Columbia)
    Jimmy Dean's Greatest Hits . . . . (Columbia)

Count On Me
Whitney Houston and CeCe Winans; *ST/Waiting To Exhale* . . . . (Arista)

Extra Pale
Goo Goo Dolls; *Dizzy Up The Girl* . . . . (Warner Sunset/Reprise)

Got Me Wrong
Alice In Chains; *Alice In Chains-MTV Unplugged* . . . . (Columbia)
    ST/Clerks . . . . (Chaos)

Got To Be Strong
Maysa; *All My Life* . . . . (Rice/N-Coded)

Hold On
Jamie Walters; *Jamie Walters* . . . . (Atlantic)

I Am Woman
Helen Reddy; *Helen Reddy's Greatest Hits* . . . . (Capitol)
    I Am Woman . . . . (Capitol)
    I Am Woman-C . . . . (Nick At Nite)
    I Don't Know How To Love Him . . . . (Capitol)

I Can't Help Myself (Sugar Pie Honey Bunch)
Four Tops; *16 #1 Hits From The Early '60s-C* . . . . (Motown)
    Billboard Top R&B Hits-1965-C . . . . (Rhino)
    Four Tops' Greatest Hits . . . . (Motown)
    Four Tops-Anthology . . . . (Motown)
    Good Feeling Music Of The Big Chill Generation-#1-C . . . . (Motown)
    Motown Story-First 25 Years-C . . . . (Motown)
    Motown Superstar Series-#14-Four Tops . . . . (Motown)
    ST/Forrest Gump . . . . (Epic/Sony Music Soundtrax)
    ST/Heaven Help Us . . . . (EMI)
    ST/Into The Night . . . . (MCA)
    ST/Where The Buffalo Roam . . . . (Backstreet)

I Didn't Know My Own Strength
Lorrie Morgan; *Lorrie Morgan's Greatest Hits* . . . . (BNA)
    Reflections-Limited Edition Greatest Hits . . . . (BNA)

I Didn't Know My Own Strength
Bobbie Cryner; *Girl Of Your Dreams* . . . . (MCA)

I Turn To You
Christina Aguilera; *Christina Aguilera* . . . . (RCA)

I Will, If You Will
John Berry; *Faces* . . . . (Capitol)

I'm Not Strong Enough To Say No
BlackHawk; *Strong Enough* . . . . (Arista)

John Henry
"Little" Jimmy Dickens; *Columbia Historic Edition-"Little" Jimmy
    Dickens* . . . . (Columbia)
Harry Belafonte; *Harry Belafonte-At Carnegie Hall* . . . . (RCA)
    Harry Belafonte-Legendary Performer . . . . (RCA)
    Harry Belafonte's All Time Greatest Hits-#1 . . . . (RCA)
Merle Travis; *Great American Train Songs-C* . . . . (C.M.H. Prod.)
Odetta; *Essential Odetta* . . . . (Vanguard)
    Greatest Folksingers Of The '60s-C . . . . (Vanguard)
Woody Guthrie; *Immortal Woody Guthrie-Golden Classics-#2* . . . (Collectables)
    Legendary Woody Guthrie . . . . (Tradition)

Love A Little Stronger
Diamond Rio; *'90s Hot Country-C* . . . . (K-Tel)
    Diamond Rio's Greatest Hits . . . . (Arista)
    Diamond Rio-Super Hits . . . . (Arista)
    Hit Country '96-C . . . . (K-Tel)
    Love A Little Stronger . . . . (Arista)

Love Is A Battlefield
Pat Benatar; *Best Shots* . . . . (Chrysalis)
    I Am Woman-C . . . . (Nick At Nite)
    Live From Earth . . . . (Chrysalis)

Love Is Stronger Than Pride
Ricochet; *Ricochet*. . . . . (Columbia)
Mighty Fortress Is Our God, A
Leontyne Price; *God Bless America* . . . . (RCA)
My Song
Jerry Cantrell; *Boggy Depot* . . . . (Columbia)
My Strongest Suit
Spice Girls; *ST/Aida* . . . . (Island)
No Man's Land
John Michael Montgomery; *John Michael Montgomery*. . . . . (Atlantic)
Only The Strong Survive
REO Speedwagon; *A Decade Of Rock And Roll 1970 To 1980* . . . . (Epic)
Nine Lives . . . . (Epic)
Only The Strong Survive
Elvis Presley; *From Elvis In Memphis* . . . . (RCA)
Memphis Record . . . . (RCA)
Jerry Butler; *Best Of Jerry Butler* . . . . (Mercury)
Best Of Jerry Butler . . . . (Rhino)
Only The Strong Survive
Tubes; *Remote Control* . . . . (A&M)
T.R.A.S.H. (Tubes Rarities And Smash Hits) . . . . (A&M)
Reach
Gloria Estefan; *Destiny* . . . . (Epic)
She Said
Collective Soul; *Dosage* . . . . (Atlantic)
ST/Scream 2 . . . .(Dimension/Capitol)
Simple Lessons
Candlebox; *Lucy* . . . . (Maverick)
Stand Up
Keb' Mo'; *The Door* . . . .(550/Epic/Okeh)
Strength Of A Woman
Carpenters; *Made In America* . . . . (A&M)
Strong Enough
Sheryl Crow; *Tuesday Night Music Club*. (A&M)
Strong Enough To Bend
Tanya Tucker; *Strong Enough To Bend*. . . . . (Liberty)
Tanya Tucker's Greatest Hits . . . . (Liberty)
Stronger
Britney Spears; *Now That's What I Call Music!-#6-C*. . . . .(Virgin)
Oops!...I Did It Again. . . . .(Jive)
Stronger Than Dirt (Ajax)
Original Soundtrack; *TeeVee Toons-The Commercials-#1-C* . . . . (TVT)
Ten Pound Hammer
Aaron Tippin; *Tool Box* . . . .(RCA)
Theme From "Mighty Mouse"
Original Soundtrack; *Television's Greatest Hits-#2-C* . . . . (TVT)
Theme From "Popeye"
Original Soundtrack; *Television's Greatest Hits-#1-C* . . . . (TVT)
Theme From "The Mighty Hercules"
Original Soundtrack; *Television's Greatest Hits-#4-Black & White*
Classics-C . . . . (TVT)
This Lil' Game We Play
Subway; *Good Times*. . . . . (Biv 10/Motown)
Too Little Too Late
Barenaked Ladies; *Maroon* . . . .(Reprise)

STUCK, Frustration, Manipulated, Stymied, Trapped
See Also: DECISIONS, ESCAPE, HOLDING ON, LOVE (various), PRISON, SLEEP, STRINGS & ROPES, WALLS

(I Can't Get No) Satisfaction
Devo; *Best Of Devo-Greatest Hits*. . . . . (Warner Bros.)
Q: Are We Not Men? A: We Are Devo! . . . . (Warner Bros.)
Otis Redding; *Best Of Otis Redding*. . . . . (Atlantic)
History Of Otis Redding . . . . (Atco)
Otis Redding . . . . (Atlantic)
The Otis Redding Story. . . . . (Atlantic)
Rolling Stones; *Big Hits (High Tide & Green Grass)* . . . . (Abkco)
Flashpoint. . . . .(Virgin)
got Live if you want it!. . . . . (Abkco)
Hot Rocks 1964-1971 . . . . (Abkco)
Out Of Our Heads . . . . (Abkco)
Singles Collection-The London Years. . . . . (Abkco)
4 Seasons Of Loneliness
Boyz II Men; *Evolution* . . . . (Motown)
Acoustic #3
Goo Goo Dolls; *Dizzy Up The Girl* . . . . (Warner Sunset/Reprise)
Ain't It The Life
Foo Fighters; *There Is Nothing Left To Lose* . . . .(Roswell/RCA)
All I Want
Offspring; *Ixnay On The Hombre* . . . . (Columbia)
All Tangled Up In Love
Gus Hardin & Earl Thomas Conley; *Collector's Series-Duets-C* . . . .(RCA)
Wall Of Tears . . . .(RCA)
All Tied Up
Ronnie McDowell; *All Tied Up In Love* . . . .(Curb/MCA)

Country Classics-#9-1984-1987-C . . . .(Universal)
Always Wanting You
Merle Haggard & The Strangers; *For The Record: Merle Haggard-43*
Legendary Hits . . . . (BNA)
Arthur's Theme (Best That You Can Do)
Christopher Cross; *ST/Arthur*. . . . . (Warner Bros.)
Baby Don't Get Hooked On Me
Mac Davis; *Mac Davis' Greatest Hits* . . . .(Columbia)
Super Hits Of The '70s-Have A Nice Day-#20-C . . . .(Rhino)
Baby's Got A Hold On Me
Nitty Gritty Dirt Band; *Hold On*. . . . . (Warner Bros.)
Beast In Me
Johnny Cash; *American Recordings*. . . . .(American)
Nick Lowe; *The Impossible Bird* . . . .(Upstart)
The Sopranos-Music From The HBO Original
Series . . . . (Sony Music Soundtrax)
Best Things
Filter; *Title Of Record* . . . . (Reprise)
Big City
Merle Haggard; *For The Record: Merle Haggard-43 Legendary Hits*. . . . (BNA)
Bitter Sweet Symphony
Verve; *Urban Hymns* . . . .(Hut/Virgin)
Bittersweet Me
R.E.M.; *New Adventures In Hi-Fi* . . . . (Warner Bros.)
Bridge Washed Out
Warner Mack; *Country's Greatest Hits-#3-C* . . . . (MCA)
MCA Records 30 Years Of Hits-1958-1988-C. . . . . (MCA)
Broken Home
Papa Roach; *Infest* . . . . (DreamWorks/SKG)
Build Me Up Buttercup
Foundations; *Billboard Top Rock 'N' Roll Hits-1969-C* . . . .(Rhino)
History Of British Rock-#9-C . . . .(Rhino)
ST/There's Something About Mary . . . .(Capitol)
Bullet With Butterfly Wings
Smashing Pumpkins; *Mellon Collie And The Infinite Sadness* . . . . (Virgin)
Can't Keep A Good Man Down
38 Special; *Special Delivery* . . . .(A&M)
Alabama; *Alabama-Live* . . . . (RCA)
Can't Let Go
Mariah Carey; *Emotions* . . . .(Columbia)
MTV Unplugged-Mariah Carey . . . .(Columbia)
Casual Affair
Tonic; *Lemon Parade*. . . . . (Polydor)
Caught In Your Web (Swear To Your Heart)
Russell Hitchcock; *ST/Arachnophobia* . . . .(Hollywood)
Caught Up In You
38 Special; *Flashback-Best Of 38 Special* . . . .(A&M)
Special Forces. . . . .(A&M)
Chain Of Fools
Aretha Franklin; *Aretha Franklin's Greatest Hits* . . . . (Atlantic)
Aretha's Gold . . . . (Atlantic)
Atlantic Rhythm & Blues 1947-1974-#6 (1966-1969)-C. . . . . (Atlantic)
Best Of Aretha Franklin . . . . (Atlantic)
Lady Of Soul . . . . (Atlantic)
Clint Black & Pointer Sisters; *Rhythm Country And Blues-C*. . . . . (MCA)
Chains
Beatles; *Please Please Me* . . . . (Parlophone)
The Early Beatles . . . . (Capitol)
Carole King; *Pearls* . . . . (Capitol)
Cookies; *Introducing...The Beatles* . . . . (Vee-Jay)
Chains
Patty Loveless; *Honky Tonk Angel*. (MCA)
Patty Loveless' Greatest Hits . . . . (MCA)
Chains
Tina Arena; *Don't Ask* . . . . (Epic)
Chains Of Love
Erasure; *Innocents* . . . . (Sire)
Just Say Yo-#2 Of Just Say Yes-C . . . . (Sire)
Chains Of Love
Big Joe Turner; *Big Joe Turner's Greatest Hits* . . . . (Atlantic)
In The Evening . . . . (Pablo)
Turns On The Blues. . . . . (Kent)
Bobby Bland; *Introspective Of The Early Years* . . . . (MCA)
Spotlighting The Man . . . . (MCA)
Mickey Gilley; *First Class* . . . .(Playboy)
Mickey Gilley's Biggest Hits . . . . (Epic)
Charlie Brown's Parents
Dishwalla; *Pet Your Friends* . . . .(A&M)
Choice In The Matter
Aimee Mann; *I'm With Stupid* . . . . (Geffen)
Complicated
Carolyn Dawn Johnson; *Room With A View* . . . .(Arista)
Dancing In The Dark
Bruce Springsteen; *Born In The U.S.A.* . . . .(Columbia)
Bruce Springsteen's Greatest Hits . . . .(Columbia)
Darned If I Don't (Danged If I Do)
Shenandoah; *In The Vicinity Of The Heart*. . . . . (Capitol)
Devil Woman
Marty Robbins; *Billboard Top Country Hits-1962-C* . . . .(Rhino)

Columbia Country Classics-#4-Nashville Sound-C . . . . (Columbia)
Lifetime Of Song-1951-1982 . . . . (Columbia)
Marty Robbins' Greatest Hits-#4 . . . . (Columbia)

Diving To Be Deeper
Sinead Lohan; *No Mermaid* . . . . (Grapevine)

Dizzy
Tommy Roe; *Original Classic Oldies Of The '60s-#10-C* . . . . (MCA)
Super Hits-#1-C . . . . (Gusto)
Tommy Roe's Greatest Hits . . . . (MCA)

Don't Be Stupid (You Know I Love You)
Shania Twain; *Come On Over* . . . . (Mercury)

Don't Keep Me Hangin' On
Sonny James; *Best Of Sonny James* . . . . (Curb)
Young Love: The Collection . . . . (Razor & Tie)

Door, The
Keb' Mo'; *The Door* . . . . (550/Epic/Okeh)

Fire
Bruce Springsteen & The E Street Band; *Bruce Springsteen & The E Street*
   Band Live/1975-85 . . . . (Legacy)
Pointer Sisters; *Cover Me (Bruce Springsteen Tribute)-C* . . . . (Rhino)
Energy . . . . (Planet)
I Am Woman-C . . . . (Nick At Nite)

Folsom Prison Blues
Brooks & Dunn with Johnny Cash; *Red Hot + Country-C* . . . . (Mercury)
Johnny Cash; *Billboard Top Country Hits-1968-C* . . . . (Rhino)
Classic Cash-Hall Of Fame Series . . . . (Mercury)
Hot Tracks-Train Super Hits-C . . . . (Epic)
Jailhouse Rock (Hits From The Big House)-C . . . . . (Sony Music Special Prod.)
Johnny Cash At Folsom Prison & San Quentin . . . . (Columbia)
Johnny Cash-Original Golden Hits-#1 . . . . (Sun)
Johnny Cash's Greatest Hits-#2 . . . . (Columbia)
Superbilly . . . . (Sun)
The Man In Black-His Greatest Hits . . . . (Legacy)

Freak On A Leash
Korn; *Follow The Leader* . . . . (Immortal/Epic)

From Hell To Paradise
Mavericks; *From Hell To Paradise* . . . . (MCA)

Girl
Beatles; *Beatles-Box Set* . . . . (Capitol)
Beatles-Love Songs . . . . (Capitol)
Rubber Soul . . . . (Capitol)
The Beatles/1962-1966 . . . . (Capitol)

Graduate
Third Eye Blind; *Third Eye Blind* . . . . (Elektra)

Greedy Fly
Bush; *Razorblade Suitcase* . . . . (Trauma)

Green Door
Jim Lowe; *Billboard Top Rock 'N' Roll Hits-1956-C* . . . . (Rhino)
Super Hits-#4-C . . . . (Gusto)

Hanginaround
Counting Crows; *This Desert Life* . . . . (David Geffen Co.)

Heart Of Gold
Neil Young; *Decade* . . . . (Reprise)
Harvest . . . . (Reprise)

Heart-Shaped Box
Nirvana; *In Utero* . . . . (David Geffen Co.)

Heavy Things
Phish; *Farmhouse* . . . . (Elektra)

Here I Am
Patty Loveless; *Patty Loveless-Classics* . . . . (Epic)
When Fallen Angels Fly . . . . (Epic)

High And Dry
Marty Brown; *High And Dry* . . . . (MCA)

Hole In My Head
Dixie Chicks; *Fly* . . . . (Monument)

Hole In My Pocket
Ricky Van Shelton; *Loving Proof* . . . . (Columbia)
Ricky Van Shelton-16 Biggest Hits . . . . (Legacy)
Ricky Van Shelton-Super Hits-#2 . . . . (Columbia)

Hotel California
Eagles; *Eagles Greatest Hits, Volume 2* . . . . (Asylum)
Eagles Live . . . . (Asylum)
Hell Freezes Over . . . . (Geffen)
Hotel California . . . . (Asylum)

I Can't Do That
Stephen Simmonds; *Spirit Tales* . . . . (Priority)

I Can't Help It (If I'm Still In Love With You)
Hank Williams With His Drifting Cowboys; *24 Of Hank Williams'*
   Greatest Hits . . . . (Polydor)
Hank Williams-40 Greatest Hits . . . . (Polydor)
Hank Williams, Jr.; *ST/Your Cheatin' Heart* . . . . . . (Sony Music Special Prod.)
Johnny Cash; *First Years* . . . . (Allegiance)
Johnny Cash & Jerry Lee Lewis; *Singing Story Teller* . . . . (Sun)
Johnny Tillotson; *Poetry In Motion: The Best Of Johnny*
   Tillotson . . . . (Varese Vintage)
Linda Ronstadt; *Heart Like A Wheel* . . . . (Capitol)
Linda Ronstadt-Retrospective . . . . (Capitol)
Ricky Nelson; *Ricky Nelson Sings Again* . . . . (Liberty)
Ricky Nelson-Legendary Masters . . . . (EMI)

I Can't Tell You Why
Brownstone; *From The Bottom Up* . . . . (MJJ/Epic)
Eagles; *Eagles Greatest Hits, Volume 2* . . . . (Asylum)
Eagles Live . . . . (Asylum)
The Long Run . . . . (Asylum)
Vince Gill; *Common Thread-Songs Of The Eagles-C* . . . . (Giant)

I Don't Live Today
Jimi Hendrix; *Concerts* . . . . (Reprise)
Essential Jimi Hendrix, Volume 2. . . . . (Reprise)
Kiss The Sky . . . . (Reprise)
Jimi Hendrix Experience; *Are You Experienced?* . . . . (Reprise)

I Never Loved A Man (The Way I Love You)
Aretha Franklin; *Aretha Franklin-30 Greatest Hits* . . . . (Rhino)
Golden Age Of Black Music-1960-1970-C . . . . (Atlantic)
ST/The Commitments . . . . (MCA)

I Remember Holding You
Boys Club; *'80s Greatest Rock Hits-Teen Idols-C* . . . . (Priority)
Boys Club . . . . (MCA)
Retro Lunchbox-Gooey Love Songs-C . . . . (ISD/Intersound)

I Shall Be Released
Band; *Music From Big Pink* . . . . (Capitol)
The Band-Anthology-#1 . . . . (Capitol)
The Last Waltz . . . . (Warner Bros.)
To Kingdom Come-The Definitive Collection. . . . . (Capitol)
Bette Midler; *Bette Midler* . . . . (Atlantic)
ST/Divine Madness . . . . (Atlantic)
Bob Dylan; *Biograph* . . . . (Columbia)
Bob Dylan At Budokan . . . . (Columbia)
Bob Dylan's Greatest Hits-#2 . . . . (Columbia)
The Bootleg Series-Volumes 1-3 [Rare & Unreleased] . . . . (Columbia)
Bob Dylan And The Band; *Before The Flood* . . . . (Columbia)
Box Tops; *Box Tops' Greatest Hits* . . . . (Rhino)
Flying Burrito Brothers; *Farther Along-Best Of The Flying Burrito*
   Brothers. . . . . (A&M)
Joan Baez; *Any Day Now: Songs Of Bob Dylan* . . . . (Vanguard)
Carry It On . . . . (Vanguard)
From Every Stage . . . . (A&M)
Joe Cocker; *With A Little Help From My Friends* . . . . (A&M)
Nina Simone; *Best Of Nina Simone* . . . . (Verve)
Rick Nelson; *Rick Nelson In Concert-Troubadour 1969.* . . . . (MCA)

I Still Haven't Found What I'm Looking For
U2; *Joshua Tree* . . . . (Island)
Rattle And Hum . . . . (Island)

I Tawt I Taw A Puddy Tat
Mel Blanc; *From The Vaults-#7-The Movies...-C* . . . . (Capitol)

I Try
Macy Gray; *Now That's What I Call Music!-#4-C* . . . . (Virgin)
On How Life Is . . . . (Epic)

I Used To Love Him
Lauryn Hill featuring Mary J. Blige; *The Miseducation Of*
   Lauryn Hill . . . . (Ruffhouse/Columbia)

I'll Never Fall In Love Again
Dionne Warwick; *Billboard Top Soft Rock Hits-1970-C* . . . . (Rhino)
Her Classic Songs-#1 . . . . (Curb)
Elvis Presley; *From Elvis Presley Boulevard, Memphis, Tennessee* . . . . . (RCA)
Mary Chapin Carpenter; *ST/My Best Friend's Wedding* . . . . (Work/Epic)

I'm A Fool
Dino, Desi & Billy; *Even More Nuggets-C* . . . . (Rhino)
Only Love-1965-1969-C. . . . . (JCI Assoc. Labels)

I'm Tired Of Living This Lie
Bob Wills & His Texas Playboys; *Bob Wills & His Texas Playboys-24*
   Great Hits . . . . (Polydor)

I'm Tired Of Texas
Nancy Walker; *I Can Cook Too.* . . . . (DRG)
Nancy Walker Sings Show Stoppers . . . . (Stet)

It's Gonna Kill Me
Filter; *Title Of Record* . . . . (Reprise)

Just A Girl
No Doubt; *Tragic Kingdom.* . . . . (Trauma)

Keepin' Up
Alabama; *For The Record: 41 Number One Hits* . . . . (RCA)

Lack Of Water
Why Store; *The Why Store* . . . . (MCA)

Last Nite
Strokes; *Is This It.* . . . . (RCA)

Laughing Out Loud
Wallflowers; *Bringing Down The Horse* . . . . (Interscope)

Lazy Eye
Goo Goo Dolls; *ST/Batman & Robin-Music From And Inspired By The*
   Motion Picture. . . . . (Jive)

Let Her Go
Mark Collie; *Hardin County Line* . . . . (MCA)

Life
K-Ci & JoJo; *It's Real* . . . . (Rock Land/Interscope)

Little White Lie
Sammy Hagar; *Marching To Mars* . . . . (MCA)

Lodi
Creedence Clearwater Revival; *1969* . . . . (Fantasy)
Creedence Clearwater Revival-Chronicle . . . . (Fantasy)

Creedence Country . . . .(Fantasy)
Green River . . . .(Fantasy)
Live In Europe . . . .(Fantasy)
More Creedence Gold. . . . .(Fantasy)
Travelin' Band . . . .(Fantasy)

Love Is A Battlefield
Pat Benatar; Best Shots . . . . (Chrysalis)
I Am Woman-C . . . .(Nick At Nite)
Live From Earth . . . . (Chrysalis)

Love's Train
Con Funk Shun; Love's Train-C . . . . (Mercury)
Smooth Grooves-A Sensual Collection-#1-C . . . . (Rhino)
To The Max . . . . (Mercury)

Manic Depression
Jimi Hendrix Experience; Are You Experienced? . . . . (Reprise)

Mary Jane's Last Dance
Tom Petty And The Heartbreakers; Playback . . . . (MCA)
Tom Petty And The Heartbreakers' Greatest Hits . . . . (MCA)

Meet Virginia
Train; Now That's What I Call Music!-#4-C . . . . (Virgin)
Train . . . . (Aware/C2/Columbia)

Million Miles
Bob Dylan; Time Out Of Mind . . . . (Columbia)

Misery
Soul Asylum; Let Your Dim Light Shine . . . . (Columbia)

Night To Remember
Joe Diffie; A Night To Remember . . . . (Epic)

No More Drama
Mary J. Blige; No More Drama . . . . (MCA)

No Way Out
Jefferson Starship; Greatest Hits-Ten Years & Change-1979-1991 . . . . . .(RCA)
Nuclear Furniture. . . . . (Grunt)

No Way Out
Stone Temple Pilots; No. 4 . . . . (Atlantic)

No Way Out
Electric Light Orchestra; Aftermath . . . . (Abkco)

No Way Out
Restless Heart; Big Dreams In A Small Town . . . .(RCA)

No Way Out
Firefall; Firefall . . . . (Rhino)

No Way Out
Oak Ridge Boys; Monongahela. . . . . (MCA)

Nothing But Heartaches
Diana Ross & The Supremes; Diana Ross & The Supremes'
Greatest Hits . . . . (Motown)
Diana Ross & The Supremes-Anthology (1962-1969) . . . . (Motown)
Motown Story-First 25 Years-C . . . . (Motown)
Motown Superstar Series-#1-Diana Ross & The Supremes . . . . . . (Motown)

Nowhere To Go
Melissa Etheridge; Your Little Secret . . . . (Island)

One Headlight
Wallflowers; Bringing Down The Horse . . . . (Interscope)

One Step Up
Bruce Springsteen; Tunnel Of Love . . . . (Columbia)

One's On The Way (Here In Topeka)
Loretta Lynn; Loretta Lynn-20 Greatest Hits . . . . (MCA)
Loretta Lynn-Greatest Hits Live . . . . (K-Tel)
Loretta Lynn's Greatest Hits-#2 . . . . (MCA)
The Country Music Hall Of Fame-Loretta Lynn . . . . (MCA)

Outside
Staind; Break The Cycle . . . . (Flip/Elektra)

Over You
Gary Puckett And The Union Gap; Best Of Gary
Puckett . . . . (Hollywood/DNA-Rounder)
Gary Puckett-Super Hits. . . . . (Legacy)

Piano Man
Billy Joel; Billy Joel-Greatest Hits, Volume I & Volume II . . . .(Columbia)
Piano Man . . . . (Columbia)
Rock Classics Of The '70s-C. (Columbia)

Pretty Noose
Soundgarden; Down On The Upside . . . . (A&M)

Prisoner Of Love
Art Tatum; Solo Masterpieces-#3 . . . . (Pablo)
Frank Sinatra; Sinatra & Strings . . . . (Reprise)
Perry Como; Como's Golden Records. . . . . (RCA)
Nipper's Greatest Hits Of The '40s-#2-C. . . . . (RCA)
Perry Como-Pure Gold. . . . . (RCA)
This Is Perry Como . . . . (RCA)

Release Me
Dolly Parton; Country & Western . . . . (Intercom Music)
Dolly Parton & Donna Fargo; Queens Of Country . . . (Intermedia)
Elvis Presley; On Stage-February, 1970 . . . . (RCA)
Welcome To My World. . . . . (RCA)
Engelbert Humperdinck; Engelbert Humperdinck-His Greatest Hits . . . . (Parrot)
Live In Concert/All Of Me. . . . . (Epic)
Release Me . . . . (Mercury)
Esther Phillips; Atlantic Rhythm & Blues 1947-1974-#5 (1962-
1966)-C . . . . (Atlantic)

Billboard Top R&B Hits-1962-C. . . . .(Rhino)
Oldies But Goodies-#9-C . . . . (Original Sound)
Kitty Wells; Kitty Wells' Greatest Hits . . . . (MCA)
The Kitty Wells Story . . . . (MCA)
Lefty Frizzell; Lefty Frizzell's Greatest Hits . . . .(Columbia)
Meli'sa Morgan; Still In Love With You . . . . (Pendulum)
Ray Price; Ray Price's Greatest Hits . . . . (Columbia)
Ray Price's Greatest Hits-#1-3 . . . . (Step One)
Wilson Phillips; Wilson Phillips . . . .(SBK)

Release Me
Angelina; Angelina . . . . (Upstairs)

Rock & A Hard Place
Rolling Stones; Flashpoint. . . . . (Virgin)
Steel Wheels . . . . (Rolling Stones)

Rocks Off
Rolling Stones; Exile On Main Street. . . . . (Virgin)
Let There Be Drums!-#3-The '70s-C. . . . .(Rhino)

Satin Sheets
Jeannie Pruett; 16 Top Country Hits-#1-C . . . . (MCA)
Country Chart-Toppers . . . .(Dominion Entert.)
Grand Ole Opry-75 Years-#2-C . . . . (MCA)
MCA Records 30 Years Of Hits-1958-1988-C. . . . . (MCA)
Shawn Colvin; Cover Girl . . . .(Columbia)

Secret Place
Megadeth; Cryptic Writings . . . . (Capitol)

Seen Enough
Crosby, Stills, Nash & Young; Looking Forward . . . . (Reprise)

Serious Hold On Me
O'Jays; Serious . . . . (EMI)

Shelf In The Room
Days Of The New; Days Of The New . . . . (Outpost/Interscope)

Silvertown Blues
Mark Knopfler; Sailing To Philadelphia . . . .(Warner Bros.)

Sitting In Limbo
Jimmy Cliff; ST/The Harder They Come . . . . (Mango)
ST/The Harder They Come . . . . (Mango)

Snowbound
Genesis; And Then There Were Three . . . . (Atlantic)

Spiderwebs
No Doubt; 1997 Grammy Nominees-C . . . . (Chronicles)
Tragic Kingdom . . . . (Trauma)

Stinkfist
Tool; Aenima . . . .(Freeworld/Capitol)

Straight Time
Bruce Springsteen; The Ghost Of Tom Joad. . . . .(Columbia)

Stuck Here Again
L7; Hungry For Stink . . . . (Slash)

Stuck In A Closet With Vanna White
"Weird Al" Yankovic; Even Worse . . . . (Scotti Bros.)

Stuck In A Moment You Can't Get Out Of
U2; All That You Can't Leave Behind . . . . (Interscope)

Stuck In The Middle With You
Stealers Wheel; Super Hits Of The '70s-Have A Nice Day-#10-C . . . . . .(Rhino)

Stuck Inside Of Mobile With The Memphis Blues Again
Bob Dylan; Blonde On Blonde . . . .(Columbia)
Bob Dylan's Greatest Hits-#2 . . . .(Columbia)
Hard Rain . . . .(Columbia)

Stuck On You
Elvis Presley; Elvis' Golden Records, Volume 3 . . . . (RCA)
Number One Hits . . . . (RCA)
Return Of The Rocker . . . . (RCA)
Worldwide 50 Gold Award Hits, Vol. 1, Parts 1 & 2 . . . . (RCA)

Stuck On You
Lionel Richie; Can't Slow Down . . . .(Motown)

Stuck With You
Huey Lewis and the News; Fore!. . . . . (Chrysalis)

Summertime Blues
Alan Jackson; Who I Am. . . . .(Arista)
Blue Cheer; Good Times Are So Hard To Find-History Of Blue
Cheer . . . .(Mercury)
Louder Than God-Best Of Blue Cheer. . . . .(Rhino)
San Francisco Nights-C . . . .(Rhino)
Brian Setzer; ST/La Bamba . . . . (Slash)
Eddie Cochran; Eddie Cochran-Legendary Masters . . . . (EMI)
Eddie Cochran's Greatest Hits . . . . (Curb)
EMI Legends Of Rock & Roll-24 Greatest Hits-C . . . . (EMI)
Joan Jett & The Blackhearts; I Love Rock 'n' Roll . . . . . . (Blackheart)
Who; Hooligans . . . . (MCA)
Live At Leeds . . . . (MCA)
Who's Last. . . . . (MCA)

Suspicious Minds
Elvis Presley; Aloha from Hawaii via Satellite. . . . . (RCA)
From Memphis To Vegas/From Vegas To Memphis . . . . (RCA)
Memphis Record . . . . (RCA)
Nipper's Greatest Hits Of The '60s-#2-C . . . . (RCA)
ST/This Is Elvis . . . . (RCA)

Sweet Dreams (Of You)
Chet Atkins & Mark Knopfler; Neck And Neck . . . .(Columbia)

Don Gibson; *Don Gibson-18 Greatest Hits* . . . . (Curb)
  Don Gibson's All-Time Greatest Hits . . . . (RCA)
Emmylou Harris; *Brand New Dance* . . . . (Reprise)
  Elite Hotel . . . . (Reprise)
  Profile/Best Of Emmylou Harris . . . .(Warner Bros.)
Jim Reeves; *Jim Reeves' Greatest Hits* . . . . (RCA)
Patsy Cline; *Patsy Cline's Greatest Hits* . . . . (MCA)
  ST/Sweet Dreams . . . .(MCA)
  The Patsy Cline Story . . . . (MCA)
Reba McEntire; *Out Of A Dream* . . . . (Mercury)

Sweet Sixteen
Destiny's Child; *The Writing's On The Wall* . . . . (Columbia)

Tangled In The Web
Lynch Mob; *Lynch Mob* . . . . (Elektra)

Tangled Up In Blue
Bob Dylan; *Biograph* . . . . (Columbia)
  Blood On The Tracks . . . . (Columbia)
  Real Live . . . . (Columbia)
  The Bootleg Series-Volumes 1-3 [Rare & Unreleased] . . . . (Columbia)

Tangled Up In Texas
Billy Burnette; *Coming Home* . . . . (Capricorn)

Tangled Up Puppet
Harry Chapin; *Gold Medal Collection* . . . . (Elektra)
  Legends Of The Lost & Found . . . . (Elektra)
  Portrait Gallery . . . . (Elektra)

Ten Cents A Dance
Eileen Farrell; *I Gotta Right To Sing The Blues* . . . . (Sony Music Classical)
Ella Fitzgerald; *Rodgers & Hart Songbook* . . . . (Verve)

Tender Trap (Love Is The)
Frank Sinatra; *At The Movies* . . . . (Capitol)
  Best Of The Capitol Years . . . . (Capitol)
  Frank Sinatra Sings The Songs Of Van Heusen & Cahn . . . . . (Reprise)
  Very Best Of Frank Sinatra . . . . (Reprise)
Sammy Cahn; *Evening With Sammy Cahn* . . . . (DRG)

Theme From "Quantum Leap"
Original Soundtrack; *Sci-Fi's Greatest Hits-#4-Defenders Of Justice* . . . . (TVT)
  Television's Greatest Hits-#7-Cable Ready-C . . . . (TVT)

There's No Easy Way
James Ingram; *It's Your Night-C* . . . . (Qwest)
  The Power Of Great Music . . . . (Warner Bros.)

Throwing Stones
Paula Cole; *This Fire* . . . . (Imago)

Tired Of Being Alone
Al Green; *Al Green's Greatest Hits* . . . . (Right Stuff)
  Tokyo...Live . . . . (Right Stuff)

Tired Of Midnight Blue
George Harrison; *Extra Texture* . . . . (Capitol)

Tired Of Waiting For You
Kinks; *History Of British Rock-#3-C* . . . . (Rhino)
  Kinda Kinks . . . . (Rhino)
  Kinks' Greatest Hits . . . . (Rhino)

Tired Of Your Jive
B.B. King; *Electric B.B. King-His Best* . . . . (MCA)
  Great Moments With B.B. King . . . . (MCA)

Too Much
Dave Matthews Band; *Crash* . . . . (RCA)

Too Much Monkey Business
Chuck Berry; *Classic Oldies From The '50s & '60s-#16-C* . . . .(MCA)
  Roll Over Beethoven . . . .(Allegiance)
  ST/Hail! Hail! Rock 'N' Roll . . . . (MCA)
  Toronto Rock 'N' Roll Revival-#2-C . . . . (Accord)
Elvis Presley; *Guitar Man* . . . . (RCA)
  Million-Dollar Quartet . . . . (RCA)
  ST/This Is Elvis . . . . (RCA)
Yardbirds; *Five Live Yardbirds* . . . . (Rhino)
  For Your Love . . . . (Accord)
  Yardbirds' Greatest Hits-#1 (1964-1966) . . . . (Rhino)

Traffic Jam
Artie Shaw; *Begin The Beguine* . . . . (Bluebird)
Ella Fitzgerald & Chick Webb; *Ella Sings/Chick Swings* . . . . (Olympic)

Traffic Jam
James Taylor; *JT* . . . . (Columbia)

Trapped
Bruce Springsteen & The E Street Band; *We Are The World-C* . . . . . (Columbia)

Trapped Again
Southside Johnny And The Asbury Jukes; *Best Of Southside Johnny And The Asbury Jukes* . . . . (Legacy)
  Havin' A Party With Southside Johnny And The Asbury Jukes . . . .(Epic)
  Hearts Of Stone . . . .(Epic)

Trapped In The Body Of A White Girl
Julie Brown; *Trapped In The Body Of A White Girl* . . . . (Sire)

Tryin' To Love Two
William Bell; *Coming Back For More* . . . . (Razor & Tie)

Trying To Love Two Women
Oak Ridge Boys; *Oak Ridge Boys' Greatest Hits* . . . .(MCA)
  Oak Ridge Boys-Collection . . . .(MCA)
  Together . . . .(MCA)

Turn Me Loose
Fabian; *Collectables Presents The History Of Rock-#6-C* . . . . (Collectables)
  Good Time Rock 'N' Roll-C . . . . (MCA)
  Teen Idols-C . . . . (Rhino)

Turn Me Loose
Loverboy; *Big Ones* . . . . (Columbia)
  Loverboy . . . . (Columbia)

Turn Me Loose
Vince Gill; *Best Of Vince Gill* . . . . (RCA)

Two Dozen Roses
Shenandoah; *30 Years Of #1 Hits-#20-C* . . . . (Columbia)
  Road Not Taken . . . . (Columbia)
  Shenandoah's Greatest Hits . . . . (Columbia)

Under My Thumb
Rolling Stones; *"Still Life" (American Concert 1981)* . . . .(Virgin)
  12 X 5 . . . .(Abkco)
  Aftermath . . . .(Abkco)
  got Live if you want it! . . . .(Abkco)
  Hot Rocks 1964-1971 . . . .(Abkco)
Who; *Odds & Sods* . . . . (MCA)
  Who's Missing . . . . (MCA)

Walk Away
Cool For August; *Grand World* . . . . (Warner Bros.)

We Gotta Get Out Of This Place
Animals; *Best Of The Animals* . . . .(Abkco)
  Greatest Hits Live!-Rip It To Shreds . . . . (I.R.S.)
  Sullivan Years-British Invasion . . . . (TVT)
Fear; *The Record* . . . .(Slash)

When A Woman's Fed Up
R. Kelly; *Now That's What I Call Music!-#2-C* . . . . (Virgin)
  R. . . . .(Jive)

Whipping Post
Allman Brothers Band; *Allman Brothers Band* . . . .(Polydor)
  At Fillmore East . . . . (Capricorn)
  Beginnings . . . .(Polydor)
  Decade Of Hits-1969-1979 . . . .(Polydor)
  Dreams . . . .(Polydor)
  The Road Goes On Forever, A Collection Of Their Greatest Recordings . . . .(Polydor)

Who Needs You Baby
Clay Walker; *Hypnotize The Moon* . . . .(Giant)

Wish You Were Here
Limp Bizkit & John Rzeznik; *America: A Tribute To Heroes-C* . . . . .(Interscope)
Pink Floyd; *Collection Of Great Dance Songs* . . . . (Columbia)
  Delicate Sound Of Thunder . . . . (Columbia)
  Wish You Were Here . . . . (Columbia)

Without You
Dixie Chicks; *Fly* . . . . (Monument)

Woman (Sensuous Woman)
Don Gibson; *Don Gibson-18 Greatest Hits* . . . . (Curb)
Mark Chesnutt; *Almost Goodbye* . . . . (MCA)

Wrapped Around Your Finger
Dan Hill; *I'm Doing Fine* . . . .(Spontaneous)

Written In The Stars
Elton John & LeAnn Rimes; *ST/Aida* . . . . (Island)

Yeah, Whatever
Splender; *Halfway Down The Sky* . . . . (Columbia)

You Keep Me Hangin' On
Diana Ross; *Evening With Diana Ross* . . . . (Motown)
Diana Ross & The Supremes; *Diana Ross & The Supremes-Anthology (1962-1969)* . . . . (Motown)
  Motown Story-First 25 Years-C . . . . (Motown)
Kim Wilde; *Another Step* . . . . (MCA)
Reba McEntire; *Starting Over* . . . . (MCA)
Supremes; *Billboard Top R&B Hits-1965-C* . . . . (Rhino)
  Diana Ross & The Supremes' Greatest Hits-#2 . . . . (Motown)
Vanilla Fudge; *Best Of Vanilla Fudge* . . . . (Atco)
  Vanilla Fudge . . . . (Atco)
Wilson Pickett; *A Man & A Half-Best Of Wilson Pickett* . . . . (Rhino)
  Wilson Pickett's Greatest Hits . . . .(Atlantic)

You Make Me Wanna...
Usher; *My Way* . . . . (LaFace)
  Totally Hits-#1-C . . . . (Arista)

You'll Never Know
Dick Haymes; *Best Of Dick Haymes* . . . . (Curb)
  You'll Never Know . . . . (MCA Special Prod.)
Dick Haymes & His Song Spinners; *Billboard Pop Memories-1940-1944-C* . . . . (Rhino)
  Billboard Top Movie Hits-1940s-C . . . . (Rhino)

You'll Never Leave Harlan Alive
Patty Loveless; *Mountain Soul* . . . . (Epic)

You've Really Got A Hold On Me
Beatles; *The Beatles-Anthology-#1* . . . . (Capitol)
Smokey Robinson & The Miracles; *Best Of Smokey Robinson & The Miracles-Anthology* . . . . (Motown)
  Great Songs & Performances That Inspired The Motown 25th Anniversary Television Special-C . . . . (Motown)
  Smokey Robinson-The Ultimate Collection . . . . (Motown)

SUICIDE

See Also: **DEATH, DESPAIR, KILL, LOW SELF-ESTEEM, SADNESS**

Adam's Song
Blink-182; *Enema Of The State* . . . . (MCA)
Alone Again (Naturally)
Gilbert O'Sullivan; *Best Of Gilbert O'Sullivan* . . . . (Rhino)
   Billboard Top Rock 'N' Roll Hits-1972-C . . . . (Rhino)
Auf Wiedersehen
Cheap Trick; *Heaven Tonight* . . . . (Epic)
Beaches Of Cheyenne
Garth Brooks; *Fresh Horses* . . . . (Capitol)
   Limited Series Box . . . . (Capitol)
Bookends
Joe Walsh; *The Smoker You Drink The Player You Get* . . . . (MCA)
Camera One
Josh Joplin Group; *Useful Music* . . . . (Artemis)
Chop Suey!
System Of A Down; *Toxicity* . . . . (American/Columbia)
Chrome Plated Suicide
Flaming Lips; *Telepathic Surgery* . . . . (Restless)
Drown Yourself
Staple Singers; *Be What You Are* . . . . (Stax)
Drunk Is Better Than Dead
Push Stars; *ST/Malcolm In The Middle* . . . . (Restless)
Falling Away From Me
Korn; *Issues* . . . . (Immortal/Epic)
Fire And Rain
James Taylor; *James Taylor's Greatest Hits* . . . . (Warner Bros.)
   Sweet Baby James . . . . (Warner Bros.)
   The Concert For New York City-C . . . . (Columbia)
Sammy Kershaw; *Red Hot + Country-C* . . . . (Mercury)
Free To Decide
Cranberries; *To The Faithful Departed* . . . . (Island)
Freshmen, The
Verve Pipe; *Villains* . . . . (RCA)
I Ain't Ever Satisfied
Gretchen Peters; *The Secret Of Life* . . . . (Purple Crayon Prod.)
Steve Earle & The Dukes; *Ain't Ever Satisfied: The Steve Earle*
   Collection . . . . (Hip-O)
   Exit 0 . . . . (MCA)
   Shut Up And Die Like An Aviator . . . . (MCA)
I Think I'm Gonna Kill Myself
Elton John; *Honky Chateau* . . . . (Rocket)
I Think I'm Gonna Kill Myself Today
Buddy Knox; *Best Of Buddy Knox* . . . . (Rhino)
Waylon Jennings; *Ol' Waylon* . . . . (RCA)
I Wonder If Heaven Got A Ghetto
2Pac; *R U Still Down (Remember Me)* . . . . (Amaru/Jive)
I'm Not Gonna Let It Bother Me Tonight
Atlanta Rhythm Section; *Are You Ready!* . . . . (Polydor)
   Champagne Jam . . . . (Polydor)
Joining You
Alanis Morissette; *Supposed Former Infatuation Junkie* . . . . (Maverick)
Jump Jump Jump
Rick Derringer; *All American Boy* . . . . (Blue Sky)
Jumper
Third Eye Blind; *Third Eye Blind* . . . . (Elektra)
   Totally Hits-#1-C . . . . (Arista)
Just Another Suicide
UFO; *Lights Out* . . . . (Chrysalis)
Kevorkian
Public Enemy; *There's A Poison Goin On* . . . . (Atomic Pop)
Kids Aren't Alright
Offspring; *Americana* . . . . (Columbia)
Killing Yourself To Live
Black Sabbath; *Sabbath Bloody Sabbath* . . . . (Warner Bros.)
Last Resort
Papa Roach; *Infest* . . . . (DreamWorks/SKG)
Let Go Of The Stone
John Anderson; *Seminole Wind* . . . . (BNA)
Letter, The
Macy Gray; *On How Life Is* . . . . (Epic)
Lighthouse's Tale
Nickel Creek; *Nickel Creek* . . . . (Sugar Hill)
Lilies Of The Field
Gretchen Peters; *Gretchen Peters* . . . . (Purple Crayon Prod.)
Little Girl, The
John Michael Montgomery; *Brand New Me* . . . . (Atlantic)
   Totally Hits-#3-C . . . . (Atlantic)
Man Who Shot Himself
Tom T. Hall; *Places I've Done Time* . . . . (RCA)
Man Who Sold The World
David Bowie; *Man Who Sold The World* . . . . (Rykodisc)
   Sound + Vision . . . . (Rykodisc)

Nirvana; *MTV Unplugged In New York* . . . . (David Geffen Co.)
Milk It
Nirvana; *In Utero* . . . . (David Geffen Co.)
Misery
Soul Asylum; *Let Your Dim Light Shine* . . . . (Columbia)
Most Peculiar Man
Simon & Garfunkel; *Sounds Of Silence* . . . . (Columbia)
Murder By Suicide
Gary Richrath; *Only The Strong Survive* . . . . (Crescendo)
My Life In The Suicide Ranks
Tears For Fears; *Saturnine Martial & Lunatic* . . . . (Fontana)
Ode To Billy Joe
Bobbi Gentry; *All-Time Country Classics-#1-C* . . . . (Capitol)
On Suicide
Art Bears; *Hopes & Fears* . . . . (Cuneiform)
Robyn Archer; *Robyn Archer* . . . . (Angel)
Once In A While
Dishwalla; *And You Think You Know What Life's About* . . . (A&M)
Peggy Suicide Is Missing
Julian Cope; *Jehovahkill* . . . . (Island)
Pennyroyal Tea
Nirvana; *In Utero* . . . . (David Geffen Co.)
   MTV Unplugged In New York . . . . (David Geffen Co.)
People Who Died
Jim Carroll Band; *Catholic Boy* . . . . (Atco)
   ST/Tuff Turf . . . . (Rhino)
Poor Poor Pitiful Me
Linda Ronstadt; *Linda Ronstadt's Greatest Hits, Volume Two* . . . . (Asylum)
   Simple Dreams . . . . (Asylum)
Terri Clark; *Just The Same* . . . . (Mercury)
Warren Zevon; *A Quiet Normal Life-Best Of* . . . . (Asylum)
   Stand In The Fire . . . . (Asylum)
Potential Suicide
Black Market Baby; *Faster & Louder-Hardcore Punk-#2-C* . . . . (Rhino)
Richard Cory
Simon & Garfunkel; *Collected Works* . . . . (Columbia)
   Sounds Of Silence . . . . (Columbia)
Wings; *Wings Over America* . . . . (Capitol)
Richard Cory Cries
Midnight Reign; *Mountain Of Metal* . . . . (Mountain)
Richard Hung Himself
D.I.; *Team Goon* . . . . (Triple X Entert.)
Rock & Roll Suicide
David Bowie; *David Live* . . . . (Rykodisc)
   Rise & Fall Of Ziggy Stardust And The Spiders From Mars . . . (Rykodisc)
   Sound + Vision . . . . (Rykodisc)
   ST/Ziggy Stardust-The Motion Picture . . . . (Rykodisc)
Save The Life Of My Child
Simon & Garfunkel; *Bookends* . . . . (Columbia)
   Collected Works . . . . (Columbia)
Six O'Clock News
John Prine; *John Prine* . . . . (Atlantic)
   John Prine-Souvenirs . . . . (Oh Boy)
Stan
Eminem; *The Marshall Mathers LP* . . . . (Aftermath/Interscope)
Suicidal Failure
Suicidal Tendencies; *Still Cyco After All These Years* . . . . . . (Epic)
   Suicidal Tendencies . . . . (Frontier)
Suicidal Heroin
Ratos De Porao; *Brasil* . . . . (Roadracer)
Suicidal Man
Uriah Heep; *Wonderworld* . . . . (Sequel)
Suicidal Mania
Suicidal Tendencies; *How Will I Laugh Tomorrow When I Can't Even Smile*
   Today . . . . (Epic)
Suicidal Maniac
Suicidal Tendencies; *Join The Army* . . . . (Caroline)
Suicidal Rage
Death Squad; *Split You At The Seams* . . . . (Ever Rat)
Suicide
Thin Lizzy; *Fighting* . . . . (Mercury)
   Live And Dangerous . . . . (Warner Bros.)
Suicide
Suzi Quatro; *If You Knew Suzi* . . . . (RSO)
Suicide
Damned; *Machine Gun Etiquette* . . . . (Roadracer)
Suicide
Dog; *Tom Troccoli's Dog* . . . . (SST)
Suicide Blonde
INXS; *Live Baby Live* . . . . (Atlantic)
   X . . . . (Atlantic)
Suicide Blues
Curtis Jones; *Trouble Blues* . . . . (Bluesville)
Leroy Carr; *Singin' The Blues* . . . . (Biograph)
Little Charlie & The Nightcats; *All The Way Crazy* . . . . . (Alligator)
Suicide Child
Nuns; *Best Of Rodney On The 'ROQ* . . . . (Posh Boy)
   Posh Hits-#1-C . . . . (Posh Boy)

Suicide Chump
Frank Zappa; *You Are What You Is* . . . . (Rykodisc)
Suicide Is Not The Way
Maurice John Vaughn; *In The Shadow Of The City* . . . . (Alligator)
Suicide Machine
Death; *Best Of Death* . . . . (Relativity)
Suicide Machine
Swell; *...Well?* . . . . (Def American)
Suicide Madness
Germs; *Germicide-Live At The Whisky-1977* . . . . (Roir)
Suicide Note
Pontiac Brothers; *Fuzzy Little Piece Of The World* . . . . (Frontier)
Suicide On Downing St.
Tim Finn; *Tim Finn* . . . . (Capitol)
Suicide Ride
Mark Brodie & Beaver Patrol; *Shreds-#2: American Underground 1994-C* . . . . (Shredder)
Suicide Solution
Ozzy Osbourne; *Blizzard Of Ozz* . . . . (Jet)
Live & Loud . . . . (Epic Portrait Assoc.)
Tribute . . . . (Epic)
Suicide Song
Loudon Wainwright III; *A Live One* . . . . (Rounder)
Album II . . . . (Atlantic)
Suicide Won't Satisfy
Johnny Winter; *Birds Can't Row Boats* . . . . (Relix)
Suicide's An Alternative/You'll Be Sorry
Suicidal Tendencies; *Still Cyco After All These Years* . . . . (Epic)
Suicidal Tendencies . . . . (Frontier)
Suzy Suicide
Spread Eagle; *Spread Eagle* . . . . (MCA)
Sweet Old World
Emmylou Harris; *Wrecking Ball* . . . . (Asylum)
Teenage Suicide
Unrest; *Kustom Karnal Blackxploitation* . . . . (Caroline)
Teenage Suicide (Don't Do It)
Don Dixon; *If I'm A Ham Well You're A Sausage* . . . . (Restless)
Theme From "M*A*S*H" (Suicide Is Painless)
Ahmad Jamal; *Digital Works* . . . . (Atlantic)
*ST/M*A*S*H* . . . . (Columbia)
Original Soundtrack; *CBS: The First 50 Years* . . . . (TVT)
Television's Greatest Hits-#3-1970s & 1980s-C . . . . (TVT)
Percy Faith & His Orchestra; *Percy Faith & His Orchestra's All-Time Greatest Hits* . . . . (Columbia)
Waltzing Matilda
Burl Ives; *Best Of Burl Ives* . . . . (MCA)
Fred Astaire; *Three Evenings With Fred Astaire* . . . . (DRG)
James Galway; *Pachebel Canon & Other Favorites* . . . . (RCA)
Original Soundtrack; *Children's Favorites* . . . . (Kid Rhino/Rhino 4 Kids)
What's This Life For
Creed; *My Own Prison* . . . . (Wind-up)
Yer Blues
Beatles; *The Beatles (White Album)* . . . . (Capitol)
Youth Of The Nation
P.O.D.; *Satellite* . . . . (Atlantic)

SUN

*See Also: **FIRE, HOT, LIGHT, MORNING, NIGHT, RAIN, SEASONS: SUMMER, SKY, SPACE, STARS***

African Sunrise
John Denver; *Dreamland Express* . . . . (RCA)
African Sunset
Tommy Page; *Tommy Page* . . . . (Sire)
Afternoon Sunshine
Edwin Starr; *Edwin Starr* . . . . (20th Century Fox)
Ain't Going Down (Til The Sun Comes Up)
Garth Brooks; *In Pieces* . . . . (Liberty)
Alaskan Sunrise
Dick Pinney; *Devil Take My Shiny Coins* . . . . (Mountain Railroad)
Always The Sun
Stranglers; *All Live & All Of The Night* . . . . (Epic)
Dreamtime . . . . (Epic)
Stranglers' Greatest Hits-1977-1990 . . . . (Epic)
Apartment #9
Melissa Etheridge; *Tammy Wynette...Remembered-C* . . . . (Asylum)
Tammy Wynette; *Tammy Wynette-Anniversary-20 Years Of Hits* . . . . . . (Epic)
Tammy Wynette's Greatest Hits . . . . (Epic)
Aquarius/Let The Sunshine In Medley
5th Dimension; *Billboard Top Rock 'N' Roll Hits-1969-C* . . . . (Rhino)
Greatest Hits On Earth . . . . (Arista)
ST/1969 . . . . (Rhino)
ST/Forrest Gump . . . . (Epic/Sony Music Soundtrax)
At Sundown
Mom & Dads; *Blue Hawaii* . . . . (Crescendo)

Because Of You
98 Degrees; *98 Degrees And Rising* . . . . (Universal)
Now That's What I Call Music!-#2-C . . . . (Virgin)
Behind The Sun
Red Hot Chili Peppers; *Uplift Mofo Party Plan* . . . . (EMI)
What Hits!? . . . . (EMI)
Behind The Sun
Eric Clapton; *Behind The Sun* . . . . (Duck/Reprise)
Black Hole Sun
Soundgarden; *Superunknown* . . . . (A&M)
Black Sunshine
White Zombie; *La Sexorcisto-Devil Music-#1* . . . . (Geffen)
Blame It On The Sun
Stevie Wonder; *Talking Book* . . . . (Motown)
Blister In The Sun
Violent Femmes; *ST/Gross Pointe Blank* . . . . (Mercury)
Blues Before Sunrise
Eric Clapton; *From The Cradle* . . . . (Duck/Reprise)
Bright Sunny South
Alison Krauss & Union Station; *New Favorite* . . . . (Rounder)
California Sun
Ramones; *All The Stuff & More-#1* . . . . (Sire)
Leave Home . . . . (Sire)
ST/Rock 'N' Roll High School . . . . (Sire)
Rivieras; *Beach Classics-All Original Recordings-C* . . . . (Dunhill Compact Classics)
Frat Rock!-#4-C . . . . (Rhino)
Summer & Sun-C . . . . (Rhino)
California Sunset
Neil Young; *Old Ways* . . . . (Geffen)
Canadian Sunset
Andy Williams; *Andy Williams-16 Most Requested Songs* . . . . (Legacy)
Etta Jones; *Etta Jones' Greatest Hits* . . . . (Prestige)
Something Nice . . . . (Original Jazz Classics)
Carolina Sun
Anne Murray; *Keeping In Touch* . . . . (Capitol)
Carolina Sunshine Girl
Geoff Muldaur & Amos Garrett; *Geoff Muldaur & Amos Garrett* . . . . (Flying Fish)
Cheap Sunglasses
ZZ Top; *Deguello* . . . . (Warner Bros.)
ST/Teachers . . . . (Capitol)
Clint Eastwood
Gorillaz; *Gorillaz* . . . . (Virgin)
Colors Of The Sun
Bonnie Koloc; *Bonnie Koloc-At Her Best* . . . . (Ovation)
You're Gonna Love Yourself In The Morning . . . . (Ovation)
Jackson Browne; *For Everyman* . . . . (Asylum)
Come Rain Or Come Shine
Ella Fitzgerald; *Harold Arlen Songbook-#2* . . . . (Verve)
Frank Sinatra; *Very Best Of Frank Sinatra* . . . . (Reprise)
Frank Sinatra & Gloria Estefan; *Frank Sinatra-Duets-C* . . . . (Capitol)
Judy Garland; *America's Treasure* . . . . (Dunhill Compact Classics)
Hits Of Judy Garland . . . . (Capitol)
Judy . . . . (Capitol)
Judy Garland-At Carnegie Hall . . . . (Capitol)
Michael Crawford; *With Love* . . . . (Atlantic)
Country Sunshine
Dottie West; *Collector's Dottie West* . . . . (RCA)
Great Moments At The Grand Ole Opry-C . . . . (RCA)
Rita Remington; *Country Girl Gold* . . . . (Plantation)
Day In The Sun
Peter Frampton; *Peter Frampton* . . . . (Relativity)
Do You Know You Are My Sunshine
Statler Brothers; *Statler Brothers-30th Anniversary Celebration* . . . . . (Mercury)
Don't Leave Your Records In The Sun
John Hartford; *Mark Twang* . . . . (Flying Fish)
Don't Let The Sun Catch You Crying
Gerry And The Pacemakers; *Best Of Gerry And The Pacemakers* . . . . . . (EMI)
Gerry And The Pacemakers' Greatest Hits . . . . (Laurie)
History Of British Rock-#1-C . . . . (Rhino)
Super Oldies Of The '60s-#5-C . . . . (Audio Fidelity)
Louis Jordan; *Best Of Louis Jordan* . . . . (MCA)
Ray Charles; *Genius Of Ray Charles* . . . . (Atlantic)
Rickie Lee Jones; *Flying Cowboys* . . . . (Geffen)
Don't Let The Sun Go Down On Me
Elton John; *Caribou* . . . . (Rocket)
Elton John's Greatest Hits . . . . (Polydor)
Live In Australia With The Melbourne Symphony Orchestra . . . . . . (MCA)
Elton John & George Michael; *Duets-C* . . . . (MCA)
George Michael & Elton John; *Two Rooms-Celebrating The Songs Of Elton John & Bernie Taupin-C* . . . . (Polydor)
Earth, The Sun, The Rain
Color Me Badd; *Now & Forever* . . . . (Giant)
East Of The Sun & West Of The Moon
Al Cohn & Zoot Sims; *RCA Victor Jazz: First Half-Century-C* . . . . (RCA)
Billie Holiday; *Billie's Best* . . . . (Verve)
Diana Krall; *When I Look In Your Eyes* . . . . (GRP)
Tommy Dorsey & Frank Sinatra; *Stardust* . . . . (Bluebird)

Electric L.A. Sunset
Al Stewart; *Al Stewart-Early Years* . . . . (Janus)
Electrolite
Michael Stipe/Mike Mills; *Tibetan Freedom Concert* . . . . (Capitol)
R.E.M.; *New Adventures In Hi-Fi* . . . . (Warner Bros.)
Every Night When The Sun Goes In
Jo Stafford; *Jo Plus Blues* . . . . (Corinthian)
Everybody's Free (To Wear Sunscreen)
Baz Luhrmann; *Now That's What I Call Music!-#2-C* . . . . (Virgin)
Something For Everybody . . . . (Capitol)
Everybody's Talkin'
Nilsson; *Everybody's Talkin': The Encore Collection* . . . . (BMG Special Prod.)
ST/Forrest Gump . . . . (Epic/Sony Music Soundtrax)
ST/Midnight Cowboy . . . . (EMI)
Willie Nelson; *Best Of Willie* . . . . (RCA)
Sweet Memories . . . . (RCA)
Faith In You
Steve Wariner; *Faith In You* . . . . (Capitol)
Father Sun
Wynonna; *Tell Me Why* . . . . (MCA)
Feel So Numb
Rob Zombie; *Sinister Urge* . . . . (Geffen)
Feels Like Love
Vince Gill; *Let's Make Sure We Kiss Goodbye* . . . . (MCA)
Fly Into The Sun
Lou Reed; *New Sensations* . . . . (RCA)
Fool On The Hill
Beatles; *Beatles-Box Set* . . . . (Capitol)
Magical Mystery Tour . . . . (Capitol)
The Beatles/1967-1970 . . . . (Capitol)
For A Change
Neal McCoy; *You Gotta Love That!* . . . . (Atlantic)
Georgia Sunshine
Jerry Reed; *Best Of Jerry Reed* . . . . (RCA)
God Of The Sun
America; *Harbor* . . . . (Warner Bros.)
Golden Apples Of The Sun
Judy Collins; *Golden Apples Of The Sun* . . . . (Elektra)
So Early In The Spring, The First 15 Years . . . . (Elektra)
Good Day Sunshine
Beatles; *Beatles-Box Set* . . . . (Capitol)
Revolver . . . . (Capitol)
Goodnight Moon
Shivaree; *I Oughtta Give You A Shot...* . . . . (Capitol)
Groovin'
Aretha Franklin; *Lady Soul* . . . . (Atlantic)
Booker T. & The M.G.s; *Best Of Booker T. & The M.G.s* . . . . (Atlantic)
Soul Shots-#3-Soul Twist-C . . . . (Rhino)
Rascals; *Groovin'* . . . . (Warner Special Prod.)
Hit Singles-1958-1977-C . . . . (Atlantic)
Rascals' Greatest Hits . . . . (Atlantic)
ST/Platoon . . . . (Atlantic)
Happier Than The Morning Sun
Stevie Wonder; *Music Of My Mind* . . . . (Motown)
Happiness Street
Georgia Gibbs; *Best Of Georgia Gibbs-The Mercury Years* . . . . . . (Chronicles)
Hard To Explain
Cowboy Junkies; *Pale Sun, Crescent Moon* . . . . (RCA)
Here Comes The Sun
Beatles; *Abbey Road* . . . . (Parlophone)
The Beatles/1967-1970 . . . . (Capitol)
George Benson; *Best Of George Benson* . . . . (A&M)
George Benson-Collection . . . . (Warner Bros.)
George Harrison; *Bangladesh* . . . . (Capitol)
Best Of George Harrison . . . . (Capitol)
High On Sunshine
Commodores; *Hot On The Tracks* . . . . (Motown)
Holidays In The Sun
Sex Pistols; *Never Mind The Bollocks, Here's The Sex Pistols* . . . (Warner Bros.)
Hot As Sun
Paul McCartney; *McCartney* . . . . (Capitol)
House Of The Rising Sun
Animals; *Animals Greatest Hits* . . . . (Allegiance)
Best Of The Animals . . . . (Abkco)
Greatest Hits Live!-Rip It To Shreds . . . . (I.R.S.)
Hank Williams, Jr.; *Hank Williams, Jr. ''Live''* . . . . (WB/Curb)
Ronnie Milsap; *Ronnie Milsap-16 Greatest Hits-#2* . . . . (Trip)
Hurry Sundown
Outlaws; *Bring It Back Alive* . . . . (Arista)
Hurry Sundown . . . . (Arista)
South's Greatest Hits-#2-C . . . . (Capricorn)
I Can See Clearly Now
Gladys Knight & The Pips; *Gladys Knight & The Pips'*
Greatest Hits . . . . (Buddah)
Imagination . . . . (Right Stuff)
On & On . . . . (Fifty One West)
Johnny Nash; *Billboard Top Rock 'N' Roll Hits-1972-C* . . . . (Rhino)
Rock Artifacts-From The Vaults-#2-C . . . . (Legacy)

I Don't Care If The Sun Don't Shine
Elvis Presley; *A Golden Celebration* . . . . (RCA)
The Sun Sessions . . . . (RCA)
I Got The Sun In The Morning
Ethel Merman/Bruce Yarnell/Original Cast; *Annie Get*
Your Gun . . . . (RCA Victor)
Ethel Merman/Ray Middleton/Original Cast; *Annie Get Your Gun* . . . . . (MCA)
Original Broadway Cast; *Annie Get Your Gun* . . . . (Angel)
I Live For The Sun
Sunrays; *Beach Classics-All Original*
Recordings-C . . . . (Dunhill Compact Classics)
Summer And Surf-C . . . . (Rhino)
I Want To Spread A Little Sunshine
Jack Norworth; *Music From The New York Stage (1890-1920)-#4-1917-*
1920-C . . . . (Pearl)
If The Sun Doesn't Shine
Smithereens; *Green Thoughts* . . . . (Capitol)
I'll Follow The Sun
Beatles; *Beatles '65* . . . . (Capitol)
Beatles-Box Set . . . . (Capitol)
Beatles-Love Songs . . . . (Capitol)
For Sale . . . . (Capitol)
In The Absence Of Sun
Duncan Sheik; *Duncan Sheik* . . . . (Atlantic)
In The Evening
Big Joe Turner; *In The Evening* . . . . (Pablo)
Joe Williams; *Everyday I Have The Blues* . . . . (Savoy)
In The Evening When The Sun Goes Down
Ella Fitzgerald; *These Are The Blues* . . . . (Verve)
Mel Torme; *Duke Ellington & Count Basie Songbook* . . . . (Verve)
Pete Seeger; *20 Golden Pieces Of Pete Seeger* . . . . (Bulldog)
Pete Seeger Sings Folk Music Of The World . . . . (Tradition)
In The Sun
Peter Gabriel; *Diana, Princess Of Wales-Tribute-C* . . . . (Columbia)
Indian Sunset
Elton John; *Madman Across The Water* . . . . (Polydor)
Island In The Sun
Weezer; *Weezer 2001* . . . . (Geffen)
It's A Great Day To Be Alive
Travis Tritt; *Down The Road I Go* . . . . (Columbia)
Itsy Bitsy Spider, The
Original Soundtrack; *Mother Goose Songs* . . . . (Madacy)
Jenny (Iowa Sunrise)
Janis Ian; *Night Trains* . . . . (Columbia)
Keep On The Sunny Side
Randy Scruggs with Earl Scruggs & Doc Watson; *Red Hot +*
Country-C . . . . (Mercury)
Whites; *ST/O Brother, Where Art Thou?* . . . . (Mercury)
Keep Searchin' (We'll Follow The Sun)
Del Shannon; *Del Shannon's Greatest Hits* . . . . (Rhino)
Del Shannon's Greatest Hits . . . . (Curb)
Kentucky Sunrise
Ringling Brothers B & B Band; *Circus Time* . . . . (MCA)
L.A. Sunshine
War; *Platinum Jazz* . . . . (Blue Note)
Life Goes On
Little Texas; *Little Texas' Greatest Hits* . . . . (Warner Bros.)
Lipstick Sunset
John Hiatt; *Bring The Family* . . . . (A&M)
Hiatt Comes Alive At Budokan . . . . (A&M)
John Hiatt's Greatest Hits-The A&M Years '87-'94 . . . . (A&M)
Look Into The Sun
Jethro Tull; *Stand Up* . . . . (Chrysalis)
Louisiana Sun
Doug Kershaw; *Louisiana Man* . . . . (Warner Bros.)
Wichita Wildcat . . . . (Fifty One West)
Mad Dogs & Englishmen
Noel Coward; *Live From Las Vegas & New York* . . . . (Columbia)
Memphis Sun
Orion; *Rockabilly* . . . . (Sun)
Midnight Girl/Sunset Town
Sweethearts Of The Rodeo; *Sweethearts Of The Rodeo* . . . . (Columbia)
Midnight Sun
Brian Culbertson; *Modern Life* . . . . (Mesa/Bluemoon)
Ella Fitzgerald; *In Rome-Birthday Concert* . . . . (Verve)
Ella Fitzgerald & Oscar Peterson; *Ella & Oscar* . . . . (Pablo)
Sarah Vaughan; *Best Of Sarah Vaughan* . . . . (Pablo)
How Long Has This Been Going On? . . . . (Pablo)
Miss Sun
Boz Scaggs; *Boz Scaggs-Hits!* . . . . (Columbia)
Miss Sun
Toto; *Toto* . . . . (Columbia)
Morning Sun
Jesse Colin Young; *Best Of Jesse Colin Young-Solo Years* . . . . . . (Rhino)
Song For Juli . . . . (Warner Bros.)
Morning Sun
Bad Company; *Burnin' Sky* . . . . (Swan Song)

Most High
Jimmy Page/Robert Plant; *Walking Into Clarksdale* (Atlantic)
Mr. Too Damn Good
Gerald Levert; *G* (East West)
My Carolina Sunshine Girl
Jimmie Rodgers; *Jimmie Rodgers-Early Years-1928-1929* (Rounder)
My Mammy
Al Jolson; *Best Of Al Jolson* (MCA)
Let Me Sing And I'm Happy (Turner Classic Movies)
The '20s-From Broadway To Hollywood-#3-C (Flapper)
Happenings; *Happenings-Golden Hits!* (B.T. Puppy)
Never Let You Go
Third Eye Blind; *Blue* (Elektra)
Totally Hits-#2-C (Elektra)
North Dakota Sunrise
Metamora; *Metamora* (Sugar Hill)
October Sunshine
First Brass; *First Brass* (M-A Music Int'l)
Jazz Horizons-Best Of M-A Music-#1-C (M-A Music Int'l)
Oklahoma Sunshine
Mayf Nutter; *Goin' Skinny Dippin'* (Crescendo)
Old Kentucky Home
Randy Newman; *12 Songs* (Reprise)
Randy Newman/Live (Warner Archives)
On The Sunny Side Of The Street
Diana Krall; *Stepping Out* (Justin Time)
Frank Sinatra; *Come Swing With Me!* (Capitol)
One More For The Road (Capitol)
Sentimental Journey (Capitol)
The Capitol Years (Capitol)
Judy Garland; *Best Of Judy Garland* (MCA)
Louis Armstrong; *Best Of Louis Armstrong* (MCA)
Chicago Concert 1956 (Columbia)
Jazz Club-Vocal (Verve)
Music Autobiography (MCA)
Ted Lewis & His Orchestra; *Charming Gents Of Stage & Screen-C* (Legacy)
Those Wonderful Years: Puttin' On The Ritz-C (JCI Assoc. Labels)
One In The Sun
Lynyrd Skynyrd; *Lynyrd Skynyrd-Legend* (MCA)
Steve Gaines; *Rockin' Southern Style-C* (MCA Special Prod.)
Other Man's Grass Is Always Greener
Petula Clark; *Petula Clark's Greatest Hits* (Crescendo)
Paper Sun
Def Leppard; *Euphoria* (Mercury)
Paper Sun
Traffic; *20th Century Masters-The Millennium Collection-The Best Of Steve Winwood-Traffic* (Island)
Best Of Traffic (Island)
Feelin' Alright-Very Best Of Traffic (Island)
Island Story 1962-1987-C (Island)
Smiling Phases (Island)
Place In The Sun
Stevie Wonder; *Looking Back* (Motown)
Stevie Wonder's Greatest Hits (Motown)
Place In The Sun
Pablo Cruise; *A Place In The Sun* (A&M)
Please Mr. Sun
Johnnie Ray; *Back To The Early '50s* (Dominion Entert.)
Johnnie Ray-16 Most Requested Songs (Legacy)
Vogues; *Vogues' Greatest Hits* (Rhino)
Powder Your Face With Sunshine (Smile!)
Guy Lombardo & His Royal Canadians; *Best Of Guy Lombardo* (Curb)
Sammy Kaye & His Orchestra; *Sammy Kaye & His Orchestra Play 22 Original Big Band Recordings* (Hindsight)
Prayin' For Daylight
Rascal Flatts; *Rascal Flatts* (Lyric Street)
Raining In My Heart
Anne Murray; *New Kind Of Feeling* (Capitol)
Buddy Holly; *Buddy Holly-20 Golden Greats* (MCA)
The Buddy Holly Collection (MCA)
Vintage Music-#6-C (MCA)
Jo-el Sonnier; *Come On Joe* (RCA)
Leo Sayer; *Leo Sayer* (Warner Bros.)
Red Red Sun
INXS; *Listen Like Thieves* (Atlantic)
Red Rubber Ball
Cyrkle; *Even More Nuggets-C* (Rhino)
Pop Classics Of The '60s-C (Columbia)
Red Rubber Ball (A Collection) (Columbia)
Red Sails In The Sunset
Big Joe Turner; *Nobody In Mind* (Pablo)
Dinah Washington; *Echoes Of An Era-Dinah Washington* (Roulette)
Jarmels; *Jarmels-Golden Classics* (Collectables)
Nat ''King'' Cole; *Unforgettable* (Capitol)
Platters; *Platters Greatest Hits* (Everest)
Saturday Sun
Nick Drake; *Five Leaves Left* (Hannibal)
Sauerkraut 'N' Solar Energy
Norman Blake & Others; *Norman Blake/Others* (Flying Fish)
Seasons In The Sun
Kingston Trio; *Capitol Collectors Series-The Kingston Trio* (Capitol)
Terry Jacks; *'70s Greatest Rock Hits-#9-#1 Hits-C* (Priority)
Super Hits Of The '70s-Have A Nice Day-#12-C (Rhino)
Set The Controls For The Heart Of The Sun
Pink Floyd; *Nice Pair* (Capitol)
Saucerful Of Secrets (Capitol)
Ummagumma (Capitol)
Works (Capitol)
Slowdown, Sundown
Steve Winwood; *Arc Of A Diver* (Island)
Softly, As In A Morning Sunrise
Artie Shaw; *Artie Shaw Plays 22 Original Big Band Recordings-1938-1939* (Hindsight)
Big Bands In Hi-Fi-#1-Let's Dance-C (Capitol)
Bing Crosby; *Bing: His Legendary Years-1931-1957* (MCA)
Bobby Darin; *That's All* (Atlantic)
Dianne Reeves; *I Remember* (Blue Note)
Sonny Rollins; *Best Of Sonny Rollins-The Blue Note Years* (Blue Note)
Staring At The Sun
U2; *Pop* (Island)
Steal My Sunshine
Len; *You Can't Stop The Bum Rush* (Work)
Sugar Magnolia
Grateful Dead; *American Beauty* (Warner Bros.)
Best Of/Skeletons From The Closet (Warner Bros.)
Europe '72 (Warner Bros.)
Grateful Dead-Live-#1 (JCI Assoc. Labels)
Sultry Sunset
Duke Ellington; *20 Golden Pieces Of Duke Ellington* (Bulldog)
Duke Ellington & His Orchestra; *Duke Ellington & His Orchestra* (Laserlight)
Sun & Moon
Original London Cast; *Miss Saigon* (Geffen)
Sun & The Rainfall
Depeche Mode; *Broken Frame* (Sire)
Sun Ain't Gonna Shine Anymore
Walker Brothers; *History Of British Rock-#7-C* (Rhino)
Love Sixties-C (JCI Assoc. Labels)
Sun Also Rises In Hell
XYZ; *Hungry* (Capitol)
Sun Always Shines On T.V.
A-Ha; *Hunting High & Low* (Warner Bros.)
Sun Comes Up, It's Tuesday
Cowboy Junkies; *Caution Horses* (RCA)
Sun Don't Shine
Inspiral Carpets; *Life* (Elektra)
Sun Don't Shine On The Same Folks All The Time
Sawyer Brown; *Sawyer Brown* (Curb)
Sun Goddess
Earth, Wind & Fire; *Eternal Dance* (Columbia)
Gratitude (Legacy)
Sun Goddess
Ramsey Lewis; *Best Of Ramsey Lewis* (Columbia)
Sun Goddess (Columbia)
Sun Goes Down
Thin Lizzy; *Life Live* (Warner Bros.)
Thunder & Lightning (Metal Blade)
Sun Hasn't Set On This Boy Yet
Nils Lofgren; *Nils Lofgren* (Rykodisc)
Nils Lofgren-Classics-#13 (A&M)
Sun In My Hand
Scorpions; *Best Of The Scorpions-#2* (RCA)
In Trance (RCA)
Sun In My Mouth
Bjork; *Vespertine* (Elektra)
Sun Is Burning
Simon & Garfunkel; *Collected Works* (Columbia)
Wednesday Morning 3 A.M. (Columbia)
Sun Is Gonna Shine Again
Graham Parker; *Best Of Graham Parker 1988-1991* (RCA)
Sun Is Out
Flora Purim & Airto Moriera; *The Sun Is Out* (Crossover)
Sun Is Shining
Elmore James; *Chess Blues Box-C* (Chess)
The Sky Is Crying-History Of Elmore James (Rhino)
Jeff Beck & The Yardbirds; *Beckology-C* (Epic)
Sun Is Shining
Bob Marley & The Wailers; *Kaya* (Tuff Gong)
Songs Of Freedom (Tuff Gong)
Sun Is Shining
Jimmy Reed; *Speak The Lyrics To Me Mama Reed* (Vee-Jay)
Sun Is Still Shining
Moody Blues; *To Our Children's Children's Children* (Polydor)
Sun King
Beatles; *Abbey Road* (Parlophone)
Beatles-Box Set (Capitol)
Sun King
Cult; *Sonic Temple* (Sire)

Sun Maid
  Soul Asylum; *Grave Dancers Union* . . . . (Columbia)
Sun Of '79
  Des'ree; *Mind Adventures* . . . . (550 Music)
Sun On The Moon
  James Taylor; *Never Die Young* . . . . (Columbia)
Sun Singer
  Paul Winter; *Anthems* . . . . (Living Music)
  Paul Winter Consort; *Sun Singer* . . . . (Living Music)
Sun Song
  Dave Grusin; *Discovered Again* . . . . (Sheffield Lab)
  Lee Ritenour; *Best Of Lee Ritenour* . . . . (Epic)
    Captain Fingers . . . . (Epic)
Sun Won't Set
  Original Cast; *A Little Night Music* . . . . (Columbia)
  Original London Cast; *A Little Night Music* . . . . (RCA)
Sun, Moon & Stars
  Nanci Griffith; *Late Night Grande Hotel* . . . . (MCA)
Sunburst
  Bob Seger; *Night Moves* . . . . (Capitol)
Sundance
  Kitaro; *Light Of The Spirit* . . . . (Geffen)
Sundance
  Danny Joe Brown Band; *Danny Joe Brown Band* . . . . (Epic)
Sundancing (For The Hopi/Navajo Energy)
  Jon Anderson; *In The City Of Angels* . . . . (Columbia)
Sunday Morning Sunshine
  Harry Chapin; *Harry Chapin-Anthology* . . . . (Elektra)
Sunday Sun
  Neil Diamond; *Glory Road-1968-1972* . . . . (MCA)
    Velvet Gloves & Spit . . . . (MCA Special Prod.)
Sunday Sunrise
  Brenda Lee; *Brenda Lee-Greatest Country Hits* . . . . (MCA)
Sundown
  Gordon Lightfoot; *Gord's Gold* . . . . (Reprise)
    Sundown . . . . (Reprise)
Sundown
  Jesus & Mary Chain; *Honey's Dead* . . . . (Def American)
Sundown Blues
  Riders In The Sky; *Riders Radio Theater* . . . . (MCA)
Sundress
  Phat Cat Players featuring Coco Brown; *Make It Phat Baby* . . . . (Parlane)
Sunface
  Tanita Tikaram; *Everybody's Angel* . . . . (Reprise)
Sunflower
  Glen Campbell; *Best Of Glen Campbell* . . . . (Capitol)
    Glen Campbell-Live . . . . (Capitol)
    Southern Nights . . . . (Capitol)
Sunless Saturday
  Fishbone; *Reality Of My Surroundings* . . . . (Columbia)
Sunlight
  Jesse Colin Young; *Best Of Jesse Colin Young-Solo Years* . . . . (Rhino)
  Youngbloods; *Best Of The Youngbloods* . . . . (RCA)
    Elephant Mountain . . . . (Mobile Fidelity Sound Lab)
    Jesse Colin Young On The Road . . . . (Warner Bros.)
    This Is The Youngbloods . . . . (RCA)
    Youngbloods . . . . (RCA)
Sunny
  Bobby Hebb; *Billboard Top R&B Hits-1965-1969-C* . . . . (Rhino)
    Oldies But Goodies-#11-C . . . . (Original Sound)
  Classics IV; *Very Best Of The Classics IV* . . . . (EMI)
  Electric Flag; *Long Time Comin'* . . . . (Columbia)
  Stevie Wonder; *For Once In My Life* . . . . (Motown)
Sunny Afternoon
  Kinks; *Compleat Collection-20th Anniversary* . . . . (Compleat)
    Kink Kronikles . . . . (Reprise)
    Kinks' Greatest Hits . . . . (Rhino)
    Kinks-Live . . . . (Reprise)
Sunny Goodge Street
  Donovan; *Catch The Wind* . . . . (Garland)
  Judy Collins; *Colors Of The Day-The Best Of Judy Collins* . . . . (Elektra)
Sunny Hills
  Bobby Caldwell; *Carry On* . . . . (Sin-Drome)
Sunny Inside
  Neil Young; *This Note's For You* . . . . (Reprise)
Sunny Monday
  Booker T. & The M.G.s; *Melting Pot* . . . . (Stax)
Sunny Side Of The Mountain
  Bill Monroe; *Bean Blossom* . . . . (MCA)
  Jimmy Martin and the Sunny Mountain Boys; *Best Of Bluegrass-C* . . . . . (K-Tel)
  Nitty Gritty Dirt Band; *Will The Circle Be Unbroken* . . . . (EMI)
Sunny Side Of The Street
  Pogues; *Essential Pogues* . . . . (Island)
    Hell's Ditch . . . . (Island)
Sunny Side To Every Situation
  Original Broadway Cast; *42nd Street* . . . . (RCA Victor)
Sunny Side Up
  Freddie Ravel; *Freddie Ravel* . . . . (GRP/VMG)

Sunny Skies
  James Taylor; *In Harmony 2-C* . . . . (Columbia)
    Sweet Baby James . . . . (Warner Bros.)
  Jerry Douglas; *Fluxedo* . . . . (Rounder)
Sunny Skies
  Teena Marie; *Emerald City* . . . . (Epic)
Sunny Tennessee
  Doc Watson; *Old Timey Concert* . . . . (Vanguard)
Sunnyland
  Elmore James; *Golden Classics-Elmore James* . . . . (Collectables)
Sunrise
  White Mountain Singers; *Best Of The White Mountain Singers* . . . . . . (Folk Era)
    Memories-Live! . . . . (Folk Era)
    Sunrise . . . . (Takoma)
Sunrise
  Jay Beckenstein; *Eye Contact* . . . . (Windham Hill)
Sunrise
  Triplets; *...Thicker Than Water* . . . . (Mercury)
Sunrise
  Uriah Heep; *Best Of Uriah Heep* . . . . (Mercury)
    Magician's Birthday . . . . (Mercury)
Sunrise
  Paul Kantner/Jefferson Starship; *Blows Against The Empire* . . . . (RCA)
Sunrise
  Joe Sample; *Carmel* . . . . (MCA)
    Joe Sample-Collection . . . . (GRP)
Sunrise
  Jimmy Cliff; *Cliff Hanger* . . . . (Columbia)
Sunrise
  Eric Carmen; *Eric Carmen-The Definitive Collection* . . . . (Arista)
Sunrise
  New Order; *Low-Life* . . . . (Qwest)
Sunrise
  Originals; *Motown Superstar Series-#10-Originals* . . . . (Motown)
Sunrise
  Chet Atkins & George Benson; *Stay Tuned* . . . . (Columbia)
Sunrise
  Seals & Crofts; *Takin' It Easy* . . . . (Warner Bros.)
Sunrise
  Grateful Dead; *Terrapin Station* . . . . (Arista)
Sunrise In La Jolla
  Kilauea; *Antigua Blue* . . . . (Brainchild)
Sunrise In Mexico
  Clifford Jordan; *Starting Time* . . . . (Jazz Land)
Sunrise Over Haleakala
  Merl Saunders & Jerry Garcia; *Blues From The Rainforest-A Musical*
    Suite . . . . (Sumertone)
Sunrise Serenade
  Frankie Carle & His Orchestra; *Big Band Instrumentals-16 Most*
    Requested . . . . (Columbia)
  Glenn Miller; *Best Of Glenn Miller* . . . . (Bluebird)
    Glenn Miller-A Legendary Performer-#1 & 2 . . . . (Bluebird)
  Glenn Miller & His Orchestra; *Glenn Miller & His Orchestra-*
    Pure Gold . . . . (Bluebird)
Sunrise, Sunset
  Original Cast; *Fiddler On The Roof* . . . . (RCA Victor)
Sun's Gonna Shine Again
  Ray Charles; *Birth Of Soul-Complete Atlantic R&B 1952-1959-C* . . . . (Atlantic)
Sunset
  Moody Blues; *Caught Live Plus Five* . . . . (Polydor)
    Days Of Future Passed . . . . (Polydor)
Sunset
  Jackie Lomax; *Is This What You Want?* . . . . (Capitol)
Sunset
  Jonathan Butler; *Jonathan Butler* . . . . (Jive)
Sunset
  Roxy Music; *Stranded* . . . . (Reprise)
Sunset
  Michael Lington; *Vivid* . . . . (Samson)
Sunset At Noon
  Kenny G; *G-Force* . . . . (Arista)
Sunset Dreams
  Clannad; *Banba* . . . . (Atlantic)
Sunset Grill
  Don Henley; *Building The Perfect Beast* . . . . (Geffen)
Sunset People
  Donna Summer; *Bad Girls* . . . . (Casablanca)
    Donna Summer's Greatest Hits . . . . (Casablanca)
    On The Radio-Greatest Hits-Volumes I & II . . . . (Casablanca)
    Walk Away-Best Of Donna Summer-1977-1980 . . . . (Casablanca)
Sunset To Sunrise
  Duprees; *Best Of The Duprees* . . . . (Rhino)
Sunshine
  Kenny Rogers; *Back Home Again* . . . . (Reprise)
  Kenny Rogers And The First Edition; *Best Of Kenny Rogers And The First*
    Edition . . . . (K-Tel)
    Kenny Rogers And The First Edition-Love Songs . . . . (MCA Special Prod.)

Sunshine
Coko; *Hot Coko* . . . . (RCA)
Sunshine
Jonathan Edwards; *Super Hits Of The '70s-Have A Nice Day-#7-C* . . . . . (Rhino)
Juice Newton; *Juice Newton's Greatest Country Hits* . . . . (Curb)
Sunshine
Timbuk 3; *Best Of Timbuk 3* . . . .(I.R.S.)
Sunshine
Alice In Chains; *Facelift* . . . . (Columbia)
Sunshine
Original Cast; *Gentlemen Prefer Blondes* . . . .(Sony Music Special Prod.)
Sunshine
Earth, Wind & Fire; *Gratitude* . . . . (Legacy)
The Eternal Dance . . . . (Columbia)
Sunshine
Alexander O'Neal; *Hearsay* . . . . (Tabu)
Sunshine
Boys; *Messages From The Boys* . . . . (Motown)
Sunshine
O'Jays; *Live In London* . . . . (Philadelphia Int'l)
O'Jays-Collector's Item . . . . (Philadelphia Int'l)
Sunshine
Babyface; *Tender Lover* . . . . (Solar)
Sunshine
Aerosmith; *Just Push Play* . . . . (Columbia)
Sunshine & Chocolate
Semisonic; *All About Chemistry* . . . .(MCA)
Sunshine Girl
Parade; *More Nuggets-C* . . . . (Rhino)
Sunshine In Their Eyes
Stevie Wonder; *Where I'm Coming From* . . . . (Motown)
Sunshine Of Your Love
Cream; *Cream-Live-#2* . . . . (Polydor)
Disraeli Gears . . . . (Polydor)
History Of British Rock-#8-C . . . . (Rhino)
Strange Brew-Very Best Of Cream . . . . (Polydor)
Eric Clapton; *24 Nights* . . . . (Duck/Reprise)
Eric Clapton-Crossroads-C . . . . (Polydor)
Knebworth-The Album-C . . . . (Polydor)
Sunshine Of Your Smile
Tommy Dorsey & Frank Sinatra; *Tommy Dorsey & Frank Sinatra's All-Time Greatest Hits-#4* . . . . (Bluebird)
Sunshine On My Shoulders
John Denver; *John Denver's Greatest Hits* . . . . (RCA)
Take Me Home, Country Roads & Other Hits . . . . (RCA)
Sunshine Saturday Morning
Jim Aikin; *Light's Broken Speech Revived* . . . .(Linden)
Sunshine Superman
Donovan; *Donovan's Greatest Hits* . . . .(Epic)
History Of British Rock-#5-C . . . . (Rhino)
Sunshine Superman . . . .(Epic)
Troubadour-Definitive Collection . . . .(Epic)
Sunshine, Lollipops & Rainbows
Lesley Gore; *Golden Hits Of Lesley Gore* . . . . (Mercury)
Lesley Gore-Anthology . . . . (Rhino)
Sunshine, Sunshine
James Taylor; *James Taylor* . . . . (Capitol)
Sunshower
Kenny Barron & John Hicks Quartet; *Rhythm-A-Ning* . . . . . . (Candid)
Sunshower
Chris Cornell; *ST/Great Expectations* . . . . (Atlantic)
Sunshower
Chuck Mangione; *Best Of Chuck Mangione* . . . . (Mercury)
Sunshower
Jeanie Bryson; *I Love Being Here With You* . . . . (Telarc)
Sunshowers
Billie Holiday; *Golden Years-#2* . . . . (Columbia)
The Billie Holiday Story-#3 . . . . (Columbia)
Swallow The Sun
Love Exchange; *Nuggets-#10-Folk Rock-C* . . . . (Rhino)
Sweet Hawaiian Sunshine
Jorma Kaukonen & Tom Hobson; *Quah* . . . . (Relix)
Tequila Sunrise
Alan Jackson; *Common Thread-Songs Of The Eagles-C* . . . . (Giant)
Eagles; *Desperado* . . . . (Asylum)
Eagles/Their Greatest Hits 1971-1975 . . . . (Asylum)
Hell Freezes Over . . . . (Geffen)
That Lucky Old Sun
Asleep At The Wheel; *Western Standard Time* . . . .(Epic)
Bing Crosby; *The Radio Years: 25 Songs* . . . .(Crescendo)
Frankie Laine; *Frankie Laine-16 Most Requested Songs* . . . . (Legacy)
Frankie Laine-Golden Hits . . . . (Mercury)
Frankie Laine's Greatest Hits . . . . (Columbia)
Jerry Garcia Band; *Jerry Garcia Band* . . . . (Arista)
Louis Armstrong; *Louis Armstrong's Greatest Hits* . . . . (Curb)
Ray Charles; *Ray Charles-Anthology* . . . . (Rhino)
Willie Nelson; *Sound In Your Mind* . . . . (Columbia)
There Goes The Neighborhood
Sheryl Crow; *The Globe Sessions* . . . . (A&M)

Third Rock From The Sun
Joe Diffie; *A Thousand Winding Roads* . . . . (Epic)
Third Stone From The Sun
Jimi Hendrix; *Essential Jimi Hendrix* . . . . (Reprise)
Kiss The Sky . . . . (Reprise)
Jimi Hendrix Experience; *Are You Experienced?* . . . . (Reprise)
This Part Of Town
Widespread Panic; *Don't Tell The Band* . . . . (Widespread/SRG)
Three Sunrises
U2; *Unforgettable Fire* . . . . (Island)
Wide Awake In America . . . . (Island)
To The Door Of The Sun
Al Martino; *Al Martino's Greatest Hits* . . . . (Curb)
Capitol Collectors Series-Al Martino . . . . (Capitol)
Tulsa (Don't Let The Sun Set On You)
Waylon Jennings; *Taker/Tulsa & Honky Tonk Heroes* . . . .(Mobile Fidelity Sound Lab)
Under The Big Black Sun
X; *Under The Big Black Sun* . . . . (Elektra)
Under The Same Sun
Scorpions; *Face The Heat* . . . . (Mercury)
Up, Up & Away
5th Dimension; *5th Dimension-Anthology 1967-1973* . . . . (Rhino)
Greatest Hits On Earth . . . . (Arista)
Wait Till The Sun Shines Nellie
Joan Morris & William Bolcom; *After The Ball* . . . . (Nonesuch)
Waiting For Sun
Jayhawks; *Hollywood Town Hall* . . . .(Def American)
Waiting For The Sun
Doors; *Best Of The Doors* . . . . (Elektra)
Doors-Classics . . . . (Elektra)
Morrison Hotel/Hard Rock Cafe . . . . (Elektra)
Waiting For The Sun To Shine
John Conlee; *In My Eyes* . . . . (MCA)
Lionel Cartwright; *Chasin' The Sun* . . . . (MCA)
Reba McEntire; *Reba Nell McEntire* . . . . (Mercury)
Ricky Skaggs; *Favorite Country Songs* . . . . (Epic)
Waiting For The Sun To Shine . . . . (Epic)
Wake Up Sunshine
Chicago; *Chicago II* . . . . (Chicago)
Walk In The Sun
Bruce Hornsby; *Hot House* . . . . (RCA)
Walkin' On The Sun
Smash Mouth; *Fush Yu Mang* . . . .(Interscope)
Walking In The Sun
Zombies; *Time Of The Zombies* . . . .(Bac-Trac)
Walking In The Sun
Rufus; *Rags To Rufus* . . . . (MCA)
Walking In The Sunshine
Roger Miller; *Best Of Roger Miller* . . . . (Mercury)
King Of The Road . . . . (Laserlight)
More Golden Hits . . . .(Smash)
Statler Brothers; *Statler Brothers Sing The Big Hits* . . . . (Columbia)
The World Of The Statler Brothers . . . . (Columbia)
Walking In The Sunshine
Frank Sinatra; *Hello Young Lovers* . . . . (Columbia)
Walking Into Sunshine
Central Line; *Full Length Funk-The 12'' Collection And More-C* . . . . (Mercury)
Walking On Sunshine
Katrina And The Waves; *Katrina And The Waves* . . . . (Capitol)
Spring Break-#2-Cold Kegs & Tan Legs . . . . (Capitol)
Walking On Sunshine
Eddy Grant; *Let's Dance-DJ's Collection* . . . . (Columbia)
Walking On Sunshine . . . . (Epic)
Warmth Of The Sun
Beach Boys; *Absolute Best-#1* . . . . (Capitol)
Beach Boys-Gift Set . . . . (Capitol)
Best Of The Beach Boys . . . . (Capitol)
Endless Summer . . . . (Capitol)
Fun Fun Fun . . . . (Capitol)
ST/Good Morning, Vietnam . . . . (A&M)
Was A Sunny Day
Paul Simon; *There Goes Rhymin' Simon* . . . . (Columbia)
Watch The Sun Go Down
X; *Ain't Love Grand* . . . . (Elektra)
Waterloo Sunset
Kinks; *Kink Kronikles* . . . . (Reprise)
Something Else . . . . (Reprise)
Way Beyond The Sun
Byrds; *The Byrds* . . . . (Columbia)
We'll Meet Again
Vera Lynn; *ST/Dr. Strangelove: Music From The Films Of Stanley Kubrick* . . . .(Silva Classics)
We'll Meet Again . . . . (Living Era)
We'll Sing In The Sunshine
Gale Garnett; *21 Country Rock & Love Songs Of The '50s & '60s-#1-C* . . . .(Laurie)
Nipper's Greatest Hits Of The '60s-#1-C . . . . (RCA)

West Coast Sunset
Billy Joe Walker, Jr.; *Life Is Good* . . . . (Liberty)
What Sundown Does To You
Loretta Lynn; *Best Of Loretta Lynn-#2* . . . . (MCA Special Prod.)
   Loretta Lynn's Greatest Hits-#2 . . . . (MCA)
When The Sun Comes Out
Barbra Streisand; *...Just For The Record* . . . . (Columbia)
   The Second Barbra Streisand Album . . . . (Columbia)
Benny Goodman; *Clarinet A La King* . . . . (Columbia)
Ella Fitzgerald; *Harold Arlen Songbook-#1* . . . . (Verve)
When The Sun Goes Down
Mark Collie; *Born & Raised In Black & White* . . . . (MCA)
When The Sun Goes Down
Fleetwood Mac; *Behind The Mask* . . . . (Warner Bros.)
When The Sun Goes Down
Count Basie & Joe Williams; *Count Basie Swings Joe Williams Sings* . . . (Verve)
When The Sun Goes Down
T-Bone Walker; *T-Bone Walker-Complete Imperial Recordings-1950-1954* . . . . (EMI)
When The Sun Goes Down
Marty Stuart; *Hillbilly Rock* . . . . (MCA)
When The Sun Goes Down In The South
Original Broadway Cast; *Big River-The Adventures Of Huckleberry Finn* . . . . (MCA)
When You Love Someone
Bryan Adams; *MTV Unplugged-Bryan Adams* . . . . (A&M)
White Sun
Doobie Brothers; *Toulouse Street* . . . . (Warner Bros.)
Windows Of The World
Burt Bacharach; *One Amazing Night* . . . . (N2K)
Dionne Warwick; *Dionne Warwick Collection-Her All-Time Greatest Hits* . . . . (Rhino)
   Dionne Warwick-Definitive Collection . . . . (Arista)
Isaac Hayes; *Live At The Sahara Tahoe* . . . . (Stax)
Mormon Tabernacle Choir; *Voices In Harmony* . . . . . (CBS Masterworks)
Pretenders; *ST/1969* . . . . (Polydor)
Without You
Charlie Wilson; *Bridging The Gap* . . . . (Major Hits)
World Is Waiting For The Sunrise
Benny Goodman; *I Like Jazz-Essence Of Benny Goodman* . . . . (Columbia)
Benny Goodman Orchestra & Quartet; *Let's Dance* . . . . (Laserlight)
Les Paul & Mary Ford; *The World Is Waiting For The Sunrise* . . . . . (Laserlight)
Roy Clark & Buck Trent; *Banjo Bandit* . . . . (MCA)
You Are My Sunshine
Bing Crosby; *Best Of Bing Crosby* . . . . (MCA)
   Bing Crosby's Greatest Hits . . . . (MCA)
Jimmie Davis; *20 Golden Souvenirs Of Music City U.S.A.-C* . . . . (Plantation)
   Best Of Jimmie Davis . . . . (MCA)
   Jimmie Davis-Golden Hits . . . . (Plantation)
   The Country Music Hall Of Fame-Jimmie Davis . . . . (MCA)
Mississippi John Hurt; *Best Of Mississippi John Hurt* . . . . (Vanguard)
Mitch Miller; *Mitch Miller-16 Most Requested Songs* . . . . (Columbia)
Norman Blake; *ST/O Brother, Where Art Thou?* . . . . (Mercury)
Ray Charles; *Ray Charles-Anthology* . . . . (Rhino)
   Ray Charles-His Greatest Hits-#2 . . . . (Dunhill Compact Classics)
Willie Nelson & Leon Russell; *One For The Road* . . . . (Columbia)
You Are The Sunshine Of My Life
Peter Nero; *Peter Nero's Greatest Hits* . . . . (Columbia)
Stevie Wonder; *20/20-C* . . . . (Motown)
   Original Musiquarium . . . . (Motown)
   Talking Book . . . . (Motown)

SWEET, Honey, Sugar

See Also: **BEST, CANDY, COMPLIMENTS, FOOD & BEVERAGES
(various), HEART, LOVE (various), SPECIAL**

Absolutely Sweet Marie
Bob Dylan; *Blonde On Blonde* . . . . (Columbia)
Ah! Sweet Mystery Of Life
Bing Crosby; *Little Bit Of Irish* . . . . (Atlantic)
Nelson Eddy; *Through The Years* . . . . (Living Era)
Ain't She Sweet?
Beatles; *History Of British Rock-#5-C* . . . . (Rhino)
   The Beatles-Anthology-#3 . . . . (Capitol)
Erroll Garner; *Body And Soul* . . . . (Legacy)
Frank Sinatra; *Sinatra and Swingin' Brass* . . . . (Reprise)
Pearl Bailey; *Pearl Bailey-16 Most Requested Songs* . . . . . . (Legacy)
Along Comes Mary
Association; *Association Greatest Hits* . . . . (Warner Bros.)
   Vintage Association . . . . (Fifty One West)
Apple Honey
Woody Herman; *Best Of Woody Herman & His Orchestra* . . . . (Curb)
   Big Band Treasures-#2-C . . . . (Dunhill Compact Classics)
   Thundering Herds-1945-1947 . . . . (Columbia)
Big Bad Bill Is Sweet William Now
Ry Cooder; *Jazz* . . . . (Warner Bros.)

Big Rock Candy Mountain
Burl Ives; *Burl Ives' Greatest Hits* . . . . (MCA)
   Poor Wayfaring Stranger . . . . (Flapper)
Harry McClintock; *ST/O Brother, Where Art Thou?* . . . . (Mercury)
John Hartford; *ST/Down From The Mountain* . . . . . . (Lost Highway/IDJMG)
Pete Seeger; *20 Golden Pieces Of Pete Seeger* . . . . (Bulldog)
Tex Ritter; *Capitol Collectors Series-Tex Ritter* . . . . (Capitol)
Bitter Sweet Symphony
Verve; *Urban Hymns* . . . . (Hut/Virgin)
Bittersweet
Big Head Todd & The Monsters; *Midnight Radio* . . . . (Giant)
   Sister Sweetly . . . . (Giant)
Bittersweet
Fuel; *Sunburn* . . . . (550 Music)
Bittersweet
Fuel; *Sunburn* . . . . (550 Music)
Bittersweet
Verve; *Urban Hymns* . . . . (Hut/Virgin)
Bittersweet
Crosby, Stills & Nash; *CSN* . . . . (Atlantic)
Bittersweet Me
R.E.M.; *New Adventures In Hi-Fi* . . . . (Warner Bros.)
Black Honey
Graham Parker; *Heart Treatment* . . . . (Mercury)
   Live! Alone In America . . . . (RCA)
Brown Sugar
Rolling Stones; *Classic Rock 1966-1988-C* . . . . (Atlantic)
   Hot Rocks 1964-1971 . . . . (Abkco)
   Made In The Shade . . . . (Rolling Stones)
   Sticky Fingers . . . . (Virgin)
Brown Sugar
D'Angelo; *Brown Sugar* . . . . (EMI)
Brown Sugar
ZZ Top; *Six Pack* . . . . (Warner Bros.)
   ZZ Top . . . . (Warner Bros.)
Candy
Cameo; *12'' Collection And More* . . . . (Mercury)
   Best Of Cameo . . . . (Mercury/Funk Essentials)
   Billboard Top R&B Hits-1987-C . . . . (Rhino)
   Greatest Hits . . . . (Chronicles)
Will Smith featuring Larry Blackmon; *Big Willie Style* . . . . (Columbia)
Candy Girl
4 Seasons; *25th Anniversary Collection* . . . . (Rhino)
   4 Seasons-Anthology . . . . (Rhino)
   Lil' Bit Of Gold 3'' CD Series-C . . . . (Rhino)
Candy Man
Fred Neil; *Little Bit Of Rain* . . . . (Elektra)
Mickey Gilley & Charly McClain; *It Takes Believers* . . . . (Epic)
Roy Orbison; *In Dreams-Greatest Hits* . . . . (Orbison)
   Roy Orbison Greatest Hits . . . . (Monument)
   Roy Orbison's All-Time Greatest Hits-#1 & 2 . . . . (Monument)
   Very Best Of Roy Orbison . . . . (Monument)
Chewy Chewy
Ohio Express; *Best Of Ohio Express & Other Bubblegum Smashes-#1* . . . . (Rhino)
   Best Of Ohio Express & Other Bubblegum Smashes-#1-C . . . . (Rhino)
   Bubblegum's Greatest Hits-#2-C . . . . (Accord)
   Fabulous Bubblegum Years-C . . . . (Fifty One West)
Cold Blue Steel & Sweet Fire
Joni Mitchell; *For The Roses* . . . . (Asylum)
Joni Mitchell with Tom Scott & The L.A. Express; *Miles Of Aisles* . . . . (Asylum)
Dust On The Bottle
David Lee Murphy; *Out With A Bang* . . . . (MCA)
Everybody's Trying To Be My Baby
Beatles; *Beatles '65* . . . . (Capitol)
   For Sale . . . . (Capitol)
   The Beatles-Anthology-#2 . . . . (Capitol)
Carl Perkins; *Blue Suede Shoes: The Very Best Of Carl Perkins* . . . (Collectables)
   Carl Perkins' Greatest Hits/Finest Performances . . . . (Sun)
   Carl Perkins-Original Sun Greatest Hits . . . . (Rhino)
Fantasy
Mariah Carey; *Daydream* . . . . (Columbia)
Fine & Dandy
Art Tatum; *Solo Masterpieces-#5* . . . . (Pablo)
Barbra Streisand; *People* . . . . (Columbia)
Chet Baker; *Out Of Nowhere* . . . . (Milestone)
Milt Jackson & Sonny Stitt; *Milt Jackson & Sonny Stitt-In The Beginning* . . . . (Galaxy)
For You Blue
Beatles; *Beatles-Box Set* . . . . (Capitol)
   Let It Be . . . . (Capitol)
George Harrison; *Best Of George Harrison* . . . . (Capitol)
Gary, Indiana
Original Cast; *ST/The Music Man* . . . . (Gold Rush)
Georgia On My Mind
Billie Holiday; *God Bless The Child* . . . . (Columbia)
   The Billie Holiday Story-#2 . . . . (Columbia)
Hoagy Carmichael; *Hoagy Carmichael-Legendary Performer* . . . . . . (RCA)
   Hoagy Sings Carmichael . . . . (EMI)

Mildred Bailey; *Harlem Lullaby* .... (ASV)
Preservation Hall Jazz Band; *Best Of The Preservation Hall Jazz Band* .... (Columbia)
Ray Charles; *Ray Charles' Greatest Hits-#2* .... (Rhino)
Ray Charles-Anthology .... (Rhino)
Willie Nelson; *Greatest Hits (& Some That Will Be)* .... (Columbia)
Stardust .... (Legacy)
Willie & Family Live .... (Columbia)

Ginger Bread
Frankie Avalon; *Gold For The Road-Carburetor Classics-C* .... (Compose)
Venus: The Very Best Of Frankie Avalon .... (Collectables)

Girls Dem Sugar
Beenie Man; *Art And Life* .... (Virgin)

God Bless America
Anita Bryant; *Golden Classics-Anita Bryant* .... (Collectables)
Bill & Gloria Gaither; *Kennedy Center Homecoming: A Celebration Of Our Faith And Heritage* .... (Springhouse Music Grp./Chordant)
Celine Dion; *America: A Tribute To Heroes-C* .... (Interscope)
God Bless America-C .... (Columbia)
Drew Carey; *ST/The Drew Carey Show* .... (Rhino)
Frank Zappa; *Uncle Meat* .... (Barking Pumpkin)
Kate Smith; *Best Of Kate Smith* .... (RCA)
God Bless America .... (Pickwick)
Kate Smith-Legendary Performer .... (RCA)
Nipper's Greatest Hits Of The '30s-#1-C .... (RCA)
Stars And Stripes Forever-#2-C .... (Volcano Entertainment)
LeAnn Rimes; *You Light Up My Life-Inspirational Songs* .... (Curb)
Lee Greenwood; *American Patriot* .... (Capitol)
Mormon Tabernacle Choir; *God Bless America* .... (Sony Music Classical)
Original Soundtrack; *ST/The Deer Hunter* .... (Capitol)
Peter Pan Kids; *I Love America Sing Along* .... (Compose)
Robert Shaw Chorale; *Battle Cry Of Freedom* .... (RCA)

Goodnight Sweetheart
David Kersh; *Goodnight Sweetheart* .... (Curb)

Goodnight Sweetheart
Guy Lombardo & His Royal Canadians; *Guy Lombardo-All Time Favorites* .... (MCA Special Prod.)

Goodnight, Sweetheart
Flamingos; *Best Of The Flamingos* .... (Rhino)
Spaniels; *Cruisin'-1957-C* .... (Increase)
Doo-Wop Ballads-#2-C .... (Rhino)
Lovin' '50s-C .... (Priority)

Goodnight, Sweetheart, Goodnight
McGuire Sisters; *McGuire Sisters-Anthology* .... (MCA)

Gum Drop
Crew-Cuts; *Best Of The Crew-Cuts-The Mercury Years* .... (Mercury)

Happy Birthday, Sweet Sixteen
Neil Sedaka; *Neil Sedaka Sings His Greatest Hits* .... (RCA)
Neil Sedaka Sings The Hits .... (RCA)
Neil Sedaka's All-Time Greatest Hits .... (RCA)

Happy Girl
Beth Nielsen Chapman; *Sand And Water* .... (Reprise)
Martina McBride; *Evolution* .... (RCA)

Hey, Sweet Darling
Iguanas; *Nuevo Boogaloo* .... (Margaritaville)

Hi De Ho (That Old Sweet Roll)
Bobby Darin; *Live At The Desert Inn* .... (Motown)

Home Sweet Home
Carl Jackson; *Songs Of The South* .... (Sugar Hill)
Doc & Merle Watson; *Home Sweet Home* .... (Sugar Hill)
Lawrence Welk; *200 Years Of American Music* .... (Ranwood)

Home Sweet Home
Motley Crue; *Theatre Of Pain* .... (Elektra)

Home Sweet Home
Peter Gabriel; *Peter Gabriel* .... (Atlantic)

Home, Sweet Oklahoma
Tom Paxton; *It Ain't Easy* .... (Flying Fish)

Honey
Mariah Carey; *Butterfly* .... (Columbia)

Honey Bun
Original Cast; *South Pacific* .... (CBS Masterworks)

Honey Can I Put On Your Clothes
Barbra Streisand; *Songbird* .... (Columbia)

Honey Child
Bad Company; *Run With The Pack* .... (Swan Song)

Honey Chile
Martha Reeves & The Vandellas; *Compact Command Performances-Martha Reeves & The Vandellas* .... (Motown)
Martha Reeves & The Vandellas-Anthology .... (Motown)
Motown Superstar Series-#11-Martha Reeves & The Vandellas .... (Motown)

Honey Don't
Beatles; *For Sale* .... (Capitol)

Honey Don't Leave L.A.
James Taylor; *JT* .... (Columbia)

Honey For The Bees
Patti Austin; *Gettin' Away With Murder* .... (Qwest)

Honey For The Bees
Alison Moyet; *Alf* .... (Columbia)

Honey Love
R. Kelly & Public Announcement; *Born Into The '90s* .... (Jive)

Honey Pie
Beatles; *The Beatles (White Album)* .... (Capitol)
The Beatles-Anthology-#3 .... (Capitol)

Honey To The Bee
Billie; *Honey To The B* .... (Virgin)

Honeycomb
Jimmie Rodgers; *Best Of Jimmie Rodgers* .... (Rhino)
Best Of Jimmie Rodgers .... (Curb)

Honeysuckle Honey
Commander Cody & His Lost Planet Airmen; *Country Casanova* ...... (MCA)

Hooch
Everything; *Super Natural* .... (Blackbird/Sire)

How Sweet It Is (To Be Loved By You)
James Taylor; *Gorilla* .... (Warner Bros.)
James Taylor-Best Live .... (Columbia)
James Taylor's Greatest Hits .... (Warner Bros.)
Junior Walker & The All Stars; *Junior Walker & The All Stars' Greatest Hits* .... (Motown)
Junior Walker & The All Stars-The Ultimate Collection .... (Motown)
Marvin Gaye; *20th Century Masters-The Millennium Collection-The Best Of Marvin Gaye-#1 (The '60s)* .... (Motown)
Marvin Gaye-Anthology .... (Motown)
Marvin Gaye's Greatest Hits/ .... (Motown)

Hush, Hush, Sweet Charlotte
Al Martino; *Best Of Al Martino* .... (Capitol)
Patti Page; *Patti Page-Greatest Songs* .... (Curb)

I Can't Help Myself (Sugar Pie Honey Bunch)
Four Tops; *16 #1 Hits From The Early '60s-C* .... (Motown)
Billboard Top R&B Hits-1965-C .... (Rhino)
Four Tops' Greatest Hits .... (Motown)
Four Tops-Anthology .... (Motown)
Good Feeling Music Of The Big Chill Generation-#1-C .... (Motown)
Motown Story-First 25 Years-C .... (Motown)
Motown Superstar Series-#14-Four Tops .... (Motown)
ST/Forrest Gump .... (Epic/Sony Music Soundtrax)
ST/Heaven Help Us .... (EMI)
ST/Into The Night .... (MCA)
ST/Where The Buffalo Roam .... (Backstreet)

I Lost My Sugar In Salt Lake City
Johnny Mercer; *Capitol Collectors Series-Johnny Mercer* .... (Capitol)

I Wanna Be A Cowboy's Sweetheart
Patsy Montana & The Prairie Ramblers; *All Time Legends Of Country Music-C* .... (Legacy)
Respect: A History Of Women In Music-C .... (Rhino)

Imitation Of Life
R.E.M.; *Reveal* .... (Warner Bros.)

Innamorata
Dean Martin; *Capitol Collectors Series-Dean Martin* .... (Capitol)
Dean Martin's All Time Greatest Hits .... (Curb)
Jerry Vale; *Essence Of Jerry Vale* .... (Legacy)
Jerry Vale-17 Most Requested Songs .... (Legacy)
Jerry Vale's Greatest Hits .... (Columbia)

Josephine
Wallflowers; *Bringing Down The Horse* .... (Interscope)

Jukebox Never Plays Home Sweet Home
Jack Greene; *45-#0016* .... (EMH)

Kisses Sweeter Than Wine
Jimmie Rodgers; *Best Of Jimmie Rodgers* .... (Rhino)
Cruisin'-1958-C .... (Increase)
Weavers; *Best Of The Weavers* .... (MCA)
Reunion-At Carnegie Hall-1963 .... (Vanguard)
Weavers At Carnegie Hall .... (Vanguard)
Weavers' Greatest Hits .... (Vanguard)

Let Me Call You Sweetheart
Bette Midler; *ST/The Rose* .... (Atlantic)
Billy Vaughn & His Orchestra; *Billy Vaughn & His Orchestra Play 22 Of His Greatest Hits* .... (Ranwood)
Bing Crosby; *Bing Crosby-Love Songs* .... (Universal)
Bob Ralston; *22 Great Organ Hits-#2* .... (Ranwood)
Gene Autry; *Gene Autry-Love Songs* .... (Varese Sarabande)
Lawrence Welk; *American Favorites* .... (Ranwood)
Peerless Quartet; *78-#1057* .... (Columbia)

Let Me Fall
Wood; *Songs From Stamford Hill* .... (Columbia)

Lips Like Sugar
Echo & The Bunnymen; *Echo & The Bunnymen* .... (Sire)
Just Say Yes...Sire's Winter CD Sampler-C .... (Sire)

Lollipop
Chordettes; *Best Of The Chordettes* .... (Rhino)
Chordettes Greatest Hits .... (Everest)
Jukebox Classics-#2-C .... (Rhino)
Lil' Bit Of Gold 3'' CD Series-C .... (Rhino)
ST/Stand By Me .... (Atlantic)

Love Me Tender
Elvis Presley; *Elvis* .... (RCA)
Elvis Aron Presley .... (RCA)
Elvis' Golden Records .... (RCA)

Elvis-A Legendary Performer, Volume 1 . . . .(RCA)
Worldwide 50 Gold Award Hits, Vol. 1, Parts 1 & 2. . . . .(RCA)

Magnolia
J.J. Cale; Naturally . . . . (MCA)

Melissa
Allman Brothers Band; An Evening With The Allman Brothers Band-
First Set . . . . (Epic)
Best Of The Allman Brothers Band . . . .(Polydor)
Decade Of Hits-1969-1979 . . . .(Polydor)
Eat A Peach . . . .(Polydor)

Milk & Honey
Original Cast; Milk & Honey . . . . (RCA Victor)

Money Honey
38 Special; Rockin' Into The Night . . . . (A&M)
Drifters; Drifters' Greatest Hits 1953-1958 . . . . (Atlantic)
Drifters-Their Greatest Recordings . . . . (Atco)
Soul Years-C . . . . (Atlantic)
Elvis Presley; Rocker. . . . .(RCA)
Little Richard; Little Richard's Greatest Hits . . . .(Everest)

Money Honey
Bay City Rollers; Bay City Rollers' Greatest Hits . . . . (Arista)
Rock & Roll Love Letters . . . . (Arista)

My Sweet Eyed Georgia Girl
Atlanta; Atlanta . . . . (MCA)

My Sweet Hunk O' Trash
Louis Armstrong; Jazz Heritage-Louis With Guest Stars-C . . . . (MCA)

My Sweet Lord
George Harrison; All Things Must Pass . . . .(Parlophone)
Best Of George Harrison . . . .(Capitol)
Concert For Bangladesh-C . . . .(Capitol)

My Sweetheart In Tennessee
Burnett & Rutherford; Ramblin' Reckless Hobo . . . . (Rounder)

My Sweetheart Lives In San Antonio
Ray Duncan; 45-#232 . . . . (Door Knob)

Need A Little Sugar In My Bowl
Hadda Brooks; Best Blues Album In The World...Ever!-C . . . .(Virgin)

No Sugar Tonight
Guess Who; American Woman . . . .(RCA)
Best Of The Guess Who . . . .(RCA)
Track Record-Collection . . . .(RCA)

Oh Me, Oh My, Sweet Baby
Diamond Rio; Close To The Edge . . . . (Arista)
George Strait; Beyond The Blue Neon . . . . (MCA)

Oklahoma Sweetheart
George Thorogood & The Destroyers; Boogie People . . . . (EMI)

Oklahoma Sweetheart Sally
Maddox Brothers & Rose; America's Most Colorful Hillbillly Band . .(Arhoolie)

One Sweet Day
Mariah Carey; Daydream . . . .(Columbia)
Mariah Carey & Boyz II Men; 1996 Grammy Nominees-C . . . .(Columbia)

One Sweet Letter From You
Benny Goodman; Roll 'Em . . . .(Columbia)

Poison Sugar
Reba McEntire; Just A Little Love . . . . (MCA)

Pour Some Sugar On Me
Def Leppard; Hysteria . . . .(Mercury)

Pure Love
Ronnie Milsap; Ronnie Milsap's Greatest Hits . . . .(RCA)
Ronnie Milsap-Super Hits . . . .(RCA)

Radio Sweetheart
Elvis Costello; Taking Liberties . . . .(Columbia)

Rollin' In My Sweet Baby's Arms
Bill Monroe; Bean Blossom . . . . (MCA)
Del McCoury Band; Appalachian Stomp: Bluegrass Classics-C . . . .(Rhino)
Dillard & Clark; Fantastic Expedition/Through The
Morning . . . . (Mobile Fidelity Sound Lab)
Flatt & Scruggs; Flatt & Scruggs At Carnegie Hall! . . . .(Koch International)
Flatt & Scruggs-20 Greatest Hits . . . .(Deluxe)
Flying Burrito Brothers; Close Encounters To The West Coast . . . .(Relix)
Leon Russell; Hank Wilson's Back, Vol. 1 . . . .(Right Stuff)
New Lost City Ramblers; Greatest Folksingers Of The '60s-C . . . . (Vanguard)
Ramblin' Jack Elliott; Hard Travelin'. . . . .(Fantasy)
Ricky Skaggs and Kentucky Thunder; History Of The Future . .(Skaggs Family)
Tony Trischka; Heartlands . . . .(Rounder)
Willie Nelson; Willie & Family Live . . . .(Columbia)

Rosabella
Original Broadway Cast; The Most Happy Fella . . . .(Sony Music Classical)

Roses Are Red
Bobby Vinton; Bobby Vinton-16 Most Requested Songs . . . .(Legacy)
Bobby Vinton's All-Time Greatest Hits . . . . (Epic)
Spring Sensations . . . . (Epic)

Sail Away Sweet Sister
Queen; The Game . . . .(Hollywood)

Shake The Sugar Tree
Pam Tillis; Homeward Looking Angel. . . . .(Arista)

She Smiled Sweetly
Rolling Stones; Between The Buttons . . . .(Abkco)

Shine On Me
Andy Griggs & Waylon Jennings; You Won't Ever Be Lonely . . . .(RCA)

Silver Medals & Sweet Memories
Statler Brothers; Best Of The Statler Brothers-Rides Again-#2 . . . . . .(Mercury)
Short Stories . . . .(Mercury)

Slow Like Honey
Fiona Apple; Tidal . . . . (Clean Slate/Work)

Soft Lights And Sweet Music
John Coltrane; John Coltrane And The Jazz Giants . . . . (Fantasy)
Victor Young & The Brunswick Orchestra with Bing Crosby; Irving Berlin:
A Hundred Years-C . . . .(Columbia)

Soft, Sweet And Warm
David Houston; 45-#10870 . . . .(Epic)

Someday Sweetheart
Bing Crosby; Here Lies Love . . . .(ASV Living Era)
Peggy Lee; You Can Depend On Me . . . .(Glendale)
Zoot Sims; Best Of Zoot Sims . . . .(Pablo)

Something Sweet About Me
Madge Crichton; Music From The New York Stage (1890-1920)-#1-1890-
1908-C . . . .(Pearl)

Stay As Sweet As You Are
Art Tatum; Art Tatum Solo Masterpieces-#1 . . . .(Pablo)
Betty Carter; It's Not About The Melody . . . .(Verve)
Jimmie Grier & His Orchestra; 78-#7307 . . . .(Brunswick)
Nat "King" Cole; Love Is The Thing . . . .(Capitol)

Stockholm Sweetnin'
Al Jarreau; 1965 . . . .(Bainbridge)
Cannonball Adderley & His Orchestra; African Waltz . . . (Original Jazz Classics)
Clifford Brown; Memorial . . . .(Prestige)
Jon Hendricks; Jazz Club-Vocal. . . . .(Verve)
Patti Austin; Real Me . . . .(Qwest)

Such Sweet Thunder
Duke Ellington; Duke Ellington-Vol. 6-Dance Dates-California-1958 . . . . (Saja)
Duke Ellington & His Orchestra; Such Sweet
Thunder . . . . (Sony Music Special Prod.)

Sugar Bee
Boozoo Chavis & The Majic Sounds; Stomp Down Zydeco-C . . . .(Rounder)
Jo-el Sonnier; Jo-el Sonnier-Complete Mercury Sessions . . . .(Mercury)
Rockin' Dopsie & The Cajun Twisters; Big Bad Zydeco . . . .(Crescendo)

Sugar Daddy
Bellamy Brothers; Bellamy Brothers' Greatest Hits . . . . (MCA)
You Can Get Crazy . . . .(WB/Curb)

Sugar Daddy
Thompson Twins; Big Trash . . . .(Red Eye)

Sugar Daddy
Fleetwood Mac; Fleetwood Mac . . . . (Reprise)

Sugar Daddy
Michigan & Smiley; Sugar Daddy . . . . (Real Authentic Sound)

Sugar Daddy
Jackson 5; Jackson 5-Anthology. . . . .(Motown)
Jackson 5's Greatest Hits . . . .(Motown)

Sugar Hill Saturday Night
Charlie Daniels Band; Midnight Wind . . . . (Epic)

Sugar Magnolia
Grateful Dead; American Beauty . . . .(Warner Bros.)
Best Of/Skeletons From The Closet . . . .(Warner Bros.)
Europe '72. . . . .(Warner Bros.)
Grateful Dead-Live-#1 . . . .(JCI Assoc. Labels)

Sugar Mama
John Lee Hooker; Blues-#2-C . . . .(Chess)
House Of The Blues . . . .(Chess)

Sugar Mama
Bonnie Raitt; Bonnie Raitt-Collection . . . .(Warner Bros.)
Home Plate . . . .(Warner Bros.)

Sugar Mice
Marillion; Clutching At Straws. . . . .(Capitol)
Thieving Magpie . . . .(Capitol)

Sugar Moon
Bob Wills & His Texas Playboys; Essential Bob Wills & His Texas
Playboys-1935-1973 . . . .(Legacy)
k.d. lang; Shadowland . . . .(Sire)

Sugar Moon
Pat Boone; Best Of Pat Boone . . . . (MCA)

Sugar Mountain
Neil Young; Decade. . . . . (Reprise)
Neil Young & Crazy Horse; Live Rust . . . . (Reprise)

Sugar On Sunday
Tommy James And The Shondells; Best Of Tommy James And The
Shondells . . . .(Roulette)
Crimson & Clover/Cellophane Symphony . . . .(Rhino)
Tommy James And The Shondells-Anthology . . . .(Rhino)

Sugar Shack
Jimmy Gilmer And The Fireballs; Billboard Top Rock 'N' Roll Hits-
1963-C . . . .(Rhino)
Golden Years-1963-C . . . .(Dominion Entert.)
Good Old Rock & Roll-C . . . .(International Mktg. Group)

Sugar Town
Nancy Sinatra; Nancy's Greatest Hits . . . . (Reprise)
Sugar . . . .(Sundazed Music)
The Hit Years . . . .(Rhino)

Sugar Walls
Sheena Easton; *Dance Mix* . . . .(EMI)
   Private Heaven . . . .(EMI)
Sugar, Sugar
Archies; *Billboard Top Rock 'N' Roll Hits-1969-C* . . . . (Rhino)
Sugarcane
Cry Of Love; *Diamonds & Debris* . . . . (Columbia)
Sugarfoot Rag
Asleep At The Wheel; *Very Best Of Asleep At The Wheel*
   Since 1970. . . . . (Relentless/Madacy)
Bill Keith; *Something Auld, Something Newgrass, Something Borrowed,*
   Something Bluegrass. . . . . (Rounder)
Porter Wagoner; *Grand Ole Opry-75 Years-#2-C* . . . .(MCA)
Suitelady
Maxwell; *Maxwell's Urban Hang Suite* . . . . (Columbia)
Sumthin' Sumthin'
Maxwell; *Maxwell's Urban Hang Suite* . . . . (Columbia)
   ST/Love Jones . . . . (Columbia)
Sunshower
Chris Cornell; *ST/Great Expectations* . . . . (Atlantic)
Sweet & Sexy Thing
Rick James; *Flag* . . . . (Motown)
Sweet Adeline
Tommy Dorsey; *Best Of Tommy Dorsey* . . . .(MCA)
Tommy Dorsey & His Orchestra; *Big Bands Greatest*
   Hits-#2-C . . . . (MCA Special Prod.)
Sweet Afton
Nickel Creek; *Nickel Creek* . . . . (Sugar Hill)
Sweet And Lovely
Bing Crosby; *Pennies From Heaven.* . . . . (Pro-Arte)
Thelonius Monk; *Monk's Dream* . . . . (Columbia)
Woody Herman; *Essential Big Bands-C.* . . . . (Verve)
Sweet Angeline
Mott The Hoople; *Mott The Hoople-Live* . . . . (Columbia)
   The Ballad Of Mott: A Retrospective . . . . (Columbia)
Sweet Angeline
David Allan Coe; *Just Divorced* . . . . (Columbia)
Sweet As Bear Meat
Johnny Hodges Orchestra; *Used To Be Duke* . . . . (Verve)
Sweet Baby
Macy Gray; *The Id* . . . .(Epic)
Sweet Baby James
James Taylor; *James Taylor's Greatest Hits* . . . .(Warner Bros.)
   Sweet Baby James . . . .(Warner Bros.)
Sweet Baby James
Highway 101; *Paint The Town* . . . .(Warner Bros.)
Sweet Becky Walker
Larry Gatlin & The Gatlin Brothers Band; *Larry Gatlin & The Gatlin*
   Brothers' Greatest Hits. . . . . (Columbia)
   Larry Gatlin & The Gatlin Brothers-17 Greatest Hits . . . . (Columbia)
Sweet Betsy From Pike
Cisco Houston; *Cowboy Ballads* . . . . (Smithsonian Folkways)
Mormon Tabernacle Choir; *This Land Is Your Land* . . . . (Columbia)
Sweet Bird
Joni Mitchell; *Hissing Of Summer Lawns.* . . . .(Asylum)
Sweet Black Angel
Rolling Stones; *Exile On Main Street* . . . . (Virgin)
Sweet Black Girl
Buddy Guy & Junior Wells; *Alone & Acoustic* . . . . (Alligator)
Sweet Caroline
Neil Diamond; *Glory Road-1968-1972* . . . .(MCA)
   Hot August Night . . . .(MCA)
   Love At The Greek . . . . (Columbia)
   Neil Diamond-Gold . . . .(MCA)
   Neil Diamond-His 12 Greatest Hits . . . .(MCA)
Sweet Cherry Wine
Tommy James And The Shondells; *Tommy James And The Shondells-*
   Anthology. . . . . (Rhino)
   Very Best Of Tommy James And The Shondells . . . . (Pair)
Sweet Chicago Home
David Bromberg; *How Late'll Ya Play 'Til?* . . . . (Fantasy)
Sweet Child O' Mine
Guns N' Roses; *Appetite For Destruction* . . . .(Geffen)
Sweet City Woman
Stampeders; *'70s Smash Hits-#5-C* . . . . (Rhino)
   Super Hits Of The '70s-Have A Nice Day-#6-C . . . . (Rhino)
Sweet Cleo Brown
Dave Brubeck; *Greatest Hits From The Fantasy Years* . . . . (Fantasy)
Sweet Country Music
Atlanta; *Pictures* . . . .(MCA)
   Today's Country Classics-C . . . . (MCA Special Prod.)
Sweet Country Woman
Johnny Duncan; *Country Music Classics-#11-Early '70s-C* . . . . (K-Tel)
   Johnny Duncan's Greatest Hits . . . . (Columbia)
   Winnin' Country . . . . (Fifty One West)
Sweet Daddy (Your Mama's Done Gone Mad)
Little Brother Montgomery; *Chicago-Living Legends-South Side*
   Blues . . . .(Riverside)

Sweet Daze
Pete.; *Pete.* . . . . (Warner Bros.)
Sweet Dream
Jethro Tull; *20 Years Of Jethro Tull* . . . . (Chrysalis)
   Bursting Out. . . . . (Chrysalis)
   Living In The Past. . . . . (Chrysalis)
   Original Masters . . . . (Chrysalis)
Sweet Dreams
Air Supply; *Air Supply's Greatest Hits* . . . . (Arista)
   The One That You Love . . . . (Arista)
Sweet Dreams
Yes; *Time And A Word* . . . .(Atlantic)
   Yesterdays . . . .(Atlantic)
Sweet Dreams
La Bouche; *Sweet Dreams.* . . . . (RCA)
   The Ultimate Dance Party-1998-C. . . . . (Arista)
Sweet Dreams (Are Made Of This)
Eurythmics; *Eurythmics' Greatest Hits.* . . . . (Arista)
   Sweet Dreams (Are Made Of This) . . . . (RCA)
Marilyn Manson; *Smells Like Children.* . . . . (Interscope)
Sweet Dreams (Of You)
Chet Atkins & Mark Knopfler; *Neck And Neck* . . . . (Columbia)
Don Gibson; *Don Gibson-18 Greatest Hits.* . . . . (Curb)
   Don Gibson's All-Time Greatest Hits. . . . . (RCA)
Emmylou Harris; *Brand New Dance* . . . . (Reprise)
   Elite Hotel . . . . (Reprise)
   Profile/Best Of Emmylou Harris. . . . . (Warner Bros.)
Jim Reeves; *Jim Reeves' Greatest Hits* . . . . (RCA)
Patsy Cline; *Patsy Cline's Greatest Hits.* . . . .(MCA)
   ST/Sweet Dreams . . . .(MCA)
   The Patsy Cline Story . . . .(MCA)
Reba McEntire; *Out Of A Dream.* . . . . (Mercury)
Sweet Eloise
Glenn Miller & His Orchestra; *Complete Glenn Miller & His*
   Orchestra. . . . . (Bluebird)
Russ Morgan & His Orchestra; *Russ Morgan & His Orchestra Play 22*
   Original Big Band Recordings . . . . (Hindsight)
Tex Beneke & The Modernaires; *Reunion* . . . .(MCA)
Sweet Emotion
Aerosmith; *ST/Armageddon-The Album.* . . . . (Columbia)
Sweet Feelin'
Doobie Brothers; *Minute By Minute* . . . . (Warner Bros.)
Sweet Fire Of Love
Robbie Robertson; *Robbie Robertson* . . . . (Geffen)
Sweet Forgiveness
Bonnie Raitt; *Sweet Forgiveness.* . . . . (Warner Bros.)
Sweet Forgiveness
Iris DeMent; *Infamous Angel* . . . . (Warner Bros.)
Sweet Freedom
Michael McDonald; *Soundtrack Smashes-'80s & More-C* . . . . (MCA)
   ST/Running Scared . . . . (MCA Special Prod.)
Sweet Georgia Brown
Anita O'Day; *Compact Jazz-Best Of The Compact Jazz Vocalists-C* . . . . (Verve)
Beatles; *The Beatles featuring Tony Sheridan-In The Beginning (Circa*
   1960). . . . . (Polydor)
Ben Bernie & His Orchestra; *78-#15002.* . . . . (Vocalion)
Bing Crosby; *Bing Crosby-16 Most Requested Songs.* . . . . (Legacy)
Coasters; *Coasters' Greatest Hits.* . . . . (Atco)
Django Reinhardt; *Djangologie USA-#1.* . . . . (Disques Swing)
   Quintet Of The Hot Club Of France . . . . (Prestige)
Ella Fitzgerald; *Ella Fitzgerald In London* . . . . (Pablo)
   Whisper Not . . . . (Verve)
Ella Fitzgerald & Count Basie; *Perfect Match* . . . . (Pablo)
Original Broadway Cast; *Bubbling Brown Sugar* . . . . (Amherst)
Stephane Grappelli; *Live In London* . . . . (Black Lion)
Tito Puente; *Out Of This World.* . . . . (Concord Picante Jazz)
Sweet Gingerbread Man
Mike Curb Congregation; *Mike Curb Congregation's Greatest Hits* . . . . . (Curb)
Sweet Girl In Texas
John Delafose & The Eunice Playboys; *Joe Pete Got Two Women* . . . . (Arhoolie)
Sweet Guava Jelly
Lee ''Scratch'' Perry; *Soundz From The Hot Line.* . . . . (Heartbeat)
Sweet Hawaiian Sunshine
Jorma Kaukonen & Tom Hobson; *Quah.* . . . .(Relix)
Sweet Hitchhiker
Creedence Clearwater Revival; *Creedence Clearwater Revival-*
   Chronicle. . . . .(Fantasy)
   Live In Europe . . . .(Fantasy)
   Mardi Gras. . . . .(Fantasy)
   More Creedence Gold . . . .(Fantasy)
Sweet Home Alabama
Alabama; *Skynyrd Frynds-C.* . . . .(MCA)
Charlie Daniels Band; *Volunteer Jam VII-C* . . . . (Epic)
Hank Williams, Jr.; *Hank Williams, Jr. ''Live''* . . . . (WB/Curb)
Lynyrd Skynyrd; *Billboard Top Rock 'N' Roll Hits-1974-C.* . . . . (Rhino)
   Gold & Platinum . . . .(MCA)
   One More From The Road . . . .(MCA)
   Second Helping . . . .(MCA)
   South's Greatest Hits-C . . . . (Capricorn)

ST/Forrest Gump . . . . (Epic/Sony Music Soundtrax)

Sweet Home Chicago
Blues Brothers; *ST/The Blues Brothers* . . . . (Atlantic)
Foghat; *Best Of Foghat-#2* . . . . (Rhino)
 Stone Blue . . . . (Rhino)
Junior Parker; *Best Of Junior Parker* . . . . (MCA)
Leon Russell & Marc Benno; *Asylum Choir II* . . . . (MCA)
Magic Sam; *Magic Sam-Live* . . . . (Delmark)
Robert Johnson; *King Of The Delta Blues Singers-#2* . . . . . . (Columbia)
 Robert Johnson-Complete Recordings . . . . (Columbia)
Taj Mahal; *Recycling The Blues & Other Related Stuff* . . . . (Columbia)
Urban Knights; *Urban Knights 3* . . . . (Narada)

Sweet Honey Sucking Bees
Miranda Sex Garden; *Madra* . . . . (Mute/Reprise)

Sweet Indiana Home
Aileen Stanley; *78-#18922* . . . . (Victor)
Marion Harris; *78-#2310* . . . . (Brunswick)

Sweet Inniscarra
Chauncey Olcott; *Music From The New York Stage (1890-1920)-#1-1890-
 1908-C* . . . . (Pearl)

Sweet Inspiration
Sweet Inspirations; *Best Of The Sweet Inspirations* . . . . (Soul Classics)
 Great R&B Female Groups-Hits Of The '60s-C . . . . (K-Tel)

Sweet Jamaica
Cat Stevens; *Izitso* . . . . (A&M)

Sweet Jane
Cowboy Junkies; *ST/Natural Born Killers* . . . . (Nothing)
 Trinity Session . . . . (RCA)
Lou Reed; *Rock N Roll Animal* . . . . (RCA)
 Walk On The Wild Side-The Best Of Lou Reed . . . . (RCA)
Mott The Hoople; *All The Young Dudes* . . . . (Columbia)
 The Ballad Of Mott: A Retrospective . . . . (Columbia)
Velvet Underground; *Live At Max's Kansas City* . . . . (Collectables)

Sweet Jesus
Sugar Minott; *Ghetto Child* . . . . (Heartbeat)

Sweet Kentucky Ham
David Frishberg; *Can't Take You Nowhere* . . . . (Fantasy)
 David Frishberg-Classics . . . . (Concord Jazz)

Sweet Kisses
Jessica Simpson; *Sweet Kisses* . . . . (Columbia)

Sweet Kisses
Van & Schenck; *Music From The New York Stage (1890-1920)-#4-1917-
 1920-C* . . . . (Pearl)

Sweet Lady
Tyrese; *Tyrese* . . . . (RCA)

Sweet Lady Mary
Rod Stewart/Faces; *Storyteller/The Complete Anthology: 1964-
 1990* . . . . (Warner Bros.)

Sweet Leilani
Bing Crosby; *Best Of Bing Crosby* . . . . (MCA)
King Sisters; *And The Winner Is-Best Movie Songs-C* . . . . (Capitol)

Sweet Life
Marie Osmond & Paul Davis; *All In Love* . . . . (Curb)
Paul Davis; *Best Of Paul Davis* . . . . (Bang)
 Singer Of Songs-Teller Of Tales . . . . (Bang)

Sweet Little '66
Steve Earle & The Dukes; *Exit 0* . . . . (MCA)

Sweet Little Angel
B.B. King; *B.B. King-16 Original Big Hits* . . . . (Fantasy)
 Back In The Alley . . . . (MCA)
 Live & Well . . . . (MCA)
 Live At The Regal . . . . (MCA)
Buddy Guy; *Best Of The Chicago Blues-C* . . . . (Vanguard)
 Man & The Blues . . . . (Vanguard)
Etta James; *Late Show* . . . . (Fantasy)
 Rocks The House . . . . (Chess)

Sweet Little Bullet From A Pretty Blue Gun
Tom Waits; *Blue Valentine* . . . . (Asylum)

Sweet Little Cafe In A Square
Lena Spencer & Others; *Welcome To Caffe Lena* . . . . (Biograph)

Sweet Little Country Girl
Charlie Daniels; *America, I Believe In You* . . . . (Liberty)

Sweet Little Flower
Sleepy John Estes; *Electric Sleep* . . . . (Delmark)

Sweet Little Girl
Stevie Wonder; *Music Of My Mind* . . . . (Motown)

Sweet Little Miss Blue Eyes
Jim & Jesse/The Virginia Boys; *Appalachian Stomp: More Bluegrass
 Classics-C* . . . . (Rhino)

Sweet Little Missy
Lynyrd Skynyrd; *Lynyrd Skynyrd-Legend* . . . . (MCA)

Sweet Little Papa
Louis Armstrong; *Hot Fives & Hot Sevens-#2* . . . . (Columbia)

Sweet Little Rock & Roller
Chuck Berry; *Chuck Berry Is On Top* . . . . (Chess)
 The Chess Box-Chuck Berry . . . . (Chess)
Richard Thompson; *Guitar/Vocal* . . . . (Hannibal)
Rod Stewart; *Absolutely Live* . . . . (Warner Bros.)

Best Of Rod Stewart . . . . (Mercury)
Storyteller/The Complete Anthology: 1964-1990 . . . . (Warner Bros.)

Sweet Little Sixteen
Beatles; *45-#1502* . . . . (Collectables)
Chuck Berry; *Best Of The Best Of Chuck Berry* . . . . . (International Mktg. Group)
 Chuck Berry-Golden Hits . . . . (Mercury)
 Chuck Berry-Greatest Hits Live . . . . (Quicksilver)
 Cruisin'-1965-C . . . . (Increase)
 Oldies But Goodies-#12-C . . . . (Original Sound)
Jerry Lee Lewis; *Jerry Lee Lewis-Original Golden Hits-#3* . . . . (Sun)
Jerry Lee Lewis & Friends; *Jerry Lee Lewis & Friends-Duets* . . . . (Sun)
John Lennon; *Lennon* . . . . (Capitol)
 Rock 'N' Roll . . . . (Capitol)

Sweet Lorraine
Art Tatum; *Solos-1940* . . . . (MCA)
 Standards . . . . (Black Lion)
Carmen McRae; *You're Lookin' At Me* . . . . (Concord Jazz)
Count Basie; *The Standards* . . . . (Verve)
Frank Sinatra; *The Reprise Collection* . . . . (Reprise)
Nat "King" Cole; *Complete After Midnight Sessions* . . . . (Capitol)
 The Nat "King" Cole Story . . . . (Capitol)
Woody Herman; *Big Band Treasures-#2-C* . . . . (Dunhill Compact Classics)

Sweet Lorraine
Uriah Heep; *Best Of Uriah Heep* . . . . (Mercury)
 Magician's Birthday . . . . (Mercury)

Sweet Louisiana
Charlie Daniels Band; *Saddle Tramp* . . . . (Epic)
 Volunteer Jam 3 & 4 . . . . (Epic)

Sweet Love
Commodores; *All The Great Love Songs-Commodores* . . . . (Motown)
 Commodores Greatest Hits . . . . (Motown)
 Lionel Richie-Composer Series . . . . (Motown)

Sweet Love
Anita Baker; *Rapture* . . . . (Elektra)

Sweet Lover Hangover
Love And Rockets; *Sweet F.A.* . . . . (American)

Sweet Lover Man
Pointer Sisters; *Best Of The Pointer Sisters 1978-1981* . . . . (RCA)
 Sweet & Soulful . . . . (RCA)

Sweet Lovin'
Poco; *Good Feelin' To Know* . . . . (Epic)
 Very Best Of Poco . . . . (Epic)

Sweet Lovin' Daddy
Betty Wright; *Golden Classics-Betty Wright* . . . . (Collectables)
Fontella Bass; *Rescued-Best Of Fontella Bass* . . . . (Chess)

Sweet Mama
Allman Brothers Band; *Win, Lose Or Draw* . . . . (Polydor)

Sweet Mama Goodtimes
Mickey Gilley; *Mickey Gilley's Greatest Hits-#2* . . . . (Epic)

Sweet Mama Hurry Home Or I'll Be Gone
Leon Redbone; *On The Track* . . . . (Warner Bros.)

Sweet Man
Jelly Roll Morton; *The Piano Rolls* . . . . (Nonesuch)

Sweet Marijuana Brown
Paula Lockheart; *It Ain't The End Of The World* . . . . (Flying Fish)

Sweet Mary
Wadsworth Mansion; *Super Hits Of The '70s-Have A Nice Day-#4-C* . . (Rhino)

Sweet Maxine
Doobie Brothers; *Stampede* . . . . (Warner Bros.)

Sweet Milwaukee Rose
Andy Badale & The Beer Garden Band; *Nashville Beer Garden* . . . . . (Ranwood)

Sweet Misery
Amel Larrieux; *Infinite Possibilities* . . . . (Epic)

Sweet Mother Texas
Eddy Raven; *Eddy Raven's Greatest Hits* . . . . (Warner Bros.)

Sweet Music Man
Dolly Parton; *Here You Come Again* . . . . (Dunhill Compact Classics)
Kenny Rogers; *Daytime Friends* . . . . (EMI)
Reba McEntire; *Reba McEntire's Greatest Hits-#3: I'm A Survivor* . . . . . (MCA)

Sweet Music Man
Millie Jackson; *Get It Out'cha System* . . . . (Spring)
 Live & Uncensored . . . . (Spring)

Sweet Music Man
Nana Mouskouri; *Song For Liberty* . . . . (Mercury)

Sweet Old Fashioned Girl, A
Teresa Brewer; *Music! Music! Music!-Best Of Teresa
 Brewer* . . . . (Varese Vintage)

Sweet Painted Lady
Elton John; *Goodbye Yellow Brick Road* . . . . (Polydor)

Sweet Pea
Tommy Roe; *Best Of Tommy Roe* . . . . (Curb)
 Cruisin'-1966-C . . . . (Increase)
 Tommy Roe's Greatest Hits . . . . (MCA)

Sweet Pear
Elvis Costello; *Mighty Like A Rose* . . . . (Warner Bros.)

Sweet Peggy O'Neill
John McCormack; *Drop Of The Irish* . . . . (Pearl Flapper)

Sweet Potato Pie
Al Jarreau; *We Got By* . . . . (Reprise)

Sweet Potato Pie
James Taylor; *Never Die Young* . . . . (Columbia)
Sweet Rain
Stan Getz; *Artistry Of-Stan Getz-Best Of Verve Years-#1* . . . . (Verve)
Stan Getz Quartet; *Sweet Rain* . . . . (Verve)
Sweet Rhode Island Red
Ike & Tina Turner; *Proud Mary-Best Of Ike & Tina Turner* . . . .(EMI)
Sweet Rosalyn
Sheryl Crow; *Sheryl Crow* . . . . (A&M)
Sweet Rosemary
Sandy Denny; *Who Knows Where The Time Goes* . . . . (Hannibal)
Sweet Savannah Sue
Fats Waller; *Turn On The Heat-Fats Waller Piano Solos* . . . . (Bluebird)
Louis Armstrong; *Louis Armstrong-Vol. 5-In New York* . . . . (Columbia)
Sweet Sensimilla
Jimmy Riley; *Put The People First* . . . . (Shanachie)
Sweet September
Buddy Merrill; *Best Of Buddy Merrill* . . . .(Accent)
Holiday For Guitars . . . .(Accent)
Sweet September Morning
Buffy Sainte-Marie; *She Used To Wanna Be A Ballerina* . . . . (Vanguard)
Sweet Sexy Eyes
Cristy Lane; *Country Classics* . . . . (Arrival)
Cristy Lane-At Her Best . . . .(EMI)
Sweet Sexy Thing
Nu Flavor; *Nu Flavor* . . . . (Reprise)
Sweet Sixteen
B.B. King; *Back In The Alley* . . . . (MCA)
Best Of B.B. King . . . . (MCA)
Electric B.B. King-His Best . . . . (MCA)
Live In Cook County Jail . . . . (MCA)
Sweet Sixteen
Destiny's Child; *The Writing's On The Wall* . . . . (Columbia)
Sweet Sixteen
Judy Garland; *Best Of Judy Garland* . . . . (MCA)
Sweet Sixteen
Big Joe Turner; *Big Joe Turner's Greatest Hits* . . . . (Atlantic)
Sweet Sixteen
Chuck Berry; *Chuck Berry's Greatest Hits* . . . . (Everest)
Sweet Sixteen Bars
Earl Gray; *Best Of Earl Gray* . . . .(MCA)
Ray Charles; *Atlantic Jazz-Piano-C* . . . . (Atlantic)
Best Of Ray Charles . . . . (Atlantic)
Great Ray Charles . . . . (Atlantic)
Sweet Song Of India
McGuire Sisters; *Best Of The McGuire Sisters* . . . . (MCA)
Sweet Soul Music
Arthur Conley; *Atlantic Soul Classics-C* . . . . (Warner Special Prod.)
Golden Age Of Black Music-1960-1970-C . . . .(Atlantic)
Sweet Sue (Just You)
Benny Goodman; *Benny Goodman-Early Years* . . . . (Biograph)
Big Joe Turner; *Rhythm & Blues Years* . . . . (Rhino)
Bing Crosby; *Crooner-Columbia Years-1928-1934.* . . . . (Columbia)
Leon Redbone; *Champagne Charlie* . . . .(Warner Bros.)
Mom & Dads; *Goodnight Sweetheart* . . . . (Crescendo)
Sweet Summer
Diamond Rio; *One More Day* . . . . (Arista)
Sweet Summer Blue And Gold
Stone Poneys Featuring Linda Ronstadt; *The Stone Poneys Featuring Linda
Ronstadt* . . . .(EMI)
Sweet Summer Day
Freddy Fender; *Before The Next Teardrop Falls* . . . . (Universal)
Sweet Summer Lovin'
Dolly Parton; *Essential Dolly Parton* . . . . (RCA)
Sweet Sunday Kinda Love
Honeys; *Capitol Collectors Series-The Honeys* . . . . (Capitol)
Sweet Surf Music
Malibooz; *Malibooz Rule* . . . . (Rhino)
Sweet Surrender
John Denver; *Back Home Again* . . . . (RCA)
Evening With John Denver . . . . (RCA)
Sweet Surrender
Sarah McLachlan; *Mirrorball.* . . . . (Arista)
Surfacing . . . . (Arista)
Sweet Surrender
Bread; *Best Of Bread-#2.* . . . . (Elektra)
Bread-Anthology . . . . (Elektra)
Sweet Suzanne
Mark O'Connor; *New Nashville Cats* . . . .(Warner Bros.)
Sweet Suzie
Johnny Burnette; *Best Of Johnny Burnette-You're Sixteen* . . . .(Gold Rush)
Sweet Sweet
Smashing Pumpkins; *Siamese Dream* . . . . (Virgin)
Sweet Talker
Richard Thompson; *ST/Sweet Talker* . . . . (Capitol)
Sweet Talkin' Guy
Chiffons; *Best Of The Chiffons* . . . . (Laurie)
Chiffons-Golden Classics . . . . (Collectables)

Collectables Presents The History Of Rock-#1-C. . . . . (Collectables)
Everything You Always Wanted . . . .(Laurie)
Sweet Talking Woman
Electric Light Orchestra; *Afterglow.* . . . . (Epic)
Box Of Their Best . . . .(Jet)
Electric Light Orchestra's Greatest Hits . . . .(Jet)
Out Of The Blue . . . .(Jet)
Sweet Thames Flow Softly
Alison Brown; *Twilight Motel.* . . . . (Vanguard)
Sweet Thing
Mary J. Blige; *Uptown MTV Unplugged* . . . .(Uptown)
Sweet Thursday
Sweet Thursday; *Sweet Thursday* . . . . (Out Of Print)
Sweet Thursday
Icicle Works; *If You Want To Defeat Your Enemy* . . . .(Beggar's Banquet)
Sweet Thursday
Helen Traubel/Original Cast; *Pipe Dream* . . . . (RCA)
Sweet Transvestite
Original London Cast; *Rocky Horror Show.* . . . . (Rhino)
Tim Curry; *ST/Rocky Horror Picture Show* . . . . (Rhino)
Tim Curry & Original Roxy Cast; *Rocky Horror Show.* . . . . (Rhino)
Sweet Tuesday Morning
Badfinger; *Straight Up* . . . . (Apple)
Sweet Violets
Mitch Miller; *Sing Along With Mitch* . . . . (Columbia)
Sweet Virginia
Rolling Stones; *Exile On Main Street* . . . .(Virgin)
Sweet Woman (From Maine)
Robert Lockwood, Jr.; *Blues Masters-#2-Post-War Chicago Blues-C* . . . (Rhino)
Sweet Woman Like You
Joe Tex; *Billboard Top R&B Hits-1965-1969-C* . . . . (Rhino)
I Believe I'm Gonna Make It!-Best Of Joe Tex . . . . (Rhino)
Joe Tex's Greatest Hits. . . . . (Curb)
Sweet Wyoming Home
Chris LeDoux; *Chris LeDoux & The Saddle Boogie Band* . . . . (Liberty)
Sweet Young America
Roger Whittaker; *Wind Beneath My Wings.* . . . . (RCA)
Sweet, Sweet Smile
Carpenters; *Carpenters-Classics-#2* . . . . (A&M)
Passage . . . . (A&M)
Yesterday Once More . . . . (A&M)
Sweeter Than Chocolate
Burning Spear; *The World Should Know* . . . . (Heartbeat)
Sweetest Days
Vanessa Williams; *The Sweetest Days* . . . . (Uptown/MCA)
Sweetest Kittens (Have The Sharpest Claws)
Meatmen; *Rock 'N' Roll Juggernaut* . . . . (Caroline)
Sweetest Sounds
Art Pepper; *Goin' Home* . . . . (Galaxy)
Barbra Streisand; *Barbra Streisand...and other musical
instruments* . . . . (Columbia)
Original Broadway Cast; *No Strings* . . . . (Angel)
Rosemary Clooney; *Rosemary Clooney Sings Rodgers, Hart &
Hammerstein* . . . . (Concord Jazz)
Sarah Vaughan; *Compact Jazz-Sarah Vaughan* . . . . (Verve)
Sweetest Taboo
Sade; *Promise.* . . . . (Portrait)
Sweetest Thing
Refugee Camp All-Stars featuring Lauryn Hill; *ST/Love Jones* . . . . . (Columbia)
Sweetest Thing
U2; *Best Of 1980-1990* . . . . (Island)
Now That's What I Call Music!-#2-C . . . .(Virgin)
Sweetest Thing (I've Ever Known)
Juice Newton; *Country Love-C* . . . . (K-Tel)
Juice Newton-Greatest Hits & More . . . . (Capitol)
Juice Newton's Greatest Country Hits . . . .(Curb)
Sweetest Victory
Touch; *ST/Rocky IV.* . . . .(Scotti Bros.)
Sweetheart
Dan Hicks & His Hot Licks; *Last Train To Hicksville.* . . . . (MCA)
Maria Muldaur; *Waitress In The Donut Shop* . . . . (Warner Archives)
Sweetheart
Thin Lizzy; *Chinatown* . . . . (Warner Bros.)
Sweetheart
Frankie & The Knockouts; *Radio Daze-Pop Hits Of The '80s-#5-C* . . . . (Rhino)
Sweetheart From Venezuela
Harry Belafonte; *Harry Belafonte-Pure Gold* . . . . (RCA)
Sweetheart Of Sigma Chi
Fred Waring's Pennsylvanians; *Very Best Of Fred Waring & The
Pennsylvanians* . . . . (Reader's Digest Music)
Gene Austin; *The Voice Of The Southland* . . . . (Living Era)
Sweetheart Of The Rodeo
Emmylou Harris; *Ballad Of Sally Rose* . . . . (Warner Bros.)
Sweetheart Of The Year
Ray Price; *Best Of Ray Price* . . . . (Columbia)
Ray Price's Greatest Hits-#3 . . . .(Step One)

Sweetheart You Done Me Wrong
Bill Monroe & His Blue Grass Boys; *Essential Bill Monroe-1945-1949* . . . . (Columbia)
Elvis Presley; *Million-Dollar Quartet* . . . . (RCA)

Sweethearts On Parade
Guy Lombardo & His Royal Canadians; *Best Of Guy Lombardo* . . . . (Curb)
Best Of Guy Lombardo . . . . (MCA)
Louis Armstrong; *Louis Armstrong-Vol. 7-You're Driving Me Crazy* . . . . (Columbia)
Pete Fountain; *Pete Fountain's New Orleans* . . . . (MCA)
Roy Eldridge; *Happy Time* . . . . (Pablo)

Sweets For My Sweet
Drifters; *1959-1965-All-Time Greatest Hits And More* . . . . (Atlantic)
Very Best Of The Drifters . . . . (Rhino)

Sweetwater Nights
Dave Grusin; *Out Of The Shadows* . . . . (GRP)

Swing Low, Sweet Cadillac
Dizzy Gillespie; *Dizzy's Diamonds-Best Of The Verve Years* . . . . (Verve)

Swing Low, Sweet Chariot
Eric Clapton; *Time Pieces-#1-The Best Of Eric Clapton* . . . . (Polydor)
Glenn Miller & His Orchestra; *Moonlight Serenade* . . . . (Ranwood)
Hi-Lo's; *Suddenly It's The Hi-Lo's* . . . . (Columbia)
Jerry Garcia Acoustic Band; *Almost Acoustic* . . . . (Grateful Dead)
Joan Baez; *From Every Stage* . . . . (A&M)
Peggy Lee; *Best Of Peggy Lee* . . . . (MCA)

Taste Of Honey
Barbra Streisand; *The Barbra Streisand Album* . . . . (Columbia)
Beatles; *Beatles-Box Set* . . . . (Capitol)
Please Please Me . . . . (Parlophone)
The Early Beatles . . . . (Capitol)
Herb Alpert; *Midnight Sun* . . . . (A&M)
Herb Alpert & The Tijuana Brass; *Herb Alpert & The Tijuana Brass' Greatest Hits* . . . . (A&M)
Herb Alpert & The Tijuana Brass-Classics-#1 . . . . (A&M)
Tony Bennett; *Forty Years-The Artistry Of Tony Bennett* . . . . (Columbia)

There's A Lump Of Sugar Down In Dixie
Al Jolson; *Music From The New York Stage (1890-1920)-#4-1917-1920-C* . . . . (Pearl)

Too Much Candy For A Dime
Eddy Raven; *Best Of Eddy Raven* . . . . (Liberty)
Right For The Flight . . . . (Liberty)

Truck Driver's Sweetheart
Karl & Harty; *Truck Driver Boogie Big Rig Hits-1939-1969-C* . . . . . . (Audium)
Marcie Dickerson; *Country Gold-Marcie Dickerson* . . . . (Plantation)

Tupelo Honey
Van Morrison; *Van Morrison* . . . . (Warner Bros.)

Tweedlee Dee
Ike & Tina Turner; *Ike & Tina Turner's Greatest Hits-#3* . . . . (Saja)
LaVern Baker; *20 Million-Dollar Memories-#1-C* . . . . (Laurie)
Billboard Top Rock 'N' Roll Hits-1955-C . . . . (Rhino)

Two Step
Dave Matthews Band; *Crash* . . . . (RCA)

Wang Dang Sweet Poontang
Ted Nugent; *Cat Scratch Fever* . . . . (Epic)
Double Live Gonzo . . . . (Epic)

What The World Needs Now Is Love
Burt Bacharach; *Burt Bacharach's Greatest Hits* . . . . (A&M)
Jackie DeShannon; *Flower Power-Psychedelic Rock Classics-C* . . . . . . (K-Tel)
Good Vibrations (Sounds Of Top 40 Radio: 1964-1967)-C . . . . . . (Capitol)
Oldies But Goodies-#14-C . . . . (Original Sound)
ST/Forrest Gump . . . . (Epic/Sony Music Soundtrax)
ST/My Best Friend's Wedding . . . . (Work/Epic)
Very Best Of Jackie DeShannon . . . . (EMI)
Luther Vandross; *Songs* . . . . (Epic)
Tom Clay; *20 Hard-To-Find Motown Classics-#2-C* . . . . (Motown)

When I Take My Sugar To Tea
Boswell Sisters; *78-#6083* . . . . (Brunswick)
Frank Sinatra; *Ring-A-Ding Ding* . . . . (Reprise)
Nat "King" Cole; *The Vocal Classics-1947-1950* . . . . (Capitol)

When My Sugar Walks Down The Street
Ella Fitzgerald; *Ella Fitzgerald-The Early Years-#2 (1939-1941)* . . . . . . (GRP)
Nat "King" Cole; *The Billy May Sessions* . . . . (Capitol)
Peggy Lee; *Capitol Sings Jimmy McHugh: I Feel A Song Comin' On-C* . . . . (Capitol)

White Honey
Graham Parker; *Howlin' Wind* . . . . (Mercury)

White Sugar
Peter Frampton; *Frampton's Camel* . . . . (A&M)

Who Will Call You Sweetheart
Stanley Brothers & The Clinch Mountain Boys; *Best Of Bluegrass-#1-Standards-C* . . . . (Mercury)

Wild Honey
Beach Boys; *Absolute Best-#2* . . . . (Capitol)
Party!/Stack-O-Tracks . . . . (Capitol)
Smiley Smile/Wild Honey . . . . (Capitol)

Wild Honey Pie
Beatles; *Beatles-Box Set* . . . . (Capitol)
The Beatles (White Album) . . . . (Capitol)

Wild Mountain Honey
Steve Miller Band; *Fly Like An Eagle* . . . . (Capitol)
Steve Miller Band's Greatest Hits-1974-78 . . . . (Capitol)

Wolverton Mountain
Claude King; *American Originals-Claude King* . . . . (Columbia)
Best Of Claude King . . . . (Gusto)
Billboard Top Country Hits-1962-C . . . . (Rhino)
Super Hits Of The '60s-C . . . . (Epic)

Your Sweetness
Good Girls; *All For Your Love* . . . . (Motown)

You're So Sweet, Horseflies Keep Hangin' Round Your Face
Neil Diamond; *Brother Love's Traveling Salvation Show* . . . . (MCA)

Yummy Yummy Yummy
Ohio Express; *Billboard Top Rock 'N' Roll Hits-1968-C* . . . . (Rhino)
Bubblegum Classics-#1-C . . . . (Varese Vintage)

TATTOO

See Also: ANATOMY: SKIN

Baby Skin Tattoo
Moist; *Creature* . . . . (Arista)

Common Disaster
Cowboy Junkies; *Lay It Down* . . . . (Geffen)

Illustrated Man
Johnny Winter; *Best Blues Album In The World...Ever!-C* . . . . (Virgin)

It's A Great Day To Be Alive
Travis Tritt; *Down The Road I Go* . . . . (Columbia)

Like A Tattoo
Sade; *Love Deluxe* . . . . (Epic)

Project Chick/Project Bitch
Cash Money Millionaires; *12'' Maxi Single* . . . . (Cash Money/Universal)

Right In Time
Lucinda Williams; *Car Wheels On A Gravel Road* . . . . (Mercury)

Rose Tattoo
David Byrne; *Rei Momo* . . . . (Luaka Bop)

Sailor's Not A Sailor ('Til A Sailor's Been Tattooed)
Various Artists; *There's No Business Like Show Business: Broadway Showstoppers-C* . . . . (Sony Broadway)

Show Me Your Tattoo
Cadillac Moon; *In The Kitchen* . . . . (Sunnyview)

Sister's Got A New Tattoo
Sawyer Brown; *Cafe On The Corner* . . . . (Curb)

Tattoo
Faster Pussycat; *Wake Me When It's Over* . . . . (Elektra)

Tattoo
Who; *Live At Leeds* . . . . (MCA)
The Who Sell Out . . . . (MCA)

Tattoo Me Now
Bobs; *Plugged* . . . . (Rounder)

Tattoo Vampire
Blue Oyster Cult; *Agents Of Fortune* . . . . (Columbia)

Tattooed Love Boys
Pretenders; *Pretenders* . . . . (Sire)

Tattooed Millionaire
Bruce Dickinson; *Alive In Studio A* . . . . (CMC Int'l)

Tattoos & Scars
Montgomery Gentry; *Tattoos & Scars* . . . . (Columbia)

Texas Tattoo
Gibson/Miller Band; *Steppin' Country-C* . . . . (Columbia)
Where There's Smoke . . . . (Epic)

Want You Bad
Offspring; *Conspiracy Of One* . . . . (Columbia)

When It All Goes Wrong Again
Everclear; *Songs From An American Movie-#2-Good Time For A Bad Attitude* . . . . (Capitol)

TAXI

See Also: CARS (various), LEAVING, TRAVELING

"Taxi Driver"-Night Piece For Orchestra
Royal Philharmonic Orchestra; *Bernard Herrmann Film Scores* . . . . . . (Milan)

Ashtray Taxi
Sam Chatmon; *Sam Chatmon's Advice* . . . . (Rounder)

Big Yellow Taxi
Amy Grant; *House Of Love* . . . . (A&M)
Joni Mitchell; *Ladies Of The Canyon* . . . . (Reprise)
Joni Mitchell with Tom Scott & The L.A. Express; *Miles Of Aisles* . . . . (Asylum)

Black Man Can't Get A Cab
U.T.F.O.; *Bag It & Bone It* . . . . (Jive)

Cab Driver
Mills Brothers; *Cab Driver* . . . . (Ranwood)
Close Harmony . . . . (Ranwood)
Mills Brothers-22 Great Hits . . . . (Ranwood)

Cabbies On Crack
Ramones; *Mondo Bizarro* . . . .(Radioactive/MCA)
Horse & Carriage
Cam'ron featuring Mase; *Confessions Of Fire* . . . . (Untertainment/Epic)
In The Back Of A Taxi
Penguin Cafe Orchestra; *Broadcasting From Home* . . . .(Editions E.G.)
Kicking Back In Amsterdam
Kevin Welch; *Life Down Here On Earth* . . . . (Dead Reckoning)
Lady Cab Driver
Prince; *1999* . . . .(Warner Bros.)
Nadine (Is It You?)
Chuck Berry; *Rock & Roll Rarities* . . . . (Chess)
Oriental Taxi
Sly Dunbar; *Sly Wicked & Slick* . . . .(Front Line)
Rainy Taxi
Jon St. James; *Enigma Variations-#2-C* . . . .(Enigma Capitol)
Red Cab To Manhattan
Stephen Bishop; *Best Of Bish* . . . . (Rhino)
Taxi
Harry Chapin; *Gold Medal Collection* . . . . (Elektra)
Greatest Stories-Live . . . . (Elektra)
Harry Chapin-Anthology . . . . (Elektra)
Heads & Tales . . . . (Elektra)
Taxi
Samples; *Last Drag* . . . .(Warfare)
Taxi
Bryan Ferry; *Taxi* . . . . (Reprise)
Taxi
Steps Ahead; *Yin-Yang* . . . . (NYC)
Taxi Blues
Bluzblasters; *Sooner Or Later* . . . . (Flying Fish)
Little Richard; *Shut Up-Collection Of Rare Tracks-1951-1964* . . . . (Rhino)
Taxi Cab
Rhythm Pigs; *Choke On This* . . . . (C/Z)
Taxi Connection
Sly & Robbie; *Street Reggae* . . . . (K-Tel)
Taxi Fare . . . . (Heartbeat)
Taxi Dancer
John Cougar; *John Cougar* . . . . (Riva)
Taxi Driver
Hanoi Rocks; *All Those Wasted Years-Live* . . . .(Geffen)
Self-Destruction Blues . . . .(Geffen)
Taxi Driver
Steel Pulse; *Rastafari Centennial-Live In Paris* . . . .(MCA)
Victims . . . .(MCA)
Taxi Driver
Joyce; *Language & Love* . . . . (Verve/Forecast)
Taxi Driver Blues
Eddie "Cleanhead" Vinson; *"Clean" Machine* . . . .(Muse)
Taxi Grabb
Jethro Tull; *Too Old To Rock 'N' Roll: Too Young To Die!* . . . .(Chrysalis)
Taxi Ride
Jane Siberry; *Speckless Sky* . . . .(Open Air)
Taxi Suite
Rare Air; *Hard To Beat* . . . .(Green Linnet)
Taxi To Heaven
Pray For Rain; *ST/Sid & Nancy* . . . .(MCA)
Taxi War Dance
Count Basie; *Essential Count Basie-#1* . . . . (Columbia)
I Like Jazz-Essence Of Count Basie . . . . (Columbia)
Theme From "Taxi"
Original Soundtrack; *Television's Greatest Hits-#3-1970s & 1980s-C* . . . (TVT)
Tijuana Taxi
Herb Alpert & The Tijuana Brass; *Four Sider* . . . . (A&M)
Herb Alpert & The Tijuana Brass' *Greatest Hits* . . . . (A&M)
Herb Alpert & The Tijuana Brass-*Classics-#1* . . . . (A&M)
You Already Drove Me There
Lisa Brokop; *Every Little Girl's Dream* . . . . (Patriot)

TEACHING VALUES

See Also: **ADVICE, BAD, CHARACTER & INTEGRITY, CHILDREN, FAITH, GOD, GOOD, PARENTS (various), RIGHT, SCHOOL, WARNINGS, WRONG**

Black Chick, White Guy
Kid Rock; *Devil Without A Cause* . . . . (Top Dog/Lava/Atlantic)
Child Of Clay
Jimmie Rodgers; *Best Of Jimmie Rodgers* . . . . (Rhino)
Everybody's Free (To Wear Sunscreen)
Baz Luhrmann; *Now That's What I Call Music!-#2-C* . . . . (Virgin)
Something For Everybody . . . . (Capitol)
Fields Have Turned Brown
Stanley Brothers & The Clinch Mountain Boys; *Bluegrass Super Hits-C* . . . . (Columbia)

Fun, Fun, Fun
Beach Boys; *Beach Boys-Gift Set* . . . . (Capitol)
Best Of The Beach Boys . . . . (Capitol)
Endless Summer . . . . (Capitol)
Made In The U.S.A. . . . . (Capitol)
The Beach Boys In Concert . . . . (Brother)
Home
Alan Jackson; *Alan Jackson-The Greatest Hits Collection* . . . . (Arista)
Here In The Real World . . . . (Arista)
Jesus Christ
Arlo Guthrie; *Tribute To Woody Guthrie-C* . . . . (Warner Bros.)
Cisco Houston; *Greatest Songs Of Woody Guthrie-C* . . . . (Vanguard)
U2; *Folkways: A Vision Shared-C* . . . . (Columbia)
Woody Guthrie; *Woody Guthrie* . . . . (Warner Bros.)
Just The Two Of Us
Will Smith; *Big Willie Style* . . . . (Columbia)
Key To Life, The
Vince Gill; *The Key* . . . . (MCA)
Kids
Original Broadway Cast; *Bye Bye Birdie* . . . . (Columbia)
Paul Lynde; *ST/Bye Bye Birdie* . . . .(RCA)
Lie On Lie
Chalk Farm; *Notwithstanding* . . . . (Columbia)
Living For The City
Stevie Wonder; *Innervisions* . . . . (Motown)
Original Musiquarium . . . . (Motown)
Love Without End, Amen
George Strait; *Livin' It Up* . . . . (MCA)
Ten Strait Hits . . . . (MCA)
Mama Tried
Grateful Dead; *Grateful Dead (Skull & Roses)* . . . . (Warner Bros.)
John Anderson & Marty Stuart; *Mama's Hungry Eyes-Merle Haggard Tribute-C* . . . . (Arista)
Merle Haggard; *Jailhouse Rock (Hits From The Big House)-C* . . . . . . (Sony Music Special Prod.)
Merle Haggard & The Strangers; *Best Of Merle Haggard & The Strangers* . . . . (Capitol)
For The Record: Merle Haggard-43 Legendary Hits . . . .(BNA)
Okie From Muskogee . . . . (Capitol)
Songs I'll Always Sing . . . . (Capitol)
Very Best Of Merle Haggard . . . . (Capitol)
Out Behind The Barn
"Little" Jimmy Dickens; *Columbia Historic Edition-"Little" Jimmy Dickens* . . . . (Columbia)
Roots Of My Raising
Merle Haggard & The Strangers; *Capitol Collectors Series-Merle Haggard & The Strangers* . . . . (Capitol)
For The Record: Merle Haggard-43 Legendary Hits . . . .(BNA)
Merle Haggard's Greatest Hits-#2 . . . . (Curb)
Shoes You're Wearing
Clint Black; *Nothin' But The Taillights* . . . . (RCA)
Song For Mama
Boyz II Men; *BET-Best Of Planet Groove-C* . . . . (Virgin)
Evolution . . . . (Motown)
ST/Soul Food . . . . (LaFace)
Swinging On A Star
Bing Crosby; *All-Time Best* . . . . (Curb)
Best Of Bing Crosby . . . . (MCA)
Dion And The Belmonts; *Dion And The Belmonts-Their Best* . . . . . . (Laurie)
Frank Sinatra; *Frank Sinatra Sings The Songs Of Van Heusen & Cahn* . . . . (Reprise)
Take Time To Know Her
Percy Sledge; *Best Of Percy Sledge* . . . . (Atlantic)
It Tears Me Up-Best Of Percy Sledge . . . . (Rhino)
Teach Your Children
Crosby, Stills & Nash; *CSN* . . . .(Atlantic)
Crosby, Stills, Nash & Young; *4 Way Street* . . . .(Atlantic)
Deja Vu . . . . (Atlantic)
So Far . . . . (Atlantic)
ST/The Wonder Years-Music From The Show & Era . . . . (Atlantic)
Suzy Bogguss/Alison Krauss/Kathy Mattea/Crosby, Stills & Nash; *Red Hot + Country-C* . . . . (Mercury)
Unconditional
Clay Davidson; *Unconditional* . . . . (Virgin)
Way Down The Line
Offspring; *Ixnay On The Hombre* . . . . (Columbia)
What Children Believe
Shenandoah; *Shenandoah 2000* . . . . (Free Falls Entert.)
What Is Truth
Johnny Cash; *The Man In Black-His Greatest Hits* . . . . (Legacy)
Ya Got Trouble
Robert Preston/Original Broadway Cast; *The Music Man* . . . . (Angel)
Robert Preston/Original Cast; *ST/The Music Man* . . . . (Warner Bros.)
The Music Man . . . . (Gold Rush)
Yakety Yak
2 Live Crew; *ST/Twins* . . . . (WTG)
Coasters; *Atlantic Rhythm & Blues 1947-1974-#3 (1955-1958)-C* . . . . .(Atlantic)
Billboard Top Rock 'N' Roll Hits-1958-C . . . . (Rhino)
Coasters' Greatest Hits . . . . (Atco)

Cruisin'-1958-C . . . . (Increase)
ST/Stand By Me . . . . (Atlantic)
You Gotta Be
Des'ree; *Diana, Princess Of Wales-Tribute-C* . . . . (Columbia)
I Ain't Movin' . . . . (550 Music)
Young Jews Be Proud
2 Live Jews; *As Kosher As They Wanna Be* . . . . (Kosher)
Your Life Is Now
John Mellencamp; *John Mellencamp* . . . . (Columbia)
You've Got To Be Carefully Taught
Original Cast; *South Pacific* . . . . (CBS Masterworks)

TEENAGERS, Adolescence

See Also: *AGES (various), AGING, BABY, CHILDREN, FAMILY (various), FAMILY PLANNING, LOVE (various), PARENTS (various), REBELS, SCHOOL, YOUNG*

16 Candles
Crests; *Alan Freed's Memory Lane-C* . . . . (MCA)
Billboard Top Rock 'N' Roll Hits-1959-C . . . . (Rhino)
Crests Greatest Hits . . . . (Collectables)
Cruisin'-1959-C . . . . (Increase)
Oldies But Goodies-#14-C . . . . (Original Sound)
Rock & Roll U.S.A.-21 Rock & Roll Favorites-#2-C . . . . (Laurie)
ST/American Graffiti . . . . (MCA)
6 Teens
Sweet; *Desolation Boulevard* . . . . (Capitol)
Adolescent Funk
Funkadelic; *Hardcore Jollies* . . . . (Warner Bros.)
All The Young Dudes
David Bowie; *David Live* . . . . (Rykodisc)
Ian Hunter; *Live/Welcome To The Club* . . . . (Chrysalis)
Mott The Hoople; *All The Young Dudes* . . . . (Columbia)
Mott The Hoople-Live . . . . (Columbia)
Mott The Hoople's Greatest Hits . . . . (Columbia)
ST/Queen's Logic . . . . (Epic)
All The Young Punks
Clash; *Give 'Em Enough Rope* . . . . (Epic)
Almost Eighteen
Roy Orbison; *Get Hot Or Go Home-Vintage
Rockabilly-C* . . . . (Country Music Foundation)
Legendary Roy Orbison . . . . (Sony Music Special Prod.)
Almost Grown
Chuck Berry; *Berry Is On Top* . . . . (Chess)
Cruisin'-1959-C . . . . (Increase)
Roll Over Beethoven . . . . (Allegiance)
ST/American Graffiti . . . . (MCA)
The Chess Box-Chuck Berry . . . . (Chess)
Angels Working Overtime
Deana Carter; *Everything's Gonna Be Alright* . . . . (Capitol)
At Seventeen
Janis Ian; *Between The Lines* . . . . (Columbia)
Super Hits Of The '70s-Have A Nice Day-#15-C . . . . (Rhino)
Baba O'Reilly (Teenage Wasteland)
Who; *Hooligans* . . . . (MCA)
ST/The Kids Are Alright . . . . (MCA)
The Concert For New York City-C . . . . (Columbia)
Who's Last . . . . (MCA)
Who's next . . . . (MCA)
Ballad Of A Teenage Queen
Johnny Cash; *Johnny Cash* . . . . (Sun)
Johnny Cash-Original Golden Hits-#2 . . . . (Sun)
Johnny Cash-Sun Years . . . . (Rhino)
ST/Harper Valley PTA . . . . (Sun)
The Legend . . . . (Plantation)
The Man In Black-His Greatest Hits . . . . (Legacy)
Be Young You
Jefferson Starship; *Dragon Fly* . . . . (RCA)
Be Young, Be Foolish, Be Happy
Tams; *Tam's Greatest Hits* . . . . (Universal)
Beat On The Brat
Ramones; *All The Stuff & More-#1* . . . . (Sire)
Mania . . . . (Sire)
Ramones . . . . (Sire)
Be-Bop-A-Lula
Everly Brothers; *Everly Brothers* . . . . (Rhino)
Gene Vincent and His Blue Caps; *Billboard Top Rock 'N' Roll Hits-
1956-C* . . . . (Rhino)
ST/Wild At Heart . . . . (Polydor)
Jerry Lee Lewis; *Monsters* . . . . (Sun)
Trio Plus . . . . (Sun)
John Lennon; *Rock 'N' Roll* . . . . (Capitol)
Because They're Young
Duane Eddy; *Compact Command Performances-Duane Eddy* . . . . . . (Motown)
Cruisin'-1960-C . . . . (Increase)
Duane Eddy-16 Greatest Hits . . . . (Jamie)

History Of Rock Instrumentals-#2-C . . . . (Rhino)
Bed Of Rose's
Statler Brothers; *Bed Of Rose's* . . . . (Mercury)
Best Day
George Strait; *Latest Greatest Straitest Hits* . . . . (MCA)
Body Bumpin'
Mytown; *Mytown* . . . . (Cherry/Universal)
Born To Run
Bruce Springsteen; *Born To Run* . . . . (Columbia)
Chimes Of Freedom . . . . (Columbia)
Bruce Springsteen & The E Street Band; *Bruce Springsteen & The E Street
Band Live/1975-85* . . . . (Legacy)
Melissa Etheridge; *The Concert For New York City-C* . . . . (Columbia)
Bow Wow (That's My Name)
Lil Bow Wow; *Beware Of Dog* . . . . (So So Def/Columbia)
Brenda's Got A Baby
Tupac; *2Pacalypse Now* . . . . (Priority)
Brothers Under The Bridges ('83)
Bruce Springsteen; *Tracks* . . . . (Columbia)
Calendar Girl
Neil Sedaka; *Neil Sedaka Sings His Greatest Hits* . . . . (RCA)
Neil Sedaka-Greatest Hits Live . . . . (K-Tel)
Neil Sedaka's All-Time Greatest Hits . . . . (RCA)
Charms
Bobby Vee; *EMI Legends Of Rock & Roll-Bobby Vee* . . . . (Gold Rush)
Chattahoochee
Alan Jackson; *A Lot About Livin' (And A Little 'Bout Love)* . . . . (Arista)
Christine 16
Kiss; *Alive II* . . . . (Casablanca)
Love Gun . . . . (Casablanca)
Come Back When You Grow Up
Bobby Vee; *Best Of Bobby Vee* . . . . (EMI)
Bobby Vee-Legendary Masters . . . . (EMI)
Good Vibrations (Sounds Of Top 40 Radio: 1964-1967)-C . . . . (Capitol)
Coming Of Age
Damn Yankees; *Damn Yankees* . . . . (Warner Bros.)
Davy The Fat Boy
Randy Newman; *Randy Newman* . . . . (Warner Archives)
Randy Newman/Live . . . . (Warner Archives)
Dirty White Boy
Foreigner; *Head Games* . . . . (Atlantic)
Records . . . . (Atlantic)
Edge Of Seventeen
Stevie Nicks; *Bella Donna* . . . . (Modern)
Excitable Boy
Warren Zevon; *Excitable Boy* . . . . (Asylum)
Quiet Normal Life-Best Of Warren Zevon . . . . (Asylum)
Stand In The Fire . . . . (Asylum)
Fancy
Bobbi Gentry; *All-Time Country Classics-#1-C* . . . . (Capitol)
Reba McEntire; *Rumor Has It* . . . . (MCA)
Fight For Your Right (To Party)
Beastie Boys; *Def Jam Classics-#1-C* . . . . (Def Jam)
Heart Of Soul-C . . . . (Columbia)
Licensed To Ill . . . . (Def Jam)
Fun, Fun, Fun
Beach Boys; *Beach Boys-Gift Set* . . . . (Capitol)
Best Of The Beach Boys . . . . (Capitol)
Endless Summer . . . . (Capitol)
Made In The U.S.A. . . . . (Capitol)
The Beach Boys In Concert . . . . (Brother)
Ginger Bread
Frankie Avalon; *Gold For The Road-Carburetor Classics-C* . . . . (Compose)
Venus: The Very Best Of Frankie Avalon . . . . (Collectables)
Girl, You'll Be A Woman Soon
Neil Diamond; *Double Gold-Neil Diamond* . . . . (Bang)
Hot August Night . . . . (MCA)
Neil Diamond-Classics (Early Years) . . . . (Columbia)
Neil Diamond's Greatest Hits . . . . (Bang)
Growin' Up
Bruce Springsteen; *Greetings From Asbury Park, N.J.* . . . . (Columbia)
Live 1975-1985 . . . . (Legacy)
Tracks . . . . (Columbia)
Bruce Springsteen & The E Street Band; *Bruce Springsteen & The E Street
Band Live/1975-85* . . . . (Legacy)
Growin' Up In The Hood
Compton's Most Wanted; *ST/Boyz N The Hood* . . . . (Qwest)
Happy Birthday, Sweet Sixteen
Neil Sedaka; *Neil Sedaka Sings His Greatest Hits* . . . . (RCA)
Neil Sedaka Sings The Hits . . . . (RCA)
Neil Sedaka's All-Time Greatest Hits . . . . (RCA)
He Would Be Sixteen
Michelle Wright; *Now & Then* . . . . (Arista)
Hey Nineteen
Steely Dan; *Gaucho* . . . . (MCA)
Steely Dan-Gold . . . . (MCA)
I Saw Her Standing There
Beatles; *Introducing...The Beatles* . . . . (Vee-Jay)

Meet The Beatles! . . . . (Capitol)
Please Please Me . . . . (Parlophone)
Rock 'N' Roll Music . . . . (Capitol)
The Beatles-Anthology-#1 . . . . (Capitol)
Paul McCartney; Tripping The Live Fantastic-Highlights! . . . . (Capitol)

I Saw Him Standing There
Tiffany; Tiffany . . . . (MCA)
Tiffany's Greatest Hits . . . . (Hip-O)

I Was A Teenage Werewolf
Cramps; Elvira Presents Haunted Hits-C . . . . (Rhino)
Songs The Lord Taught Us . . . . (I.R.S.)

I'm Already Taken
Steve Wariner; Country Cares For Kids II-C . . . . (BNA)
Two Teardrops . . . . (Capitol)

I'm Going To Be A Teenage Idol
Elton John; Don't Shoot Me I'm Only The Piano Player . . . . (Polydor)

It's Late
Ricky Nelson; Lonesome Town . . . . (CEMA Special Prod.)
Ricky Nelson Volume 1 . . . . (Gold Rush)

Jack & Diane
John Cougar; American Fool . . . . (Riva)

Juke Box Baby
Perry Como; Perry Como's Greatest Hits . . . . (RCA)

Kids
Original Broadway Cast; Bye Bye Birdie . . . . (Columbia)
Paul Lynde; ST/Bye Bye Birdie . . . . (RCA)

Kids Are Alright
Pete Townshend; Another Scoop . . . . (Atco)
Who; Meaty Beaty Big & Bouncy . . . . (MCA)
The Who Sings ''My Generation'' . . . . (MCA)

Laurie (Strange Things Happen)
Dickey Lee; Collector's Essentials-#1-1960s-C . . . . (Varese Sarabande)

Leader Of The Pack
Bette Midler; Divine Miss M . . . . (Atlantic)
ST/Divine Madness . . . . (Atlantic)
Original Cast; Leader Of The Pack . . . . (Elektra)
Shangri-Las; 21 Number One Hits-C . . . . (Original Sound)
Billboard Top Rock 'N' Roll Hits-1964-C . . . . (Rhino)
Girl Groups-Story Of A Sound-C . . . . (Rhino)
Golden Hits Of The Shangri-Las . . . . (Mercury)
Oldies But Goodies-#15-C . . . . (Original Sound)
Radio Active Hits-#2-C . . . . (Accord)
Remember The Shangri-Las At Their Best . . . . (Collectables)

Letting Go
Suzy Bogguss; Aces . . . . (Liberty)
Voices In The Wind . . . . (Liberty)

Life's A Dance
John Michael Montgomery; Life's A Dance . . . . (Atlantic)

Lonely Teenager
Dion; Collectables Presents The History Of Rock-#4-C . . . . (Collectables)
Dion-His Best . . . . (Laurie)
Everything You Always Wanted To Hear By . . . . (Laurie)
The Wanderer . . . . (Laurie)

Love, Me
Collin Raye; All I Can Be . . . . (Epic)
Greatest Country Hits Of The '90s-1992-C . . . . (Columbia)

My Back Pages
Bob Dylan; Another Side Of Bob Dylan . . . . (Columbia)
Bob Dylan's Greatest Hits-#2 . . . . (Columbia)
Byrds; 20 Essential Tracks From The Box Set . . . . (Columbia)
Byrds Play Dylan . . . . (Columbia)
The Byrds' Greatest Hits . . . . (Columbia)
Younger Than Yesterday . . . . (Columbia)

My Little Town
Paul Simon; Still Crazy After All These Years . . . . (Columbia)

Negasonic Teenage Warhead
Monster Magnet; Dopes To Infinity . . . . (A&M)

New Girl In School
Jan & Dean; Jan & Dean-Legendary Masters . . . . (EMI)
Surf City-Best Of Jan & Dean . . . . (EMI)

No Such Thing
John Mayer; Room For Squares . . . . (Aware/C2/Columbia)

Oh Julie
Crescendos; In The Still Of The Night . . . . (Capitol)
Southern Rhythm 'N' Rock-Best Of Excello-#2-C . . . . . . (Rhino)

Only Sixteen
Dr. Hook; Bankrupt . . . . (Capitol)
Dr. Hook-Greatest Hits & More . . . . (Capitol)
Great Records Of The Decade-'70s Hits-#2-C . . . . (Curb)
Little Bit More . . . . (Capitol)
Sam Cooke; Best Of Sam Cooke . . . . (RCA)
The Man And His Music . . . . (RCA)
This Is Sam Cooke . . . . (RCA)

Our Teenage Love
Torquays; 45-#66 . . . . (Original Sound)

Papa Don't Preach
Madonna; Immaculate Collection . . . . (Sire)
Royal Box . . . . (Sire)
True Blue . . . . (Sire)

Parents Just Don't Understand
D.J. Jazzy Jeff & The Fresh Prince; He's The D.J. I'm The Rapper . . . . . . (Jive)

Popular
Nada Surf; High/Low . . . . (Elektra)

Restless Youth
Swimming Pool Q's; Deep End . . . . (DB)

Restless Youth
Ian Hunter; All American Alien Boy . . . . (Columbia)

Ricky Wants A Man Of Her Own
Bruce Springsteen; Tracks . . . . (Columbia)

Rock 'N' Roll Juvenile
Cliff Richard; We Don't Talk Anymore . . . . (EMI)

Runaway Train
Soul Asylum; Grave Dancers Union . . . . (Columbia)

School Boy Romance
Danny & The Juniors; Rockin' With Danny & The
Juniors . . . . (MCA Special Prod.)

Serve The Servants
Nirvana; In Utero . . . . (David Geffen Co.)

Seventeen
Bobby Brown; Dance!...Ya Know It! . . . . (MCA)
King Of Stage . . . . (MCA)

Seventeen
Chambers Brothers; Best Of The Chambers Brothers . . . . (Fantasy)

Seventeen
Foreigner; Head Games . . . . (Atlantic)

Seventeen
Sex Pistols; Never Mind The Bollocks, Here's The Sex Pistols . . . (Warner Bros.)

Seventeen
Rusty Draper; Rusty Draper's Greatest Hits . . . . (Monument)

Seventeen
Winger; Winger . . . . (Atlantic)

Seventeen
Chris LeDoux; Radio & Rodeo Hits . . . . (Liberty)

Seventeen Come Sunday
John Wright & Catherine Perrier; Traditional Music Of
Ireland . . . . (Green Linnet)

Seventeen Goin' On 21
Brian Elliot; Brian Elliot . . . . (Warner Bros.)

Sexy + 17
Stray Cats; Best Of Stray Cats-Rock This Town . . . . (EMI)
Rant 'N' Rave With The Stray Cats . . . . (EMI)

She Is Always Seventeen
Harry Chapin; Greatest Stories-Live . . . . (Elektra)
Harry Chapin-Anthology . . . . (Elektra)

She Was Only Seventeen (He Was One Year More)
Marty Robbins; American Originals-Marty Robbins . . . . . . (Columbia)
Marty Robbins' Greatest Hits . . . . (Columbia)

She's In Love With The Boy
Trisha Yearwood; Trisha Yearwood . . . . (MCA)

She's Leaving Home
Al Jarreau; All Fly Home . . . . (Warner Bros.)
Beatles; Beatles-Box Set . . . . (Capitol)
Beatles-Love Songs . . . . (Capitol)
Sgt. Pepper's Lonely Hearts Club Band . . . . (Capitol)

She's Nineteen Years Old
Muddy Waters; Best Of Blues-#1-C . . . . (MCA Special Prod.)
The Chess Box-Muddy Waters . . . . (Chess)

Show Biz Kids
Steely Dan; Countdown To Ecstasy . . . . (MCA)
Steely Dan's Greatest Hits . . . . (MCA)

Shy Of The Moon
Wallflowers; The Wallflowers . . . . (Virgin)

Sixteen Going On Seventeen
Original Cast; The Sound Of Music . . . . (Sony Broadway)

Slide
Goo Goo Dolls; Dizzy Up The Girl . . . . (Warner Sunset/Reprise)

Smells Like Teen Spirit
Nirvana; Nevermind . . . . (David Geffen Co.)

So Young And In Love
Bruce Springsteen; Tracks . . . . (Columbia)

Spirit Of A Boy, Wisdom Of A Man
Randy Travis; Big Country Hits '99-C . . . . (K-Tel)
You And You Alone . . . . (DreamWorks/SKG)

Story Of A Teenager
America; Hearts . . . . (Warner Bros.)

Strawberry Wine
Deana Carter; Did I Shave My Legs For This? . . . . (Capitol)

Street Kids
Elton John; Rock Of The Westies . . . . (Polydor)

Summer Of '69
Bryan Adams; Reckless . . . . (A&M)

Sweet Little Sixteen
Beatles; 45-#1502 . . . . (Collectables)
Chuck Berry; Best Of The Best Of Chuck Berry . . . . (International Mktg. Group)
Chuck Berry-Golden Hits . . . . (Mercury)
Chuck Berry-Greatest Hits Live . . . . (Quicksilver)
Cruisin'-1965-C . . . . (Increase)

Oldies But Goodies-#12-C ....(Original Sound)
Jerry Lee Lewis; *Jerry Lee Lewis-Original Golden Hits-#3* ....(Sun)
Jerry Lee Lewis & Friends; *Jerry Lee Lewis & Friends-Duets* ....(Sun)
John Lennon; *Lennon* ....(Capitol)
Rock 'N' Roll ....(Capitol)

Sweet Sixteen
B.B. King; *Back In The Alley*...(MCA)
Best Of B.B. King ....(MCA)
Electric B.B. King-His Best ....(MCA)
Live In Cook County Jail...(MCA)

Sweet Sixteen
Destiny's Child; *The Writing's On The Wall* ....(Columbia)

Sweet Sixteen
Judy Garland; *Best Of Judy Garland* ....(MCA)

Sweet Sixteen
Big Joe Turner; *Big Joe Turner's Greatest Hits*. ....(Atlantic)

Sweet Sixteen
Chuck Berry; *Chuck Berry's Greatest Hits* ....(Everest)

Sweet Sixteen Bars
Earl Gray; *Best Of Earl Gray*...(MCA)
Ray Charles; *Atlantic Jazz-Piano-C*...................................(Atlantic)
Best Of Ray Charles ....(Atlantic)
Great Ray Charles ....(Atlantic)

Talking The Teenage Language
Lost Generation; *Chicago Soul* ....(Epic)

Tall Paul
Annette with the Afterbeats; *Best Of Annette Funicello* ....(Rhino)
Sherman Brothers...(Disney)
Too Cute-C ....(Dunhill Compact Classics)

Teen Age Idol
Rick Nelson; *Rick Nelson's Greatest Hits* ....(Rhino)
Ricky Nelson; *Best Of Ricky Nelson* ....(EMI)
Ricky Nelson-Legendary Masters.......................................(EMI)

Teen Age Idol
Blackfoot; *Blackfoot* ....(Atco)

Teen Angel
Dion And The Belmonts; *Everything You Always Wanted* ....(Laurie)
Rock & Roll U.S.A.-21 Rock & Roll Favorites-#2-C ....(Laurie)
Mark Dinning; *Golden Years-1959-C* ....(Dominion Entert.)
Oldies But Goodies-#7-C ....(Original Sound)
ST/American Graffiti ....(MCA)
Teenage Tragedies-C ....(Rhino)

Teen Angst (What The World Needs Now)
Cracker; *Cracker*...(Virgin)

Teen Archer
Blue Oyster Cult; *Tyranny & Mutation* ....(Columbia)

Teen Beat
Fleetwood Mac; *25 Years-The Chain* ....(Warner Bros.)

Teenage Abuse
Sicilian Vespers; *Sicilian Vespers* ....(Profile)

Teenage Brain Surgeon
Spike Jones; *In Stereo* ....(Warner Bros.)

Teenage Clone
Germs; *Germicide-Live At The Whisky-1977* ....(Roir)

Teenage Crush
Tommy Sands; *Steady Date With Tommy Sands* ....(Collectables)

Teenage Cutie
Eddie Cochran; *Eddie Cochran-Legendary Masters*.......................(EMI)

Teenage Darling
Fleetwood Mac; *Fleetwood Mac-Early Years*.............................(Pair)

Teenage Depression
Eddie & The Hot Rods; *D.I.Y.-#1-UK Punk-Anarchy In UK-1976-
   1977-C*...(Rhino)
ST/Rock 'N' Roll High School...(Sire)
Teenage Depression ....(Island)

Teenage Dirtbag
Wheatus; *Wheatus* ....(Columbia)

Teenage Eyes
Flash Cadillac & The Continental Kids; *Rock & Roll Forever* ....(Epic)

Teenage Failure
Chad & Jeremy; *History Of British Rock-#7-C* ....(Rhino)
Painted Dayglow Smile-Collection.....................................(Columbia)

Teenage Frankenstein
Alice Cooper; *Constrictor* ....(MCA)
Prince Of Darkness...(MCA)

Teenage Good Night
Chordettes; *Best Of The Chordettes*...................................(Rhino)

Teenage Heaven
Eddie Cochran; *Eddie Cochran-Legendary Masters*.......................(EMI)
Eddie Cochran's Greatest Hits..(Curb)
Johnny Cymbal; *Teen Idols-C*..(Universal)

Teenage Immigrant Welfare Mothers On Drugs
Austin Lounge Lizards; *Live Bait* ....(Sugar Hill)

Teenage Jail
Eagles; *Long Run*...(Asylum)

Teenage Lament '74
Alice Cooper; *Alice Cooper's Greatest Hits* ....(Warner Bros.)
Muscle Of Love ....(Warner Bros.)

Teenage Letter
Big Joe Turner; *Rhythm & Blues Years* ....(Rhino)
Jerry Lee Lewis; *Jerry Lee Lewis-Original Golden Hits-#1* ....(Sun)

Teenage Lobotomy
Ramones; *All The Stuff & More-#2*.....................................(Sire)
Ramones Mania..(Sire)
Rocket To Russia ....(Sire)

Teenage Love
Frankie Lymon and The Teenagers; *Best Of Frankie Lymon and The
   Teenagers*..(Rhino)

Teenage Love Affair
Rick Derringer; *All American Boy* ....(Blue Sky)
Derringer Live...(Blue Sky)

Teenage Lust
Jesus & Mary Chain; *Honey's Dead* ....(Def American)

Teenage Nervous Breakdown
Little Feat; *Hoy-Hoy!*..(Warner Bros.)
Sailin' Shoes ....(Warner Bros.)

Teenage Prostitute
Frank Zappa; *Ship arriving too late to save a drowning witch* ....(Rykodisc)

Teenage Queen
Rick Derringer; *All American Boy* ....(Blue Sky)

Teenage Suicide
Unrest; *Kustom Karnal Blackxploitation*...............................(Caroline)

Teenage Suicide (Don't Do It)
Don Dixon; *If I'm A Ham Well You're A Sausage* ....(Restless)

Teenage Vows Of Love
Dreamer; *Spotlite Series-Goldisc Records-#1-C* ....(Collectables)

Teenage Whore
Hole; *Pretty On The Inside*...(Caroline)

Teenager In Love
Dion And The Belmonts; *Classic Old & Gold-C* ....(Laurie)
Collectables Presents The History Of Rock-#6-C ....(Collectables)
Dion And The Belmonts-Their Best.....................................(Laurie)
Oldies But Goodies-#6-C ....(Original Sound)
Party Time Fifties-C ....(JCI Assoc. Labels)

Teenarama
Records; *Records* ....(Virgin)

Tenderness On The Block
Warren Zevon; *Excitable Boy* ....(Asylum)

Theme From "Clarissa Explains It All"
Original Soundtrack; *Television's Greatest Hits-#7-Cable Ready-C*.....(TVT)

Theme From "Doogie Howser, M.D."
Original Soundtrack; *Television's Greatest Hits-#7-Cable Ready-C*.....(TVT)

Theme From "Facts Of Life"
Original Soundtrack; *Television's Greatest Hits-#3-1970s & 1980s-C*....(TVT)

Theme From "Fresh Prince Of Bel-Air"
Original Soundtrack; *Television's Greatest Hits-#7-Cable Ready-C*.....(TVT)

Theme From "Gidget"
Original Soundtrack; *Television's Greatest Hits-#2-C* ....(TVT)

Theme From "James At 15"
Original Soundtrack; *Television's Greatest Hits-#6-Remote Control-C*...(TVT)

Theme From "Mod Squad"
Original Soundtrack; *Television's Greatest Hits-#1-C* ....(TVT)

Theme From "My So-Called Life"
Original Soundtrack; *Television's Greatest Hits-#7-Cable Ready-C*.....(TVT)

Theme From "Saved By The Bell"
Original Soundtrack; *Television's Greatest Hits-#7-Cable Ready-C*.....(TVT)

Theme From "Speed Racer"
Original Soundtrack; *Television's Greatest Hits-#3-1970s & 1980s-C*....(TVT)

Theme From "What's Happening?"
Original Soundtrack; *Television's Greatest Hits-#6-Remote Control-C*...(TVT)

Treat The Youths Right
Jimmy Cliff; *Rhythm Come Forward: A Reggae Anthology-C* ......(Columbia)
Special..(Columbia)

Two Sparrows In A Hurricane
Tanya Tucker; *Can't Run From Yourself*................................(Liberty)
Tanya Tucker's Greatest Hits-1990-1992 ....(Capitol)

Venus In Blue Jeans
Jimmy Clanton; *All-Star Chartbusters*.................................(Intermedia)
Golden Years-1962-C..(Dominion Entert.)

Wake Up Little Susie
Everly Brothers; *All They Had To Do Was Dream* ....(Rhino)
American Graffiti-#3-C...(MCA)
Everly Brothers ....(Rhino)
Everly Brothers' All-Time Greatest Hits ....(Curb)
Oldies But Goodies-#7-C ....(Original Sound)
Very Best Of The Everly Brothers ....(Warner Bros.)
Grateful Dead; *History Of The Grateful Dead-Vol. 1 (Bear's
   Choice)*..(Warner Bros.)
Simon & Garfunkel; *The Concert In Central Park*.......................(Warner Bros.)

Walkaway Joe
Trisha Yearwood; *Hearts In Armor* ....(MCA)
Songbook-A Collection Of Hits ....(MCA)

War Is Hell (On The Homefront Too)
T.G. Sheppard; *Perfect Stranger* ....(Warner Bros.)

T.G. Sheppard's All-Time Greatest Hits . . . . (Warner Bros.)
T.G. Sheppard's Greatest Hits . . . . (Warner Bros./Curb)
Watching Scotty Grow
Bobby Goldsboro; *Bobby Goldsboro's All-Time Greatest Hits* . . . . (Curb)
Honey-Best Of Bobby Goldsboro . . . . (EMI)
Mac Davis; *Mac Davis' Greatest Hits* . . . . (Columbia)
Way Down The Line
Offspring; *Ixnay On The Hombre* . . . . (Columbia)
We Were In Love
Toby Keith; *Dream Walkin'* . . . . (Mercury)
Toby Keith's Greatest Hits, Volume One . . . . (Mercury)
When I Was Young
Animals; *Best Of The Animals* . . . . (Abkco)
Greatest Hits Live!-Rip It To Shreds . . . . (I.R.S.)
History Of British Rock-#8-C . . . . (Rhino)
White Sport Coat (And A Pink Carnation)
Marty Robbins; *16 Most Requested Songs Of The '50s-#2-C* . . . . (Legacy)
Lifetime Of Song-1951-1982 . . . . (Columbia)
Marty Robbins' Greatest Hits . . . . (Columbia)
Wild One
Faith Hill; *Take Me As I Am* . . . . (Warner Bros.)
Yakety Yak
2 Live Crew; *ST/Twins* . . . . (WTG)
Coasters; *Atlantic Rhythm & Blues 1947-1974-#3 (1955-1958)-C* . . . . . (Atlantic)
Billboard Top Rock 'N' Roll Hits-1958-C . . . . (Rhino)
Coasters' Greatest Hits . . . . (Atco)
Cruisin'-1958-C . . . . (Increase)
ST/Stand By Me . . . . (Atlantic)
You Get What You Give
New Radicals; *Maybe You've Been Brainwashed Too* . . . . (MCA)
Now That's What I Call Music!-#2-C . . . . (Virgin)
Young Americans
David Bowie; *Changesbowie* . . . . (Rykodisc)
Sound + Vision . . . . (Rykodisc)
The Singles-1969-1993 . . . . (Rykodisc)
Young Americans . . . . (Rykodisc)
Young Blood
Bad Company; *Run With The Pack* . . . . (Swan Song)
Coasters; *Coasters' Greatest Hits* . . . . (Atco)
Coasters-Their Greatest Recordings-Early Years . . . . (Atco)
The Ultimate Coasters . . . . (Warner Special Prod.)
Young Girl
Union Gap Featuring Gary Puckett; *Billboard Top Pop Hits-1968-C* . . . (Rhino)
Young Girl Blues
Sammy Hagar; *All Night Long* . . . . (One Way)
Young Love
Sonny James; *Golden Jukebox Favorites* . . . . (Capitol)
Opry Legends-Sonny James . . . . (Capitol)
Stars Of The Grand Ole Opry-1926-1974-C . . . . (RCA)
Traditions In Country Music-C . . . . (Capitol)
Tab Hunter; *Fonzie's Make-Out Music-C* . . . . (Nick At Nite)
Teen Idols-C . . . . (Universal)
Young Man Blues
Who; *Live At Leeds* . . . . (MCA)
ST/The Kids Are Alright . . . . (MCA)
You're Sixteen
Johnny Burnette; *ST/American Graffiti* . . . . (MCA)
Ringo Starr; *Blast From Your Past* . . . . (Gold Rush)
Ringo . . . . (Capitol)
You're Still A Young Man
Tower Of Power; *Bump City* . . . . (Warner Bros.)
Live & In Living Color . . . . (Warner Bros.)
Zero And Blind Terry
Bruce Springsteen; *Tracks* . . . . (Columbia)

TELEPHONE, Answering Machines, Fax, Operator, Pager, Phone Numbers, Telegraph, Voicemail

See Also: COMMUNICATION (various), COMPUTERS, MAIL

1-900-2-COMPTON
N.W.A.; *Efil4zaggin* . . . . (Ruthless/Priority)
1-900-2LONELY
David Grey; *Signature* . . . . (JRS)
1-900-WORLD
Leaving Trains; *Lump In My Forehead* . . . . (SST)
26 Cents
Wilkinsons; *Nothing But Love* . . . . (Giant)
606-0842
B-52's; *B-52's* . . . . (Warner Bros.)
634-5789
Ry Cooder; *Borderline* . . . . (Warner Bros.)
Wilson Pickett; *Wilson Pickett's Greatest Hits* . . . . (Atlantic)
777-9311
Time; *What Time Is It?* . . . . (Warner Bros.)

867-5309/Jenny
Tommy Tutone; *Tommy Tutone-2* . . . . (Columbia)
911
Wyclef Jean featuring Mary J. Blige; *The Ecleftic-2 Sides II A Book* . . . . (Ruffhouse/Columbia)
911 Is A Joke
Public Enemy; *Fear Of A Black Planet* . . . . (Def Jam)
Yo! MTV Raps-C . . . . (Def Jam)
Ain't That Lonely Yet
Dwight Yoakam; *Last Chance For A Thousand Years-Greatest Hits From The '90s* . . . . (Reprise)
This Time . . . . (Reprise)
All Alone
Frank Sinatra; *Frank Sinatra-Complete Reprise Studio Recordings* . . . . (Reprise)
Rosemary Clooney; *Some Of The Best-Rosemary Clooney* . . . . (Laserlight)
All I Know
Screaming Trees; *Dust* . . . . (Epic)
All I've Got To Do
Beatles; *Meet The Beatles!* . . . . (Capitol)
All You Do Is Dial
Heatwave; *Too Hot To Handle* . . . . (Epic)
Annie Waits
Ben Folds; *Rockin' The Suburbs* . . . . (Epic)
Answering Machine
Rupert Holmes; *Partners In Crime* . . . . (MCA)
Answering Machine
Kinsey Report; *Edge Of The City* . . . . (Alligator)
Answering Machine
Replacements; *Let It Be* . . . . (Twin-Tone)
Apolitical Blues
Little Feat; *Last Record Album* . . . . (Warner Bros.)
Sailin' Shoes . . . . (Warner Bros.)
Waiting For Columbus . . . . (Warner Bros.)
Van Halen; *OU812* . . . . (Warner Bros.)
Area Codes
Ludacris; *Word Of Mouf* . . . . (Murder Inc./Def Jam/IDJMG)
As Soon As I Hang Up The Phone
Loretta Lynn; *Country Partners* . . . . (MCA)
Loretta Lynn & Conway Twitty; *Making Believe* . . . . (MCA)
Very Best Of Loretta Lynn & Conway Twitty . . . . (MCA)
At The Sound Of The Tone
John Schneider; *Country Classics-#7-1986-1987-C* . . . . (Universal)
John Schneider's Greatest Hits . . . . (MCA)
Take The Long Way Home . . . . (MCA Special Prod.)
Austin
Blake Shelton; *Blake Shelton* . . . . (Giant)
Baby Don't Forget My Number
Milli Vanilli; *All Or Nothing* . . . . (Arista)
Baby Hang Up The Phone
Carl Graves; *45-#1620* . . . . (A&M)
Beechwood 4-5789
Carpenters; *Made In America* . . . . (A&M)
Marvelettes; *Compact Command Performances-Marvelettes* . . . . (Motown)
Marvelettes' Greatest Hits . . . . (Motown)
Marvelettes-Anthology . . . . (Motown)
More American Graffiti-#4-C . . . . (MCA)
Beep A Freak
Gap Band; *Gap Band VI* . . . . (Total Experience)
Beep Me 911
Missy "Misdemeanor" Elliot; *Supa Dupa Fly* . . . . (East West)
Bills, Bills, Bills
Destiny's Child; *The Writing's On The Wall* . . . . (Columbia)
Boy In The Bubble
Paul Simon; *Graceland* . . . . (Warner Bros.)
Build Me Up Buttercup
Foundations; *Billboard Top Rock 'N' Roll Hits-1969-C* . . . . (Rhino)
History Of British Rock-#9-C . . . . (Rhino)
ST/There's Something About Mary . . . . (Capitol)
Call Me
Frank Sinatra; *Strangers In The Night* . . . . (Reprise)
Call Me
Blondie; *Best Of Blondie* . . . . (Chrysalis)
ST/American Gigolo . . . . (Chrysalis)
Call Me
Aretha Franklin; *Aretha Franklin's Greatest Hits* . . . . (Atlantic)
Call Me
Dennis DeYoung; *Back To The World* . . . . (A&M)
Call Me
BeBe & CeCe Winans; *BeBe & CeCe Winans* . . . . (Capitol)
Call Me
Chambers Brothers; *Best Of The Chambers Brothers* . . . . (Fantasy)
Call Me
Phil Perry; *Heart Of The Man* . . . . (Capitol)
Call Me
Skyy; *Skyy Line* . . . . (Salsoul)
Call Me (Come Back Home)
Al Green; *Al Green's Greatest Hits* . . . . (Right Stuff)

Call Me Up
Rick James; *Street Songs* . . . . (Motown)
Call My Job
Albert King; *King Albert* . . . .(Tomato)
 Masterworks . . . . (Atlantic)
Call On Me
Bobby Bland; *Best Of Bobby Bland* . . . . (MCA)
 Call On Me . . . . (MCA)
Call On Me
Chicago; *Chicago IX-Chicago's Greatest Hits* . . . . (Chicago)
 Chicago VII . . . . (Chicago)
Call On Me
Eddie Money; *Life For The Taking* . . . . (Columbia)
Call On Me
Michael Jackson; *Michael Jackson-Anthology* . . . . (Motown)
Call On Me
Bad Company; *Straight Shooter* . . . . (Swan Song)
Call On Me
Tanya Tucker; *Strong Enough To Bend* . . . . (Liberty)
Callin' Baton Rouge
Garth Brooks; *In Pieces* . . . . (Liberty)
New Grass Revival; *New Grass Revival-Anthology* . . . . . (Liberty)
Oak Ridge Boys; *Room Service* . . . . (MCA Special Prod.)
Calling Elvis
Dire Straits; *On Every Street* . . . . (Warner Bros.)
Can't Hang Up The Phone
Stonewall Jackson; *45-#42628* . . . . (Columbia)
Chantilly Lace
Big Bopper; *45s On CD-#1-1956-1959-C* . . . . (Mercury)
 Cruisin'-1958-C . . . . (Increase)
 Oldies But Goodies-#4-C . . . .(Original Sound)
 ST/American Graffiti . . . . (MCA)
Jerry Lee Lewis; *"Killer" Rocks On* . . . . (Mercury)
 Best Of Jerry Lee Lewis-#2 . . . . (Mercury)
Coconut Telegraph
Jimmy Buffett; *Boats Beaches Bars & Ballads* . . . . (Margaritaville)
 Coconut Telegraph . . . . (MCA)
Crazy Things I Do
Sammie; *From The Bottom To The Top* . . . . (Freeworld/Capitol)
Crybaby
Mariah Carey featuring Snoop Dogg; *Rainbow* . . . . (Columbia)
Dial A Hitman
Big Audio Dynamite; *No. 10 Upping St.* . . . . (Columbia)
Dial Africa
John Coltrane & Wilbur Harden; *Africa-Savoy Sessions* . . . . . . (Savoy)
 Dial Africa . . . . (Savoy)
Dial That Telephone
Eddie Rabbitt; *The Best Year Of My Life* . . . . (Warner Bros.)
Disconnected Line
John Mayall; *Hard Core Passage* . . . . (MCA)
Don't Lose My Number
Phil Collins; *No Jacket Required* . . . . (Atlantic)
 Serious Hits...Live! . . . . (Atlantic)
Easy Tonight
Five For Fighting; *America Town* . . . . (Aware/C2/Columbia)
Echo Valley 2-6809
Partridge Family; *Partridge Family's Greatest Hits* . . . . . . (Arista)
Girlfriend/Boyfriend
Blackstreet featuring Janet; *Finally* . . . . (Lil' Man/Interscope)
Had To Phone Ya
Beach Boys; *15 Big Ones* . . . . (Brother)
Hang Up And Drive
Ray Stevens; *Osama-Yo' Mama* . . . . (Curb)
Hanging On The Telephone
Blondie; *Best Of Blondie* . . . . (Chrysalis)
 Parallel Lines . . . . (Chrysalis)
He Calls Home
Candlebox; *Candlebox* . . . . (Maverick)
Hearts Of Stone
Bruce Springsteen; *Tracks* . . . . (Columbia)
Southside Johnny And The Asbury Jukes; *Best Of Southside Johnny And The*
 Asbury Jukes . . . . (Legacy)
 Cover Me (Bruce Springsteen Tribute)-C . . . . (Rhino)
 Hearts Of Stone . . . . (Epic)
He'll Have To Go
Jim Reeves; *60 Years Of Country Music-C* . . . .(RCA)
 Best Of Jim Reeves . . . .(RCA)
 Billboard Top Country Hits-1960-C . . . . (Rhino)
 Great Moments At The Grand Ole Opry-C . . . . (RCA)
 Jim Reeves' Greatest Hits . . . . (RCA)
 Nipper's Greatest Hits Of The '50s-#1-C . . . . (RCA)
Ry Cooder; *Chicken Skin Music* . . . . (Reprise)
Hello, Central, Give Me No Man's Land
Al Jolson; *Music From The New York Stage (1890-1920)-#4-1917-*
 1920-C . . . . (Pearl)
Here's A Quarter (Call Someone Who Cares)
Travis Tritt; *It's All About To Change* . . . . (Warner Bros.)

Hot Line
Black Sabbath; *Born Again* . . . . (Warner Bros.)
Hot Line
Sylvers; *Best Of The Sylvers* . . . .(Capitol)
How Come U Don't Call Me Anymore
Stephanie Mills; *Merciless* . . . . (Casablanca)
How Come You Don't Call Me
Alicia Keys; *Songs In A Minor* . . . .(J)
I Apologize
Anita Baker; *Rhythm Of Love* . . . . (Atlantic)
I Can Still Make Cheyenne
George Strait; *Blue Clear Sky* . . . . (MCA)
 Latest Greatest Straitest Hits . . . . (MCA)
I Can't Reach Her Anymore
Sammy Kershaw; *Haunted Heart* . . . .(Mercury)
I Got Your Number
Boz Scaggs; *Slow Dancer* . . . .(Columbia)
I Just Called To Say I Love You
Aretha Franklin; *Aretha Franklin's Greatest Hits* . . . . (Atlantic)
 Aretha's Gold . . . . (Atlantic)
 Best Of Aretha Franklin . . . . (Atlantic)
Stevie Wonder; *ST/Lady In Red* . . . . (Motown)
I Know
Dionne Farris; *Wild Seed - Wild Flower* . . . .(Columbia)
I Want You Back
'N Sync; *'N Sync* . . . . (RCA)
If I Needed Someone
Beatles; *Rubber Soul* . . . .(Capitol)
Is That A Tear
Tracy Lawrence; *Best Of Tracy Lawrence* . . . . (Atlantic)
 Time Marches On . . . . (Atlantic)
It Must Be Him
Vikki Carr; *Greatest Hits* . . . .(Curb)
It's Me Again Margaret
Ray Stevens; *Country Classics-#3-1984-1985-C* . . . .(Universal)
 He Thinks He's Ray Stevens . . . . (MCA)
 Ray Stevens' Greatest Hits . . . . (MCA)
It's Your Call
Reba McEntire; *It's Your Call* . . . . (MCA)
Jesus Is On The Mainline
Ry Cooder; *Paradise And Lunch* . . . . (Reprise)
 Show Time . . . . (Warner Bros.)
Just Seven Numbers
Four Tops; *Compact Command Performances-Four Tops* . . . .(Motown)
 Four Tops-Anthology . . . . (Motown)
Kiss The Rain
Billie Myers; *A Taste Of '98-C* . . . .(Universal)
 Growing Pains . . . .(Universal)
Knock It On The Head
Wood; *Songs From Stamford Hill* . . . .(Columbia)
Last Train To Clarksville
Monkees; *Monkees* . . . .(Arista)
 Monkees' Greatest Hits . . . . (Rhino)
 Monkees-Live-1967 . . . . (Rhino)
 Then & Now...The Best Of The Monkees . . . . (Arista)
Letting Go
Sozzi; *Songs From Dawson's Creek* . . . . (Sony Music Soundtrax)
Long Distance Call
Muddy Waters; *Best Of Muddy Waters* . . . . (Chess)
 The Chess Box-Muddy Waters . . . .(Chess)
Muddy Waters Blues Band; *Mud In Your Ear* . . . . (Muse)
Long Distance Love
Little Feat; *Last Record Album* . . . . (Warner Bros.)
Long Distance Operator
Bob Dylan And The Band; *Basement Tapes* . . . .(Columbia)
Long Distance Runaround
Yes; *Classic Yes* . . . . (Atlantic)
 Fragile . . . . (Atlantic)
 Yessongs . . . . (Atlantic)
Lost My Drivin' Wheel
Tom Rush; *Best Of Tom Rush: No Regrets* . . . .(Legacy)
 Tom Rush . . . .(Columbia)
Lost You In The Canyon
Marc Cohn; *Burning The Daze* . . . . (Atlantic)
Love On The Telephone
Foreigner; *Head Games* . . . . (Atlantic)
Mama Don't Forget To Pray For Me
Diamond Rio; *Diamond Rio* . . . .(Arista)
 Diamond Rio's Greatest Hits . . . . (Arista)
Memphis
Chuck Berry; *Chuck Berry* . . . . (Audio Fidelity)
 Chuck Berry-Golden Hits . . . . (Mercury)
 Chuck Berry's Greatest Hits . . . . (Everest)
 St. Louis To Liverpool . . . .(Chess)
 ST/Hail! Hail! Rock 'N' Roll . . . . (MCA)
 The Chess Box-Chuck Berry . . . . (Chess)

Toronto Rock 'N' Roll Revival-#2-C . . . . (Accord)
John Cale; *IRS Greatest Hits-#2 & #3-C* . . . .(I.R.S.)
Johnny Rivers; *Best Of Johnny Rivers* . . . .(EMI)
Johnny Rivers-Anthology 1964-1977. . . . . (Rhino)
Lonnie Mack; *Rock Instrumental Classics-#2-'60s-C* . . . . (Rhino)
Teen Beat-Instrumental Rock-1957-1965-C . . . . (Capitol)

Missing You
Brooks & Dunn; *Tight Rope* . . . . (Arista)
John Waite; *'80s Greatest Rock Hits-#1-Passion & Power-C* . . . . (Priority)
Complete John Waite-#1-Falling Backwards . . . . (EMI)
Essential John Waite-1976-1986 . . . .(Chrysalis)
Tina Turner; *Wildest Dreams* . . . . (Virgin)

Mr. Telephone Man
New Edition; *New Edition* . . . .(MCA)
New Edition's Greatest Hits, Vol. 1 . . . .(MCA)

My Favorite Girl
Dave Hollister; *Ghetto Hymns* . . . .(Def Squad/DreamWorks)

New York Telephone Conversation
Lou Reed; *Transformer* . . . . (RCA)
Walk On The Wild Side-The Best Of Lou Reed. . . . . (RCA)

No Telephone In Heaven
Doc Watson; *My Dear Old Southern Home* . . . . (Sugar Hill)

Nobody Home
Pink Floyd; *The Wall* . . . . (Columbia)
Roger Waters; *The Wall-Live In Berlin.* . . . . (Mercury)

Obscene Phone Caller
Rockwell; *Somebody's Watching Me* . . . . (Motown)

Off The Hook
Rolling Stones; *The Rolling Stones, Now!* . . . . (Abkco)

Old Man From The Mountain
Merle Haggard & The Strangers; *For The Record: Merle Haggard-43 Legendary Hits* . . . . (BNA)

On The Phone
Julian Lennon; *Valotte* . . . .(Atlantic)

One More Chance
Notorious B.I.G.; *Ready To Die* . . . . (Bad Boy/Arista)

Operator
Manhattan Transfer; *Best Of The Manhattan Transfer* . . . .(Atlantic)
The Manhattan Transfer . . . . (Rhino)

Operator
Grateful Dead; *American Beauty* . . . .(Warner Bros.)

Operator
Gladys Knight & The Pips; *Letter Full Of Tears-Golden Classics* . . . . (Collectables)

Operator
Midnight Star; *Planetary Invasion* . . . . (Solar)

Operator
Lloyd Price; *Walkin' The Track* . . . . (Specialty)

Operator (That's Not The Way It Feels)
Jim Croce; *Photographs & Memories/His Greatest Hits* . . . .(Atlantic)
Time In A Bottle/Jim Croce's Greatest Love Songs . . . . (Atlantic)
You Don't Mess Around With Jim . . . . (Lifesong)

Operator, Long Distance Please
Barbara Mandrell; *In Black & White.* . . . .(MCA)

Operator, Operator
Eddy Raven; *Best Of Eddy Raven* . . . . (RCA)

Pennsylvania 6-5000
Glenn Miller; *Glenn Miller-A Legendary Performer-#1 & 2* . . . . (Bluebird)
Memorial-1944-1969. . . . . (Bluebird)
The Glenn Miller Story . . . . (RCA)
Glenn Miller & His Orchestra; *Complete Glenn Miller & His Orchestra-#4.* . . . . (Bluebird)
Glenn Miller & His Orchestra-Pure Gold* . . . . (Bluebird)
Moonlight Serenade. . . . . (Ranwood)
The Unforgettable Glenn Miller & His Orchestra . . . . (RCA)

Phone
House Of Love; *Spy In The House Of Love.* . . . . (Fontana)
Records; *Records* . . . . (Virgin)

Phone Booth
Albert King; *I'm In A Phone Booth Baby* . . . .(Stax)
Robert Cray Band; *Bad Influence* . . . .(Hightone)
Blues Masters-#9-Postmodern Blues-C. . . . . (Rhino)

Phone Booth Man
Tuff Darts; *Tuff Darts* . . . . (Sire)

Phone Call
King Diamond; *Dark Sides.* . . . .(Roadrunner)
Them . . . . (Roadracer)

Phone Call
Joe Satriani; *Flying In A Blue Dream* . . . . (Relativity)

Phone Call
Dan Hill; *Hold On.* . . . . (20th Century Fox)

Phone Call
Pretenders; *Pretenders* . . . . (Sire)

Phone Call From Chicago
Peter Himmelman; *From Strength To Strength* . . . .(Epic)

Phone Call From God
Ray Reeves; *Comedy For The Road-#2-C* . . . .(Hollywood/DNA-Rounder)

Phone Call From Leavenworth
Chris Whitley; *Living With The Law* . . . . (Columbia)

Phone Call From The Devil
Jim Nesbitt; *Phone Call From The Devil.* . . . .(Scotti Bros.)

Phone Call From The Moon
Adrian Belew; *Young Lions* . . . .(Atlantic)

Phone Sexxx
Jimmy Z; *Muzical Madness.* . . . . (Ruthless)

Pick Up The Phone
Aaron Hall; *The Truth* . . . . (Silas)

Pick Up The Phone
Jamaica Boys; *J Boys* . . . . (Reprise)

Please Call Home
Allman Brothers Band; *Beginnings.* . . . .(Polydor)
Idlewild South. . . . .(Polydor)
Gregg Allman; *Laid Back* . . . .(Polydor)

Please Call Me, Baby
Tom Waits; *The Heart Of Saturday Night* . . . .(Asylum)

Private Number
Judy Clay & William Bell; *15 Original Big Hits-#2-C* . . . . (Stax)
Private Numbers. . . . . (Stax)
Top Of The Stax-Twenty Greatest Hits-#2-C. . . . . (Stax)

Promised Land
Band; *Moondog Matinee.* . . . . (Capitol)
Chuck Berry; *Rock 'N' Roll Rarities-20 Magic Tracks* . . . .(Chess)
The Chess Box-Chuck Berry. . . . . (Chess)
Elvis Presley; *Promised Land* . . . .(RCA)
ST/This Is Elvis . . . . (RCA)
Freddy Weller; *Country Music Classics-#11-Early '70s-C.* . . . . (K-Tel)
Freddy Weller's Greatest Hits . . . . (Columbia)
Gary Morris; *Full Moon Empty Heart* . . . . (Liberty)
Grateful Dead; *Steal Your Face.* . . . .(Grateful Dead)
James Taylor; *Walking Man* . . . .(Warner Bros.)
Kingfish; *Kingfish/Alive In Eighty Five-Double Dose.* . . . . (Relix)

Red Telephone
Love; *Forever Changes.* . . . . (Elektra)

Request Line
Zhane'; *Saturday Night* . . . .(Motown)

Rikki Don't Lose That Number
Steely Dan; *Classic Rock-#2-C* . . . . (MCA)
Decade Of Steely Dan. . . . . (MCA)
Pretzel Logic . . . .(MCA)
Steely Dan's Greatest Hits . . . . (MCA)

Ring My Phone
Tommy Sands; *Steady Date With Tommy Sands* . . . .(Collectables)

Royal Telephone
Burl Ives; *Best Of Burl Ives-#2* . . . . (MCA)
George Lewis & Eclipse Alley Five; *George Lewis Of New Orleans* . . . . (Riverside)

San Francisco Days
Chris Isaak; *San Francisco Days.* . . . .(Reprise)

She Came In Through The Bathroom Window
Beatles; *Abbey Road* . . . .(Parlophone)
Beatles-Box Set. . . . . (Capitol)
Joe Cocker; *Joe Cocker Live* . . . . (Capitol)
Joe Cocker! . . . . (A&M)
Joe Cocker-Classics-#4 . . . . (A&M)
Mad Dogs & Englishmen . . . . (A&M)

Silence On The Line
Chris LeDoux; *Cowboy.* . . . . (Capitol)

So Anxious
Ginuwine; *100 Percent Ginuwine* . . . .(550 Music)

Soon
Tanya Tucker; *Soon* . . . . (Liberty)

Spiderwebs
No Doubt; *1997 Grammy Nominees-C* . . . . (Chronicles)
Tragic Kingdom . . . .(Trauma)

Standing Outside A Broken Phone Booth With Money In My Hand
Primitive Radio Gods; *MTV Best Of The Buzz Bin-#2-C* . . . .(Mammoth)
Rocket. . . . . (Ergo)

Star 69
R.E.M.; *Monster* . . . . (Warner Bros.)

Straight Up
Chante Moore; *Exposed* . . . . (Silas)

Switchboard Susan
Nick Lowe; *Basher: Best Of* . . . . (Columbia)
Labour Of Lust. . . . . (Columbia)

Telefone (Long Distance Love Affair)
Sheena Easton; *Best Kept Secret* . . . .(EMI)
Sheena Easton's Greatest Hits . . . .(EMI Special Markets)
The World Of Sheena Easton: The Singles Collection-C . . . . (EMI)

Telephone
Diana Ross; *Endless Love* . . . .(RCA)
Swept Away . . . . (RCA)

Telephone
Chaka Khan; *The Woman I Am* . . . .(Warner Bros.)

Telephone Call From Istanbul
Tom Waits; *Big Time* .... (Island)
Frank's Wild Years-Un Operachi Romantico .... (Island)
Telephone Exchange
Angel; *Live Without A Net* .... (Casablanca)
Telephone Girl
Eddie & The Hot Rods; *Life On The Line* .... (Island)
Telephone Girl
Jade Warrior; *Jade Warrior* .... (Vertigo)
Telephone Girlie
Original Cast/Ruby Keeler; *No No Nanette* .... (RCA)
Telephone Hour
Original Cast; *Bye Bye Birdie* .... (Columbia)
Soundtrack; *Bye Bye Birdie* .... (RCA)
Telephone Line
Electric Light Orchestra; *Afterglow* .... (Epic)
E.L.O. Classics .... (Sony Music Special Prod.)
Electric Light Orchestra's Greatest Hits .... (Jet)
New World Record .... (Jet)
Telephone Man
Meri Wilson; *First Take* .... (GRT)
Super Hits Of The '70s-Have A Nice Day-#21-C .... (Rhino)
Telephone Number
3-D; *3-D* .... (Polydor)
Telephone Road
Steve Earle; *Alt. Country-C* .... (Simitar)
El Corazon .... (E Squared)
Telephone Song
Original London Cast; *Miss Saigon* .... (Geffen)
Telephone Song
Original Cast; *Cabaret* .... (Columbia)
Telephone Song
Vaughan Brothers; *Family Style* .... (Epic Portrait Assoc.)
That's The Kind Of Mood I'm In
Patty Loveless; *Strong Heart* .... (Epic)
Theme From "Midnight Caller"
Original Soundtrack; *Television's Greatest Hits-#7-Cable Ready-C* ..... (TVT)
This Is A Call
Foo Fighters; *Foo Fighters* .... (Roswell/RCA)
Three Nickels & A Dime
Ricky Lynn Gregg; *Ricky Lynn Gregg* .... (Liberty)
Trouble On The Line
Sawyer Brown; *Cafe On The Corner* .... (Curb)
Two Little Girls (911)
Ani DiFranco; *Little Plastic Castle* .... (Righteous Babe)
Uncle Albert/Admiral Halsey
Paul And Linda McCartney; *RAM* .... (Capitol)
Paul McCartney; *All The Best!* .... (Capitol)
Paul McCartney-Gift Set .... (Capitol)
Wings; *Wings Greatest* .... (Capitol)
Watin' For The Phone To Ring
Patty Loveless; *Up Against My Heart* .... (MCA)
Ronna Reeves; *What Comes Naturally* .... (Mercury)
What's A Telephone Bill
Bootsy's Rubber Band; *The Name Is Bootsy Baby* .... (Warner Bros.)
What's The 411?
Mary J. Blige; *What's The 411?* .... (Uptown)
Whenever You Call
Mariah Carey; *Butterfly* .... (Columbia)
Why Didn't You Call Me
Macy Gray; *On How Life Is* .... (Epic)
Why Don't That Telephone Ring
Tracy Byrd; *Tracy Byrd* .... (MCA)
Why Haven't I Heard From You
Reba McEntire; *Read My Mind* .... (MCA)
Reba McEntire's Greatest Hits-#3: I'm A Survivor .... (MCA)
Wichita Lineman
Dwight Yoakam; *Under The Covers* .... (Reprise)
Glen Campbell; *Best Of Glen Campbell* .... (Capitol)
Country Music Classics-#3-1965-1970-C .... (K-Tel)
Glen Campbell-Classics Collection .... (Capitol)
Glen Campbell-Live .... (Capitol)
Glen Campbell's Greatest Hits .... (Capitol)
Jimmy Webb Collection .... (Columbia)
Wrong Number
Cure; *Galore-The Singles-1987-1997* .... (Fiction/Elektra)
X-Girlfriend
Mariah Carey; *Rainbow* .... (Columbia)
You Can't Take The Telephone To Bed
Jill Hollier; *45-#28796* .... (Warner Bros.)
You Know My Name (Look Up My Number)
Beatles; *Beatles-Box Set* .... (Capitol)
Past Masters-Volume Two .... (Parlophone)
Rarities .... (Capitol)
Your Phone's Off The Hook, But You're Not
X; *Los Angeles/Wild Gift* .... (Slash)

TELEVISION, Theme Songs To Programs & Products, Video

See Also: **CARTOON CHARACTERS, HOLLYWOOD, MOVIES, NEWS, PRODUCTS & BRANDS: SPECIFIC, RADIO, SHOW BIZ**

57 Channels (And Nothin' On)
Bruce Springsteen; *Human Touch* .... (Columbia)
'70s TV
Dramarama; *Stuck In Wonderamaland* .... (Chameleon)
All Night Television
3-D; *3-D* .... (Polydor)
Animal Crackers
Steven Tyler featuring Liv Tyler and Ben Affleck; *ST/Armageddon-The Album* .... (Columbia)
Another Brick In The Wall, Part 3
Pink Floyd; *The Wall* .... (Columbia)
Bad Touch, The
Bloodhound Gang; *Hooray For Boobies* .... (Republic/Geffen)
Ballad Of Davy Crockett
Bill Hayes; *Songs Of The West-#4-Movie & Television Themes-C* ..... (Rhino)
Fess Parker; *16 Most Requested Songs Of The '50s-#1-C* .... (Legacy)
Columbia Country Classics-#3-Americana-C .... (Columbia)
Hollywood Magic-1950s-C .... (Columbia)
Kentucky HeadHunters; *Electric Barnyard* .... (Mercury)
Mac Wiseman; *45-#1240* .... (Dot)
Original Soundtrack; *Television's Greatest Hits-#4-Black & White Classics-C* .... (TVT)
Tennessee Ernie Ford; *Capitol Collectors Series-Tennessee Ernie Ford* .... (Capitol)
Ballad Of TV Violence
Cheap Trick; *Cheap Trick* .... (Epic)
Black And White Television
Ian Anderson; *Walk Into Light* .... (Chrysalis)
Blow Up Your TV
John Denver; *Aerie* .... (RCA)
Bonanza
Billy Strange; *Great Western Themes* .... (Crescendo)
Buddy Holly
Weezer; *Weezer* .... (David Geffen Co.)
Cable TV
"Weird Al" Yankovic; *Dare To Be Stupid* .... (Scotti Bros.)
Color TV Blues
Don McLean; *Prime Time* .... (Arista)
David Duchovny
Bree Sharp; *Cheap & Evil Girl* .... (Trauma)
Death From Your TV Screen
Voice Of Destruction; *Steamroller Tactics* .... (Cleopatra)
Dirty Laundry
Don Henley; *I Can't Stand Still* .... (Asylum)
El Macho
Mark Knopfler; *Sailing To Philadelphia* .... (Warner Bros.)
Freak Of The Week
Marvelous 3; *Hey Album* .... (HiFi/Elektra)
God Trying To Get Your Attention
Keb' Mo'; *Slow Down* .... (550/Epic/Okeh)
High-Tech Redneck
George Jones; *High-Tech Redneck* .... (MCA)
Hooray For Captain Spaulding
Groucho Marx; *Dr. Demento Presents The Greatest Novelty Records-#1-1940s & Before-C* .... (Rhino)
Dr. Demento Presents The Greatest Novelty Records-C .... (Rhino)
Original Soundtrack; *Television's Greatest Hits-#6-Remote Control-C* ... (TVT)
Human Video Game
D.J. Jazzy Jeff & The Fresh Prince; *He's The D.J. I'm The Rapper* .... (Jive)
I Lost On Jeopardy
"Weird Al" Yankovic; *"Weird Al" Yankovic's Greatest Hits* .... (Scotti Bros.)
In 3-D .... (Scotti Bros.)
I Saw It On TV
John Fogerty; *Centerfield* .... (Warner Bros.)
I'm The Slime
Mothers Of Invention; *Apostrophe/Overnite Sensation* .... (Rykodisc)
It's All Been Done
Barenaked Ladies; *Stunt* .... (Reprise)
Jerry Springer
"Weird Al" Yankovic; *Running With Scissors* .... (Volcano Entertainment)
Lazy Day
Moody Blues; *On The Threshold Of A Dream* .... (Polydor)
Lifestyles Of The Not-So-Rich & Famous
Tracy Byrd; *No Ordinary Man* .... (MCA)
Man In The Box
Alice In Chains; *Facelift* .... (Columbia)
Mercedes Benz
Janis Joplin; *Pearl* .... (Legacy)
ST/Janis .... (Columbia)
Mister Big Time
Jon Bon Jovi; *ST/Armageddon-The Album* .... (Columbia)

Money For Nothing
Dire Straits; *Brothers In Arms*. . . . .(Warner Bros.)
  Money For Nothing . . . .(Warner Bros.)
More News At 11
Public Enemy; *Apocalypse 91...The Enemy Strikes Black* . . (Def Jam/Columbia)
My Color TV
Young Black Teenagers; *Young Black Teenagers* . . . . (S.O.U.L.)
My Favorite Headache
Geddy Lee; *My Favorite Headache* . . . . (Anthem/Atlantic)
My TV Went Black & White On Me
Young Black Teenagers; *Young Black Teenagers* . . . . (S.O.U.L.)
News At Ten
Vapors; *New Clear Days* . . . . (Liberty)
Olympic Fanfare & Theme
Felix Slatkin Concert Band; *U.S.A.* . . . . (Angel)
John Williams; *Official Music Of The XXIIIrd Olympiad* . . . . (Columbia)
Original Soundtrack; *Television's Greatest Hits-#5-In Living Color-C* . . . (TVT)
On TV
Renegade Soundwave; *Soundclash* . . . . (Mute/Reprise)
Perry Mason
Ozzy Osbourne; *Ozzmosis* . . . .(Epic)
Playboy Channel
Negativeland; *Escape From Noise* . . . .(SST)
Prime Time
Alan Parsons Project; *Ammonia Avenue* . . . . (Arista)
  Best Of Alan Parsons Project-#2 . . . . (Arista)
Prime Time
Tubes; *Remote Control* . . . . (A&M)
  T.R.A.S.H. (Tubes Rarities And Smash Hits) . . . . (A&M)
Prime Time TV
Basia; *Time And Tide* . . . .(Epic)
Put Your Hands On The Screen
Martin Briley; *One Night With A Stranger* . . . . (Mercury)
Revolution Will Not Be Televised
Gil Scott-Heron; *Gil Scott-Heron* . . . . (Bluebird)
  Pieces Of A Man . . . . (Flying Dutchman)
  Revolution Will Not Be Televised . . . . (Flying Dutchman)
Ronny Zamora (My Friend Ron)
Deaf School; *English Boys/Working Girls* . . . .(Warner Bros.)
Roy Rogers
Elton John; *Goodbye Yellow Brick Road* . . . . (Polydor)
Satellite Blues
AC/DC; *Stiff Upper Lip* . . . . (East West)
Secret Agent Man
Devo; *Duty Now For The Future* . . . .(Warner Bros.)
Johnny Rivers; *Best Of Johnny Rivers* . . . .(EMI)
  Johnny Rivers-Anthology 1964-1977 . . . . (Rhino)
  Television's Greatest Hits-#1-C . . . . (TVT)
  Very Best Of Johnny Rivers . . . .(EMI)
She Watch Channel Zero
Public Enemy; *It Takes A Nation Of Millions To Hold Us Back* . . . . . .(Def Jam)
Sleeping With The Television On
Billy Joel; *Glass Houses* . . . . (Columbia)
Sleeping With The TV On
Dictators; *Manifest Destiny* . . . . (Asylum)
St. George & The Dragonet
Stan Freberg; *Greatest Hits-Stan Freberg* . . . . (Curb)
  Tip Of The Freberg: The Stan Freberg Collection-1951-1998 . . . . (Rhino)
Sun Always Shines On T.V.
A-Ha; *Hunting High & Low* . . . .(Warner Bros.)
T.V. Mind
Revolting Cocks; *Big Sexy Land* . . . . (Wax Trax)
T.V. On
Thompson Twins; *Big Trash* . . . .(Red Eye)
T.V. Talkin' Song
Bob Dylan; *Under The Red Sky* . . . . (Columbia)
Talk Show Shhh!
Shae Jones; *Talk Show* . . . . (Universal)
Talking Pay T.V.
Phil Ochs; *Broadside Tapes-#1* . . . . (Smithsonian Folkways)
Telecide
Tubes; *Remote Control* . . . . (A&M)
Television
Dave Edmunds; *Tracks On Wax 4* . . . . (Swan Song)
Television
Mind Over 4; *Out Here* . . . .(Triple X Entert.)
Television
Japan; *Adolescent Sex* . . . . (Ariola America)
Television Blues
Lowell Fulsom; *San Francisco Blues* . . . . (Black Lion)
Television Eye
John Mayall; *Room To Move-1969-1974-Chronicle Series* . . . .(Polydor)
Television Generation
Kursaal Flyers; *D.I.Y.-#3-UK Pop 1-Teenage Kicks-1976-1979-C* . . . . . (Rhino)
  Permanent Wave . . . .(Epic)
Television Girl
Atlantics; *Big City Rock* . . . .(MCA)

Television Kiss
Lave Love; *Aphrodisia* . . . . (Sky)
Television Man
Talking Heads; *Little Creatures* . . . .(Sire)
Television Nightmare
Madrigal; *Madrigal* . . . . (SSS International)
Television People
Psychefunkapus; *Skin* . . . .(Atlantic)
Television Station
Front 242; *Official Version* . . . . (Epic)
Television, The Drug Of The Nation
Disposable Heroes Of Hiphoprisy; *Hypocrisy Is The Greatest*
  Luxury . . . . (4th & Broadway)
Televisions On My Leg
Squirrels; *What Gives?* . . . .(Pop Llama Prod.)
Test For Echo
Rush; *Test For Echo* . . . .(Atlantic)
Test Pattern
Lime Spiders; *Volatile.* . . . . (Caroline)
Thank You For Being A Friend
Andrew Gold; *All This & Heaven Too.* . . . .(Asylum)
  Chicken Soup For The Soul: I'll Be There For You-Songs Of Friendship,
    Brotherhood And Sisterhood-C . . . . (Rhino)
  Television's Greatest Hits-#6-Remote Control-C . . . . (TVT)
  Thank You For Being A Friend: The Best Of Andrew Gold . . . . (Rhino)
Theme From "21 Jump Street"
Original Soundtrack; *Television's Greatest Hits-#7-Cable Ready-C* . . . . . (TVT)
Theme From "77 Sunset Strip"
Original Soundtrack; *Television's Greatest Hits-#1-C* . . . . (TVT)
  TV Classic Themes: 25th Anniversary Edition-C . . . .(Breakable)
Theme From "A Different World"
Original Soundtrack; *Television's Greatest Hits-#7-Cable Ready-C* . . . . . (TVT)
Theme From "ABC's Wide World Of Sports"
Original Soundtrack; *Television's Greatest Hits-#2-C* . . . . (TVT)
Theme From "Adam-12"
Original Soundtrack; *Television's Greatest Hits-#1-C* . . . . (TVT)
Theme From "Adventures Of Pete And Pete"
Original Soundtrack; *Television's Greatest Hits-#7-Cable Ready-C* . . . . . (TVT)
Theme From "Airwolf"
Original Soundtrack; *Television's Greatest Hits-#6-Remote Control-C* . . . (TVT)
Theme From "Alf"
Original Soundtrack; *Television's Greatest Hits-#6-Remote Control-C* . . . (TVT)
Theme From "Alfred Hitchcock Presents"
Original Soundtrack; *Alfred Hitchcock Presents Signature In*
  Suspense . . . .(Hip-O)
  CBS: The First 50 Years . . . . (TVT)
  Television's Greatest Hits-#1-C. . . . . (TVT)
Theme From "Alice"
Original Soundtrack; *Television's Greatest Hits-#6-Remote Control-C* . . . (TVT)
Theme From "Alien Nation"
Original Soundtrack; *Television's Greatest Hits-#7-Cable Ready-C* . . . . . (TVT)
Theme From "All In The Family"
Original Soundtrack; *CBS: The First 50 Years* . . . . (TVT)
  Television's Greatest Hits-#3-1980s-C . . . .(TVT)
Theme From "All My Children"
Original Soundtrack; *Television's Greatest Hits-#5-In Living Color-C* . . . (TVT)
Theme From "American Bandstand" (Bandstand Boogie)
Barry Manilow; *Barry Manilow's Greatest Hits-#1* . . . . (Arista)
  Trying To Get The Feeling . . . . (Arista)
Original Soundtrack; *Television's Greatest Hits-#3-1970s and 1980s-C* . . . (TVT)
Theme From "America's Most Wanted"
Original Soundtrack; *Television's Greatest Hits-#7-Cable Ready-C* . . . . . (TVT)
Theme From "Anything But Love"
Original Soundtrack; *Television's Greatest Hits-#7-Cable Ready-C* . . . . . (TVT)
Theme From "As The World Turns"
Rosemary Joyce & Bill Bartholomew; *Soap Opera Themes* . . . .(Crescendo)
Theme From "Asphalt Jungle"
Original Soundtrack; *Television's Greatest Hits-#4-Black & White*
  Classics-C . . . . (TVT)
Theme From "Augie Doggie"
Original Soundtrack; *Hanna-Barbera Classics-#1-Original Recordings Of*
  The World's Most Famous Cartoon Themes &
  Scores . . . .(Kid Rhino/Rhino 4 Kids)
  Hanna-Barbera Pic-A-Nic Basket Of Cartoon
  Classics . . . .(Kid Rhino/Rhino 4 Kids)
Theme From "B.J. And The Bear"
Original Soundtrack; *Television's Greatest Hits-#6-Remote Control-C* . . . (TVT)
Theme From "Baa Baa Black Sheep"
Original Soundtrack; *Television's Greatest Hits-#6-Remote Control-C* . . . (TVT)
Theme From "Baretta"
Original Soundtrack; *Television's Greatest Hits-#3-1970s and 1980s-C* . . . (TVT)
Theme From "Barnaby Jones"
Original Soundtrack; *CBS: The First 50 Years* . . . . (TVT)
  Television's Greatest Hits-#3-1970s and 1980s-C . . . .(TVT)
Theme From "Barney And Friends"
Original Soundtrack; *Television's Greatest Hits-#7-Cable Ready-C* . . . . . (TVT)
Theme From "Barney Miller"
Original Soundtrack; *Television's Greatest Hits-#3-1970s and 1980s-C* . . . (TVT)

Theme From "Batman"
Original Soundtrack; *Television's Greatest Hits-#1-C* . . . . (TVT)
Theme From "Battlestar Galactica"
Boston Pops Orchestra/John Williams; *Pops Out Of This World* . . . . . . (Philips)
Original Soundtrack; *Science Fiction Move Themes* . . . .(Laserlight)
Theme From "Beauty & The Beast"
Ron Perlman; *Theme From "Beauty & The Beast"* . . . . (Capitol)
Theme From "Ben Casey"
Original Soundtrack; *Television's Greatest Hits-#2-C* . . . . (TVT)
Theme From "Benson"
Original Soundtrack; *Television's Greatest Hits-#6-Remote Control-C* . . . (TVT)
Theme From "Beverly Hills 90210"
John Davis; *Beverly Hills 90210: Songs From The Peach Pit* . . . . (Rhino)
ST/Beverly Hills, 90210-College Years . . . . (Giant)
Television's Greatest Hits-#7-Cable Ready-C . . . . (TVT)
Theme From "Bewitched"
Original Soundtrack; *Television's Greatest Hits-#2-C* . . . . (TVT)
Theme From "Blossom"
Original Soundtrack; *Television's Greatest Hits-#7-Cable Ready-C* . . . . . (TVT)
Theme From "Bonanza"
Al Caiola & His Orchestra; *Songs Of The West-#4-Movie & Television
Themes-C* . . . . (Rhino)
Cincinnati Pops Orchestra/Erich Kunzel; *Round-Up* . . . . (Telarc)
Original Soundtrack; *Television's Greatest Hits-#1-C* . . . . (TVT)
TV Classic Themes: 25th Anniversary Edition-C . . . . (Breakable)
Theme From "Branded"
Original Soundtrack; *Television's Greatest Hits-#1-C* . . . . (TVT)
Theme From "Bronco"
Original Soundtrack; *Television's Greatest Hits-#4-Black & White
Classics-C* . . . . (TVT)
Theme From "Bugs Bunny Overture"
Original Soundtrack; *Television's Greatest Hits-#1-C* . . . . (TVT)
Theme From "Burke's Law"
Original Soundtrack; *Television's Greatest Hits-#4-Black & White
Classics-C* . . . . (TVT)
Theme From "Cagney & Lacey"
Original Soundtrack; *CBS: The First 50 Years* . . . . (TVT)
Television's Greatest Hits-#6-Remote Control-C . . . . (TVT)
Theme From "Captain Kangaroo"
Original Soundtrack; *CBS: The First 50 Years* . . . . (TVT)
Television's Greatest Hits-#1-C . . . . (TVT)
Theme From "Car 54, Where Are You?"
Original Soundtrack; *Television's Greatest Hits-#2-C* . . . . (TVT)
Theme From "Casper The Friendly Ghost"
Original Soundtrack; *Television's Greatest Hits-#1-C* . . . . (TVT)
Theme From "Charles In Charge"
Shandi; *Television's Greatest Hits-#6-Remote Control-C* . . . . (TVT)
Tube Tunes-#3-The '70s & '80s-C . . . . (Rhino)
Theme From "Charlie's Angels"
Original Soundtrack; *Television's Greatest Hits-#3-1970s & 1980s-C* . . . . (TVT)
TV Classic Themes: 25th Anniversary Edition-C . . . . (Breakable)
Theme From "Cheers"
Gary Portnoy; *Tube Tunes-#3-The '70s & '80s-C* . . . . (Rhino)
Original Soundtrack; *Television's Greatest Hits-#3-1970s & 1980s-C* . . . (TVT)
Theme From "Cheyenne"
Original Soundtrack; *Television's Greatest Hits-#4-Black & White
Classics-C* . . . . (TVT)
Theme From "Chicago Hope"
Original Soundtrack; *CBS: The First 50 Years* . . . . (TVT)
Theme From "CHiPs"
Original Soundtrack; *Television's Greatest Hits-#6-Remote Control-C* . . . (TVT)
Theme From "Clarissa Explains It All"
Original Soundtrack; *Television's Greatest Hits-#7-Cable Ready-C* . . . . . (TVT)
Theme From "Colt .45"
Original Soundtrack; *Television's Greatest Hits-#4-Black & White
Classics-C* . . . . (TVT)
Theme From "Combat"
Original Soundtrack; *Television's Greatest Hits-#1-C* . . . . (TVT)
Theme From "Cosby"
Original Soundtrack; *CBS: The First 50 Years* . . . . (TVT)
Theme From "Courageous Cat & Minute Mouse"
Original Soundtrack; *Television's Greatest Hits-#2-C* . . . . (TVT)
Theme From "Dallas"
Original Soundtrack; *CBS: The First 50 Years* . . . . (TVT)
Television's Greatest Hits-#3-1970s & 1980s-C . . . . (TVT)
TV Classic Themes: 25th Anniversary Edition-C . . . . (Breakable)
Theme From "Daniel Boone"
Original Soundtrack; *Television's Greatest Hits-#1-C* . . . . (TVT)
Theme From "Dark Shadows"
Original Soundtrack; *Television's Greatest Hits-#2-C* . . . . (TVT)
Theme From "Dastardly & Muttley In Their Flying Machine"
Original Soundtrack; *Hanna-Barbera Pic-A-Nic Basket Of Cartoon
Classics* . . . . (Kid Rhino/Rhino 4 Kids)
Television's Greatest Hits-#3-1970s & 1980s-C . . . . (TVT)
Theme From "Davis Rules"
Original Soundtrack; *Television's Greatest Hits-#7-Cable Ready-C* . . . . . (TVT)
Theme From "Dennis The Menace"
Original Soundtrack; *Television's Greatest Hits-#1-C* . . . . (TVT)

Theme From "Designing Women" (Georgia On My Mind)
Original Soundtrack; *Television's Greatest Hits-#7-Cable Ready-C* . . . . . (TVT)
Theme From "Diff'rent Strokes"
Original Soundtrack; *Television's Greatest Hits-#6-Remote Control-C* . . . (TVT)
Theme From "Doogie Howser, M.D."
Original Soundtrack; *Television's Greatest Hits-#7-Cable Ready-C* . . . . . (TVT)
Theme From "Dr. Kildare" (Three Stars Will Shine Tonight)
Betty Carter; *'Round Midnight* . . . . (Atlantic)
Original Soundtrack; *Television's Greatest Hits-#4-Black & White
Classics-C* . . . . (TVT)
Theme From "Dragnet"
Original Soundtrack; *Television's Greatest Hits-#1-C* . . . . (TVT)
Theme From "Duckman"
Original Soundtrack; *Television's Greatest Hits-#7-Cable Ready-C* . . . . . (TVT)
Theme From "Dudley-Do-Right"
Original Soundtrack; *Television's Greatest Hits-#3-1970s & 1980s-C* . . . (TVT)
Theme From "Dynasty"
Original Soundtrack; *Television's Greatest Hits-#3-1970s & 1980s-C* . . . . (TVT)
Theme From "Empty Nest"
Original Soundtrack; *Television's Greatest Hits-#7-Cable Ready-C* . . . . . (TVT)
Theme From "Entertainment Tonight"
Original Soundtrack; *Television's Greatest Hits-#3-1970s & 1980s-C* . . . . (TVT)
Theme From "Evening Shade"
Original Soundtrack; *Television's Greatest Hits-#7-Cable Ready-C* . . . . . (TVT)
Theme From "Everybody Loves Raymond"
Original Soundtrack; *CBS: The First 50 Years* . . . . (TVT)
Theme From "Facts Of Life"
Original Soundtrack; *Television's Greatest Hits-#3-1970s & 1980s-C* . . . . (TVT)
Theme From "Falcon Crest"
Original Soundtrack; *Television's Greatest Hits-#6-Remote Control-C* . . . (TVT)
Theme From "Fame"
Original Soundtrack; *Television's Greatest Hits-#5-In Living Color-C* . . . . (TVT)
Theme From "Family Affair"
Original Soundtrack; *Television's Greatest Hits-#5-In Living Color-C* . . . . (TVT)
Theme From "Family Feud"
Original Soundtrack; *Television's Greatest Hits-#6-Remote Control-C* . . . (TVT)
Theme From "Family Matters"
Original Soundtrack; *Television's Greatest Hits-#7-Cable Ready-C* . . . . . (TVT)
Theme From "Family Ties"
Original Soundtrack; *Television's Greatest Hits-#6-Remote Control-C* . . . (TVT)
Theme From "Fantasy Island"
Original Soundtrack; *Television's Greatest Hits-#6-Remote Control-C* . . . (TVT)
Theme From "Fat Albert And The Cosby Kids"
Original Soundtrack; *Television's Greatest Hits-#3-1970s & 1980s-C* . . . . (TVT)
Theme From "Father Knows Best"
Original Soundtrack; *Television's Greatest Hits-#4-Black & White
Classics-C* . . . . (TVT)
Theme From "Fireball XL-5"
Original Soundtrack; *Television's Greatest Hits-#1-C* . . . . (TVT)
Theme From "Fish"
Original Soundtrack; *Television's Greatest Hits-#6-Remote Control-C* . . . (TVT)
Theme From "Flipper"
Original Soundtrack; *Television's Greatest Hits-#1-C* . . . . (TVT)
Theme From "Fractured Fairy Tales"
Original Soundtrack; *Television's Greatest Hits-#3-1970s & 1980s-C* . . . . (TVT)
Theme From "Fresh Prince Of Bel-Air"
Original Soundtrack; *Television's Greatest Hits-#7-Cable Ready-C* . . . . . (TVT)
Theme From "Friends" (I'll Be There For You)
Rembrandts; *LP* . . . .(East West)
ST/Friends-Music From The TV Series . . . . (Reprise)
Theme From "F-Troop"
Original Soundtrack; *Television's Greatest Hits-#1-C* . . . . (TVT)
Theme From "Full House"
Original Soundtrack; *Television's Greatest Hits-#7-Cable Ready-C* . . . . . (TVT)
Theme From "General Hospital"
Original Soundtrack; *Television's Greatest Hits-#5-In Living Color-C* . . . (TVT)
Theme From "Gentle Ben"
Original Soundtrack; *Television's Greatest Hits-#5-In Living Color-C* . . . . (TVT)
Theme From "George Of The Jungle"
Original Soundtrack; *Television's Greatest Hits-#2-C* . . . . (TVT)
Theme From "Get Smart"
Original Soundtrack; *Television's Greatest Hits-#1-C* . . . . (TVT)
Theme From "Gidget"
Original Soundtrack; *Television's Greatest Hits-#2-C* . . . . (TVT)
Theme From "Gilligan's Island"
Original Soundtrack; *CBS: The First 50 Years* . . . . (TVT)
Television's Greatest Hits-#1-C . . . . (TVT)
Theme From "Gimme A Break"
Original Soundtrack; *Television's Greatest Hits-#3-1970s & 1980s-C* . . . . (TVT)
Theme From "Gomer Pyle, U.S.M.C."
Original Soundtrack; *Television's Greatest Hits-#2-C* . . . . (TVT)
Theme From "Good Times"
Original Soundtrack; *CBS: The First 50 Years* . . . . (TVT)
Television's Greatest Hits-#3-1970s & 1980s-C . . . . (TVT)
Theme From "Greatest American Hero"
Joey Scarbury; *Television's Greatest Hits-#3-1970s & 1980s-C* . . . . (TVT)
Tube Tunes-#3-The '70s & '80s-C . . . . (Rhino)

Theme From "Green Acres"
Eddie Albert & Eva Gabor; *ST/Son In Law* . . . . (Hollywood)
Original Soundtrack; *CBS: The First 50 Years* . . . . (TVT)
Television's Greatest Hits-#1-C . . . . (TVT)

Theme From "Growing Pains"
Original Soundtrack; *Television's Greatest Hits-#6-Remote Control-C* . . (TVT)

Theme From "Gunsmoke" (The Old Trail)
Billy Strange; *Great Western Themes* . . . .(Crescendo)
Original Soundtrack; *CBS: The First 50 Years* . . . . (TVT)
Television's Greatest Hits-#4-Black & White Classics-C . . . . (TVT)

Theme From "Happy Days"
Original Soundtrack; *Television's Greatest Hits-#3-1970s & 1980s-C* . . . (TVT)

Theme From "Hardcastle And McCormick"
Original Soundtrack; *Television's Greatest Hits-#6-Remote Control-C* . . (TVT)

Theme From "Hart To Hart"
Original Soundtrack; *Television's Greatest Hits-#3-1970s & 1980s-C* . . . (TVT)

Theme From "Have Gun Will Travel" (Ballad Of Paladin)
Duane Eddy; *Duane Eddy-Pure Gold* . . . . (RCA)
Johnny Western; *Columbia Country Classics-#3-Americana-C* . . . . (Columbia)
Television's Greatest Hits-#7-Cable Ready-C . . . . (TVT)

Theme From "Hawaii Five-O"
Original Soundtrack; *CBS: The First 50 Years* . . . . (TVT)
Television's Greatest Hits-#1-C . . . . (TVT)
Ventures; *Billboard Top Pop Hits-1969-C* . . . . (Rhino)
Drew's Famous Luau Party Music-C . . . .(Turn Up The Music)

Theme From "Here Come The Brides"
Original Soundtrack; *Television's Greatest Hits-#5-In Living Color-C* . . . (TVT)

Theme From "Highway Patrol"
Original Soundtrack; *Television's Greatest Hits-#4-Black & White Classics-C* . . . . (TVT)

Theme From "Highway To Heaven"
Original Soundtrack; *Television's Greatest Hits-#6-Remote Control-C* . . (TVT)

Theme From "Hill Street Blues"
Original Soundtrack; *Television's Greatest Hits-#3-1970s & 1980s-C* . . . (TVT)

Theme From "Hogan's Heroes"
Original Soundtrack; *CBS: The First 50 Years* . . . . (TVT)
Television's Greatest Hits-#2-C . . . . (TVT)

Theme From "Hokey Wolf"
Original Soundtrack; *Hanna-Barbera Classics-#1-Original Recordings Of The World's Most Famous Cartoon Themes & Scores* . . . .(Kid Rhino/Rhino 4 Kids)
Hanna-Barbera Pic-A-Nic Basket Of Cartoon Classics . . . . (Kid Rhino/Rhino 4 Kids)

Theme From "Home Improvement"
Original Soundtrack; *Television's Greatest Hits-#7-Cable Ready-C* . . . . . (TVT)

Theme From "Howdy Doody"
Original Soundtrack; *Television's Greatest Hits-#1-C* . . . . (TVT)

Theme From "Huckleberry Hound"
Original Soundtrack; *Hanna-Barbera Classics-#1-Original Recordings Of The World's Most Famous Cartoon Themes & Scores* . . . .(Kid Rhino/Rhino 4 Kids)
Hanna-Barbera Pic-A-Nic Basket Of Cartoon Classics . . . . (Kid Rhino/Rhino 4 Kids)
Television's Greatest Hits-#2-C . . . . (TVT)

Theme From "Hudson Street"
Original Soundtrack; *Television's Greatest Hits-#7-Cable Ready-C* . . . . . (TVT)

Theme From "Hunter"
Original Soundtrack; *Television's Greatest Hits-#6-Remote Control-C* . . (TVT)

Theme From "I Dream Of Jeannie"
Original Soundtrack; *Television's Greatest Hits-#1-C* . . . . (TVT)

Theme From "I Love Lucy"
Original Soundtrack; *CBS: The First 50 Years* . . . . (TVT)
Television's Greatest Hits-#1-C . . . . (TVT)
TV Theme Sing-Along Album . . . . (Rhino)

Theme From "I Spy"
Original Soundtrack; *Television's Greatest Hits-#2-C* . . . . (TVT)

Theme From "I'll Fly Away"
Original Soundtrack; *Television's Greatest Hits-#7-Cable Ready-C* . . . . . (TVT)

Theme From "In The Heat Of The Night"
Original Soundtrack; *Television's Greatest Hits-#7-Cable Ready-C* . . . . . (TVT)

Theme From "Inspector Gadget"
Original Soundtrack; *Television's Greatest Hits-#3-1970s & 1980s-C* . . . (TVT)

Theme From "Ironside"
Original Soundtrack; *Television's Greatest Hits-#1-C* . . . . (TVT)

Theme From "It Takes A Thief"
Original Soundtrack; *Television's Greatest Hits-#5-In Living Color-C* . . . (TVT)

Theme From "It's Garry Shandling's Show"
Original Soundtrack; *Television's Greatest Hits-#7-Cable Ready-C* . . . . . (TVT)

Theme From "James At 15"
Original Soundtrack; *Television's Greatest Hits-#6-Remote Control-C* . . (TVT)

Theme From "Jeopardy" (Think Music)
Original Soundtrack; *Television's Greatest Hits-#2-C* . . . . (TVT)

Theme From "John Larroquette Show"
Original Soundtrack; *Television's Greatest Hits-#7-Cable Ready-C* . . . . . (TVT)

Theme From "Johnny Quest"
Original Soundtrack; *Hanna-Barbera Pic-A-Nic Basket Of Cartoon Classics* . . . . (Kid Rhino/Rhino 4 Kids)
Television's Greatest Hits-#2-C . . . . (TVT)

Theme From "Josie & The Pussycats"
Original Soundtrack; *Hanna-Barbera Pic-A-Nic Basket Of Cartoon Classics* . . . .(Kid Rhino/Rhino 4 Kids)
Television's Greatest Hits-#3-1970s & 1980s-C . . . . (TVT)

Theme From "Judd For The Defense"
Original Soundtrack; *Television's Greatest Hits-#5-In Living Color-C* . . . (TVT)

Theme From "Karen"
Original Soundtrack; *Television's Greatest Hits-#4-Black & White Classics-C* . . . . (TVT)

Theme From "Kids In The Hall"
Original Soundtrack; *Television's Greatest Hits-#7-Cable Ready-C* . . . . . (TVT)

Theme From "Knots Landing"
Original Soundtrack; *CBS: The First 50 Years* . . . . (TVT)
Television's Greatest Hits-#3-1970s & 1980s-C . . . . (TVT)

Theme From "Kojak"
Henry Mancini; *Cop Show Themes* . . . . (RCA)
John Gregory; *TV's Greatest Detective Hits* . . . . (Mercury)
Original Soundtrack; *Television's Greatest Hits-#3-1970s & 1980s-C* . . . (TVT)

Theme From "Kukla, Fran And Ollie" ("Here We Are, Hop, Hop, Hop")
Original Soundtrack; *Television's Greatest Hits-#4-Black & White Classics-C* . . . . (TVT)

Theme From "L.A. Law"
Original Soundtrack; *Television's Greatest Hits-#3-1970s & 1980s-C* . . . (TVT)

Theme From "Lassie"
Original Soundtrack; *Television's Greatest Hits-#4-Black & White Classics-C* . . . . (TVT)

Theme From "Laverne & Shirley"
Original Soundtrack; *Television's Greatest Hits-#3-1970s & 1980s-C* . . . (TVT)

Theme From "Law And Order"
Original Soundtrack; *Television's Greatest Hits-#7-Cable Ready-C* . . . . . (TVT)

Theme From "Leave It To Beaver"
Original Soundtrack; *CBS: The First 50 Years* . . . . (TVT)
Television's Greatest Hits-#1-C . . . . (TVT)

Theme From "Let's Make A Deal"
Original Soundtrack; *Television's Greatest Hits-#5-In Living Color-C* . . . (TVT)

Theme From "Lifestyles Of The Rich And Famous"
Original Soundtrack; *Television's Greatest Hits-#6-Remote Control-C*. . . (TVT)

Theme From "Lippy The Lion & Hardy Har Har"
Original Soundtrack; *Hanna-Barbera Classics-#1-Original Recordings Of The World's Most Famous Cartoon Themes & Scores* . . . .(Kid Rhino/Rhino 4 Kids)
Hanna-Barbera Pic-A-Nic Basket Of Cartoon Classics . . . .(Kid Rhino/Rhino 4 Kids)

Theme From "Little House On The Prairie"
Original Soundtrack; *Television's Greatest Hits-#3-1970s & 1980s-C* . . . (TVT)

Theme From "Little Rascals"
Original Soundtrack; *Television's Greatest Hits-#1-C* . . . . (TVT)

Theme From "Lois And Clark: The New Adventures Of Superman"
Original Soundtrack; *Television's Greatest Hits-#7-Cable Ready-C* . . . . . (TVT)

Theme From "Looney Tunes"
Original Soundtrack; *Television's Greatest Hits-#2-C* . . . . (TVT)

Theme From "Lost In Space"
Neil Norman; *Greatest Science Fiction Hits-#3-C* . . . .(Crescendo)
Original Soundtrack; *CBS: The First 50 Years* . . . . (TVT)
Television's Greatest Hits-#1-C . . . . (TVT)

Theme From "Love, American Style"
Original Soundtrack; *Television's Greatest Hits-#2-C* . . . . (TVT)
TV Classic Themes: 25th Anniversary Edition-C . . . . (Breakable)

Theme From "MacGyver"
Original Soundtrack; *Television's Greatest Hits-#6-Remote Control-C*. . . (TVT)

Theme From "Mad About You"
Original Soundtrack; *Television's Greatest Hits-#7-Cable Ready-C* . . . . . (TVT)

Theme From "Magilla Gorilla"
Original Soundtrack; *Hanna-Barbera Classics-#1-Original Recordings Of The World's Most Famous Cartoon Themes & Scores* . . . .(Kid Rhino/Rhino 4 Kids)
Hanna-Barbera Pic-A-Nic Basket Of Cartoon Classics . . . .(Kid Rhino/Rhino 4 Kids)
Television's Greatest Hits-#1-C . . . . (TVT)

Theme From "Magnum P.I."
Original Soundtrack; *Television's Greatest Hits-#3-1970s & 1980s-C* . . . (TVT)

Theme From "Major Dad"
Original Soundtrack; *Television's Greatest Hits-#7-Cable Ready-C* . . . . . (TVT)

Theme From "Mannix"
Original Soundtrack; *CBS: The First 50 Years* . . . . (TVT)
Television's Greatest Hits-#1-C . . . . (TVT)
San Diego Symphony & Lalo Schifrin; *Hitchcock-Master Of Mayhem* . . . . (Pro-Arte)

Theme From "Marcus Welby, M.D."
Original Soundtrack; *Television's Greatest Hits-#3-1970s & 1980s-C* . . . (TVT)

Theme From "Mary Hartman, Mary Hartman"
Original Soundtrack; *Television's Greatest Hits-#5-In Living Color-C* . . . (TVT)

Theme From "Masterpiece Theatre"
Original Soundtrack; *Television's Greatest Hits-#5-In Living Color-C* . . . (TVT)

Theme From "Matt Houston"
Original Soundtrack; *Television's Greatest Hits-#6-Remote Control-C*. . . (TVT)

Theme From ''Maude''
Original Soundtrack; *Television's Greatest Hits-#3-1970s & 1980s-C* . . . . (TVT)
Theme From ''Maverick''
Original Soundtrack; *Television's Greatest Hits-#2-C* . . . . (TVT)
Theme From ''Max Headroom''
Original Soundtrack; *Television's Greatest Hits-#7-Cable Ready-C* . . . . . (TVT)
Theme From ''McHale's Navy''
Original Soundtrack; *Television's Greatest Hits-#1-C* . . . . (TVT)
Theme From ''Medic''
Original Soundtrack; *Television's Greatest Hits-#4-Black & White
    Classics-C* . . . . (TVT)
Theme From ''Medical Center''
Original Soundtrack; *Television's Greatest Hits-#2-C* . . . . (TVT)
Theme From ''Merrie Melodies''
Original Soundtrack; *Television's Greatest Hits-#2-C* . . . . (TVT)
Theme From ''Miami Vice''
Jan Hammer; *Escape From Television* . . . . (MCA)
    Soundtrack Smashes-'80s & More-C . . . . (MCA)
    ST/Miami Vice . . . . (MCA)
Original Soundtrack; *Television's Greatest Hits-#3-1970s & 1980s-C* . . . . (TVT)
Theme From ''Midnight Caller''
Original Soundtrack; *Television's Greatest Hits-#7-Cable Ready-C* . . . . . (TVT)
Theme From ''Mighty Mouse''
Original Soundtrack; *Television's Greatest Hits-#2-C* . . . . (TVT)
Theme From ''Mike Hammer''
Original Soundtrack; *TV Classic Themes: 25th Anniversary
    Edition-C* . . . . (Breakable)
Theme From ''Mission: Impossible''
Adam Clayton & Larry Mullen; *ST/Mission: Impossible* . . . . . . (Mother/Island)
Lalo Schifrin; *The Reel Lalo Schifrin* . . . . (Hip-O)
Original Soundtrack; *CBS: The First 50 Years* . . . . (TVT)
    Television's Greatest Hits-#1-C . . . . (TVT)
San Diego Symphony & Lalo Schifrin; *Hitchcock-Master Of
    Mayhem* . . . . (Pro-Arte)
Theme From ''Mod Squad''
Original Soundtrack; *Television's Greatest Hits-#1-C* . . . . (TVT)
Theme From ''Monday Night Football''
Original Soundtrack; *Television's Greatest Hits-#6-Remote Control-C* . . . (TVT)
Theme From ''Monty Python's Flying Circus''
Original Soundtrack; *Television's Greatest Hits-#2-C* . . . . (TVT)
Theme From ''Moonlighting''
Al Jarreau; *ST/Moonlighting* . . . . (MCA)
    Television's Greatest Hits-#6-Remote Control-C . . . . (TVT)
Theme From ''Mork & Mindy''
Original Soundtrack; *Television's Greatest Hits-#6-Remote Control-C* . . . (TVT)
Theme From ''Movin' On''
Original Soundtrack; *Television's Greatest Hits-#6-Remote Control-C* . . . (TVT)
Theme From ''Mr. Belvedere'' (According To Our New Arrivals)
Leon Redbone; *Television's Greatest Hits-#6-Remote Control-C* . . . . . . (TVT)
Theme From ''Mr. Lucky''
Original Soundtrack; *Television's Greatest Hits-#4-Black & White
    Classics-C* . . . . (TVT)
Theme From ''Mr. Magoo''
Original Soundtrack; *Television's Greatest Hits-#3-1970s & 1980s-C* . . . . (TVT)
Theme From ''Mr. Rogers' Neighborhood''
Original Soundtrack; *Television's Greatest Hits-#2-C* . . . . (TVT)
Theme From ''M-Squad''
Original Soundtrack; *Television's Greatest Hits-#4-Black & White
    Classics-C* . . . . (TVT)
Theme From ''Murder, She Wrote''
Original Soundtrack; *CBS: The First 50 Years* . . . . (TVT)
Theme From ''Murphy Brown''
Original Soundtrack; *CBS: The First 50 Years* . . . . (TVT)
Theme From ''My Favorite Martian''
Original Soundtrack; *Television's Greatest Hits-#2-C* . . . . (TVT)
Theme From ''My Mother The Car''
Original Soundtrack; *Television's Greatest Hits-#2-C* . . . . (TVT)
Theme From ''My So-Called Life''
Original Soundtrack; *Television's Greatest Hits-#7-Cable Ready-C* . . . . . (TVT)
Theme From ''My Three Sons''
Original Soundtrack; *CBS: The First 50 Years* . . . . (TVT)
    Television's Greatest Hits-#1-C . . . . (TVT)
Theme From ''My Two Dads''
Original Soundtrack; *Television's Greatest Hits-#7-Cable Ready-C* . . . . . (TVT)
Theme From ''N.Y.P.D. Blue''
Original Soundtrack; *Television's Greatest Hits-#7-Cable Ready-C* . . . . . (TVT)
Theme From ''Nanny And The Professor''
Original Soundtrack; *Television's Greatest Hits-#5-In Living Color-C* . . . (TVT)
Theme From ''Night Court''
Original Soundtrack; *Television's Greatest Hits-#6-Remote Control-C* . . . (TVT)
Theme From ''Night Gallery''
Original Soundtrack-Sonny Curtis; *Television's Greatest Hits-#5-In Living
    Color-C* . . . . (TVT)
Theme From ''Northern Exposure''
David Schwartz; *ST/Music From ''Northern Exposure''* . . . . (MCA)
Original Soundtrack; *CBS: The First 50 Years* . . . . (TVT)
Theme From ''One Day At A Time''
Original Soundtrack; *CBS: The First 50 Years* . . . . (TVT)

Theme From ''One Life To Live''
Rosemary Joyce & Bill Bartholomew; *Soap Opera Themes* . . . . (Crescendo)
Theme From ''Our Miss Brooks''
Original Soundtrack; *Television's Greatest Hits-#4-Black & White
    Classics-C* . . . . (TVT)
Theme From ''Outer Limits''
Original Soundtrack; *Television's Greatest Hits-#2-C* . . . . (TVT)
Theme From ''Paper Chase''
Original Soundtrack; *Television's Greatest Hits-#6-Remote Control-C* . . . (TVT)
Theme From ''Party Of Five'' (Closer To Free)
BoDeans; *Chicago Bulls Greatest Hits-#3-C* . . . . (Atlantic)
    Go Slow Down . . . . (Slash)
    Joe Dirt Car . . . . (Reprise)
    ST/Party Of Five . . . . (Reprise)
Theme From ''Perry Mason''
Blues Brothers; *Made In America* . . . . (Atlantic)
Jerry Goodman; *It's Alive* . . . . (Private Music)
Original Soundtrack; *CBS: The First 50 Years* . . . . (TVT)
    Television's Greatest Hits-#1-C . . . . (TVT)
    TV Theme Sing-Along Album . . . . (Rhino)
Theme From ''Petticoat Junction''
Flatt & Scruggs; *20 All-Time Great Recordings* . . . . (Columbia)
Original Soundtrack; *Television's Greatest Hits-#1-C* . . . . (TVT)
    TV Theme Sing-Along Album . . . . (Rhino)
Theme From ''Peyton Place''
Original Soundtrack; *Television's Greatest Hits-#5-In Living Color-C* . . . (TVT)
Theme From ''Pixie And Dixie''
Original Soundtrack; *Hanna-Barbera Classics-#1-Original Recordings Of
    The World's Most Famous Cartoon Themes &
    Scores* . . . . (Kid Rhino/Rhino 4 Kids)
    *Hanna-Barbera Pic-A-Nic Basket Of Cartoon
    Classics* . . . . (Kid Rhino/Rhino 4 Kids)
Theme From ''Police Story''
Original Soundtrack; *Television's Greatest Hits-#5-In Living Color-C* . . . (TVT)
Ventures; *TV Themes* . . . . (United Artists)
Theme From ''Police Woman''
Original Soundtrack; *Television's Greatest Hits-#5-In Living Color-C* . . . (TVT)
Theme From ''Promised Land''
Original Soundtrack; *CBS: The First 50 Years* . . . . (TVT)
Theme From ''Quantum Leap''
Original Soundtrack; *Sci-Fi's Greatest Hits-#4-Defenders Of Justice* . . . . (TVT)
    Television's Greatest Hits-#7-Cable Ready-C . . . . (TVT)
Theme From ''Quincy, M.E.''
Original Soundtrack; *Television's Greatest Hits-#3-1970s & 1980s-C* . . . . (TVT)
Theme From ''Rat Patrol''
Original Soundtrack; *Television's Greatest Hits-#2-C* . . . . (TVT)
Theme From ''Rawhide''
Blues Brothers; *Original Soundtrack* . . . . (Atlantic)
Frankie Laine; *CBS: The First 50 Years* . . . . (TVT)
    Cowboy Super Hits-C . . . . (Columbia)
    Television's Greatest Hits-#2-C . . . . (TVT)
Riders In The Sky; *Cowboy Songs* . . . . (Rounder)
Theme From ''Ren And Stimpy''
Original Soundtrack; *Television's Greatest Hits-#7-Cable Ready-C* . . . . . (TVT)
Theme From ''Rin Tin Tin''
Original Soundtrack; *Television's Greatest Hits-#1-C* . . . . (TVT)
Theme From ''Road Runner''
Original Soundtrack; *Television's Greatest Hits-#2-C* . . . . (TVT)
Theme From ''Roc''
Original Soundtrack; *Television's Greatest Hits-#7-Cable Ready-C* . . . . . (TVT)
Theme From ''Rockford Files''
Original Soundtrack; *Television's Greatest Hits-#3-1970s & 1980s-C* . . . . (TVT)
Theme From ''Room 222''
Original Soundtrack; *Television's Greatest Hits-#3-1970s & 1980s-C* . . . . (TVT)
Theme From ''Roots''
Original Soundtrack; *Television's Greatest Hits-#6-Remote Control-C* . . . (TVT)
Theme From ''Roseanne''
Original Soundtrack; *Television's Greatest Hits-#7-Cable Ready-C* . . . . . (TVT)
Theme From ''Route 66''
Nelson Riddle & His Orchestra; *Beat Generation* . . . . (Rhino)
    Television's Greatest Hits-#2-C . . . . (TVT)
Original Soundtrack; *CBS: The First 50 Years* . . . . (TVT)
Theme From ''Rowan And Martin's Laugh-In''
Original Soundtrack; *Television's Greatest Hits-#5-In Living Color-C* . . . (TVT)
Theme From ''Ruff And Reddy''
Original Soundtrack; *Hanna-Barbera Classics-#1-Original Recordings Of
    The World's Most Famous Cartoon Themes &
    Scores* . . . . (Kid Rhino/Rhino 4 Kids)
    *Hanna-Barbera Pic-A-Nic Basket Of Cartoon
    Classics* . . . . (Kid Rhino/Rhino 4 Kids)
Theme From ''S.W.A.T.''
Original Soundtrack; *Television's Greatest Hits-#3-1970s & 1980s-C* . . . . (TVT)
Rhythm Heritage; *Billboard Top Rock 'N' Roll Hits-1976-C* . . . . (Rhino)
Theme From ''Sanford & Son''
Original Soundtrack; *Television's Greatest Hits-#3-1970s & 1980s-C* . . . . (TVT)
Theme From ''Santa Barbara''
Original Soundtrack; *Soap Opera's Greatest Love Themes* . . . . (Scotti Bros.)
Theme From ''Saturday Night Live''
Original Soundtrack; *Television's Greatest Hits-#3-1970s & 1980s-C* . . . . (TVT)

Saturday Night Live Band; *Jazz...The Digital Age* . . . .(Pro Jazz)
Theme From "Saved By The Bell"
Original Soundtrack; *Television's Greatest Hits-#7-Cable Ready-C* . . . . . (TVT)
Theme From "Scooby Doo, Where Are You?"
Original Soundtrack; *Hanna-Barbera Classics-#1-Original Recordings Of The World's Most Famous Cartoon Themes & Scores* . . . . (Kid Rhino/Rhino 4 Kids)
Hanna-Barbera Pic-A-Nic Basket Of Cartoon Classics . . . . (Kid Rhino/Rhino 4 Kids)
Television's Greatest Hits-#3-1970s & 1980s-C . . . . (TVT)
Theme From "Sea Hunt"
Original Soundtrack; *Television's Greatest Hits-#2-C* . . . . (TVT)
Theme From "Secret Squirrel"
Original Soundtrack; *Hanna-Barbera Pic-A-Nic Basket Of Cartoon Classics* . . . . (Kid Rhino/Rhino 4 Kids)
Television's Greatest Hits-#5-In Living Color-C . . . . (TVT)
Theme From "Seinfeld"
Original Soundtrack; *Television's Greatest Hits-#7-Cable Ready-C* . . . . (TVT)
Theme From "Sesame Street"
Original Soundtrack; *Television's Greatest Hits-#3-1970s & 1980s-C* . . . (TVT)
Theme From "Silver Spoons"
Original Soundtrack; *Television's Greatest Hits-#6-Remote Control-C* . . (TVT)
Theme From "Simon And Simon"
Original Soundtrack; *Television's Greatest Hits-#3-1970s & 1980s-C* . . . (TVT)
Theme From "Siskel And Ebert"
Original Soundtrack; *Television's Greatest Hits-#6-Remote Control-C* . . (TVT)
Theme From "Sisters"
Original Soundtrack; *Television's Greatest Hits-#7-Cable Ready-C* . . . . (TVT)
Theme From "Sledge Hammer"
Original Soundtrack; *Television's Greatest Hits-#7-Cable Ready-C* . . . . (TVT)
Theme From "Soap"
Original Soundtrack; *Television's Greatest Hits-#6-Remote Control-C* . . (TVT)
Theme From "Solid Gold"
Original Soundtrack; *Television's Greatest Hits-#3-1970s & 1980s-C* . . . (TVT)
Theme From "Space Ghost Coast To Coast"
Original Soundtrack; *Television's Greatest Hits-#7-Cable Ready-C* . . . . (TVT)
Theme From "Spiderman"
Original Soundtrack; *Television's Greatest Hits-#2-C* . . . . (TVT)
Theme From "St. Elsewhere"
Dave Grusin; *Night-Lines* . . . . (GRP)
Original Soundtrack; *Television's Greatest Hits-#3-1970s & 1980s-C* . . . (TVT)
Theme From "Star Trek"
Cincinnati Pops Orchestra/Erich Kunzel; *Star Tracks II* . . . . (Telarc)
Theme From "Star Trek: The Next Generation"
Original Soundtrack; *Television's Greatest Hits-#7-Cable Ready-C* . . . . (TVT)
Theme From "Starsky & Hutch"
Original Soundtrack; *Television's Greatest Hits-#3-1970s & 1980s-C* . . . (TVT)
Theme From "Superman"
London Symphony Orchestra & John Williams; *ST/Superman-The Movie* . . . .(Warner Bros.)
Neil Norman; *Greatest Science Fiction Hits* . . . .(Crescendo)
Original Soundtrack; *Television's Greatest Hits-#1-C* . . . . (TVT)
Theme From "Surfside 6"
Original Soundtrack; *Television's Greatest Hits-#1-C* . . . . (TVT)
Theme From "T.J. Hooker"
Original Soundtrack; *Television's Greatest Hits-#6-Remote Control-C* . . (TVT)
Theme From "Tales From The Crypt"
Original Soundtrack; *Television's Greatest Hits-#7-Cable Ready-C* . . . . (TVT)
Theme From "Tarzan"
Original Soundtrack; *Television's Greatest Hits-#2-C* . . . . (TVT)
Theme From "Taxi"
Original Soundtrack; *Television's Greatest Hits-#3-1970s & 1980s-C* . . . (TVT)
Theme From "Ted Mack's Original Amateur Hour"
Original Soundtrack; *Television's Greatest Hits-#4-Black & White Classics-C* . . . . (TVT)
Theme From "Tennessee Tuxedo"
Original Soundtrack; *Television's Greatest Hits-#4-Black & White Classics-C* . . . . (TVT)
Theme From "That Girl"
Original Soundtrack; *Television's Greatest Hits-#2-C* . . . . (TVT)
Theme From "The Addams Family"
Original Soundtrack; *Television's Greatest Hits-#1-C* . . . . (TVT)
Vic Mizzy; *Elvira Presents Haunted Hits-C* . . . . (Rhino)
Haunted Hits-C . . . . (Rhino)
Original Music From "The Addams Family" . . . . (RCA)
Theme From "The Adventures Of Ozzie And Harriet"
Original Soundtrack; *Television's Greatest Hits-#4-Black & White Classics-C* . . . . (TVT)
Theme From "The Adventures Of Robin Hood"
Original Soundtrack; *Television's Greatest Hits-#2-C* . . . . (TVT)
Theme From "The Alvin Show"
Original Soundtrack; *Television's Greatest Hits-#3-1970s & 1980s-C* . . . (TVT)
Theme From "The Andy Griffith Show"
Original Soundtrack; *CBS: The First 50 Years* . . . . (TVT)
Television's Greatest Hits-#1-C . . . . (TVT)
Theme From "The Archies"
Original Soundtrack; *Television's Greatest Hits-#3-1970s & 1980s-C* . . . (TVT)

Theme From "The A-Team"
Original Soundtrack; *Television's Greatest Hits-#3-1970s & 1980s-C* . . . (TVT)
Theme From "The Atom Ant Show"
Original Soundtrack; *Hanna-Barbera Pic-A-Nic Basket Of Cartoon Classics* . . . .(Kid Rhino/Rhino 4 Kids)
Television's Greatest Hits-#5-In Living Color-C . . . . (TVT)
Theme From "The Avengers"
Original Soundtrack; *Television's Greatest Hits-#2-C* . . . . (TVT)
Theme From "The Beany & Cecil Show"
Original Soundtrack; *Television's Greatest Hits-#4-Black & White Classics-C* . . . . (TVT)
Theme From "The Beverly Hillbillies"
Original Soundtrack; *CBS: The First 50 Years* . . . . (TVT)
Television's Greatest Hits-#1-C . . . . (TVT)
Theme From "The Bionic Woman"
Original Soundtrack; *Television's Greatest Hits-#5-In Living Color-C* . . . (TVT)
Theme From "The Bob Hope Show" (Thanks For The Memories)
Original Soundtrack; *Television's Greatest Hits-#4-Black & White Classics-C* . . . . (TVT)
Theme From "The Bob Newhart Show"
Original Soundtrack; *CBS: The First 50 Years* . . . . (TVT)
Television's Greatest Hits-#3-1970s & 1980s-C . . . . (TVT)
Theme From "The Brady Bunch"
Brady Bunch Kids; *It's A Sunshine Day-Best Of The Brady Bunch Kids* . . . . (MCA)
Television's Greatest Hits-#2-C . . . . (TVT)
Theme From "The Brothers Grunt"
Original Soundtrack; *Television's Greatest Hits-#7-Cable Ready-C* . . . . (TVT)
Theme From "The Carol Burnett Show"
Original Soundtrack; *CBS: The First 50 Years* . . . . (TVT)
Theme From "The Cosby Show"
Original Soundtrack; *Television's Greatest Hits-#7-Cable Ready-C* . . . . (TVT)
Theme From "The Courtship Of Eddie's Father" (Best Friend)
Nilsson; *Television's Greatest Hits-#2-C* . . . . (TVT)
Theme From "The Dating Game"
Original Soundtrack; *Television's Greatest Hits-#5-In Living Color-C* . . . (TVT)
Theme From "The Days And Nights Of Molly Dodd"
Original Soundtrack; *Television's Greatest Hits-#7-Cable Ready-C* . . . . (TVT)
Theme From "The Dick Van Dyke Show"
Original Soundtrack; *CBS: The First 50 Years* . . . . (TVT)
Television's Greatest Hits-#1-C . . . . (TVT)
Theme From "The Donna Reed Show"
Original Soundtrack; *Donna Reed's Dinner Party-C* . . . .(Nick At Nite)
Television's Greatest Hits-#1-C . . . . (TVT)
TV Classic Themes: 25th Anniversary Edition-C . . . .(Breakable)
Theme From "The Dukes Of Hazzard"
Waylon Jennings; *Only Daddy That'll Walk The Line-The RCA Years* . . . .(RCA)
Television's Greatest Hits-#6-Remote Control-C . . . . (TVT)
Waylon Jennings' Greatest Hits-#2 . . . .(RCA)
Theme From "The Equalizer"
Original Soundtrack; *Television's Greatest Hits-#7-Cable Ready-C* . . . . (TVT)
Theme From "The F.B.I."
101 Strings Orchestra; *TV Themes* . . . . (Alshire)
Original Soundtrack; *Television's Greatest Hits-#1-C* . . . . (TVT)
Theme From "The Fall Guy"
Original Soundtrack; *Television's Greatest Hits-#6-Remote Control-C* . . . (TVT)
Theme From "The Felony Squad"
Original Soundtrack; *Television's Greatest Hits-#5-In Living Color-C* . . . (TVT)
Theme From "The Flintstones"
Original Soundtrack; *Hanna-Barbera Classics-#1-Original Recordings Of The World's Most Famous Cartoon Themes & Scores* . . . .(Kid Rhino/Rhino 4 Kids)
Hanna-Barbera Pic-A-Nic Basket Of Cartoon Classics . . . .(Kid Rhino/Rhino 4 Kids)
Television's Greatest Hits-#1-C . . . . (TVT)
Steve Hobbs; *Escape* . . . . (Cexton)
Theme From "The Flying Nun"
Original Soundtrack; *Television's Greatest Hits-#5-In Living Color-C* . . . (TVT)
Theme From "The Fugitive"
Original Soundtrack; *Television's Greatest Hits-#4-Black & White Classics-C* . . . . (TVT)
Theme From "The Ghost And Mrs. Muir"
Original Soundtrack; *Television's Greatest Hits-#5-In Living Color-C* . . . (TVT)
Theme From "The Girl From U.N.C.L.E."
Original Soundtrack; *Television's Greatest Hits-#5-In Living Color-C* . . . (TVT)
Theme From "The Green Hornet"
Original Soundtrack; *Television's Greatest Hits-#2-C* . . . . (TVT)
Theme From "The Guiding Light"
Rosemary Joyce & Bill Bartholomew; *Soap Opera Themes* . . . .(Crescendo)
Theme From "The Gumby Show"
Original Soundtrack; *Television's Greatest Hits-#4-Black & White Classics-C* . . . . (TVT)
Theme From "The Heights"
Original Soundtrack; *Television's Greatest Hits-#7-Cable Ready-C* . . . . (TVT)
Theme From "The High Chapparal"
Original Soundtrack; *Television's Greatest Hits-#5-In Living Color-C* . . . (TVT)

Theme From "The Honeymooners"
Original Soundtrack; *Television's Greatest Hits-#2-C* . . . . (TVT)
Theme From "The Jackie Gleason Show"
Original Soundtrack; *CBS: The First 50 Years* . . . . (TVT)
Television's Greatest Hits-#2-C . . . . (TVT)
Theme From "The Jeffersons"
Original Soundtrack; *CBS: The First 50 Years* . . . . (TVT)
Television's Greatest Hits-#3-1970s & 1980s-C . . . . (TVT)
Theme From "The Jetsons"
Original Soundtrack; *Hanna-Barbera Pic-A-Nic Basket Of Cartoon
Classics* . . . . (Kid Rhino/Rhino 4 Kids)
Television's Greatest Hits-#1-C . . . . (TVT)
Stunners; *ST/Jetsons-The Movie* . . . . (MCA)
Theme From "The Late Late Show"
Original Soundtrack; *Television's Greatest Hits-#1-C* . . . . . . (TVT)
Theme From "The Late Show With David Letterman"
Original Soundtrack; *CBS: The First 50 Years* . . . . (TVT)
Television's Greatest Hits-#7-Cable Ready-C . . . . (TVT)
Theme From "The Lawman"
Original Soundtrack; *Television's Greatest Hits-#4-Black & White
Classics-C* . . . . (TVT)
Theme From "The Life And Legend Of Wyatt Earp"
Original Soundtrack; *Television's Greatest Hits-#4-Black & White
Classics-C* . . . . (TVT)
Theme From "The Lone Ranger" (William Tell Overture)
Boston Pops Orchestra; *TV Classics-C* . . . . (RCA)
Boston Pops Orchestra/Arthur Fiedler; *Fiedler-Greatest Hits* . . . . (RCA)
Original Soundtrack; *Television's Greatest Hits-#7-Cable Ready-C* . . . . (TVT)
Spike Jones & His City Slickers; *Best Of Spike Jones & His City
Slickers* . . . . (RCA)
Theme From "The Love Boat"
Original Soundtrack; *Television's Greatest Hits-#3-1970s & 1980s-C* . . . . (TVT)
Theme From "The Man From U.N.C.L.E."
Challengers; *25 Greatest Instrumental Hits-C* . . . . (Crescendo)
Original Soundtrack; *Television's Greatest Hits-#1-C* . . . . . . (TVT)
The Man From U.N.C.L.E.: The Music From U.N.C.L.E. . . . . . . (Razor & Tie)
TV Classic Themes: 25th Anniversary Edition-C . . . . (Breakable)
Theme From "The Many Loves Of Dobie Gillis"
Original Soundtrack; *CBS: The First 50 Years* . . . . (TVT)
Television's Greatest Hits-#1-C . . . . (TVT)
TV Classic Themes: 25th Anniversary Edition-C . . . . (Breakable)
Theme From "The Mary Tyler Moore Show"
Original Soundtrack-Sonny Curtis; *CBS: The First 50 Years* . . . . (TVT)
Television's Greatest Hits-#2-C . . . . (TVT)
Theme From "The Monkees"
Monkees; *Monkees' Greatest Hits* . . . . (Rhino)
Original Soundtrack; *Television's Greatest Hits-#2-C* . . . . . . (TVT)
Theme From "The Munsters"
Original Soundtrack; *Television's Greatest Hits-#1-C* . . . . . . (TVT)
Theme From "The Muppet Show"
Muppets/Cast; *Muppet Hits* . . . . (Jim Henson)
Original Soundtrack; *Television's Greatest Hits-#3-1970s & 1980s-C* . . . . (TVT)
Theme From "The Name Of The Game"
Original Soundtrack; *Television's Greatest Hits-#3-1970s & 1980s-C* . . . . (TVT)
Theme From "The Nanny"
Original Soundtrack; *Television's Greatest Hits-#7-Cable Ready-C* . . . . (TVT)
Theme From "The Newlywed Game"
Original Soundtrack; *Television's Greatest Hits-#5-In Living Color-C* . . . (TVT)
Theme From "The Odd Couple"
Original Soundtrack; *Television's Greatest Hits-#7-Cable Ready-C* . . . . (TVT)
Theme From "The Patty Duke Show"
Original Soundtrack; *Just Patty: The Best Of Patty Duke* . . . . (EMI)
Television's Greatest Hits-#1-C . . . . (TVT)
Theme From "The People's Court"
Original Soundtrack; *Television's Greatest Hits-#6-Remote Control-C* . . . (TVT)
Theme From "The Price Is Right"
Original Soundtrack; *Television's Greatest Hits-#6-Remote Control-C* . . . (TVT)
Theme From "The Prisoner"
Neil Norman; *Greatest Science Fiction Hits* . . . . (Crescendo)
Theme From "The Real McCoys"
Original Soundtrack; *Television's Greatest Hits-#4-Black & White
Classics-C* . . . . (TVT)
Theme From "The Rebel"
Original Soundtrack; *Television's Greatest Hits-#2-C* . . . . . . (TVT)
Theme From "The Red Skelton Show"
Original Soundtrack; *CBS: The First 50 Years* . . . . (TVT)
Theme From "The Rifleman"
Cincinnati Pops Orchestra/Erich Kunzel; *Round-Up* . . . . (Telarc)
Original Soundtrack; *Television's Greatest Hits-#1-C* . . . . . . (TVT)
Theme From "The Rocky & Bullwinkle Show"
Original Soundtrack; *Television's Greatest Hits-#2-C* . . . . . . (TVT)
Theme From "The Rookies"
Original Soundtrack; *Television's Greatest Hits-#3-1970s & 1980s-C* . . . . (TVT)
Theme From "The Simpsons"
Original Soundtrack; *Television's Greatest Hits-#7-Cable Ready-C* . . . . (TVT)
Theme From "The Single Guy"
Original Soundtrack; *Television's Greatest Hits-#7-Cable Ready-C* . . . . (TVT)

Theme From "The Six Million Dollar Man"
Original Soundtrack; *Television's Greatest Hits-#5-In Living Color-C* . . . (TVT)
Theme From "The Smothers Brothers Comedy Hour"
Original Soundtrack; *Television's Greatest Hits-#2-C* . . . . . . (TVT)
Theme From "The Smurfs"
Original Soundtrack; *Television's Greatest Hits-#3-1970s & 1980s-C* . . . . (TVT)
Theme From "The Soupy Sales Show"
Original Soundtrack; *Television's Greatest Hits-#4-Black & White
Classics-C* . . . . (TVT)
Theme From "The Streets Of San Francisco"
Original Soundtrack; *Television's Greatest Hits-#3-1970s & 1980s-C* . . . . (TVT)
TV Cop Show Theme Songs . . . . (Laserlight)
Theme From "The Three Stooges"
Original Soundtrack; *Television's Greatest Hits-#2-C* . . . . . . (TVT)
Theme From "The Tonight Show"
Original Soundtrack; *Television's Greatest Hits-#1-C* . . . . . . (TVT)
Theme From "The Tracey Ullman Show"
Original Soundtrack; *Television's Greatest Hits-#7-Cable Ready-C* . . . . (TVT)
Theme From "The Twilight Zone"
Original Soundtrack; *CBS: The First 50 Years* . . . . (TVT)
Television's Greatest Hits-#1-C . . . . (TVT)
Theme From "The Untouchables"
Original Soundtrack; *Television's Greatest Hits-#4-Black & White
Classics-C* . . . . (TVT)
Theme From "The Virginian"
101 Strings Orchestra; *Western Themes-#1* . . . . (Alshire)
Original Soundtrack; *Television's Greatest Hits-#2-C* . . . . . . (TVT)
Theme From "The Waltons"
Original Soundtrack; *CBS: The First 50 Years* . . . . (TVT)
Television's Greatest Hits-#3-1970s & 1980s-C . . . . (TVT)
Theme From "The Woody Woodpecker Show"
Original Soundtrack; *Television's Greatest Hits-#1-C* . . . . . . (TVT)
Theme From "Three's Company"
Original Soundtrack; *Television's Greatest Hits-#3-1970s & 1980s-C* . . . . (TVT)
Theme From "Top Cat"
Original Soundtrack; *Hanna-Barbera Pic-A-Nic Basket Of Cartoon
Classics* . . . . (Kid Rhino/Rhino 4 Kids)
Television's Greatest Hits-#1-C . . . . (TVT)
Theme From "Touche Turtle"
Original Soundtrack; *Hanna-Barbera Classics-#1-Original Recordings Of
The World's Most Famous Cartoon Themes &
Scores* . . . . (Kid Rhino/Rhino 4 Kids)
*Hanna-Barbera Pic-A-Nic Basket Of Cartoon
Classics* . . . . (Kid Rhino/Rhino 4 Kids)
Theme From "Trapper John, M.D."
Original Soundtrack; *Television's Greatest Hits-#6-Remote Control-C* . . . (TVT)
Theme From "Twelve O'Clock High"
Original Soundtrack; *Television's Greatest Hits-#2-C* . . . . . . (TVT)
Theme From "Twin Peaks"
Original Soundtrack; *Television's Greatest Hits-#7-Cable Ready-C* . . . . (TVT)
Theme From "Underdog"
Original Soundtrack; *Television's Greatest Hits-#2-C* . . . . . . (TVT)
Theme From "Unsolved Mysteries"
Original Soundtrack; *Television's Greatest Hits-#7-Cable Ready-C* . . . . (TVT)
Theme From "Vegas"
Original Soundtrack; *Television's Greatest Hits-#6-Remote Control-C* . . . (TVT)
Theme From "Voyage To The Bottom Of The Sea"
Original Soundtrack; *Television's Greatest Hits-#2-C* . . . . . . (TVT)
Theme From "Wagon Train"
Original Soundtrack; *Television's Greatest Hits-#2-C* . . . . . . (TVT)
Theme From "Walker, Texas Ranger"
Original Soundtrack; *CBS: The First 50 Years* . . . . (TVT)
Theme From "Wally Gator"
Original Soundtrack; *Hanna-Barbera Classics-#1-Original Recordings Of
The World's Most Famous Cartoon Themes &
Scores* . . . . (Kid Rhino/Rhino 4 Kids)
*Hanna-Barbera Pic-A-Nic Basket Of Cartoon
Classics* . . . . (Kid Rhino/Rhino 4 Kids)
Theme From "Wayne's World"
Mike Myers & Dana Carvey; *ST/Wayne's World* . . . . (Reprise)
Theme From "Webster" (Then Came You)
Original Soundtrack; *Television's Greatest Hits-#6-Remote Control-C* . . . (TVT)
Theme From "What's Happening?"
Original Soundtrack; *Television's Greatest Hits-#6-Remote Control-C* . . . (TVT)
Theme From "Where In The World Is Carmen Sandiego?"
Original Soundtrack; *Television's Greatest Hits-#7-Cable Ready-C* . . . . (TVT)
Theme From "Wild Wild West"
Original Soundtrack; *CBS: The First 50 Years* . . . . (TVT)
Television's Greatest Hits-#1-C . . . . (TVT)
Theme From "Wings"
Original Soundtrack; *Television's Greatest Hits-#7-Cable Ready-C* . . . . (TVT)
Theme From "WKRP In Cincinnati"
Original Soundtrack; *CBS: The First 50 Years* . . . . (TVT)
Television's Greatest Hits-#3-1970s & 1980s-C . . . . (TVT)
Steve Carlisle; *Steve Carlisle Sings WKRP* . . . . (MCA)
Theme From "Wonder Woman"
Original Soundtrack; *Television's Greatest Hits-#3-1970s & 1980s-C* . . . . (TVT)

Theme From "Yakky Doodle"
Original Soundtrack; *Hanna-Barbera Classics-#1-Original Recordings Of The World's Most Famous Cartoon Themes & Scores* . . . . (Kid Rhino/Rhino 4 Kids)
Hanna-Barbera Pic-A-Nic Basket Of Cartoon Classics . . . . (Kid Rhino/Rhino 4 Kids)

Theme From "Yogi Bear"
Original Soundtrack; *Hanna-Barbera Classics-#1-Original Recordings Of The World's Most Famous Cartoon Themes & Scores* . . . . (Kid Rhino/Rhino 4 Kids)
Hanna-Barbera Pic-A-Nic Basket Of Cartoon Classics . . . . (Kid Rhino/Rhino 4 Kids)
Television's Greatest Hits-#1-C . . . . (TVT)

Theme From "Zorro"
Original Soundtrack; *Disney Collection-#2-C* . . . . (Disney)

There Ain't S... On T.V. Tonight
Minutemen; *Double Nickels On The Dime* . . . . (SST)

This Ain't Dallas
Hank Williams, Jr.; *Five-O* . . . . (WB/Curb)
Hank Williams, Jr.'s Greatest Hits III . . . . (Curb)

Top Of The Pops
Kinks; *Everybody's In Show-Biz* . . . . (Rhino)
Lola Versus Powerman And The Moneygoround, Part One . . . . . (Reprise)

Top Of The Pops
Smithereens; *Blow Up* . . . . (Capitol)

Turn It On Again
Genesis; *Duke* . . . . (Atlantic)
Three Sides Live . . . . (Atlantic)

Turn Me On
Tubes; *Remote Control* . . . . (A&M)
T.R.A.S.H. (Tubes Rarities And Smash Hits) . . . . (A&M)

TV
Dwight Twilley Band; *Sincerely* . . . . (MCA)

TV
Flying Lizards; *Flying Lizards* . . . . (Virgin)

TV Age
Joe Jackson; *Night & Day* . . . . (A&M)

TV Blues
Mick Clarke Band; *Steel & Fire* . . . . (Burnside)

TV Blues
Country Joe McDonald; *Goodbye Blues* . . . . (Fantasy)

TV Blues
Bob Mintzer Big Band; *Only In New York* . . . . (Digital Music Prod.)

TV Caesar
Procol Harum; *Grand Hotel* . . . . (Chrysalis)

TV Dinners
ZZ Top; *Eliminator* . . . . (Warner Bros.)

TV Dreams
Charlie; *Fantasy Girls* . . . . (Columbia)

TV Eye
Iggy & The Stooges; *Legends Of Rock Guitar-'70s-C* . . . . (Rhino)
Stooges; *Elektrock-Sixties-C* . . . . (Elektra)
Fun House . . . . (Elektra)

TV Guide
Graham Nash; *Earth & Sky* . . . . (Capitol)

TV Is King
Tubes; *Remote Control* . . . . (A&M)

TV Mama
Big Joe Turner; *Atlantic Blues-Guitar-C* . . . . (Atlantic)
Texas Style . . . . (Evidence Music)
Dizzy Gillespie & Others; *Trumpet Kings Meet Joe Turner* . . . . (Pablo)
Freddie King; *Freddie King* . . . . (RSO)
Johnny Winter; *Nothin' But The Blues* . . . . (Blue Sky)

TV Mama
Leon Haywood; *It's Me Again* . . . . (Casablanca)

TV Movie
Bruce Springsteen; *Tracks* . . . . (Columbia)

TV Party
Black Flag; *7-Inch Wonders Of The World-C* . . . . (SST)
Damaged . . . . (SST)
ST/Repo Man . . . . (MCA)

TV Preacher Man Blues
Glenn Sutton; *Close Encounters Of The Sutton Kind* . . . . (Mercury)

TV Private Eye
Now; *Now* . . . . (Maison De Soul)

TV Psychology
Rockwell; *Rockwell-Captured* . . . . (Motown)

TV Savage
Bow Wow Wow; *I Want Candy* . . . . (RCA)

TV Set
Cramps; *Bad Music For Bad People* . . . . (I.R.S.)
Songs The Lord Taught Us . . . . (I.R.S.)

TV Snooze
Nina Hagen; *Fearless* . . . . (Columbia)

Video
Jeff Lynne; *ST/Electric Dreams* . . . . (Epic)

Video
India.Arie; *Acoustic Soul* . . . . (Motown)

Video Blues
Hank Williams, Jr.; *Major Moves* . . . . (WB/Curb)

Video Games
Ronnie Jones; *Best Of Lollipop Records* . . . . (Hot Prod.)

Video Killed The Radio Star
Bruce Woolley & The Camera Club; *Bruce Woolley & The Camera Club* . . . . (Columbia)
Buggles; *Age Of Plastic* . . . . (Island)
Rock Of The '80s-#2-C . . . . (Priority)
The Island Story-1962-1987-25th Anniversary-C . . . . (Island)

Video Shop
Kinks; *Lost & Found-1986-1989* . . . . (MCA)
Think Visual . . . . (MCA Special Prod.)

Video Tape
Steve Goodman; *Say It In Private* . . . . (Asylum)

Video Violence
Lou Reed; *Between Thought & Expression-Anthology* . . . . (RCA)

Vidiot
Ken Nordine; *Best Of Word Jazz-#1* . . . . (Rhino)

Watching TV
Charlie; *Lines* . . . . (Janus)

Watching TV (With The Radio On)
Barefoot Jerry; *Watching TV (With The Radio On)* . . . . (Monument)

Western Movies (My Baby Loves)
Olympics; *All-Time Greatest Hits Of Rock 'N' Roll-C* . . . . (Curb)
American Graffiti-#3-C . . . . (MCA)
Best Of The Olympics . . . . (Vee-Jay)
Jumpin' Jive '50s-C . . . . (Priority)

What's On Tonight
Montell Jordan; *More...* . . . . (Mercury)

With The T.V. On
Invaders; *Singles-Great New York Singles Scene* . . . . (Roir)

You Get A Little Extra When You Watch TV
Peter Alsop; *Wha' D' Ya Wanna Do* . . . . (Flying Fish)

THINKING & KNOWING, Awareness, Beliefs, Brains, Enlightenment, Ideas, Ignorance, Information, Insight, Intelligence, Knowledge, Mentality, Mind, Opinions, Smart, Understanding

See Also: ADVICE, DECISIONS, EGO, FOOLS, LIFE, MACHINES, PRETEND, QUESTIONS & ANSWERS, REMEMBER, SCHOOL, STRANGE, WARNINGS

(This Ain't) No Thinkin' Thing
Trace Adkins; *Dreamin' Out Loud* . . . . (Capitol)

(You're The) Devil In Disguise
Elvis Presley; *Elvis' Gold Records, Volume 4* . . . . (RCA)
The Top Ten Hits . . . . (RCA)

10,000 Horses
Candlebox; *Happy Pills* . . . . (Maverick)

26 Cents
Wilkinsons; *Nothing But Love* . . . . (Giant)

Across The Universe
Beatles; *Let It Be* . . . . (Capitol)
Past Masters-Volume Two . . . . (Parlophone)
Rarities . . . . (Capitol)
The Beatles/1967-1970 . . . . (Capitol)
David Bowie; *Young Americans* . . . . (Rykodisc)

Alfie
Barbra Streisand; *What About Today* . . . . (Columbia)
Dionne Warwick; *Dionne Warwick Greatest Hits* . . . . (Everest)
Dionne Warwick-Anthology 1962-1971 . . . . (Rhino)

All At Once You Love Her
Perry Como; *Perry Como's Greatest Hits* . . . . (RCA)

All Day Thinkin'
Babyface; *The Day* . . . . (Epic)

All For You
Sister Hazel; *...Somewhere More Familiar* . . . . (Universal)
Sister Hazel . . . . (Universal)

All I Do
Somethin' For The People; *This Time It's Personal* . . . . (Warner Bros.)

All I Do Is Think Of You
Jackson 5; *Baddest Love Jams-Volume 3-After The Dance-C* . . . . (Motown)
Jackson 5-Anthology . . . . (Motown)
Troop; *Attitude* . . . . (Atlantic)

All I Know
Screaming Trees; *Dust* . . . . (Epic)

All I Know
Art Garfunkel; *Angel Clare* . . . . (Columbia)
Garfunkel . . . . (Columbia)

All I Need To Know
Kenny Chesney; *All I Need To Know* . . . . (BNA)
Kenny Chesney's Greatest Hits . . . . (BNA)

All Mixed Up
311; *311* ....(Capricorn)
Almost Home
Mary Chapin Carpenter; *Party Doll And Other Favorites* ....(Columbia)
Already Home
Marc Cohn; *Burning The Daze* ....(Atlantic)
Always On My Mind
Willie Nelson; *Always On My Mind* ....(Columbia)
Super Hits Of The '80s-C ....(Epic)
Willie Nelson-Super Hits ....(Columbia)
Always The Last To Know
Del Amitri; *Change Everything* ....(A&M)
Am I Dreaming
Ol Skool featuring Keith Sweat & Xscape; *Ol Skool* ....(Keia/Universal)
Am I Getting Through (Part I & II)
Sheryl Crow; *The Globe Sessions* ....(A&M)
Analyse
Cranberries; *Wake Up And Smell The Coffee* ....(MCA)
Another Brick In The Wall, Part 2
Class Of '99; *ST/The Faculty* ....(Columbia)
Pink Floyd; *Collection Of Great Dance Songs* ....(Columbia)
Delicate Sound Of Thunder ....(Columbia)
The Wall ....(Columbia)
Roger Waters; *The Wall-Live In Berlin* ....(Mercury)
Anthem For The Year 2000
Silverchair; *Neon Ballroom* ....(Epic)
Anytime
Brian McKnight; *Anytime* ....(Motown)
Now That's What I Call Music!-#1-C ....(Virgin)
Aquarius
Original Broadway Cast; *Hair* ....(RCA)
Are You Experienced?
Jimi Hendrix; *Kiss The Sky* ....(Reprise)
Jimi Hendrix Experience; *Are You Experienced?* ....(Reprise)
Essential Jimi Hendrix ....(Reprise)
Are You There?
Oleander; *Unwind* ....(Republic/Universal)
Army
Ben Folds Five; *The Unauthorized Biography Of Reinhold Messner* ....(550 Music)
As If You Read My Mind
Stevie Wonder; *Hotter Than July* ....(Motown)
Away
Toadies; *Rubberneck* ....(Interscope)
Back 2 Good
Matchbox Twenty; *Yourself Or Someone Like You* ....(Lava)
Bad Day
Fuel; *Now That's What I Call Music!-#8-C* ....(Virgin)
Something Like Human ....(Epic)
Beat Goes On, The
Sonny & Cher; *Best Of Sonny & Cher* ....(Atco)
Hit Singles-1958-1977-C ....(Atlantic)
Sonny & Cher-Live ....(MCA)
The Beat Goes On-Best Of Sonny & Cher ....(Rhino)
Two Of Us ....(Atco)
Beginning, The
Keb' Mo'; *The Door* ....(550/Epic/Okeh)
Bible Tells Me So
Don Cornell; *Rock 'N Roll Reunion: Class Of '55-C* ....(Madacy)
Bird Brain Baby
Mercy Dee Walton; *Back Luck 'N' Trouble* ....(Arhoolie)
Birdbrain
Tom Buffalo; *Birdbrain* ....(Beggar's Banquet)
Bird-Brain Rag
Max Morath; *The World Of Scott Joplin-#2* ....(Vanguard)
Black Chick, White Guy
Kid Rock; *Devil Without A Cause* ....(Top Dog/Lava/Atlantic)
Both Sides Now
Joni Mitchell; *Clouds* ....(Reprise)
Judy Collins; *Colors Of The Day-The Best Of Judy Collins* ....(Elektra)
So Early In The Spring, The First 15 Years ....(Elektra)
Wildflowers ....(Elektra)
Neil Diamond; *Neil Diamond-Gold* ....(MCA)
Neil Diamond-Love Songs ....(MCA)
Rainbow ....(MCA)
Touching You Touching Me ....(MCA)
Brain Damage
Pink Floyd; *Dark Side Of The Moon* ....(Capitol)
Pink Floyd-Gift Set ....(Capitol)
Works ....(Capitol)
Brain Of J.
Pearl Jam; *Yield* ....(Epic)
Brain Stew
Green Day; *Insomniac* ....(Reprise)
Brian Wilson
Barenaked Ladies; *Gordon* ....(Reprise)
Rock Spectacle ....(Reprise)

Brilliant Disguise
Bruce Springsteen; *Bruce Springsteen's Greatest Hits* ....(Columbia)
Tunnel Of Love ....(Columbia)
Burning A Hole In My Mind
Connie Smith; *Essential Connie Smith* ....(RCA)
But Anyway
Blues Traveler; *Blues Traveler* ....(A&M)
Live From The Fall ....(A&M)
By Your Side
Sade; *Lovers Rock* ....(Epic)
Can I Change My Mind
Tyrone Davis; *Soul Shots-#2-The ''In'' Crowd-Sweet Soul-C* ......(Rhino)
Tyrone Davis' Greatest Hits ....(Rhino)
Can I Get To Know You Better
Turtles; *Best Of The Turtles-Golden Archive Series.* ....(Rhino)
Turtles-20 Greatest Hits ....(Rhino)
Can't Fight The Moonlight
LeAnn Rimes; *ST/Coyote Ugly* ....(London Sire/Curb)
Carlene
Phil Vassar; *Phil Vassar* ....(Arista)
Carmen
Paula Cole; *This Fire* ....(Imago)
Casey Jones
Grateful Dead; *Best Of The Grateful Dead-Skeletons From The Closet* ....(Warner Bros.)
Bill Graham Presents The Last Days Of The Fillmore-C ....(Epic Portrait Assoc.)
Workingman's Dead ....(Warner Bros.)
Jerry Garcia Acoustic Band; *Almost Acoustic* ....(Grateful Dead)
Change My Mind
John Berry; *Faces* ....(Capitol)
Change Your Mind
Neil Young & Crazy Horse; *Sleeps With Angels* ....(Reprise)
Change Your Mind
Sister Hazel; *Fortress* ....(Universal)
Charlie Brown's Parents
Dishwalla; *Pet Your Friends* ....(A&M)
Chemistry
Semisonic; *All About Chemistry* ....(MCA)
Choose
Color Me Badd; *Time And Chance* ....(Giant)
Church Of The Poison Mind
Culture Club; *At Worst...The Best Of Boy George And Culture Club* .....(SBK)
Colour By Numbers ....(Virgin)
C'mon Marianne
4 Seasons; *25th Anniversary Collection* ....(Rhino)
4 Seasons-Anthology ....(Rhino)
Cocaine Blues
Dave Van Ronk; *Folksinger* ....(Prestige)
Inside Dave Van Ronk ....(Fantasy)
Troubadours Of The Folk Era-#1-C ....(Rhino)
David Bromberg; *My Own House* ....(Fantasy)
George Thorogood & The Destroyers; *Move It On Over* ....(Rounder)
Jackson Browne; *Running On Empty* ....(Asylum)
Johnny Cash; *Essential Johnny Cash* ....(Columbia)
Johnny Cash At Folsom Prison & San Quentin ....(Columbia)
Silver ....(Columbia)
Lonnie Mack; *Road Houses & Dance Halls* ....(Epic)
Reverend Gary Davis; *From Blues To Gospel* ....(Biograph)
Cocaine in My Brain
Dillinger; *Classic Reggae-#1-C* ....(Profile)
Planet Reggae-World Of Reggae Music ....(Rhythm Safari)
Cocoon
Bjork; *Vespertine* ....(Elektra)
Cold Cold Heart
Hank Williams; *Complete Hank Williams* ....(Mercury)
Hank Williams With His Drifting Cowboys; *24 Of Hank Williams' Greatest Hits* ....(Polydor)
Hank Williams ....(MGM)
Hank Williams-40 Greatest Hits ....(Polydor)
Live At Opry ....(MGM)
Long Gone Lonesome Blues ....(Polydor)
Jerry Lee Lewis; *Duets* ....(Sun)
Golden Cream Of Jerry Lee Lewis ....(Sun)
Jerry Lee Lewis & Friends-Duets ....(Sun)
Lucinda Williams; *Timeless: Hank Williams Tribute-C* ....(Lost Highway/IDJMG)
Tony Bennett; *Tony Bennett-16 Most Requested Songs* ....(Legacy)
Come With Me
Shai; *Blackface* ....(Gasoline Alley)
Computer Minds
Leroy Jenkins; *Live!* ....(Black Saint)
Cool Relax
Jon B.; *Cool Relax* ....(Yab Yum/550)
Couldn't Last A Moment
Collin Raye; *Tracks* ....(Epic)
Cowboy's Wild Song To His Herd
Skip Gorman; *A Cowboy's Wild Song To His Herd* ....(Rounder)

Crawling In The Dark
Hoobastank; *Hoobastank* . . . .(Island/IDJMG)
Crazy
K-Ci & JoJo; *Now That's What I Call Music!-#6-C* . . . . (Virgin)
X. . . . .(MCA)
Crazy For This Girl
Evan And Jaron; *Evan And Jaron* . . . . (Columbia)
Now That's What I Call Music!-#6-C . . . . (Virgin)
Cry Of The Wild Goose
Frankie Laine; *Frankie Laine-Golden Hits* . . . . (Mercury)
Crystal Blue Persuasion
Tommy James And The Shondells; *Best Of Tommy James And The Shondells* . . . . (Roulette)
Tommy James And The Shondells-Anthology . . . . (Rhino)
Daddy's Come Around
Paul Overstreet; *Heroes* . . . . (RCA)
Dandelion
Rolling Stones; *More Hot Rocks (big hits & fazed cookies)* . . . . (Abkco)
Through The Past, Darkly (Big Hits Vol. 2) . . . . (Abkco)
Dawn (Go Away)
4 Seasons; *25th Anniversary Collection* . . . . (Rhino)
4 Seasons-Anthology . . . . (Rhino)
Daydreamin'
Tatyana Ali; *Kiss The Sky* . . . . (MJJ Music/Work)
Deeper Than You Think
George Benson; *Absolute Benson* . . . . (GRP/VMG)
Did You Ever Have To Make Up Your Mind?
Lovin' Spoonful; *Best Of The Lovin' Spoonful* . . . . (Rhino)
Lovin' Spoonful-Anthology . . . . (Rhino)
Did You Ever Love Somebody
Jessica Simpson; *Songs From Dawson's Creek* . . . . (Sony Music Soundtrax)
Did You Ever Think
R. Kelly; *R.* . . . . (Jive)
Didn't Cha Know
Erykah Badu; *Mama's Gun* . . . . (Motown)
Diving To Be Deeper
Sinead Lohan; *No Mermaid* . . . . (Grapevine)
Do You Know (What It Takes)
Robyn; *Robyn Is Here* . . . . (RCA)
Do You Know You Are My Sunshine
Statler Brothers; *Statler Brothers-30th Anniversary Celebration* . . . . . (Mercury)
Do You Want To Know A Secret
Beatles; *Introducing...The Beatles* . . . . (Vee-Jay)
Please Please Me . . . . (Parlophone)
The Early Beatles . . . . (Capitol)
Does Your Mother Know?
Abba; *Abba Live* . . . . (Atlantic)
Abba's Greatest Hits-#2 . . . . (Atlantic)
The Singles-First 10 Years . . . . (Atlantic)
Voulez-Vous . . . . (Atlantic)
Dolphin's Thoughts
Jay B. Jay; *Dream Machine* . . . . (Innovative Comm.)
Over Seas . . . . (Innovative Comm.)
Don't Be Cruel
Cheap Trick; *Cheap Trick's Greatest Hits* . . . . (Epic)
Lap Of Luxury . . . . (Epic)
Elvis Presley; *Billboard Top Rock 'N' Roll Hits-1956-C* . . . . (Rhino)
Nipper's Greatest Hits Of The '50s-#2-C . . . . (RCA)
Number One Hits . . . . (RCA)
The Great Performances . . . . (RCA)
The Top Ten Hits . . . . (RCA)
Judds; *Heartland* . . . . (MCA)
Don't Be Stupid (You Know I Love You)
Shania Twain; *Come On Over* . . . . (Mercury)
Don't Get Me Wrong
Pretenders; *Get Close* . . . . (Sire)
Pretenders-The Singles . . . . (Sire)
Don't Know Much
Linda Ronstadt & Aaron Neville; *Chicken Soup For The Couples Soul-C* . . . . (Rhino)
Cry Like A Rainstorm-Howl Like The Wind . . . . (Elektra)
Don't Make Love To Mary
Merle Travis; *Johnny Gimble's Texas Honky-Tonk Hits-C* . . . . .(C.M.H. Prod.)
Don't Stop
Elton John; *Legacy-A Tribute To Fleetwood Mac's Rumours-C* . . . . . . (Lava)
Fleetwood Mac; *25 Years-The Chain* . . . .(Warner Bros.)
Fleetwood Mac Live . . . .(Warner Bros.)
Fleetwood Mac's Greatest Hits . . . .(Warner Bros.)
Rumours . . . .(Warner Bros.)
Don't Think I'm Not
Kandi; *Hey Kandi* . . . .(So So Def/Columbia)
Now That's What I Call Music!-#5-C . . . . (Virgin)
Don't Think You're Smart
Memphis Slim; *Raining The Blues* . . . . (Fantasy)
Don't Use Your Penis (For A Brain)
Romanovsky & Phillips; *Trouble In Paradise* . . . . (Fresh Fruit)
Don't You Get It
Mark Knopfler; *Golden Heart* . . . .(Warner Bros.)

Don't You Just Know It
Huey "Piano" Smith; *New Orleans Party Classics-C* . . . . (Rhino)
Huey "Piano" Smith And The Clowns; *Oldies But Goodies-#3-C* . . . . (Original Sound)
Don't You Know
Keb' Mo'; *The Door* . . . . (550/Epic/Okeh)
Don't You Know I Care
Cleo Laine; *Solitude* . . . . (RCA Victor)
Duke Ellington; *Black, Brown & Beige: 1944-1946 Band Recordings* . . . . (Bluebird)
Joe Williams; *Every Day: The Best Of The Verve Years* . . . . (Verve)
Don't You Know What The Night Can Do?
Steve Winwood; *Roll With It* . . . . (Virgin)
Door, The
Keb' Mo'; *The Door* . . . . (550/Epic/Okeh)
Down Low (Nobody Has To Know)
R. Kelly; *R. Kelly* . . . . (Jive)
D'You Know What I Mean
Oasis; *Be Here Now* . . . . (Epic)
E.T.I. (Extra Terrestrial Intelligence)
Blue Oyster Cult; *Agents Of Fortune* . . . . (Columbia)
Career Of Evil . . . . (Columbia)
Extraterrestrial Live . . . . (Columbia)
Some Enchanted Evening . . . . (Columbia)
Ease My Mind
Arrested Development; *Zingalamaduni* . . . . (Chrysalis)
Einstein On The Beach
Counting Crows; *August And Everything After* . . . .(David Geffen Co.)
Elderly Woman Behind The Counter In A Small Town
Pearl Jam; *Vs.* . . . . (Epic Portrait Assoc.)
End Of The Innocence
Don Henley; *The End Of The Innocence* . . . . (Geffen)
End Of The World
Skeeter Davis; *Best Of Skeeter Davis* . . . . (Gusto)
Billboard Top Country Hits-1963-C . . . . (Rhino)
Nipper's Greatest Hits Of The '60s-#1-C . . . . (RCA)
Stars Of The Grand Ole Opry-1926-1974-C . . . . (RCA)
Super Country Hits Of The '60s-C . . . . (Gusto)
Espresso Logic
Chris Rea; *Espresso Logic* . . . . (East West)
Eugene You Genius
Bryan White; *Bryan White* . . . . (Asylum)
Everlasting Glaze
Smashing Pumpkins; *Machina: The Machines Of God* . . . . (Virgin)
Every Little Thing I Do
Soul For Real; *100% Party-Hits Of The '90s-#2-C* . . . . (Priority)
Candy Rain . . . . (Uptown/MCA)
Every Morning
Keb' Mo'; *Keb' Mo'* . . . . (Okeh)
Everybody Knows
Trisha Yearwood; *Everybody Knows* . . . . (MCA)
Everybody's Talkin'
Nilsson; *Everybody's Talkin': The Encore Collection* . . . . (BMG Special Prod.)
ST/Forrest Gump . . . .(Epic/Sony Music Soundtrax)
ST/Midnight Cowboy . . . . (EMI)
Willie Nelson; *Best Of Willie* . . . . (RCA)
Sweet Memories . . . . (RCA)
Everything To Everyone
Everclear; *Ka-Boom!-C* . . . . (Beast)
So Much For The Afterglow . . . . (Capitol)
Everything You Want
Vertical Horizon; *Everything You Want* . . . . (RCA)
Totally Hits-#3-C . . . . (Atlantic)
Evil On Your Mind
Jan Howard; *Grand Ladies Of The Opry-C* . . . . (Deluxe)
Ex-Girlfriend
No Doubt; *Return Of Saturn* . . . . (Interscope)
Extra Pale
Goo Goo Dolls; *Dizzy Up The Girl* . . . .(Warner Sunset/Reprise)
Faded Love
Bob Wills & His Texas Playboys; *Bob Wills & His Texas Playboys-24 Great Hits* . . . . (Polydor)
For The Last Time . . . . (Capitol)
Tiffany Transcriptions-#2-Best Of The Tiffanys . . . . (Rhino)
Mickey Gilley; *Mickey Gilley's Greatest Hits-#1* . . . . (Epic)
Patsy Cline; *12 Greatest Hits* . . . . (MCA)
Shawn Colvin & Lyle Lovett & Asleep At The Wheel; *Ride With Bob-C* . . . . (DreamWorks/SKG)
Willie Nelson; *Greatest Hits (& Some That Will Be)* . . . . (Columbia)
Fastlove
George Michael; *Ladies & Gentlemen: The Best Of George Michael* . . . . . (Epic)
Older . . . .(DreamWorks/SKG)
Fever
Buddy Guy; *This Is Buddy Guy* . . . . (Vanguard)
Elvis Presley; *A Valentine Gift For You* . . . . (RCA)
Aloha from Hawaii via Satellite . . . . (RCA)
Elvis Presley-Pure Gold . . . . (RCA)
Little Willie John; *Best Of Little Willie John-Fever* . . . . (Rhino)

Peggy Lee; *Memories Are Made Of This-C* .... (Capitol)
Rita Coolidge; *Rita Coolidge-Classics-#5* .... (A&M)
   Rita Coolidge's Greatest Hits .... (A&M)
Fire Escape
Fastball; *All The Pain Money Can Buy* .... (Hollywood)
Fixing A Hole
Beatles; *Sgt. Pepper's Lonely Hearts Club Band* .... (Capitol)
Flyin' High In The Friendly Sky
Marvin Gaye; *What's Going On* .... (Motown)
Foggy Notion
Velvet Underground; *V.U.* .... (Verve)
For The First Time
Kenny Loggins; *ST/One Fine Day* .... (Columbia)
Four Leaf Clover
Abra Moore; *Strangest Places* .... (Arista Austin)
Free To Go
Folk Implosion; *One Part Lullaby* .... (Interscope)
Free Your Mind
En Vogue; *Funky Divas* .... (East West)
Freek'n You
Jodeci; *MTV Party To Go-#7-C* .... (Tommy Boy)
   The Show, The After-Party, The Hotel .... (Uptown/MCA)
Friday On My Mind
David Bowie; *Bowie Pin Ups* .... (Rykodisc)
Easybeats; *Best Of The Easybeats* .... (Rhino)
   Nuggets-Classic Collection From The Psychedelic '60s-C .... (Rhino)
Funny Familiar Forgotten Feelings
Don Gibson; *Best Of Don Gibson-#1* .... (Curb)
Mandy Barnett; *I've Got A Right To Cry* .... (Sire)
Tom Jones; *Back To Back-Greatest Hits* .... (Rebound)
   Country Side Of Tom Jones .... (London)
   Tom Jones-London Collector-Greatest Hits .... (London)
Gentle On My Mind
Elvis Presley; *From Elvis In Memphis* .... (RCA)
   Great Country Songs .... (RCA)
Glen Campbell; *Best Of Austin City Limits-Legends Of Country*
   Music-C .... (Legacy)
   Best Of Glen Campbell .... (Capitol)
   Glen Campbell-Best Of The Early Years .... (Curb)
John Hartford; *Me Oh My-How The Time Does Fly-Anthology* ..... (Flying Fish)
Patti Page; *Patti Page-16 Most Requested Songs* .... (Legacy)
Gentleman Is A Dope
Jo Stafford; *Jo Stafford's Greatest Hits* .... (Curb)
Morgana King; *Another Time Another Space* .... (Muse)
Georgia On My Mind
Billie Holiday; *God Bless The Child* .... (Columbia)
   The Billie Holiday Story-#2 .... (Columbia)
Hoagy Carmichael; *Hoagy Carmichael-Legendary Performer* .... (RCA)
   Hoagy Sings Carmichael .... (EMI)
Mildred Bailey; *Harlem Lullaby* .... (ASV)
Preservation Hall Jazz Band; *Best Of The Preservation Hall*
   Jazz Band .... (Columbia)
Ray Charles; *Ray Charles' Greatest Hits-#2* .... (Rhino)
   Ray Charles-Anthology .... (Rhino)
Willie Nelson; *Greatest Hits (& Some That Will Be)* ... (Columbia)
   Stardust .... (Legacy)
   Willie & Family Live .... (Columbia)
Getting To Know You
Original Broadway Cast; *The King And I* .... (RCA Victor)
Original Cast; *ST/The King And I* .... (Angel)
   The King And I .... (MCA)
Ghost-Town Of My Brain
Jim White; *No Such Place* .... (Luaka Bop)
Girl Inside My Head
Blues Traveler; *Bridge* .... (A&M)
Girl You Know It's True
Milli Vanilli; *All Or Nothing* .... (Arista)
   Girl You Know It's True .... (Arista)
Give It Up Or Let Me Go
Dixie Chicks; *Wide Open Spaces* .... (Monument)
God Knows
Debby Boone; *Best Of Debby Boone* .... (Curb)
   Best Of Debby Boone .... (MCA)
   Midstream .... (Warner Bros.)
God Knows
Bob Dylan; *Under The Red Sky* .... (Columbia)
God Knows I'm Good
David Bowie; *Space Oddity* .... (Rykodisc)
God Only Knows
Beach Boys; *Beach Boys' Greatest Hits* .... (Reprise)
   Best Of The Beach Boys-Good Vibrations .... (Reprise)
   Made In The U.S.A. .... (Capitol)
   Pet Sounds .... (Capitol)
   Stack 'O' Tracks .... (Capitol)
   The Pet Sounds Sessions: A 30th Anniversary Collection ..... (Capitol)
Goes My Mind (Pop, Pop, Pop, Pop)
Levert; *Smooth Grooves-A Sensual Collection-#8-C* ...... (Rhino)
Good Feelin' To Know
Poco; *Good Feelin' To Know* .... (Epic)

   Ride The Country .... (Epic)
   Songs Of Richie Furay .... (Epic)
   Very Best Of Poco .... (Epic)
Got You (Where I Want You)
Flys; *Holiday Man* .... (Delicious Vinyl)
   ST/Disturbing Behavior .... (Trauma)
Greatest Man I Never Knew
Reba McEntire; *For My Broken Heart* .... (MCA)
   Reba McEntire's Greatest Hits Volume Two .... (MCA)
Grey Matter
Oingo Boingo; *Boingo Alive* .... (MCA)
   Nothing To Fear .... (A&M)
   Skeletons In The Closet: The Best Of Oingo Boingo ... (A&M)
Grey Matter
An Emotional Fish; *An Emotional Fish* .... (Atlantic)
Hand Song, The
Nickel Creek; *Nickel Creek* .... (Sugar Hill)
Heart Over Mind
Lorrie Morgan; *War Paint* .... (BNA)
Hearts Don't Think (They Feel)
Natural Selection; *Natural Selection* .... (East West)
Heaven
Nu Flavor; *110% Hits-C* .... (Simitar)
   Nu Flavor .... (Reprise)
Heaven Is In Your Mind
Three Dog Night; *Captured Live At The Forum* .... (MCA)
Traffic; *Mr. Fantasy* .... (Island)
   Winwood .... (United Artists)
Heaven Knows
Donna Summer; *Live & More* .... (Casablanca)
   On The Radio-Greatest Hits-Volumes I & II ..... (Casablanca)
   Summer Collection .... (Mercury)
Heaven Knows
Grass Roots; *Grass Roots-All-Time Greatest Hits* ...... (MCA)
   Grass Roots-Anthology (1966-1975) .... (Rhino)
Heaven Knows
Commodores; *Heroes/Commodores* .... (Motown)
Heaven Knows
Lalah Hathaway; *Lalah Hathaway* .... (Virgin)
Heaven Knows
Robert Plant; *Now And Zen* .... (Es Paranza)
Heaven On Their Minds
Original Cast; *ST/Jesus Christ Superstar* .... (MCA)
Heaven Only Knows
Shangri-Las; *Best Of The Shangri-Las* .... (Mercury)
   Golden Hits Of The Shangri-Las .... (Mercury)
   Remember The Shangri-Las At Their Best .... (Collectables)
Heaven Only Knows
Emmylou Harris; *Bluebird* .... (Reprise)
Heaven Only Knows
Richard Marx; *Richard Marx* .... (Capitol)
Her Man
Gary Allan; *Cryin' Lyin' Lovin' & Leavin'-C* ...... (Universal)
   Used Heart For Sale .... (Decca)
Waylon Jennings; *The Eagle* .... (Epic)
Here I Am (Just When I Thought I Was Over You)
Air Supply; *Air Supply-The Definitive Collection* ...... (Arista)
Here In Your Bedroom
Goldfinger; *Richter* .... (Mojo Music/Universal)
He's Misstra Know-It-All
Stevie Wonder; *Innervisions* .... (Motown)
Higher Ground
Stevie Wonder; *Innervisions* .... (Motown)
   Original Musiquarium .... (Motown)
How Do I Live
LeAnn Rimes; *Absolute Dance Hits-C* .... (Curb)
   You Light Up My Life-Inspirational Songs .... (Curb)
Trisha Yearwood; *Songbook-A Collection Of Hits* .... (MCA)
How Do You Do It
Beatles; *The Beatles-Anthology-#1* .... (Capitol)
How Do You Fall In Love
Alabama; *For The Record: 41 Number One Hits* .... (RCA)
How Forever Feels
Kenny Chesney; *Everywhere We Go* .... (BNA)
   Kenny Chesney's Greatest Hits .... (BNA)
How I Know You
James Taylor; *ST/Aida* .... (Island)
How Little We Know
Frank Sinatra; *Best Of The Capitol Years* .... (Capitol)
   Capitol Collectors Series-Frank Sinatra .... (Capitol)
How Was I To Know
Reba McEntire; *Forever Reba* .... (Universal)
   What If It's You .... (MCA)
How Was I To Know
John Michael Montgomery; *What I Do The Best* ...... (Atlantic)
I Always Think I'm Up In Heaven
Watson Sisters; *Music From The New York Stage (1890-1920)-#4-1917-*
   1920-C .... (Pearl)

I Am
Train; *Train* . . . .(Aware/C2/Columbia)
I Am That Man
Brooks & Dunn; *Borderline* . . . . (Arista)
I Can See For Miles
Who; *Hooligans* . . . .(MCA)
 Join Together . . . .(MCA)
 Meaty Beaty Big & Bouncy . . . .(MCA)
 ST/The Kids Are Alright . . . .(MCA)
 The Who Sell Out . . . .(MCA)
I Can't Get You Off My Mind
Bob Dylan; *Timeless: Hank Williams Tribute-C* . . . . . . (Lost Highway/IDJMG)
Hank Williams; *Complete Hank Williams* . . . . (Mercury)
 Health & Happiness Shows . . . .(Mercury)
Patty Loveless; *If My Heart Had Windows* . . . .(MCA)
I Didn't Know My Own Strength
Lorrie Morgan; *Lorrie Morgan's Greatest Hits* . . . . (BNA)
 Reflections-Limited Edition Greatest Hits . . . . (BNA)
I Didn't Know What Time It Was
Ella Fitzgerald; *Rodgers & Hart Songbook* . . . . (Verve)
Sarah Vaughan; *Crazy & Mixed Up* . . . .(Pablo)
I Don't Even Know Your Name
Mavericks; *Trampoline* . . . .(MCA)
I Don't Know
Blues Brothers; *Best Of The Blues Brothers* . . . .(Atlantic)
 Briefcase Full Of Blues . . . .(Atlantic)
I Don't Know
Celine Dion; *Falling Into You*. . . . . (550 Music)
I Don't Know
Gretchen Peters; *Gretchen Peters*. . . . . (Purple Crayon Prod.)
I Don't Know Anybody Else
Black Box; *Dreamland* . . . . (RCA)
I Don't Know If It's Right
Evelyn ''Champagne'' King; *Dance! Dance! Dance!-#2-C* . . . . . . (RCA)
 Smooth Talk . . . . (RCA)
I Don't Know Why I Love You
House Of Love; *House Of Love* . . . .(Fontana)
I Don't Know You Anymore
Savage Garden; *Affirmation* . . . .(Columbia)
I Don't Want To Know
Fleetwood Mac; *Rumours*. . . . .(Warner Bros.)
Goo Goo Dolls; *Legacy-A Tribute To Fleetwood Mac's Rumours-C* . . . . . (Lava)
I Found The Brains Of Santa Claus
Jason & The Straptones; *Demento's Mementos* . . . . (PVC)
I Have Learned To Respect The Power Of Love
Angela Winbush; *Real Thing* . . . . (Mercury)
Stephanie Mills; *Stephanie Mills* . . . .(MCA)
I Just Don't Understand
Ann Margret; *Nipper's Greatest Hits Of The '60s-#1-C*. . . . . . (RCA)
I Just Wanted You To Know
Mark Chesnutt; *Almost Goodbye* . . . .(MCA)
I Knew I Loved You
Savage Garden; *Affirmation* . . . . (Columbia)
 Now That's What I Call Music!-#4-C . . . . (Virgin)
I Knew You Were Waiting (For Me)
Aretha Franklin & George Michael; *Aretha Franklin's Greatest Hits-1980-
 1994* . . . . (Arista)
 Billboard Top Hits-1987-C . . . .(Rhino)
 Chicken Soup For The Couples Soul-C . . . . (Rhino)
I Knew You When
Billy Joe Royal; *Billy Joe Royal's Greatest Hits*. . . . . (Columbia)
I Knew You When
Pamela Rose; *Morpheus*. . . . . (Grace)
I Know
Dionne Farris; *Wild Seed - Wild Flower* . . . .(Columbia)
I Know
Kim Richey; *Bitter Sweet* . . . .(Mercury)
I Know
Luther Vandross; *I Know* . . . .(LV/Virgin)
I Know A Heartache When I See One
Jennifer Warnes; *Best Of Jennifer Warnes* . . . .(Arista)
 Shot Through The Heart . . . .(Arista)
I Know A Little
Sammy Kershaw; *Skynyrd Frynds-C* . . . .(MCA)
I Know An Old Lady Who Swallowed A Fly
Original Soundtrack; *More Silly Songs*. . . . .(Disney)
Peter, Paul & Mary; *Peter, Paul & Mommy, Too* . . . .(Warner Bros.)
I Know She Still Loves Me
George Strait; *Platinum Country-C* . . . .(MCA)
 Strait Out Of The Box. . . . .(MCA)
I Know The Truth
Elton John & Janet Jackson; *ST/Aida* . . . . (Island)
I Know There's An Answer
Beach Boys; *Pet Sounds* . . . .(Capitol)
 The Pet Sounds Sessions: A 30th Anniversary Collection . . . . (Capitol)
I Know There's Something Going On
Frida; *Something's Going On*. . . . .(Atlantic)

I Know What Boys Like
Waitresses; *Best Of The Waitresses*. . . . .(Polydor)
 Just Can't Get Enough: New Wave Hits Of The '80s-#5-C . . . . (Rhino)
I Know What I Know
Paul Simon; *Graceland*. . . . . (Warner Bros.)
I Know Where Love Lives
Hal Ketchum; *Past The Point Of Rescue* . . . .(Curb)
I Know You Rider
Big Brother & The Holding Company; *Big Brother & The Holding
 Company Live* . . . . (Rhino)
Grateful Dead; *Europe '72* . . . . (Warner Bros.)
Hot Tuna; *Hot Tuna*. . . . . (RCA)
I Like 'Em Big & Stupid
Julie Brown; *Trapped In The Body Of A White Girl* . . . .(Sire)
I May Be Wrong
Frankie Laine; *The Uncollected Frankie Laine* . . . . (Hindsight)
I May Be Wrong (But I Think You're Wonderful)
Doris Day; *Doris Day-16 Most Requested Songs-Encore!* . . . . . . (Columbia)
Harry James; *Harry James-22 Original Big Band Recordings* . . . . . . (Hindsight)
I Need To Know
Marc Anthony; *Marc Anthony*. . . . . (Columbia)
 Now That's What I Call Music!-#4-C. . . . .(Virgin)
I Never Knew Love
Doug Stone; *More Love*. . . . . (Epic)
I Never Thought I'd Live To Be A Hundred
Moody Blues; *To Our Children's Children's Children*. . . . .(Polydor)
I Never Thought I'd Live To Be A Million
Moody Blues; *To Our Children's Children's Children*. . . . .(Polydor)
I Only Know I Love You
Four Aces; *Four Aces-More Greatest Hits* . . . .(Varese Vintage)
I Really Don't Want To Know
Charlie McCoy; *Greatest Hits Of Charlie McCoy*. . . . . (Columbia)
Eddy Arnold; *Best Of Eddy Arnold* . . . .(RCA)
 Essential Eddy Arnold . . . . (RCA)
Elvis Presley; *Elvis Country (''I'm 10,000 Years Old'')*. . . . .(RCA)
 Great Country Songs . . . . (RCA)
Les Paul; *Best Of The Capitol Masters* . . . . (Gold Rush)
Les Paul & Mary Ford; *Les Paul's Greatest Hits* . . . .(Pair)
Ronnie Dove; *Ronnie Dove-His Best* . . . .(Laurie)
Tommy Edwards; *It's All In The Game-The Complete Hits Of Tommy
 Edwards*. . . . . (Eric)
I Should Have Known Better
Beatles; *A Hard Day's Night* . . . .(Parlophone)
I Should Know
Mavericks; *Trampoline* . . . . (MCA)
I Taught Her Everything She Knows
Billy Walker; *Billy Walker's Greatest Hits* . . . . (Monument)
I Tawt I Taw A Puddy Tat
Mel Blanc; *From The Vaults-#7-The Movies...-C* . . . . (Capitol)
I Think About It All The Time
John Berry; *Standing On The Edge* . . . . (Capitol)
I Think About You
Collin Raye; *Best Of Collin Raye-Direct Hits* . . . . (Epic)
 I Think About You . . . . (Epic)
I Think God Can Explain
Splender; *ST/Dawson's Creek-#2* . . . .(C2/Columbia)
I Think I Know
Reno; *Reno* . . . . (Curb)
I Think I'll Just Stay Here And Drink
Merle Haggard; *For The Record: Merle Haggard-43 Legendary Hits* . . . .(BNA)
I Think I'm In Love With You
Jessica Simpson; *Now That's What I Call Music!-#5-C* . . . .(Virgin)
 Sweet Kisses. . . . . (Columbia)
I Think We're Alone Now
Tiffany; *Tiffany* . . . . (MCA)
 Tiffany's Greatest Hits . . . .(Hip-O)
Tommy James And The Shondells; *Best Of Tommy James And The
 Shondells* . . . . (Roulette)
 Billboard Top Rock 'N' Roll Hits-1967-C . . . . (Rhino)
 Tommy James And The Shondells-Anthology . . . .(Rhino)
I Think You Know
Todd Rundgren; *Todd* . . . . (Rhino)
I Think You Know What I Mean
Lyle Lovett; *I Love Everybody* . . . . (Curb/MCA)
I Think You've Got Your Fools Mixed Up
Brenton Wood; *Brenton Wood-18 Best*. . . . .(Original Sound)
I Thought About You
Billie Holiday; *Lady Sings The Blues* . . . . (Verve)
Dinah Washington; *What A Diff'rence A Day Makes* . . . . (Mercury)
Frank Sinatra & Nelson Riddle Orchestra; *songs for swingin'
 Lovers!*. . . . . (Capitol)
Rosemary Clooney; *Rosemary Clooney Sings The Music Of Jimmy Van
 Heusen*. . . . .(Concord Jazz)
Tony Bennett; *Perfectly Frank* . . . .(Columbia)
I Thought I'd Write To Juliet
Elvis Costello; *The Juliet Letters*. (Warner Bros.)
I Thought It Was You
Doug Stone; *I Thought It Was You* . . . . (Epic)

I Thought Of God
Porter Wagoner; *Porter Wagoner-In Person* . . . . (Koch International)

I Try To Think About Elvis
Patty Loveless; *Patty Loveless-Classics* . . . . (Epic)
When Fallen Angels Fly . . . . (Epic)

I Understand (Just How You Feel)
Four Tunes; *45-#5132* . . . . (Jubilee)
Freddie And The Dreamers; *45-#72377* . . . . (Mercury)
G-Clefs; *45-#7500* . . . . (Terrace)
Ink Spots; *ST/Trees Lounge* . . . . (MCA)

I Wanna Know
Joe; *My Name Is Joe* . . . . (Jive)
Now That's What I Call Music!-#4-C . . . . (Virgin)

I Want To Know You Before We Make Love
Conway Twitty; *Borderline* . . . . (MCA)

I Wish I Knew
Carmen McRae; *Monterey Jazz Festival: 40 Legendary*
Years-C . . . . (Warner Bros.)
Chet Baker; *Grey December* . . . . (Blue Note)
Jimmy Scott; *Lost And Found* . . . . (Rhino)
John Coltrane; *ST/The Fisher King* . . . . (MCA)

I Wonder Do You Think Of Me
Keith Whitley; *I Wonder Do You Think Of Me* . . . . (RCA)

I Would've Loved You Anyway
Trisha Yearwood; *Inside Out* . . . . (MCA)

Idiot Wind
Bob Dylan; *Blood On The Tracks* . . . . (Columbia)
Hard Rain . . . . (Columbia)
The Bootleg Series-Volumes 1-3 [Rare & Unreleased] . . . . (Columbia)

If I Fell
Beatles; *Beatles-Love Songs* . . . . (Capitol)
Something New . . . . (Capitol)
ST/A Hard Day's Night . . . . (Capitol)

If I Knew You Were Comin' I'd've Baked A Cake
Bing Crosby; *The Radio Years-#4* . . . . (Crescendo)
Ethel Merman; *The Ethel Merman Collection* . . . . (Razor & Tie)

If I Know Me
George Strait; *Livin' It Up* . . . . (MCA)

If I Only Had A Brain
Harry Connick, Jr.; *20* . . . . (Columbia)
Kay Kyser & His Orchestra; *Best Of The Big Bands-C* . . . . . . (Columbia)
Original Soundtrack; *The Wizard Of Oz-The Deluxe Edition* . . . . . (Rhino)
The Wizard Of Oz-The Story And Songs . . . . (Rhino)

If I Was A Drinkin' Man
Neal McCoy; *Neal McCoy's Greatest Hits* . . . . (Atlantic)
Neal McCoy-Super Hits . . . . (Atlantic)
You Gotta Love That! . . . . (Atlantic)

If She Knew What She Wants
Bangles; *Bangles' Greatest Hits* . . . . (Columbia)
Different Light . . . . (Columbia)

If Tomorrow Never Comes
Garth Brooks; *Garth Brooks* . . . . (Liberty)
Limited Series-Box . . . . (Capitol)
Joose; *Joose* . . . . (Flavor Unit)

If You Change Your Mind
Rosanne Cash; *King's Record Shop* . . . . (Columbia)
Rosanne Cash-Super Hits . . . . (Columbia)

If You Could Only See
Tonic; *Lemon Parade* . . . . (Polydor)
Now That's What I Call Music!-#1-C . . . . (Virgin)

If You Could Read My Mind
Gordon Lightfoot; *Gord's Gold* . . . . (Reprise)
If You Could Read My Mind . . . . (Reprise)
Sit Down Young Stranger . . . . (Reprise)

If You Don't Know Me By Now
Harold Melvin And The Blue Notes; *Harold Melvin And The Blue Notes-*
Collector's Item . . . . (Philadelphia Int'l)
Philly Ballads-#1-C . . . . (Philadelphia Int'l)
Simply Red; *New Flame* . . . . (Elektra)
Simply Red's Greatest Hits . . . . (East West)

If You Ever Change Your Mind
Crystal Gayle; *Crystal Gayle Greatest Hits* . . . . (Columbia)
These Days . . . . (Columbia)

If You Ever Have Forever In Mind
Vince Gill; *The Key* . . . . (MCA)

If You Knew Susie (Like I Know Susie)
Eddie Cantor; *Memories* . . . . (MCA)

If You Love Me (Let Me Know)
Olivia Newton-John; *Back To Basics-Essential Collection 1971-1992.* . (Geffen)
If You Love Me Let Me Know . . . . (MCA)
Olivia Newton-John's Greatest Hits . . . . (MCA)

If You Only Knew
John Charles Thomas; *Music From The New York Stage (1890-1920)-#4-*
1917-1920-C . . . . (Pearl)

If You Think You're Lonely Now
Bobby Womack; *The Poet* . . . . (Razor & Tie)
K-Ci Hailey; *ST/Jason's Lyric* . . . . (Mercury)

If Your Girl Only Knew
Aaliyah; *MTV Party To Go '98-C* . . . . (Tommy Boy)

One In A Million . . . . (BlackGround Enterp./Atlantic)

If You're Gone
Matchbox Twenty; *Mad Season By Matchbox Twenty* . . . . (Lava)

If You're Happy & You Know It
Original Soundtrack; *Children's Favorites* . . . . (Kid Rhino/Rhino 4 Kids)

Ignoreland
R.E.M.; *Automatic For The People* . . . . (Warner Bros.)

I'll Follow The Sun
Beatles; *Beatles '65* . . . . (Capitol)
Beatles-Box Set . . . . (Capitol)
Beatles-Love Songs . . . . (Capitol)
For Sale . . . . (Capitol)

I'll Know
Original Cast; *ST/Guys & Dolls* . . . . (MCA)

I'll Never Love This Way Again
Dionne Warwick; *Dionne Warwick's Greatest Hits-1979-1990* . . . . . (Arista)
Grammy's Greatest Moments-#4-C . . . . (Atlantic)

I'll Think Of Something
Mark Chesnutt; *Longnecks & Short Stories* . . . . (MCA)
Mark Chesnutt's Greatest Hits . . . . (Decca)

I'm A Believer
Monkees; *Billboard Top Rock 'N' Roll Hits-1966-C* . . . . (Rhino)
Monkees' Greatest Hits . . . . (Rhino)
More Of The Monkees . . . . (Rhino)
Oldies But Goodies-#3-C . . . . (Original Sound)
Neil Diamond; *Live In America* . . . . (Columbia)
Neil Diamond's Greatest Hits-1966-1992. . . . . (Columbia)
September Morn . . . . (Columbia)
Smash Mouth; *Now That's What I Call Music!-#8-C.* . . . . (Virgin)
ST/Shrek . . . . (Interscope)

I'm Flying
Original Cast/Mary Martin; *Peter Pan-The 1954 Broadway*
Production . . . . (RCA Victor)

I'm Like A Bird
Nelly Furtado; *Whoa Nelly!* . . . . (DreamWorks/SKG)

I'm The Fool
Mark Knopfler; *Golden Heart* . . . . (Warner Bros.)

I'm The Man Who Murdered Love
XTC; *Wasp Star (Apple Venus Volume 2)* . . . . (Idea/TVT)

I'm Thinking Tonight Of My Blue Eyes
Gene Autry; *All Time Legends Of Country Music-C* . . . . (Legacy)

Image Of A Girl
Safaris; *Brown Eyed Soul...East L.A.-#3-C* . . . . (Rhino)

Impression That I Get
Mighty Mighty Bosstones; *Let's Face It* . . . . (Big Rig/Mercury)
Live From The Middle East . . . . (Big Rig/Mercury)
Music From The X Games-#3-C . . . . (Mammoth)
Safe And Sound-C . . . . (Mercury)

In Hiding
Pearl Jam; *Yield* . . . . (Epic)

Ireland We Know
Ed Reavy; *Ed Reavy* . . . . (Rounder)

Iris
Goo Goo Dolls; *Dizzy Up The Girl* . . . . (Warner Sunset/Reprise)
ST/City Of Angels . . . . (Warner Sunset/Reprise)

Ironic
Alanis Morissette; *Jagged Little Pill* . . . . (Maverick)

It's About Time
Public Announcement; *All Work, No Play* . . . . (A&M)

It's All In Your Head
Diamond Rio; *Diamond Rio IV* . . . . (Arista)
Diamond Rio's Greatest Hits . . . . (Arista)

It's Bad You Know
R.L. Burnside; *The Sopranos-Music From The HBO Original*
Series . . . . (Sony Music Soundtrax)

It's In His Kiss (Shoop Shoop Song)
Betty Everett; *Billboard Top R&B Hits-1964-C* . . . . (Rhino)
Hits Of The Sixties-C . . . . (Intercom Music)
More American Graffiti-C . . . . (MCA)
Oldies But Goodies-#3-C . . . . (Original Sound)
Very Best Of Betty Everett . . . . (Vee-Jay)
Wonder Women-History Of Girl Group Sound-C . . . . (Rhino)
Cher; *ST/Mermaids* . . . . (Geffen)
Vonda Shepard; *ST/Songs From ''Ally McBeal'' Featuring Vonda*
Shepard . . . . (550/Epic)

It's No Good
Depeche Mode; *Ultra.* . . . . (Mute/Reprise)

It's The End Of The World As We Know It (And I Feel Fine)
R.E.M.; *Document* . . . . (EMI-Capitol Entert. Properties)

It's Wonderful
Rascals; *Nuggets-#8-Acid Rock-C* . . . . (Rhino)
Once Upon A Time . . . . (Rhino)
Rascals' Greatest Hits. . . . . (Atlantic)

I've Been Down That Road Before
Hank Williams; *Alone And Forsaken.* . . . . (Mercury)
Beyond The Sunset . . . . (Polydor)

I've Been Thinking About You
Londonbeat; *In The Blood* . . . . (Radioactive/MCA)

I've Been Thinking About You
Jocelyn Enriquez; *Freestyle Greatest Beats-The Complete Collection-#10-C* . . . . (Tommy Boy)
Jaded
Aerosmith; *Just Push Play* . . . . (Columbia)
Now That's What I Call Music!-#7-C . . . . (Virgin)
Jesus & Mama
Confederate Railroad; *Confederate Railroad* . . . . (Atlantic)
Jesus Children Of America
Stevie Wonder; *Innervisions* . . . . (Motown)
Jesus He Knows Me
Genesis; *We Can't Dance* . . . . (Atlantic)
Joe Knows How To Live
Eddy Raven; *Best Of Eddy Raven* . . . . (RCA)
Nitty Gritty Dirt Band; *Hold On* . . . . (Warner Bros.)
Jukebox In My Mind
Alabama; *Pass It On Down* . . . .(BMG Special Prod.)
Jumper
Third Eye Blind; *Third Eye Blind* . . . . (Elektra)
Totally Hits-#1-C . . . . (Arista)
Just Friends (Sunny)
Musiq Soulchild; *Aijuswanaseing* . . . .(Def Soul/IDJMG)
Kentucky Woman
Deep Purple; *Purple Passages* . . . .(Warner Bros.)
When We Rock We Rock & When We Roll We Roll . . . . . .(Warner Bros.)
Gary Puckett And The Union Gap; *Gary Puckett And The Union Gap's Greatest Hits* . . . .(Bac-Trac)
Neil Diamond; *Love At The Greek* . . . . (Columbia)
Neil Diamond-Classics (Early Years) . . . . (Columbia)
Neil Diamond-Gold . . . .(MCA)
King Of Wishful Thinking
Go West; *ST/Pretty Woman* . . . .(EMI)
Kiss An Angel Good Mornin'
Charley Pride; *Charley Pride-24 Greatest Hits* . . . .(Tee Vee)
Pride! My 6 Latest And 6 Greatest . . . .(ISD/Intersound)
The Ultimate Charley Pride . . . . (Bransounds)
Kiss The Rain
Billie Myers; *A Taste Of '98-C* . . . . (Universal)
Growing Pains . . . . (Universal)
Lady Picture Show
Stone Temple Pilots; *Tiny Music...Songs From The Vatican Gift Shop* . . . . (Atlantic)
Last Cup Of Sorrow
Faith No More; *Album Of The Year* . . . . (Reprise)
Last Night
Al Jarreau; *Tomorrow Today* . . . . (GRP/VMG)
Last Night's Letter
K-Ci & JoJo; *Love Always* . . . .(MCA)
Last Thing On My Mind
Porter Wagoner & Dolly Parton; *Essential Porter Wagoner & Dolly Parton* . . . . (RCA)
Lately
Divine; *Fairy Tales* . . . . (Pendulum)
Lateralus
Tool; *Lateralus* . . . .(Volcano Entertainment)
Let's Think About Living
Bob Luman; *Bob Luman-Classic Country* . . . . (Simitar)
Letting Go
Sozzi; *Songs From Dawson's Creek* . . . . (Sony Music Soundtrax)
Life As We Knew It
Kathy Mattea; *Class Of Country-C* . . . . (K-Tel)
Collection Of Hits . . . . (Mercury)
Untasted Honey . . . . (Polydor Country)
Little Brains, A Little Talent
Original Broadway Cast; *Damn Yankees* . . . . (RCA)
Lock And Load
Bob Seger; *It's A Mystery* . . . . (Capitol)
Lonesome, I Know You Too Well
Shawn Mullins; *Beneath The Velvet Sun* . . . . (Columbia)
Love And Understanding
Cher; *Love Hurts* . . . .(Geffen)
Love And Understanding
Blue Rodeo; *Diamond Mine* . . . . (Atlantic)
Love And Understanding
Kool & The Gang; *Kool & The Gang Spin Their Top Hits* . . . . . . (De-Lite)
Love Has A Mind Of Its Own
Donna Summer; *She Works Hard For The Money* . . . . (Mercury)
Love Has A Mind Of Its Own
Oak Ridge Boys; *Where The Fast Lane Ends* . . . .(MCA)
Love Is A Battlefield
Pat Benatar; *Best Shots* . . . .(Chrysalis)
I Am Woman-C . . . . (Nick At Nite)
Live From Earth . . . .(Chrysalis)
Love Like This
Faith Evans; *Keep The Faith* . . . . (Bad Boy/Arista)
Love On My Mind
Xscape; *Hummin' Comin' At 'Cha* . . . .(So So Def/Columbia)

Love, Love, Love
Clovers; *Clovers-Dance Party* . . . . (Collectables)
Luxury: Cococure
Maxwell; *Embrya* . . . . (Columbia)
Making Love Out Of Nothing At All
Air Supply; *Air Supply's Greatest Hits* . . . . (Arista)
Mama
Spice Girls; *Diana, Princess Of Wales-Tribute-C* . . . . (Columbia)
Spice . . . .(Virgin)
Man Smart, Woman Smarter
Harry Belafonte; *Harry Belafonte-Pure Gold* . . . .(RCA)
Robert Palmer; *Some People Can Do What They Like* . . . . (Island)
Rosanne Cash; *I Am Woman-C* . . . .(Nick At Nite)
Right Or Wrong . . . . (Columbia)
Maybe I Know
Lesley Gore; *Golden Hits Of Lesley Gore* . . . . (Mercury)
Lesley Gore-Anthology . . . . (Rhino)
Maybe I'm Amazed
Paul McCartney; *McCartney* . . . . (Capitol)
Wings; *Wings Over America* . . . . (Capitol)
Me Wise Magic
Van Halen; *Best Of Van Halen-#1* . . . . (Warner Bros.)
Meaning Of Life
Offspring; *Ixnay On The Hombre* . . . . (Columbia)
Mental Hopscotch
Missing Persons; *Best Of Missing Persons* . . . . (Capitol)
Mental Picture
Jon Secada; *Heart, Soul & A Voice* . . . . (SBK)
ST/The Specialist . . . .(Epic/Sony Music Soundtrax)
Michelle
Beatles; *Beatles-Love Songs* . . . . (Capitol)
Rubber Soul . . . . (Capitol)
The Beatles/1962-1966 . . . . (Capitol)
Mind Blowin'
D.O.C.; *No One Can Do It Better* . . . . (Ruthless)
Mind Games
John Lennon; *Mind Games* . . . . (Capitol)
John Lennon/Plastic Ono Band; *Shaved Fish* . . . . (Capitol)
Mind Playing Tricks On Me
Geto Boys; *10th Anniversary: Rap-A-Lot Records-C* . . .(Rap-A-Lot/Noo Trybe)
Misunderstanding
Genesis; *Duke* . . . .(Atlantic)
Three Sides Live . . . .(Atlantic)
Mmm Bop
Hanson; *1998 Grammy Nominees-C* . . . . (MCA)
Middle Of Nowhere . . . . (Mercury)
Now That's What I Call Music!-#1-C . . . . (Virgin)
Three Car Garage: The Independent Recordings . . . . (Mercury)
Monday Morning Quarterback
Frank Sinatra; *She Shot Me Down* . . . . (Reprise)
More Than This
10,000 Maniacs; *Love Among The Ruins* . . . . (Geffen)
Roxy Music; *Avalon* . . . . (Warner Bros.)
Street Life-20 Great Hits . . . . (Reprise)
More Than You Know
Barbra Streisand; *ST/Funny Lady* . . . . (Arista)
More Than You'll Ever Know
Travis Tritt; *The Restless Kind* . . . . (Warner Bros.)
More Than You'll Ever Know
Barbra Streisand; *Simply Streisand* . . . . (Columbia)
Billie Holiday; *Quintessential-#7-1938-1939* . . . . (Legacy)
Dinah Washington; *Jazz 'Round Midnight-Dinah Washington* . . . . . . (Verve)
Frank Sinatra; *Everything Happens To Me* . . . . (Reprise)
Johnny Mathis; *Heavenly* . . . . (Columbia)
Movie In My Mind
Original London Cast; *Miss Saigon* . . . . (Geffen)
Mr. Big Stuff
Jean Knight; *'70s Hit(s) Back Again-C* . . . . (Hip-O)
Have A Nice Decade-The '70s Pop Culture Box-C . . . . (Rhino)
Mr. Man
Alicia Keys with Jimmy Cozier; *Songs In A Minor* . . . . (J)
Mrs. Potter's Lullaby
Counting Crows; *This Desert Life* . . . .(David Geffen Co.)
My Daddy Knows Best
Marvelettes; *Compact Command Performances-Marvelettes* . . . . (Motown)
Marvelettes-Anthology . . . . (Motown)
My Head's In Mississippi
ZZ Top; *Recycler* . . . . (Warner Bros.)
ZZ Top's Greatest Hits . . . . (Warner Bros.)
My Heart Would Know
Hank Williams; *24 Of Hank Williams' Greatest Hits* . . . .(Polydor)
Hey Good Lookin' (December 1950-July 1951) . . . .(Polydor)
Mysterious
Scorpions; *Eye II Eye* . . . . (Koch International)
Navajo Know
Pixies; *Trompe Le Monde* . . . . (Elektra)
Never Ever
All Saints; *All Saints* . . . . (London)

Now That's What I Call Music!-#1-C . . . .(Virgin)

Never Is A Promise
Fiona Apple; *Tidal* . . . .(Clean Slate/Work)

Never Knew Lonely
Vince Gill; *When I Call Your Name* . . . . (MCA)

Never Let You Go
Third Eye Blind; *Blue* . . . .(Elektra)
Totally Hits-#2-C . . . .(Elektra)

New Worried Mind
Bob Wills; *Stay A Little Longer-The Original Columbia Recordings* . . . .(Roswell/RCA)

New York, I Don't Know About You
Peter Allen; *Taught By Experts* . . . . (A&M)

Nietzche's Eyes
Paula Cole; *This Fire* . . . .(Imago)

Night And Day
Bette Midler; *Some People's Lives* . . . . (Atlantic)
Billie Holiday; *Legacy Box-1933-1958* . . . .(Columbia)
Ella Fitzgerald; *Cole Porter Songbook* . . . .(Verve)
Frank Sinatra; *Nipper's Greatest Hits Of The '40s-#1-C* . . . .(RCA)
Sinatra & Strings . . . .(Reprise)
Sinatra Reprise-The Very Good Years . . . .(Reprise)
Sinatra: A Man And His Music . . . .(Reprise)
The Capitol Years . . . .(Capitol)
The Reprise Collection . . . .(Reprise)
Fred Astaire; *Cheek To Cheek* . . . .(Pro-Arte)
Steppin' Out-Astaire Sings . . . . (Verve)
Tony Bennett; *Perfectly Frank* . . . .(Columbia)
U2; *Red Hot + Blue-Tribute To Cole Porter-C* . . . .(Chrysalis)

No One Knows About A Good Thing
Curtis Mayfield; *New World Order* . . . . (Warner Bros.)

No One Needs To Know
Shania Twain; *The Woman In Me* . . . .(Mercury)

No Time To Think
Bob Dylan; *Street Legal* . . . .(Columbia)

Nobody I Know
Peter And Gordon; *History Of British Rock-#1-C* . . . .(Rhino)

Nobody Knows
Kevin Sharp; *Measure Of A Man* . . . . (143/Asylum)
Tony Rich Project; *Words* . . . .(LaFace)

Nobody Knows The Trouble I've Seen
Mahalia Jackson; *Gospels, Spirituals & Hymns* . . . .(Columbia)
Mahalia Jackson's Greatest Hits . . . .(Columbia)
Nat "King" Cole; *Every Time I Feel The Spirit* . . . .(Capitol)

Nobody Knows The Way I Feel This Morning
Aretha Franklin; *Aretha Franklin Sings The Blues* . . . .(Columbia)
Ernest "Punch" Miller; *Atlantic Jazz-New Orleans-C* . . . . . .(Atlantic)

Nobody Knows You When You're Down And Out
Bessie Smith; *Bessie Smith-The Collection* . . . .(Legacy)
Bessie Smith-The Complete Recordings-#4 . . . .(Legacy)
Derek And The Dominos; *Layla* . . . .(Polydor)
Eric Clapton; *Eric Clapton-Unplugged* . . . .(Reprise)
Otis Redding; *Soul Album* . . . .(Atco)
Rod Stewart; *Out Of Order* . . . . (Warner Bros.)

Nothing To Prove
Caroline's Spine; *Attention Please* . . . .(Hollywood)

Now I Know
Lari White; *Wishes* . . . .(RCA)

Now That I Know Love
Kenny Loggins; *The Unimaginable Life* . . . .(Columbia)

Ocean Of Thoughts & Dreams
Dramatics; *Shake It Well* . . . . (MCA)

Oh Girl (You Know Where To Find Me)
Vince Gill; *When I Call Your Name* . . . . (MCA)

Old
Paul Simon; *You're The One* . . . . (Warner Bros.)

Old Enough To Know Better
Wade Hayes; *Country Dance Hits-C* . . . .(Columbia)
Old Enough To Know Better . . . .(Columbia)
Steppin' Country-#2-C . . . .(Columbia)
Super Hits Of 1994-C . . . .(Columbia)

Om
John Coltrane; *Fire Into Music-Best Of Impulse!-#3-C* . . . .(MCA/Impulse)
Om . . . .(MCA/Impulse)

Om
Moody Blues; *In Search Of The Lost Chord* . . . . (Polydor)

On Second Thought
Eddie Rabbitt; *Country's Greatest Hits-#8-Lonely Hearts-C* . . . .(Priority)
Jersey Boy . . . .(Capitol)
Ten Years Of Greatest Hits . . . .(Capitol)

Once In A While
Tommy Dorsey; *Boogie Woogie* . . . .(Pro-Arte)

One Of Us Must Know (Sooner Or Later)
Bob Dylan; *Blonde On Blonde* . . . .(Columbia)

Only God Knows Why
Kid Rock; *Devil Without A Cause* . . . . (Top Dog/Lava/Atlantic)

Only The Lonely (Know The Way I Feel)
Roy Orbison; *For The Lonely: A Roy Orbison Anthology 1959-1965* . . . .(Rhino)

In Dreams-Greatest Hits . . . . (Orbison)
Roy Orbison's All-Time Greatest Hits-#1 & 2 . . . .(Monument)

Ooh La La
Rod Stewart; *When We Were The New Boys* . . . .(Warner Bros.)

Open Our Eyes
Earth, Wind & Fire; *Open Our Eyes* . . . .(Columbia)

Open Your Eyes
Yes; *Open Your Eyes* . . . . (Beyond)

Open Your Eyes
Doobie Brothers; *Minute By Minute* . . . .(Warner Bros.)

Out Of Sight, Out Of Mind
Five Keys; *Golden Classics-Five Keys* . . . .(Collectables)

Outtasite (Outta Mind)
Wilco; *Being There* . . . . (Reprise)

Over Now
Alice In Chains; *Alice In Chains* . . . .(Columbia)

Packed Up And Took My Mind
Little Milton; *Tin Pan Alley* . . . . (Stax)

Parents Just Don't Understand
D.J. Jazzy Jeff & The Fresh Prince; *He's The D.J. I'm The Rapper* . . . . (Jive)

Peace In Mind
Joan Armatrading; *Show Some Emotion* . . . .(A&M)

Peace Of Mind
Loggins & Messina; *Loggins & Messina-On Stage* . . . .(Columbia)
Sittin' In . . . .(Columbia)
The Best Of Friends . . . .(Columbia)

Peace Of Mind
Boston; *Boston* . . . . (Epic)

Peace Of Mind
Bad Company; *Burnin' Sky* . . . .(Swan Song)

Peace Of Mind
Neil Young; *Comes A Time* . . . . (Reprise)

Peace Of Mind
Eddy Raven; *Eddy Raven's Greatest Hits* . . . .(Warner Bros.)

Peace Of Mind
Blue Cheer; *Good Times Are So Hard To Find-History Of Blue Cheer* . . . .(Mercury)
Louder Than God-Best Of Blue Cheer . . . .(Rhino)

Peace Of Mind
Engelbert Humperdinck; *Miracles* . . . . (Epic)

Peace, Love & Understanding (What's So Funny About)
Curtis Stigers; *ST/The Bodyguard* . . . .(Arista)
Elvis Costello & The Attractions; *Armed Forces* . . . .(Rykodisc)
Best Of Elvis Costello & The Attractions . . . .(Columbia)

Penny For Your Thoughts
Peter Frampton; *Frampton Comes Alive* . . . . (A&M)
Shine On-Collection . . . . (A&M)

Penny For Your Thoughts
Tavares; *Slow Jams-The Timeless Collection-#3-C* . . . .(Right Stuff)

Penny For Your Thoughts
Willie Nelson; *Sound In Your Mind* . . . .(Columbia)

Piano Lesson & If You Don't Mind My Saying So
Shirley Jones; *ST/The Music Man* . . . .(Warner Bros.)

Pinch Me
Barenaked Ladies; *Maroon* . . . . (Reprise)
Totally Hits-#3-C . . . .(Atlantic)

Playground In My Mind
Clint Holmes; *Rock Artifacts-From The Vaults-#2-C* . . . .(Legacy)
Super Hits Of The '70s-Have A Nice Day-#11-C . . . .(Rhino)

Poison To The Mind
Pop Will Eat Itself; *This Is The Day...This Is The Hour...* . . . . (RCA)

Pretty Vacant
Joan Jett; *The Hit List* . . . .(Epic)
Sex Pistols; *Live At Chelmsford Top Security Prison* . . . .(Restless)
Never Mind The Bollocks, Here's The Sex Pistols . . . .(Warner Bros.)

Pretzel Logic
Donald Fagen & Michael McDonald; *New York Rock & Soul Revue-At The Beacon-C* . . . .(Giant)
Steely Dan; *Pretzel Logic* . . . . (MCA)
Steely Dan's Greatest Hits . . . . (MCA)

Put It On Me
Ja Rule featuring Li'l Mo And Vita; *Rule 3:36*. . . (Murder Inc./Def Jam/IDJMG)

Question
Moody Blues; *A Night At Red Rocks With The Colorado Symphony Orchestra* . . . .(Polydor)
A Question Of Balance . . . .(Polydor)
This Is The Moody Blues . . . .(Polydor)

Quiet
Paul Simon; *You're The One* . . . . (Warner Bros.)

Rain, The Park And Other Things
Cowsills; *Cowsills* . . . .(Razor & Tie)

Rambling On My Mind
Eric Clapton; *Eric Clapton-Crossroads-C* . . . .(Polydor)
John Mayall's Bluesbreakers with Eric Clapton; *John Mayall's Bluesbreakers with Eric Clapton* . . . .(Deram)
Robert Johnson; *King Of The Delta Blues Singers* . . . .(Columbia)
Robert Johnson-Complete Recordings . . . .(Columbia)
Savoy Brown; *Slow Train* . . . .(Relix)

Rebecca
Pat McGhee Band; *Shine* . . . .(Giant/Warner Bros.)
Reconsider Baby
Eric Clapton; *From The Cradle* . . . . (Duck/Reprise)
Reflections
Diana Ross & The Supremes; *Diana Ross & The Supremes' Greatest*
Hits-#3 . . . . (Motown)
Diana Ross & The Supremes-25th Anniversary . . . . (Motown)
Diana Ross & The Supremes-Anthology (1962-1969) . . . . (Motown)
Motown Story-First 25 Years-C . . . . (Motown)
Four Tops; *Four Tops-Anthology* . . . . (Motown)
Still Waters Run Deep . . . . (Motown)
Until You Love Someone: More Of The Best (1965-1970) . . . . (Rhino)
Luther Vandross; *Songs* . . . .(Epic)
Rest My Mind On Jesus
Charles Ford Band; *Charles Ford Band* . . . . (Arhoolie)
Ridiculous Thoughts
Cranberries; *No Need To Argue* . . . . (Island)
River Of Deceit
Mad Season; *Above* . . . . (Columbia)
Runaway
Bonnie Raitt; *Bonnie Raitt-Collection* . . . .(Warner Bros.)
Sweet Forgiveness . . . .(Warner Bros.)
Del Shannon; *Billboard Top Rock 'N' Roll Hits-1961-C* . . . . (Rhino)
Cruisin'-1961-C . . . .(Increase)
Del Shannon's Greatest Hits . . . . (Rhino)
Heart & Soul Of Rock 'N' Roll-#1-C . . . . (Rhino)
Little Town Flirt . . . . (Rhino)
ST/American Graffiti . . . .(MCA)
Elvis Presley; *Collector's Gold* . . . . (RCA)
Sadder & Wiser Beaver
Original Broadway Cast; *Beyond The Fringe* . . . . (Capitol)
Sadder-But-Wiser Girl For Me
Original Cast; *The Music Man* . . . .(Gold Rush)
Robert Preston; *ST/The Music Man* . . . .(Warner Bros.)
San Diego Serenade
Nanci Griffith; *Late Night Grande Hotel* . . . .(MCA)
Tom Waits; *The Heart Of Saturday Night* . . . . (Asylum)
Tom Waits-Anthology . . . . (Asylum)
Satisfied Mind
Bob Dylan; *Saved* . . . . (Columbia)
Byrds; *Turn! Turn! Turn!* . . . . (Legacy)
David Allan Coe; *Texas Moon* . . . . (Plantation)
Lindsey Buckingham; *Law And Order* . . . . (Asylum)
Porter Wagoner; *Porter Wagoner's Greatest* . . . . (Tudor)
Satisfied Mind
Ozark Mountain Daredevils; *It's Alive* . . . . (A&M)
Ozark Mountain Daredevils . . . . (A&M)
Satisfy You
Puff Daddy Featuring R. Kelly; *Forever* . . . .(Bad Boy/Arista)
Say It
Voices Of Theory; *Voices Of Theory* . . . .(H.O.L.A./Red Ant)
Secret
Madonna; *Bedtime Stories* . . . .(Maverick/Sire)
GHV2 . . . .(Warner Bros.)
Secret Of Life
Faith Hill; *Faith* . . . .(Warner Bros.)
Gretchen Peters; *The Secret Of Life* . . . . (Purple Crayon Prod.)
Shadow Knows
Coasters; *Coasters' Greatest Hits* . . . . (Atco)
Shallow End Of The Gene Pool
Austin Lounge Lizards; *Small Minds* . . . . (Sugar Hill)
Shanti/Ashtangi
Madonna; *Ray Of Light* . . . .(Maverick)
She Can't Say I Didn't Cry
Rick Trevino; *Rick Trevino* . . . . (Columbia)
She Don't Know She's Beautiful
Sammy Kershaw; *Haunted Heart* . . . . (Mercury)
She's A Woman
Beatles; *Beatles '65* . . . . (Capitol)
Beatles-Box Set . . . . (Capitol)
Compact Disc Singles Collection . . . . (Capitol)
Past Masters-Volume One . . . . (Parlophone)
The Beatles At The Hollywood Bowl . . . . (Capitol)
Jeff Beck; *Blow By Blow* . . . . (Epic)
She's Already Made Up Her Mind
Lyle Lovett; *Joshua Judges Ruth* . . . .(Curb/MCA)
She's Every Woman
Garth Brooks; *Fresh Horses* . . . . (Capitol)
She's Got a 60 Cycle Brain
Paul Buff Organization; *45-#55* . . . . (Original Sound)
Should've Asked Her Faster
Ty England; *Ty England* . . . . (RCA)
Show Me The Meaning Of Being Lonely
Backstreet Boys; *Millennium* . . . . (Jive)
Now That's What I Call Music!-#5-C . . . . (Virgin)
Sick Of Myself
Matthew Sweet; *100% Fun* . . . . (Zoo)

Sign, The
Ace Of Base; *The Sign* . . . . (Arista)
Silent Lucidity
Queensryche; *Empire* . . . . (EMI)
Sit Down I Think I Love You
Buffalo Springfield; *Buffalo Springfield-Retrospective* . . . . (Atco)
Sittin' Up In My Room
Brandy; *ST/Waiting To Exhale* . . . . (Arista)
Skellig
Loreena McKennitt; *The Book Of Secrets* . . . . (Quinlan Rd./Warner Bros.)
Sly Mongoose
Charlie Parker; *Bebop & Bird-#2* . . . . (Rhino)
Monty Alexander Ivory & Steel; *Jamboree* . . . .(Concord Picante Jazz)
So Emotional
Whitney Houston; *Whitney* . . . . (Arista)
Whitney Houston's Greatest Hits . . . . (Arista)
So You Think You're In Love
Robyn Hitchcock & The Egyptians; *Perspex Island* . . . . (A&M)
Somebody To Love
Jefferson Airplane; *2400 Fulton Street-An Anthology* . . . . (RCA)
Loves You . . . . (RCA)
Nipper's Greatest Hits Of The '60s-#1-C . . . . (RCA)
Surrealistic Pillow . . . . (RCA)
The Worst Of Jefferson Airplane . . . . (RCA)
Someday We'll Know
New Radicals; *Maybe You've Been Brainwashed Too* . . . . (MCA)
Someday, Someway
Marshall Crenshaw; *Marshall Crenshaw* . . . . (Rhino)
ST/Nightshift . . . . (Warner Bros.)
Someone To Love
Jon B.; *Bonafide* . . . .(Yab Yum/550)
Jon B. featuring Babyface; *ST/Bad Boys* . . . . (Work)
Someone You Used To Know
Collin Raye; *Big Country Hits '99-C* . . . . (K-Tel)
The Walls Came Down . . . . (Epic)
Somethin' Stupid
Frank & Nancy Sinatra; *Frank Sinatra's Greatest Hits!* . . . . (Reprise)
The World We Knew . . . . (Reprise)
Nancy Sinatra & Frank Sinatra; *Boots-Nancy Sinatra's Greatest Hits* . . . (Rhino)
Something
Beatles; *Abbey Road* . . . . (Parlophone)
Beatles 1 . . . . (Capitol)
The Beatles/1967-1970 . . . . (Capitol)
The Beatles-Anthology-#3 . . . . (Capitol)
Song For The Life
Alan Jackson; *Who I Am* . . . . (Arista)
Alison Krauss; *Too Late To Cry* . . . . (Rounder)
Jerry Jeff Walker; *A Man Must Carry On* . . . . (MCA)
John Denver; *Country Roads Collection* . . . . (RCA)
Kathy Mattea; *Walk The Way The Wind Blows* . . . . (Mercury)
Rodney Crowell; *Ain't Living Long Like This* . . . . (Warner Bros.)
Sophisticated Bitch
Public Enemy; *Yo! Bum Rush The Show* . . . .(Def Jam/Columbia)
Sophisticated Lady
Diane Schuur; *In Tribute* . . . . (GRP)
Duke Ellington; *Mood Indigo* . . . . (Pro-Arte)
Reminiscing In Tempo . . . . (Columbia)
Linda Ronstadt; *Lush Life* . . . . (Asylum)
Original Broadway Cast; *Bubbling Brown Sugar* . . . . (Amherst)
Rosemary Clooney; *Essence Of Rosemary Clooney* . . . . (Legacy)
Tito Puente & His Latin Ensemble; *On Broadway* . . . .(Concord Picante Jazz)
Special
Garbage; *Now That's What I Call Music!-#3-C* . . . .(Virgin)
Version 2.0 . . . . (Almo Sounds)
Spirit Of A Boy, Wisdom Of A Man
Randy Travis; *Big Country Hits '99-C* . . . . (K-Tel)
You And You Alone . . . .(DreamWorks/SKG)
State Of Mind
Clint Black; *No Time To Kill* . . . . (RCA)
Step Out Of Your Mind
American Breed; *Bend Me, Shape Me-Best Of The American*
Breed . . . .(Varese Vintage)
Still On Your Side
BBMak; *Sooner Or Later* . . . . (Hollywood)
Stop And Think It Over
Dale & Grace; *Rockin' '50s & '60s-C* . . . . (Jewel)
Stop Making Sense
Talking Heads; *Stop Making Sense* . . . .(Sire)
Stop! In The Name Of Love
Diana Ross & The Supremes; *16 #1 Hits From The Early '60s-C* . . . . (Motown)
Diana Ross & The Supremes' Greatest Hits . . . . (Motown)
Diana Ross & The Supremes-Anthology (1962-1969) . . . . (Motown)
Evening With Diana Ross . . . . (Motown)
Girl Groups-Story Of A Sound-C . . . . (Rhino)
Motown Superstar Series-#1-Diana Ross & The Supremes . . . . (Motown)
Hollies; *45-#89819* . . . .(Atlantic)
Supremes; *Billboard Top Pop Hits-1965-C* . . . . (Rhino)
Stupid Cupid
Connie Francis; *Very Best Of Connie Francis* . . . .(Polydor)

Neil Sedaka; *Neil Sedaka's All-Time Greatest Hits-#2* . . . . (RCA)

Stupid Einstein
Three O'Clock; *Sixteen Tambourines* . . . . (Frontier)

Stupid Girl
Rolling Stones; *Aftermath* . . . . (Abkco)
   Singles Collection-The London Years . . . . (Abkco)

Stupid Girl
Garbage; *Garbage* . . . . (Almo Sounds)

Stupid Marriage
Specials; *Specials* . . . . (Chrysalis)

Stupid War Movies
Paleface; *Paleface* . . . . (Polydor)

Summer Knows
Barbra Streisand; *Barbra Joan Streisand* . . . . (Columbia)
Frank Sinatra; *Some Nice Things I've Missed* . . . . (Reprise)
Freddie Hubbard; *Best Of Freddie Hubbard* . . . . (Pablo)
   Live At The North Sea Jazz Festival . . . . (Pablo)
Johnny Mathis; *First Time Ever I Saw Your Face* . . . . (Columbia)

Superstition
Stevie Wonder; *20/20-C* . . . . (Motown)
   Original Musiquarium . . . . (Motown)
   Talking Book . . . . (Motown)

Suspicious Minds
Elvis Presley; *Aloha from Hawaii via Satellite* . . . . (RCA)
   From Memphis To Vegas/From Vegas To Memphis . . . . (RCA)
   Memphis Record . . . . (RCA)
   Nipper's Greatest Hits Of The '60s-#2-C . . . . (RCA)
   ST/This Is Elvis . . . . (RCA)

Sweetest Thing
Refugee Camp All-Stars featuring Lauryn Hill; *ST/Love Jones* . . . . . (Columbia)

Sweetest Thing (I've Ever Known)
Juice Newton; *Country Love-C* . . . . (K-Tel)
   Juice Newton-Greatest Hits & More . . . . (Capitol)
   Juice Newton's Greatest Country Hits . . . . (Curb)

T.V. Mind
Revolting Cocks; *Big Sexy Land* . . . . (Wax Trax)

Take A Look Around
Limp Bizkit; *Chocolate Starfish & The Hotdog Flavored*
   Water . . . . (Flip/Interscope)

Take Time To Know Her
Percy Sledge; *Best Of Percy Sledge* . . . . (Atlantic)
   It Tears Me Up-Best Of Percy Sledge . . . . (Rhino)

Taking You Home
Don Henley; *Inside Job* . . . . (Warner Bros.)

Tarantella
Original Cast/Cyril Ritchard; *Peter Pan-The 1954 Broadway*
   Production . . . . (RCA Victor)

Teach The Gifted Children
Lou Reed; *Between Thought & Expression-Anthology* . . . . (RCA)

Teenage Lobotomy
Ramones; *All The Stuff & More-#2* . . . . (Sire)
   Ramones Mania . . . . (Sire)
   Rocket To Russia . . . . (Sire)

Tell Him
Exciters; *Best Of The Girl Groups-#2-C* . . . . (Rhino)
   ST/Big Chill . . . . (Motown)
   ST/My Best Friend's Wedding . . . . (Work/Epic)
   Tell Him . . . . (Collectables)
Patti Drew; *Tell Him-Golden Classics* . . . . (Collectables)
Vonda Shepard; *ST/Songs From "Ally McBeal" Featuring Vonda*
   Shepard . . . . (550/Epic)

Terms Of Psychic Warfare
Husker Du; *New Day Rising* . . . . (SST)

Thank U
Alanis Morissette; *Supposed Former Infatuation Junkie* . . . . (Maverick)

That Girl's Been Spyin' On Me
Billy Dean; *It's What I Do* . . . . (Capitol)

That's How You Know (When You're In Love)
Lari White; *Best Of Lari White* . . . . (RCA)
   Wishes . . . . (RCA)

That's How You Know It's Love
Deana Carter; *Did I Shave My Legs For This?* . . . . (Capitol)

That's Just About Right
BlackHawk; *BlackHawk* . . . . (Arista)
   The Hits-Love & Gravity . . . . (Arista)

That's Not Me
Beach Boys; *Pet Sounds* . . . . (Capitol)
   The Pet Sounds Sessions: A 30th Anniversary Collection . . . . (Capitol)

That's Why I'm Here
Kenny Chesney; *I Will Stand* . . . . (BNA)

The World I Know
Collective Soul; *Collective Soul* . . . . (Atlantic)

Theme From "Cheers"
Gary Portnoy; *Tube Tunes-#3-The '70s & '80s-C* . . . . (Rhino)
Original Soundtrack; *Television's Greatest Hits-#3-1970s and 1980s-C* . . . (TVT)

Theme From "Father Knows Best"
Original Soundtrack; *Television's Greatest Hits-#4-Black & White*
   Classics-C . . . . (TVT)

Theme From "Jeopardy" (Think Music)
Original Soundtrack; *Television's Greatest Hits-#2-C* . . . . (TVT)

Theme From "Yogi Bear"
Original Soundtrack; *Hanna-Barbera Classics-#1-Original Recordings Of*
   The World's Most Famous Cartoon Themes &
   Scores . . . . (Kid Rhino/Rhino 4 Kids)
   Hanna-Barbera Pic-A-Nic Basket Of Cartoon
   Classics . . . . (Kid Rhino/Rhino 4 Kids)
   Television's Greatest Hits-#1-C . . . . (TVT)

There Goes My Baby
Trisha Yearwood; *Where Your Road Leads* . . . . (MCA)

There She Goes
Sixpence None The Richer; *Sixpence None The Richer* . . . . . (Squint/Columbia)

There's A Place
Beatles; *Introducing...The Beatles* . . . . (Vee-Jay)
   Rarities . . . . (Capitol)

There's A Tear In My Beer
Hank Williams, Jr. & Hank Williams, Sr.; *Complete Hank Williams* . . . (Mercury)
   Hank Williams, Jr.'s Greatest Hits III . . . . (Curb)

There's A Whole Lot About A Woman (A Man Don't Know)
Jack Greene; *45-#32823* . . . . (Decca)

These Lips Don't Know How To Say Goodbye
Doug Stone; *Doug Stone* . . . . (Epic)
   Greatest Country Hits Of The '90s-1991-C . . . . (Columbia)
Forester Sisters; *Sincerely* . . . . (Warner Bros.)

They Don't Know
Tracey Ullman; *Best Of Tracey Ullman* . . . . (Rhino)
   You Broke My Heart In 17 Places . . . . (MCA)

They Don't Know
Jon B.; *Cool Relax* . . . . (Yab Yum/550)

Think
Aretha Franklin; *Aretha Franklin's Greatest Hits* . . . . (Atlantic)
   Aretha's Gold . . . . (Atlantic)
   Best Of Aretha Franklin . . . . (Atlantic)
   ST/The Blues Brothers . . . . (Atlantic)

Think About Love
Dolly Parton; *Best There Is* . . . . (RCA)

Think For Yourself
Beatles; *Beatles-Box Set* . . . . (Capitol)
   Rubber Soul . . . . (Capitol)
George Harrison; *Best Of George Harrison* . . . . (Capitol)

Think Of Me
Buck Owens & The Buckaroos; *Buck Owens Collection-1959-1990* . . . (Rhino)
   Very Best Of Buck Owens-#2 . . . . (Rhino)

Think Of Tomorrow
Chris Isaak; *Baja Sessions* . . . . (Reprise)

Think Of What You've Done
Ricky Skaggs and Kentucky Thunder; *Bluegrass Rules!* . . . . (Rounder)

Think Of You
Usher; *Usher* . . . . (LaFace)

Think Twice
Brook Benton; *Best Of Brook Benton* . . . . (Mercury)

Thinkin' About You
Trisha Yearwood; *Thinkin' About You* . . . . (MCA)

Thinkin' 'Bout It
Gerald Levert; *Love & Consequences* . . . . (East West)

Thinkin' 'Bout Your Mother
Freewheelers; *Freewheelers* . . . . (David Geffen Co.)

Thinkin' Out Loud
Band; *Cahoots* . . . . (Capitol)

Thinkin' Problem
David Ball; *Thinkin' Problem* . . . . (Warner Bros.)

Thinking About Leaving
Dwight Yoakam; *Last Chance For A Thousand Years-Greatest Hits From*
   The '90s . . . . (Reprise)

Thinking About Sex Again
Waitresses; *Best Of The Waitresses* . . . . (Polydor)

Thinking About Your Troubles
Nilsson; *The Point* . . . . (RCA)

Thinking Of You
Tony Toni Tone; *House Of Music* . . . . (Mercury)
   Tony Toni Tone-Hits . . . . (Mercury)

Thinking With The Wrong Head
Little Charlie & The Nightcats; *Captured Live* . . . . (Alligator)

This Time Around
Michael Jackson; *HIStory: Past, Present And Future-Book 1-C* . . . . . . (Epic)

Thoughts Of A Fool
George Strait; *ST/Pure Country* . . . . (MCA)

To Know Him, Is To Love Him
Dolly Parton/Emmylou Harris/Linda Ronstadt; *Trio* . . . . (Warner Bros.)
Teddy Bears; *At The Hop-'50s Rock 'N' Roll* . . . . (K-Tel)
   Phil Spector-Back To Mono 1958-1969-C . . . . (Abkco)

To Love Somebody
Bee Gees; *Bee Gees-Gold* . . . . (Polydor)
   History Of British Rock-#7-C . . . . (Rhino)
Jimmy Somerville; *Jimmy Somerville-Singles Collection-1984-1990* . . (London)
Michael Bolton; *Timeless-Classics* . . . . (Columbia)

Tomorrow Never Knows
Beatles; *Beatles-Box Set* . . . . (Capitol)
Revolver . . . . (Capitol)
Phil Collins; *Face Value* . . . .(Atlantic)

Too Busy Thinking About My Baby
Manhattan Transfer; *Tonin'* . . . .(Atlantic)
Marvin Gaye; *Every Great Motown Hit Of Marvin Gaye* . . . . (Motown)
Superhits . . . . (Motown)

Too Little Too Late
Barenaked Ladies; *Maroon.* . . . . (Reprise)

Too Soon To Know
Don Gibson; *Oh Lonesome Me* . . . . (Collectables)
Roy Orbison; *The Classic Roy Orbison-1965-1968* . . . . (Rhino)

Too Young
Donny Osmond; *Donny Osmond's Greatest Hits* . . . . (Curb)
Nat "King" Cole; *Nat "King" Cole-Greatest Hits* . . . . (Capitol)

Transcendance
Santana; *Moonflower* . . . . (Columbia)

Travelin' At The Speed Of Thought
O'Jays; *Travelin' At The Speed Of Thought* . . . . (Philadelphia Int'l)

Trouble In Mind
Bob Wills; *Stay A Little Longer-The Original Columbia
Recordings* . . . . (Roswell/RCA)

Tucker's Town
Hootie & The Blowfish; *Fairweather Johnson.* . . . .(Atlantic)

U Know What's Up
Donell Jones; *Totally Hits-#2-C* . . . . (Elektra)
Where I Wanna Be . . . . (LaFace)

U Will Know
Black Men United; *ST/Jason's Lyric* . . . . (Mercury)

Um, Um, Um, Um, Um (Curious Mind)
Major Lance; *Seems Like Yesterday-#5-Mid '60s-C* . . . . (K-Tel)

Understand Your Man
Johnny Cash; *Billboard Top Country Hits-1964-C* . . . . (Rhino)
Johnny Cash's Greatest Hits . . . . (Columbia)
The Man In Black-His Greatest Hits . . . . (Legacy)

Understanding
Xscape; *Hummin' Comin' At 'Cha* . . . .(So So Def/Columbia)

Understanding
Candlebox; *Lucy* . . . .(Maverick)

Unforgiven II
Metallica; *Reload* . . . . (Elektra)

Unglued
Stone Temple Pilots; *Purple* . . . .(Atlantic)

Untanglin' My Mind
Clint Black; *One Emotion* . . . . (RCA)

Very Thought Of You, The
Diane Schuur; *A Time For Love: Priceless Jazz-C* . . . . (GRP)
Ray Noble & His Orchestra; *The Sweetest Sounds Ever Heard-C* . . . . . . (Hip-O)
Those Wonderful Years: Puttin' On The Ritz-C . . . . (JCI Assoc. Labels)
Wynton Marsalis; *The Very Thought Of You: Jazz For Lovers-C* . . . . . . (Legacy)

Vidiot
Ken Nordine; *Best Of Word Jazz-#1* . . . . (Rhino)

Vincent
Don McLean; *American Pie* . . . .(EMI)
Best Of Don McLean . . . .(EMI)
Greatest Hits Then & Now . . . .(EMI)

Voices Inside My Head
Police; *Zenyatta Mondatta* . . . . (A&M)

Wait
Seven Mary Three; *Economy Of Sound* . . . . (Mammoth)

Wake Up & Smell The Coffee
Killbilly; *Stranger In This Place.* . . . . (Flying Fish)

Warming Up The Brain Farm
Lo Fidelity Allstars; *How To Operate With A Blown Mind.* . . . . (Skint)

Waylon Jennings
Waylon Jennings; *Greatest Country Hits Of The '90s-1990-C* . . . . (Columbia)

We Danced Anyway
Deana Carter; *Did I Shave My Legs For This?* . . . . (Capitol)

What Do I Know
Ricochet; *Pure Country-Best Of The '90s-#2-C* . . . . (Priority)
Ricochet. . . . .(Columbia)

What Do They Know
Tammy Wynette; *Without Walls-C.* . . . .(Epic)

What Goes On
Beatles; *"Yesterday"...And Today* . . . . (Capitol)

What I Didn't Know
Athenaeum; *Radiance* . . . .(Atlantic)

What It's Like
Everlast; *Whitey Ford Sings The Blues* . . . . (Tommy Boy)

What I've Got In Mind
Billie Jo Spears; *Best Of Billie Jo Spears* . . . . (Razor & Tie)

What Mattered Most
Ty Herndon; *Super Hits Of 1995-C* . . . .(Epic)
What Mattered Most . . . .(Epic)

What Part Of No
Lorrie Morgan; *Lorrie Morgan's Greatest Hits* . . . . (BNA)
Watch Me . . . . (BNA)

What She Don't Know Won't Hurt Her
Gene Watson; *Gene Watson's Greatest Hits* . . . . (MCA)

What Were You Thinkin'
Little Texas; *First Time For Everything* . . . . (Warner Bros.)

What'd I Say
Elvis Presley; *Collector's Gold* . . . .(RCA)
Elvis' Gold Records, Volume 4. . . . .(RCA)
Elvis In Concert . . . .(RCA)
Elvis-Greatest Hits, Volume One . . . .(RCA)
Jerry Lee Lewis; *Jerry Lee Lewis-Original Golden Hits-#2* . . . . (Sun)
Jerry Lee Lewis-Original Golden Hits-#2 . . . . (Sun)
Milestones . . . . (Rhino)
Rocket 88 . . . .(Tomato)
Rockin' My Life Away. . . . .(Tomato)
John Mayall's Bluesbreakers with Eric Clapton; *John Mayall's Bluesbreakers
with Eric Clapton.* . . . .(Deram)
Ray Charles; *Atlantic Rhythm & Blues 1947-1974-#4 (1958-1962)-C* . .(Atlantic)
Atlantic Soul Classics-C . . . . (Warner Special Prod.)
Frat Rock!-#3-Grandson Of Frat Rock!-C . . . . (Rhino)
Life In Music. . . . .(Atlantic)
Ray Charles-Anthology . . . . (Rhino)

What's On Your Mind (Pure Energy)
Information Society; *Information Society* . . . . (Tommy Boy)

What's The 411?
Mary J. Blige; *What's The 411?* . . . .(Uptown)

When I Think About Angels
Jamie O'Neal; *Shiver* . . . . (Mercury)

When I Think Of You
Journey; *Trial By Fire* . . . . (Columbia)

When The Heart Rules The Mind
GTR; *GTR.* . . . . (Arista)

When They're Old Enough To Know Better
Eddie Cantor; *Music From The New York Stage (1890-1920)-#4-1917-
1920-C.* . . . . (Pearl)

When U Think About Me
Voice V; *ST/Jailbait!* . . . . (MCA)

When You Talk About Love
Patti LaBelle; *Flame* . . . . (MCA)
Live! One Night Only . . . . (MCA)

When You Think Of Me
Eric Benet; *A Day In The Life* . . . . (Warner Bros.)

Where Do I Go From You
Jon Secada; *Heart, Soul & A Voice* . . . . (SBK)

Where Do You Go
No Mercy; *No Mercy.* . . . .(Arista)

Where Have All The Flowers Gone
Johnny Rivers; *Best Of Johnny Rivers.* . . . . (EMI)
Johnny Rivers-Anthology 1964-1977 . . . . (Rhino)
Kingston Trio; *Capitol Collectors Series-The Kingston Trio* . . . . (Capitol)
Songs Of Protest-C . . . . (Rhino)
Pete Seeger; *Essential Pete Seeger* . . . . (Vanguard)
Pete Seeger's Greatest Hits . . . . (Columbia)
Peter, Paul & Mary; *Peter, Paul And Mary* . . . . (Warner Bros.)
Wes Montgomery; *Wes Montgomery-Classics-#22* . . . . (A&M)

Who Are The Brain Police
Frank Zappa; *Disconnected Synapses* . . . . (Rhino)
Mothers Of Invention; *Freak Out* . . . . (Barking Pumpkin)

Who Are You
Who; *Hooligans* . . . . (MCA)
The Concert For New York City-C . . . . (Columbia)
Who Are You. . . . . (MCA)
Who Greatest Hits . . . . (MCA)
Who's Last . . . . (MCA)

Who Do You Think You Are
Spice Girls; *Spice* . . . .(Virgin)

Whole Lot To Think About
Wood; *Songs From Stamford Hill* . . . . (Columbia)

Why Didn't I Think Of That
Doug Stone; *From The Heart* . . . . (Epic)

Will I Ever Understand You
Berlin; *Best Of Berlin 1979-1988* . . . . (Geffen)
Count Three & Pray . . . . (Geffen)

Windmills Of Your Mind
Acker Bilk; *Best Of Acker Bilk* . . . .(Crescendo)
Dusty Springfield; *Dusty In Memphis* . . . . (Rhino)
Johnny Mathis; *How Do You Keep The Music Playing* . . . . (Columbia)
Mel Torme; *Best Of Mel Torme.* . . . . (Curb)
Philadelphia Orchestra & Eugene Ormandy; *Movie Love Songs.* . . . . . . (RCA)

Wiser Time
Black Crowes; *Amorica* . . . . (American)

Wishful Thinking
Dan Hill & Celine Dion; *Real Love* . . . . (Columbia)

Wishful Thinking
Wynn Stewart; *Heroes Of Country Music-#4-Legends Of The West
Coast-C* . . . . (Rhino)

Wishful Thinking
Little Anthony And The Imperials; *Best Of Little Anthony And The
Imperials* . . . . (Rhino)

Wishful Thinking
Dolly Parton & Donna Fargo; *Queens Of Country* . . . . (Intermedia)
Wishful Thinking
China Crisis; *Working With Fire & Steel*. . . . . (Warner Bros.)
With Me Part 1
Destiny's Child featuring JD; *Destiny's Child*. . . . . (Grass Roots/Columbia)
Without Expression
John Mellencamp; *Best That I Could Do-1978-1988* . . . . (Mercury)
Woman Of Heart & Mind
Joni Mitchell; *For The Roses*. . . . . (Asylum)
Joni Mitchell with Tom Scott & The L.A. Express; *Miles Of Aisles* . . . (Asylum)
Woman, Woman
Union Gap Featuring Gary Puckett; *Best Of Gary Puckett*. . . . . (Hollywood/DNA-Rounder)
Gary Puckett And The Union Gap's Greatest Hits . . . . (Columbia)
Woman's Got A Right To Change Her Mind
Rex Stewart & The Ellingtonians; *Rex Stewart & The Ellingtonians*. . . . . (Riverside)
Woman's Smarter
Jolly Boys; *Sunshine 'N' Water*. (Rykodisc)
Wonderful World
Art Garfunkel; *Watermark*. . . . . (Legacy)
Herman's Hermits; *Herman's Hermits-Their Greatest Hits* . . . . (Abkco)
Sam Cooke; *Best Of Sam Cooke* . . . . (RCA)
ST/Animal House . . . . (MCA)
This Is Sam Cooke. . . . . (RCA)
Words Of Wisdom
Wyclef Jean featuring The Refugee Allstars; *Presents The Carnival F/ Refugee Allstars*. . . . . (Ruffhouse/Columbia)
Words Of Wisdom
Christopher Cross; *Another Page* . . . . (Warner Bros.)
World I Know, The
Collective Soul; *Collective Soul* . . . . (Atlantic)
World We Knew (Over And Over)
Frank Sinatra; *Frank Sinatra's Greatest Hits!*. . . . . (Reprise)
The World We Knew . . . . (Reprise)
Worried Mind
Roy Acuff; *Night Train To Memphis* . . . . (Columbia River Entert. Group)
Yes The River Knows
Doors; *Waiting For The Sun* . . . . (Elektra)
You Better Think Twice
Vince Gill; *When Love Finds You* . . . . (MCA)
You Don't Even Know Who I Am
Patty Loveless; *Patty Loveless-Classics* . . . . (Epic)
When Fallen Angels Fly . . . . (Epic)
You Don't Know How It Feels
Tom Petty; *Wildflowers*. . . . . (Warner Bros.)
You Don't Know Me
Jerry Vale; *Jerry Vale-17 Most Requested Songs* . . . . (Legacy)
Jerry Vale's All-Time Greatest Hits . . . . (Columbia)
Jerry Vale's Greatest Hits . . . . (Columbia)
You Don't Know Me
Ray Charles; *Ray Charles-Complete Country & Western Recordings 1959-1986* . . . . (Rhino)
You Don't Know Me At All
Don Henley; *Actual Miles: Henley's Greatest Hits* . . . . (Geffen)
You Don't Understand
House Of Love; *Babe Rainbow* . . . . (Fontana)
You Have No Idea
Pamela Rose; *Morpheus* . . . . (Grace)
You Know How We Do
Ice Cube; *Lethal Injection* . . . . (Priority)
You Know Me Better Than That
George Strait; *Strait Out Of The Box* . . . . (MCA)
The Chill Of An Early Fall . . . . (MCA)
You Know My Name (Look Up My Number)
Beatles; *Beatles-Box Set* . . . . (Capitol)
Past Masters-Volume Two . . . . (Parlophone)
Rarities . . . . (Capitol)
You Know What To Do
Beatles; *The Beatles-Anthology-#1* . . . . (Capitol)
You Might Think
Cars; *Heartbeat City* . . . . (Elektra)
The Cars' Greatest Hits . . . . (Elektra)
You Never Knew About Me
Tom Powers & Dot Temple; *Music From The New York Stage (1890-1920)-#4-1917-1920-C* . . . . (Pearl)
You Oughta Know
Alanis Morissette; *1996 Grammy Nominees-C* . . . . (Columbia)
Jagged Little Pill. . . . . (Maverick)
You Should Know Better
Kenny Wayne Shepherd Band; *Live On* . . . . (Giant)
You Stupid Jerk
Angry Samoans; *Back From Samoa* . . . . (PVC)
Gimme Samoa-31 Garbage-Pit Hits. . . . . (PVC)
You Were On My Mind
We Five; *Baby Boomer Classics-Folk Sixties-C* . . . . (JCI Assoc. Labels)
Billboard Top Pop Hits-1965-C . . . . (Rhino)

You Wouldn't Believe
311; *From Chaos* . . . . (Volcano Entertainment)
You'll Never Know
Dick Haymes; *Best Of Dick Haymes* . . . .(Curb)
You'll Never Know . . . . (MCA Special Prod.)
Dick Haymes & His Song Spinners; *Billboard Pop Memories-1940-1944-C* . . . .(Rhino)
Billboard Top Movie Hits-1940s-C. . . . .(Rhino)
You'll Never Know
Mindy McCready; *If I Don't Stay The Night* . . . . (BNA)
You'll Never Never Know
Platters; *Magic Touch-An Anthology* . . . .(Mercury)
Very Best Of The Platters . . . .(Mercury)
Young Blood
Bad Company; *Run With The Pack* . . . .(Swan Song)
Coasters; *Coasters' Greatest Hits* . . . .(Atco)
Coasters-Their Greatest Recordings-Early Years. . . . .(Atco)
The Ultimate Coasters . . . .(Warner Special Prod.)
Younger Girl
Critters; *Sixties Rule! Chapter Two-C* . . . . (One Way)
Lovin' Spoonful; *Lovin' Spoonful-Anthology* . . . .(Rhino)
Your Mind Has Left Your Body
Paul Kantner, Grace Slick & David Freiberg; *Baron Von Tollbooth & The Chrome Nun* . . . . (Grunt)
Your Mother Should Know
Beatles; *Beatles-Box Set* . . . .(Capitol)
Magical Mystery Tour. . . . .(Capitol)
You're A God
Vertical Horizon; *Everything You Want* . . . . (RCA)
You're Always On My Mind
SWV; *It's About Time* . . . . (RCA)
You're Not In Kansas Anymore
Jo Dee Messina; *Jo Dee Messina* . . . .(Curb)
You're Only Lonely
J.D. Souther; *Radio Daze-Pop Hits Of The '80s-#1-C* . . . .(Rhino)
You're Only Lonely . . . . (Legacy)
You're So Vain
Carly Simon; *'70s Greatest Rock Hits-#3-High Times-C* . . . . (Priority)
Best Of Carly Simon . . . . (Elektra)
Carly Simon-Greatest Hits Live . . . . (Arista)
No Secrets . . . . (Elektra)
You're Still On My Mind
Byrds; *Sweetheart Of The Rodeo* . . . .(Columbia)

TIME: GENERAL, Clocks

See Also: **AFTERNOON, DAYS OF THE WEEK (various), DAYS: GENERAL, ETERNITY, FUTURE, HISTORY, LATE, LIFE, MIDNIGHT, MONTHS & DATES (various), MORNING, NIGHT, TIME: SPECIFIC, WAITING, YEARS: GENERAL, YEARS: SPECIFIC, YESTERDAY**

(I Believe) Our Time Is Gonna Come
REO Speedwagon; *A Decade Of Rock And Roll 1970 To 1980* . . . .(Epic)
R.E.O. . . . .(Epic)
REO Speedwagon Live/You Get What You Play For . . . .(Epic)
(I've Had) The Time Of My Life
Bill Medley; *Best Of Bill Medley* . . . .(Curb)
Bill Medley & Jennifer Warnes; *Dirty Dancing Live In Concert-C* . . . . . . (RCA)
ST/Dirty Dancing . . . . (RCA)
15 Minutes
Marc Nelson; *chocolate mood* . . . .(Columbia)
24 Hours From Tulsa
Gene Pitney; *45-#3015*. . . . .(Collectables)
Double Gold-Gene Pitney . . . .(Mustcor)
Ian & Sylvia; *Best Of Ian & Sylvia* . . . .(Vanguard)
Ian & Sylvia's Greatest Hits . . . .(Vanguard)
Play One More . . . .(Vanguard)
24/7
Kevon Edmonds; *24/7* . . . . (RCA)
5-4-3-2 (Yo! Time Is Up)
Jade; *Mind Body & Soul* . . . . (Giant)
6, 8, 12
Brian McKnight; *Back At One* . . . .(Motown)
After All This Time
Rodney Crowell; *Diamonds & Dirt* . . . .(Columbia)
After Party
Koffee Brown; *Mars/Venus* . . . . (Arista)
Ain't It The Life
Foo Fighters; *There Is Nothing Left To Lose* . . . . (Roswell/RCA)
Ain't Wastin' Time No More
Allman Brothers Band; *Decade Of Hits-1969-1979* . . . . (Polydor)
Dreams . . . . (Polydor)
Eat A Peach . . . . (Polydor)
All Along
Blessid Union Of Souls; *Home*. . . . .(EMI)

All Day And All Of The Night
Kinks; *British Rock-#1-C* . . . . (Original Sound)
   God Save The Kinks! . . . .(Castle Music America)
   History Of British Rock-#2-C . . . . (Rhino)
All I Need
Forester Sisters; *All I Need* . . . .(Warner Bros.)
All I Need
Jack Wagner; *All I Need* . . . . (Qwest)
All The Time In The World
Subdudes; *Primitive Streak* . . . . (High Street)
All Things Must Pass
George Harrison; *All Things Must Pass* . . . . (Parlophone)
All This Time
Tiffany; *Hold An Old Friend's Hand* . . . .(MCA)
   Tiffany's Greatest Hits . . . . (Hip-O)
All This Time
Reba McEntire; *If You See Him* . . . . (MCA)
All This Time
Sting; *Fields Of Gold-The Best Of Sting 1984-1994* . . . . (A&M)
   Soul Cages . . . . (A&M)
All Those Yesterdays
Pearl Jam; *Yield* . . . .(Epic)
Always On Time
Ja Rule; *Pain Is Love* . . . . (Murder Inc./Def Jam/IDJMG)
Another Nine Minutes
Yankee Grey; *Untamed* . . . . (Monument)
Any Time At All
Beatles; *Rock 'N' Roll Music* . . . . (Capitol)
   Something New . . . . (Capitol)
Any Time, Any Place
Janet Jackson; *janet.* . . . . (Virgin)
Anytime
Eddie Fisher; *Best Of Eddie Fisher* . . . . (MCA)
Eddy Arnold, The Tennessee Plowboy and his Guitar; *Nipper's Greatest Hits*
   Of The '40s-#2-C . . . . (RCA)
Patsy Cline; *Best Of Patsy Cline* . . . .(MCA Special Prod.)
Anytime
Brian McKnight; *Anytime* . . . . (Motown)
   Now That's What I Call Music!-#1-C . . . . (Virgin)
Arkansas Time Traveler
Star-Spangled Washboard Band; *Collector's Item* . . . . . . (Flying Fish)
As Time Goes By
Andy Williams; *Moon River & Other Great Movie Themes* . . . . . . (Columbia)
Barbra Streisand; *Third Album* . . . . (Columbia)
Frank Sinatra; *Point Of No Return* . . . . (Capitol)
Johnny Mathis; *Best Days Of My Life* . . . . (Columbia)
   First 25 Years-Silver Anniversary Album . . . . (Columbia)
Natalie Cole; *Take A Look* . . . . (Elektra)
Nilsson; *A Little Touch Of Schmilsson In The Night* . . . . (RCA)
   Nilsson's Greatest Hits . . . . (RCA)
Willie Nelson; *Without A Song* . . . . (Columbia)
At The Same Time
Barbra Streisand; *Higher Ground* . . . . (Columbia)
Battle Flag
Lo Fidelity Allstars; *How To Operate With A Blown Mind* . . . . . . (Skint)
Beat Goes On, The
Sonny & Cher; *Best Of Sonny & Cher* . . . . (Atco)
   Hit Singles-1958-1977-C . . . .(Atlantic)
   Sonny & Cher-Live . . . .(MCA)
   The Beat Goes On-Best Of Sonny & Cher . . . . (Rhino)
   Two Of Us . . . . (Atco)
Bidin' My Time
Original Cast; *Girl Crazy* . . . .(Sony Music Special Prod.)
Sarah Vaughan; *Sarah Vaughan Sings George Gershwin Songbook,*
   Vol. 1 . . . . (Emarcy)
Big Spender (Muriel Cigars)
Original Soundtrack; *TeeVee Toons-The Commercials-#1-C* . . . . (TVT)
Big Time
Neil Young & Crazy Horse; *Broken Arrow* . . . . (Reprise)
   Year Of The Horse . . . . (Reprise)
Bookends
Simon & Garfunkel; *Bookends* . . . . (Columbia)
   Collected Works . . . . (Columbia)
   Simon & Garfunkel's Greatest Hits . . . . (Columbia)
Borrowed Time
John Lennon; *Lennon* . . . . (Capitol)
John Lennon & Yoko Ono; *Milk & Honey* . . . . (Polydor)
Borrowed Time
Styx; *Cornerstone* . . . . (A&M)
Borrowed Time
Olivia Newton-John; *Totally Hot* . . . . (MCA)
Brand New Day
Sting; *Brand New Day* . . . . (A&M)
Buying Time
Clint Black; *The Hard Way* . . . . (RCA)
Can We Spend Some Time
Surface; *2nd Wave* . . . . (Columbia)
Cara Mia
Jay & The Americans; *I Got Rhythm-C* . . . . (K-Tel)

Jay & The Americans' *Greatest Hits* . . . . (CEMA Special Prod.)
Jay & The Americans' *Greatest Hits* . . . . (Curb)
Carry That Weight
Beatles; *Abbey Road* . . . . (Parlophone)
Child In Time
Deep Purple; *Deepest Purple/The Very Best Of Deep Purple* . . . . (Warner Bros.)
   In Rock . . . . (Warner Bros.)
   Made In Japan . . . . (Warner Bros.)
Circle Game, The
Buffy Sainte-Marie; *Best Of Buffy Sainte-Marie* . . . . (Vanguard)
   Fire & Fleet & Candlelight . . . . (Vanguard)
Ian & Sylvia; *Ian & Sylvia's Greatest Hits* . . . . (Vanguard)
Joni Mitchell; *Ladies Of The Canyon* . . . . (Reprise)
Joni Mitchell with Tom Scott & The L.A. Express; *Miles Of Aisles* . . . .(Asylum)
Tom Rush; *Classic Rush* . . . . (Elektra)
   The Circle Game . . . . (Elektra)
City
Fleetwood Mac; *Mystery To Me* . . . . (Reprise)
Coffee Time
Li'l Wally; *My Polish Girlfriend & Others* . . . . (Jay Jay)
Couldn't Last A Moment
Collin Raye; *Tracks* . . . . (Epic)
Cryin' Time
Julio Iglesias; *Starry Night* . . . . (Columbia)
Cryin' Time
Barbra Streisand; *Butterfly* . . . . (Columbia)
Cryin' Time
Kendalls; *Kendalls-20 Favorites* . . . . (Epic)
Crying Time
Buck Owens & Emmylou Harris; *Act Naturally* . . . . (Capitol)
Ray Charles; *Ray Charles' Greatest Hits* . . . . (Rhino)
   Ray Charles-Anthology . . . . (Rhino)
   Ray Charles-His Greatest Hits-#1 . . . . (Dunhill Compact Classics)
Dangerous Times
Cher; *Cher* . . . . (Geffen)
Daughters Of Time
Judy Collins; *All-Ears Review-#7-Still*
   Amazing...-C . . . . (Really Outstanding Music)
Day After Day
Def Leppard; *Euphoria* . . . . (Mercury)
Doctor Time
Rick Trevino; *Rick Trevino* . . . . (Columbia)
Does Anybody Really Know What Time It Is?
Chicago; *Chicago At Carnegie Hall* . . . . (Chicago)
   Chicago IX-Chicago's Greatest Hits . . . . (Chicago)
   Chicago Transit Authority . . . . (Chicago)
   If You Leave Me Now . . . . (Chicago)
Doin' My Time
Flatt & Scruggs; *Flatt & Scruggs-20 Greatest Hits* . . . . (Deluxe)
Johnny Cash; *Get Rhythm* . . . . (Sun)
   Johnny Cash-Original Golden Hits-#3 . . . . (Sun)
   Strawberry Cake . . . . (Sun)
Doin' Time
Spooner; *Every Corner Dance* . . . . (Mountain Railroad)
   Wildest Dreams/Every Corner Dance . . . .(Dali)
Doin' Time
Meg Christian & Cris Williamson; *Meg-Cris At*
   Carnegie Hall . . . . (Second Wave)
Doin' Time
Justin Hayward; *Songwriter* . . . .(Deram)
Don't Rush (Take Love Slowly)
K-Ci & JoJo; *Love Always* . . . . (MCA)
Don't Waste Your Time
Yarbrough & Peoples; *Best Of Yarbrough & Peoples* . . . . (Mercury)
Don't Waste Your Time
Five Stairsteps; *Five Stairsteps' Greatest Hits* . . . . (Collectables)
Drug-Stabbing Time
Clash; *Give 'Em Enough Rope* . . . . (Epic)
Dust On The Bottle
David Lee Murphy; *Out With A Bang* . . . . (MCA)
Every Day Of The Week
Jade; *Mind, Body & Song* . . . .(Giant)
   ST/Beverly Hills, 90210-College Years . . . .(Giant)
Every Once In Awhile
BlackHawk; *BlackHawk* . . . . (Arista)
Every Other Time
LFO; *Life Is Good* . . . . (J)
Every Second
Collin Raye; *All I Can Be* . . . . (Epic)
Every Time I Close My Eyes
Babyface; *The Day* . . . . (Epic)
Everything Must Change
Barbra Streisand; *Higher Ground* . . . . (Columbia)
Excuse Me Mr.
No Doubt; *Tragic Kingdom* . . . . (Trauma)
Final Hour
Lauryn Hill; *The Miseducation Of Lauryn Hill* . . . . (Ruffhouse/Columbia)

First Time Ever I Saw Your Face
Celine Dion; *All The Way...A Decade Of Song* . . . . (550 Music)
Roberta Flack; *Atlantic Rhythm & Blues 1947-1974-#6 (1966-*
1969)-C . . . . (Atlantic)
Best Of Roberta Flack . . . . (Atlantic)
First Take . . . . (Atlantic)
Fly Like An Eagle
Seal; *ST/Space Jam* . . . . (Warner Sunset)
Steve Miller; *Fly Like An Eagle* . . . . (Capitol)
ST/FM . . . . (MCA)
Steve Miller Band-Gift Set . . . . (Capitol)
Steve Miller Band-Live . . . . (Capitol)
Steve Miller Band's Greatest Hits-1974-78 . . . . (Capitol)
For A Little While
Tim McGraw; *Everywhere* . . . . (Curb)
Tim McGraw's Greatest Hits . . . . (Curb)
Forty-Five Minutes From Broadway
Mickey Finn; *Caught In The Act* . . . . (Crescendo)
Fred Jones Part 2
Ben Folds; *Rockin' The Suburbs* . . . . (Epic)
Free
Vast; *Music For People* . . . . (Elektra)
Funny How Time Slips Away
Al Green & Lyle Lovett; *Rhythm Country And Blues-C* . . . . (MCA)
Jimmy Elledge; *Nipper's Greatest Hits Of The '60s-#2-C* . . . . . . (RCA)
RCA's Greatest One-Hit Wonders-C . . . . (RCA)
Willie Nelson; *Best Of Willie Nelson* . . . . (Capitol)
Collector's Series-Willie Nelson . . . . (RCA)
Healing Hands Of Time . . . . (Liberty)
My Own Way . . . . (RCA)
San Antonio Rose . . . . (Columbia)
Willie & Family Live . . . . (Columbia)
Willie Nelson & Faron Young; *Funny How Time Slips Away* . . . . . . (Columbia)
Get Me To The World On Time
Electric Prunes; *Nuggets-Original Artyfacts From The First Psychedelic Era-*
1965-1968-C . . . . (Rhino)
Gettin' Together
Tommy James And The Shondells; *Tommy James And The Shondells-*
Anthology . . . . (Rhino)
Gimme Some Time
Natalie Cole; *Natalie Cole & Peabo Bryson: Best Of Friends* . . . . (Capitol)
Natalie Cole-Collection . . . . (Capitol)
Reaching For The Sky-Towering Soul From The '70s-C . . . . (Capitol)
Give Me Just A Little More Time
Chairmen Of The Board; *Chairmen Of The Board's Greatest Hits* . . . . . (HDH)
Given More Time
Vince Gill; *High Lonesome Sound* . . . . (MCA)
God Must Have Spent A Little More Time On You
Alabama Featuring 'N Sync; *Twentieth Century* . . . . (RCA)
'N Sync; *'N Sync* . . . . (RCA)
Totally Hits-#1-C . . . . (Arista)
Good Timin'
Jimmy Jones; *Hard To Find 45s On CD-#1-1955-1960-C* . . . . (Eric)
Got The Time
Joe Jackson; *Live 1980/86* . . . . (A&M)
Look Sharp! . . . . (A&M)
No Wave . . . . (A&M)
Graduation Day
Beach Boys; *Beach Boys-Gift Set* . . . . (Capitol)
Spirit Of America . . . . (Capitol)
Rover Boys; *Choice Voices! Pop Vocal Group Gems Of The*
'50s-C . . . . (Collector's Choice)
Hanging By A Moment
Lifehouse; *No Name Face* . . . . (DreamWorks/SKG)
Now That's What I Call Music!-#7-C . . . . (Virgin)
Haven't Got Time For The Pain
Carly Simon; *Best Of Carly Simon* . . . . (Elektra)
Hotcakes . . . . (Elektra)
Hazy Shade Of Winter
Bangles; *Bangles' Greatest Hits* . . . . (Columbia)
ST/Less Than Zero . . . . (Def Jam)
Simon & Garfunkel; *Bookends* . . . . (Columbia)
Collected Works . . . . (Columbia)
Healing Hands Of Time
Willie Nelson; *Healing Hands Of Time* . . . . (Liberty)
Hello Stranger
Barbara Lewis; *Atlantic Rhythm & Blues 1947-1974-#5 (1962-*
1966)-C . . . . (Atlantic)
Billboard Top R&B Hits-1963-C . . . . (Rhino)
Collectables Presents The History Of Rock-#5-C . . . . (Collectables)
High Times
Jamiroquai; *Traveling Without Moving* . . . . (Work/Epic)
Hour Of Gold
Emmylou Harris; *Red Dirt Girl* . . . . (Nonesuch)
How Beautiful The Days
Original Broadway Cast; *The Most Happy Fella* . . . . . . (Sony Music Classical)
How Can I Help You Say Goodbye
Patty Loveless; *Only What I Feel* . . . . (Epic)
Patty Loveless-Classics . . . . (Epic)

How Many More Times
Led Zeppelin; *Led Zeppelin* . . . . (Atlantic)
I Believe My Time Ain't Long
Fleetwood Mac; *25 Years-The Chain* . . . . (Warner Bros.)
I Can't Wait Another Minute
Hi-Five; *Hi-Five* . . . . (Jive)
I Didn't Know What Time It Was
Ella Fitzgerald; *Rodgers & Hart Songbook* . . . . (Verve)
Sarah Vaughan; *Crazy & Mixed Up* . . . . (Pablo)
I Guess That's Why They Call It The Blues
Elton John; *Elton John's Greatest Hits-1976-1986* . . . . (MCA)
Too Low For Zero . . . . (MCA)
I Hope You Dance
Lee Ann Womack; *I Hope You Dance* . . . . (MCA)
I Just Wasn't Made For These Times
Beach Boys; *Pet Sounds* . . . . (Capitol)
The Pet Sounds Sessions: A 30th Anniversary Collection . . . . . (Capitol)
I Want To Tell You
Beatles; *Revolver* . . . . (Capitol)
If I Could Be With You
Helen Humes; *Ladies Sing The Blues-#2-C* . . . . (Savoy)
Louis Armstrong; *Best Of Louis Armstrong* . . . . (MCA)
Satchmo-Musical Autobiography-#2 . . . . (MCA)
The Louis Armstrong Story-#4 . . . . (Columbia)
If I Could Turn Back The Hands Of Time
R. Kelly; *Now That's What I Call Music!-#3-C* . . . . (Virgin)
R. . . . . (Jive)
If I Could Turn Back Time
Cher; *Heart Of Stone* . . . . (Geffen)
If You've Got The Money I've Got The Time
Lefty Frizzell; *American Originals-Lefty Frizzell* . . . . (Columbia)
Columbia Country Classics-#2-Honky Tonk Heroes-C . . . . . . (Columbia)
Lefty Frizzell's Greatest Hits . . . . (Columbia)
Willie Nelson; *Greatest Hits (& Some That Will Be)* . . . . (Columbia)
Sound In Your Mind . . . . (Columbia)
Willie & Family Live . . . . (Columbia)
If You've Got The Time (Miller High Life Beer)
Original Soundtrack; *TeeVee Toons-The Commercials-#1-C* . . . . . . (TVT)
I'll Follow The Sun
Beatles; *Beatles '65* . . . . (Capitol)
Beatles-Box Set . . . . (Capitol)
Beatles-Love Songs . . . . (Capitol)
For Sale . . . . (Capitol)
I'm Not A Girl, Not Yet A Woman
Britney Spears; *Britney* . . . . (Jive)
Image Of A Girl
Safaris; *Brown Eyed Soul...East L.A.-#3-C* . . . . (Rhino)
In A New York Minute
Ronnie McDowell; *19 Hot Country Requests-#3-C* . . . . (Epic)
In A New York Minute . . . . (Epic)
Older Women & Other Greatest Hits . . . . (Epic)
In The End
Linkin Park; *Hybrid Theory* . . . . (Warner Bros.)
In The Meantime
Spacehog; *Resident Alien* . . . . (Sire)
In Times Like These
Barbara Mandrell; *Barbara Mandrell's Greatest Hits* . . . . (MCA)
Spun Gold . . . . (MCA)
Isn't It Time
Babys; *Babys-Anthology* . . . . (Chrysalis)
Broken Heart . . . . (Chrysalis)
It Only Hurts For A Little While
Ames Brothers; *Best Of The Ames Brothers* . . . . (Pair)
Anne Murray; *Croonin'* . . . . (SBK)
Margo Smith; *Best Of Margo Smith* . . . . (MCA Special Prod.)
It Takes Time
Louis Armstrong; *Pops* . . . . (Bluebird)
It Takes Time
Marshall Tucker Band; *10th* . . . . (Warner Bros.)
It Won't Be Long
Beatles; *Meet The Beatles!* . . . . (Capitol)
With The Beatles . . . . (Parlophone)
It Wouldn't Hurt To Have Wings
Mark Chesnutt; *Wings* . . . . (Decca)
It's About Time
Public Announcement; *All Work, No Play* . . . . (A&M)
It's Been A Long, Long Time
Bing Crosby; *Best Of Bing Crosby* . . . . (MCA)
Harry James & His Orchestra; *Words & Music Of World*
War II-C . . . . (Columbia)
Harry James & Kitty Kallen; *Best Of The Big Bands-C* . . . . . . (Columbia)
Jan Garber & His Orchestra; *Best Of Jan Garber* . . . . (MCA)
Louis Armstrong; *Hello Dolly! & Other Hits* . . . . (MCA)
It's Been Awhile
Staind; *Break The Cycle* . . . . (Flip/Elektra)
It's Going To Take Some Time
Carole King; *A Natural Woman: The Ode Collection-1968-1976* . . . . . (Legacy)
Music . . . . (Epic)

Carpenters; *A Song For You* .... (A&M)
  Carpenters-The Singles 1969-1973 .... (A&M)
  Yesterday Once More. .... (A&M)

It's High Time
Dottie West; *Best Of Dottie West* .... (Liberty)

It's In Your Eyes (Any Time At All)
Phil Collins; *Dance Into The Light* .... (Atlantic)

It's Just A Matter Of Time
Brook Benton; *45s On CD-#1-1956-1959-C* .... (Mercury)
  Billboard Top R&B Hits-1959-C .... (Rhino)
Glen Campbell; *It's Just A Matter Of Time* .... (Atlantic America)
Randy Travis; *No Holdin' Back* .... (Warner Bros.)
  Rock Rhythm & Blues-C .... (Warner Bros.)

It's Just A Matter Of Time
Beach Boys; *Beach Boys* .... (Caribou)

It's Late
Ricky Nelson; *Lonesome Town* .... (CEMA Special Prod.)
  Ricky Nelson Volume 1 .... (Gold Rush)

It's My Time
Martina McBride; *Emotion.* .... (RCA)

It's No Good
Depeche Mode; *Ultra* .... (Mute/Reprise)

It's Now Or Never
Elvis Presley; *Elvis Presley-Love Songs* .... (RCA)
  Heart & Soul .... (RCA)
  Worldwide 50 Gold Award Hits, Vol. 1, Parts 1 & 2 .... (RCA)

It's Time
Winans; *Return* .... (Qwest)

It's Time For Love
Don Williams; *Best Of Don Williams-#4* .... (MCA)
  Cafe Carolina .... (MCA)
  Don Williams Sings Bob McDill .... (MCA)
  Till The Rivers All Run Dry .... (MCA Special Prod.)

It's Time For Love
James Brown; *Love Overdue* .... (Scotti Bros.)

It's Time For Love
Chi-Lites; *Chi-Lites' Greatest Hits-#2* .... (Rhino)

It's Too Late
Amy Grant; *Tapestry Revisited: Tribute To Carole King-C* .. (Lava)
Carole King; *Her Greatest Hits* .... (Epic)
  Tapestry .... (Epic)
Gloria Estefan; *Hold Me, Thrill Me, Kiss Me* .... (Epic)

I've Had Enough
Regina Belle; *Believe In Me* .... (MCA)

I've Loved You For A Long Time
Spinners; *Love Trippin'* .... (Atlantic)

Just Another Day
John Mellencamp; *Mr. Happy Go Lucky* .... (Mercury)

Just In Time
Barbra Streisand; *Third Album* .... (Columbia)
Frank Sinatra; *Come Dance With Me!* .... (Capitol)
Michael Feinstein; *Michael Feinstein Sings The Jule Styne
  Songbook* .... (Nonesuch)
Tony Bennett; *Tony Bennett-16 Most Requested Songs* .... (Legacy)

Killin' Time
Clint Black; *Killin' Time.* .... (RCA)
  RCA Award Winners-C .... (RCA)

Killing Time
Destiny's Child; *ST/Men In Black.* .... (Columbia)

Large Time
Atlanta Rhythm Section; *Are You Ready!* .... (Polydor)
  Champagne Jam .... (Polydor)

Last Time Lover
Spice Girls; *Spice* .... (Virgin)

Lately
Divine; *Fairy Tales* .... (Pendulum)

Lately
Tyrese; *Tyrese* .... (RCA)

Leave A Tender Moment Alone
Billy Joel; *Innocent Man* .... (Columbia)

Let's Roll
Neil Young; *Let's Roll-CD Single* .... (Reprise)

Little More Time With You
James Taylor; *Hourglass* .... (Columbia)

Livin' On Borrowed Time
Travis Tritt; *Down The Road I Go* .... (Columbia)

Living In A Moment
Ty Herndon; *Living In A Moment* .... (Epic)
  Super Hits Of 1996-C. .... (Epic)

Long Long Long
Beatles; *The Beatles (White Album)* .... (Capitol)

Long Long Time
Linda Ronstadt; *Different Drum* .... (Capitol)
  Linda Ronstadt-Retrospective .... (Capitol)
  Linda Ronstadt's Greatest Hits .... (Asylum)
  Silk Purse. .... (Capitol)

Long Long While
Rolling Stones; *More Hot Rocks (big hits & fazed cookies)* .... (Abkco)

Long Run
Eagles; *Eagles Greatest Hits, Volume 2* .... (Asylum)
  Eagles Live .... (Asylum)
  The Long Run .... (Asylum)

Long Time
Todd Rundgren; *Runt-The Ballad Of Todd Rundgren* .... (Rhino)

Long Time
Boston; *Boston* .... (Epic)

Long Time
Molly Hatchet; *Flirtin' With Disaster* .... (Epic)

Long Time Ago
Remingtons; *Blue Frontier* .... (BNA)

Long Time Gone
Crosby, Stills & Nash; *Crosby, Stills & Nash* .... (Atlantic)
  CSN .... (Atlantic)
Crosby, Stills, Nash & Young; *4 Way Street.* .... (Atlantic)

Long Time Gone
Triumph; *Surveillance.* .... (MCA)

Long Time Gone
38 Special; *38 Special* .... (A&M)

Long Time No See
Chicago; *Chicago VIII* .... (Chicago)

Long Time No See, Baby
Glenn Miller & His Orchestra; *Complete Glenn Miller & His
  Orchestra-#5* .... (Bluebird)
  Complete Glenn Miller & His Orchestra-#9 .... (Bluebird)

Longer
Dan Fogelberg; *Dan Fogelberg/Greatest Hits* .... (Full Moon)
  Phoenix. .... (Full Moon)

Longest Time
Billy Joel; *An Innocent Man* .... (Columbia)
  Billy Joel-Greatest Hits, Volume I & Volume II .... (Columbia)

Look What Love Has Done
Patty Smyth; *ST/Junior* .... (MCA)

Love Comes To Everyone
George Harrison; *Best Of Dark Horse 1976-1989.* .... (Dark Horse)
  George Harrison .... (Dark Horse)

Love Gets Me Every Time
Shania Twain; *Come On Over* .... (Mercury)

Love Is On The Way
Celine Dion; *Let's Talk About Love-C* .... (550 Music)
Dave Koz; *Dance* .... (Capitol)

Love Remains
Collin Raye; *I Think About You* .... (Epic)

Love Takes Time
Ralph Tresvant; *Ralph Tresvant* .... (MCA)

Love Takes Time
Orleans; *Forever* .... (Infinity)

Love Takes Time
Mariah Carey; *Mariah Carey* .... (Columbia)

Lovin' Every Minute Of It
Loverboy; *Big Ones* .... (Columbia)
  Lovin' Every Minute Of It. .... (Columbia)

Making Memories
Frankie Laine; *Very Best Of The ABC Years* .... (Taragon)

Man Out Of Time
Elvis Costello; *Girls Girls Girls* .... (Columbia)
Elvis Costello & The Attractions; *Best Of Elvis Costello & The
  Attractions* .... (Columbia)
  Imperial Bedroom .... (Columbia)

Mexican Minutes
Brooks & Dunn; *Hard Workin' Man* .... (Arista)

Miles To Go (Before I Sleep)
Celine Dion; *Let's Talk About Love-C* .... (550 Music)

Minute By Minute
Doobie Brothers; *Best Of The Doobies, Volume II* .... (Warner Bros.)
  Minute By Minute .... (Warner Bros.)

Minutes To Memories
John Cougar Mellencamp; *Scarecrow.* .... (Riva)

Moment To Myself
Macy Gray; *On How Life Is* .... (Epic)

Moment, The
Kenny G; *Kenny G's Greatest Hits* .... (Arista)
  The Moment .... (Arista)

Moonlight Savings Time (There Ought To Be A)
Guy Lombardo & His Royal Canadians; *Auld Lang Syne* .... (Pro-Arte)

Morning Glory
Oasis; *(What's The Story) Morning Glory.* .... (Epic)

Motel Time
Larry Coryell; *Bolero* .... (Evidence Music)

My Baby's Got Good Timing
Dan Seals; *Best Of Dan Seals* .... (Capitol)
  Country Gold-C .... (Priority)
  Dan Seals-Classics Collection-#1 .... (Capitol)
  Early Dan Seals .... (Capitol)
  San Antone .... (EMI)

My Dark Hour
Steve Miller Band; *Best Of Steve Miller 1968-1973* .... (Capitol)

Steve Miller Band-Anthology . . . . (Capitol)
My Song
Jerry Cantrell; *Boggy Depot* . . . . (Columbia)
My Time
Gladys Knight & The Pips; *Best Of Gladys Knight & The Pips-The Columbia Years* . . . . (Columbia)
Life . . . . (Columbia)
My Time
Jane's Addiction; *Jane's Addiction* . . . . (Triple X Entert.)
My Time
Psychedelic Furs; *Mirror Moves* . . . . (Columbia)
My Time
Boz Scaggs; *My Time* . . . . (Columbia)
My Time After Awhile
Buddy Guy; *Hold That Plane* . . . . (Vanguard)
I Was Walkin' Through The Woods . . . . (Chess)
My Time After Awhile . . . . (Vanguard)
My Time Of Day
Mel Torme; *Songs Of New York* . . . . (Rhino)
Original Cast; *Guys & Dolls* . . . . (RCA Victor)
Guys & Dolls . . . . (MCA)
Never A Time
Genesis; *We Can't Dance* . . . . (Atlantic)
Never Never Land
Original Cast/Mary Martin; *Peter Pan-The 1954 Broadway Production* . . . . (RCA Victor)
Next Time
Gladys Knight; *Just For You* . . . . (MCA)
Nick Of Time
AC/DC; *Blow Up Your Video* . . . . (Atco)
Nick Of Time
Bonnie Raitt; *Nick Of Time* . . . . (Capitol)
Night Time
Ted Nugent & The Amboy Dukes; *Greatest Collection Ever* . . . . (Dunhill Compact Classics)
Night Time
J. Geils Band; *Love Stinks* . . . . (EMI)
Night Time Is Cry Time
Jimmy C. Newman; *Jimmy C. Newman's Greatest Hits* . . . . (Plantation)
Night Time Is The Right Time
Creedence Clearwater Revival; *1969* . . . . (Fantasy)
Creedence Clearwater Revival-Chronicle-#2 . . . . (Fantasy)
Green River . . . . (Fantasy)
Ray Charles; *Ray Charles-Complete Atlantic R&B Recordings-1952-1959* . . . . (Atlantic)
No Time
Guess Who; *American Woman* . . . . (RCA)
Best Of The Guess Who . . . . (RCA)
Greatest Of The Guess Who . . . . (RCA)
Track Record-Collection . . . . (RCA)
No Time At All
Original Cast; *Pippin* . . . . (Motown)
No Time For Talk
Christopher Cross; *Another Page* . . . . (Warner Bros.)
No Time To Kill
Clint Black; *No Time To Kill* . . . . (RCA)
No Time To Live
Traffic; *Traffic* . . . . (Island)
No Time To Lose
Tarney/Spencer Band; *Run For Your Life* . . . . (A&M)
No Time To Think
Bob Dylan; *Street Legal* . . . . (Columbia)
Nobody Wants To Be Lonely
Ricky Martin; *Sound Loaded* . . . . (Columbia)
Not Enough Hours In The Night
Doug Supernaw; *You Still Got Me* . . . . (Giant)
Not Enough Time
INXS; *Welcome To Wherever You Are* . . . . (Atlantic)
Nothing But Time
Jackson Browne; *Running On Empty* . . . . (Asylum)
Now's The Time To Fall In Love
Eddie Cantor; *The Eddie Cantor Radio Show-1942-1943* . . . . . . (Original Cast)
Gene Gardos & His Orchestra; *Brother Can You Spare A Dime? Great American Songs Of The Depression-C* . . . . (Pro-Arte)
Oh How The Years Go By
Vanessa Williams; *NBA At 50-A Musical Celebration-C* . . . . (Mercury)
Once In A Lifetime
Talking Heads; *Remain In Light* . . . . (Sire)
ST/Stop Making Sense. . . . . (Sire)
Once Upon A Time
Donna Summer; *Live & More* . . . . (Casablanca)
Once Upon A Time . . . . (Casablanca)
Once Upon A Time
Marvin Gaye & Mary Wells; *Marvin Gaye-Anthology* . . . . (Motown)
Together . . . . (Motown)
Once Upon A Time
Dan Fogelberg; *Nether Lands* . . . . (Full Moon)

Once Upon A Time
Simple Minds; *Once Upon A Time* . . . . (A&M)
Simple Minds Live: In The City Of Light . . . . (A&M)
Once Upon A Time
Frank Sinatra; *September Of My Years* . . . . (Reprise)
Tony Bennett; *I Left My Heart In San Francisco* . . . . (Columbia)
One Clear Moment
Little Feat; *Let It Roll* . . . . (Warner Bros.)
One Hour With You
Nelson Eddy; *When I'm Calling You* . . . . (Living Era)
One Million Billionth Of A Millisecond On A Sunday Morning
Flaming Lips; *Oh My Gawd The Flaming Lips* . . . . (Restless)
One Minute Man
Missy ''Misdemeanor'' Elliot; *Miss E...So Addictive.* . . . . (Gold Mind/East West/EEG)
Only Time
Enya; *A Day Without Rain* . . . . (Reprise)
Only Time Will Tell
Asia; *Asia* . . . . (Geffen)
Live In Moscow . . . . (Rhino)
Then & Now . . . . (Geffen)
Only Time Will Tell
Blast; *It's In My Blood* . . . . (SST)
Otherside
Red Hot Chili Peppers; *Californication* . . . . (Warner Bros.)
Our Time Has Come
Wood; *Songs From Stamford Hill* . . . . (Columbia)
Our Time Is Coming
Brooks & Dunn; *Hard Workin' Man* . . . . (Arista)
Out Of Time
Rolling Stones; *Flowers* . . . . (Abkco)
More Hot Rocks (big hits & fazed cookies) . . . . (Abkco)
Singles Collection-The London Years . . . . (Abkco)
Out Of Time
Sam Phillips; *Indescribable Wow* . . . . (Virgin)
Out Of Time
Divinyls; *Temperamental.* . . . . (Chrysalis)
Overs
Simon & Garfunkel; *Bookends.* . . . . (Columbia)
Collected Works . . . . (Columbia)
Pajama Game/Racing With The Clock
Original Cast; *Pajama Game* . . . . (Columbia)
Party Time
T.G. Sheppard; *Great Divorce Songs For Him-C* . . . . (Warner Bros.)
T.G. Sheppard's All-Time Greatest Hits . . . . (Warner Bros.)
T.G. Sheppard's Greatest Hits . . . . (Warner Bros./Curb)
Pass The Time
Cream; *Wheels Of Fire* . . . . (Polydor)
Passing Time
Bad Company; *Burnin' Sky* . . . . (Swan Song)
Peace In Our Time
Eddie Money; *Eddie Money's Greatest Hits-Sound Of Money* . . . . . (Columbia)
Peace In Our Time
Elvis Costello & The Attractions; *Goodbye Cruel World* . . . . (Columbia)
Peking Theme (So Little Time)
Andy Williams; *ST/55 Days At Peking* . . . . (Varese Sarabande)
Perpetual Blues Machine
Keb' Mo'; *Just Like You.* . . . . (Okeh)
Pledging My Time
Bob Dylan; *Blonde On Blonde.* . . . . (Columbia)
Luther ''Guitar Jr.'' Johnson; *Tangled Up In Blues-Songs Of Bob Dylan-This Ain't No Tribute-C* . . . . (House Of Blues)
Praying For Time
George Michael; *Listen Without Prejudice* . . . . (Columbia)
Precious Time
Journey; *Departure* . . . . (Columbia)
Precious Time
Pat Benatar; *Precious Time* . . . . (Chrysalis)
Precious Time
Van Morrison; *Back On Top* . . . . (Point Blank/Virgin)
Prime Time
Alan Parsons Project; *Ammonia Avenue* . . . . (Arista)
Best Of Alan Parsons Project-#2. . . . . (Arista)
Prime Time
Tubes; *Remote Control* . . . . (A&M)
T.R.A.S.H. (Tubes Rarities And Smash Hits) . . . . (A&M)
Quality Time
David Frishberg; *Quality Time.* . . . . (Sterling)
Queen Of The Hours
Electric Light Orchestra; *No Answer* . . . . (Jet)
Question Of Time
Depeche Mode; *101* . . . . (Sire)
Black Celebration . . . . (Sire)
Question Of Time
Jack Bruce; *Question Of Time* . . . . (Epic)
Quittin' Time
Mary Chapin Carpenter; *Greatest Country Hits Of The '90s-1990-C* . . . . (Columbia)

State Of The Heart . . . . (Columbia)
Raging Winds Of Time
Walking Wounded; *Raging Winds Of Time* . . . . (Chameleon)
Razorblades
Chris Stills; *100 Year Thing* . . . . (Atlantic)
Remember The Time
Michael Jackson; *Dangerous* . . . .(Epic)
Rhythm Of Time
Front 242; *Tyranny For You* . . . . (Epic)
Right In Time
Lucinda Williams; *Car Wheels On A Gravel Road* . . . . (Mercury)
Right Time Of The Night
Jennifer Warnes; *Best Of Jennifer Warnes* . . . . (Arista)
Jennifer Warnes . . . . (Arista)
Ring On Her Finger, Time On Her Hands
Lee Greenwood; *Best Of Lee Greenwood-God Bless America* . . . . (Curb)
Inside Out/You've Got A Good Love Comin' . . . . (MCA)
Lee Greenwood's Greatest Hits . . . .(MCA)
Lee Greenwood-Super Hits . . . . (Epic)
Reba McEntire; *Starting Over* . . . . (MCA)
Rock & Roll Time
Roger McGuinn; *Cardiff Rose* . . . . (Columbia)
Rocket Man
Elton John; *Elton John's Greatest Hits* . . . . (Polydor)
Here And There . . . .(Rocket)
Honky Chateau . . . .(Rocket)
Kate Bush; *Two Rooms-Celebrating The Songs Of Elton John & Bernie
Taupin-C* . . . . (Polydor)
Rockin' Time
Bunny Wailer; *Roots Radics Rockers Reggae* . . . . (Shanachie)
'Round The Clock Lovin'
Gail Davies; *Best Of Gail Davies* . . . . (Capitol)
K.T. Oslin; *This Woman* . . . . (RCA)
Running Out Of Time
Joan Osborne; *Righteous Love* . . . . (Interscope)
Sands Of Time
Howard Keel; *ST/Kismet* . . . .(Sony Music Special Prod.)
Original Cast; *Kismet* . . . . (Columbia)
Sands Of Time
Fleetwood Mac; *Future Games* . . . . (Reprise)
Say When
Lonestar; *Crazy Nights* . . . . (BNA)
Sea Of Time & Sea Of Holes
Beatles; *Beatles-Box Set* . . . . (Capitol)
Yellow Submarine . . . . (Capitol)
Seems Like A Long Time
Rod Stewart; *Every Picture Tells A Story* . . . . (Mercury)
She Don't Care About Time
Byrds; *Original Singles-#1-1965-1967* . . . . (Columbia)
The Byrds . . . . (Columbia)
She's A River
Simple Minds; *Good News From The Next World* . . . . (Virgin)
Sign O' the times
Prince; *Sign "O" The Times* . . . . (Paisley Park)
Sign Of The Times
Queensryche; *Hear In The Now Frontier* . . . . (Virgin)
Sign Of The Times
Travis Tritt; *Country Club* . . . .(Warner Bros.)
Sign Of The Times
Petula Clark; *Greatest Hits Of Petula Clark* . . . . (Crescendo)
Sign Of The Times
Bryan Ferry; *Bride Stripped Bare* . . . . (Reprise)
Since I Lost My Baby
Temptations; *Temptations' Greatest Hits-#1* . . . . (Motown)
Temptations-Anthology-The Best Of The Temptations . . . . (Motown)
Temptations-The Ultimate Collection . . . . (Motown)
Sixty Minute Man
Billy Ward & His Dominoes; *Rock & Roll Show-C* . . . . (Gusto)
Dominos; *Oldies But Goodies-#5-C* . . . . (Original Sound)
Rufus Thomas & Carla Thomas; *Rufus Thomas & Carla Thomas-
Chronicle* . . . .(Stax)
Slow Poke
Ray Conniff; *Speak To Me Of Love* . . . . (Columbia)
So Much To Say
Dave Matthews Band; *Crash* . . . . (RCA)
Something Beautiful Remains
Tina Turner; *Wildest Dreams* . . . . (Virgin)
Sometimes
Britney Spears; *...Baby One More Time* . . . . (Jive)
Now That's What I Call Music!-#3-C . . . . (Virgin)
Sooner Or Later
Eddy Raven; *Best Of Eddy Raven* . . . . (Liberty)
Temporary Sanity . . . . (Capitol)
Sooner Or Later
Grass Roots; *Grass Roots-All-Time Greatest Hits* . . . . (MCA)
Grass Roots-Anthology (1966-1975) . . . . (Rhino)
Super Hits-#2-C . . . . (Gusto)

Sooner Or Later
Barbara Cook; *Disney Album* . . . . (Disney)
Sooner Or Later
Madonna; *I'm Breathless-Music From Dick Tracy* . . . .(Sire)
Sooner Or Later
Gary Morris; *Stones* . . . . (Liberty)
Sour Times (Nobody Loves Me)
Portishead; *Dummy* . . . .(Go! Discs)
Spend A Little Time
Joan Armatrading; *Whatever's For Us* . . . . (A&M)
Spending My Time
Roxette; *Joyride* . . . . (EMI)
Squeeze Me In
Garth Brooks; *Scarecrow* . . . . (Capitol)
Stay
4 Seasons; *4 Seasons' Greatest Hits-#1.* . . . . (Rhino)
Jackson Browne; *Running On Empty* . . . .(Asylum)
Maurice Williams & The Zodiacs; *Best Of Maurice Williams & The
Zodiacs* . . . . (Collectables)
Billboard Top Rock 'N' Roll Hits-1960-C . . . . (Rhino)
Cruisin'-1960-C . . . . (Increase)
Rock & Roll Is Here To Stay-C . . . . (Gusto)
ST/Dirty Dancing . . . . (RCA)
Stay (Wasting Time)
Dave Matthews Band; *Before These Crowded Streets* . . . . (RCA)
Stay A Little Longer
Bob Wills; *Sounds Of Texas* . . . . (Capitol)
Bob Wills & His Texas Playboys; *Bob Wills & His Texas Playboys-
Anthology 1935-1973* . . . . (Rhino)
Tiffany Transcriptions-#2-Best Of The Tiffanys . . . . (Rhino)
Willie Nelson; *Greatest Hits (& Some That Will Be)* . . . . (Columbia)
Willie & Family Live . . . . (Columbia)
Still Doin' Time
George Jones; *By Request* . . . . (Epic)
George Jones-Anniversary-Ten Years Of Hits . . . . (Epic)
Greatest Country Hits Of The '80s-1981-C . . . . (Columbia)
Straight Time
Bruce Springsteen; *The Ghost Of Tom Joad* . . . . (Columbia)
Stuck In A Moment You Can't Get Out Of
U2; *All That You Can't Leave Behind* . . . .(Interscope)
Syncopated Clock
Leroy Anderson; *Best Of Leroy Anderson-Sleigh Ride* . . . . (Decca)
Take The Time
Bad Company; *Desolation Angels.* . . . . (Swan Song)
Take Time
Chris Walker; *First Time.* . . . . (Pendulum)
Take Time To Know Her
Percy Sledge; *Best Of Percy Sledge.* . . . .(Atlantic)
It Tears Me Up-Best Of Percy Sledge . . . . (Rhino)
Take Your Time
Judson Spence; *Judson Spence* . . . .(Atlantic)
Take Your Time (Do It Right) Part 1
Max-A-Million; *Club Hitz Of The '90s-#2-C* . . . .(Beast)
Take Your Time . . . . (S.O.S./Zoo)
S.O.S. Band; *Best Of The S.O.S. Band.* . . . . (Tabu)
Billboard Top Hits-1980-C . . . . (Rhino)
Club Epic-#1-C . . . . (Legacy)
S.O.S. Band. . . . . (Rhino)
Takes A Little Time
Amy Grant; *Behind The Eyes* . . . . (A&M)
Takin' My Time
Marvin Gaye; *Marvin Gaye's Greatest Hits* . . . . (Motown)
That Stubborn Kinda Fellow . . . . (Motown)
Takin' My Time
Little Feat; *Little Feat* . . . .(Warner Bros.)
Takin' My Time
Bonnie Raitt; *Sweet Forgiveness* . . . .(Warner Bros.)
Telephone Hour
Original Cast; *Bye Bye Birdie* . . . . (Columbia)
Soundtrack; *Bye Bye Birdie* . . . .(RCA)
Ten Minutes Ago
Julie Andrews & Jon Cypher; *Cinderella-The CBS Television
Production* . . . . (Columbia)
Stuart Damon & Lesley Ann Warren; *Cinderella-The CBS Television
Network Production* . . . . (Columbia)
Tender Time
Louise Mandrell; *Best Of Louise Mandrell* . . . .(BNA)
That Was Then, This Is Now
Monkees; *Listen To The Band* . . . . (Rhino)
Then & Now...The Best Of The Monkees . . . . (Arista)
Theme From "Back To The Future"
Cincinnati Pops Orchestra/Erich Kunzel; *Star Tracks II* . . . . (Telarc)
Theme From "Quantum Leap"
Original Soundtrack; *Sci-Fi's Greatest Hits-#4-Defenders Of Justice* . . . . (TVT)
Television's Greatest Hits-#7-Cable Ready-C . . . . (TVT)
Theme From "Time Tunnel"
Original Soundtrack; *Television's Greatest Hits-#2-C* . . . . (TVT)
Then Was Then & Now Is Now
Peggy Lee; *Moments Like This* . . . .(Chesky)

Randy Graff; *Doing Something Right* . . . . (Varese Sarabande)

These Are The Times
Dru Hill; *Enter The Dru* . . . . (Def Jam/RAL/Mercury/Island)

Things Will Grow
Sweethearts Of The Rodeo; *Rodeo Waltz* . . . . (Sugar Hill)

Thinkin' 'Bout It
Gerald Levert; *Love & Consequences* . . . . (East West)

This Is The Right Time
Lisa Stansfield; *Affection* . . . . (Arista)
Power Jams-Today's Hottest Hits-C . . . . (K-Tel)

This Precious Time
Grass Roots; *Grass Roots-All-Time Greatest Hits* . . . . (MCA)
Let's Live For Today . . . . (MCA Special Prod.)
P.F. Sloan; *P.F. Sloan-Anthology* . . . . (One Way)

This Precious Time
Barry McGuire; *Barry McGuire-Anthology* . . . . (One Way)

This Time
Curtis Stigers; *Time Was* . . . . (Arista)

This Time
Bryan Adams; *Cuts Like A Knife* . . . . (A&M)

This Time Around
Michael Jackson; *HIStory: Past, Present And Future-Book 1-C* . . . . (Epic)

Through The Test Of Time
Patti Austin; *GRP 10th Anniversary Collection-C.* . . . . (GRP)
Love Is Gonna Getcha . . . . (GRP)
Patti Austin-Live . . . . (GRP)

Tick Tock
Vaughan Brothers; *Family Style* . . . . (Epic Portrait Assoc.)

'Til I Gain Control Again
Crystal Gayle; *Best Of Crystal Gayle* . . . . (Warner Bros.)
True Love . . . . (Elektra)
Emmylou Harris; *Elite Hotel* . . . . (Reprise)
Rodney Crowell; *Rodney Crowell* . . . . (Warner Bros.)
Rodney Crowell-Collection . . . . (Warner Bros.)
Willie Nelson; *Greatest Hits (& Some That Will Be)* . . . . (Columbia)
Willie Nelson & Waylon Jennings; *Take It To The Limit* . . . . (Columbia)
Willie & Family Live . . . . (Columbia)
Willie Nelson & Waylon Jennings' Greatest Hits . . . . (Columbia)

'Til I Get It Right
Tammy Wynette; *Tammy Wynette's Biggest Hits* . . . . (Epic)
Tammy Wynette's Greatest Hits-#3 . . . . (Epic)
Tears Of Fire-25th Anniversary Collection . . . . (Epic)
Trisha Yearwood; *Tammy Wynette...Remembered-C* . . . . (Asylum)

'Til Something Better Comes Along
Louise Mandrell & R.C. Bannon; *Me & My R.C.* . . . . (RCA)

Till
Roger Williams; *Best Of Roger Williams* . . . . (MCA)
Tony Bennett; *Forty Years-The Artistry Of Tony Bennett* . . . . (Columbia)
Vogues; *Vogues' Greatest Hits* . . . . (Rhino)
Vogues' Greatest Hits . . . . (Reprise)

Till The End Of Time
Perry Como; *Como's Golden Records* . . . . (RCA)
Nipper's Greatest Hits Of The '40s-#2-C . . . . (RCA)
Perry Como-Pure Gold . . . . (RCA)
There Is Love-Wedding Songs-C . . . . (Scotti Bros.)

Till The End Of Time
Chicago; *Chicago XI* . . . . (Chicago)

Till The Next Goodbye
Rolling Stones; *It's Only Rock 'N Roll* . . . . (Rolling Stones)

Till Then
Mills Brothers; *Best Of The Mills Brothers* . . . . (MCA)
Cab Driver . . . . (Ranwood)
Lazy River . . . . (MCA Special Prod.)
Mills Brothers . . . . (Everest)
Mills Brothers' Greatest Hits . . . . (MCA)

Till There Was You
Beatles; *Beatles-Box Set* . . . . (Capitol)
Meet The Beatles! . . . . (Capitol)
With The Beatles . . . . (Parlophone)
Original Cast; *ST/The Music Man* . . . . (Warner Bros.)

Till We Two Are One
Eddy Howard; *Best Of Eddy Howard-The Mercury Years* . . . . (Mercury)
Georgie Shaw; *45-#28937* . . . . (Decca)
Louis Jordan; *One Guy Named Louis* . . . . (Blue Note)

Time
Pink Floyd; *Dark Side Of The Moon* . . . . (Capitol)
Delicate Sound Of Thunder . . . . (Columbia)
Pink Floyd-Gift Set . . . . (Capitol)

Time
Freddie Mercury; *Great Pretender* . . . . (Hollywood)

Time
David Bowie; *Aladdin Sane* . . . . (Rykodisc)
ST/Ziggy Stardust-The Motion Picture . . . . (Rykodisc)

Time
Tom Waits; *Big Time* . . . . (Island)
Rain Dogs . . . . (Island)

Time
Lionel Richie; *Time* . . . . (Mercury)

Time
Tesla; *Psychotic Supper* . . . . (Geffen)

Time
Edwin Starr; *Motown Superstar Series-#3-Edwin Starr* . . . . (Motown)
War & Peace . . . . (Motown)

Time
Hootie & The Blowfish; *Cracked Rear View* . . . . (Atlantic)

Time & Love
Sawyer Brown; *Dirt Road* . . . . (Curb)

Time & Love
Barbra Streisand; *Stoney End* . . . . (Columbia)
Laura Nyro; *New York Tendaberry* . . . . (Columbia)

Time & Tide
Basia; *No Boundaries* . . . . (Columbia)
Time And Tide . . . . (Epic)

Time (Clock Of The Heart)
Culture Club; *Kissing To Be Clever* . . . . (Virgin)

Time (Keeps Flowing Like A River)
Alan Parsons Project; *Best Of The Alan Parsons Project* . . . . (Arista)
Turn Of A Friendly Card . . . . (Arista)

Time After Time
Cyndi Lauper; *Chicken Soup For The Woman's Soul-C* . . . . (Rhino)
She's So Unusual . . . . (Portrait)
Twelve Deadly Cyns...And Then Some . . . . (Epic)
Everything But The Girl; *Acoustic* . . . . (Atlantic)
INOJ & So So Def Bass All-Stars; *Time After Time (Maxi Single)* . . . . (So So Def/Columbia)
Miles Davis; *Live Around The World* . . . . (Warner Bros.)
You're Under Arrest . . . . (Columbia)

Time After Time
Carly Simon; *My Romance* . . . . (Arista)
Frank Sinatra; *Frank Sinatra-16 Most Requested Songs* . . . . (Columbia)
Johnny Mathis; *Johnny Mathis-Love Songs* . . . . (Columbia)
Placido Domingo; *Domingo Songbook* . . . . (Sony Music Classical)
Sarah Vaughan; *Jazzfest Masters* . . . . (Jazz Masters)
Stephane Grappelli; *Afternoon In Paris* . . . . (Verve)
Tony Bennett; *Perfectly Frank* . . . . (Columbia)

Time After Time
Ozzy Osbourne; *Live & Loud* . . . . (Epic Portrait Assoc.)
No More Tears . . . . (Epic Portrait Assoc.)

Time After Time (Annelise)
R.E.M.; *Reckoning* . . . . (I.R.S.)

Time Ain't Money
Huey Lewis and the News; *Hard At Play* . . . . (EMI)

Time And A Word
Yes; *Time And A Word* . . . . (Atlantic)
Yesshows . . . . (Atlantic)
Yesterdays . . . . (Atlantic)

Time And Time Again
Counting Crows; *August And Everything After* . . . . (David Geffen Co.)

Time Between
Byrds; *The Byrds* . . . . (Columbia)
Younger Than Yesterday . . . . (Columbia)
Desert Rose Band; *Desert Rose Band* . . . . (Curb)

Time Bomb
Rancid; *...And Out Come The Wolves* . . . . (Epitaph)

Time Changes Everything
Bob Wills & His Texas Playboys; *Bob Wills & His Texas Playboys-Anthology 1935-1973* . . . . (Rhino)
Columbia Country Classics-#1-Golden Age-C . . . . (Columbia)
Essential Bob Wills & His Texas Playboys-1935-1973 . . . . (Legacy)
Roy Rogers; *The Country Music Hall Of Fame-Roy Rogers* . . . . (MCA)

Time Don't Run Out On Me
Anne Murray; *Anne Murray-Country Hits* . . . . (Capitol)
Anne Murray's Greatest Hits-#2 . . . . (Capitol)
Heart Over Mind . . . . (Capitol)

Time For Everything
Jethro Tull; *Benefit* . . . . (Chrysalis)

Time For Love
Shirley Horn; *Here's To Life* . . . . (Verve)
Tony Bennett; *Forty Years-The Artistry Of Tony Bennett* . . . . (Columbia)
Tony Bennett's All-Time Greatest Hits . . . . (Columbia)

Time For Love
Kenny Rogers; *They Don't Make 'Em Like They Used To* . . . . (RCA)

Time For Me To Fly
REO Speedwagon; *A Decade Of Rock And Roll 1970 To 1980* . . . . (Epic)
REO Speedwagon-The Hits . . . . (Epic)
You Can Tune A Piano But You Can't Tuna Fish . . . . (Epic)

Time Goes On
En Vogue; *Born To Sing* . . . . (Atlantic)

Time Has Come Today
Chambers Brothers; *Nuggets-#9-Acid Rock-C* . . . . (Rhino)
Rock Classics Of The '60s-C . . . . (Columbia)
The Time Has Come . . . . (Columbia)

Time Heals
Todd Rundgren; *Healing* . . . . (Rhino)
Todd Rundgren-Anthology 1968-1985 . . . . (Rhino)

Time Heals Everything
Barbara Cook; *Barbara Cook-Live At Carnegie Hall* . . . (Sony Music Classical)

Bernadette Peters; *Bernadette Peters-Live At Carnegie Hall* . . . . . . (EMI-Angel)
Original Cast; *Mack & Mabel* . . . . (MCA)

Time In A Bottle
Jim Croce; *50th Anniversary Collection* . . . . (Saja)
  Photographs & Memories/His Greatest Hits . . . . (Atlantic)
  Time In A Bottle/Jim Croce's Greatest Love Songs . . . . (Atlantic)

Time Is Here
Stomu Yamashta & Go; *Live From Paris* . . . . (Island)
  Stomu Yamashta & Go . . . . (Island)

Time Is On My Side
Irma Thomas; *Best Of New Orleans Rhythm & Blues-#1-C* . . . . (Rhino)
  Simply The Best-Live! . . . . (Rounder)
Keith Richards & The X-Pensive Winos; *Live At Hollywood Palladium-
  December 1988.* . . . . (Virgin)
Rolling Stones; *"Still Life" (American Concert 1981)* . . . . (Virgin)
  12 X 5 . . . . (Abkco)
  Big Hits (High Tide & Green Grass) . . . . (Abkco)
  got Live if you want it! . . . . (Abkco)
  Hot Rocks 1964-1971. . . . . (Abkco)
  Singles Collection-The London Years . . . . (Abkco)

Time Is Running Out
Steve Winwood; *Steve Winwood* . . . . (Island)

Time Is Tight
Booker T. & The M.G.s; *Booker T. & The M.G.s' Greatest Hits* . . . . (Stax)
  Soul Shots-#2-The "In" Crowd-Sweet Soul-C . . . . (Rhino)
  Soul Shots-#3-Soul Twist-C . . . . (Rhino)

Time Is Wasting
Carlo; *20 Great Love Songs Of The '50s & '60s-#1-C* . . . . (Laurie)
  22 Leaders Of The Pack-#1-C . . . . (Laurie)

Time Isn't Kind
Fine Young Cannibals; *Fine Young Cannibals* . . . . (I.R.S.)

Time It's Time
Talk Talk; *Colour Of Spring* . . . . (EMI)

Time Loves A Hero
Little Feat; *Time Loves A Hero* . . . . (Warner Bros.)
  Waiting For Columbus. . . . . (Warner Bros.)

Time Machine
Grand Funk Railroad; *Capitol Collectors Series-Grand Funk
  Railroad* . . . . (Capitol)
  Legends Of Rock Guitar-'70s-C . . . . (Rhino)
  Mark, Don & Mel 1969-71. . . . . (Capitol)
  On Time . . . . (Capitol)

Time Machine
T. Graham Brown; *Come As You Were* . . . . (Capitol)

Time Machine
Barbra Streisand; *Emotions* . . . . (Columbia)

Time Machine
Black Sabbath; *Dehumanizer* . . . . (Reprise)
  ST/Wayne's World . . . . (Reprise)

Time Marches On
Tracy Lawrence; *Best Of Tracy Lawrence* . . . . (Atlantic)
  Time Marches On. . . . . (Atlantic)

Time Of The Preacher Theme
Willie Nelson; *Red Headed Stranger* . . . . (Columbia)

Time Of The Season
Argent; *Argent-Anthology-Collection Of Greatest Hits* . . . . (Epic)
  Encore-Argent . . . . (Epic)
  ST/Awakenings . . . . (Reprise)
Zombies; *Billboard Top Rock 'N' Roll Hits-1969-C* . . . . (Rhino)
  Odyssey & Oracle . . . . (Rhino)
  Rock Classics-#3-C . . . . (K-Tel)
  ST/1969 . . . . (Polydor)

Time Of Your Life (Good Riddance)
Green Day; *Nimrod* . . . . (Reprise)

Time Off For Bad Behaviour
Confederate Railroad; *Confederate Railroad* . . . . (Atlantic)

Time On My Hands
Billie Holiday; *Billie Holiday* . . . . (Columbia)
  Quintessential-#8-1939-1940 . . . . (Legacy)
  The Billie Holiday Story-#2 . . . . (Columbia)
Duke Ellington; *Lullaby Of Birdland* . . . . (Intermedia)
Glenn Miller; *Best Of The Big Bands-C* . . . . (Columbia)

Time On My Hands
Sweet Honey In The Rock; *Good News* . . . . (Flying Fish)

Time Out
Joe Walsh; *Best Of Joe Walsh.* . . . . (MCA)
  Joe Walsh. . . . . (MCA Special Prod.)
  So What . . . . (MCA)
  You Can't Argue With A Sick Mind . . . . (MCA)

Time Out Of Mind
Steely Dan; *Gaucho* . . . . (MCA)

Time Passages
Al Stewart; *'70s Greatest Rock Hits-#6-FM Hits-C* . . . . (Priority)
  Best Of Al Stewart . . . . (Arista)
  Live/Indian Summer. . . . . (Arista)
  Time Passages . . . . (Arista)

Time Passed Autumn
Claus Ogerman Orchestra; *Gate Of Dreams* . . . . (Warner Bros.)

Time Passes By
Kathy Mattea; *Time Passes By* . . . . (Mercury)

Time Passes Me By
Desert Rose Band; *Pages Of Life.* . . . . (Curb)

Time Passes Slowly
Bob Dylan; *Biograph* . . . . (Columbia)
  New Morning . . . . (Columbia)
Judy Collins; *Whales & Nightingales* . . . . (Elektra)

Time Remembered
Bill Evans; *Loose Blues* . . . . (Milestone)
  Time Remembered . . . . (Milestone)

Time Stands Still
Rush; *Hold Your Fire* . . . . (Mercury)
  Rush-Chronicles. . . . . (Mercury)
  Show Of Hands . . . . (Mercury)

Time Stood Still
Vern Gosdin; *10 Years Of Greatest Hits Newly Recorded.* . . . . (Columbia)

Time The Avenger
Pretenders; *Learning To Crawl* . . . . (Sire)

Time To Cry
Paul Anka; *Paul Anka's 21 Golden Hits* . . . . (RCA)

Time To Get Alone
Beach Boys; *Friends-20/20.* . . . . (Capitol)

Time To Hide
Wings; *Wings At The Speed Of Sound* . . . . (Capitol)
  Wings Over America . . . . (Capitol)

Time To Kill
UK; *Night After Night* . . . . (Editions E.G.)
  UK . . . . (Editions E.G.)

Time To Kill
Band; *Stage Fright* . . . . (Capitol)

Time To Kill
Alice Cooper; *Raise Your Fist And Yell.* . . . . (MCA)

Time To Pay
Marc Nelson; *chocolate mood.* . . . . (Columbia)

Time Waits For No One
Rolling Stones; *It's Only Rock 'N Roll* . . . . (Rolling Stones)
  Sucking In The Seventies . . . . (Rolling Stones)

Time Waits For No One
Hilltoppers; *P.S. I Love You (The Best Of The Hilltoppers).* . . . . . (Varese Vintage)

Time Warp
Rocky Horror Picture Show Cast; *Dr. Demento Presents The Greatest
  Novelty Records-#4-1970s-C* . . . . (Rhino)
Tim Curry & Original Roxy Cast; *Rocky Horror Show.* . . . . (Rhino)

Time Was
Kate Smith; *Kate Smith-16 Most Requested Songs* . . . . (Columbia)

Time Will Reveal
DeBarge; *In A Special Way* . . . . (Motown)

Time Will Tell
Black Crowes; *Southern Harmony & Musical Companion.* . . . . . (Def American)
Bob Marley & The Wailers; *Kaya* . . . . (Tuff Gong)
  Songs Of Freedom . . . . (Tuff Gong)

Time Will Tell
Tower Of Power; *Back To Oakland.* . . . . (Warner Bros.)

Time Will Tell
Jimmy Cliff; *Reggae Spectacular-C* . . . . (A&M)
  Wonderful World, Beautiful People . . . . (A&M)

Time Will Tell
Gary Morris; *These Days.* . . . . (Capitol)

Time Won't Let Me
Smithereens; *Blown To Smithereens: Best Of The Smithereens* . . . . . . (Capitol)

Time, Love & Tenderness
Michael Bolton; *Time, Love & Tenderness* . . . . (Columbia)

Time, The
Baby Washington; *Best Of Baby Washington* . . . . (Collectables)
  Best Of Sue Records-C . . . . (Collectables)
Five Satins; *Five Satins Sing Their Greatest Hits* . . . . (Collectables)
Inez Foxx; *Stax Soul Sisters-C* . . . . (Stax)

Time, Time
Ed Ames; *Best Of Ed Ames* . . . . (RCA)
  Ed Ames-Pure Gold . . . . (RCA)

Timeless
Rick Derringer; *Guitars & Women* . . . . (Blue Sky)

Timeless & True Love
McCarters; *Country Love Songs-C* . . . . (Warner Bros.)
  The Gift. . . . . (Warner Bros.)

Times Have Changed
Supertramp; *Indelibly Stamped.* . . . . (A&M)

Times Of Your Life
Paul Anka; *Paul Anka-30th Anniversary Anthology* . . . . (Rhino)
  Paul Anka-His Best . . . . (EMI)

Times They Are A-Changin'
Billy Joel; *KOHUEPT.* . . . . (Columbia)
Bob Dylan; *Biograph* . . . . (Columbia)
  Bob Dylan At Budokan. . . . . (Columbia)
  Bob Dylan's Greatest Hits . . . . (Columbia)
  The Bootleg Series-Volumes 1-3 [Rare & Unreleased] . . . . (Columbia)
  The Times They Are A-Changin' . . . . (Columbia)

Byrds; *The Byrds* . . . . . (Columbia)
Turn! Turn! Turn! . . . . . (Legacy)
Peter, Paul & Mary; *Peter, Paul and Mary In Concert* . . . . . (Warner Bros.)
Simon & Garfunkel; *Collected Works* . . . . . (Columbia)
Wednesday Morning 3 A.M. . . . . . (Columbia)

Time's Up
Southern Pacific & Carlene Carter; *County Line* . . . . . (Warner Bros.)
Favorite Country Duets-C . . . . . (Warner Bros.)
Southern Pacific's Greatest Hits . . . . . (Warner Bros.)

To Be Loved
Curtis Stigers; *Songs From Dawson's Creek* . . . . . (Sony Music Soundtrax)

Tomorrow Is A Long Time
Bob Dylan; *Bob Dylan's Greatest Hits-#2* . . . . . (Columbia)
Chris Hillman; *Morning Sky* . . . . . (Sugar Hill)
Elvis Presley; *A Valentine Gift For You* . . . . . (RCA)
Ian & Sylvia; *Four Strong Winds* . . . . . (Vanguard)
Ian & Sylvia's Greatest Hits . . . . . (Vanguard)
Troubadours Of The Folk Era-#1-C . . . . . (Rhino)
Sandy Denny; *Who Knows Where The Time Goes* . . . . . (Hannibal)

Tomorrow Is Such A Long Time
Rod Stewart; *Every Picture Tells A Story* . . . . . (Mercury)
Rod Stewart's Greatest Hits-#2 . . . . . (Mercury)

Too Busy Thinking About My Baby
Manhattan Transfer; *Tonin'* . . . . . (Atlantic)
Marvin Gaye; *Every Great Motown Hit Of Marvin Gaye* . . . . . (Motown)
Superhits . . . . . (Motown)

Too Gone, Too Long
En Vogue; *Best Of En Vogue* . . . . . (Elektra)
EV3 . . . . . (East West)

Too Much Time On My Hands
Styx; *Caught In The Act* . . . . . (A&M)
Paradise Theater . . . . . (A&M)
Styx-Classics-#15 . . . . . (A&M)

Total Eclipse Of The Heart
Bonnie Tyler; *Billboard Top Hits-1983-C* . . . . . (Rhino)
Faster Than The Speed Of Night . . . . . (Columbia)
Seems Like Yesterday-#4-Early '80s-C . . . . . (K-Tel)
Nicki French; *Dance Hits '96 Supermix-C* . . . . . (Critique)
Secrets . . . . . (Critique)

Tulip Time
Andrews Sisters; *Capitol Collectors Series-The Andrews Sisters* . . . . . (Capitol)
John Steel; *Music From The New York Stage (1890-1920)-#4-1917-1920-C* . . . . . (Pearl)

Tulsa Time
Don Williams; *Best Of Don Williams-#2* . . . . . (MCA)
Country's Greatest Hits-#6-Superstars-C . . . . . (Priority)
Don Williams-Legends . . . . . (MCA)
Expressions . . . . . (MCA)
Eric Clapton; *Backless* . . . . . (Polydor)
Just One Night . . . . . (Polydor)

Turn Back The Hands Of Time
Tyrone Davis; *Atlantic Rhythm & Blues 1947-1974-#7 (1969-1974)-C* . . . . . (Atlantic)
Didn't It Blow Your Mind: Soul Hits Of The '70s-#2-C . . . . . (Rhino)
Sock Hop-C . . . . . (Dunhill Compact Classics)
Tyrone Davis' Greatest Hits . . . . . (Rhino)

Turn Back Time
Aqua; *Aquarium* . . . . . (MCA)
ST/Sliding Doors . . . . . (MCA)

Twenty-Five Minutes To Go
Johnny Cash; *Essential Johnny Cash* . . . . . (Columbia)
Johnny Cash At Folsom Prison & San Quentin . . . . . (Columbia)
True West . . . . . (Columbia)

Ugly Hour
David Bromberg; *Bandit In A Bathing Suit* . . . . . (Fantasy)

Unchained Melody
Elvis Presley; *Always On My Mind* . . . . . (RCA)
Moody Blue . . . . . (RCA)
The Great Performances . . . . . (RCA)
George Benson; *Livin' Inside Your Love* . . . . . (Warner Bros.)
LeAnn Rimes; *LeAnn Rimes-Early Years-Unchained Melody* . . . . . (MCG/Curb)
Platters; *Platters Greatest Hits* . . . . . (Everest)
Red Sails In The Sunset . . . . . (Allegiance)
Richard Clayderman; *Richard Clayderman Plays Love Songs Of The World* . . . . . (Columbia)
Righteous Brothers; *Righteous Brothers' Greatest Hits* . . . . . (Verve)
ST/Ghost . . . . . (Varese Sarabande)
Willie Nelson; *Stardust* . . . . . (Legacy)

Until The End Of Time
Guy & Ralna; *22 Golden Country Classics* . . . . . (Ranwood)

Wait A Minute
Ray-J; *This Ain't A Game* . . . . . (Atlantic)

Wasted On The Way
Crosby, Stills & Nash; *CSN* . . . . . (Atlantic)
Daylight Again . . . . . (Atlantic)

Wasting My Time
Default; *Fallout* . . . . . (TVT)

Wasting Time
Collective Soul; *Hints, Allegations And Things Left Unsaid* . . . . . (Atlantic)

What Time Is It?
Ken Nordine; *Best Of Word Jazz-#1* . . . . . (Rhino)

What Time Is It?
Spin Doctors; *Pocket Full Of Kryptonite* . . . . . (Epic Portrait Assoc.)

When It's Sleepy Time Down South
Billie Holiday; *Last Recordings* . . . . . (Verve)
Dizzy Gillespie; *20 Golden Pieces Of Dizzy GIllespie* . . . . . (Bulldog)
Louis Armstrong; *At The Crescendo* . . . . . (MCA)
Best Of Louis Armstrong . . . . . (MCA)
Best Of The Decca Years-#1-Hits!-C . . . . . (Decca)
Essential Louis Armstrong . . . . . (Vanguard)
I Like Jazz-Essence Of Louis Armstrong . . . . . (Columbia)
Louis Armstrong's Greatest Hits . . . . . (Legacy)
Satchmo-Musical Autobiography . . . . . (MCA)
Mel Torme; *Mel Torme* . . . . . (Glendale)
Wynton Marsalis; *Standard Time-#2-Intimacy Calling* . . . . . (Columbia)

Where Or When
Barbra Streisand; *Color Me Barbra* . . . . . (Columbia)
Benny Goodman; *Small Groups-1941-1945* . . . . . (Columbia)
Bryan Ferry; *As Time Goes By* . . . . . (Virgin)
Dion And The Belmonts; *Best Of Doo Wop Ballads-C* . . . . . (Rhino)
Complete Dion And The Belmonts . . . . . (Collector's Choice)
Ella Fitzgerald; *Ella Fitzgerald Sings The Rodgers & Hart Songbook* . . . . . (Verve)
Frank Sinatra; *Sinatra At The Sands* . . . . . (Reprise)
Johnny Mathis; *You Light Up My Life* . . . . . (Columbia)
Peggy Lee; *Peggy Lee-Complete Recordings-1941-1947* . . . . . (Legacy)
Wynton Marsalis; *Standard Time-#3-The Resolution Of Romance* . . . . . (Columbia)

Where Time Stands Still
Mary Chapin Carpenter; *Stones In The Road* . . . . . (Columbia)

Who Knows Where The Time Goes
Fairport Convention; *Circle Dance-Hokey Pokey Charity-C* . . . . . (Green Linnet)
Fairport Convention-Chronicles . . . . . (A&M)
Judy Collins; *Colors Of The Day-The Best Of Judy Collins* . . . . . (Elektra)
Who Knows Where The Time Goes . . . . . (Elektra)
Sandy Denny; *Best Of Sandy Denny* . . . . . (Hannibal)
Who Knows Where The Time Goes . . . . . (Hannibal)

Why Did You Waste My Time?
Screamin' Jay Hawkins; *Collectables Blues Collection-#1-C* . . . . . (Collectables)

Wild Hearts Run Out Of Time
Roy Orbison; *King Of Hearts* . . . . . (Virgin)

Wildest Times Of The World
Vonda Shepard; *ST/Songs From ''Ally McBeal'' Featuring Vonda Shepard* . . . . . (550/Epic)

Winter Time
Steve Miller Band; *Book Of Dreams* . . . . . (Capitol)
Steve Miller Band-Gift Set . . . . . (Capitol)
Steve Miller Band's Greatest Hits-1974-78 . . . . . (Capitol)

Wintertime Love
Doors; *Waiting For The Sun* . . . . . (Elektra)

Wiser Time
Black Crowes; *Amorica* . . . . . (American)

Work It Out
Def Leppard; *Slang* . . . . . (Mercury)

You Can Make History (Young Again)
Elton John; *Elton John-Love Songs* . . . . . (MCA)

You Don't Need The Wine To Have A Wonderful Time
Eddie Cantor; *Music From The New York Stage (1890-1920)-#4-1917-1920-C* . . . . . (Pearl)

You Should Be Mine (Don't Waste Your Time)
Brian McKnight; *Anytime* . . . . . (Motown)

Young Turks
Rod Stewart; *Absolutely Live* . . . . . (Warner Bros.)
Downtown Train-Selections From The Storyteller Anthology . . . . . (Warner Bros.)
Storyteller/The Complete Anthology: 1964-1990 . . . . . (Warner Bros.)
Tonight I'm Yours . . . . . (Warner Bros.)

Your Time Is Gonna Come
Led Zeppelin; *Led Zeppelin* . . . . . (Atlantic)
Led Zeppelin-Box Set . . . . . (Atlantic)

You're Still A Young Man
Tower Of Power; *Bump City* . . . . . (Warner Bros.)
Live & In Living Color . . . . . (Warner Bros.)

TIME: SPECIFIC, O'clock, Times Of Day

See Also: ***AFTERNOON, DAYS OF THE WEEK (various), DAYS: GENERAL, ETERNITY, FUTURE, HISTORY, LATE, LIFE, MIDNIGHT, MONTHS & DATES (various), MORNING, NIGHT, TIME: GENERAL, URGENT, WAITING, YEARS: GENERAL, YEARS: SPECIFIC, YESTERDAY***

(We're Gonna) Rock Around The Clock
Bill Haley & His Comets; *Bill Haley & His Comets' Greatest Hits* . . . . . (MCA)
Bill Haley & His Comets' Greatest Hits . . . . . (Everest)
Bill Haley & His Comets-Golden Hits . . . . . (MCA)
Billboard Top Rock 'N' Roll Hits-1955-C . . . . . (Rhino)
ST/American Graffiti . . . . . (MCA)

10:15 Saturday Night
Cure; *Boys Don't Cry* . . . . (Elektra)
   Standing On A Beach-The Singles . . . . (Elektra)
100 Years From Now
Huey Lewis and the News; *Time Flies...Best Of Huey Lewis and*
   the News . . . . (Elektra)
11 O'Clock Tick Tock
U2; *Under A Blood Red Sky* . . . . (Island)
1st Of Tha Month
Bone Thugs-N-Harmony; *E. 1999 Eternal* . . . . (Ruthless/Relativity)
2:10 Train
Rising Sons; *Rising Sons Featuring Taj Mahal & Ry Cooder* . . . . (Legacy)
Steve Gillette; *Steve Gillette* . . . . (Vanguard)
Stone Poneys Featuring Linda Ronstadt; *The Stone Poneys Featuring Linda*
   Ronstadt . . . . (EMI)
3 A.M. Eternal
KLF; *MTV Party To Go-#2-C* . . . . (Tommy Boy)
   The White Room . . . . (Arista)
3 A.M. Somewhere Out Of Beaumont
KLF; *Chill Out* . . . . (Wax Trax)
3 O'Clock...School's Out!
Full Force; *Guess Who's Comin' To The Crib?* . . . . (Columbia)
3am
Matchbox Twenty; *Yourself Or Someone Like You* . . . . (Lava)
4 A.M. In Texas
7 Seconds; *Soulforce Revolution* . . . . (Restless)
4:37 AM (Arabs With Knives & West German Skies)
Roger Waters; *Pros & Cons Of Hitchhiking* . . . . (Columbia)
5:15
Who; *Hooligans* . . . . (MCA)
   Join Together . . . . (MCA)
   ST/Quadrophenia . . . . (MCA)
   Who's Greatest Hits . . . . (MCA)
9 To 5
Dolly Parton; *9 To 5 And Odd Jobs* . . . . (RCA)
   Best There Is . . . . (RCA)
   Dolly Parton's Greatest Hits . . . . (RCA)
   I Am Woman-C . . . . (Nick At Nite)
   Nipper's Greatest Hits Of The '80s-C . . . . (RCA)
About A Quarter To Nine
Original Broadway Cast; *42nd Street* . . . . (RCA Victor)
After 12, Before 6
Sam Salter; *It's On Tonight* . . . . (LaFace)
Anniversary Song
Al Jolson; *Al Jolson-Best Of The Decca Years* . . . . (MCA)
   Cocktail Hour . . . . (Columbia River Entert. Group)
Dinah Shore; *Buttons & Bows* . . . . (ASV)
   Dinah Shore-16 Most Requested Songs-Encore! . . . . (Legacy)
Django Reinhardt; *Verve Jazz Masters 38* . . . . (Verve)
Eva Cassidy; *Time After Time* . . . . (Blix Street)
Guy Lombardo & His Royal Canadians; *Enjoy Yourself, The Hits Of Guy*
   Lombardo . . . . (MCA)
At 4 A.M.
Tom Verlaine; *Flash Light* . . . . (I.R.S.)
Blue (3 AM)
LeAnn Rimes; *Blue* . . . . (MCG/Curb)
Can't Wait One Minute More
CIV; *Box Presents Big Ones Of Alternative Rock-#1-C* . . . . (Box Tunes)
   Set Your Goals . . . . (Lava)
Chant: 13th Hour
Redbone; *Best Of Redbone* . . . . (Epic)
Clock Strikes Ten
Cheap Trick; *Cheap Trick At Budokan* . . . . (Epic)
   In Color . . . . (Epic)
Closing Time
Semisonic; *Feeling Strangely Fine* . . . . (MCA)
   Now That's What I Call Music!-#2-C . . . . (Virgin)
Cold Day In Hell
Gary Moore; *After Hours* . . . . (Charisma)
Do You Know Where Your Man Is
Pam Tillis; *Homeward Looking Angel* . . . . (Arista)
Don't Happen Twice (3 AM)
Kenny Chesney; *Kenny Chesney's Greatest Hits* . . . . (BNA)
Don't The Girls All Get Prettier At Closing Time
Mickey Gilley; *Make It Like The First Time* . . . . (ISD/Intersound)
Expressway To Your Heart (5 PM)
Blues Brothers; *Best Of The Blues Brothers* . . . . (Atlantic)
Soul Survivors; *Dick Bartley's One-Hit Wonders Of The '60s-#2-C* . . . . (Rhino)
   Oldies But Goodies-#11-C . . . . (Original Sound)
   Super Oldies Of The '60s-#6-C . . . . (Audio Fidelity)
   When The Whistle Blows Anything Goes . . . . (Collectables)
Five Minutes
Lorrie Morgan; *Lorrie Morgan's Greatest Hits* . . . . (BNA)
   Lorrie Morgan-Super Hits . . . . (RCA)
Pam Tillis; *Time-Collection* . . . . (Warner Bros.)
Five O'Clock World
Hal Ketchum; *Past The Point Of Rescue* . . . . (Curb)
Vogues; *ST/Good Morning, Vietnam* . . . . (A&M)

Vogues' Greatest Hits . . . . (SSS International)
Vogues' Greatest Hits . . . . (Rhino)
Four In The Morning
Night Ranger; *7 Wishes* . . . . (MCA)
   Night Ranger's Greatest Hits . . . . (Camel)
Four In The Morning
Faron Young; *Faron Young's Greatest Hits-#3* . . . . (Step One)
Fourteen Minutes Old
Doug Stone; *Doug Stone* . . . . (Epic)
From This Moment On
Shania Twain & Bryan White; *Come On Over* . . . . (Mercury)
From This Moment On
Anita O'Day; *Swings Cole Porter* . . . . (Verve)
Ella Fitzgerald; *Ella Fitzgerald Sings The Cole Porter Songbook* . . . . . (Verve)
Frank Sinatra; *a Swingin' Affair!* . . . . (Capitol)
Original Soundtrack; *Kiss Me Kate* . . . . (Rhino)
Glendale Train (9.30 AM)
New Riders Of The Purple Sage; *Best Of New Riders Of The*
   Purple Sage . . . . (Columbia)
   New Riders Of The Purple Sage . . . . (Columbia)
Got A Date With An Angel
Hal Kemp; *Best Of The Big Bands-C* . . . . (Columbia)
Sammy Kaye & His Orchestra; *Best Of Sammy Kaye & His Orchestra* . . (MCA)
Here & Now
Letters To Cleo; *Aurora Gory Alice* . . . . (Cherrydisc)
High Noon
Frankie Laine; *Billboard Top Movie Hits-1950-1954-C* . . . . (Rhino)
Tex Ritter; *Heroes Of Country Music-#4-Legends Of The West*
   Coast-C . . . . (Rhino)
   The Envelope Please-Academy Award Winning Songs (1946-
   1957)-C . . . . (Rhino)
I Count The Minutes
Ricky Martin; *Ricky Martin* . . . . (Columbia)
If I Could Talk I'd Tell You (9:30, 9:45, 10:15)
Lemonheads; *Car Button Cloth* . . . . (Tag/Atlantic)
In A Week Or Two
Diamond Rio; *Close To The Edge* . . . . (Arista)
   Diamond Rio's Greatest Hits . . . . (Arista)
In My Time Of Dying
Led Zeppelin; *Physical Graffiti* . . . . (Swan Song)
In The Cool, Cool, Cool Of The Evening
Bing Crosby; *Best Of Bing Crosby* . . . . (MCA)
Frank Sinatra; *Days Of Wine And Roses, Moon River, And Other Academy*
   Award Winners . . . . (Reprise)
Rosemary Clooney; *Rosemary Clooney-16 Most Requested Songs* . . . . (Legacy)
In The Midnight Hour
Rascals; *Classic Rock 1966-1988-C* . . . . (Atlantic)
   ST/More Songs From "The Big Chill" . . . . (Motown)
   Time Peace/The Rascals' Greatest Hits . . . . (Atlantic)
Roxy Music; *Flesh + Blood* . . . . (Atco)
   Street Life-20 Great Hits . . . . (Reprise)
Wilson Pickett; *Atlantic Rhythm & Blues 1947-1974-#5 (1962-*
   1966)-C . . . . (Atlantic)
   Best Of Wilson Pickett . . . . (Atlantic)
   Frat Rock!-#4-C . . . . (Rhino)
   Golden Soul-C . . . . (Atlantic)
   Soul Years-C . . . . (Atlantic)
   Wilson Pickett's Greatest Hits . . . . (Atlantic)
It's 2 A.M.
Shemekia Copeland; *Wicked* . . . . (Alligator)
It's 3 O'Clock In The Morning
Mom & Dads; *Blue Hawaii* . . . . (Crescendo)
It's Four In The Morning
Faron Young; *Faron Young-Golden Hits* . . . . (Mercury)
   Faron Young-The Hits . . . . (Mercury)
It's Now Or Never
Elvis Presley; *Elvis Presley-Love Songs* . . . . (RCA)
   Heart & Soul . . . . (RCA)
   Worldwide 50 Gold Award Hits, Vol. 1, Parts 1 & 2 . . . . . . (RCA)
Jumpin, Jumpin (11:30)
Destiny's Child; *The Writing's On The Wall* . . . . (Columbia)
Last Night
Mar-Keys; *Atlantic Rhythm & Blues 1947-1974-#4 (1958-1962)-C* . . . . (Atlantic)
   Soul Shots-#3-Soul Twist-C . . . . (Rhino)
Last Night
Az Yet; *Az Yet* . . . . (LaFace)
Last Night
Al Jarreau; *Tomorrow Today* . . . . (GRP/VMG)
Last Night
Buddy Holly/The Crickets; *Chirping Crickets* . . . . (MCA)
Last Night
Stephanie Mills; *Tantalizingly Hot* . . . . (Casablanca)
Last Night
Traveling Wilburys; *Traveling Wilburys-Volume One* . . (Wilbury/Warner Bros.)
Last Night A D.J. Saved My Life
Indeep; *Last Night A D.J. Saved My Life* . . . . (Sound Of New York)
   The Disco Years-#2-On The Beat-1978-1982-C . . . . (Rhino)
Last Night I Didn't Get To Sleep At All
5th Dimension; *Greatest Hits On Earth* . . . . (Arista)

Last Night I Had A Dream
Randy Newman; *Randy Newman/Live* . . . . (Warner Archives)
Sail Away . . . .(Reprise)
Last Night I Had The Strangest Dream
Simon & Garfunkel; *Collected Works* . . . . (Columbia)
Wednesday Morning 3 A.M. . . . .(Columbia)
Last Night Of The World
Bruce Cockburn; *Breakfast In New Orleans, Dinner In Timbuktu*. . . . (Rykodisc)
Last Night On Earth
U2; *Pop* . . . . (Island)
Last Night's Letter
K-Ci & JoJo; *Love Always* . . . . (MCA)
Last Train To Clarksville (4:30)
Monkees; *Monkees* . . . . (Arista)
Monkees' Greatest Hits . . . . (Rhino)
Monkees-Live-1967 . . . . (Rhino)
Then & Now...The Best Of The Monkees . . . . (Arista)
Lonesome Standard Time
Kathy Mattea; *Lonesome Standard Time*. . . . . (Mercury)
Lonesome, I Know You Too Well (3 AM)
Shawn Mullins; *Beneath The Velvet Sun*. . . . . (Columbia)
Love Or Something Like It (2 A.M.)
Kenny Rogers; *Kenny Rogers-Twenty Greatest Hits*. . . . . (EMI)
Love You For A Day
Ricky Martin; *Ricky Martin*. . . . . (Columbia)
Moment, The
Kenny G; *The Moment*. . . . . (Arista)
Monkey Time
Major Lance; *Back To The '60s-#3-C* . . . . (Dominion Entert.)
Groove 'N' Grind-'50s & '60s Dance Hits-C . . . . (Rhino)
Soul Shots-#2-The ''In'' Crowd-Sweet Soul-C . . . . (Rhino)
Tubes; *Best Of The Tubes* . . . . (Gold Rush)
More News At 11
Public Enemy; *Apocalypse 91...The Enemy Strikes Black* . .(Def Jam/Columbia)
Nashville 1 A.M.
Harvey Mandel; *Cristo Redentor*. . . . . (Editions E.G.)
New York Minute
Don Henley; *End Of The Innocence* . . . . (Geffen)
News At Ten
Vapors; *New Clear Days*. . . . . (Liberty)
Now And Forever
Richard Marx; *Paid Vacation* . . . . (Capitol)
Now And Forever (You And Me)
Anne Murray; *Anne Murray's Greatest Hits-#2* . . . . (Capitol)
Something To Talk About . . . . (Capitol)
Now More Than Ever
John Mellencamp; *Whenever We Wanted* . . . . (Mercury)
Oh! How I Hate To Get Up In The Morning (5 O'Clock)
Irving Berlin; *American Songbook Series-Irving
Berlin*. . . . . (Smithsonian Collection)
War Years-C. . . . . (ISD/Intersound)
One After 909
Beatles; *Let It Be* . . . . (Capitol)
The Beatles-Anthology-#1 . . . . (Capitol)
One Moment In Time
Whitney Houston; *1984 Olympics Album-C* . . . . (Arista)
Whitney Houston's Greatest Hits . . . . (Arista)
One O'clock Jump
Count Basie & His Orchestra; *Swingingest Sounds Ever Heard-C* . . . . . . (Hip-O)
One Week
Barenaked Ladies; *Stunt* . . . .(Reprise)
Totally Hits-#1-C . . . . (Arista)
Peak Hour (Lunch Break)
Moody Blues; *Caught Live Plus Five* . . . . (Polydor)
Days Of Future Passed. . . . . (Polydor)
Pumpkin Time
Darol Anger & Barbara Higbie; *Live At Montreux* . . . . (Windham Hill)
Quarter To Three
Gary U.S. Bonds; *Best Of Gary U.S. Bonds*. . . . . (Rhino)
Best Of Gary U.S. Bonds. . . . .(EMI Legends Of Rock 'N' Roll)
Rednecks, White Socks And Blue Ribbon Beer (4:30)
Johnny Russell; *Beer Redneck Mothers*. . . . . (RCA)
Country Legends-C. . . . . (Madacy)
Country's Greatest Drinking Songs-C . . . . (All-Star Music)
Rednecks, White Socks & Blue Ribbon Beer . . . . (RCA)
Right Here, Right Now
Jesus Jones; *Doubt*. . . . . (SBK)
Right Now
Van Halen; *For Unlawful Carnal Knowledge* . . . . (Warner Bros.)
Rip It Up (10 PM)
Elvis Presley; *Elvis* . . . . (RCA)
Rocker. . . . . (RCA)
Little Richard; *Big Hits* . . . . (Crescendo)
Grooviest 17 Original Hits . . . . (Specialty)
Little Richard-18 Greatest Hits . . . . (Rhino)
Little Richard's Greatest Hits . . . . (Everest)

Send Down An Angel (3 AM)
Allison Moorer; *The Hardest Part*. (MCA)
Sentimental Journey (7 O'Clock)
Dinah Shore; *Sentimental Journey: Capitol's Great Ladies Of
Song-C* . . . . (Gold Rush)
Doris Day; *Doris Day Sings 22 Great Songs-Original Big Band* . . . . .(Hindsight)
Hal McIntyre & His Orchestra; *Nipper's Greatest Hits Of The
'40s-#2-C* . . . . (RCA)
Les Brown & His Orchestra; *Best Of The Big Bands-C* . . . .(Columbia)
Seven O'Clock News
Simon & Garfunkel; *Collected Works* . . . .(Columbia)
Parsley Sage Rosemary & Thyme . . . . (Columbia)
She's Leaving Home (5 AM, 9 AM)
Al Jarreau; *All Fly Home* . . . . (Warner Bros.)
Beatles; *Beatles-Box Set*. . . . . (Capitol)
Beatles-Love Songs . . . .(Capitol)
Sgt. Pepper's Lonely Hearts Club Band . . . . (Capitol)
Shoot Your Shot (9:30)
J. Geils Band; *Blow Your Face Out* . . . .(Rhino)
Junior Walker & The All Stars; *Junior Walker & The All Stars'
Greatest Hits* . . . . (Motown)
Junior Walker & The All Stars-Anthology. . . . . (Motown)
Shotgun . . . . (Motown)
Six O'Clock
Lovin' Spoonful; *Lovin' Spoonful-Anthology* . . . .(Rhino)
Six O'Clock Train & A Girl With Green Eyes
John Hartford; *All In The Name Of Love* . . . . (Flying Fish)
Six-Thirty Sunday Morning
Peter Allen; *Taught By Experts* . . . .(A&M)
So Anxious (11:30)
Ginuwine; *100 Percent Ginuwine* . . . . (550 Music)
Spark (6:58)
Tori Amos; *From The Choirgirl Hotel* . . . . (Atlantic)
Sunset At Noon
Kenny G; *G-Force*. . . . .(Arista)
Talking In Your Sleep (3 A.M.)
Crystal Gayle; *Classic Crystal*. . . . . (EMI)
Country Gold-C. . . . . (Priority)
Crystal Gayle's All-Time Greatest Hits. . . . .(Curb)
When I Dream . . . . (Liberty)
Reba McEntire; *Starting Over* . . . . (MCA)
Ten O'Clock In Toronto
Christine Lavin; *Compass* . . . . (Philo)
The Day (That You Gave Me A Son)
Babyface; *The Day*. . . . . (Epic)
Theme From ''Howdy Doody''
Original Soundtrack; *Television's Greatest Hits-#1-C* . . . .(TVT)
This Magic Moment
Drifters; *Drifters' Greatest Hits*. . . . . (Gusto)
Drifters-Golden Hits . . . . (Atlantic)
Jay & The Americans; *Come A Little Bit Closer-Best Of Jay & The
Americans*. . . . . (Gold Rush)
Jay & The Americans' All-Time Greatest Hits . . . . (Rhino)
Marvin Gaye; *M.P.G.*. . . . . (Motown)
Three O'Clock Blues
B.B. King; *Best Blues Album In The World...Ever!-C* . . . . (Virgin)
Chart Toppers-R&B Hits Of The '50s-C . . . . (Priority)
Thunder Rolls, The (3:30am)
Garth Brooks; *Garth Brooks-Double Live* . . . . (Capitol)
No Fences . . . .(Capitol)
Tuesday At Ten
Count Basie; *Essential Count Basie-#3* . . . .(Columbia)
Twelve Thirty (Young Girls Are Coming To The Canyon)
Mamas & The Papas; *Best Of The Mamas & The Papas* . . . . (MCA)
Mamas & The Papas-16 Of Their Greatest Hits . . . . (MCA)
The Papas & The Mamas . . . . (MCA)
Twilight Time
Platters; *Pick Of The Platters* . . . . (Fifty One West)
Platters . . . . (Everest)
Platters-16 Greatest Hits . . . . (Trip)
Platters-Anthology. . . . .(Rhino)
Sold Out. . . . . (Fifty One West)
Willie Nelson; *What A Wonderful World* . . . .(Columbia)
Twilight Time
Moody Blues; *Days Of Future Passed* . . . . (Polydor)
Two Minutes To Midnight
Iron Maiden; *A Real Dead One* . . . . (Capitol)
Live After Death-World Slavery Tour . . . . (Capitol)
Powerslave. . . . .(Capitol)
Two O'Clock In The Morning
Stuart Duncan; *Stuart Duncan* . . . . (Rounder)
Two O'Clock Jump
Harry James; *All-Time Favorites By Harry James* . . . (Sony Music Special Prod.)
Harry James' Greatest Hits. . . . .(Columbia)
Two O'Clock Jump . . . .(Pro-Arte)
Wednesday Morning, 3 AM
Simon & Garfunkel; *Collected Works* . . . . (Columbia)
Wednesday Morning 3 A.M. . . . .(Columbia)

TOGETHERNESS, Reunited, United
See Also: *BROTHERHOOD, COUPLES, FRIENDS, GOD, LOVE (various), MARRIAGE, PEACE, PEOPLE*

2 Become 1
Spice Girls; *Spice* . . . . (Virgin)
After All These Years
Jim Brickman & Anne Cochran; *Visions Of Love* . . . . (Windham Hill)
Ain't Got Nothin' On Us
John Michael Montgomery; *What I Do The Best* . . . . (Atlantic)
All Through The Night
Cyndi Lauper; *She's So Unusual* . . . . (Portrait)
  Twelve Deadly Cyns...And Then Some . . . . (Epic)
Jules Shear; *Horse Of A Different Color: The Jules Shear Collection-1976-1989* . . . . (Razor & Tie)
All Together Now
Beatles; *Yellow Submarine* . . . . (Capitol)
Muppets; *Kermit Unpigged* . . . . (Jim Henson)
Alone Together
Judy Garland; *Judy Garland-At Carnegie Hall* . . . . (Capitol)
Alone With You
Faron Young; *'50s Hits-Country-#1-C* . . . . (Curb)
  Faron Young's All-Time Greatest Hits . . . . (Curb)
  Faron Young's Greatest Hits-#2 . . . . (Step One)
As Long As I'm Rockin' With You
John Conlee; *Best Of John Conlee* . . . . (Curb)
  In My Eyes . . . . (MCA)
  John Conlee-20 Greatest Hits . . . . (MCA)
  John Conlee-Legends . . . . (MCA)
At The Beginning
Richard Marx & Donna Lewis; *ST/Anastasia-Music From The Motion Picture* . . . . (Atlantic)
Back In Your Arms Again
Lorrie Morgan; *Lorrie Morgan's Greatest Hits* . . . . (BNA)
Backstreets
Bruce Springsteen; *Born To Run* . . . . (Columbia)
Be My Life's Companion
Mills Brothers; *Best Of The Mills Brothers* . . . . (MCA)
  The Mills Brothers-Best Of The Decca Years . . . . (Decca)
Rosemary Clooney; *Rosemary Clooney-16 Most Requested Songs* . . . . (Legacy)
Beauty And The Beast
Celine Dion & Peabo Bryson; *All The Way...A Decade Of Song* . . . . (550 Music)
  Celine Dion . . . . (Epic)
  ST/Beauty And The Beast . . . . (Disney)
Being With You
Smokey Robinson; *Billboard Top Hits-1981-C* . . . . (Rhino)
  Blame It On Love & All The Great Hits . . . . (Motown)
  Smokey Robinson-The Ultimate Collection . . . . (Motown)
Bent
Matchbox Twenty; *Mad Season By Matchbox Twenty* . . . . (Lava)
  Totally Hits-#3-C . . . . (Atlantic)
Between Us
Harry Connick, Jr.; *She* . . . . (Columbia)
Bigger Than The Beatles
Joe Diffie; *Life's So Funny* . . . . (Epic)
Born To Be Together
Ronettes; *Best Of The Ronettes* . . . . (Abkco)
Born To Be With You
Chordettes; *Best Of The Chordettes* . . . . (Rhino)
  Chordettes Greatest Hits . . . . (Everest)
  Lil' Bit Of Gold 3'' CD Series-C . . . . (Rhino)
Brothers Under The Bridges ('83)
Bruce Springsteen; *Tracks* . . . . (Columbia)
Caravan Of Love
Isley, Jasper, Isley; *Caravan Of Love* . . . . (CBS Associated)
Chapel Of Love
Dixie Cups; *Girl Groups-Story Of A Sound-C* . . . . (Rhino)
  Jewels-#1-C . . . . (SSS International)
  Oldies But Goodies-#11-C . . . . (Original Sound)
  Original New York Rock & Roll-C . . . . (Original Sound)
Come Again
Damn Yankees; *Damn Yankees* . . . . (Warner Bros.)
Come Go With Me
Del Vikings; *1956 Audition Tapes* . . . . (Collectables)
  Billboard Top R&B Hits-1957-C . . . . (Rhino)
  Oldies But Goodies-#3-C . . . . (Original Sound)
  ST/American Graffiti . . . . (MCA)
  ST/Stand By Me . . . . (Atlantic)
Come On Let's Go
Los Lobos; *And A Time To Dance* . . . . (Slash)
  Just Another Band From East L.A. . . . . (Slash)
  ST/La Bamba . . . . (Slash)
Ritchie Valens; *Best Of Ritchie Valens* . . . . (Rhino)
  Oldies But Goodies-#4-C . . . . (Original Sound)
  The Ritchie Valens Story . . . . (Del Fi)
Come Together
Aerosmith; *ST/Armageddon-The Album* . . . . (Columbia)

Beatles; *Abbey Road* . . . . (Parlophone)
  Beatles 1 . . . . (Capitol)
  Beatles-20 Greatest Hits . . . . (Capitol)
  The Beatles/1967-1970 . . . . (Capitol)
Ike & Tina Turner; *Proud Mary-Best Of Ike & Tina Turner* . . . . (EMI)
  Workin' Together . . . . (EMI)
John Lennon; *Live In New York City* . . . . (Capitol)
Cowboy Take Me Away
Dixie Chicks; *Fly* . . . . (Monument)
Cruisin'
D'Angelo; *Brown Sugar* . . . . (EMI)
Huey Lewis and Gwyneth Paltrow; *ST/Duets* . . . . (Hollywood)
Smokey Robinson; *Compact Command Performances-Smokey Robinson* . . . . (Motown)
  Motown Love Songs-C . . . . (Motown)
  Motown Story-First 25 Years-C . . . . (Motown)
  Where There's Smoke . . . . (Motown)
Darlin' Companion
Johnny Cash; *Johnny Cash At Folsom Prison & San Quentin* . . . . . . (Columbia)
Lovin' Spoonful; *Hums Of The Lovin' Spoonful* . . . . (Kama Sutra)
  Lovin' Spoonful-Collector's Edition-#1 . . . . (Platinum Disc)
  Lovin' Spoonful's Greatest Hits . . . . (Buddah)
Do You Believe In Us?
Jon Secada; *Jon Secada* . . . . (SBK)
Downtown
B-52's; *B-52's* . . . . (Warner Bros.)
Frank Sinatra; *Strangers In The Night* . . . . (Reprise)
Petula Clark; *Dick Clark's 21 All-Time Hits-#2-C* . . . . (Original Sound)
  Petula Clark's Greatest Hits . . . . (Crescendo)
Drive South
John Hiatt; *Slow Turning* . . . . (A&M)
Suzy Bogguss; *Voices In The Wind* . . . . (Liberty)
Embraceable You
Billie Holiday; *Body And Soul* . . . . (Verve)
Frank Sinatra; *The Capitol Years* . . . . (Capitol)
MGM Studio Orchestra; *ST/American In Paris* . . . . . (Sony Music Special Prod.)
Oleta Adams; *Glory Of Gershwin Featuring Larry Adler-C* . . . . . (Mercury)
Sarah Vaughan; *Complete Sarah Vaughan On Mercury-#1-Great Jazz Years-1954-1956* . . . . (Mercury)
End Of The Road
Boyz II Men; *Cooleyhighharmony* . . . . (Motown)
Even The Nights Are Better
Air Supply; *Air Supply's Greatest Hits* . . . . (Arista)
  Now & Forever . . . . (Arista)
Everywhere
Fleetwood Mac; *25 Years-The Chain* . . . . (Warner Bros.)
  Fleetwood Mac's Greatest Hits . . . . (Warner Bros.)
  Tango In The Night . . . . (Warner Bros.)
Faith In Me, Faith In You
Doug Stone; *Country Lovin'-Songs From The Heart-C* . . . . (Rhino)
  Faith In Me Faith In You . . . . (Columbia)
  Super Hits Of 1995-C . . . . (Epic)
Faith In You
Steve Wariner; *Faith In You* . . . . (Capitol)
Feels So Right
Alabama; *Alabama's Greatest Hits* . . . . (RCA)
  Feels So Right . . . . (RCA)
Flesh And Blood
Johnny Cash; *Johnny Cash's Biggest Hits* . . . . (Columbia)
  The Man In Black-His Greatest Hits . . . . (Legacy)
Forever Together
Randy Travis; *High Lonesome* . . . . (Warner Bros.)
Fourteen Minutes Old
Doug Stone; *Doug Stone* . . . . (Epic)
From This Moment On
Anita O'Day; *Swings Cole Porter* . . . . (Verve)
Ella Fitzgerald; *Ella Fitzgerald Sings The Cole Porter Songbook* . . . . . (Verve)
Frank Sinatra; *a Swingin' Affair!* . . . . (Capitol)
Original Soundtrack; *Kiss Me Kate* . . . . (Rhino)
Gel
Collective Soul; *Collective Soul* . . . . (Atlantic)
  ST/Jerky Boys . . . . (Atlantic)
Get A Little Closer
Ricky Lynn Gregg; *Get A Little Closer* . . . . (Liberty)
Get It Together
702; *No Doubt* . . . . (Biv 10/Motown)
Grow Old With Me
John Lennon; *The John Lennon Anthology* . . . . (Capitol)
  Wonsaponatime . . . . (Capitol)
Mary Chapin Carpenter; *Party Doll And Other Favorites* . . . . (Columbia)
Happy Together
Flo & Eddie And The Turtles; *History Of Flo & Eddie And The Turtles* . . . . (Rhino)
Turtles; *Billboard Top Rock 'N' Roll Hits-1967-C* . . . . (Rhino)
  Cruisin'-1967-C . . . . (Increase)
  Happy Together . . . . (Rhino)
  Turtles-20 Greatest Hits . . . . (Rhino)
  Turtlesized . . . . (Rhino)

Here We Are
Alabama; *Pass It On Down* . . . . (BMG Special Prod.)
Here We Are
Gloria Estefan; *Cuts Both Ways* . . . . (Epic)
High Hopes And Empty Pockets
McBride & The Ride; *McBride & The Ride* . . . . (MCA)
Holdin'
Diamond Rio; *Diamond Rio IV* . . . . (Arista)
Diamond Rio's Greatest Hits . . . . (Arista)
House At Pooh Corner
Loggins & Messina; *Loggins & Messina-On Stage* . . . . (Columbia)
Sittin' In . . . . (Columbia)
The Best Of Friends . . . . (Columbia)
Nitty Gritty Dirt Band; *Best Of The Nitty Gritty Dirt Band* . . . . (Liberty)
Best Of The Nitty Gritty Dirt Band . . . . (Liberty)
Dirt, Silver & Gold . . . . (One Way)
Uncle Charlie And His Dog Teddy . . . . (Liberty)
I Ain't Goin' Nowhere
Martina McBride; *Emotion* . . . . (RCA)
I Believe In You And Me
Whitney Houston; *ST/The Preacher's Wife* . . . . (Arista)
I Feel Fine
Beatles; *Beatles 1* . . . . (Capitol)
Beatles '65 . . . . (Capitol)
Beatles-20 Greatest Hits . . . . (Capitol)
Past Masters-Volume One . . . . (Parlophone)
The Beatles/1962-1966 . . . . (Capitol)
Sweethearts Of The Rodeo; *One Time One Night* . . . . (Columbia)
I Got You
Split Enz; *History Never Repeats-Best Of Split Enz.* . . . . (A&M)
True Colours . . . . (A&M)
I Got You
Dwight Yoakam; *Buenas Noches From A Lonely Room* . . . . (Reprise)
Just Lookin' For A Hit . . . . (Reprise)
I Got You
Shenandoah; *Extra Mile* . . . . (Columbia)
I Got You Babe
Cher with Beavis & Butt-head; *The Beavis & Butt-head*
Experience-C . . . . (Geffen)
Sonny & Cher; *I Got You Babe* . . . . (Rhino)
The Beat Goes On-Best Of Sonny & Cher. . . . . (Rhino)
UB40 & Chrissie Hynde; *Chicken Soup For The Couples Soul-C* . . . . (Rhino)
I Guess You Had To Be There
Lorrie Morgan; *To Get To You-Greatest Hits Collection.* . . . . (BNA)
Watch Me . . . . (BNA)
I Love You Always Forever
Donna Lewis; *Now In A Minute* . . . . (Atlantic)
The Absolute Hits-C . . . . (Atlantic)
I Still Believe In You
Vince Gill; *I Still Believe In You* . . . . (MCA)
I Think We're Alone Now
Tiffany; *Tiffany* . . . . (MCA)
Tiffany's Greatest Hits . . . . (Hip-O)
Tommy James And The Shondells; *Best Of Tommy James And The*
Shondells . . . . (Roulette)
Billboard Top Rock 'N' Roll Hits-1967-C . . . . (Rhino)
Tommy James And The Shondells-Anthology . . . . (Rhino)
I Wanna B With U
Fun Factory; *Close To You* . . . . (Curb)
Fun-Tastic . . . . (Curb)
I Wanna Be With You
Mandy Moore; *I Wanna Be With You* . . . . (550 Music)
Now That's What I Call Music!-#5-C . . . . (Virgin)
I Wanna Get With U
Guy; *Future* . . . . (Uptown/MCA)
If
Bread; *Best Of Bread* . . . . (Elektra)
Bread-Anthology . . . . (Elektra)
Bread-Retrospective . . . . (Rhino)
Manna. . . . . (Rhino)
I'll Be By Your Side
Stevie B; *Best Of Stevie B* . . . . (LMR)
Love & Emotion . . . . (LMR)
I'll Be Your Everything
Tommy Page; *Paintings In My Mind* . . . . (Sire)
I'll Never Find Another You
Seekers; *Best Of The Seekers* . . . . (Capitol)
History Of British Rock-#3-C . . . . (Rhino)
Sonny James; *All-Time Country Classics-#2-C* . . . . (Capitol)
Opry Legends-Sonny James . . . . (Capitol)
I'll Stand By You
Pretenders; *Last Of The Independents* . . . . (Sire)
I'll String Along With You
Diana Krall; *When I Look In Your Eyes* . . . . (GRP)
I'm Already There
Lonestar; *I'm Already There* . . . . (BNA)
I'm Gonna Make You Love Me
Jayhawks; *Smile* . . . . (American/Columbia)

I'm Not Giving You Up
Gloria Estefan; *Destiny* . . . . (Epic)
In Another's Eyes
Trisha Yearwood & Garth Brooks; *Songbook-A Collection Of Hits* . . . . . (MCA)
In Times Like These
Barbara Mandrell; *Barbara Mandrell's Greatest Hits* . . . . (MCA)
Spun Gold . . . . (MCA)
It Takes Two
Marvin Gaye & Kim Weston; *Hitsville USA-The Motown Singles Collection-*
1959-1971-C . . . . (Motown)
It's A Woman's World
Four Aces; *Best Of The Four Aces* . . . . (MCA)
I've Got This Feeling
Mavericks; *Trampoline* . . . . (MCA)
Jamboree
Naughty By Nature Featuring Zhane'; *19 Naughty Nine:*
Nature's Fury. . . . . (Arista)
Joining You
Alanis Morissette; *Supposed Former Infatuation Junkie* . . . . (Maverick)
Just Another Day In Paradise
Phil Vassar; *Phil Vassar.* . . . . (Arista)
Just As Long As I Have You
Don Williams; *One Good Well.* . . . . (RCA)
Just Between You And Me
April Wine; *Nature Of The Beast* . . . . (Capitol)
Just Between You And Me
Kinleys; *Just Between You And Me* . . . . (Epic)
Just Between You And Me
Charley Pride; *Best Of Charley Pride* . . . . (RCA)
Just Between You And Me
Chordettes; *Best Of The Chordettes* . . . . (Rhino)
Just Between You And Me
Lou Gramm; *Long Hard Look* . . . . (Atlantic)
Just The Two Of Us
Will Smith; *Big Willie Style* . . . . (Columbia)
Just The Two Of Us
Grover Washington, Jr. & Bill Withers; *Billboard Top R&B Hits-*
1981-C . . . . (Rhino)
Grover Washington, Jr.-Anthology . . . . (Elektra)
Grover Washington, Jr.-Winelight . . . . (Elektra)
Just You And I And The Moon
Jose Collins; *Music From The New York Stage (1890-1920)-#3-1913-*
1917-C . . . . (Pearl)
Keep It Together
Madonna; *Like A Prayer* . . . . (Sire)
Lazy Day
Spanky & Our Gang; *Best Of Spanky & Our Gang* . . . . (Rhino)
Let's Build A World Together
George Jones & Tammy Wynette; *George Jones & Tammy Wynette-16*
Biggest Hits . . . . (Epic/Legacy)
Let's Fall To Pieces Together
George Strait; *George Strait's Greatest Hits* . . . . (MCA)
Right Or Wrong . . . . (MCA)
Strait Out Of The Box . . . . (MCA)
Let's Get Together
Hayley Mills; *Classic Disney-#1-60 Years Of Musical Magic-C* . . . . . . (Disney)
Family Friendship Classics-The Most Memorable Songs From Film &
Television-C . . . . (Rhino)
Let's Go All The Way
Norma Jean; *Best Of Norma Jean* . . . . (Collector's Choice)
Let's Stay Home Together
Joe; *Better Days* . . . . (Jive)
Let's Stay Together
Al Green; *Al Green's Greatest Hits* . . . . (Right Stuff)
Let's Stay Together . . . . (Right Stuff)
Tokyo...Live . . . . (Right Stuff)
Let's Stay Together
Eric Benet; *True To Myself.* . . . . (Jac-Mac/Warner Bros.)
Live Forever
Oasis; *Definitely Maybe* . . . . (Epic)
Livin' On A Prayer
Bon Jovi; *America: A Tribute To Heroes-C* . . . . (Interscope)
Cross Road-14 Classic Grooves . . . . (Mercury)
Slippery When Wet . . . . (Jambco)
The Concert For New York City-C . . . . (Columbia)
Long Walk, A
Jill Scott; *Who Is Jill Scott? Words And Sounds-#1* . . . . . . (Hidden Beach/Epic)
Love Is All
Marc Anthony; *Marc Anthony* . . . . (Columbia)
Love Keep Us Together
Martin Sexton; *Black Sheep* . . . . (Eastern Front)
The American . . . . (Atlantic)
Love On Arrival
Dan Seals; *Dan Seals' Greatest Hits* . . . . (Liberty)
On Arrival . . . . (Capitol)
Love Will Keep Us Together
Captain & Tennille; *Billboard Top Hits-1975-C* . . . . (Rhino)
Captain & Tennille's Greatest Hits . . . . (A&M)

Man Of My Word
Collin Raye; *Extremes* . . . .(Epic)
Maybe I'm Amazed
Paul McCartney; *McCartney* . . . . (Capitol)
Wings; *Wings Over America* . . . . (Capitol)
Me & My Old Lady
Offspring; *Ixnay On The Hombre* . . . . (Columbia)
Me And You
Kenny Chesney; *All I Need To Know* . . . . (BNA)
Me And You . . . . (BNA)
Monday We'll Be Together
Nikki D; *Daddy's Little Girl* . . . . (Def Jam/Columbia)
Near You
Francis Craig & His Orchestra; *Cigar Classics-#1-The Standards-C* . . . . (Hip-O)
George Jones & Tammy Wynette; *George Jones & Tammy Wynette-16 Biggest Hits* . . . . (Epic/Legacy)
Next To You, Next To Me
Shenandoah; *Extra Mile* . . . . (Columbia)
Greatest Country Hits Of The '90s-#2-C . . . . (Columbia)
Shenandoah's Greatest Hits . . . . (Columbia)
Nobody I Know
Peter And Gordon; *History Of British Rock-#1-C* . . . . (Rhino)
Oh How Happy
Shades Of Blue; *Oldies But Goodies-#2-C* . . . . (Original Sound)
Oh How The Years Go By
Vanessa Williams; *NBA At 50-A Musical Celebration-C* . . . . . (Mercury)
Old Friends
Barry Manilow; *Showstoppers* . . . . (Arista)
Liza Minnelli; *Liza Minnelli-At Carnegie Hall* . . . . . . (Telarc)
Original Cast; *Merrily We Roll Along* . . . . (RCA)
Stephen Sondheim & Angela Lansbury & Co.; *Collector's Sondheim-C* . . (RCA)
Old Friends
Simon & Garfunkel; *Bookends* . . . . (Columbia)
Collected Works . . . . (Columbia)
The Concert In Central Park . . . .(Warner Bros.)
Old Friends
Willie Nelson & Roger Miller; *Old Friends* . . . . (Columbia)
Willie Nelson & Waylon Jennings; *Take It To The Limit* . . . . . . (Columbia)
Old Friends
Everything But The Girl; *Worldwide* . . . .(Atlantic)
One
Creed; *My Own Prison* . . . . (Wind-up)
One
George Jones & Tammy Wynette; *George Jones Collection* . . . . (MCA)
Grand Ole Opry-75 Years-#2-C . . . . (MCA)
One . . . .(MCA)
One Boy, One Girl
Collin Raye; *Best Of Collin Raye-Direct Hits* . . . .(Epic)
I Think About You . . . .(Epic)
One Man Woman
Judds; *Judds-Collection 1983-1990* . . . . (RCA)
River Of Time . . . . (RCA)
Only Wanna Be With You
Hootie & The Blowfish; *Cracked Rear View* . . . . (Atlantic)
Part Of Me, Part Of You
Glenn Frey; *ST/Thelma & Louise* . . . . (MCA)
Strange Weather . . . .(MCA)
Puppy Song
Nilsson; *Harry* . . . .(Dunhill Compact Classics)
ST/You've Got Mail . . . . (Atlantic)
Rendezvous
Bruce Springsteen; *Tracks* . . . . (Columbia)
Gary U.S. Bonds; *Best Of Gary U.S. Bonds* . . . (EMI Legends Of Rock 'N' Roll)
Greg Kihn; *Kihnsolidation-Best Of Greg Kihn* . . . . (Rhino)
Greg Kihn Band; *Cover Me (Bruce Springsteen Tribute)-C* . . . . (Rhino)
Reunion
Indigo Girls; *Swamp Ophelia* . . . .(Epic)
Rhapsody In The Rain
Lou Christie; *Enlightnin'ment-Best Of Lou Christie* . . . . (Rhino)
Right Beside You
Sophie B. Hawkins; *Whaler* . . . . (Columbia)
Rockin' With The Rhythm Of The Rain
Judds; *Judds' Greatest Hits* . . . .(MCA)
Rockin' With The Rhythm . . . .(MCA)
Runaway
Janet Jackson; *Design Of A Decade-1986/1996* . . . . (A&M)
Running Back To You
Vanessa Williams; *The Comfort Zone* . . . . (Wing)
Say You, Say Me
Lionel Richie; *Back To Front* . . . . (Motown)
Dancing On The Ceiling . . . . (Motown)
Side By Side
Kay Starr; *Kay Starr's Greatest Hits* . . . . (Curb)
Mitch Miller; *Mitch Miller-16 Most Requested Songs* . . . . (Columbia)
Sisters
Rosemary Clooney & Betty Clooney; *Mothers & Daughters* . . . . .(Concord Jazz)
So Close
Daryl Hall & John Oates; *Change Of Season* . . . . (Arista)

So Close
Diana Ross; *Silk Electric* . . . .(RCA)
So Much In Love
Tymes; *20th Century Rocks-#9-'60's Vocal Groups-I Got Rhythm-C* . . . . (Dominion Entert.)
Some Things Are Meant To Be
Linda Davis; *Some Things Are Meant To Be* . . . . (Arista)
Someday We'll Be Together
Diana Ross & The Supremes; *20/20-C* . . . . (Motown)
Diana Ross & The Supremes' Greatest Hits-#3 . . . . (Motown)
Diana Ross & The Supremes-Anthology (1962-1969) . . . . (Motown)
Evening With Diana Ross . . . . (Motown)
Motown Story-First 25 Years-C . . . . (Motown)
Motown Superstar Series-#1-Diana Ross & The Supremes . . . . (Motown)
Something That We Do
Clint Black; *Country Cares For Kids II-C* . . . .(BNA)
Nothin' But The Taillights . . . . (RCA)
Somewhere Other Than The Night
Garth Brooks; *The Chase* . . . . (Liberty)
Song For Mama
Boyz II Men; *BET-Best Of Planet Groove-C* . . . .(Virgin)
Evolution . . . . (Motown)
ST/Soul Food . . . .(LaFace)
Spend My Life With You
Eric Benet; *A Day In The Life* . . . . (Warner Bros.)
Standing Together
George Benson; *Standing Together* . . . .(GRP)
Stay
4 Seasons; *4 Seasons' Greatest Hits-#1* . . . . (Rhino)
Jackson Browne; *Running On Empty* . . . .(Asylum)
Maurice Williams & The Zodiacs; *Best Of Maurice Williams & The Zodiacs* . . . . (Collectables)
Billboard Top Rock 'N' Roll Hits-1960-C . . . . (Rhino)
Cruisin'-1960-C . . . . (Increase)
Rock & Roll Is Here To Stay-C . . . . (Gusto)
ST/Dirty Dancing . . . . (RCA)
Stay A Little Longer
Bob Wills; *Sounds Of Texas* . . . . (Capitol)
Bob Wills & His Texas Playboys; *Bob Wills & His Texas Playboys-Anthology 1935-1973* . . . . (Rhino)
Tiffany Transcriptions-#2-Best Of The Tiffanys . . . . (Rhino)
Willie Nelson; *Greatest Hits (& Some That Will Be)* . . . . (Columbia)
Willie & Family Live . . . . (Columbia)
Sweethearts Together
Rolling Stones; *Voodoo Lounge* . . . .(Virgin)
Texas, Me & You
Asleep At The Wheel; *Route 66* . . . . (Liberty)
Thankyou
Dido; *No Angel* . . . . (Arista)
Totally Hits 2001-C . . . . (Arista)
That Ol' Wind
Garth Brooks; *Fresh Horses* . . . . (Capitol)
Limited Series Box . . . . (Capitol)
There's A Kind Of Hush (All Over The World)
Carpenters; *A Kind Of Hush* . . . . (A&M)
Carpenters-Classics-#2 . . . . (A&M)
Yesterday Once More . . . . (A&M)
Herman's Hermits; *Herman's Hermits-Their Greatest Hits* . . . .(Abkco)
They're Playin' Our Song
Neal McCoy; *Neal McCoy's Greatest Hits* . . . .(Atlantic)
You Gotta Love That! . . . . (Atlantic)
Till I'm Holding You Again
Pirates Of The Mississippi; *Walk The Plank* . . . . (Liberty)
To Be With You
Mr. Big; *Lean Into It* . . . .(Atlantic)
To Be With You
Mavericks; *Trampoline* . . . . (MCA)
Together
Nilsson; *Aerial Ballet* . . . . (RCA)
Together Again
Buck Owens; *Buck Owens' All-Time Greatest Hits-#1* . . . .(Curb)
Very Best Of Buck Owens-#1 . . . . (Rhino)
Emmylou Harris; *Elite Hotel* . . . . (Reprise)
Profile/Best Of Emmylou Harris . . . . (Warner Bros.)
Together Again
Janet Jackson; *Now That's What I Call Music!-#1-C* . . . .(Virgin)
Velvet Rope . . . .(Virgin)
Together Again
Dave Koz; *Dance* . . . . (Capitol)
Together Always
Porter Wagoner & Dolly Parton; *Lassoes N' Spurs* . . . . (RCA)
Together Always . . . . (RCA)
Together In America
King Errisson; *Global Music* . . . . (Ichiban Int'l)
Together Wherever We Go
Original Cast; *ST/Gypsy* . . . . (Columbia)
Tomorrow
Strawberry Alarm Clock; *Best Of The Strawberry Alarm Clock-#1* . . .(Bac-Trac)

Twilight Time
Platters; *Pick Of The Platters*..........................(Fifty One West)
 Platters......................................(Everest)
 Platters-16 Greatest Hits.........................(Trip)
 Platters-Anthology..............................(Rhino)
 Sold Out....................................(Fifty One West)
Willie Nelson; *What A Wonderful World*.................(Columbia)
Two For The Road
Bruce Springsteen; *Tracks*..........................(Columbia)
Two Hearts Beat As One
U2; *War*......................................(Island)
Two Of A Kind, Workin' On A Full House
Garth Brooks; *No Fences*............................(Capitol)
Two Sparrows In A Hurricane
Tanya Tucker; *Can't Run From Yourself*.................(Liberty)
 Tanya Tucker's Greatest Hits-1990-1992..............(Capitol)
Unity
Queen Latifah; *Black Reign*.........................(Motown)
Walk This World
Heather Nova; *Oyster*..............................(Big Cat)
We Are Family
Sister Sledge; *Atlantic Records 50 Years-The Gold Anniversary*
 Collection-C.................................(Atlantic)
 Best Of Sister Sledge-1973-1985...................(Rhino)
 Chicken Soup For The Soul: I'll Be There For You-Songs Of Friendship,
 Brotherhood And Sisterhood-C.....................(Rhino)
 ST/The Full Monty............................(RCA Victor)
 We Are Family...............................(Rhino)
We Are The World
USA For Africa; *We Are The World-C*...................(Columbia)
We Belong Together
Rickie Lee Jones; *Naked Songs Live And Acoustic*..........(Reprise)
 Pirates.....................................(Warner Bros.)
We Belong Together
Robert & Johnny; *Doo Wop's Greatest Hits-C*.............(K-Tel)
We Belong Together
Peaches & Herb; *Love Is Strange-The Best Of Peaches & Herb*.......(Legacy)
We Belong Together
Spinners; *Spinners*...............................(Rhino)
We Belong Together
Los Lobos; *ST/La Bamba*...........................(Slash)
Ritchie Valens; *Brown Eyed Soul...East L.A.-#2-C*.........(Rhino)
We Don't Need Another Hero (Thunderdome)
Tina Turner; *Live In Europe*........................(Capitol)
 Simply The Best.............................(Capitol)
We Gather Together
Original Soundtrack; *School Days-Kids Classics*...........(Benson)
We Gotta Live Together
Jimi Hendrix; *Band Of Gypsys*......................(Capitol)
We'll Be Together
Sting; *...Nothing Like The Sun*.......................(A&M)
 Fields Of Gold-The Best Of Sting 1984-1994.........(A&M)
We're All Alone
Boz Scaggs; *Boz Scaggs-Hits!*.......................(Columbia)
 Slow Dancer................................(Columbia)
Rita Coolidge; *Rita Coolidge's Greatest Hits*............(A&M)
We're Gonna Hold On
George Jones & Tammy Wynette; *George Jones & Tammy Wynette-16*
 Biggest Hits................................(Epic/Legacy)
We're In This Together
Nine Inch Nails; *The Fragile*.......................(Nothing)
When Boy Meets Girl
Terri Clark; *Terri Clark*...........................(Mercury)
When I'm Sixty-Four
Beatles; *Beatles-Box Set*..........................(Capitol)
 Sgt. Pepper's Lonely Hearts Club Band..............(Capitol)
When You Need Me
Bruce Springsteen; *Tracks*.........................(Columbia)
Whenever Wherever Whatever
Maxwell; *Maxwell's Urban Hang Suite*.................(Columbia)
Where've You Been
Kathy Mattea; *Collection Of Hits*....................(Mercury)
 Willow In The Wind...........................(Mercury)
Whither Thou Goest
Les Paul & Mary Ford; *Best Of The Capitol Masters*.........(Gold Rush)
 Les Paul's All-Time Greatest Hits...............(EMI Special Markets)
Whole New World (Aladdin's Theme)
Peabo Bryson & Regina Belle; *ST/Aladdin*..............(Disney)
Regina Belle & Peabo Bryson; *Passion*.................(Columbia)
Wild Angels
Martina McBride; *Angels Among Us-C*..................(RCA)
 Wild Angels.................................(RCA)
Will You Still Be Mine
Morgana King; *Simply Eloquent*......................(Muse)
Mundell Lowe; *Mundell Lowe Quartet*..................(Riverside)
Red Garland Trio; *Groovy*..........................(Prestige)
Rosemary Clooney; *Rosemary Clooney With Love*..........(Concord Jazz)
With You
Prince; *Prince*..................................(Warner Bros.)

With You
Original Broadway Cast; *Baby*.......................(Polydor)
With You
Charly McClain; *Charly McClain's Biggest Hits*...........(Epic)
With You
Original Cast; *Pippin*.............................(Motown)
With You
Tony Terry; *Tony Terry*...........................(Epic)
With You I'm Born Again
Billy Preston & Syreeta; *15 Of Motown's Greatest Love Songs*.......(Motown)
 Endless Love-Motown's Greatest Love Songs-C.......(Motown)
 Hard-To-Find Motown Classics-#2-C...............(Motown)
 Motown Story-First 25 Years-#3-C.................(Motown)
Wouldn't It Be Nice
Beach Boys; *Absolutely Best-#2*......................(Capitol)
 Made In The U.S.A............................(Capitol)
 Pet Sounds..................................(Capitol)
 Still Cruisin'................................(Capitol)
You & Forever & Me
Little Texas; *First Time For Everything*................(Warner Bros.)
You And I
Eddie Rabbitt & Crystal Gayle; *Best Of Eddie Rabbitt/Greatest*
 Hits-II.....................................(Warner Bros.)
 Chicken Soup For The Couples Soul-C..............(Rhino)
You And Me Against The World
Helen Reddy; *Helen Reddy's Greatest Hits*..............(Capitol)
You And Me Against The World
Roy Rogers; *Best Of Roy Rogers*.....................(Curb)
You Could Be Mine
Guns N' Roses; *Use Your Illusion II*..................(Geffen)
You're The Cream In My Coffee
Lawrence Welk; *Lawrence Welk-16 Most Requested Songs*.......(Columbia)
Les Brown & His Orchestra; *Best Of Les Brown & His Orchestra*.......(MCA)

TOOLS, Cutlery, Cutting, Knives, Nails, Swords
See Also: **BUILDING & CONSTRUCTION, FIXING, MACHINES**

4:37 AM (Arabs With Knives & West German Skies)
Roger Waters; *Pros & Cons Of Hitchhiking*..............(Columbia)
Ace Of Swords
Alan Parsons Project; *Turn Of A Friendly Card*...........(Arista)
Anvil Chorus
Glenn Miller; *Memorial-1944-1969*....................(Bluebird)
 Secret Broadcasts............................(RCA Victor)
Keith Lockhart; *Runnin' Wild*.......................(RCA Victor)
Back Stabbers
O'Jays; *Billboard Top Rock 'N' Roll Hits-1972-C*..........(Rhino)
 Live In London..............................(Philadelphia Int'l)
 O'Jays-Collector's Item........................(Philadelphia Int'l)
Bag Of Hammers
Local H; *Ham Fisted*.............................(Island)
Blood On The Dance Floor
Michael Jackson; *Blood On The Dance Floor-HIStory...*.....(MJJ Music/Work)
Broadsword
Jethro Tull; *Broadsword And The Beast*................(Chrysalis)
Careful With That Axe Eugene
Pink Floyd; *Relics*..............................(Capitol)
 Ummagumma.................................(Capitol)
Clocks Don't Bring Tomorrow-Knives Don't Bring Good News
Bruce Cockburn; *Night Vision*.......................(Columbia)
Cold Hard Facts Of Life, The
Porter Wagoner; *Essential Porter Wagoner*..............(RCA)
 Porter Wagoner's Greatest Hits..................(Pair)
Country Boy's Tool Box
Aaron Tippin; *Tool Box*...........................(RCA)
Cut You In
Jerry Cantrell; *Boggy Depot*........................(Columbia)
Cuts Like A Knife
Bryan Adams; *Cuts Like A Knife*.....................(A&M)
 Live! Live! Live!.............................(A&M)
 MTV Unplugged-Bryan Adams....................(A&M)
 So Far So Good..............................(A&M)
Die By The Sword
Slayer; *Slayer-Live-Decade Of Aggression*..............(Def American)
Hammer
Bob Marley & The Wailers; *King Of Reggae*.............(Madacy)
 Reggae Fever-C..............................(Madacy)
Hammer & Nail
Forester Sisters; *More Than I Am*....................(Warner Resound)
Hammer (Keeps A Knockin')
Faye Adams; *Faye Adams-Golden Classics*..............(Collectables)
Hammer And A Nail
Indigo Girls; *Nomads, Indians, Saints*.................(Epic)
Hammer And Nail
Suzy Bogguss; *It's A Perfect Day*....................(Platinum Music)

Hammer And Nails
Radney Foster; *Del Rio, TX 1959* . . . . (Arista)
Hammer Back
Blue Oyster Cult; *Heaven Forbid* . . . . (CMC Int'l)
Hammer Blow
Skip Martin; *ST/Crime Jazz: Music In The Second Degree* . . . . (Rhino)
Hammer Blues
Charley Patton; *Founder Of The Delta Blues-1929-1934* . . . . (Yazoo)
King Of The Delta Blues: The Music Of Charley Patton . . . . (Yazoo)
Hammer Down
Billy Dean; *Billy Dean* . . . . (Liberty)
Floor Fillin', Two-Steppin', Honky Tonk Hits-#1-C . . . . (Liberty)
Hammer Going Down
Chris Knight; *Chris Knight* . . . . (Decca)
Hammer Of Love
Bad Company; *The Original Bad Company Anthology* . . . . (Elektra)
Hammer Ring
Jesse Bradley & Augustus ''Track Horse'' Haggerty; *Field Recordings-#6: Texas (1933-1958)-C* . . . . (Document)
Original Soundtrack; *Wake Up Dead Man: Black Convict Worksongs From Texas Prisons* . . . . (Rounder)
Hammer To Fall
Queen; *Classic Queen* . . . . (Hollywood)
Live At Wembley '86 . . . . (Hollywood)
Queen's Greatest Hits I & II . . . . (Hollywood)
Queen-The Works . . . . (Hollywood)
Hammer, Hammer, Hammer
Ella Jenkins; *Ella Jenkins And A Union Of Friends Pulling Together* . . . . (Smithsonian Collection)
Hammer, The
Motorhead; *Fistful Of Aces: Best Of Motorhead* . . . . (Griffin Entert. Group)
No Sleep 'Til Hammersmith . . . . (Castle Music America)
Hammer, The
Red Prysock; *Harlem Rock 'N' Blues-#3-C* . . . . (Collectables)
Hole In My Soul
Aerosmith; *Nine Lives* . . . . (Columbia)
If I Had A Hammer (The Hammer Song)
Pete Seeger; *Sing-A-Long-Live At Sanders Theatre 1980* . . . . (Smithsonian Folkways)
Peter, Paul & Mary; *10 Years Together/The Best Of Peter, Paul and Mary* . . . . (Warner Bros.)
Peter, Paul and Mary . . . . (Warner Bros.)
Peter, Paul and Mary In Concert . . . . (Warner Bros.)
Trini Lopez; *Best Of Trini Lopez* . . . . (Exact)
Weavers; *Weavers' Greatest Hits* . . . . (Vanguard)
I'll Fall With Your Knife
Peter Murphy; *Cascade* . . . . (Beggar's Banquet)
It Sure Is Monday
Mark Chesnutt; *Almost Goodbye* . . . . (MCA)
Jackhammer John
Richie Havens & Pete Seeger; *Tribute To Woody Guthrie-C* . . . . . (Warner Bros.)
Jackknife Beat
Rory Gallagher; *Calling Card* . . . . (Buddah)
Jackknife Johnny
Alice Cooper; *From The Inside* . . . . (Warner Bros.)
Jacob's Ladder
Rush; *Exit...Stage Left* . . . . (Mercury)
Permanent Waves . . . . (Mercury)
Jacob's Ladder
Mark Wills; *Mark Wills* . . . . (Mercury)
Jacob's Ladder
Huey Lewis and the News; *Fore!* . . . . (Chrysalis)
Jacob's Ladder
Bruce Hornsby & The Range; *Scenes From The Southside* . . . . (RCA)
John Deere Tractor
Judds; *Judds' Greatest Hits-#2* . . . . (MCA)
Love Can Build A Bridge . . . . (MCA)
John Deere Tractor Song
Don Walser; *Uprooted: Best Of Roots Country-C* . . . . (Shanachie)
Johnny Too Bad
Slickers; *ST/The Harder They Come* . . . . (Mango)
Taj Mahal; *Best Of Taj Mahal* . . . . (Columbia)
Mo' Roots . . . . (Legacy)
UB40; *Labour Of Love* . . . . (A&M)
Live In Moscow . . . . (A&M)
Knife Edge
Emerson, Lake & Palmer; *Best Of Emerson, Lake & Palmer* . . . . . . (Rhino)
Knife, The
Genesis; *Trespass* . . . . (MCA)
Knife's Edge
Midnight Oil; *Bird Noises* . . . . (Columbia)
Ladder
Joan Osborne; *Lilith Fair-A Celebration Of Women In Music-C* . . . . . (Arista)
Relish . . . . (Blue Gorilla/Mercury)
Last Resort
Papa Roach; *Infest* . . . . (DreamWorks/SKG)
Life And How To Live It
R.E.M.; *Fables Of The Reconstruction* . . . . (I.R.S.)

Like A Knife In The Back
Twisted Sister; *You Can't Stop Rock 'N' Roll* . . . . (Atlantic)
Mack The Knife
Bobby Darin; *Bobby Darin-At The Copa* . . . . (Bainbridge)
Hit Singles-1958-1977-C . . . . (Atlantic)
The Bobby Darin Story . . . . (Atlantic)
Frank Sinatra; *The Reprise Collection* . . . . (Reprise)
Louis Armstrong; *Best Of Louis Armstrong* . . . . (Vanguard)
Maxwell's Silver Hammer
Beatles; *Abbey Road* . . . . (Parlophone)
Monkey Wrench
Foo Fighters; *The Colour And The Shape* . . . . (Roswell/RCA)
Nine Pound Hammer
David Grisman with Doc Watson and Alan O'Bryant; *Steel Rails-Classic Railroad Songs-#1-C* . . . . (Rounder)
Merle Travis; *Great American Train Songs-C* . . . . (C.M.H. Prod.)
Old Enough To Know Better
Wade Hayes; *Country Dance Hits-C* . . . . (Columbia)
Old Enough To Know Better . . . . (Columbia)
Steppin' Country-#2-C . . . . (Columbia)
Super Hits Of 1994-C . . . . (Columbia)
Plowed
Sponge; *Rotting Pinata* . . . . (Work)
Razor Love
Neil Young; *Silver & Gold* . . . . (Reprise)
Razorblades
Chris Stills; *100 Year Thing* . . . . (Atlantic)
Right Man For The Job
Charlie Robison; *Step Right Up* . . . . (Lucky Dog)
She Twists The Knife Again
Richard Thompson; *Across A Crowded Room* . . . . (Polydor)
Shonen Knife
Shonen Knife; *712* . . . . (Rockville)
Six Blade Knife
Dire Straits; *Dire Straits* . . . . (Warner Bros.)
Slaves And Bulldozers
Soundgarden; *Badmotorfinger* . . . . (A&M)
Sledgehammer
Peter Gabriel; *So* . . . . (Geffen)
Sledgehammer
Bachman-Turner Overdrive; *Not Fragile* . . . . (Mercury)
Swing That Hammer
Lonesome River Band; *Talkin' To Myself* . . . . (Sugar Hill)
Sword Of Damocles
Lou Reed; *Magic And Loss* . . . . (Sire)
Swords And Knives
Tears For Fears; *Seeds Of Love* . . . . (Fontana)
Ten Pound Hammer
Aaron Tippin; *Tool Box* . . . . (RCA)
Teresa, Give Me That Knife
No Means No; *Small Parts Isolated And Destroyed-The Day Everything Became Nothing* . . . . (Alternative Tentacles)
Theme From ''Home Improvement''
Original Soundtrack; *Television's Greatest Hits-#7-Cable Ready-C* . . . . . (TVT)
Theme From ''Silver Spoons''
Original Soundtrack; *Television's Greatest Hits-#6-Remote Control-C* . . . (TVT)
Three Blind Mice
Van Alexander; *Small Fry-Capitol Sings Kids Songs For Grownups-C* . . . . (Capitol)
Throw Down The Sword
Wishbone Ash; *Argus* . . . . (MCA)
Live Dates . . . . (MCA)
Twist The Knife (Slowly)
Napalm Death; *ST/Mortal Kombat* . . . . (TVT)
Under The Knife
Kansas; *Freaks Of Nature* . . . . (Intersound)
Unglued
Stone Temple Pilots; *Purple* . . . . (Atlantic)
When The Hammer Falls
Sammy Hagar; *I Never Said Goodbye* . . . . (Geffen)
Year Of The Knife
Tears For Fears; *Seeds Of Love* . . . . (Fontana)
You're Lookin' At Country
Loretta Lynn; *Loretta Lynn-20 Greatest Hits* . . . . (MCA)
Loretta Lynn-Greatest Hits Live . . . . (K-Tel)
Loretta Lynn's Greatest Hits-#2 . . . . (MCA)
The Country Music Hall Of Fame-Loretta Lynn . . . . (MCA)

TOUCH

See Also: *ANATOMY: HANDS, FEELINGS, LOVE (various)*

(I'm Always Touched) By Your Presence Dear
Blondie; *Plastic Letters* . . . . (Chrysalis)
Bad Touch, The
Bloodhound Gang; *Hooray For Boobies* . . . . (Republic/Geffen)

Breathe
Faith Hill; *Breathe* . . . . (Warner Bros.)
Burn Me Down
Marty Stuart; *Tempted* . . . . (MCA)
Butterflies
Michael Jackson; *Invincible* . . . . (Epic)
Can I Touch You…There?
Michael Bolton; *Michael Bolton's Greatest Hits-1985-1995* . . . . (Columbia)
Can't Take My Eyes Off You
Frankie Valli; *25th Anniversary Collection* . . . . (Rhino)
Frankie Valli-Anthology . . . . (Rhino)
Very Best Of Frankie Valli . . . . (MCA)
Lauryn Hill; *The Miseducation Of Lauryn Hill* . . . . (Ruffhouse/Columbia)
Continental Touch, A
My Life With The Thrill Kill Kult; *Sexplosion!* . . . . (Rykodisc)
Cover You In Kisses
John Michael Montgomery; *Leave A Mark* . . . . (Atlantic)
Don't Ever Touch Me (Again)
Dionne Farris; *Wild Seed - Wild Flower* . . . . (Columbia)
Don't Feel Your Touch
Bruce Cockburn; *Big Circumstance* . . . . (Columbia)
Don't Touch Me There
Tubes; *T.R.A.S.H. (Tubes Rarities And Smash Hits)* . . . . (A&M)
What Do You Want From Live . . . . (A&M)
Young And Rich . . . . (A&M)
Don't You Feel My Leg
Maria Muldaur; *Maria Muldaur* . . . . (Reprise)
Eclipse
Pink Floyd; *Dark Side Of The Moon* . . . . (Capitol)
Works . . . . (Capitol)
Eres Tu (Touch The Wind)
Mocedades; *Super Hits Of The '70s-Have A Nice Day-#12-C* . . . . (Rhino)
Everything I Touch
Stabbing Westward; *Darkest Days* . . . . (Columbia)
Everything That Touches You
Association; *Association Greatest Hits* . . . . (Warner Bros.)
Everytime You Touch Me I Get High
Charlie Rich; *Charlie Rich's Greatest Hits* . . . . (Epic)
Eye
Smashing Pumpkins; *ST/Lost Highway* . . . . (Interscope)
Femininity
Eric Benet; *True To Myself* . . . . (Jac-Mac/Warner Bros.)
Fire Of The Newly Alive
Rosanne Cash; *The Wheel* . . . . (Columbia)
Get In Touch
Firehouse; *Hold Your Fire* . . . . (Epic)
Get In Touch With Yourself
Swing Out Sister; *Get In Touch With Yourself* . . . . (Mercury)
Goldfinger
Shirley Bassey; *13 Original James Bond Themes-C* . . . . (EMI)
Best Of Shirley Bassey . . . . (EMI)
Great Performances . . . . (Liberty)
Shirley Bassey-Live At Carnegie Hall. . . . . (United Artists)
Shirley Bassey's Greatest Hits . . . . (EMI)
ST/Goldfinger . . . . (United Artists)
He Touched Me
Elvis Presley; *Amazing Grace-His Greatest Sacred Performances* . . . . (RCA)
Human Touch
Rick Springfield; *Living In Oz* . . . . (RCA)
Rick Springfield's Greatest Hits . . . . (RCA)
Human Touch
Bruce Springsteen; *Bruce Springsteen's Greatest Hits* . . . . (Columbia)
Human Touch . . . . (Columbia)
Human Touch
Elvis Costello & The Attractions; *Get Happy!* . . . . (Rykodisc)
Human Touch
Joe Jackson; *Blaze Of Glory* . . . . (A&M)
I Have The Touch
Peter Gabriel; *Security* . . . . (Geffen)
I Have The Touch
Heather Nova; *ST/The Craft* . . . . (Columbia)
I Just Want To Touch You
Utopia; *Deface The Music* . . . . (Rhino)
I Touch Myself
Divinyls; *Divinyls* . . . . (Virgin)
I Touch Roses
Book Of Love; *Book Of Love* . . . . (Sire)
I Wanna Touch You
Def Leppard; *Adrenalize* . . . . (Mercury)
I Want To Touch You
Catherine Wheel; *Ferment.* . . . . (Fontana)
If You Let Me Make Love To You Why Can't I Touch You?
Ronnie Dyson; *Didn't It Blow Your Mind: Soul Hits Of The*
'70s-#3-C . . . . (Rhino)
If You Wanna Touch Her, Ask!
Shania Twain; *Come On Over* . . . . (Mercury)
I'm In Touch With Your World
Cars; *The Cars* . . . . (Elektra)

Invisible Touch
Genesis; *Hit Singles-1980-1988-C* . . . . (Atlantic)
Invisible Touch . . . . (Atlantic)
It's All Coming Back To Me Now
Celine Dion; *All The Way…A Decade Of Song* . . . . (550 Music)
Falling Into You . . . . (550 Music)
Just A Touch
Keith Sweat; *Keith Sweat* . . . . (Elektra)
Just A Touch
R.E.M.; *Life's Rich Pageant* . . . . (EMI-Capitol Entert. Properties)
Just A Touch Of Love
Slave; *Everybody Dance! Best Of Remixed Dance Classics-C* . . . . (Rhino)
Slide And Other Hits . . . . (Flashback)
Just Between You And Me
Kinleys; *Just Between You And Me* . . . . (Epic)
Let Me Touch You For Awhile
Alison Krauss & Union Station; *New Favorite* . . . . (Rounder)
Let's Keep In Touch While Dancing
Lynnette Perry; *Unsung Irving Berlin-C* . . . . (VSI)
Like A Virgin
Madonna; *Immaculate Collection* . . . . (Sire)
Like A Virgin . . . . (Sire)
Royal Box . . . . (Sire)
Linger
Jonatha Brooke; *Steady Pull.* . . . . (Bad Dog)
Look But You Can't Touch
Poison; *Open Up And Say…Ahh!* . . . . (Capitol)
Lost My Touch
Church; *Sometime Anywhere* . . . . (Arista)
Love Touch
Rod Stewart; *Storyteller/The Complete Anthology: 1964-1990* . . . (Warner Bros.)
Magic Touch
Aerosmith; *Permanent Vacation* . . . . (Geffen)
Magic Touch
Mike Oldfield; *Islands* . . . . (Caroline)
Magic Touch, (You've Got) The
Platters; *Enchanted-The Best Of The Platters* . . . . (Rhino)
Man With The Magic Touch
Brian Setzer Orchestra; *Guitar Slinger* . . . . (Interscope)
Memory
Original Broadway Cast; *Cats* . . . . (Geffen)
Midas Touch
Original Cast; *Bells Are Ringing* . . . . (Columbia)
Midas Touch
Midnight Star; *Anniversary Collection* . . . . (Right Stuff)
My Baby Must Be A Magician
Marvelettes; *Marvelettes-The Ultimate Collection* . . . . (Motown)
Not To Touch The Earth
Doors; *Doors' Greatest Hits* . . . . (Elektra)
Waiting For The Sun . . . . (Elektra)
Out Of Touch
Death; *Individual Thought Patterns* . . . . (Relativity)
Out Of Touch
Daryl Hall & John Oates; *Big Bam Boom* . . . . (RCA)
Out-A-Touch
Pat Benatar; *Crimes Of Passion* . . . . (Chrysalis)
Pinch Me
Barenaked Ladies; *Maroon* . . . . (Reprise)
Totally Hits-#3-C . . . . (Atlantic)
Please Don't Touch
Steve Hackett; *Please Don't Touch* . . . . (Chrysalis)
Reaching Happiness, Touching Pain
Cathedral; *Forest Of Equilibrium.* . . . . (Earache)
Skin
Madonna; *Ray Of Light* . . . . (Maverick)
So Far Away
Stabbing Westward; *Stabbing Westward* . . . . (Koch International)
Softest Touch In Town
Bobby G. Rice; *45-#031.* . . . . (Republic/Universal)
Somebody Touched Me
Bruce Cockburn; *Nothing But A Burning Light* . . . . (Columbia)
Someone To Love
Jon B.; *Bonafide* . . . . (Yab Yum/550)
Jon B. featuring Babyface; *ST/Bad Boys* . . . . (Work)
Someone To Touch
Scorpions; *Face The Heat* . . . . (Mercury)
Sometimes When We Touch
Dan Hill; *Greatest Hits And More…Let Me Show You.* . . . . (Spontaneous)
Sometimes When We Touch
Rod Stewart; *If We Fall In Love Tonight* . . . . (Warner Bros.)
Stranger's Touch
Olivia Newton-John; *Physical* . . . . (MCA)
Sweet Caroline
Neil Diamond; *Glory Road-1968-1972* . . . . (MCA)
Hot August Night. . . . . (MCA)
Love At The Greek. . . . . (Columbia)
Neil Diamond-Gold. . . . . (MCA)

Neil Diamond-His 12 Greatest Hits . . . . (MCA)
Too Hot To Handle
UFO; *Lights Out* . . . .(Chrysalis)
Strangers In The Night . . . .(Chrysalis)
Too Hot To Handle
Roosevelt Sykes; *Raining In My Heart* . . . . (Delmark)
Touch
Berlin; *Love Life* . . . .(Geffen)
Touch & Go Crazy
Lee Greenwood; *Country Classics-#12-1987-1988-C* . . . . . (Universal)
Lee Greenwood's Greatest Hits-#2 . . . .(MCA)
Touch A Four Leaf Clover
Atlantic Starr; *Atlantic Starr-Classics-#10* . . . . (A&M)
Secret Lovers: Best Of Atlantic Starr . . . . (A&M)
Yours Forever . . . . (A&M)
Touch A Hand, Make A Friend
Oak Ridge Boys; *Country's Greatest Hits-#4-C* . . . .(MCA Special Prod.)
Oak Ridge Boys' Greatest Hits 3 . . . .(MCA)
Step On Out . . . .(MCA)
Staple Singers; *15 Original Big Hits-#4-C* . . . .(Stax)
Staple Singers-Chronicle . . . .(Stax)
Top Of The Stax-Twenty Greatest Hits-#2-C . . . .(Stax)
Touch And Go
Cars; *Panorama* . . . . (Elektra)
The Cars' Greatest Hits . . . . (Elektra)
Touch And Go
Emerson, Lake & Powell; *Emerson, Lake & Powell* . . . .(Polydor)
Touch And Go
Stiff Little Fingers; *All The Best* . . . .(One Way)
Touch And Go
Storm; *Storm* . . . .(Interscope)
Touch Away, A
Deep Purple; *Purpendicular* . . . .(CMC Int'l)
Touch It
Monifah; *Mo'hogany* . . . .(Uptown)
Touch Me
Doors; *Best Of The Doors* . . . . (Elektra)
Doors 13 . . . . (Elektra)
Doors' Greatest Hits . . . . (Elektra)
Soft Parade . . . . (Elektra)
Touch Me
Solo; *4 Bruthas & A Bass* . . . . (Perspective/A&M)
Touch Me
Willie Nelson; *Best Of Willie Nelson* . . . . (Capitol)
Touch Me (All Night Long)
Cathy Dennis; *Move To This* . . . .(Polydor)
Touch Me (I Want Your Body)
Samantha Fox; *Samantha Fox's Greatest Hits* . . . .(Jive)
Touch Me (I Want Your Body) . . . .(Jive)
Touch Me Fall
Indigo Girls; *Swamp Ophelia* . . . .(Epic)
Touch Me In The Morning
Diana Ross; *12 #1 Hits From The '70s-C* . . . . (Motown)
20 Greatest Songs In Motown History-C . . . . (Motown)
Diana Ross-All The Great Hits . . . . (Motown)
Diana Ross-Anthology . . . . (Motown)
Diana Ross-The Ultimate Collection . . . . (Motown)
Evening With Diana Ross . . . . (Motown)
Touch Me In The Morning . . . . (Motown)
Touch Me Tease Me
Case Featuring Foxy Brown; *Case* . . . .(Def Jam/RAL/Mercury)
Def Jam Greatest Hits-C . . . .(Def Jam)
ST/The Nutty Professor . . . .(Def Jam)
Ultimate Hip Hop Party-1998-C . . . .(Arista)
Touch Me When We're Dancing
Alabama; *The Touch* . . . . (RCA)
Carpenters; *Carpenters-Classics-#2* . . . . (A&M)
Made In America . . . . (A&M)
Yesterday Once More . . . . (A&M)
Touch Me With Your Love
Beth Orton; *Trailerpark* . . . . (Dedicated)
Touch My Heart
Ray Price; *Ray Price's Greatest Hits-#2* . . . . (Step One)
Touch My Heart
Vinx; *I Love My Job* . . . .(Pangaea)
Touch Of Evil
Warlock; *Triumph And Agony* . . . . (Mercury)
Touch Of Grey
Grateful Dead; *Heart Of Rock-C* . . . .(Columbia)
In The Dark . . . . (Arista)
Touch Of Love, A
Cleopatra; *Comin' Atcha* . . . .(Maverick)
Touch Of Madness
Night Ranger; *Midnight Madness* . . . .(MCA)
Touch Of Your Hand, A
Nylons; *Happy Together* . . . . (Open Air)
Touch Of Your Lips
Ben Webster; *Compact Jazz-Ben Webster-The Verve Years* . . . . (Verve)

Nat "King" Cole; *Nat "King" Cole (Box Set)* . . . . (Capitol)
Tony Bennett & Bill Evans; *Tony Bennett & Bill Evans* . . . . (Fantasy)
Touch The Hand
Bryan Adams; *Waking Up The Neighbours* . . . . (A&M)
Touch The Morning
Don Gibson; *Best Of Don Gibson-#1* . . . . (Curb)
Don Gibson-18 Greatest Hits . . . . (Curb)
Touch The Night
Neil Young; *Landing On Water* . . . . (Geffen)
Touch Too Much
AC/DC; *Highway To Hell* . . . . (Atco)
Touch, Peel, And Stand
Days Of The New; *Days Of The New* . . . .(Outpost/Interscope)
X Games-#3-Music From The X Games-C . . . .(Mammoth)
Touch, The
Stan Bush; *ST/Transformers-The Movie* . . . . (Volcano Entertainment)
Touch-A, Touch-A, Touch-A, Touch Me
Rocky Horror Picture Show Cast; *ST/Rocky Horror Picture Show* . . . . . . (Rhino)
Touchdown Boy
Blink-182; *Cheshire Cat* . . . . (Cargo)
Touched
Vast; *Visual Audio Sensory Theater* . . . . (Elektra)
Touched By The Hand Of God
New Order; *Best Of New Order* . . . .(Qwest)
Touched By The Sun
Carly Simon; *Letters Never Sent* . . . . (Arista)
Touching Him
Ray Boltz; *Watch The Lamb* . . . . (Word)
Touching Tongues
Steve Vai; *Sex And Religion* . . . . (Epic)
Touchy!
A-Ha; *Stay On These Roads* . . . . (Warner Bros.)
U Can't Touch This
Hammer; *Please Hammer Don't Hurt 'Em* . . . . (Capitol)
Untouchable
Rialto; *Rialto* . . . .(Sire)
Untouchable Face
Ani DiFranco; *Dilate* . . . . (Righteous Babe)
Living In Clip . . . . (Righteous Babe)
When I Need You
Celine Dion; *Let's Talk About Love-C* . . . . (550 Music)
Leo Sayer; *'70s Greatest Rock Hits-#5-Kickin' Back-C* . . . . (Priority)
Show Must Go On-Anthology . . . . (Rhino)
When Sly Calls (Don't Touch That Phone)
Michael Franks; *Passionfruit* . . . . (Warner Bros.)
When You Put Your Hands On Me
Christina Aguilera; *Christina Aguilera* . . . .(RCA)
Why Can't I Touch It?
Buzzcocks; *Singles Going Steady* . . . . (I.R.S.)
Why Won't You Touch Me?
Capercaillie; *To The Moon* . . . . (Green Linnet)
Woman's Touch
Toby Keith; *Blue Moon* . . . .(Polydor Country)
You Still Touch Me
Sting; *Mercury Falling* . . . . (A&M)

TOYS & GAMES, Dolls, Playing Games, Puppets

See Also: **CARNIVALS, CARTOON CHARACTERS, CHILDREN,**
FUN, PRETEND, SPORTS (various), STORYBOOK CHARACTERS

"8" Ball
Slammin' Watusis; *Super Oldies Of The '60s-#7-C* . . . . (Audio Fidelity)
"8" Ball
Herb Alpert; *Wild Romance* . . . . (A&M)
"They Just Can't Stop It" (The Games People Play)
Spinners; *Best Of The Spinners* . . . .(Atlantic)
Golden Age Of Black Music-1970-1975-C . . . .(Atlantic)
(Let Me Be Your) Teddy Bear
Elvis Presley; *Elvis' Golden Records* . . . .(RCA)
Elvis In Concert . . . . (RCA)
Number One Hits . . . . (RCA)
ST/Loving You . . . . (RCA)
The Top Ten Hits . . . . (RCA)
(Peek-A-Boo) Game
Sir Mix-A-Lot; *Seminar* . . . .(Nastymix)
8 Ball
N.W.A.; *Staight Outta Compton* . . . . (Ruthless/Priority)
99 Luftballons (99 Red Balloons)
Nena; *99 Luftballons* . . . . (Epic)
All Fall Down
Emmylou Harris & George Jones; *Duets-C* . . . .(Reprise)
All Fall Down
Standells; *Best Of The Standells* . . . . (Rhino)
All Fall Down
Five Star; *Luxury Of Life* . . . .(RCA)

Ally Ally Oxen Free
Kingston Trio; *Capitol Collectors Series-The Kingston Trio* . . . . (Capitol)
Made In The U.S.A. . . . .(Pair)
Annie Get Your Yo Yo
Junior Parker; *Best Of Junior Parker* . . . . (MCA)
Little Junior Parker; *Annie Get Your Yo Yo* . . . . (MCA Special Prod.)
Apples Peaches Pumpkin Pie
Jay And The Techniques; *Cruisin'-1967-C* . . . . (Increase)
Arizona Indian Doll
Faster Pussycat; *Wake Me When It's Over* . . . . (Elektra)
Arkansas See Saw
Jerry Lee Lewis; *Keeps Rockin'* . . . . (Mercury)
As Tears Go By
Marianne Faithfull; *Marianne Faithfull's Greatest Hits* . . . . (Abkco)
Strange Weather . . . . (Island)
Rolling Stones; *Big Hits (High Tide & Green Grass)* . . . . (Abkco)
December's Children (and everybody's) . . . . (Abkco)
Hot Rocks 1964-1971 . . . . (Abkco)
Singles Collection-The London Years . . . . (Abkco)
As The Toys Go Winding Down
Primus; *Frizzle Fry* . . . . (Caroline)
Attack Of The Name Game
Stacy Lattisaw; *Sneakin' Out* . . . . (Cotillion)
Baby Doll
Tony Toni Tone; *Who?* . . . . (Wing)
Baby Doll
Bessie Smith; *Bessie Smith-The Complete Recordings-#3* . . . . (Legacy)
Baby Doll
Ella Fitzgerald; *Best Of Ella Fitzgerald* . . . . (MCA)
Baby Doll
Raindogs; *Border Drive-In Theatre* . . . . (Atco)
Baby Doll
Marvin & Johnny; *Flipped Out* . . . . (Specialty)
Baby Doll
Rita Remington; *Girls Girls Girls* . . . . (Plantation)
Baby Doll
Carlo; *La Bamba & Other Original Hits-C* . . . .(Laurie)
Baby Doll
Memphis Slim; *Raining The Blues* . . . .(Fantasy)
Baby Doll
Farmers; *Rock Angel* . . . .(Flying Fish)
Baby Doll
Devo; *Total Devo* . . . . (Enigma Capitol)
Baby Doll Polka
Frankie Yankovic & His Yanks; *America's Favorites* . . . . (Smash)
One More Time . . . . (Crescendo)
Baby Let's Play House
Elvis Presley; *A Date With Elvis* . . . . (RCA)
A Golden Celebration . . . . (RCA)
The Sun Sessions . . . . (RCA)
Babydoll
Mariah Carey; *Butterfly* . . . . (Columbia)
Bang Bang
Cher; *Cher* . . . . (Geffen)
EMI Legends Of Rock & Roll-24 Greatest Hits-C . . . . (EMI)
Barbi Doll
Barbara Weathers; *Barbara Weathers* . . . .(Reprise)
Barbie & Ken
Weathermen; *Black Album According To The
Weathermen* . . . . (Play It Again Sam)
Barbie & Ken Ferrari
John Hiatt; *Perfectly Good Guitar* . . . . (A&M)
Barbie Doll Look
Sky Saxon; *Best Of Rodney On The 'ROQ* . . . . (Posh Boy)
Barbie Girl
Aqua; *Aquarium* . . . . (MCA)
Now That's What I Call Music!-#1-C . . . .(Virgin)
Baron, The
Johnny Cash; *Columbia Records-1958-1986* . . . . (Columbia)
Greatest Country Hits Of The '80s-1981-C . . . . (Columbia)
Johnny Cash's Biggest Hits . . . . (Columbia)
Beggar's Game
Dan Fogelberg; *Phoenix* . . . . (Full Moon)
Bicycle Built For Two
Kidsongs; *Cars, Boats, Trains, Planes* . . . . (Sony Wonder)
Original Soundtrack; *School Days-Kids Classics* . . . .(Benson)
Billy The Kid (I Miss...)
Billy Dean; *Billy Dean* . . . . (Liberty)
Bingo Fever
Da Yoopers; *Camp Fever* . . . .(You Guys)
Brand New Key
Deana Carter; *Everything's Gonna Be Alright* . . . . (Capitol)
Melanie; *Best Of Melanie* . . . . (Rhino)
Super Hits Of The '70s-Have A Nice Day-#7-C . . . . (Rhino)
Brand New Toy
Hot Tuna; *Pair A Dice Found* . . . . (Epic)
Broken Toys
Jerry Jeff Walker; *Mr. Bojangles* . . . . (Bainbridge)

Broken Toys
B.J. Thomas; *Throwin' Rocks At The Moon* . . . .(Columbia)
Broken Yo-Yo
Texas Alexander; *Story Of The Blues-C* . . . .(Columbia)
Broomstick Cowboy
Bobby Goldsboro; *10th Anniversary Album-#1* . . . . (EMI)
Honey-Best Of Bobby Goldsboro . . . . (EMI)
Cannibals
Mark Knopfler; *Golden Heart* . . . . (Warner Bros.)
Carrie-Anne
Hollies; *Best Of The Hollies* . . . . (EMI)
Evolution . . . . (Epic)
Hollies-Epic Anthology From The Original Master Tapes . . . . (Epic)
The Hollies' Greatest Hits . . . . (Epic)
Catch Us If You Can
Dave Clark Five; *History Of The Dave Clark Five* . . . .(Hollywood)
Cat's In The Cradle
Harry Chapin; *Greatest Stories-Live* . . . . (Elektra)
Harry Chapin-Anthology . . . . (Elektra)
Verities & Balderdash . . . . (Elektra)
Caught In The Game
Survivor; *Caught In The Game* . . . . (Scotti Bros.)
Checkmate
Defiance; *Void Terra Firma* . . . .(Roadrunner)
Checkmate
Ernie Henry; *Presenting Ernie Henry* . . . . (Riverside)
Cherry Hill Park
Billy Joe Royal; *Billy Joe Royal's Greatest Hits* . . . .(Columbia)
Super Hits Of The '70s-Have A Nice Day-#1-C . . . .(Rhino)
Chess
Original Broadway Cast; *Chess* . . . . (RCA)
Chess Game
Jerry Jeff Walker; *Circus Maximus With* . . . .(Vanguard)
Chess Game
Original Cast; *March Of The Falsettos* . . . . (DRG)
Chess Players
Art Blakey & His Jazz Messengers; *Big Beat* . . . . (Blue Note)
Chessman's Delight
Randy Weston Trio & Cecil Payne; *Jazz A La Bohemia* . . . . (Riverside)
China Doll
Slim Whitman; *15th Anniversary* . . . .(Imperial)
Best Of Slim Whitman-Legendary Master Series . . . . (EMI)
Paloma Blanca-Best Of Slim Whitman-Legendary Masters . . . . (EMI)
China Doll
Suzanne Vega; *Deadicated-C* . . . . (Arista)
China Doll
Grateful Dead; *From The Mars Hotel* . . . . (Grateful Dead)
Reckoning . . . .(Arista)
Chinese Checkers
Booker T. & The M.G.s; *Very Best Of Booker T. & The MG's* . . . .(Rhino)
Circle Game, The
Buffy Sainte-Marie; *Best Of Buffy Sainte-Marie* . . . .(Vanguard)
Fire & Fleet & Candlelight . . . .(Vanguard)
Ian & Sylvia; *Ian & Sylvia's Greatest Hits* . . . .(Vanguard)
Joni Mitchell; *Ladies Of The Canyon* . . . . (Reprise)
Joni Mitchell with Tom Scott & The L.A. Express; *Miles Of Aisles* . . . . (Asylum)
Tom Rush; *Classic Rush* . . . . (Elektra)
The Circle Game . . . . (Elektra)
Come & Buy My Toys
David Bowie; *Starting Point* . . . . (Deram)
Come Out And Play
Offspring; *Smash* . . . . (Epitaph)
Computer Games
Yellow Magic Orchestra; *'80s New Wave-#2-Electronic '80s-C* . . . . .(Universal)
Kyoretsu Na Rhythm-Characters . . . . (Restless)
Computer Games
George Clinton; *Computer Games* . . . .(Capitol)
Computer Games
Mi Sex; *Richard Blade's Flashback Favorites-#6-C* . . . . (Oglio)
This Ain't No Disco (New Wave Dance Hits)-C . . . . (Risky Business)
Count Me In
Deana Carter; *Did I Shave My Legs For This?* . . . .(Capitol)
Cowboys To Girls
Intruders; *Intruders-Super Hits* . . . .(Philadelphia Int'l)
Soul Shots-C . . . .(Rhino)
Crossword Puzzle
Barbara Mandrell; *Clean Cut* . . . . (MCA)
Country Classics-#4-1984-1985-C . . . .(Universal)
Cry Like A Baby
Box Tops; *Billboard Top Rock 'N' Roll Hits-1968-C* . . . .(Rhino)
Box Tops' Greatest Hits . . . .(Rhino)
Super Hits-#5-C . . . .(Gusto)
WCBS FM 101 History Of Rock-'60s-#4-C . . . .(Collectables)
Crying Game
Boy George; *At Worst...The Best Of Boy George And Culture Club* . . . . . .(SBK)
Cuddly Toy
Nilsson; *Pandemonium Shadow Show* . . . . (RCA)

Cuddly Toy (Feel For Me)
Roachford; *Roachford* . . . .(Epic)
Darkness On The Playground
Desert Rose Band; *Pages Of Life* . . . . (Curb)
Dart Game
Shelly Manne & His Men; *Swinging Sounds-#4* . . . .(Contemporary)
Day Job (Frisbee)
Gin Blossoms; *Congratulations I'm Sorry* . . . . (A&M)
Outside Looking In: The Best Of The Gin Blossoms . . . . (A&M)
Days Of Sand & Shovels
Bobby Vinton; *Bobby Vinton's All-Time Greatest Hits* . . . .(Epic)
Waylon Jennings; *Best Of Waylon Jennings* . . . . (RCA)
Dear Prudence
Beatles; *The Beatles (White Album)* . . . . (Capitol)
Siouxsie And The Banshees; *Hyaena* . . . . (Geffen)
Nocturne . . . .(Geffen)
Devil's Toy
Almighty; *Soul Destruction* . . . .(Polydor)
Do The Boomerang
Junior Walker & The All Stars; *Junior Walker & The All Stars-*
Anthology . . . . (Motown)
Shotgun . . . . (Motown)
Doll Parts
Hole; *Live Through This* . . . . (David Geffen Co.)
Dollhouse
Bruce Springsteen; *Tracks* . . . . (Columbia)
Domino
Van Morrison; *Best Of Van Morrison* . . . .(Polydor)
His Band And The Street Choir . . . .(Warner Bros.)
It's Too Late To Stop Now . . . .(Warner Bros.)
Domino
Genesis; *Invisible Touch* . . . .(Atlantic)
Domino
Cramps; *Psychedelic Jungle/Gravest Hits* . . . .(I.R.S.)
Domino
Masters Of Reality; *Masters Of Reality* . . . .(Delicious Vinyl)
Domino Dancing
Pet Shop Boys; *Introspective* . . . .(EMI)
Dominoes
Flesheaters; *Destroyed By Fire-Greatest Hits* . . . .(SST)
Dominoes
Syd Barrett; *Barrett* . . . . (Capitol)
Dominoes
Robbie Nevil; *Robbie Nevil* . . . .(EMI)
Einstein At The Pool Hall
Pat McDonald & The Essentials; *Lowdown* . . . . (Mountain Railroad)
End Game
Robin Trower; *B.L.T.* . . . .(Chrysalis)
No Stopping Anytime . . . .(Chrysalis)
End Game
Ian Anderson; *Walking Into Light* . . . .(Chrysalis)
Everybody Plays The Fool
Aaron Neville; *Warm Your Heart* . . . . (A&M)
Main Ingredient; *Golden Classics-Main Ingredient* . . . . (Collectables)
Nipper's Greatest Hits Of The '70s-C . . . . (RCA)
Everyone A Puzzle Lover
10,000 Maniacs; *Wishing Chair* . . . . (Elektra)
Flavor Of The Weak (Nintendo)
American Hi-Fi; *American Hi-Fi* . . . . (Island)
Flowers On The Wall
Eric Heatherly; *Swimming In Champagne* . . . . (Mercury)
Statler Brothers; *All Time Legends Of Country Music-C* . . . . (Legacy)
Best Of The Statler Brothers . . . . (Mercury)
Billboard Top Country Hits-1966-C . . . . (Rhino)
Columbia Country Classics-#3-Americana-C . . . . (Columbia)
Pop Classics Of The '60s-C . . . . (Columbia)
Foolish Games
Jewel; *Pieces Of You* . . . .(Atlantic)
ST/Batman & Robin-Music From And Inspired By The Motion Picture . . (Jive)
VH-1 Crossroads-C . . . .(Atlantic)
Freeze Tag
Suzanne Vega; *Suzanne Vega* . . . . (A&M)
Fun & Games
Chuck Mangione; *Best Of Chuck Mangione* . . . . (A&M)
Chuck Mangione-Classics-#6 . . . . (A&M)
Fun & Games . . . . (A&M)
Fun & Games
Isley Brothers; *Showdown* . . . .(T-Neck/Columbia)
Future Games
Fleetwood Mac; *Future Games* . . . . (Reprise)
Game Is Over
John Denver; *Whose Garden Was This* . . . . (RCA)
Game Number 9
Ray Charles; *True To Life* . . . .(Atlantic)
Game Of Life
Billy Paul; *First Class* . . . . (Philadelphia Int'l)
Game Of Love
Wayne Fontana & The Mindbenders; *45s On CD-#2-1960-1966-C* . . . (Mercury)

ST/Good Morning, Vietnam . . . . (A&M)
Super Oldies Of The '60s-#10-C . . . . (Audio Fidelity)
Games
New Kids On The Block; *No More Games/Remix Album* . . . . (Columbia)
Step By Step . . . . (Columbia)
Games
Shalamar; *Circumstantial Evidence* . . . .(Solar)
Shalamar's Greatest Hits . . . .(Solar)
Games
Husker Du; *Flip Your Wig* . . . .(SST)
Games
Ann Peebles; *If This Is Heaven* . . . . (Hi)
Games
David Crosby & Graham Nash; *David Crosby & Graham Nash* . . . . . .(Atlantic)
Games People Play
Joe South; *On The Road Again-Rock's New Frontiers-C* . . . . (Capitol)
Games People Play
Alan Parsons Project; *Best Of The Alan Parsons Project* . . . . (Arista)
Turn Of A Friendly Card . . . . (Arista)
Games That Daddies Play
Conway Twitty; *Conway Twitty-Number Ones-#1* . . . . (Liberty)
Conway Twitty's Greatest Hits-#2 . . . . (MCA)
Games Without Frontiers
Peter Gabriel; *Peter Gabriel* . . . . (Geffen)
Shaking The Tree-Sixteen Golden Greats . . . . (Geffen)
Games, Games
Tavares; *Madam Butterfly* . . . . (Capitol)
Gamin' On Ya
Parliament; *Parliament Live/P. Funk Earth Tour* . . . .(Casablanca)
The Clones Of Dr. Funkenstein . . . .(Casablanca)
Get Ready
Rare Earth; *Earth Tones-Essential* . . . . (Motown)
Very Best Of Rare Earth . . . . (Motown)
Temptations; *Temptations-Anthology-The Best Of The Temptations* . . (Motown)
Temptations-The Ultimate Collection . . . . (Motown)
Girl On A Swing
Gerry And The Pacemakers; *History Of British Rock-#7-C* . . . . (Rhino)
God's Coloring Book
Dolly Parton; *Here You Come Again* . . . . (Dunhill Compact Classics)
Goin' Back
Byrds; *20 Essential Tracks From The Box Set* . . . . (Columbia)
The Byrds . . . . (Columbia)
Dusty Springfield; *Dusty Springfield-Golden Greats* . . . . (Philips)
Neil Young; *Comes A Time* . . . . (Reprise)
Nils Lofgren; *Best Of Nils Lofgren* . . . . (A&M)
Night After Night . . . . (A&M)
Nils Lofgren . . . . (Rykodisc)
Guessing Games
Daryl Hall & John Oates; *H2O* . . . . (RCA)
Head Games
Foreigner; *Head Games* . . . .(Atlantic)
Records . . . .(Atlantic)
Healing Game
Van Morrison; *The Healing Game* . . . . (A&M)
Hide & Go Seek
Big Joe Turner; *Rock This Joint* . . . . (Intermedia)
Hide & Seek
Chuck Mangione; *Evening Of Magic* . . . . (A&M)
Feels So Good . . . . (A&M)
Hide & Seek
Howard Jones; *Action Replay* . . . . (Elektra)
Human's Lib . . . . (Elektra)
Hide & Seek
Bill Haley & His Comets; *Bill Haley & His Comets-Golden Hits* . . . . . . (MCA)
Hide & Seek
Spencer Davis Group; *Greatest & Latest* . . . . (Priority)
High Hopes
Doris Day; *The Envelope Please-Academy Award Winning Songs (1934-*
1993)-C . . . . (Rhino)
Frank Sinatra; *Best Of The Capitol Years* . . . . (Capitol)
ST/Sinatra-CBS Mini-Series . . . . (Reprise)
Hole In My Head
Dixie Chicks; *Fly* . . . . (Monument)
Holiday
Bee Gees; *Bee Gees-Gold* . . . .(Polydor)
Best Of The Bee Gees-#1 . . . .(Polydor)
Honky Tonk Toys
John Conlee; *Friday Night Blues* . . . . (MCA)
Human Toy
Ready For The World; *Ready For The World* . . . . (MCA)
Human Video Game
D.J. Jazzy Jeff & The Fresh Prince; *He's The D.J. I'm The Rapper* . . . . . .(Jive)
I Don't Wanna Play House
Sara Evans; *Tammy Wynette...Remembered-C* . . . .(Asylum)
Tammy Wynette; *Tammy Wynette-Anniversary-20 Years Of Hits* . . . . . . (Epic)
Tammy Wynette's Greatest Hits . . . . (Epic)
Tammy Wynette-Super Hits . . . . (Epic)
I Don't Want To Play House
Lynn Anderson; *Rose Garden* . . . . (Columbia)

I Don't Want To Play In Your Yard
Joan Morris & William Bolcom; *After The Ball* . . . .(Nonesuch)

I Just Want To Be Your Everything
Andy Gibb; *Andy Gibb-A Collection Of His Greatest Hits* . . . . (Polydor)

I Lost On Jeopardy
"Weird Al" Yankovic; *"Weird Al" Yankovic's Greatest Hits* . . . . (Scotti Bros.)
In 3-D . . . . (Scotti Bros.)

I Throw My Toys Around
Original Soundtrack; *ST/The Rugrats Movie* . . . . (Interscope)

I Wanna Be A Toy
Dead Or Alive; *Youthquake* . . . . (Epic)

I'm Forever Blowing Bubbles
Lawrence Welk; *I'm Forever Blowing Bubbles.* . . . . (Ranwood)
Live At Lake Tahoe . . . . (Ranwood)
Reminiscing-#1 . . . . (Ranwood)

I'm Gonna Tear Your Playhouse Down
Ann Peebles; *Ann Peebles Greatest Hits* . . . . (MCA)
B.B. King; *Lucille Talks Back* . . . . (Out Of Print)
Graham Parker; *Pourin' It All Out-Mercury Years* . . . . (Mercury)
Graham Parker And The Rumour; *Stick To Me* . . . . (Mercury)
The Parkerilla . . . . (Mercury)
Paul Young; *Secret Of Association* . . . . (Columbia)

I'm In Love With My Little Red Tricycle
Napoleon XIV; *The Second Coming* . . . . (Rhino)

I'm On A Seesaw
Fats Waller; *Complete Fats Waller-#3-1935-1936* . . . . (RCA)

I'm Your Puppet
James & Bobby Purify; *Oldies But Goodies-#12-C* . . . .(Original Sound)
Soul Shots-#5-La-La Means I Love You-C . . . . (Rhino)
Sweet & Soulful '60s-C . . . . (K-Tel)

Incense And Peppermints
Strawberry Alarm Clock; *Billboard Top Rock 'N' Roll Hits-1967-C* . . . . (Rhino)
Cruisin'-1967-C . . . . (Increase)
Even More Nuggets-C . . . . (Rhino)
Nuggets-#8-Acid Rock-C . . . . (Rhino)

Indoor Games
King Crimson; *Lizard* . . . . (Editions E.G.)

It's All Been Done
Barenaked Ladies; *Stunt* . . . . (Reprise)

It's All In The Game
Four Tops; *Compact Command Performances-Four Tops* . . . . (Motown)
Four Tops-Anthology . . . . (Motown)
George Benson; *Weekend In L.A.* . . . . (Warner Bros.)
Nat "King" Cole; *Nat "King" Cole-Gift Set* . . . . (Capitol)
Tommy Edwards; *Oldies But Goodies-#7-C* . . . .(Original Sound)

It's Slinky
Original Soundtrack; *TeeVee Toons-The Commercials-#1-C* . . . . (TVT)

I've Got The World On A String
Count Basie; *Standards* . . . . (Verve)
Diana Krall; *Only Trust Your Heart.* . . . . (GRP)
Ella Fitzgerald; *Harold Arlen Songbook-#1* . . . . (Verve)
Frank Sinatra; *Capitol Collectors Series-Frank Sinatra* . . . . (Capitol)
Frank Sinatra & Liza Minnelli; *Frank Sinatra-Duets-C* . . . . (Capitol)
Sarah Vaughan; *Best Of Sarah Vaughan* . . . . (Pablo)
Stephane Grappelli & Martin Taylor; *We've Got The World On A
String* . . . . (Angel)

Jet Silver & The Dolls Of Venus
Be Bop Deluxe; *Axe Victim* . . . . (Capitol)
Best Of Be Bop Deluxe-Raiding The Divine Archive . . . . (Capitol)

Jig Saw Puzzle
Rolling Stones; *Beggars Banquet* . . . . (Abkco)

Just A Game
Triumph; *Just A Game* . . . . (RCA)

Keep The Ball Rollin'
Jay And The Techniques; *Bubblegum Classics-#4-C* . . . . (Varese Vintage)

Kick The Can
Fred Frith; *Speechless* . . . . (Ralph)

Kiss Me
Sixpence None The Richer; *Sixpence None The Richer.* . . . . . (Squint/Columbia)
Songs From Dawson's Creek . . . . (Sony Music Soundtrax)

Kite
Nick Heyward; *From Monday To Sunday* . . . . (Epic)

Lazy Day
Spanky & Our Gang; *Best Of Spanky & Our Gang* . . . . (Rhino)

Learning The Game
Andrew Gold; *What's Wrong With This Picture?* . . . . (Asylum)

Learning The Game
Buddy Holly; *Complete Buddy Holly* . . . . (MCA)
The Buddy Holly Collection . . . . (MCA)

Learning The Game
Santa Esmeralda; *Beauty* . . . . (Casablanca)

Let Me Play With Your Yo-Yo
Moses Rascoe; *Blues* . . . . (Flying Fish)

Let The Children Play
Santana; *Festival* . . . . (Columbia)
Moonflower . . . . (Columbia)

Let's Chase Each Other Around The Room
Merle Haggard; *19 Hot Country Requests-#2-C* . . . . (Epic)

For The Record: Merle Haggard-43 Legendary Hits . . . . (BNA)
It's All In The Game . . . . (Epic)

Life Is Just A Tire Swing
Jimmy Buffett; *A1A* . . . . (MCA)

Lily, Rosemary And The Jack Of Hearts
Bob Dylan; *Blood On The Tracks* . . . . (Columbia)

Lincoln Logs
Mojo Nixon & Skid Roper; *Bo-Day-Shus!!!* . . . . (I.R.S.)

Love Is A Dangerous Game
Millie Jackson; *Back To The Shit* . . . . (Jive)
Thelma Houston; *Qualifying Heat* . . . . (MCA)

Love Is Just A Game
Larry Gatlin & The Gatlin Brothers Band; *Larry Gatlin & The Gatlin
Brothers' Greatest Hits* . . . . (Columbia)
Larry Gatlin & The Gatlin Brothers-17 Greatest Hits . . . . (Columbia)
Live At 8:00 . . . . (Capitol)

Man On The Moon
R.E.M.; *Automatic For The People* . . . . (Warner Bros.)

Mental Hopscotch
Missing Persons; *Best Of Missing Persons* . . . .(Capitol)

Mind Games
John Lennon; *Mind Games.* . . . .(Capitol)
John Lennon/Plastic Ono Band; *Shaved Fish.* . . . .(Capitol)

Mind Playing Tricks On Me
Geto Boys; *10th Anniversary: Rap-A-Lot Records-C* . . .(Rap-A-Lot/Noo Trybe)

Musical Box
Genesis; *Genesis-Live* . . . . (Atlantic)
Live/The Way We Walk-Volume Two: The Longs . . . . (Atlantic)
Nursery Cryme . . . . (Atlantic)
Seconds Out. . . . . (Atlantic)

Mystical Potato Head Groove Thing
Joe Satriani; *Flying In A Blue Dream* . . . . (Relativity)

Name Game
Shirley Ellis; *Cruisin'-1965-C* . . . . (Increase)

Name Of The Game
Abba; *Abba's Greatest Hits-#2* . . . . (Atlantic)
The Album . . . . (Atlantic)

New Fool At An Old Game
Reba McEntire; *Country's Greatest Hits-#4-Sweet Country-C* . . . . . . (Priority)
Reba . . . . (MCA)
Reba McEntire-Live . . . . (MCA)

New York Broken Toy
Nazareth; *Expect No Mercy* . . . . (A&M)

New York, New York
Ryan Adams; *Gold.* . . . .(Lost Highway/IDJMG)

Night Game
Paul Simon; *Still Crazy After All These Years* . . . . (Columbia)

Night Games
Charley Pride; *Charley Pride* . . . . (RCA)
Charley Pride's Greatest Hits-#2 . . . . (RCA)
Night Games . . . . (RCA)

Night Games
Gregg Allman Band; *Just Before The Bullets Fly.* . . . . (Epic)

No Strings Attached
'N Sync; *No Strings Attached.* . . . . (Jive)

Occasional Wife
Faron Young; *Faron Young-Golden Hits.* . . . .(Mercury)

Oh You Beautiful Doll
Guy Lombardo & His Royal Canadians; *Dance To Songs Everybody
Knows.* . . . . (MCA)

Old Playground
Bruce Hornsby & The Range; *Scenes From The Southside* . . . . (RCA)

Old Rockin' Horse
Slim Dusty; *Australia Is His Name* . . . . (Philo)

Old Toy Trains
Billy Strange; *Railroad Man* . . . . (Crescendo)
Glen Campbell; *All-Star Country Christmas-C* . . . . (Capitol)
That Christmas Feeling . . . . (Capitol)
Statler Brothers; *Statler Brothers Christmas Present.* . . . . (Mercury)

Ollie Ollie Outs In Free
Carl Ravazza & His Orchestra; *The Uncollected Carl Ravazza & His
Orchestra-1941-1944.* . . . . (Hindsight)

One Night In Bangkok (Chess)
Murray Head; *Chess Pieces* . . . . (RCA)
Original Broadway Cast; *Chess* . . . . (RCA)

Only A Pawn In Their Game
Bob Dylan; *The Times They Are A-Changin'* . . . . (Columbia)

Only Game In Town
Red Rider; *As Far As Siam* . . . . (Capitol)

Oops!...I Did It Again
Britney Spears; *Oops!...I Did It Again.* . . . . (Jive)

Pac-Man Fever
Buckner & Garcia; *Pac Man Fever* . . . . (Columbia)

Paper Airplanes
Seals & Crofts; *Year Of Sunday* . . . . (Warner Bros.)

Paper Doll
Bar-Kays; *Banging The Wall* . . . . (Mercury)
Mills Brothers; *Best Of The Mills Brothers* . . . . (MCA)

Billboard Pop Memories-1940-1944-C . . . . (Rhino)
Mills Brothers' All Time Greatest Hits . . . . (MCA)
Mills Brothers' Greatest Hits . . . . (MCA)
Mills Brothers-22 Great Hits . . . . (Ranwood)
Paper Doll . . . . (MCA)
Sentimental Journey: Pop Vocal Classics-#1-1942-1946-C . . . . (Rhino)
The Mills Brothers-Best Of The Decca Years. . . . . (Decca)

Paper Doll
Fleetwood Mac; *25 Years-The Chain* . . . . (Warner Bros.)

Paper Doll
Gatlin Brothers; *Moments To Remember* . . . . (ISD/Intersound)

Pat-A-Cake
Bill Haley & His Comets; *King Of Rock & Roll* . . . . (Alshire)

Patriot Game
Clancy Brothers; *Clancy Brothers-Super Hits* . . . . (Legacy)
Clancy Brothers & Tommy Makem; *Folk, Gospel & Blues: Will The Circle
    Be Unbroken-C* . . . . (Legacy)
Judy Collins; *Whales & Nightingales* . . . . (Elektra)
Kingston Trio; *Capitol Collectors Series-The Kingston Trio* . . . . (Capitol)

Pawns In The Game
Professor Griff & His Last Asiatic Disciples; *Pawns In The Game* . . . . . . (Luke)

Peek A Boo
Cadillacs; *Best Of The Cadillacs.* . . . . (Rhino)

Peek-A-Boo
Siouxsie And The Banshees; *Peepshow* . . . . (Geffen)
Twice Upon A Time-The Singles . . . . (Geffen)

Peek-A-Boo!
Devo; *Best Of Devo-Greatest Hits* . . . . (Warner Bros.)
EZ Listening Disc. . . . . (Rykodisc)
Oh No! It's Devo . . . . (Warner Bros.)

Peking Doll
Kazumi Watanabe & Resonance Vox; *Pandora* . . . . (Gramavision)

Picture Puzzle
Kate Wolf; *Evening In Austin* . . . . (Kaleidoscope)
Give Yourself To Love . . . . (Kaleidoscope)
Lines On The Paper . . . . (Kaleidoscope)

Pinball Machine
Lonnie Irving; *Super Country Hits Of The '60s-C* . . . . (Gusto)

Pinball Wizard
Elton John; *Elton John's Greatest Hits-#2* . . . . (Polydor)
Pete Townshend; *Another Scoop* . . . . (Atco)
Pete Townshend's Deep End Live! . . . . (Atco)
Rod Stewart; *Best Of Rod Stewart* . . . . (Mercury)
Sing It Again, Rod . . . . (Mercury)
Storyteller/The Complete Anthology: 1964-1990 . . . . (Warner Bros.)
Who; *Meaty Beaty Big & Bouncy* . . . . (MCA)
ST/The Kids Are Alright . . . . (MCA)
ST/Tommy . . . . (Polydor)
Tommy . . . . (MCA)
Who Greatest Hits . . . . (MCA)
Who's Last . . . . (MCA)

Play The Game
Queen; *Play The Game* . . . . (Hollywood)
Queen's Greatest Hits I & II . . . . (Hollywood)

Play The Game
Joe Perry Project; *I've Got The Rock 'N' Rolls Again* . . . . (Columbia)

Play The Game Tonight
Kansas; *Best Of Kansas* . . . . (CBS Associated)
Vinyl Confessions . . . . (Kirshner)

Play The Game Tonight
Neil Diamond; *On The Way To The Sky* . . . . (Columbia)

Play To Win
Heaven 17; *Best Of Heaven 17-Higher & Higher* . . . . (Virgin)

Play To Win
Clash; *Cut The Crap-C* . . . . (Epic)

Play With Fire
Rolling Stones; *Hot Rocks 1964-1971* . . . . (Abkco)
Out Of Our Heads . . . . (Abkco)
Singles Collection-The London Years . . . . (Abkco)

Play With Toys
Basehead; *Plays With Toys* . . . . (Imago)

Playground
Another Bad Creation; *Coolin' At The Playground Ya' Know!* . . . . . . (Motown)
MTV Party To Go-#2-C . . . . (Tommy Boy)

Playground In My Mind
Clint Holmes; *Rock Artifacts-From The Vaults-#2-C* . . . . (Legacy)
Super Hits Of The '70s-Have A Nice Day-#11-C . . . . (Rhino)

Playin' With Fire
Lita Ford; *Dangerous Curves* . . . . (RCA)
Lita Ford's Greatest Hits . . . . (RCA)

Playin' With Fire
Vishugruv; *Vishugruv.* . . . . (Red Light)

Playing Games
Al B. Sure!; *Sexy Versus* . . . . (Warner Bros.)

Playing Marbles With Diamonds
Steve Camp; *Doing My Best-#2* . . . . (Sparrow)

Playing With Fire
Lisa Lisa & Cult Jam; *Spanish Fly* . . . . (Columbia)

Playing With Fire
David Foster; *David Foster* . . . . (Atlantic)

Playing With Fire
Sam Riney; *Playing With Fire.* . . . . (Spindletop)

Playing With Fire
Richard Marx; *Rush Street* . . . . (Capitol)

Poli High
Nilsson; *The Point.* . . . . (RCA)

Pop Goes The Weasel
Bing Crosby; *Where The Blue Of The Night Meets The Gold Of
    The Day* . . . . (Biograph)
Boston Pops Orchestra/Arthur Fiedler; *Forever Fiedler* . . . . (RCA)
Merry Macs; *Small Fry-Capitol Sings Kids Songs For Grownups-C* . . . (Capitol)

Porcelain Doll
Tony MacAlpine; *Maximum Security* . . . . (Mercury)

Puppet
Lisa Germano; *Happiness* . . . . (Capitol)

Puppet
Echo & The Bunnymen; *Songs To Learn & Sing-The Hits* . . . . (Sire)

Puppet
D.I.; *What Good Is Grief To A God* . . . . (Triple X Entert.)

Puppet Dog
Thin White Rope; *Ruby Sea* . . . . (Frontier)

Puppet Girl
Wendy James; *Now Ain't The Time For Your Tears* . . . . (David Geffen Co.)

Puppet Man
5th Dimension; *Greatest Hits On Earth* . . . . (Arista)

Puppet On A String
Elvis Presley; *ST/Girl Happy* . . . . (RCA)

Puppet Show
Danger Danger; *Screw It!* . . . . (Epic Portrait Assoc.)

Puppet Song
4 Seasons; *Rarities-#2* . . . . (Rhino)

Puppets
Depeche Mode; *Speak & Spell* . . . . (Sire)

Puppets' Dance
Jean-Luc Ponty; *Cosmic Messenger* . . . . (Rhino)

Quit Playing Games (With My Heart)
Backstreet Boys; *Backstreet Boys* . . . . (Jive)
MTV Party To Go '98-C . . . . (Tommy Boy)
The Concert For New York City-C . . . . (Columbia)

Rag Doll
4 Seasons; *25th Anniversary Collection* . . . . (Rhino)
4 Seasons' Greatest Hits-#2 . . . . (Rhino)
4 Seasons-Anthology . . . . (Rhino)
Billboard Top Rock 'N' Roll Hits-1964-C . . . . (Rhino)

Rag Doll
Aerosmith; *Big Ones.* . . . . (Geffen)
Permanent Vacation . . . . (Geffen)

Rainbow Doll
Jimmy Dell; *Get Hot Or Go Home-Vintage
    Rockabilly-C* . . . . (Country Music Foundation)

Real Toys
Altered Images; *Happy Birthday.* . . . . (Portrait)

Rebecca Lynn
Bryan White; *Bryan White* . . . . (Asylum)

Red Rubber Ball
Cyrkle; *Even More Nuggets-C* . . . . (Rhino)
Pop Classics Of The '60s-C . . . . (Columbia)
Red Rubber Ball (A Collection) . . . . (Columbia)

Redneck Games
Jeff Foxworthy; *Crank It Up: The Music Album* . . . . (Warner Bros.)
Jeff Foxworthy's Greatest Bits . . . . (Warner Bros.)

Ride My See Saw
Moody Blues; *Caught Live Plus Five* . . . . (Polydor)
In Search Of The Lost Chord . . . . (Polydor)
This Is The Moody Blues. . . . . (Polydor)

Right String But The Wrong Yo-Yo
Carl Perkins; *Carl Perkins-Original Sun Greatest Hits.* . . . . (Rhino)
Elvin Bishop; *Big Fun* . . . . (Alligator)

Ring-Around-A-Rosy Rag
Arlo Guthrie; *Alice's Restaurant.* . . . . (Reprise)

Rock 'N' Roll Is A Vicious Game
April Wine; *First Glance.* . . . . (Capitol)

Rockin' Horse
Bad English; *Bad English* . . . . (Epic)

Roll Over & Play Dead
Lizzy Borden; *Master Of Disguise* . . . . (Metal Blade)

'Round The World With The Rubber Duck
C.W. McCall; *C.W. McCall's Greatest Hits* . . . . (Polydor)

Row Of Dominoes
Joe Ely; *Lord Of The Highway* . . . . (Hightone)
Points West-New Horizons In Country-C . . . . (Hightone)

Sand Castles In The Snow
Public Image Ltd.; *9* . . . . (Virgin)

Sandbox
Too Much Joy; *Cereal Killers* . . . . (Giant)

Satan's Doll
Floyd Cramer; *Best Of Floyd Cramer* . . . .(RCA)

Satin Doll
Carmen McRae; *Great American Songbook* . . . . (Atlantic)
Count Basie & His Orchestra; *Warm Breeze* . . . . (Pablo)
Duke Ellington; *1954 Los Angeles Concert.* . . . .(Crescendo)
Jazz Party . . . . (Legacy)
Harry James; *Golden Trumpet Of Harry James.* . . . .(London)
Stephane Grappelli & Jean-Luc Ponty; *Stephane Grappelli & Jean-Luc Ponty* . . . .(Accord)
Stylistics; *All-Time Classics* . . . . (Amherst)

Secretary Is Not A Toy
New Broadway Cast; *How To Succeed In Business Without Really Trying* . . . . (RCA Victor)
Original Cast; *How To Succeed In Business Without Really Trying* . . . . . . (RCA)

See Emily Play
David Bowie; *Bowie Pin Ups* . . . .(Rykodisc)
Pink Floyd; *Relics* . . . . (Capitol)
Works . . . . (Capitol)

See Saw
Aretha Franklin; *Aretha's Gold* . . . . (Atlantic)
Don Covay; *Memphis Soul* . . . . (Warner Special Prod.)

See Saw
Pink Floyd; *Saucerful Of Secrets* . . . . (Capitol)

Shabby Doll
Elvis Costello; *Girls Girls Girls* . . . .(Columbia)
Elvis Costello & The Attractions; *Imperial Bedroom* . . . .(Columbia)

Shadow Puppets
Tor Dietrichson; *Global Village* . . . .(Global Pacific)

Shake Me I Rattle
Cristy Lane; *Cristy Lane Is The Name* . . . . (Laughing Stock)
Cristy Lane-At Her Best . . . . (EMI)

She's Playing Hard To Forget
Eddy Raven; *Eddy Raven-Greatest Country Hits* . . . .(Curb)
Eddy Raven's Greatest Hits . . . . (Warner Bros.)

Shiny Toys
Joni Mitchell; *Dog Eat Dog* . . . . (Geffen)

Show Don't Tell
Rush; *Presto* . . . . (Atlantic)
Rush-Chronicles . . . . (Mercury)

Simon Says
1910 Fruitgum Company; *Best Of The 1910 Fruitgum Company-#2-C* . . (Rhino)
Bubblegum's Greatest Hits-#2-C . . . . (Accord)
Fabulous Bubblegum Years-C . . . .(Fifty One West)

Space Invader
Pretenders; *Pretenders* . . . .(Sire)

Stop This Game
Cheap Trick; *All Shook Up* . . . . (Epic)

Sympathy For The Devil
Bryan Ferry; *These Foolish Things* . . . .(Reprise)
Jane's Addiction; *Jane's Addiction* . . . . (Triple X Entert.)
Rolling Stones; *Beggars Banquet* . . . . (Abkco)
Flashpoint. . . . . (Virgin)
Get Yer Ya-Ya's Out! . . . . (Abkco)
Hot Rocks 1964-1971 . . . . (Abkco)
Love You Live . . . . (Virgin)

Tangled Up Puppet
Harry Chapin; *Gold Medal Collection.* . . . . (Elektra)
Legends Of The Lost & Found . . . . (Elektra)
Portrait Gallery . . . . (Elektra)

Teddy Bear Song
Barbara Fairchild; *Back To The '70s-Country-C* . . . . (Dominion Entert.)
Country Superstars-C. . . . . (Dominion Entert.)

Teddy Bears
Barbra Streisand; *ST/Prince Of Tides* . . . .(Columbia)

Teddy Bears' Picnic
Anne Murray; *There's A Hippo In My Tub* . . . .(Capitol)
Frank DeVol; *Small Fry-Capitol Sings Kids Songs For Grownups-C.* . . (Capitol)

Theme From "Family Feud"
Original Soundtrack; *Television's Greatest Hits-#6-Remote Control-C* . . (TVT)

Theme From "Howdy Doody"
Original Soundtrack; *Television's Greatest Hits-#1-C* . . . . (TVT)

Theme From "Jeopardy" (Think Music)
Original Soundtrack; *Television's Greatest Hits-#2-C* . . . . (TVT)

Theme From "Kukla, Fran And Ollie" ("Here We Are, Hop, Hop, Hop")
Original Soundtrack; *Television's Greatest Hits-#4-Black & White Classics-C* . . . . (TVT)

Theme From "Let's Make A Deal"
Original Soundtrack; *Television's Greatest Hits-#5-In Living Color-C* . . (TVT)

Theme From "The Dating Game"
Original Soundtrack; *Television's Greatest Hits-#5-In Living Color-C* . . (TVT)

Theme From "The Muppet Show"
Muppets/Cast; *Muppet Hits* . . . . (Jim Henson)
Original Soundtrack; *Television's Greatest Hits-#3-1970s & 1980s-C* . . (TVT)

Theme From "The Name Of The Game"
Original Soundtrack; *Television's Greatest Hits-#3-1970s & 1980s-C* . . (TVT)

Theme From "The Newlywed Game"
Original Soundtrack; *Television's Greatest Hits-#5-In Living Color-C* . . (TVT)

Theme From "The Price Is Right"
Original Soundtrack; *Television's Greatest Hits-#6-Remote Control-C* . . .(TVT)

Theme From "Where In The World Is Carmen Sandiego?"
Original Soundtrack; *Television's Greatest Hits-#7-Cable Ready-C.* . . . . .(TVT)

This Lil' Game We Play
Subway; *Good Times.* . . . . (Biv 10/Motown)

This Masquerade
Carpenters; *Carpenters-Classics-#2* . . . .(A&M)
Now & Then . . . .(A&M)
Yesterday Once More . . . . (A&M)
David Sanborn; *Pearls.* . . . .(Elektra)
George Benson; *Breezin'* . . . . (Warner Bros.)
George Benson-Collection . . . . (Warner Bros.)
Leon Russell; *Best Of Leon Russell* . . . .(MCA)
Carney. . . . .(Right Stuff)
Gimme Shelter! The Best Of Leon Russell . . . .(Capitol)

This Used To Be My Playground
Madonna; *Something To Remember.* . . . . (Maverick/Sire)

Tic-Tac-Toe
Booker T. & The M.G.s; *Best Of Booker T. & The M.G.s* . . . . (Atlantic)
Soul Dressing . . . . (Atlantic)
Kyper; *Tic-Tac-Toe* . . . . (Atlantic)

Tin Drum
Toni Childs; *Union.* . . . . (A&M)

Tin Drum
Big Pig; *Bonk* . . . . (A&M)

Too Many Games
Maze featuring Frankie Beverly; *Can't Stop The Love* . . . .(Capitol)
Live In Los Angeles . . . . (Capitol)

Toy Heart
Bill Monroe; *Columbia Historic Edition-Bill Monroe* . . . .(Columbia)
Bill Monroe & Flatt & Scruggs; *Bill Monroe And Flatt & Scruggs* . . . .(Rounder)
Bill Monroe & His Blue Grass Boys; *Essential Bill Monroe-1945-1949* . . . .(Columbia)
Ricky Skaggs; *Family & Friends* . . . .(Rounder)

Toy Or Treasure
Kay Starr; *Capitol Collectors Series-Kay Starr* . . . .(Capitol)

Toy Soldiers
Martika; *Martika* . . . .(Columbia)

Toys Are Made For Children
Joe Stampley/The Uniques; *Joe Stampley-Golden Hits* . . . . (Paula)

Toys In The Attic
Aerosmith; *Aerosmith-Classics Live 2* . . . .(Columbia)
Live! Bootleg . . . . (Columbia)
Pandora's Box. . . . . (Columbia)
Toys In The Attic . . . . (Columbia)
R.E.M.; *Dead Letter Office* . . . . (I.R.S.)

Toytown
Walking Wounded; *New West* . . . .(Charisma)

Toytown People
Fabulous Poodles; *Mirror Stars* . . . . (Epic)

Tug Of War
Paul McCartney; *Tug Of War.* . . . . (Gold Rush)

Two Can Play That Game
Bobby Brown; *Bobby.* . . . . (MCA)
Remixes In The Key Of B . . . . (MCA)

Up In My Treehouse
Chet Atkins; *Sails.* . . . .(Columbia)

Useless Toy
Doggy Style; *Don't Hit Me Up.* . . . . (Triple X Entert.)

Victim Of The Game
Garth Brooks; *No Fences* . . . .(Capitol)
Trisha Yearwood; *Trisha Yearwood* . . . . (MCA)

Victim Of The Game
Restless Heart; *Wheels.* . . . . (RCA)

Video Games
Ronnie Jones; *Best Of Lollipop Records* . . . . (Hot Prod.)

Voodoo Doll
Soul Asylum; *Say What You Will.* . . . .(Twin-Tone)

Voodoo Sex Doll
Crisis Party; *Rude Awakening* . . . . (Metal Blade)

Waiting Game
Swing Out Sister; *Kaleidoscope World* . . . . (Fontana)

War Games
Crosby, Stills & Nash; *Allies* . . . . (Atlantic)

War Games
Paul Young; *Between Two Fires* . . . .(Columbia)

We Hide & Seek
Jerry Douglas; *Slide Rule* . . . . (Sugar Hill)

Where Do The Children Play
Cat Stevens; *Cat Stevens-Classics-#24* . . . . (A&M)
Footsteps In The Dark-Greatest Hits-#2 . . . . (A&M)
Tea For The Tillerman . . . . (A&M)

Where's The Playground Susie
Glen Campbell; *Best Of Glen Campbell.* . . . .(Capitol)

Whiskey On A Sunday (Puppet Song)
Irish Rovers; *Irish Rovers' Greatest Hits* . . . .(MCA)

Wicked Game
Chris Isaak; *Heart Shaped World* . . . . (Reprise)
ST/Wild At Heart . . . . (Polydor)
Win, Lose Or Draw
Allman Brothers Band; *Best Of The Allman Brothers Band* . . . . (Polydor)
Win, Lose Or Draw . . . . (Polydor)
Word Games
Billy Walker; *45-#10205* . . . . (RCA)
Lovin' and Losin' . . . . (RCA)
World On A String
Neil Young; *Neil Young-Unplugged.* . . . . (Reprise)
Tonight's The Night . . . . (Reprise)
Yesterday
Beatles; *"Yesterday"...And Today* . . . . (Capitol)
Beatles 1 . . . . (Capitol)
Beatles-20 Greatest Hits . . . . (Capitol)
Beatles-Box Set . . . . (Capitol)
Beatles-Love Songs . . . . (Capitol)
Compact Disc Singles Collection. . . . . (Capitol)
The Beatles/1962-1966 . . . . (Capitol)
Elvis Presley; *On Stage-February, 1970* . . . . (RCA)
En Vogue; *Funky Divas* . . . . (East West)
Frank Sinatra; *My Way* . . . . (Reprise)
Paul McCartney; *The Concert For New York City-C* . . . . (Columbia)
Placido Domingo; *Domingo Songbook.* . . . . (Sony Music Classical)
Ray Charles; *Ray Charles-His Greatest Hits-#1* . . . . . (Dunhill Compact Classics)
Supremes; *I Hear A Symphony* . . . . (Motown)
Wings; *Wings Over America* . . . . (Capitol)
Yo Yo
Kinks; *Give The People What They Want* . . . . (Arista)
Yo Yo
Billy Joe Royal; *Billy Joe Royal's Greatest Hits.* . . . . (Columbia)
You Can't Hurry Love
Diana Ross; *Diana Ross-The Ultimate Collection* . . . . (Motown)
Diana Ross & The Supremes; *16 #1 Hits From The Early '60s-C* . . . . (Motown)
Phil Collins; *Hello, I Must Be Going.* . . . . (Atlantic)
You Can't Play With My Yo-Yo
Yo-Yo & Ice Cube; *Make Way For The Motherlode* . . . . (East West)

TRAINS, Cable Cars, Hobos, Stations, Subways, Trolleys
See Also: LEAVING, RETURNING, SEARCH, SEPARATION, TRAVELING

2:10 Train
Rising Sons; *Rising Sons Featuring Taj Mahal & Ry Cooder* . . . . (Legacy)
Steve Gillette; *Steve Gillette* . . . . (Vanguard)
Stone Poneys Featuring Linda Ronstadt; *The Stone Poneys Featuring Linda Ronstadt* . . . . (EMI)
5:15
Who; *Hooligans* . . . . (MCA)
Join Together. . . . . (MCA)
ST/Quadrophenia . . . . (MCA)
Who's Greatest Hits. . . . . (MCA)
Another Journey By Train
Cure; *Standing On A Beach-The Singles.* . . . . (Elektra)
Another Train
Pete Morton; *One Big Joke.* . . . . (Green Linnet)
At The Station
Joe Walsh; *But Seriously Folks.* . . . . (Asylum)
Baby Likes To Rock It
Tractors; *Tractors.* . . . . (Arista)
Back On The Chain Gang
Pretenders; *Learning To Crawl.* . . . . (Sire)
Pretenders-The Singles . . . . (Sire)
ST/King Of Comedy . . . . (Warner Bros.)
Baggage Coach Ahead
Mac Wiseman; *Great American Train Songs-C* . . . . (C.M.H. Prod.)
The Mac Wiseman Story . . . . (C.M.H. Prod.)
Wabash Cannonball: 20 Classic Train Songs-C . . . . . (C.M.H. Prod.)
Been On A Train
Laura Nyro; *Christmas & The Beads Of Sweat.* . . . . (Columbia)
Better Than You
Metallica; *Reload.* . . . . (Elektra)
Beyond The Blue Horizon
Jeanette MacDonald; *Hollywood Sings-C* . . . . (Living Era)
Lou Christie; *ST/Rain Man* . . . . (Capitol)
Big Railroad Blues
Grateful Dead; *Grateful Dead (Skull & Roses).* . . . . (Warner Bros.)
Big Rock Candy Mountain
Burl Ives; *Burl Ives' Greatest Hits.* . . . . (MCA)
Poor Wayfaring Stranger. . . . . (Flapper)
Harry McClintock; *ST/O Brother, Where Art Thou?* . . . . (Mercury)
John Hartford; *ST/Down From The Mountain* . . . . . . (Lost Highway/IDJMG)
Pete Seeger; *20 Golden Pieces Of Pete Seeger* . . . . (Bulldog)
Tex Ritter; *Capitol Collectors Series-Tex Ritter.* . . . . (Capitol)
Big Train From Memphis
John Fogerty; *Centerfield* . . . . (Warner Bros.)

Black Train
Montrose; *Montrose* . . . . (Warner Bros.)
Blue Railroad Train
Doc Watson; *Doc Watson & Merle Watson: Southbound* . . . . (Vanguard)
Essential Doc Watson. . . . . (Vanguard)
Lonesome Road . . . . (United Artists)
Blue Train
Johnny Cash; *Classic Cash-Hall Of Fame Series* . . . . (Mercury)
Original Johnny Cash . . . . (Sun)
Story Songs Of The Trains & Rivers. . . . . (Sun)
The Man-The World-His Music. . . . . (Sun)
Marty Stuart; *Freight Train Blues-Classic Railroad Songs-#4-C* . . . . (Rounder)
Blue Train
John Coltrane; *Best Of Blue Note-#1-C.* . . . . (Blue Note)
Blue Train. . . . . (Blue Note)
Blue Train, The
Linda Ronstadt; *Feels Like Home* . . . . (Elektra)
Maura O'Connell; *Blue Is The Colour Of Hope* . . . . (Warner Bros.)
Blue Yodel #4 (California Blues)
Bill Monroe; *Columbia Historic Edition-Bill Monroe* . . . . (Columbia)
Jimmie Rodgers; *Jimmie Rodgers-Early Years-1928-1929* . . . . . . (Rounder)
Never No Mo' Blues . . . . (RCA)
This Is Jimmie Rodgers. . . . . (RCA)
Merle Haggard & The Strangers; *Train Whistle Blues* . . . . . . (Rounder)
Blues For Dixie
Asleep At The Wheel featuring Lyle Lovett; *Tribute To The Music Of Bob Wills And The Texas Playboys-C.* . . . . (Liberty)
Barry & Holly Tashian; *Harmony.* . . . . (Rounder)
Bob Wills & His Texas Playboys; *Bob Wills & His Texas Playboys-Anthology 1935-1973* . . . . (Rhino)
Tiffany Transcriptions-#8-More Of The Best . . . . (Rhino)
Merle Haggard & The Strangers; *Best Of Country Blues* . . . . . . (Curb)
Train Whistle Blues . . . . (Rounder)
Born With A Broken Heart
Kenny Wayne Shepherd; *Ledbetter Heights* . . . . (Giant)
Boxcars
Butch Hancock; *Eats Away The Night.* . . . . (Sugar Hill)
Joe Ely; *Best Of Joe Ely.* . . . . (MCA)
Freight Train Blues-Classic Railroad Songs-#4-C . . . . (Rounder)
Honky Tonk Masquerade . . . . (MCA)
Rosie Flores; *Rockabilly Filly* . . . . (Hightone)
Bringin' In The Georgia Mail
Don Reno & Bill Harrell; *Great American Train Songs-C* . . . . . (C.M.H. Prod.)
Broke Down Engine
Blind Willie McTell; *Between The Rails: America's Train Songs-C* . . . . (Crescendo)
Brother, Can You Spare A Dime
Bing Crosby; *Bing Crosby-16 Most Requested Songs.* . . . . (Legacy)
Odetta/Dr. John/John Campbell/Rufus Reid; *Strike A Deep Chord-Blues For The Homeless-C* . . . . (Justice)
Peter, Paul & Mary; *See What Tomorrow Brings* . . . . (Warner Bros.)
Weavers; *Weavers' Greatest Hits* . . . . (Vanguard)
Bummin' An Old Freight Train
Lester Flatt & The Nashville Grass; *Great American Train Songs-C* . . . . (C.M.H. Prod.)
Bumming Around
"T" Texas Tyler; *Only Country-1950-1954-C.* . . . . (JCI Assoc. Labels)
Bus Stations & Train Yards
Gutterboy; *Gutterboy.* . . . . (Mercury)
Canadian Railroad Trilogy
Gordon Lightfoot; *Best Of Gordon Lightfoot* . . . . (EMI)
Gord's Gold . . . . (Reprise)
Sunday Concert . . . . (EMI)
The Way I Feel . . . . (United Artists)
United Artists Collection . . . . (EMI)
Cannonball Blues
Grandpa Jones; *Great American Train Songs-C* . . . . (C.M.H. Prod.)
Can't You See
Alabama; *Alabama-Live* . . . . (RCA)
Charlie Daniels Band; *Volunteer Jam VII-C* . . . . (Epic)
Hank Williams, Jr.; *Hank Williams, Jr. & Friends* . . . . (Polydor)
Rebels, Renegades & Ramblers-C . . . . (Polydor)
Standing In The Shadows . . . . (Polydor)
Marshall Tucker Band; *Marshall Tucker Band* . . . . (AJK Music)
Searchin' For A Rainbow . . . . (AJK Music)
Carolina Blues
Blues Traveler; *Straight On Till Morning* . . . . (A&M)
Casey Jones
Grateful Dead; *Best Of The Grateful Dead-Skeletons From The Closet.* . . . . (Warner Bros.)
Bill Graham Presents The Last Days Of The Fillmore-C. . . . . (Epic Portrait Assoc.)
Workingman's Dead. . . . . (Warner Bros.)
Jerry Garcia Acoustic Band; *Almost Acoustic* . . . . (Grateful Dead)
Casey Jones
Fred McDowell; *Fred McDowell & Furry Lewis: When I Lay My Burden Down.* . . . . (Biograph)
Casey's Last Ride
Johnny Cash; *Rainbow* . . . . (Columbia)

Catch A Train
Free; *Best Of Free* .... (A&M)
Caution! (Do Not Stop On Tracks)
Grateful Dead; *Anthem Of The Sun* .... (Warner Bros.)
Charleston Railroad Tavern
Bobby Bare; *This Is Bobby Bare* .... (RCA)
Chattanooga Choo Choo
Asleep At The Wheel; *Train Trax-C* .... (Sony Music Special Prod.)
Billy Strange; *Railroad Man* .... (Crescendo)
Boston Pops Orchestra/Arthur Fiedler; *Boston Pops Orchestra/Arthur
    Fiedler* .... (RCA)
    Greatest Hits Of The '40s .... (RCA)
Glenn Miller; *Best Of Glenn Miller* .... (RCA)
    Decade Of The '40s-C .... (RCA)
    Glenn Miller-A Legendary Performer-#1 & 2 .... (Bluebird)
    Memorial-1944-1969 .... (Bluebird)
    Nipper's Greatest Hits Of The '40s-#1-C .... (Bluebird)
Glenn Miller & His Orchestra; *Glenn Miller & His Orchestra-
    Pure Gold* .... (Bluebird)
Tuxedo Junction; *Best Of Butterfly Records-C* .... (Hot Prod.)
    Tuxedo Junction .... (Butterfly)
Chinese Mule Train
Spike Jones; *Best Of Spike Jones-#2* .... (RCA)
Choo Choo Ch'Boogie (Jack)
Asleep At The Wheel; *All Time Legends Of Country Music-C* .... (Legacy)
    Asleep At The Wheel .... (Epic)
    Hot Tracks-Train Super Hits-C .... (Epic)
    Served Live .... (Capitol)
    Very Best Of Asleep At The Wheel Since 1970 .... (Relentless/Madacy)
Beach Boys; *Ten Years Of Harmony* .... (Caribou)
Clifton Chenier; *Alligator Stomp-#2-C* .... (Rhino)
Louis Jordan; *Best Of Louis Jordan* .... (MCA)
Quincy Jones; *Birth Of A Band-C* .... (Mercury)
Choo Choo Mama
Ten Years After; *Recorded Live* .... (Chrysalis)
    Universal .... (Chrysalis)
Choo Choo Train
Box Tops; *Box Tops' Greatest Hits* .... (Rhino)
City Of New Orleans
Arlo Guthrie; *Best Of Arlo Guthrie* .... (Warner Bros.)
    Hobo's Lullaby .... (Reprise)
    Together In Concert .... (Reprise)
HARP; *HARP* .... (Redwood)
Willie Nelson; *19 Hot Country Requests-#2-C* .... (Epic)
    City Of New Orleans .... (Columbia)
    Greatest Country Hits Of The '80s-#4-C .... (Columbia)
    Hot Tracks-Train Super Hits-C .... (Epic)
    Train Trax-C .... (Sony Music Special Prod.)
Clack Clack/Oldest Living Son
John Stewart; *Last Campaign* .... (Laserlight)
Click-Clack
Dicky Doo And The Don'ts; *Greatest Hit Singles Collection-C* ....(Laserlight)
C'mon 'N Ride It (The Train)
Quad City DJ's; *110% Hits-C* .... (Simitar)
    ESPN Presents Jock Jams-#3-C .... (Tommy Boy)
    Get On Up And Dance .... (Big Beat)
    The Ultimate Dance Party-1997-C .... (Arista)
Cocaine Train
Johnny Paycheck; *Banded Together-C* .... (Epic)
    Everybody's Got a Family .... (Epic)
Coffee Train
David Thomas; *Monster Walks The Winter Lake* .... (Twin-Tone)
Coming And The Going Of The Trains, The
Merle Haggard & The Strangers; *Train Whistle Blues* ..... (Rounder)
Crazy Train
Ozzy Osbourne; *Blizzard Of Ozz* .... (Jet)
    The Ozzman Cometh .... (Epic)
    Tribute .... (Epic)
Crescent City Crawl
Wynton Marsalis; *ST/Tune In Tomorrow...* .... (Columbia)
Cross-Tie Walker
Creedence Clearwater Revival; *1969* .... (Fantasy)
    Creedence Country .... (Fantasy)
    Green River .... (Fantasy)
Daddy, What's A Train?
Utah Phillips; *Steel Rails-Classic Railroad Songs-#1-C* .... (Rounder)
Death Train
Beat Farmers; *Glad 'N' Greasy* .... (Rhino)
Desperados Waiting For A Train
Guy Clark; *Old No. 1* .... (Sugar Hill)
Jerry Jeff Walker; *Best Of Jerry Jeff Walker* .... (MCA)
    Great Gonzos .... (MCA)
    Viva Terlingua .... (MCA)
Waylon Jennings, Willie Nelson, Johnny Cash, Kris Kristofferson;
    Highwayman .... (Columbia)
    Hot Tracks-Train Super Hits-C .... (Epic)
Detroit City
Ace Cannon; *Golden Favorites* .... (Ranwood)
Bill Anderson; *Best Of Bill Anderson* .... (Curb)

Bobby Bare; *Nipper's Greatest Hits Of The '60s-#2-C* .... (RCA)
    This Is Bobby Bare .... (RCA)
Chet Atkins; *Country Gems* .... (Pair)
Flatt & Scruggs; *20 All-Time Great Recordings* .... (Columbia)
Hank Williams, Jr.; *Live At Cobo Hall Detroit* .... (Polydor)
    Standing In The Shadows .... (Polydor)
Mel Tillis; *Best Of Mel Tillis* .... (MCA)
    Live At The Sam Houston Coliseum .... (MGM)
Solomon Burke; *Home In Your Heart-Best Of Solomon Burke* ....(Rhino)
Devil's Train
Hank Williams; *Lovesick Blues* .... (Polydor)
Roy Acuff; *Roy Acuff's Greatest Hits* .... (Columbia)
Dixie Cannonball
Red Knuckles & The Trailblazers; *Freight Train Blues-Classic Railroad
    Songs-#4-C* .... (Rounder)
Don't Forget The Trains
Asleep At The Wheel; *Route 66* .... (Liberty)
Don't Sleep In The Subway
Frank Sinatra; *Frank Sinatra* .... (Reprise)
Petula Clark; *Petula Clark's Greatest Hits* .... (Crescendo)
    Summer Of Love-#1-C .... (Rhino)
Don't You See That Train
Laurie Lewis & Kathy Kallick; *Freight Train Blues-Classic Railroad
    Songs-#4-C* .... (Rounder)
Down In The Subway
Gene Pitney; *This Is Gene Pitney* .... (Out Of Print)
Down In The Tube Station At Midnight
Jam; *Snap!* .... (Polydor)
    The Jam's Greatest Hits .... (Polydor)
Down There By The Train
Johnny Cash; *American Recordings* .... (American)
Downtown Train
Patty Smyth; *Train Trax-C* .... (Sony Music Special Prod.)
Rod Stewart; *Downtown Train-Selections From The Storyteller
    Anthology* .... (Warner Bros.)
    Storyteller/The Complete Anthology: 1964-1990 ...... (Warner Bros.)
Downtown Train
Mary Chapin Carpenter; *Hometown Girl* .... (Columbia)
Drill Ye Tarriers Drill
Weavers; *On Tour* .... (Vanguard)
Drill, Ye Tarriers
Dick & Jacquie Schuyler; *Great American Train Songs-C* ..... (C.M.H. Prod.)
Drug Train
Social Distortion; *Social Distortion* .... (Epic)
Drug Train
Cramps; *Bad Music For Bad People* .... (I.R.S.)
East Bound Train
Lester Flatt & Earl Scruggs; *Hear The
    Whistles Blow* .... (International Mktg. Group)
End Of The Line
Bob Wills & His Texas Playboys; *Bob Wills & His Texas Playboys-24
    Great Hits* .... (Polydor)
Buddy Emmons; *Buddy Emmons Sings Bob Wills* .... (Flying Fish)
Jason Roberts & Asleep At The Wheel; *Ride With Bob-C* .. (DreamWorks/SKG)
Engine #9
Midnight Star; *Headlines* .... (Solar)
Engine 143
Joan Baez; *Joan Baez, Vol. 2* .... (Vanguard)
Engine 999
Hooters; *One Way Home* .... (Columbia)
Engine Engine #9
Roger Miller; *Best Of Roger Miller-#2-King Of The Road* ....(Mercury)
    Best Of Roger Miller-His Greatest Songs .... (Curb)
    King Of The Road-Genius Of Roger Miller .... (Mercury)
    Roger Miller-Golden Hits .... (Smash)
    Roger Miller-The Hits .... (Mercury)
    Train Trax-C .... (Sony Music Special Prod.)
Engineers Don't Wave From The Trains Anymore
Earl Scruggs & Tom T. Hall; *The Storyteller & The Banjo Man* .....(Columbia)
Lynn Morris; *The Bramble And The Rose* .... (Rounder)
Every Night When The Sun Goes In
Jo Stafford; *Jo Plus Blues* .... (Corinthian)
Fast Moving Train
Restless Heart; *Best Of Restless Heart* .... (RCA)
    Fast Moving Train .... (RCA)
First Train Heading South
Johnny Horton; *Between The Rails: America's Train Songs-C* ..... (Crescendo)
First Train To California
Cryan' Shames; *Best Of The Cryan' Shames* .... (Bac-Trac)
Flint Hill Special
Flatt & Scruggs; *Golden Era* .... (Rounder)
Nitty Gritty Dirt Band; *Will The Circle Be Unbroken* .... (EMI)
Folsom Prison Blues
Brooks & Dunn with Johnny Cash; *Red Hot + Country-C* ....(Mercury)
Johnny Cash; *Billboard Top Country Hits-1968-C* .... (Rhino)
    Classic Cash-Hall Of Fame Series .... (Mercury)
    Hot Tracks-Train Super Hits-C .... (Epic)
    Jailhouse Rock (Hits From The Big House)-C .... (Sony Music Special Prod.)

Johnny Cash At Folsom Prison & San Quentin . . . . (Columbia)
Johnny Cash-Original Golden Hits-#1 . . . . (Sun)
Johnny Cash's Greatest Hits-#2 . . . . (Columbia)
Superbilly . . . . (Sun)
The Man In Black-His Greatest Hits . . . . (Legacy)

Freedom Train, The
Bing Crosby; *Bing Crosby-Complete Recordings* . . . .(MCA)
Peggy Lee; *Peggy Lee-Complete Recordings-1941-1947* . . . . (Legacy)

Freight Train
Sonny Terry & Brownie McGhee; *Back To New Orleans* . . . . (Fantasy)

Freight Train Be My Friend
John Lee Hooker; *At Newport*. . . . .(Vee-Jay)

Freight Train Blues
Bob Dylan; *Bob Dylan* . . . . (Columbia)
The Times They Are A-Changin' . . . . (Columbia)
Doc & Merle Watson; *Freight Train Blues-Classic Railroad Songs-#4-C* . . . . (Rounder)
Roy Acuff; *Columbia Historic Edition-Roy Acuff* . . . . (Columbia)
Roy Acuff's Greatest Hits . . . . (Columbia)

Freight Train Boogie
Delmore Brothers; *45-#2077* . . . . (Gusto)
Johnny Otis; *Original Johnny Otis Show-#2*. . . . . (Savoy)

Friendship Train
Gladys Knight & The Pips; *Compact Command Performances-Gladys Knight & The Pips* . . . . (Motown)
Gladys Knight & The Pips-All The Great Hits . . . . (Motown)
Gladys Knight & The Pips-Anthology . . . . (Motown)
Motown Superstar Series-#13-Gladys Knight & The Pips . . . . (Motown)

From A Moving Train
America; *Human Nature* . . . . (Oxygen)

Funiculi, Funicula
Mario Lanza; *Legendary Tenor* . . . . (RCA)

Gambler, The
Kenny Rogers; *Kenny Rogers' Greatest Hits* . . . .(EMI)
Kenny Rogers-Twenty Greatest Hits . . . .(EMI)
The Gambler . . . .(EMI)

Georgia On A Fast Train
Billy Joe Shaver; *Hot Tracks-Train Super Hits-C* . . . .(Epic)

Get A Transfer
Nashville Bluegrass Band; *Freight Train Blues-Classic Railroad Songs-#4-C* . . . . (Rounder)

Ghost Train
Counting Crows; *August And Everything After* . . . . (David Geffen Co.)

Glendale Train
New Riders Of The Purple Sage; *Best Of New Riders Of The Purple Sage*. . . . . (Columbia)
New Riders Of The Purple Sage . . . . (Columbia)

Golden Rocket
Hank Snow; *All About Trains* . . . . (RCA)
Best Of Hank Snow . . . . (RCA)
Horse Soldiers; *Between The Rails: America's Train Songs-C* . . . (Crescendo)
Willie Nelson & Hank Snow; *Brand On My Heart*. . . . . (Columbia)

Graveyard Train
Creedence Clearwater Revival; *1968-1969* . . . . (Fantasy)
Bayou Country. . . . . (Fantasy)

Green Green Grass Of Home
Burl Ives; *Best Of Burl Ives-#2* . . . .(MCA)
Elvis Presley; *Elvis Presley Today* . . . . (RCA)
Our Memories Of Elvis, Volume 2 . . . . (RCA)
George Jones; *20 Golden Pieces Of George Jones* . . . . (Bulldog)
Johnny Cash; *Johnny Cash-16 Biggest Hits-#2* . . . . (Legacy)
Tom Jones; *Country Side Of Tom Jones* . . . . (London)
Things That Matter Most To Me . . . . (Mercury)
Tom Jones-London Collector-Greatest Hits . . . . (London)

Hear My Train A'Comin'
Jimi Hendrix; *Concerts*. . . . . (Reprise)
Rainbow Bridge . . . . (Reprise)
Jimi Hendrix Experience; *Radio One* . . . . (Rykodisc)

Heartbreak Station
Cinderella; *Heartbreak Station*. . . . . (Mercury)

Heaven Bound Train
Carl Story; *Great American Train Songs-C* . . . .(C.M.H. Prod.)

Hellbound Train
Savoy Brown; *Hellbound Train* . . . . (Parrot)
Savoy Brown-London Collector. . . . . (London)
Savoy Brown's Greatest Hits-Live In Concert . . . . (Townhouse)

Here Comes The Freedom Train
Merle Haggard; *Capitol Collectors Series-Merle Haggard* . . . . (Capitol)

Hey Porter
Johnny Cash; *First Years* . . . .(Allegiance)
Johnny Cash-Legend . . . . (Sun)
Johnny Cash-Original Golden Hits-#1 . . . . (Sun)
Johnny Cash's Greatest Hits-#2 . . . . (Columbia)
Johnny Cash-Sun Years . . . . (Rhino)
Vintage Years-1955-1963 . . . . (Rhino)

Hitchcock Railway
Joe Cocker; *Joe Cocker Live* . . . . (Capitol)
Joe Cocker! . . . . (A&M)
Jose Feliciano; *Jose Feliciano's All-Time Greatest Hits* . . . . (RCA)

Hobo
Linda Ronstadt; *Different Drum* . . . . (Capitol)
Linda Ronstadt-Retrospective . . . . (Capitol)

Hobo & His Mother
Goebel Reeves; *Texas Drifter* . . . .(Glendale)

Hobo Bill's Last Ride
Merle Haggard & The Strangers; *Okie From Muskogee* . . . . (Capitol)
Same Train Different Time . . . . (Capitol)
Train Whistle Blues . . . . (Rounder)

Hobo Blues
John Lee Hooker; *Best Of John Lee Hooker* . . . .(Crescendo)
I'm John Lee Hooker . . . .(Vee-Jay)
Real Blues Brothers-C . . . . (Dunhill Compact Classics)
Lonesome River Band; *Freight Train Blues-Classic Railroad Songs-#4-C* . . . . (Rounder)

Hobo Heaven
Boxcar Willie; *Boxcar Willie* . . . . (Dot)

Hobo Jungle
Band; *Northern Lights-Southern Cross*. . . . . (Capitol)

Hobo Song
Johnny Cash; *Mystery Of Life* . . . . (Mercury)

Hobo Song
John Prine; *Bruised Orange* . . . . (Oh Boy)

Hobo, The
Merle Haggard & The Strangers; *Train Whistle Blues* . . . . (Rounder)

Hobo, You Can't Ride This Train
Louis Armstrong; *Satchmo-Musical Autobiography*. . . . . (MCA)

Hobo's Blues
Paul Simon; *Paul Simon* . . . . (Columbia)

Hobo's Lullaby
Arlo Guthrie; *Hobo's Lullaby* . . . . (Reprise)
Goebel Reeves; *Texas Drifter* . . . .(Glendale)
Joan Baez; *Tribute To Woody Guthrie-C*. . . . . (Warner Bros.)

Hobo's Meditation
Dolly Parton/Emmylou Harris/Linda Ronstadt; *Trio* . . . . (Warner Bros.)
Merle Haggard & The Strangers; *Train Whistle Blues* . . . . (Rounder)

Homeward Bound
Paul Simon; *Paul Simon In Concert/Live Rhymin'* . . . . (Columbia)
Paul Simon & George Harrison; *Nobody's Child-Romanian Angel Appeal-C* . . . . (Warner Bros.)
Simon & Garfunkel; *Collected Works*. (Columbia)
Parsley Sage Rosemary & Thyme. . . . . (Columbia)
Simon & Garfunkel's Greatest Hits . . . . (Columbia)
The Concert In Central Park . . . . (Warner Bros.)
Willie Nelson & Waylon Jennings; *Take It To The Limit* . . . . (Columbia)

Honky Tonk Train (Blues)
Emerson, Lake & Palmer; *Works, Volume 2* . . . .(Atlantic)
Meade Lux Lewis; *Atlantic Blues-Piano-C* . . . .(Atlantic)
Classic Jazz Piano . . . . (Bluebird)
Jazz Heritage-Kings & Queens Of Ivory-#1-C . . . . (MCA)
Ridin' In Rhythm-C . . . . (Disques Swing)

Hot Rails To Hell
Blue Oyster Cult; *Career Of Evil* . . . . (Columbia)
Extraterrestrial Live . . . . (Columbia)
Metal Giants-C . . . . (Columbia)
On Your Feet Or On Your Knees . . . . (Columbia)
Tyranny & Mutation . . . . (Columbia)

I Ain't Ever Satisfied
Gretchen Peters; *The Secret Of Life*. . . . . (Purple Crayon Prod.)
Steve Earle & The Dukes; *Ain't Ever Satisfied: The Steve Earle Collection* . . . . (Hip-O)
Exit 0 . . . . (MCA)
Shut Up And Die Like An Aviator . . . . (MCA)

I Am A Man Of Constant Sorrow
Ralph Stanley; *Rebel Records: 35 Years Of The Best In Bluegrass-1960-1995-C* . . . . (Rebel)
Soggy Bottom Boys featuring Dan Tyminski; *ST/O Brother, Where Art Thou?* . . . . (Mercury)
Stanley Brothers; *All Time Legends Of Country Music-C* . . . . (Legacy)

I Been To Georgia On A Fast Train
Willie Nelson; *Me & Paul* . . . . (Columbia)

I Get The Fever
Bill Anderson; *Bill Anderson's Greatest Hits* . . . . (Varese Sarabande)

I Got The Train Sittin' Waitin'
Waylon Jennings; *Between The Rails: America's Train Songs-C* . . . .(Crescendo)

I Left My Heart In San Francisco
Tony Bennett; *I Left My Heart In San Francisco*. . . . . (Columbia)
Pop Classics Of The '60s-C . . . . (Columbia)
Tony Bennett's All-Time Greatest Hits. . . . . (Columbia)

I Like Trains
Fred Eaglesmith; *Freight Train Blues-Classic Railroad Songs-#4-C* . . (Rounder)

I Packed My Suitcase, Started To The Train
Memphis Jug Band; *The Story-1927-1934* . . . . (EPM)

I Thought About You
Billie Holiday; *Lady Sings The Blues* . . . . (Verve)
Dinah Washington; *What A Diff'rence A Day Makes* . . . . (Mercury)
Frank Sinatra & Nelson Riddle Orchestra; *songs for Swingin' Lovers!*. . . . . (Capitol)

Rosemary Clooney; *Rosemary Clooney Sings The Music Of Jimmy Van Heusen* .... (Concord Jazz)
Tony Bennett; *Perfectly Frank* .... (Columbia)

I Walk The Line
Johnny Cash; *Johnny Cash At Folsom Prison & San Quentin* ...... (Columbia)
Johnny Cash-Legends .... (Dunhill Compact Classics)
Johnny Cash-Original Golden Hits-#1 .... (Sun)
Johnny Cash's Greatest Hits .... (Columbia)
Johnny Cash-Sun Years .... (Rhino)
Memphis Country-C .... (Sun)
Show Time .... (Sun)
Souvenirs Of Music City U.S.A.-C .... (Plantation)
Sun Story-C .... (Rhino)
Superbilly .... (Sun)
The Man In Black-His Greatest Hits .... (Legacy)

I Want To Work On The Railroad
Debby McClatchy; *Someday Cafe* .... (Green Linnet)

I'd Be Better Off (In A Pine Box)
Doug Stone; *Doug Stone* .... (Epic)
Greatest Country Hits Of The '90s-1990-C .... (Columbia)

I'm Moving On
Elvis Presley; *Canadian Tribute* .... (RCA)
From Elvis In Memphis .... (RCA)
Guitar Man .... (RCA)
Memphis Record .... (RCA)
Emmylou Harris; *Last Date* .... (Warner Bros.)
Profile II-The Best Of Emmylou Harris .... (Warner Bros.)
George Thorogood & The Destroyers; *Born To Be Bad* ... (Gold Rush)
Hank Snow; *60 Years Of Country Music-C* .... (RCA)
Best Of Hank Snow .... (RCA)
Great Moments At The Grand Ole Opry-C .... (RCA)
I'm Moving On & Other Great Country Hits ..... (RCA)
Nipper's Greatest Hits Of The '50s-#2-C ...... (RCA)
Rolling Stones; *December's Children (and everybody's)* .... (Abkco)

In A Station
Band; *Music From Big Pink* .... (Capitol)

In The Pines
Merle Travis & Mac Wiseman; *Great American Train Songs-C* .... (C.M.H. Prod.)

Interstate Love Song
Stone Temple Pilots; *Purple* .... (Atlantic)

It Takes A Lot To Laugh, It Takes A Train To Cry
Bob Dylan; *Highway 61 Revisited* .... (Columbia)
The Bootleg Series-Volumes 1-3 [Rare & Unreleased] .... (Columbia)
Mike Bloomfield/Al Kooper/Stephen Stills; *Super Session* .... (Columbia)

It Won't Be Long
Kathy Chiavola; *Freight Train Blues-Classic Railroad Songs-#4-C* ... (Rounder)

It's Hard To Be A Saint In The City
Bruce Springsteen; *Greetings From Asbury Park, N.J.* .... (Columbia)
Live 1975-1985 .... (Legacy)
Tracks .... (Columbia)
David Bowie; *One Step Up/Two Steps Back-The Songs Of Bruce Springsteen-C* .... (Right Stuff)

I've Been Working On The Railroad
Mitch Miller; *Sing Along With Mitch* .... (Columbia)
Original Soundtrack; *Children's Favorites* .... (Kid Rhino/Rhino 4 Kids)

Jimmie The Kid
Jimmie Rodgers; *Steel Town* .... (Flying Fish)

John Henry
''Little'' Jimmy Dickens; *Columbia Historic Edition-''Little'' Jimmy Dickens* .... (Columbia)
Harry Belafonte; *Harry Belafonte-At Carnegie Hall* .... (RCA)
Harry Belafonte-Legendary Performer .... (RCA)
Harry Belafonte's All Time Greatest Hits-#1 ... (RCA)
Merle Travis; *Great American Train Songs-C* ...... (C.M.H. Prod.)
Odetta; *Essential Odetta* .... (Vanguard)
Greatest Folksingers Of The '60s-C .... (Vanguard)
Woody Guthrie; *Immortal Woody Guthrie-Golden Classics-#2* ... (Collectables)
Legendary Woody Guthrie .... (Tradition)

Just Another Whistle Stop
Band; *Stage Fright* .... (Capitol)

Just Like This Train
Joni Mitchell; *Court & Spark* .... (Asylum)

Kansas City Railroad Blues
Nashville Bluegrass Band; *Waitin' For The Hard Times To Go* ..... (Sugar Hill)

Kansas City Southern
Pure Prairie League; *Freight Train Blues-Classic Railroad Songs-#4-C* .... (Rounder)
Takin' The Stage .... (RCA)
Two Lane Highway .... (RCA)

Keep This Train A-Rollin'
Doobie Brothers; *One Step Closer* .... (Warner Bros.)

King Of The Road
R.E.M.; *Dead Letter Office* .... (I.R.S.)
Roger Miller; *Billboard Top Country Hits-1965-C* .... (Rhino)
Cruisin'-1965-C .... (Increase)
Roger Miller-Golden Hits .... (Smash)

Land Of Hope And Dreams
Bruce Springsteen & The E Street Band; *God Bless America-C* ..... (Columbia)

Live In New York City .... (Columbia)

Last Fair Deal Gone Down
Keb' Mo'; *Just Like You* .... (Okeh)

Last Steam Engine Train
John Fahey; *Best Of John Fahey: 1959-1977* .... (Takoma)
Dance Of Death & Other Plantation Faves .... (Takoma)
Leo Kottke; *Best Of Leo Kottke* .... (Capitol)
Greenhouse .... (Capitol)
Very Best Of Leo Kottke .... (Capitol)

Last Train
Robin Trower & Jack Bruce; *Truce* .... (Chrysalis)

Last Train
Arlo Guthrie; *Best Of Arlo Guthrie* .... (Warner Bros.)

Last Train
Peter Rowan; *Steel Rails-Classic Railroad Songs-#1-C* .... (Rounder)

Last Train Done Gone Down
Marty Stuart; *Hot Tracks-Train Super Hits-C* .... (Epic)
Let There Be Country .... (Columbia)

Last Train To Clarksville
Monkees; *Monkees* .... (Arista)
Monkees' Greatest Hits .... (Rhino)
Monkees-Live-1967 .... (Rhino)
Then & Now...The Best Of The Monkees .... (Arista)

Last Train To London
Electric Light Orchestra; *Box Of Their Best* .... (Jet)
Discovery .... (Jet)

Last Train To Nuremberg
Pete Seeger; *A Link In The Chain* .... (Legacy)

Lay Down Your Arms
Chordettes; *Best Of The Chordettes* .... (Rhino)

Leavin' Train
Bruce Springsteen; *Tracks* .... (Columbia)

Let The Train Blow The Whistle
Johnny Cash; *American Recordings* .... (American)

Letter, The
Box Tops; *Billboard Top Rock 'N' Roll Hits-1967-C* .... (Rhino)
Box Tops' Greatest Hits .... (Rhino)
Cruisin'-1967-C .... (Increase)
Oldies But Goodies-#12-C .... (Original Sound)
Rockin' '60s-C .... (Priority)
Joe Cocker; *Joe Cocker Live* .... (Capitol)
Joe Cocker-Classics-#4 .... (A&M)
Joe Cocker's Greatest Hits .... (A&M)
Mad Dogs & Englishmen .... (A&M)
Vernon Green & The Medallions; *Oldies But Goodies-#1-C* ... (Original Sound)
Vernon Green & The Medallions-Golden Classics .... (Collectables)

Life's Railway To Heaven
Merle Haggard & The Strangers; *Train Whistle Blues* .... (Rounder)

Locomotion
Orchestral Manoeuvres In The Dark; *in the dark/the best of OMD* ...... (A&M)
Junk Culture .... (A&M)

Loco-Motion
Grand Funk Railroad; *Billboard Top Rock 'N' Roll Hits-1974-C* ...... (Rhino)
Caught In The Act .... (Capitol)
Grand Funk Railroad-Hits .... (Capitol)
Kylie Minogue; *Kylie* .... (Geffen)
Little Eva; *Billboard Top Rock 'N' Roll Hits-1962-C* .... (Rhino)
Groove 'N' Grind-'50s & '60s Dance Hits-C ...... (Rhino)
More American Graffiti-C .... (MCA)

Locomotive Breath
Jethro Tull; *''M.U.''-Best Of* .... (Chrysalis)
20 Years Of Jethro Tull .... (Chrysalis)
Aqualung .... (Chrysalis)
Bursting Out .... (Chrysalis)
Original Masters .... (Chrysalis)
Rock Classics-C .... (K-Tel)

Lollipop Train (You Never Had It So Good)
Grass Roots; *Grass Roots-Anthology (1966-1975)* .... (Rhino)
P.F. Sloan; *P.F. Sloan-Anthology* .... (One Way)

Lonesome Whistle
Hank Williams With His Drifting Cowboys; *Between The Rails: America's Train Songs-C* .... (Crescendo)
Hank Williams-24 Greatest Hits-#2 .... (Polydor)
Hank Williams-40 Greatest Hits .... (Polydor)
Johnny Cash; *Story Songs Of The Trains & Rivers* .... (Sun)
Little Feat; *Hoy-Hoy!* .... (Warner Bros.)

Long Train Runnin'
Doobie Brothers; *Best Of The Doobies* .... (Warner Bros.)
Captain & Me .... (Warner Bros.)
Farewell Tour .... (Warner Bros.)

Looking For My Baby
Little Milton; *Between The Rails: America's Train Songs-C* ...... (Crescendo)

Lord Of The Trains
Tom Russell; *Steel Rails-Classic Railroad Songs-#1-C* .... (Rounder)

Love In Vain
Rolling Stones; *Get Yer Ya-Ya's Out!* .... (Abkco)
Let It Bleed .... (Abkco)

Love Train
Keb' Mo'; *Big Wide Grin* .... (Sony Wonder)

O'Jays; *Billboard Top Rock 'N' Roll Hits-1973-C* . . . . (Rhino)
  O'Jays' Greatest Hits . . . . (Philadelphia Int'l)
  O'Jays-Collector's Item. . . . . (Philadelphia Int'l)
  Philadelphia Classics-C . . . . (Philadelphia Int'l)
  Train Trax-C . . . . (Sony Music Special Prod.)
Love's Train
Con Funk Shun; *Love's Train-C* . . . . (Mercury)
  Smooth Grooves-A Sensual Collection-#1-C . . . . (Rhino)
  To The Max . . . . (Mercury)
M.T.A.
Kingston Trio; *25 Years Non-Stop* . . . .(Xeres)
  Best Of The Kingston Trio . . . . (Capitol)
  Capitol Collectors Series-The Kingston Trio . . . . (Capitol)
  Scarlet Ribbons . . . . (Capitol)
  Very Best Of The Kingston Trio . . . . (Capitol)
Mama From The Train
Patti Page; *Patti Page-Golden Celebration* . . . . (Mercury)
Marrakesh Express
Crosby, Stills & Nash; *Crosby, Stills & Nash* . . . . (Atlantic)
  CSN . . . . (Atlantic)
  Replay . . . . (Atlantic)
  Woodstock Two . . . . (Atlantic)
Me And Bobby McGee
Grateful Dead; *Grateful Dead (Skull & Roses)* . . . .(Warner Bros.)
Janis Joplin; *Janis* . . . . (Legacy)
  Janis Joplin's Greatest Hits . . . . (Columbia)
  Pearl . . . . (Legacy)
  Rock Classics Of The '70s-C . . . . (Columbia)
Willie Nelson; *Willie Nelson Sings Kristofferson* . . . . (Columbia)
Mean Mama Blues
Bob Wills; *Stay A Little Longer-The Original Columbia
  Recordings* . . . . (Roswell/RCA)
Message To Michael
Dionne Warwick; *Dionne Warwick* . . . . (Everest)
  Dionne Warwick Greatest Hits . . . . (Everest)
  Dionne Warwick-Anthology 1962-1971 . . . . (Rhino)
  Hot! Live & Otherwise . . . . (Arista)
  Original Rock 'N' Roll Hits Of The '60s-C . . . . (Roulette)
Midnight Flyer
Eagles; *On The Border* . . . . (Elektra)
Osborne Brothers; *Essential Bluegrass Album* . . . .(C.M.H. Prod.)
Osborne Brothers & Mac Wiseman; *Great American Train
  Songs-C* . . . .(C.M.H. Prod.)
Midnight Mary
Joey Powers; *Dick Bartley's One-Hit Wonders Of The '60s-#1-C* . . . . . . (Rhino)
Midnight Special Train
Big Joe Turner; *Atlantic Rhythm & Blues 1947-1974-#3 (1955-
  1958)-C* . . . .(Atlantic)
  Joe Turner's Greatest Hits. . . . . (Atlantic)
Midnight Train
Jim & Jesse; *Great American Train Songs-C* . . . .(C.M.H. Prod.)
Midnight Train To Georgia
Gladys Knight & The Pips; *Billboard Top Rock 'N' Roll Hits-1973-C*. . . (Rhino)
  Gladys Knight & The Pips' Greatest Hits . . . . (Buddah)
  Imagination . . . . (Right Stuff)
  On & On. . . . . (Fifty One West)
  Radio Active Hits-C . . . . (Accord)
  Train Trax-C . . . . (Sony Music Special Prod.)
  Very Best Of Gladys Knight & The Pips. . . . . (Buddah)
Mobile & K.C. Line
Robert Shaw; *Ma Grinder* . . . . (Arhoolie)
Mobile Line
Jim Kweskin and His Jug Band; *Jim Kweskin and His Jug Band* . . . . (Vanguard)
  Jim Kweskin and His Jug Band's Greatest Hits . . . . (Vanguard)
  Troubadours Of The Folk Era-#3-C . . . . (Rhino)
Mobile/Texas Line
Tom Rush; *Blues Songs & Ballads* . . . . (Fantasy)
  Mind Ramblin'. . . . . (Prestige)
  Tom Rush. . . . . (Fantasy)
Morning Train (Nine To Five)
Sheena Easton; *Sheena Easton* . . . .(EMI)
Muskrat Ramble
Dukes Of Dixieland; *Digital Dixieland* . . . .(Pro Jazz)
Kid Ory's Creole Jazz Band; *Kid Ory's Creole Jazz Band-
  1954* . . . . (Good Time Jazz)
Louis Armstrong; *Essential Louis Armstrong.* . . . . (Vanguard)
  Louis Armstrong's Greatest Hits . . . . (Curb)
McGuire Sisters; *McGuire Sisters' Greatest Hits* . . . . (MCA)
Pete Fountain; *High Society* . . . . (Bluebird)
My Baby Thinks He's A Train
Rosanne Cash; *Rosanne Cash-Hits-1979-1989* . . . . (Columbia)
  Seven Year Ache. . . . . (Columbia)
My Baby Thinks She's A Train
Asleep At The Wheel; *Freight Train Blues-Classic Railroad
  Songs-#4-C* . . . . (Rounder)
  Very Best Of Asleep At The Wheel Since 1970 . . . . . . (Relentless/Madacy)
My Heart Is A Hobo
Rosemary Clooney; *Rosemary Clooney Sings The Music Of Jimmy Van
  Heusen* . . . .(Concord Jazz)

My Love Affair With Trains
Merle Haggard; *Between The Rails: America's Train Songs-C* . . . . .(Crescendo)
Merle Haggard & The Strangers; *Train Whistle Blues* . . . . (Rounder)
My Rough And Rowdy Ways
Merle Haggard & The Strangers; *Train Whistle Blues* . . . . (Rounder)
My Train Rolled Up In Texas
Big Joe Turner; *Things That I Used To Do* . . . . (Pablo)
Mystery Train
Band; *Moondog Matinee* . . . . (Capitol)
  The Band-Anthology-#2 . . . . (Capitol)
  The Last Waltz . . . . (Warner Bros.)
  To Kingdom Come-The Definitive Collection . . . . (Capitol)
Elvis Presley; *For LP Fans Only* . . . .(RCA)
  The Sun Sessions . . . .(RCA)
Junior Parker; *Between The Rails: America's Train Songs-C* . . . . . .(Crescendo)
Neil Young; *Neil & The Shocking Pinks* . . . . (Geffen)
Neville Brothers; *Brother's Keeper.* . . . . (A&M)
Paul Butterfield Blues Band; *Golden Butter* . . . . (Elektra)
  Paul Butterfield Blues Band . . . . (Elektra)
Sam The Sham and The Pharaohs; *Best Of Sam The Sham and The
  Pharaohs* . . . .(Polydor)
New Delhi Freight Train
Little Feat; *Time Loves A Hero* . . . . (Warner Bros.)
New Frisco Train
Washington White; *Mississippi Moaners-1927-1942* . . . .(Yazoo)
New River Train
Doc & Merle Watson; *Remembering Merle* . . . .(Sugar Hill)
White Brothers & New Kentucky Colonels; *Live In Sweden.* . . . . (Rounder)
New Timer
Bruce Springsteen; *The Ghost Of Tom Joad* . . . . (Columbia)
Next Stop Brattleboro
NRBQ; *Freight Train Blues-Classic Railroad Songs-#4-C* . . . . (Rounder)
Night Time In The Switching Yard
Warren Zevon; *Excitable Boy* . . . .(Asylum)
Night Train
James Brown; *Train Trax-C* . . . . (Sony Music Special Prod.)
James Brown And The Famous Flames; *Soul Shots-C* . . . . (Rhino)
  ST/Quadrophenia. . . . . (MCA)
Night Train
Jimmy Forrest; *Heart Of The Forest* . . . .(Palo Alto Jazz)
  Night Train . . . . (Delmark)
Night Train
U2; *The Island Story-1962-1987-25th Anniversary-C* . . . . (Island)
Night Train
Steve Winwood; *Arc Of A Diver* . . . . (Island)
Night Train
Lionel Richie; *Dancing On The Ceiling* . . . . (Motown)
Night Train
Paul Revere And The Raiders; *Legend Of Paul Revere And The
  Raiders* . . . . (Columbia)
Night Train
Rickie Lee Jones; *Rickie Lee Jones* . . . . (Warner Bros.)
Night Train To Madrid
Bertram Levy; *That Old Gut Feeling.* . . . . (Flying Fish)
Night Train To Memphis
Jerry Lee Lewis; *Rare Tracks* . . . . (Rhino)
  Taste Of Country . . . .(Sun)
Joe Maphis; *Great American Train Songs-C.* . . . . (C.M.H. Prod.)
Roy Acuff; *Best Of Roy Acuff* . . . . (Liberty)
  Essential Roy Acuff-1936-1949 . . . . (Legacy)
  Roy Acuff's Greatest Hits . . . . (Columbia)
Nighttrain
Public Enemy; *Apocalypse 91...The Enemy Strikes Black* . .(Def Jam/Columbia)
  Stanley Son Of Theodore-Music Sampler . . . . (Epic)
Nighttrain
Guns N' Roses; *Appetite For Destruction.* . . . . (Geffen)
Nine Pound Hammer
David Grisman with Doc Watson and Alan O'Bryant; *Steel Rails-Classic
  Railroad Songs-#1-C.* . . . . (Rounder)
Merle Travis; *Great American Train Songs-C* . . . . (C.M.H. Prod.)
No Leaf Clover
Metallica; *S&M.* . . . . (Elektra)
No More Trains To Ride
Merle Haggard & The Strangers; *Train Whistle Blues* . . . . (Rounder)
Nobody's Gonna Rain On Our Parade
Kathy Mattea; *Walking Away A Winner* . . . . (Mercury)
Northbound-Southbound
Wynton Marsalis; *Big Train* . . . . (Columbia)
Oh My Old Train
Lonesome Strangers; *Lonesome Strangers* . . . .(Hightone)
Old Black Choo Choo
Rose Maddox; *Rose Of The West Coast Country* . . . . (Arhoolie)
Old Toy Trains
Billy Strange; *Railroad Man.* . . . .(Crescendo)
Glen Campbell; *All-Star Country Christmas-C.* . . . . (Capitol)
  That Christmas Feeling . . . . (Capitol)
Statler Brothers; *Statler Brothers Christmas Present* . . . . (Mercury)
One After 909
Beatles; *Let It Be* . . . . (Capitol)

The Beatles-Anthology-#1 . . . . . (Capitol)
One Toke Over The Line
Brewer & Shipley; *'70s Greatest Rock Hits-#10-C* . . . . . (Priority)
Super Hits Of The '70s-Have A Nice Day-#4-C . . . . . (Rhino)
One Way Ticket (Because I Can)
LeAnn Rimes; *Blue* . . . . . (MCG/Curb)
One Way Ticket Back Home
Don Edwards with Tom Morrell & Time-Warp Tophands; *Freight Train Blues-Classic Railroad Songs-#4-C* . . . . . (Rounder)
One Way Track
Ricky Skaggs and Kentucky Thunder; *History Of The Future* . . (Skaggs Family)
Only A Hobo
Bob Dylan; *The Bootleg Series-Volumes 1-3 [Rare & Unreleased]* . . (Columbia)
Johnson Mountain Boys; *Blue Diamond* . . . . . (Rounder)
Rod Stewart; *Gasoline Alley* . . . . . (Mercury)
I Shall Be Unreleased-Songs Of Bob Dylan . . . . . (Rhino)
Mercury Anthology . . . . . (Mercury)
Vintage Rod Stewart . . . . . (Mercury)
Orange Blossom Special
Bill Monroe; *Bean Blossom* . . . . . (MCA)
Bill Monroe and His Blue Grass Boys-60 Years Of Country . . . . . (RCA)
Stars Of The Grand Ole Opry-1926-1974-C . . . . . (RCA)
Charlie Daniels Band; *Fire On The Mountain* . . . . . (Epic)
ST/Urban Cowboy 2 . . . . . (Epic)
Flatt & Scruggs; *Hear The Whistles Blow* . . . . . (International Mktg. Group)
Gordon Terry; *Disco Country* . . . . . (Plantation)
Gordon Terry-20 Golden Souvenirs . . . . . (Plantation)
Johnny Cash; *Columbia Records-1958-1986* . . . . . (Columbia)
Essential Johnny Cash . . . . . (Columbia)
Johnny Cash-16 Biggest Hits-#2 . . . . . (Legacy)
Johnny Cash's Greatest Hits . . . . . (Columbia)
The Man In Black-His Greatest Hits . . . . . (Legacy)
Train Trax-C . . . . . (Sony Music Special Prod.)
Johnson Mountain Boys; *Steel Rails-Classic Railroad Songs-#1-C* . . . (Rounder)
Nitty Gritty Dirt Band; *Will The Circle Be Unbroken* . . . . . (EMI)
Outre Risque Locomotive
Neneh Cherry; *Raw Like Sushi* . . . . . (Virgin)
Paddy On The Railway
Barley Bree; *Castles In The Air* . . . . . (Shanachie)
Paddy Works On The Railway
Pete Seeger; *Concert Folk Songs And Ballads* . . . . . (Collectables)
Pan American Boogie
Kate MacKenzie; *Steel Rails-Classic Railroad Songs-#1-C* . . . . . (Rounder)
Papa Hobo
Paul Simon; *Paul Simon* . . . . . (Columbia)
Party Train
Gap Band; *Train Trax-C* . . . . . (Sony Music Special Prod.)
Passenger
Grateful Dead; *Dead Set* . . . . . (Arista)
Terrapin Station . . . . . (Arista)
Passin' Train
Sawyer Brown; *The Boys Are Back* . . . . . (Liberty)
Passing Of The Train
Karen Tobin; *Carolina Smokey Moon* . . . . . (Atlantic)
Peace Train
Cat Stevens; *Cat Stevens Greatest Hits* . . . . . (A&M)
Cat Stevens-Classics-#24 . . . . . (A&M)
Teaser And The Firecat . . . . . (A&M)
People Get Ready
Aretha Franklin; *Aretha-Lady Soul* . . . . . (Atlantic)
Impressions; *Impressions' Greatest Hits* . . . . . (MCA)
Soul Shots-#5-La-La Means I Love You-C . . . . . (Rhino)
Train Trax-C . . . . . (Sony Music Special Prod.)
Jeff Beck; *Flash* . . . . . (Epic)
Rod Stewart; *Storyteller/The Complete Anthology: 1964-1990* . . (Warner Bros.)
Please Take That Train From My Door
Wayne Horvitz; *This New Generation* . . . . . (Elektra)
Poverty Train
Laura Nyro; *Eli And The Thirteenth Confession* . . . . . (Columbia)
Promised Land
Band; *Moondog Matinee* . . . . . (Capitol)
Chuck Berry; *Rock 'N' Roll Rarities-20 Magic Tracks* . . . . . (Chess)
The Chess Box-Chuck Berry . . . . . (Chess)
Elvis Presley; *Promised Land* . . . . . (RCA)
ST/This Is Elvis . . . . . (RCA)
Freddy Weller; *Country Music Classics-#11-Early '70s-C* . . . . . (K-Tel)
Freddy Weller's Greatest Hits . . . . . (Columbia)
Gary Morris; *Full Moon Empty Heart* . . . . . (Liberty)
Grateful Dead; *Steal Your Face* . . . . . (Grateful Dead)
James Taylor; *Walking Man* . . . . . (Warner Bros.)
Kingfish; *Kingfish/Alive In Eighty Five-Double Dose* . . . . . (Relix)
Put Me On A Train Back To Texas
Waylon Jennings & Willie Nelson; *Clean Shirt* . . . . . (Epic)
Hot Tracks-Train Super Hits-C . . . . . (Epic)
Railroad
Grand Funk Railroad; *Caught In The Act* . . . . . (Capitol)
We're An American Band . . . . . (Capitol)
Railroad Bill
Etta Baker; *One-Dime Blues* . . . . . (Rounder)
Ramblin' Jack Elliott; *Hard Travelin'* . . . . . (Fantasy)
Ramblin' Jack Elliott . . . . . (Prestige)
Railroad Blues
New Lost City Ramblers; *New Lost City Ramblers-Early Years-1958-1962* . . . . . (Smithsonian Folkways)
Norman Blake; *Blackberry Blossom* . . . . . (Flying Fish)
Railroad Boy
Joan Baez; *Ballad Book-#2* . . . . . (Vanguard)
Joan Baez, Vol. 2 . . . . . (Vanguard)
Very Best Of Joan Baez . . . . . (Vanguard)
Railroad Corral
Don Edwards; *Between The Rails: America's Train Songs-C* . . . . . (Crescendo)
Railroad Days
Poco; *From The Inside* . . . . . (Epic)
Train Trax-C . . . . . (Sony Music Special Prod.)
Very Best Of Poco . . . . . (Epic)
Railroad Lady
J.D. Crowe and the New South; *My Home Ain't In The Hall Of Fame* . . . . . (Rounder)
Jerry Jeff Walker; *A Man Must Carry On* . . . . . (MCA)
Gypsy Songman . . . . . (Rykodisc)
Jimmy Buffett; *White Sport Coat & A Pink Crustacean* . . . . . (MCA)
Willie Nelson; *Greatest Hits (& Some That Will Be)* . . . . . (Columbia)
To Lefty From Willie . . . . . (Columbia)
Railroad Song
Lynyrd Skynyrd; *Nuthin' Fancy* . . . . . (MCA)
Railroad Steel
Georgia Satellites; *Georgia Satellites* . . . . . (Elektra)
Rainy Night In Georgia
Brook Benton; *Atlantic Rhythm & Blues 1947-1974-#6 (1966-1969)-C* . . . . . (Atlantic)
Brook Benton Today . . . . . (Cotillion)
Brook Benton-Anthology . . . . . (Rhino)
Golden Age Of Black Music-1960-1970-C . . . . . (Atlantic)
Pick Of Brook Benton . . . . . (Fifty One West)
Soul Years-C . . . . . (Atlantic)
Hank Williams, Jr.; *Hank Williams, Jr.-14 Greatest Hits* . . . . . (Polydor)
Sam Moore & Conway Twitty; *Rhythm Country And Blues-C* . . . . . (MCA)
Raised By The Railroad Line
Chris LeDoux; *Sounds Of The Western Country* . . . . . (Liberty)
Ramblin' Hobo
Doc Watson; *Don Watson & Family-Treasures Untold* . . . . . (Vanguard)
Essential Doc Watson . . . . . (Vanguard)
Old Time Music At Newport . . . . . (Vanguard)
Watson Family; *Watson Family* . . . . . (Smithsonian Folkways)
Ramblin' Jack (A Lonesome Hobo)
Skip Gorman; *A Cowboy's Wild Song To His Herd* . . . . . (Rounder)
Ramblin' Man
Hank Williams; *24 Of Hank Williams' Greatest Hits* . . . . . (Polydor)
Hank Williams-16 Great Hits . . . . . (Everest)
Hank Williams-40 Greatest Hits . . . . . (Polydor)
Hank Williams, Jr.; *Rowdy* . . . . . (WB/Curb)
ST/Your Cheatin' Heart . . . . . (Sony Music Special Prod.)
Kieran Kane; *Steel Rails-Classic Railroad Songs-#1-C* . . . . . (Rounder)
Red Streamliner
Little Feat; *Hoy-Hoy!* . . . . . (Warner Bros.)
Time Loves A Hero . . . . . (Warner Bros.)
Redemption Day
Sheryl Crow; *Sheryl Crow* . . . . . (A&M)
Reuben's Train
Doc Watson & Family; *Treasures Untold-C* . . . . . (Vanguard)
Ride The Train
Alabama; *Feels So Right* . . . . . (RCA)
Ridin' On The Gravy Train
Nat "King" Cole; *Jazz Encounters* . . . . . (Blue Note)
Ridin' That Midnight Train
Ricky Skaggs and Kentucky Thunder; *Bluegrass Rules!* . . . . . (Rounder)
Ridin' The L&N
Bluegrass Cardinals; *Welcome To Virginia* . . . . . (Rounder)
Riding On A Railroad
James Taylor; *Mud Slide Slim And The Blue Horizon* . . . . . (Warner Bros.)
Riding That Midnight Train
Doc Watson; *Riding That Midnight Train* . . . . . (Sugar Hill)
Rock Island
Soundtrack; *ST/The Music Man* . . . . . (Warner Bros.)
Rock Island Line
Johnny Cash; *Johnny Cash-Sun Years* . . . . . (Rhino)
Story Songs Of The Trains & Rivers . . . . . (Sun)
Vintage Years-1955-1963 . . . . . (Rhino)
Sonny Terry & Brownie McGhee; *Hootin'* . . . . . (Muse)
Jazz Heritage . . . . . (MCA)
Weavers; *Best Of The Weavers* . . . . . (MCA)
Weavers At Carnegie Hall . . . . . (Vanguard)
Weavers' Greatest Hits . . . . . (Vanguard)
Rock Island Rocket
Tom Scott; *Best Of Tom Scott* . . . . . (Columbia)
Tom Scott & The L.A. Express; *Tom Cat* . . . . . (Epic Ode)
Rockin' Train
Joe Perry Project; *Let The Music Do The Talking* . . . . . (Columbia)

Rollin' In My Sweet Baby's Arms
Bill Monroe; *Bean Blossom* . . . . (MCA)
Del McCoury Band; *Appalachian Stomp: Bluegrass Classics-C* . . . . (Rhino)
Dillard & Clark; *Fantastic Expedition/Through The
    Morning* . . . . (Mobile Fidelity Sound Lab)
Flatt & Scruggs; *Flatt & Scruggs At Carnegie Hall!* . . . . . . (Koch International)
    Flatt & Scruggs-20 Greatest Hits . . . . (Deluxe)
Flying Burrito Brothers; *Close Encounters To The West Coast* . . . . (Relix)
Leon Russell; *Hank Wilson's Back, Vol. 1* . . . . (Right Stuff)
New Lost City Ramblers; *Greatest Folksingers Of The '60s-C* . . . . (Vanguard)
Ramblin' Jack Elliott; *Hard Travelin'* . . . . (Fantasy)
Ricky Skaggs and Kentucky Thunder; *History Of The Future* . . (Skaggs Family)
Tony Trischka; *Heartlands* . . . . (Rounder)
Willie Nelson; *Willie & Family Live* . . . . (Columbia)
Rude Boy Train
Desmond Dekker & The Aces; *Rockin' Steady-Best Of Desmond Dekker &
    The Aces* . . . . (Rhino)
Runaway Train
Soul Asylum; *Grave Dancers Union* . . . . (Columbia)
Runaway Train
Elton John featuring Eric Clapton; *The One* . . . .(MCA)
Runaway Train
Rosanne Cash; *Greatest Country Hits Of The '80s-1988-C* . . . . (Columbia)
    Hot Tracks-Train Super Hits-C . . . . (Epic)
    King's Record Shop . . . . (Columbia)
    Rosanne Cash-Retrospective . . . . (Columbia)
Runaway Train
Dawn Sears; *Nothin' But Good* . . . . (Decca)
Runaway Train
John Stewart; *Punch The Big Guy* . . . . (Cypress)
Runaway Trains
Tom Petty And The Heartbreakers; *Let Me Up (I've Had Enough)* . . . . . .(MCA)
Saint Agnes & The Burning Train
Sting; *Soul Cages* . . . . (A&M)
San Francisco Treat, The (Rice-A-Roni)
Original Soundtrack; *TeeVee Toons-The Commercials-#1-C* . . . . (TVT)
Sentimental Journey
Dinah Shore; *Sentimental Journey: Capitol's Great Ladies Of
    Song-C* . . . . (Gold Rush)
Doris Day; *Doris Day Sings 22 Great Songs-Original Big Band* . . . . (Hindsight)
Hal McIntyre & His Orchestra; *Nipper's Greatest Hits Of The
    '40s-#2-C* . . . . (RCA)
Les Brown & His Orchestra; *Best Of The Big Bands-C* . . . . (Columbia)
Silver Ghost, The
Merle Haggard & The Strangers; *Train Whistle Blues* . . . . (Rounder)
Silver Train
Johnny Winter; *Still Alive & Well* . . . . (Columbia)
Rolling Stones; *Goats Head Soup* . . . .(Rolling Stones)
Sittin' On Top Of The World
Bob Dylan; *Good As I Been To You* . . . . (Columbia)
Bob Wills & His Texas Playboys; *Bob Wills & His Texas Playboys-24
    Great Hits* . . . . (Polydor)
    Bob Wills-Anthology . . . . (Sony Music Special Prod.)
    Tiffany Transcriptions-#8-More Of The Best . . . . (Rhino)
Cream; *Wheels Of Fire* . . . . (Polydor)
Doc Watson; *Doc Watson* . . . . (Vanguard)
    Greatest Folksingers Of The '60s-C . . . . (Vanguard)
    Old Timey Concert . . . . (Vanguard)
Grateful Dead; *Grateful Dead (Skull & Roses)* . . . .(Warner Bros.)
Jerry Jeff Walker; *Will The Circle Be Unbroken-#2-C* . . . . (Uni)
Ray Charles; *20 Golden Pieces Of Ray Charles* . . . . (Bulldog)
Sweet Honey In The Rock; *Believe I'll Run On, See What The End's
    Gonna Be* . . . . (Redwood)
Six O'Clock Train & A Girl With Green Eyes
John Hartford; *All In The Name Of Love* . . . . (Flying Fish)
Slow Moving Freight Train
Hugh Moffatt; *Steel Rails-Classic Railroad Songs-#1-C* . . . . (Rounder)
Slow Train
Bob Dylan; *Slow Train Coming* . . . . (Columbia)
Bob Dylan & The Grateful Dead; *Dylan & The Dead.* . . . . (Columbia)
Slow Train Through Georgia
Norman Blake; *Whiskey Before Breakfast* . . . . (Rounder)
Slow Train To Dawn
The The & Neneh Cherry; *Infected.* . . . . (Epic)
Slow Train To Memphis
Jim Horn; *Work It Out.* . . . .(Warner Bros.)
Smokestack Lightning
George Thorogood & The Destroyers; *Born To Be Bad* . . . . (Gold Rush)
Grateful Dead; *History Of The Grateful Dead-Vol. 1 (Bear's
    Choice)* . . . .(Warner Bros.)
Howlin' Wolf; *Best Of Chess Blues-C* . . . . (Chess)
    Between The Rails: America's Train Songs-C . . . .(Crescendo)
    Blues-#1-C . . . . (Chess)
    Moanin' In The Moonlight . . . . (Chess)
Lynyrd Skynyrd; *1991* . . . . (Atlantic)
Muddy Waters; *The Chess Box-Muddy Waters* . . . . (Chess)
Soundgarden; *Ultramega OK* . . . . (SST)
Yardbirds; *Five Live Yardbirds* . . . . (Rhino)
    For Your Love . . . . (Accord)
    Yardbirds' Greatest Hits-#1 (1964-1966) . . . . (Rhino)
Southbound Train
Julie Gold; *When October Goes: Autumn Love Songs-C* . . . . (Philo)
Nanci Griffith; *Flyer* . . . . (Elektra)
Standin' At The Station
Keb' Mo'; *Just Like You* . . . . (Okeh)
Station Man
Fleetwood Mac; *25 Years-The Chain* . . . . (Warner Bros.)
    Kiln House . . . . (Reprise)
Steel Rails
Alison Krauss; *Steel Rails-Classic Railroad Songs-#1-C* . . . . (Rounder)
Stop That Train
Bob Marley & The Wailers; *Catch A Fire* . . . .(Tuff Gong)
Jerry Garcia Band; *Jerry Garcia Band* . . . . (Arista)
Peter Tosh; *Mama Africa* . . . . (EMI)
Streamlined Cannonball
Limeliters; *Alive! In Concert-#1* . . . .(Crescendo)
Roy Acuff; *Columbia Historic Edition-Roy Acuff.* . . . . (Columbia)
Subway
Alex DeGrassi; *Southern Exposure* . . . .(Windham Hill)
Subway
Vic Juris; *Bleecker Street* . . . .(Muse)
Subway
Quicksilver Messenger Service; *Sons Of Mercury* . . . . (Rhino)
Subway Heart
Massacre; *Killing Time* . . . .(Celluloid)
Subway Love
Gary Windo; *Deep Water* . . . .(Antilles)
Subway Ride
Peter Hofmann/Debbie Sasson/Michael Tilson Thomas; *Bernstein On
    Broadway* . . . . (Columbia)
Subway Ride
Sheryl Crow; *The Globe Sessions* . . . . (A&M)
Subway Rider
Pablo Moses; *In The Future* . . . .(Alligator)
Subway Song
Cure; *Boys Don't Cry* . . . . (Elektra)
Subway To Venus
Red Hot Chili Peppers; *Mother's Milk* . . . . (EMI)
Subway Train
New York Dolls; *New York Dolls* . . . . (Mercury)
    Night Of The Living Dolls. . . . . (Mercury)
Take The "A" Train
Bobby McFerrin; *The Voice* . . . . (Elektra)
Dave Brubeck Quartet; *Jazz Goes To College* . . . . (Columbia)
Duke Ellington; *20 Golden Pieces Of Duke Ellington.* . . . .(Bulldog)
    Greatest Jazz Concert In The World. . . . . (Pablo)
    Sophisticated Lady . . . . (Bluebird)
Duke Ellington & Betty Roche; *Uptown* . . . . (Columbia)
Duke Ellington & Billy Strayhorn; *Great Times* . . . . (Riverside)
Duke Ellington & Count Basie Orchestra; *First Time!-Count Meets
    The Duke* . . . . (Columbia)
Glenn Miller; *Best Of Glenn Miller-#2* . . . .(RCA)
    Glenn Miller-A Legendary Performer-#1 & 2 . . . . (Bluebird)
Glenn Miller & His Orchestra; *Complete Glenn Miller & His
    Orchestra-#6* . . . . (Bluebird)
Harry James; *Golden Trumpet Of Harry James* . . . . (London)
Mel Torme; *Duke Ellington & Count Basie Songbook* . . . . (Verve)
Sarah Vaughan; *Jazz Club-Vocal* . . . . (Verve)
Tamp 'Em Up Solid
Ry Cooder; *Paradise And Lunch.* . . . . (Reprise)
Tennessee Choo Choo
Delmore Brothers; *Best Of The Delmore Brothers* . . . . (Starday)
Terrapin Station
Grateful Dead; *Terrapin Station* . . . . (Arista)
That Same Old Train
Blind Snooks Eaglin; *Legacy Of The Blues-#2* . . . .(Crescendo)
That Train Don't Stop Here
Los Lobos; *Kiko* . . . .(Slash)
That Train Don't Stop Here Anymore
Mike Henderson; *Country Music Made Me Do It* . . . .(RCA)
Theme From "Petticoat Junction"
Flatt & Scruggs; *20 All-Time Great Recordings* . . . . (Columbia)
Original Soundtrack; *Television's Greatest Hits-#1-C* . . . . (TVT)
    TV Theme Sing-Along Album . . . . (Rhino)
This Train
Big Bill Broonzy; *Big Bill Broonzy Sings Folk Songs* . . .(Smithsonian Folkways)
Peter, Paul & Mary; *Peter, Paul and Mary* . . . . (Warner Bros.)
This Train
Bob Marley & The Wailers; *One Love* . . . . (Heartbeat)
This Train
John Hammond; *John Hammond* . . . . (Vanguard)
This Train
Bunny Wailer; *Blackheart Man.* . . . . (Island)
This Train
Kingston Trio; *American Troubadours.* . . . . (Pair)
This Train Is Bound For Glory
Arlo Guthrie; *Tribute To Woody Guthrie-C* . . . . (Warner Bros.)

This Train Revised
Indigo Girls; *Swamp Ophelia* . . . . (Epic)
Took The Last Train
David Gates; *Goodbye Girl* . . . . (Elektra)
Track Walkin'
Billy Strange; *Between The Rails: America's Train Songs-C* . . . . . . (Crescendo)
Train
Tommy Bolin; *The Ultimate Tommy Bolin* . . . . (Geffen)
Train
Mose Allison; *Back Country Suite* . . . . (Prestige)
Train
1910 Fruitgum Company; *Bubblegum's Greatest Hits-#1-C* . . . . (Accord)
Train
Leo Sayer; *Just A Boy* . . . . (Out Of Print)
Train
Bobby McFerrin; *Medicine Music* . . . . (EMI)
Train
Graham Central Station; *Now Do You U Wanta Dance* . . . . (Warner Bros.)
Train
Roches; *Roches* . . . . (Warner Bros.)
Train & The River
Jimmy Giuffre; *Jimmy Giuffre Three* . . . . (Atlantic)
Train 45
Bill Monroe; *Bean Blossom* . . . . (MCA)
Mac Wiseman; *Great American Train Songs-C* . . . . (C.M.H. Prod.)
Train 45 & A Half
Mike Auldridge; *Critic's Choice-C* . . . . (Takoma)
Dobro/Blues & Bluegrass . . . . (Takoma)
Dobro/Blues & Bluegrass . . . . (Takoma)
Train For Auschwitz
Tom Paxton; *Best Of Broadside 1962-1968: Anthems Of The American
Underground From The Pages Of Broadside
Magazine-C* . . . . (Smithsonian Folkways)
Train From Kansas City
Shangri-Las; *Golden Hits Of The Shangri-Las* . . . . (Mercury)
Train Goin' Nowhere
Steven Beasley; *Between The Rails: America's Train Songs-C.* . . . . . (Crescendo)
Train I Ride
Junior Wells; *Train Trax-C* . . . . (Sony Music Special Prod.)
Train In The Distance
Paul Simon; *Concert In The Park-August 15 1991* . . . . (Warner Bros.)
Hearts & Bones . . . . (Warner Bros.)
Negotiations And Love Songs, 1971-1986 . . . . (Warner Bros.)
Train In Vain
Clash; *London Calling* . . . . (Epic)
On Broadway . . . . (Epic)
The Story Of The Clash, Volume 1 . . . . (Epic)
Train Kept A Rollin'
Aerosmith; *Aerosmith-Classics Live* . . . . (Columbia)
Get Your Wings . . . . (Columbia)
Live Bootleg . . . . (Columbia)
Pandora's Box . . . . (Columbia)
Johnny Burnette & The Rock & Roll Trio; *Between The Rails: America's
Train Songs-C* . . . . (Crescendo)
Tiny Bradshaw; *Blues Masters-#5-Jump Blues Classics-C.* . . . . (Rhino)
Yardbirds; *Legends Of Rock Guitar-'60s-#1-C* . . . . (Rhino)
Yardbirds' Greatest Hits-#1 (1964-1966) . . . . (Rhino)
Train Leaves Here This Morning
Eagles; *Eagles* . . . . (Asylum)
Train Man
Bob Seger System; *Ramblin' Gamblin' Man* . . . . (Capitol)
Train Medley
Boxcar Willie; *45-#954* . . . . (Mainstreet)
Train No. 1262
Flatt & Scruggs; *Hear The Whistles Blow* . . . . (International Mktg. Group)
Train Of Gold
Electric Light Orchestra; *Secret Messages* . . . . (Jet)
Train Of Love
Johnny Cash; *Johnny Cash-Legend* . . . . (Sun)
Johnny Cash-Original Golden Hits-#1 . . . . (Sun)
Johnny Cash-Sun Years . . . . (Rhino)
Superbilly . . . . (Sun)
Trucks,Trains & Airplanes-C . . . . (International Mktg. Group)
Train Of Love
Neil Young; *Sleeps With Angels* . . . . (Reprise)
Train Of Memories
Kathy Mattea; *14 Country Favorites-C* . . . . (Mercury)
Collection Of Hits . . . . (Mercury)
Walk The Way The Wind Blows . . . . (Mercury)
Train Running Low On Soul Coal
XTC; *Big Express* . . . . (Geffen)
Train Song
Tom Waits; *Big Time* . . . . (Island)
Frank's Wild Years-Un Operachi Romantico . . . . (Island)
Train Song
Holly Near; *Watch Out* . . . . (Redwood)
Train That Carried My Girl From Town, The
Doc Watson; *Essential Doc Watson* . . . . (Vanguard)

Watson Family; *Watson Family* . . . . (Smithsonian Folkways)
Train To Birmingham
Kevin Welch & The Overtones; *Western Beat* . . . . (Reprise)
Train To Bombay
Christopher Max; *More Than Physical* . . . . (EMI)
Train To Johannesburg
Original Cast; *Lost In The Stars* . . . . (MCA)
Train To Nowhere
Rare Earth; *Get Ready* . . . . (Motown)
Train To Rhodesia
Big Youth; *Dreadlocks Dread* . . . . (Front Line)
Train Whistle Blues
Jimmie Rodgers; *Between The Rails: America's Train Songs-C* . . . . (Crescendo)
Merle Haggard & The Strangers; *Train Whistle Blues* . . . . (Rounder)
Train Wreck On Prom Night
Pajama Slave Dancers; *Blood Sweat & Beers* . . . . (Restless)
Train, Train
Blackfoot; *Legends Of Rock Guitar-'70s-C* . . . . (Rhino)
Strikes . . . . (Atco)
Warrant; *Cherry Pie* . . . . (Columbia)
Trains & Boats & Planes
Billy J. Kramer With The Dakotas; *Billy J. Kramer With The Dakotas-The
Definitive Collection* . . . . (EMI)
History Of British Rock-#4-C . . . . (Rhino)
Dionne Warwick; *Dionne Warwick* . . . . (Everest)
Dionne Warwick Greatest Hits . . . . (Everest)
Dionne Warwick-Anthology 1962-1971 . . . . (Rhino)
Hot! Live & Otherwise . . . . (Arista)
Trains Don't Run From Nashville
Kate Campbell; *Freight Train Blues-Classic Railroad Songs-#4-C* . . . (Rounder)
Trains/Leavin' Tennessee
Tasty Licks; *Tasty Licks* . . . . (Rounder)
Traintime
Cream; *Wheels Of Fire* . . . . (Polydor)
Trainwreck Of Emotion
Lorrie Morgan; *Essential Lorrie Morgan* . . . . (RCA)
Leave The Light On . . . . (RCA)
To Get To You-Greatest Hits Collection . . . . (BNA)
Trainwreck Of Emotion
Del McCoury Band; *Steel Rails-Classic Railroad Songs-#1-C* . . . . . . (Rounder)
Trash Train
Band Of Susans; *Band Of Susans Now* . . . . (Restless)
Trolley Song
Judy Garland; *Best Of Judy Garland* . . . . (MCA)
Judy Garland's All-Time Greatest Hits . . . . (Curb)
Original Broadway Cast; *Meet Me In St. Louis* . . . . (DRG)
Trouble In Mind
Bob Wills; *Stay A Little Longer-The Original Columbia
Recordings* . . . . (Roswell/RCA)
Trouble's Comin' Like A Train
Mark Collie; *Mark Collie* . . . . (MCA)
Two Moose In A Caboose
Stan Kenton & His Orchestra; *The Uncollected Stan Kenton & His
Orchestra-#5-1945-1947* . . . . (Hindsight)
Two Trains
Little Feat; *Dixie Chicken* . . . . (Warner Bros.)
Hoy-Hoy! . . . . (Warner Bros.)
Lowell George; *Thanks I'll Eat It Here* . . . . (Warner Bros.)
Two Trains Running
Blues Project; *No Time Like The Right Time-Best Of The Blues
Project* . . . . (Rhino)
Projections . . . . (Polydor)
Paul Butterfield Blues Band; *East-West* . . . . (Elektra)
Under The Subway
No Face; *Wake Your Daughter Up* . . . . (RAL/Columbia)
Wabash Cannonball
Billy Strange; *Between The Rails: America's Train Songs-C* . . . . . . (Crescendo)
Nitty Gritty Dirt Band; *Will The Circle Be Unbroken* . . . . (EMI)
Roy Acuff; *All Time Legends Of Country Music-C* . . . . (Legacy)
Backstage At The Grand Ole Opry-C . . . . (RCA)
Best Of Roy Acuff. . . . . (Liberty)
Columbia Historic Edition-Roy Acuff . . . . (Columbia)
Essential Roy Acuff-1936-1949 . . . . (Legacy)
Hot Tracks-Train Super Hits-C . . . . (Epic)
Roy Acuff's Greatest Hits . . . . (Columbia)
Steel Rails-Classic Railroad Songs-#1-C . . . . (Rounder)
Waitin' For A Train
Merle Haggard & The Strangers; *Train Whistle Blues* . . . . (Rounder)
Waiting For A Train
Jimmie Rodgers; *Jimmie Rodgers-Early Years-1928-1929* . . . . (Rounder)
This Is Jimmie Rodgers . . . . (RCA)
Waiting For A Train
Boz Scaggs; *Boz Scaggs.* . . . . (Atlantic)
Walkin' Down The Road
Ozark Mountain Daredevils; *Best Of The Ozark Mountain Daredevils* . . (A&M)
It'll Shine When It Shines . . . . (A&M)
It's Alive . . . . (A&M)
Watching Me Watching You
Jethro Tull; *The Broadsword And The Beast* . . . . (Chrysalis)

Wayward Wind
Gogi Grant; *'50s Jukebox Favorites-C* . . . . (K-Tel)
Collectables Presents The History Of Rock-#7-C . . . . (Collectables)
Lynn Anderson & Emmylou Harris; *Cowboy's Sweetheart* . . . . . (Laserlight)
Patsy Cline; *The Patsy Cline Story* . . . .(MCA)

When The Golden Train Comes Down
Sons Of The Pioneers; *Columbia Historic Edition-Sons Of The
Pioneers* . . . . (Columbia)
Steel Rails-Classic Railroad Songs-#1-C . . . . (Rounder)

When The Midnight Choo Choo Leaves For Alabam'
Andrews Sisters; *Best Of The Andrews Sisters-#2* . . . .(MCA)
Judy Garland & Fred Astaire; *ST/Easter Parade* . . . . (Rhino)

When The Train Comes Along
Uncle Dave Macon; *Grand Ole Opry-75 Years-#2-C*. . . . .(MCA)

Whiskey Train
Procol Harum; *Best Of Procol Harum* . . . . (A&M)
Home . . . . (A&M)
Procol Harum-Classics-#17 . . . . (A&M)
Procol Harum's Greatest Hits . . . . (A&M)

White Man Singin' The Blues
Merle Haggard & The Strangers; *Train Whistle Blues* . . . . (Rounder)

Wreck Of The Old '97
Johnny Cash; *Johnny Cash At Folsom Prison & San Quentin* . . . . . . (Columbia)
Johnny Cash-Original Golden Hits-#3 . . . . (Sun)
Story Songs Of The Trains & Rivers . . . . (Sun)
Superbilly . . . . (Sun)
The Man-The World-His Music . . . . (Sun)

Yesterday's Train
Byrds; *The Byrds (Untitled)* . . . . (Legacy)

Yodeling Hobo
Gene Autry; *Gene Autry: Blues Singer-1929-1933* . . . . (Legacy)

Zing! Went The Strings Of My Heart
Coasters; *Coasters' Greatest Hits* . . . . (Atco)
Rare Soul-Beach Music Classics-#1-C . . . . (Rhino)
Frank Sinatra; *The Reprise Collection* . . . . (Reprise)
Judy Garland; *Best Of Judy Garland* . . . .(MCA)
Best Of The Decca Years-#1-Hits!-C . . . . (Decca)
Judy Garland-At Carnegie Hall . . . . (Capitol)
Judy Garland's All-Time Greatest Hits . . . . (Curb)

TRASH, Garbage, Junk, Waste, Wasting Time

See Also: CLEAN, DIRT

(Our Love) Don't Throw It All Away
Bee Gees; *Bee Gees' Greatest* . . . . (Polydor)

Ain't It The Life
Foo Fighters; *There Is Nothing Left To Lose* . . . . (Roswell/RCA)

Alice's Restaurant Massacree
Arlo Guthrie; *Alice's Restaurant* . . . . (Reprise)
Best Of Arlo Guthrie . . . .(Warner Bros.)

Atomic Waste
Peter Alsop; *Draw The Line* . . . . (Flying Fish)

Before The Trash Truck Comes
Bob Frank; *Bob Frank* . . . . (Vanguard)

Big Jesus Trash Can
Birthday Party; *Best & Rarest*. . . . .(Missing Link)
Birthday Party-Collection . . . .(Missing Link)

Big Trash
Thompson Twins; *Big Trash* . . . .(Red Eye)

Birdman Of Alkatrash
Strawberry Alarm Clock; *Strawberry Alarm Clock-Anthology* . . . . . .(One Way)

Cash For Your Trash
Original Cast; *Ain't Misbehavin'* . . . . (RCA)

Cosmik Debris
Frank Zappa; *Apostrophe/Overnite Sensation* . . . .(Rykodisc)
You Can't Do That On Stage Anymore-#3 . . . .(Rykodisc)

Crotch Deep Trash
Soup Dragons; *Lovegod* . . . .(Big Life)

Cupid's Trash Truck
Lou & Peter Berryman; *Cupid's Trash Truck*. . . . . (Cornbelt)

Don't Pick It Up
Offspring; *Ixnay On The Hombre* . . . . (Columbia)

Don't Throw Your Life Away
Vickie Winans; *The Lady* . . . .(MCA)

Don't Throw Your Love Away
Searchers; *History Of British Rock-#2-C* . . . . (Rhino)
Searchers' Greatest Hits . . . . (Rhino)

Don't Toss Us Away
Lone Justice; *Lone Justice* . . . . (Geffen Goldline)
This World Is Not My Home . . . .(Geffen)
Patty Loveless; *Honky Tonk Angel* . . . .(MCA)
Patty Loveless' Greatest Hits . . . .(MCA)

Down In The Sewer
Stranglers; *All Live & All Of The Night* . . . .(Epic)

Elegantly Wasted
INXS; *Elegantly Wasted*. . . . . (Mercury)

Euro-Trash Girl
Cracker; *Kerosene Hat* . . . .(Virgin)

Fresh Garbage
Spirit; *Best Of Spirit* . . . . (Epic)
Spirit . . . . (Epic)
Time Circle . . . . (Epic)

Garbage
Guy Carawan; *Songs Of Struggle & Celebration* . . . .(Flying Fish)

Garbage Man
Cramps; *Bad Music For Bad People* . . . . (I.R.S.)
Songs The Lord Taught Us . . . . (I.R.S.)
Muddy Waters; *Can't Get No Grindin'* . . . . (Chess)

I Sold My Heart To The Junkman
Blue-Belles; *Super Oldies Of The '60s-#3-C* . . . . (Audio Fidelity)
Carmen McRae; *Sound Of Silence* . . . .(Atlantic)

I Threw Away The Rose
George Jones; *20 Golden Pieces Of George Jones* . . . .(Bulldog)
Hank Williams, Jr.; *Living Proof-MGM Recordings 1963-1975*. . . . . (Mercury)
Lorrie Morgan; *Mama's Hungry Eyes-Merle Haggard Tribute-C* . . . . . (Arista)
Merle Haggard; *Merle Haggard-Best Of The Early Years* . . . . (Curb)

I Threw It All Away
Bob Dylan; *Hard Rain*. . . . .(Columbia)
Nashville Skyline . . . . (Columbia)

I Threw It All Away
Elvis Costello; *Kojak Variety* . . . . (Warner Bros.)

Junk
Paul McCartney; *McCartney*. . . . . (Capitol)
Paul McCartney-Gift Set . . . . (Capitol)

Junk Cars
Mac McAnally; *Live & Learn* . . . . (MCA)

Junk Culture
Orchestral Manoeuvres In The Dark; *Junk Culture* . . . . (A&M)

Junk Mail
Circle Jerks; *Gig* . . . . (Relativity)
Golden Shower Of Hits . . . .(Avenue)

Junk Male
Five Thirty; *Bed* . . . . (Atco)

Last Worthless Evening
Don Henley; *End Of The Innocence* . . . . (Geffen)

Let's Lock The Door (And Throw Away The Key)
Jay & The Americans; *Jay & The Americans' All-Time Greatest Hits* . . . (Rhino)

My Life (Throw It Away If I Want To)
Bill Anderson; *Best Of Bill Anderson* . . . . (Curb)

My Sweet Hunk O' Trash
Louis Armstrong; *Jazz Heritage-Louis With Guest Stars-C* . . . . (MCA)

No Trash In My Trailer
Gene Watson; *From The Heart* . . . . (Row Music Group)

Nuclear Waste
Tuff Darts; *Tuff Darts* . . . .(Sire)

One Man's Trash
John McCutcheon; *What's It Like* . . . . (Rounder)

Paper In Fire
John Cougar Mellencamp; *The Lonesome Jubilee* . . . . (Mercury)
John Mellencamp; *Best That I Could Do-1978-1988* . . . . (Mercury)

Piece Of Crap
Neil Young & Crazy Horse; *Sleeps With Angels* . . . .(Reprise)

Please Mr. Junkman
Penguins; *Oldies-C* . . . . (Dooto)

Po' White Trash
White Trash; *White Trash* . . . . (Elektra)

Put Me In The Trash
Mick Jagger; *Wandering Spirit* . . . .(Atlantic)

Sarah Cynthia Sylvia Stout
Shel Silverstein; *Dr. Demento Presents The Greatest Novelty Records-#4-
1970s-C* . . . . (Rhino)
Dr. Demento: 20th Anniversary Collection-C . . . . (Rhino)
Where The Sidewalk Ends . . . . (Columbia)

Sewer Pipe Dream
Close Lobsters; *Foxheads Stalk This Land* . . . . (Enigma)

She's A River
Simple Minds; *Good News From The Next World* . . . . (Virgin)

Singalong Junk
Paul McCartney; *McCartney*. . . . . (Capitol)
Paul McCartney-Gift Set . . . . (Capitol)

Space Junk
Devo; *EZ Listening Disc* . . . .(Rykodisc)
Q: Are We Not Men? A: We Are Devo! . . . . (Warner Bros.)

Stay (Wasting Time)
Dave Matthews Band; *Before These Crowded Streets* . . . .(RCA)

Stray Cat Strut
Stray Cats; *Best Of Stray Cats-Rock This Town* . . . . (EMI)
Built For Speed. . . . . (EMI)
Rock The First-#4-C . . . . (Sandstone Music)

Take It Back
Cream; *Disraeli Gears* . . . . (Polydor)

Take Out The Garbage
Fowler Brothers; *Hunter* . . . . (Fossil)

Talkin' Trash
Tom Principato; *Smokin'* . . . . (Powerhouse)
Talkin' Trash
Chico Freeman; *Tradition In Transition* . . . . (Elektra)
That's Cool, That's Trash
Kingsmen; *Best Of The Kingsmen* . . . . (Rhino)
Theme From "Sanford & Son"
Original Soundtrack; *Television's Greatest Hits-#3-1970s & 1980s-C* . . . . (TVT)
Throw It Away
Joe Jackson; *Look Sharp!* . . . . (A&M)
Throw That Beat In The Garbage Can
B-52's; *Mesopotamia* . . . . (Warner Bros.)
Throw The Roses Away
Daryl Hall & John Oates; *Marigold Sky* . . . . (Push)
Throwaway
Mick Jagger; *Primitive Cool* . . . . (Columbia)
Throwing It All Away
Genesis; *Invisible Touch* . . . . (Atlantic)
Live/The Way We Walk-Volume One: The Shorts . . . . (Atlantic)
Total Trash
Sonic Youth; *Daydream Nation* . . . . (Blast First)
Trash
New York Dolls; *Live In NYC-1975* . . . . (Restless)
New York Dolls . . . . (Mercury)
Trash
Korn; *Issues* . . . . (Immortal/Epic)
Trash
Bobs; *Bobs* . . . . (Kaleidoscope)
Trash
Berlin; *Count Three & Pray* . . . . (Geffen)
Trash
Roxy Music; *Manifesto* . . . . (Atco)
Trash
Mondo Rock; *Mondo Rock Chemistry* . . . . (Atlantic)
Trash
Alice Cooper; *Trash* . . . . (Epic)
Trash Can Charlie
Billy Goat; *Bush Roaming Mammals* . . . . (Third Rail)
Trash Can City
Bob Florence; *Jewels* . . . . (Discovery)
Trash Can King
Nick Seeger; *Sail On Flying Dutchman* . . . . (Biograph)
Trash City
Kik Tracee; *No Rules* . . . . (RCA)
Trash Man
Jimi Hendrix; *Midnight Lightning* . . . . (Reprise)
Trash Park
T. Lavitz & Bad Habitz; *T. Lavitz & Bad Habitz* . . . . (Intima)
Trash Planet
Stewart & Gaskin; *Spin* . . . . (Rykodisc)
Trash Talkin'
Albert Collins; *Albert Collins-Complete Imperial Recordings* . . . . . . (EMI)
Trash Train
Band Of Susans; *Band Of Susans Now* . . . . (Restless)
Trash Truck
Tad; *8-Way Santa* . . . . (Sub Pop)
Trashcan Oil Drum
Pussy Galore; *Right Now!* . . . . (Caroline)
Trashed
Black Sabbath; *Born Again* . . . . (Warner Bros.)
Trashing All The Loves Of History
Snakefinger; *Greener Postures* . . . . (Ralph)
Trashmen
Phantom Opera; *Phantom Opera* . . . . (New Allegiance)
Trashpickin'
Ben Vaughn; *Blows Your Mind* . . . . (Restless)
Trashy Dog
Steve Cropper/Albert King/Pops Staples; *Jammed Together* . . . . (Stax)
Trashy Lady
Neon Judgement; *Horny As Hell* . . . . (Play It Again Sam)
Trashy Women
Confederate Railroad; *Confederate Railroad* . . . . (Atlantic)
Wash It Away
Black Lab; *Your Body Above Me* . . . . (David Geffen Co.)
Wasted Days And Wasted Nights
Freddy Fender; *Before The Next Teardrop Falls* . . . . (Universal)
Best Of Freddy Fender . . . . (MCA)
Country Comes To Carnegie Hall-C . . . . (MCA)
Happy Trails . . . . (United Artists)
Texas Country . . . . (United Artists)
The Freddy Fender Collection . . . . (MCA)
Wasted On The Way
Crosby, Stills & Nash; *CSN* . . . . (Atlantic)
Daylight Again . . . . (Atlantic)
Wasted Words
Allman Brothers Band; *Brothers & Sisters* . . . . (Polydor)
Decade Of Hits-1969-1979 . . . . (Polydor)

Dreams . . . . (Polydor)
Gregg Allman; *Laid Back* . . . . (Polydor)
Wasting My Time
Default; *Fallout* . . . . (TVT)
Wasting Time
Collective Soul; *Hints, Allegations And Things Left Unsaid* . . . . (Atlantic)
White Trash
Orchestral Manoeuvres In The Dark; *Junk Culture* . . . . (A&M)
White Trash
Redd Kross; *Born Innocent* . . . . (Frontier)
White Trash
Bellamy Brothers; *Crazy From The Heart* . . . . (MCA)
White Trash
Bad Religion; *How Could Hell Be Any Worse* . . . . (Epitaph)
White Trash
Steve Cash; *White Mansions* . . . . (A&M)
White Trash Song
Steve Young; *Honky-Tonk Man* . . . . (Rounder)
Solo/Live . . . . (Watermelon)
White Trash Wife
Exene Cervenka; *Old Wives' Tales* . . . . (Rhino)
White Trash With Cash
Southgang; *Group Therapy* . . . . (Charisma)
Who's Gonna Take The Garbage Out
Ernest Tubb & Loretta Lynn; *Ernest Tubb & Loretta Lynn* . . . . (MCA)
More Great Country Duets-C . . . . (MCA Special Prod.)
The Ernest Tubb/Loretta Lynn Story . . . . (MCA)
Your Cash Ain't Nothin' But Trash
Clovers; *Down In The Alley* . . . . (Rhino)
Huey Lewis and the News; *Four Chords & Several Years Ago* . . . . . . (Elektra)
Steve Miller Band; *The Joker* . . . . (Capitol)

TRAVELING, Drifting Along, Marching, Movin' On, Running, Stepping, Walking, Wandering

See Also: AIRPLANES, BUS, CARS (various), CITIES: A-Z, COUNTRIES: A-Z, DISTANCE, FLYING, HITCHHIKING, HOME, HOTELS, LEAVING, MOTORCYCLES, REBELS, RETURNING, ROAD, ROAD ACCIDENTS, SAILING, SEARCH, SHIPS, STATES: A-Z, TAXI, TRAINS, TRUCKS

4 Miles
Take 6; *Join The Band-C* . . . . (Reprise)
50 Ways To Leave Your Lover
Paul Simon; *Greatest Hits, Etc.* . . . . (Columbia)
Negotiations And Love Songs, 1971-1986 . . . . (Warner Bros.)
Still Crazy After All These Years . . . . (Columbia)
Simon & Garfunkel; *The Concert In Central Park* . . . . (Warner Bros.)
500 Miles Away From Home
Bobby Bare; *500 Miles Away From Home* . . . . (RCA)
Foy Willing; *Cowboy/The New Sound Of American Folk* . . . . (DRG)
Reba McEntire; *Starting Over* . . . . (MCA)
96 Miles To Birmingham
Dick Silveras; *Negro Folk Songs & Ballads* . . . . (Stinson)
Across The Great Divide
Band; *Rock Of Ages* . . . . (Capitol)
The Band . . . . (Capitol)
Against The Wind
Bob Seger & The Silver Bullet Band; *Against The Wind* . . . . (Capitol)
Nine Tonight . . . . (Capitol)
ST/Forrest Gump . . . . (Epic/Sony Music Soundtrax)
Ain't She Sweet?
Beatles; *History Of British Rock-#5-C* . . . . (Rhino)
The Beatles-Anthology-#3 . . . . (Capitol)
Erroll Garner; *Body And Soul* . . . . (Legacy)
Frank Sinatra; *Sinatra and Swingin' Brass* . . . . (Reprise)
Pearl Bailey; *Pearl Bailey-16 Most Requested Songs* . . . . (Legacy)
Alabama Bound
Doc & Merle Watson; *Ballads From Deep Gap* . . . . (Vanguard)
Leadbelly/Woody Guthrie/Cisco Houston; *Leadbelly Sings Folk
Songs* . . . . (Smithsonian Folkways)
Alabama Getaway
Grateful Dead; *Go To Heaven* . . . . (Arista)
Alabamy Bound
Tom Rush; *Blues Songs & Ballads* . . . . (Fantasy)
Tom Rush . . . . (Fantasy)
All I Want
Joni Mitchell; *Blue* . . . . (Reprise)
Joni Mitchell with Tom Scott & The L.A. Express; *Miles Of Aisles* . . . (Asylum)
All Revved Up With No Place To Go
Meat Loaf; *Bat Out Of Hell* . . . . (Epic)
All Roads Lead To You
Chicago; *The Heart Of Chicago-1967-1988-#2* . . . . (Reprise)
Amarillo By Morning
George Strait; *George Strait's Greatest Hits* . . . . (MCA)

Strait From The Heart . . . .(MCA)
America
Neil Diamond; *12 Greatest Hits-#2* . . . . (Columbia)
Hot August Night II . . . . (Columbia)
ST/The Jazz Singer . . . . (Capitol)
America
David Bowie; *The Concert For New York City-C.* . . . . (Columbia)
Paul Simon; *Paul Simon In Concert/Live Rhymin'* . . . . (Columbia)
Simon & Garfunkel; *Bookends* . . . . (Columbia)
Collected Works . . . . (Columbia)
Simon & Garfunkel's Greatest Hits . . . . (Columbia)
The Concert In Central Park . . . .(Warner Bros.)
American In Paris, An
Atlantic Brass Quintet; *By George! Gershwin's Greatest Hits* . . . (Musicmasters)
George Gershwin; *Rhapsody In Blue* . . . . (Biograph)
American Tune
Paul Simon; *Paul Simon In Concert/Live Rhymin'* . . . . (Columbia)
There Goes Rhymin' Simon . . . . (Columbia)
Simon & Garfunkel; *The Concert In Central Park* . . . .(Warner Bros.)
Amy's Back In Austin
Little Texas; *Kick A Little* . . . .(Warner Bros.)
Little Texas' Greatest Hits . . . .(Warner Bros.)
Another Journey By Train
Cure; *Standing On A Beach-The Singles* . . . . (Elektra)
Are You Gonna Go My Way
Lenny Kravitz; *Are You Gonna Go My Way* . . . . (Virgin)
Arkansas Time Traveler
Star-Spangled Washboard Band; *Collector's Item* . . . . (Flying Fish)
Arkansas Traveler
Albert Lee; *Speechless* . . . .(MCA)
Fiddlin' Red Herron; *Red, White & Bluegrass-C* . . . .(C.M.H. Prod.)
Floyd Cramer; *Country Gold-Floyd Cramer* . . . . (Step One)
Mark O'Connor; *Championship Years* . . . .(Country Music Foundation)
Michelle Shocked; *Arkansas Traveler* . . . . (Mercury)
Sam Hinton; *Newport Broadside: Newport Folk Festival-1963-C* . . . (Vanguard)
Arms Of The One Who Loves You
Xscape; *Traces Of My Lipstick* . . . . (So So Def/Columbia)
Around The World
Red Hot Chili Peppers; *Californication* . . . .(Warner Bros.)
Around The World In A Day
Prince and the Revolution; *Around The World In A Day.* . . . . (Paisley Park)
Around The World In Eighty Days
Boston Pops Orchestra/Arthur Fiedler; *Greatest Hits Of The '50s-#2* . . . . (RCA)
Frank Sinatra; *Come Fly With Me* . . . . (Capitol)
Roger Williams; *Roger Williams' Greatest Hits* . . . .(MCA)
Victor Young & His Singing Strings; *Hollywood's Greatest Hits-#2* . . . . (Telarc)
Astral Traveller
Yes; *Time And A Word* . . . . (Atlantic)
Yesterdays . . . . (Atlantic)
At The Beginning
Richard Marx & Donna Lewis; *ST/Anastasia-Music From The Motion*
Picture . . . . (Atlantic)
Baby Elephant Walk
Henry Mancini; *Henry Mancini-Pure Gold* . . . . (RCA)
Peter Gunn . . . . (RCA)
Baby Step Back
Gordon Lightfoot; *Gord's Gold-#2* . . . .(Warner Bros.)
Baby That's When I Come Runnin'
Luther Vandross; *One Night With You-The Best Of Love-#2* . . . . (LV/Epic)
Back In The Saddle Again
Gene Autry; *50th Anniversary* . . . .(Republic/Universal)
Columbia Country Classics-#1-Golden Age-C . . . . (Columbia)
Cowboy Hall Of Fame . . . .(Republic/Universal)
Cowboy Super Hits-C . . . . (Columbia)
Great American Singing Cowboys-C . . . .(Republic/Universal)
South Of The Border . . . .(Republic/Universal)
Back In The U.S.S.R.
Beatles; *Beatles-Box Set* . . . . (Capitol)
Rock 'N' Roll Music . . . . (Capitol)
The Beatles (White Album) . . . . (Capitol)
The Beatles/1967-1970 . . . . (Capitol)
Billy Joel; *KOHUEPT* . . . . (Columbia)
Ballad Of William Worthy
Phil Ochs; *Best Of Broadside 1962-1968: Anthems Of The American*
Underground From The Pages Of Broadside
Magazine-C . . . . (Smithsonian Folkways)
Band On The Run
Paul McCartney; *All The Best!* . . . . (Capitol)
Paul McCartney & Wings; *Band On The Run.* . . . . (Capitol)
Wings; *Wings Greatest* . . . . (Capitol)
Wings Over America . . . . (Capitol)
Bear Went Over The Mountain, The
Original Soundtrack; *Children's Favorites* . . . . (Kid Rhino/Rhino 4 Kids)
Beat It On Down The Line
Grateful Dead; *Grateful Dead (Skull & Roses)* . . . .(Warner Bros.)
Steal Your Face . . . . (Grateful Dead)
Jesse Fuller; *Lone Cat* . . . . (Good Time Jazz)
Before I Go
John Hiatt; *Crossing Muddy Waters* . . . . (Vanguard)

Before They Make Me Run
Rolling Stones; *Some Girls* . . . .(Virgin)
Belle, Belle, My Liberty Belle
Guy Mitchell; *Definitive Guy Mitchell* . . . . (Collector's Choice)
Guy Mitchell-16 Most Requested Songs . . . .(Legacy)
Big Log
Robert Plant; *Principle Of Moments* . . . . (Es Paranza)
Big Time
Neil Young & Crazy Horse; *Broken Arrow.* . . . .(Reprise)
Year Of The Horse . . . .(Reprise)
Blazin' Your Own Trail Again
REO Speedwagon; *You Can Tune A Piano But You Can't Tuna Fish* . . . . (Epic)
Boogie Back To Texas
Asleep At The Wheel; *Asleep At The Wheel-10* . . . . (Epic)
Swinging Best Of Asleep At The Wheel. . . . . (Epic)
Texas Super Hits-C. . . . . (Columbia)
Very Best Of Asleep At The Wheel Since 1970 . . . .(Relentless/Madacy)
Born Ready
Jesse Hunter; *A Man Like Me* . . . . (BNA)
Born To Be Wild
Steppenwolf; *Billboard Top Rock 'N' Roll Hits-1968-C.* . . . . (Rhino)
Live Steppenwolf . . . . (MCA)
Steppenwolf . . . . (MCA)
Steppenwolf-16 Greatest Hits. . . . . (MCA)
Vintage Music-#9 & 10-C. . . . . (MCA)
Born To Move
Creedence Clearwater Revival; *1970* . . . .(Fantasy)
Creedence Clearwater Revival-Chronicle-#2 . . . .(Fantasy)
Pendulum . . . .(Fantasy)
Born To Run
Bruce Springsteen; *Born To Run.* . . . . (Columbia)
Chimes Of Freedom . . . . (Columbia)
Bruce Springsteen & The E Street Band; *Bruce Springsteen & The E Street*
Band Live/1975-85 . . . .(Legacy)
Melissa Etheridge; *The Concert For New York City-C* . . . . (Columbia)
Born To Run
Emmylou Harris; *Cimarron* . . . . (Warner Bros.)
Profile II-The Best Of Emmylou Harris . . . . (Warner Bros.)
Born To Wander
Rare Earth; *20 Hard-To-Find Motown Classics-#2-C.* . . . . (Motown)
Ecology. . . . . (Motown)
Hard-To-Find Motown Classics-#2-C . . . . (Motown)
Motown Superstar Series-#16-Rare Earth . . . . (Motown)
Break My Stride
Matthew Wilder; *I Don't Speak The Language* . . . . (Private I)
Buicks To The Moon
Alan Jackson; *Everything I Love* . . . . (Arista)
By The Time I Get To Phoenix
Glen Campbell; *All-Time Country Classics-#1-C* . . . . (Capitol)
Glen Campbell-Classics Collection . . . . (Capitol)
Glen Campbell-Live . . . . (Capitol)
Glen Campbell's Greatest Hits. . . . . (Capitol)
Very Best Of Glen Campbell. . . . . (Capitol)
Reba McEntire; *Starting Over.* . . . .(MCA)
Cadillac Walk
Mink De Ville; *Mink De Ville* . . . . (Capitol)
Savoire Faire . . . . (Capitol)
California
Joni Mitchell; *Blue* . . . .(Reprise)
California Dreamin'
Beach Boys; *Made In The U.S.A.* . . . . (Capitol)
Mamas & The Papas; *At The Hop* . . . .(MCA)
Good Feeling Music Of The Big Chill Generation-#1-C . . . . (Motown)
Mamas & The Papas-20 Golden Hits . . . . (MCA)
ST/Air America . . . . (MCA)
ST/American Pop . . . . (MCA)
ST/Forrest Gump . . . .(Epic/Sony Music Soundtrax)
California Nights
Lesley Gore; *Summer & Sun-C* . . . . (Rhino)
Can I Run
L7; *Hungry For Stink* . . . .(Slash)
Can't Help But Wonder Where I'm Bound
Wyatt Rice; *Picture In A Tear* . . . . (Rounder)
Caravan
Duke Ellington; *Best Of Duke Ellington* . . . . (Capitol)
Money Jungle . . . . (Blue Note)
Ella Fitzgerald; *Montreux '75* . . . . (Pablo)
Johnny Mathis; *In A Sentimental Mood-Johnny Mathis Sings*
Ellington . . . . (Columbia)
Wynton Marsalis; *Marsalis Standard Time-#1* . . . . (Columbia)
Caravan
Van Morrison; *Moondance* . . . . (Warner Bros.)
Van Morrison & The Band; *The Last Waltz* . . . . (Warner Bros.)
Caravan To Midnight
Robin Trower; *Caravan To Midnight* . . . . (Chrysalis)
Caribbean Queen
Billy Ocean; *Billy Ocean's Greatest Hits* . . . .(Jive)
Suddenly . . . .(Jive)

Carnival
Natalie Merchant; *Tigerlily* . . . . (Elektra)
Carry Me Back
Statler Brothers; *Best Of The Statler Brothers* . . . . (Mercury)
  Carry Me Back . . . . (Mercury)
Carry Me Back To Old Virginny
Jerry Lee Lewis; *Doin' Just Fine* . . . . (Accord)
  Ole Tyme Country Music . . . . (Sun)
  Sunday Down South . . . . (Sun)
Carrying Your Love With Me
George Strait; *Carrying Your Love With Me* . . . . (MCA)
  Latest Greatest Straitest Hits . . . . (MCA)
Chant Of The Wanderer
Sons Of The Pioneers; *Sunset On The Range* . . . . (Pair)
Chariots Of Fire
Vangelis; *ST/Chariots Of Fire* . . . . (Polydor)
  Themes . . . . (Polydor)
Click-Clack
Dicky Doo And The Don'ts; *Greatest Hit Singles Collection-C* . . . . . (Laserlight)
Cold Irons Bound
Bob Dylan; *Time Out Of Mind* . . . . (Columbia)
Colorado Trail
Ian Tyson; *Ian Tyson* . . . . (Columbia)
Salli Terri; *Songs Of The American Land* . . . . (Angel)
Come Go With Me
Del Vikings; *1956 Audition Tapes* . . . . (Collectables)
  Billboard Top R&B Hits-1957-C . . . . (Rhino)
  Oldies But Goodies-#3-C . . . . (Original Sound)
  ST/American Graffiti . . . . (MCA)
  ST/Stand By Me . . . . (Atlantic)
Come On Let's Go
Los Lobos; *And A Time To Dance* . . . . (Slash)
  Just Another Band From East L.A. . . . . (Slash)
  ST/La Bamba . . . . (Slash)
Ritchie Valens; *Best Of Ritchie Valens* . . . . (Rhino)
  Oldies But Goodies-#4-C . . . . (Original Sound)
  The Ritchie Valens Story . . . . (Del Fi)
Come Running
Van Morrison; *Moondance* . . . . (Warner Bros.)
Come Running Back
Dean Martin; *Dean Martin's Greatest Hits* . . . . (Reprise)
Comin' Home
Lynyrd Skynyrd; *First & Last* . . . . (MCA)
  Gold & Platinum . . . . (MCA)
  Southern By The Grace Of God-Tribute '87 . . . . (MCA)
Comin' Home
Delaney & Bonnie; *Best Of Delaney & Bonnie* . . . . (Rhino)
  Delaney & Bonnie & Friends On Tour With Eric Clapton . . . . (Rhino)
  Eric Clapton-Crossroads-C . . . . (Polydor)
Comin' Home
Nutmegs; *Harlem Holiday-New York Rhythm & Blues-#7-C* . . . . . (Collectables)
  Nutmegs' Greatest Hits . . . . (Collectables)
Comin' Home
Bob Seger & The Silver Bullet Band; *The Distance* . . . . (Capitol)
Crawling In The Dark
Hoobastank; *Hoobastank* . . . . (Island/IDJMG)
Crawling To The U.S.A.
Elvis Costello; *ST/Americathon* . . . . (Columbia)
  Taking Liberties . . . . (Columbia)
Cross-Tie Walker
Creedence Clearwater Revival; *1969* . . . . (Fantasy)
  Creedence Country . . . . (Fantasy)
  Green River . . . . (Fantasy)
Cruisin'
D'Angelo; *Brown Sugar* . . . . (EMI)
Huey Lewis and Gwyneth Paltrow; *ST/Duets* . . . . (Hollywood)
Smokey Robinson; *Compact Command Performances-Smokey Robinson* . . . . (Motown)
  Motown Love Songs-C . . . . (Motown)
  Motown Story-First 25 Years-C . . . . (Motown)
  Where There's Smoke . . . . (Motown)
Cruisin'
Alabama; *The Touch* . . . . (RCA)
Cruisin'
Michael Nesmith; *Newer Stuff* . . . . (Rhino)
Cruisin'
Ted Nugent; *Weekend Warriors* . . . . (Epic)
Cry Of The Wild Goose
Frankie Laine; *Frankie Laine-Golden Hits* . . . . (Mercury)
Da Doo Ron Ron (When He Walked Me Home)
Crystals; *Best Of The Crystals* . . . . (Abkco)
  Good Time Rock 'N' Roll-C . . . . (MCA)
  Hits Of The Sixties-C . . . . (Intercom Music)
  Phil Spector's Greatest Hits-C . . . . (Spector)
Shaun Cassidy; *Shaun Cassidy's Greatest Hits* . . . . (Curb)
Daddy Frank (The Guitar Man)
Merle Haggard; *Best Of Merle Haggard* . . . . (Capitol)
  Capitol Collectors Series-Merle Haggard . . . . (Capitol)

Merle Haggard & The Strangers; *For The Record: Merle Haggard-43 Legendary Hits* . . . . (BNA)
  Songs I'll Always Sing . . . . (Capitol)
Days Are Numbers (The Traveller)
Alan Parsons Project; *Best Of Alan Parsons Project-#2* . . . . (Arista)
  Vulture Culture . . . . (Arista)
Destination Anywhere
Commitments; *ST/The Commitments* . . . . (MCA)
Destination Unknown
Electric Light Orchestra; *Afterglow* . . . . (Epic)
Detour (Devil Took A)
Patti Page; *Patti Page-Golden Hits* . . . . (Mercury)
Detour Ahead
Billie Holiday; *Billie's Blues* . . . . (Blue Note)
Herb Ellis; *Roll Call* . . . . (Justice)
Herb Ellis & Others; *After You've Gone* . . . . (Concord Jazz)
Sarah Vaughan; *Complete Sarah Vaughan On Mercury-#3* . . . . . (Mercury)
Stan Getz; *Essential Stan Getz Songbook* . . . . (Verve)
Did You Ever See A Dream Walking
Bing Crosby; *Crosby Classics* . . . . (Columbia)
Hal Kemp & Skinnay Ennis; *The Uncollected Hal Kemp-#2 & #3* . . . (Hindsight)
Dirt Road Blues
Bob Dylan; *Time Out Of Mind* . . . . (Columbia)
Do America
Mark Knopfler; *Sailing To Philadelphia* . . . . (Warner Bros.)
Do You Wanna Get Away
Shannon; *Do You Wanna Get Away* . . . . (Mirage)
Doggie In The Window
Patti Page; *Patti Page-16 Most Requested Songs* . . . . (Legacy)
  Patti Page-Golden Hits . . . . (Mercury)
  Patti Page's Greatest Hits . . . . (Columbia)
Don't Get Around Much Anymore
Duke Ellington; *I Like Jazz-Essence Of Duke Ellington* . . . . (Columbia)
Duke Ellington & His Orchestra; *Nipper's Greatest Hits Of The '40s-#1-C* . . . . (RCA)
Etta James; *Second Time Around* . . . . (Chess)
Harry Connick, Jr.; *ST/When Harry Met Sally* . . . . (Columbia)
Johnny Mathis; *In A Sentimental Mood-Johnny Mathis Sings Ellington* . . . . (Columbia)
Mel Torme; *Duke Ellington & Count Basie Songbook* . . . . (Verve)
Mose Allison; *Mose Allison's Greatest Hits* . . . . (Prestige)
Natalie Cole; *Unforgettable With Love* . . . . (Elektra)
Shelby Lynne; *Tough All Over* . . . . (Epic)
Don't Go Away
Oasis; *Be Here Now* . . . . (Epic)
Don't Run (Come Back To Me)
KC And The Sunshine Band; *KC And The Sunshine Band* . . . . . (Double Play)
Don't Think Twice, It's All Right
Bob Dylan; *Before The Flood* . . . . (Columbia)
  Bob Dylan's Greatest Hits-#2 . . . . (Columbia)
  Freewheelin' . . . . (Columbia)
Joan Baez; *The First 10 Years* . . . . (Vanguard)
Wonder Who?; *Anniversary* . . . . (Rhino)
Don't Turn Around
Ace Of Base; *The Sign* . . . . (Arista)
Don't Walk Away
Jade; *Jade To The Max* . . . . (Giant)
Don't You Get It
Mark Knopfler; *Golden Heart* . . . . (Warner Bros.)
Down The Line
Buddy Holly; *Rock & Roll Collection* . . . . (MCA)
  The Buddy Holly Collection . . . . (MCA)
Down Under
Men At Work; *Business As Usual* . . . . (Columbia)
Dream Walkin'
Toby Keith; *Dream Walkin'* . . . . (Mercury)
  Toby Keith's Greatest Hits, Volume One . . . . (Mercury)
Drifting Along
Jamiroquai; *Traveling Without Moving* . . . . (Work/Epic)
Drifting Like Whales In The Darkness
Sven Vath; *Accident In Paradise* . . . . (Warner Bros.)
Duck And Run
3 Doors Down; *Better Life* . . . . (Republic/Universal)
Ease On Down The Road
Grateful Dead; *Go To Heaven* . . . . (Arista)
Ease On Down The Road
Original Cast; *ST/The Wiz* . . . . (MCA)
Eight More Miles
Kieran Kane/Kevin Welch; *11/12/13: Live In Melbourne, Australia* . . . . (Dead Reckoning)
Eight More Miles To Louisville
Eric Weissberg; *Dueling Banjos From ''Deliverance''* . . . . . (Warner Bros.)
Grandpa Jones; *Truckin' On-C* . . . . (Hollywood)
Mike Auldridge; *Dobro/Blues & Bluegrass* . . . . (Takoma)
Reno & Smiley; *1983 Collector's Edition-#3* . . . . (Gusto)
  Best Of Reno & Smiley . . . . (Starday)
Elegantly Wasted
INXS; *Elegantly Wasted* . . . . (Mercury)

Embryonic Journey
Hot Tuna; *Splashdown* . . . . (Relix)
Jefferson Airplane; *2400 Fulton Street-An Anthology* . . . . (RCA)
   Surrealistic Pillow . . . . (RCA)
   The Worst Of Jefferson Airplane . . . . (RCA)
Every Little Step
Bobby Brown; *Dance!...Ya Know It!* . . . . (MCA)
   Don't Be Cruel . . . . (MCA)
Every Mother's Son
Traffic; *John Barleycorn Must Die* . . . . (Island)
Every Step Of The Way
John Waite; *Mask Of Smiles* . . . .(EMI)
Everybody's Talkin'
Nilsson; *Everybody's Talkin': The Encore Collection* . . . . . (BMG Special Prod.)
   ST/*Forrest Gump* . . . . (Epic/Sony Music Soundtrax)
   ST/*Midnight Cowboy* . . . .(EMI)
Willie Nelson; *Best Of Willie* . . . . (RCA)
   Sweet Memories . . . . (RCA)
Everywhere
Tim McGraw; *Everywhere* . . . . (Curb)
Everywhere I Go
Shawn Mullins; *Beneath The Velvet Sun* . . . . (Columbia)
Exodus
Bob Marley & The Wailers; *Babylon By Bus* . . . . (Tuff Gong)
   Exodus . . . . (Tuff Gong)
   Legend: The Best Of Bob Marley & The Wailers . . . . (Island)
Fantastic Voyage
Lakeside; *Club Epic-#1-C* . . . . (Legacy)
   Fantastic Voyage . . . . (Solar)
Fantastic Voyage
Coolio; *It Takes A Thief* . . . . (Tommy Boy)
Farther Along
Byrds; *The Byrds* . . . . (Columbia)
Elvis Presley; *Million-Dollar Quartet* . . . . (RCA)
Flying Burrito Brothers; *Farther Along-Best Of The Flying Burrito Brothers* . . . . (A&M)
Rose Maddox; *Rose Of The West Coast Country* . . . . (Arhoolie)
Fearless
Pink Floyd; *Meddle* . . . . (Capitol)
   Works . . . . (Capitol)
Fifteen Miles To Birmingham
Happy & Artie Traum/Others; *Mud Acres* . . . . (Rounder)
Find Your Way Back
Jefferson Starship; *Greatest Hits-Ten Years & Change-1979-1991* . . . . . (RCA)
   Modern Times . . . .(Grunt)
Five Miles To Texas
Stockton & Johnson; *Born By The River* . . . . (Out Of Print)
Follow You, Follow Me
Genesis; *And Then There Were Three* . . . . (Atlantic)
   Three Sides Live . . . . (Atlantic)
Food Phone Gas Lodging
Charlie King; *Food Phone Gas Lodging* . . . . (Flying Fish)
Fools Rush In (Where Angels Fear To Tread)
Brook Benton; *Super Oldies Of The '60s-#10-C* . . . .(Audio Fidelity)
Tommy Dorsey & Frank Sinatra; *Sessions-#1-February 1, 1940-July 17, 1940* . . . . (RCA)
For A Change
Neal McCoy; *You Gotta Love That!* . . . . (Atlantic)
Fort Worth Blues
Guy Clark; *Cold Dog Soup* . . . . (Sugar Hill)
Frankie
Bruce Springsteen; *Tracks* . . . . (Columbia)
Free Bird
Lynyrd Skynyrd; *Gold & Platinum* . . . .(MCA)
   One More From The Road . . . .(MCA)
   Pronounced Leh-nerd Skin-nerd . . . .(MCA)
   Southern By The Grace Of God-Tribute '87 . . . .(MCA)
Wynonna; *Skynyrd Frynds-C* . . . .(MCA)
From The Indies To The Andies In His Undies
Hoosier Hot Shots; *All Time Legends Of Country Music-C* . . . . (Legacy)
Funny Familiar Forgotten Feelings
Don Gibson; *Best Of Don Gibson-#1* . . . . (Curb)
Mandy Barnett; *I've Got A Right To Cry* . . . . (Sire)
Tom Jones; *Back To Back-Greatest Hits* . . . . (Rebound)
   Country Side Of Tom Jones . . . . (London)
   Tom Jones-London Collector-Greatest Hits . . . . (London)
Galilee Road
Marcus Hummon; *Looking For The Child* . . . . (Velvet Armadillo)
Gentle On My Mind
Elvis Presley; *From Elvis In Memphis* . . . . (RCA)
   Great Country Songs . . . . (RCA)
Glen Campbell; *Best Of Austin City Limits-Legends Of Country Music-C* . . . . (Legacy)
   Best Of Glen Campbell . . . . (Capitol)
   Glen Campbell-Best Of The Early Years . . . . (Curb)
John Hartford; *Me Oh My-How The Time Does Fly-Anthology* . . . . (Flying Fish)
Patti Page; *Patti Page-16 Most Requested Songs* . . . . (Legacy)
Get Away
Bobby Brown; *Bobby* . . . .(MCA)

Get Back
Beatles; *Beatles 1* . . . . (Capitol)
   Beatles-20 Greatest Hits . . . . (Capitol)
   Beatles-Box Set . . . . (Capitol)
   Let It Be . . . . (Capitol)
   Past Masters-Volume Two . . . . (Parlophone)
   Reel Music . . . . (Capitol)
   Rock 'N' Roll Music . . . . (Capitol)
   The Beatles/1967-1970 . . . . (Capitol)
Get Out Of Denver
Bob Seger; *Live Bullet* . . . . (Capitol)
Dave Edmunds; *Get It* . . . . (Swan Song)
Get Out The Map
Indigo Girls; *Shaming Of The Sun* . . . . (Epic)
Ghost-Town Of My Brain
Jim White; *No Such Place* . . . . (Luaka Bop)
Girl From Ipanema
Antonio Carlos Jobim; *Antonio Carlos Jobim* . . . . (Warner Bros.)
   Compact Jazz-Antonio Carlos Jobim . . . . (Verve)
Ella Fitzgerald; *Ella A Nice* . . . . (Pablo)
   Montreux '75 . . . . (Pablo)
   Pablo Today-Ella Embraces Antonio Carlos Jobim . . . . (Pablo)
Stan Getz & Astrud Gilberto; *Cruisin'-1964-C* . . . . (Increase)
   Getz/Gilberto . . . . (Verve)
Gliding Through My Memoree
Original Cast; ST/*Flower Drum Song* . . . . (Sony Music Classical)
Go The Distance
Michael Bolton; *All That Matters* . . . . (Columbia)
Go Walking Down There
Chris Isaak; *Forever Blue* . . . . (Reprise)
Go Your Own Way
Cranberries; *Legacy-A Tribute To Fleetwood Mac's Rumours-C* . . . . (Lava)
Fleetwood Mac; *25 Years-The Chain* . . . . (Warner Bros.)
   Fleetwood Mac Live . . . . (Warner Bros.)
   Fleetwood Mac's Greatest Hits . . . . (Warner Bros.)
   Rumours . . . . (Warner Bros.)
Goin' Away Blues
Eric Clapton; *From The Cradle* . . . . (Duck/Reprise)
Goin' Back
Byrds; *20 Essential Tracks From The Box Set* . . . . (Columbia)
   The Byrds . . . . (Columbia)
Dusty Springfield; *Dusty Springfield-Golden Greats* . . . . (Philips)
Neil Young; *Comes A Time* . . . . (Reprise)
Nils Lofgren; *Best Of Nils Lofgren* . . . . (A&M)
   Night After Night . . . . (A&M)
   Nils Lofgren . . . . (Rykodisc)
Goin' Back To Alabama
Kenny Rogers; *Share Your Love* . . . . (Liberty)
Goin' Back To Florida
John Hammond; *Best Of John Hammond* . . . . (Vanguard)
Lightnin' Hopkins; *Lightnin' Hopkins* . . . .(Smithsonian Folkways)
   Roots Of Lightnin' Hopkins . . . .(Smithsonian Folkways)
Goin' Back To Indiana
Jackson 5; *Goin' Back To Indiana* . . . . (Motown)
   Jackson 5-Anthology . . . . (Motown)
   Jackson 5's Greatest Hits . . . . (Motown)
   Third Album . . . . (Motown)
Goin' Back To Oakland
Isaac Scott; *San Francisco Blues Festival-#2-C* . . . .(Solid Smoke)
Tom McFarland; *Travelin' With The Blues* . . . . (Arhoolie)
Goin' Back To Old Kentucky
New Grass Revival; *Festival Tapes* . . . . (Flying Fish)
Goin' Back To Paris
Bill Collins; *Charmin' Billy* . . . . (Chestnut)
Goin' Back To Texas
Bobby Bare; *Bobby Bare's Biggest Hits* . . . . (Columbia)
Don Edwards; *Best Of Don Edwards* . . . . (Warner Western)
   Goin' Back To Texas . . . . (Warner Western)
Goin' Down Louisiana
Blues Project; *No Time Like The Right Time-Best Of The Blues Project* . . . . (Rhino)
Goin' Down To Muskogee
Jim Pepper; *Comin' & Goin'* . . . .(Antilles)
Goin' Down To Tampa
Jeff Warner & Jeff Davis; *Wilder Joy-Traditional American Folk Songs* . . . . (Flying Fish)
Goin' Home
Alvin Lee/Ten Years Later; *Ride On* . . . . (RSO)
Goin' To Cairo
Joel Mabus; *Settin' The Woods On Fire* . . . . (Flying Fish)
Goin' To Chattanooga
Ralph Willis; *East Coast Blues* . . . . (Collectables)
Goin' To Dallas To See My Pony Run
Lightnin' Hopkins; *Blues In My Bottle* . . . . (Bluesville)
   Drinkin' In The Blues-Golden Classics-#1 . . . . (Collectables)
   Lightnin' Hopkins . . . . (Everest)
Goin' To Kansas City
Furry Lewis; *Shake 'Em On Down* . . . . (Fantasy)
Jimmy Witherspoon; *'Spoon Concerts* . . . . (Fantasy)

Goin' To Las Vegas
Suicide; *1/2 Alive* .... (Roir)
Goin' To Memphis
Carl Perkins; *Best Of Carl Perkins-Jive After 5-1958-1978* .... (Rhino)
Goin' To New Orleans
Rockin' Tabby Thomas; *Rockin' With The Blues* .... (Maison De Soul)
Going Back To Alabam'
Alan Munde & Country Gazette; *Keep On Pushing* ....(Flying Fish)
Going Back To Alabama
Asa Martin; *Dr. Ginger Blue* .... (Rounder)
Going Back To Big Sur
Johnny Rivers; *Johnny Rivers-Anthology 1964-1977* .... (Rhino)
  Touch Of Gold .... (Imperial)
Going Back To Birmingham
Ten Years After; *Universal* .... (Chrysalis)
Going Back To Detroit
Platters; *Double Gold-The Platters* .... (Mustcor)
Going Back To Dublin
Eric Bogle; *Something Of Value* ....(Philo)
Going Back To Florida
Billie & De De Pierce; *New Orleans Jazz-C* ....(Arhoolie)
Going Back To Indiana
Sawyer Brown; *Sawyer Brown* .... (Curb)
Going Back To Iuka
Albert King; *Lovejoy* .... (Stax)
Koko Taylor & Her Blues Machine; *Live From Chicago-With The
  Queen* ....(Alligator)
Going Back To Liverpool
Jackie Lomax; *Is This What You Want?* ....(Capitol)
Going Back To Louisiana
Delbert McClinton; *Live From Austin* ....(Alligator)
Joey Farr; *45-#105* ....(Fairview)
Going Back To Memphis
Muddy Waters; *Muddy Brass & Blues* .... (Chess)
Going Back To Miami
Blues Brothers; *Best Of The Blues Brothers* .... (Atlantic)
  Made In America .... (Atlantic)
Wayne Cochran; *Soul Shots-#6-Blue-Eyed Soul-C* .... (Rhino)
Going Back To New Orleans
Dr. John; *Going Back To New Orleans* .... (Warner Bros.)
Going Back To Okinawa
Ry Cooder; *Get Rhythm* .... (Warner Bros.)
Going Back To Tampa
Roy Bookbinder; *Going Back To Tampa* ....(Flying Fish)
Going Back To Tennessee
Tracy Nelson; *Doin' It My Way* .... (Adelphi)
Going Back To Texas
R.C. Smith; *I Have To Paint My Face: Mississippi Blues-1960* ......(Arhoolie)
Going Back To Texas
Wayne Hancock; *Wild, Free & Reckless* .... (Ark 21)
Going Back To Virginia
Jim & Jesse; *Music Among Friends* .... (Rounder)
Going Down To Liverpool
Bangles; *All Over The Place* .... (Columbia)
  Bangles' Greatest Hits .... (Columbia)
Going Down To Mexico
ZZ Top; *Six Pack* .... (Warner Bros.)
  ZZ Top .... (Warner Bros.)
Going Down To Mississippi
Phil Ochs; *Toast To Those Who Are Gone* .... (Rhino)
Going Down To Texas
Shel Silverstein; *Great Conch Train Robbery* ....(Flying Fish)
Going Home
Osmonds; *Osmonds' Greatest Hits* .... (Polydor)
Going Home
Rolling Stones; *Aftermath* .... (Abkco)
Going Home
Elvis Presley; *Collector's Gold* ....(RCA)
Going Home
Fats Domino; *Fats Domino-Legendary Masters* .... (United Artists)
Going Home
Kenny G; *Kenny G-Live* .... (Arista)
Going Home
Buddy Guy; *Left My Blues In San Francisco* .... (Chess)
Going Home
Little Richard; *Little Richard's Greatest Hits* .... (Trip)
Going Home
Dire Straits; *Live-Alchemy* .... (Warner Bros.)
Going Home
Santana; *Lotus* .... (Columbia)
Going Home To Louisiana
Chris Thomas; *The Beginning* ....(Arhoolie)
Going Mobile
Who; *Who's next* .... (MCA)
Going To Brazil
Motorhead; *1916* .... (WTG)
Going To California
Led Zeppelin; *Led Zeppelin IV* .... (Atlantic)

  Led Zeppelin-Box Set .... (Atlantic)
Going To California
John Lee Hooker; *John Lee Hooker Sings John Lee Hooker* .... (Everest)
Going To Chicago Blues
Count Basie; *Essential Count Basie-#1* ....(Columbia)
Jimmy Rushing; *Essential Jimmy Rushing* ....(Vanguard)
Joe Williams; *Jazz Singers* .... (Prestige)
Lambert, Hendricks & Ross; *Twisted-Best Of Lambert, Hendricks
  & Ross* ....(Rhino)
Lowell Fulsom; *Let's Go Get Stoned* ....(Kent)
Going To Georgia
Johnson Mountain Boys; *At The Old Schoolhouse* ....(Rounder)
Stanley Brothers; *Shadows Of The Past* .... (Copper Creek)
Going To Louisiana
John Lee Hooker; *Berkeley Blues Festival* .... (Arhoolie)
  That's Where It's At. ....(Stax)
Going To Mexico
Steve Miller Band; *Best Of Steve Miller 1968-1973* ....(Capitol)
  Steve Miller Band-Anthology ....(Capitol)
  Steve Miller Band-Number 5 ....(Capitol)
Going To New York
Climax Blues Band; *FM/Live* .... (Sire)
Jimmy Reed; *Best Of Jimmy Reed* .... (Crescendo)
  Jimmy Reed-At Carnegie Hall ....(Vee-Jay)
  Jimmy Reed's Greatest Hits-#2 ....(Kent)
  Legend-The Man ....(Vee-Jay)
Siegel-Schwall Band; *Best Of The Siegel-Schwall Band* ....(Vanguard)
  Siegel-Schwall Band ....(Vanguard)
Going To Newport
Frankie Laine; *Frankie Laine's 16 Greatest Hits* .... (Trip)
Going To St. Louis
Yank Rachell & Others; *Chicago Style* ....(Delmark)
Going To The Country
Bruce Cockburn; *Waiting For A Miracle-Singles 1970-1987* ..... (Gold Castle)
Going To The Country
Steve Miller Band; *Best Of Steve Miller 1968-1973* ....(Capitol)
  Number 5 ....(Capitol)
  Steve Miller Band-Anthology ....(Capitol)
Going Up The Country
Canned Heat; *Best Of Canned Heat* .... (EMI)
  ST/1969 .... (Polydor)
  ST/Woodstock .... (Atlantic)
  Summer Of Love-#1-C. .... (Rhino)
Gone Till November
Wyclef Jean featuring The Refugee Allstars; *Presents The Carnival F/
  Refugee Allstars* ....(Ruffhouse/Columbia)
Good Day To Run
Darryl Worley; *Hard Rain Don't Last* .... (DreamWorks/SKG)
Good Woman Blues
Mel Tillis; *Mel Tillis' Greatest Hits* ....(Curb)
Goodbye San Francisco, Hello Amsterdam
Doug Sahm; *SDQ '98.* ....(Watermelon)
Goodnight Irene
Jim Reeves; *Jim Reeves-Pure Gold* .... (RCA)
Johnny Cash; *Rough Cut King Of Country Music* .... (Sun)
  The Man-The World-His Music. .... (Sun)
Ry Cooder; *Chicken Skin Music* .... (Reprise)
Weavers; *Best Of The Weavers* .... (MCA)
  Weavers At Carnegie Hall ....(Vanguard)
  Weavers' Greatest Hits ....(Vanguard)
Goodnight Sweetheart
David Kersh; *Goodnight Sweetheart* ....(Curb)
Gotta Travel On
Bill Monroe & His Blue Grass Boys; *20th Century Masters-The Millennium
  Collection-The Best Of Bill Monroe* ....(MCA)
  Country's Greatest Hits-#1-C .... (MCA Special Prod.)
Graceland
Paul Simon; *Graceland* ....(Warner Bros.)
Green, Green
New Christy Minstrels; *New Christy Minstrels' Greatest Hits* ......(Columbia)
Happy Wanderer
Frank Weir & His Orchestra; *Hits To Remember-C* ... (PolyGram Special Prod.)
Joey Miskulin; *Hooked On Polkas* ....(K-Tel)
Original Soundtrack; *Disney Travel Songs-C* ....(Disney)
Hard To Be A Husband, Hard To Be A Wife
Chely Wright & Brad Paisley; *Grand Ole Opry-75 Years-#2-C* .... (MCA)
He Walked On Water
Randy Travis; *No Holdin' Back* .... (Warner Bros.)
Heads Carolina, Tails California
Jo Dee Messina; *Greatest Hits Of Country Dance-C* ....(Curb)
  Jo Dee Messina ....(Curb)
Heavy Traffic Ahead
Bill Monroe & His Blue Grass Boys; *The Father Of Bluegrass: The Early
  Years-1940-1947* ....(ASV)
Ricky Skaggs with Steve Wariner; *Big Mon: The Songs Of Bill
  Monroe-C.* ....(Skaggs Family)
Here Comes My Baby
Tremeloes; *Best Of The Tremeloes* .... (Rhino)

High Time We Went
Joe Cocker; *Joe Cocker* . . . . (A&M)
  Joe Cocker Live . . . . (Capitol)
  Joe Cocker-Classics-#4 . . . . (A&M)
  Joe Cocker's Greatest Hits . . . . (A&M)
Highway Chile
Jimi Hendrix Experience; *Are You Experienced?* . . . . (Reprise)
Hillbilly Shoes
Montgomery Gentry; *Tattoos & Scars* . . . . (Columbia)
Hit The Ground Running
Jonny Lang; *Lie To Me* . . . . (A&M)
Hold My Hand
Hootie & The Blowfish; *Cracked Rear View* . . . . (Atlantic)
Home Sweet Home
Motley Crue; *Theatre Of Pain* . . . . (Elektra)
Homeward Bound
Fleetwood Mac; *Bare Trees* . . . . (Reprise)
Honey Chile
Martha Reeves & The Vandellas; *Compact Command Performances-Martha
  Reeves & The Vandellas* . . . . (Motown)
  Martha Reeves & The Vandellas-Anthology . . . . (Motown)
  Motown Superstar Series-#11-Martha Reeves & The Vandellas . . . . (Motown)
Houston (Means I'm One Day Closer To You)
Larry Gatlin & The Gatlin Brothers Band; *19 Hot Country Requests-C* . . . . (Epic)
  Greatest Country Hits Of The '80s-1983-C . . . . (Columbia)
  Larry Gatlin & The Gatlin Brothers' Greatest Hits-Encore . . . . (Capitol)
  Larry Gatlin & The Gatlin Brothers-17 Greatest Hits . . . . (Columbia)
How A Cowgirl Says Goodbye
Tracy Lawrence; *The Coast Is Clear* . . . . (Atlantic)
How I Got To Memphis
Bobby Bare; *This Is Bare Country* . . . . (Mercury)
Otis Williams & The Midnight Cowboys; *From Where I Stand: The Black
  Experience In Country Music-C* . . . . (Warner Bros.)
I Ain't Got No Home
Bob Dylan; *Tribute To Woody Guthrie-C* . . . . (Warner Bros.)
I Am A Man Of Constant Sorrow
Ralph Stanley; *Rebel Records: 35 Years Of The Best In Bluegrass-1960-
  1995-C* . . . . (Rebel)
Soggy Bottom Boys featuring Dan Tyminski; *ST/O Brother, Where Art
  Thou?* . . . . (Mercury)
Stanley Brothers; *All Time Legends Of Country Music-C* . . (Legacy)
I Can Still Make Cheyenne
George Strait; *Blue Clear Sky* . . . . (MCA)
  Latest Greatest Straitest Hits . . . . (MCA)
I Can't Get Started
Anita O'Day; *Jazz 'Round Midnight-Anita O'Day* . . . . (Verve)
Bunny Berigan & His Orchestra; *An Evening At Rao's: Songs From An
  Italian Restaurant-C* . . . . (Legacy)
  Idiot's Guide To Jazz-C . . . . (RCA Victor)
  The Pied Piper . . . . (Bluebird)
  The Swingingest Sounds Ever Heard-C . . . . (Hip-O)
Ella Fitzgerald; *Compact Jazz-Ella Fitzgerald* . . . . (Verve)
Lester Young; *Best Of Lester Young* . . . . (Pablo)
I Don't Know
Gretchen Peters; *Gretchen Peters* . . . . (Purple Crayon Prod.)
I Don't Wanna Walk Around With You
Ramones; *All The Stuff & More-#1* . . . . (Sire)
  Ramones . . . . (Sire)
I Don't Want To Walk Without You
Barry Manilow; *One Voice* . . . . (Arista)
Harry James; *Best Of The Big Bands-C* . . . . (Columbia)
Rosemary Clooney; *For The Duration* . . . . (Concord Jazz)
I Get Around
Beach Boys; *Best Of The Beach Boys* . . . . (Capitol)
  Billboard Top Rock 'N' Roll Hits-1964-C . . . . (Rhino)
  Endless Summer . . . . (Capitol)
  Made In The U.S.A. . . . . (Capitol)
  ST/Good Morning, Vietnam . . . . (A&M)
I Get The Fever
Bill Anderson; *Bill Anderson's Greatest Hits* . . . . (Varese Sarabande)
I Gotta Move
Kinks; *Kinda Kinks* . . . . (Rhino)
  Kinks-Size Kinkdom . . . . (Rhino)
Ted Nugent; *Scream Dream* . . . . (Epic)
I Packed My Suitcase, Started To The Train
Memphis Jug Band; *The Story-1927-1934* . . . . (EPM)
I Ran (So Far Away)
A Flock Of Seagulls; *A Flock Of Seagulls* . . . . (Jive)
  Best Of A Flock Of Seagulls . . . . (Jive)
I Take A Lot Of Pride In What I Am
Clint Black; *Mama's Hungry Eyes-Merle Haggard Tribute-C* . . . . (Arista)
Merle Haggard; *Capitol Collectors Series-Merle Haggard* . . . . . (Capitol)
  Merle Haggard's Greatest Hits . . . . (Curb)
I Think We're Alone Now
Tiffany; *Tiffany* . . . . (MCA)
  Tiffany's Greatest Hits . . . . (Hip-O)
Tommy James And The Shondells; *Best Of Tommy James And The
  Shondells* . . . . (Roulette)
  Billboard Top Rock 'N' Roll Hits-1967-C . . . . (Rhino)

  Tommy James And The Shondells-Anthology . . . . (Rhino)
I Try
Macy Gray; *Now That's What I Call Music!-#4-C* . . . . (Virgin)
  On How Life Is . . . . (Epic)
I Walk Alone
Marty Robbins; *Lifetime Of Song-1951-1982* . . . . (Columbia)
  Marty Robbins' All-Time Greatest Hits . . . . (Columbia)
  Marty Robbins' Greatest Hits-#3 . . . . (Columbia)
I Walk Alone
Los Lobos; *The Neighborhood* . . . . (Slash)
I Walk The Line
Johnny Cash; *Johnny Cash At Folsom Prison & San Quentin* . . . . . (Columbia)
  Johnny Cash-Legends . . . . (Dunhill Compact Classics)
  Johnny Cash-Original Golden Hits-#1 . . . . (Sun)
  Johnny Cash's Greatest Hits . . . . (Columbia)
  Johnny Cash-Sun Years . . . . (Rhino)
  Memphis Country-C . . . . (Sun)
  Show Time . . . . (Sun)
  Souvenirs Of Music City U.S.A.-C . . . . (Plantation)
  Sun Story-C . . . . (Rhino)
  Superbilly . . . . (Sun)
  The Man In Black-His Greatest Hits . . . . (Legacy)
I Walked
Wanderlust; *Prize* . . . . (RCA)
I Want To Walk You Home
Fats Domino; *Billboard Top R&B Hits-1959-C* . . . . (Rhino)
  Fats Domino's Greatest Hits . . . . (MCA)
  My Blue Heaven-Best Of Fats Domino-#1 . . . . (EMI)
I Wonder As I Wander
Barbra Streisand; *Barbra Streisand Christmas Album* . . . . . (Columbia)
Gary Morris; *Every Christmas* . . . . (Liberty)
Grover Washington, Jr.; *Breath Of Heaven-A Holiday Collection* . . . (Columbia)
Joan Baez; *Noel* . . . . (Vanguard)
Julie Andrews; *Christmas With Julie Andrews* . . . . (Columbia)
Mormon Tabernacle Choir; *This Land Is Your Land* . . . . . . (Columbia)
Peter, Paul & Mary; *Holiday Celebration* . . . . (Warner Bros.)
Philadelphia Orchestra & Eugene Ormandy; *Sleigh Ride!-Classic Christmas
  Favorites-C* . . . . (RCA)
Sandi Patty; *Gift Goes On* . . . . (Word)
Vanessa Williams; *Star Bright* . . . . (Mercury)
I Won't Let You Walk Away
Cleve Francis; *Walkin'* . . . . (Liberty)
If I Knew You Were Comin' I'd've Baked A Cake
Bing Crosby; *The Radio Years-#4* . . . . (Crescendo)
Ethel Merman; *The Ethel Merman Collection* . . . . (Razor & Tie)
If I Should Fall Behind
Bruce Springsteen; *In Concert/MTV Plugged* . . . . (Columbia)
  Lucky Town . . . . (Columbia)
Faith Hill; *Breathe* . . . . (Warner Bros.)
Linda Ronstadt; *We Ran* . . . . (Elektra)
If You Go
Jon Secada; *Heart, Soul & A Voice* . . . . (SBK)
I'll Be Back
Beatles; *Beatles '65* . . . . (Capitol)
  Beatles-Love Songs . . . . (Capitol)
I'll Follow The Sun
Beatles; *Beatles '65* . . . . (Capitol)
  Beatles-Box Set . . . . (Capitol)
  Beatles-Love Songs . . . . (Capitol)
  For Sale . . . . (Capitol)
I'll Repossess My Heart
Kitty Wells; *Kitty Wells' Greatest Hits* . . . . (Hollywood/DNA-Rounder)
I'll Walk Alone
Dinah Shore; *Dinah Shore's Greatest Hits* . . . . (Curtom)
I'm A Lonesome Fugitive
Merle Haggard; *Merle Haggard-16 Biggest Hits* . . . . (Legacy)
Merle Haggard & The Strangers; *Best Of Merle Haggard & The
  Strangers* . . . . (Capitol)
  Capitol Collectors Series-Merle Haggard & The Strangers . . . (Capitol)
  Songs I'll Always Sing . . . . (Capitol)
Roy Buchanan; *Roy Buchanan* . . . . (Polydor)
I'm Going Back To Alabama
Jerry Douglas; *Fluxology* . . . . (Rounder)
I'm Going Back To Old Kentucky
Bill Monroe; *Best Of Bill Monroe & His Blue Grass Boys* . . . . (MCA)
  Bill Monroe And Flatt & Scruggs . . . . (Rounder)
  Columbia Historic Edition-Bill Monroe . . . . (Columbia)
Bill Monroe & The Stars Of The Bluegrass Hall Of Fame; *Bill Monroe &
  The Stars Of The Bluegrass Hall Of Fame* . . . . (MCA)
Osborne Brothers; *Red, White & Bluegrass-C* . . . . (C.M.H. Prod.)
I'm Going Down To Bourbon Street
Waylon Thibodeaux; *Jimmy Buffett's Margaritaville Cafe: New
  Orleans-C* . . . . (Margaritaville)
I'm Going Home
Ten Years After; *ST/Woodstock* . . . . (Atlantic)
I'm Gonna Be (500 Miles)
Proclaimers; *ST/Benny & Joon* . . . . (BMG)
  Sunshine On Leith . . . . (Chrysalis)

I'm Moving On
Elvis Presley; *Canadian Tribute* . . . . (RCA)
　From Elvis In Memphis . . . . (RCA)
　Guitar Man . . . . (RCA)
　Memphis Record . . . . (RCA)
Emmylou Harris; *Last Date* . . . . (Warner Bros.)
　Profile II-The Best Of Emmylou Harris . . . . (Warner Bros.)
George Thorogood & The Destroyers; *Born To Be Bad* . . . . (Gold Rush)
Hank Snow; *60 Years Of Country Music-C* . . . . (RCA)
　Best Of Hank Snow . . . . (RCA)
　Great Moments At The Grand Ole Opry-C . . . . (RCA)
　I'm Moving On & Other Great Country Hits . . . . (RCA)
　Nipper's Greatest Hits Of The '50s-#2-C . . . . (RCA)
Rolling Stones; *December's Children (and everybody's)* . . . . (Abkco)

I'm Walkin'
Fats Domino; *Billboard Top R&B Hits-1957-C* . . . . (Rhino)
　Fats Domino's Greatest Hits . . . . (MCA)
　My Blue Heaven-Best Of Fats Domino-#1 . . . . (EMI)

I'm Walking Behind You
Eddie Fisher; *Very Best Of Eddie Fisher* . . . . (MCA)
Frank Sinatra; *Capitol Collectors Series-Frank Sinatra* . . . . (Capitol)
　Concepts . . . . (Capitol)
　Point Of No Return . . . . (Capitol)

I'm Walking The Dog
Webb Pierce; *Best Of Webb Pierce* . . . . (MCA)
　Webb Pierce-Golden Hits . . . . (Plantation)

In Walked Bud
Art Blakey & Thelonious Monk; *Great Moments In Jazz-C* . . . . (Atlantic)
Thelonius Monk; *Best Of Thelonius Monk* . . . . (Blue Note)
　Genius Of Modern Music-#1 . . . . (Blue Note)

Inner Light
Beatles; *Past Masters-Volume Two* . . . . (Parlophone)
　Rarities . . . . (Capitol)

Into The Great Wide Open
Tom Petty And The Heartbreakers; *Into The Great Wide Open* . . . . . . (MCA)

It Keeps You Running
Carly Simon; *Another Passenger* . . . . (Elektra)
Doobie Brothers; *Best Of The Doobies* . . . . (Warner Bros.)
　ST/FM . . . . (MCA)
　ST/Forrest Gump . . . . (Epic/Sony Music Soundtrax)
　Takin' It To The Streets . . . . (Warner Bros.)

It's A Long Way There
Little River Band; *Backstage Pass* . . . . (Capitol)
　Little River Band . . . . (Capitol)
　Little River Band's Greatest Hits . . . . (Capitol)

It's A Short Walk From Heaven To Hell
John Schneider; *Country Classics-#5-1985-1986-C* . . . . (Universal)
　John Schneider's Greatest Hits . . . . (MCA)
　Tryin' To Outrun The Wind . . . . (MCA)

I've Been Everywhere
Johnny Cash; *Unchained* . . . . (American)

Jack-Ass
Beck; *Odelay* . . . . (David Geffen Co.)

Joey, Joey, Joey
Al Jarreau; *1965* . . . . (Bainbridge)
Broadway Cast; *Most Happy Fella* . . . . (RCA)
Judy Garland; *Judy Garland-Live* . . . . (Capitol)
　One & Only . . . . (Capitol)

Journey
Jimmy Cliff; *Power & The Glory* . . . . (Columbia)

Journey
Boston; *Don't Look Back* . . . . (Epic)

Journey
Small Faces; *Ogdens' Nut Gone Flake* . . . . (Abkco)

Journey From Eden
Steve Miller Band; *Recall The Beginning* . . . . (Capitol)
　Steve Miller Band-Anthology . . . . (Capitol)

Journey From Mariabronn
Kansas; *Kansas* . . . . (Kirshner)
　Two For The Show . . . . (Kirshner)

Journey Man
Jethro Tull; *Heavy Horses* . . . . (Chrysalis)

Journey Through The Past
Neil Young; *Time Fades Away* . . . . (Reprise)

Journey To A Star
Judy Garland; *Judy Garland-Collector's Items-1936-1945* . . . . . . (MCA)

Journey To Capricorn
Stan Kenton; *Journey Into Capricorn* . . . . (Creative World)

Just A Closer Walk With Thee
Jim Nabors; *Jim Nabors-16 Most Requested Songs* . . . . (Legacy)
Kid Thomas; *Kid Thomas & His New Orleans Jazz Band* . . . . (Arhoolie)
Patsy Cline; *Best Of Patsy Cline* . . . . (Curb)
　Here's Patsy Cline . . . . (MCA)
Preservation Hall Jazz Band; *Best Of The Preservation Hall
　Jazz Band* . . . . (Columbia)
Tom Rush; *Blues Songs & Ballads* . . . . (Fantasy)

Just Walk In My Shoes
Gladys Knight & The Pips; *Gladys Knight & The Pips-Anthology* . . . . (Motown)
　Motown Legends-Gladys Knight & The Pips . . . . (Motown)

Just Walking In The Rain
Johnnie Ray; *16 Most Requested Songs Of The '50s-#1-C* . . . . (Legacy)
　Best Of Johnnie Ray . . . . (Columbia)
　Johnnie Ray-16 Most Requested Songs . . . . (Legacy)
　Johnnie Ray's Greatest Hits . . . . (Sony Music Special Prod.)

Kansas City
Beatles; *Beatles VI* . . . . (Capitol)
　Beatles-Box Set . . . . (Capitol)
　Rock 'N' Roll Music . . . . (Capitol)
　Super Oldies Of The '60s-#10-C . . . . (Audio Fidelity)
Bill Haley & His Comets; *Bill Haley & His Comets' Greatest Hits* . . . . (Everest)
Fats Domino; *Fats Domino's Greatest Hits* . . . . (Everest)
Wilbert Harrison; *American Graffiti-#3-C* . . . . (MCA)
　Billboard Top Rock 'N' Roll Hits-1959-C . . . . (Rhino)
　Cruisin'-1959-C . . . . (Increase)
　Echoes Of A Rock Era-Middle Years-C . . . . (Roulette)
　Super Oldies Of The '50s-#2-C . . . . (Audio Fidelity)

Keep On Chooglin'
Creedence Clearwater Revival; *1968-1969* . . . . (Fantasy)
　Bayou Country . . . . (Fantasy)
　Chooglin' . . . . (Fantasy)
　Live In Europe . . . . (Fantasy)

Keep On Movin'
Soul II Soul; *Keep On Movin'* . . . . (Virgin)

Keep On Running
Spencer Davis Group; *Best Of The Spencer Davis Group* . . . . (Rhino)
　Best Of The Spencer Davis Group . . . . (EMI)
　History Of British Rock-#4-C . . . . (Rhino)
　The Island Story-1962-1987-25th Anniversary-C . . . . (Island)

Keep On Running
Stevie Wonder; *Music Of My Mind* . . . . (Motown)

Keep On Truckin'
Hot Tuna; *''Howling Blues'' & Other Hits* . . . . (RCA)
　Burgers . . . . (Grunt)
　Final Vinyl . . . . (Grunt)

Keep On Truckin' (Part 1)
Eddie Kendricks; *12 #1 Hits From The '70s-C* . . . . (Motown)
　20/20-C . . . . (Motown)
　Didn't It Blow Your Mind: Soul Hits Of The '70s-#11-C . . . . . (Rhino)
　Eddie Kendricks-At His Best . . . . (Motown)
　Motown Superstar Series-#19-Eddie Kendricks . . . . (Motown)
　Motown's Biggest Pop Hits-C . . . . (Motown)

Keep On Walkin'
Cece Peniston; *Finally* . . . . (A&M)

Keep Searchin' (We'll Follow The Sun)
Del Shannon; *Del Shannon's Greatest Hits* . . . . (Rhino)
　Del Shannon's Greatest Hits . . . . (Curb)

Keep The Customer Satisfied
Simon & Garfunkel; *Bridge Over Troubled Water* . . . . (Columbia)
　Collected Works . . . . (Columbia)

Kentucky Rain
Elvis Presley; *Elvis Presley-Pure Gold* . . . . (RCA)
　Memphis Record . . . . (RCA)
　Worldwide 50 Gold Award Hits, Vol. 1, Parts 1 & 2 . . . . (RCA)

Kiss Me, I'm Gone
Marty Stuart; *Love And Luck* . . . . (MCA)

Kokomo
Beach Boys; *ST/Cocktail* . . . . (Elektra)
　Still Cruisin' . . . . (Capitol)

Leavin' Memphis, Frisco Bound
Jesse Fuller; *Frisco Bound* . . . . (Arhoolie)
　Lone Cat . . . . (Good Time Jazz)

Leaving Kansas City
George Jackson; *Sweet Down Home Delta Blues* . . . . (Amblin')

Leaving Of Liverpool
Clancy Brothers; *Clancy Brothers Greatest Hits* . . . . (Vanguard)

Leaving This Town
Beach Boys; *Holland* . . . . (Brother)
　The Beach Boys In Concert . . . . (Brother)

Legend Of A Cowgirl
Imani Coppola; *Chupacapra* . . . . (Columbia)

Let's Go
Cars; *Candy-O* . . . . (Elektra)
　The Cars' Greatest Hits . . . . (Elektra)

Let's Go
Nitty Gritty Dirt Band; *Let's Go* . . . . (Warner Bros.)

Let's Go
Wang Chung; *Mosaic* . . . . (Geffen)

Let's Go
Eurythmics; *Revenge* . . . . (RCA)

Let's Go Away For Awhile
Beach Boys; *Pet Sounds* . . . . (Capitol)
　The Pet Sounds Sessions: A 30th Anniversary Collection . . . . . (Capitol)

Let's Go To Vegas
Faith Hill; *It Matters To Me* . . . . (Warner Bros.)

Let's Go Trippin'
Beach Boys; *Surfin' U.S.A.* . . . . (Capitol)
Dick Dale And The Del-Tones; *Beach Classics-All Original
　Recordings-C* . . . . (Dunhill Compact Classics)

Dick Dale And The Del-Tones' Greatest Hits . . . . (Crescendo)
Tigers Loose . . . . (Rhino)
Let's See How Far You Get
BR549; *This Is BR549* . . . . (Lucky Dog)
Letter, The
Box Tops; *Billboard Top Rock 'N' Roll Hits-1967-C* . . . . (Rhino)
Box Tops' *Greatest Hits* . . . . (Rhino)
Cruisin'-1967-C . . . . (Increase)
Oldies But Goodies-#12-C . . . . (Original Sound)
Rockin' '60s-C . . . . (Priority)
Joe Cocker; *Joe Cocker Live* . . . . (Capitol)
Joe Cocker-Classics-#4 . . . . (A&M)
Joe Cocker's Greatest Hits . . . . (A&M)
Mad Dogs & Englishmen . . . . (A&M)
Vernon Green & The Medallions; *Oldies But Goodies-#1-C* . . (Original Sound)
Vernon Green & The Medallions-Golden Classics . . . . (Collectables)
Like A Rolling Stone
Bob Dylan; *Biograph* . . . . (Columbia)
Bob Dylan At Budokan . . . . (Columbia)
Bob Dylan's Greatest Hits . . . . (Columbia)
Highway 61 Revisited . . . . (Columbia)
More American Graffiti-#4-C . . . . (MCA)
Self Portrait . . . . (Columbia)
Bob Dylan And The Band; *Before The Flood* . . . . (Columbia)
Jimi Hendrix; *ST/Jimi Plays Monterey* . . . . (Reprise)
Jimi Hendrix Experience; *Jimi Hendrix Experience* . . . . (Reprise)
Rolling Stones; *Stripped* . . . . (Virgin)
Little Gasoline, A
Terri Clark; *Fearless* . . . . (Mercury)
Little Past Little Rock
Lee Ann Womack; *Some Things I Know* . . . . (Decca)
Little Red Rodeo
Collin Raye; *Best Of Collin Raye-Direct Hits* . . . . (Epic)
Lonesome Town
Ricky Nelson; *Best Of Ricky Nelson* . . . . (Curb)
Long May You Run
Neil Young; *Decade* . . . . (Reprise)
Neil Young-Unplugged . . . . (Reprise)
Stills/Young Band; *Long May You Run* . . . . (Reprise)
Long Road, The
Eddie Vedder; *America: A Tribute To Heroes-C* . . . . (Interscope)
Long Walk, A
Jill Scott; *Who Is Jill Scott? Words And Sounds-#1* . . . . . . (Hidden Beach/Epic)
Long Way
Dan Fogelberg; *Dan Fogelberg-Souvenirs* . . . . (Full Moon)
Long Way Around
Linda Ronstadt; *Hand Sown Home Grown* . . . . (Capitol)
Linda Ronstadt-Retrospective . . . . (Capitol)
Long Way Around
Chris Whitley; *Living With The Law* . . . . (Columbia)
Louisiana Bound
Big Joe Williams; *Shake Your Boogie* . . . . (Arhoolie)
Louisiana Rain
Tom Petty; *Playback* . . . . (MCA)
Tom Petty And The Heartbreakers; *Damn The Torpedoes* . . . . . . (MCA)
Love Can Run Faster
Robert Palmer; *Double Fun* . . . . (Island)
Love Travels
Kathy Mattea; *Love Travels* . . . . (Mercury)
Love Walked In
Chet Baker; *Chet Baker With Strings* . . . . (Columbia)
Frank Sinatra; *Sinatra Swings* . . . . (Reprise)
The Reprise Collection . . . . (Reprise)
Sarah Vaughan; *Complete Sarah Vaughan On Mercury-#2* . . . . . (Mercury)
Love Walks In
Van Halen; *5150* . . . . (Warner Bros.)
Mach 5
Presidents Of The United States Of America; *Presidents Of The United States
Of America II* . . . . (Columbia)
Mama, I'm Coming Home
Ozzy Osbourne; *No More Tears* . . . . (Epic Portrait Assoc.)
Many A Long & Lonesome Highway
Rodney Crowell; *Keys To The Highway* . . . . (Columbia)
Taste Of Texas-Songs 'Bout Texas By Texans-C . . . . (Columbia)
Many A Mile
Buffy Sainte-Marie; *Best Of Buffy Sainte-Marie* . . . . (Vanguard)
Many A Mile . . . . (Vanguard)
Many A Mile To Freedom
Traffic; *The Low Spark Of High Heeled Boys* . . . . (Island)
Many Rivers To Cross
Jimmy Cliff; *In Concert-Best Of Jimmy Cliff* . . . . (Reprise)
Reggae Spectacular-C . . . . (A&M)
ST/The Harder They Come . . . . (Mango)
Wonderful World, Beautiful People . . . . (A&M)
Linda Ronstadt; *Prisoner In Disguise* . . . . (Asylum)
UB40; *Labour Of Love* . . . . (A&M)
Marching To Mars
Sammy Hagar; *Marching To Mars* . . . . (MCA)

Marching To Pretoria
Weavers; *Weavers At Carnegie Hall, Vol. 2* . . . . (Vanguard)
Me And Julio Down By The Schoolyard
Paul Simon; *Greatest Hits, Etc.* . . . . (Columbia)
Negotiations And Love Songs, 1971-1986 . . . . (Warner Bros.)
Paul Simon . . . . (Columbia)
Paul Simon In Concert/Live Rhymin' . . . . (Columbia)
Simon & Garfunkel; *The Concert In Central Park* . . . . . . (Warner Bros.)
Me And My Arrow
Nilsson; *Nilsson's Greatest Hits* . . . . (RCA)
The Point . . . . (RCA)
Mean Mama Blues
Bob Wills; *Stay A Little Longer-The Original Columbia
Recordings* . . . . (Roswell/RCA)
Meet In The Middle
Diamond Rio; *Diamond Rio* . . . . (Arista)
Diamond Rio's Greatest Hits . . . . (Arista)
Mer Girl
Madonna; *Ray Of Light* . . . . (Maverick)
Mexico
James Taylor; *Gorilla* . . . . (Warner Bros.)
James Taylor-Live . . . . (Columbia)
James Taylor's Greatest Hits . . . . (Warner Bros.)
Mellow Rock Hits Of The '70s-Summer Breeze-C . . . . (Rhino)
Jimmy Buffett; *Barometer Soup* . . . . (Margaritaville)
Midnight Flyer
Eagles; *On The Border* . . . . (Elektra)
Osborne Brothers; *Essential Bluegrass Album* . . . . (C.M.H. Prod.)
Osborne Brothers & Mac Wiseman; *Great American Train
Songs-C* . . . . (C.M.H. Prod.)
Miles Away
Basia; *Greenpeace/Rainbow Warriors-C* . . . . (Geffen)
Time And Tide . . . . (Epic)
Miles Away
Jackson Browne; *I'm Alive* . . . . (Elektra)
Miles Away
Winger; *In The Heart Of The Young* . . . . (Atlantic)
Miles Away
Marc Cohn; *Marc Cohn* . . . . (Atlantic)
Miles Away
Fleetwood Mac; *Mystery To Me* . . . . (Reprise)
Miles To Go (Before I Sleep)
Celine Dion; *Let's Talk About Love-C* . . . . (550 Music)
Mister & Mississippi
Patti Page; *Patti Page's Greatest Hits* . . . . (Columbia)
Moonlight Mile
Rolling Stones; *Sticky Fingers* . . . . (Virgin)
Most High
Jimmy Page/Robert Plant; *Walking Into Clarksdale* . . . . . . (Atlantic)
Most Likely You'll Go Your Way & I'll Go Mine
Bob Dylan; *Biograph* . . . . (Columbia)
Blonde On Blonde . . . . (Columbia)
Bob Dylan And The Band; *Before The Flood* . . . . (Columbia)
Motor City
Randy Weeks; *Madeline* . . . . (Hightone)
Move It
Chantays; *Revenge Of The Surf Instrumentals-C* . . . . (MCA)
Move On
Bernadette Peters & Mandy Patinkin; *Collector's Sondheim-C* . . . . (RCA)
Move On
Warren Brothers; *King Of Nothing* . . . . (BNA)
Move On
An Emotional Fish; *An Emotional Fish* . . . . (Atlantic)
Move On
Santana; *Inner Secrets* . . . . (Columbia)
Move On
Abba; *The Album* . . . . (Atlantic)
Move On Down The Line
Jerry Lee Lewis; *Jerry Lee Lewis-Original Golden Hits-#1* . . . . . (Sun)
Jerry Lee Lewis-Original Golden Hits-#1 . . . . (Sun)
Milestones . . . . (Rhino)
Movin'
REO Speedwagon; *Ridin' The Storm Out* . . . . (Epic)
Movin'
Brass Construction; *Brass Construction* . . . . (United Artists)
Movin'
Wes Montgomery; *Movin' Along* . . . . (Riverside)
Movin'
Psychefunkapus; *Psychefunkapus* . . . . (Atlantic)
Movin' & Groovin'
Duane Eddy; *Compact Command Performances-Duane Eddy* . . . . (Motown)
Duane Eddy-16 Greatest Hits . . . . (Jamie)
Movin' On
Dave Dudley; *Interstate Gold* . . . . (Sun)
Trucks, Trains & Airplanes-C . . . . (International Mktg. Group)
Merle Haggard; *Capitol Collectors Series-Merle Haggard* . . . . . (Capitol)
Merle Haggard & Brooks & Dunn; *For The Record: Merle Haggard-43
Legendary Hits* . . . . (BNA)

Merle Haggard & The Strangers; *Winners* . . . . (Capitol)

Movin' On
Bad Company; *10 From 6* . . . . (Atlantic)
Bad Company . . . . (Swan Song)

Movin' Out
Aerosmith; *Aerosmith* . . . . (Columbia)
Aerosmith-Classics Live 2 . . . . (Columbia)
Pandora's Box . . . . (Columbia)

Movin' Out
Billy Joel; *Billy Joel-Greatest Hits, Volume I & Volume II* . . . . . . (Columbia)
Stranger . . . . (Columbia)

Movin' Out
Sonny Rollins; *Movin' Out* . . . . (Prestige)

Moving On
Dells; *Oh, What A Night* . . . . (Vee-Jay)

Moving On
Triumph; *Just A Game* . . . . (RCA)

Moving On
Sweet Honey In The Rock; *Other Side* . . . . (Flying Fish)

Much Too Young (To Feel This Damn Old)
Garth Brooks; *Garth Brooks-Double Live* . . . . (Capitol)

Mummer's Dance
Loreena McKennitt; *The Book Of Secrets* . . . . (Quinlan Rd./Warner Bros.)

My Daddy Was A Travelin' Man
Brenda Kaye Perry; *45-#1021* . . . . (MRC)

My Elusive Dreams
Bobby Vinton; *Autumn Memories* . . . . (Epic)
Bobby Vinton's All-Time Greatest Hits . . . . (Epic)
Charlie Rich; *Charlie Rich-16 Biggest Hits* . . . . (Legacy)
Charlie Rich's Greatest Hits . . . . (Epic)
Charlie Rich-Super Hits . . . . (Epic)
David Houston & Tammy Wynette; *Best Of David
  Houston* . . . . (Collector's Choice)
Billboard Top Country Hits-1967-C . . . . (Rhino)
Tammy Wynette's Greatest Hits . . . . (Epic)

My Heroes Have Always Been Cowboys
Willie Nelson; *All Time Legends Of Country Music-C* . . . . (Legacy)
Cowboy Super Hits-C . . . . (Columbia)
Greatest Country Hits Of The '80s-1980-C . . . . (Columbia)
Greatest Hits (& Some That Will Be) . . . . (Columbia)
ST/My Heroes Have Always Been Cowboys . . . . (RCA)
ST/The Electric Horseman . . . . (Columbia)

My Mammy
Al Jolson; *Best Of Al Jolson* . . . . (MCA)
Let Me Sing And I'm Happy . . . . (Turner Classic Movies)
The '20s-From Broadway To Hollywood-#3-C . . . . (Flapper)
Happenings; *Happenings-Golden Hits!* . . . . (B.T. Puppy)

My Shoes Keep Walking Back To You
Ray Price; *All Time Legends Of Country Music-C* . . . . (Legacy)
Essential Ray Price-1951-1962 . . . . (Columbia)
Ray Price's Greatest Hits . . . . (Columbia)

Mystic Eyes
Them featuring Van Morrison; *Here Comes The Night* . . . . (Out Of Print)
History Of British Rock-#6-C . . . . (Rhino)
*The Sopranos-Music From The HBO Original
  Series* . . . . (Sony Music Soundtrax)

Mystic Traveler
Dave Mason; *Let It Flow* . . . . (Columbia)

Never Going Back Again
Fleetwood Mac; *25 Years-The Chain* . . . . (Warner Bros.)
Fleetwood Mac Live . . . . (Warner Bros.)
Rumours . . . . (Warner Bros.)
Matchbox Twenty; *Legacy-A Tribute To Fleetwood Mac's Rumours-C* . . . (Lava)

New Timer
Bruce Springsteen; *The Ghost Of Tom Joad* . . . . (Columbia)

No One To Run With
Allman Brothers Band; *Where It All Begins* . . . . (Epic)

No Particular Place To Go
Chuck Berry; *Best Of The Best Of Chuck Berry* . . . . . (International Mktg. Group)
The Chess Box-Chuck Berry . . . . (Chess)

No Place To Go
Howlin' Wolf; *Moanin' In The Moonlight* . . . . (Chess)

No Place To Go
Charlie Daniels Band; *Fire On The Mountain* . . . . (Epic)

No Place To Run
UFO; *No Place To Run* . . . . (Chrysalis)

North Carolina Bound
Connie & Babe & The Backwoods Boys; *Backwoods Bluegrass* . . . . . (Rounder)

Northbound-Southbound
Wynton Marsalis; *Big Train* . . . . (Columbia)

Northwest Passage
Woody Herman & His Orchestra; *Best Of The Big Bands-Woody Herman &
  His Orchestra* . . . . (Legacy)
This Is Jazz-#24: Woody Herman . . . . (Legacy)

Nowhere Bound
Diamond Rio; *Diamond Rio* . . . . (Arista)

Nowhere To Run
Esther Phillips; *A Way To Say Goodbye* . . . . (Muse)

Nowhere To Run
Isley Brothers; *This Old Heart Of Mine* . . . . (Motown)

Martha & The Vandellas; *Martha Reeves & The Vandellas'
  Greatest Hits* . . . . (Motown)
Martha Reeves & The Vandellas-Anthology . . . . (Motown)
Motown Story-First 25 Years-C . . . . (Motown)
Motown Superstar Series-#11-Martha Reeves & The Vandellas . . . . (Motown)
ST/Sound Of "Murphy Brown" . . . . (MCA)

Nowhere To Run
J.J. Cale; *Naturally* . . . . (MCA)

Nowhere To Run
Pete Townshend & Ronnie Lane; *Rough Mix* . . . . (Atlantic)

Nowhere To Run
Santana; *Shango* . . . . (Columbia)

Oh, Susanna
Disneyland Cast; *Children's Favorite Songs-#1* . . . . (Disney)
James Taylor; *Sweet Baby James* . . . . (Warner Bros.)
Myron Floren; *Best Of The Wurstfest* . . . . (Ranwood)
Myron Floren . . . . (Ranwood)

Old Folks At Home
Mormon Tabernacle Choir; *Songs Of The Civil War And Stephen Foster
  Favorites* . . . . (Sony Music Classical)
Paul Robeson; *A Man & His Beliefs-Golden Classics-#2* . . . . (Collectables)

Old Man And Me
Hootie & The Blowfish; *Fairweather Johnson* . . . . (Atlantic)

On The Road Again
Willie Nelson; *Greatest Country Hits Of The '80s-1980-C* . . . . (Columbia)
Greatest Hits (& Some That Will Be) . . . . (Columbia)
Hot Country Rock-#1-C . . . . (Epic)
ST/Forrest Gump . . . . (Epic/Sony Music Soundtrax)
ST/Honeysuckle Rose . . . . (Columbia)

On The Road Again
Tom Rush; *Classic Rush* . . . . (Elektra)
Tom Rush . . . . (Elektra)

On The Road Again
Aerosmith; *Pandora's Box* . . . . (Columbia)

On The Road Again
Grateful Dead; *Reckoning* . . . . (Arista)
So Many Roads (1965-1995) . . . . (Arista)

On The Run
Pink Floyd; *Dark Side Of The Moon* . . . . (Capitol)
Pink Floyd-Gift Set . . . . (Capitol)

On The Run
Prophet; *Cycle Of The Moon* . . . . (Megaforce)

On The Run
Electric Light Orchestra; *Discovery* . . . . (Jet)

On The Run
Marshall Crenshaw; *Good Evening* . . . . (Warner Bros.)

On The Run
Balaam & The Angel; *Live Free Or Die* . . . . (Virgin)

On The Run
Judas Priest; *Point Of Entry* . . . . (Columbia)

On The Run
Blackfoot; *Tomcattin'* . . . . (Atco)

On The Sunny Side Of The Street
Diana Krall; *Stepping Out* . . . . (Justin Time)
Frank Sinatra; *Come Swing With Me!* . . . . (Capitol)
One More For The Road . . . . (Capitol)
Sentimental Journey . . . . (Capitol)
The Capitol Years . . . . (Capitol)
Judy Garland; *Best Of Judy Garland* . . . . (MCA)
Louis Armstrong; *Best Of Louis Armstrong* . . . . (MCA)
Chicago Concert 1956 . . . . (Columbia)
Jazz Club-Vocal . . . . (Verve)
Music Autobiography . . . . (Columbia)
Ted Lewis & His Orchestra; *Charming Gents Of Stage & Screen-C* . . . (Legacy)
Those Wonderful Years: Puttin' On The Ritz-C . . . . (JCI Assoc. Labels)

One After 909
Beatles; *Let It Be* . . . . (Capitol)
The Beatles-Anthology-#1 . . . . (Capitol)

One Headlight
Wallflowers; *Bringing Down The Horse* . . . . (Interscope)

One More Mile
Clarence "Gatemouth" Brown; *One More Mile* . . . . (Rounder)
Paul Butterfield Blues Band; *Golden Butter* . . . . (Elektra)

One Step At A Time
Brenda Lee; *Brenda Lee-Anthology-#1 & #2* . . . . (MCA)

One Step Closer
Doobie Brothers; *Best Of The Doobies, Volume II* . . . . (Warner Bros.)
One Step Closer . . . . (Warner Bros.)

One Step Closer
Highway 101; *Highway 101* . . . . (Warner Bros.)

One Step Closer To You
Gavin Christopher; *One Step Closer* . . . . (Manhattan)

One Step Up
Bruce Springsteen; *Tunnel Of Love* . . . . (Columbia)

One Way Ticket (Because I Can)
LeAnn Rimes; *Blue* . . . . (MCG/Curb)

One Way Ticket To Memphis
Bobby King & Terry Evans; *Rhythm Blues Soul & Grooves* .... (Rounder)
Orinoco Flow (Sail Away)
Enya; *Watermark* .... (Reprise)
Ostrich Walk
Bob Crosby & His Orchestra; *Bob Crosby-With June Christy & Polly Bergen* .... (Hindsight)
Bob Scobey's Frisco Band; *Direct From San Francisco* ..... (Good Time Jazz)
Out Of My Bones
Randy Travis; *You And You Alone* .... (DreamWorks/SKG)
Pack It Up
UFO; *Obsession* .... (Chrysalis)
Pack It Up
Pretenders; *Pretenders II* .... (Sire)
Pack Up Your Sins And Go To The Devil
Dorothy Loudon; *Broadway Baby* .... (DRG)
Ella Fitzgerald & Chick Webb; *The Early Years-#1: With Chick Webb & His Orchestra-1935-1938* .... (GRP)
Packed Up And Took My Mind
Little Milton; *Tin Pan Alley* .... (Stax)
Papa Was A Rollin' Stone
Temptations; *20/20-C* .... (Motown)
25 #1 Hits From 25 Years-C .... (Motown)
All The Million-Sellers .... (Motown)
Billboard Top Rock 'N' Roll Hits-1972-C .... (Rhino)
Compact Command Performances-Temptations .... (Motown)
Temptations-Anthology-The Best Of The Temptations ...... (Motown)
Paris, Tennessee
Dennis Robbins; *Man With A Plan* .... (Giant)
Kenny Chesney; *All I Need To Know* .... (BNA)
Tracy Lawrence; *Sticks & Stones* .... (Atlantic)
Pascagoula Run
Jimmy Buffett; *Boats Beaches Bars & Ballads* .... (Margaritaville)
Off To See The Lizard .... (MCA)
Pay You Back With Interest
Hollies; *Best Of The Hollies* .... (EMI)
History Of British Rock-#4-C .... (Rhino)
The Hollies' Greatest Hits .... (Epic)
Peaceful Journey
Fat Larry's Band; *Sweet Soul Music-Stax Groups-C* .... (Stax)
Peaceful Journey
Heavy D & The Boyz; *Peaceful Journey* .... (Uptown)
Perfect Day
Collective Soul; *Blender* .... (Atlantic)
Planet Caravan
Pantera; *Far Beyond Driven* .... (East West)
Polly-Wolly-Doodle
Leon Redbone; *Live!* .... (Pair)
On The Track .... (Warner Bros.)
Mance Lipscomb; *Mance Lipscomb-Vol. 3-Texas Songster In A Live Performance* .... (Arhoolie)
Pete Seeger/Woody Guthrie/Cisco Houston; *Lonesome Valley* .... (Smithsonian Folkways)
Poor Wayfaring Stranger
Jim Hendricks; *Appalachian Memories-Front Porch Favorites* .... (Benson)
Jo Stafford; *American Folk Songs* .... (Corinthian)
Pre-Road Downs
Crosby, Stills & Nash; *Crosby, Stills & Nash* .... (Atlantic)
Prodigal Son
Rolling Stones; *Beggars Banquet* .... (Abkco)
Promised Land
Band; *Moondog Matinee* .... (Capitol)
Chuck Berry; *Rock 'N' Roll Rarities-20 Magic Tracks* .... (Chess)
The Chess Box-Chuck Berry .... (Chess)
Elvis Presley; *Promised Land* .... (RCA)
ST/This Is Elvis .... (RCA)
Freddy Weller; *Country Music Classics-#11-Early '70s-C* .... (K-Tel)
Freddy Weller's Greatest Hits .... (Columbia)
Gary Morris; *Full Moon Empty Heart* .... (Liberty)
Grateful Dead; *Steal Your Face* .... (Grateful Dead)
James Taylor; *Walking Man* .... (Warner Bros.)
Kingfish; *Kingfish/Alive In Eighty Five-Double Dose* .... (Relix)
Ramble On
Led Zeppelin; *Led Zeppelin II* .... (Atlantic)
Led Zeppelin-Box Set .... (Atlantic)
Remasters .... (Atlantic)
Ramble On Rose
Grateful Dead; *Europe '72* .... (Warner Bros.)
What A Long Strange Trip It's Been: The Best Of The Grateful Dead .... (Warner Bros.)
Rambler
Molly Hatchet; *Beatin' The Odds* .... (Epic)
Ramblin'
Marshall Tucker Band; *Marshall Tucker Band* .... (AJK Music)
Marshall Tucker Band's Greatest Hits .... (Capricorn)
Where We All Belong .... (AJK Music)
Ramblin' Boy
Tom Paxton; *Greatest Folksingers Of The '60s-C* .... (Vanguard)
Newport Broadside: Newport Folk Festival-1963-C .... (Vanguard)

Ramblin' Boy .... (Elektra)
Troubadours Of The Folk Era-#2-C .... (Rhino)
Ramblin' Fever
Merle Haggard; *Merle Haggard's Greatest Hits* .... (MCA)
More Of The Best .... (Rhino)
Ramblin' Fever .... (MCA)
Merle Haggard & Alabama; *For The Record: Merle Haggard-43 Legendary Hits* .... (BNA)
Ramblin' Gamblin' Man
Bob Seger; *Live Bullet* .... (Capitol)
Ramblin' Hobo
Doc Watson; *Don Watson & Family-Treasures Untold* ...... (Vanguard)
Essential Doc Watson .... (Vanguard)
Old Time Music At Newport .... (Vanguard)
Watson Family; *Watson Family* .... (Smithsonian Folkways)
Ramblin' In My Shoes
Hank Williams, Jr.; *The Pressure Is On-Original Classics Collection-#7* .... (Curb)
Ramblin' Jack (A Lonesome Hobo)
Skip Gorman; *A Cowboy's Wild Song To His Herd* .... (Rounder)
Ramblin' Man
Allman Brothers Band; *Best Of The Allman Brothers Band* .... (Polydor)
Billboard Top Rock 'N' Roll Hits-1973-C .... (Rhino)
Brothers & Sisters .... (Polydor)
Decade Of Hits-1969-1979 .... (Polydor)
Dreams .... (Polydor)
Rock Classics-C .... (K-Tel)
South's Greatest Hits-C .... (Capricorn)
The Road Goes On Forever, A Collection Of Their Greatest Recordings .... (Polydor)
Wipe The Windows-Check The Oil-Dollar Gas .... (Capricorn)
Ramblin' Man
Hank Williams; *24 Of Hank Williams' Greatest Hits* ...... (Polydor)
Hank Williams-16 Great Hits .... (Everest)
Hank Williams-40 Greatest Hits .... (Polydor)
Hank Williams, Jr.; *Rowdy* .... (WB/Curb)
ST/Your Cheatin' Heart .... (Sony Music Special Prod.)
Kieran Kane; *Steel Rails-Classic Railroad Songs-#1-C* ..... (Rounder)
Ramblin' Rose
Hank Snow; *Collector's Series-Hank Snow-#2* .... (RCA)
Nat "King" Cole; *Best Of Nat "King" Cole-Vol. 1* .... (Capitol)
Memories Are Made Of This-C .... (Capitol)
Ramblin' Rose
Chuck Berry; *Chuck Berry's Greatest Hits* .... (Everest)
Ramblin' Round Your City
Linda Ronstadt; *Linda Ronstadt* .... (Capitol)
Linda Ronstadt-Retrospective .... (Capitol)
Odetta; *Greatest Songs Of Woody Guthrie-C* .... (Vanguard)
Tribute To Woody Guthrie-C .... (Warner Bros.)
Rambling On My Mind
Eric Clapton; *Eric Clapton-Crossroads-C* .... (Polydor)
John Mayall's Bluesbreakers with Eric Clapton; *John Mayall's Bluesbreakers with Eric Clapton* .... (Deram)
Robert Johnson; *King Of The Delta Blues Singers* .... (Columbia)
Robert Johnson-Complete Recordings .... (Columbia)
Savoy Brown; *Slow Train* .... (Relix)
Ready To Run
Dixie Chicks; *Fly* .... (Monument)
ST/Runaway Bride .... (Sony Music Soundtrax)
Remember (Walkin' In The Sand)
Aerosmith; *Aerosmith's Greatest Hits* .... (Columbia)
Night In The Ruts .... (Columbia)
Go-Go's; *Return To The Valley Of The Go-Go's* .... (I.R.S.)
Shangri-Las; *Girl Groups-Story Of A Sound-C* .... (Rhino)
Oldies But Goodies-#6-C .... (Original Sound)
Original Golden Hits Of The Great Groups-#1-C .... (SSS International)
ST/Goodfellas .... (Atlantic)
Restless
Carl Perkins; *Jive After Five-Best Of Carl Perkins-1959-1978* .... (Rhino)
Mark O'Connor; *Great Divorce Songs For Him-C* ...... (Warner Bros.)
The New Nashville Cats .... (Warner Bros.)
Ridin' That Midnight Train
Ricky Skaggs and Kentucky Thunder; *Bluegrass Rules!* .... (Rounder)
Right Where I Need To Be
Gary Allan; *Smoke Rings In The Dark* .... (MCA)
River And The Highway
Pam Tillis; *All Of This Love* .... (Arista)
Pam Tillis' Greatest Hits .... (Arista)
Road Less Traveled, The
George Strait; *The Road Less Traveled* .... (MCA)
Road Less Travelled
Preston Reed; *Road Less Travelled* .... (Flying Fish)
Road Runner (I'm A)
Fleetwood Mac; *Penguin* .... (Reprise)
Humble Pie; *Eat It* .... (A&M)
Smokin' .... (A&M)
Junior Walker & The All Stars; *Junior Walker & The All Stars' Greatest Hits* .... (Motown)
Junior Walker & The All Stars-Anthology .... (Motown)

Motown Superstar Series-#5-Junior Walker & The All Stars . . . . (Motown)
Shotgun . . . . (Motown)

Road To Dead
Paula Cole; *This Fire* . . . .(Imago)

Roam
B-52's; *Cosmic Thing* . . . .(Reprise)

Roamin' Wyoming
Randy Travis; *Wind In The Wire* . . . . (Warner Bros.)

Roll Me Away
Bob Seger & The Silver Bullet Band; *ST/Armageddon-The Album*. . . (Columbia)

Rollin' Home
Eric Andersen; *Best Of Eric Andersen* . . . . (Vanguard)
Peter, Paul & Mary; *Album 1700* . . . . (Warner Bros.)

Rollin' On
Doobie Brothers; *Brotherhood* . . . .(Capitol)

Rollin' Stone
Humble Pie; *Rock On* . . . . (A&M)
Rockin' The Fillmore . . . . (A&M)

Rollin' Stone
Mose Allison; *Best Of Mose Allison* . . . . (Rhino)

Rollin' Stone
Muddy Waters; *Best Of Chess Blues-C* . . . . (Chess)
Best Of Muddy Waters . . . . (Chess)

Room To Move
John Mayall; *Best Of John Mayall* . . . . (Polydor)
The Turning Point . . . . (Polydor)

'Round The World With The Rubber Duck
C.W. McCall; *C.W. McCall's Greatest Hits* . . . . (Polydor)

Route 66
Asleep At The Wheel; *Served Live* . . . . (Capitol)
Very Best Of Asleep At The Wheel Since 1970 . . . .(Relentless/Madacy)
Wheelin' & Dealin'. . . . . (Capitol)
Depeche Mode; *ST/Earth Girls Are Easy* . . . .(Sire)
George Maharis; *45-#15-2227*. (Epic)
Manhattan Transfer; *Bop doo-wopp* . . . . (Atlantic)
Nat ''King'' Cole; *Capitol Collectors Series-Nat ''King'' Cole* . . . . . . (Capitol)
The Nat ''King'' Cole Story . . . . (Capitol)
Natalie Cole; *Unforgettable With Love* . . . . (Elektra)
Rolling Stones; *December's Children (and everybody's)* . . . . (Abkco)
England's Newest Hit Makers/The Rolling Stones . . . . (Abkco)

Roving Kind, The
Guy Mitchell; *Guy Mitchell-16 Most Requested Songs* . . . . (Legacy)

Run
Collective Soul; *Dosage* . . . . (Atlantic)

Run
George Strait; *The Road Goes On Forever, A Collection Of Their Greatest Recordings* . . . . (Polydor)

Run Baby Run (Back Into My Arms)
Newbeats; *Collectables Presents The History Of Rock-#10-C* . . . . (Collectables)
Newbeats-Golden Classics Edition . . . .(Collectables)
Tremeloes; *Best Of The Tremeloes* . . . . (Rhino)

Run For Your Life
Beatles; *Beatles-Box Set* . . . . (Capitol)
Rubber Soul . . . . (Capitol)

Run From Tears
Crosby, Stills & Nash; *CSN* . . . . (Atlantic)

Run Joe
Louis Jordan; *Best Of Louis Jordan* . . . . (MCA)
Neville Brothers; *Fiyo On The Bayou* . . . . (A&M)

Run Joey Run
David Geddes; *Super Hits Of The '70s-Have A Nice Day-#15-C* . . . . (Rhino)

Run Like A Deer
Beers Family Sings; *Seasons Of Peace* . . . . (Biograph)

Run Like A Thief
Bonnie Raitt; *Home Plate* . . . . (Warner Bros.)
J.D. Souther; *J.D. Souther* . . . . (Asylum)

Run Like An Antelope
Phish; *Lawn Boy* . . . . (Elektra)

Run Like Hell
Pink Floyd; *Delicate Sound Of Thunder* . . . . (Columbia)
Knebworth-The Album-C . . . . (Polydor)
The Wall . . . . (Columbia)
Roger Waters; *The Wall-Live In Berlin* . . . . (Mercury)

Run Little Rabbit
John & Jamie Hartford; *Hartford & Hartford* . . . .(Flying Fish)

Run Possum Run!
Southern Rail; *Roadwork*. . . . .(Turquoise)

Run Red Run
Coasters; *The Ultimate Coasters* . . . . (Warner Special Prod.)

Run Run Run
Who; *Happy Jack* . . . . (MCA)
Magic Bus-The Who On Tour . . . . (MCA)

Run Samson Run
Neil Sedaka; *Neil Sedaka Sings His Greatest Hits* . . . . (RCA)
Neil Sedaka-Pure Gold . . . .(RCA)
Neil Sedaka's All-Time Greatest Hits . . . . (RCA)

Run Through The Jungle
Creedence Clearwater Revival; *1970* . . . .(Fantasy)

Cosmo's Factory. . . . . (Fantasy)
Creedence Clearwater Revival-Chronicle . . . . (Fantasy)
More Creedence Gold . . . . (Fantasy)

Run To Me
Bee Gees; *Bee Gees-Gold* . . . . (Polydor)
Here At Last...Bee Gees...Live . . . . (Polydor)

Run To Me
Animotion; *Animotion* . . . .(Mercury)

Run To Me
Dionne Warwick & Barry Manilow; *Run To Me* . . . .(Arista)

Run To Me
Angela Winbush; *Sharp* . . . .(Mercury)

Run To Mexico
Babys; *Head First* . . . .(Chrysalis)

Run To My Lovin' Arms
Jay & The Americans; *Jay & The Americans' Greatest Hits* . . . . (CEMA Special Prod.)

Run To The Water
Live; *The Distance To Here* . . . . (Radioactive/MCA)

Run To You
Bryan Adams; *Music For The Miracle-C* . . . .(Epic Portrait Assoc.)
Reckless. . . . .(A&M)

Run With The Fox
Yes; *Yesyears* . . . . (Atco)

Run With The Wolf
Blackmore's Rainbow; *Rainbow Rising*. . . . . (Polydor)

Run, Run, Run
Diana Ross & The Supremes; *Diana Ross & The Supremes' Greatest Hits* . . . . (Motown)
Diana Ross & The Supremes-Anthology (1962-1969). . . . .(Motown)

Run, Run, Run
Third Rail; *Even More Nuggets-C* . . . .(Rhino)
Rock Artifacts-From The Vaults-#3-C . . . .(Columbia)

Run, Run, Run
Concrete Blonde; *Free* . . . .(Capitol)

Run, Run, Run
Jo Jo Gunne; *Super Hits Of The '70s-Have A Nice Day-#8-C* . . . .(Rhino)

Run, Woman, Run
Tammy Wynette; *Tammy Wynette-Anniversary-20 Years Of Hits* . . . . (Epic)
Tammy Wynette's Biggest Hits . . . . (Epic)

Runaround
Fleetwoods; *Best Of The Fleetwoods* . . . . (Rhino)

Runaround
Van Halen; *For Unlawful Carnal Knowledge* . . . . (Warner Bros.)

Runaway
Corrs; *Forgiven, Not Forgotten* . . . .(143/Asylum)

Runaway
Janet Jackson; *Design Of A Decade-1986/1996* . . . .(A&M)

Runaway
Jefferson Starship; *Earth* . . . . (Grunt)
Jefferson Starship-Gold . . . . (RCA)

Runaway
Bon Jovi; *Bon Jovi* . . . .(Mercury)

Runaway
Melissa Manchester; *Melissa Manchester's Greatest Hits* . . . .(Arista)

Runaway
Damn Yankees; *Damn Yankees* . . . . (Warner Bros.)

Runner
Manfred Mann's Earth Band; *Somewhere In Afrika*. . . . .(Arista)

Runnin'
Santana; *Marathon*. . . . .(Columbia)

Runnin'
Earth, Wind & Fire; *All 'N All* . . . .(Columbia)

Runnin'
Mason Ruffner; *Gypsy Blood*. . . . .(Epic Portrait Assoc.)

Runnin'
Steve Wariner; *I Should Be With You* . . . . (MCA)

Runnin' Away
Sly & The Family Stone; *Sly & The Family Stone-Anthology* . . . .(Epic)
There's A Riot Goin' On . . . . (Epic)

Runnin' Away With My Heart
Lonestar; *Lonestar* . . . . (BNA)

Runnin' Back To Saskatoon
Guess Who; *Track Record-Collection* . . . . (RCA)

Runnin' Blue
Doors; *Soft Parade* . . . . (Elektra)
Weird Scenes Inside The Gold Mine . . . . (Elektra)

Runnin' For Your Lovin'
Brothers Johnson; *Brothers Johnson-Classics-#11* . . . . (A&M)
Right On Time . . . . (A&M)

Runnin' With The Devil
Van Halen; *Van Halen* . . . . (Warner Bros.)

Runnin' With The Wind
Eddie Rabbitt; *Jersey Boy* . . . .(Capitol)
Ten Years Of Greatest Hits . . . .(Capitol)

Running Back
Emotions; *Sunshine* . . . . (Stax)
The Emotions-Chronicle . . . . (Stax)

Running Back
Freddy Fender; *Before The Next Teardrop Falls* . . . . (Universal)
Running Back
Thin Lizzy; *Jailbreak* . . . . (Mercury)
Running Back
Eddie Money; *Playing For Keeps* . . . . (Columbia)
Running Back To You
Vanessa Williams; *The Comfort Zone* . . . . (Wing)
Running Bear
Johnny Preston; *45s On CD-#1-1956-1959-C* . . . . (Mercury)
Billboard Top Rock 'N' Roll Hits-1960-C . . . . (Rhino)
Cruisin'-1960-C . . . . (Increase)
Sonny James; *All-Time Country Classics-#1-C* . . . . (Capitol)
Running Down To Cuba
John Townley & The Press Gang; *Chesapeake Sailor's Companion* . . . (Adelphi)
Running Free
Iron Maiden; *Iron Maiden* . . . . (Capitol)
Live After Death-World Slavery Tour . . . . (Capitol)
Maiden Japan . . . . (Capitol)
Running Like The Wind
Marshall Tucker Band; *Running Like The Wind* . . . . (Warner Bros.)
Running On
Steve Winwood; *Refugees Of The Heart* . . . . (Virgin)
Running On Empty
Jackson Browne; *Running On Empty* . . . . (Asylum)
Running On Ice
Billy Joel; *The Bridge* . . . . (Columbia)
Running Out Of Reasons To Run
Rick Trevino; *Learning As You Go* . . . . (Columbia)
Sawyer Brown; *Wide Open* . . . . (Curb)
Running Scared
Roy Orbison; *For The Lonely: A Roy Orbison Anthology 1959-1965* . . . (Rhino)
In Dreams-Greatest Hits . . . . (Orbison)
Roy Orbison & Friends: Black & White Night-Live . . . . (Virgin)
Roy Orbison's All-Time Greatest Hits-#1 & 2 . . . . (Monument)
Running Up That Hill
Kate Bush; *Hounds Of Love* . . . . (EMI)
The Whole Story . . . . (EMI)
Kate Bush & David Gilmour; *Secret Policeman's Third Ball-The
Music-C* . . . . (Virgin)
Running Wild
Judas Priest; *Hell Bent For Leather* . . . . (Columbia)
Unleashed In The East . . . . (Columbia)
Running Wild
Benny Goodman Quartet; *Bluebird Sampler-C* . . . . (Bluebird)
Running Wild
Roxy Music; *Flesh + Blood* . . . . (Atco)
Running Wild
Sam Cooke; *Golden Sound Of Sam Cooke* . . . . (Trip)
Running Wild
Soup Dragons; *Hotwired* . . . . (Black Lion)
Running With The Night
Lionel Richie; *Back To Front* . . . . (Motown)
Can't Slow Down . . . . (Motown)
Music For The Miracle-C . . . . (Epic Portrait Assoc.)
Sailing To Philadelphia
Mark Knopfler; *Sailing To Philadelphia* . . . . (Warner Bros.)
Secret Journey
Police; *Ghost In The Machine* . . . . (A&M)
See The U.S.A. (Chevrolet)
Original Soundtrack; *TeeVee Toons-The Commercials-#1-C* . . . . (TVT)
Sentimental Journey
Dinah Shore; *Sentimental Journey: Capitol's Great Ladies Of
Song-C* . . . . (Gold Rush)
Doris Day; *Doris Day Sings 22 Great Songs-Original Big Band* . . . . (Hindsight)
Hal McIntyre & His Orchestra; *Nipper's Greatest Hits Of The
'40s-#2-C* . . . . (RCA)
Les Brown & His Orchestra; *Best Of The Big Bands-C* . . . . (Columbia)
Serengeti Long Walk
Stewart Copeland; *Rhythmatist* . . . . (A&M)
Serengeti Walk
Dave Grusin; *Dave Grusin-Collection* . . . . (GRP)
Out Of The Shadows . . . . (GRP)
Dave Grusin & N.Y./L.A. Dream Band; *Dave Grusin & N.Y./L.A.
Dream Band* . . . . (GRP)
Set 'Em Up Joe
Vern Gosdin; *Chiseled In Stone* . . . . (Columbia)
Greatest Country Hits Of The '80s-1988-C . . . . (Columbia)
She Walks This Earth
Sting; *Love Affair-Music Of Ivan Lins-C* . . . . (Telarc)
She's About A Mover
Sir Douglas Quintet; *Best Of The Sir Douglas Quintet* . . . . (Takoma)
Texas Music-#3-Garage Bands & Psychedelia-C . . . . (Rhino)
She's Leaving Home
Al Jarreau; *All Fly Home* . . . . (Warner Bros.)
Beatles; *Beatles-Box Set* . . . . (Capitol)
Beatles-Love Songs . . . . (Capitol)
Sgt. Pepper's Lonely Hearts Club Band . . . . (Capitol)

Show Me The Road
Bill Staines; *Going To The West* . . . . (Red House)
Shuffle Off To Buffalo
Hal Kemp; *Best Of The Big Bands-C* . . . . (Columbia)
Original Broadway Cast; *42nd Street* . . . . (RCA Victor)
Side By Side
Kay Starr; *Kay Starr's Greatest Hits* . . . . (Curb)
Mitch Miller; *Mitch Miller-16 Most Requested Songs* . . . . (Columbia)
Silent Running
Klaus Schulze; *Trancefer* . . . . (Gramavision)
Silent Running
Mike & The Mechanics; *Mike & The Mechanics* . . . . (Atlantic)
Sinner
Neil Finn; *Try Whistling This* . . . . (Work)
Six Days On The Road
Boxcar Willie; *Truck Driving Favorites* . . . . (Madacy)
Dave Dudley; *Billboard Top Country Hits-1963-C* . . . . (Rhino)
Country Music Classics-#2-1960-1965-C . . . . (K-Tel)
Legends Of Country Guitar-#2-C . . . . (Rhino)
Truck Driver Boogie Big Rig Hits-1939-1969-C . . . . (Audium)
Flying Burrito Brothers; *Cabin Fever* . . . . (Relix)
Farther Along-Best Of The Flying Burrito Brothers . . . . (A&M)
Last Of The Red Hot Burritos . . . . (A&M)
Sawyer Brown; *Six Days On The Road* . . . . (Curb)
Taj Mahal; *Giant Step/De Ole Folks At Home* . . . . (Columbia)
Legends Of Rock Guitar-'60s-#2-C . . . . (Rhino)
Skippin' In The Mississippi Dew
John Hartford; *John Hartford-Anthology* . . . . (Flying Fish)
Mark Twang . . . . (Flying Fish)
New Grass Revival; *Fly Through The Country* . . . . (Flying Fish)
Sky Fits Heaven
Madonna; *Ray Of Light* . . . . (Maverick)
Sleepwalker
Kinks; *Come Dancing With The Kinks-Best Of The Kinks 1977-1986* . . . (Arista)
Sleepwalker . . . . (Arista)
Sleepwalker
Wallflowers; *Breach* . . . . (Interscope)
Sleepwalker
Shawn Phillips; *Second Contribution* . . . . (A&M)
Sleepwalking
Daniel Cage; *Loud On Earth* . . . . (MCA)
So Much In Love
Tymes; *20th Century Rocks-#9-'60's Vocal Groups-I Got
Rhythm-C* . . . . (Dominion Entert.)
So You Ran
Orion The Hunter; *Orion The Hunter* . . . . (Portrait)
Softest Place On Earth
Xscape; *Traces Of My Lipstick* . . . . (So So Def/Columbia)
Someday Soon
Chris LeDoux; *Rodeo Songs Old & New* . . . . (Liberty)
Ian & Sylvia; *Ian & Sylvia's Greatest Hits* . . . . (Vanguard)
Northern Journey . . . . (Vanguard)
Judy Collins; *Colors Of The Day-The Best Of Judy Collins* . . . . (Elektra)
Who Knows Where The Time Goes . . . . (Elektra)
Moe Bandy; *Moe Bandy's Greatest Hits* . . . . (Columbia)
Rodeo Romeo . . . . (Columbia)
Suzy Bogguss; *Aces* . . . . (Liberty)
Suzy Bogguss' Greatest Hits . . . . (Liberty)
Somewhere In The Vicinity Of The Heart
Shenandoah; *In The Vicinity Of The Heart* . . . . (Capitol)
Now And Then . . . . (Capitol)
Pure Country-Best Of The '90s-#2-C . . . . (Priority)
Southside
Moby featuring Gwen Stefani; *12'' Maxi Single* . . . . (V2)
Play . . . . (V2)
Spanish Caravan
Doors; *Best Of The Doors* . . . . (Elektra)
Live At The Hollywood Bowl . . . . (Elektra)
Waiting For The Sun . . . . (Elektra)
Weird Scenes Inside The Gold Mine . . . . (Elektra)
St. Louis Blues
Bessie Smith; *Beauty Of The Blues* . . . . (Columbia)
Bessie Smith-The Collection . . . . (Legacy)
Big Joe Turner; *Boss Of The Blues* . . . . (Atlantic)
Billie Holiday; *Quintessential-#9-1940-1942* . . . . (Columbia)
The Billie Holiday Story-#3 . . . . (Columbia)
Bob Wills & His Texas Playboys; *Bob Wills & His Texas Playboys-24
Great Hits* . . . . (Polydor)
Cleo Laine; *Jazz* . . . . (RCA)
Dave Brubeck Quartet; *25th Anniversary Reunion* . . . . (A&M)
Dave Brubeck Quartet-At Carnegie Hall . . . . (Columbia)
Paper Moon . . . . (Concord Jazz)
Duke Ellington; *1953 Pasadena Concert* . . . . (Crescendo)
Ella Fitzgerald; *These Are The Blues* . . . . (Verve)
Louis Armstrong; *At The Crescendo* . . . . (MCA)
Louis Armstrong-Legendary Performer . . . . (RCA)
Louis Armstrong-Vol. 6-St. Louis Blues . . . . (Columbia)
Nipper's Greatest Hits Of The '30s-#2-C . . . . (RCA)

Merle Haggard & Asleep At The Wheel; *Ride With Bob*-C .... (DreamWorks/SKG)
Original Broadway Cast; *Black & Blue* ....(DRG)
Pete Fountain; *Best Of Pete Fountain* .... (MCA)
Preservation Hall Jazz Band; *Best Of The Preservation Hall Jazz Band*......................................(Columbia)
    New Orleans-#2 ....(Columbia)

Start Movin' (In My Direction)
Sal Mineo; *Hard To Find 45s On CD-#4-Late '50s*-C .... (Empire Recording Comm.)

State Of Mind
Clint Black; *No Time To Kill* ....(RCA)

Steal Away
Johnnie Taylor; *Chronicle: The 20 Greatest Hits* .... (Stax)
    Johnnie Taylor-Super Hits .... (Stax)

Steal Away
Billy Joe Royal; *Billy Joe Royal's Greatest Hits* ....(Columbia)

Steal Away
Joy; *Joy* ....(Fantasy)

Steal Away
Robbie Dupree; *Robbie Dupree*...........................(Elektra)

Steal Away
Poco; *Rose Of Cimarron* .... (MCA)

Steal Away
Whitesnake; *Snakebite* ....(Geffen)

Steal Away
Nils Lofgren; *Nils* ....(A&M)
    Nils Lofgren-Classics-#13 ....(A&M)

Step By Step
New Kids On The Block; *No More Games/Remix Album* ....(Columbia)
    Step By Step ....(Columbia)

Step By Step
Crests; *Best Of Doo Wop Uptempo-#2*-C................. (Rhino)
    Crests Greatest Hits ....(Collectables)
    Oldies But Goodies-#9-C ....(Original Sound)
    Super Oldies Of The '60s-#9-C...................(Audio Fidelity)
    WCBS FM 101 History Of Rock-'60s-#1-C ....(Collectables)

Step By Step
Eddie Rabbitt; *Best Of Eddie Rabbitt/Greatest Hits-II* .... (Warner Bros.)
    Number 1's .... (Warner Bros.)

Step By Step
Whitney Houston; *ST/The Preacher's Wife*......................(Arista)

Step By Step
Sweet Honey In The Rock; *Other Side* ....(Flying Fish)

Step By Step
Alan Parsons Project; *Eye In The Sky* ....(Arista)

Step Into The Light
Dust For Life; *Dust For Life* ....(Wind-up)

Steppin' (Out)
Gap Band; *The Gap Band II*........................... (Mercury)

Steppin' In A Slide Zone
Moody Blues; *Octave* .... (Polydor)

Steppin' Out
Joe Jackson; *Live 1980/86* .... (A&M)
    Night & Day .... (A&M)

Steppin' Out
Paul Revere And The Raiders; *Legend Of Paul Revere And The Raiders*..(Columbia)
    Paul Revere And The Raiders' Greatest Hits ....(Columbia)

Steppin' Out
Mel Tillis; *Your Body Is An Outlaw* .... (Elektra)

Steppin' Out
Michelle Shocked; *Texas Campfire Tapes*..................... (Mercury)

Steppin' Out
Electric Light Orchestra; *Out Of The Blue* ....(Jet)

Steppin' Out
Cream; *Cream-Live-#2* ....(Polydor)
    Eric Clapton-Crossroads-C ....(Polydor)

Steppin' Out
Joan Armatrading; *Back To The Night*.................. (A&M)
    Steppin' Out .... (A&M)

Stepping Stone
Lari White; *Stepping Stone* .... (Lyric Street)

Stone Free
Eric Clapton; *Eric Clapton-Unplugged*....................(Reprise)
Jimi Hendrix; *Are You Experienced?* ....(Reprise)

Straight Lines
Wood; *Songs From Stamford Hill* ....(Columbia)

Stroll, The
Diamonds; *Groove 'N' Grind-'50s & '60s Dance Hits*-C .... (Rhino)
    Partytime '50s-C ....(Priority)
    ST/American Graffiti .... (MCA)

Strollin'
Gene Harris Quartet; *Like A Lover*........................(Concord Jazz)
Horace Silver; *Horacescope* .... (Blue Note)

Strollin'
Champion Jack Dupree; *Atlantic Blues-Piano*-C .... (Atlantic)

Strollin' (With My Moose)
Edgar Meyer; *Sampler '88-#2*-C ....(MCA)

Strollin' Beale No. 1
Rufus Thomas; *Can't Get Away From This Dog* .... (Stax)

Strollin' On
Maxi Priest; *Best Of Me* ....(Charisma)

Struttin' With Some Barbecue
Louis Armstrong; *Louis Armstrong Of New Orleans*................. (MCA)
    Louis Armstrong's Greatest Hits.......................(Legacy)
Newport Jazz Festival All-Stars; *Newport Jazz Festival All-Stars* ....(Concord Jazz)
Teddy Buckner; *Salute To Louis Armstrong* .... (Crescendo)

Sukiyaki
4 P.M.; *Now's The Time*................... (Next Plateau/London/Island)
Kyu Sakamoto; *When AM Was King*-C ....(Capitol)
Taste Of Honey; *Golden Honey* ....(Capitol)
    Twice As Sweet ....(Capitol)

Sweet Betsy From Pike
Cisco Houston; *Cowboy Ballads* .... (Smithsonian Folkways)
Mormon Tabernacle Choir; *This Land Is Your Land* ....(Columbia)

Sweet Dreams (Are Made Of This)
Eurythmics; *Eurythmics' Greatest Hits* ....(Arista)
    Sweet Dreams (Are Made Of This) .... (RCA)
Marilyn Manson; *Smells Like Children* .... (Interscope)

Take A Giant Step
Taj Mahal; *Best Of Taj Mahal* ....(Columbia)
    Giant Step/De Ole Folks At Home ....(Columbia)
    Troubadours Of The Folk Era-#2-C ....(Rhino)

Take A Little Trip
Alabama; *American Pride* .... (RCA)

Take A Little Walk With Me
Big John Wrencher & Joe Carter; *Blues Masters-#4-Harmonica Classics*-C ....(Rhino)

Take It On The Run
REO Speedwagon; *A Second Decade Of Rock And Roll 1981 To 1991* .... (Epic)
    Hi Infidelity ....(Epic)
    REO Speedwagon-The Hits ....(Epic)

Take Me Back To My Old Carolina Home
Uncle Dave Macon; *Laugh Your Blues Away*.....................(Rounder)

Take Me Back To New Orleans
Chris Barber & Dr. John; *Take Me Back To New Orleans* ....(Black Lion)
Gary U.S. Bonds; *School Of Rock 'N' Roll-Best Of Gary U.S. Bonds* ....(Rhino)

Take Me Back To New York City
Si Kahn; *Unfinished Portraits* .... (Flying Fish)

Take Me Back To Old Wyoming
Chris LeDoux; *Thirty-Dollar Cowboy* ....(Liberty)

Take Me Back To Tulsa
Asleep At The Wheel; *Route 66* ....(Liberty)
    Very Best Of Asleep At The Wheel Since 1970 ....(Relentless/Madacy)
Bob Wills & His Texas Playboys; *All Time Legends Of Country Music*-C ....(Legacy)
    Bob Wills-Anthology...................... (Sony Music Special Prod.)
    Columbia Country Classics-#1-Golden Age-C ....(Columbia)
    Tiffany Transcriptions-#2-Best Of The Tiffanys ....(Rhino)
Clay Walker & Asleep At The Wheel; *Ride With Bob*-C ... (DreamWorks/SKG)

Take Me To Los Angeles
Jimmy Soul; *Best Of Jimmy Soul* ....(Rhino)

Take The Highway
Marshall Tucker Band; *Best Of The Marshall Tucker Band-The Capricorn Years* ....(Era)
    Marshall Tucker Band.................................(AJK Music)
    Where We All Belong ....(AJK Music)

Take The Long Way Home
Supertramp; *Breakfast In America*.........................(A&M)
    Paris ....(A&M)
    Supertramp-Classics-#9 ....(A&M)

Take The Long Way Home
John Schneider; *Country Classics-#8-1986-1987*-C ....(Universal)
    John Schneider's Greatest Hits ....(MCA)

Take The Money & Run
Steve Miller Band; *Fly Like An Eagle* ....(Capitol)
    Steve Miller Band-Gift Set...........................(Capitol)
    Steve Miller Band-Live...............................(Capitol)
    Steve Miller Band's Greatest Hits-1974-78 ....(Capitol)

Take The Short Way Home
Dionne Warwick; *Heartbreaker* ....(Arista)

Tennessee Traveler
Mike Auldridge; *Mike Auldridge* .... (Flying Fish)

Texas Bound
Gary Morris; *Full Moon Empty Heart* ....(Liberty)

Texas Bound And Flyin'
Jerry Reed; *ST/Smokey And The Bandit 2* ....(MCA)
    Texas Bound & Flyin' .... (RCA)

Texas Bound Blues
Margaret Thornton; *Barrelhouse Mamas: Born In The Alley, Raised In The Slums*-C .... (Yazoo)

Theme From ''Back To The Future''
Cincinnati Pops Orchestra/Erich Kunzel; *Star Tracks II* .... (Telarc)

Theme From "Have Gun Will Travel" (Ballad Of Paladin)
Duane Eddy; *Duane Eddy-Pure Gold* . . . . (RCA)
Johnny Western; *Columbia Country Classics-#3-Americana-C* . . . . (Columbia)
Television's Greatest Hits-#7-Cable Ready-C . . . . (TVT)
Theme From "Promised Land"
Original Soundtrack; *CBS: The First 50 Years* . . . . (TVT)
Theme From "Quantum Leap"
Original Soundtrack; *Sci-Fi's Greatest Hits-#4-Defenders Of Justice* . . . . (TVT)
Television's Greatest Hits-#7-Cable Ready-C . . . . (TVT)
Theme From "Route 66"
Nelson Riddle & His Orchestra; *Beat Generation* . . . . (Rhino)
Television's Greatest Hits-#2-C . . . . (TVT)
Original Soundtrack; *CBS: The First 50 Years* . . . . (TVT)
Theme From "Star Trek"
Cincinnati Pops Orchestra/Erich Kunzel; *Star Tracks II* . . . . (Telarc)
Theme From "Star Trek: The Next Generation"
Original Soundtrack; *Television's Greatest Hits-#7-Cable Ready-C* . . . . . (TVT)
Theme From "The Beverly Hillbillies"
Original Soundtrack; *CBS: The First 50 Years* . . . . (TVT)
Television's Greatest Hits-#1-C . . . . (TVT)
Theme From "Time Tunnel"
Original Soundtrack; *Television's Greatest Hits-#2-C* . . . . (TVT)
Theme From "Voyage To The Bottom Of The Sea"
Original Soundtrack; *Television's Greatest Hits-#2-C* . . . . (TVT)
Then The Morning Comes
Smash Mouth; *Astro Lounge* . . . . (Interscope)
Now That's What I Call Music!-#4-C . . . . (Virgin)
There She Goes
Bob Marley & The Wailers; *One Love* . . . . (Heartbeat)
There She Goes
Sixpence None The Richer; *Sixpence None The Richer* . . . . . (Squint/Columbia)
There She Goes
Chambers Brothers; *Best Of The Chambers Brothers* . . . . (Fantasy)
There She Goes
Jerry Wallace; *Jerry Wallace's Greatest Hits* . . . . (Curb)
There She Goes
La's; *La's* . . . . (London)
There She Goes
Beat; *ST/Caddyshack* . . . . (Columbia)
There's A Moon Out Tonight
Capris; *20 Top 10 Hits Of The '50s & '60s-C* . . . . (Laurie)
22 Leaders Of The Pack-#2-C . . . . (Laurie)
Collectables Presents The History Of Rock-#3-C . . . . (Collectables)
There's A Moon Out Tonight . . . . (Collectables)
There's No Place Like Home For The Holidays
Perry Como; *Now That's What I Call Christmas!-C* . . . . (UTV)
Perry Como's Greatest Hits . . . . (RCA)
These Boots Are Made For Walkin'
Billy Ray Cyrus; *Some Gave All* . . . . (Mercury)
Nancy Sinatra; *Billboard Top Rock 'N' Roll Hits-1966-C* . . . . (Rhino)
Boots-Nancy Sinatra's Greatest Hits . . . . (Rhino)
Thirty Nine Miles To Mobile
Charlie Daniels Band; *Charlie Daniels Band* . . . . (Capitol)
This Hard Land
Bruce Springsteen; *Bruce Springsteen's Greatest Hits* . . . . (Columbia)
Tracks . . . . (Columbia)
This Land Is Your Land
Bruce Springsteen & The E Street Band; *Bruce Springsteen & The E Street*
Band Live/1975-85 . . . . (Legacy)
Glen Campbell; *All American* . . . . (Liberty)
Lee Greenwood; *American Patriot* . . . . (Capitol)
Odetta, Arlo Guthrie & Company; *Tribute To Woody*
Guthrie-C . . . . (Warner Bros.)
Pete Seeger; *God Bless America-C* . . . . (Columbia)
Pete Seeger Sings Woody Guthrie . . . . (Smithsonian Folkways)
Pete Seeger-Complete Carnegie Hall Concert-1963 . . . . (Columbia)
Weavers; *Weavers' Greatest Hits* . . . . (Vanguard)
Woody Guthrie; *Greatest Songs Of Woody Guthrie-C* . . . . (Vanguard)
Troubadours Of The Folk Era-#1-C . . . . (Rhino)
Woody Guthrie . . . . (Vanguard)
Ticket Back To Georgia
Head East; *Flat As A Pancake* . . . . (A&M)
Ticket To Ride
Beatles; *Beatles 1* . . . . (Capitol)
Beatles-20 Greatest Hits . . . . (Capitol)
Beatles-Box Set . . . . (Capitol)
Reel Music . . . . (Capitol)
ST/Help! . . . . (Capitol)
The Beatles At The Hollywood Bowl . . . . (Capitol)
The Beatles/1962-1966 . . . . (Capitol)
Carpenters; *Carpenters-Classics-#2* . . . . (A&M)
Carpenters-The Singles 1969-1973 . . . . (A&M)
From The Top . . . . (A&M)
Ticket To Ride . . . . (A&M)
Yesterday Once More . . . . (A&M)
Vanilla Fudge; *Best Of Vanilla Fudge* . . . . (Atco)
Vanilla Fudge . . . . (Atco)
Tickets To A Better Place
7 Seconds; *Soulforce Revolution* . . . . (Restless)

'Til I Fell In Love With You
Bob Dylan; *Time Out Of Mind* . . . . (Columbia)
Tiny Steps
Elvis Costello; *Girls Girls Girls* . . . . (Columbia)
Tip-Toe Through The Tulips With Me
Tiny Tim; *Dr. Demento Presents The Greatest Novelty Records-#3-*
1960s-C . . . . (Rhino)
Silly Songs-C . . . . (K-Tel)
To Go To California Anymore (I Don't Have A Reason)
Willie Nelson; *Born For Trouble* . . . . (Columbia)
To The Moon And Back
Savage Garden; *Savage Garden* . . . . (Columbia)
To Zion
Lauryn Hill featuring Carlos Santana; *The Miseducation Of*
Lauryn Hill . . . . (Ruffhouse/Columbia)
Together Wherever We Go
Original Cast; *ST/Gypsy* . . . . (Columbia)
Tomb Of The Unknown Love
Cassell Webb; *Songs Of A Stranger* . . . . (Venture)
Kenny Rogers; *The Heart Of The Matter* . . . . (RCA)
Tomorrow I'll Be Out Of Town
Ten Years After; *Classic Performances Of Ten Years After* . . . . (Columbia)
Universal . . . . (Chrysalis)
Track Walkin'
Billy Strange; *Between The Rails: America's Train Songs-C* . . . . . . (Crescendo)
Trains & Boats & Planes
Billy J. Kramer With The Dakotas; *Billy J. Kramer With The Dakotas-The*
Definitive Collection . . . . (EMI)
History Of British Rock-#4-C . . . . (Rhino)
Dionne Warwick; *Dionne Warwick* . . . . (Everest)
Dionne Warwick Greatest Hits . . . . (Everest)
Dionne Warwick-Anthology 1962-1971 . . . . (Rhino)
Hot! Live & Otherwise . . . . (Arista)
Trains/Leavin' Tennessee
Tasty Licks; *Tasty Licks* . . . . (Rounder)
Tramp, Tramp, Tramp
Mormon Tabernacle Choir; *Songs Of The Civil War And Stephen Foster*
Favorites . . . . (Sony Music Classical)
Travel On My Way
Chambers Brothers; *Best Of The Chambers Brothers* . . . . (Fantasy)
Travelin' All Alone
Billie Holiday; *Billie Holiday* . . . . (Columbia)
Legacy Box-1933-1958 . . . . (Columbia)
Quintessential-#5-1937-1938 . . . . (Columbia)
The Billie Holiday Story-#1 . . . . (Columbia)
Travelin' At The Speed Of Thought
O'Jays; *Travelin' At The Speed Of Thought* . . . . (Philadelphia Int'l)
Travelin' Band
Creedence Clearwater Revival; *1970* . . . . (Fantasy)
Cosmo's Factory . . . . (Fantasy)
Creedence Clearwater Revival-Chronicle . . . . (Fantasy)
Live In Europe . . . . (Fantasy)
Royal Albert Hall Concert . . . . (Fantasy)
Travelin' Blues
Blind Willie McTell; *Blind Willie McTell-Early Years-1927-1932* . . . (Yazoo)
Story Of The Blues-C . . . . (Columbia)
Travelin' Light
Billie Holiday; *All Or Nothing At All* . . . . (Verve)
History Of The Real Billie Holiday . . . . (Verve)
Lady Sings The Blues . . . . (Verve)
Travelin' Light
Eric Clapton; *Reptile* . . . . (Duck/Reprise)
Travelin' Man
Lynyrd Skynyrd; *Live From Steel Town* . . . . (CMC Int'l)
One More From The Road . . . . (MCA)
Travelin' Man
Ricky Nelson; *Best Of Ricky Nelson* . . . . (EMI)
Rick Nelson's Greatest Hits . . . . (Rhino)
Travelin' Man
Doobie Brothers; *Doobie Brothers* . . . . (Warner Bros.)
Travelin' Man
Albert King; *I Wanna Get Funky* . . . . (Stax)
Travelin' Man
Bob Seger; *Beautiful Loser* . . . . (Capitol)
Live Bullet . . . . (Capitol)
Travelin' Man
Jacky Ward; *45-#47424* . . . . (Asylum)
Travelin' Man
Stevie Wonder; *Stevie Wonder's Greatest Hits-#2* . . . . (Motown)
Travelin' Prayer
Billy Joel; *Piano Man* . . . . (Columbia)
Travelin' Soldier
Bruce Robison; *Bruce Robison* . . . . (Vireo)
Traveling Blues
Loggins & Messina; *Finale* . . . . (Columbia)
Full Sail . . . . (Columbia)
Traveling Man
Dolly Parton; *Best Of Dolly Parton* . . . . (RCA)

Coat Of Many Colors . . . .(RCA)

Traveling Riverside Blues
Hindu Love Gods; *Hindu Love Gods*. . . . . (Giant)
John Hammond; *Best Of John Hammond* . . . .(Vanguard)
Led Zeppelin; *Led Zeppelin-Box Set* . . . . (Atlantic)
Robert Johnson; *King Of The Delta Blues Singers*. . . . .(Columbia)
The Slide Guitar-Bottles Knives & Steel-C . . . . (Legacy)

Traveling Without Moving
Jamiroquai; *Traveling Without Moving*. . . . . (Work/Epic)

Traveller's Prayer
George Jones & Sweethearts Of The Rodeo; *Friends In High Places-C* . . . (Epic)

Travellin' Blues
Jimmie Rodgers; *America's Blue Yodeler-1930-1931* . . . . (Rounder)
My Rough & Rowdy Ways. . . . .(RCA)
Lefty Frizzell; *Best Of Lefty Frizzell* . . . . (Rhino)

Travelling Man
Simple Minds; *Real Life* . . . . (A&M)

Trip To Flagstaff
Kornos; *On Seven Winds* . . . . (Green Linnet)

Truckin'
Mel Torme & The Mel-Tones; *Back In Town* . . . .(Verve)

Truckin'
Dwight Yoakam; *Deadicated-C* . . . . (Arista)
Grateful Dead; *American Beauty*. . . . . (Warner Bros.)
Best Of/Skeletons From The Closet. . . . . (Warner Bros.)
Europe '72 . . . . (Warner Bros.)
*What A Long Strange Trip It's Been: The Best Of The
Grateful Dead* . . . . (Warner Bros.)

Truckin'
Bread; *Best Of Bread*. . . . . (Elektra)
Bread-Anthology . . . . (Elektra)
Manna. . . . . (Rhino)

True Love Travels On A Gravel Road
Elvis Presley; *From Elvis In Memphis*. (RCA)
Memphis Record. . . . . (RCA)
Percy Sledge; *It Tears Me Up-Best Of Percy Sledge* . . . . (Rhino)

Tryin' To Get To Heaven
Bob Dylan; *Time Out Of Mind*. . . . . (Columbia)

Tulsa Time
Don Williams; *Best Of Don Williams-#2*. . . . . (MCA)
Country's Greatest Hits-#6-Superstars-C . . . . (Priority)
Don Williams-Legends . . . . (MCA)
Expressions. . . . . (MCA)
Eric Clapton; *Backless*. . . . . (Polydor)
Just One Night . . . . (Polydor)

Tumbling Tumbleweeds
Billy Vaughn; *Billy Vaughn's Greatest Hits* . . . .(Curb)
Gene Autry; *Essential Gene Autry*. . . . . (Columbia)
Meat Puppets; *Meat Puppets*. . . . . (SST)
Michael Martin Murphey; *Cowboy Songs*. . . . . (Warner Western)
Roy Rogers/K.T. Oslin/Restless Heart; *Roy Rogers Tribute-C* . . . . .(RCA)
Sons Of The Pioneers; *The Country Music Hall Of Fame-Sons Of The
Pioneers*. . . . . (MCA)

Turn The Page
Metallica; *Garage Inc.*. . . . . (Elektra)

Twenty-Five Miles
Edwin Starr; *Motown Superstar Series-#3-Edwin Starr* . . . . (Motown)
Michael Jackson; *Original Soul Of Michael Jackson* . . . . (Motown)

Twenty-Four Hours From Tulsa
Burt Bacharach; *Walk On By*. . . . . (MCA Special Prod.)
Gene Pitney; *Best Of Gene Pitney* . . . . (K-Tel)

Two For The Road
Bruce Springsteen; *Tracks*. . . . . (Columbia)

Two Of Us
Beatles; *Beatles-Box Set* . . . . (Capitol)
Let It Be. . . . . (Capitol)

Two Tickets To Paradise
Eddie Money; *Eddie Money* . . . . (Columbia)
Eddie Money's Greatest Hits-Sound Of Money . . . . (Columbia)
Unplug It In. . . . . (Columbia)

Up Around The Bend
Creedence Clearwater Revival; *1970* . . . .(Fantasy)
Cosmo's Factory. . . . . (Fantasy)
Creedence Clearwater Revival-Chronicle . . . . (Fantasy)
More Creedence Gold. . . . . (Fantasy)
Hanoi Rocks; *Two Steps From The Move* . . . . (Epic)

Up, Up & Away
5th Dimension; *5th Dimension-Anthology 1967-1973* . . . .(Rhino)
Greatest Hits On Earth. . . . . (Arista)

Vacation
Go-Go's; *Go-Go's Greatest* . . . . (I.R.S.)
Vacation . . . . (I.R.S.)

Valley Road
Bruce Hornsby & The Nitty Gritty Dirt Band; *Will The Circle Be
Unbroken-#2-C* . . . . (Uni)
Bruce Hornsby & The Range; *Scenes From The Southside*. . . . . . . (RCA)

Vaya Con Dios
Bing Crosby; *The Radio Years-#2*. . . . . (Crescendo)
Freddy Fender; *Freddy Fender-Collection* . . . . (Reprise)

Les Paul & Mary Ford; *Memories Are Made Of This-C*. . . . .(Capitol)
Roger Whittaker; *All-Time Heart-Touching Favorites* . . . .(Capitol)

Voyage
Moody Blues; *Caught Live Plus Five*. . . . . (Polydor)
On The Threshold Of A Dream . . . . (Polydor)
This Is The Moody Blues . . . . (Polydor)

Voyage
Christy Moore; *Voyage* . . . . (Atlantic)

Wabash Cannonball
Billy Strange; *Between The Rails: America's Train Songs-C* . . . . . . (Crescendo)
Nitty Gritty Dirt Band; *Will The Circle Be Unbroken* . . . .(EMI)
Roy Acuff; *All Time Legends Of Country Music-C* . . . .(Legacy)
Backstage At The Grand Ole Opry-C . . . . (RCA)
Best Of Roy Acuff. . . . . (Liberty)
Columbia Historic Edition-Roy Acuff . . . .(Columbia)
Essential Roy Acuff-1936-1949. . . . . (Legacy)
Hot Tracks-Train Super Hits-C . . . . (Epic)
Roy Acuff's Greatest Hits . . . .(Columbia)
Steel Rails-Classic Railroad Songs-#1-C . . . . (Rounder)

Walk A Mile In My Shoes
Bryan Ferry; *Another Time Another Place* . . . . (Reprise)
Elvis Presley; *On Stage-February, 1970* . . . . (RCA)
Joe South; *Best Of Joe South* . . . . (Rhino)

Walk A Thin Line
Fleetwood Mac; *25 Years-The Chain* . . . . (Warner Bros.)
Tusk . . . . (Warner Bros.)

Walk Across The Rooftops
Blue Nile; *Walk Across The Rooftops* . . . .(A&M)

Walk All Over Georgia
Louisiana Red; *Midnight Rambler* . . . . (Tomato)

Walk All Over You
AC/DC; *Highway To Hell* . . . . (Atco)

Walk Away
James Gang; *Best Of The James Gang* . . . . (MCA)
James Gang-16 Greatest Hits . . . . (MCA)
Thirds . . . . (One Way)
Joe Walsh; *Best Of Joe Walsh* . . . . (MCA)
You Can't Argue With A Sick Mind . . . . (MCA)

Walk Away
Cool For August; *Grand World* . . . . (Warner Bros.)

Walk Away
Cheap Trick; *Busted*. . . . . (Epic)

Walk Away
Dionne Warwick; *Dionne Warwick's Greatest Hits-1979-1990* . . . . . .(Arista)

Walk Away
Indigo Girls; *Strange Fire* . . . . (Epic)

Walk Away
Michael Bolton; *The Hunger* . . . .(Columbia)

Walk Away
Sisters Of Mercy; *First & Last & Always*. . . . .(Elektra)

Walk Away
Tom Kell; *One Sad Night*. . . . . (Warner Bros.)

Walk Away
Donna Summer; *Bad Girls* . . . . (Casablanca)
Dance Collection . . . . (Casablanca)
Walk Away-Best Of Donna Summer-1977-1980 . . . . (Casablanca)

Walk Away From Love
David Ruffin; *David Ruffin-At His Best* . . . . (Motown)
Jimmy & David Ruffin; *Motown Superstar Series-#8-Jimmy & David
Ruffin* . . . . (Motown)

Walk Away Renee
Four Tops; *Compact Command Performances-Four Tops* . . . .(Motown)
Four Tops Reach Out . . . . (Motown)
Four Tops-Anthology . . . . (Motown)
Left Banke; *Cruisin'-1966-C* . . . .(Increase)
History Of The Left Banke . . . . (Rhino)
Vonda Shepard; *ST/Songs From ''Ally McBeal'' Featuring Vonda
Shepard* . . . . (550/Epic)

Walk Awhile
Fairport Convention; *Full House* . . . .(Carthage)

Walk Don't Run
Ventures; *Best Of The Ventures* . . . . (EMI)
EMI Legends Of Rock & Roll-24 Greatest Hits-C . . . . (EMI)

Walk Hand In Hand
Andy Williams; *I Like Your Kind Of Love-The Best Of The Cadence
Years.* . . . . (Varese Vintage)

Walk In My Mind
Siegel-Schwall Band; *'70.* . . . .(Vanguard)
Best Of The Siegel-Schwall Band . . . .(Vanguard)

Walk In The Night
Junior Walker & The All Stars; *Junior Walker & The All Stars-All The
Great Hits* . . . . (Motown)
Junior Walker & The All Stars-Anthology. . . . . (Motown)
Motown Superstar Series-#5-Junior Walker & The All Stars . . . . (Motown)

Walk In The Sun
Bruce Hornsby; *Hot House* . . . . (RCA)

Walk Like A Man
4 Seasons; *4 Seasons' Greatest Hits-#1* . . . .(Rhino)

4 Seasons-Anthology . . . . (Rhino)
Billboard Top Rock 'N' Roll Hits-1963-C . . . . (Rhino)
ST/The Wanderers . . . .(Warner Bros.)

Walk Like A Man
Bruce Springsteen; *Tunnel Of Love* . . . . (Columbia)

Walk Like A Man
Grand Funk Railroad; *We're An American Band* . . . . (Capitol)

Walk Like An Egyptian
Bangles; *Bangles' Greatest Hits* . . . . (Columbia)
Different Light . . . . (Columbia)
Modern A Cappella . . . . (Rhino)

Walk Like I Do
William Topley; *Spanish Wells* . . . . (Mercury)

Walk My Way
Beth Nielsen Chapman; *Beth Nielsen Chapman* . . . . (Reprise)

Walk Of Life
Dire Straits; *Brothers In Arms* . . . .(Warner Bros.)
Money For Nothing . . . .(Warner Bros.)

Walk On
Sonny Terry & Brownie McGhee; *Coffeehouse Blues* . . . .(Vee-Jay)
Real Blues Brothers-C . . . .(Dunhill Compact Classics)

Walk On
U2; *America: A Tribute To Heroes-C* . . . . (Interscope)
Now That's What I Call Music!-#8-C . . . . (Virgin)

Walk On
Neil Young; *Decade* . . . . (Reprise)
On The Beach . . . . (Reprise)

Walk On
Reba McEntire; *Reba McEntire's Greatest Hits Volume Two* . . . . (MCA)
Sweet Sixteen . . . . (MCA)

Walk On By
Dionne Warwick; *Dionne Warwick-Anthology 1962-1971* . . . . (Rhino)
Hot! Live & Otherwise . . . . (Arista)
I Am Woman-C . . . . (Nick At Nite)
Oldies But Goodies-#15-C . . . . (Original Sound)
Scepter Records Story-C . . . . (Capricorn)
Isaac Hayes; *Isaac Hayes' Greatest Hit Singles* . . . . (Stax)
Melissa Manchester; *Romantic Hits Of The '80s-C* . . . . (K-Tel)
Tribute . . . . (Polydor)
Sybil; *Sybil* . . . .(Next Plateau/London/Island)

Walk On By
Leroy Van Dyke; *Billboard Top Country Hits-1961-C* . . . . (Rhino)
Country Classics-C . . . . (Sun)
Country Music Classics-#2-1960-1965-C . . . . (K-Tel)
Souvenirs Of Music City U.S.A.-C . . . . (Plantation)

Walk On Faith
Mike Reid; *Greatest Country Hits Of The '90s-1991-C* . . . . (Columbia)
Turning For Home . . . . (Columbia)

Walk On Out Of My Mind
Waylon Jennings; *Best Of Waylon Jennings* . . . . (RCA)

Walk On The Ocean
Toad The Wet Sprocket; *Fear* . . . . (Columbia)

Walk On The Water
Creedence Clearwater Revival; *1968-1969* . . . . (Fantasy)
Creedence Clearwater Revival . . . . (Fantasy)
Creedence Clearwater Revival-Chronicle-#2 . . . . (Fantasy)

Walk On The Wild Side
Edie Brickell & New Bohemians; *ST/Flashback* . . . . (WTG)
Lou Reed; *Between Thought & Expression-Anthology* . . . . (RCA)
Lou Reed Live . . . . (RCA)
Transformer . . . . (RCA)
Walk On The Wild Side-The Best Of Lou Reed . . . . (RCA)

Walk On Water
Neil Diamond; *And The Singer Sings His Song* . . . . (MCA)
Glory Road-1968-1972 . . . . (MCA)
Moods . . . . (MCA)

Walk On Water
T. Graham Brown; *Brilliant Conversationalist* . . . . (Capitol)

Walk On Water
Dio; *Lock Up The Wolves* . . . . (Reprise)

Walk On Water
Marc Cohn; *Marc Cohn* . . . . (Atlantic)

Walk On Water
Marillion; *Six Of One-Half Dozen Of The Other* . . . .(I.R.S.)

Walk On Water
Eddie Money; *Eddie Money's Greatest Hits-Sound Of Money* . . . . . (Columbia)
Nothing To Lose . . . . (Columbia)

Walk Out In The Rain
Eric Clapton; *Backless* . . . . (Polydor)
I Shall Be Unreleased-Songs Of Bob Dylan . . . . (Rhino)

Walk Right Back
Anne Murray; *Anne Murray-Country Hits* . . . . (Capitol)
Country Collection . . . . (Capitol)
Let's Keep It That Way . . . . (Liberty)
Everly Brothers; *Golden Hits Of The Everly Brothers* . . . .(Warner Bros.)
Very Best Of The Everly Brothers . . . .(Warner Bros.)

Walk Right In
Rooftop Singers; *Best Of The Rooftop Singers* . . . . (Vanguard)

Cruisin'-1963-C . . . . (Increase)
Greatest Folksingers Of The '60s-C . . . . (Vanguard)
ST/Forrest Gump . . . .(Epic/Sony Music Soundtrax)
Troubadours Of The Folk Era-#3-C . . . . (Rhino)

Walk Softly
Billy ''Crash'' Craddock; *Billy ''Crash'' Craddock Live* . . . . (MCA)
Billy ''Crash'' Craddock Sings His Greatest Hits . . . . (MCA)
Easy As Pie . . . . (MCA)

Walk Softly On The Bridge
Mel Street; *Mel Street's Greatest Hits* . . . . (GRT)

Walk Softly On This Heart Of Mine
Bill Monroe; *The Country Music Hall Of Fame-Bill Monroe* . . . . (MCA)
Joey Welz; *Lovin' My Country* . . . . (Capricorn)
Kentucky HeadHunters; *Best Of The Kentucky HeadHunters-Still*
Pickin' . . . . (Mercury)
Pickin' On Nashville . . . . (Mercury)
Ricky Skaggs and the Dixie Chicks; *Ricky Skaggs & Friends-Big Mon: Songs*
Of Bill Monroe . . . . (Skaggs Family)

Walk The Dinosaur
George Clinton & Goombas; *ST/Super Mario Brothers* . . . . (Capitol)

Walk The Dinosaur
Was (Not Was); *What Up Dog?* . . . . (Chrysalis)

Walk The Dog
Laurie Anderson; *United States Live* . . . . (Warner Bros.)

Walk The Way The Wind Blows
Hot Rize; *Traditional Ties* . . . .(Sugar Hill)
Kathy Mattea; *Collection Of Hits* . . . . (Mercury)
Walk The Way The Wind Blows . . . . (Mercury)

Walk This Way
Aerosmith; *Aerosmith-Classics Live 2* . . . . (Columbia)
Aerosmith's Greatest Hits . . . . (Columbia)
Live! Bootleg . . . . (Columbia)
Pandora's Box . . . . (Columbia)
Toys In The Attic . . . . (Columbia)
Run-D.M.C.; *Mr. Magic's Rap Attack-C* . . . .(Profile)
Raising Hell . . . .(Profile)
Rap's Biggest Hits-C . . . . (K-Tel)

Walk This World
Heather Nova; *Oyster* . . . . (Big Cat)

Walk Through This World With Me
George Jones; *Best Of George Jones-1955-1967* . . . . (Rhino)
Billboard Top Country Hits-1967-C . . . . (Rhino)
Double Gold-George Jones . . . . (Mustcor)
George Jones' All-Time Greatest Hits . . . . (Epic)

Walk Unafraid
R.E.M.; *Up* . . . . (Warner Bros.)

Walk, The
Cure; *Japanese Whispers-The Singles* . . . .(Sire)
Mixed Up . . . . (Elektra)
Standing On A Beach-The Singles . . . . (Elektra)
Walk, The . . . .(Sire)

Walk, The
Eurythmics; *Sweet Dreams (Are Made Of This)* . . . . (RCA)

Walk, The
Rufus Thomas; *That Woman Is Poison!* . . . .(Alligator)

Walk, The
Jimmy McCracklin; *Best Of Chess Rhythm & Blues-#1-C* . . . . (Chess)
Groove 'N' Grind-'50s & '60s Dance Hits-C . . . . (Columbia)
Super Oldies Of The '50s-#7-C . . . . (Audio Fidelity)

Walk, The
Time; *What Time Is It?* . . . . (Warner Bros.)

Walk, The
Sawyer Brown; *Buick* . . . . (Curb)
Dirt Road . . . . (Curb)

Walkaway Joe
Trisha Yearwood; *Hearts In Armor* . . . . (MCA)
Songbook-A Collection Of Hits . . . . (MCA)

Walkin'
Miles Davis; *Cookin' At The Plugged Nickel* . . . . (Columbia)
I Like Jazz-Essence Of Miles Davis . . . . (Columbia)
Miles Davis' Greatest Hits . . . . (Columbia)

Walkin'
Willie Nelson; *Phases & Stages* . . . .(Atlantic)

Walkin'
Bobby McFerrin; *Spontaneous Inventions* . . . . (Blue Note)

Walkin'
Cleve Francis; *Walkin'* . . . . (Liberty)

Walkin' A Broken Heart
Don Williams; *Cafe Carolina* . . . . (MCA)
Don Williams' Greatest Hits . . . . (MCA)

Walkin' After Midnight
Garth Brooks; *The Chase* . . . . (Liberty)
Loretta Lynn; *I Remember Patsy* . . . . (MCA)
Oak Ridge Boys; *Unstoppable* . . . . (RCA)
Patsy Cline; *20 Golden Pieces Of Patsy Cline* . . . . (Bulldog)
Let The Teardrops Fall . . . . (Accord)
Live At The Opry . . . . (MCA)
Patsy Cline . . . . (MCA)
Patsy Cline's Greatest Hits . . . . (MCA)

The Patsy Cline Story .... (MCA)

Walkin' All Night
Little Feat; *Dixie Chicken* .... (Warner Bros.)

Walkin' Away
Clint Black; *Killin' Time* .... (RCA)

Walkin' Away
Diamond Rio; *Diamond Rio IV* .... (Arista)
Diamond Rio's Greatest Hits .... (Arista)

Walkin' Back To Georgia
Jim Croce; *50th Anniversary Collection* .... (Saja)
Down The Highway .... (Atlantic)

Walkin' Back To San Antonio
Hank Thompson; *Here's To Country Music* .... (Step One)

Walkin' Blues
Paul Butterfield Blues Band; *East-West* .... (Elektra)
Golden Butter .... (Elektra)

Walkin' Blues
Bonnie Raitt; *Bonnie Raitt* .... (Warner Bros.)

Walkin' Blues
Hindu Love Gods; *Hindu Love Gods* .... (Giant)

Walkin' Blues
Roy Rogers; *Prime Chops-Blind Pig Sampler-C* ...... (Blind Pig)

Walkin' Blues
Robert Johnson; *Robert Johnson-Complete Recordings* .... (Columbia)

Walkin' Blues
Big Joe Williams; *Walkin' Blues* .... (Fantasy)

Walkin' Blues
Grateful Dead; *Without A Net* .... (Arista)

Walkin' By Myself
Jimmy Rogers; *Best Of Chess Blues-C* .... (Chess)
Johnny Winter; *Hot & Blue* .... (Blue Sky)
Scorchin' Blues .... (Epic Portrait Assoc.)
Walkin' By Myself .... (Relix)
White .... (Blue Sky)

Walkin' By The River
Ella Fitzgerald; *Best Of Ella Fitzgerald* .... (MCA)

Walkin' Down The Road
Ozark Mountain Daredevils; *Best Of The Ozark Mountain Daredevils* ... (A&M)
It'll Shine When It Shines .... (A&M)
It's Alive .... (A&M)

Walkin' In Jerusalem
Bill Monroe; *The Country Music Hall Of Fame-Bill Monroe* .... (MCA)
Doc Watson; *Old Timey Concert* .... (Vanguard)
Ricky Skaggs; *Love's Gonna Get Ya* .... (Epic)

Walkin' In The Rain
Grace Jones; *Island Life* .... (Island)
Nightclubbing .... (Island)

Walkin' In The Rain With The One I Love
Love Unlimited; *Didn't It Blow Your Mind: Soul Hits Of The '70s-#11-C* .... (Rhino)

Walkin' My Baby Back Home
Johnnie Ray; *Johnnie Ray-16 Most Requested Songs* .... (Legacy)
Johnnie Ray's Greatest Hits .... (Sony Music Special Prod.)
Nat "King" Cole; *Capitol Collectors Series-Nat "King" Cole* .... (Capitol)
The Nat "King" Cole Story .... (Capitol)

Walkin' On The Sun
Smash Mouth; *Fush Yu Mang* .... (Interscope)

Walkin' One & Only
Maria Muldaur; *Bread & Roses Festival Of Acoustic Music-#1-C* .... (Fantasy)
Maria Muldaur .... (Reprise)

Walkin' The Dog
Aerosmith; *Aerosmith* .... (Columbia)
Pandora's Box .... (Columbia)
Luther Allison; *Atlantic Blues-Chicago-C* .... (Atlantic)
Rolling Stones; *England's Newest Hit Makers/The Rolling Stones* ..... (Abkco)
Rufus Thomas; *Can't Get Away From This Dog* .... (Stax)
Rufus Thomas .... (Gusto)
Super Hits-#2-C .... (Gusto)
Walkin' The Dog .... (Atlantic)

Walkin' The Floor Over You
Asleep At The Wheel; *Western Standard Time* .... (Epic)
Ernest Tubb; *Legend & The Legacy* .... (First Generation)
The Ernest Tubb Story .... (MCA)
Ernest Tubb/Merle Haggard/Charlie Daniels; *Ernest Tubb Collection-C* .... (Step One)
Sandy Denny; *Who Knows Where The Time Goes* ..... (Hannibal)
Webb Pierce; *Webb Pierce-Golden Hits* .... (Plantation)

Walkin' To Freedom
Jazzmasters; *Jazzmasters II* .... (JVC Musical Industries)

Walkin', Talkin'...Beatin' Broken Heart
Highway 101; *Country's Greatest Hits-#4-Sweet Country-C* .... (Priority)
Paint The Town .... (Warner Bros.)

Walking Across Egypt
Tarwater Band; *Walking Across Egypt* .... (Flying Fish)

Walking After You
Foo Fighters; *The Colour And The Shape* .... (Roswell/RCA)

Walking Away
Information Society; *Information Society* .... (Tommy Boy)

Walking Back To Richmond
Dry Brance Fire Squad; *Fannin' The Flames* .... (Rounder)

Walking Down Madison
Kirsty MacColl; *Electric Landlady* .... (Charisma)

Walking Dream
Patsy Cline; *Forever & Always* .... (Epic)
Here's Patsy Cline .... (MCA)

Walking In A Hurricane
John Fogerty; *Blue Moon Swamp* .... (Warner Bros.)

Walking In L.A.
Missing Persons; *Best Of Missing Persons* .... (Capitol)

Walking In Memphis
Marc Cohn; *Marc Cohn* .... (Atlantic)

Walking In Space
Quincy Jones; *I Heard That!* .... (A&M)
ST/Listen Up-The Lives Of Quincy Jones .... (Qwest)
Walking In Space .... (A&M)

Walking In Space
Original Cast; *ST/Hair* .... (RCA)

Walking In The Rain
Jay & The Americans; *Come A Little Bit Closer-Best Of Jay & The Americans* .... (Gold Rush)
Jay & The Americans' All-Time Greatest Hits .... (Rhino)
Jay & The Americans' Greatest Hits .... (Curb)
Rhythm Of The Rain-C .... (Varese Vintage)
Ronettes; *Best Of The Ronettes* .... (Abkco)
Phil Spector-Back To Mono 1958-1969-C .... (Abkco)

Walking In The Rain
Marvin Gaye; *Romantically Yours* .... (Columbia)

Walking In The Shadow Of The Blues
Whitesnake; *Live In The Heart Of The City* .... (Geffen)
Love Hunter .... (Geffen)

Walking In The Sun
Zombies; *Time Of The Zombies* .... (Bac-Trac)

Walking In The Sun
Rufus; *Rags To Rufus* .... (MCA)

Walking In The Sunshine
Roger Miller; *Best Of Roger Miller* .... (Mercury)
King Of The Road .... (Laserlight)
More Golden Hits .... (Smash)
Statler Brothers; *Statler Brothers Sing The Big Hits* ..... (Columbia)
The World Of The Statler Brothers .... (Columbia)

Walking In The Sunshine
Frank Sinatra; *Hello Young Lovers* .... (Columbia)

Walking In The Wind
Traffic; *When The Eagle Flies* .... (Asylum)

Walking Into Sunshine
Central Line; *Full Length Funk-The 12" Collection And More-C* ..... (Mercury)

Walking Man
James Taylor; *James Taylor's Greatest Hits* ...... (Warner Bros.)
Walking Man .... (Warner Bros.)

Walking On A Thin Line
Huey Lewis and the News; *Sports* .... (Chrysalis)

Walking On Broken Glass
Annie Lennox; *Diva* .... (Arista)

Walking On Sunshine
Katrina And The Waves; *Katrina And The Waves* ...... (Capitol)
Spring Break-#2-Cold Kegs & Tan Legs .... (Capitol)

Walking On Sunshine
Eddy Grant; *Let's Dance-DJ's Collection* .... (Columbia)
Walking On Sunshine .... (Epic)

Walking Shoes
Tanya Tucker; *Tennessee Woman* .... (Capitol)

Walking Slow
Jackson Browne; *Late For The Sky* .... (Asylum)

Walking The Ghost
James; *Gold Mother* .... (Fontana)
James .... (Fontana)

Walking Through Fire
Mary Chapin Carpenter; *Come On Come On* .... (Columbia)

Walking To New Orleans
Fats Domino; *Fats Domino's All Time Greatest Hits* .... (Curb)
Fats Domino's Greatest Hits .... (CEMA Special Prod.)
Fats Domino's Greatest Hits .... (MCA)
My Blue Heaven-Best Of Fats Domino-#1 .... (EMI)
They Call Me The Fat Man .... (EMI)

Walks Like A Lady
Journey; *Departure* .... (Columbia)
Journey-Captured .... (Columbia)

Waltzing Matilda
Burl Ives; *Best Of Burl Ives* .... (MCA)
Fred Astaire; *Three Evenings With Fred Astaire* .... (DRG)
James Galway; *Pachebel Canon & Other Favorites* ...... (RCA)
Original Soundtrack; *Children's Favorites* .... (Kid Rhino/Rhino 4 Kids)

Wander This World
Jonny Lang; *Wander This World* .... (A&M)

Wanderer
Dion; *20 Million-Dollar Memories-#1-C* .... (Laurie)

Billboard Top Rock 'N' Roll Hits-1962-C . . . . (Rhino)
Cruisin'-1962-C . . . .(Increase)
Oldies But Goodies-#5-C . . . . (Original Sound)
ST/The Wanderers . . . . (Warner Bros.)
The Wanderer . . . . (Laurie)

Wanderer
Donna Summer; *The Wanderer* . . . .(Geffen)

Wanderin' Star
Original Broadway Cast; *Paint Your Wagon* . . . .(RCA Victor)

Wandering
James Taylor; *Gorilla* . . . .(Warner Bros.)

Wanderlust
Mark Knopfler; *Sailing To Philadelphia* . . . .(Warner Bros.)

Wanted Dead Or Alive
Bon Jovi; *Slippery When Wet* . . . .(Jambco)
The Concert For New York City-C . . . . (Columbia)

Watermelon Crawl
Tracy Byrd; *No Ordinary Man* . . . .(MCA)

Way I Walk
Jack Scott; *Jack Scott's Greatest Hits* . . . . (Curb)
Rock This Town-Rockabilly Hits-#2-C . . . . (Rhino)

Way, The
Fastball; *All The Pain Money Can Buy* . . . . (Hollywood)
Now That's What I Call Music!-#1-C . . . . (Virgin)

Wayward Wind
Gogi Grant; *'50s Jukebox Favorites-C* . . . . (K-Tel)
Collectables Presents The History Of Rock-#7-C . . . . (Collectables)
Lynn Anderson & Emmylou Harris; *Cowboy's Sweetheart* . . . . (Laserlight)
Patsy Cline; *The Patsy Cline Story* . . . .(MCA)

We Both Walk
Lorrie Morgan; *Something In Red* . . . . (RCA)

We Gonna Move To Kansas City
Walter Horton; *Fine Cuts* . . . .(Blind Pig)

We May Never Pass This Way Again
Seals & Crofts; *Diamond Girl* . . . .(Warner Bros.)
Seals & Crofts' Greatest Hits . . . .(Warner Bros.)

We're Gonna Move
Elvis Presley; *A Date With Elvis* . . . . (RCA)
Essential Elvis-The First Movies . . . . (RCA)

What About Now
Lonestar; *Lonely Grill* . . . . (BNA)

What It's Like
Everlast; *Whitey Ford Sings The Blues* . . . . (Tommy Boy)

When I Need You
Celine Dion; *Let's Talk About Love-C* . . . .(550 Music)
Leo Sayer; *'70s Greatest Rock Hits-#5-Kickin' Back-C* . . . . . . (Priority)
Show Must Go On-Anthology . . . . (Rhino)

When I Reach The Place I'm Going
Patty Loveless; *Red Hot + Country-C* . . . . (Mercury)

When My Sugar Walks Down The Street
Ella Fitzgerald; *Ella Fitzgerald-The Early Years-#2 (1939-1941)* . . . . . . (GRP)
Nat "King" Cole; *The Billy May Sessions* . . . .(Capitol)
Peggy Lee; *Capitol Sings Jimmy McHugh: I Feel A Song
Comin' On-C* . . . . (Capitol)

When The Saints Go Marching In
Al Hirt; *Best Of Al Hirt* . . . . (RCA)
Our Man-In New Orleans . . . . (Novus)
Jerry Lee Lewis; *Jerry Lee Lewis* . . . . (Rhino)
Louis Armstrong; *At The Crescendo* . . . .(MCA)
Big Bands Of The Swinging Years-#1-C . . . . (Collectables)
C'Est Si Bon . . . . (Rhino)
Essential Louis Armstrong . . . . (Vanguard)
Louis Armstrong Of New Orleans . . . .(MCA)
Original Soundtrack; *Children's Favorites* . . . . (Kid Rhino/Rhino 4 Kids)
Pete Fountain; *Best Of Pete Fountain* . . . .(MCA)
Down On Rampart Street . . . .(Intermedia)
Pete Fountain's New Orleans . . . .(MCA)
Preservation Hall Jazz Band; *Best Of The Preservation Hall
Jazz Band* . . . . (Columbia)

Where Can I Go Without You?
Nat "King" Cole; *Love Is The Thing* . . . . (Capitol)
Natalie Cole; *Stardust* . . . . (Elektra)
Peggy Lee; *Best Of The Decca Years-Peggy Lee* . . . .(MCA)

Where Do You Go
Strawbs; *Best Of The Strawbs* . . . . (A&M)
Ghosts . . . . (A&M)

Where Do You Go
Frank Sinatra; *No One Cares* . . . . (Capitol)

Where You Goin' Now
Damn Yankees; *Don't Tread* . . . .(Warner Bros.)

Wherever I May Roam
Metallica; *Metallica* . . . . (Elektra)

Which Way You Goin' Billy
Poppy Family; *Super Hits Of The '70s-Have A Nice Day-#2-C* . . . . . . (Rhino)

Whither Thou Goest
Les Paul & Mary Ford; *Best Of The Capitol Masters* . . . .(Gold Rush)
Les Paul's All-Time Greatest Hits . . . . (EMI Special Markets)

Who Can I Run To
Xscape; *Off The Hook* . . . . (So So Def/Columbia)

Smooth Love: Ultimate R&B Love Songs-C . . . . (EMI)

Who Walks In When I Walk Out
Bob Wills; *Stay A Little Longer-The Original Columbia
Recordings* . . . .(Roswell/RCA)

Why Ain't I Running
Garth Brooks; *Scarecrow* . . . . (Capitol)

Why I'm Walkin'
Stonewall Jackson; *Columbia Country Classics-#2-Honky Tonk
Heroes-C* . . . . (Columbia)
Waterloo . . . .(Laserlight)

Why Walk When You Can Fly
Mary Chapin Carpenter; *Stones In The Road* . . . . (Columbia)

Wide Open Spaces
Dixie Chicks; *Big Country Hits '99-C* . . . . (K-Tel)
Wide Open Spaces . . . . (Monument)

Widow's Walk
Suzanne Vega; *Songs In Red & Gray* . . . . (A&M)

Wild Night
John Mellencamp & Me'shell Ndegeocello; *Dance Naked* . . . . (Mercury)
Rough Harvest . . . . (Mercury)
Martha Reeves; *ST/Thelma & Louise* . . . .(MCA)
Van Morrison; *Best Of Van Morrison* . . . . (Polydor)
Tupelo Honey . . . .(Polydor)

Wild Things Run Fast
Joni Mitchell; *Wild Things Run Fast* . . . . (Geffen)

Willin'
Byrds; *The Byrds* . . . . (Columbia)
Linda Ronstadt; *Heart Like A Wheel* . . . . (Capitol)
Little Feat; *Little Feat* . . . .(Warner Bros.)
Sailin' Shoes . . . .(Warner Bros.)
Waiting For Columbus . . . .(Warner Bros.)

Winter Wonderland
Air Supply; *Air Supply Christmas Album* . . . . (Arista)
White Christmas . . . . (Word)
Alexander O'Neal; *My Gift To You* . . . . (Tabu)
Amy Grant; *Home For Christmas* . . . . (A&M)
Andrews Sisters; *Andrews Sisters-Christmas* . . . . (MCA Special Prod.)
Anne Murray; *Best Of The Season* . . . . (EMI America)
Aretha Franklin; *Rock 'N' Roll Christmas
Classics-C* . . . . (Music For Little People)
Barbara Mandrell; *Christmas At Our House* . . . . (MCA Special Prod.)
Tennessee Christmas-C . . . .(MCA)
Bing Crosby; *Bing Crosby Christmas Classics* . . . .(Capitol)
Blue Notes; *Rhythm & Blues Christmas-#1-C* . . . . (Collectables)
Brenda Lee; *Jingle Bell Rock* . . . . (MCA Special Prod.)
Carnie & Wendy Wilson; *Hey Santa!* . . . . (SBK)
Darlene Love; *Christmas Gift For You From Phil Spector-C* . . . . . . (Rhino)
Phil Spector-Back To Mono 1958-1969-C . . . . (Abkco)
Phil Spector's Christmas Album-C . . . . (Passport)
Eddy Arnold; *Christmas With Eddy Arnold* . . . . (RCA)
Elvis Presley; *If Every Day Was Like Christmas* . . . .(RCA)
Eurythmics; *Very Special Christmas-C* . . . . (A&M)
Faron Young; *Country Christmas* . . . .(Step One)
Frank Sinatra; *Christmas Songs By Sinatra* . . . . (Legacy)
George Strait; *Merry Christmas Strait To You* . . . . (MCA Special Prod.)
Hank Crawford; *We Got A Good Thing Going* . . . .(Kudo)
Johnny Mercer & The Pied Pipers; *Merry Christmas Baby-Romance &
Reindeer-C* . . . . (Capitol)
Kathie Lee Gifford; *It's Christmas Time* . . . . (Warner Bros.)
Kenny Rogers; *Christmas In America* . . . . (Reprise)
London Symphony Orchestra; *Christmas Traditions* . . . . . . (Special Music Co.)
Merle Haggard; *Merle Haggard-Christmas Gift* . . . . (Curb)
Patti LaBelle & The Blue Belles; *A Soulful Christmas-C* . . . .(Collectables)
Randy Travis; *An Old Time Christmas* . . . . (Warner Bros.)
Robert Goulet; *Essence Of Christmas* . . . . (A&M)
Rosie O'Donnell & Macy Gray; *Another Rosie Christmas-C* . . . . . . (Columbia)
Tanya Tucker; *Christmas For The '90s-#1-C* . . . . (Liberty)
Tony Bennett; *Now That's What I Call Christmas!-C* . . . . (UTV)
Travis Tritt; *Christmas-Loving Time Of The Year* . . . . . . (Warner Bros.)

Woman Walk The Line
Emmylou Harris; *Ballad Of Sally Rose* . . . . (Warner Bros.)
Highway 101; *Featuring Paulette Carlson* . . . . (Warner Bros.)
Trisha Yearwood; *Hearts In Armor* . . . .(MCA)

Women Walk More Determined
Kristin Lems; *Oh Mama!* . . . . (Carolsdatter Prod.)

Would You Like To Take A Walk?
Ella Fitzgerald; *Ella & Friends* . . . . (Decca Jazz)
Julia Sanderson/Frank Crumit/Leonard Joy; *The Song Is...Harry
Warren-C* . . . . (Living Era)
Rudy Vallee & His Connecticut Yankees; *78-#22611* . . . . (Victor)

Wrong Side Of Memphis
Matraca Berg; *Bittersweet Surrender* . . . . (RCA)
Trisha Yearwood; *Grand Ole Opry-75 Years-#1-C* . . . . (MCA)
Hearts In Armor . . . .(MCA)

Yodeling Hobo
Gene Autry; *Gene Autry: Blues Singer-1929-1933* . . . .(Legacy)

You Ain't Goin' Nowhere
Bob Dylan; *Bob Dylan's Greatest Hits-#2* . . . . (Columbia)
Bob Dylan And The Band; *Basement Tapes* . . . . (Columbia)

Byrds; *Best Of The Byrds-Greatest Hits-#2* . . . . (Columbia)
 Byrds Play Dylan . . . . (Columbia)
 Sweetheart Of The Rodeo . . . . (Columbia)
 The Byrds . . . . (Columbia)
Chris Hillman & Roger McGuinn; *Will The Circle Be Unbroken-#2-C* . . . . (Uni)
Joan Baez; *The First 10 Years* . . . . (Vanguard)

You Belong To Me
Dean Martin; *Dean Martin's All Time Greatest Hits* . . . . (Curb)
Duprees; *13 Of The Best Doo Wop Love Songs-#2-C* . . . .(Original Sound)
 Baby Boomer's Best-Mellow '60s-C . . . . (Priority)
 Best Of The Duprees . . . . (Rhino)
Jo Stafford; *Billboard Pop Memories-1950-1954-C* . . . . (Rhino)
 Jo Stafford's Greatest Hits . . . . (Curb)
Johnny Mathis; *In The Still Of The Night* . . . . (Columbia)
Patsy Cline; *Patsy Cline Sings Songs Of Love* . . . . (MCA Special Prod.)
 Sentimentally Yours . . . . (MCA)
Vonda Shepard; *ST/Songs From "Ally McBeal" Featuring Vonda*
 Shepard . . . .(550/Epic)

You Better Move On
Johnny Rivers; *Johnny Rivers-Anthology 1964-1977* . . . . (Rhino)
Rolling Stones; *December's Children (and everybody's)* . . . . (Abkco)

You Better Run
Pat Benatar; *Crimes Of Passion* . . . . (Chrysalis)
 ST/Roadie . . . . (Warner Bros.)

You Came A Long Way From St. Louis
Peggy Lee & George Shearing; *Beauty & The Beat!* . . . . (Blue Note)
Perry Como; *This Is Perry Como-#2* . . . . (RCA)

You Can Call Me Al
Paul Simon; *Concert In The Park-August 15 1991* . . . . (Warner Bros.)
 Graceland . . . . (Warner Bros.)
 Negotiations And Love Songs, 1971-1986 . . . . (Warner Bros.)

You Can't Run
Vanessa Williams; *The Sweetest Days* . . . . (Uptown/MCA)

You Can't Run From Love
Eddie Rabbitt; *Best Of Eddie Rabbitt/Greatest Hits-II* . . . . (Warner Bros.)
 Eddie Rabbitt-#1's . . . . (Warner Bros.)
 Radio Romance . . . . (Elektra)

You Don't Have To Go To Memphis
Asleep At The Wheel; *Keepin' Me Up Nights* . . . . (Arista)

You Gotta Move
Rolling Stones; *Love You Live* . . . . (Virgin)
 Sticky Fingers . . . . (Virgin)

You Keep Running Away
Four Tops; *Four Tops-Anthology* . . . . (Motown)

You Walked In
Lonestar; *Crazy Nights* . . . . (BNA)

You'll Never Walk Alone
Andy Williams; *Unchained Melody-Greatest Songs* . . . . (Curb)
Jim Nabors; *Jim Nabors-16 Most Requested Songs* . . . . (Legacy)
Judy Garland; *Best Of The Capitol Masters-One & Only Box* . . . . (Capitol)
Mormon Tabernacle Choir; *Climb Ev'ry Mountain* . . . . (Columbia)
Original Broadway Cast; *Carousel* . . . . (Angel)
Original Cast; *Carousel* . . . . (MCA)
Pink Floyd; *Meddle* . . . . (Capitol)

TREES

See Also: **COUNTRY, FLOWERS: GENERAL, JUNGLES,
MOUNTAINS, NATURE**

"Star Is Born" (Evergreen), Love Theme From "A Star Is Born"
Barbra Streisand; *Barbra Streisand's Greatest Hits* . . . . (Columbia)
 Barbra Streisand's Greatest Hits, Volume 2 . . . . (Columbia)
 Diana, Princess Of Wales-Tribute-C . . . . (Columbia)
 Memories . . . . (Columbia)
 ST/A Star Is Born . . . . (Columbia)
Luther Vandross; *Songs* . . . . (Epic)
Paul Williams; *Paul Williams-Classics* . . . . (A&M)

29 Palms
Robert Plant; *Fate Of Nations* . . . . (Es Paranza)

Alpine Milkman
Randy Erwin; *'Til The Cows Come Home/Cowboy*
 Rhythm . . . . (Really Outstanding Music)

Apple Orchard
Spirit; *Spirit* . . . . (Epic)

Apple Suckling Tree
Bob Dylan And The Band; *Basement Tapes* . . . . (Columbia)

Apple Tree
Erykah Badu; *Baduizm* . . . . (Kedar Entert./Universal)

Autumn Leaves
Barbra Streisand; *Je m'appelle Barbra* . . . . (Columbia)
Frank Sinatra; *Night We Called It A Day* . . . . (Capitol)
Nat "King" Cole; *Blossom Fell* . . . . (Capitol)
Roger Miller; *Music Of The 1950s-C* . . . . (MCA)
Roger Williams; *Best Of Roger Williams* . . . . (MCA)
 Roger Williams-Golden Hits-#2 . . . . (MCA)

Autumn Leaves
Grace Jones; *Fame* . . . . (Island)

Away
Toadies; *Rubberneck* . . . . (Interscope)

Babes In The Woods
Steve Miller Band; *Book Of Dreams* . . . . (Capitol)
 Steve Miller Band-Gift Set . . . . (Capitol)

Baby Tree
Paul Kantner/Jefferson Starship; *Blows Against The Empire* . . . . (RCA)

Bare Trees
Fleetwood Mac; *Bare Trees* . . . . (Reprise)

Birds In My Tree
Strawberry Alarm Clock; *Best Of The Strawberry Alarm Clock-#1* . . . (Bac-Trac)

Blue Spruce Woman
Foghat; *Rock & Roll Outlaws* . . . . (Rhino)

Boys In The Trees
Carly Simon; *Boys In The Trees* . . . . (Elektra)

Bury Me Beneath The Willow
Jimmie Davis; *Best Of Jimmie Davis* . . . . (MCA)
Ricky Skaggs; *Skaggs & Rice-The Essential Old-Time Country Duet*
 Recordings . . . . (Sugar Hill)
Wilma Lee Cooper; *Wilma Lee Cooper* . . . . (Rounder)
Woody Guthrie; *Woody Guthrie-#1 & 2* . . . . (Collectables)

Cactus Tree
Joni Mitchell; *Joni Mitchell* . . . . (Reprise)
Joni Mitchell with Tom Scott & The L.A. Express; *Miles Of Aisles* . . . . (Asylum)

Canadian Lumber Jack
Stompin' Tom Connors; *Bud The Spud* . . . . (EMI)

Carolina In The Pines
Michael Martin Murphey; *Best Of Michael Martin Murphey* . . . . (Liberty)
 Blue Sky-Night Thunder . . . . (Epic)

Cherry Blossom Time
Columbia Ballroom Orchestra; *Let's Dance-#7-Competition Dance* . . . (Denon)

Cherry Pink And Apple Blossom White
Fabulous Thunderbirds; *Butt Rockin'* . . . . (Chrysalis)
Perez Prado & His Orchestra; *This Is Perez Prado-Decade Of*
 The '50s . . . . (RCA)

Coconut Grove
David Lee Roth; *Crazy From The Heat* . . . . (Warner Bros.)
Lovin' Spoonful; *Lovin' Spoonful-Anthology* . . . . (Rhino)

Cypress Avenue
Van Morrison; *Astral Weeks* . . . . (Warner Bros.)
 It's Too Late To Stop Now . . . . (Warner Bros.)

Cypress Grove Blues
Skip James; *Greatest Of The Delta Blues Singers* . . . . (Biograph)
 Mississippi Blues-1927-1941 . . . . (Yazoo)
 Tribute To Skip James-#1-1964 . . . . (Biograph)

Dallas Rag/Maple Leaf Rag
David Bromberg; *How Late'll Ya Play 'Til?* . . . . (Fantasy)

Dang Me
Roger Miller; *Billboard Top Rock 'N' Roll Hits-1964-C* . . . . (Rhino)
 Cruisin'-1964-C . . . . (Increase)
 Roger Miller-Golden Hits . . . . (Smash)

Day In The Life Of A Tree
Beach Boys; *Surf's Up* . . . . (Caribou)

Don't Cut The Tree Down In Winter
Penny Little; *In A Light Garden* . . . . (Global Pacific)

Don't Sit Under The Apple Tree
Andrews Sisters; *Andrews Sisters Greatest Hits* . . . . (Curb)
 Andrews Sisters-16 Great Performances . . . . (MCA)
 Capitol Collectors Series-The Andrews Sisters . . . . (Capitol)
Glenn Miller; *Memorial-1944-1969* . . . . (Bluebird)
Glenn Miller & His Orchestra; *The Unforgettable Glenn Miller & His*
 Orchestra . . . . (RCA)

Down Among The Sheltering Pines
Barney Kessel; *Some Like It Hot* . . . . (Contemporary)
Lawrence Welk; *Champagne Music Of Lawrence Welk* . . . . (Ranwood)

East Of Ginger Trees
Seals & Crofts; *Seals & Crofts' Greatest Hits* . . . . (Warner Bros.)

Easter Tree
June Tabor; *Ashes & Diamonds* . . . . (Green Linnet)

Echoes Of The African Forest
Saka Acquaye Ensemble; *Voices Of Africa* . . . . (Nonesuch)

Eloise
David Frishberg; *Live At Vine Street* . . . . (Original Jazz Classics)

Fake Plastic Trees
Radiohead; *Bends* . . . . (Capitol)
 ST/Clueless . . . . (Capitol)

Fig Tree
Bunny Wailer; *Blackheart Man* . . . . (Island)

Fig Tree Bay
Peter Frampton; *Wind Of Change* . . . . (A&M)

Georgia Pineywoods
Osborne Brothers; *Best Of The Osborne Brothers* . . . . (MCA)
 Country Bluegrass . . . . (MCA Special Prod.)
 Red, White & Bluegrass-C . . . . (C.M.H. Prod.)

Green Leaves Of Summer
Brothers Four; *Brothers Four-Greatest Hits* . . . . (Columbia)
 Greenfields & Other Gold . . . . (First Warning)
 Hollywood Magic-1950s-C . . . . (Columbia)

Hanging Tree
Marty Robbins; *Gunfighter Ballads & Trail Songs* . . . . (Legacy)
  Hollywood Magic-1950s-C . . . . (Columbia)
  Lifetime Of Song-1951-1982 . . . . (Columbia)
  Marty Robbins' All-Time Greatest Hits . . . . (Columbia)

Hazy Shade Of Winter
Bangles; *Bangles' Greatest Hits* . . . . (Columbia)
  ST/Less Than Zero . . . .(Def Jam)
Simon & Garfunkel; *Bookends* . . . . (Columbia)
  Collected Works . . . . (Columbia)

Hickory Wind
Byrds; *Columbia Country Classics-#5-A New Tradition-C* . . . . (Columbia)
  Sweetheart Of The Rodeo . . . . (Columbia)
  The Byrds . . . . (Columbia)
Emmylou Harris; *Blue Kentucky Girl* . . . .(Warner Bros.)
Gram Parsons; *Grievous Angel* . . . . (Reprise)

Honey
Bobby Goldsboro; *Billboard Top Pop Hits-1968-C* . . . . (Rhino)
  Cruisin'-1968-C . . . .(Increase)

I Talk To The Trees
Al Hirt; *Al Hirt* . . . .(Dunhill Compact Classics)
  Showtime . . . .(Allegiance)
Alan Jay Lerner; *Alan Jay Lerner Performs His Own Songs* . . . . (DRG)
Original Broadway Cast; *Paint Your Wagon* . . . .(RCA Victor)

If I Were King Of The Forest
Bert Lahr; *ST/The Wizard Of Oz* . . . .(Sony Music Special Prod.)

In Chicago's Forest Preserve
Li'l Wally; *Polish Feelings* . . . .(Jay Jay)

In The Pines
Merle Travis & Mac Wiseman; *Great American Train
  Songs-C* . . . .(C.M.H. Prod.)

In The Valley
Marty Robbins; *Gunfighter Ballads & Trail Songs* . . . . (Legacy)

Leaves That Are Green
Country Gentlemen; *Country Gentlemen* . . . . (Vanguard)
Simon & Garfunkel; *Collected Works* . . . . (Columbia)
  Sounds Of Silence . . . . (Columbia)

Lemon Tree
Kingston Trio; *Very Best Of The Kingston Trio* . . . . (Capitol)
Peter, Paul & Mary; *10 Years Together/The Best Of Peter, Paul
  and Mary* . . . .(Warner Bros.)
  Peter, Paul and Mary . . . .(Warner Bros.)
Trini Lopez; *Best Of Trini Lopez* . . . .(Exact)

Little Willow
Paul McCartney; *Diana, Princess Of Wales-Tribute-C* . . . . (Columbia)

Lollipop Tree
Burl Ives; *A Twinkle In Your Eye* . . . . (Legacy)
Limeliters; *Through The Children's Eyes* . . . . (Folk Era)

Lullaby Of The Leaves
Various Artists; *Birdlanders-#1-C* . . . . (Original Jazz Classics)

Lumberjack
Jackyl; *Jackyl* . . . .(Geffen)

Magnolia
Tom Petty And The Heartbreakers; *You're Gonna Get It!* . . . . (Gone Gator)

Magnolia
Poco; *Crazy Eyes* . . . .(Epic)

Magnolia
Pat Travers; *Pat Travers* . . . . (Polydor)

Maple Leaf Rag
Joshua Rifkin; *Digital Ragtime-Music Of Scott Joplin* . . . . (Angel)
Scott Joplin; *Greatest Ragtime Of The Century-C* . . . . (Biograph)

Meet In The Middle
Diamond Rio; *Diamond Rio* . . . . (Arista)
  Diamond Rio's Greatest Hits . . . . (Arista)

Mummer's Dance
Loreena McKennitt; *The Book Of Secrets* . . . . (Quinlan Rd./Warner Bros.)

Oak Tree
Morris Day; *Color Of Success* . . . .(Warner Bros.)

Once A Forest
Grace Pool; *Where We Live* . . . . (Reprise)

Orange Blossom Lane
Glenn Miller & His Orchestra; *Complete Glenn Miller & His
  Orchestra* . . . . (Bluebird)
  Complete Glenn Miller & His Orchestra-#7 . . . . (Bluebird)

Orange Blossom Mandolin
Northeast Winds; *Northeast Winds In Concert* . . . . (Folk Era)

Orange Blossom Special
Bill Monroe; *Bean Blossom* . . . .(MCA)
  Bill Monroe and His Blue Grass Boys-60 Years of Country . . . . (RCA)
  Stars Of The Grand Ole Opry-1926-1974-C . . . . (RCA)
Charlie Daniels Band; *Fire On The Mountain* . . . . (Epic)
  ST/Urban Cowboy 2 . . . . (Epic)
Flatt & Scruggs; *Hear The Whistles Blow* . . . . (International Mktg. Group)
Gordon Terry; *Disco Country* . . . . (Plantation)
  Gordon Terry-20 Golden Souvenirs . . . . (Plantation)
Johnny Cash; *Columbia Records-1958-1986* . . . . (Columbia)
  Essential Johnny Cash . . . . (Columbia)
  Johnny Cash-16 Biggest Hits-#2 . . . . (Legacy)
  Johnny Cash's Greatest Hits . . . . (Columbia)

  The Man In Black-His Greatest Hits . . . . (Legacy)
  Train Trax-C . . . . (Sony Music Special Prod.)
Johnson Mountain Boys; *Steel Rails-Classic Railroad Songs-#1-C* . . . (Rounder)
Nitty Gritty Dirt Band; *Will The Circle Be Unbroken* . . . . (EMI)

Orange Blossom Time
Bing Crosby; *Crooner-Columbia Years-1928-1934* . . . . (Columbia)

Out In The Woods
Leon Russell; *Best Of Leon Russell* . . . . (MCA)
  Carney . . . . (Right Stuff)

Out Of The Woods
Nickel Creek; *Nickel Creek* . . . .(Sugar Hill)

Part Man, Part Monkey
Bruce Springsteen; *Tracks* . . . . (Columbia)

Peach Blossom Spring
Yutaka; *Yutaka* . . . . (GRP)

Peach Orchard Mamma
Big Joe Williams; *Piney Woods Blues* . . . . (Delmark)

Peach Tree
Sonny Boy Williamson; *Real Folk Blues-C* . . . . (Chess)

Peach Tree Shuffle
Panama Francis; *All-Stars 1949* . . . . (Collectables)

People Tree
Sammy Davis, Jr.; *Best Of Sammy Davis, Jr.* . . . . (Curb)

Pine Grove Blues
Nathan Abshire; *Alligator Stomp-#2-C* . . . . (Rhino)
  French Blues . . . . (Arhoolie)

Piney Woods/Coyote Howl
Skip Gorman; *A Cowboy's Wild Song To His Herd* . . . . (Rounder)

Please Mr. Sun
Johnnie Ray; *Back To The Early '50s* . . . . (Dominion Entert.)
  Johnnie Ray-16 Most Requested Songs . . . . (Legacy)
Vogues; *Vogues' Greatest Hits* . . . . (Rhino)

Plum Blossom
Vangelis; *China* . . . . (Polydor)
Yusef Lateef & Others; *Eastern Sounds* . . . . (Prestige)

Possum Up A Gum Stump
Dick Fegy; *Flatpicking Guitar Festival-C* . . . .(Shanachie)

Queen Of The Forest
Ted Nugent; *Ted Nugent* . . . . (Epic)

Rabbit In A Log
Stanley Brothers; *Long Journey Home* . . . . (Rebel)

Rain Forest
Paul Hardcastle; *Dance 2-C* . . . .(Profile)
  Paul Hardcastle . . . .(Chrysalis)
  Rain Forest . . . .(Profile)

Rain Forest
Cut To The Chase; *Cut To The Chase* . . . . (Art & Commerce)

Rain Forest
David Lanz & Paul Speer; *Narada Equinox Sampler One-C* . . . . (Narada)
  Natural States . . . . (Narada)

Rain Forest
Nelson Rangell; *Nelson Rangell* . . . . (GRP)

Rain Forest
Jeremy Steig & Eddie Gomez; *Rain Forest* . . . . (Creative Music Prod.)

Rain Forest
Jessica Williams; *Rivers Of Memory* . . . . (Clean Cuts)

Redwood Evergreen
Lorraine Duisit; *Hawks & Herons* . . . . (Flying Fish)

Redwood Hill
Vassar Clements; *Westport Drive* . . . . (Mind Dust Music)

Redwood Tree
Van Morrison; *St. Dominic's Preview* . . . .(Warner Bros.)

River In The Pines
Joan Baez; *Farewell Angelina* . . . . (Vanguard)
  Love Song Album . . . . (Vanguard)

Settin' The Woods On Fire
Hank Williams With His Drifting Cowboys; *24 Of Hank Williams'
  Greatest Hits* . . . .(Polydor)
  Hank Williams-40 Greatest Hits . . . .(Polydor)

Shade Tree Mechanic
Joe Louis Walker; *The Gift* . . . .(Hightone)
Z.Z. Hill; *I'm A Blues Man* . . . . (Malaco)
  Z.Z. Hill's Greatest Hits . . . . (Malaco)

Shady Grove
Doc Watson; *Essential Doc Watson* . . . . (Vanguard)
  Memories . . . .(Sugar Hill)
Hot Rize; *Hot Rize In Concert* . . . . (Flying Fish)
Kentucky Colonels/Clarence White/Doc Watson; *Long Journey Home-
  Newport Folk Festival-1964* . . . . (Vanguard)

Shake My Tree
Coverdale/Page; *Coverdale/Page* . . . . (Geffen)

Shake The Sugar Tree
Pam Tillis; *Homeward Looking Angel* . . . . (Arista)

Shaking The Tree
Peter Gabriel; *Shaking The Tree-Sixteen Golden Greats* . . . . (Geffen)

Shaking Your Tree (Somebody Else Been)
ZZ Top; *Six Pack* . . . .(Warner Bros.)
  ZZ Top . . . .(Warner Bros.)

She's Long, She's Tall, She Weeps Like A Willow Tree
John Lee Hooker; *Black Snake* . . . .(Fantasy)
Country Blues Of John Lee Hooker . . . . (Riverside)
Singing Tree
Elvis Presley; *ST/Clambake* . . . .(RCA)
Song Of The Evergreens
Chicago; *Chicago VII* . . . . (Chicago)
Songs From The Wood
Jethro Tull; *20 Years Of Jethro Tull*. (Chrysalis)
Bursting Out . . . . (Chrysalis)
Original Masters . . . . (Chrysalis)
Too Old To Rock 'N' Roll: Too Young To Die! . . . . (Chrysalis)
Sparrow In The Treetop
Guy Mitchell; *Guy Mitchell-16 Most Requested Songs* . . . . (Legacy)
Strange Fruit
Billie Holiday; *History Of The Real Billie Holiday* . . . . (Verve)
Lady Sings The Blues . . . . (Verve)
Songbook . . . . (Verve)
Nina Simone; *Compact Jazz-Nina Simone* . . . . (Verve)
Siouxsie And The Banshees; *Through The Looking Glass* . . . . . . (Geffen)
Strong Enough To Bend
Tanya Tucker; *Strong Enough To Bend*. . . . . (Liberty)
Tanya Tucker's Greatest Hits . . . . (Liberty)
Sycamore Leaves
A-Ha; *East Of The Sun-West Of The Moon* . . . . (Warner Bros.)
Sycamore Rag
Dick Hyman; *Scott Joplin-Greatest Hits* . . . .(RCA)
Scott Joplin; *Ragtime-#2-1900-1910*. . . . . (Biograph)
Tales From The Vienna Woods
101 Strings Orchestra; *Best Of Johann Strauss, Jr.* . . . . (Alshire)
Lawrence Welk; *22 Great Waltzes* . . . . (Ranwood)
Tall Trees In Georgia
Buffy Sainte-Marie; *Best Of Buffy Sainte-Marie-#2* . . . . (Vanguard)
I'm Gonna Be A Country Girl Again. (Vanguard)
Tall, Tall Trees
Alan Jackson; *Alan Jackson-The Greatest Hits Collection* . . . .(Arista)
George Jones; *Cup Of Loneliness-Classic Mercury Years* . . . . (Mercury)
George Jones-The Hits . . . . (Mercury)
Roger Miller; *King Of The Road-Genius Of Roger Miller*. . . . . (Mercury)
Roger Miller-The Hits . . . . (Mercury)
There Is A Tavern In The Town
Four Aces; *Four Aces-More Greatest Hits* . . . .(Varese Vintage)
Mitch Miller; *Sing Along With Mitch*. . . . . (Columbia)
Stan Wolowic & The Polka Chips; *Million-Seller Polkas* . . . . (Capitol)
There Was A Tall Oak Tree
Dorsey Burnette; *Super Hits-#1-C* . . . . (International Mktg. Group)
There's A Cabin In The Pines
Bing Crosby; *Crooner-Columbia Years-1928-1934* . . . . (Columbia)
Thorn Tree In The Garden
Derek And The Dominos; *Layla* . . . . (Polydor)
Tie A Yellow Ribbon Round The Ole Oak Tree
Dawn Featuring Tony Orlando; *'70s Party Killers-C* . . . . (Rhino)
Fantastic-#1-C . . . . (K-Tel)
Frank Sinatra; *Some Nice Things I've Missed* . . . . (Reprise)
Lawrence Welk; *Best Of Lawrence Welk-20 Great Hits* . . . . (Ranwood)
Sonny James & Karla Taylor; *Classic Country Duets-C* . . . .(Curb)
Timber I'm Falling In Love
Patty Loveless; *Country's Greatest Hits-#4-Sweet Country-C* . . . . .(Priority)
Honky Tonk Angel. . . . . (MCA)
Patty Loveless' Greatest Hits . . . . (MCA)
Timberline
Emmylou Harris; *Ballad Of Sally Rose* . . . . (Warner Bros.)
Tree Frog
Count Basie; *Best Of Count Basie & His Orchestra* . . . . (Pablo)
Count Basie & His Orchestra; *I Told You So* . . . . (Pablo)
Tree Grows In Burbank
Harry James; *The Uncollected Harry James-#5-1943-1953* . . . . (Hindsight)
Tree Hugger
Rugburns; *Taking The World By Donkey*. . . . .(Priority)
Tree In The Meadow
Lettermen; *Let It Be Me* . . . . (Capitol)
Margaret Whiting; *Capitol Collectors Series-Margaret Whiting* . . . . . (Capitol)
Great Records Of The Decade-'40s-Pop-#1-C. . . . .(Curb)
Tree In The Park
Sarah Vaughan; *Rodgers & Hart Songbook* . . . . (Emarcy)
William Bolcom & Joan Morris; *Rodgers & Hart Album* . . . .(RCA)
Tree Of Joy
Jeannie C. Riley; *Country Gold-Jeannie C. Riley* . . . . (Plantation)
Tree Of Life
Les Baxter & His Orchestra; *Brazil Now-African Blue* . . . . (Crescendo)
Tree Too Weak To Stand
Gordon Lightfoot; *Cold On The Shoulder* . . . . (Reprise)
Trees
Rush; *Exit...Stage Left* . . . . (Mercury)
Hemispheres . . . . (Mercury)
Rush-Chronicles. . . . . (Mercury)
Trees
Spaniels; *Spaniels' Golden Hits* . . . . (Juke Box Treasures)
The Acapella Collection . . . . (Juke Box Treasures)

Trees In Philadelphia
Patti Page; *Touch Of Country* . . . . (Fifty One West)
Trees Of The Ages
Laura Nyro; *Mother's Spiritual* . . . . (Columbia)
Trees They Do Grow High
Joan Baez; *Joan Baez, Vol. 2* . . . . (Vanguard)
The Joan Baez Ballad Book . . . . (Vanguard)
Under The Bamboo Tree
Marie Cahill; *Music From The New York Stage (1890-1920)-#1-1890-
1908-C* . . . . (Pearl)
Under The Sycamore Tree
Sara Hickman; *Equal Scary People* . . . .(Elektra)
Under The Willow Tree
Claude Thornhill & His Orchestra featuring Buddy Hughes; *Best Of The Big
Bands-C*. . . . . (Columbia)
Underneath The Apple Tree
Michael Franks; *Tiger In The Rain*. . . . . (Warner Bros.)
Up In My Treehouse
Chet Atkins; *Sails*. . . . . (Columbia)
Vermont Is Afire In The Autumn
Lui Collins; *Made In New England* . . . . (Green Linnet)
Wailing Of The Willow
Nilsson; *Aerial Ballet*. . . . . (RCA)
When The Golden Leaves Begin To Fall
Joe Val & The New England Bluegrass Boys; *Diamond Joe* . . . .(Rounder)
Joe Val & The New England Bluegrass Boys-Vol. 2 . . . .(Rounder)
When The World Was Young
Anita O'Day; *Mello'Day* . . . . (Crescendo)
Frank Sinatra; *Point Of No Return* . . . .(Capitol)
Whispering Pines
Johnny Horton; *Johnny Horton's Greatest Hits*. . . . . (Columbia)
Whispering Pines
Band; *The Band* . . . .(Capitol)
Wildwood Mandolin
Jack Tottle; *Rounder Bluegrass-#1-C* . . . .(Rounder)
Willow
Joan Armatrading; *Joan Armatrading-Classics-#21* . . . .(A&M)
Show Some Emotion . . . .(A&M)
Track Record . . . .(A&M)
Willow Weep For Me
Art Tatum; *Best Of Art Tatum* . . . . (Pablo)
Solo Masterpieces-#1 . . . . (Pablo)
Billie Holiday; *Billie Holiday-Live* . . . . (Verve)
Billie's Blues . . . . (Blue Note)
Lady Sings The Blues. . . . . (Verve)
Stormy Blues . . . . (Verve)
Chad & Jeremy; *Best Of Chad & Jeremy* . . . .(Capitol)
History Of British Rock-#3-C . . . .(Rhino)
Super Oldies Of The '60s-#11-C . . . . (Audio Fidelity)
Dinah Shore; *Dinah Shore-16 Most Requested Songs* . . . .(Legacy)
Lou Rawls; *Legendary Lou Rawls* . . . . (Blue Note)
Roy Eldridge; *Best Of Roy Eldridge*. . . . . (Pablo)
Steve Miller; *Born 2 B Blue* . . . . (Gold Rush)

TROUBLE, In Trouble, Problems

See Also: **DANGER & DISASTER, DECISIONS, DESPAIR,
DIFFICULT, FAITH, FRIENDS, GOD, HELP, LOVE (various),
MOTIVATION, POVERTY, SADNESS, WARNINGS**

Angel On My Shoulder
Natalie Cole; *Natalie Cole's Greatest Hits-#1* . . . .(Elektra)
Are We In Trouble Now
Mark Knopfler; *Golden Heart* . . . . (Warner Bros.)
Baby's In Black
Beatles; *Beatles '65* . . . .(Capitol)
Beatles-Box Set . . . .(Capitol)
For Sale . . . .(Capitol)
Bad Day
Fuel; *Now That's What I Call Music!-#8-C* . . . . (Virgin)
Something Like Human . . . . (Epic)
Badlands
Bruce Springsteen; *Bruce Springsteen's Greatest Hits* . . . . (Columbia)
Darkness On The Edge Of Town . . . . (Columbia)
Bruce Springsteen & The E Street Band; *Bruce Springsteen & The E Street
Band Live/1975-85* . . . . (Legacy)
Big Bright Green Pleasure Machine
Simon & Garfunkel; *Collected Works* . . . . (Columbia)
Parsley Sage Rosemary & Thyme . . . . (Columbia)
ST/The Graduate . . . . (Columbia)
Blue
Joni Mitchell; *Blue* . . . . (Reprise)
Joni Mitchell with Tom Scott & The L.A. Express; *Miles Of Aisles*. . . . (Asylum)
Bridge Over Troubled Water
Aretha Franklin; *Aretha Franklin-30 Greatest Hits* . . . .(Rhino)
Aretha Franklin's Greatest Hits . . . . (Atlantic)
Live At Fillmore West . . . . (Atlantic)

Paul Simon; *America: A Tribute To Heroes-C* . . . . (Interscope)
  Concert In The Park-August 15 1991 . . . .(Warner Bros.)
  Paul Simon In Concert/Live Rhymin' . . . . (Columbia)
Simon & Garfunkel; *Bridge Over Troubled Water* . . . . (Columbia)
  Collected Works . . . . (Columbia)
  God Bless America-C . . . . (Columbia)
  Simon & Garfunkel's Greatest Hits . . . . (Columbia)
  The Concert In Central Park . . . .(Warner Bros.)

Bring On The Rain
Jo Dee Messina with Tim McGraw; *Burn* . . . . (Curb)

Brothers Under The Bridge
Bruce Springsteen; *Tracks* . . . . (Columbia)

Casey Jones
Grateful Dead; *Best Of The Grateful Dead-Skeletons From The
  Closet* . . . .(Warner Bros.)
  *Bill Graham Presents The Last Days Of The
  Fillmore-C* . . . . (Epic Portrait Assoc.)
  Workingman's Dead . . . .(Warner Bros.)
Jerry Garcia Acoustic Band; *Almost Acoustic.* . . . . (Grateful Dead)

Cigarette
Ben Folds Five; *Whatever And Ever Amen* . . . . (Caroline/550)

Darned If I Don't (Danged If I Do)
Shenandoah; *In The Vicinity Of The Heart* . . . . (Capitol)

Deep Water
Asleep At The Wheel; *Asleep At The Wheel* . . . . (MCA Special Prod.)
Asleep At The Wheel featuring Garth Brooks; *Tribute To The Music Of Bob
  Wills And The Texas Playboys-C* . . . . (Liberty)
Bob Wills & His Texas Playboys; *Bob Wills & His Texas Playboys-
  Anthology 1935-1973* . . . . (Rhino)
  Essential Bob Wills & His Texas Playboys-1935-1973 . . . . (Legacy)
George Strait; *George Strait-Number 7* . . . . (MCA)
Willie Nelson; *San Antonio Rose* . . . . (Columbia)

Don't Tell Me Your Troubles
Doc Watson; *Memories* . . . . (Sugar Hill)
Don Gibson; *45-#7566* . . . . (RCA)
Ray Charles; *Greatest Country & Western Hits* . . . . .(Dunhill Compact Classics)

Drown
Son Volt; *Trace.* . . . .(Warner Bros.)

Everything Is Everything
Lauryn Hill; *The Miseducation Of Lauryn Hill.* . . . . (Ruffhouse/Columbia)

Get 'Em Outta Here
Sprung Monkey; *Mr. Funny Face.* . . . . (Surfdog/Hollywood)

Good Day To Run
Darryl Worley; *Hard Rain Don't Last* . . . . (DreamWorks/SKG)

Halfway Down
Patty Loveless; *When Fallen Angels Fly.* . . . .(Epic)

Handcuffed To A Fence In Mississippi
Jim White; *No Such Place.* . . . .(Luaka Bop)

Heavy Things
Phish; *Farmhouse.* . . . . (Elektra)

Hello Trouble
Desert Rose Band; *Running* . . . .(MCA)

Hold On (Change Is Comin')
Sounds Of Blackness; *Time For Healing* . . . .(Perspective/A&M)

I Am A Man Of Constant Sorrow
Ralph Stanley; *Rebel Records: 35 Years Of The Best In Bluegrass-1960-
  1995-C* . . . .(Rebel)
Soggy Bottom Boys featuring Dan Tyminski; *ST/O Brother, Where Art
  Thou?* . . . . (Mercury)
Stanley Brothers; *All Time Legends Of Country Music-C.* . . . . (Legacy)

I Got Rhythm
Ella Fitzgerald; *George & Ira Gershwin Songbook* . . . . (Verve)
Ethel Waters; *I Got Rhythm: The Smithsonian George Gershwin
  Collection-C* . . . .(Smithsonian Collection)
Happenings; *'60s Rock Classics-#1-C* . . . . (Rhino)
Judy Garland; *Judy Garland-Collector's Items-1936-1945* . . . .(MCA)
Louis Armstrong; *Essential Louis Armstrong.* . . . . (Verve)
Original Cast; *Girl Crazy* . . . . (Nonesuch)
Original London Cast; *Crazy For You* . . . . (RCA)
Robert Palmer; *Glory Of Gershwin Featuring Larry Adler-C* . . . . (Mercury)

If You've Got Trouble
Beatles; *The Beatles-Anthology-#2.* . . . . (Capitol)

In 2 Deep
Kenny Wayne Shepherd Band; *Live On* . . . .(Giant)

In The Heat Of The Night
Ray Charles; *Ray Charles-His Greatest Hits-#2* . . . .(Dunhill Compact Classics)
  ST/In The Heat Of The Night . . . . (United Artists)

Into Each Life Some Rain Must Fall
Ella Fitzgerald; *Ella & Friends.* . . . . (Decca Jazz)
Ink Spots; *Encore Of Golden Hits-Ink Spots.* . . . .(Juke Box Treasures)

It Hurts Me Too
Keb' Mo'; *The Door.* . . . . (550/Epic/Okeh)

Keep On The Sunny Side
Randy Scruggs with Earl Scruggs & Doc Watson; *Red Hot +
  Country-C* . . . . (Mercury)
Whites; *ST/O Brother, Where Art Thou?* . . . . (Mercury)

Lawyers, Guns & Money
Warren Zevon; *Excitable Boy.* . . . . (Asylum)
  Quiet Normal Life-Best Of Warren Zevon . . . . (Asylum)

  Stand In The Fire . . . .(Asylum)

Let It Be
Aretha Franklin; *Aretha Franklin's Greatest Hits* . . . .(Atlantic)
Beatles; *Beatles 1* . . . . (Capitol)
  Beatles-20 Greatest Hits . . . . (Capitol)
  Past Masters-Volume Two . . . . (Parlophone)
  Reel Music . . . . (Capitol)
  The Beatles/1967-1970. . . . . (Capitol)
Paul McCartney; *The Concert For New York City-C* . . . . (Columbia)
  Tripping The Live Fantastic-Highlights! . . . . (Capitol)
Rockestra; *Kampuchea-C* . . . .(Atlantic)

Let Your Soul Be Your Pilot
Sting; *Mercury Falling* . . . . (A&M)

Life's A Bitch
Shooter; *Songs From Dawson's Creek* . . . .(Sony Music Soundtrax)

Little Bit Of You
Lee Roy Parnell; *We All Get Lucky Sometimes* . . . .(Career)

Loose Change
Bruce Springsteen; *Tracks* . . . . (Columbia)

Mo Money Mo Problems
Notorious B.I.G.; *Jock Jams-#4-C* . . . . (Tommy Boy)
  Life After Death . . . .(Bad Boy/Arista)
  The Ultimate Dance Party-1998-C. . . . . (Arista)

Move It On Over
Hank Williams; *Complete Hank Williams.* . . . . (Mercury)

New Beginning
Tracy Chapman; *New Beginning.* . . . . (Elektra)

No One Said It Would Be Easy
Sheryl Crow; *Tuesday Night Music Club* . . . . (A&M)

Nobody
Ry Cooder; *Jazz* . . . .(Warner Bros.)

Nobody Knows The Trouble I've Seen
Mahalia Jackson; *Gospels, Spirituals & Hymns* . . . . (Columbia)
  Mahalia Jackson's Greatest Hits . . . . (Columbia)
Nat ''King'' Cole; *Every Time I Feel The Spirit* . . . . (Capitol)

One More Last Chance
Vince Gill; *I Still Believe In You* . . . . (MCA)
  The Ultimate Country Party-C . . . . (Arista)
  Vince Gill-Souvenirs . . . . (MCA)

Open My Heart
Yolanda Adams; *Mountain High Valley Low* . . . . (Elektra)

Over The Rainbow
Barbra Streisand; *Just For The Record* . . . . (Columbia)
Dave Brubeck; *Greatest Hits From The Fantasy Years* . . . . (Fantasy)
Ella Fitzgerald; *Silver Collection-Songbooks* . . . . (Verve)
Judy Garland; *Best Of The Capitol Masters-One & Only Box* . . . . . . (Capitol)
  Judy Garland-At Carnegie Hall . . . . (Capitol)
  Judy Garland's Greatest Hits . . . . (Curb)
  Miss Show Business . . . . (Capitol)
  One & Only . . . . (Capitol)
  ST/The Wizard Of Oz . . . . (Sony Music Special Prod.)

Pack Up Your Troubles In Your Old Kit Bag (And Smile, Smile, Smile)
James F. Harrison & Knickerbocker Quartet; *78-#2181* . . . . (Columbia)

Please
Chris Isaak; *Speak Of The Devil* . . . .(Reprise)

Po Lazarus
James Carter & The Prisoners; *ST/O Brother, Where Art Thou?* . . . . . (Mercury)

Promised Land
Band; *Moondog Matinee* . . . .(Capitol)
Chuck Berry; *Rock 'N' Roll Rarities-20 Magic Tracks* . . . . (Chess)
  The Chess Box-Chuck Berry . . . . (Chess)
Elvis Presley; *Promised Land* . . . . (RCA)
  ST/This Is Elvis. . . . . (RCA)
Freddy Weller; *Country Music Classics-#11-Early '70s-C.* . . . . (K-Tel)
  Freddy Weller's Greatest Hits . . . . (Columbia)
Gary Morris; *Full Moon Empty Heart.* . . . . (Liberty)
Grateful Dead; *Steal Your Face* . . . .(Grateful Dead)
James Taylor; *Walking Man* . . . .(Warner Bros.)
Kingfish; *Kingfish/Alive In Eighty Five-Double Dose.* . . . . (Relix)

Return Of The Red Baron
Royal Guardsmen; *Royal Guardsmen-Anthology* . . . . (One Way)

Rockaway The Days
Bruce Springsteen; *Tracks* . . . . (Columbia)

Second Hand News
Fleetwood Mac; *25 Years-The Chain* . . . . (Warner Bros.)
  Rumours . . . .(Warner Bros.)
Tonic; *Legacy-A Tribute To Fleetwood Mac's Rumours-C* . . . . (Lava)

Serious Juju
Sammy Hagar; *Ten 13* . . . .(Cabo Wabo/Beyond)

Shackles (Praise You)
Mary Mary; *Thankful* . . . . (C2/Columbia)

Slow Poke
Ray Conniff; *Speak To Me Of Love* . . . . (Columbia)

Somethin' Just Ain't Right
Earl Scruggs & Randy Scruggs; *Earl Scruggs And Friends-C* . . . . (MCA)

Sour Times (Nobody Loves Me)
Portishead; *Dummy* . . . . (Go! Discs)

Sparrow In The Treetop
Guy Mitchell; *Guy Mitchell-16 Most Requested Songs* . . . . (Legacy)

Stones In The Road
Mary Chapin Carpenter; *Stones In The Road*. . . . . (Columbia)
Stranded In The Jungle
Cadets; *Collectables Presents The History Of Rock-#2-C*. . . . . . (Collectables)
Cruisin'-1956-C. . . . . (Increase)
Oldies But Goodies-#1-C. . . . .(Original Sound)
Original Rock 'N' Roll Hits Of The '50s-C. . . . . (Roulette)
New York Dolls; *In Too Much Too Soon*. . . . . (Mercury)
Live In NYC-1975. . . . . (Restless)
Take A Message To Mary
Bob Dylan; *Self Portrait*. . . . . (Columbia)
Everly Brothers; *Everly Brothers-All-Time Original Hits*. . . . . (Rhino)
Everly Brothers-Cadence Classics-Their 20 Greatest Hits . . . . (Rhino)
Rockpile; *Seconds Of Pleasure* . . . . (Columbia)
Take 'Em As They Come
Bruce Springsteen; *Tracks*. . . . . (Columbia)
Thankyou
Dido; *No Angel* . . . . (Arista)
Totally Hits 2001-C . . . . (Arista)
Theme From "Car 54, Where Are You?"
Original Soundtrack; *Television's Greatest Hits-#2-C* . . . . (TVT)
Theme From "Dennis The Menace"
Original Soundtrack; *Television's Greatest Hits-#1-C* . . . . (TVT)
Theme From "Friends" (I'll Be There For You)
Rembrandts; *LP*. . . . . (East West)
ST/Friends-Music From The TV Series. . . . . (Reprise)
There's Your Trouble
Dixie Chicks; *Wide Open Spaces* . . . . (Monument)
Thing, The
Phil Harris; *The Thing About Phil Harris* . . . . (Living Era)
Thinking About Your Troubles
Nilsson; *The Point*. . . . . (RCA)
Thorn Tree In The Garden
Derek And The Dominos; *Layla* . . . . (Polydor)
Too Much Monkey Business
Chuck Berry; *Classic Oldies From The '50s & '60s-#16-C* . . . . (MCA)
Roll Over Beethoven . . . . (Allegiance)
ST/Hail! Hail! Rock 'N' Roll. . . . . (MCA)
Toronto Rock 'N' Roll Revival-#2-C. . . . . (Accord)
Elvis Presley; *Guitar Man* . . . . (RCA)
Million-Dollar Quartet. . . . . (RCA)
ST/This Is Elvis. . . . . (RCA)
Yardbirds; *Five Live Yardbirds* . . . . (Rhino)
For Your Love. . . . . (Accord)
Yardbirds' Greatest Hits-#1 (1964-1966) . . . . (Rhino)
Trouble
Lindsey Buckingham; *Law And Order* . . . . (Asylum)
Trouble
Coldplay; *Parachutes* . . . . (Nettwerk/Capitol)
Trouble In Mind
Bob Wills; *Stay A Little Longer-The Original Columbia
Recordings*. . . . . (Roswell/RCA)
Trouble In Paradise
Huey Lewis and the News; *Huey Lewis and the News*. . . . . (Chrysalis)
We Are The World-C. . . . . (Columbia)
Trouble In Paradise
Bruce Springsteen; *Tracks*. . . . . (Columbia)
Trouble In Paradise
Loretta Lynn; *Best Of Loretta Lynn-#2* . . . . (MCA Special Prod.)
Trouble In Paradise
Crests; *Crests Greatest Hits*. . . . . (Collectables)
Trouble In Paradise
Al Jarreau; *Jarreau* . . . . (Warner Bros.)
Trouble In Paradise
Princess Pang; *Princess Pang* . . . . (Metal Blade)
Trouble In Paradise
Greg Kihn; *Rockihn'* . . . . (Beserkley)
Trouble In Paradise
J.D. Souther; *You're Only Lonely* . . . . (Legacy)
Trouble Man
Angie Stone; *Black Diamond* . . . . (Arista)
Trouble With The Truth
Patty Loveless; *The Trouble With The Truth* . . . . (Epic)
Troubles
Alicia Keys; *Songs In A Minor* . . . . (J)
Trouble's Back In Town
Wilburn Brothers; *Wilburn Brothers*. . . . . (First Generation)
Two Little Girls
Ani DiFranco; *Little Plastic Castle* . . . . (Righteous Babe)
Ugly
Bubba Sparxxx; *Dark Days Bright Nights*. . . . . (Interscope)
Voice Of The Heart
Diana Ross; *Take Me Higher*. . . . . (Motown)
When God Fearin' Women Get The Blues
Martina McBride; *Martina McBride's Greatest Hits* . . . . (RCA)
Wherever You Go
Clint Black; *Clint Black-The Greatest Hits* . . . . (RCA)
One Emotion . . . . (RCA)

Wings Of A Dove
Bob Marley & The Wailers; *Birth Of A Legend 1963-
1966* . . . .(Epic Portrait Assoc.)
Ferlin Husky; *Billboard Top Country Hits-1960-C* . . . . (Rhino)
Country Music Classics-#2-1960-1965-C. . . . . (K-Tel)
Ferlin Husky's Greatest Hits. . . . . (Curb)
Without You
Van Halen; *Van Halen 3*. . . . . (Warner Bros.)
You Can Call Me Al
Paul Simon; *Concert In The Park-August 15 1991*. . . . . (Warner Bros.)
Graceland. . . . . (Warner Bros.)
Negotiations And Love Songs, 1971-1986. . . . . (Warner Bros.)
You've Got A Friend
Barbra Streisand; *Barbra Joan Streisand*. . . . . (Columbia)
Carole King; *Tapestry* . . . . (Epic)
Donny Hathaway & Roberta Flack; *Best Of Donny Hathaway* . . . . (Atco)
Jamaica Boys; *J Boys* . . . . (Reprise)
James Taylor; *James Taylor's Greatest Hits* . . . . (Warner Bros.)
Mud Slide Slim And The Blue Horizon . . . . (Warner Bros.)
Michael Jackson; *Got To Be There*. . . . . (Motown)
Original Soul Of Michael Jackson. . . . . (Motown)
Roberta Flack & Donny Hathaway; *Best Of Roberta Flack*. . . . . (Atlantic)
Roberta Flack & Donny Hathaway. . . . . (Atlantic)
You've Got Your Troubles (I've Got Mine)
Bob Kuban And The In-Men; *Look Out For The Cheater* . . . . (Collectables)

TRUCKS, Truckin'

**See Also: CARS (various), COUNTRY, FARMS, GAS STATIONS,
HITCHHIKING, ROAD, ROAD ACCIDENTS, SOCIAL CLASS:
RURAL, TRAVELING, WORK**

1959
John Anderson; *Country Love Songs-#3-C* . . . . (Warner Bros.)
John Anderson's Greatest Hits . . . . (Warner Bros.)
Alabam
Cowboy Copas; *Only Country-1960-1964-C*. . . . . (JCI Assoc. Labels)
Minnie Pearl; *Trucks,Trains & Airplanes-C* . . . .(International Mktg. Group)
Red Sovine & Minnie Pearl; *Famous Duets* . . . . (Hollywood/DNA-Rounder)
Before The Trash Truck Comes
Bob Frank; *Bob Frank* . . . . (Vanguard)
Big Joe & Phantom 309
Tom Waits; *Double Live* . . . . (Asylum)
Nighthawks At The Diner . . . . (Asylum)
Big Rig
Jimmy Buffett; *Havana Daydreamin'* . . . . (MCA)
Big Rig Rolling Man
Billy Larkin; *Blue Ribbon Country-#2-C* . . . . (Accord)
Johnny Dollar; *Truck Driver Boogie Big Rig Hits-1939-1969-C* . . . . . (Audium)
Big Wheels In The Moonlight
Dan Seals; *Dan Seals' Greatest Hits* . . . . (Liberty)
Dan Seals-Classics Collection-#2. . . . . (Liberty)
Rage On. . . . . (Capitol)
Bridge Washed Out
Warner Mack; *Country's Greatest Hits-#3-C* . . . . (MCA)
MCA Records 30 Years Of Hits-1958-1988-C. . . . . (MCA)
Brother Trucker
James Taylor; *Flag*. . . . . (Columbia)
Bud The Spud
Stompin' Tom Connors; *Bud The Spud* . . . . (EMI)
Convoy
Boxcar Willie; *Truck Driving Favorites* . . . . (Madacy)
C.W. McCall; *C.W. McCall's Greatest Hits* . . . . (Polydor)
ST/Convoy. . . . . (Polydor)
Super Hits Of The '70s-Have A Nice Day-#15-C . . . . (Rhino)
Country Club (Ford pickup)
Travis Tritt; *Country Club* . . . . (Warner Bros.)
Country Comfort
Earl Scruggs & Elton John; *Earl Scruggs And Friends-C* . . . . (MCA)
Elton John; *Tumbleweed Connection* . . . . (Polydor)
Rod Stewart; *Best Of Rod Stewart-#2* . . . . (Mercury)
Gasoline Alley . . . . (Mercury)
Sing It Again, Rod . . . . (Mercury)
Cowboy Love
John Michael Montgomery; *John Michael Montgomery* . . . . (Atlantic)
John Michael Montgomery's Greatest Hits. . . . . (Atlantic)
Cupid's Trash Truck
Lou & Peter Berryman; *Cupid's Trash Truck* . . . . (Cornbelt)
Detroit Diesel
Alvin Lee; *Detroit Diesel*. . . . . (21)
Diesel Cecil
Larry Scott; *Keep On Truckin'* . . . . (Exact)
Diesel On My Tail
Jim & Jesse; *Truckers' Jukebox-10 All-Time Radio Requests-C* . . . . . (Legacy)
Jim & Jesse/The Virginia Boys; *Truck Driver Boogie Big Rig Hits-1939-
1969-C* . . . . (Audium)

New Riders Of The Purple Sage; *Midnight Moonlight* . . . . (Relix)
Diesel Only Theme
World Famous Blue Jays; *Rig Rock Jukebox* . . . . (First Warning)
Diesel Smoke
Doyle O'Dell; *Truck Driver Boogie Big Rig Hits-1939-1969-C* . . . . . . (Audium)
Dime At A Time
Del Reeves; *Super Country Hits Of The '60s-C* . . . . (Gusto)
Don't Come Home A'Lovin' With Venison On Your Truck
Debby McClatchy; *Someday Cafe* . . . . (Green Linnet)
Drug Store Truck Drivin' Man
Byrds; *Best Of The Byrds-Greatest Hits-#2* . . . . (Columbia)
Dr. Byrds & Mr. Hyde . . . . (Legacy)
The Byrds . . . . (Columbia)
Gram Parsons & Fallen Angels; *Live 1973* . . . . (Sierra)
Joan Baez & Jeffrey Shurtleff; *ST/Woodstock* . . . . (Atlantic)
Eighteen Wheels And A Dozen Roses
Kathy Mattea; *Collection Of Hits* . . . . (Mercury)
Untasted Honey . . . . (Polydor Country)
Endless Black Ribbon
Red Simpson; *Trucks,Trains & Airplanes-C* . . . . . . (International Mktg. Group)
Red Sovine/Willis Bros./Reno & Smiley; *Heavy Haulers* . . . . . . (Power Pak)
Ethelene (The Truckstop Queen)
Ray Stevens; *I Never Made A Record I Didn't Like* . . . . (MCA)
Forty Acres
Boxcar Willie; *Truck Driving Favorites* . . . . (Madacy)
Freightline Fever
Boxcar Willie; *Truck Driving Favorites* . . . . (Madacy)
Gear Bustin' Sort Of A Feller
Bobby Braddock; *Truck Driver Boogie Big Rig Hits-1939-1969-C* . . . . (Audium)
Gear Jammer And The Hobo
Red Sovine & Johnny Bond; *Truckin' On-C* . . . . (Hollywood)
Giddy Up Go
Red Sovine; *Best Of Red Sovine* . . . . (Starday)
Truckin' On-C . . . . (Hollywood)
Red Sovine/Willis Bros./Reno & Smiley; *Heavy Haulers* . . . . . . (Power Pak)
Girl On The Billboard
Boxcar Willie; *Truck Driving Favorites* . . . . (Madacy)
Del Reeves; *101 Greatest Country Hits-#10-C* . . . . (K-Tel)
Truck Driver Boogie Big Rig Hits-1939-1969-C . . . . (Audium)
Truckin' On-C . . . . (Hollywood)
Guitar Town
Steve Earle & The Dukes; *Country Classics-#8-1986-1987-C* . . . . . (Universal)
Guitar Town . . . . (MCA)
Henry
New Riders Of The Purple Sage; *Best Of New Riders Of The Purple Sage* . . . . (Columbia)
Bill Graham Presents The Last Days Of The Fillmore-C . . . . (Epic Portrait Assoc.)
Home Home On The Road . . . . (Columbia)
New Riders Of The Purple Sage . . . . (Columbia)
Highway Man
Curtis Leach; *Truck Driver Boogie Big Rig Hits-1939-1969-C* . . . . (Audium)
How Far To Little Rock
Stanley Brothers; *Stanley Series-Vol. 1-#2* . . . . (Copper Creek)
How Fast Them Trucks Will Go
Boxcar Willie; *Truck Driving Favorites* . . . . (Madacy)
I'll Have Another Cup Of Coffee
Claude Gray; *Truckin' On-C* . . . . (Hollywood)
I'm A Truck
Red Simpson; *Red Simpson/Red Sovine/Dave Dudley-C* . . . . . . (Gusto)
I'm A Truck Driving Man
Art Gibson; *Truck Driver Boogie Big Rig Hits-1939-1969-C* . . . . (Audium)
I'm Coming Home
Johnny Horton; *Truck Driver Boogie Big Rig Hits-1939-1969-C* . . . . (Audium)
I'm Truckin'
Spirit; *Spirit* . . . . (Epic)
Time Circle . . . . (Epic)
I've Been Everywhere
Johnny Cash; *Unchained* . . . . (American)
Just Good Ol' Boys
Moe Bandy & Joe Stampley; *Just Good Ol' Boys* . . . . (Columbia)
Moe Bandy & Joe Stampley's Greatest Hits . . . . (Columbia)
Trucker's Jukebox-#2-C . . . . (Legacy)
Keep On Truckin'
Hot Tuna; *''Howling Blues'' & Other Hits* . . . . (RCA)
Burgers . . . . (Grunt)
Final Vinyl . . . . (Grunt)
Keep On Truckin' (Part 1)
Eddie Kendricks; *12 #1 Hits From The '70s-C* . . . . (Motown)
20/20-C . . . . (Motown)
Didn't It Blow Your Mind: Soul Hits Of The '70s-#11-C . . . . (Rhino)
Eddie Kendricks-At His Best . . . . (Motown)
Motown Superstar Series-#19-Eddie Kendricks . . . . . . (Motown)
Motown's Biggest Pop Hits-C . . . . (Motown)
Little Pink Mack
Kay Adams; *Truck Driver Boogie Big Rig Hits-1939-1969-C* . . . . (Audium)
Looking At The World Through A Windshield
Commander Cody; *We've Got A Live One Here!* . . . . . . (Warner Bros.)

Commander Cody & His Lost Planet Airmen; *Hot Licks, Cold Steel & Trucker's Favorites* . . . . (MCA)
Del Reeves; *Del Reeves-His Greatest Hits* . . . . (Razor & Tie)
Truckin' On-C . . . . (Hollywood)
Red Simpson; *Ramblin' Road* . . . . (Fifty One West)
Red Sovine & Del Reeves; *Red Sovine & Del Reeves* . . . . . (Exact)
Son Volt; *ST/Feeling Minnesota* . . . . (Atlantic)
Mama Hated Diesels
Commander Cody & His Lost Planet Airmen; *Hot Licks, Cold Steel & Trucker's Favorites* . . . . (MCA)
Mama Knows The Highway
Hal Ketchum; *Sure Love* . . . . (Curb)
Mammas Don't Let Your Babies Grow Up To Be Cowboys
Gibson/Miller Band; *Cowboy Super Hits-C* . . . . (Columbia)
ST/The Cowboy Way . . . . (Epic)
Waylon Jennings & Willie Nelson; *Waylon & Willie* . . . . . (RCA)
Waylon Jennings & Willie Nelson's Greatest Hits . . . . . (RCA)
Willie Nelson; *Greatest Hits (& Some That Will Be)* . . . . (Columbia)
ST/The Electric Horseman . . . . (Columbia)
Willie & Family Live . . . . (Columbia)
Midnight Hauler
Razzy Bailey; *Razzy Bailey's Greatest Hits* . . . . (RCA)
Mother Trucker
Shaver; *Rig Rock Deluxe: A Musical Salute To the American Truck Driver-C* . . . . (Upstart)
Movin' On
Dave Dudley; *Interstate Gold* . . . . (Sun)
Trucks,Trains & Airplanes-C . . . . (International Mktg. Group)
Merle Haggard; *Capitol Collectors Series-Merle Haggard* . . . . (Capitol)
Merle Haggard & Brooks & Dunn; *For The Record: Merle Haggard-43 Legendary Hits* . . . . (BNA)
Merle Haggard & The Strangers; *Winners* . . . . (Capitol)
Mutton Trucker
Larry Scott; *Keep On Truckin'* . . . . (Exact)
Nothin' But The Taillights
Clint Black; *Nothin' But The Taillights* . . . . (RCA)
Old Home Filler Up & Keep On A Truckin'
C.W. McCall; *C.W. McCall's Greatest Hits* . . . . (Polydor)
Wolf Creek Pass . . . . (MGM)
One Headlight
Wallflowers; *Bringing Down The Horse* . . . . (Interscope)
One Is A Lonely Number
George Jones; *Truckin' On-C* . . . . (Hollywood)
Papa Loved Mama
Garth Brooks; *Garth Brooks-Double Live* . . . . (Capitol)
Ropin' The Wind . . . . (Liberty)
People Like Us
Aaron Tippin; *People Like Us* . . . . (Lyric Street)
Phantom 309
Boxcar Willie; *Truck Driving Favorites* . . . . (Madacy)
Red Sovine; *Best Of Red Sovine* . . . . (Starday)
Pickup Man
Joe Diffie; *Third Rock From The Sun* . . . . (Epic)
Pinball Machine
Lonnie Irving; *Super Country Hits Of The '60s-C* . . . . . . (Gusto)
Radar Blues
Dave Dudley & Charlie Doublas; *Diesel Duets* . . . . (Sun)
Redneck Rhythm & Blues
Brooks & Dunn; *Borderline* . . . . (Arista)
Ribbon Of Darkness
Marty Robbins; *Marty Robbins' All-Time Greatest Hits* . . . (Columbia)
Marty Robbins' Greatest Hits . . . . (Columbia)
Trucker's Jukebox-#2-C . . . . (Legacy)
Ride, The
David Allan Coe; *19 Hot Country Requests-C* . . . . (Epic)
Castles In The Sand . . . . (Columbia)
David Allan Coe-17 Greatest Hits . . . . (Columbia)
For The Record-The First 10 Years . . . . (Columbia)
Trucker's Jukebox-#2-C . . . . (Legacy)
Rolaids, Doan's Pills & Preparation H
Dave Dudley; *King Of The Road* . . . . (Sun)
Roll On (Eighteen Wheeler)
Alabama; *Alabama's Greatest Hits-#2* . . . . (RCA)
Roll On . . . . (RCA)
Roll On Big Mama
Joe Stampley; *Encore-Joe Stampley* . . . . (Epic)
Joe Stampley's Biggest Hits . . . . (Epic)
Joe Stampley's Greatest Hits . . . . (Epic)
Truckers' Jukebox-10 All-Time Radio Requests-C . . . . . (Legacy)
Roll On Buddy
Ramblin' Jack Elliott; *Essential Ramblin' Jack Elliott* . . . . (Vanguard)
Roll On Truckers
Juice Newton & Silver Spur; *Juice Newton & Silver Spur* . . . (RCA)
Juice Newton-Early Years . . . . (RCA)
Roll, Truck, Roll
Red Simpson; *Hillbilly Music-Thank God!-#1-C* . . . . (Bug)
Truck Driver Boogie Big Rig Hits-1939-1969-C . . . . . . (Audium)

Semi Diesel Blues
Super Grit Cowboy Band; *If You Can't Hang-Drag Your Country Ass* . . . . (Hoodswamp)
Semi Suite
Tom Waits; *The Heart Of Saturday Night* . . . . (Asylum)
Semi-Truck
Commander Cody & His Lost Planet Airmen; *Hot Licks, Cold Steel & Trucker's Favorites* . . . . (MCA)
She's In Love With The Boy
Trisha Yearwood; *Trisha Yearwood* . . . . (MCA)
Sitting In The Cab Of My Truck
Chip Dockery; *Country Folk Songs-Americans In Vietnam* . . . . (Flying Fish)
Six Days On The Road
Boxcar Willie; *Truck Driving Favorites* . . . . (Madacy)
Dave Dudley; *Billboard Top Country Hits-1963-C* . . . . (Rhino)
Country Music Classics-#2-1960-1965-C . . . . (K-Tel)
Legends Of Country Guitar-#2-C . . . . (Rhino)
Truck Driver Boogie Big Rig Hits-1939-1969-C . . . . (Audium)
Flying Burrito Brothers; *Cabin Fever* . . . . (Relix)
Farther Along-Best Of The Flying Burrito Brothers . . . . (A&M)
Last Of The Red Hot Burritos . . . . (A&M)
Sawyer Brown; *Six Days On The Road* . . . . (Curb)
Taj Mahal; *Giant Step/De Ole Folks At Home* . . . . (Columbia)
Legends Of Rock Guitar-'60s-#2-C . . . . (Rhino)
Space Truckin'
Deep Purple; *Deepest Purple/The Very Best Of Deep Purple* . . . . (Warner Bros.)
Machine Head . . . . (Warner Bros.)
Made In Japan . . . . (Warner Bros.)
When We Rock We Rock & When We Roll We Roll . . . . (Warner Bros.)
Speedball Tucker
Jim Croce; *Down The Highway* . . . . (Atlantic)
Life & Times . . . . (Lifesong)
Spirit Of A Boy, Wisdom Of A Man
Randy Travis; *Big Country Hits '99-C* . . . . (K-Tel)
You And You Alone . . . . (DreamWorks/SKG)
Tennessee Border
Hank Williams; *Alone With His Guitar* . . . . (Mercury)
I Ain't Got Nothin' But Time-1947-1947 . . . . (Polydor)
Red Foley; *Red Foley: The Country Music Hall Of Fame* . . . . (MCA Special Prod.)
Sonny Burgess & Dave Alvin; *Tennessee Border* . . . . (Hightone)
Tennessee Ernie Ford; *Best Of Tennessee Ernie Ford-16 Tons Of Boogie* . . . . (Rhino)
Capitol Collectors Series-Tennessee Ernie Ford . . . . (Capitol)
That Ain't My Truck
Rhett Akins; *A Thousand Memories* . . . . (Decca)
Cryin' Lyin' Lovin' & Leavin'-C . . . . (Universal)
Theme From "B.J. And The Bear"
Original Soundtrack; *Television's Greatest Hits-#6-Remote Control-C* . . . (TVT)
Theme From "Movin' On"
Original Soundtrack; *Television's Greatest Hits-#6-Remote Control-C* . . . (TVT)
Thong Song
Sisqo; *Unleash The Dragon* . . . . (Dragon/Def Soul/IDJMG)
Tombstone Every Mile
Dave Dudley; *Interstate Gold* . . . . (Sun)
Dick Curless; *Truck Driver Boogie Big Rig Hits-1939-1969-C* . . . . . . (Audium)
Trash Truck
Tad; *8-Way Santa* . . . . (Sub Pop)
Truck
Larry Scott; *Keep On Truckin'* . . . . (Exact)
Truck Driver Blues
Cliff Bruner And His Boys; *Truck Driver Boogie Big Rig Hits-1939-1969-C* . . . . (Audium)
Truck Driver Divorce
Frank Zappa; *Them Or Us* . . . . (Rykodisc)
You Can't Do That On Stage Anymore-#4 . . . . (Rykodisc)
Truck Driver's Blues
Johnny Gimble & The Texas Swing Pioneers; *Johnny Gimble's Texas Honky-Tonk Hits-C* . . . . (C.M.H. Prod.)
Truck Drivers Boogie
Milo Twins; *Truck Driver Boogie Big Rig Hits-1939-1969-C* . . . . . . (Audium)
Truck Drivers Coffee Shop
Dick Reinhart & His Lone Star Boys; *Truck Driver Boogie Big Rig Hits-1939-1969-C* . . . . (Audium)
Truck Driver's Lament
Johnny Dollar; *Blue Ribbon Country-#3-C* . . . . (Accord)
Truck Drivers Night Run Blues
Joe "Cannonball" Lewis; *Truck Driver Boogie Big Rig Hits-1939-1969-C* . . . . (Audium)
Truck Driver's Prayer
Dave Dudley; *Diesel Express* . . . . (Fifty One West)
Truck Driver's Queen
Moore And Napier; *Truckin' On-C* . . . . (Hollywood)
Willis Brothers; *45-#2043* . . . . (Gusto)
Truck Driver's Sweetheart
Karl & Harty; *Truck Driver Boogie Big Rig Hits-1939-1969-C* . . . . . (Audium)
Marcie Dickerson; *Country Gold-Marcie Dickerson* . . . . (Plantation)
Truck Drivin' Cat With Nine Wives
Charlie Walker; *Truckers' Jukebox-10 All-Time Radio Requests-C* . . . . (Legacy)

Jim Nesbitt; *Truck Driver Boogie Big Rig Hits-1939-1969-C* . . . . (Audium)
Truck Drivin' Girl
Bonny Boekeker; *45-#1357* . . . . (Accent)
Truck Drivin' Man
Commander Cody & His Lost Planet Airmen; *Hot Licks, Cold Steel & Trucker's Favorites* . . . . (MCA)
Too Much Fun-Best Of Commander Cody & His Lost Planet Airmen . . . (MCA)
J. Geils Band; *Blow Your Face Out* . . . . (Rhino)
Truck Drivin' Man
Flying Burrito Brothers; *Close Encounters To The West Coast* . . . . (Relix)
Truck Drivin' Man
Hank Wilson; *Hank Wilson's Back, Vol. 1* . . . . (Right Stuff)
Truck Drivin' Man
Larry Scott; *Keep On Truckin'* . . . . (Exact)
Truck Drivin' Man
Lynyrd Skynyrd; *Lynyrd Skynyrd-Legend* . . . . (MCA)
Truck Drivin' Man
Charlie Walker; *Trucker's Jukebox-#2-C* . . . . (Legacy)
Truck Drivin' Son Of A Gun
Boxcar Willie; *Truck Driving Favorites* . . . . (Madacy)
Dave Dudley; *20 Golden Souvenirs Of Music City U.S.A.-C* . . . . . . (Plantation)
Billboard Top Country Hits-1965-C . . . . (Rhino)
Truck Driving Buddy
Red Sovine/Willis Bros./Reno & Smiley; *Heavy Haulers* . . . . (Power Pak)
Truck Driving Man
Terry Fell & The Fellers; *Truck Driver Boogie Big Rig Hits-1939-1969-C* . . . . (Audium)
Truck 'Em On Down
Stick "Horse" Hammond; *Alley Special* . . . . (Collectables)
Truck Of Love
Blitzspeer; *Saves* . . . . (Epic)
Truck On Fire
White Zombie; *Soul-Crusher* . . . . (Caroline)
Truck Stop
Mills Brothers; *Cab Driver* . . . . (Ranwood)
Truck Stop
Lenny Dee; *Best Of Lenny Dee-#2* . . . . (MCA)
Truck Stop At The End Of The World
Commander Cody; *Let's Rock* . . . . (Blind Pig)
Truck Stop Girl
Byrds; *The Byrds* . . . . (Columbia)
The Byrds (Untitled) . . . . (Legacy)
Little Feat; *Little Feat* . . . . (Warner Bros.)
Truck Stop Rock
Commander Cody & His Lost Planet Airmen; *Hot Licks, Cold Steel & Trucker's Favorites* . . . . (MCA)
Truckdrivin' Man
Boxcar Willie; *Truck Driving Favorites* . . . . (Madacy)
Trucker's Nightmare
Lawrence Hammond; *Coyote's Dream* . . . . (Takoma)
Critic's Choice-C . . . . (Takoma)
Truckers Prayer
Boxcar Willie; *Truck Driving Favorites* . . . . (Madacy)
Truckin'
Dwight Yoakam; *Deadicated-C* . . . . (Arista)
Grateful Dead; *American Beauty* . . . . (Warner Bros.)
Best Of/Skeletons From The Closet . . . . (Warner Bros.)
Europe '72 . . . . (Warner Bros.)
What A Long Strange Trip It's Been: The Best Of The Grateful Dead . . . . (Warner Bros.)
Truckin'
Mel Torme & The Mel-Tones; *Back In Town* . . . . (Verve)
Truckin'
Bread; *Best Of Bread* . . . . (Elektra)
Bread-Anthology . . . . (Elektra)
Manna . . . . (Rhino)
Truckin' Dad
Dave Dudley; *Diesel Express* . . . . (Fifty One West)
Truckin' Down The Avenue
Sonny Burgess; *Sun Rockabillies-#1-C* . . . . (Sun)
Truckin' Little Baby
John Hammond; *Solo* . . . . (Vanguard)
Truckload Of Lovin'
Albert King; *I'm In A Phone Booth Baby* . . . . (Stax)
Masterworks . . . . (Atlantic)
The Tomato Years . . . . (Tomato)
Truckload Of Lovin' . . . . (Tomato)
Where I Come From
Alan Jackson; *When Somebody Loves You* . . . . (Arista)
White Freightliner Blues
Jimmie Dale Gilmore; *Fair & Square* . . . . (Hightone)
New Grass Revival; *When The Storm Is Over* . . . . (Flying Fish)
Townes Van Zandt; *Live & Obscure* . . . . (Sugar Hill)
White Line Fever
Flying Burrito Brothers; *Close Encounters To The West Coast* . . . . (Relix)
Merle Haggard; *More Of The Best* . . . . (Rhino)
Merle Haggard & The Strangers; *Okie From Muskogee* . . . . (Capitol)

Widow Maker
Jimmy Martin; *Truck Driver Boogie Big Rig Hits-1939-1969-C* . . . . . .(Audium)
Willin'
Byrds; *The Byrds* . . . . (Columbia)
Linda Ronstadt; *Heart Like A Wheel*. (Capitol)
Little Feat; *Little Feat* . . . .(Warner Bros.)
Sailin' Shoes . . . .(Warner Bros.)
Waiting For Columbus. . . . .(Warner Bros.)
Wolverton Mountain
Claude King; *American Originals-Claude King*. . . . . (Columbia)
Best Of Claude King . . . . (Gusto)
Billboard Top Country Hits-1962-C . . . . (Rhino)
Super Hits Of The '60s-C . . . .(Epic)
Woman Behind The Man Behind The Wheel
Red Sovine; *Truckin' On-C* . . . . (Hollywood)

TRUTH, Real, True

See Also: *CHARACTER & INTEGRITY, CHEATING & LIES,*
FAITH, FAKE, LOVE (various), PROMISE, TEACHING VALUES,
THINKING & KNOWING

(Everything I Do) I Do It For You
Bryan Adams; *ST/Robin Hood: Prince Of Thieves*. . . . .(Morgan Creek)
Waking Up The Neighbours . . . . (A&M)
Ain't Nothing Like The Real Thing
Marvin Gaye & Tammi Terrell; *Every Great Motown Hit Of*
Marvin Gaye . . . . (Motown)
Marvin Gaye's Greatest Hits. . . . . (Motown)
Motown 40 Forever-C . . . . (Motown)
Vince Gill & Gladys Knight; *Rhythm Country And Blues-C* . . . .(MCA)
Alison
Elvis Costello; *Girls Girls Girls* . . . . (Columbia)
My Aim Is True . . . . (Columbia)
Elvis Costello & The Attractions; *Best Of Elvis Costello & The*
Attractions . . . . (Columbia)
Always True To You In My Fashion
Blossom Dearie; *Night & Day-Cole Porter Songbook-C* . . . . (Verve)
Original Cast; *Kiss Me Kate* . . . . (EMI-Angel)
Peggy Lee & George Shearing; *Anything Goes-Capitol Sings Cole*
Porter-C . . . . (Capitol)
Am I Dreaming
Ol Skool featuring Keith Sweat & Xscape; *Ol Skool* . . . . (Keia/Universal)
Amigone
Goo Goo Dolls; *Dizzy Up The Girl* . . . . (Warner Sunset/Reprise)
At Seventeen
Janis Ian; *Between The Lines* . . . . (Columbia)
Super Hits Of The '70s-Have A Nice Day-#15-C . . . . (Rhino)
Battle Hymn Of The Republic, The
Charlie Sexton; *Charlie Sexton*. . . . .(MCA)
Judy Collins; *Songs Of The Civil War-C*. . . . . (Columbia)
Mormon Tabernacle Choir; *God Bless America* . . . . . (Sony Music Classical)
Stars And Stripes Forever . . . . (Columbia)
National Philharmonic Orchestra & Chorus; *Stars And Stripes*
Forever-#2-C . . . .(Volcano Entertainment)
Original Soundtrack; *School Days-Kids Classics*. . . . . (Benson)
Pat Boone; *Star Spangled Banner*. . . . .(Word)
Be True
Bruce Springsteen; *Tracks* . . . . (Columbia)
Be True
Rance Allen; *Up Above My Head* . . . .(Stax)
Beautiful People
Bobby Vee; *Very Best Of Bobby Vee* . . . . (Collectables)
Brilliant Disguise
Bruce Springsteen; *Bruce Springsteen's Greatest Hits*. . . . . (Columbia)
Tunnel Of Love. . . . . (Columbia)
Call Me Irresponsible
Frank Sinatra; *Sinatra: A Man And His Music* . . . . (Reprise)
Sinatra's Sinatra . . . . (Reprise)
Jackie Gleason; *Best Of Jackie Gleason & His Orchestra* . . . . (Curb)
Robert Goulet; *Robert Goulet-16 Most Requested Songs* . . . . (Columbia)
Rosemary Clooney; *Rosemary Clooney Sings The Music Of Jimmy Van*
Heusen . . . . (Concord Jazz)
Can't Get This Stuff No More
Van Halen; *Best Of Van Halen-#1* . . . . (Warner Bros.)
Can't Take My Eyes Off You
Frankie Valli; *25th Anniversary Collection* . . . . (Rhino)
Frankie Valli-Anthology . . . . (Rhino)
Very Best Of Frankie Valli. . . . .(MCA)
Lauryn Hill; *The Miseducation Of Lauryn Hill*. . . . . . (Ruffhouse/Columbia)
Cold Hard Truth, The
George Jones; *Cold Hard Truth* . . . . (Asylum)
Jamie O'Hara; *Rise Above It* . . . . (RCA)
Come What May
Patti Page; *Patti Page Collection-The Mercury Years-#1* . . . . (Mercury)
Confessions
Destiny's Child; *The Writing's On The Wall* . . . . (Columbia)

Cornflake Girl
Tori Amos; *Under The Pink* . . . .(Atlantic)
Crush With Eyeliner
R.E.M.; *Monster* . . . . (Warner Bros.)
Do What You Gotta Do
Garth Brooks; *Sevens* . . . . (Capitol)
Every Time I Close My Eyes
Babyface; *The Day* . . . . (Epic)
Glass Onion
Beatles; *Beatles-Box Set* . . . . (Capitol)
The Beatles (White Album). . . . . (Capitol)
Go On
George Strait; *George Strait* . . . . (MCA)
God Must Have Spent A Little More Time On You
Alabama Featuring 'N Sync; *Twentieth Century*. . . . . (RCA)
'N Sync; *'N Sync* . . . . (RCA)
Totally Hits-#1-C . . . . (Arista)
He Wasn't Man Enough
Toni Braxton; *The Heat*. . . . . (LaFace)
Totally Hits-#3-C . . . .(Atlantic)
Hey Jealous Lover
Frank Sinatra; *Capitol Collectors Series-Frank Sinatra* . . . . (Capitol)
Honesty
Billy Joel; *52nd Street* . . . . (Columbia)
KOHUEPT . . . . (Columbia)
Honky Tonk Truth
Brooks & Dunn; *Brooks & Dunn-The Greatest Hits Collection* . . . . (Arista)
I Don't Want To Know
Fleetwood Mac; *Rumours* . . . . (Warner Bros.)
Goo Goo Dolls; *Legacy-A Tribute To Fleetwood Mac's Rumours-C* . . . . (Lava)
I Honestly Love You
Olivia Newton-John; *Back To The Basics-Essential Collection* . . . . (Geffen)
Back With A Heart . . . . (MCA)
If You Love Me Let Me Know . . . . (MCA)
Olivia Newton-John's Greatest Hits. (MCA)
I Know The Truth
Elton John & Janet Jackson; *ST/Aida* . . . . (Island)
I Lost It
Kenny Chesney; *Kenny Chesney's Greatest Hits* . . . .(BNA)
I Only Want To Be With You
Bay City Rollers; *Bay City Rollers' Greatest Hits*. . . . . (Arista)
Dusty Springfield; *Dusty Springfield-Anthology*. . . . . (Mercury)
Dusty Springfield-Golden Hits . . . . (Mercury)
Vonda Shepard; *ST/Songs From "Ally McBeal" Featuring Vonda*
Shepard . . . .(550/Epic)
I Turn To You
Christina Aguilera; *Christina Aguilera* . . . . (RCA)
I Wasn't With It
Jesse Powell; *'Bout It* . . . . (Silas)
I'd Lie For You (And That's The Truth)
Meat Loaf; *Welcome To The Neighborhood* . . . . (MCA)
I'm Free
Who; *Join Together*. . . . . (MCA)
Tommy . . . . (MCA)
I'm Like A Bird
Nelly Furtado; *Whoa Nelly!*. . . . .(DreamWorks/SKG)
I'm Real
Jennifer Lopez; *J. Lo* . . . . (Epic)
Now That's What I Call Music!-#8-C . . . .(Virgin)
It Takes Two
Marvin Gaye & Kim Weston; *Hitsville USA-The Motown Singles Collection-*
1959-1971-C . . . . (Motown)
It's Alright
Candlebox; *Happy Pills* . . . . (Maverick)
It's How You Say It
Al Jarreau; *Tomorrow Today*. . . . . (GRP/VMG)
Light My Fire
Doors; *Best Of The Doors* . . . . (Elektra)
Doors . . . . (Elektra)
Doors 13 . . . . (Elektra)
Doors' Greatest Hits . . . . (Elektra)
ST/The Doors . . . . (Elektra)
Jose Feliciano; *Encore-Jose Feliciano* . . . . (RCA)
Jose Feliciano's All-Time Greatest Hits. . . . . (RCA)
Love Of My Life
Jim Brickman featuring Michael W. Smith; *Destiny*. . . . .(Windham Hill)
Lullaby
Tom Rush; *Tom Rush* . . . . (Columbia)
Make It Real
Jets; *Best Of The Jets* . . . . (MCA)
Thinking About You-Modern Love Songs-C . . . . (Hip-O)
Man On The Moon
R.E.M.; *Automatic For The People*. . . . . (Warner Bros.)
More Love
Kim Carnes; *Gypsy Honeymoon-The Best Of Kim Carnes* . . . . (Gold Rush)
Smokey Robinson & The Miracles; *Smokey Robinson & The Miracles'*
Anthology . . . . (Motown)

Smokey Robinson-*The Ultimate Collection* .... (Motown)

Ms. Jackson
Outkast; *Stankonia* .... (LaFace/Arista)

My Favorite Headache
Geddy Lee; *My Favorite Headache*..................... (Anthem/Atlantic)

My One True Friend
Bette Midler; *Bathhouse Betty*........................... (Warner Bros.)

My True Story
Jive Five; *Back Seat Jams-C* .... (Dunhill Compact Classics)
 Billboard Top R&B Hits-1961-C .... (Rhino)
 Cruisin'-1961-C .... (Increase)
 Jive Five-Their Greatest Hits .... (Collectables)
 Oldies But Goodies-#4-C ....(Original Sound)

My Truly, Truly Fair
Guy Mitchell; *Guy Mitchell-16 Most Requested Songs* .... (Legacy)

N.I.B.
Primus with Ozzy; *Nativity In Black II: Tribute To Black
Sabbath-C* ....(Divine/Priority)

Never Lie
Immature; *Playtime Is Over* .... (MCA)

New York State Of Mind
Barbra Streisand; *Memories* .... (Columbia)
 Streisand Superman .... (Columbia)
Billy Joel; *America: A Tribute To Heroes-C* .... (Interscope)
 Billy Joel-Greatest Hits, Volume I & Volume II .... (Columbia)
 The Concert For New York City-C .... (Columbia)
 Turnstiles .... (Columbia)
Carmen McRae; *Ms. Magic* .... (Dunhill Compact Classics)
Tony Bennett with Billy Joel; *Playin' With My Friends-Bennett Sings The
Blues-C* .... (Columbia)

No Such Thing
John Mayer; *Room For Squares* .... (Aware/C2/Columbia)

On My Word Of Honor
Platters; *Enchanted-The Best Of The Platters* .... (Rhino)

One Belief Away
Bonnie Raitt; *Fundamental* .... (Capitol)

One Honest Heart
Reba McEntire; *If You See Him* .... (MCA)
 Reba McEntire's Greatest Hits-#3: I'm A Survivor .... (MCA)

Open Your Eyes
Doobie Brothers; *Minute By Minute* .... (Warner Bros.)

Outside
Staind; *Break The Cycle* .... (Flip/Elektra)

Pass You By
Boyz II Men; *Nathan Michael Shawn Wanya* .... (Universal)

Passin' Thru
Earl Scruggs & Don Henley & Johnny Cash; *Earl Scruggs And
Friends-C* .... (MCA)
Randy Scruggs; *Crown Of Jewels* ....(Reprise)
Randy Scruggs & Joan Osborne; *ST/Happy Texas* .... (Arista)

Promise
Jagged Edge; *J.E. Heartbreak*.................... (So So Def/Columbia)

Promises
Def Leppard; *Euphoria* .... (Mercury)

Real Life (I Never Was The Same Again)
Jeff Carson; *Real Life* .... (Curb)

Real Live Woman
Trisha Yearwood; *Real Live Woman* .... (MCA)

Real Love
Jody Watley; *Larger Than Life* .... (MCA)
 You Wanna Dance With Me? .... (MCA)

Real Love
Beatles; *The Beatles-Anthology-#2* .... (Capitol)
John Lennon; *ST/Imagine: John Lennon*..................... (Capitol)

Real Love
Dolly Parton & Kenny Rogers; *Best Of Dolly Parton-#3* .... (RCA)

Real Love
Bob Seger & The Silver Bullet Band; *Fire Inside* .... (Capitol)

Real Love
El DeBarge; *Gemini*...................................... (Motown)

Real Love
Doobie Brothers; *One Step Closer*.................. (Warner Bros.)

Real Love
Ashford & Simpson; *Real Love* .... (Capitol)

Real Love
Skyy; *Start Of A Romance* .... (Atlantic)

Real Love
Slaughter; *The Wild Life* .... (Chrysalis)

Real Love
Mary J. Blige; *What's The 411?* .... (Uptown)

Real Slim Shady
Eminem; *The Marshall Mathers LP* ....(Aftermath/Interscope)

Real World
Richard Marx; *Repeat Offender*............................. (EMI)

Real World
Matchbox Twenty; *Yourself Or Someone Like You*................ (Lava)

Real World
Bangles; *Bangles* .... (I.R.S.)

Real World
Bruce Springsteen; *Human Touch* ....(Columbia)

Real World
Mighty Lemon Drops; *Laughter* .... (Sire)

Real World
Jesus Jones; *Liquidizer*...................................(SBK)

Rose And A Baby Ruth, A
George Hamilton IV; *At The Hop*............................ (MCA)
 Vintage Music-#12-C .... (MCA)

Rose Colored Glasses
John Conlee; *Backstage At The Grand Ole Opry-C* .... (RCA)
 Grand Ole Opry-75 Years-#1-C .... (MCA)
 John Conlee-Legends .... (MCA)
 John Conlee's Greatest Hits .... (MCA)
 MCA Records 30 Years Of Hits-1958-1988-C................. (MCA)
 Rose Colored Glasses .... (Universal)

Say You, Say Me
Lionel Richie; *Back To Front*............................. (Motown)
 Dancing On The Ceiling .... (Motown)

She's Been Good To Me
Marc Anthony; *Marc Anthony* ....(Columbia)

Sincerely
McGuire Sisters; *Billboard Pop Memories-1955-1959-C* ....(Rhino)
 McGuire Sisters' Greatest Hits .... (MCA)
Moonglows; *13 Of The Best Doo Wop Love Songs-C* .... (Original Sound)
 Billboard Top Rock 'N' Roll Hits-1955-C ....(Rhino)
 Moonglows-Their Greatest Hits .... (Chess)

So In Love With You
U.N.V.; *Universal Nubian Voices* ....(Maverick/Warner Bros.)

Sour Times (Nobody Loves Me)
Portishead; *Dummy* ....(Go! Discs)

Stacked Actors
Foo Fighters; *There Is Nothing Left To Lose* .... (Roswell/RCA)

Stand And Be Counted
Crosby, Stills, Nash & Young; *Looking Forward* .... (Reprise)

Straight Up
Paula Abdul; *Disco Queens-The '80s-C*.....................(Rhino)
 First Generation: 25 Years Of Virgin Records-C .... (Virgin)
 Forever Your Girl .... (Virgin)
 Shut Up And Dance .... (Virgin)
 Shut Up And Dance (The Dance Mixes) .... (Virgin)

Straight Up
Chante Moore; *Exposed* ....(Silas)

Strong Enough To Bend
Tanya Tucker; *Strong Enough To Bend* ....(Liberty)
 Tanya Tucker's Greatest Hits ....(Liberty)

Tattva
Kula Shaker; *K*...(Columbia)

Tell It Like It Is
Aaron Neville; *Classic Aaron Neville* ....(Rounder)
 Soul Shots-#5-La-La Means I Love You-C ....(Rhino)
 Super Oldies Of The '60s-#7-C .... (Audio Fidelity)
 Tell It Like It Is ....(Curb)
 Tell it Like It Is-Golden Classics ....(Collectables)
 Treacherous: A History Of The Neville Brothers ....(Rhino)
Billy Joe Royal; *Billy Joe Royal's Greatest Hits* .... (Atlantic)
 Tell It Like It Is .... (Atlantic)
George Benson; *Best Of George Benson*......................(A&M)
UB40; *Live In Moscow* ....(A&M)
 Rat In The Kitchen ....(A&M)

Tell The Truth
Otis Redding; *Best Of Otis Redding* ....(Atco)
 Tell The Truth ....(Rhino)
 The Otis Redding Story ....(Atlantic)
Ray Charles; *Birth Of Soul-Complete Atlantic R&B 1952-1959-C* .... (Atlantic)

Tell The Truth
Derek And The Dominos; *Derek & The Dominos In Concert* .... (RSO)
 Eric Clapton-Crossroads-C .... (Polydor)
 Layla .... (Polydor)

Tell The Truth
David Lee Roth; *A Little Ain't Enough*.................... (Warner Bros.)

Tell The Truth
Lee Roy Parnell; *Tell The Truth* ....(Vanguard)

Tempted
Squeeze; *East Side Story* ....(A&M)
 Rock Of The '80s-#1-C .... (Priority)
 VH-1 The Big '80s-C .... (Rhino)

Testify
Rage Against The Machine; *The Battle Of Los Angeles*.............. (Epic)

That's For Sure
Jeffrey Osborne; *That's For Sure*..................... (Private Music)

Theme From "The Real McCoys"
Original Soundtrack; *Television's Greatest Hits-#4-Black & White
Classics-C* ....(TVT)

They Don't Know
Jon B.; *Cool Relax* . . . . (Yab Yum/550)
Three Chords And The Truth
Sara Evans; *Chicken Soup For The Woman's Soul-C* . . . . (Rhino)
To Be Loved
Curtis Stigers; *Songs From Dawson's Creek* . . . . (Sony Music Soundtrax)
Too Good To Be True
Michael Peterson; *Michael Peterson* . . . . (Reprise)
Trouble With The Truth
Patty Loveless; *The Trouble With The Truth* . . . .(Epic)
True
Spandau Ballet; *Billboard Top Hits-1983-C* . . . . (Rhino)
True
George Strait; *Latest Greatest Straitest Hits* . . . . (MCA)
One Step At A Time . . . . (MCA)
True Colors
Cyndi Lauper; *She's So Unusual/True Colors/Hat Full Of Stars (Box)* . . . .(Epic)
True Colors . . . . (Portrait)
Twelve Deadly Cyns...And Then Some . . . .(Epic)
Phil Collins; *Phil Collins-Hits* . . . . (Atlantic)
True Friends
Shannon Curfman; *Loud Guitars Big Suspicions* . . . . (Arista)
True Love
Elton John & Kiki Dee; *Duets-C* . . . . (MCA)
Four Aces; *Best Of The Four Aces* . . . . (MCA)
Johnny Mathis & Henry Mancini; *Hollywood Musicals* . . . . (Columbia)
Patsy Cline; *Always* . . . . (MCA)
The Patsy Cline Story . . . . (MCA)
Roger Whittaker; *Best Loved Ballads-#2* . . . . (Liberty)
True Love
Glenn Frey; *Soul Searchin'* . . . . (MCA)
True Love
Vince Gill; *Essential Vince Gill* . . . . (RCA)
I Never Knew Lonely . . . . (RCA)
True Love
Pat Alger & Trisha Yearwood; *True Love & Other Short
Stories-C* . . . . (Sugar Hill)
True Love
Neville Brothers; *Family Groove* . . . . (A&M)
True Love
Joan Armatrading; *Square The Circle* . . . . (A&M)
True Love
Jefferson Airplane; *Jefferson Airplane* . . . .(Epic)
True Love Never Dies
Earl Scruggs & Gary Scruggs & Travis Tritt; *Earl Scruggs And
Friends-C* . . . . (MCA)
Kevin Welch; *Kevin Welch* . . . . (Reprise)
Truly
Lionel Richie; *Back To Front* . . . . (Motown)
Lionel Richie . . . . (Motown)
Truly Madly Deeply
Savage Garden; *Savage Garden* . . . . (Columbia)
Truly, Truly
Grant Lee Buffalo; *Jubilee* . . . . (Slash)
Truth About You, The
Rosanne Cash; *The Wheel* . . . . (Columbia)
What I Really Meant To Say
Cyndi Thomson; *My World* . . . . (Capitol)
What Is Truth
Johnny Cash; *The Man In Black-His Greatest Hits* . . . . (Legacy)
What It Is
Mark Knopfler; *Sailing To Philadelphia* . . . .(Warner Bros.)
Whiter Shade Of Pale
Annie Lennox; *Medusa* . . . . (Arista)
Procol Harum; *Best Of Procol Harum* . . . . (A&M)
Billboard Top Pop Hits-1967-C . . . . (Rhino)
History Of British Rock-#8-C . . . . (Rhino)
ST/Big Chill . . . . (Motown)
Whole New You
Shawn Colvin; *Whole New You* . . . . (Columbia)
Why Don't You Believe Me?
Duprees; *Best Of The Duprees* . . . . (Rhino)
Best Of The Duprees . . . . (Collectables)
Joni James; *Platinum & Gold Hits* . . . .(Taragon)
Patti Page; *Patti Page-Golden Celebration* . . . . (Mercury)
Woman's Worth, A
Alicia Keys; *Songs In A Minor* . . . . (J)
Yes It Is
Beatles; *Beatles VI* . . . . (Capitol)
Beatles-Box Set . . . . (Capitol)
Beatles-Love Songs . . . . (Capitol)
Past Masters-Volume One . . . . (Parlophone)
You Haven't Done Nothin'
Stevie Wonder; *Fulfillingness' First Finale* . . . . (Motown)
Your Eyes
Xscape; *Traces Of My Lipstick* . . . . (So So Def/Columbia)

UFO'S, Alien Creatures, Space People
See Also: **SPACE, STARS, STRANGE**

(Radio Station) EXP
Jimi Hendrix; *Axis: Bold As Love* . . . . (Reprise)
Alien
Atlanta Rhythm Section; *Quinella* . . . . (Columbia)
Alien
Tanya Tucker; *Love Me Like You Used To* . . . . (Liberty)
Arriving U.F.O.
Yes; *Tormato* . . . .(Atlantic)
Astro Boy
Buggles; *Age Of Plastic* . . . . (Island)
Astro Man
Jimi Hendrix; *Cry Of Love* . . . . (Reprise)
Astronaut Food
Sopwith Camel; *Miraculous Hump Returns* . . . . (Reprise)
Attack Of The Radioactive Hamsters
''Weird Al'' Yankovic; *ST/UHF & Other Stuff* . . . .(Scotti Bros.)
Bermuda Triangle
Fleetwood Mac; *Heroes Are Hard To Find* . . . . (Reprise)
Bermuda Triangle Blues (Flight 45)
Blondie; *Plastic Letters* . . . . (Chrysalis)
Calling Occupants Of Interplanetary Craft
Carpenters; *Carpenters-Classics-#2* . . . . (A&M)
Passage . . . . (A&M)
Yesterday Once More . . . . (A&M)
Klaatu; *Klaatu* . . . . (Capitol)
E.T.I. (Extra Terrestrial Intelligence)
Blue Oyster Cult; *Agents Of Fortune* . . . . (Columbia)
Career Of Evil . . . . (Columbia)
Extraterrestrial Live . . . . (Columbia)
Some Enchanted Evening . . . . (Columbia)
Ewok Celebration
Meco; *45-#9045* . . . . (Arista)
Fly On U.F.O.
Chromium; *Star To Star* . . . . (Infinity)
Flying Saucers Rock 'N' Roll
Billy Lee Riley & His Little Green Men; *Legends Of Rock Guitar-
'50s-#2-C* . . . . (Rhino)
Sun Story-C . . . . (Rhino)
Have You Seen The Saucers
Jefferson Airplane; *2400 Fulton Street-An Anthology* . . . . (RCA)
30 Seconds Over Winterland . . . . (RCA)
Heartlight
Neil Diamond; *Heartlight* . . . . (Columbia)
Hot August Night II . . . . (Columbia)
I've Seen The Saucers
Elton John; *Caribou* . . . . (Rocket)
Joe Slam And The Spaceship
Harry Connick, Jr.; *She* . . . . (Columbia)
Looking For A U.F.O.
Adrian Belew; *Young Lions* . . . .(Atlantic)
Loving The Alien
David Bowie; *The Singles-1969-1993* . . . . (Rykodisc)
Martian Boogie
Brownsville Station; *Brownsville Station* . . . . (Private Stock)
Martian Hop
Ran-Dells; *Dr. Demento Presents The Greatest Novelty Records-#3-
1960s-C* . . . . (Rhino)
Elvira Presents Haunted Hits-C . . . . (Rhino)
Halloween Hits-C . . . . (Rhino)
Martian Love Song
Hypnolovewheel; *Angel Food* . . . .(Alias)
Martian Manhunter
Icepick Trotsky; *Ultraviolet Catastrophe* . . . .(SST)
Martians At The Window
Kaleidoscope; *Greetings From Kartoonistan* . . . .(Gift Horse)
Martians Go Home
Shorty Rogers; *Great Moments In Jazz-C* . . . .(Atlantic)
Maybe Angels
Sheryl Crow; *Sheryl Crow* . . . . (A&M)
Men In Black
Will Smith; *Big Willie Style* . . . . (Columbia)
ST/Men In Black . . . . (Columbia)
Planetary Invasion
Midnight Star; *Planetary Invasion* . . . .(Solar)
Praying To The Aliens
Gary Numan & Tubeway Army; *Replicas* . . . . (Atco)
Rapture
Blondie; *Autoamerican* . . . . (Chrysalis)
Best Of Blondie . . . . (Chrysalis)
Once More Into The Bleach . . . . (Chrysalis)
Rock The First-#4-C . . . . (Sandstone Music)
Saucerful Of Secrets
Pink Floyd; *Nice Pair* . . . . (Capitol)

Saucerful Of Secrets . . . . (Capitol)
Ummagumma . . . . (Capitol)
Space Lord
Monster Magnet; *Powertrip* . . . . (A&M)
Sure The Boy Was Green
Horslips; *Aliens* . . . . (DJM)
Theme From "Alf"
Original Soundtrack; *Television's Greatest Hits-#6-Remote Control-C* . . . (TVT)
Theme From "Alien Nation"
Original Soundtrack; *Television's Greatest Hits-#7-Cable Ready-C* . . . . . (TVT)
Theme From "Alien"
Boston Pops Orchestra/John Williams; *Pops Out Of This World* . . . . . (Philips)
Theme From "Close Encounters Of The Third Kind"
John Williams; *Billboard Top Movie Hits-1970s-C* . . . . (Rhino)
ST/Close Encounters Of The Third Kind . . . .(Varese Sarabande)
Original Soundtrack; *Sci-Fi's Greatest Hits-#3-The Uninvited* . . . . (TVT)
Walter Murphy; *Themes From E.T.* . . . . (MCA)
Theme From "E.T."
Boston Pops Orchestra/John Williams; *Pops Out Of This World* . . . . . (Philips)
Walter Murphy; *"E.T." Theme* . . . . (MCA)
Theme From "Mork & Mindy"
Original Soundtrack; *Television's Greatest Hits-#6-Remote Control-C* . . . (TVT)
Theme From "My Favorite Martian"
Original Soundtrack; *Television's Greatest Hits-#2-C* . . . . (TVT)
Theme From "Return Of The Jedi"
Boston Pops Orchestra/John Williams; *Pops Out Of This World* . . . . . (Philips)
Neil Norman; *Greatest Science Fiction Hits-#3-C* . . . . (Crescendo)
Theme From "U.F.O."
Neil Norman; *Greatest Science Fiction Hits-#3-C* . . . . (Crescendo)
Theme From "War Of The Worlds"
Neil Norman; *Greatest Science Fiction Hits-#3-C* . . . . (Crescendo)
Third Stone From The Sun
Jimi Hendrix; *Essential Jimi Hendrix* . . . . (Reprise)
Kiss The Sky . . . . (Reprise)
Jimi Hendrix Experience; *Are You Experienced?* . . . . (Reprise)
U.F.O.
Country Joe McDonald; *Rock & Roll Music From The Planet Earth* . . .(Fantasy)
U.F.O.
Undisputed Truth; *It Came From Outer Space…-C* . . . . (VSI)
U.F.O.
Nina Hagen; *Nunsexmonkrock* . . . . (Columbia)
U.F.O.
Reggie Knighton Band; *Reggie Knighton Band* . . . . (Columbia)
U.F.O. Story
Flaming Lips; *Telepathic Surgery* . . . . (Restless)
UFO Has Landed In The Ghetto
Ry Cooder; *The Slide Area* . . . . (Warner Bros.)
UFO Over Cairo
Nasa; *Insha-Allah!* . . . .(Sire)
UFO's Are Real
Spot 1019; *Still…Again* . . . . (Frontier)
Under The Eye
Dennis Linde; *Under The Eye* . . . . (Monument)
Unidentified Flying Tuna Trot
REO Speedwagon; *You Can Tune A Piano But You Can't Tuna Fish* . . . . . (Epic)
Vulcan Death Grip
Ugly Americans; *Stereophonic Spanish Fly* . . . . (Mercury)
Waiting For The UFO's
Graham Parker And The Rumour; *Squeezing Out Sparks* . . . . (Arista)
We Are The Other People
Mothers Of Invention; *We're Only In It For The Money* . . . . (Rykodisc)
Ziggy Stardust
David Bowie; *Changesbowie* . . . . (Rykodisc)
Rise & Fall Of Ziggy Stardust And The Spiders From Mars . . . . . . (Rykodisc)
Sound + Vision . . . . (Rykodisc)
ST/Ziggy Stardust-The Motion Picture . . . . (Rykodisc)
Stage . . . . (Rykodisc)
The Singles-1969-1993 . . . . (Rykodisc)

URGENT, Desperate, Hurry, Immediate, Right Now
See Also: BUSY, DESIRE, FAST, LATE, TIME: GENERAL, TIME: SPECIFIC, TROUBLE, WAITING

15 Minutes
Marc Nelson; *chocolate mood* . . . . (Columbia)
911
Wyclef Jean featuring Mary J. Blige; *The Ecleftic-2 Sides II*
A Book . . . . (Ruffhouse/Columbia)
Amigone
Goo Goo Dolls; *Dizzy Up The Girl* . . . . (Warner Sunset/Reprise)
Beep Me 911
Missy "Misdemeanor" Elliot; *Supa Dupa Fly* . . . . (East West)
Call The Police
Hot Chocolate; *Hot Chocolate* . . . . (Big Tree)
Nat "King" Cole; *From The Very Beginning* . . . . (MCA)

Can't Wait
Bob Dylan; *Time Out Of Mind* . . . . (Columbia)
Can't Wait One Minute More
CIV; *Box Presents Big Ones Of Alternative Rock-#1-C* . . . . (Box Tunes)
Set Your Goals . . . . (Lava)
Carolina Blues
Blues Traveler; *Straight On Till Morning* . . . . (A&M)
Come And Get It
Badfinger; *Best Of Badfinger* . . . . (Capitol)
Beatles; *The Beatles-Anthology-#3* . . . . (Capitol)
Come See About Me
Diana Ross & The Supremes; *16 #1 Hits From The Early '60s-C* . . . . .(Motown)
Diana Ross & The Supremes' Greatest Hits . . . . (Motown)
Diana Ross & The Supremes-Anthology (1962-1969) . . . . (Motown)
Diana Ross & The Supremes-At The Copa . . . . (Motown)
Every Great #1 Hit . . . . (Motown)
Girl Groups-Story Of A Sound-C . . . . (Rhino)
Motown Story-First 25 Years-C . . . . (Motown)
Motown Superstar Series-#1-Diana Ross & The Supremes . . . . . (Motown)
Darling Be Home Soon
Joe Cocker; *Joe Cocker!* . . . . (A&M)
Joe Cocker-Classics-#4. . . . . (A&M)
Joe Cocker's Greatest Hits . . . . (A&M)
Lovin' Spoonful; *Best Of The Lovin' Spoonful-#2* . . . . (Rhino)
Lovin' '60s-C . . . . (Priority)
Lovin' Spoonful-Anthology . . . . (Rhino)
Distant Drums
Jim Reeves; *Best Of The Best Of Jim Reeves* . . . . (King)
Billboard Top Country Hits-1966-C . . . . (Rhino)
Essential Jim Reeves . . . . (RCA)
Excuse Me Mr.
No Doubt; *Tragic Kingdom* . . . . (Trauma)
Fools Rush In (Where Angels Fear To Tread)
Brook Benton; *Super Oldies Of The '60s-#10-C* . . . . (Audio Fidelity)
Tommy Dorsey & Frank Sinatra; *Sessions-#1-February 1, 1940-July*
17, 1940 . . . . (RCA)
Get The Party Started
Pink; *Missundaztood* . . . . (Arista)
Heads Carolina, Tails California
Jo Dee Messina; *Greatest Hits Of Country Dance-C* . . . . (Curb)
Jo Dee Messina . . . . (Curb)
Honey, Do You Love Me, Huh
Hank Williams; *Complete Hank Williams* . . . . (Mercury)
I Don't Want To Wait
Paula Cole; *Live On Letterman-From The Late Show* . . . . (Reprise)
Songs From Dawson's Creek . . . . (Sony Music Soundtrax)
This Fire . . . . (Imago)
I Need You Now
Eddie Fisher; *Very Best Of Eddie Fisher* . . . . (MCA)
I Shall Be Released
Band; *Music From Big Pink* . . . . (Capitol)
The Band-Anthology-#1 . . . . (Capitol)
The Last Waltz. . . . . (Warner Bros.)
To Kingdom Come-The Definitive Collection . . . . (Capitol)
Bette Midler; *Bette Midler* . . . . (Atlantic)
ST/Divine Madness . . . . (Atlantic)
Bob Dylan; *Biograph* . . . . (Columbia)
Bob Dylan At Budokan . . . . (Columbia)
Bob Dylan's Greatest Hits-#2 . . . . (Columbia)
The Bootleg Series-Volumes 1-3 [Rare & Unreleased]. . . . . (Columbia)
Bob Dylan And The Band; *Before The Flood* . . . . (Columbia)
Box Tops; *Box Tops' Greatest Hits* . . . . (Rhino)
Flying Burrito Brothers; *Farther Along-Best Of The Flying Burrito*
Brothers . . . . (A&M)
Joan Baez; *Any Day Now: Songs Of Bob Dylan* . . . . (Vanguard)
Carry It On . . . . (Vanguard)
From Every Stage . . . . (A&M)
Joe Cocker; *With A Little Help From My Friends* . . . . (A&M)
Nina Simone; *Best Of Nina Simone* . . . . (Verve)
Rick Nelson; *Rick Nelson In Concert-Troubadour 1969* . . . . (MCA)
I'm In A Hurry (And Don't Know Why)
Alabama; *American Pride* . . . . (RCA)
In The Mood
Andrews Sisters; *Andrews Sisters-16 Great Performances* . . . . (MCA)
Boogie Woogie Bugle Girls . . . . (MCA)
Chesterfield Broadcasts-#1 . . . . (RCA Victor)
Bette Midler; *Bette Midler* . . . . (Atlantic)
Live At Last . . . . (Atlantic)
Glenn Miller; *Best Of Glenn Miller* . . . . (RCA)
Glenn Miller-A Legendary Performer-#1 & 2. . . . . (Bluebird)
The Glenn Miller Story . . . . (RCA)
Glenn Miller & His Orchestra; *Glenn Miller & His Orchestra-*
Pure Gold. . . . . (Bluebird)
The Unforgettable Glenn Miller & His Orchestra. . . . . (RCA)
It's About Time
Public Announcement; *All Work, No Play* . . . . (A&M)
It's My Life
Bon Jovi; *Crush* . . . . (Island/IDJMG)
Now That's What I Call Music!-#5-C . . . . (Virgin)

The Concert For New York City-C . . . . (Columbia)
It's Now Or Never
Elvis Presley; *Elvis Presley-Love Songs* . . . . (RCA)
  Heart & Soul . . . . (RCA)
  Worldwide 50 Gold Award Hits, Vol. 1, Parts 1 & 2 . . . . (RCA)
Jimmy Mack
Martha & The Vandellas; *Billboard Top R&B Hits-1967-C* . . . . (Rhino)
  Compact Command Performances-Martha Reeves & The
    Vandellas . . . . (Motown)
  Martha Reeves & The Vandellas-Anthology . . . . (Motown)
  Motown Story-First 25 Years-C . . . . (Motown)
  Motown Superstar Series-#11-Martha Reeves & The Vandellas . . . . (Motown)
  Top 10 With A Bullet-Motown Girl Groups-C . . . . (Motown)
Katie Wants A Fast One
Steve Wariner & Garth Brooks; *Faith In You* . . . . (Capitol)
Last Chance Texaco
Rickie Lee Jones; *Naked Songs Live And Acoustic* . . . . (Reprise)
  Rickie Lee Jones. . . . . (Warner Bros.)
Last Night On Earth
U2; *Pop.* . . . . (Island)
Last Train To Clarksville
Monkees; *Monkees* . . . . (Arista)
  Monkees' Greatest Hits . . . . (Rhino)
  Monkees-Live-1967 . . . . (Rhino)
  Then & Now...The Best Of The Monkees . . . . (Arista)
Lean On Me
Kirk Franklin; *The Nu Nation Project.* . . . . (Gospo Centric/Interscope)
Let's Lock The Door (And Throw Away The Key)
Jay & The Americans; *Jay & The Americans' All-Time Greatest Hits* . . . (Rhino)
Let's Roll
Neil Young; *Let's Roll-CD Single* . . . . (Reprise)
Letter, The
Box Tops; *Billboard Top Rock 'N' Roll Hits-1967-C* . . . . (Rhino)
  Box Tops' Greatest Hits . . . . (Rhino)
  Cruisin'-1967-C . . . . (Increase)
  Oldies But Goodies-#12-C . . . . (Original Sound)
  Rockin' '60s-C . . . . (Priority)
Joe Cocker; *Joe Cocker Live* . . . . (Capitol)
  Joe Cocker-Classics-#4 . . . . (A&M)
  Joe Cocker's Greatest Hits . . . . (A&M)
  Mad Dogs & Englishmen . . . . (A&M)
Vernon Green & The Medallions; *Oldies But Goodies-#1-C* . . . (Original Sound)
  Vernon Green & The Medallions-Golden Classics . . . . (Collectables)
Look What Love Has Done
Patty Smyth; *ST/Junior.* . . . . (MCA)
Love's In Need Of Love Today
Stevie Wonder featuring Take 6; *America: A Tribute To*
  Heroes-C. . . . . (Interscope)
Make It Right
Econoline Crush; *Brand New History.* . . . . (Restless)
Make Yourself Comfortable
Sarah Vaughan; *Essential Sarah Vaughan-The Great Songs* . . . . (Verve)
Meeting Across The River
Bruce Springsteen; *Born To Run.* . . . . (Columbia)
No Other Love
Perry Como; *Easy Listening* . . . . (Pair)
No, No, No
Destiny's Child; *Destiny's Child* . . . . (Grass Roots/Columbia)
Nobody Wants To Be Lonely
Ricky Martin; *Sound Loaded* . . . . (Columbia)
Only The Good Die Young
Billy Joel; *Billy Joel-Greatest Hits, Volume I & Volume II.* . . . . (Columbia)
  KOHUEPT. . . . . (Columbia)
  The Stranger . . . . (Columbia)
Radar Love
Golden Earring; *'70s Greatest Rock Hits-#1-Hard N' Heavy-C.* . . . . . . (Priority)
  Classic Rock-#1-C . . . . (MCA)
  Golden Earring-Live . . . . (MCA)
  Moontan. . . . . (MCA)
  Super Hits Of The '70s-Have A Nice Day-#13-C. . . . . (Rhino)
Razorblades
Chris Stills; *100 Year Thing* . . . . (Atlantic)
Reminiscing
Little River Band; *'70's Super Groups-C* . . . . (Rhino)
  Reminiscing: The Twentieth Anniversary Collection. . . . . (Rhino)
Right Here Waiting
Richard Marx; *Chicken Soup For The Woman's Soul-C.* . . . . (Rhino)
  Repeat Offender. . . . . (EMI)
Right Here, Right Now
Jesus Jones; *Doubt* . . . . (SBK)
Ruby
Ray Charles; *Love Songs* . . . . (Rhino)
Run
George Strait; *The Road Goes On Forever, A Collection Of Their Greatest*
  Recordings . . . . (Polydor)
Rush Over
Marcus Miller & Me'Shell Ndegeocello; *ST/Love Jones* . . . . (Columbia)
Rush Rush
Paula Abdul; *Spellbound* . . . . (Captive)

Searchin' My Soul
Vonda Shepard; *ST/Songs From "Ally McBeal" Featuring Vonda*
  Shepard . . . . (550/Epic)
  The Radical Light . . . . (Vesperally)
Slow Poke
Ray Conniff; *Speak To Me Of Love* . . . . (Columbia)
State Trooper
Bruce Springsteen; *Nebraska* . . . . (Columbia)
  The Sopranos-Music From The HBO Original
    Series . . . . (Sony Music Soundtrax)
Surrounded
Chantal Kreviazuk; *Under These Rocks And Stones* . . . . (Columbia)
Take Time To Know Her
Percy Sledge; *Best Of Percy Sledge.* . . . . (Atlantic)
  It Tears Me Up-Best Of Percy Sledge . . . . (Rhino)
Thunder Road
Bruce Springsteen; *Born To Run.* . . . . (Columbia)
  Bruce Springsteen's Greatest Hits . . . . (Columbia)
Bruce Springsteen & The E Street Band; *Bruce Springsteen & The E Street*
  Band Live/1975-85 . . . . (Legacy)
Time
Pink Floyd; *Dark Side Of The Moon* . . . . (Capitol)
  Delicate Sound Of Thunder . . . . (Columbia)
  Pink Floyd-Gift Set . . . . (Capitol)
Two Little Girls
Ani DiFranco; *Little Plastic Castle* . . . . (Righteous Babe)
Urgent
Foreigner; *Records* . . . . (Atlantic)
Want You Bad
Offspring; *Conspiracy Of One* . . . . (Columbia)
What About Now
Lonestar; *Lonely Grill* . . . . (BNA)
Wheel Of Fortune
Cardinals; *Atlantic Rhythm & Blues 1947-1974-box-C.* . . . . (Atlantic)
Kay Starr; *Capitol Collectors Series-Kay Starr* . . . . (Capitol)
When I Get Home
Beatles; *Beatles-Box Set* . . . . (Capitol)
  Something New. . . . . (Capitol)
Yes!
Chad Brock; *Yes!.* . . . . (Warner Bros.)
Your Life Is Now
John Mellencamp; *John Mellencamp* . . . . (Columbia)

WAITING

See Also: **BUSY, TIME: GENERAL, TIME: SPECIFIC, URGENT**

5-4-3-2 (Yo! Time Is Up)
Jade; *Mind Body & Soul* . . . . (Giant)
After Tonight
Mariah Carey; *Rainbow* . . . . (Columbia)
Ain't Misbehavin'
Fats Waller; *20 Golden Pieces Of Fats Waller* . . . . (Bulldog)
  Ain't Misbehavin'. . . . . (RCA)
  Fats Waller-Legendary Performer. . . . . (RCA)
  Fats Waller-Live-#2. . . . . (Giants Of Jazz)
  Piano Solos-1929-1941 . . . . (RCA)
Hank Williams, Jr.; *Five-O* . . . . (WB/Curb)
  Hank Williams, Jr.'s Greatest Hits III . . . . (Curb)
Ain't No Fun (Waiting Round To Be A Millionaire)
AC/DC; *Dirty Deeds Done Dirt Cheap* . . . . (Atlantic)
All Along
Blessid Union Of Souls; *Home* . . . . (EMI)
All My Friends
Counting Crows; *This Desert Life* . . . . (David Geffen Co.)
All The Fun
Paul Overstreet; *Best Of Paul Overstreet* . . . . (RCA)
Alone
Bee Gees; *Still Waters* . . . . (Polydor)
Amelia
Gretchen Peters; *Gretchen Peters* . . . . (Purple Crayon Prod.)
Angels In Waiting
Tammy Cochran; *Tammy Cochran* . . . . (Epic)
Angels Of The Silences
Counting Crows; *Recovering The Satellites* . . . . (David Geffen Co.)
Annie Waits
Ben Folds; *Rockin' The Suburbs* . . . . (Epic)
Another Nine Minutes
Yankee Grey; *Untamed.* . . . . (Monument)
Another Op'nin', Another Show
Original Cast; *Kiss Me Kate* . . . . (Sony Music Classical)
  Kiss Me Kate . . . . (MCA)
  Kiss Me Kate . . . . (EMI-Angel)
  There's No Business Like Show Business: Broadway
    Showstoppers-C. . . . . (Sony Broadway)
Anticipating
Britney Spears; *Britney* . . . . (Jive)

Anticipation
Carly Simon; *Anticipation* .... (Elektra)
Best Of Carly Simon .... (Elektra)

Anytime
Eddie Fisher; *Best Of Eddie Fisher* .... (MCA)
Eddy Arnold, The Tennessee Plowboy and his Guitar; *Nipper's Greatest Hits
Of The '40s-#2-C* .... (RCA)
Patsy Cline; *Best Of Patsy Cline* .... (MCA Special Prod.)

Apartment #9
Melissa Etheridge; *Tammy Wynette...Remembered-C* .... (Asylum)
Tammy Wynette; *Tammy Wynette-Anniversary-20 Years Of Hits* .... (Epic)
Tammy Wynette's Greatest Hits .... (Epic)

Auf Wiedersehn-Sweetheart
Vera Lynn; *Those Wonderful Years: Tenderly-C* .... (JCI Assoc. Labels)

Be My Baby
Linda Ronstadt; *Dedicated To The One I Love* .... (Elektra)
Melissa Etheridge; *Concert For The Rock & Roll Hall Of Fame-C* ... (Columbia)
Ronettes; *Best Of The Ronettes* .... (Abkco)
Phil Spector-Back To Mono 1958-1969-C .... (Abkco)
ST/Dirty Dancing .... (RCA)

Best Is Yet To Come
Frank Sinatra; *It Might As Well Be Swing* .... (Reprise)
Sinatra Reprise-The Very Good Years .... (Reprise)
Johnny Mathis; *I'll Buy You A Star* .... (Legacy)
Rosemary Clooney; *Girl Singer* .... (Concord Jazz)
Tony Bennett; *I Left My Heart In San Francisco* .... (Columbia)
The Ultimate Tony Bennett .... (Legacy)

Beyond The Blue Horizon
Jeanette MacDonald; *Hollywood Sings-C* .... (Living Era)
Lou Christie; *ST/Rain Man* .... (Capitol)

Bidin' My Time
Original Cast; *Girl Crazy* .... (Sony Music Special Prod.)
Sarah Vaughan; *Sarah Vaughan Sings George Gershwin Songbook,
Vol. 1* .... (Emarcy)

Blackbird
Beatles; *Beatles-Box Set* .... (Capitol)
The Beatles (White Album) .... (Capitol)
Crosby, Stills & Nash; *CSN* .... (Atlantic)
Paul McCartney; *Unplugged (The Official Bootleg)* .... (Capitol)
Wings; *Wings Over America* .... (Capitol)

Born To Fly
Sara Evans; *Born To Fly* .... (RCA)

Broadway
Goo Goo Dolls; *Dizzy Up The Girl* .... (Warner Sunset/Reprise)

Build Me Up Buttercup
Foundations; *Billboard Top Rock 'N' Roll Hits-1969-C* .... (Rhino)
History Of British Rock-#9-C .... (Rhino)
ST/There's Something About Mary .... (Capitol)

Buying Time
Clint Black; *The Hard Way* .... (RCA)

Can Heaven Wait
Luther Vandross; *Luther Vandross* .... (J)

Can't Find My Way Home
Blind Faith; *Blind Faith* .... (Polydor)
Eric Clapton-Crossroads-C .... (Polydor)
ST/1969 .... (Polydor)

Can't Wait
Bob Dylan; *Time Out Of Mind* .... (Columbia)

Can't Wait One Minute More
CIV; *Box Presents Big Ones Of Alternative Rock-#1-C* .... (Box Tunes)
Set Your Goals .... (Lava)

Carolina Blues
Blues Traveler; *Straight On Till Morning* .... (A&M)

Charmaine
Frank Sinatra; *Frank Sinatra-Complete Reprise Studio Recordings* .... (Reprise)
Mantovani; *Mantovani-Golden Hits* .... (London)
Mom & Dads; *Good Night Sweetheart* .... (Crescendo)
Tommy Dorsey; *Best Of Tommy Dorsey* .... (MCA)

Chime Bells
Elton Britt; *The RCA Years* .... (Collector's Choice)
Jody King; *Photographs & Memories* .... (Capricorn)

Come On Back
Keb' Mo'; *The Door* .... (550/Epic/Okeh)

Come See About Me
Diana Ross & The Supremes; *16 #1 Hits From The Early '60s-C* ..... (Motown)
Diana Ross & The Supremes' Greatest Hits .... (Motown)
Diana Ross & The Supremes-Anthology (1962-1969) .... (Motown)
Diana Ross & The Supremes-At The Copa .... (Motown)
Every Great #1 Hit .... (Motown)
Girl Groups-Story Of A Sound-C .... (Rhino)
Motown Story-First 25 Years-C .... (Motown)
Motown Superstar Series-#1-Diana Ross & The Supremes .... (Motown)

Come Softly To Me
Fleetwoods; *Come Softly To Me: The Very Best Of The Fleetwoods* ...... (EMI)
Only Love-1955-1959-C .... (Rhino)

Coming Back Home
Bebe Winans featuring Brian McKnight & Joe; *Love & Freedom* .... (Motown)

Coming Up
Paul McCartney; *All The Best!* .... (Capitol)

Tripping The Live Fantastic-Highlights! .... (Capitol)

Crying, Waiting, Hoping
Buddy Holly; *Buddy Holly Collection* .... (MCA)
Marshall Crenshaw; *ST/La Bamba* .... (Slash)

Darling Be Home Soon
Joe Cocker; *Joe Cocker!* .... (A&M)
Joe Cocker-Classics-#4 .... (A&M)
Joe Cocker's Greatest Hits .... (A&M)
Lovin' Spoonful; *Best Of The Lovin' Spoonful-#2* .... (Rhino)
Lovin' '60s-C .... (Priority)
Lovin' Spoonful-Anthology .... (Rhino)

Desperados Waiting For A Train
Guy Clark; *Old No. 1* .... (Sugar Hill)
Jerry Jeff Walker; *Best Of Jerry Jeff Walker* .... (MCA)
Great Gonzos .... (MCA)
Viva Terlingua .... (MCA)
Waylon Jennings, Willie Nelson, Johnny Cash, Kris Kristofferson;
Highwayman .... (Columbia)
Hot Tracks-Train Super Hits-C .... (Epic)

Detroit City
Ace Cannon; *Golden Favorites* .... (Ranwood)
Bill Anderson; *Best Of Bill Anderson* .... (Curb)
Bobby Bare; *Nipper's Greatest Hits Of The '60s-#2-C* .... (RCA)
This Is Bobby Bare .... (RCA)
Chet Atkins; *Country Gems* .... (Pair)
Flatt & Scruggs; *20 All-Time Great Recordings* .... (Columbia)
Hank Williams, Jr.; *Live At Cobo Hall Detroit* .... (Polydor)
Standing In The Shadows .... (Polydor)
Mel Tillis; *Best Of Mel Tillis* .... (MCA)
Live At The Sam Houston Coliseum .... (MGM)
Solomon Burke; *Home In Your Heart-Best Of Solomon Burke* .... (Rhino)

Don't Let The Stars Get In Your Eyes
Perry Como; *Como's Golden Records* .... (RCA)
Perry Como-Pure Gold .... (RCA)
Perry Como's All-Time Greatest Hits-#1 .... (RCA)
This Is Perry Como .... (RCA)

Don't Pass Me By
Beatles; *The Beatles (White Album)* .... (Capitol)
The Beatles-Anthology-#3 .... (Capitol)

Down So Long
Jewel; *Spirit* .... (Atlantic)

Eddie My Love
Fontane Sisters; *History Of Dot-#1-Young Love-C* .... (Varese Sarabande)

Elegantly Wasted
INXS; *Elegantly Wasted* .... (Mercury)

Engine Engine #9
Roger Miller; *Best Of Roger Miller-#2-King Of The Road* .... (Mercury)
Best Of Roger Miller-His Greatest Songs .... (Curb)
King Of The Road-Genius Of Roger Miller .... (Mercury)
Roger Miller-Golden Hits .... (Smash)
Roger Miller-The Hits .... (Mercury)
Train Trax-C .... (Sony Music Special Prod.)

Essence
Lucinda Williams; *Essence* .... (Lost Highway/IDJMG)

Everlasting Glaze
Smashing Pumpkins; *Machina: The Machines Of God* .... (Virgin)

Every Light In The House
Trace Adkins; *Dreamin' Out Loud* .... (Capitol)

Everyday
Buddy Holly; *Buddy Holly* .... (MCA)
Buddy Holly-20 Golden Greats .... (MCA)
Buddy Holly's Greatest Hits .... (MCA)
From The Original Master Tapes-Buddy Holly .... (MCA)
Legend-From The Original Master Tapes .... (MCA)
The Buddy Holly Collection .... (MCA)

Exactly Like You
Andy Williams; *Moon River-Days Of Wine And Roses* .... (Columbia)
Sarah Vaughan; *Complete Sarah Vaughan On Mercury-#1-Great Jazz Years-
1954-1956* .... (Mercury)
Willie Nelson; *Somewhere Over The Rainbow* .... (Columbia)

Excuse Me Mr.
No Doubt; *Tragic Kingdom* .... (Trauma)

Exhale (Shoop Shoop)
Whitney Houston; *ST/Waiting To Exhale* .... (Arista)
Whitney Houston's Greatest Hits .... (Arista)

Exile
Enya; *Watermark* .... (Reprise)

Factory Girl
Rolling Stones; *Beggars Banquet* .... (Abkco)

Faded
soulDecision; *No One Does It Better* .... (MCA)
Now That's What I Call Music!-#5-C .... (Virgin)

First Night
Monica; *The Boy Is Mine* .... (Arista)

Five O'Clock World
Hal Ketchum; *Past The Point Of Rescue* .... (Curb)
Vogues; *ST/Good Morning, Vietnam* .... (A&M)
Vogues' Greatest Hits .... (SSS International)
Vogues' Greatest Hits .... (Rhino)

For You I Will
Monica; *The Boy Is Mine* . . . . (Arista)
Forever
Mariah Carey; *Daydream* . . . . (Columbia)
Forever Love
Reba McEntire; *If You See Him* . . . .(MCA)
Reba McEntire's Greatest Hits-#3: I'm A Survivor . . . . (MCA)
Ghost Of Tom Joad
Bruce Springsteen; *The Ghost Of Tom Joad* . . . . (Columbia)
Go Away
Lorrie Morgan; *Lorrie Morgan-Super Hits* . . . . (RCA)
Shakin' Things Up . . . . (BNA)
To Get To You-Greatest Hits Collection . . . . (BNA)
Got Me Waiting
Heavy D & The Boyz; *Nuttin' But Love* . . . .(Uptown)
Halfway Home Cafe
Ricky Skaggs and Kentucky Thunder; *History Of The Future* . . (Skaggs Family)
Hanginaround
Counting Crows; *This Desert Life* . . . . (David Geffen Co.)
Heart Of Innocence
Jessica Simpson; *Sweet Kisses* . . . . (Columbia)
Heartbreak U.S.A.
Kitty Wells; *I Love Country-Hits Of The '60s-#1-C* . . . . (Priority)
Kitty Wells' Greatest Songs . . . . (Curb)
The Country Music Hall Of Fame-Kitty Wells . . . .(MCA Special Prod.)
Heaven Can Wait
Paul Young; *Other Voices* . . . . (Columbia)
Heaven Can Wait
Meat Loaf; *Bat Out Of Hell* . . . .(Epic)
Heaven Can Wait
Iron Maiden; *Somewhere In Time* . . . . (Capitol)
Here I Am
Patty Loveless; *Patty Loveless-Classics* . . . .(Epic)
When Fallen Angels Fly . . . . (Epic)
High Country Snows
Dan Fogelberg; *High Country Snows* . . . . (Full Moon)
High Noon
Frankie Laine; *Billboard Top Movie Hits-1950-1954-C* . . . . (Rhino)
Tex Ritter; *Heroes Of Country Music-#4-Legends Of The West*
Coast-C . . . . (Rhino)
The Envelope Please-Academy Award Winning Songs (1946-
1957)-C . . . . (Rhino)
Hit Or Miss (Waited Too Long)
New Found Glory; *New Found Glory* . . . . (Drive-Thru)
Hold On
Xscape; *Traces Of My Lipstick* . . . . (So So Def/Columbia)
Hold On! I'm A Comin'
Chuck Jackson & Maxine Brown; *Best Of Chuck Jackson* . . . . (Tomato)
Sam & Dave; *Best Of Sam & Dave* . . . .(Atlantic)
Holding Out For A Hero
Bonnie Tyler; *ST/Footloose* . . . . (Columbia)
Homeward Bound
Paul Simon; *Paul Simon In Concert/Live Rhymin'* . . . . (Columbia)
Paul Simon & George Harrison; *Nobody's Child-Romanian Angel*
Appeal-C . . . .(Warner Bros.)
Simon & Garfunkel; *Collected Works* . . . . (Columbia)
Parsley Sage Rosemary & Thyme . . . . (Columbia)
Simon & Garfunkel's Greatest Hits . . . . (Columbia)
The Concert In Central Park . . . .(Warner Bros.)
Willie Nelson & Waylon Jennings; *Take It To The Limit* . . . . (Columbia)
How Could You
K-Ci & JoJo; *Love Always* . . . .(MCA)
How Long Must I Wait For You
Joe Jackson; *Jumpin' Jive* . . . . (A&M)
I Can't Wait To Meetchu
Macy Gray; *On How Life Is* . . . .(Epic)
I Can't Wait Another Minute
Hi-Five; *Hi-Five* . . . . (Jive)
I Could Not Ask For More
Edwin McCain; *Messenger* . . . . (Lava)
I Count The Minutes
Ricky Martin; *Ricky Martin* . . . . (Columbia)
I Don't Want To Wait
Paula Cole; *Live On Letterman-From The Late Show* . . . . (Reprise)
Songs From Dawson's Creek . . . . (Sony Music Soundtrax)
This Fire . . . . (Imago)
I Finally Found Someone
Barbra Streisand & Bryan Adams; *ST/The Mirror Has Two Faces* . . (Columbia)
I Got The Train Sittin' Waitin'
Waylon Jennings; *Between The Rails: America's Train Songs-C* . . .(Crescendo)
I Have To Surrender
Ty Herndon; *Living In A Moment* . . . .(Epic)
I Hope You've Learned
Ricky Skaggs and Kentucky Thunder; *Bluegrass Rules!* . . . . (Rounder)
I Just Can't Wait To Be King
Elton John; *ST/The Lion King* . . . . (Walt Disney)
I Knew I Loved You
Savage Garden; *Affirmation* . . . . (Columbia)

Now That's What I Call Music!-#4-C . . . .(Virgin)
I Knew You Were Waiting (For Me)
Aretha Franklin & George Michael; *Aretha Franklin's Greatest Hits-1980-*
1994 . . . . (Arista)
Billboard Top Hits-1987-C . . . . (Rhino)
Chicken Soup For The Couples Soul-C . . . . (Rhino)
I Will
Beatles; *The Beatles (White Album)* . . . . (Capitol)
The Beatles-Anthology-#3 . . . . (Capitol)
Ben Taylor; *ST/Bye Bye, Love* . . . .(Giant)
Dean Martin; *Dean Martin's Greatest Hits* . . . . (EMI)
I Will Wait
Hootie & The Blowfish; *Musical Chairs* . . . .(Atlantic)
If I Should Fall Behind
Bruce Springsteen; *In Concert/MTV Plugged* . . . . (Columbia)
Lucky Town . . . . (Columbia)
Faith Hill; *Breathe* . . . . (Warner Bros.)
Linda Ronstadt; *We Ran* . . . . (Elektra)
If You Think You're Lonely Now
Bobby Womack; *The Poet* . . . . (Razor & Tie)
K-Ci Hailey; *ST/Jason's Lyric* . . . . (Mercury)
I'll Be Home
Barbra Streisand; *Stoney End* . . . . (Columbia)
Randy Newman; *Little Criminals* . . . . (Warner Bros.)
Randy Newman/Live . . . . (Warner Archives)
I'll Come Runnin'
Connie Smith; *Essential Connie Smith* . . . .(RCA)
I'm Already Taken
Steve Wariner; *Country Cares For Kids II-C* . . . .(BNA)
Two Teardrops . . . . (Capitol)
I'm Free
Who; *Join Together* . . . .(MCA)
Tommy . . . . (MCA)
I'm Gonna Knock On Your Door
Eddie Hodges; *History Of Cadence Records-#1-C* . . . .(Varese Vintage)
I'm Gonna Make You Mine
Lou Christie; *Enlightnin'ment-Best Of Lou Christie* . . . . (Rhino)
I'm Thinking Tonight Of My Blue Eyes
Gene Autry; *All Time Legends Of Country Music-C* . . . . (Legacy)
I'm Waiting For The Day
Beach Boys; *Pet Sounds* . . . . (Capitol)
The Pet Sounds Sessions: A 30th Anniversary Collection . . . . (Capitol)
I'm Waiting For The Man
Lou Reed; *Lou Reed Live* . . . .(RCA)
Velvet Underground; *Live MCMXCIII* . . . .(Sire)
The Velvet Underground & Nico . . . . (Verve)
Image Of A Girl
Safaris; *Brown Eyed Soul...East L.A.-#3-C* . . . . (Rhino)
In A Shanty In Old Shanty Town
Ink Spots; *Java Jive* . . . .(Laserlight)
In The Air Tonight
Phil Collins; *Classic Rock 1966-1988-C* . . . .(Atlantic)
Face Value . . . . (Atlantic)
Miami Vice-C . . . . (MCA)
Prince's Trust 10th Anniversary Party-C . . . . (A&M)
Serious Hits...Live! . . . . (Atlantic)
The Secret Policeman's Other Ball/The Music . . . . (Rhino)
In The Midnight Hour
Rascals; *Classic Rock 1966-1988-C* . . . .(Atlantic)
ST/More Songs From ''The Big Chill'' . . . . (Motown)
Time Peace/The Rascals' Greatest Hits . . . . (Atlantic)
Roxy Music; *Flesh + Blood* . . . . (Atco)
Street Life-20 Great Hits . . . . (Reprise)
Wilson Pickett; *Atlantic Rhythm & Blues 1947-1974-#5 (1962-*
1966)-C . . . .(Atlantic)
Best Of Wilson Pickett . . . . (Atlantic)
Frat Rock!-#4-C . . . . (Rhino)
Golden Soul-C . . . . (Atlantic)
Soul Years-C . . . . (Atlantic)
Wilson Pickett's Greatest Hits . . . . (Atlantic)
In The Mood
Andrews Sisters; *Andrews Sisters-16 Great Performances* . . . . (MCA)
Boogie Woogie Bugle Girls . . . . (MCA)
Chesterfield Broadcasts-#1 . . . . (RCA Victor)
Bette Midler; *Bette Midler* . . . . (Atlantic)
Live At Last . . . . (Atlantic)
Glenn Miller; *Best Of Glenn Miller* . . . .(RCA)
Glenn Miller-A Legendary Performer-#1 & 2 . . . . (Bluebird)
The Glenn Miller Story . . . . (RCA)
Glenn Miller & His Orchestra; *Glenn Miller & His Orchestra-*
Pure Gold . . . . (Bluebird)
The Unforgettable Glenn Miller & His Orchestra . . . . (RCA)
Isn't It Time
Babys; *Babys-Anthology* . . . . (Chrysalis)
Broken Heart . . . . (Chrysalis)
It's Now Or Never
Elvis Presley; *Elvis Presley-Love Songs* . . . .(RCA)
Heart & Soul . . . . (RCA)
Worldwide 50 Gold Award Hits, Vol. 1, Parts 1 & 2 . . . .(RCA)

Jig Saw Puzzle
Rolling Stones; *Beggars Banquet* . . . . (Abkco)
Just You Wait
Julie Andrews/Original Cast; *My Fair Lady* . . . . (Columbia)
Kansas City Song
Buck Owens; *Buck Owens Collection-1959-1990* . . . . (Rhino)
Lara's Theme
Maurice Jarre Orchestra; *Hollywood's Great Composers-C* . . . . (Columbia Special Prod.)
MGM Studio Orchestra; *ST/Dr. Zhivago* . . . . (MCA)
Lead On
George Strait; *Latest Greatest Straitest Hits* . . . . (MCA)
Lead On . . . . (MCA)
Leaving On A Jet Plane
Chantal Kreviazuk; *ST/Armageddon-The Album* . . . . (Columbia)
John Denver; *John Denver's Greatest Hits* . . . . (RCA)
Rhymes & Reasons . . . . (RCA)
Kendalls; *Super Country Hits Of The '70s-C* . . . . (Gusto)
Peter, Paul & Mary; *10 Years Together/The Best Of Peter, Paul and Mary* . . . . (Warner Bros.)
Album 1700 . . . . (Warner Bros.)
Leaving Town
Dexter Freebish; *Life Of Saturdays* . . . . (Capitol)
Life On A Chain
Pete Yorn; *Musicforthemorningafter* . . . . (Columbia)
Like Dreamers Do
Beatles; *The Beatles-Anthology-#1* . . . . (Capitol)
Lit Up
Buckcherry; *Buckcherry* . . . . (DreamWorks/SKG)
Lonely Too Long
Patty Loveless; *Patty Loveless-Classics* . . . . (Epic)
Super Hits Of 1996-C . . . . (Epic)
The Trouble With The Truth . . . . (Epic)
Long And Winding Road, The
Beatles; *Beatles 1* . . . . (Capitol)
Beatles-20 Greatest Hits . . . . (Capitol)
Beatles-Love Songs . . . . (Capitol)
Let It Be . . . . (Capitol)
Reel Music . . . . (Capitol)
The Beatles/1967-1970 . . . . (Capitol)
Paul McCartney; *Tripping The Live Fantastic-Highlights!* . . . . (Capitol)
Wings; *Wings Over America* . . . . (Capitol)
Long Long Time
Linda Ronstadt; *Different Drum* . . . . (Capitol)
Linda Ronstadt-Retrospective . . . . (Capitol)
Linda Ronstadt's Greatest Hits . . . . (Asylum)
Silk Purse . . . . (Capitol)
Look Of Love, The
Andy Williams; *Born Free-Love Andy* . . . . (Collectables)
Legend At His Best . . . . (Collectables)
Anita Baker; *Rhythm Of Love* . . . . (Atlantic)
Diana Krall; *The Look Of Love* . . . . (Impulse!)
Dionne Warwick; *Hidden Gems-Best Of Dionne Warwick-#2* . . . . (Rhino)
Neil Diamond; *As Time Goes By-The Movie Album* . . . . (Columbia)
Sergio Mendes & Brasil '66; *Sergio Mendes-Classics-#18* . . . . (A&M)
Louie Louie
Kingsmen; *Best Of The Kingsmen* . . . . (Rhino)
Billboard Top Rock 'N' Roll Hits-1963-C . . . . (Rhino)
Cruisin'-1963-C . . . . (Increase)
Frat Rock!-C . . . . (Rhino)
Oldies But Goodies-#11-C . . . . (Original Sound)
Rock & Roll Is Here To Stay-C . . . . (Gusto)
ST/Quadrophenia . . . . (MCA)
WCBS FM 101 History Of Rock-'60s-#1-C . . . . (Collectables)
Love Is On The Way
Celine Dion; *Let's Talk About Love-C* . . . . (550 Music)
Dave Koz; *Dance* . . . . (Capitol)
Love Will Be Waiting
Kevon Edmonds; *24/7* . . . . (RCA)
Love Won't Let Me Wait
Luther Vandross; *Any Love* . . . . (Epic)
Best Of Luther Vandross...The Best Of Love . . . . (Epic)
Major Harris; *Atlantic Rhythm & Blues 1947-1974-#6 (1966-1969)-C* . . . . (Atlantic)
Major Harris-Live . . . . (WMOT)
My Way . . . . (Atlantic)
Me And Bobby McGee
Grateful Dead; *Grateful Dead (Skull & Roses)* . . . . (Warner Bros.)
Janis Joplin; *Janis* . . . . (Legacy)
Janis Joplin's Greatest Hits . . . . (Columbia)
Pearl . . . . (Legacy)
Rock Classics Of The '70s-C . . . . (Columbia)
Willie Nelson; *Willie Nelson Sings Kristofferson* . . . . (Columbia)
Meeting In My Bedroom
Silk; *Tonight* . . . . (Elektra)
Miss You
Mick Jagger & Keith Richards; *The Concert For New York City-C* . . (Columbia)
Rolling Stones; *Rewind (1971-1984)* . . . . (Rolling Stones)
Some Girls . . . . (Virgin)
Flashpoint . . . . (Virgin)
Moonlight On The Colorado
Sons Of The Pioneers; *Songs Of The Trail* . . . . (Pair)
Mother's Only Sleeping
Ricky Skaggs and Kentucky Thunder; *History Of The Future* . . . (Skaggs Family)
Murder (Or A Heart Attack)
Old 97's; *Fight Songs* . . . . (Elektra)
Never Ever
All Saints; *All Saints* . . . . (London)
Now That's What I Call Music!-#1-C . . . . (Virgin)
Next Lifetime
Erykah Badu; *Baduizm* . . . . (Kedar Entert./Universal)
Ninety Nine Years (Dead Or Alive)
Guy Mitchell; *Definitive Guy Mitchell* . . . . (Collector's Choice)
No Other Love
Perry Como; *Easy Listening* . . . . (Pair)
On The Road Again
Willie Nelson; *Greatest Country Hits Of The '80s-1980-C* . . . . (Columbia)
Greatest Hits (& Some That Will Be) . . . . (Columbia)
Hot Country Rock-#1-C . . . . (Epic)
ST/Forrest Gump . . . . (Epic/Sony Music Soundtrax)
ST/Honeysuckle Rose . . . . (Columbia)
Only Waiting For You
Crosby, Stills & Nash; *After The Storm* . . . . (Atlantic)
Our Time Has Come
Wood; *Songs From Stamford Hill* . . . . (Columbia)
Paper Sun
Def Leppard; *Euphoria* . . . . (Mercury)
Patiently Waiting
Kathy Mattea; *Love Travels* . . . . (Mercury)
Please Mister Postman
Beatles; *Beatles-Box Set* . . . . (Capitol)
The Beatles' Second Album . . . . (Capitol)
With The Beatles . . . . (Parlophone)
Carpenters; *Carpenters-Classics-#2* . . . . (A&M)
Horizon . . . . (A&M)
Yesterday Once More . . . . (A&M)
Marvelettes; *Billboard Top Rock 'N' Roll Hits-1961-C* . . . . (Rhino)
Marvelettes' Greatest Hits . . . . (Motown)
Marvelettes-Anthology . . . . (Motown)
Motown Story-First 25 Years-C . . . . (Motown)
Poor Butterfly
Sarah Vaughan; *Compact Jazz-Sarah Vaughan* . . . . (Verve)
Live In Japan . . . . (Mainstream)
Sarah Vaughan-Golden Hits . . . . (Mercury)
Sonny Rollins; *Best Of Sonny Rollins-The Blue Note Years* . . . . (Blue Note)
Sonny Rollins-Vol. 2 . . . . (Blue Note)
Push Push
Paula Abdul; *Spellbound* . . . . (Captive)
Question
Moody Blues; *A Night At Red Rocks With The Colorado Symphony Orchestra* . . . . (Polydor)
A Question Of Balance . . . . (Polydor)
This Is The Moody Blues . . . . (Polydor)
Ready, Willing And Able
Lari White; *Best Of Lari White* . . . . (RCA)
Don't Fence Me In . . . . (RCA)
Real Love
Beatles; *The Beatles-Anthology-#2* . . . . (Capitol)
John Lennon; *ST/Imagine: John Lennon* . . . . (Capitol)
Reasons For Waiting
Jethro Tull; *Stand Up* . . . . (Chrysalis)
Redemption Day
Sheryl Crow; *Sheryl Crow* . . . . (A&M)
Right Here Waiting
Richard Marx; *Chicken Soup For The Woman's Soul-C* . . . . (Rhino)
Repeat Offender . . . . (EMI)
Rudiger
Mark Knopfler; *Golden Heart* . . . . (Warner Bros.)
Run Baby Run (Back Into My Arms)
Newbeats; *Collectables Presents The History Of Rock-#10-C* . . . . (Collectables)
Newbeats-Golden Classics Edition . . . . (Collectables)
Tremeloes; *Best Of The Tremeloes* . . . . (Rhino)
Runaround
Fleetwoods; *Best Of The Fleetwoods* . . . . (Rhino)
Running Bear
Johnny Preston; *45s On CD-#1-1956-1959-C* . . . . (Mercury)
Billboard Top Rock 'N' Roll Hits-1960-C . . . . (Rhino)
Cruisin'-1960-C . . . . (Increase)
Sonny James; *All-Time Country Classics-#1-C* . . . . (Capitol)
Sad Eyed Lady Of The Lowlands
Bob Dylan; *Blonde On Blonde* . . . . (Columbia)
Joan Baez; *Any Day Now: Songs Of Bob Dylan* . . . . (Vanguard)
Lovesong Album . . . . (Vanguard)
Second Class Wait Here
Slim Dusty; *Australia Is His Name* . . . . (Philo)
Second Wind
Darryl Worley; *Hard Rain Don't Last* . . . . (DreamWorks/SKG)

Ships That Don't Come In
Joe Diffie; *Regular Joe* . . . .(Epic)
Silence On The Line
Chris LeDoux; *Cowboy* . . . . (Capitol)
Sittin' On Go
Bryan White; *Between Now And Forever* . . . . (Asylum)
Sittin' Up In My Room
Brandy; *ST/Waiting To Exhale* . . . . (Arista)
Sitting In Limbo
Jimmy Cliff; *ST/The Harder They Come* . . . .(Mango)
ST/The Harder They Come . . . .(Mango)
Slow Poke
Ray Conniff; *Speak To Me Of Love* . . . . (Columbia)
Smoke! Smoke! Smoke!
Commander Cody & His Lost Planet Airmen; *Country Casanova*. . . . . . .(MCA)
Too Much Fun-Best Of Commander Cody & His Lost Planet Airmen . . .(MCA)
We've Got A Live One Here! . . . .(Warner Bros.)
Doc Watson; *Red Rocking Chair* . . . . (Flying Fish)
Johnny Bond & His Red River Valley Boys; *All Time Legends Of Country Music-C* . . . . (Legacy)
Merle Travis; *Johnny Gimble's Texas Honky-Tonk Hits-C* . . . . . .(C.M.H. Prod.)
Tex Williams; *Birth Of A Dream-Capitol's Early Hits-C*. . . . . (Capitol)
Dr. Demento Presents The Greatest Novelty Records-#1-1940s & Before-C . . . . (Rhino)
Somebody
J. Geils Band; *Monkey Island* . . . . (Atlantic)
Somewhere
Aretha Franklin; *Aretha's Jazz* . . . . (Rhino)
Barbra Streisand; *The Broadway Album* . . . . (Columbia)
Dave Brubeck; *Music From West Side Story* . . . . (Columbia)
Jose Carreras; *Amigos Para Siempre-Friends For Life* . . . . (Atlantic)
Original Cast; *ST/West Side Story* . . . .(Sony Broadway)
Tom Waits; *Tom Waits-Anthology* . . . . (Asylum)
Somewhere In My Broken Heart
Billy Dean; *Billy Dean's Greatest Hits* . . . . (Liberty)
Heart Beats-Country Lovin': Songs From The Heart-C . . . . (Rhino)
Young Man . . . . (SBK)
Randy Travis; *No Holdin' Back* . . . .(Warner Bros.)
Somewhere In The Vicinity Of The Heart
Shenandoah; *In The Vicinity Of The Heart* . . . . (Capitol)
Now And Then . . . . (Capitol)
Pure Country-Best Of The '90s-#2-C . . . . (Priority)
Soon
Tanya Tucker; *Soon* . . . . (Liberty)
Space Between, The
Dave Matthews Band; *Everyday* . . . . (RCA)
Standing In The Shadows Of Love
Barry White; *Barry White's Greatest Hits* . . . . (20th Century Fox)
I've Got So Much To Give . . . . (20th Century Fox)
Four Tops; *Four Tops' Greatest Hits* . . . . (Motown)
Four Tops Reach Out . . . . (Motown)
Four Tops-Anthology . . . . (Motown)
Motown Story-First 25 Years-C . . . . (Motown)
Motown Superstar Series-#14-Four Tops . . . . (Motown)
Rod Stewart; *Blondes Have More Fun* . . . .(Warner Bros.)
Step Into The Light
Dust For Life; *Dust For Life* . . . . (Wind-up)
Take Your Time
Judson Spence; *Judson Spence* . . . . (Atlantic)
That Girl Who Waits On Tables
Ronnie Milsap; *Collector's Series-Ronnie Milsap* . . . . (RCA)
Where My Heart Is . . . . (RCA)
There's A Fella Waitin' In Poughkeepsie
Pied Pipers; *Capitol Collectors Series-Pied Pipers* . . . . (Capitol)
These Are The Times
Dru Hill; *Enter The Dru* . . . .(Def Jam/RAL/Mercury/Island)
Tie A Yellow Ribbon Round The Ole Oak Tree
Dawn Featuring Tony Orlando; *'70s Party Killers-C* . . . . (Rhino)
Fantastic-#1-C . . . . (K-Tel)
Frank Sinatra; *Some Nice Things I've Missed* . . . . (Reprise)
Lawrence Welk; *Best Of Lawrence Welk-20 Great Hits* . . . . (Ranwood)
Sonny James & Karla Taylor; *Classic Country Duets-C* . . . . (Curb)
Till Then
Mills Brothers; *Best Of The Mills Brothers* . . . . (MCA)
Cab Driver . . . . (Ranwood)
Lazy River . . . .(MCA Special Prod.)
Mills Brothers . . . . (Everest)
Mills Brothers' Greatest Hits . . . . (MCA)
Till You Love Me
Reba McEntire; *Read My Mind* . . . . (MCA)
Time After Time
Cyndi Lauper; *Chicken Soup For The Woman's Soul-C* . . . . (Rhino)
She's So Unusual . . . . (Portrait)
Twelve Deadly Cyns...And Then Some . . . .(Epic)
Everything But The Girl; *Acoustic* . . . . (Atlantic)
INOJ & So So Def Bass All-Stars; *Time After Time (Maxi Single)* . . . .(So So Def/Columbia)
Miles Davis; *Live Around The World* . . . .(Warner Bros.)
You're Under Arrest . . . . (Columbia)

Time Is Wasting
Carlo; *20 Great Love Songs Of The '50s & '60s-#1-C* . . . .(Laurie)
22 Leaders Of The Pack-#1-C . . . .(Laurie)
Time Waits For No One
Rolling Stones; *It's Only Rock 'N Roll* . . . . (Rolling Stones)
Sucking In The Seventies . . . . (Rolling Stones)
Time Waits For No One
Hilltoppers; *P.S. I Love You (The Best Of The Hilltoppers)*. . . . .(Varese Vintage)
Tired Of Waiting For You
Kinks; *History Of British Rock-#3-C* . . . . (Rhino)
Kinda Kinks . . . . (Rhino)
Kinks' Greatest Hits . . . . (Rhino)
To Love You More
Celine Dion with The Bee Gees; *All The Way...A Decade Of Song* . . . . (550 Music)
Let's Talk About Love-C . . . .(550 Music)
To The Moon And Back
Savage Garden; *Savage Garden* . . . . (Columbia)
Tomorrow
Silverchair; *Frogstomp* . . . . (Epic)
Too Little Too Late
Barenaked Ladies; *Maroon* . . . . (Reprise)
Travelin' Soldier
Bruce Robison; *Bruce Robison* . . . . (Vireo)
Trials
Jackopierce; *Finest Hour* . . . . (A&M)
Tropicalia
Beck; *Mutations* . . . .(David Geffen Co.)
Twilight Time
Platters; *Pick Of The Platters* . . . . (Fifty One West)
Platters . . . . (Everest)
Platters-16 Greatest Hits . . . . (Trip)
Platters-Anthology . . . . (Rhino)
Sold Out . . . . (Fifty One West)
Willie Nelson; *What A Wonderful World* . . . . (Columbia)
Unchained Melody
Elvis Presley; *Always On My Mind* . . . . (RCA)
Moody Blue . . . . (RCA)
The Great Performances . . . . (RCA)
George Benson; *Livin' Inside Your Love* . . . .(Warner Bros.)
LeAnn Rimes; *LeAnn Rimes-Early Years-Unchained Melody* . . . . .(MCG/Curb)
Platters; *Platters Greatest Hits* . . . . (Everest)
Red Sails In The Sunset . . . . (Allegiance)
Richard Clayderman; *Richard Clayderman Plays Love Songs Of The World* . . . . (Columbia)
Righteous Brothers; *Righteous Brothers' Greatest Hits* . . . . (Verve)
ST/Ghost . . . .(Varese Sarabande)
Willie Nelson; *Stardust* . . . . (Legacy)
Unforgiven II
Metallica; *Reload* . . . . (Elektra)
Until She Comes
Psychedelic Furs; *World Outside* . . . . (Columbia)
Until You Come Back To Me
Aretha Franklin; *Aretha Franklin-30 Greatest Hits* . . . . (Rhino)
Best Of Aretha Franklin . . . . (Atlantic)
Golden Age Of Black Music-1970-1975-C . . . . (Atlantic)
Basia; *Brave New Hope* . . . . (Epic)
London Warsaw New York . . . . (Epic)
Hil St. Soul; *Soul Organic* . . . .(Dome/Select-O-Hits)
Miki Howard; *Miki Howard* . . . . (Atlantic)
Stevie Wonder; *Stevie Wonder-Love Songs-20 Classic Hits* . . . . (Motown)
Wait
Beatles; *Beatles-Box Set* . . . . (Capitol)
Rubber Soul . . . . (Capitol)
Wait
Sarah McLachlan; *Fumbling Towards Ecstasy* . . . . (Arista)
Wait
Huffamoose; *We've Been Had Again* . . . .(Interscope)
Wait
Seven Mary Three; *Economy Of Sound* . . . .(Mammoth)
Wait A Minute
Ray-J; *This Ain't A Game* . . . .(Atlantic)
Wait Till The Sun Shines Nellie
Joan Morris & William Bolcom; *After The Ball* . . . . (Nonesuch)
Wait Until Tomorrow
Jimi Hendrix; *Axis: Bold As Love* . . . . (Reprise)
Jimi Hendrix Experience; *Radio One* . . . . (Rykodisc)
Waitin' For A Train
Merle Haggard & The Strangers; *Train Whistle Blues* . . . . (Rounder)
Waitin' For The Bus
ZZ Top; *Best Of ZZ Top* . . . . (Warner Bros.)
Six Pack . . . . (Warner Bros.)
Tres Hombres . . . . (Warner Bros.)
Waitin' In School
Rick Nelson; *Legends Of Rock Guitar-'50s-#2-C* . . . . (Rhino)
Ricky Nelson; *Ricky Nelson-Legendary Masters* . . . . (EMI)
Waitin' In Your Welfare Line
Buck Owens & The Buckaroos; *Billboard Top Country Hits-1966-C* . . . (Rhino)

Buck Owens & The Buckaroos-Live At
Carnegie Hall . . . . (Country Music Foundation)
Buck Owens Collection-1959-1990 . . . . (Rhino)

Waiting
Nilsson; *Harry*. (Dunhill Compact Classics)

Waiting For A Star To Fall
Boy Meets Girl; *Nipper's Greatest Hits Of The '80s-C* . . . .(RCA)
Reel Life . . . .(RCA)

Waiting For A Train
Jimmie Rodgers; *Jimmie Rodgers-Early Years-1928-1929* . . . . (Rounder)
This Is Jimmie Rodgers . . . .(RCA)

Waiting For A Train
Boz Scaggs; *Boz Scaggs* . . . . (Atlantic)

Waiting For Love
Alias; *Alias* . . . . (EMI)

Waiting For Love
3T; *ST/Men In Black* . . . . (Columbia)

Waiting For Sun
Jayhawks; *Hollywood Town Hall* . . . .(Def American)

Waiting For The Day
Gerry Rafferty; *City To City* . . . . (EMI)

Waiting For The End Of The World
Elvis Costello; *My Aim Is True* . . . . (Columbia)

Waiting For The Light To Change
Tonic; *Sugar* . . . . (Universal)

Waiting For The Light To Turn Green
Gretchen Peters; *The Secret Of Life* . . . .(Purple Crayon Prod.)

Waiting For The Moon
Bruce Cockburn; *Trouble With Normal*. . . . . (Columbia)

Waiting For The Rain To Fall
Chris Isaak; *Chris Isaak*. . . . . (Warner Bros.)

Waiting For The Robert E. Lee
Al Jolson; *My Mammy*. (MCA Special Prod.)
Eddie Cantor; *Centennial Celebration* . . . .(RCA)

Waiting For The Russians
Trees; *Forrest Fires*. . . . . (Adelphi)

Waiting For The Sun
Doors; *Best Of The Doors* . . . . (Elektra)
Doors-Classics . . . . (Elektra)
Morrison Hotel/Hard Rock Cafe . . . . (Elektra)

Waiting For The Sun To Shine
John Conlee; *In My Eyes* . . . . (MCA)
Lionel Cartwright; *Chasin' The Sun* . . . . (MCA)
Reba McEntire; *Reba Nell McEntire* . . . . (Mercury)
Ricky Skaggs; *Favorite Country Songs* . . . . (Epic)
Waiting For The Sun To Shine . . . . (Epic)

Waiting For The Tide To Turn
Robert Cray Band; *Bad Influence* . . . . (Hightone)

Waiting For The UFO's
Graham Parker And The Rumour; *Squeezing Out Sparks* . . . .(Arista)

Waiting For The Worms
Pink Floyd; *The Wall* . . . . (Columbia)
Roger Waters; *The Wall-Live In Berlin* . . . . (Mercury)

Waiting For Tonight
Tom Petty; *Playback* . . . . (MCA)

Waiting For Tonight
Jennifer Lopez; *Now That's What I Call Music!-#4-C*. . . . .(Virgin)
On The 6 . . . . (Work)

Waiting Game
Swing Out Sister; *Kaleidoscope World* . . . . (Fontana)

Waiting In The Wings
BBM; *Around The Next Dream*. . . . .(Virgin)

Waiting On A Friend
Rolling Stones; *Rewind (1971-1984)*. . . . . (Rolling Stones)
Tattoo You . . . . (Virgin)

Walk On By
Leroy Van Dyke; *Billboard Top Country Hits-1961-C* . . . . (Rhino)
Country Classics-C. . . . .(Sun)
Country Music Classics-#2-1960-1965-C . . . . (K-Tel)
Souvenirs Of Music City U.S.A.-C . . . . (Plantation)

Wasting My Time
Default; *Fallout* . . . .(TVT)

Watin' For The Phone To Ring
Patty Loveless; *Up Against My Heart* . . . . (MCA)
Ronna Reeves; *What Comes Naturally* . . . . (Mercury)

Welcome To My World
Eddy Arnold; *Eddy Arnold-Pure Gold* . . . . (RCA)
The World Of Eddy Arnold . . . . (RCA)
Welcome To My World . . . . (RCA)
Elvis Presley; *Aloha from Hawaii via Satellite* . . . . (RCA)
Welcome To My World . . . . (RCA)
Jim Reeves; *Am I That Easy To Forget* . . . . (RCA)
Best Of Jim Reeves . . . . (RCA)
Jim Reeves . . . . (RCA)
Jim Reeves-Legendary Performer . . . . (RCA)

Wells Fargo Wagon
Original Broadway Cast; *The Music Man* . . . .(Angel)
Original Cast; *The Music Man*. (Gold Rush)

What A Dream
Conway Twitty; *Conway Twitty's Greatest Hits* . . . .(Curb)
Patti Page; *45-#70416* . . . .(Mercury)
Slim Harpo; *Raining In My Heart* . . . . (Hip-O)

Whatever It Takes
Sinead Lohan; *No Mermaid* . . . . (Grapevine)

When I Get Home
Beatles; *Beatles-Box Set*. . . . .(Capitol)
Something New . . . .(Capitol)

Where Did You Go?
Full Devil Jacket; *Full Devil Jacket* . . . . (Island/IDJMG)

Where The Blue Of The Night Meets The Gold Of The Day
Bing Crosby; *All-Time Best Of*. . . . .(Curb)
Best Of Bing Crosby . . . . (MCA)
Where The Blue Of The Night Meets The Gold Of The Day . . . . (Biograph)

Whispering Pines
Band; *The Band* . . . .(Capitol)

Will He Wait A Little Longer
Stanley Brothers; *Stanley Series-Vol. 1-#3* . . . . (Copper Creek)

World Is Waiting For The Sunrise
Benny Goodman; *I Like Jazz-Essence Of Benny Goodman* . . . .(Columbia)
Benny Goodman Orchestra & Quartet; *Let's Dance* . . . . (Laserlight)
Les Paul & Mary Ford; *The World Is Waiting For The Sunrise* . . . . . (Laserlight)
Roy Clark & Buck Trent; *Banjo Bandit* . . . .(MCA)

World Without Love, A
Peter And Gordon; *Billboard Top Pop Hits-1964-C* . . . .(Rhino)
History Of British Rock-#1-C . . . .(Rhino)
Peter & Gordon's Greatest Hits . . . .(CEMA Special Prod.)

Wouldn't It Be Nice
Beach Boys; *Absolutely Best-#2*. . . . .(Capitol)
Made In The U.S.A. . . . . (Capitol)
Pet Sounds. . . . . (Capitol)
Still Cruisin' . . . . (Capitol)

www.Memory
Alan Jackson; *Under The Influence* . . . .(Arista)

You Better Wait
Steve Perry; *For The Love Of Strange Medicine* . . . .(Columbia)

You Can't Hurry Love
Diana Ross; *Diana Ross-The Ultimate Collection* . . . .(Motown)
Diana Ross & The Supremes; *16 #1 Hits From The Early '60s-C* . . . . .(Motown)
Phil Collins; *Hello, I Must Be Going* . . . . (Atlantic)

Younger Girl
Critters; *Sixties Rule! Chapter Two-C* . . . . (One Way)
Lovin' Spoonful; *Lovin' Spoonful-Anthology* . . . .(Rhino)

WAITRESSES, Waiters

**See Also: BARS, FOOD & BEVERAGES (various),
RESTAURANTS, WORK**

Beer And Bones
John Michael Montgomery; *John Michael Montgomery's
Greatest Hits* . . . . (Atlantic)
Life's A Dance . . . . (Atlantic)

Chain Of Love
Clay Walker; *Live, Laugh, Love*. (Giant)

Country Bumpkin
Cal Smith; *16 Top Country Hits-#1-C* . . . . (MCA)
Country's Greatest Hits-#2-C . . . . (MCA Special Prod.)
Grand Ole Opry-75 Years-#2-C . . . . (MCA)

Easy On The Pain
Michael Martin Murphey; *Cowboy Songs Four* . . . . (Valley Entert.)

Halfway Home Cafe
Ricky Skaggs and Kentucky Thunder; *History Of The Future* . . .(Skaggs Family)

Invitation To The Blues
Holly Cole; *Temptation* . . . . (Metro Blue)
Tom Waits; *Small Change* . . . . (Asylum)

Picture Postcards From L.A.
Joshua Kadison; *Painted Desert Serenade*. . . . .(SBK)

She Works Hard For The Money
Donna Summer; *I Am Woman-C* . . . . (Nick At Nite)
She Works Hard For The Money . . . .(Mercury)
Summer Collection . . . .(Mercury)

Sweetheart
Dan Hicks & His Hot Licks; *Last Train To Hicksville* . . . . (MCA)
Maria Muldaur; *Waitress In The Donut Shop* . . . . (Warner Archives)

That Girl Who Waits On Tables
Ronnie Milsap; *Collector's Series-Ronnie Milsap*. . . . . (RCA)
Where My Heart Is . . . . (RCA)

Theme From "Alice"
Original Soundtrack; *Television's Greatest Hits-#6-Remote Control-C* . . .(TVT)

Tomb Of The Unknown Love
Cassell Webb; *Songs Of A Stranger* . . . . (Venture)
Kenny Rogers; *The Heart Of The Matter* . . . . (RCA)

WALLS

See Also: **BUILDING & CONSTRUCTION, HOUSES, PRISON, STUCK**

Another Brick In The Wall, Part 2
Class Of '99; *ST/The Faculty* . . . . (Columbia)
Pink Floyd; *Collection Of Great Dance Songs* . . . . (Columbia)
   Delicate Sound Of Thunder . . . . (Columbia)
   The Wall. . . . . (Columbia)
Roger Waters; *The Wall-Live In Berlin*. . . . . (Mercury)
Flowers On The Wall
Eric Heatherly; *Swimming In Champagne* . . . . (Mercury)
Statler Brothers; *All Time Legends Of Country Music-C* . . . . (Legacy)
   Best Of The Statler Brothers . . . . (Mercury)
   Billboard Top Country Hits-1966-C . . . . (Rhino)
   Columbia Country Classics-#3-Americana-C . . . . (Columbia)
   Pop Classics Of The '60s-C . . . . (Columbia)
Hello Walls
Faron Young; *Billboard Top Country Hits-1961-C* . . . . (Rhino)
Willie Nelson; *Essential Willie Nelson* . . . . (RCA)
   Willie Nelson-Greatest Songs . . . . (Curb)
If Walls Could Talk
Little Milton; *If Walls Could Talk* . . . . (Chess)
   Little Milton's Greatest Hits . . . . (Chess)
Ry Cooder; *Paradise And Lunch* . . . . (Reprise)
If Walls Could Talk
Celine Dion; *All The Way...A Decade Of Song*. . . . . (550 Music)
It's OK
Tracy Chapman; *Telling Stories* . . . . (Elektra)
Knock Down Walls
Tonic; *Sugar*. . . . . (Universal)
Lift Up Every Stone
John Hiatt; *Crossing Muddy Waters* . . . . (Vanguard)
Lonely
Tracy Lawrence; *Lessons Learned* . . . . (Atlantic)
Off The Wall
Jacksons; *Jacksons Live* . . . . (Epic)
Michael Jackson; *Off The Wall* . . . .(Epic)
Only God Knows Why
Kid Rock; *Devil Without A Cause*. . . . .(Top Dog/Lava/Atlantic)
Original Prankster
Offspring; *Conspiracy Of One* . . . . (Columbia)
Paper Walls
Marc Cohn; *Rainy Season*. . . . . (Atlantic)
Piss On The Wall
J. Geils Band; *Freeze-Frame* . . . .(EMI)
Walls
Tom Petty And The Heartbreakers; *ST/She's The One* . . . .(Warner Bros.)
Walls
Pamela Rose; *Morpheus* . . . . (Grace)
What Do I Know
Ricochet; *Pure Country-Best Of The '90s-#2-C* . . . . (Priority)
   Ricochet. . . . . (Columbia)
Wonderwall
Oasis; *What's The Story Morning Glory?* . . . . (Epic)
World Leader Pretend
R.E.M.; *Green* . . . .(Warner Bros.)

WAR, Army, Battles, Bombs, Military, Soldiers, Surrender, Veterans' Day

See Also: **COUNTRIES: A-Z, COUNTRIES: AMERICA, COUNTRIES: VIETNAM, DANGER & DISASTER, DEATH, DRAFT, GUNS, FIGHT, FREEDOM, HATE, HELP, HEROISM, NUCLEAR ENERGY, PATRIOTISM, PEACE, POLICE, POLITICS (various), PROTEST**

1812 Overture
New York Philharmonic & Leonard Bernstein; *Conducts*
   Tchaikovsky . . . . (Columbia)
   Great Tchaikovsky . . . . (Columbia)
   Overtures and Tone Poems . . . . (Columbia)
   Tchaikovsky's Greatest Hits-#1 . . . . (Columbia)
   Various Overtures . . . . (Columbia)
19
Paul Hardcastle; *Paul Hardcastle* . . . .(Chrysalis)
1959
John Anderson; *Country Love Songs-#3-C*. . . . .(Warner Bros.)
   John Anderson's Greatest Hits . . . .(Warner Bros.)
1983... (A Merman I Should Turn To Be)
Jimi Hendrix Experience; *Electric Ladyland* . . . . (Reprise)
50,000 Names
George Jones; *The Rock: Stone Cold Country 2001* . . . . (BNA)

Abolitionist Hymn
Hermes Nye; *Ballads Of The Civil War-#1 & 2*. . . . . . .(Smithsonian Folkways)
Ain't Gonna Study War No More
Nat ''King'' Cole; *Every Time I Feel The Spirit* . . . . (Capitol)
Weavers; *Reunion-At Carnegie Hall-1963* . . . . (Vanguard)
Alice's Restaurant Massacree
Arlo Guthrie; *Alice's Restaurant*. . . . . (Reprise)
   Best Of Arlo Guthrie. . . . . (Warner Bros.)
All Is Fair In Love And War
Ronnie Milsap; *Club* . . . .(RCA)
All Quiet Along The Potomac Tonight
Hermes Nye; *Ballads Of The Civil War-#1 & 2*. . . . . . .(Smithsonian Folkways)
Anchors Aweigh
Firehouse Five Plus Two; *Goes To Sea* . . . . (Good Time Jazz)
Original Soundtrack; *Top Ten College Fight Songs* . . . . (K-Tel)
Pat Boone; *Star Spangled Banner* . . . . (Word)
Angels Of Mercy
Glenn Miller & His Orchestra; *Complete Glenn Miller & His*
   Orchestra. . . . . (Bluebird)
Anne Frank Story
Human Sexual Response; *Fig. 15* . . . . (Eat)
Another Old Soldier
Mark Collie; *Hardin County Line* . . . . (MCA)
Another One In The Dark
Wallflowers; *The Wallflowers*. . . . .(Virgin)
Any Bonds Today?
Andrews Sisters; *Swing Out To Victory: Songs Of World*
   War II-C . . . .(ISD/Intersound)
Barry Wood; *78-#27478* . . . .(Victor)
Bing Crosby; *Original Soundtrack Sessions* . . . .(Vintage Jazz Classics)
Army
Ben Folds Five; *The Unauthorized Biography Of Reinhold*
   Messner . . . .(550 Music)
Army Air Corps
Fred Waring's Pennsylvanians; *Very Best Of Fred Waring & The*
   Pennsylvanians . . . .(Reader's Digest Music)
Glenn Miller; *Best Of The Lost Recordings And The Secret*
   Broadcasts. . . . . (RCA Victor)
   V-Disc Recordings-Glenn Miller . . . . (Collector's Choice)
Army Blues
Bobby Blue Bland; *I Pity The Fool/Duke Recordings-#1* . . . . (MCA)
Army Dreamers
Kate Bush; *Never For Ever* . . . . (EMI)
   The Whole Story . . . . (EMI)
Army Life
Leadbelly; *Easy Rider* . . . .(Smithsonian Folkways)
Army Man In Vietnam
Big Joe Williams; *Shake Your Boogie* . . . .(Arhoolie)
   Thinking Of What They Did To Me . . . .(Arhoolie)
Army Of The Free
Tennessee Ernie Ford; *Tennessee Ernie Ford Sings Songs Of The*
   Civil War . . . . (Capitol)
Army Song
Original Cast; *Threepenny Opera* . . . .(Polydor)
At War With The World
Foreigner; *Foreigner* . . . .(Atlantic)
Atlanta Burned Again Last Night
Atlanta; *Pictures* . . . . (MCA)
Atlanta's Burning Down
Dickey Betts & Great Southern; *Dickey Betts & Great Southern* . . . . (Arista)
Randy Howard; *All-American Redneck*. . . . . (Warner Bros.)
Ballad For A Soldier
Leon Russell & Marc Benno; *Asylum Choir II* . . . . (MCA)
Ballad Of Davy Crockett
Bill Hayes; *Songs Of The West-#4-Movie & Television Themes-C* . . . . . . (Rhino)
Fess Parker; *16 Most Requested Songs Of The '50s-#1-C* . . . . (Legacy)
   Columbia Country Classics-#3-Americana-C . . . . (Columbia)
   Hollywood Magic-1950s-C . . . . (Columbia)
Kentucky HeadHunters; *Electric Barnyard* . . . . (Mercury)
Mac Wiseman; *45-#1240* . . . . (Dot)
Original Soundtrack; *Television's Greatest Hits-#4-Black & White*
   Classics-C . . . . (TVT)
Tennessee Ernie Ford; *Capitol Collectors Series-Tennessee*
   Ernie Ford . . . . (Capitol)
Ballad Of Ira Hayes, The
Johnny Cash; *The Man In Black-His Greatest Hits* . . . . (Legacy)
Peter La Farge; *Best Of Broadside 1962-1968: Anthems Of The American*
   Underground From The Pages Of Broadside
   Magazine-C . . . .(Smithsonian Folkways)
Ballad Of The Green Berets
Barry Sadler; *Cruisin'-1966-C* . . . . (Increase)
   Hits Of The Sixties-C . . . . (Intercom Music)
   More American Graffiti-#4-C . . . . (MCA)
   Nipper's Greatest Hits Of The '60s-#2-C . . . . (RCA)
   Super Hits-#3-C . . . . (Gusto)
Bang The Drum Slowly
Emmylou Harris; *Red Dirt Girl* . . . . (Nonesuch)
Battle Cry Of Freedom
Mormon Tabernacle Choir; *God Bless America* . . . .(Sony Music Classical)

Mormon Tabernacle Choir's Greatest Hits . . . . (Columbia)
Songs Of The North & South 1861-1965. . . . . (Columbia)
The Mormon Tabernacle Choir Album. . . . . (Columbia)

Battle Hymn Of The Republic, The
Charlie Sexton; *Charlie Sexton* . . . . (MCA)
Judy Collins; *Songs Of The Civil War-C* . . . . (Columbia)
Mormon Tabernacle Choir; *God Bless America* . . . .(Sony Music Classical)
Stars And Stripes Forever . . . . (Columbia)
National Philharmonic Orchestra & Chorus; *Stars And Stripes*
Forever-#2-C . . . . (Volcano Entertainment)
Original Soundtrack; *School Days-Kids Classics* . . . .(Benson)
Pat Boone; *Star Spangled Banner* . . . . (Word)

Battle Of Atlanta
Reno & Smiley; *1983 Collector's Edition-#2* . . . . (Gusto)

Battle Of Bunker Hill
Jim Burroughs; *Songs Of Rebellion* . . . . (Audio Fidelity)

Battle Of Glass Tears
King Crimson; *Lizard* . . . . (Editions E.G.)

Battle Of New Orleans
Chet Atkins & The Boston Pops; *Best Of Chet Atkins & The*
Boston Pops . . . . (RCA)
Johnny Horton; *American Originals-Johnny Horton* . . . . (Columbia)
Johnny Horton's Greatest Hits . . . . (Columbia)
Radio Classics Of The '50s-C . . . . (Columbia)
Nitty Gritty Dirt Band; *Dirt, Silver & Gold* . . . . (One Way)
Dream . . . .(United Artists)
Stars And Stripes Forever . . . . (Capitol)

Battle Of Trenton
Jim Burroughs; *Songs Of Rebellion* . . . . (Audio Fidelity)

Battle Of Who Could Care Less
Ben Folds Five; *Whatever And Ever Amen* . . . . (Caroline/550)

Being At War With Each Other
Barbra Streisand; *The Way We Were* . . . . (Columbia)
Carole King; *Fantasy*. . . . . (Epic Ode)

Billy Don't Be A Hero
Bo Donaldson & The Heywoods; *Super Hits Of The '70s-Have A Nice*
Day-#13-C . . . . (Rhino)

Blow Up The Outside World
Soundgarden; *A-Sides* . . . . (A&M)
Down On The Upside . . . . (A&M)

Bomb The Russians
Fear; *More Beer*. . . . .(Enigma)

Bomb! (These Sounds Fall Into My Mind)
Bucketheads; *All In The Mind* . . . . (Big Beat/Atlantic)

Bomb, The
L7; *Hungry For Stink*. . . . . (Slash)

Bomber Medley
James Gang; *Best Of The James Gang*. . . . . (MCA)
James Gang Rides Again . . . . (MCA)

Bombs Away
Police; *Zenyatta Mondatta*. . . . . (A&M)

Bombs Away
Bob Weir; *Heaven Help The Fool* . . . . (Arista)

Bonaparte's Retreat
Chieftains; *Bonaparte's Retreat* . . . .(Shanachie)
Glen Campbell; *Glen Campbell-Classics Collection* . . . . (Capitol)
Kay Starr; *Kay Starr's Greatest Hits* . . . . (Curb)
Sons Of The Pioneers; *Country & Western Memories*. . . . .(Pair)

Boogie Woogie Bugle Boy
Andrews Sisters; *Andrews Sisters-16 Great Performances*. . . . . (MCA)
Best Of The Andrews Sisters . . . . (MCA)
Boogie Woogie Bugle Girls . . . . (MCA)
Rarities . . . . (MCA)
Bette Midler; *Divine Miss M* . . . . (Atlantic)
Live At Last . . . . (Atlantic)
ST/Divine Madness. . . . . (Atlantic)

Born In The U.S.A.
Bruce Springsteen; *Born In The U.S.A.* . . . . (Columbia)
Bruce Springsteen's Greatest Hits . . . . (Columbia)
Tracks . . . . (Columbia)
Bruce Springsteen & The E Street Band; *Bruce Springsteen & The E Street*
Band Live/1975-85 . . . . (Legacy)

Bring Them Home
Pete Seeger; *Young Vs. Old* . . . . (Out Of Print)

British Grenadiers
Cambridge Singers; *The Lark In The Clear Air* . . . . (Collegium)

Brother, Can You Spare A Dime
Bing Crosby; *Bing Crosby-16 Most Requested Songs* . . . . (Legacy)
Odetta/Dr. John/John Campbell/Rufus Reid; *Strike A Deep Chord-Blues For*
The Homeless-C . . . . (Justice)
Peter, Paul & Mary; *See What Tomorrow Brings* . . . . (Warner Bros.)
Weavers; *Weavers' Greatest Hits* . . . . (Vanguard)

Brothers Under The Bridge
Bruce Springsteen; *Tracks*. . . . . (Columbia)

Bugle Call Rag
Benny Goodman; *Stompin' At The Savoy* . . . . (Bluebird)
Enoch Light & His Light Brigade; *Big Band Hits Of The '30s-#2* . . . . (Project 3)
New Orleans Rhythm Kings; *New Orleans Rhythm Kings* . . . . (Milestone)

Burning Of Atlanta
Claude King; *American Originals-Claude King* . . . .(Columbia)

Business Goes On As Usual
Roberta Flack; *Chapter Two* . . . . (Atlantic)

California
Joni Mitchell; *Blue* . . . . (Reprise)

Car Bomb
Negativeland; *Escape From Noise* . . . . (SST)

Cast The First Stone
Angel; *On Earth As It Is In Heaven* . . . . (Casablanca)

Christmas In Vietnam
Johnny & Jon; *45-#776* . . . . (Jewel)

Civil Defense Sign, The
Mark Spoelstra; *Best Of Broadside 1962-1968: Anthems Of The American*
Underground From The Pages Of Broadside
Magazine-C . . . . (Smithsonian Folkways)

Comin' In On A Wing & A Prayer
Anita Ellis; *Songs That Won The War-C* . . . . . . (Columbia River Entert. Group)
Anne Shelton; *V-E Day 50th Anniversary-The Musical*
Memories-C . . . . (Living Era)
Four Vagabonds; *The Victory Collection: The Smithsonian Remembers When*
America Went To War-C . . . . (RCA)
Ry Cooder; *Boomer's Story* . . . . (Reprise)

Coming Home Soldier
Bobby Vinton; *Bobby Vinton's All-Time Greatest Hits* . . . .(Epic)

Conquistador
Procol Harum; *Best Of Procol Harum* . . . .(A&M)
Procol Harum Live In Concert with the Edmonton Symphony . . . . (A&M)
Procol Harum-Classics-#17 . . . .(A&M)

Cowards Over Pearl Harbor
Wilma Lee Cooper; *Wilma Lee Cooper* . . . .(Rounder)

Cruel War
Peter, Paul & Mary; *Peter, Paul and Mary*. . . . .(Warner Bros.)

Daddy's Last Letter (Private First Class John H. McCormick)
Tex Ritter; *45-#1267* . . . .(Capitol)

Davy's Dinghy
Ruth Wallis; *Dr. Demento Presents The Greatest Novelty Records-#2-*
1950s-C . . . .(Rhino)
Dr. Demento's Dementia Royale-C. . . . .(Rhino)

Days Of Our Livez
Bone Thugs-N-Harmony; *The Collection-#1*. . . . .(Ruthless)

Dear Uncle Sam
Loretta Lynn; *Honky Tonk Girl: The Loretta Lynn Collection* . . . . (MCA)
Loretta Lynn's Greatest Hits . . . . (MCA)

Deck Of Cards
"T" Texas Tyler; *45-#2060.* . . . . (Gusto)
Bill Anderson; *American Music Greatest Hits-C* . . . .(Curb)
Best Of Bill Anderson . . . .(Curb)
Tex Ritter; *Capitol Collectors Series-Tex Ritter* . . . .(Capitol)
Tex Ritter's Greatest Hits . . . . (Curb)

Desaperecidos (Central America)
Little Steven; *Voice Of America* . . . .(Razor & Tie)

Distant Drums
Jim Reeves; *Best Of The Best Of Jim Reeves* . . . .(King)
Billboard Top Country Hits-1966-C . . . .(Rhino)
Essential Jim Reeves . . . . (RCA)

Dixie
Black Oak Arkansas; *Best Of Black Oak Arkansas* . . . .(Atco)
Hot & Nasty-Best Of Black Oak Arkansas. . . . .(Rhino)
Boston Pops Orchestra/Arthur Fiedler; *American Salute* . . . .(RCA)
Lee Greenwood; *American Patriot* . . . .(Capitol)
Mormon Tabernacle Choir; *Mormon Tabernacle Choir's Greatest*
Hits-#2 . . . .(Columbia)
Songs Of The Civil War And Stephen Foster
Favorites . . . . (Sony Music Classical)
Tennessee Ernie Ford; *Tennessee Ernie Ford Sings Songs Of The*
Civil War . . . .(Capitol)

Done With Bonaparte
Mark Knopfler; *Golden Heart* . . . . (Warner Bros.)

Dreams Of Wounded Knee
Bill Miller; *The Red Road* . . . . (Warner Western)

Dying Soldier
Christy Moore; *Christy Moore*. . . . . (Atlantic)

English Civil War
Clash; *Give 'Em Enough Rope* . . . .(Epic)
The Story Of The Clash, Volume 1. . . . .(Epic)

Enlisted Men's Mess
Glenn Miller; *Major Glenn Miller/Army Air Force Band* . . . .(Bluebird)

Eve Of Destruction
Barry McGuire; *Billboard Top Rock 'N' Roll Hits-1965-C* . . . . (Rhino)
Cruisin'-1965-C . . . .(Increase)
Good Feeling Music Of The Big Chill Generation-#3-C. . . . .(Motown)
Songs Of Protest-C . . . .(Rhino)
Vintage Music-#9 & 10-C . . . . (MCA)
Dickies; *Great Dictations (Definitive Collection)* . . . .(A&M)
Incredible Shrinking Dickies. . . . .(A&M)
Turtles; *Turtle Wax-Best Of The Turtles-#2* . . . . (Rhino)
Turtlesized. . . . . (Rhino)

Fall Of Charleston
Tennessee Ernie Ford; *Tennessee Ernie Ford Sings Songs Of The Civil War*. . . . . (Capitol)
Fall Of Saigon
Original London Cast; *Miss Saigon* . . . . (Geffen)
Fightin' Side Of Me
Merle Haggard; *All American*. . . . . (Capitol)
Best Of Merle Haggard . . . . (Capitol)
Capitol Collectors Series-Merle Haggard. . . . . (Capitol)
The Fightin' Side Of Me . . . . (Capitol)
Merle Haggard & The Strangers; *Songs I'll Always Sing* . . . . (Capitol)
Folk Song Army
Tom Lehrer; *That Was The Year That Was*. . . . . (Reprise)
For Your Country And My Country
Frances Alda; *78-#64689* . . . . (Victor)
Peerless Quartet; *78-#2273*. . . . . (Columbia)
Fortress Around Your Heart
Sting; *Dream Of The Blue Turtles* . . . . (A&M)
Fields Of Gold-The Best Of Sting 1984-1994 . . . . (A&M)
Forty Thousand Headmen
Traffic; *Traffic* . . . . (Island)
Welcome To The Canteen . . . . (Island)
Foxhole
Television; *Adventure*. . . . . (Elektra)
From A Distance
Bette Midler; *Some People's Lives* . . . . (Atlantic)
Byrds; *20 Essential Tracks From The Box Set* . . . . (Columbia)
The Byrds . . . . (Columbia)
Judy Collins; *Fires Of Eden* . . . . (Columbia)
Kathy Mattea; *Time Passes By* . . . . (Mercury)
Nanci Griffith; *Lone Star State Of Mind* . . . . (MCA)
One Fair Summer Evening. . . . . (MCA)
Front Line
Stevie Wonder; *Original Musiquarium* . . . . (Motown)
Galveston Bay
Bruce Springsteen; *The Ghost Of Tom Joad* . . . . (Columbia)
General Custer
Tom Paxton; *How Come The Sun* . . . . (Out Of Print)
Goodbye Blue Sky
Pink Floyd; *The Wall* . . . . (Columbia)
Roger Waters; *The Wall-Live In Berlin*. . . . . (Mercury)
Guerrilla Radio
Rage Against The Machine; *The Battle Of Los Angeles* . . . . (Epic)
Guns Of Love
Pamela Rose; *Morpheus* . . . . (Grace)
Hawaiian War Chant
Bette Midler; *Live At Last*. . . . . (Atlantic)
Tommy Dorsey; *Complete Tommy Dorsey-#8* . . . . (RCA)
This Is Tommy Dorsey . . . . (RCA)
Hay Una Mujer Desaparecida
Holly Near; *Imagine My Surprise*. . . . . (Redwood)
Holly Near & Ronnie Gilbert; *Lifeline* . . . . (Redwood)
Heartbreak U.S.A.
Kitty Wells; *I Love Country-Hits Of The '60s-#1-C* . . . . . . (Priority)
Kitty Wells' Greatest Songs . . . . (Curb)
The Country Music Hall Of Fame-Kitty Wells . . . . (MCA Special Prod.)
Hell No, I Ain't Gonna Go
Matt Jones & Elaine Laron; *Best Of Broadside 1962-1968: Anthems Of The American Underground From The Pages Of Broadside Magazine-C* . . . . (Smithsonian Folkways)
Hiroshima
Todd Rundgren's Utopia; *Ra* . . . . (Rhino)
Hiroshima, Nagasaki Russian Roulette
Jim Page; *Best Of Broadside 1962-1968: Anthems Of The American Underground From The Pages Of Broadside Magazine-C* . . . . (Smithsonian Folkways)
I Don't Want To Be A Soldier
John Lennon/Plastic Ono Band; *Imagine* . . . . (Capitol)
I Don't Want To Wait
Paula Cole; *Live On Letterman-From The Late Show*. . . . . . (Reprise)
Songs From Dawson's Creek. . . . . (Sony Music Soundtrax)
This Fire . . . . (Imago)
I Surrender Dear
Bing Crosby; *Pennies From Heaven*. . . . . (Pro-Arte)
Where The Blue Of The Night Meets The Gold Of The Day . . . . (Biograph)
Count Basie; *Basie & Zoot* . . . . (Pablo)
Jam-#3 . . . . (Pablo)
Loose Walk . . . . (Pablo)
Count Basie & His Kansas City 3; *For The Second Time* . . . . (Pablo)
Gus Arnheim & His Orchestra featuring Bing Crosby; *78-#22618* . . . . . (Victor)
Mel Torme; *Smooth As Velvet*. . . . . (Pickwick)
Rosemary Clooney; *Rosemary Clooney Sings Bing* . . . . . . (Concord Jazz)
I'd Surrender All
Randy Travis; *High Lonesome* . . . . (Warner Bros.)
If I Had A Rocket Launcher (Central America)
Bruce Cockburn; *Stealing Fire* . . . . (Columbia)
Waiting For A Miracle-Singles 1970-1987 . . . . (Gold Castle)
If The South Woulda Won
Hank Williams, Jr.; *Wild Streak* . . . . (WB/Curb)

I-Feel-Like-I'm-Fixin'-To-Die Rag
Country Joe & The Fish; *Country Joe & The Fish-Greatest Hits* . . . . (Vanguard)
Greatest '60s Folksingers-C . . . . (Vanguard)
I-Feel-Like-I'm-Fixin'-To-Die . . . . (Vanguard)
Life & Times Of Country Joe & The Fish . . . . (Vanguard)
More American Graffiti-#4-C . . . . (MCA)
Songs Of Protest-C. . . . . (Rhino)
ST/Woodstock. . . . . (Atlantic)
I'm Getting Tired So I Can Sleep
Dinah Shore; *The Eddie Cantor Radio Show-1942-1943* . . . . . . (Original Cast)
Immigrant Song
Led Zeppelin; *Led Zeppelin III* . . . . (Atlantic)
Led Zeppelin-Box Set . . . . (Atlantic)
In Germany Before The War
Randy Newman; *Little Criminals* . . . . (Warner Bros.)
In The Army Now
Big Bill Broonzy; *News & The Blues-Telling It Like It Is-C* . . . . . (Columbia)
In The Army Now
Status Quo; *Status Quo* . . . . (Mercury)
Indian War Whoop
John Hartford; *ST/O Brother, Where Art Thou?* . . . . (Mercury)
Israelis, Terrorists And Arabs
Jackie Mason; *ST/Brand New* . . . . (Sony Broadway)
It Ain't My Fault
Silkk The Shocker; *Charge It 2 Da Game* . . . . (No Limit/Priority)
John Brown's Body
Pete Seeger; *American Favorite Ballads-#3* . . . . (Smithsonian Folkways)
Sonny Terry & Brownie McGhee; *Every Tone A Testimony-C* . . . . . . (Smithsonian Folkways)
Johnny Has Gone For A Soldier
Jo Stafford; *American Folk Songs*. . . . . (Corinthian)
Join The Army
Suicidal Tendencies; *Join The Army* . . . . (Caroline)
Joshua Fought The Battle Of Jericho
Elvis Presley; *His Hand In Mine* . . . . (RCA)
Jordanaires; *Tribute To Elvis' Favorite Spirituals* . . . . (Step One)
New Messengers Of Happiness; *Swinging Gospel* . . . . (Alshire)
Pete Seeger; *20 Golden Pieces Of Pete Seeger* . . . . (Bulldog)
Sister Rosetta Tharpe; *Live At The Hot Club De France* . . . . . (Milan)
Kansas City Bomber
Phil Ochs; *The War Is Over-Best Of Phil Ochs* . . . . (A&M)
Kids Of The Baby Boom
Bellamy Brothers; *Bellamy Brothers' Greatest Hits-#3* . . . . . (MCA)
Country Rap . . . . (MCA)
MCA #1 Hits Of The '80s-#3-C . . . . (MCA Special Prod.)
Kill For Peace
Fugs; *Best Of Broadside 1962-1968: Anthems Of The American Underground From The Pages Of Broadside Magazine-C* . . . . . . (Smithsonian Folkways)
Fugs . . . . (ESP Disk)
Fugs 4 Rounders Score . . . . (ESP Disk)
Last Night I Had The Strangest Dream
Simon & Garfunkel; *Collected Works*. . . . . (Columbia)
Wednesday Morning 3 A.M. . . . . (Columbia)
Last Train To Nuremberg
Pete Seeger; *A Link In The Chain* . . . . (Legacy)
Lay Down Your Arms
Chordettes; *Best Of The Chordettes* . . . . (Rhino)
Lie On Lie
Chalk Farm; *Notwithstanding* . . . . (Columbia)
Life During Wartime
Talking Heads; *Fear Of Music* . . . . (Sire)
Name Of This Band Is Talking Heads. . . . . (Sire)
ST/Stop Making Sense . . . . (Sire)
Like A Soldier
Johnny Cash; *American Recordings* . . . . (American)
Lili Marlene
Marlene Dietrich; *Best Of Marlene Dietrich* . . . . (Columbia)
Essential Marlene Dietrich . . . . (Capitol)
Live At The Cafe De Paris . . . . (Columbia)
This Is Art Deco-C . . . . (Columbia)
Long Live Our Love
Shangri-Las; *Best Of The Shangri-Las* . . . . (Mercury)
Longest Day
Arthur Fiedler; *Motion Picture Classics-#2* . . . . (RCA Victor)
Mitch Miller; *Mitch Miller-The Gang & Orchestra-Greatest Hits* . . . (Columbia)
Paul Anka; *Paul Anka's 21 Golden Hits* . . . . (RCA)
Love Is A Battlefield
Pat Benatar; *Best Shots* . . . . (Chrysalis)
I Am Woman-C . . . . (Nick At Nite)
Live From Earth . . . . (Chrysalis)
Lucky Man
Emerson, Lake & Palmer; *Best Of Emerson, Lake & Palmer* . . . . . (Rhino)
Emerson, Lake & Palmer . . . . (Atlantic)
Mack The Bomb
Pete Seeger; *Best Of Broadside 1962-1968: Anthems Of The American Underground From The Pages Of Broadside Magazine-C* . . . . . . (Smithsonian Folkways)
Marines' Hymn
Mormon Tabernacle Choir; *God Bless America* . . . . (Sony Music Classical)

Stars And Stripes Forever . . . . (Columbia)
Masters Of War
Bob Dylan; *Biograph.* . . . . (Columbia)
Freewheelin'. . . . . (Columbia)
Real Live . . . . (Columbia)
Me & Crippled Soldiers
Merle Haggard; *American Music Greatest Hits-C.* . . . . (Curb)
Blue Jungle . . . . (Curb)
Meadowlands
101 Strings Orchestra; *Soul Of Russia* . . . . (Madacy)
Jefferson Airplane; *Volunteers* . . . . (RCA)
Meet De Boys On The Battlefront
Wild Tchoupitoulas; *Treacherous: A History Of The Neville Brothers* . . . (Rhino)
Wild Tchoupitoulas. . . . . (Island)
Military Madness
Graham Nash; *Bread & Roses Festival Of Acoustic Music-#2-C* . . . . . (Fantasy)
Songs For Beginners. . . . . (Atlantic)
Minstrel Boy
Boston Pops Orchestra/Arthur Fiedler; *Irish Album* . . . . (RCA)
Irish Night At The Pops. . . . . (RCA)
John McDermott; *Battlefields Of Green-Songs Of Love & Loss* . . . . (Angel)
Missing The War
Ben Folds Five; *Whatever And Ever Amen* . . . . (Caroline/550)
Moratorium
Buffy Sainte-Marie; *She Used To Wanna Be A Ballerina* . . . . (Vanguard)
More Than A Name On The Wall
Statler Brothers; *Statler Brothers' Greatest Hits* . . . . (Mercury)
Mr. Custer
Larry Verne; *Collectables Presents The History Of Rock-#10-C* . . (Collectables)
Dr. Demento Presents The Greatest Novelty Records-#3-1960s-C . . . . (Rhino)
Wacky Weirdos-C. . . . . (K-Tel)
My Daddy Was A Milkman
Kentucky HeadHunters; *Pickin' On Nashville* . . . . (Mercury)
My Little Marine
Jamie Horton; *45-#118* . . . . (Eric)
Napalm For Breakfast
Rhythm Devils; *Apocalypse Now Sessions* . . . . (Rykodisc)
Navy Blue
Diane Renay; *Growin' Up Too Fast-The Girl Group Anthology-C* . . . . (Mercury)
New Orleans Wins The War
Randy Newman; *Land Of Dreams* . . . . (Reprise)
New Soldiers Joy
Kentucky Colonels featuring Roland & Clarence White; *1965-1967* . . (Rounder)
Night They Drove Old Dixie Down
Band; *Best Of The Band.* . . . . (Capitol)
Rock Of Ages. . . . . (Capitol)
The Band. . . . . (Capitol)
The Band-Anthology-#1 . . . . (Capitol)
The Band-Gift Set . . . . (Capitol)
The Last Waltz . . . . (Warner Bros.)
Bob Dylan And The Band; *Before The Flood* . . . . (Columbia)
Joan Baez; *Country Music Album* . . . . (Vanguard)
From Every Stage . . . . (A&M)
Hits/Greatest & Others. . . . . (Vanguard)
Joan Baez-Classics-#8 . . . . (A&M)
No No No To Draft & War
Minutemen; *Ballot Result* . . . . (SST)
No Surrender
Bruce Springsteen; *Born In The U.S.A.* . . . . (Columbia)
North Won The War Again Last Night, The
Cal Smith; *Cal Smith* . . . . (First Generation)
Oh! How I Hate To Get Up In The Morning
Irving Berlin; *American Songbook Series-Irving Berlin* . . . . (Smithsonian Collection)
War Years-C. . . . . (ISD/Intersound)
Soundtrack; *American Musical Theater-#2.* . . . . (Smithsonian Collection)
Ohio
Crosby, Stills & Nash; *CSN* . . . . (Atlantic)
Crosby, Stills, Nash & Young; *4 Way Street.* . . . . (Atlantic)
So Far. . . . . (Atlantic)
Neil Young; *Decade* . . . . (Reprise)
ST/Journey Through The Past . . . . (Warner Bros.)
Old Man And Me
Hootie & The Blowfish; *Fairweather Johnson* . . . . (Atlantic)
Oliver's Army
Elvis Costello; *Girls Girls Girls* . . . . (Columbia)
Elvis Costello & The Attractions; *Armed Forces* . . . . (Rykodisc)
Best Of Elvis Costello & The Attractions . . . . (Columbia)
On, Brave Old Army Team
All-Star Inter-Conference Band; *College Marches At Halftime* . . . . (Alshire)
Glenn Miller; *Pennsylvania 6-5000-Sustaining Remotes* . . . . (Vintage Jazz Classics)
Original Soundtrack; *Top Ten College Fight Songs* . . . . (K-Tel)
One Man Army
Our Lady Peace; *Happiness...Is Not A Fish That You Can Catch* . . . . (Columbia)
One Tin Soldier
Coven; *Super Hits Of The '70s-Have A Nice Day-#7-C* . . . . (Rhino)
Orange Crush
R.E.M.; *Best Of MTV's 120 Minutes-#2-C* . . . . (Rhino)

Green. . . . . (Warner Bros.)
Osama, Yo' Mama
Ray Stevens; *Osama-Yo' Mama.* . . . .(Curb)
Out To Bomb Fresh Kings
Doctor Nerve; *Armed Observation.* . . . . (Cuneiform)
Over There
Glenn Miller; *Original Recordings-#3-Army/Air Force Band* . . . . (Pair)
Glenn Miller & His Army/Air Force Band; *Glenn Miller-A Legendary Performer-#3* . . . .(Bluebird)
Mormon Tabernacle Choir; *God Bless America* . . . . (Sony Music Classical)
Pass The Hand Grenade
Eric B. & Rakim; *Don't Sweat The Technique* . . . . (MCA)
Patriot's Dream
Arlo Guthrie; *Amigo.* . . . .(Koch International)
Gordon Lightfoot; *Don Quixote* . . . . (Warner Archives)
Pinkville Helicopter
Thom Parrott; *Best Of Broadside 1962-1968: Anthems Of The American Underground From The Pages Of Broadside Magazine-C* . . . . (Smithsonian Folkways)
Planetary Invasion
Midnight Star; *Planetary Invasion.* . . . . (Solar)
Played Around & Stayed Around In Vietnam Too Long
Chuck Rosenberg & Others; *Folk Songs Of Americans In Vietnam War.* . . . . (Flying Fish)
Please Mr. Custer
Ray Stevens; *Gitarzan* . . . . (Barnaby)
Political Science
Randy Newman; *Sail Away* . . . . (Reprise)
Pop The Silo
Nazareth; *Fool Circle.* . . . .(A&M)
Porn Wars
Frank Zappa; *Meets The Mothers Of Prevention* . . . . (Rykodisc)
Post Cold War Politics
Fishbone; *In Your Face* . . . .(Columbia)
Ragged Old Flag
Johnny Cash; *Patriot* . . . .(Columbia)
We The People-C. . . . . (Folk Era)
Readjustment Blues
John Denver; *Aerie.* . . . . (RCA)
Red Army Blues
Waterboys; *Pagan Place* . . . . (Chrysalis)
Red Baron
David Benoit; *Here's To You Charlie Brown: 50th Great* . . . . (GRP/VMG)
Remember Pearl Harbor
Sammy Kaye & His Orchestra; *ST/Radio Days* . . . . (Novus)
Remember The Alamo
Johnny Cash; *We The People-C* . . . . (Folk Era)
Kingston Trio; *At Large/Here We Go Again!* . . . .(Capitol)
Remembrance Day
Bryan Adams; *Into The Fire.* . . . .(A&M)
Renegade
Styx; *Pieces Of Eight* . . . .(A&M)
Styx-Classics-#15 . . . .(A&M)
Renegade, The
Ian & Sylvia; *Ian & Sylvia's Greatest Hits.* . . . .(Vanguard)
Nashville . . . .(Vanguard)
Riding With Private Malone
David Ball; *Amigo* . . . . (Razor & Tie)
Rock Soldiers
Ace Frehley; *Frehley's Comet* . . . . (Megaforce)
Metal Mania-C . . . . (Priority)
Rockin' Chair Money
Hank Williams; *Alone With His Guitar* . . . .(Mercury)
Roland The Headless Thompson Gunner
Warren Zevon; *Excitable Boy* . . . . (Asylum)
Quiet Normal Life-Best Of Warren Zevon . . . . (Asylum)
Ruby, Don't Take Your Love To Town
Kenny Rogers; *Kenny Rogers-20 Great Years* . . . . (Reprise)
Kenny Rogers-Twenty Greatest Hits . . . .(EMI)
Ten Years Of Gold. . . . . (EMI)
Kenny Rogers And The First Edition; *Hits & Pieces* . . . . (MCA)
Kenny Rogers And The First Edition's Greatest Hits . . . .(K-Tel)
Mel Tillis; *Best Of Mel Tillis* . . . .(MCA)
Mel Tillis & The Statesiders; *Mel Tillis & The Statesiders-24 Great Hits.* . . . .(MGM)
M-M-Mel Live . . . .(MCA)
Russians
Sting; *Dream Of The Blue Turtles* . . . .(A&M)
Fields Of Gold-The Best Of Sting 1984-1994 . . . .(A&M)
Saigon Warrior
Saul Broudy & Robin Thomas; *In Country-Americans In The Vietnam War.* . . . . (Flying Fish)
Sailing Home For Christmas
Doug Stone; *First Christmas* . . . . (Epic)
Sam Stone
John Prine; *John Prine* . . . . (Atlantic)
John Prine-Souvenirs. . . . . (Oh Boy)
Prime Prine-The Best Of John Prine . . . . (Atlantic)

Send The Marines
Tom Lehrer; *That Was The Year That Was* . . . . (Reprise)
She Gave Her Heart To A Soldier Boy
Roy Rogers; *The Country Music Hall Of Fame-Roy Rogers* . . . . (MCA)
Shhh, It's A Military Secret
Glenn Miller & His Orchestra; *Complete Glenn Miller & His Orchestra* . . . . (Bluebird)
Shut Out The Light
Bruce Springsteen; *Tracks* . . . . (Columbia)
Sink The Bismarck
Johnny Horton; *American Originals-Johnny Horton* . . . . (Columbia)
Billboard Top Country Hits-1960-C . . . . (Rhino)
Johnny Horton's Greatest Hits . . . . (Columbia)
Sinner
Neil Finn; *Try Whistling This* . . . . (Work)
Skye Boat Song
King's Singers; *American Balladeer-Golden Classics-#1-C* . . . . (Collectables)
Annie Laurie-Folk Songs Of British Isles . . . . (Angel)
Roger Whittaker; *Live In Concert* . . . . (RCA)
Sloth (Drums)
Fairport Convention; *Fairport Convention-Chronicles* . . . . (A&M)
Full House . . . . (Carthage)
Sneaky Private Lee
Paice/Ashton/Lord; *Malice In Wonderland* . . . . (Warner Bros.)
Snoopy Vs. The Red Baron
Royal Guardsmen; *Best Of The Royal Guardsmen-#1* . . . . (Rhino)
Collectables Presents The History Of Rock-#9-C . . . . (Collectables)
Cruisin'-1967-C . . . . (Increase)
Million-Dollar Memories #1-C . . . . (RCA)
Super Oldies Of The '60s-#6-C . . . . (Audio Fidelity)
Soldier
Neil Young; *Decade* . . . . (Reprise)
ST/Journey Through The Past . . . . (Warner Bros.)
Soldier
Spirit; *12 Dreams Of Dr. Sardonicus* . . . . (Epic)
Soldier
Stephen Stills; *Illegal Stills* . . . . (Columbia)
Soldier
James Taylor; *Mud Slide Slim And The Blue Horizon* . . . . (Warner Bros.)
Soldier Blue
Buffy Sainte-Marie; *Native North American Child* . . . . (Vanguard)
She Used To Wanna Be A Ballerina . . . . (Vanguard)
Soldier Blue
Julian Cope; *Peggy Suicide* . . . . (Island)
Soldier Blue
Cult; *Sonic Temple* . . . . (Sire)
Soldier Boy
Shirelles; *Billboard Top Rock 'N' Roll Hits-1962-C* . . . . (Rhino)
Oldies But Goodies-#4-C . . . . (Original Sound)
Shirelles-Anthology 1959-1964 . . . . (Rhino)
ST/The Wanderers . . . . (Warner Bros.)
Soldier Boy
Small Faces; *78 In The Shade* . . . . (Atlantic)
Soldier Boy
Elvis Presley; *A Golden Celebration* . . . . (RCA)
Elvis Is Back! . . . . (RCA)
From Nashville To Memphis-The Essential '60s Masters . . . . (RCA)
Soldier In The Rain
England Dan & John Ford Coley; *Best Of England Dan & John Ford Coley* . . . . (Big Tree)
Dowdy Ferry Road . . . . (Big Tree)
Soldier Of Fortune
Joe Perry Project; *I've Got The Rock 'N' Rolls Again* . . . . (Columbia)
Soldier Of Fortune
Alan O'Day; *Appetizers* . . . . (Pacific)
Soldier Of Fortune
Thin Lizzy; *Bad Reputation* . . . . (Mercury)
Soldier Of Fortune
Manhattan Transfer; *Bodies & Souls* . . . . (Atlantic)
Soldier Of Fortune
Deep Purple; *Stormbringer* . . . . (Warner Bros.)
Soldier Of Love
Kenny Rogers; *Love Is Strange* . . . . (Reprise)
Soldier Of Love
Donny Osmond; *Donny Osmond* . . . . (Capitol)
Soldier Of Love
Lee Greenwood; *Love's On The Way* . . . . (Liberty)
Soldier Of Love
Marshall Crenshaw; *Marshall Crenshaw* . . . . (Rhino)
Soldier Of Love
Nitty Gritty Dirt Band; *Workin' Band* . . . . (Warner Bros.)
Soldier Of Love
Billy Burnette; *Soldier Of Love* . . . . (Curb)
Soldiers In The Park
Ethel Jackson; *Music From The New York Stage (1890-1920)-#1-1890-1908-C* . . . . (Pearl)
Soldier's Joy
Jimmy Driftwood; *Best Of Jimmy Driftwood* . . . . (Motown)

Marty Stuart; *Busy Bee Cafe* . . . . (Sugar Hill)
Nitty Gritty Dirt Band; *Dirt, Silver & Gold* . . . . (One Way)
Will The Circle Be Unbroken . . . . (EMI)
Tony Trischka; *Heartlands* . . . . (Rounder)
Soldier's Last Letter
Ernest Tubb; *Legend & The Legacy* . . . . (First Generation)
Living Legend . . . . (First Generation)
Ernest Tubb & Johnny Cash; *Ernest Tubb Collection-C* . . . . (Step One)
George Jones; *20 Golden Pieces Of George Jones* . . . . (Bulldog)
Merle Haggard; *Capitol Collectors Series-Merle Haggard* . . . . (Capitol)
Some Gave All
Billy Ray Cyrus; *Some Gave All* . . . . (Mercury)
Spanish Bombs
Clash; *London Calling* . . . . (Epic)
On Broadway . . . . (Epic)
The Story Of The Clash, Volume 1 . . . . (Epic)
Springtime For Hitler
Mel Brooks; *ST/High Anxiety* . . . . (Asylum)
Original Broadway Cast; *The Producers* . . . . (Sony Music Classical)
Star Spangled Banner
American Brass Band; *National Anthems* . . . . (Laserlight)
Banda Sinfonica De Madrid; *National Anthems* . . . . (International Music)
Duke Ellington; *Carnegie Hall Concert-January 23, 1943* . . . . (Prestige)
Houston Symphony Orchestra; *Celebrate America* . . . . (Pro-Arte)
Jimi Hendrix; *Essential Jimi Hendrix, Volume 2* . . . . (Reprise)
Lifelines/Jimi Hendrix Story . . . . (Reprise)
ST/Jimi Hendrix . . . . (Reprise)
ST/Woodstock . . . . (Atlantic)
Lee Greenwood; *American Patriot* . . . . (Capitol)
Marvin Gaye; *Musical Testament 1964-1984* . . . . (Motown)
Mormon Tabernacle Choir; *God Bless America* . . . . (Sony Music Classical)
God Bless America-C . . . . (Columbia)
This Is My Country . . . . (Columbia)
Original Soundtrack; *The Greatest College Fight Songs* . . . . (Laserlight)
Sandi Patty; *Stars And Stripes Forever-#2-C* . . . . (Volcano Entertainment)
Vienna State Opera Orchestra; *National Anthems Of The World* . . (Bescol, Ltd.)
Vinnie Vincent Invasion; *Head Banging Metal-C* . . . . (Priority)
Whitney Houston; *Whitney Houston's Greatest Hits* . . . . (Arista)
Still In Saigon
Charlie Daniels Band; *A Decade Of Hits* . . . . (Epic)
Windows . . . . (Epic)
Stop The War Now
Edwin Starr; *Very Best Of Edwin Starr* . . . . (Motown)
Street Soldiers
Hammer; *Too Legit To Quit* . . . . (Capitol)
Strike Up The Band
Boston Pops Orchestra/Arthur Fiedler; *Gershwin-Greatest Hits* . . . . (RCA)
Count Basie & His Orchestra; *Fancy Pants* . . . . (Pablo)
Ella Fitzgerald; *Ella Fitzgerald Sings The George & Ira Gershwin Songbook* . . . . (Verve)
Rosemary Clooney; *Rosemary Clooney Sings The Lyrics Of Ira Gershwin* . . . . (Concord Jazz)
Tony Bennett; *Fascinatin' Rhythm-Capitol Sings Gershwin-C* . . . . (Capitol)
Stupid War Movies
Paleface; *Paleface* . . . . (Polydor)
Stupid, Stupid War
D.R.I.; *Dealing With It* . . . . (Metal Blade)
Sullivan
Caroline's Spine; *Monsoon* . . . . (Hollywood)
Surrender
Cheap Trick; *Cheap Trick At Budokan* . . . . (Epic)
Cheap Trick's Greatest Hits . . . . (Epic)
Heaven Tonight . . . . (Epic)
Surrender
J. Geils Band; *J. Geils Band-Anthology-Houseparty* . . . . (Rhino)
Monkey Island . . . . (Atlantic)
Surrender
Gloria Estefan and Miami Sound Machine; *Let It Loose* . . . . (Epic)
Surrender
U2; *War* . . . . (Island)
Surrender
Elvis Presley; *Number One Hits* . . . . (RCA)
The Top Ten Hits . . . . (RCA)
Surrender Paradise
Miami Sound Machine; *Primitive Love* . . . . (Epic)
Surrounded
Chantal Kreviazuk; *Under These Rocks And Stones* . . . . (Columbia)
Swiss Army Girl
Scatterbrain; *Scamboogery* . . . . (Elektra)
Talking Old Soldiers
Elton John; *Tumbleweed Connection* . . . . (Polydor)
Talking Vietnam Pot Luck Blues
Tom Paxton; *Morning After* . . . . (Elektra)
Talking World War III Blues
Bob Dylan; *Freewheelin'* . . . . (Columbia)
Taxi War Dance
Count Basie; *Essential Count Basie-#1* . . . . (Columbia)
I Like Jazz-Essence Of Count Basie . . . . (Columbia)

Tell That To The Marines
Al Jolson; *Music From The New York Stage (1890-1920)-#4-1917-1920-C* .... (Pearl)
Terms Of Psychic Warfare
Husker Du; *New Day Rising* .... (SST)
Theme From "Airwolf"
Original Soundtrack; *Television's Greatest Hits-#6-Remote Control-C* ... (TVT)
Theme From "Baa Baa Black Sheep"
Original Soundtrack; *Television's Greatest Hits-#6-Remote Control-C* ... (TVT)
Theme From "Battlestar Galactica"
Boston Pops Orchestra/John Williams; *Pops Out Of This World* ...... (Philips)
Original Soundtrack; *Science Fiction Move Themes* .... (Laserlight)
Theme From "Combat"
Original Soundtrack; *Television's Greatest Hits-#1-C* .... (TVT)
Theme From "Exodus"
101 Strings Orchestra; *Golden Movie Themes* .... (Alshire)
Boston Pops Orchestra/Arthur Fiedler; *Motion Picture Classics-#1* .... (RCA Victor)
Ferrante & Teicher; *Grand Pianos* .... (Pair)
Theme From "F-Troop"
Original Soundtrack; *Television's Greatest Hits-#1-C* .... (TVT)
Theme From "Gomer Pyle, U.S.M.C."
Original Soundtrack; *Television's Greatest Hits-#2-C* .... (TVT)
Theme From "Gone With The Wind"
Toronto Festival Pops Orchestra; *Hooray For Hollywood* .... (Pro-Arte)
Theme From "Hogan's Heroes"
Original Soundtrack; *CBS: The First 50 Years* .... (TVT)
Television's Greatest Hits-#2-C .... (TVT)
Theme From "M*A*S*H" (Suicide Is Painless)
Ahmad Jamal; *Digital Works* .... (Atlantic)
*ST/M*A*S*H* .... (Columbia)
Original Soundtrack; *CBS: The First 50 Years* .... (TVT)
Television's Greatest Hits-#3-1970s & 1980s-C .... (TVT)
Percy Faith & His Orchestra; *Percy Faith & His Orchestra's All-Time Greatest Hits* .... (Columbia)
Theme From "Major Dad"
Original Soundtrack; *Television's Greatest Hits-#7-Cable Ready-C* ..... (TVT)
Theme From "McHale's Navy"
Original Soundtrack; *Television's Greatest Hits-#1-C* .... (TVT)
Theme From "Rat Patrol"
Original Soundtrack; *Television's Greatest Hits-#2-C* .... (TVT)
Theme From "Rin Tin Tin"
Original Soundtrack; *Television's Greatest Hits-#1-C* .... (TVT)
Theme From "Schindler's List"
John Williams & Itzhak Perlman; *ST/Schindler's List* .... (MCA)
Theme From "Star Wars"
John Williams; *ST/Star Wars* .... (Polydor)
Meco; *Best Of Meco* .... (Chronicles)
Neil Norman; *Greatest Science Fiction Hits* .... (Crescendo)
Theme From "Twelve O'Clock High"
Original Soundtrack; *Television's Greatest Hits-#2-C* .... (TVT)
Theme From "War Of The Worlds"
Neil Norman; *Greatest Science Fiction Hits-#3-C* .... (Crescendo)
There's Something About A War
Stephen Sondheim; *Collector's Sondheim-C* .... (RCA)
Thermonuclear War
Carnivore; *Carnivore* .... (Roadrunner)
They Dance Alone (Cueca Solo)
Sting; *...Nothing Like The Sun* .... (A&M)
Fields Of Gold-The Best Of Sting 1984-1994 .... (A&M)
This Ain't No Rag, It's A Flag
Charlie Daniels Band; *This Ain't No Rag, It's A Flag-CD Single* ..... (Blue Hat)
This Cold War With You
Floyd Tillman; *Columbia Country Classics-#2-Honky Tonk Heroes-C* .... (Columbia)
John Prine; *Pink Cadillac* .... (Asylum)
Merle Haggard; *Friend In California* .... (Epic)
Ray Price; *Ray Price's Greatest Hits-#4-By Request* .... (Step One)
Willie Nelson; *San Antonio Rose* .... (Columbia)
This Is The Army, Mr. Jones
Irving Berlin; *V-E Day 50th Anniversary-The Musical Memories-C* .... (Living Era)
Mel Torme & George Shearing; *Mel & George Do World War II* .... (Concord Jazz)
Mormon Tabernacle Choir; *God Bless America* .... (Sony Music Classical)
This Means War
Joan Jett & The Blackhearts; *Good Music* .... (Epic Portrait Assoc.)
This Means War
AC/DC; *Blow Up Your Video* .... (Atco)
This Means War
Pariah; *To Mock A Killingbird* .... (Geffen)
This Uncivil War
Martina McBride; *Emotion* .... (RCA)
Throw Down The Sword
Wishbone Ash; *Argus* .... (MCA)
Live Dates .... (MCA)
Tokyo Road
Bon Jovi; *7800 Degrees Fahrenheit* .... (Mercury)

Too Long A Soldier
Pat Benatar; *Wide Awake In Dreamland* .... (Chrysalis)
Too Much Monkey Business
Chuck Berry; *Classic Oldies From The '50s & '60s-#16-C* .... (MCA)
Roll Over Beethoven .... (Allegiance)
ST/Hail! Hail! Rock 'N' Roll .... (MCA)
Toronto Rock 'N' Roll Revival-#2-C .... (Accord)
Elvis Presley; *Guitar Man* .... (RCA)
Million-Dollar Quartet .... (RCA)
ST/This Is Elvis .... (RCA)
Yardbirds; *Five Live Yardbirds* .... (Rhino)
For Your Love .... (Accord)
Yardbirds' Greatest Hits-#1 (1964-1966) .... (Rhino)
Toy Soldiers
Martika; *Martika* .... (Columbia)
Train For Auschwitz
Tom Paxton; *Best Of Broadside 1962-1968: Anthems Of The American Underground From The Pages Of Broadside Magazine-C* .... (Smithsonian Folkways)
Tramp, Tramp, Tramp
Mormon Tabernacle Choir; *Songs Of The Civil War And Stephen Foster Favorites* .... (Sony Music Classical)
Travelin' Soldier
Bruce Robison; *Bruce Robison* .... (Vireo)
Tug Of War
Paul McCartney; *Tug Of War* .... (Gold Rush)
U.S. Air Force
Mormon Tabernacle Choir; *Stars And Stripes Together* .... (Columbia)
Undercover Of The Night
Rolling Stones; *Rewind (1971-1984)* .... (Rolling Stones)
Undercover .... (Rolling Stones)
Universal Soldier
Buffy Sainte-Marie; *Best Of Buffy Sainte-Marie* .... (Vanguard)
Festival Of Acoustic Music-#1 .... (Fantasy)
Troubadours Of The Folk Era-#1-C .... (Rhino)
Donovan; *Catch The Wind* .... (Garland)
History Of British Rock-#4-C .... (Rhino)
Songs Of Protest-C .... (Rhino)
The Secret Policeman's Other Ball/The Music .... (Rhino)
Unknown Soldier
Doors; *Best Of The Doors* .... (Elektra)
Doors 13 .... (Elektra)
Doors-Classics .... (Elektra)
Live At The Hollywood Bowl .... (Elektra)
Waiting For The Sun .... (Elektra)
Us & Them
Pink Floyd; *Dark Side Of The Moon* .... (Capitol)
Delicate Sound Of Thunder .... (Columbia)
Pink Floyd-Gift Set .... (Capitol)
Shine On .... (Columbia)
Vera Cruz
Warren Zevon; *Excitable Boy* .... (Asylum)
Veteran Of The Psychic Wars
Blue Oyster Cult; *Extraterrestrial Live* .... (Columbia)
Fire Of Unknown Origin .... (Columbia)
Viet Cong Blues
Junior Wells; *Best Of The Chicago Blues-C* .... (Vanguard)
Chicago/The Blues Today .... (Vanguard)
Vanguard Collector's Edition-C .... (Vanguard)
Junior Wells & His Chicago Blues Band; *Legends Of Electric Blues Guitar-#2-C* .... (Rhino)
Viet Cong Live Next Door
Left; *Last Train To Hagerstown* .... (Green World)
Vietnam
Jimmy Cliff; *In Concert-Best Of Jimmy Cliff* .... (Reprise)
Reggae Spectacular-C .... (A&M)
Wonderful World, Beautiful People .... (A&M)
Vietnam
Paul Kaplan; *Best Of Broadside 1962-1968: Anthems Of The American Underground From The Pages Of Broadside Magazine-C* .... (Smithsonian Folkways)
Vietnam Blues
Champion Jack Dupree; *Legacy Of The Blues-#3* .... (Crescendo)
Vietnam Never Again
Country Joe McDonald; *Child's Play* .... (Rag Baby)
Vietnam Veteran Still Alive
Country Joe McDonald; *Into The Fray* .... (Rag Baby)
Vietnamerica
Stranglers; *Stranglers IV* .... (I.R.S.)
Virginia's Bloody Soil
Tennessee Ernie Ford; *Tennessee Ernie Ford Sings Songs Of The Civil War* .... (Capitol)
Waist Deep In The Big Muddy
Pete Seeger; *Best Of Broadside 1962-1968: Anthems Of The American Underground From The Pages Of Broadside Magazine-C* .... (Smithsonian Folkways)
Walking On A Thin Line
Huey Lewis and the News; *Sports* .... (Chrysalis)

War
Bruce Springsteen & The E Street Band; *Bruce Springsteen & The E Street Band Live/1975-85* . . . . (Legacy)
Edwin Starr; *Billboard Top Rock 'N' Roll Hits-1970-C* . . . . (Rhino)
Didn't It Blow Your Mind: Soul Hits Of The '70s-#3-C . . . . (Rhino)
Motown Superstar Series-#3-Edwin Starr . . . . (Motown)
Songs Of Protest-C . . . . (Rhino)
War & Peace . . . . (Motown)
War A Africa
Jimmy Cliff; *Breakout* . . . . (JRS)
War Baby
''C'' Company & Terry Nelson; *Wake Up America* . . . . (Plantation)
War Baby Son Of Zorro
Daryl Hall & John Oates; *War Babies* . . . . (Atlantic)
War Child
Jethro Tull; *Repeat-The Best Of Jethro Tull, Vol. II* . . . . (Chrysalis)
Too Old To Rock 'N' Roll: Too Young To Die! . . . . (Chrysalis)
War Clouds
New Orleans Ragtime Orchestra; *New Orleans Jazz-C* . . . . (Arhoolie)
War Games
Crosby, Stills & Nash; *Allies* . . . . (Atlantic)
War Games
Paul Young; *Between Two Fires* . . . . (Columbia)
War In Babylon
Max Romeo & The Upsetters; *This Is Reggae Music-#1-C* . . . . . . (Island)
War In Babylon . . . . (Island)
War Is Coming, War Is Coming
War; *Platinum Jazz* . . . . (Blue Note)
War Is Hell (On The Homefront Too)
T.G. Sheppard; *Perfect Stranger* . . . . (Warner Bros.)
T.G. Sheppard's All-Time Greatest Hits . . . . (Warner Bros.)
T.G. Sheppard's Greatest Hits . . . . (Warner Bros./Curb)
War Is Over
Phil Ochs; *Chords Of Fame* . . . . (A&M)
Tape From California . . . . (A&M)
The War Is Over-Best Of Phil Ochs . . . . (A&M)
War Machine
Kiss; *Creatures Of The Night* . . . . (Casablanca)
War Of Man
Neil Young; *Harvest Moon* . . . . (Reprise)
War Of The Hearts
Sade; *Promise* . . . . (Portrait)
War On Drugs
2 Black 2 Strong MMG; *Doin' Hard Time On Planet Earth* . . . . (Clappers)
War Pigs
Black Sabbath; *Live Evil* . . . . (Warner Bros.)
Paranoid . . . . (Warner Bros.)
We Sold Our Soul For Rock 'N' Roll . . . . (Warner Bros.)
Faith No More; *Real Thing* . . . . (Slash)
Ozzy Osbourne; *Just Say Ozzy* . . . . (Epic Portrait Assoc.)
Speak Of The Devil . . . . (Jet)
The Ozzman Cometh . . . . (Epic)
War Song
Culture Club; *Waking Up With The House On Fire* . . . . (Virgin)
War Widow
Country Joe McDonald; *War War War* . . . . (Vanguard)
War/No More Trouble
Bob Marley & The Wailers; *Babylon By Bus* . . . . (Tuff Gong)
Rebel Music . . . . (Tuff Gong)
Warm Machine
Bush; *Science Of Things* . . . . (Trauma)
Warrior
Public Image Ltd.; *9* . . . . (Virgin)
Greatest Hits So Far . . . . (Virgin)
Warrior, The
Scandal featuring Patty Smyth; *Warrior* . . . . (Columbia)
Wars Of Germany
Clancy Brothers & Tommy Makem; *Luck Of The Irish* . . . . (Columbia)
Wartime Wedding
Original Broadway Cast; *Over Here!* . . . . (Sony Music Classical)
Was My Brother In The Battle
Kate & Anna McGarrigle; *Songs Of The Civil War-C* . . . . (Columbia)
Waterloo
Stonewall Jackson; *American Originals-Stonewall Jackson* . . . . (Columbia)
Billboard Top Country Hits-1959-C . . . . (Rhino)
Columbia Country Classics-#3-Americana-C . . . . (Columbia)
Country Music Classics-#1-1950s-C . . . . (K-Tel)
Waterloo
Abba; *Abba's Greatest Hits* . . . . (Atlantic)
Waterloo . . . . (Atlantic)
We Didn't Start The Fire
Billy Joel; *Storm Front* . . . . (Columbia)
We Got The Neutron Bombs
Weirdos; *D.I.Y.-#6-L.A. Scene-1976-1979-C* . . . . (Rhino)
We Seek No Wider War
Phil Ochs; *Best Of Broadside 1962-1968: Anthems Of The American Underground From The Pages Of Broadside Magazine-C* . . . . (Smithsonian Folkways)

Weekend Warriors
Ted Nugent; *Weekend Warriors* . . . . (Epic)
What's Happening, Brother
Marvin Gaye; *What's Going On* . . . . (Motown)
When Johnny Comes Marching Home
Marilyn Horne; *Beautiful Dreamer-Great American Songbook* . . . . (London)
Mormon Tabernacle Choir; *Songs Of The Civil War And Stephen Foster Favorites* . . . . (Sony Music Classical)
United States Military Academy Band; *Songs Of The Civil War-C* . . . (Columbia)
When The Generals Talk
Midnight Oil; *Red Sails In The Sunset* . . . . (Columbia)
Where Have All The Flowers Gone
Johnny Rivers; *Best Of Johnny Rivers* . . . . (EMI)
Johnny Rivers-Anthology 1964-1977 . . . . (Rhino)
Kingston Trio; *Capitol Collectors Series-The Kingston Trio* . . . . (Capitol)
Songs Of Protest-C . . . . (Rhino)
Pete Seeger; *Essential Pete Seeger* . . . . (Vanguard)
Pete Seeger's Greatest Hits . . . . (Columbia)
Peter, Paul & Mary; *Peter, Paul and Mary* . . . . (Warner Bros.)
Wes Montgomery; *Wes Montgomery-Classics-#22* . . . . (A&M)
White Cliffs Of Dover
Kay Kyser & His Orchestra; *16 Most Requested Songs Of The '40s-#1-C* . . . . (Legacy)
Lee Andrews And The Hearts; *Lee Andrews And The Hearts' Biggest Hits* . . . . (Collectables)
Mystics; *Mystics-16 Golden Classics* . . . . (Collectables)
Righteous Brothers; *Righteous Brothers' Greatest Hits* . . . . (Verve)
Righteous Brothers-Anthology 1962-1974 . . . . (Rhino)
Rosemary Clooney; *For The Duration* . . . . (Concord Jazz)
Wooden Ships
Crosby, Stills & Nash; *Crosby, Stills & Nash* . . . . (Atlantic)
CSN . . . . (Atlantic)
Crosby, Stills, Nash & Young; *So Far* . . . . (Atlantic)
ST/Woodstock . . . . (Atlantic)
Jefferson Airplane; *2400 Fulton Street-An Anthology* . . . . (RCA)
Flight Log (1966-1976) . . . . (Grunt)
Loves You . . . . (RCA)
Volunteers . . . . (RCA)
World War None!
Frank Sinatra; *Trilogy: Pasts, Present, Future* . . . . (Reprise)
You Don't Have To Be In The Army To Fight In The War
Mungo Jerry; *In The Summertime-Best Of Mungo Jerry* . . . . (Rhino)
You Dropped A Bomb On Me
Gap Band; *12'' Collection* . . . . (Mercury)
Gap Band IV . . . . (Mercury)
Gap Gold/Best Of The Gap Band . . . . (Mercury)
Your Squaw Is On The Warpath
Loretta Lynn; *Loretta Lynn's Greatest Hits-#2* . . . . (MCA)
Zoot Suit Riot
Cherry Poppin' Daddies; *Now That's What I Call Music!-#1-C* . . . . . . (Virgin)
Zoot Suit Riot-The Swingin' Hits Of The Cherry Poppin' Daddies . . . . (Mojo Music/Universal)

WARNINGS, Threats

See Also: **ADVICE, DANGER & DISASTER, DRUGS (various), HELP, LIGHTHOUSES, LOVE (various), TROUBLE**

(Ghost) Riders In The Sky
Gene Autry; *50th Anniversary* . . . . (Republic/Universal)
Cowboy Hall Of Fame . . . . (Republic/Universal)
Johnny Cash; *The Man In Black-His Greatest Hits* . . . . (Legacy)
Outlaws; *Ghost Riders* . . . . (Arista)
Roy Clark; *Roy Clark In Concert* . . . . (MCA)
Roy Clark's Greatest Hits . . . . (MCA)
Superpicker . . . . (MCA)
Vaughn Monroe; *Best Of Vaughn Monroe* . . . . (RCA)
This Is Vaughn Monroe/Decade Of The '40s . . . . (RCA)
(If You're Not In It...) I'm Outta Here!
Shania Twain; *The Woman In Me* . . . . (Mercury)
19th Nervous Breakdown
Rolling Stones; *Big Hits (High Tide & Green Grass)* . . . . (Abkco)
got Live if you want it! . . . . (Abkco)
Hot Rocks 1964-1971 . . . . (Abkco)
Singles Collection-The London Years . . . . (Abkco)
32 Flavors
Alana Davis; *Blame It On Me* . . . . (Elektra)
Ani DiFranco; *Living In Clip* . . . . (Righteous Babe)
Not A Pretty Girl . . . . (Righteous Babe)
American Woman
Guess Who; *American Woman* . . . . (RCA)
Best Of The Guess Who . . . . (RCA)
Greatest Of The Guess Who . . . . (RCA)
Nipper's Greatest Hits Of The '70s-C . . . . (RCA)
Rock Classics-C . . . . (K-Tel)
Lenny Kravitz; *5* . . . . (Virgin)
Now That's What I Call Music!-#3-C . . . . (Virgin)
ST/Austin Powers-The Spy Who Shagged Me . . . . (Maverick)

Angel's Eye
Aerosmith; *ST/Charlie's Angels* ....(Columbia)
Babe I'm Gonna Leave You
Led Zeppelin; *Led Zeppelin*....................... (Atlantic)
   Led Zeppelin-Box Set .... (Atlantic)
Baby Doll
Andy Williams; *Andy Williams* .... (Madacy)
Baby Don't Get Hooked On Me
Mac Davis; *Mac Davis' Greatest Hits*.....................(Columbia)
   Super Hits Of The '70s-Have A Nice Day-#20-C ....(Rhino)
Back Up Buddy
Carl Smith; *Essential Carl Smith-1950-1956* ....(Legacy)
   Trucker's Jukebox-#2-C ....(Legacy)
Bad Boyz
Shyne featuring Levy, Barrington; *Shyne* .... (Bad Boy/Arista)
Bad Moon Rising
Creedence Clearwater Revival; *1969* ....(Fantasy)
   Creedence Clearwater Revival-Chronicle ....(Fantasy)
   Creedence Clearwater Revival-Gold ....(Fantasy)
   Green River ....(Fantasy)
   Live In Europe ....(Fantasy)
Battle Flag
Lo Fidelity Allstars; *How To Operate With A Blown Mind* ....(Skint)
Be Careful
Ricky Martin & Madonna; *Ricky Martin*.....................(Columbia)
Be Careful, It's My Heart
Bing Crosby & Fred Astaire; *ST/Holiday Inn* .... (MCA)
Four Freshmen; *Puttin' On The Ritz-Capitol Sings Berlin-C*........(Capitol)
Kate Smith; *Kate Smith-16 Most Requested Songs* ....(Columbia)
Rosemary Clooney; *Rosemary Clooney Sings The Music Of Irving
   Berlin* ....(Concord Jazz)
Tommy Dorsey & Frank Sinatra; *Tommy Dorsey & Frank Sinatra's All-Time
   Greatest Hits-#1* ....(Bluebird)
Be Glad
Del Reeves; *45-#50531* ....(United Artists)
Bird Dog
Everly Brothers; *Best Of The Everly Brothers* ....(Rhino)
   Billboard Top Rock 'N' Roll Hits-1958-C ....(Rhino)
   Everly Brothers-Cadence Classics-Their 20 Greatest Hits ....(Rhino)
   Fabulous Style Of The Everly Brothers ....(Rhino)
   Very Best Of The Everly Brothers .... (Warner Bros.)
Blame It On Your Heart
Patty Loveless; *Only What I Feel* .... (Epic)
   Patty Loveless-Classics .... (Epic)
Blob, The
Five Blobs; *Elvira Presents Haunted Hits-C* ....(Rhino)
   Halloween Hits-C ....(Rhino)
Little Stevie & The McQueens; *Horror Rock Classics-#2-C*.........(Rhino)
Blood On The Dance Floor
Michael Jackson; *Blood On The Dance Floor-HIStory...* ..... (MJJ Music/Work)
Blue Suede Shoes
Carl Perkins; *Blue Suede Shoes* ....(Sun)
   Carl Perkins-Original Sun Greatest Hits ....(Rhino)
   Cruisin'-1956-1957-C .... (Dunhill Compact Classics)
   Oldies But Goodies-#4-C ....(Original Sound)
Elvis Presley; *Aloha from Hawaii via Satellite* ....(RCA)
   Elvis Presley ....(RCA)
   Elvis-A Legendary Performer, Volume 2 ....(RCA)
   From Memphis To Vegas/From Vegas To Memphis.................(RCA)
   ST/G.I. Blues....................................(RCA)
Blues In The Night
Benny Goodman; *Small Groups-1941-1945* .... (Columbia)
Bobby Bland; *Introspective Of The Early Years* .... (MCA)
Dinah Shore; *Nipper's Greatest Hits Of The '40s-#1-C* ....(RCA)
Doc Severinsen; *Best Of Doc Severinsen*. .... (MCA)
Frank Sinatra; *Frank Sinatra sings for Only The Lonely* .... (Capitol)
Jimmie Lunceford & His Orchestra; *Warner Bros.' 75 Years Entertaining
   The World-Film Music-C* .... (Rhino)
Mel Torme; *Torme*. ....(Verve)
Robins; *Best Of The Robins* ....(Crescendo)
Rosemary Clooney; *Rosemary Clooney-16 Most Requested Songs* .... (Legacy)
Tony Bennett; *Playin' With My Friends-Bennett Sings The
   Blues-C* ....(Columbia)
Woody Herman; *Blues On Parade* ....(GRP)
   Woody Herman-Best Of The Decca Years ....(Decca)
Woody Herman & His Orchestra; *Big Bands Greatest
   Hits-#3-C* .... (MCA Special Prod.)
Brain Of J.
Pearl Jam; *Yield* .... (Epic)
Break Stuff
Limp Bizkit; *Significant Other* ....(Flip/Interscope)
Breakdown
Tantric; *Tantric* .... (Maverick)
Bubblegoose
Wyclef Jean; *Chef Aid-The South Park Album* ....(Columbia)
Wyclef Jean featuring Melky Sedeck; *Presents The Carnival F/Refugee
   Allstars* .... (Ruffhouse/Columbia)
But It's Alright
J.J. Jackson; *Didn't It Blow Your Mind: Soul Hits Of The '70s-#3-C* .... (Rhino)

   Soul Shots-C ....(Rhino)
Candyman
Grateful Dead; *American Beauty* ....(Warner Bros.)
   Dead Set ....(Arista)
Careful With That Mic...
Clutch; *Pure Rock Fury* .... (Atlantic)
Catfish John
Johnny Russell; *Johnny Russell's Greatest Hits* ....(Dominion Entert.)
Caution! (Do Not Stop On Tracks)
Grateful Dead; *Anthem Of The Sun* .... (Warner Bros.)
Children Of The Korn
Korn with Ice Cube; *Follow The Leader* ....(Immortal/Epic)
Cold Contagious
Bush; *Razorblade Suitcase*. .... (Trauma)
Cold Hard Truth, The
George Jones; *Cold Hard Truth* ....(Asylum)
Jamie O'Hara; *Rise Above It* .... (RCA)
Cold Hearted
Paula Abdul; *Forever Your Girl* ....(Virgin)
   Get Up & Dance-Dance Mixes ....(Virgin)
Complicated Shadows
Elvis Costello & The Attractions; *The Sopranos-Music From The HBO
   Original Series* .... (Sony Music Soundtrax)
Crush 'Em
Megadeth; *Risk*. ....(Trauma)
   ST/Universal Soldier II: The Return ....(Arista)
Daylight Fading
Counting Crows; *Recovering The Satellites*. .... (David Geffen Co.)
Deja Vu (Uptown Baby)
Lord Tariq & Peter Gunz; *Deja Vu*. .... (Codeine/Columbia)
Detour (Devil Took A)
Patti Page; *Patti Page-Golden Hits* ....(Mercury)
Do Re Mi
Arlo Guthrie; *Tribute To Woody Guthrie-C* ....(Warner Bros.)
John Cougar Mellencamp; *Folkways: A Vision Shared-C*..........(Columbia)
Ry Cooder; *Ry Cooder* .... (Reprise)
   Show Time ....(Warner Bros.)
Woody Guthrie; *Dust Bowl Ballads* ....(Rounder)
Don't Come Home A'Drinkin' (With Lovin' On Your Mind)
Loretta Lynn; *Loretta Lynn-Greatest Hits Live* ....(K-Tel)
   Loretta Lynn's Greatest Hits .... (MCA)
   MCA Records 30 Years Of Hits-1958-1988-C. .... (MCA)
Don't Drink & Drive
James Cannings; *Music For All Seasons* .... (J.C.)
Don't Drink The Water
Dave Matthews Band; *Before These Crowded Streets* .... (RCA)
Don't Drive Drunk
Stevie Wonder; *ST/Woman In Red* ....(Motown)
Don't Eat Stuff Off The Sidewalk
Cramps; *Psychedelic Jungle/Gravest Hits* .... (I.R.S.)
Don't Leave Your Records In The Sun
John Hartford; *Mark Twang*. .... (Flying Fish)
Don't Let The Stars Get In Your Eyes
Perry Como; *Como's Golden Records* ....(RCA)
   Perry Como-Pure Gold .... (RCA)
   Perry Como's All-Time Greatest Hits-#1 ....(RCA)
   This Is Perry Como ....(RCA)
Don't Make Me Come Over There And Love You
George Strait; *George Strait*. .... (MCA)
Don't Marry Me
Original Cast; *Flower Drum Song* .... (Sony Music Classical)
Don't Mess With Bill
Marvelettes; *Compact Command Performances-Marvelettes* ....(Motown)
   Marvelettes' Greatest Hits ....(Motown)
   Marvelettes-Anthology ....(Motown)
   Top 10 With A Bullet-Motown Girl Groups-C.............(Motown)
Don't Mess With My Ducktail
Hank C. Burnette; *Don't Mess With My Ducktail*. .... (Sun)
Don't Mess With My Man
Irma Thomas; *We Got A Party-Best Of Ron Records-#1-C* ....(Rounder)
Don't Pick It Up
Offspring; *Ixnay On The Hombre*. ....(Columbia)
Don't Say
Jon B.; *Cool Relax* .... (Yab Yum/550)
Don't Start Me Talkin'
Doobie Brothers; *Farewell*. ....(Warner Bros.)
   Toulouse Street ....(Warner Bros.)
New York Dolls; *In Too Much Too Soon* ....(Mercury)
Sonny Boy Williamson; *Down & Out Blues* ....(Chess)
   Superblues-#2-All-Time Classic Blues-C ....(Stax)
Don't Touch Me There
Tubes; *T.R.A.S.H. (Tubes Rarities And Smash Hits)* ....(A&M)
   What Do You Want From Live ....(A&M)
   Young And Rich ....(A&M)
Don't You Marry The Mormon Boys
Rosalie Sorrels; *Lonesome Roving Wolves-Songs & Ballads Of
   The West* .... (Green Linnet)

Dope Show
Marilyn Manson; *Mechanical Animals* . . . .(Nothing)
Down Under
Men At Work; *Business As Usual* . . . . (Columbia)
Dream On
Depeche Mode; *Exciter* . . . . (Mute/Reprise)
Dreams
Corrs; *Legacy-A Tribute To Fleetwood Mac's Rumours-C* . . . . (Lava)
Fleetwood Mac; *25 Years-The Chain* . . . .(Warner Bros.)
Fleetwood Mac Live . . . .(Warner Bros.)
Fleetwood Mac's Greatest Hits . . . .(Warner Bros.)
Rumours . . . .(Warner Bros.)
Emotional Girl
Terri Clark; *Just The Same* . . . . (Mercury)
Eve Of Destruction
Barry McGuire; *Billboard Top Rock 'N' Roll Hits-1965-C* . . . . (Rhino)
Cruisin'-1965-C . . . .(Increase)
Good Feeling Music Of The Big Chill Generation-#3-C . . . . (Motown)
Songs Of Protest-C . . . . (Rhino)
Vintage Music-#9 & 10-C . . . . (MCA)
Dickies; *Great Dictations (Definitive Collection)*. . . . . (A&M)
Incredible Shrinking Dickies . . . . (A&M)
Turtles; *Turtle Wax-Best Of The Turtles-#2* . . . . (Rhino)
Turtlesized . . . . (Rhino)
Evil Ways
Santana; *Best Of Santana* . . . . (Legacy)
Santana . . . . (Columbia)
Santana's Greatest Hits . . . . (Columbia)
Viva Santana! . . . . (Columbia)
Fair And Tender Ladies
Whites; *A Lifetime In The Making* . . . . (Ceili Music)
Fear The Voices
Alice In Chains; *Music Bank*. . . . . (Columbia)
Fightin' Side Of Me
Merle Haggard; *All American* . . . . (Capitol)
Best Of Merle Haggard . . . . (Capitol)
Capitol Collectors Series-Merle Haggard. . . . . (Capitol)
The Fightin' Side Of Me . . . . (Capitol)
Merle Haggard & The Strangers; *Songs I'll Always Sing* . . . . . . (Capitol)
Final Hour
Lauryn Hill; *The Miseducation Of Lauryn Hill* . . . . (Ruffhouse/Columbia)
First We Take Manhattan
Jennifer Warnes; *Critics Choice-C* . . . .(Cypress)
Famous Blue Raincoat. . . . . (Private Music)
Leonard Cohen; *I'm Your Man* . . . . (Columbia)
R.E.M.; *I'm Your Fan-Songs Of Leonard Cohen* . . . . (Atlantic)
Fist City
Loretta Lynn; *Loretta Lynn-20 Greatest Hits* . . . .(MCA)
Loretta Lynn-Greatest Hits Live . . . . (K-Tel)
Loretta Lynn's Greatest Hits-#2 . . . .(MCA)
The Country Music Hall Of Fame-Loretta Lynn . . . . (MCA)
Forgive Them Father
Lauryn Hill featuring Shelly Thunder; *The Miseducation Of
Lauryn Hill* . . . . (Ruffhouse/Columbia)
Get Ready
Rare Earth; *Earth Tones-Essential* . . . . (Motown)
Very Best Of Rare Earth. . . . . (Motown)
Temptations; *Temptations-Anthology-The Best Of The Temptations* . . (Motown)
Temptations-The Ultimate Collection . . . . (Motown)
Gettin' In The Way
Jill Scott; *Who Is Jill Scott? Words And Sounds-#1* . . . .(Hidden Beach/Epic)
Go Away Little Girl
Happenings; *The Ultimate History Of Rock 'N' Roll-#6-C* . . . . (K-Tel)
Steve Lawrence; *Steve Lawrence's Greatest Hits*. . . . . (Columbia)
God's Gonna Get'cha (For That)
George Jones & Tammy Wynette; *George Jones & Tammy Wynette-16
Biggest Hits*. . . . . (Epic/Legacy)
George Jones & Tammy Wynette's Greatest Hits . . . .(Epic)
Got Your Money
Ol' Dirty Bastard; *Nigga Please* . . . . (Elektra)
Happening, The
Diana Ross; *Diana Ross-Anthology* . . . . (Motown)
Diana Ross & The Supremes; *Diana Ross & The Supremes-Superstar
Series-#1* . . . . (Motown)
He Wasn't Man Enough
Toni Braxton; *The Heat* . . . . (LaFace)
Totally Hits-#3-C . . . .(Atlantic)
Heartbreaker
Pat Benatar; *Best Shots* . . . .(Chrysalis)
In The Heat Of The Night . . . .(Chrysalis)
Live From Earth. . . . .(Chrysalis)
Hell
Squirrel Nut Zippers; *Hot* . . . . (Mammoth)
Here Today
Beach Boys; *Pet Sounds* . . . . (Capitol)
The Pet Sounds Sessions: A 30th Anniversary Collection . . . . (Capitol)
Here We Go Again
Aretha Franklin; *A Rose Is Still A Rose* . . . . (Arista)

He's A Heartache (Looking For A Place To Happen)
Janie Fricke; *19 Hot Country Requests-C* . . . . (Epic)
It Ain't Easy . . . .(Columbia)
Janie Fricke-17 Greatest Hits . . . . (Columbia)
Very Best Of Janie Fricke . . . . (Columbia)
Highwire
Rolling Stones; *Flashpoint* . . . .(Virgin)
Hold Me, Thrill Me, Kiss Me
Mel Carter; *Baby Boomer Classics-Love Sixties-C* . . . .(JCI Assoc. Labels)
Holla Holla
Ja Rule; *Venni Vetti Vecci* . . . .(Murder Inc./Def Jam/IDJMG)
Hypnotize The Moon
Clay Walker; *Hypnotize The Moon* . . . .(Giant)
I Left Something Turned On At Home
Trace Adkins; *Dreamin' Out Loud* . . . . (Capitol)
I Only Know I Love You
Four Aces; *Four Aces-More Greatest Hits* . . . .(Varese Vintage)
I Will…But
SHeDAISY; *The Whole Shebang* . . . .(Lyric Street)
I Won't Let You Do That To Me
Luther Vandross; *One Night With You-The Best Of Love-#2*. . . . . (LV/Epic)
If I Fall You're Going Down With Me
Dixie Chicks; *Fly* . . . . (Monument)
If You Can Do Anything Else
George Strait; *George Strait* . . . . (MCA)
If You Think You're Lonely Now
Bobby Womack; *The Poet*. . . . . (Razor & Tie)
K-Ci Hailey; *ST/Jason's Lyric* . . . . (Mercury)
If Your Girl Only Knew
Aaliyah; *MTV Party To Go '98-C* . . . .(Tommy Boy)
One In A Million . . . .(BlackGround Enterp./Atlantic)
It Ain't My Fault
Silkk The Shocker; *Charge It 2 Da Game* . . . . (No Limit/Priority)
It Could Happen To You
Chet Baker; *Chet Baker Sings It Could Happen
To You* . . . . (Original Jazz Classics)
Doris Day; *Best Of The Big Bands-Doris Day*. . . . . (Legacy)
Eydie Gorme; *Best Of Eydie Gorme* . . . . (Curb)
Jo Stafford; *Songs That Got Us Through WWII-#2-C* . . . . (Rhino)
Rosemary Clooney; *Rosemary Clooney Sings The Music Of Jimmy Van
Heusen*. . . . . (Concord Jazz)
Shirley Horn; *Close Enough For Love* . . . . (Verve)
Sonny Rollins; *The Sound Of Sonny* . . . . (Original Jazz Classics)
It's All Right
Impressions; *Billboard Top R&B Hits-1963-C* . . . . (Rhino)
Cruisin'-1964-C . . . .(Increase)
Impressions' Greatest Hits . . . . (MCA)
ST/The Flamingo Kid . . . . (Motown)
It's Lonely Out There
Pam Tillis; *All Of This Love* . . . . (Arista)
I've Got You Under My Skin
4 Seasons; *25th Anniversary Collection* . . . . (Rhino)
Diana Krall; *When I Look In Your Eyes* . . . . (GRP)
Frank Sinatra; *At The Sands* . . . . (Reprise)
Round #1 . . . . (Capitol)
Sinatra: A Man And His Music . . . . (Reprise)
Sinatra's Sinatra . . . . (Reprise)
The Reprise Collection . . . . (Reprise)
Frank Sinatra & Bono; *Frank Sinatra-Duets-C* . . . . (Capitol)
Frank Sinatra & Nelson Riddle Orchestra; *songs for Swingin'
Lovers!*. . . . . (Capitol)
Just You Wait
Julie Andrews/Original Cast; *My Fair Lady* . . . . (Columbia)
Kicks
Paul Revere And The Raiders; *Legend Of Paul Revere And The
Raiders* . . . . (Columbia)
Midnight Ride . . . . (Columbia)
Paul Revere And The Raiders' Greatest Hits . . . . (Columbia)
Killing The Fly
Union Underground; *…An Education In Rebellion*. . . . . (Portrait)
King Nothing
Metallica; *Load* . . . . (Elektra)
Laugh Laugh
Beau Brummels; *Best Of The Beau Brummels* . . . . (Rhino)
Heart & Soul Of Rock 'N' Roll-#1-C . . . . (Rhino)
Introducing The Beau Brummels . . . . (Rhino)
Nuggets-#7-Early San Francisco-C . . . . (Rhino)
Lay Low
Snoop Dogg; *The Last Meal* . . . .(No Limit/Priority)
Leave My Kitten Alone
Beatles; *The Beatles-Anthology-#1* . . . . (Capitol)
Elvis Costello; *Kojak Variety* . . . . (Warner Bros.)
Little Willie John; *Best Of Little Willie John-Fever* . . . . (Rhino)
Let's See How Far You Get
BR549; *This Is BR549*. . . . . (Lucky Dog)
Lickin'
Black Crowes; *Lions* . . . .(V2)
Life #9
Martina McBride; *The Way That I Am*. . . . .(RCA)

Lightning's Girl
Nancy Sinatra; *How Does That Grab You?* . . . .(Sundazed Music)
Li'l Red Riding Hood
Sam The Sham and The Pharaohs; *Best Of Sam The Sham and The*
  Pharaohs . . . . (Polydor)
  Cruisin'-1966-C . . . . (Increase)
  Pharaohization! (Best Of) . . . . (Rhino)
Lion's Den
Bruce Springsteen; *Tracks* . . . .(Columbia)
Little Black Backpack
Stroke9; *Nasty Little Thoughts* . . . .(Cherry/Universal)
Little Sister
Elvis Presley; *Elvis' Golden Records, Volume 3* . . . .(RCA)
  Elvis In Concert . . . .(RCA)
  I Was The One . . . .(RCA)
  The Top Ten Hits . . . .(RCA)
  Worldwide 50 Gold Award Hits, Vol. 1, Parts 1 & 2 . . . .(RCA)
Little Town Flirt
Del Shannon; *Del Shannon's Greatest Hits* . . . .(Rhino)
  Del Shannon's Greatest Hits . . . .(Curb)
Little White Lie
Sammy Hagar; *Marching To Mars* . . . . (MCA)
Livin' On The Edge
Aerosmith; *Get A Grip* . . . . (Geffen)
Locked & Loaded
Jackyl; *Cut The Crap-C* . . . . (Epic)
Look Into My Eyes
Bone Thugs-N-Harmony; *Art Of War* . . . . (Ruthless/Relativity)
Look What Love Has Done
Patty Smyth; *ST/Junior* . . . . (MCA)
Love Is A Dangerous Game
Millie Jackson; *Back To The Shit* . . . .(Jive)
Thelma Houston; *Qualifying Heat* . . . . (MCA)
Love You Save, The
Jackson 5; *14 Greatest Hits* . . . . (Motown)
  ABC . . . . (Motown)
  Goin' Back To Indiana . . . . (Motown)
  Jackson 5-Anthology . . . . (Motown)
  Jackson 5's Greatest Hits . . . . (Motown)
  Motown Superstar Series-#12-Jackson 5 . . . . (Motown)
  TV ST/Diana-C . . . . (Motown)
Lucky Man
Bruce Springsteen; *Tracks* . . . .(Columbia)
Mama Told Me Not To Come
Randy Newman; *12 Songs* . . . . (Reprise)
  Randy Newman/Live . . . . (Warner Archives)
Three Dog Night; *Best Of Three Dog Night* . . . . (MCA)
  Billboard Top Rock 'N' Roll Hits-1970-C . . . . (Rhino)
Wilson Pickett; *Wilson Pickett's Greatest Hits* . . . . (Atlantic)
Maneater
Daryl Hall & John Oates; *H2O* . . . . (RCA)
  Nipper's Greatest Hits Of The '80s-C . . . . (RCA)
  Rock 'N Soul, Part 1 . . . . (RCA)
Midnight Special
Creedence Clearwater Revival; *1969* . . . .(Fantasy)
  Creedence Clearwater Revival-Chronicle-#2 . . . .(Fantasy)
  Creedence Clearwater Revival-Gold . . . .(Fantasy)
  Movie Album . . . .(Fantasy)
  Willy & The Poor Boys . . . .(Fantasy)
Johnny Rivers; *Johnny Rivers-Anthology 1964-1977* . . . .(Rhino)
  Very Best Of Johnny Rivers . . . . (EMI)
Missionary Man
Eurythmics; *Eurythmics' Greatest Hits* . . . . (Arista)
  Revenge . . . .(RCA)
Must To Avoid, A
Herman's Hermits; *Herman's Hermits-Their Greatest Hits* . . . . (Abkco)
My Heart Has A History
Paul Brandt; *Calm Before The Storm* . . . .(Reprise)
My Name Is Not Susan
Whitney Houston; *I'm Your Baby Tonight* . . . . (Arista)
My Way
Limp Bizkit; *Chocolate Starfish & The Hotdog Flavored*
  Water . . . . (Flip/Interscope)
Narcolepsy
Ben Folds Five; *The Unauthorized Biography Of Reinhold*
  Messner . . . . (550 Music)
Nature's Disappearing
John Mayall; *Room To Move-1969-1974-Chronicle Series* . . . . . (Polydor)
  Wake Up Call . . . .(Silvertone)
Needle & The Damage Done
Neil Young; *Decade* . . . .(Reprise)
  Harvest . . . .(Reprise)
Neil Young & Crazy Horse; *Live Rust* . . . .(Reprise)
Negasonic Teenage Warhead
Monster Magnet; *Dopes To Infinity* . . . . (A&M)
Night Has A Thousand Eyes
Anita O'Day; *Night Has A Thousand Eyes* . . . . (Emily)
Bobby Vee; *Best Of Bobby Vee* . . . . (EMI)

  Bobby Vee-Legendary Masters . . . .(EMI)
  Golden Years-1962-C . . . .(Dominion Entert.)
No Cheap Thrill
Suzanne Vega; *Nine Objects Of Desire* . . . . (A&M)
No Depression
Johnson Mountain Boys; *Goin' Up Copper Creek-C* . . . . (Copper Creek)
Uncle Tupelo; *No Depression* . . . .(Rockville)
No, No, No
Destiny's Child; *Destiny's Child* . . . . (Grass Roots/Columbia)
Oh Well - Pt. I
Fleetwood Mac; *Then Play On* . . . . (Reprise)
Old Man From The Mountain
Merle Haggard & The Strangers; *For The Record: Merle Haggard-43*
  Legendary Hits . . . . (BNA)
One Angry Dwarf And 200 Solemn Faces
Ben Folds Five; *Whatever And Ever Amen* . . . .(Caroline/550)
Only Daddy That'll Walk The Line
Hank Williams, Jr.; *Family Tradition* . . . . (WB/Curb)
Kentucky HeadHunters; *Electric Barnyard* . . . .(Mercury)
Ricky Skaggs; *My Father's Son* . . . .(Epic)
Waylon Jennings; *Best Of Waylon Jennings* . . . .(RCA)
  Waylon Jennings' Greatest Hits . . . .(RCA)
  Waylon Jennings-Early Years . . . .(RCA)
Willie Nelson; *Willie & Family Live* . . . .(Columbia)
Over There
Glenn Miller; *Original Recordings-#3-Army/Air Force Band* . . . . . . (Pair)
Glenn Miller & His Army/Air Force Band; *Glenn Miller-A Legendary*
  Performer-#3 . . . .(Bluebird)
Mormon Tabernacle Choir; *God Bless America* . . . . . . (Sony Music Classical)
Party Up
DMX; *...And Then There Was X* . . . . (Ruff Ryders/IDJMG)
Pick Me Up On Your Way Down
Charlie Walker; *Columbia Country Classics-#2-Honky Tonk*
  Heroes-C . . . . (Columbia)
  Heroes Of Country Music-#2-Legends Of Honky Tonk-C . . . . . .(Rhino)
Harlan Howard; *All-Time Favorite Country Songwriter* . . . .(Koch International)
Pill, The
Loretta Lynn; *Loretta Lynn-20 Greatest Hits* . . . . (MCA)
  The Country Music Hall Of Fame-Loretta Lynn . . . . (MCA)
Poison Ivy
Coasters; *Atlantic Rhythm & Blues 1947-1974-#4 (1958-1962)-C* . . . .(Atlantic)
  Billboard Top R&B Hits-1959-C . . . .(Rhino)
  Coasters' Greatest Hits . . . .(Atco)
  Coasters-Their Greatest Recordings-Early Years . . . .(Atco)
  More American Graffiti-C . . . . (MCA)
Nylons; *Rockapella* . . . . (Windham Hill)
  ST/Stealing Home . . . . (Atlantic)
Rolling Stones; *More Hot Rocks (big hits & fazed cookies)* . . . . (Abkco)
Precious Time
Van Morrison; *Back On Top* . . . . (Point Blank/Virgin)
Purple Pills
D12; *Devil's Night* . . . .(Shady/Interscope)
Rain, Rain, Rain
Frankie Laine; *Frankie Laine-16 Most Requested Songs* . . . .(Legacy)
Red Football
Sinead O'Connor; *Universal Mother* . . . . (Ensign)
Return Of The Red Baron
Royal Guardsmen; *Royal Guardsmen-Anthology* . . . .(One Way)
Rev On The Red Line
Foreigner; *Head Games* . . . . (Atlantic)
Ricochet
Teresa Brewer; *Best Of Teresa Brewer* . . . . (MCA Jazz)
Roving Kind, The
Guy Mitchell; *Guy Mitchell-16 Most Requested Songs* . . . .(Legacy)
Run Away
Real McCoy; *Another Night* . . . .(Arista)
Run For Your Life
Beatles; *Beatles-Box Set* . . . .(Capitol)
  Rubber Soul . . . .(Capitol)
Runaround Sue
Dion; *Billboard Top Rock 'N' Roll Hits-1961-C* . . . .(Rhino)
  Everything You Always Wanted To Hear . . . . (Laurie)
  Million-Dollar Memories #1-C . . . . (RCA)
  Oldies But Goodies-#7-C . . . . (Original Sound)
  ST/The Flamingo Kid . . . . (Motown)
  ST/The Wanderers . . . . (Warner Bros.)
Runaround, The
Xscape; *Traces Of My Lipstick* . . . . (So So Def/Columbia)
Salvation
Cranberries; *To The Faithful Departed* . . . .(Island)
Same Script, Different Cast
Whitney Houston & Deborah Cox; *Whitney Houston's Greatest Hits* . . . .(Arista)
Save The Children
Diana Ross; *Diana Ross-Anthology* . . . .(Motown)
  Touch Me In The Morning . . . .(Motown)
Gil Scott-Heron; *Gil Scott-Heron* . . . .(Bluebird)
  Revolution Will Not Be Televised . . . .(Flying Dutchman)
Marvin Gaye; *Marvin Gaye Live At The London Palladium* . . . .(Motown)

    Marvin Gaye-Anthology . . . . (Motown)
    Musical Testament 1964-1984 . . . . (Motown)
    What's Going On . . . . (Motown)

Serious Juju
    Sammy Hagar; *Ten 13* . . . . (Cabo Wabo/Beyond)

Shake The Sugar Tree
    Pam Tillis; *Homeward Looking Angel* . . . . (Arista)

Shaky Ground
    Lacy J. Dalton & Glen Campbell; *Country Duets Two By Two-C* . . . . . (Capitol)
    Lacy J. . . . . (Capitol)

Shame, Shame
    Magic Lanterns; *Shame, Shame* . . . . (Collectables)

She Can Put Her Shoes Under My Bed (Anytime)
    Johnny Duncan; *Classic Country* . . . . (Simitar)

She's Single Again
    Janie Fricke; *19 Hot Country Requests-#3-C* . . . .(Epic)
    Greatest Country Hits Of The '80s-1985-C . . . . (Columbia)
    Janie Fricke-17 Greatest Hits . . . . (Columbia)
    Very Best Of Janie Fricke . . . . (Columbia)
    Reba McEntire; *Have I Got A Deal For You* . . . .(MCA)

Shoe Was On The Other Foot
    Patti LaBelle; *Flame* . . . . (MCA)

Shop Around
    Captain & Tennille; *Captain & Tennille's Greatest Hits* . . . . . (A&M)
    Miracles; *Greatest Hits From The Beginning* . . . . (Motown)
    Hi-We're The Miracles . . . . (Motown)
    Smokey Robinson & The Miracles; *16 #1 Hits From The Early
      '60s-C* . . . . (Motown)
    Every Great Motown Song-First 25 Years-C . . . . (Motown)
    Smokey Robinson & The Miracles' Anthology . . . . (Motown)

Skating On Thin Ice
    Tower Of Power; *Bump City* . . . .(Warner Bros.)

Slow Like Honey
    Fiona Apple; *Tidal* . . . . (Clean Slate/Work)

Smoke Gets In Your Eyes
    Bryan Ferry; *Another Time Another Place* . . . . (Reprise)
    Street Life-20 Great Hits . . . . (Reprise)
    Dinah Washington; *Golden Classics-Dinah Washington* . . . . (Collectables)
    Lawrence Welk; *Musical Memories With Lawrence Welk* . . . . . . (Ranwood)
    Patti Austin; *Real Me* . . . . (Qwest)
    Platters; *Encore Of Golden Hits-Platters* . . . . (Mercury)
    Oldies But Goodies-#14-C . . . . (Original Sound)
    Platters Greatest Hits . . . . (Everest)
    ST/Always . . . .(MCA)
    ST/American Graffiti . . . .(MCA)
    Super Oldies Of The '50s-#5-C . . . . (Audio Fidelity)

Some Kind Of Trouble
    Tanya Tucker; *What Do I Do With Me* . . . . (Capitol)

Some Of These Days
    Cab Calloway; *Masters Of Jazz-#6-Male Vocal Classics-C* . . . . (Rhino)
    Leon Redbone; *On The Track* . . . .(Warner Bros.)
    Louis Armstrong; *Louis Armstrong And The Big Bands-1928-1930* . . . . . (DRG)
    Mills Brothers; *Close Harmony* . . . . (Ranwood)
    Sophie Tucker; *Legendary Entertainers* . . . . (Pro-Arte)
    Those Wonderful Years-Roaring '20s-C . . . . (JCI Assoc. Labels)

Somebody Like Me
    Eddy Arnold; *Best Of Eddy Arnold-#2* . . . .(Dunhill Compact Classics)

Stiff Upper Lip
    AC/DC; *Stiff Upper Lip* . . . . (East West)

Still A G Thang
    Snoop Dogg; *Da Game Is To Be Sold, Not To Be Told* . . . . . (No Limit/Priority)

Stop! In The Name Of Love
    Diana Ross & The Supremes; *16 #1 Hits From The Early '60s-C* . . . . (Motown)
    Diana Ross & The Supremes' Greatest Hits . . . . (Motown)
    Diana Ross & The Supremes-Anthology (1962-1969) . . . . (Motown)
    Evening With Diana Ross . . . . (Motown)
    Girl Groups-Story Of A Sound-C . . . . (Rhino)
    Motown Superstar Series-#1-Diana Ross & The Supremes . . . . (Motown)
    Hollies; *45-#89819* . . . . (Atlantic)
    Supremes; *Billboard Top Pop Hits-1965-C* . . . . (Rhino)

Storm Warning
    Bonnie Raitt; *Longing In Their Hearts* . . . . (Capitol)

Storm, The
    Garth Brooks; *Scarecrow* . . . . (Capitol)

Straight Tequila Night
    John Anderson; *Seminole Wind* . . . . (BNA)
    Today's Hot Country-C . . . . (K-Tel)

Streets Of Fire
    Duncan Browne; *Streets Of Fire* . . . . (Sire)

Sweetest Kittens (Have The Sharpest Claws)
    Meatmen; *Rock 'N' Roll Juggernaut* . . . . (Caroline)

Sympathy For The Devil
    Bryan Ferry; *These Foolish Things* . . . . (Reprise)
    Jane's Addiction; *Jane's Addiction* . . . .(Triple X Entert.)
    Rolling Stones; *Beggars Banquet* . . . . (Abkco)
    Flashpoint . . . . (Virgin)
    Get Yer Ya-Ya's Out! . . . . (Abkco)
    Hot Rocks 1964-1971 . . . . (Abkco)
    Love You Live . . . . (Virgin)

Take It On The Run
    REO Speedwagon; *A Second Decade Of Rock And Roll 1981 To 1991* . . . . (Epic)
    Hi Infidelity . . . . (Epic)
    REO Speedwagon-The Hits . . . . (Epic)

Taker, The
    Kris Kristofferson; *The Silver Tongued Devil And I* . . . . (Columbia)
    Waylon Jennings; *Essential Waylon Jennings* . . . . (RCA)
    Only Daddy That'll Walk The Line-The RCA Years . . . . (RCA)

Talk Show Shhh!
    Shae Jones; *Talk Show* . . . . (Universal)

Teenage Suicide (Don't Do It)
    Don Dixon; *If I'm A Ham Well You're A Sausage* . . . . (Restless)

That'll Be The Day
    Buddy Holly; *ST/American Graffiti* . . . . (MCA)
    Buddy Holly/The Crickets; *Buddy Holly-20 Golden Greats* . . . . (MCA)
    Chirping Crickets . . . . (MCA)
    Crickets; *Billboard Top Rock 'N' Roll Hits-1957-C* . . . . (Rhino)
    Foghat; *Best Of Foghat-#2* . . . . (Rhino)
    Energized . . . . (Rhino)
    Linda Ronstadt; *Hasten Down The Wind* . . . .(Asylum)
    Linda Ronstadt's Greatest Hits . . . .(Asylum)

Then What
    Clay Walker; *Clay Walker's Greatest Hits* . . . .(Giant)

Thin Ice
    Pink Floyd; *Shine On* . . . . (Columbia)
    The Wall . . . . (Columbia)
    Roger Waters; *The Wall-Live In Berlin* . . . . (Mercury)

Thin Ice
    Daryl Hall & John Oates; *H2O* . . . . (RCA)

Thin Ice
    Ozark Mountain Daredevils; *Car Over The Lake Album* . . . . (A&M)

Thin Ice
    Robin Trower & Jack Bruce; *Truce* . . . . (Chrysalis)

Thing, The
    Phil Harris; *The Thing About Phil Harris* . . . . (Living Era)

This Ain't No Rag, It's A Flag
    Charlie Daniels Band; *This Ain't No Rag, It's A Flag-CD Single* . . . . . (Blue Hat)

Times They Are A-Changin'
    Billy Joel; *KOHUEPT* . . . . (Columbia)
    Bob Dylan; *Biograph* . . . . (Columbia)
    Bob Dylan At Budokan . . . . (Columbia)
    Bob Dylan's Greatest Hits . . . . (Columbia)
    The Bootleg Series-Volumes 1-3 [Rare & Unreleased] . . . . (Columbia)
    The Times They Are A-Changin' . . . . (Columbia)
    Byrds; *The Byrds* . . . . (Columbia)
    Turn! Turn! Turn! . . . . (Legacy)
    Peter, Paul & Mary; *Peter, Paul and Mary In Concert* . . . . (Warner Bros.)
    Simon & Garfunkel; *Collected Works* . . . . (Columbia)
    Wednesday Morning 3 A.M. . . . . (Columbia)

Tokyo Storm Warning
    Elvis Costello; *Girls Girls Girls* . . . . (Columbia)
    Elvis Costello & The Attractions; *Blood & Chocolate* . . . . (Columbia)

Too Close For Comfort
    Eydie Gorme; *Eydie Gorme* . . . . (Taragon)

Treat Her Like A Lady
    Cornelius Brothers & Sister Rose; *Billboard Top Rock 'N' Roll Hits-
      1971-C* . . . . (Rhino)
    Didn't It Blow Your Mind: Soul Hits Of The '70s-#5-C . . . . (Rhino)
    Johnny Lee; *Best Of Johnny Lee* . . . . (Curb)

Treat Her Like A Lady
    Joe; *My Name Is Joe* . . . . (Jive)

Treat Her Like A Lady
    Jimmy Buffett; *Boats Beaches Bars & Ballads* . . . .(Margaritaville)
    Volcano . . . . (MCA)

Treat Her Like A Lady
    Temptations; *Temptations-Anthology-The Best Of The Temptations* . . (Motown)
    Truly For You . . . . (Motown)

Treat Me Right
    Pat Benatar; *Crimes Of Passion* . . . . (Chrysalis)
    ST/An Officer And A Gentleman . . . . (Island)

T-R-O-U-B-L-E
    Elvis Presley; *A Touch Of Platinum-#2* . . . .(RCA)
    Travis Tritt; *Travis Tritt's Greatest Hits-From The Beginning* . . . (Warner Bros.)
    T-R-O-U-B-L-E . . . . (Warner Bros.)

Trouble Man
    Grover Washington, Jr.; *Grover Washington, Jr.-Anthology* . . . . . . (Motown)
    Soul Box-#1 . . . . (Motown)
    Marvin Gaye; *Every Great Motown Hit Of Marvin Gaye* . . . . (Motown)
    Marvin Gaye Live At The London Palladium . . . . (Motown)
    Marvin Gaye-Anthology . . . . (Motown)
    Marvin Gaye's Greatest Hits . . . . (Motown)
    ST/Trouble Man . . . . (Motown)

Trouble On The Line
    Sawyer Brown; *Cafe On The Corner* . . . . (Curb)

Trouble With Diamonds
    Mac McAnally; *Live & Learn* . . . . (MCA)

Trouble's Comin' Like A Train
    Mark Collie; *Mark Collie* . . . . (MCA)

True Friends
Shannon Curfman; *Loud Guitars Big Suspicions* . . . . (Arista)
Ugly
Bubba Sparxxx; *Dark Days Bright Nights* . . . . (Interscope)
Walkaway Joe
Trisha Yearwood; *Hearts In Armor* . . . . (MCA)
Songbook-A Collection Of Hits . . . . (MCA)
Walkin' On The Sun
Smash Mouth; *Fush Yu Mang* . . . . (Interscope)
Warning
Green Day; *Warning* . . . . (Reprise)
Warning Labels
Doug Stone; *From The Heart* . . . . (Epic)
Warning Sign
Talking Heads; *More Songs About Buildings & Food* . . . . (Sire)
Watch Out
Fleetwood Mac; *25 Years-The Chain* . . . . (Warner Bros.)
Watch Out For Lucy
Eric Clapton; *Backless* . . . . (Polydor)
We'll Sing In The Sunshine
Gale Garnett; *21 Country Rock & Love Songs Of The '50s &*
'60s-#1-C . . . . (Laurie)
Nipper's Greatest Hits Of The '60s-#1-C . . . . (RCA)
When God Fearin' Women Get The Blues
Martina McBride; *Martina McBride's Greatest Hits* . . . . (RCA)
When The Lights Go Out
Five; *5* . . . . (Arista)
Totally Hits-#1-C . . . . (Arista)
When You Need My Love
Darryl Worley; *Hard Rain Don't Last* . . . . (DreamWorks/SKG)
White Lines (Don't Do It)
Grandmaster Flash & Melle Mel; *Hip Hop Greats-Classic Raps-C* . . . . . (Rhino)
Who's Sorry Now
Benny Goodman; *Stompin'* . . . . (Drive)
Big Bill Broonzy; *Black, Brown & White* . . . . (Evidence Music)
Bob Crosby; *Bob Crosby & His Orchestra* . . . . (EPM)
Connie Francis; *Dick Clark's 21 All-Time Hits-#1-C* . . . . . (Original Sound)
Very Best Of Connie Francis . . . . (Polydor)
Ella Fitzgerald; *The Intimate Ella* . . . . (Verve)
Esquivel; *Space-Age Bachelor Pad Music* . . . . (Bar/None)
Glen Gray; *Moonglow: 1930-1936* . . . . (Aero Space)
Nat "King" Cole; *The Billy May Sessions* . . . . (Capitol)
Ray Anthony; *Swing Back To The '40s* . . . . (Aero Space)
Wicked Game
Chris Isaak; *Heart Shaped World* . . . . (Reprise)
ST/Wild At Heart . . . . (Polydor)
Wild World
Cat Stevens; *Cat Stevens Greatest Hits* . . . . (A&M)
Tea For The Tillerman . . . . (A&M)
Jimmy Cliff; *In Concert-Best Of Jimmy Cliff* . . . . (Reprise)
Reggae Spectacular-C . . . . (A&M)
Maxi Priest; *Best Of Me* . . . . (Charisma)
Maxi . . . . (Virgin)
Woman's Threat
R. Kelly; *TP-2.com* . . . . (Jive)
You Better Run
Pat Benatar; *Crimes Of Passion* . . . . (Chrysalis)
ST/Roadie . . . . (Warner Bros.)
You Better Think Twice
Vince Gill; *When Love Finds You* . . . . (MCA)
You Can't Do That
Beatles; *Beatles-Box Set* . . . . (Capitol)
Rock 'N' Roll Music . . . . (Capitol)
The Beatles' Second Album . . . . (Capitol)
You Should Know Better
Kenny Wayne Shepherd Band; *Live On* . . . . (Giant)
You Shouldn't Kiss Me Like This
Toby Keith; *How Do You Like Me Now?!* . . . . (DreamWorks/SKG)
You'll Never Get To Heaven (If You Break My Heart)
Dionne Warwick; *Dionne Warwick* . . . . (Everest)
Dionne Warwick Greatest Hits . . . . (Everest)
Dionne Warwick-Anthology 1962-1971 . . . . (Rhino)
Hot! Live & Otherwise . . . . (Arista)
Say A Little Prayer . . . . (Dunhill Compact Classics)
Stylistics; *Best Of The Stylistics-#2* . . . . (Amherst)
Your Cheatin' Heart
Beck; *Timeless: Hank Williams Tribute-C* . . . . (Lost Highway/IDJMG)
Elvis Presley; *Elvis For Everyone!* . . . . (RCA)
Welcome To My World . . . . (RCA)
Frankie Laine; *Frankie Laine's 16 Greatest Hits* . . . . (Trip)
Frankie Laine's Greatest Hits . . . . (Columbia)
Hank Williams With His Drifting Cowboys; *24 Of Hank Williams'*
Greatest Hits . . . . (Polydor)
Hank Williams-16 Great Hits . . . . (Everest)
Hank Williams-40 Greatest Hits . . . . (Polydor)
Hank Williams, Jr.; *Very Best Of Hank Williams, Jr.* . . . . (Polydor)
Jerry Lee Lewis; *Live At The Star Club-Hamburg 1964* . . . . (Rhino)
The Golden Hits Of Jerry Lee Lewis . . . . (Smash)
Patsy Cline; *ST/Sweet Dreams* . . . . (MCA)

The Patsy Cline Story . . . . (MCA)
Ray Charles; *Ray Charles' Greatest Hits-#2* . . . . (Rhino)
You're Going To Lose That Girl
Beatles; *ST/Help!* . . . . (Capitol)
You're Gonna Change (Or I'm Gonna Leave)
Hank Williams With His Drifting Cowboys; *Hank Williams-24 Greatest*
Hits-#2 . . . . (Polydor)
Hank Williams-40 Greatest Hits . . . . (Polydor)
Health & Happiness Shows . . . . (Mercury)
Hank Williams, Jr.; *A Tribute To My Father* . . . . (Curb)
Tom Petty; *Timeless: Hank Williams Tribute-C* . . . . . . (Lost Highway/IDJMG)
You're Gonna Get What's Coming
Bonnie Raitt; *The Glow* . . . . (Warner Bros.)
Robert Palmer; *Addictions-#2* . . . . (Island)
Double Fun . . . . (Island)
You're Gonna Get Your Fingers Burned
Alan Parsons Project; *Eye In The Sky* . . . . (Arista)
Very Best Live . . . . (RCA Victor)
You're Gonna Miss Me When I'm Gone
Flatt & Scruggs; *20 All-Time Great Recordings* . . . . (Columbia)
Muddy Waters; *Muddy Waters-Complete Plantation Recordings-1941-*
1942 . . . . (Chess)
You're Gonna Miss Me When I'm Gone
Brooks & Dunn; *Brooks & Dunn-The Greatest Hits Collection* . . . . . . (Arista)
Waitin' On Sundown . . . . (Arista)
You're Still Not Safe In A Japanese Car
Jumpin' John Goldsmith; *45-#7-89686* . . . . (Atlantic)

WATER, Waterfalls

See Also: CLEAN, DROWN, FLOOD, FOOD & BEVERAGES (various), OCEAN, RAIN, RIVERS, SAILING, SHIPS, SPORTS: SWIMMING

(Love Is) Thicker Than Water
Andy Gibb; *Andy Gibb's Greatest Hits* . . . . (RSO)
Flowing Rivers . . . . (RSO)
(You're A Fish And I'm A) Water Sign
Parliament; *Motor-Booty Affair* . . . . (Casablanca)
All Over You
Live; *Throwing Copper* . . . . (Radioactive/MCA)
Aqua Boogie (A Pscychoalphadiscobetabioaquadoloop)
Parliament; *Motor-Booty Affair* . . . . (Casablanca)
Parliament's Greatest Hits . . . . (Casablanca)
Beneath Still Waters
Emmylou Harris; *Blue Kentucky Girl* . . . . (Warner Bros.)
Profile II-The Best Of Emmylou Harris . . . . (Warner Bros.)
Black Water
Doobie Brothers; *Best Of The Doobies* . . . . (Warner Bros.)
What Were Once Vices Are Now Habits . . . . (Warner Bros.)
Blood Is Thicker Than Water
Wyclef Jean featuring G&B (The Product); *The Sopranos-Music From The*
HBO Original Series . . . . (Sony Music Soundtrax)
Blue Water
Poco; *Crazy Eyes* . . . . (Epic)
Ride The Country . . . . (Epic)
Born In The Water
Tragically Hip; *Road Apples* . . . . (MCA)
Bread & Water
Gary Morris; *Stones* . . . . (Liberty)
Bridge Over Troubled Water
Aretha Franklin; *Aretha Franklin-30 Greatest Hits* . . . . (Rhino)
Aretha Franklin's Greatest Hits . . . . (Atlantic)
Live At Fillmore West . . . . (Atlantic)
Paul Simon; *America: A Tribute To Heroes-C* . . . . (Interscope)
Concert In The Park-August 15 1991 . . . . (Warner Bros.)
Paul Simon In Concert/Live Rhymin' . . . . (Columbia)
Simon & Garfunkel; *Bridge Over Troubled Water* . . . . (Columbia)
Collected Works . . . . (Columbia)
God Bless America-C . . . . (Columbia)
Simon & Garfunkel's Greatest Hits . . . . (Columbia)
The Concert In Central Park . . . . (Warner Bros.)
Bring Me Some Water
Melissa Etheridge; *Melissa Etheridge* . . . . (Island)
California Saga
Beach Boys; *Holland* . . . . (Brother)
Ten Years Of Harmony . . . . (Caribou)
Candle On The Water
Helen Reddy; *Chicken Soup For The Soul: I'll Be There For You-Songs Of*
Friendship, Brotherhood And Sisterhood-C . . . . (Rhino)
Live In London . . . . (Capitol)
ST/Pete's Dragon . . . . (Capitol)
Chant Of The Wanderer
Sons Of The Pioneers; *Sunset On The Range* . . . . (Pair)
Choppy Water (Rocky Marriage Breakdown)
Connie Kaldor; *Small Cafe* . . . . (Philo)

Cool Cool Water
Beach Boys; *10 Years Of Harmony* . . . .(Caribou)
Sunflower. . . . .(Caribou)
Cool Water
Bob Nolan; *Sound Of A Pioneer*. (Elektra)
Frankie Laine; *Frankie Laine-16 Most Requested Songs* . . . . . (Legacy)
Jack Scott; *Capitol Collectors Series-Jack Scott* . . . . (Capitol)
Joni Mitchell; *Chalk Mark In A Rain Storm* . . . .(Geffen)
Marty Robbins; *Gunfighter Ballads & Trail Songs*. . . . . . . (Legacy)
Sons Of The Pioneers; *60 Years Of Country Music-C* . . . . . . (RCA)
Best Of The Sons Of The Pioneers . . . . (RCA)
Cool Water. . . . . (RCA)
Western Country . . . . (Granite)
Cool Water
Talking Heads; *Naked*. . . . .(Fly/Sire)
Cool, Clear Water
Bonnie Raitt; *Longing In Their Hearts* . . . . (Capitol)
Crazy Water
Elton John; *Blue Moves* . . . .(MCA)
Crossing Muddy Waters
John Hiatt; *Crossing Muddy Waters*. . . . . (Vanguard)
Danger Waters (Hold Me Tight)
Joan Baez; *Joan Baez In Concert* . . . . (Vanguard)
Lovesong Album . . . . (Vanguard)
Deep Water
Asleep At The Wheel; *Asleep At The Wheel* . . . .(MCA Special Prod.)
Asleep At The Wheel featuring Garth Brooks; *Tribute To The Music Of Bob Wills And The Texas Playboys-C* . . . . (Liberty)
Bob Wills & His Texas Playboys; *Bob Wills & His Texas Playboys-Anthology 1935-1973* . . . . (Rhino)
Essential Bob Wills & His Texas Playboys-1935-1973 . . . . (Legacy)
George Strait; *George Strait-Number 7* . . . .(MCA)
Willie Nelson; *San Antonio Rose* . . . . (Columbia)
Digital Bath
Deftones; *White Pony*. . . . .(Maverick)
Dirty Water
Standells; *Best Of The Standells* . . . . (Rhino)
Nuggets-Classic Collection From The Psychedelic '60s-C. . . . (Rhino)
Super Oldies Of The '60s-#10-C . . . .(Audio Fidelity)
Don't Drink The Water
Dave Matthews Band; *Before These Crowded Streets* . . . . . . (RCA)
Don't Go Near The Water
Beach Boys; *10 Years Of Harmony* . . . .(Caribou)
Surf's Up. . . . .(Caribou)
Down By The Water
PJ Harvey; *ST/Basketball Diaries*. . . . . (Island)
To Bring You My Love . . . . (Island)
Down To The Water
America; *Harbor* . . . .(Warner Bros.)
Down To The Waterline
Dire Straits; *Dire Straits* . . . .(Warner Bros.)
Money For Nothing . . . .(Warner Bros.)
Drink Muddy Water Leaving Tennessee
Rio Grande Band; *Rio Grande Band*. . . . . (Rounder)
Fire And Water
Free; *Best Of Free* . . . .(A&M)
Fire And Water . . . . (A&M)
Free-Live . . . . (A&M)
Fire And Water
Wilson Pickett; *Very Best Of Wilson Pickett*. . . . . (Rhino)
Flood
Jars Of Clay; *Jars Of Clay* . . . .(Silvertone)
Where Music Meets Film: Live From The Sundance Film Festival-C . . . .(Beyond)
Flood Water Blues
Lonnie Johnson; *Complete Recorded Works-#1-1937-1940* . . . .(Document)
Gimme Some Water
Eddie Money; *Life For The Taking*. . . . . (Columbia)
Givin' Water To A Drowning Man
Lee Roy Parnell; *We All Get Lucky Sometimes* . . . . (Career)
Goin' Gone
Kathy Mattea; *Collection Of Hits* . . . . (Mercury)
Untasted Honey . . . . (Polydor Country)
High Water
Bob Dylan; *''Love And Theft''* . . . . (Columbia)
Holy Water
Bad Company; *Holy Water*. . . . . (Atco)
Hot Water
Level 42; *Physical Presence-#2* . . . .(Polydor)
True Colours . . . . (Polydor)
World Machine . . . . (Polydor)
Hot Water
Jefferson Starship; *Spitfire* . . . .(Grunt)
I Asked For Water (He Gave Me Gasoline)
Lucinda Williams; *Lucinda Williams* . . . . (Koch International)
I Asked For Water (She Gave Me Gasoline)
Howlin' Wolf; *Howlin' Wolf-His Best* . . . . (Chess)
The Blues-#3-C . . . . (Chess)

I Fell In The Water
John Anderson; *On Solid Ground* . . . .(BNA)
I Need You
LeAnn Rimes; *ST/Jesus-The Epic Mini-Series* . . . . . . (Sparrow/Curb/Capitol)
Itsy Bitsy Spider, The
Original Soundtrack; *Mother Goose Songs* . . . .(Madacy)
John Deere Green
Joe Diffie; *Honky Tonk Attitude* . . . . (Epic)
Joe Diffie's Greatest Hits . . . . (Epic)
Lack Of Water
Why Store; *The Why Store* . . . . (MCA)
Let's Make The Water Turn Black
Mothers Of Invention; *Lumpy Gravy* . . . .(Rykodisc)
Like Water
Bad Company; *Burnin' Sky*. . . . . (Swan Song)
Madman Across The Water
Elton John; *Live In Australia With The Melbourne Symphony Orchestra* . . . . (MCA)
Madman Across The Water . . . .(Polydor)
May This Be Love
Emmylou Harris; *Wrecking Ball* . . . .(Asylum)
Jimi Hendrix; *Are You Experienced?* . . . . (Reprise)
Michigan Water
Gregory Hines/Original Cast; *Jelly's Last Jam* . . . . (Mercury)
Michigan Water Blues
Little Brother Montgomery & Others; *Chicago Breakdown* . . . .(Takoma)
Midnight On The Water/Dry And Dusty
Skip Gorman; *A Cowboy's Wild Song To His Herd* . . . . (Rounder)
Muddy Water
Aretha Franklin; *Aretha Sings The Blues*. . . . . (Columbia)
Sonny Terry & Brownie McGhee; *Best Of Sonny Terry & Brownie McGhee* . . . .(Prestige)
Midnight Special . . . .(Fantasy)
Muddy Water
Clint Black; *Put Yourself In My Shoes*. . . . .(RCA)
Muddy Water
Johnny Rivers; *Johnny Rivers-Anthology 1964-1977* . . . . (Rhino)
Muddy Water
Original Broadway Cast; *Big River-The Adventures Of Huckleberry Finn* . . . . (MCA)
Muddy Water
Keb' Mo'; *Slow Down*. . . . . (550/Epic/Okeh)
One Good Well
Don Williams; *One Good Well* . . . .(RCA)
Our Lady Of The Well
Jackson Browne; *For Everyman* . . . .(Asylum)
Over Rusty Water
XTC; *Rag & Bone Buffet*. . . . . (Geffen)
Peaceful Waters
Gordon Lightfoot; *Lightfoot* . . . . (EMI)
Poison In The Well
10,000 Maniacs; *Blind Man's Zoo*. . . . .(Elektra)
Raging Waters
Al Jarreau; *Al Jarreau In London* . . . .(Warner Bros.)
High Crime . . . .(Warner Bros.)
Testament; *Legacy* . . . .(Atlantic)
Ripple
Grateful Dead; *American Beauty*. . . . .(Warner Bros.)
Reckoning. . . . . (Arista)
What A Long Strange Trip It's Been: The Best Of The Grateful Dead . . . .(Warner Bros.)
Jane's Addiction; *Deadicated-C* . . . . (Arista)
Ripplin' Waters
Nitty Gritty Dirt Band; *Dirt, Silver & Gold*. . . . . (One Way)
Dream. . . . .(United Artists)
Live Two Five . . . . (Capitol)
Twenty Years Of Dirt-Best Of The Nitty Gritty Dirt Band . . . . (Warner Bros.)
Rock Me On The Water
Jackson Browne; *Jackson Browne* . . . .(Asylum)
Kathy Mattea with Jackson Browne; *Red Hot + Country-C* . . . . . . (Mercury)
Linda Ronstadt; *Different Drum* . . . .(Capitol)
Linda Ronstadt . . . . (Capitol)
Linda Ronstadt-Retrospective . . . .(Capitol)
Run To The Water
Live; *The Distance To Here* . . . .(Radioactive/MCA)
Sand And Water
Beth Nielsen Chapman; *Sand And Water* . . . .(Reprise)
Scarlet Water
Johnny Duncan; *Best Of Johnny Duncan* . . . . (Columbia)
Johnny Duncan's Greatest Hits . . . . (Columbia)
Silver Springs
Fleetwood Mac; *1998 Grammy Nominees-C* . . . .(MCA)
25 Years-The Chain . . . .(Warner Bros.)
The Dance . . . .(Reprise)
Silver Waters
Ken Stover; *Cruisers 1.0*. . . . .(Hearts Of Space)
Sir Dancelot's Dream. . . . .(Hearts Of Space)

Smoke On The Water
Deep Purple; *Deepest Purple/The Very Best Of Deep Purple* .... (Warner Bros.)
   Machine Head .... (Warner Bros.)
   Made In Japan .... (Warner Bros.)
   Nobody's Perfect .... (Mercury)
   When We Rock We Rock & When We Roll We Roll.......... (Warner Bros.)
Stars On The Water
Jimmy Buffett; *Boats Beaches Bars & Ballads* .... (Margaritaville)
   One Particular Harbour .... (MCA)
Rodney Crowell; *Rodney Crowell* .... (Warner Bros.)
   Rodney Crowell-Collection .... (Warner Bros.)
Still Water
Four Tops; *Four Tops-Anthology* .... (Motown)
   Motown Superstar Series-#14-Four Tops .... (Motown)
   Still Waters Run Deep .... (Motown)
Still Water
Sawyer Brown; *Buick* .... (Curb)
Still Water Runs The Deepest
Asleep At The Wheel featuring Willie Nelson; *Tribute To The Music Of Bob
   Wills And The Texas Playboys-C* .... (Liberty)
Tall Drink Of Water
Barbara Mandrell; *Best Of Barbara Mandrell* .... (Liberty)
Mel Tillis; *Best Of Branson U.S.A.-#2-C* .... (Curb)
   Mel Tillis' Greatest Hits .... (Curb)
Tall Drink Of Water
Matraca Berg; *Speed Of Grace* .... (RCA)
Three Coins In The Fountain
Andy Williams; *Moon River & Other Great Movie Themes* .... (Columbia)
Doris Day & Frank De Vol Orchestra; *Hooray For
   Hollywood-#2-C* .... (Columbia)
Four Aces; *Billboard Top Movie Hits-1950-1954-C* .... (Rhino)
   Four Aces' Greatest Hits .... (MCA)
Frank Sinatra; *At The Movies* .... (Capitol)
   Capitol Collectors Series-Frank Sinatra .... (Capitol)
Harry James; *Harry James Plays The Songs That Sold A Million* .... (Columbia)
Julius LaRosa; *The Envelope Please-Academy Award Winning Songs-#2
   (1946-1957)-C* .... (Rhino)
To The Last Whale Medley
Crosby, Stills & Nash; *CSN* .... (Atlantic)
   Replay................................. (Atlantic)
David Crosby & Graham Nash; *Best Of David Crosby &
   Graham Nash* .... (MCA)
   Wind On The Water .... (MCA)
Walk On The Water
Creedence Clearwater Revival; *1968-1969*..................... (Fantasy)
   Creedence Clearwater Revival .... (Fantasy)
   Creedence Clearwater Revival-Chronicle-#2 .... (Fantasy)
Walk On Water
Neil Diamond; *And The Singer Sings His Song* .... (MCA)
   Glory Road-1968-1972................................. (MCA)
   Moods................................. (MCA)
Walk On Water
T. Graham Brown; *Brilliant Conversationalist*................. (Capitol)
Walk On Water
Dio; *Lock Up The Wolves* .... (Reprise)
Walk On Water
Marc Cohn; *Marc Cohn* .... (Atlantic)
Walk On Water
Marillion; *Six Of One-Half Dozen Of The Other* .... (I.R.S.)
Walk On Water
Eddie Money; *Eddie Money's Greatest Hits-Sound Of Money* ...... (Columbia)
   Nothing To Lose .... (Columbia)
Water
Hothouse Flowers; *Home* .... (London)
Water
Sugarcubes; *Here Today, Tomorrow Next Week!* .... (Elektra)
Water
Rose Royce; *ST/Car Wash*............................. (MCA)
Water
Who; *Two's Missing* .... (MCA)
Water Boy
Roger Whittaker; *Last Farewell & Other Hits*................. (RCA)
   New World In The Morning .... (RCA)
Water Boy
John Lee Hooker; *Country Blues Of John Lee Hooker* .... (Riverside)
Water Boy
Paul Robeson; *Historic Paul Robeson-Golden Classics-#3* ...... (Collectables)
Water From The Moon
Lee Ritenour; *Earth Run* .... (GRP)
Water From The Moon
Celine Dion; *Celine Dion* .... (Epic)
Water Into Wine
Bruce Cockburn; *In The Falling Dark*..................... (True North)
Water Is Wide
Joan Baez; *Very Early Joan Baez* .... (Vanguard)
Karla Bonoff; *ST/Thirtysomething* .... (Geffen)
Roger McGuinn; *Born To Rock & Roll* .... (Columbia)
Water Of Love
Dire Straits; *Dire Straits* .... (Warner Bros.)

Judds; *Collection-1983-1990*............................. (RCA)
   River Of Time .... (RCA)
Water Runs Dry
Boyz II Men; *Boyz II Men II*......................... (Motown)
Water Sign
Gary Wright; *Light Of Smiles*......................... (Warner Bros.)
Water Under The Bridge
Dan Seals; *Dan Seals' Greatest Hits* .... (Liberty)
   On Arrival .... (Capitol)
Olivia Newton-John; *Have You Never Been Mellow* .... (MCA)
Water With The Wine
Joan Armatrading; *Joan Armatrading* .... (A&M)
Waterhole
Outlaws; *Outlaws*................................. (Arista)
Watermark
Enya; *Watermark*................................. (Reprise)
Watermark
Art Garfunkel; *Watermark* .... (Legacy)
Water's Edge
Seven Mary Three; *American Standard* .... (Mammoth)
Waterwheel
Daryl Hall & John Oates; *Whole Oats* .... (Atlantic)
When The Levee Breaks
Led Zeppelin; *Led Zeppelin IV*......................... (Atlantic)
   Led Zeppelin-Box Set .... (Atlantic)
Wine Into Water
T. Graham Brown; *Wine Into Water*..................... (ISD/Intersound)

WEEKEND

**See Also: *DAYS OF THE WEEK (various), FUN, PARTY, TIME:
GENERAL, TIME: SPECIFIC, WORK***

48 Hours Till Monday
Sawyer Brown; *Buick*................................. (Curb)
Computer Weekend
Jean-Michel Jarre; *Images: The Best Of Jean-Michel Jarre*.......... (Dreyfus)
Dance Little Sister
Rolling Stones; *It's Only Rock 'N Roll*..................... (Rolling Stones)
   Made In The Shade .... (Rolling Stones)
Drugland Weekend
Hounds; *Unleashed* .... (Columbia)
Finally Friday
George Jones; *Walls Can Fall* .... (MCA)
   Working Man's Blues-C .... (Hip-O)
Friday Night Blues
John Conlee; *John Conlee-Live At Billy Bob's*................. (Razor & Tie)
   John Conlee's Greatest Hits .... (MCA)
Sonny Throckmorton; *45-#57018* .... (Mercury)
Friday On My Mind
David Bowie; *Bowie Pin Ups*......................... (Rykodisc)
Easybeats; *Best Of The Easybeats* .... (Rhino)
   Nuggets-Classic Collection From The Psychedelic '60s-C.......... (Rhino)
Here Comes The Weekend
Dave Edmunds; *Best Of Dave Edmunds* .... (Swan Song)
   Get It .... (Swan Song)
Here Comes The Weekend
Moody Blues; *Sur La Mer* .... (Polydor)
If We're Not Back In Love By Monday
Merle Haggard; *MCA Records 30 Years Of Hits-1958-1988-C* .... (MCA)
   Merle Haggard-Legends................................. (MCA)
   Merle Haggard's Greatest Hits .... (MCA)
   More Of The Best. .... (MCA)
   Ramblin' Fever .... (MCA)
It Sure Is Monday
Mark Chesnutt; *Almost Goodbye* .... (MCA)
King Of New Orleans
Better Than Ezra; *Friction, Baby* .... (Swell/Elektra)
Livin' For The Weekend
O'Jays; *Family Reunion* .... (Philadelphia Int'l)
   O'Jays-Collector's Item .... (Philadelphia Int'l)
Lonely Weekend
Yellowjackets; *Samurai Samba* .... (Warner Bros.)
Lonely Weekends
Charlie Rich; *Charlie Rich-Complete Smash Sessions* .... (Mercury)
   Lonely Weekends. .... (Sun)
   Sun's Greatest Hits-C .... (RCA)
Shelby Lynne; *Tough All Over* .... (Epic)
Long Weekend
Horslips; *Man Who Built America* .... (DJM)
Lost Weekend
Sarah Vaughan/Lol Creme/Kevin Godley; *Consequences*.......... (Mercury)
Lost Weekend
Wall Of Voodoo; *Call Of The West* .... (I.R.S.)
Lost Weekend
Woody Herman & The Woodchoppers; *1940s-Small Groups-C*..... (Columbia)

Lost Weekend
Lloyd Cole & The Commotions; *Easy Pieces.* . . . . (Capitol)
Lost Weekend
Roy Lanham; *Legends Of Country Guitar-#1-C.* . . . . (Rhino)
Lost Weekend
Del Fuegos; *Smoking In The Fields* . . . . (RCA)
Lost Weekend
Beat Farmers; *Tales Of The New West* . . . . (Rhino)
Payday/Mine 'Til Monday
Original Broadway Cast; *Tree Grows In Brooklyn* . . . . . (Sony Music Classical)
Rock 'N' Roll The Weekend
Sammy Hagar; *All Night Long* . . . . (One Way)
  Sammy Hagar . . . . (Capitol)
Saturday Night & Sunday Morning
Phil Collins; *...But Seriously* . . . . (Atlantic)
Thank God It's Friday
Love And Kisses; *ST/Thank God It's Friday* . . . . (Casablanca)
Vegas Weekend
Thelonius Monster; *Beautiful Mess* . . . . (Capitol)
Week In A County Jail, A
Tom T. Hall; *Storyteller, Poet, Philospher* . . . . (Mercury)
  Tom T. Hall's Greatest Hits-#1 . . . . (Mercury)
Weekend
Steve Wariner; *'80s Biggest Country Hits-#3-C* . . . . (MCA Special Prod.)
  Country Classics-#10-1987-C . . . . (Universal)
  It's A Crazy World . . . . (MCA)
  Steve Wariner's Greatest Hits . . . . (MCA)
Weekend
Eddie Cochran; *Eddie Cochran-Legendary Masters* . . . . (EMI)
Weekend
Dictators; *Go Girl Crazy.* . . . . (Epic)
Weekend
Wet Willie; *Which One's Willie* . . . . (Epic)
Weekend
Russ Ballard; *Winning* . . . . (Epic)
Weekend
Kenny Lattimore; *Weekend* . . . . (Arista)
Weekend Friend
Con Hunley; *Con Hunley* . . . . (Warner Bros.)
Weekend In New England
Barry Manilow; *Barry Manilow/Live* . . . . (Arista)
  Barry Manilow's Greatest Hits-#2 . . . . (Arista)
  This One's For You . . . . (Arista)
Weekend In The Country
Original Cast; *A Little Night Music* . . . . (Columbia)
Original London Cast; *A Little Night Music* . . . . (RCA)
Weekend Love
Golden Earring; *No Promises-No Debts* . . . . (Polydor)
Weekend Love
Queen Latifah; *Black Reign* . . . . (Motown)
Weekend Of A Private Secretary
Eileen Farrell; *Eileen Farrell Sings Johnny Mercer* . . . . (Reference)
Mildred Bailey; *Her Greatest* . . . . (Columbia)
Weekend Song
Billy Joel; *Streetlife Serenade.* . . . . (Columbia)
Weekend Warriors
Ted Nugent; *Weekend Warriors* . . . . (Epic)
Weekend With Feather
Brook Benton; *This Is Brook Benton* . . . . (All Platinum)
When Country Comes To Town
Toby Keith; *How Do You Like Me Now?!* . . . . (DreamWorks/SKG)
Where The Blacktop Ends
keith urban; *keith urban* . . . . (Capitol)
Wild Week-End
Bill Anderson; *Bill Anderson-Legend.* . . . . (Masters)
  MCA Records 30 Years Of Hits-1958-1988-C . . . . (MCA)
  Still. . . . . (MCA Special Prod.)
Will You Be Staying After Sunday
Peppermint Rainbow; *Bubble Gum Classics-C* . . . . (MCA Special Prod.)
Workin' For The Weekend
Ken Mellons; *Ken Mellons* . . . . (Epic)
  Steppin' Country-#2-C . . . . (Columbia)
Working For The Weekend
Loverboy; *Big Ones* . . . . (Columbia)
  Get Lucky . . . . (Columbia)

WILD

See Also: **AMERICAN WEST, COUNTRY, DANGER & DISASTER, FREEDOM, NATURE, REBELS**

Bad Boys Running Wild
Scorpions; *Love At First Sting* . . . . (Mercury)
  Wold Wide Live . . . . (Mercury)
Born To Be Wild
Steppenwolf; *Billboard Top Rock 'N' Roll Hits-1968-C* . . . . (Rhino)
  Live Steppenwolf . . . . (MCA)

  Steppenwolf . . . . (MCA)
  Steppenwolf-16 Greatest Hits. . . . . (MCA)
  Vintage Music-#9 & 10-C. . . . . (MCA)
Buck Wild
E.U.; *Livin' Large* . . . . (Virgin)
Call Of The Wild
Aaron Tippin; *Call Of The Wild* . . . . (RCA)
Candy's Room
Bruce Springsteen; *Darkness On The Edge Of Town* . . . . (Columbia)
Bruce Springsteen & The E Street Band; *Bruce Springsteen & The E Street
  Band Live/1975-85* . . . . (Legacy)
Child Of The Wild Blue Yonder
John Hiatt; *Stolen Moments* . . . . (A&M)
Cowboy's Wild Song To His Herd
Skip Gorman; *A Cowboy's Wild Song To His Herd.* . . . . (Rounder)
Cry Of The Wild Goose
Frankie Laine; *Frankie Laine-Golden Hits* . . . . (Mercury)
Deuces Are Wild
Aerosmith; *Beavis & Butt-Head Experience.* . . . . (Geffen)
Hold Me, Thrill Me, Kiss Me, Kill Me
U2; *Number One Movie Hits-C.* . . . . (ESX Entert.)
  ST/Batman Forever . . . . (Atlantic)
Hot! Wild! Unrestricted! Crazy Love
Millie Jackson; *Imitation Of Love* . . . . (Jive)
I Go Wild
Rolling Stones; *Voodoo Lounge* . . . . (Virgin)
In Your Wildest Dreams
Tina Turner & Barry White; *Wildest Dreams* . . . . (Virgin)
Jokers Wild
Paul Hardcastle; *Hardcastle 2.* . . . . (JVC Musical Industries)
Let Sally Drive
Sammy Hagar; *Ten 13* . . . . (Cabo Wabo/Beyond)
My Wild Irish Rose
Magic Organ; *22 Great Organ Favorites* . . . . (Ranwood)
Mom & Dads; *One Dozen Roses* . . . . (Crescendo)
Out With A Bang
David Lee Murphy; *Out With A Bang* . . . . (MCA)
Pagan Poetry
Bjork; *Vespertine* . . . . (Elektra)
Restless & Wild
Accept; *Accept* . . . . (Portrait)
  Restless & Wild . . . . (Portrait)
Ride A Wild Horse
Kenny Nolan; *Night Miracles* . . . . (Casablanca)
Ride The Wild Surf
Jan & Dean; *Monster Summer Hits-Wild Surf-C* . . . . (Capitol)
  Surf City-Best Of Jan & Dean. . . . . (EMI)
  Surfin' Hits-C . . . . (Rhino)
Ridge Running Roan
Skip Gorman; *A Cowboy's Wild Song To His Herd.* . . . . (Rounder)
Run Away Child, Running Wild
Temptations; *All The Million-Sellers* . . . . (Motown)
  Cloud Nine . . . . (Motown)
  Compact Command Performances-Temptations . . . . (Motown)
  Temptations' Greatest Hits-#2 . . . . (Motown)
  Temptations-Anthology-The Best Of The Temptations . . . . (Motown)
Running Wild
Judas Priest; *Hell Bent For Leather.* . . . . (Columbia)
  Unleashed In The East . . . . (Columbia)
Running Wild
Benny Goodman Quartet; *Bluebird Sampler-C.* . . . . (Bluebird)
Running Wild
Roxy Music; *Flesh + Blood* . . . . (Atco)
Running Wild
Sam Cooke; *Golden Sound Of Sam Cooke* . . . . (Trip)
She Drives Me Wild
Michael Jackson; *Dangerous* . . . . (Epic)
Some Girls Do
Sawyer Brown; *Dirt Road* . . . . (Curb)
Something Wild
John Hiatt; *Perfectly Good Guitar.* . . . . (A&M)
Theme From "Wild Wild West"
Original Soundtrack; *CBS: The First 50 Years* . . . . (TVT)
  Television's Greatest Hits-#1-C . . . . (TVT)
Walk On The Wild Side
Edie Brickell & New Bohemians; *ST/Flashback.* . . . . (WTG)
Lou Reed; *Between Thought & Expression-Anthology* . . . . (RCA)
  Lou Reed Live . . . . (RCA)
  Transformer . . . . (RCA)
  Walk On The Wild Side-The Best Of Lou Reed . . . . (RCA)
Who's Gonna Ride Your Wild Horses
U2; *Achtung Baby* . . . . (Island)
Wild
Thompson Twins; *Big Trash* . . . . (Red Eye)
Wild
Seal; *Seal.* . . . . (Sire)

Wild & Blue
Hank Williams, Jr.; *Major Moves* .... (WB/Curb)
John Anderson; *John Anderson's Greatest Hits* .... (Warner Bros.)
   Wild & Blue .... (Warner Bros.)

Wild & Crazy Love
Mary Jane Girls; *Only Four You* .... (Motown)

Wild & Wooly
Chris LeDoux; *Radio & Rodeo Hits* .... (Liberty)
   Wild & Wooly .... (Liberty)

Wild About Me
Prairie Oyster; *Prairie Oyster* .... (RCA)

Wild About My Lovin'
Stone Poneys Featuring Linda Ronstadt; *The Stone Poneys Featuring Linda Ronstadt* .... (EMI)

Wild About You Baby
Elmore James; *Let's Cut It-Very Best Of Elmore James* .... (Flair)

Wild America
Tora Tora; *Wild America* .... (A&M)

Wild And Loose
Time; *What Time Is It?* .... (Warner Bros.)

Wild Angel
John Cougar; *Nothin' Matters And What If It Did* .... (Riva)

Wild Angels
Martina McBride; *Angels Among Us-C* .... (RCA)
   Wild Angels .... (RCA)

Wild As A Wildcat
Charlie Walker; *Charlie Walker-Golden Hits* .... (Plantation)

Wild Bill Jones
Hot Rize; *Radio Boogie* .... (Flying Fish)
Kentucky Colonels; *Appalachian Swing!* .... (Rounder)

Wild Bill's Blues
Country Gazette; *Strictly Instrumental* .... (Flying Fish)

Wild Billy's Circus Story
Bruce Springsteen; *The Wild, The Innocent & The E Street Shuffle* ... (Columbia)

Wild Boys
Duran Duran; *Arena* .... (Capitol)
   Decade .... (Capitol)

Wild Cat
UB40; *Present Arms* .... (Virgin)

Wild Cherry
Foghat; *Best Of Foghat* .... (Rhino)
   Energized .... (Rhino)

Wild Cherry
Leroy Washington; *Sound Of The Swamp-Best Of Excello-#1-C* .... (Rhino)

Wild Child
W.A.S.P.; *Head Banging Metal-C* .... (Priority)
   Last Command .... (Capitol)
   Live...In The Raw .... (Capitol)

Wild Child
Heart; *Brigade* .... (Capitol)
   Rock The House "Live" .... (Capitol)

Wild Child
Doors; *Doors 13* .... (Elektra)
   Doors-Classics .... (Elektra)
   Soft Parade .... (Elektra)

Wild Child
Lou Reed; *Walk On The Wild Side-The Best Of Lou Reed* .... (RCA)

Wild Child
Untouchables; *Wild Child* .... (MCA)

Wild Children
Van Morrison; *Hard Nose The Highway* .... (Polydor)
   It's Too Late To Stop Now .... (Warner Bros.)

Wild Cow Moan
Big Joe Turner & Sonny Boy Williamson; *Story Of The Blues-C* .... (Columbia)

Wild Dog Moan
Drivin' N' Cryin'; *Mystery Road* .... (Island)

Wild Dogs
Hank Williams, Jr.; *Bocephus Box-Collection-1979-1992* ...... (Capricorn)

Wild Dogs
Tommy Bolin; *The Ultimate Tommy Bolin* .... (Geffen)

Wild Eyed Boy From Freecloud
David Bowie; *Sound + Vision* .... (Rykodisc)
   Space Oddity .... (Rykodisc)
   ST/Ziggy Stardust-The Motion Picture .... (Rykodisc)

Wild Flowers
Jimmy Smith; *Best Of Jimmy Smith* .... (Curb)

Wild For You Baby (Goin')
Bonnie Raitt; *Bonnie Raitt-Collection* .... (Warner Bros.)
   The Glow .... (Warner Bros.)

Wild Frontier
Bruce Hornsby & The Range; *The Way It Is* .... (RCA)

Wild Frontier
Gary Moore; *Wild Frontier* .... (Virgin)

Wild Goose Grasses In Tarrytown
Weavers; *Weavers' Greatest Hits* .... (Vanguard)
   Weavers-Classics .... (Vanguard)

Wild Heart
Stevie Nicks; *Wild Heart* .... (Modern)

Wild Heart Of The Young
Karla Bonoff; *Wild Heart Of The Young* .... (Columbia)

Wild Hearted Son
Cult; *Ceremony* .... (Sire)

Wild Hearts
Roy Orbison; *Legendary Roy Orbison* .... (Sony Music Special Prod.)

Wild Hearts Run Out Of Time
Roy Orbison; *King Of Hearts* .... (Virgin)

Wild Honey
Beach Boys; *Absolute Best-#2* .... (Capitol)
   Party!/Stack-O-Tracks .... (Capitol)
   Smiley Smile/Wild Honey .... (Capitol)

Wild Honey Pie
Beatles; *Beatles-Box Set* .... (Capitol)
   The Beatles (White Album) .... (Capitol)

Wild Horses
Rolling Stones; *Hot Rocks 1964-1971* .... (Abkco)
   Made In The Shade .... (Rolling Stones)
   Singles Collection-The London Years .... (Abkco)
   Sticky Fingers .... (Virgin)

Wild Horses
Garth Brooks; *No Fences* .... (Capitol)

Wild Horses
Gino Vannelli; *Big Dreams Never Sleep* .... (Epic Portrait Assoc.)

Wild Horses
Sundays; *Blind* .... (David Geffen Co.)

Wild Horses
Flying Burrito Brothers; *Farther Along-Best Of The Flying Burrito Brothers* .... (A&M)

Wild Horses
Suzy Bogguss; *Moment Of Truth* .... (Capitol)

Wild Horses
Prefab Sprout; *Jordan-The Comeback* .... (Epic)
   Life Of Surprises-Best Of Prefab Sprout .... (Epic)

Wild In The Country
Elvis Presley; *The Other Sides-Worldwide Gold Award Hits, Vol. 2* ..... (RCA)

Wild In The Streets
Circle Jerks; *Best Of Rodney On The 'ROQ* .... (Posh Boy)
   Group Sex/Wild In The Streets .... (Frontier)

Wild In The Streets
Bon Jovi; *Slippery When Wet* .... (Jambco)

Wild Injuns
Neville Brothers; *Yellow Moon* .... (A&M)

Wild Is Love
Nat "King" Cole; *Nat "King" Cole (Box Set)* .... (Capitol)
   The Nat "King" Cole Story .... (Capitol)

Wild Is The Wind
David Bowie; *Changestwobowie* .... (RCA)
   Sound + Vision .... (Rykodisc)
   Station To Station .... (Rykodisc)

Wild Is The Wind
Johnny Mathis; *Johnny Mathis' Greatest Hits* .... (Columbia)
   Johnny Mathis-16 Most Requested Songs .... (Columbia)

Wild Kentucky Roan
Mike Auldridge; *Mike Auldridge & Old Dog* .... (Flying Fish)

Wild Kentucky Skies
Marty Brown; *Wild Kentucky Skies* .... (MCA)

Wild Kids
David Benoit; *Urban Daydreams* .... (GRP)

Wild Life
Wings; *Wild Life* .... (Capitol)

Wild Life
INXS; *Kick* .... (Atlantic)

Wild Little Willy
Ronnie Hawkins and The Hawks; *Best Of Ronnie Hawkins and The Hawks* .... (Rhino)

Wild Love
Chris Isaak; *Chris Isaak* .... (Warner Bros.)

Wild Man
Ricky Van Shelton; *Ricky Van Shelton's Greatest Hits Plus* .... (Columbia)
   Steppin' Country-C .... (Columbia)

Wild Man
J. Geils Band; *Flashback-Best Of The J. Geils Band* .... (EMI)

Wild Man Blues
Jelly Roll Morton; *Jelly's Last Jam & Other Morton Classics* .... (Bluebird)
Louis Armstrong; *Louis Armstrong-Best Of The Decca Years-#2-The Composer-C* .... (MCA)

Wild Montana Skies
John Denver; *It's About Time* .... (RCA)
   John Denver's Greatest Hits-#3 .... (RCA)
John Denver & Emmylou Harris; *Collector's Series-Duets-C* .... (RCA)

Wild Mountain Honey
Steve Miller Band; *Fly Like An Eagle* .... (Capitol)
   Steve Miller Band's Greatest Hits-1974-78 .... (Capitol)

Wild Mountain Thyme
Armstrong Family; *Wheel Of The Year-Thirty Years With The Armstrong Family* .... (Flying Fish)
Byrds; *Fifth Dimension*. .... (Columbia)
Joan Baez; *Farewell Angelina* .... (Vanguard)
Wild Night
John Mellencamp & Me'shell Ndegeocello; *Dance Naked* .... (Mercury)
Rough Harvest. .... (Mercury)
Martha Reeves; *ST/Thelma & Louise* .... (MCA)
Van Morrison; *Best Of Van Morrison*. .... (Polydor)
Tupelo Honey. .... (Polydor)
Wild Night In Odessa
Klezmorim; *Metropolis* .... (Flying Fish)
Wild Nights, Hot & Crazy Days
Judas Priest; *Metal Works-1973-1993* .... (Columbia)
Turbo. .... (Columbia)
Wild One
Faith Hill; *Take Me As I Am* .... (Warner Bros.)
Wild One, Forever
Tom Petty And The Heartbreakers; *Tom Petty & The Heartbreakers* .... (Gone Gator)
Wild Places
Dan Fogelberg; *Live-Greetings From The West* .... (Full Moon)
Wild Reaction
Gipsy Kings; *Prey*. .... (Simitar)
Wild Rice
Lee Ritenour; *Best Of Lee Ritenour* .... (Epic)
First Course. .... (Epic)
Wild Ride
Dwight Yoakam; *This Time* .... (Reprise)
Wild River
Golden Palominos; *Dead Horse* .... (Celluloid)
Our World Of Music .... (Celluloid)
Wild Rover
John Faulkner; *Kind Providence*. .... (Green Linnet)
Wild Sewerage Tickles Brazil
Squeeze; *Squeeze-Classics-#25* .... (A&M)
Wild Sex (In The Working Class)
Oingo Boingo; *Best O' Boingo* .... (MCA)
Boingo Alive. .... (MCA)
Nothing To Fear. .... (A&M)
Wild Side
Motley Crue; *Decade Of Decadence* .... (Elektra)
Girls Girls Girls. .... (Elektra)
Wild Side Of Life
Freddy Fender; *Before The Next Teardrop Falls* .... (Universal)
Best Of Freddy Fender. .... (MCA)
Hank Thompson; *Best Of The Best Of Hank Thompson* .... (Gusto)
Capitol Collectors Series-Hank Thompson .... (Capitol)
Hank Thompson's All-Time Greatest Hits .... (Curb)
Traditions In Country Music-C .... (Capitol)
Rod Stewart; *Night On The Town* .... (Warner Bros.)
Wild Strawberries
Gordon Lightfoot; *Waiting For You* .... (Reprise)
Wild Streak
Hank Williams, Jr.; *Wild Streak* .... (WB/Curb)
Wild Tales
Crosby, Stills & Nash; *CSN* .... (Atlantic)
Wild Thing
Jimi Hendrix; *Essential Jimi Hendrix, Volume 2* .... (Reprise)
Live At Winterland. .... (Rykodisc)
ST/Jimi Plays Monterey. .... (Reprise)
Tone Loc; *Loc-ed After Dark* .... (Delicious Vinyl)
Rap's Biggest Hits-C. .... (K-Tel)
Rock The First-#6-C .... (Sandstone Music)
Troggs; *Billboard Top Rock 'N' Roll Hits-1966-C* .... (Rhino)
Frat Rock!-C. .... (Rhino)
History Of British Rock-#3-C .... (Rhino)
Wild Things Run Fast
Joni Mitchell; *Wild Things Run Fast*. .... (Geffen)
Wild Turkey
Lacy J. Dalton; *Hot Country Rock-#1-C*. .... (Epic)
Wild Tyme
Jefferson Airplane; *2400 Fulton Street-An Anthology* .... (RCA)
Best Of The Jefferson Airplane .... (RCA)
Wild Week-End
Bill Anderson; *Bill Anderson-Legend*. .... (Masters)
MCA Records 30 Years Of Hits-1958-1988-C .... (MCA)
Still. .... (MCA Special Prod.)
Wild West End
Dire Straits; *Dire Straits*. .... (Warner Bros.)
Wild West Hero
Electric Light Orchestra; *Out Of The Blue* .... (Jet)
Wild West Show
Darden Smith; *Native Soil* .... (Watermelon)
Wild West Show/Dog Act
Original Broadway Cast; *Will Rogers Follies* .... (Columbia)

Wild Wild Life
Talking Heads; *Popular Favorites-1984-1992* .... (Sire)
True Stories .... (Sire)
Wild Wild West
Will Smith; *Willenium*. .... (Columbia)
Wild Wild Women
Henry Lewis; *Music From The New York Stage (1890-1920)-#4-1917-1920-C*. .... (Pearl)
Wild Women Do
Natalie Cole; *ST/Pretty Woman*. .... (EMI)
Wild World
Cat Stevens; *Cat Stevens Greatest Hits* .... (A&M)
Tea For The Tillerman .... (A&M)
Jimmy Cliff; *In Concert-Best Of Jimmy Cliff* .... (Reprise)
Reggae Spectacular-C .... (A&M)
Maxi Priest; *Best Of Me*. .... (Charisma)
Maxi .... (Virgin)
Wild, Wild West
Kool Moe Dee; *How Ya Like Me Now* .... (Jive)
Jive Presents...Yo! MTV Raps-C .... (Jive)
Kool Moe Dee's Greatest Hits .... (Jive)
Mr. Magic's Rap Attack-#4-C .... (Profile)
Wild, Wild West
Escape Club; *Rock The First-#3-C* .... (Priority)
Wild Wild West .... (Atlantic)
Wilder Days
Baillie & The Boys; *Best Of Baillie & The Boys* .... (RCA)
Wildest Dreams
Asia; *Asia* .... (Geffen)
Then & Now .... (Geffen)
Wildest Dreams
Annie Haslam; *Annie Haslam* .... (Epic)
Wildest Dreams
Dolly Parton; *Eagle When She Flies* .... (Columbia)
Wildest Times Of The World
Vonda Shepard; *ST/Songs From ''Ally McBeal'' Featuring Vonda Shepard* .... (550/Epic)
Wild-Eyed Dream
Ricky Van Shelton; *Wild-Eyed Dream* .... (Columbia)
Wild-Eyed Gypsies
John Hiatt; *Hangin' Around The Observatory*. .... (Epic)
Wild-Eyed Southern Boys
38 Special; *Wild-Eyed Southern Boys* .... (A&M)
Wildfire
Michael Martin Murphey; *'70s Greatest Rock Hits-#3-High Times-C* .. (Priority)
Best Of Michael Martin Murphey. .... (Liberty)
Blue Sky-Night Thunder. .... (Epic)
Super Hits Of The '70s-Have A Nice Day-#14-C .... (Rhino)
Wildfire Woman
Bad Company; *Straight Shooter* .... (Swan Song)
Wildflower
Skylark; *Reaching For The Sky-Towering Soul From The '70s-C* ..... (Capitol)
Super Hits Of The '70s-Have A Nice Day-#10-C .... (Rhino)
Wildflower
Carter Family; *60 Years Of Country Music-C* .... (RCA)
Wildflower
O'Jays; *Live In London* .... (Philadelphia Int'l)
O'Jays-Collector's Item .... (Philadelphia Int'l)
Wildflowers
Dolly Parton/Emmylou Harris/Linda Ronstadt; *Trio* .... (Warner Bros.)
Wildflowers In A Mason Jar
John Denver; *Some Days Are Diamonds*. .... (RCA)
Wildlife
Yellowjackets; *Four Corners* .... (MCA)
Live Wires. .... (GRP)
Wildside
Marky Mark And The Funky Bunch; *Music For The People* .... (Interscope)
Wildwood Days
Bobby Rydell; *Bobby Rydell*. .... (Big Top)
Wildwood Flower
Carter Family; *Legends Of Country Guitar-#2-C* .... (Rhino)
Chet Atkins; *Tennessee Guitar Man* .... (Pair)
Hank Thompson & Merle Travis; *Great Records Of The Decade-'50s-Pop-#1-C* .... (Curb)
Hank Thompson's Greatest Hits-#2 .... (Curb)
Kentucky Colonels; *Featuring Clarence White* .... (Rounder)
Young Thing, Wild Dreams (Rock Me)
Red Rider; *Breaking Curfew* .... (Capitol)
Your Good Girl's Gonna Go Bad
Billie Jo Spears; *Best Of Billie Jo Spears* .... (CEMA Special Prod.)
Best Of Billie Jo Spears .... (Razor & Tie)
K.T. Oslin; *Tammy Wynette...Remembered-C* .... (Asylum)
Tammy Wynette; *Tammy Wynette-Anniversary-20 Years Of Hits* ...... (Epic)
Tammy Wynette's Greatest Hits .... (Epic)
Your Good Girl's Gonna Go Bad .... (Legacy)
Your Wildest Dreams
Moody Blues; *Other Side Of Life* .... (Polydor)

WIND

*See Also: **AIR, DANGER & DISASTER, NATURE, RAIN, SAILING, SKY, SPIRITS***

Against The Wind
Bob Seger & The Silver Bullet Band; *Against The Wind* .... (Capitol)
Nine Tonight .... (Capitol)
ST/Forrest Gump .... (Epic/Sony Music Soundtrax)
Any Old Wind That Blows
Johnny Cash; *Johnny Cash-16 Biggest Hits-#2* .... (Legacy)
Any Way The Wind Blows
Frank Zappa; *Cruising With Ruben & The Jets* .... (Barking Pumpkin)
Mothers Of Invention; *Freak Out* .... (Barking Pumpkin)
Any Way The Wind Blows
Southern Pacific; *County Line* .... (Warner Bros.)
ST/Pink Cadillac .... (Warner Bros.)
Ashes In The Wind
Moe Bandy; *No Regrets* .... (Curb)
Because
Beatles; *Abbey Road* .... (Parlophone)
Beatles-Box Set .... (Capitol)
Black Throated Wind
Bob Weir; *Ace* .... (Grateful Dead)
Grateful Dead; *Steal Your Face* .... (Grateful Dead)
Blow Away
George Harrison; *Best Of Dark Horse 1976-1989* .... (Dark Horse)
George Harrison .... (Dark Horse)
ST/Nuns On The Run .... (Mercury)
Blow Away
Grateful Dead; *Built To Last* .... (Arista)
Blowin' In The Wind
Bob Dylan; *Before The Flood* .... (Columbia)
Biograph .... (Columbia)
Bob Dylan At Budokan .... (Columbia)
Bob Dylan's Greatest Hits .... (Columbia)
Freewheelin' .... (Columbia)
God Bless America-C .... (Columbia)
Greatest Folksingers Of The '60s-C .... (Vanguard)
Joan Baez; *ST/Forrest Gump* .... (Epic/Sony Music Soundtrax)
Peter, Paul & Mary; *10 Years Together/The Best Of Peter, Paul and Mary* .... (Warner Bros.)
Holiday Celebration .... (Warner Bros.)
In The Wind .... (Warner Bros.)
Peter, Paul and Mary In Concert .... (Warner Bros.)
Stevie Wonder; *Motown Year By Year-The Sound Of Young America-1966-C* .... (Motown)
Blowing Kisses In The Wind
Paula Abdul; *Spellbound* .... (Captive)
Breeze From Alabama
Max Morath; *Max Morath Plays Ragtime* .... (Vanguard)
The World Of Scott Joplin .... (Vanguard)
Scott Joplin; *The Entertainer-#4* .... (Biograph)
Bus Stop
Hollies; *Best Of The Hollies* .... (EMI)
History Of British Rock-#3-C .... (Rhino)
The Hollies' Greatest Hits .... (Epic)
Button Up Your Overcoat
Rose Murphy; *Rose Murphy Sings Again* .... (MCA)
Sarah Vaughan; *Sarah Vaughan* .... (Everest)
Call Me The Breeze
J.J. Cale; *Naturally* .... (MCA)
Lynyrd Skynyrd; *Best Of The Rest Of Lynyrd Skynyrd* .... (MCA)
One More From The Road .... (MCA)
Second Helping .... (MCA)
Southern By The Grace Of God-Tribute '87 .... (MCA)
Mavericks; *Skynyrd Frynds-C* .... (MCA)
Calling In The Wind
Judds; *Collection-1983-1990* .... (RCA)
Love Can Build A Bridge .... (MCA)
Candle In The Wind
Elton John; *Goodbye Yellow Brick Road* .... (Polydor)
Live In Australia With The Melbourne Symphony Orchestra .... (MCA)
Your Songs .... (Polydor)
Candle In The Wind 1997
Elton John; *Candle In The Wind 1997 (Diana, Princess Of Wales) (Single)* .... (Rocket)
Caribbean Breeze
Rippingtons; *Life In The Tropics* .... (Peak/Concord)
Cast Your Fate To The Wind
Sandpipers; *Guantanamera* .... (A&M)
Vince Guaraldi; *Original Jazz Classics-#1* .... (Fantasy)
Vince Guaraldi's Greatest Hits .... (Fantasy)
Catch The Wind
Donovan; *Donovan-Hits* .... (Epic)
Donovan's Greatest Hits .... (Epic)
History Of British Rock-#2-C .... (Rhino)
The Secret Policeman's Other Ball/The Music .... (Rhino)
Chasin' The Wind
Chicago; *Twenty 1* .... (Full Moon)
Chasing The Wind
Greg Karukas; *Nightshift* .... (N-Coded)
Cold Wind In August
Van Morrison; *Period Of Transition* .... (Warner Bros.)
Cold Windy City Of Chicago
Boxcar Willie; *Best Of Boxcar Willie-#1* .... (Mainstreet)
Colors Of The Wind
Judy Kuhn; *Princess Collection* .... (Disney)
Vanessa Williams; *ST/Pocahontas* .... (Hollywood)
Vanessa Williams' Greatest Hits-The First Ten Years .... (Mercury)
Devil Wind
Bob Welch; *Three Hearts* .... (Capitol)
Down In The Valley
Elvis Presley; *Reconsider Baby* .... (RCA)
Leadbelly; *Defense Blues-Golden Classics-#2* .... (Collectables)
Pete Seeger; *American Favorite Ballads-#1* .... (Smithsonian Folkways)
Drops Of Jupiter (Tell Me)
Train; *Drops Of Jupiter* .... (Aware/C2/Columbia)
Dust In The Wind
Kansas; *Best Of Kansas* .... (CBS Associated)
Point Of Know Return .... (Kirshner)
Two For The Show .... (Kirshner)
Evil Wind
Bad Company; *Desolation Angels* .... (Swan Song)
Fishin' In The Dark
Nitty Gritty Dirt Band; *Billboard Top Country Hits-1987-C* .... (Rhino)
Hold On .... (Warner Bros.)
More Great Dirt-Best Of Nitty Gritty Dirt Band .... (Warner Bros.)
Four Strong Winds
Ian & Sylvia; *Best Of Ian & Sylvia* .... (Vanguard)
Ian & Sylvia's Greatest Hits .... (Vanguard)
Neil Young; *Comes A Time* .... (Reprise)
Gone With The Wind
Art Pepper; *Intensity* .... (Contemporary)
Art Tatum; *Solo Masterpieces-#2* .... (Pablo)
Barney Kessel; *Music To Listen To Barney Kessel By* .... (Contemporary)
Clifford Brown; *Clifford Brown* .... (EMI)
Dave Brubeck; *I Like Jazz-Essence Of Dave Brubeck* .... (Columbia)
Dave Brubeck Quartet; *Gone With The Wind* .... (Columbia)
Dick Jurgens; *Best Of The Sweet Bands* .... (Hindsight)
Duprees; *Best Of The Duprees* .... (Rhino)
Ella Fitzgerald & Joe Pass; *Speak Love* .... (Pablo)
Sarah Vaughan; *Misty* .... (Mercury)
Goodnight Moon
Shivaree; *I Oughtta Give You A Shot...* .... (Capitol)
Gypsy Wind
Dan Fogelberg; *Phoenix* .... (Full Moon)
Hasten Down The Wind
Linda Ronstadt; *Different Drum* .... (Capitol)
Warren Zevon; *Warren Zevon* .... (Asylum)
Hear The Wind Howl
Leo Kottke; *Mudlark* .... (Capitol)
My Feet Are Smiling .... (Capitol)
Hickory Wind
Byrds; *Columbia Country Classics-#5-A New Tradition-C* .... (Columbia)
Sweetheart Of The Rodeo .... (Columbia)
The Byrds .... (Columbia)
Emmylou Harris; *Blue Kentucky Girl* .... (Warner Bros.)
Gram Parsons; *Grievous Angel* .... (Reprise)
Howlin' Wind
Graham Parker; *Howlin' Wind* .... (Mercury)
Pourin' It All Out-Mercury Years .... (Mercury)
I Know What I Know
Paul Simon; *Graceland* .... (Warner Bros.)
I Talk To The Wind
King Crimson; *In The Court Of The Crimson King-An Observation By King Crimson* .... (Editions E.G.)
Idiot Wind
Bob Dylan; *Blood On The Tracks* .... (Columbia)
Hard Rain .... (Columbia)
The Bootleg Series-Volumes 1-3 [Rare & Unreleased] .... (Columbia)
January Wind
Erica Wheeler; *Three Wishes* .... (Signature)
Let It All Blow
Dazz Band; *Dazz Band's Greatest Hits* .... (Motown)
Jukebox .... (Motown)
Let The Four Winds Blow
Fats Domino; *Best Of Fats Domino* .... (EMI)
Billboard Top R&B Hits-1961-C .... (Rhino)
Roy Brown; *Best Of New Orleans Rhythm & Blues-#1-C* .... (Rhino)
Lighthouse's Tale
Nickel Creek; *Nickel Creek* .... (Sugar Hill)
Lonely Wind
Kansas; *Kansas* .... (Kirshner)
Two For The Show .... (Kirshner)
Louise
Maurice Chevalier; *Louise* .... (ASV)

Man Of La Mancha
Original Cast; *Lost In The Stars* . . . .(MCA)
Original London Cast; *Man Of La Mancha* . . . .(MCA)
Mandolin Wind
Rod Stewart; *Best Of Rod Stewart-#2*. . . . . (Mercury)
Every Picture Tells A Story . . . . (Mercury)
Sing It Again, Rod . . . . (Mercury)
Storyteller/The Complete Anthology: 1964-1990 . . . .(Warner Bros.)
Many A Long & Lonesome Highway
Rodney Crowell; *Keys To The Highway*. . . . . (Columbia)
Taste Of Texas-Songs 'Bout Texas By Texans-C . . . . (Columbia)
March Winds And April Showers
Wingy Manone; *Wingy Manone Collection-#3-1934-1935* . . . . (Collector's Classics)
March Winds Gonna Blow My Blues All Away
Carter Family; *Longing For Old Virginia: Their Complete Victor Recordings-1934* . . . . (Rounder)
Midnight Wind
Charlie Daniels Band; *Midnight Wind* . . . .(Epic)
Midnight Wind
John Stewart; *Bombs Away Dream Babies* . . . . (RSO)
My Oklahoma Home (It Blowed Away)
Sis Cunningham; *Best Of Broadside 1962-1968: Anthems Of The American Underground From The Pages Of Broadside Magazine-C* . . . . (Smithsonian Folkways)
North Wind
Slim Whitman; *Slim Whitman's Greatest Hits* . . . . (Curb)
Slim Whitman-Vintage Collection . . . . (Capitol)
North Wind Blues
Big Joe Williams; *Complete Recorded Works-#1-1935-1941* . . . . . .(Document)
Northern Winds
Steve Earle; *Train A Comin'*. . . . .(Warner Bros.)
Nothin' But The Taillights
Clint Black; *Nothin' But The Taillights* . . . . (RCA)
November Winds
Friedemann; *Indian Summer*. . . . . (Narada)
Narada Equinox Sampler One-C . . . . (Narada)
Ocean Breeze
Pablo Cruise; *Pablo Cruise* . . . . (A&M)
October Winds
Bela Fleck; *Natural Bridge*. . . . . (Rounder)
Only The Wind
Pet Shop Boys; *Behavior* . . . .(EMI)
Only The Wind
Billy Dean; *Billy Dean* . . . . (Liberty)
Only The Wind
Joey Welz; *Somewhere Elvis Is Smiling* . . . . (Caprice Int'l)
People Of The Southwind
Kansas; *Monolith* . . . . (Kirshner)
Pillow Of Winds
Pink Floyd; *Meddle* . . . . (Capitol)
Pink Floyd-Gift Set . . . . (Capitol)
Pissin' In The Wind
Jerry Jeff Walker; *Ridin' High* . . . .(MCA)
Please Mr. Sun
Johnnie Ray; *Back To The Early '50s* . . . . (Dominion Entert.)
Johnnie Ray-16 Most Requested Songs . . . . (Legacy)
Vogues; *Vogues' Greatest Hits* . . . . (Rhino)
Raging Winds Of Time
Walking Wounded; *Raging Winds Of Time* . . . . (Chameleon)
Reflections In A Crystal Wind
Mimi & Richard Farina; *Best Of Mimi & Richard Farina* . . . . (Vanguard)
Reflections In A Crystal Wind . . . . (Vanguard)
Ride Like The Wind
Christopher Cross; *Christopher Cross* . . . .(Warner Bros.)
Riding On The Wind
Judas Priest; *Screaming For Vengeance* . . . . (Columbia)
Paul Horn; *China* . . . . (Kuckuck)
Sketches-Collection. . . . . (Lost Lake Arts)
Runnin' With The Wind
Eddie Rabbitt; *Jersey Boy* . . . . (Capitol)
Ten Years Of Greatest Hits . . . . (Capitol)
Running Like The Wind
Marshall Tucker Band; *Running Like The Wind* . . . .(Warner Bros.)
Saddle Tramp
Marty Robbins; *Gunfighter Ballads & Trail Songs*. . . . . (Legacy)
Marty Robbins-More Greatest Hits . . . . (Columbia)
Sailing The Wind
Loggins & Messina; *Full Sail* . . . . (Columbia)
Sea Breezes
Bryan Ferry; *Let's Stick Together*. . . . . (Virgin)
Roxy Music; *Roxy Music* . . . . (Reprise)
Siouxsie And The Banshees; *Through The Looking Glass* . . . .(Geffen)
Second Wind
Darryl Worley; *Hard Rain Don't Last* . . . . (DreamWorks/SKG)
Seminole Wind
John Anderson; *Seminole Wind* . . . . (BNA)

Shadows & The Wind
Uriah Heep; *Wonderworld* . . . .(Sequel)
Shanghai Breezes
John Denver; *John Denver's Greatest Hits-#3* . . . . (RCA)
Seasons Of The Heart. . . . .(RCA)
She's Like The Wind
Patrick Swayze; *ST/Dirty Dancing* . . . . (RCA)
Soft Summer Breeze
Diamonds; *45-#70934*. (Mercury)
Eddie Heywood; *Chart Toppers-Romantic Hits Of The '50s-C* . . . . . . (Priority)
Great Instrumental Hits Of The '50s-'80s-C . . . . (Rebound)
Someday Soon
Chris LeDoux; *Rodeo Songs Old & New*. . . . . (Liberty)
Ian & Sylvia; *Ian & Sylvia's Greatest Hits* . . . . (Vanguard)
Northern Journey . . . . (Vanguard)
Judy Collins; *Colors Of The Day-The Best Of Judy Collins* . . . . (Elektra)
Who Knows Where The Time Goes. . . . . (Elektra)
Moe Bandy; *Moe Bandy's Greatest Hits* . . . . (Columbia)
Rodeo Romeo . . . . (Columbia)
Suzy Bogguss; *Aces* . . . . (Liberty)
Suzy Bogguss' Greatest Hits. . . . . (Liberty)
Spring Wind
Shawn Phillips; *Collaboration* . . . . (A&M)
Strong Enough To Bend
Tanya Tucker; *Strong Enough To Bend*. . . . . (Liberty)
Tanya Tucker's Greatest Hits. . . . . (Liberty)
Summer Breeze
Isley Brothers; *3+3* . . . . (T-Neck/Columbia)
Forever Gold . . . . (T-Neck/Columbia)
The Isley Brothers Story-#2-The T-Neck Years-1969-1985 . . . . (Rhino)
Seals & Crofts; *Seals & Crofts' Greatest Hits*. . . . . (Warner Bros.)
Summer Breeze. . . . . (Warner Bros.)
Summer Wind
Frank Sinatra; *Frank Sinatra's Greatest Hits!*. . . . . (Reprise)
Sinatra Reprise-The Very Good Years . . . . (Reprise)
Strangers In The Night . . . . (Reprise)
Frank Sinatra & Julio Iglesias; *Frank Sinatra-Duets-C*. . . . . (Capitol)
Summer Wind
Desert Rose Band; *Running*. . . . . (MCA)
That Ol' Wind
Garth Brooks; *Fresh Horses* . . . . (Capitol)
Limited Series Box . . . . (Capitol)
Theme From "Gone With The Wind"
Toronto Festival Pops Orchestra; *Hooray For Hollywood* . . . . (Pro-Arte)
They Call The Wind Maria
Kingston Trio; *Early American Heroes*. . . . .(Pair)
Kingston Trio/From The Hungry i . . . . (Capitol)
Stereo Concert Plus . . . . (Folk Era)
Original Broadway Cast; *Paint Your Wagon*. . . . . (RCA Victor)
To The Last Whale Medley
Crosby, Stills & Nash; *CSN* . . . .(Atlantic)
Replay. . . . .(Atlantic)
David Crosby & Graham Nash; *Best Of David Crosby & Graham Nash* . . . . (MCA)
Wind On The Water . . . . (MCA)
Tradewinds
Tommy Dorsey & Frank Sinatra; *Sessions-#1-February 1, 1940-July 17, 1940* . . . . (RCA)
Tradewinds
Rod Stewart; *A Night On The Town*. . . . . (Warner Bros.)
Tradewinds
Randy Crawford; *Secret Combination* . . . . (Warner Bros.)
Up Around The Bend
Creedence Clearwater Revival; *1970* . . . . (Fantasy)
Cosmo's Factory . . . . (Fantasy)
Creedence Clearwater Revival-Chronicle . . . . (Fantasy)
More Creedence Gold . . . . (Fantasy)
Hanoi Rocks; *Two Steps From The Move* . . . . (Epic)
Valerie
Steve Winwood; *Steve Winwood-Chronicles* . . . . (Island)
Talking Back To The Night . . . . (Island)
Walk The Way The Wind Blows
Hot Rize; *Traditional Ties*. . . . . (Sugar Hill)
Kathy Mattea; *Collection Of Hits* . . . . (Mercury)
Walk The Way The Wind Blows . . . . (Mercury)
Walking In The Wind
Traffic; *When The Eagle Flies* . . . . (Asylum)
Waltz Of The Wind
Hank Williams; *I'm So Lonesome I Could Cry-1949* . . . . (Polydor)
Roy Acuff; *Best Of Roy Acuff* . . . . (Liberty)
Essential Roy Acuff-1936-1949 . . . . (Legacy)
Warmth, The
Incubus; *Make Yourself*. . . . . (Immortal/Epic)
Ways Of The Wind
PM Dawn; *Bliss Album...?* . . . .(Gee Street)
Wayward Wind
Gogi Grant; *'50s Jukebox Favorites-C* . . . . (K-Tel)
Collectables Presents The History Of Rock-#7-C. . . . . (Collectables)
Lynn Anderson & Emmylou Harris; *Cowboy's Sweetheart* . . . . . . (Laserlight)

Patsy Cline; *The Patsy Cline Story* .... (MCA)
West Texas Wind
Joe Sun; *45-#1324* .... (AMI)
What Is And What Should Never Be
Jimmy Page & Black Crowes; *Live At The Greek* .... (TVT)
Led Zeppelin; *BBC Sessions* .... (Atlantic)
Led Zeppelin II .... (Atlantic)
Led Zeppelin-Box Set .... (Atlantic)
Led Zeppelin-The Complete Studio Recordings .... (Atlantic)
What She's Doing Now
Garth Brooks; *Ropin' The Wind* .... (Liberty)
Whatever Way The Wind Blows
Kelly Willis; *One More Time-MCA Recordings* .... (MCA)
When The Wind Was Green
Frank Sinatra; *September Of My Years* .... (Reprise)
Whispering Breezes
Al H. Wilson; *Music From The New York Stage (1890-1920)-#1-1890-1908-C* .... (Pearl)
Whispering Pines
Johnny Horton; *Johnny Horton's Greatest Hits* .... (Columbia)
Whispering Wind
Mandy Barnett; *I've Got A Right To Cry* .... (Sire)
Wichita Cross Winds
John Stewart; *Centennial* .... (Homecoming)
Wild Is The Wind
David Bowie; *Changestwobowie* .... (RCA)
Sound + Vision .... (Rykodisc)
Station To Station .... (Rykodisc)
Wild Is The Wind
Johnny Mathis; *Johnny Mathis' Greatest Hits* .... (Columbia)
Johnny Mathis-16 Most Requested Songs .... (Columbia)
Wild Night
John Mellencamp & Me'shell Ndegeocello; *Dance Naked* ...... (Mercury)
Rough Harvest .... (Mercury)
Martha Reeves; *ST/Thelma & Louise* .... (MCA)
Van Morrison; *Best Of Van Morrison* .... (Polydor)
Tupelo Honey .... (Polydor)
Wind Beneath My Wings
Bette Midler; *ST/Beaches* .... (Atlantic)
Gary Morris; *Chicken Soup For The Soul: I'll Be There For You-Songs Of Friendship, Brotherhood And Sisterhood-C* .... (Rhino)
Country Love Songs-C .... (Warner Bros.)
Gary Morris-Hits .... (Warner Bros.)
Why Lady Why .... (Warner Bros.)
James Galway; *Wind Beneath My Wings* .... (RCA)
Lee Greenwood; *Somebody's Gonna Love You* .... (MCA)
Lou Rawls; *When The Night Comes* .... (Epic)
Roger Whittaker; *Roger Whittaker Greatest Hits* .... (RCA)
Wind Beneath My Wings .... (RCA)
Willie Nelson; *City Of New Orleans* .... (Columbia)
Wind Blows Her Hair
Seeds; *Nuggets-#9-Acid Rock-C* .... (Rhino)
Wind Cries Mary
Jimi Hendrix; *Essential Jimi Hendrix, Volume 2* .... (Reprise)
Jimi Hendrix Experience; *Are You Experienced?* .... (Reprise)
Smash Hits .... (Reprise)
Wind In The Wire
Randy Travis; *Wind In The Wire* .... (Warner Bros.)
Wind Of Change
Peter Frampton; *Comes Alive* .... (A&M)
Shine On-Collection .... (A&M)
Wind Of Change .... (A&M)
Wind Of Change
Bee Gees; *Bee Gees' Greatest* .... (Polydor)
Main Course .... (RSO)
Wind Of Change
Scorpions; *Crazy World* .... (Mercury)
Windmills Of Your Mind
Acker Bilk; *Best Of Acker Bilk* .... (Crescendo)
Dusty Springfield; *Dusty In Memphis* .... (Rhino)
Johnny Mathis; *How Do You Keep The Music Playing* .... (Columbia)
Mel Torme; *Best Of Mel Torme* .... (Curb)
Philadelphia Orchestra & Eugene Ormandy; *Movie Love Songs* ...(RCA)
Winds Of Change
Jefferson Starship; *Winds Of Change* .... (Grunt)
Winds Of Change
Guadalcanal Diary; *2 X 4* .... (Elektra)
Winds Of Change
Cinderella; *Heartbreak Station* .... (Mercury)
Winds Of March
Journey; *Infinity* .... (Columbia)
Windsurfer
Roy Orbison; *Mystery Girl* .... (Virgin)
Windswept
Bryan Ferry; *Boys & Girls* .... (Warner Bros.)
Windswept
John Jarvis; *Whatever Works* .... (MCA)
Windy
Association; *Association Greatest Hits* .... (Warner Bros.)

Billboard Top Rock 'N' Roll Hits-1967-C .... (Rhino)
Summer Of Love-#1-C .... (Rhino)
Vintage Association .... (Fifty One West)
Wes Montgomery; *A Day In The Life* .... (A&M)
Wes Montgomery-Classics-#22 .... (A&M)
Wes Montgomery's Greatest Hits .... (A&M)
Written On The Wind
Four Aces; *Best Of The Four Aces* .... (MCA)
Four Aces' 20 Greatest Hits .... (Everest)
Love Is A Many Splendored Thing .... (Accord)

WINDOWS

See Also: *BOTTLES, DOORS, EYES, HOUSES, INSIDE/OUTSIDE, OPEN & CLOSED, REFLECTIONS, SEEING*

Belly Button Window
Jimi Hendrix; *Cry Of Love* .... (Reprise)
Candle In The Window
Alabama; *Alabama-Christmas* .... (RCA)
Cars Hiss By My Window
Doors; *L.A. Woman* .... (Elektra)
Come To My Window
Melissa Etheridge; *The Concert For New York City-C* .... (Columbia)
Yes I Am .... (Island)
Doggie In The Window
Patti Page; *Patti Page-16 Most Requested Songs* .... (Legacy)
Patti Page-Golden Hits .... (Mercury)
Patti Page's Greatest Hits .... (Columbia)
Epistle To Dippy
Donovan; *Donovan's Greatest Hits* .... (Epic)
From A Window
Billy J. Kramer With The Dakotas; *History Of British Rock-#3-C* ....(Rhino)
Chad & Jeremy; *Best Of Chad & Jeremy* .... (One Way)
Go 'Way From My Window
Joan Baez; *Joan Baez/5* .... (Vanguard)
God Ain't No Stained Glass Window
Kathy Mattea; *Kathy Mattea* .... (Mercury)
Graceland
Paul Simon; *Graceland* .... (Warner Bros.)
Heart Hotels
Dan Fogelberg; *Dan Fogelberg/Greatest Hits* .... (Full Moon)
Phoenix .... (Full Moon)
Hello Walls
Faron Young; *Billboard Top Country Hits-1961-C* .... (Rhino)
Willie Nelson; *Essential Willie Nelson* .... (RCA)
Willie Nelson-Greatest Songs .... (Curb)
Hi-Lili, Hi-Lo
Anne Murray; *There's A Hippo In My Tub* .... (Capitol)
Ray Conniff; *Encore! 16 Most Requested Songs* .... (Legacy)
I Guess You Had To Be There
Lorrie Morgan; *To Get To You-Greatest Hits Collection* ... (BNA)
Watch Me .... (BNA)
I Saw The Light
Wynonna; *Wynonna* .... (MCA)
I Threw A Brick Through A Window
U2; *October* .... (Island)
I Want My Goodbye Back
Ty Herndon; *What Mattered Most* .... (Epic)
If My Heart Had Windows
Patty Loveless; *Country Classics-#12-1987-1988-C* ..... (Universal)
If My Heart Had Windows .... (MCA)
Patty Loveless' Greatest Hits .... (MCA)
I'm Only Sleeping
Beatles; *"Yesterday"...And Today* .... (Capitol)
Rarities .... (Capitol)
Just My Imagination (Running Away With Me)
Rolling Stones; *"Still Life" (American Concert 1981)* .... (Virgin)
Some Girls .... (Virgin)
Temptations; *12 #1 Hits From The '70s-C* .... (Motown)
20 Greatest Songs In Motown History-C .... (Motown)
25 #1 Hits From 25 Years-C .... (Motown)
All The Million-Sellers .... (Motown)
Compact Command Performances-Temptations .... (Motown)
Temptations-25th Anniversary .... (Motown)
Temptations-Anthology-The Best Of The Temptations .... (Motown)
Moon At The Window
Joni Mitchell; *Wild Things Run Fast* .... (Geffen)
My Baby Left Me
Arthur "Big Boy" Crudup; *That's All Right (Mama)* ..... (Bluebird)
Creedence Clearwater Revival; *Cosmo's Factory* .... (Fantasy)
Creedence Country .... (Fantasy)
Elvis Presley; *Elvis Recorded Live On Stage In Memphis* ... (RCA)
Open Up My Window
Christopher Cross; *Window* .... (Rhythm Safari)
Power Windows
Billy Falcon; *Pretty Blue World* .... (Jambco)

Rain, The (Supa Dupa Fly)
Missy ''Misdemeanor'' Elliot; *Supa Dupa Fly* . . . . (East West)
Rainy Day, Dream Away
Jimi Hendrix Experience; *Electric Ladyland* . . . . (Reprise)
Razor Love
Neil Young; *Silver & Gold* . . . . (Reprise)
Reflections
Diana Ross & The Supremes; *Diana Ross & The Supremes' Greatest
Hits-#3* . . . . (Motown)
Diana Ross & The Supremes-25th Anniversary . . . . (Motown)
Diana Ross & The Supremes-Anthology (1962-1969) . . . . (Motown)
Motown Story-First 25 Years-C . . . . (Motown)
Four Tops; *Four Tops-Anthology* . . . . (Motown)
Still Waters Run Deep . . . . (Motown)
Until You Love Someone: More Of The Best (1965-1970) . . . . (Rhino)
Luther Vandross; *Songs* . . . .(Epic)
Room With A View
Johnny Adams; *Room With A View Of The Blues* . . . . (Rounder)
Lou Rawls; *Legendary Lou Rawls* . . . . (Blue Note)
Lou Rawls-At Last . . . . (Blue Note)
Room With A View
Wall Of Voodoo; *Seven Days In Sammystown* . . . .(I.R.S.)
Room With A View
Noel Coward; *Live From Las Vegas & New York* . . . . (Columbia)
Room With A View
Yellowjackets; *Four Corners* . . . .(MCA)
Room With A View
Bobby Short; *Bobby Noel & Cole* . . . . (Atlantic)
Room With A View
Jeffrey Osborne; *Emotional* . . . . (A&M)
Room With A View
Carolyn Dawn Johnson; *Room With A View* . . . . (Arista)
She Came In Through The Bathroom Window
Beatles; *Abbey Road* . . . . (Parlophone)
Beatles-Box Set . . . . (Capitol)
Joe Cocker; *Joe Cocker Live* . . . . (Capitol)
Joe Cocker! . . . . (A&M)
Joe Cocker-Classics-#4 . . . . (A&M)
Mad Dogs & Englishmen . . . . (A&M)
Sign On The Window
Bob Dylan; *New Morning* . . . . (Columbia)
Smooth Criminal
Alien Ant Farm; *Alien Ant Farm-Anthology* . . . .(DreamWorks/SKG)
Michael Jackson; *Bad* . . . .(Epic)
Still Rainin'
Jonny Lang; *Wander This World* . . . . (A&M)
Summer Song
Chad & Jeremy; *Best Of Chad & Jeremy* . . . . (K-Tel)
Capitol Gold-Best Of Chad & Jeremy . . . . (Capitol)
History Of British Rock-#2-C . . . . (Rhino)
That Hound Dog In The Window
Homer & Jethro; *Duets-Collector's* . . . . (RCA)
Three Window Coupe
Rip Chords; *Rock Artifacts-From The Vaults-#4-C* . . . . (Columbia)
We're All Alone
Boz Scaggs; *Boz Scaggs-Hits!* . . . . (Columbia)
Slow Dancer . . . . (Columbia)
Rita Coolidge; *Rita Coolidge's Greatest Hits* . . . . (A&M)
When It's Over
Sugar Ray; *Sugar Ray* . . . . (Lava)
Totally Hits 2001-C . . . . (Arista)
Window
They Might Be Giants; *John Henry* . . . . (Elektra)
Window Dreamin'
Chicago; *Chicago XIII* . . . .(Chicago)
Window Eyes
Lee Andrews And The Hearts; *For Collectors Only* . . . . (Collectables)
Window Lady
Cadillacs; *Best Of The Cadillacs* . . . . (Rhino)
Window Of Hope
Oleta Adams; *Evolution* . . . . (Fontana)
Window Of My Heart
Roger Whittaker; *Awakening* . . . .(RCA Victor)
Window Of Roses
Sisters Wade; *Sisters Wade* . . . . (Blue Hat)
Window Paine
Smashing Pumpkins; *Gish* . . . . (Virgin)
Window Pane Blues
Tommie Bradley; *Violin, Sing The Blues For Me-African-American Fiddlers
1926-1949-C* . . . . (Old Hat)
Window Raisin' Granny
Gladys Knight & The Pips; *Imagination* . . . . (Right Stuff)
Window Shopper, The
John Entwistle; *Best Of John Entwistle-Thunderfingers* . . . . (Rhino)
Window Shoppin'
Hiram Bullock; *From All Sides* . . . . (Atlantic)
Window Shopping
Hank Williams; *24 Of Hank Williams' Greatest Hits* . . . . (Polydor)

Hank Williams-40 Greatest Hits . . . .(Polydor)
Live At The Grand Ole Opry . . . . (Mercury)
Window Shopping For Blinds
Beautiful South; *Quench* . . . . (Mercury)
Window Song, The
V-Roys; *All About Town* . . . . (E Squared)
Window To The World
Shawn Colvin; *Cover Girl* . . . . (Columbia)
Window To Your Soul
Average White Band; *Soul Tattoo* . . . .(Foundation)
Window Up Above
George Jones; *Cup Of Loneliness-Classic Mercury Years* . . . . (Mercury)
George Jones' All-Time Greatest Hits . . . . (Epic)
George Jones-Super Hits . . . . (Epic)
George Jones-Super Hits . . . . (Epic)
Hank Wilson; *Hank Wilson's Back, Vol. 1* . . . . (Right Stuff)
Hot Rize; *Red Knuckle-Hot Rize Live* . . . . (Flying Fish)
Johnny Cash; *Back To Back* . . . . (K-Tel)
Mickey Gilley; *Mickey Gilley's Greatest Hits-#1* . . . . (Epic)
Ten Years Of Hits . . . . (Epic)
Ralph Stanley; *Clinch Mountain Country* . . . . (Rebel)
Ricky Skaggs; *Ricky Skaggs-Country Boy* . . . . (Epic)
Wanda Jackson; *Wanda Jackson-Vintage Collection* . . . . (Capitol)
Window Washer Man
Mills Brothers; *Best Of The Decca Years-Mills Brothers* . . . . (MCA)
Window Wishing
Dionne Warwick; *From The Vaults* . . . . (Soul Classics)
Window, The
Trout Fishing In America; *Dr. Demento Gooses
Mother-C* . . . .(Kid Rhino/Rhino 4 Kids)
Window, The
Steve Miller Band; *Fly Like An Eagle* . . . . (Capitol)
Window, The
Leonard Cohen; *Recent Songs* . . . . (Columbia)
Window, The
Tish Hinojosa; *Culture Swing* . . . . (Rounder)
Windows
Utopia; *Oops! Wrong Planet* . . . . (Rhino)
Windows
Missing Persons; *Best Of 80's Rock-C* . . . . (Priority)
Best Of Missing Persons . . . . (Capitol)
Windows
Screaming Trees; *Screaming Trees-Anthology* . . . .(SST)
Windows
Roger Kellaway; *Windows* . . . . (EMI-Angel)
Windows
Chick Corea; *Best Of Chick Corea* . . . . (Blue Note)
Gary Burton; *Like Minds* . . . . (Concord Jazz)
Stan Getz Quartet; *Sweet Rain* . . . . (Verve)
Windows And Walls
Dan Fogelberg; *Windows And Walls* . . . . (Epic)
Windows Of Heaven
Jefferson Starship; *Windows Of Heaven* . . . .(CMC Int'l)
Windows Of My Room
Cypress Hill; *Latino Gangster Rappers-C* . . . . (Deff Trapp)
Windows Of The World
Burt Bacharach; *One Amazing Night* . . . . (N2K)
Dionne Warwick; *Dionne Warwick Collection-Her All-Time
Greatest Hits* . . . . (Rhino)
Dionne Warwick-Definitive Collection . . . . (Arista)
Isaac Hayes; *Live At The Sahara Tahoe* . . . . (Stax)
Mormon Tabernacle Choir; *Voices In Harmony* . . . . (CBS Masterworks)
Pretenders; *ST/1969* . . . .(Polydor)
Windows To The Soul
Steve Vai; *Ultra Zone* . . . . (Epic)

WINNING, Victory

See Also: *FAITH, FIGHT, GAMBLING, HEROISM, LOSING &
LOSS, LUCK, MONEY, MOTIVATION, SPORTS (various), TOYS &
GAMES, WAR*

#1
Nelly; *Soundtrack Single* . . . . (Priority)
7-11 (A Winner)
Li'l Wally; *Polish Carnival* . . . . (Jay Jay)
Ace In The Hole
George Strait; *Beyond The Blue Neon* . . . . (MCA)
Alright Okay You Win
Marcels; *Best Of The Marcels* . . . . (Rhino)
Peggy Lee; *Peggy Lee's Greatest Hits* . . . . (Capitol)
Tony Bennett with Diana Krall; *Playin' With My Friends-Bennett Sings The
Blues-C* . . . . (Columbia)
Blaze Of Glory
Alarm; *Declaration* . . . . (I.R.S.)
Electric Folklore . . . . (I.R.S.)

Blaze Of Glory
Joe Jackson; *Blaze Of Glory* . . . . (A&M)
Blaze Of Glory
Jon Bon Jovi; *Blaze Of Glory-ST/Young Guns II* . . . . (Mercury)
Cheaters Never Win
Love Committee; *Beachbeat Shaggin'* . . . . (Dunhill Compact Classics)
Cheaters Never Win
Moe Bandy; *It's A Cheating Situation* . . . . (Columbia)
Checkmate
Defiance; *Void Terra Firma* . . . . (Roadrunner)
Checkmate
Ernie Henry; *Presenting Ernie Henry* . . . . (Riverside)
Color Of Success
Morris Day; *Color Of Success* . . . . (Warner Bros.)
Cup Of Life
Ricky Martin; *Ricky Martin* . . . . (Columbia)
Death or Glory
Clash; *London Calling* . . . . (Epic)
Do Something
Macy Gray; *On How Life Is* . . . . (Epic)
ST/Music Of The Heart . . . . (Epic/Sony Music Soundtrax)
Dressed For Success
Roxette; *Look Sharp!* . . . . (EMI)
Easy Winners
Itzhak Perlman & Andre Previn; *Easy Winners* . . . . (Angel)
Joshua Rifkin; *Digital Ragtime-Music Of Scott Joplin* . . . . (Angel)
Marvin Hamlisch; *ST/The Sting* . . . . (MCA)
Scott Joplin; *The Entertainer* . . . . (Biograph)
Every 1's A Winner
Hot Chocolate; *Every 1's A Winner* . . . . (Infinity)
Everybody Loves A Winner
Linda Ronstadt; *Don't Cry Now* . . . . (Asylum)
Everybody Loves A Winner
Rita Coolidge; *Lady's Not For Sale* . . . . (A&M)
Everybody Loves A Winner
William Bell; *Soul Of A Bell* . . . . (Atlantic)
First Taste
Fiona Apple; *Tidal* . . . . (Clean Slate/Work)
Get A Leg Up
John Mellencamp; *Whenever We Wanted* . . . . (Mercury)
Ghetto Supastar (That Is What You Are)
Pras Michel featuring Old Dirty Bastard & Mya; *ST/Bulworth* . . . . . (Interscope)
Gold Diggers' Song (We're In The Money)
Ginger Rogers; *Lullaby Of Broadway-The Best Of Busby Berkeley At Warner
Brothers* . . . . (Rhino)
Grey Victory
10,000 Maniacs; *Hope Chest-Fredonia Recordings-1982-1983* . . . . . . (Elektra)
Wishing Chair . . . . (Elektra)
Hard Way, The
Mary Chapin Carpenter; *Come On Come On* . . . . (Columbia)
I Feel Lucky
Mary Chapin Carpenter; *Come On Come On* . . . . (Columbia)
If I Could Only Win Your Love
Emmylou Harris; *Pieces Of The Sky* . . . . (Reprise)
Profile/Best Of Emmylou Harris . . . . (Warner Bros.)
If The South Woulda Won
Hank Williams, Jr.; *Wild Streak* . . . . (WB/Curb)
Impossible Dream
Andy Williams; *Andy Williams' Greatest Hits-#2* . . . . (Columbia)
Andy Williams-16 Most Requested Songs . . . . (Legacy)
Impossible Dream . . . . (Columbia)
Ed Ames; *Best Of Ed Ames* . . . . (RCA)
Ed Ames-Pure Gold . . . . (RCA)
Impossible Dream . . . . (RCA)
This Is Ed Ames . . . . (RCA)
Jack Jones; *Best Of Jack Jones* . . . . (MCA)
Kate Smith; *Best Of Kate Smith* . . . . (RCA)
Kate Smith-Legendary Performer . . . . (RCA)
Luther Vandross; *Songs* . . . . (Epic)
Original London Cast; *Man Of La Mancha* . . . . (MCA)
Robert Goulet; *Robert Goulet's Greatest Hits* . . . . (Columbia)
Incense And Peppermints
Strawberry Alarm Clock; *Billboard Top Rock 'N' Roll Hits-1967-C* . . . . (Rhino)
Cruisin'-1967-C . . . . (Increase)
Even More Nuggets-C . . . . (Rhino)
Nuggets-#8-Acid Rock-C . . . . (Rhino)
It's Not Where You Start (It's Where You Finish)
Barbara Cook; *Dorothy Fields-Close As Pages In A Book* . . . . (DRG)
Original Broadway Cast; *See Saw* . . . . (DRG)
Just Can't Win 'Em All
Stevie Woods; *Stevie Woods* . . . . (Cotillion)
Just One Victory
Todd Rundgren; *A Wizard A True Star* . . . . (Rhino)
Todd Rundgren-Anthology 1968-1985 . . . . (Rhino)
Utopia; *Another Live* . . . . (Rhino)
Keep Your Hands Off My Baby
Trashmen; *Bird Call! The Twin City Stomp Of The
Trashmen* . . . . (Sundazed Music)

Kid's Last Fight
Frankie Laine; *Frankie Laine-16 Most Requested Songs* . . . . (Legacy)
Last Laugh
Mark Knopfler; *Sailing To Philadelphia* . . . . (Warner Bros.)
Last Song
Elton John; *The One* . . . . (MCA)
Life To Win
Motorhead; *Ace Of Spades* . . . . (Mercury)
Little Victories
Bob Seger & The Silver Bullet Band; *The Distance* . . . . (Capitol)
Long Distance Winner
Buckingham/Nicks; *Buckingham/Nicks* . . . . (Polydor)
Make It Right
Econoline Crush; *Brand New History* . . . . (Restless)
Man At The Top
Bruce Springsteen; *Tracks* . . . . (Columbia)
Moonlight Gambler
Frankie Laine; *Frankie Laine-16 Most Requested Songs* . . . . (Legacy)
Frankie Laine's Greatest Hits . . . . (Columbia)
New Orleans Wins The War
Randy Newman; *Land Of Dreams* . . . . (Reprise)
Nobody Wins
Brenda Lee; *Brenda Lee-Greatest Country Hits* . . . . (MCA)
Nobody Wins
Radney Foster; *Del Rio, TX 1959* . . . . (Arista)
Nobody Wins
Elton John; *The Fox* . . . . (Geffen)
Notre Dame Victory March
Original Soundtrack; *The Greatest College Fight Songs* . . . . (Laserlight)
Top Ten College Fight Songs . . . . (K-Tel)
University Of Notre Dame Band; *Songs Of The Fighting
Irish* . . . . (Fidelity Sound)
Paths Of Victory
Bob Dylan; *The Bootleg Series-Volumes 1-3 [Rare & Unreleased]* . . (Columbia)
Broadside Singers; *Best Of Broadside 1962-1968: Anthems Of The
American Underground From The Pages Of Broadside
Magazine-C* . . . . (Smithsonian Folkways)
Byrds; *20 Essential Tracks From The Box Set* . . . . (Columbia)
Pete Seeger; *I Shall Be Unreleased-Songs Of Bob Dylan* . . . . (Rhino)
Picture Me In Victory
K-Yze; *Without Warning* . . . . (Warner Bros.)
Place In The Sun
Pablo Cruise; *A Place In The Sun* . . . . (A&M)
Play To Win
Heaven 17; *Best Of Heaven 17-Higher & Higher* . . . . (Virgin)
Play To Win
Clash; *Cut The Crap-C* . . . . (Epic)
Playing To Win
Little River Band; *Playing To Win* . . . . (Capitol)
Playing To Win
Bonham; *Disregard Of Timekeeping* . . . . (WTG)
Quitter Never Wins, A
Jonny Lang; *Lie To Me* . . . . (A&M)
Race To Win
Blitzspeer; *Blitzspeer Live* . . . . (Epic)
Red Sox Are Winning
Earth Opera; *Elektrock-Sixties-C* . . . . (Elektra)
Rhiannon (Will You Ever Win)
Fleetwood Mac; *25 Years-The Chain* . . . . (Warner Bros.)
Fleetwood Mac . . . . (Reprise)
Fleetwood Mac Live . . . . (Warner Bros.)
Fleetwood Mac's Greatest Hits . . . . (Warner Bros.)
Right The First Time
Gamma; *Best Of Gamma* . . . . (Crescendo)
Gamma 3 . . . . (Elektra)
Same Ol' G
Ginuwine; *ST/Dr. Dolittle* . . . . (Atlantic)
She's Gonna Win Your Heart
Eddy Raven; *I Could Use Another You* . . . . (RCA)
Slow Like Honey
Fiona Apple; *Tidal* . . . . (Clean Slate/Work)
Small Victory
Faith No More; *Angel Dust* . . . . (Slash)
Speedway At Nazareth
Mark Knopfler; *Sailing To Philadelphia* . . . . (Warner Bros.)
Success
Loretta Lynn; *Loretta Lynn's Greatest Hits* . . . . (MCA)
The Country Music Hall Of Fame-Loretta Lynn . . . . (MCA)
Success
Dan Hicks & His Hot Licks; *Last Train To Hicksville* . . . . (MCA)
Success
Iggy Pop; *Lust For Life* . . . . (Virgin)
Success Has Made A Failure Of Our Home
Sinead O'Connor; *Am I Not Your Girl?* . . . . (Ensign)
So Far...The Best Of Sinead O'Connor . . . . (EMI)
Sweetest Victory
Touch; *ST/Rocky IV* . . . . (Scotti Bros.)

Theme From "The Miss America Pageant" (There She Is, Miss
America)
  Bert Parks; *Television's Greatest Hits-#4-Black & White Classics-C* .... (TVT)
This Uncivil War
  Martina McBride; *Emotion*................................. (RCA)
Thunder Road
  Bruce Springsteen; *Born To Run*.................... (Columbia)
  Bruce Springsteen's Greatest Hits....................... (Columbia)
  Bruce Springsteen & The E Street Band; *Bruce Springsteen & The E Street
    Band Live/1975-85* .... (Legacy)
Till Victory
  Patti Smith Group; *Easter*............................... (Arista)
Top Of The World
  Carpenters; *A Song For You* .... (A&M)
  Carpenters-Classics-#2 .... (A&M)
  Carpenters-The Singles 1969-1973 .... (A&M)
  Yesterday Once More............................... (A&M)
Top Of The World
  Brandy featuring Mase; *Never Say Never*.................... (Atlantic)
Top Of The World
  Lynn Anderson; *Country Superstars-C* .... (Dominion Entert.)
  Lynn Anderson's Greatest Hits-#2..................... (Columbia)
  Top Of The World .... (Columbia)
Top Of The World
  Van Halen; *For Unlawful Carnal Knowledge* .... (Warner Bros.)
Top Of The World
  James; *James* .... (Fontana)
Top Of The World
  Diana Ross; *Diana Ross-Anthology* .... (Motown)
Triumph
  Generation X; *Perfect Hits-1975-1981*..................... (Chrysalis)
Veni-Vidi-Vici (I Came, I Saw, I Conquered)
  Gaylords; *Best Of The Gaylords*........................ (Chronicles)
Victor
  Dick Dale And The Del-Tones; *Dick Dale And The Del-Tones'
    Greatest Hits*.................................... (Crescendo)
Victors, The
  Ohio State University Marching Band; *Music For Cheerleaders & Song
    Girls* ....(Fidelity Sound)
  Saturday Afternoon At Columbus ....(Fidelity Sound)
  Original Soundtrack; *College Fight Songs: The Big Ten-C* .... (K-Tel)
  The Greatest College Fight Songs .... (Laserlight)
  Top Ten College Fight Songs .... (K-Tel)
  University Of Michigan Band; *41 Great College Victory Songs* .... (Vanguard)
Victory
  Kool & The Gang; *Forever*............................ (Mercury)
Victory
  No Means No; *Day Everything Became Isolated...* ...... (Alternative Tentacles)
Victory
  Eric Johnson; *Tones* .... (Reprise)
Victory Day
  Red Rider; *Victory Day*............................ (RCA)
Victory Polka
  Glenn Miller; *Major Glenn Miller/Army Air Force Band*.......... (Bluebird)
Walking Away A Winner
  Kathy Mattea; *Walking Away A Winner* .... (Mercury)
We Are The Champions
  Big Blue Wrecking Crew; *Baseball's Greatest Hits-C*............. (Rhino)
  Queen; *Billboard Top Rock 'N' Roll Hits-1978-C* .... (Rhino)
  Live At Wembley '86 .... (Hollywood)
  Live Killers .... (Hollywood)
  News Of The World .... (Hollywood)
  Queen's Greatest Hits I & II .... (Hollywood)
We Can't Go Wrong
  Cover Girls; *We Can't Go Wrong*...................... (Capitol)
We're A Winner
  Impressions; *Billboard Top R&B Hits-1965-1969-C* .... (Rhino)
  Classic Soul-C ....(MCA)
  Impressions' Greatest Hits ....(MCA)
We're A Winner
  Rita Coolidge; *Rita Coolidge's Greatest Hits*............ (A&M)
We're Going All The Way
  Jeffrey Osborne; *Stay With Me Tonight* .... (A&M)
What Does It Take (To Win Your Love)
  Junior Walker & The All Stars; *Billboard Top R&B Hits-1965-
    1969-C* .... (Rhino)
  Junior Walker & The All Stars' Greatest Hits .... (Motown)
  Junior Walker & The All Stars-Anthology .... (Motown)
  Oldies But Goodies-#13-C........................(Original Sound)
What It Takes
  Aerosmith; *Pump* ....(Geffen)
When The Going Gets Tough, The Tough Get Going
  Billy Ocean; *Billy Ocean's Greatest Hits* .... (Jive)
  Love Zone .... (Jive)
Win
  David Bowie; *Young Americans* ....(Rykodisc)
Win Or Lose
  Earth, Wind & Fire; *Faces* .... (Columbia)

Win Or Lose
  Nitty Gritty Dirt Band; *Dirt, Silver & Gold*.................. (One Way)
Win Some, Lose Some
  Scandal; *Scandal*................................. (Columbia)
Win Some, Lose Some
  Bryan Adams; *Bryan Adams* .... (A&M)
Win, Lose Or Draw
  Allman Brothers Band; *Best Of The Allman Brothers Band* ....(Polydor)
  Win, Lose Or Draw................................(Polydor)
Winner
  Dorothy Moore; *Winner* .... (Volt)
Winner
  Circle O' Fire; *Escape Hatch* .... (Stax)
Winner
  Chris LeDoux; *Rodeo & Living Free*..................... (Liberty)
Winner Of Your Heart
  Johnnie & Jack & Their Tennessee Mountain Boys; *45-Out of print* ..... (RCA)
Winner Take All
  Natalie Cole; *I Love You So*........................ (Capitol)
  I'm Ready .... (Epic)
Winner Take All
  Platters; *Platters-Anthology* .... (Rhino)
Winner Take All
  Styx; *Best Of Styx* ....(RCA)
Winner Takes All
  Holly Near; *Journeys* .... (Redwood)
Winner Takes All
  Isley Brothers; *Winner Takes All*.................. (T-Neck/Columbia)
Winner Takes It All
  Abba; *Super Trouper* ....(Atlantic)
  Munich Philharmonic Orchestra & Leon Ives; *Munich Philharmonic
    Orchestra & Leon Ives Play Abba Classics*..................(Atlantic)
Winner Takes It All
  Sammy Hagar; *ST/Over The Top*...................... (Columbia)
Winner/Loser
  Stomu Yamashta & Go; *Live From Paris* .... (Island)
  Stomu Yamashta & Go .... (Island)
Winners
  Kleeer; *Winners*..................................(Atlantic)
Winners
  Frank Sinatra; *Ol' Blue Eyes Is Back*................... (Reprise)
Winners & Losers
  Rossington-Collins Band; *Anytime, Anyplace, Anywhere*............. (MCA)
Winning
  Santana; *Zebop!*............................... (Columbia)
Winning Streak
  Rufus Thomas; *I Ain't Getting Older I'm Getting Better*.....(American Variety)
Winning Ugly
  Rolling Stones; *Dirty Work* ....(Virgin)
Wish, The
  Bruce Springsteen; *Tracks* .... (Columbia)
World's Greatest, The
  R. Kelly; *ST/Ali* ....(Interscope)
Yesterday's Winner Is A Loser Today
  Ernest Tubb; *Ernest Tubb Collection-C* ....(Step One)
You Cannot Win If You Do Not Play
  Steve Forbert; *Alive On Arrival*............................(Nemperor)
You Win Again
  Hank Williams With His Drifting Cowboys; *24 Of Hank Williams'
    Greatest Hits* ....(Polydor)
  Hank Williams-40 Greatest Hits........................(Polydor)
  Jerry Lee Lewis; *Heartbreak*......................... (Tomato)
  Memphis Country-C .... (Sun)
  Rockin' My Life Away............................(Tomato)
  Taste Of Country .... (Sun)
  The Golden Hits Of Jerry Lee Lewis ....(Smash)
  Johnny Cash; *Johnny Cash-Original Golden Hits-#3* .... (Sun)
  Keith Richards; *Timeless: Hank Williams Tribute-C* ... (Lost Highway/IDJMG)
  Keith Whitley; *Kentucky Bluebird* ....(RCA)
  Mary Chapin Carpenter; *Greatest Country Hits Of The '90s-#2-C* ..(Columbia)
  Tommy Edwards; *It's All In The Game-The Complete Hits Of Tommy
    Edwards*...(Eric)
You Win My Love
  Shania Twain; *The Woman In Me* .... (Mercury)

WOMEN: GENERAL, Female, Girls, Ladies

See Also: ***BOSSES, CELEBRITIES: SPECIFIC, FAMILY (various),
GENDER CONFLICT, GENDER STEREOTYPES, LOVE (various),
PEOPLE, QUEENS, ROYALTY, TEENAGERS, WOMEN'S
NAMES: A-Z***

(She's) Some Kind Of Wonderful
  Drifters; *Drifters-16 Greatest Hits* ....(Trip)
  Drifters-Golden Hits.............................(Atlantic)

ST/More Dirty Dancing . . . . (RCA)
Very Best Of The Drifters . . . . (Rhino)
Huey Lewis and the News; Four Chords & Several Years Ago . . . . (Elektra)
Jay & The Americans; Sands Of Time/Wax Museum . . . . (EMI)
Marvin Gaye; I Heard It Through The Grapevine/I Want You . . . . (Motown)

(You Make Me Feel Like) A Natural Woman
Aretha Franklin; Aretha Franklin's Greatest Hits-1980-1994 . . . . (Arista)
Chicken Soup For The Woman's Soul-C . . . . (Rhino)
Carole King; Tapestry . . . . (Epic)
Celine Dion; Tapestry Revisited: Tribute To Carole King-C . . . . (Lava)

(You're The) Devil In Disguise
Elvis Presley; Elvis' Gold Records, Volume 4 . . . . (RCA)
The Top Ten Hits . . . . (RCA)

21st Century Sha La La La Girl
Def Leppard; Euphoria . . . . (Mercury)

2nd Movement: African Lady
Randy Weston; Uhuru Africa/Highlife . . . . (Roulette)

36-22-36
Bobby Bland; Best Of Bobby Bland-#2 . . . . (MCA)
Bobby Bland . . . . (MCA)
Here's The Man . . . . (MCA)

80's Ladies
K.T. Oslin; 80's Ladies . . . . (RCA)
K.T. Oslin's Greatest Hits: Songs From An Aging Sex Bomb . . . . (RCA)
Nipper's Greatest Hits Of The '80s-C . . . . (RCA)

96 Tears
? & The Mysterians; ? & The Mysterians . . . . (Collectables)
Ten Roir Years . . . . (Roir)

Aberdeen
Kenny Wayne Shepherd; Ledbetter Heights . . . . (Giant)

About A Girl
Nirvana; MTV Unplugged In New York . . . . (David Geffen Co.)

Absolutely (Story Of A Girl)
Nine Days; Maddening Crowd . . . . (550 Music)
Now That's What I Call Music!-#5-C . . . . (Virgin)

Afraid
Motley Crue; Generation Swine . . . . (Beyond)
Motley Crue's Greatest Hits . . . . (Beyond)

African Woman
Third World; Journey To Addis . . . . (Island)

After The Blackbird Sings
Wallflowers; The Wallflowers . . . . (Virgin)

Ah, Paree, Beautiful Girls
Millicent Martin; Collector's Sondheim-C . . . . (RCA)
Stephen Sondheim; Collector's Sondheim-C . . . . (RCA)

Ain't She Sweet?
Beatles; History Of British Rock-#5-C . . . . (Rhino)
The Beatles-Anthology-#3 . . . . (Capitol)
Erroll Garner; Body And Soul . . . . (Legacy)
Frank Sinatra; Sinatra and Swingin' Brass . . . . (Reprise)
Pearl Bailey; Pearl Bailey-16 Most Requested Songs . . . . (Legacy)

Alabama Lady
Wright Brothers; Easy Street . . . . (Mercury)

Alabama Woman Blues
John Hammond; John Hammond . . . . (Vanguard)

All About Me Intro
Xscape; Traces Of My Lipstick . . . . (So So Def/Columbia)

All American Girl
Daryl Hall & John Oates; Big Bam Boom . . . . (RCA)

All American Girl
Melissa Etheridge; Yes I Am . . . . (Island)

All American Girls
Sister Sledge; Best Of Sister Sledge-1973-1985 . . . . (Rhino)

All At Once You Love Her
Perry Como; Perry Como's Greatest Hits . . . . (RCA)

All Day And All Of The Night
Kinks; British Rock-#1-C . . . . (Original Sound)
God Save The Kinks! . . . . (Castle Music America)
History Of British Rock-#2-C . . . . (Rhino)

All She Wants To Do Is Dance
Don Henley; Building The Perfect Beast . . . . (Geffen)

All That She Wants
Ace Of Base; All That She Wants . . . . (Arista)

All The Fun
Paul Overstreet; Best Of Paul Overstreet . . . . (RCA)

All The Things She Said
Simple Minds; Once Upon A Time . . . . (A&M)

All The Woman I Need
Luther Vandross; Songs . . . . (Epic)

Alligator Woman
R.G. & Bayou Zydeco; Fire On The Bayou . . . . (Takoma)

Alligator Woman
Cameo; Alligator Woman . . . . (Chocolate City)

Almost A Memory Now
BlackHawk; Strong Enough . . . . (Arista)
The Hits-Love & Gravity . . . . (Arista)

Am I The Same Girl
Swing Out Sister; Get In Touch With Yourself . . . . (Mercury)

American Girl
Goo Goo Dolls; The Concert For New York City-C . . . . (Columbia)
Tom Petty And The Heartbreakers; Pack Up The Plantation!-Live! . . . . . . (MCA)
Tom Petty & The Heartbreakers . . . . (Gone Gator)
You're Gonna Get It! . . . . (Gone Gator)

American Girls
Rick Springfield; Success Hasn't Spoiled Me Yet . . . . (RCA)

American Made
Oak Ridge Boys; American Made . . . . (MCA)
Oak Ridge Boys' Greatest Hits 2 . . . . (MCA)

American Pie
Don McLean; American Pie . . . . (EMI)
Best Of Don McLean . . . . (EMI)
Greatest Hits Then & Now . . . . (EMI)
ST/Born On The Fourth Of July . . . . (MCA)
Madonna; ST/The Next Big Thing . . . . (Maverick)

American Woman
Guess Who; American Woman . . . . (RCA)
Best Of The Guess Who . . . . (RCA)
Greatest Of The Guess Who . . . . (RCA)
Nipper's Greatest Hits Of The '70s-C . . . . (RCA)
Rock Classics-C . . . . (K-Tel)
Lenny Kravitz; 5 . . . . (Virgin)
Now That's What I Call Music!-#3-C . . . . (Virgin)
ST/Austin Powers-The Spy Who Shagged Me . . . . (Maverick)

And She Was
Talking Heads; Little Creatures . . . . (Sire)

Angel Lady
Boz Scaggs; Slow Dancer . . . . (Columbia)

Angel On My Bike
Wallflowers; Bringing Down The Horse . . . . (Interscope)

Angel Woman
Andrew Gold; What's Wrong With This Picture? . . . . (Asylum)

Angels
Robbie Williams; The Egg Has Landed . . . . (Capitol)

Another Girl
Beatles; Beatles-Box Set . . . . (Capitol)
ST/Help! . . . . (Capitol)

Another One In The Dark
Wallflowers; The Wallflowers . . . . (Virgin)

Apache Woman
Rolling Stones; Made In The Shade . . . . (Rolling Stones)

April Come She Will
Simon & Garfunkel; Collected Works . . . . (Columbia)
Sounds Of Silence . . . . (Columbia)
ST/The Graduate . . . . (Columbia)
The Concert In Central Park . . . . (Warner Bros.)

Are You Ready For The Sex Girls
Gleaming Spires; Best Of Rodney On The 'ROQ . . . . (Posh Boy)

Arlington Girl
Shivaree; I Oughtta Give You A Shot... . . . . (Capitol)

Around The Way Girl
L.L. Cool J; Mama Said Knock You Out . . . . (Def Jam)

Around The World
Red Hot Chili Peppers; Californication . . . . (Warner Bros.)

Ask Any Girl
Diana Ross & The Supremes; Diana Ross & The Supremes'
Greatest Hits . . . . (Motown)
Supremes; Where Did Our Love Go . . . . (Motown)

At My Front Door
Nilsson; Son Of Schmilsson . . . . (RCA)

At Night She Sleeps
Night Ranger; Dawn Patrol . . . . (Camel)

Atlanta Lady
Marty Balin; Balin . . . . (EMI)
Balince-A Collection . . . . (Rhino)

Attack Of The Fifty-Foot Woman
Tubes; Best Of The Tubes . . . . (Gold Rush)
Completion Backward Principle . . . . (Capitol)
Elvira Presents Haunted Hits-C . . . . (Rhino)

Attractive Female Wanted
Rod Stewart; Blondes Have More Fun . . . . (Warner Bros.)

Austin
Blake Shelton; Blake Shelton . . . . (Giant)

Awful
Hole; Celebrity Skin . . . . (David Geffen Co.)

Baby Likes To Rock It
Tractors; Tractors . . . . (Arista)

Baby's Got Her Blue Jeans On
Mel McDaniel; All-Time Country Classics-#2-C . . . . (Capitol)
Let It Roll . . . . (Capitol)
Mel McDaniel's Greatest Hits . . . . (Capitol)

Baby's Smile Woman's Kiss
Johnny Duncan; Best Of Johnny Duncan . . . . (Columbia)

Back In The U.S.S.R.
Beatles; Beatles-Box Set . . . . (Capitol)
Rock 'N' Roll Music . . . . (Capitol)
The Beatles (White Album) . . . . (Capitol)

The Beatles/1967-1970 . . . . (Capitol)
Billy Joel; *KOHUEPT* . . . . (Columbia)
Bad Day
Fuel; *Now That's What I Call Music!-#8-C* . . . . (Virgin)
Something Like Human . . . .(Epic)
Bad Girl
Jon B.; *Cool Relax* . . . . (Yab Yum/550)
Bad Girls
Donna Summer; *Bad Girls* . . . . (Casablanca)
Dance Collection . . . . (Casablanca)
On The Radio-Greatest Hits-Volumes I & II . . . . . . (Casablanca)
Summer Collection . . . . (Mercury)
Walk Away-Best Of Donna Summer-1977-1980 . . . . (Casablanca)
Bag Lady
Todd Rundgren; *Hermit Of Mink Hollow* . . . . (Rhino)
Bag Lady
Erykah Badu; *Mama's Gun* . . . . (Motown)
Bag Lady
Robby Krieger; *Versions/Robby Krieger* . . . .(One Way)
Bag Lady Song, The
Accused; *Martha Splatterhead's Maddest Stories Ever Told* . . . . . . (Relativity)
Bald-Headed Woman
Lightnin' Hopkins; *Lightnin' Sam Hopkins* . . . . (Arhoolie)
Ballerina Girl
Lionel Richie; *Dancing On The Ceiling* . . . . (Motown)
Banjo Picking Girl
Lamar Grier; *Rounder Banjo-C* . . . . (Rounder)
Bayou Girl
Bob Woodruff; *Dreams & Saturday Nights* . . . . (Asylum)
Be Your Own Girl
Wallflowers; *The Wallflowers* . . . . (Virgin)
Beaches Of Cheyenne
Garth Brooks; *Fresh Horses* . . . . (Capitol)
Limited Series Box . . . . (Capitol)
Beautiful Black Girl
Quincy Jones; *Mellow Madness* . . . . (A&M)
Beautiful Disaster
311; *Live!* . . . . (Capricorn)
Transistor . . . . (Capricorn)
Beauty And The Beast
Celine Dion & Peabo Bryson; *All The Way...A Decade Of Song* . . . . (550 Music)
Celine Dion . . . . (Epic)
ST/Beauty And The Beast . . . .(Disney)
Be-Bop-A-Lula
Everly Brothers; *Everly Brothers* . . . . (Rhino)
Gene Vincent and His Blue Caps; *Billboard Top Rock 'N' Roll Hits-1956-C* . . . . (Rhino)
ST/Wild At Heart . . . . (Polydor)
Jerry Lee Lewis; *Monsters* . . . . (Sun)
Trio Plus . . . . (Sun)
John Lennon; *Rock 'N' Roll* . . . . (Capitol)
Beer Drinkin' Woman
Memphis Slim; *At The Gate Of Horn* . . . .(Vee-Jay)
Raining The Blues . . . . (Fantasy)
Behind Closed Doors
Charlie Rich; *American Originals-Charlie Rich.* . . . . (Columbia)
Behind Closed Doors . . . .(Epic)
Charlie Rich's Greatest Hits . . . .(Epic)
Columbia Country Classics-#4-Nashville Sound-C . . . . (Columbia)
Belles Of Paris
Beach Boys; *M.I.U. Album* . . . . (Brother)
Berkeley Woman
John Denver; *Farewell Andromeda* . . . . (RCA)
John Denver . . . . (RCA)
Best Man I Can Be
Ginuwine, R.L., Tyrese, Case; *ST/The Best Man* . . . (Sony Music Soundtrax)
Bette Davis Eyes
Kim Carnes; *Best Of Kim Carnes* . . . . (EMI Special Markets)
Billboard Top Hits-1981-C . . . . (Rhino)
Mistaken Identity . . . . (EMI)
Big Bad Mamma
Foxy Brown featuring Dru Hill; *Ill Na Na* . . . .(Violator)
Big Chested Girls
Prince Charles & The City Beat Band; *Stone Killers!* . . . .(Roir)
Big Fat Lady
George Benson; *Cookbook* . . . . (Columbia)
Big Fat Woman
Leadbelly; *Bourgeois Blues-Golden Classics-#1* . . . . . . (Collectables)
Tom Rush; *Blues Songs & Ballads* . . . . (Fantasy)
Big Girls Don't Cry
4 Seasons; *4 Seasons' Greatest Hits-#1* . . . . (Rhino)
4 Seasons-Anthology . . . . (Rhino)
Billboard Top Rock 'N' Roll Hits-1962-C . . . . (Rhino)
More Dirty Dancing-C . . . . (RCA)
Big River
Grateful Dead; *One From The Vault* . . . . (Grateful Dead)
Steal Your Face . . . . (Grateful Dead)
Johnny Cash; *Johnny Cash-Legend* . . . . (Sun)

Johnny Cash's Greatest Hits-#2 . . . . (Columbia)
Johnny Cash-Sun Years . . . . (Rhino)
Superbilly . . . . (Sun)
The Man In Black-His Greatest Hits . . . . (Legacy)
Rosanne Cash; *Right Or Wrong* . . . . (Columbia)
Bikini Girls With Machine Guns
Cramps; *Stay Sick!* . . . . (Enigma Capitol)
Billy Get Me A Woman
Joe Stampley; *Joe Stampley's Biggest Hits* . . . . (Epic)
Bimbombey
Jimmie Rodgers; *Best Of Jimmie Rodgers.* . . . . (Rhino)
Best Of Jimmie Rodgers . . . . (Curb)
Birdmad Girl
Cure; *Top.* . . . .(Sire)
Birthday Girl
Hi-Five; *Hi-Five's Greatest Hits* . . . .(Jive)
Bitch
Meredith Brooks; *Blurring The Edges* . . . . (Capitol)
Bitch Betta Have My Money
AMG; *Give A Dog A Bone.* . . . . (Select)
Bitch Is Back
Elton John; *Caribou* . . . . (Rocket)
Elton John's Greatest Hits-#2 . . . .(Polydor)
Here And There . . . . (Rocket)
Tina Turner; *Two Rooms-Celebrating The Songs Of Elton John & Bernie Taupin-C* . . . . (Polydor)
Black Chick, White Guy
Kid Rock; *Devil Without A Cause* . . . . . (Top Dog/Lava/Atlantic)
Black Country Woman
Led Zeppelin; *Physical Graffiti* . . . . (Swan Song)
Black Hearted Woman
Allman Brothers Band; *Allman Brothers Band* . . . .(Polydor)
Beginnings . . . .(Polydor)
The Road Goes On Forever, A Collection Of Their Greatest Recordings. . . . . (Polydor)
Black Magic Woman
Fleetwood Mac; *25 Years-The Chain* . . . . (Warner Bros.)
Vintage Years . . . .(Sire)
Santana; *Abraxas.* . . . . (Columbia)
Moonflower . . . . (Columbia)
Rock Classics Of The '70s-C . . . . (Columbia)
Santana's Greatest Hits . . . . (Columbia)
Viva Santana! . . . . (Columbia)
Black Widow
Alice Cooper; *The Alice Cooper Show* . . . . (Warner Bros.)
Welcome To My Nightmare . . . .(Atlantic)
Black Widow
Jefferson Starship; *Winds Of Change* . . . . (Grunt)
Black Widow
Lita Ford; *Dangerous Curves* . . . . (RCA)
Blistered
Johnny Cash; *Johnny Cash-16 Biggest Hits-#2.* . . . . (Legacy)
Blonde Ambition
Billy Burnette; *Soldier Of Love* . . . . (Curb)
Blue Clear Sky
George Strait; *Blue Clear Sky* . . . . (MCA)
Latest Greatest Straitest Hits . . . . (MCA)
Blue Kentucky Girl
Emmylou Harris; *Blue Kentucky Girl* . . . . (Warner Bros.)
Profile II-The Best Of Emmylou Harris . . . . (Warner Bros.)
Loretta Lynn; *Loretta Lynn's Greatest Hits* . . . . (MCA)
Blue Spruce Woman
Foghat; *Rock & Roll Outlaws* . . . . (Rhino)
Bobby Sox To Stockings
Frankie Avalon; *Best Of Frankie Avalon.* . . . . (MCA)
Collectables Presents The History Of Rock-#3-C. . . (Collectables)
Frankie Avalon's Greatest Hits . . . . (Everest)
Greatest Of Fabian and Frankie Avalon . . . . (MCA)
Pick Of Frankie Avalon . . . . (Fifty One West)
Super Oldies Of The '50s-#7-C . . . . (Audio Fidelity)
Body Bumpin'
Mytown; *Mytown* . . . . (Cherry/Universal)
Boogie On Reggae Woman
Stevie Wonder; *Fulfillingness' First Finale* . . . . (Motown)
Motown Time Capsule-#2-'70s-C . . . . (Motown)
Original Musiquarium . . . . (Motown)
Born A Woman
Sandy Posey; *Best Of Sandy Posey-With Skeeter Davis* . . . (Gusto)
Best Of Town & Country-#3-C . . . . (Gusto)
Cruisin'-1966-C. . . . . (Increase)
Sandy Posey/Skeeter Davis/Wanda Jackson . . . . (Gusto)
Super Hits-#5-C . . . . (Gusto)
Boston Lady
John Stewart; *Fire In The Wind* . . . . (RSO)
Boys + Girls
Tony Toni Tone; *Tony Toni Tone-Hits* . . . . (Mercury)
Breaking The Girl
Red Hot Chili Peppers; *Blood Sugar Sex Magik* . . . . (Warner Bros.)

Bride Of Rain Dog
Tom Waits; *Rain Dogs* . . . . (Island)
Bring Me My Bride
Original Cast; *A Funny Thing Happened On The Way To The Forum* . . . . (Angel)
Broken Wing
Martina McBride; *Evolution* . . . . (RCA)
Brown Eyed Girl
Isley Brothers; *Live It Up* . . . . (T-Neck/Columbia)
Jimmy Buffett; *One Particular Harbour* . . . . (MCA)
Van Morrison; *Bang Masters* . . . . (Epic)
  Best Of Van Morrison . . . . (Polydor)
  ST/Born On The Fourth Of July . . . . (MCA)
  ST/Sleeping With The Enemy . . . . (Columbia)
  Wonder Years-Music From Emmy Shows/Era-C . . . . (Atlantic)
Brown Eyed Woman
Grateful Dead; *Europe '72* . . . . (Warner Bros.)
  What A Long Strange Trip It's Been: The Best Of The
  Grateful Dead . . . . (Warner Bros.)
Brown Girl In The Ring
Boney M; *Nightflight To Venus* . . . . (Sire)
Brown Skin Gal
Bob Wills; *Best Of Bob Wills & His Texas Playboys* . . . . (MCA)
Brown Skin Girl
Jesse Fuller; *Brother Lowdown* . . . . (Fantasy)
  San Francisco Bay Blues . . . . (Good Time Jazz)
Brown Sugar
Rolling Stones; *Classic Rock 1966-1988-C* . . . . (Atlantic)
  Hot Rocks 1964-1971 . . . . (Abkco)
  Made In The Shade . . . . (Rolling Stones)
  Sticky Fingers . . . . (Virgin)
Brownsville Blues
Hammie Nixon; *Tappin' That Thing* . . . .(High Water)
Brownsville Girl
Bob Dylan; *Knocked Out Loaded* . . . . (Columbia)
Bus Drivin' Woman
Chicago Bob; *Hit & Run Lover* . . . . (Ichiban Int'l)
Bus Stop
Hollies; *Best Of The Hollies* . . . . (EMI)
  History Of British Rock-#3-C . . . . (Rhino)
  The Hollies' Greatest Hits . . . . (Epic)
Business With My Baby
B.B. King; *King Of The Blues* . . . . (MCA)
But It's Alright
J.J. Jackson; *Didn't It Blow Your Mind: Soul Hits Of The '70s-#3-C* . . . . (Rhino)
  Soul Shots-C . . . . (Rhino)
Buy The Bitch A Cadillac
Annie Moscow; *Wolves At My Door* . . . .(Melonball)
Cajun Girl
Oak Ridge Boys; *American Dreams* . . . . (MCA)
Cajun Girl
Little Feat; *Let It Roll* . . . . (Warner Bros.)
Calendar Girl
Neil Sedaka; *Neil Sedaka Sings His Greatest Hits* . . . . (RCA)
  Neil Sedaka-Greatest Hits Live . . . . (K-Tel)
  Neil Sedaka's All-Time Greatest Hits . . . . (RCA)
California Girl
Eddie Floyd; *15 Original Big Hits-#4-C* . . . . (Stax)
  Eddie Floyd-Chronicle . . . . (Stax)
California Girls
Beach Boys; *Beach Boys '69 (The Beach Boys Live In London)* . . . . . . (Capitol)
  Best Of The Beach Boys-#2 . . . . (Capitol)
  Endless Summer . . . . (Capitol)
  Good Vibrations-Thirty Years Of The Beach Boys . . . . (Capitol)
  The Beach Boys In Concert . . . . (Brother)
David Lee Roth; *Crazy From The Heat* . . . . (Warner Bros.)
  ST/Down & Out In Beverly Hills . . . . (Warner Bros.)
California Sun
Ramones; *All The Stuff & More-#1* . . . . (Sire)
  Leave Home . . . . (Sire)
  ST/Rock 'N' Roll High School . . . . (Sire)
Rivieras; *Beach Classics-All Original*
  Recordings-C . . . . (Dunhill Compact Classics)
  Frat Rock!-#4-C . . . . (Rhino)
  Summer & Sun-C . . . . (Rhino)
Candy Perfume Girl
Madonna; *Ray Of Light* . . . . (Maverick)
Can't Change Me
Chris Cornell; *Euphoria Morning* . . . . (A&M)
Can't Let Her Go
Boyz II Men; *Evolution* . . . . (Motown)
Can't Really Be Gone
Tim McGraw; *All I Want* . . . . (Curb)
Can't You See
Alabama; *Alabama-Live* . . . . (RCA)
Charlie Daniels Band; *Volunteer Jam VII-C* . . . . (Epic)
Hank Williams, Jr.; *Hank Williams, Jr. & Friends* . . . . (Polydor)
  Rebels, Renegades & Ramblers-C . . . . (Polydor)
  Standing In The Shadows . . . . (Polydor)

Marshall Tucker Band; *Marshall Tucker Band* . . . . (AJK Music)
  Searchin' For A Rainbow . . . . (AJK Music)
Can't You See That She's Mine
Dave Clark Five; *History Of The Dave Clark Five* . . . . (Hollywood)
Captain Of Her Heart
Double; *Blue* . . . . (A&M)
  Romantic Hits Of The '80s-C . . . . (K-Tel)
Carolina Sunshine Girl
Geoff Muldaur & Amos Garrett; *Geoff Muldaur & Amos*
  Garrett . . . . (Flying Fish)
Catholic Girls
Frank Zappa; *Joe's Garage Acts I-III* . . . . (Rykodisc)
  You Can't Do That On Stage Anymore-#6 . . . . (Rykodisc)
Catholic School Girls Rule
Red Hot Chili Peppers; *Abbey Road E.P.* . . . . (EMI)
  Freaky Styley . . . . (EMI)
  What Hits!? . . . . (EMI)
Certain Girl, A
Warren Zevon; *Bad Luck Streak In Dancing School* . . . . (Asylum)
Yardbirds; *Yardbirds' Greatest Hits-#1 (1964-1966)* . . . . (Rhino)
Chantilly Lace
Big Bopper; *45s On CD-#1-1956-1959-C* . . . . (Mercury)
  Cruisin'-1958-C . . . . (Increase)
  Oldies But Goodies-#4-C . . . . (Original Sound)
  ST/American Graffiti . . . . (MCA)
Jerry Lee Lewis; ''Killer'' *Rocks On* . . . . (Mercury)
  Best Of Jerry Lee Lewis-#2 . . . . (Mercury)
Cheatin' Woman
Lynyrd Skynyrd; *Best Of Lynyrd Skynyrd* . . . . (MCA Special Prod.)
  Nuthin' Fancy . . . . (MCA)
Molly Hatchet; *Molly Hatchet* . . . . (Epic)
Checking Out The Checkout Girl
Wazmo Nariz; *10th Anniversary-These People Are Nuts-C* . . . . (I.R.S.)
Cherchez La Femme
Dr. Buzzard's Original ''Savannah'' Band; *Nipper's Greatest Hits Of The*
  '70s-C . . . . (RCA)
Gloria Estefan; *Hold Me, Thrill Me, Kiss Me* . . . . (Epic)
Cherokee Maiden
Asleep At The Wheel; *Ride With Bob-C* . . . . (DreamWorks/SKG)
Merle Haggard; *All Time Greatest Hits Of Country-C* . . . . (Curb)
  Capitol Collectors Series-Merle Haggard . . . . (Capitol)
Chick-A-Boom (Don't Ya Jes' Love It)
Daddy Dewdrop; *'70s Smash Hits-#4-C* . . . . (Rhino)
  Super Hits Of The '70s-Have A Nice Day-#5-C . . . . (Rhino)
Chime Bells
Elton Britt; *The RCA Years* . . . . (Collector's Choice)
Jody King; *Photographs & Memories* . . . .(Capricorn)
China Girl
David Bowie; *Changesbowie* . . . . (Rykodisc)
  Let's Dance . . . . (EMI)
  The Singles-1969-1993 . . . . (Rykodisc)
China Girl
John Cougar; *American Fool* . . . . (Riva)
China Lady
Accept; *Accept* . . . . (Portrait)
  Midnight Highway . . . . (PVC)
Chocolate Girl
Whispers; *Greatest Slow Jams #1* . . . . (Right Stuff)
  Open Up Your Love . . . . (Right Stuff)
Chocolate Girl
Keith Sweat; *Keith Sweat* . . . . (Elektra)
Cincinnati Underworld Woman
Bob Coleman & The Cincinnati Jug Band; *Cincinnati Blues-1928-*
  1936 . . . . (Sony Broadway)
Cinnamon Girl
Neil Young & Crazy Horse; *Decade* . . . . (Reprise)
  Everybody Knows This Is Nowhere . . . . (Reprise)
  Live Rust . . . . (Reprise)
  WELD . . . . (Reprise)
Circus Girl
Gretchen Peters; *The Secret Of Life* . . . . (Purple Crayon Prod.)
Clean Up Woman
Betty Wright; *Atlantic Rhythm & Blues 1947-1974-#6 (1966-*
  1969)-C . . . . (Atlantic)
  Betty Wright Live . . . . (Atlantic)
  Golden Classics-Betty Wright . . . . (Collectables)
  Soul Years-C . . . . (Atlantic)
Clown Woman
Montrose; *Montrose* . . . . (Warner Bros.)
Come Back When You Grow Up
Bobby Vee; *Best Of Bobby Vee* . . . . (EMI)
  Bobby Vee-Legendary Masters . . . . (EMI)
  Good Vibrations (Sounds Of Top 40 Radio: 1964-1967)-C . . . . . . (Capitol)
Computer Lady
Allen Toussaint; *Connected* . . . . (NYNO)
Cornflake Girl
Tori Amos; *Under The Pink* . . . . (Atlantic)
Could I Be Your Girl
Jann Arden; *Living Under June* . . . . (A&M)

Country Girl
Faron Young; *Billboard Top Country Hits-1959-C* . . . . (Rhino)
Faron Young's Greatest Hits-#2 . . . . (Step One)
Country Girl
Barbara Mandrell; *Barbara Mandrell Live* . . . . (MCA)
Country Girl
Steve Earle & The Dukes; *The Hard Way* . . . . (MCA)
Country Girl
Ozark Mountain Daredevils; *Best Of The Ozark Mountain Daredevils* . . (A&M)
Ozark Mountain Daredevils . . . . (A&M)
Country Girl
Jeannie C. Riley; *Country Girl* . . . . (Plantation)
Jeannie C. Riley's Greatest Hits . . . . (Plantation)
Country Girls
John Schneider; *John Schneider's Greatest Hits* . . . . (MCA)
MCA #1 Hits Of The '80s-#1-C . . . . (MCA Special Prod.)
Today's Country Classics-C . . . . (MCA Special Prod.)
Too Good To Stop Now . . . . (MCA)
Cowboy & The Lady
John Denver; *Some Days Are Diamonds* . . . . (RCA)
Cowboy & The Lady
Johnny Duncan; *Come A Little Bit Closer* . . . . (Columbia)
Cowboys To Girls
Intruders; *Intruders-Super Hits* . . . . (Philadelphia Int'l)
Soul Shots-C . . . . (Rhino)
Cowgirl In The Sand
Crosby, Stills, Nash & Young; *4 Way Street* . . . . (Atlantic)
Neil Young; *Decade* . . . . (Reprise)
Neil Young & Crazy Horse; *Everybody Knows This Is Nowhere* . . . . . (Reprise)
Crack House Woman
George "Wild Child" Butler; *These Mean Old Blues* . . . . (Bullseye Blues)
Crazy About Her
Rod Stewart; *Out Of Order* . . . . (Warner Bros.)
Storyteller/The Complete Anthology: 1964-1990 . . . . (Warner Bros.)
Crazy 'Bout That Married Woman
Rockin' Dopsie; *Saturday Night Zydeco* . . . . (Maison De Soul)
Crazy For This Girl
Evan And Jaron; *Evan And Jaron* . . . . (Columbia)
Now That's What I Call Music!-#6-C . . . . (Virgin)
Crazy Little Mama
Eldorados; *Greatest Groups Of The '50s-#2-C* . . . . (Collectables)
Sock Hop-C . . . .(Dunhill Compact Classics)
Crazy She Calls Me
Abbey Lincoln; *Blue Series-Female Vocals-C* . . . . (Blue Note)
Aretha Franklin; *Aretha's Jazz* . . . . (Rhino)
Billie Holiday; *From The Original Decca Masters* . . . . (MCA)
Joe Mooney; *Erteguns' New York, N.Y. Cabaret Music-C* . . . (Atlantic)
Linda Ronstadt; *What's New* . . . . (Asylum)
Lurlean Hunter; *Atlantic Jazz-Singers-C* . . . . (Atlantic)
Crazy Woman
Juluka; *Stand Your Ground* . . . . (Warner Bros.)
Criminal
Fiona Apple; *1998 Grammy Nominees-C* . . . . (MCA)
Tidal . . . . (Clean Slate/Work)
Cruel Little Number
Jeff Healey Band; *Feel This* . . . . (Arista)
Curly Headed Baby
Pete Seeger; *Tribute To Woody Guthrie-C* . . . . (Warner Bros.)
Daddy's Money
Ricochet; *Ricochet* . . . . (Columbia)
Dance On Little Girl
Paul Anka; *Best Of Paul Anka* . . . . (Rhino)
Paul Anka Sings His Big 15, Vol. 2 . . . . (RCA)
Paul Anka-30th Anniversary Anthology . . . . (Rhino)
Paul Anka's 21 Golden Hits . . . . (RCA)
She's A Lady . . . . (RCA)
Dance The Night Away
Mavericks; *Trampoline* . . . . (MCA)
Danger! She's A Stranger
Five Stairsteps; *Five Stairsteps' Greatest Hits* . . . . (Collectables)
Dangerous Woman
Mississippi Jook Band; *Good Time Blues* . . . . (Columbia)
Dark Lady
Scorpions; *Best Of The Scorpions* . . . . (RCA)
Hot & Heavy . . . . (RCA)
In Trance . . . . (RCA)
Tokyo Tapes . . . . (RCA)
Dark Lady
Cher; *Cher's Greatest Hits* . . . . (MCA)
Darlin'
Beach Boys; *Absolute Best-#2* . . . . (Capitol)
Concert/'69-Live In London . . . . (Capitol)
Smiley Smile/Wild Honey . . . . (Capitol)
Sunshine Dream . . . . (Capitol)
Darling Be Home Soon
Joe Cocker; *Joe Cocker!* . . . . (A&M)
Joe Cocker-Classics-#4 . . . . (A&M)
Joe Cocker's Greatest Hits . . . . (A&M)

Lovin' Spoonful; *Best Of The Lovin' Spoonful-#2* . . . . (Rhino)
Lovin' '60s-C . . . . (Priority)
Lovin' Spoonful-Anthology . . . . (Rhino)
Daughter
Bread; *Baby I'm-A Want You* . . . . (Elektra)
Best Of Bread-#2 . . . . (Elektra)
Daughter
Pearl Jam; *Vs.* . . . . (Epic Portrait Assoc.)
Day That She Left Tulsa (In A Chevy)
Wade Hayes; *When The Wrong One Loves You Right* . . . . (Columbia/DKC)
Day Tripper
Beatles; *"Yesterday"...And Today* . . . . (Capitol)
Beatles 1 . . . . (Capitol)
Beatles-Box Set . . . . (Capitol)
Past Masters-Volume Two . . . . (Parlophone)
The Beatles/1962-1966 . . . . (Capitol)
Jimi Hendrix Experience; *Radio One* . . . . (Rykodisc)
Otis Redding; *Dictionary Of Soul* . . . . (Atco)
The Otis Redding Story . . . . (Atlantic)
Sergio Mendes & Brasil '66; *Sergio Mendes & Brasil '66's*
Greatest Hits . . . . (A&M)
Days Of The Week
Stone Temple Pilots; *Shangri-La-Dee-Da* . . . . (Atlantic)
Dead Girls Of London
Frank Zappa; *You Can't Do That On Stage Anymore-#5* . . . . (Rykodisc)
Dear Lady Twist
Gary U.S. Bonds; *Best Of Gary U.S. Bonds* . . . . (Rhino)
Deep River Woman
Lionel Richie; *Dancing On The Ceiling* . . . . (Motown)
Delta Lady
Joe Cocker; *Joe Cocker!* . . . . (A&M)
Joe Cocker-Classics-#4 . . . . (A&M)
Joe Cocker's Greatest Hits . . . . (A&M)
Mad Dogs & Englishmen . . . . (A&M)
Leon Russell; *Best Of Leon Russell* . . . . (MCA)
Leon Russell . . . . (MCA)
Detroit Girls
Starz; *Live In Action* . . . . (Metal Blade)
Starz . . . . (Metal Blade)
Devil Ain't A Lonely Woman's Friend
Red Steagall; *45-#2824* . . . . (MCA)
Devil In Her Heart
Beatles; *The Beatles' Second Album* . . . . (Capitol)
With The Beatles . . . . (Parlophone)
Donays; *Beatles Originals* . . . . (Rhino)
Devil With A Blue Dress On & Good Golly Miss Molly
Bruce Springsteen; *ST/No Nukes-Muse Concerts* . . . . (Asylum)
Mitch Ryder And The Detroit Wheels; *Frat Rock!-#4-C* . . . . . (Rhino)
Rev Up-Best Of Mitch Ryder . . . . (Rhino)
Son Of Frat Rock!-C . . . . (Rhino)
Toga Rock-C . . . . (Dunhill Compact Classics)
Devil Woman
Marty Robbins; *Billboard Top Country Hits-1962-C* . . . . (Rhino)
Columbia Country Classics-#4-Nashville Sound-C . . . . (Columbia)
Lifetime Of Song-1951-1982 . . . . (Columbia)
Marty Robbins' Greatest Hits-#4 . . . . (Columbia)
Devil Woman
Buddy Knox; *Best Of Buddy Knox* . . . . (Rhino)
Devil Woman
Hanoi Rocks; *Oriental Beat* . . . . (Geffen)
Diamonds Are A Girl's Best Friend
Carol Channing; *Broadway Magic-The 1950s-C* . . . . (Columbia)
Emmylou Harris; *White Shoes* . . . . (Warner Bros.)
Marilyn Monroe; *Goodbye Primadonna* . . . . (Accord)
Pearl Bailey; *Back On Broadway* . . . . (Roulette)
Echoes Of An Era-Pearl Bailey . . . . (Roulette)
Diamonds On The Soles Of Her Shoes
Paul Simon; *Concert In The Park-August 15 1991* . . . . . . (Warner Bros.)
Graceland . . . . (Warner Bros.)
Negotiations And Love Songs, 1971-1986 . . . . (Warner Bros.)
Did You Ever See A Dream Walking
Bing Crosby; *Crosby Classics* . . . . (Columbia)
Hal Kemp & Skinnay Ennis; *The Uncollected Hal Kemp-#2 & #3* . . . (Hindsight)
Dime Queen Of Nevada
Tom Jones; *Darlin'* . . . . (Mercury)
Dirty Little Girl
Elton John; *Goodbye Yellow Brick Road* . . . . (Polydor)
Disco Lady
Johnnie Taylor; *Mega Hits Disco Explosion-#4-C* . . . . (Priority)
Rated X-Traordinaire-Best Of Johnnie Taylor . . . . (Legacy)
Disney Girls
Art Garfunkel; *Breakaway* . . . . (Columbia)
Beach Boys; *Surf's Up* . . . . (Caribou)
Captain & Tennille; *Captain & Tennille's Greatest Hits* . . . . . . (A&M)
Distance, The
Cake; *Fashion Nugget* . . . . (Capricorn)
Do Right Woman, Do Right Man
Aretha Franklin; *Aretha Franklin-30 Greatest Hits* . . . . (Rhino)
ST/Dead Presidents . . . . (Capitol)

Commitments; *ST/The Commitments* . . . . (MCA)

Do Wah Diddy Diddy
Manfred Mann; *Best Of Manfred Mann.* . . . . (EMI Special Markets)
Billboard Top Rock 'N' Roll Hits-1964-C . . . . (Rhino)
History Of British Rock-#2-C . . . . (Rhino)

Does She Love That Man?
Breathe; *Peace Of Mind.* . . . . (A&M)

Don't Kick Her In The Butt
Bobby Taylor & Carolyn Majors; *ST/Far Out Man.* . . . . (Chameleon)

Don't Put A Tax On The Beautiful Girls
Eddie Cantor; *Rare Early Recordings-1919-1921.* . . . . (Biograph)

Don't Take Her She's All I Got
Tracy Byrd; *Big Love.* . . . . (MCA)

Don't Take The Girl
Tim McGraw; *Not A Moment Too Soon* . . . . (Curb)
Tim McGraw's Greatest Hits . . . . (Curb)

Down Home Girl
Nazareth; *Play'n' The Game* . . . . (A&M)

Down Home Girl
Rolling Stones; *The Rolling Stones, Now!* . . . . (Abkco)

Dragon Lady
Blue Oyster Cult; *Revolution By Night* . . . . (Columbia)

Dragon Lady
Germs; *Germs* . . . . (Slash)

Dragon Lady
Bob Dylan; *Infidels* . . . . (Columbia)

Dream Girl
Stephen Bishop; *ST/Animal House* . . . . (MCA)

Dream Lady
Bread; *Baby I'm-A Want You.* . . . . (Elektra)
Best Of Bread-#2 . . . . (Elektra)

Dream On Texas Ladies
John Michael Montgomery; *Life's A Dance* . . . . (Atlantic)
ST/Maverick . . . . (Atlantic)

Dream Walkin'
Toby Keith; *Dream Walkin'* . . . . (Mercury)
Toby Keith's Greatest Hits, Volume One . . . . (Mercury)

Dreams Of The Everyday Housewife
Glen Campbell; *Glen Campbell-Classics Collection* . . . . (Capitol)
Glen Campbell-Live . . . . (Capitol)
Glen Campbell's Greatest Hits . . . . (Capitol)
Very Best Of Glen Campbell . . . . (Capitol)

Drug Store Woman
John Lee Hooker; *Best Of John Lee Hooker* . . . . (Vee-Jay)
Best Of John Lee Hooker . . . . (Crescendo)

Dublin Lady
Andy M. Stewart & Manus Lunny; *Dublin Lady.* . . . . (Green Linnet)

Dude (Looks Like A Lady)
Aerosmith; *Big Ones* . . . . (Geffen)
Permanent Vacation . . . . (Geffen)

Early To Bed
Morphine; *Like Swimming.* . . . . (DreamWorks/Rykodisc)

Earth Girls Are Easy
Julie Brown; *Goddess In Progress* . . . . (Rhino)

Easter Woman
Residents; *Commercial Album* . . . . (Ralph)

Easy Lover
Phil Collins; *Phil Collins-Hits* . . . . (Atlantic)
Serious Hits...Live!. . . . . (Atlantic)
Philip Bailey & Phil Collins; *Chinese Wall* . . . . (Columbia)

Elderly Woman Behind The Counter In A Small Town
Pearl Jam; *Vs.* . . . . (Epic Portrait Assoc.)

Electric Lady
Con Funk Shun; *Electric Lady.* . . . . (Mercury)

Elvis And Andy
Confederate Railroad; *Confederate Railroad's Greatest Hits* . . . . (Atlantic)
Notorious . . . . (Atlantic)

Emotional Girl
Terri Clark; *Just The Same* . . . . (Mercury)

European Female
Stranglers; *All Live & All Of The Night* . . . . (Epic)
Feline . . . . (Epic)
Stranglers' Greatest Hits-1977-1990 . . . . (Epic)

Euro-Trash Girl
Cracker; *Kerosene Hat* . . . . (Virgin)

Every Little Girl's Dream
Lisa Brokop; *Every Little Girl's Dream* . . . . (Patriot)

Every Little Thing She Does Is Magic
Police; *Every Breath You Take-The Classics* . . . . (A&M)
Ghost In The Machine. . . . . (A&M)

Every Morning
Sugar Ray; *14:59* . . . . (Lava)

Every Woman
Dave Mason; *Best Of Dave Mason* . . . . (Columbia)

Every Woman In The World
Air Supply; *Air Supply's Greatest Hits* . . . . (Arista)
Air Supply-The Definitive Collection . . . . (Arista)
Lost In Love . . . . (Arista)

Everything She Wants
Wham! Featuring George Michael; *'80s Greatest Rock Hits-#1-Passion &*
Power-C . . . . (Priority)
Make It Happen . . . . (Columbia)

Evil Woman
Electric Light Orchestra; *Afterglow* . . . . (Epic)
Electric Light Orchestra's Greatest Hits. . . . . (Jet)
Face The Music . . . . (Jet)
Ole ELO . . . . (Jet)

Evil Woman
Doobie Brothers; *Captain & Me* . . . . (Warner Bros.)

Ex-Girlfriend
No Doubt; *Return Of Saturn.* . . . . (Interscope)

Factory Girl
Rolling Stones; *Beggars Banquet.* . . . . (Abkco)

Fair And Tender Ladies
Whites; *A Lifetime In The Making* . . . . (Ceili Music)

Falls Apart
Sugar Ray; *14:59* . . . . (Lava)
Totally Hits-#2-C . . . . (Elektra)

Fantasy Girl
38 Special; *Flashback-Best Of 38 Special* . . . . (A&M)
Wild-Eyed Southern Boys . . . . (A&M)

Fast Moving Train
Restless Heart; *Best Of Restless Heart* . . . . (RCA)
Fast Moving Train. . . . . (RCA)

Fat Bottomed Girls
Queen; *Jazz* . . . . (Hollywood)
Queen's Greatest Hits I & II . . . . (Hollywood)

Fat Lady That Bumped Me Down
Paul Kelly; *Stand On The Positive Side* . . . . (Warner Bros.)

Father Of Girls
Perry Como; *Perry Como-Legendary Performer.* . . . . (RCA)

Female Of The Species
Space; *Spiders* . . . . (Gut/Universal)

Femininity
Eric Benet; *True To Myself.* . . . . (Jac-Mac/Warner Bros.)

Find Me A Girl
Jacksons; *Goin' Places* . . . . (Epic)
Philly Ballads-#2-C. . . . . (Philadelphia Int'l)

Fire Girl
Commodores; *Natural High.* . . . . (Motown)

Fire Woman
Cult; *Sonic Temple.* . . . . (Sire)

Five O'Clock World
Hal Ketchum; *Past The Point Of Rescue* . . . . (Curb)
Vogues; *ST/Good Morning, Vietnam* . . . . (A&M)
Vogues' Greatest Hits . . . . (SSS International)
Vogues' Greatest Hits . . . . (Rhino)

Flower Lady
Peter And Gordon; *Best Of Peter And Gordon.* . . . . (Rhino)
Phil Ochs; *Chords Of Fame* . . . . (A&M)
Pleasures Of The Harbor . . . . (A&M)
The War Is Over-Best Of Phil Ochs . . . . (A&M)

Foolish Little Girl
Shirelles; *Shirelles' Greatest Hits* . . . . (Everest)
Shirelles-16 Greatest Hits . . . . (Trip)
Shirelles-Anthology 1959-1964. . . . . (Rhino)

For Me & My Gal
Bing Crosby; *The Radio Years: 25 Songs.* . . . . (Crescendo)
Judy Garland & Gene Kelly; *Best Of The Decca Years-#1-Hits!-C* . . . . . (Decca)
Nilsson; *A Little Touch Of Schmilsson In The Night.* . . . . (RCA)

Forever My Lady
Jodeci; *Forever My Lady* . . . . (Uptown)

Forever Your Girl
Paula Abdul; *Forever Your Girl.* . . . . (Virgin)
Shut Up And Dance (The Dance Mixes) . . . . (Virgin)

Foxey Lady
Jimi Hendrix; *Essential Jimi Hendrix, Volume 2* . . . . (Reprise)
ST/Jimi Plays Monterey . . . . (Reprise)
ST/Wayne's World. . . . . (Reprise)
Jimi Hendrix Experience; *Are You Experienced?* . . . . (Reprise)
Smash Hits. . . . . (Reprise)
Mary's Danish; *Circa.* . . . . (Morgan Creek)

Fraulein
Bobby Helms; *Pop-A-Dilly* . . . . (MCA)
Super Country Hits Of The '50s-C. . . . . (Gusto)
Mickey Gilley; *Mickey Gilley's Greatest Hits-#1* . . . . (Epic)

Free Girl Now
Tom Petty And The Heartbreakers; *Echo.* . . . . (Warner Bros.)

Fresno Beauties
Broadway Cast; *Most Happy Fella* . . . . (RCA)

Friend, Love, Woman, Life
Mac Davis; *Baby Don't Get Hooked On Me* . . . . (Columbia)
Mac Davis' Greatest Hits . . . . (Columbia)

Fun, Fun, Fun
Beach Boys; *Beach Boys-Gift Set.* . . . . (Capitol)
Best Of The Beach Boys. . . . . (Capitol)

Endless Summer. . . . . (Capitol)
Made In The U.S.A. . . . . (Capitol)
The Beach Boys In Concert . . . . (Brother)

Funky Cold Medina
Tone Loc; *Loc-ed After Dark* . . . .(Delicious Vinyl)

Funny Girl
Barbra Streisand; *ST/Funny Girl* . . . . (Columbia)

Gal That Got Away
Four Freshmen; *Voices In Love-Love Lost* . . . . (Collector's Choice)
Frank Sinatra; *Complete Capitol Singles Collection*. . . . . (Capitol)

Gas Station Woman
Phil Ochs; *The War Is Over-Best Of Phil Ochs*. . . . . (A&M)

Geisha Girl
Hank Locklin; *Hank Locklin-Golden Hits* . . . . (Plantation)

Gemini Girl
David Allan Coe; *Son Of The South* . . . . (Columbia)

German Nun
Sex Gang Children; *Ecstasy & Vendetta Over New York* . . . .(Roir)

Get Off My Back Woman
B.B. King; *Live & Well* . . . .(MCA)

Get Out Of My Life, Woman
Lee Dorsey; *History Of New Orleans R&B-#3-1962-1970-C* . . . . (Rhino)
Paul Butterfield Blues Band; *East-West* . . . . (Elektra)
Golden Butter . . . . (Elektra)

Ghost Of A Texas Ladies' Man
Concrete Blonde; *Walking In London*. . . . .(I.R.S.)

Girl
Beatles; *Beatles-Box Set* . . . . (Capitol)
Beatles-Love Songs . . . . (Capitol)
Rubber Soul . . . . (Capitol)
The Beatles/1962-1966 . . . . (Capitol)

Girl
Cassie; *ST/Love Jones*. . . . . (Columbia)

Girl Can't Help It
Journey; *Journey's Greatest Hits* . . . . (Columbia)
Raised On Radio . . . . (Columbia)

Girl Can't Help It, The
Little Richard; *Little Richard-18 Greatest Hits* . . . . (Rhino)
Little Richard's Greatest Hits . . . . (Everest)
Super Oldies Of The '50s-#3-C . . . .(Audio Fidelity)
Well Alright! . . . . (Specialty)

Girl Don't Tell Me
Beach Boys; *Beach Boys-Gift Set* . . . . (Capitol)
California Girls . . . . (Capitol)
Endless Summer. . . . . (Capitol)

Girl From Atlanta
Benny Carter All-Star Sax Ensemble; *Over The Rainbow* . . . . . (Musicmasters)

Girl From Baltimore
Fleshtones; *Living Legends*. . . . .(I.R.S.)

Girl From Germany
Sparks; *Profile-The Ultimate Sparks Collection*. . . . . (Rhino)

Girl From Greenland
Chet Baker; *Compact Jazz-Chet Baker*. . . . . (Emarcy)

Girl From Hiroshima
Third World; *Sense Of Purpose* . . . . (Columbia)

Girl From Ipanema
Antonio Carlos Jobim; *Antonio Carlos Jobim* . . . .(Warner Bros.)
Compact Jazz-Antonio Carlos Jobim. . . . . (Verve)
Ella Fitzgerald; *Ella A Nice*. . . . .(Pablo)
Montreux '75 . . . .(Pablo)
Pablo Today-Ella Embraces Antonio Carlos Jobim . . . .(Pablo)
Stan Getz & Astrud Gilberto; *Cruisin'-1964-C* . . . .(Increase)
Getz/Gilberto . . . . (Verve)

Girl From Key Biscayne
Diego Modena & Jean Philippe Audin; *Ocarina* . . . . (Private Music)

Girl From Knoxville
Dave Loggins; *Apprentice (In A Musical Workshop)* . . . .(Epic)

Girl From Mill Valley
Jeff Beck Group; *Beck-Ola*. . . . .(Epic)

Girl From New York City
Beach Boys; *Today/Summer Days (& Summer Nights!)*. . . . . (Capitol)

Girl From The North Country
Bob Dylan; *Freewheelin'* . . . . (Columbia)
Nashville Skyline . . . . (Columbia)
Real Live . . . . (Columbia)
Joe Cocker; *Mad Dogs & Englishmen* . . . . (A&M)
Johnny Cash with Bob Dylan; *The Man In Black-His Greatest Hits*. . . . (Legacy)

Girl From Uganda
Les Baxter & His Orchestra; *African Blue-Brazil Now*. . . . .(Crescendo)

Girl I Got My Eyes On You
Today; *Today* . . . . (Motown)

Girl I Knew Somewhere, The
Monkees; *Monkees' Greatest Hits* . . . . (Rhino)

Girl I Love
Led Zeppelin; *BBC Sessions* . . . . (Atlantic)

Girl In A T-Shirt
ZZ Top; *Antenna*. . . . . (RCA)

Girl Inside My Head
Blues Traveler; *Bridge* . . . . (A&M)

Girl Is Mine
Michael Jackson with Paul McCartney; *Thriller*. . . . . (Epic)

Girl Like You
Edwyn Collins; *Gorgeous George* . . . . (Bar/None)
ST/Empire Records. . . . . (A&M)

Girl Like You
Rascals; *Groovin'* . . . .(Warner Special Prod.)
Rascals' Greatest Hits . . . .(Atlantic)

Girl Like You
Smithereens; *11* . . . .(Enigma)

Girl Next Door
Earl Lewis &The Channels; *Harlem Holiday-New York Rhythm & Blues-#2-C*. . . . .(Collectables)
New York's Finest . . . . (Collectables)

Girl Next Door
Johnny Crawford; *Best Of Johnny Crawford*. . . . . (Rhino)

Girl Next Door
Frank Sinatra; *Frank Sinatra-Gift Set* . . . . (Capitol)

Girl Next Door
Bobby Brown; *Dance!...Ya Know It!* . . . . (MCA)
King Of Stage . . . . (MCA)

Girl Next Door
Musiq Soulchild; *Aijuswanaseing*. . . . . (Def Soul/IDJMG)

Girl Of My Dreams
Bram Tchaikovsky; *D.I.Y.-#4-UK Pop II-Starry Eyes-1978-1979-C* . . . . (Rhino)
Strange Man, Changed Man. . . . .(Polydor)

Girl Of My Dreams
Dizzy Gillespie & Stan Getz; *Diz & Getz* . . . . (Verve)

Girl Of My Dreams
Buddy Clark; *Buddy Clark-16 Most Requested Songs* . . . . (Columbia)

Girl On A Swing
Gerry And The Pacemakers; *History Of British Rock-#7-C* . . . . (Rhino)

Girl On The Billboard
Boxcar Willie; *Truck Driving Favorites* . . . .(Madacy)
Del Reeves; *101 Greatest Country Hits-#10-C* . . . . (K-Tel)
Truck Driver Boogie Big Rig Hits-1939-1969-C . . . . (Audium)
Truckin' On-C . . . . (Hollywood)

Girl Talk
Betty Carter; *Finally* . . . . (Roulette)
Ella Fitzgerald & Joe Pass; *Speak Love*. . . . . (Pablo)

Girl Thang
Tammy Wynette & Wynonna; *Without Walls-C* . . . . (Epic)

Girl That I Marry, The
Dick Haymes; *Best Of Dick Haymes* . . . . (MCA)
Doris Day/Original Cast; *Annie Get Your Gun* . . . . (Columbia)
Original Broadway Cast; *Annie Get Your Gun* . . . . (Angel)
Original Cast; *Annie Get Your Gun* . . . . (MCA)

Girl With April In Her Eyes
Chris DeBurgh; *Crusader* . . . . (A&M)

Girl With The Hungry Eyes
Jefferson Starship; *At Point Zero* . . . . (Grunt)

Girl You Know It's True
Milli Vanilli; *All Or Nothing* . . . . (Arista)
Girl You Know It's True . . . . (Arista)

Girl, I've Been Hurt
Snow; *12 Inches Of Snow* . . . . (East West)

Girl, You'll Be A Woman Soon
Neil Diamond; *Double Gold-Neil Diamond* . . . .(Bang)
Hot August Night . . . . (MCA)
Neil Diamond-Classics (Early Years) . . . . (Columbia)
Neil Diamond's Greatest Hits . . . .(Bang)

Girlfriend
Beautiful South; *Welcome To The Beautiful South* . . . . (Elektra)

Girlfriend
Matthew Sweet; *Girlfriend* . . . .(Zoo)

Girlfriend
Bobby Brown; *King Of Stage* . . . . (MCA)

Girlfriend
Wings; *London Town* . . . . (Capitol)

Girlfriend
Michael Jackson; *Off The Wall* . . . . (Epic)

Girlfriend
Mary Jane Girls; *Only Four You* . . . . (Motown)

Girlfriend
Pebbles; *Pebbles* . . . . (MCA)

Girlfriend
Alicia Keys; *Songs In A Minor* . . . . (J)

Girlfriend Is Better
Talking Heads; *Speaking In Tongues* . . . . (Sire)
ST/Stop Making Sense . . . . (Sire)

Girlfriend/Boyfriend
Blackstreet featuring Janet; *Finally*. . . . .(Lil' Man/Interscope)

Girl's Alright With Me
Temptations; *Temptations' Greatest Hits-#1* . . . . (Motown)
Temptations-Anthology-The Best Of The Temptations. . . . . (Motown)

Girl's Gotta Do (What A Girl's Gotta Do)
Mindy McCready; *Ten Thousand Angels* . . . .(BNA)
Girls In Love
Gary Lewis And The Playboys; *Gary Lewis And The Playboys-Legendary Masters Series* . . . . (EMI)
Girls Just Want To Have Fun
Cyndi Lauper; *She's So Unusual* . . . . (Portrait)
Girls Night Out
Judds; *Judds' Greatest Hits* . . . . (MCA)
Why Not Me . . . . (MCA)
Girls Nite Out
Tyler Collins; *Girls Nite Out* . . . .(RCA)
Girls Of Montreal
Artie Traum; *Life On Earth* . . . . (Rounder)
Girls Of Porn
Mr. Bungle; *Mr. Bungle* . . . . (Warner Bros.)
Girls Of Santa Fe
Bill Morrissey; *Standing Eight* . . . .(Philo)
Girls Of Summer
Original Cast; *Marry Me A Little* . . . .(RCA)
Girls On The Beach
Beach Boys; *Absolute Best-#1* . . . . (Capitol)
Endless Summer . . . . (Capitol)
Little Deuce Coupe/All Summer Long . . . .(Capitol)
Girls' School
Wings; *London Town* . . . . (Capitol)
Girls Talk
Dave Edmunds; *Best Of Dave Edmunds* . . . . (Swan Song)
Repeat When Necessary . . . .(Swan Song)
Dave Edmunds Band; *I Hear You Rockin'* . . . . (Columbia)
Elvis Costello; *Girls Girls Girls* . . . . (Columbia)
Taking Liberties . . . . (Columbia)
Linda Ronstadt; *Mad Love* . . . . (Elektra)
Girls With Guitars
Wynonna; *Tell Me Why* . . . . (MCA)
Girls, Girls
George Carroll; *Music From The New York Stage (1890-1920)-#1-1890-1908-C* . . . . (Pearl)
Girls, Girls, Girls
Jay-Z; *Girls, Girls, Girls* . . . . (Roc-A-Fella/DJMG)
Gliding Through My Memoree
Original Cast; *ST/Flower Drum Song* . . . .(Sony Music Classical)
Go Away Little Girl
Happenings; *The Ultimate History Of Rock 'N' Roll-#6-C* . . . . . . (K-Tel)
Steve Lawrence; *Steve Lawrence's Greatest Hits* . . . . (Columbia)
Go Home Girl
Ry Cooder; *Bop Till You Drop* . . . . (Warner Bros.)
God Blessed Texas
Little Texas; *Big Time* . . . . (Warner Bros.)
God Don't Make Lonely Girls
Wallflowers; *Bringing Down The Horse* . . . . (Interscope)
Gold Digger
EPMD; *Business As Usual* . . . . (Def Jam)
Gold Dust Woman
Fleetwood Mac; *25 Years-The Chain* . . . . (Warner Bros.)
Rumours . . . . (Warner Bros.)
Sister Hazel; *Legacy-A Tribute To Fleetwood Mac's Rumours-C* . . . .(Lava)
Gold Dust Woman
Hole; *ST/City Of Angels* . . . . (Warner Sunset/Reprise)
Golden Lady
Stevie Wonder; *Innervisions* . . . . (Motown)
Golf Girl
Caravan; *Best Of Caravan* . . . .(London)
Caravan-London Collector . . . .(London)
In The Land Of Grey & Pink . . . . (London)
Gone As A Girl Can Get
George Strait; *Holding My Own* . . . . (MCA)
Good Girls
Joe; *All That I Am* . . . .(Jive)
Good Girls Don't
Knack; *Get The Knack* . . . . (Capitol)
Good Girls Go To Heaven
Charlie Floyd; *Charlie Floyd* . . . . (Liberty)
Good Hearted Woman
George Jones; *I Am What I Am* . . . . (Epic)
Waylon Jennings; *Good Hearted Woman* . . . .(RCA)
The Outlaws . . . . (RCA)
Waylon Jennings' Greatest Hits . . . .(RCA)
Willie Nelson; *Greatest Hits (& Some That Will Be)* . . . . (Columbia)
Willie . . . .(RCA)
Good Morning Girl
Journey; *Departure* . . . . (Columbia)
Good Morning Little School Girl
Grateful Dead; *Grateful Dead (Skull & Roses)* . . . . (Warner Bros.)
Huey Lewis and the News; *Four Chords & Several Years Ago* . . . . (Elektra)
Johnny Winter; *Johnny Winter* . . . . (Columbia)
Live/Johnny Winter And . . . . (Columbia)
Ten Years After; *Classic Performances Of Ten Years After* . . . . . . (Columbia)

Recorded Live . . . .(Columbia)
SSSSH . . . . (Chrysalis)
Universal . . . .(Chrysalis)
Yardbirds; *Eric Clapton-Crossroads-C* . . . . (Polydor)
Five Live Yardbirds . . . . (Rhino)
Good Run Of Bad Luck
Clint Black; *No Time To Kill* . . . . (RCA)
Good Time Girl
Lee Ferrell; *Hard Times* . . . . (TMS)
Good Woman Blues
Mel Tillis; *Mel Tillis' Greatest Hits* . . . .(Curb)
Goodbye Girl
David Gates; *Bread-Retrospective* . . . .(Rhino)
Super Hits Of The '70s-Have A Nice Day-#21-C . . . . (Rhino)
Green Eyed Lady
Sugarloaf; *Sugarloaf-Spaceship Earth* . . . .(Collectables)
Gulf And The Shell
Clinton Gregory; *Clinton Gregory* . . . . (Polydor Country)
Guys & Dolls
Original Cast; *ST/Guys & Dolls* . . . . (MCA)
Gypsy Woman
Brian Hyland; *Brian Hyland's Greatest Hits* . . . .(Rhino)
Super Hits Of The '70s-Have A Nice Day-#3-C . . . . (Rhino)
Impressions; *Billboard Top R&B Hits-1961-C* . . . . (Rhino)
Impressions' Greatest Hits . . . . (MCA)
Oldies But Goodies-#12-C . . . . (Original Sound)
Vintage Music-#6-C . . . . (MCA)
Ry Cooder; *Slide Area* . . . . (Warner Bros.)
Gypsy Woman
Muddy Waters; *Real Folk Blues-C* . . . . (Chess)
The Chess Box-Muddy Waters . . . . (Chess)
Gypsy Woman (She's Homeless)
Crystal Waters; *Red Hot + Dance-C* . . . . (Columbia)
Surprise . . . . (Mercury)
Hanky Panky
Tommy James And The Shondells; *Billboard Top Rock 'N' Roll Hits-1966-C* . . . . (Rhino)
Tommy James And The Shondells-Anthology . . . . (Rhino)
Happiest Girl In The Whole U.S.A.
Donna Fargo; *Best Of Donna Fargo* . . . .(Curb)
Jeanne Pruett; *Stand By Your Man* . . . .(Allegiance)
Happiness Is A Warm Gun
Beatles; *The Beatles (White Album)* . . . .(Capitol)
Happy Girl
Beth Nielsen Chapman; *Sand And Water* . . . . (Reprise)
Martina McBride; *Evolution* . . . . (RCA)
Hard Headed Woman
Elvis Presley; *Billboard Top Rock 'N' Roll Hits-1958-C* . . . .(Rhino)
Number One Hits . . . . (RCA)
ST/King Creole . . . . (RCA)
The Top Ten Hits . . . . (RCA)
Worldwide 50 Gold Award Hits, Vol. 1, Parts 1 & 2 . . . . (RCA)
Hard Headed Woman
Cat Stevens; *Cat Stevens Greatest Hits* . . . . (A&M)
Tea For The Tillerman . . . . (A&M)
Hard Lovin' Woman
Mark Collie; *Unleashed* . . . . (MCA)
Hard Luck Woman
Garth Brooks; *Kiss My Ass-C* . . . .(Mercury)
Kiss; *Alive II.* . . . . (Casablanca)
Double Platinum . . . .(Mercury)
Rock & Roll Over . . . . (Casablanca)
Harry's House Centerpiece
Joni Mitchell; *Hissing Of Summer Lawns* . . . . (Asylum)
Have You Ever Loved A Woman
Derek And The Dominos; *Layla* . . . . (Polydor)
Have You Ever Really Loved A Woman?
Bryan Adams; *18 Til I Die* . . . .(A&M)
Number One Movie Hits-C . . . . (ESX Entert.)
ST/Don Juan De Marco . . . . (A&M)
Have You Seen Her
Chi-Lites; *Chi-Lites' Greatest Hits* . . . .(Rhino)
Hammer; *Please Hammer Don't Hurt 'Em* . . . . (Capitol)
He Stopped Loving Her Today
George Jones; *All Time Legends Of Country Music-C* . . . . (Legacy)
First Time Live! . . . . (Epic)
George Jones-Anniversary-Ten Years Of Hits . . . . (Epic)
Greatest Country Hits Of The '80s-1980-C . . . .(Columbia)
Greatest Hits From The Jukebox-C . . . . (Epic)
I Am What I Am . . . . (Epic)
He Thinks He'll Keep Her
Mary Chapin Carpenter; *Come On Come On* . . . .(Columbia)
Hearts Are Gonna Roll
Hal Ketchum; *Sure Love* . . . .(Curb)
Heart-Shaped Box
Nirvana; *In Utero* . . . . (David Geffen Co.)
Hello Hello
Talk Show; *Talk Show* . . . . (Atlantic)

Hello Little Girl
Beatles; *The Beatles-Anthology-#1* . . . . (Capitol)
Her Strut
Bob Seger & The Silver Bullet Band; *Against The Wind* . . . . (Capitol)
  Nine Tonight . . . . (Capitol)
Her Town Too
James Taylor & J.D. Souther; *Dad Loves His Work* . . . . (Columbia)
Here, There & Everywhere
Beatles; *Beatles-Box Set* . . . . (Capitol)
  Beatles-Love Songs . . . . (Capitol)
  Revolver . . . . (Capitol)
Kenny Loggins; *Kenny Loggins Alive* . . . . (Columbia)
Heroin Girl
Everclear; *Sparkle And Fade* . . . . (Capitol)
Hey Baby
No Doubt; *Rock Steady* . . . . (Interscope)
Hey Girl
Billy Joel; *Billy Joel's Greatest Hits-#3* . . . . (Columbia)
Freddie Scott; *Freddie Scott Sings And Sings And Sings* . . . . (Collectables)
Michael McDonald; *Best Of Smooth Jazz-#2-Under The*
  Covers-C . . . . (Warner Bros.)
  Blink Of An Eye . . . . (Reprise)
Righteous Brothers; *Best Of The Righteous Brothers-#2* . . . . (Curb)
Hey Girl (I Like Your Style)
Temptations; *Cloud Nine* . . . . (Motown)
  Masterpiece . . . . (Motown)
Hey Hey What Can I Do
Hootie & The Blowfish; *Encomium: Tribute To Led Zeppelin-C* . . . . . . (Atlantic)
Led Zeppelin; *Led Zeppelin-Box Set* . . . . (Atlantic)
  Led Zeppelin-The Complete Studio Recordings . . . . (Atlantic)
Hey Little Girl
Professor Longhair; *Atlantic Rhythm & Blues 1947-1974-#1 (1947-*
  1952)-C . . . . (Atlantic)
  New Orleans Piano-Blues Originals-#2 . . . . (Atlantic)
Hey Little Girl
Icehouse; *Primitive Man* . . . . (Chrysalis)
Hey Little Girl
Dee Clark; *Jukebox Classics-#1-C* . . . . (Rhino)
  Super Oldies Of The '50s-#2-C . . . . (Audio Fidelity)
High Country Snows
Dan Fogelberg; *High Country Snows* . . . . (Full Moon)
Highway Lady
UFO; *No Heavy Petting* . . . . (Chrysalis)
Hippychick
Soho; *Goddess* . . . . (Atco)
Holdin' Heaven
Tracy Byrd; *Tracy Byrd* . . . . (MCA)
Hollywood Lady
Burt Compton & Steve Mele; *Rock 'N' Roll Genius* . . . . (Wizard)
Hollywood Movie Girls
Dusty Springfield; *It Begins Again* . . . . (United Artists)
Honey Bun
Original Cast; *South Pacific* . . . . (CBS Masterworks)
Honeysuckle Honey
Commander Cody & His Lost Planet Airmen; *Country Casanova* . . . . . . (MCA)
Honky Tonk Women Love Redneck Men
Ronnie McDowell; *American Music* . . . . (Curb)
Honolulu Lulu
Jan & Dean; *Dead Man's Curve* . . . . (EMI)
  Jan & Dean-Legendary Masters . . . . (EMI)
  One Summer Night-Live . . . . (Rhino)
  Surf City-Best Of Jan & Dean . . . . (EMI)
Hospital Lady
Loudon Wainwright III; *Loudon Wainwright III* . . . . (Atlantic)
Hot Boyz
Missy ''Misdemeanor'' Elliot; *Da Real World* . . . . (East West)
  Totally Hits-#2-C . . . . (Elektra)
Hot Girls In Love
Loverboy; *Big Ones* . . . . (Columbia)
  Keep It Up . . . . (Columbia)
Hotel For Women
Nails; *Hotel For Women* . . . . (PVC)
Housewife
Leon Russell; *Americana* . . . . (Paradise)
Houston, Treat My Lady Good
Joe Stampley; *Red Wine & Blue Memories* . . . . (Epic)
How Come, How Long
Babyface & Stevie Wonder; *The Day* . . . . (Epic)
How Do You Talk To Girls
Rick Springfield; *Success Hasn't Spoiled Me Yet* . . . . (RCA)
How To Handle A Woman
Original Cast; *Camelot* . . . . (Columbia)
Richard Harris; *ST/Camelot* . . . . (Warner Bros.)
Hundred Pounds Of Clay
Gene McDaniels; *Best Of Gene McDaniels-A Hundred Pounds*
  Of Clay . . . . (Collectables)
  Rock Is Dead But It Won't Lie Down-C . . . . (Gold Rush)

Hymn To Her
Pretenders; *Diana, Princess Of Wales-Tribute-C* . . . . (Columbia)
  Get Close . . . . (Sire)
  The Isle Of View . . . . (Warner Bros.)
Hymn To Him
Audrey Hepburn; *ST/My Fair Lady* . . . . (Columbia)
Julie Andrews/Original Cast; *My Fair Lady* . . . . (Columbia)
I Am
Train; *Train* . . . . (Aware/C2/Columbia)
I Am That Man
Brooks & Dunn; *Borderline* . . . . (Arista)
I Am Woman
Helen Reddy; *Helen Reddy's Greatest Hits* . . . . (Capitol)
  I Am Woman . . . . (Capitol)
  I Am Woman-C . . . . (Nick At Nite)
  I Don't Know How To Love Him . . . . (Capitol)
I Am Your Woman
Syleena Johnson; *Chapter One: Love, Pain & Forgiveness* . . . . (Jive)
I Asked For Water (She Gave Me Gasoline)
Howlin' Wolf; *Howlin' Wolf-His Best* . . . . (Chess)
  The Blues-#3-C . . . . (Chess)
I Can't Reach Her Anymore
Sammy Kershaw; *Haunted Heart* . . . . (Mercury)
I Don't Even Know Your Name
Alan Jackson; *Alan Jackson-The Greatest Hits Collection* . . . . (Arista)
  Who I Am . . . . (Arista)
I Dream Of Women Like You
Ronnie McDowell; *Country Boy's Heart* . . . . (Epic)
  Older Women & Other Greatest Hits . . . . (Epic)
I Enjoy Being A Girl
Original Cast; *Flower Drum Song* . . . . (Sony Music Classical)
I Found My Girl In The Good Old U.S.A.
Jimmie Skinner; *45-#2095* . . . . (Gusto)
I Go Wild
Rolling Stones; *Voodoo Lounge* . . . . (Virgin)
I Got A Girl
Tripping Daisy; *I Am An Elastic Firecracker* . . . . (Island)
I Kissed A Girl
Jill Sobule; *Jill Sobule* . . . . (Lava)
  Lesbian Favorites-Women Like Us-C . . . . (Rhino)
I Knew You When
Billy Joe Royal; *Billy Joe Royal's Greatest Hits* . . . . (Columbia)
I Know An Old Lady Who Swallowed A Fly
Original Soundtrack; *More Silly Songs* . . . . (Disney)
Peter, Paul & Mary; *Peter, Paul & Mommy, Too* . . . . (Warner Bros.)
I Know She Still Loves Me
George Strait; *Platinum Country-C* . . . . (MCA)
  Strait Out Of The Box . . . . (MCA)
I Left Something Turned On At Home
Trace Adkins; *Dreamin' Out Loud* . . . . (Capitol)
I Let Her Lie
Daryle Singletary; *Daryle Singletary* . . . . (Giant)
I Like It, I Love It
Tim McGraw; *All I Want* . . . . (Curb)
  Tim McGraw's Greatest Hits . . . . (Curb)
I Like Them Girls
Tyrese; *2000 Watts* . . . . (RCA)
I Lost My Gal From Memphis
New Sunshine Jazz Band; *Too Much Mustard* . . . . (Biograph)
Tex Williams; *Tex Williams-Vintage Collections* . . . . (Capitol)
I Love You (Miss Robot)
Buggles; *Age Of Plastic* . . . . (Island)
I Met Her In Church
Box Tops; *Box Tops' Greatest Hits* . . . . (Rhino)
I Need A Hot Girl
Hot Boys; *Guerrilla Warfare* . . . . (Cash Money/Universal)
I Saw Her Again
Mamas & The Papas; *Best Of The Mamas & The Papas* . . . . (MCA)
  Farewell To The First Golden Era . . . . (MCA)
  Mamas & The Papas . . . . (MCA)
I Saw Her Standing There
Beatles; *Introducing...The Beatles* . . . . (Vee-Jay)
  Meet The Beatles! . . . . (Capitol)
  Please Please Me . . . . (Parlophone)
  Rock 'N' Roll Music . . . . (Capitol)
  The Beatles-Anthology-#1 . . . . (Capitol)
Paul McCartney; *Tripping The Live Fantastic-Highlights!* . . . . (Capitol)
I Taught Her Everything She Knows
Billy Walker; *Billy Walker's Greatest Hits* . . . . (Monument)
I Think About It All The Time
John Berry; *Standing On The Edge* . . . . (Capitol)
I Think About You
Collin Raye; *Best Of Collin Raye-Direct Hits* . . . . (Epic)
  I Think About You . . . . (Epic)
I Want A Girl (Just Like The Girl)
Al Jolson; *The Al Jolson Story-#1* . . . . (MCA)
Spike Jones & His City Slickers; *King Of Corn* . . . . (Glendale)

I Want A Little Girl
Big Joe Turner; *Atlantic Jazz-Singers-C* . . . . (Atlantic)
Ray Charles; *Life In Music* . . . . (Atlantic)
I Want To Be A Lady
Katie Barry; *Music From The New York Stage (1890-1920)-#1-1890-1908-C* . . . . (Pearl)
I Wish I Had A Girl
Henry Lee Summer; *Henry Lee Summer* . . . . (CBS Associated)
I Wonder What She's Doing Tonite
Tommy Boyce & Bobby Hart; *More Nuggets-C* . . . . (Rhino)
I Wonder Why She Kept On Saying "Si-Si-Si-Si Senor"
Al Jolson; *Music From The New York Stage (1890-1920)-#4-1917-1920-C* . . . . (Pearl)
If Drinkin' Don't Kill Me (Her Memory Will)
George Jones; *10 Years Of Hits* . . . . (Epic)
I Am What I Am . . . . (Epic)
If I Could Have Her Tonight
Neil Young; *Neil Young* . . . . (Reprise)
If I Was Your Girlfriend
Prince; *The Hits 2* . . . . (Paisley Park)
The Hits/The B-Sides . . . . (Paisley Park)
If I Were Your Woman
Gladys Knight; *At Last* . . . . (MCA)
Gladys Knight & The Pips; *Compact Command Performances-Gladys Knight & The Pips* . . . . (Motown)
Every Great Motown Song-First 25 Years-C . . . . (Motown)
Gladys Knight & The Pips-All The Great Hits . . . . (Motown)
Gladys Knight & The Pips-Anthology . . . . (Motown)
If I Were Your Woman . . . . (Motown)
Motown Superstar Series-#13-Gladys Knight & The Pips . . . . (Motown)
If She Knew What She Wants
Bangles; *Bangles' Greatest Hits* . . . . (Columbia)
Different Light . . . . (Columbia)
If Women Ruled The World
Joan Armatrading; *Square The Circle* . . . . (A&M)
If You See Her, Say Hello
Bob Dylan; *Blood On The Tracks* . . . . (Columbia)
If You See Him/If You See Her
Brooks & Dunn & Reba McEntire; *If You See Her* . . . . (Arista)
Reba McEntire & Brooks & Dunn; *If You See Him* . . . . (MCA)
Reba McEntire's Greatest Hits-#3: I'm A Survivor . . . . (MCA)
If Your Girl Only Knew
Aaliyah; *MTV Party To Go '98-C* . . . . (Tommy Boy)
One In A Million . . . . (BlackGround Enterp./Atlantic)
I'll Come Back As Another Woman
Tanya Tucker; *Girls Like Me* . . . . (Capitol)
Tanya Tucker's Greatest Hits . . . . (Liberty)
I'll Say She Does
Al Jolson; *Music From The New York Stage (1890-1920)-#4-1917-1920-C* . . . . (Pearl)
I'll Think Of A Reason Later
Lee Ann Womack; *Some Things I Know* . . . . (Decca)
I'm A Honky Tonk Girl
Loretta Lynn; *The Country Music Hall Of Fame-Loretta Lynn* . . . . . (MCA)
I'm A One- Woman Man
George Jones; *Essential George Jones-The Spirit Of Country* . . . . . . (Legacy)
George Jones-Super Hits . . . . (Epic)
One Woman Man . . . . (Epic)
Who's Gonna Fill Their Shoes . . . . (Epic)
Glen Campbell; *Still Within The Sound Of My Voice* . . . . (MCA)
Johnny Horton; *American Originals-Johnny Horton* . . . . (Columbia)
Honky Tonk Man-The Essential Johnny Horton-1956-1960 . . . . . . (Legacy)
I'm A Woman
Maria Muldaur; *Waitress In The Donut Shop* . . . . (Warner Archives)
Peggy Lee; *I Am Woman-C* . . . . (Nick At Nite)
Peggy Lee's All-Time Greatest Hits . . . . (Curb)
Reba McEntire; *Out Of A Dream* . . . . (Mercury)
I'm An Errand Girl For Rhythm
Diana Krall; *All For You (A Dedication To The Nat "King" Cole Trio)* . . . . (Impulse!)
I'm An Ordinary Man
Rex Harrison/Original Cast; *My Fair Lady* . . . . (Columbia)
I'm Every Woman
Chaka Khan; *Chicken Soup For The Soul: I'll Be There For You-Songs Of Friendship, Brotherhood And Sisterhood-C* . . . . (Rhino)
Epiphany: The Best Of Chaka Khan-#1 . . . . (Reprise)
I Am Woman-C . . . . (Nick At Nite)
Whitney Houston; *ST/The Bodyguard* . . . . (Arista)
Whitney Houston's Greatest Hits . . . . (Arista)
I'm Not A Girl, Not Yet A Woman
Britney Spears; *Britney* . . . . (Jive)
I'm Not Strong Enough To Say No
BlackHawk; *Strong Enough* . . . . (Arista)
I'm That Kind Of Girl
Patty Loveless; *On Down The Line* . . . . (MCA)
Patty Loveless' Greatest Hits . . . . (MCA)
I'm The Laziest Gal In Town
Julie Wilson; *Cole Porter Songbook* . . . . (DRG)

In China Or A Woman's Heart
Kate Wolf; *Poet's Heart* . . . . (Kaleidoscope)
In The Girls' Room
Rick James; *Wonderful* . . . . (Reprise)
In The Heart Of A Woman
Billy Ray Cyrus; *It Won't Be The Last* . . . . (Mercury)
In The Summertime
Mungo Jerry; *In The Summertime-Best Of Mungo Jerry* . . . . (Rhino)
Super Hits Of The '70s-Have A Nice Day-#3-C . . . . (Rhino)
Independent Women Pt.1
Destiny's Child; *Now That's What I Call Music!-#6-C* . . . . (Virgin)
ST/Charlie's Angels . . . . (Columbia)
Indian Girl
Rolling Stones; *Emotional Rescue* . . . . (Rolling Stones)
Indian Girl
Hollies; *Hollies-Epic Anthology From The Original Master Tapes* . . . . . . (Epic)
Indian Girl
Capris; *There's A Moon Out Tonight* . . . . (Collectables)
Indian Lady
Roger Whittaker; *Reflections Of Love* . . . . (RCA)
Indian Woman
Sons Of The Pioneers; *Western Country* . . . . (Granite)
Indian Woman
Dan Hill; *Frozen In The Night* . . . . (20th Century Fox)
Insatiable Woman
Isley, Jasper, Isley; *Caravan Of Love* . . . . (CBS Associated)
Invisible Touch
Genesis; *Hit Singles-1980-1988-C* . . . . (Atlantic)
Invisible Touch . . . . (Atlantic)
Irish Suite: Irish Washerwoman
Boston Pops Orchestra/Arthur Fiedler; *Irish Night At The Pops* . . . . . (RCA)
Is She Really Going Out With Him
Joe Jackson; *Live 1980/86* . . . . (A&M)
Look Sharp! . . . . (A&M)
Is There Life Out There
Reba McEntire; *For My Broken Heart* . . . . (MCA)
Reba McEntire's Greatest Hits Volume Two . . . . (MCA)
Island Girl
Elton John; *Billboard Top Hits-1975-C* . . . . (Rhino)
Elton John's Greatest Hits-#2 . . . . (Polydor)
Rock Of The Westies . . . . (Polydor)
Island Girl
Beach Boys; *Still Cruisin'* . . . . (Capitol)
Island Woman
Pablo Cruise; *Pablo Cruise* . . . . (A&M)
It Could've Been Me
Billy Ray Cyrus; *Some Gave All* . . . . (Mercury)
It Should've Been Me
Commander Cody & His Lost Planet Airmen; *Hot Licks, Cold Steel & Trucker's Favorites* . . . . (MCA)
It Won't Be Long
Beatles; *Meet The Beatles!* . . . . (Capitol)
With The Beatles . . . . (Parlophone)
It Won't Be Over You
Steve Wariner; *Steve Wariner-Drive* . . . . (Arista)
Italian Girls
Daryl Hall & John Oates; *H2O* . . . . (RCA)
Soulful Sounds . . . . (RCA)
Italian Girls
Rod Stewart; *Best Of Rod Stewart-#2* . . . . (Mercury)
It's A Shame To Ship Your Wife On Sunday
Fiddlin' John Carson; *The Old Hen Cackled (& The Rooster's Going To Crow)* . . . . (Rounder)
It's A Woman's World
Four Aces; *Best Of The Four Aces* . . . . (MCA)
Itsy Bitsy Teenie Weenie Yellow Polkadot Bikini
Brian Hyland; *Brian Hyland's Greatest Hits* . . . . (Rhino)
Dr. Demento Presents The Greatest Novelty Records-#3-1960s-C . . . (Rhino)
Vintage Music-#5-C . . . . (MCA)
I've Got A Gal In Kalamazoo
Glenn Miller; *Best Of Glenn Miller* . . . . (RCA)
Decade Of The '40s-C . . . . (RCA)
Glenn Miller-A Legendary Performer-#1 & 2 . . . . (Bluebird)
Memorial-1944-1969 . . . . (Bluebird)
The Glenn Miller Story . . . . (RCA)
Glenn Miller & His Orchestra; *Glenn Miller & His Orchestra-Pure Gold* . . . . (Bluebird)
The Unforgettable Glenn Miller & His Orchestra . . . . (RCA)
I've Got A Woman
Jimmy McGriff; *Best Of Sue Records-C* . . . . (Collectables)
Toast To Jimmy McGriff's Golden Classics . . . . (Collectables)
J.A.P. Rap
2 Live Jews; *As Kosher As They Wanna Be* . . . . (Kosher)
Jamaica Lady
Nitty Gritty Dirt Band; *Dirt, Silver & Gold* . . . . (One Way)
Jealous Girl
New Edition; *Candy Girl* . . . . (Streetwise)

Jersey Girl
Bruce Springsteen & The E Street Band; *Bruce Springsteen & The E Street Band Live/1975-85* . . . . (Legacy)
Tom Waits; *Heartattack & Vine* . . . . (Asylum)
Tom Waits-Anthology . . . . (Asylum)

Jessie's Girl
Rick Springfield; *Nipper's Greatest Hits Of The '80s-C*. . . . . (RCA)
Rick Springfield's Greatest Hits . . . . (RCA)
Working Class Dog . . . . (RCA)

Jet City Woman
Queensryche; *Empire* . . . .(EMI)

Johannesburg Woman
David Rudder; *1990* . . . . (Sire)

Johnny Have You Seen Her?
Rembrandts; *United* . . . . (Atco)

Just A Girl
No Doubt; *Tragic Kingdom* . . . . (Trauma)

Just Another Girl
Monica; *ST/Down To Earth* . . . .(Epic)

Just Be A Man About It
Toni Braxton; *The Heat* . . . . (LaFace)

Just Like A Woman
Bob Dylan; *Before The Flood* . . . . (Columbia)
Biograph . . . . (Columbia)
Blonde On Blonde . . . . (Columbia)
Bob Dylan At Budokan . . . . (Columbia)
Bob Dylan's Greatest Hits . . . . (Columbia)
Byrds; *The Byrds* . . . . (Columbia)

Just Like Anyone
Soul Asylum; *Let Your Dim Light Shine* . . . . (Columbia)

Just Tell Her Jim Said Hello
Elvis Presley; *Collector's Gold* . . . . (RCA)
Elvis' Gold Records, Volume 4 . . . . (RCA)
The Other Sides-Worldwide Gold Award Hits, Vol. 2 . . . . (RCA)

Just To See Her
Smokey Robinson; *One Heartbeat* . . . . (Motown)

Kansas City
Beatles; *Beatles VI* . . . . (Capitol)
Beatles-Box Set . . . . (Capitol)
Rock 'N' Roll Music . . . . (Capitol)
Super Oldies Of The '60s-#10-C . . . .(Audio Fidelity)
Bill Haley & His Comets; *Bill Haley & His Comets' Greatest Hits* . . . . (Everest)
Fats Domino; *Fats Domino's Greatest Hits* . . . . (Everest)
Wilbert Harrison; *American Graffiti-#3-C* . . . .(MCA)
Billboard Top Rock 'N' Roll Hits-1959-C . . . . (Rhino)
Cruisin'-1959-C . . . . (Increase)
Echoes Of A Rock Era-Middle Years-C . . . . (Roulette)
Super Oldies Of The '50s-#2-C . . . .(Audio Fidelity)

Kansas City Woman
Little Charlie & The Nightcats; *Big Break!* . . . . (Alligator)

Keep In Touch
Robert Palmer; *Some People Can Do What They Like* . . . . (Island)

Kentucky Woman
Deep Purple; *Purple Passages* . . . .(Warner Bros.)
When We Rock & When We Roll . . . .(Warner Bros.)
Gary Puckett And The Union Gap; *Gary Puckett And The Union Gap's Greatest Hits*. . . . . (Bac-Trac)
Neil Diamond; *Love At The Greek* . . . . (Columbia)
Neil Diamond-Classics (Early Years) . . . . (Columbia)
Neil Diamond-Gold . . . .(MCA)

Kentucky Woman
Billy Cole Reed; *Audiograph Alive-C*. . . . .(Audiograph)

Kentucky Woman
Ronnie Milsap; *Ronnie Milsap-16 Greatest Hits-#2*. . . . . (Trip)

Kicks
Paul Revere And The Raiders; *Legend Of Paul Revere And The Raiders* . . . . (Columbia)
Midnight Ride . . . . (Columbia)
Paul Revere And The Raiders' Greatest Hits . . . . (Columbia)

Knoxville Girl
Cathy Fink & Duck Donald; *Cathy Fink & Duck Donald*. . . . . (Flying Fish)
Jimmy Martin; *Me 'N Ole Pete* . . . . (International Mktg. Group)
Stanley Brothers; *Stanley Series-Vol. 1-#1* . . . . (Copper Creek)

L.A. Girls
Nazareth; *Play'n' The Game* . . . . (A&M)

L.A. Lady
New Riders Of The Purple Sage; *Adventures Of Panama Red* . . . . . . (Columbia)

L.A. Woman
Billy Idol; *Charmed Life*. . . . .(Chrysalis)
Doors; *Best Of The Doors* . . . . (Elektra)
Doors' Greatest Hits . . . . (Elektra)
L.A. Woman . . . . (Elektra)
ST/The Doors . . . . (Elektra)
Weird Scenes Inside The Gold Mine . . . . (Elektra)

Ladies Night
Kool & The Gang; *Ladies Night* . . . . (De-Lite)

Ladies Night In Buffalo
David Lee Roth; *Eat 'Em & Smile* . . . .(Warner Bros.)

Ladies Of The Canyon
Joni Mitchell; *Ladies Of The Canyon* . . . . (Reprise)

Ladies Who Lunch
Original Cast; *Company* . . . . (Columbia)

Lady
Stryper; *Against The Law* . . . . (Hollywood)
Can't Stop The Rock: The Stryper Collection-1984-1991 . . . . (Hollywood)

Lady
Styx; *Best Of Styx* . . . . (RCA)
Lady . . . . (RCA)
Nipper's Greatest Hits Of The '70s-C . . . . (RCA)
Styx-Greatest Hits . . . . (A&M)

Lady
Little River Band; *Little River Band's Greatest Hits* . . . . (Capitol)
Reminiscing: The Twentieth Anniversary Collection . . . . (Rhino)

Lady
Jack Jones; *Best Of Jack Jones* . . . . (MCA)
The Impossible Dream . . . . (Universal)

Lady
George Benson; *Breezin'* . . . . (Warner Bros.)

Lady
Kenny Rogers; *Kenny Rogers' Greatest Hits* . . . . (EMI)
Kenny Rogers-20 Great Years . . . . (Reprise)
Kenny Rogers-Love Songs . . . . (Capitol)
Kenny Rogers-Twenty Greatest Hits . . . . (EMI)
Lionel Richie; *Time* . . . . (Mercury)
Roger Williams; *Roger Williams' Greatest Hits* . . . . (Curb)

Lady
D'Angelo; *Brown Sugar* . . . . (EMI)

Lady (You Bring Me Up)
Commodores; *All The Great Love Songs-Commodores* . . . . (Motown)
Commodores-All The Great Hits . . . . (Motown)
Compact Command Performances-Commodores . . . . (Motown)

Lady Bird
Nancy Sinatra & Lee Hazlewood; *Fairy Tales & Fantasies-Best Of*. . . . (Rhino)

Lady Blue
George Benson; *Weekend In L.A.* . . . . (Warner Bros.)
Leon Russell; *Best Of Leon Russell* . . . . (MCA)
Will O' The Wisp . . . . (MCA)

Lady Bus Driver
Ultra Head; *Cement Truck*. . . . . (Imperial Stab Chamber)

Lady Cab Driver
Prince; *1999* . . . . (Warner Bros.)

Lady Came From Baltimore
Joan Baez; *Contemporary Ballad Book*. . . . . (Vanguard)
Joan . . . . (Vanguard)
John Stewart; *Neon Beach*. . . . . (Homecoming)
Johnny Cash; *Johnny Cash-16 Biggest Hits-#2*. . . . . (Legacy)
Tim Hardin; *Hang On To A Dream-Verve Recordings* . . . .(Polydor)

Lady Doctor
Graham Parker; *Howlin' Wind* . . . . (Mercury)
Graham Parker And The Rumour; *The Parkerilla* . . . . (Mercury)

Lady Down On Love
Alabama; *Alabama-Live* . . . . (RCA)
Alabama's Greatest Hits-#2 . . . . (RCA)
Closer You Get . . . . (RCA)

Lady Grinning Soul
David Bowie; *Aladdin Sane* . . . . (Rykodisc)

Lady In Red
Charlie Daniels Band; *Windows* . . . . (Epic)

Lady In Red
Joan Jett & The Blackhearts; *I Love Rock 'n' Roll*. . . . . (Blackheart)

Lady In Red
Chris DeBurgh; *Into The Light* . . . . (A&M)

Lady In Red
Stan Getz; *Stan Getz's Greatest Hits* . . . .(Prestige)

Lady Is A Tramp
Ella Fitzgerald; *Rodgers & Hart Songbook*. . . . . (Verve)
Frank Sinatra; *Sinatra Reprise-The Very Good Years* . . . . (Reprise)
The Capitol Years. . . . . (Capitol)
Frank Sinatra & Luther Vandross; *Frank Sinatra-Duets-C* . . . . (Capitol)

Lady Luck
Journey; *Evolution* . . . . (Columbia)
Journey-Captured . . . . (Columbia)

Lady Luck
Kenny Loggins; *Celebrate Me Home* . . . . (Columbia)

Lady Luck
Restless Heart; *Fast Moving Train* . . . . (RCA)

Lady Luck
David Lee Roth; *Little Ain't Enough* . . . . (Warner Bros.)

Lady Of Spain
Bing Crosby; *The Radio Years: 20 Songs* . . . .(Crescendo)
Les Paul; *Legend & The Legacy-#1-4* . . . . (Capitol)
Muppets/Amazing Marvin Suggs/Muppaphone; *Muppet Hits* . . . . .(Jim Henson)

Lady Of The Island
Crosby, Stills & Nash; *Crosby, Stills & Nash* . . . .(Atlantic)
CSN . . . .(Atlantic)

Lady Picture Show
Stone Temple Pilots; *Tiny Music...Songs From The Vatican*
Gift Shop . . . . (Atlantic)
Lady Sings The Blues
Billie Holiday; *All Or Nothing At All* . . . . (Verve)
Essential Billie Holiday-Carnegie Hall Concert . . . . (Verve)
History Of The Real Billie Holiday . . . . (Verve)
Lady Sings The Blues . . . . (Verve)
Lady Stardust
David Bowie; *Rise & Fall Of Ziggy Stardust And The Spiders
From Mars* . . . . (Rykodisc)
Lady Starlight
Scorpions; *Animal Magnetism* . . . . (Mercury)
Lady Takes The Cowboy Every Time
Larry Gatlin & The Gatlin Brothers Band; *Houston To Denver* . . . . . (Columbia)
The Gatlin Brothers' Biggest Hits . . . . (Columbia)
Lady Writer
Dire Straits; *Communique* . . . . (Warner Bros.)
Lady's In Love With You
Annie Ross & Gerry Mulligan; *Annie Ross Sings A Song With Gerry
Mulligan* . . . . (EMI)
Shirley Ross; *Thanks For The Memories* . . . . (Decca)
Lay Lady Lay
Bob Dylan; *Biograph* . . . . (Columbia)
Bob Dylan's Greatest Hits-#2 . . . . (Columbia)
Hard Rain . . . . (Columbia)
Nashville Skyline . . . . (Columbia)
Bob Dylan And The Band; *Before The Flood* . . . . (Columbia)
Byrds; *The Byrds* . . . . (Columbia)
Leader Of Men
Nickelback; *State* . . . . (Roadrunner)
Legs
ZZ Top; *Eliminator* . . . . (Warner Bros.)
Let Her Cry
Hootie & The Blowfish; *1996 Grammy Nominees-C* . . . . (Columbia)
Cracked Rear View . . . . (Atlantic)
Let Her Down Easy
Terence Trent D'Arby; *Symphony Or Damn* . . . . (Columbia)
Life Is A Lady
Santana; *Inner Secrets* . . . . (Columbia)
Life Is A Woman
Original Cast/Sammy Davis, Jr.; *Stop The World I Want To
Get Off* . . . . (Warner Bros.)
Lightning's Girl
Nancy Sinatra; *How Does That Grab You?* . . . . (Sundazed Music)
Little Dutch Girl
George Morgan; *American Originals-George Morgan* . . . . (Columbia)
Little Girl
Monkees; *Monkee Flips* . . . . (Rhino)
Present . . . . (Rhino)
Little Girl
Stephen Bishop; *Love Shouldn't Hurt-C* . . . . (Qwest)
Little Girl
Ritchie Valens; *Best Of Ritchie Valens* . . . . (Rhino)
History Of Ritchie Valens . . . . (Rhino)
Little Girl
Steve Miller Band; *Steve Miller Band-Anthology* . . . . (Capitol)
Your Saving Grace . . . . (Capitol)
Little Girl
Reba McEntire; *Sweet Sixteen* . . . . (MCA)
Little Girl Blue
Ella Fitzgerald; *Rodgers & Hart Songbook* . . . . (Verve)
Little Girl From Little Rock
Original Cast; *Gentlemen Prefer Blondes* . . . . (Sony Music Special Prod.)
Little Girl Of Mine
Cleftones; *Original Rock 'N' Roll Hits Of The '50s-C* . . . . . . (Roulette)
Dion; *Bronx Blues-Columbia Recordings 1962-1965* . . . . . . (Columbia)
Little Girls
Original Broadway Cast; *Annie* . . . . (Columbia)
Little Girls
Patti LaBelle; *Best Of Patti LaBelle* . . . . (Epic)
Little Girls, Goodbye
John Charles Thomas; *Music From The New York Stage (1890-1920)-#4-
1917-1920-C* . . . . (Pearl)
Little Hollywood Girl
Crickets; *Liberty Years* . . . . (EMI)
Little Lady Preacher
Tom T. Hall; *Tom T. Hall's Greatest Hits-#2* . . . . (Mercury)
Little Miss Can't Be Wrong
Spin Doctors; *Homebelly Groove* . . . . (Epic Portrait Assoc.)
Pocket Full Of Kryptonite . . . . (Epic Portrait Assoc.)
Up For Grabs...Live . . . . (Epic Portrait Assoc.)
Little Miss Love
Eldorados; *45-#1451* . . . . (Collectables)
Little Miss Lover
Jimi Hendrix; *Axis: Bold As Love* . . . . (Reprise)
Essential Jimi Hendrix . . . . (Reprise)

Little Miss Magic
Jimmy Buffett; *Boats Beaches Bars & Ballads* . . . . (Margaritaville)
Coconut Telegraph . . . . (MCA)
Little Old Lady (From Pasadena)
Beach Boys; *Concert/'69-Live In London* . . . . (Capitol)
Jan & Dean; *Best Of Jan & Dean* . . . . (EMI)
Billboard Top Rock 'N' Roll Hits-1964-C . . . . (Rhino)
Dead Man's Curve . . . . (EMI)
Surf City-Best Of Jan & Dean . . . . (EMI)
Little Wing
Derek And The Dominos; *Layla* . . . . (Polydor)
Jimi Hendrix; *Axis: Bold As Love* . . . . (Reprise)
Concerts . . . . (Reprise)
Essential Jimi Hendrix . . . . (Reprise)
Lifelines/Jimi Hendrix Story . . . . (Reprise)
Sting; *...Nothing Like The Sun* . . . . (A&M)
Little Woman
Bobby Sherman; *Bobby Sherman's Greatest Hits* . . . . (K-Tel)
Bubblegum Classics-#3-C . . . . (Varese Vintage)
Livin' La Vida Loca
Ricky Martin; *Ricky Martin* . . . . (Columbia)
Living Dead Girl
Rob Zombie; *Hellbilly Deluxe* . . . . (Geffen)
Living Loving Maid
Led Zeppelin; *Led Zeppelin II* . . . . (Atlantic)
Living On The Edge Of The World
Bruce Springsteen; *Tracks* . . . . (Columbia)
Lizard Lady
Residents; *Duck Stab/Buster & Glenn/Goosebump* . . . . (East Side Digital)
Lolly Pop Mama
Wynonie Harris; *Risque Blues: Sixty Minute Man-C* . . . . (King)
Lollypop Mama
Clarence Samuels; *Chess Blues Box-C* . . . . (Chess)
London Girl
Jam; *This Is The Modern World* . . . . (Polydor)
London Girls
Vibrators; *Pure Mania* . . . . (Columbia)
London Lady
Stranglers; *All Live & All Of The Night* . . . . (Epic)
Rattus Norvegicus . . . . (A&M)
London You're A Lady
Pogues; *Peace & Love* . . . . (Island)
Lonely Girls
Lucinda Williams; *Essence* . . . . (Lost Highway/IDJMG)
Lonely Woman
Branford Marsalis; *Random Abstract* . . . . (Columbia)
Chris Connors; *Atlantic Jazz-Singers-C* . . . . (Atlantic)
Modern Jazz Quartet; *Lonely Woman* . . . . (Atlantic)
Sarah Vaughan; *Complete Sarah Vaughan On Mercury-#1-Great Jazz Years-
1954-1956* . . . . (Mercury)
Sylvia Sims; *Atlantic Jazz-Singers-C* . . . . (Atlantic)
Lonely Women Make Good Lovers
Bob Luman; *Bob Luman-Classic Country* . . . . (Simitar)
Steve Wariner; *Best Of Steve Wariner* . . . . (RCA)
Midnight Fire . . . . (RCA)
Steve Wariner's Greatest Hits . . . . (RCA)
Steve Wariner-Super Hits . . . . (RCA)
Long Cool Woman In A Black Dress
Hollies; *Best Of The Hollies* . . . . (EMI)
Best Of The Hollies-#2 . . . . (EMI)
Billboard Top Rock 'N' Roll Hits-1972-C . . . . (Rhino)
Distant Light . . . . (Epic)
Hollies-Epic Anthology From The Original Master Tapes . . . . . (Epic)
The Hollies' Greatest Hits . . . . (Epic)
Lookin' In The Same Direction
Ken Mellons; *Ken Mellons* . . . . (Epic)
Louisiana Lady
New Riders Of The Purple Sage; *Best Of New Riders Of The
Purple Sage* . . . . (Columbia)
New Riders Of The Purple Sage . . . . (Columbia)
Louisiana Woman
Catfish Hodge; *Bout With The Blues* . . . . (Adelphi)
R.G. & Bayou Zydeco; *Fire On The Bayou* . . . . (Takoma)
Rockin' Tabby Thomas; *King Of Swamp Blues* . . . . (Maison De Soul)
Louisiana Woman, Mississippi Man
Loretta Lynn & Conway Twitty; *Louisiana Woman Mississippi Man* . . . . (MCA)
Very Best Of Loretta Lynn & Conway Twitty . . . . (MCA)
Louisiana Women
J.J. Cale; *Really* . . . . (Mercury)
Wayne Stewart; *Aspen Skyline* . . . . (Briar)
Love Makes A Woman
Barbara Acklin; *Soul Shots-#2-The "In" Crowd-Sweet Soul-C* . . . . (Rhino)
Love Of A Woman
Travis Tritt; *Down The Road I Go* . . . . (Columbia)
Love Will Bring Her Around
Rob Crosby; *Solid Ground* . . . . (Arista)
Lovergirl
Teena Marie; *Club Epic-#1-C* . . . . (Legacy)

Starchild . . . .(Epic)
Luck Be A Lady
Frank Sinatra; *Sinatra Reprise-The Very Good Years* . . . . (Reprise)
The Reprise Collection. . . . . (Reprise)
Original Cast; *Guys & Dolls* . . . .(MCA)
Lullaby
Shawn Mullins; *Soul's Core* . . . . (Columbia)
Lyin' Ass Bitch
Fishbone; *Fishbone* . . . . (Columbia)
Lyin' Eyes
Eagles; *Eagles/Their Greatest Hits 1971-1975.* . . . . (Asylum)
One Of These Nights . . . . (Asylum)
ST/Urban Cowboy . . . . (Asylum)
Macon Georgia Bad Girl
Jeannie C. Riley; *Jeannie C. Riley & Fancy Friends* . . . . (Plantation)
Maid In Heaven
Be Bop Deluxe; *Best Of Be Bop Deluxe-Raiding The Divine Archive* . . (Capitol)
Live! In The Air Age. . . . . (Harvest)
Mail Order Woman
Champion Jack Dupree; *Blues For Everybody* . . . . . (International Mktg. Group)
Make Me The Woman That You Go Home To
Gladys Knight & The Pips; *Compact Command Performances-Gladys Knight
& The Pips* . . . . (Motown)
Gladys Knight & The Pips-All The Great Hits. . . . . (Motown)
Gladys Knight & The Pips-Anthology . . . . (Motown)
Standing Ovation. . . . . (S.O.U.L.)
Maker Said Take Her
Alabama; *In Pictures* . . . . (RCA)
Mama Don't Get Dressed Up For Nothing
Brooks & Dunn; *Borderline* . . . . (Arista)
Mambo No. 5 (A Little Bit Of…)
Lou Bega; *A Little Bit Of Mambo* . . . . (RCA)
Totally Hits-#2-C. . . . . (Elektra)
Man Ain't Supposed To Cry
Public Announcement; *Don't Hold Back* . . . . (RCA)
Man Holdin' On (To A Woman Lettin' Go)
Ty Herndon; *Big Hopes* . . . .(Epic)
Man Overboard
Blink-182; *The Mark, Tom & Travis Show-The Enema Strikes Back* . . . . .(MCA)
Man Smart, Woman Smarter
Harry Belafonte; *Harry Belafonte-Pure Gold.* . . . . (RCA)
Robert Palmer; *Some People Can Do What They Like* . . . . (Island)
Rosanne Cash; *I Am Woman-C* . . . . (Nick At Nite)
Right Or Wrong . . . . (Columbia)
Man! I Feel Like A Woman
Shania Twain; *Come On Over* . . . . (Mercury)
VH-1 Divas Live-C. . . . .(Epic)
Maneater
Daryl Hall & John Oates; *H2O* . . . . (RCA)
Nipper's Greatest Hits Of The '80s-C . . . . (RCA)
Rock 'N Soul, Part 1. . . . . (RCA)
Married Lady
Bill Anderson; *Ladies Choice* . . . .(MCA)
Married Woman
Frankie Lee Sims; *Lucy Mae Blues.* . . . . (Specialty)
This Is How It All Began-#1-C. . . . . (Specialty)
Marry A Woman Uglier Than You
King's Singers; *10th Anniversary Concert-#2* . . . . (Mojo Music/Universal)
Material Girl
Madonna; *Immaculate Collection.* . . . . (Sire)
Like A Virgin . . . . (Sire)
Royal Box. . . . . (Sire)
Maybe He'll Notice Her Now
Mindy McCready; *Ten Thousand Angels* . . . . (BNA)
Medicine Woman
Paul Davis; *Southern Tracks & Fantasies* . . . . (Bang)
Meeting In The Ladies Room
Klymaxx; *Meeting In The Ladies Room* . . . .(Constellation)
ST/Secret Admirer . . . .(MCA)
Memphis Belle
Hank Williams, Jr.; *Pure Hank* . . . . (WB/Curb)
Mer Girl
Madonna; *Ray Of Light.* . . . .(Maverick)
Midnight Girl/Sunset Town
Sweethearts Of The Rodeo; *Sweethearts Of The Rodeo* . . . . (Columbia)
Midnight Tennessee Woman
Jack Greene; *Jack Greene Sings His Best* . . . . (Step One)
Minneapolis Girls
Joel Johnson; *City Music* . . . .(Blue Loon)
Minnesota Girl
American Girls; *Welcome To Our Love Sick Porch* . . . . (Manifesto)
Miss Texas 1967
Colourfield; *Deception* . . . .(Chrysalis)
Missing
Everything But The Girl; *Amplified Heart* . . . . (Atlantic)
MTV Party To Go-#9-C . . . . (Tommy Boy)
The Absolute Hits-C. . . . . (Atlantic)
The Ultimate Dance Party-1997-C . . . . (Arista)

Mississippi Lady
Jim Croce; *Down The Highway.* . . . .(Atlantic)
Mississippi Woman
Willie Nelson; *Longhorn Jamboree* . . . . (Plantation)
Willie Nelson & His Friends. . . . . (Plantation)
Mistress Of The Salmon Salt
Blue Oyster Cult; *Tyranny & Mutation* . . . . (Columbia)
Mixed Up, Shook Up Girl
Mink De Ville; *Mink De Ville* . . . . (Capitol)
Mockingbird Girl
Magnificent Bastards; *ST/Tank Girl* . . . . (Elektra)
Modern Girl
Sheena Easton; *Best Of Sheena Easton* . . . . (EMI)
Sheena Easton . . . . (EMI)
Sheena Easton's Greatest Hits . . . . (EMI Special Markets)
The World Of Sheena Easton: The Singles Collection-C . . . . (EMI)
Modern Maiden's Prayer, The
Eddie Cantor; *Music From The New York Stage (1890-1920)-#4-1917-
1920-C.* . . . . (Pearl)
Money In The Bank
John Anderson; *On Solid Ground* . . . .(BNA)
Moon Over Georgia
Shenandoah; *Extra Mile* . . . . (Columbia)
Shenandoah's Greatest Hits . . . . (Columbia)
Moonlight Lady
Julio Iglesias; *1100 Bel Air Place* . . . . (Columbia)
More Pretty Girls Than One
Tom Rush; *Blues Songs & Ballads* . . . .(Fantasy)
Woody Guthrie; *One Of A Kind.* . . . .(Pair)
Morning Side Of The Mountain, The
Tommy Edwards; *It's All In The Game-The Complete Hits Of Tommy
Edwards.* . . . .(Eric)
Most Beautiful Girl
Charlie Rich; *Behind Closed Doors* . . . . (Epic)
Charlie Rich's Greatest Hits . . . . (Epic)
Columbia Country Classics-#4-Nashville Sound-C . . . . (Columbia)
Most Beautiful Girl In The World
Frank Sinatra; *Strangers In The Night.* . . . . (Reprise)
Tony Bennett; *Rodgers & Hart Songbook.* . . . .(DRG)
Tony Bennett Sings More Great Rodgers & Hart . . . . (Improv)
Most Beautiful Girl In The World
Prince; *The Gold Experience.* . . . . (NPG)
Most Girls
Pink; *Can't Take Me Home* . . . . (LaFace)
Totally Hits-#3-C. . . . .(Atlantic)
Motorcycle Cowboy
Merle Haggard; *Merle Haggard-Live At Billy Bob's.* . . . . (Razor & Tie)
Multi Colored Lady
Gregg Allman; *Laid Back* . . . .(Polydor)
Murder In High Heels
Kiss; *Animalize* . . . . (Mercury)
Music To Watch Girls By
Andy Williams; *Andy Williams' Greatest Hits-#2* . . . . (Columbia)
Must To Avoid, A
Herman's Hermits; *Herman's Hermits-Their Greatest Hits* . . . .(Abkco)
My Beautiful Irish Maid
Chauncey Olcott; *Music From The New York Stage (1890-1920)-#1-1890-
1908-C.* . . . . (Pearl)
My Best Friend's Girl
Cars; *The Cars.* . . . . (Elektra)
The Cars' Greatest Hits . . . . (Elektra)
My Carolina Sunshine Girl
Jimmie Rodgers; *Jimmie Rodgers-Early Years-1928-1929* . . . . (Rounder)
My Favorite Girl
Dave Hollister; *Ghetto Hymns.* . . . . (Def Squad/DreamWorks)
My Girl
Mamas & The Papas; *Best Of The Mamas & The Papas* . . . . (MCA)
Otis Redding; *Best Of Otis Redding* . . . . (Atco)
Rolling Stones; *Flowers* . . . .(Abkco)
Temptations; *All The Million-Sellers* . . . . (Motown)
ST/Big Chill . . . . (Motown)
Temptations' Greatest Hits-#1. . . . . (Motown)
Temptations-25th Anniversary . . . . (Motown)
Temptations-Anthology-The Best Of The Temptations. . . . . (Motown)
My Girl
Aerosmith; *Pump* . . . . (Geffen)
My Girl Josephine
Fats Domino; *Fats Domino's Greatest Hits* . . . . (MCA)
They Call Me The Fat Man. . . . . (EMI)
My Girlfriend Is A Waitress
Iguanas; *Nuevo Boogaloo* . . . .(Margaritaville)
My Kind Of Girl
Collin Raye; *Best Of Collin Raye-Direct Hits* . . . . (Epic)
Extremes . . . . (Epic)
My Kinda Girl
Babyface; *Closer Look* . . . . (Solar)
Tender Lover. . . . . (Solar)

My Little Girl
Crickets; *EMI Legends Of Rock & Roll-24 Greatest Hits-C* . . . . (EMI)
   Liberty Years . . . . (EMI)
My Little Girl
Crescendos; *Excello Vocal Groups-C* . . . . (Excello)
My Little Girl
Spike Jones & His City Slickers; *King Of Corn* . . . . (Glendale)
My Little Girl
Roxy Music; *Manifesto* . . . . (Atco)
My Little Girl In Tennessee
Lester Flatt, Earl Scruggs & The Foggy Mountain Boys; *Lester Flatt,*
   Earl Scruggs & The Foggy Mountain Boys-Complete Mercury
   Sessions . . . . (Mercury)
My Little Lady
Jimmie Rodgers; *Jimmie Rodgers-Early Years-1928-1929* . . . . (Rounder)
Roy Rogers; *Columbia Historic Edition-Roy Rogers* . . . . (Columbia)
My Little Miss America
Gary U.S. Bonds; *45-#1034* . . . . (LeGrand)
My Lovely Lady
Jimmy Buffett; *White Sport Coat & A Pink Crustacean* . . . . (MCA)
My Melancholy Baby
Barbra Streisand; *Third Album* . . . . (Columbia)
Bing Crosby; *Hits Of 1939-C* . . . . (Living Era)
Coleman Hawkins; *Genius Of Coleman Hawkins* . . . . (Verve)
Dorothy Loudon; *Saloon* . . . . (DRG)
Frank Sinatra; *Voice: The Columbia Years-1943-1952* . . . . (Columbia)
Gene Austin; *78-#21015* . . . . (Victor)
Jan Garber & His Orchestra; *Jan Garber & His Orchestra Play 22 Original*
   Big Band Favorites . . . . (Hindsight)
Kate Smith; *Kate Smith-16 Most Requested Songs* . . . . (Columbia)
Leon Redbone; *Double Time* . . . . (Warner Bros.)
Marcels; *Best Of The Marcels* . . . . (Rhino)
My North Dakota Girl
Dakota Harmony; *My North Dakota Girl-45* . . . . (Accent)
My Polish Girlfriend
Li'l Wally; *My Polish Girlfriend & Others* . . . . (Jay Jay)
My Sunday Gal
Duke Ellington; *Great Ellington Units* . . . . (Bluebird)
My Sweet Eyed Georgia Girl
Atlanta; *Atlanta* . . . . (MCA)
My Tennessee Baby
Ernest Tubb; *45-#46173* . . . . (Decca)
My Wife & My Dead Wife
Robyn Hitchcock & The Egyptians; *Fegmania* . . . . (Slash)
My Wife, She Got Drunk
Li'l Wally; *All American Polkas* . . . . (Jay Jay)
My Woman, My Woman, My Wife
Marty Robbins; *Lifetime Of Song-1951-1982* . . . . (Columbia)
   Marty Robbins' All-Time Greatest Hits . . . . (Columbia)
Nashville Women's Blues
Bessie Smith; *Bessie Smith-The Complete Recordings-#2* . . . . (Legacy)
National Working Woman's Holiday
Sammy Kershaw; *Feelin' Good Train* . . . . (Mercury)
Naughty Girls Need Love Too
Samantha Fox; *Samantha Fox* . . . . (Jive)
New Girl In School
Jan & Dean; *Jan & Dean-Legendary Masters* . . . . (EMI)
   Surf City-Best Of Jan & Dean . . . . (EMI)
New Orleans Ladies
Louisiana's Le Roux; *'70s Greatest Rock Hits-#4-C* . . . . (Priority)
   Louisiana's Le Roux . . . . (Capitol)
New Pollution
Beck; *Odelay* . . . . (David Geffen Co.)
New York Girls
Kingston Trio; *Kingston Trio/From The Hungry i* . . . . (Capitol)
New York Lady
Burt Bacharach; *Burt Bacharach-Classics-#23* . . . . (A&M)
Next Time You See Her
Eric Clapton; *Slowhand* . . . . (Polydor)
Night In Summer Long Ago
Mark Knopfler; *Golden Heart* . . . . (Warner Bros.)
No Man's Woman
Sinead O'Connor; *Faith & Courage* . . . . (Atlantic)
No Way To Treat A Lady
Bonnie Raitt; *Bonnie Raitt-Collection* . . . . (Warner Bros.)
   Nine Lives . . . . (Warner Bros.)
No Woman, No Cry
Bob Marley; *Bob Marley & The Wailers-Live* . . . . (Tuff Gong)
Bob Marley & The Wailers; *Legend: The Best Of Bob Marley & The*
   Wailers . . . . (Island)
   Natty Dread . . . . (Tuff Gong)
   Songs Of Freedom . . . . (Tuff Gong)
Londonbeat; *In The Blood* . . . . (Radioactive/MCA)
Norfolk Girls
John Townley & The Press Gang; *Chesapeake Sailor's Companion* . . (Adelphi)
North Country Girl
Pete Townshend; *Pete Townshend Live* . . . . (Platinum Music)

Northeast Texas Women
David Bromberg; *Bandit In A Bathing Suit* . . . . (Fantasy)
Jerry Jeff Walker; *Lone Wolf: The Best Of Jerry Jeff Walker Elektra*
   Sessions . . . . (Warner Archives)
Willis Alan Ramsey; *Willis Alan Ramsey* . . . . (Dunhill Compact Classics)
Norwegian Girl
Vernon Castle; *Polka Update* . . . . (Taggart)
Norwegian Wood (This Bird Has Flown)
Beatles; *Beatles-Box Set* . . . . (Capitol)
   Beatles-Love Songs . . . . (Capitol)
   Rubber Soul . . . . (Capitol)
   The Beatles/1962-1966 . . . . (Capitol)
November Girl
Carmen McRae; *November Girl* . . . . (Jazz Man)
Occasional Wife
Faron Young; *Faron Young-Golden Hits* . . . . (Mercury)
Oh Girl
Paul Young; *Other Voices* . . . . (Columbia)
Oh Girl
Boy Meets Girl; *Boy Meets Girl* . . . . (A&M)
Oh Girl (You Know Where To Find Me)
Vince Gill; *When I Call Your Name* . . . . (MCA)
Oh You Beautiful Doll
Guy Lombardo & His Royal Canadians; *Dance To Songs Everybody*
   Knows . . . . (MCA)
Oh, Lady Be Good
Benny Goodman; *Benny Goodman-Live At Carnegie Hall* . . . . (London)
Count Basie; *Essential Count Basie-#1* . . . . (Columbia)
Count Basie Trio; *For The First Time* . . . . (Pablo)
Ella Fitzgerald; *Compact Jazz-Ella Live!* . . . . (Verve)
   Essential Ella Fitzgerald-The Great Songs . . . . (Verve)
Erroll Garner; *Original Misty* . . . . (Mercury)
Lionel Hampton & His Orchestra; *Jazz Club-Big Band* . . . . (Verve)
Pete Fountain; *Best Of Pete Fountain* . . . . (MCA)
Supersax; *Supersax Plays Bird* . . . . (Blue Note)
Oh, My Mysterious Lady
Original Cast; *Peter Pan-The 1954 Broadway Production* . . . . . . (RCA Victor)
Oh, Pretty Woman
2 Live Crew; *As Clean As They Wanna Be* . . . . (Luke)
Al Green; *Al Green's Greatest Hits-#2* . . . . (Motown)
   I'm Still In Love With You . . . . (Right Stuff)
Ricky Van Shelton; *RVS III* . . . . (Columbia)
Roy Orbison; *In Dreams-Greatest Hits* . . . . (Orbison)
   Roy Orbison's All-Time Greatest Hits-#1 & 2 . . . . (Monument)
   ST/Pretty Woman . . . . (EMI)
Van Halen; *Diver Down* . . . . (Warner Bros.)
Oh, Pretty Woman
Gary Moore; *Blues Alive* . . . . (Virgin)
   Still Got The Blues . . . . (Charisma)
Oh, Pretty Woman (Can't Make You Love Me)
Albert King; *The Ultimate Collection-Albert King* . . . . (Rhino)
Oh, What A Girl!
Sam Ash; *Music From The New York Stage (1890-1920)-#4-1917-*
   1920-C . . . . (Pearl)
Oklahoma Borderline
Vince Gill; *Best Of Vince Gill* . . . . (RCA)
Oklahoma Country Girl
Elvin Bishop; *Big Fun* . . . . (Alligator)
Old Flames Have New Names
Mark Chesnutt; *Longnecks & Short Stories* . . . . (MCA)
Old Maid Boogie
Eddie "Cleanhead" Vinson; *Late Show* . . . . (Fantasy)
On A Good Night
Wade Hayes; *On A Good Night* . . . . (Columbia)
   Super Hits Of 1996-C . . . . (Epic)
One
Original Broadway Cast; *A Chorus Line* . . . . (Columbia)
One Boy, One Girl
Collin Raye; *Best Of Collin Raye-Direct Hits* . . . . (Epic)
   I Think About You . . . . (Epic)
One Good Woman
Billy Squier; *Emotions In Motion* . . . . (Capitol)
One Hell Of A Woman
Mac Davis; *Mac Davis' Greatest Hits* . . . . (Columbia)
One Man Woman
Judds; *Judds-Collection 1983-1990* . . . . (RCA)
   River Of Time . . . . (RCA)
One Too Many Girlfriends
REO Speedwagon; *A Second Decade Of Rock And Roll 1981 To 1991* . . . . (Epic)
   Life As We Know It . . . . (Epic)
One Woman Man
Dave Hollister; *Chicago '85 The Movie* . . . . (Def Squad/DreamWorks)
Only Sixteen
Dr. Hook; *Bankrupt* . . . . (Capitol)
   Dr. Hook-Greatest Hits & More . . . . (Capitol)
   Great Records Of The Decade-'70s Hits-#2-C . . . . (Curb)
   Little Bit More . . . . (Capitol)
Sam Cooke; *Best Of Sam Cooke* . . . . (RCA)

The Man And His Music . . . . (RCA)
This Is Sam Cooke . . . . (RCA)
Only Women Bleed
Alice Cooper; *The Alice Cooper Show* . . . .(Warner Bros.)
Welcome To My Nightmare . . . . (Atlantic)
Lita Ford; *Stiletto* . . . . (RCA)
Opium Bride
Annabouboula; *Greek Fire* . . . . (Shanachie)
Orange Lady
Weather Report; *Weather Report* . . . . (Columbia)
Orphan Girl
Emmylou Harris; *Wrecking Ball* . . . . (Asylum)
Gillian Welch; *Revival* . . . . (Almo Sounds)
Tim O'Brien; *Away Out On The Mountain* . . . . (Sugar Hill)
Other Woman
Ray Parker Jr.; *Ray Parker Jr.'s Greatest Hits* . . . . (Arista)
Other Woman
Loretta Lynn; *Loretta Lynn's Greatest Hits* . . . .(MCA)
Our Lady Of The Well
Jackson Browne; *For Everyman* . . . .(Asylum)
Outlaw Women
Hank Williams, Jr.; *Bocephus Box-Collection-1979-1992* . . . . (Capricorn)
Whiskey Bent & Hell Bound . . . . (WB/Curb)
Pack Up Her Trunk Blues
Tommy Bradley; *Complete Recorded Works-1928-1932* . . . . (Document)
Parachute Woman
Rolling Stones; *Beggars Banquet* . . . .(Abkco)
Paradise
Nat "King" Cole; *Nat "King" Cole-Gift Set* . . . . (Capitol)
The Nat "King" Cole Story . . . . (Capitol)
Ray Conniff; *'S Awful Nice* . . . . (Columbia)
Russ Colombo; *Nipper's Greatest Hits Of The '30s-#2-C* . . . . (RCA)
Party Doll
Buddy Knox; *Best Of Buddy Knox* . . . . (Rhino)
Billboard Top Rock 'N' Roll Hits-1957-C . . . . (Rhino)
ST/American Graffiti . . . . (MCA)
Party Girl
Elvis Costello; *Girls Girls Girls* . . . . (Columbia)
Elvis Costello & The Attractions; *Armed Forces* . . . .(Rykodisc)
Linda Ronstadt; *Mad Love* . . . . (Elektra)
Party Girl
Bernadette Carroll; *20 Million-Dollar Memories-#2-C* . . . . (Laurie)
22 Leaders Of The Pack-#1-C . . . . (Laurie)
Party Girl
T-Bone Walker; *T-Bone Walker* . . . . (Blue Note)
T-Bone Walker-Complete Imperial Recordings-1950-1954 . . . . . .(EMI)
Party Girl
U2; *Under A Blood Red Sky* . . . . (Island)
Party Girls
Rick James Presents The Stone City Band; *In 'n' Out* . . . . (Gordy)
Party Girls
Mink De Ville; *Mink De Ville* . . . . (Capitol)
Partyin' Gal
Charlie Daniels Band; *Windows* . . . .(Epic)
Perfect Day
Collective Soul; *Blender* . . . .(Atlantic)
Pink Cocktail For A Blue Lady
Glenn Miller & His Orchestra; *Complete Glenn Miller & His
Orchestra* . . . . (Bluebird)
Complete Glenn Miller & His Orchestra-#9 . . . . (Bluebird)
Pisces Apple Lady
Leon Russell; *Leon Russell* . . . .(MCA)
Planet Of Women
ZZ Top; *Afterburner* . . . .(Warner Bros.)
ZZ Top's Greatest Hits . . . .(Warner Bros.)
Plano Texas Girl
Steve Wariner; *I Got Dreams* . . . .(MCA)
Play Lady Play
Fourplay; *Best Of Fourplay* . . . .(Warner Bros.)
Elixir . . . .(Warner Bros.)
Jazz Central Station-Global Poll Winners-#1-C . . . . (N2K)
Please Don't Go Girl
New Kids On The Block; *Hangin' Tough* . . . . (Columbia)
No More Games/Remix Album . . . . (Columbia)
Please Don't Tell Her
Big Head Todd & The Monsters; *Beautiful World* . . . . (Revolution)
Live Monsters . . . .(Revolution)
PMS
Mary J. Blige; *No More Drama* . . . .(MCA)
Poetry In Motion
Johnny Tillotson; *10 Top Ten Hits-#1* . . . . (Laurie)
American Graffiti-#3-C . . . .(MCA)
Jukebox Classics-#1-C . . . . (Rhino)
Mellow '60s-C . . . . (Priority)
Million-Dollar Memories-#2-C . . . . (RCA)
Police Woman
Henry Mancini; *Cop Show Themes* . . . . (RCA)
Poor Little Rich Girl
Count Basie & Tony Bennett; *Basie Swings Bennett Sings* . . . . (Roulette)

Judy Garland; *Best Of Judy Garland* . . . . (MCA)
Poor Little Rich Girl
Uriah Heep; *Equator* . . . . (Columbia)
Poor Little Rich Girl
Romantics; *National Breakout* . . . .(Nemperor)
Portland Woman
New Riders Of The Purple Sage; *New Riders Of The Purple Sage* . . . (Columbia)
Vintage NRPS . . . .(Relix)
Portuguese Washerwoman
Astrud Gilberto; *Look To The Rainbow* . . . . (Verve)
Buddy Merrill; *Holiday For Guitars* . . . . (Accent)
Power Of Love
Celine Dion; *All The Way...A Decade Of Song* . . . .(550 Music)
The Colour Of My Love . . . .(550 Music)
Pretend You Don't See Her
Jerry Vale; *Jerry Vale-17 Most Requested Songs* . . . . (Legacy)
Jerry Vale's All-Time Greatest Hits . . . . (Columbia)
Jerry Vale's Greatest Hits . . . . (Columbia)
Pretending She's You
Jimmie Davis; *Jimmie Davis-Golden Hits-#2* . . . . (Plantation)
Pretty Blue Eyes
Steve Lawrence; *Best Of Steve Lawrence* . . . . (Taragon)
Pretty Girl
Jon B.; *Bonafide* . . . .(Yab Yum/550)
Pretty Girl Is Like A Melody, A
John Steel; *Music From The New York Stage (1890-1920)-#4-1917-
1920-C* . . . .(Pearl)
Pretty Girl Milking A Cow
Judy Garland; *Best Of Judy Garland* . . . . (MCA)
One & Only . . . . (Capitol)
Pretty Girls And Cadillacs
Nighthawks; *Backtrack* . . . .(Varrick)
Pretty Girls Don't Cry
Chris Isaak; *Silvertone* . . . . (Warner Bros.)
Pretty Girls Everywhere
Eugene Church & The Fellows; *Spotlite Series-Class
Records-#1-C* . . . . (Collectables)
Pretty Girls In Chicago Polka
Li'l Wally; *Brings Happiness To You* . . . . (Jay Jay)
Pretty Girls Make Graves
Smiths; *Smiths* . . . .(Sire)
Pretty Lady
Original Broadway Cast; *Pacific Overtures* . . . .(RCA)
Pretty Litle Lady From Beaumont, Texas
George Jones; *One Woman Man* . . . . (Epic)
Texas Super Hits-C . . . . (Columbia)
Pretty Woman
Duke Ellington & His Orchestra; *Duke Ellington & His Orchestra Play 22
Original Big Band Recordings* . . . . (Hindsight)
Pretty Women
Original Cast; *Sweeney Todd* . . . .(RCA)
Pretty Women/Ladies Who Lunch
Barbra Streisand; *The Broadway Album* . . . .(Columbia)
Prison Women
REO Speedwagon; *Jailhouse Rock (Hits From The Big
House)-C* . . . . (Sony Music Special Prod.)
Private Conversation
Lyle Lovett; *The Road To Ensenada* . . . . (MCA)
Promise Her Anything
Burt Bacharach; *The Look Of Love-The Burt Bacharach Collection* . . . . . (Rhino)
Punk Bitch
Too $hort; *Short Dog's In The House* . . . .(Jive)
Puppet Girl
Wendy James; *Now Ain't The Time For Your Tears* . . . . (David Geffen Co.)
Pure Morning
Placebo; *Without You I'm Nothing* . . . .(Virgin)
Quiche Woman In A Barbecue Town
Tarwater Band; *Walking Across Egypt* . . . .(Flying Fish)
Quicksilver Girl
Steve Miller Band; *Best Of Steve Miller 1968-1973* . . . . (Capitol)
More Songs From "The Big Chill" Soundtrack-C . . . . (Motown)
Sailor . . . . (Capitol)
Radio Dream Girl
Roger Voudouris; *Radio Dream Girl* . . . . (Warner Bros.)
Radio Girl
John Hiatt; *Slug Line* . . . . (MCA)
Y'All Caught? Ones That Got Away, 1979-85 . . . . (Geffen)
Radio Girl
Marshall Crenshaw; *Good Evening* . . . . (Warner Bros.)
Rag Doll
4 Seasons; *25th Anniversary Collection* . . . . (Rhino)
4 Seasons' Greatest Hits-#2 . . . . (Rhino)
4 Seasons-Anthology . . . . (Rhino)
Billboard Top Rock 'N' Roll Hits-1964-C . . . . (Rhino)
Rag Doll
Aerosmith; *Big Ones* . . . . (Geffen)
Permanent Vacation . . . . (Geffen)

Railroad Lady
J.D. Crowe and the New South; *My Home Ain't In The Hall Of Fame* . . . . (Rounder)
Jerry Jeff Walker; *A Man Must Carry On* . . . . (MCA)
Gypsy Songman . . . . (Rykodisc)
Jimmy Buffett; *White Sport Coat & A Pink Crustacean* . . . . (MCA)
Willie Nelson; *Greatest Hits (& Some That Will Be)* . . . . (Columbia)
To Lefty From Willie . . . . (Columbia)

Rain, The Park And Other Things
Cowsills; *Cowsills* . . . . (Razor & Tie)

Rainy Day Woman
Waylon Jennings; *Ramblin' Man* . . . . (RCA)
Waylon Live . . . . (RCA)

Rainy Day Women #12 & 35
Bob Dylan; *Blonde On Blonde* . . . . (Columbia)
Bob Dylan's Greatest Hits . . . . (Columbia)
Rock Classics Of The '60s-C . . . . (Columbia)
ST/Forrest Gump . . . . (Epic/Sony Music Soundtrax)
Bob Dylan And The Band; *Before The Flood* . . . . (Columbia)

Real Live Woman
Trisha Yearwood; *Real Live Woman* . . . . (MCA)

Rebel Girl
Joe Glazer; *Songs Of Joe Hill* . . . . (Smithsonian Folkways)

Rebel Girl
Outlaws; *Los Hombres Malo* . . . . (Arista)

Red Dirt Girl
Emmylou Harris; *Red Dirt Girl* . . . . (Nonesuch)

Red Hot
Billy Lee Riley & His Little Green Men; *Red Hot: The Very Best Of Billy Lee Riley* . . . . (Collectables)
Rock This Town-Rockabilly Hits-#1-C . . . . (Rhino)
Robert Gordon; *Rock This Town-Rockabilly Hits-#2-C* . . . . (Rhino)
Robert Gordon & Link Wray; *Robert Gordon & Link Wray* . . . . (RCA)

Red Roses For A Blue Lady
Al Martino; *Best Of Al Martino* . . . . (Capitol)
Capitol Collectors Series-Al Martino . . . . (Capitol)
Andy Williams; *Andy Williams-16 Most Requested Songs* . . . . (Legacy)
Mom & Dads; *Best Of The Mom & Dads* . . . . (Crescendo)
Roger Whittaker; *All-Time Heart-Touching Favorites* . . . . (Capitol)
Roger Whittaker-Classics Collection-#1 . . . . (Capitol)
Vaughn Monroe; *Best Of Vaughn Monroe* . . . . (RCA)

Redneck Girl
Bellamy Brothers; *America's Country: Good Time Country-C* . . . . . . (Madacy)
Bellamy Brothers' Greatest Hits . . . . (MCA)
Bellamy Brothers' Greatest Hits-#1 . . . . (Curb)
Bellamy Brothers-At Their Best . . . . (EMI Special Markets)

Redneck Girl
Kentucky HeadHunters; *Best Of The Kentucky HeadHunters-Still Pickin'* . . . . (Mercury)

Redneck Woman From Planet Mars
Horny Mormons; *Can Of Pork-C* . . . . (Lookout)

Reefer Head Woman
Aerosmith; *Night In The Ruts* . . . . (Columbia)

Reno
Doug Supernaw; *Red And Rio Grande* . . . . (BNA)

Restless Nights
Bruce Springsteen; *Tracks* . . . . (Columbia)
Rocking Chairs; *One Step Up/Two Steps Back-The Songs Of Bruce Springsteen-C* . . . . (Right Stuff)

Rhumba Girl
Nicolette Larson; *Nicolette* . . . . (Warner Bros.)

Rich Bitch
D.O.A.; *War On 45/Bloodied But Unbowed* . . . . (Restless)

Rich Girl
Daryl Hall & John Oates; *Bigger Than Both Of Us* . . . . (RCA)
Billboard Top Rock 'N' Roll Hits-1977-C . . . . (Rhino)
Livetime . . . . (RCA)
Nipper's Greatest Hits Of The '70s-C . . . . (RCA)
Rock 'N Soul, Part 1 . . . . (RCA)
Soulful Sounds . . . . (RCA)

Rich Little Bitch
Dash Rip Rock; *Boiled Alive!* . . . . (Mammoth)
Not Of This World . . . . (Mammoth)

Rich Woman
Fabulous Thunderbirds; *Fabulous Thunderbirds* . . . . (Chrysalis)

Richland Woman Blues
Mississippi John Hurt; *Best Of Mississippi John Hurt* . . . . (Vanguard)

Right On The Money
Alan Jackson; *Big Country Hits '99-C* . . . . (K-Tel)
High Mileage . . . . (Arista)

Rip Her To Shreds
Blondie; *Best Of Blondie* . . . . (Chrysalis)
Blondie . . . . (Chrysalis)

River And The Highway
Pam Tillis; *All Of This Love* . . . . (Arista)
Pam Tillis' Greatest Hits . . . . (Arista)

Robot Girl
Was (Not Was); *What Up Dog?* . . . . (Chrysalis)

Rock & Roll Widow
Wishbone Ash; *Live Dates* . . . . (MCA)
Wishbone Four . . . . (MCA)

Rock & Roll Woman
Buffalo Springfield; *Buffalo Springfield* . . . . (Atco)
Buffalo Springfield Again . . . . (Atco)
Buffalo Springfield-Retrospective . . . . (Atco)

Rock & Roll Women
Whitesnake; *Love Hunter* . . . . (Geffen)

Rock & Roll Women
Brinsley Schwarz; *Brinsley Schwarz* . . . . (Capitol)

Rock My World (Little Country Girl)
Brooks & Dunn; *Hard Workin' Man* . . . . (Arista)

Rock Show, The
Blink-182; *Now That's What I Call Music!-#8-C* . . . . (Virgin)
Take Off Your Pants And Jacket . . . . (MCA)

Rock-N-Roll Lady
Rick Nelson; *Best Of Rick Nelson 1963-1975* . . . . (MCA)

Rodeo Girl
Rickie Lee Jones; *Flying Cowboys* . . . . (Geffen)

Rodeo Girls
Tanya Tucker; *Best Of Tanya Tucker* . . . . (MCA)

Roll Me Away
Bob Seger & The Silver Bullet Band; *ST/Armageddon-The Album* . . . (Columbia)

Roots Woman
Jimmy Cliff; *Power & The Glory* . . . . (Columbia)

Rope The Moon
John Michael Montgomery; *Kickin' It Up* . . . . (Atlantic)

Roving Kind, The
Guy Mitchell; *Guy Mitchell-16 Most Requested Songs* . . . . (Legacy)

Rumor Has It
Reba McEntire; *Reba McEntire's Greatest Hits Volume Two* . . . . . (MCA)
Rumor Has It . . . . (MCA)

Run For Your Life
Beatles; *Beatles-Box Set* . . . . (Capitol)
Rubber Soul . . . . (Capitol)

Run, Woman, Run
Tammy Wynette; *Tammy Wynette-Anniversary-20 Years Of Hits* . . . (Epic)
Tammy Wynette's Biggest Hits . . . . (Epic)

Runaway Girl
Dion; *Runaround Sue* . . . . (Collectables)
Dion And The Belmonts; *Dion And The Belmonts-20 Golden Classics* . . . . (Collectables)
Everything You Always Wanted To Hear . . . . (Laurie)

Runnin' Away With My Heart
Lonestar; *Lonestar* . . . . (BNA)

Russian Lady
Karen Alexander; *Isn't It Always Love* . . . . (Asylum)

Sad Eyed Lady Of The Lowlands
Bob Dylan; *Blonde On Blonde* . . . . (Columbia)
Joan Baez; *Any Day Now: Songs Of Bob Dylan* . . . . (Vanguard)
Lovesong Album . . . . (Vanguard)

Sadder-But-Wiser Girl For Me
Original Cast; *The Music Man* . . . . (Gold Rush)
Robert Preston; *ST/The Music Man* . . . . (Warner Bros.)

Sail Away Ladies
Kingston Trio; *Hidden Treasures* . . . . (Folk Era)
Odetta; *At The Gate Of Horn* . . . . (Vanguard)
Movin' It On . . . . (Rose Quartz)
One Grain Of Sand . . . . (Vanguard)

Sales Tax On The Woman
New Lost City Ramblers; *New Lost City Ramblers-Early Years-1958-1962* . . . . (Smithsonian Folkways)

Salesgirl Blues
Rick Parker; *Wicked World* . . . . (Geffen)

Same Old Fashioned Girl
Gene Autry; *Columbia Historic Edition-Gene Autry* . . . . (Columbia)

San Antonio Girl
Steve Earle & The Dukes; *Exit 0* . . . . (MCA)

San Antonio Girl
Lyle Lovett; *Lyle Lovett Anthology-#1-Cowboy Man* . . . . (MCA)

San Francisco Girls
Fever Tree; *Best Of Fever Tree* . . . . (Bac-Trac)
Nuggets-#11-Pop-Part 4-C . . . . (Rhino)
Sixties Rule! Chapter 1-C . . . . (One Way)

Sanctified Lady
Marvin Gaye; *Dream Of A Lifetime* . . . . (Columbia)

Santa Ana Woman
Bobs; *Songs For Tomorrow Morning* . . . . (Kaleidoscope)

Savannah Woman
Tommy Bolin; *Teaser* . . . . (Columbia)

Savannah Woman
Brother Noland; *Pacific Bad Boy* . . . . (Mountain Apple)

Scarborough Fair/Canticle
Simon & Garfunkel; *Collected Works* . . . . (Columbia)
Parsley Sage Rosemary & Thyme . . . . (Columbia)
Simon & Garfunkel's Greatest Hits . . . . (Columbia)
ST/The Graduate . . . . (Columbia)

The Concert In Central Park . . . .(Warner Bros.)

Scarlet Ribbons (For Her Hair)
Harry Belafonte; *Harry Belafonte-Legendary Performer* . . . . . . (RCA)
Harry Belafonte's All Time Greatest Hits-#1 . . . . (RCA)
This Is Harry Belafonte . . . . (RCA)
Jim Ed Brown & Maxine Brown; *Essential Jim Ed Brown* . . . . (RCA)
Kingston Trio; *At Large/Here We Go Again!* . . . . (Capitol)
Capitol Collectors Series-The Kingston Trio . . . . (Capitol)
Lennon Sisters; *Best Of The Lennon Sisters* . . . .(Ranwood)
Les Paul; *Legend & The Legacy-#1-4* . . . . (Capitol)
NRBQ; *Diggin' Uncle Q* . . . . (Rounder)
Patti Page; *Patti Page-16 Most Requested Songs* . . . . (Legacy)
Roger Whittaker; *Roger Whittaker-Classics Collection-#2* . . . . . . (Liberty)

Searchin'
Coasters; *50 Coastin' Classics-C* . . . . (Rhino)
All-Star Chartbusters . . . .(Intermedia)
Coasters' Greatest Hits . . . . (Atco)
Golden Years-1957-C . . . . (Dominion Entert.)
Oldies But Goodies-#8-C . . . . (Original Sound)
The Ultimate Coasters . . . . (Warner Special Prod.)
Very Best Of The Coasters . . . . (Rhino)
Spencer Davis Group; *Best Of The Spencer Davis Group* . . . .(EMI)
Best Of The Spencer Davis Group . . . . (Rhino)

Seasons For Girls
Trammps; *Trammps III* . . . .(Atlantic)

Second-Hand Woman
Steve Winwood; *Arc Of A Diver* . . . . (Island)

Secret Garden
Bruce Springsteen; *Bruce Springsteen's Greatest Hits* . . . . (Columbia)
ST/*Jerry Maguire* . . . .(Epic/Sony Music Soundtrax)

Senorita
Don Williams; *Don Williams' Greatest Country Hits* . . . . (Curb)
New Moves . . . . (Capitol)

Senorita With A Necklace Of Tears
Paul Simon; *You're The One* . . . .(Warner Bros.)

Sentimental Lady
Fleetwood Mac; *25 Years-The Chain* . . . .(Warner Bros.)
Bare Trees . . . . (Reprise)

Senza Una Donna (Without A Woman)
Paul Young; *From Time To Time-The Singles Collection* . . . . . . (Columbia)
Zucchero & Paul Young; *Zucchero & Paul Young* . . . .(London)

September Girls
Bangles; *Different Light* . . . . (Columbia)

September Girls
Big Star; *Big Star Live* . . . .(Rykodisc)

Seven Little Girls Sitting In The Back Seat
Paul Evans; *Music To Remember-C* . . . . (Dominion Entert.)

Sex And Candy
Marcy Playground; *Marcy Playground* . . . . (Capitol)
Now That's What I Call Music!-#1-C . . . .(Virgin)

Sexy + 17
Stray Cats; *Best Of Stray Cats-Rock This Town* . . . .(EMI)
Rant 'N' Rave With The Stray Cats . . . .(EMI)

Sexy Girl
Lillo Thomas; *Lillo Thomas* . . . . (Capitol)

Sexy Girl
Glenn Frey; *Allnighter* . . . .(MCA)

Sexy Lady
Carl Carlton; *Carl Carlton* . . . . (20th Century Fox)
Ear Candy-#2-C . . . . (20th Century Fox)

Sexy Lady
Rick James; *Come Get It!* . . . . (Motown)

Sexy Lady
Commodores; *Midnight Magic* . . . . (Motown)

Sexy Mexican Maid
Red Hot Chili Peppers; *Mother's Milk* . . . .(EMI)

Shady River Gal/Alabama Gals
Beverly Cotton; *Clogging Lessons* . . . . (Flying Fish)

Shake It Like A White Girl
E.U.; *Livin' Large* . . . . (Virgin)

She
Kiss; *Alive!* . . . . (Mercury)
Double Platinum . . . . (Mercury)
Dressed To Kill . . . . (Mercury)

She
Green Day; *Dookie* . . . . (Reprise)

She
Emmylou Harris; *Luxury Liner* . . . .(Warner Bros.)
Gram Parsons; *GP/Grievous Angel* . . . . (Reprise)

She
Jacksons; *2300 Jackson Street* . . . .(Epic)

She
Roy Orbison; *Classic-1965-1968* . . . . (Rhino)

She
Del Shannon; *Liberty Years (Runaway)* . . . .(EMI)

She
Monkees; *Monkees' Greatest Hits* . . . . (Rhino)

She
Harry Connick, Jr.; *She* . . . . (Columbia)

She
Edie Brickell & New Bohemians; *Shooting Rubberbands At The Stars* . . . . (Geffen)

She
Tommy James And The Shondells; *Tommy James And The Shondells-Anthology* . . . . (Rhino)

She Ain't Got No Hair
Professor Longhair; *Mardi Gras In Baton Rouge* . . . . (Rhino)

She Ain't The Girl For You
Kinleys; *Kinleys II* . . . . (Epic)

She Ain't Ugly
Gary B.B. Coleman; *Romance Without Finance Is A Nuisance* . . . (Ichiban Int'l)

She Ain't Worth It
Glenn Medeiros; *Glenn Medeiros With Bobby Brown* . . . . (MCA)

She Ain't Your Ordinary Girl
Alabama; *Alabama-Super Hits-#2* . . . . (RCA)
In Pictures . . . . (RCA)

She Bangs The Drums
Stone Roses; *The Stone Roses* . . . .(Silvertone)

She Believes In Me
Kenny Rogers; *Kenny Rogers-20 Great Years* . . . . (Reprise)

She Blinded Me With Science
Thomas Dolby; *Golden Age Of Wireless* . . . . (Capitol)

She Brakes For Rainbows
B-52's; *Bouncing Off The Satellites* . . . . (Warner Bros.)

She Came In Through The Bathroom Window
Beatles; *Abbey Road* . . . .(Parlophone)
Beatles-Box Set . . . . (Capitol)
Joe Cocker; *Joe Cocker Live* . . . . (Capitol)
Joe Cocker! . . . . (A&M)
Joe Cocker-Classics-#4 . . . . (A&M)
Mad Dogs & Englishmen . . . . (A&M)

She Can Put Her Shoes Under My Bed (Anytime)
Johnny Duncan; *Classic Country* . . . . (Simitar)

She Can't Say I Didn't Cry
Rick Trevino; *Rick Trevino* . . . . (Columbia)

She Can't Say That Anymore
John Conlee; *Friday Night Blues* . . . . (MCA)
John Conlee's Greatest Hits . . . . (MCA)

She Caught The Katy & Left Me A Mule To Ride
Blues Brothers; *Best Of The Blues Brothers* . . . .(Atlantic)
ST/*The Blues Brothers* . . . .(Atlantic)
Taj Mahal; *Best Of Taj Mahal* . . . . (Columbia)
Natch'l Blues . . . . (Columbia)

She Closed Her Eyes
Chris Rea; *Espresso Logic* . . . . (East West)

She Comes In Colors
Hooters; *Nervous Night* . . . . (Columbia)

She Comes In Colors
Love; *Best Of Love* . . . . (Rhino)

She Cooks Me Cabbage
Champion Jack Dupree; *Blues For Everybody* . . . . . (International Mktg. Group)

She Couldn't Change Me
Montgomery Gentry; *Carrying On* . . . . (Columbia)

She Cried
Jay & The Americans; *Come A Little Bit Closer-Best Of Jay & The Americans* . . . . (Gold Rush)
Jay & The Americans' All-Time Greatest Hits . . . . (Rhino)
Jay & The Americans' Greatest Hits . . . . (Curb)

She Cried
Toad The Wet Sprocket; *Pale* . . . . (Columbia)

She Deserves You
Baillie & The Boys; *Best Of Baillie & The Boys* . . . . (RCA)
Turn The Tide . . . . (RCA)

She Didn't Lie
Garland Jeffreys; *One-Eyed Jack* . . . . (A&M)

She Doesn't Cry Anymore
Shenandoah; *Road Not Taken* . . . . (Columbia)
Shenandoah . . . . (Columbia)

She Doesn't Need Me Anymore
Peter Cetera; *You're The Inspiration-A Collection* . . . . (River North)

She Don't Care About Time
Byrds; *Original Singles-#1-1965-1967* . . . . (Columbia)
The Byrds . . . . (Columbia)

She Don't Get The Blues
Alan Jackson; *Here In The Real World* . . . . (Arista)

She Don't Have A License
Porter Wagoner; *45-#7-29772* . . . . (Warner Bros.)

She Don't Know She's Beautiful
Sammy Kershaw; *Haunted Heart* . . . . (Mercury)

She Don't Look Back
Dan Fogelberg; *Exiles* . . . .(Full Moon)

She Don't Love Nobody
Desert Rose Band; *Running* . . . . (MCA)

She Don't Love Nobody
Nick Lowe; *Basher: Best Of* . . . . (Columbia)

She Don't Talk Like Us No More
K.T. Oslin; *This Woman* . . . . (RCA)

She Dreams
Mark Chesnutt; *What A Way To Live* . . . . (Decca)
She Drives Me Crazy
Fine Young Cannibals; *Raw & The Cooked* . . . . (I.R.S.)
Raw & The Remix . . . . (MCA)
Rock The First-#1-C . . . . (Sandstone Music)
She Drives Me Madagascar
Chi; *Jet Stream* . . . . (Sonic Atmospheres)
She Drives Me Wild
Michael Jackson; *Dangerous* . . . . (Epic)
She Even Woke Me Up To Say Goodbye
Jerry Lee Lewis; *Best Of Jerry Lee Lewis* . . . . (Smash)
Heartbreak . . . . (Tomato)
Kenny Rogers And The First Edition; *Kenny Rogers And The First Edition-Love Songs* . . . . (MCA Special Prod.)
She Gave Her Heart To A Soldier Boy
Roy Rogers; *The Country Music Hall Of Fame-Roy Rogers* . . . . (MCA)
She Gave Her Heart To Jethro
Tom T. Hall; *Essential Tom T. Hall-20th Anniversary Collection* . . . . . (Mercury)
She Gets Too High
Rob Rule; *Rob Rule* . . . . (Mercury)
She Gives It All To Me (I Can't Believe)
Conway Twitty; *Conway Twitty-Number Ones-#1* . . . . (Liberty)
Very Best Of Conway Twitty . . . . (MCA)
She Gives Me Religion
Van Morrison; *Beautiful Vision* . . . . (Warner Bros.)
She Goes Down
Motley Crue; *Dr. Feelgood* . . . . (Elektra)
She Goes Down
Billy Squier; *Creatures Of Habit* . . . . (Capitol)
She Gonna Come Home Wit' Me
Original Broadway Cast; *Most Happy Fella* . . . . (Sony Music Classical)
She Got A Mule Kick
Harry Crafton; *Harry Crafton* . . . . (Collectables)
She Got Me (When She Got Her Dress On)
Masters Of Reality; *Sunrise On The Sufferbus* . . . . (Chrysalis)
She Got The Goldmine (I Got The Shaft)
Jerry Reed; *14 #1 Country Hits-C* . . . . (RCA)
Jerry Reed's Greatest Hits . . . . (RCA)
Solid Country Gold-C . . . . (RCA)
She Got The Radio
Cory Hart; *First Offense* . . . . (EMI)
She Has Eyes
L7; *Hungry For Stink* . . . . (Slash)
She Has Funny Cars
Allman Brothers Band/Second Coming; *Dreams* . . . . (Polydor)
Jefferson Airplane; *2400 Fulton Street-An Anthology* . . . . (RCA)
Loves You . . . . (RCA)
Surrealistic Pillow . . . . (RCA)
She Has No Memory Of Me
Moe Bandy; *Moe Bandy's Greatest Hits* . . . . (Curb)
She Hung The Moon
George Jones; *Shine On* . . . . (Epic)
She Is A Diamond
Original Cast; *Evita* . . . . (MCA)
She Is Always Seventeen
Harry Chapin; *Greatest Stories-Live* . . . . (Elektra)
Harry Chapin-Anthology . . . . (Elektra)
She Is His Only Need
Wynonna; *Wynonna* . . . . (MCA)
Wynonna-Collection . . . . (Curb)
She Is Still A Mystery
Lovin' Spoonful; *Lovin' Spoonful-Anthology* . . . . (Rhino)
She Keeps The Home Fires Burning
Ronnie Milsap; *Essential Ronnie Milsap* . . . . (RCA)
She Kept Chewing Gum
Donald Jacob; *Zydeco Blues 'N' Boogie* . . . . (Rykodisc)
She Left Me A Mule To Ride
Big Joe Williams; *Shake Your Boogie* . . . . (Arhoolie)
She Loves Austin
Johnny Rodriguez; *Gracias* . . . . (Capitol)
She Loves My Automobile
ZZ Top; *Deguello* . . . . (Warner Bros.)
She Loves My Car
Ronnie Milsap; *One More Try For Love* . . . . (RCA)
She Loves My Car
Bobby Caldwell; *August Moon* . . . . (Sin-Drome)
She Loves The Jerk
John Hiatt; *Riding With The King* . . . . (Geffen)
Y'All Caught? Ones That Got Away, 1979-85 . . . . (Geffen)
Rodney Crowell; *Street Language* . . . . (Columbia)
She Loves You
Beatles; *Beatles 1* . . . . (Capitol)
Beatles-20 Greatest Hits . . . . (Capitol)
Beatles-Box Set . . . . (Capitol)
Past Masters-Volume One . . . . (Parlophone)
The Beatles At The Hollywood Bowl . . . . (Capitol)
The Beatles' Second Album . . . . (Capitol)

The Beatles/1962-1966 . . . . (Capitol)
She Makes Me Shake Like A Soul Machine
Unrest; *Kustom Karnal Blackxploitation* . . . . (Caroline)
She Makes The Coming Home Worth The Being Gone
Shenandoah; *Extra Mile* . . . . (Columbia)
She Misses Him
Tim Rushlow; *Tim Rushlow* . . . . (Atlantic)
She Misses Him On Sunday The Most
Diamond Rio; *Diamond Rio IV* . . . . (Arista)
Diamond Rio's Greatest Hits . . . . (Arista)
She Moved Through The Fair
Art Garfunkel; *Watermark* . . . . (Legacy)
James Galway & The Chieftains; *In Ireland* . . . . (RCA)
She Moves Me
Muddy Waters; *Best Of Muddy Waters* . . . . (Chess)
Rolling Stone . . . . (Chess)
She Needs Someone To Hold Her (When She Cries)
Conway Twitty; *Best Of Conway Twitty-#2* . . . . (MCA Special Prod.)
Conway Twitty's Greatest Hits-#2 . . . . (MCA)
She Never Lets It Go To Her Heart
Tim McGraw; *All I Want* . . . . (Curb)
Tim McGraw's Greatest Hits . . . . (Curb)
She Put Her Hand Where My Money Was
John Lee; *Down At The Depot* . . . . (Rounder)
She Put The Sad In All His Songs
Alabama; *Closer You Get* . . . . (RCA)
She Runs Hot
Little Village; *Little Village* . . . . (Reprise)
She Said
Collective Soul; *Dosage* . . . . (Atlantic)
ST/Scream 2 . . . . (Dimension/Capitol)
She Said She Said
Beatles; *Beatles-Box Set* . . . . (Capitol)
Revolver . . . . (Capitol)
She Said The Same Things To Me
John Hiatt; *Warming Up To The Ice Age* . . . . (Geffen)
Y'All Caught? Ones That Got Away, 1979-85 . . . . (Geffen)
She Said Yeah
Rolling Stones; *December's Children (and everybody's)* . . . . (Abkco)
Wilson Pickett; *A Man & A Half-Best Of Wilson Pickett* . . . . (Rhino)
She Said Yes
Rhett Akins; *A Thousand Memories* . . . . (Decca)
She Say (Oom Dooby Doom)
Diamonds; *Best Of The Diamonds* . . . . (Rhino)
She Smiled Sweetly
Rolling Stones; *Between The Buttons* . . . . (Abkco)
She Suits Me To A Tee
Buddy Guy; *Left My Blues In San Francisco* . . . . (Chess)
Very Best Of Buddy Guy . . . . (Rhino)
She Sure Got Away With My Heart
John Anderson; *Eye Of A Hurricane* . . . . (Warner Bros.)
John Anderson's Greatest Hits-#2 . . . . (Warner Bros.)
She Takes My Breath Away
Eddie Money; *Right Here* . . . . (Columbia)
She Thinks His Name Was John
Reba McEntire; *Read My Mind* . . . . (MCA)
Reba McEntire's Greatest Hits-#3: I'm A Survivor . . . . (MCA)
She Thinks I Still Care
Elvis Presley; *Moody Blue* . . . . (RCA)
George Jones; *Best Of George Jones-1955-1967* . . . . (Rhino)
Billboard Top Country Hits-1962-C . . . . (Rhino)
George Jones' All-Time Greatest Hits . . . . (Epic)
George Jones-Super Hits-#2 . . . . (Epic)
She Thinks My Tractor's Sexy
Kenny Chesney; *Everywhere We Go* . . . . (BNA)
She Took It Like A Man
Confederate Railroad; *Confederate Railroad* . . . . (Atlantic)
She Took You For A Ride
Aaron Neville; *Aaron Neville's Greatest Hits* . . . . (Curb)
Tell it Like It Is-Golden Classics . . . . (Collectables)
She Used To Be Mine
Brooks & Dunn; *Hard Workin' Man* . . . . (Arista)
She Used To Be Somebody's Baby
Larry Gatlin & The Gatlin Brothers Band; *Greatest Country Hits Of The '80s-1986-C* . . . . (Columbia)
The Gatlin Brothers' Biggest Hits . . . . (Columbia)
She Used To Sing On Sunday
Larry Gatlin & The Gatlin Brothers Band; *Larry Gatlin & The Gatlin Brothers' Greatest Hits-#2* . . . . (Columbia)
Larry Gatlin & The Gatlin Brothers-17 Greatest Hits . . . . (Columbia)
She Walks This Earth
Sting; *Love Affair-Music Of Ivan Lins-C* . . . . (Telarc)
She Wants To Dance With Me
Rick Astley; *Hold Me In Your Arms* . . . . (RCA)
She Was Hot
Rolling Stones; *Undercover* . . . . (Rolling Stones)
She Was Only Seventeen (He Was One Year More)
Marty Robbins; *American Originals-Marty Robbins* . . . . (Columbia)

Marty Robbins' Greatest Hits . . . . (Columbia)

She Watch Channel Zero
Public Enemy; *It Takes A Nation Of Millions To Hold Us Back* . . . . . . (Def Jam)

She Wears Red Feathers
Guy Mitchell; *Guy Mitchell-16 Most Requested Songs* . . . . (Legacy)

She Won't Be Lonely Long
Lee Roy Parnell; *Hits And Highways Ahead*. (Arista)

She Wore A Yellow Ribbon
Mitch Miller; *Sing Along With Mitch* . . . . (Columbia)

She Works Hard For The Money
Donna Summer; *I Am Woman-C*. . . . . (Nick At Nite)
   She Works Hard For The Money . . . . (Mercury)
   Summer Collection . . . . (Mercury)

She'd Give Anything
Boy Howdy; *She'd Give Anything* . . . . (Curb)

She'd Rather Be With Me
Turtles; *Best Of The Turtles-Golden Archive Series* . . . . (Rhino)
   Oldies But Goodies-#3-C . . . . (Original Sound)
   Turtles-20 Greatest Hits . . . . (Rhino)

She'll Be Coming 'Round The Mountain
Four Freshmen & Stan Kenton & Orchestra; *Live At Butler*
   University . . . . (Creative World)
Mormon Tabernacle Choir; *This Land Is Your Land* . . . . (Columbia)
Original Soundtrack; *Children's Favorites* . . . . (Kid Rhino/Rhino 4 Kids)
   School Days-Kids Classics . . . . (Benson)

She's A Carnival
Siouxsie And The Banshees; *Kiss In The Dream House* . . . . (Geffen)

She's A Fool
Lesley Gore; *Golden Hits Of Lesley Gore* . . . . (Mercury)
   Lesley Gore-Anthology . . . . (Rhino)

She's A Heartbreaker
Gene Pitney; *Best Of Gene Pitney*. . . . . (K-Tel)
   Gene Pitney-Anthology 1961-1968 . . . . (Rhino)

She's A Heartbreaker
ZZ Top; *Six Pack* . . . . (Warner Bros.)
   Tejas . . . . (Warner Bros.)

She's A Hum Dum Dinger
Jimmie Davis; *The Roots Of Rap-Classic Recordings-C* . . . . (Yazoo)

She's A Latin From Manhattan
Al Jolson; *Lullaby Of Broadway-Music Of H. Warren* . . . . (Pearl Flapper)

She's A Little Past Forty
Ronnie McDowell; *Best Of Ronnie McDowell* . . . . (Curb)

She's A Miracle
Exile; *19 Hot Country Requests-#3-C*. . . . . (Epic)
   Exile's Greatest Hits . . . . (Epic)
   Kentucky Hearts. . . . . (Epic)

She's A Mystery To Me
Roy Orbison; *Mystery Girl* . . . . (Virgin)

She's A Natural
Rob Crosby; *Solid Ground* . . . . (Arista)

She's A Rainbow
Rolling Stones; *Get Yer Ya-Ya's Out!* . . . . (Abkco)
   More Hot Rocks (big hits & fazed cookies) . . . . (Abkco)
   Singles Collection-The London Years . . . . (Abkco)
   Their Satanic Majesties Request . . . . (Abkco)
   Through The Past, Darkly (Big Hits Vol. 2) . . . . (Abkco)

She's A River
Simple Minds; *Good News From The Next World* . . . . (Virgin)

She's A Woman
Beatles; *Beatles '65* . . . . (Capitol)
   Beatles-Box Set . . . . (Capitol)
   Compact Disc Singles Collection. . . . . (Capitol)
   Past Masters-Volume One . . . . (Parlophone)
   The Beatles At The Hollywood Bowl . . . . (Capitol)
Jeff Beck; *Blow By Blow*. . . . . (Epic)

She's About A Mover
Sir Douglas Quintet; *Best Of The Sir Douglas Quintet* . . . . (Takoma)
   Texas Music-#3-Garage Bands & Psychedelia-C . . . . (Rhino)

She's All I Ever Had
Ricky Martin; *Ricky Martin* . . . . (Columbia)

She's All I Got
Johnny Paycheck; *Johnny Paycheck-16 Biggest Hits* . . . . (Epic)
   Johnny Paycheck's Biggest Hits . . . . (Epic)

She's All I Got
Jimmy Cozier; *Jimmy Cozier* . . . . (J)

She's Already Made Up Her Mind
Lyle Lovett; *Joshua Judges Ruth* . . . . (Curb/MCA)

She's Always A Woman
Billy Joel; *Billy Joel-Greatest Hits, Volume I & Volume II*. . . . . (Columbia)
   The Stranger . . . . (Columbia)

She's Always Right
Clay Walker; *Live, Laugh, Love* . . . . (Giant)

She's Coming Back Some Cold Rainy Day
Georgia Cotton Pickers; *The Greatest In Country Blues (1929-*
   1956)-#3-C . . . . (Sony Broadway)

She's Crazy For Leavin'
Rodney Crowell; *30 Years Of #1 Hits-#19-C* . . . . (Columbia)
   Diamonds & Dirt . . . . (Columbia)

Greatest Country Hits Of The '80s-1989-C . . . . (Columbia)
Steve Wariner; *Life's Highway* . . . . (MCA)

She's Crying For Me
New Orleans Rhythm Kings; *RCA Victor Jazz: First Half-Century-C* . . . . (RCA)

She's Every Woman
Garth Brooks; *Fresh Horses* . . . . (Capitol)

She's Funny That Way (I Got A Woman Crazy For Me)
Art Tatum; *Solo Masterpieces-#8* . . . . (Pablo)
Count Basie Jam; *Montreux '77-C* . . . . (Pablo)
Frank Sinatra; *At The Movies* . . . . (Capitol)
   Nice 'N' Easy . . . . (Capitol)
Jackie Gleason; *Lush Moods* . . . . (Pair)
Nat "King" Cole; *Big Band Cole* . . . . (Blue Note)

She's Gone
Daryl Hall & John Oates; *Abandoned Luncheonette* . . . . (Atlantic)
   Rock 'N Soul, Part 1 . . . . (RCA)

She's Gone
Eric Clapton; *Pilgrim* . . . . (Duck/Reprise)

She's Gone To L.A. Again
Oak Ridge Boys; *Fancy Free* . . . . (MCA)

She's Gone, Gone, Gone
Lefty Frizzell; *American Originals-Lefty Frizzell*. . . . . (Columbia)
   Best Of Lefty Frizzell . . . . (Rhino)

She's Gonna Fly
Collin Raye; *Tracks*. . . . . (Epic)

She's Gonna Make It
Garth Brooks; *Sevens* . . . . (Capitol)

She's Gonna Win Your Heart
Eddy Raven; *I Could Use Another You* . . . . (RCA)

She's Got a 60 Cycle Brain
Paul Buff Organization; *45-#55* . . . . (Original Sound)

She's Got A Cause
Ministry; *With Sympathy* . . . . (Arista)

She's Got A Way
Billy Joel; *Billy Joel-Greatest Hits, Volume I & Volume II* . . . . (Columbia)
   Cold Spring Harbor . . . . (Columbia)
   Songs In The Attic . . . . (Columbia)

She's Got Another Pair Of Shoes
Little Richard; *Grooviest 17 Original Hits* . . . . (Specialty)

She's Got Issues
Offspring; *Americana* . . . . (Columbia)

She's Got It
Little Richard; *Here's Little Richard*. . . . . (Specialty)
   Little Richard-His Best. . . . . (Dominion Entert.)

She's Got Rhythm
Beach Boys; *M.I.U. Album* . . . . (Brother)

She's Got The Rhythm (And I Got The Blues)
Alan Jackson; *A Lot About Livin' (And A Little 'Bout Love)* . . . . (Arista)

She's Hot
Fabulous Thunderbirds; *Powerful Stuff*. . . . . (Epic Portrait Assoc.)

She's In Love
Mark Wills; *Wish You Were Here* . . . . (Mercury)

She's In Love With A Rodeo Man
Chris LeDoux; *Songs Of Rodeo & Country*. . . . . (Liberty)
Don Williams; *Don Williams' Greatest Hits* . . . . (MCA)

She's In Love With The Boy
Trisha Yearwood; *Trisha Yearwood* . . . . (MCA)

She's Just A Drifter
Marty Robbins; *El Paso City*. . . . . (Columbia)
   Marty Robbins' Biggest Hits . . . . (Columbia)

She's Just A Groupie
Bobby Nunn; *Second To Nunn* . . . . (Motown)

She's Just Killing Me
ZZ Top; *Rhythmeen*. . . . . (RCA)
   ST/From Dusk Till Dawn . . . . (Epic/Sony Music Soundtrax)

She's Leaving Home
Al Jarreau; *All Fly Home* . . . . (Warner Bros.)
Beatles; *Beatles-Box Set* . . . . (Capitol)
   Beatles-Love Songs . . . . (Capitol)
   Sgt. Pepper's Lonely Hearts Club Band . . . . (Capitol)

She's Like Heroin To Me
Gun Club; *Fire Of Love* . . . . (Slash)

She's Like The Wind
Patrick Swayze; *ST/Dirty Dancing* . . . . (RCA)

She's Long, She's Tall, She Weeps Like A Willow Tree
John Lee Hooker; *Black Snake* . . . . (Fantasy)
   Country Blues Of John Lee Hooker . . . . (Riverside)

She's Lookin' Good
Rodger Collins; *Soul Shots-#2-The "In" Crowd-Sweet Soul-C* . . . . (Rhino)
Wilson Pickett; *Very Best Of Wilson Pickett* . . . . (Rhino)
   Wilson Pickett's Greatest Hits . . . . (Atlantic)

She's Lying
Lee Greenwood; *Inside Out/You've Got A Good Love Comin'* . . . . (MCA)
   Lee Greenwood's Greatest Hits . . . . (MCA)

She's Mine Tonight
Jay Ferguson; *White Noise* . . . . (Capitol)

She's More
Andy Griggs; *You Won't Ever Be Lonely* . . . . (RCA)

She's My Baby
Traveling Wilburys; *Traveling Wilburys-Vol. 3* . . . . (Wilbury/Warner Bros.)
Wings; *Wings At The Speed Of Sound* . . . . (Capitol)
She's My Cadillac
Santa Fe; *Santa Fe* . . . . (Creative Indep. Artists)
She's My Girl
Turtles; *'60s Sound Explosion-C* . . . . (K-Tel)
Nuggets-#9-Acid Rock-C . . . . (Rhino)
Turtles-20 Greatest Hits . . . . (Rhino)
She's My Machine
David Lee Roth; *Your Filthy Little Mouth* . . . . (Reprise)
She's My Rock
George Jones; *19 Hot Country Requests-#2-C* . . . . (Epic)
First Time Live! . . . . (Epic)
Ladies Choice . . . . (Epic)
She's My Saturday Night Special
Ronnie McDowell; *Unchained Melody* . . . . (Curb)
Wayne Newton; *Best Of Wayne Newton-Now* . . . . (Curb)
She's My Summer Girl
Jan & Dean; *Surf City-Best Of Jan & Dean* . . . . (EMI)
She's Nineteen Years Old
Muddy Waters; *Best Of Blues-#1-C* . . . . (MCA Special Prod.)
The Chess Box-Muddy Waters . . . . (Chess)
She's No Lady
Lyle Lovett; *Great Records Of The Decade-'80s Hits-Country-C* . . . . . . (Curb)
Pontiac . . . . (MCA)
She's Not Cryin' Anymore
Billy Ray Cyrus; *Some Gave All* . . . . (Mercury)
She's Not Just Another Woman
Biz Markie; *Diabolical-The Biz Never Sleeps* . . . . (Cold Chillin')
She's Not Just Another Woman
M.C. Peaches; *More Than Just A Pretty Face* . . . . (East West)
She's Not Just Another Woman
8th Day; *Didn't It Blow Your Mind: Soul Hits Of The '70s-#5-C* . . . . . (Rhino)
She's Not On The Menu
SNFU; *Last Of The Big Time Suspenders* . . . . (Cargo)
She's Not There
Santana; *Moonflower* . . . . (Columbia)
Viva Santana! . . . . (Columbia)
Vanilla Fudge; *Vanilla Fudge* . . . . (Atco)
Zombies; *Best & The Rest Of The Zombies* . . . . (Epic)
Billboard Top Rock 'N' Roll Hits-1964-C . . . . (Rhino)
History Of British Rock-#1-C . . . . (Rhino)
Time Of The Zombies . . . . (Bac-Trac)
She's Not You
Elvis Presley; *Elvis' Golden Records, Volume 3* . . . . (RCA)
The Top Ten Hits . . . . (RCA)
She's Only Happy When She's Dancin'
Bryan Adams; *Reckless* . . . . (A&M)
She's Out Of My Life
Jacksons; *Jacksons Live* . . . . (Epic)
Michael Jackson; *Off The Wall* . . . . (Epic)
She's Playing Hard To Forget
Eddy Raven; *Eddy Raven-Greatest Country Hits* . . . . (Curb)
Eddy Raven's Greatest Hits . . . . (Warner Bros.)
She's Playing Hell Trying To Get Me To Heaven
George Strait; *Strait Country* . . . . (MCA)
She's Pulling Me Back Again
Mickey Gilley; *Ten Years Of Hits* . . . . (Epic)
She's Ready For Someone To Love Her
Kenny Rogers; *I Prefer The Moonlight* . . . . (RCA)
Kenny Rogers' Greatest Hits . . . . (RCA)
She's Single Again
Janie Fricke; *19 Hot Country Requests-#3-C* . . . . (Epic)
Greatest Country Hits Of The '80s-1985-C . . . . (Columbia)
Janie Fricke-17 Greatest Hits . . . . (Columbia)
Very Best Of Janie Fricke . . . . (Columbia)
Reba McEntire; *Have I Got A Deal For You* . . . . (MCA)
She's So Cold
Rolling Stones; *Emotional Rescue* . . . . (Rolling Stones)
She's So High
Marc Tanner Band; *No Escape* . . . . (Elektra)
She's So Modern
Boomtown Rats; *Boomtown Rats' Greatest Hits* . . . . (Columbia)
Tonic For The Troops . . . . (Columbia)
She's Still Here
Shenandoah; *Shenandoah* . . . . (Columbia)
She's Sure Taking It Well
Kevin Sharp; *Measure Of A Man* . . . . (143/Asylum)
She's Taken
Billy Dean; *Young Man* . . . . (SBK)
She's Taken A Shine
John Berry; *Faces* . . . . (Capitol)
She's The One
Bruce Springsteen; *Born To Run* . . . . (Columbia)
She's Vibrator Dependent
Mojo Nixon & Skid Roper; *Root Hog Or Die* . . . . (I.R.S.)

Shimmer
Fuel; *Sunburn* . . . . (550 Music)
Shipoopi
Original Broadway Cast; *The Music Man* . . . . (Angel)
Original Cast; *The Music Man* . . . . (Gold Rush)
Shoot Her If She Runs
Climax Blues Band; *Tightly Knit* . . . . (Sire)
Short Skirt/Long Jacket
Cake; *Comfort Eagle* . . . . (Columbia)
Show Her
Ronnie Milsap; *Collector's Series-Ronnie Milsap* . . . . (RCA)
Keyed Up . . . . (RCA)
Ronnie Milsap's Greatest Hits-#2 . . . . (RCA)
Shy Guy
Diana King; *ST/Bad Boys* . . . . (Work)
Tougher Than Love . . . . (Work)
Shy Of The Moon
Wallflowers; *The Wallflowers* . . . . (Virgin)
Silence Is Golden
4 Seasons; *25th Anniversary Collection* . . . . (Rhino)
4 Seasons-Anthology . . . . (Rhino)
Tremeloes; *Best Of The Tremeloes* . . . . (Rhino)
History Of British Rock-#7-C . . . . (Rhino)
Rock Artifacts-From The Vaults-#4-C . . . . (Columbia)
Simply Irresistible
Robert Palmer; *Super Nova* . . . . (Island)
Single White Female
Chely Wright; *Single White Female* . . . . (MCA)
Single Women
Dolly Parton; *Heartbreak Express* . . . . (RCA)
Six O'Clock Train & A Girl With Green Eyes
John Hartford; *All In The Name Of Love* . . . . (Flying Fish)
Slave Girl
Goo Goo Dolls; *A Boy Named Goo* . . . . (Metal Blade)
Sleepy Time Gal
Glenn Miller; *Best Of The Big Bands-C* . . . . (Columbia)
Harry James; *All-Time Favorites By Harry James* . . . (Sony Music Special Prod.)
Liberace; *Encore-Liberace* . . . . (American Variety)
Liberace . . . . (American Variety)
Piano Memories . . . . (American Variety)
Mose Allison; *Creek Bank* . . . . (Prestige)
Small Town Girl
Steve Wariner; *It's A Crazy World* . . . . (MCA)
Steve Wariner's Greatest Hits . . . . (MCA)
Small Town Girl
Larry Carlton; *Larry Carlton-Collection* . . . . (GRP)
Small Town Girl
John Cafferty And The Beaver Brown Band; *Tough All Over* . . . . . (Scotti Bros.)
So Fine
Fiestas; *Baby Boomer Classics-Party Time Fifties-C* . . . . . . (JCI Assoc. Labels)
Baby Boomer's Best-Jumpin' Jive 50's-C . . . . (Priority)
So Help Me Girl
Gary Barlow; *Open Road* . . . . (Arista)
Joe Diffie; *Third Rock From The Sun* . . . . (Epic)
Soft Lips
Hank Thompson and His Brazos Valley Boys; *45-#40211* . . . . (Capitol)
Soft Lips And Hard Liquor
Charlie Walker; *45-#0870* . . . . (RCA)
Soft, Sweet And Warm
David Houston; *45-#10870* . . . . (Epic)
Some Girls
Rolling Stones; *Some Girls* . . . . (Virgin)
Some Girls Do
Sawyer Brown; *Dirt Road* . . . . (Curb)
Some Kinda Woman
Traffic; *Far From Home* . . . . (Virgin)
Somebody
Depeche Mode; *101* . . . . (Sire)
Catching Up With Depeche Mode . . . . (Sire)
Some Great Reward . . . . (Sire)
Somebody
Fleetwood Mac; *Mystery To Me* . . . . (Reprise)
Somebody Stole My Gal
Benny Goodman; *B.G. In Hi-Fi* . . . . (Blue Note)
Best Of The Big Bands-C . . . . (Columbia)
Somebody's Baby
Jackson Browne; *ST/Fast Times At Ridgemont High* . . . . (Elektra)
The Next Voice You Hear-Best Of Jackson Browne . . . . (Elektra)
Somethin' 4 Da Honeyz
Montell Jordan; *This Is How We Do It* . . . . (PMP/RAL)
Something
Beatles; *Abbey Road* . . . . (Parlophone)
Beatles 1 . . . . (Capitol)
The Beatles/1967-1970 . . . . (Capitol)
The Beatles-Anthology-#3 . . . . (Capitol)
Something Like That
Tim McGraw; *A Place In The Sun* . . . . (Curb)
Tim McGraw's Greatest Hits . . . . (Curb)

Something So Feminine About A Mandolin
Jimmy Buffett; *Havana Daydreamin'* . . . . (MCA)
Sometimes She Forgets
Steve Earle; *Train A Comin'* . . . .(Warner Bros.)
Travis Tritt; *Greatest Hits-From The Beginning* . . . .(Warner Bros.)
Sophisticated Bitch
Public Enemy; *Yo! Bum Rush The Show* . . . . (Def Jam/Columbia)
Sophisticated Lady
Diane Schuur; *In Tribute* . . . . (GRP)
Duke Ellington; *Mood Indigo* . . . .(Pro-Arte)
Reminiscing In Tempo . . . . (Columbia)
Linda Ronstadt; *Lush Life* . . . . (Asylum)
Original Broadway Cast; *Bubbling Brown Sugar* . . . . (Amherst)
Rosemary Clooney; *Essence Of Rosemary Clooney* . . . . (Legacy)
Tito Puente & His Latin Ensemble; *On Broadway* . . . . . . (Concord Picante Jazz)
Sour Girl
Stone Temple Pilots; *No. 4* . . . .(Atlantic)
South City Midnight Lady
Doobie Brothers; *Best Of The Doobies* . . . .(Warner Bros.)
Captain & Me . . . .(Warner Bros.)
South Dakota Lady
Buddy Red Bow; *Buddy Red Bow* . . . . (First Warning)
Spanish Eyes
Ricky Martin; *Ricky Martin* . . . . (Columbia)
Spanish Is The Loving Tongue
Bob Dylan; *Dylan* . . . . (Columbia)
Emmylou Harris; *Cimarron* . . . .(Warner Bros.)
Evangeline . . . .(Warner Bros.)
Ian & Sylvia; *Four Strong Winds* . . . . (Vanguard)
Ian & Sylvia's Greatest Hits . . . . (Vanguard)
Michael Martin Murphey; *Cowboy Songs* . . . . . . (Warner Western)
Spanish Lady
John Handy; *Monterey* . . . . (Columbia)
Sparkling Brown Eyes
Webb Pierce with the Wilburn Brothers; *King Of The Honky-Tonk: From The*
Original Decca Masters-1952-1959 . . . .(Country Music Foundation)
Webb Pierce-Greatest Hits/Finest Performances . . . . (Sun)
Spilled Perfume
Pam Tillis; *Sweetheart's Dance* . . . . (Arista)
St. Louis Blues
Bessie Smith; *Beauty Of The Blues* . . . . (Columbia)
Bessie Smith-The Collection . . . . (Legacy)
Big Joe Turner; *Boss Of The Blues* . . . .(Atlantic)
Billie Holiday; *Quintessential-#9-1940-1942* . . . . (Columbia)
The Billie Holiday Story-#3 . . . . (Columbia)
Bob Wills & His Texas Playboys; *Bob Wills & His Texas Playboys-24*
Great Hits . . . . (Polydor)
Cleo Laine; *Jazz* . . . . (RCA)
Dave Brubeck Quartet; *25th Anniversary Reunion* . . . . (A&M)
Dave Brubeck Quartet-At Carnegie Hall . . . . (Columbia)
Paper Moon . . . .(Concord Jazz)
Duke Ellington; *1953 Pasadena Concert* . . . .(Crescendo)
Ella Fitzgerald; *These Are The Blues* . . . . (Verve)
Louis Armstrong; *At The Crescendo* . . . .(MCA)
Louis Armstrong-Legendary Performer . . . . (RCA)
Louis Armstrong-Vol. 6-St. Louis Blues . . . . (Columbia)
Nipper's Greatest Hits Of The '30s-#2-C . . . . (RCA)
Merle Haggard & Asleep At The Wheel; *Ride With*
Bob-C . . . . (DreamWorks/SKG)
Original Broadway Cast; *Black & Blue* . . . . (DRG)
Pete Fountain; *Best Of Pete Fountain* . . . .(MCA)
Preservation Hall Jazz Band; *Best Of The Preservation Hall*
Jazz Band . . . . (Columbia)
New Orleans-#2 . . . . (Columbia)
Stairway To Heaven
Led Zeppelin; *Led Zeppelin IV* . . . .(Atlantic)
Led Zeppelin-Box Set . . . .(Atlantic)
Remasters . . . .(Atlantic)
ST/The Song Remains The Same . . . . (Swan Song)
Stanley Jordan; *Best Of Stanley Jordan* . . . . (Blue Note)
Flying Home . . . .(EMI)
Standing On The Corner
Broadway Cast; *Most Happy Fella* . . . . (RCA)
Dean Martin; *Best Of Dean Martin* . . . . (CEMA Special Prod.)
Four Lads; *Four Lads-16 Most Requested Songs* . . . . (Legacy)
Original Broadway Cast; *Most Happy Fella* . . . . (Sony Music Classical)
Steppin' Out With My Baby
Fred Astaire; *Cheek To Cheek: The Irving Berlin Songbook-C* . . . . (Verve)
Fred Astaire At MGM . . . . (Rhino)
ST/Easter Parade . . . . (Rhino)
Steppin' Out-Astaire Sings . . . . (Verve)
Tony Bennett; *MTV Unplugged-Tony Bennett* . . . . (Columbia)
Steppin' Out . . . . (Columbia)
Still She Cries
Journey; *Trial By Fire* . . . . (Columbia)
Straight Tequila Night
John Anderson; *Seminole Wind* . . . .(BNA)
Today's Hot Country-C . . . . (K-Tel)

Strange Kind Of Woman
Deep Purple; *Deepest Purple/The Very Best Of Deep Purple* . . . . (Warner Bros.)
Fireball . . . .(Warner Bros.)
Made In Japan . . . .(Warner Bros.)
Nobody's Perfect . . . . (Mercury)
Streamline Woman
Muddy Waters; *Blues Sky* . . . . (Epic Portrait Assoc.)
The Chess Box-Muddy Waters . . . . (Chess)
Strength Of A Woman
Carpenters; *Made In America* . . . . (A&M)
Stupid Girl
Rolling Stones; *Aftermath* . . . .(Abkco)
Singles Collection-The London Years . . . .(Abkco)
Stupid Girl
Garbage; *Garbage* . . . . (Almo Sounds)
Sugar Magnolia
Grateful Dead; *American Beauty* . . . .(Warner Bros.)
Best Of/Skeletons From The Closet . . . . (Warner Bros.)
Europe '72 . . . .(Warner Bros.)
Grateful Dead-Live-#1 . . . . (JCI Assoc. Labels)
Sugar, Sugar
Archies; *Billboard Top Rock 'N' Roll Hits-1969-C* . . . . (Rhino)
Suicide Blonde
INXS; *Live Baby Live* . . . .(Atlantic)
X . . . .(Atlantic)
Suitelady
Maxwell; *Maxwell's Urban Hang Suite* . . . . (Columbia)
Sullen Girl
Fiona Apple; *Tidal* . . . .(Clean Slate/Work)
Summer Girls
LFO; *Summer Girls-CD Single* . . . . (Logic)
Totally Hits-#1-C . . . . (Arista)
Sun Maid
Soul Asylum; *Grave Dancers Union* . . . . (Columbia)
Sunday Girl
Blondie; *Best Of Blondie* . . . . (Chrysalis)
Parallel Lines . . . . (Chrysalis)
Sunday Kind Of Woman
Charlie Rich; *Behind Closed Doors* . . . . (Epic)
Sunshine Girl
Parade; *More Nuggets-C* . . . . (Rhino)
Superwoman
Lil' Mo; *Based On A True Story* . . . . (Gold Mind/East West/EEG)
Superwoman
Karyn White; *Karyn White* . . . . (Warner Bros.)
Stevie Wonder; *Music Of My Mind* . . . . (Motown)
Original Musiquarium . . . . (Motown)
Surfer Girl
Beach Boys; *American Graffiti-#3-C* . . . . (MCA)
Best Of The Beach Boys . . . . (Capitol)
Endless Summer . . . . (Capitol)
Made In The U.S.A. . . . . (Capitol)
Oldies But Goodies-#2-C . . . . (Original Sound)
Sushi Girl
Tubes; *Best Of The Tubes* . . . . (Gold Rush)
Completion Backward Principle . . . . (Capitol)
Sweet Black Angel
Rolling Stones; *Exile On Main Street* . . . .(Virgin)
Sweet Black Girl
Buddy Guy & Junior Wells; *Alone & Acoustic* . . . . (Alligator)
Sweet City Woman
Stampeders; *'70s Smash Hits-#5-C* . . . . (Rhino)
Super Hits Of The '70s-Have A Nice Day-#6-C . . . . (Rhino)
Sweet Country Woman
Johnny Duncan; *Country Music Classics-#11-Early '70s-C* . . . . (K-Tel)
Johnny Duncan's Greatest Hits . . . . (Columbia)
Winnin' Country . . . . (Fifty One West)
Sweet Girl In Texas
John Delafose & The Eunice Playboys; *Joe Pete Got Two Women* . . . .(Arhoolie)
Sweet Lady
Tyrese; *Tyrese* . . . . (RCA)
Sweet Little Girl
Stevie Wonder; *Music Of My Mind* . . . . (Motown)
Sweet Little Miss Blue Eyes
Jim & Jesse/The Virginia Boys; *Appalachian Stomp: More Bluegrass*
Classics-C . . . . (Rhino)
Sweet Little Rock & Roller
Chuck Berry; *Chuck Berry Is On Top* . . . . (Chess)
The Chess Box-Chuck Berry . . . . (Chess)
Richard Thompson; *Guitar/Vocal* . . . .(Hannibal)
Rod Stewart; *Absolutely Live* . . . . (Warner Bros.)
Best Of Rod Stewart . . . . (Mercury)
Storyteller/The Complete Anthology: 1964-1990 . . . . (Warner Bros.)
Sweet Little Sixteen
Beatles; *45-#1502* . . . . (Collectables)
Chuck Berry; *Best Of The Best Of Chuck Berry* . . . . (International Mktg. Group)
Chuck Berry-Golden Hits . . . . (Mercury)
Chuck Berry-Greatest Hits Live . . . .(Quicksilver)
Cruisin'-1965-C . . . . (Increase)

Oldies But Goodies-#12-C . . . .(Original Sound)
Jerry Lee Lewis; *Jerry Lee Lewis-Original Golden Hits-#3* . . . .(Sun)
Jerry Lee Lewis & Friends; *Jerry Lee Lewis & Friends-Duets* . . . .(Sun)
John Lennon; *Lennon* . . . .(Capitol)
Rock 'N' Roll . . . .(Capitol)

Sweet Old Fashioned Girl, A
Teresa Brewer; *Music! Music! Music!-Best Of Teresa
Brewer* . . . .(Varese Vintage)

Sweet Sexy Thing
Nu Flavor; *Nu Flavor* . . . .(Reprise)

Sweet Sixteen
B.B. King; *Back In The Alley* . . . . (MCA)
Best Of B.B. King . . . . (MCA)
Electric B.B. King-His Best . . . . (MCA)
Live In Cook County Jail. . . . . (MCA)

Sweet Sixteen
Chuck Berry; *Chuck Berry's Greatest Hits* . . . . (Everest)

Sweet Sixteen
Judy Garland; *Best Of Judy Garland* . . . . (MCA)

Sweet Sixteen
Big Joe Turner; *Big Joe Turner's Greatest Hits.* . . . . (Atlantic)

Sweet Talking Woman
Electric Light Orchestra; *Afterglow* . . . . (Epic)
Box Of Their Best . . . .(Jet)
Electric Light Orchestra's Greatest Hits . . . .(Jet)
Out Of The Blue . . . .(Jet)

Sweet Woman (From Maine)
Robert Lockwood, Jr.; *Blues Masters-#2-Post-War Chicago Blues-C* . . . (Rhino)

Sweet Woman Like You
Joe Tex; *Billboard Top R&B Hits-1965-1969-C* . . . . (Rhino)
I Believe I'm Gonna Make It!-Best Of Joe Tex . . . . (Rhino)
Joe Tex's Greatest Hits . . . .(Curb)

Swimsuit Issue
Sonic Youth; *Dirty.* . . . .(David Geffen Co.)

Swingin'
Tom Petty And The Heartbreakers; *Echo* . . . . (Warner Bros.)

Swiss Army Girl
Scatterbrain; *Scamboogery* . . . . (Elektra)

Swiss Maid
Del Shannon; *Del Shannon-Legends* . . . .(Laurie)
Del Shannon's Greatest Hits . . . .(Rhino)

Swiss Miss
Fred Astaire; *Crazy Feet!* . . . . (ASV Living Era)

Take Back Your Mink
Original Cast; *Guys & Dolls* . . . . (MCA)

Take Time To Know Her
Percy Sledge; *Best Of Percy Sledge* . . . . (Atlantic)
It Tears Me Up-Best Of Percy Sledge . . . . (Rhino)

Talkin' 'Bout Women Obviously
Buddy Guy/Junior Mance/Junior Wells; *Buddy & The Juniors.* . . . . . . (MCA)

Tallahassee Lassie
Freddy Cannon; *14 Booming Hits* . . . . (Rhino)
Freddy Cannon-His Latest & Greatest . . . . (Critique)
Partytime '50s-C . . . .(Priority)

Tarot Woman
Blackmore's Rainbow; *Rainbow Rising* . . . . (Polydor)

Tear For The Girl
Martha Reeves & The Vandellas; *Live Wire! Singles-1962-1972* . . . . . (Motown)

Telephone Girl
Eddie & The Hot Rods; *Life On The Line* . . . . (Island)

Telephone Girl
Jade Warrior; *Jade Warrior.* . . . .(Vertigo)

Telephone Girlie
Original Cast/Ruby Keeler; *No No Nanette* . . . .(RCA)

Television Girl
Atlantics; *Big City Rock.* . . . . (MCA)

Tell Her About It
Billy Joel; *An Innocent Man* . . . .(Columbia)
Billy Joel-Greatest Hits, Volume I & Volume II . . . .(Columbia)

Tell Her No
Juice Newton; *Dirty Looks* . . . .(Capitol)
Juice Newton-Greatest Hits & More. . . . .(Capitol)
Zombies; *Best Of The Rest Of The Zombies.* . . . .(Bac-Trac)
History Of British Rock-#2-C . . . .(Rhino)
Live On The BBC . . . .(Rhino)
Time Of The Zombies . . . .(Bac-Trac)

Ten Girls Ago
Graham Parker; *Best Of Graham Parker 1988-1991* . . . .(RCA)

Tennessee Girl
Charley Pride; *Charley Pride Live.* . . . .(RCA)

Tennessee Whiskey & Texas Women
Rayburn Anthony; *Audiograph Alive-C* . . . . (Audiograph)
Dance Floor Crystal Ball . . . . (Audiograph)

Texas Tattoo
Gibson/Miller Band; *Steppin' Country-C* . . . .(Columbia)
Where There's Smoke . . . . (Epic)

Texas Tornado
Tracy Lawrence; *Best Of Tracy Lawrence.* . . . . (Atlantic)
I See It Now . . . . (Atlantic)

Texas Twister
Little Feat; *Representing The Mambo* . . . .(Warner Bros.)

Texas Woman Blues
Taj Mahal; *Recycling The Blues & Other Related Stuff* . . . .(Columbia)

Texas Women
Hank Williams, Jr.; *Hank Williams, Jr.'s Greatest Hits* . . . .(WB/Curb)
Rowdy . . . .(WB/Curb)

Texas Women (Don't Stay Lonely Long)
Brooks & Dunn; *Hard Workin' Man* . . . .(Arista)

Thank God For Believers
Mark Chesnutt; *Thank God For Believers* . . . .(Decca)

Thank Heaven For Little Girls
Maurice Chevalier; *ST/Gigi* . . . . (Sony Music Special Prod.)
Merle Haggard & Janie Fricke; *It's All In The Game* . . . .(Epic)

Thank You Girl
Beatles; *Beatles-Box Set.* . . . .(Capitol)
Past Masters-Volume One. . . . . (Parlophone)
The Beatles' Second Album . . . .(Capitol)

Thank You Girl
John Hiatt; *Bring The Family* . . . .(A&M)

Thank You Pretty Baby
Brook Benton; *Brook Benton-At His Best* . . . . (Pair)
It's Just A Matter Of Time-His Greatest Hits . . . .(Mercury)
Professor Longhair; *'Fess-Anthology* . . . .(Rhino)

That Girl
Crosby, Stills, Nash & Young; *American Dream.* . . . . (Atlantic)

That Girl
Maxi Priest featuring Shaggy; *Man With The Fun* . . . . (Virgin)
Reggae Party 1999-C . . . .(Island)

That Girl
Bad Company; *Fame & Fortune* . . . . (Atlantic)

That Girl
Glenn Frey; *No Fun Aloud* . . . . (Asylum)

That Girl
Stevie Wonder; *Original Musiquarium* . . . .(Motown)

That Girl Belongs To Yesterday
Gene Pitney; *Gene Pitney-Anthology 1961-1968.* . . . .(Rhino)

That Girl Could Sing
Jackson Browne; *Hold Out.* . . . . (Asylum)

That Girl Wants To Dance With Me
Gregory Hines; *Gregory Hines* . . . . (Epic)

That Girl Who Waits On Tables
Ronnie Milsap; *Collector's Series-Ronnie Milsap* . . . . (RCA)
Where My Heart Is . . . . (RCA)

That Girl's A Slut
Just-Ice; *Rapmasters 7-Best Of The Laughs-C* . . . . (Priority)

That Girl's Been Spyin' On Me
Billy Dean; *It's What I Do* . . . .(Capitol)

That Kind Of Woman
Eric Clapton; *Nobody's Child-Romanian Angel Appeal-C* . . . . . .(Warner Bros.)
Gary Moore; *Still Got The Blues* . . . .(Charisma)

That Lady
Isley Brothers; *Isley Brothers' Greatest Hits* . . . .(T-Neck/Columbia)
Rock Artifacts-From The Vaults-#1-C. . . . .(Columbia)
The Isley Brothers Story-#2-The T-Neck Years-1969-1985. . . . .(Rhino)

That Summer
Garth Brooks; *The Chase* . . . .(Liberty)

That Thing You Do!
Wonders; *ST/That Thing You Do!* . . . . (Epic)

That's All She Wrote
Rick Nelson; *Garden Party* . . . .(MCA Special Prod.)
Rick Nelson Sings ''For You''. . . . . (MCA)

That's All She Wrote
Ghetto Girlz; *Ain't Takin' No S@#T* . . . .(Heat Wave)

That's All She Wrote
Marty Robbins; *Come Back To Me* . . . .(Columbia)

That's All She Wrote
Conway Twitty; *Hello Darlin'.* . . . .(MCA Special Prod.)

That's All She Wrote
Reba McEntire; *Rumor Has It* . . . . (MCA)

That's Another Song
Bryan White; *Between Now And Forever* . . . . (Asylum)

That's Not Her Style
Billy Joel; *Storm Front.* . . . .(Columbia)

That's What Girls Are Made For
Spinners; *One Of A Kind Love Affair-Anthology* . . . .(Rhino)
Tammi Terrell; *Irresistible.* . . . .(Motown)

That's Where My Money Goes
101 Strings Orchestra; *Beer Drinkin' Sing Alongs!!* . . . .(Alshire)

Theme From ''Charlie's Angels''
Original Soundtrack; *Television's Greatest Hits-#3-1970s & 1980s-C* . . . .(TVT)
TV Classic Themes: 25th Anniversary Edition-C . . . . (Breakable)

Theme From ''Designing Women'' (Georgia On My Mind)
Original Soundtrack; *Television's Greatest Hits-#7-Cable Ready-C* . . . . . .(TVT)

Theme From ''Golden Girls''
Original Soundtrack; *Television's Greatest Hits-#6-Remote Control-C* . . .(TVT)

Theme From ''Police Woman''
Original Soundtrack; *Television's Greatest Hits-#5-In Living Color-C* . . . .(TVT)

Theme From "That Girl"
Original Soundtrack; *Television's Greatest Hits-#2-C* . . . . (TVT)
Theme From "The Bionic Woman"
Original Soundtrack; *Television's Greatest Hits-#5-In Living Color-C* . . . (TVT)
Theme From "The Girl From U.N.C.L.E."
Original Soundtrack; *Television's Greatest Hits-#5-In Living Color-C* . . . (TVT)
Theme From "The Miss America Pageant" (There She Is, Miss America)
Bert Parks; *Television's Greatest Hits-#4-Black & White Classics-C* . . . . (TVT)
Then I Kissed Her
Beach Boys; *California Girls* . . . . (Capitol)
 Sunshine Dream . . . . (Capitol)
 Today/Summer Days (& Summer Nights!) . . . . (Capitol)
There Is Nothin' Like A Dame
Original Cast; *South Pacific* . . . . (CBS Masterworks)
There Once Was A Man
Original Cast; *Pajama Game* . . . . (Columbia)
 ST/Pajama Game . . . . (Collectables)
There She Goes
Bob Marley & The Wailers; *One Love* . . . . (Heartbeat)
There She Goes
Sixpence None The Richer; *Sixpence None The Richer* . . . . . (Squint/Columbia)
There She Goes
Babyface; *Face 2 Face* . . . . (Arista)
There She Goes
Chambers Brothers; *Best Of The Chambers Brothers* . . . . (Fantasy)
There She Goes
Jerry Wallace; *Jerry Wallace's Greatest Hits* . . . . (Curb)
There She Goes
La's; *La's* . . . . (London)
There She Goes
Beat; *ST/Caddyshack* . . . . (Columbia)
There's A Girl
Original Broadway Cast; *Secret Garden* . . . . (Columbia)
There's A Tennessee Woman/Ben's Song
Tanya Tucker; *Tennessee Woman* . . . . (Capitol)
There's A Whole Lot About A Woman (A Man Don't Know)
Jack Greene; *45-#32823* . . . . (Decca)
There's The Girl
Heart; *Bad Animals* . . . . (Capitol)
They Don't Make 'Em Like That Anymore
Boy Howdy; *She'd Give Anything* . . . . (Curb)
They'll Never Take Her Love From Me
Emmylou Harris; *Blue Kentucky Girl* . . . . (Warner Bros.)
George Jones; *George Jones Sings The Great Songs Of Leon
 Payne* . . . . (Hollywood/DNA-Rounder)
Hank Williams With His Drifting Cowboys; *Hank Williams-24 Greatest
 Hits-#2* . . . . (Polydor)
 Hank Williams-40 Greatest Hits . . . . (Polydor)
This Ain't Tennessee & She Ain't You
Tom Jones; *Don't Let Our Dreams Die Young* . . . . (Mercury)
This Girl Is A Woman Now
Gary Puckett And The Union Gap; *Best Of Gary
 Puckett* . . . . (Hollywood/DNA-Rounder)
 Gary Puckett And The Union Gap's Greatest Hits . . . . (Columbia)
 Looking Glass-Collection . . . . (Columbia)
This Girl's In Love With You
Dionne Warwick; *Dionne Warwick-At Her Very Best* . . . . (Pair)
Petula Clark; *Greatest Hits Of Petula Clark* . . . . (Crescendo)
This Little Girl
Dion; *Bronx Blues-Columbia Recordings 1962-1965* . . . . (Columbia)
 Dion-24 Original Classics . . . . (Arista)
Gary U.S. Bonds; *Cover Me (Bruce Springsteen Tribute)-C* . . . . (Rhino)
Gary U.S. Bonds & Bruce Springsteen; *Dedication* . . . . (Razor & Tie)
This Little Girl Of Mine
Everly Brothers; *Everly Brothers-Cadence Classics-Their 20
 Greatest Hits* . . . . (Rhino)
Herbie Mann; *Best Of Herbie Mann* . . . . (Atlantic)
Ray Charles; *Atlantic Rhythm & Blues 1947-1974-#2 (1952-1955)-C* . . (Atlantic)
 Birth Of Soul-Complete Atlantic R&B 1952-1959-C . . . . (Atlantic)
 Life In Music . . . . (Atlantic)
This Woman
K.T. Oslin; *K.T. Oslin's Greatest Hits: Songs From An Aging
 Sex Bomb* . . . . (RCA)
 This Woman . . . . (RCA)
This Woman
Kenny Rogers; *Eyes That See In The Dark* . . . . (RCA)
This Woman And This Man
Clay Walker; *If I Could Make A Living* . . . . (Giant)
This Woman Needs
SHeDAISY; *The Whole Shebang* . . . . (Lyric Street)
This Woman's Work
Kate Bush; *Sensual World* . . . . (Columbia)
 ST/She's Having A Baby . . . . (I.R.S.)
This Year's Girl
Elvis Costello; *2 1/2 Years* . . . . (Rykodisc)
 Girls Girls Girls . . . . (Columbia)
 This Year's Model . . . . (Rykodisc)

Thorn Tree In The Garden
Derek And The Dominos; *Layla* . . . . (Polydor)
Three Drunken Maidens
Maddy Prior & Tim Hart; *Summer Solstice* . . . . (Shanachie)
Three Girls From Detroit
Will & The Bushmen; *Will & The Bushmen* . . . . (SBK)
Three Times A Lady
Commodores; *All The Great Love Songs-Commodores* . . . . (Motown)
 Commodores Greatest Hits . . . . (Motown)
 Commodores-All The Great Hits . . . . (Motown)
 Endless Love-Motown's Greatest Love Songs-C . . . . (Motown)
 Natural High . . . . (Motown)
Thundercrack
Bruce Springsteen; *Tracks* . . . . (Columbia)
Ticket To Ride
Beatles; *Beatles 1* . . . . (Capitol)
 Beatles-20 Greatest Hits . . . . (Capitol)
 Beatles-Box Set . . . . (Capitol)
 Reel Music . . . . (Capitol)
 ST/Help! . . . . (Capitol)
 The Beatles At The Hollywood Bowl . . . . (Capitol)
 The Beatles/1962-1966 . . . . (Capitol)
Carpenters; *Carpenters-Classics-#2* . . . . (A&M)
 Carpenters-The Singles 1969-1973 . . . . (A&M)
 From The Top . . . . (A&M)
 Ticket To Ride . . . . (A&M)
 Yesterday Once More . . . . (A&M)
Vanilla Fudge; *Best Of Vanilla Fudge* . . . . (Atco)
 Vanilla Fudge . . . . (Atco)
Tiger In A Dress
Dan Reed Network; *Slam* . . . . (Mercury)
Tiger Woman
Claude King; *American Originals-Claude King* . . . . (Columbia)
 Claude King's Best . . . . (Gusto)
To All The Girls I've Loved Before
Julio Iglesias & Willie Nelson; *1100 Bel Air Place* . . . . (Columbia)
Merle Haggard & Janie Fricke; *It's All In The Game* . . . . (Epic)
Willie Nelson & Julio Iglesias; *Greatest Country Hits Of The '80s-
 1984-C* . . . . (Columbia)
 Half Nelson-C . . . . (Columbia)
To Ev'ry Girl-To Ev'ry Boy (The Meaning Of Love)
Johnnie Ray; *45-#40252* . . . . (Columbia)
Tomorrow's Girls
Donald Fagen; *Kamakiriad* . . . . (Reprise)
Tonight Carmen
Marty Robbins; *American Originals-Marty Robbins* . . . . (Columbia)
 Essential Marty Robbins-1951-1982 . . . . (Columbia)
 Marty Robbins' All-Time Greatest Hits . . . . (Columbia)
Too Busy Thinking About My Baby
Manhattan Transfer; *Tonin'* . . . . (Atlantic)
Marvin Gaye; *Every Great Motown Hit Of Marvin Gaye* . . . . (Motown)
 Superhits . . . . (Motown)
Too Good To Be True
Michael Peterson; *Michael Peterson* . . . . (Reprise)
Trailer Park Woman
Pinkard & Bowden; *Cousins Cattle & Other Love Stories* . . . . . . (Warner Bros.)
Train That Carried My Girl From Town, The
Doc Watson; *Essential Doc Watson* . . . . (Vanguard)
Watson Family; *Watson Family* . . . . (Smithsonian Folkways)
Trapped In The Body Of A White Girl
Julie Brown; *Trapped In The Body Of A White Girl* . . . . (Sire)
Trashy Lady
Neon Judgement; *Horny As Hell* . . . . (Play It Again Sam)
Trashy Women
Confederate Railroad; *Confederate Railroad* . . . . (Atlantic)
Travelin' Man
Ricky Nelson; *Best Of Ricky Nelson* . . . . (EMI)
 Rick Nelson's Greatest Hits . . . . (Rhino)
Treat Her Like A Lady
Cornelius Brothers & Sister Rose; *Billboard Top Rock 'N' Roll Hits-
 1971-C* . . . . (Rhino)
 Didn't It Blow Your Mind: Soul Hits Of The '70s-#5-C . . . . (Rhino)
Johnny Lee; *Best Of Johnny Lee* . . . . (Curb)
Treat Her Like A Lady
Celine Dion; *Let's Talk About Love-C* . . . . (550 Music)
Treat Her Like A Lady
Joe; *My Name Is Joe* . . . . (Jive)
Treat Her Like A Lady
Jimmy Buffett; *Boats Beaches Bars & Ballads* . . . . (Margaritaville)
 Volcano . . . . (MCA)
Treat Her Like A Lady
Temptations; *Temptations-Anthology-The Best Of The Temptations* . . (Motown)
 Truly For You . . . . (Motown)
Treat Her Right
Commitments; *ST/The Commitments* . . . . (MCA)
George Thorogood & The Destroyers; *Born To Be Bad* . . . . (Gold Rush)
Roy Head And The Traits; *Billboard Top Rock 'N' Roll Hits-1965-C* . . . (Rhino)
Treat Her Right
Sawyer Brown; *This Thing Called Wantin' & Havin' It All* . . . . (Curb)

Trials
Jackopierce; *Finest Hour* . . . . (A&M)
T-R-O-U-B-L-E
Elvis Presley; *A Touch Of Platinum-#2* . . . . (RCA)
Travis Tritt; *Travis Tritt's Greatest Hits-From The Beginning* . . . (Warner Bros.)
T-R-O-U-B-L-E . . . . (Warner Bros.)
Trouble Man
Angie Stone; *Black Diamond* . . . . (Arista)
Truck Drivin' Girl
Bonny Boekeker; *45-#1357.* . . . . (Accent)
Truck Stop Girl
Byrds; *The Byrds* . . . . (Columbia)
The Byrds (Untitled) . . . . (Legacy)
Little Feat; *Little Feat* . . . . (Warner Bros.)
Trying To Love Two Women
Oak Ridge Boys; *Oak Ridge Boys' Greatest Hits* . . . . (MCA)
Oak Ridge Boys-Collection. . . . . (MCA)
Together . . . . (MCA)
Tupelo Honey
Van Morrison; *Van Morrison* . . . . (Warner Bros.)
Twelve Thirty (Young Girls Are Coming To The Canyon)
Mamas & The Papas; *Best Of The Mamas & The Papas* . . . . (MCA)
Mamas & The Papas-16 Of Their Greatest Hits . . . . (MCA)
The Papas & The Mamas . . . . (MCA)
Twentieth Century Fox
Doors; *Doors* . . . . (Elektra)
Twenty-Nine Ways (To My Baby's Door)
Koko Taylor; *Koko Taylor.* . . . . (Chess)
South Side Lady . . . . (Evidence Music)
Marc Cohn; *Marc Cohn.* . . . . (Atlantic)
Willie Dixon; *The Chess Box-Willie Dixon* . . . . (Chess)
Twist, Twist Senora
Gary U.S. Bonds; *Best Of Gary U.S. Bonds* . . . . (Rhino)
Let's Twist!-C . . . . (K-Tel)
School Of Rock 'N' Roll-Best Of Gary U.S. Bonds . . . . (Rhino)
Two Hot Girls (On A Hot Summer Night)
Carly Simon; *Carly Simon-Greatest Hits Live.* . . . . (Arista)
Coming Around Again . . . . (Arista)
Two Ladies
Original Cast; *Cabaret.* . . . . (Columbia)
Two Little Girls
Ani DiFranco; *Little Plastic Castle* . . . . (Righteous Babe)
Ugliest Girl In The World
Bob Dylan; *Down In The Groove* . . . . (Columbia)
Ugly Girl
Fleming & John; *The Way We Are.* . . . . (Universal)
Under My Thumb
Rolling Stones; *"Still Life" (American Concert 1981).* . . . . (Virgin)
12 X 5 . . . . (Abkco)
Aftermath . . . . (Abkco)
got Live if you want it!. . . . . (Abkco)
Hot Rocks 1964-1971 . . . . (Abkco)
Who; *Odds & Sods* . . . . (MCA)
Who's Missing . . . . (MCA)
Undun
Guess Who; *American Woman, These Eyes & Other Hits* . . . . (RCA)
Best Of The Guess Who. . . . . (RCA)
Union Maid
Judy Collins; *Tribute To Woody Guthrie-C* . . . . (Warner Bros.)
Unlucky Girl
Big Mama Thornton; *Ball N' Chain* . . . . (Arhoolie)
Until She Comes
Psychedelic Furs; *World Outside.* . . . . (Columbia)
Unusually Unusual
Lonestar; *I'm Already There* . . . . (BNA)
Uptown Girl
Billy Joel; *An Innocent Man* . . . . (Columbia)
Billy Joel-Greatest Hits, Volume I & Volume II . . . . (Columbia)
KOHUEPT . . . . (Columbia)
Vagabond Virgin
Traffic; *Traffic.* . . . . (Island)
Venom Wearin' Denim
Junior Brown; *Semi Crazy.* . . . . (Curb)
Venus In Blue Jeans
Jimmy Clanton; *All-Star Chartbusters* . . . . (Intermedia)
Golden Years-1962-C. . . . . (Dominion Entert.)
Volcano Girls
Veruca Salt; *Eight Arms To Hold You* . . . . (Geffen)
Voodoo Woman
Koko Taylor; *I Got What It Takes* . . . . (Alligator)
Voodoo Woman
Bobby Goldsboro; *Honey-Best Of Bobby Goldsboro* . . . . (EMI)
Waitress In The Sky
Replacements; *Tim* . . . . (Sire)
Walk This Way
Aerosmith; *Aerosmith-Classics Live 2* . . . . (Columbia)
Aerosmith's Greatest Hits. . . . . (Columbia)
Live! Bootleg . . . . (Columbia)

Pandora's Box. . . . . (Columbia)
Toys In The Attic . . . . (Columbia)
Run-D.M.C.; *Mr. Magic's Rap Attack-C* . . . . (Profile)
Raising Hell. . . . . (Profile)
Rap's Biggest Hits-C . . . . (K-Tel)
Walks Like A Lady
Journey; *Departure* . . . . (Columbia)
Journey-Captured . . . . (Columbia)
Wannagirl
Jeremy Jordan; *Try My Love* . . . . (Giant)
War Widow
Country Joe McDonald; *War War War* . . . . (Vanguard)
Warm Beer & Cold Women
Tom Waits; *Nighthawks At The Diner* . . . . (Asylum)
Watch The Girl Destroy Me
Possum Dixon; *Possum Dixon* . . . . (Interscope)
Way She Loves Me
Richard Marx; *Paid Vacation.* . . . . (Capitol)
Ways Of A Woman In Love
Johnny Cash; *Best Of Johnny Cash* . . . . (Curb)
Essential Johnny Cash . . . . (Columbia)
Johnny Cash-Sun Years. . . . . (Rhino)
We Gotta Get You A Woman
Todd Rundgren; *Runt.* . . . . (Rhino)
Todd Rundgren-Anthology 1968-1985 . . . . (Rhino)
West End Girls
Pet Shop Boys; *Disco.* . . . . (EMI)
Discography-Complete Singles Collection . . . . (EMI)
Please . . . . (EMI)
West Texas Women
Whistlin' Alex Moore; *I'm Wild About My Lovin'-1928-1930* . . . . . (Historical)
Western Girls
Marty Stuart; *Hillbilly Rock* . . . . (MCA)
What A Girl Wants
Christina Aguilera; *Christina Aguilera* . . . . (RCA)
Totally Hits-#3-C . . . . (Atlantic)
What A Way To Go
Ray Kennedy; *What A Way To Go* . . . . (Atlantic)
What Does A Woman See In A Man
Jimmy Webb; *Suspending Disbelief.* . . . . (Elektra)
What It Feels Like For A Girl
Madonna; *GHV2* . . . . (Warner Bros.)
Music. . . . . (Maverick)
What She Don't Know Won't Hurt Her
Gene Watson; *Gene Watson's Greatest Hits* . . . . (MCA)
What She Is (Is A Woman In Love)
Earl Thomas Conley; *Heart Of It All* . . . . (RCA)
What She Said
Smiths; *Meat Is Murder* . . . . (Sire)
Rank . . . . (Sire)
What She's Doing Now
Garth Brooks; *Ropin' The Wind* . . . . (Liberty)
What The Cowgirls Do
Vince Gill; *When Love Finds You* . . . . (MCA)
What You Want
DMX; *...And Then There Was X* . . . . (Ruff Ryders/IDJMG)
What's New Pussycat
Tom Jones; *Tom Jones-London Collector-Greatest Hits* . . . . (London)
What's Your Name
Lynyrd Skynyrd; *Gold & Platinum* . . . . (MCA)
Skynyrd's Innards-Their Greatest Hits . . . . (MCA)
Street Survivors. . . . . (MCA)
What's Your Name . . . . (MCA Special Prod.)
When A Man Loves A Woman
Bette Midler; *ST/The Rose* . . . . (Atlantic)
Michael Bolton; *Time, Love & Tenderness* . . . . (Columbia)
Percy Sledge; *Atlantic Rhythm & Blues 1947-1974-#5 (1962-*
1966)-C . . . . (Atlantic)
Atlantic Soul Classics-C . . . . (Warner Special Prod.)
Best Of Percy Sledge. . . . . (Atlantic)
Golden Age Of Black Music-1960-1970-C . . . . (Atlantic)
ST/Platoon . . . . (Atlantic)
When A Man Loves A Woman
Barbara Mandrell; *Best Of Barbara Mandrell* . . . . (Liberty)
Key's In The Mailbox . . . . (Capitol)
When A Woman Doesn't Want You
Elton John; *The One.* . . . . (MCA)
When A Woman Loves A Man
Lee Roy Parnell; *We All Get Lucky Sometimes* . . . . (Career)
When A Woman's Fed Up
R. Kelly; *Now That's What I Call Music!-#2-C* . . . . (Virgin)
R. . . . . (Jive)
When Boy Meets Girl
Terri Clark; *Terri Clark* . . . . (Mercury)
When God Fearin' Women Get The Blues
Martina McBride; *Martina McBride's Greatest Hits* . . . . (RCA)
When It Comes To You
John Anderson; *Seminole Wind* . . . . (BNA)

When It Comes To You
Dire Straits; *On Every Street*. . . . .(Warner Bros.)
When My Baby Smiles At Me
Pete Fountain; *Best Of Pete Fountain* . . . .(MCA)
Ted Lewis & His Orchestra; *Music From The New York Stage (1890-1920)-*
#4-1917-1920-C . . . . (Pearl)
When She Cries
Restless Heart; *Big Iron Horses* . . . . (RCA)
Restless Heart's Greatest Hits . . . . (RCA)
Today's Number One Country-C . . . . (K-Tel)
When She Was My Girl
Four Tops; *When She Was My Girl* . . . . (Casablanca)
When You Love A Woman
Journey; *Trial By Fire* . . . . (Columbia)
Whenever You Come Around
Vince Gill; *When Love Finds You* . . . .(MCA)
Where The Blue Of The Night Meets The Gold Of The Day
Bing Crosby; *All-Time Best Of* . . . . (Curb)
Best Of Bing Crosby . . . .(MCA)
Where The Blue Of The Night Meets The Gold Of The Day . . . .(Biograph)
Where's The Love
Hanson; *Middle Of Nowhere* . . . . (Mercury)
Whiskey And Wimmen
John Lee Hooker; *Best Of John Lee Hooker* . . . .(Vee-Jay)
Best Of John Lee Hooker . . . .(Crescendo)
Infinite Boogie . . . . (Rhino)
Real Blues Brothers-C . . . .(Dunhill Compact Classics)
World's Greatest Blues Singer . . . . (Vee-Jay)
Whiskey, If You Were A Woman
Highway 101; *Highway 101* . . . .(Warner Bros.)
Highway 101's Greatest Hits . . . .(Warner Bros.)
White Trash Wife
Exene Cervenka; *Old Wives' Tales* . . . . (Rhino)
Who Needs You Baby
Clay Walker; *Hypnotize The Moon* . . . . (Giant)
Who's That Girl
Madonna; *ST/Who's That Girl* . . . . (Sire)
Wicker Man
Iron Maiden; *Brave New World* . . . . (Portrait)
Wide Open Spaces
Dixie Chicks; *Big Country Hits '99-C* . . . . (K-Tel)
Wide Open Spaces . . . . (Monument)
Wife & The Whore
Kristin Lems; *Born A Woman* . . . . (Flying Fish)
Wild One
Faith Hill; *Take Me As I Am* . . . .(Warner Bros.)
Wild Thing
Jimi Hendrix; *Essential Jimi Hendrix, Volume 2* . . . . (Reprise)
Live At Winterland . . . .(Rykodisc)
ST/Jimi Plays Monterey . . . . (Reprise)
Tone Loc; *Loc-ed After Dark* . . . .(Delicious Vinyl)
Rap's Biggest Hits-C . . . . (K-Tel)
Rock The First-#6-C . . . . (Sandstone Music)
Troggs; *Billboard Top Rock 'N' Roll Hits-1966-C* . . . . (Rhino)
Frat Rock!-C . . . . (Rhino)
History Of British Rock-#3-C . . . . (Rhino)
Wild Wild Women
Henry Lewis; *Music From The New York Stage (1890-1920)-#4-1917-*
1920-C . . . . (Pearl)
Wild Women Do
Natalie Cole; *ST/Pretty Woman* . . . .(EMI)
Wildfire Woman
Bad Company; *Straight Shooter* . . . . (Swan Song)
Wind Blows Her Hair
Seeds; *Nuggets-#9-Acid Rock-C* . . . . (Rhino)
Wink
Neal McCoy; *No Doubt About It* . . . .(Atlantic)
Witchy Woman
Eagles; *Eagles* . . . . (Asylum)
Eagles/Their Greatest Hits 1971-1975 . . . . (Asylum)
Without Her
Nilsson; *Pandemonium Shadow Show* . . . . (RCA)
Wives Are In Connecticut
Carly Simon; *Spoiled Girl* . . . .(Epic)
Woman
John Lennon; *ST/Imagine: John Lennon* . . . . (Capitol)
The John Lennon Collection . . . . (Capitol)
John Lennon & Yoko Ono; *Double Fantasy* . . . . (Capitol)
Woman
Peter And Gordon; *Best Of Peter And Gordon* . . . . (Rhino)
History Of British Rock-#4-C . . . . (Rhino)
Woman
James Gang; *Best Of The James Gang* . . . .(MCA)
James Gang Rides Again . . . .(MCA)
James Gang-16 Greatest Hits . . . .(MCA)
Woman
Scorpions; *Face The Heat* . . . . (Mercury)
Woman
Womack & Womack; *Love Wars* . . . . (Elektra)

Woman
Simple Minds; *Real Life* . . . . (A&M)
Woman (Sensuous Woman)
Don Gibson; *Don Gibson-18 Greatest Hits* . . . . (Curb)
Mark Chesnutt; *Almost Goodbye* . . . .(MCA)
Woman At Home
Country Joe McDonald; *Tribute To Woody Guthrie-C* . . . . (Warner Bros.)
Woman Before Me
Trisha Yearwood; *Trisha Yearwood* . . . . (MCA)
Woman Behind The Man Behind The Wheel
Red Sovine; *Truckin' On-C* . . . . (Hollywood)
Woman From Tokyo
Deep Purple; *Deepest Purple/The Very Best Of Deep Purple* . . . . (Warner Bros.)
Nobody's Perfect . . . . (Mercury)
When We Rock We Rock & When We Roll We Roll. . . . . (Warner Bros.)
Who Do You Think We Are . . . . (Warner Bros.)
Woman In Love
Barbra Streisand; *A Collection: Greatest Hits...And More* . . . . (Columbia)
Guilty . . . . (Columbia)
Woman In Love
Frankie Laine; *Frankie's Gold-Greatest Hits-#2* . . . .(Playback)
Woman In Love
Ronnie Milsap; *Ronnie Milsap's Greatest Hits-#3* . . . . (RCA)
Stranger Things Have Happened . . . . (RCA)
Woman In Me
Jessica Simpson featuring Destiny's Child; *Sweet Kisses* . . . . (Columbia)
Woman In Me (Needs The Man In You)
Shania Twain; *Woman In Me* . . . . (Mercury)
Woman In Texas
Jerry Jeff Walker; *Live At Gruene Hall* . . . . (Rykodisc)
Woman Is The Nigger Of The World
John Lennon; *Live In New York City* . . . . (Capitol)
John Lennon/Plastic Ono Band; *Lennon* . . . . (Capitol)
Shaved Fish . . . . (Capitol)
Some Time In New York City . . . . (Capitol)
Woman Loves
Steve Wariner; *I Am Ready* . . . . (Arista)
Woman Of Heart & Mind
Joni Mitchell; *For The Roses*. . . . .(Asylum)
Joni Mitchell with Tom Scott & The L.A. Express; *Miles Of Aisles* . . . .(Asylum)
Woman Of The Year
Original Cast; *Woman Of The Year* . . . .(Bay Cities)
Woman Power
Yoko Ono; *Walking On Thin Ice Compilation* . . . . (Rykodisc)
Woman To Woman
Tammy Wynette; *Tammy Wynette-Anniversary-20 Years Of Hits* . . . . (Epic)
Tammy Wynette's Greatest Hits-#3 . . . . (Epic)
Tears Of Fire-25th Anniversary Collection . . . . (Epic)
Wynonna; *Tammy Wynette...Remembered-C* . . . . (Asylum)
Woman To Woman
Jewell; *ST/Murder Was The Case* . . . . (Death Row/Interscope)
Woman To Woman
Beverley Craven; *Beverley Craven* . . . . (Epic)
Woman To Woman
Joe Cocker; *Joe Cocker-Classics-#4* . . . . (A&M)
Joe Cocker's Greatest Hits. . . . . (A&M)
Woman To Woman
Shirley Brown; *Didn't It Blow Your Mind: Soul Hits Of The*
'70s-#15-C. . . . . (Rhino)
Top Of The Stax-Twenty Greatest Hits-C . . . . (Stax)
Woman To Woman . . . . (Stax)
Woman Tonight
America; *Hearts* . . . . (Warner Bros.)
History-Greatest Hits. . . . . (Warner Bros.)
Woman Walk The Line
Emmylou Harris; *Ballad Of Sally Rose* . . . . (Warner Bros.)
Highway 101; *Featuring Paulette Carlson* . . . . (Warner Bros.)
Trisha Yearwood; *Hearts In Armor* . . . . (MCA)
Woman, A Lover, A Friend
Jackie Wilson; *Jackie Wilson's Greatest Hits-#2* . . . . (Brunswick)
Mr. Excitement . . . . (Rhino)
Otis Redding; *The Otis Redding Story*. . . . . (Atlantic)
Woman, Woman
Union Gap Featuring Gary Puckett; *Best Of Gary*
Puckett. . . . .(Hollywood/DNA-Rounder)
Gary Puckett And The Union Gap's Greatest Hits . . . . (Columbia)
Woman's Got A Right To Change Her Mind
Rex Stewart & The Ellingtonians; *Rex Stewart & The*
Ellingtonians . . . . (Riverside)
Woman's Gotta Have It
LV; *How Long*. . . . .(Loud)
Woman's Needs, A
Tammy Wynette & Elton John; *Without Walls-C* . . . . (Epic)
Woman's Point Of View
Shirley Murdock; *Woman's Point Of View* . . . . (Elektra)
Woman's Prerogative
Pearl Bailey; *Pearl Bailey-16 Most Requested Songs* . . . . (Legacy)

Woman's Smarter
Jolly Boys; *Sunshine 'N' Water* . . . . (Rykodisc)
Woman's Threat
R. Kelly; *TP-2.com* . . . . (Jive)
Woman's Touch
Toby Keith; *Blue Moon* . . . . (Polydor Country)
Woman's Worth, A
Alicia Keys; *Songs In A Minor* . . . . (J)
Women Be Wise
Bonnie Raitt; *Bonnie Raitt* . . . . (Warner Bros.)
Women Walk More Determined
Kristin Lems; *Oh Mama!* . . . . (Carolsdatter Prod.)
Women Will Rule The World
Ry Cooder; *Get Rhythm* . . . . (Warner Bros.)
Women's Love Rights
Laura Lee; *Laura Lee's Greatest Hits* . . . . (HDH)
Words Of Love
Mamas & The Papas; *Best Of The Mamas & The Papas* . . . . (MCA)
Farewell To The First Golden Era . . . . (MCA)
Mamas & The Papas-16 Of Their Greatest Hits . . . . (MCA)
Mama's Big Ones-Her Greatest Hits . . . . (MCA)
XXX's And OOO's
Trisha Yearwood; *Thinkin' About You* . . . . (MCA)
Yankee Rose
David Lee Roth; *Eat 'Em & Smile* . . . . (Warner Bros.)
Yellow Gal
Leadbelly; *Leadbelly* . . . . (Fantasy)
Legend Of Leadbelly . . . . (Tradition)
Memorial-#2 . . . . (Stinson)
Take This Hammer . . . . (Smithsonian Folkways)
Yellow Rose Of Texas
Hoyt Axton; *Songs Of The Civil War-C* . . . . (Columbia)
Michael Martin Murphey; *Cowboy Songs* . . . . (Warner Western)
Mitch Miller; *Mitch Miller-16 Most Requested Songs* . . . . (Columbia)
Roy Rogers; *Great American Singing Cowboys-C* . . . . . (Republic/Universal)
Yellow Woman's Door Bells
Leadbelly; *Leadbelly* . . . . (Fantasy)
Leadbelly . . . . (Everest)
Yes!
Chad Brock; *Yes!* . . . . (Warner Bros.)
Yessir, That's My Baby
Frank Sinatra; *Strangers In The Night* . . . . (Reprise)
Milt Jackson; *Best Of Milt Jackson* . . . . (Pablo)
Mom & Dads; *Dance With The Mom & Dads* . . . . (Crescendo)
Very Best Of The Mom & Dads . . . . (Crescendo)
Yesterday's Girl
Hank Thompson; *Hank Thompson-20 Greatest Hits* . . . . (Deluxe)
Hank Thompson's Greatest Songs-#1 . . . . (Curb)
You Ain't Much Fun
Toby Keith; *Boomtown* . . . . (Polydor Country)
You Are My Lady
Freddie Jackson; *Greatest Hits Of Freddie Jackson* . . . . (Capitol)
You Are The Woman
Firefall; *Firefall* . . . . (Rhino)
Firefall's Greatest Hits . . . . (Rhino)
You Gotta Love That
Neal McCoy; *Neal McCoy's Greatest Hits* . . . . (Atlantic)
Today's Country Love-C . . . . (K-Tel)
You Gotta Love That! . . . . (Atlantic)
You Need A Woman Tonight
Captain & Tennille; *Dreams* . . . . (A&M)
You Should Hear How She Talks About You
Melissa Manchester; *Hey Ricky* . . . . (Arista)
Melissa Manchester's Greatest Hits . . . . (Arista)
Young And Beautiful
Elvis Presley; *A Valentine Gift For You* . . . . (RCA)
Heart & Soul . . . . (RCA)
The Other Sides-Worldwide Gold Award Hits, Vol. 2 . . . . (RCA)
Young And Beautiful
Peter And Gordon; *Woman/Lady Godiva* . . . . (Collectables)
Young Girl
Union Gap Featuring Gary Puckett; *Billboard Top Pop Hits-1968-C* . . . . (Rhino)
Young Girl Blues
Sammy Hagar; *All Night Long* . . . . (One Way)
Young Lust
Pink Floyd; *1980-1981 Wall Live-Is There Anybody Out There* . . . . (Columbia)
The Wall . . . . (Columbia)
Roger Waters & Bryan Adams; *The Wall-Live In Berlin* . . . . (Mercury)
Young Man, Older Woman
Millie Jackson; *Very Best Of Millie Jackson* . . . . (Jive)
Young Woman's Blues
Bessie Smith; *Bessie Smith-The Collection* . . . . (Legacy)
Bessie Smith-The Complete Recordings-#3 . . . . (Legacy)
Younger Girl
Critters; *Sixties Rule! Chapter Two-C* . . . . (One Way)
Lovin' Spoonful; *Lovin' Spoonful-Anthology* . . . . (Rhino)
Your Good Girl's Gonna Go Bad
Billie Jo Spears; *Best Of Billie Jo Spears* . . . . (CEMA Special Prod.)

Best Of Billie Jo Spears . . . . (Razor & Tie)
K.T. Oslin; *Tammy Wynette...Remembered-C* . . . . (Asylum)
Tammy Wynette; *Tammy Wynette-Anniversary-20 Years Of Hits* . . . . . . (Epic)
Tammy Wynette's Greatest Hits . . . . (Epic)
Your Good Girl's Gonna Go Bad . . . . (Legacy)
Your Woman
White Town; *MTV The Grind-#1-C* . . . . (Tommy Boy)
Women In Technology . . . . (Chrysalis)
You're A Big Girl Now
Bob Dylan; *Blood On The Tracks* . . . . (Columbia)
You're A Man Of Words, I'm A Woman
Betty LaVette; *Lost Soul-#1-C* . . . . (Epic)
You're Going To Lose That Girl
Beatles; *ST/Help!* . . . . (Capitol)
You're Lost, Little Girl
Doors; *Doors 13* . . . . (Elektra)
Strange Days . . . . (Elektra)
You've Got It Bad Girl
Quincy Jones; *Best Of Quincy Jones-#2* . . . . (A&M)
Quincy Jones-Classics-#3 . . . . (A&M)
Stevie Wonder; *Talking Book* . . . . (Motown)

WOMEN'S NAMES: A

See Also: CELEBRITIES: SPECIFIC, FAMILY (various),
WOMEN: GENERAL

Abigail Beecher
Freddy Cannon; *14 Booming Hits* . . . . (Rhino)
Big Blast From Boston: The Best Of Freddy ''Boom Boom''
Cannon . . . . (Rhino)
Adalida
George Strait; *Latest Greatest Straitest Hits* . . . . (MCA)
Lead On . . . . (MCA)
Adelaide's Lament
Original Cast; *Guys & Dolls* . . . . (MCA)
Guys & Dolls . . . . (Motown)
Adia
Sarah McLachlan; *Mirrorball* . . . . (Arista)
Surfacing . . . . (Arista)
Alberta
Doc Watson; *Essential Doc Watson* . . . . (Vanguard)
Southbound . . . . (Vanguard)
Alberta
John Lee Hooker; *Alone* . . . . (Specialty)
Alberta
Leadbelly; *Leadbelly* . . . . (Columbia)
Alberta
Maxwell Street Jimmy; *Rare Blues* . . . . (Takoma)
Alberta
Blind Snooks Eaglin; *Rural Blues* . . . . (Fantasy)
Alexis From Texas
Red Steagall; *Lone Star Beer & Bob Wills Music* . . . . (MCA)
Alice Blue Gown
Edith Day; *Music From The New York Stage (1890-1920)-#4-1917-*
1920-C . . . . (Pearl)
Nipper's Greatest Hits Of The '20s-C . . . . (RCA)
Alice In Wonderland
Neil Sedaka; *Neil Sedaka's All-Time Greatest Hits* . . . . (RCA)
Alice You've Made Dallas (Paradise)
Lee Ferrell; *Hard Times* . . . . (TMS)
Alice's Restaurant Massacree
Arlo Guthrie; *Alice's Restaurant* . . . . (Reprise)
Best Of Arlo Guthrie . . . . (Warner Bros.)
Alison
Elvis Costello; *Girls Girls Girls* . . . . (Columbia)
My Aim Is True . . . . (Columbia)
Elvis Costello & The Attractions; *Best Of Elvis Costello & The*
Attractions . . . . (Columbia)
All My Ex's Live In Texas (Allison)
George Strait; *Country Classics-#10-1987-C* . . . . (Universal)
George Strait's Greatest Hits-#2 . . . . (MCA)
Ocean Front Property . . . . (MCA)
All The Girls Love Alice
Elton John; *Goodbye Yellow Brick Road* . . . . (Polydor)
Allison Road
Gin Blossoms; *New Miserable Experience* . . . . (A&M)
Amanda
Don Williams; *Don Williams' Greatest Hits* . . . . (MCA)
Volume One . . . . (MCA)
Waylon Jennings; *Waylon Jennings' Greatest Hits* . . . . (RCA)
Amanda
Dionne Warwick; *Dionne Warwick-Anthology 1962-1971* . . . . (Rhino)
Amanda
Boston; *Third Stage* . . . . (MCA)
Amanda Jewell
Ricky Skaggs and Kentucky Thunder; *Bluegrass Rules!* . . . . (Rounder)

Amelia
  Gretchen Peters; *Gretchen Peters* . . . . (Purple Crayon Prod.)
Amelia Earhart
  BTO; *Rock 'N' Roll Nights* . . . . (Mercury)
American Pie
  Don McLean; *American Pie* . . . .(EMI)
    Best Of Don McLean . . . .(EMI)
    Greatest Hits Then & Now . . . .(EMI)
    ST/Born On The Fourth Of July . . . .(MCA)
  Madonna; *ST/The Next Big Thing* . . . .(Maverick)
Amie
  Pure Prairie League; *Bustin' Out* . . . . (RCA)
    Jukebox Saturday Night-C . . . . (RCA)
    Let Me Love You Tonight & Other Hits . . . . (RCA)
    Takin' The Stage . . . . (RCA)
Amoreena
  Elton John; *Tumbleweed Connection* . . . . (Polydor)
Amphetamine Annie
  Canned Heat; *Best Of Canned Heat* . . . .(EMI)
    Boogie With . . . . (Liberty)
Amy's Back In Austin
  Little Texas; *Kick A Little* . . . .(Warner Bros.)
    Little Texas' Greatest Hits . . . .(Warner Bros.)
Ana's Song (Open Fire)
  Silverchair; *Neon Ballroom* . . . .(Epic)
Angel Angelina
  George Strait; *Beyond The Blue Neon* . . . .(MCA)
Angelia
  Richard Marx; *Repeat Offender* . . . .(EMI)
Angeline Is Coming Home
  Badlees; *River Songs* . . . . (Atlas)
Angie
  Rolling Stones; *Goats Head Soup* . . . .(Rolling Stones)
    Made In The Shade . . . .(Rolling Stones)
    Rewind (1971-1984) . . . .(Rolling Stones)
Angie Baby
  Helen Reddy; *Helen Reddy's Greatest Hits* . . . . (Capitol)
Angie Girl
  Stevie Wonder; *Motown Legends-Stevie Wonder* . . . . (Motown)
    My Cherie Amour . . . . (Motown)
Anita Goes To China
  David Hayes; *Logos Through A Sideman* . . . . (Gold Castle)
Anita, You're Dreaming
  Waylon Jennings; *Best Of Waylon Jennings* . . . . (RCA)
    Waylon Jennings-Early Years . . . . (RCA)
Anna
  Beatles; *Beatles-Box Set* . . . . (Capitol)
    Please Please Me . . . . (Parlophone)
    The Early Beatles . . . . (Capitol)
Anna
  Toto; *Seventh One* . . . . (Columbia)
Anna Begins
  Counting Crows; *August And Everything After* . . . . (David Geffen Co.)
Anna In Indiana
  Eddie Cantor; *Rare Early Recordings-1919-1921* . . . .(Biograph)
Annalee The Healer
  Beach Boys; *Friends-20/20* . . . . (Capitol)
Anne Frank Story
  Human Sexual Response; *Fig. 15* . . . .(Eat)
Annie Get Your Yo Yo
  Junior Parker; *Best Of Junior Parker* . . . .(MCA)
  Little Junior Parker; *Annie Get Your Yo Yo* . . . .(MCA Special Prod.)
Annie Had A Baby
  Hank Ballard And The Midnighters; *Cruisin'-1955-C* . . . .(Increase)
Annie Laurie
  King's Singers; *Annie Laurie-Folk Songs Of British Isles* . . . . (Angel)
Annie Mae's Cafe
  Little Milton; *Annie Mae's Cafe* . . . . (Malaco)
Annie Waits
  Ben Folds; *Rockin' The Suburbs* . . . .(Epic)
Annie's Song
  John Denver; *Back Home Again* . . . . (RCA)
    Evening With John Denver . . . . (RCA)
    John Denver's Greatest Hits-#2 . . . . (RCA)
Arizona
  Mark Lindsay; *Super Hits Of The '70s-Have A Nice Day-#1-C* . . . . (Rhino)
Aubrey
  Bread; *Best Of Bread-#2* . . . .(Elektra)
    Bread-Anthology . . . . (Elektra)
Aunt Alicia
  Original Cast; *ST/Gigi* . . . .(Sony Music Special Prod.)
Aunt Avis
  Widespread Panic; *Bombs & Butterflies* . . . . (Capricorn)
Ava Adore
  Smashing Pumpkins; *Adore* . . . . (Virgin)
Avenging Annie
  Andy Pratt; *Andy Pratt* . . . . (Columbia)
  Roger Daltrey; *Best Bits* . . . .(MCA)

Dallas Alice
  Doug Sahm; *She's About A Mover: The Best Of Doug Sahm* . . . .(Edsel)
  Sir Douglas Quintet; *The Crazy Cajun Recordings* . . . .(Edsel)
Don't Look Back
  Bruce Springsteen; *Tracks* . . . . (Columbia)
  Knack; *One Step Up/Two Steps Back-The Songs Of Bruce*
    Springsteen-C . . . . (Right Stuff)
    Retrospective-Best Of The Knack . . . . (Gold Rush)
Don't Look Back (Angel)
  Bruce Springsteen; *Tracks* . . . . (Columbia)
  Knack; *One Step Up/Two Steps Back-The Songs Of Bruce*
    Springsteen-C . . . . (Right Stuff)
    Retrospective-Best Of The Knack . . . . (Gold Rush)
Dreamboat Annie
  Heart; *Dreamboat Annie* . . . . (Capitol)
    Heart's Greatest Hits/Live . . . . (Epic)
Flaming Agnes
  Original Broadway Cast; *I Do! I Do!* . . . . (RCA Victor)
Gentle Annie
  Kate & Anna McGarrigle; *The McGarrigle Hour* . . . .(Hannibal)
  Linda Ronstadt; *Linda Ronstadt-Box Set* . . . . (Elektra)
  Makem & Clancy; *The Makem & Clancy Collection* . . . .(Shanachie)
Has Anybody Seen Amy
  John & Audrey Wiggins; *John & Audrey* . . . . (Mercury)
Heartbreaker (Annie)
  Led Zeppelin; *Led Zeppelin II* . . . .(Atlantic)
    Led Zeppelin-The Complete Studio Recordings . . . .(Atlantic)
Isn't She Lovely (Aiesha)
  Keb' Mo'; *Big Wide Grin* . . . . (Sony Wonder)
  Lee Ritenour; *Best Of Lee Ritenour* . . . . (Epic)
  Stevie Wonder; *Original Musiquarium* . . . . (Motown)
    Songs In The Key Of Life . . . . (Motown)
Living Next Door To Alice
  Johnny Carver; *Best Of Johnny Carver* . . . . (MCA)
Louisiana Anna
  Maines Brothers Band; *High Rollin'* . . . . (Mercury)
Mail Order Annie
  Harry Chapin; *Gold Medal Collection* . . . . (Elektra)
    Short Stories . . . . (Elektra)
Miami, My Amy
  Keith Whitley; *Keith Whitley's Greatest Hits* . . . . (RCA)
    L.A. To Miami . . . . (RCA)
    Star Spangled Country-C . . . . (RCA)
Miss Amanda Jones
  Rolling Stones; *Between The Buttons* . . . .(Abkco)
Miss America
  Styx; *Caught In The Act* . . . . (A&M)
    Grand Illusion . . . . (A&M)
    Styx-Classics-#15 . . . . (A&M)
Miss America
  Mark Lindsay; *Mark Lindsay: Golden Classics* . . . . (Collectables)
Miss America
  Big Dish; *Satellites* . . . . (East West)
My Angeline
  Bing Crosby; *Crooner-Columbia Years-1928-1934* . . . . (Columbia)
My Antonia
  Emmylou Harris; *Red Dirt Girl* . . . . (Nonesuch)
My Baby You (Arianna)
  Marc Anthony; *Marc Anthony* . . . . (Columbia)
Once In Love With Amy
  Barry Manilow; *Showstoppers* . . . . (Arista)
  Lawrence Welk; *My Personal Favorites* . . . . (Ranwood)
  Mel Torme; *Swings Shubert Alley* . . . . (Verve)
Polk Salad Annie
  Elvis Presley; *Elvis As Recorded At Madison Square Garden* . . . .(RCA)
  Tony Joe White; *Soul Shots-#6-Blue-Eyed Soul-C* . . . . (Rhino)
    Swingin' Country Favorites-C . . . . (Warner Bros.)
Pretty Little Adriana
  Vince Gill; *High Lonesome Sound* . . . . (MCA)
Ragtime Annie
  Byron Berline; *Dad's Favorites* . . . . (Rounder)
  Mason Williams; *Fresh Fish-C* . . . . (Flying Fish)
Saint Agnes & The Burning Train
  Sting; *Soul Cages* . . . . (A&M)
Skin & Bone (Annie)
  Kinks; *Celluloid Heroes* . . . . (RCA)
    Everybody's In Show-Biz . . . . (Rhino)
    Muswell Hillbillies . . . . (VelVel)
    The Kinks' Greatest-Celluloid Heroes . . . . (RCA)
Smooth Criminal (Annie)
  Alien Ant Farm; *Alien Ant Farm-Anthology* . . . .(DreamWorks/SKG)
  Michael Jackson; *Bad* . . . . (Epic)
Sweet Adeline
  Tommy Dorsey; *Best Of Tommy Dorsey* . . . . (MCA)
  Tommy Dorsey & His Orchestra; *Big Bands Greatest*
    Hits-#2-C . . . . (MCA Special Prod.)
Sweet Angeline
  Mott The Hoople; *Mott The Hoople-Live* . . . . (Columbia)

One Of The Boys . . . . (MCA)

The Ballad Of Mott: A Retrospective . . . . (Columbia)
Sweet Angeline
David Allan Coe; *Just Divorced* . . . . (Columbia)
Texas Ann
Joe Beck; *Beck & Sanborn* . . . . (CBS Associated)
Theme From "Alice"
Original Soundtrack; *Television's Greatest Hits-#6-Remote Control-C* . . . (TVT)
Time After Time (Annelise)
R.E.M.; *Reckoning* . . . . (I.R.S.)
Wax Ecstatic (To Sell Angeline)
Sponge; *Wax Ecstatic* . . . . (Columbia)
White Rabbit
Damned; *Best Of The Damned* . . . . (Roadracer)
Machine Gun Etiquette . . . . (Roadracer)
George Benson; *George Benson-Collection* . . . . (Warner Bros.)
White Rabbit . . . . (CBS Associated)
Jefferson Airplane; *2400 Fulton Street-An Anthology* . . . . (RCA)
Flight Log (1966-1976) . . . . (Grunt)
Loves You . . . . (RCA)
ST/Platoon . . . . (Atlantic)
Surrealistic Pillow . . . . (RCA)
The Worst Of Jefferson Airplane . . . . (RCA)
Work With Me Annie
Hank Ballard And The Midnighters; *Best Of Hank Ballard And The
Midnighters-Sexy Ways* . . . . (Rhino)
Royals; *Risque Rhythms: Nasty '50s R&B-C* . . . . (Rhino)
Wrong Way (Annie)
Sublime; *Sublime* . . . . (Gasoline Alley)
Yes, Anastasia
Tori Amos; *Under The Pink* . . . . (Atlantic)

WOMEN'S NAMES: B

**See Also: CELEBRITIES: SPECIFIC, FAMILY (various),
WOMEN: GENERAL**

1959 (Betty)
John Anderson; *Country Love Songs-#3-C* . . . . (Warner Bros.)
John Anderson's Greatest Hits . . . . (Warner Bros.)
Aunt Bee
Andy Griffith; *The Andy Griffith Show* . . . . (EMI Special Markets)
Ballad Of Bonnie And Clyde
Georgie Fame; *History Of British Rock-#8-C* . . . . (Rhino)
Barbara Allen
Joan Baez; *Ballad Book-#2* . . . . (Vanguard)
Joan Baez, Vol. 2 . . . . (Vanguard)
The Joan Baez Ballad Book . . . . (Vanguard)
Tom Rush; *Blues Songs & Ballads* . . . . (Fantasy)
Tom Rush . . . . (Fantasy)
Barbara Ann
Beach Boys; *Beach Boys '69 (The Beach Boys Live In London)* . . . . . . (Capitol)
Beach Boys-Gift Set . . . . (Capitol)
Best Of The Beach Boys-#2 . . . . (Capitol)
Frat Rock!-C . . . . (Rhino)
Spirit Of America . . . . (Capitol)
Regents; *Cruisin'-1961-C* . . . . (Increase)
Original Rock 'N' Roll Hits Of The '60s-C . . . . (Roulette)
ST/American Graffiti . . . . (MCA)
Who; *Who's Missing* . . . . (MCA)
Barbi Doll
Barbara Weathers; *Barbara Weathers* . . . . (Reprise)
Barbie & Ken
Weathermen; *Black Album According To The
Weathermen* . . . . (Play It Again Sam)
Barbie & Ken Ferrari
John Hiatt; *Perfectly Good Guitar* . . . . (A&M)
Barbie Doll Look
Sky Saxon; *Best Of Rodney On The 'ROQ* . . . . (Posh Boy)
Barbie Girl
Aqua; *Aquarium* . . . . (MCA)
Now That's What I Call Music!-#1-C . . . . (Virgin)
Becky Is Back In The Ballet
Fanny Brice; *Music From The New York Stage (1890-1920)-#4-1917-
1920-C* . . . . (Pearl)
Belle
Al Green; *Belle Album* . . . . (Motown)
Tokyo...Live . . . . (Right Stuff)
Belle, Belle, My Liberty Belle
Guy Mitchell; *Definitive Guy Mitchell* . . . . (Collector's Choice)
Guy Mitchell-16 Most Requested Songs . . . . (Legacy)
Bernadette
Four Tops; *Compact Command Performances-Four Tops* . . . . (Motown)
Four Tops' Greatest Hits . . . . (Motown)
Four Tops Reach Out . . . . (Motown)
Four Tops-Anthology . . . . (Motown)
Motown Superstar Series-#14-Four Tops . . . . (Motown)

Bess You Is My Woman Now
Miles Davis & His Orchestra; *Porgy & Bess* . . . . (Columbia)
Original Cast; *Porgy & Bess* . . . . (MCA)
Beth
Kiss; *Alive II.* . . . . (Casablanca)
Destroyer. . . . . (Casablanca)
Double Platinum . . . . (Mercury)
Smashes, Thrashes & Hits. . . . . (Mercury)
Bette Davis Eyes
Kim Carnes; *Best Of Kim Carnes* . . . . (EMI Special Markets)
Billboard Top Hits-1981-C . . . . (Rhino)
Mistaken Identity . . . . (EMI)
Betty Lou's Gettin' Out Tonight
Bob Seger & The Silver Bullet Band; *Against The Wind* . . . . (Capitol)
Nine Tonight . . . . (Capitol)
Betty's Bein' Bad
Sawyer Brown; *Best Of Country Rock-C* . . . . (K-Tel)
Sawyer Brown's Greatest Hits . . . . (Curb)
Shakin' . . . . (Curb)
Billie Jean
Michael Jackson; *Thriller* . . . . (Epic)
Billie's Blues
Billie Holiday; *Billie's Blues* . . . . (Blue Note)
Essential Billie Holiday-Carnegie Hall Concert . . . . (Verve)
I Like Jazz-Essence Of Billie Holiday . . . . (Columbia)
Songbook . . . . (Verve)
Billie's Bounce
Charlie Parker; *The Charlie Parker Story* . . . . (Savoy Jazz)
Count Basie & His Orchestra; *Best Of Count Basie & His Orchestra* . . . (Pablo)
Shelly Manne; *The Tree & The Two* . . . . (Contemporary)
Stan Getz; *Artistry Of Stan Getz-#2* . . . . (Verve)
Blackberry
Black Crowes; *Three Snakes And One Charm* . . . . (American)
Bobbie Ann Mason
Rick Trevino; *Looking For The Light* . . . . (Columbia)
Bobby Jean
Bruce Springsteen; *Born In The U.S.A.* . . . . (Columbia)
Bruce Springsteen & The E Street Band; *Bruce Springsteen & The E Street
Band Live/1975-85.* . . . . (Legacy)
Bonnie Jean (Little Sister)
David Lynn Jones; *Best Of Country Rock-C* . . . . (K-Tel)
Hard Times On Easy Street . . . . (Mercury)
Brandy
Looking Glass; *Billboard Top Rock 'N' Roll Hits-1972-C* . . . . (Rhino)
Rock Artifacts-From The Vaults-#2-C . . . . (Legacy)
Brenda's Got A Baby
Tupac; *2Pacalypse Now* . . . . (Priority)
Build Me Up Buttercup
Foundations; *Billboard Top Rock 'N' Roll Hits-1969-C* . . . . (Rhino)
History Of British Rock-#9-C . . . . (Rhino)
ST/There's Something About Mary . . . . (Capitol)
Come Back To Us Barbara Lewis Hare Krisha Beauregard
John Prine; *Common Sense* . . . . (Atlantic)
Great Days-Anthology . . . . (Rhino)
Prime Prine-The Best Of John Prine . . . . (Atlantic)
Happy Birthday, Mrs. J.J. Brown
Original Cast; *The Unsinkable Molly Brown* . . . . (EMI-Angel)
I'll Go Home With Bonnie Jean
Original Cast; *Brigadoon.* . . . . (RCA)
Kid's Last Fight
Frankie Laine; *Frankie Laine-16 Most Requested Songs* . . . . (Legacy)
Legend Of Bonnie And Clyde
Merle Haggard & The Strangers; *For The Record: Merle Haggard-43
Legendary Hits* . . . . (BNA)
Meanwhile Back At The Ranch (Blanche)
Clark Family Experience; *Meanwhile Back At The Ranch* . . . . (Curb)
Miss Blue
Filter; *Title Of Record* . . . . (Reprise)
Mrs. Brown You've Got A Lovely Daughter
Herman's Hermits; *Herman's Hermits-Their Greatest Hits* . . . . (Abkco)
Something Good Again . . . . (Abkco)
My Bonnie Lies Over The Ocean
Beatles With Tony Sheridan; *History Of British Rock-#5-C* . . . . . . (Rhino)
*The Beatles featuring Tony Sheridan-In The Beginning (Circa
1960)* . . . . (Polydor)
Ed McCurdy; *Best Of Ed McCurdy* . . . . (Tradition)
Mitch Miller; *Favorite Irish Sing-Alongs.* . . . . (Legacy)
My Name Is Barbra
Barbra Streisand; *Lazy Afternoon.* . . . . (Columbia)
Pictures Of Bernadette
Talk Talk; *45-#8326.* . . . . (EMI)
Please Don't Ask About Barbara
Bobby Vee; *Best Of Bobby Vee* . . . . (EMI)
Bobby Vee-Golden Greats. . . . . (Liberty)
Bobby Vee-Legendary Masters . . . . (EMI)
Very Best Of Bobby Vee. . . . . (Collectables)
Please Take A Letter Miss Brown
Ink Spots; *Best Of The Ink Spots.* . . . . (MCA)

Pucker Up Buttercup
Junior Walker & The All Stars; *Junior Walker & The All Stars'*
Greatest Hits . . . . (Motown)
Suite Madame Blue
Styx; *Caught In The Act* . . . . (A&M)
Equinox . . . . (A&M)
Styx-Classics-#15 . . . . (A&M)
Sweet Becky Walker
Larry Gatlin & The Gatlin Brothers Band; *Larry Gatlin & The Gatlin*
Brothers' Greatest Hits . . . . (Columbia)
Larry Gatlin & The Gatlin Brothers-17 Greatest Hits . . . . . (Columbia)
Sweet Betsy From Pike
Cisco Houston; *Cowboy Ballads* . . . . (Smithsonian Folkways)
Mormon Tabernacle Choir; *This Land Is Your Land* . . . . (Columbia)
Theme From ''Our Miss Brooks''
Original Soundtrack; *Television's Greatest Hits-#4-Black & White*
Classics-C . . . . (TVT)
Unfortunate Miss Bailey
Kingston Trio; *At Large/Here We Go Again!* . . . . (Capitol)
You Can Call Me Al (Betty)
Paul Simon; *Concert In The Park-August 15 1991* . . . .(Warner Bros.)
Graceland . . . .(Warner Bros.)
Negotiations And Love Songs, 1971-1986 . . . .(Warner Bros.)

WOMEN'S NAMES: C

See Also: **CELEBRITIES: SPECIFIC, FAMILY (various),**
WOMEN: GENERAL

Caldonia (What Makes Your Big Head So Hard?)
Louis Jordan; *No Moe! Louis Jordan's Greatest Hits* . . . . (Verve)
Original Cast; *Five Guys Named Moe* . . . . (Columbia)
Woody Herman & His Orchestra; *Verve Jazz Masters 54* . . . . (Verve)
Candida
Dawn; *Candida* . . . . (Razor & Tie)
Candy
Cameo; *12'' Collection And More* . . . . (Mercury)
Best Of Cameo . . . . (Mercury/Funk Essentials)
Billboard Top R&B Hits-1987-C . . . . (Rhino)
Greatest Hits . . . .(Chronicles)
Will Smith featuring Larry Blackmon; *Big Willie Style* . . . . (Columbia)
Candy Girl
4 Seasons; *25th Anniversary Collection* . . . . (Rhino)
4 Seasons-Anthology . . . . (Rhino)
Lil' Bit Of Gold 3'' CD Series-C . . . . (Rhino)
Candy-O
Cars; *Candy-O* . . . . (Elektra)
Just What I Needed: The Cars Anthology. . . . . (Rhino)
Candy's Room
Bruce Springsteen; *Darkness On The Edge Of Town* . . . . (Columbia)
Bruce Springsteen & The E Street Band; *Bruce Springsteen & The E Street*
Band Live/1975-85 . . . . (Legacy)
Carlene
Phil Vassar; *Phil Vassar* . . . . (Arista)
Carmelita
Linda Ronstadt; *Simple Dreams* . . . . (Asylum)
Warren Zevon; *Warren Zevon* . . . . (Asylum)
Carmen
Paula Cole; *This Fire* . . . . (Imago)
Carol
Chuck Berry; *Berry Is On Top* . . . . (Chess)
Chuck Berry-Golden Hits . . . . (Mercury)
Chuck Berry's Greatest Hits . . . . (Everest)
Roll Over Beethoven . . . .(Allegiance)
Rolling Stones; *England's Newest Hit Makers/The Rolling Stones* . . . . . (Abkco)
Get Yer Ya-Ya's Out! . . . . (Abkco)
Carolina Blues
Blues Traveler; *Straight On Till Morning* . . . . (A&M)
Caroline
Fleetwood Mac; *Tango In The Night* . . . .(Warner Bros.)
Caroline, No
Beach Boys; *Pet Sounds* . . . . (Capitol)
The Pet Sounds Sessions: A 30th Anniversary Collection . . . . . . (Capitol)
Caroline's Still In Georgia
Mac Davis; *Soft Talk.* . . . . (Casablanca)
Carolyn
Merle Haggard & The Strangers; *For The Record: Merle Haggard-43*
Legendary Hits . . . . (BNA)
Carrie
Michael Bolton; *Michael Bolton.* . . . . (Columbia)
Carrie
Europe; *Final Countdown.* . . . .(Epic)
Carrie-Anne
Hollies; *Best Of The Hollies* . . . .(EMI)
Evolution . . . .(Epic)
Hollies-Epic Anthology From The Original Master Tapes . . . .(Epic)
The Hollies' Greatest Hits . . . .(Epic)

Cathy's Clown
Everly Brothers; *Billboard Top Rock 'N' Roll Hits-1960-C* . . . . (Rhino)
Golden Hits Of The Everly Brothers . . . . (Warner Bros.)
The Reunion Concert-Live At Albert Hall 1983 . . . . (Mercury)
Very Best Of The Everly Brothers . . . . (Warner Bros.)
Reba McEntire; *Sweet Sixteen* . . . . (MCA)
Cecilia
Simon & Garfunkel; *Bridge Over Troubled Water* . . . . (Columbia)
Collected Works . . . . (Columbia)
Simon & Garfunkel's Greatest Hits . . . . (Columbia)
Charlotte The Harlot
Iron Maiden; *Iron Maiden* . . . . (Capitol)
Charlotte's Web
Statler Brothers; *10th Anniversary* . . . . (Mercury)
Charmaine
Frank Sinatra; *Frank Sinatra-Complete Reprise Studio Recordings* . . . . (Reprise)
Mantovani; *Mantovani-Golden Hits* . . . .(London)
Mom & Dads; *Good Night Sweetheart* . . . .(Crescendo)
Tommy Dorsey; *Best Of Tommy Dorsey* . . . . (MCA)
Cherry, Cherry
Neil Diamond; *Bang & Shout* . . . . (Bang)
Hot August Night . . . . (MCA)
Hot August Night II. . . . . (Columbia)
Neil Diamond-Classics (Early Years) . . . . (Columbia)
Neil Diamond-Gold . . . . (MCA)
Neil Diamond's Greatest Hits . . . . (Bang)
Shilo . . . . (Bang)
Cheryl
Charlie Parker; *Bird At The Hi-Hat* . . . . (Blue Note)
George Shearing & Don Thompson; *Live At The Cafe Carlyle* . . . (Concord Jazz)
Chewy Chewy
Ohio Express; *Best Of Ohio Express & Other Bubblegum*
Smashes-#1-C . . . . (Rhino)
Best Of Ohio Express & Other Bubblegum Smashes-#1-C . . . . (Rhino)
Bubblegum's Greatest Hits-#2-C . . . . (Accord)
Fabulous Bubblegum Years-C . . . . (Fifty One West)
Chloe
Al Jolson; *Music From The New York Stage (1890-1920)-#4-1917-*
1920-C . . . .(Pearl)
Christine
Broadside Singers & Tom Paxton; *Best Of Broadside 1962-1968: Anthems*
Of The American Underground From The Pages Of Broadside
Magazine-C . . . .(Smithsonian Folkways)
Christine 16
Kiss; *Alive II* . . . .(Casablanca)
Love Gun . . . .(Casablanca)
Cinderella
Britney Spears; *Britney* . . . .(Jive)
Cindy, Oh Cindy
Beach Boys; *Surfin' Safari-Surfin' Usa (Remasterd With Bonus*
Tracks). . . . . (Capitol)
Cindy's Birthday
Johnny Crawford; *Best Of Johnny Crawford.* . . . . (Rhino)
Super Oldies Of The '60s-#8-C . . . . (Audio Fidelity)
Cinnamon
Derek; *Rock Artifacts-From The Vaults-#3-C* . . . . (Columbia)
Clair
Gilbert O'Sullivan; *Super Hits Of The '70s-Have A Nice Day-#9-C* . . . . . (Rhino)
Claudette
Dwight Yoakam; *Under The Covers* . . . .(Reprise)
Everly Brothers; *Everly Brothers' Greatest Hits.* . . . .(Delta)
Everly Brothers-Cadence Classics-Their 20 Greatest Hits . . . . (Rhino)
Roy Orbison; *Roy Orbison-The Sun Years* . . . . (Rhino)
Very Best Of Roy Orbison. . . . . (Virgin)
Clementine
Bobby Darin; *Bobby Darin-At The Copa* . . . . (Bainbridge)
The Bobby Darin Story. . . . .(Atlantic)
Original Soundtrack; *Children's Favorites* . . . .(Kid Rhino/Rhino 4 Kids)
Cleopatra, Queen Of Denial
Pam Tillis; *Homeward Looking Angel* . . . . (Arista)
Cleopatra's Cat
Spin Doctors; *Turn It Upside Down* . . . . (Epic)
Close To Cathy
Mike Clifford; *'60s Dance Party-#2-C* . . . . (Dominion Entert.)
Cruisin'-1962-C . . . . (Increase)
Corrina, Corrina
Asleep At The Wheel featuring Brooks & Dunn; *Tribute To The Music Of*
Bob Wills And The Texas Playboys-C . . . .(Liberty)
Big Joe Turner; *Best Of Big Joe Turner.* . . . . (Pablo)
Big Joe Turner's Greatest Hits . . . .(Atlantic)
Bob Dylan; *Freewheelin'* . . . . (Columbia)
Ray Peterson; *Good Old Rock & Roll-C* . . . . (International Mktg. Group)
Super Hits-#1-C . . . . (Gusto)
Steppenwolf; *Live Steppenwolf.* . . . . (MCA)
Cynthia
Bruce Springsteen; *Tracks* . . . . (Columbia)
Don't Cry Cherie
Glenn Miller & His Orchestra; *Complete Glenn Miller & His*
Orchestra-#6 . . . . (Bluebird)

Don't Kill It Carol
Manfred Mann's Earth Band; *Angel Station* . . . . (Warner Bros.)
Happy Birthday Caroline
Concrete Blonde; *Free* . . . .(Capitol)
Recollection: The Best Of Concrete Blonde . . . .(Capitol)
Hey, Cinderella
Suzy Bogguss; *Something Up My Sleeve* . . . .(Liberty)
Hot Cherie
Hardline; *Double Eclipse* . . . . (MCA)
Hush, Hush, Sweet Charlotte
Al Martino; *Best Of Al Martino* . . . .(Capitol)
Patti Page; *Patti Page-Greatest Songs* . . . .(Curb)
I Want Candy
Bow Wow Wow; *Best Of Bow Wow Wow* . . . .(RCA)
I Want Candy . . . .(RCA)
Strangeloves; *Frat Rock!-#3-Grandson Of Frat Rock!-C* . . . .(Rhino)
John Deere Green (Charlene)
Joe Diffie; *A Thousand Winding Roads* . . . . (Epic)
Kiss For Cinderella
Michael Tilson Thomas; *Of Thee I Sing/Let 'Em Eat Cake* . . . . (Columbia)
Lawdy Miss Clawdy
Elvis Presley; *A Golden Celebration* . . . .(RCA)
Elvis . . . .(RCA)
Elvis Recorded Live On Stage In Memphis . . . .(RCA)
For LP Fans Only . . . .(RCA)
Rocker . . . .(RCA)
Joe Cocker; *Joe Cocker!* . . . .(A&M)
Lloyd Price; *Best Of New Orleans Rhythm & Blues-#2-C* . . . .(Rhino)
History Of New Orleans R&B-#1-1950-1958-C . . . .(Rhino)
Mrs. Clara Sullivan's Letter
Pete Seeger; *Best Of Broadside 1962-1968: Anthems Of The American*
Underground From The Pages Of Broadside
Magazine-C . . . .(Smithsonian Folkways)
Oh! Carol
Neil Sedaka; *Neil Sedaka Sings His Greatest Hits* . . . .(RCA)
Neil Sedaka's All-Time Greatest Hits . . . .(RCA)
Nipper's Greatest Hits Of The '50s-#1-C . . . .(RCA)
One Headlight (Cinderella)
Wallflowers; *Bringing Down The Horse* . . . . (Interscope)
Planet Claire
B-52's; *B-52's* . . . . (Warner Bros.)
Powder River/Carrie's Gone To Kansas City
Bill Shute & Lisa Null; *American Primitive* . . . . (Green Linnet)
Searchin' For Celine
Blue Oyster Cult; *Spectres* . . . .(Columbia)
Sweet Caroline
Neil Diamond; *Glory Road-1968-1972* . . . . (MCA)
Hot August Night . . . . (MCA)
Love At The Greek . . . . (Columbia)
Neil Diamond-Gold . . . . (MCA)
Neil Diamond-His 12 Greatest Hits . . . . (MCA)
Sweet Cleo Brown
Dave Brubeck; *Greatest Hits From The Fantasy Years* . . . .(Fantasy)
Tell It To Carrie
Romantics; *The Romantics* . . . .(Columbia)
What I Like About You (And Other Romantic Hits) . . . .(Nemperor)
Theme From "Cagney & Lacey"
Original Soundtrack; *CBS: The First 50 Years* . . . .(TVT)
Television's Greatest Hits-#6-Remote Control-C . . . .(TVT)
Theme From "Clarissa Explains It All"
Original Soundtrack; *Television's Greatest Hits-#7-Cable Ready-C* . . . . .(TVT)
Theme From "Cleopatra Jones"
Joe Simon featuring The Mainstreeters; *Didn't It Blow Your Mind: Soul Hits*
Of The '70s-#12-C . . . . (Rhino)
Super Bad On Celluloid: Music From '70s Black Cinema-C . . . .(Hip-O)
Theme From "The Carol Burnett Show"
Original Soundtrack; *CBS: The First 50 Years* . . . .(TVT)
Theme From "The Patty Duke Show" (Cathy)
Original Soundtrack; *Just Patty: The Best Of Patty Duke* . . . . (EMI)
Theme From "Where In The World Is Carmen Sandiego?"
Original Soundtrack; *Television's Greatest Hits-#7-Cable Ready-C* . . . . .(TVT)
They Don't Dance Like Carmen No More
Jimmy Buffett; *Boats Beaches Bars & Ballads* . . . . (Margaritaville)
White Sport Coat & A Pink Crustacean . . . . (MCA)

WOMEN'S NAMES: D

See Also: **CELEBRITIES: SPECIFIC, FAMILY (various),**
WOMEN: GENERAL

All My Ex's Live In Texas (Dimples)
George Strait; *Country Classics-#10-1987-C* . . . .(Universal)
George Strait's Greatest Hits-#2 . . . . (MCA)
Ocean Front Property . . . . (MCA)
Bicycle Built For Two (Daisy)
Kidsongs; *Cars, Boats, Trains, Planes* . . . .(Sony Wonder)

Daisy Jane
America; *America In Concert* . . . .(Capitol)
America Live . . . . (Warner Bros.)
Hearts . . . . (Warner Bros.)
History-Greatest Hits . . . . (Warner Bros.)
Dallas
Alan Jackson; *Don't Rock The Jukebox* . . . .(Arista)
Dancy's Dream
Restless Heart; *Fast Moving Train* . . . . (RCA)
Dandelion
Rolling Stones; *More Hot Rocks (big hits & fazed cookies)* . . . . (Abkco)
Through The Past, Darkly (Big Hits Vol. 2) . . . . (Abkco)
Dandy
Herman's Hermits; *Herman's Hermits-Their Greatest Hits* . . . . (Abkco)
Darlene
T. Graham Brown; *Come As You Were* . . . .(Capitol)
T. Graham Brown's Greatest Hits . . . .(Capitol)
Darlene
Led Zeppelin; *Coda* . . . . (Atlantic)
Dawn (Go Away)
4 Seasons; *25th Anniversary Collection* . . . .(Rhino)
4 Seasons-Anthology . . . .(Rhino)
Deborah
Dave Edmunds; *Best Of Dave Edmunds* . . . .(Swan Song)
Tracks On Wax 4 . . . .(Swan Song)
Dede Dinah
Frankie Avalon; *Frankie Avalon's Greatest Hits* . . . .(Everest)
Pick Of Frankie Avalon . . . . (Fifty One West)
Delia's Gone
Johnny Cash; *American Recordings* . . . .(American)
Delilah
Glenn Miller; *Best Of Glenn Miller-#3* . . . . (RCA)
Platters; *Platters-16 Greatest Hits* . . . . (Trip)
Tom Jones; *Live In Las Vegas* . . . .(Parrot)
Tom Jones-London Collector-Greatest Hits . . . . (London)
Delores
Mavericks; *Trampoline* . . . . (MCA)
Delta Dawn
Bette Midler; *Divine Miss M* . . . . (Atlantic)
Live At Last . . . . (Atlantic)
Helen Reddy; *Helen Reddy's Greatest Hits* . . . .(Capitol)
Tanya Tucker; *Tanya Tucker Live* . . . . (MCA Special Prod.)
Tanya Tucker-Greatest Hits Encore . . . . (Gold Rush)
Tanya Tucker's Greatest Hits . . . .(Columbia)
Denise
Randy & The Rainbows; *Doo-Wop Uptempo-#2-C* . . . .(Rhino)
Super Oldies Of The '60s-#4-C . . . . (Audio Fidelity)
WCBS FM 101 History Of Rock-'60s-#1-C . . . .(Collectables)
Desiree
Neil Diamond; *12 Greatest Hits-#2* . . . .(Columbia)
I'm Glad You're Here With Me Tonight . . . .(Columbia)
Diana
Paul Anka; *21 Legendary Superstars-C* . . . . (Original Sound)
Billboard Top Rock 'N' Roll Hits-1957-C . . . .(Rhino)
Paul Anka's 21 Golden Hits . . . . (RCA)
Diana
Eugene Wilde; *Serenade* . . . .(Phil World)
Diane
Bachelors; *Hard To Find 45s On CD-#2-1961-'64-C* . . . . (Eric)
Diane
Kentucky HeadHunters; *Electric Barnyard* . . . .(Mercury)
Dinah
Bing Crosby; *Bing Crosby-16 Most Requested Songs* . . . .(Legacy)
Cab Calloway; *Best Of The Big Bands-C* . . . .(Columbia)
Cliff Edwards; *Singin' In The Rain* . . . .(ASV)
Count Basie & Ethel Waters; *Tribute To Black Entertainers-C* . . . . . .(Columbia)
Duke Ellington; *Jubilee Stomp* . . . .(Bluebird)
Ethel Waters; *Am I Blue?* . . . .(ASV)
Fats Waller; *Ain't Misbehavin': 25 Greatest Hits* . . . . (Living Era)
Lionel Hampton & His Orchestra; *Tempo & Swing* . . . .(Bluebird)
Louis Armstrong; *Louis Armstrong-Vol. 6-St. Louis Blues* . . . .(Columbia)
Mills Brothers; *50th Anniversary* . . . .(Ranwood)
Dinah Flo
Boz Scaggs; *Hits!* . . . .(Columbia)
My Time . . . .(Columbia)
My Time: A Boz Scaggs Anthology-1969-1997 . . . .(Legacy)
Dirty Diana
Michael Jackson; *Bad* . . . . (Epic)
Dominique
Singing Nun; *Billboard Top Pop Hits-1963-C* . . . .(Rhino)
Donna
Los Lobos; *ST/La Bamba* . . . . (Slash)
Ritchie Valens; *American Graffiti-#3-C* . . . . (MCA)
Best Of Ritchie Valens . . . .(Rhino)
Heart & Soul Of Rock 'N' Roll-#1-C . . . .(Rhino)
History Of Latino Rock-#1-C . . . .(Rhino)
History Of Ritchie Valens . . . .(Rhino)
Donna Everywhere
Too Much Joy; *Mutiny* . . . . (Giant)

Donna From Mobile
Anne Hills; *Don't Panic (Panic Is On/Don't Explain)* . . . . (Hogeye)
Donna Lee
Art Pepper; *Arthur's Blues* . . . . (Galaxy)
Charlie Parker; *Genius Of Charlie Parker* . . . . (Savoy Jazz)
Claude Thornhill; *Be-Bop Era* . . . . (Columbia)
Donna The Prima Donna
Dion; *Bronx Blues-Columbia Recordings 1962-1965* . . . . (Columbia)
Dion-24 Original Classics . . . . (Arista)
Dulcinea
Original Cast; *ST/Man Of La Mancha* . . . . (MCA)
Dynamo Humm
Mothers; *Over-nite Sensation* . . . . (Rykodisc)
Hello Donna
Carol Channing/Original Cast; *Hello Dolly!.* . . . . (RCA)
Louis Armstrong; *Essential Louis Armstrong.* . . . . (Vanguard)
Vintage Music-#16-C. . . . . (MCA)
Original Cast; *Hello Dolly!.* . . . . (RCA)
Hey Donna
Rythm Syndicate; *Rythm Syndicate* . . . . (Impact)
I've Been Working On The Railroad (Dinah)
Mitch Miller; *Sing Along With Mitch* . . . . (Columbia)
Pete Seeger; *20 Golden Pieces Of Pete Seeger* . . . . (Bulldog)
Jack & Diane
John Cougar; *American Fool* . . . . (Riva)
Little Diane
Dion; *Dion-24 Original Classics* . . . . (Arista)
Dion And The Belmonts; *Everything You Always Wanted To Hear By* . . (Laurie)
Reunion-Live At Madison Square Garden 1972 . . . . (Rhino)
Oh Diane
Fleetwood Mac; *25 Years-The Chain* . . . . (Warner Bros.)
Pretty Donna
Collective Soul; *Hints, Allegations And Things Left Unsaid* . . . . (Atlantic)
Sam & Delilah
Original Cast; *Girl Crazy* . . . . (Sony Music Special Prod.)
Samson & Delilah
Blind Gary Davis; *Harlem Street Singer.* . . . . (Bluesville)
Reverend Gary Davis; *From Blues To Gospel* . . . . (Biograph)
Samson & Delilah
Blasters; *Blasters-Collection* . . . . (Slash)
Samson & Delilah
Grateful Dead; *Dead Set* . . . . (Arista)
Terrapin Station. . . . . (Arista)
Since Dolly Dimple Made A Hit
Grace Cameron; *Music From The New York Stage (1890-1920)-#1-1890-*
1908-C . . . . (Pearl)
Theme From ''The Donna Reed Show''
Original Soundtrack; *Donna Reed's Dinner Party-C* . . . . (Nick At Nite)
Television's Greatest Hits-#1-C . . . . (TVT)
TV Classic Themes: 25th Anniversary Edition-C. . . . . (Breakable)
Theme From ''The Dukes Of Hazzard''
Waylon Jennings; *Only Daddy That'll Walk The Line-The RCA Years* . . . (RCA)
Television's Greatest Hits-#6-Remote Control-C . . . . (TVT)
Waylon Jennings' Greatest Hits-#2 . . . . (RCA)
Tutti Frutti
Elvis Presley; *Elvis Presley* . . . . (RCA)
Rocker. . . . . (RCA)
Little Richard; *Greatest Hits Recorded Live* . . . . (Epic)
Little Richard. . . . . (Specialty)
Little Richard-18 Greatest Hits . . . . (Rhino)
More American Graffiti-C . . . . (MCA)
This Is How It All Began-#2-C. . . . . (Specialty)
Tribute To Black Entertainers-C . . . . (Columbia)
Queen; *Live At Wembley '86.* . . . . (Hollywood)
Waltz For Debby
Bill Evans; *Bill Evans-Complete Riverside Recordings* . . . . (Riverside)
New Jazz Conceptions . . . . (Riverside)
Bill Evans & Cannonball Adderley; *Know What I Mean?* . . . . (Riverside)
Tony Bennett; *Forty Years-The Artistry Of Tony Bennett.* . . . . (Columbia)
Tony Bennett & Bill Evans; *Tony Bennett & Bill Evans.* . . . . (Fantasy)
Toots Thielemans; *East Coast West Coast* . . . . (Private Music)
Who's Holding Donna Now
DeBarge; *DeBarge's Greatest Hits* . . . . (Motown)
Rhythm Of The Night . . . . (Motown)
Wild Horses (Diane)
Garth Brooks; *No Fences* . . . . (Capitol)

WOMEN'S NAMES: E

See Also: **CELEBRITIES: SPECIFIC, FAMILY (various),**
WOMEN: GENERAL

Check Yes Or No (Emmylou Hayes)
George Strait; *Strait Out Of The Box* . . . . (MCA)
Come On Eileen
Dexy's Midnight Runners; *Too-Rye-Ay* . . . . (Mercury)

Edna
Vernon Green & The Medallions; *Vernon Green & The Medallions-Golden*
Classics . . . . (Collectables)
Eileen
Keith Richards; *Main Offender* . . . . (Virgin)
Eleanor Rigby
Beatles; *Beatles 1* . . . . (Capitol)
Revolver. . . . . (Capitol)
The Beatles/1962-1966. . . . . (Capitol)
Ray Charles; *Ray Charles' Greatest Hits-#2.* . . . . (Rhino)
Ray Charles-Anthology . . . . (Rhino)
Elena
Marc Tanner Band; *No Escape* . . . . (Elektra)
Elenore
Turtles; *Best Of The Turtles-Golden Archive Series* . . . . (Rhino)
Oldies But Goodies-#7-C . . . . (Original Sound)
Super Oldies Of The '60s-#7-C . . . . (Audio Fidelity)
Turtles-20 Greatest Hits . . . . (Rhino)
Elizabeth
Statler Brothers; *Statler Brothers' Greatest Hits.* . . . . (Mercury)
Statler Brothers Today . . . . (Mercury)
Eloise
Kay Thompson; *Dr. Demento Presents The Greatest Novelty Records-#2-*
1950s-C . . . . (Rhino)
Eloise
David Frishberg; *Live At Vine Street* . . . . (Original Jazz Classics)
Eloise
Damned; *Light At The End Of The Tunnel.* . . . . (MCA)
Elsa
Bill Evans; *Compact Jazz-Bill Evans* . . . . (Verve)
Bill Evans & Eddie Gomez; *Montreux III* . . . . (Fantasy)
Elvira
Murry Kellum; *Country Comedy-20 Country Comedy Hits* . . . . (Plantation)
Oak Ridge Boys; *Fancy Free* . . . . (MCA)
MCA Records 30 Years Of Hits-1958-1988-C . . . . (MCA)
Oak Ridge Boys' Greatest Hits 2 . . . . (MCA)
Emily
Frank Sinatra; *Softly, As I Leave You.* . . . . (Reprise)
The Reprise Collection . . . . (Reprise)
Emily
Beth Nielsen Chapman; *Beth Nielsen Chapman* . . . . (Reprise)
Emily
Los Lobos; *Neighborhood.* . . . . (Slash)
Emily
4 Seasons; *Rarities-#2.* . . . . (Rhino)
Emily
Fear Of God; *Within The Veil* . . . . (Warner Bros.)
Emma
Hot Chocolate; *Super Hits Of The '70s-Have A Nice Day-#14-C* . . . . . (Rhino)
Emma Jean's Guitar
Chely Wright; *Let Me In* . . . . (MCA)
Erica
Jesse Colin Young; *Highway is For Heroes* . . . . (Cypress)
Ethelene (The Truckstop Queen)
Ray Stevens; *I Never Made A Record I Didn't Like.* . . . . (MCA)
Eva Braun (I Never Loved)
Boomtown Rats; *Tonic For The Troops* . . . . (Columbia)
Evangelina
Hoyt Axton; *Bread & Roses Festival Of Acoustic Music-#1-C* . . . . . . (Fantasy)
Evangeline
Emmylou Harris & The Band; *Duets-C.* . . . . (Reprise)
The Last Waltz . . . . (Warner Bros.)
Evangeline
Matthew Sweet; *Girlfriend* . . . . (Zoo)
Evangeline
Los Lobos; *How Will The Wolf Survive* . . . . (Slash)
Evangeline
Jerry Garcia Band; *Jerry Garcia Band* . . . . (Arista)
For Emily, Wherever I May Find Her
Simon & Garfunkel; *Collected Works* . . . . (Columbia)
Parsley Sage Rosemary & Thyme. . . . . (Columbia)
Simon & Garfunkel's Greatest Hits . . . . (Columbia)
In Memory Of Elizabeth Reid
Allman Brothers Band; *At Fillmore East* . . . . (Capricorn)
Beginnings . . . . (Polydor)
Decade Of Hits-1969-1979 . . . . (Polydor)
Letter To Elise
Cure; *Wish.* . . . . (Fiction/Elektra)
Miss Emily's Picture
John Conlee; *Country Gold-C.* . . . . (Priority)
John Conlee With Love. . . . . (MCA)
John Conlee's Greatest Hits. . . . . (MCA)
See Emily Play
David Bowie; *Bowie Pin Ups* . . . . (Rykodisc)
Pink Floyd; *Relics* . . . . (Capitol)
Works . . . . (Capitol)
Streak, The (Ethel)
Ray Stevens; *Ray Stevens' Greatest Hits.* . . . . (MCA)

Ray Stevens' Greatest Hits ....(RCA)
Ray Stevens-All-Time Greatest Comic Hits ....(Curb)
Super Hits Of The '70s-Have A Nice Day-#12-C ....(Rhino)
Sweet Eloise
Glenn Miller & His Orchestra; *Complete Glenn Miller & His*
Orchestra..(Bluebird)
Russ Morgan & His Orchestra; *Russ Morgan & His Orchestra Play 22*
Original Big Band Recordings.........................(Hindsight)
Tex Beneke & The Modernaires; *Reunion*....................(MCA)
Who's That Girl
Eve; *Scorpion* .... (Ruff Ryders/IDJMG)

WOMEN'S NAMES: F

See Also: **CELEBRITIES: SPECIFIC, FAMILY (various),**
WOMEN: GENERAL

El Paso (Felina)
Grateful Dead; *Steal Your Face*.......................(Grateful Dead)
Marty Robbins; *Billboard Top Country Hits-1960-C* .....(Rhino)
Gunfighter Ballads & Trail Songs.......................(Legacy)
Marty Robbins' Biggest Hits.........................(Columbia)
Radio Classics Of The '50s-C.........................(Columbia)
Fancy
Bobbi Gentry; *All-Time Country Classics-#1-C* ....(Capitol)
Reba McEntire; *Rumor Has It* .... (MCA)
Fancy Free
Oak Ridge Boys; *Fancy Free* .... (MCA)
Oak Ridge Boys' Greatest Hits 2 .... (MCA)
Fanny
Bee Gees; *Bee Gees' Greatest* .... (Polydor)
Main Course .... (RSO)
Fanny Mae
Buster Brown; *Billboard Top R&B Hits-1960-C*..........(Rhino)
Cruisin'-1960-C.................................... (Increase)
New King Of The Blues.............................(Collectables)
ST/American Graffiti............................... (MCA)
Elvin Bishop; *Alligator Records 20th Anniversary Collection-C* .....(Alligator)
Don't Let The Bossman Get You Down................(Alligator)
Joey Dee & the Starliters; *Hey Let's Twist! Best Of Joey Dee & The*
Starliters .... (Rhino)
Frances Farmer Will Have Her Revenge On Seattle
Nirvana; *In Utero*..............................(David Geffen Co.)
Frankie
Bruce Springsteen; *Tracks*...........................(Columbia)
Frankie & Johnny
Brook Benton; *Endlessly-The Best Of Brook Benton*...........(Rhino)
Doc Watson; *Favorites-Doc Watson* ....(Liberty)
Jerry Lee Lewis; *Jerry Lee's Greatest!* ....(Rhino)
Frankie & Johnny Blues
Glenn Yarbrough; *Best Of Glenn Yarbrough*....................(RCA)
Kay Starr; *Kay Starr-Country* ....(Crescendo)
Short Fat Fannie
Larry Williams; *Original Rock Oldies-Golden Hits-#1-C* .... (Specialty)
The Ultimate '50s Party-C .... (Era)
This Is How It All Began-#2-C ....(Specialty)
Theme From "Kukla, Fran And Ollie" ("Here We Are, Hop,
Hop, Hop")
Original Soundtrack; *Television's Greatest Hits-#4-Black & White*
Classics-C .... (TVT)
Theme From "The Flintstones"
Original Soundtrack; *Hanna-Barbera Classics-#1-Original Recordings Of*
The World's Most Famous Cartoon Themes &
Scores .... (Kid Rhino/Rhino 4 Kids)
Hanna-Barbera Pic-A-Nic Basket Of Cartoon
Classics .... (Kid Rhino/Rhino 4 Kids)
Television's Greatest Hits-#1-C....................... (TVT)
Steve Hobbs; *Escape*.................................. (Cexton)
They Were Doin' The Mambo (Flo)
Vaughn Monroe; *Very Best Of Vaughn Monroe* .... (Taragon)
They're Hanging Me Tonight (Flo)
Marty Robbins; *Gunfighter Ballads & Trail Songs* ....(Legacy)

WOMEN'S NAMES: G

See Also: **CELEBRITIES: SPECIFIC, FAMILY (various),**
WOMEN: GENERAL

Georgia On My Mind
Billie Holiday; *God Bless The Child* ....(Columbia)
The Billie Holiday Story-#2 ....(Columbia)
Hoagy Carmichael; *Hoagy Carmichael-Legendary Performer*..........(RCA)

Hoagy Sings Carmichael...............................(EMI)
Mildred Bailey; *Harlem Lullaby* ....(ASV)
Preservation Hall Jazz Band; *Best Of The Preservation Hall*
Jazz Band...(Columbia)
Ray Charles; *Ray Charles' Greatest Hits-#2* ....(Rhino)
Ray Charles-Anthology..............................(Rhino)
Willie Nelson; *Greatest Hits (& Some That Will Be)* ......(Columbia)
Stardust ....(Legacy)
Willie & Family Live ....(Columbia)
Georgy Girl
Seekers; *History Of British Rock-#4-C* ....(Rhino)
Gigi
Charles Boyer; *Romantic Songs Of Love* ....(Everest)
Louis Jordan; *ST/Gigi* .... (Sony Music Special Prod.)
Gina
Johnny Mathis; *Johnny Mathis' All-Time Greatest Hits* ....(Columbia)
Johnny Mathis-16 Most Requested Songs ....(Columbia)
Gina
Stray Cats; *Blast Off*............................... (EMI)
Gina
Michael Bolton; *Hunger* ....(Columbia)
Ginny The Flying Girl
Janis Ian; *In Harmony 2-C* ....(Columbia)
Gloria
Doors; *Alive She Cried*.............................. (Elektra)
Jimi Hendrix; *Essential Jimi Hendrix, Volume 2* .... (Reprise)
Shadows Of Knight; *Nuggets-#2-Punk-C* ....(Rhino)
Van Morrison; *It's Too Late To Stop Now* .... (Warner Bros.)
Van Morrison & Them; *Best Of Van Morrison* .... (Polydor)
Gloria
Manhattan Transfer; *Best Of The Manhattan Transfer*............. (Atlantic)
Manhattan Transfer-Live .... (Atlantic)
The Manhattan Transfer ....(Rhino)
Gloria
U2; *October* ....(Island)
Under A Blood Red Sky ....(Island)
Gloria
Escorts; *Original Classic Oldies Of The '50s & '60s-#13-C* .... (MCA)
Gloria
Laura Branigan; *Branigan* .... (Atlantic)
Dance Traxx-C .... (Atlantic)
Gloria Ann
Steve Laury; *Vineland Dreams* .... (CTI)
Gloria: The Enchantment Medley
Jesse Powell; *Jesse Powell* ....(Silas)
Guantanamera
Wyclef Jean featuring Celia Cruz & Jeni Fujita; *Presents The Carnival F/*
Refugee Allstars ....(Ruffhouse/Columbia)
Guenevere
Original Cast; *Camelot*...............................(Columbia)
Original Soundtrack; *ST/Camelot* .... (Warner Bros.)
Guinnevere
Crosby, Stills & Nash; *Crosby, Stills & Nash*..............(Atlantic)
CSN .... (Atlantic)
Crosby, Stills, Nash & Young; *So Far* ....(Atlantic)
Woodstock Two .... (Atlantic)
Lady Godiva
Peter And Gordon; *History Of British Rock-#4-C* ....(Rhino)
Little Green
Joni Mitchell; *Blue*............................... (Reprise)
Livin' On A Prayer (Gina)
Bon Jovi; *America: A Tribute To Heroes-C*.............. (Interscope)
Cross Road-14 Classic Grooves ....(Mercury)
Slippery When Wet ....(Jambco)
The Concert For New York City-C...................(Columbia)
Madame George
Van Morrison; *Astral Weeks* .... (Warner Bros.)
Bang Masters ....(Epic)
Sam's Place (Gina)
Buck Owens & The Buckaroos; *Billboard Top Country Hits-1967-C* ....(Rhino)
Sweet Georgia Brown
Anita O'Day; *Compact Jazz-Best Of The Compact Jazz Vocalists-C.* .....(Verve)
Beatles; *The Beatles featuring Tony Sheridan-In The Beginning (Circa*
1960) .... (Polydor)
Ben Bernie & His Orchestra; *78-#15002* .... (Vocalion)
Bing Crosby; *Bing Crosby-16 Most Requested Songs* .... (Legacy)
Coasters; *Coasters' Greatest Hits* ....(Atco)
Django Reinhardt; *Djangologie USA-#1* ....(Disques Swing)
Quintet Of The Hot Club Of France .... (Prestige)
Ella Fitzgerald; *Ella Fitzgerald In London* ....(Pablo)
Whisper Not.......................................(Verve)
Ella Fitzgerald & Count Basie; *Perfect Match* .... (Pablo)
Original Broadway Cast; *Bubbling Brown Sugar* ....(Amherst)
Stephane Grappelli; *Live In London* ....(Black Lion)
Tito Puente; *Out Of This World* ....(Concord Picante Jazz)
Theme From "Gidget"
Original Soundtrack; *Television's Greatest Hits-#2-C* ....(TVT)

WOMEN'S NAMES: H

See Also: **CELEBRITIES: SPECIFIC, FAMILY (various), WOMEN: GENERAL**

Aunt Hagar's Blues
Art Tatum; *Solo Masterpieces-#4*................................(Pablo)
Kid Ory's Creole Jazz Band; *This Kid's The Greatest* .... (Good Time Jazz)
Graduation (Friends Forever) (Heather)
Vitamin C; *Totally Hits-#3-C*...................................(Atlantic)
   Vitamin C...(Elektra)
Grandma Harp
Merle Haggard; *18 Rare Classics* .... (Curb)
Harriet Tubman
Holly Near & Ronnie Gilbert; *Lifeline* ....(Redwood)
   Redwood Collection..(Redwood)
Harriet Tubman's Gonna Carry Me Home
Long Ryders; *Two-Fisted Tales* .... (Island)
Heather Honey
Tommy Roe; *Sheila* .... (Accord)
   Tommy Roe's Greatest Hits ....(MCA)
Helen Wheels
Paul McCartney & Wings; *Band On The Run*................... (Capitol)
Henrietta
Jimmy Dee And The Off-Beats; *Loud, Fast & Out Of Control: The Wild
   Sounds Of '50s Rock-C* .... (Rhino)
   The History Of Dot-#2-Come Go With Me-C........... (Varese Sarabande)
Holly Holy
Neil Diamond; *Hot August Night* ....(MCA)
   Hot August Night II .... (Columbia)
   Love At The Greek .... (Columbia)
   Neil Diamond-Gold ....(MCA)
   Neil Diamond-His 12 Greatest Hits ....(MCA)
   Touching You Touching Me ....(MCA)
Hooray For Hazel
Tommy Roe; *Original Rock 'N' Roll Hits Of The '60s-C* .... (Roulette)
   Sheila.. (Accord)
   Tommy Roe's Greatest Hits ....(MCA)
I'm Not Running Anymore (Holly)
John Mellencamp; *John Mellencamp* .... (Columbia)
Little Miss Honky Tonk
Brooks & Dunn; *Waitin' On Sundown* .... (Arista)
Long Legged Hannah (From Butte, Montana)
Jesse Hunter; *A Man Like Me* .... (BNA)
Louisiana Hannah
Webb Wilder; *Hybrid Vigor* .... (Island)
Please, Mrs. Henry
Bob Dylan And The Band; *Basement Tapes*................... (Columbia)
Sam's Place (Hattie)
Buck Owens & The Buckaroos; *Billboard Top Country Hits-1967-C* ... (Rhino)
Soft Hearted Hana
George Harrison; *George Harrison* .... (Dark Horse)
Theme From "Hart To Hart"
Original Soundtrack; *Television's Greatest Hits-#3-1970s & 1980s-C* ... (TVT)
Theme From "Hazel"
Original Soundtrack; *Television's Greatest Hits-#4-Black & White
   Classics-C*... (TVT)
Theme From "The Adventures Of Ozzie And Harriet"
Original Soundtrack; *Television's Greatest Hits-#4-Black & White
   Classics-C*... (TVT)

WOMEN'S NAMES: I

See Also: **CELEBRITIES: SPECIFIC, FAMILY (various), WOMEN: GENERAL**

All My Ex's Live In Texas (Irene)
George Strait; *Country Classics-#10-1987-C*................... (Universal)
   George Strait's Greatest Hits-#2..............................(MCA)
   Ocean Front Property...(MCA)
Angels Working Overtime (Indiana)
Deana Carter; *Everything's Gonna Be Alright* .... (Capitol)
Goodnight Irene
Jim Reeves; *Jim Reeves-Pure Gold* .... (RCA)
Johnny Cash; *Rough Cut King Of Country Music*............... (Sun)
   The Man-The World-His Music .... (Sun)
Ry Cooder; *Chicken Skin Music* .... (Reprise)
Weavers; *Best Of The Weavers* ....(MCA)
   Weavers At Carnegie Hall .... (Vanguard)
   Weavers' Greatest Hits .... (Vanguard)
Ida Red
Asleep At The Wheel featuring Jody Nix, Huey Lewis & Willie Nelson;
   Tribute To The Music Of Bob Wills And The Texas Playboys-C .... (Liberty)
Bob Wills & His Texas Playboys; *Bob Wills & His Texas Playboys-
   Greatest Hits*... (Curb)

Iesha
   Tiffany Transcriptions-#2-Best Of The Tiffanys .... (Rhino)
Iesha
Another Bad Creation; *Coolin' At The Playground Ya' Know!*....... (Motown)
Imelda
Mark Knopfler; *Golden Heart*........................... (Warner Bros.)
Irma La Douce
Katherine Kovar; *Love Echoes* .... (Accent)
Original Cast; *Irma La Douce* .... (Sony Music Special Prod.)
Isabella's Eyes
Kenny Loggins; *Back To Avalon* .... (Columbia)
Isabelle
Mary Lou Williams; *Jazz Pioneers* ....(Prestige)
Oye Isabel
Iguanas; *Nuevo Boogaloo* ....(Margaritaville)
Sexy Ida
Ike & Tina Turner; *Proud Mary-Best Of Ike & Tina Turner* .... (EMI)
Taste Of India
Aerosmith; *Nine Lives* .... (Columbia)
Video (India)
India.Arie; *Acoustic Soul*................................. (Motown)

WOMEN'S NAMES: J

See Also: **CELEBRITIES: SPECIFIC, FAMILY (various), WOMEN: GENERAL**

(Just Like) Romeo & Juliet
Reflections; *'60s Dance Party-C*.................... (Dominion Entert.)
   Sensational '60s-#1-C .... (Dominion Entert.)
867-5309/Jenny
Tommy Tutone; *Tommy Tutone-2*........................ (Columbia)
Angry Johnny (Jezebel)
Poe; *Hello* ....(Modern)
Arkansas Jane
Kong Cotton; *Bo Diddley Beats* .... (Rhino)
Baby Jane
Rod Stewart; *Body Wishes*........................... (Warner Bros.)
   Storyteller/The Complete Anthology: 1964-1990..... (Warner Bros.)
Back In Judy's Jungle
Brian Eno; *Desert Island Selection* .... (Editions E.G.)
   Taking Tiger Mountain By Strategy .... (Editions E.G.)
Blue Jean
David Bowie; *Changesbowie* .... (Rykodisc)
   The Singles-1969-1993................................. (Rykodisc)
   Tonight .... (EMI)
Cousin Jane
Troggs; *Archeology-1967-1977* ....(Polydor)
Dammit Janet
Barry Bostwick; *ST/Rocky Horror Picture Show* .... (Rhino)
Original London Cast; *Rocky Horror Show*.................... (Rhino)
Dance Little Jean
Nitty Gritty Dirt Band; *Let's Go* .... (Warner Bros.)
   Twenty Years Of Dirt-Best Of The Nitty Gritty Dirt Band ..... (Warner Bros.)
Daydream Believer (Jean)
Anne Murray; *Anne Murray's Greatest Hits*................... (Capitol)
   I'll Always Love You.. (Capitol)
Monkees; *Billboard Top Rock 'N' Roll Hits-1967-C* .... (Rhino)
   Mellow '60s-C .... (Priority)
   Monkees' Greatest Hits .... (Rhino)
Dear Jean (I'm Nervous)
City Boy; *Young Men Gone West* .... (Mercury)
Death Of Queen Jane
Joan Baez; *Joan Baez/5* .... (Vanguard)
   Love Song Album .... (Vanguard)
Don't Cry Joni
Conway Twitty; *Conway Twitty-Number Ones-#1* .... (Liberty)
   Conway Twitty's Greatest Hits-#1 .... (MCA)
   Very Best Of Conway Twitty................................. (MCA)
Electric Aunt Jemima
Frank Zappa; *Uncle Meat* .... (Barking Pumpkin)
Have You Met Miss Jones
Art Tatum; *Best Of Art Tatum* .... (Pablo)
Coleman Hawkins; *April In Paris* .... (Bluebird)
Ella Fitzgerald; *Silver Collection-Songbooks* .... (Verve)
Frank Sinatra; *Swing Along With Me*........................ (Reprise)
Louis Armstrong; *American Songbook* .... (Verve)
Tony Bennett; *Jazz* .... (Columbia)
   Rodgers & Hart Songbook ....(DRG)
I Dream Of Jeanie With Light Brown Hair
Al Jolson; *The Al Jolson Story-#5* .... (MCA)
Joan Baez; *Diamonds & Rust* .... (A&M)
Mormon Tabernacle Choir; *Beautiful Dreamer* .... (Columbia)
   Mormon Tabernacle Choir's Greatest Hits-#3 .... (Columbia)
   Old Beloved Songs .... (Columbia)
I Thought I'd Write To Juliet
Elvis Costello; *The Juliet Letters* .... (Warner Bros.)

It's My Party (Judy)
Lesley Gore; *Billboard Top Rock 'N' Roll Hits-1963-C* . . . . (Rhino)
   Golden Hits Of Lesley Gore . . . . (Mercury)
   Good Time Rock 'N' Roll-C . . . . (MCA)
   Lesley Gore-Anthology . . . . (Rhino)
   Oldies But Goodies-#3-C . . . .(Original Sound)
Jack And Jill
Ray Parker Jr.; *Chartbusters* . . . . (Arista)
   Ray Parker Jr.'s Greatest Hits . . . . (Arista)
Raydio; *Raydio* . . . . (Arista)
Jackie Blue
Ozark Mountain Daredevils; *Best Of The Ozark Mountain Daredevils* . . . (A&M)
   Billboard Top Hits-1975-C . . . . (Rhino)
   It'll Shine When It Shines . . . . (A&M)
   It's Alive . . . . (A&M)
   Super Hits Of The '70s-Have A Nice Day-#14-C . . . . (Rhino)
Jamie
Ray Parker Jr.; *Chartbusters* . . . . (Arista)
Jane
Jefferson Starship; *Freedom At Point Zero* . . . . (Grunt)
   Greatest Hits-Ten Years & Change-1979-1991 . . . .(RCA)
Jane Doe
Alicia Keys; *Songs In A Minor* . . . . (J)
Jane, Jane, Jane
Kingston Trio; *Capitol Collectors Series-The Kingston Trio* . . . . (Capitol)
   Hidden Treasures . . . . (Folk Era)
   Very Best Of The Kingston Trio . . . . (Capitol)
Jane's Getting Serious
John Astley; *Everyone Loves The Pilot Except The Crew* . . . . . (Atlantic)
Janet
Commodores; *Nightshift* . . . . (Motown)
Janey Don't You Lose Heart
Bruce Springsteen; *Tracks* . . . . (Columbia)
Janie Baker
Shenandoah; *Under The Kudzu* . . . .(RCA)
Janie's Got A Gun
Aerosmith; *Pump* . . . . (Geffen)
Jean
Jim Nabors; *Jim Nabors-16 Most Requested Songs* . . . . (Legacy)
Oliver; *Billboard Top Movie Hits-1960s-C* . . . . (Rhino)
Jean Genie
David Bowie; *Aladdin Sane* . . . . (Rykodisc)
   Changesbowie . . . . (Rykodisc)
   David Live . . . . (Rykodisc)
   The Singles-1969-1993 . . . . (Rykodisc)
Jeannie Needs A Shooter
Warren Zevon; *Bad Luck Streak In Dancing School* . . . . (Asylum)
   Stand In The Fire . . . . (Asylum)
Jennie Lee
Jan & Dean; *Jan & Dean-Legendary Masters* . . . . (EMI)
Jennifer
Eurythmics; *Sweet Dreams (Are Made Of This)* . . . . (RCA)
Jennifer Eccles
Hollies; *Best Of The Hollies-#2* . . . . (EMI)
   Hollies-Epic Anthology From The Original Master Tapes . . . . (Epic)
Jenny
Marty Robbins; *Marty Robbins' Biggest Hits* . . . . (Columbia)
Jenny
Chicago; *Chicago VI* . . . . (Chicago)
Jenny
Harry Chapin; *Living Room Suite* . . . . (Elektra)
Jenny (Iowa Sunrise)
Janis Ian; *Night Trains* . . . . (Columbia)
Jenny Says
Cowboy Mouth; *Are You With Me?* . . . . (MCA)
   Word Of Mouth . . . .(Monkey Hill)
Jenny Take A Ride
Mitch Ryder And The Detroit Wheels; *Mitch Ryder And The Detroit Wheels'*
   Greatest Hits . . . . (Roulette)
   Original Rock 'N' Roll Hits Of The '60s-C . . . . (Roulette)
   Rev Up-Best Of Mitch Ryder . . . . (Rhino)
   Toga Rock-C . . . . (Dunhill Compact Classics)
Jenny, Jenny
Little Richard; *Compact Command Performances-Little Richard* . . . . (Motown)
   Grooviest 17 Original Hits . . . . (Specialty)
   Little Richard . . . . (Specialty)
   Little Richard-18 Greatest Hits . . . . (Rhino)
   Tutti Frutti . . . . (Accord)
Jessica
Allman Brothers Band; *Best Of The Allman Brothers Band* . . . . (Polydor)
   Brothers & Sisters . . . . (Polydor)
   Decade Of Hits-1969-1979 . . . . (Polydor)
   Dreams . . . . (Polydor)
Jewel Eyed Judy
Fleetwood Mac; *Kiln House* . . . . (Reprise)
Joan Crawford
Blue Oyster Cult; *Extraterrestrial Live* . . . . (Columbia)
   Fire Of Unknown Origin . . . . (Columbia)

Joanna
Kool & The Gang; *Everything Is-Greatest Hits* . . . .(Mercury)
   In The Heart . . . . (De-Lite)
Joanne
Michael Nesmith; *Compilation* . . . . (Pacific Arts)
Wall Of Voodoo; *Happy Planet* . . . . (I.R.S.)
Jody Girl
Bob Seger; *Beautiful Loser* . . . .(Capitol)
   Live Bullet . . . .(Capitol)
Jody Like A Melody
David Allan Coe; *David Allan Coe-17 Greatest Hits* . . . .(Columbia)
   For The Record-The First 10 Years . . . . (Columbia)
Johanna
Angela Lansbury & Len Cariou; *Sweeney Todd* . . . . (RCA)
Jolene
Dolly Parton; *Best Of Dolly Parton* . . . . (RCA)
   Best There Is . . . . (RCA)
   Jolene . . . . (RCA)
   RCA Years-1967-1986 . . . . (RCA)
Sherrie Austin; *Followin' A Feelin'* . . . .(We/Madacy)
Joli Girl
Marty Robbins; *Marty Robbins' All-Time Greatest Hits* . . . .(Columbia)
Josephine
Wayne King & His Orchestra; *Best Of Wayne King* . . . . (MCA)
   Nipper's Greatest Hits Of The '30s-#1-C . . . . (RCA)
Josephine
Wallflowers; *Bringing Down The Horse* . . . . (Interscope)
Josie
Steely Dan; *Aja* . . . . (MCA)
   Steely Dan's Greatest Hits . . . . (MCA)
Joy
Nilsson; *Son Of Schmilsson* . . . . (RCA)
Judith
A Perfect Circle; *Mer De Noms* . . . . (Virgin)
Judy In Disguise (With Glasses)
John Fred & His Playboy Band; *Billboard Top Rock 'N' Roll Hits-*
   1968-C . . . .(Rhino)
   Cruisin'-1967-C . . . .(Increase)
   ST/Drugstore Cowboy . . . .(Novus)
   Super Oldies Of The '60s-#7-C . . . . (Audio Fidelity)
Judy's Turn To Cry
Lesley Gore; *'60s Dance Party-#2-C* . . . .(Dominion Entert.)
   Golden Hits Of Lesley Gore . . . .(Mercury)
   Lesley Gore-Anthology . . . .(Rhino)
Julia
Beatles; *Beatles-Box Set* . . . .(Capitol)
   ST/Imagine: John Lennon . . . . (Capitol)
   The Beatles (White Album) . . . . (Capitol)
Julia
Conway Twitty; *Borderline* . . . . (MCA)
   Conway Twitty's Greatest Hits-#3 . . . . (MCA)
Julia
Eurythmics; *ST/1984-For The Love Of Big Brother* . . . . (RCA)
Julie, Do Ya Love Me
Bobby Sherman; *Rock & Roll Is Here To Stay-C* . . . .(Gusto)
   Super Hits Of The '70s-Have A Nice Day-#3-C . . . .(Rhino)
Julie's In The Drug Squad
Clash; *Give 'Em Enough Rope* . . . . (Epic)
Juliet
Oak Ridge Boys; *Country Classics-#2-Today's Country Classics-C* . .(Universal)
   Country Classics-#6-1985-1986-C . . . . (Universal)
   Seasons . . . . (MCA)
Juliet
Neil Diamond; *And The Singer Sings His Song* . . . . (MCA)
   Neil Diamond-Love Songs . . . . (MCA)
Juliet
Stevie Nicks; *Other Side Of The Mirror* . . . . (Modern)
Lady Jane
Rolling Stones; *Aftermath* . . . . (Abkco)
   Flowers . . . . (Abkco)
   got Live if you want it! . . . . (Abkco)
   More Hot Rocks (big hits & fazed cookies) . . . . (Abkco)
Little Jeannie
Elton John; *21 At 33* . . . . (Polydor)
   Elton John's Greatest Hits-1976-1986 . . . . (MCA)
Love Theme From "Romeo & Juliet"
101 Strings Orchestra; *World's Greatest Standards* . . . .(Alshire)
Andre Kostelanetz; *Andre Kostelanetz-16 Most Requested Songs* . . . .(Columbia)
Andy Williams & The Royal Philharmonic Orchestra; *Greatest Love*
   Classics . . . . (Capitol)
Percy Faith & His Orchestra; *Percy Faith & His Orchestra-16 Most*
   Requested Songs . . . . (Columbia)
Me & Baby Jane
Leon Russell; *Carney* . . . . (Right Stuff)
Me & Mrs. Jones
Billy Paul; *Ten Years Of #1 Hits-C* . . . .(Philadelphia Int'l)
Ms. Jackson
Outkast; *Stankonia* . . . . (LaFace/Arista)

My Girl Josephine
Fats Domino; *Fats Domino's Greatest Hits* . . . .(MCA)
They Call Me The Fat Man . . . .(EMI)

North To Alaska (Jenny)
Dwight Yoakam; *Under The Covers*. . . . . (Reprise)
Johnny Horton; *American Originals-Johnny Horton*. . . . . (Columbia)
Billboard Top Country Hits-1961-C . . . . (Rhino)
Johnny Horton's Greatest Hits . . . . (Columbia)
Super Hits Of The '60s-C . . . .(Epic)

Oh Julie
Crescendos; *In The Still Of The Night* . . . . (Capitol)
Southern Rhythm 'N' Rock-Best Of Excello-#2-C . . . . (Rhino)

Poor Jenny
Everly Brothers; *All They Had To Do Was Dream* . . . . (Rhino)
Everly Brothers . . . . (Rhino)
Fabulous Style Of The Everly Brothers . . . . (Rhino)

Portrait Of Jennie
Nat ''King'' Cole; *Unforgettable* . . . . (Capitol)
Red Garland & Ray Barretto; *Manteca*. . . . .(Prestige)

Queen Jane Approximately
4 Seasons; *The 4 Seasons Sing Big Hits By Bacharach/David/Dylan* . . . . (Rhino)
Bob Dylan; *Highway 61 Revisited* . . . . (Columbia)
Bob Dylan & The Grateful Dead; *Dylan & The Dead*. . . . . (Columbia)

Ride On Josephine
George Thorogood & The Destroyers; *George Thorogood & The Destroyers*. . . . . (Rounder)

Romeo & Juliet
Chambers Brothers; *The Time Has Come* . . . . (Columbia)

Romeo & Juliet
Dire Straits; *Live-Alchemy* . . . .(Warner Bros.)
Making Movies. . . . .(Warner Bros.)
Money For Nothing . . . .(Warner Bros.)
Indigo Girls; *Rites Of Passage* . . . .(Epic)

Running Gun (Jeannie)
Marty Robbins; *Gunfighter Ballads & Trail Songs*. . . . . (Legacy)

Suite: Judy Blue Eyes
Crosby, Stills & Nash; *Crosby, Stills & Nash* . . . .(Atlantic)
CSN . . . .(Atlantic)
ST/Woodstock . . . .(Atlantic)
Crosby, Stills, Nash & Young; *So Far* . . . .(Atlantic)

Sweet Jane
Cowboy Junkies; *ST/Natural Born Killers* . . . .(Nothing)
Trinity Session . . . . (RCA)
Lou Reed; *Rock N Roll Animal* . . . . (RCA)
Walk On The Wild Side-The Best Of Lou Reed. . . . . (RCA)
Mott The Hoople; *All The Young Dudes* . . . . (Columbia)
The Ballad Of Mott: A Retrospective . . . . (Columbia)
Velvet Underground; *Live At Max's Kansas City* . . . . (Collectables)

Tarzan & Jane
Sparks; *Angst In My Pants* . . . .(Atlantic)

Theme From ''I Dream Of Jeannie''
Original Soundtrack; *Television's Greatest Hits-#1-C* . . . . (TVT)

Theme From ''Josie & The Pussycats''
Original Soundtrack; *Hanna-Barbera Pic-A-Nic Basket Of Cartoon Classics*. . . . . (Kid Rhino/Rhino 4 Kids)
Television's Greatest Hits-#3-1970s & 1980s-C . . . . (TVT)

Theme From ''The Jetsons''
Original Soundtrack; *Hanna-Barbera Pic-A-Nic Basket Of Cartoon Classics*. . . . . (Kid Rhino/Rhino 4 Kids)
Television's Greatest Hits-#1-C . . . . (TVT)
Stunners; *ST/Jetsons-The Movie* . . . .(MCA)

This Romeo Ain't Got Julie Yet
Diamond Rio; *Close To The Edge*. . . . . (Arista)

Visions Of Johanna
Bob Dylan; *Biograph* . . . . (Columbia)
Blonde On Blonde . . . . (Columbia)

Youngstown (Jenny)
Bruce Springsteen; *The Ghost Of Tom Joad* . . . . (Columbia)

WOMEN'S NAMES: K

See Also: CELEBRITIES: SPECIFIC, FAMILY (various), WOMEN: GENERAL

Grandma Klump
Eddie Murphy; *Eddie Murphy-Greatest Comedy Hits* . . . . (Columbia)

If You See Kay
Memphis Slim/Tampa Red/Lonnie Johnson; *Bawdy Blues* . . . . (Bluesville)

I'll Take You Home Again Kathleen
Billy Shepherd Singers; *Irish Sing-Along*. . . . .(MCA)
Bing Crosby; *When Irish Eyes Are Smiling* . . . .(MCA)
Slim Whitman; *Paloma Blanca-Best Of Slim Whitman-Legendary Masters* . . . .(EMI)

Kate
Ben Folds Five; *Whatever And Ever Amen*. . . . .(Caroline/550)

Kathleen
Willie Nelson; *Partners* . . . . (Columbia)

Kathleen
Blasters; *Blasters-Collection*. . . . .(Slash)

Kathleen
Roachford; *Roachford*. . . . . (Epic)

Kathleen (Catholicism Made Easier)
Randy Newman; *Little Criminals* . . . . (Warner Bros.)

Kathleen Mavourneen
Mormon Tabernacle Choir; *Songs Of The Civil War And Stephen Foster Favorites* . . . . (Sony Music Classical)

Kathy's Song
Simon & Garfunkel; *Collected Works*. . . . . (Columbia)
Simon & Garfunkel's Greatest Hits . . . . (Columbia)
Sounds Of Silence . . . . (Columbia)

Katie Left Memphis
Tangle Eye; *Roots Of The Blues* . . . . (Nightwork)

Katie Wants A Fast One
Steve Wariner & Garth Brooks; *Faith In You* . . . . (Capitol)

Katie, My Southern Rose
William H. Thompson; *Music From The New York Stage (1890-1920)-#1-1890-1908-C* . . . .(Pearl)

Kiddio
Brook Benton; *Best Of Brook Benton* . . . . (Mercury)
Brook Benton-Golden Hits . . . . (Mercury)
Endlessly-The Best Of Brook Benton . . . . (Rhino)

Kitty's Back
Bruce Springsteen; *The Wild, The Innocent & The E Street Shuffle*. . . (Columbia)

Kyrie
Mr. Mister; *Welcome To The Real World* . . . . (RCA)

She's In Love With The Boy (Katie)
Trisha Yearwood; *Trisha Yearwood* . . . . (MCA)

Shimmy Like Kate
Olympics; *Meet The Marathons* . . . . (Collectables)
Official Record Album Of The Olympics. . . . . (Rhino)

Terence's Farewell To Kathleen
John McCormack; *Ireland Of Treasures-Voices & Melodies-C* . . . . . . (Capitol)

Theme From ''Karen''
Original Soundtrack; *Television's Greatest Hits-#4-Black & White Classics-C* . . . . (TVT)

WOMEN'S NAMES: L

See Also: CELEBRITIES: SPECIFIC, FAMILY (various), WOMEN: GENERAL

Ah Leah
Donnie Iris; *Back On The Streets*. . . . . (MCA)

Change In Louise
Joe Cocker; *With A Little Help From My Friends* . . . . (A&M)

Climb That Hill (Lucy)
Tom Petty And The Heartbreakers; *ST/She's The One* . . . . (Warner Bros.)

Darling Lorraine
Paul Simon; *You're The One*. . . . . (Warner Bros.)

Dizzy Miss Lizzy
Beatles; *Beatles VI* . . . . (Capitol)
Rock 'N' Roll Music . . . . (Capitol)
The Beatles At The Hollywood Bowl. (Capitol)
Ronnie Hawkins and The Hawks; *Best Of Ronnie Hawkins and The Hawks* . . . . (Rhino)

Donald And Lydia
John Prine; *John Prine*. . . . .(Atlantic)
John Prine-Souvenirs. . . . .(Oh Boy)
Prime Prine-The Best Of John Prine . . . .(Atlantic)

Get Back (Loretta)
Beatles; *Beatles 1* . . . . (Capitol)
Beatles-20 Greatest Hits . . . . (Capitol)
Beatles-Box Set. . . . . (Capitol)
Let It Be . . . . (Capitol)
Past Masters-Volume Two . . . . (Parlophone)
Reel Music . . . . (Capitol)
Rock 'N' Roll Music . . . . (Capitol)
The Beatles/1967-1970. . . . . (Capitol)

Honolulu Lulu
Jan & Dean; *Dead Man's Curve* . . . . (EMI)
Jan & Dean-Legendary Masters . . . . (EMI)
One Summer Night-Live . . . . (Rhino)
Surf City-Best Of Jan & Dean. . . . . (EMI)

I Believe
Blessid Union Of Souls; *Home* . . . . (EMI)

I Saw Linda Yesterday
Dickey Lee; *45s On CD-#2-1960-1966-C* . . . . (Mercury)

I'm Not Lisa
Jessi Colter; *Heartbreak Hotel-C* . . . . (EMI)
Super Hits Of The '70s-Have A Nice Day-#15-C . . . . (Rhino)

It All Depends On Linda
Johnny Burnette; *Best Of Johnny Burnette-You're Sixteen* . . . . (Gold Rush)

Lara's Theme
Maurice Jarre Orchestra; *Hollywood's Great
 Composers-C* . . . . (Columbia Special Prod.)
MGM Studio Orchestra; *ST/Dr. Zhivago* . . . . (MCA)

Laura
Frank Sinatra; *Night We Called It A Day* . . . . (Capitol)
 Where Are You? . . . . (Capitol)
Sammy Davis, Jr.; *Capitol Collectors Series-Sammy Davis, Jr.* . . . . (Capitol)
Spike Jones & His City Slickers; *Best Of Spike Jones & His City
 Slickers* . . . . (RCA)

Laurie (Strange Things Happen)
Dickey Lee; *Collector's Essentials-#1-1960s-C* . . . . (Varese Sarabande)

Layla
Derek And The Dominos; *Classic Rock 1966-1988-C* . . . . (Atlantic)
 Eric Clapton-Crossroads-C . . . . (Polydor)
 Layla . . . . (Polydor)
 ST/Goodfellas . . . . (Atlantic)
Eric Clapton; *Eric Clapton-Unplugged* . . . . (Reprise)

Leah
Roy Orbison; *In Dreams-Greatest Hits* . . . . (Orbison)
 Roy Orbison-Anthology: 1956-1965 . . . . (Rhino)
 Roy Orbison's All-Time Greatest Hits-#1 & 2 . . . . (Monument)

Lida Rose/Will I Ever Tell You?
Original Broadway Cast; *The Music Man* . . . . (Angel)
Original Cast; *The Music Man* . . . . (Gold Rush)
Soundtrack; *ST/The Music Man* . . . . (Warner Bros.)

Lili Marlene
Marlene Dietrich; *Best Of Marlene Dietrich* . . . . (Columbia)
 Essential Marlene Dietrich . . . . (Capitol)
 Live At The Cafe De Paris . . . . (Columbia)
 This Is Art Deco-C . . . . (Columbia)

Lilly Dale
Bob Wills & His Texas Playboys; *The Country Music Hall Of Fame-Bob
 Wills* . . . . (Universal)

Lily Was Here
Candy Dulfer & Dave Stewart; *ST/Lily Was Here* . . . . (Arista)

Lily, Rosemary And The Jack Of Hearts
Bob Dylan; *Blood On The Tracks* . . . . (Columbia)

Linda Let Me Be The One
Bruce Springsteen; *Tracks* . . . . (Columbia)

Linda On My Mind
Conway Twitty; *Conway Twitty's Greatest Hits-#2* . . . . (MCA)
 Conway's #1 Classics-#2 . . . . (Warner Bros.)
 Songwriter . . . . (MCA)
 Very Best Of Conway Twitty . . . . (MCA)

Lisa
Cat Stevens; *Tea For The Tillerman* . . . . (A&M)

Lisa, Listen To Me
Blood, Sweat & Tears; *Blood, Sweat & Tears Greatest Hits* . . . . (Columbia)

Liza Jane
Vince Gill; *Pocket Full Of Gold* . . . . (MCA)

Liza Jane
David Bowie; *Love You Till Tuesday* . . . . (London)

Loddy Lo
Chubby Checker; *Chubby Checker's Dance Party* . . . . (K-Tel)
 Chubby Checker's Greatest Hits . . . . (Everest)

Lola
Kinks; *Come Dancing With The Kinks-Best Of The Kinks 1977-1986* . . . (Arista)
 Everybody's In Show-Biz . . . . (Rhino)
 Kink Kronikles . . . . (Reprise)
 Lola Versus Powerman And The Moneygoround, Part One . . . . (Reprise)
 One For The Road . . . . (Arista)
 Second Time Around . . . . (RCA)

Loola Loo
Keb' Mo'; *The Door* . . . . (550/Epic/Okeh)

Losing Lisa
Ben Folds; *Rockin' The Suburbs* . . . . (Epic)

Louie Louie
Kingsmen; *Best Of The Kingsmen* . . . . (Rhino)
 Billboard Top Rock 'N' Roll Hits-1963-C . . . . (Rhino)
 Cruisin'-1963-C . . . . (Increase)
 Frat Rock!-C . . . . (Rhino)
 Oldies But Goodies-#11-C . . . . (Original Sound)
 Rock & Roll Is Here To Stay-C . . . . (Gusto)
 ST/Quadrophenia . . . . (MCA)
 WCBS FM 101 History Of Rock-'60s-#1-C . . . . (Collectables)

Louise
Bonnie Raitt; *Bonnie Raitt-Collection* . . . . (Warner Bros.)
 Sweet Forgiveness . . . . (Warner Bros.)
Leo Kottke; *Greenhouse* . . . . (Capitol)
 My Feet Are Smiling . . . . (Capitol)
 Very Best Of Leo Kottke . . . . (Capitol)
Linda Ronstadt; *Linda Ronstadt-Retrospective* . . . . (Capitol)
 Silk Purse . . . . (Capitol)
Paul Siebel; *Woodsmoke & Oranges* . . . . (Elektra)

Louise
Maurice Chevalier; *Louise* . . . . (ASV)

Louise, Louise
Pamela Rose; *Morpheus* . . . . (Grace)

Love Theme From "Eyes Of Laura Mars"
Barbra Streisand; *Barbra Streisand's Greatest Hits* . . . . (Columbia)
 Lazy Afternoon . . . . (Columbia)

Lucille
Everly Brothers; *Golden Hits Of The Everly Brothers* . . . . (Warner Bros.)
 The Reunion Concert-Live At Albert Hall 1983 . . . . (Mercury)
 Very Best Of The Everly Brothers . . . . (Warner Bros.)
Little Richard; *American Graffiti-#3-C* . . . . (MCA)
 Big Hits . . . . (Crescendo)
 Little Richard's Greatest Hits . . . . (Everest)
 Oldies But Goodies-#12-C . . . . (Original Sound)

Lucille
Kenny Rogers; *Kenny Rogers* . . . . (United Artists)
 Kenny Rogers' Greatest Hits . . . . (EMI)
 Kenny Rogers-Twenty Greatest Hits . . . . (EMI)
 Ten Years Of Gold . . . . (EMI)

Lucky
Britney Spears; *Now That's What I Call Music!-#5-C* . . . . (Virgin)
 Oops!...I Did It Again . . . . (Jive)

Lucy In The Sky With Diamonds
Beatles; *Sgt. Pepper's Lonely Hearts Club Band* . . . . (Capitol)
 The Beatles/1967-1970 . . . . (Capitol)
 Yellow Submarine . . . . (Capitol)
Elton John; *All This & World War 2* . . . . (20th Century Fox)
 Elton John's Greatest Hits-#2 . . . . (Polydor)
John Lennon; *Lennon* . . . . (Capitol)

Luka
Suzanne Vega; *Solitude Standing* . . . . (A&M)

Lump
Presidents Of The United States Of America; *Pure Frosting* . . . . (Columbia)
 The Presidents Of The United States Of America . . . . (Columbia)

Lynda
Steve Wariner; *Country Classics-#11-1987-1988-C* . . . . (Universal)
 It's A Crazy World . . . . (MCA)
 MCA #1 Hits Of The '80s-#3-C . . . . (MCA Special Prod.)
 Steve Wariner's Greatest Hits . . . . (MCA)

Miseducation Of Lauryn Hill
Lauryn Hill; *The Miseducation Of Lauryn Hill* . . . . (Ruffhouse/Columbia)

Norwegian Waltz/Liza Lynn
Jackie Daly & Seamus & Manus McGuire; *Buttons & Bows* . . . . . (Green Linnet)

Pearl Of The Quarter (Louise)
Steely Dan; *Countdown To Ecstasy* . . . . (MCA)

Pictures Of Lily
Pete Townshend; *Another Scoop* . . . . (Atco)
Who; *Magic Bus-The Who On Tour* . . . . (MCA)
 Meaty Beaty Big & Bouncy . . . . (MCA)

Princess Leia's Theme
John Williams; *ST/Star Wars* . . . . (Polydor)

Queen Lucy
Original Cast; *You're A Good Man, Charlie Brown* . . . . (Polydor)

Quiche Lorraine
B-52's; *Tame Yourself-C* . . . . (Rhino)
 Wild Planet . . . . (Warner Bros.)

Red Dirt Girl (Lillian)
Emmylou Harris; *Red Dirt Girl* . . . . (Nonesuch)

Shanghai Lil
Guy Lombardo & His Royal Canadians; *Guy Lombardo-16 Most Requested
 Songs* . . . . (Legacy)

Sweet Leilani
Bing Crosby; *Best Of Bing Crosby* . . . . (MCA)
King Sisters; *And The Winner Is-Best Movie Songs-C* . . . . (Capitol)

Sweet Lorraine
Art Tatum; *Solos-1940* . . . . (MCA)
 Standards . . . . (Black Lion)
Carmen McRae; *You're Lookin' At Me* . . . . (Concord Jazz)
Count Basie; *The Standards* . . . . (Verve)
Frank Sinatra; *The Reprise Collection* . . . . (Reprise)
Nat "King" Cole; *Complete After Midnight Sessions* . . . . (Capitol)
 The Nat "King" Cole Story . . . . (Capitol)
Woody Herman; *Big Band Treasures-#2-C* . . . . . (Dunhill Compact Classics)

Sweet Lorraine
Uriah Heep; *Best Of Uriah Heep* . . . . (Mercury)
 Magician's Birthday . . . . (Mercury)

Tell Laura I Love Her
Ray Peterson; *Nipper's Greatest Hits Of The '60s-#1-C* . . . . (RCA)
 Teenage Tragedies-C . . . . (Rhino)

Thanks For Leaving, Lucille
Sherri Jerrico; *Best Of Town & Country-#3-C* . . . . . (International Mktg. Group)

Theme From "Cagney & Lacey"
Original Soundtrack; *CBS: The First 50 Years* . . . . (TVT)
 Television's Greatest Hits-#6-Remote Control-C . . . . (TVT)

Theme From "I Love Lucy"
Original Soundtrack; *CBS: The First 50 Years* . . . . (TVT)
 Television's Greatest Hits-#1-C . . . . (TVT)
 TV Theme Sing-Along Album . . . . (Rhino)

Theme From "Laverne & Shirley"
Original Soundtrack; *Television's Greatest Hits-#3-1970s & 1980s-C* . . . (TVT)

Theme From "Lois And Clark: The New Adventures Of Superman"
Original Soundtrack; *Television's Greatest Hits-#7-Cable Ready-C* . . . . (TVT)

Think Of Laura
Christopher Cross; *Another Page* (Warner Bros.)
Soap Opera's Greatest Love Themes (Scotti Bros.)
Twistin' With Linda
Isley Brothers; *Scepter Records Story-C* (Capricorn)
The Isley Brothers Story-#1-Rockin' Soul-1959-1968 (Rhino)
Utah Carol (Lenore)
Harry K. McClintock; *Cowboy Songs On Folkways-C* (Smithsonian Folkways)
Marty Robbins; *Gunfighter Ballads & Trail Songs* (Legacy)
Visions Of Johanna
Bob Dylan; *Biograph* (Columbia)
Blonde On Blonde (Columbia)
Watch Out For Lucy
Eric Clapton; *Backless* (Polydor)
Watch What Happens (Lola's Theme)
Frank Sinatra; *My Way* (Reprise)
Henry Mancini; *Mancini Magic* (Pair)
Sergio Mendes; *Foursider* (A&M)
Who Stole The Jukebox (From Lucy's Perfume Parlor)
Johnny Bond; *Johnny Gimble's Texas Honky-Tonk Hits-C* (C.M.H. Prod.)

WOMEN'S NAMES: M

See Also: ***CELEBRITIES: SPECIFIC, FAMILY (various), WOMEN: GENERAL***

(Margie's At) The Lincoln Park Inn
Bobby Bare; *Ryman Country Homecoming 1-C* (Springhouse Music Grp./Chordant)
(Marie's The Name) His Latest Flame
Elvis Presley; *Elvis' Golden Records, Volume 3* (RCA)
ST/This Is Elvis (RCA)
The Other Sides-Worldwide Gold Award Hits, Vol. 2 (RCA)
The Top Ten Hits (RCA)
Absolutely Sweet Marie
Bob Dylan; *Blonde On Blonde* (Columbia)
Adrian (Mary)
Jewel; *Pieces Of You* (Atlantic)
All The Way To Birmingham/Roaring Mary
Celtic Thunder; *Celtic Thunder* (Green Linnet)
Along Comes Mary
Association; *Association Greatest Hits* (Warner Bros.)
Vintage Association (Fifty One West)
Bloody Mary
Original Cast; *South Pacific* (CBS Masterworks)
Soundtrack; *South Pacific* (RCA)
Bloody Mary
Whitesnake; *Snakebite* (Geffen)
Bony Moronie
John Lennon; *Rock 'N' Roll* (Capitol)
Larry Williams; *Cruisin'-1957-C* (Increase)
Let The Good Times Roll-C (Capitol)
Original Rock Oldies-Golden Hits-#2-C (Specialty)
ST/Christine (Motown)
This Is Larry Williams-How It All Began-#2 (Specialty)
Bring On The Night
Bruce Springsteen; *Tracks* (Columbia)
Cherry Hill Park (Mary Hill)
Billy Joe Royal; *Billy Joe Royal's Greatest Hits* (Columbia)
Super Hits Of The '70s-Have A Nice Day-#1-C (Rhino)
C'mon Marianne
4 Seasons; *25th Anniversary Collection* (Rhino)
4 Seasons-Anthology (Rhino)
Cockles & Mussels (Molly)
Emily Mitchell; *The Irish Album* (RCA)
Cousin Mary
John Coltrane; *Best Of John Coltrane* (Rhino)
Giant Steps (Rhino)
Dear John & Marsha Letter
Stan Freberg; *Capitol Collectors Series-Stan Freberg* (Capitol)
Deep Inside
Mary J. Blige; *Mary* (MCA)
Devil With A Blue Dress On & Good Golly Miss Molly
Bruce Springsteen; *ST/No Nukes-Muse Concerts* (Asylum)
Mitch Ryder And The Detroit Wheels; *Frat Rock!-#4-C* (Rhino)
Rev Up-Best Of Mitch Ryder (Rhino)
Son Of Frat Rock!-C (Rhino)
Toga Rock-C (Dunhill Compact Classics)
Devil Woman (Mary)
Marty Robbins; *Billboard Top Country Hits-1962-C* (Rhino)
Columbia Country Classics-#4-Nashville Sound-C (Columbia)
Lifetime Of Song-1951-1982 (Columbia)
Marty Robbins' Greatest Hits-#4 (Columbia)
Distant Drums (Mary)
Jim Reeves; *Best Of The Best Of Jim Reeves* (King)
Billboard Top Country Hits-1966-C (Rhino)
Essential Jim Reeves (RCA)
Don't Make Love To Mary
Merle Travis; *Johnny Gimble's Texas Honky-Tonk Hits-C* (C.M.H. Prod.)
Elvis & Marilyn
Leon Russell; *Americana* (Paradise)
From The Vine Came The Grape (Marie)
Gaylords; *X-tra Cheese-Originals By The Originals-C* (Compose)
Good Golly, Miss Molly
Creedence Clearwater Revival; *1968-1969* (Fantasy)
Bayou Country (Fantasy)
Creedence Clearwater Revival-Chronicle-#2 (Fantasy)
Little Richard; *Big Hits* (Crescendo)
Cruisin'-1958-C (Increase)
Greatest Hits Recorded Live (Epic)
Little Richard-18 Greatest Hits (Rhino)
Little Richard-His Greatest Hits (Vee-Jay)
ST/The Flamingo Kid (Motown)
Super Oldies Of The '50s-#2-C (Audio Fidelity)
Goodbye Earl (Mary Anne)
Dixie Chicks; *Fly* (Monument)
Green Green Grass Of Home (Mary)
Burl Ives; *Best Of Burl Ives-#2* (MCA)
Elvis Presley; *Elvis Presley Today* (RCA)
Our Memories Of Elvis, Volume 2 (RCA)
George Jones; *20 Golden Pieces Of George Jones* (Bulldog)
Tom Jones; *Country Side Of Tom Jones* (London)
Things That Matter Most To Me (Mercury)
Tom Jones-London Collector-Greatest Hits (London)
Have You Seen Mary
Sponge; *Wax Ecstatic* (Columbia)
Hello Mary Lou
Creedence Clearwater Revival; *Creedence Country* (Fantasy)
Rick Nelson; *Rick Nelson In Concert-Troubadour 1969* (MCA)
Rick Nelson-Souvenirs (EMI)
Ricky Nelson; *Best Of Ricky Nelson* (EMI)
Rick Nelson's Greatest Hits (Rhino)
Statler Brothers; *14 Country Favorites-C* (Mercury)
Pardners In Rhyme (Mercury)
I Shall Call You Mary
Montage; *Nuggets-#11-Pop-Part 4-C* (Rhino)
I'm Mandy Fly Me
10 CC; *10 CC's Greatest Hits-1972-1978* (Polydor)
How Dare You! (Mercury)
Live & Let Live (Mercury)
Is Zat You, Myrtle
Carlisles; *45-#70174* (Mercury)
Louvin Brothers; *Live At New River Ranch* (Copper Creek)
It's Me Again Margaret
Ray Stevens; *Country Classics-#3-1984-1985-C* (Universal)
He Thinks He's Ray Stevens (MCA)
Ray Stevens' Greatest Hits (MCA)
Killer Joe (Marie)
Rocky Fellers; *Scepter Records Story-C* (Capricorn)
Lady Madonna
Beatles; *Beatles 1* (Capitol)
Hey Jude (Capitol)
Past Masters-Volume Two (Parlophone)
The Beatles/1967-1970 (Capitol)
Wings; *Wings Over America* (Capitol)
Lady Marmalade
Christina Aguilera, Lil' Kim, Mya & Pink; *ST/Moulin Rouge* (Interscope)
Labelle; *Nightbirds* (Epic)
Patti LaBelle; *Best Of Patti LaBelle* (Epic)
Sheila E.; *Sex Cymbal* (Warner Bros.)
Little Maggie
Kingston Trio; *Tom Dooley* (Capitol)
Ricky Skaggs and Kentucky Thunder; *Bluegrass Rules!* (Rounder)
Little Marie
Chuck Berry; *Rock 'N' Roll Rarities-20 Magic Tracks* (Chess)
St. Louis To Liverpool (Chess)
The Chess Box-Chuck Berry (Chess)
Little Martha
Allman Brothers Band; *Best Of The Allman Brothers Band* (Polydor)
Decade Of Hits-1969-1979 (Polydor)
Eat A Peach (Polydor)
Long Tall Sally
Beatles; *Past Masters-Volume One* (Parlophone)
Rock 'N' Roll Music (Capitol)
The Beatles At The Hollywood Bowl (Capitol)
The Beatles' Second Album (Capitol)
Little Richard; *Billboard Top R&B Hits-1956-C* (Rhino)
Here's Little Richard (Specialty)
Little Richard-18 Greatest Hits (Rhino)
Little Richard's Greatest Hits (Everest)
Oldies But Goodies-#3-C (Original Sound)
ST/Heaven Help Us (EMI)
Super Oldies Of The '50s-#3-C (Audio Fidelity)
Tutti Frutti (Accord)

Looking For Mary Jane
Charlie Daniels Band; *Whiskey* . . . . (Epic)
Macarena
Los Del Rio; *Club Cutz* . . . .(RCA)
Macarena Mix . . . . (Ariola America)
Maggie Mae
Beatles; *Let It Be* . . . . (Capitol)
Maggie May
Rod Stewart; *Absolutely Live* . . . . (Warner Bros.)
Best Of Rod Stewart . . . . (Mercury)
Billboard Top Rock 'N' Roll Hits-1971-C . . . . (Rhino)
Every Picture Tells A Story . . . . (Mercury)
Rod Stewart's Greatest Hits . . . . (Warner Bros.)
Sing It Again, Rod . . . . (Mercury)
Storyteller/The Complete Anthology: 1964-1990 . . . . (Warner Bros.)
Maggie's Dream
Don Williams; *Cafe Carolina* . . . . (MCA)
Country Classics-#4-1984-1985-C . . . . (Universal)
Maggie's Farm
Bob Dylan; *Bob Dylan At Budokan* . . . .(Columbia)
Bob Dylan's Greatest Hits-#2 . . . . (Columbia)
Bringing It All Back Home . . . . (Columbia)
Hard Rain . . . . (Columbia)
Real Live . . . . (Columbia)
Magnolia
Tom Petty And The Heartbreakers; *You're Gonna Get It!* . . . .(Gone Gator)
Magnolia
J.J. Cale; *Naturally* . . . . (MCA)
Magnolia
Poco; *Crazy Eyes* . . . . (Epic)
Magnolia
Pat Travers; *Pat Travers* . . . . (Polydor)
Mame
Louis Armstrong; *Mr. Music* . . . .(Accord)
Original Cast; *Mame* . . . . (Columbia)
Mandy
Barry Manilow; *Barry Manilow II* . . . . (Arista)
Barry Manilow's Greatest Hits-#1 . . . . (Arista)
Live On Broadway . . . . (Arista)
Mandy
Eddie Cantor; *Irving Berlin: A Hundred Years-C* . . . . (Columbia)
Fats Waller; *Breakin' The Ice: The Early Years, Part 1 (1934-*
1935) . . . .(Bluebird)
Van & Schenck; *Music From The New York Stage (1890-1920)-#4-1917-*
1920-C . . . .(Pearl)
Margaret's Waltz
Buttons & Bows; *The Celts Rise Again-C* . . . . (Green Linnet)
Margie
Cab Calloway; *More Big Band Greatest Hits-C* . . . . (RCA Victor)
Eddie Cantor; *Eddie Cantor-The Columbia Years: 1922-1940* . . . . (Legacy)
Jimmy Lunceford; *Big Bands Of The Swinging Years-#2-C* . . . . . . (Collectables)
Maria
Original Cast; *ST/West Side Story* . . . . (Sony Broadway)
Maria
Ricky Martin; *Ricky Martin* . . . .(Columbia)
Maria
Original Cast; *The Sound Of Music* . . . . (Broadway Angel)
The Sound Of Music . . . . (Sony Broadway)
Maria
Blondie; *No Exit* . . . . (Beyond)
Maria
Johnny Mathis; *Johnny Mathis' All-Time Greatest Hits* . . . . (Columbia)
Maria
Marvin Gaye; *Romantically Yours* . . . . (Columbia)
Maria Elena
Indios Tabajaras; *Nipper's Greatest Hits Of The '60s-#1-C* . . . . .(RCA)
Maria Elena
Smithereens; *11* . . . .(Enigma)
Maria Elena
Jimmy Dorsey & His Orchestra; *Jimmy Dorsey & His Orchestra's*
Greatest Hits . . . . (MCA)
Maria Maria
Santana; *Supernatural* . . . .(Arista)
Totally Hits-#2-C . . . . (Elektra)
Marian The Librarian
Original Broadway Cast; *The Music Man* . . . . (Angel)
Robert Preston; *ST/The Music Man* . . . . (Warner Bros.)
Marie
Bachelors; *History Of British Rock-#6-C* . . . . (Rhino)
Marie
Tommy Dorsey & His Orchestra; *Seventeen Number Ones* . . . . (RCA)
Marie
Randy Newman; *Good Old Boys* . . . .(Reprise)
Marlena
4 Seasons; *25th Anniversary Collection* . . . . (Rhino)
4 Seasons-Anthology . . . . (Rhino)
Marlena
Bobby Goldsboro; *10th Anniversary Album-#2* . . . .(United Artists)

Marlene
Todd Rundgren; *Something/Anything?* . . . .(Rhino)
Marlene On The Wall
Suzanne Vega; *Suzanne Vega* . . . .(A&M)
Martha My Dear
Beatles; *Beatles-Box Set* . . . .(Capitol)
The Beatles (White Album) . . . .(Capitol)
Martha Say
John Cougar Mellencamp; *Big Daddy* . . . .(Mercury)
Mary
Sarah McLachlan; *Fumbling Towards Ecstasy* . . . .(Arista)
Mary Had A Little Lamb
Garth Brooks; *The Magic Of Christmas: Songs From Call Me Claus* . . .(Capitol)
Original Soundtrack; *Sesame Street: Kids' Favorite Songs-#2* . . .(Sony Wonder)
Stevie Ray Vaughan and Double Trouble; *Live Alive* . . . .(Epic)
Texas Flood . . . .(Epic)
Wings; *Wild Life* . . . . (Capitol)
Mary In The Morning
Al Martino; *Al Martino's Greatest Hits* . . . .(EMI Special Markets)
Mary Jane's Last Dance
Tom Petty And The Heartbreakers; *Playback* . . . . (MCA)
Tom Petty And The Heartbreakers' Greatest Hits . . . . (MCA)
Mary Lou
Bruce Springsteen; *Tracks* . . . .(Columbia)
Mary Mary
Classics IV; *Spooky* . . . . (Liberty)
Very Best Of The Classics IV . . . . (EMI)
Mary Mary
Monkees; *More Of The Monkees* . . . .(Rhino)
Mary Mary
Run-D.M.C.; *Tougher Than Leather* . . . . (Profile)
Mary Queen Of Arkansas
Bruce Springsteen; *Greetings From Asbury Park, N.J.* . . . .(Columbia)
Tracks . . . .(Columbia)
Mary's Boy Child
Andy Williams; *Merry Christmas* . . . .(Columbia)
Anne Murray; *Anne Murray Christmas* . . . .(Liberty)
Harry Belafonte; *Billboard's Greatest Christmas Hits-C* . . . .(Rhino)
This Is Christmas-C . . . . (RCA)
Kiri Te Kanawa; *Christmas With Kiri Te Kanawa* . . . . (London)
Mary's Prayer
Danny Wilson; *Meet Danny Wilson* . . . . (Virgin)
Matilda Matilda
Harry Belafonte; *Harry Belafonte-At Carnegie Hall* . . . . (RCA)
Harry Belafonte-Legendary Performer . . . . (RCA)
Harry Belafonte-Pure Gold . . . . (RCA)
This Is Harry Belafonte . . . . (RCA)
Maxine
Donald Fagen; *The Nightfly* . . . . (Warner Bros.)
Maybelline
Chuck Berry; *Chuck Berry-Golden Hits* . . . .(Mercury)
Chuck Berry's Greatest Hits . . . .(Everest)
Cruisin'-1955-C . . . . (Increase)
Oldies But Goodies-#11-C . . . . (Original Sound)
Super Oldies Of The '50s-#5-C . . . . (Audio Fidelity)
Johnny Rivers; *Johnny Rivers-Anthology 1964-1977* . . . .(Rhino)
Very Best Of Johnny Rivers . . . . (EMI)
Melissa
Allman Brothers Band; *An Evening With The Allman Brothers Band-*
First Set . . . . (Epic)
Best Of The Allman Brothers Band . . . . (Polydor)
Decade Of Hits-1969-1979 . . . . (Polydor)
Eat A Peach . . . . (Polydor)
Memphis (Marie)
Chuck Berry; *Chuck Berry* . . . . (Audio Fidelity)
Chuck Berry-Golden Hits . . . .(Mercury)
Chuck Berry's Greatest Hits . . . .(Everest)
St. Louis To Liverpool . . . . (Chess)
ST/Hail! Hail! Rock 'N' Roll . . . . (MCA)
The Chess Box-Chuck Berry . . . . (Chess)
Toronto Rock 'N' Roll Revival-#2-C . . . .(Accord)
John Cale; *IRS Greatest Hits-#2 & #3-C* . . . . (I.R.S.)
Johnny Rivers; *Best Of Johnny Rivers* . . . . (EMI)
Johnny Rivers-Anthology 1964-1977 . . . . (Rhino)
Lonnie Mack; *Teen Beat-Instrumental Rock-1957-1965-C* . . . .(Capitol)
Michelle
Beatles; *Beatles-Love Songs* . . . .(Capitol)
Rubber Soul . . . .(Capitol)
The Beatles/1962-1966 . . . . (Capitol)
Midnight Mary
Joey Powers; *Dick Bartley's One-Hit Wonders Of The '60s-#1-C* . . . . . .(Rhino)
Mimi
Maurice Chevalier; *Early Movie Hits* . . . . (DRG)
Nipper's Greatest Hits Of The '30s-#1-C . . . . (RCA)
ST/Pepe . . . . (DRG)
Miniskirt Minnie
Wilson Pickett; *A Man & A Half-Best Of Wilson Pickett* . . . .(Rhino)

Minnie The Moocher
Cab Calloway; *Best Of The Big Bands-C* . . . . (Columbia)
   Cab Calloway . . . . (Glendale)
   Dr. Demento Presents The Greatest Novelty Records-#1-1940s &
     Before-C . . . . (Rhino)
   Jazz Heritage: Mr. Hi-De-Ho . . . .(MCA)
   ST/The Blues Brothers . . . . (Atlantic)

Molly
Sponge; *Rotting Pinata* . . . .(Work)

Molly O
Chauncey Olcott; *Music From The New York Stage (1890-1920)-#1-1890-*
   1908-C . . . . (Pearl)

Mona
Bo Diddley; *Legends Of Rock Guitar-'50s-#1-C* . . . . (Rhino)
   Vintage Music-#6-C . . . .(MCA)
Quicksilver Messenger Service; *Happy Trails* . . . . (Capitol)
   Quicksilver Messenger Service-Anthology . . . . (Capitol)
   Sons Of Mercury . . . . (Rhino)
Rolling Stones; *The Rolling Stones, Now!* . . . . (Abkco)

Mona
James Taylor; *That's Why I'm Here* . . . . (Columbia)

Mona
Original Cast; *Pump Boys & Dinettes On Broadway* . . . . (Columbia)

Mona
Wall Of Voodoo; *Seven Days In Sammystown* . . . .(I.R.S.)

Mona Lisa
Carl Mann; *Original Memphis Rock & Roll* . . . . (Sun)
   Sun Story-C . . . . (Rhino)
Elvis Presley; *Elvis-A Legendary Performer, Volume 4* . . . . (RCA)
Jim Reeves; *Jim Reeves-Pure Gold* . . . . (RCA)
Nat ''King'' Cole; *Best Of Nat ''King'' Cole-Vol. 1* . . . . (Capitol)
   Capitol Collectors Series-Nat ''King'' Cole . . . . (Capitol)
   The Nat ''King'' Cole Story . . . . (Capitol)
   Unforgettable . . . . (Capitol)
Neville Brothers; *Fiyo On The Bayou* . . . . (A&M)

Monie In The Middle
Monie Love & True Image; *Down To Earth* . . . .(Warner Bros.)

Mony Mony
Billy Idol; *Don't Stop* . . . .(Chrysalis)
   Vital Idol . . . .(Chrysalis)
   Whiplash Smile . . . .(Chrysalis)
Tommy James And The Shondells; *Billboard Top Rock 'N' Roll Hits-*
   1968-C . . . . (Rhino)
   Frat Rock!-#4-C . . . . (Rhino)
   Tommy James And The Shondells-Anthology . . . . (Rhino)

Mother Mary
UFO; *Force It* . . . .(Chrysalis)
   Strangers In The Night . . . .(Chrysalis)

Mother Mary
Julian Lennon; *Mr. Jordan* . . . .(Atlantic)

Mother Mary
Sheila E.; *Sex Cymbal* . . . .(Warner Bros.)

My Blue Heaven
Artie Shaw; *Complete Artie Shaw-#4* . . . . (RCA)
   This Is Artie Shaw . . . . (Bluebird)
Fats Domino; *Fats Domino-Legendary Masters* . . . . (United Artists)
   Fats Domino's Greatest Hits . . . . (Everest)
   My Blue Heaven-Best Of Fats Domino-#1 . . . . (EMI)
   Oldies But Goodies-#10-C . . . . (Original Sound)
Frank Sinatra; *Frank Sinatra-Gift Set* . . . . (Capitol)
   Sinatra's Swingin' Session!!! . . . . (Capitol)

My Irish Molly-O
De Danann; *Best Of De Danann* . . . . (Shanachie)

My Maria
B.W. Stevenson; *Nipper's Greatest Hits Of The '70s-C* . . . . (RCA)
   Super Hits Of The '70s-Have A Nice Day-#11-C . . . . (Rhino)
Brooks & Dunn; *Borderline* . . . . (Arista)

Ob-La-Di, Ob-La-Da (Desmond & Molly Jones)
Beatles; *Beatles-Box Set* . . . . (Capitol)
   The Beatles (White Album) . . . . (Capitol)
   The Beatles/1967-1970 . . . . (Capitol)

Oh Marie
Sheryl Crow; *Sheryl Crow* . . . . (A&M)

Oh Mary Don't You Weep
Pete Seeger; *Live At Newport* . . . . (Vanguard)

Prairie Wedding (Mary)
Mark Knopfler; *Sailing To Philadelphia* . . . .(Warner Bros.)

Proud Mary
Creedence Clearwater Revival; *1968-1969* . . . . (Fantasy)
   Bayou Country . . . . (Fantasy)
   Creedence Clearwater Revival-Chronicle . . . . (Fantasy)
   Creedence Clearwater Revival-Gold . . . . (Fantasy)
   Live In Europe . . . . (Fantasy)
George Jones & Johnny Paycheck; *My Very Special Guests* . . . .(Epic)
Ike & Tina Turner; *Best Of Ike & Tina Turner* . . . . (EMI)
   Didn't It Blow Your Mind: Soul Hits Of The '70s-#4-C . . . . . . (Rhino)
   EMI Legends Of Rock & Roll-24 Greatest Hits-C . . . .(EMI)

   Ike & Tina Turner's Greatest Hits . . . . (Curb)

Put The Blame On Mame
Mark Murphy; *Singin' In The Rain-Capitol Sings Hollywood-C* . . . . . (Capitol)

Riding With Mary
X; *Live At The Whisky A Go-Go* . . . . (Elektra)
   Under The Big Black Sun . . . . (Elektra)

River, The (Mary)
Bruce Springsteen; *The River* . . . . (Columbia)

Robin And Marian
Nickel Creek; *Nickel Creek* . . . .(Sugar Hill)

Saint Joe On The School Bus (Mary)
Marcy Playground; *Marcy Playground* . . . . (Capitol)

San Francisco Mabel Joy
Joan Baez; *Country Music Album* . . . . (Vanguard)
John Denver; *Some Days Are Diamonds* . . . . (RCA)
Kenny Rogers; *The Gambler* . . . . (EMI)
Mickey Newbury; *Bread & Roses Festival Of Acoustic Music-#1-C* . . . (Fantasy)
   Heaven Help The Child . . . . (Elektra)
   Live At Montezuma Hall . . . . (Elektra)

Searching For Madge
Fleetwood Mac; *Then Play On* . . . . (Reprise)

Skinny Minnie
Bill Haley & His Comets; *Bill Haley & His Comets' Greatest Hits* . . . . (MCA)
   Bill Haley & His Comets-Golden Hits . . . . (MCA)

Sleepy Maggie
Ashley MacIsaac; *Hi How Are You Today?* . . . . (A&M)

Suddenly Mary
Posies; *Dear 23* . . . . (David Geffen Co.)

Superwoman (Mary)
Stevie Wonder; *Music Of My Mind* . . . . (Motown)
   Original Musiquarium . . . . (Motown)

Sweet Afton (Mary)
Nickel Creek; *Nickel Creek* . . . .(Sugar Hill)

Sweet Lady Mary
Rod Stewart/Faces; *Storyteller/The Complete Anthology: 1964-*
   1990 . . . . (Warner Bros.)

Sweet Little Missy
Lynyrd Skynyrd; *Lynyrd Skynyrd-Legend* . . . . (MCA)

Sweet Mary
Wadsworth Mansion; *Super Hits Of The '70s-Have A Nice Day-#4-C* . . . (Rhino)

Sweet Maxine
Doobie Brothers; *Stampede* . . . .(Warner Bros.)

Take A Letter Maria
R.B. Greaves; *Didn't It Blow Your Mind: Soul Hits Of The '70s-#1-C* . . . (Rhino)

Take A Message To Mary
Bob Dylan; *Self Portrait* . . . . (Columbia)
Everly Brothers; *Everly Brothers-All-Time Original Hits* . . . . (Rhino)
   Everly Brothers-Cadence Classics-Their 20 Greatest Hits . . . . . . (Rhino)
Rockpile; *Seconds Of Pleasure* . . . . (Columbia)

Theme From ''Mary Hartman, Mary Hartman''
Original Soundtrack; *Television's Greatest Hits-#5-In Living Color-C* . . . (TVT)

Theme From ''Maude''
Original Soundtrack; *Television's Greatest Hits-#3-1970s & 1980s-C* . . . (TVT)

Theme From ''Mork & Mindy''
Original Soundtrack; *Television's Greatest Hits-#6-Remote Control-C* . . . (TVT)

Theme From ''Murphy Brown''
Original Soundtrack; *CBS: The First 50 Years* . . . . (TVT)

Theme From ''My Little Margie''
Original Soundtrack; *Television's Greatest Hits-#4-Black & White*
   Classics-C . . . . (TVT)

Theme From ''The Days And Nights Of Molly Dodd''
Original Soundtrack; *Television's Greatest Hits-#7-Cable Ready-C* . . . (TVT)

Theme From ''The Ghost And Mrs. Muir''
Original Soundtrack; *Television's Greatest Hits-#5-In Living Color-C* . . . (TVT)

Theme From ''The Mary Tyler Moore Show''
Original Soundtrack-Sonny Curtis; *CBS: The First 50 Years* . . . . (TVT)
   Television's Greatest Hits-#2-C . . . . (TVT)

Theme From ''The Real McCoys''
Original Soundtrack; *Television's Greatest Hits-#4-Black & White*
   Classics-C . . . . (TVT)

They Call The Wind Maria
Kingston Trio; *Early American Heroes* . . . .(Pair)
   Kingston Trio/From The Hungry i . . . . (Capitol)
   Stereo Concert Plus . . . . (Folk Era)
Original Broadway Cast; *Paint Your Wagon* . . . . (RCA Victor)

Three Marlenas
Wallflowers; *Bringing Down The Horse* . . . .(Interscope)

Thunder Road (Mary)
Bruce Springsteen; *Born To Run* . . . . (Columbia)
   Bruce Springsteen's Greatest Hits . . . . (Columbia)
Bruce Springsteen & The E Street Band; *Bruce Springsteen & The E Street*
   Band Live/1975-85 . . . . (Legacy)

Til Melinda Comes Around
Gene Watson; *Old Loves Never Die* . . . . (MCA)

To M.G. (Wherever She May Be)
John Cougar; *Nothin' Matters And What If It Did* . . . . (Riva)

Waltzing Matilda
Burl Ives; *Best Of Burl Ives* . . . . (MCA)
Fred Astaire; *Three Evenings With Fred Astaire* . . . .(DRG)
James Galway; *Pachebel Canon & Other Favorites* . . . .(RCA)
Original Soundtrack; *Children's Favorites* . . . . (Kid Rhino/Rhino 4 Kids)
What Will My Mary Say
Jay & The Americans; *Come A Little Bit Closer-Best Of Jay & The*
Americans . . . . (Gold Rush)
Johnny Mathis; *Johnny Mathis' All-Time Greatest Hits* . . . . (Columbia)
Johnny Mathis-16 Most Requested Songs . . . . (Columbia)
What's The New Mary Jane
Beatles; *The Beatles-Anthology-#3* . . . . (Capitol)
Whiskey In The Jar (Molly)
Metallica; *Garage Inc.* . . . . (Elektra)
Who Put The Benzedrine In Mrs. Murphy's Ovaltine?
Harry Gibson; *Dr. Demento's Delights-C* . . . . (Warner Bros.)
Who Threw The Overalls In Mrs. Murphy's Chowder
Bing Crosby; *Shillelaghs & Shamrocks* . . . . (MCA)
Wind Cries Mary
Jimi Hendrix; *Essential Jimi Hendrix, Volume 2* . . . .(Reprise)
Jimi Hendrix Experience; *Are You Experienced?* . . . .(Reprise)
Smash Hits . . . .(Reprise)

WOMEN'S NAMES: N

See Also: **CELEBRITIES: SPECIFIC, FAMILY (various),**
WOMEN: GENERAL

99
Toto; *Hydra* . . . . (Columbia)
Candle In The Wind (Norma Jean)
Elton John; *Goodbye Yellow Brick Road* . . . . (Polydor)
Live In Australia With The Melbourne Symphony Orchestra . . . . (MCA)
Your Songs . . . . (Polydor)
Little Joe The Wrangler's Sister Nell
Skip Gorman; *A Cowboy's Wild Song To His Herd* . . . . (Rounder)
Lullaby For Nancy Carol
Chuck Mangione; *Best Of Chuck Mangione* . . . . (Mercury)
Land Of Make Believe . . . . (Mercury)
Together . . . . (Mercury)
Nadine (Is It You?)
Chuck Berry; *Rock & Roll Rarities* . . . . (Chess)
Nancy (With The Laughing Face)
Frank Sinatra; *Sinatra Reprise-The Very Good Years* . . . .(Reprise)
Sinatra's Sinatra . . . .(Reprise)
John Coltrane; *The Gentle Side Of John Coltrane* . . . .(GRP)
Tony Bennett; *Perfectly Frank* . . . . (Columbia)
Nancy Whiskey
Ian & Sylvia; *Ian & Sylvia* . . . . (Vanguard)
Ian & Sylvia's Greatest Hits . . . . (Vanguard)
Irish Rovers; *Irish Rovers' Greatest Hits.* . . . . (MCA)
Nikita
Elton John; *Elton John's Greatest Hits-1976-1986* . . . . (MCA)
Ice On Fire . . . . (MCA)
Nina
Bobby Short; *Bobby, Noel & Cole* . . . . (Atlantic)
Norma Jean Riley
Diamond Rio; *Diamond Rio* . . . . (Arista)
Diamond Rio's Greatest Hits . . . . (Arista)
Rocky Raccoon (Nancy)
Beatles; *Beatles-Box Set* . . . . (Capitol)
The Beatles (White Album) . . . . (Capitol)
Teenage Dirtbag (Noel)
Wheatus; *Wheatus* . . . . (Columbia)
Wait Till The Sun Shines Nellie
Joan Morris & William Bolcom; *After The Ball* . . . . (Nonesuch)
Why Don't You Get A Job? (Nana)
Offspring; *Americana* . . . . (Columbia)

WOMEN'S NAMES: O

See Also: **CELEBRITIES: SPECIFIC, FAMILY (various),**
WOMEN: GENERAL

Cry Ophelia
Adam Cohen; *Songs From Dawson's Creek* . . . . (Sony Music Soundtrax)
Ophelia
Band; *Best Of The Band* . . . . (Capitol)
Northern Lights-Southern Cross. . . . . (Capitol)
The Last Waltz . . . . (Warner Bros.)
To Kingdom Come-The Definitive Collection . . . . (Capitol)

Ophelia
Jesse Colin Young; *Best Of Jesse Colin Young-Solo Years* . . . .(Rhino)

WOMEN'S NAMES: P

See Also: **CELEBRITIES: SPECIFIC, FAMILY (various),**
WOMEN: GENERAL

Cool Pearl
Capitols; *Golden Classics-Capitols* . . . . (Collectables)
Dear Prudence
Beatles; *The Beatles (White Album)* . . . .(Capitol)
Siouxsie And The Banshees; *Hyaena.* . . . . (Geffen)
Nocturne . . . . (Geffen)
Hey Paula
Paul & Paula; *Cruisin'-1963-C* . . . . (Increase)
ST/Animal House . . . . (MCA)
WCBS FM 101 History Of Rock-'60s-#1-C . . . .(Collectables)
John Brown's Body (Polly)
Pete Seeger; *American Favorite Ballads-#3* . . . . (Smithsonian Folkways)
Sonny Terry & Brownie McGhee; *Every Tone A*
Testimony-C . . . . (Smithsonian Folkways)
Lilies Of The Field (Penny)
Gretchen Peters; *Gretchen Peters* . . . . (Purple Crayon Prod.)
Mrs. Potter's Lullaby
Counting Crows; *This Desert Life* . . . . (David Geffen Co.)
My Name Is Petula
Petula Clark; *Petula Clark* . . . . (Crescendo)
Patricia
Perez Prado & His Orchestra; *Nipper's Greatest Hits Of The*
'50s-#2-C . . . . (RCA)
Perry Como; *Perry Como's Greatest Hits* . . . . (RCA)
Patty On The Turnpike
Don Stover; *Things In Life* . . . . (Rounder)
Peg
Steely Dan; *Aja* . . . . (MCA)
Decade Of Steely Dan . . . . (MCA)
Steely Dan's Greatest Hits . . . . (MCA)
Peggy Day
Bob Dylan; *Nashville Skyline.* . . . . (Columbia)
Peggy Sue
Buddy Holly; *Billboard Top Rock 'N' Roll Hits-1957-C* . . . .(Rhino)
Buddy Holly. . . . . (MCA)
Buddy Holly-20 Golden Greats . . . . (MCA)
Buddy Holly's Greatest Hits . . . . (MCA)
More American Graffiti-C . . . . (MCA)
Oldies But Goodies-#4-C . . . . (Original Sound)
Rock & Roll Collection . . . . (MCA)
Peggy Sue Got Married
Buddy Holly; *Buddy Holly-20 Golden Greats* . . . . (MCA)
Rock & Roll Collection . . . . (MCA)
Peggy Suicide Is Missing
Julian Cope; *Jehovahkill* . . . .(Island)
Peggy's Kitchen Wall
Bruce Cockburn; *Stealing Fire.* . . . .(Columbia)
Penny
Joe Stampley; *Best Of Joe Stampley.* . . . . (Varese Sarabande)
Penny Lover
Lionel Richie; *Back To Front.* . . . .(Motown)
Can't Slow Down . . . .(Motown)
Polythene Pam
Beatles; *Abbey Road* . . . . (Parlophone)
Beatles-Box Set . . . .(Capitol)
Pretty Penny
Stone Temple Pilots; *Purple.* . . . . (Atlantic)
Pretty Polly
Judy Collins; *Who Knows Where The Time Goes.* . . . .(Elektra)
Stanley Brothers; *Complete Columbia Stanley Brothers* . . . .(Legacy)
Folk Classics: Roots Of American Folk Music-C . . . .(Columbia)
Long Journey Home . . . . (Rebel)
Swee' Pea
Count Basie; *Best Of Count Basie & His Orchestra.* . . . . (Pablo)
Sweet Pea
Tommy Roe; *Best Of Tommy Roe* . . . .(Curb)
Cruisin'-1966-C . . . .(Increase)
Tommy Roe's Greatest Hits . . . . (MCA)
Sweet Peggy O'Neill
John McCormack; *Drop Of The Irish.* . . . . (Pearl Flapper)
Theme From "The Partridge Family"
Original Soundtrack; *Television's Greatest Hits-#2-C* . . . .(TVT)
Theme From "The Patty Duke Show"
Original Soundtrack; *Just Patty: The Best Of Patty Duke* . . . .(EMI)
Television's Greatest Hits-#1-C . . . .(TVT)
Who Played Poker With Pocahontas?
Fannie Watson; *Music From The New York Stage (1890-1920)-#4-1917-*
1920-C . . . . (Pearl)

WOMEN'S NAMES: R

See Also: **CELEBRITIES: SPECIFIC, FAMILY (various), FLOWERS: ROSES, WOMEN: GENERAL**

All My Ex's Live In Texas (Rosanna)
George Strait; *Country Classics-#10-1987-C* . . . . (Universal)
   George Strait's Greatest Hits-#2 . . . . (MCA)
   Ocean Front Property . . . . (MCA)
Arizona Rose
Waco Brothers; *Do You Think About Me* . . . . (Bloodshot)
Aunt Rhody
Burl Ives; *Poor Wayfaring Stranger* . . . . (Flapper)
Baby Ruth
John Prine; *Storm Windows* . . . . (Asylum)
Bed Of Rose's
Screaming Trees; *Uncle Anesthesia* . . . . (Epic)
Bed Of Rose's
Kenny Rogers; *Back Home Again* . . . . (Reprise)
Bed Of Rose's
Statler Brothers; *Bed Of Rose's* . . . . (Mercury)
Big City Miss Ruth Ann
Gallery; *Super Hits Of The '70s-Have A Nice Day-#11-C* . . . . (Rhino)
Company Time (Ruthie)
Linda Davis; *Shoot For The Moon* . . . . (Arista)
Cracklin' Rosie
Neil Diamond; *Hot August Night* . . . . (MCA)
   Hot August Night II . . . . (Columbia)
   Neil Diamond-His 12 Greatest Hits . . . . (MCA)
   Tap Root Manuscript . . . . (MCA)
Dear Mrs. Roosevelt
Bob Dylan; *Tribute To Woody Guthrie-C* . . . .(Warner Bros.)
Feet Up (Pat Him On The Po-Po) (Rosie)
Guy Mitchell; *Definitive Guy Mitchell* . . . . (Collector's Choice)
Give My Love To Rose
George Jones; *George Jones Sings The Hits Of His Country*
   Cousins . . . . (Razor & Tie)
Johnny Cash; *Johnny Cash-Sun Years* . . . . (Rhino)
Help Me Rhonda
Beach Boys; *Billboard Top Rock 'N' Roll Hits-1965-C* . . . . (Rhino)
   California Girls . . . . (Capitol)
   Dance Dance Dance . . . . (Capitol)
   Endless Summer . . . . (Capitol)
   Made In The U.S.A. . . . . (Capitol)
It's The Truth Ruth
Big Bopper; *Hellooo Baby! Best Of The Big Bopper-1954-1959* . . . . (Rhino)
Jacob's Ladder (Rachel)
Mark Wills; *Mark Wills* . . . . (Mercury)
Li'l Red Riding Hood
Sam The Sham and The Pharaohs; *Best Of Sam The Sham and The*
   Pharaohs . . . . (Polydor)
   Cruisin'-1966-C . . . . (Increase)
   Pharaohization! (Best Of) . . . . (Rhino)
Lily, Rosemary And The Jack Of Hearts
Bob Dylan; *Blood On The Tracks* . . . . (Columbia)
Little Rachel
Eric Clapton; *There's One In Every Crowd* . . . . (Polydor)
Lovely Rita
Beatles; *Sgt. Pepper's Lonely Hearts Club Band* . . . . (Capitol)
Me And Julio Down By The Schoolyard (Rosie)
Paul Simon; *Greatest Hits, Etc.* . . . . (Columbia)
   Negotiations And Love Songs, 1971-1986 . . . .(Warner Bros.)
   Paul Simon . . . . (Columbia)
   Paul Simon In Concert/Live Rhymin'. . . . . (Columbia)
Simon & Garfunkel; *The Concert In Central Park* . . . .(Warner Bros.)
Mrs. Robinson
Simon & Garfunkel; *Bookends* . . . . (Columbia)
   Collected Works . . . . (Columbia)
   Hollywood Magic-1960s-C . . . . (Columbia)
   Simon & Garfunkel's Greatest Hits . . . . (Columbia)
   ST/Forrest Gump . . . .(Epic/Sony Music Soundtrax)
   ST/The Graduate . . . . (Columbia)
   The Concert In Central Park . . . .(Warner Bros.)
My Brown Eyed Texas Rose
Tex Ritter; *Arizona Days* . . . .(MCA Special Prod.)
   The Country Music Hall Of Fame-Tex Ritter . . . .(MCA)
New San Antonio Rose
Bob Wills & His Texas Playboys; *Bob Wills & His Texas Playboys-*
   Greatest Hits . . . . (Curb)
   Columbia Country Classics-#1-Golden Age-C . . . . (Columbia)
   Essential Bob Wills & His Texas Playboys-1935-1973 . . . . (Legacy)
Dwight Yoakam & Asleep At The Wheel; *Ride With*
   Bob-C . . . . (DreamWorks/SKG)
One More Time Around Rosie
Manhattan Transfer; *Jukin'.* . . . . (Capitol)
Paper Rosie
Don Walser; *Here's To Country Music.* . . . . (Sire)
Gene Watson; *Gene Watson's Greatest Hits* . . . . (Curb)

Osborne Brothers; *Hillbilly Fever* . . . . (C.M.H. Prod.)
Picture Postcards From L.A.
Joshua Kadison; *Painted Desert Serenade* . . . . (SBK)
Rachel
Al Martino; *Capitol Collectors Series-Al Martino* . . . . (Capitol)
Rachel
Jolly Boys; *Sunshine 'N' Water.* . . . . (Rykodisc)
Rachel
Buddy & Julie Miller; *Buddy & Julie Miller* . . . .(Hightone)
Rachel's Dream
Benny Goodman; *I Like Jazz-Essence Of Benny Goodman* . . . . (Columbia)
   Yale Recordings-#5-Private Collection . . . . (Musicmasters)
Ramble On Rose
Grateful Dead; *Europe '72* . . . . (Warner Bros.)
   What A Long Strange Trip It's Been: The Best Of The
   Grateful Dead . . . . (Warner Bros.)
Ramblin' Rose
Hank Snow; *Collector's Series-Hank Snow-#2.* . . . . (RCA)
Nat "King" Cole; *Best Of Nat "King" Cole-Vol. 1* . . . . (Capitol)
   Memories Are Made Of This-C . . . . (Capitol)
Ramblin' Rose
Chuck Berry; *Chuck Berry's Greatest Hits* . . . . (Everest)
Ramona
Ramones; *All The Stuff & More-#2* . . . . (Sire)
   Rocket To Russia . . . . (Sire)
Ramona From Daytona
Dave Holladay; *Ramona From Daytona* . . . . (Step One)
Ravishing Ruby
Tom T. Hall; *Essential Tom T. Hall-20th Anniversary Collection* . . . . (Mercury)
   Tom T. Hall's Greatest Hits-#2 . . . . (Mercury)
Rebecca
Pat McGhee Band; *Shine.* . . . . (Giant/Warner Bros.)
Rebecca Lynn
Bryan White; *Bryan White* . . . . (Asylum)
Rhiannon (Will You Ever Win)
Fleetwood Mac; *25 Years-The Chain* . . . . (Warner Bros.)
   Fleetwood Mac. . . . . (Reprise)
   Fleetwood Mac Live. . . . . (Warner Bros.)
   Fleetwood Mac's Greatest Hits . . . . (Warner Bros.)
Ricky Wants A Man Of Her Own
Bruce Springsteen; *Tracks* . . . . (Columbia)
Rikki Don't Lose That Number
Steely Dan; *Classic Rock-#2-C* . . . . (MCA)
   Decade Of Steely Dan . . . . (MCA)
   Pretzel Logic . . . . (MCA)
   Steely Dan's Greatest Hits . . . . (MCA)
Rock & Roll Ruby
Warren Smith; *Memphis Country-C* . . . . (Sun)
   Original Memphis Rock & Roll . . . . (Sun)
Rocky
Austin Roberts; *Super Hits Of The '70s-Have A Nice Day-#15-C.* . . . . . (Rhino)
Roni
Bobby Brown; *Dance!...Ya Know It!* . . . . (MCA)
   Don't Be Cruel . . . . (MCA)
Ronnie
4 Seasons; *25th Anniversary Collection* . . . . (Rhino)
   4 Seasons' Greatest Hits-#1 . . . . (Rhino)
   4 Seasons-Anthology . . . . (Rhino)
Rosa De San Antonio
Santiago Jimenez, Jr.; *Mero Mero De San Antonio* . . . . (Arhoolie)
Rosa Parks
Outkast; *Aquemini.* . . . .(LaFace/Arista)
Rosabella
Original Broadway Cast; *The Most Happy Fella.* . . . .(Sony Music Classical)
Rosalinda's Eyes
Billy Joel; *52nd Street.* . . . . (Columbia)
Rosalita
Bruce Springsteen; *The Wild, The Innocent & The E Street Shuffle.* . . (Columbia)
Bruce Springsteen & The E Street Band; *Bruce Springsteen & The E Street*
   Band Live/1975-85 . . . . (Legacy)
Rosanna
Toto; *'80s Greatest Rock Hits-#1-Passion & Power-C.* . . . . (Priority)
   Past To Present 1977-1990 . . . . (Columbia)
   Toto IV . . . . (Columbia)
Rose
James Horner; *ST/Titanic* . . . .(Sony Music Classical)
Rose Goes To Yale
Jefferson Starship; *Nuclear Furniture.* . . . . (Grunt)
Rose Of Old Monterey
Happy Polkateers; *Happy Polkateers* . . . .(Crescendo)
Rose Of San Antone
Bashful Brother Oswald; *Don't Say Aloha* . . . . (Rounder)
Rose, Rose I Love You
Frankie Laine; *Frankie Laine's Greatest Hits* . . . . (Columbia)
Rose, The
Bette Midler; *Hit Singles-1980-1988-C* . . . .(Atlantic)
   ST/The Rose . . . .(Atlantic)
Conway Twitty; *Dream Maker* . . . . (Elektra)

Latest Greatest Hits-#1 . . . . (Warner Bros.)
Number One's: The Warner Bros. Years . . . . (Warner Bros.)
Rosemary
Grateful Dead; *Aoxomoxoa* . . . . (Warner Bros.)
Best Of/Skeletons From The Closet. (Warner Bros.)
Rosemary
Lenny Kravitz; *Let Love Rule* . . . .(Virgin)
Rose's Turn
Original Cast; *Gypsy* . . . . (Columbia)
Original London Cast; *Gypsy* . . . .(RCA)
Rosey From Jersey
Li'l Wally; *I Love To Polka* . . . . (Jay Jay)
Rosie
Dick Van Dyke; *ST/Bye Bye Birdie* . . . .(RCA)
Original Cast; *Bye Bye Birdie* . . . . (Columbia)
Rosie
Joan Armatrading; *Joan Armatrading-Classics-#21* . . . . (A&M)
Track Record . . . . (A&M)
Rosie
Johnny & The Distractions; *My Desire* . . . .(Burnside)
Rosie
Jackson Browne; *Running On Empty* . . . . (Asylum)
Rosie
Richie Sambora; *Stranger In This Town* . . . . (Mercury)
Rosie
Beat Farmers; *The Pursuit Of Happiness*. . . . .(Curb)
Rosie Strikes Back
Eliza Gilkyson; *Texas-A Musical Celebration-150 Years* . . . .(Tomato)
Rosanne Cash; *King's Record Shop* . . . . (Columbia)
Roxanne
Police; *Every Breath You Take-The Classics* . . . . (A&M)
Outlandos D'Amour . . . . (A&M)
Sting; *The Secret Policeman's Other Ball/The Music* . . . .(Rhino)
Ruby Ann
Marty Robbins; *American Originals-Marty Robbins* . . . . (Columbia)
Billboard Top Country Hits-1963-C. . . . .(Rhino)
Essential Marty Robbins-1951-1982 . . . . (Columbia)
Ruby Baby
Beatles; *The Beatles featuring Tony Sheridan-In The Beginning (Circa 1960)* . . . . (Polydor)
Dion; *Bronx Blues-Columbia Recordings 1962-1965* . . . . (Columbia)
Dion-24 Original Classics . . . . (Arista)
Donald Fagen; *The Nightfly* . . . . (Warner Bros.)
Drifters; *Atlantic Rhythm & Blues 1947-1974-#3 (1955-1958)-C* . . . . (Atlantic)
Drifters-Their Greatest Recordings . . . . (Atco)
Let The Boogie Woogie Roll-Greatest Hits . . . . (Atlantic)
Ruby Tuesday
Rolling Stones; *Between The Buttons* . . . . (Abkco)
Flashpoint. . . . .(Virgin)
Flowers . . . . (Abkco)
Hot Rocks 1964-1971 . . . . (Abkco)
Singles Collection-The London Years. (Abkco)
Through The Past, Darkly (Big Hits Vol. 2) . . . . (Abkco)
Ruby, Don't Take Your Love To Town
Kenny Rogers; *Kenny Rogers-20 Great Years* . . . . (Reprise)
Kenny Rogers-Twenty Greatest Hits. . . . . (EMI)
Ten Years Of Gold . . . . (EMI)
Kenny Rogers And The First Edition; *Hits & Pieces*. . . . . (MCA)
Kenny Rogers And The First Edition's Greatest Hits . . . . (K-Tel)
Mel Tillis; *Best Of Mel Tillis* . . . . (MCA)
Mel Tillis & The Statesiders; *Mel Tillis & The Statesiders-24 Great Hits* . . . . (MGM)
M-M-Mel Live . . . . (MCA)
Ruby's Golden Wedding
Danny Wilson; *Meet Danny Wilson* . . . .(Virgin)
San Antonio Rose
Asleep At The Wheel; *Western Standard Time* . . . . (Epic)
Bob Wills; *Best Of Bob Wills-#2* . . . . (MCA)
Sounds Of Texas . . . . (Capitol)
Texas State Of Mind-C . . . . (Capitol)
Floyd Cramer; *Billboard Top Country Hits-1961-C* . . . .(Rhino)
Country Love . . . .(Step One)
Patsy Cline; *The Patsy Cline Story* . . . . (MCA)
Ricky Skaggs; *Comin' Home To Stay* . . . . (Epic)
Willie Nelson; *What A Wonderful World*. . . . . (Columbia)
Second Hand Rose
Barbra Streisand; *A Happening In Central Park* . . . . (Columbia)
Barbra Streisand...and other musical instruments . . . . (Columbia)
Barbra Streisand's Greatest Hits . . . . (Columbia)
Just For The Record . . . . (Columbia)
My Name Is Barbra, Two . . . . (Columbia)
See Ruby Fall
Johnny Cash; *Essential Johnny Cash* . . . . (Columbia)
Set Me Free (Rosa Lee)
Los Lobos; *By The Light Of The Moon* . . . . (Slash)
She's Taken A Shine (Rosie)
John Berry; *Faces* . . . . (Capitol)
Sister Rosa
Neville Brothers; *Yellow Moon* . . . . (A&M)

Sweet Milwaukee Rose
Andy Badale & The Beer Garden Band; *Nashville Beer Garden* . . . . . (Ranwood)
Sweet Rosalyn
Sheryl Crow; *Sheryl Crow* . . . .(A&M)
Sweet Rosemary
Sandy Denny; *Who Knows Where The Time Goes* . . . . (Hannibal)
Take Him Back, Rachel
Basia; *London Warsaw New York* . . . .(Epic)
Theme From "Roseanne"
Original Soundtrack; *Television's Greatest Hits-#7-Cable Ready-C* . . . . .(TVT)
To Ramona
Bob Dylan; *Another Side Of Bob Dylan* . . . .(Columbia)
Biograph . . . .(Columbia)
Flying Burrito Brothers; *Flying Burrito Brothers* . . (Mobile Fidelity Sound Lab)
Texas Tornados; *Hangin' On By A Thread* . . . . (Reprise)
Tokyo Rose
Van Dyke Parks; *Tokyo Rose* . . . . (Warner Bros.)
Tokyo Rose
Shok Paris; *Steel & Starlight* . . . . (I.R.S.)
Walk Away Renee
Four Tops; *Compact Command Performances-Four Tops* . . . . (Motown)
Four Tops Reach Out . . . . (Motown)
Four Tops-Anthology . . . . (Motown)
Left Banke; *Cruisin'-1966-C*. . . . . (Increase)
History Of The Left Banke. . . . . (Rhino)
Vonda Shepard; *ST/Songs From "Ally McBeal" Featuring Vonda Shepard* . . . . (550/Epic)
Who I Am (Rosemary)
Jessica Andrews; *Who I Am* . . . . (DreamWorks/SKG)

WOMEN'S NAMES: S

See Also: CELEBRITIES: SPECIFIC, FAMILY (various), WOMEN: GENERAL

4th Of July, Asbury Park (Sandy)
Bruce Springsteen; *The Wild, The Innocent & The E Street Shuffle* . . .(Columbia)
Bruce Springsteen & The E Street Band; *Bruce Springsteen & The E Street Band Live/1975-85* . . . .(Legacy)
Callin' Baton Rouge (Samantha)
Garth Brooks; *In Pieces* . . . . (Liberty)
New Grass Revival; *New Grass Revival-Anthology*. . . . . (Liberty)
Oak Ridge Boys; *Room Service* . . . . (MCA Special Prod.)
Crocodile Rock (Susie)
Elton John; *Don't Shoot Me I'm Only The Piano Player* . . . . (Polydor)
Elton John's Greatest Hits . . . . (Polydor)
Here And There . . . .(Rocket)
Dead Flowers (Susie)
Rolling Stones; *Sticky Fingers* . . . . (Virgin)
Steve Earle & The Dukes; *Shut Up And Die Like An Aviator* . . . . (MCA)
Eggs And Sausage (In A Cadillac With Susan Michelson)
Tom Waits; *Nighthawks At The Diner* . . . . (Asylum)
Fire And Rain (Suzanne)
James Taylor; *James Taylor's Greatest Hits* . . . .(Warner Bros.)
Sweet Baby James . . . . (Warner Bros.)
Sammy Kershaw; *Red Hot + Country-C* . . . .(Mercury)
Hang On Sloopy
McCoys; *21 Oldies But Goodies-C* . . . . (Original Sound)
Billboard Top Rock 'N' Roll Hits-1965-C. . . . .(Rhino)
Frat Rock!-C. . . . .(Rhino)
Oldies But Goodies-#14-C . . . . (Original Sound)
Ramsey Lewis; *Greatest Hits Of Ramsey Lewis*. . . . . (Chess)
Vintage Music-#20-C . . . . (MCA)
Happy Birthday To Little Sally Spingel Spungel Sporn
Dr. Seuss; *The Cat In The Hat Songbook* . . . . (RCA Special Prod.)
I Like It Like That, Part 1 (Sally) (Sue)
Chris Kenner; *Billboard Top Rock 'N' Roll Hits-1961-C*. . . . .(Rhino)
ST/Full Metal Jacket . . . .(Warner Bros.)
If You Knew Susie (Like I Know Susie)
Eddie Cantor; *Memories* . . . . (MCA)
Just Friends (Sarah)
Musiq Soulchild; *Aijuswanaseing* . . . .(Def Soul/IDJMG)
Lady Came From Baltimore (Susan Moore)
Joan Baez; *Contemporary Ballad Book* . . . .(Vanguard)
Joan. . . . .(Vanguard)
John Stewart; *Neon Beach* . . . .(Homecoming)
Johnny Cash; *Johnny Cash-16 Biggest Hits-#2* . . . .(Legacy)
Tim Hardin; *Hang On To A Dream-Verve Recordings* . . . . (Polydor)
Las Vegas Turnaround (Sarah)
Daryl Hall & John Oates; *Abandoned Luncheonette* . . . . (Atlantic)
No Goodbyes. . . . . (Atlantic)
Lay Down Sally
Eric Clapton; *Eric Clapton-Crossroads-C*. . . . . (Polydor)
Just One Night. . . . . (Polydor)
Slowhand . . . . (Polydor)
Time Pieces-#1-The Best Of Eric Clapton. . . . . (Polydor)

Leaving October (Sara)
Sons Of The Desert; *Whatever Comes First* . . . .(Epic)
Let Sally Drive
Sammy Hagar; *Ten 13* . . . . (Cabo Wabo/Beyond)
Little Miss Strange
Jimi Hendrix Experience; *Electric Ladyland* . . . . (Reprise)
Little Sadie
Bob Dylan; *Self Portrait* . . . . (Columbia)
Little Sally Tease
Standells; *Best Of The Standells* . . . . (Rhino)
Little Sally, The Super Sex Star
Camille Yarborough; *Iron Pot Cooker* . . . . (Vanguard)
Long Tall Sally
Beatles; *Past Masters-Volume One* . . . . (Parlophone)
　Rock 'N' Roll Music . . . . (Capitol)
　The Beatles At The Hollywood Bowl . . . . (Capitol)
　The Beatles' Second Album . . . . (Capitol)
Little Richard; *Billboard Top R&B Hits-1956-C* . . . . (Rhino)
　Here's Little Richard . . . .(Specialty)
　Little Richard-18 Greatest Hits . . . . (Rhino)
　Little Richard's Greatest Hits . . . . (Everest)
　Oldies But Goodies-#3-C . . . . (Original Sound)
　ST/Heaven Help Us . . . .(EMI)
　Super Oldies Of The '50s-#3-C . . . .(Audio Fidelity)
　Tutti Frutti . . . . (Accord)
Looking For Suzanne
Waylon Jennings; *Waylon Jennings' Greatest Hits-#2.* . . . . (RCA)
Me & Sarah Jane
Genesis; *Abacab* . . . .(Atlantic)
　Three Sides Live . . . .(Atlantic)
Mellow Yellow (Saffron)
Donovan; *Donovan's Greatest Hits* . . . .(Epic)
　Seems Like Yesterday-#5-Mid '60s-C . . . . (K-Tel)
Miss Sun
Boz Scaggs; *Boz Scaggs-Hits!* . . . . (Columbia)
Miss Sun
Toto; *Toto* . . . . (Columbia)
Mrs. Steven Rudy
Mark McGuinn; *Mark McGuinn.* . . . . (VFR)
Mustang Sally
Rascals; *Rascals' Greatest Hits* . . . .(Atlantic)
Wilson Pickett; *A Man & A Half-Best Of Wilson Pickett* . . . . (Rhino)
　Atlantic Rhythm & Blues 1947-1974-#6 (1966-1969)-C . . . .(Atlantic)
　Best Of Wilson Pickett . . . .(Atlantic)
　Wilson Pickett's Greatest Hits . . . .(Atlantic)
　Wilson Pickett-Super Hits . . . .(Atlantic)
Young Rascals; *The Young Rascals* . . . . (Warner Special Prod.)
My Gal Sal
Madge Crichton; *Music From The New York Stage (1890-1920)-#1-1890-*
　1908-C . . . . (Pearl)
My Girl Sunday
Chieli Minucci; *Sweet On You* . . . .(Shanachie)
My Name Is Not Susan
Whitney Houston; *I'm Your Baby Tonight* . . . . (Arista)
My Sharona
Knack; *Billboard Top Hits-1979-C* . . . . (Rhino)
　Get The Knack . . . . (Capitol)
　Rock Of The '80s-C . . . . (Priority)
My True Story (Sue)
Jive Five; *Back Seat Jams-C* . . . .(Dunhill Compact Classics)
　Billboard Top R&B Hits-1961-C . . . . (Rhino)
　Cruisin'-1961-C . . . . (Increase)
　Jive Five-Their Greatest Hits . . . . (Collectables)
　Oldies But Goodies-#4-C . . . . (Original Sound)
Nobody Doesn't Like Sara Lee
Original Soundtrack; *TeeVee Toons-The Commercials-#1-C.* . . . . (TVT)
Oh Sheila
Ready For The World; *Oh Sheila-Greatest Hits* . . . .(MCA)
　Ready For The World. . . . .(MCA)
Oh, Sherrie
Steve Perry; *MTV's Rock 'N' Roll To Go-C* . . . . (Elektra)
　Street Talk . . . . (Columbia)
Oh, Susanna
Disneyland Cast; *Children's Favorite Songs-#1.* . . . . (Disney)
James Taylor; *Sweet Baby James* . . . .(Warner Bros.)
Myron Floren; *Best Of The Wurstfest* . . . .(Ranwood)
　Myron Floren. . . . .(Ranwood)
Oklahoma Sweetheart Sally
Maddox Brothers & Rose; *America's Most Colorful Hillbillly Band* . . (Arhoolie)
Please Don't Squeeze My Sharmon
Charlie Walker; *Charlie Walker-Golden Hits.* . . . . (Plantation)
　Country Music Classics-#10-Late '60s-C . . . . (K-Tel)
Road Goes On Forever, The (Sherry)
Joe Ely; *Love & Danger* . . . .(MCA)
Rock 'N' Roll Susie
Pat Travers; *Makin' Magic* . . . . (Polydor)
Runaround Sue
Dion; *Billboard Top Rock 'N' Roll Hits-1961-C* . . . . (Rhino)

　Everything You Always Wanted To Hear . . . . (Laurie)
　Million-Dollar Memories #1-C . . . . (RCA)
　Oldies But Goodies-#7-C . . . . (Original Sound)
　ST/The Flamingo Kid . . . . (Motown)
　ST/The Wanderers . . . . (Warner Bros.)
Sadie
Spinners; *Best Of The Spinners* . . . .(Atlantic)
　One Of A Kind Love Affair-Anthology . . . . (Rhino)
Sadie Was A Lady
Johnny Bond; *How I Love Them Old Songs* . . . . (Lamb & Lion)
Sadie, Sadie
Barbra Streisand; *ST/Funny Girl* . . . . (Columbia)
Sally
Stetsasonic; *Rapmasters 1-Best Of The Jam-C* . . . . (Priority)
Sally (That Girl)
Gucci Crew II; *Super Bass-20 Boomin' All-Time Bass Hits-C* . . . .(Record Guys)
Sally Ann
Flatt & Scruggs; *20 All-Time Great Recordings* . . . . (Columbia)
Sally Ann 28th Of January
Fuzzy Mountain String Band; *Fuzzy Mountain String Band* . . . . (Rounder)
Sally Can't Dance
Lou Reed; *Sally Can't Dance* . . . .(RCA)
　Walk On The Wild Side-The Best Of Lou Reed . . . . (RCA)
Sally Go Round The Roses
Jaynettes; *Best Of Chess Rock 'N' Roll-#1-C* . . . . (Chess)
　Cruisin'-1963-C . . . . (Increase)
　Girl Groups-Story Of A Sound-C . . . . (Rhino)
　Wonder Women-History Of Girl Group Sound-C. . . . . (Rhino)
Yvonne Elliman; *Night Flight* . . . . (RSO)
Sally Goodin
Bob Wills & His Texas Playboys; *Tiffany Transcriptions-#6-Sally*
　Goodin. . . . . (Rhino)
Doc Watson; *Out In The Country* . . . . (Intermedia)
Hot Rize; *Hot Rize In Concert.* . . . . (Flying Fish)
John Hickman; *Don't Mean Maybe.* . . . . (Rounder)
Sally Johnson
Mark O'Connor; *Championship Years* . . . . (Country Music Foundation)
　Mark O'Connor . . . . (Rounder)
Sally's Got A Friend In New York City
Larry McCray; *Ambition* . . . . (Charisma)
Sam
Meat Puppets; *Forbidden Places.* . . . . (London)
Samantha
Count Basie & His Orchestra; *Fancy Pants.* . . . . (Pablo)
Sandy
Dion; *Dion-His Best* . . . . (Laurie)
　Dion-Legends. . . . . (Laurie)
Dion And The Belmonts; *Dion And The Belmonts-20 Golden*
　Classics . . . . (Collectables)
Larry Hall; *Sandy & Other Golden Classics* . . . . (Collectables)
Sara
Starship; *Greatest Hits-Ten Years & Change-1979-1991* . . . . (RCA)
　Knee Deep In The Hoopla . . . . (Grunt)
Sara
Fleetwood Mac; *25 Years-The Chain* . . . . (Warner Bros.)
　Fleetwood Mac Live . . . . (Warner Bros.)
　Fleetwood Mac's Greatest Hits . . . . (Warner Bros.)
　Tusk . . . . (Warner Bros.)
Sara
Bob Dylan; *Desire.* . . . . (Columbia)
Sara Smile
After 7; *Very Best Of After 7* . . . .(Virgin)
Daryl Hall & John Oates; *Best Of Daryl Hall & John Oates* . . . . (RCA)
　Daryl Hall & John Oates . . . . (RCA)
　Livetime . . . . (RCA)
　Rock 'N Soul, Part 1 . . . . (RCA)
　Soulful Sounds . . . . (RCA)
Sarafina
Original Broadway Cast; *Sarafina! (The Music Of Liberation).* . . . . (RCA)
Sarah Cynthia Sylvia Stout
Shel Silverstein; *Dr. Demento Presents The Greatest Novelty Records-#4-*
　1970s-C. . . . . (Rhino)
　Dr. Demento: 20th Anniversary Collection-C . . . . (Rhino)
　Where The Sidewalk Ends . . . . (Columbia)
Sarah Jane
Bob Dylan; *Dylan* . . . . (Columbia)
Sarah, Sarah
Jonathan Butler; *Best Of Jonathan Butler* . . . . (Jive)
Saro Jane
Country Gazette; *Hello Operator...This Is Country Gazette.* . . . . . . (Flying Fish)
Kingston Trio; *From The Hungry i* . . . . (Capitol)
Radio Flyer; *Old Strings New Strings* . . . . (Turquoise)
Red Clay Ramblers; *Rambler* . . . . (Sugar Hill)
Sassy Mae
Memphis Slim; *Legacy Of The Blues-#7.* . . . . (Crescendo)
Memphis Slim & The House Rockers; *U.S.A.* . . . . (Pearl)
Satisfy Suzie
Lonnie Mack; *Attack Of The Killer V* . . . . (Alligator)
　Strike Like Lightning . . . . (Alligator)

Scarlet Fever
Kenny Rogers; *We've Got Tonight* . . . . (Razor & Tie)
Sexy Sadie
Beatles; *Beatles-Box Set* . . . . (Capitol)
The Beatles (White Album) . . . . (Capitol)
Sheena Is A Punk Rocker
Ramones; *Leave Home* . . . .(Sire)
Loco Live . . . .(Sire)
Mania . . . .(Sire)
Rocket To Russia . . . .(Sire)
Sheila
Tommy Roe; *Billboard Top Rock 'N' Roll Hits-1962-C* . . . . (Rhino)
Golden Years-1962-C . . . . (Dominion Entert.)
Original Rock 'N' Roll Hits Of The '60s-C . . . . (Roulette)
Sheila . . . . (Accord)
Tommy Roe's Greatest Hits . . . . (MCA)
Sherry
4 Seasons; *4 Seasons' Greatest Hits-#1* . . . . (Rhino)
4 Seasons-Anthology . . . . (Rhino)
ST/The Wanderers . . . . (Warner Bros.)
Sherry
Bobby Caldwell; *August Moon* . . . . (Sin-Drome)
Sherry Darling
Bruce Springsteen; *The River* . . . . (Columbia)
Shirley
L7; *Hungry For Stink* . . . . (Slash)
Shirley Jean
Foghat; *Rock & Roll Outlaws* . . . . (Rhino)
Shirley Lee
Ricky Nelson; *Ricky Nelson-Legendary Masters* . . . . (EMI)
Sidewalk Annie
Wallflowers; *The Wallflowers* . . . .(Virgin)
Silicone Sally
Slammin' Gladys; *Slammin' Gladys* . . . .(Priority)
Silky Sam
Spirit; *Time Circle* . . . . (Epic)
Sioux City Sue
Bob Wills & His Texas Playboys; *Tiffany Transcriptions-#8-More Of*
The Best . . . . (Rhino)
Gene Autry; *The Country Music Hall Of Fame-Gene Autry-15 Of His All-*
Time Greatest Hits . . . . (Columbia)
Jimmy C. Newman; *Cajun Cowboy* . . . . (Plantation)
Mom & Dads; *In The Good Old Summertime* . . . . (Crescendo)
Willie Nelson & Leon Russell; *One For The Road* . . . . (Columbia)
Sneakin' Sally Through The Alley
Robert Palmer; *Addictions-#2* . . . . (Island)
Sneakin' Sally Through The Alley . . . . (Island)
Song For Sharon
Joni Mitchell; *Hejira* . . . . (Asylum)
Spanish Eyes
Ricky Martin; *Ricky Martin* . . . . (Columbia)
Spooky
Atlanta Rhythm Section; *Underdog* . . . . (Polydor)
Classics IV; *Ghastly Grooves-C* . . . . (K-Tel)
Good Vibrations (Sounds Of Top 40 Radio: 1964-1967)-C . . . . (Capitol)
Spooky . . . . (Liberty)
Very Best Of The Classics IV . . . . (EMI)
Stella By Starlight
Bill Evans; *Jazzhouse* . . . . (Milestone)
Frank Sinatra; *Rarities-Columbia Years* . . . . (Columbia)
George Benson; *Tenderly* . . . . (Warner Bros.)
Joe Pass; *Virtuoso* . . . . (Pablo)
Keith Jarrett; *Standards Live* . . . . (ECM)
Miles Davis; *Cookin' At The Plugged Nickel* . . . . (Columbia)
Red Garland; *Red Alert* . . . . (Galaxy)
Stan Getz; *Stan Getz Plays* . . . . (Verve)
Tony Bennett; *Jazz* . . . . (Columbia)
Stormy
Classics IV; *Back To The '60s-#4-C* . . . . (Dominion Entert.)
Spring Break-#2-Cold Kegs & Tan Legs . . . . (Capitol)
Very Best Of The Classics IV . . . . (EMI)
Santana; *Inner Secrets* . . . . (Columbia)
Sue's Gotta Be Mine
Del Shannon; *Del Shannon-Legends* . . . .(Laurie)
Runaway . . . .(Pair)
Runaway Hits! . . . . (Rhino)
Sullivan
Caroline's Spine; *Monsoon* . . . . (Hollywood)
Sunny
Bobby Hebb; *Billboard Top R&B Hits-1965-1969-C* . . . . (Rhino)
Oldies But Goodies-#11-C . . . .(Original Sound)
Classics IV; *Very Best Of The Classics IV* . . . . (EMI)
Electric Flag; *Long Time Comin'* . . . . (Columbia)
Stevie Wonder; *For Once In My Life* . . . . (Motown)
Sunny Came Home
Shawn Colvin; *1998 Grammy Nominees-C* . . . . (MCA)
A Few Small Repairs . . . . (Columbia)
Sunshine
Aerosmith; *Just Push Play* . . . . (Columbia)

Susan
Buckinghams; *Buckinghams' Greatest Hits* . . . .(Columbia)
Rock Artifacts-From The Vaults-#3-C . . . .(Columbia)
Susan
Statler Brothers; *Best Of The Statler Brothers* . . . .(Mercury)
Susannah
Lionel Cartwright; *Chasin' The Sun* . . . . (MCA)
Susannah's Still Alive
Kinks; *Kink Kronikles* . . . . (Reprise)
Susie
John Lee Hooker; *Mr. Lucky* . . . . (Point Blank/Virgin)
Susie Cincinnati
Beach Boys; *15 Big Ones* . . . . (Brother)
Susie Darlin'
Robin Luke; *Great Records Of The Decade-'50s-Pop-#1-C* . . . . (Curb)
More '50s Jukebox Favorites-C . . . .(K-Tel)
Susie Q
Creedence Clearwater Revival; *1968-1969* . . . . (Fantasy)
Chooglin' . . . . (Fantasy)
Creedence Clearwater Revival . . . . (Fantasy)
Creedence Clearwater Revival-Chronicle . . . . (Fantasy)
Creedence Clearwater Revival-Gold . . . . (Fantasy)
Live In Europe . . . . (Fantasy)
Dale Dawkins; *Collectables Presents The History Of Rock-#3-C* . .(Collectables)
Legends Of Rock Guitar-'50s-#1-C . . . . (Rhino)
Rockin' Rebels-C . . . .(K-Tel)
Jose Feliciano; *Jose Feliciano's All-Time Greatest Hits* . . . . (RCA)
Susy Is A Headbanger
Ramones; *All The Stuff & More-#1* . . . . (Sire)
Leave Home . . . . (Sire)
Suzanne
Neil Diamond; *Neil Diamond-Love Songs* . . . . (MCA)
Stones . . . . (MCA)
Suzanne
Randy Newman; *12 Songs* . . . . (Reprise)
Suzanne
Leonard Cohen; *Best Of Leonard Cohen* . . . .(Columbia)
Suzanne
Pearls Before Swine; *Best Of Pearls Before Swine* . . . . (Adelphi)
Suzanne
Judy Collins; *In My Life* . . . .(Elektra)
Suzie-You Are
Maxi Priest; *Maxi Priest* . . . . (Virgin)
Suzy Suicide
Spread Eagle; *Spread Eagle* . . . . (MCA)
Sweet Savannah Sue
Fats Waller; *Turn On The Heat-Fats Waller Piano Solos* . . . .(Bluebird)
Louis Armstrong; *Louis Armstrong-Vol. 5-In New York* . . . .(Columbia)
Sweet Sue (Just You)
Benny Goodman; *Benny Goodman-Early Years* . . . . (Biograph)
Big Joe Turner; *Rhythm & Blues Years* . . . .(Rhino)
Bing Crosby; *Crooner-Columbia Years-1928-1934* . . . . (Columbia)
Leon Redbone; *Champagne Charlie* . . . . (Warner Bros.)
Mom & Dads; *Goodnight Sweetheart* . . . . (Crescendo)
Sweet Suzanne
Mark O'Connor; *New Nashville Cats* . . . .(Warner Bros.)
Sweet Suzie
Johnny Burnette; *Best Of Johnny Burnette-You're Sixteen* . . . . . . (Gold Rush)
Switchboard Susan
Nick Lowe; *Basher: Best Of* . . . .(Columbia)
Labour Of Lust . . . .(Columbia)
Sylvia
BoDeans; *Home* . . . . (Slash)
Sylvia
Stevie Wonder; *Down To Earth* . . . .(Motown)
Sylvia
Elvis Presley; *Elvis Now* . . . . (RCA)
Sylvia
Eurythmics; *We Too Are One* . . . .(Arista)
Sylvia's Mother
Dr. Hook; *Dr. Hook & The Medicine Show Revisited* . . . .(Columbia)
Dr. Hook-Greatest Hits & More . . . .(Capitol)
Super Hits Of The '70s-Have A Nice Day-#8-C . . . .(Rhino)
Sylvie
Leadbelly & Anne Graham; *Folkways-Original*
Vision . . . . (Smithsonian Folkways)
Matthews' Southern Comfort; *Best Of Matthews' Southern Comfort* . . . . (MCA)
Weavers; *Best Of The Weavers* . . . . (MCA)
Tender Hearted Sue
Rambling Rogue; *45-#6747* . . . . (Okeh)
Tequila Sheila
Bobby Bare; *Bobby Bare's Biggest Hits* . . . .(Columbia)
Encore-Bobby Bare . . . .(Columbia)
Mac Davis; *It's Hard To Be Humble* . . . . (Casablanca)
That's My Little Suzie
Ritchie Valens; *Best Of Ritchie Valens* . . . .(Rhino)

Theme From "Laverne & Shirley"
Original Soundtrack; *Television's Greatest Hits-#3-1970s & 1980s-C* . . . (TVT)
Theme From "The Simpsons"
Original Soundtrack; *Television's Greatest Hits-#7-Cable Ready-C* . . . . . (TVT)
Theme From "The Smurfs"
Original Soundtrack; *Television's Greatest Hits-#3-1970s & 1980s-C* . . . (TVT)
There Goes The Neighborhood (Sally)
Sheryl Crow; *The Globe Sessions* . . . . (A&M)
Tra La La La Suzy
Dean & Jean; *22 Leaders Of The Pack-#1-C* . . . . (Laurie)
Classic Old & Gold-C . . . . (Laurie)
Tutti Frutti (Sue)
Elvis Presley; *Elvis Presley* . . . . (RCA)
Rocker . . . . (RCA)
Little Richard; *Greatest Hits Recorded Live* . . . .(Epic)
Little Richard . . . .(Specialty)
Little Richard-18 Greatest Hits . . . . (Rhino)
More American Graffiti-C . . . . (MCA)
This Is How It All Began-#2-C . . . .(Specialty)
Tribute To Black Entertainers-C . . . . (Columbia)
Queen; *Live At Wembley '86* . . . . (Hollywood)
Wake Up Little Susie
Everly Brothers; *All They Had To Do Was Dream* . . . . (Rhino)
American Graffiti-#3-C . . . .(MCA)
Everly Brothers . . . . (Rhino)
Everly Brothers' All-Time Greatest Hits . . . . (Curb)
Oldies But Goodies-#7-C . . . . (Original Sound)
Very Best Of The Everly Brothers . . . . (Warner Bros.)
Grateful Dead; *History Of The Grateful Dead-Vol. 1 (Bear's
Choice)* . . . . (Warner Bros.)
Simon & Garfunkel; *The Concert In Central Park* . . . .(Warner Bros.)
Wake Up Susan
Spinners; *Happiness Is Being With The Detroit Spinners* . . . . (Atlantic)
One Of A Kind Love Affair-Anthology . . . . (Rhino)
Way Down The Line (Shannon)
Offspring; *Ixnay On The Hombre* . . . . (Columbia)
When Sunny Gets Blue
Barbra Streisand; *Simply Streisand* . . . . (Columbia)
Johnny Mathis; *First 25 Years-Silver Anniversary Album* . . . (Columbia)
Johnny Mathis' All-Time Greatest Hits . . . . (Columbia)
Johnny Mathis' Greatest Hits . . . . (Columbia)
Johnny Mathis-Love Songs . . . . (Columbia)
Kenny Rankin; *The Kenny Rankin Album* . . . .(Little David)
Steve Miller; *Born 2 B Blue* . . . . (Gold Rush)
Where's The Playground Susie
Glen Campbell; *Best Of Glen Campbell* . . . . (Capitol)
Zak And Sara
Ben Folds; *Rockin' The Suburbs* . . . .(Epic)

WOMEN'S NAMES: T

**See Also: CELEBRITIES: SPECIFIC, FAMILY (various),
WOMEN: GENERAL**

Aunt Thomasina
Sir Mix-A-Lot; *Return Of The Bumpasaurus* . . . . (American)
Backstreets (Terry)
Bruce Springsteen; *Born To Run* . . . . (Columbia)
Big Tulsa Tillie
Donnie Rohrs; *Country Music USA* . . . .(Pacific Challenger)
Just A Pimp (Tina)
Angie Stone; *Black Diamond* . . . . (Arista)
Letter From Tina
Ike & Tina Turner; *Best Of Ike & Tina Turner* . . . .(EMI)
Ike & Tina Turner-Golden Classics . . . . (Collectables)
Sad Theresa
Warrant; *Dog Eat Dog* . . . . (Columbia)
Tammy
Columbia Ballroom Orchestra; *Let's Dance-#7-Competition Dance* . . . . (Denon)
Debbie Reynolds; *Best Of Debbie Reynolds* . . . . (Curb)
Tammy . . . .(MCA Special Prod.)
Roger Williams; *Roger Williams' Greatest Hits* . . . .(MCA)
Tanya
Rockin' Dopsie & The Cajun Twisters; *Hold On* . . . .(Crescendo)
Teresa
J. Geils Band; *J. Geils Band-Anthology-Houseparty* . . . . (Rhino)
Theme From "The Tracey Ullman Show"
Original Soundtrack; *Television's Greatest Hits-#7-Cable Ready-C* . . . . . (TVT)
Tina
Frank Sinatra; *The Reprise Collection* . . . . (Reprise)
Weavers; *Weavers-Classics* . . . . (Vanguard)
Toot Toot Tootsie (Goo'Bye)
Al Jolson; *Al Jolson-Best Of The Decca Years* . . . .(MCA)
Best Of Al Jolson . . . .(MCA)

Liza Minnelli; *Liza Minnelli-At Carnegie Hall* . . . . (Telarc)
Tracey's World
Smithereens; *Beauty & Sadness* . . . . (Capitol)
Tracy
Cuff Links; *Super Hits Of The '70s-Have A Nice Day-#1-C* . . . . (Rhino)
Tracy In The Bathroom Killing Thrills
Mary's Danish; *Circa* . . . . (Morgan Creek)
Experience-Live + Foxey Lady . . . .(Chameleon)
Trudy
Charlie Daniels Band; *Fire On The Mountain* . . . . (Epic)
Trudy & Dave
John Hiatt; *Slow Turning* . . . . (A&M)
Trudy Sings The Blues
Trudy Lynn; *Trudy Sings The Blues* . . . . (Ichiban Int'l)
Zero And Blind Terry
Bruce Springsteen; *Tracks* . . . . (Columbia)

WOMEN'S NAMES: V

**See Also: CELEBRITIES: SPECIFIC, FAMILY (various),
WOMEN: GENERAL**

I'm Coming Virginia
Bix Beiderbecke; *Bix Beiderbecke-#1-Singin' The Blues* . . . . (Legacy)
Coleman Hawkins & Benny Carter; *Coleman Hawkins & Benny
Carter* . . . . (Disques Swing)
Stephane Grappelli; *Compact Jazz-Stephane Grappelli* . . . . (Verve)
Leave Virginia Alone
Rod Stewart; *A Spanner In The Works* . . . . (Warner Bros.)
Meet Virginia
Train; *Now That's What I Call Music!-#4-C* . . . .(Virgin)
Train . . . .(Aware/C2/Columbia)
Story Of Vanna White
Lawndale; *Beyond Barbecue* . . . .(SST)
Stuck In A Closet With Vanna White
"Weird Al" Yankovic; *Even Worse* . . . .(Scotti Bros.)
Sweet Virginia
Rolling Stones; *Exile On Main Street* . . . .(Virgin)
Utah Carroll (Varo)
Skip Gorman; *A Cowboy's Wild Song To His Herd* . . . . (Rounder)
Valerie
Marshall Crenshaw; *Good Evening* . . . . (Warner Bros.)
Valerie
Steve Winwood; *Steve Winwood-Chronicles* . . . . (Island)
Talking Back To The Night . . . . (Island)
Valerie
Marty Balin; *Balince-A Collection* . . . . (Rhino)
Valerie
Richard Thompson; *Daring Adventures* . . . .(Polydor)
Valerie
Bad Company; *Fame & Fortune* . . . .(Atlantic)
Valerie
Mello-Kings; *Mello-Kings' Greatest Hits* . . . . (Collectables)
Valerie
Quarterflash; *Quarterflash* . . . . (Geffen)
Valerie Loves Me
Material Issue; *International Pop Overthrow* . . . . (Mercury)
Valleri
Monkees; *Birds Bees & The Monkees* . . . . (Rhino)
Missing Links . . . . (Rhino)
More Greatest Hits Of The Monkees . . . . (Arista)
Nuggets-Classic Collection From The Psychedelic '60s-C . . . . (Rhino)
Valotte
Julian Lennon; *Valotte* . . . .(Atlantic)
Venus
Frankie Avalon; *21 Oldies But Goodies-C* . . . . (Original Sound)
'50s Sock Hop-C . . . .(K-Tel)
Billboard Top Rock 'N' Roll Hits-1959-C . . . . (Rhino)
Oldies But Goodies-#10-C . . . . (Original Sound)
Venus
Shocking Blue; *'70s Smash Hits-#1-C* . . . . (Rhino)
Billboard Top Rock 'N' Roll Hits-1970-C . . . . (Rhino)
Oldies But Goodies-#15-C . . . . (Original Sound)
Super Hits Of The '70s-Have A Nice Day-#1-C . . . . (Rhino)
Veronica
Elvis Costello; *Spike* . . . . (Warner Bros.)
Vicki
Leaving Trains; *Kill Tunes* . . . .(SST)
Victoria
Kinks; *Arthur Or The Decline And Fall Of The British Empire* . . . .(Reprise)
Kink Kronikles . . . .(Reprise)
Vidalia
Sammy Kershaw; *Politics Religion & Her* . . . . (Mercury)
Virginia Woolf
Indigo Girls; *Rites Of Passage* . . . . (Epic)

WOMEN'S NAMES: W

See Also: **CELEBRITIES: SPECIFIC, FAMILY (various), WOMEN: GENERAL**

Born To Run (Wendy)
Bruce Springsteen; *Born To Run* . . . . (Columbia)
  Chimes Of Freedom . . . . (Columbia)
Bruce Springsteen & The E Street Band; *Bruce Springsteen & The E Street Band/1975-85* . . . . (Legacy)
Goodbye Earl (Wanda)
Dixie Chicks; *Fly* . . . . (Monument)
Running Bear (White Dove)
Johnny Preston; *45s On CD-#1-1956-1959-C* . . . . (Mercury)
  Billboard Top Rock 'N' Roll Hits-1960-C . . . . (Rhino)
  Cruisin'-1960-C . . . . (Increase)
Sonny James; *All-Time Country Classics-#1-C* . . . . (Capitol)
Theme From "The Waltons"
Original Soundtrack; *CBS: The First 50 Years* . . . . (TVT)
  Television's Greatest Hits-#3-1970s & 1980s-C . . . . (TVT)
Theme From "Wonder Woman"
Original Soundtrack; *Television's Greatest Hits-#3-1970s & 1980s-C* . . . . (TVT)
Wendy
Beach Boys; *Absolute Best-#1* . . . . (Capitol)
  All Summer Long . . . . (Capitol)
  Beach Boys-Gift Set . . . . (Capitol)
  Best Of The Beach Boys . . . . (Capitol)
  Endless Summer . . . . (Capitol)
Wendy
Original Cast/Mary Martin; *Peter Pan-The 1954 Broadway Production* . . . . (RCA Victor)
Windy
Association; *Association Greatest Hits* . . . . (Warner Bros.)
  Billboard Top Rock 'N' Roll Hits-1967-C . . . . (Rhino)
  Summer Of Love-#1-C . . . . (Rhino)
  Vintage Association . . . . (Fifty One West)
Wes Montgomery; *A Day In The Life* . . . . (A&M)
  Wes Montgomery-Classics-#22 . . . . (A&M)
  Wes Montgomery's Greatest Hits . . . . (A&M)
Wynona's Big Brown Beaver
Primus; *Tales From The Punchbowl* . . . . (Interscope)

WOMEN'S NAMES: Y

See Also: **CELEBRITIES: SPECIFIC, FAMILY (various), WOMEN: GENERAL**

Ballad Of John And Yoko
Beatles; *Beatles 1* . . . . (Capitol)
  Beatles-Box Set . . . . (Capitol)
  Hey Jude . . . . (Capitol)
  Past Masters-Volume Two . . . . (Parlophone)
  ST/Imagine: John Lennon . . . . (Capitol)
  The Beatles/1967-1970 . . . . (Capitol)
Jambalaya (On The Bayou) (Yvonne)
Blue Ridge Rangers; *Blue Ridge Rangers* . . . . (Fantasy)
Fats Domino; *Fats Domino's Greatest Hits* . . . . (MCA)
Hank Williams With His Drifting Cowboys; *24 Of Hank Williams' Greatest Hits* . . . . (Polydor)
  Hank Williams-16 Great Hits . . . . (Everest)
  Hank Williams-40 Greatest Hits . . . . (Polydor)
Hank Williams, Jr.; *ST/Your Cheatin' Heart* . . . . . . (Sony Music Special Prod.)
Jerry Lee Lewis; *Twenty Classic Hits* . . . . (Sun)
Nitty Gritty Dirt Band; *All The Good Times* . . . . (United Artists)
  Stars And Stripes Forever . . . . (Capitol)

WORK, Unions, Working Class

See Also: **BOSSES, BUILDING & CONSTRUCTION, BUSINESS & INDUSTRY, FARMS, MINING, MONEY, MOTIVATION, POLITICS (various), POVERTY, PROTEST, SOCIAL CLASS (various), WAITRESSES, WEEKEND**

(Just Like) Romeo & Juliet
Reflections; *'60s Dance Party-C* . . . . (Dominion Entert.)
  Sensational '60s-#1-C . . . . (Dominion Entert.)
1040 Blues
Robert Cray Band; *Shame + Sin* . . . . (Mercury)
15 Minutes
Marc Nelson; *chocolate mood* . . . . (Columbia)
1913 Massacre
Arlo Guthrie; *Hobo's Lullaby* . . . . (Reprise)
Jack Elliot; *Tribute To Woody Guthrie-C* . . . . (Warner Bros.)
Ramblin' Jack Elliott; *Greatest Songs Of Woody Guthrie-C* . . . . . . (Vanguard)

  Woody Guthrie; *Struggle* . . . . (Smithsonian Folkways)
9 To 5
Dolly Parton; *9 To 5 And Odd Jobs* . . . . (RCA)
  Best There Is . . . . (RCA)
  Dolly Parton's Greatest Hits . . . . (RCA)
  I Am Woman-C . . . . (Nick At Nite)
  Nipper's Greatest Hits Of The '80s-C . . . . (RCA)
Adam Raised A Cain
Bruce Springsteen; *Darkness On The Edge Of Town* . . . . (Columbia)
Addicted To A Dollar
Doug Stone; *More Love* . . . . (Epic)
Against The Wind
Bob Seger & The Silver Bullet Band; *Against The Wind* . . . . (Capitol)
  Nine Tonight . . . . (Capitol)
  ST/Forrest Gump . . . . (Epic/Sony Music Soundtrax)
All The Small Things
Blink-182; *Enema Of The State* . . . . (MCA)
  Now That's What I Call Music!-#4-C . . . . (Virgin)
Allentown
Billy Joel; *Billy Joel-Greatest Hits, Volume I & Volume II* . . . . (Columbia)
  KOHUEPT . . . . (Columbia)
  Nylon Curtain . . . . (Columbia)
Another Day
Paul McCartney; *All The Best!* . . . . (Capitol)
Wings; *Wings Greatest* . . . . (Capitol)
Another Day Another Dollar
Alison Krauss & Union Station; *Every Time You Say Goodbye* . . . . (Rounder)
Back On The Chain Gang
Pretenders; *Learning To Crawl* . . . . (Sire)
  Pretenders-The Singles . . . . (Sire)
  ST/King Of Comedy . . . . (Warner Bros.)
Banana Boat (Day-O)
Harry Belafonte; *Belafonte '89* . . . . (EMI)
  Nipper's Greatest Hits Of The '50s-#1-C . . . . (RCA)
Kinks; *Everybody's In Show-Biz* . . . . (Rhino)
Been A Long Day
Original Cast; *How To Succeed In Business Without Really Trying* . . . . . . (RCA)
Big Bad John
Jimmy Dean; *American Originals-Jimmy Dean* . . . . (Columbia)
  Billboard Top Country Hits-1961-C . . . . (Rhino)
  Columbia Country Classics-#3-Americana-C . . . . (Columbia)
  Jimmy Dean's Greatest Hits . . . . (Columbia)
Big Boss Man
B.B. King; *Six Silver Strings* . . . . (MCA)
Elvis Presley; *ST/Clambake* . . . . (RCA)
Grateful Dead; *Grateful Dead (Skull & Roses)* . . . . (Warner Bros.)
Jimmy Reed; *Best Of Jimmy Reed* . . . . (Crescendo)
  Oldies But Goodies-#1-C . . . . (Original Sound)
John Hammond; *Best Of John Hammond* . . . . (Vanguard)
  So Many Roads . . . . (Vanguard)
Big City
Merle Haggard; *For The Record: Merle Haggard-43 Legendary Hits* . . . . (BNA)
Blue Collar
Bachman-Turner Overdrive; *Best Of B.T.O.-So Far* . . . . (Mercury)
Blue Collar Man
Styx; *Caught In The Act* . . . . (A&M)
  Pieces Of Eight . . . . (A&M)
  Styx-Classics-#15 . . . . (A&M)
Blue Money
Van Morrison; *His Band And The Street Choir* . . . . (Warner Bros.)
Born In The U.S.A.
Bruce Springsteen; *Born In The U.S.A.* . . . . (Columbia)
  Bruce Springsteen's Greatest Hits . . . . (Columbia)
  Tracks . . . . (Columbia)
Bruce Springsteen & The E Street Band; *Bruce Springsteen & The E Street Band Live/1975-85* . . . . (Legacy)
Bruised Orange
John Prine; *Bruised Orange* . . . . (Oh Boy)
Busy Man
Billy Ray Cyrus; *Shot Full Of Love* . . . . (Mercury)
Cadillac Assembly Line
Albert King; *Masterworks* . . . . (Atlantic)
  Truckload Of Lovin' . . . . (Tomato)
Cafe On The Corner
Sawyer Brown; *Cafe On The Corner* . . . . (Curb)
Call My Job
Albert King; *King Albert* . . . . (Tomato)
  Masterworks . . . . (Atlantic)
Car Wash
Rose Royce; *Best Of Rose Royce* . . . . (Omni)
  Billboard Top Hits-1977-C . . . . (Rhino)
  Rose Royce's Greatest Hits . . . . (Whitfield)
  The Disco Years-#1-Turn The Beat Around-1974-1978-C . . . . (Rhino)
Chain Gang
Nylons; *Happy Together* . . . . (Open Air)
Otis Redding; *Best Of Otis Redding* . . . . (Atco)
  The Otis Redding Story . . . . (Atlantic)
Persuasions; *We Came To Play* . . . . (Capitol)
Sam Cooke; *Best Of Sam Cooke* . . . . (RCA)

Nipper's Greatest Hits Of The '60s-#1-C .... (RCA)
The Man And His Music .... (RCA)

Clean Up Woman
Betty Wright; *Atlantic Rhythm & Blues 1947-1974-#6 (1966-1969)-C* .... (Atlantic)
Betty Wright Live .... (Atlantic)
Golden Classics-Betty Wright .... (Collectables)
Soul Years-C .... (Atlantic)

Common Man
John Conlee; *Best Of John Conlee* .... (Curb)
Busted .... (MCA Special Prod.)
John Conlee-20 Greatest Hits .... (MCA)
John Conlee's Greatest Hits .... (MCA)

Company Man
James Taylor; *Flag* .... (Columbia)

Company Time
Linda Davis; *Shoot For The Moon* .... (Arista)

Computer Took My Job
Maurice John Vaughn; *Generic Blues Album* .... (Alligator)

Darlington County
Bruce Springsteen; *Born In The U.S.A.* .... (Columbia)

Day Job
Gin Blossoms; *Congratulations I'm Sorry* .... (A&M)
Outside Looking In: The Best Of The Gin Blossoms .... (A&M)

Daysleeper
R.E.M.; *Up* .... (Warner Bros.)

Deportee (Plane Wreck At Los Gatos)
Arlo Guthrie & Pete Seeger; *Together In Concert* .... (Reprise)
Byrds; *The Byrds* .... (Columbia)
Cisco Houston; *Greatest Songs Of Woody Guthrie-C* ...... (Vanguard)
Gene Clark & Carla Olson; *So Rebellious A Lover* .... (Rhino)
Judy Collins; *Tribute To Woody Guthrie-C* .... (Warner Bros.)
Waylon Jennings, Willie Nelson, Johnny Cash, Kris Kristofferson; *Highwayman* .... (Columbia)

Detroit City
Ace Cannon; *Golden Favorites* .... (Ranwood)
Bill Anderson; *Best Of Bill Anderson* .... (Curb)
Bobby Bare; *Nipper's Greatest Hits Of The '60s-#2-C* .... (RCA)
This Is Bobby Bare .... (RCA)
Chet Atkins; *Country Gems* .... (Pair)
Flatt & Scruggs; *20 All-Time Great Recordings* .... (Columbia)
Hank Williams, Jr.; *Live At Cobo Hall Detroit* .... (Polydor)
Standing In The Shadows .... (Polydor)
Mel Tillis; *Best Of Mel Tillis* .... (MCA)
Live At The Sam Houston Coliseum .... (MGM)
Solomon Burke; *Home In Your Heart-Best Of Solomon Burke* ... (Rhino)

Did Beethoven Do The Dishes
Reilly & Maloney; *Profiles* .... (Freckle)

Dirt Road, The
Sawyer Brown; *Dirt Road* .... (Curb)

Dirty Business
New Riders Of The Purple Sage; *New Riders Of The Purple Sage* ... (Columbia)

Dirty Work
Fabulous Thunderbirds; *What's The Word* .... (Chrysalis)

Dirty Work
Steely Dan; *Can't Buy A Thrill* .... (MCA)

Dirty Work
Rolling Stones; *Dirty Work* .... (Virgin)

Do Re Mi
Arlo Guthrie; *Tribute To Woody Guthrie-C* .... (Warner Bros.)
John Cougar Mellencamp; *Folkways: A Vision Shared-C* ... (Columbia)
Ry Cooder; *Ry Cooder* .... (Reprise)
Show Time .... (Warner Bros.)
Woody Guthrie; *Dust Bowl Ballads* .... (Rounder)

Do You Want My Job
Little Village; *Little Village* .... (Reprise)

Don't Give Up
Peter Gabriel; *Shaking The Tree-Sixteen Golden Greats* ..... (Geffen)
So .... (Geffen)

Don't Need No Job
Lightnin' Hopkins; *Herald Recordings-#2* .... (Collectables)

Drill Ye Tarriers Drill
Weavers; *On Tour* .... (Vanguard)

Drinking On The Job
Rainmakers; *Rainmakers* .... (Mercury)

El Picket Sign
Dr. Loco's Rockin' Jalepeno Band; *Movimento Music* ...... (Flying Fish)
El Teatro Campesino; *Best Of Broadside 1962-1968: Anthems Of The American Underground From The Pages Of Broadside Magazine-C* .... (Smithsonian Folkways)

Erie Canal
Burl Ives; *Best Of Burl Ives* .... (MCA)
Weavers; *Greatest Folksingers Of The '60s-C* .... (Vanguard)
Weavers' Greatest Hits .... (Vanguard)
Weavers-Classics .... (Vanguard)

Everybody Works In China
Judy Collins; *Home Again* .... (Elektra)

Ex-Factor
Lauryn Hill; *The Miseducation Of Lauryn Hill* ...... (Ruffhouse/Columbia)

Factory
Bruce Springsteen; *Darkness On The Edge Of Town* ...... (Columbia)

Factory Girl
Rolling Stones; *Beggars Banquet* .... (Abkco)

Fakin' It
Simon & Garfunkel; *Bookends* .... (Columbia)
Collected Works .... (Columbia)

Fast Times
Heart; *Private Audition* .... (Epic)

Feel Like A Number
Bob Seger & The Silver Bullet Band; *Nine Tonight* .... (Capitol)
Stranger In Town .... (Capitol)

Field Worker
David Crosby & Graham Nash; *Wind On The Water* ...... (MCA)

Finally Friday
George Jones; *Walls Can Fall* .... (MCA)
Working Man's Blues-C .... (Hip-O)

Five O'Clock World
Hal Ketchum; *Past The Point Of Rescue* .... (Curb)
Vogues; *ST/Good Morning, Vietnam* .... (A&M)
Vogues' Greatest Hits .... (SSS International)
Vogues' Greatest Hits .... (Rhino)

Forty Hour Week (For A Livin')
Alabama; *Alabama's Greatest Hits* .... (RCA)
Forty Hour Week .... (RCA)

Fred Jones Part 2
Ben Folds; *Rockin' The Suburbs* .... (Epic)

Friday On My Mind
David Bowie; *Bowie Pin Ups* .... (Rykodisc)
Easybeats; *Best Of The Easybeats* .... (Rhino)
Nuggets-Classic Collection From The Psychedelic '60s-C .... (Rhino)

Friends In Low Places
Garth Brooks; *Garth Brooks-Double Live* .... (Capitol)
No Fences .... (Capitol)

Galveston Bay
Bruce Springsteen; *The Ghost Of Tom Joad* .... (Columbia)

Get A Job
Sha Na Na; *Best Of Sha Na Na* .... (Pair)
Silhouettes; *Best Of Doo Wop Uptempo-#1-C* .... (Rhino)
Billboard Top Rock 'N' Roll Hits-1958-C .... (Rhino)
ST/American Graffiti .... (MCA)
ST/Stand By Me .... (Atlantic)

Get Up
Amel Larrieux; *Infinite Possibilities* .... (Epic)

Go To Work On Monday
Si Kahn; *Doing My Job* .... (Flying Fish)

God Have Mercy On The Workin' Man
Randy Newman; *Good Old Boys* .... (Reprise)

Gone Till November
Wyclef Jean featuring The Refugee Allstars; *Presents The Carnival F/ Refugee Allstars* .... (Ruffhouse/Columbia)

Gonna Go To Work On Monday One More Time
Fiction Brothers; *Things Are Coming My Way* .... (Flying Fish)

Good Day To Run
Darryl Worley; *Hard Rain Don't Last* .... (DreamWorks/SKG)

Good Morning Good Morning
Beatles; *Beatles-Box Set* .... (Capitol)
Sgt. Pepper's Lonely Hearts Club Band .... (Capitol)

Got A Job
Miracles; *Greatest Hits From The Beginning* .... (Motown)
Smokey Robinson & The Miracles; *Smokey Robinson & The Miracles' Anthology* .... (Motown)

Gotta Serve Somebody
Bob Dylan; *Biograph* .... (Columbia)
Slow Train Coming .... (Columbia)
The Sopranos-Music From The HBO Original Series .... (Sony Music Soundtrax)
Bob Dylan & The Grateful Dead; *Dylan & The Dead* ...... (Columbia)

Government Center
Jonathan Richman & The Modern Lovers; *Beserkley Years-Best Of* .... (Rhino)
Chartbusters-Best Of Beserkley-1975-1978-C .... (Rhino)

Grandpa Was A Carpenter
John Prine; *John Prine-Souvenirs* .... (Oh Boy)

Grapes Of Wrath
Charlie Daniels Band; *Midnight Wind* .... (Epic)

Graveyard Shift
Sawyer Brown; *Out Goin' Cattin'* .... (Capitol)

Graveyard Shift
Bobby "Boris" Pickett & The Crypt-Kickers; *Monster Mash* .... (Out Of Print)

Hallelujah, I'm A Bum
Al Jolson; *You Ain't Heard Nothin' Yet.* .... (Legacy)
Bobby Short; *Bobby Short Celebrates Rodgers & Hart* ...... (Atlantic)

Hands Of A Working Man
Ty Herndon; *Big Hopes* .... (Epic)

Hard Day's Night, A
Beatles; *Beatles 1* .... (Capitol)
Beatles-20 Greatest Hits .... (Capitol)
ST/A Hard Day's Night .... (Capitol)
The Beatles At The Hollywood Bowl .... (Capitol)

The Beatles/1962-1966 . . . . (Capitol)
Hard Life
Little River Band; *Backstage Pass* . . . . (Capitol)
First Under The Wire . . . . (Capitol)
Hard Life
Roger Daltrey; *Daltrey* . . . . (MCA)
Hard Lovin' Woman
Mark Collie; *Unleashed* . . . . (MCA)
Hard Way, The
Mary Chapin Carpenter; *Come On Come On* . . . . (Columbia)
Hard Way, The
Clint Black; *The Hard Way* . . . . (RCA)
Hard Work
John Handy; *The ABC's Of Soul-#3-C* . . . . (Hip-O)
Hard Work
Passion Fodder; *Fat Tuesday* . . . . (Island)
Hard Work & No Play
Country Joe McDonald; *Leisure Suite* . . . .(Fantasy)
Hard Workin' Man
Brooks & Dunn; *Hard Workin' Man* . . . . (Arista)
Hard Workin' Man
Jack Nitzsche; *ST/Blue Collar* . . . . (MCA)
Harriet Tubman
Holly Near & Ronnie Gilbert; *Lifeline* . . . . (Redwood)
Redwood Collection . . . . (Redwood)
Harriet Tubman's Gonna Carry Me Home
Long Ryders; *Two-Fisted Tales* . . . . (Island)
Harry's House Centerpiece
Joni Mitchell; *Hissing Of Summer Lawns* . . . . (Asylum)
He Thinks He'll Keep Her
Mary Chapin Carpenter; *Come On Come On* . . . . (Columbia)
He Will, She Knows
Kenny Rogers; *There You Go Again* . . . .(Dreamcatcher)
Hell On High Heels
Motley Crue; *New Tattoo* . . . . (Motley/Beyond)
Highwayman
Glen Campbell; *Highwayman* . . . . (Capitol)
Johnny Cash with Waylon Jennings, Kris Kristofferson, Willie Nelson; *The Man In Black-His Greatest Hits* . . . . (Legacy)
Waylon Jennings, Willie Nelson, Johnny Cash, Kris Kristofferson; *Columbia Country Classics-#3-Americana-C* . . . . (Columbia)
Johnny Cash-16 Biggest Hits-#2 . . . . (Legacy)
Willie Nelson; *Greatest Country Hits Of The '80s-1985-C* . . . . (Columbia)
Honey, I'm Home
Shania Twain; *Come On Over* . . . . (Mercury)
Hooch
Everything; *Super Natural* . . . . (Blackbird/Sire)
Housewife
Leon Russell; *Americana* . . . . (Paradise)
I Ain't Goin' Down
Nashville Bluegrass Band; *Waitin' For The Hard Times To Go* . . . . .(Sugar Hill)
I Ain't Got No Home
Bob Dylan; *Tribute To Woody Guthrie-C* . . . . (Warner Bros.)
I Am A Simple Man
Ricky Van Shelton; *Backroads* . . . . (Columbia)
I Keep On Gettin' Paid The Same
Joe Ely; *Must Notta Gotta Lotta* . . . . (MCA)
I Want To Work On The Railroad
Debby McClatchy; *Someday Cafe* . . . . (Green Linnet)
If I Could Make A Living
Clay Walker; *Clay Walker's Greatest Hits* . . . . (Giant)
If I Could Make A Living . . . . (Giant)
If I Were A Carpenter
Bobby Darin; *Live At The Desert Inn* . . . . (Motown)
Four Tops; *Compact Command Performances-Four Tops* . . . . (Motown)
Four Tops Reach Out . . . . (Motown)
Four Tops-Anthology . . . . (Motown)
Johnny Cash & June Carter; *The Man In Black-His Greatest Hits* . . . . . . (Legacy)
Tim Hardin; *Memorial Album* . . . . (Polydor)
If It Wasn't For The Union
Matt McGinn; *Best Of Broadside 1962-1968: Anthems Of The American Underground From The Pages Of Broadside Magazine-C* . . . .(Smithsonian Folkways)
I'm An Errand Girl For Rhythm
Diana Krall; *All For You (A Dedication To The Nat "King" Cole Trio)* . . . .(Impulse!)
I'm In A Hurry (And Don't Know Why)
Alabama; *American Pride* . . . .(RCA)
I'm Tryin'
Trace Adkins; *Chrome* . . . . (Capitol)
In The Highways
Sarah, Hannah And Leah Peasall; *ST/O Brother, Where Art Thou?* . . . (Mercury)
Internationale, The
Ani DiFranco & Utah Phillips; *Fellow Workers* . . . . (Righteous Babe)
It Goes Like It Goes (Theme From "Norma Rae")
Jennifer Warnes; *Best Of Jennifer Warnes* . . . . (Arista)
The Envelope Please-Academy Award Winning Songs-#4 (1970-1981)-C . . . . (Rhino)

It Sure Is Monday
Mark Chesnutt; *Almost Goodbye* . . . . (MCA)
It's Better With A Union Man
Barbra Streisand; *Pins And Needles* . . . .(Columbia)
It's My Job
Jimmy Buffett; *Coconut Telegraph* . . . . (MCA)
I've Been Working
Van Morrison; *His Band And The Street Choir* . . . .(Warner Bros.)
It's Too Late To Stop Now . . . .(Warner Bros.)
I've Been Working
Bob Seger; *Live Bullet* . . . .(Capitol)
I've Been Working
Luther Vandross; *Never Too Much* . . . . (Epic)
I've Been Working On The Railroad
Mitch Miller; *Sing Along With Mitch* . . . .(Columbia)
Original Soundtrack; *Children's Favorites* . . . . . . (Kid Rhino/Rhino 4 Kids)
I've Got My Captain Working For Me Now
Eddie Cantor; *Music From The New York Stage (1890-1920)-#4-1917-1920-C* . . . . (Pearl)
Jackhammer John
Richie Havens & Pete Seeger; *Tribute To Woody Guthrie-C* . . . . . (Warner Bros.)
Jackson Cage
Bruce Springsteen; *The River* . . . .(Columbia)
Jesus Christ
Arlo Guthrie; *Tribute To Woody Guthrie-C* . . . . (Warner Bros.)
Cisco Houston; *Greatest Songs Of Woody Guthrie-C* . . . . (Vanguard)
U2; *Folkways: A Vision Shared-C* . . . .(Columbia)
Woody Guthrie; *Woody Guthrie* . . . . (Warner Bros.)
Joe Hill
Arlo Guthrie & Pete Seeger; *Together In Concert* . . . . (Reprise)
Joan Baez; *Carry It On* . . . .(Vanguard)
From Every Stage . . . . (A&M)
One Day At A Time . . . . (Vanguard)
ST/Woodstock . . . . (Atlantic)
Johnny 99
Bruce Springsteen; *Nebraska* . . . .(Columbia)
Bruce Springsteen & The E Street Band; *Bruce Springsteen & The E Street Band Live/1975-85* . . . . (Legacy)
Johnny Cash; *Cover Me (Bruce Springsteen Tribute)-C* . . . .(Rhino)
Just A Job To Do
Genesis; *Genesis* . . . . (Atlantic)
Just Got Paid
ZZ Top; *Best Of ZZ Top* . . . . (Warner Bros.)
Rio Grande Mud . . . . (Warner Bros.)
Six Pack . . . . (Warner Bros.)
Just Got Paid
'N Sync; *No Strings Attached* . . . . (Jive)
Keep On Working
Pete Townshend; *Empty Glass* . . . .(Atco)
Keep The Customer Satisfied
Simon & Garfunkel; *Bridge Over Troubled Water* . . . .(Columbia)
Collected Works . . . .(Columbia)
Keepin' Up
Alabama; *For The Record: 41 Number One Hits* . . . . (RCA)
King Of The Road
R.E.M.; *Dead Letter Office* . . . .(I.R.S.)
Roger Miller; *Billboard Top Country Hits-1965-C* . . . .(Rhino)
Cruisin'-1965-C . . . . (Increase)
Roger Miller-Golden Hits . . . . (Smash)
Labor Of Love
Radney Foster; *Labor Of Love* . . . .(Arista)
Last Fair Deal Gone Down
Keb' Mo'; *Just Like You* . . . . (Okeh)
Let's Work
Mick Jagger; *Primitive Cool* . . . .(Columbia)
Let's Work
Prince; *Controversy* . . . . (Warner Bros.)
Life And How To Live It
R.E.M.; *Fables Of The Reconstruction* . . . .(I.R.S.)
Life Is A Lemon And I Want My Money Back
Meat Loaf; *Bat Out Of Hell II: Back Into Hell* . . . . (MCA)
Links On The Chain
Broadside Singers & Phil Ochs; *Best Of Broadside 1962-1968: Anthems Of The American Underground From The Pages Of Broadside Magazine-C* . . . . (Smithsonian Folkways)
Little Shoe Maker
Eddie Fisher; *Very Best Of Eddie Fisher* . . . . (Taragon)
Gaylords; *Choice Voices! Pop Vocal Group Gems Of The '50s-C* . . . .(Collector's Choice)
Long Hard Road (Sharecropper's Dream)
Nitty Gritty Dirt Band; *Live Two Five* . . . .(Capitol)
Plain Dirt Fashion . . . . (Warner Bros.)
Twenty Years Of Dirt-Best Of The Nitty Gritty Dirt Band . . . . . (Warner Bros.)
Loosen Up My Strings
Clint Black; *Nothin' But The Taillights* . . . . (RCA)
Lord Have Mercy On The Working Man
Travis Tritt; *T-R-O-U-B-L-E* . . . . (Warner Bros.)

Love, Me
Collin Raye; *All I Can Be* . . . .(Epic)
Greatest Country Hits Of The '90s-1992-C . . . . (Columbia)
Lunch Hour
Rupert Holmes; *Partners In Crime* . . . .(MCA)
Maggie's Farm
Bob Dylan; *Bob Dylan At Budokan* . . . . (Columbia)
Bob Dylan's Greatest Hits-#2 . . . . (Columbia)
Bringing It All Back Home . . . . (Columbia)
Hard Rain . . . . (Columbia)
Real Live . . . . (Columbia)
Man At The Top
Bruce Springsteen; *Tracks* . . . . (Columbia)
Midnight Shift
Commander Cody & His Lost Planet Airmen; *Lost In The Ozone* . . . .(MCA)
Migrant's Song, The
Luis Valdez & Augustin Lira; *Best Of Broadside 1962-1968: Anthems*
Of The American Underground From The Pages Of Broadside
Magazine-C . . . . (Smithsonian Folkways)
Mill Worker
James Taylor; *Flag* . . . . (Columbia)
Minimum Wage
They Might Be Giants; *Flood* . . . . (Elektra)
Monday Morning Secretary
Statler Brothers; *Statler Brothers* . . . . (Mercury)
Monday Thru' Friday
Cliff Richard; *We Don't Talk Anymore* . . . .(EMI)
More Than A Paycheck
Sweet Honey In The Rock; *We All...Every One Of Us* . . . . (Flying Fish)
Morning Train (Nine To Five)
Sheena Easton; *Sheena Easton* . . . .(EMI)
Mr. Businessman
Ray Stevens; *Ray Stevens' Greatest Hits* . . . . (RCA)
Ray Stevens' Greatest Hits-#2 . . . . (MCA)
Very Best Of Ray Stevens . . . . (Barnaby)
Mr. President (Have Pity On The Working Man)
Randy Newman; *Good Old Boys* . . . . (Reprise)
ST/Forrest Gump . . . . (Epic/Sony Music Soundtrax)
Mrs. Clara Sullivan's Letter
Pete Seeger; *Best Of Broadside 1962-1968: Anthems Of The American*
Underground From The Pages Of Broadside
Magazine-C . . . . (Smithsonian Folkways)
My Hometown
Bruce Springsteen; *Born In The U.S.A.* . . . . (Columbia)
Bruce Springsteen's Greatest Hits . . . . (Columbia)
National Working Woman's Holiday
Sammy Kershaw; *Feelin' Good Train* . . . . (Mercury)
New Career In A New Town
David Bowie; *Low* . . . .(Rykodisc)
Nice Work If You Can Get It
Billie Holiday; *Compact Jazz-Billie Holiday* . . . . (Verve)
Carmen McRae; *Greatest Of Carmen McRae* . . . .(MCA)
Ella Fitzgerald; *George & Ira Gershwin Songbook* . . . . (Verve)
Frank Sinatra; *My Kind Of Broadway* . . . . (Reprise)
Original Cast; *My One And Only* . . . .(Atlantic)
Sting; *Glory Of Gershwin Featuring Larry Adler-C* . . . . (Mercury)
Night
Bruce Springsteen; *Born To Run* . . . . (Columbia)
Night Shift
Bob Marley & The Wailers; *Rastaman Vibration* . . . . (Tuff Gong)
Foghat; *Best Of Foghat* . . . . (Rhino)
Night Shift . . . . (Rhino)
Nightshift
Commodores; *Nightshift* . . . . (Motown)
No Can Do
Mark Knopfler; *Golden Heart* . . . .(Warner Bros.)
No Job Blues
Ramblin' Thomas; *Ramblin' Mind Blues* . . . . (Biograph)
Occupation
Sparks; *Introducing Sparks* . . . . (Out Of Print)
Old Enough To Know Better
Wade Hayes; *Country Dance Hits-C* . . . . (Columbia)
Old Enough To Know Better . . . . (Columbia)
Steppin' Country-#2-C . . . . (Columbia)
Super Hits Of 1994-C . . . . (Columbia)
Old Man From The Mountain
Merle Haggard & The Strangers; *For The Record: Merle Haggard-43*
Legendary Hits . . . . (BNA)
One Bourbon One Scotch One Beer
George Thorogood & The Destroyers; *George Thorogood & The*
Destroyers . . . . (Rounder)
George Thorogood & The Destroyers-Live . . . .(EMI)
John Lee Hooker; *Best Of Chess Blues-C* . . . .(Chess)
John Lee Hooker-The Ultimate Collection-1948-1990 . . . . (Rhino)
Real Folk Blues-C . . . .(Chess)
One Of Those Nights Tonight
Lorrie Morgan; *Shakin' Things Up* . . . . (BNA)
To Get To You-Greatest Hits Collection . . . . (BNA)

One Piece At A Time
Johnny Cash; *The Man In Black-His Greatest Hits* . . . . (Legacy)
Oney
Johnny Cash; *Johnny Cash-16 Biggest Hits-#2* . . . . (Legacy)
Ooh! My Feet!
Original Broadway Cast; *Most Happy Fella* . . . . (Sony Music Classical)
Other Side Of The Game
Erykah Badu; *Baduizm* . . . . (Kedar Entert./Universal)
Out Of Work
Gary U.S. Bonds; *On The Line* . . . . EMI)
Paddy Works On The Railway
Pete Seeger; *Concert Folk Songs And Ballads* . . . . (Collectables)
Pajama Game/Racing With The Clock
Original Cast; *Pajama Game.* . . . . (Columbia)
Paperback Writer
Beatles; *Beatles 1* . . . . (Capitol)
Beatles-20 Greatest Hits . . . . (Capitol)
Beatles-Box Set. . . . . (Capitol)
Hey Jude . . . . (Capitol)
Past Masters-Volume Two . . . . (Parlophone)
The Beatles/1962-1966. . . . . (Capitol)
Paul McCartney; *Paul Is Live* . . . . (Capitol)
Pastures Of Plenty
Tom Paxton; *Tribute To Woody Guthrie-C* . . . . (Warner Bros.)
Payday/Mine 'Til Monday
Original Broadway Cast; *Tree Grows In Brooklyn* . . . . . . (Sony Music Classical)
Peak Hour (Lunch Break)
Moody Blues; *Caught Live Plus Five* . . . .(Polydor)
Days Of Future Passed . . . .(Polydor)
Penny Lane
Beatles; *Beatles 1* . . . . (Capitol)
Magical Mystery Tour . . . . (Capitol)
The Beatles/1967-1970. . . . . (Capitol)
The Beatles-Anthology-#2 . . . . (Capitol)
Pittsburgh Town
Pete Seeger; *American Industrial Ballads* . . . . (Smithsonian Folkways)
Play It All Night Long
Warren Zevon; *Bad Luck Streak In Dancing School* . . . .(Asylum)
Quiet Normal Life-Best Of Warren Zevon . . . .(Asylum)
Promised Land
Bruce Springsteen; *Darkness On The Edge Of Town* . . . . (Columbia)
Bruce Springsteen & The E Street Band; *Bruce Springsteen & The E Street*
Band Live/1975-85 . . . . (Legacy)
Prove It All Night
Bruce Springsteen; *Darkness On The Edge Of Town* . . . . (Columbia)
Quitting Time
Asleep At The Wheel; *Keepin' Me Up Nights* . . . . (Arista)
John Anderson; *Blue Skies Again* . . . .(MCA)
Keith Whitley; *L.A. To Miami* . . . .(RCA)
Redneck Rhythm & Blues
Brooks & Dunn; *Borderline* . . . .(Arista)
Rex Bob Lowenstein
Mark Germino; *Rank & File* . . . . (Winter Harvest Entert.)
Right Man For The Job
Charlie Robison; *Step Right Up.* . . . . (Lucky Dog)
Right Where I Need To Be
Gary Allan; *Smoke Rings In The Dark.* . . . .(MCA)
River, The
Bruce Springsteen; *Bruce Springsteen's Greatest Hits* . . . . (Columbia)
The River . . . . (Columbia)
Bruce Springsteen & The E Street Band; *Bruce Springsteen & The E Street*
Band Live/1975-85 . . . . (Legacy)
Roy Rogers
Elton John; *Goodbye Yellow Brick Road.* . . . .(Polydor)
Runnin' Behind
Tracy Lawrence; *Sticks & Stones* . . . .(Atlantic)
Sailing To Philadelphia
Mark Knopfler; *Sailing To Philadelphia* . . . . (Warner Bros.)
Salt Of The Earth
Mick Jagger & Keith Richards; *The Concert For New York City-C* . . (Columbia)
Rolling Stones; *Beggars Banquet* . . . .(Abkco)
Sassin' The Boss
Glen Gray; *The Uncollected Glen Gray & The Casa Loma Orchestra-1939-*
1940. . . . . (Hindsight)
Saturday Boy
Billy Bragg; *Back To Basics* . . . . (Elektra)
Save The Overtime (For Me)
Gladys Knight & The Pips; *Best Of Gladys Knight & The Pips-The Columbia*
Years . . . . (Columbia)
Soul Survivors-Best Of Gladys Knight & The Pips-1973-1988 . . . . . . (Rhino)
Visions . . . . (Columbia)
Scentless Apprentice
Nirvana; *In Utero* . . . . (David Geffen Co.)
Secretary Is Not A Toy
New Broadway Cast; *How To Succeed In Business Without Really*
Trying . . . . (RCA Victor)
Original Cast; *How To Succeed In Business Without Really Trying* . . . . . .(RCA)

Sell Sell Sell
Barenaked Ladies; *Maroon* . . . . (Reprise)
Seven-And-A-Half Cents
John Raitt; *ST/Pajama Game* . . . . (Collectables)
Original Cast; *Pajama Game* . . . . (Columbia)
Sexual Harassment In The Workplace
Frank Zappa; *Guitar* . . . . (Rykodisc)
She Works Hard For The Money
Donna Summer; *I Am Woman-C* . . . . (Nick At Nite)
She Works Hard For The Money . . . . (Mercury)
Summer Collection . . . . (Mercury)
Sinaloa Cowboys
Bruce Springsteen; *The Ghost Of Tom Joad* . . . . (Columbia)
Sittin' On Top Of The World
Bob Dylan; *Good As I Been To You* . . . . (Columbia)
Bob Wills & His Texas Playboys; *Bob Wills & His Texas Playboys-24 Great Hits* . . . . (Polydor)
Bob Wills-Anthology . . . . (Sony Music Special Prod.)
Tiffany Transcriptions-#8-More Of The Best . . . . (Rhino)
Cream; *Wheels Of Fire* . . . . (Polydor)
Doc Watson; *Doc Watson* . . . . (Vanguard)
Greatest Folksingers Of The '60s-C . . . . (Vanguard)
Old Timey Concert . . . . (Vanguard)
Grateful Dead; *Grateful Dead (Skull & Roses)* . . . . (Warner Bros.)
Jerry Jeff Walker; *Will The Circle Be Unbroken-#2-C* . . . . (Uni)
Ray Charles; *20 Golden Pieces Of Ray Charles* . . . . (Bulldog)
Sweet Honey In The Rock; *Believe I'll Run On, See What The End's Gonna Be* . . . . (Redwood)
Sixteen Tons
Cactus Brothers; *Cactus Brothers* . . . . (Liberty)
Tennessee Ernie Ford; *Best Of Tennessee Ernie Ford-16 Tons Of Boogie* . . . . (Rhino)
Capitol Collectors Series-Tennessee Ernie Ford . . . . (Capitol)
When AM Was King-C . . . . (Capitol)
Weavers; *Weavers' Greatest Hits* . . . . (Vanguard)
Some Days You Gotta Dance
Dixie Chicks; *Fly* . . . . (Monument)
Sometimes It's A Bitch
Stevie Nicks; *TimeSpace-The Best Of Stevie Nicks* . . . . (Modern)
Summertime Blues
Alan Jackson; *Who I Am* . . . . (Arista)
Blue Cheer; *Good Times Are So Hard To Find-History Of Blue Cheer* . . . . (Mercury)
Louder Than God-Best Of Blue Cheer . . . . (Rhino)
San Francisco Nights-C . . . . (Rhino)
Brian Setzer; *ST/La Bamba* . . . . (Slash)
Eddie Cochran; *Eddie Cochran-Legendary Masters* . . . . (EMI)
Eddie Cochran's Greatest Hits . . . . (Curb)
EMI Legends Of Rock & Roll-24 Greatest Hits-C . . . . (EMI)
Joan Jett & The Blackhearts; *I Love Rock 'n' Roll* . . . . (Blackheart)
Who; *Hooligans* . . . . (MCA)
Live At Leeds . . . . (MCA)
Who's Last . . . . (MCA)
Sweat (Till You Get Wet)
System; *Sweat (Till You Get Wet)* . . . . (Mirage)
Sweat (Till You Get Wet)
Oingo Boingo; *Best O' Boingo* . . . . (MCA)
Sweat (Till You Get Wet)
Brick; *Summer Heat* . . . . (Bang)
Synchronicity II
Police; *Synchronicity* . . . . (A&M)
Take A Letter Maria
R.B. Greaves; *Didn't It Blow Your Mind: Soul Hits Of The '70s-#1-C* . . . (Rhino)
Take This Job And Shove It
David Allan Coe; *David Allan Coe-17 Greatest Hits* . . . . (Columbia)
Johnny Paycheck; *Johnny Paycheck's Biggest Hits* . . . . (Epic)
Johnny Paycheck's Greatest Hits-#2 . . . . (Epic)
Take This Job And Shove It . . . . (Epic)
Truckers' Jukebox-10 All-Time Radio Requests-C . . . . (Legacy)
Take This Job And Shove It Too
David Allan Coe; *I've Got Something To Say* . . . . (Columbia)
Talking Union
Pete Seeger; *Pete Seeger's Greatest Hits* . . . . (Columbia)
Pete Seeger & Others; *Songs Of America's Working People* . . . . (Flying Fish)
Ten Cents A Dance
Eileen Farrell; *I Gotta Right To Sing The Blues* . . . . (Sony Music Classical)
Ella Fitzgerald; *Rodgers & Hart Songbook* . . . . (Verve)
Tenth Avenue Freeze-Out
Bruce Springsteen; *Born To Run* . . . . (Columbia)
Bruce Springsteen & The E Street Band; *Bruce Springsteen & The E Street Band Live/1975-85* . . . . (Legacy)
That's My Job
Conway Twitty; *Borderline* . . . . (MCA)
Country Classics-#12-1987-1988-C . . . . (Universal)
Silver Anniversary Collection . . . . (MCA)
Theme From "Anything But Love"
Original Soundtrack; *Television's Greatest Hits-#7-Cable Ready-C* . . . . (TVT)
Theme From "Designing Women" (Georgia On My Mind)
Original Soundtrack; *Television's Greatest Hits-#7-Cable Ready-C* . . . . (TVT)
Theme From "Hazel"
Original Soundtrack; *Television's Greatest Hits-#4-Black & White Classics-C* . . . . (TVT)
Theme From "Laverne & Shirley"
Original Soundtrack; *Television's Greatest Hits-#3-1970s & 1980s-C* . . . . (TVT)
Theme From "Moonlighting"
Al Jarreau; *ST/Moonlighting* . . . . (MCA)
Television's Greatest Hits-#6-Remote Control-C . . . . (TVT)
Theme From "Mr. Belvedere" (According To Our New Arrivals)
Leon Redbone; *Television's Greatest Hits-#6-Remote Control-C* . . . . (TVT)
Theme From "Taxi"
Original Soundtrack; *Television's Greatest Hits-#3-1970s & 1980s-C* . . . . (TVT)
Theme From "Who's The Boss"
Original Soundtrack; *Television's Greatest Hits-#6-Remote Control-C* . . . (TVT)
There It Is
Ginuwine; *Life* . . . . (Epic)
There's No Business Like Show Business
Ethel Merman; *Irving Berlin 100th Anniversary Collection-C* . . . . (MCA)
Merman Sings Merman . . . . (London)
Original Cast; *Annie Get Your Gun* . . . . (MCA)
Things Are Tough All Over
Shelby Lynne; *Greatest Country Hits Of The '90s-#2-C* . . . . (Columbia)
Tough All Over . . . . (Epic)
This Woman's Work
Kate Bush; *Sensual World* . . . . (Columbia)
ST/She's Having A Baby . . . . (I.R.S.)
Tombstone Blues
Bob Dylan; *Biograph* . . . . (Columbia)
Highway 61 Revisited . . . . (Columbia)
Real Live . . . . (Columbia)
Tomorrow We'll See
Sting; *Brand New Day* . . . . (A&M)
Too Lazy To Work, Too Nervous To Steal
BR549; *This Is BR549* . . . . (Lucky Dog)
Try A Little Harder
Rolling Stones; *Singles Collection-The London Years* . . . . (Abkco)
Two Pump Texaco
Diamond Rio; *Unbelievable* . . . . (Arista)
Typewriter, The
101 Strings Orchestra; *Strings Have Fun!* . . . . (Alshire)
Rochester Pops Orchestra; *Leroy Anderson's Greatest Hits* . . . . (Pro-Arte)
Rochester Pops Orchestra & Erich Kunzel; *Syncopated Clock* . . . . (Pro-Arte)
Under Pressure
David Bowie & Queen; *Bowie-The Singles-1969-1993* . . . . (Rykodisc)
Queen & David Bowie; *Classic Queen* . . . . (Hollywood)
Hot Space . . . . (Hollywood)
Queen's Greatest Hits I & II . . . . (Hollywood)
Union Maid
Judy Collins; *Tribute To Woody Guthrie-C* . . . . (Warner Bros.)
Wat About Di Workin' Class?
Linton Kwesi Johnson; *Linton Kwesi Johnson In Concert With The Dub Band* . . . . (Shanachie)
We Can Work It Out
Beatles; *"Yesterday"...And Today* . . . . (Capitol)
Beatles 1 . . . . (Capitol)
Beatles-20 Greatest Hits . . . . (Capitol)
Beatles-Box Set . . . . (Capitol)
Past Masters-Volume Two . . . . (Parlophone)
The Beatles/1962-1966 . . . . (Capitol)
Paul McCartney; *Unplugged (The Official Bootleg)* . . . . (Capitol)
Stevie Wonder; *Beatles Songs By Greatest Stars* . . . . (Motown)
Signed Sealed & Delivered . . . . (Motown)
Stevie Wonder's Greatest Hits-#2 . . . . (Motown)
Top 10 With A Bullet-Motown Solo Stars-C . . . . (Motown)
We Work The Black Seam
Sting; *Bring On The Night* . . . . (A&M)
Dream Of The Blue Turtles . . . . (A&M)
Weight, The
Band; *Best Of The Band* . . . . (Capitol)
Music From Big Pink . . . . (Capitol)
Rock Of Ages . . . . (Capitol)
The Last Waltz . . . . (Warner Bros.)
Staple Singers; *Soul Folk In Action* . . . . (Stax)
Staple Singers & Marty Stuart; *Rhythm Country And Blues-C* . . . . (MCA)
Welcome To The Working Week
Elvis Costello; *My Aim Is True* . . . . (Columbia)
Well Respected Man
Kinks; *History Of British Rock-#4-C* . . . . (Rhino)
Kinks' Greatest Hits . . . . (Rhino)
Kinks-Size Kinkdom . . . . (Rhino)
West Virginia Mine Disaster
Betsy Rutherford; *Betsy Rutherford* . . . . (Biograph)
Cindy Mangsen; *Long Time Traveling* . . . . (Hogeye)
When I Lay My Burden Down
Fred McDowell & Furry Lewis; *When I Lay My Burden Down* . . . . (Biograph)
Roy Acuff; *Columbia Historic Edition-Roy Acuff* . . . . (Columbia)
When The Work's All Done This Fall
Doc Watson; *On Stage (Featuring Merle Watson)* . . . . (Vanguard)

Michael Martin Murphey; *Cowboy Songs* . . . . (Warner Western)
Whistle While You Work
NRBQ; *Peek-A-Boo-Best Of-1969-1989* . . . . (Rhino)
Whistle While You Work/Heigh Ho
Adriana Caselotti; *Disney Collection-#1-C* . . . .(Disney)
Mormon Tabernacle Choir & Columbia Symphony Orchestra; *When You Wish Upon A Star-A Tribute To Walt Disney* . . . .(CBS Masterworks)
Why Don't You Get A Job?
Offspring; *Americana* . . . . (Columbia)
Wild Sex (In The Working Class)
Oingo Boingo; *Best O' Boingo* . . . .(MCA)
Boingo Alive . . . .(MCA)
Nothing To Fear . . . . (A&M)
Wood And Wire
George Jones; *The Rock: Stone Cold Country 2001* . . . . (BNA)
Work For All
Juluka; *Stand Your Ground* . . . .(Warner Bros.)
Work In The Mines
Bill Shute & Lisa Null; *American Primitive* . . . .(Green Linnet)
Work Shy
Fabulous Poodles; *Mirror Stars* . . . .(Epic)
Work That Sucker To Death
Xavier; *Point Of Pleasure* . . . . (Liberty)
Work To Do
Average White Band; *Average White Band* . . . .(Atlantic)
Pick Up The Pieces-Best Of The Average White Band . . . . (Rhino)
Isley Brothers; *The Isley Brothers Story-#2-The T-Neck Years-1969-1985* . . . . (Rhino)
Worker Man
PAtra; *Queen Of The Pack* . . . .(Epic)
Workin' At The Car Wash Blues
Jim Croce; *50th Anniversary Collection* . . . .(Saja)
Greatest Character Songs . . . .(Lifesong)
I Got A Name . . . .(Lifesong)
Photographs & Memories/His Greatest Hits . . . .(Atlantic)
Workin' For A Livin'
Huey Lewis and the News; *The Heart Of Rock & Roll-The Best Of Huey Lewis and the News* . . . .(Chrysalis)
Workin' For The Weekend
Ken Mellons; *Ken Mellons* . . . .(Epic)
Steppin' Country-#2-C . . . . (Columbia)
Workin' It
Don Henley; *Inside Job* . . . .(Warner Bros.)
Workin' Man
Creedence Clearwater Revival; *1968-1969* . . . . (Fantasy)
Creedence Clearwater Revival . . . . (Fantasy)
Workin' Man Blues
Diamond Rio/Lee Roy Parnell/Steve Wariner; *Mama's Hungry Eyes-Merle Haggard Tribute-C* . . . . (Arista)
Gary Morris; *These Days* . . . . (Capitol)
Merle Haggard & The Strangers; *Best Of Country Blues* . . . (Curb)
Capitol Collectors Series-Merle Haggard & The Strangers . . . . (Capitol)
For The Record: Merle Haggard-43 Legendary Hits . . . . (BNA)
Okie From Muskogee . . . . (Capitol)
Songs I'll Always Sing . . . . (Capitol)
Ricky Van Shelton; *Wild-Eyed Dream* . . . . (Columbia)
Working Class Hero
John Lennon; *Lennon* . . . . (Capitol)
John Lennon/Plastic Ono Band; *John Lennon/Plastic Ono Band* . . . . . (Capitol)
Marianne Faithfull; *Broken English* . . . . (Island)
Working Class Hero
Alan Jackson; *Don't Rock The Jukebox* . . . . (Arista)
Working Class Hero
Johnny Holm; *Work's Many Voices-#1 & 2-C* . . . . (Arhoolie)
Working Class Man
Jimmy Barnes; *Jimmy Barnes* . . . .(Geffen)
Lacy J. Dalton; *Highway Diner* . . . . (Columbia)
Working Class Whore
Pulley; *Pulley* . . . . (Epitaph)
Working Day & Night
Michael Jackson; *Off The Wall* . . . .(Epic)
Working For MCA
Hank Williams, Jr.; *Hank Williams, Jr. ''Live''* . . . . (WB/Curb)
Lynyrd Skynyrd; *Best Of The Rest Of Lynyrd Skynyrd* . . . .(MCA)
One More From The Road . . . .(MCA)
Second Helping . . . .(MCA)
Working For The Japanese
Ray Stevens; *#1 With A Bullet* . . . . (Curb)
Top Ten Records . . . . (Curb)
Working For The Man
Roy Orbison; *For The Lonely: A Roy Orbison Anthology 1959-1965* . . . (Rhino)
In Dreams-Greatest Hits . . . .(Orbison)
Roy Orbison-More Greatest Hits . . . .(Monument)
Roy Orbison's All-Time Greatest Hits-#1 & 2 . . . .(Monument)
Working For The Weekend
Loverboy; *Big Ones* . . . .(Columbia)
Get Lucky . . . .(Columbia)
Working In The Coal Mine
Devo; *Best Of Devo-Greatest Hits* . . . .(Warner Bros.)

Devo's Greatest Hits . . . .(Warner Bros.)
New Traditionalists . . . . (Warner Bros.)
Now It Can Be Told (Devo At The Palace) . . . .(Enigma)
ST/Heavy Metal . . . .(Asylum)
Judds; *Collection-1983-1990* . . . .(RCA)
Rockin' With The Rhythm . . . . (MCA)
Lee Dorsey; *Best Of New Orleans Rhythm & Blues-#2-C* . . . . (Rhino)
Golden Classics-Lee Dorsey . . . . (Collectables)
History Of New Orleans R&B-#3-1962-1970-C . . . . (Rhino)
Holy Cow . . . . (Arista)
New Orleans Jazz & Heritage Festival-1976-C . . . . (Rhino)
Working Man
Rush; *All The World's A Stage* . . . . (Mercury)
Archives . . . .(Mercury)
Rush . . . . (Mercury)
Rush-Chronicles . . . . (Mercury)
Working Man
John Conlee; *Blue Highway* . . . . (MCA)
John Conlee-20 Greatest Hits . . . . (MCA)
Songs For The Working Man . . . . (MCA)
Working Man
Otis Rush; *Mourning In The Morning* . . . .(Atlantic)
Working Man
Glenn Frey; *Soul Searchin'* . . . . (MCA)
Working Man Can't Get Nowhere Today
Merle Haggard; *18 Rare Classics* . . . .(Curb)
Merle Haggard & The Strangers; *Working Man Can't Get Nowhere Today* . . . . (Capitol)
Working Man's Ph.D.
Aaron Tippin; *Call Of The Wild* . . . . (RCA)
Working My Way Back To You
4 Seasons; *25th Anniversary Collection* . . . . (Rhino)
4 Seasons-Anthology . . . . (Rhino)
Working My Way Back To You/Forgive Me, Girl
Spinners; *Billboard Top Hits-1980-C* . . . . (Rhino)
One Of A Kind Love Affair-Anthology . . . . (Rhino)
Very Best Of The Spinners . . . . (Rhino)
Working On A Building
Blue Ridge Rangers; *Blue Ridge Rangers* . . . .(Fantasy)
Kentucky Colonels featuring Clarence White; *Kentucky Colonels featuring Clarence White* . . . . (Rounder)
Working On It
Chris Rea; *New Light Through Old Windows* . . . .(Atlantic)
Working On The Highway
Bruce Springsteen; *Born In The U.S.A.* . . . . (Columbia)
Bruce Springsteen & The E Street Band; *Bruce Springsteen & The E Street Band Live/1975-85* . . . . (Legacy)
Working On The Road
Ten Years After; *Cricklewood Green* . . . .(Chrysalis)
Working Too Hard
Beat; *Beat* . . . . (Columbia)
Yakety Yak
2 Live Crew; *ST/Twins* . . . . (WTG)
Coasters; *Atlantic Rhythm & Blues 1947-1974-#3 (1955-1958)-C* . . . . .(Atlantic)
Billboard Top Rock 'N' Roll Hits-1958-C . . . . (Rhino)
Coasters' Greatest Hits . . . . (Atco)
Cruisin'-1958-C . . . .(Increase)
ST/Stand By Me . . . .(Atlantic)
You Ain't Much Fun
Toby Keith; *Boomtown* . . . .(Polydor Country)
You Don't Even Know Who I Am
Patty Loveless; *Patty Loveless-Classics* . . . . (Epic)
When Fallen Angels Fly . . . . (Epic)
Youngstown
Bruce Springsteen; *The Ghost Of Tom Joad* . . . . (Columbia)

WORLD

See Also: AIR, EARTH, GOD, LIFE, NATURE, NIGHT, POLITICS (various), PEACE, SKY, SPACE, STARS, SUN

(What This World Needs Is) A Few More Rednecks
Charlie Daniels; *The Roots Remain* . . . . (Legacy)
1-900-WORLD
Leaving Trains; *Lump In My Forehead* . . . .(SST)
A World Without Love
Peter And Gordon; *Billboard Top Pop Hits-1964-C* . . . . (Rhino)
Absolutely (Story Of A Girl)
Nine Days; *Maddening Crowd* . . . .(550 Music)
Now That's What I Call Music!-#5-C . . . . (Virgin)
Acoustic #3
Goo Goo Dolls; *Dizzy Up The Girl* . . . .(Warner Sunset/Reprise)
Across The Universe
Beatles; *Let It Be* . . . . (Capitol)
Past Masters-Volume Two . . . .(Parlophone)
Rarities . . . . (Capitol)
The Beatles/1967-1970 . . . . (Capitol)
David Bowie; *Young Americans* . . . . (Rykodisc)

Ain't Nuthin' In The World
Miki Howard; *Miki Howard* . . . . (Atlantic)
All Around The World
Little Richard; *Grooviest 17 Original Hits* . . . . (Specialty)
    Little Richard . . . . (Specialty)
    Little Richard-18 Greatest Hits . . . . (Rhino)
    Little Richard-His Biggest Hits . . . . (Specialty)
All Around The World
Oasis; *Be Here Now* . . . . (Epic)
All Around The World
Lisa Stansfield; *Affection* . . . . (Arista)
All Around The World
Edwin Starr; *War & Peace* . . . . (Motown)
All Around The World Or The Myth Of Fingerprints
Paul Simon; *Graceland* . . . . (Warner Bros.)
All Over The World
Nat "King" Cole; *Capitol Collectors Series-Nat "King" Cole* . . . . . . (Capitol)
    Ramblin' Rose . . . . (Capitol)
All Over The World
Electric Light Orchestra; *ST/Xanadu* . . . . (MCA)
All The Crying In The World
Jody Miller; *45-#2398* . . . . (Capitol)
All The Love In The World
Dionne Warwick; *Heartbreaker* . . . . (Arista)
All The Love In The World
Outfield; *Play Deep* . . . . (Columbia)
All The Time In The World
Subdudes; *Primitive Streak* . . . . (High Street)
Another Green World
Brian Eno; *Another Green World* . . . . (Editions E.G.)
Another World
Gary Morris & Crystal Gayle; *Favorite Country Duets-C* . . . . . . (Warner Bros.)
    Gary Morris' Greatest Hits-#2 . . . . (Warner Bros.)
Another World
Richard Hell & The Voidoids; *Blank Generation* . . . .(Sire)
Another World
Roches; *Another World* . . . . (Warner Bros.)
Another World
Hoodoo Gurus; *Magnum Come Louder* . . . .(RCA)
Another World
Joe Jackson; *Night & Day* . . . . (A&M)
Another World, Another Day
Soul Asylum; *Made To Be Broken* . . . . (Twin-Tone)
Anthem For The Year 2000
Silverchair; *Neon Ballroom* . . . . (Epic)
Any World
Steely Dan; *Katy Lied* . . . . (MCA)
Around The World
Weavers; *Weavers At Carnegie Hall* . . . . (Vanguard)
    Weavers' Greatest Hits . . . . (Vanguard)
Around The World
Red Hot Chili Peppers; *Californication* . . . . (Warner Bros.)
Around The World
Neil Young; *Lucky Thirteen* . . . . (Geffen)
Around The World
Bing Crosby; *Heart Beats-Closer Than A Kiss-Crooner Classics-C* . . . . . (Rhino)
Frank Sinatra; *Come Fly With Me* . . . . (Capitol)
McGuire Sisters; *McGuire Sisters-Anthology* . . . . (MCA)
Around The World
Jeff Kashiwa; *Another Door Opens* . . . . (Native Language)
Around The World (La La La...)
ATC; *Now That's What I Call Music!-#6-C* . . . .(Virgin)
    Planet Pop . . . . (Republic/Universal)
Around The World In A Day
Prince and the Revolution; *Around The World In A Day* . . . . (Paisley Park)
Around The World In Eighty Days
Boston Pops Orchestra/Arthur Fiedler; *Greatest Hits Of The '50s-#2* . . . . .(RCA)
Frank Sinatra; *Come Fly With Me* . . . . (Capitol)
Roger Williams; *Roger Williams' Greatest Hits* . . . . (MCA)
Victor Young & His Singing Strings; *Hollywood's Greatest Hits-#2* . . . . (Telarc)
As The World Falls Down
David Bowie; *ST/Labyrinth* . . . . (EMI)
At War With The World
Foreigner; *Foreigner* . . . . (Atlantic)
Baby, Now That I've Found You
Alison Krauss & Union Station; *Best Of Austin City Limits-Country Music's*
    Finest Hour-C . . . . (Legacy)
    Now That I've Found You: A Collection . . . . (Rounder)
Foundations; *Best Of Rock 'N Soul-C* . . . . (Priority)
    History Of British Rock-#6-C . . . . (Rhino)
Back To The World
Tevin Campbell; *Back To The World* . . . . (Qwest)
Ball Of Confusion (That's What The World Is Today)
Temptations; *All The Million-Sellers* . . . . (Motown)
    Compact Command Performances-Temptations . . . . (Motown)
    Songs Of Protest-C . . . . (Rhino)
    Temptations' Greatest Hits-#2 . . . . (Motown)
    Temptations-Anthology-The Best Of The Temptations . . . . (Motown)

    Top 10 With A Bullet-Motown Male Groups-C . . . . (Motown)
Beautiful Day
U2; *All That You Can't Leave Behind* . . . . (Interscope)
    Now That's What I Call Music!-#6-C . . . .(Virgin)
Beautiful People
Bobby Vee; *Very Best Of Bobby Vee* . . . .(Collectables)
Because
Beatles; *Abbey Road* . . . . (Parlophone)
    Beatles-Box Set . . . .(Capitol)
Best Of All Possible Worlds
Leonard Bernstein; *Bernstein Songbook* . . . .(Columbia)
Original Cast; *Candide* . . . .(Columbia)
Best Of Both Worlds
Midnight Oil; *Red Sails In The Sunset* . . . .(Columbia)
Best Of Both Worlds
Van Halen; *5150* . . . . (Warner Bros.)
Best Of Both Worlds
Robert Palmer; *Double Fun* . . . .(Island)
Biggest Airport In The World
Moe Bandy; *Best Of Moe Bandy-Vol. 1* . . . .(Columbia)
Black Balloon
Goo Goo Dolls; *Dizzy Up The Girl* . . . . (Warner Sunset/Reprise)
Blow Up The Outside World
Soundgarden; *A-Sides* . . . .(A&M)
    Down On The Upside . . . .(A&M)
Brain Of J.
Pearl Jam; *Yield* . . . . (Epic)
Brave New World
Steve Miller Band; *Brave New World* . . . .(Capitol)
Brave New World
Public Image Ltd.; *9* . . . . (Virgin)
Brave New World
Choirboys; *Big Bad Noise* . . . . (WTG)
Broadway
Goo Goo Dolls; *Dizzy Up The Girl* . . . . (Warner Sunset/Reprise)
Can't Change Me
Chris Cornell; *Euphoria Morning* . . . .(A&M)
Can't Stop My Heart From Loving You
Aaron Neville; *The Tattooed Heart* . . . .(A&M)
O'Kanes; *Greatest Country Hits Of The '80s-1987-C* . . . .(Columbia)
    More Hot Country Requests-#2-C . . . . (Epic)
    O'Kanes . . . .(Columbia)
Change The World
Eric Clapton; *ST/Phenomenon* . . . . (Reprise)
Change The World
Offspring; *Ixnay On The Hombre* . . . .(Columbia)
Children Of The World
Bee Gees; *Bee Gees' Greatest* . . . . (Polydor)
    Children Of The World . . . .(RSO)
Children Of The World
Amy Grant; *House Of Love* . . . .(A&M)
Children Of The World
Wailers Band; *I.D.* . . . . (Atlantic)
Children Of The World
Third World; *Sense Of Purpose* . . . .(Columbia)
Children Of The World Unite
Angela Bofill; *Angie* . . . .(GRP)
Cold Cold World
Teddy Pendergrass; *Life Is A Song Worth Singing* . . . .(Philadelphia Int'l)
Color My World
Petula Clark; *Petula Clark's Greatest Hits* . . . . (Crescendo)
Colour My World
Chicago; *Chicago At Carnegie Hall* . . . .(Chicago)
    Chicago II . . . .(Chicago)
    Chicago IX-Chicago's Greatest Hits . . . .(Chicago)
Computer Incantations For World Peace
Jean-Luc Ponty; *Individual Choice* . . . .(Rhino)
    Le Voyage: The Jean-Luc Ponty Anthology . . . .(Rhino)
Computer World
Kraftwerk; *Computer World* . . . . (Elektra)
Cops Of The World
Phil Ochs; *Phil Ochs In Concert* . . . . (Elektra)
    There But For Fortune . . . . (Elektra)
Criminal World
David Bowie; *Let's Dance* . . . . (EMI)
Cup Of Life
Ricky Martin; *Ricky Martin* . . . .(Columbia)
Dark Side Of The World
Diana Ross; *Ain't No Mountain High Enough* . . . . (Motown)
Marvin Gaye; *Musical Testament 1964-1984* . . . . (Motown)
Different Worlds
Maureen McGovern; *Maureen McGovern* . . . . (Warner Bros.)
Different Worlds
Vandenberg; *Best Of Vandenberg* . . . .(Atco)
Doggy Dogg World
Snoop Doggy Dogg; *Doggystyle* . . . .(Death Row)
Don't Build Your World Around It
Jim Lauderdale; *Every Second Counts* . . . . (Atlantic)

Don't Drop That Bomb On Me
Bryan Adams; *Waking Up The Neighbours* . . . . (A&M)
Don't Wanna Change The World
Phyllis Hyman; *Prime Of My Life* . . . . (PIR)
Dream World
Jerry Butler; *Nothing Says I Love You Like I Love You* . . . . . (Philadelphia Int'l)
Drowned World (My Substitute For Love)
Madonna; *GHV2* . . . .(Warner Bros.)
Ray Of Light . . . .(Maverick)
Duck And Run
3 Doors Down; *Better Life* . . . .(Republic/Universal)
Elegantly Wasted
INXS; *Elegantly Wasted* . . . . (Mercury)
End Of The World
Skeeter Davis; *Best Of Skeeter Davis* . . . . (Gusto)
Billboard Top Country Hits-1963-C . . . . (Rhino)
Nipper's Greatest Hits Of The '60s-#1-C . . . . (RCA)
Stars Of The Grand Ole Opry-1926-1974-C . . . . (RCA)
Super Country Hits Of The '60s-C . . . . (Gusto)
End Of The World
Vonda Shepard; *ST/Songs From "Ally McBeal" Featuring Vonda
Shepard* . . . . (550/Epic)
End Of The World
Cold; *13 Ways To Bleed On Stage* . . . . (Flip/Geffen/Interscope)
Every Woman In The World
Air Supply; *Air Supply's Greatest Hits* . . . . (Arista)
Air Supply-The Definitive Collection . . . . (Arista)
Lost In Love . . . . (Arista)
Everybody Wants To Rule The World
Tears For Fears; *Knebworth-The Album-C* . . . . (Polydor)
Music For The Miracle-C . . . . (Epic Portrait Assoc.)
Songs From The Big Chair . . . . (Mercury)
Eyes Of The World
Grateful Dead; *One From The Vault* . . . . (Grateful Dead)
Wake Of The Flood . . . . (Grateful Dead)
Without A Net . . . . (Arista)
Eyes Of The World
Fleetwood Mac; *25 Years-The Chain* . . . .(Warner Bros.)
Mirage . . . .(Warner Bros.)
Five O'Clock World
Hal Ketchum; *Past The Point Of Rescue* . . . . (Curb)
Vogues; *ST/Good Morning, Vietnam* . . . . (A&M)
Vogues' Greatest Hits . . . . (SSS International)
Vogues' Greatest Hits . . . . (Rhino)
Fool On The Hill
Beatles; *Beatles-Box Set* . . . . (Capitol)
Magical Mystery Tour . . . . (Capitol)
The Beatles/1967-1970 . . . . (Capitol)
Get Me To The World On Time
Electric Prunes; *Nuggets-Original Artyfacts From The First Psychedelic Era-
1965-1968-C* . . . . (Rhino)
Goodbye Cruel World
James Darren; *Best Of James Darren* . . . . (Rhino)
Billboard Top Rock 'N' Roll Hits-1961-C . . . . (Rhino)
Half The World
Rush; *Test For Echo* . . . . (Atlantic)
Hand Me Down World
Guess Who; *Best Of The Guess Who* . . . . (RCA)
Greatest Of The Guess Who . . . . (RCA)
Heart-Shaped World
Chris Isaak; *Heart-Shaped World* . . . . (Reprise)
Here At The Western World
Steely Dan; *Steely Dan's Greatest Hits* . . . . (MCA)
Here In The Real World
Alan Jackson; *Here In The Real World* . . . . (Arista)
He's Got The Whole World In His Hands
Laurie London; *Rock 'N Roll's Greatest Hits Of All Time-#10-
'50s-C* . . . . (Platinum Disc)
Mormon Tabernacle Choir; *Mormon Tabernacle Choir's Greatest
Hits-#2* . . . . (Columbia)
Odetta; *Essential Odetta* . . . . (Vanguard)
Hey Pretty
Poe; *Haunted* . . . . (FEI/Atlantic)
Hey Young World II
Macy Gray featuring Slick Rick; *The Id* . . . . (Epic)
Higher Ground
Stevie Wonder; *Innervisions* . . . . (Motown)
Original Musiquarium . . . . (Motown)
Hope In A Hopeless World
Widespread Panic; *Bombs & Butterflies* . . . . (Capricorn)
Hot Love Cold World
Bob Welch; *French Kiss* . . . . (Capitol)
I Ain't Got No Home
Bob Dylan; *Tribute To Woody Guthrie-C* . . . .(Warner Bros.)
I Am The Light Of This World
Jorma Kaukonen & Tom Hobson; *Quah.* . . . . (Relix)
I Don't Want To Set The World On Fire
Ink Spots; *Best Of The Ink Spots* . . . .(MCA)

I Saved The World Today
Eurythmics; *Peace* . . . . (Arista)
I Try
Macy Gray; *Now That's What I Call Music!-#4-C* . . . .(Virgin)
On How Life Is . . . . (Epic)
I Want To Make The World Turn Around
Steve Miller Band; *Living In The 20th Century* . . . . (Capitol)
I Watched It All (On My Radio)
Lionel Cartwright; *I Watched It All On The Radio* . . . . (MCA)
I Wouldn't Have Missed It For The World
Ronnie Milsap; *Ronnie Milsap's Greatest Hits-#2* . . . . (RCA)
There's No Gettin' Over Me . . . . (RCA)
I.G.Y. (What A Beautiful World)
Donald Fagen; *The Nightfly* . . . . (Warner Bros.)
I'd Like To Buy The World A Coke (Coca-Cola)
Original Soundtrack; *TeeVee Toons-The Commercials-#1-C* . . . . (TVT)
I'd Like To Teach The World To Sing (In Perfect Harmony)
New Seekers; *Chicken Soup For The Soul-Celebrating Life-C* . . . . (Rhino)
I'd Love To Change The World
Ten Years After; *A Space In Time* . . . . (Columbia)
Classic Performances Of Ten Years After . . . . (Columbia)
Universal . . . . (Chrysalis)
If I Could Build My Whole World Around You
Marvin Gaye & Tammi Terrell; *Every Great Motown Hit Of
Marvin Gaye* . . . . (Motown)
Marvin Gaye & Tammi Terrell's Greatest Hits . . . . (Motown)
Marvin Gaye-Anthology . . . . (Motown)
Motown Superstar Series-#2-Marvin Gaye . . . . (Motown)
United . . . . (Motown)
If I Ruled The World
NaS; *It Was Written* . . . . (Columbia)
If I Ruled The World
Diana Ross & The Supremes; *Diana Ross & The Supremes-25th
Anniversary* . . . . (Motown)
If I Ruled The World
Tony Bennett; *Forty Years-The Artistry Of Tony Bennett* . . . . (Columbia)
If I Ruled The World
Stevie Wonder; *Looking Back* . . . . (Motown)
If I Ruled The World
Sammy Davis, Jr.; *Sammy Davis, Jr.'s Greatest Hits* . . . . (Reprise)
If I Ruled The World
James Brown; *Sex Machine* . . . .(Polydor)
If The World Had A Front Porch
Tracy Lawrence; *Best Of Tracy Lawrence* . . . .(Atlantic)
I See It Now . . . .(Atlantic)
If This World Were Mine
Cheryl Lynn; *Instant Love* . . . . (Columbia)
Luther Vandross & Cheryl Lynn; *Best Of Luther Vandross...The Best
Of Love* . . . . (Epic)
Marvin Gaye & Tammi Terrell; *All The Great Motown Love Song
Duets-C* . . . . (Motown)
Classic Duets-Marvin Gaye & His Women-C . . . . (Motown)
Marvin Gaye & Tammi Terrell's Greatest Hits . . . . (Motown)
Marvin Gaye-Anthology . . . . (Motown)
Motown Superstar Series-#2-Marvin Gaye . . . . (Motown)
United . . . . (Motown)
If Women Ruled The World
Joan Armatrading; *Square The Circle* . . . . (A&M)
If You Were The Only Boy (In The World)
Barbra Streisand; *My Name Is Barbra* . . . . (Columbia)
I'll Kiss The World Goodbye
J.J. Cale; *Really* . . . . (Mercury)
I'm In A Different World
Four Tops; *Four Tops-Anthology* . . . . (Motown)
I'm Not Gonna Let It Bother Me Tonight
Atlanta Rhythm Section; *Are You Ready!* . . . .(Polydor)
Champagne Jam . . . .(Polydor)
I'm Sitting On Top Of The World
Al Jolson; *Jolson Sang 'Em* . . . .(Biograph)
The Al Jolson Story-#3 . . . . (MCA)
In A Perfect World
Lorrie Morgan; *Shakin' Things Up* . . . .(BNA)
In A Perfect World
Gretchen Peters; *Gretchen Peters* . . . .(Purple Crayon Prod.)
In Another World
Joe Diffie; *In Another World* . . . . (Monument)
It's A Lovely Lovely World
Gail Davies; *Gail Davies' Greatest Hits* . . . .(Little Chickadee)
It's A Man's Man's Man's World
James Brown; *Billboard Top R&B Hits-1966-C* . . . . (Rhino)
James Brown's Greatest Hits . . . . (Rhino)
It's A Small World
Various Artists; *Disney's Theme Park Sing-Along* . . . . (Disney)
It's A Woman's World
Four Aces; *Best Of The Four Aces* . . . . (MCA)
It's Such A Small World
Rodney Crowell & Rosanne Cash; *Dynamic Duets-Super Hits-C* . . . (Columbia)
Rodney Crowell-Super Hits . . . . (Columbia)

It's The End Of The World As We Know It (And I Feel Fine)
R.E.M.; *Document*. . . . . (EMI-Capitol Entert. Properties)
I've Got The World On A String
Count Basie; *Standards* . . . . (Verve)
Diana Krall; *Only Trust Your Heart*. . . . . (GRP)
Ella Fitzgerald; *Harold Arlen Songbook-#1* . . . . (Verve)
Frank Sinatra; *Capitol Collectors Series-Frank Sinatra* . . . . (Capitol)
Frank Sinatra & Liza Minnelli; *Frank Sinatra-Duets-C* . . . . (Capitol)
Sarah Vaughan; *Best Of Sarah Vaughan* . . . . (Pablo)
Stephane Grappelli & Martin Taylor; *We've Got The World On A
String* . . . . (Angel)
Joy To The World
Three Dog Night; *Best Of Three Dog Night*. . . . . (MCA)
Good Feeling Music Of The Big Chill Generation-#2-C . . . . (Motown)
Good Feeling Music Of The Big Chill Generation-#3-C . . . . (Motown)
Joy To The World-Greatest Hits . . . . (MCA)
ST/Big Chill . . . . (Motown)
ST/Forrest Gump . . . . (Epic/Sony Music Soundtrax)
King Of All The World
Old 97's; *Satellite Rides* . . . . (Elektra)
King Of The Night Time World
Kiss; *Alive II* . . . .(Casablanca)
Destroyer . . . . (Casablanca)
King Of The World
Steely Dan; *Countdown To Ecstasy*. . . . . (MCA)
Steely Dan-Gold . . . . (MCA)
Kiss The World Goodbye
Kris Kristofferson; *Border Lord* . . . . (Columbia)
Let The Rest Of The World Go By
Mitch Miller; *Sing Along With Mitch*. . . . . (Columbia)
Mom & Dads; *Down The River Of Golden Dreams* . . . . (Crescendo)
Let's Build A World Together
George Jones & Tammy Wynette; *George Jones & Tammy Wynette-16
Biggest Hits* . . . . (Epic/Legacy)
Life Gets Away
Clint Black; *Clint Black-The Greatest Hits* . . . . (RCA)
One Emotion. . . . . (RCA)
Life Goes On
Little Texas; *Little Texas' Greatest Hits* . . . . (Warner Bros.)
Light Of The World
Original Cast; *ST/Godspell* . . . . (Arista)
Living In The Material World
George Harrison; *Living In The Material World* . . . . (Capitol)
Living On The Edge Of The World
Bruce Springsteen; *Tracks*. . . . . (Columbia)
Looking At The World Through A Windshield
Commander Cody; *We've Got A Live One Here!* . . . . (Warner Bros.)
Commander Cody & His Lost Planet Airmen; *Hot Licks, Cold Steel &
Trucker's Favorites* . . . . (MCA)
Del Reeves; *Del Reeves-His Greatest Hits* . . . . (Razor & Tie)
Truckin' On-C . . . . (Hollywood)
Red Simpson; *Ramblin' Road* . . . . (Fifty One West)
Red Sovine & Del Reeves; *Red Sovine & Del Reeves* . . . . (Exact)
Son Volt; *ST/Feeling Minnesota* . . . . (Atlantic)
Lost In A Lost World
Moody Blues; *Seventh Sojourn* . . . . (Polydor)
Lost In The Neon World
Be Bop Deluxe; *Modern Music* . . . . (Capitol)
Love Makes The World Go Round
Deon Jackson; *Deon Jackson-Golden Classics* . . . . (Collectables)
Oldies But Goodies-#15-C . . . . (Original Sound)
Soul Shots-#2-The ''In'' Crowd-Sweet Soul-C . . . . (Rhino)
Super Oldies Of The '60s-#7-C . . . . (Audio Fidelity)
Love Makes The World Go Round
Madonna; *True Blue* . . . .(Sire)
Love Makes The World Go Round
Jo Basile; *Hit Broadway Musicals*. (Audio Fidelity)
Original Broadway Cast; *Me & My Girl* . . . . (MCA)
Original Cast; *Me & My Girl* . . . . (EMI)
Love The World Away
Kenny Rogers; *Kenny Rogers' Greatest Hits* . . . . (EMI)
Kenny Rogers-Twenty Greatest Hits. . . . . (EMI)
ST/Urban Cowboy . . . . (Asylum)
Love, Love, Love
Clovers; *Clovers-Dance Party*. . . . . (Collectables)
Make The World Go Away
Eddy Arnold; *Best Of Eddy Arnold* . . . . (RCA)
Billboard Top Country Hits-1965-C. . . . . (Rhino)
Eddy Arnold-Pure Gold . . . . (RCA)
Nipper's Greatest Hits Of The '60s-#1-C . . . . (RCA)
World Of Hits . . . . (MGM)
Ray Price; *Ray Price-16 Biggest Hits* . . . . (Legacy)
Ray Price-20 Hits . . . . (Tee Vee)
Man Of The World
Fleetwood Mac; *25 Years-The Chain* . . . . (Warner Bros.)
Man Who Sold The World
David Bowie; *Man Who Sold The World* . . . . (Rykodisc)
Sound + Vision . . . . (Rykodisc)
Nirvana; *MTV Unplugged In New York*. . . . . (David Geffen Co.)

Mean Old World
Bobby Bland & B.B. King; *Together Again Live* . . . . (MCA)
Climax Blues Band; *Climax Chicago Blues Band* . . . . (Sire)
Duane Allman & Eric Clapton; *Duane Allman-An Anthology* . . . .(Capricorn)
Eric Clapton-Crossroads-C . . . . (Polydor)
Robert Palmer; *Secrets* . . . .(Island)
Money Song
Original Cast; *Cabaret* . . . .(Columbia)
Most Beautiful Girl In The World
Frank Sinatra; *Strangers In The Night* . . . . (Reprise)
Tony Bennett; *Rodgers & Hart Songbook* . . . . (DRG)
Tony Bennett Sings More Great Rodgers & Hart . . . .(Improv)
Most Beautiful World In The World
Nilsson; *Son Of Schmilsson* . . . . (RCA)
My Whole World Ended (The Moment You Left Me)
David Ruffin; *David Ruffin-At His Best* . . . .(Motown)
Motown Year By Year-The Sound Of Young America-1969-C . . . . .(Motown)
Spinners; *Best Of The Spinners* . . . .(Motown)
My World
Descendants; *I Don't Wanna Grow Up* . . . . (SST)
My World
Bee Gees; *Bee Gees-Gold* . . . . (Polydor)
My World
Guns N' Roses; *Use Your Illusion II* . . . . (Geffen)
My World Begins & Ends With You
Dave & Sugar; *Stay With Me/Golden Tears* . . . . (RCA)
Eddy Arnold; *Collector's Series-Eddy Arnold*. . . . . (RCA)
My World Is Empty Without You
Diana Ross; *Diana Ross-Anthology* . . . .(Motown)
Evening With Diana Ross . . . . (Motown)
Stevie Wonder; *Down To Earth* . . . .(Motown)
New World
X; *Live At The Whisky A Go-Go* . . . .(Elektra)
More Fun In The New World . . . .(Elektra)
New World
Cause & Effect; *Another Minute* . . . . (Zoo)
New World
Strawbs; *Grave New World* . . . .(A&M)
New World
Saigon Kick; *Saigon Kick*. . . . . Third Stone)
New World
Boston; *Third Stage* . . . . (MCA)
New World In The Morning
Roger Whittaker; *Best Of Roger Whittaker* . . . . (RCA)
Last Farewell & Other Hits . . . . (RCA)
Live In Concert . . . . (RCA)
New World In The Morning . . . . (RCA)
New World Man
Rush; *Rush-Chronicles* . . . .(Mercury)
Signals. . . . . (Mercury)
Three Decades Of Rock ('60s, '70s, '80s)-C . . . . (Priority)
New World Order
Curtis Mayfield; *New World Order* . . . . (Warner Bros.)
New World Rising
Electric Light Orchestra; *On The Third Day* . . . . (Jet)
No Such Thing
John Mayer; *Room For Squares*. . . . . (Aware/C2/Columbia)
Not Enough Love In The World
Don Henley; *Building The Perfect Beast* . . . . (Geffen)
Oldest Baby In The World
John Prine; *Aimless Love* . . . . (Oh Boy)
Great Days-Anthology . . . . (Rhino)
John Prine-Live. . . . . (Oh Boy)
On Top Of The World
Cheap Trick; *Heaven Tonight* . . . .(Epic)
One World
Utopia; *Swing To The Right* . . . . (Rhino)
Utopia-Anthology 1974-1985 . . . . (Rhino)
One World
Anthrax; *Among The Living* . . . .(Island)
One World
Dire Straits; *Brothers In Arms* . . . . (Warner Bros.)
One World
John Denver; *One World* . . . . (RCA)
Ordinary World
Duran Duran; *Duran Duran (The Wedding Album)* . . . .(Capitol)
Out Of This World
Ella Fitzgerald; *Harold Arlen Songbook-#2*. . . . .(Verve)
Rosemary Clooney; *Rosemary Clooney Sings The Music Of Harold
Arlen*. . . . . (Concord Jazz)
Tito Puente; *Out Of This World* . . . .(Concord Picante Jazz)
Tony Bennett; *Jazz*. . . . .(Columbia)
Outta The World
Ashford & Simpson; *Solid*. . . . .(Capitol)
Solid Plus Seven . . . .(Capitol)
Panic In The World
Be Bop Deluxe; *Best Of And The Rest Of Be Bop Deluxe*. . . . .(Capitol)
Best Of Be Bop Deluxe-Raiding The Divine Archive . . . .(Capitol)

Drastic Plastic . . . . (Capitol)
Passin' Thru
　Earl Scruggs & Don Henley & Johnny Cash; *Earl Scruggs And*
　　Friends-C . . . .(MCA)
　Randy Scruggs; *Crown Of Jewels* . . . . (Reprise)
　Randy Scruggs & Joan Osborne; *ST/Happy Texas* . . . . (Arista)
Peaceful World
　Rascals; *Peaceful World* . . . . (Columbia)
Peaceful World
　John Mellencamp; *Cuttin' Heads* . . . . (Columbia)
　God Bless America-C . . . . (Columbia)
　The Concert For New York City-C . . . . (Columbia)
Perfect World
　Tevin Campbell; *T.E.V.I.N.* . . . . (Qwest)
Perfect World
　Talking Heads; *Little Creatures* . . . . (Sire)
Perfect World
　Roger Daltrey; *Rocks In My Head* . . . .(Atlantic)
Perfect World
　Huey Lewis and the News; *Small World* . . . .(Chrysalis)
Place In This World
　Michael W. Smith; *Go West Young Man* . . . . (Reunion)
Pretty World
　Sergio Mendes & Brasil '66; *Sergio Mendes & Brasil '66's*
　　Greatest Hits . . . . (A&M)
　Sergio Mendes-Classics-#18 . . . . (A&M)
Rainy Night In Georgia
　Brook Benton; *Atlantic Rhythm & Blues 1947-1974-#6 (1966-*
　　1969)-C . . . .(Atlantic)
　Brook Benton Today . . . . (Cotillion)
　Brook Benton-Anthology . . . . (Rhino)
　Golden Age Of Black Music-1960-1970-C . . . .(Atlantic)
　Pick Of Brook Benton . . . . (Fifty One West)
　Soul Years-C . . . .(Atlantic)
　Hank Williams, Jr.; *Hank Williams, Jr.-14 Greatest Hits* . . . . . (Polydor)
　Sam Moore & Conway Twitty; *Rhythm Country And Blues-C* . . . .(MCA)
Reach Out And Touch
　Diana Ross; *Diana Ross-All The Great Hits* . . . . (Motown)
　Diana Ross-Anthology . . . . (Motown)
　Live At Caesar's Palace . . . . (Motown)
　Most Played Songs On America's Jukeboxes . . . . (Motown)
　Motown Story-First 25 Years-C . . . . (Motown)
Real World
　Richard Marx; *Repeat Offender* . . . .(EMI)
Real World
　Matchbox Twenty; *Yourself Or Someone Like You* . . . . (Lava)
Real World
　Bangles; *Bangles* . . . .(I.R.S.)
Real World
　Bruce Springsteen; *Human Touch* . . . . (Columbia)
Real World
　Mighty Lemon Drops; *Laughter* . . . . (Sire)
Real World
　Jesus Jones; *Liquidizer* . . . . (SBK)
Rhythm Saved The World
　Bunny Berigan & His Boys; *Take It Bunny* . . . . (Sony Music Special Prod.)
Richest Man On Earth
　Paul Overstreet; *Sowin' Love* . . . . (RCA)
Rock & Roll Music To The World
　Ten Years After; *Classic Performances Of Ten Years After* . . . . (Columbia)
Rock My World (Little Country Girl)
　Brooks & Dunn; *Hard Workin' Man* . . . . (Arista)
Rock The World
　Third World; *Rock The World* . . . . (Columbia)
Rock You All Around The World
　Judas Priest; *Priest...Live!* . . . . (Columbia)
　Turbo . . . . (Columbia)
Rockin' In The Free World
　Bon Jovi; *One Wild Night: Live 1985-2001* . . . . (Island)
　Neil Young; *Freedom* . . . . (Reprise)
　Neil Young & Crazy Horse; *WELD* . . . . (Reprise)
　Pearl Jam; *8/12/00: Tampa, Florida* . . . . (Epic)
Room At The Top
　Tom Petty And The Heartbreakers; *Echo* . . . .(Warner Bros.)
Rose Tint In My World
　Tim Curry & Original Roxy Cast; *Rocky Horror Show* . . . . (Rhino)
'Round The World With The Rubber Duck
　C.W. McCall; *C.W. McCall's Greatest Hits* . . . . (Polydor)
Sail Around The World
　David Gates; *First* . . . . (Elektra)
Santa Monica (Watch The World Die)
　Everclear; *Sparkle And Fade* . . . . (Capitol)
Saturday Night At The World
　Mason Williams; *Music-1968-1971* . . . . (Vanguard)
　Mason Williams & Mannheim Steamroller;
　　Classical Gas . . . .(American Gramaphone)
Save The World
　George Harrison; *Greenpeace-C* . . . . (A&M)

Somewhere In England . . . .(Dark Horse)
Separate Ways (Worlds Apart)
　Journey; *Frontiers* . . . . (Columbia)
　Journey's Greatest Hits . . . . (Columbia)
Sittin' On Top Of The World
　Bob Dylan; *Good As I Been To You* . . . . (Columbia)
　Bob Wills & His Texas Playboys; *Bob Wills & His Texas Playboys-24*
　　Great Hits . . . .(Polydor)
　Bob Wills-Anthology . . . . (Sony Music Special Prod.)
　Tiffany Transcriptions-#8-More Of The Best . . . . (Rhino)
　Cream; *Wheels Of Fire* . . . .(Polydor)
　Doc Watson; *Doc Watson* . . . . (Vanguard)
　Greatest Folksingers Of The '60s-C . . . . (Vanguard)
　Old Timey Concert . . . . (Vanguard)
　Grateful Dead; *Grateful Dead (Skull & Roses)* . . . . (Warner Bros.)
　Jerry Jeff Walker; *Will The Circle Be Unbroken-#2-C* . . . . (Uni)
　Ray Charles; *20 Golden Pieces Of Ray Charles* . . . .(Bulldog)
　Sweet Honey In The Rock; *Believe I'll Run On, See What The End's*
　　Gonna Be . . . . (Redwood)
Sitting On Top Of The World
　Cream; *Goodbye* . . . .(Polydor)
　Very Best Of Cream . . . .(Polydor)
　Wheels Of Fire . . . .(Polydor)
　Howlin' Wolf; *Real Folk Blues-C* . . . . (Chess)
　The Chess Box-Howlin' Wolf . . . . (Chess)
Small World
　Johnny Mathis; *Johnny Mathis' All-Time Greatest Hits* . . . . (Columbia)
　Johnny Mathis-16 Most Requested Songs . . . . (Columbia)
　Original Cast; *Gypsy* . . . . (Columbia)
　Original London Cast; *Gypsy* . . . . (RCA)
Small World
　Huey Lewis and the News; *Greenpeace/Rainbow Warriors-C* . . . . (Geffen)
　Small World . . . . (Chrysalis)
Small World
　Adrian Belew; *Young Lions* . . . .(Atlantic)
Somethin' Just Ain't Right
　Earl Scruggs & Randy Scruggs; *Earl Scruggs And Friends-C* . . . . (MCA)
Songs Of Freedom
　Santana; *Freedom* . . . . (Columbia)
Spirits In The Material World
　Police; *Every Breath You Take-The Classics* . . . . (A&M)
　Ghost In The Machine . . . . (A&M)
State Of The World
　Janet Jackson; *Janet Jackson's Rhythm Nation 1814* . . . . (A&M)
Stop The World
　Extreme; *III Sides To Every Story* . . . . (A&M)
Stop The World
　Clash; *On Broadway* . . . . (Epic)
Stop The World
　Teena Marie; *Robbery* . . . . (Epic)
Stop The World (& Let Me Off)
　Merle Haggard; *Big City* . . . . (Epic)
　Patsy Cline; *20 Golden Pieces Of Patsy Cline* . . . .(Bulldog)
　Forever & Always . . . . (Epic)
　Here's Patsy Cline . . . . (MCA)
　Waylon Jennings; *Waylon Jennings-Early Years* . . . . (RCA)
Stop The World Right Here
　Temptations; *Back To Basics* . . . . (Motown)
Take Me To Your World
　George Jones; *Tammy Wynette...Remembered-C* . . . . (Asylum)
　Tammy Wynette; *Tammy Wynette-16 Biggest Hits* . . . . (Legacy)
　Tammy Wynette's Greatest Hits . . . . (Epic)
Teen Angst (What The World Needs Now)
　Cracker; *Cracker* . . . .(Virgin)
Tell The World
　Dells; *Harlem New York-Ballad Era-C* . . . . (Collectables)
Tell The World
　Ratt; *Ratt & Roll 8191* . . . .(Atlantic)
Tell The World How I Feel About 'Cha Baby
　Harold Melvin And The Blue Notes; *Wake Up Everybody* . . . (Philadelphia Int'l)
Test For Echo
　Rush; *Test For Echo* . . . . (Atlantic)
Thank You World
　Statler Brothers; *Best Of The Statler Brothers* . . . . (Mercury)
That's The Way Of The World
　Earth, Wind & Fire; *Best Of Earth, Wind & Fire-#1* . . . . (Legacy)
　Eternal Dance . . . . (Columbia)
　Love Shouldn't Hurt-C . . . . (Qwest)
　Pop Classics Of The '70s-C . . . . (Columbia)
　That's The Way Of The World . . . . (Legacy)
That's The Way That The World Goes Round
　John Prine; *Bruised Orange* . . . . (Oh Boy)
　Great Days-Anthology . . . . (Rhino)
　John Prine-Live . . . . (Oh Boy)
The World I Know
　Collective Soul; *Collective Soul* . . . .(Atlantic)
Theme From "A Different World"
　Original Soundtrack; *Television's Greatest Hits-#7-Cable Ready-C* . . . . . (TVT)

Theme From "ABC's Wide World Of Sports"
Original Soundtrack; *Television's Greatest Hits-#2-C* . . . . (TVT)
Theme From "As The World Turns"
Rosemary Joyce & Bill Bartholomew; *Soap Opera Themes* . . . . (Crescendo)
Theme From "Walt Disney's Wonderful World Of Color"
Original Soundtrack; *Television's Greatest Hits-#4-Black & White
Classics-C* . . . . (TVT)
Theme From "War Of The Worlds"
Neil Norman; *Greatest Science Fiction Hits-#3-C* . . . . (Crescendo)
Theme From "Wayne's World"
Mike Myers & Dana Carvey; *ST/Wayne's World* . . . . (Reprise)
Theme From "Where In The World Is Carmen Sandiego?"
Original Soundtrack; *Television's Greatest Hits-#7-Cable Ready-C* . . . . . (TVT)
There Must Be A Better World Somewhere
B.B. King; *King Of The Blues* . . . . (MCA)
There Must Be A Better World Somewhere . . . . (MCA)
There's A Kind Of Hush (All Over The World)
Carpenters; *A Kind Of Hush* . . . . (A&M)
Carpenters-Classics-#2 . . . . (A&M)
Yesterday Once More . . . . (A&M)
Herman's Hermits; *Herman's Hermits-Their Greatest Hits* . . . . (Abkco)
There's A Place In The World For A Gambler
Dan Fogelberg; *Dan Fogelberg-Souvenirs* . . . . (Full Moon)
Live-Greetings From The West . . . . (Full Moon)
ST/FM . . . . (MCA)
There's No Reason In The World
Original Cast; *Milk & Honey* . . . . (RCA Victor)
Third Stone From The Sun
Jimi Hendrix; *Essential Jimi Hendrix* . . . . (Reprise)
Kiss The Sky . . . . (Reprise)
Jimi Hendrix Experience; *Are You Experienced?* . . . . (Reprise)
This Funny World
Tony Bennett; *Rodgers & Hart Songbook* . . . . (DRG)
This Whole World
Beach Boys; *Sunflower* . . . . (Caribou)
This World
Staple Singers; *Staple Singers' Greatest Hits* . . . . (Fantasy)
Staple Singers-Chronicle . . . . (Stax)
This World
Rosanne Cash; *Interiors* . . . . (Columbia)
This World Of Ours
Eddy Arnold; *The World Of Eddy Arnold* . . . . (RCA)
Till The End Of The World Rolls 'Round
Flatt & Scruggs; *Columbia Historic Edition-Flatt & Scruggs* . . . . (Columbia)
Golden Era . . . . (Rounder)
Today My World Slipped Away
George Strait; *Carrying Your Love With Me* . . . . (MCA)
Latest Greatest Straitest Hits . . . . (MCA)
Vern Gosdin; *10 Years Of Greatest Hits Newly Recorded* . . . . (Columbia)
Legends Of The Silver Eagle-C . . . . (King Biscuit Entert.)
Today My World Slipped Away . . . . (AMI)
Top Of The World
Carpenters; *A Song For You* . . . . (A&M)
Carpenters-Classics-#2 . . . . (A&M)
Carpenters-The Singles 1969-1973 . . . . (A&M)
Yesterday Once More . . . . (A&M)
Top Of The World
Brandy featuring Mase; *Never Say Never* . . . . (Atlantic)
Top Of The World
Lynn Anderson; *Country Superstars-C* . . . . (Dominion Entert.)
Lynn Anderson's Greatest Hits-#2 . . . . (Columbia)
Top Of The World . . . . (Columbia)
Top Of The World
Van Halen; *For Unlawful Carnal Knowledge* . . . . (Warner Bros.)
Top Of The World
James; *James* . . . . (Fontana)
Top Of The World
Diana Ross; *Diana Ross-Anthology* . . . . (Motown)
Tracey's World
Smithereens; *Beauty & Sadness* . . . . (Capitol)
Truck Stop At The End Of The World
Commander Cody; *Let's Rock* . . . . (Blind Pig)
Trying To Throw Your Arms Around The World
U2; *Achtung Baby* . . . . (Island)
Two Different Worlds
Robert Goulet; *My Love Forgive Me-Sincerely Yours Robert
Goulet* . . . . (Collector's Choice)
Two Less Lonely People In The World
Air Supply; *Now & Forever* . . . . (Arista)
Ugliest Girl In The World
Bob Dylan; *Down In The Groove* . . . . (Columbia)
Universal Heart-Beat
Juliana Hatfield; *Box Presents Big Ones Of Alternative
Rock-#1-C* . . . . (Box Tunes)
Only Everything . . . . (Mammoth)
Universe
Savage Garden; *Savage Garden* . . . . (Columbia)

Uno Mundo
Buffalo Springfield; *Buffalo Springfield* . . . . (Atco)
Until The End Of The World
U2; *Achtung Baby* . . . . (Island)
ST/Until The End Of The World . . . . (Warner Bros.)
Waiting For The End Of The World
Elvis Costello; *My Aim Is True* . . . . (Columbia)
Wake The World
Beach Boys; *Concert/'69-Live In London* . . . . (Capitol)
Friends-20/20 . . . . (Capitol)
Walk This World
Heather Nova; *Oyster* . . . . (Big Cat)
Walk Through This World With Me
George Jones; *Best Of George Jones-1955-1967* . . . . (Rhino)
Billboard Top Country Hits-1967-C . . . . (Rhino)
Double Gold-George Jones . . . . (Mustcor)
George Jones' All-Time Greatest Hits . . . . (Epic)
Wander This World
Jonny Lang; *Wander This World* . . . . (A&M)
Watching The World Go By
Gun; *Gallus* . . . . (A&M)
Way Of The World
Genesis; *We Can't Dance* . . . . (Atlantic)
Way Of The World
Roger Daltrey; *Daltrey* . . . . (MCA)
Way Of The World
Cheap Trick; *Dream Police* . . . . (Epic)
Way Of The World
Tina Turner; *Simply The Best* . . . . (Capitol)
We Are The Champions
Big Blue Wrecking Crew; *Baseball's Greatest Hits-C* . . . . (Rhino)
Queen; *Billboard Top Rock 'N' Roll Hits-1978-C* . . . . (Rhino)
Live At Wembley '86 . . . . (Hollywood)
Live Killers . . . . (Hollywood)
News Of The World . . . . (Hollywood)
Queen's Greatest Hits I & II . . . . (Hollywood)
We Are The World
USA For Africa; *We Are The World-C* . . . . (Columbia)
We Can Change The World
Graham Nash; *Songs For Beginners* . . . . (Atlantic)
We Can Change The World
Jacksons; *Victory* . . . . (Epic)
We Didn't Start The Fire
Billy Joel; *Storm Front* . . . . (Columbia)
We Don't Want The World
Jack Greene & Jeannie Seely; *Jack Greene's
Greatest Hits* . . . . (International Mktg. Group)
Jeannie Seely; *Best Of Town & Country-#3-C* . . . . . (International Mktg. Group)
Weight Of The World
Ringo Starr; *Time Takes Time* . . . . (Private Music)
Welcome To My World
Eddy Arnold; *Eddy Arnold-Pure Gold* . . . . (RCA)
The World Of Eddy Arnold . . . . (RCA)
Welcome To My World . . . . (RCA)
Elvis Presley; *Aloha from Hawaii via Satellite* . . . . (RCA)
Welcome To My World . . . . (RCA)
Jim Reeves; *Am I That Easy To Forget* . . . . (RCA)
Best Of Jim Reeves . . . . (RCA)
Jim Reeves . . . . (RCA)
Jim Reeves-Legendary Performer . . . . (RCA)
What A Wonderful World
Louis Armstrong; *ST/Good Morning, Vietnam* . . . . (A&M)
Vocalists-Jazz Masters-C . . . . (Bluebird)
What A Wonderful World . . . . (Decca Jazz)
Mormon Tabernacle Choir; *Songs From America's Heartland* . . . . . . (London)
Willie Nelson; *What A Wonderful World* . . . . (Columbia)
What The World Needs Now Is Love
Burt Bacharach; *Burt Bacharach's Greatest Hits* . . . . (A&M)
Jackie DeShannon; *Flower Power-Psychedelic Rock Classics-C* . . . . . (K-Tel)
Good Vibrations (Sounds Of Top 40 Radio: 1964-1967)-C . . . . . . (Capitol)
Oldies But Goodies-#14-C . . . . (Original Sound)
ST/Forrest Gump . . . . (Epic/Sony Music Soundtrax)
ST/My Best Friend's Wedding . . . . (Work/Epic)
Very Best Of Jackie DeShannon . . . . (EMI)
Luther Vandross; *Songs* . . . . (Epic)
Tom Clay; *20 Hard-To-Find Motown Classics-#2-C* . . . . (Motown)
What's Going On In Your World
George Strait; *Beyond The Blue Neon* . . . . (MCA)
Ten Strait Hits . . . . (MCA)
**When The World Is Running Down, You Make The Best Of What's
Still Around**
Police; *Zenyatta Mondatta* . . . . (A&M)
When The World Was Young
Anita O'Day; *Mello'Day* . . . . (Crescendo)
Frank Sinatra; *Point Of No Return* . . . . (Capitol)
When Two Worlds Collide
Rex Allen, Jr.; *20 Golden Souvenirs Of Music City U.S.A.-C* . . . . . (Plantation)
Roger Miller; *Best Of Roger Miller-His Greatest Songs* . . . . (Curb)

When You Love A Woman
Journey; *Trial By Fire*. . . . . (Columbia)
When You're Smiling (The Whole World Smiles With You)
Frank Sinatra; *Sinatra's Swingin' Session!!!* . . . . (Capitol)
Judy Garland; *Judy Garland-At Carnegie Hall* . . . . (Capitol)
Judy Garland's Greatest Hits . . . . (Curb)
One & Only . . . . (Capitol)
Louis Armstrong; *Best Of Louis Armstrong* . . . .(MCA)
Louis Armstrong-Vol. 4-In New York. . . . . (Columbia)
Musical Autobiography-#2 . . . .(MCA)
Where Were You (When The World Stopped Turning)
Alan Jackson; *Alan Jackson-Drive* . . . . (Arista)
White Cliffs Of Dover
Kay Kyser & His Orchestra; *16 Most Requested Songs Of The
'40s-#1-C* . . . . (Legacy)
Lee Andrews And The Hearts; *Lee Andrews And The Hearts'
Biggest Hits*. . . . . (Collectables)
Mystics; *Mystics-16 Golden Classics* . . . . (Collectables)
Righteous Brothers; *Righteous Brothers' Greatest Hits*. . . . . (Verve)
Righteous Brothers-Anthology 1962-1974 . . . . (Rhino)
Rosemary Clooney; *For The Duration* . . . .(Concord Jazz)
Whole New World (Aladdin's Theme)
Peabo Bryson & Regina Belle; *ST/Aladdin* . . . .(Disney)
Regina Belle & Peabo Bryson; *Passion* . . . . (Columbia)
Whole Wide World
A'me Lorain/Family Affair; *Starring In...Standing In A Monkey Sea* . . . . (RCA)
Whole Wide World
Soup Dragons; *Hang Ten* . . . . (Sire)
Wicked World
Rick Parker; *Wicked World*. . . . .(Geffen)
Wicked World
Black Sabbath; *Black Sabbath* . . . .(Warner Bros.)
Wicked World
Jimmy Nail; *Growing Up In Public* . . . .(Atlantic)
Wide World Of Sports
Instant Funk; *Instant Funk* . . . . (Salsoul)
Wild World
Cat Stevens; *Cat Stevens Greatest Hits*. . . . . (A&M)
Tea For The Tillerman . . . . (A&M)
Jimmy Cliff; *In Concert-Best Of Jimmy Cliff* . . . . (Reprise)
Reggae Spectacular-C . . . . (A&M)
Maxi Priest; *Best Of Me* . . . . (Charisma)
Maxi . . . . (Virgin)
Wildest Times Of The World
Vonda Shepard; *ST/Songs From "Ally McBeal" Featuring Vonda
Shepard*. . . . . (550/Epic)
Window To The World
Shawn Colvin; *Cover Girl* . . . . (Columbia)
Windows Of The World
Burt Bacharach; *One Amazing Night* . . . . (N2K)
Dionne Warwick; *Dionne Warwick Collection-Her All-Time
Greatest Hits* . . . . (Rhino)
Dionne Warwick-Definitive Collection . . . . (Arista)
Isaac Hayes; *Live At The Sahara Tahoe* . . . .(Stax)
Mormon Tabernacle Choir; *Voices In Harmony* . . . .(CBS Masterworks)
Pretenders; *ST/1969* . . . . (Polydor)
Winter World Of Love
Engelbert Humperdinck; *Engelbert Humperdinck* . . . . (Parrot)
Engelbert Humperdinck-His Greatest Hits . . . . (Parrot)
Woman Is The Nigger Of The World
John Lennon; *Live In New York City* . . . . (Capitol)
John Lennon/Plastic Ono Band; *Lennon*. . . . . (Capitol)
Shaved Fish . . . . (Capitol)
Some Time In New York City . . . . (Capitol)
Women Will Rule The World
Ry Cooder; *Get Rhythm* . . . .(Warner Bros.)
Wonderful World
Art Garfunkel; *Watermark* . . . . (Legacy)
Herman's Hermits; *Herman's Hermits-Their Greatest Hits* . . . .(Abkco)
Sam Cooke; *Best Of Sam Cooke* . . . . (RCA)
ST/Animal House . . . .(MCA)
This Is Sam Cooke . . . . (RCA)
Wonderful World, Beautiful People
Jimmy Cliff; *In Concert-Best Of Jimmy Cliff* . . . . (Reprise)
Reggae Spectacular-C . . . . (A&M)
Wonderful World, Beautiful People . . . . (A&M)
World
Bee Gees; *Here At Last...Bee Gees...Live* . . . . (Polydor)
World Anthem
Frank Marino & Mahogany Rush; *Frank Marino & Mahogany Rush-
Live* . . . . (Columbia)
World Anthem . . . . (Columbia)
World Full Of Strangers
B.B. King; *Midnight Believer* . . . .(MCA)
World I Know, The
Collective Soul; *Collective Soul* . . . .(Atlantic)
World I Used To Know
Glenn Yarbrough; *Best Of Glenn Yarbrough* . . . . (RCA)

World In Motion
Jackson Browne; *World In Motion* . . . . (Elektra)
World In My Eyes
Depeche Mode; *Violator* . . . .(Sire)
World Is A Concerto
Barbra Streisand; *Barbra Streisand...and other musical
instruments* . . . . (Columbia)
World Is A Ghetto
George Benson; *In Flight* . . . . (Warner Bros.)
War; *Best Of War...And More-#2* . . . . (Avenue)
The Music Band . . . . (MCA)
The Music Band 2 . . . . (MCA)
The World Is A Ghetto . . . . (Avenue)
War-Anthology (1970-1994) . . . .(Avenue)
World Is A Little Bit Under The Weather
Meters; *Trick Bag* . . . .(Reprise)
World Is Africa
Black Uhuru; *Sinsemilla* . . . . (Mango)
World Is Changing Hands
Dave Davies; *Dave Davies* . . . . (RCA)
World Is Round
Rufus Thomas & Carla Thomas; *Rufus Thomas & Carla Thomas-
Chronicle* . . . . (Stax)
World Is So Cold
Ginuwine; *The Bachelor* . . . .(550 Music)
World Is Upside Down
Joe Higgs; *This Is Reggae Music-#1-C* . . . . (Island)
World Is Waiting For The Sunrise
Benny Goodman; *I Like Jazz-Essence Of Benny Goodman* . . . . (Columbia)
Benny Goodman Orchestra & Quartet; *Let's Dance* . . . .(Laserlight)
Les Paul & Mary Ford; *The World Is Waiting For The Sunrise* . . . . . (Laserlight)
Roy Clark & Buck Trent; *Banjo Bandit* . . . .(MCA)
World Keeps Spinning
Behan Johnson; *Behan Johnson* . . . . (RCA)
World Leader Pretend
R.E.M.; *Green* . . . . (Warner Bros.)
World Needs A Melody
George Jones & Tammy Wynette; *George Jones' Greatest Hits-#2* . . . . . (Epic)
Kenny Rogers; *Love Lifted Me* . . . . (EMI)
World Of Our Own
Seekers; *Best Of Today* . . . . (Curb)
Capitol Collectors Series-The Seekers . . . . (Capitol)
World Of Our Own
Mickey Gilley; *Mickey Gilley* . . . .(Paula)
World Of Our Own
Elvis Presley; *ST/It Happened At The World's Fair* . . . . (RCA)
World Of Our Own
Surface; *Best Of Surface...A Nice Time 4 Lovin'*. . . . . (Columbia)
World Of Pain
Cream; *Disraeli Gears* . . . .(Polydor)
World Of Stone
George Harrison; *Extra Texture* . . . . (Capitol)
World Of Trouble
Lou Rawls; *Best From Lou Rawls* . . . . (Capitol)
Legendary Lou Rawls. . . . . (Blue Note)
World On A String
Neil Young; *Neil Young-Unplugged* . . . . (Reprise)
Tonight's The Night . . . . (Reprise)
World Tonight
Paul McCartney; *Flaming Pie* . . . . (Capitol)
World Turning
Fleetwood Mac; *Fleetwood Mac* . . . . (Reprise)
World War None!
Frank Sinatra; *Trilogy: Pasts, Present, Future* . . . . (Reprise)
World We Knew (Over And Over)
Frank Sinatra; *Frank Sinatra's Greatest Hits!*. . . . . (Reprise)
The World We Knew . . . . (Reprise)
World's A Masquerade
Earth, Wind & Fire; *Head To The Sky* . . . . (Columbia)
Worlds Apart
Vince Gill; *High Lonesome Sound* . . . . (MCA)
Worlds Away
BoDeans; *Home* . . . .(Slash)
Worlds Away
Pablo Cruise; *Worlds Away* . . . . (A&M)
World's Greatest Lover
Bellamy Brothers; *Bellamy Brothers' Greatest Hits-#2* . . . . (MCA)
Bellamy Brothers' Greatest Hits-#2 . . . . (Curb)
World's Greatest, The
R. Kelly; *ST/Ali* . . . .(Interscope)
Worlds In A Triangle
Fleetwood Mac; *In Chicago* . . . . (Sire)
You And Me Against The World
Helen Reddy; *Helen Reddy's Greatest Hits*. . . . . (Capitol)
You And Me Against The World
Roy Rogers; *Best Of Roy Rogers* . . . . (Curb)
You Can Tell The World
Simon & Garfunkel; *Collected Works* . . . . (Columbia)

Wednesday Morning 3 A.M. . . . . (Columbia)
You Mean The World To Me
Toni Braxton; *Toni Braxton* . . . . (LaFace)
You Rock My World
Michael Jackson; *Invincible* . . . . (Epic)
Young World
Rick Nelson; *Rick Nelson's Greatest Hits* . . . . (Rhino)
Ricky Nelson; *All My Best* . . . . (MCA)
Best Of Rick Nelson-#2 . . . . (EMI)
Teenage Idol . . . . (Liberty)
You're My World
Cilla Black; *History Of British Rock-#2-C* . . . . (Rhino)

WRONG, Not The Way Things Should Be, Unfair, Wrong Circumstances

See Also: **BAD, GUILT, LOVE: SOMEBODY DONE SOMEBODY WRONG, MISTAKES, MISTREATMENT, POLITICS: SOCIAL INJUSTICE, PREJUDICE, PROTEST, RIGHT**

(Hey Won't You Play) Another Somebody Done Somebody Wrong Song
B.J. Thomas; *Class Of Country-1975-1979-C* . . . . (Hip-O)
All Out Of Love
Air Supply; *Air Supply's Greatest Hits* . . . . (Arista)
Air Supply-The Definitive Collection . . . . (Arista)
Lost In Love . . . . (Arista)
Am I Wrong
Keb' Mo'; *Keb' Mo'* . . . . (Okeh)
Amigone
Goo Goo Dolls; *Dizzy Up The Girl* . . . . (Warner Sunset/Reprise)
Anything But Strong
Eurythmics; *Peace* . . . . (Arista)
Baby Come Back
Player; *Billboard Top Hits-1978-C* . . . . (Rhino)
Mellow Rock Hits Of The '70s-Ventura Highway-C . . . . (Rhino)
Super Hits Of The '70s-Have A Nice Day-#21-C . . . . (Rhino)
Beat It
Michael Jackson; *Thriller* . . . . (Epic)
Bodies
Drowning Pool; *Sinner* . . . . (Wind-up)
Couldn't Get It Right
Climax Blues Band; *Billboard Top Hits-1977-C* . . . . (Rhino)
Gold Plated . . . . (Sire)
Mellow Rock Hits Of The '70s-Ventura Highway-C . . . . (Rhino)
Desperately Wanting
Better Than Ezra; *Friction, Baby* . . . . (Swell/Elektra)
Didn't Cha Know
Erykah Badu; *Mama's Gun* . . . . (Motown)
Do Right
Jimmie's Chicken Shack; *Bring Your Own Stereo* . . . . (Rocket)
Don't Get Me Wrong
Pretenders; *Get Close* . . . . (Sire)
Pretenders-The Singles . . . . (Sire)
Don't Seem Right
Steve James; *Two Track Mind* . . . . (Antone's)
Drown
Son Volt; *Trace* . . . . (Warner Bros.)
Easy Tonight
Five For Fighting; *America Town* . . . . (Aware/C2/Columbia)
Expressway To Your Heart
Blues Brothers; *Best Of The Blues Brothers* . . . . (Atlantic)
Soul Survivors; *Dick Bartley's One-Hit Wonders Of The '60s-#2-C* . . . . . (Rhino)
Oldies But Goodies-#11-C . . . . (Original Sound)
Super Oldies Of The '60s-#6-C . . . . (Audio Fidelity)
When The Whistle Blows Anything Goes . . . . (Collectables)
Fixing A Hole
Beatles; *Sgt. Pepper's Lonely Hearts Club Band* . . . . (Capitol)
Got Me Wrong
Alice In Chains; *Alice In Chains-MTV Unplugged* . . . . (Columbia)
ST/Clerks . . . . (Chaos)
How Come, How Long
Babyface & Stevie Wonder; *The Day* . . . . (Epic)
How You Remind Me
Nickelback; *Silver Side Up* . . . . (Roadrunner)
I Did It
Dave Matthews Band; *Everyday* . . . . (RCA)
I May Be Wrong
Frankie Laine; *The Uncollected Frankie Laine* . . . . (Hindsight)
I May Be Wrong (But I Think You're Wonderful)
Doris Day; *Doris Day-16 Most Requested Songs-Encore!* . . . . (Columbia)
Harry James; *Harry James-22 Original Big Band Recordings* . . . . . . (Hindsight)
I Was Wrong
Social Distortion; *White Light White Heat White Trash* . . . . (550 Music)
I Was Wrong
Keb' Mo'; *Slow Down* . . . . (550/Epic/Okeh)

I'll Be On My Way
Beatles; *Live At The BBC* . . . . (Apple)
I'm A Honky Tonk Girl
Loretta Lynn; *The Country Music Hall Of Fame-Loretta Lynn* . . . . (MCA)
It Hurts Me Too
Keb' Mo'; *The Door* . . . . (550/Epic/Okeh)
It Isn't Right
Platters; *Enchanted-The Best Of The Platters* . . . . (Rhino)
Magic Touch-An Anthology . . . . (Mercury)
It's Not Right But It's Okay
Whitney Houston; *My Love Is Your Love* . . . . (Arista)
I've Been Wrong Before
Deborah Allen; *Cheat The Night* . . . . (RCA)
Last Resort
Papa Roach; *Infest* . . . . (DreamWorks/SKG)
Leave It Behind
Offspring; *Ixnay On The Hombre* . . . . (Columbia)
Lessons To Be Learned
Barbra Streisand; *Higher Ground* . . . . (Columbia)
Light Years
Pearl Jam; *Binaural* . . . . (Epic)
Little Bit Me, A Little Bit You
Monkees; *Monkees' Greatest Hits* . . . . (Rhino)
Little Darlin'
Diamonds; *Best Of The Diamonds* . . . . (Rhino)
Billboard Top Rock 'N' Roll Hits-1957-C . . . . (Rhino)
Cruisin'-1957-C . . . . (Increase)
Good Time Rock 'N' Roll-C . . . . (MCA)
Oldies But Goodies-#11-C . . . . (Original Sound)
ST/American Graffiti . . . . (MCA)
Lonely Too Long
Patty Loveless; *Patty Loveless-Classics* . . . . (Epic)
Super Hits Of 1996-C . . . . (Epic)
The Trouble With The Truth . . . . (Epic)
Look What Followed Me Home
David Ball; *Thinkin' Problem* . . . . (Warner Bros.)
Losing Lisa
Ben Folds; *Rockin' The Suburbs* . . . . (Epic)
Love Is Stronger Than Pride
Ricochet; *Ricochet* . . . . (Columbia)
Maryland
Vonda Shepard; *ST/Songs From ''Ally McBeal'' Featuring Vonda Shepard* . . . . (550/Epic)
Matchbox
Beatles; *Past Masters-Volume Two* . . . . (Parlophone)
Rock 'N' Roll Music . . . . (Capitol)
Something New . . . . (Capitol)
Mississippi
Bob Dylan; *''Love And Theft''* . . . . (Columbia)
Sheryl Crow; *The Globe Sessions* . . . . (A&M)
Never Let You Go
Third Eye Blind; *Blue* . . . . (Elektra)
Totally Hits-#2-C . . . . (Elektra)
Nevertheless
Frank Sinatra; *Best Of The Columbia Years-1943-1952* . . . . (Columbia)
McGuire Sisters; *McGuire Sisters-Anthology* . . . . (MCA)
Right Or Wrong
George Strait; *George Strait's Greatest Hits* . . . . (MCA)
Right Or Wrong . . . . (MCA)
Strait Out Of The Box . . . . (MCA)
Reba McEntire & Asleep At The Wheel; *Ride With Bob-C* . . . . (DreamWorks/SKG)
Rock And Roll Waltz
Kay Starr; *Capitol Collectors Series-Kay Starr* . . . . (Capitol)
Rock Island Line
Johnny Cash; *Johnny Cash-Sun Years* . . . . (Rhino)
Story Songs Of The Trains & Rivers . . . . (Sun)
Vintage Years-1955-1963 . . . . (Rhino)
Sonny Terry & Brownie McGhee; *Hootin'* . . . . (Muse)
Jazz Heritage . . . . (MCA)
Weavers; *Best Of The Weavers* . . . . (Vanguard)
Weavers At Carnegie Hall . . . . (Vanguard)
Weavers' Greatest Hits . . . . (Vanguard)
Runaway
Bonnie Raitt; *Bonnie Raitt-Collection* . . . . (Warner Bros.)
Sweet Forgiveness . . . . (Warner Bros.)
Del Shannon; *Billboard Top Rock 'N' Roll Hits-1961-C* . . . . (Rhino)
Cruisin'-1961-C . . . . (Increase)
Del Shannon's Greatest Hits . . . . (Rhino)
Heart & Soul Of Rock 'N' Roll-#1-C . . . . (Rhino)
Little Town Flirt . . . . (Rhino)
ST/American Graffiti . . . . (MCA)
Elvis Presley; *Collector's Gold* . . . . (RCA)
Stand Up
Keb' Mo'; *The Door* . . . . (550/Epic/Okeh)
Still On Your Side
BBMak; *Sooner Or Later* . . . . (Hollywood)

Streets Of Laredo
Buck Owens & The Buckaroos; *Buck Owens & The Buckaroos-Live At Carnegie Hall* . . . .(Country Music Foundation)
Marty Robbins; *Cowboy Super Hits-C* . . . . (Columbia)
Marty Robbins' All-Time Greatest Hits . . . . (Columbia)
Marty Robbins-More Greatest Hits . . . . (Columbia)
More Gunfighter Ballads & Trail Songs . . . . (Columbia)
Rex Allen; *Great American Singing Cowboys-C* . . . .(Republic/Universal)

There's A Whole Lot About A Woman (A Man Don't Know)
Jack Greene; *45-#32823* . . . . (Decca)

Thinking With The Wrong Head
Little Charlie & The Nightcats; *Captured Live* . . . . (Alligator)

This Ain't A Love Song
Bon Jovi; *These Days* . . . . (Mercury)

Trouble
Coldplay; *Parachutes* . . . . (Nettwerk/Capitol)

Wages Of Sin
Bruce Springsteen; *Tracks* . . . . (Columbia)

We Can Work It Out
Beatles; *"Yesterday"...And Today* . . . . (Capitol)
Beatles 1 . . . . (Capitol)
Beatles-20 Greatest Hits . . . . (Capitol)
Beatles-Box Set . . . . (Capitol)
Past Masters-Volume Two . . . . (Parlophone)
The Beatles/1962-1966 . . . . (Capitol)
Paul McCartney; *Unplugged (The Official Bootleg)* . . . . (Capitol)
Stevie Wonder; *Beatles Songs By Greatest Stars* . . . . (Motown)
Signed Sealed & Delivered . . . . (Motown)
Stevie Wonder's Greatest Hits-#2 . . . . (Motown)
Top 10 With A Bullet-Motown Solo Stars-C . . . . (Motown)

When It All Goes Wrong Again
Everclear; *Songs From An American Movie-#2-Good Time For A Bad Attitude* . . . . (Capitol)

When The Lights Go Out
Bruce Springsteen; *Tracks* . . . . (Columbia)

Without You
Van Halen; *Van Halen 3* . . . .(Warner Bros.)

Wrong Again
Martina McBride; *Big Country Hits '99-C* . . . . (K-Tel)
Country Cares For Kids II-C . . . . (BNA)
Evolution . . . . (RCA)

Wrong End Of The Rainbow
Anne Murray; *Yes I Do* . . . . (Liberty)
You Will . . . . (Liberty)

Wrong End Of The Rainbow
Tom Rush; *Wrong End Of The Rainbow* . . . . (Columbia)

Wrong Night
Reba McEntire; *If You See Him* . . . .(MCA)

Wrong Number
Cure; *Galore-The Singles-1987-1997* . . . . (Fiction/Elektra)

Wrong Side Of Memphis
Matraca Berg; *Bittersweet Surrender* . . . . (RCA)
Trisha Yearwood; *Grand Ole Opry-75 Years-#1-C* . . . .(MCA)
Hearts In Armor . . . .(MCA)

Wrong Way
Sublime; *Sublime* . . . . (Gasoline Alley)

You May Be Right
Billy Joel; *Billy Joel-Greatest Hits, Volume I & Volume II* . . . . (Columbia)
Glass Houses . . . . (Columbia)

YEARS: GENERAL

See Also: AGING, ANNIVERSARY, BIRTHDAY, FUTURE, HISTORY, MONTHS & DATES (various), REMEMBER, TIME: GENERAL, YEARS: SPECIFIC

100 Years From Now
Huey Lewis and the News; *Time Flies...Best Of Huey Lewis and the News* . . . . (Elektra)

30 Years In The Bathroom
Wonderstuff; *Hup!* . . . . (Polydor)

4 Seasons Of Loneliness
Boyz II Men; *Evolution* . . . . (Motown)

After All These Years
Jim Brickman & Anne Cochran; *Visions Of Love* . . . .(Windham Hill)

All These Years
Sawyer Brown; *Cafe On The Corner* . . . . (Curb)

All Those Years Ago
George Harrison; *Best Of Dark Horse 1976-1989* . . . . (Dark Horse)
Somewhere In England . . . . (Dark Horse)

Another Football Year
Jeannie C. Riley; *45-#14666* . . . . (MGM)

Best Year Of My Life
Eddie Rabbitt; *Number 1's* . . . .(Warner Bros.)
The Best Year Of My Life . . . .(Warner Bros.)

First Year Blues
Hank Williams; *Alone With His Guitar* . . . . (Mercury)

Five Long Years
Eric Clapton; *From The Cradle* . . . . (Duck/Reprise)

Forgotten Years
Midnight Oil; *Blue Sky Mining* . . . . (Columbia)

Golden Years
David Bowie; *Changesonebowie* . . . .(RCA)
Station To Station . . . . (Rykodisc)
The Singles-1969-1993 . . . . (Rykodisc)

Good Year For The Roses
George Jones & Alan Jackson; *The Bradley Barn Sessions* . . . . (MCA)

Holding Back The Years
Simply Red; *Picture Book* . . . . (Elektra)
Simply Red's Greatest Hits . . . . (East West)

I'm Gonna Make You Love Me
Jayhawks; *Smile* . . . .(American/Columbia)

It Was A Very Good Year
Frank Sinatra; *Frank Sinatra-The Very Good Years* . . . .(Reprise)
September Of My Years . . . .(Reprise)
The Reprise Collection . . . .(Reprise)
The Sopranos-Music From The HBO Original Series . . . .(Sony Music Soundtrax)
Frank Sinatra with Count Basie & The Orchestra; *Sinatra At The Sands* . . . .(Reprise)

Last Cowboy Song
Ed Bruce; *16 Top Country Hits-#2-C* . . . . (MCA)
Ed Bruce's Greatest Hits . . . . (MCA)
Waylon Jennings, Willie Nelson, Johnny Cash, Kris Kristofferson; *Cowboy Super Hits-C* . . . . (Columbia)
Highwayman . . . . (Columbia)

Light Years
Pearl Jam; *Binaural* . . . . (Epic)

Living Years, The
Mike & The Mechanics; *Living Years* . . . .(Atlantic)

Losing A Whole Year
Third Eye Blind; *Third Eye Blind* . . . . (Elektra)

My Next Thirty Years
Tim McGraw; *A Place In The Sun* . . . . (Curb)
Tim McGraw's Greatest Hits . . . . (Curb)

Next Year
Foo Fighters; *There Is Nothing Left To Lose* . . . .(Roswell/RCA)

Ninety-Nine
Bill Anderson; *45-#30914* . . . . (Decca)

Oh How The Years Go By
Vanessa Williams; *NBA At 50-A Musical Celebration-C* . . . . (Mercury)

Painted Perfect
One Way Ride; *Strait Up!* . . . . (Refuge/MCA)

Rockin' Years
Dolly Parton & Ricky Van Shelton; *Eagle When She Flies* . . . . (Columbia)
Ricky Van Shelton & Dolly Parton; *Backroads* . . . . (Columbia)

September Of My Years
Frank Sinatra; *At The Sands* . . . .(Reprise)
Frank Sinatra Sings The Songs Of Van Heusen & Cahn . . . .(Reprise)
Frank Sinatra's Greatest Hits-#2 . . . .(Reprise)
September Of My Years . . . .(Reprise)
Sinatra: A Man And His Music . . . .(Reprise)

Seven Year Ache
Rosanne Cash; *Columbia Country Classics-#5-A New Tradition-C* . . (Columbia)
Greatest Country Hits Of The '80s-1981-C . . . . (Columbia)
Hits-1979-1989 . . . . (Columbia)
Seven Year Ache . . . . (Columbia)

Still Crazy After All These Years
Paul Simon; *Greatest Hits, Etc.* . . . . (Columbia)
Negotiations And Love Songs, 1971-1986 . . . . (Warner Bros.)
Still Crazy After All These Years . . . . (Columbia)
Simon & Garfunkel; *The Concert In Central Park* . . . . (Warner Bros.)

Sweetheart Of The Year
Ray Price; *Best Of Ray Price* . . . . (Columbia)
Ray Price's Greatest Hits-#3 . . . .(Step One)

Tender Years
George Jones; *Best Of George Jones-1955-1967* . . . . (Rhino)
Billboard Top Country Hits-1961-C . . . . (Rhino)
Essential George Jones-The Spirit Of Country . . . . (Legacy)

Thirteen Years In Prison
Big Leon Brooks' Blues Harp Band; *Living Chicago Blues-#4* . . . .(Alligator)

Thirty Years Of Tears
John Hiatt; *Stolen Moments* . . . . (A&M)

This Is My Year For Mexico
Crystal Gayle; *Crystal Gayle* . . . .(United Artists)

This Year's Girl
Elvis Costello; *2 1/2 Years* . . . . (Rykodisc)
Girls Girls Girls . . . . (Columbia)
This Year's Model . . . . (Rykodisc)

This Year's Kisses
Billie Holiday; *Quintessential-#3-1936-1937* . . . . (Columbia)
June Christy; *Misty June Christy* . . . . (Blue Note)
Lester Young & Roy Eldridge; *Jazz Giants* . . . . (Verve)

Two Years In Chicago
Robin Trower; *1st Dibs* . . . . (Flying Fish)

Two Years Of Torture
Lou Rawls; *Lou Rawls-At Last* . . . .(Blue Note)
Percy Mayfield; *Please Send Me Someone To Love*. . . . . (Intermedia)
Year Of The Cat
Al Stewart; *'70s Greatest Rock Hits-#5-Kickin' Back-C* . . . .(Priority)
Best Of Al Stewart . . . .(Arista)
Year Of The Cat . . . .(Arista)

YEARS: SPECIFIC

See Also: AGES (various), ANNIVERSARY, BIRTHDAY, FUTURE, HISTORY, MONTHS & DATES (various), REMEMBER, TIME: SPECIFIC, YEARS: GENERAL

1812 Overture
New York Philharmonic & Leonard Bernstein; *Conducts*
Tchaikovsky . . . .(Columbia)
Great Tchaikovsky . . . .(Columbia)
Overtures and Tone Poems . . . .(Columbia)
Tchaikovsky's Greatest Hits-#1 . . . .(Columbia)
Various Overtures . . . .(Columbia)
1913 Massacre
Arlo Guthrie; *Hobo's Lullaby* . . . .(Reprise)
Jack Elliot; *Tribute To Woody Guthrie-C* . . . . (Warner Bros.)
Ramblin' Jack Elliott; *Greatest Songs Of Woody Guthrie-C* . . . . (Vanguard)
Woody Guthrie; *Struggle*. . . . .(Smithsonian Folkways)
1941
Nilsson; *Pandemonium Shadow Show*. . . . .(RCA)
1952 Vincent Black Lightning
Richard Thompson; *Richard Thompson-Best Of Capitol Years* . . . .(Capitol)
1959
John Anderson; *Country Love Songs-#3-C* . . . . (Warner Bros.)
John Anderson's Greatest Hits. . . . . (Warner Bros.)
1970 #1 Song Cadillac
Terry Radigan; *Pawnbroker's Daughter* . . . . (Asylum)
1979
Smashing Pumpkins; *Mellon Collie And The Infinite Sadness*. . . . .(Virgin)
The Aeroplane Flies High . . . .(Virgin)
1983... (A Merman I Should Turn To Be)
Jimi Hendrix Experience; *Electric Ladyland* . . . .(Reprise)
1984
David Bowie; *Changestwobowie*. . . . .(RCA)
David Live . . . . (Rykodisc)
Diamond Dogs . . . . (Rykodisc)
Fame & Fashion . . . .(RCA)
Tina Turner; *Private Dancer* . . . .(Capitol)
1984
Spirit; *Best Of Spirit*. . . . . (Epic)
Spirit Of '84 . . . .(Mercury)
1984
Van Halen; *1984* . . . . (Warner Bros.)
1999
Prince; *1999*. . . . . (Warner Bros.)
59 Chevy
Geronimo Black; *Geronimo Black* . . . . (One Way)
'70s TV
Dramarama; *Stuck In Wonderamaland* . . . .(Chameleon)
80's Ladies
K.T. Oslin; *80's Ladies* . . . .(RCA)
K.T. Oslin's Greatest Hits: Songs From An Aging Sex Bomb . . . .(RCA)
Nipper's Greatest Hits Of The '80s-C. . . . .(RCA)
Acapulco 1922
Herb Alpert & The Tijuana Brass; *Lonely Bull* . . . .(A&M)
Solid Brass . . . .(A&M)
America The Beautiful, 1976
Charlie Rich; *Charlie Rich's Greatest Hits* . . . . (Epic)
American Bad Ass ('65 Chevelle)
Kid Rock; *History Of Rock* . . . . (Top Dog/Lava/Atlantic)
American Beat '84
Fleshtones; *Living Legends* . . . .(I.R.S.)
Anthem For The Year 2000
Silverchair; *Neon Ballroom*. . . . . (Epic)
Anti-Sex Backlash Of The '80s
Roches; *Speak* . . . .(MCA)
April 2031
Warrant; *Dog Eat Dog*. . . . .(Columbia)
April 24, 1981
Rick Springfield; *Success Hasn't Spoiled Me Yet* . . . .(RCA)
August 1967
Holy Modal Rounders; *Last Round* . . . . (Adelphi)
Biko (September 1977)
Peter Gabriel; *Peter Gabriel* . . . . (Geffen)
Peter Gabriel/Plays Live . . . . (Geffen)
Shaking The Tree-Sixteen Golden Greats. . . . . (Geffen)
Born In Chicago (1941)
George Thorogood & The Destroyers; *Boogie People* . . . . (EMI)

Paul Butterfield Blues Band; *Golden Butter*. . . . .(Elektra)
Paul Butterfield Blues Band . . . .(Elektra)
Born In The Fifties
Police; *Outlandos D'Amour* . . . .(A&M)
Born Late '58
Mott The Hoople; *Mott The Hoople's Greatest Hits* . . . .(Columbia)
The Ballad Of Mott: A Retrospective. . . . .(Columbia)
Buick '55
Johnny & The Distractions; *My Desire* . . . . (Burnside)
Buick '59
Vernon Green & The Medallions; *Best Vocal Group In Rhythm &*
Blues. . . . .(Dooto)
Vernon Green & The Medallions . . . .(Dooto)
Vernon Green & The Medallions-Golden Classics . . . .(Collectables)
Candy Cain (1958)
Steve Miller; *Steve Miller-Box Set* . . . .(Capitol)
Case Of The Ex (Whatcha Gonna Do) (1996)
Mya; *Fear Of Flying* . . . . (University/Interscope)
Now That's What I Call Music!-#5-C . . . . (Virgin)
Child Of The Fifties
Statler Brothers; *Legend Goes On* . . . .(Mercury)
Class Of '57
Statler Brothers; *Best Of The Statler Brothers* . . . .(Mercury)
Dayton Ohio 1903
Randy Newman; *Sail Away* . . . . (Reprise)
December, 1963 (Oh, What A Night)
4 Seasons; *25th Anniversary Collection* . . . .(Rhino)
4 Seasons-Anthology . . . .(Rhino)
Oh What A Night . . . .(Curb)
Easter '88
Urge Overkill; *Americruiser/Jesus Urge Superstar* . . . .(Touch & Go)
Emma Jean's Guitar (1950, 1964)
Chely Wright; *Let Me In*. . . . . (MCA)
Everybody's Free (To Wear Sunscreen) (1999)
Baz Luhrmann; *Now That's What I Call Music!-#2-C* . . . . (Virgin)
Something For Everybody . . . .(Capitol)
Flood Of '57
Stanley Brothers & The Clinch Mountain Boys; *Classic Bluegrass-Stanley*
Brothers & The Clinch Mountain Boys. . . . .(Rebel)
Flood Of '93
David Olney; *High, Wide And Lonesome* . . . . (Philo)
Happy Birthday 1975
Joni Mitchell; *Mingus* . . . .(Elektra)
Happy Birthday Dear America/In 1776
Ella Jenkins; *We Are All America's Children* . . . . (Smithsonian Folkways)
Hillbilly Rock (1953)
Marty Stuart; *Hillbilly Rock* . . . . (MCA)
Homecoming '63
Keith Whitley; *L.A. To Miami* . . . . (RCA)
How Bizarre ('69 Chevy)
OMC; *How Bizarre* . . . . (Huh!/Mercury)
I Don't Want To Wait (1944)
Paula Cole; *Live On Letterman-From The Late Show* . . . . (Reprise)
Songs From Dawson's Creek . . . . (Sony Music Soundtrax)
This Fire . . . .(Imago)
I Just Shot John Lennon (1980)
Cranberries; *To The Faithful Departed* . . . .(Island)
I Walk The Line (Revisted) (1956)
Rodney Crowell; *The Houston Kid* . . . . (Sugar Hill)
I Walk The Line (Revisted) ('49 Ford)
Rodney Crowell; *The Houston Kid* . . . . (Sugar Hill)
In The Year 2525 (Exordium & Terminus)
Zager & Evans; *Nipper's Greatest Hits Of The '60s-#2-C* . . . . (RCA)
June The 15, 1967
Gary Burton; *Artist's Choice* . . . .(Bluebird)
Justice And Independence '85
John Cougar Mellencamp; *Scarecrow* . . . .(Riva)
Last Time I Saw Richard (1968)
Joni Mitchell; *Blue*. . . . . (Reprise)
Leaving October ('89)
Sons Of The Desert; *Whatever Comes First*. . . . . (Epic)
Lighthouse Act 1911
Steinbecks; *From The Wrestling Chair To The Sea* . . . .(Summershine)
Lost In The Fifties Tonight
Ronnie Milsap; *Lost In The Fifties Tonight* . . . . (RCA)
Ronnie Milsap's Greatest Hits-#2 . . . .(RCA)
Louisiana 1927
Aaron Neville; *Warm Your Heart* . . . .(A&M)
Jo-el Sonnier; *Come On Joe* . . . . (RCA)
Randy Newman; *Good Old Boys* . . . . (Reprise)
ST/Blaze . . . .(A&M)
Love, Me (1923)
Collin Raye; *All I Can Be* . . . . (Epic)
Greatest Country Hits Of The '90s-1992-C . . . .(Columbia)
Miami 2017
Billy Joel; *Songs In The Attic* . . . .(Columbia)
The Concert For New York City-C . . . .(Columbia)
Turnstiles . . . .(Columbia)

Miss Texas 1967
Colourfield; *Deception* . . . .(Chrysalis)
Mustang Sally (1965)
Wilson Pickett; *A Man & A Half-Best Of Wilson Pickett* . . . . (Rhino)
Atlantic Rhythm & Blues 1947-1974-#6 (1966-1969)-C . . . (Atlantic)
Best Of Wilson Pickett . . . .(Atlantic)
Wilson Pickett-Super Hits . . . .(Atlantic)
My Niece From Pittsburgh In 1992
PFS; *Illustrative Problems* . . . .(Cuneiform)
New York Mining Disaster 1941 (Mr. Jones)
Bee Gees; *Bee Gees-Gold* . . . .(Polydor)
Here At Last...Bee Gees...Live . . . .(Polydor)
History Of British Rock-#8-C . . . . (Rhino)
North To Alaska (1901)
Dwight Yoakam; *Under The Covers.* . . . . (Reprise)
Johnny Horton; *American Originals-Johnny Horton* . . . . . (Columbia)
Billboard Top Country Hits-1961-C . . . . (Rhino)
Johnny Horton's Greatest Hits . . . . (Columbia)
Super Hits Of The '60s-C . . . .(Epic)
November 22, 1963
Original Cast; *Assassins* . . . . (RCA)
October 17, 1988
Keith Jarrett; *Paris Concert* . . . . (ECM)
Ol' '55
Eagles; *On The Border* . . . . (Elektra)
Tom Waits; *Tom Waits-Anthology* . . . . (Asylum)
Old Farm 1939
Randy Newman; *ST/The Natural* . . . .(Warner Bros.)
On Saturday Afternoons In 1963
Rickie Lee Jones; *Rickie Lee Jones* . . . .(Warner Bros.)
One I Loved Back Then (Corvette Song) (1963)
George Jones; *19 Hot Country Requests-#3-C* . . . .(Epic)
George Jones-Super Hits. . . . .(Epic)
Greatest Country Hits Of The '80s-1986-C . . . . (Columbia)
Who's Gonna Fill Their Shoes . . . .(Epic)
One Piece At A Time (1949 and many other years)
Johnny Cash; *The Man In Black-His Greatest Hits.* . . . . (Legacy)
Pittsburgh 1901
Mark Isham; *Sampler '86-C* . . . .(Windham Hill)
Windham Hill-First Ten Years-C . . . .(Windham Hill)
Racing In The Street ('69 Chevrolet)
Bruce Springsteen; *Darkness On The Edge Of Town* . . . . (Columbia)
Bruce Springsteen & The E Street Band; *Bruce Springsteen & The E Street Band Live/1975-85* . . . . (Legacy)
Radar Gun ('86 T-Bird)
Bottle Rockets; *The Brooklyn Side* . . . .(East Side Digital)
Ragtop Cadillac ('65 Chevy)
Lonestar; *Lonestar* . . . . (BNA)
Rainbow '65
Gene Chandler; *Hits From The Legendary Vee-Jay Records-C* . . . . . . (Motown)
Rainbow '80
Gene Chandler; *Ear Candy-#2-C* . . . . (20th Century Fox)
Gene Chandler '80. . . . . (20th Century Fox)
Riding With Private Malone (1966)
David Ball; *Amigo* . . . . (Razor & Tie)
Rock Radio Into The Nineties & Beyond
KLF; *Chill Out* . . . . (Wax Trax)
Rockabilly Blues (Texas 1955)
Johnny Cash; *Texas Super Hits-C* . . . . (Columbia)
September 1979
Bill Barron; *Variations In Blue.* . . . .(Muse)
Sex In The '90s
Gloria Estefan; *Into The Light.* . . . .(Epic)
Shades Of '45
Gary O'; *Strange Behavior* . . . . (RCA)
Someday (1967)
Steve Earle & The Dukes; *Guitar Town* . . . .(MCA)
Shut Up And Die Like An Aviator. . . . .(MCA)
Stompin' In The '90s
Yo-Yo; *Make Way For The Motherlode* . . . . (East West)
Summer Of '69
Bryan Adams; *Reckless* . . . . (A&M)
Sun Of '79
Des'ree; *Mind Adventures* . . . . (550 Music)
Sweet Little '66
Steve Earle & The Dukes; *Exit 0.* . . . .(MCA)
Teenage Lament '74
Alice Cooper; *Alice Cooper's Greatest Hits.* . . . .(Warner Bros.)
Muscle Of Love . . . .(Warner Bros.)
Texas In 1880
Foster & Lloyd; *Foster & Lloyd* . . . . (RCA)
Texas, 1947
Guy Clark; *Guy Clark's Greatest Hits* . . . . (RCA)
Old No. 1 . . . . (Sugar Hill)
Steel Rails-Classic Railroad Songs-#1-C . . . .(Rounder)
Theme From "2001: A Space Odyssey"
Boston Pops Orchestra/John Williams; *Pops Out Of This World* . . . . . .(Philips)
Neil Norman; *Greatest Science Fiction Hits.* . . . .(Crescendo)

Original Soundtrack; *2001: A Space Odyssey Theme* . . . .(MGM)
Theme From "Summer Of '42"
George Benson; *Best Of George Benson.* . . . . (CBS Associated)
White Rabbit. . . . . (CBS Associated)
Peter Nero; *"Summer Of '42" Theme.* . . . . (Columbia)
Peter Nero's Greatest Hits. . . . . (Columbia)
Waist Deep In The Big Muddy (1942)
Pete Seeger; *Best Of Broadside 1962-1968: Anthems Of The American Underground From The Pages Of Broadside Magazine-C.* . . . .(Smithsonian Folkways)
War Is Hell (On The Homefront Too) (1942)
T.G. Sheppard; *Perfect Stranger.* . . . . (Warner Bros.)
T.G. Sheppard's All-Time Greatest Hits. . . . . (Warner Bros.)
T.G. Sheppard's Greatest Hits. . . . .(Warner Bros./Curb)
Warsaw 1943 (I Never Betrayed The Revolution)
Johnny Clegg & Savuka; *Cruel, Crazy, Beautiful World* . . . . (Capitol)
What Mattered Most (1964)
Ty Herndon; *Super Hits Of 1995-C.* . . . . (Epic)
What Mattered Most. . . . . (Epic)
Will 2K
Will Smith; *Willenium.* . . . . (Columbia)
Wrong Side Of Memphis ('69 Tempest)
Matraca Berg; *Bittersweet Surrender* . . . . (RCA)
Trisha Yearwood; *Grand Ole Opry-75 Years-#1-C* . . . .(MCA)
Hearts In Armor. . . . . (MCA)
Year 2003 Minus 25
Waylon Jennings & Willie Nelson; *Waylon & Willie* . . . .(RCA)
You Win My Love ('55 Chevy)
Shania Twain; *The Woman In Me* . . . . (Mercury)

YESTERDAY

See Also: **HISTORY, REMEMBER, TIME: GENERAL, TIME: SPECIFIC**

After The Love Is Gone
Earth, Wind & Fire; *Best Of Earth, Wind & Fire-#2* . . . . (Columbia)
Earth, Wind & Fire-Greatest Hits-#1 . . . . (Legacy)
All Mixed Up
311; *311.* . . . . (Capricorn)
Angel
Jimi Hendrix; *Cry Of Love* . . . .(Reprise)
Experience Hendrix: The Best Of Jimi Hendrix . . . . (MCA)
First Rays Of The New Rising Sun . . . . (MCA)
Rod Stewart; *Best Of Rod Stewart.* . . . . (Mercury)
Angels Rejoiced Last Night
Gram Parsons & The Flying Burrito Brothers; *Sleepless Nights* . . . . (A&M)
Another You
David Kersh; *Goodnight Sweetheart.* . . . .(Curb)
Atlanta Burned Again Last Night
Atlanta; *Pictures* . . . . (MCA)
Big Man
Four Preps; *Best Of The Four Preps* . . . .(Curb)
Capitol Collectors Series-Four Preps . . . .(Collectables)
Born In The Dark
Doug Stone; *Faith In Me Faith In You* . . . . (Columbia)
Steppin' Country-#2-C . . . . (Columbia)
Born Yesterday
Everly Brothers; *Born Yesterday.* . . . . (Mercury)
Bubba Shot The Jukebox
Mark Chesnutt; *Longnecks & Short Stories* . . . . (MCA)
Don't Stop
Elton John; *Legacy-A Tribute To Fleetwood Mac's Rumours-C* . . . . (Lava)
Fleetwood Mac; *25 Years-The Chain* . . . . (Warner Bros.)
Fleetwood Mac Live. . . . . (Warner Bros.)
Fleetwood Mac's Greatest Hits. . . . . (Warner Bros.)
Rumours. . . . . (Warner Bros.)
Fire And Rain
James Taylor; *James Taylor's Greatest Hits.* . . . . (Warner Bros.)
Sweet Baby James. . . . . (Warner Bros.)
The Concert For New York City-C. . . . . (Columbia)
Sammy Kershaw; *Red Hot + Country-C.* . . . . (Mercury)
Funny How Time Slips Away
Al Green & Lyle Lovett; *Rhythm Country And Blues-C* . . . . (MCA)
Jimmy Elledge; *Nipper's Greatest Hits Of The '60s-#2-C* . . . . (RCA)
RCA's Greatest One-Hit Wonders-C . . . . (RCA)
Willie Nelson; *Best Of Willie Nelson.* . . . . (Capitol)
Collector's Series-Willie Nelson . . . . (RCA)
Healing Hands Of Time . . . . (Liberty)
My Own Way . . . . (RCA)
San Antonio Rose . . . . (Columbia)
Willie & Family Live . . . . (Columbia)
Willie Nelson & Faron Young; *Funny How Time Slips Away* . . . . . . (Columbia)
Hopeless
Dionne Farris; *ST/Love Jones* . . . . (Columbia)
I Can't Stop Loving You
Don Gibson; *60 Years Of Country Music-C* . . . . (RCA)

Collector's Series-Don Gibson . . . . (RCA)
Stars Of The Grand Ole Opry-1926-1974-C . . . . (RCA)
Elvis Presley; *Aloha from Hawaii via Satellite* . . . . (RCA)
Elvis As Recorded At Madison Square Garden . . . . (RCA)
Elvis Recorded Live On Stage In Memphis . . . . (RCA)
From Memphis To Vegas/From Vegas To Memphis . . . . (RCA)
Ray Charles; *Ray Charles' Greatest Hits-#2* . . . . (Rhino)
Ray Charles-Anthology . . . . (Rhino)
Roy Orbison; *Best Of Roy Orbison-Loved Standards* . . . . (Monument)
Legendary Roy Orbison . . . . (Sony Music Special Prod.)

I Dreamed About Mama Last Night
Hank Williams; *Complete Hank Williams* . . . . (Mercury)
Johnny Cash; *Timeless: Hank Williams Tribute-C* . . . . (Lost Highway/IDJMG)

I Had A Dream Last Night
Buddy Guy; *Best Of The Chicago Blues-C* . . . . (Vanguard)
This Is Buddy Guy . . . . (Vanguard)

I Had Too Much To Dream (Last Night)
Electric Prunes; *Even More Nuggets-C* . . . . (Rhino)
Nuggets-#1-The Hits-C . . . . (Rhino)
Summer Of Love-#1-C . . . . (Rhino)

I Saw Her Again
Mamas & The Papas; *Best Of The Mamas & The Papas* . . . . (MCA)
Farewell To The First Golden Era . . . . (MCA)
Mamas & The Papas . . . . (MCA)

I Saw Linda Yesterday
Dickey Lee; *45s On CD-#2-1960-1966-C* . . . . (Mercury)

I Wasn't Born Yesterday
Daryl Hall; *Three Hearts In The Happy Ending Machine* . . . . (RCA)

I Wasn't Born Yesterday
Allan Clarke; *I Wasn't Born Yesterday* . . . . (Atlantic)

I Wasn't Born Yesterday
Safire; *I Wasn't Born Yesterday* . . . . (Mercury)

It Seems Like Yesterday
Louise Gunning; *Music From The New York Stage (1890-1920)-#1-1890-1908-C* . . . . (Pearl)

It's So Hard To Say Goodbye To Yesterday
Boyz II Men; *Cooleyhighharmony* . . . . (Motown)
G.C. Cameron; *Motown Memories-#3-C* . . . . (Motown)

Last Night
Mar-Keys; *Atlantic Rhythm & Blues 1947-1974-#4 (1958-1962)-C* . . . (Atlantic)
Soul Shots-#3-Soul Twist-C . . . . (Rhino)

Last Night
Az Yet; *Az Yet* . . . . (LaFace)

Last Night
Al Jarreau; *Tomorrow Today* . . . . (GRP/VMG)

Last Night
Buddy Holly/The Crickets; *Chirping Crickets* . . . . (MCA)

Last Night
Stephanie Mills; *Tantalizingly Hot* . . . . (Casablanca)

Last Night
Traveling Wilburys; *Traveling Wilburys-Volume One* . . (Wilbury/Warner Bros.)

Last Night A D.J. Saved My Life
Indeep; *Last Night A D.J. Saved My Life* . . . . (Sound Of New York)
The Disco Years-#2-On The Beat-1978-1982-C . . . . (Rhino)

Last Night I Didn't Get To Sleep At All
5th Dimension; *Greatest Hits On Earth* . . . . (Arista)

Last Night I Had A Dream
Randy Newman; *Randy Newman/Live* . . . . (Warner Archives)
Sail Away . . . . (Reprise)

Last Night I Had The Strangest Dream
Simon & Garfunkel; *Collected Works* . . . . (Columbia)
Wednesday Morning 3 A.M. . . . . (Columbia)

Last Night's Letter
K-Ci & JoJo; *Love Always* . . . . (MCA)

Like There Ain't No Yesterday
BlackHawk; *Strong Enough* . . . . (Arista)
The Hits-Love & Gravity . . . . (Arista)

Michelangelo
Emmylou Harris; *Red Dirt Girl* . . . . (Nonesuch)

More Today Than Yesterday
Spiral Staircase; *CBS Classics-Pop Classics Of The '60s-C* . . . . (Columbia)
Rock Artifacts-From The Vaults-#1-C . . . . (Columbia)
Super Hits Of The '70s-Have A Nice Day-#1-C . . . . (Rhino)

Never Too Far
Mariah Carey; *Glitter* . . . . (Virgin)

New Day Yesterday, A
Jethro Tull; *Best Of Jethro Tull-The Anniversary Collection* . . . . (Chrysalis)
Stand Up . . . . (Chrysalis)

Night Before
Beatles; *Beatles-Box Set* . . . . (Capitol)
Rock 'N' Roll Music . . . . (Capitol)
ST/Help! . . . . (Capitol)

No Sign Of Yesterday
Men At Work; *Brazil* . . . . (Columbia)
Cargo . . . . (Columbia)

North Won The War Again Last Night, The
Cal Smith; *Cal Smith* . . . . (First Generation)

She's My Girl
Turtles; *'60s Sound Explosion-C* . . . . (K-Tel)
Nuggets-#9-Acid Rock-C . . . . (Rhino)
Turtles-20 Greatest Hits . . . . (Rhino)

Stronger
Britney Spears; *Now That's What I Call Music!-#6-C* . . . . (Virgin)
Oops!...I Did It Again . . . . (Jive)

That Girl Belongs To Yesterday
Gene Pitney; *Gene Pitney-Anthology 1961-1968* . . . . (Rhino)

Today's Lonely Fool
Tracy Lawrence; *Sticks & Stones* . . . . (Atlantic)

What A Crying Shame
Mavericks; *Best Of The Mavericks-Super Colossal Smash Hits Of The '90s* . . . . (Mercury)
What A Crying Shame . . . . (MCA)

Yester Love
Smokey Robinson & The Miracles; *Best Of Smokey Robinson & The Miracles-Anthology* . . . . (Motown)
Smokey Robinson-The Ultimate Collection . . . . (Motown)

Yesterday
Beatles; *"Yesterday"...And Today* . . . . (Capitol)
Beatles 1 . . . . (Capitol)
Beatles-20 Greatest Hits . . . . (Capitol)
Beatles-Box Set . . . . (Capitol)
Beatles-Love Songs . . . . (Capitol)
Compact Disc Singles Collection . . . . (Capitol)
The Beatles/1962-1966 . . . . (Capitol)
Elvis Presley; *On Stage-February, 1970* . . . . (RCA)
En Vogue; *Funky Divas* . . . . (East West)
Frank Sinatra; *My Way* . . . . (Reprise)
Paul McCartney; *The Concert For New York City-C* . . . . (Columbia)
Placido Domingo; *Domingo Songbook* . . . . (Sony Music Classical)
Ray Charles; *Ray Charles-His Greatest Hits-#1* . . . . (Dunhill Compact Classics)
Supremes; *I Hear A Symphony* . . . . (Motown)
Wings; *Wings Over America* . . . . (Capitol)

Yesterday
Shanice; *Shanice* . . . . (LaFace)

Yesterday Once More
Carpenters; *Carpenters-Classics-#2* . . . . (A&M)
Carpenters-The Singles 1969-1973 . . . . (A&M)
Now & Then . . . . (A&M)
Yesterday Once More . . . . (A&M)

Yesterday, I Heard The Rain
Bill Evans; *Tokyo Concert* . . . . (Fantasy)
Tony Bennett; *Essence Of Tony Bennett* . . . . (Columbia)

Yesterday, Today And Tomorrow
Small Faces; *From The Beginning* . . . . (Polydor)
Small Faces-Anthology-1965-1967 . . . . (Polydor)

Yesterday, When I Was Young
Roy Clark; *Roy Clark's Greatest Hits* . . . . (Varese Vintage)

Yesterdays
Guns N' Roses; *Use Your Illusion II* . . . . (Geffen)

Yesterdays
Art Tatum; *Art Tatum Solo Masterpieces-#3* . . . . (Pablo)
Billie Holiday; *Verve Jazz Masters 12* . . . . (Verve)
Billy Kirsch; *Southern Fried* . . . . (Artifex)
Dinah Shore; *More Of The Best* . . . . (Laserlight)
Frank Sinatra; *Sinatra & Strings* . . . . (Reprise)
Jo Stafford; *Capitol Sings Jerome Kern: The Song Is You-C* . . . . (Capitol)
Kevin Eubanks; *Guitarist* . . . . (Discovery)
Miles Davis; *Best Of Miles Davis: The Capitol And Blue Note Years* . . . . (Blue Note)
Stan Getz; *At The Opera House* . . . . (Verve)
Tito Puente; *Mambo Beat-The Progressive Side Of Tito Puente* . . . . (RCA Int'l)
Wynton Marsalis; *Standard Time-#2-Intimacy Calling* . . . . (Columbia)

Yesterday's Dreams
Four Tops; *Four Tops-Anthology* . . . . (Motown)

Yesterday's Girl
Hank Thompson; *Hank Thompson-20 Greatest Hits* . . . . (Deluxe)
Hank Thompson's Greatest Songs-#1 . . . . (Curb)

Yesterday's Gone
Chad & Jeremy; *Best Of Chad & Jeremy* . . . . (One Way)

Yesterday's Gone Forever
Little Texas; *Little Texas* . . . . (Warner Bros.)
Little Texas-Super Hits . . . . (Warner Bros.)

Yesterday's Hero
Bay City Rollers; *Bay City Rollers' Greatest Hits* . . . . (Arista)

Yesterday's Hero
Gene Pitney; *Gene Pitney's Greatest Hits* . . . . (Evergreen Music)

Yesterday's News Just Hit Home Today
Johnny Paycheck; *Johnny Paycheck's Biggest Hits* . . . . (Epic)

Yesterday's Paper
Tish Hinojosa; *Destiny's Gate* . . . . (Warner Bros.)

Yesterday's Papers
Rolling Stones; *Between The Buttons* . . . . (Abkco)

Yesterday's Rain
Spanky & Our Gang; *Spanky & Our Gang's Greatest Hits* . . . . (Mercury)

Yesterday's Songs
Neil Diamond; *12 Greatest Hits-#2* . . . . (Columbia)
On The Way To The Sky . . . . (Columbia)

Yesterday's Train
Byrds; *The Byrds (Untitled)* .... (Legacy)
Yesterday's Wine
Merle Haggard & George Jones; *By Request* ....(Epic)
   Greatest Country Hits Of The '80s-1982-C .... (Columbia)
   Taste Of Yesterday's Wine ....(Epic)
   Walking The Line ....(Epic)
Willie Nelson; *Best Of Willie* ....(RCA)
   Collector's Series-Willie Nelson ....(RCA)
   The Outlaws ....(RCA)
Yesterday's Winner Is A Loser Today
Ernest Tubb; *Ernest Tubb Collection-C* ....(Step One)
Yester-Me, Yester-You, Yesterday
Stevie Wonder; *My Cherie Amour* .... (Motown)
   Stevie Wonder's Greatest Hits-#2 ....(Motown)

YOUNG

*See Also: **AGES (various), AGING, BABY, CHILDREN, LOVE:
YOUNG LOVE, OLD, PARENTS: CONCERNED ABOUT TEEN
LOVE, TEENAGERS***

All The Young Dudes
David Bowie; *David Live* ....(Rykodisc)
Ian Hunter; *Live/Welcome To The Club* ....(Chrysalis)
Mott The Hoople; *All The Young Dudes* .... (Columbia)
   Mott The Hoople-Live .... (Columbia)
   Mott The Hoople's Greatest Hits .... (Columbia)
   ST/Queen's Logic ....(Epic)
All The Young Punks
Clash; *Give 'Em Enough Rope* ....(Epic)
Angry Young Man
Steve Earle & The Dukes; *Exit 0* ....(MCA)
Angry Young Man
Corey Hart; *Fields Of Fire* ....(EMI)
Angry Young Man
Billy Joel; *KOHUEPT* .... (Columbia)
   Turnstiles .... (Columbia)
Anthem For The Year 2000
Silverchair; *Neon Ballroom* ....(Epic)
Be Young You
Jefferson Starship; *Dragon Fly* .... (RCA)
Because They're Young
Duane Eddy; *Compact Command Performances-Duane Eddy* ...... (Motown)
   Cruisin'-1960-C ....(Increase)
   Duane Eddy-16 Greatest Hits ....(Jamie)
   History Of Rock Instrumentals-#2-C .... (Rhino)
Believe Me If All Those Endearing Young Charms
Bronn Journey; *Celtic Journey* ....(Phileo)
Mitch Miller; *Favorite Irish Sing-Alongs* ....(Legacy)
Roger Whittaker; *Danny Boy & Other Irish Favorites* ....(RCA Victor)
Big Time
Neil Young & Crazy Horse; *Broken Arrow* .... (Reprise)
   Year Of The Horse .... (Reprise)
Blame It On My Youth
Nat "King" Cole; *Complete After Midnight Sessions* .... (Capitol)
Bookends
Simon & Garfunkel; *Bookends* .... (Columbia)
   Collected Works .... (Columbia)
   Simon & Garfunkel's Greatest Hits .... (Columbia)
Brown Sugar
Rolling Stones; *Classic Rock 1966-1988-C* .... (Atlantic)
   Hot Rocks 1964-1971 ....(Abkco)
   Made In The Shade ....(Rolling Stones)
   Sticky Fingers .... (Virgin)
Dance With Me
Debelah Morgan; *Dance With Me* .... (Atlantic)
   Totally Hits-#3-C .... (Atlantic)
Die Young, Stay Pretty
Blondie; *Eat To The Beat* ....(Chrysalis)
Electric Youth
Debbie Gibson; *Electric Youth* .... (Atlantic)
Flaming Youth
Kiss; *Destroyer* .... (Casablanca)
Flower & The Young Man
Strawbs; *Grave New World* .... (A&M)
Forever Young
Johnny Cash; *Red Hot + Country-C* .... (Mercury)
Forever Young
Chris Isaak; *Heart Shaped World* .... (Reprise)
Forever Young
Rod Stewart; *Downtown Train-Selections From The Storyteller
   Anthology* ....(Warner Bros.)
   If We Fall In Love Tonight ....(Warner Bros.)
   Storyteller/The Complete Anthology: 1964-1990 ....(Warner Bros.)
Forever Young
Alphaville; *Alphaville-The Singles Collection* .... (Atlantic)

Forever Young ....(Atlantic)
Forever Young
Band; *Best Of The Band-#2* .... (Rhino)
   The Last Waltz .... (Warner Bros.)
Bob Dylan; *Biograph* .... (Columbia)
   Bob Dylan At Budokan .... (Columbia)
   Bob Dylan's Greatest Hits-#3 .... (Columbia)
   Planet Waves .... (Columbia)
Joan Baez; *From Every Stage* ....(A&M)
   Joan Baez's Greatest Hits ....(A&M)
Pretenders; *ST/Free Willy 2: The Adventure Home* ..... (MJJ Music/Work)
   ST/With Honors .... (Maverick)
Gray Haired Young Man
Don Potter; *Over The Rainbow* ....(Mirror)
Heroes Die Young
Sleeze Beez; *Screwed Blued & Tattooed* ....(Atlantic)
Heroes Die Young
Waysted; *Save Your Prayers* .... (Capitol)
Hey Young World II
Macy Gray featuring Slick Rick; *The Id* .... (Epic)
If The Good Die Young
Tracy Lawrence; *Alibis* ....(Atlantic)
J.A.R. (Jason Andrew Relva)
Green Day; *ST/Angus* .... (Reprise)
Keep Young And Beautiful
Annie Lennox; *Diva* .... (Arista)
Kisses Sweeter Than Wine
Jimmie Rodgers; *Best Of Jimmie Rodgers* .... (Rhino)
   Cruisin'-1958-C .... (Increase)
Weavers; *Best Of The Weavers* .... (MCA)
   Reunion-At Carnegie Hall-1963 .... (Vanguard)
   Weavers At Carnegie Hall .... (Vanguard)
   Weavers' Greatest Hits .... (Vanguard)
Love Is A Battlefield
Pat Benatar; *Best Shots* .... (Chrysalis)
   I Am Woman-C ....(Nick At Nite)
   Live From Earth ....(Chrysalis)
Love You Down
INOJ; *So So Def Bass All-Stars-#2-C* .... (So So Def/Columbia)
   Total Dance Explosion-C .... (Columbia)
Much Too Young (To Feel This Damn Old)
Garth Brooks; *Garth Brooks-Double Live* .... (Capitol)
My Back Pages
Bob Dylan; *Another Side Of Bob Dylan* .... (Columbia)
   Bob Dylan's Greatest Hits-#2 .... (Columbia)
Byrds; *20 Essential Tracks From The Box Set* .... (Columbia)
   Byrds Play Dylan .... (Columbia)
   The Byrds' Greatest Hits .... (Columbia)
   Younger Than Yesterday .... (Columbia)
My Generation
Who; *Live At Leeds* .... (MCA)
   Meaty Beaty Big & Bouncy .... (MCA)
   ST/The Kids Are Alright .... (MCA)
   The Who Sings "My Generation" .... (MCA)
   Who Greatest Hits .... (MCA)
Night Is Still Young
Billy Joel; *Billy Joel-Greatest Hits, Volume I & Volume II* .... (Columbia)
Not For You
Pearl Jam; *Vitalogy* .... (Epic)
Not Too Young To Get Married
Bob B. Soxx/Blue Jeans; *Phil Spector-Back To Mono 1958-1969-C* ....(Abkco)
Darlene Love; *Best Of Darlene Love* ....(Abkco)
Ochone! When I Used To Be Young
Joseph O'Mara; *Music From The New York Stage (1890-1920)-#1-1890-
   1908-C* ....(Pearl)
Old Enough To Know Better
Wade Hayes; *Country Dance Hits-C* .... (Columbia)
   Old Enough To Know Better .... (Columbia)
   Steppin' Country-#2-C .... (Columbia)
   Super Hits Of 1994-C .... (Columbia)
Only Sixteen
Dr. Hook; *Bankrupt* .... (Capitol)
   Dr. Hook-Greatest Hits & More .... (Capitol)
   Great Records Of The Decade-'70s Hits-#2-C .... (Curb)
   Little Bit More .... (Capitol)
Sam Cooke; *Best Of Sam Cooke* .... (RCA)
   The Man And His Music .... (RCA)
   This Is Sam Cooke .... (RCA)
Only The Good Die Young
Billy Joel; *Billy Joel-Greatest Hits, Volume I & Volume II* ...... (Columbia)
   KOHUEPT .... (Columbia)
   The Stranger .... (Columbia)
Puppy Love
Lil Bow Wow Featuring Jagged Edge; *Beware Of Dog* .. (So So Def/Columbia)
Smashing Young Man
Collective Soul; *Collective Soul* ....(Atlantic)
So Young And In Love
Bruce Springsteen; *Tracks* .... (Columbia)

Streets Of Laredo
Buck Owens & The Buckaroos; *Buck Owens & The Buckaroos-Live At Carnegie Hall* . . . . . (Country Music Foundation)
Marty Robbins; *Cowboy Super Hits-C* . . . . . (Columbia)
Marty Robbins' All-Time Greatest Hits . . . . . (Columbia)
Marty Robbins-More Greatest Hits . . . . . (Columbia)
More Gunfighter Ballads & Trail Songs . . . . . (Columbia)
Rex Allen; *Great American Singing Cowboys-C* . . . . . (Republic/Universal)
Sweet Young America
Roger Whittaker; *Wind Beneath My Wings* . . . . . (RCA)
Take Me Back To Tulsa
Asleep At The Wheel; *Route 66* . . . . . (Liberty)
Very Best Of Asleep At The Wheel Since 1970 . . . . . (Relentless/Madacy)
Bob Wills & His Texas Playboys; *All Time Legends Of Country Music-C* . . . . . (Legacy)
Bob Wills-Anthology . . . . . (Sony Music Special Prod.)
Columbia Country Classics-#1-Golden Age-C . . . . . (Columbia)
Tiffany Transcriptions-#2-Best Of The Tiffanys . . . . . (Rhino)
Clay Walker & Asleep At The Wheel; *Ride With Bob-C* . . . (DreamWorks/SKG)
Tattoos & Scars
Montgomery Gentry; *Tattoos & Scars* . . . . . (Columbia)
Theme From "21 Jump Street"
Original Soundtrack; *Television's Greatest Hits-#7-Cable Ready-C* . . . . . (TVT)
Theme From "The Monkees"
Monkees; *Monkees' Greatest Hits* . . . . . (Rhino)
Original Soundtrack; *Television's Greatest Hits-#2-C* . . . . . (TVT)
Till I'm Too Old To Die Young
Moe Bandy; *Great Records Of The Decade-'80s Hits-Country-C* . . . . . (Curb)
Moe Bandy's Greatest Hits . . . . . (Curb)
Times They Are A-Changin'
Billy Joel; *KOHUEPT* . . . . . (Columbia)
Bob Dylan; *Biograph* . . . . . (Columbia)
Bob Dylan At Budokan . . . . . (Columbia)
Bob Dylan's Greatest Hits . . . . . (Columbia)
The Bootleg Series-Volumes 1-3 [Rare & Unreleased] . . . . . (Columbia)
The Times They Are A-Changin' . . . . . (Columbia)
Byrds; *The Byrds* . . . . . (Columbia)
Turn! Turn! Turn! . . . . . (Legacy)
Peter, Paul & Mary; *Peter, Paul and Mary In Concert* . . . . . (Warner Bros.)
Simon & Garfunkel; *Collected Works* . . . . . (Columbia)
Wednesday Morning 3 A.M. . . . . . (Columbia)
Too Old To Rock 'N' Roll: Too Young To Die
Jethro Tull; *Bursting Out* . . . . . (Chrysalis)
Classic Case with the London Symphony Orchestra . . . . . (RCA)
Original Masters . . . . . (Chrysalis)
Repeat-The Best Of Jethro Tull, Vol. II . . . . . (Chrysalis)
Twelve Thirty (Young Girls Are Coming To The Canyon)
Mamas & The Papas; *Best Of The Mamas & The Papas* . . . . . (MCA)
Mamas & The Papas-16 Of Their Greatest Hits . . . . . (MCA)
The Papas & The Mamas . . . . . (MCA)
Two Little Girls
Ani DiFranco; *Little Plastic Castle* . . . . . (Righteous Babe)
We Die Young
Alice In Chains; *Facelift* . . . . . (Columbia)
What Is Truth
Johnny Cash; *The Man In Black-His Greatest Hits* . . . . . (Legacy)
When I Was Young
Animals; *Best Of The Animals* . . . . . (Abkco)
Greatest Hits Live!-Rip It To Shreds . . . . . (I.R.S.)
History Of British Rock-#8-C . . . . . (Rhino)
When The World Was Young
Anita O'Day; *Mello'Day* . . . . . (Crescendo)
Frank Sinatra; *Point Of No Return* . . . . . (Capitol)
Wild Heart Of The Young
Karla Bonoff; *Wild Heart Of The Young* . . . . . (Columbia)
Yesterday, When I Was Young
Roy Clark; *Roy Clark's Greatest Hits* . . . . . (Varese Vintage)
You Can Make History (Young Again)
Elton John; *Elton John-Love Songs* . . . . . (MCA)
Young Americans
David Bowie; *Changesbowie* . . . . . (Rykodisc)
Sound + Vision . . . . . (Rykodisc)
The Singles-1969-1993 . . . . . (Rykodisc)
Young Americans . . . . . (Rykodisc)
Young And Beautiful
Elvis Presley; *A Valentine Gift For You* . . . . . (RCA)
Heart & Soul . . . . . (RCA)
The Other Sides-Worldwide Gold Award Hits, Vol. 2 . . . . . (RCA)
Young And Beautiful
Peter And Gordon; *Woman/Lady Godiva* . . . . . (Collectables)
Young And Foolish
Eddie Fisher; *Very Best Of Eddie Fisher* . . . . . (MCA)
Four Tops; *Lost & Found: Breaking Through* . . . . . (Motown)
Joe Williams; *Here's To Life* . . . . . (Telarc)
Nancy Kelly; *Singin' & Swingin'* . . . . . (Amherst)
Tony Bennett & Bill Evans; *The Tony Bennett & Bill Evans Album* . . . . . (Original Jazz Classics)
Young And Healthy
Bing Crosby with Guy Lombardo & His Royal Canadians; *The Song Is...Harry Warren-C* . . . . . (Living Era)
Dick Powell & Toby Wing; *Lullaby Of Broadway-The Best Of Busby Berkeley At Warner Brothers* . . . . . (Rhino)
Guy Lombardo & His Royal Canadians; *Guy Lombardo-16 Most Requested Songs* . . . . . (Legacy)
Original Broadway Cast; *42nd Street* . . . . . (RCA Victor)
Young Blood
Bad Company; *Run With The Pack* . . . . . (Swan Song)
Coasters; *Coasters' Greatest Hits* . . . . . (Atco)
Coasters-Their Greatest Recordings-Early Years . . . . . (Atco)
The Ultimate Coasters . . . . . (Warner Special Prod.)
Young Blood
Rickie Lee Jones; *Naked Songs Live And Acoustic* . . . . . (Reprise)
Rickie Lee Jones . . . . . (Warner Bros.)
Young Dreams
Elvis Presley; *ST/King Creole* . . . . . (RCA)
The Other Sides-Worldwide Gold Award Hits, Vol. 2 . . . . . (RCA)
Young Girl
Union Gap Featuring Gary Puckett; *Billboard Top Pop Hits-1968-C* . . . . (Rhino)
Young Girl Blues
Sammy Hagar; *All Night Long* . . . . . (One Way)
Young Guns
Wham! Featuring George Michael; *Fantastic* . . . . . (Columbia)
Young Hearts Run Free
Candi Staton; *The Disco Years-#3-Boogie Fever-C* . . . . . (Rhino)
Young Hearts Run Free: The Best Of Candi Staton . . . . . (Warner Bros.)
Young Love
Sonny James; *Golden Jukebox Favorites* . . . . . (Capitol)
Opry Legends-Sonny James . . . . . (Capitol)
Stars Of The Grand Ole Opry-1926-1974-C . . . . . (RCA)
Traditions In Country Music-C . . . . . (Capitol)
Tab Hunter; *Fonzie's Make-Out Music-C* . . . . . (Nick At Nite)
Teen Idols-C . . . . . (Universal)
Young Love
Janet Jackson; *Janet Jackson* . . . . . (A&M)
Young Love
Teena Marie; *Baddest Love Jams-Volume 1-Quite Storm-C* . . . . . (Motown)
Best Of Teena Marie . . . . . (Motown)
Young Lust
Pink Floyd; *1980-1981 Wall Live-Is There Anybody Out There* . . . . . (Columbia)
The Wall . . . . . (Columbia)
Roger Waters & Bryan Adams; *The Wall-Live In Berlin* . . . . . (Mercury)
Young Man, Older Woman
Millie Jackson; *Very Best Of Millie Jackson* . . . . . (Jive)
Young 'N' Russian
Korgis; *Korgis* . . . . . (Warner Bros.)
Young Thing, Wild Dreams (Rock Me)
Red Rider; *Breaking Curfew* . . . . . (Capitol)
Young Turks
Rod Stewart; *Absolutely Live* . . . . . (Warner Bros.)
Downtown Train-Selections From The Storyteller Anthology . . . (Warner Bros.)
Storyteller/The Complete Anthology: 1964-1990 . . . . . (Warner Bros.)
Tonight I'm Yours . . . . . (Warner Bros.)
Young Woman's Blues
Bessie Smith; *Bessie Smith-The Collection* . . . . . (Legacy)
Bessie Smith-The Complete Recordings-#3 . . . . . (Legacy)
Young World
Rick Nelson; *Rick Nelson's Greatest Hits* . . . . . (Rhino)
Ricky Nelson; *All My Best* . . . . . (MCA)
Best Of Rick Nelson-#2 . . . . . (EMI)
Teenage Idol . . . . . (Liberty)
Young, Gifted And Black
Aretha Franklin; *Young, Gifted And Black* . . . . . (Atlantic & Atco Remasters)
Bob & Marcia; *Archive Reggae-C* . . . . . (Rialto)
Nina Simone; *The Tomato Collection* . . . . . (Tomato)
Young-At-Heart
Bing Crosby with Guy Lombardo & His Royal Canadians; *The Radio Years: 20 Songs* . . . . . (Crescendo)
Frank Sinatra; *At The Movies* . . . . . (Capitol)
Capitol Collectors Series-Frank Sinatra . . . . . (Capitol)
Classic Sinatra . . . . . (Capitol)
Sinatra's Sinatra . . . . . (Reprise)
Ray Price; *Portrait Of A Singer* . . . . . (Step One)
Rosemary Clooney; *Essence Of Rosemary Clooney* . . . . . (Legacy)
Younger Girl
Critters; *Sixties Rule! Chapter Two-C* . . . . . (One Way)
Lovin' Spoonful; *Lovin' Spoonful-Anthology* . . . . . (Rhino)
Younger Than Springtime
Original Cast; *South Pacific* . . . . . (CBS Masterworks)
You're Still A Young Man
Tower Of Power; *Bump City* . . . . . (Warner Bros.)
Live & In Living Color . . . . . (Warner Bros.)
Youth Of The Nation
P.O.D.; *Satellite* . . . . . (Atlantic)

In the alphabetical index listings, **MAIN CATEGORIES** appear in boldface upper case; their associated **subcategories** appear with them in boldface upper/lower case. Main categories may be followed by *"See Also"* references to other relevant categories. Example:

ADVICE, Lecturing, Recommendations, Suggestions
    See Also DRUGS (various), MOTIVATION, SCHOOL,
    TEACHING VALUES, THINKING & KNOWING,
    WARNINGS

Subcategories are also listed alphabetically, in boldface upper/lower case. *"See"* refers to the main category with which the subcategory is associated. Subcategories may have *"See Also"* references to other relevant categories. Example:

Lecturing *See* ADVICE
    See Also SCHOOL

Additional search terms appear in upper/lower case. *"See"* refers to the suggested main category/categories. Example:

Lessons *See* ADVICE, SCHOOL

(various) refers to a group of main categories. Example:

AGES (various) refers to AGES: 16, AGES: 17, AGES: SPECIFIC

1 *See* NUMBERS: 1 *988*
1,000's *See* NUMBERS: THOUSANDS *1007*
1-2-3 *See* COUNTING SONGS *262*, NUMBERS: 1 *988*,
    NUMBERS: 2 *998*, NUMBERS: 3 *1001*
10 *See* NUMBERS: 10 *994*
100's *See* NUMBERS: HUNDREDS *1006*
11-99 *See* NUMBERS: 11-99 *994*
12 Midnight *See* MIDNIGHT *901*
14 Karat *See* GOLD *533*
16 *See* AGES: 16 *10*, NUMBERS: 11-99 *994*
17 *See* AGES: 17 *11*, NUMBERS: 11-99 *994*
2 *See* NUMBERS: 2 *998*
20th Century *See* HISTORY *603*
24 Hours *See* DAYS: GENERAL *334*, TIME:
    GENERAL *1360*
3 *See* NUMBERS: 3 *1001*
4 *See* NUMBERS: 4 *1002*
411 (information) *See* TELEPHONE *1339*
42nd Street *See* CITIES: NEW YORK *198*, STREETS:
    SPECIFIC *1314*
4th Of July *See* COUNTRIES: AMERICA *263*,
    FREEDOM *499*, MONTHS & DATES: JULY *916*,
    PATRIOTISM *1043*
5 *See* NUMBERS: 5 *1003*
6 *See* NUMBERS: 6 *1004*
7 *See* NUMBERS: 7 *1004*
8 *See* NUMBERS: 8 *1005*
9 *See* NUMBERS: 9 *1005*
9 To 5 *See* WORK *1494*
911 (emergency) *See* DANGER & DISASTER *323*,
    HELP *590*, TELEPHONE *1339*, URGENT *1420*

A

A.M. *See* MORNING *924*
Abandon *See* ESCAPE *412*, LEAVING *654*
Abandoned *See* LONELY *684*, LOVE (various) *701*,
    MISTREATMENT *905*
Abandoned Children *See* CHILDREN *148*, DOMESTIC
    ABUSE *377*, PARENTS: SINGLE, STEP, ABSENT *1037*
ABC's *See* SCHOOL *1181*, SPELLING SONGS *1269*
Ability *See* MOTIVATION *928*, POWER & CONTROL *1068*
Abnormal *See* STRANGE *1308*
Abolition *See* FREEDOM *499*, SLAVERY *1242*, WAR *1427*
Abortion *See* FAMILY PLANNING *432*
Above *See* FLYING *479*, MOUNTAINS *937*, SKY *1239*
Absent-minded *See* CRAZY *290*, THINKING &
    KNOWING *1349*
Absentee Parent *See* PARENTS: SINGLE, STEP,
    ABSENT *1037*
Absolution *See* FAITH *425*, GOD *522*, GUILT *544*
Abuse *See* DOMESTIC ABUSE *377*, MISTREATMENT *905*
Abused Substances *See* ALCOHOL *19*, DRUGS (various) *388*
Academics *See* SCHOOL *1181*
Access *See* DOORS *378*, INSIDE/OUTSIDE *626*
Accidents *See* DANGER & DISASTER *323*, PAIN &
    HEALING *1025*, ROAD ACCIDENTS *1159*
Acclaim *See* COMPLIMENTS *256*
Accommodate *See* CHANGES *135*
Accuracy *See* TRUTH *1417*
Accuse *See* GUILT *544*, LAW & ORDER *652*
Aches *See* PAIN & HEALING *1025*
Acid Rain *See* NATURE *961*, RAIN *1116*
Active Duty *See* DRAFT *380*, WAR *1427*
Actors *See* MOVIES *941*
    See Also SHOW BIZ, TELEVISION
Actresses *See* MOVIES *941*
    See Also SHOW BIZ, TELEVISION
Adapt *See* CHANGES *135*
Add *See* COUNTING SONGS *262*
Addictions *See* DRUGS: GENERAL *389*
    See Also ALCOHOL, ALCOHOL: RECOVERING
    ALCOHOLIC, DRUGS: COCAINE,
    DRUGS: MARIJUANA
Addresses *See* STREETS: SPECIFIC *1314*
Adjust *See* CHANGES *135*
Admonish *See* ADVICE *1*, WARNINGS *1433*
Adolescence *See* TEENAGERS *1336*
Adoption *See* FAMILY PLANNING *432*
    See Also FAMILY (various)
Adornments *See* RIBBONS *1148*
Adrift *See* LOST & MISPLACED *699*
    See Also TRAVELING
Adulation *See* COMPLIMENTS *256*
Adults *See* PEOPLE *1046*
    See Also FAMILY (various), PARENTS (various)
Adventure *See* FUN *508*
Adversity *See* DIFFICULT *364*, LOSING & LOSS *696*, PAIN
    & HEALING *1025*, POVERTY *1063*, TROUBLE *1412*
Advertising *See* NEWS *964*, SHOPPING *1228*
ADVICE *1* **Lecturing, Recommendations, Suggestions**
    See Also DRUGS (various), MOTIVATION, SCHOOL,
    TEACHING VALUES, THINKING &
    KNOWING, WARNINGS

Brittle   *See* BREAK *108*

Broadcasters   *See* NEWS *964*

Broadway   *See* CITIES: NEW YORK *198*
   See Also SHOW BIZ

Broke   *See* POVERTY *1063*

Broken   *See* BREAK *108*

Broken Heart   *See* HEART *571*, LOVE (various) *701*, PAIN &
   HEALING *1025*, SADNESS *1169*

Broken Home   *See* DIVORCE *375*, HOME *608*, PARENTS:
   SINGLE, STEP, ABSENT *1037*

Broken Marriage   *See* DIVORCE *375*

Broken Promises   *See* CHEATING & LIES *140*

Bronx   *See* CITIES: NEW YORK *198*

Brooklyn   *See* CITIES: NEW YORK *198*

Brooks   *See* RIVERS *1149*

Brooms   *See* CLEAN *211*, DIRT *371*

BROTHERHOOD *111*   **Sisterhood**
   See Also FAMILY (various), FEMINISM, GOD, HELP,
   PEACE, POLITICS: POLITICAL CLASSICS, PROTEST,
   TOGETHERNESS, WORK (unions)

Brotherly Love   *See* BROTHERHOOD *111*, CHARACTER &
   INTEGRITY *137*, FAITH *425*, FAMILY: BROTHERS *433*,
   GOD *522*, LOVE (various) *701*

Brothers   *See* BROTHERHOOD *111*, FAMILY:
   BROTHERS *433*

Brow   *See* EYES *418*

Brown   *See* COLORS: BROWN *228*

Bruises   *See* DOMESTIC ABUSE *377*, FIGHT *461*, PAIN &
   HEALING *1025*

Brunette   *See* ANATOMY: HAIR *31*

Brush (hair)   *See* ANATOMY: HAIR *31*

Brush Fire   *See* FIRE *465*, TREES *1410*

Bubble Gum   *See* FOOD & BEVERAGES: GENERAL *486*

BUBBLES *112*
   See Also ALCOHOL, CLEAN

Buccaneers   *See* PIRATES *1049*

Buckets   *See* BOTTLES *106*

Buddha   *See* GOD *522*

Buddies   *See* COUPLES *285*, FRIENDS *503*

Buffalo   *See* AMERICAN WEST *25*, ANIMALS: B *45*

Bugs   *See* ANIMALS: INSECTS *61*

BUILDING & CONSTRUCTION *112*
   See Also BUSINESS & INDUSTRY, FIXING, HOUSES,
   TOOLS, WORK

Bulldozers   *See* BUILDING & CONSTRUCTION *112*

Bulletins   *See* NEWS *964*

Bullets   *See* GUNS *550*

Bullfights   *See* SPORTS: GENERAL *1273*

Bulls   *See* ANIMALS: B *45*

Bums   *See* INSULTS *627*, POVERTY *1063*, SOCIAL
   OUTCASTS *1262*

Bunnies   *See* ANIMALS: RABBITS *66*

Burden   *See* BAGGAGE & WEIGHT *83*

Burglars   *See* CRIME *297*

Burial   *See* DEATH *336*

Buried Treasure   *See* PIRATES *1049*

Burned   *See* FIRE *465*, PAIN & HEALING *1025*

Burned Out   *See* BORED *105*, CRAZY *290*

Burning   *See* FIRE *465*

Bury   *See* DEATH *336*

BUS *113*
   See Also CARS (various), GAS STATIONS, LEAVING,
   MOTORCYCLES, ROAD, ROAD ACCIDENTS, TAXI,
   TRAVELING, TRUCKS

BUSINESS & INDUSTRY *114*   **Technology**
   See Also BOSSES, BUILDING & CONSTRUCTION,
   COMPUTERS, MACHINES, MONEY, NATURE,
   PROTEST, RECORD BUSINESS, SHOPPING, SHOW
   BIZ, WORK

Busted   *See* BREAK *108*
   See Also POVERTY

BUSY *115*
   See Also FAST, LATE, RELAX, TIME: GENERAL,
   URGENT, WAITING

Busybody   *See* GOSSIP *540*

Butterflies   *See* ANIMALS: INSECTS *61*

Buttocks   *See* ANATOMY: REAR *38*

Buttons   *See* CLOTHES *213*, RIBBONS *1148*

Buying   *See* SHOPPING *1228*
   See Also LOVE: LOVE & MONEY, MONEY

By Oneself   *See* LONELY *684*, SOLITUDE *1263*

C

C.I.A.   *See* POLICE *1055*

Cabarets   *See* BARS *84*

Cabins   *See* HOUSES *621*

Cable (TV)   *See* TELEVISION *1342*

Cable Cars   *See* TRAINS *1383*

Cabs   *See* TAXI *1334*

Cactus   *See* FLOWERS: GENERAL *473*

Cadillac   *See* CARS: CADILLAC *123*

Cafes   *See* RESTAURANTS *1141*

Caffeine   *See* FOOD & BEVERAGES: COFFEE *482*

Caged   *See* PRISON *1082*, STUCK *1318*

Calamity   *See* DANGER & DISASTER *323*

California   *See* STATES: CALIFORNIA *1282*

Call   *See* TELEPHONE *1339*

Call Up   *See* DRAFT *380*, WAR *1427*

Calling Out   *See* COMMUNICATION: SAY *239*

Calm   *See* PEACE *1044*

Camelot   *See* BOOKS *101*, PARADISE *1034*, PLACES *1049*

Cameras   *See* ART & PHOTOGRAPHY *71*

Campaigns   *See* POLITICS: POLITICS &
   GOVERNMENT *1061*

Campus   *See* SCHOOL *1181*

Can't Explain   *See* DIFFICULT *364*, QUESTIONS &
   ANSWERS *1097*, REASONS *1124*, STRANGE *1308*

Can't Find The Words   *See* LOVE: LOOKING FOR THE
   WORDS *809*
   See Also COMMUNICATION: WORDS, DIFFICULT

Can't Get Over You   *See* LOVE: CAN'T GET OVER
   YOU *702*, STUCK *1318*

Can't Let Go   *See* HOLDING ON *605*, LOVE (various) *701*,
   STUCK *1318*

Can't Resist   *See* LOVE: TEMPTATION *843*

Canada   *See* COUNTRIES: CANADA *270*

Candles   *See* FIRE *465*

CITIES: I *187*
See Also CITIES: GENERAL, COUNTRIES: A-Z,
STATES: A-Z

CITIES: J *187*
See Also CITIES: GENERAL, COUNTRIES: A-Z,
STATES: A-Z

CITIES: K *187*
See Also CITIES: GENERAL, CITIES: KANSAS CITY,
COUNTRIES: A-Z, STATES: A-Z

CITIES: KANSAS CITY *188*
See Also STATES: KANSAS, STATES: MISSOURI

CITIES: L *188*
See Also CITIES: GENERAL, CITIES: LAS VEGAS,
LONDON, LOS ANGELES, COUNTRIES: A-Z,
STATES: A-Z

CITIES: LAS VEGAS *189*
See Also GAMBLING, LUCK, STATES: NEVADA

CITIES: LONDON *189*
See Also COUNTRIES: ENGLAND

CITIES: LOS ANGELES *190* **L.A. Suburbs**
See Also CELEBRITIES: SPECIFIC, HOLLYWOOD,
MOVIES, SHOW BIZ, STATES: CALIFORNIA

CITIES: M *192*
See Also CITIES: GENERAL, CITIES: MEMPHIS, MIAMI,
MOBILE, MOSCOW, NEW YORK (Manhattan)

CITIES: MEMPHIS *193*
See Also STATES: TENNESSEE

CITIES: MIAMI *194*
See Also STATES: FLORIDA

CITIES: MOBILE *195*
See Also STATES: ALABAMA

CITIES: MOSCOW *195*
See Also COUNTRIES: RUSSIA

CITIES: N *195*
See Also CITIES: GENERAL, CITIES: NASHVILLE,
NEW ORLEANS, NEW YORK, COUNTRIES: A-Z,
STATES: A-Z

CITIES: NASHVILLE *195*
See Also MUSIC, RECORD BUSINESS,
STATES: TENNESSEE

CITIES: NEW ORLEANS *196*
See Also CARNIVALS, STATES: LOUISIANA

CITIES: NEW YORK *198* **Broadway, Bronx, Brooklyn,
Harlem, Manhattan, Queens (N.Y.C.), Staten Island**
See Also SHOW BIZ, STATES: NEW YORK,
STREETS: SPECIFIC

CITIES: O *202*
See Also CITIES: GENERAL, COUNTRIES: A-Z,
STATES: A-Z

CITIES: P *202*
See Also CITIES: GENERAL, CITIES: PARIS, CITIES:
PHILADELPHIA, COUNTRIES: A-Z, STATES: A-Z

CITIES: PARIS *203*
See Also COUNTRIES: FRANCE

CITIES: PHILADELPHIA *204*
See Also STATES: PENNSYLVANIA

CITIES: R *204*
See Also CITIES: GENERAL, CITIES: RIO DE JANEIRO,
COUNTRIES: A-Z, STATES: A-Z

CITIES: RIO DE JANEIRO *205*
See Also COUNTRIES: BRAZIL

CITIES: ROME *205*
See Also COUNTRIES: ITALY

CITIES: S *205*
See Also CITIES: GENERAL, CITIES: SAN ANTONIO,
SAN FRANCISCO, SANTA FE, SAVANNAH, ST. LOUIS,
COUNTRIES: A-Z, STATES: A-Z

CITIES: SAN ANTONIO *207*
See Also AMERICAN WEST, COWBOYS,
STATES: TEXAS

CITIES: SAN FRANCISCO *207* **San Francisco Suburbs**
See Also BRIDGES, HIPPIES, STATES: CALIFORNIA

CITIES: SANTA FE *208*
See Also AMERICAN WEST, COWBOYS, STATES:
NEW MEXICO

CITIES: SAVANNAH *208*
See Also STATES: GEORGIA

CITIES: ST. LOUIS *209*
See Also STATES: MISSOURI

CITIES: T *209*
See Also CITIES: GENERAL, CITIES: TOKYO, CITIES:
TULSA, COUNTRIES: A-Z, STATES: A-Z

CITIES: TOKYO *210*
See Also COUNTRIES: JAPAN

CITIES: TULSA *210*
See Also STATES: OKLAHOMA

CITIES: U *210*
See Also CITIES: GENERAL, COUNTRIES: A-Z,
STATES: A-Z

CITIES: V *210*
See Also CITIES: GENERAL, CITIES: VIENNA,
COUNTRIES: A-Z, STATES: A-Z

CITIES: VIENNA *211*
See Also COUNTRIES: A

CITIES: W *211*
See Also CITIES: GENERAL, COUNTRIES: A-Z,
STATES: A-Z

CITIES: Y *211*
See Also CITIES: GENERAL, COUNTRIES: A-Z,
STATES: A-Z

Citizenship *See* PATRIOTISM *1043*

City *See* CITIES: GENERAL *183*

City Slums *See* CITIES: A-Z *174*, HARD CITY LIFE *566*,
POVERTY *1063*

Civil Service *See* POLITICS: POLITICS &
GOVERNMENT *1061*, WORK *1494*

Civil War *See* COUNTRIES: AMERICA *263*,
SLAVERY *1242*, WAR *1427*

Class Differences *See* SOCIAL CLASS: GENERAL *1259*
See Also LOVE: FORBIDDEN LOVE

Classifieds *See* NEWS *964*, SHOPPING *1228*

Classrooms *See* SCHOOL *1181*

Classy *See* SOCIAL CLASS: GENERAL *1259*

CLEAN *211* **Laundry, Soap, Wash**
See Also BATHROOMS, DIRT, TRASH

Clear Skies *See* SKY *1239*

Cliche *See* ADVICE *1*, COMMUNICATION: WORDS *253*

Cliffs *See* MOUNTAINS *937*

CLIMBING *213* **Ladders, Stairs**
See Also DISTANCE, MOTIVATION,
MOUNTAINS, TRAVELING

Clinics *See* PAIN & HEALING *1025*

Clocks *See* TIME: GENERAL *1360*

Close *See* DISTANCE *373*

Close (shut) *See* DOORS *378*, ENDINGS *408*, OPEN &
CLOSED *1016*, STOP *1304*

Closeness   *See* FRIENDS *503*, LOVE (various) *701*, TOGETHERNESS *1371*

Cloth   *See* CLOTHES *213*, FABRICS *424*

CLOTHES *213* **Blue Jeans, Fashion, Swimsuits**
   See Also CLEAN (laundry), FABRICS, HATS, RIBBONS, SHOES, SHOPPING

Cloudburst   *See* RAIN *1116*

Clouds   *See* SKY *1239*
   See Also RAIN

Clowns   *See* CARNIVALS *121*

Clubs   *See* BARS *84*

Coal Mine   *See* MINING *903*

Coast   *See* OCEAN *1008*

Coast Guard   *See* SHIPS *1224*, WAR *1427*

Coats   *See* CLOTHES *213*

Cocaine   *See* DRUGS: COCAINE *388*

Cocktail Lounges   *See* BARS *84*

Cocktails   *See* ALCOHOL *19*

Coffee   *See* FOOD & BEVERAGES: COFFEE *482*

Coffee Breaks   *See* WORK *1494*

Coffee Shops   *See* RESTAURANTS *1141*

Coffins   *See* DEATH *336*

Coins   *See* MONEY *906*

COLD *217* **Freezing, Frost, Frozen, Ice**
   See Also CHRISTMAS, COOL, MONTHS & DATES (various), SEASONS: WINTER, SNOW

Cold (illness)   *See* PAIN & HEALING *1025*

Cold (unfeeling)   *See* INSULTS *627*, MISTREATMENT *905*

Cold Cream   *See* COSMETICS *261*

Cold Feet   *See* FEAR & COURAGE *453*

Cold Turkey   *See* ALCOHOL: RECOVERING ALCOHOLIC *25*, DRUGS: GENERAL *389*

Cold War   *See* WAR *1427*

College   *See* SCHOOL *1181*

College Fight Songs   *See* SCHOOL *1181*, SPORTS: FOOTBALL *1272*, STATES: A-Z *1281*

Cologne (perfume)   *See* COSMETICS *261*

Colorado   *See* STATES: COLORADO *1285*

Coloring Books   *See* COLORS: GENERAL *229*, TOYS & GAMES *1377*

Colorless   *See* COLORS: WHITE *236*

COLORS: BLACK *219* **Ebony**
   See Also COLORS (various)

COLORS: BLUE *222*
   See Also COLORS (various), LOVE (various), SADNESS

COLORS: BROWN *228* **Tan**
   See Also ANATOMY: HAIR (brunette), COLORS (various)

COLORS: GENERAL *229* **Multiple Colors**
   See Also COLORS (various), RAINBOWS

COLORS: GREEN *230*
   See Also COLORS (various)

COLORS: GREY *231*
   See Also COLORS (various)

COLORS: ORANGE *232*
   See Also COLORS (various), FOOD & BEVERAGES: FRUIT

COLORS: PINK *232*
   See Also COLORS (various)

COLORS: PURPLE *233*
   See Also COLORS (various)

COLORS: RED *233* **Crimson, Scarlet**
   See Also ANATOMY: HAIR (redhead), COLORS (various)

COLORS: WHITE *236* **Ivory, Pale**
   See Also COLORS (various)

COLORS: YELLOW *238*
   See Also ANATOMY: HAIR (blonde), COLORS (various)

Comb   *See* ANATOMY: HAIR *31*

Combat   *See* WAR *1427*

Come   *See* TRAVELING *1392*

Come Alive   *See* LIFE *662*

Come Back   *See* LOVE: DON'T WANT TO BREAK UP *748*

Come In   *See* DOORS *378*, HELLO *588*

Comedians   *See* SHOW BIZ *1230*, SMILE *1254*

Comets   *See* STARS *1277*

Comfort   *See* HELP *590*

Comfortable   *See* RELAX *1132*

Comic Book Characters   *See* CARTOON CHARACTERS *130*

Comical   *See* FOOLS *494*, SMILE *1254*

Coming   *See* FUTURE *511*

Coming Apart   *See* BITS & PIECES *100*, BREAK *108*, CRAZY *290*

Coming Back   *See* RETURNING *1142*
   See Also CIRCLES

Coming Home   *See* HOME *608*, RETURNING *1142*, TRAVELING *1392*

Coming Of Age   *See* AGING *12*, BIRTHDAY *99*, TEENAGERS *1336*

Coming Out   *See* HOMOSEXUALS *616*

Command   *See* POWER & CONTROL *1068*

Commandments   *See* GOD *522*

Commemorate   *See* REMEMBER *1133*

Commend   *See* COMPLIMENTS *256*

Comment   *See* COMMUNICATION: SAY *239*

Commerce   *See* BUSINESS & INDUSTRY *114*

Commitment   *See* LOVE: DEVOTION *738*
   See Also CHARACTER & INTEGRITY, PROMISE

Common Man   *See* MEN: GENERAL *867*, WORK *1494*

Common Sense   *See* ADVICE *1*, THINKING & KNOWING *1349*

Communicable Diseases   *See* AIDS *16*, PAIN & HEALING *1025*, SEX *1213*

COMMUNICATION: CONVERSATION *239* **Discussion, Voices**
   See Also COMMUNICATION (various), GOSSIP

COMMUNICATION: SAY *239* **Calling Out**
   See Also COMMUNICATION (various), GOSSIP

COMMUNICATION: SCREAM *244* **Howl**
   See Also COMMUNICATION (various)

COMMUNICATION: SHOUT *244* **Crying Out**
   See Also COMMUNICATION (various)

COMMUNICATION: TALK *245* **Speak**
   See Also COMMUNICATION (various), GOSSIP

COMMUNICATION: TELL *249*
   See Also COMMUNICATION (various), GOSSIP

COMMUNICATION: WHISPER *253*
   See Also COMMUNICATION (various), GOSSIP

COMMUNICATION: WORDS *253* **Language**
   See Also COMMUNICATION (various), GOSSIP, LOVE: LOOKING FOR THE WORDS

Communism   *See* POLITICS: POLITICS & GOVERNMENT *1061*

Companions   *See* COUPLES *285*, FRIENDS *503*, TOGETHERNESS *1371*

Company (corporation)   *See* BUSINESS & INDUSTRY *114*, WORK *1494*

Disappear *See* INVISIBLE *632*

Disappointment *See* SADNESS *1169*

Disapprove *See* ANGER *44*, COMPLAINTS *255*, INSULTS *627*

Disarm *See* GUNS *550*, PROTEST *1091*, WAR *1427*

Disaster *See* DANGER & DISASTER *323*

Disc Jockeys *See* MUSIC *942*, RADIO *1113*

Discipline *See* BOSSES *105*, POWER & CONTROL *1068*

Disclose *See* COMMUNICATION: TELL *249*, SECRETS *1201*

Disco *See* DANCE *311*

Discomforts *See* PAIN & HEALING *1025*

Discontent *See* ANGER *44*, COMPLAINTS *255*, SADNESS *1169*

Discontinued *See* ENDINGS *408*

Discouragement *See* SADNESS *1169*
     See Also LOW SELF-ESTEEM

Discovery *See* BEGINNINGS *92*
     See Also FINDING

Discovery Of Love *See* LOVE: FALLING IN LOVE *755*

Discrimination *See* POLITICS: SOCIAL INJUSTICE *1061*, PREJUDICE *1071*

Discussion *See* COMMUNICATION: CONVERSATION *239*
     See Also COMMUNICATION: TALK

Diseases *See* PAIN & HEALING *1025*

Disgraceful *See* BAD *79*, GUILT *544*

Disguise *See* PRETEND *1074*
     See Also HIDING

Disgusting *See* BAD *79*

Disillusionment *See* SADNESS *1169*

Disintegrate *See* BITS & PIECES *100*, BREAK *108*

Disorders *See* CRAZY *290*, PAIN & HEALING *1025*

Disoriented *See* CRAZY *290*, STRANGE *1308*

Disparage *See* COMPLAINTS *255*, INSULTS *627*

Dispensary *See* DRUGS: GENERAL *389*

Dispose Of *See* TRASH *1391*

Disreputable *See* BAD *79*, SLEAZY *1242*

Dissatisfied *See* SADNESS *1169*, STUCK *1318*

Dissent *See* PROTEST *1091*

DISTANCE *373* **Close, Deeper, Far, Feet, Inches, Measurements, Miles, Near**
     See Also EXTREMES, LONELY, SEPARATION, TRAVELING

Distracted *See* CRAZY *290*

Distressed *See* PAIN & HEALING *1025*, SADNESS *1169*

Districts *See* PLACES *1049*

Disturbed *See* CRAZY *290*

Diversity *See* BROTHERHOOD *111*, POLITICS: POLITICAL CLASSICS *1058*, POLITICS: SOCIAL INJUSTICE *1061*, PROTEST *1091*

Diving *See* SPORTS: SWIMMING *1276*

DIVORCE *375* **Broken Marriage**
     See Also CHEATING & LIES, LOVE (various), MARRIAGE, PARENTS: SINGLE, STEP, ABSENT

Divulge *See* COMMUNICATION: TELL *249*, HIDING *600*, SECRETS *1201*

Dixie *See* DIRECTIONS: SOUTH *368*

Dizzy *See* CRAZY *290*

DJs *See* RADIO *1113*
     See Also MUSIC

Do Good *See* CHARACTER & INTEGRITY *137*, GOOD *536*, HELP *590*

Doctors *See* PAIN & HEALING *1025*

Dogs *See* ANIMALS: DOGS *53*

Doing Better Now *See* BACK ON MY FEET *78*

Doing Time *See* PRISON *1082*

Dollars *See* MONEY *906*

Dolls *See* TOYS & GAMES *1377*

Dolphins *See* ANIMALS: DOLPHINS *56*

DOMESTIC ABUSE *377* **Domestic Violence**
     See Also ANGER, CRIME, FAMILY (various), FIGHT, MISTREATMENT

Domestic Life *See* HOME *608*, LIFE *662*, MARRIAGE *860*

Domestic Violence *See* DOMESTIC ABUSE *377*

Domination *See* POWER & CONTROL *1068*

Don't Disturb *See* SOLITUDE *1263*

Don't Forget *See* REMEMBER *1133*

Don't Give Up *See* MOTIVATION *928*

Don't Go *See* LOVE: DON'T WANT TO BREAK UP *748*

Don't Know *See* THINKING & KNOWING *1349*

Don't Know Myself *See* IDENTITY CRISIS *626*

Don't Love You Anymore *See* LOVE: PAINFUL BREAK-UP *822*

Don't Want To Be Alone *See* LONELY *684*, LOVE (various) *701*

Don't Want To Break Up *See* LOVE: DON'T WANT TO BREAK UP *748*

Don't Worry *See* CAREFREE *118*, HELP *590*

Done *See* ENDINGS *408*

Doom *See* DANGER & DISASTER *323*

Doorbells *See* BELLS *93*, DOORS *378*

DOORS *378* **Gates, Keys, Locks**
     See Also HOUSES, LEAVING, SECRETS

Dope Addicts *See* DRUGS (various) *388*

Double *See* COUPLES *285*, NUMBERS: 2 *998*

Doves *See* ANIMALS: BIRDS *46*, PEACE *1044*

Down (sad) *See* SADNESS *1169*

Down & Out *See* DESPAIR *361*
     See Also POVERTY

Download *See* COMPUTERS *259*

Downstream *See* RIVERS *1149*

Downtown *See* CITIES: GENERAL *183*

Dozen *See* NUMBERS: 11-99 *994*

DRAFT *380* **Draft Resistance, Enlistment**
     See Also COUNTRIES: AMERICA, PATRIOTISM, POLITICS (various), PROTEST, WAR

Draft Resistance *See* DRAFT *380*
     See Also POLITICS: POLITICAL CLASSICS

Drag (bad situation) *See* COMPLAINTS *255*, SADNESS *1169*, TROUBLE *1412*

Drag Racing *See* SPORTS: CAR RACING *1271*
     See Also CARS: GENERAL, ROAD ACCIDENTS

Dragons *See* MONSTERS *913*

Drains *See* BATHROOMS *87*, CLEAN *211*

Drama *See* LIFE *662*, SHOW BIZ *1230*

Drawbacks *See* DIFFICULT *364*, TROUBLE *1412*

Drawings *See* ART & PHOTOGRAPHY *71*

DREAMS *380* **Daydreaming, Nightmares**
     See Also DESIRE, FAITH, LOVE (various), MOTIVATION, NIGHT, OPTIMISM, PRETEND, SLEEP

Dress *See* CLOTHES *213*

Drifters *See* POVERTY *1063*, TRAINS (hobos) *1383*

Drifting (on water) *See* OCEAN *1008*

E

F

Galaxies   *See* SPACE *1265*, STARS *1277*
Gallery   *See* ART & PHOTOGRAPHY *71*
Gallows   *See* CAPITAL PUNISHMENT *117*
GAMBLING *515* **Betting, Card Games, Casino Games, Chance, Dice, Risk**
    See Also CITIES: LAS VEGAS, LOSING & LOSS, LUCK, SPORTS (various), WINNING
Game Hunting   *See* GUNS *550*
Games   *See* GAMBLING *515*, SPORTS (various) *1271*, TOYS & GAMES *1377*
Gangs   *See* CRIME *297*, HARD CITY LIFE *566*
Gangsta Life   *See* HARD CITY LIFE *566*
Gangsters   *See* CRIME *297*
Garage   *See* CARS: GENERAL *125*
Garbage   *See* TRASH *1391*
Garden Of Eden   *See* FLOWERS: GENERAL *473*, NATURE *961*, PARADISE *1034*
Gardens   *See* FLOWERS: GENERAL *473*
Gas   *See* ENERGY *411*
Gas Chamber   *See* CAPITAL PUNISHMENT *117*
GAS STATIONS *518* **Car Repair, Gasoline**
    See Also CARS (various), ENERGY, MOTORCYCLES, ROAD, TRAVELING, TRUCKS
Gasoline   *See* GAS STATIONS *518*
Gates   *See* DOORS *378*
Gay   *See* HOMOSEXUALS *616*
Gaze   *See* EYES *418*, SEEING *1204*
Gear   *See* TOOLS *1374*
Gems   *See* JEWELRY *637*
Gender Competition   *See* GENDER CONFLICT *519*
GENDER CONFLICT *519* **Gender Competition, Man-hating, Misogyny**
    See Also FEMINISM, GENDER STEREOTYPES
GENDER STEREOTYPES *519* **Traditional Female, Traditional Male**
    See Also FEMINISM, GENDER CONFLICT
General Store   *See* SHOPPING *1228*
Generals (Armed Forces)   *See* WAR *1427*
Generous   *See* CHARACTER & INTEGRITY *137*, HELP *590*
Genie   *See* SPIRITS *1269*
Genius   *See* THINKING & KNOWING *1349*
GENTLE *521* **Delicate, Soft, Tender**
    See Also CHARACTER & INTEGRITY, HELP, LOVE (various)
Gentleman   *See* CHARACTER & INTEGRITY *137*, MEN: GENERAL *867*, SOCIAL CLASS: GENERAL *1259*
Genuine   *See* TRUTH *1417*
Georgia   *See* STATES: GEORGIA *1286*
Germany   *See* COUNTRIES: GERMANY *273*
Germs   *See* CLEAN *211*, DIRT *371*, PAIN & HEALING *1025*
Get A Job   *See* WORK *1494*
Get Around   *See* TRAVELING *1392*
Get Back At   *See* REVENGE *1145*
Get Down   *See* DANCE *311*, PARTY *1038*
Get Help   *See* CRAZY *290*, HELP *590*, PAIN & HEALING *1025*
Get Lost   *See* INSULTS *627*, LOVE: GET LOST! *803*
Get Mad   *See* ANGER *44*, FIGHT *461*
Get Married   *See* MARRIAGE *860*

Get Out   *See* ESCAPE *412*, LEAVING *654*, LOVE: GET LOST! *803*
Get Up   *See* MORNING *924*, SLEEP *1243*
Get Well   *See* BACK ON MY FEET *78*, PAIN & HEALING *1025*
Getaway   *See* ESCAPE *412*, FREEDOM *499*, LEAVING *654*, REBELS *1126*, TRAVELING *1392*
Getting Acquainted   *See* HELLO *588*
Getting Drunk   *See* ALCOHOL *19*
Getting Even   *See* REVENGE *1145*
Getting High   *See* DRUGS (various) *388*
Getting Older   *See* AGING *12*, OLD *1012*
Getting Paid   *See* MONEY *906*
Getting Stoned   *See* DRUGS: MARIJUANA *393*
Getting To Know You   *See* HELLO *588*
Ghetto   *See* POVERTY *1063*
    See Also HARD CITY LIFE
Ghosts   *See* SPIRITS *1269*
Giant   *See* BIG *96*
Giants   *See* MONSTERS *913*
Gifted (smart)   *See* THINKING & KNOWING *1349*
Gigantic   *See* BIG *96*
Gigolos   *See* PROSTITUTES *1090*
Girlfriends   *See* FRIENDS *503*, LOVE (various) *701*
Girls   *See* WOMEN: GENERAL *1449*
    See Also CHILDREN
Give Birth   *See* BABY *74*
Give One's Word   *See* LOVE: DEVOTION *738*, PROMISE *1088*
Give Orders   *See* BOSSES *105*, POWER & CONTROL *1068*
Give Up   *See* DESPAIR *361*, ENDINGS *408*, LOSING & LOSS *696*
Glad   *See* HAPPINESS *555*, SMILE *1254*
Glass   *See* WINDOWS *1446*
Glitter   *See* GOLD *533*, JEWELRY *637*, LIGHT *679*
Gloating   *See* BRAGGING *107*
Global   *See* COUNTRIES: A-Z *263*, EARTH *394*, NATURE *961*, WORLD *1499*
Gloomy   *See* RAIN *1116*, SADNESS *1169*
Glut   *See* EXTREMES *417*
Go Crazy   *See* CRAZY *290*
Go On   *See* LIFE *662*, MOTIVATION *928*
Go To The Bathroom   *See* BATHROOMS *87*
Goal-seeking   *See* MOTIVATION *928*
Goblins   *See* SPIRITS *1269*
GOD *522* **Church, Faiths Of The World, Jesus Christ, Prayer, Religion**
    See Also ANGELS, BAD (sin), CHARACTER & INTEGRITY, CHRISTMAS, EASTER, FAITH, FORGIVE, GRATITUDE, HEAVEN, HELL, MARRIAGE, TEACHING VALUES
Goddess   *See* GOD *522*
Going   *See* LEAVING *654*
Going Back   *See* RETURNING *1142*
    See Also TRAVELING
Going Home   *See* HOME *608*, RETURNING *1142*
Going Out   *See* LOVE (various) *701*
Going Out On The Town   *See* PARTY *1038*
    See Also FUN
GOLD *533* **Golden**
    See Also JEWELRY, MINING, MONEY, SILVER
Golden   *See* GOLD *533*

Hanukkah   *See* GOD *522*

HAPPINESS *555* **Feeling Good, High Consciousness, High On Life, Joy, Liking The Way Things Are, Natural High**
See Also BEST, CAREFREE, FUN, GOOD, GRATITUDE, LOVE (various), PAIN & HEALING, OPTIMISM, PARTY, RELAX, SMILE, THINKING & KNOWING (enlightenment)

Happy Anniversary   *See* ANNIVERSARY *71*, HAPPINESS *555*, MARRIAGE *860*

Happy Birthday   *See* BIRTHDAY *99*

Happy-go-lucky   *See* CAREFREE *118*, RELAX *1132*

Harassment   *See* FEMINISM *460*, PREJUDICE *1071*

Harbor   *See* OCEAN *1008*

HARD CITY LIFE *566* **Gangsta Life**
See Also CITIES: A-Z, CITIES: GENERAL, POVERTY (ghetto)

Hard Drugs   *See* DRUGS (various) *388*

Hard Feelings   *See* ANGER *44*

Hard Luck   *See* LUCK *849*, TROUBLE *1412*

Hard Times   *See* POVERTY *1063*
See Also TROUBLE

Hard To Do   *See* DIFFICULT *364*

Hard To Find   *See* FINDING *464*

Hard Work   *See* WORK *1494*

Hardships   *See* DIFFICULT *364*, TROUBLE *1412*

Hare Krishna   *See* GOD *522*

Harlem   *See* CITIES: NEW YORK *198*

Harm   *See* DOMESTIC ABUSE *377*, FIGHT *461*, MISTREATMENT *905*, WAR *1427*

Harmony   *See* BROTHERHOOD *111*, MUSIC *942*, PEACE *1044*

Harvest   *See* FARMS *450*, SEASONS: AUTUMN *1190*

Hashish   *See* DRUGS: MARIJUANA *393*

Hassle   *See* COMPLAINTS *255*, DIFFICULT *364*, FIGHT *461*

Hasty   *See* BUSY *115*, URGENT *1420*

Hatchets   *See* TOOLS *1374*

HATE *567*
See Also ANGER, BROTHERHOOD, DIVORCE, FEELINGS, FIGHT, GENDER CONFLICT, LOVE (various), MISTREATMENT, POLITICS (various), PREJUDICE, PROTEST, REVENGE, WAR

Hate Oneself   *See* LOW SELF-ESTEEM *848*

HATS *567* **Berets, Veils**
See Also ANATOMY: HEAD, CLOTHES, FABRICS, SHOES, SHOPPING

Haunted   *See* SPIRITS *1269*

Haute Couture   *See* CLOTHES *213*

Havana   *See* CITIES: HAVANA *186*

Have An Attitude   *See* EGO *398*

Have An Urge   *See* DESIRE *346*

Have Control Over   *See* POWER & CONTROL *1068*

Haven't Got Time   *See* BUSY *115*, URGENT *1420*

Having Sex   *See* SEX *1213*

Havoc   *See* DANGER & DISASTER *323*

Hawaii   *See* STATES: HAWAII *1287*

Hazards   *See* DANGER & DISASTER *323*, DIFFICULT *364*, WARNINGS *1433*

Head   *See* ANATOMY: HEAD *35*

Headaches   *See* PAIN & HEALING *1025*

Headlines   *See* NEWS *964*

Healing   *See* PAIN & HEALING *1025*

Health   *See* PAIN & HEALING *1025*

Healthy   *See* PAIN & HEALING *1025*

HEAR *568* **Ears, Listen, Sound**
See Also COMMUNICATION (various), SILENCE, SOUNDS

HEART *571* **Valentines**
See Also BREAK, CHARACTER & INTEGRITY, FEELINGS, LOVE (various), MARRIAGE, MOTIVATION, PAIN & HEALING, SWEET

Heartache   *See* PAIN & HEALING *1025*
See Also HEART

Heartbeat   *See* HEART *571*

Heartbreak   *See* BREAK *108*, HEART *571*, LOVE (various) *701*, PAIN & HEALING *1025*, SADNESS *1169*

Heartland   *See* COUNTRY *282*, FARMS *450*, HEART *571*, SMALL TOWN LIFE *1253*

Heartless   *See* BAD *79*

Heat   *See* HOT *616*

HEAVEN *583* **Afterlife**
See Also ANGELS, DEATH, DEVILS, FAITH, GOD, HAPPINESS, HELL, PARADISE

Heavy   *See* BAGGAGE & WEIGHT *83*

Heights   *See* MOUNTAINS *937*

Helicopters   *See* AIRPLANES *17*

HELL *587*
See Also ANGELS, BAD (sin), DEATH, DEVILS, GOD, HEAVEN

HELLO *588* **Getting To Know You, Greetings, Meeting, Welcome**
See Also BEGINNINGS, LEAVING, MORNING, RETURNING

HELP *590* **Comfort, Compassion, Protect, Reassure, Rescue, Safe, Save, Shelter, Support, Sympathy**
See Also ANGELS, CHARACTER & INTEGRITY, DANGER & DISASTER, DESIRE, DESPAIR, FAITH, FEELINGS, FORGIVE, FRIENDS, GOD, GRATITUDE, HOLDING ON, HUG, LOVE (various), MOTIVATION, OPTIMISM, PAIN & HEALING, PROMISE, SADNESS, TROUBLE

Help Wanted Ads   *See* NEWS *964*, WORK *1494*

Helpless   *See* HELP *590*, STUCK *1318*

Herbs & Spices   *See* FOOD & BEVERAGES: GENERAL *486*

Here   *See* PLACES *1049*

Heritage   *See* HISTORY *603*

Heroin   *See* DRUGS: GENERAL *389*

Heroines   *See* HEROISM *597*

HEROISM *597*
See Also CHARACTER & INTEGRITY, DANGER & DISASTER, FEAR & COURAGE, HELP, PATRIOTISM, WAR, WINNING

Hide & Seek   *See* HIDING *600*, SEARCH *1186*, TOYS & GAMES *1377*

HIDING *600* **Conceal, Sneak**
See Also CHEATING & LIES, CRIME, ESCAPE, FEAR & COURAGE, FINDING, LAW & ORDER, LOVE: FORBIDDEN LOVE, LOW SELF-ESTEEM, PRETEND, REBELS, SEARCH, SECRETS, TOYS & GAMES

High   *See* AIR *16*, AIRPLANES *17*, ANIMALS: BIRDS *46*, DRUGS (various) *388*, FLYING *479*, MOUNTAINS *937*, SKY *1239*

High Class   *See* MONEY *906*, SOCIAL CLASS: GENERAL *1259*

High Consciousness   *See* HAPPINESS *555*

High Heels   *See* SHOES *1226*

I

M

Pools *See* SPORTS: SWIMMING *1276*

Poor *See* POVERTY *1063*

Poor Health *See* PAIN & HEALING *1025*

Poor Self-esteem *See* LOW SELF-ESTEEM *848*

Popular *See* COOL *260*

Pornography *See* ART & PHOTOGRAPHY *71*, NEWS (magazines) *964*, PROSTITUTES *1090*, SEX *1213*

Porpoises *See* ANIMALS: DOLPHINS *56*

Porters (train) *See* TRAINS *1383*

Portraits *See* ART & PHOTOGRAPHY *71*

Position *See* PLACES *1049*

Positive Attitude *See* OPTIMISM *1023*

Possessed *See* CRAZY *290*, DEVILS *362*

Possible *See* DREAMS *380*, EASY *396*, MOTIVATION *928*, PRETEND *1074*

Post Office *See* MAIL *857*

Potential *See* MOTIVATION *928*, NEW *963*

Pots & Pans *See* FOOD & BEVERAGES: GENERAL *486*

Pounds (British) *See* MONEY *906*

Pounds (weight) *See* BAGGAGE & WEIGHT *83*, FAT *452*

POVERTY *1063* **Broke, Ghetto, Hard Times, Homeless, Poor**
See Also DIFFICULT, GAMBLING, HARD CITY LIFE, LOVE: LOVE & MONEY, LUCK, MONEY, POLITICS (various), ROYALTY, SLAVERY, SOCIAL CLASS: GENERAL, SOCIAL CLASS: RURAL, TRAINS, TROUBLE, WORK

Powder *See* COSMETICS *261*

Power (nuclear) *See* NUCLEAR ENERGY *987*

Power (political) *See* POLITICS (various) *1058*, PROTEST *1091*

POWER & CONTROL *1068* **Authority, Force**
See Also BOSSES, BUSINESS & INDUSTRY, EGO, ENERGY, KINGS, LAW & ORDER, MACHINES, MONEY, MOTIVATION, POLICE, POLITICS (various), QUEENS, ROYALTY, SOCIAL CLASS: GENERAL, STRONG, STUCK

Power Of Love *See* LOVE: GENERAL *766*, POWER & CONTROL *1068*

Prairie *See* COUNTRY *282*
See Also AMERICAN WEST

Praise *See* COMPLIMENTS *256*

Prayer *See* GOD *522*

Preach *See* ADVICE *1*, GOD *522*, WARNINGS *1433*

Precious *See* SPECIAL *1267*

Precious Stones *See* JEWELRY *637*

Predicament *See* STUCK *1318*, TROUBLE *1412*

Predictions *See* FUTURE *511*

Prefer *See* DECISIONS *343*

Pregnant *See* BABY *74*
See Also BEGINNINGS, FAMILY PLANNING, PARENTS (various)

PREJUDICE *1071* **Bigotry, Segregation**
See Also BROTHERHOOD, GENDER CONFLICT, GENDER STEREOTYPES, HARD CITY LIFE, HATE, HISTORY, LOVE: FORBIDDEN LOVE, MISTREATMENT, POLITICS (various), PROTEST, SLAVERY, SOCIAL CLASS: GENERAL, SOCIAL CLASS: RURAL

Premonition *See* DREAMS *380*, WARNINGS *1433*

Prescriptions *See* DRUGS: GENERAL *389*
See Also PAIN & HEALING

PRESIDENTS *1073*
See Also CELEBRITIES: SPECIFIC, COUNTRIES: A-Z, COUNTRIES: AMERICA, HISTORY, KINGS, MEN'S NAMES: A-Z, PATRIOTISM, POLITICS (various), POWER & CONTROL, QUEENS, ROYALTY, WOMEN'S NAMES: A-Z

Press (newspaper) *See* NEWS *964*

Pressures *See* FEAR & COURAGE *453*, TROUBLE *1412*

PRETEND *1074* **Disguise, Fantasy, Imagine, Virtual, Wish, Wonder**
See Also CHARACTER & INTEGRITY, CHEATING & LIES, DESIRE, DREAMS, FAKE, HIDING, QUESTIONS & ANSWERS, SECRETS, STRANGE, TRUTH

Pretty *See* BEAUTY *88*

Prices *See* MONEY *906*, SHOPPING *1228*

Pride *See* EGO *398*

Priests *See* GOD *522*

Primary *See* NUMBERS: 1 *988*

Prince Charming *See* KINGS *646*, LOVE (various) *701*, STORYBOOK CHARACTERS *1306*

Princes *See* KINGS *646*

Princesses *See* QUEENS *1095*

Principals *See* SCHOOL *1181*

Principles *See* ADVICE *1*, CHARACTER & INTEGRITY *137*, TEACHING VALUES *1335*

Printing *See* BOOKS *101*

Priority *See* URGENT *1420*

Prisms *See* COLORS: GENERAL *229*

PRISON *1082* **Chains, Doing Time**
See Also CAPITAL PUNISHMENT, CRIME, ESCAPE, FREEDOM, LAW & ORDER, POLICE, POLITICS (various), PROTEST, REBELS, STRINGS & ROPE, STUCK, WALLS

Private *See* SECRETS *1201*
See Also HIDING

Private Eyes *See* POLICE *1055*

Private Parts *See* ANATOMY: SEXUAL *38*

Privates (Army) *See* WAR *1427*

Problems *See* TROUBLE *1412*
See Also DIFFICULT

PRODUCTS & BRANDS: SPECIFIC *1085*
See Also BUSINESS & INDUSTRY, CARS: CADILLAC, CARS: SPECIFIC MAKES & MODELS, FOOD & BEVERAGES (various), SHOPPING, TELEVISION (theme songs)

Professionals *See* BUSINESS & INDUSTRY *114*, WORK *1494*

Prognosis *See* FUTURE *511*, PAIN & HEALING *1025*

Programs (computer) *See* COMPUTERS *259*

Progress *See* BUSINESS & INDUSTRY *114*, CHANGES *135*

Projects (slums) *See* HARD CITY LIFE *566*, POVERTY *1063*

PROMISE *1088* **Pledge, Swear**
See Also CHARACTER & INTEGRITY, CHEATING & LIES, DECISIONS, FAITH, GOD, HELP, LOVE: DEVOTION, MARRIAGE, MOTIVATION, SEX: RESISTING TEMPTATION, TOGETHERNESS, TRUTH

Promised Land *See* GOD *522*, HEAVEN *583*, PLACES *1049*

Proms *See* PARTY *1038*, SCHOOL *1181*

Propaganda *See* POLITICS (various) *1058*

Prophets *See* FUTURE *511*

Propose *See* LOVE: CHOOSE ME *711*, MARRIAGE *860*

PROSTITUTES *1090* **Exotic Dancers, Gigolos, Pimps, Strippers**
    See Also DANCE, LOVE: COMMITTED OR NOT?, SEX

Protect *See* HELP *590*

PROTEST *1091* **Political Demonstrations, Revolution**
    See Also BROTHERHOOD, COUNTRIES: A-Z, COUNTRIES: AMERICA, DRAFT, FIGHT, FREEDOM, LAW & ORDER, NATURE, NUCLEAR ENERGY, PATRIOTISM, POLITICS (various), POWER & CONTROL, PREJUDICE, WAR, WORK

Proud *See* EGO *398*

Provincial *See* COUNTRY *282*, SMALL TOWN LIFE *1253*

Psychedelics *See* DRUGS: GENERAL *389*

Psychiatry *See* CRAZY *290*

Psychics *See* ASTROLOGY *74*, FUTURE *511*, SPIRITS *1269*

Psychotic *See* CRAZY *290*

Public Transportation *See* AIRPLANES *17*, BUS *113*, FLYING *479*, SAILING *1179*, SHIPS *1224*, TAXI *1334*, TRAINS *1383*, TRAVELING *1392*

Publicity *See* NEWS *964*, SHOW BIZ *1230*

Pubs *See* BARS *84*

Pull Through *See* BACK ON MY FEET *78*, LIFE *662*, MOTIVATION *928*, PAIN & HEALING *1025*

Punishment *See* CRIME *297*, LAW & ORDER *652*, PRISON *1082*

Punks *See* CRIME *297*, REBELS *1126*

Puppets *See* TOYS & GAMES *1377*

Puppies *See* ANIMALS: DOGS *53*

Puppy Love *See* LOVE: YOUNG LOVE *846*

Purple *See* COLORS: PURPLE *233*

Pursue *See* CHASING *139*, MOTIVATION *928*, SEARCH *1186*

Pushers *See* DRUGS (various) *388*

Put Back Together *See* BACK ON MY FEET *78*, BITS & PIECES *100*, FIXING *471*, LOVE: BACK TOGETHER *701*

Put Into Words *See* COMMUNICATION: WORDS *253*, LOVE: LOOKING FOR THE WORDS *809*

Put To Death *See* CAPITAL PUNISHMENT *117*

Puzzled *See* CRAZY *290*, STRANGE *1308*, THINKING & KNOWING *1349*

Puzzles *See* TOYS & GAMES *1377*

Q

Quality *See* BEST *94*
    See Also GOOD, SPECIAL

Quandary *See* DECISIONS *343*, DIFFICULT *364*

Quantity *See* COUNTING SONGS *262*

QUEENS *1095* **Princesses**
    See Also BOSSES, CELEBRITIES: SPECIFIC, COUNTRIES: A-Z, KINGS, POLITICS (various), POWER & CONTROL, PRESIDENTS, PROTEST, ROYALTY, SOCIAL CLASS: GENERAL, WOMEN'S NAMES: A-Z

Queens (N.Y.C.) *See* CITIES: NEW YORK *198*

QUESTIONS & ANSWERS *1097*
    See Also COMMUNICATION (various), DECISIONS, DESIRE, PRETEND, REASONS, STRANGE, THINKING & KNOWING

Quick *See* FAST *451*

Quiet *See* SILENCE *1235*

Quit *See* ENDINGS *408*, STOP *1304*, WORK *1494*

R

R & B *See* MUSIC *942*, RHYTHM *1146*

Rabbits *See* ANIMALS: RABBITS *66*

Race Cars *See* CARS: GENERAL *125*, SPORTS: CAR RACING *1271*

Race Differences (love) *See* LOVE: FORBIDDEN LOVE *764*

Racehorses *See* ANIMALS: HORSES *59*, SPORTS: GENERAL *1273*

Racetrack (car) *See* SPORTS: CAR RACING *1271*

Racetrack (horses) *See* SPORTS: GENERAL *1273*

Racing *See* SPORTS (various) *1271*

Racism *See* PREJUDICE *1071*

Radar *See* MACHINES *851*
    See Also AIRPLANES, POLICE

Radiation *See* NUCLEAR ENERGY *987*

RADIO *1113* **DJs, Radio Stations**
    See Also CARS (various), FUN, HEAR, JUKEBOX, MUSIC, PARTY, RECORD BUSINESS, ROCK & ROCKING, SHOW BIZ, TELEVISION

Radio Stations *See* RADIO *1113*

Radioactive *See* NUCLEAR ENERGY *987*

Rage *See* ANGER *44*, FIGHT *461*

Ragged *See* BREAK *108*

Rags *See* CLOTHES *213*, POVERTY *1063*

Railroad *See* TRAINS *1383*

RAIN *1116* **Fog, Hurricanes, Lightning, Storms, Thunder, Tornado**
    See Also CRYING, DANGER & DISASTER, DROWN, FLOOD, LIGHTHOUSES, NATURE, OCEAN, RAINBOWS, RIVERS, SADNESS, SAILING, SHIPS, SKY, SUN, TROUBLE, WARNINGS, WATER, WIND

RAINBOWS *1123*
    See Also COLORS (various), HAPPINESS, NATURE, RAIN

Rainforest *See* JUNGLES *641*, NATURE *961*

Raising A Family *See* FAMILY (various) *433*

Raising Hell *See* REBELS *1126*

Rally *See* PROTEST *1091*

Rambling *See* TRAVELING *1392*

Ranch *See* COWBOYS *286*

Range *See* AMERICAN WEST *25*, ANIMALS: HORSES *59*, COWBOYS *286*

Rare *See* SPECIAL *1267*

Rat Race *See* LIFE *662*, WORK *1494*

Rational *See* THINKING & KNOWING *1349*

Rats *See* ANIMALS: RATS *66*

Raunchy *See* SEX *1213*

Raving *See* CRAZY *290*

Raze *See* BITS & PIECES *100*, BUILDING & CONSTRUCTION *112*

Reach A Decision *See* DECISIONS *343*

Reach Out *See* HELP *590*, HOLDING ON *605*

Reading *See* BOOKS *101*

Real *See* TRUTH *1417*
    See Also FAKE

Rhythm & Blues *See* MUSIC *942*
RIBBONS *1148* **Adornments**
   See Also ANATOMY: HAIR, CLOTHES, COSMETICS,
   FABRICS, HATS
Rich *See* MONEY *906*
Rich & Famous *See* CELEBRITIES: SPECIFIC *133*,
   MONEY *906*, SHOW BIZ *1230*
Ride *See* ANIMALS: HORSES *59*, HITCHHIKING *605*,
   ROAD *1154*, TRAVELING *1392*
Rides *See* CARNIVALS *121*
Ridges *See* MOUNTAINS *937*
Ridiculous *See* FOOLS *494*
Riding *See* ANIMALS: HORSES *59*
Riding In Cars *See* CARS: GENERAL *125*
Rifles *See* GUNS *550*
RIGHT *1148*
   See Also WRONG
Right From Wrong *See* TEACHING VALUES *1335*
Right Now *See* URGENT *1420*
Rights *See* POLITICS (various) *1058*
Ring (bells) *See* BELLS *93*
Ring (telephone) *See* TELEPHONE *1339*
Rings *See* JEWELRY *637*
   See Also ANATOMY: HANDS, GOLD, MARRIAGE
Rio De Janeiro *See* CITIES: RIO DE JANEIRO *205*
Riot *See* DANGER & DISASTER *323*, PROTEST *1091*
Rip *See* BREAK *108*
Risk *See* GAMBLING *515*
   See Also DANGER & DISASTER
Riverboat Gambling *See* GAMBLING *515*
Riverboats *See* RIVERS *1149*, SHIPS *1224*
RIVERS *1149* **Bayou, Creeks, Delta, Streams**
   See Also DANGER & DISASTER, DROWN, FLOOD,
   OCEAN, RAIN, SAILING, SHIPS, SPORTS:
   SWIMMING, WATER
ROAD *1154* **Highway, Trail**
   See Also BUS, CARS (various), DIRECTIONS (various),
   DISTANCE, HITCHHIKING, LEAVING,
   MOTORCYCLES, REBELS, RETURNING, ROAD
   ACCIDENTS, SPORTS: CAR RACING, SIGNS,
   STREETS: GENERAL, STREETS: SPECIFIC, TAXI,
   TRAVELING, TRUCKS
ROAD ACCIDENTS *1159* **Wrecks**
   See Also CARS (various), DANGER & DISASTER,
   DEATH, MOTORCYCLES, ROAD, TRUCKS
Roadhouse *See* BARS *84*
Roaming *See* TRAVELING *1392*
Roar *See* COMMUNICATION: SHOUT *244*
Robbery *See* CRIME *297*
Robots *See* MACHINES *851*
Rock 'n' Roll *See* ROCK & ROCKING *1160*
ROCK & ROCKING *1160* **Rock & Roll, Rock 'n' Roll**
   See Also BABY, DANCE, ELVIS, FUN, MOUNTAINS,
   MUSIC, MUSICAL INSTRUMENTS (various), PARTY,
   RADIO, RECORD BUSINESS, RHYTHM, SEX, SHOW
   BIZ, STONES
Rock & Roll *See* ROCK & ROCKING *1160*
Rock Star *See* MUSIC *942*, RECORD BUSINESS *1130*,
   ROCK & ROCKING *1160*, SHOW BIZ *1230*
Rockets *See* SPACE *1265*
Rocking Chairs *See* FURNITURE *510*, ROCK &
   ROCKING *1160*

Rocks *See* STONES *1303*
Rodents *See* ANIMALS: A-Z *45*
RODEO *1167*
   See Also AMERICAN WEST, ANIMALS: COWS,
   ANIMALS: HORSES, COWBOYS
Rogues *See* REBELS *1126*
Roller coaster *See* CARNIVALS *121*
Roller Skating *See* SPORTS: GENERAL *1273*
Romance *See* LOVE: GENERAL *766*
Rome *See* CITIES: ROME *205*
Roofs *See* HOUSES *621*
Room (hotel) *See* HOTELS *619*
Rooms *See* HOUSES *621*
   See Also HOME
Roosters *See* ANIMALS: BIRDS *46*
Rope *See* STRINGS & ROPE *1316*
Roses *See* FLOWERS: ROSES *476*
Rotate *See* CIRCLES *170*
Roulette *See* GAMBLING *515*
Round *See* CIRCLES *170*
Route *See* ROAD *1154*, TRAVELING *1392*
Rowboats *See* SHIPS *1224*
Rowdy *See* REBELS *1126*
ROYALTY *1168* **Castles, Nobility**
   See Also BOSSES, KINGS, MONEY, POLITICS (various),
   POWER & CONTROL, PREJUDICE, PRESIDENTS,
   PROTEST, QUEENS, SOCIAL CLASS: GENERAL
Rubbish *See* TRASH *1391*
Rubies *See* JEWELRY *637*
Rugged *See* DIFFICULT *364*
Ruin *See* DANGER & DISASTER *323*
Rulers *See* KINGS *646*, QUEENS *1095*, ROYALTY *1168*
Rules & Regulations *See* LAW & ORDER *652*, POLICE *1055*,
   POLITICS: POLITICS & GOVERNMENT *1061*
Ruling Class *See* SOCIAL CLASS: GENERAL *1259*
Rumors *See* GOSSIP *540*
Run (control) *See* POWER & CONTROL *1068*
Run (exercise) *See* SPORTS: GENERAL *1273*
Run Out *See* ENDINGS *408*, ESCAPE *412*, LEAVING *654*
Runaround *See* CHEATING & LIES *140*, LOVE (various) *701*
Runaways *See* REBELS *1126*
   See Also CHILDREN LEAVING HOME, DOMESTIC
   ABUSE, SOCIAL OUTCASTS, TEENAGERS,
   TRAVELING, TROUBLE
Running *See* TRAVELING *1392*
Running Wild *See* REBELS *1126*
Rural *See* COUNTRY *282*, FARMS *450*
Rural Living *See* SMALL TOWN LIFE *1253*
   See Also SOCIAL CLASS: RURAL
Rush *See* BUSY *115*, FAST *451*, URGENT *1420*
Russia *See* COUNTRIES: RUSSIA *279*
Rustic *See* COUNTRY *282*, FARMS *450*, SOCIAL CLASS:
   RURAL *1261*

S

S.O.S. *See* DANGER & DISASTER *323*, HELP *590*
Sabbath *See* DAYS OF THE WEEK: SATURDAY *329*, DAYS
   OF THE WEEK: SUNDAY *331*, GOD *522*
Sacred *See* GOD *522*

Self-confidence *See* MOTIVATION *928*

Self-control *See* POWER & CONTROL *1068*

Self-criticism *See* LOW SELF-ESTEEM *848*

Self-doubt *See* LOW SELF-ESTEEM *848*

Self-esteem Issues *See* LOW SELF-ESTEEM *848*

Self-hatred *See* LOW SELF-ESTEEM *848*

Self-respect *See* EGO *398*
 See Also CHARACTER & INTEGRITY

Selfishness *See* EGO *398*
 See Also GREED

Selling *See* SHOPPING *1228*

Semi (trucks) *See* TRUCKS *1414*

Send *See* MAIL *857*

Senior High *See* SCHOOL *1181*, TEENAGERS *1336*

Senior Prom *See* PARTY *1038*, SCHOOL *1181*,
 TEENAGERS *1336*

Sensational *See* BEST *94*, COMPLIMENTS *256*,
 SPECIAL *1267*

Sense *See* THINKING & KNOWING *1349*

Sensitivity *See* FEELINGS *456*
 See Also CHARACTER & INTEGRITY

Sentence (jail) *See* LAW & ORDER *652*, PRISON *1082*

Sentimental *See* REMEMBER *1133*
 See Also LOVE (various)

SEPARATION *1210* **Being Apart**
 See Also DISTANCE, DIVORCE, LEAVING, LOVE
 (various), LONELY, RETURNING, SADNESS,
 SOLITUDE, TRAVELING, WAITING

September *See* MONTHS & DATES: SEPTEMBER *919*

Serenity *See* PEACE *1044*

Sermons *See* ADVICE *1*, GOD *522*

Servants *See* ROYALTY *1168*, SLAVERY *1242*

Servers *See* WAITRESSES *1426*

Settle *See* DECISIONS *343*

Seven *See* NUMBERS: 7 *1004*

Seventeen *See* AGES: 17 *11*, NUMBERS: 11-99 *994*

Seventh *See* NUMBERS: 7 *1004*

Sewer *See* TRASH *1391*

SEX *1213* **Having Sex, Impotence, Lust, Sex Appeal, Sexy**
 See Also AIDS, ANATOMY (various), DESIRE, FAMILY
 PLANNING, KISSING, LOVE (various), PROSTITUTES,
 SEX: RESISTING TEMPTATION

Sex Appeal *See* SEX *1213*

Sex Organs *See* ANATOMY: SEXUAL *38*

SEX: RESISTING TEMPTATION *1222*
 See Also AIDS, CHARACTER & INTEGRITY, FAMILY
 PLANNING, LOVE (various), PARENTS: CONCERNED
 ABOUT TEEN LOVE, SEX

Sex Roles *See* GENDER STEREOTYPES *519*

Sexual Assault *See* CRIME *297*

Sexual Reproduction *See* ANATOMY: SEXUAL *38*, FAMILY
 PLANNING *432*, SEX *1213*

Sexual Variations *See* HOMOSEXUALS *616*

Sexuality *See* HOMOSEXUALS *616*, SEX *1213*

Sexually Transmitted Diseases *See* AIDS *16*, FAMILY
 PLANNING *432*, PAIN & HEALING *1025*, SEX *1213*,
 SEX: RESISTING TEMPTATION *1222*

Sexy *See* SEX *1213*
 See Also BEAUTY, DESIRE

Shackles *See* PRISON *1082*, STRINGS & ROPE *1316*

Shade *See* SHADOWS *1222*, TREES *1410*

SHADOWS *1222* **Eclipse**
 See Also ECHOES, LIGHT, REFLECTIONS

Shaking *See* DANCE *311*
 See Also EARTHQUAKE

Shame *See* GUILT *544*

Shampoo *See* ANATOMY: HAIR *31*, CLEAN *211*

Sharecroppers *See* FARMS *450*, POVERTY *1063*,
 SLAVERY *1242*

Sharks *See* ANIMALS: FISH *57*

Shatter *See* BREAK *108*

Sheep *See* ANIMALS: SHEEP *69*

Sheiks *See* KINGS *646*, ROYALTY *1168*

Shelter *See* HELP *590*
 See Also HOME, HOUSES

Shepherds *See* ANIMALS: SHEEP *69*

Sheriff *See* POLICE *1055*

Shhh! *See* COMMUNICATION: WHISPER *253*,
 SILENCE *1235*

Shine *See* LIGHT *679*

Shins *See* ANATOMY: LEGS *36*

SHIPS *1224* **Boats, Shipwrecks, Submarines**
 See Also ANIMALS (various), DROWNING,
 LIGHTHOUSES, OCEAN, PIRATES, RIVERS, SAILING,
 TRAVELING, WAR, WATER

Shipwrecks *See* SHIPS *1224*
 See Also DANGER & DISASTER

Shirts *See* CLOTHES *213*

Shiver *See* COLD *217*

Shock *See* CRAZY *290*

Shock (electric) *See* ENERGY *411*

SHOES *1226* **Boots**
 See Also ANATOMY: FEET, CLOTHES, HATS,
 SHOPPING, TRAVELING

Shooting *See* GUNS *550*
 See Also CRIME, KILL

Shooting Up *See* DRUGS (various) *388*

Shoplifting *See* CRIME *297*, SHOPPING *1228*

SHOPPING *1228* **Buying, Selling, Stores**
 See Also BUSINESS & INDUSTRY, LOVE: LOVE &
 MONEY, MONEY, NEWS, PRODUCTS & BRANDS:
 SPECIFIC, RADIO, TELEVISION

Shore *See* OCEAN *1008*

Short *See* SMALL *1247*

Shotguns *See* GUNS *550*

Shoulder *See* ANATOMY: SHOULDER *39*

Shout *See* COMMUNICATION: SHOUT *244*

SHOW BIZ *1230* **Fame, Stardom**
 See Also BUSINESS & INDUSTRY, CITIES: A-Z,
 CITIES: NEW YORK (Broadway), COUNTRY, ELVIS,
 HOLLYWOOD, MONEY, MOVIES, MUSIC, RADIO,
 RECORD BUSINESS, ROCK & ROCKING, STREETS:
 SPECIFIC, TELEVISION

Show Off *See* BRAGGING *107*, EGO *398*

Shower *See* BATHROOMS *87*

Showers *See* RAIN *1116*

Shriek *See* COMMUNICATION: SCREAM *244*

Shuffle *See* DANCE *311*

Shut *See* OPEN & CLOSED *1016*

Shy *See* FEAR & COURAGE *453*

Sickness *See* PAIN & HEALING *1025*

Side By Side *See* COUPLES *285*

Side Show *See* CARNIVALS *121*

Stepfamily *See* FAMILY (various) *433*, PARENTS: SINGLE, STEP, ABSENT *1037*

Stepping *See* TRAVELING *1392*

Stereotypes *See* GENDER STEREOTYPES *519*, PREJUDICE *1071*

Stick To *See* HOLDING ON *605*

Still Miss You *See* LOVE: CAN'T GET OVER YOU *702*, LOVE: LONG GONE *806*

Stillness *See* SILENCE *1235*

Stimulants *See* ALCOHOL *19*, DRUGS: GENERAL *389*

Sting *See* ANIMALS: INSECTS *61*, PAIN & HEALING *1025*

Stockade *See* PRISON *1082*

Stockings *See* CLOTHES *213*

Stocks & Bonds *See* MONEY *906*

Stomach *See* ANATOMY: BODY *28*

STONES *1303* **Bricks, Rocks**
    See Also MOUNTAINS, ROCK & ROCKING

STOP *1304*
    See Also BEGINNINGS, ENDINGS, OPEN & CLOSED

Stores *See* SHOPPING *1228*

Stories *See* BOOKS *101*

Storms *See* RAIN *1116*

STORYBOOK CHARACTERS *1306*
    See Also BOOKS, CARTOON CHARACTERS

Straightforward *See* CHARACTER & INTEGRITY *137*, EASY *396*, TRUTH *1417*

STRANGE *1308* **Mystery, Strangers, Unknown**
    See Also MAGIC, PEOPLE, PRETEND, QUESTIONS & ANSWERS, REASONS, SECRETS, SPIRITS, THINKING & KNOWING, UFO'S

Strangers *See* STRANGE *1308*

Strangle *See* KILL *642*

Straw *See* FARMS *450*

Stray *See* LOST & MISPLACED *699*, TRAVELING *1392*

Streamlined *See* EASY *396*

Streams *See* RIVERS *1149*

Street Corners *See* STREETS: GENERAL *1312*

Street Life *See* HARD CITY LIFE *566*, POVERTY *1063*, SOCIAL OUTCASTS *1262*

Street Racing *See* SPORTS: CAR RACING *1271*
    See Also CARS: GENERAL

STREETS: GENERAL *1312* **Sidewalks**
    See Also BUS, CARS (various), CITIES: A-Z, DIRECTIONS (various), HITCHHIKING, MOTORCYCLES, PLACES, ROAD, ROAD ACCIDENTS, STREETS: SPECIFIC, TAXI, TRAVELING, TRUCKS

STREETS: SPECIFIC *1314* **Addresses**
    See Also CITIES: A-Z, CITIES: NEW YORK (Broadway), PLACES, STREETS: GENERAL

Streetwalkers *See* PROSTITUTES *1090*

Strength *See* STRONG *1317*

Stress *See* CRAZY *290*

Strike (hit) *See* FIGHT *461*

Strike Back *See* REVENGE *1145*

Strikes (workers) *See* POLITICS: POLITICAL CLASSICS *1058*, POLITICS: SOCIAL INJUSTICE *1061*, WORK *1494*

Stringed Instruments *See* MUSICAL INSTRUMENTS: FIDDLES & VIOLINS *956*, MUSICAL INSTRUMENTS: GUITARS *957*, MUSICAL INSTRUMENTS: MANDOLINS *958*

STRINGS & ROPE *1316*
    See Also CAPITAL PUNISHMENT, HOLDING ON, LOVE: CAN'T GET OVER YOU, PRISON, STUCK

Strip-mining *See* MINING *903*, NATURE *961*

Strippers *See* PROSTITUTES *1090*
    See Also SEX

Striving *See* MOTIVATION *928*

Strolling *See* TRAVELING *1392*

STRONG *1317* **Tough**
    See Also CHARACTER & INTEGRITY, EGO, FAITH, FEAR & COURAGE, FEMINISM, HEROISM, MOTIVATION, POWER & CONTROL

Structures *See* BUILDING & CONSTRUCTION *112*

Struggle *See* FIGHT *461*

Struggling *See* DIFFICULT *364*, POVERTY *1063*

STUCK *1318* **Frustration, Manipulated, Stymied, Trapped**
    See Also DECISIONS, ESCAPE, HOLDING ON, LOVE (various), PRISON, SLEEP, STRINGS & ROPES, WALLS

Student Demonstrations *See* PROTEST *1091*

Students *See* SCHOOL *1181*

Stuffed Animals *See* TOYS & GAMES *1377*

Stumbling Blocks *See* DIFFICULT *364*, MOTIVATION *928*, TROUBLE *1412*

Stunned *See* CRAZY *290*

Stupid *See* FOOLS *494*
    See Also THINKING & KNOWING

Stylish *See* COOL *260*
    See Also CLOTHES

Stymied *See* STUCK *1318*

Submarines *See* SHIPS *1224*

Submerged *See* DROWN *388*, OCEAN *1008*, RIVERS *1149*, SHIPS *1224*

Substance Abuse *See* ALCOHOL *19*, ALCOHOL: RECOVERING ALCOHOLIC *25*, DRUGS (various) *388*

Substantial *See* BIG *96*

Substitute *See* FAKE *430*, PRETEND *1074*

Subways *See* TRAINS *1383*

Success *See* WINNING *1447*

Sudden *See* FAST *451*

Sue (bring suit) *See* LAW & ORDER *652*

Suede *See* CLOTHES *213*, FABRICS *424*

Suffer A Loss *See* LOSING & LOSS *696*

Suffering *See* PAIN & HEALING *1025*
    See Also DOMESTIC ABUSE, LOVE (various), MISTREATMENT

Sugar *See* SWEET *1328*

Suggestions *See* ADVICE *1*

SUICIDE *1322*
    See Also DEATH, DESPAIR, KILL, LOW SELF-ESTEEM, SADNESS

Suitcases *See* BAGGAGE & WEIGHT *83*

Suits *See* CLOTHES *213*

Sultans *See* KINGS *646*

Sum Up *See* COUNTING SONGS *262*

Summer *See* SEASONS: SUMMER *1195*

SUN *1323*
    See Also FIRE, HOT, LIGHT, MORNING, NIGHT, RAIN, SEASONS: SUMMER, SKY, SPACE, STARS

Sunday *See* DAYS OF THE WEEK: SUNDAY *331*, WEEKEND *1440*

Sunglasses *See* EYES *418*

Sunlight   *See* SUN *1323*

Syphilis   *See* PAIN & HEALING *1025*

Sunrise   *See* MORNING *924*
   See Also SUN

Sunset   *See* SUN *1323*

Superb   *See* BEST *94*

Superheroes   *See* CARTOON CHARACTERS *130*,
   HEROISM *597*, STORYBOOK CHARACTERS *1306*,
   TELEVISION *1342*

Superiority   *See* BEST *94*

Superlatives   *See* BEST *94*
   See Also SPECIAL

Supermarkets   *See* SHOPPING *1228*

Supernatural   *See* MAGIC *853*
   See Also STRANGE

Superstars   *See* SHOW BIZ *1230*

Superstition   *See* MAGIC *853*

Supervise   *See* BOSSES *105*, WORK *1494*

Supper   *See* FOOD & BEVERAGES: GENERAL *486*

Support   *See* HELP *590*

Suppress   *See* POWER & CONTROL *1068*

Supremely   *See* BEST *94*, EXTREMES *417*, SPECIAL *1267*

Surfing   *See* SPORTS: SURFING *1275*

Surprise   *See* URGENT *1420*

Surrender   *See* WAR *1427*
   See Also LOSING & LOSS

Surround   *See* CIRCLES *170*

Survive   *See* LIFE *662*
   See Also BACK ON MY FEET, FAITH, HELP,
   MOTIVATION, PAIN & HEALING

Suspicion   *See* CHEATING & LIES *140*, HIDING *600*,
   SECRETS *1201*

Swamp   *See* OCEAN *1008*

Swap Meets   *See* SHOPPING *1228*

Sway   *See* POWER & CONTROL *1068*

Swear   *See* PROMISE *1088*
   See Also LOVE: DEVOTION

Sweat   *See* HOT *616*

Sweden   *See* COUNTRIES: SWEDEN *281*

Sweep   *See* CLEAN *211*, DIRT *371*

SWEET *1328* **Honey, Sugar**
   See Also BEST, CANDY, COMPLIMENTS, FOOD &
   BEVERAGES (various), HEART, LOVE
   (various), SPECIAL

Sweet Sixteen   *See* AGES: 16 *10*, BIRTHDAY *99*

Sweetheart   *See* LOVE (various) *701*

Swimming   *See* SPORTS: SWIMMING *1276*

Swimsuits   *See* CLOTHES *213*

Swindler   *See* CHEATING & LIES *140*, CRIME *297*

Swing (music)   *See* MUSIC *942*

Swirl   *See* CIRCLES *170*

Switch   *See* CHANGES *135*

Switchboard   *See* TELEPHONE *1339*

Switzerland   *See* COUNTRIES: SWITZERLAND *281*

Swords   *See* TOOLS *1374*
   See Also WAR

Symbols   *See* SIGNS *1235*

Sympathy   *See* HELP *590*

Symphony   *See* MUSIC *942*

Symptoms   *See* PAIN & HEALING *1025*, SIGNS *1235*

Syncopation   *See* MUSIC *942*, RHYTHM *1146*

Synthetic   *See* FAKE *430*

T

T.V.   *See* TELEVISION *1342*

Tabloids   *See* NEWS *964*

Tact   *See* CHARACTER & INTEGRITY *137*

Take A Bath   *See* BATHROOMS *87*

Take A Chance   *See* GAMBLING *515*

Take A Trip   *See* TRAVELING *1392*

Take Charge   *See* POWER & CONTROL *1068*

Take Comfort   *See* HELP *590*

Take It Easy   *See* RELAX *1132*

Take Me Back   *See* LOVE: DON'T WANT TO
   BREAK UP *748*

Take The Train   *See* LEAVING *654*, TRAINS *1383*,
   TRAVELING *1392*

Taking A Stand   *See* EGO *398*
   See Also CHARACTER & INTEGRITY,
   MOTIVATION, PROTEST

Tales   *See* BOOKS *101*

Talk   *See* COMMUNICATION: TALK *245*

Talk Over   *See* COMMUNICATION: CONVERSATION *239*

Talk Shows   *See* TELEVISION *1342*

Tall   *See* BIG *96*

Tame   *See* POWER & CONTROL *1068*, REBELS *1126*,
   WILD *1441*

Tan   *See* COLORS: BROWN *228*

Tangled   *See* STUCK *1318*

Tarot   *See* ASTROLOGY *74*
   See Also FUTURE

Tasting   *See* FOOD & BEVERAGES: GENERAL *486*

TATTOO *1334*
   See Also ANATOMY: SKIN

Taverns   *See* BARS *84*

Taxes   *See* MONEY *906*
   See Also POLITICS: POLITICS & GOVERNMENT

TAXI *1334*
   See Also CARS (various), LEAVING, TRAVELING

Tea   *See* FOOD & BEVERAGES: COFFEE *482*

Teachers   *See* SCHOOL *1181*

TEACHING VALUES *1335*
   See Also ADVICE, BAD, CHARACTER & INTEGRITY,
   CHILDREN, FAITH, GOD, GOOD, PARENTS (various),
   RIGHT, SCHOOL, WARNINGS, WRONG

Team Songs   *See* SCHOOL *1181*, SPORTS: FOOTBALL *1272*,
   STATES: A-Z *1281*

Teams   *See* COUPLES *285*, SPORTS (various) *1271*,
   TOGETHERNESS *1371*

Tear Apart   *See* BREAK *108*

Tears   *See* CRYING *300*

Technicolor   *See* COLORS: GENERAL *229*, MOVIES *941*

Technology   *See* BUSINESS & INDUSTRY *114*
   See Also COMPUTERS

Teddy Bears   *See* ANIMALS: BEARS *46*, TOYS &
   GAMES *1377*

Teen Idols   *See* SHOW BIZ *1230*

Teen Love   *See* LOVE: YOUNG LOVE *846*
   See Also PARENTS: CONCERNED ABOUT TEEN LOVE

Troubled Times *See* DANGER & DISASTER *323,*
    POVERTY *1063,* WAR *1427*
Truce *See* PEACE *1044,* WAR *1427*
Truck Stops *See* RESTAURANTS *1141*
Truckin' *See* TRUCKS *1414*
TRUCKS *1414* **Truckin'**
    See Also CARS (various), COUNTRY, FARMS, GAS
    STATIONS, HITCHHIKING, ROAD, ROAD ACCIDENTS,
    SOCIAL CLASS: RURAL, TRAVELING, WORK
True *See* TRUTH *1417*
True Love *See* LOVE: DEVOTION *738*
Trust *See* FAITH *425*
Trustworthy *See* CHARACTER & INTEGRITY *137*
TRUTH *1417* **Real, True**
    See Also CHARACTER & INTEGRITY, CHEATING
    & LIES, FAITH, FAKE, LOVE (various), PROMISE,
    TEACHING VALUES, THINKING & KNOWING
Try *See* MOTIVATION *928*
Tube (subway) *See* TRAINS *1383*
Tubs *See* BATHROOMS *87*
Tuesday *See* DAYS OF THE WEEK: TUESDAY *333*
Tulsa *See* CITIES: TULSA *210*
Tumbleweeds *See* AMERICAN WEST *25*
Tunes *See* MUSIC *942*
Turmoil *See* DANGER & DISASTER *323*
Turn *See* CHANGES *135*
Turn Back *See* RETURNING *1142*
Turnabout *See* REVENGE *1145*
Turned On *See* DESIRE *346,* SEX *1213*
Turning *See* CIRCLES *170*
Turnpike *See* ROAD *1154*
Turtles *See* ANIMALS: REPTILES *67*
TV Movies *See* MOVIES *941*
Twice *See* NUMBERS: 2 *998*
Twilight *See* NIGHT *966*
Two *See* NUMBERS: 2 *998*
Two Sides *See* OPPOSITES *1017*
Twosomes *See* COUPLES *285,* LOVE (various) *701*
Tycoons *See* MONEY *906*
Typewriters *See* BOOKS *101,* WORK *1494*
Tyranny *See* PROTEST *1091*

U

U.K. *See* COUNTRIES: ENGLAND *272*
U.S.A. *See* COUNTRIES: AMERICA *263*
U.S.S.R. *See* COUNTRIES: RUSSIA *279*
UFO'S *1419* **Alien Creatures, Space People**
    See Also SPACE, STARS, STRANGE
Ugly *See* BEAUTY *88*
    See Also INSULTS
Ultimate Sacrifice *See* HEROISM *597,* WAR *1427*
Umbrellas *See* RAIN *1116*
Unaware *See* THINKING & KNOWING *1349*
Unbalanced *See* CRAZY *290*
Unceasing *See* ETERNITY *414*
Uncivilized *See* WILD *1441*
Uncles *See* FAMILY: UNCLES *449*

Uncomplicated *See* EASY *396*
Uncontrollable *See* POWER & CONTROL *1068,*
    REBELS *1126,* WILD *1441*
Undecided *See* DECISIONS *343*
Under The Influence *See* ALCOHOL *19,* DRUGS
    (various) *388*
Under The Weather *See* PAIN & HEALING *1025*
Underbelly Of Life *See* SLEAZY *1242*
Undercover *See* HIDING *600,* POLICE *1055,* SECRETS *1201*
Underground (subway) *See* TRAINS *1383*
Understanding *See* THINKING & KNOWING *1349*
Underwear *See* CLOTHES *213*
Underworld *See* CRIME *297,* SLEAZY *1242*
Undressed *See* ANATOMY: BODY *28,* CLOTHES *213*
Undying *See* ETERNITY *414*
Uneasy *See* FEAR & COURAGE *453*
Unemployment *See* WORK *1494*
Unending *See* ETERNITY *414*
Unequal *See* POLITICS: SOCIAL INJUSTICE *1061,*
    PREJUDICE *1071,* PROTEST *1091*
Unexplained *See* STRANGE *1308*
Unfair *See* WRONG *1506*
    See Also POLITICS: SOCIAL INJUSTICE
Unfaithful *See* CHEATING & LIES *140*
    See Also LOVE (various), MARRIAGE
Unforgettable *See* REMEMBER *1133*
Unfortunate *See* LUCK *849,* SADNESS *1169*
Unfulfilled *See* STUCK *1318*
Unhappy *See* SADNESS *1169*
Unhealthy *See* PAIN & HEALING *1025*
Unidentified Flying Objects *See* UFO'S *1419*
Uninhabited *See* EMPTY *407*
Uninhibited *See* WILD *1441*
Uninterested *See* BORED *105*
Unions *See* WORK *1494*
    See Also POLITICS: POLITICAL CLASSICS, POLITICS:
    SOCIAL INJUSTICE
Unique *See* SPECIAL *1267*
United *See* TOGETHERNESS *1371*
United Kingdom *See* COUNTRIES: ENGLAND *272*
United States Of America *See* COUNTRIES: AMERICA *263*
Universe *See* SPACE *1265*
University *See* SCHOOL *1181*
Unknown *See* STRANGE *1308*
Unlawful *See* CRIME *297,* LAW & ORDER *652*
Unlike *See* OPPOSITES *1017*
Unlovable *See* LOW SELF-ESTEEM *848*
Unlucky *See* LUCK *849*
Unoccupied *See* EMPTY *407*
Unplanned Pregnancy *See* FAMILY PLANNING *432*
    See Also PARENTS (various)
Unpredictable *See* FUTURE *511,* GAMBLING *515*
Unruly *See* WILD *1441*
Unsafe *See* DANGER & DISASTER *323,* FEAR &
    COURAGE *453,* WARNINGS *1433*
Unsaid *See* COMMUNICATION: SAY *239*
Unsatisfied *See* SADNESS *1169*
Unsophisticated *See* SOCIAL CLASS: GENERAL *1259*
Unstable *See* CRAZY *290*
Untamed *See* WILD *1441*
Until *See* TIME: GENERAL *1360*

Unusual *See* SPECIAL *1267*, STRANGE *1308*

Unwed Parents *See* FAMILY PLANNING *432*
See Also PARENTS: SINGLE, STEP, ABSENT

Unwell *See* PAIN & HEALING *1025*

Unwieldy *See* DIFFICULT *364*

Upheaval *See* CHANGES *135*, DANGER & DISASTER *323*, PROTEST *1091*

Uphill *See* MOUNTAINS *937*

Uphill Battle *See* DIFFICULT *364*, MOTIVATION *928*

Uproar *See* COMMUNICATION: SHOUT *244*

Upset *See* ANGER *44*, CRAZY *290*

Upstairs *See* CLIMBING *213*

Upstanding *See* CHARACTER & INTEGRITY *137*

Uptown *See* CITIES: GENERAL *183*

Uranium *See* NUCLEAR ENERGY *987*

Urban *See* CITIES: GENERAL *183*

Urban Poor *See* HARD CITY LIFE *566*, POVERTY *1063*

URGENT *1420* **Desperate, Hurry, Immediate, Right Now**
See Also BUSY, DESIRE, FAST, LATE, TIME: GENERAL, TIME: SPECIFIC, TROUBLE, WAITING

Us *See* COUPLES *285*, TOGETHERNESS *1371*

Us Against The World *See* LOVE: US AGAINST THE WORLD *845*

Used *See* SHOPPING *1228*

Used (mistreated) *See* MISTREATMENT *905*

User (drugs) *See* ALCOHOL *19*, ALCOHOL: RECOVERING ALCOHOLIC *25*, CIGARETTES *169*, DRUGS (various) *388*

Utah *See* STATES: UTAH *1302*

Utensils *See* TOOLS *1374*

Utopia *See* PARADISE *1034*

V

V.D. *See* PAIN & HEALING *1025*, SEX *1213*

V.I.P. *See* CELEBRITIES: SPECIFIC *133*

Vacant *See* EMPTY *407*

Vacation *See* CHRISTMAS *154*, TRAVELING *1392*

Vagabonds *See* POVERTY *1063*, TRAINS *1383*, TRAVELING *1392*

Valentines *See* HEART *571*
See Also DESIRE, LOVE (various), MONTHS & DATES: FEBRUARY

Valleys *See* MOUNTAINS *937*

Values *See* CHARACTER & INTEGRITY *137*
See Also PATRIOTISM, TEACHING VALUES

Vampires *See* MONSTERS *913*

Vanity *See* EGO *398*

Varsity *See* SCHOOL *1181*

Vary *See* CHANGES *135*

VCR *See* TELEVISION *1342*

Vegetables *See* FOOD & BEVERAGES: FRUIT *483*, FOOD & BEVERAGES: VEGETABLES *493*

Veils *See* HATS *567*

Veins *See* BLOOD *101*

Velvet *See* CLOTHES *213*, FABRICS *424*

Venereal Disease *See* PAIN & HEALING *1025*, SEX *1213*

Vengeance *See* REVENGE *1145*

Venom *See* ANIMALS: REPTILES *67*, POISON *1055*

Verbal *See* COMMUNICATION (various) *239*, COMMUNICATION: WORDS *253*

Verdict *See* LAW & ORDER *652*

Vermont *See* STATES: VERMONT *1302*

Verse *See* BOOKS *101*, MUSIC *942*

Vertigo *See* CRAZY *290*

Vestibule *See* HOUSES *621*

Veterans' Day *See* WAR *1427*
See Also CHARACTER & INTEGRITY, COUNTRIES: AMERICA, FEAR & COURAGE, PATRIOTISM

Vicious *See* ANGER *44*, BAD *79*

Victims *See* CRIME *297*, DEATH *336*

Victory *See* WINNING *1447*
See Also LOSING & LOSS, WAR

Video *See* TELEVISION *1342*

Video Games *See* TOYS & GAMES *1377*

Vienna *See* CITIES: VIENNA *211*

Vietnam *See* COUNTRIES: VIETNAM *282*

Vietnam War *See* WAR *1427*

Vigor *See* ENERGY *411*

Village *See* CITIES: GENERAL *183*
See Also SMALL TOWN LIFE

Villains *See* BAD *79*, CRIME *297*, REBELS *1126*

Violence *See* FIGHT *461*
See Also CRIME, DANGER & DISASTER, DOMESTIC ABUSE, KILL, WAR

Violins *See* MUSICAL INSTRUMENTS: FIDDLES & VIOLINS *956*

Virginia *See* STATES: VIRGINIA *1302*

Virtual *See* PRETEND *1074*
See Also COMPUTERS

Virtue *See* CHARACTER & INTEGRITY *137*, SEX: RESISTING TEMPTATION *1222*, TEACHING VALUES *1335*

Vision *See* EYES *418*, SEEING *1204*

Visitation Rights *See* PARENTS: SINGLE, STEP, ABSENT *1037*

Vital *See* URGENT *1420*

Vitality *See* ENERGY *411*, LIFE *662*

Vocabulary *See* COMMUNICATION: WORDS *253*

Vocation *See* WORK *1494*

Voicemail *See* TELEPHONE *1339*

Voices *See* COMMUNICATION: CONVERSATION *239*

Void *See* EMPTY *407*

Volcanoes *See* MOUNTAINS *937*

Voodoo *See* MAGIC *853*

Vows *See* LOVE: DEVOTION *738*, MARRIAGE *860*, PROMISE *1088*

Voyage *See* SHIPS *1224*, TRAVELING *1392*

Vulnerable *See* FEAR & COURAGE *453*

W

Wacky *See* CRAZY *290*, SMILE *1254*

Wages *See* MONEY *906*, WORK *1494*

Wagon Train *See* AMERICAN WEST *25*, COWBOYS *286*

Wail *See* COMMUNICATION: SCREAM *244*, CRYING *300*

Waiters *See* WAITRESSES *1426*

Work Out *See* SPORTS: GENERAL *1273*
Work Week *See* DAYS OF THE WEEK (various) *327*,
    WORK *1494*
Working Class *See* WORK *1494*
WORLD *1499*
    See Also AIR, EARTH, GOD, LIFE, NATURE, NIGHT,
    POLITICS (various), PEACE, SKY, SPACE, STARS, SUN
World War *See* WAR *1427*
World Wide Web *See* COMPUTERS *259*
Worry *See* FEAR & COURAGE *453*
    See Also CAREFREE
Worship *See* GOD *522*
Worst *See* BAD *79*, EXTREMES *417*
Worthless *See* BAD *79*, MONEY *906*, TRASH *1391*
Worthy *See* CHARACTER & INTEGRITY *137*
Wounded *See* PAIN & HEALING *1025*
Wranglers *See* COWBOYS *286*
Wrath *See* ANGER *44*
Wreak Havoc *See* DANGER & DISASTER *323*
Wrecks *See* ROAD ACCIDENTS *1159*
    See Also DANGER & DISASTER
Wretched *See* BAD *79*, DESPAIR *361*, SADNESS *1169*
Wrists *See* ANATOMY: HANDS *32*
Wristwatch *See* TIME: GENERAL *1360*
Write *See* MAIL *857*
Writing *See* BOOKS *101*
WRONG *1506* **Not The Way Things Should Be, Unfair,**
    Wrong Circumstances
    See Also BAD, GUILT, LOVE: SOMEBODY DONE
    SOMEBODY WRONG, MISTAKES, MISTREATMENT,
    POLITICS: SOCIAL INJUSTICE, PREJUDICE,
    PROTEST, RIGHT
Wrong Circumstances *See* WRONG *1506*
Wrongdoing *See* CRIME *297*
Wronged *See* GUILT *544*, LOVE (various) *701*,
    MISTREATMENT *905*, WRONG *1506*
WW I *See* WAR *1427*
WW II *See* WAR *1427*
Wyoming *See* STATES: WYOMING *1303*

Y

Yankee *See* DIRECTIONS: NORTH *367*
Yardage *See* DISTANCE *373*
Yearn *See* DESIRE *346*
YEARS: GENERAL *1507*
    See Also AGING, ANNIVERSARY, BIRTHDAY,
    FUTURE, HISTORY, MONTHS & DATES (various),
    REMEMBER, TIME: GENERAL, YEARS: SPECIFIC
YEARS: SPECIFIC *1508*
    See Also AGES (various), ANNIVERSARY, BIRTHDAY,
    FUTURE, HISTORY, MONTHS & DATES (various),
    REMEMBER, TIME: SPECIFIC, YEARS: GENERAL
Yell *See* COMMUNICATION: SHOUT *244*
Yellow *See* COLORS: YELLOW *238*
YESTERDAY *1509*
    See Also HISTORY, REMEMBER, TIME: GENERAL,
    TIME: SPECIFIC
You & Me *See* COUPLES *285*, LOVE (various) *701*,
    TOGETHERNESS *1371*

You Can Do It *See* MOTIVATION *928*, OPTIMISM *1023*
You're Not My Type *See* LOVE: GET LOST! *803*
YOUNG *1511*
    See Also AGES (various), AGING, BABY, CHILDREN,
    LOVE: YOUNG LOVE, OLD, PARENTS: CONCERNED
    ABOUT TEEN LOVE, TEENAGERS
Young Love *See* LOVE: YOUNG LOVE *846*

Z

Zen *See* CIRCLES *170*, GOD *522*
Zodiac *See* ASTROLOGY *74*
Zombies *See* MONSTERS *913*
Zone *See* PLACES *1049*
Zoos *See* ANIMALS: GENERAL *58*

NOTES

NOTES

NOTES

NOTES

NOTES